PETERSON'S

Graduate Programs in Business, Education, Health, Information Studies, Law & Social Work

1999

THIRTY-THIRD EDITION

Book 6

Peterson's

Princeton, New Jersey

About Peterson's

Peterson's is the country's largest educational information/communications company, providing the academic, consumer, and professional communities with books, software, and online services in support of lifelong education access and career choice. Well-known references include Peterson's annual guides to private schools, summer programs, colleges and universities, graduate and professional programs, financial aid, international study, adult learning, and career guidance. Peterson's Web site at petersons.com is the only comprehensive—and most heavily traveled—education resource on the Internet. The site carries all of Peterson's fully searchable major databases and includes financial aid sources, test-prep help, job postings, direct inquiry and application features, and specially created Virtual Campuses for every accredited academic institution and summer program in the U.S. and Canada that offers in-depth narratives, announcements, and multimedia features.

The colleges and universities represented in this book recognize that federal laws, where applicable, require compliance with Title IX (Education Amendments of 1972), Title VII (Civil Rights Act of 1964), and Section 504 of the Rehabilitation Act of 1973 as amended, prohibiting discrimination on the basis of sex, race, color, handicap, or national or ethnic origin in their educational programs and activities, including admissions and employment.

Editorial inquiries concerning this book should be addressed to:
Editor, Peterson's, P.O. Box 2123, Princeton, New Jersey 08543-2123

ISSN 1088-9442
ISBN 1-56079-986-2

Composition and design by Peterson's

Printed in the United States of America

10 9 8 7 6 5 4 3 2 1

Contents

Introduction

How to Use These Guides

OVERVIEW

The six volumes of Peterson's Annual Guides to Graduate Study, the only annually updated reference work of its kind, provide wide-ranging information on the graduate and professional programs offered by accredited colleges and universities in the United States and U.S. territories and by those institutions in Canada, Mexico, Europe, and Africa that are accredited by U.S. accrediting bodies. More than 36,000 individual academic and professional programs at more than 1,700 institutions are listed. Peterson's Annual Guides to Graduate Study have been used for more than thirty years by prospective graduate and professional students, placement counselors, faculty advisers, and all others interested in postbaccalaureate education.

Book 1, *Graduate & Professional Programs: An Overview*, contains information on institutions as a whole. Books 2 through 6 are devoted to specific academic and professional fields:

- Book 2—*Graduate Programs in the Humanities, Arts & Social Sciences*
- Book 3—*Graduate Programs in the Biological Sciences*
- Book 4—*Graduate Programs in the Physical Sciences, Mathematics, Agricultural Sciences, the Environment & Natural Resources*
- Book 5—*Graduate Programs in Engineering & Applied Sciences*
- Book 6—*Graduate Programs in Business, Education, Health, Information Studies, Law & Social Work*

The books may be used individually or as a set. For example, if you have chosen a field of study but do not know what institution you want to attend or if you have a college or university in mind but have not chosen an academic field of study, the best place to begin is Book 1.

Book 1 presents several directories to help you identify programs of study that might interest you; you can then research those programs further in Books 2 through 6. The Directory of Graduate and Professional Programs by Field lists the 396 fields for which there are program directories in Books 2 through 6 and gives the names of those institutions that offer graduate degree programs in each. Degrees granted are also indicated.

For geographical or financial reasons, you may be interested in attending a particular institution and will want to know what it has to offer. You should turn to the Directory of Institutions and Their Offerings, which lists the degree programs available at each institution, again, in the 396 academic and professional fields for which Books 2 through 6 have program directories. As in the Graduate and Professional Programs by Field directory, the level of degrees offered is also indicated.

Finally, the Directory of Combined-Degree Programs lists the areas in which two graduate degrees may be earned concurrently and the schools that offer them.

CLASSIFICATION OF PROGRAMS

After you identify the particular programs and institutions that interest you, use both Book 1 and the specialized volumes to obtain detailed information—Book 1 for information on the institutions overall and Books 2 through 6 for details about the individual graduate units and their degree programs.

Books 2 through 6 are divided into sections that contain one or more directories devoted to programs in a particular field. If you do not find a directory devoted to your field of interest in a specific book, consult the Index of Directories and Subject Areas in Books 2–6; this index appears at the end of each book. After you have identified the correct book, consult the Index of Directories and Subject Areas in This Book, which shows (as does the more general directory) what directories cover subjects not specifically named in a directory or section title. This index in Book 2, for example, will tell you that if you are interested in sculpture, you should see the directory entitled Art/Fine Arts. The Art/Fine Arts entry will direct you to the proper page.

Books 2 through 6 have a number of general directories. These directories have entries for the largest unit at an institution granting graduate degrees in that field. For example, the general Engineering and Applied Sciences directory in Book 5 consists of profiles for colleges, schools, and departments of engineering and applied sciences.

General directories are followed by other directories, or sections, in Books 3, 5, and 6, that give more detailed information about programs in particular areas of the general field that has been covered. The general Psychology directory, in the example above, is followed by fourteen directories in specific areas of psychology, such as Clinical Psychology, Health Psychology, and School Psychology.

Because of the broad nature of many fields, any system of organization is bound to involve a certain amount of overlap. Environmental studies, for example, is a field whose various aspects are studied in several types of departments and schools. Readers interested in such studies will find information on relevant programs in Book 3 under Ecology and Environmental Biology; in Book 4 under Environmental Policy and Resource Management and Natural Resources; in Book 5 under Energy Management and Policy and Environmental Engineering; and in Book 6 under Environmental and Occupational Health. To help you find all of the programs of interest to you, the introduction to each section of Books 2 through 6 includes, if applicable, a paragraph suggesting other sections and directories with information on related areas of study to consult.

In addition, this book contains more than 330 listings of academic centers and institutes, including information about the graduate students served, affiliated faculty members, and research budgets. This information can be found in the Research and Training Opportunities section in this volume.

SCHOOL AND PROGRAM INFORMATION

In all of the books, information is presented in three forms: profiles—capsule summaries of basic information—and the short announcements and in-depth descriptions written by graduate school and program administrators. The format of the profiles is constant, making it easy to compare one institution with another and one program with another. A description of the information in the profiles in Books 2 through 6 may be found below; the Book 1 profile description is found immediately preceding the profiles in Book 1. A number of graduate school and program administrators have attached brief announcements to the end of their profile listings. In them you will find information that an institution or program wants to emphasize. The in-depth descriptions are by their very nature more expansive and flexible than the profiles, and the administrators who have written them may emphasize different aspects of their programs. All of these in-depth descriptions are organized in the same way, and in each one you will find information on the same basic topics, such as programs of study, research facilities, tuition and fees, financial aid, and application procedures. If an institution or program has submitted an in-depth description, a boldface cross-reference appears below its profile. As with the profile announcements, all of the in-depth descriptions in the guides have been submitted by choice of administrators; the absence of an announcement or in-depth description does not reflect any type of editorial judgment on the part of Peterson's.

Interdisciplinary Programs

In addition to the regular directories that present profiles of programs in each field of study, many sections in Books 2 through 6 contain special notices under the heading Cross-Discipline Announcements. Appearing at the end of the profiles in many sections, these Cross-Discipline Announcements inform you about programs that you may find of interest described in a different section. A biochemistry department, for example, may place a notice under Cross-Discipline Announcements in the Chemistry section (Book 4) to alert chemistry students to their current description in the Biochemistry section of Book 3. Cross-discipline announcements, also written by administrators to highlight their programs, will be helpful to you not only in finding out about programs in fields related to your own but also in locating departments that are actively recruiting students with a specific undergraduate major.

Profiles of Graduate Units (Books 2–6)

The profiles found in the 396 directories in Books 2 through 6 provide basic data about the graduate units in capsule form for quick reference. To make these directories as useful as possible, profiles are generally listed for an institution's smallest academic unit within a subject area. In other words, if an institution has a College of Liberal Arts that administers many related programs, the profile for the individual program (e.g., Program in History), not the entire College, appears in the directory.

There are some programs that do not fit into any current directory and are not given individual profiles. The directory structure is reviewed annually in order to keep this number to a minimum and to accommodate major trends in graduate education.

The following outline describes the profile information found in the guides and explains how best to use that information. Any item that does not apply to or was not provided by a graduate unit is omitted from its listing.

Identifying Information. The institution's name, in boldface type, is followed by a complete listing of the administrative structure for that field of study. (For example, **University of Akron,** Buchtel College of Arts and Sciences, Department of Mathematical Sciences and Statistics, Program in Mathematics.) The last unit listed is the one to which all information in the profile pertains. The institution's address follows.

Offerings. Each field of study offered by the unit is listed with all postbaccalaureate degrees awarded. Degrees that are not preceded by a specific concentration are awarded in the general field listed in the unit name. Frequently, fields of study are broken down into subspecializations, and those appear following the degrees awarded; for example, "Offerings in secondary education (M Ed), including English education, mathematics education, science education." Students enrolled in the M.Ed. program would be able to specialize in any of the three fields mentioned.

Professional Accreditation. Profiles indicate whether a program is professionally accredited. Specific information on the accreditation status of a unit is obtained directly from the accreditation agency's most current listing at the time of publication. However, because it is possible for a program to receive or lose professional accreditation at any time, students entering fields in which accreditation is important to a career should verify the status of programs by contacting either the chairperson or the appropriate accrediting association (see Accreditation and Accrediting Agencies in each book).

Restricted and Suspended Admissions. Some programs admit only certain groups (such as students who were undergraduates at the institution), and other programs have suspended or permanently terminated admissions. Notes to this effect are printed after the list of degrees offered. Institutions that have restricted admission are often unable to handle queries, and some have requested that Peterson's discourage applicants from writing directly to them; readers are advised, therefore, to write only if they qualify for admission under the stated restrictions. In many cases, programs with suspended admissions still have students completing degrees; enrollment figures as well as degree requirements are printed here in order to give an accurate reflection of each program's current status. Interested students should contact the unit head or dean to determine when and if admissions will be resumed if the profile states that the situation is temporary.

Jointly Offered Degrees. Explanatory statements concerning programs that are offered in cooperation with other institutions also follow the list of degrees offered. This occurs most commonly on a regional basis (for example, two state universities offering a cooperative Ph.D. in special education) or where the specialized nature of the institutions encourages joint efforts (a J.D./M.B.A. offered by a law school at an institution with no formal business programs and an institution with a business school but lacking a law school). Only programs that are truly cooperative are listed; those involving only limited course work at another institution are not. Interested students should contact the heads of such units for further information.

Part-Time and Evening/Weekend Programs. When information regarding the availability of part-time or evening/weekend study appears in the profile, it means that students are able to earn a degree exclusively through such study.

Postbaccalaureate Distance Learning Degrees. A postbaccalaureate distance learning degree program signifies that course requirements can be fulfilled with minimal or no on-campus study. If these programs require minimal on-campus study or no on-campus study it may be indicated here.

Faculty. Figures on the number of faculty members actively involved with graduate students through teaching or research are separated into full-and part-time as well as men and women whenever the information has been supplied.

Matriculated Students. Figures for the number of students enrolled in graduate and professional programs pertain to the semester of highest enrollment from the 1997–98 academic year. These figures are broken down into full- and part-time and men and women whenever the data have been supplied. Information on the number of matriculated students enrolled in the unit who are members of a minority group or are international students appears here. The average age of the matriculated students is followed by the number of applicants and the percentage accepted for fall 1997.

Degrees Awarded. In addition to the number of degrees awarded in the 1997 calendar year, this section contains information on the percentages of students who have gone on to continue full-time study, entered university research or teaching, or chosen other work related to their field and information on the average amount of time required to earn the degree for full-time and part-time students. Many doctoral programs offer a terminal master's degree if students leave the program after completing only part of the requirements for a doctoral degree; that is indicated here. All degrees are classified into one of four types: master's, doctoral, first professional, and other advanced degrees. A unit may award one or several degrees at a given level; however, the data are only collected by type and may therefore represent several different degree programs.

Degree Requirements. The information in this section is also broken down by type of degree, and all information for a degree level pertains to all degrees of that type unless otherwise specified. Degree requirements are collected in a simplified form to provide some very basic information on the nature of the program and on foreign language, computer language, and thesis or dissertation requirements. Many units also provide a short list of additional requirements, such as fieldwork or an internship. No information is listed on the number of courses or credits required for completion or whether a minimum or maximum number of years or semesters is needed. For complete information on graduation requirements, contact the graduate school or program directly.

Entrance Requirements. Entrance requirements are broken down into the four degree levels of master's, doctoral, first professional, and other advanced degrees. Within each level, information may be provided in two basic categories, entrance exams and other requirements. The entrance exams use the standard acronyms used by the testing agencies, unless they are not well known; a complete list of these acronyms appears in each volume in the appendix Abbreviations Used in the Guides. Additional information on each of the common tests is provided in the section Tests Required of Applicants. The usual format in this part of the profile is a test name followed by a minimum score and an average score if provided. When a minimum or average combined score is given for the GRE General Test, it is for the verbal and quantitative sections combined (without the analytical section) unless otherwise specified. More information on the scale and other aspects of the test may be obtained directly from the testing agency. Other entrance requirements are quite varied, but they often contain an undergraduate or graduate grade point average (GPA). Unless otherwise stated, the GPA is calculated on a 4.0 scale and is listed as a minimum required for admission. The standard application deadline, any nonrefundable application fee, and whether electronic applications are accepted may be listed here. Note that the deadline should be used for reference only; these dates are subject to change, and students interested in applying should contact the graduate unit directly about application procedures and deadlines.

Expenses. The cost of study for the 1998–99 academic year is given in two basic categories, tuition and fees. It is not possible to represent the complete tuition and fees schedule for each graduate unit, so a simplified version of the cost of studying in that unit is provided. In general, the costs of both full- and part-time study are listed if the unit allows for both types of programs and lists separate costs. For public institutions, the tuition and fees are listed for both state residents and nonresidents. Cost of study may be quite complex at a graduate institution. There are often sliding scales for part-time study, a different cost for first-year students, and other variables that make it impossible to completely cover the cost of study for each graduate program. To provide the most usable information, figures are given for full-time study for a full year where available and for part-time study in terms of a per-unit rate (per credit, per semester hour, etc.). If the tuition cannot be expressed in these terms, a minimum figure is provided for part-time study. This figure usually represents the minimum cost associated with one three-credit course for one semester or quarter. Minimum figures are for comparison purposes only—your actual cost of study may differ. Expenses are usually subject to change; for exact costs at any given time, contact your chosen schools and programs directly. Keep in mind that the tuition of Canadian institutions is usually given in Canadian dollars.

Financial Aid. This section contains data on the number of awards that are administered by the institution and were given to graduate students during the 1997–98 academic year. The first figure given represents the total number of students receiving financial aid enrolled in that unit. If the unit has provided information on graduate appointments, these are broken down into four major categories: *fellowships* give money to graduate students to cover the cost of study and living expenses and are not based on a work obligation or research commitment, *research assistantships* provide stipends to graduate students for assistance in a formal research project with a faculty member, *teaching assistantships* provide stipends to graduate students for teaching or for assisting faculty members in teaching undergraduate classes, and *other appointments* include a variety of awards that schools define and fund in their own way. Within each category, figures are given for the total number of awards, the number of awards given to first-year students, the average monthly stipend, and the total amount awarded.

In addition to graduate appointments, the availability of several other financial aid sources is covered in this section. *Tuition waivers* are routinely part of a graduate appointment, but units sometimes waive part or all of a student's tuition even if a graduate appointment is not available. *Federal Work-Study* is made available to students who demonstrate need and meet the federal guidelines; this form of aid normally includes 10 or more hours of work per week in an office of the institution. *Institutionally sponsored loans* are low-interest loans available to graduate students to cover both educational and living expenses. *Career-related internships* or *fieldwork* offer money to students who are participating in a formal off-campus research project or practicum. The availability of financial aid to part-time students is also indicated here.

Some programs list the financial aid application deadline and the forms that need to be completed for students to be eligible for financial aid. There are two forms: FAFSA, the Free Application for Federal Student Aid, which is required for federal aid; and the CSS Financial Aid PROFILE, if required.

Faculty Research. Each unit has the opportunity to list several keyword phrases describing the current research involving faculty members and graduate students. Space limitations prevent the unit from listing complete information on all research programs. The total expenditure for funded research from the previous academic year may also be included.

Unit Head and Application Contact. The head of the graduate program for each unit is listed with the academic title and telephone, fax, and e-mail numbers if available. In addition to the unit head, many graduate programs list separate contacts for application and admission information, which follows the listing for the unit head. If no unit head or application contact is given, you should contact the overall institution for information on graduate admissions.

Data Collection and Editorial Procedures

DIRECTORIES AND PROFILES

The information published in the directories and profiles of all the books is collected through Peterson's Annual Survey of Graduate Institutions. The survey is sent each spring and summer to more than 1,700 institutions offering postbaccalaureate degree programs, including accredited institutions in the United States and U.S. territories and those institutions in Canada, Mexico, Europe, and Africa that are accredited by U.S. accrediting bodies. Deans and other administrators complete these surveys, providing information on programs in the 396 academic and professional fields covered in the guides as well as overall institutional information. Peterson's staff then goes over each returned survey carefully and verifies or revises responses after further research and discussion with administrators at the institutions. Extensive files on past responses are kept from year to year.

While every effort has been made to ensure the accuracy and completeness of the data, information is sometimes unavailable or changes occur after publication deadlines. All usable information received in time for publication has been included. The omission of any particular item from a directory or profile signifies either that the item is not applicable to the institution or program or that information was not available. Profiles of programs scheduled to begin during the 1998–99 academic year cannot, obviously, include statistics on enrollment or, in many cases, the number of faculty members. If no usable data were submitted by an institution, its name, address, and program name where appropriate nonetheless appear in order to indicate the existence of graduate work.

ANNOUNCEMENTS AND IN-DEPTH DESCRIPTIONS

The announcements and in-depth descriptions are supplementary insertions submitted by deans, chairs, and other administrators who wish to make an additional, more individualized statement to readers. Those who have chosen to write these insertions are responsible for the accuracy of the content, but Peterson's editors have reserved the right to delete irrelevant material or questionable self-appraisals and to edit for style. Statements regarding a university's objectives and accomplishments are a reflection of its own beliefs and are not the opinions of the editors. Since inclusion of announcements and descriptions is by choice, their presence or absence in the guides should not be taken as an indication of status, quality, or approval.

The Graduate Adviser

This section consists of two essays and information on admissions tests and accreditation. The first essay, Applying to Graduate and Professional Schools, is by Jane E. Levy of Cornell University and Elinor R. Workman of the University of Chicago. It covers a number of points of interest to students considering postbaccalaureate work, including types of degrees, choosing a specialization and researching programs, applying, and some issues for returning, part-time, and international students. The second essay is Financing Your Graduate and Professional Education, by Patricia McWade of Georgetown University. It discusses how and when to apply for aid, determining financial need, and types of aid available as it relates to degree programs in business, education, health, information studies, law, and social work. Both essays appear in each of the six Graduate Guides. Tests Required of Applicants lists all standardized admissions tests that are relevant to programs in business, education, health, and law. Accreditation and Accrediting Agencies gives information on accreditation and its purpose and lists first institutional accrediting agencies and then specialized accrediting agencies relevant to business, education, health, information studies, law, and social work. This section is filled with crucial information for all students; it is addressed to the reader who is still in college but also contains information specifically for returning, part-time, and international students.

Applying to Graduate and Professional Schools

The decision to attend graduate school and the choice of an institution and degree program require serious consideration. The time, money, and energy you will expend doing graduate work are significant, and you will want to analyze your options carefully. Before you begin filing applications, you should evaluate your interests and goals, know what programs are available, and be clear about your reasons for pursuing a particular degree.

There are two excellent reasons for attending graduate school, and if your decision is based on one of these, you probably have made the right choice. There are careers such as medicine, law, and college and university teaching that require specialized training and, therefore, necessitate advanced education. Another motivation is to specialize in a subject that you have decided is of great importance, either for career goals or for personal satisfaction.

Degrees

Traditionally, graduate education has involved acquiring and communicating knowledge gained through original research in a particular academic field. The highest earned academic degree, which requires the pursuit of original research, is the Doctor of Philosophy (Ph.D.). In contrast, professional training stresses the practical application of knowledge and skills; this is true, for example, in the fields of business, law, and medicine. At the doctoral level, degrees in these areas include the Doctor of Business Administration (D.B.A.), Juris Doctor (J.D.), and the Doctor of Medicine (M.D.).

Master's degrees are offered in most fields and may also be academic or professional in orientation. In many fields, the master's degree may be the only professional degree needed for employment. This is the case, for example, in fine arts (M.F.A.), library science (M.L.S.), and social work (M.S.W.). (For a list of the graduate and professional degrees currently being offered in the United States and Canada, readers may refer to the appendix of degree abbreviations.)

Some people decide to earn a master's degree at one institution and then select a different university or a somewhat different program of study for doctoral work. This can be a way of acquiring a broad background: you can choose a master's program with one emphasis or orientation and a doctoral program with another. The total period of graduate study may be somewhat lengthened by proceeding this way, but probably not by much.

In recent years, the distinctions between traditional academic programs and professional programs have become blurred. The course of graduate education has changed direction in the last thirty years, and many programs have redefined their shape and focus. There are centers and institutes for research, many graduate programs are now interdepartmental and interdisciplinary, off-campus graduate programs have multiplied, and part-time graduate programs have increased. Colleges and universities have also established combined-degree programs, in many cases in order to enable students to combine academic and professional studies. As a result of such changes, you now have considerable freedom in determining the program best suited to your current needs as well as your long-term goals.

Choosing a Specialization and Researching Programs

There are several sources of information you should make use of in choosing a specialization and a program. A good way to begin is to consult the appropriate directories in these guides, which will tell you what programs exist in the field or fields you are interested in and, for each one, will give you information on degrees, research facilities, the faculty, financial aid resources, tuition and other costs, application requirements, and so on.

Talk with your college adviser and professors about your areas of interest and ask for their advice about the best programs to research. Besides being very well informed themselves, these faculty members may have colleagues at institutions you are investigating, and they can give you inside information about individual programs and the kind of background they seek in candidates for admission.

The valuable perspective of educators should not be overlooked. If the faculty members you know through your courses are not involved in your field of interest, do not hesitate to contact other appropriate professors at your institution or neighboring institutions to ask for advice on programs that might suit your goals. In addition, talk to graduate students studying in your field of interest; their advice can be valuable also.

Your decision about a field of study may be determined by your research interests or, if you choose to enter a professional school, by the appeal of a particular career. In either case, as you attempt to limit the number of institutions you will apply to, you will want to familiarize yourself with publications describing current research in your discipline. Find related professional journals and note who is publishing in the areas of specialization that interest you, as well as where they are teaching. Take note of the institutions represented on the publications' editorial boards (they are usually listed on the inside cover); such representation usually reflects strength in the discipline.

Being aware of who the top people are and where they are will pay off in a number of ways. A graduate department's reputation rests heavily on the reputation of its faculty, and in some disciplines it is more important to study under someone of note than it is to study at a college or university with a prestigious name. In addition, in certain fields graduate funds are often tied to a particular research project and, as a result, to the faculty member directing that project. Finally, most Ph.D. candidates (and nonprofessional master's degree candidates) must pick an adviser and one or more other faculty members who form a committee that directs and approves their work. Many times this choice must be made during the first semester, so it is important to learn as much as you can about faculty members before you begin your studies. As you research the faculties of various departments, keep in mind the following questions: What is their academic training? What are their research activities? What kind of concern do they have for teaching and student development?

There are other important factors to consider in judging the educational quality of a program. First, what kind of students enroll in the program? What are their academic abilities, achievements, skills, geographic representation, and level of professional success upon completion of the program? Second, what are the program's resources? What kind of financial support does it have? How complete is the library? What laboratory equipment and computer facilities are available? And third, what does the program have to offer in terms of both curriculum and services? What are its purposes, its course offerings, and its job placement and student advisement services? What is the student-faculty ratio, and what kind of interaction is there between students and professors? What internships, assistantships, and other experiential education opportunities are available?

When evaluating a particular institution's reputation in a given field, you may also want to look at published graduate program ratings. There is no single rating that is universally accepted, so you would be well advised to read several and not place too much importance on any one. Most consist of what are known as "peer ratings"; that is, they are the results of polls of respected scholars who are asked to rate graduate departments in their field of expertise. Many academicians feel that these ratings are too heavily based upon traditional concepts of what constitutes quality—such as the publications of the faculty—and that they perpetuate the notion of a research-oriented department as the only model of excellence in graduate education. Depending on whether your own goals are research-oriented, you may want to attribute more or less importance to this type of rating.

If possible, visit the institutions that interest you and talk with faculty members and currently enrolled students. Be sure, however, to write or call the admissions office a week in advance to give the person in charge a chance to set up appointments for you with faculty members and students.

Another invaluable tool for researching programs is the Internet. In addition to an institution's Web site, dig deeper to find the "unofficial" information, such as: student reviews of faculty; editorials in the student newspaper; crime statistics; and alumni homepages. E-mail, listservs, newsgroups, bulletin boards, and chat rooms are all effective tools you should employ in your search for a graduate school program.

The Application Process

TIMETABLE

It is important to start gathering information early to be able to complete your applications on time. Most people should start the process a full year and a half before their anticipated date of matriculation. There are, however, some exceptions to this rule. The time frame will be different if you are applying for national scholarships or if your undergraduate institution has an evaluation committee through which you are applying, for example, to a health-care program. In such a situation, you may have to begin the process two years before your date of matriculation in order to take your graduate admission test and arrange for letters of recommendation early enough to meet deadlines.

Application deadlines may range from August (a year prior to matriculation) for early decision programs at medical schools using the American Medical College Application Service (AMCAS) to late spring or summer (when beginning graduate school in the fall) for a few programs with rolling admissions. Most deadlines for entry in the fall are between January and March. You should in all cases plan to meet formal deadlines; beyond this, you should be aware of the fact that many schools with rolling admissions encourage and act upon early applications. Applying early to a school with rolling admissions is usually advantageous, as it shows your enthusiasm for the program and gives admissions committees more time to evaluate the subjective components of your application, rather than just the "numbers." Applicants are not rejected early unless they are clearly below an institution's standards.

The timetable that appears below represents the ideal for most applicants.

Six months prior to applying

- Research areas of interest, institutions, and programs.
- Talk to advisers about application requirements.
- Register and prepare for appropriate graduate admission tests.
- Investigate national scholarships.
- If appropriate, obtain letters of recommendation.

Three months prior to applying

- Take required graduate admission tests.
- Write for application materials.
- Write your application essay.
- Check on application deadlines and rolling admissions policies.
- For medical, dental, osteopathy, podiatry, or law school, you may need to register for the national application or data assembly service most programs use.

Fall, a year before matriculating

- Obtain letters of recommendation.
- Take graduate admission tests if you haven't already.
- Send in completed applications.

Winter, before matriculating in the fall

- Complete the Free Application for Federal Student Aid (FAFSA) and Financial Aid PROFILE, if required.

Spring, before matriculating in the fall

- Check with all institutions before their deadlines to make sure your file is complete.
- Visit institutions that accept you.
- Send a deposit to your institution of choice.
- Notify other colleges and universities that accepted you of your decision so that they can admit students on their waiting list.
- Send thank-you notes to people who wrote your recommendation letters, informing them of your success.

You may not be able to adhere to this timetable if your application deadlines are very early, as is the case with medical schools, or if you decide to attend graduate school at the last minute. In any case, keep in mind the various application requirements and be sure to meet all deadlines. If deadlines are impossible to meet, call the institution to see if a late application will be considered.

OBTAINING APPLICATION FORMS AND INFORMATION

To obtain the materials you need, send a neatly typed or handwritten postcard requesting an application, a bulletin, and financial aid information to the address provided in this Guide. However, you may want to request an application by writing a formal letter directly to the department chair in which you briefly describe your training, experience, and specialized research interests. If you want to write to a particular faculty member about your background and interests in order to explore the possibility of an assistantship, you should also feel free to do so. However, do not ask a faculty member for an application, as this may cause a significant delay in your receipt of the forms.

NATIONAL APPLICATION SERVICES

In a few professional fields, there are national services that provide assistance with some part of the application process. These services are the Law School Data Assembly Service (LSDAS), American Medical College Application Service (AMCAS), American Association of Colleges of Osteopathic Medicine Application Service (AACOMAS), American Association of Colleges of Podiatric Medicine Application Service (AACPMAS), and American Association of Dental Schools Application Service (AADSAS). Many programs require applicants to use these services because they simplify the application process for both the professional programs' admissions committees and the applicant. The role these services play varies from one field to another. The LSDAS, for example, analyzes your transcript(s) and submits the analysis to the law schools to which you are applying, while the other services provide a more complete application service. More information and applications for these services can be obtained from your undergraduate institution.

Going to Business School? Use GradAdvantage

GradAdvantage is a new service developed by Educational Testing Service and Peterson's, and sponsored by the Graduate Management Admission Council (GMAC). GradAdvantage allows you to apply online to as many business schools as you wish, enter most of your personal data only once, and have your application arrive at the admissions office with your secure Graduate Management Admission Test (GMAT) score attached. The GradAdvantage Web site, gradadvantage.org, also has a wealth of information about business schools, financing options, and GMAT registration and preparation.

With GradAdvantage, you can complete your applications online, save your work, and make revisions any time you are on the Web. You save time and avoid the headaches of conventional applications, like typing or printing onto pre-set paper forms, and sending your application by express mail services. The advantages for business schools include speed, security, and cost-effectiveness. The cost to you is $12.00 per application, and you can pay online by credit card. The platform- and browser-independent service requires no substantial upgrades in hardware or software. All you have to do is remember the URL: gradadvantage.org.

MEETING APPLICATION REQUIREMENTS

Requirements vary from one field to another and from one institution to another. Read each program's requirements carefully; the importance of this cannot be overemphasized.

Graduate Admission Tests

Colleges and universities usually require a specific graduate admission test, and departments sometimes have their own requirements as well. Scores are used in evaluating the likelihood of your success in a particular program (based upon the success rate of past students with similar scores). Most programs will not accept scores more than three to five years old. The various tests are described a little later in this book.

Transcripts

Admissions committees require official transcripts of your grades to evaluate your academic preparation for graduate study. Grade point averages are important but are not examined in isolation; the rigor of the courses you have taken, your course load, and the reputation of the undergraduate institution you have attended are also scrutinized. To have your college transcript sent to graduate institutions, contact your college registrar.

Letters of Recommendation

Choosing people to write recommendations can be difficult, and most graduate schools require two or three letters. While recommendations from faculty members are essential for academically oriented programs, professional programs may seriously consider nonacademic recommendations from professionals in the field. Indeed, often these nonacademic recommendations are as respected as those from faculty members.

To begin the process of choosing references, identify likely candidates from among those you know through your classes, extracurricular activities, and jobs. A good reference will meet several of the following criteria: he or she has a high opinion of you, knows you well in more than one area of your life, is familiar with the institutions to which you are applying as well as the kind of study you are pursuing, has taught or worked with a large number of students and can make a favorable comparison of you with your peers, is known by the admissions committee and is regarded as someone whose judgment should be given weight, and has good written communication skills. No one person is likely to satisfy all these criteria, so choose those people who come closest to the ideal.

Once you have decided whom to ask for letters, you may wonder how to approach them. Ask them if they think they know you well enough to write a meaningful letter. Be aware that the later in the semester you ask, the more likely they are to hesitate because of time constraints; ask early in the fall semester of your senior year. Once those you ask to write letters agree in a suitably enthusiastic manner, make an appointment to talk with them. Go to the appointment with recommendation forms in hand, being sure to include addressed, stamped envelopes for their convenience. In addition, give them other supporting materials that will assist them in writing a good, detailed letter on your behalf. Such documents as transcripts, a résumé, a copy of your application essay, and a copy of a research paper can help them write a thorough recommendation.

On the recommendation form, you will be asked to indicate whether you wish to waive or retain the right to see the recommendation. Before you decide, discuss the confidentiality of the letter with each writer. Many faculty members will not write a letter unless it is confidential. This does not necessarily mean that they will write a negative letter but, rather, that they believe it will carry more weight as part of your application if it is confidential. Waiving the right to see a letter does, in fact, usually increase its validity.

If you will not be applying to graduate school as a senior but you plan to pursue further education in the future, open a credentials file if your college or university offers this service. Letters of recommendation can be kept on file for you until you begin the application process. If you are returning to school after working for several years and did not establish a credentials file, it may be difficult to obtain letters of recommendation from professors at your undergraduate institution. In this case, contact the graduate schools you are applying to and ask what their policies are regarding your situation. They may waive the requirement of recommendation letters, allow you to substitute letters from employment supervisors, or suggest you enroll in relevant courses at a nearby institution and obtain letters from professors upon completion of the course work. Program policies vary considerably, so it is best to check with each school.

Application Essays

Writing an essay, or personal statement, is often the most difficult part of the application process. Requirements vary widely in this regard. Some programs request only one or two paragraphs about why you want to pursue graduate study, while others require five or six separate essays in which you are expected to write at length about your motivation for graduate study, your strengths and weaknesses, your greatest achievements, and solutions to hypothetical problems. Business schools are notorious for requiring several time-consuming essays.

An essay or personal statement for an application should be essentially a statement of your ideas and goals. Usually it includes a certain amount of personal history, but, unless an institution specifically requests autobiographical information, you do not have to supply any. Even when the requirement is a "personal statement," the possibilities are almost unlimited. There is no set formula to follow, and, if you do write an autobiographical piece, it does not have to be arranged chronologically. Your aim should be a clear, succinct statement showing that you have a definite sense of what you want to do and enthusiasm for the field of study you have chosen. Your essay should reflect your writing abilities; more important, it should reveal the clarity, the focus, and the depth of your thinking.

Before writing anything, stop and consider what your reader might be looking for; the general directions or other parts of the application may give you an indication of this. Admissions committees may be trying to evaluate a number of things from your statement, including the following things about you:

- Motivation and commitment to a field of study
- Expectations with regard to the program and career opportunities
- Writing ability
- Major areas of interest
- Research or work experience
- Educational background
- Immediate and long-term goals
- Reasons for deciding to pursue graduate education in a particular field and at a particular institution
- Maturity
- Personal uniqueness—what you would add to the diversity of the entering class

There are two main approaches to organizing an essay. You can outline the points you want to cover and then expand on them, or you can put your ideas down on paper as they come to you, going over them, eliminating certain sentences, and moving others around until you achieve a logical sequence. Making an outline will probably lead to a well-organized essay, whereas writing spontaneously may yield a more inspired piece of writing. Use the approach you feel most comfortable with. Whichever approach you use, you will want someone to critique your essay. Your adviser and those who write your letters of recommendation may be very helpful to you in this regard. If they are in the field you plan to pursue, they will be able to tell you what things to stress and what things to keep brief. Do not be surprised, however, if you get differing opinions on the content of your essay. In the end, only you can decide on the best way of presenting yourself.

If there is information in your application that might reflect badly on you, such as poor grades or a low admission test score, it is better not to deal with it in your essay unless you are asked to. Keep your essay positive. You will need to explain anything that could be construed as negative in your application, however, as failure to do so may eliminate you from consideration. You can do this on a separate sheet entitled "Addendum," which you attach to the application, or in a cover letter that you enclose. In either form, your explanation should be short and to the point, avoiding long, tedious excuses. In addition to supplying your own explanation, you may find it appropriate to ask one or more of your recommenders to address the issue in their recommendation letter. Ask them to do this only if they are already familiar with your problem and could talk about it from a positive perspective.

In every case, essays should be word processed or typed. It is usually acceptable to attach pages to your application if the space provided is insufficient. Neatness, spelling, and grammar are important.

Interviews, Portfolios, and Auditions

Some graduate programs will require you to appear for an interview. In certain fields, you will have to submit a portfolio of your work or schedule an audition.

Interviews. Interviews are usually required by medical schools and are often required or suggested by business schools and other programs. An interview can be a very important opportunity for you to persuade an institution's admissions officer or committee that you would be an excellent doctor, dentist, manager, etc.

Interviewers will be interested in the way you think and approach problems and will probably concentrate on questions that enable them to assess your thinking skills, rather than questions that call upon your grasp of technical knowledge. Some interviewers will ask controversial questions, such as "What is your viewpoint on abortion?" or give you a hypothetical situation and ask how you would handle it. Bear in mind that the interviewer is more interested in how you think than in what you think. As in your essay, you may be asked to address such topics as your motivation for graduate study, personal philosophy, career goals, related research and work experience, and areas of interest.

You should prepare for a graduate school interview as you would for a job interview. Think about the questions you are likely to be asked and practice verbalizing your answers. Think too about what you want interviewers to know about you so that you can present this information when the opportunity is given. Dress as you would for an employment interview.

Portfolios. Many graduate programs in art, architecture, journalism, environmental design, and other fields involving visual creativity may require a portfolio as part of the application. The function of the portfolio is to show your skills and ability to do further work in a particular field, and it should reflect the scope of your cumulative training and experience. If you are applying to a program in graphic design, you may be required to submit a portfolio showing advertisements, posters, pamphlets, and illustrations you have prepared. In fine arts, applicants must submit a portfolio with pieces related to their proposed major.

Individual programs have very specific requirements regarding what your portfolio should contain and how it should be arranged and labeled. Many programs request an interview and ask you to present your portfolio at that time. They may not want you to send the portfolio in advance or leave it with them after the interview, as they are not insured against its loss. If you do send it, you usually do so at your own risk, and you should label all pieces with your name and address.

Auditions. Like a portfolio, the audition is a demonstration of your skills and talent, and it is often required by programs in music, theater, and dance. Although all programs require a reasonable level of proficiency, standards vary according to the field of study. In a nonperformance area like music education, you need only show that you have attained the level of proficiency normally acquired through an undergraduate program in that field. For a performance major, however, the audition is the most important element of the graduate application. Programs set specific requirements as to what material is appropriate, how long the performance should be, whether it should be memorized, and so on. The audition may be live or taped, but a live performance is usually preferred. In the case of performance students, a committee of professional musicians will view the audition and evaluate it according to prescribed standards.

SUBMITTING COMPLETED APPLICATIONS

Graduate schools have established a wide variety of procedures for filing applications, so read each institution's instructions carefully. Some may request that you send all application materials in one package (including letters of recommendation). Others—medical schools, for example—may have a two-step application process. This system requires the applicant to file a preliminary application; if this is reviewed favorably, he or she submits a second set of documents and a second application fee. Pay close attention to each school's instructions.

Graduate schools generally require an application fee. Sometimes this fee may be waived if you meet certain financial criteria. Check with your undergraduate financial aid office and the graduate schools to which you are applying to see if you qualify.

ADMISSION DECISIONS

At most institutions, once the graduate school office has received all of your application materials, your file is sent directly to the academic department. A faculty committee (or the department chairperson) then makes a recommendation to the chief graduate school officer (usually a graduate dean or vice president), who is responsible for the final admission decision. Professional schools at most institutions act independently of the graduate school office; applications are submitted to them directly, and they make their own admission decisions.

Usually a student's grade point average, letters of recommendation, and graduate admission test scores are the primary factors considered by admissions committees. The appropriateness of the undergraduate degree, an interview, and evidence of creative talent may also be taken into account. Normally the student's total record is examined closely, and the weight assigned to specific factors fluctuates from program to program. Few, if any, institutions base their decisions purely on numbers, that is, admission test scores and grade point average. A study by the Graduate Record Examinations Board found that grades and recommendations by known faculty members were considered to be somewhat more important than GRE General Test scores and that GRE Subject Test scores were rated as relatively unimportant (Oltman and Hartnett, 1984). This indicates that some graduate admission test scores may be of less importance than is commonly believed, but this will of course differ from program to program.

Some of the common reasons applicants are rejected for admission to graduate schools are inappropriate undergraduate curriculum; poor grades or lack of academic prerequisites; low admission test scores; weak or ineffective recommendation letters; a poor interview, portfolio, or audition; and lack of extracurricular activities, volunteer experience, or research activities. To give yourself the best chances of being admitted where you apply, try to make a realistic assessment of an institution's admission standards and your own qualifications. Remember, too, that missing deadlines and filing an incomplete application can also be a cause for rejection; be sure that your transcripts and recommendation letters are received on time.

Returning Students

Many graduate programs not only accept the older, returning student but actually prefer these "seasoned" candidates. Programs in business administration, social work, and other professional fields value mature applicants with work experience, for they have found that these students often show a higher level of motivation and commitment and work harder than 21-year-olds. Many programs also seek the diversity older students bring to the student body, as differences in perspective and experience make for interesting—and often intense—class discussions. Nonprofessional programs also view older students favorably if their academic and experiential preparation is recent enough and sufficient for the proposed fields of study.

Many institutions have programs designed to make the transition to academic life easier for the returning student. Such programs include low-cost child-care centers, emotional support programs for both the returning student and his or her spouse, and review courses of various kinds.

Other than making the necessary changes in their life-style, older students report that the most difficult aspect of returning to school is recovering, or developing, appropriate study habits. Initially, older students often feel at a disadvantage compared to students fresh out of an undergraduate program who are accustomed to preparing research papers and taking tests. This feeling can be overcome by taking advantage of noncredit courses in study skills and time management and review courses in math and writing, as well as by taking a tour of the library and becoming thoroughly familiar with it. By the end of the graduate program, most returning students feel that their life experience gave them an edge, because they could use concrete experiences to help them understand academic theory.

If you choose to go back to school, you are not alone. A significant number of adults are currently enrolled in some kind of educational program in order to make their lives or careers more rewarding.

Part-Time Students

As graduate education has changed over the past thirty years, the number of part-time graduate programs has increased. Traditionally, graduate programs were completed by full-time students. Graduate schools instituted residence requirements, demanding that students take a full course load for a certain number of consecutive semesters. It was felt that total immersion in the field of study and extensive interaction with the faculty were necessary to achieve mastery of an academic area.

In most academic Ph.D. programs as well as many health-care fields, this is still the only approach. However, many other programs now admit part-time students or allow a portion of the requirements to be completed on a part-time basis. Professional schools are more likely to allow part-time study because many students work full-time in the field and pursue their degree in order to enhance their career credentials. Other applicants choose part-time study because of financial considerations. By continuing to work full-time while attending school, they take fewer economic risks.

Part-time programs vary considerably in quality and admissions standards. When evaluating a part-time program, use the same criteria you would use in judging the reputation of any graduate program. Some schools use more adjunct faculty members with weaker academic training for their night and weekend courses, and this could lower the quality of the program; however, adjunct lecturers often have excellent experiential knowledge. Admissions standards may be lower for a part-time program than for an equivalent full-time program at the same school, but, again, your fellow students in the part-time program may be practicing in the field and may have much to add to class discussions. Another concern is placement opportunities upon completion of the program. Some schools may not offer placement services to part-time students, and many employers do not value part-time training as highly as a full-time education. However, if a part-time program is the best option for you, do not hesitate to enroll after carefully researching available programs.

International Students

If you are an international student, you will follow the same application procedures as other graduate school applicants. However, you will have to meet additional requirements.

Since your success as a graduate student will depend on your ability to understand, write, read, and speak English, if English is not your native language, you will be required to take the Test of English as a Foreign Language (TOEFL), or a similar test. Some schools will waive the language test requirement, however, if you have a degree from a college or university in a country where the native language is English or if you have studied two or more years in an undergraduate or graduate program in a country where the native language is English. As for all other tests, score requirements vary, but some schools admit students with lower scores on the condition that they enroll in an intensive English program before or during their graduate study. You should ask each school or department about its policies.

In addition to scores on your English test, or proof of competence in English, your formal application must be accompanied by a certified English translation of your academic transcripts. You may also be required to submit records of immunization and certain health certificates as well as documented evidence of financial support at the time of application. However, since you may apply for financial assistance from graduate schools as well as other sources, some institutions require evidence of financial support only as the last step in your formal admittance and may grant you conditional acceptance first.

Once you have been formally admitted into a graduate program and have submitted evidence of your source or sources of financial support, the school will send you Form I-20 or Form IAP-66, Certificate of Eligibility for Non-Immigrant Status. You must present this document, along with a passport from your own government, and evidence of financial support (some schools will require evidence of support for the entire course of study, while others require evidence of support only for the first year of study, if there is also documentation to show reasonable expectation of continued support) to a U.S. embassy or consulate to obtain an international student visa (F-1 with the Form I-20 or J-1 with the Form IAP-66).

Your own government may have other requirements you must meet to study in the United States. Be sure to investigate those requirements as well.

Once all the paperwork has been completed and approved, you are ready to make your travel arrangements. If your port of entry into the United States will be New York's Kennedy Airport, you can arrange, for a fee, to be met and assisted by a representative of the YMCA Arrivals Program. This person will help you through customs and assist you in making travel connections. He or she can also help you find temporary overnight accommodations, if needed. To inquire about fees for this service, contact the Arrivals Program by phone (212-727-8800 Ext. 130), fax (212-727-8814), or e-mail (jholt@ymcanyc.org). If you decide to take advantage of this assistance, you must provide the Arrivals Program with the following information: your name, age, sex, date and time of arrival, airline and flight number, college or university you will be attending, sponsoring agency (if any), and connecting flight information. Include a photo to help identify you, and note if you need overnight accommodations in New York. This information should be sent well in advance to YMCA Arrivals Program, 71 West 23rd Street, Suite 1904, New York, New York 10010.

When you arrive on your American college campus, you will want to contact the international student adviser. This person's job is to help international students in their academic and social adjustment. The adviser often coordinates special orientation programs for new students, which may consist of lectures on American culture, intensive language instruction, campus tours, academic placement examinations, and visits to places of cultural interest in the community. This adviser will also help you with travel and employment questions as well as financial concerns and will keep copies of your visa documents on file, which is required by U.S. immigration law.

A number of nonprofit educational organizations are available throughout the world to assist international students in planning graduate study in the United States. To learn how to get in touch with these organizations for detailed information, contact the U.S. embassy in your country.

Jane E. Levy
Senior Associate Director
University Career Center
Cornell University
and
Elinor R. Workman
Director of Career Services
Graduate School of Business
University of Chicago

Financing Your Graduate and Professional Education

If you're considering attending graduate school but fear you don't have enough money, don't despair. Financial support for graduate study does exist, although, admittedly, the information about support sources can be difficult to find.

Support for graduate study can take many forms, depending upon the field of study and program you pursue. For example, some 60 percent of doctoral students receive support in the form of either grants/fellowships or assistantships, whereas most students in master's programs rely on loans to pay for their graduate study. In addition, doctoral candidates are more likely to receive grants/fellowships and assistantships than master's degree students, and students in the sciences are more likely to receive aid than those in the arts and humanities.

For those of you who have experience with financial aid as an undergraduate, there are some differences for graduate students you'll notice right away. For one, aid to undergraduates is based primarily on need (although the number of colleges that now offer undergraduate merit-based aid is increasing). But graduate aid is often based on academic merit, especially in the arts and sciences. Second, as a graduate student, you are automatically "independent" for federal financial aid purposes, meaning your parents' income and assest information is not required in assessing your need for federal aid. And third, at some graduate schools, the awarding of aid may be administered by the academic departments or the graduate school itself, not the financial aid office. This means that at some schools, you may be involved with as many as three offices: a central financial aid office, the graduate school, *and* your academic department.

FINANCIAL AID MYTHS

- **Financial aid is just for poor people.**
- **Financial aid is just for smart people.**
- **Financial aid is mainly for minority students.**
- **I have a job, so I must not be eligible for aid.**
- **If I apply for aid, it will affect whether or not I'm admitted.**
- **Loans are not financial aid.**

Be Prepared

Being prepared for graduate school means you should put together a financial plan. So, before you enter graduate school, you should have answers to these questions:

- What should I be doing now to prepare for the cost of my graduate education?
- What can I do to minimize my costs once I arrive on campus?
- What financial aid programs are available at each of the schools to which I am applying?
- What financial aid programs are available outside the university, at the federal, state, or private level?
- What financing options do I have if I cannot pay the full cost from my own resources and those of my family?
- What should I know about the loans I am being offered?
- What impact will these loans have on me when I complete my program?

You'll find your answers in three guiding principles: think ahead, live within your means, and keep your head above water.

Think Ahead

The first step to putting together your financial plan comes from thinking about the future: the loss of your income while you're attending school, your projected income after you graduate, the annual rate of inflation, additional expenses you will incur as a student and after you graduate, and any loss of income you may experience later from unintentional periods of unemployment, pregnancy, or disability. The cornerstone of thinking ahead is following a step-by-step process.

1. *Set your goals.* Decide what and where you want to study, whether you will attend full- or part-time, whether you'll work while attending, and what an appropriate level of debt would be. Consider whether you would attend full-time if you had enough financial aid or whether keeping your full-time job is an important priority in your life. Keep in mind that some employers have tuition reimbursement plans for full-time employees.
2. *Take inventory.* Collect your financial information and add up your assets—bank accounts, stocks, bonds, real estate, business and personal property. Then subtract your liabilities—money owed on your assets including credit card debt and car loans—to yield your net worth.
3. *Calculate your need.* Compare your net worth with the costs at the schools you are considering to get a rough estimate of how much of your assets you can use for your schooling.
4. *Create an action plan.* Determine how much you'll earn while in school, how much you think you will receive in grants and scholarships, and how much you plan to borrow. Don't forget to consider inflation and possible life changes that could affect your overall financial plan.
5. *Review your plan regularly.* Measure the progress of your plan every year and make adjustments for such things as increases in salary or other changes in your goals or circumstances.

Live Within Your Means

The second step in being prepared is knowing how much you spend now so you can determine how much you'll spend when you're in school. Use the standard cost of attendance budget published by your school as a guide. But don't be surprised if your estimated budget is higher than the one the school provides, especially if you've been out of school for a while. Once you've figured out your budget, see if you can pare down your current costs and financial obligations so the lean years of graduate school don't come as too large a shock.

Keep Your Head Above Water

Finally, the third step is managing the debt you'll accrue as a graduate student. Debt is manageable only when considered in terms of five things:

1. Your future income
2. The amount of time it takes to repay the loan
3. The interest rate you are being charged
4. Your personal lifestyle and expenses after graduation
5. Unexpected circumstances that change your income or your ability to repay what you owe

To make sure your educational debt is manageable, you should borrow an amount that requires payments of between 8 and 15 percent of your starting salary.

The approximate monthly installments for repaying borrowed principal at 5, 8–10, and 12 percent are indicated on the next page.

Estimated Loan Repayment Schedule
Monthly Payments for Every $1000 Borrowed

Rate	5 years	10 years	15 years	20 years	25 years
5%	$18.87	$10.61	$ 7.91	$ 6.60	$ 5.85
8%	20.28	12.13	9.56	8.36	7.72
9%	20.76	12.67	10.14	9.00	8.39
10%	21.74	13.77	10.75	9.65	9.09
12%	22.24	14.35	12.00	11.01	10.53

You can use this table to estimate your monthly payments on a loan for any of the five repayment periods (5, 10, 15, 20, and 25 years). The amounts listed are the monthly payments for a $1000 loan for each of the interest rates. To estimate your monthly payment, choose the closest interest rate and multiply the amount of the payment listed by the total amount of your loan and then divide by 1,000. For example, for a total loan of $15,000 at 9 percent to be paid back over ten years, multiply $12.67 times 15,000 (190,050) divided by 1,000. This yields $190.05 per month.

If you're wondering just how much of a loan payment you can afford monthly without running into payment problems, consult the chart below.

HOW MUCH CAN YOU AFFORD TO REPAY?

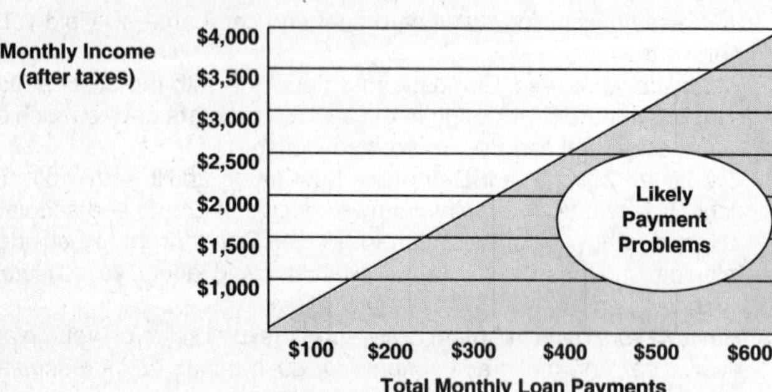

This graph shows the monthly cash-flow outlook based on your total monthly loan payments in comparison with your monthly income earned after taxes. Ideally, to eliminate likely payment problems, your monthly loan payment should be less than 15 percent of your monthly income.

Of course, the best way to manage your debt is to borrow less. While cutting your personal budget may be one option, there are a few others you may want to consider:

- *Ask Your Family for Help:* Although the federal government considers you "independent," your parents and family may still be willing and able to help pay for your graduate education. If your family is not open to just giving you money, they may be open to making a low-interest (or deferred-interest) loan. Family loans usually have more attractive interest rates and repayment terms than commercial loans. They may also have tax consequences, so you may want to check with a tax adviser.
- *Push to Graduate Early:* It's possible to reduce your total indebtedness by completing your program ahead of schedule. You can either take more courses per semester or during the summer. Keep in mind, though, that these options reduce the time you have available to work.
- *Work More, Attend Less:* Another alternative is to enroll part-time, leaving more time to work. Remember, though, to qualify for aid, you must be enrolled at least half-time, which is usually considered 6 credits per term. And if you're enrolled less than half-time, you'll have to start repaying your loans once the grace period has expired.

Roll Your Loans into One

There's a good chance that as a graduate student you will have two or more loans included in your aid package, plus any money you borrowed as an undergraduate. That means when you start repaying, you could be making loan payments to several different lenders. Not only can the recordkeeping be a nightmare, but with each loan having a minimum payment, your total monthly payments may be more than you can handle. If that is the case, you may want to consider consolidating your federal loans.

There is no minimum or maximum on the amount of loans you must have in order to consolidate. Also, there is no consolidation fee. The interest rate varies annually, is adjusted every July 1, and is capped at 8.25 percent. Your repayment can also be extended to up to thirty years, depending on the total amount you borrow, which will make your monthly payments lower (of course, you'll also be paying more total interest). With a consolidated loan, some lenders offer graduated or income-sensitive repayment options. Consult with your lender or the U.S. Department of Education about the types of consolidation provisions offered.

Plastic Mania

Any section on managing debt would be incomplete if it didn't mention the responsible use of credit cards. Most graduate students hold one or more credit cards, and many students find themselves in financial difficulties because of them. Here are two suggestions: use credit cards only for convenience, never for extended credit; and, if you have more than one credit card, keep only the one that has the lowest finance charge and the lowest limit.

Credit: Don't Let Your Past Haunt You

Many schools will check your credit history before they process any private educational loans for you. To make sure your credit rating is accurate, you may want to request a copy of your credit report before you start graduate school. You can get a copy of your report by sending a signed, written request to one of the four national credit reporting agencies at the address listed below. Include your full name, social security number, current address, any previous addresses for the past five years, date of birth, and daytime phone number. Call the agency before you request your report so you know whether there is a fee for this report. Note that you are entitled to a free copy of your credit report if you have been denied credit within the last sixty days. In addition, Experian currently provides complimentary credit reports once every twelve months.

Credit criteria used to review and approve student loans can include the following:

- Absence of negative credit
- No bankruptcies, foreclosures, repossessions, charge-offs, or open judgments
- No prior educational loan defaults, unless paid in full or making satisfactory repayments
- Absence of excessive past due accounts; that is, no 30-, 60-, or 90-day delinquencies on consumer loans or revolving charge accounts within the past two years

CREDIT REPORTING AGENCIES

Experian
P.O. Box 9530
Allen, Texas 75013
888-397-3742

Equifax
P.O. Box 105873

Atlanta, Georgia 30348
800-685-1111

CSC Credit Services
Consumer Assistance Center
P.O. Box 674402
Houston, Texas 77267-4402
800-759-5979

Trans Union Corporation
P.O. Box 390
Springfield, Pennsylvania 19064-0390
800-888-4213

Types of Aid Available

There are three types of aid: money given to you (grants, scholarships, and fellowships), money you earn through work, and loans.

GRANTS, SCHOLARSHIPS, AND FELLOWSHIPS

Most grants, scholarships, and fellowships are outright awards that require no service in return. Often they provide the cost of tuition and fees plus a stipend to cover living expenses. Some are based exclusively on financial need, some exclusively on academic merit, and some on a combination of need and merit. As a rule, grants are awarded to those with financial need, although they may require the recipient to have expertise in a certain field. Fellowships and scholarships often connote selectivity based on ability—financial need is usually not a factor.

Federal Support

Several federal agencies fund fellowship and trainee programs for graduate and professional students. The amounts and types of assistance offered vary considerably by field of study.

Education

Jacob Javits Fellowship. This is a grant program for students in the arts, humanities, and social sciences to use at the school of their choice. Graduate students apply directly to the U.S. Department of Education. The application deadline is in February. The school the Javits Fellow attends receives up to $10,222 toward the cost of tuition. If the tuition exceeds $10,222, the school is obliged to cover the additional cost in the form of a grant. Javits Fellows receive as much as $15,000 in stipend, depending on financial need and available funding. No funding is guaranteed beyond this current 1998 fiscal year. For more information, call 202-708-8596.

National Institutes of Health (NIH). NIH sponsors many different fellowship opportunities. For example, it offers training grants administered through schools' research departments. Training grants provide tuition plus a twelve-month stipend of $11,496. For more information, call 301-435-0714.

Federal Scholarships for Students with Exceptional Financial Need (EFN) and Federal Assistance for Disadvantaged Health Professions Students (FADHPS). Some medical schools receive funding in the Health and Human Services Department for two scholarship programs. EFN and FADHPS are targeted for very needy students who are interested in primary care. These scholarships carry a service obligation and recipients complete a primary residency within four years of graduation as well as practice primary health care for five years following residency. Contact the medical school financial aid office for more information.

Service Scholarships. One of the most popular service scholarships is the **National Health Services Corps Scholarship Program** administered by the Public Health Service. The program offers full tuition assistance, reimbursement for books and supplies, and a monthly stipend for living expenses in exchange for a service commitment after graduation and residency. If you are concerned about the burden of taking on the amount of student debt many medical students assume, you may want to consider applying for a service scholarship. You can contact the Public Health Service directly by writing to National Health Service Corps Scholarship Program, 1010 Wayne Avenue, Suite 240, Silver Spring, Maryland 20910, or by calling 800-638-0824.

Veterans' Benefits. Veterans may use their educational benefits for training at the graduate and professional levels. Contact your regional office of the Veterans Administration for more details.

State Support

Some states offer grants for graduate study, with California, Michigan, New York, North Carolina, Texas, and Virginia offering the largest programs. States grant approximately $2.9 billion per year to graduate students. Due to fiscal constraints, however, some states have had to reduce or eliminate their financial aid programs for graduate study. To qualify for a particular state's aid you must be a resident of that state. Residency is established in most states after you have lived there for at least twelve consecutive months prior to enrolling in school. Many states provide funds for in-state students only; that is, funds are not transferable out of state. Contact your state scholarship office to determine what aid it offers.

Institutional Aid

Educational institutions using their own funds provide more than $3 billion in graduate assistance in the form of fellowships, tuition waivers, and assistantships. Consult each school's catalog for information about aid programs.

Corporate Aid

Some corporations provide graduate student support as part of the employee benefits package. Most employees who receive aid study at the master's level or take courses without enrolling in a particular degree program.

Aid from Foundations

Most foundations provide support in areas of interest to them. For example, for those studying for the Ph.D., the Howard Hughes Institute funds students in the biomedical sciences, while the Spencer Foundation funds dissertation research in the field of education.

The Foundation Center of New York City publishes several reference books on foundation support for graduate study. For more information, call 212-620-4230 or access their Web site at http://fdncenter.org.

Financial Aid for Minorities and Women

Patricia Roberts Harris Fellowships. This federal award provides support for minorities and women. Awards are made to schools, and the schools decide who receives these funds. Fellows receive a stipend of $14,400 for up to four years, and their institutions receive up to $9493 per year. Consult the graduate school for more information. No funding is guaranteed beyond the 1998 fiscal year.

Bureau of Indian Affairs. The Bureau of Indian Affairs (BIA) offers aid to students who are at least one quarter American Indian or native Alaskan and from a federally recognized tribe. Contact your tribal education officer, BIA area office, or call the Bureau of Indian Affairs at 202-208-3710.

The Ford Foundation Doctoral Fellowship for Minorities. Provides three-year doctoral fellowships and one-year dissertation fellowships. Predoctoral fellowships include an annual stipend of $14,000 to the fellow and an annual institutional grant of $7500 to the fellowship institution in lieu of tuition and fees. Dissertation fellows receive a stipend of $18,000 for a twelve-month period. Applications are due in early November. For more information, contact the Fellowship Office, National Research Council at 202-334-2872.

The Council on Legal Education Opportunity (CLEO) helps economically and educationally disadvantaged students attend law school. It also sponsors summer institutes for preparatory work. Contact the law school you want to attend and ask if the school participates in the CLEO program. In addition, below are some books available that describe financial aid opportunities for women and minorities.

The Directory of Financial Aids for Women by Gail Ann Schlachter (Reference Service Press, 1997) lists sources of support and identifies foundations and other organizations interested in helping women secure funding for graduate study.

The Association for Women in Science publishes *Grants-at-a-Glance,* a booklet highlighting fellowships for women in science. It can be ordered by calling 202-326-8940, or visit their Web site at http://www.awis.org.

Books such as the *Financial Aid for Minorities* (Garrett Park, MD: Garrett Park Press, 1998) describe financial aid opportunities for minority students. For more information, call 301-946-2553.

Reference Service Press also publishes four directories specifically for minorities: *Financial Aid for African Americans, Financial Aid for Asian Americans, Financial Aid for Hispanic Americans,* and *Financial Aid for Native Americans.*

Also, visit the Minority On-Line Information Service (MOLIS) Web site at http://web.fie.com/web/mol/.

Disabled students are eligible to receive aid from a number of organizations. *Financial Aid for the Disabled and Their Families, 1996–98* by Gail Ann Schlachter and David R. Weber (Reference Service Press) lists aid opportunities for disabled students. The Vocational Rehabilitation Services in your home state can also provide information.

Researching Grants and Fellowships

The books listed below are good sources of information on grant and fellowship support for graduate education and should be consulted before you resort to borrowing. Keep in mind that grant support varies dramatically from field to field.

Annual Register of Grant Support: A Directory of Funding Sources, Wilmette, Illinois: National Register Publishing Co. This is a comprehensive guide to grants and awards from government agencies, foundations, and business and professional organizations.

Corporate Foundation Profiles, 10th ed. New York: Foundation Center, 1998. This is an in-depth, analytical profile of 250 of the largest company-sponsored foundations in the United States. Brief descriptions of all 700 company-sponsored foundations are also included. There is an index of subjects, types of support, and geographical locations.

The Foundation Directory. Edited by Stan Olsen. New York: Foundation Center, 1998. This directory, with a supplement, gives detailed information on U.S. foundations with brief descriptions of the purpose and activities of each.

The Grants Register 1998, 16th ed. Edited by Lisa Williams. New York: St. Martin's, 1998. This lists grant agencies alphabetically and gives information on awards available to graduate students, young professionals, and scholars for study and research.

Peterson's Grants for Graduate and Postdoctoral Study 5th ed. Princeton: Peterson's, 1998. This book includes information on more than 1,400 grants, scholarships, awards, fellowships, and prizes. Originally compiled by the Office of Research Affairs at the Graduate School of the University of Massachusetts at Amherst, this guide is updated periodically by Peterson's.

Graduate schools sometimes publish listings of support sources in their catalogs, and some provide separate publications, such as the *Graduate Guide to Grants,* compiled by the Harvard Graduate School of Arts and Sciences. For more information, call 617-495-1814.

THE INTERNET AS A SOURCE OF FUNDING INFORMATION

If you have not explored the financial resources on the World Wide Web (the Web, for short), your research is not complete. Now available on the Web is a wealth of information ranging from loan and entrance applications to minority grants and scholarships.

University-Specific Information on the Web

Many universities have Web financial aid directories. Florida, Virginia Tech, Massachusetts, Emory, and Georgetown are just a few. Applications of admission can now be downloaded from the Web to start the graduate process. After that, detailed information can be obtained on financial aid processes, forms, and deadlines. University-specific grant and scholarship information can also be found, and more may be learned about financing information by using the Web than by an actual visit. Questions can be answered on line.

Scholarships on the Web

When searching for scholarship opportunities, one can search the Web. Many benefactors and other scholarship donors have pages on the Web listing pertinent information with regard to their specific scholarship. You can reach this information through a variety of methods. For example, you can find a directory listing minority scholarships, quickly look at the information on line, decide if it applies to you, and then move on. New scholarship pages are being added to the Web daily. Library and Web resources are productive and—free.

The Web also lists many services that will look for scholarships for you. Some of these services cost money, and advertise more scholarships per dollar than any other service. While some of these might be helpful, beware. Check references to make sure a bona fide service is being offered. Your best bet initially is to surf the Web and use the traditional library resources on available scholarships.

Bank and Loan Information on the Web

Banks and loan servicing centers have pages on the Web, making it easier to access loan information on the Web. Having the information on screen in front of you instantaneously is more convenient than being put on hold on the phone. Any loan information such as interest rate variations, descriptions of loans, loan consolidation programs, and repayment charts can all be found on the Web.

WORK PROGRAMS

Certain types of support, such as teaching, research, and administrative assistantships, require recipients to provide service to the university in exchange for a salary or stipend; sometimes tuition is also provided or waived.

Teaching Assistantships

Because science and engineering classes are taught at the undergraduate level, you stand a good chance of securing a teaching assistantship. These positions usually involve conducting small classes, delivering lectures, correcting class work, grading papers, counseling students, and supervising laboratory groups. Usually about 20 hours of work is required each week.

Teaching assistantships provide excellent educational experience as well as financial support. TAs generally receive a salary (now considered taxable income). Sometimes tuition is provided or waived as well. In addition, at some schools, TAs can be declared state residents, qualifying them for the in-state tuition rates. Appointments are based on academic qualifications and are subject to the availability of funds within a department. If you are interested in a teaching assistantship, contact the academic department. Ordinarily you are not considered for such positions until you have been admitted to the graduate school.

Research Assistantships

Research Assistantships usually require that you assist in the research activities of a faculty member. Appointments are ordinarily made for the academic year. They are rarely offered to first-year students. Contact the academic department, describing your particular research interests. As is the case with teaching assistantships, research assistantships provide excellent academic training as well as practical experience and financial support.

Administrative Assistantships

These positions usually require 10 to 20 hours of work each week in an administrative office of the university. For example, those seeking a graduate degree in education may work in the admissions, financial aid, student affairs, or placement office of the school they are attending. Some administrative assistantships provide a tuition waiver, others a salary. Details concerning these positions can be found in the school catalog or by contacting the academic department directly.

Federal Work-Study Program (FWS)

This federally funded program provides eligible students with employment opportunities, usually in public and private nonprofit organizations. Federal funds pay up to 75 percent of the wages, with the remainder paid by the employing agency. FWS is available to graduate students who demonstrate financial need. Not all schools have these funds, and some only award undergraduates. Each school sets its application deadline and work-study earnings limits. Wages vary and are related to the type of work done.

Additional Employment Opportunities

Many schools provide on-campus employment opportunities that do not require demonstrated financial need. The student employment office on most campuses assists students in securing jobs both on and off the campus.

LOANS

Most needy graduate students, except those pursuing Ph.D.'s in certain fields, borrow to finance their graduate programs. There are basically two sources of student loans–the federal government and private loan programs. You should read and understand the terms of these loan programs before submitting your loan application.

FEDERAL LOANS

Federal Stafford Loans. The Federal Stafford Loan Program offers government-sponsored, low-interest loans to students through a private lender such as a bank, credit union, or savings and loan association.

There are two components of the Federal Stafford Loan program. Under the *subsidized* component of the program, the federal government pays the interest accruing on the loan while you are enrolled in graduate school on at least a half-time basis. Under the *unsubsidized* component of the program, you pay the interest on the loan from the day proceeds are issued. Eligibility for the federal subsidy is based on demonstrated financial need as determined by the financial aid office from the information you provide on the Free Application for Federal Student Aid (FAFSA). A cosigner is not required, since the loan is not based on creditworthiness.

Although Unsubsidized Federal Stafford Loans may not be as desirable as Subsidized Federal Stafford Loans from the consumer's perspective, they are a useful source of support for those who may not qualify for the subsidized loans or who need additional financial assistance.

Graduate students may borrow up to $18,500 per year through the Stafford Loan Program, up to a maximum of $138,500, including undergraduate borrowing. This may include up to $8500 in Subsidized Stafford Loans, depending on eligibility, up to a maximum of $65,000, including undergraduate borrowing. The amount of the loan borrowed through the Unsubsidized Stafford Program equals the total amount of the loan (as much $18,500) minus your eligibility for a Subsidized Stafford Loan (as much as $8500). You may borrow up to the cost of the school in which you are enrolled or will attend, minus estimated financial assistance from other federal, state, and private sources, up to a maximum of $18,500.

The interest rate for the Federal Stafford Loans varies annually and is set every July. The rate during in-school, grace, and deferment periods is based on the 91-Day U.S. Treasury Bill rate plus 2.5 percent, capped at 8.25 percent. The rate in repayment is based on the 91-Day U.S. Treasury Bill rate plus 3.1 percent, capped at 8.25 percent. However, the interest rate may soon be based on the ten-year Treasury Bill, pending current legislation.

Two fees are deducted from the loan proceeds upon disbursement: a guarantee fee of up to 1 percent, which is deposited in an insurance pool to ensure repayment to the lender if the borrower defaults, and a federally mandated 3 percent origination fee, which is used to offset the administrative cost of the Federal Stafford Loan Program.

Under the *subsidized* Federal Loan Program, repayment begins six months after your last enrollment on at least a half-time basis. Under the *unsubsidized* program, repayment of interest begins within thirty days from disbursement of the loan proceeds, and repayment of the principal begins six months after your last enrollment on at least a half-time basis. Some lenders may require that some payments may be made even while you are in school, although most lenders will allow you to defer payments and will add the accrued interest to the loan balance. Under both components of the program repayment may extend over a maximum of ten years with no prepayment penalty.

Federal Direct Loans. Some schools are participating in the Department of Education's Direct Lending Program instead of offering Federal Stafford Loans. The two programs are essentially the same except with the Direct Loans, schools themselves originate the loans with funds provided from the federal government. Terms and interest rates are virtually the same except that there are a few more repayment options with Federal Direct Loans.

Federal Perkins Loans. The Federal Perkins Loan is a long-term loan available to students demonstrating financial need and is administered directly by the school. Not all schools have these funds, and some may award them to undergraduates only. Eligibility is determined from the information you provide on the FAFSA. The school will notify you of your eligibility.

Eligible graduate students may borrow up to $5000 per year, up to a maximum of $30,000, including undergraduate borrowing (even if your previous Perkins Loans have been repaid.) The interest rate for Federal Perkins Loans is 5 percent, and no interest accrues while you remain in school at least half-time. There are no guarantee, loan, or disbursement fees. Repayment begins nine months after your last enrollment on at least a half-time basis and may extend over a maximum of ten years with no prepayment penalty.

Deferring Your Federal Loan Repayments. If you borrowed under the Federal Stafford Loan Program or the Federal Perkins Loan Program for previous undergraduate or graduate study, some of your repayments may be deferred (i.e., suspended) when you return to graduate school, depending on when you borrowed and under which program.

There are other deferment options available if you are temporarily unable to repay your loan. Information about these deferments is provided at your entrance and exit interviews. If you believe you are eligible for a deferment of your loan repayments, you must contact your lender to complete a deferment form. The deferment must be filed prior to the time your repayment is due, and it must be refiled when it expires if you remain eligible for deferment at that time.

Supplemental Loans

Many lending institutions offer supplemental loan programs and other financing plans, such as the ones described below, to students seeking assistance in meeting their expected contribution toward educational expenses.

If you are considering borrowing through a supplemental loan program, you should carefully consider the terms of the program and be sure to "read the fine print." Check with the program sponsor for the most current terms that will be applicable to the amounts you intend to borrow for graduate study. Most supplemental loan programs for graduate study offer unsubsidized, credit-based loans. In general, a credit-ready borrower is one who has a satisfactory credit history or no credit history at all. A creditworthy borrower generally must pass a credit test to be eligible to borrow or act as a cosigner for the loan funds.

Many supplemental loan programs have a minimum annual loan limit and a maximum annual loan limit. Some offer amounts equal to the cost of attendance minus any other aid you will receive for graduate study. If you are planning to borrow for several years of graduate study, consider whether there is a cumulative or aggregate limit on the amount you may borrow. Often this cumulative or aggregate limit will include any amounts you borrowed and have not repaid for undergraduate or previous graduate study.

The combination of the annual interest rate, loan fees, and the repayment terms you choose will determine how much the amount is that you will repay over time. Compare these features in combination before you decide which loan program to use. Some loans offer interest rates that are adjusted monthly, some quarterly, some annually. Some offer interest rates that are lower during the in-school, grace, and deferment periods, and then increase when you begin repayment. Most programs include a loan "origination" fee, which is usually deducted from the principal amount you receive when the loan is disbursed, and must be repaid along with the interest and other principal when you graduate, withdraw from school, or drop below half-time study. Sometimes the loan fees are reduced if you borrow with a qualified cosigner. Some programs allow you to defer interest and/or principal payments while you are enrolled in graduate school. Many programs allow you to capitalize your interest payments; the interest due on your loan is added to the outstanding balance of your loan, so you don't have to repay immediately, but this increases the amount you owe. Other programs allow you to pay the interest as you go, which will reduce the amount you later have to repay.

For more information about supplemental loan programs or to obtain applications, call the customer service phone numbers of the organizations listed below, access the sponsor's site on the World Wide Web, or visit your school's financial aid office.

American Express Alternative Loan. An unsubsidized, credit-based loan for credit-ready graduate students enrolled at least half-time, sponsored by American Express/California Higher Education Loan Authority (800-255-8374).

CitiAssist Graduate Loan. An unsubsidized, credit-based loan for graduate students in all disciplines, sponsored by Citibank (800-745-5473 or 800-946-4019; World Wide Web: http://www.citibank.com/student).

CollegeReserve Loan. An unsubsidized, credit-based loan for creditworthy graduate students enrolled at least half-time, sponsored by USA Group (800-538-8492; World Wide Web: http://www.usagroup.com).

EXCEL Loan. An unsubsidized, credit-based loan for borrowers who are not credit-ready or who would prefer to borrow with a creditworthy cosigner to obtain a more attractive interest rate, sponsored by Nellie Mae (888-2TUITION).

GradAchiever Loan. An unsubsidized, credit-based loan for graduate students enrolled at least half-time, sponsored by Key Education Resources (800-KEY-LEND; World Wide Web: http://www.key.com/education/grad.html).

GradEXCEL Loan. An unsubsidized, credit-based loan for credit-ready graduate students enrolled at least half-time, sponsored by Nellie Mae (888-2TUITION).

Graduate Access Loan. An unsubsidized, credit-based loan for creditworthy graduate students enrolled at least half-time, sponsored by the Access Group (800-282-1550; World Wide Web: http://www.accessgroup.org).

Signature Student Loan. An unsubsidized, credit-based loan for graduate students enrolled at least half-time, sponsored by Sallie Mae (888-272-5543; World Wide Web: http://www.salliemae.com).

Business Loans

Business Access Loans. The minimum loan amount is $500. The maximum total outstanding educational debt is $120,000 (including undergraduate and graduate debt). The interest rate for the in-school period varies quarterly based on the 91-Day U.S. Treasury Bill rate plus 3 percent. Interest is capitalized once—at repayment. The guarantee fee is 6 percent at disbursement. An additional fee of between 1.5 and 6.9 percent is added to the principal of the loan immediately prior to repayment. There is no origination fee. Repayment begins nine months after graduation or after your enrollment status drops to less than half-time. You have up to twenty years to repay. For information, contact The Access Group at 800-282-1550.

MBAchiever. The minimum loan amount is $500. The maximum total outstanding educational debt is $120,000 (including undergraduate and graduate debt). You may borrow up to the total cost of education minus other financial aid. The interest rate prior to repayment varies quarterly based on the 91-Day U.S. Treasury Bill rate plus 3.25 percent. At repayment, the interest rate varies based on the 91-Day U.S. Treasury Bill rate plus 3.4 percent. Interest is capitalized once—at repayment. An initial loan fee of 6 percent is deducted from each disbursement. A supplemental loan fee (not to exceed 6.9 percent) will be added to your loan balance prior to repayment. Repayment begins nine months after graduation or after you cease to be enrolled at least half-time. You have up to twenty years to repay. For information, contact Key Education Resources at 800-KEY-LEND.

MBAEXCEL. The maximum total outstanding educational debt is $82,000. The interest rate is based on the prime rate. There is a guarantee fee of 7 percent with a co-borrower, 10 percent without a co-borrower. There is a 2 percent capitalization fee. With a co-borrower, you may borrow up to the total cost of attendance, and without a co-borrower, you may borrow up to $12,000. For more information, contact Nellie Mae at 800-FOR-TUITION.

MBA Loans. M.B.A. students attending AACSB-accredited institutions at least half-time can now borrow through a program called MBA Loans. Designed specifically for M.B.A. students, this program offers a two-in-one application form to apply for Federal Stafford Loans and an alternative loan through the Tuition Loan Program (TLP). For information contact your school's financial aid office.

Law Loans

Law Access Loans. The Access Group has a loan program that provides law students with access to private loans. The minimum loan amount is $500. The maximum total outstanding debt is $130,000 (including undergraduate and graduate debt). The interest rate varies quarterly based on the 91-Day U.S. Treasury Bill rate plus 2.9 percent. Interest is capitalized once—at repayment. The guarantee fee is 6 percent at disbursement. An additional fee of between 1.5 and 6.9 percent is added to the principal of the loan immediately prior to repayment. There is no origination fee. Repayment begins nine months after graduation, or when your student status drops to less than half-time, with up to twenty years to repay. For more information, call The Access Group at 800-282-1550.

LawEXCEL. The maximum total outstanding educational debt is $105,000. The interest rate is based on the prime rate. There is a guarantee fee of 7 percent with a co-borrower, 10 percent without a co-borrower. There is a 2 percent capitalization fee. With a co-borrower, you may borrow up to the total cost of attendance, and without a co-borrower, you may borrow up to $12,000. For more information, contact Nellie Mae at 800-FOR-TUITION.

LawLoans. LawLoans provide up to the cost of education, with a cumulative LawLoans limit of $75,000 and a total educational debt limit of $150,000 with a cosigner, $125,000 without a cosigner. The interest rate is based on the 91-Day U.S. Treasury Bill rate plus 3.25 percent. For more information, call 800-366-5626.

Medicine/Health-Care Loans

Dental Access Loans. The minimum loan amount is $500. The maximum total outstanding educational debt is $195,000 (including undergraduate and graduate debt). The interest rate varies quarterly based on the 91-Day U.S. Treasury Bill rate plus 2.75 percent. Interest is capitalized once, just prior to repayment. The guarantee fee is 6 percent at disbursement. An additional fee of between 1.5 and 6.9 percent is added to the principal of the loan immediately prior to repayment. There is no origination fee. Repayment begins nine months after graduation or after your student status drops to less than half-time or after completion of a required dental residency or postdoctoral program. You have up to twenty years to repay. For more information, contact The Access Group at 800-282-1550.

Health Education Assistance Loans. The Health Education Assistance Loan (HEAL) provides loans to medical and other health professions students through participating banks. Application forms, available from your school's financial aid office, refer you to a participating lender. Students may borrow up to $20,000 each year, up to a total of $80,000. HEAL interest rates are variable and are tied to the 91-Day U.S. Treasury Bill rate plus 3 percent. HEAL borrowers pay an insurance premium of 8 percent. The lender must permit you to defer all payments toward interest and principal until you enter the repayment period. Instead of allowing the interest to capitalize, you can choose to pay it on an ongoing basis, which markedly decreases the overall cost of the loan. Repayment begins nine months after the completion of training or withdrawal from school. You have up to twenty-five years to repay, excluding deferment periods.

MedDentEXCEL. The maximum total outstanding educational debt is $145,000 for medical students and $80,000 for dental students. The interest rate is based on the prime rate. There is a guarantee fee of 7 percent with a co-borrower, 9 percent for medical students without a co-borrower, 10 percent for dental students without a co-borrower. There is a 2 percent capitalization fee. With a co-borrower, you may borrow up to the total cost of attendance, and without a co-borrower, you may borrow up to $15,000. You may opt for interest-only payments during a residency program or full-time postgraduate training. In the final year of medical/dental school, you may borrow up to $5,000 in addition to the regular loan amount. For more information, contact Nellie Mae at 800-FOR-TUITION.

Medical Access Loans. The minimum loan amount is $500. The maximum total outstanding educational debt is $195,000 (including undergraduate and graduate debt). The interest rate varies quarterly based on the 91-Day U.S. Treasury Bill rate plus 2.5 percent. Interest is capitalized once, just prior to repayment. The guarantee fee is 6 percent at disbursement. An additional fee of 1.5 percent is added to the principal of the loan immediately prior to repayment. There is no origination fee. Repayment begins nine months after graduation, or after your student status drops to less than half-time, or after completion of a required residency program, not to exceed forty-eight months. You have up to twenty years to repay. For more information, contact The Access Group at 800-282-1550.

MedLoans, Alternative Loan Program (ALP). MedLoans was developed by the Association of American Medical Colleges (AAMC). The interest rate is variable and determined quarterly on the 91-Day U.S. Treasury Bill plus 2.5 percent. The annual loan limit is the cost of attendance, minus other financial aid. There are residency deferment options available for three to four years after graduation. For more information, contact AAMC at 2450 N Street, NW, Washington, D.C. 20037, or call 800-858-5050.

Primary Care Loans. Primary Care Loans, formerly the Health Professions Student Loan (HPSL), are available to full-time graduate students enrolled in programs of study in the health professions, health administration, clinical psychology or public health. Primary Care Loans are administered by the school but are not offered by all schools. You may borrow up to the cost of tuition plus $2500 or the amount of your financial need, whichever is less. The current interest rate is 5 percent. Repayment begins one year after you complete or cease to pursue full-time study.

International Education and Study Abroad

A variety of funding sources are offered for study abroad and for foreign nationals studying in the United States. The Institute of International Education in New York assists students in locating such aid. It publishes *Funding for U.S. Study—A Guide for International Students and Professionals* and *Financial Resources for International Study,* a guide to organizations offering awards for overseas study. The Council on International Educational Exchange in New York publishes the *Student Travel Catalogue,* which lists fellowship sources and explains the council's services both for United States students traveling abroad and for foreign students coming to the United States.

The U.S. Department of Education administers programs that support fellowships related to international education. Foreign Language and Area Studies Fellowships and Fulbright-Hays Doctoral Dissertation Awards were established to promote knowledge and understanding of other countries and cultures. They offer support to graduate students interested in foreign languages and international relations. Discuss these and other foreign study opportunities with the financial aid officer or someone in the graduate school dean's office at the school you will attend.

How to Apply

All applicants for federal aid must complete the Free Application for Federal Student Aid (FAFSA). This application must be submitted *after* January 1 preceding enrollment in the fall. It is a good idea to submit the FAFSA as soon as possible after this date. On this form you report your income and asset information for the preceding calendar year and specify which schools will receive the data. Two to four weeks later you'll receive an acknowledgment, the Student Aid Report (SAR), on which you can make any corrections. The schools you've designated will also receive the information and may begin asking you to send them documents, usually your U.S. income tax return, verifying what you reported.

In addition to the FAFSA, some graduate schools want additional information and will ask you to complete the CSS Financial Aid PROFILE. If your school requires this form, it will be listed in the PROFILE registration form available in college financial aid offices. Other schools use their own supplemental application. Check with your financial aid office to confirm which forms they require.

If you have already filed your federal income tax for the year, it will be much easier for you to complete these forms. If not, use estimates, but be certain to notify the financial aid office if your estimated figures differ from the actual ones once you have calculated them.

APPLICATION DEADLINES

Application deadlines vary. Some schools require you to apply for aid when applying for admission; others require that you be admitted before applying for aid. Aid application instructions and deadlines should be clearly stated in each school's application material. The FAFSA must be filed after January 1 of the year you are applying for aid but the Financial Aid PROFILE can be completed earlier, in October or November.

Determining Financial Need

Eligibility for need-based financial aid is based on your income during the calendar year prior to the academic year in which you apply for aid. Prior-year income is used because it is a good predictor of current-year income and is verifiable. If you have a significant reduction in income or assets after your aid application is completed, consult a financial aid counselor. If, for example, you are returning to school after working, you should let the financial aid counselor know your projected income for the year you will be in school. Aid counselors may use their "professional judgment" to revise your financial need, based on the actual income you will earn while you are in graduate school.

Need is determined by examining the difference between the cost of attendance at a given institution and the financial resources you bring to the table. Eligibility for aid is calculated by subtracting your resources from the total cost of attendance budget. These standard student budgets are generally on the low side of the norm. So if your expenses are higher because of medical bills, higher research travel, or more costly books, for example, a financial aid counselor can make an adjustment. Of course, you'll have to document any unusual expenses. Also, keep in mind that with limited grant and scholarship aid, a higher budget will probably mean either more loan or more working hours for you.

Tax Issues

Since the passage of the Tax Reform Act of 1986, grants, scholarships, and fellowships may be considered taxable income. That portion of the grant used for payment of tuition and course-required fees, books, supplies, and equipment is excludable from taxable income. Grant support for living expenses is taxable. A good rule of thumb for determining the tax liability for grants and scholarships is to view anything that exceeds the actual cost of tuition, required fees, books, supplies related to courses, and required equipment as taxable.

- If you are employed by an educational institution or other organization that gives tuition reimbursement, you must pay tax on the value that exceeds $5250.
- If your tuition is waived in exchange for working at the institution, the tuition waiver is taxable. This includes waivers that come with teaching or research assistantships.
- Other student support, such as stipends and wages paid to research assistants and teaching assistants, is also taxable income. Student loans, however, are not taxable.
- If you are an international student you may or may not owe taxes depending upon the agreement the U.S. has negotiated with your home country. The United States has tax treaties with more than forty countries. You are responsible for making sure that the school you attend follows the terms of the tax treaty. If your country does not have a tax treaty with the U.S., you may have as much as 30 percent withheld from your paycheck.

A Final Note

While amounts and eligibility criteria vary from field to field as well as from year to year, with thorough research you can uncover many opportunities for graduate financial assistance. If you are interested in graduate study, discuss your plans with faculty members and advisers. Explore all options. Plan ahead, complete forms on time, and be tenacious in your search for support. No matter what your financial situation, if you are academically qualified and knowledgeable about the different sources of aid, you should be able to attend the graduate school of your choice.

Patricia McWade
Dean of Student Financial Services
Georgetown University

Tests Required of Applicants

Many graduate schools require that applicants submit scores on one or more standardized tests, often the Graduate Record Examinations (GRE) or the Miller Analogies Test (MAT). Professional schools usually require that applicants take a specific admission test, such as the Dental Admission Test (DAT), the Graduate Management Admission Test (GMAT), the Law School Admission Test (LSAT), the Medical College Admission Test (MCAT), the Optometry Admission Test (OAT), the Pharmacy College Admission Test (PCAT), or the Veterinary College Admission Test (VCAT). Many graduate schools of education ask applicants to take the Praxis Series tests. Virtually all graduate and professional schools ask students whose native language is not English to take the Test of English as a Foreign Language (TOEFL), and some also ask for TOEFL's Test of Written English (TWE) or the Test of Spoken English (TSE).

Brief descriptions of these tests and the addresses to write to for additional information are given below.

DENTAL ADMISSION TESTING

The DAT Program is conducted by the Department of Testing Services of the American Dental Association. The testing program consists of four examinations covering natural sciences (biology, general chemistry, and organic chemistry), reading comprehension, quantitative reasoning, and perceptual ability. The entire test requires one half day. In 1999, the DAT will be given at Sylvan Technology Centers in each of the fifty states, the District of Columbia, and Puerto Rico. The DAT will be administered on regular business days. The fee for the examination is $150. All fees must be paid with a certified check or money order. The fee for each official report of scores, requested after the time of application, is $5. This fee must be paid with a certified check or money order.

Additional information is available from the Department of Testing Services, American Dental Association, 211 East Chicago Avenue, Suite 1840, Chicago, Illinois 60611-2678. Information about test centers and test application procedures is available by telephone (312-440-2689).

GRADUATE MANAGEMENT ADMISSION TEST

The GMAT is designed to help graduate management schools assess the qualifications of applicants for graduate-level programs in business and management. The GMAT is now administered as a computer-adaptive test (CAT).

The GMAT measures general verbal, mathematical, and analytical writing skills that are developed over a long period of time and are associated with success in the first year of study at graduate schools of management. The quantitative sections of the test measure basic mathematical skills and understanding of elementary concepts and the ability to reason quantitatively, solve quantitative problems, and interpret graphic data. The verbal sections of the test measure the ability to understand and evaluate what is read and to recognize basic conventions of standard written English. The analytical writing sections of the test measure the ability to think critically and communicate complex ideas through writing.

Information about how to register and prepare for the GMAT, as well as a list of test centers, is available on the Web site at http://www.gmat.org.

Peterson's offers *GMAT Success*, a complete guide to the GMAT. Visit your local bookstore or contact Peterson's at 800-225-0261.

GRADUATE RECORD EXAMINATIONS

The GRE General Test and Subject Tests are designed to assess academic knowledge and skills relevant to graduate study. The General Test measures verbal, quantitative, and analytical reasoning skills, and the Subject Tests measure achievement in particular fields of study. The GRE tests are administered worldwide by Educational Testing Service (ETS) of Princeton, New Jersey, under policies established by the Graduate Record Examinations Board, an independent board affiliated with the Association of Graduate Schools and the Council of Graduate Schools.

Currently, the General Test is offered both as a computer-based test (CBT) and a paper-based test. However, GRE plans to phase out the paper-based General Test after April 1999 and introduce a Writing Test. Subject Tests, offered only as paper-based tests, are available in fourteen areas: biochemistry, cell and molecular biology; biology; chemistry; computer science; economics; engineering; geology; history; literature in English; mathematics; music; physics; psychology; and sociology.

While the paper-based General Test is not offered in many international locations, the CBT General Test is offered year-round at more than 600 test centers around the world. The CBT offers convenient scheduling, immediate viewing of unofficial scores, and faster score reporting. To schedule an appointment in the U.S., U.S. Territories, or Canada, call 800-GRE-CALL. For international testing, refer to the 1998–99 *GRE Information and Registration Bulletin* or the GRE Web site (http://www.gre.org) for a list of the regional registration centers. The *GRE Bulletin* contains registration and program services information for both CBT and paper-based testing.

The 1998–99 GRE paper-based test dates are November 7, December 12, and April 10. The General Test is offered on the November and April test dates only. Subject Tests are offered on all three dates; however, the economics, geology, history, music, and sociology tests will not be offered on the November test date.

Fees for the CBT General Test and the paper-based General Test and Subject Tests are $96 for testing in the U.S. and U.S. Territories and $120 in all other locations. Fees are subject to change.

Nonstandard testing accommodations are available for test takers with disabilities through both the CBT and paper-based testing programs. Students who cannot test on Saturdays for religious reasons may request a Monday paper-based administration immediately following a regular Saturday test date. Refer to the *GRE Bulletin* for more information.

Test takers can register by phone or fax for computer-based testing, by mail for both computer-based and paper-based testing, or on line for paper-based testing. Test takers should consider admission deadlines and register early to get their preferred test dates.

Further information on registration is available from the GRE Web site or by writing to GRE-ETS, P.O. Box 6000, Princeton, New Jersey 08541-6000 or by calling 609-771-7670.

Peterson's offers *GRE Success*, a complete guide to the GRE. Visit your local bookstore or contact Peterson's at 800-225-0261.

LAW SCHOOL ADMISSION TEST

The Law School Admission Test is a half-day standardized test required for admission to all 195 Law School Admission Council-member law schools. It consists of five 35-minute sections of multiple-choice questions. Four of the five sections contribute to the test taker's score. These sections include one reading comprehension section, one analytical reasoning section, and two logical reasoning sections. The fifth section typically is used to pretest new test items and to preequate new test forms. A 30-minute writing sample is administered at the end of the test. The writing sample is not scored by the Council; however, copies of the writing sample are sent to all law schools to which you apply. Scores on the LSAT range from 120 to 180; 120 is the lowest possible score and 180 is the highest.

The LSAT is designed to measure skills that are considered essential for success in law school, such as the reading and comprehension of complex texts with accuracy and insight; the organization and management of information and the ability to draw reasonable inferences from it; the ability to reason critically; and the analysis and evaluation of the reasoning and argument of others.

The LSAT provides a standard measure of acquired reading and verbal reasoning skills that law schools can use as one of several factors in assessing applicants.

The LSAT is administered at test centers in each of the fifty states, the District of Columbia, Puerto Rico, and Canada and many other countries. It is not given at every test center on every test date. The 1998–99 test dates for the LSAT are December 5 and 7, February 6 and 8, June 14, and October 2 and 4. Members of recognized religious groups observing the Sabbath on Saturday may make special arrangements to take the test on the Monday following a Saturday administration (except in June). In addition, special testing accommodations are available for those with disabilities.

The LSAT is offered by the Law School Admission Council. The LSAT fee is $86 (fee subject to change), and must be paid each time an individual registers to take the test.

Peterson's offers *LSAT Success*, a complete guide to the LSAT. Visit your local bookstore or contact Peterson's at 800-225-0261.

MEDICAL COLLEGE ADMISSION TEST

The Medical College Admission Test (MCAT) is designed to help admission committees predict which of their applicants will be successful in medical school and to encourage students interested in medicine to pursue broad undergraduate study in the natural and social sciences and in the humanities. The MCAT assesses mastery of basic biology, chemistry, and physics concepts; facility with scientific problem solving and critical thinking; and writing skills. Four separate scores are reported. The Verbal Reasoning, Physical Sciences, and Biological Sciences sections of the test are composed of multiple-choice items; scores are reported on a scale ranging from 1 (lowest) to 15 (highest). The Writing Sample section consists of two 30-minute essays; the score is reported on a scale of J (lowest) to T (highest).

Verbal Reasoning draws upon materials from the humanities, social sciences, and natural sciences to assess students' abilities to comprehend, reason, and think critically. The Verbal Reasoning Section does not test subject-matter knowledge. The two science sections—Biological Sciences, which assesses biology and biologically related chemistry concepts and Physical Sciences, which assesses physics and physically related chemistry topics—consist entirely of science problems and assess knowledge of basic, introductory-level science concepts through their application to the solution of science problems. Essay questions on the Writing Sample provide specific topics requiring an expository response. Topics are designed to assess skill in the development of a central idea, synthesis of concepts and ideas, cohesive and logical presentation of ideas, and clear writing.

The MCAT is offered twice a year; the 1999 test dates are April 17 and August 21. The test is given at test centers located in all of the states, the District of Columbia, Puerto Rico, the Virgin Islands, and selected countries. Individuals can arrange for Sunday test dates by presenting evidence that their religious convictions prevent them from taking the examination on Saturday, or they have an unavoidable conflict. Additional information may be found on the AAMC Web site at http://www.aamc.org.

Peterson's offers *MCAT Success*, a complete guide to the MCAT. Visit your local bookstore or contact Peterson's at 800-225-0261.

MILLER ANALOGIES TEST

The MAT is published and administered by The Psychological Corporation, a division of Harcourt Brace & Company. The MAT is a high-level mental ability test that requires the solution of 100 problems stated in the form of analogies. The MAT is accepted by more than 2,300 graduate school programs as part of their admission process. The test items use different types of analogies to sample general information and a variety of fields, such as fine arts, literature, mathematics, natural science, and social science. Examinees are allowed 50 minutes to complete the test.

The MAT is offered at more than 600 test centers in the United States and Canada. For examinee convenience, the test is given on an as-needed basis at most test centers. Fees are also determined by each test center.

Additional information about the MAT, including preparatory materials and test center locations, is available from The Psychological Corporation, 555 Academic Court, San Antonio, Texas 78204. Telephone: 210-299-1061 or 800-622-3231 (7 a.m. to 7 p.m., Monday through Friday, Central time).

OPTOMETRY ADMISSION TEST

The OAT is prepared and administered by the Optometry Admission Testing Program for applicants seeking admission to schools and colleges of optometry. Given two times each year at established testing centers in the United States and Canada, the test is designed to measure general academic ability and scientific knowledge. The test includes sections on a survey of the natural sciences (biology, general chemistry, and organic chemistry), reading comprehension, quantitative reasoning, and physics.

In 1999, the test will be administered on February 6 and October 23. The examination fee for applicants taking the test at centers in the United States and Canada is $80; applicants requesting special testing arrangements must pay a total of $170. There is a late fee charge of $15. The fee for individuals registering at regular test centers on the day of the test is $160. All fees must be paid with a certified check or money order. The fee for each official report of scores, requested after the time of application, is $5. This fee must be paid with a certified check or money order.

All correspondence and requests for information concerning the OAT should be directed to Optometry Admission Testing Program, 211 East Chicago Avenue, Suite 1846, Chicago, Illinois 60611-2678. Telephone: 312-440-2693.

PHARMACY COLLEGE ADMISSION TEST

The PCAT is published and administered by The Psychological Corporation, a division of Harcourt Brace & Company, under the auspices of the American Association of Colleges of Pharmacy. Designed to measure general academic ability and scientific knowledge, the test includes sections on verbal ability, quantitative ability, reading comprehension, and knowledge of biology and chemistry. The test is given three times each year, January, April, and October, at established testing centers in the United States and Canada. Sunday testing may be arranged for applicants presenting satisfactory evidence that their religious convictions prevent their taking the examination on Saturday. The examination fee is $40; additional fees are charged for standby registration.

Additional information about the PCAT and test application materials are available from colleges of pharmacy or The Psychological Corporation, 555 Academic Court, San Antonio, Texas 78204. Telephone: 210-299-1061 or 800-622-3231 (7 a.m. to 7 p.m., Monday through Friday, Central time).

THE PRAXIS SERIES TESTS

The Praxis Series tests include the continuing NTE Programs Core Battery tests, the Specialty Area tests, and the Pre-Professional Skills Tests (PPST) of reading, mathematics, and writing. In addition, The Praxis Series offers Subject Assessments and the computer-based Academic Skills Assessments.

The tests are standardized, secure examinations that provide objective measures of academic achievement for college students entering or completing teacher education programs and for advanced candidates who have received additional training in specific fields.

ETS conducts the program, but it is assisted and advised by professional educators from all sections of the country. The tests themselves are developed and revised periodically with the assistance of committees of recognized authorities in specific subject fields. These committees are usually appointed from nominations made by appropriate national professional associations.

The Core Battery includes three 2-hour tests of communication skills, general knowledge, and professional knowledge. During 1999, the tests are administered on January 23, March 13, April 24, and June 12. The registration fee is $35. Please refer to the 1998–99 Praxis registration bulletin for the test fees.

Specialty Area and Subject Assessments tests measure understanding of content and methods applicable to the separate subject areas. More than 140 Specialty Area and Subject Assessments tests are administered on January 23, March 13, April 24, and June 12. The fees for the 1-hour and 2-hour multiple choice tests are $45 and $60, respectively. The fees for the 1-hour and 2-hour constructed response tests are $50 and $65, respectively.

The Pre-Professional Skills Tests consist of three separate 1-hour tests of basic proficiency in communication and computation skills—reading, mathematics, and writing (including an essay). Four Pre-Professional Skills Tests are scheduled for 1999: January 23, March 13, April 24, and June 12. Test fees are $18 for each test.

The computer-based Academic Skills Assessments are available at selected institutional sites and at Sylvan Learning Centers by appointment. Test fees are $70, $90, and $110 for one, two, or three tests, respectively, taken on the same test date.

Additional information is available from The Praxis Series, P.O. Box 6051, Educational Testing Service, Princeton, New Jersey 08541-6051. Telephone: 609-771-7395. World Wide Web: http//www.ets.org/praxis/.

TEST OF ENGLISH AS A FOREIGN LANGUAGE

The purpose of the TOEFL test is to evaluate the English proficiency of people whose native language is not English.

Beginning in July 1998, TOEFL will be administered as a computer-based test throughout most of the world. The computer-based TOEFL test is available year-round by appointment only. It is not necessary to have previous computer experience to take the test. Examinees will be given all the instructions and practice needed to perform the necessary computer tasks before the actual test begins. The test consists of four sections—listening, reading, structure, and writing. Total testing time is approximately 4 hours. The fee for the computer-based TOEFL test is $100, which must be paid in U.S. dollars. The *Information Bulletin for Computer-Based Testing* contains information about the new testing format, registration procedures, and testing sites.

TOEFL will remain paper-based in Bangladesh, Bhutan, Cambodia, Hong Kong, India, Japan, Korea, Laos, Macau, Pakistan, People's Republic of China, Taiwan, Thailand, and Vietnam. For 1998–99, in these countries tests will be offered on December 18, January 16, February 27, March 19, April 17, May 15, and June 11.

The paper-based TOEFL test consists of three sections—listening comprehension, structure and written expression, and reading comprehension. Testing time is approximately 3 hours. In December, February, and May, the Test of Written English (TWE) will also be given. TWE is a 30-minute essay that measures the examinee's ability to compose in English. Examinees receive a TWE score separate from their TOEFL score. The fee for the paper-based TOEFL test is $75, which must be paid in U.S. dollars. There is no additional charge for TWE. The *Information Bulletin* contains information on local fees and registration procedures.

The TOEFL test is given at many test centers throughout the world and is administered by Educational Testing Service (ETS) under the general direction of a policy council established by the College Board and the Graduate Record Examinations Board.

Additional information and registration material is available from the TOEFL Program Office, P.O. Box 6151, Princeton, New Jersey 08541-6151. Telephone: 609-771-7100. E-mail: toefl@ets.org. World Wide Web: http://www.toefl.org.

Peterson's offers *TOEFL Success*, a complete guide to the TOEFL. Visit your local bookstore or contact Peterson's at 800-225-0261.

TEST OF SPOKEN ENGLISH

The major purpose of the TSE is to evaluate the spoken English proficiency of people whose native language is not English. The test, which takes about 30 minutes, requires examinees to demonstrate their ability to speak English by answering a variety of questions presented in printed and recorded form. All the answers to test questions are recorded on tape; no writing is required. TSE is given at selected TOEFL test centers worldwide. The test is administered by Educational Testing Service (ETS) under the general direction of a policy council established by the College Board and the Graduate Record Examinations Board.

The 1998–99 test dates are December 18, January 16, February 27, March 19, April 17, May 15, and June 11. The registration fee is $125, which must be paid in U.S. dollars.

Additional information and registration material can be found in the *Information Bulletin for the Test of Spoken English,* available from the TOEFL Program Office, P.O. Box 6151, Princeton, New Jersey 08541-6151, U.S.A. Telephone: 609-771-7100.

VETERINARY COLLEGE ADMISSION TEST

The VCAT is published and administered by The Psychological Corporation, a division of Harcourt Brace & Company, for applicants seeking admission to schools and colleges of veterinary medicine. The test contains sections on verbal ability, biology, chemistry, quantitative ability, and reading comprehension.

The VCAT is offered in January, October, and November at established testing centers in the United States and Canada. Sunday testing may be arranged for applicants presenting satisfactory evidence that their religious convictions prevent their taking the examination on Saturday. The regular examination fee is $60; additional fees are charged for standby registration. Additional information about the VCAT and test application materials are available from colleges of veterinary medicine or The Psychological Corporation, 555 Academic Court, San Antonio, Texas 78204. Telephone: 210-299-1061 or 800-622-3231 (7 a.m. to 7 p.m., Monday through Friday, Central time).

Accreditation and Accrediting Agencies

Colleges and universities in the United States, and their individual academic and professional programs, are accredited by nongovernmental agencies concerned with monitoring the quality of education in this country. Agencies with both regional and national jurisdictions grant accreditation to institutions as a whole, while specialized bodies acting on a nationwide basis—often national professional associations—grant accreditation to departments and programs in specific fields.

Institutional and specialized accrediting agencies share the same basic concerns: the purpose an academic unit—whether university or program—has set for itself and how well it fulfills that purpose, the adequacy of its financial and other resources, the quality of its academic offerings, and the level of services it provides. Agencies that grant institutional accreditation take a broader view, of course, and examine universitywide or collegewide services that a specialized agency may not concern itself with.

Both types of agencies follow the same general procedures when considering an application for accreditation. The academic unit prepares a self-evaluation, focusing on the concerns mentioned above and usually including an assessment of both its strengths and weaknesses; a team of representatives of the accrediting body reviews this evaluation, visits the campus, and makes its own report; and finally, the accrediting body makes a decision on the application. Often, even when accreditation is granted, the agency makes a recommendation regarding how the institution or program can improve. All institutions and programs are also reviewed every few years to determine whether they continue to meet established standards; if they do not, they may lose their accreditation.

Accrediting agencies themselves are reviewed and evaluated periodically by the U.S. Department of Education and the Council for Higher Education Accreditation (CHEA). Agencies recognized adhere to certain standards and practices, and their authority in matters of accreditation is widely accepted in the educational community.

This does not mean, however, that accreditation is a simple matter, either for schools wishing to become accredited or for students deciding where to apply. Indeed, in certain fields the very meaning and methods of accreditation are the subject of a good deal of debate. For their part, those applying to graduate school should be aware of the safeguards provided by regional accreditation, especially in terms of degree acceptance and institutional longevity. Beyond this, applicants should understand the role that specialized accreditation plays in their field, as this varies considerably from one discipline to another. In certain professional fields, it is necessary to have graduated from a program that is accredited in order to be eligible for a license to practice, and in some fields the federal government also makes this a hiring requirement. In other disciplines, however, accreditation is not as essential, and there can be excellent programs that are not accredited. In fact, some programs choose not to seek accreditation, although most do.

Institutions and programs that present themselves for accreditation are sometimes granted the status of candidate for accreditation, or what is known as "preaccreditation." This may happen, for example, when an academic unit is too new to have met all the requirements for accreditation. Such status signifies initial recognition and indicates that the school or program in question is working to fulfill all requirements; it does not, however, guarantee that accreditation will be granted.

Readers are advised to contact agencies directly for answers to their questions about accreditation. The names and addresses of all agencies recognized by the U.S. Department of Education and the Council for Higher Education Accreditation are listed below.

Institutional Accrediting Agencies—Regional

MIDDLE STATES ASSOCIATION OF COLLEGES AND SCHOOLS
Accredits institutions in Delaware, District of Columbia, Maryland, New Jersey, New York, Pennsylvania, Puerto Rico, and the Virgin Islands.
Jean Avnet Morse, Executive Director
Commission on Higher Education
3624 Market Street
Philadelphia, Pennsylvania 19104-2680
Telephone: 215-662-5606
Fax: 215-662-5950
E-mail: jamorse@msache.org

NEW ENGLAND ASSOCIATION OF SCHOOLS AND COLLEGES
Accredits institutions in Connecticut, Maine, Massachusetts, New Hampshire, Rhode Island, and Vermont.
Charles M. Cook, Director
Commission on Institutions of Higher Education
209 Burlington Road
Bedford, Massachusetts 01730-1433
Telephone: 781-271-0022
Fax: 781-271-0950
E-mail: ccook@neasc.org

NORTH CENTRAL ASSOCIATION OF COLLEGES AND SCHOOLS
Accredits institutions in Arizona, Arkansas, Colorado, Illinois, Indiana, Iowa, Kansas, Michigan, Minnesota, Missouri, Nebraska, New Mexico, North Dakota, Ohio, Oklahoma, South Dakota, West Virginia, Wisconsin, and Wyoming.
Steve Crow, Executive Director
Commission on Institutions of Higher Education
30 North LaSalle, Suite 2400
Chicago, Illinois 60602-2504
Telephone: 312-263-0456
Fax: 312-263-7462
E-mail: crow@ncacihe.org

NORTHWEST ASSOCIATION OF SCHOOLS AND COLLEGES
Accredits institutions in Alaska, Idaho, Montana, Nevada, Oregon, Utah, and Washington.
Sandra E. Elman, Executive Director
Commission on Colleges
11130 Northeast 33rd Place, Suite 120
Seattle, Washington 98004
Telephone: 425-827-2005
Fax: 425-827-3395
E-mail: selman@u.washington.edu

SOUTHERN ASSOCIATION OF COLLEGES AND SCHOOLS
Accredits institutions in Alabama, Florida, Georgia, Kentucky, Louisiana, Mississippi, North Carolina, South Carolina, Tennessee, Texas, and Virginia.
James T. Rogers, Executive Director
Commission on Colleges
1866 Southern Lane
Decatur, Georgia 30033-4097
Telephone: 404-679-4500
Fax: 404-679-4558
E-mail: jrogers@sacscoc.org

WESTERN ASSOCIATION OF SCHOOLS AND COLLEGES
Accredits institutions in California, Guam, and Hawaii.
Ralph A. Wolff, Executive Director
Accrediting Commission for Senior Colleges and Universities
Mills College
P.O. Box 9990
Oakland, California 94613-0990
Telephone: 510-632-5000
Fax: 510-632-8361
E-mail: rwolff@wasc.mills.edu

Institutional Accrediting Agencies—Other

ACCREDITING COUNCIL FOR INDEPENDENT COLLEGES AND SCHOOLS
Stephen D. Parker, Executive Director
750 First Street, NE, Suite 980
Washington, D.C. 20002-4241
Telephone: 202-336-6780
Fax: 202-842-2593
E-mail: acics@digex.net
World Wide Web: http://www.acics.org

DISTANCE EDUCATION AND TRAINING COUNCIL
Michael P. Lambert, Executive Secretary
1601 Eighteenth Street, NW
Washington, D.C. 20009-2529
Telephone: 202-234-5100
Fax: 202-332-1386
E-mail: detc@detc.org
World Wide Web: http://www.detc.org

Specialized Accrediting Agencies

[Only Book 1 of Peterson's Annual Guides to Graduate Study includes the complete list of specialized accrediting groups recognized by the U.S. Department of Education and the Council on Higher Education Accreditation (CHEA). The lists in Books 2, 4, 5, and 6 are abridged, and there are no such recognized specialized accrediting bodies for the programs in Book 3.]

ACUPUNCTURE
Dort S. Bigg, Executive Director
Accreditation Commission for Acupuncture and Oriental Medicine
1010 Wayne Avenue, Suite 1270
Silver Spring, Maryland 20910
Telephone: 301-608-9680
Fax: 301-608-9576
E-mail: 73352.2467@compuserve.com

CHIROPRACTIC
Paul D. Walker, Executive Director
The Council on Chiropractic Education
7975 North Hayden Road, Suite A-210
Scottsdale, Arizona 85258
Telephone: 602-443-8877
Fax: 602-483-7333
E-mail: cceoffice@aol.com

CLINICAL LABORATORY SCIENCE
Cynthia Wells, Chairman
National Accrediting Agency for Clinical Laboratory Sciences
8410 West Bryn Mawr Avenue, Suite 670
Chicago, Illinois 60631
Telephone: 312-714-8880
Fax: 312-714-8886
E-mail: naacls@msc.net

DENTISTRY
James J. Koelbl, Associate Executive Director, Education
American Dental Association
211 East Chicago Avenue, 18th Floor
Chicago, Illinois 60611
Telephone: 312-440-2500
Fax: 312-440-2915
World Wide Web: http://www.ada.org

EDUCATION
Arthur Wise, President
National Council for Accreditation of Teacher Education
2010 Massachusetts Avenue, NW
Washington, D.C. 20036-1023
Telephone: 202-466-7496
Fax: 202-296-6620
E-mail: ncate@ncate.org

ENVIRONMENT
Gary Silverman
National Environmental Health Science and Protection Accreditation Council
102 Health Center
College of Health and Human Services
Bowling Green State University
Bowling Green, Ohio 43403-0280
Telephone: 419-372-7774
Fax: 419-372-2897
E-mail: silverma@bgnet.bgsu.edu

HEALTH SERVICES ADMINISTRATION
Patrick M. Sobczak, President
Accrediting Commission on Education for Health Services Administration
1911 North Fort Myer Drive, Suite 503
Arlington, Virginia 22209-1603
Telephone: 703-524-0511
Fax: 703-525-4791
E-mail: accredcom@aol.com

LAW
Carl Monk, Executive Vice President
Accreditation Committee
Association of American Law Schools
1201 Connecticut Avenue, NW, Suite 800
Washington, D.C. 20036-2605
Telephone: 202-296-8851
Fax: 202-296-8869
E-mail: cmonk@aals.org
World Wide Web: http://www.aals.org

James P. White, Consultant on Legal Education
American Bar Association
Indiana University
550 West North Street
Indianapolis, Indiana 46202
Telephone: 317-264-8340
Fax: 317-264-8355
E-mail: jwhite@iupui.edu

LIBRARY
Mary Taylor, Acting Director
Committee on Accreditation
American Library Association
50 East Huron Street
Chicago, Illinois 60611
Telephone: 800-545-2433 Ext. 2436
Fax: 312-280-2433
E-mail: mtaylor@ala.org

MEDICINE
Liaison Committee on Medical Education
The LCME is administered in even-numbered years, beginning each July 1, by:
Donald G. Kassebaum, M.D., Secretary
Association of American Medical Colleges
2450 N Street, NW
Washington, D.C. 20037
Telephone: 202-828-0596
Fax: 202-828-1125
E-mail: dgkassebaum@aamc.org
World Wide Web: http://www.aamc.org

The LCME is administered in odd-numbered years, beginning each July 1, by:
Harry S. Jonas, M.D., Secretary
American Medical Association
515 North State Street
Chicago, Illinois 60610
Telephone: 312-464-4657
Fax: 312-464-5830
E-mail: harry_jonas@ama-assn.org
World Wide Web: http://www.ama-assn.org

NATUROPATHIC MEDICINE
Robert Lofft, Executive Director
Council on Naturopathic Medical Education
P.O. Box 11426
Eugene, Oregon 97440-3626
Telephone: 541-484-6028
E-mail: crest@clipper.net

NURSE ANESTHESIA
Betty J. Horton, Director of Accreditation
Council on Accreditation of Nurse Anesthetists Educational Programs
222 South Prospect Avenue, Suite 304
Park Ridge, Illinois 60068-4010
Telephone: 847-692-7050
Fax: 847-693-7137
E-mail: 75777.1576@compuserve.com

NURSE MIDWIFERY
Helen Varney Burst, Chair
Division of Accreditation
American College of Nurse-Midwives
818 Connecticut Avenue, NW, Suite 900
Washington, D.C. 20006
Telephone: 202-728-9877
Fax: 202-728-9897
E-mail: lslatter@acnm.org

NURSING
Geraldene Felton, Executive Director
National League for Nursing
350 Hudson Street
New York, New York 10014
Telephone: 800-669-1656
Fax: 212-989-3710
E-mail: gfelton@nln.org

OCCUPATIONAL THERAPY
Doris Gordon, Director
American Occupational Therapy Association
4720 Montgomery Lane
P.O. Box 31220
Bethesda, Maryland 20824-1220
Telephone: 301-652-2682
Fax: 301-652-7711
E-mail: DORISG@AOTA.ORG

OPTOMETRY
Joyce Urbeck, Administrative Director
Council on Optometric Education
American Optometric Association
243 North Lindbergh Boulevard
St. Louis, Missouri 63141
Telephone: 314-991-4100
Fax: 314-991-4101
E-mail: urbeckcoe@aol.com

OSTEOPATHIC MEDICINE
Konrad Retz, Executive Director
Bureau of Professional Education, Council on Predoctoral Education
American Osteopathic Association
142 East Ontario Street
Chicago, Illinois 60611
Telephone: 312-280-5840
Fax: 312-280-3860

PHARMACY
Daniel A. Nona, Executive Director
American Council on Pharmaceutical Education
311 West Superior Street
Chicago, Illinois 60610
Telephone: 312-664-3575
Fax: 312-664-4652
E-mail: acpe@compuserve.com

PHYSICAL THERAPY
Virginia Nieland, Director
Department of Accreditation
American Physical Therapy Association
Trans Potomac Plaza
1111 North Fairfax Street
Alexandria, Virginia 22314
Telephone: 703-684-3245
Fax: 703-684-7343
E-mail: vnieland@apta.org

PODIATRIC MEDICINE
Alan R. Tinkleman, Director
Council on Podiatric Medical Education
American Podiatric Medical Association
9312 Old Georgetown Road
Bethesda, Maryland 20814-2752
Telephone: 301-571-9200
Fax: 301-581-9299
E-mail: artinkleman@apma.org

PUBLIC HEALTH
Patricia Evans, Executive Director
Council on Education for Public Health
1015 Fifteenth Street, NW, Suite 403
Washington, D.C. 20005
Telephone: 202-789-1050
Fax: 202-789-1895
E-mail: evan0015@cdc.gov

REHABILITATION EDUCATION
Jeanne Patterson, Executive Director
Council on Rehabilitation Education
Commission on Standards and Accreditation
1835 Rohlwing Road, Suite E
Rolling Meadows, Illinois 60008
Telephone: 847-394-1785
Fax: 847-394-2108
E-mail: patters@polaris.net

SOCIAL WORK
Nancy Randolph, Director
Council on Social Work Education
1600 Duke Street, Suite 300
Alexandria, Virginia 22314
Telephone: 703-683-8080
Fax: 703-683-8099
E-mail: accred@cswe.org
World Wide Web: http://www.cswe.org

SPEECH-LANGUAGE PATHOLOGY AND AUDIOLOGY
Sharon Goldsmith, Director
American Speech-Language-Hearing Association
10801 Rockville Pike
Rockville, Maryland 20852
Telephone: 301-897-5700
Fax: 301-571-0457
E-mail: sgoldsmith@asha.org
World Wide Web: http://www.asha.org/

VETERINARY MEDICINE
Donald G. Simmons, Director of Education and Research Division
American Veterinary Medical Association
1931 North Meacham Road, Suite 100
Schaumburg, Illinois 60173
Telephone: 847-925-8070
Fax: 847-925-1329
E-mail: dsimmons@avma.org

Directory of Institutions with Programs in Business, Education, Health, Information Studies, Law, and Social Work

This directory lists institutions in alphabetical order and includes beneath each name the academic fields in business, education, health, information studies, law, and social work in which each institution offers graduate programs. The degree level in each field is also indicated, provided that the institution has supplied that information in response to Peterson's Annual Survey of Graduate Institutions. An *M* indicates that a master's degree program is offered; a *D* indicates that a doctoral degree program is offered; a *P* indicates that the first professional degree is offered; an *O* signifies that other advanced degrees (e.g., certificates or specialist degrees) are offered; and an * (asterisk) indicates that an in-depth description and/or announcement is located in this volume. See the index for the page number of the in-depth description and/or announcement.

ABILENE CHRISTIAN UNIVERSITY
Accounting M
Business Administration and Management M
Counselor Education M
Education M
Educational Administration M
Educational Measurement and Evaluation M
Elementary Education M
Human Resources Development M
Human Services M
Nursing M
Reading Education M
Religious Education M
Secondary Education M

ACADEMY OF CHINESE CULTURE AND HEALTH SCIENCES
Oriental Medicine and Acupuncture M*

ACADIA UNIVERSITY
Counselor Education M
Curriculum and Instruction M
Education M,O
Educational Administration M
Special Education M

ADAMS STATE COLLEGE
Counselor Education M
Education M*
Elementary Education M
Health Education M
Physical Education M
Recreation and Park Management M
Secondary Education M
Special Education M

ADELPHI UNIVERSITY
Accounting M
Art Education M
Business Administration and Management M,O*
Communication Disorders M,D
Early Childhood Education M
Education M,D,O*
Educational Measurement and Evaluation O
Elementary Education M
English as a Second Language M,O
English Education M
Exercise and Sports Science O
Finance and Banking M,O
Foreign Languages Education M
Health Education M,O
Human Resources Management O
Maternal/Child-Care Nursing M,O
Mathematics Education M
Medical/Surgical Nursing M,O
Multilingual and Multicultural Education M
Music Education M
Nursing M,D,O*
Nursing Administration M,O
Nursing Education M,O
Physical Education M,O
Psychiatric Nursing M,O
Reading Education M,O
Science Education M
Secondary Education M
Social Sciences Education M
Social Work M,D,O*
Special Education M,O
Sports Administration O

AGNES SCOTT COLLEGE
English Education M

AIR FORCE INSTITUTE OF TECHNOLOGY
Logistics M
Management Information Systems M

ALABAMA AGRICULTURAL AND MECHANICAL UNIVERSITY
Art Education M
Business Administration and Management M
Communication Disorders M
Counselor Education M,O
Early Childhood Education M,O
Education M,O
Educational Administration M
Elementary Education M,O
Finance and Banking M
Human Resources Management M
Marketing M
Music Education M
Physical Education M
Secondary Education M,O
Social Work M
Special Education M
Vocational and Technical Education M

ALABAMA STATE UNIVERSITY
Accounting M
Allied Health M
Business Administration and Management M
Counselor Education M,O
Early Childhood Education M,O
Education M,O
Educational Administration M,O
Educational Media/Instructional Technology M,O
Elementary Education M,O
English Education M
Mathematics Education M
Music Education M
Physical Education M,O
Physical Therapy M
Science Education M,O
Secondary Education M,O
Social Sciences Education M
Special Education M

ALASKA PACIFIC UNIVERSITY
Business Administration and Management M
Education M
Elementary Education M
Middle School Education M

ALBANY COLLEGE OF PHARMACY OF UNION UNIVERSITY
Pharmacy P

ALBANY LAW SCHOOL OF UNION UNIVERSITY
Law P

ALBANY MEDICAL COLLEGE
Allopathic Medicine P
Nurse Anesthesia M

ALBANY STATE UNIVERSITY
Business Administration and Management M
Business Education M
Early Childhood Education M
Education M,O
Educational Administration M,O
English Education M
Health Education M
Human Resources Management M
Mathematics Education M
Middle School Education M
Music Education M
Nursing M
Physical Education M
Reading Education M
Science Education M
Secondary Education M
Special Education M

ALBERTUS MAGNUS COLLEGE
Business Administration and Management M

ALCORN STATE UNIVERSITY
Agricultural Education M
Counselor Education M
Education M,O
Educational Administration M
Elementary Education M,O
Health Education M
Nursing M
Physical Education M
Secondary Education M
Special Education M
Vocational and Technical Education M

ALDERSON–BROADDUS COLLEGE
Allied Health M
Emergency Medical Services M
Physician Assistant Studies M

ALFRED UNIVERSITY
Business Administration and Management M
Business Education M
Counselor Education M
Education M
Elementary Education M
English Education M
Mathematics Education M
Reading Education M
Science Education M
Secondary Education M
Social Sciences Education M

ALLEGHENY UNIVERSITY OF THE HEALTH SCIENCES
Allied Health M,D*
Allopathic Medicine P
Emergency Medical Services M
Health Education M
Health Physics/Radiological Health M,D
Medical Physics M,D
Nursing M,O
Physical Therapy M,D*
Public Health M*
Veterinary Sciences M

ALLENTOWN COLLEGE OF ST. FRANCIS DE SALES
Business Administration and Management M
Computer Education M
Education M
English Education M
Mathematics Education M
Nursing M
Physician Assistant Studies M
Science Education M

ALVERNO COLLEGE
Curriculum and Instruction M
Education M

AMBER UNIVERSITY
Business Administration and Management M
Human Resources Development M
Human Resources Management M

AMERICAN BIBLE COLLEGE AND SEMINARY
Religious Education M

AMERICAN COLLEGE (PA)
Business Administration and Management M
Finance and Banking M

AMERICAN COLLEGE OF TRADITIONAL CHINESE MEDICINE
Oriental Medicine and Acupuncture M

AMERICAN INTERCONTINENTAL UNIVERSITY (CA)
International Business M
Management Information Systems M

AMERICAN INTERCONTINENTAL UNIVERSITY (GA)
International Business M
Management Information Systems M

AMERICAN INTERCONTINENTAL UNIVERSITY (UNITED KINGDOM)
Business Administration and Management M
International Business M

AMERICAN INTERNATIONAL COLLEGE
Business Administration and Management M*
Education M,D,O
Educational Administration M,O
Educational Psychology M,D
Elementary Education M,O
English Education M
Human Resources Development M,O
Mathematics Education M
Organizational Behavior M
Physical Therapy M
Reading Education M,O
Secondary Education M,O
Social Sciences Education M
Special Education M,O

AMERICAN UNIVERSITY
Accounting M
Business Administration and Management M*
Education M,D*
Educational Administration M
Elementary Education M
English as a Second Language M,O
Entrepreneurship M
Exercise and Sports Science M*
Finance and Banking M
Human Resources Management M
International and Comparative Education M
International Business M
Law P,M
Legal and Justice Studies M
Management Information Systems M
Marketing M
Mathematics Education D
Organizational Behavior M
Real Estate M
Secondary Education M
Special Education M
Taxation M

AMERICAN UNIVERSITY IN CAIRO
Business Administration and Management M,O
English as a Second Language M,O
Foreign Languages Education M

ANDOVER NEWTON THEOLOGICAL SCHOOL
Religious Education M

ANDREWS UNIVERSITY
Allied Health M
Business Administration and Management M
Curriculum and Instruction M,D,O
Education M,D,O
Educational Administration M,D,O
Educational Psychology M,D
Elementary Education M
English as a Second Language M
English Education M
Foreign Languages Education M
Management Information Systems M
Marketing M
Nursing M
Physical Therapy M
Reading Education M
Religious Education M,D,O
Science Education M
Secondary Education M
Social Sciences Education M
Social Work M

ANGELO STATE UNIVERSITY
Accounting M
Business Administration and Management M
Counselor Education M
Curriculum and Instruction M
Education M
Educational Administration M
Educational Measurement and Evaluation M
Kinesiology and Movement Studies M
Music Education M
Nursing M
Physical Education M
Reading Education M

ANGLO-EUROPEAN COLLEGE OF CHIROPRACTIC
Chiropractic M

ANNA MARIA COLLEGE
Business Administration and Management M
Education M
Environmental and Occupational Health M

ANTIOCH NEW ENGLAND GRADUATE SCHOOL
Business Administration and Management M*
Early Childhood Education M
Education M*
Educational Administration M
Elementary Education M
Foundations and Philosophy of Education M
Human Services M
Science Education M

ANTIOCH SOUTHERN CALIFORNIA/LOS ANGELES
Business Administration and Management M
Entrepreneurship M
Human Resources Development M
Organizational Behavior M

ANTIOCH SOUTHERN CALIFORNIA/SANTA BARBARA
Organizational Behavior M

ANTIOCH UNIVERSITY SEATTLE
Business Administration and Management M
Education M
Organizational Behavior M

APPALACHIAN STATE UNIVERSITY
Accounting M
Adult Education M,O
Business Administration and Management M
Communication Disorders M
Counselor Education M,O
Early Childhood Education M
Education M,D,O

- Educational Administration — M,D
- Educational Media/Instructional Technology — M
- Elementary Education — M
- Exercise and Sports Science — M
- Foundations and Philosophy of Education — M
- Higher Education — M,O
- Human Resources Management — M
- Library Science — M,O
- Music Education — M
- Physical Education — M
- Reading Education — M,O
- Secondary Education — M
- Special Education — M
- Sports Administration — M
- Vocational and Technical Education — M

AQUINAS COLLEGE (MI)

- Business Administration and Management — M
- Education — M

ARIZONA STATE UNIVERSITY

- Accounting — M,D
- Business Administration and Management — M,D*
- Communication Disorders — M,D
- Counselor Education — M
- Curriculum and Instruction — M,D
- Education — M,D*
- Educational Administration — M,D
- Educational Media/Instructional Technology — M,D
- Educational Psychology — M,D
- English as a Second Language — M
- Exercise and Sports Science — M,D
- Finance and Banking — D
- Foundations and Philosophy of Education — M
- Health Services Management and Hospital Administration — M*
- Health Services Research — D
- Higher Education — M,D
- Law — P
- Legal and Justice Studies — M,D
- Logistics — D
- Management Information Systems — M,D
- Marketing — D
- Nursing — M
- Physical Education — M
- Recreation and Park Management — M
- Social Work — M,D
- Special Education — M
- Taxation — M
- Transportation Management — O

ARIZONA STATE UNIVERSITY EAST

- Management Information Systems — M
- Transportation Management — M

ARIZONA STATE UNIVERSITY WEST

- Accounting — O
- Business Administration and Management — M
- Education — M
- Educational Administration — M
- Elementary Education — M
- Secondary Education — M
- Special Education — M

ARKANSAS STATE UNIVERSITY

- Business Administration and Management — M
- Business Education — M,O
- Communication Disorders — M
- Counselor Education — M,O
- Curriculum and Instruction — M,O
- Early Childhood Education — M
- Education — M,D,O
- Educational Administration — M,D,O
- Education of the Gifted — M
- Elementary Education — M,O
- English Education — M,O
- Music Education — M,O
- Nursing — M
- Physical Education — M,O
- Reading Education — M,O
- Science Education — M,O
- Secondary Education — M,D,O
- Special Education — M

ARKANSAS TECH UNIVERSITY

- Curriculum and Instruction — M
- Education — M,D
- Educational Administration — M
- Educational Media/Instructional Technology — M
- Education of the Gifted — M
- Elementary Education — M
- English Education — M
- Health Education — M,D
- Mathematics Education — M
- Physical Education — M,D
- Social Sciences Education — M

ARMSTRONG ATLANTIC STATE UNIVERSITY

- Education — M
- Elementary Education — M
- Health Services Management and Hospital Administration — M
- Middle School Education — M
- Nursing — M
- Physical Therapy — M
- Public Health — M
- Secondary Education — M
- Special Education — M

ARMSTRONG UNIVERSITY

- Accounting — M
- Business Administration and Management — M*
- Finance and Banking — M
- International Business — M
- Marketing — M

ART ACADEMY OF CINCINNATI

- Art Education — M

ARTHUR D. LITTLE SCHOOL OF MANAGEMENT

- Business Administration and Management — M

ASBURY THEOLOGICAL SEMINARY

- Religious Education — M

ASHLAND UNIVERSITY

- Business Administration and Management — M
- Business Education — M
- Computer Education — M
- Curriculum and Instruction — M
- Early Childhood Education — M
- Education — M
- Educational Administration — M
- Education of the Gifted — M
- Exercise and Sports Science — M
- Reading Education — M
- Religious Education — M
- Special Education — M

ASSUMPTION COLLEGE

- Business Administration and Management — M,O
- Education — M
- Religious Education — M
- Special Education — M

ATHABASCA UNIVERSITY

- Business Administration and Management — M,O
- Education — M

ATLANTIC UNION COLLEGE

- Education — M

AUBURN UNIVERSITY

- Accounting — M
- Adult Education — M,D,O
- Business Administration and Management — M,D*
- Communication Disorders — M
- Counselor Education — M,D,O
- Curriculum and Instruction — M,D,O
- Early Childhood Education — M,D,O
- Education — M,D,O*
- Educational Administration — M,D,O
- Educational Media/Instructional Technology — M
- Educational Psychology — D
- Elementary Education — M,D,O
- English Education — M,D,O
- Foreign Languages Education — M
- Health Education — M,D,O
- Higher Education — M,D,O
- Human Resources Management — D*
- Management Information Systems — M,D*
- Mathematics Education — M,D,O
- Music Education — M,D,O
- Pharmaceutical Sciences — M,D
- Pharmacy — P
- Physical Education — M,D,O
- Reading Education — D,O
- Science Education — M,D,O
- Secondary Education — M,D,O
- Social Sciences Education — M,D,O
- Special Education — M,D,O
- Veterinary Medicine — P
- Veterinary Sciences — M,D
- Vocational and Technical Education — M,D,O

AUBURN UNIVERSITY MONTGOMERY

- Business Administration and Management — M
- Counselor Education — M,O
- Early Childhood Education — M,O
- Education — M,O
- Educational Administration — M,O
- Elementary Education — M,O
- Physical Education — M,O
- Reading Education — M,O
- Secondary Education — M,O
- Special Education — M,O

AUDREY COHEN COLLEGE

- Business Administration and Management — M

AUGSBURG COLLEGE

- Business Administration and Management — M
- Social Work — M

AUGUSTANA COLLEGE (SD)

- Computer Education — M
- Education — M
- Nursing — M
- Special Education — M

AUGUSTA STATE UNIVERSITY

- Business Administration and Management — M
- Counselor Education — M,O
- Early Childhood Education — M,O
- Education — M,O
- Educational Administration — M,O
- Middle School Education — M,O
- Secondary Education — M,O
- Special Education — M,O

AURORA UNIVERSITY

- Business Administration and Management — M
- Education — M
- Educational Administration — M
- Leisure Studies — M
- Recreation and Park Management — M
- Social Work — M

AUSTIN COLLEGE

- Education — M
- Elementary Education — M
- Secondary Education — M

AUSTIN PEAY STATE UNIVERSITY

- Advertising and Public Relations — M
- Counselor Education — M,O
- Curriculum and Instruction — M
- Education — M,O
- Educational Administration — M,O
- Educational Psychology — O
- Elementary Education — M,O
- Health Education — M
- Music Education — M
- Physical Education — M
- Reading Education — M
- Secondary Education — O
- Special Education — M

AVERETT COLLEGE

- Business Administration and Management — M
- Curriculum and Instruction — M
- Education — M
- Reading Education — M

AVILA COLLEGE

- Business Administration and Management — M
- Education — M

AZUSA PACIFIC UNIVERSITY

- Business Administration and Management — M
- Curriculum and Instruction — M
- Education — M,D
- Educational Administration — M,D
- Educational Media/Instructional Technology — M
- English as a Second Language — M,O
- Higher Education — M
- Human Resources Development — M
- International Business — M
- Management Strategy and Policy — M
- Multilingual and Multicultural Education — M
- Music Education — M
- Nursing — M
- Physical Education — M
- Physical Therapy — M
- Special Education — M

BABSON COLLEGE

- Business Administration and Management — M*
- International Business — M

BAKER COLLEGE CENTER FOR GRADUATE STUDIES

- Business Administration and Management — M
- Health Services Management and Hospital Administration — M
- Human Resources Management — M
- Industrial and Manufacturing Management — M
- International Business — M
- Recreation and Park Management — M

BAKER UNIVERSITY

- Business Administration and Management — M
- Education — M

BALDWIN-WALLACE COLLEGE

- Business Administration and Management — M
- Education — M
- Educational Administration — M
- Health Services Management and Hospital Administration — M
- International Business — M*
- Reading Education — M
- Special Education — M

BALL STATE UNIVERSITY

- Accounting — M
- Actuarial Science — M
- Adult Education — M,D
- Advertising and Public Relations — M
- Art Education — M
- Business Administration and Management — M
- Business Education — M
- Communication Disorders — M,O
- Curriculum and Instruction — M,O
- Early Childhood Education — M,D
- Education — M,D,O
- Educational Administration — M,D,O
- Educational Psychology — M,D,O
- Elementary Education — M,D
- Exercise and Sports Science — D
- Health Education — M
- Health Promotion — M
- Mathematics Education — M
- Middle School Education — M
- Music Education — M,D
- Nursing — M
- Physical Education — M,D
- Reading Education — M,D
- Science Education — D
- Secondary Education — M
- Special Education — M,D,O
- Vocational and Technical Education — M

BANK STREET COLLEGE OF EDUCATION

- Early Childhood Education — M
- Education — M,O*
- Educational Administration — M
- Educational Media/Instructional Technology — M,O
- Elementary Education — M
- Mathematics Education — M
- Multilingual and Multicultural Education — M
- Reading Education — M
- Special Education — M

BAPTIST BIBLE COLLEGE OF PENNSYLVANIA

- Counselor Education — M
- Religious Education — M

BARAT COLLEGE

- Education — M

BARRY UNIVERSITY

- Advanced Practice Nursing — M
- Advertising and Public Relations — M
- Business Administration and Management — M
- Counselor Education — M,D,O
- Early Childhood Education — M
- Education — M,D,O
- Educational Administration — M,D,O
- Educational Media/Instructional Technology — M,D,O
- Education of the Gifted — M,D,O
- Elementary Education — M
- Exercise and Sports Science — M
- Health Services Management and Hospital Administration — M
- Higher Education — M,D

Barry University (continued)

Human Resources Development M,D
Nurse Anesthesia M
Nursing D
Nursing Administration M
Nursing Education M
Physician Assistant Studies M
Podiatric Medicine P*
Reading Education M,O
Social Work M,D
Special Education M,D,O
Sports Administration M

BARUCH COLLEGE OF THE CITY UNIVERSITY OF NEW YORK

Accounting M,D
Business Administration and Management M,D,O*
Early Childhood Education M
Education M
Educational Administration M
Elementary Education M
Finance and Banking M,D
Health Services Management and Hospital Administration M
Higher Education M
Human Resources Management M
Industrial and Manufacturing Management M
International Business M
Management Information Systems M
Management Strategy and Policy M,D
Marketing M,D
Organizational Behavior M,D
Taxation M

BASTYR UNIVERSITY

Naturopathic Medicine D*
Oriental Medicine and Acupuncture M*

BAYLOR COLLEGE OF DENTISTRY

Dental Hygiene M
Dentistry P
Health Education M
Oral and Dental Sciences P,M,D,O

BAYLOR COLLEGE OF MEDICINE

Allopathic Medicine P
Communication Disorders D
Nurse Anesthesia M
Nurse Midwifery M
Physician Assistant Studies M

BAYLOR UNIVERSITY

Accounting M
Advanced Practice Nursing M
Allied Health M
Business Administration and Management M*
Communication Disorders M
Curriculum and Instruction M,D,O
Education M,D,O
Educational Administration M,D,O
Educational Psychology M,D,O
Health Education M
Health Services Management and Hospital Administration M
Human Services M
International Business M
Law P
Management Information Systems M
Maternal/Child-Care Nursing M
Music Education M
Nursing M
Nursing Administration M
Physical Education M
Physical Therapy M
Recreation and Park Management M

BEAVER COLLEGE

Art Education M
Computer Education M,O
Curriculum and Instruction O
Early Childhood Education M,O
Education M,O*
Educational Administration M,O
Educational Media/Instructional Technology M
Educational Psychology O
Elementary Education M,O
English Education M,O
Health Education M
Mathematics Education M,O
Music Education M
Physical Therapy M
Physician Assistant Studies M
Reading Education M,O
Science Education M,O
Secondary Education M,O
Social Sciences Education M
Special Education M,O

BELHAVEN COLLEGE

Business Administration and Management M

BELLARMINE COLLEGE

Business Administration and Management M
Early Childhood Education M
Education M
Elementary Education M
Middle School Education M
Nursing M
Nursing Administration M
Nursing Education M
Public Health Nursing M
Special Education M

BELLEVUE UNIVERSITY

Business Administration and Management M
Health Services Management and Hospital Administration M
Human Services M
Management Information Systems M

BELMONT ABBEY COLLEGE

Business Administration and Management M
Education M
Elementary Education M
Middle School Education M
Special Education M

BELMONT UNIVERSITY

Business Administration and Management M
Education M
Educational Administration M
Elementary Education M
English Education M
Music Education M
Nursing M
Occupational Therapy M
Physical Therapy M

BEMIDJI STATE UNIVERSITY

Computer Education M
Curriculum and Instruction M
Education M
Educational Administration M
Mathematics Education M
Physical Education M
Science Education M
Special Education M
Vocational and Technical Education M

BENEDICTINE COLLEGE

Business Administration and Management M
Educational Administration M

BENEDICTINE UNIVERSITY

Business Administration and Management M
Curriculum and Instruction M
Education M
Elementary Education M
Exercise and Sports Science M*
Management Information Systems M
Organizational Behavior M,D
Public Health M
Special Education M

BENNINGTON COLLEGE

Education M

BENTLEY COLLEGE

Accounting M,O*
Business Administration and Management M*
Entrepreneurship M
Finance and Banking M*
Industrial and Manufacturing Management M
International Business M
Management Information Systems M
Marketing M
Taxation M*

BERRY COLLEGE

Business Administration and Management M
Curriculum and Instruction O
Early Childhood Education M
Education M,O
Middle School Education M
Reading Education M

BETHANY COLLEGE OF THE ASSEMBLIES OF GOD

Education M

BETHEL COLLEGE (IN)

Business Administration and Management M

BETHEL COLLEGE (MN)

Education M
Nursing M
Organizational Behavior M

BETHEL COLLEGE (TN)

Education M

BETHEL THEOLOGICAL SEMINARY

Religious Education P,M

BIOLA UNIVERSITY

Education M
English as a Second Language M,O
Religious Education M,D

BIRMINGHAM–SOUTHERN COLLEGE

Accounting M
Business Administration and Management M

BISHOP'S UNIVERSITY

Education M,O
English as a Second Language O

BLACK HILLS STATE UNIVERSITY

Curriculum and Instruction M
Education M*
Hospitality Management M
Travel and Tourism M

BLOOMSBURG UNIVERSITY OF PENNSYLVANIA

Accounting M
Business Administration and Management M
Business Education M
Communication Disorders M
Curriculum and Instruction M
Early Childhood Education M
Education M
Educational Media/Instructional Technology M
Elementary Education M
Exercise and Sports Science M
Nursing M
Reading Education M
Science Education M
Special Education M

BLUFFTON COLLEGE

Education M

BOISE STATE UNIVERSITY

Accounting M
Art Education M
Business Administration and Management M*
Counselor Education M
Curriculum and Instruction M,D
Early Childhood Education M
Education M,D
Educational Media/Instructional Technology M
Exercise and Sports Science M
Management Information Systems M
Mathematics Education M
Music Education M
Public Health M
Reading Education M
Science Education M
Social Work M
Special Education M
Sports Administration M

BORICUA COLLEGE

Human Services M

BOSTON COLLEGE

Accounting M
Business Administration and Management M,D*
Curriculum and Instruction M,D,O
Early Childhood Education M
Education M,D,O*
Educational Administration M,D,O
Educational Measurement and Evaluation M,D,O
Educational Psychology M,D
Education of the Multiply Handicapped M
Elementary Education M
English Education M
Finance and Banking M,D
Foreign Languages Education M
Gerontological Nursing M
Higher Education M,D
Human Resources Management M,D*
Law P

Management Information Systems M
Management Strategy and Policy M
Marketing M
Maternal/Child-Care Nursing M
Mathematics Education M
Medical/Surgical Nursing M
Nursing M,D
Organizational Behavior M,D*
Psychiatric Nursing M
Public Health Nursing M
Reading Education M,O
Religious Education M,D
Science Education M
Secondary Education M
Social Sciences Education M
Social Work M,D*
Special Education M,D,O

BOSTON CONSERVATORY

Music Education M

BOSTON UNIVERSITY

Accounting D
Actuarial Science M
Adult Education M,D,O
Advertising and Public Relations M
Allied Health M,D,O*
Allopathic Medicine P
Art Education M
Business Administration and Management M,D*
Communication Disorders M,D,O*
Counselor Education M,O
Curriculum and Instruction D
Dental Hygiene M,D,O*
Dentistry P*
Early Childhood Education M,D,O
Education M,D,O*
Educational Administration M,D,O
Educational Media/Instructional Technology M,D,O
Elementary Education M
English as a Second Language M,O
English Education M,D,O
Environmental and Occupational Health M,D*
Epidemiology M,D*
Finance and Banking M,D*
Foreign Languages Education M
Health Education M,O
Health Promotion M*
Health Services Management and Hospital Administration M*
Higher Education M
Human Resources Management M,D,O
Industrial and Manufacturing Management D
International and Comparative Education M
International Business M*
International Health M,O*
Kinesiology and Movement Studies M,D,O*
Law P,M
Legal and Justice Studies M*
Leisure Studies M,O
Management Information Systems M,D*
Management Strategy and Policy M*
Marketing D
Maternal and Child Health M,O*
Mathematics Education M,D,O
Multilingual and Multicultural Education M,D,O
Music Education M,D
Nonprofit Management M*
Nurse Midwifery O*
Occupational Therapy M,D,O*
Oral and Dental Sciences M,D,O*
Organizational Behavior D
Physical Education M,D,O
Physical Therapy M,D*
Public Health M,D,O*
Reading Education M,D,O
Science Education M,D,O
Social Sciences Education M,D,O
Social Work M,D
Special Education M,D,O
Taxation M

BOWIE STATE UNIVERSITY

Advanced Practice Nursing M
Business Administration and Management M
Counselor Education M
Education M
Educational Administration M
Elementary Education M
Human Resources Development M
Management Information Systems M,O
Nursing M
Nursing Administration M
Nursing Education M

Reading Education M
Secondary Education M
Special Education M

BOWLING GREEN STATE UNIVERSITY

Accounting M
Business Administration and Management M
Business Education M
Communication Disorders M,D
Counselor Education M
Education M,D,O
Educational Administration M,D,O
Elementary Education M
English as a Second Language M
Foreign Languages Education M
Higher Education D
Kinesiology and Movement Studies M
Leisure Studies M
Mathematics Education O
Music Education M
Organizational Behavior M
Public Health M
Reading Education M,O
Recreation and Park Management M
Science Education M,D
Secondary Education M
Special Education M
Sports Administration M
Vocational and Technical Education M

BRADLEY UNIVERSITY

Accounting M
Business Administration and Management M*
Counselor Education M
Curriculum and Instruction M
Education M
Educational Administration M
Nursing M
Special Education M

BRANDEIS UNIVERSITY

Business Administration and Management M*
Finance and Banking M,D*
Health Services Management and Hospital Administration M
Human Services M
International Business M,D*

BRANDON UNIVERSITY

Counselor Education M
Curriculum and Instruction M
Education M,O
Educational Administration M
Music Education M
Special Education M

BRENAU UNIVERSITY

Advanced Practice Nursing M
Business Administration and Management M
Early Childhood Education M,O
Education M,O
Middle School Education M,O
Nursing M
Special Education M

BRESCIA COLLEGE

Business Administration and Management M

BRIDGEWATER STATE COLLEGE

Art Education M
Counselor Education M
Early Childhood Education M
Education M,O
Educational Administration M,O
Educational Media/Instructional Technology M
Elementary Education M
Health Promotion M
Mathematics Education M
Physical Education M
Reading Education M
Science Education M
Secondary Education M
Special Education M

BRIERCREST BIBLICAL SEMINARY

Business Administration and Management M
Finance and Banking M
Higher Education M
Human Resources Management M
Organizational Behavior M

BRIGHAM YOUNG UNIVERSITY

Accounting M
Art Education M
Business Administration and Management M*
Communication Disorders M
Counselor Education M,D
Education M,D,O
Educational Administration M,D
Educational Media/Instructional Technology M,D
Educational Psychology M,D
Elementary Education M
English as a Second Language M,O
Exercise and Sports Science M,D
Foreign Languages Education M
Foundations and Philosophy of Education M,D
Health Education M
Health Promotion M
Law P,M
Management Information Systems M
Music Education M
Nursing M
Organizational Behavior M
Physical Education M,D
Reading Education D
Recreation and Park Management M
Science Education M
Social Work M
Special Education M,D
Vocational and Technical Education M

BROCK UNIVERSITY

Education M
English as a Second Language M

BROOKLYN COLLEGE OF THE CITY UNIVERSITY OF NEW YORK

Accounting M
Art Education M
Communication Disorders M
Community Health M
Counselor Education M,O
Early Childhood Education M
Education M,O
Educational Administration O
Elementary Education M
English Education M
Exercise and Sports Science M
Foreign Languages Education M
Health Education M
Health Services Management and Hospital Administration M
Home Economics Education M
Mathematics Education M
Multilingual and Multicultural Education M
Music Education M
Physical Education M
Public Health M
Reading Education M
Science Education M
Secondary Education M
Social Sciences Education M
Special Education M
Sports Administration M

BROOKLYN LAW SCHOOL

Law P

BROWN UNIVERSITY

Allopathic Medicine P
Community Health M,D
Education M
Elementary Education M
English Education M
Epidemiology M,D*
Health Services Research M,D
Multilingual and Multicultural Education M
Science Education M
Secondary Education M
Social Sciences Education M

BRYANT COLLEGE

Accounting M,O
Business Administration and Management M,O*
Finance and Banking M,O
Health Services Management and Hospital Administration M,O
Industrial and Manufacturing Management M,O
International Business M
Management Information Systems M,O
Marketing M,O
Taxation M,O

BRYN MAWR COLLEGE

Social Work M,D*

BUCKNELL UNIVERSITY

Accounting M
Business Administration and Management M
Counselor Education M
Curriculum and Instruction M
Education M
Educational Administration M
Educational Measurement and Evaluation M
Finance and Banking M
Industrial and Manufacturing Management M
Marketing M
Quantitative Analysis M
Reading Education M

BUENA VISTA UNIVERSITY

Counselor Education M
Education M
Educational Administration M

BUTLER UNIVERSITY

Business Administration and Management M
Counselor Education M,O
Education M,O
Educational Administration M,O
Elementary Education M
Music Education M
Pharmaceutical Sciences P,M
Pharmacy P,M
Reading Education M
Secondary Education M
Special Education M

CABRINI COLLEGE

Education M

CALDWELL COLLEGE

Accounting M
Business Administration and Management M
Curriculum and Instruction M
Education O
Educational Administration M

CALIFORNIA BAPTIST COLLEGE

Business Administration and Management M
Curriculum and Instruction M
Education M
Educational Administration M
English Education M
Exercise and Sports Science M
Multilingual and Multicultural Education M
Reading Education M
Special Education M
Vocational and Technical Education M

CALIFORNIA COLLEGE FOR HEALTH SCIENCES

Health Promotion M
Health Services Management and Hospital Administration M

CALIFORNIA COLLEGE OF PODIATRIC MEDICINE

Podiatric Medicine P,M

CALIFORNIA INSTITUTE OF INTEGRAL STUDIES

Organizational Behavior M

CALIFORNIA LUTHERAN UNIVERSITY

Business Administration and Management M
Counselor Education M
Education M
Educational Administration M
Entrepreneurship M
Finance and Banking M
Health Services Management and Hospital Administration M
International Business M
Management Information Systems M
Marketing M
Organizational Behavior M
Reading Education M
Special Education M

CALIFORNIA POLYTECHNIC STATE UNIVERSITY, SAN LUIS OBISPO

Business Administration and Management M
Counselor Education M
Curriculum and Instruction M
Education M
Educational Administration M
Industrial and Manufacturing Management M
Kinesiology and Movement Studies M
Physical Education M
Reading Education M
Special Education M

CALIFORNIA SCHOOL OF PROFESSIONAL PSYCHOLOGY–LOS ANGELES

Health Services Management and Hospital Administration M

CALIFORNIA STATE POLYTECHNIC UNIVERSITY, POMONA

Business Administration and Management M
Education M
Kinesiology and Movement Studies M

CALIFORNIA STATE UNIVERSITY, BAKERSFIELD

Business Administration and Management M
Counselor Education M
Curriculum and Instruction M
Early Childhood Education M
Education M
Educational Administration M
Health Services Management and Hospital Administration M
Multilingual and Multicultural Education M
Nursing M
Reading Education M
Social Work M
Special Education M

CALIFORNIA STATE UNIVERSITY, CHICO

Accounting M
Business Administration and Management M
Communication Disorders M
Curriculum and Instruction M
Education M
Educational Media/Instructional Technology M
Health Services Management and Hospital Administration M
Multilingual and Multicultural Education M
Nursing M
Physical Education M
Reading Education M
Recreation and Park Management M
Special Education M

CALIFORNIA STATE UNIVERSITY, DOMINGUEZ HILLS

Business Administration and Management M
Clinical Laboratory Sciences M,O
Computer Education M,O
Counselor Education M
Curriculum and Instruction M
Education M,O
Educational Administration M
English as a Second Language O
Management Information Systems M
Multilingual and Multicultural Education M
Nursing M
Physical Education M
Quality Management M
Special Education M

CALIFORNIA STATE UNIVERSITY, FRESNO

Advanced Practice Nursing M
Business Administration and Management M
Communication Disorders M
Counselor Education M
Curriculum and Instruction M
Early Childhood Education M
Education M
Educational Administration M,D
English as a Second Language M
Environmental and Occupational Health M
Exercise and Sports Science M
Health Promotion M
Health Services Management and Hospital Administration M
Kinesiology and Movement Studies M
Music Education M
Nursing M
Physical Therapy M
Public Health M
Reading Education M
Social Work M
Special Education M

CALIFORNIA STATE UNIVERSITY, FULLERTON

Accounting M
Advertising and Public Relations M

California State University, Fullerton (continued)

Business Administration and Management M
Communication Disorders M
Counselor Education M
Education M
Educational Administration M
Elementary Education M
English as a Second Language M
Finance and Banking M
International Business M
Management Information Systems M
Marketing M
Mathematics Education M
Multilingual and Multicultural Education M
Music Education M
Physical Education M
Reading Education M
Science Education M
Special Education M
Taxation M

CALIFORNIA STATE UNIVERSITY, HAYWARD

Accounting M
Business Administration and Management M
Communication Disorders M
Counselor Education M
Education M
Educational Administration M
Entrepreneurship M
Finance and Banking M
Human Resources Management M
International Business M
Management Information Systems M
Marketing M
Physical Education M
Quantitative Analysis M
Special Education M
Taxation M

CALIFORNIA STATE UNIVERSITY, LONG BEACH

Art Education M
Business Administration and Management M
Communication Disorders M
Counselor Education M,O
Education M,O
Educational Administration M
Educational Psychology M
Elementary Education M
Epidemiology M
Foundations and Philosophy of Education M
Health Education M
Health Services Management and Hospital Administration M,O
Kinesiology and Movement Studies M
Leisure Studies M
Medical Technology M
Nurse Anesthesia M
Nursing M
Physical Education M
Recreation and Park Management M
Secondary Education M
Social Work M
Special Education M
Vocational and Technical Education M

CALIFORNIA STATE UNIVERSITY, LOS ANGELES

Accounting M
Adult Education M
Art Education M
Business Administration and Management M
Communication Disorders M
Computer Education M
Counselor Education M
Education M,D
Educational Administration M
Educational Media/Instructional Technology M
Education of the Gifted M
Elementary Education M
English as a Second Language M
Finance and Banking M
Foundations and Philosophy of Education M
Health Education M
Health Services Management and Hospital Administration M
International Business M
Management Information Systems M
Marketing M
Multilingual and Multicultural Education M
Music Education M
Nursing M
Physical Education M
Reading Education M
Secondary Education M
Social Work M
Special Education M,D
Taxation M
Vocational and Technical Education M

CALIFORNIA STATE UNIVERSITY, NORTHRIDGE

Accounting M
Business Administration and Management M
Business Education M
Communication Disorders M
Counselor Education M,O
Early Childhood Education M
Education M,O
Educational Administration M
Educational Psychology M
Education of the Gifted M
Elementary Education M
Environmental and Occupational Health M
Finance and Banking M
Foundations and Philosophy of Education M
Health Education M
Health Services Management and Hospital Administration M
Insurance M
Kinesiology and Movement Studies M
Leisure Studies M
Marketing M
Music Education M
Physical Therapy M
Public Health M
Real Estate M
Recreation and Park Management M
Secondary Education M
Special Education M
Taxation M

CALIFORNIA STATE UNIVERSITY, SACRAMENTO

Accounting M
Business Administration and Management M
Communication Disorders M
Counselor Education M
Curriculum and Instruction M
Early Childhood Education M
Education M
Educational Administration M
English as a Second Language M
Human Resources Development M
Human Resources Management M
Human Services M
Management Information Systems M
Multilingual and Multicultural Education M
Nursing M
Physical Education M
Reading Education M
Real Estate M
Recreation and Park Management M
Social Work M
Special Education M

CALIFORNIA STATE UNIVERSITY, SAN BERNARDINO

Business Administration and Management M
Counselor Education M
Education M
Educational Administration M
Educational Media/Instructional Technology M
Elementary Education M
English as a Second Language M
English Education M
Health Services Management and Hospital Administration M
Multilingual and Multicultural Education M
Reading Education M
Science Education M
Secondary Education M
Social Sciences Education M
Social Work M
Special Education M
Vocational and Technical Education M

CALIFORNIA STATE UNIVERSITY, SAN MARCOS

Business Administration and Management M
Education M

CALIFORNIA STATE UNIVERSITY, STANISLAUS

Business Administration and Management M
Counselor Education M
Curriculum and Instruction M
Education M
Educational Administration M
Educational Media/Instructional Technology M
Elementary Education M
English as a Second Language M
Multilingual and Multicultural Education M
Physical Education M
Reading Education M
Secondary Education M
Social Sciences Education M
Social Work M
Special Education M

CALIFORNIA UNIVERSITY OF PENNSYLVANIA

Business Administration and Management M
Communication Disorders M
Computer Education M
Counselor Education M
Early Childhood Education M
Education M
Educational Administration M
Elementary Education M
Exercise and Sports Science M
Mathematics Education M
Reading Education M
Science Education M
Social Work M
Special Education M
Vocational and Technical Education M

CALIFORNIA WESTERN SCHOOL OF LAW

Law P*

CALVIN COLLEGE

Curriculum and Instruction M
Education M
Educational Administration M
Reading Education M
Special Education M

CALVIN THEOLOGICAL SEMINARY

Religious Education M

CAMBRIDGE COLLEGE (MA)

Business Administration and Management M
Education M

CAMERON UNIVERSITY

Business Administration and Management M
Education M

CAMPBELLSVILLE UNIVERSITY

Education M
Music Education M

CAMPBELL UNIVERSITY

Business Administration and Management M
Counselor Education M
Education M
Educational Administration M
Elementary Education M
English Education M
Law P
Mathematics Education M
Middle School Education M
Pharmacy P
Physical Education M
Religious Education M
Secondary Education M
Social Sciences Education M

CANADIAN COLLEGE OF NATUROPATHIC MEDICINE

Naturopathic Medicine D

CANADIAN MEMORIAL CHIROPRACTIC COLLEGE

Chiropractic P,O

CANADIAN THEOLOGICAL SEMINARY

Religious Education M

CANISIUS COLLEGE

Accounting M
Business Administration and Management M
Counselor Education M,O
Education M,O
Educational Administration M,O
Physical Education M
Reading Education M
Secondary Education M
Special Education M
Sports Administration M

CAPITAL UNIVERSITY

Business Administration and Management M
Law P,M
Nursing M
Nursing Administration M
Taxation M

CAPITOL COLLEGE

Management Information Systems M

CARDINAL STRITCH UNIVERSITY

Business Administration and Management M*
Computer Education M
Education M,D*
Educational Administration M,D
English as a Second Language M
Health Services Management and Hospital Administration M
International Business M
Reading Education M
Religious Education M
Special Education M

CARLETON UNIVERSITY

Business Administration and Management M,D
Legal and Justice Studies M
Social Work M

CARLOW COLLEGE

Advanced Practice Nursing M,O
Art Education M
Early Childhood Education M
Education M
Educational Administration M
Health Services Management and Hospital Administration M
Human Resources Development M
Nonprofit Management M
Nursing M,O
Nursing Administration M,O

CARNEGIE MELLON UNIVERSITY

Accounting D
Business Administration and Management M
Education D
Finance and Banking D
Health Services Management and Hospital Administration M
Industrial and Manufacturing Management M,D
Marketing D
Organizational Behavior M,D

CARROLL COLLEGE (WI)

Education M
Physical Therapy M

CARSON-NEWMAN COLLEGE

Counselor Education M
Curriculum and Instruction M
Education M
Elementary Education M
English as a Second Language M
Secondary Education M

CARTHAGE COLLEGE

Art Education M
Counselor Education M
Education M,O
Education of the Gifted M
English Education M
Reading Education M,O
Science Education M
Social Sciences Education M

CASE WESTERN RESERVE UNIVERSITY

Accounting M,D
Advanced Practice Nursing M
Allopathic Medicine P
Art Education M
Bioethics M
Business Administration and Management M,D,O*
Communication Disorders M,D,O
Dentistry P
Epidemiology M,D*
Finance and Banking M,D
Gerontological Nursing M
Health Services Research M,D
Human Resources Management M,D
Law P,M
Legal and Justice Studies M
Management Information Systems M,D*
Management Strategy and Policy M,D
Marketing M,D

Maternal/Child-Care Nursing M
Medical/Surgical Nursing M
Music Education M,D
Nonprofit Management M,O*
Nurse Anesthesia M
Nurse Midwifery M
Nursing M,D*
Oncology Nursing M
Oral and Dental Sciences M,O
Organizational Behavior M,D
Psychiatric Nursing M
Public Health Nursing M
Quality Management M
Social Work M,D,O*
Taxation M

CASTLETON STATE COLLEGE

Curriculum and Instruction M
Education M,O
Educational Administration M,O
Reading Education M,O
Special Education M

CATAWBA COLLEGE

Education M
English Education M
Mathematics Education M

THE CATHOLIC UNIVERSITY OF AMERICA

Accounting M
Advanced Practice Nursing M
Business Administration and Management M,D
Clinical Laboratory Sciences M,D
Counselor Education M
Curriculum and Instruction M
Education M,D
Educational Administration M,D
Educational Psychology D
English as a Second Language M
Finance and Banking M
Gerontological Nursing M
Human Resources Management M
Industrial and Manufacturing Management D
Information Studies M*
Law P
Legal and Justice Studies D,O
Library Science M*
Maternal/Child-Care Nursing M
Medical/Surgical Nursing M
Music Education M,D
Nursing M,D
Nursing Administration M
Nursing Education M
Psychiatric Nursing M
Religious Education M,D
Social Work M,D*

CENTENARY COLLEGE

Accounting M
Education M
Educational Administration M

CENTENARY COLLEGE OF LOUISIANA

Business Administration and Management M
Curriculum and Instruction M
Education M
Educational Administration M
Elementary Education M

CENTER FOR HUMANISTIC STUDIES

Educational Psychology M,O

CENTRAL CONNECTICUT STATE UNIVERSITY

Art Education M
Business Administration and Management M
Business Education M
Counselor Education M
Curriculum and Instruction M
Early Childhood Education M
Education M,O
Educational Administration M,O
Educational Media/Instructional Technology M
Elementary Education M
English as a Second Language M
Exercise and Sports Science M
Foundations and Philosophy of Education M
Industrial and Manufacturing Management M
International Business M
Music Education M
Physical Education M
Reading Education M,O
Secondary Education M
Special Education M
Vocational and Technical Education M

CENTRAL METHODIST COLLEGE

Education M

CENTRAL MICHIGAN UNIVERSITY

Accounting M
Business Administration and Management M
Business Education M
Communication Disorders M,D
Counselor Education M,O
Early Childhood Education M
Education M,O
Educational Administration M,O
Educational Media/Instructional Technology M
Elementary Education M
English as a Second Language M
Exercise and Sports Science M,O
Finance and Banking M
Health Promotion M
Health Services Management and Hospital Administration M,O
Hospitality Management M
Human Resources Management M,O
Industrial and Manufacturing Management M
Leisure Studies M
Management Information Systems M,O
Marketing M
Middle School Education M
Music Education M
Physical Education M,O
Physical Therapy M
Physician Assistant Studies M
Recreation and Park Management M
Science Education M
Secondary Education M
Social Work M
Special Education M
Sports Administration M
Vocational and Technical Education M

CENTRAL MISSOURI STATE UNIVERSITY

Accounting M
Adult Education M
Art Education M
Business Administration and Management M
Communication Disorders M
Counselor Education M,O
Curriculum and Instruction M,O
Education M,D,O
Educational Administration M,D,O
Elementary Education M
English as a Second Language M
English Education M
Environmental and Occupational Health M,O
Exercise and Sports Science M
Industrial and Manufacturing Management M
Industrial Hygiene M
Information Studies M
Library Science M,O
Mathematics Education M
Physical Education M,O
Reading Education M
Secondary Education M
Social Sciences Education M
Special Education M,O
Vocational and Technical Education M,O

CENTRAL STATE UNIVERSITY

Education M
Educational Administration M
Educational Media/Instructional Technology M
Reading Education M

CENTRAL WASHINGTON UNIVERSITY

Business Education M
Counselor Education M
Curriculum and Instruction M
Education M
Educational Administration M
Elementary Education M
English as a Second Language M
English Education M
Health Education M
Home Economics Education M
Physical Education M
Reading Education M
Recreation and Park Management M
Special Education M

CHADRON STATE COLLEGE

Business Administration and Management M
Business Education M

Counselor Education M,O
Education M,O
Educational Administration M,O
Elementary Education M
English Education M
Secondary Education M
Social Sciences Education M

CHAMINADE UNIVERSITY OF HONOLULU

Business Administration and Management M
Education M
International Business M
Social Sciences Education M

CHAPMAN UNIVERSITY

Business Administration and Management M
Counselor Education M
Curriculum and Instruction M
Education M
Educational Administration M
Educational Psychology M
English as a Second Language M
English Education M
Health Services Management and Hospital Administration M
Human Resources Development M
Human Resources Management M
Law P*
Organizational Behavior M
Physical Therapy M
Reading Education M
Special Education M

CHARLES R. DREW UNIVERSITY OF MEDICINE AND SCIENCE

Allopathic Medicine P

CHARLESTON SOUTHERN UNIVERSITY

Accounting M
Business Administration and Management M
Education M
Educational Administration M
Elementary Education M
English Education M
Finance and Banking M
Health Services Management and Hospital Administration M
Marketing M
Organizational Behavior M
Science Education M
Secondary Education M
Social Sciences Education M

CHATHAM COLLEGE

Allied Health M
Business Administration and Management M
Education M
Occupational Therapy M*
Physical Therapy M*
Physician Assistant Studies M*

CHESTNUT HILL COLLEGE

Early Childhood Education M
Educational Media/Instructional Technology M
Elementary Education M

CHEYNEY UNIVERSITY OF PENNSYLVANIA

Adult Education M
Education M
Educational Administration M
Elementary Education M
Special Education M

CHICAGO STATE UNIVERSITY

Counselor Education M
Curriculum and Instruction M
Early Childhood Education M
Education M
Educational Administration M
Educational Media/Instructional Technology M
Elementary Education M
Library Science M
Multilingual and Multicultural Education M
Physical Education M
Reading Education M
Secondary Education M
Special Education M
Vocational and Technical Education M

CHICAGO THEOLOGICAL SEMINARY

Religious Education D

CHRISTIAN BROTHERS UNIVERSITY

Business Administration and Management M
Management Information Systems M

CHRISTIAN THEOLOGICAL SEMINARY

Religious Education M

CHRISTOPHER NEWPORT UNIVERSITY

Education M
Mathematics Education M
Nursing M
Reading Education M
Science Education M

CINCINNATI BIBLE COLLEGE AND SEMINARY

Religious Education M

THE CITADEL, THE MILITARY COLLEGE OF SOUTH CAROLINA

Business Administration and Management M
Counselor Education M
Curriculum and Instruction M
Education M,O
Educational Administration M,O
Health Education M
Mathematics Education M
Physical Education M
Reading Education M
Science Education M
Secondary Education M
Social Sciences Education M
Special Education M

CITY COLLEGE OF THE CITY UNIVERSITY OF NEW YORK

Art Education M
Counselor Education M
Early Childhood Education M
Education M,O
Educational Administration M,O
Elementary Education M
English Education M
Mathematics Education M
Multilingual and Multicultural Education M
Reading Education M,O
Science Education M
Secondary Education M
Social Sciences Education M
Special Education M
Vocational and Technical Education M

CITY UNIVERSITY

Business Administration and Management M,O
Curriculum and Instruction M
Education M,O
Educational Administration M,O
Educational Media/Instructional Technology M
English as a Second Language M,O
Finance and Banking M,O
Human Resources Development M
Management Information Systems M,O
Marketing M,O
Project Management M,O
Special Education M

CITY UNIVERSITY OF NEW YORK SCHOOL OF LAW AT QUEENS COLLEGE

Law P

CLAREMONT GRADUATE UNIVERSITY

Accounting M
Business Administration and Management M,D,O*
Curriculum and Instruction M,D
Education M,D*
Educational Administration M,D
Educational Measurement and Evaluation M,D
Finance and Banking M
Higher Education M,D
Human Resources Management M*
International and Comparative Education M,D
International Business M
Management Information Systems M,D
Management Strategy and Policy M
Marketing M
Mathematics Education M
Music Education M
Organizational Behavior M
Reading Education M,D
Social Sciences Education M,D

CLARION UNIVERSITY OF PENNSYLVANIA
Business Administration and Management M
Communication Disorders M
Education M
Elementary Education M
Library Science M
Mathematics Education M
Nursing M
Reading Education M
Science Education M
Special Education M

CLARK ATLANTA UNIVERSITY
Business Administration and Management M
Counselor Education M,D
Curriculum and Instruction M,O
Education M,D,O
Educational Administration M,D,O
Educational Psychology M,D
Education of the Gifted M,O
Finance and Banking M
Information Studies M,O
International Business M
Library Science M,O
Marketing M
Quantitative Analysis M
Science Education D
Social Work M,D

CLARKE COLLEGE
Business Administration and Management M
Education M
Educational Administration M
Educational Media/Instructional Technology M
Nursing M
Physical Therapy M
Reading Education M

CLARKSON COLLEGE
Advanced Practice Nursing M
Health Services Management and Hospital Administration M
Nursing M
Nursing Administration M
Nursing Education M

CLARKSON UNIVERSITY
Business Administration and Management M*
Human Resources Management M*
Industrial and Manufacturing Management M
Management Information Systems M*

CLARK UNIVERSITY
Business Administration and Management M*
Education M
Finance and Banking M
Health Services Management and Hospital Administration M

CLEMSON UNIVERSITY
Accounting M
Agricultural Education M
Business Administration and Management M,D*
Counselor Education M
Curriculum and Instruction D
Education M,D,O
Educational Administration M,D,O
Elementary Education M
English Education M
Foundations and Philosophy of Education M
Health Services Management and Hospital Administration M
Human Resources Development M
Industrial and Manufacturing Management M,D*
Mathematics Education M
Nursing M
Reading Education M
Recreation and Park Management M,D
Science Education M
Secondary Education M
Social Sciences Education M
Special Education M
Travel and Tourism M,D
Vocational and Technical Education M,D

CLEVELAND CHIROPRACTIC COLLEGE OF KANSAS CITY (MO)
Chiropractic P*

CLEVELAND CHIROPRACTIC COLLEGE OF LOS ANGELES (CA)
Chiropractic P*

CLEVELAND STATE UNIVERSITY
Accounting M
Adult Education M
Business Administration and Management M,D*
Communication Disorders M
Computer Education M
Counselor Education M,O
Curriculum and Instruction M
Early Childhood Education M
Education M,D,O*
Educational Administration M,O
Educational Measurement and Evaluation M
Education of the Gifted M
Education of the Multiply Handicapped M
Elementary Education M
English as a Second Language M
Exercise and Sports Science M
Health Education M
Human Resources Management M
Law P,M
Management Information Systems M,D
Middle School Education M
Multilingual and Multicultural Education M
Music Education M
Physical Education M
Reading Education M
Recreation and Park Management M
Secondary Education M
Social Work M
Special Education M
Sports Administration M
Urban Education D

COASTAL CAROLINA UNIVERSITY
Early Childhood Education M
Education M
Elementary Education M
Secondary Education M

COE COLLEGE
Education M

COLGATE UNIVERSITY
Education M
Secondary Education M

COLLEGE FOR FINANCIAL PLANNING
Finance and Banking M

COLLEGE MISERICORDIA
Business Administration and Management M
Curriculum and Instruction M
Education M
Nursing M
Occupational Therapy M
Physical Therapy M

COLLEGE OF INSURANCE
Actuarial Science M*
Business Administration and Management M*
Finance and Banking M*
Insurance M*

COLLEGE OF MOUNT ST. JOSEPH
Art Education M
Business Education M
Early Childhood Education M
Education M
Elementary Education M
Foundations and Philosophy of Education M
Reading Education M
Special Education M

COLLEGE OF MOUNT SAINT VINCENT
Allied Health M,O
Education M
Gerontological Nursing M
Health Education M
Health Services Management and Hospital Administration M,O
Medical/Surgical Nursing M
Multilingual and Multicultural Education M
Nursing M
Nursing Administration M
Rehabilitation Nursing M
Urban Education M

THE COLLEGE OF NEW JERSEY
Communication Disorders M
Counselor Education M
Education M,O
Educational Administration M
Educational Media/Instructional Technology O
Elementary Education M
English as a Second Language M,O
Health Education M
Nursing M
Physical Education M
Reading Education M
Secondary Education M
Special Education M

COLLEGE OF NEW ROCHELLE
Art Education M
Early Childhood Education M
Education M,O
Educational Administration M,O
Education of the Gifted M,O
Elementary Education M
English as a Second Language M
Human Resources Development M,O
Nursing M,O
Reading Education M
Special Education M

COLLEGE OF NOTRE DAME
Art Education M
Business Administration and Management M
Early Childhood Education M
Education M,O
Educational Media/Instructional Technology M
Elementary Education M,O
English Education M
Foreign Languages Education M
Management Information Systems M
Multilingual and Multicultural Education M
Music Education M
Religious Education M
Science Education M
Secondary Education M,O
Social Sciences Education M

COLLEGE OF NOTRE DAME OF MARYLAND
Business Administration and Management M
Education M
Educational Administration M

COLLEGE OF OUR LADY OF THE ELMS
Early Childhood Education M
Education M
Educational Administration M
Elementary Education M
English as a Second Language M
English Education M
Foreign Languages Education M
Reading Education M
Science Education M
Secondary Education M
Special Education M

COLLEGE OF ST. CATHERINE
Education M
Information Studies M
Library Science M
Nursing M
Occupational Therapy M
Organizational Behavior M
Physical Therapy M
Social Work M

COLLEGE OF SAINT ELIZABETH
Business Administration and Management M
Education M
Educational Administration M
Educational Media/Instructional Technology M
Health Services Management and Hospital Administration M

COLLEGE OF ST. JOSEPH
Education M
Elementary Education M
Reading Education M
Special Education M

THE COLLEGE OF SAINT ROSE
Accounting M
Art Education M
Business Administration and Management M
Communication Disorders M
Counselor Education M
Early Childhood Education M
Education M,O
Educational Administration M,O
Educational Psychology M
Elementary Education M
Music Education M
Reading Education M
Secondary Education M
Special Education M

COLLEGE OF ST. SCHOLASTICA
Business Administration and Management M
Education M
Exercise and Sports Science M
Nursing M
Occupational Therapy M
Physical Therapy M

COLLEGE OF SANTA FE
Business Administration and Management M
Counselor Education M
Education M
Educational Administration M
Multilingual and Multicultural Education M
Special Education M

COLLEGE OF STATEN ISLAND OF THE CITY UNIVERSITY OF NEW YORK
Education M,O
Educational Administration O
Elementary Education M
Secondary Education M
Special Education M

COLLEGE OF THE SOUTHWEST
Counselor Education M
Curriculum and Instruction M
Education M
Educational Administration M

COLLEGE OF WILLIAM AND MARY
Business Administration and Management M
Counselor Education M,D
Curriculum and Instruction M
Education M,D
Educational Administration M,D
Education of the Gifted M
Law P,M
Special Education M

COLORADO CHRISTIAN UNIVERSITY
Business Administration and Management M
Curriculum and Instruction M

THE COLORADO COLLEGE
Education M
Elementary Education M
Mathematics Education M
Science Education M
Secondary Education M

COLORADO STATE UNIVERSITY
Accounting M
Advertising and Public Relations M*
Business Administration and Management M*
English Education M
Environmental and Occupational Health M,D*
Exercise and Sports Science M
Finance and Banking M
Health Physics/Radiological Health M,D
Management Information Systems M
Marketing M
Music Education M
Occupational Therapy M
Recreation and Park Management M,D
Social Work M
Taxation M
Veterinary Medicine P
Veterinary Sciences M,D
Vocational and Technical Education M,D

COLORADO TECHNICAL UNIVERSITY
Business Administration and Management M,D
Health Services Management and Hospital Administration M
Human Resources Management M
Logistics M
Management Information Systems M

COLUMBIA COLLEGE (IL)
Education M
Elementary Education M
English Education M
Multilingual and Multicultural Education M
Urban Education M

COLUMBIA COLLEGE (MO)
Business Administration and Management M
Education M

COLUMBIA COLLEGE (SC)

Elementary Education M

COLUMBIA INTERNATIONAL UNIVERSITY

Curriculum and Instruction M
Education M,D
Educational Administration M
English as a Second Language M
Religious Education P,M,D

COLUMBIA UNIVERSITY

Accounting M,D
Advanced Practice Nursing M,O
Allopathic Medicine P
Business Administration and Management M,D
Community Health M,D
Dentistry P
Entrepreneurship M
Environmental and Occupational Health M,D
Epidemiology M,D
Finance and Banking M,D
Gerontological Nursing M,O
Health Services Management and Hospital Administration M,D
Human Resources Management M
International Business M
Law P,M,D
Marketing M,D
Maternal and Child Health M
Maternal/Child-Care Nursing M,O
Medical Physics M,D
Medical/Surgical Nursing M,O
Nurse Anesthesia M
Nurse Midwifery M
Nursing M,D,O*
Occupational Therapy M*
Oncology Nursing M,O
Oral and Dental Sciences M
Physical Therapy M*
Psychiatric Nursing M,O
Public Health M,D*
Real Estate M
Social Work M,D*

COLUMBUS STATE UNIVERSITY

Art Education M
Business Administration and Management M
Counselor Education M,O
Early Childhood Education M,O
Education M,O
Educational Administration M,O
English Education M,O
Mathematics Education M,O
Middle School Education M,O
Music Education M
Physical Education M
Reading Education M,O
Science Education M,O
Secondary Education M,O
Social Sciences Education M,O
Special Education M,O

CONCORDIA UNIVERSITY (CA)

Curriculum and Instruction M
Educational Administration M

CONCORDIA UNIVERSITY (IL)

Computer Education M,O
Counselor Education M,O
Curriculum and Instruction M,O
Early Childhood Education M,O
Educational Administration M,O
Human Services M,O
Mathematics Education M,O
Reading Education M,O
Urban Education M

CONCORDIA UNIVERSITY (NE)

Early Childhood Education M
Education M
Educational Administration M
Elementary Education M
Reading Education M
Religious Education M

CONCORDIA UNIVERSITY (OR)

Curriculum and Instruction M
Education M
Educational Administration M
Elementary Education M
Secondary Education M

CONCORDIA UNIVERSITY (CANADA)

Accounting O
Adult Education O
Art Education M,D,O
Business Administration and Management M,D,O
Early Childhood Education O
Education M,D,O
Educational Media/Instructional Technology M,D,O
Library Science O
Mathematics Education M,O
Sports Administration O
Transportation Management M

CONCORDIA UNIVERSITY AT ST. PAUL (MN)

Business Administration and Management M
Early Childhood Education M
Education M
Elementary Education M
Organizational Behavior M

CONCORDIA UNIVERSITY WISCONSIN

Advanced Practice Nursing M
Business Administration and Management M
Counselor Education M
Curriculum and Instruction M
Early Childhood Education M
Education M
Educational Administration M
Finance and Banking M
Gerontological Nursing M
Health Services Management and Hospital Administration M
Human Resources Management M
International Business M
Management Information Systems M
Marketing M
Nursing M
Nursing Education M
Occupational Therapy M
Physical Therapy M
Reading Education M

CONNECTICUT COLLEGE

Education M
Elementary Education M
English Education M
Foreign Languages Education M
Mathematics Education M
Music Education M
Science Education M
Secondary Education M

CONVERSE COLLEGE

Curriculum and Instruction O
Education M,O
Educational Administration O
Education of the Gifted M
Elementary Education M
Music Education M
Secondary Education M
Special Education M

COPPIN STATE COLLEGE

Adult Education M
Curriculum and Instruction M
Education M
Special Education M

CORNELL UNIVERSITY

Accounting D
Adult Education M,D
Agricultural Education M,D
Business Administration and Management M,D
Curriculum and Instruction M,D
Education M,D
Educational Administration M,D
Educational Measurement and Evaluation M,D
Educational Psychology M,D
Epidemiology M
Facilities Management M
Finance and Banking D
Health Services Management and Hospital Administration M*
Health Services Research M
Hospitality Management M,D*
Human Resources Management M,D
Human Services M,D
Law P,M,D
Management Information Systems D
Marketing D
Mathematics Education M
Organizational Behavior M,D
Quantitative Analysis D
Real Estate M*
Science Education M
Veterinary Medicine P
Veterinary Sciences M,D

CORNELL UNIVERSITY MEDICAL COLLEGE

Allopathic Medicine P

COVENANT COLLEGE

Education M*

CREIGHTON UNIVERSITY

Allied Health P,D
Allopathic Medicine P
Business Administration and Management M
Counselor Education M
Dentistry P
Education M
Educational Administration M
Law P
Nursing M
Occupational Therapy D
Pharmaceutical Sciences M
Pharmacy P
Physical Therapy D

CUMBERLAND COLLEGE

Early Childhood Education M
Education M,O
Educational Administration O
Elementary Education M,O
Middle School Education M
Reading Education M
Secondary Education M,O
Special Education M

CUMBERLAND UNIVERSITY

Business Administration and Management M
Education M
Human Resources Management M

CURRY COLLEGE

Adult Education M,O
Education M,O
Reading Education M,O
Special Education M,O

DAEMEN COLLEGE

Advanced Practice Nursing M
Education M
Nursing M
Physical Therapy M
Special Education M

DALHOUSIE UNIVERSITY

Adult Education M
Allopathic Medicine P
Business Administration and Management M
Communication Disorders M
Community Health M
Curriculum and Instruction M
Dental Hygiene O
Dentistry P
Education M,D
Educational Administration M
Educational Psychology M
Epidemiology M
Foundations and Philosophy of Education M,D
Health Education M
Health Services Management and Hospital Administration M
Information Studies M
Kinesiology and Movement Studies M
Law M,D
Leisure Studies M
Library Science M
Nursing M
Oral and Dental Sciences
Pharmaceutical Sciences M,D
Social Work M

DALLAS BAPTIST UNIVERSITY

Accounting M
Business Administration and Management M
Counselor Education M
Early Childhood Education M
Education M
Educational Administration M
Elementary Education M
Finance and Banking M
Higher Education M
Human Resources Management M
International Business M
Management Information Systems M
Marketing M
Organizational Behavior M
Reading Education M

DALLAS THEOLOGICAL SEMINARY

Religious Education M,D

DARTMOUTH COLLEGE

Allopathic Medicine P
Business Administration and Management M
Health Services Research M,D

DAVID LIPSCOMB UNIVERSITY

Education M

DEFIANCE COLLEGE

Business Administration and Management M
Education M
Organizational Behavior M

DELAWARE STATE UNIVERSITY

Business Administration and Management M
Curriculum and Instruction M
Education M
Science Education M
Social Work M
Special Education M

DELTA STATE UNIVERSITY

Accounting M
Business Administration and Management M
Counselor Education M
Education M,D,O
Educational Administration M,O
Elementary Education M,O
English Education M
Marketing M
Mathematics Education M
Music Education M
Nursing M
Physical Education M
Recreation and Park Management M
Social Sciences Education M
Social Work M
Special Education M
Transportation Management M

DENVER PARALEGAL INSTITUTE

Legal and Justice Studies O

DENVER TECHNICAL COLLEGE

Project Management M

DEPAUL UNIVERSITY

Accounting P,M
Advanced Practice Nursing M
Business Administration and Management P,M*
Counselor Education M
Curriculum and Instruction M
Education M*
Educational Administration M
Elementary Education M
Entrepreneurship M
Finance and Banking M,O*
Health Services Management and Hospital Administration M*
Higher Education M
Human Resources Management M
Human Services M
Industrial and Manufacturing Management M
International Business M*
Law P,M*
Legal and Justice Studies M*
Management Information Systems M
Management Strategy and Policy M
Marketing M
Mathematics Education M
Multilingual and Multicultural Education M
Music Education M
Nonprofit Management M,O*
Nurse Anesthesia M
Nursing M
Physical Education M
Reading Education M
Science Education M
Secondary Education M
Social Sciences Education M
Special Education M
Taxation M
Urban Education M

DETROIT COLLEGE OF BUSINESS (DEARBORN)

Accounting M
Business Administration and Management M

DETROIT COLLEGE OF LAW AT MICHIGAN STATE UNIVERSITY

Law P*

THE DICKINSON SCHOOL OF LAW OF THE PENNSYLVANIA STATE UNIVERSITY

Law P,M

DOANE COLLEGE

Business Administration and Management M
Counselor Education M
Curriculum and Instruction M
Education M

Doane College (continued)

Educational Administration	M

DR. WILLIAM M. SCHOLL COLLEGE OF PODIATRIC MEDICINE

Podiatric Medicine	P

DOMINICAN COLLEGE OF BLAUVELT

Education	M
Occupational Therapy	M
Special Education	M

DOMINICAN COLLEGE OF SAN RAFAEL

Business Administration and Management	M
Curriculum and Instruction	M
Education	M,O
International Business	M*
Management Strategy and Policy	M

DOMINICAN UNIVERSITY

Accounting	M
Business Administration and Management	M
Early Childhood Education	M
Education	M
Educational Administration	M
Information Studies	M,O*
Library Science	M,O*
Management Information Systems	M
Organizational Behavior	M
Special Education	M

DONGGUK–ROYAL UNIVERSITY

Oriental Medicine and Acupuncture	M

DORDT COLLEGE

Education	M

DOWLING COLLEGE

Business Administration and Management	M,O*
Education	M,O*
Educational Administration	O
Educational Media/Instructional Technology	O
Elementary Education	M
Finance and Banking	M,O
Quality Management	M,O
Reading Education	M
Secondary Education	M
Special Education	M
Transportation Management	M,O

DRAKE UNIVERSITY

Adult Education	M,D,O
Business Administration and Management	M
Counselor Education	M,D
Curriculum and Instruction	M,D,O
Education	M,D,O
Educational Administration	M,D,O
Elementary Education	M
Higher Education	M,D,O
Law	P*
Music Education	M
Nursing	M
Pharmacy	P
Secondary Education	M
Special Education	M
Vocational and Technical Education	M

DREW UNIVERSITY

Bioethics	M,O

DREXEL UNIVERSITY

Accounting	M,D
Business Administration and Management	M,D,O*
Curriculum and Instruction	M
Education	M
Finance and Banking	M,D
Information Studies	M,D,O*
Library Science	M,D,O*
Management Strategy and Policy	D
Marketing	M,D
Organizational Behavior	D
Quantitative Analysis	M,D
Taxation	M

DRURY COLLEGE

Business Administration and Management	M
Education	M
Education of the Gifted	M
Elementary Education	M
Human Services	M
International Business	M
Middle School Education	M
Physical Education	M
Secondary Education	M

DUKE UNIVERSITY

Advanced Practice Nursing	M
Allopathic Medicine	P
Business Administration and Management	M,D
Clinical Laboratory Sciences	M
Education	M
Gerontological Nursing	M,O
Health Services Management and Hospital Administration	M
Law	P,M,D
Maternal/Child-Care Nursing	M,O
Medical/Surgical Nursing	M,O
Nursing	M,O
Nursing Administration	M,O
Oncology Nursing	M,O
Physical Therapy	M
Physician Assistant Studies	M

DUQUESNE UNIVERSITY

Advanced Practice Nursing	M
Allied Health	M
Bioethics	M,D
Business Administration and Management	M*
Communication Disorders	M
Counselor Education	M
Curriculum and Instruction	D
Education	M,D,O
Educational Administration	M,D
Elementary Education	M
Foundations and Philosophy of Education	M
Health Services Management and Hospital Administration	M*
Law	P
Management Information Systems	M
Music Education	M
Nursing	M,D
Nursing Administration	M
Nursing Education	M
Occupational Therapy	M
Pharmaceutical Sciences	M,D*
Pharmacy	P
Physical Therapy	M
Physician Assistant Studies	M
Reading Education	M
Secondary Education	M
Special Education	M
Taxation	M

D'YOUVILLE COLLEGE

Advanced Practice Nursing	M
Business Administration and Management	M
Education	M
Elementary Education	M
Health Services Management and Hospital Administration	M
International Business	M
Nursing	M
Physical Therapy	M
Secondary Education	M
Special Education	M

EAST CAROLINA UNIVERSITY

Accounting	M
Adult Education	M
Allied Health	M,D
Allopathic Medicine	P
Business Administration and Management	M
Communication Disorders	M,D
Counselor Education	M,O
Education	M,D,O
Educational Administration	M,D,O
Educational Media/Instructional Technology	M,O
Elementary Education	M
Environmental and Occupational Health	M
Exercise and Sports Science	M
Finance and Banking	M
Health Education	M
Library Science	M,O
Marketing	M
Medical Physics	M
Middle School Education	M
Music Education	M
Nursing	M
Occupational Therapy	M
Physical Therapy	M
Reading Education	M
Rehabilitation Sciences	M
Science Education	M
Social Sciences Education	M
Social Work	M
Special Education	M
Vocational and Technical Education	M

EAST CENTRAL UNIVERSITY

Counselor Education	M
Education	M
Human Resources Management	M

EASTERN COLLEGE

Accounting	M
Business Administration and Management	M
Counselor Education	M
Education	M,O*
Educational Psychology	M
English as a Second Language	O
Finance and Banking	M
Health Education	M
Marketing	M
Multilingual and Multicultural Education	M
Nonprofit Management	M

EASTERN CONNECTICUT STATE UNIVERSITY

Early Childhood Education	M
Education	M
Elementary Education	M
Mathematics Education	M
Organizational Behavior	M
Reading Education	M
Science Education	M

EASTERN ILLINOIS UNIVERSITY

Business Administration and Management	M
Business Education	M
Communication Disorders	M
Counselor Education	M,O
Education	M,O
Educational Administration	M,O
Educational Psychology	M,O
Elementary Education	M
Mathematics Education	M
Middle School Education	M
Physical Education	M
Special Education	M

EASTERN KENTUCKY UNIVERSITY

Advanced Practice Nursing	M
Agricultural Education	M
Allied Health	M
Art Education	M
Business Administration and Management	M
Business Education	M
Communication Disorders	M
Counselor Education	M,O
Education	M,O
Educational Administration	M,O
Elementary Education	M
English Education	M
Health Education	M
Health Services Management and Hospital Administration	M
Higher Education	M
Home Economics Education	M
Mathematics Education	M
Music Education	M
Nursing	M
Occupational Therapy	M
Physical Education	M
Reading Education	M
Recreation and Park Management	M
Science Education	M
Secondary Education	M
Social Sciences Education	M
Special Education	M,O
Sports Administration	M
Vocational and Technical Education	M

EASTERN MENNONITE UNIVERSITY

Business Administration and Management	M
Education	M

EASTERN MICHIGAN UNIVERSITY

Accounting	M
Art Education	M
Business Administration and Management	M*
Business Education	M
Communication Disorders	M
Counselor Education	M,O
Curriculum and Instruction	M
Early Childhood Education	M
Education	M,D,O
Educational Administration	M,D,O
Educational Psychology	M
Elementary Education	M
English as a Second Language	M
Finance and Banking	M
Foundations and Philosophy of Education	M
Human Resources Management	M
Industrial and Manufacturing Management	M
International Business	M
Management Information Systems	M
Marketing	M
Middle School Education	M
Multilingual and Multicultural Education	M
Nursing Education	M
Occupational Therapy	M
Organizational Behavior	M
Physical Education	M
Quality Management	M
Reading Education	M
Science Education	M
Secondary Education	M
Social Work	M
Special Education	M,O
Vocational and Technical Education	M

EASTERN NAZARENE COLLEGE

Early Childhood Education	M,O
Education	M,O
Educational Administration	M,O
Elementary Education	M,O
English as a Second Language	M,O
Middle School Education	M,O
Multilingual and Multicultural Education	M,O
Music Education	M,O
Physical Education	M,O
Reading Education	M,O
Secondary Education	M,O
Special Education	M,O

EASTERN NEW MEXICO UNIVERSITY

Business Administration and Management	M
Communication Disorders	M
Counselor Education	M
Education	M
Physical Education	M
Special Education	M

EASTERN OREGON UNIVERSITY

Education	M
Elementary Education	M
Secondary Education	M

EASTERN VIRGINIA MEDICAL SCHOOL

Allopathic Medicine	P
Public Health	M

EASTERN WASHINGTON UNIVERSITY

Adult Education	M
Art Education	M
Business Administration and Management	M
Business Education	M
Communication Disorders	M
Community College Education	M
Computer Education	M
Counselor Education	M
Curriculum and Instruction	M
Early Childhood Education	M
Education	M
Educational Administration	M
Educational Media/Instructional Technology	M
Elementary Education	M
Foreign Languages Education	M
Foundations and Philosophy of Education	M
Higher Education	M
Mathematics Education	M
Medical Technology	M
Music Education	M
Nursing	M
Nursing Education	M
Physical Education	M
Physical Therapy	M
Reading Education	M
Science Education	M
Social Sciences Education	M
Social Work	M
Special Education	M
Vocational and Technical Education	M

EAST STROUDSBURG UNIVERSITY OF PENNSYLVANIA

Communication Disorders	M
Education	M
Elementary Education	M
Exercise and Sports Science	M
Health Education	M
Physical Education	M
Public Health	M
Reading Education	M
Rehabilitation Sciences	M
Science Education	M
Secondary Education	M
Special Education	M
Sports Administration	M

EAST TENNESSEE STATE UNIVERSITY

Accounting	M
Advanced Practice Nursing	O
Allied Health	M
Allopathic Medicine	P
Business Administration and Management	M
Communication Disorders	M
Counselor Education	M
Early Childhood Education	M
Education	M,D,O
Educational Administration	M,D,O

Educational Media/Instructional Technology M
Elementary Education M
Environmental and Occupational Health M
Music Education M
Nursing M,O
Physical Education M
Public Health M
Reading Education M
Secondary Education M
Special Education M

EAST TEXAS BAPTIST UNIVERSITY
Business Administration and Management M

ÉCOLE DES HAUTES ÉTUDES COMMERCIALES
Accounting M,O
Business Administration and Management M,D,O*
Finance and Banking M,O
Human Resources Management M
Industrial and Manufacturing Management M
International Business M
Management Information Systems M
Management Strategy and Policy M
Marketing M
Taxation O

EDGEWOOD COLLEGE
Business Administration and Management M
Education M,O
Educational Administration M,O
Nursing M
Special Education M,O

EDINBORO UNIVERSITY OF PENNSYLVANIA
Advanced Practice Nursing M
Communication Disorders M
Counselor Education M
Early Childhood Education M
Education M,O
Educational Administration M,O
Educational Psychology M
Elementary Education M
English Education M
Health Education O
Mathematics Education M
Middle School Education M
Nursing M
Physical Education O
Reading Education M,O
Science Education M
Secondary Education M
Social Sciences Education M
Special Education M

ELMIRA COLLEGE
Adult Education M
Education M
Elementary Education M
Reading Education M
Secondary Education M

ELON COLLEGE
Business Administration and Management M
Education M
Elementary Education M
Physical Therapy M
Special Education M

EMBRY–RIDDLE AERONAUTICAL UNIVERSITY (FL)
Business Administration and Management M
Transportation Management M

EMBRY–RIDDLE AERONAUTICAL UNIVERSITY, EXTENDED CAMPUS
Business Administration and Management M
Transportation Management M

EMERSON COLLEGE
Advertising and Public Relations M
Communication Disorders M,D
Public Health M*

EMMANUEL COLLEGE (MA)
Business Administration and Management M
Education M
Educational Media/Instructional Technology M
Human Resources Management M

EMORY UNIVERSITY
Advanced Practice Nursing M
Allied Health M
Allopathic Medicine P
Business Administration and Management M
Community Health M*
Early Childhood Education M
Education M,D,O*
Environmental and Occupational Health M*
Epidemiology M,D*
Gerontological Nursing M
Health Physics/Radiological Health M,D
Health Services Management and Hospital Administration M
International Health M*
Law P,M
Maternal/Child-Care Nursing M
Medical/Surgical Nursing M
Middle School Education M
Nurse Anesthesia M
Nurse Midwifery M
Nursing M
Oncology Nursing M
Oral and Dental Sciences O
Physical Therapy M
Physician Assistant Studies M
Psychiatric Nursing M
Public Health M,D*
Secondary Education M
Vision Sciences M

EMPEROR'S COLLEGE OF TRADITIONAL ORIENTAL MEDICINE
Oriental Medicine and Acupuncture M

EMPORIA STATE UNIVERSITY
Business Administration and Management M*
Business Education M
Counselor Education M
Curriculum and Instruction M
Early Childhood Education M
Education M,O
Educational Administration M
Educational Media/Instructional Technology M
Education of the Gifted M
Elementary Education M
Finance and Banking M
Information Studies M,D
Library Science M,D
Marketing M
Music Education M
Physical Education M
Reading Education M
Secondary Education M
Social Sciences Education M
Special Education M

ENDICOTT COLLEGE
Art Education M
Elementary Education M
Reading Education M
Special Education M

THE EVERGREEN STATE COLLEGE
Education M

FAIRFIELD UNIVERSITY
Accounting M,O
Advanced Practice Nursing M,O
Business Administration and Management M,O*
Counselor Education M,O
Early Childhood Education M,O
Education M,O*
Educational Media/Instructional Technology M,O
Elementary Education M
English as a Second Language M,O
Finance and Banking M,O
Foundations and Philosophy of Education M,O
Human Resources Management M,O
International Business M,O
Marketing M,O
Multilingual and Multicultural Education M,O
Nursing M,O
Special Education M,O
Taxation M,O

FAIRLEIGH DICKINSON UNIVERSITY, FLORHAM–MADISON CAMPUS
Accounting M
Business Administration and Management M*
Education M
Finance and Banking M
Human Resources Management M*

Industrial and Manufacturing Management M
International Business M
Marketing M
Organizational Behavior M
Quantitative Analysis M
Taxation M

FAIRLEIGH DICKINSON UNIVERSITY, TEANECK–HACKENSACK CAMPUS
Accounting M
Business Administration and Management M*
Curriculum and Instruction M
Education M
Elementary Education M
English as a Second Language M
English Education M
Finance and Banking M
Human Resources Management M
Industrial and Manufacturing Management M
International Business M
Management Information Systems M
Marketing M
Mathematics Education M
Multilingual and Multicultural Education M
Nursing M
Physical Education M
Quantitative Analysis M
Science Education M
Social Sciences Education M
Special Education M
Taxation M

FAULKNER UNIVERSITY
Law P

FAYETTEVILLE STATE UNIVERSITY
Business Administration and Management M
Education D
Educational Administration M
Elementary Education M
Mathematics Education M
Middle School Education M
Science Education M
Secondary Education M
Social Sciences Education M
Special Education M

FELICIAN COLLEGE
Advanced Practice Nursing M
Nursing M

FERRIS STATE UNIVERSITY
Business Administration and Management M
Education M
Management Information Systems M
Optometry P
Pharmacy P
Vocational and Technical Education M

FIELDING INSTITUTE
Educational Administration D
Human Services M,D
Organizational Behavior M,D

FINCH UNIVERSITY OF HEALTH SCIENCES/THE CHICAGO MEDICAL SCHOOL
Allied Health M*
Allopathic Medicine P
Clinical Laboratory Sciences M*
Health Services Management and Hospital Administration M*
Medical Physics M,D
Physical Therapy M*
Physician Assistant Studies M*

FITCHBURG STATE COLLEGE
Art Education M
Business Administration and Management M
Counselor Education M,O
Early Childhood Education M
Education M,O*
Educational Administration M,O
Elementary Education M
English Education M
Mathematics Education M
Middle School Education M
Nursing M*
Science Education M
Secondary Education M
Social Sciences Education M
Special Education M
Vocational and Technical Education M

FIVE BRANCHES INSTITUTE: COLLEGE OF TRADITIONAL CHINESE MEDICINE
Oriental Medicine and Acupuncture M

FIVE TOWNS COLLEGE
Music Education M

FLORIDA AGRICULTURAL AND MECHANICAL UNIVERSITY
Accounting M
Adult Education M
Agricultural Education M
Business Administration and Management M
Business Education M
Counselor Education M
Early Childhood Education M
Education M
Educational Administration M
Elementary Education M
Finance and Banking M
Health Education M
Management Information Systems M
Marketing M
Pharmaceutical Sciences M,D*
Pharmacy P
Physical Education M
Recreation and Park Management M
Secondary Education M
Vocational and Technical Education M

FLORIDA ATLANTIC UNIVERSITY
Accounting M
Adult Education M,D,O
Advanced Practice Nursing M,O
Allied Health M
Art Education M
Business Administration and Management M,D
Communication Disorders M
Counselor Education M,O
Curriculum and Instruction D,O
Early Childhood Education M
Education M,D,O
Educational Administration M,D,O
Educational Media/Instructional Technology M
Elementary Education M,D
Exercise and Sports Science M
Foreign Languages Education M
Foundations and Philosophy of Education M
Maternal/Child-Care Nursing M,O
Medical/Surgical Nursing M,O
Nursing M,O
Nursing Administration M
Physical Therapy M
Reading Education M
Special Education M,D
Taxation M

FLORIDA GULF COAST UNIVERSITY
Allied Health M
Business Administration and Management M
Counselor Education M
Curriculum and Instruction M
Education M
Educational Administration M
Elementary Education M
Physical Therapy M
Social Work M
Special Education M

FLORIDA INSTITUTE OF TECHNOLOGY
Business Administration and Management M*
Computer Education M,D,O
Health Services Management and Hospital Administration M
Human Resources Management M
International Business M
Logistics M
Management Information Systems M
Mathematics Education M,D,O
Science Education M,D,O

FLORIDA INTERNATIONAL UNIVERSITY
Accounting M,D
Adult Education M
Art Education M
Business Administration and Management M,D*
Community College Education D
Counselor Education M
Curriculum and Instruction D,O
Early Childhood Education M
Education M,D,O
Educational Administration D,O
Elementary Education M
English as a Second Language M

Florida International University (continued)

- English Education M
- Finance and Banking M,D
- Foreign Languages Education M
- Health Education M
- Health Services Management and Hospital Administration M
- Home Economics Education M
- Hospitality Management M
- Human Resources Development M
- International and Comparative Education M
- International Business M,D
- Management Information Systems M
- Marketing M,D
- Mathematics Education M
- Medical Technology M
- Music Education M
- Nursing M
- Occupational Therapy M
- Physical Education M
- Physical Therapy M
- Public Health M
- Reading Education M
- Recreation and Park Management M
- Science Education M
- Social Sciences Education M
- Social Work M,D
- Special Education M,D
- Taxation M,D
- Urban Education M
- Vocational and Technical Education M

FLORIDA METROPOLITAN UNIVERSITY–FORT LAUDERDALE COLLEGE

- Business Administration and Management M

FLORIDA METROPOLITAN UNIVERSITY–ORLANDO COLLEGE, NORTH

- Accounting M
- Business Administration and Management M
- International Business M
- Management Information Systems M
- Marketing M

FLORIDA METROPOLITAN UNIVERSITY–TAMPA COLLEGE

- Business Administration and Management M
- Human Resources Management M
- International Business M

FLORIDA SOUTHERN COLLEGE

- Accounting M
- Business Administration and Management M

FLORIDA STATE UNIVERSITY

- Accounting M
- Adult Education M,D,O
- Advanced Practice Nursing M
- Art Education M,D,O
- Business Administration and Management M,D
- Communication Disorders M,D
- Counselor Education M,O
- Early Childhood Education M,D,O
- Education M,D,O
- Educational Administration M,D,O
- Educational Measurement and Evaluation M,D,O
- Educational Media/Instructional Technology M,D,O
- Educational Psychology M,D,O
- Elementary Education M,D,O
- English Education M,D,O
- Exercise and Sports Science M
- Foundations and Philosophy of Education M,D,O
- Health Education M
- Higher Education M,D,O
- Human Services M,D,O
- Information Studies M,D*
- International and Comparative Education M,D,O
- Kinesiology and Movement Studies M,D
- Law P
- Library Science M,D*
- Mathematics Education M,D,O
- Multilingual and Multicultural Education M,D,O
- Music Education M,D
- Nursing M
- Nursing Education M
- Physical Education M,D,O
- Reading Education M,D,O
- Recreation and Park Management M
- Science Education M,D,O
- Social Sciences Education M,D,O
- Social Work M,D
- Special Education M,D,O
- Sports Administration M,D,O
- Vocational and Technical Education D,O

FONTBONNE COLLEGE

- Business Administration and Management M
- Communication Disorders M
- Computer Education M
- Education M
- Taxation M

FORDHAM UNIVERSITY

- Accounting M
- Adult Education M
- Business Administration and Management M,O*
- Counselor Education M,O
- Curriculum and Instruction M,D
- Early Childhood Education M
- Education M,D,O*
- Educational Administration M,D,O
- Educational Psychology M,D,O
- Elementary Education M
- English as a Second Language M
- Finance and Banking M
- Human Resources Management M
- Law P,M*
- Management Information Systems M
- Marketing M
- Multilingual and Multicultural Education M
- Quality Management O
- Reading Education M,O
- Religious Education M,O
- Secondary Education M
- Social Work M,D
- Special Education M,O
- Taxation M

FORT HAYS STATE UNIVERSITY

- Accounting M
- Business Administration and Management M
- Communication Disorders M
- Computer Education M
- Counselor Education M
- Education M,O
- Educational Administration M,O
- Educational Media/Instructional Technology M
- Elementary Education M
- Finance and Banking M
- Health Education M
- Management Information Systems M
- Mathematics Education M
- Nursing M
- Physical Education M
- Recreation and Park Management M
- Secondary Education M
- Special Education M

FORT VALLEY STATE UNIVERSITY

- Counselor Education M,O
- Early Childhood Education M
- Middle School Education M

FRAMINGHAM STATE COLLEGE

- Business Administration and Management M
- Education M
- Educational Administration M
- English Education M
- Health Services Management and Hospital Administration M
- Home Economics Education M
- Human Resources Management M
- Mathematics Education M
- Reading Education M
- Social Sciences Education M
- Special Education M

FRANCISCAN UNIVERSITY OF STEUBENVILLE

- Business Administration and Management M
- Education M
- Educational Administration M

FRANCIS MARION UNIVERSITY

- Business Administration and Management M
- Early Childhood Education M
- Education M
- Elementary Education M
- Secondary Education M
- Special Education M

FRANKLIN PIERCE COLLEGE

- Business Administration and Management M

FRANKLIN PIERCE LAW CENTER

- Law P,M,O

FRANKLIN UNIVERSITY

- Business Administration and Management M
- Human Services M
- Marketing M

FREED–HARDEMAN UNIVERSITY

- Counselor Education M
- Curriculum and Instruction M
- Education M

FRESNO PACIFIC UNIVERSITY

- Business Administration and Management M
- Counselor Education M
- Curriculum and Instruction M
- Education M
- Educational Administration M
- Educational Media/Instructional Technology M
- Education of the Multiply Handicapped M
- English as a Second Language M
- Mathematics Education M
- Multilingual and Multicultural Education M
- Reading Education M
- Science Education M
- Special Education M

FRIENDS UNIVERSITY

- Business Administration and Management M
- Educational Administration M
- Elementary Education M
- Human Resources Development M
- Management Information Systems M
- Quality Management M
- Secondary Education M

FROSTBURG STATE UNIVERSITY

- Business Administration and Management M
- Counselor Education M
- Curriculum and Instruction M
- Education M
- Educational Administration M
- Elementary Education M
- Health Education M
- Physical Education M
- Reading Education M
- Recreation and Park Management M
- Science Education M
- Secondary Education M

FURMAN UNIVERSITY

- Education M
- Educational Administration M
- Elementary Education M
- Exercise and Sports Science M
- Health Education M
- Reading Education M
- Social Sciences Education M
- Special Education M

GALLAUDET UNIVERSITY

- Communication Disorders M,D
- Counselor Education M
- Early Childhood Education M,O
- Education M,D,O
- Educational Administration M,D,O
- Educational Measurement and Evaluation M
- Education of the Multiply Handicapped M,O
- Elementary Education M,O
- Secondary Education M,O
- Social Work M
- Special Education M,D,O

GANNON UNIVERSITY

- Accounting O
- Advanced Practice Nursing M,O
- Business Administration and Management M,O
- Curriculum and Instruction M
- Early Childhood Education M,O
- Education M,O
- Educational Media/Instructional Technology M
- Finance and Banking O
- Gerontological Nursing M
- Health Services Management and Hospital Administration M,O
- Human Resources Management O
- Medical/Surgical Nursing M
- Nurse Anesthesia M
- Nursing M,O
- Nursing Administration M
- Physical Therapy M
- Reading Education M,O
- Science Education M,O
- Secondary Education M

GARDNER–WEBB UNIVERSITY

- Business Administration and Management M
- Education M
- Educational Administration M
- Elementary Education M
- English Education M
- Middle School Education M
- Physical Education M

GENEVA COLLEGE

- Education M
- Higher Education M*
- Organizational Behavior M

GEORGE FOX UNIVERSITY

- Business Administration and Management M
- Education M
- Religious Education M

GEORGE MASON UNIVERSITY

- Accounting M
- Advanced Practice Nursing M
- Business Administration and Management M
- Community College Education D
- Counselor Education M
- Early Childhood Education M
- Education M,D
- Educational Administration M
- Educational Media/Instructional Technology M
- English as a Second Language M
- Exercise and Sports Science M
- Human Resources Management M
- Law P
- Medical/Surgical Nursing M
- Middle School Education M
- Multilingual and Multicultural Education M
- Music Education M
- Nursing M,D
- Nursing Administration M
- Organizational Behavior M
- Reading Education M
- Secondary Education M
- Special Education M
- Taxation M

GEORGETOWN COLLEGE

- Education M

GEORGETOWN UNIVERSITY

- Allopathic Medicine P
- Business Administration and Management M*
- English as a Second Language M,O
- Epidemiology M*
- Health Physics/Radiological Health M
- Law P,M,D
- Multilingual and Multicultural Education O
- Nursing M*
- Taxation M

THE GEORGE WASHINGTON UNIVERSITY

- Accounting M,D
- Allopathic Medicine P
- Business Administration and Management M,D*
- Communication Disorders M
- Community Health M*
- Counselor Education M,D,O
- Curriculum and Instruction M,D,O
- Early Childhood Education M
- Education M,D,O*
- Educational Administration M,D,O
- Educational Media/Instructional Technology M
- Elementary Education M
- Environmental and Occupational Health M*
- Epidemiology M,D*
- Exercise and Sports Science M*
- Finance and Banking M,D*
- Foundations and Philosophy of Education M
- Health Promotion M*
- Health Services Management and Hospital Administration M,O*
- Higher Education M,D,O
- Hospitality Management M
- Human Resources Development M,D,O
- Human Resources Management M
- Industrial and Manufacturing Management M
- International and Comparative Education M
- International Business M,D

International Health M*
Law P,M,D
Logistics M
Management Information Systems M
Management Strategy and Policy M,D
Marketing M,D
Maternal and Child Health M*
Organizational Behavior M
Project Management M
Public Health M,D*
Real Estate M
Secondary Education M
Special Education M,D,O
Sports Administration M
Taxation M
Travel and Tourism M

GEORGIA COLLEGE AND STATE UNIVERSITY

Business Administration and Management M
Early Childhood Education M,O
Education M,O
Educational Administration M,O
Educational Media/Instructional Technology M
Foundations and Philosophy of Education M,O
Health Education M,O
Logistics M
Middle School Education M,O
Nursing M
Physical Education M,O
Secondary Education M,O
Special Education M

GEORGIA INSTITUTE OF TECHNOLOGY

Business Administration and Management M,D
Health Physics/Radiological Health M,D
Health Services Management and Hospital Administration M

GEORGIAN COURT COLLEGE

Business Administration and Management M
Education M
Educational Administration M
Reading Education M
Special Education M

GEORGIA SOUTHERN UNIVERSITY

Accounting M
Adult Education M
Advanced Practice Nursing M,O
Allied Health M,O
Art Education M,O
Business Administration and Management M
Business Education M
Counselor Education M,O
Curriculum and Instruction D
Early Childhood Education M,O
Education M,D,O
Educational Administration M,D,O
Educational Media/Instructional Technology M,O
English Education M,O
Foreign Languages Education M
Health Education M,O
Kinesiology and Movement Studies M
Mathematics Education M,O
Middle School Education M,O
Music Education M,O
Nursing M,O
Physical Education M,O
Public Health Nursing M
Reading Education M,O
Recreation and Park Management M
Science Education M,O
Social Sciences Education M,O
Special Education M,O
Sports Administration M
Vocational and Technical Education M,O

GEORGIA SOUTHWESTERN STATE UNIVERSITY

Business Administration and Management M
Business Education M
Early Childhood Education M,O
Education M,O
Health Education M
Management Information Systems M
Middle School Education M,O
Physical Education M
Reading Education M
Secondary Education M

GEORGIA STATE UNIVERSITY

Accounting M,D
Actuarial Science M
Allied Health M,D
Art Education M,O
Business Administration and Management M,D
Business Education M
Communication Disorders M
Counselor Education M,D,O
Curriculum and Instruction D
Early Childhood Education M,D,O
Education M,D,O*
Educational Administration M,D,O
Educational Measurement and Evaluation M,D
Educational Media/Instructional Technology M,D,O
Educational Psychology M,D
Education of the Multiply Handicapped M
English as a Second Language M
English Education M,D,O
Exercise and Sports Science M,D
Finance and Banking M,D
Foundations and Philosophy of Education M,D
Gerontological Nursing M
Health Services Management and Hospital Administration M
Higher Education D
Human Resources Development M,D
Human Resources Management M,D*
Insurance M,D
International Business M
Law P*
Management Information Systems M,D
Marketing M,D
Maternal/Child-Care Nursing M,D
Mathematics Education M,D,O
Medical Technology M
Middle School Education M,O
Music Education M,O
Nonprofit Management M
Nursing M,D
Nursing Education D
Physical Education M,O
Physical Therapy M
Psychiatric Nursing M
Public Health Nursing D
Reading Education M,O
Real Estate M,D
Science Education M,D,O
Social Sciences Education M,D,O
Special Education M,D,O
Sports Administration M
Taxation M
Transportation Management M
Vocational and Technical Education M,D,O

GMI ENGINEERING & MANAGEMENT INSTITUTE (SEE KETTERING UNIVERSITY)

GODDARD COLLEGE

Education M

GOLDEN GATE BAPTIST THEOLOGICAL SEMINARY

Religious Education M

GOLDEN GATE UNIVERSITY

Accounting M
Advertising and Public Relations M,O
Business Administration and Management M,D,O*
Entrepreneurship M
Finance and Banking M,O
Health Services Management and Hospital Administration M,O
Hospitality Management M
Human Resources Management M,O
Industrial and Manufacturing Management M,O
International Business M,O
Law P,M,D*
Legal and Justice Studies M,D*
Logistics M,O
Management Information Systems M,O
Marketing M
Organizational Behavior M
Project Management M,O
Taxation M,O*
Travel and Tourism M

GOLDEY–BEACOM COLLEGE

Accounting M
Business Administration and Management M
Finance and Banking M
Human Resources Management M

GONZAGA UNIVERSITY

Accounting M
Art Education M
Business Administration and Management M
Computer Education M
Curriculum and Instruction M
Education M,D
Educational Administration M,D
Law P
Nurse Anesthesia M
Nursing M
Organizational Behavior M
Social Sciences Education M
Special Education M
Sports Administration M

GOODING INSTITUTE OF NURSE ANESTHESIA

Nurse Anesthesia M

GORDON COLLEGE (MA)

Education M*

GORDON-CONWELL THEOLOGICAL SEMINARY

Religious Education M

GOUCHER COLLEGE

Education M

GOVERNORS STATE UNIVERSITY

Accounting M
Allied Health M
Business Administration and Management M
Communication Disorders M
Counselor Education M
Education M
Educational Administration M
Educational Media/Instructional Technology M
Health Services Management and Hospital Administration M
Legal and Justice Studies M
Nursing M
Occupational Therapy M
Physical Therapy M
Social Work M
Special Education M

GRACELAND COLLEGE

Advanced Practice Nursing M,O
Nursing M,O
Nursing Administration M
Nursing Education M

GRACE UNIVERSITY

Religious Education M

GRADUATE SCHOOL AND UNIVERSITY CENTER OF THE CITY UNIVERSITY OF NEW YORK

Accounting D
Business Administration and Management D
Communication Disorders D
Educational Psychology D
Finance and Banking D
Management Information Systems D
Organizational Behavior D
Social Work D

THE GRADUATE SCHOOL OF AMERICA

Business Administration and Management M,D
Education M,D
Human Services M,D
Organizational Behavior D

GRADUATE THEOLOGICAL UNION

Religious Education M

GRAMBLING STATE UNIVERSITY

Business Administration and Management M
Curriculum and Instruction D
Early Childhood Education M
Education M,D
Educational Administration D
Elementary Education M
Nursing M
Science Education M
Social Sciences Education M
Social Work M
Sports Administration M

GRAND CANYON UNIVERSITY

Business Administration and Management M
Education M
Elementary Education M
English as a Second Language M
Reading Education M
Secondary Education M

GRAND RAPIDS BAPTIST SEMINARY

Religious Education P,M,D

GRAND VALLEY STATE UNIVERSITY

Allied Health M
Business Administration and Management M
Early Childhood Education M
Education M
Educational Administration M
Educational Media/Instructional Technology M
Education of the Gifted M
Elementary Education M
English Education M
Mathematics Education M
Nursing M
Occupational Therapy M
Physical Therapy M
Physician Assistant Studies M
Reading Education M
Science Education M
Social Sciences Education M
Social Work M
Special Education M
Taxation M

GRATZ COLLEGE

Education M
Library Science O
Religious Education M,O
Social Work M,O

GROVE CITY COLLEGE

Accounting M

GWYNEDD–MERCY COLLEGE

Advanced Practice Nursing M
Counselor Education M
Education M
Educational Administration M
Gerontological Nursing M
Maternal/Child-Care Nursing M
Medical/Surgical Nursing M
Nursing M
Oncology Nursing M
Reading Education M

HAMLINE UNIVERSITY

Business Administration and Management M
Education M,D
Law P*
Nonprofit Management M

HAMPTON UNIVERSITY

Business Administration and Management M
Communication Disorders M*
Counselor Education M
Education M
Elementary Education M
Nursing M
Special Education M

HARDING UNIVERSITY

Education M
Educational Administration M
Elementary Education M
Secondary Education M

HARDIN–SIMMONS UNIVERSITY

Business Administration and Management M
Counselor Education M
Education M
Education of the Gifted M
Elementary Education M
Foreign Languages Education M
Music Education M
Nursing M
Physical Education M
Physical Therapy M
Reading Education M
Recreation and Park Management M
Secondary Education M
Social Sciences Education M
Sports Administration M

HARVARD UNIVERSITY

Adult Education D
Allopathic Medicine P
Art Education M
Business Administration and Management M,D,O*
Communication Disorders D*
Community Health M
Curriculum and Instruction M,D,O
Dentistry P
Education M,D,O*
Educational Administration M,D,O
Educational Media/Instructional Technology M
Educational Psychology M,D,O

Harvard University (continued)
- Elementary Education D
- Environmental and Occupational Health M,D*
- Epidemiology M,D
- Foundations and Philosophy of Education M,D,O
- Health Promotion M,D
- Health Services Management and Hospital Administration M,D
- Higher Education D
- Industrial Hygiene M,D
- International and Comparative Education M,D
- International Health M,D
- Law P,M,D
- Maternal and Child Health M,D
- Mathematics Education M,O
- Medical Physics D
- Oral and Dental Sciences M,D,O
- Organizational Behavior D
- Public Health M,D,O*
- Reading Education M,D,O
- Science Education M,O
- Secondary Education D
- Urban Education D

HASTINGS COLLEGE
- Education M

HAWAII PACIFIC UNIVERSITY
- Accounting M
- Advanced Practice Nursing M
- Business Administration and Management M*
- Finance and Banking M
- Human Resources Management M
- International Business M
- Management Information Systems M
- Marketing M
- Nursing M
- Organizational Behavior M
- Public Health Nursing M
- Quality Management M

HEBREW COLLEGE
- Education M
- Religious Education M

HEBREW UNION COLLEGE–JEWISH INSTITUTE OF RELIGION (CA)
- Education M,D
- Religious Education M,D
- Social Work M,O

HEBREW UNION COLLEGE–JEWISH INSTITUTE OF RELIGION (NY)
- Education M
- Religious Education M

HEIDELBERG COLLEGE
- Business Administration and Management M
- Counselor Education M
- Education M

HENDERSON STATE UNIVERSITY
- Art Education M
- Business Administration and Management M
- Counselor Education M
- Early Childhood Education M
- Education M
- Educational Administration M
- Elementary Education M
- English Education M
- Mathematics Education M
- Physical Education M
- Science Education M
- Secondary Education M
- Social Sciences Education M
- Special Education M

HERITAGE COLLEGE
- Counselor Education M
- Early Childhood Education M
- Education M
- Educational Administration M
- English as a Second Language M
- Human Resources Development M
- Multilingual and Multicultural Education M
- Special Education M

HIGH POINT UNIVERSITY
- Business Administration and Management M
- International Business M

HOFSTRA UNIVERSITY
- Accounting M
- Art Education M
- Business Administration and Management M*
- Communication Disorders M
- Counselor Education M,O
- Early Childhood Education M
- Education M,D,O*
- Educational Administration M,D,O
- Educational Measurement and Evaluation M
- Elementary Education M
- English as a Second Language M
- English Education M,O
- Finance and Banking M
- Foundations and Philosophy of Education M,O
- Health Education M
- Health Services Management and Hospital Administration M
- International Business M
- Law P
- Management Information Systems M
- Marketing M
- Mathematics Education M
- Multilingual and Multicultural Education M
- Music Education M
- Physical Education M
- Quantitative Analysis M
- Reading Education M,D,O
- Science Education M
- Secondary Education M
- Special Education M,O
- Taxation M

HOLLINS UNIVERSITY
- Education M

HOLY FAMILY COLLEGE
- Education M
- Elementary Education M
- Nursing M
- Reading Education M
- Secondary Education M

HOLY NAMES COLLEGE
- Advanced Practice Nursing M
- Business Administration and Management M
- Education M,O
- English as a Second Language O
- Music Education M,O
- Nursing M
- Public Health Nursing M

HOOD COLLEGE
- Business Administration and Management M
- Curriculum and Instruction M
- Early Childhood Education M
- Education M
- Educational Administration M
- Elementary Education M
- Mathematics Education M
- Reading Education M
- Science Education M
- Secondary Education M
- Special Education M

HOPE INTERNATIONAL UNIVERSITY
- Business Administration and Management M
- Education M
- International Business M
- Nonprofit Management M

HOUSTON BAPTIST UNIVERSITY
- Accounting M
- Advanced Practice Nursing M
- Business Administration and Management M
- Counselor Education M
- Education M
- Educational Administration M
- Educational Measurement and Evaluation M
- Elementary Education M
- Finance and Banking M
- Health Services Management and Hospital Administration M
- Human Resources Management M
- Management Information Systems M
- Marketing M
- Multilingual and Multicultural Education M
- Nursing M
- Reading Education M
- Secondary Education M
- Special Education M

HOWARD UNIVERSITY
- Advanced Practice Nursing O
- Allopathic Medicine P
- Business Administration and Management M
- Communication Disorders M,D
- Counselor Education M,D,O
- Dentistry P,O
- Early Childhood Education M,O
- Education M,D,O*
- Educational Administration M,O
- Educational Psychology M,D,O
- Elementary Education M
- Exercise and Sports Science M
- Health Education M
- Health Services Management and Hospital Administration M
- International and Comparative Education M,O
- Law P,M
- Leisure Studies M
- Music Education M
- Nursing M,O
- Pharmacy P
- Reading Education M,O
- Recreation and Park Management M
- Secondary Education M,O
- Social Work M,D*
- Special Education M,O

HUMBOLDT STATE UNIVERSITY
- Business Administration and Management M
- Physical Education M

HUMPHREYS COLLEGE
- Law P

HUNTER COLLEGE OF THE CITY UNIVERSITY OF NEW YORK
- Advanced Practice Nursing M,O
- Communication Disorders M
- Counselor Education M
- Early Childhood Education M
- Education M,O
- Educational Administration O
- Elementary Education M
- English as a Second Language M
- English Education M
- Environmental and Occupational Health M
- Foreign Languages Education M
- Gerontological Nursing M
- Maternal/Child-Care Nursing M,O
- Mathematics Education M
- Medical/Surgical Nursing M
- Multilingual and Multicultural Education M
- Music Education M
- Nursing M,O
- Nursing Administration M
- Psychiatric Nursing M
- Public Health M
- Public Health Nursing M
- Reading Education M
- Science Education M
- Secondary Education M
- Social Sciences Education M
- Social Work M,D
- Special Education M

HUNTINGTON COLLEGE
- Religious Education M

HURON INTERNATIONAL UNIVERSITY
- Business Administration and Management M

HURON UNIVERSITY
- Business Administration and Management M

HUSSON COLLEGE
- Advanced Practice Nursing M
- Business Administration and Management M
- Nursing M
- Physical Therapy M
- Psychiatric Nursing M

ICR GRADUATE SCHOOL
- Science Education M

IDAHO STATE UNIVERSITY
- Allied Health M,D,O
- Business Administration and Management M
- Communication Disorders M
- Counselor Education M,D,O
- Curriculum and Instruction M
- Early Childhood Education M
- Education M,D,O
- Educational Administration M,D,O
- Health Promotion M
- Health Services Management and Hospital Administration M,D
- Home Economics Education M
- Nursing M,O
- Occupational Therapy M
- Pharmaceutical Sciences M,D
- Pharmacy P,M,D
- Physical Therapy M
- Public Health M
- Reading Education M
- Special Education M,O
- Sports Administration M
- Vocational and Technical Education M

ILLINOIS COLLEGE OF OPTOMETRY
- Optometry P

ILLINOIS INSTITUTE OF TECHNOLOGY
- Business Administration and Management M,D*
- Finance and Banking M*
- Human Resources Development M
- Industrial and Manufacturing Management M
- Law P,M
- Marketing M*
- Medical Physics M,D

ILLINOIS SCHOOL OF PROFESSIONAL PSYCHOLOGY, CHICAGO CAMPUS
- Health Services Management and Hospital Administration M*

ILLINOIS STATE UNIVERSITY
- Accounting M
- Art Education D
- Business Administration and Management M*
- Communication Disorders M
- Counselor Education M
- Curriculum and Instruction M,D
- Education M,D
- Educational Administration M,D
- Educational Psychology M
- Health Education M
- Higher Education D
- Mathematics Education D
- Physical Education M
- Reading Education M
- Special Education M,D

IMC–INTERNATIONAL MANAGEMENT CENTRES
- Business Administration and Management M,D

IMMACULATA COLLEGE
- Counselor Education O
- Educational Administration M,D,O
- Elementary Education O
- Multilingual and Multicultural Education M

INDIANA STATE UNIVERSITY
- Business Administration and Management M,D,O
- Business Education M,D,O
- Clinical Laboratory Sciences M
- Communication Disorders M,D,O
- Counselor Education M,D,O
- Curriculum and Instruction M,D,O
- Early Childhood Education M,D,O
- Education M,D,O
- Educational Administration M,D,O
- Educational Media/Instructional Technology M,D,O
- Educational Psychology M,D,O
- Education of the Gifted M,O
- Elementary Education M,D,O
- Exercise and Sports Science M
- Facilities Management M
- Health Education M
- Health Services Management and Hospital Administration M
- Higher Education M
- Human Resources Development M
- Music Education M
- Nursing M
- Physical Education M
- Reading Education M,D,O
- Science Education M
- Secondary Education M,D,O
- Special Education M,D,O
- Vocational and Technical Education M,D

INDIANA UNIVERSITY BLOOMINGTON
- Accounting D
- Art Education M
- Business Administration and Management M,D*
- Communication Disorders M,D
- Counselor Education M,D
- Curriculum and Instruction M,D,O
- Early Childhood Education M,O
- Education M,D,O*
- Educational Administration M,D,O
- Educational Media/Instructional Technology M,D,O
- Educational Psychology M,D,O
- Elementary Education M,O
- English as a Second Language M,D,O
- English Education M
- Entrepreneurship M
- Exercise and Sports Science M,D
- Finance and Banking M,D

Foreign Languages Education M
Foundations and Philosophy of Education M,D
Health Education M,O
Health Promotion M
Higher Education M,D
Human Resources Development M
Human Resources Management M
Information Studies M,D,O*
International and Comparative Education M
International Business M
Kinesiology and Movement Studies M,D,O
Law P,M,D
Leisure Studies D
Library Science M,D,O*
Management Information Systems M,D
Marketing M,D
Mathematics Education M
Optometry P
Organizational Behavior D
Physical Education M,D,O
Public Health M,D,O
Reading Education M,D,O
Recreation and Park Management M,D,O
Science Education M
Secondary Education M,O
Social Sciences Education M
Special Education M,D,O
Sports Administration M
Vision Sciences M,D*

INDIANA UNIVERSITY KOKOMO

Business Administration and Management M
Education M
Elementary Education M

INDIANA UNIVERSITY NORTHWEST

Accounting M,O
Business Administration and Management M,O
Education M
Elementary Education M
Health Services Management and Hospital Administration M
Human Services M
Nonprofit Management O
Secondary Education M
Social Work M

INDIANA UNIVERSITY OF PENNSYLVANIA

Adult Education M
Business Administration and Management M
Business Education M
Communication Disorders M
Counselor Education M
Early Childhood Education M
Education M,D,O
Educational Administration M,D,O
Educational Psychology M,O
Elementary Education D
English as a Second Language M
English Education M
Environmental and Occupational Health M
Exercise and Sports Science M
Facilities Management M
Health Education M
Higher Education M
Mathematics Education M
Music Education M
Nursing M
Physical Education M
Reading Education M,O
Science Education M
Special Education M
Sports Administration M

INDIANA UNIVERSITY–PURDUE UNIVERSITY FORT WAYNE

Business Administration and Management M
Counselor Education M
Education M
Educational Administration M
Elementary Education M
Nursing Administration M
Secondary Education M

INDIANA UNIVERSITY–PURDUE UNIVERSITY INDIANAPOLIS

Allopathic Medicine P
Art Education M
Business Administration and Management M
Counselor Education M
Dentistry P
Education M
Educational Administration M
Elementary Education M
Foreign Languages Education M
Health Services Management and Hospital Administration M*
Law P
Nursing M,D*
Oral and Dental Sciences M,D
Secondary Education M
Social Work M,D
Special Education M

INDIANA UNIVERSITY SOUTH BEND

Accounting M
Business Administration and Management M
Counselor Education M
Education M
Elementary Education M
Music Education M
Secondary Education M
Social Work M
Special Education M

INDIANA UNIVERSITY SOUTHEAST

Counselor Education M
Education M
Elementary Education M
Secondary Education M

INDIANA WESLEYAN UNIVERSITY

Business Administration and Management M
Counselor Education M
Curriculum and Instruction M
Education M
Nursing M
Nursing Education M
Public Health Nursing M

INSTITUTE FOR CHRISTIAN STUDIES (CANADA)

Education M

INSTITUTE FOR CLINICAL SOCIAL WORK

Social Work D

INSTITUTE FRANCAIS DE CHIROPRACTIE

Chiropractic P

INSTITUTO CENTROAMERICANO DE ADMINISTRACIÓN DE EMPRESAS

Business Administration and Management M

INSTITUTO TECNOLÓGICO Y DE ESTUDIOS SUPERIORES DE MONTERREY

Business Administration and Management M,D
Finance and Banking M
International Business M
Marketing M
Science Education M

INSTITUTO TECNOLÓGICO Y DE ESTUDIOS SUPERIORES DE MONTERREY, CHIHUAHUA CAMPUS

International Business M

INSTITUTO TECNOLÓGICO Y DE ESTUDIOS SUPERIORES DE MONTERREY, CIUDAD DE MÉXICO CAMPUS

Business Administration and Management M,D
Finance and Banking M

INSTITUTO TECNOLÓGICO Y DE ESTUDIOS SUPERIORES DE MONTERREY, ESTADO DE MÉXICO CAMPUS

Business Administration and Management M
Education M
Finance and Banking M
Management Information Systems M
Marketing M
Quality Management M

INSTITUTO TECNOLÓGICO Y DE ESTUDIOS SUPERIORES DE MONTERREY, GUADALAJARA CAMPUS

Business Administration and Management M
Finance and Banking M

INSTITUTO TECNOLÓGICO Y DE ESTUDIOS SUPERIORES DE MONTERREY, LAGUNA CAMPUS

Business Administration and Management M
Management Information Systems M

INSTITUTO TECNOLÓGICO Y DE ESTUDIOS SUPERIORES DE MONTERREY, LEÓN CAMPUS

Business Administration and Management M

INSTITUTO TECNOLÓGICO Y DE ESTUDIOS SUPERIORES DE MONTERREY, MORELOS CAMPUS

Business Administration and Management M
Finance and Banking M
Human Resources Management M
International Business M
Marketing M

INSTITUTO TECNOLÓGICO Y DE ESTUDIOS SUPERIORES DE MONTERREY, QUERÉTARO CAMPUS

Business Administration and Management M

INSTITUTO TECNOLÓGICO Y DE ESTUDIOS SUPERIORES DE MONTERREY, SONORA NORTE CAMPUS

Business Administration and Management M
Education M

INSTITUTO TECNOLÓGICO Y DE ESTUDIOS SUPERIORES DE MONTERREY, TOLUCA CAMPUS

Business Administration and Management M

INTER AMERICAN UNIVERSITY OF PUERTO RICO, METROPOLITAN CAMPUS

Accounting M
Business Administration and Management M
Business Education M
Counselor Education M
Education M,D
Educational Administration M
Educational Media/Instructional Technology M
Elementary Education M
English as a Second Language M
Finance and Banking M
Health Education M
Higher Education M
Human Resources Development M
Human Resources Management M
Industrial and Manufacturing Management M
Law P
Marketing M
Medical Technology M
Optometry P
Physical Education M
Science Education M
Social Work M
Special Education M
Vocational and Technical Education M

INTER AMERICAN UNIVERSITY OF PUERTO RICO, SAN GERMÁN CAMPUS

Accounting M
Business Administration and Management M
Business Education M
Counselor Education M
Curriculum and Instruction M
Education M
Educational Administration M
English as a Second Language M
Finance and Banking M
Higher Education M
Human Resources Development M
Human Resources Management M
Kinesiology and Movement Studies M
Library Science M
Marketing M
Medical Technology O
Physical Education M
Science Education M
Special Education M

INTERNATIONAL COLLEGE OF THE CAYMAN ISLANDS

Business Administration and Management M

INTERNATIONAL INSTITUTE OF CHINESE MEDICINE

Oriental Medicine and Acupuncture M,O*

IONA COLLEGE (NEW ROCHELLE)

Accounting M
Advertising and Public Relations M
Business Administration and Management M,O*
Business Education M
Educational Administration M,O
Educational Media/Instructional Technology M,O
Elementary Education M
English Education M
Finance and Banking M,O
Foreign Languages Education M
Health Services Management and Hospital Administration M,O
Human Resources Management M,O
Industrial and Manufacturing Management M,O
International Business M,O
Management Information Systems M,O
Marketing M,O
Mathematics Education M
Multilingual and Multicultural Education M
Science Education M
Secondary Education M
Social Sciences Education M

IOWA STATE UNIVERSITY OF SCIENCE AND TECHNOLOGY

Adult Education M,D
Agricultural Education M,D
Business Administration and Management M*
Counselor Education M
Curriculum and Instruction M,D
Education M,D
Educational Administration M,D
Educational Measurement and Evaluation M
Educational Media/Instructional Technology M,D
Elementary Education M
Foundations and Philosophy of Education M
Health Education M
Higher Education M,D
Home Economics Education M,D
Hospitality Management M,D
International and Comparative Education M
Mathematics Education M
Physical Education M
Secondary Education M
Special Education M
Transportation Management M
Veterinary Medicine P
Veterinary Sciences M,D
Vocational and Technical Education M,D

ISIM UNIVERSITY

Business Administration and Management M
Health Services Management and Hospital Administration M
Management Information Systems M

ITHACA COLLEGE

Allied Health M
Communication Disorders M
Exercise and Sports Science M
Music Education M
Occupational Therapy M
Physical Therapy M

JACKSON STATE UNIVERSITY

Accounting M,D
Business Administration and Management M,D
Business Education M
Communication Disorders M
Counselor Education M,O
Early Childhood Education M,D,O
Education M,D,O
Educational Administration M,D,O
Educational Media/Instructional Technology M
Elementary Education M,D,O
English Education M
Health Education M
Management Information Systems M
Music Education M
Physical Education M
Science Education M
Secondary Education M,O
Social Work M,D
Special Education M,O
Vocational and Technical Education M

JACKSONVILLE STATE UNIVERSITY

- Business Administration and Management M
- Counselor Education M
- Early Childhood Education M
- Education M,O
- Educational Administration M,O
- Educational Media/Instructional Technology M
- Elementary Education M
- Health Education M
- Music Education M
- Physical Education M
- Secondary Education M
- Special Education M

JACKSONVILLE UNIVERSITY

- Art Education M
- Business Administration and Management M
- Computer Education M
- Early Childhood Education O
- Education M,O*
- Educational Administration M
- Educational Media/Instructional Technology M
- Education of the Gifted O
- Elementary Education M
- English Education M
- Foreign Languages Education M
- Mathematics Education M
- Music Education M
- Reading Education M
- Secondary Education O
- Special Education O

JAMES MADISON UNIVERSITY

- Accounting M
- Art Education M
- Business Administration and Management M
- Communication Disorders M
- Early Childhood Education M
- Education M
- Educational Administration M
- Educational Media/Instructional Technology M
- Health Education M
- Kinesiology and Movement Studies M
- Middle School Education M
- Music Education M
- Reading Education M
- Secondary Education M
- Special Education M
- Vocational and Technical Education M

JEWISH HOSPITAL COLLEGE OF NURSING AND ALLIED HEALTH

- Advanced Practice Nursing M
- Gerontological Nursing M
- Maternal/Child-Care Nursing M
- Medical/Surgical Nursing M
- Nursing M
- Nursing Education M

JEWISH THEOLOGICAL SEMINARY OF AMERICA

- Religious Education M,D

JEWISH UNIVERSITY OF AMERICA

- Religious Education M,D

JOHN BROWN UNIVERSITY

- Counselor Education M

JOHN CARROLL UNIVERSITY

- Business Administration and Management M
- Counselor Education M,O
- Education M
- Educational Administration M
- Educational Psychology M
- Elementary Education M
- Secondary Education M

JOHN F. KENNEDY UNIVERSITY

- Business Administration and Management M,O
- Education M
- Health Education M
- Human Resources Development M,O
- Law P
- Organizational Behavior O

JOHN JAY COLLEGE OF CRIMINAL JUSTICE, THE CITY UNIVERSITY OF NEW YORK

- Legal and Justice Studies D
- Organizational Behavior D

JOHN MARSHALL LAW SCHOOL

- International Business M
- Law P,M
- Legal and Justice Studies M
- Management Information Systems M
- Real Estate M
- Taxation M

JOHNS HOPKINS UNIVERSITY

- Advanced Practice Nursing M,O*
- Allopathic Medicine P
- Business Administration and Management M,O
- Clinical Laboratory Sciences M,D
- Counselor Education M,D,O
- Early Childhood Education M
- Education M,D,O*
- Educational Administration M,D,O
- Educational Media/Instructional Technology M,O
- Education of the Gifted M,O
- Elementary Education M
- Environmental and Occupational Health M,D*
- Epidemiology M,D
- Finance and Banking O
- Health Physics/Radiological Health M,D*
- Health Services Management and Hospital Administration M,D,O*
- Health Services Research M,D
- Human Resources Development M
- International Health M,D
- Management Information Systems M,O
- Marketing M
- Maternal and Child Health M,D
- Maternal/Child-Care Nursing M,O*
- Medical/Surgical Nursing M,O*
- Nursing M,D,O*
- Nursing Administration M*
- Oncology Nursing M*
- Public Health M,D*
- Public Health Nursing M*
- Reading Education M,O
- Real Estate M
- Secondary Education M
- Special Education M,D,O

JOHNSON & WALES UNIVERSITY (RI)

- Accounting M
- Business Administration and Management M
- Business Education M
- Education M
- Educational Administration D
- Educational Media/Instructional Technology M
- Hospitality Management M
- International Business M

JOHNSON BIBLE COLLEGE

- Educational Media/Instructional Technology M

JOHNSON STATE COLLEGE

- Counselor Education M
- Curriculum and Instruction M
- Early Childhood Education M
- Education M
- Educational Administration M
- Education of the Gifted M
- Reading Education M
- Special Education M

JUDGE ADVOCATE GENERAL'S SCHOOL, U.S. ARMY

- Law M

KANSAS STATE UNIVERSITY

- Accounting M
- Adult Education M,D
- Business Administration and Management M
- Counselor Education M,D
- Curriculum and Instruction D
- Education M,D
- Educational Administration M,D
- Educational Psychology M,D
- Elementary Education M
- Foundations and Philosophy of Education M,D
- Hospitality Management M,D
- Human Services M,D
- Kinesiology and Movement Studies M
- Secondary Education M
- Special Education M,D
- Veterinary Medicine P
- Veterinary Sciences M

KANSAS WESLEYAN UNIVERSITY

- Business Administration and Management M

KEAN UNIVERSITY

- Art Education M
- Communication Disorders M
- Counselor Education M,O
- Curriculum and Instruction M,O
- Early Childhood Education M
- Education M,O
- Educational Administration M,O
- Educational Psychology M
- English as a Second Language M,O
- Health Services Management and Hospital Administration M
- Management Information Systems M
- Mathematics Education M
- Multilingual and Multicultural Education M,O
- Nursing M
- Reading Education M,O
- Science Education M
- Social Work M
- Special Education M

KEENE STATE COLLEGE

- Counselor Education M
- Curriculum and Instruction M
- Education M
- Educational Administration M
- Special Education M

KELLER GRADUATE SCHOOL OF MANAGEMENT

- Accounting M
- Business Administration and Management M
- Finance and Banking M
- Human Resources Management M
- Management Information Systems M
- Project Management M

KENNESAW STATE UNIVERSITY

- Accounting M
- Advanced Practice Nursing M
- Business Administration and Management M
- Early Childhood Education M
- Education M
- Elementary Education M
- Entrepreneurship M
- Finance and Banking M
- Human Resources Development M
- Human Resources Management M
- Management Information Systems M
- Marketing M
- Middle School Education M
- Nursing M
- Special Education M

KENT STATE UNIVERSITY

- Accounting M,D
- Art Education M
- Business Administration and Management M*
- Communication Disorders M,D
- Counselor Education M,D,O
- Curriculum and Instruction M,D,O
- Early Childhood Education M
- Education M,D,O
- Educational Administration M,D,O
- Educational Measurement and Evaluation M,D
- Educational Media/Instructional Technology M,D
- Educational Psychology M
- Education of the Gifted M
- Education of the Multiply Handicapped M
- Elementary Education M
- Exercise and Sports Science M,D
- Finance and Banking D
- Foundations and Philosophy of Education M,D
- Health Education M
- Higher Education M,D,O
- Library Science M
- Management Information Systems D
- Marketing D
- Maternal/Child-Care Nursing M
- Medical/Surgical Nursing M
- Music Education M,D
- Nursing M
- Nursing Administration M
- Nursing Education M
- Physical Education M,D
- Psychiatric Nursing M
- Reading Education M
- Secondary Education M
- Special Education M,D,O
- Vocational and Technical Education M

KETTERING UNIVERSITY

- Industrial and Manufacturing Management M

KING'S COLLEGE

- Accounting M
- Business Administration and Management M
- Finance and Banking M
- Health Services Management and Hospital Administration M
- Reading Education M
- Taxation M

KIRKSVILLE COLLEGE OF OSTEOPATHIC MEDICINE

- Allied Health M
- Exercise and Sports Science M
- Occupational Therapy M
- Osteopathic Medicine P,M*
- Physical Therapy M
- Physician Assistant Studies M

KNOWLEDGE SYSTEMS INSTITUTE

- Computer Education M
- Management Information Systems M

KUTZTOWN UNIVERSITY OF PENNSYLVANIA

- Art Education M
- Business Administration and Management M
- Counselor Education M
- Curriculum and Instruction M
- Education M
- Educational Administration M
- Elementary Education M
- English Education M
- Library Science M
- Mathematics Education M
- Reading Education M
- Science Education M
- Secondary Education M
- Social Sciences Education M

KYUNG SAN UNIVERSITY USA

- Oriental Medicine and Acupuncture M

LAGRANGE COLLEGE

- Business Administration and Management M
- Early Childhood Education M
- Education M
- Middle School Education M

LAKE ERIE COLLEGE

- Business Administration and Management M
- Education M
- Reading Education M

LAKE ERIE COLLEGE OF OSTEOPATHIC MEDICINE

- Osteopathic Medicine P

LAKE FOREST GRADUATE SCHOOL OF MANAGEMENT

- Business Administration and Management M

LAKEHEAD UNIVERSITY

- Curriculum and Instruction M
- Education M
- Educational Administration M
- Exercise and Sports Science M
- Physical Education M
- Social Work M

LAKELAND COLLEGE

- Business Administration and Management M
- Education M

LAKE SUPERIOR STATE UNIVERSITY

- Business Administration and Management M

LAMAR UNIVERSITY

- Business Administration and Management M
- Communication Disorders M
- Counselor Education M
- Education M,O
- Educational Administration M
- Elementary Education M,O
- Kinesiology and Movement Studies M
- Music Education M
- Secondary Education M,O
- Special Education M,D,O

LANDER UNIVERSITY

- Art Education M
- Education M
- Elementary Education M
- English Education M
- Science Education M

LANGSTON UNIVERSITY

- Education M

LA ROCHE COLLEGE

- Advanced Practice Nursing M

Gerontological Nursing M
Human Resources Management M
Medical/Surgical Nursing M
Nurse Anesthesia M
Nursing M
Nursing Administration M
Public Health Nursing M
Science Education M

LA SALLE UNIVERSITY
Advanced Practice Nursing M
Business Administration and Management M,O
Education M
Medical/Surgical Nursing M
Nursing M
Nursing Administration M
Nursing Education M
Public Health Nursing M

LA SIERRA UNIVERSITY
Business Administration and Management M
Counselor Education M,O
Curriculum and Instruction M,D,O
Education M,D,O
Educational Administration M,D,O
Educational Psychology M,O
Religious Education M
Special Education M

LAURENTIAN UNIVERSITY
Business Administration and Management M
Communication Disorders M
Social Work M

LAWRENCE TECHNOLOGICAL UNIVERSITY
Business Administration and Management M
Education M
Industrial and Manufacturing Management M
Management Information Systems M
Science Education M

THE LEADERSHIP INSTITUTE OF SEATTLE
Business Administration and Management M
Management Information Systems M

LEBANON VALLEY COLLEGE
Business Administration and Management M

LEE UNIVERSITY (TN)
Education M

LEHIGH UNIVERSITY
Business Administration and Management M,D
Counselor Education M,O
Curriculum and Instruction D
Education M,D,O
Educational Administration M,D,O
Educational Media/Instructional Technology M,D
Elementary Education M,D,O
Human Services M
Multilingual and Multicultural Education M
Secondary Education M,O
Special Education M,D,O

LEHMAN COLLEGE OF THE CITY UNIVERSITY OF NEW YORK
Accounting M
Business Education M
Communication Disorders M
Counselor Education M
Early Childhood Education M
Education M
Elementary Education M
English as a Second Language M
English Education M
Gerontological Nursing M
Health Education M
Health Promotion M
Maternal/Child-Care Nursing M
Mathematics Education M
Medical/Surgical Nursing M
Multilingual and Multicultural Education M
Nursing M
Reading Education M
Recreation and Park Management M
Science Education M
Social Sciences Education M
Special Education M

LE MOYNE COLLEGE
Business Administration and Management M
Education M

LEMOYNE–OWEN COLLEGE
Education M

LENOIR–RHYNE COLLEGE
Business Administration and Management M
Counselor Education M,O
Early Childhood Education M
Education M,O
Education of the Gifted M
Elementary Education M
Middle School Education M
Reading Education M

LESLEY COLLEGE
Art Education M,O
Business Administration and Management M*
Computer Education M,O
Curriculum and Instruction M,O
Early Childhood Education M
Education M,D,O*
Educational Administration M,O
Elementary Education M
Health Education M
Health Services Management and Hospital Administration M
Human Resources Development M
Human Resources Management M
Human Services M
International and Comparative Education M
Management Information Systems M
Middle School Education M
Multilingual and Multicultural Education M
Nonprofit Management M
Project Management M
Reading Education M,O
Special Education M,O

LETOURNEAU UNIVERSITY
Business Administration and Management M

LEWIS & CLARK COLLEGE
Communication Disorders M
Education M,O*
Educational Administration O
Elementary Education M
Law P,M
Music Education M
Secondary Education M
Special Education M

LEWIS UNIVERSITY
Business Administration and Management M
Education M,O
Educational Administration O
Nursing M,O
Nursing Administration M,O
Nursing Education M
Public Health Nursing M

LIBERTY UNIVERSITY
Education M
Educational Administration M
Elementary Education M
Reading Education M
Secondary Education M

LIFE CHIROPRACTIC COLLEGE WEST
Chiropractic P*

LIFE UNIVERSITY
Chiropractic P*
Exercise and Sports Science M

LINCOLN MEMORIAL UNIVERSITY
Business Administration and Management M
Education M,O

LINCOLN UNIVERSITY (CA)
Business Administration and Management M

LINCOLN UNIVERSITY (MO)
Business Administration and Management M
Counselor Education M
Education M
Educational Administration M
Elementary Education M
Secondary Education M

LINCOLN UNIVERSITY (PA)
Human Services M

LINDENWOOD UNIVERSITY
Business Administration and Management M
Education M
Health Services Management and Hospital Administration M
Human Resources Management M
Human Services M
Marketing M

LINDSEY WILSON COLLEGE
Educational Psychology M
Human Services M

LOCK HAVEN UNIVERSITY OF PENNSYLVANIA
Curriculum and Instruction M
Education M
Physician Assistant Studies M

LOGAN COLLEGE OF CHIROPRACTIC
Chiropractic P*

LOMA LINDA UNIVERSITY
Allied Health M,D
Allopathic Medicine P
Bioethics M
Communication Disorders M
Dentistry P
Environmental and Occupational Health M
Epidemiology M,D*
Gerontological Nursing M
Health Education M,D
Health Promotion M,D
Health Services Management and Hospital Administration M
International Health M
Maternal/Child-Care Nursing M
Nursing M,O
Nursing Administration M,O
Oral and Dental Sciences M,O
Physical Therapy M,D
Public Health M,D
Social Work M

LONG ISLAND UNIVERSITY, BROOKLYN CAMPUS
Accounting M
Advanced Practice Nursing M
Business Administration and Management M
Communication Disorders M
Community Health M
Counselor Education M,O
Education M,O
Educational Administration M,O
Educational Media/Instructional Technology M,O
Elementary Education M
English as a Second Language M
English Education M
Exercise and Sports Science M
Health Education M
Health Services Management and Hospital Administration M
Mathematics Education M
Multilingual and Multicultural Education M
Nursing M
Pharmaceutical Sciences M,D
Pharmacy P
Physical Education M
Physical Therapy M
Reading Education M
Special Education M
Taxation M

LONG ISLAND UNIVERSITY, C.W. POST CAMPUS
Accounting M,O
Advanced Practice Nursing M,O
Allied Health M,O
Art Education M
Business Administration and Management M,O*
Clinical Laboratory Sciences M
Communication Disorders M
Computer Education M,O
Counselor Education M
Education M,O
Educational Administration M,O
Elementary Education M
English as a Second Language M
English Education M
Finance and Banking M,O
Foreign Languages Education M
Health Services Management and Hospital Administration M,O
Human Resources Management M
Information Studies M,D,O
International Business M
Library Science M,D,O*
Management Information Systems M
Marketing M
Mathematics Education M
Middle School Education M
Multilingual and Multicultural Education M
Music Education M
Nursing M,O
Pharmaceutical Sciences M
Reading Education M
Science Education M
Secondary Education M
Social Sciences Education M
Special Education M
Taxation M

LONG ISLAND UNIVERSITY, SOUTHAMPTON COLLEGE
Education M
Elementary Education M
Reading Education M

LONGWOOD COLLEGE
Counselor Education M
Education M
Educational Administration M
Educational Media/Instructional Technology M
Elementary Education M
English Education M
Physical Education M
Reading Education M
Social Sciences Education M
Special Education M

LORAS COLLEGE
Counselor Education M
Curriculum and Instruction M
Educational Administration M
Physical Education M

LOS ANGELES COLLEGE OF CHIROPRACTIC
Chiropractic P*

LOUISIANA STATE UNIVERSITY AND AGRICULTURAL AND MECHANICAL COLLEGE
Accounting M,D
Agricultural Education M,D
Business Administration and Management M,D
Business Education M
Communication Disorders M,D
Counselor Education M,O
Curriculum and Instruction M,D,O
Education M,D,O
Educational Administration M,D,O
Educational Measurement and Evaluation D
Elementary Education M
Finance and Banking M,D
Home Economics Education M
Information Studies M,O
International and Comparative Education M,D
Kinesiology and Movement Studies M,D
Law P,M
Library Science M,O
Management Information Systems M,D
Marketing M,D
Music Education D
Secondary Education M
Social Work M,D
Veterinary Medicine P,M,D
Veterinary Sciences P,M,D
Vocational and Technical Education M,D

LOUISIANA STATE UNIVERSITY IN SHREVEPORT
Business Administration and Management M
Education M,O
Science Education M

LOUISIANA STATE UNIVERSITY MEDICAL CENTER
Advanced Practice Nursing M
Allied Health M
Allopathic Medicine P
Communication Disorders M
Dentistry P
Maternal/Child-Care Nursing M
Medical/Surgical Nursing M,D
Nursing M,D
Nursing Administration M,D
Physical Therapy M
Psychiatric Nursing M,D
Public Health M
Public Health Nursing M,D

LOUISIANA TECH UNIVERSITY
- Accounting M,D
- Business Administration and Management M,D
- Business Education M
- Communication Disorders M
- Counselor Education M,O
- Curriculum and Instruction M,D
- Education M,D,O
- Educational Administration D
- English Education M
- Finance and Banking M,D
- Foreign Languages Education M
- Health Education M
- Marketing M,D
- Mathematics Education M
- Physical Education M
- Quantitative Analysis M,D
- Reading Education O
- Science Education M
- Secondary Education M
- Social Sciences Education M
- Special Education M

LOUISVILLE PRESBYTERIAN THEOLOGICAL SEMINARY
- Religious Education M

LOYOLA COLLEGE
- Business Administration and Management M*
- Communication Disorders M,O
- Counselor Education M,O
- Curriculum and Instruction M,O
- Education M,O
- Educational Administration M,O
- Finance and Banking M
- Foundations and Philosophy of Education M,O
- International Business M
- Marketing M
- Quantitative Analysis M
- Reading Education M,O
- Special Education M,O

LOYOLA MARYMOUNT UNIVERSITY
- Business Administration and Management M*
- Counselor Education M
- Education M
- Educational Administration M
- Educational Psychology M
- Elementary Education M
- English as a Second Language M
- English Education M
- Foreign Languages Education M
- Law P
- Mathematics Education M
- Multilingual and Multicultural Education M
- Reading Education M
- Science Education M
- Secondary Education M
- Social Sciences Education M
- Special Education M

LOYOLA UNIVERSITY CHICAGO
- Accounting M
- Advanced Practice Nursing M
- Allopathic Medicine P
- Business Administration and Management M*
- Counselor Education M
- Curriculum and Instruction M,D
- Early Childhood Education M,D
- Education M,D
- Educational Administration M,D
- Educational Measurement and Evaluation M,D
- Educational Psychology M,D
- Foundations and Philosophy of Education M,D
- Higher Education D
- Human Resources Development M
- Human Resources Management M
- International and Comparative Education M,D
- Law P,M,D
- Management Information Systems M
- Maternal/Child-Care Nursing M
- Medical/Surgical Nursing M
- Nursing M,D
- Nursing Administration M
- Oncology Nursing M
- Organizational Behavior M
- Rehabilitation Nursing M
- Religious Education M
- Social Work M,D
- Special Education M

LOYOLA UNIVERSITY NEW ORLEANS
- Advanced Practice Nursing M
- Business Administration and Management M
- Counselor Education M
- Education M
- Elementary Education M
- Law P
- Nursing M
- Quality Management M
- Reading Education M
- Secondary Education M

LUTHER RICE BIBLE COLLEGE AND SEMINARY
- Religious Education P,M

LYNCHBURG COLLEGE
- Business Administration and Management M
- Counselor Education M
- Curriculum and Instruction M
- Early Childhood Education M
- Education M
- Educational Administration M
- English Education M
- Human Resources Management M
- Industrial and Manufacturing Management M
- Middle School Education M
- Physical Education M
- Reading Education M
- Secondary Education M
- Special Education M

LYNDON STATE COLLEGE
- Counselor Education M
- Curriculum and Instruction M
- Education M
- Reading Education M
- Science Education M
- Special Education M

LYNN UNIVERSITY
- Business Administration and Management M
- Education M,D
- Educational Administration D
- English as a Second Language M
- Health Services Management and Hospital Administration M,O
- Hospitality Management M
- International and Comparative Education D
- International Business M
- Special Education M
- Sports Administration M

MADONNA UNIVERSITY
- Business Administration and Management M
- Education M
- Educational Administration M
- Health Services Management and Hospital Administration M
- International Business M
- Medical/Surgical Nursing M
- Nursing M
- Nursing Administration M
- Quality Management M
- Reading Education M
- Special Education M

MAHARISHI UNIVERSITY OF MANAGEMENT
- Business Administration and Management M,D
- Education M
- Elementary Education M
- Foundations and Philosophy of Education M
- Secondary Education M

MAINE MARITIME ACADEMY
- Logistics M,O
- Transportation Management M,O

MALONE COLLEGE
- Business Administration and Management M
- Counselor Education M
- Curriculum and Instruction M
- Early Childhood Education M
- Education M
- Educational Administration M
- Educational Media/Instructional Technology M
- Exercise and Sports Science M
- Middle School Education M
- Physical Education M
- Reading Education M
- Special Education M

MANCHESTER COLLEGE
- Accounting M

MANHATTAN COLLEGE
- Accounting M
- Business Administration and Management M*
- Counselor Education M,O
- Education M,O*
- Educational Administration M,O
- Finance and Banking M
- International Business M
- Management Information Systems M
- Marketing M
- Special Education M,O

MANHATTANVILLE COLLEGE
- Art Education M
- Education M
- Educational Administration M
- Elementary Education M
- English as a Second Language M
- English Education M
- Foreign Languages Education M
- Human Resources Development M
- Management Strategy and Policy M
- Mathematics Education M
- Music Education M
- Organizational Behavior M
- Reading Education M
- Science Education M
- Secondary Education M
- Social Sciences Education M
- Special Education M

MANKATO STATE UNIVERSITY
- Advanced Practice Nursing M
- Allied Health M,O
- Art Education M
- Business Administration and Management M
- Business Education M
- Communication Disorders M
- Community Health M
- Counselor Education M
- Curriculum and Instruction M,O
- Early Childhood Education M
- Education M,O
- Educational Administration M,O
- Educational Media/Instructional Technology M,O
- Education of the Gifted M
- Education of the Multiply Handicapped M
- Elementary Education M,O
- English Education M
- Health Education M
- Higher Education M
- Human Services M
- Mathematics Education M
- Multilingual and Multicultural Education M
- Nursing M
- Nursing Administration M
- Nursing Education M
- Physical Education M,O
- Reading Education M
- Secondary Education M,O
- Social Sciences Education M
- Special Education M
- Vocational and Technical Education M

MANSFIELD UNIVERSITY OF PENNSYLVANIA
- Art Education M
- Education M
- Elementary Education M
- Music Education M
- Secondary Education M
- Special Education M

MARIAN COLLEGE OF FOND DU LAC
- Business Administration and Management M
- Education M
- Educational Administration M
- Organizational Behavior M
- Quality Management M

MARIETTA COLLEGE
- Education M

MARIST COLLEGE
- Business Administration and Management M,O*
- Educational Psychology M

MARLBORO COLLEGE
- Computer Education M*

MARQUETTE UNIVERSITY
- Advanced Practice Nursing M
- Advertising and Public Relations M
- Business Administration and Management M
- Communication Disorders M
- Dentistry P
- Education M,D,O
- Gerontological Nursing O
- Human Resources Development M
- Human Resources Management M
- Law P
- Maternal/Child-Care Nursing M,O
- Mathematics Education M
- Medical/Surgical Nursing M,O
- Nurse Midwifery M,O
- Nursing M,O
- Oral and Dental Sciences M
- Physical Therapy M
- Physician Assistant Studies M

MARSHALL UNIVERSITY
- Adult Education M
- Allopathic Medicine P
- Business Administration and Management M
- Communication Disorders M
- Counselor Education M,O
- Early Childhood Education M
- Education M,D,O
- Educational Administration M,D,O
- Educational Media/Instructional Technology M
- Elementary Education M
- Exercise and Sports Science M
- Health Education M
- Health Services Management and Hospital Administration M
- Human Resources Management M
- Nursing M
- Physical Education M
- Reading Education M,O
- Secondary Education M
- Social Sciences Education M
- Special Education M
- Vocational and Technical Education M

MARY BALDWIN COLLEGE
- Education M
- Elementary Education M

MARYCREST INTERNATIONAL UNIVERSITY
- Early Childhood Education M
- Education M
- Reading Education M

MARYGROVE COLLEGE
- Early Childhood Education M
- Education M
- Educational Administration M
- Foreign Languages Education M
- Human Resources Management M
- Reading Education M
- Special Education M

MARYLAND INSTITUTE, COLLEGE OF ART
- Art Education M

MARYLHURST UNIVERSITY
- Business Administration and Management M

MARYMOUNT UNIVERSITY
- Advanced Practice Nursing M
- Allied Health M
- Business Administration and Management M*
- Counselor Education M
- Education M
- Elementary Education M
- English as a Second Language M
- Health Promotion M
- Health Services Management and Hospital Administration M
- Human Resources Management M
- Legal and Justice Studies M
- Management Information Systems M
- Medical/Surgical Nursing M
- Nursing M
- Nursing Administration M
- Nursing Education M
- Organizational Behavior M
- Physical Therapy M
- Secondary Education M
- Special Education M

MARYVILLE UNIVERSITY OF SAINT LOUIS
- Art Education M
- Business Administration and Management M
- Early Childhood Education M
- Education M
- Education of the Gifted M
- Elementary Education M
- Middle School Education M
- Multilingual and Multicultural Education M
- Science Education M
- Secondary Education M

MARYWOOD UNIVERSITY

Art Education M
Business Administration and Management M
Communication Disorders M
Counselor Education M
Early Childhood Education M
Education M
Educational Administration M
Educational Media/Instructional Technology M
Elementary Education M
Finance and Banking M
Health Services Management and Hospital Administration M
Management Information Systems M
Music Education M
Reading Education M
Social Work M*
Special Education M

MASSACHUSETTS COLLEGE OF ART

Art Education M

MASSACHUSETTS COLLEGE OF LIBERAL ARTS

Curriculum and Instruction M
Education M
Educational Administration M
Reading Education M
Special Education M

MASSACHUSETTS COLLEGE OF PHARMACY AND ALLIED HEALTH SCIENCES

Pharmaceutical Sciences M,D*

MASSACHUSETTS INSTITUTE OF TECHNOLOGY

Business Administration and Management M,D
Communication Disorders D*
Health Physics/Radiological Health M,D*
Industrial and Manufacturing Management M
Logistics M
Medical Physics D
Real Estate M
Transportation Management M,D

MAYO MEDICAL SCHOOL

Allopathic Medicine P

MAYO SCHOOL OF HEALTH-RELATED SCIENCES

Nurse Anesthesia M
Physical Therapy M

MCGILL UNIVERSITY

Allopathic Medicine P
Art Education M
Bioethics M
Business Administration and Management M,D*
Communication Disorders M,D
Community Health M
Curriculum and Instruction M
Dentistry P
Education M,D,O
Educational Administration M
Educational Psychology M,D
English as a Second Language M
Environmental and Occupational Health M,D
Epidemiology M,D,O
Foreign Languages Education M
Foundations and Philosophy of Education M,D
Health Physics/Radiological Health M,D
Health Services Management and Hospital Administration M
Industrial and Manufacturing Management M
Information Studies M,D,O
Law M,D,O
Library Science M,D,O
Medical Physics M,D
Music Education M,D
Nursing M,D
Oral and Dental Sciences M,D
Physical Education M
Reading Education M
Rehabilitation Sciences M,D
Social Work M,D
Transportation Management M

THE MCGREGOR SCHOOL OF ANTIOCH UNIVERSITY

Business Administration and Management M

MCMASTER UNIVERSITY

Allopathic Medicine P
Business Administration and Management M,D
Education M
Health Physics/Radiological Health M
Health Services Research M,D
Human Resources Management M,D
Kinesiology and Movement Studies M,D
Management Information Systems D
Nursing M,D
Social Work M

MCNEESE STATE UNIVERSITY

Business Administration and Management M
Business Education M
Counselor Education M
Early Childhood Education M
Education M,O
Educational Administration M,O
Educational Media/Instructional Technology M
Elementary Education M
English Education M
Health Education M
Mathematics Education M
Music Education M
Nursing M
Physical Education M
Reading Education M
Science Education M
Secondary Education M
Social Sciences Education M
Special Education M

MEADVILLE/LOMBARD THEOLOGICAL SCHOOL

Religious Education M

MEDAILLE COLLEGE

Business Administration and Management M*
Education M*

MEDICAL COLLEGE OF GEORGIA

Advanced Practice Nursing M
Allied Health M
Allopathic Medicine P
Dental Hygiene M
Dentistry P
Maternal/Child-Care Nursing M
Medical/Surgical Nursing M
Medical Technology M
Nurse Anesthesia M
Nursing M,D
Occupational Therapy M
Oral and Dental Sciences M,D
Physical Therapy M
Psychiatric Nursing M
Public Health Nursing M

MEDICAL COLLEGE OF OHIO

Advanced Practice Nursing M
Allied Health M
Allopathic Medicine P
Environmental and Occupational Health M,O*
Health Physics/Radiological Health M
Nursing M,O
Occupational Therapy M
Oral and Dental Sciences M
Physician Assistant Studies M
Public Health M

MEDICAL COLLEGE OF WISCONSIN

Allopathic Medicine P
Bioethics M
Environmental and Occupational Health M
Epidemiology M
Public Health M

MEDICAL UNIVERSITY OF SOUTH CAROLINA

Advanced Practice Nursing M
Allied Health M,D,O
Allopathic Medicine P
Clinical Laboratory Sciences M
Communication Disorders M
Dentistry P
Epidemiology M,D
Gerontological Nursing M
Health Education M
Health Services Management and Hospital Administration M,D,O
Maternal/Child-Care Nursing M
Medical/Surgical Nursing M
Medical Technology M
Nurse Anesthesia M
Nurse Midwifery M
Nursing M,D
Nursing Administration M
Occupational Therapy M
Oral and Dental Sciences M
Pharmaceutical Sciences D
Pharmacy P
Physical Therapy M
Psychiatric Nursing M
Rehabilitation Sciences M

MEHARRY MEDICAL COLLEGE

Allopathic Medicine P
Community Health M
Dentistry P
Environmental and Occupational Health M
Health Services Management and Hospital Administration M

MEIJI COLLEGE OF ORIENTAL MEDICINE

Oriental Medicine and Acupuncture M*

MEMORIAL UNIVERSITY OF NEWFOUNDLAND

Adult Education M
Allopathic Medicine P
Business Administration and Management M
Community Health M,D,O
Education M
Educational Administration M
Educational Psychology M
Epidemiology M,D,O
Nursing M
Pharmaceutical Sciences M
Physical Education M
Social Work M,D

MENNONITE COLLEGE OF NURSING

Nursing M

MERCER UNIVERSITY (MACON)

Allopathic Medicine P,M
Business Administration and Management M
Early Childhood Education M,O
Education M,O
English Education M
Law P
Mathematics Education M
Middle School Education M,O
Reading Education M
Science Education M
Social Sciences Education M

MERCER UNIVERSITY, CECIL B. DAY CAMPUS

Business Administration and Management M
Early Childhood Education M,O
Education M,O
Health Services Management and Hospital Administration M
Middle School Education M,O
Pharmaceutical Sciences D
Pharmacy P

MERCY COLLEGE

Business Administration and Management M
Education M
Educational Media/Instructional Technology M
Finance and Banking M
Human Resources Management M
Nursing M
Occupational Therapy M
Organizational Behavior M
Oriental Medicine and Acupuncture M
Physical Therapy M

MERCYHURST COLLEGE

Multilingual and Multicultural Education M
Organizational Behavior M,O
Special Education M

MEREDITH COLLEGE

Business Administration and Management M
Education M

MERRIMACK COLLEGE

Education M

MESA STATE COLLEGE

Business Administration and Management M

METROPOLITAN STATE UNIVERSITY

Business Administration and Management M
Finance and Banking M
Human Resources Management M
International Business M
Management Information Systems M
Marketing M
Nursing M
Organizational Behavior M

MGH INSTITUTE OF HEALTH PROFESSIONS

Allied Health M,O
Communication Disorders M*
Health Services Research M*
Nursing M,O*
Physical Therapy M*

MIAMI UNIVERSITY

Accounting M
Art Education M
Business Administration and Management M*
Communication Disorders M
Curriculum and Instruction M
Education M,D,O
Educational Administration M,D
Educational Psychology M,O
Elementary Education M
English Education M
Exercise and Sports Science M
Finance and Banking M
Management Information Systems M
Marketing M
Music Education M
Reading Education M
Secondary Education M
Special Education M

MICHIGAN STATE UNIVERSITY

Accounting M,D
Adult Education M,D
Advertising and Public Relations M
Agricultural Education M,D
Allopathic Medicine P
Business Administration and Management M,D
Clinical Laboratory Sciences M
Communication Disorders M,D
Community College Education M
Counselor Education M,D
Curriculum and Instruction M,D,O
Education M,D,O*
Educational Administration M,D,O
Educational Measurement and Evaluation D
Educational Psychology M,D
English as a Second Language M
English Education M
Epidemiology M*
Exercise and Sports Science M,D
Facilities Management M
Finance and Banking M,D
Foreign Languages Education M
Home Economics Education M
Hospitality Management M
Human Resources Management M,D
Industrial and Manufacturing Management M,D
Logistics M
Management Strategy and Policy D
Marketing M,D
Mathematics Education M,D
Medical Technology M
Music Education M,D
Nursing M*
Organizational Behavior D
Osteopathic Medicine P
Physical Education M,D
Reading Education M
Recreation and Park Management M,D
Science Education M,D
Social Sciences Education M
Social Work M,D
Special Education M,D
Transportation Management D
Travel and Tourism M,D
Veterinary Medicine P
Veterinary Sciences M,D*

MICHIGAN TECHNOLOGICAL UNIVERSITY

Business Administration and Management M
Industrial and Manufacturing Management M

MICHIGAN THEOLOGICAL SEMINARY

Religious Education M

MIDAMERICA NAZARENE UNIVERSITY

Business Administration and Management M
Curriculum and Instruction M
Education M

MIDDLE TENNESSEE SCHOOL OF ANESTHESIA
- Nurse Anesthesia M

MIDDLE TENNESSEE STATE UNIVERSITY
- Accounting M
- Business Administration and Management M
- Business Education M
- Counselor Education M,O
- Curriculum and Instruction M,O
- Early Childhood Education M
- Education M,D,O
- Educational Administration M,O
- Elementary Education M,O
- Finance and Banking M,D
- Foreign Languages Education M
- Health Education M,D
- Management Information Systems M
- Mathematics Education M
- Middle School Education M
- Physical Education M,D
- Reading Education M
- Recreation and Park Management M,D
- Science Education M
- Secondary Education M,O
- Special Education M
- Transportation Management M
- Vocational and Technical Education M

MIDWESTERN BAPTIST THEOLOGICAL SEMINARY
- Religious Education M

MIDWESTERN STATE UNIVERSITY
- Advanced Practice Nursing M
- Business Administration and Management M
- Counselor Education M
- Education M
- Educational Administration M
- Elementary Education M
- Health Physics/Radiological Health M
- Nursing M
- Nursing Education M
- Physical Education M
- Reading Education M
- Secondary Education M
- Special Education M

MIDWESTERN UNIVERSITY
- Allied Health M
- Occupational Therapy M*
- Osteopathic Medicine P*
- Pharmacy P*
- Physical Therapy M*
- Physician Assistant Studies M*

MILLERSVILLE UNIVERSITY OF PENNSYLVANIA
- Art Education M
- Counselor Education M
- Education M,O
- Education of the Gifted M
- Elementary Education M
- English Education M
- Foreign Languages Education M
- Mathematics Education M
- Nursing M
- Reading Education M
- Special Education M
- Vocational and Technical Education M

MILLIGAN COLLEGE
- Education M
- Occupational Therapy M

MILLSAPS COLLEGE
- Accounting M
- Business Administration and Management M

MILLS COLLEGE
- Curriculum and Instruction M
- Early Childhood Education M
- Education M,D
- Educational Administration D
- Elementary Education M
- English Education M
- Mathematics Education M
- Science Education M
- Secondary Education M
- Social Sciences Education M

MINOT STATE UNIVERSITY
- Business Administration and Management M
- Communication Disorders M
- Educational Psychology O
- Education of the Multiply Handicapped M
- Elementary Education M
- English Education M
- Mathematics Education M
- Music Education M
- Science Education M
- Special Education M

MISSISSIPPI COLLEGE
- Accounting M
- Art Education M
- Business Administration and Management M
- Business Education M
- Computer Education M
- Counselor Education M,O
- Education M,O
- Educational Administration M
- Elementary Education M
- Health Services Management and Hospital Administration M
- Law P
- Mathematics Education M
- Music Education M
- Science Education M
- Secondary Education M

MISSISSIPPI STATE UNIVERSITY
- Accounting M
- Agricultural Education M,D,O
- Business Administration and Management M,D*
- Business Education M
- Counselor Education M,D
- Education M,D,O
- Educational Administration M,D,O
- Educational Measurement and Evaluation M
- Educational Media/Instructional Technology M
- Educational Psychology M,D
- Elementary Education M,D,O
- Exercise and Sports Science M
- Health Education M
- Health Promotion M
- Management Information Systems M
- Music Education M
- Physical Education M
- Secondary Education M,D,O
- Special Education M,D,O
- Sports Administration M
- Taxation M
- Veterinary Medicine P
- Veterinary Sciences M,D
- Vocational and Technical Education M

MISSISSIPPI UNIVERSITY FOR WOMEN
- Communication Disorders M
- Education M
- Education of the Gifted M
- Nursing M,O

MISSISSIPPI VALLEY STATE UNIVERSITY
- Education M
- Elementary Education M
- Environmental and Occupational Health M

MOLLOY COLLEGE
- Advanced Practice Nursing M,O
- Maternal/Child-Care Nursing M,O
- Medical/Surgical Nursing M,O
- Nursing M,O
- Nursing Administration O
- Nursing Education O
- Psychiatric Nursing M,O

MONMOUTH UNIVERSITY
- Advertising and Public Relations O
- Business Administration and Management M*
- Education M,O*
- Educational Administration M,O
- Elementary Education M
- Nursing M*
- Reading Education M,O
- Special Education M,O

MONTANA STATE UNIVERSITY–BILLINGS
- Counselor Education M
- Curriculum and Instruction M
- Early Childhood Education M
- Education M
- Educational Media/Instructional Technology M
- Education of the Multiply Handicapped M
- Health Services Management and Hospital Administration M
- Information Studies M
- Reading Education M
- Secondary Education M
- Special Education M

MONTANA STATE UNIVERSITY–BOZEMAN
- Accounting M
- Business Education M
- Education M,D,O
- Health Services Management and Hospital Administration M
- Nursing M*
- Project Management M

MONTANA STATE UNIVERSITY–NORTHERN
- Counselor Education M
- Education M
- Elementary Education M
- Science Education M
- Vocational and Technical Education M

MONTANA TECH OF THE UNIVERSITY OF MONTANA
- Industrial Hygiene M
- Project Management M

MONTCLAIR STATE UNIVERSITY
- Accounting M
- Business Administration and Management M
- Business Education M
- Communication Disorders M
- Counselor Education M
- Education M
- Educational Administration M
- Educational Psychology M
- Environmental and Occupational Health M
- Exercise and Sports Science M
- Finance and Banking M
- Health Education M
- Home Economics Education M
- International Business M
- Legal and Justice Studies M
- Marketing M
- Mathematics Education M
- Music Education M
- Physical Education M
- Quantitative Analysis M
- Reading Education M
- Science Education M
- Social Sciences Education M
- Special Education M
- Sports Administration M
- Vocational and Technical Education M

MONTEREY INSTITUTE OF INTERNATIONAL STUDIES
- Business Administration and Management M*
- English as a Second Language M
- Foreign Languages Education M
- International Business M*

MONTREAT COLLEGE
- Business Administration and Management M

MOORHEAD STATE UNIVERSITY
- Art Education M
- Business Administration and Management M
- Communication Disorders M
- Counselor Education M
- Curriculum and Instruction M
- Education M,O
- Educational Administration M,O
- Elementary Education M
- Human Services M
- Music Education M
- Reading Education M
- Special Education M

MORAVIAN COLLEGE
- Business Administration and Management M

MOREHEAD STATE UNIVERSITY
- Adult Education M,O
- Art Education M
- Business Administration and Management M
- Counselor Education M,O
- Curriculum and Instruction D,O
- Education M,D,O
- Educational Administration O
- Educational Measurement and Evaluation D
- Educational Psychology D
- Elementary Education M
- Health Education M,D
- Higher Education M,O
- Middle School Education M
- Music Education M
- Physical Education M,D
- Reading Education M
- Recreation and Park Management M,D
- Secondary Education M
- Special Education M,D
- Sports Administration M
- Vocational and Technical Education M,D

MOREHOUSE SCHOOL OF MEDICINE
- Allopathic Medicine P
- Public Health M

MORGAN STATE UNIVERSITY
- Business Administration and Management M
- Education M,D
- Educational Administration M,D
- Elementary Education M
- Middle School Education M
- Transportation Management M
- Urban Education D

MORNINGSIDE COLLEGE
- Computer Education M
- Education M
- Elementary Education M
- Reading Education M
- Special Education M

MOUNT MARTY COLLEGE
- Nurse Anesthesia M
- Nursing M

MOUNT MARY COLLEGE
- Education M
- Health Education M
- Occupational Therapy M

MOUNT SAINT MARY COLLEGE
- Advanced Practice Nursing M
- Business Administration and Management M
- Education M
- Elementary Education M
- Medical/Surgical Nursing M
- Nursing M
- Nursing Administration M
- Nursing Education M
- Secondary Education M
- Special Education M

MOUNT ST. MARY'S COLLEGE
- Education M
- Educational Administration M
- Elementary Education M
- Physical Therapy M
- Secondary Education M
- Special Education M

MOUNT SAINT MARY'S COLLEGE AND SEMINARY
- Business Administration and Management M
- Education M

MOUNT SAINT VINCENT UNIVERSITY
- Adult Education M
- Curriculum and Instruction M
- Education M
- Educational Psychology M
- Elementary Education M
- Foundations and Philosophy of Education M
- Reading Education M

MOUNT SINAI SCHOOL OF MEDICINE OF THE CITY UNIVERSITY OF NEW YORK
- Allopathic Medicine P

MOUNT VERNON COLLEGE
- Business Administration and Management M
- Early Childhood Education M
- English as a Second Language M

MOUNT VERNON NAZARENE COLLEGE
- Education M

MURRAY STATE UNIVERSITY
- Business Administration and Management M
- Communication Disorders M
- Counselor Education M,O
- Early Childhood Education M
- Education M,D,O
- Educational Administration O
- Elementary Education M,O
- English as a Second Language M
- Environmental and Occupational Health M
- Human Services M
- Middle School Education M,O
- Music Education M
- Nurse Anesthesia M
- Nursing M
- Physical Education M
- Reading Education M
- Secondary Education M,O
- Special Education M
- Vocational and Technical Education M

MUSKINGUM COLLEGE
Education M

THE NATIONAL COLLEGE OF CHIROPRACTIC
Chiropractic P*

NATIONAL COLLEGE OF NATUROPATHIC MEDICINE
Naturopathic Medicine D*
Oriental Medicine and Acupuncture M*

NATIONAL–LOUIS UNIVERSITY
Adult Education M,D,O
Business Administration and Management M
Curriculum and Instruction M,D,O
Early Childhood Education M,O
Education M,D,O
Educational Administration M,D,O
Educational Media/Instructional Technology M,O
Educational Psychology M,D,O
Elementary Education M
English Education M,O
Human Resources Development M
Human Resources Management M
Human Services M,O
Mathematics Education M,O
Reading Education M,D,O
Science Education M,O
Secondary Education M
Special Education M,O

NATIONAL TECHNOLOGICAL UNIVERSITY
Health Physics/Radiological Health M
International Business M

NATIONAL UNIVERSITY
Adult Education M
Business Administration and Management M
Counselor Education M
Curriculum and Instruction M
Education M
Educational Administration M
Educational Media/Instructional Technology M
Health Services Management and Hospital Administration M
Human Resources Management M
Human Services M
International Business M
Multilingual and Multicultural Education M
Special Education M

NAVAL POSTGRADUATE SCHOOL
Management Information Systems M,D

NAZARENE THEOLOGICAL SEMINARY
Religious Education M

NAZARETH COLLEGE OF ROCHESTER
Art Education M
Business Administration and Management M
Business Education M
Communication Disorders M
Computer Education M
Early Childhood Education M
Education M
Elementary Education M
English as a Second Language M
Gerontological Nursing M
Music Education M
Nursing M
Reading Education M
Secondary Education M
Special Education M

NEBRASKA METHODIST COLLEGE OF NURSING AND ALLIED HEALTH
Health Promotion M

NEUMANN COLLEGE
Education M
Nursing M
Physical Therapy M

NEW COLLEGE OF CALIFORNIA
Law P*

NEW ENGLAND COLLEGE
Business Administration and Management M,O
Health Services Management and Hospital Administration M,O
Human Resources Management O
Human Services M

NEW ENGLAND COLLEGE OF OPTOMETRY
Optometry P*

NEW ENGLAND SCHOOL OF ACUPUNCTURE
Oriental Medicine and Acupuncture M,O*

NEW ENGLAND SCHOOL OF LAW
Law P

NEW HAMPSHIRE COLLEGE
Accounting M,O
Business Administration and Management M,O*
Business Education M
Finance and Banking M,O
Health Services Management and Hospital Administration O
Human Resources Management O
International Business M,D,O
Management Information Systems M,O
Taxation O

NEW JERSEY CITY UNIVERSITY
Art Education M
Early Childhood Education M
Education M,O
Educational Administration M
Educational Psychology M,O
English as a Second Language M
Health Education M
Health Services Management and Hospital Administration M
Mathematics Education M
Multilingual and Multicultural Education M
Music Education M
Reading Education M
Special Education M
Urban Education M

NEW JERSEY INSTITUTE OF TECHNOLOGY
Industrial and Manufacturing Management M,D*
Transportation Management M,D

NEWMAN THEOLOGICAL COLLEGE
Religious Education M,O

NEWMAN UNIVERSITY
Adult Education M
Education M
Educational Administration M
Elementary Education M
English as a Second Language M
Middle School Education M
Nursing M
Organizational Behavior M
Social Work M

NEW MEXICO HIGHLANDS UNIVERSITY
Business Administration and Management M
Counselor Education M
Curriculum and Instruction M
Education M
Educational Administration M
Exercise and Sports Science M
Physical Education M
Social Work M
Special Education M

NEW MEXICO INSTITUTE OF MINING AND TECHNOLOGY
Science Education M

NEW MEXICO STATE UNIVERSITY
Accounting M
Agricultural Education M
Business Administration and Management M,D
Communication Disorders M
Counselor Education M,D,O
Curriculum and Instruction M,D,O
Education M,D,O
Educational Administration M,D,O
Nursing M
Public Health M
Reading Education O
Social Work M
Special Education M

NEW ORLEANS BAPTIST THEOLOGICAL SEMINARY
Religious Education P,M,D

NEW SCHOOL UNIVERSITY
Business Administration and Management M,D,O*
Education M*
Health Services Management and Hospital Administration M,O
Human Resources Development O
Human Resources Management M,O
Nonprofit Management M
Secondary Education M*

NEW YORK CHIROPRACTIC COLLEGE
Chiropractic P*

NEW YORK COLLEGE OF PODIATRIC MEDICINE
Podiatric Medicine P*

NEW YORK INSTITUTE OF TECHNOLOGY
Business Administration and Management M
Education M,O
Educational Media/Instructional Technology M,O
Elementary Education M
Human Resources Management M,O
Osteopathic Medicine P*

NEW YORK LAW SCHOOL
Law P

NEW YORK MEDICAL COLLEGE
Allopathic Medicine P
Emergency Medical Services M
Environmental and Occupational Health M*
Epidemiology M*
Health Promotion M
Health Services Management and Hospital Administration M*
International Health M
Maternal and Child Health M
Physical Therapy M*
Public Health M*

NEW YORK UNIVERSITY
Accounting M,D,O
Advanced Practice Nursing M,O
Allopathic Medicine P
Art Education M,D
Business Administration and Management M,D,O
Business Education M,D,O
Communication Disorders M,D
Counselor Education M,D,O
Dentistry P
Early Childhood Education M,D,O
Education M,D,O*
Educational Administration M,D,O
Educational Measurement and Evaluation M
Educational Media/Instructional Technology M,D,O
Elementary Education M,D,O
English as a Second Language M,D,O
English Education M,D,O
Environmental and Occupational Health M,D
Epidemiology D
Finance and Banking M,D,O
Foreign Languages Education M,O
Foundations and Philosophy of Education M,D
Gerontological Nursing M,O
Health Education M,D,O*
Health Physics/Radiological Health D
Health Services Management and Hospital Administration M,D,O
Higher Education M,D
Hospitality Management M,D*
Human Resources Management M,O
Industrial and Manufacturing Management M
International and Comparative Education M,D
International Business M,D,O
Kinesiology and Movement Studies M
Law P,M,D
Legal and Justice Studies D
Leisure Studies M,D,O
Management Information Systems M,D,O*
Marketing M,D,O*
Maternal/Child-Care Nursing M,O
Mathematics Education M,D
Medical/Surgical Nursing M,O
Multilingual and Multicultural Education M,D,O
Music Education M,D,O
Nonprofit Management M,O
Nurse Midwifery M,O
Nursing M,D,O*
Nursing Education M
Occupational Therapy M,D*
Oral and Dental Sciences M,O
Physical Therapy M,D
Psychiatric Nursing M,O
Public Health M,D,O*
Quantitative Analysis O
Reading Education M,D
Real Estate M*
Recreation and Park Management M,D,O
Science Education M
Social Sciences Education M,D
Social Work M,D
Special Education M,O
Taxation M,D,O
Travel and Tourism M*

NIAGARA UNIVERSITY
Advanced Practice Nursing M
Business Administration and Management M
Counselor Education M,O
Education M,O
Educational Administration M,O
Elementary Education M
Foundations and Philosophy of Education M
Nursing M
Science Education M
Secondary Education M

NICHOLLS STATE UNIVERSITY
Business Administration and Management M
Counselor Education M,O
Curriculum and Instruction M
Education M
Educational Administration M

NICHOLS COLLEGE
Accounting M
Business Administration and Management M
Finance and Banking M
International Business M
Marketing M

NORFOLK STATE UNIVERSITY
Early Childhood Education M
Education M
Educational Administration M
Education of the Gifted M
Education of the Multiply Handicapped M
Music Education M
Secondary Education M
Social Work M,D
Urban Education M

NORTH CAROLINA AGRICULTURAL AND TECHNICAL STATE UNIVERSITY
Adult Education M
Agricultural Education M
Art Education M
Counselor Education M
Early Childhood Education M
Education M
Educational Administration M
Educational Media/Instructional Technology M
Elementary Education M
English Education M
Health Education M
Human Resources Development M
Human Resources Management M
Mathematics Education M
Middle School Education M
Physical Education M
Reading Education M
Science Education M
Social Sciences Education M
Social Work M
Vocational and Technical Education M

NORTH CAROLINA CENTRAL UNIVERSITY
Business Administration and Management M
Communication Disorders M
Counselor Education M
Education M
Educational Administration M
Educational Media/Instructional Technology M
Elementary Education M
Information Studies M
Law P
Library Science M
Physical Education M
Recreation and Park Management M
Special Education M

NORTH CAROLINA STATE UNIVERSITY
Accounting M
Adult Education M,D
Agricultural Education M,O
Business Administration and Management M,D
Community College Education M,D
Counselor Education M,D,O
Curriculum and Instruction M,D
Education M,D,O
Epidemiology M,D
Management Information Systems M
Mathematics Education M,D
Middle School Education M
Quality Management M
Recreation and Park Management M
Science Education M,D
Special Education M
Sports Administration M
Travel and Tourism M
Veterinary Medicine P
Veterinary Sciences M,D
Vocational and Technical Education M,D,O

NORTH CENTRAL COLLEGE
Business Administration and Management M
Education M
Management Information Systems M

NORTH DAKOTA STATE UNIVERSITY
Agricultural Education M
Business Administration and Management M
Counselor Education M
Education M,O
Educational Administration M,O
Home Economics Education M
Pharmaceutical Sciences M,D
Physical Education M
Sports Administration M
Veterinary Sciences M,D

NORTHEASTERN ILLINOIS UNIVERSITY
Accounting M
Business Administration and Management M
Counselor Education M
Education M
Educational Administration M
Education of the Gifted M
English Education M
Exercise and Sports Science M
Finance and Banking M
Human Resources Development M
Marketing M
Mathematics Education M
Multilingual and Multicultural Education M
Reading Education M
Rehabilitation Sciences M
Special Education M
Urban Education M

NORTHEASTERN OHIO UNIVERSITIES COLLEGE OF MEDICINE
Allopathic Medicine P

NORTHEASTERN STATE UNIVERSITY
Business Administration and Management M
Counselor Education M
Curriculum and Instruction M
Early Childhood Education M
Education M
Educational Administration M
Elementary Education M
Higher Education M
Industrial and Manufacturing Management M
Optometry P
Reading Education M
Secondary Education M
Special Education M

NORTHEASTERN UNIVERSITY
Accounting M,O*
Advanced Practice Nursing M,O*
Business Administration and Management M,O*
Communication Disorders M*
Counselor Education M
Curriculum and Instruction M
Education M*
Educational Measurement and Evaluation M
Educational Psychology M
Exercise and Sports Science M*
Finance and Banking M
Health Services Management and Hospital Administration M*
Law P
Legal and Justice Studies M,D
Maternal/Child-Care Nursing M,O*
Medical Technology M,D*
Nurse Anesthesia M*
Nursing M,O*
Nursing Administration M*
Pharmaceutical Sciences M,D*
Pharmacy P*
Physician Assistant Studies M*
Psychiatric Nursing M,O*
Public Health Nursing M,O*
Reading Education M
Science Education M,D
Special Education M*
Taxation M,O*

NORTHEAST LOUISIANA UNIVERSITY
Business Administration and Management M
Communication Disorders M
Counselor Education M,O
Curriculum and Instruction D
Education M,D,O
Educational Administration M,D,O
Elementary Education M,O
English Education M
Health Education M
Pharmaceutical Sciences M,D
Physical Education M
Reading Education M
Secondary Education M,O
Special Education M

NORTHERN ARIZONA UNIVERSITY
Allied Health M
Business Administration and Management M
Communication Disorders M
Counselor Education M,D
Curriculum and Instruction D
Early Childhood Education M
Education M,D
Educational Administration M,D
Educational Psychology D
Elementary Education M
English as a Second Language M,D
Health Education M
Health Promotion M
Management Information Systems M
Multilingual and Multicultural Education M
Nursing M
Physical Education M
Physical Therapy M
Public Health M
Reading Education M
Science Education M
Secondary Education M
Special Education M
Vocational and Technical Education M

NORTHERN ILLINOIS UNIVERSITY
Accounting M
Adult Education M,D*
Business Administration and Management M*
Communication Disorders M
Counselor Education M,D
Curriculum and Instruction M,D
Early Childhood Education M
Education M,D,O
Educational Administration M,D,O*
Educational Media/Instructional Technology M,D*
Educational Psychology M,D
Elementary Education M
Finance and Banking M
Foundations and Philosophy of Education M*
Industrial and Manufacturing Management M
Law P
Management Information Systems M
Nursing M
Physical Education M
Public Health M
Reading Education M,D
Special Education M,D
Taxation M

NORTHERN KENTUCKY UNIVERSITY
Business Administration and Management M
Education M
Elementary Education M
Law P
Nursing M
Secondary Education M

NORTHERN MICHIGAN UNIVERSITY
Allied Health M
Communication Disorders M
Education M
Educational Administration M
Elementary Education M
Exercise and Sports Science M
Mathematics Education M
Nursing M
Science Education M
Secondary Education M
Special Education M

NORTHERN STATE UNIVERSITY
Counselor Education M
Education M
Educational Administration M
Elementary Education M
English Education M
Health Education M
Physical Education M
Reading Education M
Secondary Education M
Special Education M

NORTH GEORGIA COLLEGE & STATE UNIVERSITY
Advanced Practice Nursing M
Art Education M
Early Childhood Education M
Education M
English Education M
Foreign Languages Education M
Mathematics Education M
Middle School Education M
Nursing M
Physical Education M
Physical Therapy M
Science Education M
Secondary Education M
Social Sciences Education M
Special Education M

NORTH PARK THEOLOGICAL SEMINARY
Religious Education M

NORTH PARK UNIVERSITY
Business Administration and Management M
Education M
Nursing M

NORTHWESTERN COLLEGE OF CHIROPRACTIC
Chiropractic P*

NORTHWESTERN OKLAHOMA STATE UNIVERSITY
Counselor Education M
Education M
Educational Measurement and Evaluation M
Educational Media/Instructional Technology M
Elementary Education M
Reading Education M
Secondary Education M

NORTHWESTERN STATE UNIVERSITY OF LOUISIANA
Business Education M
Counselor Education M,O
Early Childhood Education M
Education M,O
Educational Administration M,O
Elementary Education M,O
English Education M
Health Promotion M
Home Economics Education M
Mathematics Education M
Nursing M
Reading Education M,O
Science Education M
Secondary Education M,O
Social Sciences Education M
Special Education M,O
Sports Administration M*

NORTHWESTERN UNIVERSITY
Accounting D
Advertising and Public Relations M*
Allopathic Medicine P
Business Administration and Management M
Communication Disorders M,D*
Education M,D*
Educational Administration M
Educational Media/Instructional Technology M,D*
Elementary Education M
Environmental and Occupational Health M,D
Finance and Banking D
Health Physics/Radiological Health M,D
Health Services Management and Hospital Administration M
Higher Education M
Industrial and Manufacturing Management M
Law P,M,D
Logistics M
Management Information Systems M*
Management Strategy and Policy D
Marketing M,D*
Music Education M,D
Nonprofit Management M
Organizational Behavior D
Physical Therapy M
Project Management M
Public Health M
Real Estate M
Secondary Education M
Special Education M,D*
Transportation Management M

NORTHWEST INSTITUTE OF ACUPUNCTURE AND ORIENTAL MEDICINE
Oriental Medicine and Acupuncture M,O*

NORTHWEST MISSOURI STATE UNIVERSITY
Accounting M
Agricultural Education M
Art Education M
Business Administration and Management M
Business Education M
Computer Education M
Counselor Education M
Early Childhood Education M
Education M,O
Educational Administration M,O
Elementary Education M
English Education M
Health Education M
Mathematics Education M
Middle School Education M
Music Education M
Physical Education M
Reading Education M
Science Education M
Secondary Education M
Social Sciences Education M
Special Education M
Vocational and Technical Education M

NORTHWEST NAZARENE COLLEGE
Business Administration and Management M
Counselor Education M
Curriculum and Instruction M
Education M
Educational Administration M

NORTHWOOD UNIVERSITY (MI)
Business Administration and Management M

NOTRE DAME COLLEGE
Counselor Education M
Curriculum and Instruction M
Education M
Educational Administration M
Elementary Education M
English as a Second Language M
Reading Education M
Secondary Education M
Special Education M

NOTRE DAME COLLEGE OF OHIO
Education M

NOVA SCOTIA COLLEGE OF ART AND DESIGN
Art Education M

NOVA SOUTHEASTERN UNIVERSITY
Accounting M
Adult Education D
Allied Health M,D
Business Administration and Management M,D*
Communication Disorders M,D
Computer Education M,D,O
Dentistry P
Early Childhood Education M,D,O
Education M,D,O
Educational Administration M,D,O
Educational Media/Instructional Technology M,D,O*
Elementary Education M,O
English as a Second Language M,O
English Education M,O
Health Education D
Health Services Management and Hospital Administration M
Higher Education D
Human Resources Management M
International Business M,D
Law P
Management Information Systems M,D*
Mathematics Education M,O
Middle School Education D
Occupational Therapy M,D
Optometry P
Osteopathic Medicine P
Pharmacy P

Physical Therapy M
Reading Education M,O
Science Education M,O
Social Sciences Education M,O
Special Education M,O
Vocational and Technical Education D

NYACK COLLEGE
Religious Education P

OAKLAND CITY UNIVERSITY
Business Administration and Management M

OAKLAND UNIVERSITY
Accounting M
Allied Health M
Business Administration and Management M
Counselor Education M,O
Curriculum and Instruction M,O
Early Childhood Education M,O
Education M,D,O
Educational Administration M,O
Educational Media/Instructional Technology O
Exercise and Sports Science M
Human Resources Development M
Medical Physics D
Medical/Surgical Nursing M
Nurse Anesthesia M
Nursing M
Nursing Administration M
Physical Therapy M
Reading Education M,D,O
Special Education M,O

OCCIDENTAL COLLEGE
Education M*
Elementary Education M
English Education M
Foreign Languages Education M
Mathematics Education M
Music Education M
Science Education M
Secondary Education M
Social Sciences Education M

OGLALA LAKOTA COLLEGE
Business Administration and Management M

OGLETHORPE UNIVERSITY
Business Administration and Management M
Early Childhood Education M
Education M
Middle School Education M

OHIO COLLEGE OF PODIATRIC MEDICINE
Podiatric Medicine P

OHIO NORTHERN UNIVERSITY
Law P*

THE OHIO STATE UNIVERSITY
Accounting M,D
Agricultural Education M,D
Allied Health M
Allopathic Medicine P
Art Education M,D
Business Administration and Management M,D*
Communication Disorders M,D
Curriculum and Instruction M,D
Dentistry P
Education M,D,O*
Educational Administration M,D,O
Foundations and Philosophy of Education M,D
Health Education M,D
Health Services Management and Hospital Administration M,D*
Home Economics Education M,D
Hospitality Management M,D
Human Resources Management M,D
Law P
Management Information Systems M,D
Nursing M,D
Optometry P
Oral and Dental Sciences M,D
Pharmaceutical Sciences M,D*
Pharmacy P*
Physical Education M,D
Public Health M,D*
Recreation and Park Management M,D
Social Work M,D
Veterinary Medicine P
Veterinary Sciences M,D
Vocational and Technical Education D

OHIO UNIVERSITY
Accounting M
Art Education M
Business Administration and Management M*
Communication Disorders M,D
Computer Education M
Counselor Education M,D
Early Childhood Education M
Education M,D,O
Educational Administration M,D,O
Educational Measurement and Evaluation M,D
Educational Media/Instructional Technology M
Education of the Gifted M
Elementary Education M
Exercise and Sports Science M
Health Services Management and Hospital Administration M
Higher Education M,D
Mathematics Education M,D
Middle School Education M
Osteopathic Medicine P
Physical Education M
Physical Therapy M
Reading Education M,D
Secondary Education M
Social Sciences Education M,D
Special Education M
Sports Administration M

OKLAHOMA CITY UNIVERSITY
Accounting M
Advertising and Public Relations M
Business Administration and Management M
Early Childhood Education M
Education M
Education of the Gifted M
Elementary Education M
English as a Second Language M
Finance and Banking M
Health Services Management and Hospital Administration M
International Business M
Law P
Management Information Systems M
Marketing M
Religious Education M
Secondary Education M

OKLAHOMA STATE UNIVERSITY
Accounting M,D
Agricultural Education M,D
Business Administration and Management M,D*
Communication Disorders M
Computer Education D
Counselor Education M,D
Curriculum and Instruction M,D,O
Education M,D,O
Educational Administration M,D,O
Educational Psychology M,D
Finance and Banking M,D
Health Education M,D
Higher Education M,D,O
Hospitality Management M,D
Leisure Studies M,D
Marketing M,D
Physical Education M,D
Veterinary Medicine P
Veterinary Sciences M,D
Vocational and Technical Education M,D,O

OKLAHOMA STATE UNIVERSITY COLLEGE OF OSTEOPATHIC MEDICINE
Osteopathic Medicine P

OLD DOMINION UNIVERSITY
Accounting M
Allied Health M,D,O
Business Administration and Management M,D*
Business Education M
Communication Disorders M
Community Health M
Counselor Education M,O
Dental Hygiene M
Early Childhood Education M
Education M,D,O
Educational Administration M,O
Educational Media/Instructional Technology M
Elementary Education M
Environmental and Occupational Health M
Health Services Management and Hospital Administration D,O
Medical Technology M
Nursing M,O
Physical Education M
Physical Therapy M
Public Health M,O
Reading Education M
Recreation and Park Management M
Secondary Education M
Special Education M
Sports Administration M
Taxation M
Urban Education D
Vocational and Technical Education M

OLIVET NAZARENE UNIVERSITY
Business Administration and Management M
Curriculum and Instruction M
Education M
Elementary Education M
Secondary Education M

ORAL ROBERTS UNIVERSITY
Accounting M
Business Administration and Management M
Curriculum and Instruction M
Early Childhood Education M
Education M
Educational Administration M
English as a Second Language M
Finance and Banking M
International Business M
Marketing M
Religious Education M

OREGON COLLEGE OF ORIENTAL MEDICINE
Oriental Medicine and Acupuncture M*

OREGON GRADUATE INSTITUTE OF SCIENCE AND TECHNOLOGY
Business Administration and Management M,O*

OREGON HEALTH SCIENCES UNIVERSITY
Advanced Practice Nursing M,O
Allopathic Medicine P
Dentistry P
Epidemiology M
Gerontological Nursing M,D,O
Maternal/Child-Care Nursing M,O
Medical/Surgical Nursing M,O
Nurse Midwifery M,O
Nursing M,D,O
Oral and Dental Sciences M,O
Psychiatric Nursing M,O
Public Health Nursing M,O

OREGON STATE UNIVERSITY
Adult Education M
Agricultural Education M
Business Administration and Management M,O
Counselor Education M,D
Education M,D
Educational Administration M
Elementary Education M
English Education M
Environmental and Occupational Health M
Exercise and Sports Science M,D
Health Education M
Health Physics/Radiological Health M
Health Services Management and Hospital Administration M
Home Economics Education M
Kinesiology and Movement Studies M
Mathematics Education M,D
Music Education M
Pharmaceutical Sciences P,M,D
Physical Education M
Public Health M
Science Education M,D
Veterinary Medicine P
Veterinary Sciences M,D
Vocational and Technical Education M

OTTAWA UNIVERSITY
Education M
Human Resources Development M
Human Resources Management M

OTTERBEIN COLLEGE
Advanced Practice Nursing O
Business Administration and Management M
Education M
Medical/Surgical Nursing M,O
Nursing M,O
Nursing Administration M

OUR LADY OF HOLY CROSS COLLEGE
Counselor Education M
Curriculum and Instruction M
Education M
Educational Administration M
Reading Education M

OUR LADY OF THE LAKE UNIVERSITY OF SAN ANTONIO
Business Administration and Management M
Communication Disorders M
Counselor Education M
Curriculum and Instruction M
Education M,D
Educational Administration M
Educational Media/Instructional Technology M
Finance and Banking M
Health Services Management and Hospital Administration M
International Business M
Social Work M
Special Education M

PACE UNIVERSITY
Accounting M
Business Administration and Management M,D,O*
Curriculum and Instruction M
Education M,O*
Educational Administration M,O
Finance and Banking M
Health Services Management and Hospital Administration M
International Business M
Law P,M,D*
Management Information Systems M
Marketing M
Marketing Research M
Nonprofit Management M
Nursing M,O*
Taxation M

PACIFIC COLLEGE OF ORIENTAL MEDICINE
Oriental Medicine and Acupuncture M,O*

PACIFIC LUTHERAN UNIVERSITY
Advanced Practice Nursing M
Business Administration and Management M
Curriculum and Instruction M
Education M
Educational Administration M
Educational Media/Instructional Technology M
Elementary Education M
Gerontological Nursing M
Nursing M
Nursing Administration M
Reading Education M
Secondary Education M
Special Education M

PACIFIC STATES UNIVERSITY
Business Administration and Management D
Finance and Banking M
International Business M

PACIFIC UNION COLLEGE
Education M
Elementary Education M

PACIFIC UNIVERSITY
Early Childhood Education M
Education M
Elementary Education M
Middle School Education M
Occupational Therapy M
Optometry P
Physical Therapy M
Physician Assistant Studies M
Secondary Education M
Vision Sciences M

PALM BEACH ATLANTIC COLLEGE
Business Administration and Management M
Counselor Education M
Education M
Elementary Education M
Human Resources Development M

PALMER COLLEGE OF CHIROPRACTIC
Chiropractic P*

PALMER COLLEGE OF CHIROPRACTIC WEST
Chiropractic P*

PARK COLLEGE

Business Administration and Management M
Education M

PARKER COLLEGE OF CHIROPRACTIC

Chiropractic P*

PENNSYLVANIA COLLEGE OF OPTOMETRY

Optometry P
Rehabilitation Sciences M
Special Education M
Vision Sciences M*

PENNSYLVANIA STATE UNIVERSITY AT ERIE, THE BEHREND COLLEGE

Business Administration and Management M

PENNSYLVANIA STATE UNIVERSITY GREAT VALLEY SCHOOL OF GRADUATE PROFESSIONAL STUDIES

Business Administration and Management M,O
Curriculum and Instruction M
Education M*
Educational Media/Instructional Technology M
Health Services Management and Hospital Administration M*
Special Education M

PENNSYLVANIA STATE UNIVERSITY HARRISBURG CAMPUS OF THE CAPITAL COLLEGE

Adult Education D
Business Administration and Management M
Curriculum and Instruction M
Education M,D
Health Education M
Health Services Management and Hospital Administration M
Management Information Systems M

PENNSYLVANIA STATE UNIVERSITY MILTON S. HERSHEY MEDICAL CENTER

Allopathic Medicine P
Veterinary Sciences M

PENNSYLVANIA STATE UNIVERSITY UNIVERSITY PARK CAMPUS

Accounting M,D
Adult Education M,D
Agricultural Education M,D
Art Education M,D
Business Administration and Management M,D
Communication Disorders M,D*
Counselor Education M,D
Curriculum and Instruction M,D
Early Childhood Education M,D
Education M,D
Educational Administration M,D
Educational Media/Instructional Technology M,D
Educational Psychology M,D
Elementary Education M,D
English as a Second Language M
Finance and Banking M,D
Foundations and Philosophy of Education M,D
Health Services Management and Hospital Administration M,D*
Higher Education M,D
Hospitality Management M*
Human Resources Development M
Industrial and Manufacturing Management M,D
Insurance M,D
Kinesiology and Movement Studies M,D*
Leisure Studies M,D*
Logistics M,D
Management Information Systems M
Marketing M,D
Multilingual and Multicultural Education M,D
Music Education M,D
Nursing M*
Quality Management M
Reading Education M,D
Real Estate M,D
Science Education M,D
Social Sciences Education M,D
Special Education M,D
Veterinary Sciences M,D*
Vocational and Technical Education M,D

PEPPERDINE UNIVERSITY (CULVER CITY)

Business Administration and Management M
Education M,D*
Educational Administration M,D
Educational Media/Instructional Technology M,D
International Business M
Organizational Behavior M

PEPPERDINE UNIVERSITY (MALIBU)

Business Administration and Management M*
International Business M
Law P

PERU STATE COLLEGE

Education M

PFEIFFER UNIVERSITY

Business Administration and Management M
Organizational Behavior M
Religious Education M

PHILADELPHIA COLLEGE OF BIBLE

Education M
Organizational Behavior M

PHILADELPHIA COLLEGE OF OSTEOPATHIC MEDICINE

Osteopathic Medicine P
Physician Assistant Studies M

PHILADELPHIA COLLEGE OF TEXTILES AND SCIENCE

Accounting M
Business Administration and Management M
Computer Education M
Finance and Banking M
Health Services Management and Hospital Administration M
International Business M
Management Information Systems M
Marketing M
Nurse Midwifery M
Occupational Therapy M
Taxation M

PHILLIPS GRADUATE INSTITUTE

Organizational Behavior M

PHILLIPS UNIVERSITY

Business Administration and Management M
Education M
Elementary Education M
Secondary Education M

PIEDMONT COLLEGE

Early Childhood Education M
Education M
Secondary Education M

PIKEVILLE COLLEGE

Osteopathic Medicine P

PINE MANOR COLLEGE

Early Childhood Education M
Education M
Elementary Education M

PITTSBURG STATE UNIVERSITY

Accounting M
Business Administration and Management M
Community College Education O
Counselor Education M
Education M,O
Educational Administration M,O
Elementary Education M,O
Human Resources Development M
Music Education M
Nursing M
Physical Education M
Reading Education O
Secondary Education M,O
Special Education M
Vocational and Technical Education M,O

PLATTSBURGH STATE UNIVERSITY OF NEW YORK

Communication Disorders M
Counselor Education M,O
Education M,O
Educational Administration M,O
Elementary Education M
English Education M
Foreign Languages Education M
Mathematics Education M
Reading Education M
Science Education M
Secondary Education M
Social Sciences Education M
Special Education M

PLYMOUTH STATE COLLEGE OF THE UNIVERSITY SYSTEM OF NEW HAMPSHIRE

Art Education M
Business Administration and Management M*
Computer Education M
Counselor Education M
Education M*
Educational Administration M
Elementary Education M
Health Education M
Mathematics Education M
Reading Education M
Science Education M
Secondary Education M
Social Sciences Education M

POINT LOMA NAZARENE UNIVERSITY

Education M,D,O

POINT PARK COLLEGE

International Business M*

POLYTECHNIC UNIVERSITY, BROOKLYN CAMPUS

Business Administration and Management M
Environmental and Occupational Health M
Finance and Banking M
Industrial and Manufacturing Management M
Organizational Behavior M
Transportation Management M

POLYTECHNIC UNIVERSITY, FARMINGDALE CAMPUS

Business Administration and Management M
Finance and Banking M
Industrial and Manufacturing Management M

POLYTECHNIC UNIVERSITY, WESTCHESTER GRADUATE CENTER

Business Administration and Management M
Finance and Banking M
Industrial and Manufacturing Management M
Organizational Behavior M
Transportation Management M

PONCE SCHOOL OF MEDICINE

Allopathic Medicine P

PONTIFICAL CATHOLIC UNIVERSITY OF PUERTO RICO

Business Administration and Management M
Education M
Law P,M
Medical/Surgical Nursing M
Nursing M
Psychiatric Nursing M
Social Work M

PORTLAND STATE UNIVERSITY

Adult Education D
Business Administration and Management M,D*
Communication Disorders M
Counselor Education M
Curriculum and Instruction M,D
Early Childhood Education M
Education M,D
Educational Administration M,D
Educational Media/Instructional Technology M
Elementary Education M
English as a Second Language M
Health Education M
Health Promotion M
Health Services Management and Hospital Administration M
Higher Education D
International Business M*
Mathematics Education D
Music Education M
Public Health M
Reading Education M
Science Education M
Secondary Education M
Social Sciences Education M
Social Work M,D
Special Education M
Taxation M

PRAIRIE VIEW A&M UNIVERSITY

Business Administration and Management M
Counselor Education M
Curriculum and Instruction M
Education M
Educational Administration M
Educational Media/Instructional Technology M
Health Education M
Physical Education M
Special Education M

PRATT INSTITUTE

Art Education M
Facilities Management M
Information Studies M,O*
Library Science M,O*
Special Education M

PRESCOTT COLLEGE

Education M
English as a Second Language M
Multilingual and Multicultural Education M
Science Education M

PRINCETON UNIVERSITY

Community College Education D
Social Sciences Education D

PROVIDENCE COLLEGE

Business Administration and Management M*
Counselor Education M
Education M
Educational Administration M
Mathematics Education M
Religious Education M
Special Education M

PROVIDENCE COLLEGE AND THEOLOGICAL SEMINARY

English as a Second Language O
Religious Education M

PURDUE UNIVERSITY

Accounting M,D
Agricultural Education M,D,O
Art Education D
Business Administration and Management M,D*
Communication Disorders M,D*
Counselor Education M,D,O
Curriculum and Instruction M,D,O
Education M,D,O
Educational Administration M,D,O
Educational Media/Instructional Technology M,D,O
Educational Psychology M,D
Education of the Gifted M
Elementary Education M
English Education M,D,O
Environmental and Occupational Health M,D*
Epidemiology M,D
Exercise and Sports Science M,D
Finance and Banking M,D
Foreign Languages Education M,D,O
Foundations and Philosophy of Education M
Health Physics/Radiological Health M,D*
Health Promotion M,D
Home Economics Education M,D,O
Hospitality Management M*
Human Resources Management M,D
Industrial and Manufacturing Management M
Industrial Hygiene M,D*
Management Information Systems M,D
Management Strategy and Policy M,D
Marketing M,D
Mathematics Education M,D,O
Medical Physics M,D*
Organizational Behavior M,D
Pharmaceutical Sciences M,D*
Pharmacy P
Physical Education M
Quantitative Analysis M,D
Reading Education M,D,O
Science Education M,D,O
Social Sciences Education M,D,O
Special Education M
Travel and Tourism M
Veterinary Medicine P
Veterinary Sciences M,D
Vocational and Technical Education M,D,O

PURDUE UNIVERSITY CALUMET

Business Administration and Management M
Counselor Education M
Curriculum and Instruction M
Education M
Educational Administration M
Educational Media/Instructional Technology M
Elementary Education M
Nursing M
Secondary Education M

PURDUE UNIVERSITY NORTH CENTRAL
Education M
Elementary Education M

QUEENS COLLEGE
Business Administration and Management M
Education M
Elementary Education M
Nursing M
Nursing Administration M

QUEENS COLLEGE OF THE CITY UNIVERSITY OF NEW YORK
Art Education M
Communication Disorders M
Counselor Education M
Education M,O
Educational Administration O
Elementary Education M,O
English as a Second Language M
English Education M,O
Exercise and Sports Science M
Foreign Languages Education M,O
Home Economics Education M
Information Studies M,O
Library Science M,O
Mathematics Education M,O
Multilingual and Multicultural Education M
Music Education M,O
Physical Education M
Reading Education M
Science Education M,O
Secondary Education M,O
Social Sciences Education M,O
Special Education M

QUEEN'S UNIVERSITY AT KINGSTON
Allopathic Medicine P
Business Administration and Management M,D
Community Health M
Education M
Environmental and Occupational Health M
Epidemiology M
Exercise and Sports Science M,D
Health Services Management and Hospital Administration M
Law P,M
Nursing M
Rehabilitation Sciences M

QUINCY UNIVERSITY
Business Administration and Management M
Education M

QUINNIPIAC COLLEGE
Accounting M
Advanced Practice Nursing M*
Allied Health M
Business Administration and Management M*
Clinical Laboratory Sciences M*
Education M*
English Education M
Finance and Banking M
Foreign Languages Education M
Health Services Management and Hospital Administration M*
International Business M
Law P*
Management Information Systems M
Marketing M
Mathematics Education M
Middle School Education M*
Nursing M*
Physical Therapy M*
Physician Assistant Studies M*
Science Education M
Secondary Education M*
Social Sciences Education M

RADFORD UNIVERSITY
Art Education M
Business Administration and Management M
Communication Disorders M
Counselor Education M
Curriculum and Instruction M
Education M
Educational Administration M
Educational Media/Instructional Technology M
Leisure Studies M
Music Education M
Nursing M
Physical Education M
Reading Education M
Social Work M
Special Education M

REFORMED THEOLOGICAL SEMINARY (MS)
Religious Education P,M

REGENT UNIVERSITY
Business Administration and Management M
Counselor Education M,D
Education M,O
Law P
Organizational Behavior M,D

REGIS COLLEGE
Education M
Nursing M,O

REGIS UNIVERSITY
Allied Health M
Business Administration and Management M
Education M
Management Information Systems M
Nonprofit Management M,O
Nursing M
Physical Therapy M

RENSSELAER AT HARTFORD
Business Administration and Management M

RENSSELAER POLYTECHNIC INSTITUTE
Accounting M,D
Business Administration and Management M,D*
Entrepreneurship M
Finance and Banking M,D
Human Resources Development D
Human Resources Management M,D
Industrial and Manufacturing Management M,D
Management Information Systems M,D
Management Strategy and Policy D
Marketing M
Organizational Behavior M
Quantitative Analysis M

RESEARCH COLLEGE OF NURSING
Advanced Practice Nursing M
Nursing M

RHODE ISLAND COLLEGE
Art Education M
Counselor Education M,O
Curriculum and Instruction O
Early Childhood Education M
Education D
Educational Administration M,O
Educational Psychology M
Elementary Education M
English as a Second Language M
Foreign Languages Education M
Health Education M
Multilingual and Multicultural Education M
Music Education M
Reading Education M,O
Science Education M
Secondary Education M
Social Work M
Special Education M,O
Vocational and Technical Education M

RHODE ISLAND SCHOOL OF DESIGN
Art Education M

RHODES COLLEGE
Accounting M

RICE UNIVERSITY
Business Administration and Management M*
Education M

THE RICHARD STOCKTON COLLEGE OF NEW JERSEY
Business Administration and Management M
Educational Media/Instructional Technology M
Nursing M
Physical Therapy M

RICHMOND, THE AMERICAN INTERNATIONAL UNIVERSITY IN LONDON
Business Administration and Management M
Management Information Systems M

RIDER UNIVERSITY
Business Administration and Management M
Business Education M
Counselor Education M,O
Curriculum and Instruction M
Education M,O
Educational Administration M
Human Services M
Reading Education M

RIVIER COLLEGE
Business Administration and Management M
Computer Education M
Counselor Education M
Early Childhood Education M
Education M
Educational Administration M
Elementary Education M
Foreign Languages Education M
Human Resources Management M
Nursing M
Reading Education M
Secondary Education M
Special Education M

ROBERT MORRIS COLLEGE (PA)
Accounting M
Business Administration and Management M
Business Education M
Educational Administration M
Finance and Banking M
Health Services Management and Hospital Administration M
Management Information Systems M
Marketing M
Sports Administration M
Taxation M

ROBERTS WESLEYAN COLLEGE
Business Administration and Management M
Education M
Human Services M
Social Work M

ROCHESTER INSTITUTE OF TECHNOLOGY
Accounting M
Art Education M
Business Administration and Management M
Educational Media/Instructional Technology M
Finance and Banking M
Health Services Management and Hospital Administration M,O*
Hospitality Management M
Human Resources Development M
Industrial and Manufacturing Management M
International Business M
Secondary Education M
Special Education M,O
Travel and Tourism M

ROCKFORD COLLEGE
Art Education M
Business Administration and Management M
Education M
Elementary Education M
English Education M
Reading Education M
Secondary Education M
Social Sciences Education M
Special Education M

ROCKHURST COLLEGE
Business Administration and Management M
Occupational Therapy M
Physical Therapy M

ROGER WILLIAMS UNIVERSITY
Law P*

ROLLINS COLLEGE
Business Administration and Management M*
Counselor Education M
Education M
Elementary Education M
English Education M
Human Resources Development M
Human Resources Management M
Mathematics Education M
Music Education M
Secondary Education M

ROOSEVELT UNIVERSITY
Accounting M
Actuarial Science M
Business Administration and Management M
Counselor Education M
Early Childhood Education M
Education M,D
Educational Administration M,D
Elementary Education M
Hospitality Management M
International Business M
Management Information Systems M
Music Education M,O
Reading Education M
Secondary Education M

ROSEMONT COLLEGE
Business Administration and Management M
Computer Education O
Counselor Education M
Educational Media/Instructional Technology M,O
Human Services M
Middle School Education M

ROWAN UNIVERSITY
Advertising and Public Relations M
Art Education M
Business Administration and Management M
Computer Education O
Curriculum and Instruction M,O
Education M,D,O
Educational Administration M,D,O
Educational Media/Instructional Technology M,O
Elementary Education M,O
English as a Second Language O
Health Education M,O
Higher Education M
Mathematics Education M,O
Music Education M
Physical Education M,O
Reading Education M
Science Education M
Secondary Education M
Special Education M,O

RUSH UNIVERSITY
Advanced Practice Nursing M,D
Allopathic Medicine P
Bioethics M*
Communication Disorders M*
Gerontological Nursing M,D
Health Services Management and Hospital Administration M*
Maternal/Child-Care Nursing M,D
Medical Physics M,D
Medical/Surgical Nursing M,D
Nurse Anesthesia M,D
Nursing M,D*
Occupational Therapy M*
Psychiatric Nursing M,D
Public Health Nursing M,D
Rehabilitation Nursing M,D

RUTGERS, THE STATE UNIVERSITY OF NEW JERSEY, CAMDEN
Business Administration and Management M
Health Services Management and Hospital Administration M
Law P
Physical Therapy M

RUTGERS, THE STATE UNIVERSITY OF NEW JERSEY, NEWARK
Accounting M,D
Advanced Practice Nursing M
Business Administration and Management M,D
Finance and Banking M,D
Gerontological Nursing M
Health Services Management and Hospital Administration M
Human Resources Management M
International Business M,D
Law P
Management Information Systems M,D
Marketing M,D
Maternal/Child-Care Nursing M
Medical/Surgical Nursing M
Nursing M,D
Organizational Behavior M
Psychiatric Nursing M
Public Health Nursing M

RUTGERS, THE STATE UNIVERSITY OF NEW JERSEY, NEW BRUNSWICK
Adult Education M,D
Early Childhood Education M,D,O

Rutgers, The State University of New Jersey, New Brunswick (continued)

Education M,D,O
Educational Administration M,D,O
Educational Measurement and Evaluation M,D
Educational Psychology M,D
Elementary Education M,D,O
English as a Second Language M,D
English Education M
Foreign Languages Education M,D,O
Foundations and Philosophy of Education M,D,O
Human Resources Management M,D*
Information Studies M,D
Legal and Justice Studies D
Library Science M,D
Mathematics Education M,D,O
Pharmaceutical Sciences M,D
Pharmacy P
Public Health M,D*
Quality Management M
Reading Education M,D,O
Science Education M,D,O
Social Sciences Education M,D,O
Social Work M,D
Special Education M,D
Vocational and Technical Education M,D,O

SACRED HEART UNIVERSITY

Business Administration and Management M
Education M,O
Educational Administration O
Elementary Education M
Health Services Management and Hospital Administration M
Nursing M
Nursing Administration M
Physical Therapy M
Secondary Education M

SAGE GRADUATE SCHOOL

Advanced Practice Nursing M
Business Administration and Management M
Community Health M
Counselor Education M,O
Education M,O
Elementary Education M
Finance and Banking M
Health Education M
Health Services Management and Hospital Administration M
Human Resources Management M
Human Services M
Marketing M
Medical/Surgical Nursing M
Nursing M,O
Psychiatric Nursing M
Public Health Nursing M
Reading Education M
Secondary Education M,O
Special Education M

SAGINAW VALLEY STATE UNIVERSITY

Advanced Practice Nursing M
Business Administration and Management M
Early Childhood Education M
Education M,O
Educational Administration M,O
Elementary Education M
Middle School Education M
Nursing M
Nursing Administration M
Nursing Education M
Organizational Behavior M
Reading Education M
Science Education M
Secondary Education M
Special Education M

ST. AMBROSE UNIVERSITY

Accounting M
Business Administration and Management M
Health Services Management and Hospital Administration M
Physical Therapy M
Social Work M
Special Education M

ST. BONAVENTURE UNIVERSITY

Accounting M
Business Administration and Management M,O
Counselor Education M,O
Curriculum and Instruction M
Education M,O
Educational Administration M,O
Finance and Banking M
Marketing M
Reading Education M
Secondary Education M
Special Education M

ST. CLOUD STATE UNIVERSITY

Accounting M
Art Education M
Business Administration and Management M
Communication Disorders M
Counselor Education M
Education M,O
Educational Administration M,O
Educational Media/Instructional Technology M
Education of the Gifted M
Elementary Education M
English as a Second Language M
Exercise and Sports Science M
Finance and Banking M
Marketing M
Middle School Education M
Music Education M
Physical Education M
Reading Education M
Secondary Education M
Special Education M,O
Sports Administration M

ST. EDWARD'S UNIVERSITY

Accounting O
Business Administration and Management M,O*
Education M
Human Services M*

SAINT FRANCIS COLLEGE (PA)

Business Administration and Management M
Education M
Educational Administration M
Human Resources Management M*
Occupational Therapy M
Physical Therapy M
Physician Assistant Studies M

ST. FRANCIS XAVIER UNIVERSITY

Adult Education M
Education M,O

ST. JOHN FISHER COLLEGE

Advanced Practice Nursing O
Business Administration and Management M
Human Resources Development M
Mathematics Education M
Nursing M,O
Science Education M

ST. JOHN'S UNIVERSITY (NY)

Accounting M,O
Business Administration and Management M,O
Communication Disorders M
Counselor Education M
Education M,D,O
Educational Administration M,D,O
Elementary Education M
English as a Second Language M
Finance and Banking M,O
Health Services Management and Hospital Administration M
Higher Education M
Information Studies M,O
Law P
Library Science M,O
Management Information Systems M,O
Marketing M,O
Medical Technology M
Multilingual and Multicultural Education M
Pharmaceutical Sciences M,D
Pharmacy P
Quantitative Analysis M,O
Reading Education M,O
Secondary Education M
Special Education M,O
Taxation M,O

SAINT JOSEPH COLLEGE (CT)

Counselor Education M,O
Early Childhood Education M
Education M,O
Elementary Education M
Maternal/Child-Care Nursing M
Nursing M
Psychiatric Nursing M
Science Education M
Secondary Education M
Special Education M

SAINT JOSEPH'S COLLEGE (ME)

Health Services Management and Hospital Administration M
Nursing M

ST. JOSEPH'S COLLEGE, SUFFOLK CAMPUS

Early Childhood Education M
Education M

SAINT JOSEPH'S UNIVERSITY

Accounting M
Adult Education M
Business Administration and Management M
Education M,O
Environmental and Occupational Health M
Finance and Banking M
Health Education M
Health Services Management and Hospital Administration M
International Business M
Management Information Systems M
Marketing M
Mathematics Education M
Nurse Anesthesia M
Reading Education M
Science Education M
Secondary Education M
Special Education M

ST. LAWRENCE UNIVERSITY

Counselor Education M,O
Education M,O
Educational Administration M,O

SAINT LEO COLLEGE

Business Administration and Management M
Education M

ST. LOUIS COLLEGE OF PHARMACY

Health Services Management and Hospital Administration M
Pharmaceutical Sciences M
Pharmacy P

SAINT LOUIS UNIVERSITY

Accounting M,D
Advanced Practice Nursing M,O
Allied Health M
Allopathic Medicine P
Bioethics D
Business Administration and Management M,D
Communication Disorders M
Community Health M
Counselor Education M,D
Curriculum and Instruction M,D
Education M,D,O
Educational Administration M,D,O
Finance and Banking M,D
Foundations and Philosophy of Education M,D
Gerontological Nursing M,O
Health Services Management and Hospital Administration M
Health Services Research D
Higher Education M,D,O
International Business M,D*
Law P,M*
Management Information Systems M,D
Marketing M,D
Maternal/Child-Care Nursing M,O
Medical/Surgical Nursing M,O
Nursing D
Nursing Administration M,O
Oral and Dental Sciences M
Physical Therapy M
Psychiatric Nursing M,O
Public Health M,D
Public Health Nursing M,O
Quantitative Analysis M,D
Social Work M
Special Education M

SAINT MARTIN'S COLLEGE

Advanced Practice Nursing M
Business Administration and Management M
Computer Education M
Counselor Education M
Curriculum and Instruction M
Education M
Nursing M
Nursing Administration M
Reading Education M
Special Education M

SAINT MARY COLLEGE

Business Administration and Management M
Education M

SAINT MARY'S COLLEGE OF CALIFORNIA

Business Administration and Management M
Counselor Education M
Early Childhood Education M
Education M
Educational Administration M
Health Education M
Health Services Management and Hospital Administration M
International Business M
Physical Education M
Reading Education M
Special Education M

SAINT MARY'S UNIVERSITY

Business Administration and Management M

SAINT MARY'S UNIVERSITY OF MINNESOTA

Business Administration and Management M
Education M
Educational Administration M,D
Health Services Management and Hospital Administration M
Nurse Anesthesia M
Special Education M

ST. MARY'S UNIVERSITY OF SAN ANTONIO

Business Administration and Management M
Education M
Educational Administration M
Human Services M,D,O
Law P
Management Information Systems M
Reading Education M

SAINT MEINRAD SCHOOL OF THEOLOGY

Religious Education M

SAINT MICHAEL'S COLLEGE

Business Administration and Management M,O
Curriculum and Instruction M,O
Education M,O
Educational Administration M,O
Educational Media/Instructional Technology M
English as a Second Language M
Reading Education M
Special Education M,O

ST. NORBERT COLLEGE

Education M

SAINT PETER'S COLLEGE (JERSEY CITY)

Accounting M,O
Business Administration and Management M
Curriculum and Instruction M,O
Education M,O
Educational Administration M,O
Elementary Education O
International Business M
Management Information Systems M
Nursing M
Reading Education M
Urban Education M

ST. THOMAS AQUINAS COLLEGE

Business Administration and Management M
Education M
Elementary Education M
Finance and Banking M
Marketing M
Reading Education M
Secondary Education M
Special Education M

ST. THOMAS UNIVERSITY

Accounting M
Business Administration and Management M,O
Counselor Education M,O
Education M,O
Elementary Education M
Health Services Management and Hospital Administration M,O
Human Resources Management M,O
International Business M,O
Law P
Sports Administration M

SAINT VINCENT SEMINARY

Religious Education M

ST. VLADIMIR'S ORTHODOX THEOLOGICAL SEMINARY

Religious Education M

SAINT XAVIER UNIVERSITY

Advanced Practice Nursing M,O

- Business Administration and Management M,O
- Communication Disorders M
- Curriculum and Instruction M
- Education M,O
- Educational Administration M
- Finance and Banking M,O
- Health Services Management and Hospital Administration M,O
- Marketing M
- Medical/Surgical Nursing M
- Nursing M,O
- Nursing Administration M
- Psychiatric Nursing M
- Public Health Nursing M
- Reading Education M
- Special Education M
- Taxation M,O

SALEM COLLEGE

- Early Childhood Education M
- Education M
- Elementary Education M
- Reading Education M
- Special Education M

SALEM STATE COLLEGE

- Business Administration and Management M
- Counselor Education M
- Early Childhood Education M
- Education M
- Educational Administration M
- Educational Media/Instructional Technology M
- Elementary Education M
- English as a Second Language M
- English Education M
- Mathematics Education M
- Nursing M
- Reading Education M
- Science Education M
- Social Sciences Education M
- Social Work M
- Special Education M

SALEM–TEIKYO UNIVERSITY

- Education M
- Elementary Education M
- Secondary Education M

SALISBURY STATE UNIVERSITY

- Business Administration and Management M
- Early Childhood Education M
- Education M
- Educational Administration M
- Educational Media/Instructional Technology M
- Elementary Education M
- English as a Second Language M
- English Education M
- Mathematics Education M
- Music Education M
- Nursing M
- Reading Education M
- Science Education M
- Secondary Education M
- Social Sciences Education M

SALVE REGINA UNIVERSITY

- Accounting M
- Business Administration and Management M
- Education M
- Health Services Management and Hospital Administration M
- Human Resources Management M
- Medical Technology M

SAMFORD UNIVERSITY

- Business Administration and Management M
- Early Childhood Education M,O
- Education M,O
- Educational Administration M,O
- Elementary Education M,O
- Law P
- Music Education M
- Nursing M
- Pharmacy P

SAM HOUSTON STATE UNIVERSITY

- Agricultural Education M
- Art Education M
- Business Administration and Management M
- Counselor Education M
- Curriculum and Instruction D
- Early Childhood Education M
- Education M,D,O
- Educational Administration M
- Elementary Education M,O
- English as a Second Language O
- Health Education M
- Kinesiology and Movement Studies M
- Library Science M
- Multilingual and Multicultural Education O
- Music Education M
- Reading Education M
- Secondary Education M,O
- Special Education M
- Vocational and Technical Education M

SAMRA UNIVERSITY OF ORIENTAL MEDICINE

- Oriental Medicine and Acupuncture M*

SAMUEL MERRITT COLLEGE

- Advanced Practice Nursing O
- Nurse Anesthesia O
- Nursing M,O
- Nursing Administration M
- Occupational Therapy M
- Physical Therapy M

SAN DIEGO STATE UNIVERSITY

- Accounting M
- Advertising and Public Relations M
- Business Administration and Management M
- Communication Disorders M,D
- Counselor Education M
- Education M,D
- Educational Administration M
- Educational Media/Instructional Technology M
- Elementary Education M
- Environmental and Occupational Health M
- Epidemiology M,D
- Exercise and Sports Science M
- Finance and Banking M
- Health Physics/Radiological Health M
- Health Promotion M
- Health Services Management and Hospital Administration M
- Industrial Hygiene M
- International Business M
- Management Information Systems M
- Marketing M
- Mathematics Education D
- Multilingual and Multicultural Education M
- Nursing M
- Public Health M,D
- Reading Education M
- Science Education D
- Secondary Education M
- Social Work M
- Special Education M

SAN FRANCISCO STATE UNIVERSITY

- Adult Education M,O
- Advanced Practice Nursing M
- Business Administration and Management M
- Clinical Laboratory Sciences M
- Communication Disorders M
- Counselor Education M
- Early Childhood Education M
- Education M,D,O
- Educational Administration M,O
- Educational Media/Instructional Technology M,O
- Elementary Education M
- English as a Second Language M
- English Education O
- Health Education M
- Leisure Studies M
- Mathematics Education M
- Nonprofit Management M
- Nursing M
- Nursing Administration M
- Nursing Education M
- Physical Education M
- Physical Therapy M
- Reading Education O
- Recreation and Park Management M
- Secondary Education M,O
- Social Work M
- Special Education M,D,O
- Taxation M

SAN JOAQUIN COLLEGE OF LAW

- Law P
- Taxation M

SAN JOSE STATE UNIVERSITY

- Accounting M
- Advanced Practice Nursing M
- Art Education M
- Business Administration and Management M
- Communication Disorders M
- Counselor Education M
- Education M,O
- Educational Administration M,O
- Educational Media/Instructional Technology M,O
- Elementary Education M
- English as a Second Language M
- Gerontological Nursing M
- Health Services Management and Hospital Administration O
- Higher Education M,O
- Information Studies M
- Leisure Studies M
- Library Science M
- Nursing M
- Nursing Administration M
- Nursing Education M
- Occupational Therapy M
- Physical Education M
- Public Health M,O
- Public Health Nursing M
- Quality Management M
- Recreation and Park Management M
- Secondary Education M
- Social Work M
- Special Education M
- Taxation M
- Transportation Management M

SANTA BARBARA COLLEGE OF ORIENTAL MEDICINE

- Oriental Medicine and Acupuncture M

SANTA CLARA UNIVERSITY

- Business Administration and Management M*
- Counselor Education M
- Education M,O
- Educational Administration M
- Law P,M,O
- Special Education M

SARAH LAWRENCE COLLEGE

- Education M
- Public Health M*

SCHILLER INTERNATIONAL UNIVERSITY

- Business Administration and Management M
- Hospitality Management M*
- International Business M*
- Travel and Tourism M*

SCHILLER INTERNATIONAL UNIVERSITY (PARIS, FRANCE)

- Business Administration and Management M
- International Business M

SCHILLER INTERNATIONAL UNIVERSITY (STRASBOURG, FRANCE)

- Business Administration and Management M
- International Business M

SCHILLER INTERNATIONAL UNIVERSITY (GERMANY)

- Business Administration and Management M
- International Business M

SCHILLER INTERNATIONAL UNIVERSITY (SPAIN)

- Business Administration and Management M
- International Business M

SCHILLER INTERNATIONAL UNIVERSITY (UNITED KINGDOM)

- Hospitality Management M*
- International Business M*
- Travel and Tourism M*

SCHILLER INTERNATIONAL UNIVERSITY, AMERICAN COLLEGE OF SWITZERLAND

- Business Administration and Management M
- International Business M

SCHOOL FOR INTERNATIONAL TRAINING

- Business Administration and Management M
- English as a Second Language M
- Foreign Languages Education M
- International Business M
- Multilingual and Multicultural Education M

SCHOOL OF THE ART INSTITUTE OF CHICAGO

- Art Education M,O

SCHREINER COLLEGE

- Education M

SEATTLE PACIFIC UNIVERSITY

- Advanced Practice Nursing M
- Business Administration and Management M*
- Counselor Education M
- Curriculum and Instruction M
- Education M,D
- Educational Administration M,D
- English as a Second Language M
- Management Information Systems M
- Nursing M
- Reading Education M
- Secondary Education M

SEATTLE UNIVERSITY

- Adult Education M
- Business Administration and Management M,O*
- Counselor Education M
- Curriculum and Instruction M
- Education M,D,O
- Educational Administration M,D,O
- Educational Measurement and Evaluation O
- English as a Second Language M
- Finance and Banking M,O
- International Business M,O
- Law P
- Nonprofit Management M
- Nursing M,O

SETON HALL UNIVERSITY

- Accounting M,O
- Advanced Practice Nursing M
- Allied Health M,D
- Business Administration and Management M,O*
- Communication Disorders M
- Counselor Education M
- Education M,D,O
- Educational Administration M,D,O
- Educational Media/Instructional Technology M,O
- Elementary Education M
- English as a Second Language M,O
- Finance and Banking M
- Gerontological Nursing M
- Health Services Management and Hospital Administration M*
- Higher Education D,O
- Human Resources Management M
- International Business M,O
- Law P,M
- Management Information Systems M
- Marketing M
- Maternal/Child-Care Nursing M
- Medical/Surgical Nursing M
- Multilingual and Multicultural Education M,O
- Nonprofit Management M*
- Nursing M
- Nursing Administration M
- Nursing Education M
- Occupational Therapy M
- Physician Assistant Studies M
- Quantitative Analysis M
- Secondary Education M,O
- Sports Administration M
- Taxation M,O

SETON HILL COLLEGE

- Elementary Education M,O*
- Special Education M,O*

SHENANDOAH UNIVERSITY

- Business Administration and Management M
- Computer Education M
- Education M
- Music Education M,D
- Nursing M
- Occupational Therapy M
- Pharmacy P
- Physical Therapy M

SHERMAN COLLEGE OF STRAIGHT CHIROPRACTIC

- Chiropractic P*

SHIPPENSBURG UNIVERSITY OF PENNSYLVANIA

- Business Administration and Management M
- Business Education M

Shippensburg University of Pennsylvania (continued)

Computer Education M
Counselor Education M
Education M
Educational Administration M
Elementary Education M
Mathematics Education M
Reading Education M
Special Education M

SIENA COLLEGE

Accounting M
Business Administration and Management M

SIENA HEIGHTS UNIVERSITY

Counselor Education M
Curriculum and Instruction M
Early Childhood Education M
Education M
Elementary Education M
Human Resources Development M
Middle School Education M
Reading Education M
Secondary Education M

SIERRA NEVADA COLLEGE

Education O
Elementary Education O
Secondary Education O

SILVER LAKE COLLEGE

Business Administration and Management M
Education M

SIMMONS COLLEGE

Advanced Practice Nursing M,O*
Business Administration and Management M*
Education M*
Elementary Education M
English as a Second Language M
Health Promotion M
Health Services Management and Hospital Administration M,O*
Information Studies M,D*
Library Science M,D*
Middle School Education M
Nursing M,O*
Physical Therapy M*
Secondary Education M
Social Work M,D*
Special Education M

SIMON FRASER UNIVERSITY

Accounting M
Business Administration and Management M
Counselor Education M
Curriculum and Instruction M,D
Education M,D
Educational Administration M
Educational Psychology M,D
Finance and Banking M
International Business M
Kinesiology and Movement Studies M,D
Management Information Systems M
Management Strategy and Policy M
Marketing M
Organizational Behavior M

SIMPSON COLLEGE AND GRADUATE SCHOOL (CA)

Curriculum and Instruction M

SINTE GLESKA UNIVERSITY

Education M
Elementary Education M

SLIPPERY ROCK UNIVERSITY OF PENNSYLVANIA

Accounting M
Allied Health M
Business Administration and Management M
Counselor Education M
Early Childhood Education M
Education M
Elementary Education M
Mathematics Education M
Nursing M
Physical Education M
Physical Therapy D
Reading Education M
Recreation and Park Management M
Science Education M
Secondary Education M
Special Education M

SMITH COLLEGE

Art Education M
Early Childhood Education M
Education M
Elementary Education M
English Education M
Exercise and Sports Science M
Foreign Languages Education M
Mathematics Education M
Music Education M
Science Education M
Secondary Education M
Social Sciences Education M
Social Work M,D*
Special Education M

SONOMA STATE UNIVERSITY

Advanced Practice Nursing M
Business Administration and Management M
Counselor Education M
Curriculum and Instruction M
Early Childhood Education M
Education M
Educational Administration M
Kinesiology and Movement Studies M
Reading Education M
Special Education M

SOUTH BAYLO UNIVERSITY

Oriental Medicine and Acupuncture M

SOUTH CAROLINA STATE UNIVERSITY

Business Administration and Management M
Business Education M
Communication Disorders M
Counselor Education M
Early Childhood Education M
Education M,D,O
Educational Administration D,O
Elementary Education M
English Education M
Home Economics Education M
Mathematics Education M
Science Education M
Secondary Education M
Social Sciences Education M
Special Education M
Vocational and Technical Education M

SOUTH DAKOTA STATE UNIVERSITY

Counselor Education M
Curriculum and Instruction M
Education M
Educational Administration M
Health Education M
Nursing M
Pharmaceutical Sciences M
Pharmacy P
Physical Education M
Recreation and Park Management M

SOUTHEASTERN BAPTIST THEOLOGICAL SEMINARY

Religious Education P,M

SOUTHEASTERN LOUISIANA UNIVERSITY

Business Administration and Management M
Counselor Education M,O
Education M,O
Educational Administration M,O
Elementary Education M,O
Health Education M
Kinesiology and Movement Studies M
Nursing M
Reading Education M
Secondary Education M
Special Education M

SOUTHEASTERN OKLAHOMA STATE UNIVERSITY

Business Administration and Management M
Counselor Education M
Education M
Educational Administration M
Elementary Education M
Industrial and Manufacturing Management M
Secondary Education M

SOUTHEASTERN UNIVERSITY

Accounting M
Business Administration and Management M
Finance and Banking M
Health Services Management and Hospital Administration M
International Business M
Management Information Systems M

Marketing M
Taxation M

SOUTHEAST MISSOURI STATE UNIVERSITY

Business Administration and Management M
Business Education M
Communication Disorders M
Counselor Education M
Educational Administration M,D,O
Elementary Education M
English as a Second Language M
Health Services Management and Hospital Administration M
Human Resources Management M
Middle School Education M
Music Education M
Nursing M
Physical Education M
Science Education M
Secondary Education M
Special Education M

SOUTHERN ADVENTIST UNIVERSITY

Business Administration and Management M
Counselor Education M
Education M
Health Services Management and Hospital Administration M

SOUTHERN ARKANSAS UNIVERSITY–MAGNOLIA

Business Administration and Management M
Counselor Education M
Education M
Educational Media/Instructional Technology M
Education of the Gifted M
Elementary Education M
Health Education M
Kinesiology and Movement Studies M
Mathematics Education M
Reading Education M
Science Education M
Special Education M

SOUTHERN BAPTIST THEOLOGICAL SEMINARY

Religious Education P,M,D

SOUTHERN CALIFORNIA COLLEGE

Education M*

SOUTHERN CALIFORNIA COLLEGE OF OPTOMETRY

Optometry P

SOUTHERN COLLEGE OF OPTOMETRY

Optometry P

SOUTHERN CONNECTICUT STATE UNIVERSITY

Art Education M
Business Administration and Management M
Communication Disorders M
Counselor Education M,O
Early Childhood Education M
Education M,O
Educational Administration O
Educational Measurement and Evaluation M
Educational Media/Instructional Technology M*
Elementary Education M
English as a Second Language M
Foundations and Philosophy of Education O
Health Education M
Information Studies O*
Leisure Studies M
Library Science M,O*
Mathematics Education M
Multilingual and Multicultural Education M
Nursing M
Physical Education M
Public Health M
Reading Education M,O
Recreation and Park Management M
Science Education M,O
Secondary Education M
Social Work M
Special Education M,O

SOUTHERN ILLINOIS UNIVERSITY AT CARBONDALE

Accounting M,D
Allopathic Medicine P
Business Administration and Management M,D*

Communication Disorders M
Counselor Education M,D
Curriculum and Instruction M,D
Education M,D
Educational Administration M,D
Educational Measurement and Evaluation D
Educational Psychology M,D
English as a Second Language M
Health Education M,D
Higher Education M
Law P
Music Education M
Physical Education M
Recreation and Park Management M
Social Work M
Special Education M
Vocational and Technical Education M,D

SOUTHERN ILLINOIS UNIVERSITY AT EDWARDSVILLE

Accounting M
Advanced Practice Nursing M
Business Administration and Management M
Business Education M
Communication Disorders M
Curriculum and Instruction D
Dentistry P
Education M,D,O
Educational Administration M,O
Educational Media/Instructional Technology M
Elementary Education M
English as a Second Language M
English Education M
Health Education M
Management Information Systems M
Marketing Research M
Medical/Surgical Nursing M
Nurse Anesthesia M
Nursing M
Physical Education M
Psychiatric Nursing M
Public Health Nursing M
Recreation and Park Management M
Secondary Education M
Social Work M
Special Education M

SOUTHERN METHODIST UNIVERSITY

Business Administration and Management M*
Law P,M,D
Taxation M

SOUTHERN NAZARENE UNIVERSITY

Business Administration and Management M
Education M

SOUTHERN NEW ENGLAND SCHOOL OF LAW

Law P

SOUTHERN OREGON UNIVERSITY

Business Administration and Management M
Counselor Education M
Early Childhood Education M
Education M
Educational Administration M
Elementary Education M
Reading Education M
Science Education M
Secondary Education M
Special Education M

SOUTHERN POLYTECHNIC STATE UNIVERSITY

Quality Management M

SOUTHERN UNIVERSITY AND AGRICULTURAL AND MECHANICAL COLLEGE

Accounting M
Business Administration and Management M
Counselor Education M
Education M
Educational Administration M
Educational Media/Instructional Technology M
Elementary Education M
Law P*
Nursing M
Recreation and Park Management M
Secondary Education M
Special Education M,D

SOUTHERN UNIVERSITY AT NEW ORLEANS
Social Work	M

SOUTHERN UTAH UNIVERSITY
Accounting	M
Education	M
Elementary Education	M
Secondary Education	M

SOUTHERN WESLEYAN UNIVERSITY
Business Administration and Management	M

SOUTH TEXAS COLLEGE OF LAW AFFILIATED WITH TEXAS A&M UNIVERSITY
Law	P

SOUTHWEST ACUPUNCTURE COLLEGE
Oriental Medicine and Acupuncture	M

SOUTHWEST BAPTIST UNIVERSITY
Accounting	M
Business Administration and Management	M
Education	M
Educational Administration	M
Health Services Management and Hospital Administration	M
Physical Therapy	M

SOUTHWEST COLLEGE OF NATUROPATHIC MEDICINE AND HEALTH SCIENCES
Naturopathic Medicine	D*
Oriental Medicine and Acupuncture	O*

SOUTHWESTERN ADVENTIST UNIVERSITY
Accounting	M
Business Administration and Management	M
Education	M
Elementary Education	M

SOUTHWESTERN ASSEMBLIES OF GOD UNIVERSITY
Education	M

SOUTHWESTERN BAPTIST THEOLOGICAL SEMINARY
Religious Education	M,D

SOUTHWESTERN COLLEGE (KS)
Education	M

SOUTHWESTERN COLLEGE (NM)
Counselor Education	M

SOUTHWESTERN OKLAHOMA STATE UNIVERSITY
Business Administration and Management	M
Counselor Education	M
Early Childhood Education	M
Education	M
Educational Administration	M
Educational Measurement and Evaluation	M
Educational Media/Instructional Technology	M
Elementary Education	M
Health Education	M
Physical Education	M
Recreation and Park Management	M
Secondary Education	M
Special Education	M

SOUTHWESTERN UNIVERSITY SCHOOL OF LAW
Law	P

SOUTHWEST MISSOURI STATE UNIVERSITY
Accounting	M
Business Administration and Management	M
Communication Disorders	M
Counselor Education	M
Education	M,O
Educational Administration	M,O
Elementary Education	M
Health Promotion	M
Management Information Systems	M
Nurse Anesthesia	M
Nursing	M
Reading Education	M
Science Education	M
Secondary Education	M
Social Work	M
Special Education	M

SOUTHWEST STATE UNIVERSITY
Business Administration and Management	M
Education	M

SOUTHWEST TEXAS STATE UNIVERSITY
Accounting	M
Agricultural Education	M
Allied Health	M
Business Administration and Management	M
Communication Disorders	M
Counselor Education	M
Education	M
Educational Administration	M
Elementary Education	M
Foreign Languages Education	M
Health Education	M
Health Services Management and Hospital Administration	M
Health Services Research	M
Music Education	M
Physical Education	M
Physical Therapy	M
Reading Education	M
Secondary Education	M
Social Sciences Education	M,D
Social Work	M
Special Education	M
Vocational and Technical Education	M

SPALDING UNIVERSITY
Advanced Practice Nursing	M
Counselor Education	M
Education	M,D
Educational Administration	M,D
Elementary Education	M
Higher Education	M
Library Science	M
Middle School Education	M
Nursing	M
Nursing Administration	M
Reading Education	M
Social Work	M

SPERTUS INSTITUTE OF JEWISH STUDIES
Human Services	M
Religious Education	M

SPRING ARBOR COLLEGE
Business Administration and Management	M
Education	M

SPRINGFIELD COLLEGE (MA)
Counselor Education	M,O
Education	M
Educational Administration	M,O
Exercise and Sports Science	M,O
Health Education	M
Health Promotion	M,O
Health Services Management and Hospital Administration	M
Human Services	M
Kinesiology and Movement Studies	M
Occupational Therapy	M,O
Physical Education	M,D,O
Physical Therapy	M
Recreation and Park Management	M
Secondary Education	M
Social Work	M
Sports Administration	M,O

SPRING HILL COLLEGE
Business Administration and Management	M
Early Childhood Education	M
Education	M
Elementary Education	M
Reading Education	M

STANFORD UNIVERSITY
Allopathic Medicine	P
Business Administration and Management	M,D*
Curriculum and Instruction	M,D
Education	M,D*
Educational Administration	M,D
Educational Psychology	M,D
English Education	M
Epidemiology	M,D
Foreign Languages Education	M,D
Foundations and Philosophy of Education	D
Health Services Research	M
Higher Education	M,D
International and Comparative Education	M,D
Law	P,M,D
Mathematics Education	M
Multilingual and Multicultural Education	M,D
Religious Education	D
Science Education	M
Social Sciences Education	M,D

STATE UNIVERSITY OF NEW YORK AT ALBANY
Accounting	M
Business Administration and Management	M,D
Counselor Education	O
Curriculum and Instruction	M,D,O
Education	M,D,O
Educational Administration	M,D,O
Educational Measurement and Evaluation	D
Educational Media/Instructional Technology	M,O
Educational Psychology	M,D,O
Environmental and Occupational Health	M,D
Epidemiology	M,D
Finance and Banking	M
Health Services Management and Hospital Administration	M
Human Resources Management	M
Information Studies	M,O
Library Science	M,O
Management Information Systems	M
Marketing	M
Mathematics Education	M
Organizational Behavior	D
Public Health	M,D*
Reading Education	M,D,O
Secondary Education	M
Social Work	M,D
Special Education	M
Taxation	M

STATE UNIVERSITY OF NEW YORK AT BINGHAMTON
Accounting	M,D
Business Administration and Management	M,D
Early Childhood Education	M
Education	M,D
Elementary Education	M
English Education	M
Finance and Banking	M,D
Foreign Languages Education	M
Foundations and Philosophy of Education	D
Health Services Management and Hospital Administration	M
Mathematics Education	M
Nursing	M,D,O
Reading Education	M
Science Education	M
Secondary Education	M
Social Sciences Education	M
Special Education	M

STATE UNIVERSITY OF NEW YORK AT BUFFALO
Allied Health	M,D
Allopathic Medicine	P
Business Administration and Management	M,D
Clinical Laboratory Sciences	M
Communication Disorders	M,D
Community Health	D
Counselor Education	M,D,O
Dentistry	P
Early Childhood Education	M,D
Education	M,D,O*
Educational Administration	M,D,O
Educational Psychology	M,D,O
Elementary Education	M,D
English as a Second Language	M,D
English Education	D
Epidemiology	M,D
Exercise and Sports Science	M,D
Foreign Languages Education	D
Foundations and Philosophy of Education	D
Information Studies	M,O
Law	P
Library Science	M,O
Maternal/Child-Care Nursing	M
Mathematics Education	D
Medical/Surgical Nursing	M
Multilingual and Multicultural Education	M
Music Education	M,O
Nurse Anesthesia	M
Nursing	M,D
Occupational Therapy	M,D
Oral and Dental Sciences	M,D,O
Pharmaceutical Sciences	M,D
Pharmacy	P
Reading Education	M,D
Rehabilitation Sciences	D
Science Education	D
Secondary Education	M,D
Social Work	M,D

STATE UNIVERSITY OF NEW YORK AT NEW PALTZ
Art Education	M
Business Administration and Management	M
Communication Disorders	M
Early Childhood Education	M
Education	M,O
Educational Administration	M,O
Elementary Education	M
English as a Second Language	M
Gerontological Nursing	M
Music Education	M
Nursing	M
Reading Education	M
Science Education	M
Secondary Education	M
Special Education	M

STATE UNIVERSITY OF NEW YORK AT OSWEGO
Art Education	M
Business Administration and Management	M
Education	M,D,O
Educational Administration	M,D,O
Elementary Education	M
Human Services	M
Reading Education	M
Secondary Education	M
Special Education	M
Vocational and Technical Education	M

STATE UNIVERSITY OF NEW YORK AT STONY BROOK
Advanced Practice Nursing	O
Allopathic Medicine	P
Business Administration and Management	M
Dentistry	P,O
Educational Administration	O
Educational Media/Instructional Technology	O
English as a Second Language	M,D
English Education	M
Environmental and Occupational Health	O
Foreign Languages Education	M
Gerontological Nursing	M
Health Services Management and Hospital Administration	M,O
Maternal/Child-Care Nursing	M,O
Medical/Surgical Nursing	M,O
Nurse Midwifery	M,O
Nursing	M,O
Oral and Dental Sciences	D,O
Physical Education	O
Psychiatric Nursing	M,O
Science Education	M
Social Sciences Education	M
Social Work	M,D*

STATE UNIVERSITY OF NEW YORK COLLEGE AT BROCKPORT
Counselor Education	M,O
Education	M
Educational Administration	M,O
Elementary Education	M
English Education	M
Health Education	M
Leisure Studies	M
Mathematics Education	M
Multilingual and Multicultural Education	M
Physical Education	M
Reading Education	M
Recreation and Park Management	M
Science Education	M
Secondary Education	M
Social Sciences Education	M

STATE UNIVERSITY OF NEW YORK COLLEGE AT BUFFALO
Art Education	M
Business Education	M
Communication Disorders	M
Computer Education	M
Educational Administration	M,O
Elementary Education	M
English Education	M
Mathematics Education	M
Multilingual and Multicultural Education	M
Reading Education	M
Science Education	M
Social Sciences Education	M
Special Education	M
Vocational and Technical Education	M

STATE UNIVERSITY OF NEW YORK COLLEGE AT CORTLAND
Education	M,O
Educational Administration	O

State University of New York College at Cortland (continued)

Elementary Education M
English Education M
Foreign Languages Education M
Health Education M
Mathematics Education M
Physical Education M
Reading Education M
Recreation and Park Management M
Science Education M
Secondary Education M
Social Sciences Education M

STATE UNIVERSITY OF NEW YORK COLLEGE AT FREDONIA

Business Administration and Management M
Communication Disorders M
Education M,O
Educational Administration O
Elementary Education M
Music Education M
Reading Education M
Secondary Education M

STATE UNIVERSITY OF NEW YORK COLLEGE AT GENESEO

Communication Disorders M
Education M
Elementary Education M
Reading Education M
Secondary Education M
Special Education M

STATE UNIVERSITY OF NEW YORK COLLEGE AT ONEONTA

Business Administration and Management M
Counselor Education M,O
Education M,O
Elementary Education M
English Education M
Home Economics Education M
Mathematics Education M
Nursing Education M
Reading Education M
Science Education M
Secondary Education M
Social Sciences Education M

STATE UNIVERSITY OF NEW YORK COLLEGE AT POTSDAM

Education M
Educational Media/Instructional Technology M
Elementary Education M
Music Education M
Reading Education M
Secondary Education M
Special Education M

STATE UNIVERSITY OF NEW YORK COLLEGE OF OPTOMETRY

Optometry P
Vision Sciences M,D

STATE UNIVERSITY OF NEW YORK EMPIRE STATE COLLEGE

Business Administration and Management M

STATE UNIVERSITY OF NEW YORK HEALTH SCIENCE CENTER AT BROOKLYN

Advanced Practice Nursing M,O
Allopathic Medicine P
Nursing M,O

STATE UNIVERSITY OF NEW YORK HEALTH SCIENCE CENTER AT SYRACUSE

Allied Health M
Allopathic Medicine P
Medical Technology M
Nursing M
Physical Therapy M

STATE UNIVERSITY OF NEW YORK INSTITUTE OF TECHNOLOGY AT UTICA/ROME

Accounting M
Advanced Practice Nursing M,O
Business Administration and Management M
Nursing M,O
Nursing Administration M

STATE UNIVERSITY OF NEW YORK MARITIME COLLEGE

Transportation Management M

STATE UNIVERSITY OF WEST GEORGIA

Accounting M
Art Education M
Business Administration and Management M
Business Education M,O
Counselor Education M,O
Early Childhood Education M,O
Education M,D,O
Educational Administration M,D,O
Educational Media/Instructional Technology M,O
Middle School Education M,O
Music Education M
Physical Education M,O
Reading Education M,O
Secondary Education M,O
Special Education M,O

STEPHEN F. AUSTIN STATE UNIVERSITY

Accounting M
Agricultural Education M
Business Administration and Management M
Communication Disorders M
Counselor Education M
Early Childhood Education M
Education M,D
Educational Administration M,D
Elementary Education M
Health Education M
Marketing M
Mathematics Education M
Physical Education M
Secondary Education M,D
Social Work M
Special Education M

STEPHENS COLLEGE

Business Administration and Management M
Counselor Education M
Education M
Special Education M

STETSON UNIVERSITY

Accounting M
Business Administration and Management M
Counselor Education M
Education M,O
Educational Administration M,O
Elementary Education M
Law P*
Special Education M

STEVENS INSTITUTE OF TECHNOLOGY

Business Administration and Management M,D,O*
Industrial and Manufacturing Management M,O
Management Information Systems M,D,O
Management Strategy and Policy M
Project Management M,O

STRAYER UNIVERSITY

Accounting M
Business Administration and Management M
Management Information Systems M

SUFFOLK UNIVERSITY

Accounting M,O*
Adult Education M,O
Business Administration and Management M,O*
Counselor Education M,O
Education M,O*
Educational Administration M,O
Entrepreneurship M*
Finance and Banking M*
Health Services Management and Hospital Administration M*
Human Resources Development M,O
Human Resources Management M
International Business M*
Law P
Nonprofit Management M
Secondary Education M
Taxation M

SULLIVAN COLLEGE

Business Administration and Management M

SUL ROSS STATE UNIVERSITY

Art Education M
Business Administration and Management M
Counselor Education M
Education M
Educational Administration M
Educational Measurement and Evaluation M
Elementary Education M
International Business M
Multilingual and Multicultural Education M
Physical Education M
Reading Education M
Secondary Education M
Vocational and Technical Education M

SYRACUSE UNIVERSITY

Accounting M,D
Advertising and Public Relations M
Art Education M,O
Business Administration and Management M,D*
Communication Disorders M,D
Counselor Education M,D,O
Curriculum and Instruction M,D,O
Early Childhood Education M
Education M,D,O*
Educational Administration M,D,O
Educational Measurement and Evaluation M,D,O
Elementary Education M,O
English Education M,D,O
Exercise and Sports Science M,O
Finance and Banking M,D
Foundations and Philosophy of Education M,D,O
Health Education M,O
Higher Education M,D,O
Human Resources Management M
Human Services M
Industrial and Manufacturing Management M,D
Information Studies M,D*
International Business M
Law P
Library Science M,O*
Logistics M
Management Information Systems M,D*
Management Strategy and Policy D
Marketing M,D
Mathematics Education M,D,O
Music Education M
Nursing M
Organizational Behavior M,D
Physical Education M,O
Reading Education M,D,O
Science Education M,D,O
Social Sciences Education M,O
Social Work M
Special Education M,D
Transportation Management M

TAI HSUAN FOUNDATION: COLLEGE OF ACUPUNCTURE AND HERBAL MEDICINE

Oriental Medicine and Acupuncture M

TARLETON STATE UNIVERSITY

Business Administration and Management M
Counselor Education M
Education M,O
Educational Administration M,O
Elementary Education M,O
Health Education M,O
Physical Education M,O
Reading Education O
Secondary Education M,O
Special Education O

TEACHERS COLLEGE, COLUMBIA UNIVERSITY

Adult Education M,D
Art Education M,D
Communication Disorders M,D
Computer Education M
Curriculum and Instruction M,D
Early Childhood Education M,D
Education M,D*
Educational Administration M,D
Educational Measurement and Evaluation M,D
Educational Media/Instructional Technology M,D
Educational Psychology M,D
Education of the Gifted M,D
Elementary Education M
English as a Second Language M,D
English Education M,D
Foreign Languages Education M,D
Foundations and Philosophy of Education M,D
Health Education M,D
Higher Education M,D
International and Comparative Education M,D
Kinesiology and Movement Studies M,D
Mathematics Education M,D
Multilingual and Multicultural Education M
Music Education M,D
Nursing Education M,D
Physical Education M,D
Reading Education M
Religious Education M,D
Science Education M,D
Social Sciences Education M,D
Special Education M,D

TEMPLE UNIVERSITY (PHILADELPHIA)

Accounting M,D
Actuarial Science M
Allied Health M,D*
Allopathic Medicine P
Art Education M
Business Administration and Management M,D*
Communication Disorders M
Community Health M*
Counselor Education M
Dentistry P
Early Childhood Education M,O
Education M,D,O*
Educational Administration M,D
Educational Psychology M,D
Elementary Education M,O
Environmental and Occupational Health M
Finance and Banking M,D
Health Education M,D*
Health Services Management and Hospital Administration M*
Hospitality Management M*
Human Resources Management M,D
Insurance M
International Business M
Kinesiology and Movement Studies D*
Law P,M*
Legal and Justice Studies M
Leisure Studies M*
Management Information Systems M
Management Strategy and Policy M,D
Marketing M,D
Mathematics Education M,D
Music Education M,D
Nursing M*
Occupational Therapy M*
Oral and Dental Sciences M,O
Pharmaceutical Sciences M,D*
Pharmacy P
Physical Education M,D*
Physical Therapy M,D*
Podiatric Medicine P
Public Health M*
Reading Education M,D
Real Estate M
Recreation and Park Management M*
Science Education M,D
Secondary Education M,O
Social Work M
Special Education M
Sports Administration M*
Taxation M*
Travel and Tourism M*
Urban Education M,D
Vocational and Technical Education M

TENNESSEE STATE UNIVERSITY

Adult Education M
Allied Health M
Business Administration and Management M
Counselor Education M
Curriculum and Instruction D
Education M,D
Educational Administration M,D
Educational Media/Instructional Technology M
Elementary Education M,D
Health Education M
Music Education M
Nursing M
Physical Education M
Reading Education M
Recreation and Park Management M
Secondary Education M,D
Special Education M,D

TENNESSEE TECHNOLOGICAL UNIVERSITY

Business Administration and Management M*
Curriculum and Instruction M,O
Early Childhood Education M,O
Education M,O
Educational Administration M,O
Educational Psychology M,O
Elementary Education M,O
Health Education M
Physical Education M
Reading Education M,O
Secondary Education M,O
Special Education M,O

TENNESSEE TEMPLE UNIVERSITY

Education M
Educational Administration M

TEXAS A&M INTERNATIONAL UNIVERSITY

Accounting M*
Business Administration and Management M
Business Education M
Counselor Education M
Early Childhood Education M
Education M
Educational Administration M
Education of the Gifted M
Elementary Education M
Finance and Banking M*
International Business M*
Logistics M*
Management Information Systems M*
Multilingual and Multicultural Education M
Reading Education M
Secondary Education M

TEXAS A&M UNIVERSITY (COLLEGE STATION)

Accounting M,D
Adult Education M,D
Agricultural Education M,D
Allopathic Medicine P
Business Administration and Management M,D*
Curriculum and Instruction M,D
Education M,D*
Educational Administration M,D
Educational Measurement and Evaluation M,D
Educational Media/Instructional Technology M
Educational Psychology M,D
Education of the Gifted M
Epidemiology M
Finance and Banking M,D
Foundations and Philosophy of Education M,D
Health Education M,D
Health Physics/Radiological Health M*
Human Resources Development M,D
Industrial Hygiene M
Kinesiology and Movement Studies M,D
Management Information Systems M,D
Marketing M,D
Mathematics Education M,D
Multilingual and Multicultural Education M,D
Physical Education M,D
Project Management M,D
Reading Education M,D
Recreation and Park Management M,D
Science Education M,D
Special Education M,D
Veterinary Medicine P
Veterinary Sciences M,D*
Vocational and Technical Education M,D

TEXAS A&M UNIVERSITY–COMMERCE

Agricultural Education M
Business Administration and Management M
Counselor Education M,D
Early Childhood Education M
Education M,D
Educational Administration M,D
Educational Media/Instructional Technology M
Educational Psychology D
Elementary Education M,D
English Education D
Health Education M
Higher Education M,D
Music Education M
Physical Education M
Reading Education M
Secondary Education M,D
Social Sciences Education M
Special Education M,D
Vocational and Technical Education M

TEXAS A&M UNIVERSITY–CORPUS CHRISTI

Accounting M
Business Administration and Management M
Counselor Education M
Curriculum and Instruction M
Education M,D
Educational Administration M,D
Elementary Education M
Nursing M
Nursing Administration M
Secondary Education M
Special Education M
Vocational and Technical Education M

TEXAS A&M UNIVERSITY–KINGSVILLE

Adult Education M
Agricultural Education M
Business Administration and Management M
Communication Disorders M
Counselor Education M
Early Childhood Education M
Education M,D
Educational Administration M,D
Elementary Education M
English as a Second Language M
Health Education M
Higher Education D
Kinesiology and Movement Studies M
Multilingual and Multicultural Education M,D
Music Education M
Reading Education M
Secondary Education M
Special Education M

TEXAS A&M UNIVERSITY–TEXARKANA

Business Administration and Management M
Education M
Elementary Education M
Secondary Education M
Special Education M

TEXAS CHIROPRACTIC COLLEGE

Chiropractic P*

TEXAS CHRISTIAN UNIVERSITY

Accounting M
Business Administration and Management M
Communication Disorders M
Education M
Educational Administration M
Educational Measurement and Evaluation M
Elementary Education M
Kinesiology and Movement Studies M
Music Education M
Physical Education M
Secondary Education M
Special Education M

TEXAS SOUTHERN UNIVERSITY

Business Administration and Management M
Business Education M
Counselor Education M,D
Curriculum and Instruction M,D
Early Childhood Education M
Education M,D
Educational Administration M,D
Educational Media/Instructional Technology M
Elementary Education M
Health Education M
Higher Education M,D
Home Economics Education M
Law P
Multilingual and Multicultural Education M
Pharmacy P
Physical Education M
Reading Education M
Secondary Education M
Special Education M
Urban Education D

TEXAS TECH UNIVERSITY

Accounting M,D
Agricultural Education M
Art Education M,O
Business Administration and Management M,D,O*
Counselor Education M,D,O
Curriculum and Instruction M,D,O
Early Childhood Education M,O
Education M,D,O
Educational Administration M,D,O
Educational Media/Instructional Technology M,D
Educational Psychology M,D,O
Elementary Education M,D,O
Exercise and Sports Science M
Finance and Banking M,D
Health Services Management and Hospital Administration M,O*
Higher Education M,D
Home Economics Education M,D
Hospitality Management M
Industrial and Manufacturing Management D
Law P
Management Information Systems M,D
Marketing M,D
Multilingual and Multicultural Education M,D
Music Education M,O
Physical Education M,O*
Quantitative Analysis M,D
Reading Education M,D,O
Secondary Education M,D,O
Special Education M,D,O
Taxation M

TEXAS TECH UNIVERSITY HEALTH SCIENCES CENTER

Advanced Practice Nursing M
Allied Health M*
Allopathic Medicine P
Communication Disorders M
Gerontological Nursing M
Nursing M
Nursing Administration M
Nursing Education M
Physical Therapy M
Public Health Nursing M

TEXAS WESLEYAN UNIVERSITY

Business Administration and Management M
Education M
Law P
Nurse Anesthesia M

TEXAS WOMAN'S UNIVERSITY

Advanced Practice Nursing M,D
Art Education M
Business Administration and Management M
Communication Disorders M
Counselor Education M
Early Childhood Education M,D
Education M,D
Educational Administration M
Elementary Education M
Exercise and Sports Science M,D
Health Education M,D
Health Services Management and Hospital Administration M
Hospitality Management M
Information Studies M,D*
Kinesiology and Movement Studies M,D
Library Science M,D*
Maternal/Child-Care Nursing M
Medical/Surgical Nursing M,D
Music Education M
Nursing M,D
Occupational Therapy M,D
Physical Education M,D
Physical Therapy M,D
Psychiatric Nursing M
Public Health Nursing M
Reading Education M,D
Science Education M
Special Education M,D
Vocational and Technical Education M,D

THOMAS COLLEGE (ME)

Business Administration and Management M
Computer Education M

THOMAS EDISON STATE COLLEGE

Business Administration and Management M

THOMAS JEFFERSON SCHOOL OF LAW

Law P

THOMAS JEFFERSON UNIVERSITY

Allopathic Medicine P
Nursing M
Occupational Therapy M
Physical Therapy M

THOMAS M. COOLEY LAW SCHOOL

Law P

THOMAS MORE COLLEGE

Business Administration and Management M

THUNDERBIRD, THE AMERICAN GRADUATE SCHOOL OF INTERNATIONAL MANAGEMENT

Health Services Management and Hospital Administration M*
International Business M*
International Health M*

TIFFIN UNIVERSITY

Business Administration and Management M

TOCCOA FALLS COLLEGE

Religious Education M

TOURO COLLEGE

Health Services Management and Hospital Administration O
Law P,M
Occupational Therapy M
Physical Therapy M

TOWSON UNIVERSITY

Accounting M
Allied Health M
Art Education M
Communication Disorders M
Early Childhood Education M,O
Education M
Educational Media/Instructional Technology M
Elementary Education M,O
Human Resources Development M
Industrial and Manufacturing Management M
Management Information Systems M
Music Education M,O
Occupational Therapy M
Project Management M
Reading Education M,O
Secondary Education M,O

TRADITIONAL ACUPUNCTURE INSTITUTE

Oriental Medicine and Acupuncture M

TREVECCA NAZARENE UNIVERSITY

Counselor Education M
Curriculum and Instruction M
Education M
Educational Administration M
Elementary Education M
Organizational Behavior M
Physician Assistant Studies M

TRI-COLLEGE UNIVERSITY (SEE NORTH DAKOTA STATE UNIVERSITY)

TRINITY COLLEGE (DC)

Business Administration and Management M
Community Health M
Counselor Education M
Curriculum and Instruction M
Early Childhood Education M
Education M
Educational Administration M
Elementary Education M
Entrepreneurship M
Health Promotion M
Human Resources Development M
Human Resources Management M
Nonprofit Management M
Reading Education M
Secondary Education M
Special Education M
Urban Education M

TRINITY COLLEGE OF VERMONT

Education M,O

TRINITY INTERNATIONAL UNIVERSITY

Bioethics M
Law P
Religious Education M,D

TRINITY UNIVERSITY

Accounting M
Education M
Educational Administration M
Health Services Management and Hospital Administration M*

TROY STATE UNIVERSITY (TROY)

Business Administration and Management M
Counselor Education M
Early Childhood Education M,O
Education M,O
Educational Administration M
Elementary Education M,O
Foundations and Philosophy of Education M
Human Resources Management M
Nursing M
Secondary Education M,O
Special Education M,O

TROY STATE UNIVERSITY DOTHAN

Accounting M
Business Administration and Management M
Business Education M
Counselor Education M,O
Early Childhood Education M,O
Education M,O
Educational Administration M,O
Elementary Education M,O
Finance and Banking M

Troy State University Dothan (continued)

Foundations and Philosophy of Education M
Human Resources Management M
Management Information Systems M
Quantitative Analysis M
Secondary Education M
Special Education M

TROY STATE UNIVERSITY MONTGOMERY

Adult Education M
Business Administration and Management M
Counselor Education M,O
Education M,O
Educational Administration O
Elementary Education M
Human Resources Management M
Management Information Systems M

TRUMAN STATE UNIVERSITY

Accounting M
Communication Disorders M
Education M

TUFTS UNIVERSITY

Allopathic Medicine P
Dentistry P
Early Childhood Education M
Education M,O*
Elementary Education M
Environmental and Occupational Health M,D
Middle School Education M
Nonprofit Management O
Occupational Therapy M,O
Oral and Dental Sciences M,O
Public Health M*
Secondary Education M
Veterinary Medicine P
Veterinary Sciences M

TULANE UNIVERSITY

Allopathic Medicine P,M,D,O
Business Administration and Management M,D*
Education O
Environmental and Occupational Health M,D
Epidemiology M,D
Health Education M
Health Services Management and Hospital Administration M,D*
International Health M,D
Law P,M,D
Maternal and Child Health M,D
Public Health M,D,O*
Social Work M,D,O*

TUSCULUM COLLEGE

Adult Education M
Business Administration and Management M
Education M

TUSKEGEE UNIVERSITY

Counselor Education M
Education M
Educational Administration M
Science Education M
Veterinary Medicine P
Veterinary Sciences M
Vocational and Technical Education M

UNIFORMED SERVICES UNIVERSITY OF THE HEALTH SCIENCES

Advanced Practice Nursing M
Allopathic Medicine P
International Health M
Nurse Anesthesia M
Nursing M
Public Health M,D

UNION COLLEGE (KY)

Education M
Educational Administration O
Elementary Education M
Health Education M
Middle School Education M
Music Education M
Reading Education M
Secondary Education M
Special Education M

UNION COLLEGE (NY)

Accounting M
Business Administration and Management M*
Computer Education M
Education M
English Education M
Foreign Languages Education M
Health Services Management and Hospital Administration M
Industrial and Manufacturing Management M
International Business M
Law
Management Information Systems M
Mathematics Education M
Science Education M
Social Sciences Education M

UNION THEOLOGICAL SEMINARY AND PRESBYTERIAN SCHOOL OF CHRISTIAN EDUCATION

Religious Education M,D,O

UNION UNIVERSITY

Business Administration and Management M
Education M

UNITED STATES INTERNATIONAL UNIVERSITY

Business Administration and Management M,D
Education M,D
Educational Administration M,D
Educational Media/Instructional Technology M,D
English as a Second Language M,D
Finance and Banking D
International Business M,D
Management Strategy and Policy D
Marketing D

UNITED STATES INTERNATIONAL UNIVERSITY–AFRICA

Business Administration and Management M
Finance and Banking M
Marketing M

UNITED STATES INTERNATIONAL UNIVERSITY–MEXICO

Business Administration and Management M
International Business M

UNITED STATES SPORTS ACADEMY

Exercise and Sports Science M*
Physical Education M*
Sports Administration M,D*

UNIVERSIDAD CENTRAL DEL CARIBE, ESCUELA DE MEDICINA

Allopathic Medicine P

UNIVERSIDAD DE LAS AMÉRICAS–PUEBLA

Business Administration and Management M
Clinical Laboratory Sciences M
Education M
Finance and Banking M

UNIVERSIDAD DEL TURABO

Accounting M
Business Administration and Management M
Education M
Educational Administration M
English as a Second Language M
Human Resources Development M
Human Resources Management M
Human Services M
Logistics M
Marketing M
Multilingual and Multicultural Education M
Special Education M

UNIVERSIDAD METROPOLITANA

Accounting M
Business Administration and Management M
Education M
Educational Administration M
Marketing M
Science Education M

UNIVERSITÉ DE MONCTON

Business Administration and Management M
Counselor Education M
Education M
Educational Administration M
Educational Psychology M
Law P,O
Social Work M

UNIVERSITÉ DE MONTRÉAL

Allopathic Medicine P
Bioethics O
Communication Disorders M
Community Health M,D,O
Curriculum and Instruction M,D
Dentistry P
Education M,D,O
Educational Administration M,D,O
Educational Psychology M,D
Emergency Medical Services
Environmental and Occupational Health M,O
Health Services Management and Hospital Administration M
Human Services D
Information Studies M,D
Kinesiology and Movement Studies M,D
Law P,M,D,O
Library Science M,D
Medical Technology
Nurse Anesthesia
Nursing M,D
Optometry P
Oral and Dental Sciences M,O
Pharmaceutical Sciences M,D
Physical Education M,D
Social Work M,D,O
Sports Administration M
Veterinary Medicine P
Veterinary Sciences M,D,O
Vision Sciences M

UNIVERSITÉ DE SHERBROOKE

Accounting M
Adult Education O
Allopathic Medicine P
Business Administration and Management M,O
Clinical Laboratory Sciences M,D
Counselor Education M
Education M,O
Educational Administration M
Elementary Education M,O
Finance and Banking M
Higher Education M,O
Human Resources Management M
Kinesiology and Movement Studies M
Law P,M,O
Management Information Systems M
Marketing M
Physical Education M,O
Social Work M
Special Education M,O
Taxation M,O

UNIVERSITÉ DU QUÉBEC À CHICOUTIMI

Business Administration and Management M
Education M,D
Project Management M

UNIVERSITÉ DU QUÉBEC À HULL

Adult Education O
Education M,D
Educational Psychology M,O
Project Management M

UNIVERSITÉ DU QUÉBEC À MONTRÉAL

Accounting M,O
Actuarial Science O
Business Administration and Management M,D,O
Education M,D,O
Elementary Education M
Environmental and Occupational Health O
Finance and Banking O
Foundations and Philosophy of Education O
Kinesiology and Movement Studies M
Law M
Management Information Systems M
Project Management M,O
Science Education O
Social Work M

UNIVERSITÉ DU QUÉBEC À RIMOUSKI

Education M,D
Project Management M

UNIVERSITÉ DU QUÉBEC À TROIS-RIVIÈRES

Accounting O
Business Administration and Management M,D
Education M,D
Educational Administration O
Educational Psychology M,O
Entrepreneurship M
Finance and Banking O
Industrial Hygiene M
Leisure Studies M
Physical Education M
Project Management M

UNIVERSITÉ DU QUÉBEC, ÉCOLE NATIONALE D'ADMINISTRATION PUBLIQUE

International Business O

UNIVERSITÉ DU QUÉBEC EN ABITIBI-TÉMISCAMINGUE

Business Administration and Management M
Education M,D
Project Management M
Social Work O

UNIVERSITÉ LAVAL

Allopathic Medicine P
Business Administration and Management M,D,O
Community Health M
Counselor Education M,D
Curriculum and Instruction M,D
Dentistry P
Education M,D,O
Educational Administration M,D,O
Educational Measurement and Evaluation M,D
Educational Media/Instructional Technology M,D
Educational Psychology M,D,O
Environmental and Occupational Health O
Epidemiology M,D
Law M,D,O
Nursing M
Oral and Dental Sciences M,O
Pharmaceutical Sciences M,D,O
Physical Education M,D
Social Work M,D

UNIVERSITY COLLEGE OF CAPE BRETON

Business Administration and Management M

THE UNIVERSITY OF AKRON

Accounting M
Business Administration and Management M
Communication Disorders M
Counselor Education M
Education M,D
Educational Administration M,D
Elementary Education M,D
Exercise and Sports Science M
Finance and Banking M
Higher Education M
Human Resources Management M
International Business M
Law P
Management Information Systems M
Marketing M
Music Education M
Nursing M
Nursing Administration M
Nursing Education M
Physical Education M
Secondary Education M,D
Social Work M
Special Education M
Taxation M
Vocational and Technical Education M

THE UNIVERSITY OF ALABAMA (TUSCALOOSA)

Accounting M,D
Advertising and Public Relations M,D
Art Education M
Business Administration and Management M,D
Communication Disorders M
Counselor Education D,O
Curriculum and Instruction D
Early Childhood Education M,O
Education M,D,O
Educational Administration M,D,O
Educational Measurement and Evaluation D
Educational Psychology M,D,O
Elementary Education M,D,O
English as a Second Language M
Finance and Banking M,D
Health Education M,D,O
Health Promotion M,D
Higher Education M,D,O
Hospitality Management M
Industrial and Manufacturing Management M,D
Information Studies M,O
Law P,M*
Library Science M,O
Marketing M,D
Music Education M,D,O
Secondary Education M,D,O
Social Work M,D

Special Education M,D,O
Taxation M

THE UNIVERSITY OF ALABAMA AT BIRMINGHAM

Allied Health M,D,O
Allopathic Medicine P,M,D
Art Education M,O
Business Administration and Management M,D
Clinical Laboratory Sciences M
Counselor Education M
Dentistry P,M,D
Early Childhood Education M,D,O
Education M,D,O
Educational Administration M,D,O
Elementary Education M,O
Environmental and Occupational Health M,D*
Epidemiology M,D*
Health Education M,D,O
Health Promotion D,O*
Health Services Management and Hospital Administration M,D*
Industrial Hygiene M,D*
International Health M,D*
Maternal and Child Health M*
Music Education M
Nurse Anesthesia M
Nursing M,D*
Occupational Therapy M
Optometry P,M,D
Oral and Dental Sciences M
Physical Education M,O
Physical Therapy M
Public Health M,D*
Secondary Education M,O
Special Education M,O
Vision Sciences M,D

THE UNIVERSITY OF ALABAMA IN HUNTSVILLE

Accounting M
Business Administration and Management M
Nursing M
Vision Sciences D

UNIVERSITY OF ALASKA ANCHORAGE

Adult Education M
Business Administration and Management M
Counselor Education M
Education M
Educational Administration M
Nursing M
Social Work M
Special Education M
Vocational and Technical Education M

UNIVERSITY OF ALASKA FAIRBANKS

Business Administration and Management M
Counselor Education M
Curriculum and Instruction M
Education M,O
Educational Administration M
English Education M
Mathematics Education M,D
Multilingual and Multicultural Education M,O
Music Education M
Science Education M,D

UNIVERSITY OF ALASKA SOUTHEAST

Business Administration and Management M
Early Childhood Education M
Education M
Elementary Education M
Secondary Education M

UNIVERSITY OF ALBERTA

Accounting D
Adult Education M
Allopathic Medicine P
Business Administration and Management M,D
Communication Disorders M
Counselor Education M
Dental Hygiene O
Dentistry P
Educational Administration M,D,O
Educational Media/Instructional Technology M
Educational Psychology M,D
Elementary Education M,D
English as a Second Language M
Environmental and Occupational Health M,D
Epidemiology M,D
Exercise and Sports Science M,D
Finance and Banking M,D
Foundations and Philosophy of Education M,D,O
Health Physics/Radiological Health M,D
Health Promotion M,O
Health Services Management and Hospital Administration M,D,O
Health Services Research M
Information Studies M
International and Comparative Education M,D
International Business M
Law P,M,O
Library Science M
Marketing D
Medical Physics M,D
Medical Technology M,D
Multilingual and Multicultural Education M,D
Nursing M,D
Occupational Therapy M
Oral and Dental Sciences M,D,O
Organizational Behavior D
Pharmaceutical Sciences M,D
Physical Education M,D
Physical Therapy M
Public Health M,D,O
Recreation and Park Management M,D
Rehabilitation Sciences D
Secondary Education M,D
Special Education M,D
Sports Administration M
Vision Sciences M,D

THE UNIVERSITY OF ARIZONA

Accounting M
Agricultural Education M
Allopathic Medicine P
Art Education M
Business Administration and Management M,D
Communication Disorders M,D
Education M,D,O*
Educational Administration M,D,O
Educational Psychology M,D
Elementary Education M,D
English as a Second Language M,D
English Education D
Epidemiology M,D
Exercise and Sports Science M
Finance and Banking M
Health Education M
Higher Education M,D
Home Economics Education M
Information Studies M,D
Law P,M
Library Science M,D
Management Information Systems M
Management Strategy and Policy M
Marketing M
Multilingual and Multicultural Education M,D,O
Music Education M,D
Nursing M,D
Pharmaceutical Sciences M,D
Pharmacy P,M,D
Public Health M*
Reading Education M,D,O
Secondary Education M,D,O
Special Education M,D,O
Veterinary Sciences M,D

UNIVERSITY OF ARKANSAS (FAYETTEVILLE)

Accounting M
Adult Education M,D,O
Agricultural Education M
Business Administration and Management M,D*
Communication Disorders M
Counselor Education M,D,O
Curriculum and Instruction D
Early Childhood Education M
Education M,D,O
Educational Administration M,D,O
Educational Media/Instructional Technology M
Elementary Education M
Health Education M,D
Higher Education M,D,O
Kinesiology and Movement Studies M,D
Law P,M
Logistics M
Management Information Systems M
Mathematics Education M
Middle School Education M
Music Education M
Physical Education M
Recreation and Park Management M
Secondary Education M
Special Education M
Transportation Management M
Vocational and Technical Education M,D,O

UNIVERSITY OF ARKANSAS AT LITTLE ROCK

Adult Education M
Art Education M
Business Administration and Management M
Counselor Education M
Early Childhood Education M,O
Education M,D,O
Educational Administration M,D,O
Educational Media/Instructional Technology M
Education of the Gifted M
Education of the Multiply Handicapped M
Elementary Education M,O
Health Services Management and Hospital Administration M
Higher Education D
Law P
Reading Education M,O
Secondary Education M
Social Work M
Special Education M

UNIVERSITY OF ARKANSAS AT MONTICELLO

Education M
Elementary Education M
Secondary Education M

UNIVERSITY OF ARKANSAS AT PINE BLUFF

Education M
Elementary Education M
English Education M
Mathematics Education M
Physical Education M
Science Education M
Secondary Education M
Social Sciences Education M

UNIVERSITY OF ARKANSAS FOR MEDICAL SCIENCES

Allopathic Medicine P
Communication Disorders M
Environmental and Occupational Health M
Nursing M,D
Pharmaceutical Sciences P,M
Pharmacy P,M

UNIVERSITY OF BALTIMORE

Accounting M
Business Administration and Management M
Finance and Banking M
Law P,M
Legal and Justice Studies M
Management Information Systems M
Taxation M

UNIVERSITY OF BRIDGEPORT

Business Administration and Management M*
Chiropractic P*
Computer Education M,O
Early Childhood Education M,O
Education M,D,O*
Educational Administration D,O
Elementary Education M,O
Human Resources Development M*
Human Services M*
International and Comparative Education M,O
Naturopathic Medicine D*
Reading Education M,O
Secondary Education M,O

UNIVERSITY OF BRITISH COLUMBIA

Accounting D
Adult Education M
Allopathic Medicine P,M
Art Education M,D
Business Administration and Management M,D
Business Education M
Communication Disorders M,D
Community Health M
Curriculum and Instruction M,D
Dentistry P
Early Childhood Education M
Education M,D,O
Educational Administration M,D
Educational Measurement and Evaluation M
Educational Psychology M,D
English as a Second Language M,D
English Education M,D
Environmental and Occupational Health M,D
Epidemiology M,D
Finance and Banking M,D
Foundations and Philosophy of Education M,D
Health Services Management and Hospital Administration M
Health Services Research M,D
Higher Education M
Home Economics Education M,D
Information Studies M,O
Kinesiology and Movement Studies M,D
Law M,D
Library Science M,O
Logistics M
Management Information Systems M,D
Management Strategy and Policy D
Marketing D
Mathematics Education M,D
Music Education M,D
Nursing M,D
Oral and Dental Sciences M,D,O
Organizational Behavior D
Pharmaceutical Sciences M,D
Pharmacy P
Reading Education M,D
Rehabilitation Sciences M
Science Education M,D
Social Sciences Education M,D
Social Work M
Special Education M,D
Transportation Management M
Vocational and Technical Education M,D

THE UNIVERSITY OF CALGARY

Adult Education M,D
Allopathic Medicine P
Business Administration and Management M,D*
Community Health M,D
Curriculum and Instruction M,D
Education M,D
Educational Administration M,D
Educational Media/Instructional Technology M,D
Educational Psychology M,D
Epidemiology M,D
Kinesiology and Movement Studies M
Law P,M
Nursing M,D
Social Work M,D
Special Education M,D

UNIVERSITY OF CALIFORNIA, BERKELEY

Accounting D
Business Administration and Management M,D*
Education M,D,O
Educational Administration M,D
Educational Measurement and Evaluation M,D
English Education O
Environmental and Occupational Health M,D
Epidemiology M,D
Finance and Banking D
Foundations and Philosophy of Education M,D
Health Education M
Health Services Management and Hospital Administration M,D
Information Studies M,D
Law P,M,D
Legal and Justice Studies D
Marketing D
Maternal and Child Health M
Mathematics Education M,D
Multilingual and Multicultural Education M,D,O
Optometry P
Organizational Behavior D
Public Health M,D
Reading Education M,D,O
Science Education M,D
Social Work M,D
Special Education D
Vision Sciences M,D

UNIVERSITY OF CALIFORNIA, DAVIS

Allopathic Medicine P
Business Administration and Management M*
Curriculum and Instruction D
Education M,D
Educational Psychology D
Epidemiology M,D
Exercise and Sports Science M
Law P,M
Transportation Management M,D
Veterinary Medicine P
Veterinary Sciences M,O

UNIVERSITY OF CALIFORNIA, HASTINGS COLLEGE OF THE LAW

Law P

UNIVERSITY OF CALIFORNIA, IRVINE

Allopathic Medicine P
Business Administration and Management M,D*
Education D
Educational Administration D
Environmental and Occupational Health M,D

UNIVERSITY OF CALIFORNIA, LOS ANGELES

Allopathic Medicine P
Business Administration and Management M,D*
Community Health M,D
Dentistry P,O
Education M,D
Educational Administration D
English as a Second Language M,O
Environmental and Occupational Health M,D*
Epidemiology M,D
Health Services Management and Hospital Administration M,D
Information Studies M,D,O
Law P,M
Library Science M,D,O
Medical Physics M,D
Nursing M,D
Oral and Dental Sciences M,D
Public Health M,D
Science Education M
Social Work M,D
Special Education D

UNIVERSITY OF CALIFORNIA, RIVERSIDE

Business Administration and Management M*
Education M,D

UNIVERSITY OF CALIFORNIA, SAN DIEGO

Allopathic Medicine P
Communication Disorders D
Education M
Epidemiology D
Public Health D

UNIVERSITY OF CALIFORNIA, SAN FRANCISCO

Allopathic Medicine P,D
Dentistry P
Nursing M,D
Oral and Dental Sciences M,D
Pharmaceutical Sciences D*
Pharmacy P*
Physical Therapy M

UNIVERSITY OF CALIFORNIA, SANTA BARBARA

Communication Disorders M,D
Education M,D

UNIVERSITY OF CALIFORNIA, SANTA CRUZ

Education M,O

UNIVERSITY OF CENTRAL ARKANSAS

Business Administration and Management M
Business Education M
Communication Disorders M
Counselor Education M
Early Childhood Education M
Education M,O
Educational Administration M,O
Educational Media/Instructional Technology M
Elementary Education M
Health Education M
Kinesiology and Movement Studies M
Library Science M
Music Education M
Nursing M
Occupational Therapy M
Physical Therapy M,D
Reading Education M
Secondary Education M
Special Education M

UNIVERSITY OF CENTRAL FLORIDA

Accounting M
Art Education M
Business Administration and Management M,D*
Business Education M
Communication Disorders M
Counselor Education M
Curriculum and Instruction D,O
Education M,D,O
Educational Administration M,D,O
Educational Media/Instructional Technology M,D
Elementary Education M
English as a Second Language M
English Education M
Finance and Banking D
Foreign Languages Education M
Health Services Management and Hospital Administration M
Mathematics Education M
Music Education M
Nursing M
Physical Education M
Reading Education M
Science Education M
Secondary Education M
Social Sciences Education M
Social Work M
Special Education M
Taxation M
Vocational and Technical Education M

UNIVERSITY OF CENTRAL OKLAHOMA

Adult Education M
Business Administration and Management M
Communication Disorders M
Computer Education M
Counselor Education M
Early Childhood Education M
Education M
Educational Administration M
Educational Media/Instructional Technology M
Elementary Education M
Health Education M
Higher Education M
Mathematics Education M
Music Education M
Reading Education M
Secondary Education M
Special Education M

UNIVERSITY OF CENTRAL TEXAS

Business Administration and Management M

UNIVERSITY OF CHARLESTON

Business Administration and Management M
Human Resources Management M

UNIVERSITY OF CHARLESTON, SOUTH CAROLINA

Accounting M
Business Administration and Management M
Early Childhood Education M
Education M
Elementary Education M
Legal and Justice Studies M
Special Education M

UNIVERSITY OF CHICAGO

Accounting M
Allopathic Medicine P
Business Administration and Management M,D
Education M,O
Finance and Banking M
Health Services Management and Hospital Administration M,O*
International Business M
Law P,M,D
Medical Physics M,D*
Social Work M,D*
Vision Sciences M,D

UNIVERSITY OF CINCINNATI

Accounting M,D
Advanced Practice Nursing M
Allopathic Medicine P
Art Education M
Business Administration and Management M,D
Communication Disorders M,D
Counselor Education M,D,O
Curriculum and Instruction M,D
Early Childhood Education M
Education M,D,O*
Educational Administration M,D,O
Elementary Education M,D
Environmental and Occupational Health M,D*
Epidemiology M*
Finance and Banking M,D
Foundations and Philosophy of Education M,D
Health Education M
Health Physics/Radiological Health M,D
Health Services Management and Hospital Administration M
Industrial and Manufacturing Management M,D
Industrial Hygiene M*
International Business M
Law P
Management Information Systems M,D
Marketing M,D
Maternal/Child-Care Nursing M
Mathematics Education M
Medical/Surgical Nursing M
Music Education M,D
Nurse Anesthesia M
Nurse Midwifery M
Nursing M,D
Nursing Administration M
Pharmaceutical Sciences M,D*
Pharmacy P*
Psychiatric Nursing M
Public Health Nursing M
Quantitative Analysis M,D
Reading Education M,D
Real Estate M
Secondary Education M
Social Work M
Special Education M,D

UNIVERSITY OF COLORADO AT BOULDER

Accounting M
Business Administration and Management M,D*
Communication Disorders M,D
Curriculum and Instruction M,D
Education M,D
Educational Measurement and Evaluation D
Educational Psychology M,D
Entrepreneurship M
Finance and Banking M,D
Kinesiology and Movement Studies M,D
Law P
Marketing M,D
Medical Physics D
Multilingual and Multicultural Education M,D
Music Education M,D
Organizational Behavior M,D
Physical Education M
Taxation M

UNIVERSITY OF COLORADO AT COLORADO SPRINGS

Accounting M
Advanced Practice Nursing M
Business Administration and Management M
Counselor Education M
Curriculum and Instruction M
Education M
Finance and Banking M
Human Services M
Industrial and Manufacturing Management M
Management Information Systems M
Marketing M
Maternal/Child-Care Nursing M
Medical/Surgical Nursing M
Nursing M
Organizational Behavior M
Special Education M

UNIVERSITY OF COLORADO AT DENVER

Accounting M
Business Administration and Management M*
Counselor Education M
Curriculum and Instruction M
Early Childhood Education M
Education M,D,O
Educational Administration M,D,O
Educational Media/Instructional Technology M
Educational Psychology M
English as a Second Language M*
Finance and Banking M
Health Education D
Health Services Management and Hospital Administration M*
International Business M
Management Information Systems M
Marketing M
Special Education M

UNIVERSITY OF COLORADO HEALTH SCIENCES CENTER

Allopathic Medicine P
Clinical Laboratory Sciences D
Dentistry P
Medical Physics M
Nursing M,D*
Pharmaceutical Sciences M,D*
Pharmacy P
Physical Therapy M
Physician Assistant Studies M
Public Health M*

UNIVERSITY OF CONNECTICUT

Accounting M,D
Adult Education M,D
Allied Health M
Business Administration and Management M,D*
Communication Disorders M,D
Curriculum and Instruction M,D
Education M,D
Educational Administration M,D
Educational Measurement and Evaluation M,D
Educational Media/Instructional Technology M,D
Educational Psychology M,D
Education of the Gifted M,D
Elementary Education M,D
English Education M,D
Exercise and Sports Science M,D
Finance and Banking D
Foreign Languages Education M,D
Foundations and Philosophy of Education M,D
Health Services Management and Hospital Administration M
Higher Education M,D
Human Resources Management M
International Business
Law P
Leisure Studies M,D
Marketing M,D
Mathematics Education M,D
Multilingual and Multicultural Education M,D
Music Education M,D
Nursing M,D
Nursing Administration M
Nursing Education M
Oral and Dental Sciences M
Pharmaceutical Sciences M,D*
Public Health M
Reading Education M,D
Science Education M,D
Secondary Education M,D
Social Sciences Education M,D
Social Work M
Special Education M,D
Vocational and Technical Education M,D

UNIVERSITY OF CONNECTICUT HEALTH CENTER

Allopathic Medicine P
Dentistry P
Oral and Dental Sciences M,D
Public Health M

UNIVERSITY OF DALLAS

Business Administration and Management M*
Finance and Banking M
Health Services Management and Hospital Administration M
Human Resources Management M
Industrial and Manufacturing Management M
International Business M
Management Information Systems M
Marketing M

UNIVERSITY OF DAYTON

Business Administration and Management M
Counselor Education M
Education M,D,O
Educational Administration M,D,O
Law P
Physical Education M
Social Work M

UNIVERSITY OF DELAWARE

Accounting M
Advanced Practice Nursing M,O
Business Administration and Management M*
Counselor Education M
Curriculum and Instruction M,D
Education M,D
Educational Administration M,D
Educational Measurement and Evaluation M,D
English as a Second Language M
English Education M
Exercise and Sports Science M
Foreign Languages Education M
Gerontological Nursing M,O
Health Promotion M
Higher Education M
Kinesiology and Movement Studies M,D
Maternal/Child-Care Nursing M,O
Multilingual and Multicultural Education M
Nursing M,O
Nursing Administration M,O
Oncology Nursing M,O
Physical Education M
Physical Therapy M
Rehabilitation Sciences M
Secondary Education M
Special Education M

UNIVERSITY OF DENVER

- Accounting M
- Adult Education M,D
- Advertising and Public Relations M
- Business Administration and Management M*
- Curriculum and Instruction M,D
- Education M,D,O
- Educational Administration M,D
- Educational Measurement and Evaluation M,D
- Finance and Banking M
- Health Services Management and Hospital Administration M
- Higher Education M,D
- Hospitality Management M
- Information Studies M
- Law P,M
- Legal and Justice Studies M
- Library Science M
- Management Information Systems M
- Marketing M
- Music Education M
- Public Health M
- Real Estate M
- Social Sciences Education M
- Social Work M,D*
- Sports Administration M
- Taxation M*
- Travel and Tourism M

UNIVERSITY OF DETROIT MERCY

- Allied Health M
- Business Administration and Management M*
- Counselor Education M
- Curriculum and Instruction M
- Dentistry P,M,O
- Early Childhood Education M
- Education M,O*
- Educational Administration M,O
- Health Education M
- Health Services Management and Hospital Administration M
- Law P
- Management Information Systems M
- Mathematics Education M
- Nurse Anesthesia M
- Oral and Dental Sciences M,O
- Physician Assistant Studies M*
- Special Education M

UNIVERSITY OF DUBUQUE

- Business Administration and Management M
- Education M
- Special Education M
- Transportation Management M

UNIVERSITY OF EVANSVILLE

- Counselor Education M
- Education M
- Health Services Management and Hospital Administration M
- Nursing M
- Special Education M

THE UNIVERSITY OF FINDLAY

- Business Administration and Management M
- Early Childhood Education M
- Education M
- Educational Administration M
- Educational Media/Instructional Technology M
- Elementary Education M
- English as a Second Language M
- Finance and Banking M
- Human Resources Management M
- International Business M
- Marketing M
- Multilingual and Multicultural Education M
- Special Education M

UNIVERSITY OF FLORIDA

- Accounting M,D
- Advertising and Public Relations M,D
- Agricultural Education M
- Allied Health M,D
- Allopathic Medicine P
- Art Education M
- Business Administration and Management M,D
- Communication Disorders M,D
- Computer Education M,D,O
- Counselor Education M,D,O
- Dentistry P
- Early Childhood Education M,D,O
- Education M,D,O*
- Educational Administration M,D,O
- Educational Measurement and Evaluation M,D,O
- Educational Media/Instructional Technology M,D,O
- Educational Psychology M,D,O
- Elementary Education M,D,O
- English as a Second Language O
- English Education M,D,O
- Exercise and Sports Science M,D
- Finance and Banking M,D
- Foreign Languages Education M,D,O
- Foundations and Philosophy of Education M,D,O
- Health Education M,D
- Health Physics/Radiological Health M,D
- Health Services Management and Hospital Administration M,D
- Higher Education D,O
- Human Resources Management D
- International and Comparative Education M,D,O
- Law P,M
- Management Information Systems M,D
- Management Strategy and Policy D
- Marketing M,D
- Mathematics Education M,D,O
- Medical Physics M,D
- Middle School Education M,D,O
- Multilingual and Multicultural Education M,D,O
- Music Education M,D
- Nursing M,D
- Occupational Therapy M
- Oral and Dental Sciences M,D
- Pharmaceutical Sciences M,D
- Pharmacy P
- Physical Education D
- Physical Therapy M
- Physician Assistant Studies M
- Reading Education M,D,O
- Real Estate M,D
- Recreation and Park Management M,D
- Rehabilitation Sciences D
- Science Education M,D,O
- Secondary Education M,D,O
- Social Sciences Education M,D,O
- Special Education M,D,O
- Taxation M
- Veterinary Medicine P
- Veterinary Sciences M,D

UNIVERSITY OF GEORGIA

- Accounting M
- Adult Education M,D,O
- Agricultural Education M
- Art Education M,D,O
- Business Administration and Management M,D*
- Business Education M
- Communication Disorders M,D,O
- Computer Education M
- Counselor Education M,D
- Early Childhood Education M,D,O
- Education M,D,O
- Educational Administration M,D,O
- Educational Media/Instructional Technology M,D,O
- Educational Psychology M,D,O
- Education of the Gifted D
- Elementary Education M,D,O
- English Education M,O
- Environmental and Occupational Health M
- Exercise and Sports Science M,D,O
- Foreign Languages Education M,D,O
- Health Education M,D,O
- Health Promotion M,D,O
- Health Services Management and Hospital Administration M,D*
- Higher Education D
- Home Economics Education M
- Human Resources Development M*
- Law P,M
- Leisure Studies M,D
- Marketing Research M
- Mathematics Education M,D,O
- Middle School Education M,D,O
- Music Education M,D,O
- Pharmaceutical Sciences M,D*
- Pharmacy P
- Physical Education M,D,O
- Reading Education M,D,O
- Recreation and Park Management M,D
- Science Education M,D,O
- Secondary Education M,D,O
- Social Sciences Education M,D,O
- Social Work M,D*
- Special Education M,D,O
- Veterinary Medicine P
- Veterinary Sciences M,D
- Vocational and Technical Education M,D,O

UNIVERSITY OF GREAT FALLS

- Counselor Education M
- Curriculum and Instruction M
- Education M
- Educational Administration M
- Elementary Education M
- Secondary Education M

UNIVERSITY OF GUAM

- Business Administration and Management M
- Counselor Education M
- Education M
- Educational Administration M
- English as a Second Language M
- Reading Education M
- Secondary Education M
- Special Education M

UNIVERSITY OF GUELPH

- Epidemiology M,D
- Hospitality Management M
- Medical Technology M,D
- Veterinary Medicine M,D
- Veterinary Sciences M,D,O
- Vision Sciences M,D

UNIVERSITY OF HARTFORD

- Accounting M
- Business Administration and Management M
- Counselor Education M,O
- Early Childhood Education M
- Education M,D,O
- Educational Administration M,D,O
- Educational Media/Instructional Technology M
- Elementary Education M
- Finance and Banking M
- Human Resources Management M
- Industrial and Manufacturing Management M
- Insurance M
- International Business M
- Management Information Systems M
- Management Strategy and Policy M
- Marketing M
- Music Education M,D
- Nursing M
- Organizational Behavior M
- Quantitative Analysis M
- Secondary Education M
- Special Education M
- Taxation M

UNIVERSITY OF HAWAII AT MANOA

- Accounting M
- Advanced Practice Nursing M
- Allopathic Medicine P
- Business Administration and Management M
- Communication Disorders M
- Community Health M
- Counselor Education M
- Curriculum and Instruction D
- Education M,D
- Educational Administration M,D
- Educational Measurement and Evaluation D
- Educational Media/Instructional Technology M
- Educational Psychology M,D
- Elementary Education M
- English as a Second Language M,D
- Environmental and Occupational Health M
- Epidemiology M,D
- Foreign Languages Education D
- Foundations and Philosophy of Education M,D
- Health Education M
- Health Promotion D
- Health Services Management and Hospital Administration M
- Hospitality Management M
- Information Studies M,D,O*
- International Business D
- International Health M
- Law P
- Library Science M,D,O
- Maternal and Child Health M
- Medical/Surgical Nursing M
- Nursing M,O
- Nursing Administration M
- Public Health M,D
- Public Health Nursing M
- Secondary Education M
- Social Work M,D
- Special Education M,D
- Travel and Tourism M

UNIVERSITY OF HEALTH SCIENCES

- Osteopathic Medicine P*

UNIVERSITY OF HOUSTON

- Accounting M,D
- Advertising and Public Relations M
- Art Education M
- Business Administration and Management M,D*
- Communication Disorders M
- Curriculum and Instruction M,D
- Early Childhood Education M
- Education M,D
- Educational Administration M,D
- Educational Psychology M,D
- Education of the Gifted M
- Elementary Education M
- English as a Second Language M
- Entrepreneurship M,D
- Exercise and Sports Science M
- Finance and Banking M,D
- Foundations and Philosophy of Education M,D
- Health Education M,D
- Health Services Management and Hospital Administration M
- Higher Education M
- Hospitality Management M*
- Industrial and Manufacturing Management M,D
- International Business M
- Law P,M
- Management Information Systems M,D
- Marketing M,D
- Mathematics Education M
- Multilingual and Multicultural Education M
- Music Education M,D
- Optometry P*
- Pharmaceutical Sciences M,D
- Pharmacy P,M
- Physical Education M,D
- Reading Education M
- Science Education M
- Secondary Education M
- Social Sciences Education M
- Social Work M,D
- Special Education M,D
- Taxation M,D
- Vision Sciences M,D*

UNIVERSITY OF HOUSTON–CLEAR LAKE

- Accounting M
- Business Administration and Management M
- Counselor Education M
- Curriculum and Instruction M
- Early Childhood Education M
- Education M
- Educational Administration M
- Educational Media/Instructional Technology M
- Exercise and Sports Science M
- Finance and Banking M
- Health Services Management and Hospital Administration M
- Human Resources Management M
- Multilingual and Multicultural Education M
- Reading Education M
- Secondary Education M

UNIVERSITY OF HOUSTON–VICTORIA

- Business Administration and Management M
- Education M

UNIVERSITY OF IDAHO

- Accounting M
- Adult Education M,D
- Agricultural Education M
- Art Education M
- Business Administration and Management M
- Business Education M
- Counselor Education M,D,O
- Education M,D,O
- Educational Administration M,D,O
- Elementary Education M
- English as a Second Language M
- English Education M
- Foreign Languages Education M
- Law P
- Mathematics Education M
- Physical Education M,D
- Recreation and Park Management M
- Science Education M
- Secondary Education M
- Social Sciences Education M
- Special Education M,O
- Veterinary Sciences M,D
- Vocational and Technical Education M,D,O

UNIVERSITY OF ILLINOIS AT CHICAGO

- Accounting M
- Allied Health M,D
- Allopathic Medicine P
- Business Administration and Management M*
- Clinical Laboratory Sciences M
- Community Health M,D
- Curriculum and Instruction M,D
- Dentistry P
- Education M,D
- Educational Administration M,D
- Elementary Education M
- English as a Second Language M
- English Education M
- Environmental and Occupational Health M,D
- Epidemiology M,D
- Finance and Banking D
- Health Education M
- Health Services Management and Hospital Administration M,D
- Human Resources Management D
- Kinesiology and Movement Studies M
- Management Information Systems M,D
- Marketing D
- Maternal/Child-Care Nursing M
- Mathematics Education M
- Medical/Surgical Nursing M
- Nurse Midwifery M
- Nursing M,D
- Nursing Administration M
- Occupational Therapy M
- Oral and Dental Sciences M
- Pharmaceutical Sciences M,D
- Pharmacy P
- Physical Therapy M
- Psychiatric Nursing M
- Public Health M,D
- Public Health Nursing M
- Reading Education M
- Secondary Education M
- Social Work M,D
- Special Education M,D

UNIVERSITY OF ILLINOIS AT SPRINGFIELD

- Accounting M
- Business Administration and Management M
- Educational Administration M
- Legal and Justice Studies M
- Management Information Systems M
- Public Health M

UNIVERSITY OF ILLINOIS AT URBANA–CHAMPAIGN

- Accounting M,D*
- Advertising and Public Relations M
- Agricultural Education M
- Allopathic Medicine
- Art Education M,D
- Business Administration and Management M,D*
- Communication Disorders M,D*
- Community Health M,D
- Curriculum and Instruction M,D,O
- Education M,D,O*
- Educational Administration M,D,O
- Educational Psychology M,D,O
- English as a Second Language M
- Finance and Banking M,D*
- Foreign Languages Education M
- Foundations and Philosophy of Education M,D,O
- Health Physics/Radiological Health M,D
- Human Resources Management M,D*
- Information Studies M,D,O*
- Kinesiology and Movement Studies M,D*
- Law P,M,D
- Leisure Studies M,D
- Library Science M,D,O*
- Mathematics Education M
- Rehabilitation Sciences M
- Social Work M,D
- Special Education M,D,O
- Veterinary Medicine P
- Veterinary Sciences M,D*
- Vocational and Technical Education M,D,O

UNIVERSITY OF INDIANAPOLIS

- Accounting M
- Art Education M
- Business Administration and Management M
- Education M
- Elementary Education M
- English Education M
- Occupational Therapy M
- Physical Therapy M
- Secondary Education M
- Social Sciences Education M

THE UNIVERSITY OF IOWA

- Accounting M,D
- Allopathic Medicine P
- Art Education M,D
- Business Administration and Management M,D*
- Communication Disorders M,D
- Community Health M
- Counselor Education M,D,O
- Curriculum and Instruction O
- Dentistry P
- Early Childhood Education M,D,O
- Education M,D,O
- Educational Administration M,D,O
- Educational Measurement and Evaluation M,D,O
- Educational Media/Instructional Technology M,D,O
- Educational Psychology M,D,O
- Elementary Education M,D,O
- English Education D
- Environmental and Occupational Health M,D
- Epidemiology M,D
- Exercise and Sports Science M,D
- Finance and Banking D
- Foundations and Philosophy of Education M,D
- Health Services Management and Hospital Administration M,D*
- Higher Education M,D,O
- Human Resources Management D
- Industrial Hygiene M
- Information Studies M
- Law P,M
- Leisure Studies M
- Library Science M
- Management Information Systems M
- Marketing D
- Music Education M,D
- Nursing M,D
- Oral and Dental Sciences M,D,O
- Organizational Behavior D
- Pharmaceutical Sciences M,D
- Pharmacy P
- Physical Education M,D
- Physical Therapy M,D
- Physician Assistant Studies M
- Public Health M
- Quality Management M
- Science Education M,D
- Secondary Education M,D,O
- Social Work M,D
- Special Education M,D,O

UNIVERSITY OF JUDAISM

- Business Administration and Management M
- Education M
- Nonprofit Management M

UNIVERSITY OF KANSAS

- Accounting M,D
- Allied Health M,D
- Allopathic Medicine P
- Art Education M
- Business Administration and Management M*
- Communication Disorders M,D
- Early Childhood Education M,D
- Education M,D,O
- Educational Administration M,D,O
- Education of the Gifted M,D,O
- English as a Second Language M,D
- Finance and Banking D
- Foundations and Philosophy of Education M,D
- Health Education M,D
- Health Services Management and Hospital Administration M
- Higher Education M,D
- Law P
- Marketing D
- Music Education M,D
- Nurse Anesthesia M
- Nursing M,D
- Occupational Therapy M
- Pharmaceutical Sciences M,D*
- Physical Education M,D
- Physical Therapy M
- Public Health M
- Reading Education M,D,O
- Social Work M,D
- Special Education M,D,O

UNIVERSITY OF KENTUCKY

- Accounting M
- Allied Health M
- Allopathic Medicine P
- Art Education M
- Business Administration and Management M,D*
- Communication Disorders M
- Curriculum and Instruction M,D
- Dentistry P,M
- Education M,D,O
- Educational Administration D,O
- Educational Measurement and Evaluation M,D
- Educational Psychology M,D,O
- Foundations and Philosophy of Education M,D
- Health Physics/Radiological Health M
- Health Promotion M,D
- Health Services Management and Hospital Administration M
- Higher Education M
- International Business M
- Kinesiology and Movement Studies M,D
- Law P
- Library Science M
- Medical Physics M*
- Nursing M,D*
- Oral and Dental Sciences M
- Pharmaceutical Sciences M,D
- Pharmacy P
- Physical Therapy M
- Public Health M
- Social Work M,D
- Special Education M,D,O
- Veterinary Sciences M,D*
- Vocational and Technical Education M,D,O

UNIVERSITY OF LA VERNE

- Business Administration and Management M
- Counselor Education M
- Education M,O
- Educational Administration M,D,O
- Health Services Management and Hospital Administration M
- Industrial and Manufacturing Management M
- Law P*
- Organizational Behavior M
- Reading Education M
- Special Education M

UNIVERSITY OF LETHBRIDGE

- Education M

UNIVERSITY OF LOUISVILLE

- Allied Health M
- Allopathic Medicine P
- Art Education M
- Business Administration and Management M
- Business Education M
- Communication Disorders M
- Counselor Education M,D,O
- Dentistry P
- Early Childhood Education M
- Education M,D,O
- Educational Administration M,D,O
- Educational Measurement and Evaluation D
- Elementary Education M,O
- Exercise and Sports Science M
- Foreign Languages Education M
- Higher Education M,O
- Law P
- Middle School Education M
- Music Education M
- Nursing M
- Oral and Dental Sciences M
- Physical Education M
- Reading Education M
- Secondary Education M,O
- Social Work M,D*
- Special Education M,D,O
- Vision Sciences D
- Vocational and Technical Education M

UNIVERSITY OF MAINE (ORONO)

- Business Administration and Management M*
- Communication Disorders M
- Counselor Education M,O
- Education M,D,O*
- Educational Administration M,D,O
- Elementary Education M,O
- Foreign Languages Education M
- Higher Education M,O
- Kinesiology and Movement Studies M,O
- Nursing M,O
- Physical Education M,O
- Reading Education M,D,O
- Science Education M,O
- Secondary Education M,O
- Social Sciences Education M,O
- Social Work M
- Special Education M,O

UNIVERSITY OF MAINE SCHOOL OF LAW (SEE UNIVERSITY OF SOUTHERN MAINE)

UNIVERSITY OF MANITOBA

- Accounting M
- Actuarial Science M
- Art Education M
- Business Administration and Management M
- Business Education M
- Community Health M,D
- Counselor Education M
- Curriculum and Instruction M
- Dentistry P
- Early Childhood Education M
- Education M,D
- Educational Administration M,D
- Educational Measurement and Evaluation M
- Educational Media/Instructional Technology M
- English as a Second Language M
- Finance and Banking M
- Foreign Languages Education M
- Foundations and Philosophy of Education M
- Health Education M
- Home Economics Education M
- Law M
- Legal and Justice Studies M
- Marketing M
- Mathematics Education M
- Music Education M
- Nursing M
- Oral and Dental Sciences M,D,O
- Pharmaceutical Sciences M,D
- Physical Education M
- Reading Education M
- Recreation and Park Management M
- Rehabilitation Sciences M
- Science Education M
- Social Sciences Education M
- Social Work M
- Special Education M
- Vocational and Technical Education M

UNIVERSITY OF MARY

- Advanced Practice Nursing M
- Business Administration and Management M
- Education M
- Educational Administration M
- Elementary Education M
- Higher Education M
- Nursing M
- Nursing Administration M
- Nursing Education M
- Physical Therapy M
- Secondary Education M
- Special Education M

UNIVERSITY OF MARY HARDIN–BAYLOR

- Business Administration and Management M
- Education M
- Educational Administration M
- Educational Psychology M
- Health Services Management and Hospital Administration M
- Reading Education M

UNIVERSITY OF MARYLAND, BALTIMORE

- Allopathic Medicine P
- Bioethics M
- Dental Hygiene M
- Dentistry P
- Epidemiology M,D
- Gerontological Nursing M
- Health Services Management and Hospital Administration D
- Law P
- Maternal/Child-Care Nursing M
- Medical/Surgical Nursing M
- Medical Technology M*
- Nursing M,D
- Nursing Administration M
- Nursing Education M
- Oral and Dental Sciences M,D
- Pharmaceutical Sciences M,D
- Pharmacy P,M,D
- Psychiatric Nursing M
- Public Health Nursing M
- Social Work M,D*

UNIVERSITY OF MARYLAND, BALTIMORE COUNTY

- Education M
- Educational Media/Instructional Technology M
- Epidemiology M
- Health Education M
- Health Services Management and Hospital Administration M

UNIVERSITY OF MARYLAND, COLLEGE PARK

- Advertising and Public Relations M,D
- Agricultural Education M,D,O
- Business Administration and Management M,D*
- Business Education M,D,O

Communication Disorders M,D
Counselor Education M,D,O
Early Childhood Education M,D,O
Education M,D,O
Educational Administration M,D
Educational Measurement and Evaluation M,D
Educational Media/Instructional Technology M,D
Educational Psychology M,D,O
English as a Second Language M
Foundations and Philosophy of Education M,D,O
Health Education M,D
Information Studies M,D*
Kinesiology and Movement Studies M,D
Law
Library Science M,D*
Music Education M,D
Reading Education M,D,O
Recreation and Park Management M,D
Science Education M,D,O
Secondary Education M,D,O
Special Education M,D,O
Vocational and Technical Education M,D,O

UNIVERSITY OF MARYLAND EASTERN SHORE

Agricultural Education M
Counselor Education M
Education M
Physical Therapy M
Special Education M

UNIVERSITY OF MARYLAND UNIVERSITY COLLEGE

Business Administration and Management M*
International Business M
Management Information Systems M

UNIVERSITY OF MASSACHUSETTS AMHERST

Business Administration and Management M,D
Communication Disorders M,D
Counselor Education M,D,O
Curriculum and Instruction M,D,O
Early Childhood Education M,D,O
Education M,D,O*
Educational Administration M,D,O
Educational Measurement and Evaluation M,D,O
Educational Media/Instructional Technology M,D,O
Elementary Education M,D,O
Exercise and Sports Science M,D
Foreign Languages Education M
Higher Education M,D,O
Hospitality Management M
International and Comparative Education M,D,O
Multilingual and Multicultural Education M,D,O
Nursing M,D
Physical Education M,D,O
Public Health M,D
Reading Education M,D,O
Secondary Education M,D,O
Special Education M,D,O
Travel and Tourism M
Veterinary Sciences M,D

UNIVERSITY OF MASSACHUSETTS BOSTON

Business Administration and Management M
Counselor Education M,O
Curriculum and Instruction M
Education M,D,O
Educational Administration M,D,O
Elementary Education M
English as a Second Language M
Higher Education D
Human Services M
Multilingual and Multicultural Education M
Nursing M,D
Secondary Education M
Special Education M
Urban Education D

UNIVERSITY OF MASSACHUSETTS DARTMOUTH

Art Education M
Business Administration and Management M
Education M
Nursing M

UNIVERSITY OF MASSACHUSETTS LOWELL

Allied Health M,D
Business Administration and Management M
Clinical Laboratory Sciences M
Curriculum and Instruction M,D,O
Education M,D,O*
Educational Administration M,D,O
Gerontological Nursing M
Health Physics/Radiological Health M,D
Health Promotion D
Health Services Management and Hospital Administration M
Industrial and Manufacturing Management M
Mathematics Education D
Music Education M
Nursing M,D
Nursing Administration D
Physical Therapy M
Psychiatric Nursing M
Public Health Nursing M
Reading Education M,D,O
Science Education D

UNIVERSITY OF MASSACHUSETTS MEDICAL CENTER AT WORCESTER

Advanced Practice Nursing M
Allopathic Medicine P
Medical Physics D
Medical/Surgical Nursing M,O
Nursing M,D,O
Public Health Nursing M,O

UNIVERSITY OF MEDICINE AND DENTISTRY OF NEW JERSEY

Allied Health M,D,O*
Allopathic Medicine P
Dentistry P,O
Health Education M*
Nurse Midwifery O*
Nursing M,O
Oral and Dental Sciences M
Osteopathic Medicine P
Physical Therapy M*
Physician Assistant Studies M*
Public Health M,D*

THE UNIVERSITY OF MEMPHIS

Accounting M,D
Adult Education D
Business Administration and Management M,D*
Communication Disorders M,D
Counselor Education M,D
Curriculum and Instruction M,D
Early Childhood Education M,D
Education M,D,O
Educational Administration M,D,O
Educational Measurement and Evaluation M,D
Educational Media/Instructional Technology M,D
Educational Psychology M,D
Elementary Education M
Exercise and Sports Science M
Finance and Banking M,D
Health Promotion M
Health Services Management and Hospital Administration M
Higher Education D
Human Resources Management M
International Business M*
Law P
Leisure Studies M
Management Information Systems M,D
Marketing M,D
Music Education M,D
Nonprofit Management M
Reading Education M,D
Real Estate M
Secondary Education M
Special Education M,D
Taxation M

UNIVERSITY OF MIAMI

Accounting M
Advanced Practice Nursing M
Advertising and Public Relations M
Allopathic Medicine P
Business Administration and Management M,D,O*
Early Childhood Education M,O
Education M,D,O*
Educational Administration M,D,O
Educational Measurement and Evaluation M,D
Elementary Education M,O
English as a Second Language M,O
Environmental and Occupational Health M
Epidemiology D*
Exercise and Sports Science M,D*
Health Physics/Radiological Health M
Health Services Management and Hospital Administration O
Higher Education M,D
International Business M
Law P,M
Management Information Systems M,O
Medical/Surgical Nursing M
Music Education M,D,O
Nurse Midwifery M
Nursing M,D
Physical Therapy M,D
Public Health M*
Reading Education M,D,O
Special Education M,D,O
Sports Administration M,D*
Taxation M

UNIVERSITY OF MICHIGAN

Advanced Practice Nursing M
Allopathic Medicine P
Business Administration and Management M,D
Computer Education M,D
Curriculum and Instruction M
Dentistry P
Early Childhood Education M,D
Education M,D*
Educational Administration M,D
Educational Measurement and Evaluation D
English Education M,D
Environmental and Occupational Health M,D*
Epidemiology M,D*
Finance and Banking M
Foreign Languages Education M
Foundations and Philosophy of Education M,D
Gerontological Nursing M
Health Physics/Radiological Health M
Health Promotion M,D*
Health Services Management and Hospital Administration M,D*
Health Services Research M
Higher Education M
Industrial Hygiene M,D*
Information Studies M,D*
International Health M*
Kinesiology and Movement Studies M,D,O*
Law P,M,D
Library Science M,D*
Maternal/Child-Care Nursing M
Mathematics Education M,D
Medical/Surgical Nursing M
Music Education D
Nurse Midwifery M
Nursing M,D,O
Nursing Administration M
Oral and Dental Sciences M,D,O
Pharmaceutical Sciences M,D
Pharmacy P
Psychiatric Nursing M
Public Health M,D*
Public Health Nursing M
Reading Education M,D
Science Education M,D
Social Sciences Education M
Social Work M,D*
Special Education M*

UNIVERSITY OF MICHIGAN–DEARBORN

Adult Education M
Business Administration and Management M
Education M
Special Education M

UNIVERSITY OF MICHIGAN–FLINT

Business Administration and Management M
Health Education M
Nurse Anesthesia M
Physical Therapy M

UNIVERSITY OF MINNESOTA, DULUTH

Allopathic Medicine P
Business Administration and Management M
Communication Disorders M
Educational Psychology M
Music Education M
Social Work M

UNIVERSITY OF MINNESOTA, TWIN CITIES CAMPUS

Accounting M,D
Adult Education M
Advanced Practice Nursing M
Agricultural Education M
Allopathic Medicine P
Art Education M,D
Business Administration and Management M,D*
Business Education M
Clinical Laboratory Sciences M*
Communication Disorders M,D
Community Health M
Curriculum and Instruction M,D
Dentistry P
Early Childhood Education M,D
Education M,D,O*
Educational Administration M,D,O
Educational Measurement and Evaluation M,D
Educational Psychology M,D,O
Elementary Education M,D
English Education M
Environmental and Occupational Health M,D*
Epidemiology M,D*
Finance and Banking M,D
Gerontological Nursing M
Health Services Management and Hospital Administration M,D*
Health Services Research M,D*
Higher Education M,D
Human Resources Management M,D*
Industrial and Manufacturing Management M,D
Industrial Hygiene M,D*
International and Comparative Education M,D
Kinesiology and Movement Studies M,D
Law P,M
Leisure Studies M,D
Logistics M,D
Management Information Systems M,D
Management Strategy and Policy M,D
Marketing M,D
Maternal and Child Health M*
Maternal/Child-Care Nursing M
Mathematics Education M,D
Medical Physics M,D*
Medical/Surgical Nursing M
Multilingual and Multicultural Education M,D
Nurse Midwifery M
Nursing M,D
Nursing Administration M
Nursing Education M
Oncology Nursing M
Oral and Dental Sciences M,D
Pharmaceutical Sciences M,D
Pharmacy P
Physical Therapy M,D
Public Health M,D*
Public Health Nursing M,D
Quantitative Analysis M,D
Reading Education M
Recreation and Park Management M,D
Rehabilitation Sciences M,D
Science Education M,D
Social Sciences Education M,D
Social Work M,D
Special Education M
Taxation M
Veterinary Medicine P
Veterinary Sciences M,D
Vocational and Technical Education M

UNIVERSITY OF MISSISSIPPI

Accounting M,D
Art Education M
Business Administration and Management M*
Communication Disorders M
Curriculum and Instruction M,D,O
Education M,D,O
Educational Administration M,D,O
Educational Psychology M,D,O
Exercise and Sports Science M,D
Higher Education M
Law P
Leisure Studies M,D
Management Information Systems M
Pharmaceutical Sciences M,D
Pharmacy P
Secondary Education M
Taxation M

UNIVERSITY OF MISSISSIPPI MEDICAL CENTER

Allopathic Medicine P
Clinical Laboratory Sciences M,D
Dentistry P
Epidemiology M,D
Nursing M

UNIVERSITY OF MISSOURI–COLUMBIA

Accounting M,D
Adult Education M,D,O
Allopathic Medicine P

University of Missouri–Columbia (continued)

- Business Administration and Management M,D*
- Communication Disorders M
- Community Health M
- Curriculum and Instruction M,D,O
- Education M,D,O
- Educational Administration M,D,O
- Educational Psychology M,D,O
- Exercise and Sports Science M,D
- Health Physics/Radiological Health M
- Health Services Management and Hospital Administration M
- Higher Education M,D,O
- Hospitality Management M
- Information Studies M
- Law P
- Library Science M
- Medical Physics M
- Nursing M,D*
- Physical Therapy M
- Recreation and Park Management M
- Social Work M
- Special Education M,D,O
- Veterinary Medicine P
- Veterinary Sciences M,D
- Vocational and Technical Education M,D,O

UNIVERSITY OF MISSOURI–KANSAS CITY

- Accounting M
- Advanced Practice Nursing M
- Allopathic Medicine P
- Business Administration and Management M
- Counselor Education M,D,O
- Curriculum and Instruction M,D,O
- Dental Hygiene M
- Dentistry P
- Education M,D,O
- Educational Administration M,D,O
- Educational Measurement and Evaluation M
- Educational Psychology M
- Elementary Education M
- Law P,M
- Maternal/Child-Care Nursing M
- Medical/Surgical Nursing M
- Music Education M,D
- Nursing M,D*
- Oral and Dental Sciences M,D,O
- Pharmaceutical Sciences M
- Pharmacy P
- Reading Education M,O
- Secondary Education M
- Special Education M
- Taxation M

UNIVERSITY OF MISSOURI–ROLLA

- Mathematics Education M
- Science Education M

UNIVERSITY OF MISSOURI–ST. LOUIS

- Accounting M
- Business Administration and Management M
- Counselor Education M
- Education M,D
- Educational Administration M
- Elementary Education M
- Finance and Banking M
- Human Resources Management O
- Management Information Systems M
- Marketing M,O
- Music Education M
- Nursing M,D
- Optometry P
- Organizational Behavior M
- Quantitative Analysis M
- Secondary Education M
- Social Work O
- Special Education M
- Taxation O
- Vision Sciences M,D

UNIVERSITY OF MOBILE

- Business Administration and Management M
- Education M
- Nursing M
- Physical Therapy M

THE UNIVERSITY OF MONTANA–MISSOULA

- Accounting M
- Business Administration and Management M*
- Counselor Education M,D,O
- Curriculum and Instruction M,O
- Education M,D,O
- Educational Administration M,O
- English Education M
- Health Education M
- Law P
- Mathematics Education M,D
- Music Education M
- Pharmaceutical Sciences M,D*
- Physical Education M
- Physical Therapy M
- Recreation and Park Management M
- Science Education M

UNIVERSITY OF MONTEVALLO

- Communication Disorders M
- Counselor Education M
- Early Childhood Education M,O
- Education M,O
- Educational Administration O
- Elementary Education M,O
- Health Education M,O
- Home Economics Education M
- Physical Education M,O
- Recreation and Park Management M,O
- Secondary Education M,O

UNIVERSITY OF NEBRASKA AT KEARNEY

- Art Education M
- Business Administration and Management M
- Business Education M
- Communication Disorders M
- Counselor Education M,O
- Curriculum and Instruction M
- Early Childhood Education M
- Education M,O
- Educational Administration M,O
- Educational Media/Instructional Technology M
- Education of the Gifted M
- Elementary Education M
- English Education M
- Exercise and Sports Science M
- Foreign Languages Education M
- Mathematics Education M
- Middle School Education M
- Music Education M
- Physical Education M
- Reading Education M
- Science Education M
- Social Sciences Education M
- Special Education M

UNIVERSITY OF NEBRASKA AT OMAHA

- Accounting M
- Business Administration and Management M*
- Communication Disorders M
- Counselor Education M
- Education M,D,O
- Educational Administration M,D,O
- Educational Psychology M
- Elementary Education M
- Health Education M
- Physical Education M
- Reading Education M
- Recreation and Park Management M
- Secondary Education M
- Social Work M
- Special Education M
- Urban Education M

UNIVERSITY OF NEBRASKA–LINCOLN

- Accounting M,D
- Actuarial Science M
- Adult Education M
- Agricultural Education M
- Business Administration and Management M,D
- Communication Disorders M
- Curriculum and Instruction M,D,O
- Education M,D,O
- Educational Administration M,D,O
- Educational Psychology M,O
- Finance and Banking M,D
- Health Education M
- Law P
- Legal and Justice Studies M
- Marketing M,D
- Physical Education M
- Recreation and Park Management M
- Special Education M
- Veterinary Sciences M,D
- Vocational and Technical Education M

UNIVERSITY OF NEBRASKA MEDICAL CENTER

- Allied Health M
- Allopathic Medicine P
- Dentistry P,O
- Nursing M,D
- Oral and Dental Sciences M
- Pharmaceutical Sciences M,D
- Pharmacy P
- Physical Therapy M
- Physician Assistant Studies M

UNIVERSITY OF NEVADA, LAS VEGAS

- Accounting M
- Advanced Practice Nursing M
- Business Administration and Management M
- Curriculum and Instruction M,D,O
- Education M,D,O
- Educational Administration M,D,O
- Educational Measurement and Evaluation D
- Educational Media/Instructional Technology M
- Educational Psychology M
- Elementary Education M
- English as a Second Language M
- English Education M
- Exercise and Sports Science M
- Health Physics/Radiological Health M
- Higher Education M
- Hospitality Management M,D*
- Kinesiology and Movement Studies M
- Leisure Studies M*
- Mathematics Education M
- Middle School Education M
- Music Education M
- Nursing M
- Secondary Education M
- Social Work M
- Special Education M,D,O
- Vocational and Technical Education M

UNIVERSITY OF NEVADA, RENO

- Accounting M
- Allopathic Medicine P
- Business Administration and Management M
- Communication Disorders M,D
- Counselor Education M,D,O
- Curriculum and Instruction M,D,O
- Education M,D,O
- Educational Administration M,D,O
- Educational Psychology M,D,O
- Elementary Education M
- English as a Second Language M
- Environmental and Occupational Health M,D
- Legal and Justice Studies M
- Mathematics Education M
- Nursing M
- Physical Education M
- Secondary Education M
- Social Work M
- Special Education M

UNIVERSITY OF NEW BRUNSWICK (FREDERICTON)

- Adult Education M
- Business Administration and Management M
- Counselor Education M
- Curriculum and Instruction M
- Education M
- Educational Administration M
- Educational Psychology M
- Law P
- Physical Education M
- Recreation and Park Management M
- Special Education M
- Vocational and Technical Education M

UNIVERSITY OF NEW BRUNSWICK (SAINT JOHN)

- Business Administration and Management M
- International Business M

UNIVERSITY OF NEW ENGLAND

- Education M
- Nurse Anesthesia M
- Osteopathic Medicine P
- Physician Assistant Studies M
- Social Work M*

UNIVERSITY OF NEW HAMPSHIRE

- Business Administration and Management M*
- Communication Disorders M
- Counselor Education M
- Early Childhood Education M
- Education M,D,O
- Educational Administration M,O
- Elementary Education M
- English Education M
- Health Services Management and Hospital Administration M*
- Kinesiology and Movement Studies M
- Mathematics Education D
- Music Education M
- Nursing M
- Occupational Therapy M
- Reading Education M,D
- Secondary Education M
- Social Work M
- Special Education M
- Vocational and Technical Education M

UNIVERSITY OF NEW HAVEN

- Accounting M
- Advertising and Public Relations M
- Business Administration and Management M
- Education M,O
- Environmental and Occupational Health M
- Finance and Banking M
- Health Services Management and Hospital Administration M
- Hospitality Management M
- Human Resources Management M
- Industrial Hygiene M
- International Business M
- Logistics M,O
- Management Information Systems M,D
- Management Strategy and Policy M
- Marketing M
- Organizational Behavior M
- Taxation M
- Travel and Tourism M

UNIVERSITY OF NEW MEXICO

- Accounting M
- Advanced Practice Nursing M,O
- Allopathic Medicine P
- Art Education M
- Business Administration and Management M*
- Communication Disorders M
- Curriculum and Instruction O
- Education M,D,O
- Educational Administration M,D,O
- Educational Media/Instructional Technology M,D,O
- Educational Psychology M,D
- Elementary Education M
- Finance and Banking M
- Foundations and Philosophy of Education M,D
- Gerontological Nursing M
- Health Education M,D
- Human Resources Management M
- International Business M
- Law P
- Management Information Systems M
- Marketing M
- Maternal/Child-Care Nursing M
- Medical/Surgical Nursing M
- Multilingual and Multicultural Education D,O
- Nurse Midwifery M
- Nursing M,O
- Nursing Administration M,O
- Pharmaceutical Sciences M,D
- Pharmacy P
- Physical Education M,D,O
- Psychiatric Nursing M
- Public Health M
- Public Health Nursing M
- Recreation and Park Management M,D,O
- Secondary Education M
- Special Education M,D,O
- Taxation M

UNIVERSITY OF NEW ORLEANS

- Accounting M
- Business Administration and Management M
- Counselor Education M,D,O
- Curriculum and Instruction M,D,O
- Education M,D,O
- Educational Administration M,D,O
- Exercise and Sports Science M
- Foundations and Philosophy of Education M,D,O
- Health Education M,O
- Physical Education M,O
- Science Education M
- Special Education M,D,O
- Sports Administration M
- Taxation M

UNIVERSITY OF NORTH ALABAMA

- Business Administration and Management M
- Counselor Education M
- Early Childhood Education M
- Education M,O
- Educational Administration M,O
- Elementary Education M
- Reading Education M
- Secondary Education M
- Special Education M

THE UNIVERSITY OF NORTH CAROLINA AT CHAPEL HILL

- Accounting M,D
- Allied Health M

Allopathic Medicine	P
Business Administration and Management	M,D
Communication Disorders	M
Counselor Education	M
Curriculum and Instruction	M,D
Dental Hygiene	M*
Dentistry	P
Early Childhood Education	D
Education	M,D
Educational Administration	M,D
Educational Psychology	M,D
Elementary Education	M
English Education	M
Epidemiology	M,D*
Exercise and Sports Science	M
Finance and Banking	D
Foreign Languages Education	M
Health Education	M,D*
Health Services Management and Hospital Administration	M,D
Information Studies	M,D,O
Kinesiology and Movement Studies	M
Law	P
Leisure Studies	M
Library Science	M,D,O
Management Information Systems	D
Management Strategy and Policy	D
Marketing	D
Maternal and Child Health	M,D
Mathematics Education	M
Music Education	M
Nursing	M,D
Occupational Therapy	M
Oral and Dental Sciences	M,D*
Organizational Behavior	D
Pharmaceutical Sciences	M,D*
Physical Education	M
Physical Therapy	M
Public Health	M,D*
Public Health Nursing	M
Quantitative Analysis	D
Reading Education	D
Recreation and Park Management	M
Science Education	M
Secondary Education	M
Social Sciences Education	M
Social Work	M,O
Special Education	M
Sports Administration	M

UNIVERSITY OF NORTH CAROLINA AT CHARLOTTE

Accounting	M
Business Administration and Management	M*
Counselor Education	M
Education	M,D,O
Educational Administration	M,D,O
Educational Media/Instructional Technology	M
Elementary Education	M
English as a Second Language	M
Health Education	M
Health Services Management and Hospital Administration	M
Mathematics Education	M
Middle School Education	M
Nursing	M
Reading Education	M
Secondary Education	M
Special Education	M

UNIVERSITY OF NORTH CAROLINA AT GREENSBORO

Accounting	M
Art Education	M
Business Administration and Management	M,O
Business Education	M
Communication Disorders	M
Community Health	M
Counselor Education	M,D,O
Curriculum and Instruction	D
Education	M,D,O
Educational Administration	M,D,O
Educational Measurement and Evaluation	M,D
Elementary Education	M
English Education	M,D
Exercise and Sports Science	M,D
Gerontological Nursing	O
Higher Education	M
Home Economics Education	M,D
Hospitality Management	M,D
Information Studies	M
International Business	O
Library Science	M
Management Information Systems	M
Marketing	M,D
Middle School Education	M
Music Education	M,D
Nurse Anesthesia	M,O
Nursing	M,O
Nursing Administration	M
Recreation and Park Management	M
Secondary Education	M
Social Work	M
Special Education	M

UNIVERSITY OF NORTH CAROLINA AT PEMBROKE

Business Administration and Management	M
Counselor Education	M
Education	M
Educational Administration	M
Elementary Education	M
English Education	M
Mathematics Education	M
Middle School Education	M
Organizational Behavior	M
Reading Education	M

UNIVERSITY OF NORTH CAROLINA AT WILMINGTON

Accounting	M
Business Administration and Management	M
Education	M
Educational Administration	M
Elementary Education	M
Reading Education	M
Special Education	M

UNIVERSITY OF NORTH DAKOTA

Allopathic Medicine	P
Business Administration and Management	M
Business Education	M
Communication Disorders	M
Early Childhood Education	M
Education	M,D,O
Educational Administration	M,D,O
Educational Measurement and Evaluation	D
Elementary Education	M,D
Industrial and Manufacturing Management	M
Kinesiology and Movement Studies	M
Law	P
Medical Technology	M
Music Education	M
Nursing	M
Physical Therapy	M
Reading Education	M
Secondary Education	D
Social Work	M
Special Education	M,D
Vocational and Technical Education	M

UNIVERSITY OF NORTHERN COLORADO

Advanced Practice Nursing	M
Communication Disorders	M
Community Health	M
Counselor Education	M,D
Early Childhood Education	M
Education	M,D,O
Educational Administration	M,D,O
Educational Media/Instructional Technology	M
Educational Psychology	M,D
Elementary Education	M,D
Kinesiology and Movement Studies	M,D
Mathematics Education	M,D
Music Education	M,D
Nursing	M
Nursing Education	M
Physical Education	M,D
Public Health	M
Reading Education	M
Science Education	M,D
Special Education	M,D

UNIVERSITY OF NORTHERN IOWA

Art Education	M
Business Administration and Management	M
Communication Disorders	M
Computer Education	M
Counselor Education	M,D
Curriculum and Instruction	M,D
Early Childhood Education	M
Education	M,D,O
Educational Administration	M,D
Educational Media/Instructional Technology	M
Educational Psychology	M,O
Education of the Gifted	M
English as a Second Language	M
Health Education	M
Leisure Studies	M
Mathematics Education	M
Middle School Education	M
Music Education	M
Physical Education	M
Reading Education	M
Science Education	M,O
Special Education	M
Vocational and Technical Education	M,D

UNIVERSITY OF NORTH FLORIDA

Accounting	M
Advanced Practice Nursing	M
Allied Health	M,O
Business Administration and Management	M
Counselor Education	M
Education	M,D
Educational Administration	M,D
Elementary Education	M
Exercise and Sports Science	M
Health Services Management and Hospital Administration	M
Human Resources Management	M
Mathematics Education	M
Music Education	M
Science Education	M
Secondary Education	M
Special Education	M

UNIVERSITY OF NORTH TEXAS

Accounting	M,D
Art Education	M,D
Business Administration and Management	M,D
Communication Disorders	M
Community Health	M
Computer Education	M
Counselor Education	M,D
Curriculum and Instruction	D
Early Childhood Education	M,D
Education	M,D,O
Educational Administration	M,D
Educational Measurement and Evaluation	D
Elementary Education	M
Facilities Management	M
Finance and Banking	M,D
Health Promotion	M
Health Services Management and Hospital Administration	M
Higher Education	D
Hospitality Management	M
Industrial and Manufacturing Management	M,D
Information Studies	M,D
Insurance	M,D
Kinesiology and Movement Studies	M
Leisure Studies	M,O
Library Science	M,D
Management Information Systems	M,D
Marketing	M,D
Music Education	M,D
Organizational Behavior	D
Reading Education	M,D
Real Estate	M,D
Recreation and Park Management	M,O
Rehabilitation Sciences	M
Secondary Education	M
Special Education	M,D
Vocational and Technical Education	M,D,O

UNIVERSITY OF NORTH TEXAS HEALTH SCIENCE CENTER AT FORT WORTH

Osteopathic Medicine	P
Public Health	M*

UNIVERSITY OF NOTRE DAME

Accounting	M
Business Administration and Management	M
Law	P,M,D
Nonprofit Management	M

UNIVERSITY OF OKLAHOMA

Accounting	M
Adult Education	M,D
Advertising and Public Relations	M
Business Administration and Management	M,D*
Counselor Education	M
Curriculum and Instruction	M,D
Early Childhood Education	M,D
Education	M,D
Educational Administration	M,D
Educational Psychology	M,D
Elementary Education	M,D
English Education	M,D
Environmental and Occupational Health	M
Exercise and Sports Science	M
Foundations and Philosophy of Education	M,D
Higher Education	M,D
Human Services	M
Information Studies	M,O
Law	P
Library Science	M,O
Mathematics Education	M,D
Music Education	M,D
Reading Education	M,D
Science Education	M,D
Secondary Education	M,D
Social Sciences Education	M,D
Social Work	M
Special Education	M,D
Sports Administration	M

UNIVERSITY OF OKLAHOMA HEALTH SCIENCES CENTER

Allied Health	M,D,O
Allopathic Medicine	P
Communication Disorders	M,D,O
Dentistry	P
Environmental and Occupational Health	M,D
Epidemiology	M,D
Health Physics/Radiological Health	M,D
Health Promotion	M,D
Health Services Management and Hospital Administration	M,D
Medical Physics	M,D
Nursing	M
Oral and Dental Sciences	M
Pharmaceutical Sciences	M,D
Pharmacy	P
Public Health	M,D
Rehabilitation Sciences	M
Special Education	M

UNIVERSITY OF OREGON

Accounting	D
Business Administration and Management	M,D
Communication Disorders	M,D
Education	M,D
Educational Administration	M,D
Educational Media/Instructional Technology	D
Exercise and Sports Science	M,D
Finance and Banking	M,D
Foundations and Philosophy of Education	M,D
Higher Education	M
Human Resources Development	M
Human Resources Management	M
Kinesiology and Movement Studies	M,D
Law	P
Management Information Systems	M
Marketing	M,D
Music Education	M,D
Quantitative Analysis	M,D
Special Education	M,D

UNIVERSITY OF OSTEOPATHIC MEDICINE AND HEALTH SCIENCES

Health Services Management and Hospital Administration	M
Osteopathic Medicine	P
Physical Therapy	M
Podiatric Medicine	P*

UNIVERSITY OF OTTAWA

Allopathic Medicine	M,D
Business Administration and Management	M
Communication Disorders	M
Community Health	M
Education	M,D
Epidemiology	M
Health Services Management and Hospital Administration	M
International Business	M
Kinesiology and Movement Studies	M
Law	M,D,O
Legal and Justice Studies	O
Nursing	M
Social Work	M

UNIVERSITY OF PENNSYLVANIA

Accounting	M,D
Advanced Practice Nursing	M,O
Allopathic Medicine	P
Business Administration and Management	M,D
Dentistry	P
Early Childhood Education	M
Education	M,D*
Educational Administration	M,D
Educational Measurement and Evaluation	M,D
Elementary Education	M
English as a Second Language	M,D
Epidemiology	M,D
Finance and Banking	D
Foundations and Philosophy of Education	M,D

University of Pennsylvania (continued)

Gerontological Nursing M
Health Services Management and Hospital Administration M,D
Higher Education M,D
Insurance M,D
International Business M
Law P,M,D
Legal and Justice Studies M
Management Information Systems M,D
Marketing D
Maternal/Child-Care Nursing M,O
Medical/Surgical Nursing M
Multilingual and Multicultural Education M
Nurse Midwifery M
Nursing M,D,O
Nursing Administration M,D
Oncology Nursing M
Organizational Behavior M
Psychiatric Nursing M
Reading Education M,D
Real Estate M
Secondary Education M
Social Work M,D*
Veterinary Medicine P

UNIVERSITY OF PHOENIX

Advanced Practice Nursing M
Business Administration and Management M
Counselor Education M
Education M
Educational Administration M
International Business M
Nursing M
Nursing Administration M
Organizational Behavior M

UNIVERSITY OF PITTSBURGH

Advanced Practice Nursing M*
Allopathic Medicine P
Bioethics M
Business Administration and Management M,D*
Clinical Laboratory Sciences M*
Communication Disorders M,D*
Community Health M*
Counselor Education M
Dentistry P
Early Childhood Education M
Education M,D
Educational Administration M,D
Educational Measurement and Evaluation M,D
Educational Psychology D
Elementary Education M
English Education M,D
Environmental and Occupational Health M,D*
Epidemiology M,D*
Exercise and Sports Science M,D
Foreign Languages Education M,D
Foundations and Philosophy of Education M,D
Health Education M
Health Physics/Radiological Health O
Health Promotion M
Health Services Management and Hospital Administration M,D,O*
Information Studies M,D,O*
International and Comparative Education M,D
International Business
Kinesiology and Movement Studies M,D
Law P,M
Legal and Justice Studies O
Library Science M,D,O*
Management Information Systems M,O
Maternal/Child-Care Nursing M*
Mathematics Education M,D
Nurse Anesthesia M*
Nursing M,D*
Nursing Administration M*
Nursing Education M*
Occupational Therapy M*
Oral and Dental Sciences M,O
Pharmaceutical Sciences M,D
Pharmacy P
Physical Therapy M*
Psychiatric Nursing M*
Public Health M,D,O*
Reading Education M,D
Rehabilitation Sciences M,D,O*
Science Education M,D
Secondary Education M,D
Social Sciences Education M,D
Social Work M,D
Special Education M,D

UNIVERSITY OF PORTLAND

Advanced Practice Nursing O
Business Administration and Management M
Early Childhood Education M
Education M
Music Education M
Nursing M,O
Nursing Administration O
Religious Education M
Secondary Education M
Special Education M

UNIVERSITY OF PRINCE EDWARD ISLAND

Veterinary Medicine P
Veterinary Sciences M,D

UNIVERSITY OF PUERTO RICO, MAYAGÜEZ CAMPUS

Agricultural Education M
Business Administration and Management M

UNIVERSITY OF PUERTO RICO, MEDICAL SCIENCES CAMPUS

Allied Health M
Allopathic Medicine P
Clinical Laboratory Sciences M
Communication Disorders M
Dentistry P
Environmental and Occupational Health M
Epidemiology M
Health Education M
Health Services Management and Hospital Administration M
Health Services Research M
Industrial Hygiene M
Maternal and Child Health M
Nurse Anesthesia M
Nursing M
Nursing Administration M
Nursing Education M
Oral and Dental Sciences M,O
Pharmacy M
Public Health M
Special Education O

UNIVERSITY OF PUERTO RICO, RÍO PIEDRAS

Business Administration and Management M
Counselor Education M,D
Curriculum and Instruction M,D
Early Childhood Education M
Education M,D
Educational Administration M,D
Educational Measurement and Evaluation M
Elementary Education M
English as a Second Language M
English Education M
Foreign Languages Education M
Home Economics Education M
Law P
Library Science M
Mathematics Education M
Science Education M
Secondary Education M
Social Sciences Education M
Social Work M
Special Education M

UNIVERSITY OF PUGET SOUND

Counselor Education M
Education M
Educational Administration M
Elementary Education M
Occupational Therapy M
Physical Therapy M
Reading Education M
Secondary Education M

UNIVERSITY OF REDLANDS

Business Administration and Management M
Communication Disorders M
Curriculum and Instruction M
Education M
Educational Administration M
Management Information Systems M

UNIVERSITY OF REGINA

Business Administration and Management M
Curriculum and Instruction M,O
Education M,D,O
Educational Administration M,O
Educational Psychology M,D,O
Health Services Management and Hospital Administration M
Physical Education M
Social Work M
Vocational and Technical Education M,O

UNIVERSITY OF RHODE ISLAND

Accounting M
Adult Education M
Business Administration and Management M,D*
Clinical Laboratory Sciences M
Communication Disorders M
Education M*
Elementary Education M
Finance and Banking M
Health Education M
Home Economics Education M
Industrial and Manufacturing Management M
Information Studies M
International Business M
Library Science M
Management Information Systems M
Marketing M
Nursing M,D*
Nursing Administration M*
Nursing Education M*
Pharmaceutical Sciences M,D
Pharmacy P
Physical Education M
Physical Therapy M
Quantitative Analysis D
Reading Education M
Recreation and Park Management M
Secondary Education M
Sports Administration M

UNIVERSITY OF RICHMOND

Business Administration and Management M
Early Childhood Education M
Education M
Elementary Education M
Law P
Reading Education M
Secondary Education M
Special Education M

UNIVERSITY OF RIO GRANDE

Art Education M
Education M
Mathematics Education M
Reading Education M
Special Education M

UNIVERSITY OF ROCHESTER

Allopathic Medicine P
Business Administration and Management M,D*
Education M,D*
Environmental and Occupational Health M
Health Services Research D*
Music Education M,D
Nursing M,D
Oral and Dental Sciences M
Public Health M*

UNIVERSITY OF ST. AUGUSTINE FOR HEALTH SCIENCES

Occupational Therapy M
Physical Therapy M,D

UNIVERSITY OF ST. FRANCIS (IL)

Business Administration and Management M
Education M
Health Services Management and Hospital Administration M,O
Middle School Education M

UNIVERSITY OF SAINT FRANCIS (IN)

Business Administration and Management M
Counselor Education M
Education M
Nursing M
Reading Education M
Special Education M

UNIVERSITY OF ST. THOMAS (MN)

Accounting M,O
Advertising and Public Relations O
Business Administration and Management M,O*
Curriculum and Instruction M,O
Education M,D,O
Educational Administration M,D,O
Educational Media/Instructional Technology M,O
Education of the Gifted M
Finance and Banking M,O
Health Services Management and Hospital Administration M,O
Human Resources Management M,O
Industrial and Manufacturing Management M
Insurance M
International Business M,O
Management Information Systems M
Marketing M,O
Music Education M
Nonprofit Management M,O
Real Estate M
Religious Education M
Social Work M
Special Education M
Sports Administration M

UNIVERSITY OF ST. THOMAS (TX)

Business Administration and Management M
Education M

UNIVERSITY OF SAN DIEGO

Advanced Practice Nursing M
Business Administration and Management M*
Counselor Education M
Curriculum and Instruction M
Education M,D
Educational Administration M,D
Law P,M,O
Legal and Justice Studies M
Nursing M,D
Nursing Administration M
Public Health Nursing M
Religious Education M
Special Education M
Taxation M,O

UNIVERSITY OF SAN FRANCISCO

Advanced Practice Nursing M
Business Administration and Management M
Counselor Education M
Curriculum and Instruction M,D
Education M,D*
Educational Administration M,D
English as a Second Language M
Finance and Banking M
Health Services Management and Hospital Administration M
Human Resources Development M
International and Comparative Education M,D
International Business M
Law P
Marketing M
Medical/Surgical Nursing M
Multilingual and Multicultural Education M,D
Nonprofit Management M
Nursing M
Nursing Administration M
Organizational Behavior M
Religious Education O
Sports Administration M

UNIVERSITY OF SARASOTA

Business Administration and Management M,D
Counselor Education M,D
Curriculum and Instruction M,D
Education M,D
Educational Administration M,D
Human Services M,D

UNIVERSITY OF SASKATCHEWAN

Accounting M
Allopathic Medicine P
Business Administration and Management M,D
Community Health M,D
Curriculum and Instruction M,D,O
Dentistry P
Education M,D,O
Educational Administration M,D,O
Educational Psychology M,D,O
Epidemiology M,D
Finance and Banking M
Foundations and Philosophy of Education M,D,O
Law P,M
Marketing M
Nursing M
Organizational Behavior M
Pharmaceutical Sciences M,D
Physical Education M,D
Special Education M,D,O
Veterinary Medicine P
Veterinary Sciences M,D,O

UNIVERSITY OF SCRANTON

Accounting M
Advanced Practice Nursing M
Business Administration and Management M
Counselor Education M
Education M
Educational Administration M
Elementary Education M
Finance and Banking M
Health Services Management and Hospital Administration M
Human Resources Development M
Human Resources Management M
International Business M
Marketing M
Nursing M
Organizational Behavior M

Reading Education M
Secondary Education M

UNIVERSITY OF SIOUX FALLS

Business Administration and Management M
Education M
Educational Administration M
Educational Media/Instructional Technology M
Reading Education M

UNIVERSITY OF SOUTH ALABAMA

Accounting M
Allied Health M,D
Allopathic Medicine P
Art Education M
Business Administration and Management M
Business Education M
Communication Disorders M,D
Counselor Education M,O
Early Childhood Education M,O
Education M,D,O
Educational Administration M,O
Educational Media/Instructional Technology M,D,O
Education of the Gifted M
Education of the Multiply Handicapped M
Elementary Education M,O
Exercise and Sports Science M
Foundations and Philosophy of Education M,O
Health Education M
Leisure Studies M
Maternal/Child-Care Nursing M
Medical/Surgical Nursing M
Music Education M
Nursing M
Physical Education M,O
Physician Assistant Studies M
Psychiatric Nursing M
Reading Education M
Recreation and Park Management M
Science Education M
Secondary Education M,O
Special Education M,O

UNIVERSITY OF SOUTH CAROLINA (COLUMBIA)

Accounting M
Advanced Practice Nursing O
Allopathic Medicine P
Art Education M
Business Administration and Management M,D*
Communication Disorders M,D
Counselor Education M,D,O
Curriculum and Instruction D
Early Childhood Education M,D
Education M,D,O
Educational Administration M,D,O
Educational Measurement and Evaluation M,D
Educational Media/Instructional Technology M
Elementary Education M,D
English as a Second Language O
English Education M
Environmental and Occupational Health M,D
Epidemiology M,D
Exercise and Sports Science M,D
Foreign Languages Education M
Foundations and Philosophy of Education D
Health Education M,D,O
Health Promotion M,D,O
Health Services Management and Hospital Administration M,D
Higher Education M
Hospitality Management M
Human Resources Management M
Industrial Hygiene M,D
Information Studies M,O
International Business M*
Law P
Library Science M,O
Mathematics Education M
Music Education M,D
Nurse Anesthesia M
Nursing M,D
Nursing Administration M,O
Pharmaceutical Sciences M,D
Pharmacy P
Physical Education M,D
Psychiatric Nursing M
Public Health M
Public Health Nursing M
Reading Education M,D
Science Education M
Secondary Education M,D
Social Sciences Education M
Social Work M,D
Special Education M,D

Taxation M
Travel and Tourism M
Vocational and Technical Education M

UNIVERSITY OF SOUTH CAROLINA–AIKEN

Education M
Elementary Education M

UNIVERSITY OF SOUTH CAROLINA SPARTANBURG

Early Childhood Education M
Education M
Elementary Education M

UNIVERSITY OF SOUTH DAKOTA

Accounting M
Allied Health M
Allopathic Medicine P
Business Administration and Management M
Communication Disorders M
Counselor Education M,D,O
Curriculum and Instruction M,D,O
Education M,D,O
Educational Administration M,D,O
Educational Psychology M,D,O
Elementary Education M
Health Education M
Law P
Occupational Therapy M
Physical Education M
Physical Therapy M
Secondary Education M
Special Education M

UNIVERSITY OF SOUTHERN CALIFORNIA

Accounting M
Advertising and Public Relations M
Allied Health M,D,O
Allopathic Medicine P
Business Administration and Management M,D
Curriculum and Instruction M,D
Dentistry P,O
Education M,D,O*
Educational Administration M,D
Educational Media/Instructional Technology M
Educational Psychology M,D
English as a Second Language M
Epidemiology M,D
Exercise and Sports Science M,D
Finance and Banking M
Health Promotion M
Health Services Management and Hospital Administration M
Health Services Research D*
International and Comparative Education M
International Business M*
Kinesiology and Movement Studies M,D
Law P
Management Information Systems M
Music Education M,D
Nursing M,O
Occupational Therapy M,D
Oral and Dental Sciences M,D
Pharmaceutical Sciences M,D*
Pharmacy P
Physical Therapy M,D
Public Health M*
Reading Education D
Real Estate M*
Social Work M,D
Special Education M
Taxation M

UNIVERSITY OF SOUTHERN COLORADO

Business Administration and Management M

UNIVERSITY OF SOUTHERN INDIANA

Accounting M
Business Administration and Management M
Education M
Elementary Education M
Industrial and Manufacturing Management M
Nursing M
Secondary Education M
Social Work M

UNIVERSITY OF SOUTHERN MAINE

Adult Education M,O
Business Administration and Management M
Counselor Education M,O
Education M,O
Educational Administration M,O

English as a Second Language M,O
Health Services Management and Hospital Administration M
Industrial and Manufacturing Management M
Law P
Medical/Surgical Nursing M,O
Nursing M,O
Nursing Administration M
Psychiatric Nursing M,O
Reading Education M,O
Special Education M
Vocational and Technical Education M

UNIVERSITY OF SOUTHERN MISSISSIPPI

Accounting M
Adult Education M,D,O
Advertising and Public Relations M
Art Education M
Business Administration and Management M
Communication Disorders M,D
Curriculum and Instruction M,D,O
Early Childhood Education M,O
Education M,D,O
Educational Administration M,D,O
Education of the Gifted M,D,O
Elementary Education M,D,O
Environmental and Occupational Health M
Foreign Languages Education M
Health Education M
Health Services Management and Hospital Administration M
Library Science M,O
Medical Technology M
Music Education M,D
Nursing M
Nursing Administration M
Physical Education M,D
Psychiatric Nursing M
Public Health M
Public Health Nursing M
Reading Education M,O
Recreation and Park Management M,D
Science Education M,D
Secondary Education M,D,O
Social Work M
Special Education M,D,O
Vocational and Technical Education M

UNIVERSITY OF SOUTH FLORIDA

Accounting M
Adult Education M,D,O
Allopathic Medicine P
Art Education M
Business Administration and Management M,D
Business Education M
Communication Disorders M
Community College Education M
Community Health M,D
Counselor Education M
Early Childhood Education M,D
Education M,D,O*
Educational Administration M,D,O
Educational Measurement and Evaluation M,D,O
Educational Media/Instructional Technology M,D
Education of the Gifted M
Elementary Education M,D,O
English as a Second Language M
English Education M,D,O
Environmental and Occupational Health M,D
Epidemiology M,D
Foreign Languages Education M
Health Services Management and Hospital Administration M,D
Higher Education M,D,O
Information Studies M
Library Science M
Management Information Systems M
Mathematics Education M,D,O
Middle School Education M
Music Education M,D
Nursing M,D
Physical Education M
Public Health M,D
Reading Education M,D,O
Science Education M,D,O
Secondary Education D
Social Sciences Education M
Social Work M
Special Education M,D,O
Vocational and Technical Education M,D,O

UNIVERSITY OF SOUTHWESTERN LOUISIANA

Business Administration and Management M
Communication Disorders M
Counselor Education M
Curriculum and Instruction M
Education M
Educational Administration M
Education of the Gifted M
Health Services Management and Hospital Administration M
Music Education M
Nursing M

THE UNIVERSITY OF TAMPA

Advanced Practice Nursing M
Business Administration and Management M
Nursing M
Nursing Administration M

UNIVERSITY OF TENNESSEE AT CHATTANOOGA

Accounting M
Advanced Practice Nursing M
Business Administration and Management M
Counselor Education M
Curriculum and Instruction M
Early Childhood Education M
Education M
Educational Administration M
Finance and Banking M
Industrial and Manufacturing Management M
Marketing M
Medical/Surgical Nursing M
Nurse Anesthesia M
Nursing M
Nursing Administration M
Nursing Education M
Organizational Behavior M
Physical Education M
Physical Therapy M
Reading Education M
Secondary Education M
Special Education M

THE UNIVERSITY OF TENNESSEE AT MARTIN

Accounting M
Business Administration and Management M
Counselor Education M
Education M

UNIVERSITY OF TENNESSEE, KNOXVILLE

Accounting M,D
Adult Education M,D
Advertising and Public Relations M,D
Agricultural Education M
Art Education M
Bioethics M,D
Business Administration and Management M,D*
Communication Disorders M,D
Community Health M,D*
Counselor Education M,O
Curriculum and Instruction M,D,O
Early Childhood Education M,D
Education M,D,O
Educational Administration M,D,O
Educational Measurement and Evaluation D
Educational Media/Instructional Technology M,D,O
Educational Psychology M,D
Elementary Education M,D,O
English as a Second Language M,D,O
English Education M,D,O
Entrepreneurship M
Exercise and Sports Science M,D
Finance and Banking M,D
Foreign Languages Education M,D,O
Foundations and Philosophy of Education M
Health Education M,D*
Health Promotion M*
Higher Education M,D
Hospitality Management M*
Human Resources Development M,D*
Industrial and Manufacturing Management M
Information Studies M*
International Business M
Law P
Library Science M*
Logistics M,D
Marketing M,D
Mathematics Education M,D,O
Multilingual and Multicultural Education M,D
Music Education M

University of Tennessee, Knoxville (continued)

Nursing M,D
Public Health M*
Reading Education M,D,O
Recreation and Park Management M*
Science Education M,D,O
Social Sciences Education M,D,O
Social Work M,D
Special Education M,D
Sports Administration M
Transportation Management M,D
Travel and Tourism M*
Veterinary Medicine P

UNIVERSITY OF TENNESSEE, MEMPHIS

Allied Health M
Allopathic Medicine P
Dentistry P,M
Nursing D
Pharmaceutical Sciences M,D
Pharmacy P,M,D
Physical Therapy M

THE UNIVERSITY OF TEXAS AT ARLINGTON

Accounting M
Business Administration and Management M,D*
Education M
Finance and Banking M
Health Physics/Radiological Health M
Human Resources Management M
Management Information Systems M,D
Marketing M
Marketing Research M
Nursing M
Nursing Administration M
Nursing Education M
Real Estate M
Social Work M,D*
Taxation M

THE UNIVERSITY OF TEXAS AT AUSTIN

Accounting M,D
Advertising and Public Relations M,D
Art Education M
Business Administration and Management M,D
Communication Disorders M,D
Curriculum and Instruction M,D
Education M,D
Educational Administration M,D
Educational Psychology M,D
Finance and Banking D
Foreign Languages Education M,D
Health Education M,D
Information Studies M,D
Kinesiology and Movement Studies M,D
Law P,M
Library Science M,D
Management Information Systems D
Marketing D
Mathematics Education M,D
Nursing M,D
Pharmaceutical Sciences M,D
Pharmacy P
Science Education M,D
Social Work M,D
Special Education M,D

THE UNIVERSITY OF TEXAS AT BROWNSVILLE

Business Administration and Management M
Counselor Education M
Curriculum and Instruction M
Early Childhood Education M
Education M,D
Educational Administration M
Educational Media/Instructional Technology M
Elementary Education M
English as a Second Language M
Reading Education M
Special Education M

THE UNIVERSITY OF TEXAS AT DALLAS

Business Administration and Management M,D*
Communication Disorders M
International Business M,D
Mathematics Education M
Science Education M

THE UNIVERSITY OF TEXAS AT EL PASO

Accounting M
Advanced Practice Nursing M
Allied Health M
Business Administration and Management M
Communication Disorders M
Education M,D
Educational Administration D
Educational Psychology M
Exercise and Sports Science M
Foundations and Philosophy of Education D
Kinesiology and Movement Studies M
Maternal/Child-Care Nursing M
Medical/Surgical Nursing M
Music Education M
Nurse Midwifery M
Nursing M
Nursing Administration M
Psychiatric Nursing M
Public Health Nursing M

THE UNIVERSITY OF TEXAS AT SAN ANTONIO

Accounting M
Business Administration and Management M
Education M
English as a Second Language M
Mathematics Education M
Multilingual and Multicultural Education M
Taxation M

THE UNIVERSITY OF TEXAS AT TYLER

Business Administration and Management M
Early Childhood Education M
Education M,O
Educational Administration M,O
Elementary Education M,O
English Education M,O
Exercise and Sports Science M
Health Education M
Health Services Management and Hospital Administration M
Kinesiology and Movement Studies M
Mathematics Education M,O
Nursing M
Reading Education M,O
Science Education M,O
Secondary Education M,O
Social Sciences Education M,O
Special Education M,O
Vocational and Technical Education M

THE UNIVERSITY OF TEXAS HEALTH SCIENCE CENTER AT SAN ANTONIO

Allopathic Medicine P
Dentistry P,M,O
Health Physics/Radiological Health M,D
Nursing M,D
Oral and Dental Sciences M,O

THE UNIVERSITY OF TEXAS–HOUSTON HEALTH SCIENCE CENTER

Allopathic Medicine P
Dentistry P
Gerontological Nursing M
Maternal/Child-Care Nursing M
Medical Physics M,D
Nurse Anesthesia M
Nursing M
Oncology Nursing M
Oral and Dental Sciences M
Psychiatric Nursing M
Public Health M,D

THE UNIVERSITY OF TEXAS MEDICAL BRANCH AT GALVESTON

Allied Health M
Allopathic Medicine P
Community Health M,D
Health Education M
Health Promotion M
Nursing M,D
Physical Therapy M

THE UNIVERSITY OF TEXAS OF THE PERMIAN BASIN

Accounting M
Business Administration and Management M
Counselor Education M
Early Childhood Education M
Education M
Educational Administration M
Elementary Education M
Physical Education M
Reading Education M
Secondary Education M
Special Education M

THE UNIVERSITY OF TEXAS–PAN AMERICAN

Business Administration and Management M,D*
Communication Disorders M
Counselor Education M
Early Childhood Education M
Education M,D
Educational Administration M
Educational Measurement and Evaluation M
Educational Psychology M
Education of the Gifted M
Elementary Education M
English as a Second Language M
Kinesiology and Movement Studies M
Multilingual and Multicultural Education M
Nursing M
Reading Education M
Secondary Education M
Social Work M
Special Education M

THE UNIVERSITY OF TEXAS SOUTHWESTERN MEDICAL CENTER AT DALLAS

Allopathic Medicine P

UNIVERSITY OF THE ARTS

Art Education M
Music Education M

UNIVERSITY OF THE DISTRICT OF COLUMBIA

Business Administration and Management M
Communication Disorders M
Counselor Education M
Early Childhood Education M
Education M
English Education M
Law P

UNIVERSITY OF THE INCARNATE WORD

Adult Education M
Business Administration and Management M
Early Childhood Education M
Education M
Educational Measurement and Evaluation M
Elementary Education M
International Business M
Nursing M
Physical Education M
Reading Education M
Secondary Education M
Special Education M
Sports Administration M

UNIVERSITY OF THE PACIFIC

Business Administration and Management M
Communication Disorders M
Counselor Education M
Curriculum and Instruction M,D
Dentistry P
Education M,D
Educational Administration M,D
Educational Measurement and Evaluation M
Educational Psychology M,D
Exercise and Sports Science M
Foundations and Philosophy of Education M,D
Law P,M
Legal and Justice Studies M
Oral and Dental Sciences M
Pharmaceutical Sciences M,D*
Pharmacy P*
Physical Therapy M
Special Education M,D

UNIVERSITY OF THE SACRED HEART

Advertising and Public Relations M
Business Administration and Management M
Education M
Educational Media/Instructional Technology M
Human Resources Management M
Management Information Systems M
Marketing M
Medical Technology O
Taxation M

UNIVERSITY OF THE SCIENCES IN PHILADELPHIA

Health Services Management and Hospital Administration M,D*
Pharmaceutical Sciences M,D*
Pharmacy P
Physical Therapy M
Science Education M

UNIVERSITY OF THE VIRGIN ISLANDS

Business Administration and Management M
Education M

UNIVERSITY OF TOLEDO

Accounting M
Art Education M
Business Administration and Management M*
Business Education M
Communication Disorders M
Counselor Education M,D,O
Curriculum and Instruction M,D,O
Early Childhood Education M
Education M,D,O
Educational Administration M,D,O
Educational Measurement and Evaluation M,D
Educational Media/Instructional Technology M
Educational Psychology M,D
Elementary Education M
English as a Second Language M
Exercise and Sports Science M
Finance and Banking M
Foundations and Philosophy of Education M,D
Health Education M,D
Higher Education M,D
Industrial and Manufacturing Management M,D
International Business M
Law P
Leisure Studies M
Management Information Systems M,D
Marketing M
Music Education M
Pharmaceutical Sciences M,D
Pharmacy P
Physical Education M,D
Public Health M
Recreation and Park Management M
Secondary Education M
Special Education M
Vocational and Technical Education M

UNIVERSITY OF TORONTO

Accounting M,D
Allopathic Medicine P
Bioethics M,D
Business Administration and Management M,D
Communication Disorders M,D
Community Health M,D
Dentistry P
Education M,D
Information Studies M,D
Law P,M,D
Library Science M,D
Nursing M,D
Oral and Dental Sciences M,D,O
Pharmaceutical Sciences M,D
Rehabilitation Sciences M
Social Work M,D

UNIVERSITY OF TULSA

Accounting M
Business Administration and Management M
Communication Disorders M
Education M
Law P
Management Information Systems M
Mathematics Education M
Music Education M
Nursing Administration M
Science Education M
Taxation M

UNIVERSITY OF UTAH

Accounting M,D
Allopathic Medicine P
Art Education M
Business Administration and Management M,D
Communication Disorders M,D
Education M,D
Educational Administration M,D
Educational Psychology M,D
Elementary Education M
Exercise and Sports Science M,D
Finance and Banking M,D
Foreign Languages Education M
Foundations and Philosophy of Education M,D
Gerontological Nursing M,O
Health Education M,D
Health Promotion M,D
Human Resources Management M
Law P,M
Leisure Studies M,D
Marketing M,D
Medical Technology M
Nursing M,D
Pharmaceutical Sciences M,D
Pharmacy P,M
Physical Therapy M

Public Health M
Recreation and Park Management M,D
Science Education M
Secondary Education M
Social Work M,D
Special Education M,D

UNIVERSITY OF VERMONT

Allied Health M
Allopathic Medicine P
Business Administration and Management M
Counselor Education M
Curriculum and Instruction M
Education M,D
Educational Administration M,D
English Education M
Foreign Languages Education M
Mathematics Education M
Medical Technology M
Nursing M
Physical Therapy M
Reading Education M
Science Education M,D
Social Sciences Education M
Social Work M
Special Education M
Vocational and Technical Education M

UNIVERSITY OF VICTORIA

Art Education M
Business Administration and Management M
Counselor Education M
Curriculum and Instruction M
Education M,D
Educational Administration M
Educational Psychology M,D
English Education M,D
Exercise and Sports Science M
Finance and Banking M
Industrial and Manufacturing Management M
Law P
Leisure Studies M
Mathematics Education M
Music Education M
Physical Education M
Science Education M
Social Sciences Education M
Social Work M
Special Education M

UNIVERSITY OF VIRGINIA

Accounting M*
Allopathic Medicine P,M
Bioethics M
Business Administration and Management M,D
Communication Disorders M
Counselor Education M,D,O
Curriculum and Instruction M,D,O
Education M,D,O*
Educational Administration M,D,O
Educational Measurement and Evaluation M,D
Educational Psychology M,D,O
Epidemiology M*
Foreign Languages Education M
Health Education M,D
Health Services Management and Hospital Administration M*
Health Services Research M*
Higher Education D,O
Law P,M,D
Management Information Systems M*
Nursing M,D
Physical Education M,D
Science Education M
Special Education M,D,O
Transportation Management M,D

UNIVERSITY OF WASHINGTON

Allopathic Medicine P
Bioethics M,D
Business Administration and Management M,D
Clinical Laboratory Sciences M
Communication Disorders M,D
Counselor Education M,D
Curriculum and Instruction M,D
Dentistry P
Education M,D
Educational Administration M,D
Educational Measurement and Evaluation M,D
English as a Second Language M
Environmental and Occupational Health M,D*
Epidemiology M,D*
Health Services Management and Hospital Administration M*
Industrial Hygiene M,D*
Law P,M,D
Library Science M
Music Education M,D
Nursing M,D
Occupational Therapy M
Oral and Dental Sciences M,D
Pharmaceutical Sciences M,D*
Pharmacy P
Physical Therapy M
Public Health M,D*
Rehabilitation Sciences M
Social Work M,D
Special Education M,D
Taxation M

UNIVERSITY OF WATERLOO

Accounting M,D
Actuarial Science M,D
Educational Psychology M
Finance and Banking M
Health Education M,D
Kinesiology and Movement Studies M,D
Leisure Studies M,D
Management Information Systems M,D
Optometry P
Recreation and Park Management M,D
Taxation M
Vision Sciences M,D

THE UNIVERSITY OF WEST ALABAMA

Adult Education M
Counselor Education M
Early Childhood Education M
Education M
Educational Administration M
Educational Media/Instructional Technology M
Elementary Education M
English Education M
Foundations and Philosophy of Education M
Mathematics Education M
Physical Education M
Science Education M
Secondary Education M
Social Sciences Education M
Special Education M

THE UNIVERSITY OF WESTERN ONTARIO

Allopathic Medicine P,M
Business Administration and Management M,D*
Communication Disorders M
Counselor Education M
Curriculum and Instruction M
Dentistry P
Education M
Educational Administration M
Educational Psychology M
Epidemiology M,D
Information Studies M,D*
Kinesiology and Movement Studies M,D
Law P,O
Library Science M,D*
Nursing M
Occupational Therapy M
Oral and Dental Sciences M
Physical Therapy M
Special Education M

UNIVERSITY OF WEST FLORIDA

Accounting M
Business Administration and Management M
Curriculum and Instruction D,O
Early Childhood Education M
Education M,D,O
Educational Administration M,O
Elementary Education M
Health Education M
Leisure Studies M
Mathematics Education M
Middle School Education M
Physical Education M
Reading Education M
Science Education M
Special Education M
Vocational and Technical Education M

UNIVERSITY OF WEST LOS ANGELES

Law P

UNIVERSITY OF WINDSOR

Business Administration and Management M
Education M
Kinesiology and Movement Studies M
Nursing M
Social Work M

UNIVERSITY OF WISCONSIN–EAU CLAIRE

Allied Health M
Business Administration and Management M
Communication Disorders M
Education M
Elementary Education M
English Education M
Environmental and Occupational Health M
Mathematics Education M
Nursing M
Public Health M
Reading Education M
Science Education M
Secondary Education M
Social Sciences Education M
Special Education M

UNIVERSITY OF WISCONSIN–GREEN BAY

Business Administration and Management M
Educational Administration M

UNIVERSITY OF WISCONSIN–LA CROSSE

Business Administration and Management M
Community Health M
Education M
Educational Administration M
Elementary Education M
Exercise and Sports Science M
Health Education M
Nurse Anesthesia M
Physical Education M
Physical Therapy M
Public Health M
Reading Education M
Recreation and Park Management M
Rehabilitation Sciences M
Secondary Education M
Social Work M
Special Education M
Sports Administration M

UNIVERSITY OF WISCONSIN–MADISON

Accounting M,D
Actuarial Science M,D
Adult Education M,D
Allopathic Medicine P
Art Education M
Business Administration and Management M,D
Communication Disorders M,D
Counselor Education M
Curriculum and Instruction M,D
Education M,D*
Educational Administration M,D
Educational Psychology M,D
English Education M
Epidemiology M,D
Finance and Banking M,D
Foreign Languages Education M
Foundations and Philosophy of Education M,D
Health Services Management and Hospital Administration M,D
Health Services Research M,D
Human Resources Management M
Industrial and Manufacturing Management M,D
Information Studies M,D,O
Insurance M,D
International Business M
Kinesiology and Movement Studies M,D
Law P,M,D
Legal and Justice Studies M
Library Science M,D,O
Logistics M
Management Information Systems M,D
Marketing M
Marketing Research M
Mathematics Education M
Medical Physics M,D
Music Education M,D
Nursing M,D
Pharmaceutical Sciences D*
Pharmacy P,M,D*
Real Estate M,D
Rehabilitation Sciences M
Science Education M
Social Sciences Education M
Social Work M,D
Special Education M,D
Veterinary Medicine P
Veterinary Sciences M,D
Vocational and Technical Education M,D

UNIVERSITY OF WISCONSIN–MILWAUKEE

Allied Health M
Art Education M
Business Administration and Management M,D
Clinical Laboratory Sciences M
Communication Disorders M
Curriculum and Instruction M
Early Childhood Education M
Education M,D
Educational Administration M
Educational Psychology M
Elementary Education M
Foundations and Philosophy of Education M
Information Studies M,O
Kinesiology and Movement Studies M
Library Science M,O
Middle School Education M
Nursing M,D
Occupational Therapy M
Reading Education M
Secondary Education M
Social Work M
Special Education M
Urban Education M,D

UNIVERSITY OF WISCONSIN–OSHKOSH

Advanced Practice Nursing M
Business Administration and Management M
Communication Disorders M
Counselor Education M
Curriculum and Instruction M
Early Childhood Education M
Education M
Educational Administration M
Health Services Management and Hospital Administration M
Mathematics Education M
Nursing M
Reading Education M
Science Education M
Special Education M

UNIVERSITY OF WISCONSIN–PARKSIDE

Business Administration and Management M

UNIVERSITY OF WISCONSIN–PLATTEVILLE

Adult Education M
Counselor Education M
Education M
Elementary Education M
Industrial and Manufacturing Management M
Middle School Education M
Secondary Education M
Vocational and Technical Education M

UNIVERSITY OF WISCONSIN–RIVER FALLS

Agricultural Education M
Communication Disorders M
Counselor Education M
Education M
Elementary Education M
English Education M
Mathematics Education M
Reading Education M
Science Education M
Social Sciences Education M

UNIVERSITY OF WISCONSIN–STEVENS POINT

Advertising and Public Relations M
Business Administration and Management M
Communication Disorders M
Counselor Education M
Education M
Educational Administration M
Elementary Education M
Music Education M
Reading Education M

UNIVERSITY OF WISCONSIN–STOUT

Counselor Education M,O
Education M
Educational Media/Instructional Technology M
Hospitality Management M
Human Resources Development M
Travel and Tourism M
Vocational and Technical Education M,O

UNIVERSITY OF WISCONSIN–SUPERIOR

Art Education M
Counselor Education M
Curriculum and Instruction M
Education M
Educational Administration M,O
Reading Education M
Special Education M

UNIVERSITY OF WISCONSIN–WHITEWATER
- Accounting M
- Business Administration and Management M*
- Business Education M
- Communication Disorders M
- Counselor Education M
- Curriculum and Instruction M
- Education M
- Educational Administration M
- Reading Education M
- Special Education M

UNIVERSITY OF WYOMING
- Adult Education M,D,O
- Business Administration and Management M
- Communication Disorders M
- Education M,D,O
- Educational Administration M,D,O
- Finance and Banking M
- Health Education M
- Law P
- Music Education M
- Nursing M
- Physical Education M
- Recreation and Park Management M
- Science Education M
- Social Work M

UPPER IOWA UNIVERSITY
- Business Administration and Management M
- Human Resources Management M
- Quality Management M

URSULINE COLLEGE
- Education M
- Educational Administration M
- Nursing M

UTAH STATE UNIVERSITY
- Accounting M
- Agricultural Education M
- Business Administration and Management M
- Business Education M,D
- Communication Disorders M,O
- Curriculum and Instruction D
- Education M,D,O
- Educational Measurement and Evaluation D
- Educational Media/Instructional Technology M,D,O
- Elementary Education M
- Health Education M
- Human Resources Management M
- Management Information Systems M,D
- Physical Education M
- Recreation and Park Management M,D
- Secondary Education M
- Special Education M,D
- Veterinary Sciences M,D
- Vocational and Technical Education M

VALDOSTA STATE UNIVERSITY
- Adult Education D
- Art Education M
- Business Administration and Management M
- Business Education M,D,O
- Communication Disorders M
- Counselor Education M,O
- Curriculum and Instruction D
- Early Childhood Education M,O
- Education M,D,O
- Educational Administration M,D,O
- Educational Media/Instructional Technology M
- Education of the Multiply Handicapped M,O
- Health Education M
- Human Services M
- Middle School Education M,O
- Music Education M
- Nursing M
- Nursing Administration M
- Physical Education M
- Public Health Nursing M
- Reading Education M,O
- Secondary Education M,D,O
- Social Work M
- Special Education M,O
- Vocational and Technical Education M,D,O

VALPARAISO UNIVERSITY
- Curriculum and Instruction M
- Education M
- Law P,M
- Nursing M
- Special Education M

VANDERBILT UNIVERSITY
- Advanced Practice Nursing M
- Allopathic Medicine P,M
- Business Administration and Management M,D
- Communication Disorders M,D
- Counselor Education M
- Curriculum and Instruction M
- Early Childhood Education M,D
- Education M,D,O*
- Educational Administration M,D,O
- Educational Measurement and Evaluation M,D
- Elementary Education M,D
- English Education M,D
- Finance and Banking D
- Gerontological Nursing M
- Health Education M
- Higher Education M,D,O
- Human Resources Development M,D
- Industrial and Manufacturing Management D
- International Business M
- Law P
- Marketing D
- Maternal/Child-Care Nursing M
- Mathematics Education M,D
- Medical/Surgical Nursing M
- Nurse Midwifery M
- Nursing M,D
- Organizational Behavior D
- Psychiatric Nursing M
- Public Health M
- Reading Education M,D
- Science Education M,D
- Secondary Education M
- Social Sciences Education M,D
- Special Education M,D,O

VANDERCOOK COLLEGE OF MUSIC
- Music Education M

VERMONT LAW SCHOOL
- Law P
- Legal and Justice Studies M

VILLA JULIE COLLEGE
- Management Information Systems M

VILLANOVA UNIVERSITY
- Advanced Practice Nursing O
- Business Administration and Management M
- Counselor Education M
- Education M
- Educational Administration M
- Elementary Education M
- Health Services Management and Hospital Administration M
- Human Resources Development M
- Human Services M
- Law P,M
- Maternal/Child-Care Nursing M
- Mathematics Education M
- Medical/Surgical Nursing M
- Nurse Anesthesia M,O
- Nursing M,O*
- Nursing Administration M,O
- Nursing Education M
- Secondary Education M
- Taxation M

VIRGINIA COMMONWEALTH UNIVERSITY
- Accounting D
- Adult Education M
- Advanced Practice Nursing O
- Advertising and Public Relations M
- Allied Health M,D,O
- Allopathic Medicine P
- Art Education M
- Business Administration and Management M,D,O
- Clinical Laboratory Sciences M
- Counselor Education M
- Curriculum and Instruction M
- Dentistry P
- Early Childhood Education M
- Education M,D,O
- Educational Administration M
- Environmental and Occupational Health M
- Finance and Banking M,D
- Health Services Management and Hospital Administration M,D*
- Health Services Research D*
- Human Resources Management M
- Insurance M
- International Business D
- Management Information Systems M,D,O
- Marketing M,D
- Maternal/Child-Care Nursing M
- Mathematics Education M
- Medical/Surgical Nursing M
- Middle School Education M
- Music Education M
- Nurse Anesthesia M
- Nurse Midwifery M
- Nursing M,D,O
- Nursing Administration M
- Occupational Therapy M
- Pharmaceutical Sciences M,D*
- Pharmacy P
- Physical Education M
- Physical Therapy M,D
- Psychiatric Nursing M
- Public Health M
- Quantitative Analysis M,D
- Reading Education M
- Real Estate M,O
- Recreation and Park Management M
- Secondary Education M,O
- Social Work M,D
- Special Education M
- Taxation M,D
- Urban Education D

VIRGINIA POLYTECHNIC INSTITUTE AND STATE UNIVERSITY
- Accounting M,D*
- Adult Education M,D,O
- Business Administration and Management M,D*
- Curriculum and Instruction M,D,O
- Education M,D,O
- Educational Administration M,D,O
- Educational Measurement and Evaluation D
- Exercise and Sports Science M,D
- Finance and Banking D
- Health Education M
- Hospitality Management M,D
- Human Resources Development M,D
- Kinesiology and Movement Studies M,D
- Marketing D
- Physical Education M
- Recreation and Park Management M,D
- Special Education D,O
- Veterinary Medicine P
- Veterinary Sciences M,D
- Vocational and Technical Education M,D,O

VIRGINIA STATE UNIVERSITY
- Business Administration and Management M
- Counselor Education M
- Education M
- Educational Administration M
- Educational Media/Instructional Technology M
- Elementary Education M
- Finance and Banking M
- Mathematics Education M
- Special Education M
- Vocational and Technical Education M,O

VITERBO COLLEGE
- Education M
- Nursing M

WAGNER COLLEGE
- Advanced Practice Nursing O
- Business Administration and Management M
- Education M
- Elementary Education M
- Finance and Banking M
- International Business M
- Marketing M
- Nursing M
- Secondary Education M
- Special Education M

WAKE FOREST UNIVERSITY
- Accounting M
- Allopathic Medicine P
- Business Administration and Management M
- Counselor Education M
- Education M*
- Epidemiology M*
- Exercise and Sports Science M
- Health Services Research M
- Law P,M
- Secondary Education M

WALDEN UNIVERSITY
- Business Administration and Management D
- Education D
- Educational Media/Instructional Technology M
- Health Services Management and Hospital Administration D
- Human Services D

WALLA WALLA COLLEGE
- Counselor Education M
- Curriculum and Instruction M
- Education M
- Educational Administration M
- Reading Education M
- Social Work M
- Special Education M

WALSH COLLEGE OF ACCOUNTANCY AND BUSINESS ADMINISTRATION
- Accounting M
- Business Administration and Management M*
- Finance and Banking M
- Management Information Systems M
- Taxation M

WALSH UNIVERSITY
- Business Administration and Management M
- Counselor Education M
- Education M
- Physical Therapy M

WASHBURN UNIVERSITY OF TOPEKA
- Business Administration and Management M
- Curriculum and Instruction M
- Education M
- Educational Administration M
- Law P
- Reading Education M
- Special Education M

WASHINGTON AND LEE UNIVERSITY
- Law P

WASHINGTON STATE UNIVERSITY
- Accounting M
- Business Administration and Management M,D*
- Communication Disorders M
- Curriculum and Instruction D
- Education M,D
- Educational Administration M,D
- Educational Psychology M,D
- Elementary Education M,D
- English Education M
- Kinesiology and Movement Studies M
- Leisure Studies M
- Nursing M
- Pharmacy P
- Recreation and Park Management M
- Secondary Education M,D
- Veterinary Medicine P
- Veterinary Sciences M,D

WASHINGTON UNIVERSITY IN ST. LOUIS
- Allied Health M,D
- Allopathic Medicine P
- Business Administration and Management M,D
- Communication Disorders M,D*
- Early Childhood Education M,O
- Education M,D,O*
- Educational Measurement and Evaluation D
- Elementary Education M,O
- Health Services Management and Hospital Administration M*
- Kinesiology and Movement Studies D
- Law P,M,D*
- Mathematics Education M
- Occupational Therapy M*
- Physical Therapy M,D
- Secondary Education M
- Social Work M,D*

WAYLAND BAPTIST UNIVERSITY
- Business Administration and Management M
- Education M

WAYNESBURG COLLEGE
- Business Administration and Management M

WAYNE STATE COLLEGE
- Art Education M
- Business Administration and Management M
- Business Education M
- Counselor Education M
- Curriculum and Instruction M
- Education M,O
- Educational Administration M,O
- Elementary Education M
- English as a Second Language M
- English Education M
- Health Education M
- Mathematics Education M
- Music Education M
- Physical Education M
- Science Education M
- Social Sciences Education M

- Special Education M
- Vocational and Technical Education M

WAYNE STATE UNIVERSITY

- Advanced Practice Nursing M,O
- Advertising and Public Relations M
- Allied Health M
- Allopathic Medicine P
- Business Administration and Management M*
- Clinical Laboratory Sciences M
- Communication Disorders M,D
- Community Health M,O
- Counselor Education M,D,O
- Curriculum and Instruction D,O
- Education M,D,O*
- Educational Administration M,D,O
- Educational Measurement and Evaluation M,D
- Educational Media/Instructional Technology M,D,O
- Educational Psychology M,D,O
- Elementary Education M
- Environmental and Occupational Health M
- Foundations and Philosophy of Education D
- Health Education M
- Health Physics/Radiological Health M,D
- Higher Education D
- Human Services O
- Industrial Hygiene M
- Information Studies M,O
- Law P,M*
- Library Science M,O
- Maternal/Child-Care Nursing M,O
- Medical Physics D
- Medical/Surgical Nursing M
- Medical Technology M
- Music Education M
- Nurse Anesthesia M
- Nursing M,D,O
- Nursing Administration M
- Nursing Education O
- Occupational Therapy M
- Pharmaceutical Sciences M,D*
- Pharmacy P,M
- Physical Education M
- Physical Therapy M
- Physician Assistant Studies M
- Psychiatric Nursing M
- Public Health Nursing M
- Reading Education D,O
- Recreation and Park Management M
- Rehabilitation Sciences M
- Science Education O
- Secondary Education M
- Social Sciences Education O
- Social Work M,O*
- Special Education M,D,O
- Sports Administration M
- Taxation M

WEBBER COLLEGE

- Business Administration and Management M

WEBB INSTITUTE

- Transportation Management M

WEBER STATE UNIVERSITY

- Accounting M
- Business Administration and Management M
- Curriculum and Instruction M
- Education M

WEBSTER UNIVERSITY

- Business Administration and Management M,D
- Computer Education M
- Early Childhood Education M
- Education M
- Finance and Banking M
- Health Services Management and Hospital Administration M
- Human Resources Development M
- Human Resources Management M
- International Business M
- Legal and Justice Studies M,O
- Management Information Systems M
- Marketing M
- Mathematics Education M
- Music Education M
- Nurse Anesthesia M
- Nursing M
- Real Estate M
- Science Education M
- Social Sciences Education M
- Special Education M

WESLEYAN COLLEGE

- Early Childhood Education M
- Education M
- Mathematics Education M
- Middle School Education M
- Science Education M

WESLEY COLLEGE (DE)

- Curriculum and Instruction M
- Education M
- Middle School Education M
- Secondary Education M

WEST CHESTER UNIVERSITY OF PENNSYLVANIA

- Business Administration and Management M
- Communication Disorders M
- Counselor Education M
- Education M
- Educational Measurement and Evaluation M
- Educational Media/Instructional Technology M
- Elementary Education M
- English as a Second Language M
- Exercise and Sports Science M
- Finance and Banking M
- Foreign Languages Education M
- Health Education M
- Health Services Management and Hospital Administration M
- Kinesiology and Movement Studies M,O
- Music Education M
- Nursing M
- Physical Education M,O
- Public Health Nursing M
- Reading Education M
- Secondary Education M
- Social Work M
- Special Education M
- Sports Administration M

WESTERN CAROLINA UNIVERSITY

- Accounting M
- Art Education M
- Business Administration and Management M
- Communication Disorders M
- Community College Education M
- Counselor Education M
- Education M,D,O
- Educational Administration M,D,O
- Elementary Education M
- English Education M
- Health Services Management and Hospital Administration M
- Home Economics Education M
- Human Resources Development M
- Mathematics Education M
- Middle School Education M
- Physical Education M
- Physical Therapy M
- Project Management M
- Reading Education M
- Science Education M
- Secondary Education M
- Social Sciences Education M
- Special Education M

WESTERN CONNECTICUT STATE UNIVERSITY

- Business Administration and Management M
- Counselor Education M
- Education M
- Elementary Education M
- Music Education M
- Nursing M
- Reading Education M
- Secondary Education M

WESTERN ILLINOIS UNIVERSITY

- Accounting M
- Business Administration and Management M
- Communication Disorders M
- Counselor Education M
- Education M,O
- Educational Administration M,O
- Educational Media/Instructional Technology M
- Elementary Education M
- Foundations and Philosophy of Education M
- Health Education M
- Health Promotion M
- Physical Education M
- Reading Education M
- Recreation and Park Management M
- Special Education M
- Sports Administration M
- Travel and Tourism M

WESTERN INTERNATIONAL UNIVERSITY

- Accounting M
- Business Administration and Management M
- Finance and Banking M
- Health Services Management and Hospital Administration M
- International Business M
- Management Information Systems M
- Marketing M

WESTERN KENTUCKY UNIVERSITY

- Accounting M
- Art Education M
- Business Administration and Management M
- Business Education M
- Communication Disorders M
- Counselor Education M,O
- Early Childhood Education M
- Education M,D,O
- Educational Administration M,D,O
- Educational Media/Instructional Technology M
- Elementary Education M,O
- English as a Second Language M
- English Education M
- Environmental and Occupational Health M
- Foreign Languages Education M
- Health Education M
- Health Services Management and Hospital Administration M
- Home Economics Education M
- Marketing M
- Mathematics Education M
- Middle School Education M
- Music Education M
- Nursing M
- Physical Education M
- Public Health M
- Reading Education M
- Recreation and Park Management M
- Science Education M
- Secondary Education M,O
- Social Sciences Education M
- Special Education M

WESTERN MARYLAND COLLEGE

- Counselor Education M
- Education M
- Educational Administration M
- Educational Media/Instructional Technology M
- Elementary Education M
- Library Science M
- Physical Education M
- Reading Education M
- Secondary Education M
- Special Education M

WESTERN MICHIGAN UNIVERSITY

- Accounting M
- Business Administration and Management M
- Communication Disorders M
- Counselor Education M,D
- Early Childhood Education M
- Education M,D,O
- Educational Administration M,D,O
- Elementary Education M
- Exercise and Sports Science M
- Home Economics Education M
- Mathematics Education M,D
- Middle School Education M
- Occupational Therapy M
- Physical Education M
- Reading Education M
- Science Education M,D
- Social Work M
- Special Education M,D
- Sports Administration M
- Vocational and Technical Education M

WESTERN NEW ENGLAND COLLEGE

- Accounting M
- Business Administration and Management M
- Finance and Banking M
- Health Services Management and Hospital Administration M
- Human Resources Development M
- Human Resources Management M
- International Business M
- Law P
- Management Information Systems M
- Marketing M

WESTERN NEW MEXICO UNIVERSITY

- Business Administration and Management M*
- Counselor Education M
- Education M
- Educational Administration M
- Elementary Education M
- Reading Education M
- Secondary Education M
- Special Education M

WESTERN OREGON UNIVERSITY

- Early Childhood Education M
- Education M
- Educational Media/Instructional Technology M
- Education of the Multiply Handicapped M
- Elementary Education M
- English as a Second Language M
- Mathematics Education M
- Middle School Education M
- Reading Education M
- Science Education M
- Secondary Education M
- Social Sciences Education M
- Special Education M

WESTERN SEMINARY

- Religious Education P,M

WESTERN STATES CHIROPRACTIC COLLEGE

- Chiropractic P*

WESTERN STATE UNIVERSITY COLLEGE OF LAW

- Law P*

WESTERN UNIVERSITY OF HEALTH SCIENCES

- Advanced Practice Nursing M
- Allied Health M,O
- Health Education M
- Nursing M
- Osteopathic Medicine P
- Pharmacy P
- Physical Therapy M
- Physician Assistant Studies O

WESTERN WASHINGTON UNIVERSITY

- Adult Education M
- Art Education M
- Business Administration and Management M
- Communication Disorders M
- Counselor Education M
- Education M
- Educational Administration M
- Educational Media/Instructional Technology M
- Elementary Education M
- Environmental and Occupational Health M
- Physical Education M
- Reading Education M
- Science Education M
- Secondary Education M
- Special Education M

WESTFIELD STATE COLLEGE

- Early Childhood Education M
- Education M,O
- Educational Administration M,O
- Educational Media/Instructional Technology M
- Elementary Education M
- Middle School Education M
- Reading Education M
- Secondary Education M
- Special Education M
- Vocational and Technical Education M

WESTMINSTER COLLEGE (PA)

- Counselor Education M,O
- Curriculum and Instruction M,O
- Education M,O
- Educational Administration M,O
- Elementary Education M,O
- Reading Education M,O

WESTMINSTER COLLEGE OF SALT LAKE CITY

- Business Administration and Management M
- Education M
- Nursing M

WEST TEXAS A&M UNIVERSITY

- Accounting M
- Business Administration and Management M
- Counselor Education M
- Curriculum and Instruction M
- Education M
- Educational Administration M
- Educational Measurement and Evaluation M
- Educational Media/Instructional Technology M
- Elementary Education M
- Exercise and Sports Science M
- Finance and Banking M
- Nursing M
- Reading Education M
- Secondary Education M

WEST VIRGINIA SCHOOL OF OSTEOPATHIC MEDICINE

- Osteopathic Medicine P

WEST VIRGINIA UNIVERSITY
Accounting M
Advanced Practice Nursing O
Agricultural Education M
Allopathic Medicine P
Art Education M
Business Administration and Management M
Communication Disorders M
Community Health M
Curriculum and Instruction M,D
Dentistry P
Education M,D
Educational Administration M,D
Educational Psychology M,D
Elementary Education M
English as a Second Language M
Exercise and Sports Science M
Health Promotion M
Law P*
Medical Technology M
Nursing M,O
Occupational Therapy M
Oral and Dental Sciences M
Pharmaceutical Sciences M,D
Pharmacy P
Physical Education M,D
Physical Therapy M
Public Health M
Reading Education M
Recreation and Park Management M
Secondary Education M
Social Work M
Special Education M,D
Veterinary Sciences M
Vocational and Technical Education M,D

WEST VIRGINIA WESLEYAN COLLEGE
Business Administration and Management M

WHEATON COLLEGE (IL)
Education M
English as a Second Language O
Religious Education M
Secondary Education M

WHEELING JESUIT UNIVERSITY
Accounting M
Business Administration and Management M
Mathematics Education M
Nursing M
Physical Therapy M
Science Education M

WHEELOCK COLLEGE
Early Childhood Education M,O
Education M,O*
Educational Administration M,O
Elementary Education M
Maternal and Child Health M,O
Reading Education M,O
Social Work M
Special Education M,O

WHITTIER COLLEGE
Early Childhood Education M
Education M
Educational Administration M
Elementary Education M
Law P
Secondary Education M

WHITWORTH COLLEGE
Business Administration and Management M
Counselor Education M
Education M
Educational Administration M
Education of the Gifted M
English as a Second Language M
International Business M
Physical Education M
Reading Education M
Special Education M
Sports Administration M

WICHITA STATE UNIVERSITY
Accounting M
Allied Health M
Art Education M
Business Administration and Management M
Communication Disorders M,D
Counselor Education M
Curriculum and Instruction M
Education M,D,O
Educational Administration M,D
Educational Psychology M
Exercise and Sports Science M
Maternal/Child-Care Nursing M
Medical/Surgical Nursing M
Music Education M
Nursing M
Nursing Administration M
Nursing Education M
Physical Education M
Physical Therapy M
Psychiatric Nursing M
Public Health M
Special Education M
Sports Administration M

WIDENER UNIVERSITY
Accounting M
Business Administration and Management M
Education M,D
Health Services Management and Hospital Administration M
Human Resources Management M
Law P,M*
Nursing M,D,O
Physical Therapy M
Social Work M*
Taxation M

WILFRID LAURIER UNIVERSITY
Business Administration and Management M
Social Work M,D

WILKES UNIVERSITY
Accounting M
Business Administration and Management M
Computer Education M
Education M
Educational Administration M
Educational Measurement and Evaluation M
Elementary Education M
English Education M
Finance and Banking M
Health Services Management and Hospital Administration M
Human Resources Management M
International Business M
Management Information Systems M
Marketing M
Mathematics Education M
Nursing M
Pharmacy P
Science Education M
Secondary Education M
Social Sciences Education M

WILLAMETTE UNIVERSITY
Business Administration and Management M*
Education M
Law P*

WILLIAM CAREY COLLEGE
Business Administration and Management M
Education M
Educational Administration M
Education of the Gifted M
Elementary Education M
Secondary Education M
Special Education M

WILLIAM MITCHELL COLLEGE OF LAW
Law P,M

WILLIAM PATERSON UNIVERSITY OF NEW JERSEY
Business Administration and Management M
Communication Disorders M
Counselor Education M
Education M
Elementary Education M
Nursing M
Reading Education M
Special Education M

WILLIAM WOODS UNIVERSITY
Business Administration and Management M
Curriculum and Instruction M
Education M
Educational Administration M

WILMINGTON COLLEGE (DE)
Advanced Practice Nursing M
Business Administration and Management M
Counselor Education M
Education M,D
Educational Administration M,D
Elementary Education M
Human Resources Management M
Nursing M
Special Education M

WINEBRENNER THEOLOGICAL SEMINARY
Religious Education P,M

WINGATE UNIVERSITY
Business Administration and Management M
Education M
Elementary Education M
Secondary Education M

WINONA STATE UNIVERSITY
Business Administration and Management M
Business Education M
Counselor Education M
Early Childhood Education M
Education M,O
Educational Administration M,O
Elementary Education M
Nursing M*
Physical Education M
Special Education M

WINTHROP UNIVERSITY
Art Education M
Business Administration and Management M
Business Education M
Counselor Education M
Curriculum and Instruction O
Education M,O
Educational Administration M,O
Educational Media/Instructional Technology M
Elementary Education M,O
Home Economics Education M
Music Education M
Physical Education M
Reading Education M
Secondary Education M,O
Special Education M,O

WOODBURY UNIVERSITY
Business Administration and Management M*

WORCESTER POLYTECHNIC INSTITUTE
Business Administration and Management M
Industrial and Manufacturing Management M
Management Information Systems M
Marketing M

WORCESTER STATE COLLEGE
Communication Disorders M
Early Childhood Education M
Education M,O
Educational Administration M
Elementary Education M
English Education M
Health Education M
Middle School Education M,O
Nonprofit Management M
Occupational Therapy M
Physical Therapy M
Reading Education M,O
Secondary Education M,O
Social Sciences Education M

WRIGHT STATE UNIVERSITY
Accounting M
Advanced Practice Nursing M
Allopathic Medicine P
Business Administration and Management M*
Business Education M
Counselor Education M
Early Childhood Education M
Education M,D,O
Educational Administration M,O
Education of the Gifted M
Education of the Multiply Handicapped M
Elementary Education M
English as a Second Language M
Finance and Banking M
Health Education M
Health Services Management and Hospital Administration M
Industrial and Manufacturing Management M
International Business M
Logistics M
Management Information Systems M
Marketing M
Maternal/Child-Care Nursing M
Medical Physics M
Medical/Surgical Nursing M
Music Education M
Nursing M
Nursing Administration M
Nursing Education M
Physical Education M
Project Management M
Public Health Nursing M
Recreation and Park Management M
Science Education M
Secondary Education M
Special Education M
Vocational and Technical Education M

XAVIER UNIVERSITY
Art Education M
Business Administration and Management M
Counselor Education M
Early Childhood Education M
Education M
Educational Administration M
Education of the Gifted M
Education of the Multiply Handicapped M
Elementary Education M
English Education M
Health Services Management and Hospital Administration M*
Human Resources Development M
Mathematics Education M
Multilingual and Multicultural Education M
Music Education M
Nursing M
Nursing Administration M
Occupational Therapy O
Reading Education M
Religious Education M
Secondary Education M
Special Education M
Sports Administration M

XAVIER UNIVERSITY OF LOUISIANA
Counselor Education M
Curriculum and Instruction M
Education M
Educational Administration M
Nurse Anesthesia M
Pharmacy P*

YALE UNIVERSITY
Accounting D
Allopathic Medicine P
Business Administration and Management M,D*
Environmental and Occupational Health M,D*
Epidemiology M,D*
Finance and Banking D
Health Services Management and Hospital Administration M,D*
International Health M*
Law P,M,D
Marketing D
Nursing M,D,O*
Physician Assistant Studies O
Public Health M,D*

YESHIVA UNIVERSITY
Allopathic Medicine P
Educational Administration M,D,O
Law P
Religious Education M,D,O
Social Work M,D

YORK COLLEGE OF PENNSYLVANIA
Business Administration and Management M

YORK UNIVERSITY
Business Administration and Management M,D*
Education M
Exercise and Sports Science M
Law P,M,D
Social Work M

YO SAN UNIVERSITY OF TRADITIONAL CHINESE MEDICINE
Oriental Medicine and Acupuncture M

YOUNGSTOWN STATE UNIVERSITY
Accounting M
Business Administration and Management M
Counselor Education M
Early Childhood Education M
Education M,D
Educational Administration M,D
Education of the Gifted M
Elementary Education M
Finance and Banking M
Health Services Management and Hospital Administration M
Human Services M
Marketing M
Middle School Education M
Music Education M
Nursing M
Reading Education M
Secondary Education M
Special Education M

Academic and Professional Programs in Business

This part of Book 6 consists of twenty sections covering business. Each section has a table of contents (listing the program directories, announcements, and in-depth descriptions); program directories, which consist of brief profiles of programs in the relevant fields (and 50-word or 100-word announcements following the profiles, if programs have chosen to include them); Cross-Discipline Announcements, if programs have chosen to submit such entries; and in-depth descriptions, which are more individualized statements included, if programs have chosen to submit them.

Section 1
Business Administration and Management

This section contains a general directory of institutions that have programs in business administration and management, followed by in-depth entries submitted by institutions that chose to prepare detailed program descriptions. Additional information about programs listed in the directory but not augmented by an in-depth entry may be obtained by writing directly to the dean of a graduate school or chair of a department at the address given in the directory.

For programs offering related work, see also in this book Sections 2–20 and Education (Business Education), Health Services, Nursing (Nursing Administration), and Sports Administration. In Book 2, see Art and Art History (Arts Administration), Economics, Home Economics and Family Studies (Consumer Economics), Political Science and International Affairs, Psychology (Industrial and Organizational Psychology), and Public, Regional, and Industrial Affairs (Industrial and Labor Relations). In Book 4, see Environmental Sciences and Management (Environmental Policy and Resource Management) and Mathematical Sciences; and in Book 5, Computer Science and Information Technology, Civil and Environmental Engineering (Construction Engineering and Management), Industrial Engineering, and Management of Engineering and Technology.

CONTENTS

Program Directory

Announcements

Cross-Discipline Announcements

In-Depth Descriptions

Business Administration and Management—General

Abilene Christian University, College of Business Administration, Program in Business Administration, Abilene, TX 79699-9100. Awards MBA. Part-time programs available. Faculty: 10 part-time (0 women). Students: 7 full-time (2 women), 7 part-time (4 women); includes 2 minority (both African Americans), 2 international. 21 applicants, 29% accepted. In 1997, 8 degrees awarded. *Degree requirements:* Comprehensive exam required, foreign language and thesis not required. *Entrance requirements:* GMAT or GRE General Test. Application deadline: 4/1 (priority date; rolling processing; 11/1 for spring admission). Application fee: $25 ($45 for international students). *Expenses:* Tuition $308 per credit hour. Fees $430 per year full-time, $85 per semester (minimum) part-time. *Financial aid:* Teaching assistantships, Federal Work-Study available. Aid available to part-time students. Financial aid application deadline: 4/1. *Faculty research:* Organizational structure, financial management, cost accounting, unit analysis management. • Application contact: Dr. Carley Dodd, Graduate Dean, 915-674-2354. Fax: 915-674-6717. E-mail: gradinfo@nicanor.acu.edu.

Adelphi University, School of Management and Business, Certificate Programs in Management, Garden City, NY 11530. Offerings in banking (Certificate), human resource management (Certificate), management for non-business majors (Certificate), management for women (Certificate). Part-time and evening/weekend programs available. Students: 11 part-time (8 women). Average age 30. In 1997, 3 degrees awarded. *Average time to degree:* other advanced degree–2 years full-time, 2.5 years part-time. *Application deadline:* 8/15 (priority date; rolling processing; 12/15 for spring admission). *Application fee:* $50. *Expenses:* Tuition $16,000 per year full-time, $485 per credit part-time. Fees $500 per year full-time, $150 per semester part-time. *Financial aid:* Application deadline 3/1. • Application contact: Jennifer Spiegel, Associate Director of Admissions, 516-877-3055.

See in-depth description on page 133.

Adelphi University, School of Management and Business, Department of Administrative Sciences, Garden City, NY 11530. Awards MBA. Part-time and evening/weekend programs available. Faculty: 10 full-time (2 women), 14 part-time (1 woman). Students: 8 full-time (5 women), 347 part-time (168 women). Average age 28. In 1997, 135 degrees awarded. *Degree requirements:* Computer language required, foreign language and thesis not required. *Average time to degree:* master's–2.5 years full-time, 5 years part-time. *Entrance requirements:* GMAT (minimum score 450), TOEFL (minimum score 550). Application deadline: 8/15 (priority date; rolling processing; 12/15 for spring admission). Application fee: $50. *Expenses:* Tuition $16,000 per year full-time, $485 per credit part-time. Fees $500 per year full-time, $150 per semester part-time. *Financial aid:* In 1997–98, 1 grant was awarded; career-related internships or fieldwork also available. Financial aid application deadline: 3/1. • Dr. Allan Ashley, Chairperson, 516-877-4640. Application contact: Jennifer Spiegel, Associate Director of Admissions, 516-877-3055.

See in-depth description on page 133.

Alabama Agricultural and Mechanical University, School of Business, Department of Management and Marketing, PO Box 1357, Normal, AL 35762-1357. Awards MBA. Part-time and evening/weekend programs available. Faculty: 13 full-time (2 women), 4 part-time (0 women). Students: 34 full-time (18 women), 74 part-time (47 women); includes 68 minority (64 African Americans, 4 Asian Americans), 17 international. Average age 28. In 1997, 37 degrees awarded. *Degree requirements:* Comprehensive exam required, thesis optional, foreign language not required. *Entrance requirements:* GMAT, TOEFL (minimum score 500), minimum undergraduate GPA of 2.5. Application deadline: 5/1 (priority date; rolling processing). Application fee: $15 ($20 for international students). *Expenses:* Tuition $2782 per year full-time, $565 per semester (minimum) part-time for state residents; $5164 per year full-time, $1015 per semester (minimum) part-time for nonresidents. Fees $560 per year full-time, $390 per year part-time. *Financial aid:* Research assistantships, Federal Work-Study, institutionally sponsored loans, and career-related internships or fieldwork available. Financial aid application deadline: 4/1. *Faculty research:* Consumer behavior of blacks, small business marketing, economics of education, China in transition, international economics, intergenerational economics/eco-demographics. • Dr. Herman Mixon, Chair, 205-851-5088. Application contact: Dr. Marsha D. Griffin, Coordinator, 205-851-5494.

Alabama State University, School of Graduate Studies, College of Business Administration, Montgomery, AL 36101-0271. Awards MS. *Application deadline:* 7/15 (rolling processing; 12/15 for spring admission). *Application fee:* $10. *Expenses:* Tuition $85 per credit hour for state residents; $170 per credit hour for nonresidents. Fees $486 per year. • Dr. Percy Vaughn, Dean, 334-229-4124.

Alaska Pacific University, Graduate Programs, Business Administration Department, Program in Business Administration, 4101 University Drive, Anchorage, AK 99508-4672. Awards MBA. Faculty: 5 full-time (1 woman), 1 part-time (0 women), 5.33 FTE. Students: 8 full-time (3 women), 24 part-time (14 women); includes 8 minority (2 African Americans, 2 Asian Americans, 1 Hispanic, 3 Native Americans), 2 international. Average age 36. 18 applicants, 50% accepted. In 1997, 16 degrees awarded. *Degree requirements:* Thesis optional, foreign language not required. *Entrance requirements:* GMAT or GRE, minimum GPA of 3.0. Application deadline: 4/1 (priority date; rolling processing; 12/15 for spring admission). Application fee: $25. *Expenses:* Tuition $6600 per year full-time, $370 per credit hour part-time. Fees $80 per year. *Financial aid:* In 1997–98, 5 research assistantships (1 to a first-year student) totaling $18,900, 9 grants, scholarships (3 to first-year students) totaling $112,500 were awarded; Federal Work-Study and career-related internships or fieldwork also available. Aid available to part-time students. Financial aid application deadline: 3/15. • Dr. Fred Barbee, Director, 907-564-8251. Fax: 907-562-4276. E-mail: busadapu@corecom.net. Application contact: Kirsty Gladkoff, Associate Director of Admissions, 907-564-8248. Fax: 907-564-8317. E-mail: apu@corecom.net.

Albany State University, School of Business, Albany, GA 31705-2717. Awards MBA. Part-time programs available. Faculty: 9 full-time (2 women). Students: 44 part-time (19 women); includes 12 minority (all African Americans), 1 international. Average age 28. 25 applicants, 100% accepted. In 1997, 17 degrees awarded. *Degree requirements:* Comprehensive exam. *Entrance requirements:* GMAT (minimum score 450), minimum GPA of 2.5. Application deadline: 9/1. Application fee: $10. *Financial aid:* In 1997–98, 1 scholarship (to a first-year student) was awarded; Federal Work-Study and career-related internships or fieldwork also available. Aid available to part-time students. Financial aid application deadline: 4/1. *Faculty research:* Economic impacts, employment opportunities. • Dr. Mollie Brown, Interim Dean, 912-430-4772. Fax: 912-430-5119. E-mail: mbrown@fld94.alsnet.peachnet.edu.

Albertus Magnus College, Program in Management, New Haven, CT 06511-1189. Awards MSM. Faculty: 3 full-time, 15 part-time. Students: 200. 120 applicants, 83% accepted. *Degree requirements:* Thesis. *Entrance requirements:* TOEFL (minimum score 600), 3 years of management or related experience, minimum GPA of 2.5. Application deadline: rolling. Application fee: $75. *Expenses:* Tuition $948 per course (minimum). Fees $20 per year. *Financial aid:* Available to part-time students. • Dr. Samuel Brown, Director, 203-773-0800.

Alfred University, Graduate School, College of Business, Alfred, NY 14802-1205. Awards MBA. Part-time programs available. Faculty: 15 full-time (4 women). Students: 15 full-time (4 women), 15 part-time (6 women). Average age 25. 27 applicants, 67% accepted. In 1997, 12 degrees awarded. *Entrance requirements:* GMAT, TOEFL. Application deadline: rolling. Application fee: $50. *Expenses:* Tuition $20,376 per year full-time, $390 per credit hour (minimum) part-time. Fees $546 per year. *Financial aid:* Research assistantships and career-related internships or fieldwork available. Aid available to part-time students. Financial aid applicants required to submit FAFSA. *Faculty research:* Regional economic development, activity-based costing, nonprofit consumer behavior. • Dr. Daniel D. Acton, Director of MBA Program, 607-871-2204. E-mail: facton@bigvax.alfred.edu. Application contact: Cathleen R. Johnson, Assistant Director of Admissions, 607-871-2141. Fax: 607-871-2198. E-mail: johnsonc@bigvax.alfred.edu.

Allentown College of St. Francis de Sales, Graduate Division, Department of Business, Center Valley, PA 18034-9568. Offers program in business administration (MBA). Offered jointly with Gwynedd-Mercy College. Part-time and evening/weekend programs available. Faculty: 10 full-time (1 woman), 17 part-time (2 women). Students: 410 part-time (245 women); includes 3 minority (2 African Americans, 1 Hispanic). 80 applicants, 75% accepted. In 1997, 47 degrees awarded. *Average time to degree:* master's–3 years part-time. *Entrance requirements:* Minimum GPA of 3.0. Application deadline: rolling. Application fee: $35. *Tuition:* $410 per credit. *Financial aid:* Career-related internships or fieldwork available. *Faculty research:* Quality improvement, executive development, productivity, cross-cultural managerial differences, leadership. • Dr. Mohamed Latib, Director, 610-282-1100 Ext. 1365. E-mail: latib@faculty-1.allencol.edu. Application contact: Debra Hockenberry, Coordinator, 610-282-1100 Ext. 1451. Fax: 610-282-2254.

Amber University, Graduate School, Department of Business Administration, Garland, TX 75041-5595. Offers programs in general business (MBA), management (MBA). Part-time and evening/weekend programs available. Faculty: 16 full-time (7 women), 45 part-time (20 women). Students: 40 full-time (15 women), 250 part-time (150 women); includes 71 minority (44 African Americans, 1 Asian American, 25 Hispanics, 1 Native American), 20 international. Average age 35. 325 applicants, 98% accepted. In 1997, 165 degrees awarded. *Entrance requirements:* GMAT, GRE, or MAT, minimum GPA of 3.0. Application fee: $25 ($100 for international students). *Expenses:* Tuition $150 per semester hour. Fees $25 per year. • Dr. Algia Allen, Academic Dean, Graduate School, 972-279-6511 Ext. 135. Fax: 972-279-9773.

American College, Richard D. Irwin Graduate School of Management, Bryn Mawr, PA 19010-2105. Awards MSM. Part-time and evening/weekend programs available. Postbaccalaureate distance learning degree programs offered (minimal on-campus study). Faculty: 27 full-time (3 women), 8 part-time (0 women). Students: 500 part-time. *Degree requirements:* Thesis required, foreign language not required. *Application deadline:* rolling. *Application fee:* $275. *Tuition:* $490 per course. *Faculty research:* Management of innovation, business ethics. • Dr. G. Steven McMillan, Director of Graduate Administration, 610-526-1368. E-mail: stevem@amercoll.edu. Application contact: Joanne F. Patterson, Associate Director of Graduate Administration, 610-526-1366. Fax: 610-526-1310. E-mail: joannep@amercoll.edu.

American InterContinental University, Program in Business Administration, London W1M 3DB, United Kingdom. Offers international business (MBA). Faculty: 4 full-time (2 women). Students: 50 full-time, 10 part-time. Average age 24. *Entrance requirements:* GMAT or interview. Application fee: $35. *Financial aid:* Fellowships, research assistantships, teaching assistantships available. • Dr. Andrew Hageman, Dean, School of Business. Application contact: Study Abroad Office, 800-255-6839.

American International College, School of Continuing Education and Graduate Studies, School of Business Administration, Springfield, MA 01109-3189. Awards MBA. Faculty: 7 full-time. Students: 24 full-time (11 women), 67 part-time (29 women); includes 8 minority (2 African Americans, 5 Asian Americans, 1 Hispanic), 9 international. Average age 28. 150 applicants, 40% accepted. In 1997, 34 degrees awarded. *Entrance requirements:* GMAT. Application fee: $15 ($25 for international students). *Expenses:* Tuition $363 per credit hour. Fees $25 per semester. *Financial aid:* Federal Work-Study and career-related internships or fieldwork available. • Dr. Adam Zielinski, Dean, 413-747-6230.

See in-depth description on page 135.

American University, Kogod College of Business Administration, Washington, DC 20016-8001. Awards MBA, MS, JD/MBA, MBA/MA. MBA/MA offered jointly with the School of International Service. Part-time and evening/weekend programs available. Postbaccalaureate distance learning degree programs offered. Faculty: 57 full-time (13 women), 13 part-time (5 women). Students: 229 full-time (98 women), 273 part-time (114 women); includes 90 minority (41 African Americans, 31 Asian Americans, 17 Hispanics, 1 Native American), 135 international. 624 applicants, 79% accepted. In 1997, 214 degrees awarded. *Entrance requirements:* GMAT. Application deadline: 2/1 (priority date). Application fee: $50. *Expenses:* Tuition $19,080 per year full-time, $687 per credit hour (minimum) part-time. Fees $180 per year full-time, $110 per year part-time. *Financial aid:* Fellowships, research assistantships, administrative fellowships, Federal Work-Study, institutionally sponsored loans, and career-related internships or fieldwork available. Aid available to part-time students. Financial aid application deadline: 2/1. • Dr. Stevan R. Holmberg, Acting Dean, 202-885-1985.

See in-depth description on page 137.

American University in Cairo, Graduate Studies, School of Business, Economics and Communication, Department of Management, Cairo, Egypt. Awards MBA, MPA, Diploma. Part-time programs available. *Entrance requirements:* For master's, GMAT (MBA), English entrance exam and/or TOEFL. Application fee: $35. *Faculty research:* Privatization, public sector management, Islamic banking, information systems management, role of private sector in economic development.

Andrews University, School of Graduate Studies, School of Business, Department of Management and Marketing, Berrien Springs, MI 49104. Awards MBA, MSA. *Degree requirements:* Computer language required, foreign language and thesis not required. *Entrance requirements:* GMAT (minimum score 400), TOEFL (minimum score 550). Application deadline: 8/15 (rolling processing). Application fee: $30. *Expenses:* Tuition $290 per quarter hour (minimum). Fees $75 per quarter. • Dr. Allen Stembridge, Chair, 616-471-3339.

Angelo State University, College of Professional Studies, Department of Business Administration, San Angelo, TX 76909. Offers program in management (MBA). Part-time and evening/weekend programs available. Faculty: 10 full-time (2 women). Students: 21 full-time (7 women), 40 part-time (14 women); includes 9 minority (4 African Americans, 1 Asian American, 3 Hispanics, 1 Native American), 3 international. Average age 32. 37 applicants, 68% accepted. In 1997, 8 degrees awarded. *Degree requirements:* Comprehensive exam required, thesis optional, foreign language not required. *Entrance requirements:* GMAT, minimum GPA of 2.5. Application deadline: 8/7 (priority date; rolling processing; 1/2 for spring admission). Application fee: $25 ($50 for international students). *Expenses:* Tuition $1022 per year full-time, $36 per semester hour part-time for state residents; $7382 per year full-time, $246 per semester hour part-time for nonresidents. Fees $1140 per year full-time, $165 per semester (minimum) part-time. *Financial aid:* In 1997–98, 13 fellowships were awarded; teaching assistantships, graduate assistantships, partial tuition waivers, Federal Work-Study also available. Aid available to part-time students. Financial aid application deadline: 8/1. • Dr. W. O. Smith, Head, 915-942-2383.

Anna Maria College, Program in Business Administration, Paxton, MA 01612. Awards MBA. Part-time and evening/weekend programs available. Faculty: 34. In 1997, 75 degrees awarded. *Degree requirements:* Comprehensive exam required, foreign language and thesis not required. *Entrance requirements:* GMAT. Application fee: $30. *Tuition:* $730 per course. *Financial aid:*

Directory: Business Administration and Management—General

Anna Maria College (continued)

Available to part-time students. *Faculty research:* Management organization. • Bernard Wood, Director, 508-849-3339.

Antioch New England Graduate School, Graduate School, Department of Organization and Management, Program in Management, 40 Avon Street, Keene, NH 03431-3516. Awards MS. Faculty: 1 (woman) full-time, 18 part-time (9 women). Students: 39 full-time (29 women), 10 part-time (3 women). Average age 40. In 1997, 28 degrees awarded. *Degree requirements:* Practicum required, foreign language and thesis not required. *Entrance requirements:* Previous course work and work experience in organization and management. Application deadline: 8/1 (rolling processing; 12/1 for spring admission). Application fee: $40. *Expenses:* Tuition $12,700 per year full-time, $330 per credit part-time. Fees $165 per year. *Financial aid:* 31 students received aid; Federal Work-Study and career-related internships or fieldwork available. Financial aid applicants required to submit FAFSA. *Faculty research:* Developing a collaborative CEO performance evaluation process, search conference process as change mechanism, implementing workflow designs to increase organizational competitiveness. • Application contact: Carolyn Bassett, Co-Director of Admissions, 603-357-6265 Ext. 287. Fax: 603-357-0718. E-mail: cbassett@antiochne.edu.

Announcement: Adult graduate programs emphasizing continuous learning, self-knowledge, collaboration, and leadership training in a practice-oriented, values-based curriculum. Degrees offered: Master of Science (MS) in management, Master of Human Services Administration (MHSA), and Master of Education (M Ed) in administration and supervision. In order to meet the needs of working adults, classes are scheduled, usually 1 day per week, at 3 convenient sites: Keene, New Hampshire; Bennington, Vermont; and Portsmouth, New Hampshire. Weekend master's programs also offered in Keene.

Antioch Southern California/Los Angeles, Program in Organizational Management, 13274 Fiji Way, Marina del Rey, CA 90292-7090. Offers entrepreneurship (MA), human resource development (MA), organizational behavior (MA). Part-time and evening/weekend programs available. Faculty: 2 full-time (1 woman), 5 part-time (3 women). Students: 5 full-time (3 women), 23 part-time (20 women); includes 9 minority (4 African Americans, 5 Hispanics), 1 international. Average age 43. 11 applicants, 82% accepted. In 1997, 13 degrees awarded. *Degree requirements:* Computer language, thesis required, foreign language not required. *Entrance requirements:* TOEFL (minimum score 600), interview. Application deadline: 8/8 (priority date; 2/6 for spring admission). Application fee: $50. *Financial aid:* Federal Work-Study and career-related internships or fieldwork available. Aid available to part-time students. Financial aid application deadline: 8/5; applicants required to submit CSS PROFILE or FAFSA. *Faculty research:* Systems thinking and chaos theory, technology and organizational structure, nonprofit management, organizational development and change. • Scott Schroeder, Chair, 310-578-1080. Fax: 310-822-4824. E-mail: scott_schroeder@antiochla.edu. Application contact: MeHee Hyun, Director of Admissions, 310-578-1090. Fax: 310-822-4842. E-mail: mehee_hyun@antiochla.edu.

Antioch University Seattle, Program in Management, 2326 Sixth Avenue, Seattle, WA 98121-1814. Offers environment and community (MS), management (MS). Evening/weekend programs available. Faculty: 3 full-time (1 woman), 2 part-time (1 woman). Students: 43 full-time, 36 part-time; includes 1 international. Average age 30. 28 applicants, 79% accepted. In 1997, 18 degrees awarded. *Application deadline:* 8/15 (rolling processing; 2/3 for spring admission). *Application fee:* $50. *Expenses:* Tuition $12,900 per year. Fees $30 per quarter full-time, $15 per quarter part-time. *Financial aid:* Federal Work-Study, institutionally sponsored loans available. Financial aid application deadline: 6/15. • Donald Comstock, Director, 206-441-5352. Application contact: Vicki Tolbert, Admissions Officer, 206-441-5352.

Appalachian State University, John A. Walker College of Business, Program in Business Administration, Boone, NC 28608. Offers business administration (MBA), industrial organization/human resource management (MA). Faculty: 15 full-time (5 women), 1 part-time (0 women). Students: 41 full-time (13 women), 47 part-time (23 women); includes 20 minority (all African Americans), 4 international. 57 applicants, 70% accepted. In 1997, 64 degrees awarded. *Degree requirements:* Comprehensive exam required, foreign language and thesis not required. *Entrance requirements:* GMAT (minimum score 450; average 510). Application deadline: 5/31 (priority date; rolling processing). Application fee: $35. *Tuition:* $1811 per year full-time, $354 per semester (minimum) part-time for state residents; $9081 per year full-time, $2171 per semester (minimum) part-time for nonresidents. *Financial aid:* In 1997–98, 7 assistantships were awarded; fellowships, research assistantships, teaching assistantships, and career-related internships or fieldwork also available. Aid available to part-time students. • Dr. Rickey C. Kirkpatrick, Assistant Dean for Graduate and External Programs, 704-262-6127. Fax: 704-262-2925. E-mail: kirkprc@appstate.edu.

Aquinas College, Graduate Management Program, Grand Rapids, MI 49506-1799. Awards M Mgt. Part-time and evening/weekend programs available. Faculty: 12 full-time (3 women), 10 part-time (4 women). Students: 20 full-time (13 women), 277 part-time (140 women); includes 18 minority (12 African Americans, 3 Asian Americans, 3 Hispanics), 2 international. Average age 34. 117 applicants, 100% accepted. In 1997, 88 degrees awarded. *Entrance requirements:* GMAT (score in 40th percentile or higher), minimum undergraduate GPA of 2.75, 2 years of work experience. Application deadline: rolling. Application fee: $35. *Tuition:* $310 per credit hour. *Financial aid:* Available to part-time students. Financial aid application deadline: 3/15. • Dr. Joyce McNally, Dean of Graduate Studies, 616-459-8281 Ext. 5427.

Arizona State University, College of Business, Program in Business Administration, Tempe, AZ 85287. Awards MBA, PhD, JD/MBA, MBA/M Arch, MBA/MHSA, MBA/MIM. Offerings include accountancy (PhD), business administration (MBA), finance (PhD), health services research (PhD), information management (PhD), management (PhD), marketing (PhD), supply chain management (PhD). MBA/MIM offered jointly with Thunderbird, The American Graduate School of International Management and Groupe École Supéieure de Commerce, Toulouse, France. Faculty: 93 full-time (21 women), 10 part-time (1 woman). Students: 814 full-time (226 women), 35 part-time (15 women); includes 103 minority (17 African Americans, 38 Asian Americans, 41 Hispanics, 7 Native Americans), 82 international. Average age 31. 1,100 applicants, 60% accepted. In 1997, 283 master's, 14 doctorates awarded. *Degree requirements:* For master's, thesis optional; for doctorate, dissertation. *Entrance requirements:* For master's, GMAT. Application fee: $45. *Expenses:* Tuition $2088 per year full-time, $110 per hour part-time for state residents; $9040 per year full-time, $377 per hour part-time for nonresidents. Fees $72 per year full-time, $18 per semester (minimum) part-time. *Faculty research:* Purchasing and logistics management. • Dr. Lee R. McPheters, Associate Dean, 602-965-9377. Fax: 602-965-3368. Application contact: Judy Heilala, Director of MBA, 602-965-3331.

See in-depth description on page 139.

Arizona State University West, School of Management, Program in Business, Phoenix, AZ 85069-7100. Awards MBA, MBA/MIM. MBA/MIM offered jointly with Thunderbird, The American Graduate School of International Management. Part-time and evening/weekend programs available. Faculty: 16 full-time (2 women), 1 part-time (0 women), 16.5 FTE. Students: 54 full-time (17 women), 314 part-time (99 women); includes 36 minority (5 African Americans, 18 Asian Americans, 12 Hispanics, 1 Native American), 27 international. Average age 34. 155 applicants, 57% accepted. In 1997, 75 degrees awarded. *Entrance requirements:* GMAT (average 590), TOEFL. Application deadline: 7/15 (priority date; rolling processing; 11/15 for spring admission). Application fee: $40. *Expenses:* Tuition $2088 per year full-time, $330 per course part-time for state residents; $9040 per year full-time, $1131 per course part-time for nonresidents. Fees $10 per year (minimum). *Financial aid:* Full and partial tuition waivers and career-related internships or fieldwork available. Financial aid applicants required to submit FAFSA. *Faculty research:* Services management, executive leadership, corporate control, culture and marketing, human factors in management information systems. • Application contact: Jon Delany, Academic Adviser, 602-543-6123. Fax: 602-543-6220.

Arkansas State University, College of Business, Department of Economics and Decision Sciences, State University, AR 72467. Offers program in business administration (MBA). Part-time programs available. Faculty: 29 full-time (3 women). Students: 33 full-time (8 women), 56 part-time (24 women); includes 7 minority (5 African Americans, 2 Asian Americans), 26 international. Average age 30. In 1997, 45 degrees awarded. *Degree requirements:* Thesis or alternative, comprehensive exam required, foreign language not required. *Entrance requirements:* GMAT, appropriate bachelor's degree. Application deadline: 7/1 (priority date; rolling processing; 11/15 for spring admission). Application fee: $15 ($25 for international students). *Expenses:* Tuition $2760 per year full-time, $115 per credit hour part-time for state residents; $6936 per year full-time, $289 per credit hour part-time for nonresidents. Fees $506 per year full-time, $44 per semester (minimum) part-time. *Financial aid:* Teaching assistantships available. Aid available to part-time students. Financial aid application deadline: 7/1; applicants required to submit FAFSA. • Dr. Christopher Brown, Chair, 870-972-3416. Fax: 870-972-3868. E-mail: crbrown@cherokee.astate.edu.

Armstrong University, Graduate School of Business Administration, Oakland, CA 94612. Offers programs in finance and accounting (MBA), including accounting, finance; international business (MBA); marketing and management (MBA), including management, marketing. Part-time and evening/weekend programs available. Faculty: 23 full-time, 35 part-time. Students: 658 full-time (263 women). Average age 26. In 1997, 280 degrees awarded. *Degree requirements:* Thesis required, foreign language not required. *Average time to degree:* master's–2 years full-time. *Entrance requirements:* Minimum GPA of 2.5. Application deadline: 8/15 (priority date; rolling processing; 1/1 for spring admission). Application fee: $50. • Dr. Jilla Behnam, Director, 510-835-7900. E-mail: info@armstrong-u.edu. Application contact: Judy Battle, Director of Admissions, 510-835-7900. Fax: 510-835-8935. E-mail: info@armstrong-u.edu.

See in-depth description on page 141.

Arthur D. Little School of Management, Chestnut Hill, MA 02167. Awards MSM. Faculty: 1 full-time (0 women), 22 part-time (6 women). Students: 63 full-time (9 women); includes 1 minority (African American), 57 international. Average age 32. 149 applicants, 78% accepted. In 1997, 59 degrees awarded. *Average time to degree:* master's–1 year full-time. *Entrance requirements:* TOEFL (minimum score 550), GMAT (minimum score 550), 5 years of management experience. Application deadline: rolling. Application fee: $50. *Tuition:* $29,000 per year. *Financial aid:* 1 student received aid; partial tuition waivers available. Financial aid application deadline: 6/1; applicants required to submit FAFSA. *Faculty research:* Management for international development. • Dr. William K. Harper, Dean, 617-552-2838. Fax: 617-552-2141. Application contact: William G. Makris, Director of Marketing, 617-522-2835. Fax: 517-522-2051.

Ashland University, College of Business Administration and Economics, Ashland, OH 44805-3702. Awards MBA. Part-time and evening/weekend programs available. Faculty: 22 full-time, 13 part-time. Students: 126 full-time (48 women), 404 part-time (142 women); includes 23 minority (14 African Americans, 5 Asian Americans, 4 Hispanics), 44 international. Average age 34. 132 applicants, 95% accepted. In 1997, 148 degrees awarded. *Degree requirements:* Thesis or alternative required, foreign language not required. *Entrance requirements:* GMAT if undergraduate GPA is below 2.75. Application deadline: 8/1 (priority date; rolling processing). Application fee: $25. *Tuition:* $350 per credit hour. *Faculty research:* Statistical quality control, total quality management, management information systems, business law and ethics, global issues, human resource issues. • Dr. Paul A. Sears, Dean, 419-289-5212. E-mail: psears@ashland.edu. Application contact: Stephen W. Krispinsky, Executive Director of MBA Program, 419-289-5236. Fax: 419-289-5910.

Assumption College, Department of Business Studies, 500 Salisbury Street, PO Box 15005, Worcester, MA 01615-0005. Awards MBA, CPS. Part-time and evening/weekend programs available. *Entrance requirements:* For master's, GMAT, TOEFL. Application deadline: rolling. Application fee: $20. *Expenses:* Tuition $297 per credit hour. Fees $10 per semester.

Athabasca University, Centre for Innovative Management, Athabasca, AB T9S 3A3, Canada. Offers programs in business administration (MBA), management (Advanced Diploma). Part-time programs available. Faculty: 6 full-time (3 women), 35 part-time. Students: 385 part-time (103 women). Average age 39. 177 applicants, 81% accepted. In 1997, 22 master's awarded. *Degree requirements:* For master's, thesis or alternative required, foreign language not required. *Application deadline:* 6/30 (priority date; rolling processing; 2/28 for spring admission). *Application fee:* $100. Electronic applications accepted. *Tuition:* $8500 per year. • Dr. Lindsay Redpath, Acting Executive Director, 403-459-1144. Fax: 403-459-2093. E-mail: stephenm@cs.athabascau.ca. Application contact: Shelley Lynes, Manager, Registrations, Records, and Graduate Student Affairs, 800-561-4650. Fax: 800-561-4660. E-mail: aumba@cs.athabascau.ca.

Auburn University, College of Business, Department of Management, Auburn University, AL 36849-0001. Offers programs in human relations management (PhD), management (MS), management information systems (MMIS, PhD). Part-time programs available. Faculty: 25 full-time (3 women). Students: 20 full-time (10 women), 17 part-time (3 women); includes 5 minority (4 African Americans, 1 Hispanic), 3 international. 21 applicants, 33% accepted. In 1997, 12 master's, 2 doctorates awarded. *Degree requirements:* For master's, thesis (MS); for doctorate, dissertation. *Entrance requirements:* For master's, GMAT, GRE General Test (MS), TOEFL; for doctorate, GMAT, GRE General Test, TOEFL. Application deadline: 9/1 (rolling processing; 3/1 for spring admission). Application fee: $25 ($50 for international students). *Expenses:* Tuition $2760 per year full-time, $76 per credit hour part-time for state residents; $8280 per year full-time, $228 per credit hour part-time for nonresidents. Fees $30 per year full-time, $160 per quarter part-time for state residents; $30 per year full-time, $480 per quarter part-time for nonresidents. *Financial aid:* Teaching assistantships, Federal Work-Study available. Aid available to part-time students. Financial aid application deadline: 3/15. • Dr. Robert E. Niebuhr, Head, 334-844-4071. Application contact: Dr. John F. Pritchett, Dean of the Graduate School, 334-844-4700.

See in-depth description on page 143.

Auburn University, College of Business, Program in Business Administration, Auburn University, AL 36849-0001. Awards MBA. Part-time programs available. Students: 121 full-time (38 women), 145 part-time (38 women); includes 16 minority (11 African Americans, 3 Asian Americans, 2 Hispanics), 15 international. 180 applicants, 39% accepted. In 1997, 88 degrees awarded. *Entrance requirements:* GMAT. Application deadline: 9/1 (rolling processing; 3/1 for spring admission). Application fee: $25 ($50 for international students). *Expenses:* Tuition $2760 per year full-time, $76 per credit hour part-time for state residents; $8280 per year full-time, $228 per credit hour part-time for nonresidents. Fees $30 per year full-time, $160 per quarter part-time for state residents; $30 per year full-time, $480 per quarter part-time for nonresidents. *Financial aid:* Federal Work-Study available. Aid available to part-time students. Financial aid application deadline: 3/15. • Dr. Daniel M. Gropper, Director, 334-844-4060. Application contact: Dr. John F. Pritchett, Dean of the Graduate School, 334-844-4700.

See in-depth description on page 143.

Auburn University Montgomery, School of Business, Montgomery, AL 36124-4023. Awards MBA. Part-time and evening/weekend programs available. Faculty: 34 full-time (6 women), 4 part-time (0 women). Students: 116 full-time (47 women), 101 part-time (44 women); includes 46 minority (29 African Americans, 13 Asian Americans, 4 Hispanics), 18 international. Average age 30. 79 applicants, 77% accepted. In 1997, 83 degrees awarded. *Degree requirements:* Comprehensive exam required, foreign language and thesis not required. *Entrance requirements:* GMAT (minimum score 400). Application deadline: 9/1 (priority date; rolling processing; 3/28 for spring admission). Application fee: $25. Electronic applications accepted. *Tuition:* $2664 per year full-time, $85 per quarter hour part-time for state residents; $7080 per year full-time, $255 per quarter hour part-time for nonresidents. *Financial aid:* In 1997–98, 5 teaching assistantships were awarded. Aid available to part-time students. • Dr. Keith Lantz, Dean, 334-244-3478. Application contact: Dr. Jane Goodson, Graduate Coordinator, 334-244-3565.

Audrey Cohen College, Program in Administration, 75 Varick Street, New York, NY 10013. Awards MS. Evening/weekend programs available. Faculty: 6 full-time (1 woman), 9 part-time (3 women). Students: 94 full-time (56 women); includes 66 minority (53 African Americans, 1 Asian American, 10 Hispanics, 2 Native Americans). Average age 37. *Entrance requirements:* Appropriate work experience, interview, minimum GPA of 2.7. Application deadline: 8/15 (priority date; rolling processing; 12/15 for spring admission). Application fee: $30. *Tuition:* $9760 per year. *Financial aid:* In 1997–98, scholarships totaling $47,000 were awarded. *Faculty research:* Transnational politics and culture, women and social policy, confidentiality in the human services, concepts of marginality, ethics in social policy. • Steven K. Lenhart, Director of Admissions, 212-343-1234 Ext. 2700. Fax: 212-343-8470.

Augsburg College, Program in Leadership, Minneapolis, MN 55454-1351. Awards MA. Part-time and evening/weekend programs available. *Degree requirements:* Thesis or alternative. *Entrance requirements:* MAT, minimum GPA of 3.0. Application deadline: 8/9 (priority date; rolling processing; 3/7 for spring admission). Application fee: $25. *Faculty research:* Soviet leaders, artificial intelligence, homelessness.

Augusta State University, College of Business Administration, Augusta, GA 30904-2200. Awards MBA. Part-time and evening/weekend programs available. Faculty: 10 full-time (4 women). Students: 45 full-time (16 women), 36 part-time (13 women); includes 13 minority (10 African Americans, 3 Asian Americans), 1 international. Average age 35. 45 applicants, 73% accepted. In 1997, 35 degrees awarded. *Degree requirements:* Comprehensive exam required, foreign language and thesis not required. *Entrance requirements:* GMAT (minimum score 400; average 505), minimum GPA of 2.5. Application deadline: 7/15 (priority date; rolling processing; 12/1 for spring admission). Application fee: $10. *Tuition:* $2260 per year full-time, $83 per credit hour part-time for state residents; $8260 per year full-time, $333 per credit hour part-time for nonresidents. *Financial aid:* In 1997–98, 20 research assistantships (7 to first-year students) totaling $45,500 were awarded; Federal Work-Study, institutionally sponsored loans also available. Aid available to part-time students. Financial aid application deadline: 4/1; applicants required to submit FAFSA. • Jackson K. Widener, Dean, 706-737-1418. E-mail: jwidener@aug.edu. Application contact: Dr. Richard Bramblett, Director, MBA Office, 706-737-1562. Fax: 706-667-4064. E-mail: rbramble@aug.edu.

Aurora University, School of Business and Professional Studies, Aurora, IL 60506-4892. Awards MBA. Part-time and evening/weekend programs available. Faculty: 6 full-time (2 women), 3 part-time (1 woman). Students: 25 full-time (13 women), 68 part-time (22 women). 80 applicants, 75% accepted. In 1997, 33 degrees awarded. *Degree requirements:* Computer language required, foreign language and thesis not required. *Entrance requirements:* Minimum GPA of 2.75. Application deadline: 9/1 (priority date; rolling processing). Application fee: $25. *Tuition:* $408 per semester hour. *Financial aid:* Fellowships, teaching assistantships, partial tuition waivers, institutionally sponsored loans, and career-related internships or fieldwork available. Aid available to part-time students. • Dr. Forest Etheridge, Dean, 630-844-5401. Application contact: Office of Admissions, 630-844-5533. Fax: 630-844-5463.

Averett College, Program in Business Administration, Danville, VA 24541-3692. Awards MBA. Part-time and evening/weekend programs available. Postbaccalaureate distance learning degree programs offered (no on-campus study). Faculty: 8 full-time (3 women), 79 part-time. Students: 391 full-time (169 women), 371 part-time (152 women); includes 170 minority (144 African Americans, 12 Asian Americans, 10 Hispanics, 4 Native Americans). Average age 35. *Degree requirements:* Research project required, foreign language and thesis not required. *Average time to degree:* master's–2 years part-time. *Entrance requirements:* Minimum undergraduate GPA of 3.0. Application deadline: rolling. Application fee: $20. *Tuition:* $225 per credit hour. • Dr. Brian Satterlee, Dean of Adult Education, 804-791-5650. Fax: 804-791-5898.

Avila College, Department of Business and Economics, Kansas City, MO 64145-1698. Awards MBA. Part-time and evening/weekend programs available. Faculty: 8 full-time (4 women), 9 part-time (3 women). Students: 10 full-time (6 women), 82 part-time (37 women); includes 6 minority (5 African Americans, 1 Hispanic), 10 international. Average age 35. 17 applicants, 82% accepted. In 1997, 40 degrees awarded (100% found work related to degree). *Degree requirements:* Final exam required, thesis not required. *Average time to degree:* master's–3 years full-time, 5 years part-time. *Entrance requirements:* GMAT, TOEFL (minimum score 550), minimum GPA of 3.0. Application deadline: 4/30 (priority date; rolling processing; 11/30 for spring admission). Application fee: $0. *Expenses:* Tuition $295 per credit hour. Fees $160 per year full-time, $6 per year part-time. *Financial aid:* Career-related internships or fieldwork available. Aid available to part-time students. Financial aid applicants required to submit FAFSA. *Faculty research:* Leadership characteristics, financial hedging, group dynamics. • Wendy Acker, Director, MBA Program, 816-942-8400 Ext. 2321. Fax: 816-942-3362. E-mail: ackerwl@mail.avila.edu.

Azusa Pacific University, School of Business and Management, Azusa, CA 91702-7000. Offers programs in business administration (MBA), human resource development (MHRD), international business (MBA), organizational management (MAOM), strategic management (MBA). Part-time and evening/weekend programs available. Faculty: 11 full-time (2 women), 6 part-time (1 woman). Students: 134. Average age 32. In 1997, 34 degrees awarded. *Degree requirements:* Thesis (for some programs), final project required, foreign language not required. *Average time to degree:* master's–1 year full-time, 3 years part-time. *Entrance requirements:* GMAT (minimum score 450), minimum GPA of 3.0. Application deadline: 8/15 (priority date; rolling processing). Application fee: $45 ($65 for international students). *Expenses:* Tuition $405 per unit. Fees $57 per year. *Financial aid:* Limited scholarships available. *Faculty research:* Gender issues, financial risk, leadership and ethics, marketing strategy. • Dr. Phillip Lewis, Dean, 626-812-3090. Application contact: Kim Gara, Academic Adviser, 626-812-3818. Fax: 626-815-3802.

Babson College, F. W. Olin Graduate School of Business, Babson Park, MA 02157-0310. Offers programs in business administration (MBA), international business (MBA). Part-time and evening/weekend programs available. Faculty: 151 full-time (42 women), 53 part-time (24 women). Students: 390 full-time (126 women), 1,254 part-time (429 women); includes 83 minority (24 African Americans, 37 Asian Americans, 21 Hispanics, 1 Native American), 140 international. Average age 29. 900 applicants, 44% accepted. In 1997, 424 degrees awarded. *Entrance requirements:* GMAT, TOEFL, 2 years of work experience, resume. Application deadline: rolling. Application fee: $50. Electronic applications accepted. *Expenses:* Tuition $21,940 per year full-time, $2046 per course part-time. Fees $660 per year. *Financial aid:* In 1997–98, 95 students received aid, including 32 fellowships (18 to first-year students) totaling $512,250, 32 graduate assistantships (16 to first-year students); partial tuition waivers, Federal Work-Study, and career-related internships or fieldwork also available. Financial aid application deadline: 3/15; applicants required to submit FAFSA. *Faculty research:* Entrepreneurship, innovation and quality management, artificial intelligence. Total annual research expenditures: $120,000. • Thomas Moore, Dean, 781-239-4542. Application contact: Rita S. Edmunds, Director of Graduate Admissions, 781-239-5591. Fax: 781-239-4194. E-mail: edmundsr@babson.edu.

See in-depth description on page 145.

Baker College Center for Graduate Studies, Programs in Business, Flint, MI 48507. Offerings in general business (EMBA, MBA), health and recreation services management (MBA), health care management (EMBA, MBA), human resource management (EMBA, MBA), industrial management (EMBA, MBA), international business (EMBA, MBA), leadership (EMBA, MBA). MBA (health and recreation services management) enrollment limited to international students. Part-time and evening/weekend programs available. Faculty: 8 full-time, 73 part-time. Students: 500. *Degree requirements:* Portfolio required, foreign language not required. *Entrance requirements:* 3 years of work experience, minimum undergraduate GPA of 2.5, writing sample. Application deadline: rolling. Application fee: $25. *Tuition:* $215 per quarter hour. • Dr. Michael Heberling, President, 800-469-3165. Application contact: Chuck Gurden, Director of Admissions, 800-469-3165. Fax: 810-766-4399.

Baker University, Programs in Business, Baldwin City, KS 66006-0065. Awards MBA, MSM. Students: 422 full-time (203 women); includes 53 minority (36 African Americans, 8 Asian Americans, 8 Hispanics, 1 Native American), 3 international. 150 applicants, 99% accepted. In 1997, 230 degrees awarded. *Degree requirements:* Thesis, applied management project (MBA) required, foreign language not required. *Entrance requirements:* 3 years of work experience, minimum age 25. Application deadline: rolling. Application fee: $20. *Expenses:* Tuition $310 per credit hour (minimum). Fees $40 per year. • Application contact: Jeff Driskill, Director of Marketing, 913-491-4432. Fax: 913-491-0470.

Baldwin-Wallace College, Division of Business Administration, Program in Business Management, Berea, OH 44017-2088. Awards MBA. Part-time and evening/weekend programs available. Faculty: 18 full-time (3 women), 23 part-time (4 women). Students: 223 part-time (117 women). Average age 32. 136 applicants, 62% accepted. In 1997, 140 degrees awarded. *Average time to degree:* master's–2 years part-time. *Entrance requirements:* GMAT (minimum score 500), interview, work experience. Application deadline: 8/1 (priority date; rolling processing; 4/1 for spring admission). Application fee: $15. Electronic applications accepted. *Financial aid:* Career-related internships or fieldwork available. Aid available to part-time students. Financial aid applicants required to submit FAFSA. • Application contact: Peggy Shepard, Graduate Coordinator, 440-826-2196. Fax: 440-826-3868. E-mail: pshepard@bw.edu.

Baldwin-Wallace College, Division of Business Administration, Program in Executive Management, Berea, OH 44017-2088. Awards MBA. Faculty: 11 full-time (1 woman), 5 part-time (1 woman). Students: 75 part-time (24 women); includes 5 African Americans. Average age 39. 48 applicants, 88% accepted. In 1997, 21 degrees awarded. *Degree requirements:* Project required, foreign language and thesis not required. *Entrance requirements:* Interview, work experience. Application deadline: 8/1 (priority date; rolling processing; 4/1 for spring admission). Application fee: $15. • Thomas W. Donahue, Director, 440-826-2060. Application contact: Linda Suffron, Graduate Coordinator, 440-826-2064. Fax: 440-826-3868. E-mail: lsuffron@bw.edu.

Ball State University, College of Business, Department of Management, 2000 University Avenue, Muncie, IN 47306-1099. Awards MS. Admissions temporarily suspended. Faculty: 13. Students: 0. *Expenses:* Tuition $3454 per year full-time, $518 per semester (minimum) part-time for state residents; $9316 per year full-time, $1221 per semester (minimum) part-time for nonresidents. Fees $242 per year full-time, $18 per semester (minimum) part-time. • Ray Montagno, Chairperson, 765-285-5300.

Ball State University, College of Business, Interdepartmental Program in Business Administration, 2000 University Avenue, Muncie, IN 47306-1099. Awards MBA. Students: 14 full-time (6 women), 152 part-time (46 women); includes 11 minority (3 African Americans, 7 Asian Americans, 1 Hispanic), 8 international. Average age 28. 78 applicants, 67% accepted. In 1997, 66 degrees awarded. *Entrance requirements:* GMAT. Application fee: $15 ($25 for international students). *Expenses:* Tuition $3454 per year full-time, $518 per semester (minimum) part-time for state residents; $9316 per year full-time, $1221 per semester (minimum) part-time for nonresidents. Fees $242 per year full-time, $18 per semester (minimum) part-time. • Tamara Estep, Graduate Coordinator, 765-285-1931.

Barry University, School of Business, Miami Shores, FL 33161-6695. Awards MBA, MBA/MS, MBA/MSN. MBA/MS (sport management) offered through the School of Human Performance and Leisure Sciences. Part-time and evening/weekend programs available. Faculty: 20 full-time (6 women), 20 part-time (10 women). Students: 38 full-time (17 women), 124 part-time (53 women). Average age 33. 132 applicants, 79% accepted. In 1997, 71 degrees awarded. *Entrance requirements:* GMAT (minimum score 400), minimum GPA of 3.0. Application deadline: 5/1 (priority date; rolling processing). *Tuition:* $450 per credit (minimum). *Financial aid:* 57 students received aid; research assistantships and career-related internships or fieldwork available. Aid available to part-time students. Financial aid application deadline: 5/1; applicants required to submit FAFSA. *Faculty research:* Northern Ireland tourism and marketing; marketing in Lithuania; Latin American economic development; equal opportunity requirements, cultural diversity. • Dr. Jack Scarborough, Dean, 800-892-1111. E-mail: jscarboro@mail.barry.edu. Application contact: José Poza, Director of Marketing, 800-892-1111. Fax: 305-892-6412. E-mail: poza@aquinas.barry.edu.

Baruch College of the City University of New York, School of Business, 17 Lexington Avenue, New York, NY 10010-5585. Awards EMBA, EMSF, MBA, MS, PhD, Certificate, JD/MBA. JD/MBA offered jointly with Brooklyn Law School. Part-time and evening/weekend programs available. Faculty: 133 full-time (25 women), 61 part-time (9 women). Students: 806 full-time (374 women), 1,129 part-time (455 women); includes 427 minority (79 African Americans, 284 Asian Americans, 62 Hispanics, 2 Native Americans), 430 international. Average age 28. 1,697 applicants, 58% accepted. In 1997, 627 master's, 3 doctorates awarded. Terminal master's awarded for partial completion of doctoral program. *Degree requirements:* For doctorate, computer language, dissertation required, foreign language not required. *Average time to degree:* master's–2 years full-time, 4 years part-time. *Entrance requirements:* For master's, TOEFL (minimum score 570), TWE (4.5). Application deadline: 6/15. Application fee: $40. *Expenses:* Tuition $4350 per year full-time, $185 per credit part-time for state residents; $7600 per year full-time, $320 per credit part-time for nonresidents. Fees $53 per year. *Financial aid:* In 1997–98, 249 students received aid, including 132 research assistantships (60 to first-year students) averaging $555 per month and totaling $660,000; fellowships, Federal Work-Study, and career-related internships or fieldwork also available. Aid available to part-time students. Financial aid application deadline: 5/3; applicants required to submit FAFSA. • Sidney I. Lirtzman, Dean, 212-802-6550. Application contact: Michael S. Wynne, Office of Graduate Admissions, 212-802-2330. Fax: 212-802-2335. E-mail: graduate_admissions@baruch.cuny.edu.

See in-depth description on page 147.

Baruch College of the City University of New York, School of Business, Executive Education Programs, Executive MBA Program, 17 Lexington Avenue, Box 255, New York, NY 10010. Awards EMBA. *Degree requirements:* Thesis or alternative. *Average time to degree:* master's–2 years full-time. *Entrance requirements:* GMAT (minimum score 500 required, 540 average), 5 years management-level work experience. Application deadline: 7/1 (priority date; rolling processing). Application fee: $40. • Karen E. Dennis, Director, Executive Education Programs, 212-802-6700. Fax: 212-802-6705. E-mail: xedbb@cunyvm.cuny.edu.

Announcement: The Executive MBA Program enables seasoned professionals with at least 5 years of managerial-level experience to earn their degree in 2 years. Program focus in strategic management. With classes scheduled once a week on alternating Fridays and Saturdays from September to June, the full-time program enables working executives to complete their degree requirements with minimal disruption to their career. A required 7- to 10-day International Study Tour is included. Innovative 1-year Executive MS Program in Finance permits busy executives to complete the highly focused program with minimal disruption to their career. Classes are scheduled Saturdays and 1 night per week.

Baylor University, Hankamer School of Business, Program in Business Administration, Waco, TX 76798. Awards MBA, JD/MBA. Part-time programs available. Students: 171 full-time (57 women), 4 part-time (1 woman); includes 10 minority (4 African Americans, 2 Asian Americans, 4 Hispanics), 13 international. In 1997, 103 degrees awarded. *Entrance requirements:* GMAT (minimum score 450), minimum AACSB index of 1050. Application deadline: 8/1 (rolling processing; 12/1 for spring admission). Application fee: $25. *Expenses:* Tuition $7392 per year full-time, $308 per semester hour part-time. Fees $1024 per year. *Financial aid:* Research assistantships, teaching assistantships, Federal Work-Study, institutionally sponsored loans,

Directory: Business Administration and Management—General

Baylor University (continued)

and career-related internships or fieldwork available. • Dr. Donald F. Cunningham, Associate Dean, 254-710-3718.

See in-depth description on page 149.

Belhaven College, Program in Business, Jackson, MS 39202-1789. Awards MBA. Faculty: 8. Students: 100. *Application deadline:* rolling. *Application fee:* $100. *Tuition:* $4745 per year full-time, $255 per semester hour part-time. • Dr. James Park, Chair, 601-968-5965. Application contact: Frank Tamboli, Director of Marketing, 601-968-5988.

Bellarmine College, W. Fielding Rubel School of Business, Louisville, KY 40205-0671. Awards EMBA, MBA. Part-time and evening/weekend programs available. Faculty: 13 full-time (2 women). Students: 26 full-time (6 women), 196 part-time (83 women); includes 8 minority (4 African Americans, 2 Asian Americans, 2 Hispanics). Average age 29. 52 applicants, 77% accepted. In 1997, 31 degrees awarded. *Entrance requirements:* GMAT, TOEFL. Application deadline: 8/1 (priority date; rolling processing; 12/15 for spring admission). Application fee: $25. Electronic applications accepted. *Tuition:* $375 per credit hour. *Financial aid:* In 1997–98, 1 graduate assistantship was awarded; career-related internships or fieldwork also available. Aid available to part-time students. Financial aid application deadline: 7/1. *Faculty research:* Marketing, management, small business and entrepreneurship, finance, economics. • Laura Richardson, Director, 502-452-8240.

Bellevue University, Graduate School, Bellevue, NE 68005-3098. Offers programs in business (MBA), computer information systems (MS), health care administration (MS), human services (MS), leadership (MA), management (MA). MA is delivered in an accelerated executive format. Part-time and evening/weekend programs available. Postbaccalaureate distance learning degree programs offered (no on-campus study). Faculty: 22 full-time (9 women), 13 part-time (5 women). Students: 357 full-time (149 women), 153 part-time (56 women); includes 62 minority (40 African Americans, 11 Asian Americans, 7 Hispanics, 4 Native Americans), 77 international. Average age 33. 157 applicants, 85% accepted. In 1997, 140 degrees awarded. *Degree requirements:* Thesis or project. *Average time to degree:* master's–2 years full-time, 3 years part-time. *Entrance requirements:* GMAT, GRE General Test, or MAT; TOEFL (minimum score 500), minimum GPA of 2.5 in last 60 hours. Application deadline: 7/15 (priority date; rolling processing; 11/15 for spring admission). Application fee: $50. *Financial aid:* Available to part-time students. Financial aid applicants required to submit FAFSA. • Dr. Douglas Frost, Dean, 402-293-2025. E-mail: frostd@scholars.bellevue.edu. Application contact: Elizabeth Wall, Director of Marketing and Enrollment, 402-293-3702. Fax: 402-293-3730. E-mail: eaw@scholars.bellevue.edu.

Belmont Abbey College, School of Graduate Studies, Division of Business and Professional Studies, Belmont, NC 28012-1802. Awards MBA. Part-time and evening/weekend programs available. Average age 36. *Application deadline:* 6/1 (rolling processing; 11/1 for spring admission). *Application fee:* $20. *Expenses:* Tuition $795 per course. Fees $43 per semester (minimum). *Financial aid:* Available to part-time students. Financial aid application deadline: 8/1; applicants required to submit FAFSA. • Dr. Henry Loehr, Director of Graduate Studies in Business, 704-825-6223. Application contact: Julia Gunter, Director of Adult Admissions, 704-825-6671. Fax: 704-825-6658.

Belmont University, Jack C. Massey Graduate School of Business, Nashville, TN 37212-3757. Awards M Acc, MBA. Part-time and evening/weekend programs available. Faculty: 15 full-time (4 women), 9 part-time (1 woman). Students: 246 part-time (118 women); includes 17 minority (15 African Americans, 2 Hispanics), 4 international. Average age 32. 106 applicants, 84% accepted. In 1997, 74 degrees awarded. *Average time to degree:* master's–2 years part-time. *Entrance requirements:* GMAT (minimum score 500; average 521), 2 years of work experience (MBA). Application deadline: 6/1 (priority date; rolling processing; 11/1 for spring admission). Application fee: $50. *Tuition:* $560 per credit hour. *Financial aid:* In 1997–98, 67 students received aid, including 6 research assistantships; career-related internships or fieldwork also available. Aid available to part-time students. Financial aid application deadline: 7/15. *Faculty research:* Music business, strategy, ethics, finance, accounting systems. • Dr. James Clapper, Dean, 615-460-6784. Application contact: Recruitment Director, 615-460-6480. Fax: 615-460-6455.

Benedictine College, Program in Executive Business Administration, 1020 North 2nd Street, Atchison, KS 66002-1499. Awards EMBA. Faculty: 7 part-time (0 women), 2 FTE. Students: 29 (2 women). Average age 38. *Entrance requirements:* 5 years of management experience. Application deadline: 7/1. Application fee: $100. *Tuition:* $12,500 per year. *Financial aid:* Federal Work-Study available. Aid available to part-time students. Financial aid application deadline: 3/1; applicants required to submit FAFSA. *Faculty research:* Banking, strategic planning, ethics, leadership and entrepreneurship. • Dr. Richard Miller, Chair, 913-367-5340 Ext. 2589. E-mail: rmiller@raven.benedictine.edu.

Benedictine University, Department of Executive Business, Lisle, IL 60532-0900. Awards MBA. Faculty: 2 full-time (1 woman). Students: 16 (8 women). *Application deadline:* 9/1. *Application fee:* $30. • Dr. Ruth Ann Althaus, Co-Director, 630-829-6229. Application contact: Dr. Al Rosenbloom, Co-Director, 630-829-6225. Fax: 630-960-1126.

Benedictine University, Program in Business Administration, Lisle, IL 60532-0900. Awards MBA, MBA/MS, MBA/MPH. Part-time and evening/weekend programs available. Faculty: 3 full-time (0 women), 21 part-time (4 women). Students: 311 (121 women). *Entrance requirements:* GMAT. Application fee: $30. *Financial aid:* Available to part-time students. • Bruce Buchowicz, Director, 630-829-6210. Fax: 630-829-6226.

Benedictine University, Program in Management and Organizational Behavior, Lisle, IL 60532-0900. Awards MS, MBA/MS, MPH/MS. Part-time and evening/weekend programs available. Faculty: 2 full-time (1 woman), 45 part-time (13 women). Students: 164 (112 women). *Entrance requirements:* GMAT. Application fee: $30. *Faculty research:* Organizational change, transformation, development, learning organizations, career transitions for academics. • Dr. Peter F. Sorensen, Director, 630-829-6220. Application contact: Dr. Ralph Meeker, Director of Graduate Admissions, 630-829-6200. Fax: 630-960-1126.

Bentley College, Graduate School of Business, Full Time MBA Cohort Program, 175 Forest Street, Waltham, MA 02154-4705. Awards MBA. Program new for fall 1999. Faculty: 70 full-time (21 women), 22 part-time (8 women). *Degree requirements:* Computer language required, foreign language and thesis not required. *Entrance requirements:* GMAT, TOEFL (minimum score 580). Application deadline: 6/1 (rolling processing). Application fee: $50. *Expenses:* Tuition $20,500 per year full-time, $2050 per course part-time. Fees $65 per year full-time, $15 per semester part-time. *Financial aid:* Research assistantships, departmental assistantships available. Financial aid application deadline: 4/15. • Dr. Judith B. Kamm, Director, 781-891-3433. Application contact: Sharon M. Oliver, Director of Graduate Admissions, 781-891-2108. Fax: 781-891-2464. E-mail: soliver@bentley.edu.

See in-depth description on page 151.

Bentley College, Graduate School of Business, Self-paced MBA Program, 175 Forest Street, Waltham, MA 02154-4705. Offers accountancy (MBA), advanced accountancy (MBA), business communication (MBA), business data analysis (MBA), business economics (MBA), business ethics (MBA), entrepreneurial studies (MBA), finance (MBA), international business (MBA), management (MBA), management information systems (MBA), management of technology (MBA), marketing (MBA), operations management (MBA), taxation (MBA). Part-time and evening/weekend programs available. Faculty: 70 full-time (21 women), 22 part-time (8 women). Students: 180 full-time (69 women), 887 part-time (421 women); includes 50 minority (10 African Americans, 31 Asian Americans, 8 Hispanics, 1 Native American), 107 international. Average age 30. 798 applicants, 63% accepted. In 1997, 352 degrees awarded (100% found work related to degree). *Degree requirements:* Computer language required, foreign language and thesis not required. *Entrance requirements:* GMAT (average 540), TOEFL (minimum score 580). Application deadline: 6/1 (priority date; rolling processing; 11/1 for spring admission). Application fee: $50. *Expenses:* Tuition $20,500 per year full-time, $2050 per course part-time. Fees $65 per year full-time, $15 per semester part-time. *Financial aid:* In 1997–98, 182 students received aid, including 32 research assistantships (16 to first-year students) averaging $376 per month; departmental assistantships, Federal Work-Study, and career-related internships or fieldwork also available. Aid available to part-time students. Financial aid application deadline: 4/15; applicants required to submit CSS PROFILE or FAFSA. *Faculty research:* Information technology for high performance teams, electronic commerce, mergers and acquistions, workforce diversity, accounting profession. • Dr. Judith B. Kamm, Director, 781-891-3433. Application contact: Holly Chase, Associate Director, 781-891-2108. Fax: 781-891-2464. E-mail: hchase@bentley.edu.

Announcement: Bentley College Graduate School of Business offers both a full-time MBA program and a self-paced MBA program. The full-time MBA is a 2-year program that provides an integrated view of the entire enterprise while developing key managerial skills to create competitive advantage in today's information economy. The self-paced MBA provides a strong foundation in business concepts as well as the analytical and practical techniques crucial to management. It allows students to draw on previous business knowledge to customize their curriculum through a flexible format and selection of 1 of 15 areas of concentration, including accountancy, advanced accountancy, business communication, business data analysis, business economics, business ethics, entrepreneurial studies, finance, international business, management, management information systems, management of technology, marketing, operations management, and taxation. Full-time students in the self-paced MBA program with full advanced standing credit may complete their degree in 1 year. The College also offers an advanced graduate business certificate.

See in-depth description on page 151.

Berry College, School of Business, Mount Berry, GA 30149-0159. Awards MBA. Part-time and evening/weekend programs available. Faculty: 6 part-time (2 women), 1.9 FTE. Students: 27 part-time (12 women); includes 1 minority (Hispanic). Average age 32. 11 applicants, 64% accepted. In 1997, 5 degrees awarded (100% found work related to degree). *Average time to degree:* master's–2 years full-time, 3 years part-time. *Entrance requirements:* GMAT, minimum GPA of 2.5. Application deadline: 7/29 (rolling processing; 12/16 for spring admission). Application fee: $25 ($30 for international students). *Tuition:* $364 per semester hour. *Financial aid:* In 1997–98, 6 students received aid, including 1 assistantship (to a first-year student) averaging $600 per month and totaling $6,000. Aid available to part-time students. Financial aid application deadline: 4/1; applicants required to submit FAFSA. *Faculty research:* Consumer preference as a function of lifestyle imaging, team rewards, effects of tenure by employment timing issues, effects on decision making by ordering of electronic information, evaluation of new accounting curriculum models. Total annual research expenditures: $1290. • Bettyann O'Neill, Assistant Dean, Graduate Studies in Business, 706-232-5374 Ext. 1751. Application contact: George Gaddie, Dean of Admissions, 706-236-2215. Fax: 706-290-2178.

Bethel College, Program in Business Administration, Mishawaka, IN 46545-5591. Awards MBA. Part-time programs available. Faculty: 6 part-time (1 woman). Students: 1 (woman) full-time, 45 part-time (19 women). *Application deadline:* rolling. *Application fee:* $25. *Tuition:* $300 per semester hour. • Dr. Robert Laurent, Director, Division of Graduate Studies, 219-257-3353.

Birmingham–Southern College, Program in Public and Private Management, Birmingham, AL 35254. Awards MPPM. Part-time and evening/weekend programs available. Faculty: 20 full-time (4 women), 8 part-time (2 women). Students: 95 full-time (38 women); includes 35 minority (34 African Americans, 1 Hispanic). Average age 36. 19 applicants, 37% accepted. In 1997, 33 degrees awarded. *Degree requirements:* Thesis optional, foreign language not required. *Entrance requirements:* GMAT (minimum score 500). Application deadline: 8/1 (rolling processing; 12/31 for spring admission). Application fee: $25. *Expenses:* Tuition $7740 per year full-time, $1290 per course part-time. Fees $16 per course. *Financial aid:* Scholarships available. Aid available to part-time students. • Dr. E. Byron Chew, Dean-Partner, 205-226-4893. Application contact: Eleanor F. Terry, Director of Graduate Studies, 205-226-4840. Fax: 205-226-4843. E-mail: eterry@bsc.edu.

Bloomsburg University of Pennsylvania, School of Graduate Studies, College of Business, Program in Business Administration, Bloomsburg, PA 17815-1905. Awards MBA. Faculty: 33 full-time (7 women). Students: 7 full-time (2 women), 32 part-time (14 women); includes 2 minority (1 African American, 1 Asian American), 3 international. Average age 30. 11 applicants, 100% accepted. In 1997, 34 degrees awarded. *Entrance requirements:* GMAT (minimum score 500), minimum QPA of 2.5. Application deadline: rolling. Application fee: $25. *Expenses:* Tuition $3468 per year full-time, $193 per credit part-time for state residents; $6236 per year full-time, $346 per credit part-time for nonresidents. Fees $748 per year full-time, $166 per semester (minimum) part-time. • David Martin, Coordinator, 717-389-4762. Fax: 717-389-2071.

Boise State University, College of Business and Economics, Program in Business Administration, Boise, ID 83725-0399. Awards MBA. Part-time programs available. Faculty: 54 full-time (8 women), 12 part-time (1 woman). Students: 69 full-time (29 women), 128 part-time (52 women); includes 7 minority (2 Asian Americans, 5 Hispanics), 38 international. Average age 32. 94 applicants, 95% accepted. In 1997, 37 degrees awarded. *Entrance requirements:* GMAT (minimum score 475), TOEFL (minimum score 550), minimum GPA of 2.9. Application deadline: 7/26 (priority date; rolling processing; 11/29 for spring admission). Application fee: $20 ($30 for international students). Electronic applications accepted. *Tuition:* $3020 per year full-time, $135 per credit part-time for state residents; $8900 per year full-time, $135 per credit part-time for nonresidents. *Financial aid:* In 1997–98, 11 students received aid, including 11 graduate assistantships; Federal Work-Study, institutionally sponsored loans, and career-related internships or fieldwork also available. Aid available to part-time students. Financial aid application deadline: 3/1. • Dr. Harry White, Coordinator, 208-385-1126. Application contact: J. Renee Anchustegui, Adviser, 208-385-1126. Fax: 208-385-1135.

See in-depth description on page 153.

Boston College, Wallace E. Carroll Graduate School of Management, Chestnut Hill, MA 02167-9991. Awards MBA, MSF, PhD, JD/MBA, MBA/MA, MBA/MS, MBA/MSF, MBA/PhD, MSW/MBA. Part-time and evening/weekend programs available. Faculty: 87 full-time, 45 part-time. Students: 232 full-time, 696 part-time; includes 55 international. Average age 27. 980 applicants, 42% accepted. In 1997, 271 master's, 3 doctorates awarded. *Degree requirements:* For doctorate, dissertation required, foreign language not required. *Average time to degree:* master's–2 years full-time. *Entrance requirements:* For master's, GMAT (average 610), TOEFL (minimum score 600; average 630). Application deadline: 4/1 (priority date; rolling processing; 11/15 for spring admission). Application fee: $45. Electronic applications accepted. *Expenses:* Tuition $22,134 per year full-time, $714 per semester hour part-time. Fees $80 per year (minimum) full-time, $30 per semester part-time. *Financial aid:* In 1997–98, 81 research assistantships (39 to first-year students) were awarded; fellowships, teaching assistantships, administrative assistantships, full and partial tuition waivers, Federal Work-Study, institutionally sponsored loans, and career-related internships or fieldwork also available. Financial aid application deadline: 3/1; applicants required to submit FAFSA. *Faculty research:* Capital structure, mergers, organizational transformation, management of professionals, management of service organizations. • Dr. Hassell McClellan, Associate Dean, 617-552-3773. Fax: 617-552-0514. E-mail: hassell.mcclellan@bc.edu. Application contact: Simone Marthers, Director of Admissions, 617-552-3920. Fax: 617-552-8078.

See in-depth description on page 155.

Boston University, School of Management, Boston, MA 02215. Awards Exec MBA, MBA, MSMIS, DBA, JD/MBA, MBA/MA, MBA/MS, MBA/MPH, MBA/MSMIS. Programs in accounting

(DBA); business administration (Exec MBA); finance (DBA); general management (MBA); health-care management (MBA); management information systems (MSMIS, DBA); management policy (DBA); marketing (DBA); operations management (DBA); organizational behavior (DBA); public and nonprofit management (MBA), including nonprofit management, public management. Part-time and evening/weekend programs available. Faculty: 110 full-time, 54 part-time. Students: 627 full-time (225 women), 743 part-time (277 women); includes 116 minority (15 African Americans, 86 Asian Americans, 14 Hispanics, 1 Native American), 264 international. Average age 30. 1,368 applicants, 57% accepted. In 1997, 451 master's, 7 doctorates awarded. *Degree requirements:* For doctorate, dissertation required, foreign language not required. *Entrance requirements:* For master's, GMAT (average 608); for doctorate, GMAT or GRE General Test. Application deadline: 5/1 (rolling processing). Application fee: $50. Electronic applications accepted. *Expenses:* Tuition $22,830 per year full-time, $713 per credit part-time. Fees $218 per year full-time, $40 per semester part-time. *Financial aid:* 312 students received aid; partial tuition waivers, Federal Work-Study, institutionally sponsored loans, and career-related internships or fieldwork available. Aid available to part-time students. Financial aid applicants required to submit FAFSA. *Faculty research:* Pricing strategy, corporate takeovers, mentoring, strategic planning, management of organizational change. • Therese M. Hofmann, Assistant Dean, 617-353-2673. Application contact: Peter G. Kelly, Director of Admissions and Financial Aid, 617-353-2670. Fax: 617-353-7368. E-mail: mba@bu.edu.

Boston University, Metropolitan College, Program in Administrative Studies, Boston, MA 02215. Offers financial economics (MSAS), innovation and technology (MSAS), multinational commerce (MSAS), organizational policy (MSAS). Part-time and evening/weekend programs available. Faculty: 7 full-time (2 women), 25 part-time (5 women). Students: 126 full-time (66 women), 164 part-time (83 women); includes 33 minority (3 African Americans, 20 Asian Americans, 9 Hispanics, 1 Native American), 141 international. Average age 28. 60% of applicants accepted. In 1997, 60 degrees awarded (2% entered university research/teaching, 88% found other work related to degree, 10% continued full-time study). *Degree requirements:* Thesis optional, foreign language not required. *Average time to degree:* master's–1 year full-time, 2 years part-time. *Entrance requirements:* TOEFL (minimum score 550). Application deadline: rolling. Application fee: $50. *Expenses:* Tuition $15,488 per year full-time, $484 per credit part-time. Fees $218 per year full-time, $40 per semester part-time. *Financial aid:* In 1997–98, 5 students received aid, including 5 research assistantships; Federal Work-Study and career-related internships or fieldwork also available. *Faculty research:* International business, innovative process. • Dr. Kip Becker, Chairman. E-mail: adminsc@bu.edu. Application contact: Department of Administrative Sciences, 617-353-3016. Fax: 617-353-6840. E-mail: adminsc@bu.edu.

See in-depth description on page 537.

Bowie State University, Program in Administrative Management, 14000 Jericho Park Road, Bowie, MD 20715. Offers business administration (M Adm Mgt), public administration (M Adm Mgt). Part-time and evening/weekend programs available. *Degree requirements:* Research paper, written comprehensive exam required, thesis optional. *Application fee:* $30. *Expenses:* Tuition $169 per credit hour for state residents; $304 per credit hour for nonresidents. Fees $171 per year.

Bowling Green State University, College of Business Administration, Graduate Studies in Business Program, Bowling Green, OH 43403. Awards MBA. Faculty: 59 full-time (18 women). Students: 109 full-time (35 women), 188 part-time (49 women); includes 29 minority (5 African Americans, 18 Asian Americans, 5 Hispanics, 1 Native American), 68 international. 254 applicants, 56% accepted. In 1997, 56 degrees awarded. *Degree requirements:* Research project required, foreign language and thesis not required. *Entrance requirements:* GMAT, TOEFL (minimum score 550), minimum GPA of 3.0. Application deadline: 8/1. Application fee: $30. Electronic applications accepted. *Tuition:* $6070 per year full-time, $284 per credit hour part-time for state residents; $11,358 per year full-time, $536 per credit hour part-time for nonresidents. *Financial aid:* In 1997–98, 58 assistantships were awarded; research assistantships, teaching assistantships, Federal Work-Study, institutionally sponsored loans, and career-related internships or fieldwork also available. Financial aid application deadline: 2/15; applicants required to submit FAFSA. *Faculty research:* Management of change processes, supply chain management, impacts of money on society, corporate financing strategies, macro-marketing/management of sales staff and services. • Dr. Ronald V. Hartley, Associate Dean, 419-372-2488.

Bradley University, College of Business Administration, Program in Business Administration, Peoria, IL 61625-0002. Awards MBA. *Degree requirements:* Comprehensive exam required, foreign language and thesis not required. *Entrance requirements:* GMAT (minimum score 500), TOEFL (minimum score 500), minimum undergraduate GPA of 2.75 in major. Application deadline: 7/1 (priority date; rolling processing; 11/1 for spring admission). Application fee: $35. *Tuition:* $13,240 per year full-time, $359 per semester hour (minimum) part-time.

Announcement: Bradley University offers a new health-care administration (HCA) concentration in the MBA program—12 credit hours of elective courses with an emphasis in the critical health areas of economics and finance, marketing, legal issues, human resource management and employment law, quality management and operations, critical health issues, and organizational change. MBA common body courses in the functional areas of business in combination with the HCA concentration provide the health-care professional with strong management decision-making tools for facing the everchanging environment of health-care administration. Required health-care professional development projects complete the program focus. Special modular, preparatory courses provide the general business background for those with clinical or other nonbusiness undergraduate degrees. The program is accredited by AACSB–The International Association for Management Education and is offered entirely in the evening.

Brandeis University, The Heller Graduate School, Program in Management, Waltham, MA 02454-2728. Offers child, youth, and family services (MBA, MM); health care administration (MBA, MM); human services (MBA, MM). Part-time and evening/weekend programs available. Students: 39 full-time (31 women), 40 part-time (25 women); includes 6 minority (2 African Americans, 1 Asian American, 3 Hispanics), 1 international. Average age 30. 70 applicants, 71% accepted. In 1997, 35 degrees awarded (100% found work related to degree). *Average time to degree:* master's–1 year full-time, 3 years part-time. *Entrance requirements:* GRE General Test or GMAT (MM), GRE General Test (MBA). Application fee: $50. *Expenses:* Tuition $22,390 per year full-time, $1940 per course part-time. Fees $45 per year (minimum). *Financial aid:* In 1997–98, 20 students received aid, including 20 fellowships (all to first-year students); partial tuition waivers, institutionally sponsored loans also available. Financial aid application deadline: 2/15; applicants required to submit CSS PROFILE or FAFSA. • Application contact: Karen Cooney, Admissions Officer, 781-736-3820. Fax: 781-736-3881. E-mail: cooney@binah.cc.brandeis.edu.

See in-depth description on page 157.

Brenau University, Department of Business, Gainesville, GA 30501-3697. Awards MBA. Part-time and evening/weekend programs available. Faculty: 9 full-time (0 women), 8 part-time (0 women). Students: 87 full-time (30 women), 216 part-time (94 women); includes 67 minority (56 African Americans, 6 Asian Americans, 3 Hispanics, 2 Native Americans), 4 international. Average age 35. *Entrance requirements:* GMAT, GRE General Test, or MAT. Application deadline: rolling. Application fee: $30. *Tuition:* $249 per semester hour. *Financial aid:* Career-related internships or fieldwork available. Financial aid application deadline: 6/1. *Faculty research:* Banking, public policy. • Dr. Earl Boatwright, Chair, 770-538-4707. Application contact: Kathy Cobb, Director of Graduate Admissions, 770-534-6162. Fax: 770-538-4306. E-mail: kcobb@lib.brenau.edu.

Brescia College, Program in Management, Owensboro, KY 42301-3023. Awards MSM. Part-time and evening/weekend programs available. Faculty: 5 full-time (2 women), 1 part-time (0 women), 5.25 FTE. Students: 42 part-time (23 women); includes 1 minority (Hispanic). Average age 38. 37 applicants, 73% accepted. In 1997, 9 degrees awarded. *Average time to degree:* master's–2.4 years part-time. *Entrance requirements:* GMAT, minimum GPA of 3.0. Application deadline: 7/15 (rolling processing). Application fee: $35. *Tuition:* $150 per credit hour. *Financial aid:* 2 students received aid; institutionally sponsored loans available. Aid available to part-time students. Financial aid application deadline: 5/1; applicants required to submit FAFSA. • Dr. Dorn Fowler, Director, 502-686-4274. Fax: 502-686-4266. E-mail: dornf@brescia.edu. Application contact: Rick Eber, Director of Admissions, 502-686-4241. Fax: 502-686-4201. E-mail: ricke@brescia.edu.

Briercrest Biblical Seminary, Program in Leadership and Management, Caronport, SK S0H 0S0, Canada. Offers financial leadership (MA), higher education (MA), human resource management (MA), organizational leadership (MA). *Degree requirements:* Thesis optional, foreign language not required. *Application fee:* $25. *Tuition:* $471 per course. • Application contact: Michael Penner, Enrollment Management Officer, 306-756-3200. Fax: 306-756-7366.

Brigham Young University, Marriott School of Management, Executive Program in Business Administration, Provo, UT 84602-1001. Awards MBA. Evening/weekend programs available. Students: 129 full-time (14 women); includes 7 minority (3 Asian Americans, 4 Hispanics). Average age 32. 158 applicants, 47% accepted. In 1997, 117 degrees awarded (100% found work related to degree). *Average time to degree:* master's–2 years full-time. *Entrance requirements:* GMAT, 3 years of management experience, minimum undergraduate GPA of 3.0. Application deadline: 5/1 (priority date; rolling processing). Application fee: $30. *Faculty research:* Quantitative business analysis, career planning, security markets and investments, marketing and consumer behavior, international business. • Dr. Gil Bertelson, Director, 801-378-3721. Fax: 801-378-7837. E-mail: emba@byu.edu.

See in-depth description on page 159.

Brigham Young University, Marriott School of Management, Program in Business Administration, Provo, UT 84602-1001. Awards MBA, JD/MBA, MBA/MA, MBA/MS. MBA/MA offered jointly with the Center for International and Area Studies; MBA/MS offered jointly with the Department of Mechanical Engineering. Evening/weekend programs available. Faculty: 47 full-time (5 women). Students: 264 full-time (49 women); includes 15 minority (11 Asian Americans, 2 Hispanics, 2 Native Americans), 49 international. Average age 26. 475 applicants, 48% accepted. In 1997, 121 degrees awarded. *Average time to degree:* master's–2 years full-time. *Entrance requirements:* GMAT (minimum score 570; average 620), TOEFL (minimum score 570), minimum GPA of 3.0 in last 60 hours. Application deadline: 1/15 (priority date; rolling processing). Application fee: $30. *Financial aid:* In 1997–98, 19 research assistantships, 7 teaching assistantships, 99 scholarships (98 to first-year students) totaling $217,500 were awarded; institutionally sponsored loans and career-related internships or fieldwork also available. *Faculty research:* Quantitative business analysis, career planning, security markets and investments, marketing and consumer behavior, international business. • Dr. Gary F. McKinnon, Director, 801-378-3500. Application contact: Merlene Reeder, Administrator, 801-378-3509. Fax: 801-378-4808. E-mail: mba@byu.edu.

See in-depth description on page 159.

Bryant College, College of Business Administration, Smithfield, RI 02917-1284. Offers programs in accounting (MBA, MSA, CAGS), computer information systems (MBA, CAGS), finance (MBA, CAGS), general business (MBA), health services management and hospital administration (MBA, CAGS), international business (MBA), management (MBA, CAGS), marketing (MBA, CAGS), operations management (MBA, CAGS), taxation (MST, CAGS). Part-time and evening/weekend programs available. Faculty: 45 full-time (6 women), 43 part-time (8 women). Students: 52 full-time (27 women), 490 part-time (198 women); includes 17 minority (3 African Americans, 11 Asian Americans, 2 Hispanics, 1 Native American), 18 international. Average age 33. 192 applicants, 66% accepted. In 1997, 142 master's, 9 CAGSs awarded. *Entrance requirements:* For master's, GMAT (minimum score 480; average 520). Application deadline: 7/1 (priority date; rolling processing; 11/15 for spring admission). Application fee: $55 ($70 for international students). *Tuition:* $1025 per course. *Financial aid:* In 1997–98, 57 students received aid, including 13 research assistantships; graduate assistantships and career-related internships or fieldwork also available. Aid available to part-time students. Financial aid applicants required to submit FAFSA. • Cathy Lalli, Assistant Director of Graduate Programs, Graduate School, 401-232-6230. Fax: 401-232-6494. E-mail: gradprog@bryant.edu.

See in-depth description on page 161.

Bucknell University, College of Arts and Sciences, Department of Management, Lewisburg, PA 17837. Offers programs in accounting (MSBA), managerial finance and economics (MSBA), marketing (MSBA), quantitative methods and operations management (MSBA). Faculty: 12 full-time. Students: 6 full-time (2 women), 11 part-time (6 women). *Degree requirements:* Thesis required, foreign language not required. *Entrance requirements:* GMAT, TOEFL (minimum score 550), minimum GPA of 2.8. Application deadline: 6/1 (priority date; rolling processing; 12/1 for spring admission). Application fee: $25. *Tuition:* $2410 per course. *Financial aid:* Assistantships available. Financial aid application deadline: 3/1. • Dr. Mark Bettner, Head, 717-524-1306.

Butler University, College of Business Administration, Indianapolis, IN 46208-3485. Awards MBA. Part-time and evening/weekend programs available. Faculty: 16 full-time (3 women), 9 part-time (0 women), 18.1 FTE. Students: 20 full-time (12 women), 326 part-time (122 women); includes 11 minority (5 African Americans, 4 Asian Americans, 2 Hispanics), 15 international. Average age 31. 85 applicants, 88% accepted. In 1997, 86 degrees awarded. *Degree requirements:* Computer language required, foreign language and thesis not required. *Average time to degree:* master's–2 years full-time, 5 years part-time. *Entrance requirements:* GMAT, minimum AACSB index of 950. Application deadline: 8/15 (priority date; rolling processing). Application fee: $25. *Tuition:* $320 per credit hour. *Financial aid:* 16 students received aid; institutionally sponsored loans and career-related internships or fieldwork available. Aid available to part-time students. Financial aid application deadline: 7/15. • Dr. Lee Dahringer, Dean, 317-940-9221. Application contact: Dr. William Rieber, Director of Graduate Studies, 317-940-9846. Fax: 317-940-9455.

Caldwell College, Graduate Studies, Program in Contemporary Management, Caldwell, NJ 07006-6195. Awards MS. Program new for fall 1998. *Application deadline:* rolling. *Application fee:* $25. *Tuition:* $365 per credit. • Bernard C. O'Rourke, Coordinator, 973-228-4424 Ext. 409. Fax: 973-228-3855. E-mail: borourke@caldwell.edu. Application contact: Dr. Rina Spano, Director of Graduate Studies, 973-228-4424 Ext. 408. Fax: 973-364-7618. E-mail: rspano@caldwell.edu.

California Baptist College, Graduate Program in Business Administration, Riverside, CA 92504-3206. Awards MBA. Part-time and evening/weekend programs available. Faculty: 6 part-time (0 women). Students: 42 full-time, 6 part-time. *Degree requirements:* Thesis or alternative, comprehensive business plan. *Application deadline:* rolling. *Application fee:* $40. *Expenses:* Tuition $275 per unit. Fees $100 per year. *Financial aid:* Federal Work-Study available. Aid available to part-time students. Financial aid applicants required to submit FAFSA. • Dr. Bob Jabs, Chair, 909-689-5771. Application contact: Gail Ronveaux, Director of Graduate Services, 909-343-4249. Fax: 909-351-1808. E-mail: gradser@cal.baptist.edu.

California Lutheran University, School of Business Administration, Thousand Oaks, CA 91360-2787. Offers programs in finance (MBA), healthcare management (MBA), international business (MBA), management information systems (MBA), marketing (MBA), organizational behavior (MBA), small business/entrepreneurship (MBA). Faculty: 8 full-time (3 women), 29 part-time (4 women). Students: 131 full-time (121 women), 234 part-time (115 women). Average age 30. 73 applicants, 88% accepted. In 1997, 104 degrees awarded. *Entrance*

Directory: Business Administration and Management—General

California Lutheran University (continued)

requirements: GMAT, minimum GPA of 3.0, interview. Application deadline: 8/1 (priority date; rolling processing). Application fee: $50. *Tuition:* $395 per unit. • Dr. Ronald Hagler, Director, 805-493-3371.

California Polytechnic State University, San Luis Obispo, College of Business, San Luis Obispo, CA 93407. Offers programs in agribusiness management (MBA); engineering management (MBA/MS); industrial technology (MA), including industrial and technical studies. MBA/MS offered jointly with the College of Engineering. Faculty: 53 full-time, 32 part-time. Students: 85 full-time (23 women), 21 part-time (7 women); includes 10 Asian Americans. Average age 26. 112 applicants, 58% accepted. In 1997, 46 degrees awarded. *Average time to degree:* master's–2 years full-time, 5 years part-time. *Entrance requirements:* GRE General Test (combined average of 1650 on three sections), GMAT (minimum score 530; average 558). Application deadline: 7/1 (rolling processing). Application fee: $55. *Expenses:* Tuition $0 for state residents; $164 per unit for nonresidents. Fees $2102 per year full-time, $1632 per year part-time. *Financial aid:* Federal Work-Study, institutionally sponsored loans, and career-related internships or fieldwork available. Aid available to part-time students. Financial aid application deadline: 3/2; applicants required to submit FAFSA. *Faculty research:* Management of high-tech firms, Pacific Rim, capital market structures, economics of environmental policy, marketing of services. • Dr. William Boynton, Dean, 805-756-2705. Fax: 805-756-1473. Application contact: Dr. David Peach, Director, Graduate Management Programs, 805-756-7187. Fax: 805-756-0110. E-mail: di415@academic.calpoly.edu.

California Polytechnic University, Pomona, College of Business Administration, Pomona, CA 91768-2557. Awards MBA, MSBA. Part-time programs available. Students: 54 full-time (22 women), 234 part-time (96 women); includes 103 minority (6 African Americans, 73 Asian Americans, 24 Hispanics), 55 international. 232 applicants, 47% accepted. In 1997, 96 degrees awarded. *Degree requirements:* Computer language, thesis, project report required, foreign language not required. *Entrance requirements:* GMAT. Application deadline: rolling. Application fee: $55. *Expenses:* Tuition $0 for state residents; $164 per unit for nonresidents. Fees $1953 per year full-time, $1287 per year part-time. *Financial aid:* In 1997–98, 20 students received aid, including 5 research assistantships, 3 teaching assistantships; Federal Work-Study, institutionally sponsored loans, and career-related internships or fieldwork also available. Aid available to part-time students. Financial aid application deadline: 3/2; applicants required to submit FAFSA. *Faculty research:* Business strategy; investment, cash flow, and cost of capital; entrepreneurship; trade with China; creativity and innovation. • Dr. Eric J. McLaughlin, Director, 909-869-2362. E-mail: ejmclaughlin@csupomona.edu.

California State University, Bakersfield, School of Business and Public Administration, Program in Business Administration, 9001 Stockdale Highway, Bakersfield, CA 93311-1099. Awards MBA. Students: 41 full-time (17 women), 46 part-time (20 women); includes 22 minority (2 African Americans, 16 Asian Americans, 4 Hispanics), 16 international. 60 applicants, 100% accepted. *Entrance requirements:* GMAT. Application deadline: rolling. Application fee: $55. *Expenses:* Tuition $0 for state residents; $246 per unit full-time, $164 per unit part-time for nonresidents. Fees $1584 per year full-time, $918 per year part-time. • Tom Mishoe, Graduate Coordinator, 805-664-3099. Fax: 805-664-2438.

California State University, Chico, College of Business, Program in Business Administration, Chico, CA 95929-0041. Awards MBA. Students: 36 full-time (6 women), 24 part-time (12 women); includes 4 minority (1 African American, 2 Asian Americans, 1 Hispanic), 7 international. Average age 30. 35 applicants, 43% accepted. In 1997, 25 degrees awarded. *Degree requirements:* Thesis or alternative. *Entrance requirements:* GMAT (minimum score 500). Application deadline: 4/1 (rolling processing; 10/15 for spring admission). Application fee: $55. *Expenses:* Tuition $0 for state residents; $246 per unit for nonresidents. Fees $2108 per year full-time, $1442 per year part-time. *Financial aid:* Federal Work-Study and career-related internships or fieldwork available. Aid available to part-time students. Financial aid applicants required to submit FAFSA. • Graduate Coordinator, 530-898-4425. Fax: 530-898-4584.

California State University, Dominguez Hills, School of Management, Program in Business Administration, Carson, CA 90747-0001. Offers computer information systems (MBA). Faculty: 21 full-time (2 women), 1 part-time (0 women). Students: 82 full-time (35 women), 142 part-time (57 women); includes 84 minority (37 African Americans, 35 Asian Americans, 12 Hispanics), 77 international. Average age 32. 176 applicants, 99% accepted. In 1997, 50 degrees awarded. *Degree requirements:* Computer language required, foreign language and thesis not required. *Entrance requirements:* GMAT (minimum score 450), minimum GPA of 2.75. Application deadline: 6/1. Application fee: $55. *Expenses:* Tuition $0 for state residents; $246 per unit for nonresidents. Fees $1896 per year full-time, $1230 per year part-time. *Faculty research:* Management. • Dr. Robert Dowling, Coordinator, 310-243-3465.

California State University, Fresno, Division of Graduate Studies, Sid Craig School of Business, Program in Business Administration, 5241 North Maple Avenue, Fresno, CA 93740. Awards MBA. Part-time programs available. Faculty: 31 full-time (9 women). Students: 43 full-time (21 women), 115 part-time (41 women); includes 33 minority (5 African Americans, 19 Asian Americans, 6 Hispanics, 3 Native Americans), 19 international. Average age 31. 116 applicants, 66% accepted. In 1997, 40 degrees awarded. *Degree requirements:* Thesis or alternative required, foreign language not required. *Average time to degree:* master's–3.5 years full-time. *Entrance requirements:* GMAT, TOEFL (minimum score 550), minimum GPA of 2.53. Application deadline: 6/1 (priority date; rolling processing; 10/1 for spring admission). Application fee: $55. Electronic applications accepted. *Expenses:* Tuition $0 for state residents; $246 per unit for nonresidents. Fees $1872 per year full-time, $1206 per year part-time. *Financial aid:* In 1997–98, 14 graduate assistantships, scholarships totaling $31,661 were awarded; fellowships, research assistantships, Federal Work-Study, and career-related internships or fieldwork also available. Financial aid application deadline: 3/1; applicants required to submit FAFSA. *Faculty research:* International trade development, entrepreneurial outreach. • Dr. Donald Stengel, Coordinator, 209-278-2107. Fax: 209-278-4911. E-mail: donald_stengel@csufresno.edu.

California State University, Fullerton, School of Business Administration and Economics, Department of Management, PO Box 34080, Fullerton, CA 92834-9480. Awards MBA. Part-time and evening/weekend programs available. Faculty: 21 full-time (2 women), 21 part-time, 27.2 FTE. Students: 4 full-time (2 women), 15 part-time (6 women); includes 3 minority (1 Asian American, 2 Hispanics), 9 international. Average age 28. 26 applicants, 54% accepted. In 1997, 4 degrees awarded. *Degree requirements:* Computer language, project or thesis required, foreign language not required. *Entrance requirements:* GMAT (minimum score 950), minimum AACSB index of 950. Application fee: $55. *Expenses:* Tuition $0 for state residents; $246 per unit for nonresidents. Fees $1947 per year full-time, $1281 per year part-time. *Financial aid:* Teaching assistantships, state grants, Federal Work-Study, institutionally sponsored loans available. Aid available to part-time students. Financial aid application deadline: 3/1. • Dr. Farouk Abdelwahed, Chair, 714-278-2251. Application contact: Robert Miyake, Assistant Dean, 714-278-2211.

California State University, Fullerton, School of Business Administration and Economics, Program in Business Administration, PO Box 34080, Fullerton, CA 92834-9480. Awards MBA. Part-time and evening/weekend programs available. Students: 23 full-time (14 women), 174 part-time (71 women); includes 57 minority (46 Asian Americans, 10 Hispanics, 1 Native American), 44 international. Average age 30. 182 applicants, 53% accepted. In 1997, 37 degrees awarded. *Degree requirements:* Computer language, project or thesis required, foreign language not required. *Entrance requirements:* GMAT (minimum score 950). Application fee: $55. *Expenses:* Tuition $0 for state residents; $246 per unit for nonresidents. Fees $1947 per year full-time, $1281 per year part-time. *Financial aid:* Teaching assistantships, state grants, Federal Work-Study, institutionally sponsored loans available. Aid available to part-time students. Financial aid application deadline: 3/1. • Application contact: Robert Miyake, Assistant Dean, 714-278-2211.

California State University, Hayward, School of Business and Economics, Hayward, CA 94542-3000. Awards MA, MBA, MS. Part-time and evening/weekend programs available. Faculty: 67 full-time (14 women). Students: 154 full-time (94 women), 416 part-time (191 women); includes 216 minority (18 African Americans, 164 Asian Americans, 29 Hispanics, 5 Native Americans), 80 international. 188 applicants, 62% accepted. In 1997, 195 degrees awarded. *Degree requirements:* Thesis or alternative required, foreign language not required. *Entrance requirements:* GMAT (MBA, MS), minimum GPA of 2.75. Application deadline: 4/19 (priority date; rolling processing; 1/5 for spring admission). Application fee: $55. *Expenses:* Tuition $0 for state residents; $164 per unit for nonresidents. Fees $1827 per year full-time, $1161 per year part-time. *Financial aid:* Federal Work-Study, institutionally sponsored loans, and career-related internships or fieldwork available. Aid available to part-time students. Financial aid application deadline: 3/1. • Dr. Jay Tontz, Dean, 510-885-3291. Application contact: Dr. Donna L. Wiley, Director of Graduate Programs, 510-885-3964.

California State University, Long Beach, College of Business Administration, Long Beach, CA 90840-8501. Awards MBA. Part-time programs available. Students: 96 full-time (45 women), 295 part-time (96 women); includes 90 minority (16 African Americans, 47 Asian Americans, 24 Hispanics, 3 Native Americans), 72 international. Average age 32. 484 applicants, 39% accepted. In 1997, 78 degrees awarded. *Entrance requirements:* GMAT. Application deadline: 8/1 (rolling processing; 12/1 for spring admission). Application fee: $55. *Expenses:* Tuition $0 for state residents; $246 per unit for nonresidents. Fees $1846 per year full-time, $1180 per year part-time. *Financial aid:* Application deadline 3/2. *Faculty research:* Attitude formation theory, consumer motivation, gift giving, derivative and synthetic securities, financial applications of artificial intelligence. • Dr. C. J. Walter, Dean, 562-985-5306. Application contact: Dr. Jack Gregg, Director, MBA Program, 562-985-1797. Fax: 562-985-5543. E-mail: pchong@csulb.edu.

California State University, Los Angeles, School of Business and Economics, Los Angeles, CA 90032-8530. Awards MA, MBA, MS. Part-time and evening/weekend programs available. Faculty: 72 full-time, 46 part-time. Students: 85 full-time (45 women), 190 part-time (83 women); includes 133 minority (17 African Americans, 87 Asian Americans, 27 Hispanics, 2 Native Americans), 77 international. In 1997, 90 degrees awarded. *Entrance requirements:* GMAT, TOEFL (minimum score 550), minimum GPA of 2.5 during previous 2 years. Application deadline: 6/30 (rolling processing; 11/30 for spring admission). Application fee: $55. *Expenses:* Tuition $0 for state residents; $164 per unit for nonresidents. Fees $1763 per year full-time, $1097 per year part-time. *Financial aid:* 29 students received aid; fellowships, Federal Work-Study, and career-related internships or fieldwork available. Aid available to part-time students. Financial aid application deadline: 3/1. • Dr. Hugh Warren, Acting Dean, 213-343-2800.

California State University, Northridge, College of Business Administration and Economics, Department of Management, Northridge, CA 91330. Awards MBA. Part-time programs available. Faculty: 14 full-time, 10 part-time. 7 applicants, 71% accepted. *Degree requirements:* Thesis or alternative required, foreign language not required. *Entrance requirements:* GMAT (score in 50th percentile or higher), TOEFL, minimum GPA of 3.0 in last 60 units. Application deadline: 11/31. Application fee: $55. *Expenses:* Tuition $0 for state residents; $246 per unit for nonresidents. Fees $1970 per year full-time, $1304 per year part-time. *Financial aid:* Application deadline 3/1. • Dr. Alan Glassman, Chair, 818-677-2457. Application contact: Dr. Richard Moore, Director of Graduate Programs, 818-677-2467.

California State University, Northridge, College of Business Administration and Economics, Department of Management Science, Northridge, CA 91330. Offers programs in management science (MBA), production and management systems analysis (MS). Part-time programs available. Faculty: 14 full-time, 10 part-time. *Degree requirements:* Thesis or alternative required, foreign language not required. *Entrance requirements:* GMAT (score in 50th percentile or higher), TOEFL, minimum GPA of 3.0 in last 60 units. Application deadline: 11/30. Application fee: $55. *Expenses:* Tuition $0 for state residents; $246 per unit for nonresidents. Fees $1970 per year full-time, $1304 per year part-time. *Financial aid:* Application deadline 3/1. *Faculty research:* Management assessment. • Dr. Richard Gunther, Chair, 818-677-2470. Application contact: Dr. Richard Moore, Director of Graduate Programs, 818-677-2467.

California State University, Northridge, College of Business Administration and Economics, Program in Business Administration, Northridge, CA 91330. Awards MBA. Students: 35 full-time (12 women), 248 part-time (91 women); includes 62 minority (8 African Americans, 40 Asian Americans, 12 Hispanics, 2 Native Americans), 20 international. Average age 33. 228 applicants, 57% accepted. *Degree requirements:* Thesis or alternative required, foreign language not required. *Entrance requirements:* GMAT (score in 50th percentile or higher), TOEFL, minimum GPA of 3.0 in last 60 units. Application deadline: 11/30. Application fee: $55. *Expenses:* Tuition $0 for state residents; $246 per unit for nonresidents. Fees $1970 per year full-time, $1304 per year part-time. *Financial aid:* Application deadline 3/1. • Dr. Richard Moore, Director of Graduate Programs, 818-677-2467. Application contact: Carol Cook, Assistant Director of Graduate Programs, 818-677-2467.

California State University, Sacramento, School of Business Administration, Program in Business Administration, Sacramento, CA 95819-6048. Offers business administration (MBA), human resources (MBA), urban land development (MBA). Part-time programs available. *Degree requirements:* Thesis or alternative, writing proficiency exam required, foreign language not required. *Entrance requirements:* GMAT, TOEFL (minimum score 550). Application deadline: 4/15 (11/1 for spring admission). Application fee: $55. *Expenses:* Tuition $0 for state residents; $246 per unit for nonresidents. Fees $2012 per year full-time, $1346 per year part-time. *Financial aid:* Research assistantships, teaching assistantships, Federal Work-Study, and career-related internships or fieldwork available. Aid available to part-time students. Financial aid application deadline: 3/1. • Application contact: Dr. Herbert Blake, Graduate Adviser, 916-278-6771.

California State University, San Bernardino, Graduate Studies, School of Business and Public Administration, Program in Business Administration, San Bernardino, CA 92407-2397. Awards MBA. Part-time and evening/weekend programs available. Students: 189 full-time (82 women), 121 part-time (69 women); includes 39 minority (12 African Americans, 14 Asian Americans, 13 Hispanics), 163 international. 220 applicants, 84% accepted. In 1997, 91 degrees awarded. *Application deadline:* 8/31 (priority date; rolling processing). *Application fee:* $55. *Expenses:* Tuition $0 for state residents; $164 per unit for nonresidents. Fees $1922 per year full-time, $1256 per year part-time. *Financial aid:* Federal Work-Study, institutionally sponsored loans, and career-related internships or fieldwork available. Aid available to part-time students. Financial aid application deadline: 3/1. • Sue Greenfeld, Director, 909-880-5784. Fax: 909-880-7026.

California State University, San Marcos, Graduate Program in Business Administration, San Marcos, CA 92096. Offers business management (MBA), government management (MBA). Evening/weekend programs available. Faculty: 21 full-time (4 women), 5 part-time (2 women). Students: 150; includes 31 minority (6 African Americans, 16 Asian Americans, 9 Hispanics). Average age 35. 162 applicants, 51% accepted. In 1997, 70 degrees awarded. *Degree requirements:* Project required, foreign language and thesis not required. *Average time to degree:* master's–1.5 years full-time. *Entrance requirements:* GMAT (average 535). Application deadline: 11/2 (priority date; rolling processing). Application fee: $55. *Tuition:* $11,171 per year for state residents; $21,575 per year for nonresidents. *Financial aid:* In 1997–98, 35 students received aid, including 1 research assistantship averaging $800 per month and totaling $4,000; teaching assistantships, Federal Work-Study also available. Aid available to part-time students. Financial aid applicants required to submit FAFSA. • Newton Marqulies, Dean, College of Business Administration, 760-750-4241. Fax: 760-750-4250. Application contact: Office of Graduate Programs, 760-750-4267. Fax: 760-750-4263. E-mail: mba@csusm.edu.

California State University, Stanislaus, School of Business Administration, Turlock, CA 95382. Awards MBA. Part-time and evening/weekend programs available. Students: 82 (36 women); includes 25 minority (2 African Americans, 12 Asian Americans, 9 Hispanics, 2 Native Americans). 62 applicants, 84% accepted. In 1997, 23 degrees awarded. *Degree requirements:* Computer language, thesis or alternative. *Entrance requirements:* GMAT (minimum score 450), TOEFL (minimum score 550). Application fee: $55. *Expenses:* Tuition $0 for state residents; $246 per unit for nonresidents. Fees $1779 per year full-time, $1113 per year part-time. *Financial aid:* Federal Work-Study available. Financial aid application deadline: 3/2; applicants required to submit FAFSA. • Dr. Gordon L. Patzer, Dean, 209-667-3287. Fax: 209-667-3333.

California University of Pennsylvania, School of Science and Technology, Program in Business Administration, 250 University Avenue, California, PA 15419-1394. Awards MS. Part-time and evening/weekend programs available. Faculty: 10 part-time (2 women). Students: 37 full-time (14 women), 35 part-time (21 women); includes 5 minority (1 African American, 3 Asian Americans, 1 Hispanic), 8 international. 35 applicants, 86% accepted. In 1997, 26 degrees awarded. *Degree requirements:* Comprehensive exam required, foreign language and thesis not required. *Entrance requirements:* GMAT, TOEFL (minimum score 550), work experience in business. Application deadline: rolling. Application fee: $25. *Expenses:* Tuition $3468 per year full-time, $193 per credit part-time for state residents; $6236 per year full-time, $346 per credit part-time for nonresidents. Fees $886 per year full-time, $153 per semester (minimum) part-time. *Financial aid:* Graduate assistantships and career-related internships or fieldwork available. • Dr. Mahmood Omarzai, Graduate Coordinator, 724-938-4371.

Cambridge College, Graduate Studies, Program in Management, Cambridge, MA 02138-5304. Awards M Mgt. Part-time and evening/weekend programs available. Faculty: 9 full-time (3 women), 9 part-time (6 women). Students: 171 full-time (52 women), 9 part-time (3 women); includes 60 minority (35 African Americans, 16 Asian Americans, 9 Hispanics), 3 international. Average age 39. 52 applicants, 90% accepted. In 1997, 50 degrees awarded. *Degree requirements:* Computer language, thesis. *Average time to degree:* master's–1.5 years full-time. *Application deadline:* 9/10 (priority date; rolling processing; 1/10 for spring admission). *Application fee:* $30. *Expenses:* Tuition $315 per credit. Fees $60 per semester. *Financial aid:* Teaching assistantships, Federal Work-Study, and career-related internships or fieldwork available. Financial aid applicants required to submit FAFSA. • Application contact: Jacqueline Tynes, Senior Admissions Representative, 617-868-1000 Ext. 140. Fax: 617-349-3561. E-mail: admit@idea.cambridge.edu.

Cameron University, School of Graduate and Professional Studies, Program in Business Administration, Lawton, OK 73505-6377. Awards MBA. Part-time and evening/weekend programs available. Faculty: 10 full-time (2 women). Students: 13 full-time (7 women), 21 part-time (8 women); includes 8 minority (5 African Americans, 1 Asian American, 1 Hispanic, 1 Native American). Average age 38. In 1997, 16 degrees awarded. *Degree requirements:* Comprehensive exams required, thesis optional, foreign language not required. *Average time to degree:* master's–2 years full-time, 3 years part-time. *Entrance requirements:* GMAT, minimum GPA of 2.75 (undergraduate), 3.0 (graduate). Application deadline: 8/18 (priority date; rolling processing; 1/9 for spring admission). Application fee: $15. *Tuition:* $78 per semester hour for state residents; $180 per semester hour for nonresidents. *Financial aid:* Research assistantships, Federal Work-Study, and career-related internships or fieldwork available. Aid available to part-time students. Financial aid application deadline: 4/15; applicants required to submit FAFSA. • Dr. Jack Amyx, Associate Dean, 580-581-2267. Fax: 580-581-2253. E-mail: jacka@cameron.edu. Application contact: Suzanne Cartwright, Admissions Coordinator, 580-581-2986. Fax: 580-581-5532. E-mail: suzannea@cameron.edu.

Campbell University, Lundy-Fetterman School of Business, Buies Creek, NC 27506. Awards MBA. Part-time and evening/weekend programs available. Faculty: 8 full-time (3 women), 4 part-time (1 woman). Students: 32 full-time (12 women), 319 part-time (118 women); includes 18 minority (all African Americans), 27 international. Average age 30. 116 applicants, 48% accepted. In 1997, 100 degrees awarded. *Degree requirements:* Oral exam required, foreign language and thesis not required. *Entrance requirements:* GMAT (minimum score 450), TOEFL, minimum GPA of 2.7. Application deadline: rolling. Application fee: $15. *Tuition:* $168 per credit hour (minimum). *Faculty research:* Agricultural economics, statistics, investments. • Thomas H. Folwell Jr., Dean, 910-893-1380. Fax: 910-893-1392. Application contact: James S. Farthing, Director of Graduate Admissions, 910-893-1200 Ext. 1318. Fax: 910-893-1288.

Canisius College, Wehle School of Business, Program in Business Administration, Buffalo, NY 14208-1098. Awards MBA, MBAPA. MBAPA new for fall 1998. Faculty: 22 full-time (2 women). Average age 31. In 1997, 21 degrees awarded. *Degree requirements:* Computer language required, foreign language and thesis not required. *Average time to degree:* master's–4.5 years part-time. *Entrance requirements:* GMAT. Application deadline: 7/1 (priority date; rolling processing; 11/1 for spring admission). Application fee: $20. *Expenses:* Tuition $499 per credit hour. Fees $10 per credit hour. *Financial aid:* 7 students received aid; graduate assistantships available. Financial aid application deadline: 6/15. • Daniel W. Sullivan, Associate Dean, 716-888-2140. Fax: 716-888-3211. E-mail: dsully@wehle.canisius.edu.

Capital University, Graduate School of Administration, Columbus, OH 43209-2394. Awards MBA, JD/MBA, MBA/MSN. Part-time and evening/weekend programs available. Faculty: 7 full-time (1 woman), 20 part-time (4 women). Students: 320 part-time. *Degree requirements:* Research project required, foreign language and thesis not required. *Entrance requirements:* GMAT (minimum score 450), 2 years of work experience. Application deadline: 8/1 (priority date; rolling processing; 4/1 for spring admission). Application fee: $25. *Tuition:* $260 per credit hour. *Financial aid:* Available to part-time students. Financial aid application deadline: 8/1. • Dr. John Wellington, Dean, 614-236-6679. Fax: 614-236-6540.

Cardinal Stritch University, College of Business and Management, Programs in Management for Adults, Milwaukee, WI 53217-3985. Offerings in business administration (MBA), health services administration (MS), international business (MBA), management (MS). Students: 691; includes 85 minority (68 African Americans, 6 Asian Americans, 10 Hispanics, 1 Native American), 2 international. Average age 37. *Application deadline:* 4/1 (priority date; rolling processing). *Application fee:* $20. *Expenses:* Tuition $338 per credit. Fees $25 per semester. *Financial aid:* Federal Work-Study available. Financial aid applicants required to submit FAFSA. • Application contact: Shirley Hansen, Director of Marketing, 414-410-4315.

Announcement: The College of Business and Management of Cardinal Stritch University offers innovative solutions to the busy schedules of working professionals. Master's degree programs are offered in management, health services administration, and business administration. Classes meet 1 night a week for 4 hours both on and off campus.

Carleton University, Faculty of Social Sciences, School of Business, Ottawa, ON K1S 5B6, Canada. Offers programs in management (PhD), management studies (MMS). *Degree requirements:* For master's, thesis; for doctorate, dissertation, comprehensive exam. *Entrance requirements:* For master's, GMAT, TOEFL (minimum score 550), honors degree; for doctorate, TOEFL (minimum score 550). Application deadline: 3/1 (priority date; rolling processing). Application fee: $35. *Faculty research:* Business information systems, finance, international business, marketing, production and operations.

Carnegie Mellon University, Graduate School of Industrial Administration, Pittsburgh, PA 15213-3891. Offerings include business management and software engineering (MBMSE). School faculty: 86 full-time (15 women), 12 part-time (2 women). *Average time to degree:* master's–2 years full-time, 2.7 years part-time. *Application fee:* $50. • Douglas Dunn, Dean, 412-268-2265. Application contact: Director of Admissions, 412-268-2272.

Case Western Reserve University, Weatherhead School of Management, Cleveland, OH 44106. Awards M Acc, MBA, MNO, MS, MSM, EDM, PhD, CNM, JD/MBA, JD/MNO, MBA/MS, MBA/MSM, MSN/MBA, MSSA/MNO. Part-time and evening/weekend programs available. Faculty: 87 full-time (13 women), 19 part-time (3 women), 95 FTE. Students: 834 full-time (352 women), 654 part-time (251 women); includes 157 minority (74 African Americans, 69 Asian Americans, 9 Hispanics, 5 Native Americans), 298 international. Average age 28. 1,058 applicants, 42% accepted. In 1997, 428 master's awarded; 13 doctorates awarded (90% entered university research/teaching, 10% found other work related to degree). *Degree requirements:* For doctorate, dissertation required, foreign language not required. *Average time to degree:* master's–2 years full-time, 5 years part-time; doctorate–4.5 years full-time. *Entrance requirements:* For master's, GMAT (average 603); for doctorate and CNM, GMAT. Application deadline: rolling. Application fee: $50. *Tuition:* $20,900 per year full-time, $871 per credit hour part-time. *Financial aid:* In 1997–98, 2 fellowships (1 to a first-year student) totaling $8,000, 232 awards, scholarships (94 to first-year students) totaling $1.89 million were awarded; full and partial tuition waivers, Federal Work-Study, institutionally sponsored loans, and career-related internships or fieldwork also available. Aid available to part-time students. Financial aid application deadline: 5/1; applicants required to submit FAFSA. *Faculty research:* Health systems management, technology management, nonprofit management, entrepreneurship, management assessment. Total annual research expenditures: $1.85 million. • Kim S. Cameron, Dean, 216-368-2046. Application contact: Linda S. Gaston, Director of Marketing and Admissions, 216-368-2030. Fax: 216-368-5548. E-mail: lxg10@po.cwru.edu.

See in-depth description on page 163.

Case Western Reserve University, Frances Payne Bolton School of Nursing, MSN/MBA Program, Cleveland, OH 44106. Awards MSN/MBA. Offered jointly with Weatherhead School of Management. Students: 0. Average age 35. 1 applicant, 100% accepted. *Application deadline:* 6/1 (priority date; rolling processing). *Application fee:* $75. *Tuition:* $18,400 per year full-time, $767 per credit hour part-time. *Financial aid:* Application deadline 6/30. *Faculty research:* Organizational costs and length of stay, organizational structure and policy, professionals in bureaucratic organizations. • Application contact: Molly Blank, Admission Counselor, 216-368-2529. Fax: 216-368-3542. E-mail: mab44@po.cwru.edu.

Case Western Reserve University, Weatherhead School of Management, Executive Doctorate Program, Cleveland, OH 44106. Awards EDM. Faculty: 9 full-time (2 women). Students: 39 full-time (15 women); includes 7 minority (5 African Americans, 2 Asian Americans), 4 international. Average age 46. 35 applicants, 40% accepted. *Degree requirements:* Dissertation required, foreign language not required. *Average time to degree:* doctorate–3 years full-time. *Entrance requirements:* GMAT. Application deadline: 5/30. Application fee: $50. *Tuition:* $23,100 per year. *Financial aid:* In 1997–98, 11 fellowships (4 to first-year students) totaling $101,000 were awarded. Financial aid application deadline: 5/1. • John D. Aram, Program Director, 216-368-6935. Application contact: Sue Nartker, Assistant Director, 216-368-1943. Fax: 216-368-4793. E-mail: san2@po.cwru.edu.

The Catholic University of America, School of Arts and Sciences, Department of Economics and Business, Washington, DC 20064. Awards MA, PhD, JD/MA. Programs in accounting (MA), comparative economic systems and planning (PhD), economic development (PhD), economics (MA, PhD), financial management (MA), human resource management (MA), industrial organization (PhD), international economics (PhD), international political economics (MA), quantitative economics (PhD). PhD admissions temporarily suspended. Part-time and evening/weekend programs available. Faculty: 11 full-time (4 women), 5 part-time (2 women), 13 FTE. Students: 11 full-time (7 women), 15 part-time (6 women); includes 4 minority (3 Asian Americans, 1 Hispanic), 14 international. Average age 30. 29 applicants, 59% accepted. In 1997, 14 master's, 3 doctorates awarded. Terminal master's awarded for partial completion of doctoral program. *Degree requirements:* For master's, computer language, comprehensive exam required, foreign language and thesis not required; for doctorate, 2 foreign languages, computer language, dissertation, comprehensive exam. *Entrance requirements:* For master's, GRE General Test, TOEFL. Application deadline: 8/1 (priority date; rolling processing; 12/1 for spring admission). Application fee: $50. *Expenses:* Tuition $17,325 per year full-time, $668 per credit hour part-time. Fees $680 per year full-time, $360 per year part-time. *Financial aid:* Teaching assistantships, scholarships, full and partial tuition waivers, Federal Work-Study, institutionally sponsored loans, and career-related internships or fieldwork available. Aid available to part-time students. Financial aid application deadline: 2/1. • Dr. Ernest M. Zampelli, Chair, 202-319-6683. Fax: 202-319-4426. E-mail: zampelli@cua.edu.

Centenary College of Louisiana, School of Business, Shreveport, LA 71134-1188. Awards MBA. Part-time and evening/weekend programs available. Faculty: 8 full-time (3 women), 6 part-time (2 women). Students: 1 (woman) full-time, 80 part-time (35 women); includes 12 minority (9 African Americans, 1 Asian American, 2 Hispanics), 1 international. In 1997, 24 degrees awarded. *Degree requirements:* Computer language required, foreign language and thesis not required. *Average time to degree:* master's–4 years part-time. *Entrance requirements:* GMAT. Application fee: $20. *Tuition:* $600 per course. • Dr. Barrie Richardson, Dean, 318-869-5141.

Central Connecticut State University, School of Business, New Britain, CT 06050-4010. Awards MBA, MS. Part-time and evening/weekend programs available. Faculty: 9 full-time (2 women), 5 part-time (1 woman), 10.5 FTE. Students: 26 full-time (9 women), 47 part-time (31 women); includes 5 minority (1 African American, 3 Asian Americans, 1 Native American), 15 international. Average age 33. 86 applicants, 59% accepted. In 1997, 17 degrees awarded. *Degree requirements:* Thesis or alternative. *Entrance requirements:* TOEFL (minimum score 550), minimum GPA of 2.7. Application deadline: 6/1 (priority date; rolling processing; 12/1 for spring admission). Application fee: $40. *Expenses:* Tuition $4458 per year full-time, $175 per credit hour part-time for state residents; $9943 per year full-time, $175 per credit hour part-time for nonresidents. Fees $45 per semester. *Financial aid:* Research assistantships, Federal Work-Study available. Financial aid application deadline: 3/15; applicants required to submit FAFSA. *Faculty research:* Business/marketing education, organizational management, international business. • Dr. John Hampton, Dean, 860-832-3205.

Central Michigan University, College of Business Administration, Mount Pleasant, MI 48859. Awards MA, MBA, MBE. Part-time programs available. Faculty: 56 full-time (10 women). Students: 42 full-time (18 women), 120 part-time (49 women); includes 12 minority (4 African Americans, 6 Asian Americans, 2 Native Americans), 38 international. In 1997, 71 degrees awarded. *Entrance requirements:* GMAT. Application deadline: 3/1 (priority date; rolling processing). Application fee: $30. *Expenses:* Tuition $139 per credit hour (minimum) for state residents; $276 per credit hour (minimum) for nonresidents. Fees $260 per year full-time, $150 per semester part-time. *Financial aid:* In 1997–98, 12 research assistantships (6 to first-year students), 4 teaching assistantships (2 to first-year students) were awarded; fellowships, Federal Work-Study, and career-related internships or fieldwork also available. Financial aid application deadline: 3/7. • Dr. Terry Arndt, Dean, 517-774-7412. E-mail: 3inmjt3@cmich.edu. Application contact: Dr. Daniel Vetter, Director of MBA Program, 517-774-3337. Fax: 517-774-7713. E-mail: edward.grant@cmich.edu.

Central Michigan University, Interdisciplinary Programs, Program in Administration, Mount Pleasant, MI 48859. Awards MSA. Faculty: 2 full-time (0 women). Students: 62 full-time (44 women), 52 part-time (34 women); includes 9 minority (5 African Americans, 1 Asian American, 1 Hispanic, 2 Native Americans), 68 international. Average age 28. 161 applicants, 49% accepted. In 1997, 39 degrees awarded. *Degree requirements:* Thesis or alternative required, foreign language not required. *Entrance requirements:* Minimum undergraduate GPA of 2.5. Application deadline: 3/1 (priority date). Application fee: $30. *Expenses:* Tuition $139 per credit hour (minimum) for state residents; $276 per credit hour (minimum) for nonresidents. Fees $260 per year full-time, $150 per semester part-time. *Financial aid:* Federal Work-Study available. Financial aid application deadline: 3/7. • Sue Smith, Director, 517-774-6525. Fax: 517-774-3439. E-mail: 346ws7i@cmich.edu.

Central Missouri State University, Harmon College of Business Administration, Department of Management, Warrensburg, MO 64093. Awards MBA. Part-time programs available. Faculty: 10 full-time. Students: 44 full-time (13 women), 26 part-time (13 women). In 1997, 25 degrees awarded. *Entrance requirements:* GMAT, TOEFL (minimum score 550), minimum GPA of 2.5. Application deadline: 6/30 (priority date; rolling processing). Application fee: $25 ($50 for

Directory: Business Administration and Management—General

Central Missouri State University (continued)

international students). *Tuition:* $3288 per year full-time, $137 per credit hour part-time for state residents; $5928 per year full-time, $274 per credit hour part-time for nonresidents. *Financial aid:* In 1997–98, 14 research assistantships, 1 teaching assistantship, 7 administrative and laboratory assistantships were awarded; Federal Work-Study and career-related internships or fieldwork also available. Aid available to part-time students. Financial aid application deadline: 3/1; applicants required to submit FAFSA. • Dr. Karen Waner, Chair, 660-543-4247. Fax: 660-543-8885. E-mail: waner@cmsu2.cmsu.edu.

Chadron State College, Department of Business and Economics, Chadron, NE 69337. Awards MBA. Offered jointly with the University of Nebraska–Lincoln. Part-time and evening/weekend programs available. Students: 55. *Entrance requirements:* GRE General Test (minimum score 350 on verbal section, 410 on quantitative, 390 on analytical). Application deadline: rolling. *Expenses:* Tuition $1788 per year full-time, $75 per credit hour part-time for state residents; $3588 per year full-time, $149 per credit hour part-time for nonresidents. Fees $388 per year full-time, $1232 per year part-time. *Financial aid:* Graduate assistantships, Federal Work-Study, and career-related internships or fieldwork available. Aid available to part-time students. • Dr. Margaret Crouse, Dean, 308-432-6367. Fax: 308-432-6369. E-mail: mcrouse@csc1.csc.edu.

Chaminade University of Honolulu, Program in Business Administration, Honolulu, HI 96816-1578. Awards MBA, MBA/MSJBS. Part-time and evening/weekend programs available. Faculty: 9 full-time (3 women), 7 part-time (2 women). Students: 120 full-time, 60 part-time. Average age 31. 70 applicants, 99% accepted. In 1997, 83 degrees awarded. *Degree requirements:* Computer language required, foreign language and thesis not required. *Average time to degree:* master's–1.5 years full-time, 3 years part-time. *Entrance requirements:* GMAT, TOEFL (minimum score 550), minimum GPA of 3.0. Application deadline: 9/1 (priority date; rolling processing; 3/1 for spring admission). Application fee: $50. *Financial aid:* 44 students received aid; Federal Work-Study, institutionally sponsored loans, and career-related internships or fieldwork available. Aid available to part-time students. Financial aid application deadline: 3/1. *Faculty research:* Environmental development, total quality management, international finance. • John A. Steelquist, Director, 808-739-4612. Application contact: James Moses, Assistant MBA Director, 808-739-4612. Fax: 808-735-4734. E-mail: mba@chaminade.edu.

Chapman University, School of Business and Economics, Orange, CA 92866. Awards Exec MBA, MBA. Faculty: 18 full-time (1 woman). Students: 172. In 1997, 40 degrees awarded. *Degree requirements:* Comprehensive exam required, thesis not required. *Entrance requirements:* GMAT. Application deadline: rolling. Application fee: $40. *Tuition:* $9810 per year full-time, $545 per credit part-time. *Financial aid:* Application deadline 3/1. • Dr. Richard McDowell, Dean, 714-997-6684. Application contact: Dr. Homa Shabahang, Associate Dean, 714-997-6684.

Charleston Southern University, Program in Business, Charleston, SC 29423-8087. Offers accounting (MBA), finance (MBA), health care administration (MBA), marketing (MBA), organizational development (MBA). Part-time and evening/weekend programs available. Faculty: 8 full-time (0 women), 1 (woman) part-time, 8.33 FTE. Students: 104 (51 women). Average age 35. 64 applicants, 70% accepted. In 1997, 22 degrees awarded (95% found work related to degree, 5% continued full-time study). *Entrance requirements:* GMAT. Application deadline: rolling. Application fee: $25. *Tuition:* $9821 per year full-time, $173 per hour (minimum) part-time. *Financial aid:* Research assistantships, Federal Work-Study available. *Faculty research:* Economic forecasting. • Dr. Al Parish, MBA Director, 803-863-7904. Fax: 803-863-7919. E-mail: aparish@awdd.com. Application contact: Terri Jordan, MBA Coordinator, 803-863-7955. Fax: 803-863-7922.

Chatham College, School of Graduate Studies, Program in Management, Pittsburgh, PA 15232-2826. Awards MM. Part-time and evening/weekend programs available. Faculty: 2 full-time (1 woman), 3 part-time (2 women). Students: 5 part-time (all women). 4 applicants, 100% accepted. *Entrance requirements:* Resume. Application deadline: rolling. Application fee: $35. Electronic applications accepted. *Tuition:* $15,792 per year full-time, $395 per credit part-time. *Financial aid:* 4 students received aid. Aid available to part-time students. Financial aid applicants required to submit FAFSA. • Dr. Ruthann Fagan, Dean of Continuing Education, 412-365-1859. Application contact: Melinda Robbins, Evening and Weekend Studies, 412-365-1155. Fax: 412-365-1720. E-mail: admissions@chatham.edu.

Christian Brothers University, Graduate Programs, School of Business, Memphis, TN 38104-5581. Offers programs in business administration (MBA), telecommunications and information systems management (MS). Part-time and evening/weekend programs available. Faculty: 11 full-time (2 women), 5 part-time (2 women). Students: 55 full-time (24 women), 155 part-time (64 women); includes 32 minority (29 African Americans, 3 Asian Americans), 4 international. Average age 32. 140 applicants, 85% accepted. In 1997, 37 degrees awarded. *Entrance requirements:* GMAT (minimum score 450; average 510). Application deadline: rolling. Application fee: $25. *Expenses:* Tuition $325 per hour. Fees $30 per semester. *Financial aid:* Institutionally sponsored loans available. Aid available to part-time students. *Faculty research:* Business ethics. • Dr. Ray S. House, Dean, 901-321-3316. Application contact: Michael T. Smith, Director, MBA Program, 901-321-3317. Fax: 901-321-3494.

The Citadel, The Military College of South Carolina, Department of Business Administration, Charleston, SC 29409. Awards MBA. Faculty: 11 full-time (4 women). Students: 22 full-time (3 women), 121 part-time (40 women); includes 10 minority (8 African Americans, 2 Asian Americans), 5 international. In 1997, 36 degrees awarded. *Entrance requirements:* GRE, MAT, or 12 hours of graduate course work with a minimum GPA of 3.0. Application deadline: rolling. Application fee: $25. *Expenses:* Tuition $130 per credit hour for state residents; $260 per credit hour for nonresidents. Fees $30 per semester. *Financial aid:* In 1997–98, 2 incentive fellowships were awarded. • Dr. Mark Bebensee, Head, 803-953-5056. Application contact: Dr. Shiela Foster-Stinnett, MBA Program Director.

City University, School of Business and Management Professions, Bellevue, WA 98004-6442. Offerings include general business administration (MBA), management (MA, Certificate), managerial leadership (MBA, Certificate). Postbaccalaureate distance learning degree programs offered (no on-campus study). School faculty: 14 full-time (6 women), 689 part-time (247 women). *Application deadline:* rolling. *Application fee:* $75 ($175 for international students). Electronic applications accepted. *Tuition:* $280 per credit hour. • Dr. Roman Borboa, Dean, 425-637-1010 Ext. 3759. Fax: 425-277-2439. E-mail: rborboa@cityu.edu. Application contact: Nabil El-Khatib, Vice President, Admissions, 800-426-5596. Fax: 425-277-2437. E-mail: nel-khatib@cityu.edu.

City University, School of Human Services and Applied Behavioral Sciences, Bellevue, WA 98004-6442. Offerings include management and leadership (XMA). Postbaccalaureate distance learning degree programs offered (no on-campus study). School faculty: 6 full-time (2 women), 59 part-time (38 women). *Application deadline:* rolling. *Application fee:* $75 ($175 for international students). Electronic applications accepted. *Tuition:* $280 per credit hour. • Dr. Roman Borboa, Dean, 425-637-1010 Ext. 3759. Fax: 425-277-2439. E-mail: rborboa@cityu.edu. Application contact: Nabil El-Khatib, Vice President, Admissions, 800-426-5596. Fax: 425-277-2437. E-mail: nel-khatib@cityu.edu.

Claremont Graduate University, Peter F. Drucker Graduate Management Center, Program in Executive Management, Claremont, CA 91711-6163. Awards AEMBA, EMBA, MA, PhD, Certificate. Part-time programs available. Students: 9 full-time (2 women), 163 part-time (36 women); includes 16 minority (11 Asian Americans, 5 Hispanics), 2 international. Average age 44. 62 applicants, 77% accepted. In 1997, 32 master's, 8 doctorates awarded. Terminal master's awarded for partial completion of doctoral program. *Degree requirements:* For doctorate, dissertation required, foreign language not required. *Entrance requirements:* For master's, GMAT or GRE General Test (EMBA); for doctorate, GMAT or GRE General Test. Application deadline: 2/15 (priority date; rolling processing). Application fee: $40. Electronic applications accepted. *Expenses:* Tuition $20,250 per year full-time, $913 per unit part-time. Fees $130 per year. *Financial aid:* Federal Work-Study, institutionally sponsored loans available. Aid available to part-time students. Financial aid application deadline: 2/15; applicants required to submit FAFSA. *Faculty research:* Strategy and leadership, brand management, cost management and control, organizational transformation, general management. • Donald McCrea, Director, 909-621-8073. Application contact: Felicia Hazelton, Coordinator, 909-621-8073. Fax: 909-621-8543.

See in-depth description on page 165.

Claremont Graduate University, Peter F. Drucker Graduate Management Center, Program in Management, Claremont, CA 91711-6163. Offers applied economics (MBA); business administration (MBA); finance (MBA), including accounting control; information systems (MBA); international business (MBA); marketing (MBA); organizational behavior (MBA); public policy (MBA); strategic management (MBA). Part-time programs available. Students: 141 full-time (52 women), 59 part-time (22 women); includes 47 minority (5 African Americans, 36 Asian Americans, 6 Hispanics), 83 international. Average age 29. 243 applicants, 69% accepted. In 1997, 87 degrees awarded. *Entrance requirements:* GMAT, TOEFL. Application deadline: 2/15 (priority date; rolling processing). Application fee: $40. Electronic applications accepted. *Expenses:* Tuition $20,250 per year full-time, $913 per unit part-time. Fees $130 per year. *Financial aid:* Fellowships, research assistantships, teaching assistantships, Federal Work-Study, institutionally sponsored loans, and career-related internships or fieldwork available. Aid available to part-time students. Financial aid application deadline: 2/15; applicants required to submit FAFSA. *Faculty research:* Strategy and leadership, brand management, cost management and control, organizational transformation, general management. • Dr. Jeffrey Decker, Director, 909-621-8073. Fax: 909-621-8390. E-mail: jeff.decker@cgu.edu. Application contact: Kathy Hubener, Admissions Coordinator, 909-621-8073. Fax: 909-621-8543. E-mail: mba@cgu.edu.

See in-depth description on page 165.

Clarion University of Pennsylvania, College of Business Administration, Clarion, PA 16214. Awards MBA. Part-time and evening/weekend programs available. Faculty: 31 full-time (5 women). Students: 15 full-time (5 women), 11 part-time (5 women); includes 1 minority (Asian American), 4 international. 43 applicants, 65% accepted. In 1997, 13 degrees awarded. *Entrance requirements:* GMAT, minimum QPA of 2.75. Application deadline: 8/1 (priority date; rolling processing). Application fee: $25. *Expenses:* Tuition $3468 per year full-time, $193 per credit hour part-time for state residents; $6236 per year full-time, $346 per credit hour part-time for nonresidents. Fees $921 per year full-time, $90 per credit hour part-time for state residents; $921 per year full-time, $89 per credit hour part-time for nonresidents. *Financial aid:* In 1997–98, 10 research assistantships (3 to first-year students) averaging $533 per month were awarded; career-related internships or fieldwork also available. Aid available to part-time students. Financial aid application deadline: 5/1. • Dr. Robert Balough, Coordinator, 814-226-2628.

Clark Atlanta University, School of Business Administration, Atlanta, GA 30314. Awards MBA. Part-time programs available. Students: 87 full-time (48 women), 8 part-time (7 women); includes 92 minority (90 African Americans, 2 Hispanics), 3 international. In 1997, 54 degrees awarded. *Entrance requirements:* GMAT. Application deadline: 4/1 (rolling processing; 11/1 for spring admission). Application fee: $40. *Expenses:* Tuition $9672 per year full-time, $403 per credit hour part-time. Fees $200 per year. *Financial aid:* Fellowships, Federal Work-Study, and career-related internships or fieldwork available. Aid available to part-time students. Financial aid application deadline: 4/30. *Faculty research:* Transportation activities, minority business management. • Dr. Edward Davis, Acting Dean, 404-880-8451. Application contact: Michelle Clark-Davis, Graduate Program Assistant, 404-880-8709.

Clarke College, Program in Management, Dubuque, IA 52001-3198. Awards MS. Part-time programs available. Students: 22 part-time (8 women). Average age 38. 26 applicants, 85% accepted. *Degree requirements:* Computer language required, thesis optional, foreign language not required. *Entrance requirements:* GMAT, GRE General Test or MAT, minimum GPA of 3.0 in last 60 hours, previous undergraduate course work in business. Application deadline: rolling. Application fee: $25. Electronic applications accepted. *Expenses:* Tuition $12,688 per year full-time, $315 per credit hour part-time. Fees $240 per year. *Financial aid:* Career-related internships or fieldwork available. Aid available to part-time students. Financial aid applicants required to submit FAFSA. • Dr. Gayle Schou, Director, 319-588-8147. Application contact: Admissions Office, 800-383-2345. Fax: 319-588-6789. E-mail: graduate@clarke.edu.

Clarkson University, School of Business, Department of Business Administration, Potsdam, NY 13699. Awards MBA. Faculty: 11 full-time (1 woman). Students: 68 full-time (28 women), 12 part-time (5 women); includes 7 minority (3 African Americans, 3 Asian Americans, 1 Hispanic), 14 international. Average age 26. 138 applicants, 61% accepted. In 1997, 51 degrees awarded (100% found work related to degree). *Entrance requirements:* GMAT, TOEFL. Application deadline: rolling. Application fee: $25 ($35 for international students). *Expenses:* Tuition $19,075 per year full-time, $635 per credit hour part-time. Fees $178 per year. *Financial aid:* In 1997–98, 54 teaching assistantships were awarded; research assistantships also available. *Faculty research:* Industrial organization and regulated industries, end-user computing, systems analysis and design, technological marketing, leadership development. • Application contact: Dr. Fredric C. Menz, Director, Graduate Program, 315-268-6427. Fax: 315-268-3810. E-mail: menzf@icarus.som.clarkson.edu.

See in-depth description on page 167.

Clark University, Graduate School of Management, Business Administration Program, Worcester, MA 01610-1477. Awards MBA. Part-time and evening/weekend programs available. Students: 122 full-time (42 women), 179 part-time (84 women). 353 applicants, 69% accepted. In 1997, 109 degrees awarded. *Degree requirements:* Computer language required, thesis optional, foreign language not required. *Entrance requirements:* GMAT. Application deadline: 7/31 (priority date; rolling processing). Application fee: $40. *Financial aid:* Fellowships, research assistantships, teaching assistantships, Federal Work-Study, institutionally sponsored loans, and career-related internships or fieldwork available. Aid available to part-time students. Financial aid application deadline: 5/31. *Faculty research:* Organizational development, accounting, marketing, finance, human resource management. • Application contact: Admissions Director, 508-793-7406.

See in-depth description on page 169.

Clemson University, College of Business and Public Affairs, Department of Management, Clemson, SC 29634. Offers programs in industrial management (MS, PhD), management science (PhD). Part-time programs available. Students: 30 full-time (12 women), 7 part-time (2 women); includes 4 minority (all African Americans), 11 international. Average age 25. 28 applicants, 32% accepted. In 1997, 8 master's, 3 doctorates awarded. Terminal master's awarded for partial completion of doctoral program. *Degree requirements:* For doctorate, dissertation required, foreign language not required. *Entrance requirements:* For master's, GMAT, GRE General Test, TOEFL, minimum GPA of 3.0; for doctorate, GRE General Test, TOEFL, minimum GPA of 3.5. Application deadline: 2/1 (10/1 for spring admission). Application fee: $35. *Expenses:* Tuition $3154 per year full-time, $130 per credit hour part-time for state residents; $6452 per year full-time, $264 per credit hour part-time for nonresidents. Fees $190 per year. *Financial aid:* Fellowships, research assistantships, teaching assistantships, institutionally sponsored loans available. *Faculty research:* Production/operations, strategic management, organizational behavior, management information systems. • Dr. David Grigsby, Chair, 864-656-2011. E-mail: grigsby@clemson.edu. Application contact: Dr. R. L. LaForge, Graduate Coordinator, 864-656-2011. Fax: 864-656-2015. E-mail: rllafg@clemson.edu.

See in-depth description on page 171.

Clemson University, College of Business and Public Affairs, Program in Business Administration, Clemson, SC 29634. Awards MBA. Part-time and evening/weekend programs available.

Students: 80 full-time (23 women), 215 part-time (71 women); includes 10 minority (5 African Americans, 1 Asian American, 4 Hispanics), 60 international. Average age 29. 324 applicants, 47% accepted. In 1997, 122 degrees awarded. *Degree requirements:* Computer language required, foreign language and thesis not required. *Average time to degree:* master's–2 years full-time, 3 years part-time. *Entrance requirements:* GMAT, TOEFL. Application deadline: 5/1 (priority date; rolling processing). Application fee: $35. *Expenses:* Tuition $3154 per year full-time, $130 per credit hour part-time for state residents; $6452 per year full-time, $264 per credit hour part-time for nonresidents. Fees $190 per year. *Financial aid:* Fellowships, research assistantships, institutionally sponsored loans, and career-related internships or fieldwork available. Aid available to part-time students. Financial aid application deadline: 5/1; applicants required to submit FAFSA. • Dr. Dudley W. Blair, Director, 864-656-3975. E-mail: dudley@clemson.edu. Application contact: Martha Duke, Associate Director, 864-656-3975. Fax: 864-656-0947. E-mail: dmartha@clemson.edu.

See in-depth description on page 171.

Cleveland State University, James J. Nance College of Business Administration, Business Administration Program, Cleveland, OH 44115-2440. Awards MBA, DBA, JD/MBA. Offerings include business administration (MBA, DBA), health care administration (MBA). Part-time and evening/weekend programs available. Faculty: 28 full-time (5 women). Students: 277 full-time (120 women), 544 part-time (200 women); includes 85 minority (45 African Americans, 30 Asian Americans, 10 Hispanics), 191 international. Average age 31. 606 applicants, 63% accepted. In 1997, 309 master's, 2 doctorates awarded. *Degree requirements:* For master's, computer language required, foreign language and thesis not required; for doctorate, computer language, dissertation required, foreign language not required. *Entrance requirements:* GMAT. Application deadline: 9/1 (priority date; rolling processing). Application fee: $25. *Expenses:* Tuition $5252 per year full-time, $202 per credit hour part-time for state residents; $10,504 per year full-time, $404 per credit hour part-time for nonresidents. Fees $2.25 per credit hour (minimum). *Financial aid:* Research assistantships, teaching assistantships, administrative assistantships, full tuition waivers available. • Dr. S. R. Rao, Associate Dean, 216-687-3786. Fax: 216-687-9354.

See in-depth description on page 173.

College Misericordia, Division of Professional Studies, Program in Organizational Management, Dallas, PA 18612-1098. Awards MS. Part-time and evening/weekend programs available. Faculty: 3 full-time (2 women), 9 part-time (2 women). Students: 38 part-time (21 women). 13 applicants, 92% accepted. In 1997, 11 degrees awarded. *Degree requirements:* Thesis or alternative, practicum required, foreign language not required. *Entrance requirements:* GRE or MAT, minimum GPA of 2.5. Application deadline: 8/1 (priority date; rolling processing). Application fee: $20. *Tuition:* $410 per credit. *Financial aid:* In 1997–98, 2 research assistantships were awarded; fellowships, institutionally sponsored loans, and career-related internships or fieldwork also available. Aid available to part-time students. Financial aid application deadline: 5/1. • Dr. John Kachurick, Director, 717-674-6301.

College of Insurance, Graduate Programs, Program in Business Administration, New York, NY 10007-2165. Offers actuarial science (MBA), financial management (MBA), financial management of risk (MBA), insurance (MBA), risk management (MBA). Part-time and evening/weekend programs available. Faculty: 12 full-time (1 woman), 12 part-time (1 woman). Students: 43 full-time (19 women), 56 part-time (22 women); includes 24 minority (9 African Americans, 9 Asian Americans, 6 Hispanics), 33 international. Average age 28. 87 applicants, 62% accepted. In 1997, 51 degrees awarded. *Degree requirements:* Computer language required, thesis optional, foreign language not required. *Entrance requirements:* GMAT (minimum score 500), TOEFL (minimum score 550). Application deadline: 7/15 (priority date; rolling processing; 11/1 for spring admission). Application fee: $30 ($50 for international students). *Expenses:* Tuition $554 per credit. Fees $15 per credit. *Financial aid:* Graduate assistantships, Federal Work-Study, and career-related internships or fieldwork available. Aid available to part-time students. Financial aid application deadline: 5/15. • Application contact: Theresa C. Marro, Director of Admissions, 212-815-9232. Fax: 212-964-3381. E-mail: admissions@tci.edu.

See in-depth description on page 523.

College of Notre Dame, Department of Business Administration, Belmont, CA 94002-1997. Awards MBA. Part-time and evening/weekend programs available. Faculty: 4 full-time, 10 part-time. Students: 12 full-time (8 women), 119 part-time (65 women); includes 29 minority (2 African Americans, 18 Asian Americans, 8 Hispanics, 1 Native American), 9 international. Average age 31. 61 applicants, 70% accepted. In 1997, 35 degrees awarded. *Entrance requirements:* GMAT, TOEFL (minimum score 550), minimum GPA of 2.5. Application deadline: rolling. Application fee: $50 ($500 for international students). *Tuition:* $460 per unit. *Financial aid:* Available to part-time students. • Dr. Franklin Burroughs, Chair, 650-508-3542.

College of Notre Dame of Maryland, Program in Management, Baltimore, MD 21210-2476. Awards MA. Part-time and evening/weekend programs available. *Degree requirements:* Thesis optional, foreign language not required. *Entrance requirements:* Watson-Glaser Critical Thinking Appraisal, writing test, interview. Application deadline: 8/15 (priority date; rolling processing; 1/15 for spring admission). Application fee: $25. *Tuition:* $248 per credit. *Financial aid:* Institutionally sponsored loans and career-related internships or fieldwork available. Aid available to part-time students. Financial aid application deadline: 6/30; applicants required to submit FAFSA. • Application contact: Irma Kalkowski, Graduate Admissions Secretary, 410-532-5317. Fax: 410-532-5333. E-mail: gradadm@ndm.edu.

College of Saint Elizabeth, Department of Business Administration/Economics, Morristown, NJ 07960-6989. Offers program in management (MS). Part-time and evening/weekend programs available. Faculty: 7 full-time (3 women), 3 part-time (1 woman). Students: 29 part-time (22 women); includes 2 minority (1 African American, 1 Hispanic). Average age 35. 51 applicants, 82% accepted. *Degree requirements:* Capstone Seminar required, foreign language and thesis not required. *Entrance requirements:* Minimum GPA of 3.0. Application deadline: 7/15 (priority date; 11/15 for spring admission). Application fee: $35. *Expenses:* Tuition $364 per credit. Fees $455 per year full-time, $70 per semester part-time. *Financial aid:* Research assistantships, teaching assistantships, and career-related internships or fieldwork available. Aid available to part-time students. Financial aid application deadline: 3/15; applicants required to submit FAFSA. *Faculty research:* American business history, business developments in Eastern Europe, MIS/programming languages, marketing strategy, strategic planning. • Dr. Andrew Hrechak, Chair, 973-290-4083. Fax: 973-290-4177. E-mail: business@liza.st-elizabeth.edu.

The College of Saint Rose, School of Business, Business Administration Department, Albany, NY 12203-1419. Awards MBA, JD/MBA. JD/MBA offered jointly with Albany Law School of Union University. Part-time and evening/weekend programs available. Faculty: 14 full-time (7 women), 1 (woman) part-time. Students: 8 full-time (1 woman), 89 part-time (45 women); includes 2 minority (both Native Americans). Average age 32. In 1997, 47 degrees awarded. *Entrance requirements:* GMAT, graduate degree, or minimum undergraduate GPA of 3.0. Application deadline: 7/15 (priority date; rolling processing; 12/1 for spring admission). Application fee: $30. *Expenses:* Tuition $338 per credit. Fees $60 per year. *Financial aid:* Research assistantships, partial tuition waivers available. Aid available to part-time students. Financial aid application deadline: 3/1; applicants required to submit FAFSA. • Dr. Susan Raynis, Head, 518-454-2031. Application contact: Graduate Office, 518-454-5136. Fax: 518-458-5479. E-mail: ace@rosnet.strose.edu.

College of St. Scholastica, Program in Management, Duluth, MN 55811-4199. Awards MA. Part-time and evening/weekend programs available. Postbaccalaureate distance learning degree programs offered (minimal on-campus study). Faculty: 9 full-time (2 women), 3 part-time (1 woman). Students: 75 part-time (41 women); includes 5 minority (2 African Americans, 3 Native Americans), 1 international. Average age 35. 8 applicants, 75% accepted. In 1997, 18 degrees awarded. *Degree requirements:* Thesis. *Entrance requirements:* Interview. Application deadline: rolling. Application fee: $50. *Tuition:* $7968 per year full-time, $332 per credit part-time. *Financial aid:* 32 students received aid. Aid available to part-time students. Financial aid applicants required to submit FAFSA. *Faculty research:* Violence in higher education and workplace, screening and selection procedures in law enforcement, Internet use in criminal justice, stress management in law enforcement. • Dr. Barbara Edwards, Director, 218-723-6150. Application contact: Pat Jones, 218-723-6415. Fax: 218-723-6290. E-mail: pjones@css.edu.

College of Santa Fe, Department of Business Administration, Santa Fe, NM 87505-7634. Awards MBA. Program also available at Albuquerque campus. Part-time and evening/weekend programs available. Faculty: 4 full-time (0 women), 7 part-time (0 women). Students: 32 full-time (20 women), 69 part-time (36 women). Average age 38. 23 applicants, 100% accepted. In 1997, 25 degrees awarded. *Entrance requirements:* Minimum GPA of 3.0 in last 60 hours preferred. Application deadline: rolling. Application fee: $25. *Expenses:* Tuition $237 per credit hour. Fees $25 per year. *Financial aid:* Federal Work-Study available. Financial aid applicants required to submit FAFSA. • Dr. Ali Arshad, Chair, 505-473-6212. Application contact: Debbie A. Aragon, Administrative Secretary, 505-473-6211. Fax: 505-473-6504.

College of William and Mary, School of Business, Williamsburg, VA 23187-8795. Awards MBA, JD/MBA, MBA/MPP. MBA/MPP offered jointly with the Thomas Jefferson Program in Public Policy; JD/MBA offered jointly with the Marshall-Wythe School of Law. Part-time and evening/weekend programs available. Faculty: 45 full-time (8 women), 2 part-time (0 women). Students: 237 full-time (65 women), 153 part-time (35 women); includes 27 minority (7 African Americans, 12 Asian Americans, 7 Hispanics, 1 Native American), 13 international. Average age 30. 423 applicants, 61% accepted. In 1997, 160 degrees awarded. *Degree requirements:* Field studies project required, foreign language and thesis not required. *Average time to degree:* master's–2 years full-time, 4 years part-time. *Entrance requirements:* GMAT (minimum score 600; average 620), TOEFL (minimum score 600; average 610). Application deadline: 5/1 (priority date; rolling processing). Application fee: $50. *Financial aid:* In 1997–98, 170 students received aid, including 50 research assistantships (10 to first-year students) averaging $400 per month and totaling $70,000; career-related internships or fieldwork also available. Financial aid application deadline: 3/1; applicants required to submit FAFSA. *Faculty research:* Finance, economics, marketing leadership and change, accounting. • Dr. Lawrence Pulley, Interim Dean, 757-221-4100. Application contact: Susan G. Rivera, Director of Admissions and Financial Aid, 757-221-4100. Fax: 757-221-2937.

Colorado Christian University, Graduate Division, 180 South Garrison Street, Lakewood, CO 80226-7499. Offerings include management (MSM). Division faculty: 29 (13 women). *Application deadline:* 8/15 (1/10 for spring admission). *Application fee:* $35. • Thomas Varney, Director of Graduate Studies, 303-697-8135. Application contact: Director of Graduate Admissions, 303-202-0100 Ext. 520. Fax: 303-235-0617.

Colorado State University, College of Business, Department of Management, Fort Collins, CO 80523-0015. Awards MBA, MS. Faculty: 19 full-time (8 women). Students: 3 full-time (1 woman), 16 part-time (10 women); includes 2 minority (both Hispanics), 1 international. 27 applicants, 59% accepted. In 1997, 7 degrees awarded. *Degree requirements:* Thesis optional, foreign language not required. *Entrance requirements:* GMAT, TOEFL, minimum GPA of 3.0. Application deadline: 2/1 (priority date; rolling processing). Application fee: $30. Electronic applications accepted. *Tuition:* $2920 per year (minimum) full-time, $328 per credit hour (minimum) part-time for state residents; $9000 per year (minimum) full-time, $368 per credit hour (minimum) part-time for nonresidents. *Financial aid:* In 1997–98, 8 research assistantships were awarded; traineeships also available. Financial aid application deadline: 2/1. *Faculty research:* Production planning and control, labor, strategic management, work force diversity. • Application contact: Dr. Steve Bolander, Chair, 970-491-5636.

See in-depth description on page 175.

Colorado State University, College of Business, MBA Program, Fort Collins, CO 80523-0015. Awards MBA. Students: 76 full-time (34 women), 347 part-time (97 women); includes 35 minority (9 African Americans, 9 Asian Americans, 15 Hispanics, 2 Native Americans), 53 international. Average age 29. 452 applicants, 61% accepted. In 1997, 126 degrees awarded. *Degree requirements:* Thesis optional, foreign language not required. *Entrance requirements:* GMAT, TOEFL, minimum GPA of 3.0. Application deadline: 2/1 (priority date; rolling processing). Application fee: $30. Electronic applications accepted. *Tuition:* $2920 per year (minimum) full-time, $328 per credit hour (minimum) part-time for state residents; $9000 per year (minimum) full-time, $368 per credit hour (minimum) part-time for nonresidents. *Financial aid:* Application deadline 2/1. • Application contact: Dr. Jon Clark, Associate Dean, 970-491-6471. Fax: 970-491-0596.

See in-depth description on page 175.

Colorado Technical University, Graduate Studies, Program in Management, 4435 North Chestnut Street, Colorado Springs, CO 80907-3896. Offers business administration (MBA), business administration and management (DM), business management (MSM), health science management (MSM), human resources management (MSM), logistics management (MSM), management information systems (MSM), systems management (MSM). Part-time and evening/weekend programs available. Faculty: 8 full-time (2 women), 8 part-time (1 woman), 12 FTE. Students: 255 full-time (71 women); includes 36 minority (19 African Americans, 4 Asian Americans, 12 Hispanics, 1 Native American). Average age 34. 114 applicants, 84% accepted. In 1997, 79 master's awarded (100% found work related to degree). *Degree requirements:* For master's, thesis or alternative required, foreign language not required; for doctorate, dissertation required, foreign language not required. *Average time to degree:* master's–2 years full-time. *Entrance requirements:* For master's, minimum undergraduate GPA of 3.0; for doctorate, minimum graduate GPA of 3.0, 5 years of related work experience. Application deadline: 10/4 (rolling processing; 4/5 for spring admission). Application fee: $100. *Expenses:* Tuition $230 per quarter hour. Fees $6 per quarter. *Financial aid:* Career-related internships or fieldwork available. Financial aid applicants required to submit FAFSA. • Dr. Mark Pieffer, Dean, 719-590-6765. Application contact: Judy Galante, Graduate Admissions, 719-590-6720. Fax: 719-598-3740.

Columbia College, Program in Business Administration, Columbia, MO 65216-0002. Awards MBA. Part-time and evening/weekend programs available. Faculty: 4 full-time (0 women), 2 part-time (1 woman), 5 FTE. Students: 6 full-time (2 women), 15 part-time (7 women); includes 5 minority (2 African Americans, 2 Hispanics, 1 Native American), 1 international. Average age 34. 38 applicants, 79% accepted. *Degree requirements:* Culminating experience, final exams, portfolio required, foreign language and thesis not required. *Entrance requirements:* Minimum GPA of 3.0. Application deadline: rolling. Application fee: $25 ($50 for international students). *Tuition:* $180 per credit hour. *Financial aid:* Federal Work-Study available. Financial aid applicants required to submit FAFSA. • Chair, Evening and Graduate Division, 573-875-7615. Fax: 573-875-7209. Application contact: Virginia Wilson, Assistant Director, Admissions, 573-875-7339. Fax: 573-875-7506. E-mail: vlwilson@ccishp.ccis.edu.

Columbia University, Graduate School of Business, Doctoral Program in Business, New York, NY 10027. Offers business (PhD), including accounting (PhD), finance and economics (PhD), management of organizations (PhD), management science/operations research (PhD), marketing (PhD). Faculty: 105 full-time (15 women), 86 part-time (15 women). Students: 94 full-time (34 women); includes 4 minority (2 African Americans, 2 Asian Americans), 65 international. Average age 30. 462 applicants, 7% accepted. In 1997, 9 degrees awarded (70% entered university research/teaching, 30% found other work related to degree). *Degree requirements:* Dissertation, teacher training seminars, research paper, oral exam required, foreign language not required. *Average time to degree:* doctorate–4 years full-time. *Entrance requirements:* GMAT or GRE, TOEFL or TSE. Application deadline: 2/1. Application fee: $50. *Expenses:* Tuition is $26,520 per year, fees of $1,250 per year, and students receive tuition and fee exemptions for a maximum of 12 terms. *Financial aid:* 94 students received aid; fellowships, research assistantships, teaching assistantships, institutionally sponsored loans

Directory: Business Administration and Management—General

Columbia University (continued)

available. Financial aid application deadline: 2/1. • Application contact: Elizabeth Elam, Administrative Director, 212-854-2836. Fax: 212-932-2359.

Columbia University, Graduate School of Business, Executive MBA Program, New York, NY 10027. Awards MBA. Faculty: 105 full-time (15 women), 86 part-time (15 women). Students: 360 full-time (80 women); includes 65 minority (25 African Americans, 25 Asian Americans, 15 Hispanics), 90 international. Average age 34. 385 applicants, 58% accepted. In 1997, 180 degrees awarded. *Average time to degree:* master's–1.6 years part-time. *Entrance requirements:* GMAT, essay, company sponsorship. Application deadline: 5/1 (priority date; rolling processing; 10/1 for spring admission). Application fee: $125. *Expenses:* Tuition is $83,000 for entire two-year program. *Financial aid:* Institutionally sponsored loans available. • Dr. Dina Consolini, Assistant Dean for the Executive MBA and Summer MBA Programs, 212-854-2211. Fax: 212-854-8998.

Columbia University, Graduate School of Business, MBA Program, New York, NY 10027. Awards MBA, JD/MBA, MBA/MA, MBA/MS, MBA/MIA, MBA/MPH. Offerings include accounting (MBA); construction management (MBA); entrepreneurship (MBA); finance and economics (MBA); human resource management (MBA); international business (MBA); management of organizations (MBA); management science (MBA); marketing (MBA); media, entertainment and communications (MBA); production and operations management (MBA); public and nonprofit management (MBA); real estate (MBA). Faculty: 105 full-time (15 women), 86 part-time (15 women). Students: 1,269 full-time (470 women); includes 293 minority (89 African Americans, 139 Asian Americans, 63 Hispanics, 2 Native Americans), 355 international. Average age 27. 5,275 applicants, 13% accepted. In 1997, 599 degrees awarded. *Entrance requirements:* GMAT, TOEFL (minimum score 610). Application deadline: 4/20 (rolling processing; 11/1 for spring admission). Application fee: $125 ($150 for international students). *Expenses:* Tuition $26,520 per year. Fees $1250 per year. *Financial aid:* Fellowships, research assistantships, teaching assistantships, Federal Work-Study, institutionally sponsored loans, and career-related internships or fieldwork available. Financial aid application deadline: 2/1; applicants required to submit FAFSA. • Prof. Safwan Masri, Vice Dean of Students and the MBA Program, 212-854-8716. Fax: 212-854-0545. E-mail: smm1@columbia.edu. Application contact: Linda Meehan, Assistant Dean and Executive Director of Admissions and Financial Aid, 212-854-1961. Fax: 212-662-6754. E-mail: gohermes@claven.gsb.columbia.edu.

Columbia University, Graduate School of Business, Summer MBA Program, New York, NY 10027. Awards MBA. Faculty: 105 full-time (15 women), 86 part-time (15 women). Students: 125 full-time (31 women); includes 11 minority (3 African Americans, 4 Asian Americans, 4 Hispanics), 13 international. Average age 24. 50 applicants, 70% accepted. In 1997, 30 degrees awarded (100% found work related to degree). *Entrance requirements:* GMAT, TOEFL (minimum score 656), company sponsorship. Application deadline: 2/1 (rolling processing). Application fee: $100. *Expenses:* Tuition is $69,000 for entire three-year program. • Dr. Dina Consolini, Assistant Dean for the Executive MBA and Summer MBA Programs, 212-854-2211. Application contact: Susan Roth, Coordinator, 212-854-2719. Fax: 212-854-8998.

Columbus State University, College of Business, Columbus, GA 31907-5645. Awards MBA. Part-time and evening/weekend programs available. Faculty: 15 full-time (1 woman). Students: 46 full-time (16 women), 29 part-time (10 women); includes 20 minority (15 African Americans, 3 Asian Americans, 2 Hispanics), 6 international. Average age 35. 24 applicants, 92% accepted. In 1997, 19 degrees awarded. *Average time to degree:* master's–1.5 years full-time, 3 years part-time. *Entrance requirements:* GMAT. Application deadline: 7/10 (priority date; rolling processing; 10/23 for spring admission). Application fee: $20. *Tuition:* $1718 per year full-time, $151 per semester hour part-time for state residents; $6218 per year full-time, $401 per semester hour part-time for nonresidents. *Financial aid:* In 1997–98, 5 research assistantships were awarded; teaching assistantships, full tuition waivers, Federal Work-Study, institutionally sponsored loans, and career-related internships or fieldwork also available. Aid available to part-time students. Financial aid application deadline: 7/15; applicants required to submit FAFSA. • Dr. Robert S. Johnson, Dean, 706-568-2044. E-mail: johnson_robert@colstate.edu. Application contact: Katie Thornton, Graduate Admissions, 706-568-2279. Fax: 706-568-2462. E-mail: thornton_katie@colstate.edu.

Concordia University, Faculty of Commerce and Administration, Montréal, PQ H3G 1M8, Canada. Offers programs in accounting (Diploma), including institutional administration, sports administration; administration (M Sc, PhD); business administration (Aviation MBA), including airline and aviation; business adminstration (EMBA); management accounting (Certificate). PhD offered jointly with École des Hautes Études Commerciales, McGill University, and the Université du Québec à Montréal. Part-time and evening/weekend programs available. Students: 458 full-time (213 women), 321 part-time (156 women); includes 37 international. In 1997, 135 master's, 5 doctorates, 164 other advanced degrees awarded. *Degree requirements:* For master's, 1 foreign language, computer language, thesis (for some programs), research project; for doctorate, 1 foreign language, computer language, dissertation; for other advanced degree, 1 foreign language, computer language. *Entrance requirements:* For master's, GMAT (minimum score 500), TOEFL; for doctorate, GMAT. Application fee: $30. *Expenses:* Tuition $56 per credit (minimum) for Canadian residents; $249 per credit (minimum) for nonresidents. Fees $152 per year full-time, $111 per year (minimum) part-time. *Financial aid:* Fellowships and career-related internships or fieldwork available. *Faculty research:* General business, capital markets, international business. • Dr. M. Anvari, Dean, 514-848-2700. Fax: 514-848-4502. Application contact: Dale Doreen, Director, 514-848-2958. Fax: 514-848-4208.

Concordia University at St. Paul, Program in Organizational Management, St. Paul, MN 55104-5494. Awards MA. Part-time and evening/weekend programs available. Faculty: 6 full-time (1 woman), 13 part-time (4 women), 9 FTE. Students: 62 full-time. Average age 41. 55 applicants, 95% accepted. *Entrance requirements:* MAT, interview, minimum GPA of 2.5. Application deadline: rolling. Application fee: $20. *Tuition:* $225 per semester hour. *Financial aid:* Research assistantships, teaching assistantships available. Financial aid applicants required to submit FAFSA. *Faculty research:* Creativity, self-directed learning, organizational collaboration, productivity and quality. • Dr. Robert DeWerff, Dean of Graduate and Continuing Studies, 612-641-8277. Fax: 612-659-0207. E-mail: dewerff@luther.csp.edu. Application contact: Dr. Tom Hanson, Director of the School of Accelerated Learning, 612-641-8844. Fax: 612-641-8807. E-mail: hanson@luther.csp.edu.

Concordia University Wisconsin, Division of Graduate Studies, MBA Program, Mequon, WI 53097-2402. Offers church administration (MBA), finance (MBA), health care administration (MBA), human resource management (MBA), international business (MBA), management (MBA), management information services (MBA), managerial communications (MBA), marketing (MBA), public administration (MBA), risk management (MBA). Postbaccalaureate distance learning degree programs offered (minimal on-campus study). *Degree requirements:* Thesis or alternative, comprehensive exam. *Average time to degree:* master's–2 years part-time. *Entrance requirements:* TOEFL (minimum score 550). Application deadline: 8/1 (priority date; rolling processing; 1/15 for spring admission). Application fee: $50. *Tuition:* $300 per credit. *Financial aid:* Application deadline 8/1. • David Borst, Director, 414-243-4298. Fax: 414-243-4428. E-mail: dborst@bach.cuw.edu.

Cornell University, Professional Field of the Johnson Graduate School of Management, Ithaca, NY 14853-0001. Awards MBA, JD/MBA, MBA/MILR, M Eng/MBA. Faculty: 43 full-time (9 women), 1 part-time (0 women). Students: 565 full-time (172 women). Average age 26. In 1997, 266 degrees awarded. *Entrance requirements:* GMAT. Application deadline: 4/1. Application fee: $80 ($120 for international students). *Expenses:* Tuition $24,300 per year. Fees $48 per year. *Financial aid:* Fellowships, research assistantships, full and partial tuition waivers, Federal Work-Study, institutionally sponsored loans, and career-related internships or fieldwork available. Financial aid application deadline: 2/15. • Alan G. Merten, Dean, 607-255-6418. Application contact: Admissions Office, 800-847-2082. Fax: 607-254-8886. E-mail: mba@johnson.cornell.edu.

Cornell University, Graduate Field of Management, Ithaca, NY 14853-0001. Offers programs in accounting (PhD), behavioral decision theory (PhD), finance (PhD), management information systems (PhD), managerial economics (PhD), marketing (PhD), organizational behavior (PhD), production and operations management (PhD), quantitative analysis (PhD). Faculty: 43 full-time. Students: 35 full-time (11 women); includes 5 minority (1 African American, 3 Asian Americans, 1 Hispanic), 21 international. 248 applicants, 4% accepted. In 1997, 3 doctorates awarded. Terminal master's awarded for partial completion of doctoral program. *Degree requirements:* For doctorate, dissertation required, foreign language not required. *Entrance requirements:* For doctorate, GMAT or GRE General Test, TOEFL. Application deadline: 1/10 (priority date). Application fee: $65. *Expenses:* Tuition $24,300 per year. Fees $48 per year. *Financial aid:* In 1997–98, 34 students received aid, including 4 fellowships (1 to a first-year student), 23 research assistantships (3 to first-year students), 7 teaching assistantships; full and partial tuition waivers, institutionally sponsored loans also available. Financial aid applicants required to submit FAFSA. *Faculty research:* Operations and manufacturing. • Director of Graduate Studies, 607-255-3669. Application contact: Graduate Field Assistant, 607-255-3669. Fax: 607-254-4590. E-mail: maria@johnson.cornell.edu.

Creighton University, Eugene C. Eppley College of Business Administration, Omaha, NE 68178-0001. Awards MBA, MSITM, JD/MBA. Evening/weekend programs available. Faculty: 40 full-time, 1 part-time. Students: 31 full-time (9 women), 123 part-time (50 women); includes 12 minority (5 African Americans, 3 Asian Americans, 3 Hispanics, 1 Native American), 16 international. In 1997, 65 degrees awarded. *Entrance requirements:* GMAT, TOEFL (minimum score 550). Application deadline: 3/1 (rolling processing). Application fee: $30. *Expenses:* Tuition $402 per credit hour. Fees $536 per year full-time, $28 per semester part-time. *Financial aid:* Graduate assistantships and career-related internships or fieldwork available. *Faculty research:* Small business issues. • Dr. Robert Pitts, Dean, 402-280-2852. Application contact: Michelle O'Connor, Coordinator, 402-280-2829.

Cumberland University, Division of Graduate Studies, Program in Business Administration, Lebanon, TN 37087-3554. Awards MBA. Part-time and evening/weekend programs available. Faculty: 5 part-time (1 woman). Students: 51 part-time (12 women); includes 4 minority (2 African Americans, 2 Asian Americans), 2 international. In 1997, 19 degrees awarded. *Average time to degree:* master's–2 years part-time. *Entrance requirements:* GMAT or GRE. Application fee: $50. *Financial aid:* Institutionally sponsored loans and career-related internships or fieldwork available. Aid available to part-time students. Financial aid application deadline: 8/1; applicants required to submit FAFSA. • Dr. Jack Forrest, Assistant Professor of Business and Mathematics, 615-444-2562 Ext. 1263. Application contact: Stephanie Walker, Director of Admissions, 615-444-2562 Ext. 1120. Fax: 615-444-2569. E-mail: swalker@cumberland.edu.

Dalhousie University, Faculty of Management, School of Business Administration, Halifax, NS B3H 3J5, Canada. Awards MBA, LL B/MBA. Part-time programs available. Faculty: 34 full-time. Students: 156 full-time (56 women), 122 part-time (51 women). Average age 26. 504 applicants, 38% accepted. *Entrance requirements:* GMAT (minimum score 550), TOEFL (minimum score 580). Application deadline: 6/1 (rolling processing). Application fee: $55. *Financial aid:* 12 students received aid; fellowships, teaching assistantships available. *Faculty research:* International business, quantitative methods, operations research, MIS, marketing, finance. • Dr. R. Klapstein, Director, 902-494-7080. Application contact: P. Rees, Graduate Coordinator, 902-494-1823. Fax: 902-494-1107. E-mail: philip.rees@dal.ca.

Dallas Baptist University, College of Business, Business Administration Program, Dallas, TX 75211-9299. Offers accounting (MBA), business administration (MBA), finance (MBA), international business (MBA), management (MBA), management information systems (MBA), marketing (MBA). Part-time and evening/weekend programs available. Faculty: 15 full-time (4 women), 26 part-time (5 women). Students: 61 full-time (22 women), 276 part-time (103 women). Average age 36. 271 applicants, 80% accepted. In 1997, 86 degrees awarded. *Entrance requirements:* GMAT, TOEFL (minimum score 550). Application deadline: rolling. Application fee: $25. *Tuition:* $285 per hour. *Financial aid:* In 1997–98, 15 grants, scholarships (3 to first-year students) totaling $18,787 were awarded; institutionally sponsored loans and career-related internships or fieldwork also available. *Faculty research:* Sports management, services marketing, retailing, strategic management, financial planning/investments. • Annette Hoffman, Director of Graduate Business Programs, 214-333-5280. Application contact: Travis Bundrick, Director of Graduate Programs, 214-333-5243. Fax: 214-333-5579. E-mail: graduate@dbu.edu.

Dartmouth College, Amos Tuck School of Business Administration, Hanover, NH 03755. Awards MBA, MBA/MALD, MBA/MEM, MD/MBA. MBA/MALD offered jointly with the Fletcher School of Law and Diplomacy at Tufts University. Faculty: 34 full-time (4 women), 11 part-time. Students: 374 full-time (105 women); includes 70 international. Average age 27. 3,194 applicants, 11% accepted. In 1997, 181 degrees awarded. *Entrance requirements:* GMAT. Application deadline: 4/21 (rolling processing). Application fee: $100. *Financial aid:* In 1997–98, 240 students received aid, including 167 fellowships (133 to first-year students) totaling $1; Federal Work-Study, institutionally sponsored loans also available. Financial aid applicants required to submit FAFSA. • Paul Danos, Dean, 603-646-2460. Fax: 603-646-1308. Application contact: Sally O. Jaeger, Director of Admissions, 603-646-3162. Fax: 603-646-1441.

Defiance College, Program in Business and Organizational Leadership, Defiance, OH 43512-1610. Awards MBOL. Part-time and evening/weekend programs available. Students: 20 part-time (11 women). Average age 28. *Degree requirements:* Thesis required (for some programs), foreign language not required. *Application deadline:* 8/1 (rolling processing). *Application fee:* $25. *Expenses:* Tuition $255 per credit hour. Fees $25 per semester. • Dale Sullivan, Coordinator, 419-784-4010. Application contact: Sally Bissell, Director of Continuing Education, 419-784-4010.

Delaware State University, Department of Economics and Business Administration, Program in Business Administration, Dover, DE 19901-2277. Awards MBA. Part-time and evening/weekend programs available. *Entrance requirements:* GMAT, minimum GPA of 3.0 in major; 2.75 overall in business, economics, calculus, and computing. Application deadline: 6/30 (priority date; rolling processing). Application fee: $10. *Faculty research:* Managerial economics, strategic management, qualitative effort, finance.

Delta State University, School of Business, Cleveland, MS 38733-0001. Awards MBA, MCA, MPA. Part-time and evening/weekend programs available. Faculty: 14 full-time (2 women), 2 part-time (0 women), 15.5 FTE. Students: 40 full-time (17 women), 88 part-time (45 women); includes 35 minority (27 African Americans, 7 Asian Americans, 1 Hispanic). Average age 31. 63 applicants, 98% accepted. In 1997, 21 degrees awarded. *Entrance requirements:* GMAT (minimum score 380). Application deadline: 8/1 (priority date; rolling processing). Application fee: $0. *Tuition:* $2596 per year full-time, $121 per semester hour part-time for state residents; $5546 per year full-time, $285 per semester hour part-time for nonresidents. *Financial aid:* Research assistantships, Federal Work-Study, institutionally sponsored loans, and career-related internships or fieldwork available. Aid available to part-time students. Financial aid application deadline: 6/1. • Dr. William Stewart, Dean, 601-846-4200. Application contact: Dr. John Thornell, Dean of Graduate Studies and Continuing Education, 601-846-4310. Fax: 601-846-4016. E-mail: thornell@dsu.deltast.edu.

DePaul University, Charles H. Kellstadt Graduate School of Business, Chicago, IL 60604-2287. Awards PMSA, MA, M Acc, MBA, MSA, MSF, MSMIS, MST, JD/MBA. Part-time and evening/weekend programs available. Faculty: 105 full-time (23 women), 115 part-time (24 women). Students: 1,223 full-time (449 women), 1,280 part-time (464 women); includes 342 minority (106 African Americans, 167 Asian Americans, 66 Hispanics, 3 Native Americans), 68 international. Average age 30. 1,132 applicants, 66% accepted. In 1997, 710 master's awarded. *Entrance requirements:* For master's, GMAT. Application deadline: rolling. Application fee: $40. Electronic applications accepted. *Expenses:* Tuition $1593 per course. Fees $30 per year. *Financial aid:* Research assistantships, full and partial tuition waivers, Federal Work-Study, and career-related internships or fieldwork available. Aid available to part-time students. • Dr.

Ronald J. Patten, Dean, 312-362-6781. Application contact: Christine Munoz, Director of Admissions, 312-362-8810. Fax: 312-362-6677. E-mail: mbainfo@wppost.depaul.edu.

See in-depth description on page 177.

Detroit College of Business, Graduate Studies Division, 4801 Oakman Boulevard, Dearborn, MI 48126-3799. Offers programs in accounting (MBA), management (MBA). Postbaccalaureate distance learning degree programs offered. Faculty: 5 full-time (2 women), 28 part-time (4 women). Students: 175 part-time (122 women); includes 109 minority (99 African Americans, 6 Asian Americans, 4 Hispanics). Average age 37. 50 applicants, 100% accepted. *Entrance requirements:* Minimum GPA of 2.7, previous course work in accounting and statistics. Application deadline: 8/12 (priority date; rolling processing; 4/17 for spring admission). Application fee: $50. *Financial aid:* In 1997–98, 90 students received aid, including 44 tuition grants (all to first-year students) totaling $68,461; Federal Work-Study also available. Aid available to part-time students. Financial aid application deadline: 8/1; applicants required to submit FAFSA. • Dr. James J. Krolik, Dean, 313-581-4400 Ext. 372. E-mail: dbjkrol@dcb.edu. Application contact: Ofelia Tabarez, Graduate Admissions Representative, 313-581-4400 Ext. 3781. Fax: 313-581-6822. E-mail: dbaotabarez@dcb.edu.

Doane College, Program in Management, Crete, NE 68333-2430. Awards MAA, MAM. MAA being phased out; applicants no longer accepted. Part-time and evening/weekend programs available. In 1997, 5 degrees awarded. *Degree requirements:* Thesis required, foreign language not required. *Average time to degree:* master's–2.7 years part-time. *Entrance requirements:* Minimum GPA of 2.5. Application deadline: rolling. Application fee: $25. *Tuition:* $185 per credit hour. • Application contact: Deryl E. Merritt, Associate Dean, 402-464-1223. Fax: 402-466-4228. E-mail: dmerritt@doane.edu.

Dominican College of San Rafael, School of Liberal and Professional Studies, Program in Strategic Leadership, San Rafael, CA 94901-2298. Awards MBA. Faculty: 1 full-time (0 women), 3 part-time (1 woman), 1.75 FTE. Students: 32 part-time (16 women); includes 4 minority (2 African Americans, 2 Asian Americans). 26 applicants, 85% accepted. *Degree requirements:* Thesis or alternative, practicum required, foreign language not required. *Entrance requirements:* Minimum GPA of 3.0. Application fee: $25. *Financial aid:* Application deadline 3/2. • Alister Milroy, Co-Chair, 415-257-0191. Fax: 415-485-3214.

Dominican University, Graduate School of Business, River Forest, IL 60305-1099. Awards MBA, MSA, MSMIS, MSOM, JD/MBA, MBA/MLIS. Programs in accounting (MSA), business administration (MBA), management information systems (MSMIS), organization management (MSOM). JD/MBA offered jointly with John Marshall Law School. Part-time and evening/weekend programs available. Faculty: 52 (15 women). Students: 96 full-time (49 women), 211 part-time (120 women); includes 41 minority (22 African Americans, 10 Asian Americans, 9 Hispanics), 98 international. Average age 31. 143 applicants, 55% accepted. In 1997, 79 degrees awarded. *Entrance requirements:* GMAT (average 500), TOEFL (minimum score 550). Application deadline: 8/1 (priority date; rolling processing). Application fee: $25. *Financial aid:* Graduate assistantships, partial tuition waivers, and career-related internships or fieldwork available. Aid available to part-time students. Financial aid applicants required to submit FAFSA. *Faculty research:* Entrepreneurship, small business finance, business ethics, marketing strategy. • Dr. Molly Burke, Dean, 708-524-6810. E-mail: burkemg@email.dom.edu. Application contact: Dr. Dan Condon, Director Admissions and Advising, 708-524-6223. Fax: 708-366-5360. E-mail: condond@email.dom.edu.

Dowling College, School of Business, Oakdale, NY 11769-1999. Offers programs in aviation management (MBA, Certificate), banking and finance (MBA, Certificate), general management (MBA), public management (MBA, Certificate), total quality management (MBA, Certificate). Part-time and evening/weekend programs available. Faculty: 17 full-time, 75 part-time. Students: 10 full-time (3 women), 709 part-time (283 women); includes 114 minority (40 African Americans, 42 Asian Americans, 28 Hispanics, 4 Native Americans), 5 international. Average age 32. In 1997, 280 master's, 4 Certificates awarded. *Degree requirements:* For master's, thesis optional, foreign language not required. *Entrance requirements:* For master's, GMAT, TOEFL. Application deadline: rolling. Application fee: $0. Electronic applications accepted. *Financial aid:* Research assistantships, Federal Work-Study, and career-related internships or fieldwork available. Aid available to part-time students. Financial aid application deadline: 4/30. *Faculty research:* Quality management, international finance, computer applications, labor relations, executive development. • Dr. Anthony F. Libertella, Interim Dean, 516-244-3355. Fax: 516-589-6644. Application contact: Kate Rowe, Director of Admissions, 516-244-3030. Fax: 516-563-3827. E-mail: rowek@dowling.edu.

Announcement: Dowling College, located on the South Shore of Long Island, 50 miles from New York City, is The Personal College®, committed to an environment for learning that recognizes and provides for the development of each individual's potential. This environment maximizes the individualized attention and opportunities for Dowling's 5,998 graduate and undergraduate students. The Master of Business Administration degree is offered in general management, aviation management, total quality management, public management, and banking and finance. Post-master's certificates are also offered in aviation management, banking and finance, public management, and total quality management. Flexible scheduling, including evenings, weekends, and an accelerated Saturdays-only program, ensures that students are able to continue their career development while working toward their MBA.

See in-depth description on page 179.

Drake University, College of Business and Public Administration, Des Moines, IA 50311-4516. Awards MBA, MPA, JD/MBA, JD/MPA, Pharm D/MBA. Pharm D/MBA offered jointly with the College of Pharmacy and Health Sciences. Part-time and evening/weekend programs available. Postbaccalaureate distance learning degree programs offered (no on-campus study). Faculty: 29 full-time (7 women). Students: 14 full-time (6 women), 498 part-time (217 women); includes 16 minority (3 African Americans, 10 Asian Americans, 3 Hispanics), 26 international. Average age 29. 210 applicants, 98% accepted. In 1997, 178 degrees awarded. *Average time to degree:* master's–1.5 years full-time, 3.5 years part-time. *Entrance requirements:* GMAT (MBA). Application deadline: 7/15 (priority date; rolling processing; 12/1 for spring admission). Application fee: $25. *Tuition:* $16,000 per year full-time, $260 per hour (minimum) part-time. *Financial aid:* Institutionally sponsored loans and career-related internships or fieldwork available. Aid available to part-time students. Financial aid application deadline: 3/1; applicants required to submit FAFSA. *Faculty research:* Measuring partnership interest, ethics in insurance industry, security credit regulation, management-personnel evaluation systems. • Antone F. Alber Jr., Dean, 515-271-2871. Application contact: Thomas M. Pursel, Director, 515-271-2188. Fax: 515-271-4518.

Drexel University, College of Business and Administration, Program in Business Administration, 3141 Chestnut Street, Philadelphia, PA 19104-2875. Offers business administration (MBA, PhD, APC), including accounting (MBA, PhD), decision sciences (PhD), economics (MBA, PhD), finance (MBA, PhD), legal studies (MBA), management (MBA), marketing (MBA, PhD), organizational sciences (PhD), quantitative methods (MBA), strategic management (PhD); decision sciences (MS). Part-time and evening/weekend programs available. Students: 294 full-time (114 women), 494 part-time (178 women); includes 67 minority (28 African Americans, 28 Asian Americans, 10 Hispanics, 1 Native American), 220 international. Average age 31. 675 applicants, 57% accepted. In 1997, 214 master's, 10 doctorates awarded. Terminal master's awarded for partial completion of doctoral program. *Degree requirements:* For master's and doctorate, computer language required, foreign language and thesis/dissertation not required. *Entrance requirements:* For master's, GMAT, TOEFL (minimum score 570), minimum GPA of 2.75; for doctorate, GMAT, TOEFL (minimum score 570). Application deadline: 8/21 (rolling processing; 3/5 for spring admission). Application fee: $35. *Expenses:* Tuition $494 per credit hour. Fees $121 per quarter full-time, $65 per quarter part-time. *Financial aid:* Research assistantships, teaching assistantships, graduate assistantships, and career-related internships or fieldwork available. Financial aid application deadline: 2/1. *Faculty research:* Decision support systems, individual and group behavior, operations research, techniques and strategy. • Dr. Jerold B. Muskin, Director of Master's Programs in Business, 215-895-2115. Application contact: Denise Bigham, Director of Admissions, 215-895-6700. Fax: 215-895-5969.

See in-depth description on page 181.

Drury College, Breech School of Business Administration, Springfield, MO 65802-3791. Awards MBA, MBA/MIM. Part-time and evening/weekend programs available. Faculty: 10 full-time (2 women). Students: 3 full-time (1 woman), 79 part-time (32 women); includes 2 minority (both Hispanics), 3 international. Average age 30. 80 applicants, 44% accepted. In 1997, 20 degrees awarded. *Average time to degree:* master's–1 year full-time, 2.3 years part-time. *Entrance requirements:* GMAT, TOEFL. Application deadline: rolling. Application fee: $25. *Expenses:* Tuition $242 per credit hour. Fees $190 per year. *Financial aid:* In 1997–98, 4 students received aid, including 2 research assistantships; career-related internships or fieldwork also available. • Dr. Tom Zimmerer, Director, 417-873-7241. Fax: 417-873-7537. E-mail: tzimmere@lib.drury.edu.

Duke University, Fuqua School of Business, Durham, NC 27708-0586. Awards MBA, WEMBA, PhD, JD/MBA, MBA/MS, MBA/AM, MBA/MEM, MBA/MF, MBA/MPP, MBA/MSN, MD/MBA. PhD offered in cooperation with the Graduate School. Evening/weekend programs available. Faculty: 80 full-time (16 women), 23 part-time (1 woman). Students: 680 full-time (211 women); includes 128 minority (58 African Americans, 57 Asian Americans, 11 Hispanics, 2 Native Americans), 167 international. Average age 27. 3,045 applicants, 19% accepted. In 1997, 417 master's awarded. *Degree requirements:* For doctorate, dissertation required, foreign language not required. *Average time to degree:* master's–2 years full-time. *Entrance requirements:* For master's, GMAT, TOEFL, 1 semester of calculus. Application deadline: 4/28 (priority date). Application fee: $125. Electronic applications accepted. *Expenses:* Tuition $25,250 per year. Fees $1235 per year. *Financial aid:* In 1997–98, 554 students received aid, including 262 fellowships (158 to first-year students); research assistantships, teaching assistantships, Federal Work-Study, institutionally sponsored loans, and career-related internships or fieldwork also available. Financial aid application deadline: 3/1; applicants required to submit FAFSA. *Faculty research:* Finance, management, economics, marketing, management decision sciences, operations accounting, health services management, communications management. • Blair H. Sheppard, Senior Associate Dean for Academic Programs, 919-660-8020. Fax: 919-684-8742. E-mail: bsheppar@mail.duke.edu. Application contact: Robert R. Williams, Director of Admissions, 919-660-7705. Fax: 919-681-8026.

Duke University, Graduate School, Department of Business Administration, Durham, NC 27708-0586. Awards PhD. Faculty: 71 full-time, 3 part-time. Students: 36 full-time (16 women); includes 4 minority (all African Americans), 14 international. 198 applicants, 11% accepted. In 1997, 5 doctorates awarded. Terminal master's awarded for partial completion of doctoral program. *Degree requirements:* For doctorate, dissertation. *Entrance requirements:* For doctorate, GMAT or GRE General Test. Application deadline: 12/31. Application fee: $75. *Expenses:* Tuition $16,632 per year full-time, $693 per unit part-time. Fees $2884 per year. *Financial aid:* In 1997–98, 25 fellowships (10 to first-year students) averaging $940 per month were awarded; research assistantships, teaching assistantships, Federal Work-Study, institutionally sponsored loans, and career-related internships or fieldwork also available. Financial aid application deadline: 12/31; applicants required to submit FAFSA. • James Bettman, Director of Graduate Studies, 919-660-7862.

Duquesne University, Graduate School of Business Administration, Pittsburgh, PA 15282-0001. Awards MBA, MS, JD/MBA, MBA/MS, MBA/MALS, MBA/MSHMS, MSN/MBA. Programs in business administration (MBA), information systems management (MS), taxation (MS). Part-time and evening/weekend programs available. Faculty: 28 full-time (2 women), 14 part-time (2 women), 32 FTE. Students: 121 full-time (50 women), 482 part-time (198 women); includes 33 minority (13 African Americans, 15 Asian Americans, 5 Hispanics), 66 international. Average age 30. 318 applicants, 76% accepted. In 1997, 182 degrees awarded. *Average time to degree:* master's–2 years full-time, 3.5 years part-time. *Entrance requirements:* GMAT (average 510), average GPA of 3.1. Application deadline: 6/1 (priority date; rolling processing; 11/1 for spring admission). Application fee: $40. *Expenses:* Tuition $481 per credit. Fees $39 per credit. *Financial aid:* In 1997–98, 28 students received aid, including 28 graduate assistantships (12 to first-year students) averaging $150 per month; career-related internships or fieldwork also available. Aid available to part-time students. Financial aid application deadline: 7/1; applicants required to submit FAFSA. *Faculty research:* International business, total quality management, activity-based costing, business ethics, technology management, supply chair management, business strategy. • Thomas J. Murrin, Dean, 412-396-5157. Application contact: Dr. William Presutti, Associate Dean and Director, 412-396-6269. Fax: 412-396-5304.

Announcement: The renaissance spirit pervades Duquesne's MBA program. Duquesne believes that the narrowly educated technical professional is inadequately prepared to meet the needs of a business world dominated by global influences. Leaders with a broad-based education that includes technical competence are crucial for the success of the business enterprises of today and tomorrow. Consequently, Duquesne seeks to develop in its graduates an appreciation of how a broad-based education contributes to effective performance. The ability to think critically and expansively and to draw on a broad spectrum of human knowledge is the hallmark of a graduate business education from Duquesne.

D'Youville College, Division of Business, Buffalo, NY 14201-1084. Offers programs in health services administration (MS), international business (MS). MS (international business) new for fall 1998. Part-time and evening/weekend programs available. Faculty: 3 full-time (all women), 9 part-time (3 women). Students: 21 full-time, 64 part-time; includes 5 minority (3 African Americans, 1 Hispanic, 1 Native American), 10 international. Average age 33. In 1997, 18 degrees awarded. *Degree requirements:* Computer language, thesis required, foreign language not required. *Entrance requirements:* Minimum GPA of 3.0 in major. Application deadline: rolling. Application fee: $25. *Expenses:* Tuition $357 per credit hour. Fees $350 per year. *Financial aid:* In 1997–98, 1 research assistantship (to a first-year student) totaling $3,000, 17 scholarships (9 to first-year students) totaling $13,600 were awarded; Federal Work-Study and career-related internships or fieldwork also available. Aid available to part-time students. Financial aid application deadline: 3/1; applicants required to submit FAFSA. • Dr. Jayanti Sen, Interim Director, 716-881-3200. Application contact: Joseph Syracuse, Graduate Admissions Director, 716-881-7676. Fax: 716-881-7790.

East Carolina University, School of Business, Greenville, NC 27858-4353. Offers programs in accounting (MSA), decision sciences (MBA), finance (MBA), management (MBA), marketing (MBA). Part-time and evening/weekend programs available. Faculty: 39 full-time (4 women). Students: 202 full-time (94 women), 138 part-time (56 women); includes 22 minority (11 African Americans, 7 Asian Americans, 3 Hispanics, 1 Native American), 8 international. Average age 28. 229 applicants, 76% accepted. In 1997, 122 degrees awarded. *Entrance requirements:* GMAT, TOEFL. Application deadline: 6/1 (priority date; rolling processing). Application fee: $40. *Tuition:* $1886 per year full-time, $472 per semester (minimum) part-time for state residents; $9156 per year full-time, $2289 per semester (minimum) part-time for nonresidents. *Financial aid:* Research assistantships, teaching assistantships, Federal Work-Study available. Aid available to part-time students. Financial aid application deadline: 6/1. • Donald B. Boldt, Director of Graduate Studies, 252-328-6970. Fax: 252-328-6664. E-mail: boldtd@mail.ecu.edu. Application contact: Dr. Paul D. Tschetter, Associate Dean, 252-328-6012. Fax: 252-328-6071. E-mail: grad@mail.ecu.edu.

Eastern College, Graduate Business Programs, St. Davids, PA 19087-3696. Awards MBA, MS, M Div/MBA, M Div/MS. Offerings include business administration (MBA), including accounting, economics, finance, management, marketing; economic development (MBA, MS); nonprofit management (MBA, MS). M Div/MS and M Div/MBA offered jointly with Eastern Baptist Theological Seminary. Part-time and evening/weekend programs available. Faculty: 32 full-time (18

Directory: Business Administration and Management—General

Eastern College (continued)

women), 14 part-time (12 women). Average age 37. In 1997, 123 degrees awarded. *Degree requirements:* Thesis required (for some programs), foreign language not required. *Entrance requirements:* GMAT (MBA), minimum GPA of 2.5. Application deadline: rolling. Application fee: $35. *Financial aid:* Research assistantships, partial tuition waivers, Federal Work-Study, and career-related internships or fieldwork available. *Faculty research:* Micro-level economic development, China-welfare and economic development, macroethics, micro- and macro-level economic development in transitional economics, organizational effectiveness. • Dr. John Stapleford, Chair, 610-341-5848. Application contact: Megan Miscioscia, Graduate Admissions Representative, 610-341-5972. Fax: 610-341-1466.

Eastern Illinois University, Lumpkin College of Business and Applied Sciences, Program in Business Administration, 600 Lincoln Avenue, Charleston, IL 61920-3099. Awards MBA. Part-time programs available. Faculty: 35 full-time (8 women). Students: 50 full-time (13 women), 140 part-time (63 women); includes 13 minority (8 African Americans, 2 Asian Americans, 3 Hispanics). In 1997, 56 degrees awarded. *Entrance requirements:* GMAT. Application deadline: 7/31 (priority date; rolling processing). Application fee: $25. *Expenses:* Tuition $3459 per year full-time, $96 per semester hour part-time for state residents; $10,377 per year full-time, $288 per semester hour part-time for nonresidents. Fees $1566 per year full-time, $37 per semester hour part-time. *Financial aid:* In 1997–98, 12 research assistantships were awarded. • Application contact: Dr. Jane Wayland, Coordinator, 217-581-3028. Fax: 217-581-6029. E-mail: cfjpw@eiu.edu.

Eastern Kentucky University, College of Business, Richmond, KY 40475-3101. Awards MBA. Part-time programs available. Students: 25 full-time (12 women), 106 part-time (41 women). In 1997, 27 degrees awarded. *Entrance requirements:* GMAT (minimum score 400), minimum GPA of 2.5. Application fee: $0. *Tuition:* $2390 per year full-time, $133 per credit hour part-time for state residents; $6630 per year full-time, $365 per credit hour part-time for nonresidents. *Financial aid:* Research assistantships, teaching assistantships, Federal Work-Study available. Aid available to part-time students. • Dr. Jack Dyer, Coordinator, 606-622-1775.

Eastern Mennonite University, Program in Business Administration, Harrisonburg, VA 22802-2462. Awards MBA. Program new for spring 1999. *Application deadline:* rolling. *Application fee:* $25. *Tuition:* $325 per credit hour. • Application contact: Don A. Yoder, Director of Seminary and Graduate Programs, 540-432-4257. Fax: 540-432-4444. E-mail: yoderda@emu.edu.

Eastern Michigan University, College of Business, Program in Business Administration, Ypsilanti, MI 48197. Offers business administration (MBA), international business (MBA). Part-time and evening/weekend programs available. In 1997, 167 degrees awarded. *Entrance requirements:* GMAT (minimum score 450), TOEFL (minimum score 550). Application deadline: 5/15 (rolling processing; 3/15 for spring admission). Application fee: $30. *Expenses:* Tuition $2691 per year full-time, $150 per credit hour part-time for state residents; $6300 per year full-time, $350 per credit hour part-time for nonresidents. Fees $368 per year full-time, $88 per semester (minimum) part-time. *Financial aid:* Fellowships, teaching assistantships available. Aid available to part-time students. Financial aid application deadline: 3/15; applicants required to submit FAFSA. • Dr. William Whitmire, Coordinator, 734-487-4444.

See in-depth description on page 183.

Eastern New Mexico University, College of Business, Portales, NM 88130. Awards MBA. Part-time and evening/weekend programs available. Faculty: 7 full-time (1 woman), 4 part-time (2 women). Students: 9 full-time (4 women), 23 part-time (13 women); includes 6 minority (3 African Americans, 3 Hispanics), 5 international. Average age 34. 9 applicants, 100% accepted. In 1997, 10 degrees awarded. *Degree requirements:* Computer language required, foreign language and thesis not required. *Entrance requirements:* GMAT, minimum GPA of 2.5. Application deadline: rolling. Application fee: $10. *Tuition:* $1956 per year full-time, $82 per credit hour part-time for state residents; $6702 per year full-time, $280 per credit hour part-time for nonresidents. *Financial aid:* In 1997–98, 9 research assistantships (3 to first-year students) were awarded; fellowships, teaching assistantships, Federal Work-Study also available. Aid available to part-time students. Financial aid application deadline: 4/1. • Dr. Dolores Martin, Dean, 505-562-2342.

Eastern Washington University, College of Business Administration, Business Administration Program, Cheney, WA 99004-2431. Awards MBA, MBA/MPA. Faculty: 21 full-time (8 women). Students: 14 full-time (6 women), 23 part-time (8 women); includes 1 minority (Asian American), 4 international. 55 applicants, 42% accepted. In 1997, 26 degrees awarded. *Degree requirements:* Comprehensive exam required, thesis optional, foreign language not required. *Entrance requirements:* GMAT (minimum score 500), minimum GPA of 3.0. Application deadline: 4/1 (priority date; rolling processing; 1/15 for spring admission). Application fee: $35. *Tuition:* $4200 per year full-time, $140 per credit part-time for state residents; $12,780 per year full-time, $415 per credit part-time for nonresidents. *Financial aid:* Research assistantships, teaching assistantships available. Financial aid application deadline: 2/1. • Dr. Morag Stewart, Director, 509-358-2227. E-mail: mstewart@ewu.edu.

East Tennessee State University, College of Business, Department of Management and Marketing, Johnson City, TN 37614-0734. Offers program in business administration (MBA). Part-time and evening/weekend programs available. Faculty: 27 full-time (2 women). Students: 34 full-time (10 women), 87 part-time (41 women); includes 5 minority (3 African Americans, 1 Asian American, 1 Hispanic), 7 international. Average age 32. 81 applicants, 57% accepted. In 1997, 34 degrees awarded. *Degree requirements:* Written comprehensive exam required, foreign language and thesis not required. *Entrance requirements:* GMAT (minimum score 450), TOEFL (minimum score 550), minimum GPA of 2.5. Application deadline: 7/1 (priority date; rolling processing; 12/1 for spring admission). Application fee: $25 ($35 for international students). *Tuition:* $2944 per year full-time, $158 per credit hour part-time for state residents; $7770 per year full-time, $369 per credit hour part-time for nonresidents. *Financial aid:* In 1997–98, 11 research assistantships (5 to first-year students), 1 tuition scholarship were awarded. Financial aid application deadline: 8/15. • Dr. Glen Riecken, Chair, 423-439-4422. Fax: 423-439-8297.

East Texas Baptist University, Program in Business Administration, Marshall, TX 75670-1498. Awards MBA. Faculty: 5. Students: 13 full-time, 16 part-time. *Application deadline:* rolling. *Application fee:* $25 ($50 for international students). *Expenses:* Tuition $245 per semester hour. Fees $600 per year full-time, $20 per semester hour part-time. • Dr. Alex Liebling, Dean of the School of Business, 903-935-7963, Ext. 280. Application contact: Caroline Olson, Recruitment Coordinator, 903-935-7963 Ext. 400.

École des Hautes Études Commerciales, School of Business Administration, Montréal, PQ H3T 2A7, Canada. Offers programs in administration (PhD), administration studies (Diploma), applied economics (M Sc), business administration and management (MBA), controllership (M Sc), decision and model-making (M Sc), energy sector management (Diploma), finance (M Sc, Diploma), financial engineering (M Sc), human resources management (M Sc), information systems (M Sc), international business (M Sc), management (M Sc, Diploma), management of cultural organizations (Diploma), marketing (M Sc), production and operations management (M Sc), public accounting (Diploma), taxation (Diploma). PhD offered jointly with Concordia University, McGill University, and the Université du Québec à Montréal. Diploma (administration studies) being phased out; applicants no longer accepted. Most courses are given in French. Part-time and evening/weekend programs available. Faculty: 166 full-time (36 women). Students: 761 full-time (337 women), 1,149 part-time (535 women). Average age 31. *Degree requirements:* For master's, 1 foreign language; for doctorate, 1 foreign language, dissertation; for Diploma, 1 foreign language required, thesis not required. *Application fee:* $40. *Financial aid:* Fellowships, research assistantships, teaching assistantships available. *Faculty research:* Entrepreneurship, art management, transportation, new technologies, business policy. • Dr. Jean-Marie Toulouse, Director, 514-340-6110. Application contact: Nicole Rivet, Registrar, 514-340-6110. Fax: 514-340-5640. E-mail: nicole.rivet@hec.ca.

See in-depth description on page 185.

Edgewood College, Program in Business, Madison, WI 53711-1998. Awards MBA. Part-time and evening/weekend programs available. Faculty: 9 full-time (1 woman), 9 part-time (3 women), 12 FTE. Students: 294. In 1997, 43 degrees awarded. *Average time to degree:* master's–6 years part-time. *Entrance requirements:* GMAT. Application deadline: 8/1 (priority date; rolling processing). Application fee: $25. *Tuition:* $330 per credit. *Financial aid:* Career-related internships or fieldwork available. • Dr. Gary Schroeder, Chair, 608-257-4861 Ext. 3374. Application contact: Sr. Lucille Marie Frost, Assistant Dean of Graduate Programs, 608-254-4861 Ext. 2382. Fax: 608-257-1455.

Elon College, Program in Business Administration, Elon College, NC 27244. Awards MBA. Part-time and evening/weekend programs available. Faculty: 17 full-time (2 women). Students: 13 full-time (6 women), 75 part-time (33 women); includes 7 minority (3 African Americans, 2 Asian Americans, 2 Hispanics), 5 international. Average age 32. 52 applicants, 56% accepted. In 1997, 46 degrees awarded. *Degree requirements:* Computer language required, foreign language and thesis not required. *Entrance requirements:* GMAT (average 532). Application deadline: 8/1 (priority date; rolling processing; 1/5 for spring admission). Application fee: $25. *Tuition:* $256 per credit hour. *Financial aid:* 8 students received aid; Federal Work-Study available. Aid available to part-time students. Financial aid application deadline: 8/1; applicants required to submit FAFSA. • Dr. Kevin J. O'Mara, Chair, 336-584-2494. Fax: 336-538-2643. E-mail: omarak@numen.elon.edu. Application contact: Alice N. Essen, Director of Graduate Admissions, 800-334-8448. Fax: 336-538-3986. E-mail: essen@numen.elon.edu.

Embry–Riddle Aeronautical University, Department of Business Administration, Daytona Beach, FL 32114-3900. Offers program in business administration in aviation (MBAA). Part-time and evening/weekend programs available. Faculty: 13 full-time (2 women), 1 part-time (0 women). Students: 51 full-time (8 women), 37 part-time (9 women); includes 5 minority (1 African American, 3 Asian Americans, 1 Hispanic), 37 international. Average age 28. 54 applicants, 80% accepted. In 1997, 21 degrees awarded. *Degree requirements:* Thesis or alternative required, foreign language not required. *Entrance requirements:* GRE General Test (minimum combined score of 1000), TOEFL (minimum score 550), minimum GPA of 2.5. Application deadline: rolling. Application fee: $30 ($50 for international students). *Expenses:* Tuition $425 per credit hour. Fees $290 per year. *Financial aid:* In 1997–98, 1 fellowship, 9 research assistantships averaging $950 per month, 7 teaching assistantships averaging $950 per month, 1 administrative assistantship averaging $950 per month were awarded; Federal Work-Study and career-related internships or fieldwork also available. Aid available to part-time students. Financial aid application deadline: 4/15; applicants required to submit FAFSA. *Faculty research:* NASA joint venture in space, human factors considerations in air traffic management. Total annual research expenditures: $271,000. • Dr. Bijah Vasigh, Program Chair, 904-226-6722. Fax: 904-226-6696. E-mail: vasighb@cts.db.erau.edu. Application contact: Ginny Tait, Graduate Admissions Specialist, 904-226-6115. Fax: 904-226-6299. E-mail: taitg@cts.db.erau.edu.

Embry–Riddle Aeronautical University, Extended Campus, Department of Business Administration, Daytona Beach, FL 32114-3900. Offers programs in aviation administration and management (MBAA), technical management (MS). Part-time and evening/weekend programs available. Postbaccalaureate distance learning degree programs offered (minimal on-campus study). Students: 2 full-time (1 woman), 536 part-time (81 women); includes 114 minority (58 African Americans, 23 Asian Americans, 28 Hispanics, 5 Native Americans). Average age 33. 90 applicants, 100% accepted. In 1997, 288 degrees awarded. *Degree requirements:* Thesis optional, foreign language not required. *Entrance requirements:* GMAT (minimum score 500). Application deadline: rolling. Application fee: $30 ($50 for international students). Electronic applications accepted. *Tuition:* $220 per credit hour. *Financial aid:* Available to part-time students. Financial aid applicants required to submit FAFSA. • Dr. Vance Mitchell, Chair, 360-375-1986. E-mail: mitchelv@cts.db.erau.edu. Application contact: Pam Thomas, Director of Admissions and Records, 904-226-6910. Fax: 904-226-6984. E-mail: ecinfo@ec.db.erau.edu.

Emmanuel College, Program in Management, Boston, MA 02115. Awards MSM. Faculty: 40. Students: 120. *Entrance requirements:* Interview. Application deadline: 9/7 (priority date; rolling processing). Application fee: $50. • Audrey Ashton-Savage, Director, 617-735-9844. Fax: 617-735-9877. Application contact: Lorene Ashton-Reed, Graduate Program Assistant, 617-735-9844.

Emory University, Roberto C. Goizueta Business School, Atlanta, GA 30322-1100. Awards EMBA, MBA, JD/MBA, MBA/MPH, M Div/MBA. Part-time and evening/weekend programs available. Faculty: 56 full-time (14 women), 7 part-time (3 women). Students: 292 full-time (75 women), 148 part-time (55 women); includes 58 minority (30 African Americans, 19 Asian Americans, 7 Hispanics, 2 Native Americans), 52 international. Average age 27. 975 applicants, 39% accepted. In 1997, 231 degrees awarded. *Average time to degree:* master's–2 years full-time, 3 years part-time. *Entrance requirements:* GMAT, TOEFL, previous course work in calculus or statistics. Application deadline: 4/15 (priority date; rolling processing). Application fee: $45. *Tuition:* $24,000 per year. *Financial aid:* In 1997–98, 194 students received aid, including 123 fellowships (61 to first-year students), 40 research assistantships (20 to first-year students); Federal Work-Study, institutionally sponsored loans, and career-related internships or fieldwork also available. Aid available to part-time students. Financial aid application deadline: 3/1; applicants required to submit CSS PROFILE or FAFSA. *Faculty research:* International finance, banking and financial markets, marketing segmentation, evolution of technology, leadership and career change. • Ronald E. Frank, Dean, 404-727-6377. Fax: 404-727-0868. E-mail: ron_frank@bus.emory.edu. Application contact: Julie Barefoot, Assistant Dean, 404-727-6311. Fax: 404-727-4612. E-mail: admissions@bus.emory.edu.

Emporia State University, School of Graduate Studies, School of Business, Emporia, KS 66801-5087. Awards MBA, MS. Part-time programs available. Faculty: 16 full-time (3 women), 1 part-time (0 women). Students: 37 full-time (10 women), 28 part-time (14 women); includes 3 minority (2 African Americans, 1 Asian American), 19 international. 26 applicants, 88% accepted. In 1997, 25 degrees awarded. *Entrance requirements:* TOEFL (minimum score 550). Application deadline: 8/15 (priority date; rolling processing). Application fee: $30 ($75 for international students). Electronic applications accepted. *Tuition:* $2300 per year full-time, $103 per credit hour part-time for state residents; $6012 per year full-time, $258 per credit hour part-time for nonresidents. *Financial aid:* In 1997–98, 2 fellowships averaging $667 per month, 2 research assistantships averaging $558 per month, 7 teaching assistantships averaging $522 per month were awarded; Federal Work-Study, institutionally sponsored loans, and career-related internships or fieldwork also available. Financial aid application deadline: 3/15; applicants required to submit FAFSA. • Dr. Sajjad Hashmi, Dean, 316-341-5274. E-mail: hashmisa@emporia.edu.

See in-depth description on page 187.

Fairfield University, School of Business, Fairfield, CT 06430-5195. Offers programs in accounting (MBA, CAS), finance (MBA, CAS), financial management (MSFM), human resource management (MBA, CAS), information technology (MBA, CAS), international business (MBA, CAS), marketing (MBA, CAS), taxation (MBA, CAS). Part-time and evening/weekend programs available. Faculty: 36 full-time (12 women), 4 part-time (2 women), 37.3 FTE. Students: 15 full-time (4 women), 270 part-time (114 women); includes 8 minority (4 African Americans, 2 Asian Americans, 1 Hispanic, 1 Native American), 12 international. Average age 27. 93 applicants, 86% accepted. In 1997, 32 master's awarded (100% found work related to degree). *Degree requirements:* For master's, thesis or alternative required, foreign language not required. *Average time to degree:* master's–2 years full-time, 3.5 years part-time. *Entrance requirements:* For master's, GMAT (minimum score 500), TOEFL (minimum score 550). Application deadline: 8/1 (priority date; rolling processing; 12/1 for spring admission). Application fee: $40. *Expenses:*

Tuition $15,000 per year full-time, $450 per credit hour part-time. Fees $40 per year. *Financial aid:* In 1997–98, 3 students received aid, including 2 research assistantships (both to first-year students) totaling $30,000; scholarships also available. *Faculty research:* Optimal investment strategies, diversity management, organization structure, shareholder value creation, international investment, international finance, strategic management, ethical strategies. • Dr. Walter G. Ryba Jr., Acting Dean, 203-254-4070. Application contact: Cynthia S. Chegwidden, Director of Graduate Programs, 203-254-4070. Fax: 203-254-4105. E-mail: cchegwidden@fairl.fairfield.edu.

See in-depth description on page 189.

Fairleigh Dickinson University, Florham–Madison Campus, Samuel J. Silberman College of Business Administration, 285 Madison Avenue, Madison, NJ 07940-1099. Awards MA, MBA, MS. Part-time and evening/weekend programs available. Faculty: 37 full-time (5 women), 75 part-time (10 women). Students: 103 full-time (46 women), 1,008 part-time (468 women); includes 53 minority (20 African Americans, 25 Asian Americans, 4 Hispanics, 4 Native Americans), 21 international. Average age 31. 381 applicants, 67% accepted. In 1997, 262 degrees awarded. *Degree requirements:* Thesis optional, foreign language not required. *Application deadline:* rolling. *Application fee:* $35. *Expenses:* Tuition $522 per credit. Fees $302 per year full-time, $138 per year part-time. *Financial aid:* Fellowships, research assistantships, teaching assistantships, Federal Work-Study, and career-related internships or fieldwork available. Aid available to part-time students. • Dr. Paul Lerman, Dean, 973-443-8801.

See in-depth description on page 191.

Fairleigh Dickinson University, Teaneck–Hackensack Campus, Samuel J. Silberman College of Business Administration, 1000 River Road, Teaneck, NJ 07666-1914. Awards MAS, MBA, MPA, MS. Part-time programs available. Faculty: 43 full-time, 59 part-time. Students: 110 full-time (51 women), 529 part-time (264 women); includes 93 minority (33 African Americans, 36 Asian Americans, 23 Hispanics, 1 Native American), 65 international. Average age 32. In 1997, 282 degrees awarded. *Degree requirements:* Computer language required, foreign language not required. *Entrance requirements:* GMAT. Application deadline: rolling. Application fee: $35. *Expenses:* Tuition $522 per credit. Fees $302 per year full-time, $138 per year part-time. *Financial aid:* Fellowships, research assistantships, Federal Work-Study, and career-related internships or fieldwork available. • Dr. Paul Lerman, Dean, 201-692-7200. Fax: 201-692-7199. E-mail: lerman@alpha.fdu.edu.

See in-depth description on page 191.

Fayetteville State University, Program in Business Administration, 1200 Murchison Road, Fayetteville, NC 28301-4298. Awards MBA. Part-time and evening/weekend programs available. *Degree requirements:* Comprehensive exams, internships required, foreign language and thesis not required. *Entrance requirements:* GMAT, minimum GPA of 2.5. Application deadline: 8/1 (rolling processing; 12/15 for spring admission). Application fee: $20. *Tuition:* $1498 per year full-time, $327 per semester (minimum) part-time for state residents; $8768 per year full-time, $2144 per semester (minimum) part-time for nonresidents. *Faculty research:* Accounting systems, management information systems, marketing, operations research, transportation.

Ferris State University, College of Business, Big Rapids, MI 49307-2742. Awards MS. Part-time and evening/weekend programs available. Faculty: 3 full-time (0 women), 4 part-time (0 women). Students: 55 full-time (17 women), 57 part-time (24 women); includes 10 minority (9 African Americans, 1 Hispanic), 31 international. In 1997, 58 degrees awarded (10% entered university research/teaching, 90% found other work related to degree). *Degree requirements:* Thesis or alternative required, foreign language not required. *Entrance requirements:* Minimum GPA of 3.0 in CIS and business core, 2.75 overall; writing sample. Application deadline: 8/1. Application fee: $20. *Expenses:* Tuition $220 per credit hour for state residents; $450 per credit hour for nonresidents. Fees $100 per year. *Financial aid:* In 1997–98, 50 research assistantships (32 to first-year students) averaging $495 per month were awarded; career-related internships or fieldwork also available. Aid available to part-time students. *Faculty research:* Computer accounting, systems accounting, auditing, LAN/WAN administration, quality improvement. • Joseph Rallo, Dean, 616-592-2422.

Fitchburg State College, Program in Business Administration, Fitchburg, MA 01420-2697. Awards MBA. Part-time and evening/weekend programs available. *Entrance requirements:* GMAT (minimum score 400), minimum GPA of 2.8. Application deadline: rolling. Application fee: $10. *Expenses:* Tuition $147 per credit. Fees $55 per semester. *Financial aid:* Graduate assistantships, Federal Work-Study available. Aid available to part-time students. Financial aid application deadline: 3/30; applicants required to submit FAFSA. • Janette Purcell, Chair, 978-665-3567. Fax: 978-665-3658. E-mail: dgce@fsc.edu. Application contact: James DuPont, Director of Admissions, 978-665-3144. Fax: 978-665-4540. E-mail: admissions@fsc.edu.

Florida Agricultural and Mechanical University, Division of Graduate Studies, Research, and Continuing Education, School of Business and Industry, Tallahassee, FL 32307-3200. Offers programs in accounting (MBA), finance (MBA), management information systems (MBA), marketing (MBA). Students: 111 (64 women); includes 106 minority (105 African Americans, 1 Asian American). In 1997, 12 degrees awarded. *Entrance requirements:* GRE General Test (minimum combined score of 1000), minimum GPA of 3.0. Application deadline: 5/13. Application fee: $20. *Expenses:* Tuition $140 per credit hour for state residents; $484 per credit hour for nonresidents. Fees $130 per year. *Financial aid:* Fellowships, grants, Federal Work-Study available. • Dr. Sybil Mobley, Dean, 850-599-3565.

Florida Atlantic University, College of Business, MBA Program in Business Administration, Boca Raton, FL 33431-0991. Awards Exec MBA, MBA. Part-time and evening/weekend programs available. Faculty: 83 full-time (23 women), 4 part-time (0 women). Students: 97 full-time (44 women), 244 part-time (110 women); includes 67 minority (14 African Americans, 16 Asian Americans, 36 Hispanics, 1 Native American). Average age 27. 207 applicants, 65% accepted. In 1997, 136 degrees awarded. *Degree requirements:* Communications program required, thesis optional, foreign language not required. *Average time to degree:* master's–1.5 years full-time, 2 years part-time. *Entrance requirements:* GMAT (minimum score 500), minimum GPA of 3.0. Application deadline: 6/1 (rolling processing; 10/1 for spring admission). Application fee: $20. *Expenses:* Tuition $2520 per year full-time, $140 per credit hour part-time for state residents; $8712 per year full-time, $484 per credit hour part-time for nonresidents. Fees $5 per year (minimum). *Financial aid:* In 1997–98, 30 students received aid, including 9 research assistantships (3 to first-year students); teaching assistantships, partial tuition waivers, Federal Work-Study, institutionally sponsored loans, and career-related internships or fieldwork also available. Aid available to part-time students. Financial aid application deadline: 3/1. *Faculty research:* Personnel and human resources, information processing models, marketing, retailing, advertising strategies. • Dr. Kenneth Wiant, Director, 954-762-5233. Fax: 954-762-5245. E-mail: wiant@acc.fau.edu. Application contact: Ella Smith, Graduate Adviser, 561-297-3650. Fax: 561-297-3978. E-mail: smith@acc.fau.edu.

Florida Atlantic University, College of Business, PhD Program in Business Administration, Boca Raton, FL 33431-0991. Awards PhD. Offered jointly with Florida International University. Faculty: 46 full-time (10 women), 4 part-time (0 women). Students: 21 full-time (5 women), 8 part-time (3 women); includes 9 minority (2 African Americans, 4 Asian Americans, 2 Hispanics, 1 Native American). Average age 32. 36 applicants, 28% accepted. In 1997, 4 degrees awarded (75% entered university research/teaching, 25% found other work related to degree). *Degree requirements:* Dissertation, comprehensive exam required, foreign language not required. *Average time to degree:* doctorate–3 years full-time, 5 years part-time. *Entrance requirements:* GMAT (minimum score 560), minimum graduate GPA of 3.5. Application deadline: 6/1 (rolling processing; 10/1 for spring admission). Application fee: $20. *Expenses:* Tuition $2520 per year full-time, $140 per credit hour part-time for state residents; $8712 per year full-time, $484 per credit hour part-time for nonresidents. Fees $5 per year (minimum). *Financial aid:* In 1997–98, 21 students received aid, including 1 fellowship (to a first-year student), 4 research assistantships (all to first-year students), 14 teaching assistantships; full and partial tuition waivers, institutionally sponsored loans also available. Aid available to part-time students. Financial aid application deadline: 3/1. *Faculty research:* Management strategy, marketing policy, corporate finance, organizational behavior, information systems. • Dr. Jeff Madura, Director, 954-762-5248. Fax: 954-762-5245. E-mail: maduraj@acc.fau.edu. Application contact: Judith Benson, Graduate Adviser, 954-762-5248. Fax: 762-355-5245. E-mail: benson@acc.fau.edu.

Florida Gulf Coast University, College of Business, Master of Business Administration Program, Fort Myers, FL 33965-6565. Awards MBA. Part-time and evening/weekend programs available. Students: 13 full-time (5 women), 75 part-time (35 women); includes 9 minority (1 African American, 4 Asian Americans, 4 Hispanics), 3 international. Average age 30. 60 applicants, 57% accepted. *Entrance requirements:* GMAT (average 530). Application deadline: 7/1 (priority date; rolling processing; 11/15 for spring admission). Application fee: $20. Electronic applications accepted. *Financial aid:* In 1997–98, 25 students received aid, including 8 graduate assistantships (4 to first-year students); Federal Work-Study and career-related internships or fieldwork also available. Aid available to part-time students. Financial aid application deadline: 5/1; applicants required to submit FAFSA. *Faculty research:* Fraud in audits, production planning in cell manufacturing systems, collaborative learning in distance courses, characteristics of minority and women-owned businesses. • Dr. Karen Eastwood, Coordinator, 941-590-7300. Fax: 941-590-7330. E-mail: eastwood@fgcu.edu.

Florida Institute of Technology, School of Business, Melbourne, FL 32901-6975. Awards MBA, MHA, MS, MSM. MHA, MS, and MSM being phased out; applicants no longer accepted. Part-time and evening/weekend programs available. Faculty: 14 full-time (3 women), 13 part-time (1 woman). Students: 23 full-time (11 women), 45 part-time (14 women); includes 7 minority (2 African Americans, 4 Asian Americans, 1 Native American), 18 international. Average age 33. 37 applicants, 49% accepted. In 1997, 47 degrees awarded. *Degree requirements:* Thesis optional, foreign language not required. *Entrance requirements:* GMAT (minimum score 425; average 480), minimum GPA of 3.0. Application deadline: rolling. Application fee: $50. *Tuition:* $550 per credit hour. *Financial aid:* In 1997–98, 2 research assistantships averaging $600 per month and totaling $4,800, 1 teaching assistantship (to a first-year student) averaging $713 per month and totaling $2,850, 3 tuition remissions (1 to a first-year student) averaging $1,199 per month and totaling $14,391 were awarded. Financial aid application deadline: 3/1; applicants required to submit FAFSA. *Faculty research:* Investment analysis, total quality management, production and operations management, marketing research, strategy analysis. Total annual research expenditures: $4263. • Dr. A. Thomas Hollingsworth, Dean, 407-674-7327. Fax: 407-674-8896. E-mail: aholling@fit.edu. Application contact: Carolyn P. Farrior, Associate Dean of Graduate Admissions, 407-674-7118. Fax: 407-723-9468. E-mail: cfarrior@fit.edu.

See in-depth description on page 193.

Florida Institute of Technology, School of Extended Graduate Studies, Program in Management, Melbourne, FL 32901-6975. Offers acquisition and contract management (MS, PMBA), global management (PMBA), health management (MS), human resources management (MS, PMBA), information systems (PMBA), logistics management (MS), management (MS), materials acquisition management (MS), operations research (MS), research (PMBA), space systems (MS), space systems management (MS). *Entrance requirements:* GMAT (minimum score 425), minimum GPA of 2.75. Application fee: $50. *Tuition:* $550 per credit hour. *Financial aid:* Application deadline 3/1; applicants required to submit FAFSA. • Application contact: Carolyn P. Farrior, Associate Dean of Graduate Admissions, 407-674-7118. Fax: 407-723-9468. E-mail: cfarrior@fit.edu.

Florida International University, College of Business Administration, Department of Marketing and Business Environment, Miami, FL 33199. Awards MBA, PhD. Faculty: 16 full-time (4 women), 2 part-time (0 women), 16.62 FTE. Students: 145 full-time (43 women), 224 part-time (87 women); includes 224 minority (22 African Americans, 24 Asian Americans, 178 Hispanics), 42 international. 338 applicants, 36% accepted. In 1997, 127 master's, 1 doctorate awarded. *Degree requirements:* For master's, computer language required, thesis not required; for doctorate, computer language, dissertation. *Entrance requirements:* For master's, GMAT, minimum AACSB index of 1000, minimum GPA of 3.0; for doctorate, GMAT (minimum score 560), minimum GPA of 3.0. Application fee: $20. *Expenses:* Tuition $138 per credit hour for state residents; $482 per credit hour for nonresidents. Fees $46 per semester. • Dr. John A. Nicholls, Chairperson, 305-348-2571. Fax: 305-348-3792. E-mail: nicholls@fiu.edu.

Florida International University, College of Business Administration, Department of Management and International Business, Program in Management, Miami, FL 33199. Awards PhD. Part-time and evening/weekend programs available. Students: 1 (woman) full-time, 1 (woman) part-time; includes 1 minority (African American). Average age 50. 10 applicants, 0% accepted. In 1997, 1 degree awarded. *Degree requirements:* Computer language, dissertation required, foreign language not required. *Entrance requirements:* GMAT (minimum score 560), minimum GPA of 3.0. Application deadline: 4/1 (priority date; rolling processing; 10/1 for spring admission). Application fee: $20. *Expenses:* Tuition $138 per credit hour for state residents; $482 per credit hour for nonresidents. Fees $46 per semester. *Financial aid:* Research assistantships, teaching assistantships available. *Faculty research:* Whole brain learning approach, management style. • Dr. Gary Dessler, Chairperson, Department of Management and International Business, 305-348-2792. E-mail: desslerg@fiu.edu.

See in-depth description on page 195.

Florida Metropolitan University–Fort Lauderdale College, MBA Program, Fort Lauderdale, FL 33304-2522. Awards MBA. Faculty: 5. Students: 46. *Application deadline:* rolling. *Application fee:* $25. *Expenses:* Tuition $263 per credit. Fees $25 per quarter. • Dr. Rhonda Polak, Chairperson. Application contact: Tony Wallace, Director of Admissions, 954-568-1600. Fax: 954-568-2008.

Florida Metropolitan University–Orlando College, North, Division of Business Administration, 5421 Diplomat Circle, Orlando, FL 32810-5674. Offers programs in accounting (MBA), information systems (MBA), international business (MBA), management analysis (MBA), marketing analysis (MBA). Part-time and evening/weekend programs available. Faculty: 7. Students: 68. *Degree requirements:* Thesis or alternative. *Application deadline:* rolling. *Application fee:* $25. *Tuition:* $263 per credit hour. *Financial aid:* Federal Work-Study available. Aid available to part-time students. • Director of Graduate Studies, 407-851-2525. Application contact: Annette Gallina, Director of Admissions, 407-851-2525 Ext. 30. Fax: 407-851-1477.

Florida Metropolitan University–Tampa College, Department of Business Administration, 3319 West Hillsborough Avenue, Tampa, FL 33614-5899. Offers programs in human resources (MBA), international business (MBA). Part-time and evening/weekend programs available. Faculty: 1 full-time, 5 part-time. Students: 65 full-time, 25 part-time. Average age 32. *Degree requirements:* Thesis optional, foreign language not required. *Entrance requirements:* GMAT (minimum score 470) or GRE, minimum GPA of 3.0. Application deadline: rolling. Application fee: $25. *Expenses:* Tuition $250 per credit hour. Fees $100 per year. *Financial aid:* Available to part-time students. • Daniel Palladino, Director of Graduate Studies, 813-879-6000 Ext. 51. Application contact: Foster Thomas, Director of Admissions, 813-879-6000 Ext. 36. Fax: 813-871-2483.

Florida Southern College, Program in Business Administration, Lakeland, FL 33801-5698. Offers programs in accounting (MBA), business administration (MBA). Part-time programs available. Faculty: 13 full-time (2 women), 10 part-time (3 women). Students: 3 full-time (2 women), 54 part-time (15 women); includes 1 minority (Hispanic), 1 international. Average age 35. 21 applicants, 62% accepted. In 1997, 17 degrees awarded. *Average time to degree:* master's–3 years part-time. *Entrance requirements:* GMAT (minimum score 450) or GRE General Test (minimum combined score of 850), minimum GPA of 2.75. Application deadline: 8/1 (rolling processing; 12/1 for spring admission). Application fee: $30. Electronic applications accepted. *Tuition:* $280 per credit hour. *Financial aid:* Available to part-time students. • Dr. Lawrence Ross, Head, 941-680-4285. Fax: 941-680-4355. E-mail: lross@flsouthern.edu.

Directory: Business Administration and Management—General

Florida Southern College (continued)

Application contact: Bill Walker, Coordinator of External Programs, 941-680-4205. Fax: 941-680-3088. E-mail: hwalker@flsouthern.edu.

Florida State University, College of Business, Tallahassee, FL 32306. Awards M Acc, MBA, MS, PhD, JD/MBA. Programs in accounting (M Acc), business administration (MBA, PhD), management (MS). Part-time and evening/weekend programs available. Faculty: 85 full-time. Students: 135 full-time (65 women), 123 part-time (48 women); includes 44 minority (29 African Americans, 9 Asian Americans, 5 Hispanics, 1 Native American), 3 international. Average age 31. 378 applicants, 57% accepted. In 1997, 88 master's awarded; 26 doctorates awarded (100% entered university research/teaching). Terminal master's awarded for partial completion of doctoral program. *Degree requirements:* For doctorate, dissertation. *Average time to degree:* master's–1 year full-time, 2.5 years part-time; doctorate–4.5 years full-time. *Entrance requirements:* For master's, GMAT (minimum score 500; average 570), minimum GPA of 3.0, average 3.3; for doctorate, GMAT (minimum score 550; average 630), minimum graduate GPA of 3.25, average 3.7. Application deadline: rolling. Application fee: $20. *Tuition:* $139 per credit hour for state residents; $482 per credit hour for nonresidents. *Financial aid:* In 1997–98, 71 students received aid, including 31 fellowships (8 to first-year students), 12 research assistantships, 29 teaching assistantships, 30 graduate assistantships (all to first-year students); career-related internships or fieldwork also available. • Dr. Pamela L. Perrewé, Associate Dean for Graduate Studies, 850-644-3090. Application contact: Scheri L. Martin, Coordinator of Graduate Programs, 850-644-6458. E-mail: smartin@cob.fsu.edu.

Fontbonne College, MBA Options, St. Louis, MO 63105-3098. Awards MBA. Evening/weekend programs available. Faculty: 55 part-time (21 women). Students: 221 full-time (103 women), 64 part-time (31 women); includes 75 minority (67 African Americans, 2 Asian Americans, 5 Hispanics, 1 Native American). Average age 31. In 1997, 103 degrees awarded. *Degree requirements:* Computer language, applied management project required, foreign language not required. *Average time to degree:* master's–2 years full-time. *Application deadline:* 8/1 (priority date; rolling processing). *Application fee:* $20. *Expenses:* Tuition $10,650 per year full-time, $346 per credit hour part-time. Fees $160 per year full-time, $7 per credit hour part-time. *Financial aid:* Available to part-time students. • Dr. Richard Maclin, Associate Dean, 314-889-4587. Fax: 314-889-1451. E-mail: rmaclin@fontbonne.edu.

Fontbonne College, Program in Management, St. Louis, MO 63105-3098. Awards MM. Faculty: 16 part-time (9 women). Students: 56 full-time (33 women); includes 11 minority (10 African Americans, 1 Hispanic), 1 international. Average age 38. *Application deadline:* 8/1 (priority date; rolling processing). *Application fee:* $20. *Expenses:* Tuition $10,650 per year full-time, $346 per credit hour part-time. Fees $160 per year full-time, $7 per credit hour part-time. • Dr. Joan Lescinski, CSJ, Vice President and Dean for Academic Affairs, Graduate Programs, 314-889-1401. E-mail: jlescins@fontbonne.edu. Application contact: Peggy Musen, Director of Admissions, 314-889-1400. Fax: 314-889-1451. E-mail: pmusen@fontbonne.edu.

Fontbonne College, Department of Business Administration, Program in Business Administration, St. Louis, MO 63105-3098. Awards MBA. Part-time and evening/weekend programs available. Students: 29 full-time (13 women), 59 part-time (26 women); includes 26 minority (25 African Americans, 1 Asian American), 13 international. Average age 48. In 1997, 50 degrees awarded. *Degree requirements:* Computer language, thesis required, foreign language not required. *Application deadline:* 8/1 (priority date; rolling processing). *Application fee:* $20. *Expenses:* Tuition $10,650 per year full-time, $346 per credit hour part-time. Fees $160 per year full-time, $7 per credit hour part-time. • Dr. Hans Helbling, Chairperson, Department of Business Administration, 314-889-4520. Fax: 314-889-1451. E-mail: hhelblin@fontbonne.edu.

Fordham University, Graduate School of Business Administration, New York, NY 10023. Awards GPMBA, MBA, MS, TMBA, Certificate, JD/MBA, MBA/MS. Programs in accounting (GPMBA, MBA), business administration (TMBA), communications and media management (GPMBA, MBA), finance (GPMBA, MBA), information and communication systems (GPMBA, MBA), management (MBA), management systems (GPMBA), marketing (GPMBA, MBA), taxation (MS), total quality management (Certificate). Part-time and evening/weekend programs available. Faculty: 85 full-time (22 women), 95 part-time (12 women). Students: 236 full-time (98 women), 1,358 part-time (558 women); includes 120 international. Average age 28. 925 applicants, 47% accepted. In 1997, 499 master's awarded. *Average time to degree:* master's–2 years full-time, 3 years part-time. *Entrance requirements:* For master's, GMAT (average 570). Application deadline: 6/1 (priority date; rolling processing; 11/1 for spring admission). Application fee: $50. *Financial aid:* In 1997–98, 3 fellowships, 248 research assistantships, 91 administrative assistantships averaging $795 per month were awarded; teaching assistantships, institutionally sponsored loans, and career-related internships or fieldwork also available. Aid available to part-time students. Financial aid application deadline: 5/1; applicants required to submit FAFSA. • Dr. Ernest J. Scalberg, Dean, 212-636-6111. Fax: 212-307-1779. Application contact: Kathy Pattison, Assistant Dean of Admission, 212-636-6200. Fax: 212-636-7076. E-mail: admission@bschool.bnet.fordham.edu.

See in-depth description on page 197.

Fort Hays State University, College of Business, Department of Business Administration, Hays, KS 67601-4099. Offers programs in accounting (MBA), computer information systems (MBA), economics (MBA), finance (MBA). Faculty: 14 full-time (2 women). Students: 3 full-time (2 women), 26 part-time (14 women); includes 1 African American, 12 Asian Americans. Average age 31. 43 applicants, 65% accepted. In 1997, 15 degrees awarded. *Degree requirements:* Thesis optional, foreign language not required. *Entrance requirements:* GMAT. Application deadline: 7/1 (priority date; rolling processing). Application fee: $25 ($35 for international students). *Tuition:* $94 per credit hour for state residents; $249 per credit hour for nonresidents. *Financial aid:* Research assistantships, teaching assistantships, full tuition waivers, institutionally sponsored loans available. Aid available to part-time students. *Faculty research:* Organizational behavior and performance appraisal, data processing, international marketing. • Dr. Dale McKemey, Acting Director, 785-628-4201.

Framingham State College, Graduate Programs, Program in Business Administration, Framingham, MA 01701-9101. Awards MA. Part-time and evening/weekend programs available. Faculty: 4 full-time, 4 part-time. Students: 114 part-time. In 1997, 19 degrees awarded. *Entrance requirements:* GMAT, GRE, or MAT. *Tuition:* $4184 per year full-time, $523 per course part-time for state residents; $4848 per year full-time, $606 per course part-time for nonresidents. • Dr. Charles White, Chairperson, 508-626-4892. Application contact: Graduate Office, 508-626-4550.

Franciscan University of Steubenville, Department of Business, Steubenville, OH 43952-6701. Awards MBA. Part-time and evening/weekend programs available. Students: 9 full-time (3 women), 37 part-time (9 women). 25 applicants, 84% accepted. In 1997, 9 degrees awarded. *Degree requirements:* Research paper required, foreign language and thesis not required. *Average time to degree:* master's–3 years full-time, 6 years part-time. *Entrance requirements:* GMAT (minimum score 460), minimum undergraduate GPA of 2.5. Application deadline: 7/1 (rolling processing; 12/15 for spring admission). Application fee: $20. *Expenses:* Tuition $280 per credit hour. Fees $10 per credit hour. *Financial aid:* Federal Work-Study available. Aid available to part-time students. Financial aid application deadline: 7/1; applicants required to submit FAFSA. • Dr. Don Kissinger, Chairman, 740-283-6270. Application contact: Mark McGuire, Associate Director of Graduate Admissions, 800-783-6220. Fax: 740-283-6472.

Francis Marion University, School of Business, Florence, SC 29501-0547. Awards MBA. Part-time and evening/weekend programs available. Faculty: 20 full-time (2 women). Students: 2 full-time (both women), 53 part-time (25 women); includes 7 minority (4 African Americans, 3 Asian Americans), 2 international. In 1997, 14 degrees awarded. *Entrance requirements:* GMAT. Application deadline: 8/21 (priority date; rolling processing; 1/4 for spring admission). Application fee: $25. *Financial aid:* Graduate assistantships available. Aid available to part-time students. Financial aid application deadline: 3/1. *Faculty research:* Ethics, directions of MBA, international business, regional economics, environmental issues. • Dr. Robert T. Barrett, Coordinator, 803-661-1435. Fax: 803-661-1432.

Franklin Pierce College, Graduate Studies, College Road, PO Box 60, Rindge, NH 03461-0060. Offers program in leadership (MBA). Faculty: 8 full-time, 18 part-time. Students: 750. *Entrance requirements:* Minimum GPA of 2.5. Application deadline: rolling. Application fee: $0. *Tuition:* $270 per credit. • Gerri F. Luke, Dean of Graduate and Professional Studies. Application contact: Dr. Duncan G. LaBay, MBA Coordinator, 603-898-1263. Fax: 603-898-0827.

Franklin University, Graduate School of Business, Columbus, OH 43215-5399. Awards MBA. Part-time and evening/weekend programs available. Faculty: 7 full-time (2 women), 12 part-time (3 women), 17 FTE. Students: 362 (161 women); includes 43 minority (29 African Americans, 10 Asian Americans, 4 Native Americans), 14 international. Average age 33. 217 applicants, 82% accepted. In 1997, 127 degrees awarded. *Degree requirements:* Computer language required, foreign language and thesis not required. *Application deadline:* 7/15 (priority date; rolling processing). *Application fee:* $30 ($40 for international students). *Expenses:* Tuition $280 per credit hour. Fees $25 per trimester. *Financial aid:* Institutionally sponsored loans available. Financial aid application deadline: 6/30; applicants required to submit FAFSA. • Application contact: MBA Associate, 614-341-6387. Fax: 614-221-7723.

Fresno Pacific University, Graduate School, Program in Administrative Leadership, Fresno, CA 93702-4709. Awards MA. Faculty: 4 full-time (1 woman), 3 part-time (0 women). Students: 47 part-time (20 women). *Degree requirements:* Thesis or alternative required, foreign language not required. *Application fee:* $75. *Tuition:* $250 per unit. *Faculty research:* Ethics, servant leadership, communication, creative problem solving. • Dr. James N. Holm Jr., Director, 209-453-3668. Fax: 209-453-2001.

Friends University, Graduate Programs, College of Business, Program in Executive Business Administration, Wichita, KS 67213. Awards EMBA. Evening/weekend programs available. Students: 53. *Application deadline:* 8/15 (priority date; rolling processing). *Application fee:* $125. *Expenses:* Tuition $326 per credit hour (minimum). Fees $215 per year. • Dr. Bill Wunder, Director, 800-794-6945 Ext. 5591. Application contact: Director of Graduate Admissions, 800-794-6945 Ext. 5530.

Friends University, Graduate Programs, College of Business, Program in Management, Wichita, KS 67213. Awards MS. Evening/weekend programs available. Students: 83. *Application deadline:* 8/15 (priority date; rolling processing). *Application fee:* $125. *Expenses:* Tuition $326 per credit hour (minimum). Fees $215 per year. • Prof. D. Litherland, Director, 800-794-6945 Ext. 5858. Application contact: Director of Graduate Admissions, 800-794-6945 Ext. 5834.

Frostburg State University, School of Business, Frostburg, MD 21532-1099. Awards MBA, M Ed. Part-time and evening/weekend programs available. *Application deadline:* 7/15 (rolling processing). *Application fee:* $30. *Faculty research:* Cooperative teaching methods, strategic change processes, political marketing.

Gannon University, School of Graduate Studies, College of Humanities, Business, and Education, School of Business, Program in Business Administration, Erie, PA 16541. Awards MBA, Certificate. Part-time and evening/weekend programs available. Students: 16 full-time (9 women), 158 part-time (59 women); includes 8 minority (3 African Americans, 2 Asian Americans, 3 Hispanics), 4 international. Average age 32. 48 applicants, 90% accepted. In 1997, 30 master's awarded. *Degree requirements:* For master's, thesis, computer workshop, research project. *Entrance requirements:* GMAT, TOEFL. Application deadline: rolling. Application fee: $25. *Expenses:* Tuition $405 per credit. Fees $200 per year full-time, $8 per credit part-time. *Financial aid:* Administrative assistantships, scholarships and career-related internships or fieldwork available. Aid available to part-time students. Financial aid application deadline: 3/1; applicants required to submit FAFSA. • Application contact: Beth Nemenz, Director of Admissions, 814-871-7240. Fax: 814-871-5803. E-mail: admissions@gannon.edu.

Gannon University, School of Graduate Studies, College of Sciences, Engineering, and Health Sciences, School of Health Sciences, MSN/MBA Program, Erie, PA 16541. Awards MSN/MBA. Part-time and evening/weekend programs available. Students: 2 part-time (both women). Average age 30. *Application deadline:* 4/15 (priority date). *Application fee:* $25. *Financial aid:* Career-related internships or fieldwork available. Aid available to part-time students. Financial aid application deadline: 3/1; applicants required to submit FAFSA. • Application contact: Beth Nemenz, Director of Admissions, 814-871-7240. Fax: 814-871-5803. E-mail: admissions@gannon.edu.

Gardner–Webb University, Broyhill School of Management, Boiling Springs, NC 28017. Awards MBA. Part-time and evening/weekend programs available. Faculty: 11 full-time (2 women), 1 part-time (0 women). Students: 85 full-time (36 women), 86 part-time (38 women); includes 14 minority (11 African Americans, 3 Asian Americans), 2 international. Average age 33. 72 applicants, 83% accepted. In 1997, 37 degrees awarded. *Entrance requirements:* GMAT (minimum score 400; average 470), 1 semester each of economics and statistics, 2 semesters of accounting. Application deadline: 8/29 (rolling processing; 1/13 for spring admission). Application fee: $30. *Tuition:* $205 per semester hour. *Financial aid:* In 1997–98, 25 students received aid, including 2 assistantships averaging $450 per month. • Dr. Anthony Negbenebor, Director, 704-434-4622. E-mail: anegbenebor@gardner-webb.edu. Application contact: Melissa L. Swofford, Director of Admissions, 704-434-4489. Fax: 704-434-4738. E-mail: mswofford@gardner-webb.edu.

George Fox University, Business Administration Program, Newberg, OR 97132-2697. Awards MBA. Part-time and evening/weekend programs available. Faculty: 10 full-time (2 women), 4 part-time (1 woman), 13 FTE. Students: 90 part-time (30 women); includes 14 minority (5 African Americans, 2 Asian Americans, 2 Hispanics, 5 Native Americans). Average age 35. 80 applicants, 76% accepted. In 1997, 33 degrees awarded. *Degree requirements:* Project required, foreign language and thesis not required. *Average time to degree:* master's–2 years part-time. *Entrance requirements:* Minimum undergraduate GPA of 3.0 during previous 2 years. Application deadline: 7/1 (rolling processing). Application fee: $25. • Dr. Asbjorn Osland, Director, 800-765-4369 Ext. 2817. E-mail: josland@georgefox.edu. Application contact: Jan Cain, Graduate Admissions Counselor, 800-631-0921. Fax: 503-538-7234. E-mail: jcain@georgefox.edu.

George Mason University, School of Management, Program in Business Administration, Fairfax, VA 22030-4444. Awards EMBA, MBA. Part-time and evening/weekend programs available. Faculty: 67 full-time (15 women), 29 part-time (8 women), 76.5 FTE. Students: 219 full-time (82 women), 442 part-time (164 women); includes 100 minority (35 African Americans, 49 Asian Americans, 16 Hispanics), 41 international. Average age 31. 574 applicants, 73% accepted. In 1997, 197 degrees awarded. *Entrance requirements:* GMAT (minimum score 500; average 575), TOEFL (minimum score 575), 2 years of work experience. Application deadline: 5/1 (rolling processing; 11/1 for spring admission). Application fee: $30. Electronic applications accepted. *Tuition:* $4344 per year full-time, $181 per credit hour part-time for state residents; $12,504 per year full-time, $521 per credit hour part-time for nonresidents. *Financial aid:* Fellowships, research assistantships, teaching assistantships, Federal Work-Study, and career-related internships or fieldwork available. Aid available to part-time students. Financial aid application deadline: 3/1; applicants required to submit FAFSA. *Faculty research:* Electronic commerce, marketing information systems, group decision making, corporate governance, risk management. • Robert Johnson, Director, 703-993-3725. Fax: 703-993-1870. Application contact: Sandy Mitchell, Director of Graduate Admissions, 703-993-2136. Fax: 703-993-1886.

Georgetown University, School of Business, Washington, DC 20057. Awards MBA, JD/MBA, MBA/MS, MBA/MPP, MD/MBA. Program in business administration (MBA). *Entrance* *requirements:* GMAT, TOEFL (minimum score 550). Application deadline: 2/1 (priority date). Application fee: $65. *Expenses:* Tuition $23,880 per year. Fees $99 (one-time charge).

See in-depth description on page 199.

The George Washington University, School of Business and Public Management, Department of Management Science, Washington, DC 20052. Offers programs in human resources management (MBA); information systems (MSIS); information systems management (MBA); logistics, operations, and materials management (MBA, MPA); management and organizations (PhD); management decision making (MBA, PhD); management of science, technology, and innovation (MBA); organizational behavior and development (MBA); project management (MS). Part-time and evening/weekend programs available. Faculty: 29 full-time (3 women), 23 part-time (5 women), 35 FTE. Students: 152 full-time (57 women), 415 part-time (179 women); includes 112 minority (55 African Americans, 45 Asian Americans, 12 Hispanics), 106 international. Average age 33. 539 applicants, 71% accepted. In 1997, 145 master's, 2 doctorates awarded. *Degree requirements:* For master's, computer language required, foreign language and thesis not required; for doctorate, computer language, dissertation required, foreign language not required. *Entrance requirements:* For master's, GMAT, TOEFL (minimum score 550); for doctorate, GMAT or GRE, TOEFL (minimum score 550). Application deadline: 4/1 (priority date; rolling processing; 10/1 for spring admission). Application fee: $50. *Expenses:* Tuition $680 per semester hour. Fees $35 per semester hour. *Financial aid:* Fellowships, teaching assistantships, Federal Work-Study, institutionally sponsored loans, and career-related internships or fieldwork available. Financial aid application deadline: 4/1. *Faculty research:* Artificial intelligence, technological entrepreneurship, expert systems, strategic planning/management. • Dr. Erik K. Winslow, Chair, 202-994-7375. Application contact: Lilly Hastings, Graduate Admissions, 202-994-6584. Fax: 202-994-6382.

See in-depth description on page 201.

Georgia College and State University, School of Business, Milledgeville, GA 31061. Awards MBA, MIS. Part-time and evening/weekend programs available. Faculty: 24 full-time (6 women). Students: 52 full-time (14 women), 83 part-time (41 women); includes 16 minority (12 African Americans, 2 Asian Americans, 2 Hispanics), 10 international. Average age 32. In 1997, 65 degrees awarded. *Degree requirements:* Computer language required, thesis not required. *Entrance requirements:* GMAT (minimum score 450), TOEFL (minimum score 550), minimum AACSB index of 1000, minimum GPA of 2.5. Application deadline: 7/31 (priority date; rolling processing). Application fee: $10. *Financial aid:* In 1997–98, 18 assistantships were awarded; Federal Work-Study and career-related internships or fieldwork also available. Aid available to part-time students. Financial aid application deadline: 4/15. *Faculty research:* Work-related stress inventory for professionals, entrepreneurship success, accounting education, return behavior of newly listed stocks, performance measures on stock analysts' forecasts. • Dr. Melinda McCannon, Graduate Director, 912-445-5115.

Georgia Institute of Technology, Dupree College of Management, Program in Management, Atlanta, GA 30332-0001. Awards MS, MS Mgt, PhD. Students: 199 full-time (51 women), 17 part-time (5 women); includes 33 minority (17 African Americans, 12 Asian Americans, 4 Hispanics), 51 international. Average age 27. 614 applicants, 38% accepted. In 1997, 104 master's, 5 doctorates awarded. *Degree requirements:* For doctorate, dissertation, comprehensive and oral exams required, foreign language not required. *Entrance requirements:* GMAT, TOEFL (minimum score 600). Application deadline: 3/1 (rolling processing). Application fee: $50. *Expenses:* Tuition $2670 per year full-time, $98 per credit hour part-time for state residents; $10,680 per year full-time, $298 per credit hour part-time for nonresidents. Fees $681 per year full-time, $23 per credit hour (minimum) part-time. *Financial aid:* In 1997–98, research assistantships averaging $670 per month and totaling $6,000, teaching assistantships averaging $670 per month and totaling $6,000 were awarded; partial tuition waivers, Federal Work-Study, institutionally sponsored loans, and career-related internships or fieldwork also available. Aid available to part-time students. *Faculty research:* MIS, management of technology, international business, entrepreneurship, operations management. • Application contact: Ann Johnston Scott, Director of MS Mgt Program/PhD Admissions, 404-894-8722.

Georgian Court College, Program in Business Administration, Lakewood, NJ 08701-2697. Awards MBA. *Application deadline:* 8/25 (rolling processing; 1/15 for spring admission). *Application fee:* $30. *Tuition:* $350 per credit. • Application contact: Renee Loew, Director of Graduate Admissions and Records, 732-367-1717. Fax: 732-364-4516.

Georgia Southern University, College of Business, Program in Business Administration, Statesboro, GA 30460-8126. Awards MBA. Part-time and evening/weekend programs available. *Degree requirements:* Computer language, terminal exams required, foreign language and thesis not required. *Entrance requirements:* GMAT. Application deadline: 7/15 (priority date; rolling processing; 11/15 for spring admission). Application fee: $0. Electronic applications accepted. *Tuition:* $2619 per year full-time, $287 per semester (minimum) part-time for state residents; $8619 per year full-time, $1037 per semester (minimum) part-time for nonresidents. *Financial aid:* Application deadline 4/15. • Application contact: Dr. John R. Diebolt, Associate Graduate Dean, 912-681-5384. Fax: 912-681-0740. E-mail: gradschool@gsvms2.cc.gasou.edu.

Georgia Southwestern State University, School of Business, Americus, GA 31709-4693. Offers programs in business administration (MSA), computer information systems (MSA), social administration (MSA). Students: 20 full-time (12 women), 25 part-time (13 women); includes 10 minority (8 African Americans, 1 Asian American, 1 Hispanic), 3 international. *Entrance requirements:* GMAT (minimum score 500) or GRE General Test (minimum score 400 on each section), minimum GPA of 2.5. Application deadline: 9/1 (rolling processing; 3/15 for spring admission). Application fee: $10. *Financial aid:* Application deadline 9/1. • Dr. John Bates, Acting Chair, 912-931-2090. Application contact: Chris Laney, Graduate Admissions Specialist, 912-931-2027. Fax: 912-931-2059. E-mail: claney@gsw1500.gsw.peachnet.edu.

Georgia State University, College of Business Administration, Department of Management, Atlanta, GA 30303-3083. Awards MBA, MS, PhD. Part-time and evening/weekend programs available. Faculty: 29 full-time, 6 part-time. Students: 94 full-time (41 women), 91 part-time (31 women); includes 17 minority (15 African Americans, 2 Asian Americans), 3 international. Average age 34. In 1997, 42 master's, 1 doctorate awarded. Terminal master's awarded for partial completion of doctoral program. *Degree requirements:* For doctorate, dissertation required, foreign language not required. *Entrance requirements:* For master's, GMAT (average 566), TOEFL; for doctorate, GMAT (average 670), TOEFL. Application deadline: 5/1 (rolling processing; 10/1 for spring admission). Application fee: $25. *Expenses:* Tuition $2673 per year full-time, $99 per semester hour part-time for state residents; $10,692 per year full-time, $396 per semester hour part-time for nonresidents. Fees $228 per year. *Financial aid:* Fellowships, research assistantships, teaching assistantships, partial tuition waivers, and career-related internships or fieldwork available. Aid available to part-time students. Financial aid applicants required to submit FAFSA. • Dr. Michael Jay Jedel Jr., Chair, 404-651-3596. Fax: 404-651-2804. Application contact: Office of Academic Assistance and Master's Admissions, 404-651-1913. Fax: 404-651-0219.

Georgia State University, College of Business Administration, Executive MBA Program, Atlanta, GA 30303-3083. Offers economics (MBA), general business (MBA). Evening/weekend programs available. Students: 55 full-time (19 women); includes 6 minority (4 African Americans, 2 Hispanics), 4 international. Average age 39. 124 applicants, 44% accepted. In 1997, 45 degrees awarded. *Entrance requirements:* GMAT (average 566), TOEFL. Application deadline: 5/1 (priority date; rolling processing). Application fee: $25. *Expenses:* Tuition $30,500 per year full-time. Fees $228 per year. • Maury C. Kalnitz, Director, 404-651-3760. Application contact: Marketing Director, 404-651-3760. Fax: 404-651-1439.

Georgia State University, College of Business Administration, Program in General Business Administration, Atlanta, GA 30303-3083. Awards MBA. Part-time and evening/weekend programs available. Students: 73 full-time (25 women), 73 part-time (23 women); includes 16 minority (9 African Americans, 4 Asian Americans, 3 Hispanics), 9 international. Average age 31. In 1997, 71 degrees awarded. *Entrance requirements:* GMAT (average 566), TOEFL. Application deadline: 5/1 (rolling processing; 10/1 for spring admission). Application fee: $25. *Expenses:* Tuition $2673 per year full-time, $99 per semester hour part-time for state residents; $10,692 per year full-time, $396 per semester hour part-time for nonresidents. Fees $228 per year. *Financial aid:* Research assistantships, partial tuition waivers available. Aid available to part-time students. Financial aid application deadline: 5/1; applicants required to submit FAFSA. • Application contact: Office of Academic Assistance and Master's Admissions, 404-651-1913. Fax: 404-651-0219.

Golden Gate University, School of Business, San Francisco, CA 94105-2968. Awards EMBA, M Ac, MBA, MS, DBA, Certificate, JD/MBA. Programs in accounting (M Ac, MBA), business administration (EMBA, DBA), economics (MS), entrepreneurship (MBA), finance (MBA, MS), financial engineering (MS), financial planning (Certificate), human resource management (MBA, MS), human resources management (Certificate), information systems (MBA), international business (MBA), management (MBA), manufacturing management (MS, Certificate), marketing (MBA, MS), operations management (MBA), organizational behavior and development (MBA, MS), procurement and logistics management (MS, Certificate), professional export management (Certificate), project and systems management (MS, Certificate), public relations (MS, Certificate), telecommunications (MBA). MBA (telecommunications, management information systems) offered jointly with the School of Technology and Industry. Part-time and evening/weekend programs available. Students: 550 full-time (261 women), 915 part-time (414 women); includes 374 minority (65 African Americans, 237 Asian Americans, 67 Hispanics, 5 Native Americans), 356 international. Average age 33. 761 applicants, 75% accepted. In 1997, 629 master's, 4 doctorates awarded. *Degree requirements:* For doctorate, dissertation required, foreign language not required. *Average time to degree:* master's–2.5 years full-time. *Entrance requirements:* For master's, GMAT (MBA), TOEFL (minimum score 550), minimum GPA of 2.5 (MS). Application deadline: 7/1 (priority date; rolling processing). Application fee: $55 ($70 for international students). *Tuition:* $996 per course (minimum). *Financial aid:* Federal Work-Study, institutionally sponsored loans, and career-related internships or fieldwork available. Aid available to part-time students. Financial aid applicants required to submit FAFSA. • Dr. Hamid Shomali, Dean, 415-442-6500. Fax: 415-442-6579. Application contact: Enrollment Services, 415-442-7800. Fax: 415-442-7807. E-mail: info@ggu.edu.

See in-depth description on page 203.

Goldey–Beacom College, MBA Program, 4701 Limestone Road, Wilmington, DE 19808-1999. Offers programs in accounting (MBA), business administration (MBA), financial management (MBA), human resource management (MBA). MBA (accounting) new for fall 1998. Part-time and evening/weekend programs available. Faculty: 6 full-time (3 women), 4 part-time (1 woman). Students: 18 full-time (8 women), 171 part-time (88 women); includes 20 minority (8 African Americans, 9 Asian Americans, 3 Hispanics), 26 international. Average age 33. 60 applicants, 83% accepted. *Average time to degree:* master's–2 years full-time, 3 years part-time. *Entrance requirements:* GMAT (minimum score 450; average 507), TOEFL (minimum score 525), minimum GPA of 3.0. Application deadline: 8/20 (rolling processing; 5/15 for spring admission). Application fee: $30. Electronic applications accepted. *Expenses:* Tuition $6030 per year full-time, $335 per credit hour part-time. Fees $5 per credit hour. *Financial aid:* 10 students received aid; research assistantships, Federal Work-Study, and career-related internships or fieldwork available. Aid available to part-time students. Financial aid application deadline: 4/1; applicants required to submit FAFSA. • Bruce D. Marsland, Director, 302-998-8814 Ext. 276. Fax: 302-998-8631. E-mail: graduate@goldey.gbc.edu.

Gonzaga University, Graduate School, School of Business Administration, Program in Business Administration, Spokane, WA 99258-0001. Awards MBA, JD/MBA. *Entrance requirements:* GMAT (minimum score 450), TOEFL (minimum score 550). Application deadline: 7/20 (priority date; rolling processing; 11/1 for spring admission). Application fee: $40. *Tuition:* $7380 per year (minimum) full-time, $410 per credit (minimum) part-time. *Financial aid:* Teaching assistantships available. Financial aid application deadline: 3/1. • Application contact: Dr. Larry Lewis, Assistant Dean, 509-328-4220 Ext. 3430.

Governors State University, College of Business and Public Administration, Program in Business Administration, University Park, IL 60466. Awards MBA. Evening/weekend programs available. Faculty: 14 full-time (6 women), 27 part-time (9 women). In 1997, 51 degrees awarded. *Degree requirements:* Computer language, competency exams in elementary and intermediate algebra required, thesis optional, foreign language not required. *Entrance requirements:* GMAT (minimum AACSB index of 950). Application deadline: 7/15 (priority date; rolling processing; 11/10 for spring admission). Application fee: $0. *Expenses:* Tuition $1140 per trimester full-time, $95 per credit hour part-time for state residents; $3420 per trimester full-time, $285 per credit hour part-time for nonresidents. Fees $95 per trimester. *Financial aid:* Research assistantships, scholarships, full and partial tuition waivers, Federal Work-Study, institutionally sponsored loans available. Aid available to part-time students. Financial aid application deadline: 5/1. • Application contact: Mike Witak, Adviser, 708-534-4390.

Graduate School and University Center of the City University of New York, Program in Business, New York, NY 10036-8099. Offers accounting (PhD), behavioral science (PhD), finance (PhD), management planning systems (PhD). Faculty: 66 full-time (5 women). Students: 62 full-time (24 women), 2 part-time (1 woman); includes 4 minority (all Asian Americans), 29 international. Average age 37. 106 applicants, 20% accepted. In 1997, 13 doctorates awarded. Terminal master's awarded for partial completion of doctoral program. *Degree requirements:* For doctorate, dissertation required, foreign language not required. *Entrance requirements:* For doctorate, GMAT. Application deadline: 3/1. Application fee: $40. *Expenses:* Tuition $4350 per year full-time, $185 per credit (minimum) part-time for state residents; $7600 per year full-time, $320 per credit (minimum) part-time for nonresidents. Fees $69 per year. *Financial aid:* In 1997–98, 24 students received aid, including 17 fellowships (2 to first-year students), 2 research assistantships (both to first-year students); teaching assistantships, full and partial tuition waivers, Federal Work-Study, institutionally sponsored loans, and career-related internships or fieldwork also available. Financial aid application deadline: 2/1; applicants required to submit FAFSA. • Dr. Gloria Thomas, Executive Officer, 212-802-6580.

The Graduate School of America, Graduate School, Management Field, Minneapolis, MN 55401. Offers programs in management (MS); organization and management (PhD), including communications technology. Part-time and evening/weekend programs available. Postbaccalaureate distance learning degree programs offered (minimal on-campus study). Faculty: 2 full-time (0 women), 15 part-time (6 women). Students: 145 full-time (54 women); includes 24 minority (17 African Americans, 3 Asian Americans, 2 Hispanics, 2 Native Americans). Average age 45. In 1997, 1 master's awarded. Terminal master's awarded for partial completion of doctoral program. *Degree requirements:* For master's, project required, thesis optional, foreign language not required; for doctorate, dissertation required, foreign language not required. *Entrance requirements:* For master's, TOEFL (minimum score 550), minimum GPA of 2.7; for doctorate, TOEFL (minimum score 550), minimum GPA of 3.0. Application deadline: rolling. Application fee: $50. Electronic applications accepted. *Expenses:* Tuition $7160 per year (minimum). Fees $795 per year (minimum). *Financial aid:* 28 students received aid; institutionally sponsored loans available. *Faculty research:* Statistics; quantitative methods; business policies; strategic, corporate, and financial management. • Dr. Frank DeCaro, Chair, 612-339-8650. E-mail: fdecaro@worldnet.att.net. Application contact: Associate Director of Admissions, 800-987-1133. Fax: 612-337-5396. E-mail: tgsainfo@tgsa.edu.

Grambling State University, College of Business, Grambling, LA 71245. Offers program in general administration (MBA). Program being phased out; applicants no longer accepted. Part-time programs available. *Degree requirements:* Computer language required, thesis not required. *Tuition:* $1960 per year full-time, $297 per semester (minimum) part-time for state residents; $7110 per year full-time, $297 per semester (minimum) part-time for nonresidents. *Financial aid:* Research assistantships, graduate assistantships, Federal Work-Study available. • Dr. Karim Dhanani, Dean, 318-274-2275.

Directory: Business Administration and Management—General

Grand Canyon University, College of Business, Phoenix, AZ 85017-3030. Awards MBA. Part-time and evening/weekend programs available. Faculty: 7 full-time (1 woman), 1 (woman) part-time. Students: 16 full-time (7 women), 47 part-time (20 women); includes 12 minority (6 African Americans, 3 Asian Americans, 2 Hispanics, 1 Native American), 9 international. In 1997, 36 degrees awarded. *Average time to degree:* master's–2 years part-time. *Entrance requirements:* GMAT, TOEFL. Application deadline: rolling. Application fee: $25. *Financial aid:* Institutionally sponsored loans available. Aid available to part-time students. Financial aid application deadline: 3/15; applicants required to submit FAFSA. • Dr. Rob Jones, Director, MBA Program, 602-589-2867. Fax: 602-589-2532.

Grand Valley State University, Seidman School of Business, Program in Business Administration, Allendale, MI 49401-9403. Awards MBA. Part-time and evening/weekend programs available. Faculty: 27 full-time (3 women), 1 part-time (0 women). Students: 16 full-time (11 women), 282 part-time (90 women); includes 8 minority (2 African Americans, 4 Asian Americans, 2 Native Americans), 12 international. Average age 33. 86 applicants, 88% accepted. In 1997, 74 degrees awarded (100% found work related to degree). *Entrance requirements:* GMAT (minimum score 450), minimum AACSB index of 1000. Application deadline: 6/1 (priority date; rolling processing; 12/1 for spring admission). Application fee: $20. *Financial aid:* In 1997–98, 33 students received aid, including 2 fellowships (1 to a first-year student) totaling $16,000, 3 research assistantships (all to first-year students) totaling $28,500. Financial aid application deadline: 4/1. • Claudia J. Bajema, Director, 616-771-6695. Fax: 616-771-6801. E-mail: bajemac@gvsu.edu.

Hamline University, Graduate School of Public Administration and Management, St. Paul, MN 55104-1284. Offerings include management (MAM). JD/MANM and JD/MAM new for fall 1998. School faculty: 4 full-time, 25 part-time. *Application deadline:* 7/15 (priority date; rolling processing; 12/15 for spring admission). *Application fee:* $30. *Tuition:* $983 per course. • Dr. Jane McPeak, Dean, 651-523-2799. Fax: 651-523-2987. Application contact: Christine Wolf, Program Assistant, 651-523-2284.

Hampton University, Program in Business, Hampton, VA 23668. Awards MBA. Part-time and evening/weekend programs available. Faculty: 7 full-time (0 women). Students: 13 full-time (8 women), 5 part-time (1 woman); includes 16 minority (15 African Americans, 1 Asian American), 1 international. In 1997, 16 degrees awarded. *Entrance requirements:* GRE General Test (minimum score 450 on verbal section). Application deadline: 6/1 (priority date; rolling processing; 11/1 for spring admission). Application fee: $25. *Expenses:* Tuition $9038 per year full-time, $220 per credit part-time. Fees $70 per year. *Financial aid:* Teaching assistantships available. Aid available to part-time students. Financial aid application deadline: 5/1; applicants required to submit FAFSA. • Dr. Francisco Coronel, Director, 757-727-5762. Application contact: Erika Henderson, Director, Graduate Programs, 757-727-5454. Fax: 757-727-5084.

Hardin–Simmons University, School of Business and Finance, Abilene, TX 79698-0001. Awards MBA. Admissions temporarily suspended. Part-time and evening/weekend programs available. Faculty: 6 full-time (0 women), 1 part-time (0 women). Students: 7 full-time (1 woman), 9 part-time (3 women); includes 7 minority (2 African Americans, 5 Hispanics). Average age 32. In 1997, 11 degrees awarded. *Degree requirements:* Thesis or alternative required, foreign language not required. *Expenses:* Tuition $280 per semester hour. Fees $630 per year full-time. *Financial aid:* Full and partial tuition waivers, Federal Work-Study, and career-related internships or fieldwork available. Aid available to part-time students. Financial aid applicants required to submit FAFSA. *Faculty research:* Gender-based roles, impact of cultural values, accounting, information systems, international business ethics. • Dr. Lynn Gillette, Dean, 915-670-1357. Fax: 915-670-1523.

Harvard University, Extension School, Cambridge, MA 02138-3722. Offerings include special studies in administration and management (CSS). School faculty: 400 part-time. *Application deadline:* rolling. *Application fee:* $75. • Michael Shinagel, Dean. Application contact: Program Director, 617-495-4024. Fax: 617-495-9176.

Harvard University, Graduate School of Business Administration, Doctoral Program in Management, Boston, MA 02163. Offers business administration (DBA), business economics (PhD), organizational behavior (PhD). PhD offered jointly with the Graduate School of Arts and Sciences. Faculty: 200 full-time. Students: 94 full-time (25 women); includes 7 minority (3 African Americans, 3 Asian Americans, 1 Hispanic), 33 international. Average age 26. 529 applicants, 6% accepted. In 1997, 18 degrees awarded (78% entered university research/teaching, 22% found other work related to degree). *Degree requirements:* Dissertation required, foreign language not required. *Entrance requirements:* GRE General Test or GMAT, TOEFL. Application deadline: 12/30. Application fee: $75. *Financial aid:* 60 students received aid; fellowships, research assistantships, teaching assistantships, full tuition waivers, institutionally sponsored loans, and career-related internships or fieldwork available. • Jay Lorsch, Doctoral Programs Chair, 617-495-6101. Application contact: Doctoral Programs Office, 617-495-6101.

See in-depth description on page 205.

Harvard University, Graduate School of Business Administration, Master's Program in School of Business Administration, Boston, MA 02163. Awards MBA, JD/MBA. Faculty: 194 full-time. Students: 1,784 full-time (429 women); includes 461 international. Average age 27. 7,469 applicants. In 1997, 882 degrees awarded. *Entrance requirements:* GMAT, TOEFL. Application deadline: 3/1. Application fee: $160. *Financial aid:* Fellowships available. • Steven Wheelwright, MBA Program Chair, 617-495-6127. Application contact: Jill Fadule, MBA Admissions Director, 617-495-6127. Fax: 617-496-9272. E-mail: admissions@hbs.edu.

Hawaii Pacific University, School of Business Administration, 1166 Fort Street, Honolulu, HI 96813-2785. Offers programs in accounting (MBA), finance (MBA), human resource management (MA, MBA), information systems management (MSIS), information systems technology (MSIS), international business (MBA), management (MA, MBA), marketing (MBA), organizational change (MA), quality management (MBA). Part-time and evening/weekend programs available. Faculty: 30 full-time (3 women), 12 part-time (1 woman), 38 FTE. Students: 640 full-time (300 women), 464 part-time (170 women); includes 339 minority (45 African Americans, 260 Asian Americans, 30 Hispanics, 4 Native Americans), 491 international. Average age 31. 463 applicants, 83% accepted. In 1997, 337 degrees awarded. *Degree requirements:* Computer language, thesis required, foreign language not required. *Average time to degree:* master's–2 years full-time, 4 years part-time. *Application deadline:* rolling. *Application fee:* $50. Electronic applications accepted. *Tuition:* $7920 per year full-time, $330 per credit part-time. *Financial aid:* 169 students received aid; research assistantships, graduate assistantships, Federal Work-Study, and career-related internships or fieldwork available. Aid available to part-time students. Financial aid application deadline: 3/1; applicants required to submit FAFSA. *Faculty research:* Statistical control process as used by management, studies in comparative cross-cultural management styles, not-for-profit management. • Dr. Richard Ward, Dean for Graduate Management Studies, 808-544-0279. Application contact: Leina Danao, Admissions Coordinator, 808-544-1120. Fax: 808-544-0280. E-mail: gradservctr@hpu.edu.

See in-depth description on page 207.

Heidelberg College, Graduate Programs, Program in Business Administration, Tiffin, OH 44883-2462. Awards MBA. Part-time and evening/weekend programs available. Faculty: 13 full-time (2 women), 4 part-time (2 women). Students: 6 full-time (3 women), 30 part-time (15 women); includes 4 minority (1 African American, 3 Asian Americans), 3 international. Average age 36. 32 applicants, 66% accepted. *Degree requirements:* Internship, practicum required, foreign language and thesis not required. *Entrance requirements:* GMAT, TOEFL (minimum score 550), previous undergraduate course work in business. Application deadline: 8/10 (rolling processing). Application fee: $35. *Tuition:* $350 per semester hour. *Financial aid:* Available to part-time students. Financial aid application deadline: 4/15; applicants required to submit FAFSA. *Faculty research:* Marketing and strategic groups, initial public offerings, small business economics and finance, local economic development. • Dr. Henry G. Rennie, Director of Graduate Studies in Business, 419-448-2221. Fax: 419-448-2124. E-mail: hrennie@nike.heidelberg.edu.

Henderson State University, School of Business Administration, Arkadelphia, AR 71999-0001. Awards MBA. Part-time programs available. Postbaccalaureate distance learning degree programs offered (minimal on-campus study). Faculty: 15 full-time (4 women). Students: 5 full-time (2 women), 27 part-time (16 women); includes 3 international. Average age 33. In 1997, 14 degrees awarded. *Entrance requirements:* GMAT (minimum score 400), minimum AACSB index of 1000, minimum GPA of 2.5. Application deadline: 7/31 (priority date; rolling processing). Application fee: $0. Electronic applications accepted. *Expenses:* Tuition $120 per credit hour for state residents; $240 per credit hour for nonresidents. Fees $105 per semester (minimum) full-time, $52 per semester (minimum) part-time. *Financial aid:* Research assistantships, Federal Work-Study, institutionally sponsored loans available. Aid available to part-time students. Financial aid application deadline: 7/31. • Dr. Louis Dawkins, Dean, 870-230-5303. Fax: 870-230-5286. E-mail: dawkins@holly.hus.edu. Application contact: Dr. Johnnie Roebuck, Graduate Dean, 870-230-5126. Fax: 870-230-5144. E-mail: roebuckj@holly.hsu.edu.

High Point University, Graduate Studies, University Station, Montlieu Avenue, High Point, NC 27262-3598. Offers programs in business administration (MBA), international management (MS), management (MS). Part-time and evening/weekend programs available. Faculty: 11 full-time (1 woman). Students: 13 full-time (5 women), 133 part-time (68 women); includes 31 minority (27 African Americans, 2 Asian Americans, 1 Hispanic, 1 Native American), 5 international. Average age 34. 62 applicants, 84% accepted. In 1997, 18 degrees awarded (100% found work related to degree). *Degree requirements:* Computer language required, thesis optional, foreign language not required. *Average time to degree:* master's–2 years full-time. *Entrance requirements:* GMAT. Application deadline: 4/1 (priority date; 10/1 for spring admission). Application fee: $35 ($50 for international students). *Tuition:* $849 per course. *Financial aid:* 42 students received aid; institutionally sponsored loans available. Aid available to part-time students. Financial aid application deadline: 3/1; applicants required to submit FAFSA. • Dr. Alberta Herron, Dean, 336-841-9198. Fax: 336-841-4599. E-mail: aherron@acme.highpoint.edu.

Hofstra University, Frank G. Zarb School of Business, Hempstead, NY 11549. Awards Exec MBA, MBA, JD/MBA. Part-time and evening/weekend programs available. Postbaccalaureate distance learning degree programs offered (no on-campus study). Faculty: 77 full-time (22 women), 17 part-time (6 women). Students: 154 full-time (53 women), 542 part-time (206 women); includes 40 minority (12 African Americans, 12 Asian Americans, 14 Hispanics, 2 Native Americans), 72 international. Average age 29. 433 applicants, 60% accepted. In 1997, 208 degrees awarded. *Degree requirements:* Computer language required, foreign language not required. *Entrance requirements:* GMAT (average 580). Application deadline: rolling. Application fee: $40 ($75 for international students). *Expenses:* Tuition $10,968 per year full-time, $457 per credit hour part-time. Fees $670 per year full-time, $112 per semester (minimum) part-time. *Financial aid:* 150 students received aid; fellowships, research assistantships, partial tuition waivers, Federal Work-Study, and career-related internships or fieldwork available. Financial aid application deadline: 4/1; applicants required to submit FAFSA. • Dr. Ralph Polimeni, Dean of Academics, 516-463-5015. E-mail: bizrsp@hofstra.edu. Application contact: Susan McTiernan, Senior Assistant Dean, 516-463-5683. Fax: 516-463-5268. E-mail: bizsmm@hofstra.edu.

See in-depth description on page 209.

Holy Names College, Department of Business Administration and Economics, 3500 Mountain Boulevard, Oakland, CA 94619-1699. Offers program in management (MBA). Part-time and evening/weekend programs available. Faculty: 6 full-time (2 women), 1 part-time (0 women). Students: 5 full-time (2 women), 21 part-time (13 women); includes 15 minority (9 African Americans, 6 Asian Americans), 4 international. 13 applicants, 100% accepted. In 1997, 2 degrees awarded. *Average time to degree:* master's–1 year full-time, 2 years part-time. *Entrance requirements:* TOEFL (minimum score 550), minimum undergraduate GPA of 2.6 overall, 3.0 in major. Application deadline: 8/1 (rolling processing; 12/1 for spring admission). Application fee: $35. *Tuition:* $7650 per year full-time, $425 per unit part-time. *Financial aid:* 4 students received aid; Federal Work-Study and career-related internships or fieldwork available. Aid available to part-time students. Financial aid application deadline: 3/2; applicants required to submit FAFSA. *Faculty research:* Business ethics, sustainable economics, accounting models. • Dr. Marcia Frideger, Program Director, 510-436-1205. Application contact: Graduate Admissions Office, 800-430-1321. Fax: 510-436-1317. E-mail: garner@admin.hnc.edu.

Hood College, Department of Economics and Management, Frederick, MD 21701-8575. Offers program in administration and management (MBA). Part-time and evening/weekend programs available. Students: 12 full-time (8 women), 112 part-time (59 women); includes 13 minority (5 African Americans, 7 Asian Americans, 1 Hispanic), 3 international. Average age 33. In 1997, 53 degrees awarded. *Degree requirements:* Computer language required, foreign language and thesis not required. *Entrance requirements:* GMAT, minimum GPA of 2.5. Application deadline: rolling. Application fee: $30. *Tuition:* $285 per credit. *Financial aid:* Partial tuition waivers, institutionally sponsored loans, and career-related internships or fieldwork available. Aid available to part-time students. Financial aid applicants required to submit FAFSA. *Faculty research:* Stock splits and firm ownership, impact of corporate responsibility on share prices, option pricing framework of financial distress, memory effects of advertising, relationship advertising. • Dr. Larry Bitner, Program Director, 301-696-3685. Fax: 301-696-3597. E-mail: lbitner@nimue.hood.edu.

Hope International University, Graduate Studies, MBA Program, Fullerton, CA 92831-3138. Offers international development (MS); management (MBA), including international development, non-profit organizations management; non-profit organizations management (MS). Part-time programs available. Faculty: 2 full-time (0 women), 23 part-time (4 women). Students: 89. *Degree requirements:* Computer language, thesis required, foreign language not required. *Average time to degree:* master's–1.5 years full-time, 2 years part-time. *Entrance requirements:* Minimum GPA of 3.0. Application deadline: rolling. Application fee: $100. Electronic applications accepted. *Financial aid:* Available to part-time students. Financial aid application deadline: 3/31; applicants required to submit FAFSA. • Dr. Raj Singh, Director, 800-762-1294 Ext. 633. Application contact: Connie Born, Director of Admissions, 800-762-1294 Ext. 626. Fax: 714-738-4564. E-mail: cborn@pacificcc.edu.

Houston Baptist University, College of Business and Economics, Program in Business Administration, Houston, TX 77074-3298. Awards EMBA. Part-time and evening/weekend programs available. Faculty: 6 full-time (1 woman), 14 part-time (2 women). Students: 56 full-time (13 women); includes 15 minority (4 African Americans, 7 Asian Americans, 4 Hispanics). In 1997, 33 degrees awarded. *Entrance requirements:* GMAT (minimum score 450), minimum GPA of 2.5, work experience. Application deadline: 7/1 (priority date; rolling processing; 1/1 for spring admission). Application fee: $25 ($85 for international students). *Expenses:* Tuition $14,750 per year. Fees $705 per year. *Financial aid:* Federal Work-Study available. Financial aid application deadline: 6/1. • Dr. Carter L. Franklin II, Associate Dean, College of Business and Economics, 281-649-3429. Application contact: Laura Motal, Program Assistant, 281-649-3322.

Houston Baptist University, College of Business and Economics, Program in Management, Houston, TX 77074-3298. Offers accounting (MBA), finance (MBA), marketing (MBA). Part-time and evening/weekend programs available. Faculty: 9 full-time (1 woman), 7 part-time (1 woman). Students: 88 full-time (41 women), 41 part-time (19 women); includes 37 minority (13 African Americans, 16 Asian Americans, 7 Hispanics, 1 Native American), 9 international. In 1997, 45 degrees awarded (100% found work related to degree). *Entrance requirements:* GMAT (minimum score 450), minimum GPA of 2.5, work experience. Application deadline: 6/1 (priority date; rolling processing; 1/1 for spring admission). Application fee: $25 ($85 for international students). *Expenses:* Tuition $300 per semester hour. Fees $235 per quarter.

Financial aid: Federal Work-Study available. Financial aid application deadline: 6/1. • Dr. Carter L. Franklin II, Associate Dean, College of Business and Economics, 281-649-3429. Application contact: Karen Murray, Program Assistant, 281-649-3306.

Howard University, School of Business, 2400 Sixth Street, NW, Washington, DC 20059-0002. Awards MBA, JD/MBA. Part-time and evening/weekend programs available. *Degree requirements:* Computer language required, foreign language and thesis not required. *Entrance requirements:* GMAT. Application deadline: 4/1. Application fee: $45. *Expenses:* Tuition $10,200 per year full-time, $567 per credit hour part-time. Fees $405 per year. *Financial aid:* Fellowships, research assistantships, teaching assistantships, grants, institutionally sponsored loans, and career-related internships or fieldwork available. Financial aid application deadline: 4/1. • Dr. Barron Harvey, Dean, 202-806-1508.

Humboldt State University, College of Professional Studies, Department of Business Administration, Arcata, CA 95521-8299. Awards MBA. Part-time and evening/weekend programs available. Faculty: 11 full-time (2 women), 6 part-time (2 women). Students: 7 full-time (4 women), 8 part-time (3 women); includes 2 minority (1 Asian American, 1 Hispanic). Average age 33. 11 applicants, 55% accepted. In 1997, 7 degrees awarded. *Degree requirements:* Thesis or alternative required, foreign language not required. *Entrance requirements:* GMAT, TOEFL (minimum score 550), minimum GPA of 2.5. Application deadline: rolling. Application fee: $55. *Expenses:* Tuition $0 for state residents; $246 per unit for nonresidents. Fees $1996 per year full-time, $1330 per year part-time. *Financial aid:* Fellowships, Federal Work-Study available. Aid available to part-time students. Financial aid application deadline: 3/1. *Faculty research:* International business development, small town entrepreneurship, international trade: Pacific Rim. • Dr. Colleen Mullery, Coordinator, 707-826-6026.

Huron International University, Program in Business Administration, San Diego, CA 92108-3801. Awards MBA. Students: 21. *Application deadline:* rolling. *Application fee:* $100. *Tuition:* $275 per unit. *Financial aid:* Institutionally sponsored loans available. • Kamal Boulazareg, Head, 619-298-9040. Application contact: Susan Edyburne, Admissions Coordinator, 619-298-9040.

Huron University, School of Business, 333 9th Street SW, Huron, SD 57350-2798. Awards MBA. Faculty: 8. Students: 70. *Application deadline:* rolling. *Application fee:* $50. *Tuition:* $8100 per year. • Dr. Billie Sargent, Chair, 605-352-8721, Ext. 25. Application contact: Dr. John Zingg, Vice President of Academic Affairs, 605-352-8721.

Husson College, Program in Business, Bangor, ME 04401-2999. Awards MSB. Part-time and evening/weekend programs available. Faculty: 21. Students: 270. *Degree requirements:* Thesis optional, foreign language not required. *Entrance requirements:* GMAT, minimum GPA of 2.5. Application deadline: rolling. Application fee: $25. *Tuition:* $545 per course. *Financial aid:* Career-related internships or fieldwork available. • Application contact: Dr. Robert M. Smith, Dean, 207-941-7062.

Idaho State University, College of Business, Pocatello, ID 83209. Awards MBA. Part-time and evening/weekend programs available. Faculty: 18 full-time (2 women), 1 part-time (0 women). Students: 42 full-time (11 women), 74 part-time (25 women); includes 4 minority (1 Asian American, 1 Hispanic, 2 Native Americans), 4 international. Average age 33. In 1997, 39 degrees awarded. *Entrance requirements:* GMAT, GRE General Test. Application deadline: 7/1 (priority date; rolling processing; 12/1 for spring admission). Application fee: $30. *Tuition:* $3130 per year full-time, $136 per credit hour part-time for state residents; $9370 per year full-time, $226 per credit hour part-time for nonresidents. *Financial aid:* 10 students received aid; teaching assistantships, full and partial tuition waivers, Federal Work-Study available. Aid available to part-time students. • William Stratton, Dean, 208-236-2135.

Illinois Institute of Technology, Stuart School of Business, Chicago, IL 60661-3691. Awards MBA, MS, PhD, JD/MBA, JD/MS, MBA/MS, MBA/MPA. Programs in business administration (MBA), environmental management (MS), financial markets and trading (MS), management science (PhD), marketing communication (MS), operations and technology management (MS). Part-time and evening/weekend programs available. Faculty: 21 full-time (1 woman), 49 part-time (6 women). Students: 138 full-time (31 women), 505 part-time (128 women); includes 153 minority (36 African Americans, 98 Asian Americans, 19 Hispanics), 77 international. 593 applicants, 77% accepted. In 1997, 220 master's, 1 doctorate awarded. Terminal master's awarded for partial completion of doctoral program. *Degree requirements:* For master's, comprehensive exam required, foreign language and thesis not required; for doctorate, dissertation, comprehensive exam required, foreign language not required. *Entrance requirements:* GMAT, TOEFL (minimum score 550). Application deadline: 8/1 (rolling processing; 4/15 for spring admission). Application fee: $30. Electronic applications accepted. *Tuition:* $1620 per course. *Financial aid:* Fellowships, teaching assistantships, graduate assistantships, tuition scholarships, Federal Work-Study, institutionally sponsored loans available. Financial aid application deadline: 3/1. *Faculty research:* Quality management, capacity planning models, forecasting models, organization effectiveness. Total annual research expenditures: $44,000. • Dr. M. Zia Hassan, Dean, 312-906-6515. E-mail: hassan@stuart.iit.edu. Application contact: Lynn Miller, Director, Admission, 312-906-6544. Fax: 312-906-6549. E-mail: degrees@stuart.iit.edu.

See in-depth description on page 211.

Illinois State University, College of Business, Program in Business Administration, Normal, IL 61790-2200. Awards MBA. Part-time programs available. Faculty: 19 full-time (5 women), 1 part-time (0 women), 19.5 FTE. Students: 54 full-time (15 women), 102 part-time (44 women); includes 14 minority (11 African Americans, 2 Asian Americans, 1 Hispanic), 27 international. 62% of applicants accepted. In 1997, 69 degrees awarded. *Degree requirements:* Thesis optional. *Entrance requirements:* GMAT (minimum score 450), TOEFL (minimum score 600), minimum GPA of 2.75 during previous 2 years. Application deadline: rolling. Application fee: $0. *Expenses:* Tuition $2454 per year full-time, $102 per hour part-time for state residents; $7362 per year full-time, $307 per hour part-time for nonresidents. Fees $1048 per year full-time, $44 per hour part-time. *Financial aid:* In 1997–98, 10 research assistantships averaging $513 per month, 2 assistantships were awarded; teaching assistantships, full tuition waivers also available. Financial aid application deadline: 4/1. • Dr. Dixie Mills, Director of Graduate Programs and Research, 309-438-8386. Application contact: Admissions and Records Office, 309-438-2181.

Announcement: Illinois State has an affordable MBA program distinguishing itself in 3 ways. First, small class sizes encourage personal interaction. Second, the 200 students have diverse academic and professional backgrounds. Part-time and full-time students collaborate on class projects, presentations, and reports through a curriculum blending analysis and writing. Third, faculty members are active in research and consulting yet are committed to teaching excellence. There are excellent library and computer facilities. Elective concentrations include accounting, agribusiness, finance, insurance, international business, management, and marketing. Evening classes, foundation courses (for nonbusiness majors) taught at the graduate level, graduate assistantships, and tuition waivers are available. World Wide Web: http://www.ilstu.edu/depts/MBA

IMC–International Management Centres, Programs in Business Administration, Buckingham MK18 1BP, United Kingdom. Awards MBA, M Phil, DBA, D Phil. Postbaccalaureate distance learning degree programs offered (no on-campus study).

Indiana State University, School of Business, Terre Haute, IN 47809-1401. Awards MA, MBA, MS, PhD, Ed S, MBA/MS. MBA/MS offered jointly with the School of Nursing. Part-time and evening/weekend programs available. Faculty: 32 full-time (12 women), 2 part-time (0 women). Students: 27 full-time (5 women), 53 part-time (22 women); includes 4 minority (all African Americans), 28 international. Average age 30. 102 applicants, 62% accepted. In 1997, 33 master's awarded. *Entrance requirements:* For master's, GMAT. Application deadline: rolling. Application fee: $20. *Tuition:* $143 per credit hour for state residents; $325 per credit hour for nonresidents. *Financial aid:* In 1997–98, 19 research assistantships (5 to first-year students) were awarded; career-related internships or fieldwork also available. Financial aid application deadline: 3/1. *Faculty research:* Small business and entrepreneurial sciences, production and operations management. • Dr. Donald Bates, Dean, 812-237-2000.

Indiana University Bloomington, School of Business, Doctoral Programs in Business, Bloomington, IN 47405. Awards DBA, PhD, DBA/MIS, PhD/MIS. Offerings include accounting (DBA, PhD), business economics and public policy (DBA, PhD), finance (DBA, PhD), information and decision systems (DBA, PhD), management (DBA, PhD), marketing (DBA, PhD), operations management (DBA, PhD), organizational behavior (DBA, PhD). PhD offered through the University Graduate School. Students: 45 full-time (11 women), 40 part-time (10 women); includes 7 minority (4 African Americans, 1 Asian American, 1 Hispanic, 1 Native American), 24 international. In 1997, 16 degrees awarded. *Degree requirements:* Computer language, dissertation required, foreign language not required. *Entrance requirements:* GMAT (minimum score 600), GRE General Test. Application deadline: 3/1. Application fee: $35. *Expenses:* Tuition $261 per credit hour for state residents; $523 per credit hour for nonresidents. Fees $343 per year. *Financial aid:* Fellowships, research assistantships, teaching assistantships available. Financial aid application deadline: 3/1. • Dr. Janet Near, Chairperson, 812-855-3476. Application contact: Barbara Clark, Program Secretary and Assistant to Chairperson, 812-855-3476. Fax: 812-855-8679. E-mail: bclark@ucs.indiana.edu.

Indiana University Bloomington, School of Business, Program in Business Administration, Bloomington, IN 47405. Awards MBA, JD/MBA. Offerings include entrepreneurship (MBA), finance (MBA), human resources (MBA), international business (MBA), management (MBA), management information systems (MBA), marketing (MBA), operations management (MBA). Self-designed programs available. Students: 590 full-time (153 women), 45 part-time (11 women); includes 84 minority (30 African Americans, 30 Asian Americans, 23 Hispanics, 1 Native American), 146 international. In 1997, 361 degrees awarded. *Entrance requirements:* GMAT, TOEFL (minimum score 580). Application deadline: 3/1. Application fee: $50 ($65 for international students). *Expenses:* Tuition $8232 per year for state residents; $16,470 per year for nonresidents. Fees $343 per year. *Financial aid:* Fellowships, research assistantships, teaching assistantships, full and partial tuition waivers, institutionally sponsored loans, and career-related internships or fieldwork available. Financial aid application deadline: 3/1; applicants required to submit FAFSA. • Dr. George Hettenhouse, Chair, 812-855-8006. Application contact: Dr. James J. Holmen, Director of Admissions and Financial Aid, 812-855-8006. Fax: 812-855-9039.

See in-depth description on page 213.

Indiana University Kokomo, Division of Business and Economics, Kokomo, IN 46904-9003. Awards MBA. Part-time and evening/weekend programs available. Faculty: 15 full-time (5 women). Students: 11 full-time (4 women), 108 part-time (34 women); includes 16 minority (1 African American, 10 Asian Americans, 4 Hispanics, 1 Native American), 5 international. Average age 32. 21 applicants, 90% accepted. In 1997, 4 degrees awarded. *Degree requirements:* Research project required, thesis optional, foreign language not required. *Average time to degree:* master's–2 years full-time, 4 years part-time. *Application deadline:* 8/1 (rolling processing; 12/15 for spring admission). *Application fee:* $35 ($50 for international students). *Financial aid:* 2 students received aid; partial tuition waivers and career-related internships or fieldwork available. *Faculty research:* MIS, finance, marketing, human resources, international business, accounting. • Dr. Thomas Von der Embse, Dean, 765-455-9446. E-mail: tvondere@iuk.edu. Application contact: Dr. Dilip Pendse, Director of MBA Program, 765-455-9279. Fax: 765-455-9348. E-mail: dpendse@iuk.edu.

Indiana University Northwest, Division of Business and Economics, Gary, IN 46408-1197. Offers programs in accountancy (M Acc), accounting (Certificate), business administration (MBA). M Acc offered jointly with Purdue University. Part-time and evening/weekend programs available. Faculty: 19 full-time (2 women), 3 part-time (1 woman), 20 FTE. Students: 6 full-time (3 women), 305 part-time (118 women); includes 48 minority (30 African Americans, 4 Asian Americans, 13 Hispanics, 1 Native American), 1 international. Average age 30. 54 applicants, 72% accepted. In 1997, 50 master's awarded. *Average time to degree:* master's–2 years full-time, 4 years part-time. *Entrance requirements:* For master's, GMAT (average 500). Application deadline: 7/15 (priority date; rolling processing; 11/15 for spring admission). Application fee: $25 ($40 for international students). *Financial aid:* In 1997–98, 9 students received aid, including 6 graduate assistantships (2 to first-year students); Federal Work-Study, institutionally sponsored loans also available. Aid available to part-time students. Financial aid application deadline: 7/15. *Faculty research:* International finance, wellness in the workplace, handicapped employment, MIS, regional economic forecasting. • Dr. Donald Coffin, Dean, 219-980-6633. Fax: 219-980-6579. Application contact: Kathryn M. Lantz, Director of Graduate Programs, 219-980-6635. Fax: 219-980-6916.

Indiana University of Pennsylvania, College of Business, Program in Business Administration, Indiana, PA 15705-1087. Awards MBA. Part-time programs available. Students: 102 full-time (35 women), 64 part-time (24 women); includes 4 minority (2 African Americans, 2 Asian Americans), 64 international. Average age 30. 156 applicants, 62% accepted. In 1997, 100 degrees awarded. *Degree requirements:* Thesis optional, foreign language not required. *Entrance requirements:* GMAT (minimum score 450), TOEFL (minimum score 500). Application deadline: 7/1 (priority date; rolling processing; 11/1 for spring admission). Application fee: $30. *Expenses:* Tuition $3468 per year full-time, $193 per credit part-time for state residents; $6236 per year full-time, $346 per credit part-time for nonresidents. Fees $313 per year (minimum) full-time, $84 per year part-time. *Financial aid:* Research assistantships, Federal Work-Study, and career-related internships or fieldwork available. Aid available to part-time students. Financial aid application deadline: 3/15. • Dr. Krish Krishnan, Graduate Coordinator, 724-357-2522. E-mail: krishnan@grove.iup.edu.

Indiana University–Purdue University Fort Wayne, School of Business and Management Sciences, Fort Wayne, IN 46805-1499. Offers program in business (MBA). Part-time and evening/weekend programs available. Faculty: 16 full-time (2 women), 1 part-time (0 women), 16.25 FTE. Students: 14 full-time (4 women), 165 part-time (50 women); includes 16 minority (2 African Americans, 9 Asian Americans, 3 Hispanics, 2 Native Americans), 4 international. Average age 25. 54 applicants, 59% accepted. In 1997, 35 degrees awarded (100% found work related to degree). *Degree requirements:* Computer language required, thesis optional, foreign language not required. *Entrance requirements:* GMAT (minimum score 450). Application deadline: 7/1 (11/1 for spring admission). Application fee: $30. *Expenses:* Tuition $2356 per year full-time, $131 per credit hour part-time for state residents; $5253 per year full-time, $292 per credit hour part-time for nonresidents. Fees $183 per year full-time, $10.15 per credit hour part-time. *Financial aid:* In 1997–98, 7 students received aid, including 7 research assistantships (2 to first-year students). Financial aid application deadline: 3/1. • Michael R. Lane, Dean, 219-481-6061. E-mail: lanem@ipfw.edu. Application contact: Ali Rassuli, Director, Graduate Business Studies, 219-481-6498. Fax: 219-481-5472. E-mail: rassuli@ipfw.edu.

Indiana University–Purdue University Indianapolis, School of Business, Indianapolis, IN 46202-2896. Awards MBA, JD/MBA, MBA/MHA. Part-time and evening/weekend programs available. Faculty: 28 full-time (6 women). Students: 304 part-time (75 women); includes 31 minority (12 African Americans, 16 Asian Americans, 3 Hispanics), 4 international. Average age 29. 124 applicants, 43% accepted. In 1997, 105 degrees awarded (100% found work related to degree). *Entrance requirements:* GMAT, previous course work in accounting, statistics. Application deadline: 5/1 (11/1 for spring admission). Application fee: $35 ($50 for international students). *Financial aid:* Federal Work-Study available. Aid available to part-time students. Financial aid application deadline: 3/1; applicants required to submit FAFSA. • Roger W. Schmenner, Associate Dean–Indianapolis Programs, 317-274-4895. Application contact: Richard J. Magjuka, Chairman of Graduate Studies, 317-274-4895. Fax: 317-274-2483. E-mail: mbaindy@iupui.edu.

Directory: Business Administration and Management—General

Indiana University South Bend, Division of Business and Economics, Program in Business Administration, South Bend, IN 46634-7111. Awards MBA. *Entrance requirements:* GMAT (minimum score 450), TOEFL (minimum score 550). Application deadline: 6/1 (11/1 for spring admission). Application fee: $35 ($40 for international students). *Expenses:* Tuition $3648 per year full-time, $152 per credit hour part-time for state residents; $8640 per year full-time, $360 per credit hour part-time for nonresidents. Fees $222 per year full-time, $34 per semester (minimum) part-time. *Financial aid:* Application deadline 3/1. • Application contact: Graduate Director, 219-237-4183. Fax: 219-237-6549.

Indiana Wesleyan University, Adult and Professional Studies Program, Program in Business Administration, Marion, IN 46953-4999. Awards MBA. Faculty: 137 part-time (22 women). Students: 730 full-time (280 women); includes 110 minority (82 African Americans, 18 Asian Americans, 7 Hispanics, 3 Native Americans). Average age 35. 569 applicants, 82% accepted. In 1997, 317 degrees awarded. *Entrance requirements:* Minimum GPA of 2.5, related experience. Application deadline: rolling. Application fee: $20. *Tuition:* $239 per hour. • David Rose, Director, 765-677-2345. Fax: 765-677-2380. Application contact: Jerry Shepherd, Marketing Manager, 765-677-2362.

Indiana Wesleyan University, Adult and Professional Studies Program, Program in Management, Marion, IN 46953-4999. Awards MS. Evening/weekend programs available. Faculty: 137 part-time (22 women). Students: 228 full-time (120 women); includes 46 minority (40 African Americans, 2 Asian Americans, 2 Hispanics, 2 Native Americans). Average age 37. 192 applicants, 86% accepted. In 1997, 104 degrees awarded. *Average time to degree:* master's–2 years full-time. *Entrance requirements:* Minimum GPA of 2.5, related experience. Application deadline: rolling. Application fee: $20. *Tuition:* $239 per hour. *Financial aid:* Available to part-time students. Financial aid applicants required to submit FAFSA. • David Rose, Director, 765-677-2345. Fax: 765-677-2380. Application contact: Jerry Shepherd, Marketing Manager, 765-677-2362.

Instituto Centroamericano de Administración de Empresas, Program in Business, SJO 1358, PO Box 025216, Miami, FL 33102-5216. Awards EMBA, MBA. *Entrance requirements:* Fluency in Spanish, interview, minimum one year work experience. Application deadline: 6/16 (rolling processing). *Faculty research:* Competitiveness, sustainable development, production.

Instituto Tecnológico y de Estudios Superiores de Monterrey, Graduate School of Management and Leadership, Program in Business Administration, Monterrey, Nuevo León 64849, Mexico. Offers business administration (MA, MBA), finance (M Sc), international business (M Sc), marketing (M Sc). MBA offered jointly with the University of California, Los Angeles and the University of Texas at Austin. Part-time programs available. *Degree requirements:* 1 foreign language, thesis. *Entrance requirements:* GMAT, TOEFL. Application deadline: 4/30 (priority date). *Faculty research:* Technology management, quality management, organizational theory and behavior.

Instituto Tecnológico y de Estudios Superiores de Monterrey, Graduate School of Management and Leadership, Program in Management, Monterrey, Nuevo León 64849, Mexico. Awards PhD. Part-time programs available. *Degree requirements:* 1 foreign language, dissertation. *Average time to degree:* doctorate–4 years full-time. *Entrance requirements:* GMAT, TOEFL. Application deadline: 3/30. Application fee: $0. *Faculty research:* Quality management, manufacturing and technology management, information systems, managerial economics, business policy.

Instituto Tecnológico y de Estudios Superiores de Monterrey, Ciudad de México Campus, Graduate Programs, Calle del Puente Num 222, Tlalpan, Ciudad de Mexico, D.F. 14380, Mexico. Offers programs in administration (PhD), administration/finance/economy (MBA), business administration (EMBA). EMBA jointly offered with The University of Texas at Austin. Part-time and evening/weekend programs available. *Average time to degree:* master's–3 years part-time; doctorate–2 years full-time, 3.3 years part-time. *Entrance requirements:* For master's, ITESM exam; for doctorate, ITESM exam, GMAT. Application deadline: 10/13 (4/5 for spring admission). Application fee: $65.

Instituto Tecnológico y de Estudios Superiores de Monterrey, Estado de México Campus, Graduate Division, Atizapán de Zaragoza 52926, Mexico. Offerings include business administration (MBA). Postbaccalaureate distance learning degree programs offered (minimal on-campus study). Institute faculty: 19 full-time (3 women), 32 part-time (3 women). *Average time to degree:* master's–2 years full-time, 3.3 years part-time. *Application deadline:* 1/12 (priority date; rolling processing; 4/4 for spring admission). *Application fee:* $72. • Emilio Alvarado Badillo, Headmaster, 5-326-5500. Fax: 5-326-5507. E-mail: ealvarad@campus.cem.itesm.mx. Application contact: Lourdes Turrubiates, Admissions Officer, 5-326-5776. E-mail: lturrubi@campus.cem.itesm.mx.

Instituto Tecnológico y de Estudios Superiores de Monterrey, Guadalajara Campus, Program in Business Administration, Zapopan, Jalisco 44100, Mexico. Awards MBA. Part-time and evening/weekend programs available. Postbaccalaureate distance learning degree programs offered. Faculty: 9 full-time (2 women), 23 part-time (2 women). Students: 240. Average age 30. 54 applicants, 74% accepted. In 1997, 55 degrees awarded. *Degree requirements:* 1 foreign language required, thesis not required. *Average time to degree:* master's–1.5 years full-time, 2.5 years part-time. *Entrance requirements:* ITESM admission test. Application deadline: 8/1 (rolling processing; 3/1 for spring admission). Application fee: $40. *Financial aid:* 112 students received aid; fellowships, Federal Work-Study, institutionally sponsored loans, and career-related internships or fieldwork available. Financial aid application deadline: 8/1. *Faculty research:* Strategic alliances in small business, family business practice in Mexico, competitiveness under NAFTA for Mexican firms. Total annual research expenditures: $670,000. • Jaime Navarro, Director, 3-669-3099. E-mail: jnavarro@campus.gda.itesm.mx. Application contact: Marcela Tapia, Administrative Coordinator, MBA Program, 3-669-3095. Fax: 3-669-3093. E-mail: mtapia@campus.gda.itesm.mx.

Instituto Tecnológico y de Estudios Superiores de Monterrey, Laguna Campus, Graduate School, Torreón, Coahuila 32583, Mexico. Offers programs in business administration (MBA), industrial engineering (MIE), management information systems (MS). Part-time programs available. *Degree requirements:* Computer language required, foreign language and thesis not required. *Entrance requirements:* GMAT (minimum score 450). Application deadline: 7/31 (priority date). Application fee: $0. *Faculty research:* Computer communications from home to the University.

Instituto Tecnológico y de Estudios Superiores de Monterrey, León Campus, Program in Business Administration, León, Guanajuato 37190, Mexico. Awards MBA. Part-time programs available. *Entrance requirements:* Entrance exam of graduate students (minimum score 450). Application deadline: 6/30.

Instituto Tecnológico y de Estudios Superiores de Monterrey, Morelos Campus, Programs in Business Administration, Cuernavaca, Morelos 62589, Mexico. Offerings in finance (MA), human resources management (MA), international business (MA), marketing (MA).

Instituto Tecnológico y de Estudios Superiores de Monterrey, Querétaro Campus, School of Business, Querétaro, Querétaro 76000, Mexico. Awards MBA. *Degree requirements:* Computer language required, thesis not required. *Entrance requirements:* Aptitude Test of College Board (minimum score 400). Application deadline: 1/11 (priority date; rolling processing; 3/29 for spring admission). Application fee: $50. *Faculty research:* Organizational analysis, industrial marketing, international trade.

Instituto Tecnológico y de Estudios Superiores de Monterrey, Sonora Norte Campus, Program in Business, Hermosillo, Sonora 83000, Mexico. Awards MA. *Entrance requirements:* GMAT (minimum score 400). Application deadline: 8/30 (rolling processing; 12/13 for spring admission).

Instituto Tecnológico y de Estudios Superiores de Monterrey, Toluca Campus, Graduate Programs, Toluca, Estado de Mexico 50000, Mexico. Awards MBA. Part-time and evening/weekend programs available. *Degree requirements:* 1 foreign language, computer language, high proficiency in English required, thesis not required. *Entrance requirements:* Master's admission test. Application deadline: 8/20 (priority date). Application fee: $100. *Faculty research:* Management in the industrial valley of Toluca.

Inter American University of Puerto Rico, Metropolitan Campus, Division of Economics and Business Administration, San Juan, PR 00919-1293. Offers programs in accounting (MBA), business education (MA), finance (MBA), human resources (MBA), industrial management (MBA), labor relations (MA), marketing (MBA). Part-time and evening/weekend programs available. Faculty: 16 full-time, 45 part-time. Students: 479 full-time (282 women), 757 part-time (424 women); includes 1,236 minority (all Hispanics). *Degree requirements:* Comprehensive exam required, foreign language and thesis not required. *Entrance requirements:* GRE or PAEG, interview. Application deadline: 5/15 (priority date; rolling processing; 11/15 for spring admission). Application fee: $31. Electronic applications accepted. *Expenses:* Tuition $3272 per year full-time, $1740 per year part-time. Fees $328 per year full-time, $176 per year part-time. *Financial aid:* Federal Work-Study available. • Dr. Angel Ruiz, Dean, 787-250-1912 Ext. 2285. Application contact: Dr. Antonio Llorens, Director, 787-250-1912 Ext. 2320. Fax: 787-250-0361.

Inter American University of Puerto Rico, San Germán Campus, Department of Business Administration, San Germán, PR 00683-5008. Offers programs in business administration (MBA), including accounting, finance, human resources, industrial relations, marketing; business education (MA). Part-time and evening/weekend programs available. Faculty: 11 full-time (3 women), 15 part-time (1 woman). In 1997, 85 degrees awarded. *Degree requirements:* Comprehensive exam required, foreign language and thesis not required. *Entrance requirements:* Minimum GPA of 3.0, GRE General Test, or PAEG. Application deadline: 4/30 (priority date; rolling processing; 11/15 for spring admission). Application fee: $31. *Expenses:* Tuition $150 per credit. Fees $177 per semester. *Financial aid:* Teaching assistantships available. • Joseph Devaris, Coordinator of Graduate Programs, 787-264-1912 Ext. 7357. Application contact: Mildred Camacho, Admissions Director, 787-892-3090. Fax: 787-892-6350.

International College of the Cayman Islands, Graduate Program in Management, Newlands, Grand Cayman, Cayman Islands. Offers programs in business administration (MBA), management (MS). Part-time and evening/weekend programs available. Faculty: 6 full-time (3 women), 3 part-time (0 women). Students: 19 full-time (11 women), 22 part-time (14 women). Average age 36. In 1997, 9 degrees awarded. *Degree requirements:* Comprehensive exam required, foreign language and thesis not required. *Application deadline:* 6/1 (priority date; rolling processing; 10/1 for spring admission). *Application fee:* $38. *Expenses:* Tuition $3000 per year full-time, $100 per credit part-time. Fees $450 per year. *Financial aid:* Teaching assistantships and career-related internships or fieldwork available. *Faculty research:* International human resources administration. • Dr. Eileen Dounce, Director of Graduate Studies, 345-947-1100. Fax: 345-947-1210.

Iona College, Hagan Graduate School of Business, 715 North Avenue, New Rochelle, NY 10801-1890. Awards MBA, PMC. Part-time and evening/weekend programs available. Faculty: 32 full-time (5 women), 9 part-time (2 women). Students: 21 full-time (12 women), 182 part-time (84 women); includes 12 minority (4 African Americans, 4 Asian Americans, 3 Hispanics, 1 Native American). Average age 31. In 1997, 105 master's, 2 PMCs awarded. *Degree requirements:* For master's, computer language required, foreign language and thesis not required. *Average time to degree:* master's–2 years full-time, 3.5 years part-time. *Entrance requirements:* For master's, GMAT. Application deadline: rolling. Application fee: $50. *Expenses:* Tuition $480 per credit hour. Fees $25 per semester. *Financial aid:* In 1997–98, 4 graduate assistantships (3 to first-year students) averaging $560 per month were awarded; partial tuition waivers, Federal Work-Study also available. Aid available to part-time students. *Faculty research:* Artificial intelligence, financial services, value-based management, public policy, business ethics. • Dr. Nicholas J. Beutell, Dean, 914-633-2256. Application contact: Carol Shea, Director of MBA Admissions, 914-633-2288.

See in-depth description on page 215.

Iowa State University of Science and Technology, College of Business, Ames, IA 50011. Awards MBA, MS, MBA/MS, MBA/MCRP. Faculty: 53 full-time. Students: 92 full-time (31 women), 127 part-time (33 women); includes 8 minority (6 African Americans, 1 Asian American, 1 Hispanic), 55 international. 268 applicants, 45% accepted. In 1997, 85 degrees awarded. *Entrance requirements:* GMAT, TOEFL, resumé. Application deadline: 5/1 (priority date; 11/1 for spring admission). Application fee: $20 ($30 for international students). *Expenses:* Tuition $3166 per year full-time, $230 per credit part-time for state residents; $9324 per year full-time, $572 per credit part-time for nonresidents. Fees $200 per year. *Financial aid:* In 1997–98, 51 research assistantships (21 to first-year students), 1 teaching assistantship, 14 scholarships (2 to first-year students) were awarded; fellowships also available. • Dr. Benjamin J. Allen, Dean, 515-294-2422. E-mail: ballen@iastate.edu. Application contact: Dr. Labh S. Hira, Associate Dean of Graduate Programs, 515-294-8118. E-mail: busgrad@iastate.edu.

See in-depth description on page 217.

ISIM University, Programs in Information Management, Program in Business Administration, Denver, CO 80246. Offers business administration (MBA), health care management (MBA). Postbaccalaureate distance learning degree programs offered (no on-campus study). *Application deadline:* rolling. *Application fee:* $50. Electronic applications accepted.

Jackson State University, School of Business, Department of Economics, Finance and General Business, Jackson, MS 39217. Offers program in business administration (MBA, PhD). PhD new for fall 1998. Part-time and evening/weekend programs available. Faculty: 11 full-time (3 women). Students: 41 full-time (29 women), 69 part-time (37 women); includes 85 minority (84 African Americans, 1 Asian American), 8 international. 61 applicants, 61% accepted. In 1997, 20 master's awarded. *Degree requirements:* For master's, thesis, comprehensive exam. *Entrance requirements:* For master's, GRE General Test (minimum combined score of 1000), TOEFL (minimum score 550). Application deadline: 3/1 (priority date; rolling processing; 10/1 for spring admission). Application fee: $20. *Tuition:* $2688 per year (minimum) full-time, $150 per semester hour part-time for state residents; $5546 per year (minimum) full-time, $309 per semester hour part-time for nonresidents. *Financial aid:* Full and partial tuition waivers, Federal Work-Study available. Financial aid application deadline: 3/1. • Dr. Jessie C. Pennington, Director, 601-982-6315. Fax: 601-982-6124. Application contact: Mae Robinson, Admissions Coordinator, 601-968-2455. Fax: 601-968-8246. E-mail: mrobinson@ccaix.jsums.edu.

Jacksonville State University, College of Commerce and Business Administration, Jacksonville, AL 36265-9982. Awards MBA. Part-time and evening/weekend programs available. Faculty: 22 full-time (5 women). Students: 23 full-time (7 women), 50 part-time (17 women); includes 6 minority (5 African Americans, 1 Hispanic), 22 international. In 1997, 25 degrees awarded. *Degree requirements:* Thesis optional. *Entrance requirements:* GMAT. Application deadline: rolling. Application fee: $20. *Expenses:* Tuition $2140 per year full-time, $107 per semester hour part-time for state residents; $4280 per year full-time, $214 per semester hour part-time for nonresidents. Fees $30 per semester. *Financial aid:* Available to part-time students. Financial aid application deadline: 4/1. • Application contact: College of Graduate Studies and Continuing Education, 205-782-5329.

Jacksonville University, College of Business, Executive Masters in Business Administration Program, 2800 University Boulevard North, Jacksonville, FL 32211-3394. Awards Exec MBA. Part-time and evening/weekend programs available. *Entrance requirements:* TOEFL, 5 years of managerial or professional experience. Application deadline: 7/1 (priority date; rolling processing). Application fee: $50. *Faculty research:* Economic impact, vicarious learning, psychology and advertising.

Jacksonville University, College of Business, Master's in Business Administration Program, 2800 University Boulevard North, Jacksonville, FL 32211-3394. Awards MBA. Part-time and evening/weekend programs available. *Entrance requirements:* GMAT (minimum score 450; average 505), TOEFL (minimum score 550). Application deadline: 8/1 (rolling processing; 12/1 for spring admission). Application fee: $25.

James Madison University, College of Business, Program in Business Administration, Harrisonburg, VA 22807. Awards MBA. Part-time and evening/weekend programs available. Faculty: 14 full-time (3 women). Students: 18 full-time (5 women), 73 part-time (25 women); includes 2 minority (1 Hispanic, 1 Native American), 6 international. Average age 30. In 1997, 62 degrees awarded. *Entrance requirements:* GMAT. Application deadline: 7/1 (priority date; rolling processing). Application fee: $50. *Tuition:* $134 per credit hour for state residents; $404 per credit hour for nonresidents. *Financial aid:* In 1997–98, 2 teaching assistantships totaling $17,280, 8 assistantships totaling $68,103 were awarded; fellowships, Federal Work-Study also available. Financial aid application deadline: 2/15; applicants required to submit FAFSA. • Dr. Robert D. Reid, Dean, College of Business, 540-568-3252.

John Carroll University, School of Business, University Heights, OH 44118-4581. Awards MBA. Part-time and evening/weekend programs available. Faculty: 35 full-time (8 women), 3 part-time (1 woman). Students: 211 part-time (87 women); includes 6 minority (4 African Americans, 1 Asian American, 1 Hispanic), 3 international. Average age 30. 68 applicants, 81% accepted. In 1997, 51 degrees awarded (100% found work related to degree). *Average time to degree:* master's–3.8 years part-time. *Entrance requirements:* GMAT. Application deadline: 8/15 (priority date; rolling processing; 1/3 for spring admission). Application fee: $25 ($35 for international students). *Financial aid:* In 1997–98, 3 students received aid, including 3 research assistantships (1 to a first-year student). Financial aid application deadline: 3/1; applicants required to submit FAFSA. • Dr. James M. Daley, Associate Dean, 216-397-4391. E-mail: jdaley@jcvaxa.jcu.edu.

John F. Kennedy University, School of Management, Program in Business Administration, Orinda, CA 94563-2689. Offers business administration (MBA), organizational leadership (Certificate). Part-time and evening/weekend programs available. Students: 10 full-time (4 women), 64 part-time (37 women); includes 23 minority (12 African Americans, 3 Asian Americans, 7 Hispanics, 1 Native American). Average age 37. 18 applicants, 72% accepted. In 1997, 24 master's, 6 Certificates awarded. *Degree requirements:* For master's, thesis or alternative. *Entrance requirements:* For master's, TOEFL (minimum score 550), interview. Application deadline: rolling. Application fee: $50. *Expenses:* Tuition $316 per unit. Fees $9 per quarter. *Financial aid:* Application deadline 3/2. • Jeffrey Newcomb, Chair, 925-295-0600. Application contact: Ellena Bloedorn, Director of Admissions, 925-258-2213. Fax: 925-254-6964.

John F. Kennedy University, School of Management, Program in Management, Orinda, CA 94563-2689. Offers executive management (Certificate), management (MA). Part-time and evening/weekend programs available. Students: 37 full-time (24 women), 17 part-time (13 women); includes 12 minority (6 African Americans, 2 Asian Americans, 4 Hispanics). 14 applicants, 100% accepted. In 1997, 24 master's awarded. *Degree requirements:* For master's, thesis or alternative. *Entrance requirements:* For master's, TOEFL (minimum score 550), interview. Application deadline: rolling. Application fee: $50. *Expenses:* Tuition $1554 per course. Fees $9 per quarter. *Financial aid:* Application deadline 3/2. • Nancy Southern, Chair, 925-295-0600. Application contact: Ellena Bloedorn, Director of Admissions, 925-258-2213. Fax: 925-254-6964.

Johns Hopkins University, School of Continuing Studies, Division of Business and Management, Baltimore, MD 21218-2699. Offers programs in business (MS); change management (Certificate); information and telecommunication systems for business (MS, Certificate); investments (Certificate); leadership development for minority managers (Certificate); marketing (MS); nursing and business (MSN/MS); organizational development and human resources (MS); real estate (MS); skilled facilitator (Certificate); the business of medicine (Certificate); the business of nursing (Certificate); women, leadership, and change (Certificate). Part-time and evening/weekend programs available. Faculty: 12 full-time, 190 part-time. Students: 42 full-time (25 women), 2,452 part-time (1,189 women); includes 504 minority (338 African Americans, 112 Asian Americans, 52 Hispanics, 2 Native Americans), 14 international. Average age 35. 1,159 applicants, 90% accepted. In 1997, 590 master's, 64 Certificates awarded. *Degree requirements:* For master's, project required, foreign language and thesis not required. *Entrance requirements:* For master's, minimum GPA of 3.0. Application deadline: rolling. Application fee: $50. *Financial aid:* 459 students received aid; Federal Work-Study available. Aid available to part-time students. Financial aid application deadline: 7/1; applicants required to submit FAFSA. • Dr. Jon Heggan, Director, 410-516-0755. Application contact: Lenora Henry, Admissions Coordinator, 410-872-1234. Fax: 410-872-1251. E-mail: adv_mail@jhuvms.hcf.jhu.edu.

Johnson & Wales University, Graduate School, Program in Management, 8 Abbott Park Place, Providence, RI 02903-3703. Awards MBA. Part-time and evening/weekend programs available. Faculty: 5 full-time (2 women), 6 part-time (1 woman). Students: 95 full-time (41 women), 82 part-time (21 women); includes 9 minority (7 African Americans, 2 Hispanics), 53 international. Average age 25. 128 applicants, 68% accepted. In 1997, 70 degrees awarded. *Degree requirements:* Thesis optional. *Average time to degree:* master's–1.5 years full-time, 2.7 years part-time. *Entrance requirements:* Minimum GPA of 2.75. Application deadline: 8/21 (priority date; rolling processing). Application fee: $0. *Expenses:* Tuition $194 per quarter hour (minimum). Fees $477 per year. *Financial aid:* In 1997–98, 14 graduate assistantships (7 to first-year students) averaging $735 per month were awarded; partial tuition waivers also available. Aid available to part-time students. Financial aid application deadline: 5/1. *Faculty research:* Human resource management, marketing, organization. • Application contact: Dr. Allan G. Freedman, Director of Graduate Admissions, 401-598-1015. Fax: 401-598-4773. E-mail: clifb@jwu.edu.

Kansas State University, College of Business Administration, Department of Business Administration, Manhattan, KS 66506. Awards MBA. Faculty: 20 full-time (2 women). Students: 47 full-time (20 women), 22 part-time (11 women); includes 10 minority (1 African American, 7 Asian Americans, 2 Hispanics). Average age 28. 42 applicants, 62% accepted. In 1997, 31 degrees awarded. *Degree requirements:* Comprehensive exam required, foreign language not required. *Entrance requirements:* GMAT (minimum score 500; average 539), minimum undergraduate GPA of 3.0. Application deadline: 6/1 (rolling processing; 11/1 for spring admission). Application fee: $45. *Tuition:* $2218 per year full-time, $401 per semester (minimum) part-time for state residents; $6336 per year full-time, $1087 per semester (minimum) part-time for nonresidents. *Faculty research:* International marketing, finance management, MIS. • Cynthia S. McCahon, Director, 785-532-7190. Fax: 785-532-7216. E-mail: cmccahan@business.cba.ksu.edu.

Kansas Wesleyan University, Program in Business Administration, Salina, KS 67401-6196. Awards MBA. Part-time and evening/weekend programs available. Faculty: 5 full-time (2 women), 1 part-time (0 women). Students: 26 full-time (15 women), 15 part-time (9 women); includes 18 minority (17 Asian Americans, 1 Hispanic). Average age 36. 26 applicants, 77% accepted. In 1997, 5 degrees awarded. *Degree requirements:* Thesis or alternative required, foreign language not required. *Entrance requirements:* GMAT (minimum score 425), minimum graduate GPA of 3.0, or minimum undergraduate GPA of 3.25. Application deadline: 8/1 (priority date; rolling processing). Application fee: $30. *Tuition:* $340 per credit hour. *Financial aid:* 10 students received aid. Aid available to part-time students. Financial aid applicants required to submit FAFSA. • Dr. Carol Ahlvers, Director, 785-827-5541. E-mail: mba@diamond.kwu.edu. Application contact: Jeffery Miller, Director of Admissions, 785-827-5541 Ext. 1283. Fax: 785-827-0927.

Keller Graduate School of Management, 1 Tower Lane, Oak Brook Terrace, IL 60181. Offers programs in accounting and financial management (MAFM), business administration (MBA), human resources management (MHRM), information systems management (MISM), project management (MPM), telecommunications management (MTM). Part-time and evening/weekend programs available. Faculty: 604. Students: 3,856. *Degree requirements:* Business plan (MBA), Capstone Project (MHRM, MPM) required, foreign language and thesis not required. *Average time to degree:* master's–3 years part-time. *Entrance requirements:* GMAT, GRE General Test, or institutional assessment, interview. Application deadline: rolling. Application fee: $0. *Tuition:* $1235 per course. • Dr. Sherrill Hole, Director, Academic Affairs, 630-574-1894. Application contact: Michael J. Alexander, Director, Central Services, 630-574-1957. Fax: 630-574-1969.

Kennesaw State University, Michael J. Coles College of Business, Program in Business Administration, Kennesaw, GA 30144-5591. Offers accounting (M Acc, MBA), business administration (MBA, MBA-EP, MBA-PE), business information systems management (MBA), entrepreneurship (MBA), finance (MBA), human resources management and development (MBA), marketing (MBA). Part-time and evening/weekend programs available. Faculty: 54 full-time (18 women), 5 part-time (0 women). Students: 393 full-time (134 women), 400 part-time (163 women); includes 171 minority (113 African Americans, 35 Asian Americans, 22 Hispanics, 1 Native American), 57 international. Average age 34. 344 applicants, 69% accepted. In 1997, 221 degrees awarded. *Entrance requirements:* GMAT (minimum score 450) or GRE General Test (minimum combined score of 1350 on three sections), minimum GPA of 2.5, work experience. Application deadline: 7/1 (rolling processing; 2/20 for spring admission). Application fee: $20. *Expenses:* Tuition $2398 per year full-time, $83 per credit hour part-time for state residents; $8398 per year full-time, $333 per credit hour part-time for nonresidents. Fees $338 per year. *Financial aid:* Federal Work-Study available. Aid available to part-time students. Financial aid application deadline: 6/15; applicants required to submit FAFSA. • Dr. Rodney Alsup, Assistant Dean, 770-423-6087. Fax: 770-423-6141. E-mail: ralsup@ksumail.kennesaw.edu. Application contact: Susan N. Barrett, Administrative Specialist, Admissions, 770-423-6500. Fax: 770-423-6541. E-mail: sbarrett@ksumail.kennesaw.edu.

Kent State University, Graduate School of Management, Master's Program in Business Administration, Kent, OH 44242-0001. Awards MBA. Part-time and evening/weekend programs available. Faculty: 43 full-time (9 women), 3 part-time (0 women). Students: 139 full-time (52 women), 211 part-time (71 women); includes 23 minority (15 African Americans, 6 Asian Americans, 2 Hispanics), 32 international. Average age 29. 212 applicants, 69% accepted. In 1997, 73 degrees awarded. *Average time to degree:* master's–1.5 years full-time, 3.5 years part-time. *Entrance requirements:* GMAT (average 520), minimum GPA of 2.75. Application deadline: 7/1 (rolling processing; 12/15 for spring admission). Application fee: $30. *Tuition:* $4752 per year full-time, $216 per credit hour part-time for state residents; $9213 per year full-time, $419 per credit hour part-time for nonresidents. *Financial aid:* In 1997–98, 43 research assistantships (18 to first-year students) averaging $500 per month were awarded; Federal Work-Study, institutionally sponsored loans, and career-related internships or fieldwork also available. Financial aid application deadline: 4/1; applicants required to submit FAFSA. • Application contact: Louise M. Ditchey, Associate Director, 330-672-2282 Ext. 235. Fax: 330-672-7303. E-mail: gradbus@bsa3.kent.edu.

See in-depth description on page 219.

King's College, William G. McGowan School of Business, Wilkes-Barre, PA 18711-0801. Offers programs in finance (MS), including accounting/taxation, finance; health care administration (MS). Part-time and evening/weekend programs available. Faculty: 7 full-time (1 woman), 3 part-time (0 women). Students: 124 part-time (76 women); includes 4 minority (1 African American, 2 Asian Americans, 1 Native American), 2 international. Average age 35. 34 applicants, 97% accepted. In 1997, 26 degrees awarded. *Average time to degree:* master's–2.5 years part-time. *Entrance requirements:* GMAT. Application deadline: 7/31 (priority date; rolling processing; 12/1 for spring admission). Application fee: $35. *Tuition:* $460 per credit. • Dr. Edward J. Schoen, Dean, 717-208-5932. Fax: 717-826-5989. E-mail: ejschoen@rs01.kings.edu. Application contact: Dr. Elizabeth S. Lott, Director of Graduate Programs, 717-208-5991. Fax: 717-825-9049. E-mail: eslott@rs02.kings.edu.

Kutztown University of Pennsylvania, Graduate School, College of Business, Program in Business Administration, Kutztown, PA 19530. Awards MBA. Part-time and evening/weekend programs available. Faculty: 7 full-time (0 women). Students: 10 full-time (5 women), 46 part-time (16 women); includes 6 minority (2 African Americans, 3 Asian Americans, 1 Hispanic). Average age 33. In 1997, 16 degrees awarded. *Entrance requirements:* GMAT, TOEFL, TSE. Application deadline: 3/1 (8/1 for spring admission). Application fee: $25. *Tuition:* $4111 per year full-time, $225 per credit hour part-time for state residents; $6879 per year full-time, $393 per credit hour part-time for nonresidents. *Financial aid:* Graduate assistantships, partial tuition waivers, Federal Work-Study, and career-related internships or fieldwork available. Financial aid application deadline: 3/15; applicants required to submit FAFSA. • Theodore Hartz, Dean, College of Business, 610-683-4575. Fax: 610-683-4573. E-mail: hartz@kutztown.edu.

LaGrange College, Program in Business Administration, LaGrange, GA 30240-2999. Awards MBA. Part-time and evening/weekend programs available. Faculty: 2 full-time (0 women), 6 part-time (1 woman). Students: 10 full-time (1 woman), 22 part-time (6 women); includes 5 minority (all African Americans), 1 international. Average age 33. 6 applicants, 83% accepted. In 1997, 8 degrees awarded (100% found work related to degree). *Degree requirements:* Comprehensive exam. *Entrance requirements:* GMAT (minimum score 450), minimum GPA of 2.5. Application deadline: 8/1 (priority date; rolling processing). Application fee: $20 ($25 for international students). *Expenses:* Tuition $219 per quarter hour. Fees $80 per quarter hour. *Financial aid:* Fellowships, teaching assistantships, and career-related internships or fieldwork available. *Faculty research:* International marketing, small business management. • Dr. Jon Birkeli, Chairman, 706-812-7282. Application contact: Andy Geeter, Director of Admissions, 706-812-7260. Fax: 706-812-7348. E-mail: ageeter@mentor.lgc.peachnet.edu.

Lake Erie College, Division of Management Studies, Painesville, OH 44077-3389. Awards MBA. Part-time and evening/weekend programs available. Faculty: 7 full-time (2 women), 2 part-time (1 woman). Students: 84 part-time; includes 7 minority (all African Americans). Average age 35. 30 applicants, 83% accepted. In 1997, 18 degrees awarded (100% found work related to degree). *Average time to degree:* master's–3 years part-time. *Application deadline:* 8/1 (priority date; rolling processing; 12/15 for spring admission). *Application fee:* $20 ($50 for international students). *Expenses:* Tuition $391 per credit hour. Fees $20 per credit hour. *Financial aid:* Career-related internships or fieldwork available. Financial aid applicants required to submit FAFSA. *Faculty research:* Organizational effectiveness. • Dr. William Blanchard, Associate Dean, 440-639-7845. Application contact: Director of Admissions, 440-639-7879. Fax: 440-352-3533.

Lake Forest Graduate School of Management, Program at Chicago, 230 South LaSalle Street, Chicago, IL 60604-1413. Awards MBA. Part-time and evening/weekend programs available. Faculty: 139 part-time (21 women). Students: 86 part-time (31 women); includes 13 minority (10 African Americans, 1 Asian American, 2 Hispanics). Average age 32. 53 applicants, 72% accepted. In 1997, 16 degrees awarded (100% found work related to degree). *Degree requirements:* Minimum GPA of 2.7 required, foreign language and thesis not required. *Average time to degree:* master's–3.5 years part-time. *Entrance requirements:* GMAT or GRE, 4 years of work experience in field. Application deadline: 8/1 (priority date; rolling processing; 3/27 for spring admission). Application fee: $35. Electronic applications accepted. *Tuition:* $12,280 per year full-time, $6140 per year part-time. *Financial aid:* 16 students received aid. Aid available to part-time students. Financial aid applicants required to submit FAFSA. • John Popoli, Vice President and Academic Dean, 847-234-5005. Fax: 847-295-3656. E-mail: jpopoli@lfgsm.edu. Application contact: Steve Zimmerman, Director of Admissions, 312-435-5330. Fax: 312-435-5333. E-mail: admiss@lfgsm.edu.

Lake Forest Graduate School of Management, Program at Lake Forest, Lake Forest, IL 60045-2497. Awards MBA. Part-time and evening/weekend programs available. Faculty: 139 part-time (21 women). Students: 405 part-time (137 women); includes 44 minority (11 African Americans, 21 Asian Americans, 12 Hispanics). Average age 32. 131 applicants, 98% accepted.

Directory: Business Administration and Management—General

Lake Forest Graduate School of Management (continued)

In 1997, 123 degrees awarded (100% found work related to degree). *Degree requirements:* Minimum GPA of 2.7 required, foreign language and thesis not required. *Average time to degree:* master's–3.5 years part-time. *Entrance requirements:* GMAT or GRE, 4 years of work experience in field. Application deadline: 8/1 (priority date; rolling processing; 3/27 for spring admission). Application fee: $35. Electronic applications accepted. *Tuition:* $12,280 per year full-time, $6140 per year part-time. *Financial aid:* 52 students received aid. Aid available to part-time students. Financial aid applicants required to submit FAFSA. • John Popoli, Vice President and Academic Dean, 847-234-5005. E-mail: jpopoli@lfgsm.edu. Application contact: Carolyn S. Brune, Director of Admissions, 847-234-5080. Fax: 847-295-3656. E-mail: admiss@lfgsm.edu.

Lake Forest Graduate School of Management, Program at Schaumburg, 1295 East Algonquin Road, Schaumburg, IL 60196. Awards MBA. Part-time and evening/weekend programs available. Faculty: 139 part-time (21 women). Students: 239 part-time (77 women); includes 33 minority (6 African Americans, 18 Asian Americans, 9 Hispanics). Average age 32. 69 applicants, 86% accepted. In 1997, 62 degrees awarded (100% found work related to degree). *Degree requirements:* Minimum GPA of 2.7 required, foreign language and thesis not required. *Average time to degree:* master's–3.5 years part-time. *Entrance requirements:* GMAT or GRE, 4 years of work experience in field. Application deadline: 8/1 (priority date; rolling processing; 3/27 for spring admission). Application fee: $35. Electronic applications accepted. *Tuition:* $12,280 per year full-time, $6140 per year part-time. *Financial aid:* 21 students received aid. Aid available to part-time students. Financial aid applicants required to submit FAFSA. • John Popoli, Vice President and Academic Dean, 847-234-5005. Fax: 847-295-3656 Ext. IFGS. E-mail: jpopoli@lfgsm.edu. Application contact: Sheryle Dirks, Director of Admissions, 847-576-1212. Fax: 847-576-1213. E-mail: admiss@lfgsm.edu.

Lakeland College, Graduate Studies Division, Program in Business Administration, Sheboygan, WI 53082-0359. Awards MBA. *Entrance requirements:* GMAT (minimum score 450). Application deadline: rolling. Application fee: $25. *Tuition:* $230 per credit hour. • Application contact: Rebecca Hagan, Graduate Program Coordinator, 414-565-1256. Fax: 414-565-1206.

Lake Superior State University, Program in Business Administration, Sault Sainte Marie, MI 49783-1629. Awards MBA. Part-time and evening/weekend programs available. Postbaccalaureate distance learning degree programs offered (minimal on-campus study). Faculty: 35 (6 women). Students: 9 full-time (3 women), 96 part-time (44 women); includes 4 minority (1 Hispanic, 3 Native Americans), 22 international. Average age 34. 26 applicants, 69% accepted. In 1997, 36 degrees awarded. *Entrance requirements:* GMAT (minimum score 280), TOEFL. Application deadline: 8/1 (priority date; rolling processing). Application fee: $25. *Tuition:* $172 per credit hour. *Financial aid:* Career-related internships or fieldwork available. Aid available to part-time students. Financial aid application deadline: 4/1. • Ray Adams, Dean of College of Engineering, Mathematics,,and Business, 906-635-2207. Fax: 906-635-2111. Application contact: Kevin Pollock, Director of Admissions, 906-635-2231. Fax: 906-635-6669. E-mail: admissions@lakers.lssu.edu.

Lamar University, College of Business, Beaumont, TX 77710. Awards MBA. Part-time and evening/weekend programs available. Faculty: 22 full-time (3 women). Students: 18 full-time (8 women), 47 part-time (18 women); includes 14 minority (7 African Americans, 2 Asian Americans, 5 Hispanics), 12 international. Average age 32. 125 applicants, 60% accepted. In 1997, 26 degrees awarded. *Degree requirements:* Thesis optional, foreign language not required. *Average time to degree:* master's–1.5 years full-time, 4 years part-time. *Entrance requirements:* GMAT (minimum score 450; average 530), TOEFL. Application deadline: rolling. Application fee: $0. *Expenses:* Tuition $1296 per year full-time, $360 per year part-time for state residents; $6432 per year full-time, $1608 per year part-time for nonresidents. Fees $238 per year full-time, $103 per year part-time. *Financial aid:* In 1997–98, 12 students received aid, including 3 fellowships, 3 research assistantships, 6 scholarships; partial tuition waivers, Federal Work-Study, institutionally sponsored loans, and career-related internships or fieldwork also available. Aid available to part-time students. Financial aid application deadline: 4/1; applicants required to submit FAFSA. *Faculty research:* Marketing, accounting, management, finance, quantitative methods. Total annual research expenditures: $200,000. • Dr. Robert A. Swerdlow, Associate Dean, 409-880-8604. Fax: 409-880-8088. E-mail: swerdlowra@hal.lamar.edu.

La Salle University, Business Administration Program, 1900 West Olney Avenue, Philadelphia, PA 19141-1199. Awards MBA, Certificate, MSN/MBA. Part-time and evening/weekend programs available. Faculty: 44 full-time (10 women), 5 part-time (0 women). Students: 56 full-time (23 women), 647 part-time (265 women); includes 63 minority (42 African Americans, 14 Asian Americans, 7 Hispanics). Average age 32. 379 applicants, 70% accepted. In 1997, 140 master's awarded. *Average time to degree:* master's–1 year full-time, 4 years part-time. *Entrance requirements:* For master's, GMAT (average 480), TOEFL (minimum score 550); for Certificate, MBA. Application deadline: 8/30 (priority date; rolling processing; 1/10 for spring admission). Application fee: $30. Electronic applications accepted. *Financial aid:* In 1997–98, 10 students received aid, including 7 research assistantships totaling $5,400; career-related internships or fieldwork also available. Financial aid application deadline: 8/15. *Faculty research:* Small business development, unemployment insurance costs, nonprofit business, transfer pricing, forecasting. • Joseph Y. Ugras, Associate Dean, 215-951-1057. E-mail: ugras@lasalle.edu. Application contact: Brian W. Niles, Director of Marketing/Graduate Enrollment, 215-951-1057. Fax: 215-951-1886. E-mail: niles@lasalle.edu.

La Sierra University, School of Business and Management, Riverside, CA 92515-8247. Offers program in business administration and management (MBA). Faculty: 7 full-time (1 woman), 5 part-time (0 women). Students: 18 full-time (7 women), 3 part-time (all women); includes 19 minority (6 African Americans, 12 Asian Americans, 1 Hispanic). 42 applicants, 64% accepted. In 1997, 12 degrees awarded. *Degree requirements:* Research project required, foreign language and thesis not required. *Entrance requirements:* GMAT (minimum score 400), TOEFL (minimum score 550), minimum GPA of 3.0. Application deadline: 8/31 (priority date; rolling processing). Application fee: $30. Electronic applications accepted. *Financial aid:* 15 students received aid; partial tuition waivers, Federal Work-Study available. Financial aid application deadline: 6/15. • Dr. Henry E. Felder, Dean, 909-785-2064. Application contact: Myrna Costa-Casado, Director of Admissions, 909-785-2176. Fax: 909-785-2447. E-mail: mcosta@lasierra.edu.

Laurentian University, School of Commerce and Administration, Sudbury, ON P3E 2C6, Canada. Awards MBA. Part-time programs available. Faculty: 12 full-time (2 women), 1 part-time (0 women). Students: 11 full-time (8 women), 40 part-time (14 women); includes 1 international. 48 applicants, 33% accepted. In 1997, 12 degrees awarded. *Entrance requirements:* GMAT (minimum score 500), 2 years of work experience. Application deadline: 5/31 (priority date; 1/31 for spring admission). Application fee: $50. *Expenses:* Tuition $4977 per year full-time, $830 per course part-time for Canadian residents; $9072 per year full-time, $3024 per course part-time for nonresidents. Fees $194 per year full-time, $15 per year part-time. *Financial aid:* In 1997–98, 5 teaching assistantships (2 to first-year students) averaging $812 per month and totaling $32,500, scholarships totaling $12,691 were awarded; institutionally sponsored loans also available. *Faculty research:* Small business and entrepreneurship, business start-ups in Northern Ontario, emerging markets, service enterprises. • Dr. Huguette Blanco, Director, 705-675-1151 Ext. 2123. Application contact: Office of Admissions, 705-675-1151 Ext. 3917. Fax: 705-675-4843.

Lawrence Technological University, College of Management, 21000 West Ten Mile Road, Southfield, MI 48075-1058. Offers programs in business administration (MBA), industrial operations (MS), information systems (MS). Part-time and evening/weekend programs available. Faculty: 7 full-time (2 women), 22 part-time (5 women), 17 FTE. Students: 3 full-time (2 women), 459 part-time (165 women). Average age 32. 134 applicants, 82% accepted. In 1997, 121 degrees awarded. *Average time to degree:* master's–3 years part-time. *Entrance requirements:* GMAT. Application deadline: 8/1 (priority date; rolling processing; 1/1 for spring admission). Application fee: $50. Electronic applications accepted. *Expenses:* Tuition $11,400 per year full-time, $380 per credit hour part-time. Fees $100 per year. *Financial aid:* Institutionally sponsored loans available. Aid available to part-time students. Financial aid application deadline: 3/1. • Dr. Lou DeGennaro, Dean, 248-204-3050. E-mail: degennaro@ltu.edu. Application contact: Paul Kinder, Director of Admissions, 248-204-3160. Fax: 248-204-3188. E-mail: admissions@ltu.edu.

The Leadership Institute of Seattle, School of Applied Behavioral Science, Managing and Consulting Track, Bellevue, WA 98004-6934. Awards MAABS. Offered jointly with Bastyr University. Faculty: 4 full-time (2 women), 10 part-time (7 women). Students: 103 full-time (60 women), 69 part-time (25 women); includes 16 minority (10 African Americans, 2 Asian Americans, 1 Hispanic, 3 Native Americans), 16 international. Average age 40. *Degree requirements:* Thesis or alternative, oral exams required, foreign language not required. *Average time to degree:* master's–2 years full-time. *Application deadline:* 8/1 (priority date; rolling processing). *Application fee:* $65. *Tuition:* $359 per unit. *Financial aid:* Scholarships available. Financial aid applicants required to submit FAFSA. *Faculty research:* Cross-functional work teams, communication, management authority, employee influence, systems theory. • Dr. Jack Fontaine, Head, 425-635-1187. Application contact: Lynn Morrison, Admissions Director, 425-635-1187 Ext. 253. Fax: 425-635-1188.

Lebanon Valley College, MBA Program, Annville, PA 17003-0501. Awards MBA. Part-time and evening/weekend programs available. Faculty: 30. Students: 210 part-time; includes 15 minority (8 African Americans, 6 Asian Americans, 1 Hispanic). Average age 33. *Entrance requirements:* GMAT. Application deadline: rolling. Application fee: $25. *Tuition:* $277 per credit. • James W. Mentzer, Director, 717-867-6337. Application contact: Cheryl L. Batdorf, Academic Adviser, 717-867-6335. Fax: 717-867-6018.

Lehigh University, College of Business and Economics, Bethlehem, PA 18015-3094. Offers programs in business (MBA, MS, PhD), including business administration (MBA), business and economics (PhD), management of technology (MS); economics (MS, PhD). Part-time and evening/weekend programs available. Postbaccalaureate distance learning degree programs offered (minimal on-campus study). Faculty: 41 full-time (6 women), 10 part-time (0 women). Students: 65 full-time (27 women), 349 part-time (102 women); includes 4 minority (2 African Americans, 2 Asian Americans), 22 international. Average age 32. 268 applicants, 63% accepted. In 1997, 88 master's, 2 doctorates awarded. Terminal master's awarded for partial completion of doctoral program. *Degree requirements:* For doctorate, dissertation required, foreign language not required. *Average time to degree:* master's–1.5 years full-time, 3.5 years part-time; doctorate–3.5 years full-time. *Entrance requirements:* For master's, TOEFL (minimum score 570; average 616); for doctorate, GMAT or GRE, TOEFL (minimum score 570; average 604). Application deadline: 7/15 (rolling processing; 12/1 for spring admission). Application fee: $40. *Expenses:* Tuition $600 per credit. Fees $12 per semester full-time, $6 per semester part-time. *Financial aid:* In 1997–98, 72 students received aid, including 2 fellowships averaging $1,100 per month, 1 research assistantship, 24 teaching assistantships (7 to first-year students) averaging $1,200 per month; full and partial tuition waivers and career-related internships or fieldwork also available. Aid available to part-time students. Financial aid application deadline: 1/15. *Faculty research:* Public finance, energy, investments, activity-based costing, management information systems, supply chain management. • Patti Ota, Dean, 610-758-3402. Application contact: Deborah Gibbs, Coordinator, 610-758-4450. Fax: 610-758-5283.

Le Moyne College, Department of Business, Syracuse, NY 13214-1399. Awards MBA. Part-time and evening/weekend programs available. Faculty: 24 full-time (4 women), 5 part-time (2 women). Students: 10 full-time (2 women), 265 part-time (91 women); includes 12 minority (5 African Americans, 6 Asian Americans, 1 Hispanic), 1 international. Average age 37. 80 applicants, 50% accepted. In 1997, 100 degrees awarded. *Entrance requirements:* GMAT (average 510), interview, average GPA of 3.0. Application deadline: rolling. Application fee: $0. *Tuition:* $373 per credit hour. *Financial aid:* 15 students received aid; partial tuition waivers and career-related internships or fieldwork available. Aid available to part-time students. Financial aid applicants required to submit FAFSA. *Faculty research:* Fuzzy logic, neural network forecasting, international finance, not-for-profit marketing. • Dr. Wally Elmer, Director of MBA Program, 315-445-4786. Fax: 315-445-4787. E-mail: elmer@palm.lemoyne.edu.

Lenoir–Rhyne College, Division of Graduate Programs, Department of Business, Hickory, NC 28601. Awards MBA. Students: 3 full-time (1 woman), 15 part-time (8 women). *Degree requirements:* Thesis optional, foreign language not required. *Entrance requirements:* Minimum GPA of 2.7. Application deadline: 8/1 (12/1 for spring admission). Application fee: $25. *Tuition:* $210 per credit hour. • Dr. Robert Simmons, Chair, 828-328-7199.

Lesley College, School of Management, Cambridge, MA 02138-2790. Offers programs in fundraising management (MSM), health services management (MSM), human resources management (MSM), management (MSM), management of information technology (MSM), training and development (MS). Part-time and evening/weekend programs available. Postbaccalaureate distance learning degree programs offered (no on-campus study). Faculty: 10 full-time (4 women), 204 part-time (78 women). Students: 224 full-time, 283 part-time; includes 62 minority (35 African Americans, 16 Asian Americans, 10 Hispanics, 1 Native American), 5 international. Average age 38. In 1997, 282 degrees awarded. *Degree requirements:* Thesis (for some programs), internship required, foreign language not required. *Entrance requirements:* Minimum GPA of 2.5, 3 years of work experience. Application deadline: rolling. Application fee: $45. *Tuition:* $425 per credit. *Financial aid:* Graduate assistantships available. Aid available to part-time students. Financial aid application deadline: 5/1. *Faculty research:* Total quality management, diversity in the workplace, international management, technology. • Dr. Earl Potter, Dean, 617-349-8682. Fax: 617-349-8678. Application contact: Marilyn Gove, Associate Director, 617-349-8690. Fax: 617-349-8313. E-mail: mgove@mail.lesley.edu.

See in-depth description on page 221.

LeTourneau University, Program in Business Administration, Longview, TX 75607-7001. Awards MBA, MSM. Evening/weekend programs available. Faculty: 6 full-time (1 woman), 12 part-time. Students: 323 full-time; includes 79 minority (52 African Americans, 10 Asian Americans, 15 Hispanics, 2 Native Americans), 8 international. 587 applicants, 93% accepted. In 1997, 79 degrees awarded. *Average time to degree:* master's–2 years full-time. *Entrance requirements:* TOEFL (minimum score 600), minimum GPA of 2.8, 3 years of full-time work experience. Application deadline: rolling. Application fee: $50. • Dr. H. Glenn Sumrall, Vice President for Academic Affairs, 903-233-3200. Application contact: Dr. Don Connors, Associate Dean of Graduate, Adult and Continuing Studies, 903-233-3250. Fax: 903-233-3227.

Lewis University, College of Business, Romeoville, IL 60446. Awards MBA. Part-time and evening/weekend programs available. Faculty: 16 (3 women). Students: 6 full-time, 396 part-time; includes 44 minority (33 African Americans, 5 Asian Americans, 5 Hispanics, 1 Native American), 5 international. Average age 33. 142 applicants, 80% accepted. In 1997, 87 degrees awarded (100% found work related to degree). *Entrance requirements:* GMAT. Application deadline: 8/15 (priority date; rolling processing). Application fee: $35. *Financial aid:* Available to part-time students. • Suzanne Benson, Executive Director of Graduate School of Management, 800-897-9000. Fax: 815-838-3330.

Lincoln Memorial University, Program in Business Administration, Cumberland Gap Parkway, Harrogate, TN 37752-1901. Awards MBA. Part-time and evening/weekend programs available. Faculty: 4 full-time (0 women), 1 (woman) part-time. Students: 12 full-time (5 women), 49 part-time (21 women); includes 1 international. Average age 27. 68 applicants, 31% accepted. In 1997, 15 degrees awarded (100% found work related to degree). *Degree requirements:* Comprehensive exam required, thesis optional, foreign language not required. *Average time to degree:* master's–1.5 years full-time, 2 years part-time. *Entrance requirements:* GMAT, minimum GPA of 2.5 in business, 3.0 overall, interview, sample of written work. Application deadline:

8/10 (priority date; rolling processing). Application fee: $25. *Expenses:* Tuition $7800 per year full-time, $210 per semester hour part-time. Fees $300 per year full-time, $100 per year part-time. *Financial aid:* In 1997–98, 10 students received aid, including 1 graduate assistantship (to a first-year student); career-related internships or fieldwork also available. Aid available to part-time students. Financial aid application deadline: 4/1; applicants required to submit FAFSA. • Chet Brisley, Dean, 423-869-6348. Fax: 423-869-6406. Application contact: Barbara McCune, Senior Assistant, Graduate Office, 423-869-6374. Fax: 423-869-6261.

Lincoln University, Business Administration Program, 281 Masonic Avenue, San Francisco, CA 94118-4498. Awards MBA. Faculty: 6 full-time (1 woman), 6 part-time (1 woman), 9 FTE. Students: 137 full-time (60 women); includes 2 minority (1 Asian American, 1 Hispanic), 135 international. Average age 27. 60 applicants, 97% accepted. In 1997, 98 degrees awarded (100% found work related to degree). *Degree requirements:* Thesis required, foreign language not required. *Average time to degree:* master's–2 years full-time. *Entrance requirements:* Minimum GPA of 2.7. Application deadline: 8/31 (priority date; rolling processing; 1/10 for spring admission). Application fee: $50. Electronic applications accepted. *Financial aid:* Tuition scholarships and career-related internships or fieldwork available. • Dr. Clarence W. Rippel, President, 415-221-1212. Application contact: Dr. Pete Bogue, Director of Admissions/Registrar, 415-221-1212. Fax: 415-387-9730. E-mail: luadm@best.com.

Lincoln University, Graduate School, College of Business, Jefferson City, MO 65102. Awards MBA. Part-time and evening/weekend programs available. Faculty: 5 part-time (0 women). Students: 14 full-time (7 women), 21 part-time (10 women). Average age 33. In 1997, 15 degrees awarded. *Entrance requirements:* GMAT, minimum GPA of 2.75 in major, 2.5 overall. Application deadline: 7/25 (priority date; rolling processing; 12/15 for spring admission). Application fee: $17. *Expenses:* Tuition $117 per credit hour for state residents; $234 per credit hour for nonresidents. Fees $552 per year (minimum) for state residents; $1104 per year (minimum) for nonresidents. *Financial aid:* Fellowships available. • Wayne Linhardt, Interim Dean, College of Business, 573-681-5489.

Lindenwood University, Department of Business Administration, St. Charles, MO 63301-1695. Awards MBA, MS. Part-time programs available. Faculty: 9 full-time (1 woman), 6 part-time (2 women). Students: 66 full-time (37 women), 279 part-time (139 women); includes 57 minority (35 African Americans, 12 Asian Americans, 5 Hispanics, 5 Native Americans), 40 international. Average age 36. *Degree requirements:* Thesis required (for some programs), foreign language not required. *Entrance requirements:* Interview, minimum GPA of 3.0, sample of written work. Application deadline: 6/30 (rolling processing; 11/30 for spring admission). Application fee: $25. Electronic applications accepted. *Tuition:* $5880 per year full-time, $245 per credit hour part-time. *Financial aid:* Partial tuition waivers, Federal Work-Study, institutionally sponsored loans, and career-related internships or fieldwork available. Financial aid application deadline: 6/30. • Nancy Matheny, Dean, 314-949-4907. Application contact: John Guffey, Director of Graduate Admissions, 314-949-4933. Fax: 314-949-4910.

Lindenwood University, Programs in Individualized Education, St. Charles, MO 63301-1695. Offerings include administration (MSA), business administration (MBA), management (MSA). Faculty: 10 full-time (7 women), 23 part-time (6 women). *Application deadline:* 6/30 (priority date; rolling processing; 12/1 for spring admission). *Application fee:* $25. *Tuition:* $5880 per year full-time, $245 per credit hour part-time. • Dr. Dan Kemper, Dean, 314-916-9125. Application contact: John Guffey, Director of Graduate Admissions, 314-949-4933. Fax: 314-949-4910.

Long Island University, Brooklyn Campus, School of Business and Public Administration, Program in Business Administration, Brooklyn, NY 11201-8423. Awards MBA. Part-time and evening/weekend programs available. Faculty: 11 full-time (2 women), 20 part-time. Students: 64 full-time (29 women), 99 part-time (57 women); includes 125 minority (84 African Americans, 26 Asian Americans, 14 Hispanics, 1 Native American). 145 applicants, 66% accepted. In 1997, 45 degrees awarded. *Entrance requirements:* GMAT or GRE General Test. Application deadline: rolling. Application fee: $30. Electronic applications accepted. *Expenses:* Tuition $480 per credit. Fees $415 per year full-time, $73 per semester (minimum) part-time. • Harry Stucke, Chair, 718-488-1070. Application contact: Bernard W. Sullivan, Associate Director of Admissions, 718-488-1011.

Long Island University, C.W. Post Campus, College of Management, School of Business, Brookville, NY 11548-1300. Awards MBA, CAS, JD/MBA. Part-time and evening/weekend programs available. Faculty: 26 full-time (5 women), 35 part-time (7 women). Students: 210 full-time (83 women), 486 part-time (210 women). Average age 28. 239 applicants, 70% accepted. In 1997, 187 master's, 4 CASs awarded. *Entrance requirements:* For master's, GMAT. Application deadline: 8/15 (priority date; rolling processing; 12/15 for spring admission). Application fee: $30. Electronic applications accepted. *Expenses:* Tuition $480 per credit. Fees $316 per year full-time, $71 per semester (minimum) part-time. *Financial aid:* Fellowships, research assistantships, graduate assistantships, partial tuition waivers available. Aid available to part-time students. Financial aid application deadline: 5/15; applicants required to submit FAFSA. • Mary K. Dillon, Coordinator, 516-299-2722. Fax: 516-299-3131. E-mail: mdillon@hornet.liunet.edu. Application contact: Sally Luzader, Associate Director of Graduate Admissions, 516-299-2417. Fax: 516-299-2137. E-mail: admissions@collegehall.liunet.edu.

Announcement: The College of Management at the C.W. Post Campus of Long Island University offers full- and part-time programs. MBA degrees are awarded in business administration with concentrations in finance, general business, international business, management, management information systems, and marketing. MPA degrees are awarded in public administration and health-care administration. Dual JD/MPA and JD/MBA degrees are offered with Touro Law Center. MS degrees are awarded in criminal justice with concentrations in planning and management, prevention and treatment, and security administration. MS degrees are also awarded in accounting, strategic management accounting, and taxation. Advanced certificates are offered in international accounting and taxation, business, and gerontology. Other continuing studies programs include fraud examination, accounting, taxation, taxation employee benefits, and strategic management accounting. Contact 516-299-3017 (telephone), jwolf@titan.liu.edu (e-mail), or http://www.liu.edu/com.htm (World Wide Web).

Louisiana State University and Agricultural and Mechanical College, College of Business Administration, Baton Rouge, LA 70803. Awards MBA, MPA, MS, PhD, JD/MPA. Part-time and evening/weekend programs available. Faculty: 108 full-time, 2 part-time. Students: 400 full-time (160 women), 246 part-time (105 women); includes 85 minority (54 African Americans, 18 Asian Americans, 10 Hispanics, 3 Native Americans), 112 international. Average age 29. 646 applicants, 43% accepted. In 1997, 208 master's, 10 doctorates awarded. Terminal master's awarded for partial completion of doctoral program. *Degree requirements:* For doctorate, dissertation required, foreign language not required. *Application deadline:* 1/25 (priority date; rolling processing). *Application fee:* $25. *Tuition:* $2736 per year full-time, $285 per semester (minimum) part-time for state residents; $6636 per year full-time, $460 per semester (minimum) part-time for nonresidents. *Financial aid:* In 1997–98, 2 fellowships, 45 research assistantships (10 to first-year students), 23 teaching assistantships, 69 service assistantships (14 to first-year students) were awarded; Federal Work-Study, institutionally sponsored loans, and career-related internships or fieldwork also available. • Dr. Thomas D. Clark Jr., Dean, 504-388-5297. Application contact: Dr. Kathleen Bosworth, Graduate Adviser, 504-388-8867.

Louisiana State University in Shreveport, College of Business Administration, Shreveport, LA 71115-2399. Awards MBA. Part-time and evening/weekend programs available. Faculty: 18 full-time (4 women). Students: 3 full-time (2 women), 117 part-time (63 women); includes 18 minority (15 African Americans, 3 Asian Americans), 2 international. Average age 30. 62 applicants, 81% accepted. In 1997, 26 degrees awarded (100% found work related to degree). *Average time to degree:* master's–1.5 years full-time, 3 years part-time. *Entrance requirements:* GMAT (average 480). Application deadline: 7/15 (rolling processing; 12/15 for spring admission). Application fee: $10 ($20 for international students). *Financial aid:* In 1997–98, 25 students received aid, including 1 research assistantship (to a first-year student) averaging $480 per month and totaling $4,320; career-related internships or fieldwork also available. Aid available to part-time students. Financial aid application deadline: 6/15. *Faculty research:* Total quality management, real estate, organizational behavior, finance, operations research, communication. • Dr. Charlotte Jones, Interim Dean, 318-797-5383. E-mail: cjones@pilot.lsus.edu. Application contact: Dr. Lorraine Krajewski, Director, 318-797-5276. Fax: 318-797-5208. E-mail: lkrajews@pilot.lsus.edu.

Louisiana Tech University, College of Administration and Business, Ruston, LA 71272. Awards MBA, MPA, DBA. Part-time programs available. Faculty: 39 full-time (3 women). Students: 113 full-time (39 women), 63 part-time (18 women); includes 7 minority (5 African Americans, 1 Asian American, 1 Hispanic), 42 international. Average age 27. In 1997, 65 master's, 11 doctorates awarded. *Degree requirements:* For master's, computer language required, foreign language and thesis not required; for doctorate, computer language, dissertation required, foreign language not required. *Entrance requirements:* GMAT. Application deadline: 7/29 (2/3 for spring admission). Application fee: $20 ($30 for international students). *Tuition:* $2382 per year full-time, $223 per quarter (minimum) part-time for state residents; $5307 per year full-time, $223 per quarter (minimum) part-time for nonresidents. *Financial aid:* Fellowships, research assistantships, teaching assistantships available. • Dr. Anthony Inman, Interim Graduate Director, 318-257-4528.

Loyola College, Sellinger School of Business and Management, Program in Executive Business Administration, Baltimore, MD 21210-2699. Awards MBA, XMBA. Part-time and evening/weekend programs available. Students: 178 full-time (53 women); includes 19 minority (11 African Americans, 5 Asian Americans, 2 Hispanics, 1 Native American), 4 international. 101 applicants, 77% accepted. In 1997, 61 degrees awarded. *Entrance requirements:* GMAT, TOEFL. Application fee: $35. *Tuition:* $19,950 per year. • John Moran, Associate Dean, 410-617-2457.

See in-depth description on page 223.

Loyola College, Sellinger School of Business and Management, Programs in Business Administration, Baltimore, MD 21210-2699. Offerings in decision sciences (MBA), economics (MBA), finance (MBA), international business (MIB), marketing/management (MBA). Part-time and evening/weekend programs available. Students: 36 full-time (15 women), 722 part-time (277 women); includes 58 minority (24 African Americans, 25 Asian Americans, 9 Hispanics), 27 international. In 1997, 215 degrees awarded. *Entrance requirements:* GMAT, TOEFL. Application deadline: 7/20 (11/20 for spring admission). Application fee: $35. *Tuition:* $365 per credit. • Dr. Peter Lorenzi, Dean, Sellinger School of Business and Management, 410-617-2301.

See in-depth description on page 223.

Loyola Marymount University, College of Business Administration, Los Angeles, CA 90045-8350. Awards MBA, JD/MBA. Part-time and evening/weekend programs available. Faculty: 43 full-time (6 women), 30 part-time (4 women). Students: 340 full-time (159 women), 121 part-time (51 women); includes 128 minority (16 African Americans, 71 Asian Americans, 38 Hispanics, 3 Native Americans), 48 international. 397 applicants, 62% accepted. In 1997, 118 degrees awarded. *Degree requirements:* Thesis required (for some programs), foreign language not required. *Entrance requirements:* GMAT, TOEFL (minimum score 600), minimum AACSB index of 1125. Application fee: $35. Electronic applications accepted. *Expenses:* Tuition $620 per unit. Fees $211 per year full-time, $128 per year part-time. *Financial aid:* In 1997–98, 140 students received aid, including 3 fellowships (1 to a first-year student) totaling $19,798, 18 research assistantships (6 to first-year students) totaling $73,211, 27 grants, scholarships (15 to first-year students) totaling $38,054; Federal Work-Study also available. Aid available to part-time students. Financial aid application deadline: 3/2; applicants required to submit FAFSA. *Faculty research:* International management, business ethics, strategy implementation. • Dr. John T. Wholihan, Dean, 310-338-2731. Application contact: Dr. Rachelle Katz, Associate Dean and Director of MBA Program, 310-338-2848.

See in-depth description on page 225.

Loyola University Chicago, Graduate School of Business, 820 North Michigan Avenue, Chicago, IL 60611-2196. Awards MBA, MS, JD/MBA, MSN/MBA. Programs in accountancy (MS), business administration (MBA), information systems management (MS). Part-time and evening/weekend programs available. Faculty: 68 full-time (9 women), 3 part-time (1 woman). Students: 224 full-time (99 women), 740 part-time (329 women); includes 133 minority (39 African Americans, 60 Asian Americans, 34 Hispanics), 161 international. Average age 26. 578 applicants, 60% accepted. In 1997, 328 degrees awarded. *Average time to degree:* master's–1.2 years full-time, 4 years part-time. *Entrance requirements:* GMAT, TOEFL. Application deadline: 6/31 (rolling processing; 11/30 for spring admission). Application fee: $35. *Tuition:* $1985 per course. *Financial aid:* Research assistantships, Federal Work-Study, institutionally sponsored loans, and career-related internships or fieldwork available. Aid available to part-time students. Financial aid application deadline: 4/15; applicants required to submit FAFSA. *Faculty research:* Financial markets, strategic planning, production management, marketing research, futures and options. • Paul Davidovitch, Director, MBA Program, 312-915-6120. Application contact: Carmen Santiago, Admissions Coordinator, 312-915-6120.

See in-depth description on page 227.

Loyola University New Orleans, Joseph A. Butt, S.J., College of Business Administration, Program in Business Administration, New Orleans, LA 70118-6195. Awards MBA, JD/MBA. Part-time and evening/weekend programs available. Postbaccalaureate distance learning degree programs offered. Faculty: 16 full-time (6 women), 2 part-time (0 women). Students: 24 full-time (10 women), 64 part-time (23 women). Average age 30. 66 applicants, 48% accepted. In 1997, 59 degrees awarded. *Entrance requirements:* GMAT, TOEFL (minimum score 580), minimum GPA of 3.0, resumé. Application deadline: 6/15 (priority date; rolling processing; 11/30 for spring admission). Application fee: $20. *Expenses:* Tuition $450 per credit hour. Fees $556 per year full-time, $164 per year part-time. *Financial aid:* 35 students received aid; research assistantships, Federal Work-Study, and career-related internships or fieldwork available. Aid available to part-time students. Financial aid application deadline: 5/1; applicants required to submit FAFSA. *Faculty research:* Environment, ethics, international business. Total annual research expenditures: $150,000. • Application contact: Dr. Pam Van Epps, Graduate Coordinator, 504-865-3477. Fax: 504-865-3496. E-mail: vanepps@loyno.edu.

Lynchburg College, School of Business, Lynchburg, VA 24501-3199. Offers programs in administration (M Ad), including industrial management, personnel management; business (MBA). Evening/weekend programs available. *Entrance requirements:* GMAT (minimum score 450) or GRE General Test (minimum score 450 on each section, 1350 on three sections), GRE Subject Test. Application fee: $20.

Lynn University, School of Graduate Studies, School of Business, Boca Raton, FL 33431-5598. Offers program in international management (MBA). Part-time and evening/weekend programs available. Faculty: 5 full-time (0 women), 2 part-time (1 woman). Students: 29 full-time (16 women), 21 part-time (11 women); includes 6 international. 53 applicants, 74% accepted. In 1997, 5 degrees awarded. *Average time to degree:* master's–1.9 years full-time, 2.8 years part-time. *Entrance requirements:* GMAT (minimum score 400 required, 4.0 on written portion), minimum undergraduate GPA of 3.0. Application deadline: rolling. Application fee: $50. Electronic applications accepted. *Expenses:* Tuition $375 per credit hour. Fees $60 per year. *Financial aid:* In 1997–98, 18 students received aid, including 3 graduate assistantships (all to first-year students); partial tuition waivers and career-related internships or fieldwork also available. Financial aid application deadline: 6/15; applicants required to submit FAFSA. *Faculty research:* Total quality management, international capital markets, motivation, entrepreneurship. • Dr. James P. Miller, Dean, 561-994-0770 Ext. 250. Application contact: Peter Gallo, Graduate Admissions Counselor, 800-544-8035. Fax: 561-241-3552. E-mail: admission@lynn.edu.

Directory: Business Administration and Management—General

Madonna University, Program in Business Administration, Livonia, MI 48150-1173. Awards MSBA, MSN/MSBA. Offerings include international business (MSBA), leadership studies (MSBA), quality and operations management (MSBA). Part-time and evening/weekend programs available. Postbaccalaureate distance learning degree programs offered (minimal on-campus study). Faculty: 8 full-time (2 women), 13 part-time (2 women). Students: 54 full-time (25 women), 164 part-time (92 women). In 1997, 39 degrees awarded (100% found work related to degree). *Degree requirements:* Thesis required (for some programs), foreign language not required. *Entrance requirements:* GMAT, GRE General Test, minimum GPA of 3.0. Application deadline: 8/1 (priority date; rolling processing; 4/1 for spring admission). *Expenses:* Tuition $260 per credit hour (minimum). Fees $50 per semester. *Financial aid:* Career-related internships or fieldwork available. *Faculty research:* Management, women in management, future studies. • Dr. Stuart Arends, Dean of Business School, 734-432-5366. Fax: 734-432-5364. E-mail: arends@smtp.munet.edu. Application contact: Sandra Kellums, Coordinator of Graduate Admissions, 734-432-5666. Fax: 734-432-5393. E-mail: kellums@smtp.munet.edu.

Maharishi University of Management, Program in Business Administration, Fairfield, IA 52557. Awards MBA, PhD. Evening/weekend programs available. Faculty: 30 (5 women). Students: 49 full-time (18 women), 10 part-time (1 woman); includes 3 minority (2 Hispanics, 1 Native American), 39 international. Average age 25. In 1997, 17 master's awarded. *Degree requirements:* For doctorate, dissertation. *Entrance requirements:* For master's, GMAT, TOEFL (minimum score 600), minimum GPA of 3.0; for doctorate, minimum GPA of 3.0. Application deadline: 4/15 (priority date; rolling processing). Application fee: $40. *Financial aid:* Full and partial tuition waivers, Federal Work-Study, and career-related internships or fieldwork available. Financial aid application deadline: 4/30. *Faculty research:* Leadership, effects of the group dynamics of consciousness on the economy, innovation, employee development, cooperative strategy. • Dr. Robert Stowe, Director, 515-472-1191. Application contact: Harry Bright, Director of Admissions, 515-472-1166.

Malone College, Graduate School, Program in Business, Canton, OH 44709-3897. Awards MBA. Part-time and evening/weekend programs available. Faculty: 9 full-time (1 woman), 3 part-time (2 women), 9.78 FTE. Students: 84 part-time (37 women); includes 3 minority (2 African Americans, 1 Native American). Average age 38. 100 applicants, 100% accepted. In 1997, 15 degrees awarded. *Entrance requirements:* GMAT, minimum GPA of 2.5. Application deadline: 8/20 (priority date; rolling processing; 12/20 for spring admission). Application fee: $20. *Tuition:* $334 per credit hour. *Financial aid:* 25 students received aid. Financial aid application deadline: 6/30; applicants required to submit FAFSA. *Faculty research:* Leadership and decision-making, diversified information systems portfolios, operations management: scheduling and routing. • Dr. John P. Harris II, Acting Director, 330-471-8247. Fax: 330-471-8478. E-mail: jharris@malone.edu. Application contact: Dan Depasquale, Director of Graduate Student Services, 800-257-4723. Fax: 330-471-8343. E-mail: depasquale@malone.edu.

Manhattan College, Program in Business Administration, Riverdale, NY 10471. Offers accounting (MBA), finance (MBA), international business (MBA), management (MBA), management information systems (MBA), marketing (MBA). Part-time and evening/weekend programs available. Faculty: 18 full-time (3 women), 8 part-time (0 women). Students: 200. Average age 30. 88 applicants, 83% accepted. In 1997, 40 degrees awarded. *Degree requirements:* Computer language, thesis or alternative. *Entrance requirements:* GMAT, minimum GPA of 2.8. Application deadline: 8/10 (priority date; rolling processing; 1/7 for spring admission). Application fee: $50. *Expenses:* Tuition $440 per credit. Fees $100 per year. *Financial aid:* In 1997–98, 4 scholarships (2 to first-year students) were awarded. Financial aid application deadline: 2/1. • Dr. Charles E. Brunner, Director, 718-862-7222. Fax: 718-862-8023. Application contact: William J. Bisset Jr., Dean of Admissions/Financial Aid, 718-862-7200. Fax: 718-863-8019. E-mail: admit@manhattan.edu.

Announcement: The MBA program at Manhattan College is aimed at working professionals. Courses are offered on Saturdays and weekday evenings. The program is composed of 6 prerequisite courses (18 credits) and 13 graduate courses (39 credits). Concentrations are available in finance, international business, management, and marketing. The program has 200 students. Typical students complete the program in 2–3 years by taking 1 or 2 courses per semester and during summer session. Work experience together with GMAT scores and undergraduate index are criteria for acceptance to the program. See in-depth description in Book 1 of this series. For further information, contact the MBA Program Office at 718-862-7222.

Mankato State University, College of Business, Program in Business Administration, South Rd and Ellis Ave, PO Box 8400, Mankato, MN 56002-8400. Awards MBA. Program being phased out; applicants no longer accepted. Part-time and evening/weekend programs available. Students: 28 full-time (8 women), 16 part-time (8 women); includes 3 minority (all Asian Americans), 6 international. Average age 32. 25 applicants, 28% accepted. In 1997, 32 degrees awarded. *Degree requirements:* Computer language, thesis or alternative, comprehensive exam required, foreign language not required. *Tuition:* $126 per credit (minimum) for state residents; $200 per credit for nonresidents. *Financial aid:* Research assistantships, teaching assistantships, Federal Work-Study, institutionally sponsored loans, and career-related internships or fieldwork available. Aid available to part-time students. Financial aid applicants required to submit FAFSA. • Dr. Gayle Stelter, Graduate Coordinator, 507-389-5426. Application contact: Joni Roberts, Admissions Coordinator, 507-389-2321. Fax: 507-389-5974. E-mail: grad@mankato.msus.edu.

Marian College of Fond du Lac, Business Division, 45 South National Avenue, Fond du Lac, WI 54935-4699. Offers program in organizational leadership and quality (MS). Part-time and evening/weekend programs available. Postbaccalaureate distance learning degree programs offered (no on-campus study). Faculty: 3 full-time (0 women), 15 part-time (3 women). Students: 77 part-time (37 women); includes 5 minority (1 African American, 4 Hispanics), 1 international. Average age 40. 40 applicants, 80% accepted. In 1997, 32 degrees awarded (100% found work related to degree). *Degree requirements:* Comprehensive group project required, foreign language and thesis not required. *Average time to degree:* master's–1.6 years part-time. *Entrance requirements:* 3 years of managerial experience. Application deadline: rolling. Application fee: $25. *Tuition:* $275 per credit hour. *Financial aid:* Institutionally sponsored loans available. Aid available to part-time students. Financial aid applicants required to submit FAFSA. *Faculty research:* Organizational values, statistical decision making, learning organization, quality planning, customer research. • Richard M. Dienesch, Assistant Dean of Evening/Weekend Programs, 920-923-8125. Fax: 920-923-7167.

Marist College, School of Management, Business Administration Program, 290 North Road, Poughkeepsie, NY 12601-1387. Awards MBA, PGC. Part-time and evening/weekend programs available. Faculty: 10 full-time (2 women), 3 part-time (0 women). Students: 4 full-time (2 women), 103 part-time (43 women). Average age 29. 60 applicants, 47% accepted. In 1997, 20 master's awarded (100% found work related to degree). *Entrance requirements:* For master's, GMAT. Application deadline: 8/1 (priority date; rolling processing; 12/15 for spring admission). Application fee: $30. *Expenses:* Tuition $419 per credit hour. Fees $50 per year (minimum). *Financial aid:* Partial tuition waivers, Federal Work-Study available. Aid available to part-time students. Financial aid application deadline: 8/15; applicants required to submit FAFSA. *Faculty research:* International trade law, process management, AIDS and the medical provider, mid-Hudson region economics, time quality management and organizational behavior. • Gregory Tully, Director, 914-575-3225. Application contact: Dr. H. Griffin Walling, Dean of Graduate and Continuing Education, 914-575-3530. Fax: 914-575-3640.

Announcement: The capable full-time faculty members and rigorous curriculum that distinguish Marist's weeknight MBA program are now available on the Internet. The 8-week online course schedule allows students the flexibility to take classes at their convenience. Emphases are available in accounting, finance, health services administration, human resources, and information systems. For more detailed information, refer to *Peterson's Guide to MBA Programs.*

Marquette University, College of Business Administration, Program in Business Administration, Milwaukee, WI 53201-1881. Awards MBA, JD/MBA. Part-time and evening/weekend programs available. Faculty: 42 full-time (7 women), 3 part-time (0 women). Students: 46 full-time (15 women), 467 part-time (140 women); includes 32 international. Average age 29. 231 applicants, 88% accepted. In 1997, 131 degrees awarded. *Entrance requirements:* GMAT, TOEFL (minimum score 550). Application fee: $40. *Tuition:* $510 per credit. *Financial aid:* In 1997–98, 4 research assistantships (1 to a first-year student), 13 teaching assistantships (3 to first-year students) were awarded; scholarships, full and partial tuition waivers, Federal Work-Study, institutionally sponsored loans also available. Aid available to part-time students. Financial aid application deadline: 2/15. *Faculty research:* Ethics in the professions, services marketing, technology impact on decision making, mentoring. Total annual research expenditures: $167,999. • Joseph P. Fox, Director of Graduate Programs, 414-288-7145. Fax: 414-288-1660.

Marshall University, College of Business, Huntington, WV 25755-2020. Awards MBA. Evening/weekend programs available. Faculty: 31 (7 women). Students: 29 full-time (10 women), 84 part-time (30 women); includes 4 minority (2 African Americans, 2 Asian Americans), 4 international. In 1997, 47 degrees awarded. *Degree requirements:* Thesis optional. *Entrance requirements:* GMAT. *Tuition:* $2364 per year full-time, $132 per hour part-time for state residents; $6894 per year full-time, $383 per hour part-time for nonresidents. • Dr. Calvin Kent, Dean, 304-696-2315. Application contact: Dr. James Harless, Director of Admissions, 304-696-3160.

Marshall University, Graduate School of Management, South Charleston, WV 25303-1600. Awards MBA, MSIR, MSM. Part-time and evening/weekend programs available. Faculty: 8 full-time (0 women), 2 part-time (0 women). Students: 25 full-time (13 women), 238 part-time (130 women); includes 21 minority (14 African Americans, 5 Asian Americans, 1 Hispanic, 1 Native American). Average age 35. In 1997, 70 degrees awarded. *Degree requirements:* Comprehensive exam required, foreign language and thesis not required. *Entrance requirements:* GMAT (minimum score 450) or GRE General Test (minimum combined score of 1000), minimum GPA of 2.5. Application deadline: 8/1 (priority date; rolling processing). Application fee: $0. *Financial aid:* Full tuition waivers and career-related internships or fieldwork available. Aid available to part-time students. Financial aid applicants required to submit FAFSA. • Dr. Kurt Olmosk, Associate Dean, 304-746-1958. Fax: 304-746-2503.

Marylhurst University, Graduate Program in Management, Marylhurst, OR 97036-0261. Awards MBA, MS. Part-time and evening/weekend programs available. Postbaccalaureate distance learning degree programs offered (minimal on-campus study). Faculty: 29 part-time (6 women). Students: 10 full-time (5 women), 120 part-time (64 women). In 1997, 35 degrees awarded (100% found work related to degree). *Degree requirements:* Thesis or alternative. *Average time to degree:* master's–3 years part-time. *Entrance requirements:* GMAT. Application deadline: 8/15 (priority date; rolling processing; 3/1 for spring admission). Application fee: $80. *Financial aid:* Federal Work-Study available. Aid available to part-time students. • Application contact: Dorothy Deline, Assistant to Graduate Director, 503-699-6246 Ext. 3397. E-mail: ddeline@marylhurst.edu.

Marymount University, School of Business Administration, Program in Business Administration, Arlington, VA 22207-4299. Awards MBA. Part-time and evening/weekend programs available. Students: 325. In 1997, 98 degrees awarded. *Degree requirements:* Thesis optional, foreign language not required. *Entrance requirements:* GMAT, interview. Application deadline: rolling. Application fee: $35. *Expenses:* Tuition $465 per credit hour. Fees $120 per year full-time, $5 per credit hour part-time. *Financial aid:* Career-related internships or fieldwork available. Aid available to part-time students. Financial aid applicants required to submit FAFSA. • Dr. Art Meiners, Associate Dean, 703-284-5910. Fax: 703-527-3815. E-mail: art.meiners@marymount.edu.

Announcement: Marymount is a comprehensive Catholic university offering 23 graduate degree programs, including a Master of Business Administration; Master of Science programs in computer science, health care management, health promotion management, information management, organizational leadership and innovation, and a full-time physical therapy program; Master of Science in Nursing programs, with specializations in critical care, administration, education, and primary care family practitioner; Master of Education programs (with areas of specialization); and Master of Arts programs in human performance systems, human resource management, interior design, legal administration, organization development, and counseling. Marymount's small classes, excellent teaching faculty, strong professional programs, and proximity to Washington, D.C., make the University ideal for individuals seeking to enhance their careers through graduate study.

Maryville University of Saint Louis, The John E. Simon School of Business, St. Louis, MO 63141-7299. Offers programs in business administration and management (MBA), management (MSM). Part-time and evening/weekend programs available. Faculty: 15 full-time (8 women), 5 part-time (2 women). Students: 38 full-time (20 women), 179 part-time (91 women); includes 10 minority (4 African Americans, 2 Asian Americans, 2 Hispanics, 2 Native Americans), 19 international. Average age 34. 68 applicants, 100% accepted. In 1997, 62 degrees awarded (100% found work related to degree). *Average time to degree:* master's–1.5 years full-time, 2.5 years part-time. *Entrance requirements:* GMAT (minimum score 430; average 485), GRE General Test (minimum combined score of 1000), minimum AACSB index of 950. Application deadline: 8/1 (priority date; rolling processing; 12/1 for spring admission). Application fee: $35. *Expenses:* Tuition $11,480 per year full-time, $345 per credit hour part-time. Fees $120 per year full-time, $60 per year part-time. *Financial aid:* In 1997–98, 1 student received aid, including 1 assistantship totaling $650; career-related internships or fieldwork also available. Financial aid application deadline: 7/23; applicants required to submit FAFSA. *Faculty research:* Behavioral simulations, executive development, information systems, database marketing. • Dr. Pamela Horwitz, Dean, 314-529-9418. E-mail: business@maryville.edu. Application contact: Dr. Patricia Parker, Director of Graduate Admissions and Enrollment, 314-529-9382. Fax: 314-529-9975. E-mail: business@maryville.edu.

Marywood University, Graduate School of Arts and Sciences, Department of Business and Managerial Science, Scranton, PA 18509-1598. Offers programs in finance and investments (MBA), general management (MBA), management information systems (MBA, MS). Part-time and evening/weekend programs available. Faculty: 4 full-time (1 woman), 6 part-time (0 women). Students: 7 full-time (4 women), 51 part-time (24 women); includes 2 minority (1 African American, 1 Asian American). Average age 33. 18 applicants, 72% accepted. In 1997, 28 degrees awarded. *Degree requirements:* Computer language, comprehensive exam required, foreign language and thesis not required. *Entrance requirements:* GMAT, TOEFL (minimum score 550; average 590). Application deadline: 7/15 (priority date; rolling processing; 12/1 for spring admission). Application fee: $20. *Expenses:* Tuition $449 per credit hour. Fees $530 per year full-time, $180 per year part-time. *Financial aid:* Research assistantships, scholarships/tuition reductions, partial tuition waivers, and career-related internships or fieldwork available. Aid available to part-time students. Financial aid application deadline: 2/15; applicants required to submit FAFSA. *Faculty research:* Problem formulation in ill-structured situations, corporate tax structures. • Dr. Samir Dagher, Chair, 717-348-6274. Application contact: Deborah M. Flynn, Coordinator of Admissions, 717-340-6002. Fax: 717-961-4745.

Massachusetts Institute of Technology, Sloan School of Management, Cambridge, MA 02139-4307. Awards MBA, SM, PhD. Postbaccalaureate distance learning degree programs offered. Faculty: 119 full-time (17 women), 2 part-time (0 women). Students: 722 full-time (203 women); includes 137 minority (42 African Americans, 61 Asian Americans, 32 Hispanics, 2 Native Americans), 236 international. Average age 28. 3,394 applicants, 14% accepted. In 1997, 290 master's, 26 doctorates awarded. *Degree requirements:* For master's, thesis (SM) required, foreign language not required; for doctorate, computer language, dissertation, exams required, foreign language not required. *Average time to degree:* master's–2 years full-time; doctorate–5 years full-time. *Entrance requirements:* For master's, GMAT, TOEFL, previous course work in calculus and economics; for doctorate, GMAT, GRE or TOEFL, previous course work in calculus and economics. Application deadline: 1/31. Application fee: $150 ($175 for international students). Electronic applications accepted. *Tuition:* $27,100 per year. *Financial aid:* In 1997–98, 175 students received aid, including 22 fellowships (15 to first-year students) totaling $195,000, 45 research assistantships (13 to first-year students), 108 teaching assistantships (6 to first-year students) totaling $480,000; institutionally sponsored loans also available. *Faculty research:* Financial engineering; entrepreneurship; applied economics, finance, and accounting; behavioral and policy sciences; management science. Total annual research expenditures: $12 million. • Dr. Glen L. Urban, Dean, 617-253-6615. Fax: 617-258-6617. E-mail: urban@mit.edu. Application contact: Rod Garcia, Director of Master's Admissions, 617-258-5434. Fax: 617-253-6405. E-mail: masters@sloan.mit.edu.

McGill University, Faculty of Graduate Studies and Research, Faculty of Management, Montreal, PQ H3A 1G5, Canada. Awards MBA, MMM, PhD, MBA/Diploma, MBA/LL B, MBA/M Sc, MD/MBA. MMM offered jointly with the Faculty of Engineering. PhD offered jointly with Concordia University, École des Hautes Études Commerciales, Université de Montréal, and Université du Quebec à Montréal. Part-time programs available. Students: 292 full-time (83 women), 382 part-time (119 women); includes 117 international. 704 applicants, 46% accepted. In 1997, 190 master's awarded. *Degree requirements:* For master's, computer language required, thesis not required; for doctorate, computer language, dissertation. *Entrance requirements:* For master's, GMAT (minimum score 550; average 620), TOEFL (minimum score 600), minimum undergraduate GPA of 3.0; for doctorate, GMAT (minimum score 550), TOEFL (minimum score 600). Application deadline: rolling. Application fee: $100. *Expenses:* Tuition $1668 per year for Canadian residents; $8268 per year for nonresidents. Fees $828 per year for Canadian residents; $1216 per year for nonresidents. *Financial aid:* 33 students received aid; fellowships, research assistantships available. Financial aid application deadline: 2/1. • Wallace Crowston, Dean. Application contact: Susanne Major, Director of Recruiting, 514-398-4000 Ext. 3196. Fax: 514-398-2499. E-mail: mba@management.mcgill.ca.

See in-depth description on page 229.

The McGregor School of Antioch University, Graduate Management Program, 800 Livermore Street, Yellow Springs, OH 45387-1609. Awards MA. Evening/weekend programs available. Faculty: 4 full-time (2 women), 18 part-time (0 women). Students: 93 full-time. *Average time to degree:* master's–2 years full-time. *Application deadline:* 8/1 (priority date; rolling processing). *Application fee:* $50. *Tuition:* $291 per credit hour. • Rosemary Hartigan, Co-Director, 937-767-6321. Application contact: Terri Haney, Director of Admissions, 937-767-6325. Fax: 937-767-6461.

McMaster University, Faculty of Business, Hamilton, ON L8S 4M2, Canada. Awards MBA, PhD. Part-time and evening/weekend programs available. Faculty: 49 full-time, 2 part-time. Students: 256 full-time, 226 part-time; includes 4 international. In 1997, 135 master's, 4 doctorates awarded. *Degree requirements:* For doctorate, computer language, dissertation, comprehensive exam required, foreign language not required. *Entrance requirements:* For master's, GMAT; for doctorate, GMAT or GRE, master's degree. Application deadline: 6/1. Application fee: $50. *Expenses:* Tuition $4422 per year full-time, $1590 per year part-time for Canadian residents; $12,000 per year full-time, $6165 per year part-time for nonresidents. Fees $257 per year full-time, $188 per year part-time. *Financial aid:* Fellowships, research assistantships, teaching assistantships, and career-related internships or fieldwork available. • Dr. David W. Conrath, Dean.

McNeese State University, College of Business, Department of Business Administration, Lake Charles, LA 70609-2495. Awards MBA. Evening/weekend programs available. Faculty: 8 full-time (1 woman). Students: 18 full-time (12 women), 52 part-time (24 women). In 1997, 7 degrees awarded. *Degree requirements:* Computer language, written exam required, foreign language and thesis not required. *Entrance requirements:* GMAT (minimum AACSB index of 950). Application deadline: 7/15 (priority date; rolling processing). Application fee: $10 ($25 for international students). *Tuition:* $2118 per year full-time, $344 per semester (minimum) part-time for state residents; $7308 per year full-time, $344 per semester (minimum) part-time for nonresidents. *Financial aid:* Research assistantships, teaching assistantships, Federal Work-Study available. Aid available to part-time students. Financial aid application deadline: 5/1. *Faculty research:* Management development, integrating technology into the work force, union/management relations, economic development. • Dr. Bruce Swindle, Director, 318-475-5576.

Medaille College, Program in Business Administration, Buffalo, NY 14214-2695. Awards MBA. Evening/weekend programs available. Faculty: 4. *Financial aid:* Federal Work-Study, institutionally sponsored loans available. • Dr. Michael Lillis, Chairperson, 716-884-3281. Application contact: Kevin Reed, Graduate Admissions Counselor, 716-884-3281 Ext. 323. Fax: 716-884-0291.

Announcement: Medaille College's Master of Business Administration (MBA) program provides graduate training in strategic decision making to business professionals. Unique characteristics include concentrations in strategic human resource management and strategic management, applying multimedia technology, use of laptop computers for the duration of the program, and a 9-week modular evening delivery system.

Memorial University of Newfoundland, School of Graduate Studies, Faculty of Business Administration, St. John's, NF A1C 5S7, Canada. Awards MBA. Students: 58 full-time (25 women), 124 part-time (60 women); includes 1 international. Average age 31. 129 applicants, 47% accepted. In 1997, 34 degrees awarded. *Entrance requirements:* GMAT (minimum score 500; average 580). Application deadline: 6/15 (priority date; rolling processing; 3/1 for spring admission). Application fee: $40. *Expenses:* Tuition $1896 per year (minimum). Fees $60 per year for Canadian residents; $621 per year for nonresidents. *Financial aid:* Fellowships available. • Dr. R. W. Blake, Dean, 709-737-8851. E-mail: bblake@morgan.ucs.mun.ca. Application contact: Dr. Herb Mackenzie, Associate Dean, 709-737-8522. E-mail: hmackenz@morgan.ucs.mun.ca.

Mercer University, Stetson School of Business and Economics, 1400 Coleman Avenue, Macon, GA 31207-0003. Awards MBA, MSM, JD/MBA. Part-time and evening/weekend programs available. Faculty: 14 full-time (2 women). Students: 27 full-time (8 women), 76 part-time (24 women); includes 12 minority (6 African Americans, 3 Asian Americans, 3 Hispanics), 7 international. Average age 32. 44 applicants, 100% accepted. In 1997, 55 degrees awarded. *Degree requirements:* Computer language required, foreign language and thesis not required. *Entrance requirements:* GMAT (average 482). Application deadline: rolling. Application fee: $35 ($50 for international students). *Tuition:* $277 per credit hour. *Financial aid:* Grants, partial tuition waivers, Federal Work-Study available. Aid available to part-time students. *Faculty research:* Federal Reserve System, management of nurses, sales promotion, systems for common stock selection, interest rate premiums. • Dr. W. Carl Joiner, Dean, 912-752-2832.

Mercer University, Cecil B. Day Campus, Stetson School of Business and Economics, 3001 Mercer University Drive, Atlanta, GA 30341-4155. Awards MBA, MS, XMBA, MBA/Pharm D. Programs in business administration (MBA, XMBA), health care policy and administration (MS), technology management (MS). Part-time and evening/weekend programs available. Faculty: 24 full-time (11 women), 14 part-time (5 women). Students: 224 full-time (115 women), 441 part-time (220 women); includes 172 minority (133 African Americans, 26 Asian Americans, 12 Hispanics, 1 Native American), 119 international. Average age 32. 291 applicants, 95% accepted. In 1997, 293 degrees awarded. *Degree requirements:* Oral exam (health care policy and administration) required, foreign language and thesis not required. *Average time to degree:* master's–1.5 years full-time, 2.5 years part-time. *Entrance requirements:* GMAT (average 450). Application deadline: 8/1 (rolling processing; 12/1 for spring admission). Application fee: $35 ($50 for international students). *Tuition:* $327 per semester hour. *Financial aid:* Federal Work-Study available. *Faculty research:* Entrepreneurship, market studies, international business strategy, financial analysis. • Dr. W. Carl Joiner, Dean, 912-752-2832. Application contact: Dr. Victoria Johnson, Associate Dean, 770-986-3235. Fax: 770-986-3337. E-mail: johnson_v@mercer.edu.

Mercy College, Department of Business, Dobbs Ferry, NY 10522-1189. Offers programs in banking (MS), organizational leadership (MS). Students: 47 full-time (30 women). *Entrance requirements:* Interview. Application fee: $60. *Tuition:* $390 per credit. • Dr. Tom Milton, Director, 914-693-4500. Fax: 914-674-7304. Application contact: Andrew Joppa, Assistant Director, 914-693-4500.

Meredith College, Department of Business and Economics, Raleigh, NC 27607-5298. Offers program in business administration (MBA). Part-time and evening/weekend programs available. Faculty: 5 full-time (1 woman), 3 part-time (0 women). Students: 80 full-time (all women), 55 part-time (all women); includes 19 minority (16 African Americans, 3 Native Americans), 9 international. Average age 28. 54 applicants, 56% accepted. In 1997, 54 degrees awarded. *Degree requirements:* Thesis optional. *Entrance requirements:* GMAT (minimum score 350), interview, minimum GPA of 2.5, 2 years of work experience. Application deadline: 8/1 (priority date; rolling processing; 12/1 for spring admission). Application fee: $50. *Tuition:* $4680 per year full-time, $260 per credit hour part-time. *Financial aid:* Application deadline 2/15. • Dr. Rebecca Oatsvall, Head, 919-829-8484. Fax: 919-829-8470. Application contact: Sally Davis, Coordinator, 919-829-2281. Fax: 919-829-2898.

Mesa State College, Professional Studies, Grand Junction, CO 81502-2647. Awards MBA. Faculty: 6. Students: 36. *Application deadline:* rolling. *Application fee:* $50. *Expenses:* Tuition $2644 per year for state residents; $8924 per year for nonresidents. Fees $504 per year. • Bill Phillips, Dean. Application contact: Dr. Tim Hatten, MBA Coordinator, 970-248-1731. Fax: 970-248-1730. E-mail: thatten@mesastate.edu.

Metropolitan State University, Management and Administration Program, St. Paul, MN 55106-5000. Offers finance (MBA), human resource management (MBA), international business (MBA), law enforcement (MMA), management information systems (MBA), manpower administration (MMA), marketing (MBA), organizational studies (MBA), purchasing management (MBA). MMA (law enforcement) new for fall 1998. Part-time and evening/weekend programs available. Faculty: 17 full-time (5 women), 150 part-time. Students: 354; includes 56 minority (25 African Americans, 25 Asian Americans, 3 Hispanics, 3 Native Americans), 50 international. Average age 36. 42 applicants, 90% accepted. In 1997, 110 degrees awarded. *Degree requirements:* Thesis required, foreign language not required. *Entrance requirements:* GMAT. Application deadline: rolling. Application fee: $20. *Tuition:* $133 per credit for state residents; $208 per credit for nonresidents. *Financial aid:* 36 students received aid; research assistantships, Federal Work-Study, and career-related internships or fieldwork available. Aid available to part-time students. Financial aid applicants required to submit FAFSA. *Faculty research:* Yugoslav economic system, workers' cooperatives, participative management and job enrichment, global business systems. • Gary Seiler, Graduate Coordinator, 612-373-2754. E-mail: seiler@msus1.msus.edu. Application contact: Gloria Marcus, Recruiter/Admissions Adviser, 612-373-2724. Fax: 612-373-2888. E-mail: marcusg@msus1.msus.edu.

Miami University, Richard T. Farmer School of Business Administration, Oxford, OH 45056. Offers programs in accountancy (M Acct), decision sciences (MBA), economics (MA), finance (MBA), general management (MBA), management information systems (MBA), marketing (MBA). Part-time programs available. Faculty: 50. Students: 59 full-time (22 women), 69 part-time (24 women); includes 10 minority (7 African Americans, 3 Asian Americans), 18 international. 134 applicants, 78% accepted. In 1997, 50 degrees awarded. *Entrance requirements:* GMAT (minimum score 475), minimum undergraduate GPA of 3.0 during previous 2 years or 2.75 overall. Application deadline: 3/1 (priority date; rolling processing). Application fee: $35. *Tuition:* $5932 per year full-time, $255 per credit hour part-time for state residents; $12,392 per year full-time, $524 per credit hour part-time for nonresidents. *Financial aid:* Fellowships, research assistantships, full tuition waivers, Federal Work-Study available. Financial aid application deadline: 3/1. • Judy Barille, Director of Graduate Programs, 513-529-6643.

See in-depth description on page 231.

Michigan State University, Eli Broad Graduate School of Management, East Lansing, MI 48824-1020. Awards MA, MBA, MS, PhD, MS/MBA. Part-time and evening/weekend programs available. Faculty: 128 (20 women). Students: 715 (203 women); includes 72 minority (23 African Americans, 34 Asian Americans, 14 Hispanics, 1 Native American), 216 international. In 1997, 258 master's, 21 doctorates awarded. Terminal master's awarded for partial completion of doctoral program. *Degree requirements:* For doctorate, dissertation required, foreign language not required. *Application deadline:* rolling. *Application fee:* $30 ($40 for international students). Electronic applications accepted. *Expenses:* Tuition $4609 per year full-time, $223 per credit hour (minimum) part-time for state residents; $8704 per year full-time, $450 per credit hour (minimum) part-time for nonresidents. Fees $576 per year full-time, $476 per year part-time. *Financial aid:* Fellowships, research assistantships, teaching assistantships, graduate assistantships, Federal Work-Study, institutionally sponsored loans, and career-related internships or fieldwork available. Aid available to part-time students. Financial aid applicants required to submit FAFSA. • Dr. James Henry, Dean, 517-355-8377. Application contact: Dr. James Rainey, Associate Dean, Academic Programs, 517-432-3433.

Michigan Technological University, School of Business and Economics, Houghton, MI 49931-1295. Awards MS. Part-time programs available. Faculty: 25 full-time (3 women). Students: 5 full-time (1 woman); includes 1 minority (Asian American), 2 international. Average age 34. 6 applicants, 100% accepted. In 1997, 6 degrees awarded. *Degree requirements:* Thesis required, foreign language not required. *Entrance requirements:* GMAT (minimum score 500) or GRE General Test (combined average 1110), TOEFL (minimum score 500; average 575), bachelor's degree in business, economics, engineering, or science. Application deadline: 3/15 (priority date; rolling processing). Application fee: $30 ($35 for international students). *Expenses:* Tuition $3867 per year full-time, $216 per credit hour part-time for state residents; $8307 per year full-time, $462 per credit hour part-time for nonresidents. Fees $360 per year (minimum) full-time, $120 per quarter (minimum) part-time. *Financial aid:* Federal Work-Study and career-related internships or fieldwork available. Aid available to part-time students. *Total annual research expenditures:* $30,000. • Dr. R. Eugene Klippel, Dean, 906-487-2669. Fax: 906-487-2944. E-mail: reklippe@mtu.edu. Application contact: Dr. Terry Monson, Associate Dean, 906-487-3174. Fax: 906-487-1863. E-mail: tmonson@mtu.edu.

MidAmerica Nazarene University, Graduate Studies in Management, Olathe, KS 66062-1899. Awards MBA. Evening/weekend programs available. Faculty: 8 full-time (4 women), 2 part-time (1 woman). Students: 92 full-time (32 women); includes 19 minority (11 African Americans, 5 Hispanics, 3 Native Americans), 1 international. Average age 36. 92 applicants, 100% accepted. In 1997, 34 degrees awarded. *Degree requirements:* Integrated portfolio project required, foreign language and thesis not required. *Average time to degree:* master's–1.8 years full-time. *Entrance requirements:* TOEFL (minimum score 600), minimum undergraduate GPA of 3.0, math assessment, sample of written work. Application deadline: 8/1 (priority date; rolling processing; 2/1 for spring admission). Application fee: $75. Electronic applications accepted. *Tuition:* $7500 per year. *Financial aid:* 27 students received aid. Financial aid applicants required to submit FAFSA. • Dr. Mark Stenger, Director, 913-791-3276. E-mail: mstenger@mnu.edu. Application contact: Karen Bevis, Administrative Assistant, 913-791-3276. Fax: 913-791-3409. E-mail: mba@mnu.edu.

Middle Tennessee State University, College of Basic and Applied Sciences, Department of Aerospace, Murfreesboro, TN 37132. Offerings include asset management (MS). MS new for fall 1998. Department faculty: 3 full-time (0 women), 2 part-time (0 women). *Application deadline:* 8/1 (priority date). *Application fee:* $5. *Expenses:* Tuition $2560 per year full-time, $129 per semester hour part-time for state residents; $7386 per year full-time, $340 per

Directory: Business Administration and Management—General

Middle Tennessee State University (continued)
semester hour part-time for nonresidents. Fees $486 per year full-time, $17 per semester (minimum) part-time. • Ronald J. Ferrara, Chair, 615-898-3515. E-mail: rferrara@frank.mtsu.edu.

Middle Tennessee State University, College of Business, Program in Business Administration, Murfreesboro, TN 37132. Offers business administration (MBA), business education (MBE). MBE offered jointly with the Department of Educational Leadership. Faculty: 26 full-time (9 women). Students: 82 full-time (41 women), 339 part-time (147 women); includes 35 minority (32 African Americans, 2 Asian Americans, 1 Hispanic), 24 international. Average age 29. 252 applicants, 41% accepted. In 1997, 84 degrees awarded. *Degree requirements:* Comprehensive exams required, foreign language and thesis not required. *Entrance requirements:* GMAT. Application deadline: 8/1 (priority date). Application fee: $5. *Expenses:* Tuition $2560 per year full-time, $129 per semester hour part-time for state residents; $7386 per year full-time, $340 per semester hour part-time for nonresidents. Fees $486 per year full-time, $17 per semester (minimum) part-time. *Financial aid:* Teaching assistantships, institutionally sponsored loans available. Aid available to part-time students. Financial aid application deadline: 5/1; applicants required to submit FAFSA. • Dr. Jill Austin, Chair, 615-898-2736. Fax: 615-898-5308. E-mail: jaustin@mtsu.edu.

Midwestern State University, Division of Business Administration, Wichita Falls, TX 76308-2096. Awards MBA. Part-time and evening/weekend programs available. Faculty: 14 full-time (1 woman). Students: 5 full-time (all women), 19 part-time (13 women); includes 3 minority (1 African American, 1 Asian American, 1 Hispanic). Average age 35. 35 applicants, 40% accepted. In 1997, 10 degrees awarded. *Degree requirements:* Thesis required (for some programs), foreign language not required. *Entrance requirements:* GMAT (minimum score 400), TOEFL (minimum score 550). Application deadline: 8/7 (12/15 for spring admission). Application fee: $0 ($50 for international students). *Expenses:* Tuition $44 per hour for state residents; $259 per hour for nonresidents. Fees $90 per year (minimum) full-time, $9 per semester (minimum) part-time. *Financial aid:* In 1997–98, 2 teaching assistantships, 2 assistantships were awarded; partial tuition waivers, Federal Work-Study, institutionally sponsored loans, and career-related internships or fieldwork also available. Aid available to part-time students. *Faculty research:* Small business management, health care personnel administration, Pacific Rim trade, AIDS in the workplace, technology transfer. • Dr. Yoshi Fukasawa, Director, 940-397-4248. Fax: 940-397-4280. Application contact: Dr. Henry Van Geem, Graduate Adviser, 940-397-4248.

Millsaps College, School of Management, Jackson, MS 39210-0001. Offers programs in accounting (M Acc), business administration (MBA). Part-time and evening/weekend programs available. Faculty: 21 full-time (4 women), 5 part-time (1 woman). Students: 36 full-time (22 women), 104 part-time (38 women); includes 13 minority (9 African Americans, 4 Asian Americans), 8 international. Average age 29. 82 applicants, 90% accepted. In 1997, 45 degrees awarded. *Average time to degree:* master's–1.2 years full-time, 3.2 years part-time. *Entrance requirements:* GMAT (minimum score 500; average 540), TOEFL (minimum score 550). Application deadline: 7/1 (priority date; rolling processing; 11/15 for spring admission). Application fee: $25. *Tuition:* $540 per semester hour. *Financial aid:* 73 students received aid; research assistantships, scholarships, partial tuition waivers, Federal Work-Study, institutionally sponsored loans, and career-related internships or fieldwork available. Aid available to part-time students. Financial aid application deadline: 7/1; applicants required to submit FAFSA. • Dr. Walter Neely, Acting Dean, 601-974-1250. Application contact: Bart Herridge, Director of Graduate Business Admissions, 601-974-1253. Fax: 601-974-1260.

Minot State University, Program in Management, Minot, ND 58707-0002. Awards MS. Faculty: 14 full-time (3 women). Students: 23 part-time (14 women). *Degree requirements:* Thesis optional, foreign language not required. *Entrance requirements:* Minimum GPA of 3.0, GMAT, or GRE General Test (minimum combined score of 1100). Application deadline: rolling. Application fee: $25. *Tuition:* $2714 per year for state residents; $3235 per year (minimum) for nonresidents. *Financial aid:* In 1997–98, 1 teaching assistantship totaling $2,000 was awarded. *Faculty research:* Distance education. • Dr. Robert Sando, Chairperson, 701-858-3110. Fax: 701-858-3111. E-mail: sando@warple.cs.misu.nodak.edu. Application contact: Tammy White, Administrative Secretary, 701-858-3250. Fax: 701-839-6933.

Mississippi College, School of Business Administration, Department of Business Administration, Clinton, MS 39058. Awards MBA, JD/MBA. *Degree requirements:* Oral and written comprehensive exams required, foreign language and thesis not required. *Entrance requirements:* GMAT, minimum GPA of 2.5, 24 hours of undergraduate course work in business. Application deadline: 8/15 (priority date; rolling processing). Application fee: $25 ($75 for international students). *Expenses:* Tuition $6624 per year full-time, $276 per hour part-time. Fees $230 per year full-time, $35 per semester (minimum) part-time. *Financial aid:* Application deadline 4/1. • Dr. Randall Robbins, Chair, 601-925-3416.

Mississippi State University, College of Business and Industry, Program in Business Administration, Mississippi State, MS 39762. Awards MBA, DBA. Part-time programs available. Faculty: 48 full-time (11 women). Students: 94 full-time (38 women), 51 part-time (22 women); includes 10 minority (8 African Americans, 1 Asian American, 1 Native American), 22 international. Average age 31. 74 applicants, 64% accepted. In 1997, 61 master's awarded; 7 doctorates awarded (100% entered university research/teaching). *Degree requirements:* For doctorate, dissertation, comprehensive oral or written exam required, foreign language not required. *Entrance requirements:* For master's, GMAT (minimum score 500), TOEFL (minimum score 575), minimum QPA of 4.0 in last 60 hours, 3.0 overall; for doctorate, GMAT (minimum score 550), TOEFL (minimum score 575), minimum QPA of 4.0 in last 60 undergraduate hours and in graduate course work, 3.0 overall. Application deadline: 7/1 (priority date; rolling processing; 11/1 for spring admission). Application fee: $0 ($25 for international students). *Tuition:* $3017 per year full-time, $168 per credit hour part-time for state residents; $6119 per year full-time, $340 per credit hour part-time for nonresidents. *Financial aid:* In 1997–98, 23 research assistantships, 22 teaching assistantships, 13 service assistantships were awarded; Federal Work-Study, institutionally sponsored loans also available. Aid available to part-time students. Financial aid application deadline: 3/15. • Garry D. Smith, Acting Dean, College of Business and Industry, 601-325-3928. Application contact: Dr. Barbara A. Spencer, Acting Head, Department of Management and Information Systems, 601-325-1891. Fax: 601-325-8161. E-mail: gsb@cobilan.msstate.edu.

See in-depth description on page 233.

Monmouth University, School of Business Administration, West Long Branch, NJ 07764-1898. Awards MBA. Part-time and evening/weekend programs available. Faculty: 23 full-time (4 women), 3 part-time (0 women). Students: 16 full-time (6 women), 294 part-time (127 women); includes 16 minority (2 African Americans, 11 Asian Americans, 3 Hispanics), 5 international. Average age 33. 96 applicants, 77% accepted. In 1997, 97 degrees awarded. *Entrance requirements:* GMAT (minimum score 450), minimum GPA of 2.75. Application deadline: 8/1 (priority date; rolling processing; 12/1 for spring admission). Application fee: $35. *Expenses:* Tuition $459 per credit. Fees $274 per semester full-time, $137 per semester part-time. *Financial aid:* In 1997–98, 38 students received aid, including 10 assistantships averaging $606 per month and totaling $45,450; partial tuition waivers, Federal Work-Study, and career-related internships or fieldwork also available. Aid available to part-time students. Financial aid application deadline: 3/1; applicants required to submit FAFSA. *Faculty research:* Information technology and marketing, behavioral research in accounting, human resources, management of technology. • Dr. William Dempsey, Dean, 732-571-3423. Fax: 732-263-5105. Application contact: Office of Graduate Admissions, 732-571-3452. Fax: 732-571-5123.

Announcement: The MBA program prepares students to succeed in a competitive business environment. The curriculum, taught by faculty members who bring real-world expertise to the classroom, provides practical skills, innovative theory, and a foundation in business ethics. MBA graduates are creative thinkers and problem solvers positioned for more rewarding careers in business.

Montclair State University, School of Business, Program in Business Administration, Upper Montclair, NJ 07043-1624. Offers accounting (MBA), business economics (MBA), finance (MBA), international business (MBA), management (MBA), marketing (MBA), quantitative analysis (MBA). Part-time and evening/weekend programs available. Faculty: 57 full-time. Students: 21 full-time (8 women), 56 part-time (29 women); includes 16 international. In 1997, 30 degrees awarded. *Entrance requirements:* GMAT. Application deadline: 4/1 (rolling processing; 11/1 for spring admission). Application fee: $40. *Expenses:* Tuition $201 per credit for state residents; $257 per credit for nonresidents. Fees $22.05 per credit. *Financial aid:* Research assistantships available. Aid available to part-time students. Financial aid application deadline: 3/1; applicants required to submit FAFSA. • Dr. Eileen Kaplan, Director, 973-655-4306.

Monterey Institute of International Studies, Fisher Graduate School of International Business, 425 Van Buren Street, Monterey, CA 93940-2691. Awards MBA. Faculty: 10 full-time (1 woman), 11 part-time (2 women), 14 FTE. Students: 114 full-time (48 women), 4 part-time (2 women); includes 17 Asian Americans, 4 Hispanics, 51 international. Average age 26. 183 applicants, 79% accepted. In 1997, 67 degrees awarded. *Degree requirements:* 1 foreign language, thesis. *Average time to degree:* master's–2 years full-time. *Entrance requirements:* GMAT, TOEFL (minimum score 550), minimum GPA of 3.0, proficiency in a foreign language. Application deadline: 6/1 (priority date; rolling processing). Application fee: $50. *Expenses:* Tuition $18,200 per year full-time, $760 per semester hour part-time. Fees $45 per year. *Financial aid:* Federal Work-Study, institutionally sponsored loans, and career-related internships or fieldwork available. Financial aid application deadline: 3/15; applicants required to submit FAFSA. *Faculty research:* International trade, organizational behavior, international marketing. • Dr. William Pendergast, Dean, 408-647-4140. Fax: 408-647-6506. Application contact: Admissions Office, 408-647-4123. Fax: 408-647-6405. E-mail: admit@miis.edu.

See in-depth description on page 547.

Montreat College, Business Division, Montreat, NC 28757-1267. Awards MBA. Evening/weekend programs available. Faculty: 5 full-time (1 woman). Students: 61 full-time (26 women); includes 12 minority (all African Americans). Average age 36. 140 applicants, 69% accepted. *Degree requirements:* Computer language, research project required, foreign language and thesis not required. *Entrance requirements:* GMAT. Application deadline: rolling. Application fee: $25. *Tuition:* $240 per semester hour. *Financial aid:* Available to part-time students. Financial aid applicants required to submit FAFSA. • Dr. Abiola Fapetu, Chair, 704-669-8012 Ext. 3653. Fax: 704-669-9554. E-mail: afapetu@montreat.edu. Application contact: Joe Sharp, Director of Recruitment, 800-436-2777. Fax: 704-357-0176. E-mail: jsharp@montreat.edu.

Moorhead State University, Department of Business Administration, Moorhead, MN 56563-0002. Awards MBA. Part-time and evening/weekend programs available. Faculty: 12 full-time (3 women). Students: 2 full-time (0 women), 27 part-time (11 women); includes 1 minority (Native American), 4 international. 10 applicants, 100% accepted. In 1997, 4 degrees awarded. *Degree requirements:* Final oral exam required, foreign language and thesis not required. *Entrance requirements:* GMAT, TOEFL (minimum score 550), minimum GPA of 2.75. Application deadline: 5/1 (priority date; rolling processing; 9/1 for spring admission). Application fee: $20 ($35 for international students). Electronic applications accepted. *Tuition:* $145 per credit hour for state residents; $220 per credit hour for nonresidents. *Financial aid:* In 1997–98, 3 administrative assistantships were awarded; Federal Work-Study also available. Financial aid application deadline: 7/15. *Faculty research:* Union decertification, small business development, business innovation, pedagogy, curriculum design. • Dr. Molly Moore, Chairperson, 218-236-4648. Application contact: Sam H. Roy, Coordinator, 218-236-4647.

Moravian College, Division of Continuing Studies, Program in Business Administration, Bethlehem, PA 18018-6650. Awards MBA. Part-time and evening/weekend programs available. Faculty: 10 full-time (2 women), 5 part-time (2 women). Students: 4 full-time (2 women), 114 part-time (39 women); includes 11 minority (2 African Americans, 7 Asian Americans, 2 Hispanics). Average age 34. 40 applicants, 85% accepted. In 1997, 26 degrees awarded (100% found work related to degree). *Entrance requirements:* GMAT (minimum AACSB index of 950), TOEFL. Application deadline: rolling. Application fee: $30. *Tuition:* $1254 per course. *Faculty research:* Marketing, interest rate, labor relations, personnel and public administration, strategic planning. • Dr. Santo D. Marabella, Director, 610-807-4444. Fax: 610-861-1466.

Morehead State University, College of Business, Program in Business and Management, Morehead, KY 40351. Awards MBA. Part-time and evening/weekend programs available. Faculty: 21 full-time (4 women). Students: 38 full-time (11 women), 116 part-time (58 women); includes 3 minority (1 African American, 2 Asian Americans), 13 international. Average age 25. 90 applicants, 100% accepted. In 1997, 47 degrees awarded. *Degree requirements:* Final comprehensive exam required, foreign language and thesis not required. *Entrance requirements:* GMAT (minimum score 400), minimum AACSB index of 950, minimum GPA of 2.5. Application deadline: 8/1 (priority date; rolling processing; 12/1 for spring admission). Application fee: $0. *Tuition:* $2470 per year full-time, $138 per semester hour part-time for state residents; $6710 per year full-time, $373 per semester hour part-time for nonresidents. *Financial aid:* In 1997–98, 9 teaching assistantships (all to first-year students) averaging $471 per month and totaling $36,000 were awarded; research assistantships, Federal Work-Study also available. Financial aid application deadline: 4/1; applicants required to submit FAFSA. *Faculty research:* Regional economic development, accounting systems, banking market structures, macroeconomics, distance learning. • Ancil Lewis, Coordinator, 606-783-2723. Fax: 606-783-5025. Application contact: Betty Cowsert, Graduate Admissions Officer, 606-783-2039. Fax: 606-783-5061.

Morgan State University, Earl G. Graves School of Business and Management, Baltimore, MD 21251. Awards MBA. Part-time and evening/weekend programs available. Faculty: 41 full-time (9 women), 8 part-time (2 women). Students: 96 full-time (21 women), 90 part-time (44 women). Average age 28. 93 applicants, 70% accepted. In 1997, 36 degrees awarded. *Degree requirements:* Comprehensive exams required, foreign language not required. *Entrance requirements:* GMAT. Application deadline: 7/1 (rolling processing; 11/1 for spring admission). Application fee: $0. *Expenses:* Tuition $160 per credit hour for state residents; $286 per credit hour for nonresidents. Fees $326 per year. *Financial aid:* Application deadline 4/1. *Faculty research:* Total quality management, disaster management, impact of globalization, marketing of services. • Dr. Otis A. Thomas, Dean, 410-319-3160. Application contact: Dr. Mildred Glover, Assistant Dean/Graduate Program Director, 410-319-3396. Fax: 410-319-3358.

Mount Saint Mary College, Division of Business, Newburgh, NY 12550-3494. Awards MBA. Part-time and evening/weekend programs available. Faculty: 7 full-time (2 women), 5 part-time (1 woman). Students: 3 full-time (2 women), 62 part-time (36 women); includes 11 minority (6 African Americans, 3 Asian Americans, 2 Hispanics). Average age 34. In 1997, 15 degrees awarded. *Degree requirements:* Computer language, thesis required, foreign language not required. *Entrance requirements:* GMAT. Application fee: $20. *Expenses:* Tuition $367 per credit. Fees $30 per year. *Faculty research:* International dimensions of organizational behavior, financial reform. • Dr. Mattson Atsunyo, Coordinator, 914-569-3121. Fax: 914-562-6762. E-mail: atsunyo@msmc.edu.

Mount Saint Mary's College and Seminary, Graduate Program in Business, Emmitsburg, MD 21727-7799. Awards MBA. Part-time and evening/weekend programs available. Faculty: 17 part-time (2 women). Students: 28 full-time (9 women), 150 part-time (52 women); includes 5 minority (2 African Americans, 1 Asian American, 1 Hispanic, 1 Native American), 37 international. Average age 30. In 1997, 54 degrees awarded. *Degree requirements:* Research project required, foreign language and thesis not required. *Entrance requirements:* GMAT, minimum AACSB index of 950. Application deadline: rolling. Application fee: $20. *Expenses:* Tuition $250 per credit hour. Fees $100 per year (minimum) full-time, $5 per credit hour part-time. *Financial aid:* Research assistantships and career-related internships or fieldwork available. *Faculty research:* Communication skills, international business, business ethics, computer science. • Dr. Raymond Speciale, Director, 301-447-5326. Fax: 301-447-5335. E-mail: speciale@msmary.edu.

Mount Vernon College, Graduate School, Washington, DC 20007. Offerings include business administration (MBA). *Average time to degree:* master's–1.5 years full-time, 3 years part-time. *Application deadline:* rolling. *Application fee:* $35.

Murray State University, College of Business and Public Affairs, Business Affairs Program, Murray, KY 42071-0009. Awards MBA. Part-time and evening/weekend programs available. Faculty: 16 full-time (4 women). Students: 64 full-time (25 women), 97 part-time (43 women); includes 5 African Americans, 1 Native American, 29 international. 54 applicants, 80% accepted. In 1997, 71 degrees awarded. *Degree requirements:* Computer language required, foreign language and thesis not required. *Entrance requirements:* GMAT, TOEFL (minimum score 525). Application deadline: rolling. Application fee: $20. *Expenses:* Tuition $2500 per year full-time, $124 per hour part-time for state residents; $6740 per year full-time, $357 per hour part-time for nonresidents. Fees $360 per year full-time, $180 per year part-time. *Financial aid:* Research assistantships, teaching assistantships, Federal Work-Study available. Financial aid application deadline: 4/1. • LaDonna McCuan, MBA Coordinator, 502-762-4187. Fax: 502-762-3482.

National-Louis University, College of Management and Business, Program in Business Administration, 2840 Sheridan Road, Evanston, IL 60201-1730. Awards MBA. Program new for fall 1998. *Degree requirements:* Thesis required, foreign language not required. *Entrance requirements:* GRE, MAT, or Watson-Glaser Critical Thinking Appraisal, minimum GPA of 3.0. Application deadline: rolling. Application fee: $25. *Tuition:* $411 per semester hour. • Dr. Edward Weiss, Coordinator, 847-475-1100 Ext. 4418. Application contact: Dr. David McCulloch, Vice President for University Services, 800-443-5522 Ext. 5127. Fax: 847-465-0593. E-mail: dmcc@wheeling1.nl.edu.

National-Louis University, College of Management and Business, Program in Managerial Leadership, 2840 Sheridan Road, Evanston, IL 60201-1730. Awards MS. Evening/weekend programs available. Students: 170 full-time (95 women), 20 part-time (13 women); includes 78 minority (63 African Americans, 4 Asian Americans, 10 Hispanics, 1 Native American). Average age 40. In 1997, 182 degrees awarded. *Degree requirements:* Thesis required, foreign language not required. *Entrance requirements:* GRE, MAT, or Watson-Glaser Critical Thinking Appraisal, minimum GPA of 3.0. Application deadline: rolling. Application fee: $25. *Tuition:* $411 per semester hour. *Financial aid:* Available to part-time students. Financial aid applicants required to submit FAFSA. • Dr. Robert Skenes, Coordinator, 703-749-3000 Ext. 6843. Application contact: Dr. David McCulloch, Vice President for University Services, 800-443-5522 Ext. 5127. Fax: 847-465-0593. E-mail: dmcc@wheeling1.nl.edu.

National University, School of Management and Technology, Department of Business Studies, La Jolla, CA 92037-1011. Offers programs in business administration (MBA), global business administration (GMBA), international business (MA). GMBA new for fall 1998. Part-time and evening/weekend programs available. Students: 550 full-time (211 women), 256 part-time (93 women); includes 249 minority (74 African Americans, 100 Asian Americans, 68 Hispanics, 7 Native Americans), 235 international. Average age 34. *Entrance requirements:* Interview, minimum GPA of 2.5. Application deadline: rolling. Application fee: $60 ($100 for international students). *Tuition:* $7830 per year full-time, $870 per course part-time. *Financial aid:* Federal Work-Study, institutionally sponsored loans available. Financial aid application deadline: 5/1. • Donald Schwartz, Chair, 619-642-8420. Application contact: Nancy Rohland, Director of Enrollment Management, 619-563-7100. Fax: 619-563-7393.

National University, School of Management and Technology, Department of Professional Studies, Program in Management, La Jolla, CA 92037-1011. Awards MA. Students: 88 full-time (32 women), 36 part-time (15 women); includes 30 minority (11 African Americans, 9 Asian Americans, 9 Hispanics, 1 Native American), 30 international. Average age 34. *Entrance requirements:* Interview, minimum GPA of 2.5. Application deadline: rolling. Application fee: $60 ($100 for international students). *Tuition:* $7830 per year full-time, $870 per course part-time. *Financial aid:* Application deadline 5/1. • Application contact: Nancy Rohland, Director of Enrollment Management, 619-563-7100. Fax: 619-563-7393.

Nazareth College of Rochester, Graduate Studies, Department of Business, Program in Management, Rochester, NY 14618-3790. Awards MS. Part-time and evening/weekend programs available. Faculty: 3 full-time (0 women), 8 part-time (1 woman). Students: 85 part-time (45 women); includes 9 minority (8 African Americans, 1 Hispanic). 22 applicants, 100% accepted. In 1997, 6 degrees awarded. *Entrance requirements:* GMAT, minimum GPA of 2.7. Application deadline: 6/1 (11/1 for spring admission). Application fee: $40. *Expenses:* Tuition $436 per credit hour. Fees $20 per semester. • Application contact: Dr. Kay F. Marshman, Dean, 716-389-2815. Fax: 716-389-2452.

New England College, Program in Organizational Management, 7 Main Street, Henniker, NH 03242-3293. Offers programs in business (MS), community mental health counseling (MS), health care (MS), health care management (Certificate), human resource management (Certificate), human services (MS). Part-time and evening/weekend programs available. Faculty: 7 full-time, 13 part-time. Students: 75 part-time. *Degree requirements:* For master's, independent research project required, foreign language not required. *Application deadline:* rolling. *Application fee:* $25. *Expenses:* Tuition $175 per credit. Fees $20 per semester. • Dr. Patricia Prinz, Director of Graduate and Continuing Studies, 603-428-2252. Fax: 603-428-2266. Application contact: Robert Godard, Associate Director, 603-428-2483.

New Hampshire College, Graduate School of Business, Program in Business Administration, Manchester, NH 03106-1045. Awards MBA, Certificate, MBA/Certificate. Offerings include accounting (Certificate), artificial intelligence (Certificate), business administration (MBA), finance (Certificate), government administration (Certificate), health administration (Certificate), human resource management (Certificate), international business (Certificate), operations management (Certificate), taxation (Certificate), training and development (Certificate). Part-time and evening/weekend programs available. Faculty: 7 full-time (1 woman), 66 part-time (11 women), 47 FTE. Students: 239 full-time (80 women), 1,203 part-time (486 women); includes 95 international. Average age 32. In 1997, 459 master's awarded. *Degree requirements:* For master's, thesis or alternative required, foreign language not required. *Average time to degree:* master's–1.5 years full-time, 4.5 years part-time. *Entrance requirements:* For master's, minimum GPA of 2.7 during previous 2 years, 2.5 overall. Application deadline: rolling. Application fee: $0. *Expenses:* Tuition $17,044 per year full-time, $945 per course part-time. Fees $530 per year full-time, $80 per year part-time. *Financial aid:* In 1997–98, 4 research assistantships (all to first-year students) were awarded; Federal Work-Study, institutionally sponsored loans, and career-related internships or fieldwork also available. Aid available to part-time students. • Dr. Paul Schneiderman, Acting Dean, Graduate School of Business, 603-644-3102. Fax: 603-644-3150.

See in-depth description on page 235.

New Mexico Highlands University, School of Business, Las Vegas, NM 87701. Awards MBA. Faculty: 12 full-time (5 women), 1 part-time (0 women), 12.5 FTE. Students: 19 full-time (12 women), 26 part-time (14 women); includes 39 minority (1 Asian American, 36 Hispanics, 2 Native Americans), 3 international. Average age 32. In 1997, 8 degrees awarded. *Degree requirements:* Thesis or alternative required, foreign language not required. *Entrance requirements:* Minimum undergraduate GPA of 3.0. Application deadline: 8/1 (priority date; rolling processing). Application fee: $15. *Expenses:* Tuition $1816 per year full-time, $227 per hour part-time for state residents; $7468 per year full-time, $227 per hour part-time for nonresidents. Fees $10 per year. *Financial aid:* Federal Work-Study available. Financial aid application deadline: 3/1. • Dr. Ronald Maestas, Dean, 505-454-3344. Fax: 505-454-3354. E-mail: ronmaestas@merlin.nmhu.edu. Application contact: Dr. Glen W. Davidson, Academic Vice President, 505-454-3311. Fax: 505-454-3558. E-mail: glendavidson@venus.nmhu.edu.

New Mexico State University, College of Business Administration and Economics, Program in Business Administration, Las Cruces, NM 88003-8001. Awards MBA, PhD. *Degree requirements:* For doctorate, dissertation required, foreign language not required. *Entrance requirements:* For master's, GMAT, TOEFL; for doctorate, GMAT (minimum score 550) or GRE, TOEFL (minimum score 550). Application deadline: 7/1 (priority date; rolling processing; 11/1 for spring admission). Application fee: $15 ($35 for international students). *Tuition:* $2514 per year full-time, $105 per credit hour part-time for state residents; $7848 per year full-time, $327 per credit hour part-time for nonresidents. *Financial aid:* Application deadline 3/1. • Application contact: Joe Benson, Director, 505-646-8003. Fax: 505-646-7977. E-mail: joeb@nmsu.edu.

New School University, Robert J. Milano Graduate School of Management and Urban Policy, New York, NY 10011-8603. Awards MS, PhD, Adv C. Part-time and evening/weekend programs available. Faculty: 25 full-time (10 women), 151 part-time (96 women). Students: 181 full-time (158 women), 602 part-time (491 women); includes 234 minority (156 African Americans, 31 Asian Americans, 47 Hispanics), 14 international. Average age 31. 288 applicants, 90% accepted. In 1997, 275 master's awarded. *Degree requirements:* For master's, computer language, thesis required, foreign language not required. *Average time to degree:* master's–2 years full-time, 3.5 years part-time. *Entrance requirements:* For master's, interview. Application deadline: 9/1 (priority date; rolling processing). Application fee: $30. *Tuition:* $622 per credit. *Financial aid:* In 1997–98, 244 students received aid, including 22 fellowships (10 to first-year students) totaling $148,000, 16 teaching assistantships totaling $24,000, 213 scholarships (79 to first-year students) totaling $105,200; full and partial tuition waivers, Federal Work-Study, and career-related internships or fieldwork also available. Aid available to part-time students. Financial aid application deadline: 3/1; applicants required to submit FAFSA. *Faculty research:* Community development, national urban policy, health policy and financing, leadership development. • James A. Krauskopf, Dean, 212-229-5400. E-mail: jkrausko@newschool.edu. Application contact: Susan Morris, Assistant Dean, 212-229-5388. Fax: 212-229-8935. E-mail: smorris@newschool.edu.

See in-depth description on page 237.

New York Institute of Technology, School of Management, Program in Business Administration, Old Westbury, NY 11568-8000. Awards MBA, DO/MBA. DO/MBA offered through the New York College of Osteopathic Medicine. Part-time and evening/weekend programs available. Faculty: 13 full-time (0 women), 11 part-time (0 women). Students: 221 full-time (69 women), 314 part-time (104 women); includes 113 minority (52 African Americans, 47 Asian Americans, 12 Hispanics, 2 Native Americans), 234 international. Average age 30. 289 applicants, 80% accepted. In 1997, 197 degrees awarded. *Degree requirements:* Thesis required (for some programs), foreign language not required. *Average time to degree:* master's–3 years part-time. *Entrance requirements:* GMAT (minimum score 400; average 550), GRE General Test, TOEFL (minimum score 550), minimum QPA of 2.85. Application deadline: rolling. Application fee: $50. *Tuition:* $413 per credit. *Financial aid:* In 1997–98, 9 graduate assistantships (2 to first-year students) were awarded; fellowships, research assistantships, full and partial tuition waivers, institutionally sponsored loans also available. Aid available to part-time students. *Faculty research:* Instructor performance appraisal; relationship between TOEFL, GMAT, GRE, and performance in foreign students. • William Lawrence, Director, 212-261-1706. Application contact: Glenn Berman, Executive Director of Admissions, 516-686-7519. Fax: 516-626-0419. E-mail: gberman@iris.nyit.edu.

New York University, Leonard N. Stern School of Business, New York, NY 10006. Awards MBA, MS, PhD, APC, JD/MBA, MBA/MA, MBA/Certificate. MBA/Certificate offered jointly with the Community of European Management Schools. Part-time and evening/weekend programs available. Faculty: 208 full-time (34 women), 160 part-time (26 women). Students: 1,242 full-time (367 women), 2,324 part-time (761 women); includes 537 minority (58 African Americans, 379 Asian Americans, 95 Hispanics, 5 Native Americans), 415 international. Average age 28. 4,244 applicants, 20% accepted. In 1997, 1,235 master's, 23 doctorates, 10 APCs awarded. Terminal master's awarded for partial completion of doctoral program. *Degree requirements:* For master's, computer language required, foreign language and thesis not required; for doctorate, computer language, dissertation required, foreign language not required. *Entrance requirements:* For master's, GMAT, TOEFL (minimum score 600); for doctorate, GMAT. Application deadline: 3/15 (rolling processing). Application fee: $75. *Financial aid:* In 1997–98, 967 students received aid, including 30 fellowships, 90 research assistantships, 185 teaching assistantships (2 to first-year students), 233 scholarships (141 to first-year students); partial tuition waivers, Federal Work-Study, and career-related internships or fieldwork also available. Financial aid application deadline: 1/15; applicants required to submit FAFSA. • George G. Daly, Dean, 212-998-0900. Application contact: Mary Miller, Director, Graduate Admissions, 212-998-0600. Fax: 212-995-4231. E-mail: sternmba@stern.nyu.edu.

Niagara University, Graduate Division of Business Administration, Niagara University, NY 14109. Offers programs in business (MBA), commerce (MBA). Part-time and evening/weekend programs available. Faculty: 6 full-time (2 women), 1 part-time (0 women). Students: 36 full-time (13 women), 88 part-time (34 women); includes 6 minority (5 African Americans, 1 Native American), 9 international. Average age 30. 89 applicants, 73% accepted. In 1997, 36 degrees awarded. *Degree requirements:* Computer language required, foreign language and thesis not required. *Entrance requirements:* GMAT, TOEFL. Application deadline: 8/1 (rolling processing; 11/1 for spring admission). Application fee: $30. *Expenses:* Tuition $7740 per year full-time, $430 per credit hour part-time. Fees $25 per semester. *Financial aid:* In 1997–98, 3 fellowships (1 to a first-year student), 2 research assistantships were awarded; Federal Work-Study and career-related internships or fieldwork also available. Aid available to part-time students. Financial aid application deadline: 8/1; applicants required to submit FAFSA. *Faculty research:* Capital flows, Federal Reserve policy, human resource management, public policy, issues in marketing. • Dr. Charles G. Smith, Director, 716-286-8179.

Nicholls State University, College of Business Administration, Thibodaux, LA 70310. Awards MBA. Part-time and evening/weekend programs available. Faculty: 28 full-time (7 women). Students: 50 full-time (19 women), 78 part-time (38 women). In 1997, 29 degrees awarded (90% found work related to degree, 10% continued full-time study). *Entrance requirements:* GMAT, TOEFL. Application deadline: 8/1 (priority date; rolling processing). Application fee: $10 ($25 for international students). *Tuition:* $2136 per year full-time, $283 per semester (minimum) part-time for state residents; $5376 per year full-time, $283 per semester (minimum) part-time for nonresidents. *Financial aid:* Research assistantships available. Financial aid application deadline: 6/1. • Dr. Ridley Gros, Dean, 504-448-4170. Fax: 504-448-4922.

Nichols College, Graduate Program in Business Administration, Dudley, MA 01571. Offers programs in accounting (MBA), finance (MBA), international business (MBA), management (MBA), marketing (MBA). Part-time and evening/weekend programs available. Faculty: 21 full-time (3 women), 6 part-time (2 women). Students: 6 full-time (3 women), 417 part-time (170 women); includes 25 minority (3 African Americans, 13 Asian Americans, 9 Hispanics), 9 international. Average age 29. *Degree requirements:* Computer language required, foreign language and thesis not required. *Entrance requirements:* GMAT, TOEFL, minimum AACSB index of 950. Application deadline: rolling. Application fee: $25. *Tuition:* $1050 per course. *Financial aid:* Career-related internships or fieldwork available. • William F. Keith, Director, 508-213-2207. E-mail: keithwf@nichols.edu.

North Carolina Central University, Division of Academic Affairs, School of Business, Durham, NC 27707-3129. Awards MBA, JD/MBA. Part-time and evening/weekend programs available. Faculty: 33 full-time (10 women), 6 part-time (1 woman). Students: 10 full-time (6 women), 20 part-time (10 women); includes 27 minority (23 African Americans, 4 Asian Americans). Average age 30. 17 applicants, 65% accepted. In 1997, 11 degrees awarded. *Degree requirements:* Computer language, thesis required, foreign language not required. *Entrance requirements:* GMAT. Application deadline: 8/1. Application fee: $30. *Tuition:* $2027 per year full-time, $508 per semester (minimum) part-time for state residents; $9155 per year full-time, $2290 per semester (minimum) part-time for nonresidents. *Financial aid:* Teaching assistantships, Federal

Directory: Business Administration and Management—General

North Carolina Central University (continued)

Work-Study, institutionally sponsored loans available. Aid available to part-time students. Financial aid application deadline: 5/1. *Faculty research:* Small business issues, research of pedagogy, African business environment. • Dr. Sundar Flemming, Dean, 919-560-6458. Application contact: Raphael Thompson, Associate Dean, 919-560-6175.

North Carolina State University, College of Management, Raleigh, NC 27695. Offers programs in accounting (MAC); economics (MA, M Econ, PhD); management (MS), including biotechnology, computer science, engineering, forest resources management, general business, management information systems, operations research, statistics, telecommunications systems engineering, textile management, total quality management. Part-time programs available. Faculty: 90 full-time (12 women), 18 part-time (0 women). Students: 184 full-time (60 women), 184 part-time (45 women); includes 42 minority (21 African Americans, 19 Asian Americans, 1 Hispanic, 1 Native American), 37 international. Average age 32. 363 applicants, 53% accepted. In 1997, 141 master's, 8 doctorates awarded. Terminal master's awarded for partial completion of doctoral program. *Degree requirements:* For doctorate, dissertation required, foreign language not required. *Entrance requirements:* GRE General Test (for aid only), TOEFL (minimum score 550). Application deadline: rolling. Application fee: $45. *Tuition:* $2370 per year full-time, $517 per semester (minimum) part-time for state residents; $11,536 per year full-time, $2809 per semester (minimum) part-time for nonresidents. *Financial aid:* In 1997–98, 1 fellowship (to a first-year student) totaling $986, 1 research assistantship averaging $4,757 per month and totaling $21,407, 39 teaching assistantships (21 to first-year students) totaling $11,044 were awarded. *Total annual research expenditures:* $274,920. • Dr. Richard J. Lewis, Dean, 919-515-5560. E-mail: lewis@econbus2.econ.ncsu.edu. Application contact: Christine Miller, Administrative Assistant, 919-515-5560. Fax: 919-515-5564. E-mail: christine_miller@ncsu.edu.

North Central College, Graduate Programs, Department of Business Administration, Naperville, IL 60566-7063. Offers programs in business administration (MBA), management information systems (MS). Faculty: 15. Students: 162. In 1997, 78 degrees awarded. *Degree requirements:* Project required, thesis not required. *Entrance requirements:* GMAT or GRE General Test, minimum GPA of 2.75. Application deadline: 8/15 (rolling processing). Application fee: $25. *Financial aid:* Available to part-time students. • Dr. Kenneth Campbell, Chairman, 630-637-5840. Fax: 630-637-5844.

North Dakota State University, College of Business Administration, Fargo, ND 58105. Awards MBA. Part-time and evening/weekend programs available. Faculty: 16 full-time (3 women). Students: 25 full-time (8 women), 36 part-time (13 women); includes 6 minority (all Asian Americans), 5 international. Average age 25. 18 applicants, 89% accepted. In 1997, 12 degrees awarded. *Degree requirements:* Final exam required, thesis optional, foreign language not required. *Average time to degree:* master's–1.5 years full-time, 4 years part-time. *Entrance requirements:* GMAT (minimum score 450), TOEFL (minimum score 550). Application deadline: 7/15 (priority date; rolling processing; 11/15 for spring admission). Application fee: $25. *Tuition:* $2572 per year full-time, $107 per credit part-time for state residents; $6868 per year full-time, $286 per credit part-time for nonresidents. *Financial aid:* In 1997–98, 13 students received aid, including 13 research assistantships (5 to first-year students) averaging $290 per month and totaling $33,800; teaching assistantships, Federal Work-Study, institutionally sponsored loans, and career-related internships or fieldwork also available. Aid available to part-time students. Financial aid application deadline: 3/15; applicants required to submit FAFSA. *Faculty research:* International finance, nonprofit organizations, agency, Internet marketing. • Dr. Jay Leitch, Dean, 701-231-7577.

Northeastern Illinois University, College of Business and Management, Chicago, IL 60625-4699. Offers programs in accounting (MBA), finance (MBA), management (MBA), marketing (MBA). Part-time and evening/weekend programs available. Faculty: 26 full-time (3 women), 14 part-time (6 women). Students: 7 full-time (3 women), 56 part-time (28 women); includes 11 minority (2 African Americans, 7 Asian Americans, 2 Hispanics), 7 international. Average age 31. 47 applicants, 51% accepted. In 1997, 19 degrees awarded. *Degree requirements:* Thesis optional, foreign language not required. *Entrance requirements:* GMAT (minimum score 450), TOEFL (minimum score 550), minimum GPA of 2.75. Application deadline: 3/18 (priority date; rolling processing; 9/30 for spring admission). Application fee: $0. *Expenses:* Tuition $2226 per year full-time, $93 per credit hour part-time for state residents; $6678 per year full-time, $278 per credit hour part-time for nonresidents. Fees $358 per year full-time, $14.90 per credit hour part-time. *Financial aid:* In 1997–98, 20 students received aid, including 8 research assistantships averaging $450 per month; full and partial tuition waivers, Federal Work-Study, institutionally sponsored loans, and career-related internships or fieldwork also available. Aid available to part-time students. *Faculty research:* Perception of accountants and non-accountants toward future of the accounting industry, asynchronous learning outcomes, cost and efficiency of financial markets, impact of deregulation on airline industry, analysis of derivational instruments, product structures and inventory management efficiency. • Dr. Charles Falk, Dean, 773-583-4050 Ext. 5247. Application contact: Dr. Kathleen Carlson, Coordinator, 773-583-4050.

Northeastern State University, College of Business and Industry, Program in Business Administration, Tahlequah, OK 74464-2399. Awards MBA. Faculty: 15 part-time (3 women). Students: 41 (16 women); includes 3 international. In 1997, 9 degrees awarded. *Degree requirements:* Thesis or alternative, comprehensive oral exam required, foreign language not required. *Entrance requirements:* GMAT, minimum GPA of 2.5. Application deadline: 6/1 (priority date; rolling processing). Application fee: $0. *Expenses:* Tuition $74 per credit hour for state residents; $176 per credit hour for nonresidents. Fees $30 per year. *Financial aid:* Federal Work-Study available. Financial aid application deadline: 3/1. • Dr. Tom Carment, Coordinator, 918-456-5511 Ext. 2905.

Northeastern University, Graduate School of Business Administration, Boston, MA 02115-5096. Awards EMBA, MBA, MSF, MST, CAS, JD/MBA, JD/MS/MBA, MS/MBA. Part-time and evening/weekend programs available. Faculty: 90 full-time, 30 part-time. Students: 392 full-time (153 women), 600 part-time (224 women). Average age 25. 801 applicants, 60% accepted. In 1997, 374 master's awarded. *Average time to degree:* master's–2 years full-time, 3 years part-time. *Entrance requirements:* For master's, GMAT; for CAS, MBA. Application deadline: rolling. Application fee: $50. *Expenses:* Tuition $500 per credit hour. Fees $55 per quarter full-time, $13.25 per quarter part-time. *Financial aid:* In 1997–98, 12 fellowships (8 to first-year students) totaling $34,000, 55 research assistantships (22 to first-year students), 18 teaching assistantships (10 to first-year students) averaging $970 per month, 42 administrative assistantships (20 to first-year students) averaging $970 per month were awarded; Federal Work-Study, institutionally sponsored loans, and career-related internships or fieldwork also available. Aid available to part-time students. Financial aid application deadline: 3/1. *Faculty research:* Investing in bankruptcy, planning for technology-based companies, organizational leadership, characteristics of small business managers. • William I. Kelly, Interim Dean of Graduate Programs, 617-373-2714. E-mail: gsba@neu.edu. Application contact: Program Director, 617-373-2714. Fax: 617-373-8564. E-mail: gsba@neu.edu.

Announcement: For nearly 50 years, Northeastern University's Graduate School of Business Administration has provided students all over the world with what many feel is the best practice-oriented business curriculum in the nation. The focus is on practical learning that leverages relevant real-world experience to hone marketable skills. Five MBA programs and a Master of Science in finance are offered, with flexible full- and part-time scheduling available to fit the student's objectives, work schedule, and lifestyle. The College of Business Administration is accredited by AACSB–The International Association for Management Education.

See in-depth description on page 239.

Northeast Louisiana University, College of Business Administration, Monroe, LA 71209-0001. Awards MBA. Part-time and evening/weekend programs available. *Entrance requirements:* GMAT, TOEFL, minimum GPA of 2.5, minimum AACSB index of 950. Application deadline: 6/1 (11/1 for spring admission). Application fee: $15 ($25 for international students). *Tuition:* $2028 per year full-time, $240 per semester (minimum) part-time for state residents; $6852 per year full-time, $240 per semester (minimum) part-time for nonresidents.

Northern Arizona University, College of Business Administration, Flagstaff, AZ 86011. Offers programs in general management (MBA), management information systems (MBA). Part-time programs available. Faculty: 52 full-time (9 women), 1 (woman) part-time. Students: 24 full-time (8 women), 17 part-time (5 women); includes 3 minority (1 Asian American, 2 Native Americans), 11 international. 74 applicants, 34% accepted. In 1997, 30 degrees awarded. *Degree requirements:* Computer language required, foreign language and thesis not required. *Entrance requirements:* GMAT. Application deadline: 3/1 (priority date; rolling processing; 10/15 for spring admission). Application fee: $45. *Expenses:* Tuition $2088 per year full-time, $330 per semester (minimum) part-time for state residents; $8004 per year full-time, $1002 per semester (minimum) part-time for nonresidents. Fees $72 per year full-time, $18 per semester (minimum) part-time. *Financial aid:* In 1997–98, 15 research assistantships, 7 teaching assistantships were awarded; full and partial tuition waivers, Federal Work-Study, institutionally sponsored loans also available. *Faculty research:* Data processing applications to business situations and problems, accounting fraud, effects of sales tactics, self-efficacy and performance. • Dr. Patricia Meyers, Dean, 520-523-7345. Application contact: Dr. Mason Gerety, MBA Director, 520-523-7342.

Northern Illinois University, College of Business, MBA Program, De Kalb, IL 60115-2854. Awards MBA. Part-time and evening/weekend programs available. Postbaccalaureate distance learning degree programs offered (no on-campus study). Faculty: 58 full-time (10 women), 3 part-time (1 woman). Students: 89 full-time (23 women), 487 part-time (171 women); includes 48 minority (13 African Americans, 24 Asian Americans, 9 Hispanics, 2 Native Americans), 4 international. Average age 33. 243 applicants, 65% accepted. In 1997, 151 degrees awarded. *Entrance requirements:* GMAT, TOEFL (minimum score 550), minimum GPA of 2.75. Application deadline: 6/1 (rolling processing; 11/1 for spring admission). Application fee: $30. *Tuition:* $3984 per year full-time, $154 per credit hour part-time for state residents; $8160 per year full-time, $328 per credit hour part-time for nonresidents. *Financial aid:* Fellowships, research assistantships, teaching assistantships, staff assistantships, full tuition waivers, Federal Work-Study, and career-related internships or fieldwork available. Aid available to part-time students. • Dr. Larry Jacobs, Director of Graduate Studies, 815-753-6301.

See in-depth description on page 241.

Northern Kentucky University, Program in Business Administration, Highland Heights, KY 41099. Awards MBA, JD/MBA. Evening/weekend programs available. Faculty: 25 full-time (8 women). Students: 10 full-time (3 women), 167 part-time (61 women); includes 7 minority (3 African Americans, 3 Asian Americans, 1 Hispanic), 2 international. Average age 34. 84 applicants, 71% accepted. In 1997, 31 degrees awarded. *Entrance requirements:* GMAT (minimum score 450). Application deadline: 8/15 (priority date; rolling processing). Application fee: $25. *Tuition:* $2420 per year full-time, $132 per semester hour part-time for state residents; $6660 per year full-time, $368 per semester hour part-time for nonresidents. *Financial aid:* In 1997–98, 2 students received aid, including 2 research assistantships (1 to a first-year student); institutionally sponsored loans also available. Aid available to part-time students. • Nina Thomas, Director, 606-572-6657. Application contact: Peg Griffin, Coordinator, Graduate Program, 606-572-6364.

North Park University, Center for Management Education, Chicago, IL 60625-4895. Awards MBA, MM, MBA/MS. Part-time and evening/weekend programs available. Faculty: 5 full-time (0 women), 6 part-time (0 women), 6.4 FTE. Students: 11 full-time (6 women), 201 part-time (93 women); includes 44 minority (18 African Americans, 15 Asian Americans, 10 Hispanics, 1 Native American), 25 international. Average age 34. 101 applicants, 69% accepted. In 1997, 23 degrees awarded. *Entrance requirements:* GMAT (average 500). Application deadline: 9/1 (priority date; rolling processing). Application fee: $20. *Financial aid:* In 1997–98, 98 students received aid, including 61 grants totaling $75,517. Aid available to part-time students. Financial aid application deadline: 8/15. • Dean A. Lundgren, Director, 773-784-3000. Fax: 773-784-4366. Application contact: Christopher Nicholson, Associate Director for Graduate and Continuing Education, 773-244-5518. Fax: 773-255-4953. E-mail: cln@gumby.npcts.edu.

Northwestern University, J. L. Kellogg Graduate School of Management, Programs in Management, Evanston, IL 60208. Awards MM, MMM, JD/MM, MD/MM, MM/MSN. Offerings include business management (MM), health services management (MM), manufacturing management (MMM), public and nonprofit management (MM), real estate management (MM), transportation management (MM). MMM offered jointly with the Robert R. McCormick School of Engineering and Applied Science; MM/MSN offered jointly with Rush Presbyterian Hospital. Part-time and evening/weekend programs available. Faculty: 129 full-time (24 women), 89 part-time (15 women). Students: 1,200 full-time (372 women), 1,300 part-time (416 women); includes 404 minority (105 African Americans, 234 Asian Americans, 59 Hispanics, 6 Native Americans), 483 international. Average age 27. 6,107 applicants, 16% accepted. *Entrance requirements:* GMAT, TOEFL, interview. Application deadline: 3/16. Application fee: $125. *Tuition:* $25,872 per year. *Financial aid:* Fellowships, grants, institutionally sponsored loans, and career-related internships or fieldwork available. Aid available to part-time students. Financial aid application deadline: 2/1; applicants required to submit FAFSA. • Michele Rogers, Assistant Dean of Admissions and Financial Aid, 847-491-3308. Fax: 847-491-4960.

Northwest Missouri State University, College of Professional and Applied Studies, Program in Business Administration, 800 University Drive, Maryville, MO 64468-6001. Awards MBA. Faculty: 15 full-time (2 women). Students: 24 full-time (15 women), 38 part-time (15 women). 25 applicants, 96% accepted. In 1997, 9 degrees awarded. *Degree requirements:* Comprehensive exam required, foreign language and thesis not required. *Entrance requirements:* GMAT, TOEFL (minimum score 550), minimum GPA of 2.5. Application deadline: 7/1 (rolling processing; 12/1 for spring admission). Application fee: $0 ($50 for international students). *Expenses:* Tuition $113 per credit hour for state residents; $197 per credit hour for nonresidents. Fees $3 per credit hour. *Financial aid:* In 1997–98, 12 students received aid, including 3 research assistantships averaging $585 per month, 3 teaching assistantships averaging $585 per month, 6 administrative assistantships averaging $585 per month. Financial aid application deadline: 3/1. • Application contact: Dr. Frances Shipley, Dean of Graduate School, 816-562-1145. E-mail: gradsch@acad.nwmissouri.edu.

Northwest Nazarene College, Department of Graduate Studies, Program in Business Administration, Nampa, ID 83686-5897. Awards MBA. Students: 40 full-time (8 women). *Entrance requirements:* GMAT, minimum GPA of 3.0. Application fee: $25. • Dr. Ron Galloway, Coordinator, 208-467-8545.

Northwood University, Richard DeVos Graduate School of Management, Midland, MI 48640-2398. Awards EMBA, MBA. Part-time programs available. Faculty: 6 full-time (1 woman), 2 part-time (both women). Students: 44 full-time (14 women), 165 part-time (47 women); includes 34 minority (21 African Americans, 5 Asian Americans, 7 Hispanics, 1 Native American), 26 international. Average age 33. 170 applicants, 68% accepted. *Average time to degree:* master's–1.5 years full-time, 2.5 years part-time. *Entrance requirements:* GMAT, TOEFL (minimum score 550), interview (EMBA). Application deadline: 7/1 (priority date; rolling processing). Application fee: $25. Electronic applications accepted. *Tuition:* $18,000 per year. *Financial aid:* 23 students received aid; fellowships, full and partial tuition waivers, and career-related internships or fieldwork available. Financial aid application deadline: 2/15; applicants required to submit FAFSA. • Dr. William T. Busby, Dean, 517-837-4488. Application contact: Lisa Marie Boyd, Director of Graduate Admissions, 517-837-4488. Fax: 517-837-4800. E-mail: mba@northwood.edu.

Nova Southeastern University, School of Business and Entrepreneurship, Doctoral Program in Business Administration, Fort Lauderdale, FL 33314-7721. Awards DBA. Part-time and evening/weekend programs available. Students: 25 full-time (8 women), 382 part-time (95 women). Average age 45. 330 applicants, 73% accepted. In 1997, 44 degrees awarded. *Degree requirements:* Dissertation. *Entrance requirements:* GMAT. Application deadline: rolling. Application fee: $50. *Tuition:* $270 per credit hour (minimum). • Dr. Richard Kelsey, Director, 954-262-5136. Fax: 054-262-3849. E-mail: kelsey@sbe.nova.edu. Application contact: Kristie Tetrault, 954-262-5036. E-mail: kristie@sbe.nova.edu.

See in-depth description on page 243.

Nova Southeastern University, School of Business and Entrepreneurship, Master's Program in Business Administration, Fort Lauderdale, FL 33314-7721. Awards MBA, JD/MBA. Offerings include business administration (MBA). Evening/weekend programs available. Students: 69 full-time (36 women), 1,136 part-time (578 women); includes 309 minority (151 African Americans, 30 Asian Americans, 125 Hispanics, 3 Native Americans), 217 international. 415 applicants, 80% accepted. In 1997, 564 degrees awarded. *Entrance requirements:* GMAT (minimum score 450). Application deadline: rolling. Application fee: $50. *Tuition:* $270 per credit hour (minimum). • Dr. Preston Jones, Director, 954-262-5127. Application contact: Shane Strum, Marketing Manager, 954-262-5035.

See in-depth description on page 243.

Oakland City University, School of Adult Programs and Professional Studies, Oakland City, IN 47660-1099. Awards MS Mgt. Evening/weekend programs available. Students: 50 full-time (14 women), 14 part-time (3 women); includes 9 minority (8 African Americans, 1 Hispanic). Average age 35. 20 applicants, 100% accepted. In 1997, 23 degrees awarded. *Degree requirements:* Thesis or alternative. *Average time to degree:* master's–1.5 years full-time. *Entrance requirements:* GMAT, GRE, or MAT; TOEFL, appropriate bachelor's degree, computer literacy. Application deadline: rolling. Application fee: $25. *Tuition:* $7200 per year. *Financial aid:* Available to part-time students. Financial aid applicants required to submit FAFSA. • Dr. Randall Brown, Dean, 812-749-1409. Fax: 812-749-1294.

Oakland University, School of Business Administration, Rochester, MI 48309-4401. Offers programs in accounting (M Acc), business administration (MBA). Part-time and evening/weekend programs available. Faculty: 47 full-time. Students: 22 full-time (9 women), 372 part-time (131 women); includes 19 minority (7 African Americans, 8 Asian Americans, 4 Hispanics), 17 international. Average age 30. 230 applicants, 81% accepted. In 1997, 80 degrees awarded. *Degree requirements:* Computer language required, foreign language and thesis not required. *Entrance requirements:* GMAT (minimum score 500), minimum GPA of 3.0 for unconditional admission. Application deadline: 7/15 (3/15 for spring admission). Application fee: $30. *Expenses:* Tuition $3852 per year full-time, $214 per credit hour part-time for state residents; $8532 per year full-time, $474 per credit hour part-time for nonresidents. Fees $420 per year. *Financial aid:* Full tuition waivers, Federal Work-Study, institutionally sponsored loans, and career-related internships or fieldwork available. Financial aid application deadline: 3/1; applicants required to submit FAFSA. *Faculty research:* Health care, economics, auto industry forecasting, computers in management. • Dr. John Gardner, Dean, 248-370-3286. Application contact: Sheryl Clark, Coordinator, 248-370-3287.

Oglala Lakota College, Program in Lakota Leadership and Management, Kyle, SD 57752-0490. Awards MA. Part-time and evening/weekend programs available. Faculty: 1 full-time (0 women), 21 part-time (7 women). Students: 17 part-time (9 women); includes 17 minority (all Native Americans). Average age 43. 6 applicants, 100% accepted. In 1997, 7 degrees awarded. *Degree requirements:* Thesis. *Application deadline:* 8/25 (priority date; rolling processing). *Application fee:* $0. *Financial aid:* 4 students received aid; full and partial tuition waivers available. • Ed Starr, Director, 605-455-2321. Fax: 605-455-2787.

Oglethorpe University, Division of Business Administration, Atlanta, GA 30319-2797. Awards MBA. Faculty: 3 full-time (0 women). Students: 11 full-time (5 women), 30 part-time (15 women). Average age 33. 12 applicants, 67% accepted. *Degree requirements:* Thesis required, foreign language not required. *Entrance requirements:* GMAT, GRE General Test. Application deadline: 8/15. Application fee: $30. *Tuition:* $1380 per course. • William Steely, Director, 404-364-8353. Application contact: Bill Price, Graduate Admissions Counselor, 404-364-8307. Fax: 404-364-8500.

The Ohio State University, Max M. Fisher College of Business, Program in Business Administration, Columbus, OH 43210. Awards MA, MBA, PhD, JD/MBA, MBA/MS, MHA/MBA. Faculty: 64. Students: 433 full-time (114 women), 10 part-time (3 women); includes 56 minority (17 African Americans, 28 Asian Americans, 11 Hispanics), 86 international. 1,832 applicants, 23% accepted. In 1997, 203 master's, 10 doctorates awarded. *Degree requirements:* For doctorate, dissertation required, foreign language not required. *Entrance requirements:* For master's, GMAT, TOEFL (minimum score 575); for doctorate, GMAT, TOEFL. Application deadline: 8/15 (rolling processing). Application fee: $30 ($40 for international students). *Tuition:* $6018 per year full-time, $635 per quarter (minimum) part-time for state residents; $14,835 per year full-time, $1514 per quarter (minimum) part-time for nonresidents. *Financial aid:* Fellowships, research assistantships, teaching assistantships, administrative assistantships, Federal Work-Study, institutionally sponsored loans available. Aid available to part-time students. • H. Rao Unnava, Graduate Studies Committee Chair, 614-292-1506. E-mail: unnava.1@osu.edu. Application contact: Cindy Holodnak, Director, Graduate Programs, 614-292-8531. Fax: 614-292-1651. E-mail: holodnak.1@osu.edu.

See in-depth description on page 245.

Ohio University, Graduate Studies, College of Business, Graduate Program for Executives in Business Administration, Athens, OH 45701-2979. Awards EMBA. Part-time and evening/weekend programs available. Students: 66 part-time (23 women); includes 3 minority (all African Americans). Average age 34. 77 applicants, 65% accepted. In 1997, 31 degrees awarded. *Entrance requirements:* GMAT (minimum score 450), minimum GPA of 2.5, work experience in management. Application deadline: 6/1. Application fee: $30. *Tuition:* $5430 per year full-time, $216 per quarter hour part-time for state residents; $10,431 per year full-time, $423 per quarter hour part-time for nonresidents. *Financial aid:* Application deadline 3/15. • Dr. Kahandas Nandola, Director, 740-593-2028. Fax: 740-593-0319. E-mail: nandola@oak.cats.ohiou.edu.

See in-depth description on page 247.

Ohio University, Graduate Studies, College of Business, Graduate Program for the Master of Business Administration, Athens, OH 45701-2979. Awards MBA. Part-time and evening/weekend programs available. Faculty: 43 full-time (12 women), 11 part-time (5 women). Students: 35 full-time (17 women), 4 part-time (2 women); includes 1 minority (African American), 19 international. 144 applicants, 34% accepted. In 1997, 30 degrees awarded. *Average time to degree:* master's–1.5 years full-time, 2 years part-time. *Entrance requirements:* GMAT (minimum score 500), minimum GPA of 3.0. Application deadline: 3/1 (priority date). Application fee: $30. *Tuition:* $5430 per year full-time, $216 per quarter hour part-time for state residents; $10,431 per year full-time, $423 per quarter hour part-time for nonresidents. *Financial aid:* In 1997–98, 25 associateships were awarded; full and partial tuition waivers, Federal Work-Study, institutionally sponsored loans, and career-related internships or fieldwork also available. Financial aid application deadline: 3/1. • Dr. Frank Barone, Director, 740-593-2007. Application contact: Jan Ross, Graduate Services Coordinator, 740-593-2007. Fax: 740-593-9823. E-mail: rossj@ouvaxa.cats.ohiou.edu.

See in-depth description on page 247.

Oklahoma City University, School of Management and Business Sciences, Program in Business Administration, Oklahoma City, OK 73106-1402. Awards MBA, JD/MBA. Offerings include arts and public service/management (MBA), finance (MBA), health administration (MBA), information systems management (MBA), international business (MBA), management (MBA), marketing and advertising (MBA). Part-time and evening/weekend programs available. Students: 456 full-time (153 women), 761 part-time (288 women); includes 127 minority (67 African Americans, 17 Asian Americans, 28 Hispanics, 15 Native Americans), 616 international. In 1997, 461 degrees awarded. *Degree requirements:* Comprehensive exam required, foreign language and thesis not required. *Entrance requirements:* TOEFL, minimum GPA of 2.5. Application deadline: rolling. Application fee: $35 ($55 for international students). *Expenses:* Tuition $350 per hour. Fees $124 per year. *Financial aid:* Fellowships, partial tuition waivers, Federal Work-Study, institutionally sponsored loans, and career-related internships or fieldwork available. Aid available to part-time students. Financial aid application deadline: 8/1. • Application contact: Laura L. Rahhal, Director of Graduate Admissions, 800-633-7242 Ext. 2. Fax: 405-521-5356. E-mail: lrahhal1@frodo.okcu.edu.

Oklahoma State University, College of Business Administration, Stillwater, OK 74078. Awards MBA, MS, PhD. Faculty: 73 full-time (12 women), 4 part-time (0 women), 74.75 FTE. Students: 271 full-time (90 women), 377 part-time (136 women); includes 64 minority (21 African Americans, 20 Asian Americans, 11 Hispanics, 12 Native Americans), 126 international. Average age 32. In 1997, 177 master's, 8 doctorates awarded. *Degree requirements:* For doctorate, dissertation required, foreign language not required. *Entrance requirements:* For master's, GMAT (MBA), TOEFL (minimum score 550); for doctorate, TOEFL (minimum score 550). Application deadline: 7/1 (priority date). Application fee: $25. *Financial aid:* In 1997–98, 86 students received aid, including 6 research assistantships (1 to a first-year student) totaling $48,480, 79 teaching assistantships (23 to first-year students) totaling $640,641; partial tuition waivers, Federal Work-Study, and career-related internships or fieldwork also available. Aid available to part-time students. Financial aid application deadline: 3/1. • Dr. Gary L. Trennepohl, Dean, 405-744-5064.

Announcement: Oklahoma State University's MBA program has been recognized as the 8th-best value-added MBA program in the country (*Journal of Business*, January 1997). The fully accredited AACSB program offers integrative, cross-functional courses, as well as opportunities for specialization in traditional and emerging business areas. Classroom models and theories are complemented by experiential learning through real-world applications with corporate partners. While emphasizing pragmatism and organizational reality, the innovative 2-year curriculum balances quantitative and behavioral courses. Learning methods include case analyses, simulations, lectures, and field projects. Classroom learning is also enhanced by internships, professional development seminars, and an annual case competition.

Old Dominion University, College of Business and Public Administration, Doctoral Program in Business Administration, Norfolk, VA 23529. Awards PhD. Students: 24 full-time (10 women), 21 part-time (8 women); includes 6 minority (4 African Americans, 2 Native Americans), 17 international. Average age 37. In 1997, 2 degrees awarded. *Degree requirements:* Dissertation, comprehensive exams required, foreign language not required. *Entrance requirements:* GMAT (minimum score 580; average 610). Application deadline: 2/1. Application fee: $30. *Expenses:* Tuition $180 per credit hour for state residents; $477 per credit hour for nonresidents. Fees $140 per year full-time, $32 per semester part-time. *Financial aid:* In 1997–98, 19 students received aid, including 1 fellowship totaling $4,064, 16 research assistantships (1 to a first-year student) totaling $142,242, 1 tuition grant (to a first-year student) totaling $3,456; partial tuition waivers and career-related internships or fieldwork also available. Financial aid application deadline: 2/15; applicants required to submit FAFSA. *Faculty research:* International business, buyer behavior, financial markets, strategy, operations research. • Dr. C. P. Rao, Director, 757-683-5138. E-mail: crao@odu.edu.

See in-depth description on page 249.

Old Dominion University, College of Business and Public Administration, Master's Program in Business Administration, Norfolk, VA 23529. Awards MBA. Part-time and evening/weekend programs available. Postbaccalaureate distance learning degree programs offered (no on-campus study). Faculty: 1 full-time (0 women). Students: 111 full-time (43 women), 293 part-time (111 women); includes 47 minority (25 African Americans, 11 Asian Americans, 11 Hispanics), 61 international. Average age 31. In 1997, 102 degrees awarded. *Entrance requirements:* GMAT (average 520). Application deadline: 7/1 (rolling processing; 11/1 for spring admission). Application fee: $30. Electronic applications accepted. *Expenses:* Tuition $180 per credit hour for state residents; $477 per credit hour for nonresidents. Fees $140 per year full-time, $32 per semester part-time. *Financial aid:* In 1997–98, 86 students received aid, including 1 fellowship totaling $600, 30 research assistantships (6 to first-year students) totaling $200,550, 37 grants (10 to first-year students) totaling $111,668; teaching assistantships, partial tuition waivers, and career-related internships or fieldwork also available. Aid available to part-time students. Financial aid application deadline: 2/15; applicants required to submit FAFSA. *Faculty research:* International business, buyer behavior, financial markets, strategy, operation research. Total annual research expenditures: $10,277. • Dr. Bruce Rubin, Director, 757-683-3585. E-mail: brubin@odu.edu. Application contact: Jean Turpin, Program Manager and Adviser, 757-683-3585. Fax: 757-683-6082. E-mail: jturpin@odu.edu.

See in-depth description on page 249.

Olivet Nazarene University, Department of Business, Kankakee, IL 60901-0592. Offers program in business administration (MBA). Evening/weekend programs available. *Degree requirements:* Thesis or alternative required, foreign language not required. *Application deadline:* rolling. *Application fee:* $20.

Oral Roberts University, School of Business, Tulsa, OK 74171-0001. Offers programs in accounting (MBA), business administration (MBA), finance (MBA), international business (MBA), management (MBA), marketing (MBA). Part-time and evening/weekend programs available. *Degree requirements:* Computer language required, thesis optional, foreign language not required. *Entrance requirements:* GMAT (minimum score 400; average 500). Application deadline: 7/31 (priority date; rolling processing; 12/31 for spring admission). Application fee: $35. Electronic applications accepted. *Faculty research:* Investments, stock market, strategic long-range planning, entrepreneurship, free enterprise.

Oregon Graduate Institute of Science and Technology, Department of Management in Science and Technology, Portland, OR 97291-1000. Offers programs in computational finance (Certificate), management in science and technology (MS). Part-time and evening/weekend programs available. Faculty: 3 full-time (0 women), 9 part-time (1 woman). Students: 11 full-time (2 women), 42 part-time (12 women); includes 5 minority (4 Asian Americans, 1 Hispanic), 5 international. Average age 37. 29 applicants, 79% accepted. In 1997, 22 master's awarded. *Entrance requirements:* For master's, TOEFL (minimum score 650). Application deadline: rolling. Application fee: $50. Electronic applications accepted. *Tuition:* $17,000 per year full-time, $425 per credit part-time. • Dr. Fred Young Phillips, Head, 503-690-1353. Fax: 503-690-1268. E-mail: fphillips@admin.ogi.edu. Application contact: Frances M. Hewitt, Enrollment Manager, 800-685-2423. Fax: 503-690-1285.

See in-depth description on page 251.

Oregon State University, Graduate School, College of Business, Corvallis, OR 97331. Awards MAIS, MBA, Certificate. Part-time programs available. Faculty: 27 full-time (4 women). Students: 63 full-time (23 women), 18 part-time (9 women); includes 7 minority (5 Asian Americans, 2 Hispanics), 25 international. Average age 28. 188 applicants, 56% accepted. In 1997, 43 master's awarded. *Degree requirements:* For master's, minimum GPA of 3.0, portfolio required, foreign language and thesis not required. *Entrance requirements:* For master's, GMAT (minimum score 500), TOEFL (minimum score 575), minimum GPA of 3.0 in last 90 hours. Application deadline: 3/15 (rolling processing). Application fee: $50. *Tuition:* $6207 per year full-time, $810 per quarter (minimum) part-time for state residents; $10,551 per year full-time, $1293 per quarter (minimum) part-time for nonresidents. *Financial aid:* In 1997–98, 15 teaching assistantships were awarded; fellowships, Federal Work-Study, institutionally sponsored loans, and career-related internships or fieldwork also available. Financial aid application deadline: 2/1. *Faculty research:* Financial and account services, market analysis and planning, innovation,

Directory: Business Administration and Management—General

Oregon State University (continued)
family business, tourism. • Dr. Donald F. Parker, Dean, 541-737-6022. Application contact: Clara Horne, Head Adviser, 541-737-3716. Fax: 541-737-4890.

Otterbein College, Department of Business, Accounting and Economics, Westerville, OH 43081. Awards MBA. Students: 39. *Entrance requirements:* GMAT. Application deadline: rolling. Application fee: $35. *Tuition:* $5216 per quarter. • Dr. Dan Eskew, Interim Chair. Application contact: Dr. Gail Arch, Director, 614-823-3210. Fax: 614-823-1014. E-mail: mba@otterbein.edu.

Our Lady of the Lake University of San Antonio, School of Business and Public Administration, 411 Southwest 24th Street, San Antonio, TX 78207-4689. Offers programs in general (MBA), including finance, international business, management; health care management (MBA). Part-time and evening/weekend programs available. Faculty: 15 full-time (2 women), 15 part-time (2 women). Students: 36 full-time (14 women), 522 part-time (275 women); includes 210 minority (52 African Americans, 22 Asian Americans, 132 Hispanics, 4 Native Americans), 3 international. Average age 38. In 1997, 168 degrees awarded. *Degree requirements:* Thesis optional. *Entrance requirements:* GMAT, GRE General Test, or MAT. Application deadline: rolling. Application fee: $15. *Expenses:* Tuition $371 per credit hour. Fees $57 per semester full-time, $32 per semester part-time. *Financial aid:* 40 students received aid; fellowships available. Financial aid application deadline: 4/15. *Faculty research:* International marketing, employee benefits, decision process. • Dr. W. Earl Walker, Dean, 210-434-6711 Ext. 281. Application contact: Quentin W. Korte, MBA Adviser, 210-434-6711 Ext. 491. Fax: 210-434-0821.

Pace University, Lubin School of Business, New York, NY 10038. Awards MBA, MS, DPS, APC, JD/MBA. Part-time and evening/weekend programs available. *Degree requirements:* For doctorate, computer language, dissertation, oral and written exams required, foreign language not required. *Entrance requirements:* For master's, GMAT; for doctorate, GMAT, interview. Application deadline: 7/31 (priority date; rolling processing; 11/30 for spring admission). Application fee: $60. *Expenses:* Tuition $545 per credit. Fees $360 per year full-time, $53 per semester (minimum) part-time.

Announcement: Pace University's Lubin School of Business' state-of-the-art graduate programs integrate theory and practical applications and offer exciting opportunities for experiential and team learning. Expanding facilities and ever-changing, revitalized curricula reflect Pace's continuing commitment to remaining in the forefront of business education and the development of global business management.

See in-depth description on page 253.

Pacific Lutheran University, School of Business Administration and Management, Tacoma, WA 98447. Offers program in business administration (MBA), including technology and innovation management. Part-time and evening/weekend programs available. Faculty: 10 full-time (1 woman), 4 part-time (1 woman). Students: 56 full-time (18 women), 35 part-time (14 women); includes 5 minority (1 African American, 3 Asian Americans, 1 Hispanic), 15 international. Average age 33. 39 applicants, 79% accepted. In 1997, 27 degrees awarded. *Degree requirements:* Thesis or alternative required, foreign language not required. *Entrance requirements:* GMAT (minimum score 470), TOEFL (minimum score 550). Application deadline: rolling. Application fee: $35. *Tuition:* $490 per semester hour. *Financial aid:* Fellowships, research assistantships, scholarships, Federal Work-Study available. Financial aid application deadline: 3/1. • Dr. Joseph McCann, Dean, 253-535-7250. Application contact: Jan Dempsey, Director, 253-535-7250.

Pacific States University, College of Business, Doctoral Program in Business Administration, Los Angeles, CA 90006. Awards DBA. Students: 12. *Entrance requirements:* TOEFL (minimum score 450), interview, minimum GPA of 2.5 (undergraduate) or 3.0 (graduate). Application deadline: 6/15 (12/15 for spring admission). Application fee: $150. *Tuition:* $240 per unit. • Dr. Jonathan Kline, Director, 888-200-0383.

Palm Beach Atlantic College, Rinker School of Business, West Palm Beach, FL 33416-4708. Awards MBA. Part-time and evening/weekend programs available. Faculty: 2 full-time (1 woman), 4 part-time (0 women). Students: 62 full-time (24 women), 50 part-time (17 women); includes 13 minority (4 African Americans, 1 Asian American, 8 Hispanics), 5 international. Average age 33. 47 applicants, 87% accepted. In 1997, 33 degrees awarded. *Entrance requirements:* GMAT (minimum score 450; average 474), minimum GPA of 3.0. Application deadline: 7/15 (priority date; rolling processing; 11/15 for spring admission). Application fee: $35. *Tuition:* $280 per credit hour. *Financial aid:* Career-related internships or fieldwork available. Aid available to part-time students. Financial aid applicants required to submit FAFSA. • Dr. David Luhrsen Jr., Dean, 561-803-2450. Fax: 561-803-2186. Application contact: Carolanne M. Brown, Director of Graduate Admissions, 800-281-3466. Fax: 561-803-2115. E-mail: grad@pbac.edu.

Park College, Graduate Program in Business Administration, Parkville, MO 64152-4358. Awards MBA. Students: 26. *Entrance requirements:* Minimum GPA of 2.5. Application deadline: 8/1 (priority date; rolling processing). Application fee: $25. *Tuition:* $210 per credit hour. • Dr. J'Noel Ball, Director, 816-741-2000 Ext. 6307.

Pennsylvania State University at Erie, The Behrend College, Program in Business Administration, Erie, PA 16563. Awards MBA. Students: 4 full-time (2 women), 134 part-time (48 women). Average age 33. In 1997, 24 degrees awarded. *Entrance requirements:* GMAT. Application deadline: 7/26. Application fee: $40. • Dr. John Magenau, Director, 814-898-6107.

Pennsylvania State University Great Valley School of Graduate Professional Studies, Graduate Studies and Continuing Education, Program in Management, Malvern, PA 19355-1488. Awards M Mgt, Post Master's Certificate, M Eng/M Mgt. Students: 29 full-time (16 women), 450 part-time (189 women). Average age 34. In 1997, 173 master's awarded. *Entrance requirements:* For master's, GRE General Test or GMAT. Application fee: $40. • Dr. David Fritzsche, Director, 610-648-3246.

Pennsylvania State University Harrisburg Campus of the Capital College, School of Business Administration, Program in Business Administration, Middletown, PA 17057-4898. Awards MBA. Students: 10 full-time (7 women), 177 part-time (64 women). Average age 33. In 1997, 27 degrees awarded. *Entrance requirements:* GMAT, TOEFL (minimum score 550). Application deadline: 7/26. Application fee: $40. *Expenses:* Tuition $6534 per year full-time, $276 per credit part-time for state residents; $12,516 per year full-time, $523 per credit part-time for nonresidents. Fees $232 per year (minimum) full-time, $40 per semester (minimum) part-time. • Dr. Gayle Yaverbaum, Director of Graduate Studies, 717-948-6140.

Pennsylvania State University University Park Campus, The Mary Jean and Frank P. Smeal College of Business Administration, PhD Programs in Business Administration, University Park, PA 16802-1503. Offerings in accounting (PhD), finance/insurance and real estate (PhD), management and organization (PhD), management science/operations/logistics (PhD), marketing and distribution (PhD). *Degree requirements:* Dissertation. *Entrance requirements:* GMAT. Application fee: $40. *Expenses:* Tuition $6534 per year full-time, $276 per credit part-time for state residents; $13,460 per year full-time, $561 per credit part-time for nonresidents. Fees $252 per year (minimum) full-time, $43 per semester (minimum) part-time. • Dr. Kenneth M. Lusht, Director and Associate Dean for Research, 814-865-7669. Application contact: Office of PhD and MS Programs, 814-865-1225.

Pennsylvania State University University Park Campus, The Mary Jean and Frank P. Smeal College of Business Administration, Program in Business Administration, University Park, PA 16802-1503. Awards MBA. Students: 328 full-time (89 women), 43 part-time (13 women). In 1997, 171 degrees awarded. *Degree requirements:* Thesis or alternative required, foreign language not required. *Entrance requirements:* GMAT. Application fee: $40. *Expenses:* Tuition $6534 per year full-time, $276 per credit part-time for state residents; $13,460 per year full-time, $561 per credit part-time for nonresidents. Fees $252 per year (minimum) full-time, $43 per semester (minimum) part-time. • Dr. Rocki-Lee DeWitt, Associate Dean for Professional Master's Programs, 814-863-3798. Application contact: James H. Hoy, MBA Admissions/Marketing Manager, 814-863-0474.

Pepperdine University, School of Business and Management, Culver City, CA 90230-7615. Offers programs in business (MBA, MIB), including business administration (MBA), international business (MIB); executive business administration (MBAA); organizational development (MSOD); technology management (MSTM). Part-time and evening/weekend programs available. Faculty: 72 full-time (10 women), 38 part-time (5 women). Students: 172 full-time (43 women), 1,675 part-time (649 women); includes 434 minority (85 African Americans, 211 Asian Americans, 135 Hispanics, 3 Native Americans), 42 international. Average age 35. 660 applicants, 78% accepted. In 1997, 609 degrees awarded. *Entrance requirements:* GMAT or MAT. Application deadline: 5/1. Application fee: $45. *Financial aid:* In 1997–98, 155 graduate assistantships, scholarships were awarded; institutionally sponsored loans and career-related internships or fieldwork also available. Aid available to part-time students. • Dr. Otis Baskin, Dean, 310-568-5500. Application contact: Dianna Sadlouskos, Director of Career Development and Student Recruitment.

Pepperdine University, Malibu Graduate Business Programs, Malibu, CA 90263-0001. Awards MBA, MIB, JD/MBA. Offerings include business administration (MBA), international business (MIB). MBA and MIB offered jointly with the School of Business and Management at the Culver City campus. Students: 179 full-time (78 women), 4 part-time (1 woman); includes 27 minority (8 African Americans, 12 Asian Americans, 6 Hispanics, 1 Native American), 64 international. Average age 28. 384 applicants, 60% accepted. In 1997, 103 degrees awarded. *Degree requirements:* Foreign language (MIB) required, thesis not required. *Entrance requirements:* GMAT, MAT, TOEFL. Application deadline: 5/1 (rolling processing). Application fee: $45. *Financial aid:* 105 students received aid; graduate assistantships, scholarships, institutionally sponsored loans, and career-related internships or fieldwork available. Financial aid application deadline: 6/1. • Dr. James A. Goodrich, Associate Dean, 310-456-4100. Application contact: Dianna Sadlouskos, Director of Career Development and Student Recruitment, 310-456-4044. Fax: 310-456-4126.

See in-depth description on page 255.

Pfeiffer University, Program in Business Administration, Charlotte, NC 28209. Awards MBA, MS, MBA/MHA. Offerings include business administration (MBA), organizational management (MS). Part-time and evening/weekend programs available. Postbaccalaureate distance learning degree programs offered. Faculty: 11 full-time (2 women), 8 part-time (4 women), 15 FTE. Students: 550. *Entrance requirements:* GMAT (minimum score 500), minimum GPA of 3.0. Application deadline: 8/21. Application fee: $50. *Tuition:* $245 per hour (minimum). *Financial aid:* Assistantships available. Aid available to part-time students. • Dr. Muhammed Abdullah, Director, 704-521-9116. Fax: 704-521-8617.

Philadelphia College of Textiles and Science, School of Business, Program in Business, Philadelphia, PA 19144-5497. Awards MBA, MBA/MS. Offerings include accounting (MBA), business administration (MBA), finance (MBA), health care management (MBA), international business (MBA), marketing (MBA). Part-time and evening/weekend programs available. *Entrance requirements:* GMAT, minimum GPA of 2.85. Application deadline: rolling. Application fee: $35. *Tuition:* $448 per credit hour. *Financial aid:* Research assistantships, graduate assistantships, residential assistantships, Federal Work-Study, and career-related internships or fieldwork available. Financial aid applicants required to submit FAFSA. • Rita Powell, Director, 215-951-2950. Fax: 215-951-2652. E-mail: powellr@phila.col.edu. Application contact: Robert J. Reed, Director of Graduate Admissions, 215-951-2943. Fax: 215-951-2907. E-mail: gradadm@phila.col.edu.

Phillips University, School of Business, 100 South University Avenue, Enid, OK 73701-6439. Awards MBA. Part-time programs available. Faculty: 5 full-time (0 women), 2 part-time (0 women). Students: 6 full-time, 13 part-time. In 1997, 12 degrees awarded. *Degree requirements:* Thesis (for some programs), oral exam required, foreign language not required. *Entrance requirements:* GMAT, minimum GPA of 2.5. Application deadline: 8/1 (1/1 for spring admission). Application fee: $20. *Expenses:* Tuition $97 per credit hour. Fees $10 per credit hour. *Financial aid:* Scholarships, full and partial tuition waivers, Federal Work-Study, institutionally sponsored loans, and career-related internships or fieldwork available. Aid available to part-time students. Financial aid application deadline: 6/1; applicants required to submit FAFSA. • Dean, 405-237-4433 Ext. 365.

Pittsburg State University, Gladys A. Kelce School of Business and Economics, Department of Management and Marketing, Pittsburg, KS 66762-5880. Offers program in general administration (MBA). Faculty: 8 full-time (1 woman). Students: 71 full-time (29 women), 25 part-time (12 women); includes 2 minority (1 Asian American, 1 Hispanic), 58 international. In 1997, 46 degrees awarded. *Degree requirements:* Thesis or alternative required, foreign language not required. *Entrance requirements:* GMAT. Application fee: $40. *Tuition:* $2418 per year full-time, $103 per credit hour part-time for state residents; $6130 per year full-time, $258 per credit hour part-time for nonresidents. *Financial aid:* Research assistantships, teaching assistantships, Federal Work-Study, and career-related internships or fieldwork available. Financial aid application deadline: 3/1. *Faculty research:* Consumer behavior, productions management, forecasting interest rate swaps, strategy management. • Dr. Henry Crouch, Chairperson, 316-235-4588.

Plymouth State College of the University System of New Hampshire, Department of Business Studies, Plymouth, NH 03264-1595. Awards MBA. Part-time and evening/weekend programs available. Faculty: 22 full-time (3 women). Students: 25 full-time (10 women), 125 part-time (49 women); includes 8 minority (7 Asian Americans, 1 Native American), 2 international. Average age 35. 59 applicants, 76% accepted. In 1997, 51 degrees awarded. *Entrance requirements:* GMAT, minimum GPA of 2.5. Application deadline: 9/1 (priority date; rolling processing). Application fee: $25 ($35 for international students). *Tuition:* $819 per course full-time, $816 per course part-time for state residents; $897 per course for nonresidents. *Financial aid:* In 1997–98, 5 graduate assistantships averaging $445 per month were awarded; institutionally sponsored loans also available. Aid available to part-time students. Financial aid application deadline: 3/15; applicants required to submit FAFSA. • Dr. Colleen Brickley, Director, 603-535-2739. Application contact: Maryann Szabadics, Administrative Secretary, 603-535-2636. Fax: 603-535-2572. E-mail: for.grad@psc.plymouth.edu.

See in-depth description on page 257.

Polytechnic University, Brooklyn Campus, Department of Management, Six Metrotech Center, Brooklyn, NY 11201-2990. Offers programs in financial engineering (MS), management (MS), management of technology (MS), operations management (MS), organizational behavior (MS), telecommunications and computing management (MS). Part-time and evening/weekend programs available. Students: 125. 125 applicants, 73% accepted. In 1997, 67 degrees awarded. *Degree requirements:* Thesis or alternative. *Entrance requirements:* GMAT, minimum B average in undergraduate course work. Application deadline: rolling. Application fee: $45. Electronic applications accepted. *Expenses:* Tuition $19,530 per year full-time, $675 per credit part-time. Fees $600 per year full-time, $135 per semester part-time. • Mel Horwitch, Head, 718-260-3610. Fax: 718-260-3874. E-mail: horwitch@poly.edu. Application contact: John S. Kerge, Dean of Admissions, 718-260-3200. Fax: 718-260-3446. E-mail: admitme@poly.edu.

Polytechnic University, Farmingdale Campus, Graduate Programs, Department of Management, Route 110, Farmingdale, NY 11735-3995. Offers programs in financial engineering (MS), management (MS), operations management (MS). Part-time and evening/weekend programs available. Students: 38. 14 applicants, 86% accepted. In 1997, 41 degrees awarded. *Application deadline:* rolling. *Application fee:* $45. Electronic applications accepted. *Expenses:*

Tuition $19,530 per year full-time, $675 per credit part-time. Fees $600 per year full-time, $135 per semester part-time. *Financial aid:* Institutionally sponsored loans available. Aid available to part-time students. Financial aid applicants required to submit FAFSA. • Dr. Mel Horwitch, Head, 718-260-3610. Fax: 718-260-3874. E-mail: horwitch@poly.edu. Application contact: John S. Kerge, Dean of Admissions, 718-260-3200. Fax: 718-260-3446. E-mail: admitme@poly.edu.

Polytechnic University, Westchester Graduate Center, Division of Management, Hawthorne, NY 10532-1507. Offers programs in financial engineering (MS), management (MS), management of technology (MS), operations management (MS), organizational behavior (MS), telecommunication and computing management (MS). Part-time and evening/weekend programs available. Faculty: 6. Students: 157 part-time. 110 applicants, 95% accepted. In 1997, 65 degrees awarded. *Degree requirements:* Computer language. *Application deadline:* rolling. *Application fee:* $45. Electronic applications accepted. *Expenses:* Tuition $19,530 per year full-time, $675 per credit part-time. Fees $600 per year full-time, $135 per semester part-time. *Financial aid:* Institutionally sponsored loans available. Aid available to part-time students. Financial aid applicants required to submit FAFSA. • Mel Horwitch, Dean, 718-260-3610. Fax: 718-260-3874. E-mail: horwitch@poly.edu. Application contact: John S. Kerge, Dean of Admissions, 718-260-3200. Fax: 718-260-3446. E-mail: admitme@poly.edu.

Pontifical Catholic University of Puerto Rico, College of Business Administration, Ponce, PR 00731-6382. Awards MBA, JD/MBA. Part-time and evening/weekend programs available. Faculty: 6 full-time (3 women), 4 part-time (2 women). Students: 41 full-time (26 women), 217 part-time (111 women); includes 258 minority (all Hispanics). Average age 34. 88 applicants, 100% accepted. In 1997, 60 degrees awarded. *Degree requirements:* Thesis. *Entrance requirements:* Interview, minimum GPA of 2.5. Application deadline: 4/30 (priority date; rolling processing). Application fee: $15. Electronic applications accepted. *Financial aid:* Fellowships, partial tuition waivers, Federal Work-Study available. Aid available to part-time students. Financial aid application deadline: 7/15. • Dr. Kenya Carrasquillo, Chairperson, 787-841-2000 Ext. 335. Application contact: Manuel Luciano, Director of Admissions, 787-841-2000 Ext. 426. Fax: 787-840-4295.

Portland State University, School of Business Administration, Portland, OR 97207-0751. Awards MBA, MIM, M Tax, PhD. PhD offered in conjunction with the Systems Science Program. Part-time and evening/weekend programs available. Postbaccalaureate distance learning degree programs offered (minimal on-campus study). Faculty: 57 full-time (17 women), 34 part-time (9 women), 60 FTE. Students: 132 full-time (61 women), 220 part-time (86 women); includes 32 minority (5 African Americans, 18 Asian Americans, 6 Hispanics, 3 Native Americans), 45 international. Average age 30. 428 applicants, 52% accepted. In 1997, 152 master's awarded. *Degree requirements:* For doctorate, dissertation. *Entrance requirements:* For master's, GMAT, TOEFL (minimum score 550). Application deadline: 4/1 (priority date). Application fee: $50. *Tuition:* $6101 per year full-time, $689 per semester (minimum) part-time for state residents; $10,445 per year full-time, $689 per semester (minimum) part-time for nonresidents. *Financial aid:* In 1997–98, 25 research assistantships (4 to first-year students) were awarded; teaching assistantships, Federal Work-Study, institutionally sponsored loans, and career-related internships or fieldwork also available. Aid available to part-time students. Financial aid application deadline: 3/1; applicants required to submit FAFSA. • Dr. Roger Ahlbrandt, Dean, 503-725-3721. Fax: 503-725-5850. E-mail: rogera@sba.pdx.edu.

See in-depth description on page 259.

Portland State University, Systems Science Program, Portland, OR 97207-0751. Offerings include systems science/business administration (PhD). Program faculty: 3 full-time (0 women), 1 part-time (0 women), 3.4 FTE. *Degree requirements:* Variable foreign language requirement, computer language, dissertation. *Entrance requirements:* GMAT (score in 75th percentile or higher), GRE General Test (score in 75th percentile or higher), TOEFL (minimum score 575), minimum undergraduate GPA of 3.0. Application deadline: 2/1 (11/1 for spring admission). Application fee: $50. *Tuition:* $6101 per year full-time, $689 per semester (minimum) part-time for state residents; $10,445 per year full-time, $689 per semester (minimum) part-time for nonresidents. • Dr. Nancy Perrin, Interim Director and Vice Provost, 503-725-4960. Application contact: Dawn Kuenle, 503-725-4960. E-mail: dawn@sysc.pdx.edu.

Prairie View A&M University, College of Business, Prairie View, TX 77446-0188. Offers program in general business administration (MBA). Part-time and evening/weekend programs available. Faculty: 13 full-time (2 women). Students: 30 full-time (12 women), 38 part-time (20 women); includes 50 minority (48 African Americans, 2 Asian Americans), 8 international. Average age 29. In 1997, 7 degrees awarded (100% found work related to degree). *Average time to degree:* master's–2.5 years full-time, 4 years part-time. *Entrance requirements:* GMAT (average 400), minimum GPA of 2.75. Application deadline: 7/1 (priority date; rolling processing; 11/1 for spring admission). Application fee: $10. *Tuition:* $2202 per year full-time, $336 per semester (minimum) part-time for state residents; $6000 per year full-time, $963 per semester (minimum) part-time for nonresidents. *Financial aid:* Federal Work-Study, institutionally sponsored loans available. Financial aid application deadline: 6/31. • Dr. David Kruegel, Interim Dean, 409-857-4310. Application contact: Dr. G. W. Nelson, Coordinator, 409-857-4310. Fax: 409-857-2797.

Providence College, Department of Business Administration, Providence, RI 02918. Awards MBA. Part-time and evening/weekend programs available. Faculty: 14 full-time (4 women), 8 part-time (0 women). Students: 23 full-time (6 women), 112 part-time (45 women); includes 1 international. Average age 33. 81 applicants, 85% accepted. In 1997, 64 degrees awarded. *Degree requirements:* Thesis optional, foreign language not required. *Entrance requirements:* GMAT (average 500), TOEFL. Application deadline: 8/12 (priority date; rolling processing; 12/1 for spring admission). Application fee: $40. *Tuition:* $729 per course. *Financial aid:* In 1997–98, 9 students received aid, including 2 graduate assistantships averaging $650 per month and totaling $15,600; institutionally sponsored loans also available. Aid available to part-time students. Financial aid applicants required to submit FAFSA. • Dr. John Shaw, Director, 401-865-2332.

See in-depth description on page 261.

Purdue University, Krannert Graduate School of Management, West Lafayette, IN 47907. Awards MS, MSIA, MSM, PhD. Evening/weekend programs available. Faculty: 84 full-time (9 women). Students: 503 full-time (142 women), 76 part-time (21 women); includes 67 minority (24 African Americans, 33 Asian Americans, 9 Hispanics, 1 Native American), 206 international. 2,039 applicants, 24% accepted. In 1997, 311 master's, 13 doctorates awarded. Terminal master's awarded for partial completion of doctoral program. *Degree requirements:* For doctorate, dissertation required, foreign language not required. *Entrance requirements:* For master's, GMAT, TOEFL (minimum score 575); for doctorate, GMAT or GRE General Test, TOEFL (minimum score 575). Application fee: $30. Electronic applications accepted. *Tuition:* $3500 per year full-time, $126 per credit hour part-time for state residents; $11,720 per year full-time, $387 per credit hour part-time for nonresidents. *Financial aid:* Fellowships, research assistantships, teaching assistantships, and career-related internships or fieldwork available. Aid available to part-time students. Financial aid application deadline: 2/15; applicants required to submit FAFSA. • Dr. Dennis J. Weidenaar, Dean, 765-494-4366.

See in-depth description on page 263.

Purdue University Calumet, School of Professional Studies, Department of Management, Hammond, IN 46323-2094. Awards MS. Evening/weekend programs available. *Entrance requirements:* GMAT, TOEFL. Application fee: $30.

Queens College, McColl School of Business, 1900 Selwyn Avenue, Charlotte, NC 28274-0002. Awards MBA. Part-time and evening/weekend programs available. Faculty: 7 full-time (1 woman), 4 part-time (1 woman). Students: 78 full-time (31 women), 206 part-time (94 women); includes 27 minority (21 African Americans, 3 Asian Americans, 2 Hispanics, 1 Native American). Average age 31. 89 applicants, 90% accepted. In 1997, 67 degrees awarded. *Entrance requirements:* GMAT (minimum score 450; average 520). Application deadline: rolling. Application fee: $25. *Expenses:* Tuition $260 per credit hour. Fees $40 per year. *Financial aid:* In 1997–98, 30 fellowships (12 to first-year students) were awarded; institutionally sponsored loans also available. Aid available to part-time students. • Dr. Sid Adkins, Dean, 704-337-2234. Application contact: Katie M. Wireman, Director of Admissions, 704-337-2224. Fax: 704-337-2594.

Queen's University at Kingston, School of Business, Program in Business Administration, Kingston, ON K7L 3N6, Canada. Awards MBA, MIR/MBA. *Degree requirements:* Research project required, thesis optional, foreign language not required. *Entrance requirements:* GMAT, TOEFL (minimum score 550; average 580). Application deadline: 2/28 (priority date). Application fee: $60. *Tuition:* $3803 per year (minimum) full-time, $1901 per year (minimum) part-time for Canadian residents; $7330 per year (minimum) for nonresidents. *Financial aid:* Fellowships, research assistantships, teaching assistantships available. Financial aid application deadline: 3/1. • Dr. Margot Northey, Dean, School of Business, 613-545-2305.

Queen's University at Kingston, School of Business, Program in Business Administration in Science and Technology, Kingston, ON K7L 3N6, Canada. Awards MBA. *Degree requirements:* Research project required, thesis optional, foreign language not required. *Entrance requirements:* GMAT, TOEFL (minimum score 550; average 580), bachelor's degree in engineering or science, 5 years of work experience in field. Application deadline: 2/28 (priority date). Application fee: $60. *Tuition:* $3803 per year (minimum) full-time, $1901 per year (minimum) part-time for Canadian residents; $7330 per year (minimum) for nonresidents. *Financial aid:* Fellowships, research assistantships, teaching assistantships available. Financial aid application deadline: 3/1. • Dr. Margot Northey, Dean, School of Business, 613-545-2305.

Queen's University at Kingston, School of Business, Program in Management, Kingston, ON K7L 3N6, Canada. Awards M Sc, PhD. M Sc and PhD administered by the School of Graduate Studies and Research. Students: 38 full-time (16 women), 3 part-time (0 women). In 1997, 7 doctorates awarded. *Degree requirements:* For master's, research project required, thesis optional, foreign language not required; for doctorate, dissertation, comprehensive exam required, foreign language not required. *Entrance requirements:* For master's, GMAT, TOEFL (minimum score 550; average 580); for doctorate, GMAT, TOEFL (minimum score 550; average 640). Application deadline: 2/28 (priority date). Application fee: $60. Electronic applications accepted. *Tuition:* $3803 per year (minimum) full-time, $1901 per year (minimum) part-time for Canadian residents; $7330 per year (minimum) for nonresidents. *Financial aid:* Fellowships, research assistantships, teaching assistantships available. Financial aid application deadline: 3/1. • Application contact: Dr. P. A. Todd, Graduate Coordinator, 613-545-6687.

Quincy University, Division of Business, Quincy, IL 62301-2699. Awards MBA. Part-time and evening/weekend programs available. Faculty: 5 full-time (1 woman). Students: 43 part-time (18 women). Average age 28. In 1997, 15 degrees awarded. *Entrance requirements:* GMAT, previous course work in accounting, economics, finance, management, marketing, and statistics. Application fee: $25. *Tuition:* $380 per credit hour. *Financial aid:* 6 students received aid. Aid available to part-time students. Financial aid applicants required to submit FAFSA. *Faculty research:* Macroeconomic forecasting, business ethics/social responsibility. • Dr. Ronny Richardson, Director, MBA Program, 217-228-5394.

Quinnipiac College, School of Business, Program in Business Administration, Hamden, CT 06518-1904. Awards MBA, JD/MBA. Offerings include accounting (MBA), computer information systems (MBA), economics (MBA), finance (MBA), health management (MBA), international business (MBA), management (MBA), marketing (MBA). Part-time and evening/weekend programs available. Faculty: 17 full-time (2 women), 4 part-time (1 woman). Students: 56 full-time (26 women), 130 part-time (66 women); includes 11 minority (2 African Americans, 5 Asian Americans, 4 Hispanics), 1 international. Average age 30. 91 applicants, 65% accepted. In 1997, 39 degrees awarded (100% found work related to degree). *Degree requirements:* Thesis optional, foreign language not required. *Average time to degree:* master's–2 years full-time, 4 years part-time. *Entrance requirements:* GMAT (minimum score 400; average 470), interview, minimum GPA of 2.5. Application deadline: 8/1 (priority date; rolling processing). Application fee: $45. Electronic applications accepted. *Expenses:* Tuition $395 per credit hour. Fees $380 per year full-time. *Financial aid:* In 1997–98, 5 research assistantships (3 to first-year students) were awarded; career-related internships or fieldwork also available. Aid available to part-time students. Financial aid applicants required to submit FAFSA. *Faculty research:* Taxation, labor relations, financial institutions, consumer satisfaction, international capital market efficiency. • Dr. Earl Chrysler, Director, 203-281-8799. Fax: 203-281-8664. E-mail: chrysler@quinnipiac.edu. Application contact: Scott Farber, Director of Graduate Admissions, 203-281-8795. Fax: 203-287-5238. E-mail: qcgradadmi@quinnipiac.edu.

See in-depth description on page 265.

Radford University, Graduate College, College of Business and Economics, Program in Business Administration, Radford, VA 24142. Awards MBA. Part-time programs available. Postbaccalaureate distance learning degree programs offered (minimal on-campus study). Faculty: 2 full-time (0 women). Students: 31 full-time (8 women), 56 part-time (27 women); includes 6 minority (4 African Americans, 2 Asian Americans), 17 international. Average age 30. 93 applicants, 70% accepted. In 1997, 18 degrees awarded. *Degree requirements:* Comprehensive exam required, foreign language and thesis not required. *Entrance requirements:* GMAT, TOEFL (minimum score 550), minimum GPA of 2.7. Application deadline: 2/1 (priority date; rolling processing; 10/1 for spring admission). Application fee: $25. Electronic applications accepted. *Expenses:* Tuition $2302 per year full-time, $147 per credit hour part-time for state residents; $5672 per year full-time, $287 per credit hour part-time for nonresidents. Fees $1222 per year full-time. *Financial aid:* In 1997–98, 4 fellowships totaling $10,214, 15 research assistantships totaling $44,606, 31 scholarships/grants totaling $114,790 were awarded; teaching assistantships, Federal Work-Study, institutionally sponsored loans, and career-related internships or fieldwork also available. Financial aid application deadline: 2/1; applicants required to submit FAFSA. • Dr. R. Wayne Saubert, Director, 540-831-5258. Fax: 540-831-6103. E-mail: wsaubert@runet.edu.

Regent University, Graduate School, School of Business, Virginia Beach, VA 23464-9800. Awards MA, MBA, JD/MA, JD/MBA, MBA/MA, MBA/M Ed, M Div/MA, M Div/MBA. Programs in business administration (MBA), management (MA). Part-time and evening/weekend programs available. Faculty: 7 full-time (0 women), 1 part-time (0 women). Students: 76 full-time (26 women), 168 part-time (47 women); includes 62 minority (41 African Americans, 12 Asian Americans, 6 Hispanics, 3 Native Americans). Average age 35. 115 applicants, 63% accepted. In 1997, 63 degrees awarded. *Average time to degree:* master's–2 years full-time, 3.5 years part-time. *Entrance requirements:* GMAT, minimum undergraduate GPA of 2.75. Application deadline: 6/1 (priority date; rolling processing). Application fee: $40. *Expenses:* Tuition $325 per credit hour. Fees $18 per semester. *Financial aid:* 46 students received aid; full and partial tuition waivers and career-related internships or fieldwork available. Financial aid application deadline: 5/1. *Faculty research:* Leadership development, managing nonprofit organizations, small entrepreneurial business developments in U.S. and ex-communist lands, financial planning, Christian business ethics. • Dr. John E. Mulford, Dean, 757-226-4351. E-mail: johnmul@regent.edu. Application contact: Tom Stansbury, Enrollment Manager, 757-226-4356. Fax: 757-226-4349. E-mail: tomstan@regent.edu.

Regis University, Program in Business, Denver, CO 80221-1099. Awards MBA. Offered at Colorado Springs Campus, Northwest Denver Campus, Southeast Denver Campus, and Fort Collins Campus. Part-time and evening/weekend programs available. Postbaccalaureate distance learning degree programs offered (no on-campus study). Students: 337 full-time, 480 part-time; includes 73 minority (23 African Americans, 17 Asian Americans, 26 Hispanics, 7 Native Americans), 20 international. Average age 36. In 1997, 178 degrees awarded. *Degree requirements:* Thesis optional, foreign language not required. *Average time to degree:* master's–2 years full-time, 4 years part-time. *Entrance requirements:* GMAT, interview, 2 years of work

Directory: Business Administration and Management—General

Regis University (continued)

experience. Application deadline: rolling. Application fee: $75. *Tuition:* $322 per semester hour (minimum). *Financial aid:* Federal Work-Study available. Aid available to part-time students. Financial aid applicants required to submit FAFSA. *Faculty research:* Finance, accounting, information systems, operations management, marketing. • Michael Goess, Chair, 303-458-4302. Application contact: Richard Boorom, Director of Marketing and Admissions, 800-677-9270. Fax: 303-964-5538. E-mail: admarg@regis.edu.

Regis University, Program in Management, Denver, CO 80221-1099. Awards MSM. Offered at Boulder Campus, Fort Collins Campus, Northwest Denver Campus, Southeast Denver Campus, and Colorado Springs Campus. Part-time and evening/weekend programs available. Students: 123 full-time, 87 part-time; includes 29 minority (9 African Americans, 1 Asian American, 16 Hispanics, 3 Native Americans). Average age 41. In 1997, 49 degrees awarded. *Degree requirements:* Final research project required, foreign language and thesis not required. *Average time to degree:* master's–2 years full-time, 4 years part-time. *Entrance requirements:* 3 years of experience in management. Application deadline: rolling. Application fee: $75. *Tuition:* $270 per semester hour. *Financial aid:* Federal Work-Study available. Aid available to part-time students. Financial aid applicants required to submit FAFSA. *Faculty research:* Organizational behavior, leadership, change, quality control, global economics. • Bonnie Johnson, Chair. Application contact: Richard Boorom, Director of Marketing and Admissions, 800-677-9270. Fax: 303-964-5538. E-mail: admarg@regis.edu.

Rensselaer at Hartford, Lally School of Management and Technology, Program in Management, Hartford, CT 06120-2991. Awards MBA, MS. Part-time and evening/weekend programs available. Faculty: 16 full-time (2 women), 57 part-time (9 women). Students: 879; includes 55 minority (19 African Americans, 28 Asian Americans, 8 Hispanics). Average age 30. *Entrance requirements:* TOEFL (minimum score 570). Application deadline: 8/6 (priority date; rolling processing). Application fee: $25. *Tuition:* $535 per credit hour. *Financial aid:* Research assistantships, student assistantships, full and partial tuition waivers available. Aid available to part-time students. Financial aid applicants required to submit FAFSA. • Application contact: Rebecca Danchak, Admissions Office, 860-548-2420. Fax: 860-548-7823. E-mail: beckyd@hgc.edu.

Rensselaer Polytechnic Institute, Lally School of Management and Technology, Troy, NY 12180-3590. Awards MBA, MS, PhD, JD/MBA, MBA/M Eng. Programs in accounting/finance (PhD); applied economics (PhD); business administration (MBA, PhD), including finance and accounting (MBA), information systems management (MBA), management (PhD), management of technology and entrepreneurships (MBA), manufacturing management (MBA), marketing management (MBA), operations research (MBA), organizational behavior and human resource management (MBA), statistical methods for management (MBA); business policy and strategy (PhD); environmental management and policy (MS, PhD); human resource (PhD); management information systems (PhD); managerial economics (PhD); manufacturing (PhD). Part-time and evening/weekend programs available. Postbaccalaureate distance learning degree programs offered (no on-campus study). Faculty: 36 full-time (5 women), 6 part-time (0 women). Students: 316 full-time (87 women), 135 part-time (44 women); includes 44 minority (9 African Americans, 24 Asian Americans, 10 Hispanics, 1 Native American), 164 international. 458 applicants, 69% accepted. In 1997, 137 master's, 5 doctorates awarded. *Degree requirements:* For master's, computer language required, foreign language and thesis not required; for doctorate, computer language, dissertation required, foreign language not required. *Entrance requirements:* For master's, GMAT, TOEFL (minimum score 570); for doctorate, GMAT or GRE General Test, TOEFL (minimum score 570). Application deadline: 2/1 (priority date; rolling processing). Application fee: $35. *Expenses:* Tuition $630 per credit hour. Fees $1000 per year. *Financial aid:* 104 students received aid; fellowships, research assistantships, teaching assistantships, full and partial tuition waivers, institutionally sponsored loans, and career-related internships or fieldwork available. Financial aid application deadline: 2/1. *Faculty research:* Entrepreneurship, operations management, product development, information systems, financial technology. Total annual research expenditures: $600,000. • Dr. Joseph G. Ecker, Dean, 518-276-6802. Application contact: Michele Martens, Manager of Enrollment Services, 518-276-4800. Fax: 518-276-8661.

See in-depth description on page 267.

Rice University, Jesse H. Jones Graduate School of Management, 6100 Main Street, Houston, TX 77005-1892. Awards MBA, MBA/M Eng. Program in business administration (MBA). Faculty: 24 full-time (3 women), 32 part-time (6 women), 30 FTE. Students: 267 full-time (75 women); includes 31 minority (2 African Americans, 22 Asian Americans, 7 Hispanics), 31 international. Average age 28. 526 applicants, 45% accepted. In 1997, 97 degrees awarded (100% found work related to degree). *Average time to degree:* master's–2 years full-time. *Entrance requirements:* GMAT (average 632), TOEFL (average 620). Application deadline: 3/1 (priority date; rolling processing). Application fee: $25. Electronic applications accepted. *Tuition:* $15,750 per year full-time. *Financial aid:* In 1997–98, 187 students received aid, including 131 scholarships (73 to first-year students) totaling $357,000; full and partial tuition waivers, Federal Work-Study, institutionally sponsored loans, and career-related internships or fieldwork also available. Financial aid application deadline: 6/1; applicants required to submit FAFSA. *Faculty research:* Capital markets, market reaction to accounting changes, marketing strategy, mergers and acquisitions, computer-human interface. • Dr. Gilbert R. Whitaker Jr., Dean, 713-527-4838. Application contact: Jill L. Deutser, Director of Admissions, 713-527-4918. Fax: 713-737-5838. E-mail: enterjgs@rice.edu.

See in-depth description on page 269.

The Richard Stockton College of New Jersey, Graduate Programs, Program in Business Studies, Pomona, NJ 08240-9988. Awards MBS. Students: 30 part-time (16 women); includes 3 minority (all Asian Americans). Average age 35. 65 applicants, 58% accepted. *Entrance requirements:* GMAT. Application deadline: rolling. Application fee: $35. *Financial aid:* 9 students received aid; Federal Work-Study and career-related internships or fieldwork available. Aid available to part-time students. Financial aid application deadline: 3/1; applicants required to submit FAFSA. *Faculty research:* Business ethics, marketing channels development, event studies, total quality management. • Dr. Dee Henderson, Dean of Professional Studies, 609-652-4518. Application contact: Alison Henry, Associate Director of Admissions, 609-652-4261. Fax: 609-748-5541. E-mail: siprod42@pollux.stockton.edu.

Richmond, The American International University in London, MBA Program, Richmond, Surrey TW10 6JP, United Kingdom. Awards MBA. Part-time and evening/weekend programs available. Faculty: 12 full-time (2 women), 14 part-time (2 women), 17 FTE. Students: 50 full-time (26 women), 38 part-time (20 women). Average age 26. 132 applicants, 27% accepted. In 1997, 35 degrees awarded (100% found work related to degree). *Degree requirements:* Minimum GPA of 3.0 (no course may be lower than C-) required, thesis not required. *Average time to degree:* master's–1.2 years full-time, 3 years part-time. *Entrance requirements:* TOEFL (minimum score 550; average 580), minimum GPA of 3.0. Application deadline: 9/10 (priority date; rolling processing; 1/14 for spring admission). Application fee: $58. *Expenses:* Tuition $15,675 per year (minimum). Fees $990 per year (minimum). *Financial aid:* In 1997–98, 6 students received aid, including 6 administrative assistantships/scholarships totaling $52,288; career-related internships or fieldwork also available. Financial aid application deadline: 7/20. *Faculty research:* International business, intercultural management skills, international finance, international marketing. • Clive Bateson, Dean, School of Business, 171-368-8488. Fax: 171-938-3037. E-mail: batesoc@staff.richmond.ac.uk. Application contact: Catherine Byrne, Assistant Dean of Graduate Admissions, 171-368-8475. Fax: 171-376-0836. E-mail: grad@richmond.staff.uk.

Rider University, College of Business Administration, Lawrenceville, NJ 08648-3001. Awards M Acc, MBA. Part-time and evening/weekend programs available. Faculty: 47 full-time (16 women), 8 part-time (6 women), 48.7 FTE. Students: 54 full-time, 377 part-time. Average age 28. 125 applicants, 79% accepted. In 1997, 119 degrees awarded (100% found work related to degree). *Entrance requirements:* GMAT, TOEFL, minimum AACSB index of 1100. Application deadline: 8/1 (priority date; rolling processing; 12/1 for spring admission). Application fee: $35. *Tuition:* $420 per credit hour. *Financial aid:* In 1997–98, 7 students received aid, including 7 research assistantships (all to first-year students); career-related internships or fieldwork also available. Financial aid application deadline: 4/1; applicants required to submit FAFSA. *Faculty research:* Ethics, international business, marketing to Latinos in the U.S., gender differences in career progression, entrepreneurship, health care management, diversity. • Tom Kelly, Associate Dean, 609-896-5127. Application contact: Dr. John Carpenter, Dean, Continuing Studies, 609-896-5036. Fax: 609-896-5261.

Rivier College, Department of Business Administration, Nashua, NH 03060-5086. Offers programs in business administration (MBA), employee relations (MBA), human resources management (MBA, MS). Part-time and evening/weekend programs available. *Entrance requirements:* GMAT. Application deadline: rolling. Application fee: $25.

Robert Morris College, Program in Business Administration, 881 Narrows Run Road, Moon Township, PA 15108-1189. Offers accounting (MBA, MS), computer information systems (MBA, MS), finance (MBA, MS), health services management (MBA, MS), management (MBA), marketing (MBA, MS), sport management (MBA, MS). Only part-time programs offered. Part-time and evening/weekend programs available. Faculty: 35 full-time (6 women), 35 part-time (5 women). Students: 665 part-time. In 1997, 188 degrees awarded. *Entrance requirements:* GMAT (minimum score 450), minimum GPA of 2.5. Application deadline: 8/1 (priority date; rolling processing; 11/30 for spring admission). Application fee: $25 ($35 for international students). *Expenses:* Tuition $328 per credit. Fees $15 per credit. *Financial aid:* Assistantships available. Aid available to part-time students. Financial aid application deadline: 5/1; applicants required to submit FAFSA. • Dr. Joseph F. Constable, Dean, School of Management, 412-262-8451. Fax: 412-262-8494. E-mail: constabl@robert-morris.edu. Application contact: Vincent J. Kane, Recruiting Coordinator, 412-262-8535. Fax: 412-299-2425.

Roberts Wesleyan College, Division of Business and Management, Program in Organizational Management, Rochester, NY 14624-1997. Awards MS. Evening/weekend programs available. Faculty: 16 full-time (4 women), 6 part-time (2 women). Students: 48 full-time (24 women); includes 7 minority (4 African Americans, 1 Asian American, 2 Hispanics). Average age 34. 45 applicants, 89% accepted. *Degree requirements:* Thesis or alternative required, foreign language not required. *Entrance requirements:* GMAT (minimum score 400; average 490), minimum GPA of 2.75, verifiable work experience. Application deadline: rolling. Application fee: $35. *Tuition:* $450 per credit hour. *Financial aid:* 15 students received aid. *Faculty research:* Nonprofit management; small business entrepreneurship, church management. • Application contact: Kathy Merz, Admissions Secretary, 716-594-6600. Fax: 716-594-6585.

Rochester Institute of Technology, College of Business, Department of Business Administration, Executive MBA Program, Rochester, NY 14623-5604. Awards Exec MBA. Students: 54 full-time (22 women); includes 8 minority (5 African Americans, 3 Hispanics), 1 international. 25 applicants, 100% accepted. In 1997, 20 degrees awarded. *Entrance requirements:* GMAT, minimum GPA of 2.5. Application deadline: 3/1 (priority date; rolling processing). Application fee: $40. • Donald Zrebiec, Director, 716-475-2244.

Rochester Institute of Technology, College of Business, Department of Business Administration, Program in Business Administration, Rochester, NY 14623-5604. Awards MBA. Students: 149 full-time (48 women), 211 part-time (99 women); includes 25 minority (10 African Americans, 11 Asian Americans, 3 Hispanics, 1 Native American), 105 international. 344 applicants, 71% accepted. In 1997, 154 degrees awarded. *Entrance requirements:* GMAT, minimum GPA of 2.5. Application deadline: 3/1 (priority date; rolling processing). Application fee: $40. *Expenses:* Tuition $18,765 per year full-time, $527 per credit hour part-time. Fees $126 per year full-time. *Financial aid:* Research assistantships and career-related internships or fieldwork available. • Patricia Sorce, Associate Dean, Department of Business Administration, 716-475-2313.

Rockford College, Program in Business Administration, Rockford, IL 61108-2393. Awards MBA. Part-time and evening/weekend programs available. Faculty: 7 full-time, 4 part-time, 8 FTE. Students: 91 part-time (40 women); includes 4 minority (all African Americans). Average age 35. 13 applicants, 85% accepted. In 1997, 16 degrees awarded. *Entrance requirements:* GMAT. Application deadline: rolling. Application fee: $35. *Tuition:* $15,500 per year full-time, $400 per credit part-time. • Jeff Fahrenwald, Head, 815-226-4178. Fax: 815-226-4119.

Rockhurst College, School of Management, Kansas City, MO 64110-2561. Awards MBA. Part-time and evening/weekend programs available. Faculty: 22 full-time (5 women), 7 part-time (1 woman). Students: 17 full-time (3 women), 441 part-time (181 women); includes 19 minority (5 African Americans, 7 Asian Americans, 6 Hispanics, 1 Native American), 5 international. Average age 30. 193 applicants, 67% accepted. In 1997, 145 degrees awarded. *Entrance requirements:* GMAT, TOEFL (minimum score 550). Application deadline: 7/25 (priority date; rolling processing; 12/15 for spring admission). Application fee: $0. *Expenses:* Tuition $335 per semester hour. Fees $15 per year. *Financial aid:* 66 students received aid; career-related internships or fieldwork available. Aid available to part-time students. Financial aid application deadline: 4/1; applicants required to submit FAFSA. *Faculty research:* Self-managed work teams, asset management, co-integration of emerging markets, Japanese investment strategies. • Thomas L. Lyon, Interim Dean, 816-501-4201. E-mail: lyon@vax2.rockhurst.edu. Application contact: Ronald L. Logan, Associate Dean, 816-501-4090. Fax: 816-501-4650. E-mail: logan@vax2.rockhurst.edu.

Rollins College, Crummer Graduate School of Business, Winter Park, FL 32789-4499. Awards MBA. Part-time and evening/weekend programs available. Faculty: 16 full-time (1 woman), 5 part-time (0 women), 18 FTE. Students: 232 full-time (83 women), 134 part-time (36 women); includes 32 minority (9 African Americans, 11 Asian Americans, 11 Hispanics, 1 Native American), 27 international. Average age 28. 483 applicants, 42% accepted. In 1997, 175 degrees awarded (100% found work related to degree). *Degree requirements:* Thesis optional. *Entrance requirements:* GMAT. Application deadline: 4/1 (priority date; rolling processing; 12/1 for spring admission). Application fee: $40. *Tuition:* $16,000 per year full-time, $7840 per year part-time. *Financial aid:* 177 students received aid; fellowships, research assistantships, grants, full tuition waivers, Federal Work-Study, and career-related internships or fieldwork available. • Dr. Edward A. Moses, Dean, 407-646-2249. Fax: 407-646-1550. Application contact: Stephen L. Gauthier, Assistant Dean for Internal Affairs, 407-646-2405.

See in-depth description on page 271.

Roosevelt University, Walter E. Heller College of Business Administration, Program in Business Administration, Chicago, IL 60605-1394. Awards MBA. Part-time and evening/weekend programs available. Students: 442 (211 women); includes 112 minority (71 African Americans, 21 Asian Americans, 20 Hispanics), 38 international. In 1997, 72 degrees awarded. *Entrance requirements:* GMAT. Application deadline: 6/1 (priority date; rolling processing). Application fee: $25 ($35 for international students). *Expenses:* Tuition $445 per credit hour. Fees $100 per year. *Financial aid:* Application deadline 2/15. • Marilyn Nance, Head, 312-341-3844. Application contact: Joanne Canyon-Heller, Coordinator of Graduate Admissions, 312-341-3612.

Rosemont College, College of Graduate Studies, Accelerated Program in Management, Rosemont, PA 19010-1699. Awards MS. Part-time and evening/weekend programs available. Students: 49 (31 women); includes 11 minority (9 African Americans, 1 Asian American, 1 Hispanic). Average age 33. 25 applicants, 80% accepted. *Degree requirements:* Thesis or alternative required, foreign language not required. *Entrance requirements:* GRE or MAT. Application deadline: rolling. Application fee: $50. *Tuition:* $6300 per year full-time, $350 per credit part-time. • Rennie Andrews, Director, 610-527-0200 Ext. 2380. Fax: 610-526-2987. Application contact: Stan Rostkowski, Enrollment Coordinator, 610-527-0200 Ext. 2187. Fax: 610-526-2964. E-mail: roscolgrad@rosemont.edu.

Directory: Business Administration and Management—General

Rowan University, College of Business Administration, Program in Business Administration, Glassboro, NJ 08028-1701. Awards MBA. Part-time and evening/weekend programs available. Students: 67 (31 women); includes 3 minority (1 African American, 2 Asian Americans). 41 applicants, 32% accepted. In 1997, 25 degrees awarded. *Degree requirements:* Thesis. *Entrance requirements:* GMAT, minimum GPA of 2.8. Application deadline: 11/1 (priority date; rolling processing; 4/1 for spring admission). Application fee: $50. *Tuition:* $5728 per year full-time, $258 per credit hour part-time for state residents; $8968 per year full-time, $393 per credit hour part-time for nonresidents. *Financial aid:* Federal Work-Study available. Aid available to part-time students. • Dr. Dilip Mirchandani, Adviser, 609-256-4048.

Rutgers, The State University of New Jersey, Camden, School of Business, Camden, NJ 08102-1401. Awards MBA. Part-time and evening/weekend programs available. Faculty: 23 full-time (6 women), 1 (woman) part-time. Students: 20 full-time (5 women), 203 part-time (60 women); includes 24 minority (10 African Americans, 13 Asian Americans, 1 Native American). Average age 27. 266 applicants, 75% accepted. In 1997, 43 degrees awarded. *Degree requirements:* Computer language required, foreign language and thesis not required. *Entrance requirements:* GMAT (minimum score 500; average 566), minimum GPA of 2.5. Application deadline: 8/1 (priority date; rolling processing; 12/1 for spring admission). Application fee: $40. *Expenses:* Tuition $9000 per year full-time, $373 per credit part-time for state residents; $13,420 per year full-time, $557 per credit part-time for nonresidents. Fees $966 per year full-time, $205 per semester (minimum) part-time. *Faculty research:* Behavioral accounting, retail marketing, financial markets, international business, management strategy. • Milton Leontiades, Dean, 609-225-6217. Application contact: Izzet Kenis, Director, 609-225-6216. Fax: 609-225-6231.

Rutgers, The State University of New Jersey, Newark, Graduate School of Management, Newark, NJ 07102-3192. Awards MA, MBA, PhD, JD/MBA, MBA/MS, MPH/MBA. JD/MBA offered jointly with the Schools of Law at Rutgers, The State University of New Jersey, Camden and Newark. Part-time and evening/weekend programs available. Faculty: 124 full-time (22 women), 71 part-time (19 women). Students: 387 full-time (143 women), 1,159 part-time (391 women). Average age 29. 998 applicants, 72% accepted. In 1997, 372 master's awarded. Terminal master's awarded for partial completion of doctoral program. *Degree requirements:* For master's, computer language required, thesis not required. *Average time to degree:* master's–1.5 years full-time, 4 years part-time. *Entrance requirements:* For master's, GMAT (average 566), TOEFL (average 602); for doctorate, GMAT, TOEFL. Application deadline: 6/1 (rolling processing). Application fee: $40. *Financial aid:* 215 students received aid; fellowships, full and partial tuition waivers, Federal Work-Study, institutionally sponsored loans, and career-related internships or fieldwork available. Aid available to part-time students. Financial aid application deadline: 3/15; applicants required to submit FAFSA. *Faculty research:* Finance/economics, accounting, international business, operations research, marketing, organizational behavior. • Dr. P. George Benson, Dean, Faculty of Management, 973-353-5128. Fax: 973-353-1345. E-mail: gbenson@gsmack.rutgers.edu. Application contact: Director of Admissions, 973-353-1234. Fax: 973-353-1592. E-mail: admit@gsmack.rutgers.edu.

Rutgers, The State University of New Jersey, Newark, Department of Management, Newark, NJ 07102-3192. Offers programs in accounting (PhD), accounting information systems (PhD), computer information systems (PhD), finance (PhD), information technology (PhD), international business (PhD), management science (PhD), marketing (PhD), organization management (PhD). Offered jointly with New Jersey Institute of Technology. Faculty: 113 full-time (13 women), 3 part-time (1 woman). Students: 88 full-time (27 women), 97 part-time (25 women); includes 16 minority (5 African Americans, 6 Asian Americans, 5 Hispanics), 95 international. Average age 32. 127 applicants, 37% accepted. In 1997, 10 doctorates awarded (100% entered university research/teaching). Terminal master's awarded for partial completion of doctoral program. *Degree requirements:* For doctorate, dissertation, cumulative exams required, foreign language not required. *Average time to degree:* doctorate–5 years full-time, 7 years part-time. *Entrance requirements:* For doctorate, GMAT or GRE, minimum undergraduate B average. Application deadline: 4/1 (rolling processing; 11/1 for spring admission). Application fee: $40. *Expenses:* Tuition $6248 per year full-time, $257 per credit part-time for state residents; $9160 per year full-time, $380 per credit part-time for nonresidents. Fees $738 per year full-time, $107 per semester (minimum) part-time. *Financial aid:* In 1997–98, 49 students received aid, including 9 fellowships (3 to first-year students) totaling $12,000, 9 research assistantships (2 to first-year students) totaling $11,000, 31 teaching assistantships (5 to first-year students) totaling $11,000; institutionally sponsored loans also available. Aid available to part-time students. Financial aid application deadline: 2/15. *Faculty research:* Technology management, leadership and teams, consumer behavior, financial and markets, logistics, multi-national firms, accounting information. • Glenn R. Shafer, Director, 973-353-1604. E-mail: gshafer@andromeda.rutgers.edu. Application contact: Ana Gonzalez, Program Secretary, 973-353-5371. Fax: 973-353-5691. E-mail: anag@gsmack.rutgers.edu.

Sacred Heart University, College of Business, 5151 Park Avenue, Fairfield, CT 06432-1000. Awards MA, MBA, MSN/MBA. Programs in business administration (MBA), health care administration (MBA), health systems management (MA). MA new for fall 1998. Part-time and evening/weekend programs available. Faculty: 24 full-time (4 women), 38 part-time (10 women). Students: 29 full-time (12 women), 577 part-time (285 women); includes 55 minority (29 African Americans, 14 Asian Americans, 12 Hispanics), 11 international. Average age 32. 80 applicants, 98% accepted. In 1997, 164 degrees awarded. *Degree requirements:* Computer language, thesis or alternative. *Application deadline:* rolling. *Application fee:* $40 ($100 for international students). *Expenses:* Tuition $395 per credit. Fees $78 per semester. *Financial aid:* Research assistantships available. *Faculty research:* Computers in curriculum, management of organizations. • Scott Colvin, Director, 203-371-7850. Application contact: Brian Ihlefeld, Graduate Admissions Counselor, 203-371-7880. Fax: 203-365-4732. E-mail: gradstudies@sacredheart.edu.

Sage Graduate School, Graduate School, Division of Management Studies, Program in Business Administration, Troy, NY 12180-4115. Awards MBA, MBA/JD, MBA/MS. Offerings include finance (MBA), human resources management (MBA), management (MBA), marketing (MBA). MBA/JD offered jointly with Albany Law School of Union University. Part-time and evening/weekend programs available. Faculty: 1 full-time (0 women), 10 part-time (1 woman). Students: 10 full-time (5 women), 105 part-time (54 women). *Entrance requirements:* Minimum GPA of 2.75. Application fee: $25. *Expenses:* Tuition $360 per credit hour. Fees $50 per semester. *Financial aid:* Career-related internships or fieldwork available. Aid available to part-time students. Financial aid application deadline: 7/1; applicants required to submit FAFSA. • Application contact: Melissa Robertson, Associate Director of Admissions, 518-244-6878. Fax: 518-244-6880. E-mail: sgsadm@sage.edu.

Saginaw Valley State University, College of Business and Management, University Center, MI 48710. Awards MBA. Part-time and evening/weekend programs available. Faculty: 14 full-time (3 women). Students: 14 full-time (6 women), 109 part-time (45 women); includes 10 minority (5 African Americans, 4 Asian Americans, 1 Hispanic), 13 international. 43 applicants, 86% accepted. In 1997, 44 degrees awarded. *Degree requirements:* Thesis optional, foreign language not required. *Entrance requirements:* GMAT. Application deadline: rolling. Application fee: $25. *Expenses:* Tuition $159 per credit hour for state residents; $311 per credit hour for nonresidents. Fees $8.70 per credit hour. *Financial aid:* Federal Work-Study available. Financial aid applicants required to submit FAFSA. *Faculty research:* International business, commercial banking, multicultural management, product sourcing, strategic management. • Dr. Severin C. Carlson, Dean, 517-790-4064. E-mail: cbmdean@tardis.svsu.edu. Application contact: Dr. Jill L. Wetmore, Assistant Dean, 517-790-4064. Fax: 517-249-1960. E-mail: cbmdean@tardis.svsu.edu.

St. Ambrose University, College of Business, Program in Business Administration, Davenport, IA 52803-2898. Offers management generalist (MBA), technical management (MBA). Part-time and evening/weekend programs available. *Degree requirements:* Capstone Seminar required, foreign language and thesis not required. *Average time to degree:* master's–4 years part-time. *Entrance requirements:* GMAT. Application deadline: 8/15 (priority date; rolling processing). Application fee: $25. Electronic applications accepted.

St. Bonaventure University, School of Business Administration, St. Bonaventure, NY 14778-2284. Awards MBA, Adv C, MBA/MA. Programs in accounting and finance (MBA), business administration (Adv C), management and marketing (MBA). Part-time and evening/weekend programs available. Faculty: 19 full-time (2 women), 3 part-time (0 women). Students: 121 full-time (59 women), 90 part-time (34 women); includes 20 minority (3 African Americans, 9 Asian Americans, 1 Hispanic, 7 Native Americans), 10 international. Average age 26. 70 applicants, 97% accepted. In 1997, 111 master's awarded. *Average time to degree:* master's–1.5 years full-time, 3 years part-time. *Entrance requirements:* For master's, GMAT (minimum score 400), TOEFL (minimum score 600). Application deadline: 8/1 (rolling processing). Application fee: $35. *Tuition:* $8100 per year full-time, $450 per credit hour part-time. *Financial aid:* In 1997–98, 7 students received aid, including 5 research assistantships (2 to first-year students) totaling $71,400; Federal Work-Study and career-related internships or fieldwork also available. Aid available to part-time students. *Faculty research:* Stock options, small business, market relationships, auditing, taxes. • Dr. Michael Fischer, Dean, 716-375-2200. Application contact: Brian C. McAllister, MBA Director, 716-375-2098. Fax: 716-375-2191. E-mail: bmac@sbu.edu.

St. Cloud State University, College of Business, St. Cloud, MN 56301-4498. Awards MBA, MS. Part-time programs available. Faculty: 55 full-time (12 women), 1 part-time (0 women). Students: 40 full-time (16 women), 44 part-time (15 women). In 1997, 30 degrees awarded. *Degree requirements:* Comprehensive exam required, foreign language and thesis not required. *Entrance requirements:* GMAT (minimum score 470), minimum GPA of 2.75. Application fee: $20 ($100 for international students). *Expenses:* Tuition $128 per credit for state residents; $203 per credit for nonresidents. Fees $16.32 per credit. *Financial aid:* In 1997–98, 17 graduate assistantships were awarded; Federal Work-Study also available. Financial aid application deadline: 3/1. • Dr. Wayne Wells, Coordinator of Graduate Programs, 320-255-3212. Application contact: Ann Anderson, Graduate Studies Office, 320-255-2113. Fax: 320-654-5371. E-mail: anna@grad.stcloud.msus.edu.

St. Edward's University, School of Business Administration, Austin, TX 78704-6489. Offers programs in accounting (Certificate), business administration (MBA). Part-time and evening/weekend programs available. Faculty: 13 full-time (3 women), 12 part-time (1 woman). Students: 39 full-time (18 women), 361 part-time (132 women); includes 84 minority (17 African Americans, 28 Asian Americans, 38 Hispanics, 1 Native American), 33 international. Average age 32. 165 applicants, 82% accepted. In 1997, 109 master's awarded. *Average time to degree:* master's–1.5 years full-time, 2.7 years part-time. *Entrance requirements:* For master's, GMAT (minimum score 500), GRE General Test (minimum combined score of 1000), TOEFL (minimum score 500), minimum GPA of 2.75. Application deadline: 8/1 (priority date; rolling processing; 12/1 for spring admission). Application fee: $25. *Financial aid:* In 1997–98, 9 scholarships totaling $4,624 were awarded; institutionally sponsored loans also available. Aid available to part-time students. Financial aid application deadline: 3/1; applicants required to submit FAFSA. • Dr. David Kendall, Dean, 512-448-8696. E-mail: davidk@admin.stedwards.edu. Application contact: Tom Evans, Director of Graduate Admissions, 512-448-8600. Fax: 512-448-8492. E-mail: seu.grad@admin.stedwards.edu.

Announcement: The MBA program is designed specifically for working adults. Classes are offered in the evening, and most students complete the degree on a part-time basis. Concentrations are available in general business, management, telecommunications management, management information systems, public administration, accounting, and sports management.

Saint Francis College, Business Administration Program, Loretto, PA 15940-0600. Awards MBA. Part-time programs available. Faculty: 7 full-time (1 woman), 8 part-time (2 women). Students: 8 full-time (5 women), 119 part-time (40 women). Average age 33. 30 applicants, 83% accepted. In 1997, 26 degrees awarded. *Average time to degree:* master's–2 years full-time, 4 years part-time. *Entrance requirements:* GMAT. Application deadline: 8/15 (priority date; rolling processing; 12/31 for spring admission). Application fee: $30. *Financial aid:* 6 students received aid; research assistantships, teaching assistantships, Federal Work-Study, and career-related internships or fieldwork available. • Randy L. Frye, Director, 814-472-3087. E-mail: rfrye@sfcpa.edu. Application contact: Roxane Hogue, Administrative Assistant, 814-472-3087. Fax: 814-472-3044. E-mail: rhogue@sfcpa.edu.

St. John Fisher College, School of Adult and Graduate Education, Management Program, Rochester, NY 14618-3597. Awards MBA. Part-time and evening/weekend programs available. Faculty: 11 full-time (1 woman), 9 part-time (1 woman). Students: 9 full-time (5 women), 158 part-time (67 women); includes 9 minority (7 African Americans, 2 Hispanics). Average age 34. 45 applicants, 64% accepted. In 1997, 28 degrees awarded. *Average time to degree:* master's–2 years full-time, 4 years part-time. *Entrance requirements:* GMAT. Application deadline: 8/1 (priority date; rolling processing; 1/1 for spring admission). Application fee: $30. *Tuition:* $17,100 per year full-time, $475 per credit hour part-time. • Dr. Selim Ilter, Director, 716-385-8079. Fax: 716-385-8094. E-mail: ilter@sjfc.edu. Application contact: Steven T. Hoskins, Director, Graduate Admissions, 716-385-8161. Fax: 716-385-8344. E-mail: hoskins@sjfc.edu.

St. John's University, College of Business Administration, Jamaica, NY 11439. Awards MBA, Adv C, JD/MBA. Part-time and evening/weekend programs available. Faculty: 98 full-time (14 women), 17 part-time (4 women). Students: 126 full-time (48 women), 908 part-time (371 women); includes 208 minority (79 African Americans, 68 Asian Americans, 58 Hispanics, 3 Native Americans), 116 international. Average age 29. 592 applicants, 69% accepted. In 1997, 329 master's, 4 Adv Cs awarded. *Degree requirements:* For master's, thesis optional, foreign language not required. *Entrance requirements:* For master's, GMAT. Application deadline: 6/1 (rolling processing; 10/1 for spring admission). Application fee: $40. *Expenses:* Tuition $600 per credit. Fees $150 per year. *Financial aid:* In 1997–98, 30 research assistantships (13 to first-year students) averaging $667 per month were awarded; Federal Work-Study also available. Aid available to part-time students. Financial aid application deadline: 3/1; applicants required to submit FAFSA. • Peter J. Tobin, Dean, 718-990-6417. Fax: 718-990-5727. Application contact: Shamus J. McGrenra, TOR, Associate Director, Graduate Admissions, 718-990-6107. Fax: 718-990-5736. E-mail: mcgrenrs@stjohns.edu.

Saint Joseph's University, Erivan K. Haub School of Business, Philadelphia, PA 19131-1395. Awards MBA, MS, DO/MBA. Part-time and evening/weekend programs available. Students: 1,332 (498 women). In 1997, 385 degrees awarded. *Entrance requirements:* GMAT, TOEFL. *Tuition:* $470 per credit hour. *Financial aid:* Research assistantships, graduate assistantships, Federal Work-Study, institutionally sponsored loans, and career-related internships or fieldwork available. Aid available to part-time students. Financial aid applicants required to submit FAFSA. • Dr. Gregory G. Dell'Omo, Dean, 610-660-1645. Fax: 610-660-1649. E-mail: gdellomo@sju.edu. Application contact: Adele C. Foley, Associate Dean, 610-660-1690. Fax: 610-660-1599. E-mail: afoley@sju.edu.

Saint Leo College, Graduate Business Studies, Saint Leo, FL 33574-2008. Awards MBA. Part-time and evening/weekend programs available. Faculty: 5 full-time (1 woman), 6 part-time (4 women). Students: 129 full-time (73 women), 18 part-time (10 women); includes 13 minority (3 African Americans, 3 Asian Americans, 7 Hispanics), 1 international. Average age 37. In 1997, 33 degrees awarded. *Average time to degree:* master's–2 years full-time, 3 years part-time. *Entrance requirements:* GMAT. Application deadline: rolling. Application fee: $45. *Tuition:* $200 per credit hour. *Financial aid:* Available to part-time students. Financial aid applicants required to submit FAFSA. • Dr. Susan Steiner, Director, 352-588-8311. Fax: 352-588-8312. Application contact: Gary Bracken, Dean of Admissions and Financial Aid, 352-588-8283. Fax: 352-588-8257. E-mail: admissns@saintleo.edu.

Saint Louis University, School of Business and Administration, Department of Management, 3674 Lindell Boulevard, St. Louis, MO 63108. Awards MBA, M Mgt, PhD. Faculty: 8 full-time (2 women), 2 part-time (1 woman). Students: 1 (woman) full-time, 5 part-time (1 woman); includes 1 international. Average age 26. 3 applicants, 33% accepted. In 1997, 3 master's, 3

Directory: Business Administration and Management—General

Saint Louis University (continued)
doctorates awarded. *Degree requirements:* For master's, oral exam required, thesis not required; for doctorate, dissertation. *Average time to degree:* master's–1.5 years full-time, 3 years part-time; doctorate–5 years full-time, 6 years part-time. *Entrance requirements:* For master's, GMAT, TOEFL; for doctorate, GMAT. Application fee: $40. • Dr. Scott R. Safranski, Chairman, 314-977-7156. Fax: 314-977-3897.

Saint Louis University, School of Business and Administration, Master's Program in Business Administration, 3674 Lindell Boulevard, St. Louis, MO 63108. Awards MBA. Part-time and evening/weekend programs available. Faculty: 55 full-time (7 women), 7 part-time (1 woman). Students: 140 full-time (59 women), 283 part-time (105 women); includes 25 minority (11 African Americans, 11 Asian Americans, 3 Hispanics), 97 international. Average age 26. 301 applicants, 63% accepted. In 1997, 217 degrees awarded. *Average time to degree:* master's–1.5 years full-time, 3 years part-time. *Entrance requirements:* GMAT, TOEFL. Application deadline: 7/15 (rolling processing; 11/15 for spring admission). Application fee: $40. Electronic applications accepted. *Financial aid:* Fellowships, research assistantships, teaching assistantships, Federal Work-Study available. Aid available to part-time students. • Dr. Stephen W. Miller, Associate Dean and Director, Graduate and Professional Programs, 314-977-3800. Fax: 314-977-3897.

Saint Louis University, School of Business and Administration, PhD Program in Business Administration, 3674 Lindell Boulevard, St. Louis, MO 63108. Awards PhD. Part-time and evening/weekend programs available. Faculty: 55 full-time (7 women), 7 part-time (1 woman). Students: 15 full-time (8 women), 19 part-time (8 women); includes 3 minority (2 African Americans, 1 Hispanic), 7 international. Average age 30. 16 applicants, 38% accepted. In 1997, 9 degrees awarded. *Degree requirements:* Dissertation. *Average time to degree:* doctorate–5 years full-time, 6 years part-time. *Entrance requirements:* GMAT. Application fee: $30. *Tuition:* $542 per credit hour. *Financial aid:* Fellowships, research assistantships, teaching assistantships available. • Dr. Stephen W. Miller, Associate Dean and Director, Graduate and Professional Programs, 314-977-3800. Fax: 314-977-3897.

Saint Martin's College, Graduate Programs, Department of Economics and Business Administration, Lacey, WA 98503-7500. Offers programs in business administration (MBA), economics and business administration (MBA). Evening/weekend programs available. Faculty: 6 full-time (1 woman), 8 part-time (0 women). Students: 85 full-time (25 women), 22 part-time (8 women); includes 15 minority (6 African Americans, 6 Asian Americans, 2 Hispanics, 1 Native American), 4 international. Average age 36. In 1997, 28 degrees awarded (100% found work related to degree). *Entrance requirements:* GMAT, TOEFL (minimum score 525). Application deadline: 7/1 (rolling processing). Application fee: $25. *Financial aid:* In 1997–98, 1 scholarship (to a first-year student) was awarded; Federal Work-Study and career-related internships or fieldwork also available. Aid available to part-time students. Financial aid application deadline: 3/1. • Haldron D. Wilson Jr., Director, 360-438-4326. Application contact: Linda Newman, Administrative Assistant, 360-438-4512. Fax: 360-438-4522.

Saint Mary College, Graduate Programs, Program in Management, Leavenworth, KS 66048-5082. Awards MS. *Degree requirements:* Thesis required, foreign language not required. *Application deadline:* rolling. *Application fee:* $20. • Dr. Sandra Van Hoose, Vice President for Academic Affairs and Graduate Dean, Graduate Programs, 913-798-6115. Fax: 913-798-6297.

Saint Mary's College of California, School of Economics and Business Administration, Evening MBA Program, Moraga, CA 94575. Awards MBA. Part-time and evening/weekend programs available. Faculty: 5 full-time (0 women), 20 part-time (4 women). Students: 155 part-time (56 women); includes 25 minority (2 African Americans, 14 Asian Americans, 9 Hispanics). Average age 29. 62 applicants, 77% accepted. In 1997, 39 degrees awarded (100% found work related to degree). *Degree requirements:* Attendance at 4 half-day management practica required, foreign language and thesis not required. *Average time to degree:* master's–3 years part-time. *Entrance requirements:* GMAT (minimum score 500), TOEFL (minimum score 550). Application deadline: rolling. Application fee: $40. *Tuition:* $1425 per course. *Financial aid:* Career-related internships or fieldwork available. Aid available to part-time students. Financial aid application deadline: 3/2; applicants required to submit FAFSA. • Nelson Shelton, Director of Graduate Business Programs, 925-631-4500. Application contact: Tracey Fanelli, Director of Admissions, 925-631-4504. Fax: 925-376-6521. E-mail: smcmba@stmarys-ca.edu.

Saint Mary's College of California, School of Economics and Business Administration, Executive MBA Program, Moraga, CA 94575. Awards MBA. Evening/weekend programs available. Faculty: 10 full-time (1 woman), 15 part-time (2 women). Students: 192 full-time (56 women); includes 43 minority (10 African Americans, 20 Asian Americans, 11 Hispanics, 2 Native Americans), 3 international. Average age 37. 87 applicants, 63% accepted. In 1997, 109 degrees awarded (100% found work related to degree). *Average time to degree:* master's–1.7 years full-time. *Entrance requirements:* GMAT (minimum score 500), TOEFL (minimum score 550), 5 years of business experience, managerial position. Application deadline: rolling. Application fee: $40. *Tuition:* $3258 per quarter (minimum). *Financial aid:* Available to part-time students. Financial aid application deadline: 3/2; applicants required to submit FAFSA. • Nelson Shelton, Director of Graduate Business Programs, 925-631-4500. Application contact: Tracey Fanelli, Director of Admissions, 925-631-4504. Fax: 925-376-6521. E-mail: smcmba@stmarys-ca.edu.

Saint Mary's University, Faculty of Commerce, Halifax, NS B3H 3C3, Canada. Awards MBA. Part-time and evening/weekend programs available. Faculty: 37 full-time (6 women), 13 part-time (4 women), 41.3 FTE. Students: 147 full-time (54 women), 120 part-time (48 women). Average age 33. 278 applicants, 77% accepted. In 1997, 101 degrees awarded. *Degree requirements:* Research project required, foreign language and thesis not required. *Entrance requirements:* GMAT, minimum B average. Application deadline: 7/1 (rolling processing). Application fee: $30. *Tuition:* $788 per course. *Financial aid:* Institutionally sponsored loans available. Financial aid application deadline: 4/30. • Dr. Paul Dixon, Dean, 902-420-5421. Application contact: Greg C. Ferguson, Director of Admissions, 902-420-5414. Fax: 902-420-5103. E-mail: gferguso@admin.stmarys.ca.

Saint Mary's University of Minnesota, Program in Management, Minneapolis, MN 55404. Awards MA, MA/MA, MS/MA. MA/MA offered jointly with the Program in Human and Health Services Administration; MS/MA offered jointly with the Program in Telecommunications. Part-time and evening/weekend programs available. *Degree requirements:* Thesis, colloquium required, foreign language not required. *Entrance requirements:* Interview, minimum GPA of 2.75. Application deadline: rolling. Application fee: $20.

St. Mary's University of San Antonio, School of Business Administration, San Antonio, TX 78228-8507. Awards MBA, JD/MBA. Part-time and evening/weekend programs available. *Degree requirements:* Computer language required, foreign language and thesis not required. *Entrance requirements:* GMAT. Application deadline: 8/1 (priority date; rolling processing). Application fee: $15. *Expenses:* Tuition $383 per credit hour (minimum). Fees $217 per year full-time, $58 per semester part-time. *Faculty research:* International operations, job satisfaction, total quality management, taxation, stress management.

Saint Michael's College, Program in Administration and Management, Colchester, VT 05439. Awards MSA, CAMS. Part-time and evening/weekend programs available. Faculty: 1 full-time (0 women), 37 part-time (13 women). Students: 14 full-time (4 women), 209 part-time (114 women); includes 6 minority (2 African Americans, 2 Asian Americans, 1 Hispanic, 1 Native American), 12 international. Average age 33. 63 applicants, 79% accepted. In 1997, 50 master's awarded. *Degree requirements:* For master's, thesis or alternative required, foreign language not required. *Entrance requirements:* For master's, TOEFL (minimum score 550), 3 years of work experience, minimum undergraduate GPA of 2.8. Application deadline: rolling. Application fee: $25. *Financial aid:* In 1997–98, 1 graduate assistantship was awarded; Federal Work-Study also available. Aid available to part-time students. Financial aid application deadline: 4/15. *Faculty research:* Learnership/leadership, international banking, top-quality management and organizational changes, national health care, management and ethics. • Robert Letovsky, Director, 802-654-2100. Fax: 802-654-2664.

Saint Peter's College, MBA Programs, 2641 Kennedy Boulevard, Jersey City, NJ 07306-5997. Awards MBA, MBA/MS. Offerings include international business (MBA), management (MBA), management information systems (MBA). Part-time and evening/weekend programs available. Faculty: 15 full-time (0 women), 16 part-time (5 women). Students: 54 full-time (22 women), 174 part-time (65 women); includes 55 minority (14 African Americans, 23 Asian Americans, 18 Hispanics), 22 international. Average age 31. 109 applicants, 92% accepted. In 1997, 58 degrees awarded. *Degree requirements:* Exit presentation. *Entrance requirements:* GMAT (minimum score 400) or MAT (minimum score 40). Application deadline: 8/1 (priority date; rolling processing). Application fee: $20. *Tuition:* $516 per credit. *Faculty research:* International finance, operations research, expert systems, networking, decision support systems. • Sr. Jeanne Gilligan, Associate Vice President for Academic Affairs, 201-915-7252. Fax: 201-946-7528. E-mail: gilliganj@spcvxa.spc.edu. Application contact: Nancy P. Campbell, Associate Vice President for Enrollment, 201-915-9213. Fax: 201-432-5860. E-mail: amissions@spcvxa.spc.edu.

St. Thomas Aquinas College, Division of Business Administration, Sparkill, NY 10976. Offers programs in finance (MBA), management (MBA), marketing (MBA). Part-time and evening/weekend programs available. Faculty: 7 full-time (2 women), 8 part-time (0 women). Students: 59 part-time (21 women); includes 6 minority (1 African American, 2 Asian Americans, 3 Hispanics). Average age 28. 28 applicants, 82% accepted. In 1997, 14 degrees awarded. *Entrance requirements:* GMAT. Application deadline: rolling. Application fee: $35. Electronic applications accepted. *Expenses:* Tuition $390 per credit. Fees $10 per year. *Financial aid:* 7 students received aid; partial tuition waivers available. Aid available to part-time students. Financial aid application deadline: 2/15; applicants required to submit FAFSA. • Barbara Donn, Chairperson, 914-398-4113. Fax: 914-359-8136. Application contact: Joseph L. Chillo, Executive Director of Enrollment Services, 914-398-4100. Fax: 914-398-4224. E-mail: joestacenroll@rockland.net.

St. Thomas University, School of Graduate Studies, Department of Business Administration, Miami, FL 33054-6459. Awards M Acc, MBA, Certificate. Part-time and evening/weekend programs available. *Degree requirements:* For master's, comprehensive exam required, foreign language and thesis not required. *Average time to degree:* master's–1.5 years full-time. *Entrance requirements:* For master's, TOEFL (minimum score 550). Application deadline: rolling. Application fee: $30. *Tuition:* $410 per credit.

St. Thomas University, School of Graduate Studies, Department of Professional Management, Specialization in Management, Miami, FL 33054-6459. Awards MBA. Part-time and evening/weekend programs available. *Degree requirements:* Comprehensive exam required, foreign language and thesis not required. *Average time to degree:* master's–1 year full-time. *Entrance requirements:* TOEFL (minimum score 550), interview, minimum GPA of 3.0 or GMAT. Application deadline: 6/15 (priority date; rolling processing; 11/15 for spring admission). Application fee: $30. *Tuition:* $410 per credit.

Saint Xavier University, Graham School of Management, Chicago, IL 60655-3105. Offers programs in certified financial planner (MBA, Certificate), finance (MBA), financial trading and practice (MBA, Certificate), generalist/administration (MBA), health care management (MBA), healthcare management (Certificate), management (MBA), marketing (MBA), taxation (MBA, Certificate). Part-time and evening/weekend programs available. Faculty: 15 full-time (2 women), 6 part-time (3 women). Students: 168; includes 13 international. Average age 35. In 1997, 51 master's awarded (100% found work related to degree). *Entrance requirements:* For master's, GMAT, minimum GPA of 3.0, 2 years of work experience. Application deadline: 8/15. Application fee: $35. *Expenses:* Tuition $455 per hour. Fees $50 per year. *Financial aid:* Career-related internships or fieldwork available. Aid available to part-time students. Financial aid applicants required to submit FAFSA. • Dr. John Eber, Dean, 773-298-3601. Fax: 773-298-3610. E-mail: eber@sxu.edu. Application contact: Sr. Evelyn McKenna, Vice President of Enrollment Management, 773-298-3050. Fax: 773-298-3076. E-mail: mckenna@sxu.edu.

Salem State College, Program in Business Administration, Salem, MA 01970-5353. Awards MBA, MBA/MSN. Evening/weekend programs available. *Entrance requirements:* GMAT. Application deadline: rolling. Application fee: $25. *Expenses:* Tuition $140 per credit hour for state residents; $230 per credit hour for nonresidents. Fees $20 per credit hour.

Salisbury State University, Program in Business Administration, Salisbury, MD 21801-6837. Awards MBA. Part-time and evening/weekend programs available. Faculty: 14 full-time (1 woman), 1 part-time (0 women). Students: 25 full-time (9 women), 81 part-time (40 women); includes 10 minority (all African Americans), 10 international. Average age 28. 44 applicants, 68% accepted. In 1997, 35 degrees awarded. *Average time to degree:* master's–1 year full-time, 3 years part-time. *Entrance requirements:* GMAT (average 500). Application deadline: 8/1 (rolling processing; 1/1 for spring admission). Application fee: $30. *Expenses:* Tuition $158 per credit hour for state residents; $310 per credit hour for nonresidents. Fees $4 per credit hour. *Financial aid:* 5 students received aid; research assistantships, institutionally sponsored loans available. Aid available to part-time students. • Wayne Bradford, Director, 410-546-6215. Fax: 410-546-6208. E-mail: wabradford@ssu.edu.

Salve Regina University, Program in Business Administration, Newport, RI 02840-4192. Awards MBA. Part-time and evening/weekend programs available. Faculty: 2 full-time (1 woman), 4 part-time (0 women), 3 FTE. Students: 5 part-time (3 women). Average age 37. 24 applicants, 63% accepted. In 1997, 9 degrees awarded. *Average time to degree:* master's–2 years full-time, 3 years part-time. *Entrance requirements:* GMAT, GRE General Test, or MAT. Application deadline: rolling. Application fee: $35. *Expenses:* Tuition $275 per credit hour. Fees $70 per year. *Financial aid:* Federal Work-Study and career-related internships or fieldwork available. Aid available to part-time students. Financial aid application deadline: 3/1. • Dr. John W. Britton, Director, 401-847-6650 Ext. 3140. Fax: 401-847-0372. Application contact: Laura E. McPhie, Dean of Enrollment Services, 401-847-6650 Ext. 2908. Fax: 401-848-2823. E-mail: sruadmis@salve.edu.

Samford University, School of Business, Birmingham, AL 35229-0002. Awards M Acc, MBA, JD/MBA, JD/M Acc, MBA/M Acc, MBA/MSN, M Div/MBA. Part-time and evening/weekend programs available. Faculty: 21 full-time (5 women), 8 part-time (0 women). Students: 10 full-time (3 women), 117 part-time (49 women); includes 10 minority (7 African Americans, 1 Asian American, 1 Hispanic, 1 Native American). Average age 31. 112 applicants, 89% accepted. In 1997, 59 degrees awarded. *Entrance requirements:* GMAT. Application deadline: 7/15 (priority date; rolling processing; 12/15 for spring admission). Application fee: $25. *Tuition:* $344 per credit hour. *Financial aid:* 40 students received aid; institutionally sponsored loans and career-related internships or fieldwork available. Aid available to part-time students. Financial aid applicants required to submit FAFSA. *Faculty research:* Community banking, health care, organizational behavior, strategy formulation. • Dr. Carl Bellas, Dean, 205-870-2364. Fax: 205-870-2464. E-mail: cjbellas@samford.edu. Application contact: Francoise Horn, Director of Graduate Programs, 205-870-2931. Fax: 205-870-2540. E-mail: fhhorn@samford.edu.

Sam Houston State University, College of Business Administration, Huntsville, TX 77341. Awards MBA. Part-time and evening/weekend programs available. Students: 25 full-time (11 women), 78 part-time (41 women); includes 7 minority (5 African Americans, 2 Hispanics), 6 international. Average age 27. In 1997, 30 degrees awarded. *Entrance requirements:* GMAT. Application deadline: 6/30 (rolling processing; 9/30 for spring admission). Application fee: $15. *Tuition:* $1810 per year full-time, $297 per semester (minimum) part-time for state residents; $6922 per year full-time, $924 per semester (minimum) part-time for nonresidents. *Financial aid:* Research assistantships, assistantships, Federal Work-Study, institutionally sponsored loans available. *Faculty research:* Banking, environmental accounting, information economics, management of services, ecology and business. • Dr. R. Dean Lewis, Dean, 409-294-1254.

San Diego State University, Graduate School of Business, San Diego, CA 92182. Awards MBA, MS, MBA/MA. Part-time and evening/weekend programs available. Students: 287 full-time (116 women), 477 part-time (164 women); includes 146 minority (11 African Americans, 86 Asian Americans, 46 Hispanics, 3 Native Americans), 82 international. Average age 28. 1,006 applicants, 37% accepted. In 1997, 262 degrees awarded. *Degree requirements:* Thesis or alternative required, foreign language not required. *Average time to degree:* master's–2 years full-time, 3.5 years part-time. *Entrance requirements:* GMAT (average 565), TOEFL (minimum score 570). Application deadline: 4/15 (priority date; rolling processing; 11/1 for spring admission). Application fee: $55. Electronic applications accepted. *Expenses:* Tuition $0 for state residents; $246 per unit for nonresidents. Fees $1932 per year full-time, $1266 per year part-time. *Financial aid:* Fellowships, research assistantships, teaching assistantships, Federal Work-Study, and career-related internships or fieldwork available. Aid available to part-time students. *Faculty research:* International business, entrepreneurship, leadership, management of technology. Total annual research expenditures: $490,000. • Dr. Michael Hergert, Associate Dean, College of Business Administration, 619-594-8073. E-mail: michael.hergert@.sdsu.edu. Application contact: Patricia Martin, Director of Admissions, 619-594-5217. Fax: 619-594-1863. E-mail: sdsumba@mail.sdsu.edu.

San Francisco State University, College of Business, Program in Business Administration, San Francisco, CA 94132-1722. Awards MBA. *Degree requirements:* Computer language, thesis, essay test required, foreign language not required. *Entrance requirements:* GMAT (minimum score 470), minimum GPA of 2.5 in last 60 units. Application deadline: 6/1 (priority date; rolling processing; 11/30 for spring admission). Application fee: $55. *Expenses:* Tuition $0 for state residents; $246 per unit for nonresidents. Fees $1982 per year full-time, $1316 per year part-time.

San Jose State University, College of Business, Program in Business Administration, San Jose, CA 95192-0001. Awards MBA. Students: 45 full-time (21 women), 180 part-time (76 women); includes 100 minority (1 African American, 85 Asian Americans, 11 Hispanics, 3 Native Americans), 19 international. Average age 30. 438 applicants, 56% accepted. In 1997, 139 degrees awarded. *Degree requirements:* Computer language, thesis or alternative, comprehensive exam required, foreign language not required. *Entrance requirements:* GMAT, minimum GPA of 3.0. Application deadline: 6/1 (rolling processing). Application fee: $59. *Expenses:* Tuition $0 for state residents; $246 per unit for nonresidents. Fees $2017 per year full-time, $1351 per year part-time. • Dr. Lee Jerrell, Director, Graduate Programs, 408-924-3420.

Santa Clara University, Leavey School of Business and Administration, Program in Business Administration, Santa Clara, CA 95053-0001. Awards MBA, JD/MBA. Part-time programs available. Students: 149 full-time (73 women), 933 part-time (310 women); includes 322 minority (12 African Americans, 275 Asian Americans, 31 Hispanics, 4 Native Americans), 86 international. Average age 32. 505 applicants, 39% accepted. In 1997, 301 degrees awarded. *Degree requirements:* Computer language required, foreign language and thesis not required. *Entrance requirements:* GMAT, TOEFL (minimum score 580), TSE (minimum score 4). Application deadline: 7/1 (rolling processing). Application fee: $55 ($75 for international students). *Tuition:* $458 per unit. *Financial aid:* Fellowships, research assistantships, institutionally sponsored loans, and career-related internships or fieldwork available. Financial aid application deadline: 5/1. • Dr. Edward McQuarrie, Associate Dean, 408-554-4500.

Announcement: The Santa Clara University MBA program is Silicon Valley's premier MBA program for working professionals and is located in the midst of one of the world's greatest concentrations of technological and scientific talent. The University's mission is to develop men and women for competence, conscience, and compassion who can provide leadership in technologically advanced and rapidly changing global environments.

See in-depth description on page 273.

Schiller International University, MBA Programs, 453 Edgewater Drive, Dunedin, FL 34698-7532. Offers programs in international business (MBA), international hotel and tourism management (MBA). Part-time and evening/weekend programs available. Faculty: 5 full-time (0 women), 10 part-time (1 woman). Students: 55. *Degree requirements:* Thesis optional, foreign language not required. *Entrance requirements:* GMAT, bachelor's degree or equivalent. Application deadline: rolling. Application fee: $35. *Expenses:* Tuition $11,800 per year. Fees $210 per year. *Financial aid:* Administrative assistantships available. Aid available to part-time students. Financial aid application deadline: 3/30. • Dr. Pat Dugan, Director, 813-736-5082. Application contact: Muriel Jault, Admissions Representative, 813-736-5082. Fax: 813-734-0359. E-mail: siuadmis@aol.com.

Schiller International University, MBA Program, 32 Boulevard de Vaugirard, Paris 75015, France. Offers programs in international business (MBA), international relations and diplomacy (MA). Bilingual French/English MBA available for native French speakers. Part-time and evening/weekend programs available. Faculty: 5 full-time (1 woman), 10 part-time (5 women). Students: 36 full-time, 23 part-time. In 1997, 13 degrees awarded. *Degree requirements:* Thesis optional, foreign language not required. *Entrance requirements:* GMAT, bachelor's degree or equivalent. Application deadline: 8/1 (priority date; rolling processing; 12/1 for spring admission). Application fee: $35. *Expenses:* Tuition $12,800 per year. Fees $210 per year. *Financial aid:* 16 students received aid; administrative assistantships, partial tuition waivers available. Aid available to part-time students. Financial aid application deadline: 3/30. • John Lynch, Adviser, 1-4538-6501. Application contact: Muriel Jault, Admissions Representative, 813-736-5082. Fax: 813-734-0359. E-mail: siuadmis@aol.com.

Schiller International University, MBA Program, Chateau Pourtales, 161 rue Melanie, Strasbourg 6700, France. Offers program in international business (MBA). Part-time and evening/weekend programs available. Faculty: 2 full-time (0 women), 5 part-time (1 woman). Students: 4 full-time, 11 part-time. Average age 28. In 1997, 11 degrees awarded. *Degree requirements:* Thesis optional, foreign language not required. *Entrance requirements:* GMAT, bachelor's degree or equivalent. Application deadline: 8/1 (priority date; rolling processing; 12/1 for spring admission). Application fee: $35. *Expenses:* Tuition $12,800 per year. Fees $210 per year. *Financial aid:* Administrative assistantships, partial tuition waivers available. Aid available to part-time students. Financial aid application deadline: 3/30. • Hanns Blasius, Adviser, 94-43-43. Fax: 94-22-55. Application contact: Muriel Jault, Admissions Representative, 813-736-5082. Fax: 813-734-0359. E-mail: siuadmis@aol.com.

Schiller International University, MBA Program, Bergstrasse 106, Heidelberg 69121, Germany. Offers program in international business (MBA, MIM). Part-time and evening/weekend programs available. Faculty: 10 full-time (6 women), 13 part-time (4 women), 13 FTE. Students: 38 full-time, 30 part-time. Average age 28. In 1997, 42 degrees awarded. *Degree requirements:* Thesis optional, foreign language not required. *Entrance requirements:* GMAT, bachelor's degree or equivalent. Application deadline: 8/1 (priority date; rolling processing; 12/1 for spring admission). Application fee: $35. *Expenses:* Tuition $12,800 per year. Fees $210 per year. *Financial aid:* 32 students received aid; administrative assistantships, partial tuition waivers available. Aid available to part-time students. Financial aid application deadline: 3/30. *Faculty research:* Leadership, international economy, foreign direct investment. • Lisa Evans, Director, 49-6221-49159. Application contact: Muriel Jault, Admissions Representative, 813-736-5082. Fax: 813-734-0359. E-mail: siuadmis@aol.com.

Schiller International University, MBA Program, San Bernardo 97-99, Edif. Colomina, Madrid 28015, Spain. Offers program in international business (MBA). Part-time and evening/weekend programs available. Faculty: 6 full-time, 4 part-time. Students: 13 full-time, 2 part-time. Average age 28. In 1997, 9 degrees awarded. *Degree requirements:* Thesis optional, foreign language not required. *Entrance requirements:* GMAT, bachelor's degree or equivalent. Application deadline: 8/1 (priority date; rolling processing; 12/1 for spring admission). Application fee: $35. *Expenses:* Tuition $12,800 per year. Fees $210 per year. *Financial aid:* Administrative assistantships, partial tuition waivers available. Aid available to part-time students. Financial aid application deadline: 3/30. • Terrance Reynolds, Adviser, 1-446-2349. Fax: 341-593-4446. Application contact: Muriel Jault, Admissions Representative, 813-736-5082. Fax: 813-734-0359. E-mail: siuadmis@aol.com.

Schiller International University, American College of Switzerland, MBA Program, CH-1854 Leysin, Switzerland. Offers program in international business (MBA). *Degree requirements:* Thesis or alternative, comprehensive exams required, foreign language not required. *Entrance requirements:* GMAT. Application deadline: rolling. Application fee: $50.

School for International Training, Program in International and Intercultural Management, Brattleboro, VT 05302-0676. Awards MIIM. Faculty: 8 full-time (6 women), 12 part-time (5 women). Students: 95 full-time (62 women), 91 part-time (75 women). Average age 28. 258 applicants, 80% accepted. In 1997, 90 degrees awarded. *Degree requirements:* 1 foreign language, thesis. *Entrance requirements:* TOEFL (minimum score 550). Application deadline: rolling. Application fee: $45. *Expenses:* Tuition $18,000 per year (minimum). Fees $1283 per year (minimum). *Financial aid:* In 1997–98, 58 students received aid, including 51 grants, scholarships (all to first-year students); Federal Work-Study, institutionally sponsored loans, and career-related internships or fieldwork also available. Financial aid application deadline: 4/1; applicants required to submit FAFSA. *Faculty research:* Intercultural communication, conflict resolution, advising and training, world issues, international business. • Karen Blanchard, Program Chair, 802-257-7751 Ext. 3322. Application contact: Marshall Brewer, Admissions Counselor, 802-258-3265. Fax: 802-258-3500.

Seattle Pacific University, School of Business and Economics, Seattle, WA 98119-1997. Offers programs in business and economics (MBA), information systems management (MS). Part-time and evening/weekend programs available. Faculty: 17 full-time (4 women), 12 part-time (3 women). Students: 23 full-time (11 women), 102 part-time (48 women); includes 13 minority (11 Asian Americans, 1 Hispanic, 1 Native American), 27 international. 55 applicants, 87% accepted. In 1997, 60 degrees awarded. *Average time to degree:* master's–2 years full-time, 4 years part-time. *Entrance requirements:* GMAT (MBA), minimum AACSB index of 1050. Application deadline: 8/1 (priority date; rolling processing; 2/1 for spring admission). Application fee: $35. *Tuition:* $412 per credit. *Financial aid:* In 1997–98, 5 students received aid, including 2 research assistantships; career-related internships or fieldwork also available. Aid available to part-time students. • Gary Karns, Associate Dean, 206-281-2948. Application contact: Debbie Wysomierski, Admissions Coordinator, 206-281-2753. Fax: 206-281-2733. E-mail: mba@spu.edu.

See in-depth description on page 275.

Seattle University, Albers School of Business and Economics, Program in Business Administration, Seattle, WA 98122. Awards MBA, Certificate, JD/MBA. Certificate and JD/MBA new for fall 1998. Part-time and evening/weekend programs available. Faculty: 42 full-time (16 women), 14 part-time (7 women). Students: 111 full-time (44 women), 476 part-time (193 women); includes 59 minority (7 African Americans, 41 Asian Americans, 9 Hispanics, 2 Native Americans), 75 international. Average age 31. 279 applicants, 61% accepted. In 1997, 137 master's awarded. *Entrance requirements:* For master's, GMAT (minimum score 500; average 560), TOEFL (minimum score 580), minimum GPA of 3.0, 1 year of related work experience. Application deadline: 8/20 (priority date; rolling processing; 2/20 for spring admission). Application fee: $55. *Expenses:* Tuition $440 per credit hour. Fees $70 per year. *Financial aid:* Federal Work-Study and career-related internships or fieldwork available. Aid available to part-time students. Financial aid applicants required to submit FAFSA. • Mary Carpenter, Director, 206-296-5700. Fax: 206-296-5795. E-mail: carpms@seattleu.edu. Application contact: Michael McKeon, Dean of Admissions, 206-296-5900. Fax: 206-296-5656. E-mail: admissions@seattleu.edu.

See in-depth description on page 277.

Seton Hall University, W. Paul Stillman School of Business, South Orange, NJ 07079-2692. Awards MBA, MS, Certificate, JD/MBA, MBA/MS. Part-time and evening/weekend programs available. Postbaccalaureate distance learning degree programs offered (no on-campus study). Faculty: 56 full-time (9 women), 17 part-time (1 woman). Students: 94 full-time (37 women), 771 part-time (300 women); includes 14 international. Average age 29. 532 applicants, 57% accepted. In 1997, 166 master's awarded. *Degree requirements:* For master's, thesis optional, foreign language not required. *Average time to degree:* master's–2 years full-time, 4 years part-time. *Entrance requirements:* For master's, GMAT (minimum score 500), TOEFL (minimum score 550); for Certificate, master's degree. Application deadline: 6/1 (priority date; rolling processing). Application fee: $50. *Expenses:* Tuition $538 per credit. Fees $185 per semester. *Financial aid:* Research assistantships and career-related internships or fieldwork available. Aid available to part-time students. Financial aid applicants required to submit FAFSA. • Sheldon Epstein, Dean, 973-761-9013. Fax: 973-275-2465. E-mail: epsteish@shu.edu. Application contact: Student Information Office, 973-761-9222. Fax: 973-761-9217. E-mail: busgrad@shu.edu.

See in-depth description on page 279.

Shenandoah University, Byrd School of Business, 1460 University Drive, Winchester, VA 22601-5195. Awards MBA. Part-time and evening/weekend programs available. Faculty: 10 full-time (2 women), 7 part-time (1 woman). Students: 30 full-time (15 women), 49 part-time (19 women); includes 3 minority (1 African American, 1 Hispanic, 1 Native American), 25 international. Average age 34. 44 applicants, 95% accepted. In 1997, 47 degrees awarded. *Entrance requirements:* GMAT. Application deadline: 3/1 (priority date; rolling processing). Application fee: $30. Electronic applications accepted. *Tuition:* $470 per credit. *Financial aid:* In 1997–98, 33 students received aid, including 2 fellowships (1 to a first-year student) averaging $222 per month, 2 graduate assistantships (1 to a first-year student); career-related internships or fieldwork also available. Aid available to part-time students. Financial aid application deadline: 3/15; applicants required to submit FAFSA. *Faculty research:* Fiscal policy, consumer expenditures, international business education, monetary policy, economic education. • Dr. Daniel A. Pavsek, Dean, 540-665-4572. Fax: 540-665-5437. E-mail: dpavsek@su.edu. Application contact: Michael Carpenter, Director of Admissions, 540-665-4581. Fax: 540-665-4627. E-mail: admit@su.edu.

Shippensburg University of Pennsylvania, College of Business, Shippensburg, PA 17257-2299. Offers program in business education/office administration (M Ed), including business education. Part-time programs available. Faculty: 2 full-time (1 woman). Students: 0. In 1997, 6 degrees awarded. *Degree requirements:* Thesis optional, foreign language not required. *Entrance requirements:* MAT or minimum GPA of 2.5. Application deadline: rolling. Application fee: $25. Electronic applications accepted. *Expenses:* Tuition $3468 per year full-time, $193 per credit hour part-time for state residents; $6236 per year full-time, $346 per credit hour part-time for nonresidents. Fees $678 per year full-time, $108 per semester (minimum) part-time. *Financial aid:* Graduate assistantships available. Aid available to part-time students. Financial aid application deadline: 3/1. • Dr. James A. Pope III, Dean, 717-532-1435.

Siena College, Business Division, Loudonville, NY 12211-1462. Offers program in professional accountancy (MBA). Part-time and evening/weekend programs available. Faculty: 10 part-time (3 women). Students: 3 full-time (2 women), 36 part-time (22 women); includes 1 minority (Asian American). Average age 32. 15 applicants, 93% accepted. *Degree requirements:* Community service, minimum GPA of 3.0 required, foreign language and thesis not required. *Entrance requirements:* GMAT, previous course work in accounting, economics, finance, business law, business statistics. Application deadline: 6/15 (priority date; rolling processing; 12/15 for spring admission). Application fee: $50. *Faculty research:* Valuation of businesses, management of family owned businesses, ethical issues in business. Total annual research expenditures: $8000. • Leonard Stokes, Director, MBA Program, 518-786-5015. E-mail: stokes@

Directory: Business Administration and Management—General

Siena College (continued)

siena.edu. Application contact: Allison Hastings, Assistant Director, MBA Program, 518-786-5015. Fax: 518-786-5040. E-mail: hastings@siena.edu.

Silver Lake College, Graduate Studies, Program in Management and Organizational Behavior, Manitowoc, WI 54220-9319. Awards MS. Part-time and evening/weekend programs available. Postbaccalaureate distance learning degree programs offered (minimal on-campus study). Faculty: 19 part-time (7 women), 6 FTE. Students: 57 full-time (22 women), 110 part-time (77 women). Average age 35. In 1997, 145 degrees awarded. *Degree requirements:* Thesis optional, foreign language not required. *Average time to degree:* master's–2 years full-time, 3.5 years part-time. *Entrance requirements:* TOEFL, interview, minimum undergraduate GPA of 3.0. Application deadline: rolling. Application fee: $30. *Expenses:* Tuition $4140 per year full-time, $230 per credit (minimum) part-time. Fees $100 per year. *Financial aid:* Federal Work-Study, institutionally sponsored loans, and career-related internships or fieldwork available. Aid available to part-time students. Financial aid application deadline: 4/15; applicants required to submit FAFSA. • Dr. Alan Heffner, Director, 920-686-6189. Fax: 920-684-9734. Application contact: Sandra Schwartz, Director of Admissions, 920-684-5955. Fax: 920-684-7082.

Simmons College, Graduate School of Management, Boston, MA 02115. Awards MBA. Part-time and evening/weekend programs available. Faculty: 12 full-time, 3 part-time. Students: 36 full-time (all women), 153 part-time (all women); includes 14 minority (6 African Americans, 4 Asian Americans, 4 Hispanics), 17 international. Average age 32. 209 applicants. In 1997, 101 degrees awarded (100% found work related to degree). *Entrance requirements:* GMAT (minimum score 550), TOEFL (minimum score 550). Application deadline: 3/30 (priority date; rolling processing; 11/15 for spring admission). Application fee: $75. *Financial aid:* In 1997–98, 35 students received aid, including 35 grants, scholarships (32 to first-year students); Federal Work-Study, institutionally sponsored loans, and career-related internships or fieldwork also available. Aid available to part-time students. Financial aid application deadline: 3/1; applicants required to submit FAFSA. • Dr. Patricia O'Brien, Dean, 617-521-3817. Application contact: Shelley Conley, Director of Admissions, 617-521-3840. Fax: 617-521-3880. E-mail: gsmadm@simmons.edu.

See in-depth description on page 281.

Simon Fraser University, Faculty of Business Administration, Burnaby, BC V5A 1S6, Canada. Awards EMBA, MBA, MBA/MRM. Programs in accounting (MBA), business administration (EMBA), decision support systems (MBA), finance (MBA), international business (MBA), management science (MBA), marketing (MBA), organization behavior (MBA), policy analysis (MBA). Part-time and evening/weekend programs available. Faculty: 48 full-time (12 women). Students: 293 full-time (107 women), 8 part-time (1 woman). Average age 27. In 1997, 99 degrees awarded. *Degree requirements:* Thesis or written project. *Entrance requirements:* GMAT, TOEFL (minimum score 570), TWE (minimum score 5) or International English Language Test (minimum score 7.5), minimum GPA of 3.0. Application fee: $55. *Expenses:* Tuition $2400 per year (minimum). Fees $207 per year. *Financial aid:* In 1997–98, 41 fellowships were awarded; research assistantships, teaching assistantships, scholarships also available. *Faculty research:* Management science and information systems, collective bargaining. • S. McShane, Director, 604-291-3639. Application contact: Program Assistant, 604-291-3047. Fax: 604-291-3404. E-mail: mba@sfu.ca.

Slippery Rock University of Pennsylvania, College of Information Science and Business Administration, Slippery Rock, PA 16057. Awards MS. *Entrance requirements:* GMAT or GRE, CPA Certificate. Application deadline: 7/1 (11/1 for spring admission). Application fee: $25. *Tuition:* $4484 per year full-time, $247 per credit part-time for state residents; $7667 per year full-time, $423 per credit part-time for nonresidents.

Sonoma State University, School of Business and Economics, Department of Business Administration, Rohnert Park, CA 94928-3609. Awards MBA. Part-time and evening/weekend programs available. Faculty: 16 full-time (5 women), 20 part-time (6 women). Students: 11 full-time (7 women), 49 part-time (25 women); includes 9 minority (5 Asian Americans, 3 Hispanics, 1 Native American), 1 international. 53 applicants, 40% accepted. In 1997, 7 degrees awarded. *Degree requirements:* Thesis or alternative required, foreign language not required. *Entrance requirements:* GMAT (average 500). Application deadline: 1/31 (rolling processing; 8/31 for spring admission). Application fee: $55. *Expenses:* Tuition $0 for state residents; $246 per unit for nonresidents. Fees $2130 per year full-time, $1464 per year part-time. *Financial aid:* In 1997–98, 1 fellowship was awarded; Federal Work-Study, institutionally sponsored loans, and career-related internships or fieldwork also available. Aid available to part-time students. Financial aid application deadline: 3/2. • Duane Dove, Chair, 707-664-2377. E-mail: duane.dove@sonoma.edu.

South Carolina State University, School of Business, 300 College Street Northeast, Orangeburg, SC 29117-0001. Offers program in agribusiness and economics (MS), including agribusiness. Part-time and evening/weekend programs available. Faculty: 8 full-time (0 women). Students: 15 full-time (5 women), 10 part-time (5 women); includes 21 minority (all African Americans). Average age 24. In 1997, 10 degrees awarded (100% found work related to degree). *Degree requirements:* Departmental qualifying exam required, thesis optional, foreign language not required. *Average time to degree:* master's–2 years full-time. *Entrance requirements:* GMAT or GRE, minimum GPA of 2.8. Application deadline: 7/15 (rolling processing; 11/10 for spring admission). Application fee: $25. *Tuition:* $2974 per year full-time, $165 per credit hour part-time. *Financial aid:* In 1997–98, 10 research assistantships (7 to first-year students) averaging $650 per month were awarded; fellowships, scholarships, Federal Work-Study, institutionally sponsored loans, and career-related internships or fieldwork also available. Financial aid application deadline: 6/1. *Faculty research:* Rural development, agriculture, international trade and development. Total annual research expenditures: $300,000. • Dr. Lucy J. Rueben, Dean, 803-536-8186.

Southeastern Louisiana University, College of Business, Hammond, LA 70402. Awards MBA. Part-time and evening/weekend programs available. Faculty: 29 full-time, 3 part-time. Students: 54 full-time (13 women), 89 part-time (37 women); includes 30 minority (5 African Americans, 20 Asian Americans, 3 Hispanics, 2 Native Americans), 20 international. Average age 25. In 1997, 67 degrees awarded. *Degree requirements:* Computer language required, foreign language and thesis not required. *Entrance requirements:* GMAT (average 475), TOEFL (minimum score 500), minimum AACSB index of 950. Application deadline: 7/15 (priority date; rolling processing; 12/15 for spring admission). Application fee: $10 ($25 for international students). Electronic applications accepted. *Expenses:* Tuition $2010 per year full-time, $287 per semester (minimum) part-time for state residents; $5232 per year full-time, $287 per semester (minimum) part-time for nonresidents. Fees $5 per year. *Financial aid:* Research assistantships, teaching assistantships, administrative assistantships, Federal Work-Study available. Aid available to part-time students. Financial aid application deadline: 5/1; applicants required to submit FAFSA. *Faculty research:* Capital structure, utility rate making, consumer behavior, organizational behavior, marketing theory. Total annual research expenditures: $20,000. • Dr. Michael Budden, Dean, 504-549-2258. Fax: 504-549-5038. Application contact: Dr. Brad S. O'Hara, Director of MBA Program, 504-549-2146. Fax: 504-549-2258. E-mail: bohara@selu.edu.

Southeastern Oklahoma State University, School of Business, Durant, OK 74701-0609. Awards MBA. Part-time and evening/weekend programs available. Faculty: 15 full-time (5 women). Students: 7 full-time (1 woman), 54 part-time (29 women); includes 9 minority (1 African American, 1 Asian American, 2 Hispanics, 5 Native Americans), 6 international. Average age 33. 38 applicants, 79% accepted. In 1997, 12 degrees awarded. *Degree requirements:* Computer language required, thesis optional, foreign language not required. *Entrance requirements:* Minimum GPA of 3.0 in last 60 hours or 2.75 overall. Application deadline: 8/1. *Tuition:* $76 per credit hour for state residents; $178 per credit hour for nonresidents. *Financial aid:* In 1997–98, 30 students received aid, including 1 teaching assistantship (to a first-year student) averaging $500 per month and totaling $4,100; Federal Work-Study, institutionally sponsored loans also available. Aid available to part-time students. Financial aid application deadline: 6/15. • Dr. Robert Masters, Dean, 580-924-0121 Ext. 2706. Fax: 580-970-7479.

Southeastern University, Program in Business Management, Washington, DC 20024-2788. Offers international management (MBA), management (MBA). Part-time and evening/weekend programs available. Faculty: 4 full-time (1 woman), 17 part-time (1 woman). Students: 14 full-time (4 women), 17 part-time (11 women); includes 31 international. Average age 28. 8 applicants, 75% accepted. In 1997, 37 degrees awarded. *Degree requirements:* Computer language required, thesis optional, foreign language not required. *Entrance requirements:* TOEFL. Application deadline: rolling. Application fee: $45. *Expenses:* Tuition $228 per credit hour. Fees $175 per quarter. *Financial aid:* Federal Work-Study, institutionally sponsored loans, and career-related internships or fieldwork available. Aid available to part-time students. Financial aid applicants required to submit FAFSA. • Dr. Mohammed Safa, Head, 202-488-8162. Application contact: Jack Flinter, Director of Admissions, 202-265-5343. Fax: 202-488-8093.

Southeast Missouri State University, College of Business, Cape Girardeau, MO 63701-4799. Awards MBA. *Application deadline:* 4/1 (priority date; rolling processing; 11/21 for spring admission). *Application fee:* $20 ($100 for international students). *Tuition:* $2034 per year full-time, $113 per credit hour part-time for state residents; $3672 per year full-time, $204 per credit hour part-time for nonresidents. • Kenneth Heitschmidt, Director, 573-651-5116.

Southern Adventist University, School of Business, Collegedale, TN 37315-0370. Offers programs in executive management (MBA), health care administration (MBA). *Application fee:* $25. *Tuition:* $275 per credit hour. • Don Van Ornam, Dean, 423-238-2750.

Southern Arkansas University–Magnolia, Program in Business Administration, Magnolia, AR 71753. Awards MBA. Offered jointly with the University of Arkansas at Little Rock. *Expenses:* Tuition $95 per hour for state residents; $138 per hour for nonresidents. Fees $2 per hour.

Southern Connecticut State University, School of Business, New Haven, CT 06515-1355. Awards MBA. Faculty: 6 full-time. Students: 10 part-time (2 women); includes 3 minority (2 African Americans, 1 Hispanic). 120 applicants, 39% accepted. In 1997, 11 degrees awarded. *Entrance requirements:* GMAT, interview. Application deadline: 7/1 (priority date; rolling processing). Application fee: $40. *Expenses:* Tuition $2632 per year full-time, $188 per credit part-time for state residents; $7200 per year full-time, $188 per credit part-time for nonresidents. Fees $1806 per year full-time, $45 per semester part-time for state residents; $2703 per year full-time, $45 per semester part-time for nonresidents. • Dr. James Finlay, Dean, 203-392-5632. Application contact: Dan Mitchell, Coordinator, 203-392-5881.

Southern Illinois University at Carbondale, College of Business and Administration, Department of Business Administration, Carbondale, IL 62901-6806. Awards MBA, DBA, JD/MBA, MBA/MA, MBA/MS. Faculty: 41 full-time (4 women). Students: 134 full-time (52 women), 22 part-time (11 women); includes 9 minority (6 African Americans, 3 Asian Americans), 70 international. Average age 26. 151 applicants, 51% accepted. In 1997, 88 master's, 9 doctorates awarded. *Degree requirements:* For master's, computer language required, foreign language and thesis not required; for doctorate, computer language, dissertation required, foreign language not required. *Entrance requirements:* For master's, GMAT, TOEFL (minimum score 550), minimum GPA of 2.7; for doctorate, GMAT, TOEFL (minimum score 600), minimum graduate GPA of 3.25. Application deadline: 6/15 (priority date; rolling processing). Application fee: $20. *Expenses:* Tuition $2964 per year full-time, $99 per semester hour part-time for state residents; $8892 per year full-time, $270 per semester hour part-time for nonresidents. Fees $1034 per year full-time, $298 per semester (minimum) part-time. *Financial aid:* In 1997–98, 2 fellowships, 42 research assistantships, 49 teaching assistantships were awarded; full tuition waivers, Federal Work-Study, institutionally sponsored loans also available. Aid available to part-time students. *Faculty research:* Marketing, corporate finance, organizational behavior, accounting, MIS, international business. Total annual research expenditures: $200,000. • Marcia Cornett, Associate Dean, 618-453-3328. E-mail: mbagp@siu.edu. Application contact: Barbara Humphrey, Administrative Aide, 618-453-3030. Fax: 618-453-7961. E-mail: barbh@siu.edu.

See in-depth description on page 283.

Southern Illinois University at Edwardsville, School of Business, Edwardsville, IL 62026-0001. Awards MA, MBA, MMR, MS, MSA, MS Ed. MS Ed (business education) offered jointly with the School of Education. Part-time programs available. Faculty: 65 full-time (17 women), 14 part-time (6 women). Students: 170 full-time (75 women), 141 part-time (64 women); includes 21 minority (13 African Americans, 6 Asian Americans, 1 Hispanic, 1 Native American), 28 international. 194 applicants, 55% accepted. In 1997, 107 degrees awarded. *Degree requirements:* Final exam required, foreign language and thesis not required. *Entrance requirements:* GMAT. Application deadline: 7/24. Application fee: $25. *Expenses:* Tuition $1716 per year full-time, $95 per credit hour part-time for state residents; $5149 per year full-time, $286 per credit hour part-time for nonresidents. Fees $463 per year full-time, $433 per year part-time. *Financial aid:* In 1997–98, 1 fellowship, 18 research assistantships, 28 assistantships were awarded; teaching assistantships, Federal Work-Study, institutionally sponsored loans also available. Aid available to part-time students. • Dr. M. Robert Carver, Dean, 618-692-3412. Application contact: Dr. Maurice Hirsch, Associate Dean, 618-692-3412.

Southern Methodist University, Edwin L. Cox School of Business, Dallas, TX 75275. Awards Exec MBA, MBA, JD/MBA, MBA/MA. MBA/MA offered jointly with the Center for Arts Administration. Part-time and evening/weekend programs available. Faculty: 36 full-time (11 women), 12 part-time (1 woman). Students: 432 full-time (126 women), 403 part-time (92 women); includes 110 minority (34 African Americans, 54 Asian Americans, 22 Hispanics), 76 international. Average age 32. In 1997, 270 degrees awarded. *Degree requirements:* Community service project, oral and written proficiency exams required, foreign language and thesis not required. *Entrance requirements:* GMAT, TOEFL (minimum score 600). Application deadline: 5/15 (priority date; rolling processing; 10/15 for spring admission). Application fee: $40. *Financial aid:* Research assistantships, full and partial tuition waivers, Federal Work-Study, and career-related internships or fieldwork available. Aid available to part-time students. Financial aid application deadline: 3/1; applicants required to submit FAFSA. *Faculty research:* Merger and acquisition activity in retailing, computer-integrated manufacturing for competitiveness, executive learning for global competitiveness. • Dr. Albert Neimi Jr., Dean, 214-768-3012. Application contact: Keith Pendergrass, Director of Graduate Admissions, 214-768-3149.

See in-depth description on page 285.

Southern Nazarene University, School of Business, Bethany, OK 73008-2694. Awards MBA, MS Mgt. Part-time and evening/weekend programs available. Faculty: 5 full-time (0 women), 11 part-time (1 woman). Students: 164 full-time (73 women). Average age 27. In 1997, 86 degrees awarded. *Degree requirements:* Thesis optional, foreign language not required. *Entrance requirements:* GMAT, English proficiency exam, minimum GPA of 3.0 in last 60 hours/major, 2.5 overall. Application deadline: 8/1 (priority date; rolling processing). Application fee: $25 ($35 for international students). • Dr. Scott Morris, Chair, 405-491-6358.

Southern Oregon University, School of Business, Ashland, OR 97520. Awards MA Ed, MBA, MS Ed. Students: 10 full-time (3 women), 17 part-time (10 women); includes 2 minority (both Asian Americans), 2 international. Average age 33. 11 applicants, 73% accepted. In 1997, 18 degrees awarded. *Degree requirements:* Comprehensive exam required, foreign language and thesis not required. *Entrance requirements:* GMAT. Application deadline: rolling. Application fee: $50. *Tuition:* $5187 per year full-time, $586 per quarter (minimum) part-time for state residents; $9228 per year full-time, $586 per quarter (minimum) part-time for nonresidents. *Financial aid:* Career-related internships or fieldwork available. • Dr. John Laughlin, Director, 541-552-6484.

Southern University and Agricultural and Mechanical College, College of Business, Baton Rouge, LA 70813. Offers program in professional accountancy (MPA). Faculty: 1 (woman) full-time, 1 (woman) part-time. Students: 8 full-time (6 women), 5 part-time (all women); includes 5 international. Average age 25. 10 applicants, 50% accepted. In 1997, 5 degrees awarded. *Degree requirements:* Thesis optional. *Entrance requirements:* GMAT or GRE General Test, TOEFL. Application deadline: 6/1 (priority date; rolling processing; 11/1 for spring admission). Application fee: $5. *Tuition:* $2226 per year full-time, $267 per semester (minimum) part-time for state residents; $6262 per year full-time, $267 per semester (minimum) part-time for nonresidents. *Financial aid:* Application deadline 4/15. • Dr. Brenda Birkett, Dean, 504-771-5640. Fax: 504-771-5262.

Southern Wesleyan University, Program in Management, Central, SC 29630-1020. Awards MS. Part-time and evening/weekend programs available. Faculty: 8 full-time (0 women), 7 part-time (1 woman). Students: 49 full-time. *Degree requirements:* Comprehensive exam required, foreign language and thesis not required. *Average time to degree:* master's–2 years full-time. *Entrance requirements:* GMAT, GRE, or MAT. Application deadline: rolling. Application fee: $25. *Expenses:* Total cost of $10,020 in tuition and required fees for complete 18-month program. • Dr. Jim Mahony, Director, 864-639-2453 Ext. 401. Fax: 864-639-0826.

Southwest Baptist University, School of Graduate Studies, School of Business, 1600 University Avenue, Bolivar, MO 65613-2597. Offers program in administration (MS), including accounting, business administration, health services. Faculty: 11 part-time (3 women). Students: 54 full-time, 87 part-time; includes 1 minority (Asian American), 3 international. Average age 30. 17 applicants, 82% accepted. In 1997, 16 degrees awarded (100% found work related to degree). *Average time to degree:* master's–1.2 years full-time. *Entrance requirements:* Interviews, minimum GPA of 2.75. Application deadline: rolling. Application fee: $25. *Tuition:* $145 per credit hour. • Dr. Michael Awad, Interim Dean, 417-326-1751. Fax: 417-326-1887. E-mail: business@sbuniv.edu. Application contact: Dr. Rodney Oglesby, Director of Graduate Studies, 417-326-1756.

Southwestern Adventist University, Program in Business Administration, Keene, TX 76059. Offers accounting (MBA). Part-time and evening/weekend programs available. Faculty: 3 full-time (0 women), 3 part-time (0 women), 5 FTE. Students: 7 full-time (3 women), 12 part-time (6 women); includes 8 minority (3 African Americans, 4 Hispanics, 1 Native American), 3 international. Average age 28. 40 applicants, 75% accepted. *Degree requirements:* Capstone Course required, thesis not required. *Entrance requirements:* GMAT (minimum score 400), GRE General Test (minimum combined score of 850). Application deadline: 8/24 (priority date; rolling processing; 12/28 for spring admission). Application fee: $0. *Tuition:* $3300 per year full-time, $275 per hour part-time. • Dr. José Goris, Director, 817-645-3921 Ext. 226. Application contact: Dr. Marie Redwine, Graduate Dean, 817-645-3921 Ext. 211. Fax: 817-556-4744. E-mail: redwinem@swau.edu.

Southwestern Oklahoma State University, School of Business, Weatherford, OK 73096-3098. Awards MBA. MBA distance learning degree program offered to Oklahoma residents only. Part-time and evening/weekend programs available. Postbaccalaureate distance learning degree programs offered (no on-campus study). Students: 2 full-time (0 women), 12 part-time (7 women); includes 1 minority (African American), 1 international. 2 applicants, 100% accepted. In 1997, 5 degrees awarded. *Degree requirements:* Comprehensive exam required, foreign language and thesis not required. *Entrance requirements:* GMAT or GRE General Test, TOEFL (minimum score 550), minimum GPA of 2.5. Application deadline: rolling. Application fee: $15. *Expenses:* Tuition $60 per credit hour (minimum) for state residents; $147 per credit hour (minimum) for nonresidents. Fees $109 per year full-time, $24 per semester (minimum) part-time. *Financial aid:* Research assistantships, teaching assistantships, partial tuition waivers, Federal Work-Study, institutionally sponsored loans available. Aid available to part-time students. Financial aid application deadline: 3/1; applicants required to submit FAFSA. • Dr. Ralph May, Director, 580-774-3279.

Southwest Missouri State University, College of Business Administration, Program in Business Administration, Springfield, MO 65804-0094. Awards MBA. Part-time and evening/weekend programs available. Faculty: 56 full-time (13 women), 1 part-time (0 women). Students: 113 full-time (49 women), 96 part-time (52 women); includes 6 minority (3 African Americans, 1 Asian American, 2 Hispanics), 74 international. Average age 25. In 1997, 44 degrees awarded. *Degree requirements:* Comprehensive exam required, thesis optional, foreign language not required. *Entrance requirements:* GMAT (minimum score 450), minimum GPA of 2.75. Application deadline: 8/6 (priority date; rolling processing; 1/4 for spring admission). Application fee: $25. *Expenses:* Tuition $1980 per year full-time, $110 per credit hour part-time for state residents; $3960 per year full-time, $220 per credit hour part-time for nonresidents. Fees $274 per year full-time, $73 per semester part-time. *Financial aid:* In 1997–98, 22 graduate assistantships averaging $583 per month and totaling $71,875 were awarded; research assistantships, institutionally sponsored loans, and career-related internships or fieldwork also available. Aid available to part-time students. • Application contact: Dr. D. Michael Fields, Director, 417-836-6346. Fax: 417-836-6337. E-mail: dmf603f@wpgate.smsu.edu.

Southwest State University, Department of Business Administration, Marshall, MN 56258-1598. Awards MS. Faculty: 11 full-time (2 women). Students: 1 full-time (0 women), 38 part-time (28 women). 18 applicants. In 1997, 1 degree awarded (100% found work related to degree). *Degree requirements:* Thesis required, foreign language not required. *Average time to degree:* master's–2.3 years part-time. *Application deadline:* rolling. *Application fee:* $20. Electronic applications accepted. *Expenses:* Tuition $128 per credit full-time, $120 per credit part-time for state residents; $190 per credit for nonresidents. Fees $389 per semester. • Dr. Joann Abbott, Head, 507-537-6223. Application contact: Rich Shearer, Director of Admissions, 507-537-6286.

Southwest Texas State University, School of Business, Program in Business Administration, San Marcos, TX 78666. Awards MBA. Part-time programs available. Faculty: 24 full-time (4 women), 1 part-time (0 women). Students: 61 full-time (20 women), 201 part-time (79 women); includes 50 minority (12 African Americans, 3 Asian Americans, 33 Hispanics, 2 Native Americans), 16 international. Average age 30. In 1997, 75 degrees awarded. *Degree requirements:* Thesis (for some programs), comprehensive exam required, foreign language not required. *Entrance requirements:* GMAT (minimum score 400), TOEFL (minimum score 550), TSE (minimum score 220). Application deadline: 7/15 (priority date; rolling processing; 11/15 for spring admission). Application fee: $25 ($50 for international students). *Expenses:* Tuition $648 per year full-time, $120 per semester (minimum) part-time for state residents; $4500 per year full-time, $750 per semester (minimum) part-time for nonresidents. Fees $1264 per year full-time, $314 per semester (minimum) part-time. *Financial aid:* Federal Work-Study, institutionally sponsored loans available. Aid available to part-time students. Financial aid application deadline: 4/1; applicants required to submit FAFSA. *Faculty research:* Organizational change and communication, artificial intelligence systems. • Dr. Robert J. Olney, Associate Dean, 512-245-2311. Fax: 512-245-8375. E-mail: ro02@swt.edu.

Spring Arbor College, School of Business and Management, Spring Arbor, MI 49283-9799. Awards MBA. Part-time and evening/weekend programs available. Faculty: 3 full-time (0 women), 11 part-time (2 women), 4.9 FTE. Students: 32 full-time (16 women), 51 part-time (27 women); includes 3 minority (all African Americans), 1 international. Average age 36. 27 applicants, 100% accepted. In 1997, 3 degrees awarded. *Average time to degree:* master's–3 years full-time. *Application deadline:* rolling. *Application fee:* $45. *Expenses:* Tuition $265 per credit hour (minimum). Fees $75 per year (minimum). *Financial aid:* 11 students received aid; partial tuition waivers, Federal Work-Study, and career-related internships or fieldwork available. Aid available to part-time students. Financial aid application deadline: 8/25; applicants required to submit FAFSA. • Dr. Richard Wallace, Dean, 517-750-6476. E-mail: rwallace@admin.arbor.edu. Application contact: Denise B. Schonhard, Admissions Representative, 517-750-6536. Fax: 517-750-1604. E-mail: schonard@admin.arbor.edu.

Spring Hill College, Graduate Programs, Program in Business Administration, Mobile, AL 36608-1791. Awards MBA. Part-time and evening/weekend programs available. Faculty: 8 full-time (2 women), 3 part-time (1 woman). Students: 10 full-time (1 woman), 36 part-time (16 women). In 1997, 20 degrees awarded. *Degree requirements:* Comprehensive exam required, foreign language and thesis not required. *Average time to degree:* master's–3 years part-time. *Entrance requirements:* GMAT, minimum undergraduate GPA of 3.0. Application deadline: rolling. Application fee: $25. *Tuition:* $245 per credit hour. *Financial aid:* Available to part-time students. Financial aid applicants required to submit FAFSA. • Dr. Lynn Stallworth, Director, 334-380-4119. E-mail: stallworth@shc.edu. Application contact: Joyce Genz, Director of Graduate Programs Administration, 334-380-3094. Fax: 334-460-2190. E-mail: jgenz@shc.edu.

Stanford University, Graduate School of Business, Stanford, CA 94305-9991. Awards MBA, PhD, JD/MBA. Faculty: 85 full-time (13 women). Students: 807 full-time (240 women), 64 part-time (15 women); includes 203 minority (38 African Americans, 114 Asian Americans, 46 Hispanics, 5 Native Americans), 241 international. Average age 28. 7,088 applicants, 7% accepted. In 1997, 403 master's, 9 doctorates awarded. *Degree requirements:* For doctorate, dissertation required, foreign language not required. *Entrance requirements:* For master's, GMAT; for doctorate, GMAT, GRE. Application deadline: 3/9. Application fee: $125. *Financial aid:* Fellowships, institutionally sponsored loans, and career-related internships or fieldwork available. Financial aid applicants required to submit FAFSA. • A. Michael Spence, Dean, 650-723-2167. Fax: 650-723-1322. E-mail: fspence@lira.stanford.edu. Application contact: Marie Mookini, Admissions Director, 650-723-2766. Fax: 650-725-7831.

See in-depth description on page 287.

State University of New York at Albany, School of Business, Albany, NY 12222-0001. Awards MBA, MS, PhD. Part-time and evening/weekend programs available. Faculty: 55 full-time (16 women), 10 part-time (2 women). Students: 195 full-time (96 women), 157 part-time (64 women); includes 27 minority (13 African Americans, 9 Asian Americans, 5 Hispanics), 38 international. Average age 26. 402 applicants, 52% accepted. In 1997, 132 master's, 3 doctorates awarded. Terminal master's awarded for partial completion of doctoral program. *Degree requirements:* For master's, project; for doctorate, dissertation. *Entrance requirements:* For master's, GMAT; for doctorate, GMAT or GRE. Application deadline: 7/1 (priority date; rolling processing). Application fee: $50. *Expenses:* Tuition $5100 per year full-time, $213 per credit hour part-time for state residents; $8416 per year full-time, $351 per credit hour part-time for nonresidents. Fees $705 per year full-time, $26.85 per credit hour part-time. *Financial aid:* Fellowships, research assistantships, minority fellowships, Federal Work-Study, and career-related internships or fieldwork available. Financial aid application deadline: 4/1. • Donald Bourque, Interim Dean, 518-442-4910. Application contact: Jeffrey Collins, Assistant Director, Graduate Admissions, 518-442-3980.

State University of New York at Binghamton, School of Management, Program in Business Administration, Binghamton, NY 13902-6000. Awards MBA, PhD, MBA/MA. Offerings include business administration (MBA, PhD), health care professional executive (MBA). MBA/MA offered jointly with the Department of History. In 1997, 56 master's, 1 doctorate awarded. *Degree requirements:* For master's, computer language required, thesis not required; for doctorate, dissertation. *Entrance requirements:* For master's, GMAT, TOEFL; for doctorate, GRE General Test, GRE Subject Test, TOEFL. Application deadline: 4/15 (priority date; rolling processing; 11/1 for spring admission). Application fee: $50. Electronic applications accepted. *Expenses:* Tuition $5100 per year full-time, $213 per credit hour part-time for state residents; $8416 per year full-time, $351 per credit hour part-time for nonresidents. Fees $654 per year full-time, $75 per semester (minimum) part-time. *Financial aid:* In 1997–98, 41 students received aid, including 2 fellowships (1 to a first-year student) averaging $811 per month and totaling $16,224, 1 research assistantship (to a first-year student) averaging $200 per month and totaling $2,000, 12 teaching assistantships (3 to first-year students) totaling $63,472, 23 graduate assistantships (9 to first-year students) totaling $125,430; Federal Work-Study, institutionally sponsored loans, and career-related internships or fieldwork also available. Aid available to part-time students. Financial aid application deadline: 2/15. • Frances Yammarino, Coordinator of Graduate Admissions, 607-777-2306.

State University of New York at Buffalo, Graduate School, School of Management, Buffalo, NY 14260. Awards MBA, PhD, JD/MBA, MA/MBA, M Arch/MBA. Part-time and evening/weekend programs available. Faculty: 55 full-time (9 women), 3 part-time (1 woman). Students: 357 full-time (115 women), 316 part-time (100 women); includes 53 minority (14 African Americans, 26 Asian Americans, 12 Hispanics, 1 Native American), 146 international. Average age 27. 847 applicants, 45% accepted. In 1997, 245 master's, 10 doctorates awarded. *Degree requirements:* For master's, computer language required, foreign language and thesis not required; for doctorate, computer language, dissertation required, foreign language not required. *Entrance requirements:* For master's, GMAT (average 580), TOEFL (minimum score 550; average 580); for doctorate, GMAT, TOEFL (minimum score 550). Application deadline: 7/1 (priority date; rolling processing; 12/15 for spring admission). Application fee: $50. Electronic applications accepted. *Tuition:* $5935 per year full-time, $271 per credit hour part-time for state residents; $9251 per year full-time, $409 per credit hour part-time for nonresidents. *Financial aid:* In 1997–98, 208 students received aid, including 16 fellowships (7 to first-year students), 22 research assistantships (4 to first-year students), 11 teaching assistantships, 48 graduate assistantships (19 to first-year students); Federal Work-Study, institutionally sponsored loans, and career-related internships or fieldwork also available. Financial aid application deadline: 2/15; applicants required to submit FAFSA. *Faculty research:* Accounting, marketing, organizational and human resources, finance, MIS. Total annual research expenditures: $890,000. • John M. Thomas, Interim Dean, 716-645-3221. Fax: 716-645-5926. Application contact: Katherine M. Gerstle, Administrative Director of the MBA Program, 716-645-3204. Fax: 716-645-2341. E-mail: gerstle@mgt.buffalo.edu.

State University of New York at New Paltz, Faculty of Engineering and Business, Department of Business Administration, New Paltz, NY 12561-2499. Awards MS. Students: 17 full-time (10 women), 25 part-time (7 women); includes 7 minority (1 African American, 1 Asian American, 5 Hispanics), 7 international. In 1997, 5 degrees awarded. *Entrance requirements:* GMAT, minimum GPA of 3.0. Application deadline: 3/15 (priority date; rolling processing). Application fee: $50. *Expenses:* Tuition $5100 per year full-time, $213 per credit hour part-time for state residents; $8416 per year full-time, $351 per credit hour part-time for nonresidents. Fees $493 per year full-time, $48 per semester (minimum) part-time. • Dr. Hadi Salavitabar, Associate Dean, 914-257-2930.

State University of New York at Oswego, School of Business, Program in Business Administration, Oswego, NY 13126. Offers business administration (MBA), management (MS). MS (management) being phased out; applicants no longer accepted. Faculty: 15 full-time, 8 part-time. Students: 32 full-time (13 women), 74 part-time (28 women); includes 9 minority (7 African Americans, 2 Asian Americans), 7 international. Average age 32. 74 applicants, 89% accepted. In 1997, 49 degrees awarded. *Entrance requirements:* GMAT, minimum GPA of 2.6. Application deadline: 7/1. Application fee: $50. *Expenses:* Tuition $5100 per year full-time, $213 per credit hour part-time for state residents; $8416 per year full-time, $351 per credit hour part-time for nonresidents. Fees $135 per year (minimum). *Financial aid:* In 1997–98, 1 teaching assistantship (to a first-year student) was awarded. *Faculty research:* Marketing, industrial finance, technology. • Dr. Charles Spector, Coordinator, 315-341-2911.

State University of New York at Stony Brook, College of Engineering and Applied Sciences, W. Averell Harriman School for Management and Policy, Stony Brook, NY 11794. Awards MS. Part-time and evening/weekend programs available. Faculty: 13 full-time, 10 part-time. Students: 49 full-time (26 women), 57 part-time (22 women); includes 17 minority (1 African American, 14 Asian Americans, 2 Hispanics), 34 international. 110 applicants, 67% accepted. In 1997, 46 degrees awarded. *Degree requirements:* Internship required, foreign language not required. *Entrance requirements:* GMAT or GRE General Test, TOEFL. Application deadline: 1/15. Application fee: $50. *Expenses:* Tuition $5100 per year full-time, $213 per credit hour part-time for state residents; $8416 per year full-time, $351 per credit hour part-time for nonresidents. Fees $529 per year full-time, $77 per semester (minimum) part-time. *Financial aid:* In 1997–98, 1 research assistantship, 2 teaching assistantships were awarded; fellowships and career-related internships or fieldwork also available. Financial aid application deadline: 4/1. *Faculty*

Directory: Business Administration and Management—General

State University of New York at Stony Brook (continued)

research: Economic development policies, entrepreneurship, decision support systems, worker-owned firms. Total annual research expenditures: $378,903. • Dr. Thomas Sexton, Director, 516-632-7180. Application contact: Thomas Gjerde, Director of Graduate Studies, 516-632-7163.

State University of New York College at Fredonia, Program in Business Administration, Fredonia, NY 14063. Awards MBA. Offered jointly with the State University of New York at Buffalo. *Application deadline:* 7/5. *Application fee:* $50. *Expenses:* Tuition $5100 per year full-time, $213 per credit hour part-time for state residents; $8416 per year full-time, $351 per credit hour part-time for nonresidents. Fees $725 per year full-time, $30 per credit hour part-time. *Financial aid:* Application deadline 3/15. • Dr. Thomas Rywick, Interim Dean, Natural and Social Sciences and Professional Studies, Graduate Studies, 716-673-3173. Application contact: Elizabeth Curtin-O'Brien, Admissions Counselor, 716-673-3251.

State University of New York College at Oneonta, Department of Economics and Business, Oneonta, NY 13820-4015. Offers program in business (MS). Students: 4 full-time (2 women), 9 part-time (4 women); includes 1 minority (Asian American). *Entrance requirements:* GMAT or GRE General Test. Application deadline: 4/15. Application fee: $50. *Expenses:* Tuition $5100 per year full-time, $213 per credit hour part-time for state residents; $8416 per year full-time, $351 per credit hour part-time for nonresidents. Fees $482 per year full-time, $6.85 per credit hour part-time. • Dr. Wade Thomas, Chairman, 607-436-3458.

State University of New York Empire State College, Program in Business and Policy Studies, Saratoga Springs, NY 12866-4391. Awards MA. Part-time and evening/weekend programs available. Postbaccalaureate distance learning degree programs offered (minimal on-campus study). Faculty: 1 full-time (0 women), 10 part-time (2 women). Students: 3 full-time, 103 part-time. *Degree requirements:* Thesis, exam required, foreign language not required. *Entrance requirements:* Proficiency in statistics. Application deadline: 7/15 (priority date; rolling processing; 11/15 for spring admission). *Tuition:* $5245 per year full-time, $915 per semester (minimum) part-time for state residents; $8561 per year full-time, $1467 per semester (minimum) part-time for nonresidents. *Financial aid:* Fellowships, Federal Work-Study, and career-related internships or fieldwork available. Aid available to part-time students. Financial aid application deadline: 7/1; applicants required to submit FAFSA. *Faculty research:* Business history, applied business statistics, labor/management relations, American social problems and business, effect of government economic policies on business. • Dr. Jim Savitt, Chair, 518-587-2100 Ext. 429. E-mail: jsavitt@sescua.esc.edu. Application contact: Patricia Ryan, Assistant Director of Student Services for Graduate Studies, 518-587-2100. Fax: 518-587-4382.

State University of New York Institute of Technology at Utica/Rome, School of Business, Program in Business Management, PO Box 3050, Utica, NY 13504-3050. Awards MS. Part-time and evening/weekend programs available. Faculty: 13 full-time (2 women), 4 part-time (0 women). Students: 28 full-time (13 women), 69 part-time (37 women); includes 7 minority (4 African Americans, 2 Asian Americans, 1 Hispanic), 1 international. Average age 35. 37 applicants, 65% accepted. In 1997, 30 degrees awarded. *Degree requirements:* Comprehensive exam required, thesis optional, foreign language not required. *Average time to degree:* master's–2 years full-time, 4 years part-time. *Entrance requirements:* GMAT (average 457), TOEFL (minimum score 550), minimum GPA of 3.0. Application deadline: 6/15 (priority date; rolling processing). Application fee: $50. *Expenses:* Tuition $5100 per year full-time, $213 per credit hour part-time for state residents; $8416 per year full-time, $351 per credit hour part-time for nonresidents. Fees $570 per year full-time, $17.60 per credit hour part-time. *Financial aid:* In 1997–98, 56 students received aid, including 1 fellowship, 3 research assistantships; Federal Work-Study and career-related internships or fieldwork also available. Aid available to part-time students. Financial aid applicants required to submit FAFSA. *Faculty research:* Small business development, entrepreneurial training. Total annual research expenditures: $204,365. • Application contact: Marybeth Lyons, Director of Admissions, 315-792-7500. Fax: 315-792-7837. E-mail: smbl@sunyit.edu.

State University of West Georgia, College of Business, Program in Business Administration, Carrollton, GA 30118. Awards MBA. Part-time and evening/weekend programs available. Faculty: 18 full-time (3 women). Students: 32 full-time (14 women), 22 part-time (7 women); includes 5 minority (3 African Americans, 2 Asian Americans), 14 international. Average age 28. In 1997, 18 degrees awarded. *Degree requirements:* Comprehensive exam required, foreign language and thesis not required. *Entrance requirements:* GMAT, minimum GPA of 2.5. Application deadline: 8/30 (rolling processing). Application fee: $15. *Expenses:* Tuition $2428 per year full-time, $83 per semester hour part-time for state residents; $8428 per year full-time, $250 per semester hour part-time for nonresidents. Fees $428 per year. *Financial aid:* Research assistantships, assistantships, and career-related internships or fieldwork available. Aid available to part-time students. Financial aid applicants required to submit FAFSA. • John R. Wells, Director, MBA Program, 770-836-6467. Fax: 770-836-6774. E-mail: jwells@sbf.bus.westga.edu. Application contact: Dr. Jack O. Jenkins, Dean, Graduate School, 770-836-6419. Fax: 770-836-2301. E-mail: jjenkins@cob.as.westga.edu.

Stephen F. Austin State University, College of Business, Program in Business Administration, Nacogdoches, TX 75962. Offers business (MBA), management and marketing (MBA). Part-time and evening/weekend programs available. Faculty: 23 full-time (5 women). Students: 25 full-time (9 women), 42 part-time (23 women); includes 6 minority (4 African Americans, 1 Asian American, 1 Hispanic), 2 international. 27 applicants, 81% accepted. In 1997, 10 degrees awarded. *Degree requirements:* Computer language, comprehensive exam required, foreign language and thesis not required. *Entrance requirements:* GMAT, minimum AACSB index of 1000. Application deadline: 7/15 (rolling processing; 11/15 for spring admission). Application fee: $0 ($25 for international students). *Tuition:* $1465 per year full-time, $263 per semester (minimum) part-time for state residents; $5299 per year full-time, $890 per semester (minimum) part-time for nonresidents. *Financial aid:* Research assistantships, teaching assistantships, Federal Work-Study, institutionally sponsored loans available. Financial aid application deadline: 3/1. *Faculty research:* Strategic implications, information search, multinational firms, philosophical guidance. • Dr. Warren Fisher, Graduate Director, 409-468-3101.

Stephens College, School of Graduate and Continuing Education, Department of Business Administration, 1200 East Broadway, Columbia, MO 65215-0002. Awards MBA. Part-time programs available. Postbaccalaureate distance learning degree programs offered (minimal on-campus study). Faculty: 5 full-time (3 women). Students: 7 part-time (all women). *Degree requirements:* Thesis required, foreign language not required. *Entrance requirements:* GMAT (minimum score 500), TOEFL (minimum score 550), minimum GPA of 3.0 in last 60 hours. Application deadline: rolling. Application fee: $25. *Tuition:* $690 per course. • Dr. Chris Prestigiacomo, Director, 573-442-2211 Ext. 139. E-mail: chrisp@wc.stephens.edu. Application contact: Dr. Joan T. Rines, Director of Graduate Programs, 800-388-7579. Fax: 573-876-7248. E-mail: joanr@wc.stephens.edu.

Stetson University, School of Business Administration, Program in Business Administration, 421 North Woodland Boulevard, DeLand, FL 32720-3781. Awards MBA, JD/MBA. Part-time and evening/weekend programs available. Students: 24 full-time (5 women), 91 part-time (48 women); includes 20 minority (6 African Americans, 5 Asian Americans, 9 Hispanics), 2 international. Average age 29. 120 applicants, 97% accepted. In 1997, 28 degrees awarded. *Degree requirements:* Computer language required, foreign language and thesis not required. *Entrance requirements:* GMAT. Application deadline: 7/1. Application fee: $25. *Tuition:* $370 per credit hour. *Financial aid:* Application deadline 3/15. • Dr. Frank DeZoort, Director, 904-822-7410.

Stevens Institute of Technology, Wesley J. Howe School of Technology Management, Hoboken, NJ 07030. Awards M Eng, MIM, MS, MTM, PhD, Certificate. Part-time and evening/weekend programs available. Postbaccalaureate distance learning degree programs offered. 499 applicants, 89% accepted. Terminal master's awarded for partial completion of doctoral program. *Degree requirements:* For doctorate, computer language, dissertation; for Certificate, computer language required, foreign language not required. *Entrance requirements:* For master's and doctorate, GMAT, GRE, TOEFL. Application deadline: rolling. Application fee: $45. Electronic applications accepted. *Expenses:* Tuition $13,500 per year full-time, $675 per credit part-time. Fees $160 per year. *Financial aid:* Fellowships, research assistantships, teaching assistantships, assistantships, Federal Work-Study, institutionally sponsored loans available. *Faculty research:* Total quality management, company and industry profitability analysis, expert systems. Total annual research expenditures: $400,000. • Dr. James Teitjen, Head, 201-216-5384. Fax: 201-216-5385.

See in-depth description on page 289.

Strayer University, Graduate School, 1025 15th Street, NW, Washington, DC 20005-2603. Offers programs in business administration (MS), information systems (MS), professional accounting (MS). Part-time and evening/weekend programs available. Postbaccalaureate distance learning degree programs offered (minimal on-campus study). Faculty: 76 full-time (3 women), 49 part-time (10 women). Students: 656 full-time (296 women), 574 part-time (270 women); includes 483 minority (332 African Americans, 86 Asian Americans, 62 Hispanics, 3 Native Americans), 188 international. Average age 32. In 1997, 302 degrees awarded. *Degree requirements:* Thesis required, foreign language not required. *Entrance requirements:* GMAT (minimum score 450), GRE General Test (minimum combined score of 1000), minimum GPA of 2.75. Application deadline: 9/28 (priority date; rolling processing; 4/6 for spring admission). Application fee: $25. Electronic applications accepted. *Tuition:* $6750 per year full-time, $250 per credit hour part-time. *Financial aid:* Federal Work-Study, institutionally sponsored loans available. Aid available to part-time students. Financial aid applicants required to submit FAFSA. • Dr. Samad Hafazi, Director of Graduate Studies, 202-408-2400. Application contact: Michael Williams, Campus Coordinator, 202-408-2400. Fax: 202-289-1831.

Suffolk University, Sawyer School of Management, Programs in Business Administration, Boston, MA 02108-2770. Awards EMBA, MBA, APC, JD/MBA. Part-time and evening/weekend programs available. Faculty: 28 full-time (6 women), 19 part-time (5 women). Students: 107 full-time (52 women), 636 part-time (266 women). Average age 30. 383 applicants, 80% accepted. In 1997, 271 master's awarded. *Entrance requirements:* For master's, GMAT (average 500), minimum undergraduate GPA of 2.75 (MBA), 5 years of managerial experience (EMBA). Application deadline: 6/15 (priority date; rolling processing; 11/15 for spring admission). Application fee: $50. *Expenses:* Tuition $17,490 per year full-time, $1749 per course part-time. Fees $50 per year full-time, $20 per year part-time. *Financial aid:* In 1997–98, 150 students received aid, including 75 fellowships; Federal Work-Study, institutionally sponsored loans, and career-related internships or fieldwork also available. Aid available to part-time students. Financial aid applicants required to submit FAFSA. *Faculty research:* Foreign investments; career strategies and boundaryless careers; corporate ethics codes; interest rates, inflations, and growth options; innovation and product development performance. • Richard Torrissi, Associate Dean, 617-573-8088. Application contact: Judy Reynolds, Acting Director of Graduate Admissions, 617-573-8302. Fax: 617-523-0116. E-mail: grad.admission@admin.suffolk.edu.

See in-depth description on page 291.

Sullivan College, School of Business, PO Box 33-308, 3101 Bardstown Road, Louisville, KY 40205. Awards MBA. Faculty: 7. Students: 50. *Application deadline:* rolling. *Application fee:* $75. *Tuition:* $246 per credit hour. • Dr. John Padgett, Dean of Academics, 502-456-6504. Application contact: Admissions Office, 502-456-6505.

Sul Ross State University, Rio Grande College of Sul Ross State University, Alpine, TX 79832. Offerings include business administration (MBA). College faculty: 16 full-time (2 women), 2 part-time (1 woman). *Application deadline:* rolling. *Application fee:* $0 ($50 for international students). *Expenses:* Tuition $864 per year full-time, $120 per semester (minimum) part-time for state residents; $5976 per year full-time, $747 per semester (minimum) part-time for nonresidents. Fees $754 per year full-time, $105 per semester (minimum) part-time. • Dr. Frank Abbott, Dean, 512-278-3339. Fax: 512-278-3330.

Sul Ross State University, Department of Business Administration, Alpine, TX 79832. Offers programs in international trade (MBA), management (MBA). Part-time and evening/weekend programs available. Faculty: 4 full-time (0 women), 2 part-time (0 women). Students: 6 full-time (5 women), 5 part-time (4 women); includes 4 minority (all Hispanics), 4 international. Average age 31. In 1997, 4 degrees awarded. *Degree requirements:* Thesis optional, foreign language not required. *Entrance requirements:* GMAT (minimum score 400) or GRE General Test (minimum combined score of 850), minimum GPA of 2.5 in last 60 hours of undergraduate work. Application deadline: rolling. Application fee: $0 ($50 for international students). *Expenses:* Tuition $864 per year full-time, $120 per semester (minimum) part-time for state residents; $5976 per year full-time, $747 per semester (minimum) part-time for nonresidents. Fees $754 per year full-time, $105 per semester (minimum) part-time. *Financial aid:* Teaching assistantships, Federal Work-Study, institutionally sponsored loans, and career-related internships or fieldwork available. Aid available to part-time students. Financial aid application deadline: 5/1; applicants required to submit FAFSA. *Faculty research:* Cross-cultural comparisons, U.S.-Mexico management relations. • William G. Green, Chair, 915-837-8066. Fax: 915-837-8003.

Syracuse University, School of Management, Syracuse, NY 13244-0003. Awards MBA, MPS, MS Acct, PhD, JD/MBA, JD/PhD, JD/MS Acct. MPS offered jointly with S. I. Newhouse School of Public Communications. Part-time and evening/weekend programs available. Faculty: 57 full-time, 24 part-time. Students: 196 full-time (65 women), 257 part-time (76 women); includes 45 minority (16 African Americans, 15 Asian Americans, 11 Hispanics, 3 Native Americans), 109 international. 751 applicants, 47% accepted. In 1997, 161 master's, 7 doctorates awarded. *Entrance requirements:* For master's, GMAT; for doctorate, GMAT (minimum score 600). Application deadline: 2/1. Application fee: $40. *Tuition:* $13,320 per year full-time, $555 per credit hour part-time. *Financial aid:* In 1997–98, 15 research assistantships, 30 teaching assistantships were awarded; fellowships, partial tuition waivers, Federal Work-Study also available. Financial aid application deadline: 3/1. • George Burman, Dean, 315-443-3715. Application contact: Associate Dean, 315-443-3850.

See in-depth description on page 293.

Tarleton State University, College of Business Administration, Stephenville, TX 76402. Awards MBA. Part-time and evening/weekend programs available. Postbaccalaureate distance learning degree programs offered (minimal on-campus study). Faculty: 14 full-time (3 women). Students: 8 full-time (4 women), 229 part-time (135 women); includes 28 minority (10 African Americans, 17 Hispanics, 1 Native American). 29 applicants, 90% accepted. In 1997, 53 degrees awarded. *Degree requirements:* Comprehensive exam required, foreign language and thesis not required. *Entrance requirements:* GMAT or GRE General Test, minimum GPA of 2.75. Application deadline: 8/5 (priority date; rolling processing; 12/1 for spring admission). Application fee: $25 ($100 for international students). *Expenses:* Tuition $46 per hour for state residents; $249 per hour for nonresidents. Fees $49 per hour. *Financial aid:* Research assistantships, teaching assistantships, Federal Work-Study, institutionally sponsored loans, and career-related internships or fieldwork available. Aid available to part-time students. Financial aid application deadline: 5/1; applicants required to submit FAFSA. • Dan Collins, Dean, 254-968-9047.

Temple University, School of Business and Management, Doctoral Program in Business Administration, Philadelphia, PA 19122-6096. Offers accounting (PhD), finance (PhD), general and strategic management (PhD), human resource administration (PhD), marketing (PhD). Students: 11 (3 women); includes 2 minority (both Asian Americans), 8 international. 7 applicants, 43% accepted. *Degree requirements:* Dissertation, preliminary exams required, foreign language not required. *Entrance requirements:* GMAT, TOEFL (minimum score 600), master's degree, minimum GPA of 3.5. Application deadline: 1/15 (rolling processing). Application fee: $40.

Expenses: Tuition $323 per semester hour for state residents; $444 per semester hour for nonresidents. Fees $170 per year full-time, $28 per semester (minimum) part-time. *Financial aid:* Fellowships, teaching assistantships, full and partial tuition waivers, institutionally sponsored loans available. Financial aid application deadline: 2/1. • Dr. Roland Lipka, Director, 215-204-8125. Fax: 215-204-5574. Application contact: Linda Whelan, Director, 215-204-7678. Fax: 215-204-8300.

See in-depth description on page 295.

Temple University, School of Business and Management, Master's Program in Business Administration, Philadelphia, PA 19122-6096. Awards MBA, MS, DMD/MBA, JD/MBA, MBA/MS. Offerings include accounting (MBA, MS); actuarial science (MBA); chemistry (MBA); computer and information sciences (MBA, MS); economics (MBA, MS); finance (MBA, MS); general and strategic management (MBA); healthcare management (MBA, MS), including healthcare financial management (MS), healthcare management (MBA); human resource administration (MBA, MS); international business (MS); international business administration (MBA); legal studies (MBA); management science/operations management (MBA, MS); marketing (MBA, MS); physical distribution (MBA); real estate and urban land studies (MBA, MS); risk management insurance (MBA, MS); statistics (MBA). Evening/weekend programs available. Faculty: 72 full-time (13 women). Students: 1,034 (393 women); includes 184 minority (78 African Americans, 86 Asian Americans, 16 Hispanics, 4 Native Americans), 80 international. 1,415 applicants, 55% accepted. In 1997, 310 degrees awarded. *Entrance requirements:* GMAT (average 540), TOEFL (minimum score 575). Application fee: $40. *Expenses:* Tuition $323 per semester hour for state residents; $444 per semester hour for nonresidents. Fees $170 per year full-time, $28 per semester (minimum) part-time. • Application contact: Linda Whelan, Director, 215-204-7678. Fax: 215-204-8300. E-mail: linda@astro.ocis.temple.edu.

See in-depth description on page 295.

Tennessee State University, College of Business, Nashville, TN 37209-1561. Awards MBA. Part-time and evening/weekend programs available. Faculty: 25 full-time (4 women), 1 part-time. Students: 29 full-time (13 women), 108 part-time (22 women); includes 60 minority (49 African Americans, 10 Asian Americans, 1 Hispanic), 26 international. Average age 30. 154 applicants, 66% accepted. In 1997, 38 degrees awarded. *Degree requirements:* Computer language required, foreign language and thesis not required. *Entrance requirements:* GMAT (minimum score 400; average 500). Application deadline: rolling. Application fee: $15. *Tuition:* $2962 per year full-time, $182 per credit hour part-time for state residents; $7788 per year full-time, $393 per credit hour part-time for nonresidents. *Financial aid:* In 1997–98, 10 research assistantships (7 to first-year students) averaging $800 per month were awarded. *Faculty research:* International business, small business development and management, information systems, taxation, technology transfer. • Dr. Tilden J. Curry, Dean, 615-963-7121. Application contact: G. Bruce Hartmann, Coordinator, 615-963-7145. Fax: 615-963-7139.

Tennessee Technological University, College of Business Administration, Cookeville, TN 38505. Awards MBA. Part-time and evening/weekend programs available. Faculty: 28 full-time (5 women). Students: 62 full-time (30 women), 58 part-time (28 women); includes 22 minority (4 African Americans, 12 Asian Americans, 6 Hispanics). Average age 25. 110 applicants, 65% accepted. In 1997, 39 degrees awarded. *Entrance requirements:* GMAT, TOEFL (minimum score 525), interview. Application deadline: 3/1 (priority date; 8/1 for spring admission). Application fee: $25 ($30 for international students). *Tuition:* $2960 per year full-time, $147 per semester hour part-time for state residents; $7786 per year full-time, $358 per semester hour part-time for nonresidents. *Financial aid:* In 1997–98, 34 students received aid, including 3 fellowships (1 to a first-year student), 31 research assistantships (21 to first-year students); teaching assistantships also available. Aid available to part-time students. Financial aid application deadline: 4/1. • Dr. Virginia Moore, Director, 615-372-3600. Fax: 615-372-6249. E-mail: vmoore@tntech.edu. Application contact: Dr. Rebecca F. Quattlebaum, Dean of the Graduate School, 615-372-3233. Fax: 615-372-3497. E-mail: rquattlebaum@tntech.edu.

See in-depth description on page 297.

Texas A&M International University, Division of Business Administration, 5201 University Boulevard, Laredo, TX 78041-1900. Offers programs in business administration (MBA), information systems (MSIS), international banking (MBA), international logistics (MSIL), international trade (MBA), professional accountancy (MP Acc). Part-time and evening/weekend programs available. *Entrance requirements:* GMAT or GRE General Test. Application deadline: 7/15 (priority date; rolling processing; 11/12 for spring admission). Application fee: $0.

Texas A&M University, Lowry Mays Graduate School of Business, Department of Management, College Station, TX 77843-4113. Awards MS, PhD. Faculty: 34 full-time (10 women), 4 part-time (0 women). Students: 53 full-time (22 women); includes 8 international. Average age 31. 76 applicants, 28% accepted. In 1997, 8 master's awarded (100% found work related to degree); 5 doctorates awarded. Terminal master's awarded for partial completion of doctoral program. *Degree requirements:* For master's, oral comprehensive exam required, foreign language and thesis not required; for doctorate, dissertation required, foreign language not required. *Average time to degree:* master's–1.5 years full-time; doctorate–4 years full-time. *Entrance requirements:* For master's, GMAT or GRE, TOEFL (minimum score 600); for doctorate, GMAT or GRE General Test, TOEFL. Application deadline: 3/1 (priority date; rolling processing; 8/1 for spring admission). Application fee: $35 ($75 for international students). *Financial aid:* 25 students received aid; fellowships, research assistantships, teaching assistantships, institutionally sponsored loans, and career-related internships or fieldwork available. Financial aid application deadline: 2/1. *Faculty research:* Strategic and human resource management, business and public policy, organizational behavior, organizational theory. • Ricky W. Griffin, Head, 409-845-4851. Application contact: Leonard Bierman, Adviser, 409-845-3233. Fax: 409-845-9641. E-mail: len-bierman@tamu.edu.

See in-depth description on page 299.

Texas A&M University, Lowry Mays Graduate School of Business, MBA Program, College Station, TX 77843-4113. Awards MBA. Faculty: 109 full-time. Students: 203 full-time (59 women). Average age 26. 530 applicants, 38% accepted. In 1997, 101 degrees awarded. *Average time to degree:* master's–1.7 years full-time. *Entrance requirements:* GMAT, TOEFL (minimum score 600). Application deadline: 3/1 (priority date; rolling processing). Application fee: $35 ($75 for international students). *Financial aid:* 89 students received aid; fellowships, research assistantships, Federal Work-Study, institutionally sponsored loans, and career-related internships or fieldwork available. Financial aid application deadline: 2/1. • Winston T. Shearon Jr., Director, 409-845-4714. Fax: 409-862-2393. E-mail: inquiries@mba-lab.tamu.edu.

See in-depth description on page 299.

Texas A&M University–Commerce, College of Business and Technology, Department of General Business and Systems Management, Commerce, TX 75429-3011. Offers program in business administration (MBA). Faculty: 17 full-time (3 women), 1 part-time (0 women). Students: 79 full-time (40 women), 70 part-time (34 women); includes 20 minority (11 African Americans, 2 Asian Americans, 4 Hispanics, 3 Native Americans), 70 international. In 1997, 31 degrees awarded. *Degree requirements:* Thesis (for some programs), oral comprehensive exam required, foreign language not required. *Entrance requirements:* GMAT. Application deadline: rolling. Application fee: $0 ($25 for international students). *Tuition:* $2382 per year full-time, $343 per semester (minimum) part-time for state residents; $7518 per year full-time, $343 per semester (minimum) part-time for nonresidents. *Financial aid:* Research assistantships, teaching assistantships, Federal Work-Study, institutionally sponsored loans available. • Dr. Edgar Manton, Head, 903-886-5692. Application contact: Pam Hammonds, Graduate Admissions Adviser, 903-886-5167. Fax: 903-886-5165.

Texas A&M University–Corpus Christi, College of Business Administration, Corpus Christi, TX 78412-5503. Offers programs in accounting (M Acc), management (MBA). Part-time and evening/weekend programs available. Students: 34 full-time (17 women), 106 part-time (45 women); includes 53 minority (4 African Americans, 5 Asian Americans, 42 Hispanics, 2 Native Americans), 3 international. Average age 34. In 1997, 57 degrees awarded. *Entrance requirements:* GMAT. Application deadline: 7/15 (priority date; rolling processing; 11/15 for spring admission). Application fee: $10 ($30 for international students). *Expenses:* Tuition $648 per year full-time, $120 per semester (minimum) part-time for state residents; $4482 per year full-time, $747 per semester (minimum) part-time for nonresidents. Fees $1010 per year full-time, $205 per semester part-time. *Financial aid:* Federal Work-Study, institutionally sponsored loans, and career-related internships or fieldwork available. Aid available to part-time students. Financial aid application deadline: 3/15; applicants required to submit FAFSA. • Dr. Moustafa H. Abdelsamad, Dean, 512-994-2655. E-mail: addba001@tamucc.edu. Application contact: Mary Margaret Dechant, Director of Admissions, 512-994-2624. Fax: 512-994-5887.

Texas A&M University–Kingsville, College of Business Administration, Kingsville, TX 78363. Awards MBA, MS. Part-time and evening/weekend programs available. Faculty: 14 full-time. Students: 20 full-time (8 women), 33 part-time (14 women); includes 16 minority (2 African Americans, 2 Asian Americans, 12 Hispanics), 15 international. Average age 30. In 1997, 10 degrees awarded (100% found work related to degree). *Degree requirements:* Computer language, thesis or alternative, comprehensive exam required, foreign language not required. *Entrance requirements:* GMAT (minimum score 490), TOEFL (minimum score 525), minimum GPA of 2.5. Application deadline: 6/1 (rolling processing; 11/15 for spring admission). Application fee: $15 ($25 for international students). *Tuition:* $1822 per year full-time, $281 per semester (minimum) part-time for state residents; $6934 per year full-time, $908 per semester (minimum) part-time for nonresidents. *Financial aid:* Federal Work-Study available. Aid available to part-time students. Financial aid application deadline: 5/15. *Faculty research:* Capital budgeting, international trade. • Dr. Darvin Hoffman, Graduate Coordinator, 512-593-3802.

Texas A&M University–Texarkana, Division of Behavioral Sciences and Business Administration, Texarkana, TX 75505-5518. Awards MBA, MS. Part-time and evening/weekend programs available. Faculty: 10 full-time (1 woman). Students: 76. 91% of applicants accepted. In 1997, 40 degrees awarded. *Degree requirements:* Thesis or alternative required, foreign language not required. *Entrance requirements:* GMAT (minimum score 450), bachelor's degree from a regionally accredited institution. Application deadline: rolling. Application fee: $0 ($25 for international students). *Tuition:* $2136 per year for state residents; $7248 per year for nonresidents. *Financial aid:* Career-related internships or fieldwork available. • Dr. David Bejou, Head, 903-223-3011. Application contact: Pat Black, Registrar, 903-223-3068. Fax: 903-832-8890. E-mail: pat.black@tamut.edu.

Texas Christian University, M. J. Neeley School of Business, Program in Business Administration, Fort Worth, TX 76129-0002. Awards MBA. Part-time and evening/weekend programs available. Faculty: 31 full-time (4 women), 1 part-time (0 women). Students: 287 (82 women); includes 16 minority (3 African Americans, 4 Asian Americans, 9 Hispanics), 62 international. In 1997, 129 degrees awarded. *Average time to degree:* master's–2 years full-time, 3 years part-time. *Entrance requirements:* GMAT, TOEFL (minimum score 550), 6 hours in economics, 3 hours in college algebra. Application deadline: 4/30 (priority date; rolling processing). Application fee: $50. Electronic applications accepted. *Expenses:* Tuition $10,350 per year full-time, $345 per credit hour part-time. Fees $1240 per year full-time, $50 per credit hour part-time. *Financial aid:* Graduate assistantships, Federal Work-Study, institutionally sponsored loans, and career-related internships or fieldwork available. Aid available to part-time students. Financial aid application deadline: 5/1; applicants required to submit FAFSA. *Faculty research:* Emerging financial markets, derivative trading activity, salesforce deployment, examining sales activity, litigation against tax practitioners, effects of accounting information on capital markets. Total annual research expenditures: $2.5 million. • Application contact: Peggy Conway, Director, MBA Admissions, 817-257-7531. Fax: 817-257-7227. E-mail: p.conway@tcu.edu.

Texas Southern University, School of Business, Program in Business Administration, Houston, TX 77004-4584. Awards MBA, JD/MBA. Part-time and evening/weekend programs available. Students: 67 full-time (37 women), 45 part-time (21 women). In 1997, 27 degrees awarded. *Degree requirements:* Computer language, comprehensive exam required, foreign language and thesis not required. *Entrance requirements:* GMAT (minimum AACSB index of 950), minimum GPA of 2.5. Application deadline: 7/15 (priority date; rolling processing). Application fee: $35 ($75 for international students). *Financial aid:* Application deadline 5/1. • Dr. Priscilla Slade, Dean, School of Business, 713-313-7215.

Texas Tech University, Graduate School, College of Business Administration, Lubbock, TX 79409. Awards MBA, MSA, MSBA, PhD, Certificate, JD/MBA, M Agr/MBA, MBA/MSN, MD/MBA. Part-time programs available. Faculty: 50 full-time (7 women). Students: 404 full-time (129 women), 54 part-time (17 women); includes 34 minority (6 African Americans, 6 Asian Americans, 22 Hispanics), 96 international. Average age 28. 349 applicants, 60% accepted. In 1997, 170 master's awarded (10% entered university research/teaching, 90% found other work related to degree); 13 doctorates awarded. *Degree requirements:* For master's, computer language, comprehensive exam required, foreign language and thesis not required; for doctorate, computer language, dissertation, qualifying exams required, foreign language not required. *Entrance requirements:* For master's, GMAT (average 560); for doctorate, GMAT (minimum score 580; average 620). Application deadline: 4/15 (priority date; rolling processing). Application fee: $25 ($50 for international students). *Expenses:* Tuition $864 per year full-time, $120 per semester (minimum) part-time for state residents; $5976 per year full-time, $747 per semester (minimum) part-time for nonresidents. Fees $2321 per year full-time, $302 per semester (minimum) part-time. *Financial aid:* Fellowships, research assistantships, teaching assistantships, Federal Work-Study, and career-related internships or fieldwork available. Aid available to part-time students. Financial aid applicants required to submit FAFSA. *Total annual research expenditures:* $1 million. • Dr. Roy D. Howell, Interim Dean, 806-742-3188. Fax: 806-742-1092. E-mail: dean@coba.ttu.edu. Application contact: Nancy Dodge, Director, 806-742-3184. Fax: 806-742-3958.

See in-depth description on page 301.

Texas Wesleyan University, Program in Business Administration, Fort Worth, TX 76105-1536. Awards MBA. Faculty: 5 part-time (1 woman). Students: 26 full-time (10 women), 53 part-time (27 women); includes 23 minority (15 African Americans, 2 Asian Americans, 6 Hispanics), 6 international. Average age 34. *Entrance requirements:* GMAT, minimum GPA of 3.0 in final 60 hours of undergraduate course work. Application deadline: rolling. Application fee: $20. *Expenses:* Tuition $275 per hour. Fees $200 per semester. *Financial aid:* 36 students received aid. Aid available to part-time students. Financial aid application deadline: 3/15; applicants required to submit FAFSA. • Robert McMurrian, Director, 817-531-6500. Fax: 817-531-6585.

Texas Woman's University, College of Arts and Sciences, Department of Business and Economics, Denton, TX 76204. Offers program in business administration (MBA). Part-time and evening/weekend programs available. Faculty: 12 full-time (7 women), 8 part-time (4 women), 16 FTE. Students: 6 full-time (all women), 34 part-time (29 women); includes 10 minority (5 African Americans, 2 Asian Americans, 3 Hispanics), 9 international. Average age 34. 35 applicants, 60% accepted. In 1997, 3 degrees awarded. *Degree requirements:* Thesis or alternative required, foreign language not required. *Average time to degree:* master's–1.5 years full-time, 5 years part-time. *Entrance requirements:* GMAT (minimum score 400), minimum GPA of 3.0. Application fee: $25. *Financial aid:* In 1997–98, 2 research assistantships (1 to a first-year student) were awarded; teaching assistantships also available. Financial aid application deadline: 4/1. *Faculty research:* Organizational behavior, accounting theory, financial analysis, health economics, marketing, taxation. • Dr. Reg Rezac, Chair, 940-898-2111.

Thomas College, Programs in Business, Waterville, ME 04901-5097. Offerings in business (MBA), computer technology education (MS). Part-time and evening/weekend programs available. Faculty: 13 full-time, 17 part-time. Students: 20 full-time (6 women), 132 part-time

Directory: Business Administration and Management—General

Thomas College (continued)
(52 women); includes 1 international. Average age 35. 60 applicants, 90% accepted. *Average time to degree:* master's–3 years full-time, 4.5 years part-time. *Entrance requirements:* GMAT or minimum GPA of 3.3 in first 3 graduate level courses. Application deadline: rolling. Application fee: $40. *Tuition:* $450 per course. *Financial aid:* Career-related internships or fieldwork available. Aid available to part-time students. • Robert M. Whitcomb, Dean, Graduate and Continuing Education, Graduate School, 207-877-0102. Application contact: Dr. Nelson Madore, Graduate Adviser, 207-873-0771 Ext. 323. Fax: 207-877-0114.

Thomas Edison State College, Graduate Studies, Trenton, NJ 08608-1176. Awards MSM. Faculty: 14 part-time (4 women). Students: 49 part-time (23 women); includes 12 minority (9 African Americans, 1 Asian American, 2 Hispanics). Average age 42. *Degree requirements:* Thesis required, foreign language not required. *Application deadline:* rolling. *Application fee:* $75. Electronic applications accepted. *Tuition:* $289 per credit hour. *Financial aid:* 5 students received aid. Aid available to part-time students. • Dr. Esther Taitsman, Director, 609-292-5143. Fax: 609-777-2956. E-mail: ammartini@call.tesc.edu.

Thomas More College, Department of Business Administration, Crestview Hills, KY 41017-3495. Awards MBA. Evening/weekend programs available. Faculty: 11 full-time (3 women), 1 (woman) part-time, 11.25 FTE. Students: 96 full-time (36 women). *Degree requirements:* Comprehensive exam, final project. *Entrance requirements:* Minimum GPA of 2.5, 2 years of related work experience. Application deadline: rolling. *Faculty research:* Computer information systems, comparison level and consumer satisfaction, history of U.S. business development, share price reaction, quality and competition. Total annual research expenditures: $18,000. • Don Ostasiewski, Chair. Application contact: Dale Myers, Vice President of Graduate and Continuing Education, 606-341-4554. Fax: 606-578-3589. E-mail: myersd@thomasmore.edu.

Tiffin University, Program in Business Administration, Tiffin, OH 44883-2161. Awards MBA. Part-time and evening/weekend programs available. Faculty: 13 full-time (3 women), 2 part-time (1 woman). Students: 74 full-time (26 women), 30 part-time (10 women); includes 15 minority (8 African Americans, 6 Asian Americans, 1 Hispanic), 5 international. Average age 36. 42 applicants, 90% accepted. In 1997, 23 degrees awarded (100% found work related to degree). *Degree requirements:* Computer language required, foreign language and thesis not required. *Average time to degree:* master's–2 years full-time, 4 years part-time. *Entrance requirements:* Minimum undergraduate GPA of 3.0 in last 2 years, 3 years of work experience. Application deadline: 8/10 (priority date; rolling processing; 1/5 for spring admission). Application fee: $30. Electronic applications accepted. *Tuition:* $12,000 per year full-time, $3000 per year part-time. *Financial aid:* 13 students received aid. Aid available to part-time students. Financial aid application deadline: 7/31; applicants required to submit FAFSA. *Faculty research:* Small business, executive development operations, research and statistical analysis, market research, MIS. • Dr. Ellen S. Jordan, Dean of the Graduate School, 419-448-3401. E-mail: ejordan@tiffin.edu. Application contact: Allen Lowery, Director of Recruitment, 800-968-6446 Ext. 3403. Fax: 419-443-5002. E-mail: alowery@tiffin.edu.

Trinity College, School of Professional Studies, Programs in Administration, Washington, DC 20017-1094. Offerings in administration in non-profit management (MA); educational administration (MSA), including instructional leadership, principalship; human resources (MSA), including entrepreneurial development, human resource development, human resource management. Part-time programs available. Faculty: 4 full-time (1 woman), 4 part-time (all women). *Degree requirements:* Thesis or alternative. *Entrance requirements:* Minimum GPA of 2.8. Application deadline: rolling. Application fee: $35. *Tuition:* $460 per credit hour. *Financial aid:* Career-related internships or fieldwork available. Financial aid applicants required to submit FAFSA. • Dr. Sheri Levin, Division Chair, Human Services, 202-884-9553. Application contact: Karen Goodwin, Director of Graduate Admissions, 202-884-9400. Fax: 202-884-9229.

Troy State University, Graduate School, University College, Sorrell College of Business and Commerce, Troy, AL 36082. Offers programs in business administration (MBA), management (MS), personnel management (MS). Part-time and evening/weekend programs available. Students: 268 full-time (110 women), 370 part-time (170 women); includes 169 minority (142 African Americans, 6 Asian Americans, 19 Hispanics, 2 Native Americans), 8 international. Average age 30. In 1997, 469 degrees awarded. *Degree requirements:* Comprehensive exam required, foreign language and thesis not required. *Entrance requirements:* GMAT, minimum GPA of 2.5. Application deadline: rolling. Application fee: $20. Electronic applications accepted. *Expenses:* Tuition $2040 per year full-time, $68 per hour part-time for state residents; $4200 per year full-time, $140 per hour part-time for nonresidents. Fees $240 per year full-time, $27 per quarter (minimum) part-time. *Financial aid:* Career-related internships or fieldwork available. Aid available to part-time students. Financial aid applicants required to submit FAFSA. • Dr. Thomas Ratcliffe, Dean, 334-670-3299. Fax: 334-670-3592. Application contact: Dr. Rodney Cox, Dean, University College, 334-670-3457. Fax: 334-670-3770. E-mail: rcox@trojan.troyst.edu.

Troy State University Dothan, School of Business, Dothan, AL 36304-0368. Awards MBA, MS. Part-time and evening/weekend programs available. Students: 32 (8 women). In 1997, 38 degrees awarded. *Entrance requirements:* Minimum GPA of 2.5. Application deadline: rolling. Application fee: $20. *Expenses:* Tuition $68 per credit hour for state residents; $140 per credit hour for nonresidents. Fees $2 per credit hour. • Dr. Adair Gilbert, Interim Dean, 334-983-6556. Application contact: Reta Cordell, Director of Admissions and Records, 334-983-6556. Fax: 334-983-6322. E-mail: rcordell@tsud.edu.

Troy State University Montgomery, Division of Business, Program in Business Administration, PO Drawer 4419, Montgomery, AL 36103-4419. Awards MBA. Part-time and evening/weekend programs available. In 1997, 40 degrees awarded. *Degree requirements:* Thesis or alternative. *Entrance requirements:* GMAT or GRE, TOEFL, BS in business. Application deadline: rolling. Application fee: $20. *Expenses:* Tuition $52 per quarter hour for state residents; $104 per quarter hour for nonresidents. Fees $30 per year. • Dr. Freda Hartman, Dean, Division of Business, 334-241-9597. Fax: 334-241-9734. E-mail: fhartman@tsum.edu.

Tulane University, A. B. Freeman School of Business, New Orleans, LA 70118-5669. Awards EMBA, M Acct, MBA, PhD, JD/MBA, MBA/MA, MBA/MPH. MBA/MA jointly administered with the Roger Thayer Stone Center for Latin American Studies. Part-time and evening/weekend programs available. Faculty: 38 full-time (6 women), 23 part-time (3 women), 47.00 FTE. Students: 288 full-time (77 women), 197 part-time (67 women); includes 60 minority (42 African Americans, 5 Asian Americans, 13 Hispanics), 72 international. 778 applicants, 34% accepted. In 1997, 209 master's awarded. Terminal master's awarded for partial completion of doctoral program. *Entrance requirements:* For master's, GMAT (average 637), TOEFL (average 622), interviews. Application deadline: 5/1 (rolling processing; 12/1 for spring admission). Application fee: $40 ($50 for international students). *Expenses:* Tuition $21,719 per year full-time, $724 per credit hour part-time. Fees $1576 per year full-time, $119 per semester (minimum) part-time. *Financial aid:* Fellowships, research assistantships, teaching assistantships, full and partial tuition waivers, Federal Work-Study, and career-related internships or fieldwork available. Aid available to part-time students. Financial aid application deadline: 4/15; applicants required to submit FAFSA. • James McFarland, Dean, 504-865-5407. Application contact: John Silbernagel, Assistant Dean for Admissions and Financial Aid, 504-865-5410. Fax: 504-865-6770. E-mail: admissions@freeman.tulane.edu.

See in-depth description on page 303.

Tusculum College, Graduate School, Program in Organizational Management, Greeneville, TN 37743-9997. Awards MAOM. Students: 118 full-time, 3 part-time. *Degree requirements:* Thesis or alternative required, foreign language not required. *Average time to degree:* master's–1.3 years full-time. *Entrance requirements:* GMAT, GRE Subject Test, MAT (minimum score 30), minimum GPA of 2.75, 3 years of work experience. Application fee: $0. *Tuition:* $190 per credit hour (minimum). • Application contact: Don Stout, Executive Director of Professional Studies, 423-636-7330 Ext. 612. Fax: 423-638-5181.

Union College, Graduate and Continuing Studies, Graduate Management Institute, Program in Business Administration, Schenectady, NY 12308-2311. Awards MBA. Evening/weekend programs available. Students: 19 full-time (6 women), 30 part-time (7 women); includes 1 minority (Asian American), 1 international. 15 applicants, 93% accepted. In 1997, 19 degrees awarded. *Degree requirements:* Computer language, comprehensive exam required, foreign language and thesis not required. *Entrance requirements:* GMAT. Application deadline: 5/15 (rolling processing). Application fee: $35. *Tuition:* $1434 per course. *Financial aid:* Fellowships, research assistantships, full and partial tuition waivers available. Financial aid application deadline: 5/15. • Dr. R. Alan Bowman, Director, 518-388-6297. Application contact: Carolyn Micklas, Recruiting and Admissions Coordinator, 518-388-6239.

See in-depth description on page 305.

Union University, School of Business Administration, Jackson, TN 38305-3697. Awards MBA. Also available at Germantown campus. Evening/weekend programs available. Faculty: 9 full-time (2 women). Students: 94 full-time (44 women), 18 part-time (6 women); includes 5 African Americans, 1 Hispanic, 1 international. Average age 32. 190 applicants, 59% accepted. In 1997, 13 degrees awarded. *Degree requirements:* Oral comprehensive exam required, foreign language and thesis not required. *Average time to degree:* master's–2 years full-time. *Entrance requirements:* GMAT, minimum GPA of 2.5. Application deadline: 8/1 (priority date; rolling processing; 2/5 for spring admission). Application fee: $25 ($50 for international students). Electronic applications accepted. *Tuition:* $275 per hour. *Financial aid:* Career-related internships or fieldwork available. Financial aid applicants required to submit FAFSA. *Faculty research:* Total quality management, self efficacy, cost of quality, electronic meeting systems. Total annual research expenditures: $8000. • Dr. Donald Lester, Dean, 901-661-5367. E-mail: dlester@buster.uu.edu. Application contact: Debbie Newell, MBA Director, 901-661-5363. Fax: 901-661-5366. E-mail: dnewell@buster.uu.edu.

United States International University, College of Business Administration, San Diego, CA 92131-1799. Offers programs in business administration (MBA); international business (MIBA, DBA), including finance (DBA), marketing (DBA); strategic business (DBA). Part-time and evening/weekend programs available. Faculty: 13 full-time (4 women), 14 part-time (6 women), 20 FTE. Students: 73 full-time (26 women), 147 part-time (59 women); includes 61 minority (19 African Americans, 15 Asian Americans, 25 Hispanics, 2 Native Americans), 122 international. Average age 27. 252 applicants, 45% accepted. In 1997, 40 master's awarded (10% entered university research/teaching, 70% found other work related to degree, 20% continued full-time study); 8 doctorates awarded (75% entered university research/teaching, 25% found other work related to degree). Terminal master's awarded for partial completion of doctoral program. *Degree requirements:* For master's, computer language required, foreign language and thesis not required; for doctorate, computer language, dissertation required, foreign language not required. *Average time to degree:* master's–1.5 years full-time, 2.5 years part-time; doctorate–3 years full-time, 5 years part-time. *Entrance requirements:* For master's, GMAT (minimum score 350; average 490), minimum GPA of 3.0; for doctorate, GMAT (minimum score 490; average 560), minimum GPA of 3.3. Application deadline: rolling. Application fee: $40. Electronic applications accepted. *Expenses:* Tuition $360 per unit. Fees $120 per year. *Financial aid:* In 1997–98, 73 students received aid, including 9 research assistantships averaging $750 per month, 16 teaching assistantships averaging $750 per month; partial tuition waivers, Federal Work-Study, institutionally sponsored loans, and career-related internships or fieldwork also available. Aid available to part-time students. Financial aid application deadline: 4/2; applicants required to submit FAFSA. *Faculty research:* Cross-cultural management. • Dr. Mink H. Stavenga, Dean, 619-635-4695. Fax: 619-635-4528. E-mail: mstaveng@usiu.edu. Application contact: Susan Topham, Assistant Director of Admissions, 619-635-4885. Fax: 619-635-4739. E-mail: admissions@usiu.edu.

United States International University–Africa, College of Business Administration, PO Box 14634, Nairobi, Kenya. Offers programs in finance (MBA, MIBA), integrated studies (MBA, MIBA), management and organizational development (MS), marketing (MBA, MIBA). Faculty: 15 full-time (2 women), 50 part-time (5 women). Students: 94 full-time (36 women), 126 part-time (62 women). 653 applicants, 69% accepted. In 1997, 83 degrees awarded. *Entrance requirements:* GRE General Test, GMAT. Application deadline: (2/8 for spring admission). Application fee: $55. *Financial aid:* In 1997–98, 18 research assistantships averaging $129 per month and totaling $21,140, 1 director's grant totaling $140 were awarded; partial tuition waivers, institutionally sponsored loans, and career-related internships or fieldwork also available. Aid available to part-time students. *Faculty research:* Marketing in small business enterprises, total quality management in Kenya. • Application contact: Office of Admissions, 254-2-802532. Fax: 254-2-803764. E-mail: usiu_adm@usiu.edu.

United States International University–Mexico, Programs in Business, Alvaro Obregon #110, Colonia Roma, Mexico City CP06700, Mexico. Offerings in business administration (MBA), international business administration (MIBA), management and organizational development (MS). Part-time programs available. Faculty: 1 full-time (0 women), 11 part-time (3 women). Students: 16 full-time (5 women), 16 part-time (4 women); includes 10 Hispanics, 16 international. Average age 32. 17 applicants, 41% accepted. In 1997, 8 degrees awarded. *Degree requirements:* Computer language, thesis or alternative required, foreign language not required. *Entrance requirements:* GMAT. Application deadline: 8/15 (priority date; rolling processing). Application fee: $35. *Faculty research:* Environmental impact and business in Mexico. • Application contact: Clarisa Desouches, Admissions Officer, 525-264-2187. Fax: 525-264-2188. E-mail: cristina@intmex.com.

Universidad de las Américas–Puebla, Division of Graduate Studies, School of Business Administration, Cholula 72820, Mexico. Awards MBA. Part-time and evening/weekend programs available. Faculty: 8 full-time (2 women), 2 part-time (1 woman). Students: 11 full-time (3 women), 107 part-time (31 women); includes 100 minority (all Hispanics). Average age 26. 40 applicants, 75% accepted. In 1997, 5 degrees awarded. *Degree requirements:* 1 foreign language, thesis. *Average time to degree:* master's–1.5 years full-time, 2.5 years part-time. *Application deadline:* 7/18 (rolling processing; 1/31 for spring admission). *Application fee:* $0. *Expenses:* Tuition $5400 per year full-time, $113 per year part-time. Fees $361 per year. *Financial aid:* 30 students received aid; research assistantships available. Aid available to part-time students. Financial aid application deadline: 5/15. *Faculty research:* System dynamics, information technology, marketing, international business, strategic planning, quality. Total annual research expenditures: $33,000. • Roberto Solano, Dean, 22-29-20-62. Fax: 22-29-24-73. E-mail: rsolano@mail.udlap.mx. Application contact: Mauricio Villegas, Chair of Admissions Office, 22-29-20-17. Fax: 22-29-20-18. E-mail: admision@mail.udlap.mx.

Universidad del Turabo, Programs in Business Administration, Gurabo, PR 00778-3030. Offerings in accounting (MBA), human resources (MBA), logistics and materials management (MBA), management (MBA), marketing (MBA). Part-time and evening/weekend programs available. *Entrance requirements:* GRE, PAEG, interview. Application deadline: 8/5. Application fee: $25.

Universidad Metropolitana, School of Business Administration, Río Piedras, PR 00928-1150. Offers programs in accounting (MBA), management (MBA), marketing (MBA). Part-time and evening/weekend programs available. Faculty: 4 full-time (2 women), 24 part-time (10 women). Students: 120 full-time (70 women), 160 part-time (90 women); includes 280 minority (all Hispanics). Average age 28. 400 applicants, 63% accepted. In 1997, 80 degrees awarded (20% entered university research/teaching, 70% found other work related to degree, 10% continued full-time study). *Average time to degree:* master's–1.5 years full-time, 3 years part-time. *Entrance requirements:* GMAT (score in 70th percentile or higher), PAEG (score in 60th percentile or higher). Application deadline: 8/31 (priority date; rolling processing; 1/15 for spring admission). Application fee: $0. *Financial aid:* In 1997–98, 2 research assistantships (both to first-year students) were awarded; Federal Work-Study also available. Aid available to part-time students. Financial aid application deadline: 5/1. *Faculty research:* Latin American trade, international investments, central city business development, Hispanic consumer research, Caribbean and Asian trade cooperation. • Pedro Hernández, Dean, 787-766-1717 Ext. 6255.

Université de Moncton, Faculty of Administration, Moncton, NB E1A 3E9, Canada. Awards MBA, LL B/MBA. Part-time programs available. Postbaccalaureate distance learning degree programs offered (no on-campus study). Faculty: 10 full-time (1 woman), 2 part-time (0 women). Students: 43 full-time (27 women), 17 part-time (10 women); includes 13 international. Average age 32. 92 applicants, 47% accepted. In 1997, 25 degrees awarded (100% found work related to degree). *Degree requirements:* 1 foreign language, computer language required, thesis not required. *Application deadline:* 6/1. *Application fee:* $30. *Financial aid:* In 1997–98, 13 students received aid, including 7 fellowships, 2 teaching assistantships; institutionally sponsored loans and career-related internships or fieldwork also available. Aid available to part-time students. Financial aid application deadline: 5/30. *Faculty research:* Entrepreneurship, international management, industrial development, accounting, computer technology, marketing of services. Total annual research expenditures: $25,000. • George Wybouw, Dean, 506-858-4205. Fax: 506-858-4093. Application contact: Nicole Savoie, Conseillière à l'àdmission, 506-858-4115. Fax: 506-858-4544. E-mail: savoien@umoncton.ca.

Université de Sherbrooke, Faculty of Administration, Program in Business Administration, Sherbrooke, PQ J1K 2R1, Canada. Awards EMBA, MBA, Diploma. *Application fee:* $15.

Université du Québec à Chicoutimi, Program in Small and Medium-Sized Organization Management, Chicoutimi, PQ G7H 2B1, Canada. Awards M Sc. Offered jointly with the Université du Québec en Abitibi-Témiscamingue. Part-time programs available. *Degree requirements:* Thesis. *Entrance requirements:* Appropriate bachelor's degree, proficiency in French. Application deadline: 5/1. Application fee: $30.

Université du Québec à Montréal, PhD Program in Business Administration, Montréal, PQ H3C 3P8, Canada. Awards PhD. Offered jointly with the École des Hautes Études Commerciales, McGill University, and Concordia University. Part-time programs available. *Degree requirements:* Dissertation required, foreign language not required. *Entrance requirements:* Appropriate master's degree or equivalent and proficiency in French. Application deadline: 5/1 (priority date). Application fee: $50.

Université du Québec à Montréal, Program in Business Administration (Professional), Montréal, PQ H3C 3P8, Canada. Offers business administration (MBA), management consultant (Diploma). Part-time programs available. *Entrance requirements:* Appropriate bachelor's degree or equivalent and proficiency in French. Application deadline: 5/1 (priority date). Application fee: $50.

Université du Québec à Montréal, Program in Business Administration (Research), Montréal, PQ H3C 3P8, Canada. Awards MBA. Part-time programs available. *Entrance requirements:* Appropriate bachelor's degree or equivalent and proficiency in French. Application deadline: 5/1 (priority date). Application fee: $50.

Université du Québec à Trois-Rivières, Program in Business Administration, Trois-Rivières, PQ G9A 5H7, Canada. Awards DBA. Offered jointly with University of Sherbrooke; program new for fall 1998. *Degree requirements:* Dissertation. *Application deadline:* 2/1 (rolling processing). *Application fee:* $30. • Jean Lorrain, Director, 819-376-5080 Ext. 3104. Fax: 819-376-5012. E-mail: jean_lorrain@uqtr.uquebec.ca. Application contact: Suzanne Camirand, Admissions Officer, 819-376-5045 Ext. 2591. Fax: 819-376-5210. E-mail: suzanne_camirand@uqtr.uquebec.ca.

Université du Québec à Trois-Rivières, Program in Management of Small and Medium-Sized Enterprises and Their Environment, Trois-Rivières, PQ G9A 5H7, Canada. Awards M Sc. Part-time programs available. Students: 23 full-time (9 women), 5 part-time (3 women). 97 applicants, 77% accepted. *Degree requirements:* Research report required, thesis not required. *Entrance requirements:* Appropriate bachelor's degree, proficiency in French. Application deadline: 2/1. Application fee: $30. *Financial aid:* Fellowships, research assistantships, teaching assistantships available. • Yvon Bigras, Director, 819-376-5080 Ext. 3127. Fax: 819-376-5012. E-mail: yvon_bigras@uqtr.uquebec.ca. Application contact: Suzanne Camirand, Admissions Officer, 819-376-5045 Ext. 2591. Fax: 819-376-5210. E-mail: suzanne_camirand@uqtr.uquebec.ca.

Université du Québec en Abitibi-Témiscamingue, Program in Organization Management, Rouyn-Noranda, PQ J9X 5E4, Canada. Awards M Sc. Offered jointly with the Université du Québec à Chicoutimi. Part-time programs available. *Degree requirements:* Thesis. *Entrance requirements:* Appropriate bachelor's degree, proficiency in French. Application deadline: 4/1. Application fee: $30.

Université Laval, Faculty of Administrative Sciences, Sainte-Foy, PQ G1K 7P4, Canada. Awards MBA, M Sc, PhD, Diploma. MBA offered jointly with York University. Students: 375 full-time (145 women), 314 part-time (129 women); includes 148 international. Average age 30. 781 applicants, 60% accepted. In 1997, 153 master's, 4 doctorates, 34 Diplomas awarded. *Application deadline:* 3/1. *Application fee:* $30. *Expenses:* Tuition $1334 per year (minimum) full-time, $56 per credit (minimum) part-time for Canadian residents; $5966 per year (minimum) full-time, $249 per credit (minimum) part-time for nonresidents. Fees $150 per year full-time, $6.25 per credit part-time. • Bernard Garnier, Dean, 418-656-2131 Ext. 2216. Fax: 418-656-2624. E-mail: bernard.garnier@fas.ulaval.ca.

Université Laval, Interdisciplinary Programs, Program in Organizations Management, Sainte-Foy, PQ G1K 7P4, Canada. Awards Diploma. 71 applicants, 56% accepted. In 1997, 2 degrees awarded. *Application deadline:* 3/1. *Application fee:* $30. *Expenses:* Tuition $1334 per year (minimum) full-time, $56 per credit (minimum) part-time for Canadian residents; $5966 per year (minimum) full-time, $249 per credit (minimum) part-time for nonresidents. Fees $150 per year full-time, $6.25 per credit part-time. • Pierre Dionne, Director, 418656-2131 Ext. 5666. Fax: 418-656-3176. E-mail: pierre.dionne@mng.ulaval.ca.

University College of Cape Breton, School of Business, Sydney, NS B1P 6L2, Canada. Offers program in community economic development (MBA). Faculty: 10. Students: 12 full-time (5 women), 8 part-time (4 women). *Application fee:* $80. *Expenses:* Tuition $800 per course. Fees $1700 per year (minimum) for nonresidents. • Dr. Gertrude MacIntyre, Director, Community Economic Development Institute, 902-563-1467. Fax: 902-562-0119.

The University of Akron, College of Business Administration, Department of Management, Akron, OH 44325-0001. Awards MBA, MSM, JD/MBA. Programs in management (MBA), management-human resources (MSM), management-information systems (MSM). Part-time and evening/weekend programs available. Students: 39 full-time (16 women), 143 part-time (40 women); includes 4 minority (2 African Americans, 2 Asian Americans), 24 international. Average age 31. In 1997, 47 degrees awarded. *Entrance requirements:* GMAT (minimum score 450), minimum GPA of 2.75. Application deadline: 8/15 (rolling processing). Application fee: $25 ($50 for international students). *Expenses:* Tuition $178 per credit hour for state residents; $333 per credit hour for nonresidents. Fees $145 per year full-time, $32 per semester (minimum) part-time. *Financial aid:* In 1997–98, 19 students received aid, including 7 research assistantships, 2 teaching assistantships; partial tuition waivers, Federal Work-Study, and career-related internships or fieldwork also available. Financial aid application deadline: 4/30. *Faculty research:* Quality control, health service management, inventory management, information systems. • Dr. Kenneth Dunning, Acting Chair, 330-972-7037. E-mail: kdunning@uakron.edu. Application contact: Dr. J. Daniel Williams, Director of Graduate Business Programs, 330-972-7043. E-mail: jwilliams@uakron.edu.

The University of Alabama, The Manderson Graduate School of Business, Executive MBA Program, Tuscaloosa, AL 35487. Awards Exec MBA. Faculty: 73 full-time (8 women). Students: 54 full-time (13 women); includes 4 minority (3 African Americans, 1 Hispanic), 11 international. *Entrance requirements:* GMAT (minimum score 550), TOEFL. Application deadline: rolling. Application fee: $25. *Tuition:* $2684 per year full-time, $594 per semester (minimum) part-time for state residents; $7216 per year full-time, $1248 per semester (minimum) part-time for nonresidents. • Robert J. Allen, Director, 205-348-0954. Fax: 205-348-2951. E-mail: rallen@alston.cba.ua.edu.

The University of Alabama, The Manderson Graduate School of Business, Program in Business Administration, Tuscaloosa, AL 35487. Awards MBA, JD/MBA. Faculty: 73 full-time (8 women). Students: 105 full-time (29 women); includes 14 minority (12 African Americans, 2 Hispanics), 4 international. Average age 25. 180 applicants, 48% accepted. In 1997, 49 degrees awarded. *Average time to degree:* master's–2 years full-time. *Entrance requirements:* GMAT (minimum score 500; average 600), TOEFL (minimum score 550), minimum GPA of 3.0, average 3.3. Application deadline: 2/12 (priority date; rolling processing; 5/15 for spring admission). Application fee: $25. *Tuition:* $2684 per year full-time, $594 per semester (minimum) part-time for state residents; $7216 per year full-time, $1248 per semester (minimum) part-time for nonresidents. *Financial aid:* In 1997–98, 25 students received aid, including 18 research assistantships (14 to first-year students) averaging $431 per month and totaling $72,000; Federal Work-Study, institutionally sponsored loans, and career-related internships or fieldwork also available. Financial aid application deadline: 2/12. *Faculty research:* Economic development, organizational effectiveness, leveraging technology in organizations, small business management issues. • Patti Rice Eggers, Interim Director, 205-348-6517. Application contact: Carey Albritton, Interim Coordinator of Graduate Recruiting, 205-348-6517. Fax: 205-348-4504. E-mail: mba@alston.cba.ua.edu.

The University of Alabama, The Manderson Graduate School of Business, Department of Management Science, Management Science Program, Tuscaloosa, AL 35487. Offers management science (MA, MBA, PhD), manufacturing management (MA, MBA, PhD), production management (MA, MBA, PhD). Faculty: 9 full-time (1 woman). Students: 6 full-time (0 women), 4 part-time (1 woman); includes 6 international. Average age 27. 10 applicants, 50% accepted. In 1997, 1 master's, 5 doctorates awarded. Terminal master's awarded for partial completion of doctoral program. *Degree requirements:* For master's, comprehensive exam required, thesis optional, foreign language not required; for doctorate, 1 foreign language (computer language can substitute), dissertation, comprehensive exam. *Average time to degree:* master's–2 years full-time; doctorate–5 years full-time. *Entrance requirements:* For master's, GMAT (average 625), TOEFL (minimum score 550); for doctorate, TOEFL. Application deadline: 7/6 (rolling processing). Application fee: $25. *Tuition:* $2684 per year full-time, $594 per semester (minimum) part-time for state residents; $7216 per year full-time, $1248 per semester (minimum) part-time for nonresidents. *Financial aid:* In 1997–98, 2 teaching assistantships averaging $845 per month and totaling $15,210 were awarded; fellowships, research assistantships, and career-related internships or fieldwork also available. *Faculty research:* Supply chain management, production and inventory modeling, scheduling. • Dr. Charles P. Schmidt, Coordinator, 205-348-8914. Fax: 205-348-0560. E-mail: cschmidt@cba.ua.edu.

The University of Alabama at Birmingham, Graduate School, Graduate School of Management, Birmingham, AL 35294. Awards M Acct, MBA, PhD, MBA/MPH, MBA/MSN. Students: 245 full-time (90 women), 206 part-time (88 women); includes 85 minority (45 African Americans, 32 Asian Americans, 7 Hispanics, 1 Native American). 408 applicants, 74% accepted. In 1997, 202 master's awarded. *Entrance requirements:* For master's, GMAT. Application deadline: rolling. Application fee: $30 ($60 for international students). Electronic applications accepted. *Expenses:* Tuition $99 per credit hour for state residents; $198 per credit hour for nonresidents. Fees $516 per year (minimum) full-time, $73 per quarter (minimum) part-time for state residents; $516 per year (minimum) full-time, $73 per unit (minimum) part-time for nonresidents. *Financial aid:* Fellowships and career-related internships or fieldwork available. • Dr. W. Jack Duncan, Interim Dean, 205-934-8800.

The University of Alabama in Huntsville, College of Administrative Science, Huntsville, AL 35899. Offers programs in accountancy (M Acc), management (MSM). M Acc new for fall 1998. Part-time and evening/weekend programs available. Faculty: 24 full-time (3 women), 7 part-time (1 woman), 25.75 FTE. Students: 32 full-time (12 women), 120 part-time (47 women); includes 11 minority (8 African Americans, 2 Asian Americans, 1 Native American), 16 international. Average age 32. 70 applicants, 87% accepted. In 1997, 33 degrees awarded. *Degree requirements:* Written exams required, thesis optional, foreign language not required. *Entrance requirements:* GMAT (minimum score 450), GRE General Test (minimum combined score of 1500 on three sections), minimum GPA of 3.0, minimum AACSB index of 950. Application deadline: 7/24 (priority date; rolling processing; 11/15 for spring admission). Application fee: $20. Electronic applications accepted. *Tuition:* $2886 per year full-time, $540 per semester (minimum) part-time for state residents; $5298 per year full-time, $1098 per semester (minimum) part-time for nonresidents. *Financial aid:* In 1997–98, 10 students received aid, including 1 research assistantship averaging $638 per month and totaling $5,742, 9 teaching assistantships (5 to first-year students) averaging $638 per month and totaling $37,323; fellowships, grants, scholarships, full and partial tuition waivers, Federal Work-Study, institutionally sponsored loans, and career-related internships or fieldwork also available. Aid available to part-time students. Financial aid application deadline: 4/1; applicants required to submit FAFSA. *Faculty research:* Technology transfer, labor economics, financial institutions, systems analysis, management of technology. Total annual research expenditures: $178,720. • Dr. C. David Billings, Dean, 205-890-6735. Fax: 205-890-6328. E-mail: billind@email.uah.edu.

University of Alaska Anchorage, College of Business and Public Policy, Program in Business Administration, Anchorage, AK 99508-8060. Awards MBA. Part-time programs available. Students: 26 full-time (13 women), 54 part-time (16 women); includes 18 minority (6 African Americans, 4 Asian Americans, 2 Hispanics, 6 Native Americans). 37 applicants, 59% accepted. In 1997, 14 degrees awarded. *Entrance requirements:* GMAT, TOEFL (minimum score 550). Application deadline: rolling. Application fee: $45. *Expenses:* Tuition $2988 per year full-time, $1990 per year part-time for state residents; $5814 per year full-time, $3876 per year part-time for nonresidents. Fees $298 per year. *Financial aid:* Research assistantships, Federal Work-Study available. Aid available to part-time students. Financial aid application deadline: 4/1. *Faculty research:* Complex global environments. • Dr. George Geistauts, Chair, 907-786-4154. Fax: 907-786-4119. Application contact: Linda Berg Smith, Associate Vice Chancellor for Enrollment Services, 907-786-1529.

University of Alaska Fairbanks, Graduate School, College of Natural Resource Development and Management, School of Management, Department of Business Administration, Fairbanks, AK 99775-7480. Awards MBA. Part-time programs available. Faculty: 11 full-time (3 women), 4 part-time (1 woman). Students: 10 full-time (7 women), 6 part-time (3 women); includes 7 minority (2 African Americans, 1 Asian American, 1 Hispanic, 3 Native Americans). Average age 30. In 1997, 25 degrees awarded. *Entrance requirements:* GMAT, TOEFL (minimum score 550). Application deadline: 8/1 (rolling processing). Application fee: $35. *Expenses:* Tuition $162 per credit for state residents; $316 per credit for nonresidents. Fees $520 per year full-time, $45 per semester (minimum) part-time. *Financial aid:* Research assistantships, teaching assistantships, and career-related internships or fieldwork available. • Dr. Jacob Joseph, Director, 907-474-6534. Application contact: Dr. Harikumar Sankaram, Director, 907-474-6534.

University of Alaska Southeast, Program in Business Administration, Juneau, AK 99801-8625. Awards MBA. *Degree requirements:* Comprehensive exam or project required, foreign language and thesis not required. *Entrance requirements:* Minimum GPA of 3.0. Application deadline: 8/15 (priority date; rolling processing; 2/15 for spring admission). Application fee: $35. Electronic applications accepted. *Tuition:* $162 per credit for state residents; $316 per credit for nonresidents. *Financial aid:* Federal Work-Study, institutionally sponsored loans, and career-related internships or fieldwork available. Aid available to part-time students. • Application contact: Greg Wagner, Recruiter, 907-465-6239. Fax: 907-465-6365. E-mail: jngaw@acad1.alaska.edu.

University of Alberta, Faculty of Graduate Studies and Research, Doctoral Program in Business, Edmonton, AB T6G 2E1, Canada. Awards PhD, MBA/PhD. Offerings include accounting (PhD), finance (PhD), industrial relations (PhD), management science (PhD), marketing

Directory: Business Administration and Management—General

University of Alberta (continued)

(PhD), organizational analysis (PhD). Faculty: 34 full-time (5 women). Students: 28 full-time (17 women), 10 part-time (5 women); includes 11 international. Average age 34. 115 applicants, 7% accepted. In 1997, 7 doctorates awarded (86% entered university research/teaching, 14% found other work related to degree). Terminal master's awarded for partial completion of doctoral program. *Degree requirements:* For doctorate, dissertation required, foreign language not required. *Average time to degree:* doctorate–6 years full-time, 8.5 years part-time. *Entrance requirements:* For doctorate, GMAT (average 675), TOEFL (minimum score 600; average 627). Application deadline: 3/1 (priority date). Application fee: $60. *Expenses:* Tuition $390 per course for Canadian residents; $781 per course for nonresidents. Fees $500 per year full-time, $184 per year part-time. *Financial aid:* In 1997–98, 27 fellowships (6 to first-year students) averaging $888 per month and totaling $191,830, 12 research assistantships (5 to first-year students) averaging $1,240 per month and totaling $113,950, 2 teaching assistantships averaging $793 per month and totaling $12,368, 28 scholarships, tuition scholarships (8 to first-year students) averaging $1,250 per month and totaling $105,000 were awarded. *Faculty research:* Accounting and management information systems, capital markets and corporate finance, organizational change and human resource management, marketing and business economics, industrial and legal relations. Total annual research expenditures: $474,474. • Dr. Michael Gibbins, Director, 403-492-2361. Application contact: Jeanette Gosine, Department Office, 403-492-2361. Fax: 403-492-3325. E-mail: jgosine@gpu.srv.ualberta.ca.

University of Alberta, Faculty of Graduate Studies and Research, Executive MBA Program, Edmonton, AB T6G 2E1, Canada. Offers business administration (Exec MBA). Offered jointly with the University of Calgary. Students: 16 full-time (2 women). *Entrance requirements:* GMAT (minimum score 500; average 600), TOEFL (minimum score 600). Application fee: $60. *Expenses:* Tuition $18,573 per year. Fees $177 per year. • Kay Devine, Associate Dean, 403-492-5414. E-mail: kay.devine@ualberta.ca. Application contact: Darren Bondar, Assistant Director, MBA Programs, 403-492-3946. Fax: 403-492-7825. E-mail: darren.bondar@ualberta.ca.

University of Alberta, Faculty of Graduate Studies and Research, Program in Business Administration, Edmonton, AB T6G 2E1, Canada. Awards MBA, MBA/M Eng, MBA/LL B, MBA/M Ag, MBA/MF, MBA/PhD. Offerings include educational administration (MBA), health administration (MBA), international business (MBA), leisure and sport management (MBA), public management (MBA). Part-time and evening/weekend programs available. Students: 122 full-time (54 women), 104 part-time (46 women); includes 9 international. Average age 28. 206 applicants, 1% accepted. *Degree requirements:* Thesis or alternative required, foreign language not required. *Entrance requirements:* GMAT, TOEFL. Application deadline: 5/31 (priority date; rolling processing). Application fee: $60. *Expenses:* Tuition $390 per course for Canadian residents; $781 per course for nonresidents. Fees $500 per year full-time, $184 per year part-time. *Financial aid:* In 1997–98, research assistantships averaging $400 per month, teaching assistantships averaging $400 per month, 3 tuition scholarships were awarded; career-related internships or fieldwork also available. • Dr. Kay Devine, Associate Dean, 403-492-3946. E-mail: kay.devine@ualberta.ca. Application contact: Darren Bondar, Assistant Director, 403-492-3946. Fax: 403-492-7825. E-mail: darren.bondar@ualberta.ca.

The University of Arizona, College of Business and Public Administration, Karl Eller Graduate School of Management, Tucson, AZ 85721. Awards MA, M Ac, MBA, MS, PhD, JD/MA, JD/MBA, JD/PhD. Programs in accounting (M Ac); business administration (MBA); economics (MA, PhD); finance (MS); management (PhD), including accounting, finance, management, management information systems, marketing; management and policy (MS); management information systems (MS); marketing (MS). Evening/weekend programs available. *Degree requirements:* For doctorate, dissertation required, foreign language not required. *Entrance requirements:* For master's, GRE General Test, TOEFL (minimum score 550), minimum GPA of 3.0; for doctorate, GRE General Test, GRE Subject Test, TOEFL (minimum score 550), minimum GPA of 3.0. Application fee: $35. *Tuition:* $2162 per year full-time, $337 per semester (minimum) part-time for state residents; $6860 per year full-time, $1138 per semester (minimum) part-time for nonresidents.

University of Arkansas, College of Business Administration, Program in Business Administration, Fayetteville, AR 72701-1201. Awards MBA, PhD. Faculty: 43 full-time (0 women). Students: 126 full-time (48 women), 28 part-time (8 women); includes 14 minority (6 African Americans, 4 Asian Americans, 2 Hispanics, 2 Native Americans), 28 international. 166 applicants, 40% accepted. In 1997, 76 master's, 11 doctorates awarded. *Degree requirements:* For doctorate, dissertation. *Entrance requirements:* GMAT. Application fee: $25 ($35 for international students). *Tuition:* $3144 per year full-time, $173 per credit hour part-time for state residents; $7140 per year full-time, $395 per credit hour part-time for nonresidents. *Financial aid:* Research assistantships, teaching assistantships, Federal Work-Study, and career-related internships or fieldwork available. Aid available to part-time students. Financial aid application deadline: 4/1; applicants required to submit FAFSA. • Dr. William Curington, Associate Dean, 501-575-2851. Application contact: Carol Reeves, MBA Director, 501-575-2851.

See in-depth description on page 307.

University of Arkansas at Little Rock, College of Business Administration, Little Rock, AR 72204-1099. Awards MBA, JD/MBA. Part-time and evening/weekend programs available. Students: 51 full-time (15 women), 164 part-time (71 women); includes 15 minority (9 African Americans, 3 Asian Americans, 2 Hispanics, 1 Native American), 29 international. Average age 30. 229 applicants, 60% accepted. In 1997, 57 degrees awarded. *Entrance requirements:* GMAT (minimum score 450), minimum undergraduate GPA of 2.7. Application deadline: 8/1 (priority date; rolling processing; 12/1 for spring admission). Application fee: $25 ($30 for international students). *Expenses:* Tuition $2466 per year full-time, $137 per credit hour part-time for state residents; $5256 per year full-time, $292 per credit hour part-time for nonresidents. Fees $216 per year full-time, $36 per semester (minimum) part-time. *Financial aid:* Research assistantships, graduate assistantships, Federal Work-Study, institutionally sponsored loans available. Aid available to part-time students. • Dr. William C. Goolsby, Dean, 501-569-3356. Application contact: Dr. Kenneth Galchus, Coordinator, 501-569-3356.

University of Baltimore, School of Business, Program in Business Administration, Baltimore, MD 21201-5779. Awards MBA, JD/MBA, MBA/MSN. MBA/MSN offered jointly with the University of Maryland, Baltimore. Part-time and evening/weekend programs available. Faculty: 65 full-time (15 women), 17 part-time (2 women). Students: 136 full-time (56 women), 382 part-time (128 women); includes 89 minority (62 African Americans, 22 Asian Americans, 4 Hispanics, 1 Native American), 63 international. Average age 31. 312 applicants, 75% accepted. In 1997, 166 degrees awarded. *Degree requirements:* Computer language required, foreign language and thesis not required. *Average time to degree:* master's–2 years full-time. *Entrance requirements:* GMAT. Application deadline: 7/15 (priority date; rolling processing; 11/15 for spring admission). Application fee: $30. *Expenses:* Tuition $5736 per year full-time, $239 per credit part-time for state residents; $8544 per year full-time, $356 per credit part-time for nonresidents. Fees $550 per year full-time, $208 per semester (minimum) part-time. *Financial aid:* In 1997–98, 16 research assistantships (7 to first-year students) were awarded; fellowships, Federal Work-Study, and career-related internships or fieldwork also available. Aid available to part-time students. Financial aid application deadline: 4/1; applicants required to submit FAFSA. *Total annual research expenditures:* $1.509 million. • Judy Sabalauskas, Graduate Adviser, 410-837-4944. Application contact: Tracey Jamison, Assistant Director of Admissions, 410-837-4809. Fax: 410-837-4793. E-mail: admissions@ubmail.ubalt.edu.

University of Bridgeport, College of Graduate and Undergraduate Studies, School of Business, Program in Business Administration, 380 University Avenue, Bridgeport, CT 06601. Awards MBA. Faculty: 13 full-time (0 women), 15 part-time (1 woman), 18 FTE. Students: 65 full-time (22 women), 120 part-time (58 women); includes 34 minority (11 African Americans, 21 Asian Americans, 2 Hispanics), 106 international. Average age 31. 297 applicants, 81% accepted. In 1997, 67 degrees awarded. *Degree requirements:* Thesis optional. *Entrance requirements:* GMAT, TOEFL. Application fee: $35 ($50 for international students). *Expenses:* Tuition $350 per credit. Fees $590 per year full-time, $75 per year part-time. *Financial aid:* 92 students received aid; research assistantships and career-related internships or fieldwork available. Financial aid application deadline: 6/1; applicants required to submit FAFSA. • Dr. Llewellyn Mullings, Director, 203-576-4363.

See in-depth description on page 309.

University of British Columbia, Faculty of Commerce and Business Administration, Doctoral Program in Commerce and Business Administration, Vancouver, BC V6T 1Z2, Canada. Offers accounting (PhD), finance (PhD), management information systems (PhD), management science (PhD), marketing (PhD), organizational behavior (PhD), policy analysis and strategy (PhD), urban land economics (PhD). *Degree requirements:* Dissertation required, foreign language not required. *Entrance requirements:* GMAT or GRE, TOEFL. Application deadline: 12/31 (priority date; rolling processing). Application fee: $60.

University of British Columbia, Faculty of Commerce and Business Administration, MBA Program, Vancouver, BC V6T 1Z2, Canada. Awards MBA. *Average time to degree:* master's–1.5 years full-time. *Entrance requirements:* GMAT (average 620), TOEFL (minimum score 600), minimum B+ average in undergraduate course work. Application fee: $100. *Faculty research:* Financial economics and reporting, human resources, information systems, management science, marketing, policy analysis transportation and logistics, urban land.

University of British Columbia, Faculty of Commerce and Business Administration, Program in Business Administration, Vancouver, BC V6T 1Z2, Canada. Offers finance (M Sc), management information systems (M Sc), management science (M Sc), transport and logistics (M Sc), urban land economics policy (M Sc). *Degree requirements:* Thesis required (for some programs), foreign language not required. *Average time to degree:* master's–2 years full-time. *Entrance requirements:* GMAT (average 620), TOEFL (minimum score 600). Application fee: $100. *Faculty research:* Financial economics and reporting, human resources, information systems, management science, marketing policy analysis, transportation and logistics, urban land.

The University of Calgary, Faculty of Management, Doctoral Program in Management, Calgary, AB T2N 1N4, Canada. Awards PhD. Faculty: 34 full-time. Students: 32 full-time (12 women); includes 1 international. Average age 33. 18 applicants, 33% accepted. In 1997, 5 degrees awarded. *Degree requirements:* Computer language, dissertation, candidacy exam required, foreign language not required. *Average time to degree:* doctorate–5.5 years full-time. *Entrance requirements:* GMAT (minimum score 570), TOEFL (minimum score 580), minimum GPA of 3.3. Application deadline: 3/1 (priority date; rolling processing). Application fee: $60. *Expenses:* Tuition $5448 per year full-time, $908 per course part-time for Canadian residents; $10,896 per year full-time, $1816 per course part-time for nonresidents. Fees $285 per year full-time, $119 per semester (minimum) part-time. *Financial aid:* In 1997–98, 5 research assistantships (1 to a first-year student) averaging $980 per month and totaling $17,640, 22 teaching assistantships (4 to first-year students) averaging $1,303 per month and totaling $120,445, 1 scholarship were awarded. Financial aid application deadline: 2/1. *Faculty research:* Technology management, tourism, international business, financial services management, energy resource management. Total annual research expenditures: $400,000. • Dr. James C. Chrisman, Associate Dean (Research) and Director, MBA Thesis and PhD Programs, 403-220-7247. E-mail: chrisman@acs.ucalgary.ca. Application contact: Lori Gibson, Graduate Program Administrator, 403-220-3803. Fax: 403-282-0095. E-mail: lgibson@acs.ucalgary.ca.

Announcement: The University of Calgary, Faculty of Management, a leader in management education and research, focuses on the development of superior business leaders. The PhD program integrates teaching and research in individualized programs. New initiatives include entrepreneurship, tourism, financial services management, energy resource management, international business, technology management, and family enterprise.

See in-depth description on page 311.

The University of Calgary, Faculty of Management, Program in Business Administration, Calgary, AB T2N 1N4, Canada. Awards EMBA, MBA. Part-time and evening/weekend programs available. Students: 106 full-time, 249 part-time. Average age 31. 295 applicants, 40% accepted. In 1997, 135 degrees awarded. *Average time to degree:* master's–2 years full-time, 4 years part-time. *Entrance requirements:* GMAT (minimum score 500; average 610), minimum GPA of 3.0. Application deadline: 5/1 (rolling processing). Application fee: $65. *Expenses:* Tuition $5448 per year full-time, $908 per course part-time for Canadian residents; $10,896 per year full-time, $1816 per course part-time for nonresidents. Fees $285 per year full-time, $119 per semester (minimum) part-time. *Financial aid:* Research assistantships available. Financial aid application deadline: 2/1. • Dr. Amy Pablo, Director, Enterprise MBA Program, 403-220-7152. Fax: 403-282-0095 Ext. 22.

See in-depth description on page 311.

University of California, Berkeley, Haas School of Business and Boalt Hall School of Law, Concurrent JD/MBA Program, Berkeley, CA 94720-1500. Awards JD/MBA. Faculty: 76 (12 women). Students: 6 full-time (3 women). Average age 27. 43 applicants, 16% accepted. *Average time to degree:* first professional–4 years full-time. *Application deadline:* 2/1. *Application fee:* $40. *Expenses:* Tuition $0 for state residents; $9384 per year for nonresidents. Fees $4409 per year. *Financial aid:* Fellowships, research assistantships, teaching assistantships available. • Dr. David H. Downes, Director, MBA Programs, 510-642-1405. Fax: 510-643-6659. E-mail: downes@haas.berkeley.edu. Application contact: JD Office of Admissions, 510-642-2274. Fax: 510-643-6222. E-mail: admissions@boalt.berkeley.edu.

University of California, Berkeley, Haas School of Business and Group in International and Area Studies, Concurrent MBA/MA Program in International and Area Studies, Berkeley, CA 94720-1500. Awards MBA/MA. Students spend the first year of matriculation in MBA program. Students: 4 full-time (1 woman). *Application deadline:* 4/1. *Application fee:* $40. *Expenses:* Tuition $0 for state residents; $9384 per year for nonresidents. Fees $4409 per year. *Financial aid:* Research assistantships, teaching assistantships available. Financial aid application deadline: 3/1. • Malcolm Feeley, Chair, 510-642-4466. Fax: 510-642-2951. E-mail: mmf@uclink.berkeley.edu. Application contact: MBA Admissions Office, 510-642-1405. Fax: 510-643-6659. E-mail: mbaadms@haas.berkeley.edu.

University of California, Berkeley, Haas School of Business and Group in Asian Studies, Concurrent MBA/MA Program with Asian Studies, Berkeley, CA 94720-1500. Awards MBA/MA. Faculty: 78 (19 women). Students: 1 full-time (0 women); includes 1 minority (Asian American). Average age 30. 8 applicants, 13% accepted. *Application deadline:* 12/15. *Application fee:* $40. *Expenses:* Tuition $0 for state residents; $9384 per year for nonresidents. Fees $4409 per year. *Financial aid:* Fellowships, research assistantships, teaching assistantships, Federal Work-Study, institutionally sponsored loans, and career-related internships or fieldwork available. Financial aid application deadline: 3/2; applicants required to submit FAFSA. • Robert R. Reed, Chair, Group in Asian Studies, 510-642-0333. Fax: 510-643-7062. Application contact: Sue Pruyn, Graduate Assistant, 510-642-0333. Fax: 510-643-5814. E-mail: asranst@uclink4.berkeley.edu.

University of California, Berkeley, Haas School of Business and School of Public Health, Concurrent MBA/MPH Program, Berkeley, CA 94720-1500. Awards MBA/MPH. Faculty: 11 full-time (3 women). Students: 14 full-time (11 women). Average age 25. 40 applicants, 10% accepted. *Application deadline:* 3/31. *Application fee:* $40. *Expenses:* Tuition $0 for state residents; $9384 per year for nonresidents. Fees $4409 per year. *Financial aid:* In 1997–98, 8 fellowships (4 to first-year students) were awarded; research assistantships, teaching assistantships, Federal Work-Study, institutionally sponsored loans, and career-related internships or fieldwork also available. Financial aid application deadline: 1/31. • Dr. Thomas Rundall, Director, Health Services Management Program, 510-642-5023. Fax: 510-643-6981. E-mail: trundall@

uclink2.berkeley.edu. Application contact: Lee Forgue, Program Assistant, 510-642-5023. Fax: 510-643-6659. E-mail: ellis@haas.berkeley.edu.

University of California, Berkeley, Haas School of Business, Doctoral Program in Business, Berkeley, CA 94720-1500. Offers accounting (PhD), business and public policy (PhD), finance (PhD), marketing (PhD), organizational behavior and industrial relations (PhD). Faculty: 64 full-time (11 women). Students: 73 full-time (19 women); includes 21 international. Average age 28. 400 applicants, 8% accepted. In 1997, 10 degrees awarded. *Degree requirements:* Dissertation, oral exam, written preliminary exams required, foreign language not required. *Entrance requirements:* GMAT or GRE, TOEFL, minimum GPA of 3.0. Application deadline: 2/10. Application fee: $40. *Expenses:* Tuition $0 for state residents; $9384 per year for nonresidents. Fees $4409 per year. *Financial aid:* In 1997–98, 25 fellowships (23 to first-year students), 13 research assistantships, 11 teaching assistantships were awarded; full tuition waivers, Federal Work-Study, institutionally sponsored loans, and career-related internships or fieldwork also available. Financial aid application deadline: 1/5; applicants required to submit FAFSA. • Dr. David C. Mowery, Director, 510-643-9992. E-mail: jan@haas.berkeley.edu. Application contact: Jan Price Greenough, Coordinator, 510-642-1409. Fax: 510-643-6659. E-mail: jan@haas.berkeley.edu.

Announcement: The Haas School of Business offers the Doctor of Philosophy degree in 5 fields: accounting, business and public policy, finance, marketing, and organizational behavior/industrial relations. Consistent with Berkeley's purpose of training men and women for careers in the research, study, and teaching of business administration, many graduates accept positions in leading universities in the United States and abroad. The PhD program takes 4 years to complete in 3 stages: course work, directed study, and individual research. The Haas School, in conjunction with the regular aid programs of the University, seeks to provide financial assistance to PhD students.

University of California, Berkeley, Haas School of Business, Evening MBA Program, Berkeley, CA 94720-1500. Awards MBA. Part-time and evening/weekend programs available. Faculty: 67 full-time (9 women), 76 part-time (13 women). Students: 281 part-time (67 women); includes 8 international. Average age 30. 447 applicants, 30% accepted. In 1997, 102 degrees awarded (100% found work related to degree). *Degree requirements:* Academic retreat required, foreign language and thesis not required. *Entrance requirements:* GMAT, TOEFL, minimum GPA of 3.0. Application deadline: 4/1 (priority date; 9/1 for spring admission). Application fee: $40. *Expenses:* Tuition $0 for state residents; $4692 per year for nonresidents. Fees $18,485 per year. *Financial aid:* 40 students received aid. Aid available to part-time students. Financial aid application deadline: 3/2; applicants required to submit FAFSA. • Diane Dimeff, Director, 510-642-1406. E-mail: evmbaadm@haas.berkeley.edu. Application contact: Laura Parks, Graduate Assistant for Admission, 510-642-1406. Fax: 510-643-5902. E-mail: evmbaadm@haas.berkeley.edu.

University of California, Berkeley, Haas School of Business, Master's Program in Business Administration, Berkeley Campus, Berkeley, CA 94720-1500. Awards MBA. Faculty: 67 full-time (9 women), 86 part-time (16 women). Students: 480 full-time (155 women); includes 169 international. Average age 28. 4,000 applicants, 11% accepted. In 1997, 241 degrees awarded (100% found work related to degree). *Degree requirements:* Project or thesis required, foreign language not required. *Average time to degree:* master's–2 years full-time. *Entrance requirements:* GMAT, TOEFL, minimum GPA of 3.0. Application deadline: 3/31 (rolling processing). Application fee: $40. *Expenses:* Tuition $0 for state residents; $9384 per year for nonresidents. Fees $10,408 per year. *Financial aid:* Fellowships, research assistantships, teaching assistantships, Federal Work-Study, institutionally sponsored loans, and career-related internships or fieldwork available. Aid available to part-time students. Financial aid application deadline: 3/2; applicants required to submit FAFSA. • Dr. David H. Downes, Director, MBA Programs, 510-642-1405. E-mail: downes@haas.berkeley.edu. Application contact: MBA Admissions Office, 510-642-1405. Fax: 510-643-6659. E-mail: mbaadms@haas.berkeley.edu.

University of California, Davis, Graduate School of Management, Davis, CA 95616. Awards MBA, JD/MBA, MBA/MS, MD/MBA, M Engr/MBA. Part-time programs available. Faculty: 23 full-time (2 women), 9 part-time (1 woman). Students: 126 full-time (47 women); includes 22 minority (2 African Americans, 14 Asian Americans, 5 Hispanics, 1 Native American), 8 international. Average age 27. 345 applicants, 30% accepted. In 1997, 103 degrees awarded (95% found work related to degree, 5% continued full-time study). *Average time to degree:* master's–2 years full-time, 4 years part-time. *Entrance requirements:* GMAT, TOEFL (minimum score 600). Application deadline: 2/1 (priority date; rolling processing). Application fee: $40. *Fees:* $10,468 per year for state residents; $19,452 per year for nonresidents. *Financial aid:* 60 students received aid; research assistantships, teaching assistantships, full tuition waivers, Federal Work-Study, institutionally sponsored loans, and career-related internships or fieldwork available. Aid available to part-time students. Financial aid application deadline: 3/1; applicants required to submit FAFSA. *Faculty research:* Accounting, organizational behavior, statistics, information systems, finance. • Robert H. Smiley, Dean, 530-752-7366. Application contact: Holly Bishop-Green, Administrative Assistant, 530-752-7363. Fax: 530-752-2924. E-mail: hbbishopgreen@ucdavis.edu.

See in-depth description on page 313.

University of California, Irvine, Graduate School of Management, Irvine, CA 92697. Awards MBA, PhD. Part-time and evening/weekend programs available. Faculty: 34 full-time (7 women), 37 part-time (2 women). Students: 246 full-time (79 women), 555 part-time (170 women); includes 189 minority (18 African Americans, 133 Asian Americans, 33 Hispanics, 5 Native Americans), 71 international. In 1997, 205 master's awarded; 8 doctorates awarded (75% entered university research/teaching, 25% found other work related to degree). Terminal master's awarded for partial completion of doctoral program. *Degree requirements:* For doctorate, dissertation required, foreign language not required. *Average time to degree:* master's–2 years full-time, 2.5 years part-time; doctorate–6 years full-time. *Entrance requirements:* For master's, GMAT, minimum GPA of 3.0; for doctorate, GMAT or GRE, minimum GPA of 3.0. Application deadline: rolling. Application fee: $40. Electronic applications accepted. *Financial aid:* Fellowships, research assistantships, teaching assistantships, full and partial tuition waivers, institutionally sponsored loans, and career-related internships or fieldwork available. Financial aid application deadline: 3/2; applicants required to submit FAFSA. *Faculty research:* Organizational behavior, finance, information technology, marketing, accounting. Total annual research expenditures: $919,390. • David H. Blake, Dean, 949-824-8470. Fax: 949-824-8469. Application contact: Victoria Ongie, Administrative Advising Assistant, 949-824-4949. Fax: 949-824-2235. E-mail: vongie@uci.edu.

See in-depth description on page 315.

University of California, Los Angeles, John E. Anderson Graduate School of Management, Los Angeles, CA 90095. Awards MBA, MS, PhD, JD/MBA, MBA/MA, MBA/MS, MBA/MLIS, MBA/MPH, MBA/MSN, MD/PhD, MD/MBA. Part-time programs available. Faculty: 72 (8 women). Students: 711 (196 women); includes 165 minority (31 African Americans, 103 Asian Americans, 30 Hispanics, 1 Native American), 148 international. 3,964 applicants, 16% accepted. *Degree requirements:* For master's, thesis (MS) required, foreign language not required; for doctorate, dissertation, oral and written qualifying exams required, foreign language not required. *Entrance requirements:* For master's, GMAT (MBA), GMAT or GRE General Test (MS), minimum GPA of 3.0; for doctorate, GMAT or GRE General Test, minimum undergraduate GPA of 3.0. Application fee: $40. *Financial aid:* In 1997–98, 547 students received aid, including fellowships totaling $846,887, research assistantships totaling $683,026, teaching assistantships totaling $344,084, federal fellowships and scholarships totaling $14,870; full and partial tuition waivers, Federal Work-Study, institutionally sponsored loans, and career-related internships or fieldwork also available. Financial aid application deadline: 3/1. • Dr. John Mamer, Dean, 310-825-6944. Application contact: Departmental Office, 310-825-6121.

See in-depth description on page 317.

University of California, Riverside, Graduate Division, Graduate School of Management, Riverside, CA 92521-0102. Awards MBA. Part-time and evening/weekend programs available. Faculty: 24 full-time (4 women), 7 part-time (2 women). Students: 130 full-time (64 women), 21 part-time (2 women); includes 38 minority (4 African Americans, 25 Asian Americans, 9 Hispanics), 66 international. Average age 27. 296 applicants, 55% accepted. In 1997, 46 degrees awarded. *Degree requirements:* Thesis optional, foreign language not required. *Average time to degree:* master's–2 years full-time. *Entrance requirements:* GMAT, TOEFL (minimum score 550). Application deadline: 5/1 (rolling processing; 12/1 for spring admission). Application fee: $40. *Financial aid:* Fellowships, research assistantships, teaching assistantships, full tuition waivers, Federal Work-Study, institutionally sponsored loans, and career-related internships or fieldwork available. Financial aid application deadline: 2/1; applicants required to submit FAFSA. *Faculty research:* Option pricing, consumer attribution, feminization of management styles, artificial intelligence, new technologies in cost accounting. • David Mayer, Interim Dean, 909-787-4237. Application contact: Gary J. Kuzas, Director of MBA Admissions, 909-787-4551. Fax: 909-787-3970. E-mail: gary.kuzas@ucr.edu.

See in-depth description on page 319.

University of Central Arkansas, College of Business Administration, Conway, AR 72035-0001. Awards MBA. Part-time programs available. Faculty: 21 full-time (4 women), 2 part-time (1 woman), 21.66 FTE. Students: 33 full-time (15 women), 33 part-time (12 women); includes 4 minority (3 African Americans, 1 Hispanic), 20 international. 76 applicants, 66% accepted. In 1997, 58 degrees awarded. *Entrance requirements:* GMAT (minimum score 400), minimum GPA of 2.7. Application deadline: 3/1 (priority date; rolling processing; 10/1 for spring admission). Application fee: $15 ($40 for international students). *Expenses:* Tuition $161 per credit hour for state residents; $298 per credit hour for nonresidents. Fees $50 per year full-time, $30 per year part-time. *Financial aid:* In 1997–98, 13 assistantships were awarded; Federal Work-Study also available. Financial aid application deadline: 2/15. *Faculty research:* Structural equation modes of individual entrepreneur's propensities. • Dr. Joe Horton, Dean, 501-450-3106. Fax: 501-450-5302. E-mail: jhorton@mail.uca.edu.

University of Central Florida, College of Business Administration, Program in Business Administration, Orlando, FL 32816. Offers business administration (MBA), finance (PhD). Part-time and evening/weekend programs available. Faculty: 61. Students: 409 full-time (171 women), 140 part-time (67 women); includes 83 minority (18 African Americans, 30 Asian Americans, 34 Hispanics, 1 Native American), 64 international. Average age 31. 258 applicants, 64% accepted. In 1997, 189 master's, 3 doctorates awarded. *Degree requirements:* For doctorate, dissertation, departmental candidacy exam. *Entrance requirements:* GMAT. Application deadline: 6/15 (rolling processing; 11/1 for spring admission). Application fee: $20. *Expenses:* Tuition $3288 per year full-time, $137 per credit hour part-time for state residents; $11,520 per year full-time, $480 per credit hour part-time for nonresidents. Fees $105 per year. *Financial aid:* Assistantships, Federal Work-Study, institutionally sponsored loans, and career-related internships or fieldwork available. Aid available to part-time students. • Application contact: Dr. Robert L. Pennington, Graduate Coordinator, 407-823-3922.

See in-depth description on page 321.

University of Central Oklahoma, College of Business Administration, Program in Business Administration, Edmond, OK 73034-5209. Awards MBA. *Degree requirements:* Thesis optional, foreign language not required. *Entrance requirements:* GMAT (minimum score 375). Application deadline: 8/18. Application fee: $15. *Tuition:* $76 per credit hour for state residents; $178 per credit hour for nonresidents.

University of Central Texas, Division of Management, Business and Technology, PO Box 1416, Killeen, TX 76540-1416. Offers programs in business administration (MBA); general studies (MS); management science (MS), including public administration. Part-time and evening/weekend programs available. Faculty: 11 full-time (1 woman), 5 part-time (3 women). Students: 219 (110 women); includes 83 minority (53 African Americans, 11 Asian Americans, 17 Hispanics, 2 Native Americans), 10 international. Average age 34. In 1997, 80 degrees awarded. *Degree requirements:* Computer language required, foreign language and thesis not required. *Entrance requirements:* GMAT, GRE General Test (minimum combined score of 900), or MAT, minimum GPA of 2.5 during previous 2 years. Application deadline: 8/30 (priority date; rolling processing; 1/17 for spring admission). Application fee: $0 ($100 for international students). *Tuition:* $150 per hour. *Financial aid:* Federal Work-Study available. Aid available to part-time students. *Faculty research:* Introversion and extroversion as related to attention to detail, student perception survey. • Dr. Robin Smith, Lead Faculty, 254-526-8262. Application contact: Pam Asmus, Admissions Adviser, 254-526-8262 Ext. 261. Fax: 254-526-8403.

University of Charleston, Jones-Benedum Division of Business, Program in Business Administration, Charleston, WV 25304-1099. Awards MBA. Part-time and evening/weekend programs available. Faculty: 10. Students: 44 part-time (15 women). *Entrance requirements:* GMAT or GRE General Test, 4 years of related experience. Application deadline: 8/1. Application fee: $40. *Faculty research:* International trade, operations technology. • Armando Alcazar, Director, 304-357-4884. Application contact: Lynn Jackson, Director of Admissions, 304-357-4750. Fax: 304-357-4715.

University of Charleston, South Carolina, School of Business and Economics, Charleston, SC 29424-0001. Awards MS. Faculty: 9 full-time (3 women). Students: 16 full-time (10 women), 17 part-time (11 women); includes 1 minority (African American), 1 international. Average age 34. 21 applicants, 81% accepted. In 1997, 13 degrees awarded. *Entrance requirements:* GMAT (minimum score 500), minimum GPA of 3.0 in last 60 hours of undergraduate course work; 24 hours of accounting course work with 6 hours of elementary accounting, 6 hours of intermediate accounting, 3 hours of cost accounting, 3 hours of individual taxation accounting, 3 hours o. Application deadline: rolling. Application fee: $35. *Expenses:* Tuition $2568 per year full-time, $438 per semester (minimum) part-time for state residents; $4596 per year full-time, $876 per semester (minimum) part-time for nonresidents. Fees $51 per year full-time, $21 per semester (minimum) part-time. *Financial aid:* In 1997–98, 2 research assistantships (1 to a first-year student) totaling $7,100 were awarded. Aid available to part-time students. Financial aid applicants required to submit FAFSA. • Dr. Clarence Condon III, Dean, 843-953-1356. Fax: 843-953-5697. Application contact: Laura H. Hines, Graduate School Coordinator, 843-953-5614. Fax: 843-953-1434. E-mail: hinesl@cofc.edu.

University of Chicago, Graduate School of Business, Chicago, IL 60637-1513. Awards EMBA, IEMBA, IMBA, MBA, PhD, JD/MBA, MBA/AM, MBA/MPP, MD/MBA, SM/MBA. Programs in accounting (MBA), business administration (EMBA, MBA, PhD), international business administration (IEMBA, IMBA). IEMBA offered through the University of Chicago at Barcelona, Spain. Part-time and evening/weekend programs available. Faculty: 114 full-time (17 women), 48 part-time (6 women). Students: 1,108 full-time (238 women), 1,654 part-time (421 women); includes 444 minority (77 African Americans, 316 Asian Americans, 47 Hispanics, 4 Native Americans), 329 international. Average age 28. 3,432 applicants, 26% accepted. In 1997, 1,168 master's, 9 doctorates awarded. Terminal master's awarded for partial completion of doctoral program. *Degree requirements:* For master's, variable foreign language requirement; for doctorate, dissertation required, foreign language not required. *Average time to degree:* master's–2 years full-time, 5 years part-time; doctorate–5.5 years full-time. *Entrance requirements:* GMAT or GRE General Test, TOEFL (minimum score 600). Application deadline: 3/17 (priority date; rolling processing). Application fee: $125. *Financial aid:* Fellowships, research assistantships, teaching assistantships, Federal Work-Study, institutionally sponsored loans, and career-related internships or fieldwork available. Aid available to part-time students. Financial aid application deadline: 2/1; applicants required to submit FAFSA. *Faculty research:* Regulation, finance, decision making, marketing, international trade. • Robert S. Hamada, Dean, 773-702-7121. Application contact: Donald Martin, Director of Admissions and Financial Aid, 773-702-7369. Fax: 773-702-9085.

University of Cincinnati, College of Business Administration, Cincinnati, OH 45221. Awards MBA, MS, PhD, JD/MBA, MBA/MA, MBA/MS, MBA/MSN. Part-time and evening/weekend

Directory: Business Administration and Management—General

University of Cincinnati (continued)
programs available. Faculty: 47 full-time. Students: 106 full-time (42 women), 305 part-time (102 women); includes 46 minority (20 African Americans, 21 Asian Americans, 4 Hispanics, 1 Native American), 39 international. 203 applicants, 39% accepted. In 1997, 142 master's, 16 doctorates awarded. *Degree requirements:* For doctorate, computer language, dissertation. *Average time to degree:* master's–2.2 years full-time; doctorate–5.8 years full-time. *Entrance requirements:* GMAT. Application fee: $30. *Tuition:* $7228 per year full-time, $185 per credit hour part-time for state residents; $13,812 per year full-time, $352 per credit hour part-time for nonresidents. *Financial aid:* Fellowships, research assistantships, teaching assistantships, graduate assistantships, full tuition waivers available. Aid available to part-time students. Financial aid application deadline: 2/15. *Faculty research:* Group and organizational behavior, accounting and information analysis, business economics and public policy, technological innovation. • Dr. Frederick Russ, Dean, 513-556-7001. E-mail: frederick.russ@uc.edu. Application contact: James Bast, Assistant Dean, Graduate Programs, 513-556-7020. Fax: 513-556-4891. E-mail: james.bast@uc.edu.

University of Colorado at Boulder, Graduate School of Business Administration, Boulder, CO 80309. Awards MBA, MS, PhD, JD/MBA, MBA/MS. Programs in accounting (MS), business administration (MBA, PhD), business self designed (MBA), finance (MBA, PhD), marketing (MBA, PhD), organization management (MBA, PhD), taxation (MS), technology and innovation management (MBA). Evening/weekend programs available. Faculty: 66 full-time (12 women). Students: 309 full-time (107 women), 8 part-time (4 women); includes 32 minority (5 African Americans, 17 Asian Americans, 9 Hispanics, 1 Native American), 25 international. Average age 30. 592 applicants, 41% accepted. In 1997, 95 master's, 11 doctorates awarded. *Degree requirements:* For master's, computer language required, foreign language not required; for doctorate, dissertation, research internship. *Entrance requirements:* GMAT. Application deadline: 3/1 (priority date; rolling processing). Application fee: $40 ($60 for international students). *Expenses:* Tuition $3594 per year (minimum) full-time, $597 per semester (minimum) part-time for state residents; $14,868 per year (minimum) full-time, $2478 per semester (minimum) part-time for nonresidents. Fees $667 per year full-time, $130 per semester (minimum) part-time. *Financial aid:* Fellowships, research assistantships, teaching assistantships available. Financial aid application deadline: 3/1. *Total annual research expenditures:* $2.2 million. • Larry Singell, Dean, 303-492-1809. Fax: 303-492-7676. E-mail: larry.singell@colorado.edu. Application contact: Diana Marinaro, Graduate Student Admissions, 303-492-1831. Fax: 303-492-1727. E-mail: busgrad@spot.colorado.edu.

See in-depth description on page 323.

University of Colorado at Colorado Springs, Graduate School of Business Administration, Colorado Springs, CO 80933-7150. Offers programs in accounting (MBA), finance (MBA), information systems (MBA), marketing (MBA), organizational management (MBA), production management (MBA). Part-time and evening/weekend programs available. Faculty: 24 full-time (4 women). Students: 207 full-time (86 women), 110 part-time (46 women); includes 23 minority (3 African Americans, 13 Asian Americans, 5 Hispanics, 2 Native Americans), 27 international. Average age 29. 83 applicants, 81% accepted. In 1997, 98 degrees awarded (100% found work related to degree). *Entrance requirements:* GMAT. Application deadline: 6/1 (priority date; 11/1 for spring admission). Application fee: $50. *Expenses:* Tuition $2860 per year full-time, $121 per credit hour part-time for state residents; $10,254 per year full-time, $420 per credit hour part-time for nonresidents. Fees $399 per year (minimum) full-time, $106 per year (minimum) part-time. *Financial aid:* Federal Work-Study, institutionally sponsored loans, and career-related internships or fieldwork available. Aid available to part-time students. Financial aid application deadline: 4/1; applicants required to submit FAFSA. *Faculty research:* Motivation of high-technology personnel, consumer information, stress management, artificial intelligence, entrepreneurship. • Dr. Richard Dicenza, Dean, 719-262-3113. E-mail: rdicenz@mail.uccs.edu. Application contact: Diane Belger, Adviser, 719-262-3408. Fax: 719-262-3494. E-mail: dbelger@mail.uccs.edu.

University of Colorado at Denver, Graduate School of Business Administration, Division of Management, Denver, CO 80217-3364. Awards MS, MBA/MS. Part-time and evening/weekend programs available. Faculty: 11 full-time. Students: 76. In 1997, 40 degrees awarded. *Entrance requirements:* GMAT (minimum score 400; average 520), TOEFL (minimum score 525; average 560). Application deadline: 7/1 (priority date; rolling processing; 11/1 for spring admission). Application fee: $50 ($60 for international students). *Expenses:* Tuition $3754 per year full-time, $225 per semester hour part-time for state residents; $12,962 per year full-time, $777 per semester hour part-time for nonresidents. Fees $252 per year. *Financial aid:* Application deadline 4/1. *Faculty research:* Human resource management, management of catastrophe, turnaround strategies. • Gary Giese, Director, 303-556-5842. Fax: 303-556-5899. Application contact: Lori Cain, Graduate Business Admissions Office, 303-556-5900. Fax: 303-556-5904. E-mail: lori_cain@maroon.cudenver.edu.

See in-depth description on page 325.

University of Colorado at Denver, Graduate School of Business Administration, Executive MBA Program, Denver, CO 80248-0006. Awards Exec MBA. Evening/weekend programs available. Faculty: 16 full-time (2 women). Students: 46 full-time (17 women); includes 9 minority (6 Asian Americans, 2 Hispanics, 1 Native American), 1 international. Average age 38. 97 applicants, 52% accepted. In 1997, 38 degrees awarded. *Entrance requirements:* GMAT (minimum score 400), TOEFL (minimum score 525; average 560). Application deadline: 6/15 (priority date; rolling processing). Application fee: $0. Electronic applications accepted. *Financial aid:* 15 students received aid; partial tuition waivers, institutionally sponsored loans available. Financial aid application deadline: 6/1; applicants required to submit CSS PROFILE or FAFSA. • W. Scott Guthrie, Director, 303-623-1888. Fax: 303-623-6228. E-mail: sguthrie@conan.cudenver.edu.

See in-depth description on page 325.

University of Colorado at Denver, Graduate School of Business Administration, Master of Business Administration Program, Denver, CO 80217-3364. Awards MBA, MBA/MS, MBA/MIM. MBA/MIM offered jointly with Thunderbird, The American Graduate School of International Management. MBA/MS (nursing administration) offered jointly with the University of Colorado Health Sciences Center. Part-time and evening/weekend programs available. Faculty: 59 full-time. Students: 603. Average age 32. 329 applicants, 65% accepted. In 1997, 176 degrees awarded. *Entrance requirements:* GMAT (minimum score 400; average 520), TOEFL (minimum score 525; average 560). Application deadline: 7/1 (priority date; rolling processing; 11/1 for spring admission). Application fee: $50 ($60 for international students). *Expenses:* Tuition $3754 per year full-time, $225 per semester hour part-time for state residents; $12,962 per year full-time, $777 per semester hour part-time for nonresidents. Fees $252 per year. *Financial aid:* Application deadline 4/1. • Sue Keaveney, Director, 303-556-5821. Application contact: Lori Cain, Graduate Business Admissions Office, 303-556-5900. Fax: 303-556-5904. E-mail: lori_cain@maroon.cudenver.edu.

See in-depth description on page 325.

University of Connecticut, School of Business Administration, Storrs, CT 06269. Awards MBA, PhD, JD/MBA, MA/MBA, MBA/MSW. Programs in accounting (MBA, PhD), finance (PhD), general business administration (MBA), health care management (MBA), human resources management (MBA), international studies and business administration (MA/MBA), management (MBA, PhD), marketing (MBA, PhD). Faculty: 63. Students: 320 full-time (102 women), 830 part-time (325 women); includes 91 minority (37 African Americans, 30 Asian Americans, 20 Hispanics, 4 Native Americans), 146 international. Average age 32. 586 applicants, 63% accepted. In 1997, 350 master's, 8 doctorates awarded. *Degree requirements:* For doctorate, dissertation. *Entrance requirements:* For master's, GMAT; for doctorate, GMAT, TOEFL. Application deadline: 6/1 (priority date; rolling processing; 11/1 for spring admission). Application fee: $40 ($45 for international students). *Expenses:* Tuition $5272 per year full-time, $293 per credit part-time for state residents; $13,696 per year full-time, $761 per credit part-time for nonresidents. Fees $948 per year full-time, $640 per year part-time. *Financial aid:* In 1997–98, 11 fellowships totaling $14,448, 59 research assistantships (14 to first-year students) totaling $619,249, 14 teaching assistantships (4 to first-year students) totaling $85,171 were awarded; career-related internships or fieldwork also available. Financial aid application deadline: 2/15. • Thomas G. Gutteridge, Dean, 860-486-3096. Application contact: David W. Palmer, Chairperson, 860-486-3096.

See in-depth description on page 327.

University of Dallas, Graduate School of Management, Irving, TX 75062-4799. Awards MBA, MM. Part-time programs available. Faculty: 20 full-time (1 woman), 59 part-time (13 women). Students: 317 full-time (139 women), 1,099 part-time (424 women); includes 256 minority (99 African Americans, 77 Asian Americans, 74 Hispanics, 6 Native Americans), 338 international. Average age 33. 680 applicants, 85% accepted. In 1997, 483 degrees awarded. *Entrance requirements:* GMAT (minimum score 400), TOEFL (average 520), minimum GPA of 3.0. Application deadline: 8/6 (priority date; rolling processing; 12/8 for spring admission). Application fee: $25 ($50 for international students). *Expenses:* Tuition $380 per credit hour. Fees $125 per year. *Financial aid:* 181 students received aid; graduate assistantships, partial tuition waivers available. Financial aid application deadline: 2/15; applicants required to submit FAFSA. • Dr. Glen E. Thurow, Provost, 972-721-5242. Fax: 972-721-5130. Application contact: Roxanne Del Rio, Director of Admissions, 972-721-5174. Fax: 972-721-4009. E-mail: admiss@gsm.udallas.edu.

See in-depth description on page 329.

University of Dayton, School of Business Administration, Dayton, OH 45469-1611. Awards MBA, JD/MBA. Part-time and evening/weekend programs available. Faculty: 44 full-time (6 women), 6 part-time (1 woman). Students: 83 full-time (31 women), 459 part-time (184 women); includes 52 minority (19 African Americans, 22 Asian Americans, 11 Hispanics), 36 international. Average age 29. 215 applicants, 80% accepted. In 1997, 169 degrees awarded. *Degree requirements:* Computer language required, foreign language and thesis not required. *Average time to degree:* master's–1.5 years full-time, 2.5 years part-time. *Entrance requirements:* GMAT (minimum score 400; average 720), TOEFL (minimum score 550; average 575), minimum GPA of 2.5. Application deadline: 8/1 (priority date; rolling processing; 12/1 for spring admission). Application fee: $30. *Financial aid:* In 1997–98, 10 fellowships (4 to first-year students) totaling $7,646, 13 research assistantships (10 to first-year students) averaging $608 per month and totaling $62,910 were awarded; career-related internships or fieldwork also available. Aid available to part-time students. Financial aid application deadline: 4/15; applicants required to submit FAFSA. *Faculty research:* MIS, economics, finance, production operations management, marketing. • Dr. Sam Gould, Dean, 937-229-3731. Application contact: Dr. E. James Dunne, Associate Dean and Director, MBA Program, 937-229-3733. Fax: 937-229-3301. E-mail: dunne@udayton.edu.

University of Delaware, College of Business and Economics, Program in Business Administration, Newark, DE 19716. Awards MBA, MA/MBA. Part-time and evening/weekend programs available. Students: 119 full-time, 286 part-time; includes 59 international. Average age 27. 296 applicants, 65% accepted. In 1997, 96 degrees awarded (100% found work related to degree). *Average time to degree:* master's–2 years full-time, 4 years part-time. *Entrance requirements:* TOEFL (minimum score 585). Application deadline: 5/31 (priority date; rolling processing; 11/1 for spring admission). Application fee: $45. Electronic applications accepted. *Expenses:* Tuition $4250 per year full-time, $236 per credit hour part-time for state residents; $12,250 per year full-time, $681 per credit hour part-time for nonresidents. Fees $466 per year full-time, $15 per semester (minimum) part-time. *Financial aid:* In 1997–98, 6 fellowships, 32 graduate assistantships were awarded; research assistantships, teaching assistantships, full and partial tuition waivers, Federal Work-Study, and career-related internships or fieldwork also available. Financial aid application deadline: 2/1. • Scott Jones, Associate Dean, 302-831-2221.

See in-depth description on page 331.

University of Denver, Daniels College of Business, Denver, CO 80208. Awards M Acc, MBA, MIM, MRECM, MS, MSF, MSM, MSMC, MSMGEN, MSRTM, JD/MBA, JD/MIM. Part-time and evening/weekend programs available. Faculty: 76 full-time (15 women). Students: 759 (294 women); includes 58 minority (10 African Americans, 21 Asian Americans, 25 Hispanics, 2 Native Americans), 154 international. Average age 28. 692 applicants, 88% accepted. In 1997, 344 degrees awarded. *Average time to degree:* master's–1.7 years full-time, 2.7 years part-time. *Application deadline:* 5/1 (priority date; rolling processing; 1/1 for spring admission). *Application fee:* $50. *Expenses:* Tuition $18,216 per year full-time, $506 per credit hour part-time. Fees $159 per year. *Financial aid:* In 1997–98, 300 students received aid, including 32 teaching assistantships averaging $426 per month and totaling $124,232, 166 grants, scholarships totaling $158,725; research assistantships, Federal Work-Study, institutionally sponsored loans, and career-related internships or fieldwork also available. Aid available to part-time students. Financial aid application deadline: 2/15; applicants required to submit FAFSA. • James R. Griesemer, Dean, 303-871-3411. Application contact: Jan Johnson, Executive Director, Student Services, 303-871-3416. Fax: 303-871-4466. E-mail: dcb@du.edu.

See in-depth description on page 333.

University of Detroit Mercy, College of Business Administration, Program in Business Administration, Detroit, MI 48219-0900. Awards MBA, JD/MBA. Part-time and evening/weekend programs available. *Degree requirements:* Thesis or alternative required, foreign language not required. *Entrance requirements:* GMAT (minimum score 400), minimum GPA of 2.75. Application deadline: 8/1 (priority date; rolling processing). Application fee: $25 ($35 for international students).

See in-depth description on page 335.

University of Dubuque, Program in Business Administration, 2000 University Avenue, Dubuque, IA 52001-5050. Offers aviation management (MBA), business administration (MBA). Part-time and evening/weekend programs available. Faculty: 10 full-time (6 women), 18 part-time (2 women). Students: 108 full-time (31 women), 147 part-time (58 women); includes 187 international. Average age 33. In 1997, 67 degrees awarded (100% found work related to degree). *Degree requirements:* Computer language required, foreign language and thesis not required. *Average time to degree:* master's–1.5 years full-time, 3 years part-time. *Entrance requirements:* GMAT, TOEFL (minimum score 550). Application deadline: 8/15 (priority date; rolling processing). Application fee: $25. *Financial aid:* Federal Work-Study available. Aid available to part-time students. Financial aid application deadline: 4/1; applicants required to submit FAFSA. • John Wiemers, Director, 319-589-3300. Fax: 319-589-3184. E-mail: mbaprogm@univ.dbq.edu.

The University of Findlay, College of Professional Studies, MBA Program, 1000 North Main Street, Findlay, OH 45840-3653. Offers financial management (MBA), human resource management (MBA), international management (MBA), management (MBA), marketing (MBA), public management (MBA). Part-time and evening/weekend programs available. Postbaccalaureate distance learning degree programs offered (minimal on-campus study). Faculty: 9 full-time (0 women), 6 part-time (0 women), 11 FTE. Students: 50 full-time (20 women), 261 part-time (104 women); includes 10 minority (all African Americans), 35 international. Average age 28. In 1997, 82 degrees awarded. *Degree requirements:* Cumulative project. *Average time to degree:* master's–1.5 years full-time, 2.5 years part-time. *Entrance requirements:* GMAT, TOEFL. Application deadline: 8/15 (rolling processing; 12/15 for spring admission). Application fee: $25. *Tuition:* $299 per semester hour. *Financial aid:* Graduate assistantships available. Aid available to part-time students. Financial aid applicants required to submit FAFSA. *Faculty research:* Health care management, operations and logistics management. • Dr. Theodore C. Alex, Director, 419-424-4704. Fax: 419-424-4822.

University of Florida, College of Business Administration, Department of Management, Gainesville, FL 32611. Offers programs in human resources management (PhD), management (MA, PhD), strategy (PhD). Faculty: 8. Students: 6 full-time (4 women), 1 part-time (0 women); includes 2 minority (1 African American, 1 Hispanic). 38 applicants, 5% accepted. In 1997, 2 doctorates awarded. *Degree requirements:* Thesis/dissertation required, foreign language not required. *Entrance requirements:* GMAT or GRE General Test, minimum GPA of 3.0. Application deadline: 2/16 (rolling processing). Application fee: $20. *Tuition:* $138 per credit hour for state residents; $481 per credit hour for nonresidents. *Financial aid:* In 1997–98, 3 fellowships averaging $1,296 per month, 5 teaching assistantships averaging $780 per month were awarded; research assistantships, graduate assistantships also available. *Faculty research:* Organizational behavior, organizational theory, strategy and business policy. • Dr. Virginia Maurer, Chair, 352-392-0163. E-mail: maurer@dale.cba.ufl.edu. Application contact: Dr. Henry Tosi, Graduate Coordinator, 352-392-6147. Fax: 352-392-6020. E-mail: tosi@nervm.nerdc.ufl.edu.

University of Florida, College of Business Administration, Program in Business Administration, Gainesville, FL 32611. Awards MBA, JD/MBA, MBA/MESS, MBA/MHA, MBA/Pharm D. Students: 307 full-time (77 women), 107 part-time (30 women); includes 56 minority (14 African Americans, 19 Asian Americans, 23 Hispanics), 30 international. 472 applicants, 50% accepted. In 1997, 136 degrees awarded. *Entrance requirements:* GMAT (average 605), minimum GPA of 3.0, interview. Application deadline: 4/1 (rolling processing). Application fee: $20. Electronic applications accepted. *Tuition:* $138 per credit hour for state residents; $481 per credit hour for nonresidents. *Financial aid:* In 1997–98, 27 students received aid, including 16 fellowships averaging $1,274 per month, 4 research assistantships averaging $574 per month, 1 teaching assistantship averaging $1,024 per month, 6 graduate assistantships averaging $386 per month; career-related internships or fieldwork also available. Financial aid application deadline: 2/1. *Faculty research:* Accounting, finance, insurance, management, real estate and urban analysis marketing. • Dr. T. Craig Tapley, Director, 352-392-1065. E-mail: tapley@nervm.nerdc.ufl.edu. Application contact: Todd Reale, Graduate Coordinator, 352-392-7992. Fax: 352-392-8791. E-mail: realetd@dale.cba.ufl.edu.

University of Georgia, Terry College of Business, Program in Business Administration, Athens, GA 30602. Awards MA, MBA, PhD, JD/MBA. Faculty: 78 full-time (12 women). Students: 220 full-time, 14 part-time (3 women); includes 26 minority (17 African Americans, 5 Asian Americans, 3 Hispanics, 1 Native American), 53 international. 877 applicants, 15% accepted. In 1997, 106 master's, 15 doctorates awarded. *Degree requirements:* For master's, thesis (MA) required, foreign language not required; for doctorate, dissertation required, foreign language not required. *Entrance requirements:* For master's, GMAT (MBA), GRE General Test (MA); for doctorate, GMAT or GRE General Test. Application deadline: 7/1 (priority date; 11/15 for spring admission). Application fee: $30. Electronic applications accepted. *Tuition:* $3290 per year full-time, $643 per semester (minimum) part-time for state residents; $11,300 per year full-time, $1645 per semester (minimum) part-time for nonresidents. *Financial aid:* Fellowships, research assistantships, teaching assistantships, assistantships available. • Dr. Kay L. Keck, Graduate Coordinator, 706-542-5671. Fax: 706-542-5351. E-mail: kkeck@cba.uga.edu.

See in-depth description on page 337.

University of Guam, College of Business and Public Administration, 303 University Drive, UOG Station, Mangilao, GU 96923. Awards MBA, MPA. Part-time and evening/weekend programs available. *Degree requirements:* Thesis required, foreign language not required. *Entrance requirements:* GMAT. Application deadline: 5/31. Application fee: $31 ($56 for international students). *Faculty research:* Economic development, international business.

University of Hartford, Barney School of Business and Public Administration, West Hartford, CT 06117-1599. Awards EMBA, MBA, MSI, MSOB, MSPA, MST, MSN/MSOB. Part-time and evening/weekend programs available. Faculty: 39 full-time (10 women), 27 part-time (2 women). Students: 195 full-time (88 women), 330 part-time (148 women); includes 150 international. Average age 26. 263 applicants, 78% accepted. In 1997, 264 degrees awarded. *Average time to degree:* master's–1.5 years full-time, 3 years part-time. *Entrance requirements:* TOEFL. Application deadline: 7/1 (priority date; rolling processing; 12/1 for spring admission). Application fee: $35 ($50 for international students). Electronic applications accepted. *Financial aid:* Fellowships, research assistantships, institutionally sponsored loans, and career-related internships or fieldwork available. Aid available to part-time students. Financial aid application deadline: 5/1. • Corine T. Norgaard, Dean, 860-768-4243. Fax: 860-768-4198. Application contact: Claire Silverstein, Assistant Director, 860-768-4900. Fax: 860-768-4821. E-mail: silverste@unavax.hartford.edu.

University of Hawaii at Manoa, College of Business Administration, Executive Business Administration Program, Honolulu, HI 96822. Offers business administration (EMBA), China focused business administration (EMBA), Japan focused business administration (EMBA). Part-time programs available. *Entrance requirements:* GMAT (minimum score 500; average 580), minimum GPA of 3.0. Application fee: $25 ($50 for international students). *Tuition:* $4029 per year full-time, $214 per credit hour part-time for state residents; $9957 per year full-time, $461 per credit hour part-time for nonresidents. • Application contact: Program Office, 808-956-3260. Fax: 808-956-3251.

University of Hawaii at Manoa, College of Business Administration, Program in Business Administration, Honolulu, HI 96822. Awards MBA. Part-time programs available. *Entrance requirements:* GMAT (minimum score 500; average 580), minimum GPA of 3.0. Application fee: $25 ($50 for international students). *Tuition:* $4029 per year full-time, $214 per credit hour part-time for state residents; $9957 per year full-time, $461 per credit hour part-time for nonresidents. • Application contact: Office of Student Academic Services, 808-956-8266. Fax: 808-956-9890.

University of Houston, College of Business Administration, 4800 Calhoun, Houston, TX 77204-2163. Awards MBA, MS Accy, MS Admin, PhD, JD/MBA, MBA/MA, MBA/MIE, MBA/MIM, MBA/MSW. MBA/MIM offered jointly with Thunderbird, The American Graduate School of International Management. Part-time and evening/weekend programs available. Faculty: 73 full-time (16 women), 22 part-time (7 women). Students: 479 full-time (181 women), 633 part-time (194 women); includes 211 minority (50 African Americans, 111 Asian Americans, 47 Hispanics, 3 Native Americans), 189 international. Average age 32. In 1997, 312 master's, 3 doctorates awarded. *Degree requirements:* For master's, computer language required, foreign language and thesis not required; for doctorate, computer language, dissertation, comprehensive exam required, foreign language not required. *Average time to degree:* master's–2 years full-time, 4.5 years part-time; doctorate–4 years full-time. *Entrance requirements:* For master's, GMAT (average 575), TOEFL (minimum score 620); for doctorate, GMAT or GRE. Application deadline: 5/1 (rolling processing; 10/1 for spring admission). Application fee: $50 ($125 for international students). *Expenses:* Tuition $1152 per year full-time, $120 per semester (minimum) part-time for state residents; $4482 per year full-time, $249 per credit hour part-time for nonresidents. Fees $977 per year full-time, $119 per semester (minimum) part-time. *Financial aid:* Research assistantships, teaching assistantships, Federal Work-Study, institutionally sponsored loans, and career-related internships or fieldwork available. Aid available to part-time students. Financial aid application deadline: 3/1; applicants required to submit FAFSA. *Total annual research expenditures:* $1.991 million. • Dr. Sara M. Freedman, Dean, 713-743-4600. Fax: 713-743-4622. E-mail: sara@rics1.cba.uh.edu. Application contact: Office of Student Services, 713-743-4900. Fax: 713-743-4942. E-mail: oss@cba.uh.edu.

See in-depth description on page 339.

University of Houston–Clear Lake, School of Business and Public Administration, Program in Business Administration, Houston, TX 77058-1098. Awards MBA, MHA/MBA. Faculty: 25. Students: 243 full-time, 478 part-time; includes 137 minority (37 African Americans, 68 Asian Americans, 32 Hispanics), 86 international. Average age 32. 424 applicants, 85% accepted. In 1997, 209 degrees awarded. *Degree requirements:* Thesis optional, foreign language not required. *Entrance requirements:* GMAT (average 510). Application deadline: 8/1 (rolling processing; 12/1 for spring admission). Application fee: $30 ($60 for international students). *Tuition:* $207 per credit hour for state residents; $336 per credit hour for nonresidents. *Financial aid:* Federal Work-Study, institutionally sponsored loans, and career-related internships or fieldwork available. Financial aid application deadline: 5/1. • Dr. R. McGlashan, Head, 281-283-3102. Application contact: Dr. Sue Neeley, Associate Dean, 281-283-3110.

University of Houston–Victoria, Division of Business Administration, 2506 East Red River, Victoria, TX 77901-4450. Awards MBA. Part-time and evening/weekend programs available. Postbaccalaureate distance learning degree programs offered (no on-campus study). Faculty: 8 full-time (1 woman), 4 part-time (0 women), 9.2 FTE. Students: 36 full-time (17 women), 59 part-time (22 women); includes 13 minority (5 African Americans, 4 Asian Americans, 4 Hispanics), 33 international. Average age 33. In 1997, 40 degrees awarded. *Degree requirements:* Computer language required, foreign language and thesis not required. *Entrance requirements:* GRE General Test (minimum combined score of 800). Application deadline: rolling. *Expenses:* Tuition $1026 per year full-time, $57 per semester hour part-time for state residents; $4464 per year full-time, $248 per semester hour part-time for nonresidents. Fees $540 per year full-time, $30 per semester hour part-time. *Financial aid:* Research assistantships, teaching assistantships, Federal Work-Study, and career-related internships or fieldwork available. Aid available to part-time students. *Faculty research:* MIS, health care, economic development, small business. • Charles Bullock, Chair, 512-788-6228.

University of Idaho, College of Graduate Studies, College of Business and Economics, Moscow, ID 83844-4140. Awards M Acct, MS. Faculty: 8 full-time (3 women). Students: 5 full-time (2 women), 6 part-time (2 women); includes 1 minority (African American), 3 international. In 1997, 1 degree awarded. *Degree requirements:* Comprehensive exam required, foreign language not required. *Entrance requirements:* Minimum GPA of 2.8. Application deadline: 8/1 (12/15 for spring admission). Application fee: $35 ($45 for international students). *Expenses:* Tuition $0 for state residents; $6000 per year full-time, $95 per credit part-time for nonresidents. Fees $2676 per year full-time, $134 per credit part-time. *Financial aid:* In 1997–98, 1 teaching assistantship (to a first-year student) averaging $1,556 per month and totaling $14,007 was awarded; scholarships, Federal Work-Study also available. Aid available to part-time students. Financial aid application deadline: 2/15. • Dr. Byron Dangerfield, Dean, 208-885-6478.

University of Illinois at Chicago, College of Business Administration, Graduate Professional Business Program, Chicago, IL 60607-7128. Awards MBA, MBA/MA, MBA/MS, MBA/MPH. Part-time programs available. Students: 162 full-time (70 women), 299 part-time (116 women); includes 91 minority (33 African Americans, 34 Asian Americans, 21 Hispanics, 3 Native Americans), 100 international. 443 applicants, 46% accepted. In 1997, 140 degrees awarded. *Entrance requirements:* GMAT, TOEFL (minimum score 570), minimum GPA of 3.75 on a 5.0 scale. Application deadline: 5/1. Application fee: $40 ($50 for international students). *Financial aid:* In 1997–98, 10 research assistantships, 8 teaching assistantships were awarded; fellowships, full tuition waivers, Federal Work-Study, institutionally sponsored loans, and career-related internships or fieldwork also available. Aid available to part-time students. Financial aid application deadline: 2/15. • John Albanese, Assistant Director, 312-996-4573.

See in-depth description on page 341.

University of Illinois at Springfield, School of Business and Management, Program in Business Administration, Springfield, IL 62794-9243. Awards MBA. Part-time and evening/weekend programs available. Faculty: 10 full-time (1 woman). Students: 31 full-time (15 women), 126 part-time (47 women); includes 5 minority (4 African Americans, 1 Hispanic), 4 international. Average age 32. 73 applicants, 67% accepted. In 1997, 36 degrees awarded. *Entrance requirements:* GMAT (minimum score 400). Application deadline: rolling. Application fee: $0. *Expenses:* Tuition $99 per credit hour for state residents; $296 per credit hour for nonresidents. Fees $242 per year full-time, $63 per semester (minimum) part-time. *Financial aid:* In 1997–98, 45 students received aid, including 8 assistantships averaging $606 per month; research assistantships, partial tuition waivers, Federal Work-Study, and career-related internships or fieldwork also available. Aid available to part-time students. Financial aid application deadline: 6/1; applicants required to submit FAFSA. *Faculty research:* Finance, marketing, organizational behavior, strategic planning. • Richard Judd, Director, 217-786-6780.

University of Illinois at Urbana–Champaign, College of Commerce and Business Administration, Department of Business Administration, Urbana, IL 61801. Awards MBA, MSBA, PhD, JD/MBA, M Arch/MBA. Faculty: 47 full-time (7 women). Students: 699 full-time (194 women); includes 107 minority (51 African Americans, 39 Asian Americans, 14 Hispanics, 3 Native Americans), 296 international. 1,186 applicants, 44% accepted. In 1997, 349 master's, 10 doctorates awarded. *Degree requirements:* For doctorate, dissertation required, foreign language not required. *Entrance requirements:* GMAT. Application deadline: rolling. Application fee: $40 ($50 for international students). *Financial aid:* In 1997–98, 12 fellowships, 109 research assistantships, 66 teaching assistantships were awarded; full and partial tuition waivers also available. Financial aid application deadline: 2/15. • Kent B. Monroe, Head, 217-333-4240.

See in-depth descriptions on pages 343 and 345.

University of Indianapolis, Graduate Business Programs, Indianapolis, IN 46227-3697. Offerings in accounting (M Acc), business administration (MBA). Part-time and evening/weekend programs available. *Average time to degree:* master's–2 years full-time, 4 years part-time. *Entrance requirements:* GMAT, interview, minimum GPA of 2.8. Application deadline: rolling. Application fee: $30. *Faculty research:* Integration of microcomputers into decision making, communication skills, application of synthesized theories.

The University of Iowa, College of Business Administration, Department of Accounting, Iowa City, IA 52242-1316. Offerings include business administration (PhD). Terminal master's awarded for partial completion of doctoral program. Department faculty: 13 full-time (2 women), 2 part-time (1 woman), 14 FTE. *Degree requirements:* Dissertation, thesis defense required, foreign language not required. *Average time to degree:* master's–1.5 years full-time, 3 years part-time; doctorate–5 years full-time. *Entrance requirements:* GMAT (minimum score 600), TOEFL (minimum score 600). Application deadline: 7/15 (priority date; rolling processing; 12/1 for spring admission). Application fee: $30 ($50 for international students). *Expenses:* Tuition $3166 per year full-time, $176 per semester hour part-time for state residents; $10,202 per year full-time, $176 per semester hour part-time for nonresidents. Fees $202 per year full-time, $52 per year (minimum) part-time. • Daniel W. Collins, Chair, 319-335-0910. E-mail: daniel-collins@uiowa.edu. Application contact: Steve Reimer, Lecturer/Adviser, 319-335-0918. Fax: 319-335-1956. E-mail: steven-reimer@uiowa.edu.

The University of Iowa, College of Business Administration, Department of Management and Organizations, Iowa City, IA 52242-1316. Offerings include business administration (PhD). Terminal master's awarded for partial completion of doctoral program. Department faculty: 11 full-time (3 women), 4 part-time (2 women). *Degree requirements:* Computer language, dissertation required, foreign language not required. *Average time to degree:* doctorate–4 years full-time, 5 years part-time. *Entrance requirements:* GMAT (minimum score 600; average 650). Application deadline: 3/1. Application fee: $30 ($50 for international students). *Expenses:* Tuition $3166 per year full-time, $176 per semester hour part-time for state residents; $10,202 per year full-time, $176 per semester hour part-time for nonresidents. Fees $202 per year full-time, $52 per year (minimum) part-time. • Michael Mount, Chair, 319-335-0927. E-mail: michael-mount@uiowa.edu. Application contact: Murray Barrick, Associate Professor, 319-335-0924. Fax: 319-335-1956. E-mail: mbarrick@uiowa.edu.

The University of Iowa, College of Business Administration, School of Management, Iowa City, IA 52242-1316. Awards MBA, JD/MBA, MBA/MA, MBA/MSN. MBA/MA offered jointly with the School of Library and Information Science and the Program in Hospital and Health Administration. MBA/MSN offered jointly with the College of Nursing. Part-time and evening/weekend programs available. Faculty: 60 full-time (12 women). Students: 181 full-time (56 women), 476 part-time (176 women). Average age 27. 762 applicants, 34% accepted. In 1997, 179 degrees awarded. *Average time to degree:* master's–2 years full-time, 5 years part-time.

Directory: Business Administration and Management—General

The University of Iowa (continued)

Entrance requirements: GMAT (average 610), TOEFL (minimum score 600; average 634). Application deadline: 4/15 (priority date; rolling processing). Application fee: $30 ($50 for international students). Electronic applications accepted. *Financial aid:* In 1997–98, 82 students received aid, including 44 fellowships (26 to first-year students) averaging $252 per month, 54 research assistantships (28 to first-year students) averaging $740 per month; teaching assistantships, Federal Work-Study, and career-related internships or fieldwork also available. Aid available to part-time students. Financial aid application deadline: 4/15; applicants required to submit FAFSA. • Gary J. Gaeth, Associate Dean, MBA Program, 800-622-4692. Application contact: Mary Spreen, Director of MBA Admissions and Financial Aid, 800-622-4692. Fax: 319-335-3604. E-mail: iowamba@uiowa.edu.

See in-depth description on page 347.

The University of Iowa, College of Business Administration, Department of Management Sciences, Doctoral Program in Management Sciences, Iowa City, IA 52242-1316. Awards PhD. Students: 9 full-time (2 women); includes 8 international. Average age 34. 36 applicants, 6% accepted. In 1997, 2 doctorates awarded. Terminal master's awarded for partial completion of doctoral program. *Degree requirements:* For doctorate, dissertation required, foreign language not required. *Average time to degree:* doctorate–4.5 years full-time. *Entrance requirements:* For doctorate, GRE General Test (minimum combined score of 1230) or GMAT (minimum score 600), minimum GPA of 3.0. Application deadline: 3/1 (rolling processing). Application fee: $30 ($50 for international students). *Expenses:* Tuition $3166 per year full-time, $176 per semester hour part-time for state residents; $10,202 per year full-time, $176 per semester hour part-time for nonresidents. Fees $202 per year full-time, $52 per year (minimum) part-time. *Financial aid:* In 1997–98, 7 students received aid, including 7 fellowships averaging $2,200 per month and totaling $107,800, research assistantships averaging $1,278 per month and totaling $6,389, teaching assistantships averaging $1,278 per month and totaling $83,325; career-related internships or fieldwork also available. Financial aid application deadline: 3/1. *Faculty research:* Information systems, operations management, quantitative methods. • Philip C. Jones, Chair, Department of Management Sciences, 319-335-3737. E-mail: philip-c-jones@uiowa.edu. Application contact: Judy Putney, Graduate Secretary, 319-335-0858. Fax: 319-335-0297. E-mail: judy-putney@uiowa.edu.

University of Judaism, Graduate School, David Lieber School of Graduate Studies, Program in Business Administration, 15600 Mulholland Drive, Bel Air, CA 90077-1599. Offers general nonprofit administration (MBA), Jewish nonprofit administration (MBA). Part-time and evening/weekend programs available. Faculty: 5 full-time (0 women), 10 part-time (4 women). Students: 17 full-time (14 women), 15 part-time (10 women). Average age 28. 11 applicants, 82% accepted. In 1997, 8 degrees awarded. *Degree requirements:* Thesis, internship required, foreign language not required. *Entrance requirements:* GMAT or GRE General Test, interview, minimum undergraduate GPA of 3.0. Application deadline: 3/31 (priority date; rolling processing; 11/1 for spring admission). Application fee: $35. *Expenses:* Tuition $13,910 per year full-time, $580 per unit part-time. Fees $465 per year. *Financial aid:* Institutional scholarships, full and partial tuition waivers, Federal Work-Study, institutionally sponsored loans, and career-related internships or fieldwork available. Financial aid application deadline: 3/2; applicants required to submit FAFSA. • Dr. Beryl Geber, Director, 310-476-9777. Application contact: Tamara Greenebaum, Dean of Admissions, 310-476-9777. Fax: 310-471-3657.

University of Kansas, School of Business, Program in Business Administration and Management, Lawrence, KS 66045. Awards MBA, JD/MBA. Students: 171 full-time (60 women), 285 part-time (90 women); includes 28 minority (6 African Americans, 14 Asian Americans, 5 Hispanics, 3 Native Americans), 30 international. In 1997, 160 degrees awarded. *Entrance requirements:* GMAT. Application deadline: 5/1 (priority date; rolling processing). Application fee: $50. *Expenses:* Tuition $2400 per year full-time, $100 per credit hour part-time for state residents; $7890 per year full-time, $329 per credit hour part-time for nonresidents. Fees $428 per year full-time, $31 per credit hour part-time. • Barry Baysinger, Director, 785-864-7596.

See in-depth description on page 349.

University of Kentucky, Graduate School Programs from the College of Business and Economics, Program in Business Administration, Lexington, KY 40506-0032. Awards MBA, PhD. Faculty: 39 full-time (6 women). Students: 204 full-time (69 women), 114 part-time (42 women); includes 38 minority (26 African Americans, 9 Asian Americans, 1 Hispanic, 2 Native Americans), 56 international. 384 applicants, 46% accepted. In 1997, 95 master's, 15 doctorates awarded. *Degree requirements:* For master's, comprehensive exam required, foreign language and thesis not required; for doctorate, dissertation, comprehensive exam required, foreign language not required. *Entrance requirements:* For master's, GMAT, minimum undergraduate GPA of 2.5; for doctorate, GMAT, minimum graduate GPA of 3.0. Application deadline: 7/19 (rolling processing; 12/5 for spring admission). Application fee: $30 ($35 for international students). *Financial aid:* In 1997–98, 24 fellowships, 22 teaching assistantships were awarded; research assistantships, Federal Work-Study, institutionally sponsored loans also available. Aid available to part-time students. Financial aid application deadline: 3/15. *Faculty research:* Expert systems in manufacturing, knowledge acquisition and management, financial institutions, market in service organizations, strategic planning. Total annual research expenditures: $75,000. • Dr. Michael G. Tearney, Associate Dean for Academic Affairs, 606-257-1876. Fax: 606-257-3654. E-mail: tearny@ukcc.uky.edu. Application contact: Dr. Constance L. Wood, Associate Dean, 606-257-4613. Fax: 606-323-1928.

See in-depth description on page 351.

University of La Verne, School of Business and Economics, La Verne, CA 91750-4443. Offers programs in business administration (MBA), business organizational management (MS), operations management (MS). Part-time and evening/weekend programs available. *Entrance requirements:* GMAT (minimum score 450), TOEFL (minimum score 550), minimum GPA of 3.0. Application fee: $25. *Expenses:* Tuition $335 per unit. Fees $60 per year.

University of Louisville, College of Business and Public Administration, School of Business, Louisville, KY 40292-0001. Awards MBA, JD/MBA. Faculty: 40 full-time (4 women), 6 part-time (0 women), 42 FTE. Students: 168 full-time (66 women), 351 part-time (142 women); includes 45 minority (18 African Americans, 22 Asian Americans, 5 Hispanics), 105 international. Average age 31. In 1997, 183 degrees awarded. *Entrance requirements:* GMAT, TOEFL. Application deadline: rolling. Application fee: $25. • Dr. Robert L. Taylor, Dean, College of Business and Public Administration, 508-852-6443.

University of Maine, College of Business, Public Policy and Health, The Maine Business School, Orono, ME 04469. Awards MBA. Part-time and evening/weekend programs available. Faculty: 16 full-time. Students: 72 (20 women). Average age 31. 86 applicants, 71% accepted. In 1997, 30 degrees awarded. *Degree requirements:* Computer language required, foreign language and thesis not required. *Entrance requirements:* GMAT, TOEFL (minimum score 550). Application deadline: 2/1 (priority date; rolling processing; 10/15 for spring admission). Application fee: $50. *Expenses:* Tuition $194 per credit hour for state residents; $548 per credit hour for nonresidents. Fees $378 per year full-time, $33 per semester (minimum) part-time. *Financial aid:* In 1997–98, 7 research assistantships (5 to first-year students) were awarded; full and partial tuition waivers, Federal Work-Study, institutionally sponsored loans also available. Financial aid application deadline: 3/1. *Faculty research:* Human resource management, investment management, international markets, decision support systems, strategic planning. • Application contact: Scott Delcourt, Director of the Graduate School, 207-581-3218. Fax: 207-581-3232. E-mail: graduate@maine.edu.

See in-depth description on page 353.

University of Manitoba, Faculty of Management, Winnipeg, MB R3T 2N2, Canada. Awards MA, MBA, M Sc. *Degree requirements:* Thesis or alternative.

University of Mary, Program in Management, 7500 University Drive, Bismarck, ND 58504-9652. Awards M Mgmt. Part-time and evening/weekend programs available. Faculty: 8 full-time (3 women), 70 part-time (35 women). Students: 75 full-time (30 women), 31 part-time (13 women); includes 3 minority (all Native Americans). In 1997, 30 degrees awarded (100% found work related to degree). *Entrance requirements:* GRE General Test (minimum combined score of 1200), minimum GPA of 2.75. Application deadline: 8/15 (rolling processing). Application fee: $15. *Tuition:* $265 per credit. *Financial aid:* Career-related internships or fieldwork available. Aid available to part-time students. Financial aid application deadline: 8/1; applicants required to submit FAFSA. • Lawrence P. Brown, Director, 701-255-7500. Application contact: Dr. Diane Fladeland, Director, Graduate Programs, 701-255-7500. Fax: 701-255-7687.

University of Mary Hardin–Baylor, School of Business, Belton, TX 76513. Awards MBA. Part-time and evening/weekend programs available. Faculty: 7 full-time (1 woman), 1 part-time (0 women). Students: 7 full-time (4 women), 19 part-time (10 women). Average age 33. 7 applicants, 100% accepted. In 1997, 13 degrees awarded (100% found work related to degree). *Degree requirements:* Computer language required, foreign language and thesis not required. *Average time to degree:* master's–1 year full-time, 2 years part-time. *Entrance requirements:* GMAT (average 498), minimum GPA of 2.5. Application deadline: 8/1 (priority date; rolling processing; 1/2 for spring admission). Application fee: $35. *Expenses:* Tuition $270 per semester hour. Fees $15 per semester hour. *Financial aid:* Available to part-time students. Financial aid application deadline: 6/1. • Dr. Lee E. Baldwin, Dean, 254-295-4644. Fax: 254-295-4535. E-mail: lbaldwin@umhb.edu.

University of Maryland, College Park, Joint Program in Business and Management/Public Management, College Park, MD 20742-5045. Awards MBA/MPM. Students: 3 full-time (2 women), 5 part-time (2 women); includes 1 international. 9 applicants, 22% accepted. *Application deadline:* rolling. *Application fee:* $50 ($70 for international students). *Expenses:* Tuition $272 per credit hour for state residents; $400 per credit hour for nonresidents. Fees $564 per year full-time, $342 per year part-time. *Financial aid:* Fellowships, research assistantships, teaching assistantships available. • Application contact: John Mollish, Director, Graduate Admissions and Records, 301-405-4198. Fax: 301-314-9305.

University of Maryland, College Park, Robert H. Smith School of Business, College Park, MD 20742-5045. Awards MBA, MS, DBA, PhD, JD/MBA, MBA/MPM. Part-time and evening/weekend programs available. Postbaccalaureate distance learning degree programs offered. Faculty: 79 full-time (14 women), 32 part-time (5 women). Students: 549 full-time (195 women), 444 part-time (160 women); includes 128 minority (39 African Americans, 68 Asian Americans, 21 Hispanics), 242 international. 2,062 applicants, 28% accepted. In 1997, 258 master's, 13 doctorates awarded. *Degree requirements:* For doctorate, variable foreign language requirement, dissertation. *Entrance requirements:* For master's, GMAT, minimum GPA of 3.0; for doctorate, GMAT. Application deadline: rolling. Application fee: $50 ($70 for international students). *Expenses:* Tuition $272 per credit hour for state residents; $400 per credit hour for nonresidents. Fees $564 per year full-time, $342 per year part-time. *Financial aid:* In 1997–98, 27 fellowships, 1 research assistantship, 178 teaching assistantships were awarded. *Faculty research:* Marketing, organizational behavior and industrial relations, business and public policy, finance, accounting. • Dr. Howard Frank, Dean, 301-405-2308. Fax: 301-314-9120. Application contact: John Mollish, Director, Graduate Admissions and Records, 301-405-4198. Fax: 301-314-9305.

See in-depth description on page 355.

University of Maryland, College Park, Robert H. Smith School of Business, Program in Business Management/Law, College Park, MD 20742-5045. Awards JD/MBA. Offered jointly with the University of Maryland, Baltimore. Students: 4 full-time (2 women), 2 part-time (0 women); includes 1 minority (African American), 2 international. 16 applicants, 56% accepted. *Application deadline:* rolling. *Application fee:* $50 ($70 for international students). *Expenses:* Tuition $272 per credit hour for state residents; $400 per credit hour for nonresidents. Fees $564 per year full-time, $342 per year part-time. *Financial aid:* In 1997–98, 1 fellowship was awarded. • Dr. Mark Wellman, Assistant Dean, Graduate Programs, 301-405-2028. Application contact: John Mollish, Director, Graduate Admissions and Records, 301-405-4198. Fax: 301-314-9305.

University of Maryland University College, Graduate School of Management and Technology, College Park, MD 20742-1600. Awards Exec MGA, Exec MIM, Exec MS, MGA, MIM, MS, M Sw E, Senior Exec MGA. Offered evenings and weekends only. Part-time and evening/weekend programs available. Postbaccalaureate distance learning degree programs offered (no on-campus study). Faculty: 121 part-time (15 women), 40 FTE. Students: 233 full-time (124 women), 3,308 part-time (1,594 women); includes 1,350 minority (970 African Americans, 267 Asian Americans, 107 Hispanics, 6 Native Americans), 156 international. Average age 36. 900 applicants, 97% accepted. In 1997, 732 degrees awarded. *Application deadline:* rolling. *Application fee:* $50. Electronic applications accepted. *Tuition:* $277 per semester hour for state residents; $367 per semester hour for nonresidents. *Financial aid:* Grants, scholarships, Federal Work-Study available. Aid available to part-time students. Financial aid application deadline: 5/1; applicants required to submit FAFSA. • Nicholas H. Allen, Dean, 301-985-7040. Fax: 301-985-4611. Application contact: Director of Graduate Admissions, 301-985-7155. Fax: 301-985-7175. E-mail: gradschool@europa.umuc.edu.

See in-depth description on page 357.

University of Massachusetts Amherst, School of Management, Program in Management, Amherst, MA 01003-0001. Awards MBA, MS, PhD. Students: 88 full-time (34 women), 36 part-time (16 women); includes 8 minority (2 African Americans, 4 Asian Americans, 2 Hispanics), 45 international. Average age 31. 408 applicants, 20% accepted. In 1997, 41 master's, 3 doctorates awarded. *Degree requirements:* For doctorate, dissertation, oral and written exams required, foreign language not required. *Entrance requirements:* GMAT, minimum GPA of 3.0. Application deadline: 3/1 (priority date; rolling processing). Application fee: $40. *Expenses:* Tuition $2640 per year full-time, $110 per credit part-time for state residents; $3690 per year (minimum) full-time, $165 per credit (minimum) part-time for nonresidents. Fees $2856 per year full-time, $422 per semester part-time for state residents; $3204 per year full-time, $480 per semester part-time for nonresidents. *Financial aid:* Fellowships, research assistantships, teaching assistantships, Federal Work-Study available. Aid available to part-time students. Financial aid application deadline: 3/1. • Ronald Karren, Director, 413-545-5659.

University of Massachusetts Amherst, School of Management, Program in Professional Master's of Business Administration, Amherst, MA 01003-0001. Awards PMBA. Students: 8 full-time (1 woman), 224 part-time (103 women); includes 9 minority (1 African American, 6 Asian Americans, 2 Hispanics). Average age 35. 84 applicants, 100% accepted. In 1997, 50 degrees awarded. *Entrance requirements:* GMAT, minimum GPA of 3.0. Application deadline: 3/1 (priority date; rolling processing). Application fee: $40. *Expenses:* Tuition $2640 per year full-time, $110 per credit part-time for state residents; $3690 per year (minimum) full-time, $165 per credit (minimum) part-time for nonresidents. Fees $2856 per year full-time, $422 per semester part-time for state residents; $3204 per year full-time, $480 per semester part-time for nonresidents. *Financial aid:* Federal Work-Study available. Aid available to part-time students. Financial aid application deadline: 3/1. • Steven Demski, Director, 413-545-5652.

University of Massachusetts Boston, College of Management, Program in Business Administration, Boston, MA 02125-3393. Awards MBA, MS/MBA. Students: 68 full-time (40 women), 296 part-time (117 women); includes 43 minority (12 African Americans, 25 Asian Americans, 6 Hispanics), 43 international. 316 applicants, 48% accepted. In 1997, 56 degrees awarded. *Entrance requirements:* GMAT, minimum GPA of 3.0. Application deadline: 3/1 (priority date; 11/1 for spring admission). Application fee: $25 ($35 for international students). *Expenses:* Tuition $2640 per year full-time, $110 per credit part-time for state residents; $8930 per year full-time, $373 per credit part-time for nonresidents. Fees $2650 per year full-time, $420 per semester (minimum) part-time for state residents; $2736 per year full-time, $420 per semester (minimum) part-time for nonresidents. *Financial aid:* In 1997–98, 9 research assistantships (2 to first-year students) averaging $225 per month and totaling $18,000, 2 teaching assistantships (both to first-year students) averaging $225 per month and totaling $4,000 were awarded; administrative assistantships also available. Financial aid application deadline: 3/1; applicants required to submit FAFSA. • Daniel Robb, Acting Director, 617-287-7720. Application contact: Lisa Lavely, Director of Graduate Admissions and Records, 617-287-6400. Fax: 617-287-6236.

University of Massachusetts Dartmouth, Graduate School, College of Business and Industry, Program in Business Administration, North Dartmouth, MA 02747-2300. Awards MBA. Part-time programs available. Faculty: 14 full-time (5 women). Students: 29 full-time (12 women), 51 part-time (32 women); includes 1 Asian American, 25 international. 78 applicants, 77% accepted. In 1997, 33 degrees awarded. *Entrance requirements:* GMAT (minimum score 450), TOEFL. Application deadline: 6/1 (priority date; rolling processing; 10/1 for spring admission). Application fee: $40. *Expenses:* Tuition $2950 per year full-time, $82 per credit part-time for state residents; $10,249 per year full-time, $285 per credit part-time for nonresidents. Fees $5002 per year full-time, $143 per credit part-time for state residents; $6830 per year full-time, $194 per credit part-time for nonresidents. *Financial aid:* In 1997–98, 1 research assistantship totaling $1,680, 1 teaching assistantship totaling $2,800, 9 graduate assistantships totaling $39,000 were awarded; Federal Work-Study also available. Aid available to part-time students. Financial aid application deadline: 3/15; applicants required to submit FAFSA. *Faculty research:* Accounting in Third World, corporate culture, operational research applications, microcomputers in marketing. • Dr. Omar Khalil, Director, 508-999-8443. Application contact: Carol A. Novo, Graduate Admissions Office, 508-999-8604. Fax: 508-999-8375. E-mail: graduate@umassd.edu.

University of Massachusetts Lowell, College of Management, Program in Business Administration, 1 University Avenue, Lowell, MA 01854-2881. Awards MBA. Part-time and evening/weekend programs available. Students: 45 full-time (18 women), 198 part-time (52 women); includes 25 minority (5 African Americans, 17 Asian Americans, 2 Hispanics, 1 Native American), 24 international. 181 applicants, 69% accepted. In 1997, 31 degrees awarded. *Degree requirements:* Computer language required, foreign language and thesis not required. *Entrance requirements:* GMAT. Application deadline: 4/1 (priority date; rolling processing; 10/1 for spring admission). Application fee: $20 ($35 for international students). *Tuition:* $4867 per year full-time, $618 per semester (minimum) part-time for state residents; $10,276 per year full-time, $1294 per semester (minimum) part-time for nonresidents. *Financial aid:* Fellowships, teaching assistantships, Federal Work-Study, institutionally sponsored loans, and career-related internships or fieldwork available. Aid available to part-time students. Financial aid application deadline: 4/1. • Application contact: Dr. Norma Powell, Coordinator, 978-934-2848. E-mail: norma_powell@woods.uml.edu.

The University of Memphis, Fogelman College of Business and Economics, Program in Business Administration, Memphis, TN 38152. Awards MBA, MS, PhD, JD/MBA. Offerings include accounting (MBA, PhD); economics (MBA, PhD); executive business administration (MBA); finance (PhD); finance, insurance, and real estate (MBA, MS); international business administration (MBA); management (MBA, MS, PhD); management information systems (MBA, MS); management information systems and decision sciences (PhD); management science (MBA); marketing (MBA, MS, PhD); real estate development (MS). Faculty: 92 full-time (15 women), 2 part-time (0 women). Students: 374 full-time (115 women), 330 part-time (109 women); includes 89 minority (70 African Americans, 14 Asian Americans, 5 Hispanics), 176 international. Average age 31. 619 applicants, 54% accepted. In 1997, 194 master's, 19 doctorates awarded. *Degree requirements:* For master's, comprehensive exams required, thesis not required; for doctorate, dissertation, comprehensive exams. *Entrance requirements:* For master's, GMAT (minimum score 430; average 535), GRE General Test; for doctorate, GMAT (average 633), interview, minimum GPA of 3.4. Application deadline: 8/1 (12/1 for spring admission). Application fee: $25 ($50 for international students). *Tuition:* $2862 per year full-time, $166 per credit hour part-time for state residents; $6696 per year full-time, $379 per credit hour part-time for nonresidents. *Financial aid:* In 1997–98, 180 students received aid, including 92 research assistantships totaling $295,000, 50 teaching assistantships totaling $225,000, 30 service assistantships totaling $100,000; career-related internships or fieldwork also available. *Faculty research:* Government contracts and tax policy, medical economics, interest rates and monetary policy, mergers, econometrics. • Application contact: Dr. Ravinder Nath, Associate Dean of Academic Programs, 901-678-3721. Fax: 901-678-4705. E-mail: fcbegp@memphis.edu.

See in-depth description on page 359.

University of Miami, School of Business Administration, Coral Gables, FL 33124. Awards Exec MBA, MA, MBA, MIBS, MPA, MP Acc, MS, MS Tax, PhD, Certificate, JD/MBA, MBA/MSIE, MPA/MPH. Part-time and evening/weekend programs available. Faculty: 53 full-time (8 women), 3 part-time (0 women). Students: 304 full-time (112 women), 101 part-time (44 women); includes 133 international. Average age 26. 749 applicants, 36% accepted. In 1997, 250 master's awarded. Terminal master's awarded for partial completion of doctoral program. *Degree requirements:* For doctorate, dissertation required, foreign language not required. *Entrance requirements:* For master's and Certificate, TOEFL (minimum score 550); for doctorate, GRE General Test (minimum combined score of 1100), TOEFL (minimum score 550), minimum GPA of 3.1. Application deadline: 6/30 (priority date; rolling processing). Application fee: $35. *Expenses:* Tuition $815 per credit hour. Fees $174 per year. *Financial aid:* Fellowships, research assistantships, teaching assistantships, partial tuition waivers, Federal Work-Study, institutionally sponsored loans, and career-related internships or fieldwork available. Aid available to part-time students. Financial aid application deadline: 3/1. *Faculty research:* Calculating efficiency of multinational operations, efficiency and effectiveness of retail locations, evolution of contractual intent. • Dr. Harold W. Berkman, Vice Dean, 305-284-2510. Fax: 305-284-5905. Application contact: Dierdre Lacativa, Director of Admissions, 305-284-4607. Fax: 305-284-1878.

See in-depth description on page 361.

University of Michigan, School of Business Administration, Doctoral Program in Business Administration, Ann Arbor, MI 48109. Awards PhD. Offered through the Horace H. Rackham School of Graduate Studies. Students: 73 full-time (24 women); includes 8 minority (5 African Americans, 2 Asian Americans, 1 Hispanic), 30 international. 368 applicants, 9% accepted. In 1997, 16 degrees awarded (100% entered university research/teaching). *Degree requirements:* Dissertation, oral defense of dissertation, preliminary exam required, foreign language not required. *Average time to degree:* doctorate–5 years full-time. *Application deadline:* 1/15. *Application fee:* $55. • Dr. Gautam Kaul, Associate Dean, 734-764-2343. Fax: 734-647-2133. E-mail: umbusphd@umich.edu. Application contact: Martha Boron, Assistant Director, 734-764-2343. Fax: 734-647-8133. E-mail: umbusphd@umich.edu.

University of Michigan, School of Business Administration, Program in Business Administration, Ann Arbor, MI 48109. Awards MBA, JD/MBA, MBA/M Arch, MBA/M Eng, MBA/MS, MBA/AM, MBA/MM, MBA/MPP, MBA/MSE, MHSA/MBA, MLA/MBA, MSW/MBA. Students: 862 full-time (221 women), 1,055 part-time (241 women); includes 350 minority (89 African Americans, 191 Asian Americans, 65 Hispanics, 5 Native Americans), 403 international. Average age 27. 4,150 applicants, 22% accepted. *Entrance requirements:* GMAT. Application deadline: 12/1. Application fee: $100. *Financial aid:* 500 students received aid; full and partial tuition waivers, Federal Work-Study, institutionally sponsored loans, and career-related internships or fieldwork available. Aid available to part-time students. Financial aid application deadline: 3/15; applicants required to submit FAFSA. • Jeanne Wilt, Director, 734-763-5796. Application contact: Admissions and Student Services, 734-763-5796. Fax: 734-763-7804. E-mail: umbusmba@umich.edu.

University of Michigan–Dearborn, School of Management, 4901 Evergreen Road, Dearborn, MI 48128-1491. Awards MBA, MBA/MSE. Part-time and evening/weekend programs available. Faculty: 29 full-time (7 women), 1 part-time (0 women). Students: 15 full-time (6 women), 336 part-time (77 women); includes 51 minority (7 African Americans, 37 Asian Americans, 7 Hispanics). Average age 31. 160 applicants, 71% accepted. In 1997, 47 degrees awarded. *Average time to degree:* master's–2 years full-time, 4 years part-time. *Entrance requirements:* GMAT (average 555), previous course work in calculus, computer applications. Application deadline: 8/1 (priority date; rolling processing; 4/1 for spring admission). Application fee: $55. *Expenses:* Tuition $4536 per year full-time, $252 per credit hour part-time for state residents; $13,086 per year full-time, $727 per credit hour part-time for nonresidents. Fees $480 per year (minimum). *Financial aid:* Federal Work-Study and career-related internships or fieldwork available. *Faculty research:* Entrepreneurship, cultural diversity, buyer-supplier relations, error detection in data, economic evolution of the Asia Pacific region. • Dr. Eric Brucker, Dean, 313-593-5248. E-mail: ebrucker@umd.umich.edu. Application contact: Julie A. Dziekan-Schueren, Director, 313-593-5248. Fax: 313-593-5636. E-mail: jdziekan@fob-f1.umd.umich.edu.

University of Michigan–Flint, School of Management, Flint, MI 48502-1950. Awards MBA. Part-time and evening/weekend programs available. Postbaccalaureate distance learning degree programs offered (minimal on-campus study). Faculty: 15 full-time (2 women), 9 part-time (1 woman). Students: 267 part-time (95 women); includes 38 minority (19 African Americans, 9 Asian Americans, 5 Hispanics, 5 Native Americans). Average age 30. 65 applicants, 89% accepted. In 1997, 94 degrees awarded. *Average time to degree:* master's–2.8 years part-time. *Entrance requirements:* GMAT (average 530), 1 semester of calculus or finite mathematics. Application deadline: 7/1 (priority date; rolling processing). Application fee: $20. *Financial aid:* 25 students received aid; research assistantships, scholarships, Federal Work-Study available. Aid available to part-time students. Financial aid application deadline: 4/1. *Faculty research:* Forecasting, financial reporting, continuous quality improvement, industrial/international marketing, mergers and acquisitions. • Dr. Rod McGraw, Interim Dean, 810-762-3160. Fax: 810-762-3282. E-mail: mcgraw_r@crob.flint.umich.edu. Application contact: Kathleen L. Gasper, Coordinator, 810-762-3163. Fax: 810-762-0736. E-mail: gasper_k@crob.flint.umich.edu.

University of Minnesota, Duluth, Graduate School, School of Business and Economics, Department of Business Administration, Duluth, MN 55812-2496. Awards MBA. Part-time programs available. Faculty: 33 full-time (6 women). Students: 4 full-time (3 women), 48 part-time (19 women). Average age 30. 10 applicants, 80% accepted. In 1997, 15 degrees awarded (100% found work related to degree). *Average time to degree:* master's–2.5 years full-time, 4.5 years part-time. *Entrance requirements:* GMAT (minimum score 500; average 550), minimum GPA of 3.0; previous course work in accounting, business administration, and economics. Application deadline: 7/15 (rolling processing; 10/1 for spring admission). Application fee: $40 ($50 for international students). *Financial aid:* In 1997–98, 14 students received aid, including 14 fellowships (4 to first-year students) totaling $9,800; Federal Work-Study, institutionally sponsored loans, and career-related internships or fieldwork also available. Aid available to part-time students. Financial aid applicants required to submit FAFSA. *Faculty research:* Regional economic analysis, marketing, management, human resources, organizational behavior. • Dr. Thomas B. Duff, Director of Graduate Studies, 218-726-8759. Fax: 218-726-6338.

University of Minnesota, Twin Cities Campus, Carlson School of Management, Minneapolis, MN 55455-0213. Awards MA, MBA, MBT, MHA, MS, MSMOT, PhD, MHA/MBA. Part-time and evening/weekend programs available. Terminal master's awarded for partial completion of doctoral program. *Degree requirements:* For doctorate, dissertation required, foreign language not required. *Faculty research:* Management information systems, operations management, decision sciences, marketing.

Announcement: Admission is based on potential for research and teaching and commitment to a career based on the PhD degree. Students in the doctoral program represent a wide range of undergraduate and graduate disciplines. A combination of fellowships and teaching and research assistantships provide a minimum of 4 years of funding to all matriculants. Applications should be submitted by mid-January.

University of Mississippi, Graduate School, School of Business Administration, Program in Business Administration, University, MS 38677-9702. Awards MBA, JD/MBA. Faculty: 26 full-time (7 women). Students: 88 full-time (25 women), 17 part-time (2 women); includes 12 minority (7 African Americans, 3 Asian Americans, 1 Hispanic, 1 Native American), 46 international. In 1997, 70 degrees awarded. *Entrance requirements:* GMAT, TOEFL, minimum GPA of 3.0. Application deadline: 8/1 (rolling processing). Application fee: $0 ($25 for international students). *Financial aid:* Fellowships, assistantships available. Financial aid application deadline: 3/1. • Dr. Randy Boxx, Dean, School of Business Administration, 601-232-5820.

Announcement: John N. Palmer Fellowships ($4000) and Assistantships ($3000) are available for a limited number of qualified students who have excelled in undergraduate work. Minority fellowships are offered to qualified members of minority groups. Both provide a waiver of tuition charges. Contact the Program Director for additional information or visit the Web site (http://www.bus.olemiss.edu).

University of Missouri–Columbia, College of Business and Public Administration, School of Business, Columbia, MO 65211. Awards MBA, PhD. Faculty: 37 full-time (5 women). Students: 102 full-time (27 women), 40 part-time (17 women); includes 7 minority (5 African Americans, 1 Asian American, 1 Native American), 36 international. In 1997, 39 master's, 2 doctorates awarded. *Degree requirements:* For doctorate, dissertation required, foreign language not required. *Entrance requirements:* For master's, GMAT, minimum GPA of 3.0; for doctorate, minimum GPA of 3.0. Application deadline: rolling. Application fee: $25 ($50 for international students). *Expenses:* Tuition $3240 per year full-time, $180 per credit hour part-time for state residents; $9108 per year full-time, $506 per credit hour part-time for nonresidents. Fees $55 per year full-time. • Dr. Lori Franz, Director of Graduate Studies, 573-882-2750.

See in-depth description on page 363.

University of Missouri–Kansas City, School of Business and Public Administration, Division of Business Administration, Kansas City, MO 64110-2499. Awards MBA, JD/MBA. Part-time and evening/weekend programs available. Faculty: 25 full-time (4 women), 6 part-time (1 woman). Students: 139 full-time (52 women), 302 part-time (137 women); includes 36 minority (15 African Americans, 13 Asian Americans, 7 Hispanics, 1 Native American), 93 international. Average age 31. 377 applicants, 56% accepted. In 1997, 143 degrees awarded. *Entrance requirements:* GMAT (minimum score 500; average 550). Application deadline: 5/1 (priority date; 10/1 for spring admission). Application fee: $25. *Expenses:* Tuition $182 per credit hour for state residents; $508 per credit hour for nonresidents. Fees $60 per year. *Financial aid:* Fellowships, research assistantships, teaching assistantships, full and partial tuition waivers, Federal Work-Study, institutionally sponsored loans, and career-related internships or fieldwork available. Aid available to part-time students. Financial aid applicants required to submit FAFSA. *Faculty research:* Strategy, leadership, human resources, quality, finance. Total annual research expenditures: $45,000. • Dr. George Pinches, Director, 816-235-2334. Application contact: Admissions Office, 816-235-1111.

University of Missouri–St. Louis, School of Business Administration, Program in Business Administration, St. Louis, MO 63121-4499. Offers accounting (MBA), finance (MBA), management information science (MBA), marketing (MBA), organizational behavior (MBA), quantitative management science (MBA). Part-time and evening/weekend programs available. Faculty: 19 (3 women). Students: 42 full-time (14 women), 221 part-time (93 women); includes 27 minority (15 African Americans, 7 Asian Americans, 4 Hispanics, 1 Native American), 13 international. 160 applicants, 63% accepted. In 1997, 49 degrees awarded. *Entrance requirements:* GMAT (minimum score 500; average 554). Application deadline: 7/1 (rolling processing; 11/1 for spring admission). Application fee: $0. Electronic applications accepted. *Expenses:* Tuition $3903 per year full-time, $167 per credit hour part-time for state residents; $11,745 per year full-time, $489 per credit hour part-time for nonresidents. Fees $816 per year

Directory: Business Administration and Management—General

University of Missouri–St. Louis (continued)
full-time, $34 per credit hour part-time. *Financial aid:* In 1997–98, 11 research assistantships, 2 teaching assistantships were awarded; Federal Work-Study, institutionally sponsored loans, and career-related internships or fieldwork also available. Aid available to part-time students. Financial aid application deadline: 4/1; applicants required to submit FAFSA. *Faculty research:* Human resources, strategic management, marketing strategy, consumer behavior product development, advertising, international marketing. • Application contact: Graduate Admissions, 314-516-5458. Fax: 314-516-6759. E-mail: gradadm@umslvma.umsl.edu.

University of Mobile, Graduate Programs, Program in Business Administration, Mobile, AL 36663-0220. Awards MBA. Part-time and evening/weekend programs available. Faculty: 10 full-time (5 women), 4 part-time (0 women). Students: 6 full-time (1 woman), 54 part-time (27 women); includes 18 minority (14 African Americans, 1 Asian American, 3 Hispanics). Average age 32. 37 applicants, 51% accepted. In 1997, 12 degrees awarded (100% found work related to degree). *Degree requirements:* Comprehensive exams. *Average time to degree:* master's–1 year full-time, 2 years part-time. *Entrance requirements:* GMAT (minimum score 400), TOEFL (minimum score 550). Application deadline: 8/3 (priority date; rolling processing; 12/23 for spring admission). Application fee: $30. *Tuition:* $160 per semester hour. *Financial aid:* Federal Work-Study available. Aid available to part-time students. Financial aid application deadline: 8/1. *Faculty research:* Management, personnel management, small business, diversity. • Dr. Anne B. Lowery, Dean, School of Business, 334-675-5990 Ext. 219. E-mail: lowerys@gulftel.com. Application contact: Kaye F. Brown, Dean, Graduate and Special Programs, 334-675-5990 Ext. 270. Fax: 334-675-9816.

The University of Montana–Missoula, School of Business Administration, Program in Business Administration, Missoula, MT 59812-0002. Awards MBA. Students: 53 full-time (22 women), 78 part-time (43 women). Average age 30. In 1997, 72 degrees awarded. *Degree requirements:* Thesis optional, foreign language not required. *Entrance requirements:* GMAT (average 580), TOEFL (minimum score 580). Application deadline: 3/1 (priority date; 9/1 for spring admission). Application fee: $30. *Tuition:* $2499 per year (minimum) full-time, $376 per semester (minimum) part-time for state residents; $6528 per year (minimum) full-time, $1048 per semester (minimum) part-time for nonresidents. *Financial aid:* Application deadline 3/1. • Application contact: Dr. Teresa K. Beed, Director of Graduate Programs, 406-243-4983. Fax: 406-243-2086.

See in-depth description on page 365.

University of Nebraska at Kearney, College of Business and Technology, Department of Business, Kearney, NE 68849-0001. Offers program in business administration (MBA). Part-time and evening/weekend programs available. Faculty: 17 full-time (3 women). Students: 11 full-time (2 women), 63 part-time (32 women); includes 9 international. In 1997, 19 degrees awarded. *Degree requirements:* Thesis optional. *Entrance requirements:* GMAT. Application deadline: 8/1 (priority date; rolling processing; 12/15 for spring admission). Application fee: $35. *Expenses:* Tuition $1494 per year full-time, $83 per credit hour part-time for state residents; $2826 per year full-time, $157 per credit hour part-time for nonresidents. Fees $229 per year full-time, $11.25 per semester (minimum) part-time. *Financial aid:* In 1997–98, 5 research assistantships, 3 teaching assistantships were awarded; career-related internships or fieldwork also available. Aid available to part-time students. Financial aid application deadline: 3/1; applicants required to submit FAFSA. • Bruce Elder, Director, 308-865-8346.

University of Nebraska at Omaha, College of Business Administration, Department of Business Administration, Omaha, NE 68182. Awards MBA. Part-time programs available. Faculty: 22 full-time (4 women). Students: 34 full-time (15 women), 281 part-time (115 women); includes 30 minority (4 African Americans, 20 Asian Americans, 5 Hispanics, 1 Native American), 16 international. Average age 34. 176 applicants, 55% accepted. In 1997, 112 degrees awarded. *Degree requirements:* Capstone Course, comprehensive exam required, foreign language and thesis not required. *Entrance requirements:* GMAT (minimum score 450), minimum AACSB index of 1040, minimum GPA of 3.0. Application deadline: 7/1 (priority date; rolling processing; 12/1 for spring admission). Application fee: $35. *Expenses:* Tuition $1670 per year full-time, $94 per credit hour part-time for state residents; $4082 per year full-time, $227 per credit hour part-time for nonresidents. Fees $302 per year full-time, $108 per semester (minimum) part-time. *Financial aid:* 47 students received aid; research assistantships, full tuition waivers, institutionally sponsored loans available. Aid available to part-time students. Financial aid application deadline: 3/1; applicants required to submit FAFSA. • Application contact: Lex Kaczmarek, Adviser, 402-554-2303.

Announcement: The University of Nebraska at Omaha offers a dynamic, challenging MBA program designed to help students acquire the knowledge, perspective, and skills necessary for success in the marketplace. The goal of the program is to develop leaders who have the ability to incorporate change, use information technology to resolve problems, and make sound business decisions. The MBA program received 2 prestigious Exxon Awards for innovative programming and was nationally recognized for excellence in computing resources. The curriculum contains a unique blend of theory, experience, and application. It focuses on results, with an emphasis on how to excel in a rapidly changing world. Through a team-oriented approach and interaction with area businesses, students learn to think on their feet and recognize challenges and opportunities.

University of Nebraska–Lincoln, College of Business Administration, Interdepartmental Area of Business, Lincoln, NE 68588. Awards MA, MBA, PhD, JD/MA, JD/MBA, M Arch/MBA. Programs in accountancy (PhD); business (MBA); finance (MA, PhD), including business; management (MA, PhD), including business; marketing (MA, PhD), including business. Part-time programs available. Faculty: 26 full-time (2 women), 2 part-time (0 women), 27.05 FTE. Students: 114 full-time (30 women), 119 part-time (46 women); includes 13 minority (3 African Americans, 4 Asian Americans, 5 Hispanics, 1 Native American), 48 international. Average age 32. 190 applicants, 33% accepted. In 1997, 69 master's, 23 doctorates awarded. *Degree requirements:* For doctorate, dissertation, comprehensive exams required, foreign language not required. *Average time to degree:* doctorate–5.2 years full-time. *Entrance requirements:* For master's, GMAT, TOEFL (minimum score 500 required for MA, 550 for MBA); for doctorate, GMAT, TOEFL (minimum score 500). Application deadline: 5/15 (10/15 for spring admission). Application fee: $35. Electronic applications accepted. *Expenses:* Tuition $110 per credit hour for state residents; $270 per credit hour for nonresidents. Fees $480 per year full-time, $110 per semester part-time. *Financial aid:* In 1997–98, 14 fellowships totaling $55,800 were awarded; research assistantships, teaching assistantships, Federal Work-Study also available. Aid available to part-time students. Financial aid application deadline: 2/15. *Total annual research expenditures:* $2115. • Dr. Gordon Karels, Graduate Committee Chair, 402-472-9500. Fax: 402-472-5180. E-mail: gradadv@cbamail.unl.edu.

University of Nevada, Las Vegas, College of Business, Program in Business Administration, Las Vegas, NV 89154-9900. Awards MBA. Part-time and evening/weekend programs available. Faculty: 43 full-time (3 women). Students: 65 full-time (26 women), 152 part-time (52 women); includes 21 minority (4 African Americans, 10 Asian Americans, 7 Hispanics), 30 international. 150 applicants, 73% accepted. In 1997, 56 degrees awarded. *Entrance requirements:* GMAT, minimum GPA of 2.75. Application deadline: 6/1 (11/15 for spring admission). Application fee: $40 ($95 for international students). *Expenses:* Tuition $93 per credit for state residents; $93 per credit full-time, $190 per credit part-time for nonresidents. Fees $5570 per year full-time for nonresidents. *Financial aid:* In 1997–98, 3 research assistantships, 12 teaching assistantships were awarded. Financial aid application deadline: 3/1. • Dr. Nassar Daneshvary, Interim Director, 702-895-3655. Application contact: Graduate College Admissions Evaluator, 702-895-3320.

University of Nevada, Reno, College of Business Administration, Department of Business Administration, Reno, NV 89557. Awards MBA. Part-time and evening/weekend programs available. Faculty: 13 (2 women). Students: 38 full-time (16 women), 95 part-time (38 women); includes 15 minority (13 Asian Americans, 2 Hispanics), 13 international. Average age 34. 75 applicants, 49% accepted. In 1997, 45 degrees awarded. *Degree requirements:* Thesis optional, foreign language not required. *Entrance requirements:* GMAT (minimum score 450), TOEFL (minimum score 500), minimum GPA of 2.75. Application deadline: 2/1 (priority date; rolling processing; 11/1 for spring admission). Application fee: $40. *Expenses:* Tuition $0 for state residents; $5770 per year full-time, $200 per credit part-time for nonresidents. Fees $93 per credit. *Financial aid:* Research assistantships, teaching assistantships, Federal Work-Study, institutionally sponsored loans available. Financial aid application deadline: 3/1. • Dr. Brent Bowman, Associate Dean, 702-784-4912. E-mail: bowman@unr.edu.

University of New Brunswick, Faculty of Administration, Fredericton, NB E3B 5A3, Canada. Awards MBA, MPA. Part-time programs available. *Entrance requirements:* TOEFL, TWE. Application deadline: 3/1 (priority date; rolling processing). Application fee: $25.

University of New Brunswick, Faculty of Business, Saint John, NB E2L 4L5, Canada. Offers programs in administration (MBA), international business (MBA). Part-time programs available. Faculty: 19 full-time (4 women). Students: 20 full-time (5 women), 28 part-time (9 women). In 1997, 7 degrees awarded. *Degree requirements:* Thesis optional. *Entrance requirements:* GMAT. Application deadline: 3/15. Application fee: $100. *Expenses:* Tuition $18,000 per year. Fees $50 per year full-time, $15 per year part-time. *Financial aid:* Fellowships, research assistantships, teaching assistantships, and career-related internships or fieldwork available. • Dr. John Chalykoff, Dean, 506-648-5571. Application contact: Dr. Robert Chanteloup, Associate Dean of Graduate Studies, 506-648-5673. Fax: 506-648-5528. E-mail: graduate@unbsj.ca.

University of New Hampshire, Whittemore School of Business and Economics, Program in Business Administration, Durham, NH 03824. Awards MBA. Faculty: 33 full-time. Students: 41 full-time (15 women), 63 part-time (23 women); includes 2 minority (both Asian Americans), 16 international. Average age 33. 158 applicants, 84% accepted. In 1997, 24 degrees awarded. *Entrance requirements:* GMAT. Application deadline: 7/1 (priority date; rolling processing). Application fee: $50. *Financial aid:* In 1997–98, 1 research assistantship, 23 teaching assistantships (9 to first-year students), 7 scholarships (3 to first-year students) were awarded; full and partial tuition waivers, Federal Work-Study, and career-related internships or fieldwork also available. Financial aid application deadline: 2/15. • Dr. Craig Wood, Associate Professor, 603-862-3355. Application contact: George Abraham, 603-862-1367.

See in-depth description on page 367.

University of New Hampshire, Whittemore School of Business and Economics, Program in Executive Business Administration, Durham, NH 03824. Awards MBA. Evening/weekend programs available. Students: 56 full-time (13 women); includes 1 minority (Hispanic). Average age 38. 40 applicants, 90% accepted. In 1997, 31 degrees awarded. *Entrance requirements:* GMAT. Application deadline: 7/1 (priority date; rolling processing). Application fee: $50. *Financial aid:* Scholarships available. Financial aid application deadline: 2/15. • Dr. Craig Wood, Associate Professor, 603-862-3355. Application contact: George Abraham, 603-862-1367.

See in-depth description on page 367.

University of New Haven, School of Business, Executive Program in Business Administration, West Haven, CT 06516-1916. Awards EMBA. Students: 98 part-time (28 women); includes 16 minority (10 African Americans, 3 Asian Americans, 3 Hispanics). *Application deadline:* rolling. *Application fee:* $50. *Financial aid:* Application deadline 5/1. • James E. Shapiro, Director, 203-932-7386.

University of New Haven, School of Business, Program in Business Administration, West Haven, CT 06516-1916. Awards MBA, MBA/MPA, MBA/MSIE. Offerings include accounting (MBA), business policy and strategy (MBA), computer and information science (MBA), finance (MBA), health care management (MBA), health care marketing (MBA), hotel and restaurant management (MBA), human resources management (MBA), international business logistics (MBA), management and organization (MBA), management science (MBA), marketing (MBA), operations research (MBA), public relations (MBA), telecommunications (MBA), travel and tourism administration (MBA). Part-time and evening/weekend programs available. Students: 116 full-time (52 women), 434 part-time (176 women); includes 36 minority (19 African Americans, 13 Asian Americans, 2 Hispanics, 2 Native Americans), 64 international. 167 applicants, 74% accepted. *Degree requirements:* Thesis or alternative required, foreign language not required. *Application deadline:* rolling. *Application fee:* $50. *Expenses:* Tuition $1125 per course. Fees $13 per trimester. *Financial aid:* Federal Work-Study available. Aid available to part-time students. Financial aid application deadline: 5/1. • Dr. Omid Nodoushani, Coordinator, 203-932-7123.

University of New Mexico, Robert O. Anderson Graduate School of Management, Albuquerque, NM 87131-1221. Awards EMBA, M Acc, MBA, JD/MBA, MBA/MALAS. Programs in accounting (M Acc, MBA), business administration (EMBA), financial management (MBA), general management (MBA), human resources management (MBA), international management (MBA), international management in Latin America (MBA), management information systems (MBA), management of technology (EMBA, MBA), marketing management (MBA), operations and management science (MBA), policy and planning (MBA), tax accounting (MBA). Part-time and evening/weekend programs available. Faculty: 50 full-time (11 women). Students: 461 (193 women); includes 79 minority (6 African Americans, 13 Asian Americans, 49 Hispanics, 11 Native Americans), 23 international. Average age 32. 184 applicants, 54% accepted. In 1997, 104 degrees awarded. *Degree requirements:* Computer language required, foreign language and thesis not required. *Entrance requirements:* GMAT (minimum score 540), TOEFL (minimum score 550). Application deadline: 7/1 (priority date; rolling processing; 11/15 for spring admission). Application fee: $25. *Expenses:* Tuition $2442 per year full-time, $103 per credit hour part-time for state residents; $8691 per year full-time, $103 per credit hour (minimum) part-time for nonresidents. Fees $32 per year. *Financial aid:* 45 students received aid; fellowships, research assistantships, teaching assistantships, full and partial scholarships, graduate assistantships, Federal Work-Study, and career-related internships or fieldwork available. • Howard L. Smith, Dean, 505-277-6471. Fax: 505-277-7108. Application contact: Sue Podeyn, MBA Program Director, 505-277-3147. Fax: 505-277-9356. E-mail: podeyn@unm.edu.

Announcement: Located in Albuquerque, New Mexico, the Robert O. Anderson Graduate School of Management (AGSM) offers the opportunity to live and study in the beautiful, historic, and culturally diverse Southwest. The AGSM MBA is a broad, competency-based degree. One course of study consists of a 42-credit-hour core curriculum designed to provide a solid foundation in business plus 15 credit hours of elective courses that can be applied to meet concentration requirements. Other options are available. The AGSM dual-degree MBA/MA in Latin American studies has been recognized nationally as a top program in international management. Community outreach efforts include the Management Development Center's weekend Executive MBA program, designed for working middle managers; the Small Business Institute; the Economic Development Assistance program; and the Western States School of Banking. AGSM has an active, professionally staffed Career Planning and Placement Center.

University of New Orleans, College of Business Administration, Program in Business Administration, New Orleans, LA 70148. Awards MBA. Students: 202 full-time (83 women), 471 part-time (207 women); includes 135 minority (91 African Americans, 21 Asian Americans, 22 Hispanics, 1 Native American), 141 international. Average age 31. 395 applicants, 81% accepted. In 1997, 107 degrees awarded. *Entrance requirements:* GMAT (minimum score 400). Application deadline: 7/1 (priority date; rolling processing). Application fee: $20. *Expenses:* Tuition $2362 per year full-time, $373 per semester (minimum) part-time for state residents; $7888 per year full-time, $1423 per semester (minimum) part-time for nonresidents. Fees $170 per year full-time, $25 per semester (minimum) part-time. *Financial aid:* Fellowships, research assistantships, teaching assistantships, Federal Work-Study available. • Application contact: Dr. Paul Hensel, Associate Dean, 504-280-6393. Fax: 504-280-6958. E-mail: pjhmk@uno.edu.

University of North Alabama, College of Business, Florence, AL 35632-0001. Awards MBA. Part-time and evening/weekend programs available. Faculty: 12 part-time (2 women). Students: 25 full-time (11 women), 71 part-time (35 women); includes 5 minority (3 African Americans, 2 Native Americans), 1 international. Average age 30. In 1997, 19 degrees awarded. *Degree requirements:* Computer language required, foreign language and thesis not required. *Entrance requirements:* GMAT (minimum score 450), minimum GPA of 2.75 in last 60 hours, 2.5 overall on a 3.0 scale; 27 hours in business and economics. Application deadline: 7/1 (priority date; rolling processing; 12/1 for spring admission). Application fee: $25. *Expenses:* Tuition $2448 per year full-time, $102 per credit hour part-time for state residents; $4896 per year full-time, $204 per credit hour part-time for nonresidents. Fees $3 per semester. *Financial aid:* Federal Work-Study available. Aid available to part-time students. Financial aid application deadline: 4/1. • Dr. Michael Butler, Dean, 205-765-4261. Application contact: Dr. Sue Wilson, Dean of Enrollment Management, 205-765-4316.

The University of North Carolina at Chapel Hill, Kenan-Flagler Business School, Doctoral Program in Business Administration, Chapel Hill, NC 27599. Offers accounting (PhD), business policy/strategy (PhD), finance (PhD), marketing (PhD), operations management/quantitative methods (PhD), organizational behavior (PhD). Faculty: 79 full-time (15 women), 29 part-time (6 women). Students: 58 full-time (29 women); includes 6 minority (2 African Americans, 3 Asian Americans, 1 Hispanic), 14 international. Average age 29. 320 applicants, 9% accepted. In 1997, 13 degrees awarded (100% entered university research/teaching). *Degree requirements:* Dissertation required, foreign language not required. *Average time to degree:* doctorate–4 years full-time. *Entrance requirements:* GMAT (average 657) or GRE General Test (minimum combined score of 1350). Application deadline: 1/1 (priority date; rolling processing). Application fee: $55. Electronic applications accepted. *Expenses:* Tuition $1428 per year for state residents; $10,414 per year for nonresidents. Fees $787 per year. *Financial aid:* In 1997–98, 3 fellowships (1 to a first-year student), 51 research assistantships, 7 teaching assistantships were awarded; institutionally sponsored loans also available. Financial aid application deadline: 3/1. *Faculty research:* Corporate governance, crisis management, employee stock options, initial public offerings, service leadership. • Ann Marucheck, Associate Dean for PhD Programs, 919-962-3193. Application contact: Liz Griffin, Director, 919-962-1657. E-mail: kfphd_app@unc.edu.

The University of North Carolina at Chapel Hill, Kenan-Flagler Business School, Executive MBA Program, Chapel Hill, NC 27599. Awards MBA. Evening/weekend programs available. Postbaccalaureate distance learning degree programs offered (minimal on-campus study). Faculty: 19 full-time (0 women), 11 part-time (3 women). Students: 127 full-time (32 women); includes 23 minority (6 African Americans, 11 Asian Americans, 5 Hispanics, 1 Native American), 3 international. Average age 33. 149 applicants, 60% accepted. In 1997, 63 degrees awarded (100% found work related to degree). *Degree requirements:* Exams, project required, foreign language and thesis not required. *Average time to degree:* master's–2 years part-time. *Entrance requirements:* GMAT (average 610), 5 years of full-time work experience, interview. Application deadline: 3/6 (rolling processing). Application fee: $60. *Tuition:* $14,900 per year. *Financial aid:* In 1997–98, 6 fellowships were awarded. Financial aid application deadline: 3/1; applicants required to submit FAFSA. *Faculty research:* Mergers and acquisitions, corporate governance, initial public offerings, service leadership, employee stock options. • Penny Oslund, Director, 800-453-9515. Fax: 919-962-0551. E-mail: penny_oslund@unc.edu.

The University of North Carolina at Chapel Hill, Kenan-Flagler Business School, MBA Programs, Chapel Hill, NC 27599. Awards MBA, JD/MBA, MBA/MHA, MBA/MRP. Faculty: 79 full-time (15 women), 29 part-time (6 women). Students: 448 full-time (140 women); includes 61 minority (29 African Americans, 9 Asian Americans, 23 Hispanics), 89 international. Average age 27. 2,025 applicants, 18% accepted. In 1997, 198 degrees awarded. *Degree requirements:* Exams, practicum required, foreign language and thesis not required. *Average time to degree:* master's–2 years full-time. *Entrance requirements:* GMAT (average 640), TOEFL (minimum score 600), interview, minimum 2 years of work experience. Application deadline: 3/1 (rolling processing). Application fee: $60. Electronic applications accepted. *Expenses:* Tuition $1428 per year for state residents; $13,144 per year for nonresidents. Fees $1937 per year. *Financial aid:* In 1997–98, 244 students received aid, including 80 fellowships (43 to first-year students); institutionally sponsored loans and career-related internships or fieldwork also available. Financial aid application deadline: 3/1; applicants required to submit FAFSA. *Faculty research:* Mergers and acquisitions, corporate governance, crisis management, employee stock options. • James Danko, Executive Director, 919-962-3236. Application contact: Anne-Marie Summers, Chairperson, Admissions Committee, 919-962-3236. Fax: 919-962-0898. E-mail: mba_info@unc.edu.

University of North Carolina at Charlotte, College of Business Administration, Program in Business Administration, Charlotte, NC 28223-0001. Awards MBA. Part-time and evening/weekend programs available. Faculty: 41 full-time (11 women). Students: 72 full-time (22 women), 362 part-time (143 women); includes 50 minority (31 African Americans, 16 Asian Americans, 2 Hispanics, 1 Native American), 35 international. Average age 30. 214 applicants, 82% accepted. In 1997, 107 degrees awarded. *Entrance requirements:* GMAT, minimum GPA of 3.0 in undergraduate major, 2.8 overall. Application deadline: 7/1. Application fee: $25. *Tuition:* $1786 per year full-time, $339 per semester (minimum) part-time for state residents; $8914 per year full-time, $2121 per semester (minimum) part-time for nonresidents. *Financial aid:* Federal Work-Study available. Financial aid application deadline: 4/1. • Dr. Virginia S. Geurin, Associate Dean for Graduate Studies and Research, 704-547-2569. Application contact: Kathy Barringer, Assistant Director of Graduate Admissions, 704-547-3366. Fax: 704-547-3279. E-mail: gradadm@email.uncc.edu.

See in-depth description on page 369.

University of North Carolina at Greensboro, Joseph M. Bryan School of Business and Economics, Program in Business Administration, Greensboro, NC 27412-0001. Offers business administration (MBA, Certificate), international business administration (Certificate). Students: 118 full-time (42 women), 113 part-time (44 women); includes 16 minority (10 African Americans, 5 Asian Americans, 1 Hispanic), 11 international. 135 applicants, 55% accepted. In 1997, 74 master's awarded. *Degree requirements:* For master's, computer language required, foreign language and thesis not required. *Entrance requirements:* For master's, GMAT, TOEFL, managerial experience. Application deadline: 7/1 (priority date; rolling processing; 11/1 for spring admission). Application fee: $35. *Expenses:* Tuition $1842 per year full-time, $370 per semester (minimum) part-time for state residents; $10,296 per year full-time, $2484 per semester (minimum) part-time for nonresidents. Fees $806 per year full-time, $111 per semester (minimum) part-time. *Financial aid:* In 1997–98, 29 students received aid, including 1 fellowship totaling $5,000, 17 research assistantships totaling $42,800; teaching assistantships also available. • Dr. Richard Ehrhardt, Director, 336-334-5390.

University of North Carolina at Pembroke, Graduate Studies, Department of Business Administration and Economics, Program in Business Administration, Pembroke, NC 28372-1510. Awards MBA. Part-time and evening/weekend programs available. Faculty: 8 full-time (0 women). Students: 2 full-time (both women), 23 part-time (18 women); includes 11 minority (6 African Americans, 5 Native Americans). In 1997, 7 degrees awarded. *Degree requirements:* Thesis optional, foreign language not required. *Average time to degree:* master's–1.5 years full-time, 2.5 years part-time. *Entrance requirements:* GMAT, minimum GPA of 3.0 in major or 2.5 overall. Application deadline: rolling. Application fee: $25. *Tuition:* $1554 per year full-time, $610 per semester (minimum) part-time for state residents; $8824 per year full-time, $2122 per semester (minimum) part-time for nonresidents. *Financial aid:* In 1997–98, 1 graduate assistantship averaging $700 per month and totaling $5,600 was awarded. Aid available to part-time students. • Dr. Stephen Bukowy, Director, 910-521-6214. Application contact: Dean of Graduate Studies, 910-521-6271. Fax: 910-521-6497.

University of North Carolina at Wilmington, School of Business, Program in Business Administration, Wilmington, NC 28403-3201. Awards MBA. Part-time and evening/weekend programs available. Faculty: 9 full-time (1 woman), 2 part-time (0 women). Students: 1 full-time (0 women), 98 part-time (33 women); includes 7 minority (all African Americans), 5 international. 113 applicants, 53% accepted. In 1997, 93 degrees awarded. *Degree requirements:* Comprehensive exam required, thesis not required. *Entrance requirements:* GMAT, 1 year of appropriate work experience. Application deadline: 7/1 (rolling processing). Application fee: $35. *Tuition:* $1748 per year full-time, $270 per semester (minimum) part-time for state residents; $8882 per year full-time, $2058 per semester (minimum) part-time for nonresidents. *Financial aid:* In 1997–98, 3 teaching assistantships were awarded; Federal Work-Study and career-related internships or fieldwork also available. Aid available to part-time students. Financial aid application deadline: 3/15. • Dr. Drew Rosen, Chair, 910-962-3677. Application contact: Neil F. Hadley, Dean, Graduate School, 910-962-4117.

University of North Dakota, College of Business and Public Administration, Business Administration Program, Grand Forks, ND 58202. Awards MBA. Part-time and evening/weekend programs available. Postbaccalaureate distance learning degree programs offered (minimal on-campus study). Faculty: 26 full-time (2 women). Students: 15 full-time (8 women), 68 part-time (19 women). 28 applicants, 82% accepted. In 1997, 26 degrees awarded. *Degree requirements:* Computer language required, foreign language and thesis not required. *Entrance requirements:* GMAT (minimum score 450), TOEFL (minimum score 550), minimum GPA of 3.0. Application deadline: 3/1 (priority date; rolling processing). Application fee: $20. *Financial aid:* In 1997–98, 20 students received aid, including 1 fellowship totaling $2,400, 18 teaching assistantships totaling $70,688, 1 assistantship totaling $72,500; research assistantships, full and partial tuition waivers, Federal Work-Study, institutionally sponsored loans also available. Financial aid application deadline: 3/15. • Dr. Jacob Wambsganss, Director, 701-777-2975. Fax: 701-777-5099. E-mail: wambsgan@badlands.nodak.edu.

University of Northern Iowa, School of Business Administration, Program in Business Administration, Cedar Falls, IA 50614. Awards MBA. Part-time and evening/weekend programs available. Faculty: 33 full-time. Students: 37 full-time (15 women), 50 part-time (22 women); includes 5 minority (2 African Americans, 3 Asian Americans), 16 international. Average age 33. 35 applicants, 91% accepted. In 1997, 27 degrees awarded. *Entrance requirements:* GMAT. Application deadline: 8/1 (priority date; rolling processing). Application fee: $20 ($30 for international students). *Expenses:* Tuition $3166 per year full-time, $176 per hour part-time for state residents; $7805 per year full-time, $176 per hour part-time for nonresidents. Fees $194 per year full-time, $12.50 per semester (minimum) part-time. *Financial aid:* Scholarships, full and partial tuition waivers, Federal Work-Study, and career-related internships or fieldwork available. Aid available to part-time students. Financial aid application deadline: 3/1. • Dr. Peter G. Goulet, Director, 319-273-2556.

University of North Florida, College of Business Administration, Department of Management, Marketing, and Logistics, Jacksonville, FL 32224-2645. Offers programs in business administration (MBA), personnel management (MHRM). Faculty: 33 full-time (4 women). Students: 115 full-time (42 women), 361 part-time (157 women); includes 71 minority (33 African Americans, 20 Asian Americans, 17 Hispanics, 1 Native American), 24 international. Average age 31. 145 applicants, 68% accepted. In 1997, 102 degrees awarded. *Degree requirements:* Computer language required, thesis not required. *Entrance requirements:* GMAT, minimum GPA of 3.0. Application deadline: rolling. Application fee: $20. *Tuition:* $3388 per year full-time, $141 per credit hour part-time for state residents; $11,634 per year full-time, $485 per credit hour part-time for nonresidents. • Dr. Robert Pickhardt, Chair, 904-646-2780.

University of North Texas, College of Business Administration, Denton, TX 76203-6737. Awards MBA, MS, PhD. Part-time and evening/weekend programs available. Faculty: 85 full-time (13 women), 13 part-time (3 women). Students: 225 full-time (94 women), 397 part-time (158 women). Average age 31. In 1997, 149 master's, 23 doctorates awarded. *Degree requirements:* For master's, computer language required, foreign language and thesis not required; for doctorate, computer language, dissertation required, foreign language not required. *Entrance requirements:* For master's, GMAT, TOEFL; for doctorate, GMAT or GRE General Test, TOEFL. Application deadline: 7/17. Application fee: $25 ($50 for international students). *Tuition:* $2063 per year full-time, $815 per year part-time for state residents; $5897 per year full-time, $2100 per year part-time for nonresidents. *Financial aid:* Fellowships, research assistantships, teaching assistantships, Federal Work-Study, institutionally sponsored loans, and career-related internships or fieldwork available. *Faculty research:* Oil and gas accounting, expert systems, stock returns, occupational safety, service marketing. • Dr. Henry Hays, Dean, 940-565-2011. Application contact: Denise Galubenski, Counselor, 940-565-3027.

University of Notre Dame, College of Business Administration, Executive Program in Business Administration, Notre Dame, IN 46556. Awards EMBA. Evening/weekend programs available. Postbaccalaureate distance learning degree programs offered (minimal on-campus study). Faculty: 15 full-time (1 woman), 1 part-time (0 women). Students: 116 full-time (23 women); includes 15 minority (7 African Americans, 2 Asian Americans, 6 Hispanics), 4 international. Average age 35. 112 applicants, 77% accepted. In 1997, 45 degrees awarded. *Average time to degree:* master's–2 years full-time. *Entrance requirements:* GMAT, 5 years of work experience. Application deadline: 5/15 (priority date; rolling processing). Application fee: $50. *Tuition:* $24,900 per year. *Financial aid:* Applicants required to submit CSS PROFILE. • Arnie Ludwig, Assistant Dean for Executive Education, 219-631-3622. Fax: 219-631-6783. E-mail: arnold.f.ludwig.1@nd.edu.

University of Notre Dame, College of Business Administration, Program in Business Administration, Notre Dame, IN 46556. Awards MBA. Faculty: 60 full-time (7 women), 8 part-time (4 women). Students: 257 full-time (54 women); includes 28 minority (9 African Americans, 7 Asian Americans, 10 Hispanics, 2 Native Americans), 54 international. Average age 26. 512 applicants, 42% accepted. In 1997, 152 degrees awarded. *Average time to degree:* master's–1.5 years full-time. *Entrance requirements:* GMAT (average 615), TOEFL (minimum score 616), 2 years of work experience. Application deadline: 5/8 (priority date; rolling processing). Application fee: $75. *Financial aid:* In 1997–98, 117 students received aid, including 117 fellowships (60 to first-year students) totaling $1.4 million; full and partial tuition waivers, Federal Work-Study, and career-related internships or fieldwork also available. Financial aid application deadline: 2/20; applicants required to submit FAFSA. • Rebecca S. Mela, Assistant Dean, 219-631-8488. E-mail: rebecca.s.mela.2@nd.edu. Application contact: Brian T. Lohr, Assistant Director of Admissions, 219-631-8488. Fax: 219-631-8800. E-mail: brian.lohr.1@nd.edu.

University of Oklahoma, College of Business Administration, Program in Business Administration, Norman, OK 73019-0390. Awards MBA, PhD, JD/MBA, MBA/MA, MBA/MS, MBA/MLIS, MBA/MPH. MBA/MA offered jointly with the Department of Modern Languages. MBA/MS offered jointly with the Department of Mathematics and the Division of Construction Science. MBA/MPH and MBA/MS (health administration, pharmacy administration) offered jointly with the University of Oklahoma Health Sciences Center. Students: 142 full-time (50 women), 116 part-time (42 women); includes 31 minority (6 African Americans, 9 Asian Americans, 3 Hispanics, 13 Native Americans), 52 international. In 1997, 73 master's, 7 doctorates awarded. *Degree requirements:* For doctorate, dissertation. *Entrance requirements:* For master's, TOEFL (minimum score 550), minimum GPA of 3.0 in last 60 hours; for doctorate, TOEFL (minimum score 550). Application fee: $25. *Expenses:* Tuition $1920 per year full-time, $80 per credit hour part-time for state residents; $6108 per year full-time, $255 per credit hour part-time for nonresidents. Fees $468 per year full-time, $12 per semester (minimum) part-time. *Financial aid:* Research assistantships, teaching assistantships available. • Dr. Richard Cosier, Dean, College of Business Administration, 405-325-3612. Application contact: Alice Watkins, Coordinator, Graduate Programs, 405-325-4107. Fax: 405-325-2096.

See in-depth description on page 371.

Directory: Business Administration and Management—General

University of Oregon, Graduate School, Charles H. Lundquist College of Business, Department of Management, Eugene, OR 97403. Awards MA, MS, PhD. Part-time programs available. Faculty: 9 full-time (1 woman), 4 part-time (2 women), 11.47 FTE. Students: 6 full-time (2 women), 2 part-time (0 women); includes 4 international. 9 applicants, 11% accepted. In 1997, 1 doctorate awarded (100% entered university research/teaching). Terminal master's awarded for partial completion of doctoral program. *Degree requirements:* For master's, computer language required, foreign language not required; for doctorate, computer language, dissertation, 2 comprehensive exams required, foreign language not required. *Average time to degree:* doctorate–5 years full-time. *Entrance requirements:* GMAT, TOEFL (minimum score 600). Application deadline: 3/1. Application fee: $50. *Tuition:* $6429 per year full-time, $873 per quarter (minimum) part-time for state residents; $10,857 per year full-time, $1360 per quarter (minimum) part-time for nonresidents. *Financial aid:* In 1997–98, 6 teaching assistantships (1 to a first-year student) were awarded; Federal Work-Study and career-related internships or fieldwork also available. • James Terborg, Head, 541-346-3339. Application contact: Linda Johnson, Graduate Secretary, 541-346-3306.

University of Oregon, Graduate School, Charles H. Lundquist College of Business, Department of Management: General Business, Eugene, OR 97403. Awards MBA. Faculty: 4 full-time (0 women), 1 part-time (0 women), 4.75 FTE. Students: 215 full-time (68 women), 51 part-time (9 women); includes 25 minority (2 African Americans, 12 Asian Americans, 7 Hispanics, 4 Native Americans), 57 international. Average age 27. 332 applicants, 60% accepted. In 1997, 107 degrees awarded (100% found work related to degree). *Degree requirements:* Computer language required, foreign language and thesis not required. *Average time to degree:* master's–2 years full-time, 4 years part-time. *Entrance requirements:* GMAT, TOEFL (minimum score 600). Application deadline: 3/1. Application fee: $50. *Tuition:* $6429 per year full-time, $873 per quarter (minimum) part-time for state residents; $10,857 per year full-time, $1360 per quarter (minimum) part-time for nonresidents. *Financial aid:* In 1997–98, 37 teaching assistantships (3 to first-year students) were awarded; fellowships, research assistantships, Federal Work-Study, and career-related internships or fieldwork also available. • Dan Poston, Director, 541-346-3251. Application contact: Linda Johnson, Graduate Secretary, 541-346-3306.

University of Ottawa, Faculty of Administration, Business Administration Program, Ottawa, ON K1N 6N5, Canada. Awards MBA. Part-time and evening/weekend programs available. Faculty: 42 full-time. Students: 164 full-time (59 women), 389 part-time (158 women); includes 30 international. Average age 31. In 1997, 167 degrees awarded. *Degree requirements:* Thesis optional, foreign language not required. *Entrance requirements:* GMAT, bachelor's degree or equivalent, minimum B average. Application deadline: 4/15. Application fee: $60. *Expenses:* Tuition $4677 per year for Canadian residents; $9900 per year for nonresidents. Fees $230 per year. *Financial aid:* Fellowships, research assistantships, teaching assistantships, full tuition waivers, Federal Work-Study, and career-related internships or fieldwork available. • François Julien, Director, 613-562-5884. Application contact: Diane Sarrazin, Administrator, 613-562-5800 Ext. 4713. Fax: 613-562-5164.

University of Ottawa, Faculty of Administration, Executive Business Administration Program, Ottawa, ON K1N 6N5, Canada. Awards EMBA. Evening/weekend programs available. Faculty: 42 full-time. Students: 184 full-time (50 women). Average age 39. In 1997, 84 degrees awarded. *Degree requirements:* Computer language, thesis or alternative, major research project required, foreign language not required. *Entrance requirements:* GMAT, bachelor's degree or equivalent, minimum B average, previous business experience. Application deadline: 7/31. Application fee: $150. *Tuition:* $6423 per year for Canadian residents; $18,000 per year for nonresidents. • André de Carufel, Director, 613-564-2926. Fax: 613-564-9927.

University of Pennsylvania, Wharton School, Management Department, Philadelphia, PA 19104. Awards MBA, PhD. Faculty: 36 full-time (7 women), 8 part-time (3 women). *Entrance requirements:* For master's, GMAT; for doctorate, GMAT or GRE. Application fee: $125. *Faculty research:* Cross-cultural leadership, international technology transfers, human resource management, financial services. • Peter Cappelli, Chairman, 215-898-7722. Fax: 215-898-0401.

University of Pennsylvania, Wharton School, Wharton Doctoral Programs Division, Philadelphia, PA 19104. Offers programs in accounting (PhD), finance (PhD), health care systems (PhD), management (PhD), marketing (PhD), operations and information management operations research (PhD), public policy and management (PhD), risk and insurance (PhD), statistics (PhD). Students: 181 full-time (41 women); includes 84 international. 646 applicants, 15% accepted. In 1997, 26 degrees awarded. *Degree requirements:* Dissertation. *Entrance requirements:* GMAT or GRE. Application deadline: 2/1. Application fee: $65. • Dr. Mark Pauly, Director, 215-898-4877. Application contact: Mallory Hiatt, Coordinator, 215-898-4877.

University of Pennsylvania, Wharton School, Wharton Executive MBA Program, Philadelphia, PA 19104. Awards Exec MBA. Evening/weekend programs available. Students: 197 full-time. Average age 34. In 1997, 98 degrees awarded. *Entrance requirements:* GMAT. Application deadline: 2/1 (priority date; 2/1 for spring admission). Application fee: $90. *Tuition:* $43,800 per year. *Financial aid:* In 1997–98, 6 students received aid, including 5 fellowships totaling $45,000; institutionally sponsored loans also available. Financial aid application deadline: 4/30. • Dr. Howard Kaufold, Director, 215-898-5887. Application contact: Catherine Molony, Associate Director, 215-898-5887. Fax: 215-898-2598.

University of Pennsylvania, Wharton School, Wharton MBA Program, Philadelphia, PA 19104. Awards MBA. Faculty: 180 full-time, 34 part-time. Students: 1,558 full-time (623 women); includes 370 minority (121 African Americans, 173 Asian Americans, 70 Hispanics, 6 Native Americans), 538 international. Average age 27. 7,461 applicants, 15% accepted. In 1997, 718 degrees awarded. *Entrance requirements:* GMAT. Application deadline: 4/10 (rolling processing). Application fee: $125. *Financial aid:* Fellowships, research assistantships, teaching assistantships, Federal Work-Study, institutionally sponsored loans, and career-related internships or fieldwork available. Financial aid application deadline: 6/1; applicants required to submit FAFSA. • Application contact: Robert J. Alig, Director of Admissions, 215-898-3430. Fax: 215-898-0120.

University of Phoenix, Graduate Programs, Business Administration and Management Programs, 4615 East Elwood St, PO Box 52069, Phoenix, AZ 85072-2069. Offerings in business administration (MBA), global management (MBA), organizational management (MAOM), technology management (MBA). Evening/weekend programs available. Postbaccalaureate distance learning degree programs offered (no on-campus study). Students: 9,198 full-time (4,139 women); includes 3,119 minority (1,113 African Americans, 736 Asian Americans, 1,187 Hispanics, 83 Native Americans). Average age 34. In 1997, 2,117 degrees awarded. *Degree requirements:* Thesis or alternative required, foreign language not required. *Entrance requirements:* TOEFL (minimum score 520), minimum undergraduate GPA of 2.5, 3 years of work experience, comprehensive cognitive assessment (COCA). Application deadline: rolling. Application fee: $50. *Tuition:* $248 per credit hour. • Beverly Downey, Dean, 602-966-9577. Application contact: Campus Information Center, 602-966-9577.

University of Pittsburgh, Joseph M. Katz Graduate School of Business, Pittsburgh, PA 15260. Awards EMBA, MBA, MHA, MS, PhD, MBA/JD, MBA/MA, MBA/MS, MBA/M Div, MBA/MIB, MBA/MPIA, MPH/MHA. Part-time and evening/weekend programs available. Faculty: 70 full-time (13 women), 24 part-time (7 women). Students: 452 full-time (123 women), 522 part-time (159 women); includes 87 minority (35 African Americans, 43 Asian Americans, 9 Hispanics), 164 international. In 1997, 468 master's, 17 doctorates awarded. *Degree requirements:* For doctorate, dissertation, comprehensive exam required, foreign language not required. *Average time to degree:* master's–1 year full-time, 3 years part-time; doctorate–4 years full-time. *Entrance requirements:* For master's, GMAT, TOEFL (minimum score 600); for doctorate, GMAT or GRE General Test, TOEFL (minimum score 680). Application deadline: rolling. *Expenses:* Tuition $463 per credit for state residents; $867 per credit for nonresidents. Fees $480 per year full-time, $180 per year part-time. *Financial aid:* Fellowships, assistantships, full and partial tuition waivers, Federal Work-Study, institutionally sponsored loans, and career-related internships or fieldwork available. Financial aid applicants required to submit FAFSA. *Total annual research expenditures:* $2.1 million. • Dr. Frederick W. Winter, Dean, 412-648-1561. Fax: 412-648-1552. E-mail: rickwinter@katz.business.pitt.edu.

See in-depth description on page 373.

University of Portland, School of Business Administration, Portland, OR 97203-5798. Awards MBA. Part-time and evening/weekend programs available. Faculty: 24 full-time (5 women). Students: 26 full-time (15 women), 99 part-time (34 women). 195 applicants, 63% accepted. In 1997, 54 degrees awarded. *Entrance requirements:* GMAT (minimum score 450), TOEFL (minimum score 570), minimum GPA of 2.75. Application deadline: 8/1 (priority date; rolling processing; 12/1 for spring admission). Application fee: $40. *Tuition:* $540 per semester hour. *Financial aid:* Partial tuition waivers, Federal Work-Study, institutionally sponsored loans available. Aid available to part-time students. Financial aid application deadline: 3/15. • Dr. Ronald P. Hill, Dean, 503-283-7224. E-mail: hill@up.edu. Application contact: Dr. Todd M. Shank, Graduate Program Director, 503-283-7226 Ext. 7279. E-mail: shank@up.edu.

University of Puerto Rico, Mayagüez Campus, College of Business Administration, Mayagüez, PR 00681-5000. Awards MBA. Part-time and evening/weekend programs available. Faculty: 17 full-time (1 woman), 3 part-time (2 women). Students: 40 full-time (26 women), 48 part-time (30 women); includes 83 minority (all Hispanics), 5 international. 64 applicants, 58% accepted. In 1997, 19 degrees awarded. *Degree requirements:* Computer language, comprehensive exam required, foreign language and thesis not required. *Entrance requirements:* GMAT (minimum score 350), PAEG (minimum score 475). Application deadline: 2/28 (rolling processing; 9/15 for spring admission). Application fee: $15. *Expenses:* Tuition $75 per credit for commonwealth residents; $75 per credit (minimum) for nonresidents. Fees $35 per semester (minimum). *Financial aid:* In 1997–98, 26 students received aid, including 17 fellowships (5 to first-year students) averaging $200 per month, 9 teaching assistantships averaging $700 per month; research assistantships, Federal Work-Study, institutionally sponsored loans also available. *Faculty research:* Organizational studies, marketing, finance, management, accounting. • Prof. Jaime Pabón, Dean, 787-265-3800. Fax: 787-832-5320. Application contact: Dr. Luis Cruz, Director, 787-265-3887.

University of Puerto Rico, Río Piedras, Graduate School of Business Administration, San Juan, PR 00931. Awards MBA. Part-time and evening/weekend programs available. *Degree requirements:* Thesis or alternative, research project required, foreign language not required. *Entrance requirements:* GMAT or PAEG, minimum GPA of 3.0. Application deadline: 2/21. Application fee: $17.

University of Redlands, Alfred North Whitehead College for Lifelong Learning, Program in Adult Education, PO Box 3080, Redlands, CA 92373-0999. Offers adult education (MAHRM, MBA), information systems (MBA). Evening/weekend programs available. Students: 558 full-time (190 women), 2 part-time (1 woman); includes 173 minority (66 African Americans, 53 Asian Americans, 50 Hispanics, 4 Native Americans). Average age 36. In 1997, 205 degrees awarded. *Degree requirements:* Thesis required, foreign language not required. *Entrance requirements:* Minimum GPA of 3.0. Application deadline: 9/1 (priority date; rolling processing; 3/1 for spring admission). Application fee: $40. Electronic applications accepted. • Dr. Hubbard Segur, Head, 909-793-2121 Ext. 4143.

University of Regina, Faculty of Graduate Studies and Research, Faculty of Administration, Department of Business Administration, Regina, SK S4S 0A2, Canada. Awards M Admin, MBA. M Admin being phased out; applicants no longer accepted. Part-time and evening/weekend programs available. Students: 4 full-time, 56 part-time. 33 applicants, 61% accepted. In 1997, 15 degrees awarded. *Entrance requirements:* GMAT, TOEFL (minimum score 580). Application deadline: rolling. Application fee: $0. *Tuition:* $196 per credit for Canadian residents; $383 per credit for nonresidents. *Financial aid:* Application deadline 6/15. • Application contact: Dr. J. Ito, Graduate Coordinator, 306-585-4714. Fax: 306-585-4805. E-mail: jack.ito@uregina.ca.

University of Rhode Island, College of Business Administration, Kingston, RI 02881. Offers programs in accounting (MS); applied mathematics (PhD); finance (MBA); international business (MBA); international sports management (MBA); management (MBA); management science (MBA), including management information systems, manufacturing; marketing (MBA). *Entrance requirements:* GMAT, TOEFL (minimum score 575). Application deadline: 4/15 (priority date; rolling processing). Application fee: $35. *Expenses:* Tuition $3446 per year full-time, $191 per credit part-time for state residents; $9850 per year full-time, $547 per credit part-time for nonresidents. Fees $1276 per year full-time, $135 per semester (minimum) part-time.

See in-depth description on page 375.

University of Richmond, The E. Claiborne Robins School of Business, Richard S. Reynolds Graduate School, University of Richmond, VA 23173. Awards MBA, JD/MBA. Part-time and evening/weekend programs available. Faculty: 42 full-time (6 women), 7 part-time (1 woman). Students: 6 full-time (4 women), 261 part-time (96 women); includes 22 minority (7 African Americans, 11 Asian Americans, 3 Hispanics, 1 Native American), 2 international. Average age 29. 52 applicants, 48% accepted. In 1997, 58 degrees awarded. *Average time to degree:* master's–2 years full-time, 3 years part-time. *Entrance requirements:* GMAT (minimum score 525; average 623), TOEFL (minimum score 550; average 580). Application deadline: 7/1 (11/1 for spring admission). Application fee: $25. *Tuition:* $18,695 per year full-time, $320 per credit hour part-time. *Financial aid:* In 1997–98, 22 students received aid, including 6 research assistantships totaling $106,020. Aid available to part-time students. Financial aid application deadline: 7/1; applicants required to submit FAFSA. • Dr. Robert W. Phillips, Associate Dean and Director, 804-289-8553. Fax: 804-287-6544. E-mail: rphillips@richmond.edu.

University of Rochester, William E. Simon Graduate School of Business Administration, Doctoral Program in Business Administration, Rochester, NY 14627-0001. Awards PhD. Students: 41 full-time (8 women); includes 31 international. 276 applicants, 17% accepted. In 1997, 7 doctorates awarded. Terminal master's awarded for partial completion of doctoral program. *Degree requirements:* For doctorate, dissertation, qualifying exam required, foreign language not required. *Entrance requirements:* For doctorate, GMAT or GRE, previous course work in calculus. Application deadline: 2/1 (rolling processing). Application fee: $75. *Financial aid:* Fellowships, research assistantships, teaching assistantships, scholarships available. Financial aid application deadline: 2/1. • Dr. Ross Watts, Committee Chair, 716-275-2959. Application contact: Lynne M. Mitchell, Program Assistant, 716-275-5672.

See in-depth description on page 377.

University of Rochester, William E. Simon Graduate School of Business Administration, Master's Program in Business Administration, Rochester, NY 14627-0001. Awards MBA, MS. Part-time and evening/weekend programs available. Students: 572 full-time (132 women), 267 part-time (77 women); includes 89 minority (23 African Americans, 49 Asian Americans, 15 Hispanics, 2 Native Americans), 217 international. 1,420 applicants, 32% accepted. In 1997, 301 degrees awarded. *Entrance requirements:* GMAT, TOEFL, previous course work in calculus. Application deadline: 6/1 (11/15 for spring admission). Application fee: $75. *Financial aid:* Fellowships, research assistantships, teaching assistantships, scholarships, institutionally sponsored loans available. Financial aid application deadline: 3/1. • Pamela Black-Colton, Assistant Dean, 716-275-3533.

See in-depth description on page 377.

University of St. Francis, Graduate Studies, Program in Business Administration, Joliet, IL 60435-6188. Awards MBA, MSM. Faculty: 1 full-time (0 women), 8 part-time (3 women). Students: 8 full-time (2 women), 33 part-time (14 women). Average age 30. In 1997, 2 degrees awarded. *Degree requirements:* Computer language. *Average time to degree:* master's–3 years part-time. *Entrance requirements:* GMAT or 2 years of management experience, minimum GPA of 2.75. Application deadline: rolling. Application fee: $25. • Dr. F. William Kelley Jr., Dean, Graduate Studies, 800-735-4723. Fax: 815-740-3537. E-mail: grdinfo@stfrancis.edu.

University of Saint Francis, Department of Business Administration, Fort Wayne, IN 46808-3994. Awards MBA, MSBA. Part-time and evening/weekend programs available. Faculty: 4 full-time, 2 part-time. Students: 20 full-time, 34 part-time; includes 11 international. Average age 32. In 1997, 23 degrees awarded. *Average time to degree:* master's–2.5 years full-time, 4.5 years part-time. *Entrance requirements:* GMAT (minimum score 400; average 486), minimum AACSB index of 900, minimum GPA of 2.5. Application deadline: 7/1 (priority date; rolling processing; 11/1 for spring admission). Application fee: $20. *Expenses:* Tuition $350 per semester hour. Fees $390 per year full-time, $69 per semester (minimum) part-time. • Dr. J. Jain, Head, 219-434-3272. E-mail: jjain@sfc.edu. Application contact: Scott Flanagan, Director of Admissions, 219-434-3264. Fax: 219-434-3183. E-mail: sflanagan@sfc.edu.

University of St. Thomas, Graduate School of Business, Day MBA Program, St. Paul, MN 55105-1096. Offers accounting (MBA), environmental management (MBA), finance (MBA), financial services management (MBA), franchise management (MBA), government contracts (MBA), health care management (MBA), human resource management (MBA), information management (MBA), insurance and risk management (MBA), management (MBA), manufacturing systems (MBA), marketing (MBA), nonprofit management (MBA), sports and entertainment management (MBA), venture management (MBA). Faculty: 13 part-time. Students: 30 full-time (12 women); includes 2 minority (1 African American, 1 Asian American), 2 international. Average age 26. 35 applicants, 71% accepted. *Degree requirements:* Computer language required, foreign language and thesis not required. *Entrance requirements:* GMAT (score in 50th percentile or higher). Application deadline: 5/1 (priority date; rolling processing). Application fee: $30. *Tuition:* $473 per credit hour. *Financial aid:* In 1997–98, 8 grants (4 to first-year students) totaling $10,344 were awarded; career-related internships or fieldwork also available. Financial aid application deadline: 4/1; applicants required to submit FAFSA. • Application contact: Jim O'Connor, Student Adviser, 612-962-4233. Fax: 612-962-4260.

See in-depth description on page 379.

University of St. Thomas, Graduate School of Business, Evening MBA Program, St. Paul, MN 55105-1096. Offers accounting (MBA, Certificate), environmental management (MBA), finance (MBA), financial services management (MBA), franchise management (MBA, Certificate), government contracts (MBA, Certificate), health care management (MBA, Certificate), human resource management (MBA, Certificate), information management (MBA), insurance and risk management (MBA, Certificate), management (MBA), manufacturing systems (MBA), marketing (MBA), nonprofit management (MBA, Certificate), sports and entertainment management (MBA), venture management (MBA, Certificate). Part-time and evening/weekend programs available. Faculty: 16 full-time (2 women), 89 part-time (17 women). Students: 53 full-time (21 women), 1,799 part-time (712 women); includes 72 minority (22 African Americans, 40 Asian Americans, 8 Hispanics, 2 Native Americans), 45 international. Average age 32. 625 applicants, 89% accepted. In 1997, 382 master's, 35 Certificates awarded. *Degree requirements:* For master's, computer language required, foreign language and thesis not required. *Entrance requirements:* For master's, GMAT (score in 50th percentile or higher). Application deadline: 8/1 (priority date; rolling processing; 12/1 for spring admission). Application fee: $30. *Tuition:* $416 per credit hour. *Financial aid:* In 1997–98, 33 grants (3 to first-year students) totaling $62,897 were awarded; career-related internships or fieldwork also available. Aid available to part-time students. Financial aid application deadline: 4/1; applicants required to submit FAFSA. • Dr. Stanford Nyquist, MBA Director, 612-962-4242. Application contact: Martha Ballard, Director of Student Services, 612-962-4226. Fax: 612-962-4260.

See in-depth description on page 379.

University of St. Thomas, Graduate School of Business, Executive MBA Program, St. Paul, MN 55105-1096. Awards MBA. Part-time and evening/weekend programs available. Faculty: 2 full-time (1 woman), 17 part-time (6 women). Students: 70 part-time (21 women); includes 1 minority (African American). Average age 40. 20 applicants, 100% accepted. In 1997, 32 degrees awarded. *Entrance requirements:* MAT. Application deadline: rolling. Application fee: $30. *Tuition:* $585 per credit hour. *Financial aid:* In 1997–98, 2 grants totaling $3,630 were awarded; career-related internships or fieldwork also available. Aid available to part-time students. Financial aid application deadline: 4/1; applicants required to submit FAFSA. • Bill Monson, Director, 612-962-4231. Application contact: Nick Lauer, Associate Director, 612-962-4205. Fax: 612-962-4235. E-mail: nclauer@stthomas.edu.

See in-depth description on page 379.

University of St. Thomas, Cameron School of Business, Houston, TX 77006-4696. Awards MBA, MIB, MSA. Part-time and evening/weekend programs available. Faculty: 18 full-time, 26 part-time. Students: 123 full-time (59 women), 313 part-time (134 women). *Degree requirements:* Computer language required, foreign language and thesis not required. *Entrance requirements:* GMAT, minimum GPA of 2.5. Application deadline: 6/30 (priority date; rolling processing; 10/31 for spring admission). Application fee: $35. *Expenses:* Tuition $410 per credit hour. Fees $33 per year full-time, $22.50 per year part-time. *Financial aid:* Fellowships, Federal Work-Study, institutionally sponsored loans available. Aid available to part-time students. Financial aid application deadline: 3/1. *Faculty research:* Trade theory, development theory, financial institutions, monetary and accounting theory. • Dr. Yhi-Min Ho, Dean, 713-525-2100. Fax: 713-525-2110. E-mail: yhiminho@stthom.edu.

University of San Diego, School of Business Administration, San Diego, CA 92110-2492. Awards MBA, MIB, JD/MBA, JD/MIB, MBA/MIB, MBA/MSN, MIB/MSN. MBA/MIB offered jointly with Instituto Tecnológico y de Estudios Superiores de Monterrey. Part-time and evening/weekend programs available. Faculty: 55 full-time (15 women). Students: 164 full-time (55 women), 250 part-time (110 women); includes 56 minority (1 African American, 25 Asian Americans, 29 Hispanics, 1 Native American), 66 international. Average age 28. 490 applicants, 52% accepted. In 1997, 149 degrees awarded. *Entrance requirements:* GMAT, TOEFL (minimum score 580), TWE (minimum score 4.5), minimum GPA of 3.0. Application deadline: 5/1 (priority date; rolling processing; 11/15 for spring admission). Application fee: $45. *Expenses:* Tuition $585 per unit (minimum). Fees $50 per year full-time, $30 per year part-time. *Financial aid:* Fellowships, assistantships, Federal Work-Study, institutionally sponsored loans, and career-related internships or fieldwork available. Aid available to part-time students. Financial aid application deadline: 5/1; applicants required to submit FAFSA. *Faculty research:* Business management, production, purchasing, quantitative methods, accounting. Total annual research expenditures: $104,000. • Dr. Curtis Cook, Dean, 619-260-4886. Fax: 619-260-4891. E-mail: sbadean@acusd.edu. Application contact: Mary Jane Tiernan, Director of Graduate Admissions, 619-260-4524. Fax: 619-260-4158. E-mail: grads@acusd.edu.

See in-depth description on page 381.

University of San Francisco, McLaren School of Business, Program in Business Administration, San Francisco, CA 94117-1080. Awards MBA, JD/MBA, MSN/MBA. Offerings include finance and banking (MBA), international business (MBA), management (MBA), marketing (MBA), telecommunications management and policy (MBA). Faculty: 33 full-time (7 women), 27 part-time (3 women). Students: 311 full-time (136 women), 216 part-time (102 women); includes 85 minority (3 African Americans, 69 Asian Americans, 12 Hispanics, 1 Native American), 167 international. Average age 30. 567 applicants, 83% accepted. In 1997, 204 degrees awarded. *Entrance requirements:* GMAT (average 540), TOEFL (minimum score 600), minimum undergraduate GPA of 3.2. Application deadline: 7/1 (priority date; rolling processing; 11/30 for spring admission). Application fee: $40 ($50 for international students). *Tuition:* $658 per unit (minimum). *Financial aid:* 163 students received aid; fellowships available. Financial aid application deadline: 3/2. *Faculty research:* International financial markets, technology transfer licensing, international marketing, strategic planning. Total annual research expenditures: $50,000. • Cathy Fusco, Director, 415-422-6314. Fax: 415-422-2502. E-mail: mbausf@usfca.edu.

University of San Francisco, McLaren School of Business, Program in Executive Business Administration, San Francisco, CA 94117-1080. Awards EMBA. Faculty: 5 full-time (1 woman). Students: 46 full-time (19 women); includes 3 minority (all African Americans). Average age 38. 34 applicants, 88% accepted. In 1997, 32 degrees awarded. *Degree requirements:* Practicum required, foreign language and thesis not required. *Entrance requirements:* GMAT (average 540), TOEFL (minimum score 600), minimum undergraduate GPA of 3.2. Application deadline: 7/1 (priority date; rolling processing; 11/30 for spring admission). *Financial aid:* 12 students received aid. Financial aid application deadline: 3/2. *Faculty research:* International finance, technology transfer licensing, international marketing, strategic management. Total annual research expenditures: $50,000. • Dr. Denis Neilson, Director, 415-422-2526. Fax: 415-422-2502.

University of Sarasota, College of Business, Program in Business, Sarasota, FL 34235-8246. Awards MBA, DBA. Part-time and evening/weekend programs available. Postbaccalaureate distance learning degree programs offered (minimal on-campus study). Faculty: 4 full-time (2 women), 7 part-time (1 woman). Students: 115 full-time (51 women), 300 part-time (151 women). Terminal master's awarded for partial completion of doctoral program. *Degree requirements:* For doctorate, dissertation, comprehensive exam required, foreign language not required. *Average time to degree:* master's–2 years full-time, 3 years part-time; doctorate–3 years full-time, 4 years part-time. *Entrance requirements:* For master's, TOEFL (minimum score 500); for doctorate, TOEFL (minimum score 550), minimum undergraduate GPA of 3.0. Application deadline: rolling. Application fee: $50. *Tuition:* $321 per credit hour (minimum). *Financial aid:* Available to part-time students. Financial aid applicants required to submit FAFSA. • Application contact: Kathy Ketterer, Admissions Representative, 800-331-5995. Fax: 941-371-8910. E-mail: kathy_kitterer@embanet.com.

University of Saskatchewan, College of Commerce, Saskatoon, SK S7N 5A2, Canada. Awards MBA, M Sc, PhD. Part-time programs available. *Degree requirements:* For master's, thesis (for some programs); for doctorate, dissertation. *Entrance requirements:* For master's, GMAT, TOEFL; for doctorate, TOEFL. Application deadline: 7/1 (priority date; rolling processing). Application fee: $0.

University of Scranton, Program in Business Administration, Scranton, PA 18510-4622. Offers accounting (MBA), finance (MBA), general business administration (MBA), international business (MBA), marketing (MBA), personnel/labor (MBA). Part-time and evening/weekend programs available. Faculty: 39 full-time (9 women), 1 part-time (0 women). Students: 43 full-time (13 women), 95 part-time (39 women); includes 7 minority (2 African Americans, 4 Asian Americans, 1 Hispanic), 29 international. Average age 29. 117 applicants, 96% accepted. In 1997, 34 degrees awarded. *Entrance requirements:* GMAT, TOEFL (minimum score 500), minimum GPA of 2.75. Application deadline: rolling. Application fee: $35. *Expenses:* Tuition $465 per credit. Fees $25 per semester. *Financial aid:* In 1997–98, 15 students received aid, including 14 teaching assistantships (1 to a first-year student) averaging $648 per month and totaling $75,206, 1 teaching fellowship averaging $864 per month and totaling $7,780; Federal Work-Study and career-related internships or fieldwork also available. Aid available to part-time students. Financial aid application deadline: 3/1. *Faculty research:* Financial markets, strategic impact of total quality management, internal accounting controls, consumer preference, information systems and the Internet. • Dr. Wayne H. J. Cunningam, Director, 717-941-4043. Fax: 717-941-4342. E-mail: cunninghamw1@uofs.edu.

University of Sioux Falls, Program in Business Administration, Sioux Falls, SD 57105-1699. Awards MBA. Part-time and evening/weekend programs available. *Degree requirements:* Project. *Entrance requirements:* GMAT or GRE General Test, TOEFL, minimum GPA of 3.0. Application fee: $25. *Tuition:* $3960 per year. *Financial aid:* Scholarships, institutionally sponsored loans available. • Dr. Jeff Tschetter, Director, 605-331-6707. E-mail: mba@thecoo.edu.

University of South Alabama, College of Business and Management Studies, Program in Business Management, Mobile, AL 36688-0002. Awards MBA. Part-time and evening/weekend programs available. Faculty: 9 full-time (4 women). Students: 82 full-time (31 women), 52 part-time (22 women); includes 14 minority (6 African Americans, 6 Asian Americans, 2 Hispanics), 44 international. 96 applicants, 51% accepted. In 1997, 69 degrees awarded. *Degree requirements:* Oral comprehensive exams required, foreign language and thesis not required. *Entrance requirements:* GMAT, minimum undergraduate GPA of 3.0. Application deadline: 9/1 (priority date; rolling processing). Application fee: $25. *Financial aid:* In 1997–98, 7 research assistantships were awarded. Aid available to part-time students. Financial aid application deadline: 4/1. • Dr. Ed Harrison, Chairman, 334-460-6411.

University of South Carolina, Graduate School, College of Business Administration, Columbia, SC 29208. Awards IMBA, MA, M Acc, MBA, MHR, MIBS, MS, M Tax, PhD, JD/MA, JD/MBA, JD/MS, JD/M Acc, JD/MHR, JD/MIBS. Programs in accounting (M Acc), business administration (IMBA, MBA, MS, PhD), economics (MA, PhD), human resources (MHR), international business (MIBS), taxation (M Tax). Part-time and evening/weekend programs available. Faculty: 97 full-time (10 women). Students: 666 full-time (253 women), 419 part-time (124 women); includes 49 minority (16 African Americans, 21 Asian Americans, 11 Hispanics, 1 Native American), 142 international. Average age 29. In 1997, 399 master's, 19 doctorates awarded. *Degree requirements:* For doctorate, 1 foreign language, dissertation. *Entrance requirements:* For master's, GMAT (minimum score 550; average 586), minimum GPA of 3.0; for doctorate, GMAT (minimum score 650). Application deadline: 2/1 (priority date; rolling processing). Application fee: $35. Electronic applications accepted. *Financial aid:* In 1997–98, 62 fellowships (40 to first-year students), 185 research assistantships (100 to first-year students), 70 teaching assistantships were awarded; Federal Work-Study, institutionally sponsored loans, and career-related internships or fieldwork also available. Financial aid application deadline: 2/1. *Faculty research:* Finance, marketing, strategic management, international management, operations. Total annual research expenditures: $485,000. • Dr. David L. Shrock, Dean, 803-777-3178. Fax: 803-777-9123. E-mail: shrock@darla.badm.sc.edu. Application contact: Carol Williams, Director of Admissions, 803-777-6749. Fax: 803-777-0414. E-mail: carol@darla.badm.sc.edu.

See in-depth description on page 383.

University of South Dakota, School of Business, Department of Business Administration, Vermillion, SD 57069-2390. Awards MBA, JD/MBA. Students: 52 full-time (15 women), 104 part-time (33 women); includes 14 minority (2 African Americans, 11 Asian Americans, 1 Native American), 12 international. 90 applicants, 72% accepted. In 1997, 72 degrees awarded. *Entrance requirements:* GMAT. Application deadline: rolling. Application fee: $15. *Expenses:* Tuition $1530 per year full-time, $85 per credit hour part-time for state residents; $4518 per year full-time, $251 per credit hour part-time for nonresidents. Fees $792 per year full-time, $44 per credit hour part-time. • Dr. Diane Hoadley, Director of Graduate Studies, 605-677-5232.

University of Southern California, Graduate School, Marshall School of Business, Los Angeles, CA 90089. Awards M Acc, MBA, MBT, MS, PhD, DDS/MBA, JD/MBA, JD/MBT, MBA/MA, MBA/MS, MBA/M Pl, MBA/MRED, Pharm D/MBA. Students: 995 full-time (280 women), 287 part-time (91 women); includes 441 minority (48 African Americans, 302 Asian Americans, 86 Hispanics, 5 Native Americans), 131 international. Average age 30. 2,237 applicants, 41% accepted. In 1997, 456 master's, 9 doctorates awarded. *Degree requirements:* For doctorate, dissertation. *Entrance requirements:* For master's, GMAT; for doctorate, GMAT or GRE General Test. *Expenses:* Tuition $16,944 per year full-time, $706 per unit part-time. Fees $414 per year full-time, $32 per year part-time. *Financial aid:* In 1997–98, 145 fellowships, 3 research assistantships, 1 teaching assistantship, 30 scholarships were awarded; Federal Work-Study, institutionally sponsored loans also available. Aid available to part-time

Directory: Business Administration and Management—General

University of Southern California (continued)
students. Financial aid application deadline: 2/15; applicants required to submit FAFSA. • Dr. Randolph Westerfield, Dean, 213-740-6422.

University of Southern Colorado, School of Business, Pueblo, CO 81001-4901. Awards MBA. Part-time and evening/weekend programs available. Faculty: 6 full-time (0 women), 2 part-time (0 women). Students: 59 full-time (21 women), 72 part-time (45 women); includes 10 minority (3 African Americans, 5 Hispanics, 2 Native Americans), 57 international. Average age 31. 80 applicants, 75% accepted. In 1997, 55 degrees awarded. *Degree requirements:* Thesis optional, foreign language not required. *Average time to degree:* master's–1.5 years full-time, 2.5 years part-time. *Entrance requirements:* GMAT (average 500), TOEFL (minimum score 550), minimum GPA of 2.7. Application deadline: 8/15 (priority date; rolling processing; 1/10 for spring admission). Application fee: $15. *Financial aid:* 4 students received aid; research assistantships available. *Faculty research:* Total quality management, leadership, small business studies, case research and writing. Total annual research expenditures: $44,000. • Bart Ward, Dean, 719-549-2142. Fax: 719-549-2909. E-mail: bward@uscolo.edu. Application contact: Christie Kangas, Director of Admissions, 719-549-2461. Fax: 719-549-2419. E-mail: kangas@uscolo.edu.

University of Southern Indiana, Graduate Studies, School of Business, Program in Business Administration, Evansville, IN 47712-3590. Awards MBA. Part-time and evening/weekend programs available. Faculty: 25 full-time (5 women), 1 (woman) part-time. Students: 4 full-time (2 women), 108 part-time (31 women); includes 1 minority (Native American), 2 international. Average age 33. 26 applicants, 77% accepted. In 1997, 21 degrees awarded. *Entrance requirements:* GMAT (minimum score 450), minimum GPA of 2.5. Application deadline: 8/15 (rolling processing). Application fee: $25. *Tuition:* $129 per credit hour for state residents; $260 per credit hour for nonresidents. • Dr. Joy Van Eck Peluchette, Director, 812-464-1803.

University of Southern Maine, School of Business, Portland, ME 04104-9300. Awards MBA. Part-time and evening/weekend programs available. Faculty: 17 full-time (3 women). Students: 60 full-time (26 women), 58 part-time (24 women); includes 2 minority (1 Asian American, 1 Hispanic). Average age 32. 56 applicants, 79% accepted. In 1997, 37 degrees awarded. *Average time to degree:* master's–1.5 years full-time, 3 years part-time. *Entrance requirements:* GMAT (minimum score 500), TOEFL (minimum score 550), minimum AACSB index of 1100. Application deadline: 8/1 (priority date; rolling processing; 12/1 for spring admission). Application fee: $25. *Expenses:* Tuition $178 per credit hour for state residents; $267 per credit hour (minimum) for nonresidents. Fees $282 per year full-time, $83 per semester (minimum) part-time. *Financial aid:* In 1997–98, 3 research assistantships (all to first-year students), 3 teaching assistantships (all to first-year students) were awarded; Federal Work-Study and career-related internships or fieldwork also available. Aid available to part-time students. Financial aid application deadline: 3/15; applicants required to submit FAFSA. *Faculty research:* Economic development, organizational behavior, human resource management, MIS, country risk analysis. • John M. Burt, Dean, 207-780-4020. Application contact: Dr. John J. Voyer, Co-Director, MBA Program, 207-780-4184. Fax: 207-780-4662. E-mail: mba@usm.maine.edu.

University of Southern Mississippi, College of Business Administration, Department of Marketing and Finance, Hattiesburg, MS 39406-5167. Offers program in business administration (MBA). Part-time and evening/weekend programs available. Faculty: 32 full-time (4 women), 5 part-time (2 women). Students: 45 full-time (24 women), 27 part-time (9 women); includes 8 minority (3 African Americans, 5 Asian Americans), 11 international. Average age 29. 112 applicants, 67% accepted. In 1997, 50 degrees awarded. *Entrance requirements:* GMAT, TOEFL (minimum score 550), minimum GPA of 2.75. Application deadline: 8/9 (priority date). Application fee: $0 ($25 for international students). *Tuition:* $2870 per year full-time, $137 per credit hour part-time for state residents; $5972 per year full-time, $172 per credit hour part-time for nonresidents. *Financial aid:* Research assistantships, Federal Work-Study, institutionally sponsored loans available. Aid available to part-time students. Financial aid application deadline: 3/15. *Faculty research:* Inflation accounting, self-esteem training, international trade policy, health care marketing, ethics in strategic planning. Total annual research expenditures: $100,000. • Dr. Alvin Williams, Chair, 601-266-4627. Application contact: Mary Schlottman, Manager of Graduate Business Programs, 601-266-4664. Fax: 601-266-5814.

University of South Florida, College of Business Administration, Department of Management, Tampa, FL 33620-9951. Awards MS. Part-time and evening/weekend programs available. Faculty: 19 full-time (6 women). Students: 2 full-time (1 woman), 22 part-time (12 women). Average age 30. 38 applicants, 55% accepted. In 1997, 1 degree awarded. *Entrance requirements:* GMAT (minimum score 450), GRE General Test (minimum combined score of 1000). Application deadline: 5/15. Application fee: $20. Electronic applications accepted. *Tuition:* $142 per credit hour for state residents; $486 per credit hour for nonresidents. *Financial aid:* Federal Work-Study, institutionally sponsored loans available. Aid available to part-time students. Financial aid applicants required to submit FAFSA. • Alan Balfour, Chairperson, 813-974-4155. Fax: 813-974-1734. E-mail: abalfour@bsn01.bsn.usf.edu.

University of South Florida, College of Business Administration, Doctoral Program in Business, Tampa, FL 33620-9951. Awards PhD. Students: 19 full-time (9 women), 12 part-time (4 women); includes 8 minority (7 African Americans, 1 Hispanic), 4 international. 32 applicants, 9% accepted. In 1997, 6 degrees awarded. *Degree requirements:* Computer language, dissertation required, foreign language not required. *Entrance requirements:* GMAT (preferred) or GRE. Application deadline: 2/1 (priority date). Application fee: $20. *Tuition:* $142 per credit hour for state residents; $486 per credit hour for nonresidents. *Financial aid:* In 1997–98, 2 fellowships averaging $895 per month, 10 research assistantships averaging $1,037 per month, 12 teaching assistantships averaging $1,250 per month were awarded. • Rick Meyer, Associate Dean of Graduate Studies, 813-974-2081. Fax: 813-974-4518. E-mail: rmeyer@coba.usf.edu. Application contact: Cathy Slagle, Assistant, 813-974-3335. Fax: 813-974-4578. E-mail: cslagle@coba.usf.edu.

University of South Florida, College of Business Administration, Executive Program in Business Administration, Tampa, FL 33620-9951. Awards Exec MBA. Evening/weekend programs available. Faculty: 17 full-time (2 women), 1 (woman) part-time. Students: 61 full-time (18 women); includes 4 minority (2 African Americans, 1 Asian American, 1 Hispanic). Average age 37. 71 applicants, 54% accepted. In 1997, 25 degrees awarded. *Average time to degree:* master's–2 years full-time. *Entrance requirements:* GRE General Test (minimum combined score of 1050), GMAT (minimum score 500), 7 or more years of work experience. Application deadline: 5/15 (priority date; rolling processing). Application fee: $20. Electronic applications accepted. *Tuition:* $142 per credit hour for state residents; $486 per credit hour for nonresidents. • Steve Baumgarten, Director, MBA Programs, 813-974-4517. Fax: 813-974-4518. E-mail: sbaumgar@bsn01.bsn.usf.edu. Application contact: Katie Knoth, Coordinator, Executive Programs, 813-974-4876. Fax: 813-974-6604. E-mail: kknoth@bsn01.bsn.usf.edu.

University of South Florida, College of Business Administration, Executive Program in Business Administration for Physicians, Tampa, FL 33620-9951. Awards Exec MBA. Evening/weekend programs available. Faculty: 19 full-time (3 women), 1 (woman) part-time. Students: 71 full-time (10 women); includes 22 minority (5 African Americans, 14 Asian Americans, 3 Hispanics), 2 international. Average age 44. 46 applicants, 65% accepted. In 1997, 38 degrees awarded. *Average time to degree:* master's–2 years full-time. *Entrance requirements:* 6 years of clinical experience, MD or DO. Application deadline: 5/15 (priority date; rolling processing). Application fee: $20. Electronic applications accepted. *Tuition:* $142 per credit hour for state residents; $486 per credit hour for nonresidents. • Steve Baumgarten, Director, MBA Programs, 813-974-4517. Fax: 813-974-4518. E-mail: sbaumgar@coba.usf.edu. Application contact: Susan Stevens, Director, 813-974-2626. Fax: 813-975-6604. E-mail: sstevens@bsn01.bsn.usf.edu.

University of South Florida, College of Business Administration, Program in Business Administration, Tampa, FL 33620-9951. Awards MBA. Part-time and evening/weekend programs available. Students: 168 full-time (72 women), 383 part-time (149 women); includes 58 minority (14 African Americans, 19 Asian Americans, 25 Hispanics), 47 international. Average age 31. 346 applicants, 64% accepted. In 1997, 184 degrees awarded. *Entrance requirements:* GMAT (minimum score 500), GRE General Test (minimum combined score of 1050), minimum GPA of 3.0 in last 2 years. Application deadline: 5/15 (10/15 for spring admission). Application fee: $20. Electronic applications accepted. *Tuition:* $142 per credit hour for state residents; $486 per credit hour for nonresidents. *Financial aid:* In 1997–98, 1 research assistantship (to a first-year student) averaging $708 per month, 11 teaching assistantships (2 to first-year students) averaging $708 per month, 19 graduate assistantships (7 to first-year students) averaging $708 per month were awarded; fellowships, Federal Work-Study, institutionally sponsored loans also available. Aid available to part-time students. Financial aid applicants required to submit FAFSA. • Steve Baumgarten, Director, MBA Programs, 813-974-3335. E-mail: sbaumgar@coba.usf.edu. Application contact: Wendy Baker, Assistant Director of Graduate Programs, 813-974-3335. Fax: 813-974-4518. E-mail: wbaker@coba.usf.edu.

University of Southwestern Louisiana, College of Business Administration, Lafayette, LA 70503. Offers programs in business administration (MBA), health care administration (MBA), health care certification (MBA). Part-time programs available. Faculty: 41 full-time (8 women). Students: 57 full-time (23 women), 94 part-time (40 women); includes 5 minority (2 African Americans, 1 Asian American, 2 Hispanics), 22 international. 91 applicants, 73% accepted. In 1997, 40 degrees awarded. *Degree requirements:* Computer language required, foreign language and thesis not required. *Entrance requirements:* GMAT (minimum score 425), minimum GPA of 2.75. Application deadline: 8/15. Application fee: $5 ($15 for international students). *Tuition:* $2012 per year full-time, $300 per semester (minimum) part-time for state residents; $7244 per year full-time, $300 per semester (minimum) part-time for nonresidents. *Financial aid:* Research assistantships, Federal Work-Study available. Aid available to part-time students. Financial aid application deadline: 5/1. • Dr. C. William Roe, Graduate Coordinator, 318-482-5882.

The University of Tampa, College of Business, MBA Program, Tampa, FL 33606-1490. Awards MBA. Part-time and evening/weekend programs available. Faculty: 36 full-time (7 women), 1 part-time (0 women). Students: 78 full-time (39 women), 361 part-time (158 women); includes 50 minority (8 African Americans, 9 Asian Americans, 31 Hispanics, 2 Native Americans), 57 international. Average age 31. 196 applicants, 78% accepted. In 1997, 95 degrees awarded. *Average time to degree:* master's–2 years full-time, 3.5 years part-time. *Entrance requirements:* GMAT (minimum score 450; average 510), TOEFL (minimum score 550; average 573). Application deadline: 8/15 (priority date; rolling processing). Application fee: $35. *Financial aid:* Assistantships and career-related internships or fieldwork available. Aid available to part-time students. Financial aid applicants required to submit FAFSA. *Faculty research:* Ethics audit, macroeconomic significance of total quality management, computer virus prevention, use and trends of information technology by Florida industries, risk of accounting practitioners. • Application contact: Fernando Nolasco, Director of Graduate Admissions, 813-258-7409. Fax: 813-259-5403. E-mail: fnolasco@alpha.utampa.edu.

University of Tennessee at Chattanooga, School of Business Administration, Program in Business Administration, Chattanooga, TN 37403-2598. Offers business administration (MBA), economics (MBA), finance (MBA), marketing (MBA), operations/production (MBA), organizational management (MBA). Part-time and evening/weekend programs available. Students: 56 full-time (29 women), 336 part-time (135 women); includes 34 minority (22 African Americans, 6 Asian Americans, 5 Hispanics, 1 Native American), 30 international. Average age 31. 229 applicants, 85% accepted. In 1997, 104 degrees awarded. *Entrance requirements:* GMAT (average 527). Application deadline: rolling. Application fee: $25. *Tuition:* $2864 per year full-time, $160 per credit hour part-time for state residents; $6806 per year full-time, $379 per credit hour part-time for nonresidents. *Financial aid:* Fellowships, research assistantships, Federal Work-Study, institutionally sponsored loans available. Aid available to part-time students. Financial aid application deadline: 4/1. • Ashley Williams, Director, 423-755-4169. Fax: 423-755-5255. Application contact: Dr. Deborah Arfken, Assistant Provost for Graduate Studies, 423-755-4667. Fax: 423-755-4478.

The University of Tennessee at Martin, School of Business Administration, Program in Business Administration, Martin, TN 38238-1000. Awards MBA. Part-time and evening/weekend programs available. Postbaccalaureate distance learning degree programs offered (no on-campus study). Students: 24 full-time (8 women), 103 part-time (46 women); includes 6 minority (all African Americans). 86 applicants, 90% accepted. In 1997, 47 degrees awarded. *Degree requirements:* Computer language required, foreign language and thesis not required. *Entrance requirements:* GMAT (minimum score 400), minimum GPA of 2.5. Application deadline: rolling. Application fee: $25 ($50 for international students). *Tuition:* $2962 per year full-time, $165 per semester hour part-time for state residents; $7788 per year full-time, $434 per semester hour part-time for nonresidents. *Financial aid:* In 1997–98, 7 students received aid, including 5 graduate assistantships (2 to first-year students) averaging $545 per month and totaling $27,035; fellowships, research assistantships, teaching assistantships, partial tuition waivers, and career-related internships or fieldwork also available. Aid available to part-time students. Financial aid application deadline: 3/1. • Dr. Richard Griffin, Coordinator, 901-587-7308. Fax: 901-587-7241. E-mail: bagrad@utm.edu.

University of Tennessee, Knoxville, College of Business Administration, Program in Business Administration, Knoxville, TN 37996. Awards Exec MBA, MBA, PMBA, PhD, JD/MBA, MS/MBA. Offerings include accounting (PhD), business administration (Exec MBA, PMBA), economics (MBA), entrepreneurship/new venture analysis (MBA), environmental management (MBA), finance (MBA, PhD), forest industries management (MBA), global business (MBA), logistics and transportation (MBA, PhD), management (MBA, PhD), manufacturing management (MBA), marketing (MBA, PhD), statistics (MBA, PhD). MS/MBA offered jointly with the College of Engineering. Postbaccalaureate distance learning degree programs offered. Faculty: 51 full-time (6 women). Students: 219 full-time (65 women), 16 part-time (5 women); includes 18 minority (15 African Americans, 1 Asian American, 1 Hispanic, 1 Native American), 32 international. 600 applicants, 26% accepted. In 1997, 87 master's, 14 doctorates awarded. *Degree requirements:* For master's, computer language, thesis or alternative required, foreign language not required; for doctorate, computer language, dissertation required, foreign language not required. *Entrance requirements:* GMAT, TOEFL (minimum score 550), minimum GPA of 2.7. Application deadline: 2/1 (priority date). Application fee: $35. Electronic applications accepted. *Tuition:* $3354 per year full-time, $181 per semester hour part-time for state residents; $8410 per year full-time, $462 per semester hour part-time for nonresidents. *Financial aid:* In 1997–98, 8 fellowships, 15 research assistantships, 39 teaching assistantships, 48 graduate assistantships were awarded; Federal Work-Study, institutionally sponsored loans, and career-related internships or fieldwork also available. Financial aid application deadline: 2/1. • Dr. Gary Dicer, Director, 423-974-5033. E-mail: gdicer@utk.edu. Application contact: Donald Potts, Graduate Representative, 423-974-5033. Fax: 423-974-3826. E-mail: dpotts@utk.edu.

See in-depth description on page 385.

University of Tennessee, Knoxville, College of Business Administration, Program in Management Science, Knoxville, TN 37996. Awards MS, PhD. Students: 10 full-time (2 women), 7 part-time (4 women); includes 10 international. 22 applicants, 41% accepted. In 1997, 6 master's, 1 doctorate awarded. *Degree requirements:* For master's, thesis or alternative required, foreign language not required; for doctorate, dissertation required, foreign language not required. *Entrance requirements:* GMAT or GRE General Test, TOEFL (minimum score 550), minimum GPA of 2.7. Application deadline: 2/1 (priority date; rolling processing). Application fee: $35. Electronic applications accepted. *Tuition:* $3354 per year full-time, $181 per semester hour part-time for state residents; $8410 per year full-time, $462 per semester hour part-time for nonresidents. *Financial aid:* Fellowships, Federal Work-Study, institutionally sponsored loans, and career-related internships or fieldwork available. Financial aid application deadline: 2/1. • Dr. Oscar Fowler, Head, 423-974-4116. Fax: 423-974-3163. E-mail: ofowler@utk.edu. Application contact: Dr. Mandyam Srinivasan, Director, 423-974-4116. E-mail: merini@utk.edu.

See in-depth description on page 385.

The University of Texas at Arlington, College of Business Administration, Program in Business Administration, Arlington, TX 76019-0407. Offers business administration (PhD), finance (MBA), information systems (MBA), management (MBA), management sciences (MBA), marketing (MBA), real estate (MBA). Students: 228 full-time (82 women), 314 part-time (99 women); includes 52 minority (8 African Americans, 26 Asian Americans, 15 Hispanics, 3 Native Americans), 167 international. 476 applicants, 51% accepted. In 1997, 158 master's, 18 doctorates awarded. *Degree requirements:* For master's, computer language required, foreign language not required; for doctorate, computer language, dissertation. *Entrance requirements:* For master's, GMAT (minimum score 480; average 550), minimum GPA of 2.9; for doctorate, GMAT (minimum score 580), TSE, minimum GPA of 3.0 (undergraduate), 3.4 (graduate). Application deadline: rolling. Application fee: $25 ($50 for international students). *Tuition:* $3206 per year full-time, $468 per semester (minimum) part-time for state residents; $8612 per year full-time, $1137 per semester (minimum) part-time for nonresidents. *Financial aid:* Fellowships, research assistantships, teaching assistantships, Federal Work-Study, and career-related internships or fieldwork available. • Application contact: Dr. James E. Walther, Graduate Adviser, 817-272-3004. Fax: 817-794-5799.

See in-depth description on page 387.

The University of Texas at Austin, Graduate School, College of Business Administration, Department of Management, Austin, TX 78712. Awards PhD. Students: 23 (8 women); includes 2 minority (1 Hispanic, 1 Native American), 11 international. 52 applicants, 15% accepted. In 1997, 3 degrees awarded (100% entered university research/teaching). *Degree requirements:* Dissertation. *Average time to degree:* doctorate–5 years full-time. *Entrance requirements:* GMAT or GRE. Application deadline: 2/1. Application fee: $50 ($75 for international students). Electronic applications accepted. *Expenses:* Tuition $2592 per year full-time, $324 per semester (minimum) part-time for state residents; $7704 per year full-time, $963 per semester (minimum) part-time for nonresidents. Fees $778 per year full-time, $161 per semester (minimum) part-time. *Financial aid:* Fellowships, research assistantships, teaching assistantships available. Financial aid application deadline: 2/1. • Victor L. Arnold, Chairman, 512-471-3638. E-mail: varnold@mail.utexas.edu. Application contact: Janet Dukerich, Graduate Adviser, 512-471-7876. Fax: 512-471-3937. E-mail: janet.dukerich@mail.utexas.edu.

The University of Texas at Austin, Graduate School, College of Business Administration, Graduate School of Business, Austin, TX 78712. Awards MBA, JD/MBA, MBA/MA, MBA/MP Aff, MBA/MSE, MBA/MSN. MBA/MA offered jointly with the Center for Asian Studies, Center for Latin American Studies, Center for Middle Eastern Studies, College of Communication, and Program in Post-Soviet and East European Studies. Faculty: 110 full-time, 20 part-time. Students: 838 full-time (205 women); includes 157 minority (43 African Americans, 36 Asian Americans, 76 Hispanics, 2 Native Americans), 132 international. Average age 27. 3,360 applicants, 27% accepted. In 1997, 557 degrees awarded. *Average time to degree:* master's–2 years full-time. *Entrance requirements:* GMAT (minimum score 550; average 630), minimum 2 years of full-time work experience. Application deadline: 1/1 (priority date; rolling processing). Application fee: $75 ($100 for international students). Electronic applications accepted. *Expenses:* Tuition $2592 per year full-time, $324 per semester (minimum) part-time for state residents; $7704 per year full-time, $963 per semester (minimum) part-time for nonresidents. Fees $778 per year full-time, $161 per semester (minimum) part-time. *Financial aid:* In 1997–98, 120 research assistantships averaging $749 per month, 210 teaching assistantships averaging $877 per month were awarded; fellowships and career-related internships or fieldwork also available. Financial aid application deadline: 2/1; applicants required to submit FAFSA. • Victor Arnold, Associate Dean, 512-471-7603. Fax: 512-471-4131. E-mail: bgvla@vtxdp.dp.utexas.edu. Application contact: Fran Forbes, Director of Admissions, 512-471-7612. Fax: 512-471-4243. E-mail: texasmba@bus.utexas.edu.

The University of Texas at Brownsville, Graduate Studies, School of Business, Brownsville, TX 78520-4991. Awards MBA. Accredited by ACBSP. Part-time and evening/weekend programs available. Faculty: 14 full-time (4 women). In 1997, 30 degrees awarded. *Degree requirements:* Thesis optional, foreign language not required. *Entrance requirements:* GMAT (minimum score 400), TOEFL (minimum score 550). Application deadline: 8/1 (priority date; rolling processing; 1/1 for spring admission). Application fee: $15. *Expenses:* Tuition $648 per year full-time, $120 per semester hour part-time for state residents; $4698 per year full-time, $783 per semester hour part-time for nonresidents. Fees $593 per year full-time, $109 per year part-time. *Financial aid:* Available to part-time students. Financial aid application deadline: 4/3; applicants required to submit FAFSA. *Faculty research:* Binational and international business. • Dr. Betsy V. Boze, Dean, 956-982-0161. Application contact: Dr. Scott Roberts, MBA Director, 956-982-0230. Fax: 956-982-0159.

The University of Texas at Dallas, School of Management, Cohort MBA Program, Richardson, TX 75083-0688. Awards MBA. Faculty: 49 full-time (9 women), 21 part-time (16 women). Students: 54 full-time (20 women), 2 part-time (1 woman); includes 3 minority (1 African American, 2 Asian Americans), 30 international. Average age 28. 28 applicants, 93% accepted. *Degree requirements:* Minimum GPA of 3.0 required, foreign language and thesis not required. *Entrance requirements:* GMAT. Application deadline: 7/15 (rolling processing). *Financial aid:* Application deadline 11/1. • Dr. Gurumurthy Kalyanaram, Program Director, 972-883-6822. Fax: 972-883-6823. E-mail: kalyang@utdallas.edu.

See in-depth description on page 389.

The University of Texas at Dallas, School of Management, Executive MBA Program, Richardson, TX 75083-0688. Awards MBA. Part-time and evening/weekend programs available. Faculty: 49 full-time (9 women). Students: 31 full-time (3 women), 31 part-time (6 women); includes 14 minority (4 African Americans, 6 Asian Americans, 4 Hispanics), 4 international. Average age 39. 40 applicants, 100% accepted. In 1997, 27 degrees awarded. *Entrance requirements:* 10 years of business experience. Application deadline: 7/15 (rolling processing; 11/15 for spring admission). *Financial aid:* Federal Work-Study available. Aid available to part-time students. Financial aid application deadline: 11/1. • Dr. David Springate, Associate Dean for Executive Program, 972-883-2028. E-mail: spring8@utdallas.edu.

See in-depth description on page 389.

The University of Texas at Dallas, School of Management, Program in Management, Richardson, TX 75083-0688. Offers management (MBA), management and administrative sciences (MS), management and administrative services (MS). Part-time and evening/weekend programs available. Faculty: 49 full-time (9 women). Students: 210 full-time (106 women), 644 part-time (281 women); includes 178 minority (30 African Americans, 110 Asian Americans, 36 Hispanics, 2 Native Americans), 133 international. Average age 31. 357 applicants, 92% accepted. In 1997, 267 degrees awarded. *Degree requirements:* Minimum GPA of 3.0 required, thesis optional, foreign language not required. *Entrance requirements:* GMAT (minimum AACSB index of 1100), TOEFL (minimum score 550). Application deadline: 7/15 (rolling processing; 11/15 for spring admission). Application fee: $25 ($75 for international students). *Financial aid:* Fellowships, research assistantships, teaching assistantships, Federal Work-Study available. Aid available to part-time students. Financial aid application deadline: 11/1. *Faculty research:* Integrated and detailed knowledge of functional areas of management, as well as analytical tools for effective appraisal and decision making. • Dr. Diane McNulty, Associate Dean and College Master, 972-883-2705. Fax: 972-883-2799. E-mail: dmcnulty@utdallas.edu. Application contact: Dr. Gary Horton, Advising Coordinator, 972-883-2707. Fax: 972-883-6425. E-mail: ghorton@utdallas.edu.

See in-depth description on page 389.

The University of Texas at Dallas, School of Management, Programs in Management Science, Richardson, TX 75083-0688. Awards PhD. Part-time and evening/weekend programs available. Faculty: 49 full-time (9 women). Students: 21 full-time (6 women), 22 part-time (10 women); includes 8 minority (2 African Americans, 6 Asian Americans), 17 international. Average age 33. 26 applicants, 69% accepted. In 1997, 6 degrees awarded. *Degree requirements:* Dissertation, minimum GPA of 3.0 required, foreign language not required. *Entrance requirements:* GMAT (minimum score 550 required, minimum AACSB index of 1100), TOEFL (minimum score 550), minimum GPA 0f 3.0. Application deadline: 7/15 (rolling processing; 11/15 for spring admission). Application fee: $25 ($75 for international students). *Financial aid:* Fellowships, research assistantships, teaching assistantships, Federal Work-Study available. Aid available to part-time students. Financial aid application deadline: 11/1. *Faculty research:* Empirical generalizations in marketing, diffusion of generations of technology, stochastic brand-choice theory, acceptance of trade deals by supermarkets, nonparametric estimations of market share response. • Dr. Frank M. Bass, Head, 972-883-2745. E-mail: mzjb@utdallas.edu. Application contact: Betty Sullivan, 972-883-2745.

See in-depth description on page 389.

The University of Texas at El Paso, College of Business Administration, Department of Business Administration, 500 West University Avenue, El Paso, TX 79968-0001. Awards MBA. *Entrance requirements:* GMAT, TOEFL (minimum score 550), minimum GPA of 2.7. Application deadline: 7/1 (priority date; rolling processing; 11/1 for spring admission). Application fee: $15 ($65 for international students). Electronic applications accepted. *Tuition:* $2063 per year full-time, $284 per credit hour part-time for state residents; $5753 per year full-time, $425 per credit hour part-time for nonresidents.

The University of Texas at San Antonio, College of Business, San Antonio, TX 78249-0617. Offers programs in accounting (MP Acct), business administration (MBA), management of technology (MSMOT), taxation (MT). Part-time and evening/weekend programs available. Faculty: 72 full-time (18 women), 40 part-time (9 women). Students: 118 full-time (38 women), 379 part-time (136 women); includes 127 minority (7 African Americans, 19 Asian Americans, 98 Hispanics, 3 Native Americans), 32 international. Average age 34. 310 applicants, 59% accepted. In 1997, 154 degrees awarded. *Entrance requirements:* GMAT (minimum score 500). Application deadline: 7/1 (rolling processing). Application fee: $20. *Expenses:* Tuition $2476 per year full-time, $309 per semester (minimum) part-time for state residents; $7584 per year full-time, $948 per semester (minimum) part-time for nonresidents. Fees $361 per year full-time, $133 per semester (minimum) part-time. *Financial aid:* Federal Work-Study available. Aid available to part-time students. Financial aid application deadline: 3/31. • James F. Gaertner, Dean, 210-458-4313. Application contact: Dr. John H. Brown, Director of Admissions and Registrar, 210-458-4530.

The University of Texas at Tyler, School of Business Administration, Tyler, TX 75799-0001. Awards MBA, MSN/MBA. Programs in business administration (MBA), health care (MBA). Part-time and evening/weekend programs available. Faculty: 12 full-time (3 women), 1 part-time (0 women). Students: 7 full-time (1 woman), 111 part-time (41 women); includes 8 minority (2 African Americans, 4 Asian Americans, 2 Hispanics), 6 international. Average age 30. In 1997, 17 degrees awarded. *Degree requirements:* Computer language required, thesis optional, foreign language not required. *Entrance requirements:* Minimum AACSB index of 1000. Application fee: $0 ($50 for international students). *Tuition:* $2144 per year full-time, $337 per semester (minimum) part-time for state residents; $7256 per year full-time, $964 per semester (minimum) part-time for nonresidents. *Financial aid:* Research assistantships and career-related internships or fieldwork available. Financial aid application deadline: 7/1. *Faculty research:* Business ethics, financial policy, policy and strategy, economic multipliers, tax policy. • Dr. Jim Tarter, Dean, 903-566-7360. Application contact: Martha D. Wheat, Director of Admissions and Student Records, 903-566-7201. Fax: 903-566-7068.

The University of Texas of the Permian Basin, Graduate School, School of Business, Program in Management, Odessa, TX 79762-0001. Awards MBA. *Degree requirements:* Thesis required, foreign language not required. *Entrance requirements:* GMAT. *Expenses:* Tuition $1314 per year full-time, $73 per hour part-time for state residents; $4896 per year full-time, $272 per hour part-time for nonresidents. Fees $383 per year full-time, $111 per semester (minimum) part-time.

The University of Texas–Pan American, College of Business Administration, Edinburg, TX 78539-2999. Awards MBA, PhD. Part-time and evening/weekend programs available. *Degree requirements:* For master's, computer language, thesis or alternative, comprehensive exam required, foreign language not required; for doctorate, 1 foreign language, dissertation, internship. *Entrance requirements:* For master's, GMAT, TOEFL (minimum score 600), minimum AACSB index of 1000 (based on last 60 semester hours); for doctorate, GMAT (score in 75th percentile or higher), TOEFL (minimum score 600). Application deadline: 7/19 (11/16 for spring admission). Application fee: $0. *Tuition:* $2156 per year full-time, $283 per semester (minimum) part-time for state residents; $6788 per year full-time, $862 per semester (minimum) part-time for nonresidents.

See in-depth description on page 391.

University of the District of Columbia, College of Professional Studies, School of Business and Public Administration, Department of Management and Office Systems, Program in Business Administration, 4200 Connecticut Avenue, NW, Washington, DC 20008-1175. Awards MBA. *Degree requirements:* Comprehensive exam required, thesis optional, foreign language not required. *Average time to degree:* master's–2 years full-time, 3 years part-time. *Entrance requirements:* GMAT, writing proficiency exam. Application deadline: 6/14 (priority date; rolling processing; 11/15 for spring admission). Application fee: $20. *Expenses:* Tuition $3564 per year full-time, $198 per credit part-time for district residents; $5922 per year full-time, $329 per credit part-time for nonresidents. Fees $990 per year full-time, $55 per credit part-time.

University of the Incarnate Word, School of Graduate Studies, College of Professional Studies, Program in Business Administration, San Antonio, TX 78209-6397. Awards MBA, MBA/MSN. Part-time and evening/weekend programs available. Faculty: 16 full-time (5 women), 2 part-time (0 women). *Average time to degree:* master's–1.5 years full-time, 3 years part-time. *Entrance requirements:* GMAT (minimum score 450), TOEFL (minimum score 550). Application deadline: 8/15 (priority date; rolling processing; 12/31 for spring admission). Application fee: $20. *Expenses:* Tuition $350 per semester hour. Fees $180 per year full-time, $111 per semester (minimum) part-time. *Financial aid:* Partial tuition waivers, Federal Work-Study, institutionally sponsored loans, and career-related internships or fieldwork available. Aid available to part-time students. Financial aid application deadline: 5/31. *Faculty research:* Small business, Mexico/U.S. business organizational development. • Victor Prosper, Coordinator, 210-829-3185. Fax: 210-829-3169. Application contact: Brian F. Dalton, Dean of Enrollment Services, 210-829-6005. Fax: 210-829-3921. E-mail: briand@universe.uiwtx.edu.

University of the Incarnate Word, School of Graduate Studies, College of Professional Studies, Programs in Administration, San Antonio, TX 78209-6397. Offerings in general management (MAA), international administration (MAA), organization development (MAA), sports management (MAA). *Entrance requirements:* GMAT, GRE, MAT, TOEFL (minimum score 550). Application deadline: 8/15 (priority date; rolling processing; 12/31 for spring admission). Application fee: $20. *Expenses:* Tuition $350 per semester hour. Fees $180 per year full-time, $111 per semester (minimum) part-time. • Victor Prosper, Coordinator, 210-829-3185. Fax: 210-829-3169. Application contact: Brian F. Dalton, Dean of Enrollment Services, 210-829-6005. Fax: 210-829-3921. E-mail: briand@the-college.iwctx.edu.

University of the Pacific, Eberhardt School of Business, Stockton, CA 95211-0197. Awards MBA, JD/MBA. Part-time programs available. Faculty: 24 full-time (4 women), 4 part-time (2 women), 26 FTE. Students: 25 full-time (12 women), 65 part-time (22 women); includes 4 international. 77 applicants, 75% accepted. In 1997, 42 degrees awarded. *Entrance requirements:* GMAT. Application deadline: 7/31 (priority date; rolling processing; 11/30 for spring admission). Application fee: $50. *Expenses:* Tuition $19,000 per year full-time, $594 per unit part-time. Fees $30 per year (minimum). *Financial aid:* Fellowships, research assistantships, Federal Work-Study, institutionally sponsored loans available. Aid available to part-time students. Financial aid application deadline: 3/1; applicants required to submit FAFSA. • Mark

Directory: Business Administration and Management—General

University of the Pacific (continued)
Plovnick, Dean, 209-946-2466. E-mail: mplovnick@uop.edu. Application contact: Ronald Hoverstad, MBA Program Director, 209-946-2476. Fax: 209-946-2586. E-mail: rhoverstad@uop.edu.

University of the Sacred Heart, Graduate Programs, Department of Business Administration, San Juan, PR 00914-0383. Offers programs in human resource management (MBA), management information systems (MBA), marketing (MBA), taxation (MBA). Part-time and evening/weekend programs available. Faculty: 6 full-time (3 women), 11 part-time (1 woman), 9.67 FTE. Students: 6 full-time (4 women), 200 part-time (90 women). 92 applicants, 53% accepted. In 1997, 6 degrees awarded. *Degree requirements:* Computer language, thesis. *Entrance requirements:* PAEG, minimum undergraduate GPA of 2.5. Application deadline: 5/15. Application fee: $25. *Expenses:* Tuition $150 per credit. Fees $240 per credit. • Yesmin Hernández, Director, 787-728-1515 Ext. 2274. Fax: 787-728-1515 Ext. 2273. E-mail: y_hernandez@uscac1.usc.clu.edu. Application contact: Dr. Blanca Villamil, Acting Director, Admissions Office, 787-728-1515 Ext. 3237. Fax: 787-728-2066. E-mail: b_villami@uscsi.usc.clu.edu.

University of the Virgin Islands, Division of Business Administration, Charlotte Amalie, St. Thomas, VI 00802-9990. Awards MBA. Part-time and evening/weekend programs available. Faculty: 6 full-time (0 women), 1 part-time (0 women). Students: 11 full-time (5 women), 43 part-time (31 women); includes 46 minority (44 African Americans, 1 Asian American, 1 Hispanic), 2 international. Average age 33. In 1997, 18 degrees awarded. *Degree requirements:* Comprehensive exam or thesis required, foreign language not required. *Entrance requirements:* GMAT, minimum GPA of 2.5. Application deadline: 4/30 (11/30 for spring admission). Application fee: $20. *Tuition:* $205 per credit for territory residents; $410 per credit for nonresidents. *Financial aid:* Application deadline 4/15. *Faculty research:* MIS. • David Boyd, Chairperson, 340-693-1301. Fax: 340-693-1311. E-mail: dboyd@uvi.edu. Application contact: Judith Edwin, Director of Enrollment Management, 340-693-1151. Fax: 340-693-1155. E-mail: jedwin@uvi.edu.

University of Toledo, Graduate School of Business, Department of Management, Toledo, OH 43606-3398. Awards MBA. Part-time and evening/weekend programs available. Faculty: 16 full-time (2 women). Students: 17 full-time (6 women), 221 part-time (80 women); includes 10 minority (2 African Americans, 6 Asian Americans, 2 Hispanics), 35 international. Average age 30. 138 applicants, 64% accepted. In 1997, 85 degrees awarded. *Entrance requirements:* GMAT (minimum score 450), TOEFL (minimum score 550). Application deadline: 8/1 (priority date; rolling processing). Application fee: $30. *Tuition:* $5907 per year full-time, $246 per hour part-time for state residents; $11,835 per year full-time, $493 per hour part-time for nonresidents. *Financial aid:* In 1997–98, 1 research assistantship was awarded; full tuition waivers, Federal Work-Study, institutionally sponsored loans, and career-related internships or fieldwork also available. Aid available to part-time students. Financial aid application deadline: 4/1; applicants required to submit FAFSA. *Faculty research:* Stress, deviation, work place, globalization, recruitment. Total annual research expenditures: $65,000. • Dr. Bhal Bhatt, Chair, 419-530-2366. Application contact: Dr. Bruce Kuhlman, MBA Director, 419-530-2774. Fax: 419-530-7260. E-mail: mba0001@uoft01.utoledo.edu.

See in-depth description on page 393.

University of Toronto, School of Graduate Studies, Social Sciences Division, Collaborative Program in Management and Economics, Toronto, ON M5S 1A1, Canada. Awards PhD. *Degree requirements:* Dissertation. *Application fee:* $75. *Expenses:* Tuition $4070 per year for Canadian residents; $7870 per year for nonresidents. Fees $628 per year. • M. Evans, Head.

University of Toronto, School of Graduate Studies, Social Sciences Division, Faculty of Management, Toronto, ON M5S 1A1, Canada. Awards MBA, MMPA, PhD, LL B/MBA, MBA/MA. Part-time and evening/weekend programs available. Faculty: 50. Students: 368 full-time (147 women), 315 part-time (87 women); includes 66 international. 1,114 applicants, 37% accepted. In 1997, 259 master's, 8 doctorates awarded. *Degree requirements:* For doctorate, dissertation. *Application fee:* $100. *Expenses:* Tuition $4070 per year for Canadian residents; $7870 per year for nonresidents. Fees $628 per year. *Financial aid:* Fellowships, research assistantships, teaching assistantships, and career-related internships or fieldwork available. *Faculty research:* Natural resources, organizational behavior, finance. • P. J. Halpern, Interim Dean, 416-978-3422. Application contact: Secretary, 416-978-3499. Fax: 416-978-5812. E-mail: mba.prog@fmgmt.mgmt.utoronto.ca.

University of Tulsa, College of Business Administration, Program in Business Administration, Tulsa, OK 74104-3189. Awards MBA, JD/MBA, MNA/MBA. Part-time and evening/weekend programs available. Faculty: 28 full-time (4 women). Students: 57 full-time (25 women), 123 part-time (50 women); includes 22 minority (4 African Americans, 9 Asian Americans, 2 Hispanics, 7 Native Americans), 23 international. Average age 29. 115 applicants, 87% accepted. In 1997, 42 degrees awarded. *Entrance requirements:* GMAT, TOEFL (minimum score 575). Application deadline: rolling. Application fee: $30. Electronic applications accepted. *Expenses:* Tuition $480 per credit hour. Fees $2 per credit hour. *Financial aid:* In 1997–98, 27 students received aid, including 3 research assistantships (all to first-year students) totaling $42,023, 24 teaching assistantships (8 to first-year students) totaling $282,140; fellowships, partial tuition waivers, Federal Work-Study also available. Aid available to part-time students. Financial aid application deadline: 2/1; applicants required to submit FAFSA. *Faculty research:* International trade and development, expert systems, leadership, creativity, entrepreneurship. • Dr. Richard C. Burgess, Assistant Dean/Director of Graduate Business Studies, 918-631-2242. Fax: 918-631-2142.

University of Utah, Graduate School of Business, Salt Lake City, UT 84112-1107. Awards MBA, MHRM, M Pr A, MS, M Stat, PhD, JD/MBA, M Arch/MBA, MBA/MS. Part-time and evening/weekend programs available. Faculty: 60 full-time (12 women), 24 part-time (4 women). Students: 260 full-time (76 women), 169 part-time (54 women); includes 25 minority (1 African American, 17 Asian Americans, 6 Hispanics, 1 Native American), 35 international. Average age 31. In 1997, 167 master's, 8 doctorates awarded. *Degree requirements:* For master's, computer language required, foreign language not required; for doctorate, computer language, dissertation, oral qualifying exams, written qualifying exams required, foreign language not required. *Entrance requirements:* GMAT, TSE, TOEFL (minimum score 500). Application deadline: 2/15. Application fee: $30 ($50 for international students). *Tuition:* $2045 per year full-time, $562 per semester (minimum) part-time for state residents; $6129 per year full-time, $1607 per semester (minimum) part-time for nonresidents. *Financial aid:* In 1997–98, 30 teaching assistantships were awarded; fellowships, Federal Work-Study, and career-related internships or fieldwork also available. *Faculty research:* Auditing, taxation, information systems, investment, risk management. • John Seybolt, Dean, 801-581-7347. Fax: 801-581-7214. E-mail: mgtjws@buo.bus.utah.edu. Application contact: Diana Hirschi, Director, Master's Programs, 801-581-7785.

University of Vermont, School of Business Administration, Burlington, VT 05405-0160. Awards MBA. Part-time programs available. Faculty: 25. Students: 74; includes 1 minority (Hispanic), 12 international. 95 applicants, 79% accepted. In 1997, 17 degrees awarded. *Degree requirements:* Computer language required, foreign language and thesis not required. *Entrance requirements:* GMAT, TOEFL (minimum score 550). Application deadline: 4/1 (priority date; rolling processing). Application fee: $25. *Expenses:* Tuition $302 per credit for state residents; $755 per credit for nonresidents. Fees $434 per year full-time, $46 per semester (minimum) part-time. *Financial aid:* Fellowships, teaching assistantships, Federal Work-Study available. Financial aid application deadline: 3/1. • Dr. Larry E. Shirland, Dean, 802-656-3177. Application contact: Dr. Gene Laber, Coordinator, 802-656-3177.

University of Victoria, Faculty of Business, Victoria, BC V8W 2Y2, Canada. Awards MBA, MBA/LL B. Part-time programs available. Faculty: 17 full-time (2 women), 6 part-time (0 women). Students: 134 full-time (61 women), 40 part-time (22 women); includes 32 international. Average age 30. 197 applicants, 36% accepted. In 1997, 38 degrees awarded. *Average time to degree:* master's–1.9 years full-time. *Entrance requirements:* GMAT (average 600), TOEFL (minimum score 575; average 620), minimum B average. Application deadline: 5/31 (rolling processing). Application fee: $50. *Tuition:* $5647 per year. *Financial aid:* In 1997–98, 2 fellowships (both to first-year students) totaling $22,000, research assistantships totaling $22,000 were awarded; teaching assistantships, awards, Federal Work-Study, institutionally sponsored loans, and career-related internships or fieldwork also available. Financial aid application deadline: 2/15. *Faculty research:* Organizational design and analysis, negotiation and conflict management, human resources management, entrepreneurship, international marketing and tourism. • Dr. Ignace Ng, Director, 250-721-6073. Fax: 250-721-7066. E-mail: ing@business.uvic.ca. Application contact: Nicholas James, Admissions Officer, 250-721-6414. Fax: 250-721-6067. E-mail: njames@business.uvic.ca.

University of Victoria, Faculty of Human and Social Development, School of Public Administration, Victoria, BC V8W 2Y2, Canada. Offerings include management science (MPA). School faculty: 14 full-time (1 woman), 13 part-time (6 women), 18 FTE. *Degree requirements:* Report required, foreign language and thesis not required. *Average time to degree:* master's–4 years full-time. *Entrance requirements:* GMAT or GRE General Test, TOEFL (minimum score 550). Application deadline: 5/1 (rolling processing; 10/15 for spring admission). Application fee: $50. *Tuition:* $2080 per year full-time, $557 per semester part-time. • Dr. B. Wharf, Acting Director, 250-721-8054. Application contact: Dr. B. Bish, Graduate Adviser, 250-721-8065.

University of Virginia, Colgate Darden Graduate School of Business Administration, Charlottesville, VA 22903. Awards MBA, DBA, PhD, JD/MBA, MBA/MA, ME/MBA, MSN/MBA. Faculty: 55 full-time (15 women), 3 part-time (2 women), 57 FTE. Students: 504 full-time (149 women), 1 part-time (0 women); includes 80 minority (33 African Americans, 30 Asian Americans, 17 Hispanics), 91 international. Average age 28. 3,028 applicants, 14% accepted. In 1997, 241 master's, 1 doctorate awarded. *Degree requirements:* For doctorate, dissertation required, foreign language not required. *Entrance requirements:* GMAT. Application deadline: 3/15. Application fee: $75. *Tuition:* $4921 per year for state residents; $15,869 per year for nonresidents. *Financial aid:* Fellowships and career-related internships or fieldwork available. • Edward A. Snyder Jr., Dean, 804-924-7481. Application contact: A. Jon Megibow, Director of Admissions, 804-924-7281. E-mail: darden@virginia.edu.

University of Virginia, Graduate School of Arts and Sciences, McIntire School of Commerce, Charlottesville, VA 22903. Awards MS, JD/MS. Programs in accounting (MS), management information systems (MS). Faculty: 52 full-time (12 women), 7 part-time (3 women), 54 FTE. Students: 48 full-time (18 women), 4 part-time (3 women); includes 8 minority (3 African Americans, 4 Asian Americans, 1 Hispanic), 5 international. Average age 26. 79 applicants, 66% accepted. In 1997, 43 degrees awarded. *Entrance requirements:* GMAT, TOEFL. Application deadline: 7/15 (rolling processing; 12/1 for spring admission). Application fee: $40. *Tuition:* $4876 per year for state residents; $15,824 per year for nonresidents. *Financial aid:* Fellowships, research assistantships, teaching assistantships, Federal Work-Study, and career-related internships or fieldwork available. • Robert S. Kemp, Director of Graduate Studies. Application contact: Duane J. Osheim, Associate Dean, 804-924-7184.

University of Washington, School of Business Administration, Seattle, WA 98195. Awards MBA, MP Acc, PhD, JD/MBA, MBA/MAIS, MBA/MHA, MBA/MSE. Evening/weekend programs available. Faculty: 98 full-time (15 women), 6 part-time (3 women). Students: 407 full-time (143 women), 94 part-time (29 women); includes 62 minority (7 African Americans, 47 Asian Americans, 6 Hispanics, 2 Native Americans), 95 international. Average age 29. 1,484 applicants, 33% accepted. In 1997, 209 master's, 10 doctorates awarded. *Degree requirements:* For master's, computer language, thesis or alternative required, foreign language not required; for doctorate, computer language, dissertation required, foreign language not required. *Entrance requirements:* For master's, GMAT (average 632), TOEFL (minimum score 600; average 620), minimum GPA of 3.0; for doctorate, GMAT, TOEFL (minimum score 580), minimum GPA of 3.0. Application deadline: 3/27 (priority date; rolling processing). Application fee: $45. *Tuition:* $5433 per year full-time, $775 per quarter (minimum) part-time for state residents; $13,479 per year full-time, $1925 per quarter (minimum) part-time for nonresidents. *Financial aid:* 282 students received aid; fellowships, research assistantships, teaching assistantships, Federal Work-Study, and career-related internships or fieldwork available. Financial aid applicants required to submit FAFSA. • William Bradford, Dean, 206-543-4750. Application contact: David Williams, Acting Director, MBA Program, 206-543-4661. Fax: 206-616-7351. E-mail: mba@washington.edu.

The University of Western Ontario, Ivey Business School, London, ON N6A 5B8, Canada. Awards EMBA, MBA, PhD, LL B/MBA. Faculty: 81 full-time (13 women). Students: 450 full-time (100 women). Average age 29. 925 applicants, 22% accepted. In 1997, 200 master's, 50 doctorates awarded. *Degree requirements:* For master's, thesis required (for some programs), foreign language not required; for doctorate, dissertation required, foreign language not required. *Average time to degree:* master's–2 years full-time; doctorate–4 years full-time. *Entrance requirements:* For master's, GMAT (minimum score 560; average 633), TOEFL (minimum score 600), 2 years of full-time work experience; for doctorate, GMAT, TOEFL (minimum score 600). Application deadline: 5/15 (rolling processing). Application fee: $100. *Financial aid:* Scholarships, full tuition waivers, Federal Work-Study, institutionally sponsored loans, and career-related internships or fieldwork available. *Faculty research:* Policy, organizational behavior, international business, finance, operations management. • L. G. Tapp, Dean. Application contact: L. Gamula, Admissions Director, 519-661-3212. Fax: 519-661-3431. E-mail: lgamula@ivey.uwo.ca.

See in-depth description on page 395.

University of West Florida, College of Business, Department of Business Administration, Pensacola, FL 32514-5750. Awards MBA. Part-time and evening/weekend programs available. Students: 54 full-time (26 women), 150 part-time (56 women); includes 26 minority (12 African Americans, 7 Asian Americans, 7 Hispanics), 8 international. Average age 31. 93 applicants, 80% accepted. In 1997, 67 degrees awarded. *Degree requirements:* Computer language required, thesis optional. *Entrance requirements:* GMAT (minimum score 450; average 550). Application deadline: 7/1 (rolling processing; 11/1 for spring admission). Application fee: $20. *Tuition:* $131 per credit hour (minimum) for state residents; $436 per credit hour (minimum) for nonresidents. *Financial aid:* Fellowships, Federal Work-Study, and career-related internships or fieldwork available. Aid available to part-time students. Financial aid application deadline: 4/1; applicants required to submit FAFSA. *Faculty research:* Robotics, corporate behavior, international trade, franchising, counterfeiting. • Dr. J. Lew Cox, Chairperson, 850-474-2309. Application contact: Mary F. Dowhal, Program Assistant, 850-474-2352.

University of Windsor, Faculty of Business Administration, Windsor, ON N9B 3P4, Canada. Awards MBA, MBA/LL B. Part-time and evening/weekend programs available. *Degree requirements:* Thesis optional. *Entrance requirements:* GMAT (minimum score 500), TOEFL (minimum score 550), minimum B average. Application deadline: 6/1 (priority date; rolling processing). Application fee: $50. *Expenses:* Tuition $4370 per year (minimum) full-time, $345 per course (minimum) part-time for Canadian residents; $8453 per year (minimum) full-time, $915 per course (minimum) part-time for nonresidents. Fees $462 per year (minimum) full-time, $141 per year (minimum) part-time. *Faculty research:* Accounting, administrative studies, finance, marketing, business policy and strategy.

University of Wisconsin–Eau Claire, College of Business, Program in Business Administration, Eau Claire, WI 54702-4004. Awards MBA. Students: 5 full-time (1 woman), 39 part-time (17 women); includes 3 minority (1 African American, 2 Native Americans). Average age 32. In 1997, 4 degrees awarded. *Application deadline:* 7/1 (rolling processing; 12/1 for spring admission). *Application fee:* $45. • Robert Erffmeyer, Head, 715-836-4644.

University of Wisconsin–Green Bay, Program in Administrative Science, Green Bay, WI 54311-7001. Awards MS. Part-time programs available. Faculty: 11 full-time (2 women), 4 part-time (1 woman). Students: 2 full-time (1 woman), 26 part-time (16 women); includes 3 minority (1 African American, 2 Native Americans). Average age 34. In 1997, 5 degrees awarded. *Degree requirements:* Thesis required, foreign language not required. *Entrance requirements:* GMAT or GRE General Test, minimum GPA of 3.0. Application deadline: 8/1 (rolling processing; 11/1 for spring admission). Application fee: $35. *Tuition:* $3774 per year full-time, $183 per credit part-time for state residents; $11,418 per year full-time, $425 per credit part-time for nonresidents. *Financial aid:* Research assistantships, teaching assistantships, Federal Work-Study, institutionally sponsored loans, and career-related internships or fieldwork available. Financial aid application deadline: 7/15; applicants required to submit FAFSA. *Faculty research:* Planning methods, budgeting, decision making, organizational behavior and theory, management. • Dr. David Littig, Coordinator, 920-465-2081. E-mail: littigd@uwgb.edu.

University of Wisconsin–La Crosse, College of Business Administration, La Crosse, WI 54601-3742. Awards MBA. Part-time and evening/weekend programs available. Faculty: 27 full-time (5 women). Students: 21 full-time (6 women), 71 part-time (22 women); includes 4 minority (2 Hispanics, 2 Native Americans), 19 international. Average age 31. 34 applicants, 94% accepted. In 1997, 36 degrees awarded (83% found work related to degree, 11% continued full-time study). *Average time to degree:* master's–1.5 years full-time, 3.5 years part-time. *Entrance requirements:* GMAT (average 530), minimum GPA of 2.85. Application deadline: 5/1 (priority date; rolling processing; 10/1 for spring admission). Application fee: $38. *Expenses:* Tuition $3772 per year full-time, $210 per credit hour part-time for state residents; $11,481 per year full-time, $639 per credit hour part-time for nonresidents. Fees $400 per year full-time, $30 per credit hour part-time. *Financial aid:* In 1997–98, 12 students received aid, including 8 research assistantships (5 to first-year students) averaging $780 per month and totaling $49,119; Federal Work-Study also available. Aid available to part-time students. Financial aid application deadline: 3/1; applicants required to submit FAFSA. *Faculty research:* Policy, organizational behavior, international business, insurance, finance. • Rex Fuller, Dean, 608-785-8091. Application contact: Amelia Dittman, Assistant to the Dean, 608-785-8092. Fax: 608-785-6700. E-mail: dittman@mail.uwlax.edu.

University of Wisconsin–Madison, School of Business, Madison, WI 53706-1380. Awards MA, M Acc, MBA, MS, PhD. Part-time and evening/weekend programs available. Terminal master's awarded for partial completion of doctoral program. *Degree requirements:* For doctorate, dissertation. *Entrance requirements:* For doctorate, GMAT. Application fee: $38. Electronic applications accepted. *Tuition:* $5950 per year full-time, $1118 per semester (minimum) part-time for state residents; $16,230 per year full-time, $3044 per semester (minimum) part-time for nonresidents. *Faculty research:* Leadership, working in teams, ethics, market psychology, health insurance, international accounting standards.

University of Wisconsin–Milwaukee, School of Business Administration, Milwaukee, WI 53201-0413. Awards MBA, MS, PhD. Part-time and evening/weekend programs available. Faculty: 55 full-time (12 women). Students: 159 full-time (68 women), 595 part-time (232 women); includes 47 minority (15 African Americans, 27 Asian Americans, 4 Hispanics, 1 Native American), 96 international. 483 applicants, 64% accepted. In 1997, 141 master's, 6 doctorates awarded. *Degree requirements:* For master's, computer language required, foreign language and thesis not required; for doctorate, computer language, dissertation, comprehensive exams required, foreign language not required. *Entrance requirements:* GMAT or GRE General Test. Application deadline: 1/1 (priority date; rolling processing; 9/1 for spring admission). Application fee: $45 ($75 for international students). *Tuition:* $6038 per year full-time, $1225 per semester (minimum) part-time for state residents; $16,274 per year full-time, $3145 per semester (minimum) part-time for nonresidents. *Financial aid:* In 1997–98, 2 fellowships, 1 research assistantship, 32 teaching assistantships, 9 project assistantships were awarded; Federal Work-Study and career-related internships or fieldwork also available. Aid available to part-time students. Financial aid application deadline: 4/15. *Faculty research:* Applied management research in finance, MIS, marketing, operations research, organizational sciences. • Charles Kroncke, Dean, 414-229-4235. Application contact: Velagapudi K. Prasad, Associate Dean, 414-229-4235.

University of Wisconsin–Oshkosh, College of Business Administration, Oshkosh, WI 54901-8602. Awards MBA. Offered jointly with University of Wisconsin–Green Bay and University of Wisconsin–Stevens Point. Part-time and evening/weekend programs available. Faculty: 41 full-time (7 women). Students: 27 full-time (9 women), 508 part-time (200 women); includes 19 minority (2 African Americans, 13 Asian Americans, 2 Hispanics, 2 Native Americans), 11 international. Average age 31. 160 applicants, 83% accepted. In 1997, 99 degrees awarded. *Entrance requirements:* GMAT (minimum score 450; average 540), minimum undergraduate GPA of 2.75. Application deadline: 7/1 (priority date; rolling processing; 12/1 for spring admission). Application fee: $45. *Tuition:* $4054 per year full-time, $678 per semester (minimum) part-time for state residents; $11,698 per year full-time, $1953 per semester (minimum) part-time for nonresidents. *Financial aid:* Federal Work-Study and career-related internships or fieldwork available. Aid available to part-time students. Financial aid application deadline: 3/15. *Faculty research:* Portfolio analysis, entrepreneurship, human resource management and leadership, decision support systems, total quality management. • Dr. E. Alan Hartman, Dean, 920-424-1424. Application contact: Dr. Donald R. Simons, MBA Coordinator, 920-424-3472.

University of Wisconsin–Parkside, School of Business and Technology, Kenosha, WI 53141-2000. Awards MBA. Part-time and evening/weekend programs available. Faculty: 14 full-time (4 women). Students: 115 part-time (52 women); includes 11 minority (4 African Americans, 4 Asian Americans, 2 Hispanics, 1 Native American), 2 international. Average age 32. In 1997, 19 degrees awarded (100% found work related to degree). *Entrance requirements:* GMAT (minimum score 450; average 500), minimum undergraduate GPA of 2.75. Application deadline: 8/1 (priority date; 12/1 for spring admission). Application fee: $45. *Faculty research:* Business strategy, ethics in accounting and finance, mutual funds, decision analysis and neural networks, management skills. • Dr. Richard Stolz, Dean, 414-595-2243. E-mail: stolz@uwp.edu. Application contact: Brad Piazza, Assistant to the Dean, 414-595-2046. Fax: 414-595-2680. E-mail: piazza@uwp.edu.

University of Wisconsin–Stevens Point, College of Letters and Science, Division of Business and Economics, Stevens Point, WI 54481-3897. Awards MBA. Offered jointly with the University of Wisconsin–Oshkosh. Faculty: 9 (1 woman). *Application deadline:* rolling. *Application fee:* $38. *Tuition:* $3702 per year full-time, $664 per semester (minimum) part-time for state residents; $11,346 per year full-time, $1938 per semester (minimum) part-time for nonresidents. *Financial aid:* Application deadline 5/1; applicants required to submit FAFSA. • Dr. Randy Cray, Chair, 715-346-2728.

University of Wisconsin–Whitewater, College of Business and Economics, Program in Business Administration, Whitewater, WI 53190-1790. Awards MBA. Part-time and evening/weekend programs available. *Degree requirements:* Computer language required, foreign language and thesis not required. *Entrance requirements:* GMAT, minimum AACSB index of 1000, minimum GPA of 2.75. Application deadline: rolling. Application fee: $45.

Announcement: Whitewater's Master of Business Administration (MBA) program provides advanced academic work in the functional aspects of public and private organizations. This professional degree program provides students with general competencies for overall management and allows a degree of specialization in the areas of accounting, decision support systems, finance, international business, management, marketing, production management, technology and training, and health care. Internationalization and globalization are important ingredients of courses. A variety of teaching methods are used. Problem-solving and communication skills are emphasized through projects, case studies, and formal and informal presentations. There is diversity among students and faculty members. Many students are employed full-time. There are a significant number of international students. MBA courses are available over the Internet. Also offered are a Master of Professional Accountancy (MPA) degree, which prepares students for the CPA exam, and a Master of Science in Management Computer Systems (MSMCS) degree, which provides information systems professionals with higher-level information systems management skills.

University of Wyoming, College of Business, Program in Business Administration, Laramie, WY 82071. Awards MBA. Part-time and evening/weekend programs available. Postbaccalaureate distance learning degree programs offered (minimal on-campus study). Faculty: 38 (7 women). Students: 18 full-time (11 women), 49 part-time (24 women); includes 4 minority (1 Asian American, 2 Hispanics, 1 Native American), 5 international. 75 applicants, 36% accepted. In 1997, 29 degrees awarded. *Degree requirements:* Thesis or alternative required, foreign language not required. *Average time to degree:* master's–2 years full-time, 4 years part-time. *Entrance requirements:* GMAT (minimum score 500; average 560), minimum GPA of 3.0. Application deadline: 4/15 (priority date; rolling processing). Application fee: $40. *Expenses:* Tuition $2430 per year full-time, $135 per credit hour part-time for state residents; $7518 per year full-time, $418 per credit hour part-time for nonresidents. Fees $386 per year full-time, $9.25 per credit hour part-time. *Financial aid:* In 1997–98, 1 fellowship was awarded; research assistantships, teaching assistantships, Federal Work-Study, institutionally sponsored loans, and career-related internships or fieldwork also available. Financial aid application deadline: 3/1; applicants required to submit FAFSA. *Faculty research:* Natural resource marketing and product development, work place violence. • Dr. Martin Greller, Director, 307-766-2449. E-mail: mba@uwyo.edu. Application contact: Program Office, 307-766-2449. Fax: 307-766-4028. E-mail: mba@uwyo.edu.

Upper Iowa University, Program in Business Leadership, Fayette, IA 52142-1857. Offers human resource management (MA), quality management (MA). Also available at Des Moines, Iowa campus; Madison, Wisconsin campus; and Waterloo, Iowa campus. Part-time and evening/weekend programs available. Postbaccalaureate distance learning degree programs offered (no on-campus study). Faculty: 40. Students: 22 full-time (13 women), 85 part-time (46 women); includes 20 minority (6 African Americans, 14 Asian Americans). Average age 35. 50 applicants, 80% accepted. In 1997, 12 degrees awarded. *Degree requirements:* Thesis optional, foreign language not required. *Entrance requirements:* GMAT, GRE, or minimum GPA of 2.5 during last 60 hours. Application deadline: 8/26 (rolling processing). Application fee: $50. *Tuition:* $200 per credit. *Financial aid:* Career-related internships or fieldwork available. Aid available to part-time students. *Faculty research:* Total quality management, CQI, teams, organization culture and climate, management. • Dr. Patrick Langan, Director, 800-773-9298. Fax: 319-425-5383.

Utah State University, College of Business, Program in Business Administration, Logan, UT 84322. Awards MBA. Part-time and evening/weekend programs available. Faculty: 43 full-time (4 women). Students: 210 full-time (39 women), 40 part-time (8 women); includes 5 minority (1 African American, 2 Hispanics, 2 Native Americans), 26 international. Average age 29. 250 applicants, 62% accepted. In 1997, 81 degrees awarded. *Degree requirements:* Computer language required, foreign language not required. *Average time to degree:* master's–1 year full-time, 2 years part-time. *Entrance requirements:* GMAT (score in 40th percentile or higher), TOEFL (minimum score 550), minimum GPA of 3.0. Application deadline: 4/15 (priority date; rolling processing; 10/15 for spring admission). Application fee: $40. *Expenses:* Tuition $1448 per year full-time, $624 per year part-time for state residents; $5082 per year full-time, $2192 per year part-time for nonresidents. Fees $421 per year full-time, $165 per year part-time. *Financial aid:* Fellowships, teaching assistantships, additional tuition waivers, full and partial tuition waivers, Federal Work-Study, institutionally sponsored loans, and career-related internships or fieldwork available. Financial aid application deadline: 4/1. *Faculty research:* Marketing strategy, technology and innovation, public utility finance, international competitiveness. • Michael Parent, Associate Dean and Director, 435-797-2360. Application contact: Anita Lowe, Assistant Director, 435-797-1773. Fax: 435-797-3995.

Valdosta State University, College of Business Administration, Valdosta, GA 31698. Awards M Acc, MBA. Part-time programs available. Faculty: 13 full-time (3 women). Students: 21 full-time (8 women), 10 part-time (5 women); includes 3 minority (2 African Americans, 1 Asian American), 2 international. Average age 27. 65 applicants, 69% accepted. In 1997, 13 degrees awarded. *Average time to degree:* master's–2 years full-time. *Entrance requirements:* GMAT (minimum score 450), minimum GPA of 2.75. Application deadline: 8/1 (rolling processing). Application fee: $10. *Expenses:* Tuition $2472 per year full-time, $83 per semester hour part-time for state residents; $8472 per year full-time, $333 per semester hour part-time for nonresidents. Fees $236 per year full-time. *Financial aid:* Graduate assistantships available. • Dr. Kenneth L. Stanley, Dean, 912-333-5991. Fax: 912-245-6498. E-mail: kstanley@grits.valdosta.peachnet.edu.

Vanderbilt University, Owen Graduate School of Management, Business Administration Program, Nashville, TN 37240-1001. Awards MBA, JD/MBA, MBA/MA, MBA/M Eng, MBA/MSN. MBA/MSN offered jointly with the School of Nursing. MBA/MA offered jointly with the Program in Latin American Studies. MBA/M Eng offered jointly with the Program in Management of Technology. Evening/weekend programs available. Faculty: 47 full-time (6 women), 16 part-time (4 women). Students: 426 full-time (121 women); includes 38 minority (18 African Americans, 13 Asian Americans, 6 Hispanics, 1 Native American), 96 international. Average age 27. 1,313 applicants, 38% accepted. In 1997, 211 degrees awarded. *Entrance requirements:* GMAT, TOEFL, previous course work in calculus. Application deadline: 3/15 (priority date; rolling processing). Application fee: $50. *Financial aid:* In 1997–98, 20 fellowships totaling $100,000, scholarships totaling $1.7 million were awarded; full and partial tuition waivers, Federal Work-Study, institutionally sponsored loans, and career-related internships or fieldwork also available. Financial aid applicants required to submit FAFSA. *Faculty research:* Financial markets, services marketing, operations, human resources, electronic commerce. • Director of MBA Program, 615-322-6469. Application contact: Hayden Estrada, Director of MBA Admissions, 615-322-6469. Fax: 615-343-1175.

Vanderbilt University, Owen Graduate School of Management, Executive Business Administration Program, Nashville, TN 37240-1001. Awards MBA. Evening/weekend programs available. Students: 103 full-time (15 women); includes 8 minority (4 African Americans, 3 Asian Americans, 1 Hispanic). Average age 35. 106 applicants, 60% accepted. In 1997, 50 degrees awarded (100% found work related to degree). *Average time to degree:* master's–2 years full-time. *Entrance requirements:* GMAT (average 580). Application fee: $50. *Faculty research:* Management, business policy, finance, marketing, operations management. • Thomas Hambury, Director, 615-322-2513. E-mail: tom.hambury@owen.vanderbilt.edu. Application contact: Becky Fritts, Coordinator, 615-322-0745. Fax: 615-343-2293. E-mail: becky.fritts@owen.vanderbilt.edu.

Vanderbilt University, Owen Graduate School of Management and Graduate School, Program in Management, Nashville, TN 37240-1001. Offers finance (PhD), marketing (PhD), operations management (PhD), organizational studies (PhD). PhD offered through the Graduate School. Students: 11 full-time (2 women); includes 8 international. Average age 28. In 1997, 1 degree awarded. *Degree requirements:* Dissertation required, foreign language not required. *Entrance requirements:* GMAT (minimum score 650), GRE, TOEFL (minimum score 600). Application deadline: 1/15. Application fee: $50. *Tuition:* $871 per semester hour. *Financial aid:* 11 students received aid; fellowships, full and partial tuition waivers, Federal Work-Study, institutionally sponsored loans, and career-related internships or fieldwork available. Financial aid applicants required to submit FAFSA. • Bruce Barry, Director, 615-322-3489. Application contact: Maureen Writesman, 615-343-1989. Fax: 615-343-7177. E-mail: owenphd@ctrvax.vanderbilt.edu.

Villanova University, College of Commerce and Finance, Business Administration Program, Villanova, PA 19085-1699. Awards MBA, JD/MBA. Part-time and evening/weekend programs available. Faculty: 38 full-time (9 women), 3 part-time (0 women). Students: 41 full-time (9 women), 578 part-time (194 women); includes 13 minority (7 African Americans, 3 Asian Americans, 3 Hispanics), 7 international. Average age 28. 273 applicants, 69% accepted. In 1997, 143 degrees awarded. *Degree requirements:* Computer language required, foreign language and thesis not required. *Average time to degree:* master's–2 years full-time, 4 years part-time. *Entrance requirements:* GMAT (average 585). Application deadline: 6/30 (rolling processing; 11/15 for spring admission). Application fee: $25. *Financial aid:* In 1997–98, 16 students received aid, including 16 research assistantships (8 to first-year students) averaging $1,000 per month. Aid available to part-time students. Financial aid application deadline: 3/15.

Directory: Business Administration and Management—General

Villanova University (continued)

Faculty research: Technology management, marketing of services, tax accounting, asset liability management. • Melinda B. German, Director of Graduate Studies in Business, 610-519-4336. Fax: 610-519-6273. E-mail: mba@email.vill.edu.

Virginia Commonwealth University, School of Business, Richmond, VA 23284-9005. Offers programs in accountancy (PhD), including accounting/taxation; business administration and management (MBA, PhD), including business administration; decision sciences (MS, PhD); economics (MA, MS, PhD); finance (MS, PhD); human resources management and industrial relations (MS); information systems (MS, PhD, Certificate); international business (PhD); marketing and business law (MS, PhD); real estate and urban land development (MS, Certificate); risk management and insurance (MS); taxation (M Tax, PhD), including accounting/taxation (PhD), taxation (M Tax). Part-time and evening/weekend programs available. Faculty: 114 (16 women). *Degree requirements:* For doctorate, dissertation. *Entrance requirements:* For doctorate, GMAT. Application deadline: rolling. Application fee: $30 ($0 for international students). *Tuition:* $4960 per year full-time, $257 per credit part-time for state residents; $12,652 per year full-time, $684 per credit part-time for nonresidents. *Financial aid:* Fellowships, research assistantships, teaching assistantships, full and partial tuition waivers, Federal Work-Study, institutionally sponsored loans available. Aid available to part-time students. Financial aid application deadline: 3/15. • Dr. Howard P. Tuckman, Dean, 804-828-1595. E-mail: hptuckma@busnet.bus.vcu.edu. Application contact: Dr. Edward L. Millner, Associate Dean of Graduate Studies, 804-828-1741. Fax: 804-828-7174. E-mail: gsib@vcu.edu.

Virginia Polytechnic Institute and State University, Pamplin College of Business, Department of Management, Blacksburg, VA 24061. Offers program in business administration/management (PhD). Faculty: 17 full-time (1 woman). Students: 10 full-time (3 women), 1 part-time (0 women); includes 2 minority (1 African American, 1 Native American). Average age 32. 12 applicants, 8% accepted. In 1997, 1 degree awarded (100% entered university research/teaching). *Degree requirements:* Dissertation required, foreign language not required. *Entrance requirements:* GMAT, TOEFL (minimum score 575). Application deadline: 12/1 (priority date; rolling processing). Application fee: $25. *Tuition:* $4927 per year full-time, $792 per semester (minimum) part-time for state residents; $7537 per year full-time, $1227 per semester (minimum) part-time for nonresidents. *Financial aid:* In 1997–98, 2 research assistantships were awarded; teaching assistantships, assistantships, institutionally sponsored loans, and career-related internships or fieldwork also available. Financial aid application deadline: 4/1. *Faculty research:* Compensation, organization effectiveness, selection, strategic planning, labor/management relations. • Dr. Robert J. Litschert, Head, 540-231-6353. Application contact: Dr. Frederick S. Hills, Director of Graduate Programs, 540-231-6345.

See in-depth description on page 397.

Virginia Polytechnic Institute and State University, Pamplin College of Business, Department of Management Science, Blacksburg, VA 24061. Offers program in business administration/management science (PhD). Faculty: 13 full-time. Students: 5 full-time (1 woman), 3 part-time (0 women). Average age 26. 2 applicants, 0% accepted. *Degree requirements:* Dissertation. *Entrance requirements:* GMAT or GRE, TOEFL (minimum score 600). Application deadline: 12/1 (priority date; rolling processing). Application fee: $25. *Tuition:* $4927 per year full-time, $792 per semester (minimum) part-time for state residents; $7537 per year full-time, $1227 per semester (minimum) part-time for nonresidents. *Financial aid:* Teaching assistantships, graduate assistantships, partial tuition waivers, institutionally sponsored loans available. Financial aid application deadline: 4/1. *Faculty research:* Mathematical programming, computer simulation, decision support systems, production/operations research. • Dr. Bernard W. Taylor III, Head, 540-231-6596.

See in-depth description on page 397.

Virginia Polytechnic Institute and State University, Pamplin College of Business, Program in Business Administration, Blacksburg, VA 24061. Awards MBA. Students: 221 full-time (61 women), 394 part-time (133 women); includes 61 minority (19 African Americans, 37 Asian Americans, 5 Hispanics), 73 international. 440 applicants, 49% accepted. In 1997, 154 degrees awarded. *Entrance requirements:* GMAT, TOEFL. Application deadline: 12/1 (priority date; rolling processing). Application fee: $25. *Tuition:* $4927 per year full-time, $792 per semester (minimum) part-time for state residents; $7537 per year full-time, $1227 per semester (minimum) part-time for nonresidents. *Financial aid:* Application deadline 4/1. • Dr. Ronald D. Johnson, Director, 540-231-6152.

See in-depth description on page 397.

Virginia State University, School of Business, 1 Hayden Drive, Petersburg, VA 23806-2096. Awards MA. Part-time programs available. Faculty: 6 full-time (0 women). In 1997, 8 degrees awarded. *Entrance requirements:* GRE General Test. Application deadline: 8/15 (rolling processing). Application fee: $25. *Tuition:* $3739 per year full-time, $133 per credit hour part-time for state residents; $9056 per year full-time, $364 per credit hour part-time for nonresidents. *Financial aid:* 1 student received aid; fellowships, Federal Work-Study available. Financial aid application deadline: 5/1. • Dr. Sadie Gregory, Dean, 804-524-5166. Application contact: Dr. Wayne F. Virag, Dean, Graduate Studies and Continuing Education, 804-524-5985. Fax: 804-524-5104. E-mail: wvirag@vsu.edu.

Wagner College, Department of Business Administration, Staten Island, NY 10301. Offers programs in finance and banking (MBA), international business (MBA), management (Exec MBA, MBA), marketing (MBA). Part-time and evening/weekend programs available. Faculty: 10 full-time (3 women), 7 part-time (1 woman). Students: 71 full-time (21 women), 65 part-time (30 women); includes 28 minority (8 African Americans, 18 Asian Americans, 2 Hispanics). 68 applicants, 82% accepted. In 1997, 27 degrees awarded. *Degree requirements:* Thesis optional, foreign language not required. *Entrance requirements:* Minimum GPA of 2.6. Application deadline: 8/1 (priority date; rolling processing; 12/10 for spring admission). Application fee: $50 ($65 for international students). *Tuition:* $580 per credit. *Financial aid:* In 1997–98, 9 alumni fellowships (3 to first-year students) were awarded; teaching assistantships, partial tuition waivers also available. • Dr. James Michael, Director, MBA Program, 718-390-3427. Application contact: Admissions Office, 718-390-3411.

Wake Forest University, Babcock Graduate School of Management, Evening MBA Program–Charlotte, Winston-Salem, NC 27109. Awards MBA. Part-time and evening/weekend programs available. Faculty: 33 full-time (3 women), 14 part-time (4 women). Students: 77 part-time (19 women); includes 6 minority (4 African Americans, 2 Asian Americans). Average age 30. 84 applicants, 75% accepted. In 1997, 26 degrees awarded. *Entrance requirements:* GMAT. Application fee: $75. *Expenses:* Tuition $20,400 per year. Fees $100 per year. *Financial aid:* 27 students received aid; institutionally sponsored loans available. Aid available to part-time students. Financial aid application deadline: 6/1; applicants required to submit FAFSA. *Faculty research:* Yield management, strategic management, international business, financial analysis, banking, risk management, consumer behavior, product management. • Mary Lai, Director, 888-925-3622. Fax: 704-365-3511. E-mail: mary_lai@mail.mba.wfu.edu.

Wake Forest University, Babcock Graduate School of Management, Evening MBA Program–Winston-Salem, Winston-Salem, NC 27109. Awards MBA. Part-time and evening/weekend programs available. Faculty: 33 full-time (3 women), 14 part-time (4 women). Students: 203 part-time (52 women); includes 17 minority (14 African Americans, 3 Hispanics). Average age 32. 76 applicants, 72% accepted. In 1997, 54 degrees awarded. *Entrance requirements:* GMAT. Application deadline: 5/1 (priority date; rolling processing; 9/1 for spring admission). Application fee: $75. Electronic applications accepted. *Expenses:* Tuition $20,400 per year. Fees $100 per year. *Financial aid:* 58 students received aid; institutionally sponsored loans available. Aid available to part-time students. Financial aid application deadline: 7/1; applicants required to submit FAFSA. *Faculty research:* Product management, yield management, strategic management and international business, financial analysis, banking, risk management, consumer behavior. • Jamie Barnes, Director, 336-758-5830. E-mail: jamie_barnes@mail.mba.wfu.edu.

Wake Forest University, Babcock Graduate School of Management, Executive MBA Program, Winston-Salem, NC 27109. Awards MBA. Part-time and evening/weekend programs available. Faculty: 33 full-time (3 women), 14 part-time (4 women). Students: 103 part-time (21 women); includes 8 African Americans, 6 Asian Americans. Average age 37. 116 applicants, 64% accepted. In 1997, 51 degrees awarded. *Average time to degree:* master's–2 years part-time. *Entrance requirements:* GMAT. Application deadline: rolling. Application fee: $75. Electronic applications accepted. *Expenses:* Tuition $20,400 per year. Fees $100 per year. *Financial aid:* 40 students received aid; institutionally sponsored loans available. Aid available to part-time students. Financial aid application deadline: 7/1; applicants required to submit FAFSA. *Faculty research:* Yield management, strategic management and international business, financial analysis and banking, consumer behavior, product management. • Jamie Barnes, Director, 800-428-6012. Fax: 336-758-5830. E-mail: jamie_barnes@mail.mba.wfu.edu.

Wake Forest University, Babcock Graduate School of Management, Full-time MBA Program, Winston-Salem, NC 27109. Awards MBA, JD/MBA, MD/MBA. Part-time and evening/weekend programs available. Faculty: 33 full-time (3 women), 14 part-time (4 women). Students: 242 full-time (61 women); includes 34 minority (14 African Americans, 13 Asian Americans, 6 Hispanics, 1 Native American), 43 international. Average age 26. 610 applicants, 44% accepted. In 1997, 106 degrees awarded (97% found work related to degree, 3% continued full-time study). *Average time to degree:* master's–2 years full-time. *Entrance requirements:* GMAT (average 615), TOEFL (minimum score 600). Application deadline: 4/1 (priority date; rolling processing). Application fee: $50. Electronic applications accepted. *Expenses:* Tuition $20,400 per year. Fees $100 per year. *Financial aid:* In 1997–98, 160 grants, scholarships, student assistantships (60 to first-year students) were awarded; full and partial tuition waivers, Federal Work-Study, institutionally sponsored loans, and career-related internships or fieldwork also available. Aid available to part-time students. Financial aid application deadline: 4/1; applicants required to submit FAFSA. *Faculty research:* Yield management, strategic management, banking, foreign exchange, risk management, consumer behavior, product management. • Application contact: Mary Goss, Assistant Dean, 336-759-5422. Fax: 336-759-5830. E-mail: mary_goss@mail.mba.wfu.edu.

Walden University, Graduate Programs, Program in Administration/Management, 155 Fifth Avenue South, Minneapolis, MN 55401. Awards PhD. Part-time and evening/weekend programs available. Postbaccalaureate distance learning degree programs offered. *Degree requirements:* Dissertation, brief dispersed residency sessions required, foreign language not required. *Entrance requirements:* 3 years of professional experience, master's degree. Application deadline: rolling. Application fee: $50. Electronic applications accepted. *Tuition:* $3125 per quarter.

Walsh College of Accountancy and Business Administration, Program in Business Administration, Troy, MI 48007-7006. Awards MBA. Program new for fall 1998. *Entrance requirements:* TOEFL (minimum score 550), minimum GPA of 2.75, previous course work in business. Application deadline: rolling. Application fee: $25. *Expenses:* Tuition $273 per credit hour. Fees $75 per semester. • Application contact: Sherree Hyde, Director, Enrollment Services, 248-689-8282 Ext. 215. Fax: 248-524-2520.

Announcement: A 75-year reputation for high-quality business education gives graduate students an edge with the MBA and Master of Science degree programs in finance, information management and communication, management, professional accountancy, or taxation. Practically based curriculum, focused concentrations of study, and hands-on learning combine to make graduate study valuable for advancement.

Walsh College of Accountancy and Business Administration, Program in Management, Troy, MI 48007-7006. Awards MSM. Part-time and evening/weekend programs available. Faculty: 4 full-time (0 women), 14 part-time (4 women). *Degree requirements:* Computer language required, foreign language and thesis not required. *Entrance requirements:* TOEFL (minimum score 550), minimum GPA of 2.75, previous course work in business. Application deadline: rolling. Application fee: $25. *Expenses:* Tuition $273 per credit hour. Fees $75 per semester. *Financial aid:* Federal Work-Study available. Aid available to part-time students. • Thomas Courneya, Interim Director, 248-689-8282. Fax: 248-689-9066. Application contact: Sherree Hyde, Director, Enrollment Services, 248-689-8282 Ext. 215. Fax: 248-524-2520.

Walsh University, Graduate Studies, Program in Management, North Canton, OH 44720-3396. Awards MA. Part-time and evening/weekend programs available. Faculty: 2 full-time (0 women), 4 part-time (1 woman). Students: 33 part-time. *Degree requirements:* Computer language required, foreign language and thesis not required. *Average time to degree:* master's–4 years part-time. *Entrance requirements:* GMAT. Application deadline: 7/15 (priority date; rolling processing). Application fee: $25. *Expenses:* Tuition $363 per credit hour. Fees $10 per credit hour. *Financial aid:* Fellowships available. • Dr. Carole Curtis Mount, Director, 330-490-7048. Application contact: Brett Freshour, Dean of Enrollment Management, 330-490-7171. Fax: 330-490-7165.

Washburn University of Topeka, School of Business, Topeka, KS 66621. Awards MBA. Part-time and evening/weekend programs available. Faculty: 19 full-time (6 women), 5 part-time (0 women). Students: 46 full-time, 132 part-time; includes 31 minority (5 African Americans, 22 Asian Americans, 4 Hispanics), 31 international. Average age 32. 49 applicants, 69% accepted. In 1997, 61 degrees awarded. *Entrance requirements:* GMAT (minimum score 400; average 500), minimum GPA of 2.6. Application deadline: 7/1 (priority date; rolling processing; 11/15 for spring admission). Application fee: $0 ($40 for international students). *Financial aid:* 38 students received aid. Aid available to part-time students. Financial aid application deadline: 3/1; applicants required to submit FAFSA. *Faculty research:* Firm value, capital structure and industry, advertising-evoked mental imagery, forensic economics. Total annual research expenditures: $30,000. • Dr. Juliann Mazachek, Dean, 785-231-1010 Ext. 1308. E-mail: zzdpbu@washburn.edu. Application contact: Dr. Russell Smith, Director of Graduate Program, 785-231-1010 Ext. 1307. Fax: 785-231-1063. E-mail: mba@washburn.edu.

Washington State University, College of Business and Economics, Programs in Business, Department of Business Administration, Pullman, WA 99164-1610. Awards MBA, PhD. Faculty: 38. Students: 100 full-time (39 women), 17 part-time (6 women); includes 8 minority (3 African Americans, 3 Asian Americans, 1 Hispanic, 1 Native American), 53 international. In 1997, 79 master's awarded; 5 doctorates awarded (100% entered university research/teaching). *Degree requirements:* For master's, oral exam required, thesis not required; for doctorate, dissertation, oral exam required, foreign language not required. *Average time to degree:* master's–1.5 years full-time; doctorate–4.5 years full-time. *Entrance requirements:* For master's, GMAT (minimum score 550), TOEFL (minimum score 580), minimum GPA of 3.0; for doctorate, GMAT (minimum score 600), minimum GPA of 3.0. Application deadline: 3/1 (priority date; rolling processing). Application fee: $35. *Tuition:* $5334 per year full-time, $267 per credit hour part-time for state residents; $13,380 per year full-time, $677 per credit hour part-time for nonresidents. *Financial aid:* In 1997–98, 4 research assistantships, 56 teaching assistantships, 5 teaching associateships were awarded; partial tuition waivers, Federal Work-Study, institutionally sponsored loans, and career-related internships or fieldwork also available. Financial aid application deadline: 4/1; applicants required to submit FAFSA. • Dr. Val Miskin, Director, Programs in Business, 509-335-7617. Fax: 509-335-4735. E-mail: mba@wsu.edu.

Announcement: Both the MBA and the M Acc programs are nationally recognized and have accreditation by the AACSB–The International Association for Management Education. The PhD program is highly research oriented and leads to high-level academic competence. Maximum flexibility in course work and research is provided, and most M Acc and PhD candidates receive financial support.

Washington University in St. Louis, John M. Olin School of Business, St. Louis, MO 63130-4899. Awards EMBA, MBA, PhD, JD/MBA, M Arch/MBA, MAUD/MBA, MBA/MA, MBA/MHA, MBA/MIM, MBA/MSW. MBA/MA offered jointly with the Program in East Asian Studies.

Part-time and evening/weekend programs available. Faculty: 69 full-time (14 women), 27 part-time (2 women), 84.7 FTE. Students: 296 full-time (86 women), 345 part-time (85 women); includes 53 minority (20 African Americans, 29 Asian Americans, 4 Hispanics), 120 international. Average age 27. 1,165 applicants, 39% accepted. In 1997, 255 master's awarded; 2 doctorates awarded (100% entered university research/teaching). Terminal master's awarded for partial completion of doctoral program. *Degree requirements:* For doctorate, dissertation required, foreign language not required. *Average time to degree:* master's–2 years full-time, 3 years part-time; doctorate–5 years full-time. *Entrance requirements:* For master's, GMAT (average 606); for doctorate, GMAT (average 700). Application deadline: 3/30 (priority date; rolling processing). Application fee: $80. Electronic applications accepted. *Tuition:* $23,800 per year full-time, $670 per credit hour part-time. *Financial aid:* 189 students received aid; fellowships, research assistantships, full and partial tuition waivers, Federal Work-Study, and career-related internships or fieldwork available. Aid available to part-time students. Financial aid application deadline: 3/31; applicants required to submit FAFSA. *Faculty research:* Value of accounting information, power and politics in organizations, manufacturing policy, venture capital financing, competitive strategy in retailing. Total annual research expenditures: $12.3 million. • Stuart I. Greenbaum, Dean, 314-935-6344. Fax: 314-935-4074. E-mail: greenbaum@wuolin.wustl.edu. Application contact: Deborah F. Booker, Director of MBA Admissions, 314-935-7301. Fax: 314-935-6309. E-mail: mba@olin.wustl.edu.

Wayland Baptist University, Program in Management, Plainview, TX 79072-6998. Awards MBA. Part-time and evening/weekend programs available. Faculty: 11 full-time (0 women), 27 part-time (10 women). Students: 12 full-time (5 women), 135 part-time (51 women); includes 31 minority (20 African Americans, 1 Asian American, 10 Hispanics), 1 international. Average age 37. 49 applicants, 96% accepted. In 1997, 58 degrees awarded. *Entrance requirements:* GMAT, GRE, minimum GPA of 2.7. Application deadline: rolling. Application fee: $35. *Expenses:* Tuition $225 per semester hour. Fees $350 per year full-time, $40 per semester part-time. *Financial aid:* Federal Work-Study available. Aid available to part-time students. Financial aid application deadline: 5/1; applicants required to submit FAFSA. • Dr. Benjamin Akande, Chairman, 806-296-4727.

Waynesburg College, Graduate Program in Business Administration, Waynesburg, PA 15370-1222. Awards MBA. Part-time and evening/weekend programs available. Faculty: 11 part-time (1 woman). Students: 100. *Average time to degree:* master's–1 year full-time, 3 years part-time. *Entrance requirements:* GMAT. Application deadline: 8/1 (priority date; rolling processing). Application fee: $15. *Tuition:* $320 per credit. *Financial aid:* Available to part-time students. Financial aid application deadline: 5/1. • Dr. Joseph A. Graff, Director, 412-854-3600.

Wayne State College, Division of Business, Wayne, NE 68787. Awards MBA. Faculty: 10 part-time (2 women). Students: 7 full-time (1 woman), 63 part-time (31 women); includes 3 minority (all Hispanics). Average age 34. In 1997, 17 degrees awarded. *Entrance requirements:* GMAT. Application deadline: rolling. Application fee: $10. *Expenses:* Tuition $1788 per year full-time, $75 per credit hour part-time for state residents; $3576 per year full-time, $149 per credit hour part-time for nonresidents. Fees $360 per year full-time, $15 per credit hour part-time. *Financial aid:* In 1997–98, 4 teaching assistantships (2 to first-year students) were awarded; career-related internships or fieldwork also available. Financial aid application deadline: 5/1; applicants required to submit FAFSA. *Faculty research:* Microcomputers in business education, vocational education, small business profitability. • Dr. Vaughn Benson, Head, 402-375-7245.

Wayne State University, School of Business Administration, Detroit, MI 48202. Awards MBA, MS, JD/MBA. Programs in business administration (MBA), taxation (MS). Part-time and evening/weekend programs available. Faculty: 117. Students: 189 full-time (74 women), 1,441 part-time (584 women). 621 applicants, 66% accepted. In 1997, 376 degrees awarded. *Degree requirements:* Thesis optional, foreign language not required. *Entrance requirements:* GMAT. Application deadline: 8/1 (4/1 for spring admission). Application fee: $20 ($30 for international students). *Expenses:* Tuition $163 per credit hour for state residents; $355 per credit hour for nonresidents. Fees $498 per year full-time, $114 per semester (minimum) part-time. *Financial aid:* Research assistantships, teaching assistantships, scholarships, Federal Work-Study, and career-related internships or fieldwork available. Aid available to part-time students. Financial aid applicants required to submit FAFSA. • Dr. Harvey Kahalos, Dean, 313-577-4500. Fax: 313-577-4557. Application contact: Linda S. Zaddach, Assistant Dean, 313-577-4510. Fax: 313-577-5299. E-mail: lzaddach@cms.cc.wayne.edu.

See in-depth description on page 399.

Webber College, Graduate Division, Babson Park, FL 33827-0096. Awards MBA. Part-time and evening/weekend programs available. Students: 10 full-time (7 women), 4 part-time (3 women); includes 3 international. Average age 31. 18 applicants, 83% accepted. *Degree requirements:* Computer language, thesis or alternative. *Average time to degree:* master's–1.6 years full-time, 3.2 years part-time. *Application deadline:* 5/15 (priority date; rolling processing). *Application fee:* $50 ($75 for international students). *Financial aid:* 7 students received aid. Aid available to part-time students. Financial aid application deadline: 8/15; applicants required to submit FAFSA. • Dr. Nikos Orphanoudakis, Dean, 941-638-2925. Application contact: Jeanne Sobierajski, MBA Marketing Director, 941-638-2927. Fax: 941-638-2823.

Weber State University, College of Business and Economics, Ogden, UT 84408-3803. Awards MP Acc. Part-time programs available. Faculty: 11 full-time (2 women). Students: 40 full-time (19 women), 20 part-time (10 women); includes 3 minority (2 Asian Americans, 1 Hispanic), 5 international. Average age 31. 44 applicants, 89% accepted. In 1997, 35 degrees awarded. *Average time to degree:* master's–1 year full-time, 3 years part-time. *Entrance requirements:* GMAT (minimum AACSB index of 1050). Application deadline: 3/1 (priority date; rolling processing). Application fee: $30 ($35 for international students). *Financial aid:* 13 students received aid; research assistantships, teaching assistantships, scholarships, full and partial tuition waivers, Federal Work-Study, institutionally sponsored loans available. Financial aid application deadline: 3/1. *Faculty research:* Quality, environment, taxation, education, logistics. • Dr. Michael Vaughan, Dean, 801-626-6063. E-mail: mvaughan@weber.edu. Application contact: Dr. James G. Swearingen, Coordinator, 801-626-6897. Fax: 801-626-7423. E-mail: jswearingen@weber.edu.

Webster University, School of Business and Technology, Department of Business, St. Louis, MO 63119-3194. Offers programs in business (MA, MBA), computer resources and information management (MA, MBA), computer science/distributed systems (MS), finance (MA, MBA), health care management (MA), health services management (MA, MBA), human resources development (MA, MBA), human resources management (MA), international business (MA, MBA), management (MA, MBA), marketing (MA, MBA), procurement and acquisitions management (MA, MBA), public administration (MA), real estate management (MA, MBA), security management (MA, MBA), space systems management (MA, MBA, MS), telecommunications management (MA, MBA). Faculty: 5 full-time (1 woman). Students: 5,773 full-time (2,565 women), 2,819 part-time (1,271 women); includes 2,617 minority (1,854 African Americans, 249 Asian Americans, 474 Hispanics, 40 Native Americans), 353 international. 1,325 applicants, 95% accepted. *Application deadline:* rolling. *Application fee:* $25 ($50 for international students). *Tuition:* $350 per credit hour. *Financial aid:* Federal Work-Study available. Aid available to part-time students. Financial aid application deadline: 4/1; applicants required to submit FAFSA. • Lucille Berry, Chair, 314-968-7022. Fax: 314-968-7077. E-mail: berrylm@webster.edu. Application contact: Beth Russell, Director of Graduate Admissions, 314-968-7089. Fax: 314-968-7166. E-mail: russellmb@webster.edu.

Webster University, School of Business and Technology, Program in Management, St. Louis, MO 63119-3194. Awards MA, DM. Faculty: 5 full-time (0 women). Students: 8 full-time (3 women), 37 part-time (19 women); includes 9 minority (8 African Americans, 1 Native American). 1,193 applicants, 95% accepted. *Degree requirements:* For doctorate, dissertation, written exam required, foreign language not required. *Entrance requirements:* For doctorate, GMAT, 3 years of work experience, MBA. Application deadline: rolling. Application fee: $25 ($50 for international students). *Tuition:* $350 per credit hour. *Financial aid:* Federal Work-Study available. Aid available to part-time students. Financial aid application deadline: 4/1; applicants required to submit FAFSA. • Dr. James Brasfield, Director, 314-968-7063. Fax: 314-968-7077. E-mail: brasfijm@webster.edu. Application contact: Beth Russell, Director of Graduate Admissions, 314-968-7089. Fax: 314-968-7166. E-mail: russellmb@webster.edu.

West Chester University of Pennsylvania, School of Business and Public Affairs, Program in Business Administration, West Chester, PA 19383. Offers economics/finance (MBA), executive business administration (MBA), general business (MBA), management (MBA). Part-time and evening/weekend programs available. Faculty: 2 part-time. Students: 12 full-time (5 women), 205 part-time (79 women); includes 33 minority (23 African Americans, 7 Asian Americans, 2 Hispanics, 1 Native American), 7 international. Average age 33. 89 applicants, 75% accepted. In 1997, 65 degrees awarded. *Degree requirements:* Comprehensive exam required, thesis optional, foreign language not required. *Entrance requirements:* GMAT, interview, minimum GPA of 3.0. Application deadline: 4/15 (priority date; rolling processing; 10/15 for spring admission). Application fee: $25. *Expenses:* Tuition $3468 per year full-time, $193 per credit part-time for state residents; $6236 per year full-time, $346 per credit part-time for nonresidents. Fees $660 per year full-time, $38 per credit part-time. *Financial aid:* In 1997–98, 1 research assistantship was awarded. Aid available to part-time students. Financial aid application deadline: 2/15. • Dr. Jim Hamilton, Graduate Coordinator, 610-436-2608.

Western Carolina University, College of Business, Program in Business Administration, Cullowhee, NC 28723. Awards MBA. Part-time and evening/weekend programs available. Students: 39 full-time (11 women), 76 part-time (35 women); includes 2 minority (1 Asian American, 1 Hispanic), 18 international. 89 applicants, 56% accepted. In 1997, 56 degrees awarded. *Degree requirements:* Comprehensive exam required, foreign language and thesis not required. *Entrance requirements:* GMAT. Application deadline: rolling. Application fee: $35. *Tuition:* $1799 per year full-time, $144 per credit hour (minimum) part-time for state residents; $9069 per year full-time, $1053 per credit hour (minimum) part-time for nonresidents. *Financial aid:* In 1997–98, 35 students received aid, including 15 research assistantships (6 to first-year students) totaling $57,280, 20 teaching assistantships (14 to first-year students) totaling $80,625; fellowships also available. Financial aid application deadline: 3/15. • Gary A. Williams, Director, 828-227-7401. Application contact: Kathleen Owen, Assistant to the Dean, 828-227-7398. Fax: 828-227-7480.

Western Connecticut State University, Ancell School of Business and Public Administration, Danbury, CT 06810-6885. Awards MBA, MHA, MSA. Part-time and evening/weekend programs available. Faculty: 14 full-time (3 women), 2 part-time (1 woman). Students: 17 full-time (11 women), 121 part-time (69 women). In 1997, 19 degrees awarded. *Degree requirements:* Computer language, comprehensive exam, research project required, thesis not required. *Entrance requirements:* GMAT (minimum score 500), minimum GPA of 3.0. Application deadline: 8/1 (priority date; rolling processing). Application fee: $40. *Expenses:* Tuition $4127 per year (minimum) full-time, $178 per credit hour part-time for state residents; $9581 per year (minimum) full-time, $178 per credit hour part-time for nonresidents. Fees $25 per year part-time. *Financial aid:* In 1997–98, 4 fellowships (all to first-year students) were awarded; Federal Work-Study and career-related internships or fieldwork also available. Aid available to part-time students. Financial aid application deadline: 5/1. • Dr. Ronald Benson, Acting Dean, 203-837-8650.

Western Illinois University, College of Business and Technology, Program in Business Administration, Macomb, IL 61455-1390. Awards MBA. Part-time programs available. Faculty: 38 full-time (6 women). Students: 64 full-time (21 women), 39 part-time (8 women); includes 1 minority (African American), 31 international. Average age 29. 76 applicants, 55% accepted. In 1997, 43 degrees awarded. *Degree requirements:* Thesis or alternative required, foreign language not required. *Entrance requirements:* GMAT (minimum score 450), minimum GPA of 2.5. Application deadline: rolling. Application fee: $0 ($25 for international students). *Expenses:* Tuition $2304 per year full-time, $96 per semester hour part-time for state residents; $6912 per year full-time, $288 per semester hour part-time for nonresidents. Fees $944 per year full-time, $33 per semester hour part-time. *Financial aid:* In 1997–98, 35 students received aid, including 35 research assistantships averaging $610 per month; full tuition waivers also available. Financial aid applicants required to submit FAFSA. *Faculty research:* International business. • Larry Wall, Director, 309-298-2442. Application contact: Barbara Baily, Director of Graduate Studies, 309-298-1806. Fax: 309-298-2245. E-mail: barb_baily@ccmail.wiu.edu.

Western International University, Graduate Programs in Business, 9215 North Black Canyon Highway, Phoenix, AZ 85021-2718. Awards MBA, MPA, MS. Evening/weekend programs available. Faculty: 27 part-time (6 women). Students: 375 full-time (135 women); includes 48 minority (16 African Americans, 1 Asian American, 30 Hispanics, 1 Native American), 105 international. Average age 35. In 1997, 179 degrees awarded. *Degree requirements:* Thesis, research project. *Average time to degree:* master's–1 year full-time. *Entrance requirements:* GMAT (strongly recommended), minimum GPA of 2.75. Application deadline: rolling. Application fee: $50 ($100 for international students). *Financial aid:* 103 students received aid. Financial aid applicants required to submit FAFSA. • Donna Stout, Director of Academic Affairs, 602-943-2311. Application contact: Enrollment Department, 602-943-2311. Fax: 602-371-8637.

Western Kentucky University, College of Business Administration, Bowling Green, KY 42101-3576. Awards MA, MA Ed, MBA, MPA. Part-time and evening/weekend programs available. Faculty: 46 full-time (6 women). Students: 19 full-time (9 women), 87 part-time (37 women); includes 6 minority (2 African Americans, 3 Asian Americans, 1 Hispanic), 8 international. Average age 30. 89 applicants, 47% accepted. In 1997, 13 degrees awarded. *Application deadline:* 8/1 (priority date; rolling processing; 12/1 for spring admission). *Application fee:* $20. *Tuition:* $2460 per year full-time, $133 per credit hour part-time for state residents; $6700 per year full-time, $369 per credit hour part-time for nonresidents. *Financial aid:* In 1997–98, 15 service awards (6 to first-year students) averaging $430 per month and totaling $46,400 were awarded; research assistantships, Federal Work-Study, institutionally sponsored loans also available. Aid available to part-time students. Financial aid application deadline: 4/1; applicants required to submit FAFSA. • Dr. Robert Jefferson, Dean, 502-745-6311. Fax: 502-745-3893.

Western Kentucky University, Interdisciplinary Program in Administration, Bowling Green, KY 42101-3576. Awards MA. Offered in cooperation with the College of Business Administration. Part-time and evening/weekend programs available. Students: 1 full-time (0 women), 3 part-time (2 women); includes 1 minority (Asian American). Average age 46. 4 applicants, 75% accepted. In 1997, 2 degrees awarded. *Degree requirements:* Thesis or alternative required, foreign language not required. *Entrance requirements:* GMAT or GRE General Test (minimum combined score of 1150), minimum GPA of 2.5. Application deadline: 8/1 (priority date; rolling processing; 12/1 for spring admission). Application fee: $20. *Tuition:* $2460 per year full-time, $133 per credit hour part-time for state residents; $6700 per year full-time, $369 per credit hour part-time for nonresidents. *Financial aid:* Federal Work-Study, institutionally sponsored loans available. Aid available to part-time students. Financial aid application deadline: 4/1; applicants required to submit FAFSA. • Dr. Elmer Gray, Dean, Graduate Studies, 502-745-2446. Fax: 502-745-5442. E-mail: graduate.studies@wku.edu.

Western Michigan University, Haworth College of Business, Program in Business Administration, Kalamazoo, MI 49008. Awards MBA. Students: 95 full-time (43 women), 547 part-time (201 women); includes 19 minority (6 African Americans, 11 Asian Americans, 1 Hispanic, 1 Native American), 142 international. 265 applicants, 69% accepted. In 1997, 208 degrees awarded. *Degree requirements:* Computer language required, thesis not required. *Entrance requirements:* GMAT. Application deadline: 2/15 (priority date; rolling processing). Application fee: $25. *Expenses:* Tuition $154 per credit hour for state residents; $372 per credit hour for nonresidents. Fees $602 per year full-time, $132 per semester part-time. *Financial aid:* Fellowships, research assistantships, teaching assistantships, Federal Work-Study available. Financial aid application deadline: 2/15; applicants required to submit FAFSA. • Dr. Richard Hodges, Director, 616-387-6060. Application contact: Paula J. Boodt, Coordinator, Graduate Admissions and Recruitment, 616-387-2000. E-mail: paulaboodt@wmich.edu.

Directory: Business Administration and Management—General

Western New England College, School of Business, Program in Business Administration, Springfield, MA 01119-2654. Awards MBA. *Application deadline:* rolling. *Application fee:* $30. *Expenses:* Tuition $353 per credit hour. Fees $44 per semester (minimum). *Financial aid:* Application deadline 4/1. • Application contact: Rod Pease, Director of Student Administrative Services, 413-796-2080.

Western New England College, School of Business, Program in Business Administration (weekend), Springfield, MA 01119-2654. Awards MBA. Part-time and evening/weekend programs available. Faculty: 10 full-time (2 women). Students: 44 part-time (14 women). Average age 37. 102 applicants, 43% accepted. *Average time to degree:* master's–1 year part-time. *Entrance requirements:* 3 years of related experience, interview. Application deadline: rolling. Application fee: $30. *Financial aid:* Available to part-time students. Financial aid application deadline: 4/1; applicants required to submit FAFSA. *Faculty research:* Organizational behavior, information systems, managerial communication. • Application contact: Dr. Anil Gulati, Coordinator, 413-782-1711. Fax: 413-796-2068.

Western New Mexico University, Department of Business Administration and Economics, Silver City, NM 88062-0680. Offers program in business (MBA). Evening/weekend programs available. Faculty: 6 full-time (3 women), 2 part-time (1 woman), 6.5 FTE. Students: 3 full-time, 15 part-time. In 1997, 3 degrees awarded. *Entrance requirements:* GMAT. Application deadline: rolling. Application fee: $10. *Tuition:* $1516 per year full-time, $55 per credit part-time for state residents; $5604 per year full-time, $55 per credit part-time for nonresidents. *Financial aid:* Partial tuition waivers, institutionally sponsored loans, and career-related internships or fieldwork available. Aid available to part-time students. Financial aid application deadline: 4/1. • Dr. Curtis Hayes, Chair, 505-538-6321.

See in-depth description on page 401.

Western Washington University, College of Business and Economics, Bellingham, WA 98225-5996. Awards MBA. Part-time and evening/weekend programs available. Faculty: 32 (3 women). Students: 35 full-time (16 women), 11 part-time (3 women). 11 applicants, 45% accepted. In 1997, 24 degrees awarded. *Degree requirements:* Comprehensive exam required, foreign language and thesis not required. *Entrance requirements:* GMAT, TOEFL (average 567), minimum GPA of 3.0 in last 60 semester hours or last 90 quarter hours. Application deadline: 6/1 (rolling processing). Application fee: $35. *Expenses:* Tuition $4200 per year full-time, $140 per credit part-time for state residents; $12,780 per year full-time, $426 per credit part-time for nonresidents. Fees $249 per year full-time, $83 per quarter part-time. *Financial aid:* Teaching assistantships, partial tuition waivers, Federal Work-Study, institutionally sponsored loans available. Aid available to part-time students. Financial aid application deadline: 3/31. • Dr. Dennis R. Murphy, Dean, 360-650-3896. Application contact: Dr. Stephen Senge, Graduate Adviser, 360-650-4894.

Westminster College of Salt Lake City, The Bill and Vieve Gore School of Business, Master of Business Administration Program, Salt Lake City, UT 84105-3697. Awards MBA. Part-time and evening/weekend programs available. Faculty: 15 full-time (2 women), 8 part-time (1 woman), 16 FTE. Students: 101 full-time (43 women), 274 part-time (92 women); includes 29 minority (5 African Americans, 16 Asian Americans, 7 Hispanics, 1 Native American), 13 international. Average age 33. 173 applicants, 89% accepted. In 1997, 59 degrees awarded. *Average time to degree:* master's–3 years full-time, 4 years part-time. *Entrance requirements:* Minimum GPA of 3.0, business experience or GMAT, resume. Application deadline: 8/1 (priority date; rolling processing). Application fee: $25. Electronic applications accepted. *Expenses:* Tuition $448 per credit hour. Fees $200 per year full-time, $65 per semester (minimum) part-time. *Financial aid:* In 1997–98, 217 students received aid, including 15 scholarships, tuition remissions (1 to a first-year student) totaling $36,480; Federal Work-Study also available. Aid available to part-time students. Financial aid applicants required to submit FAFSA. • Dr. Jerry Van Os, Director, 801-488-4230. Fax: 801-484-3767. E-mail: j-vanos@wcslc.edu. Application contact: Philip J. Alletto, Vice President for Student Development and Enrollment Management, 801-488-4200. Fax: 801-484-3252. E-mail: admispub@wcslc.edu.

West Texas A&M University, T. Boone Pickens College of Business, Department of Management, Marketing, and General Business, Canyon, TX 79016-0001. Offers program in business administration (MBA). Part-time and evening/weekend programs available. Postbaccalaureate distance learning degree programs offered (minimal on-campus study). Faculty: 6 full-time (1 woman), 3 part-time (1 woman). Students: 33 full-time (14 women), 90 part-time (33 women); includes 6 minority (1 African American, 3 Asian Americans, 2 Hispanics), 19 international. Average age 34. 45 applicants, 24% accepted. In 1997, 24 degrees awarded. *Average time to degree:* master's–3 years full-time, 6 years part-time. *Entrance requirements:* GMAT (minimum score 450; average 530). Application deadline: rolling. Application fee: $0 ($50 for international students). Electronic applications accepted. *Expenses:* Tuition $46 per semester hour for state residents; $259 per semester hour for nonresidents. Fees $156 per semester (minimum). *Financial aid:* Research assistantships, teaching assistantships, partial tuition waivers, Federal Work-Study, institutionally sponsored loans, and career-related internships or fieldwork available. Aid available to part-time students. Financial aid applicants required to submit CSS PROFILE or FAFSA. *Faculty research:* Human resources, international business. • Dr. Joan Rivera, Interim Head, 806-651-2500. Application contact: Dr. Ron Hiner, Graduate Adviser, 806-651-2517. Fax: 806-651-2927. E-mail: ron.hiner@wtamu.edu.

West Virginia University, College of Business and Economics, Program in Business Administration, Morgantown, WV 26506. Awards MBA, JD/MBA. Part-time and evening/weekend programs available. Faculty: 16 full-time (4 women), 1 part-time (0 women). Students: 32 full-time (10 women), 205 part-time (84 women); includes 18 minority (5 African Americans, 10 Asian Americans, 2 Hispanics, 1 Native American), 7 international. Average age 35. 247 applicants, 48% accepted. In 1997, 55 degrees awarded. *Average time to degree:* master's–1.2 years full-time, 2.5 years part-time. *Entrance requirements:* GMAT (average 580), TOEFL (minimum score 580). Application deadline: 2/1 (priority date; rolling processing). Application fee: $45. *Tuition:* $3130 per year for state residents; $8554 per year for nonresidents. *Financial aid:* In 1997–98, 3 teaching assistantships (1 to a first-year student), 1 graduate administrative assistantship (to a first-year student) were awarded; Federal Work-Study, institutionally sponsored loans, and career-related internships or fieldwork also available. Financial aid application deadline: 2/1; applicants required to submit FAFSA. *Faculty research:* Financial management, managerial accounting, marketing, planning, corporate finance. • Dr. Paul J. Speaker, Director, 304-293-5408. Fax: 304-293-2385.

West Virginia Wesleyan College, Faculty of Business, Buckhannon, WV 26201. Awards MBA. Part-time and evening/weekend programs available. Faculty: 4 full-time (0 women), 5 part-time (0 women). Students: 7 full-time (4 women), 58 part-time (17 women); includes 7 minority (2 African Americans, 5 Asian Americans). Average age 32. 66 applicants, 98% accepted. In 1997, 13 degrees awarded (100% found work related to degree). *Degree requirements:* Exit evaluation required, foreign language and thesis not required. *Entrance requirements:* GMAT. Application fee: $15. *Financial aid:* Federal Work-Study available. Aid available to part-time students. • David W. McCauley, Director, MBA Program, 304-473-8MBA. Fax: 304-473-8479. E-mail: mccauley@wvwc.edu.

Wheeling Jesuit University, Graduate Business Program, Wheeling, WV 26003-6295. Offers accounting (MS), business administration (MBA). Part-time and evening/weekend programs available. Faculty: 10 full-time (1 woman), 8 part-time (1 woman), 13.5 FTE. Students: 11 full-time (5 women), 111 part-time (39 women); includes 2 minority (both African Americans), 1 international. Average age 33. In 1997, 56 degrees awarded. *Average time to degree:* master's–2 years full-time, 4 years part-time. *Entrance requirements:* GMAT (minimum score 475), minimum undergraduate GPA of 2.75. Application deadline: 8/1 (priority date; rolling processing; 12/15 for spring admission). Application fee: $25. *Tuition:* $360 per credit hour. *Financial aid:* In 1997–98, 21 students received aid, including 21 assistantships (5 to first-year students) averaging $400 per month; Federal Work-Study also available. Financial aid application deadline: 5/1; applicants required to submit FAFSA. *Faculty research:* International business, consumer behavior, accounting systems, social psychology, technology management. • Dr. Edward W. Younkins, Director, 304-243-2255. Fax: 304-243-2243. Application contact: Carol Carroll, Graduate Secretary, 304-243-2344. Fax: 304-243-4441.

Whitworth College, Department of International Management, Spokane, WA 99251-2704. Awards MIM. Part-time and evening/weekend programs available. Faculty: 4 full-time (1 woman), 14 part-time (5 women), 4.8 FTE. Students: 46 full-time (18 women); includes 16 minority (1 African American, 13 Asian Americans, 2 Hispanics), 3 international. Average age 32. 40 applicants, 75% accepted. In 1997, 24 degrees awarded (4% entered university research/teaching, 92% found other work related to degree, 4% continued full-time study). *Degree requirements:* 1 foreign language, practicum required, thesis not required. *Average time to degree:* master's–1.2 years full-time, 2 years part-time. *Entrance requirements:* GMAT or GRE, TOEFL (minimum score 550), TWE (minimum score 4), minimum GPA of 3.0. Application deadline: 3/1 (11/1 for spring admission). Application fee: $35. *Financial aid:* 11 students received aid; grants, merit scholarships and career-related internships or fieldwork available. Financial aid application deadline: 4/1. *Faculty research:* International business finance, risk management, strategic planning, cross-cultural management. Total annual research expenditures: $25,000. • Dr. Dan Sanford, Director, 509-777-3742. E-mail: dsanford@whitworth.edu. Application contact: Michelle-Lynn Morimoto, Assistant Director, 509-777-3742. Fax: 509-777-3723. E-mail: mmorimoto@whitworth.edu.

Wichita State University, W. Frank Barton School of Business, Wichita, KS 67260. Awards EMBA, MA, MBA, MPA, MS, MSN/MBA. Programs in accountancy (MPA), including professional accountancy; business (EMBA, MBA, MS); economics (MA), including business economics, economic analysis. Part-time and evening/weekend programs available. Faculty: 53 full-time (10 women), 10 part-time (5 women). Students: 116 full-time (47 women), 290 part-time (106 women); includes 12 minority (4 African Americans, 4 Asian Americans, 1 Hispanic, 3 Native Americans), 86 international. Average age 33. 328 applicants, 48% accepted. In 1997, 141 degrees awarded. *Degree requirements:* Computer language required, foreign language not required. *Entrance requirements:* TOEFL (minimum score 550), minimum GPA of 2.75. Application deadline: 7/1 (priority date; rolling processing; 1/1 for spring admission). Application fee: $25 ($40 for international students). Electronic applications accepted. *Expenses:* Tuition $2303 per year full-time, $96 per credit hour part-time for state residents; $7691 per year full-time, $321 per credit hour part-time for nonresidents. Fees $490 per year full-time, $75 per semester (minimum) part-time. *Financial aid:* In 1997–98, 6 research assistantships averaging $546 per month and totaling $28,717, 33 teaching assistantships averaging $555 per month and totaling $129,354, 8 assistantships averaging $604 per month and totaling $32,499 were awarded; Federal Work-Study, institutionally sponsored loans also available. Aid available to part-time students. Financial aid applicants required to submit FAFSA. *Faculty research:* Small business development strategies, real estate decision making, managerial productivity, entrepreneurial venture creation, refinement of service marketing strategy. • Dr. Gerald H. Graham, Dean, 316-978-3525. E-mail: grahama@twsuvm.uc.twsu.edu. Application contact: Dr. Nancy Bereman, Associate Dean, 316-978-3200. Fax: 316-978-3845. E-mail: bereman@twsuvm.uc.twsu.edu.

Widener University, School of Business Administration, Chester, PA 19013-5792. Awards MBA, MHA, MS, JD/MBA, MD/MBA, MD/MHA, ME/MBA, Psy D/MBA, Psy D/MHA. Part-time and evening/weekend programs available. Faculty: 39 full-time (13 women), 38 part-time, 52 FTE. Students: 63 full-time, 461 part-time; includes 10 minority (6 African Americans, 2 Asian Americans, 2 Hispanics), 27 international. Average age 31. 202 applicants, 83% accepted. In 1997, 182 degrees awarded. *Average time to degree:* master's–2 years full-time, 4 years part-time. *Application deadline:* 8/1 (priority date; rolling processing; 12/1 for spring admission). *Application fee:* $25 ($300 for international students). *Tuition:* $455 per credit. *Financial aid:* Research assistantships, traineeships, Federal Work-Study, and career-related internships or fieldwork available. Aid available to part-time students. *Faculty research:* Cost containment in health care, human resource management, productivity, globalization. • Lisa Bussom Jr., Director, Graduate Programs in Business, 610-499-4305. Fax: 610-499-4615. E-mail: gradbus.advise@widener.edu.

Wilfrid Laurier University, School of Business and Economics, Program in Business Administration, Waterloo, ON N2L 3C5, Canada. Awards MBA. Faculty: 49 full-time. Students: 79 full-time, 235 part-time. 373 applicants, 34% accepted. In 1997, 113 degrees awarded. *Entrance requirements:* GMAT (minimum score 550), minimum 2 years of business experience. Application deadline: 5/1 (rolling processing). Application fee: $100. • Dr. A. Scott Carson, Dean, School of Business and Economics, 519-884-1970 Ext. 2054.

Wilkes University, Programs in Business Administration, Wilkes-Barre, PA 18766-0002. Offerings in accounting (MBA), finance (MBA), health care (MBA), human resource management (MBA), international business (MBA), management (MBA), management information systems (MBA), marketing (MBA). MBA (management, management information systems) being phased out; applicants no longer accepted. Evening/weekend programs available. Faculty: 11 full-time, 2 part-time. Students: 20 full-time (14 women), 94 part-time (36 women); includes 11 minority (all Asian Americans). In 1997, 30 degrees awarded. *Entrance requirements:* GMAT. Application deadline: rolling. Application fee: $30. *Expenses:* Tuition $12,552 per year full-time, $523 per credit hour part-time. Fees $240 per year full-time, $10 per credit hour part-time. *Financial aid:* Career-related internships or fieldwork available. Financial aid application deadline: 2/28; applicants required to submit FAFSA. • Dr. Robert Seeley, Director, 717-408-4717.

Willamette University, Geo. H. Atkinson Graduate School of Management, Salem, OR 97301-3931. Awards MM, JD/MM. Part-time and evening/weekend programs available. Faculty: 13 full-time (2 women), 6 part-time (2 women). Students: 131 full-time (43 women), 33 part-time (11 women); includes 18 minority (1 African American, 10 Asian Americans, 3 Hispanics, 4 Native Americans), 39 international. Average age 28. 148 applicants, 91% accepted. In 1997, 73 degrees awarded. *Average time to degree:* master's–2 years full-time, 5 years part-time. *Entrance requirements:* GMAT (average 550) or GRE, TOEFL (minimum score 550). Application deadline: 4/1 (priority date; rolling processing). Application fee: $50. *Financial aid:* In 1997–98, 106 students received aid, including 11 research assistantships totaling $14,000, 62 scholarships (39 to first-year students) totaling $384,200; partial tuition waivers, Federal Work-Study, and career-related internships or fieldwork also available. Aid available to part-time students. Financial aid application deadline: 3/1; applicants required to submit FAFSA. *Faculty research:* General management, finance, marketing, human resources, international management. • Dr. Steven Maser, Interim Dean, 503-370-6440. Application contact: Judy O'Neill, Assistant Dean/Director of Admissions, 503-370-6167. Fax: 503-370-3011. E-mail: joneill@willamette.edu.

See in-depth description on page 403.

William Carey College, School of Business, Hattiesburg, MS 39401-5499. Awards MBA. Part-time and evening/weekend programs available. Faculty: 10 full-time (3 women). Students: 110 part-time (48 women); includes 25 minority (all African Americans). Average age 35. In 1997, 36 degrees awarded. *Average time to degree:* master's–1.5 years part-time. *Entrance requirements:* GMAT, work experience. Application deadline: 7/15 (priority date; rolling processing; 2/15 for spring admission). Application fee: $25 ($40 for international students). *Tuition:* $130 per semester hour. *Financial aid:* Federal Work-Study available. Aid available to part-time students. Financial aid application deadline: 6/15; applicants required to submit FAFSA. *Faculty research:* Health care, production management. • Dr. Ben Hawkins, Dean, 601-582-6199. Fax: 601-582-6281.

William Paterson University of New Jersey, College of Business, Wayne, NJ 07470-8420. Awards MBA. Part-time and evening/weekend programs available. Faculty: 7 full-time (0 women), 4 part-time (0 women). Students: 8 full-time (5 women), 88 part-time (33 women); includes 9 minority (2 African Americans, 5 Asian Americans, 2 Hispanics). Average age 28. 57 applicants, 56% accepted. In 1997, 16 degrees awarded. *Degree requirements:* Computer language required, foreign language and thesis not required. *Entrance requirements:* GMAT, minimum AACSB index of 950. Application deadline: 4/1 (rolling processing; 10/15 for spring admission). Application fee: $35. *Expenses:* Tuition $230 per credit for state residents; $327 per credit for nonresidents. Fees $3.25 per credit. *Financial aid:* In 1997–98, 3 students received aid, including 1 graduate assistantship totaling $6,000; research assistantships also available. Aid available to part-time students. Financial aid application deadline: 4/1; applicants required to submit FAFSA. *Faculty research:* Appropriate marketing variables for international food retail chains, racial attitudes among corporate managers in northern New Jersey. • Frank Grippo, Dean, 973-720-2435. Fax: 973-720-2809. Application contact: Office of Graduate Studies, 973-720-2237. Fax: 973-720-2035.

William Woods University, College of Graduate and Adult Studies, Program in Business, Fulton, MO 65251-1098. Awards MBA. Evening/weekend programs available. Faculty: 7 full-time (1 woman), 32 part-time (12 women). Students: 270 full-time (118 women); includes 40 minority (5 African Americans, 34 Asian Americans, 1 Hispanic). Average age 32. 200 applicants, 91% accepted. In 1997, 95 degrees awarded. *Degree requirements:* Thesis or alternative required, foreign language not required. *Average time to degree:* master's–2 years full-time. *Entrance requirements:* 2 years of work experience; minimum GPA of 2.5; minimum age of 23; previous course work in accounting, algebra, and economics. Application deadline: rolling. Application fee: $25. Electronic applications accepted. *Tuition:* $290 per credit. • Brian Lemons, Chair, 573-592-4576. Application contact: Mary Henley, Director of Recruitment, 800-995-3199. Fax: 573-592-1164. E-mail: cgas@iris.wmwoods.edu.

Wilmington College, Division of Business, New Castle, DE 19720-6491. Offers programs in business administration (MBA), human resource management (MS), management (MS), public administration (MS). Part-time and evening/weekend programs available. *Average time to degree:* master's–3 years part-time. *Entrance requirements:* Work experience. Application deadline: rolling. Application fee: $25. *Expenses:* Tuition $4410 per year full-time, $735 per course part-time. Fees $50 per year. • Dr. John Camp, Chair, 302-328-9401. Application contact: Michael Lee, Director of Admissions and Financial Aid, 302-328-9401 Ext. 102.

Wingate University, School of Business, Wingate, NC 28174. Awards MBA. Part-time programs available. Faculty: 8 full-time (2 women), 2 part-time (1 woman). Students: 2 full-time (0 women), 73 part-time (24 women); includes 13 minority (all African Americans), 2 international. Average age 29. 50 applicants, 80% accepted. In 1997, 20 degrees awarded. *Degree requirements:* Computer language required, thesis not required. *Average time to degree:* master's–4 years part-time. *Entrance requirements:* GMAT, work experience. Application deadline: 8/15 (priority date; rolling processing; 12/15 for spring admission). Application fee: $25. *Financial aid:* 7 students received aid; Federal Work-Study available. Aid available to part-time students. Financial aid application deadline: 8/1; applicants required to submit FAFSA. • Charles F. Palmer, Dean, 704-233-8148. Application contact: Katherine Rowe, Secretary, 704-233-8148. Fax: 704-233-8146.

Winona State University, Graduate Studies, College of Business, Department of Management and Marketing, Winona, MN 55987-5838. Offers program in business administration (MBA). Part-time and evening/weekend programs available. Faculty: 17 full-time (7 women). Students: 7 full-time (4 women), 20 part-time (7 women); includes 6 international. 10 applicants, 60% accepted. In 1997, 11 degrees awarded. *Entrance requirements:* GMAT. Application deadline: 8/8 (priority date; rolling processing; 2/17 for spring admission). Application fee: $20. *Financial aid:* Assistantships, Federal Work-Study available. Aid available to part-time students. • Dr. Kenneth Gorman, Dean, College of Business, 507-457-5014. E-mail: kgorman@vax2.winona.msus.edu.

Winthrop University, School of Business Administration, Rock Hill, SC 29733. Awards MBA. Part-time and evening/weekend programs available. Postbaccalaureate distance learning degree programs offered (no on-campus study). Faculty: 31 full-time (9 women). Students: 90 full-time (35 women), 96 part-time (52 women); includes 34 minority (27 African Americans, 3 Asian Americans, 2 Hispanics, 2 Native Americans), 21 international. Average age 33. In 1997, 77 degrees awarded. *Entrance requirements:* GMAT (minimum score 400), TOEFL (minimum score 550). Application deadline: 7/15 (priority date; rolling processing; 12/1 for spring admission). Application fee: $35. *Tuition:* $3928 per year full-time, $164 per credit hour part-time for state residents; $7060 per year full-time, $294 per credit hour part-time for nonresidents. *Financial aid:* Graduate assistantships, graduate scholarships, Federal Work-Study available. Aid available to part-time students. Financial aid application deadline: 2/1; applicants required to submit FAFSA. • Dr. Roger Weikle, Dean, 803-323-2186. Fax: 803-323-3960. E-mail: weikler@winthrop.edu. Application contact: Sharon Johnson, Director of Graduate Studies, 803-323-2204. Fax: 803-323-2292. E-mail: johnsons@winthrop.edu.

Woodbury University, Business Administration Program, Burbank, CA 91510. Awards MBA. Part-time and evening/weekend programs available. Faculty: 8 full-time (2 women), 9 part-time (0 women). Students: 63 full-time (27 women), 93 part-time (41 women); includes 57 minority (6 African Americans, 28 Asian Americans, 23 Hispanics), 71 international. Average age 31. 97 applicants, 70% accepted. In 1997, 98 degrees awarded. *Average time to degree:* master's–1 year full-time, 2 years part-time. *Entrance requirements:* GMAT, TOEFL (minimum score 570). Application deadline: 8/1 (priority date; rolling processing; 12/1 for spring admission). Application fee: $35 ($50 for international students). *Expenses:* Tuition $550 per unit. Fees $360 per year. *Financial aid:* 32 students received aid; career-related internships or fieldwork available. Aid available to part-time students. Financial aid application deadline: 7/15; applicants required to submit FAFSA. *Faculty research:* Total quality management, leadership. • Richard King, Dean of Business and Management, 818-767-0888. Application contact: Linda Parks, Graduate Admissions Assistant, 818-767-0888 Ext. 264. Fax: 818-767-0032. E-mail: mba@vaxb.woodbury.edu.

See in-depth description on page 405.

Worcester Polytechnic Institute, Department of Management, Worcester, MA 01609-2280. Offers programs in administration and management (MBA, MSM), business administration (MBA), engineering management (MBA, MSM), manufacturing management (MS), marketing and technological innovation (MS), operations and information technology (MS). MBA, MSM (administration and management, engineering management), MS (manufacturing management) being phased out; applicants no longer accepted. Part-time and evening/weekend programs available. Faculty: 15 full-time (4 women), 7 part-time (1 woman). Students: 16 full-time (6 women), 109 part-time (26 women); includes 9 minority (4 African Americans, 3 Asian Americans, 2 Hispanics), 13 international. 55 applicants, 95% accepted. In 1997, 27 degrees awarded. *Degree requirements:* Thesis optional, foreign language not required. *Entrance requirements:* GMAT (average 560 for MBA), GMAT or GRE General Test (MS), TOEFL (minimum score 550; average 610). Application deadline: 2/15 (priority date; rolling processing; 10/15 for spring admission). Application fee: $50. Electronic applications accepted. *Tuition:* $636 per credit hour. *Financial aid:* In 1997–98, 2 students received aid, including 2 fellowships totaling $30,000; institutionally sponsored loans and career-related internships or fieldwork also available. Financial aid application deadline: 2/15. *Faculty research:* Quality control in information handling processes, supply chain management, financial distress, environmentally conscious manufacturing, strategy and new venture teams, re-engineering business education. • Dr. McRae Banks, Head, 508-831-5218. E-mail: macb@wpi.edu. Application contact: Norm Wilkinson, Director, 508-831-5218. Fax: 508-831-5720. E-mail: nwilkins@wpi.edu.

Wright State University, College of Business and Administration, Dayton, OH 45435. Awards M Acc, MBA, MS, MBA/MS. Part-time and evening/weekend programs available. Students: 153 full-time (67 women), 349 part-time (138 women); includes 53 minority (28 African Americans, 18 Asian Americans, 7 Hispanics), 71 international. Average age 30. 270 applicants, 67% accepted. In 1997, 217 degrees awarded. *Entrance requirements:* TOEFL (minimum score 550). Application fee: $25. *Tuition:* $5109 per year full-time, $161 per credit hour part-time for state residents; $9039 per year full-time, $282 per credit hour part-time for nonresidents. *Financial aid:* In 1997–98, 52 fellowships (50 to first-year students), 3 teaching assistantships, 48 graduate assistantships were awarded; research assistantships, Federal Work-Study, institutionally sponsored loans, and career-related internships or fieldwork also available. Aid available to part-time students. Financial aid applicants required to submit FAFSA. • Dr. Rishi Kumar, Dean, 937-775-3242. Application contact: James Crawford, Director of Graduate Programs, 937-775-2437. Fax: 937-775-3301.

See in-depth description on page 407.

Xavier University, College of Business Administration, Master of Business Administration Program, Cincinnati, OH 45207-2111. Awards Exec MBA, MBA, MBA/MHSA. Part-time and evening/weekend programs available. Faculty: 50 full-time (16 women), 32 part-time (9 women), 58 FTE. Students: 256 full-time (79 women), 964 part-time (353 women); includes 116 minority (52 African Americans, 48 Asian Americans, 14 Hispanics, 2 Native Americans), 40 international. Average age 32. 420 applicants, 88% accepted. In 1997, 365 degrees awarded. *Entrance requirements:* GMAT (average 520), TOEFL (minimum score 550), minimum GPA of 2.5. Application deadline: rolling. Application fee: $35. *Tuition:* $400 per credit hour. *Financial aid:* In 1997–98, grants totaling $57,500 were awarded; research assistantships, full and partial tuition waivers, institutionally sponsored loans, and career-related internships or fieldwork also available. Aid available to part-time students. Financial aid application deadline: 4/1. *Faculty research:* Finance, accounting, marketing, international business, quality management, entrepreneurial studies. • Dr. James Brodeinski, Associate Dean, 513-745-3525. Fax: 513-745-2929. E-mail: brodein@xavier.xu.edu.

Yale University, School of Management and Graduate School of Arts and Sciences, Doctoral Program in Management, New Haven, CT 06520. Offers accounting (PhD), financial economics (PhD), marketing (PhD). Faculty: 36 full-time (4 women). Students: 16 full-time (4 women); includes 14 international. Average age 27. 99 applicants, 8% accepted. In 1997, 2 doctorates awarded (50% entered university research/teaching, 50% found other work related to degree). Terminal master's awarded for partial completion of doctoral program. *Degree requirements:* For doctorate, dissertation required, foreign language not required. *Average time to degree:* doctorate–5 years full-time. *Entrance requirements:* For doctorate, GMAT or GRE General Test (GRE preferred). Application deadline: 1/2. Application fee: $65. *Expenses:* Tuition waived upon acceptance into program. *Financial aid:* 11 students received aid; fellowships, research assistantships, teaching assistantships, tuition scholarships, full tuition waivers, institutionally sponsored loans available. Financial aid application deadline: 1/2. *Faculty research:* Pricing of options and futures, term structure of interest rates, use of accounting numbers in debt contracts, product differentiation. • Application contact: Subrata Sen, Director of Graduate Studies, 203-432-6028. Fax: 203-432-6974. E-mail: subrata.sen@yale.edu.

See in-depth description on page 409.

Yale University, School of Management, Program in Business Administration, New Haven, CT 06520. Awards MBA, JD/MBA, M Div/MBA, MES/MBA, MFA/MBA, MFS/MBA, MBA/MA, MBA/M Arch, MBA/MPH, MBA/MS, MSN/MBA. Faculty: 44 full-time (5 women), 38 part-time (4 women), 54 FTE. Students: 439 full-time (125 women); includes 86 minority (5 African Americans, 71 Asian Americans, 10 Hispanics), 108 international. Average age 28. 1,620 applicants, 26% accepted. In 1997, 218 degrees awarded. *Average time to degree:* master's–2 years full-time. *Entrance requirements:* GMAT, GRE General Test, TOEFL. Application deadline: 3/16. Application fee: $120. *Financial aid:* 300 students received aid; institutionally sponsored loans and career-related internships or fieldwork available. Financial aid application deadline: 5/1; applicants required to submit FAFSA. *Faculty research:* Use of derivative securities to manage risk, regulation of telecommunications, corporate governance, competitive strategy. • Application contact: Richard A. Silverman, Executive Director of Admissions, 203-432-5932. Fax: 203-432-9991. E-mail: som.admissions@yale.edu.

York College of Pennsylvania, Department of Business Administration, York, PA 17405-7199. Awards MBA. Part-time and evening/weekend programs available. Faculty: 19 full-time (4 women), 3 part-time (0 women). Students: 37 full-time (10 women), 174 part-time (62 women); includes 9 minority (5 African Americans, 4 Asian Americans), 3 international. Average age 32. 72 applicants, 89% accepted. In 1997, 23 degrees awarded (100% found work related to degree). *Entrance requirements:* GMAT (average 494). Application deadline: 7/15 (priority date; rolling processing; 12/15 for spring admission). Application fee: $30. *Expenses:* Tuition $292 per credit hour. Fees $100 per year full-time, $60 per year part-time. *Financial aid:* Available to part-time students. Financial aid application deadline: 4/15; applicants required to submit FAFSA. • John F. Barbor, MBA Coordinator, 717-815-1491. Fax: 717-849-1619. E-mail: jbarbor@ycp.edu.

York University, Schulich School of Business, Toronto, ON M3J 1P3, Canada. Awards IMBA, MBA, MPA, PhD, MBA/LL B, MPA/LL B. Part-time and evening/weekend programs available. Faculty: 67 full-time (15 women), 62 part-time (16 women). Students: 628 full-time (276 women), 652 part-time (219 women); includes 25 international. Average age 29. 1,604 applicants, 38% accepted. In 1997, 8 doctorates awarded. *Degree requirements:* For doctorate, 1 foreign language (computer language can substitute), dissertation, comprehensive exams. *Average time to degree:* master's–1.6 years full-time, 4 years part-time; doctorate–4.5 years full-time. *Entrance requirements:* For master's, GMAT (minimum score 580; average 610), minimum GPA of 3.0; for doctorate, GMAT (minimum score 600; average 620), minimum GPA of 3.0. Application deadline: 5/1 (rolling processing). Application fee: $100. *Financial aid:* Fellowships, research assistantships, teaching assistantships, fee bursaries, institutionally sponsored loans, and career-related internships or fieldwork available. Financial aid application deadline: 6/1. • D. W. Horvàth, Dean, 416-736-5070. Fax: 416-736-5763. E-mail: dhorvath@bus.yorku.ca. Application contact: Carol Pattenden, Admissions Officer, 416-736-5060. Fax: 416-736-5687. E-mail: admissions@bus.yorku.ca.

See in-depth description on page 411.

Youngstown State University, Warren P. Williamson Jr. College of Business Administration, Youngstown, OH 44555-0002. Awards EMBA, MBA. Part-time and evening/weekend programs available. Faculty: 24 full-time (3 women), 9 part-time (0 women). Students: 72 full-time (31 women), 83 part-time (26 women); includes 5 minority (3 African Americans, 1 Asian American, 1 Hispanic), 12 international. 51 applicants, 88% accepted. In 1997, 37 degrees awarded. *Degree requirements:* Computer language required, thesis optional, foreign language not required. *Entrance requirements:* GMAT (minimum score 450), TOEFL (minimum score 550), minimum GPA of 2.7. Application deadline: 8/15 (priority date; rolling processing; 2/15 for spring admission). Application fee: $30 ($75 for international students). *Expenses:* Tuition $90 per credit hour for state residents; $144 per credit hour (minimum) for nonresidents. Fees $528 per year full-time, $244 per year (minimum) part-time. *Financial aid:* In 1997–98, 41 students received aid, including 13 research assistantships averaging $666 per month and totaling $110,760, 28 scholarships totaling $23,994; fellowships, teaching assistantships, Federal Work-Study, institutionally sponsored loans also available. Aid available to part-time students. Financial aid application deadline: 3/1. *Faculty research:* Taxation and compliance, business ethics, operations management, organizational behavior, gender issues. • Dr. Betty Jo Licata, Dean, 330-742-3064. Fax: 330-742-1459. Application contact: Dr. Peter J. Kasvinsky, Dean of Graduate Studies, 330-742-3091. Fax: 330-742-1580. E-mail: amgrad03@ysub.ysu.edu.

Cross-Discipline Announcements

Arizona State University, College of Engineering and Applied Sciences, Del E. Webb School of Construction, Tempe, AZ 85287-0204.

Arizona State's Del E. Webb School of Construction offers a Master of Science degree in construction. The program focuses on providing cross-disciplinary management education specific to the construction industry. The degree is highly desirable for those who wish to work in the construction industry as management professionals and need professional management education focused upon the construction industry. Students with architecture, business, and civil engineering backgrounds have found the program to offer significant benefits in advancing their professional careers in the construction industry.

California School of Professional Psychology–Los Angeles, Program in Organizational Psychology, Alhambra, CA 91803-1360.

Organizational psychology and management programs at the California School of Professional Psychology incorporate a strong practical component in addition to solid research and theory components. The programs train students to grasp the similarities and unique features of organizational problems and how to implement cost-effective and creative solutions. See the in-depth description in *Peterson's Guide to Graduate Programs in the Humanities, Arts and Social Sciences.*

Carnegie Mellon University, School of Computer Science, Department of Human-Computer Interaction, Pittsburgh, PA 15213-3891.

The Master of Human-Computer Interaction Program, a 1-year interdisciplinary program at Carnegie Mellon, prepares students to participate in the design and implementation of software that can be used easily, effectively, and enjoyably. Graduates become broadly knowledgeable about interaction design, software implementation, and analysis and evaluation and acquire a specialization in one of these areas. An extensive multidisciplinary team project provides real-world experience.

Case Western Reserve University, Mandel School of Applied Social Sciences, Cleveland, OH 44106.

The Mandel School of Applied Social Sciences awards a master's degree in social work, a dual degree in social work and managing nonprofit organizations, and a PhD degree in social welfare for students with an undergraduate degree in related areas who have taken considerable social science course work. Social work career options include direct practice and management. Contact MSASS at 10900 Euclid Avenue, Cleveland, OH 44106-7164. Telephone: 800-944-2290 Ext. 2280 (toll-free).

Cornell University, Graduate Fields of Industrial and Labor Relations, Ithaca, NY 14853-0001.

In addition to the MILR, long considered the top professional degree in the country in human resources and labor relations, the School also offers MS and PhD degrees in such areas as collective bargaining, labor law, labor history, labor economics, organizational behavior, human resource studies, economic and social statistics, and international and comparative labor.

Duquesne University, Bayer School of Natural and Environmental Sciences, Environmental Science and Management Program, Pittsburgh, PA 15282-0001.

The MS program is designed to meet the educational needs of the contemporary environmental professional in industry, government, academe, and the public policy arena. The curriculum combines a strong foundation in the environmental sciences with courses in business and behavioral sciences, public policy, and law. Joint 5-year BS/MS-ESM programs are offered with chemistry, biology, and microbiology. Joint MBA/MS-ESM and JD/MS-ESM graduate programs are also offered. See in-depth description in Book 4.

George Mason University, School of Information Technology and Engineering, Department of Operations Research Engineering, Fairfax, VA 22030-4444.

Graduate study available in operations research and management science in growing school centered on information technology. A 30-semester-hour MS program stressing the application of quantitative methods in a complex and computer-oriented world. No specific undergraduate degree required, but mathematics and computer prerequisites are asked of students not well prepared. Program offers subspecialties in optimization, applied probability, decision analysis, operations engineering, and military operations research. Primary faculty research foci include computational operations research, optimization, decision analysis, and stochastic modeling.

Georgia Institute of Technology, Ivan Allen College of Policy and International Affairs, Sam Nunn School of International Affairs, Atlanta, GA 30332-0001.

The Sam Nunn School of International Affairs at Georgia Tech offers a 2-year master's degree in international affairs that enables graduates to assume professional positions within business, government, and international organizations. The program is built around a core of 6 courses that provide strong theoretical and methodological skills and an understanding of the major issues in international security and international political economy. Students also have the opportunity to tailor the program to their individual interests through elective offerings within the School and interdisciplinary work in economics, management, public policy, computer science, engineering, and other fields.

Milwaukee School of Engineering, School of Business, Milwaukee, WI 53202-3109.

MSOE's Master of Science in Engineering Management is for potential or practicing managers in organizations oriented to technology, manufacturing, production, engineering, or construction. Specializations in operations management, quality management, marketing, program management, and organizational management are offered. Classes meet in the evenings in Milwaukee, Appleton, and other southeastern Wisconsin locations. Master's degrees in architectural engineering, environmental engineering, perfusion, and medical informatics are also available.

Northwestern University, Robert R. McCormick School of Engineering and Applied Science, Department of Industrial Engineering and Management Sciences, Evanston, IL 60208.

Department of Industrial Engineering and Management Science offers master's and doctoral programs in applied probability, economics and production (including manufacturing engineering), logistics, optimization (mathematical programming), organization theory, statistics and decision analysis, and systems analysis and design. See in-depth description in Industrial Engineering section of Book 5.

Northwestern University, School of Speech, Department of Communication Studies, Communication Systems Program, Evanston, IL 60208.

The Communication Systems Program offers an interdisciplinary course of study leading to a Master of Science in Communication degree. The Communication Systems Program is designed to provide graduate training for working professionals whose effective use of information technology is critical to organizational performance. While covering the basic principles of information technology, the program stresses the larger managerial perspectives required to develop information products and services and to manage information systems within organizations. Faculty members are drawn from the Departments of Communication Studies, Electrical and Computer Engineering, and Industrial Engineering and Management Science.

The Ohio State University, Max M. Fisher College of Business, Program in Labor and Human Resources, Columbus, OH 43210.

The Master of Labor and Human Resources program provides students with a historical and theoretical grounding in human resource management and industrial relations. It also provides training on the cutting edge, preparing students for employment in private firms or government agencies. The PhD program prepares students for teaching and research positions in colleges, universities, and other research-oriented institutions.

Pace University, School of Computer Science and Information Systems, New York, NY 10038.

Recognizing the need for advanced training in these fields, the School of Computer Science and Information Systems offers Master of Science degrees in computer science, information systems, and telecommunications. In addition, certificate programs are available in computer communications and networks, telecommunications, computing for teachers, and object-oriented programming.

Pace University, Dyson College of Arts and Sciences, Department of Public Administration, New York, NY 10038.

The Master of Public Administration degree, with concentrations in the management of government, health-care, and nonprofit organizations, is offered at the Graduate Center in White Plains, New York. Two years of full-time study or 3 to 4 years of part-time study are usually needed to complete the 39- to 48-credit curriculum.

Pennsylvania State University University Park Campus, College of Health and Human Development, University Park, PA 16802-1503.

Penn State offers an MBA/MHA concurrent program designed to produce graduates well grounded in basic management and health services knowledge, with skills and expertise for application in specialized institutional or functional areas of health services management. Both degrees, including residency, are completed with 21 months of full-time study.

Pepperdine University, School of Public Policy, Malibu, CA 90263-0001.

Pepperdine University's School of Public Policy offers a Master of Public Policy degree, which may be considered an alternative or complement to an MBA, a nonprofit management program, or a law degree. The School plans to offer joint-degree programs with the JD, MBA, and Master of Dispute Resolution. It is the School's firm belief that public policy itself is not limited to the study of government solutions but is broadened to embrace a full range of community-based and free-market approaches to public policy problems. For detailed information, see Book 2 of this series, contact 310-317-7493 or 888-456-1177 (toll-free), fax: 310-317-7494, e-mail: npapen@pepperdine.edu, or visit the Web site: http://www.pepperdine.edu/PublicPolicy

Rensselaer Polytechnic Institute, Lally School of Management and Technology, Program in Environmental Management and Policy, Troy, NY 12180-3590.

Environmental Management and Policy (EMP) is a Master of Science program that integrates technical course work with managerial and policy studies to develop management capability for decision-making positions in industry, environmental consulting firms, government, public-interest groups, and research institutions. The practice-oriented EMP program trains candidates to integrate better, cheaper, cleaner solutions to environmental challenges both in the US and overseas.

State University of New York at Albany, School of Public Health, Executive Park South, Albany, NY 12203-3727.

The MS in health policy, management, and behavior and the MPH with concentrations in health administration and behavioral science combine the teaching of theory with contemporary public health practice. The participation of the NYS Department of Health provides outstanding training for careers in health policy analysis and program development and evaluation. MS students can select from 3 tracks: health systems, management, and social behavior and community health. See the in-depth description of the School of Public Health.

Suffolk University, College of Liberal Arts and Sciences, Department of Economics, Boston, MA 02108-2770.

The Master of Science in International Economics (MSIE) program applies economic theory and quantitative methods to the study of international economic issues and the analysis of economic data for estimation and forecasting. The degree requires the successful completion of twelve 3-credit courses, including a thesis. Full-time students with the appropriate background can complete the program in 1 calendar year. See in-depth description in Book 2 of this series.

University of Chicago, Graduate Program in Health Administration and Policy, 969 East 60th Street, Office 6011, Chicago, IL 60637-1513.

The Graduate Program in Health Administration and Policy is an accredited, certificate-granting program completed through the normal course load required for the MBA in business.

University of Illinois at Urbana–Champaign, Institute of Labor and Industrial Relations, Urbana, IL 61801.

The Institute uses a multidisciplinary approach to the broad field of human resources management and labor and industrial relations, encompassing all aspects of employment relationships. Master's degree leads to professional careers in business, labor and education organizations, and government agencies. PhD leads primarily to university and college teaching and research.

University of Miami, School of Architecture, Coral Gables, FL 33124.

The University of Miami School of Architecture offers the professional degree for college graduates who desire a degree in architecture and the postprofessional degree program for the development of a specialization in suburb and town design and in computing.

University of Nebraska–Lincoln, College of Arts and Sciences, Department of Computer Science and Engineering, Lincoln, NE 68588.

The University of Nebraska–Lincoln offers master's degrees focusing on enterprise software engineering and information systems (IS) in the JD Edwards Honors Program in Computer Science and Management. Students obtain a high level of technical expertise and a strong understanding of the business problems and organizational needs that information systems serve. Students learn from rich experiences in business settings and take business courses with strong IS content. Courses and faculty members are from the College of Business Administration and the Department of Computer Science and Engineering. In the JD Edwards Program, fellowships and scholarships provide substantial student support.

University of New Hampshire, School of Health and Human Services, Department of Health Management and Policy, Durham, NH 03824.

The department offers the Master of Health Administration degree primarily for students working full-time in the health field. Classes are held on alternate Fridays and Saturdays from September through May, plus 2 residential weeks, 1 in late August and the other in late May. See in-depth description in Section 28 of this volume.

University of Pittsburgh, School of Information Sciences, Department of Information Science and Telecommunications, Pittsburgh, PA 15260.

The department awards graduate degrees in information science and telecommunications. Information science specialties include systems analysis and design, graphics and visualization, human-computer interface, information storage and retrieval, and cognitive science. Telecommunications specialties include telecommunications systems engineering, computer networking, telecommunications regulation, and network administration. See in-depth description in the Engineering and Applied Sciences volume of this series.

University of Southern California, Graduate School, Leonard Davis School of Gerontology, Los Angeles, CA 90089.

The University of Southern California's Leonard Davis School of Gerontology offers a dual-master's-degree program in gerontology and business administration. The MSG/MBA program prepares individuals for work in both profit and nonprofit businesses or organizations that respond to the needs of an aging population. Positions for graduates exist in a variety of settings, ranging from administration of employee benefits and retirement planning programs to health-care administration to the development and marketing of products and services for the elderly. The program features an outstanding faculty, a strong alumni network, and a wide variety of funding options.

University of Southern California, Graduate School, Annenberg School for Communication, School of Communication, Program in Communication Management, Los Angeles, CA 90089.

The master's in communication management has concentrations in strategic and corporate communication management, marketing communication, entertainment management, communication and information technologies, and communication law and policy. Students may take cognate courses in other units such as business, cinema/television, or engineering. Communication management program graduates pursue careers in such areas as marketing, market research, strategic planning, training and development, consulting, media and entertainment management, telecommunications, and information systems management.

University of Waterloo, Faculty of Engineering, Department of Management Sciences, Waterloo, ON N2L 3G1, Canada.

The Department of Management Sciences provides MASc and PhD programs in applied operations research, management information systems, and the management of technology. It also offers MOT@Distance, an innovative distance learning version of its MASc in management of technology, which can be completed from any home or office in North America.

Walden University, Graduate Programs, 155 Fifth Avenue South, Minneapolis, MN 55401.

Nationally recognized faculty members mentor experienced professionals through residency-based and computer-mediated instruction in Walden University's distance learning programs. Degrees are offered in applied management and decision sciences (PhD), education (MS, PhD), health services (PhD), human services (PhD), and psychology (MS, PhD). Accredited by the North Central Association of Colleges and Schools. For more information, see Book 1 of this series.

Washington University in St. Louis, School of Medicine, Graduate Programs in Medicine, Health Administration Program, St. Louis, MO 63110.

The health administration program at Washington University School of Medicine in St. Louis is a 2-year graduate program that awards the Master of Health Administration (MHA) degree. Optional paid 12-month postgraduate fellowship, active alumni placement services, and a network of more than 1,000 program graduates provide excellent career opportunities.

ADELPHI UNIVERSITY

School of Management and Business

Programs of Study

The School of Management and Business offers graduate curricula leading to the Master of Business Administration, Master of Business Administration with a Certified Public Accountant sequence, and Master of Science in Accounting degrees. The School also offers a graduate curriculum leading to the Master of Science in Finance and Banking.

The M.B.A. degree program requires a minimum of 39 credits and a maximum of 66 credits. This flexibility is intended to accommodate students with varied academic backgrounds, including those who have already earned an advanced degree and are now seeking a graduate business degree. The curriculum meets all national accreditation standards. The M.B.A. degree program offers eight areas of concentration: accounting, banking and financial markets, corporate finance and investments, hospital and health-care management, human resource management and personnel administration, international business, management, and marketing. The program also is currently being offered in Huntington, Long Island, at the Huntington Center and at the Manhattan Center in New York City.

The M.B.A./CPA program is designed for students without prior accounting knowledge who desire to obtain CPA certification within the context of a graduate M.B.A. program. Successful completion of this program qualifies a student to sit for the New York State CPA examination and reduces the CPA work experience requirement to one year.

The 42-credit Master of Science in Accounting degree program is designed to prepare highly qualified men and women to enter the field of public or private accounting. Successful completion of the program may reduce New York State's CPA work experience requirement to one year.

The 48-credit Master of Science in Finance and Banking combines essential management principles with highly specialized course work. Students can select either a microfinance option, which focuses on managerial finance and investments, or a macrofinance option, which deals with financial institutions and markets.

The School of Management and Business offers four graduate certificate programs. The Certificate Program in Human Resource Management requires the completion of 15 credits; the Certificate Program in Management for Nonbusiness Majors, 33 credits; the Certificate Program in Management for Women, 33 credits; and the Certificate Program in Banking, 24 credits. Credits earned in these certificate programs may be applied toward the M.B.A. or M.S. degree upon acceptance to the degree program.

Classes are scheduled during evening hours, Saturdays, and the summer.

Research Facilities

The School houses the Buchanan Computer Center, which has one of the largest mainframe computer installations on Long Island; in addition, there are more than 450 IBM and Macintosh personal computers available for student use. Internet and a large variety of CD-ROM databases are also available. In addition, Swirbul Library contains a fine collection of economics, banking, and business reference texts as well as the largest collection of reference materials on real estate appraisal in the United States. The library is completely computerized. It houses approximately 470,000 volumes and an ever-growing collection of electronic resources based on CD-ROM technology.

Financial Aid

Students may take advantage of assistance resources that include company tuition-refund plans, a University deferred-payment plan, and loans from the New York State Higher Education Services Corporation.

Cost of Study

Tuition for Adelphi University was $465 per credit hour in 1997–98. Both full- and part-time programs are available. University fees ranged from $75 to $250.

Living and Housing Costs

Adelphi University assists both single and married students in finding suitable accommodations whenever possible. The cost of living is dependent upon the specific location as well as the number of rooms rented by the student.

Student Group

There are approximately 400 students enrolled in the business, finance, and certificate programs. Within this population, there are 40 international students. The student body has varied undergraduate preparation and professional experience.

Location

Adelphi, a community of scholars and students, is part of the metropolitan community of New York City. Thus, it can draw upon the city's cultural and social resources as well as its own extensive program in the arts.

The University and The School

Adelphi University is set within a beautifully landscaped campus of 67 acres in the attractive residential community of Garden City, Long Island.

The University's Career Planning and Placement Center offers a career-planning service to all students and alumni interested in obtaining employment. Assistance is given in securing career information, writing resumes, interviewing, and planning job campaigns. Internships are available.

Applying

All degree-granting and certificate programs are available on a competitive basis to students holding a bachelor's degree in any major from an accredited college or university. The School of Management and Business admits students for the fall, spring, and summer semesters.

Students applying to the M.S. in Accounting program should have completed an undergraduate accounting curriculum that satisfies the New York State CPA education requirements.

Students must submit an application for admission and the required supporting credentials to the Graduate Admissions Office. The application fee is $50. The Graduate Management Admission Test is required of all degree applicants. International students whose native language is not English are required to take the Test of English as a Foreign Language and file a financial affidavit.

Correspondence and Information

Graduate Admissions Office
Adelphi University
1 South Avenue
Garden City, New York 11530

Telephone: 800-ADELPHI (toll-free)
Fax: 516-877-3039
E-mail: admissions@adelphi.edu
World Wide Web: http://www.adelphi.edu

Adelphi University

THE FACULTY

SCHOOL OF MANAGEMENT AND BUSINESS

Department of Accounting and Law

Grace M. Conway, M.A., Associate Professor of Accounting and Chairperson; CPA.

Jack Angel, M.S., Assistant Professor of Accounting; CPA.
Alan Kreitzman, M.B.A., Assistant Professor of Accounting; CPA.
Neil Novins, M.B.A., Assistant Professor of Accounting; CPA.
Winston Waters, J.D., Assistant Professor of Law.

Department of Administrative Sciences

Allan Ashley, Ph.D., Professor of Management and Management Science and Chairperson.

Detelen Elenkov, Ph.D., Assistant Professor of Management and Business Policy.
Gunther R. Geiss, Ph.D., Professor of Data Processing.
Jeffrey Goldstein, Ph.D., Assistant Professor of Organizational Behavior.
Rakesh C. Gupta, Ph.D. candidate, Assistant Professor of Management and Business Policy and Dean.
Gregory Gutman, M.B.A., Professor of Marketing and Management.
Zhimin Huang, Ph.D., Associate Professor of Production/Operations Management.
Susan Li, Ph.D., Assistant Professor of Management and Information Systems.
Rachel Mather, D.A., Assistant Professor of Business Communications.
Alvin Rosenstein, Ph.D., Professor of Marketing.
Joseph Ruocco, Ph.D., Associate Professor of Personnel and Human Resource Management.

Department of Banking, Economics, and Finance

Robert Felheim, Ph.D., Associate Professor of Finance and Chairperson.

Joseph Chorun, Ph.D., Associate Professor of Economics and Finance.
Harvey Heinowitz, M.B.A., Assistant Professor of Banking, Economics, and Finance.
Joseph Mascia, M.B.A., M.S., M.P.A., Associate Professor of Banking, Economics, and Finance.
Lawrence Nowicki, Ph.D., Assistant Professor of International Economics and Finance.
James Patchias, M.A., M.Ph., Associate Professor of Economics and Finance.
Bruce Swenson, Ph.D., Assistant Professor of Finance.

AMERICAN INTERNATIONAL COLLEGE

School of Business Administration

Program of Study

At American International College (AIC) students can earn an M.B.A. degree on either a full- or part-time basis. Both day and evening programs are offered with the same academic standards and requirements. M.B.A. courses are taught year round, which allows students to accelerate their progress. M.B.A. candidates must complete a total of 36 credit hours of graduate-level courses. Students lacking adequate undergraduate preparation in business may be required to complete a maximum of 18 credit hours of foundation course work. A full-time student who has a degree in business can complete degree requirements in four semesters or twelve months.

In addition to a general business plan, M.B.A. concentrations exist in accounting, finance, international business, management, and marketing. AIC is the first college in Massachusetts to offer an M.B.A. concentration in materials/operations management.

Research Facilities

Good library and other research facilities are available for all areas of graduate work. AIC is one of eight members of the Cooperating Colleges of Greater Springfield. Through this consortium, students can enroll in courses at member institutions and use their libraries and other research facilities.

The academic computer system consists of a cluster of VAX microcomputers, which are accessed by personal computers of the 386, 486, and Pentium types available to students and faculty members seven days a week. A variety of printers are also available for student use, including a PostScript laser printer. Students can produce documents that contain text, graphics, databases, spreadsheets, and video images. A variety of computer equipment is also available in the Shea Library for scholarly research.

A diverse selection of software is available, including WordPerfect, Quattro Pro, Peachtree Complete Accounting, PC Globe, D Base, Paradox, Microsoft Office, COBOL, Microsoft Windows, SPSS, and a number of programs chosen by faculty members for use in their courses.

Financial Aid

Graduate students with demonstrated financial need may apply for aid from the Federal Perkins Loan Program or the Federal Work-Study Program. These are administered by the Financial Aid Office, which helps students find the best combination of financing available. Information about VA benefits is available at the Registrar's Office. Many corporations help employees continue their education; prospective students should check with their company personnel office for details.

Cost of Study

Tuition is $343 per credit hour in 1998–99. Tuition rates are the same for all students, regardless of nationality or residence.

Living and Housing Costs

The estimated cost of living for a full-time resident is approximately $7900 per academic year. This includes room and board, books, and personal expenditures. Since classes are held in the morning, afternoon, and evening, many students organize their schedules so that they can work part-time.

Student Group

Approximately 100 men and women are both full- and part-time M.B.A. students. Many have prior work experience, and their educational backgrounds range from music to business. The majority are in their mid-to-late 20s, although many enter the M.B.A. program directly from college. A handful of degree candidates are in their 40s and 50s. This cross section of ages, background, and training enriches discussions as students bring their life experiences to the classroom. An increasing number of women and international students are entering the program, adding yet more perspectives to the study of business administration.

Location

Springfield is the major center of economic activity in western Massachusetts. The Boston Symphony Orchestra summers in nearby Tanglewood, and the Jacob's Pillow Dance Troupe and Lenox Arts Center are also located in proximity.

Although the city's population is 152,000, Springfield has retained a small-town flavor and manageability. Many features and attractions usually found only in large cities are also available in Springfield; these include the Stage West Theatre, the Basketball Hall of Fame, the Civic Center, WGBY-TV (a public television station), the Springfield Symphony, the Museum Quadrangle complex, the Springfield Historical Society, and Forest Park, a 750-acre city park.

Many AIC alumni are employed by local businesses and major corporations (such as Massachusetts Mutual Life, Friendly Ice Cream, Milton Bradley Company, Moore Company, United Technologies, and Hamilton Standard) with home offices in greater Springfield. In the downtown area, old factory buildings and brownstones are being converted into apartments and stores. Riverfront Park attracts many with open-air fairs and concerts, and international cuisine and shops can be found in Springfield's ethnic neighborhoods.

The College

AIC is a small private college dedicated to the individual student and excellence in teaching. Since its founding in 1885, the College has given students professional and career preparation based in a solid tradition of liberal arts. Respect for the integrity of each person and concern for his or her well-being and growth are hallmarks of the College's philosophy. The College has nearly 18,000 alumni.

AIC's M.B.A. program is dedicated to providing graduates who are skilled in their major field of study and who concurrently appreciate the need for the modern executive to become comfortable with interdisciplinary knowledge. To this end, such M.B.A. courses as the "World of Business Through the Eyes of Literature" and "Issues in Business Ethics" are periodically offered.

AIC has three schools—Arts and Sciences, Psychology and Education, and Business Administration—and Divisions of Nursing, Physical Therapy, and Occupational Therapy. Each school offers both undergraduate and graduate degree programs.

Applying

Qualified men and women with bachelor's degrees from accredited colleges and universities are considered for admission. Admission is based on an evaluation of undergraduate transcripts, personal references, GMAT scores, and work experience. Applications are accepted throughout the year, and students can enter the M.B.A. program at the start of the fall, spring, intersession, or summer semesters.

Correspondence and Information

Dr. Adam Zielinski, Dean
School of Business Administration
American International College
1000 State Street, Box 2A
Springfield, Massachusetts 01109

Telephone: 413-747-6230
Fax: 413-737-2803
E-mail: business@www.aic.edu

American International College

THE FACULTY

The date in parentheses at the end of each entry indicates the first year of affiliation with the College.

Salvatore Anzalotti Jr., Professor of Accounting and Chair, Department of Accounting; M.B.A., American International, 1963; CPA (Massachusetts). (1963)

Robert D. Calcasola, Assistant Professor of Accounting; M.B.A., Western New England, 1977. (1997)

Paul C. Desmarais, Associate Professor of Mathematics and Chair, Department of Mathematics; Ph.D. (mathematics), Massachusetts, 1974. (1975)

Marshall B. Epstein, Assistant Professor of Business Administration and Chair, Department of Marketing; M.B.A., Hartford, 1978. (1981)

Keith G. Gauthier, Assistant Professor of Accounting; M.S. (taxation), Hartford, 1984; CPA (Massachusetts). (1986)

Mark N. Hagopian, Professor of Political Science; Ph.D. (political science), Boston University, 1969. (1966)

Clayton Hillyer, Assistant Professor of Marketing; M.B.A. (marketing), Lowell, 1984. (1993)

Keff T. Lagoditz, Assistant Professor of Business Administration; M.B.A. (business), Western New England, 1982. (1982)

Gary L. LeFort, Assistant Professor of International Business; M.B.A. (business), Boston University, 1977. (1997)

Bonnie L. Orcutt, Assistant Professor of Economics; Ph.D. (economics), Clark, 1993. (1991)

Michael T. Peterson, Assistant Professor of Management and Chair, Department of Management; M.S. (procurement and contracting), George Washington, 1968. (1994)

Donald W. Sharpe, Lecturer of Management Information Systems; M.B.A., Western New England, 1973. (1997).

Ira Smolowitz, Professor of Finance and Dean of the Bureau of Business Research and Program Development; M.B.A. (finance and investments), CUNY, Baruch, 1965; Ph.D. (urban and environmental studies), Rensselaer, 1984. (1988)

Adam Zielinski, Professor of International Business and Dean, School of Business Administration; M.B.A. (finance), Berkeley, 1964; Ph.D. (adult and vocational education), Connecticut, 1989. (1996)

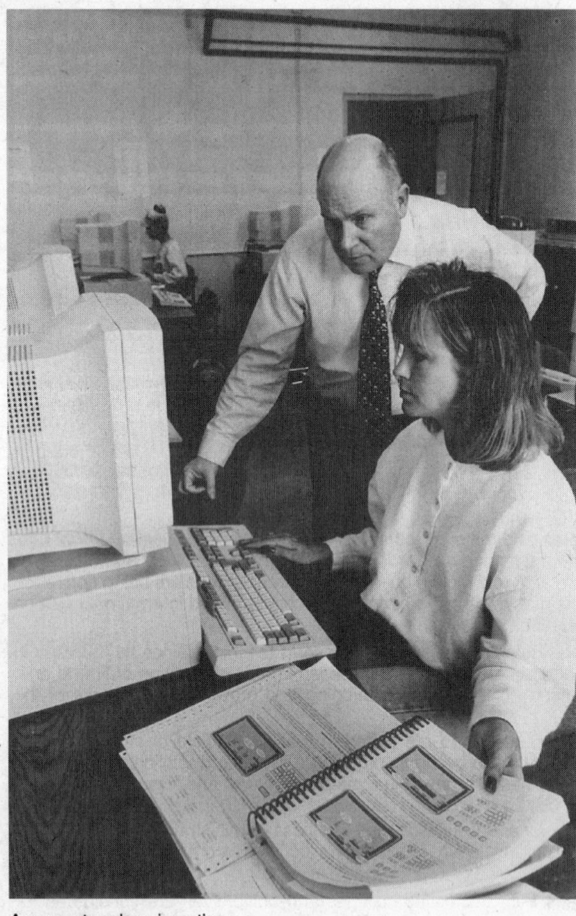

A computer class in action.

Students working together in a small group setting.

Experiential learning at AIC.

AMERICAN UNIVERSITY

Kogod College of Business Administration

Programs of Study

The Kogod College of Business Administration offers programs of graduate study leading to the Master of Business Administration and Master of Science degrees. All programs are available on a full- or part-time basis. Both the business and accounting programs of the Kogod College are accredited by the AACSB–The International Association for Management Education.

The primary purpose of the M.B.A. program is to prepare men and women for management positions in business, government, and other types of organizations. The M.B.A. program is a 54-credit-hour program. Up to 13 credit hours may be waived for students who have completed equivalent undergraduate or graduate courses within the previous seven years. Areas of concentration are available in accounting, finance, international business, marketing, management of global information technology, human resource management, entrepreneurship and management, and economic development. Students may also work with a faculty adviser to design their own concentration.

The Master of Science degree is offered to provide advanced study in accounting, finance, and taxation. In addition, the Kogod College offers joint degrees with the Washington College of Law (J.D./M.B.A.) and the School of International Service (M.A.I.A./M.B.A).

Research Facilities

Resources of the University library support graduate curriculum and research of the American University. Library services, collections, and study facilities are located in the Jack I. and Dorothy G. Bender Library and in the Music Library in the Kreeger Building. Collections include more than 675,000 volumes, 3,000 periodical titles, and more than 940,000 microforms as well as 36,000 items in a variety of media formats. ALADIN, the online information system, provides access to all of the collections at American University as well as to materials at six other universities in the Washington Research Library Consortium (WRLC). In addition, ALADIN offers access to many other resources, including indexes to newspapers and periodicals, a document delivery service, Electronic Books in Print, and WorldCat, an online database of materials in more than 9,000 libraries. A new World Wide Web version of ALADIN provides links to electronic reserves, the *Encyclopedia Britannica* on line, business statistics through Stat USA, electronic journals, and art images. Registered students may sign up for LEXIS/NEXIS, an electronic service that provides full text of news, business, and legal resources. Graduate students have borrowing privileges at WRLC libraries. For materials outside the WRLC, American University students may use interlibrary loan and document delivery services or visit more than 500 special libraries in the Washington, D.C., area.

The University operates twenty-two computer laboratories. The Office of Information Technology (OIT) provides general purpose computing in the Mary Graydon Center and Anderson Computing Complex and specialized computing support in three other facilities: the Social Science Research Lab, the McCabe Center for Computers and Writing, and the New Media Center. Other departments and offices provide specialized laboratories in the areas of business, chemistry, communication, computer science, graphic design, economics, foreign languages, law, learning services, physics, psychology, social science research, and writing. The University's high-speed network, EagleNet, provides each residence hall, classroom, and department with a direct connection to campus computing resources and the global resources of the Internet. EagleNet provides access to a wide range of site-licensed software, the online library catalog of the Washington Research Library Consortium, the mainframe and other specialized servers supporting intensive computation, and group software, such as Lotus Notes, which is the University's standard for electronic messaging and productivity. The University's mainframe computer, an IBM 9672-R51 that runs both OS/390 (MVS) and VM/ESA, provides batch and interactive services. The University's computing resources are accessible on campus from computing labs, residence hall rooms, and administrative offices via EagleNet and from off campus via modem for those who have access to the Internet through other service providers.

Financial Aid

Graduate study scholarships and graduate assistantships are available to full-time students. Special opportunity awards for members of minority groups (African American, Hispanic American, Asian and Pacific Islander American, American Indian, and Alaskan Native American) parallel the regular honor awards and take the form of assistantships and scholarships.

Cost of Study

The tuition fee for the Kogod College of Business Administration of American University in 1998–99 is $9540 per semester for full-time M.B.A. students and $687 per credit hour for part-time M.B.A. students.

Living and Housing Costs

Although many graduate students live off campus, the University provides graduate dormitory rooms and apartments. The Off-Campus Housing Office maintains a referral file of rooms and apartments; two housing workshop clinics provide personal assistance to graduate students seeking housing. Housing costs in Washington, D.C., are comparable to those in other major metropolitan areas; rates vary with distance from campus and the extent to which facilities are shared.

Student Group

Students at the Kogod College come from all fifty states and 120 countries and represent nearly all age groups and interests. Many part-time students are already successful executives who bring relevant experience with them to the classroom. Career and placement services are provided by the College and the University Career Centers.

Location

The national capital offers students a variety of educational, governmental, and cultural resources unsurpassed in the United States. The 85-acre campus, located in one of the city's most beautiful residential areas, is only minutes from downtown Washington by local bus or subway.

The University

The College of Business Administration at the American University was the first such college in the nation's capital, and the Master of Business Administration program has been offered since 1949. Opportunities for research, internships, cooperative education placement, and part-time jobs exist in every discipline, from accounting to real estate, enriching the student's degree program with opportunities for practical application of theoretical studies. Every major corporation, labor union, professional organization, and consumer group has an office in Washington.

Applying

Applicants for graduate programs must possess a baccalaureate degree from a regionally accredited institution, a satisfactory score on the Graduate Management Admission Test (GMAT), and a satisfactory grade point average for the last 60 hours of academic work. Applicants who are not native speakers of English must be certified by the University's English Language Institute.

The deadlines for applying are June 1 for the fall semester, November 1 for the spring semester, and March 15 for the summer term. Priority consideration for merit awards will be given to students who apply by February 1.

Correspondence and Information

Director of Graduate Admissions and Financial Aid
Kogod College of Business Administration—PG
American University
4400 Massachusetts Avenue, NW
Washington, D.C. 20016-8044

Telephone: 202-885-1913
800-AN-AU-MBA (toll-free)
Fax: 202-885-1078
E-mail: aumbams@american.edu
World Wide Web: http://www.kogod.american.edu

American University

THE FACULTY

Myron J. Roomkin, Dean; Ph.D., Wisconsin.
William H. DeLone, Associate Dean for Graduate Programs; Ph.D., UCLA.
Patricia Cleveland, Associate Dean for Undergraduate Programs; Ph.D., Kansas.
Firouz Bahrampour, Assistant Dean for Administration; Ph.D., American.
August Schomburg, Director of Graduate Programs; Ph.D., Maryland.
Judith Sugarman, Director of Graduate Admissions and Financial Aid; M.Ed., American.
Robert Warmkessel, Director of Graduate Business Placement; M.B.A., Syracuse.

The faculty is the real strength of the College. Full-time faculty members are primarily committed to high standards of teaching but are also actively engaged in research. The faculty members have published numerous books and articles. They serve as consultants to major corporations in the United States as well as in other countries, maintaining close ties with both domestic and international firms. This enables them to bring to students a sense of current issues and state-of-the-art solutions to the problems facing industry today.

Adjunct faculty members have top-level experience in business and professional and government communities.

Accounting and Taxation
Ajay Adhikari, Ph.D., Virginia Commonwealth; CPA.
Luis Betancourt, Ph.D., Central Florida; CPA.
Donald R. Brenner, J.D., Ohio State.
Gary Bulmash, D.B.A., Maryland; CPA.
Augustine Duru, Ph.D., Maryland; CPA.
Philip F. Jacoby, Ph.D., George Washington; CPA.
Michael A. Mass, J.D., Georgetown.
Anne C. Riley, D.B.A., George Washington; CPA.
Michael P. Sampson, LL.M., Georgetown; CPA.
Donald T. Williamson, LL.M., Georgetown; CPA.

Finance and Real Estate
Robert L. Losey, Chairperson; Ph.D., Kentucky.
H. Kent Baker, D.B.A., Maryland.
John D. Benjamin, Ph.D., LSU.
Peter Chinloy, Ph.D., Harvard.
Richard B. Edelman, D.B.A., Maryland.
P. C. Kumar, Ph.D., Penn State.
Leigh A. Riddick, Ph.D., Wisconsin.
Chera Sayers, Ph.D., Wisconsin.

International Business
Anne C. Perry, Chairperson; Ph.D., George Washington.
Jessica M. Bailey, Ph.D., Missouri.
Frank L. Dubois, Ph.D., South Carolina.
Dara Khambata, D.B.A., George Washington.
Tomasz Mroczkowski, Ph.D., Academy of Economics, Krakow.

Management (includes human resource management, management of global information technology, and entrepreneurship and management)
Edward A. Wasil Jr., Chairperson; Ph.D., Maryland.
Barbara J. Bird, Ph.D., USC.
Erran Carmel, Ph.D., Arizona.
William H. DeLone, Ph.D., UCLA.
Thomas V. Dibacco, Ph.D., American.
Kathleen A. Getz, Ph.D., Pittsburgh.
Stevan R. Holmberg; D.B.A., Indiana.
David C. Jacobs, Ph.D., Cornell.
Richard G. Linowes, D.B.A., Harvard.
David C. Martin, Ph.D., Maryland.
Victor Selman, D.Sc., George Washington.
Francis D. Tuggle, Ph.D., Carnegie Mellon.
Roger Volkema, Ph.D., Wisconsin.

Marketing
John Swasy, Chairperson; Ph.D., UCLA.
Gary T. Ford, Ph.D., SUNY at Buffalo.
Manoj Hastak, D.B.A., Penn State.
Michael B. Mazis, Ph.D., Penn State.
Anusree Mitra, Ph.D., Florida.
Mary Anne Raymond, Ph.D., Georgia.

The future home of the Kogod College of Business Administration.

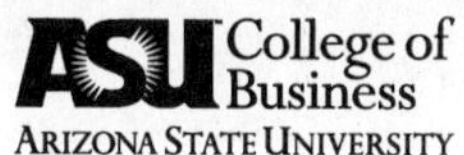

ARIZONA STATE UNIVERSITY

College of Business

Programs of Study

Arizona State University (ASU) offers highly qualified students opportunities for advanced study in all of the graduate business and economic disciplines. Degree program offerings include the Master of Business Administration, Master of Accountancy, Master of Taxation, Master of Health Services Administration, Master of Science in Economics, Master of Science in Information Management, and a special M.B.A. program for executives. In addition, Ph.D. degrees are available in business administration and economics.

The ASU M.B.A. full-time program consists of an intense first-year core with the options of a career track, certificate, or second master's to be completed in the second year. Students applying to the program must be computer literate and proficient in calculus, have demonstrated strong quantitative ability, and have a minimum of two years of full-time work experience. Students may travel abroad for a semester and enroll for international course work at ESC Toulouse, France; and Carlos III, Spain.

The College of Business offers formal concurrent degree programs with the University's College of Law (J.D./M.B.A.), the School of Health Administration and Policy (M.B.A./M.H.S.A.), and the School of Architecture (M.B.A./M.Arch.). The College of Business also offers the following concurrent degrees: M.B.A./M.S.I.M., M.B.A./M.S.Ecn., M.B.A./M.Acc., and M.B.A./M.Tax.

Dual-degree programs have been arranged with the American Graduate School of International Management (Thunderbird), ESC Toulouse in France, and Carlos III in Spain. Students enrolled in this program receive both a Master of Business Administration from ASU and a Master of International Management (M.B.A./M.I.M.).

Research Facilities

The College of Business houses the L. William Seidman Research Institute, which includes the Arizona Real Estate Center, the Bank One Economic Outlook Center, the Center for Advanced Purchasing, the Center for the Advancement of Small Business, the Center for Business Research, the Center for Services Marketing and Management, the Center for the Study of Finance, and the Joan and David Lincoln Center for Applied Ethics.

ASU libraries rank thirty-first among the largest research libraries in the United States and Canada, according to the Association of Research Libraries. ASU has six libraries on campus; business and economics holdings are housed in the Charles Trumbull Hayden Library, the University's main library.

The College of Business offers one of the most modern and sophisticated environments available for professional graduate study. The Business College provides attractive and comfortable classrooms, computer systems, and study areas as well as a television studio, modern auditoriums, and a graduate student center. Computer facilities are available to graduate students throughout the two business buildings, in a designated ASU M.B.A. computer project room, and in the University's state-of-the-art Computing Commons.

Financial Aid

Graduate assistantships are available that waive out-of-state tuition (for nonresidents) and pay a stipend that is highly competitive with those of other universities. Graduate tuition scholarships are available on a competitive basis, as are academic scholarships and sponsored scholarships. Loans are available through the Financial Assistance Office of the University.

Cost of Study

In 1998–99, registration fees and tuition are $4158 for Arizona residents and $11,110 for nonresidents per year.

Living and Housing Costs

Graduate housing is available on campus and off campus. There are numerous apartments and houses in the Tempe, Mesa, and Phoenix areas. Rental information may be obtained through the Tenants' Association. On-campus housing costs average $450 per month. Off-campus housing costs average about $600 per month (including utilities), depending upon the student's lifestyle.

Student Group

There are approximately 895 students in the ASU M.B.A. program. Roughly 40 percent are full-time students. ASU M.B.A. evening students attend classes two evenings a week and work full-time. The average age of business graduate students is 27. More than one third of the students are women. Active student groups, including the M.B.A. Association, the Graduate Women in Business Organization, the Black Student M.B.A. Association, the International Business Association, and the Hispanic M.B.A. Student Association, sponsor professional development seminars, career placement activities, and social functions, such as the ASU M.B.A. Olympics and the "Roast and Toast."

Location

Arizona State University is located in the city of Tempe, a part of the Phoenix metropolitan area. Phoenix is currently the sixth-largest city in the nation and is continuing to grow at a rapid rate. Numerous service and high-technology corporations, including American Express, Intel, Honeywell, Motorola, and Allied Signal, have established major facilities in the area. It is an easy drive from the Phoenix area to the 87 percent of Arizona that is protected for public recreation. This territory includes the Grand Canyon, the Petrified Forest, several ski areas (water and snow), and numerous lakes and state parks.

The University

Arizona State University's 700-acre main campus is landscaped with shade trees, stately palms, semitropical gardens, and modern architecture. A prominent campus feature is Gammage Center for the Performing Arts, the last major design achievement of architect Frank Lloyd Wright. The Student Recreation Center houses three swimming pools, tennis courts, weight rooms, and exercise facilities. An eighteen-hole golf course is open year round. Pedestrian malls with gardens, fountains, and bike paths connect the major building areas.

ASU, with an enrollment of 44,500 students, is the youngest and the largest university in the prestigious Pacific-10 Conference and is recognized as a Research I academic institution. Graduate students make up nearly one third of the University's on-campus enrollment.

Applying

Applications are accepted for the fall term for both day and evening programs. Applications and transcripts must be sent to the Graduate College for processing one month prior to the ASU M.B.A. Program Office deadline of May 1 for the fall term. Letters of recommendation and a statement of purpose should be sent to the ASU M.B.A. Program.

Correspondence and Information

Graduate College
Wilson Hall
Arizona State University
P.O. Box 871003
Tempe, Arizona 85287-1003
Telephone: 602-965-6113

ASU M.B.A. Program Office
College of Business
Arizona State University-Main
P.O. Box 874906
Tempe, Arizona 85287-4906
Telephone: 602-965-3332
Fax: 602-965-8569
E-mail: asu.mba@asu.edu
World Wide Web: http://www.cob.asu.edu/mba

Arizona State University

THE FACULTY AND THEIR RESEARCH

Business Administration. John Pearson, Ph.D., Acting Chair.
Four areas of business administration are the focus of 28 faculty members. These areas are business law, purchasing and logistics management, real estate, and management communication.

Economics. Arthur Blakemore, Ph.D., Chair.
The economics department has 35 faculty members, whose fields of specialization include international economics, labor economics, public-sector economics, urban and regional economics, econometrics, industrial organization, comparative systems, and law and economics. The department offers an M.S. degree program and a Ph.D. in economics.

Finance. Herbert M. Kaufman, Ph.D., Chair.
Interests of the 16 finance faculty members focus on corporate finance, investments, financial markets, and banking.

Management. William H. Glick, Ph.D., Chair.
The management department has 31 full-time faculty members whose research and teaching are focused on strategic management and human resources management.

Marketing. Michael P. Mokwa, Ph.D., Chair.
The marketing department has 23 full-time faculty members, whose major focuses of teaching and research are services marketing, advertising, distribution channels, and buyer behavior.

SCHOOL OF ACCOUNTANCY AND INFORMATION MANAGEMENT. Philip Reckers, Ph.D., Director.
The mission of the School of Accountancy and Information Management is to prepare students for successful careers in accounting and computer information systems, to expand and disseminate knowledge, and to serve the academic, accounting, and business communities. Forty-three full-time faculty members and six full-time staff members attend to this mission. The School offers bachelor's and master's degrees in accountancy, taxation, and computer information systems as well as doctoral degrees in business administration with concentrations in both accountancy and computer information systems. The School has a national reputation, the accounting programs rank in the top twenty in the nation (per *public accounting report*), and the computer information systems technology M.B.A. is ranked in the top twenty-five (per *Computerworld*). More information about the School can be found on the World Wide Web (http://www.cob.asu.edu/acct).

SCHOOL OF HEALTH ADMINISTRATION AND POLICY. Eugene S. Schneller, Ph.D., Director.
The School's 6 faculty members have expertise in a variety of academic and professional fields, such as economics, strategic planning, organizational behavior, policy analysis, management, financial planning, and medical sociology. The School offers both an M.H.S.A. degree and an M.B.A./M.H.S.A. dual degree. More information about the School can be found on the World Wide Web (http://www.cob.asu.edu/hap/index.html).

Entrance to Hayden Library.

Computing Commons.

The College of Business.

ARMSTRONG UNIVERSITY

Graduate School of Business Administration

Programs of Study

The Graduate School of Business Administration at Armstrong University offers day and evening classes that lead to the Master of Business Administration (M.B.A.) degree in accounting, finance, international business, management, and marketing. All programs are available on a full- or part-time basis.

From the moment students arrive, they make professional presentations in small, nonintimidating classes of 3 to 10 students. The M.B.A. curriculum emphasizes communication skills and application of knowledge to the workplace. A rigorous presentation skills class is part of the core curriculum, and students give oral presentations and produce professional reports in every class.

Small classes encourage student-teacher interaction and provide a supportive learning environment. Outside the classroom, students have easy access to faculty and administrative staff members who are eager to help students reach their educational goals. While the academic standards are very high, the University accommodates students with a wide range of backgrounds and offers the personal attention they need to meet these standards. The average class size is 7 students; the student-faculty ratio is 5:1. The University is committed to seeing students graduate. The full-time academic adviser takes the time to work with students individually to help them achieve their objectives.

In addition to the communication skills focus and emphasis on workplace application, the curriculum brings students the latest in global business trends, opportunities, and challenges. The University's experience in educating a diverse international student body highly qualifies it to serve a multicultural community and the global business community. Every class is a multinational meeting, with students from more than forty countries represented in the student body.

The M.B.A. program consists of three components: prerequisites, which can be waived by examination or based on undergraduate background; a business core; and concentration (major) courses. The core includes survey courses that establish a solid conceptual base in finance, management, marketing, quantitative methods, managerial economics, operations management, strategic information systems, and marketing. It also includes a presentations skills course and a capstone course in policymaking and executive action. The concentration focuses critical attention on the techniques and concepts of a dynamic area of business. Majors that are currently available are accounting, finance, international business, management, and marketing. During their last semester, students are required to complete the graduate project and the seminar in career management. Students carry out individual case studies under the supervision of a faculty adviser. The objective is for students to learn how to design and conduct research and how to defend a thesis. The seminar in career management provides students with such skills as resume writing, conducting an interview and being interviewed, negotiating skills, and professional image. The program normally takes three semesters of full-time study to complete and requires the completion of a minimum of 36 semester units.

The Career Management Office helps students acquire the skills needed to strategically manage an immediate job search and long-term career. The office provides personalized placement services to meet graduates' and employers' needs for internships and permanent employment. Armstrong University's ties with the community provide internship opportunities in local companies. Students gain insight into the business world and make valuable contacts by working full- or part-time for a twelve-week period in a job that is directly related to the student's field of study.

Research Facilities

Armstrong University is equipped with a fully networked state-of-the-art computer learning center. Microcomputers give every student easy access to a broad range of software. This configuration allows students to operate the equipment in a local-area network and to access a variety of software applications. A large screen connected to the computer network is available for demonstrations.

The library collection of 10,000 books, 200 periodical subscriptions, and 800 annual reports of corporations reflects the dedication of Armstrong University to provide an up-to-date library facility. The University library is fully computerized and provides access to many electronic references and research information sources. A variety of CD-ROMs provide the latest indexing and abstracting of periodicals and newspapers, with an emphasis on business. The Internet is now an integral part of the library and provides global information to students.

Financial Aid

Financial aid is available for U.S. students. Students should contact the University for more information.

Cost of Study

Graduate tuition in 1998–99 is $350 per semester unit; the minimum full-time course load is 6 units per semester ($2100 per semester, plus a $15 registration fee). Students are encouraged to pay tuition on the installment plan of three payments per semester. Books and instructional supplies cost about $350 per year for full-time students.

Living and Housing Costs

The University does not have residence facilities; rental housing is available in the immediate area. Housing and other living expenses vary widely, depending on the type of accommodations and lifestyle. The average cost for students who share an apartment and cook their own meals is $7500 per academic year.

Student Group

Students from more than forty countries create an international atmosphere and the opportunity to develop an international perspective. Students with varied academic, work, and cultural backgrounds contribute to a stimulating classroom experience.

Location

Armstrong University is located in downtown Oakland, adjacent to Berkeley and just across the bay from San Francisco. The Bay Area is a center for high technology, industry, and professional and scientific activity and is famous for its year-round pleasant climate. Armstrong's urban campus is in the East Bay's center of cultural entertainment and recreational opportunities and in proximity to the limitless opportunities of San Francisco. Oakland is also one of the most culturally diverse areas in the United States, where students from every country can find groups and activities in their native culture and language.

The University

Founded in 1918, Armstrong is a small, independent university. Its faculty members, most of whom are involved in demonstrating their expertise in today's business world, reflect Armstrong University's practical approach to education for a career in business. Education at Armstrong is a very personal matter. The multicultural student body creates a diverse and stimulating learning environment and gives students an opportunity to develop the international perspective that is vital to success in today's business world. In addition, students benefit from a worldwide network of other students and alumni who are involved in international business.

Applying

Admission is based on demonstrated academic ability. Personal qualities, such as maturity and motivation, are also considered. Applicants to the Graduate School must have earned a bachelor's degree from an approved college or university, with at least a 2.5 GPA. All applicants are required to submit an application for admission, have official transcripts sent to the admissions office from every college and university attended, and pay a nonrefundable fee of $35 for U.S. students and $50 for international students. International students must submit an official TOEFL score. Applications for admission are accepted throughout the year, and students may enter in the fall, spring, or summer sessions.

Correspondence and Information

Graduate Enrollment Services
Armstrong University
1608 Webster Street
Oakland, California 94612-3312

Telephone: 510-835-7900
Fax: 510-835-8935
E-mail: admin@armstrong-u.edu

Armstrong University

THE FACULTY

The faculty members are qualified to teach on the basis of their master's and doctorate degrees, but in addition, they are practicing professionals with real-world skills instead of being ivory tower academics. Armstrong University looks for expertise in a particular field, commitment as teachers, and especially practical knowledge that can be brought to the classroom. Many have owned, or currently own, their own successful businesses. All are active in scholarly or applied research, consulting, and service to the University and the community. The faculty members are also experienced curriculum developers and are adept at translating theoretical concepts into practical applications. Their instructional methods include the use of media, case study, and group interactions. They are highly qualified to teach managers whose time is valuable and whose expectations are high. The faculty's expertise covers all areas of business.

AUBURN UNIVERSITY

College of Business

Programs of Study

The College of Business offers seven graduate programs: the Master of Business Administration, the Master of Accountancy, the Master of Management Information Systems, the Master of Science in business administration, the Master of Science in Economics, and Ph.D. programs in economics and management. The graduate programs in business are accredited by the AACSB–The International Association for Management Education.

The objective of the M.B.A. degree is to prepare the talented and strongly motivated student for a leadership role in a highly competitive and volatile environment. The program generally encompasses fifteen to eighteen months of course work in five to six quarters. During the M.B.A. program, students earn a 15-hour concentration in a wide variety of functional areas, including economics, finance, human resource management, marketing, operations management, management information systems, and management of technology. The M.B.A. is also available off-campus through the Video-based Graduate Outreach Program; for more information, students should call 334-844-5300.

The M.Ac. is a 45-hour degree program with concentrations in taxation, financial/auditing, and accounting systems. This professional, nonthesis degree program is available to students with the equivalent of an undergraduate major in accounting.

The M.M.I.S. program is a 50-hour nonthesis degree program for students who wish to prepare for careers in management information systems.

Students who desire a research orientation may prefer the M.S.B.A., which requires a minimum of 45 hours and a thesis in a selected area of study. M.S.B.A. concentrations are currently offered in human resource management, production/operations management, marketing, and finance.

The M.S. in economics is a 45-hour program, plus thesis. Graduate study in economics is designed to prepare students for careers in business, government, teaching, and, in the case of the Ph.D., scholarly research.

The Ph.D. program in management is designed to prepare graduates to conduct high-quality research in universities, consulting organizations, government, and business. Doctoral students choose one of three areas of concentration: organizational analysis and change, management information systems, or human resource management. The Ph.D. is an interdepartmental program that requires a minimum of 80 quarter hours beyond the baccalaureate, plus successful completion of a dissertation. Students admitted to the program prior to receiving a master's degree may bypass the thesis requirement.

Research Facilities

Research facilities for students in the College of Business include the main library and computer system. The library is a member of the Association of Research Libraries and currently holds more than 2.5 million bound volumes and 2.4 million items on microformat. The library is a depository for U.S. government documents and lists among its subscriptions more than 10,000 serials. Eight public and one private computing sites are equipped with IBM PC-compatible and Macintosh microcomputers and laser printers. Each site is connected to AUNET, the campuswide network, and has access to the University's IBM 3090-200J mainframe computer, the Alabama Supercomputer Network, and other networks throughout the United States and around the world.

Financial Aid

A limited number of graduate assistantships are available. Each is awarded competitively based on scholastics, credentials, GMAT results, and experience. Students holding assistantships of one-quarter or more pay in-state tuition. All need-based financial assistance is processed through the Student Financial Aid Office.

Cost of Study

Tuition for fall 1997 was $785 per quarter for full-time resident students and $2355 for nonresidents per quarter. The cost of books and supplies was estimated at $250 per quarter.

Living and Housing Costs

The number of on-campus apartments available for single and married graduate students is limited. In 1997–98, the minimum cost per calendar year for a one-bedroom, furnished University apartment was $2600 (excluding the cost of electricity). A wide variety of off-campus housing is available within walking distance of the University.

Student Group

In spring 1997, 264 M.B.A., 5 M.S.B.A., 9 M.M.I.S., 49 M.Ac., 4 M.S.Ec., and 16 Ph.D. students were enrolled. The average age was 27. Sixty-three percent of the students were men. Approximately 25 percent were married. Ten percent were international students or students from minority groups. Approximately 70 percent of the M.B.A. students had undergraduate majors other than business; 50 percent received undergraduate degrees from institutions outside of Alabama.

Location

The city of Auburn has a population of approximately 32,500, including resident students. Located on Interstate 85 in east Alabama, the University has a beautiful 1,900-acre campus, and the students have easy access to major metropolitan areas. Atlanta, Georgia, and Birmingham, Alabama, are within approximately 2 hours' driving time; Columbus, Georgia, and Montgomery, Alabama, are within 1 hour's drive. The Alabama and Florida Gulf coasts are each about a 4-hour drive from the campus.

The University

Chartered in 1856, the University now carries out its mission through a graduate school and twelve colleges and schools oriented to particular areas of study. The fall 1997 enrollment on the main campus numbered 21,505, of whom 2,772 were business students. About 57 percent of Auburn students are from out of state.

Applying

Applications are accepted on a rolling basis. Applicants for the business programs must provide satisfactory scores on the Graduate Management Admission Test. Applicants for the M.S. and Ph.D. programs in economics must submit satisfactory scores on the General Test of the Graduate Record Examinations. For admission to all programs, international students are required to submit scores on the Test of English as a Foreign Language (TOEFL). Application forms can be obtained from the Graduate School office in Hargis Hall; the graduate catalog can be accessed via the Internet (http://www.grad.auburn.edu).

Correspondence and Information

Dr. Amit Mitra, Associate Dean
College of Business
415 West Magnolia Avenue
Auburn University, Alabama 36849-5240
Telephone: 334-844-4060

Auburn University

THE FACULTY

Administrative
C. Wayne Alderman, Dean; D.B.A., Tennessee; CPA.
Amit Mitra, Associate Dean; Ph.D., Clemson.
Daniel M. Gropper, M.B.A. Director; Ph.D., Florida State.
J. Philip Cook, Assistant Dean; M.Ac., Auburn; CPA.

Accounting
C. Wayne Alderman, Professor and Dean; D.B.A., Tennessee; CPA.
Barry Bryan, Assistant Professor; Ph.D., Texas A&M; CPA.
Ronald L. Clark, Professor and Director; Ph.D., Alabama.
Kent Fields, Professor; Ph.D., Texas A&M; CPA.
Norman Godwin, Assistant Professor; Ph.D., Michigan State.
Jeff Jones, Assistant Professor; Ph.D., Florida State.
Charles Price; Professor; Ph.D., Georgia; CPA.
Ronald Rasch, Associate Professor; Ph.D., Texas; CPA.
James Smith, Assistant Professor; J.D., Samford.
Robert Smith, Associate Professor; Ph.D., Texas Tech; CPA.
Sarah Stanwick, Associate Professor; Ph.D., Florida State; CPA.
Richard Tabor, Professor; Ph.D., Florida; CPA.
Arlette Wilson, Professor; Ph.D., Arkansas; CPA.
James Worthington, Associate Professor; Ph.D., Missouri; CPA.

Economics
Richard Ault, Associate Professor; Ph.D., Virginia.
Andy Barnett, Professor; Ph.D., Virginia.
Randy Beard, Associate Professor; Ph.D., Vanderbilt.
Richard Beil Jr., Associate Professor; Ph.D., Texas A&M.
Steven Caudill, Professor; Ph.D., Florida.
Robert Ekelund, Lowder Eminent Professor; Ph.D., LSU.
Roger Garrison, Professor; Ph.D., Virginia.
Daniel Gropper, Associate Professor; Ph.D., Florida State.
Robert Hebert, Russell Professor; Ph.D., LSU.
John Jackson, Professor; Ph.D., Claremont.
Dave Kaserman, Professor; Ph.D., Florida.
David Laband, Professor and Head; Ph.D., Virginia Tech.
James Long, Professor; Ph.D., Florida State.
Richard Saba, Associate Professor; Ph.D., Texas A&M.
Henry Thompson, Professor; Ph.D., Houston.
John Wells, Assistant Professor; Ph.D., Texas A&M.
David Whitten, Professor; Ph.D., Tulane.

Finance
James Barth, Lowder Eminent Professor; Ph.D., Ohio State.
Lee Colquitt, Assistant Professor; Ph.D., Georgia.
Claire Crutchley, Associate Professor; Ph.D., Virginia Tech.
Carl Hudson, Associate Professor; Ph.D., Arizona State.
John Jahera, Colonial Bank Professor and Head; Ph.D., Georgia.
Marlin Jensen, Associate Professor; Ph.D., Texas A&M.
Daniel Page, Professor; Ph.D., Georgia.
William Pugh, Associate Professor; Ph.D., Florida State.

Management
Achilles Armenakis, Torchmark Professor; D.B.A., Mississippi State.
William Boulton, Olan-Mills Professor; D.B.A., Harvard.
Terry Byrd, Associate Professor; Ph.D., South Carolina.
Houston Carr, Alumni Professor; Ph.D., Texas at Arlington.
Kerry Davis, Associate Professor; Ph.D., Georgia.
H. Field Jr., Lowder Professor; Ph.D., Georgia.
Nelson Ford, Associate Professor; Ph.D., Alabama.
Lorraine Gardiner, Associate Professor; Ph.D., Georgia.
Stanley Gardiner, Associate Professor; Ph.D., Georgia.
William Giles, Professor; Ph.D., Tennessee.
Stanley Harris, Associate Professor; Ph.D., Michigan.
William Holley, Lowder Professor; Ph.D., Alabama.
Thomas Marshall, Assistant Professor; Ph.D., North Texas.
Amit Mitra, Lowder Professor and Associate Dean; Ph.D., Clemson.
David Nembhard, Assistant Professor; Ph.D., Michigan.
Robert Niebuhr, Associate Professor and Head; Ph.D., Ohio State.
Dwight Norris, Associate Professor; Ph.D., Georgia.
Sharon Oswald, Associate Professor; Ph.D., Alabama.
Kelly Rainer, Associate Professor; Ph.D., Georgia.
Jennie Raymond, Associate Professor; Ph.D., Vanderbilt.
Chetan Sankar, Professor; Ph.D., Pennsylvania.
Scott Shafer, Associate Professor; Ph.D., Cincinnati.
Charles Snyder, Professor; Ph.D., Nebraska.
Peter Stanwick, Assistant Professor; Ph.D., Florida State.
Charlotte Sutton, Associate Professor; Ph.D., Texas A&M.
Paul Swamidass, Professor; Ph.D., Washington (Seattle).
M. V. Uzumeri, Assistant Professor; Ph.D., RPI.
Roger Wolters, Associate Professor; Ph.D., Illinois.

Marketing
Avery Abernethy, Associate Professor; Ph.D., South Carolina.
Daniel Butler, Associate Professor and Chair; Ph.D., South Carolina.
Hugh Guffey, Associate Professor; Ph.D., Georgia.
James Harris, Associate Professor; Ph.D., Florida.
Michael LaTour, Professor; Ph.D., Mississippi.
Ford Laumer, Associate Professor; Ph.D., Georgia.
Hokey Min, Associate Professor; Ph.D., Ohio State.
Rajan Nataraajan, Associate Professor; Ph.D., Drexel.
Chris Norek, Assistant Professor; Ph.D., Ohio State.
Herbert Rotfeld, Professor; Ph.D., Illinois.

The new five-story College of Business building contains state-of-the-art classroom facilities, computer equipment, and audiovisual systems.

BABSON COLLEGE

Franklin W. Olin Graduate School of Business

Programs of Study

The F. W. Olin Graduate School of Business at Babson College offers three programs of study: the Two-Year M.B.A., the One-Year M.B.A. for business graduates, and the Evening M.B.A. for working professionals.

The innovative Two-Year M.B.A. program, which began in fall 1993, emphasizes creative problem solving with a distinct cross-disciplinary approach. Based on the theme of entrepreneurial leadership in a changing global environment, the first year of the program provides an integrated exposure to complex business problems through a modular curriculum. The business mentoring program enables students to work with a local business on a team with 5 or 6 other M.B.A. students. As part of the second year elective options, students will be required to participate in an international experience. Enrollment is limited to 150 students each year. Competence in a foreign language is preferred but not required.

The One-Year M.B.A. program for business graduates begins in May of each year. This accelerated full-time program is designed for candidates who have attended an undergraduate program in business administration accredited by AACSB–The International Association for Management Education. Students enroll in a series of integrated modules over the first semester, then join the second-year M.B.A. students.

The Evening M.B.A. program, consisting of twelve required and eight elective courses, is designed for those who choose to work during the day and take evening classes. A student must complete a minimum of ten courses in residence at Babson. The College offers cluster courses, which allow students to complete the M.B.A. with fewer class sessions. Persons who have completed course work in business may be eligible for advanced standing credit. The program includes exposure to accounting, economics, entrepreneurial studies, finance, international business management, management communications, management information systems, marketing, production and operation management, quantitative methods, and taxation.

Babson takes pride in its international perspective. International business courses have been in its curriculum since the 1970s, and more than 30 percent of students in the full-time programs come from countries other than the United States. A formal concentration in international business is available for those who participate in an international internship, demonstrate proficiency in a language other than their native tongue, and complete the required international courses. International exchanges are available with schools in Japan, Spain, Norway, France, England, Ecuador, and Venezuela. Babson offers three-week offshore electives in France, Switzerland, Czechoslovakia, Russia, China, and Latin America. The International Management Internship Program provides 60 to 70 second-year M.B.A. students with the opportunity to work abroad for three months. Babson interns work on professionally demanding projects for which they receive credit for two graduate courses. Babson provides students with round-trip airfare, living accommodations, and an allowance for meals.

In the Management Consulting Field Experience, students analyze managerial problems and make recommendations to business firms, government bodies, and nonprofit organizations. Consulting teams work under a faculty adviser to produce a written report and an oral presentation to the client organization.

Research Facilities

The Horn Library houses 120,000 volumes, 1,000 periodicals, and a collection of business and financial statements from 10,000 corporations. This facility also has a fully developed media center, a 24-hour reading room, seating for more than 500, twelve group study rooms, and an exhibition center. Online search services provide access to more than 250 databases covering bibliographical and statistical information, plus texts of 35 newspapers and 100 magazines. The Horn Computer Center is equipped with 150 computer workstations, 125 of which are IBM-compatible computers that run a diversified library of business-oriented programs off a menu-driven system. There is a separate lab with 25 Macintosh SE computers.

Financial Aid

Merit-based fellowships, assistantships, and loans are offered. Resident students may apply to be residence directors. Part-time work is also available. Students applying for financial aid must complete the Free Application for Federal Student Aid (FAFSA).

Cost of Study

Full-time tuition for the 1998–99 academic year is $20,460; each 3-credit course costs $2046.

Living and Housing Costs

Some on-campus housing for both single and married students is available, yet most graduate students live off campus in the Wellesley area. The Office of Campus Life maintains a listing of off-campus housing.

Student Group

The M.B.A. program enrolls 390 full-time and 1,254 part-time students, 34 percent of whom are women. International students constitute 30 percent of the full-time graduate student population.

Student Outcomes

For the M.B.A. class of 1997, the average starting salary was $59,670—up 5.4 percent from the previous year. Eighty-nine percent of the class was employed or had offers three months after graduation; recruiting opportunities increased by 73 percent. Contacts for career networking are an integral part of Babson's career services and include industry information panel discussions and alumni referrals for informational interviews.

Location

Babson College is located on a 450-acre campus in Wellesley, Massachusetts. Just 12 miles from Boston, Babson offers an ideal setting for study. Students are within 20 minutes of Boston's financial and industrial districts; its world-renowned symphony, museums and galleries; and its professional sporting events.

The College

Founded in 1919 by financier Roger W. Babson, Babson College is an independent, nonsectarian, professional college of management offering programs of study at the undergraduate, graduate, and executive management education levels; its programs are accredited by AACSB–The International Association for Management Education. Served by about 151 full-time faculty members, the College currently enrolls 3,336 students. Babson's tenth president, Leo I. Higdon, describes the College's mission as "preparing students for successful careers in management; developing breadth of perspective, curiosity, and the ability to meet the demands of a changing world."

Applying

Two years of postgraduate work experience and an undergraduate degree are prerequisites. GMAT scores, official transcripts of all graduate and undergraduate work, two letters of recommendation, and a resume are required. Non-English-speaking international students must furnish TOEFL scores and official English translations of all pertinent academic documents. The Two-Year M.B.A. program begins in September and has a final application deadline of April 15; the One-Year M.B.A. program begins in May, with a final application deadline of January 15; and the Evening M.B.A. program begins in September and January and has June 15 and December 1 application deadlines, respectively. Applications are encouraged before the deadlines.

Correspondence and Information

F. W. Olin Graduate School of Business
Babson College
Babson Park, Massachusetts 02157-0310

Telephone: 617-239-5591
800-488-4512 (toll-free within the United States)
Fax: 617-239-4194
E-mail: mbaadmission@babson.edu

Babson College

THE FACULTY

Accountancy and Law

Lawrence P. Carr, Associate Professor and Nicholas J. Trivisonno Term Chair; M.B.A., Ph.D, Union (New York). William H. Coyle, Assistant Professor; M.B.A., Cornell; Ph.D., Texas A&M; CPA. Craig P. Ehrlich, Assistant Professor; J.D., Illinois. Michael L. Fetters, Professor and Chair, Accounting/Law Division; M.B.A., Ph.D., Wisconsin; CPA. Christopher P. Hennessey, Associate Professor; J.D., Suffolk; LL.M., Boston University; CPA. Descom D. Hoagland III, Associate Professor; M.B.A., Babson; CPA. Robert E. Holmes, Murata Dean and Associate Vice President for Academic Affairs; M.B.A., North Texas; Ph.D., Arkansas. Carolyn Hotchkiss, Associate Professor; J.D., Columbia. William C. Lawler, Associate Professor; Ph.D., Massachusetts Amherst. Toni Lester, Associate Professor; J.D., Georgetown. John L. Livingstone, Adjunct Professor; M.B.A., Ph.D., Stanford. Paul J. McMann, Visiting Lecturer; M.S., Bentley; D.B.A. candidate, Boston University. Carol J. McNair, Associate Professor; M.B.A., Ph.D., Columbia. Alfred J. Nanni Jr., Professor and Marriott Term Chair; M.S.B.A., Ph.D., Massachusetts. Ross D. Petty, Associate Professor and Roger A. Enrico Term Chair; M.B.A., Rochester; J.D., Michigan; M.P.A., Harvard. Donald B. Rotfort, Associate Professor; M.B.A., Columbia; J.D., Suffolk; LL.M., Boston University; CPA. John K. Shank, Visiting Professor, M.B.A., Pittsburgh; Ph.D., Ohio State. Virginia E. Soybel, Assistant Professor; M.B.A., Ph.D., Columbia. Robert M. Turner, Assistant Professor and Lowell Schulman Term Chair; M.B.A., Boston College; D.B.A., Boston University. Joanne D. Williams, Associate Professor; M.B.A., Ph.D., Texas A&M; CPA.

Business Communication

Kathleen A. Kelly, Associate Professor and C. J. McCarthy Family Term Chair; Ph.D., Ohio State. Sydel Sokuvitz, Associate Professor; Ph.D., Ohio State.

Economics

Kostas Axarloglou, Assistant Professor; Ph.D., Michigan. Arthur A. Bayer, Professor; M.B.A., Columbia; Ph.D., Michigan State. William L. Casey Jr., Professor; Ph.D., Boston College. Dominique Christin-Kruithof, Visiting Assistant Professor; M.S., Ph.D., Arizona State. Kent A. Jones, Professor and Edward A. Madden Term Chair; M.A.L.D., Tufts; Ph.D., Geneva (Switzerland). David Joulfaian, Visiting Professor; Ph.D., Northeastern. John E. Marthinsen, Professor and Chair, Economics Division; Ph.D., Connecticut. Robert E. McAuliffe Jr., Associate Professor; Ph.D., Virginia. Maria A. Minniti, Assistant Professor; M.S., Auburn; Ph.D., NYU. Laurence S. Moss, Professor; Ph.D., Columbia; J.D., Suffolk. Lidija Polutnik, Assistant Professor; Ph.D., Georgia State. Joseph M. Ricciardi, Associate Professor and William J. Anderson Term Chair; Ph.D, Texas at Austin. Mark Tomass, Visiting Assistant Professor; M.A., Ph.D., Northeastern.

Finance

Fernando Alvarez, Assistant Professor; Ph.D., NYU. Jennifer Bethel, Assistant Professor; Ph.D., UCLA. John C. Edmunds, Associate Professor; M.B.A., Boston University; D.B.A., Harvard. Steven P. Feinstein, Assistant Professor; M.A., M.Phil., Ph.D., Yale. Diana R. Harrington, Professor; M.S.B.A., Boston University; D.B.A., Virginia. Kathleen Thomas Hevert, Assistant Professor and Edith Babson Mustard Term Chair; Ph.D., North Carolina. Michael J. Ho, Assistant Professor; S.M., MIT; Ph.D., Virginia. Ralph C. Kimball, Associate Professor; Ph.D., Berkeley. Benoit F. Leleux, Assistant Professor; M.B.A., Virginia Tech; Ph.D., European Institute of Business Administration (INSEAD). Shirley G. Love, Visiting Assistant Professor; M.B.A., Baylor; Ph.D., Texas A&M. Richard P. Mandel, Associate Professor and Chair, Finance Division; J.D., Harvard. Catherine McDonough, Associate Professor; Ph.D., NYU. James D. Parrino, Assistant Professor; M.B.A., George Washington; Ph.D., Virginia. Mark E. Potter, Visiting Instructor; M.B.A., Boston College; Ph.D. candidate, Massachusetts Amherst. Erik R. Sirri, Assistant Professor and McDermott Term Chair; M.B.A., Ph.D., UCLA. Linda A. Stoller, Senior Lecturer; J.D., Boston College; LL.M. (taxation), Boston University; CPA.

History and Philosophy

Albert A. Anderson, Professor; Ph.D., Boston University. James E. Hoopes, Professor and Chair, History and Society Division; Ph.D., Johns Hopkins. Robert M. McKeon, Professor; B.Ph., Montreal; Licentia in Scholastic Philosophy, Institut Catholique de Paris; Docteur en Histoire, Paris.

Management

Stephen A. Allen III, Professor; M.B.A., D.B.A., Harvard. William S. Brown, Assistant Professor; M.B.A., Fairleigh Dickinson; Ph.D., Pittsburgh. William D. Bygrave, Frederic C. Hamilton Professor of Free Enterprise; D.Phil., Oxford; M.B.A., Northeastern; D.B.A., Boston University. Kishore Chakraborty, Assistant Professor; D.Ed., Harvard. Allan R. Cohen, Professor, Vice President of Academic Affairs, and Dean of Faculty; M.B.A., D.B.A., Harvard. Anne Donnellon, Associate Professor; Ph.D., Penn State. R. Jeffery Ellis, Associate Professor and Ralph Z. Sorenson Term Chair; Ph.D., Cranfield Institute of Technology (England). Susan West Engelkemeyer, Assistant Professor and Academic Quality Officer; M.B.A., East Carolina; Ph.D., Clemson. Steven E. Eriksen, Professor; Ph.D., MIT; M.B.A., Boston University. Daniel H. Gray, Senior Lecturer; Ph.D. (economics and law), MIT. Wendy C. Handler, Assistant Professor; M.B.A., D.B.A., Boston University. James M. Hunt, Assistant Professor; D.B.A., Boston University. William F. Johnston, Senior Lecturer; Sc.B. (engineering), Brown; M.B.A., Babson; Advanced Management Program, Harvard Business School. J. B. M. Kassarjian, Professor; M.B.A., D.B.A., Harvard. Elaine Landry, Assistant Professor; Ed.M., Ed.D., Harvard. Julian Lange, Executive-in-Residence in Entrepreneurship; M.B.A., Ph.D., Harvard. Nan S. Langowitz, Associate Professor; M.B.A., NYU; D.B.A., Harvard. Mark C. Maletz, Adjunct Associate Professor; Ph.D., Michigan. Dennis F. X. Mathaisel, Associate Professor; Ph.D., MIT. Ivor Morgan, Associate Professor; M.B.A., Western Ontario (Canada); D.B.A., Harvard. William C. Nemitz, Associate Professor and Chair, Management Division; M.B.A., Northeastern; Ph.D., Boston College. John W. Newman, Senior Lecturer; M.B.A., Harvard. Patricia O'Brien, Associate Professor; M.B.A., Simmons; D.B.A., Harvard. Farshad Rafii, Associate Professor; M.S.E.E., Cornell; M.B.A., D.B.A., Harvard. U. Srinivasa Rangan, Assistant Professor and Kingsbury Term Chair; M.Sc., Madurai (India); M.Sc., London School of Economics; M.B.A., International Institute for Management Development (IMD); D.B.A., Harvard. Jay Rao, Assistant Professor; M.S., Kentucky; Ph.D. candidate, UCLA. Paul D. Reynolds, Paul T. Babson Professor of Entrepreneurial Studies; M.B.A., Ph.D., Stanford. Phyllis Fineman Schlesinger, Assistant Professor; M.S.T., Wisconsin–Oshkosh; Ed.D., Boston University. Joel M. Shulman, Associate Professor and Weissman Term Chair; M.B.A., Ph.D., Michigan State. Stephen Spinelli Jr., Assistant Professor; Ph.D., London. John H. Stamm, Professor; M.E., M.S., Stevens; D.B.A., Harvard. Natalie Tabb Taylor, Associate Professor; M.B.A., D.B.A., Harvard. Neal E. Thornberry, Associate Professor; Ph.D., Bowling Green State. Jeffry Timmons, F. W. Olin Distinguished Professor of Entrepreneurship; M.B.A., D.B.A., Harvard. J. Stewart Ward, Assistant Professor; M.B.A., Columbia; J.D., Massachusetts. Joseph R. Weintraub, Associate Professor; Ph.D., Bowling Green State.

Marketing

Kathleen B. Doran, Assistant Professor; M.B.A., Virginia; Ph.D. candidate, McGill. Philip A. Dover, Associate Professor; Ph.D., Penn State. Robert J. Eng, Associate Professor; M.B.A., Syracuse; D.B.A., Indiana. Carol A. Fiske, Assistant Professor; Ph.D. candidate, South Carolina. Morton Galper, Associate Professor; M.B.A., Dartmouth; D.B.A., Harvard. Norman A. P. Govoni, Professor; M.B.A., Syracuse; Ph.D., Missouri–Columbia. H. David Hennessey, Associate Professor; M.B.A., Clark; Ph.D., NYU. H. Lawrence Isaacson, Professor; M.B.A., D.B.A., Harvard; Ph.D., Yale. Jean-Pierre Jeannet, Walter H. Carpenter Professor; M.B.A., Ph.D., Massachusetts. Robert J. Kopp, Associate Professor and Chair, Marketing Division; M.B.A., Columbia; D.B.A., Harvard. Kenichi Matsuno, Assistant Professor; M.B.A., Virginia; Ph.D., Tennessee. William H. Murphy, Assistant Professor; M.S., Ph.D., Wisconsin. Kathleen Seiders, Assistant Professor; M.B.A., Babson; Ph.D. candidate, Texas A&M. Douglas J. Tigert, Charles Clarke Reynolds Professor of Retail Marketing; M.B.A., Northwestern; Ph.D., Purdue. Suzanne B. Walchli, Assistant Professor; M.B.A., Pennsylvania (Wharton); Ph.D., Northwestern.

Mathematics/Science

Joseph F. Aieta, Senior Lecturer and Director, Math Resource Center; M.A.T., Harvard; M.A., Bowdoin. Nancy S. Balaguer, Assistant Professor; M.B.A., Ph.D., RPI. Edward G. Cale Jr., Associate Professor; M.B.A., D.B.A., Harvard. Ismael G. Dambolena, Professor; Ph.D., Massachusetts Amherst. Dawna Dewire, Visiting Lecturer; M.B.A., Northeastern; M.S., SUNY. Steven Gordon, Associate Professor and James Perry Term Chair; Ph.D., MIT. Theodore Grossman, Senior Lecturer; M.S., Northeastern. David P. Kopsco, Professor; Ph.D., Rutgers. John D. McKenzie Jr., Associate Professor; Ph.D., Michigan. Charles S. Osborn, Assistant Professor and Wallace Term Chair; M.B.A., Pennsylvania (Wharton). Gordon Prichett, Professor and Chair, Math/Science Division; Ph.D., Wisconsin. Ashok Rao, Professor; M.S.E.E., Ph.D., Iowa. William H. Rybolt, Associate Professor; Ph.D., MIT. John Saber, Professor; Ph.D., Brandeis. Stephen J. Schiffman, Associate Professor and Dean, Undergraduate Curriculum; Ph.D., Dartmouth. Noreen R. Sharpe, M.S., North Carolina; Ph.D., Virginia. Donna B. Stoddard, Assistant Professor and Constantine Simonides Term Chair; M.B.A., North Carolina; D.B.A., Harvard. Stephen J. Turner, Associate Professor; Ph.D., Massachusetts Amherst.

BARUCH COLLEGE OF THE CITY UNIVERSITY OF NEW YORK

Graduate Studies in Business

Programs of Study

Baruch College's graduate business programs, including the Master of Business Administration (M.B.A.), the Master of Science (M.S.) in business, and the Executive M.B.A. and M.S. programs provide exceptional opportunities to prepare for greater career responsibility, advance present skills and acquire new expertise, and gain a better understanding of the effective functioning of a complex and competitive society. Classes for the traditional M.B.A. and M.S. programs are scheduled Monday through Thursday during the day and evening, and students can pursue most degrees on a part- or full-time basis.

The traditional M.B.A. program is cohort in style and can be completed in either two years (full-time) or four years (part-time). Students follow a prescribed sequence of introductory courses before selecting a specialization from one of the following areas: accounting, computer information systems, economics, finance and investments, general business, health-care administration (a joint program with the Mt. Sinai School of Medicine), industrial/organizational psychology, international business, management, marketing, operations research, statistics, and taxation.

The Master of Science programs in accounting, business computer information systems, marketing, operations research, statistics, and taxation are available for students who seek concentrated, in-depth study in a subject area.

Baruch's Executive M.B.A. program is designed for high-achieving individuals who need an alternative to the traditional M.B.A. program. Classes are held on alternating Fridays and Saturdays, permitting students to finish the program in two years. Executive M.S. programs are available in finance and taxation.

The City University of New York's Ph.D. program in business is located at Baruch and comprises five specializations: accounting, finance, management planning systems, marketing, and organization and policy studies. Baruch also houses the University's Ph.D. subprogram in industrial/organizational psychology.

Research Facilities

The William and Anita Newman Library provides the Baruch community with one of the most technologically advanced facilities in New York. In addition to its traditional holdings of books and periodicals, the library maintains local area networks that provide access to information resources in CD-ROM format and to several hundred online databases through the Dow Jones News/Retrieval, LEXIS/NEXIS, and DIALOG services. Baruch students, faculty, and staff also have access to the 4.5 million volumes in the CUNY library system and to the collections of the world-famous New York Public Library.

The Baruch Computing and Technology Center provides computing hardware ranging from microcomputers to mainframes, a wide variety of software packages, and access to the global Internet.

Financial Aid

A number of graduate research assistantships are awarded, on the basis of merit, to qualified full-time master's degree students. The assistantships carry an annual stipend of $5000 and are renewable for one year; they do not include a tuition waiver. The Mitsui USA Foundation awards $5000 scholarships in the fall to two newly admitted full-time students pursuing an M.B.A. degree in international business. Applicants for the Mitsui Scholarships must be U.S. citizens or permanent residents. The Carl Spielvogel '56 Scholarship in International Marketing provides annual support of $5000 to one or more graduate students who intend to study international marketing and pursue a career in that field. The scholarship is renewable for one year. Financial aid also is available to graduate students through a variety of state, federal, and College programs. International students are eligible to apply for graduate assistantships and College work-study. Prospective doctoral students should contact the Admissions Office at the City University Graduate Center (listed below) for financial aid information.

Cost of Study

The 1997–98 tuition for graduate courses was $185 per credit for New York State residents and $320 for out-of-state students, but the total per semester did not exceed $2175 and $3800, respectively. Prospective doctoral students should contact the Admissions Office at the City University Graduate Center for tuition information. Tuition and fees are subject to change without notice.

Living and Housing Costs

Students at Baruch provide for their own room and board. A single student should anticipate spending approximately $900 per month for housing, food, utilities, books, transportation, entertainment, and incidental expenses.

Student Group

With an earned reputation for excellence that extends to all parts of the world, Baruch attracts students from New York, neighboring states, and abroad. The more than 2,000 men and women doing graduate work at Baruch hold undergraduate degrees from more than 200 colleges and universities. There are more than 400 international graduate students, who represent approximately fifty countries.

Student Outcomes

Graduates of Baruch's programs are in demand at all levels in business, government, and nonprofit sectors. Top recruiters of students include Deloitte & Touche, Andersen Consulting, Coopers & Lybrand, Bell Atlantic, Pepsi-Cola, Republic National Bank, Con Edison, Johnson & Johnson, KPMG Peat Marwick, and the United States, New York State, and New York City governments.

Location

Baruch occupies seven buildings in the Gramercy Park area of Manhattan, the heart of one of the world's most dynamic cultural and financial centers.

The College

Baruch College has evolved from the innovative School of Business and Civic Administration, established in 1919 by the trustees of the City College of New York. The first master's degree program in business administration was offered by the school in 1920. In 1954, the name of the school was changed to the Bernard M. Baruch School of Business and Public Administration, in honor of the distinguished financier and statesman who was an alumnus and a trustee of the City College. In 1968, the school became an independent senior college of The City University of New York. Baruch College is accredited by AACSB–The International Association for Management Education and by the Middle States Association of Colleges and Schools.

Applying

For the master's degree programs, a student must have a baccalaureate from a regionally accredited college or its equivalent. Applicants must submit scores from the Graduate Management Admission Test (GMAT), although the GRE may be used for M.S. applicants in business computer information systems, industrial/organizational psychology, operations research, or statistics. Applicants for the Ph.D. in business must have a baccalaureate degree from an accredited college or university. A master's degree is not necessary, but most applicants enter with an M.B.A. degree. The GMAT is required. Students in organization and policy studies or marketing may substitute the GRE General Test. Those who are applying for the Ph.D. in industrial/organizational psychology must take the GRE General Test and Subject Test in psychology.

Correspondence and Information

For M.B.A. and M.S. programs:
Office of Graduate Admissions
Baruch College/CUNY
Zicklin School of Business
17 Lexington Avenue, Box H-0880
New York, New York 10010-5585
Telephone: 212-802-2330

For the Executive M.B.A. program:
Executive M.B.A. Program
Baruch College/CUNY
17 Lexington Avenue, Box F-1215
New York, New York 10010-5585
Telephone: 212-802-6700

For doctoral degree programs:
Admissions Office
Graduate School and University Center
The City University of New York
33 West 42 Street
New York, New York 10036
Telephone:
212-802-6580 (business)
212-387-1541 (industrial/organizational psychology)

Baruch College of the City University of New York

FACULTY HEADS AND AREAS OF RESEARCH

Sidney I. Lirtzman, Dean of the Zicklin School of Business; Ph.D., Columbia.
Gloria Penn Thomas, Executive Officer of the Doctoral Program in Business; Ph.D., Temple.
Joel Lefkowitz, Executive Officer of the Doctoral Subprogram in Industrial/Organizational Psychology; Ph.D., Case Western Reserve.

The Zicklin School of Business faculty members in every department continue to develop major research contributions over a wide range of topics. During the academic year, faculty members published more than 30 text and reference books, contributed scholarly pieces that appeared in more than 40 additional books, and published nearly 200 articles in many of the leading professional journals. During this period, faculty members also held major editorial positions with more than fifty business journals and research publications.

Department of Accountancy
Steven B. Lilien, Ph.D., Chair. Major areas of research include financial accounting, managerial accounting, auditing, and taxation. Both theoretical and applied research are conducted, with most of the faculty members emphasizing basic research. The department stresses high-quality research targeted to the most selective publications. Recent research interests include auditing standards, derivative and hedge accounting, auditing professionalism, disclosure of earnings estimates, accounting information, estate and gift taxation, leasing and the cost of capital, CEO compensation, mandated accounting changes and managerial discretion, insider trading and analysts' earnings forecasts, accounting ethics, statement analysis, pension accounting and corporate takeovers, and the poetry and politics of accounting.

Department of Economics and Finance
Avner S. Wolf, Ph.D., Chair. The department's faculty members conduct both applied and theoretical research, broadly covering many areas of economics and finance. The department has a particular research strength in derivative markets, financial institutions, and investment theory. Examples of recent work include operational efficiency in banking, treasury yield curve, stock market reaction to dividend changes, valuation of interest rate–sensitive securities, buy-write securities, investment analysis software, asset pricing implications, equity derivatives, options and valuation of inventory, foreign acquisitions in the United States, foreign ownership restrictions and premiums for international investments, economies of scale and cost complementaries in commercial banking, future markets efficiency, and import and hedging uncertainty in international trade.

Department of Law
Elliot Axelrod, J.D., Chair. Major areas of research include practically all areas of business law, including heavy emphasis on contract law, corporations, partnerships, computer law, real estate law, international trade law, health-care law, the Uniform Commercial Code, antitrust law, and employment law, as well as some areas of constitutional, intellectual property, environmental, consumer, and criminal law.

Department of Management
Harry Rosen, Ph.D., Chair. Major areas of research include strategic management, temporal issues in strategy, competitive dynamics and industry structure, social issues in management, business ethics, operations management, international and comparative management, organizational behavior, work and family, economic justification of advanced manufacturing systems, technology and strategy, flexible manufacturing systems, inspection policy design, critical thinking, managing strategic flexibility, linking strategies with work redesign, ethical preferences and future orientations of business executives, optimal maintenance policies, the ceiling effect on work motivation, effects of failure on group performance, repeat purchase behavior as a criterion of teaching effectiveness, human dilemmas in work organizations, research and development in biotechnology firms, black economic empowerment in post-apartheid South Africa, and vehicle routing systems.

Department of Marketing
Gary Soldow, Ph.D., Chair. Major areas of research include advertising and marketing communications, consumer behavior, marketing research, international marketing, marketing management, retailing and sales, direct marketing, and all areas of international business. Recent research interests have included the conceptual domain of international business, the consequences of whistle-blowing, casual inferences in consumer safety judgments, how consumers assess the value of advertising, gender effects in consumer research, marketing strategies of Japanese auto manufacturers, social and governmental environment of business, comparative institutional analysis of marketing systems, globalization and quality of life considerations, entrepreneurship education for minorities, environmental standards and European consumer goods marketing, consumer marketing relationship programs, managing imitative strategies, geographical market diffusion, analysis of price and exposure of network prime-time advertising, and managing cultural differences.

Department of Psychology
Walter Reichman, Ph.D., Chair. Major areas of research include the application of stress management and biofeedback intervention coupled with modern analytic group techniques in the amelioration of stress-related health conditions; cerebral and cardiovascular psychophysiology; stress reactivity; psychologized trauma adjustment; sleep deprivation and insomnia treatment; impact of life-threatening illnesses on emotion and behavior; health implications of the doctor-patient relationship; leadership in groups and organizations; organizational training and evaluation; research methods and statistics; employment testing, training, and performance evaluation; job analysis; equal opportunity and gender issues; clinical psychology; adult development; psychology and the family; cross-cultural psychology; psychometric theory and multivariate statistics; human thinking and reasoning and its development; history and philosophy of the science of psychology; career development in the changing work environment; substance abuse in the workplace; motivation to work; women's issues in management; multicultural programs; and college counseling, loneliness, and family therapy.

Department of Statistics and Computer Information Systems
Albert Crocker, Ph.D., Chair. Major areas of research include database systems; information retrieval; telecommunications and networks; privacy; multimedia systems; organizational diffusion of information technologies; information systems in the human service and nonprofit sectors; information system ethics; control and audit of information systems; electronic commerce; financial information systems; system development methodologies; computer simulation; Bayesian analysis; business application of linear and integer programming; generalized assignment problem; health-care systems; nonparametric data analysis; categorical data analysis; expert systems; mathematical programming applied to information technology; combinatorics; polyhedral theory; cryptology; group decision support systems; Meta Analysis; statistics in sports; statistics in auditing; sampling theory; medical statistics; incomplete, censored, and truncated data; total quality management; bootstrap and Gibbs sampling; legal statistics; time series analysis; robust methods; and experimental design.

BAYLOR UNIVERSITY

Hankamer School of Business

Programs of Study

The Hankamer School of Business offers several programs of study, including a Master of Business Administration, a Master of International Management, a Master of Accountancy, a Master of Taxation, a Master of Science in economics, and a Master of Science in information systems. Within the M.B.A., students may concentrate in traditional business fields of study as well as international management and information systems. The School also offers two joint programs with the Baylor School of Law that lead to the J.D./M.B.A. and the J.D./M.Tax. The M.B.A. program at the Hankamer School is currently undergoing an ambitious and innovative restructuring. Students studying the "focus firm" evaluate business problems and create solutions in a real-time/real-life context. For more information on the M.B.A. program, students should contact the Director of Graduate Admissions at the address listed below.

Two tracks are available within the M.B.A. program. The accelerated M.B.A. program is offered to undergraduate business majors who meet specific academic requirements. This 36-hour program allows qualified candidates to complete the M.B.A. degree in three semesters (one year). For nonbusiness undergraduates, the Integrated Management Seminar is offered. This first-semester intensive seminar satisfies the requirements of ten prerequisite courses. This popular module allows students to complete the M.B.A. program in four semesters.

Students with less than two years of work experience are required to participate in a one-semester graduate-level internship program. The Career Services Center serves the students as a resource in obtaining internship positions.

Graduate and undergraduate programs at the Hankamer School of Business are fully accredited by AACSB–The International Association for Management Education.

Research Facilities

Graduate students have access to computer facilities housed in the Hankamer School of Business building. These include seventy IBM personal computers and twenty Macintosh computers. The IBM labs run off network, which provides a variety of software, including Microsoft Word for Windows, Excel, Powerpoint, Access, Arts & Letters, SAS for Windows, and a number of course-specific software packages. Laser printers, a color printer, and a scanner are provided. Students also have free access to the Internet and e-mail.

Financial Aid

The Hankamer School of Business awards merit-based graduate assistantships. These assistantships pay for 50 to 100 percent of tuition, with a monthly stipend of $315. The stipend requires student work assignments of 15 hours per week as a research assistant. Additional information on financial aid at Baylor University may be obtained by contacting the Financial Aid Office by phone at 254-710-2611 or via e-mail (financial_aid@baylor.edu).

Cost of Study

Tuition in 1998–99 at Baylor is $308 per semester hour. The University's endowment permits tuition to be among the lowest in the nation for major private universities.

Living and Housing Costs

Graduate and married student housing is available on a limited basis. The cost for a single is $252 per month; a double is $340 per month. The majority of graduate students live in off-campus apartments and houses. Housing guides are available by contacting the Director of Graduate Admissions at the address listed below.

Student Group

Programs, by choice, are relatively small. Only about 160 students are enrolled in the graduate programs in business. Seminars average between 15 and 20 students each. The average GMAT score for entering students is 580 and the average undergraduate GPA is 3.23 (on a 4.0 scale).

Student Outcomes

In the 1997–98 academic year, 93 students graduated from the Hankamer School of Business. Ninety-two percent of these graduates were employed within three months of graduation. The average starting salary for these graduates was $43,000. Industries chosen by 1997–98 graduates include (but are not limited to) consulting, finance, management information systems, management, marketing, and operations/production.

Location

Located on the banks of the Brazos River in central Texas, Baylor University is located in a metropolitan area of approximately 200,000. The city is near the population and geographical core of the state and only a few hours' drive from Dallas, Houston, Austin, and San Antonio.

The University

Baylor University, the oldest Texas university in continuous existence since its founding, was chartered by the Republic of Texas in 1845. Today, Baylor is one of the nation's major church-related universities and provides both liberal arts and professional education. By today's standards, Baylor is a medium-sized university, with approximately 12,000 students on the main campus. *U.S. News & World Report* ranked Baylor as twenty-third in its list of Best "Sticker Price" College Values.

Applying

The Hankamer School of Business encourages applications from individuals holding a bachelor's degree from an accredited college or university. All major fields of study are welcome. The deadline for application is April 1 for the summer term, July 1 for the fall semester, and November 1 for the spring semester. Decisions are made on a rolling basis.

The Graduate Management Admission Test (GMAT) is required. The GRE is accepted for the M.I.M. and the M.S. in economics programs.

In order to be considered for financial assistance, international students should observe the following deadlines: April 1 for the fall semester, September 1 for the spring semester, and February 1 for the summer term. International students whose native language is not English must score at least 600 on the TOEFL.

Correspondence and Information

Director of Graduate Admissions
Hankamer School of Business
Baylor University
P.O. Box 98001
Waco, Texas 76798-8001
Telephone: 254-710-3718
800-583-0622 (toll-free)
E-mail: mba@hsb.baylor.edu
World Wide Web: http://hsb.baylor.edu/mba

For students interested in the M.S. in economics degree:
Dr. Jim Truitt, Chair
Department of Economics
Baylor University
P.O. Box 98003
Waco, Texas 76798-8003
E-mail: jim_truitt@baylor.edu
World Wide Web: http://hsb.baylor.edu/html/dept/eco

Baylor University

THE FACULTY

Suzanne Abbe, M.B.A., Baylor; CPA. Accounting.
Martha Agee, J.D., Baylor; CPA. Business law.
A. Dale Allen Jr., D.B.A., Colorado. Management.
Kendall W. Artz, Ph.D., Purdue. Management.
D. Ray Bagby, Ph.D., South Carolina. Entrepreneurship.
Jane N. Baldwin, Ph.D., Arkansas; CPA (Arkansas). Accounting.
Mahamudu Bawumia, Ph.D., Simon Fraser. Economics.
Judy C. Bowman, M.S., Baylor. Economics.
Gary R. Carini, Ph.D., Pennsylvania. Management.
Michael N. Cassell, Ph.D., Georgia. Accounting.
Delton L. Chesser, Ph.D., Arkansas. Accounting.
Richard C. Chewning, Ph.D., Washington (Seattle). Management.
Lawrence B. Chonko, Ph.D., Houston. Marketing.
Curtis Clements, Ph.D., Texas A&M. Accounting.
Lane G. Collins, D.B.A., USC; CPA (Texas). Accounting.
Alan N. Cook, Ph.D., Arkansas. Finance.
Marjorie J. Cooper, Ph.D., Texas A&M. Marketing.
Joe Allen Cox, Ph.D., Oklahoma State. Management.
Donald F. Cunningham, Ph.D., Ohio State. Finance.
Charles E. Davis, Ph.D., North Carolina. Accounting.
Elizabeth Davis, Ph.D., Duke. Accounting.
Roger Davis, M.B.A., Baylor. Marketing.
Charles J. Delaney, Ph.D., Florida. Real estate.
Dovalee Dorsett, Ph.D., SMU. Information systems.
Mark G. Dunn, Ph.D., Mississippi. Marketing.
L. M. Dyson Jr., Ph.D., Florida. Real estate.
Richard W. Easley, Ph.D., South Carolina. Marketing.
Donald R. Edwards, Ph.D., Arizona State. Management.
Paul R. Erickson, J.D., Idaho; CPA (Arizona). Accounting.
Mark Fuller, Ph.D., Arizona. Information systems.
H. Stephen Gardner, Ph.D., Berkeley. Economics.
L. Kent Gilbreath, Ph.D., Florida. Economics.
Van D. Gray, Ph.D., North Texas. Management.
Steven L. Green, Ph.D., Brown. Economics.
Walter T. Harrison, Ph.D., Michigan State. Accounting.
James W. Henderson, Ph.D., SMU. Economics.
Danny P. Hollingsworth, D.B.A., Memphis State. Accounting.
R. Duane Ireland, Ph.D., Texas Tech. Management.
Jerry W. Johnson, Ph.D., Arkansas. Marketing.
Karen R. Johnson, M.I.M., Baylor. Economics.
Becky Jones, M.B.A., Baylor; CPA. Business law.
Timothy Kayworth, Ph.D., Florida State. Information systems.
Thomas M. Kelly, Ph.D., Oklahoma State. Economics.
Blake LeCrone, LL.B., Oklahoma. Business law.
Dorothy E. Leidner, Ph.D., Texas. Information systems.
Helen Ligon, Ph.D., Texas A&M; CDP. Information systems.
Linda P. Livingstone, Ph.D., Oklahoma State. Management.
Terry Loe, Ph.D., Memphis. Marketing.
Charles S. Madden, Ph.D., Nebraska–Lincoln. Marketing.
Terry S. Maness, Dean; D.B.A., Indiana. Finance.
Roger C. Mayer, Ph.D., Purdue. Management.
Joseph A. McKinney, Ph.D., Michigan State. Economics.
Helen Miller, M.B.A., Baylor; CPA. Accounting.
Carlos W. Moore, Ph.D., Texas A&M. Marketing.
Kris K. Moore, Ph.D., Texas A&M. Information systems.
Heather Newsome, M.S., Baylor. Economics.
Patricia M. Norman, Ph.D., North Carolina. Management.
Patricia Nunley, J.D., Baylor. Business law.
Thomas A. Odegaard, M.A., Rice. Economics.
Leslie E. Palich, Ph.D., Arizona State. Management.
J. William Petty, Ph.D., Texas. Entrepreneurship.
John L. Pisciotta, Ph.D., Texas at Austin. Economics.
J. Franklin Potts, Ph.D., LSU. Finance.
Tom L. Potts, Ph.D., Illinois. Finance.
Daniel Rajaratnam, Ph.D., Texas A&M. Marketing.
Reagan M. Ramsower, Ph.D., Minnesota. Information systems.
Raymond L. Read, Ph.D., Texas at Austin. Management.
William R. Reichenstein, Ph.D., Notre Dame. Finance.
Steve Rich, Ph.D., Indiana. Finance.
James A. Roberts, Ph.D., Nebraska. Marketing.
Michael A. Robinson, Ph.D., Texas. Accounting.
John T. Rose, Ph.D., Washington (St. Louis). Finance.
Donald R. Schreiber, M.S., Washington State. Marketing.
John W. Seaman, Ph.D., Texas at Dallas. Information systems.
Samuel L. Seaman III, Ph.D., Florida. Information systems.
Mark Serva, Ph.D., Texas. Information systems.
J. Allen Seward, Ph.D., Pennsylvania. Insurance and finance.
Charlene W. Spoede, Ph.D., Texas at Austin. Accounting.
Charles William Stanley, Ph.D., Oklahoma State; CPA (Texas). Accounting.
John F. Tanner, Ph.D., Georgia. Marketing.
Becky A. Taylor, Ph.D., Purdue. Economics.
Elisabeth J. Teal, Ph.D., Georgia. Management.
C. William ("Bill") Thomas, Ph.D., Texas at Austin; CPA (Texas). Accounting.
James M. Tipton, Ph.D., Florida. Finance.
Jonathan K. Trower, Ph.D., Minnesota. Information systems.
W. James Truitt, Ph.D., Illinois. Economics.
M. Michael Umble, Ph.D., LSU. Management.
Nancy B. Upton, Ph.D., Baylor. Psychology.
Philip M. Van Auken, D.B.A., Texas Tech. Management.
Randal L. Vaughn, Ph.D., Texas at Arlington. Information systems.
William Weeks, D.B.A., Indiana. Marketing.
Betsy Willis, M.B.A., Baylor; CPA. Accounting.
G. W. K. Willis, Ph.D., Texas A&M; CDP. Information systems.
Dean Max Young, Ph.D., Texas at Dallas. Information systems.

BENTLEY COLLEGE

Graduate School of Business

Programs of Study

Bentley College Graduate School of Business offers a full-time Master of Business Administration (M.B.A.), a self-paced M.B.A. with fifteen concentrations, and Master of Science programs in accountancy (M.S.A.), accounting information systems (M.S.A.I.S.), business economics (M.S.B.E.), computer information systems (M.S.C.I.S.), finance (M.S.F.), personal financial planning (M.S.P.F.P.), and taxation (M.S.T.). With full advanced-standing credit or an appropriate undergraduate business background, students in the self-paced M.B.A. and M.S. programs can complete their degrees in as few as ten courses in one year of full-time study or two years of part-time study. The full-time M.B.A. is a two-year program that provides an integrated view of the entire enterprise while developing key managerial skills to create a competitive advantage in today's information economy. The self-paced M.B.A. provides a strong foundation in business concepts as well as the analytical and practical techniques that are crucial to management and allows students to draw on previous business knowledge to customize their curriculum through a flexible format. The M.S.A. program is designed to provide a strong accounting foundation for those with little prior accounting course work or to provide in-depth, advanced courses for those who wish to build on an undergraduate accounting degree to expand their knowledge and meet certification requirements. The M.S.A.I.S. program focuses on the full range of information technologies that firms use as part of their financial and accounting decision-making processes. The M.S.B.E. degree is an innovative degree for individuals interested in using economic analysis in areas such as pricing, forecasting, planning, and business conditions analysis. Combining graduate business courses with graduate economics courses, the M.S.B.E. teaches the skills needed to use economics in the business world. The M.S.C.I.S. program is designed for people who possess managerial skills but who wish to develop their technical skills and for people who have technical skills but who want to enhance their managerial skills in order to further or change their careers. The M.S.F. program is an intensive course of study designed for those who want to expand their knowledge of corporate finance. Generally, M.S.F. candidates have a strong accounting background, already hold a position in the field of accounting or corporate finance, and are interested in those aspects of finance that are important in managerial decision making. The M.S.P.F.P. is designed for the financial planner of the next century and provides students with a strong background in the practical areas of financial planning, including estate planning, investment advising, retirement counseling, insurance practice, and tax consulting. The M.S.T. is designed to meet the needs of people with taxation, accounting, or legal experience who want to specialize as tax advisers, consultants, or tax executives. Many practicing tax professionals enroll to enhance their careers. All the graduate programs are designed to accommodate students with no prior business education as well as those with undergraduate business degrees. The College also offers a selection of advanced graduate business certificate programs.

Research Facilities

The library houses more than 200,000 volumes, receives more than 1,700 periodicals, and has 155,000 microform titles. Study rooms and computer terminals are available for students' use, as are the various databases (e.g., LEXIS-NEXIS, Dow Jones, and INFOTRAC) and the up-to-date Media Services Department, which provides television facilities, films, conferencing telephones, video conferencing, and recordings for both instruction and group-work support. The computer facilities at the College are state-of-the-art and include the CIS Case Lab, which supports object-oriented development, database development, groupware applications using Lotus Notes, and Web-based applications. Bentley also has a broad-based network to interact with terminals, microcomputers, and other computer systems, allowing students to communicate with students in other countries, utilize the Internet, and access e-mail. In addition, Bentley's new on-site Trading Room serves as a practical vehicle through which students, from a variety of disciplines, learn financial risk management.

Financial Aid

Financial assistance is available in the form of grants, loans, and employment. All awards are based on financial need and academic performance. In addition, full-time students are eligible for merit-based graduate assistantships, with a maximum award of full tuition remission or full tuition remission plus a stipend. In exchange, graduate assistants work with faculty members and administrators in a variety of educational, research, and administrative activities.

Cost of Study

Tuition is $2050 per course for the 1998–99 academic year. There is a $15 activity fee per semester for part-time students and a $32.50 fee per semester for full-time students. Books cost an average of $100 per course.

Living and Housing Costs

A limited number of modern, fully furnished one- and two-bedroom apartments and single dormitory rooms are available to full-time graduate students on a first-come, first-served basis. Prices vary depending on selection. A one-bedroom apartment costs approximately $4400 per semester for one person. The Office of Residence Life maintains a list of housing available in the local area.

Student Group

The Graduate School enrolls approximately 1,800 students representing fifty-four countries: 250 full-time, 1,550 part-time. Students generally have had five to seven years' work experience. Full-time students tend to have had less work experience than part-time students.

Location

Bentley is ideally located in Waltham, Massachusetts, at the heart of a high-technology region. The 110-acre campus is minutes from Boston's financial center and Cambridge's culturally diverse Harvard Square.

The College

Founded in 1917 by Harry C. Bentley, a pioneer in American business education, the College is an independent, coeducational institution recognized internationally for its excellence in professional business education. In addition to the students at the Graduate School, Bentley College also enrolls more than 3,000 undergraduates in nine business majors. While most undergraduates study full-time, a significant number of working students enroll in the Division of Continuing Education. Bentley College is accredited nationally by AACSB–The International Association for Management Education and regionally by the New England Association of Schools and Colleges (NEASC).

Applying

Applications for the self-paced M.B.A. and for the M.S. programs are accepted for the fall and spring semesters and the summer term. Applications for the full-time M.B.A. program are accepted only for the fall term. All applicants must submit an application form, official transcripts of all academic work beyond high school, scores on the Graduate Management Admission Test (GMAT), and two letters of recommendation. A resume and an interview are also required for full-time M.B.A. applicants. M.S.P.F.P. and M.S.T. applicants may submit evidence of successful completion of the CPA or bar examination or receipt of an appropriate master's or doctoral degree in lieu of GMAT scores. International students must submit their scores on the TOEFL and must complete an International Student Data Form (ISDF). There is a $50 nonrefundable application fee.

Correspondence and Information

Bentley College
Graduate School of Business
Waltham, Massachusetts 02154-4705

Telephone: 781-891-2108
800-442-4723 (toll-free)
Fax: 781-891-2464
E-mail: gradadm@bentley.edu
World Wide Web: http://www.bentley.edu/admissions/graduate

Bentley College

THE FACULTY

Bentley is a practitioner-oriented institution where excellence in teaching is valued and rewarded. All classes are taught by faculty members; none are taught by teaching assistants. Faculty members maintain professional working relationships with executives in the business world to stay abreast of current developments. The majority of the faculty publish articles in leading business publications, make professional presentations, and conduct applied research. Their commitment to scholarly pursuits and professional involvement supports classroom excellence.

As one of the largest nationally accredited graduate business schools in the United States, Bentley has a critical mass of faculty in each discipline. Graduate School courses are primarily taught by full-time faculty members drawn from a pool of more than 130 people. They are supplemented by working professionals who serve as adjunct professors when appropriate. Listed below are the directors for each of the School's seven master's degree programs. For a complete listing of the faculty currently teaching in the Graduate School, students should request a copy of the Bentley Graduate School of Business *Catalogue*.

Judith B. Kamm, Professor of Management and Director of the Master of Business Administration Program; D.B.A., Harvard.

Scott J. Callan, Associate Professor of Economics and Director of the Master of Science in Business Economics Program; Ph.D., Texas A&M.

Jay Cooprider, Associate Professor of Computer Information Systems and Director of the Master of Science in Computer Information Systems Program; Ph.D., MIT.

Glenn E. Frank, Assistant Professor of Taxation and Director of the Master of Science in Personal Financial Planning Program; M.S.T., Bentley; M.B.A., West Virginia; CPA.

David B. Milton, Assistant Professor of Finance and Director of the Master of Science in Finance Program; M.S.T., M.B.A., Bentley.

David L. Schwarzkopf, Professor of Accountancy and Coordinator of Graduate Programs in Accountancy; M.S.A., Bentley; CPA.

Frank Wolpe, Professor of Taxation, Founding Director of the Center for Tax Studies, and Director of the Master of Science in Taxation Program; J.D., Suffolk; CPA.

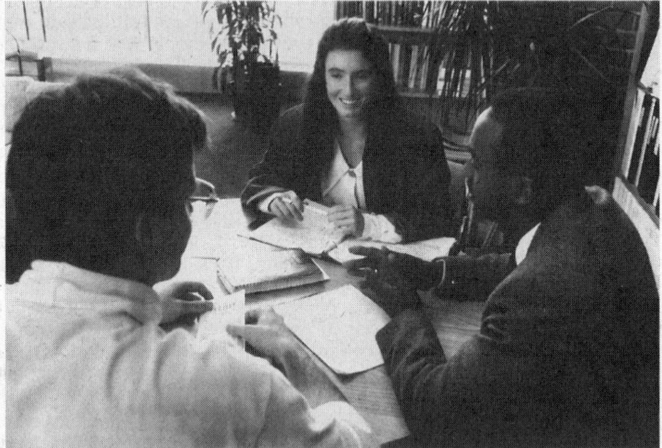

Bentley was the first business school in the country to receive U.S. Department of Education funding for its service-learning activities. Graduate students are encouraged to apply classroom theory to community service needs.

Bentley is one of only six institutions in the nation to have an on-site Trading Room that simulates a trading and risk management environment.

Kenneth Kames (center), Vice President, New Business Development Group of the Gillette Company, speaks with participants during an Executive Speaker Series session.

BOISE STATE UNIVERSITY

College of Business and Economics

Program of Study

The College of Business and Economics offers a program of study leading to the Master of Business Administration (M.B.A.), Master of Science in Accountancy (M.S.A.), Master of Science in Taxation (M.S.T.), and Master of Science in Information Systems (M.S.I.S.) degrees. These high-quality academic programs are designed to assist in the development of tomorrow's business leaders. It provides a general management perspective that enables students to target problems, select viable alternatives, and take appropriate action.

The M.B.A. requires a minimum of 33 semester credit hours and a maximum of 54 semester credit hours; the exact number of credits required depends upon the student's prior academic experience. While there is no major available in the M.B.A. program, once students satisfy the functional core of courses, they can emphasize an area of concentration with their elective credits. This specialty may extend beyond business to such areas as public administration or health policy.

Research Facilities

The College is housed in its own building. This facility provides IBM and Hewlett-Packard mainframe computers with fifty terminals, as well as three microcomputer labs with approximately seventy AT&T Pentium computers that can be linked to the mainframe and seventy-five IBM PCs. The University library houses more than 456,000 bound volumes, nearly 5,000 periodical subscriptions, and more than 1.3 million documents on microfilm, as well as numerous special collections and documents. In addition students have access to a variety of financial and economic databases and time series.

Financial Aid

Scholarships and loans are available. A limited number of assistantships are awarded each year. Assistantships cover tuition and fees and pay a stipend of approximately $7800 per academic year.

Cost of Study

Idaho residents pay no tuition; nonresident full-time students pay $5495 per semester in 1998–99. Other expenses include miscellaneous institutional fees of $1408 per semester and approximately $800 per term for books and supplies.

Living and Housing Costs

The University Housing Office assists students in locating satisfactory housing. On-campus room and board are estimated to cost $5600 for both semesters in 1998–99. Off-campus housing is also available.

Student Group

Boise State University has more than 15,000 students; more than 250 are in the M.B.A. program. Students come from all parts of the world and from diverse academic and professional backgrounds. The M.B.A. Association provides an opportunity for students to promote and improve the M.B.A. program through personal involvement.

Location

Set against a backdrop of mountains where the Boise River flows out of its lava canyons into a fertile valley, Idaho's capital city, Boise, is one of the most appealing metropolitan areas in the West. Named for the Boise River (La Rivière Boisée), present-day Boise is a green tribute to the magic of irrigation with its parks, greenbelt, tree-lined neighborhood streets, golf courses, and University campus. Boise has a pleasant, four-season climate; it is one of the premiere locations in the country for those who like the outdoors.

Boise is the commercial, financial, health-care, and government center of Idaho, allowing students to reach beyond the classroom for experiences not available elsewhere in the state.

The University and The College

Founded in 1932 as a private community college, today Boise State University has the largest enrollment in Idaho.

The College of Business and Economics is an accredited member of AACSB–The International Association for Management Education. The College has six departments and offers thirteen undergraduate majors as well as four graduate degrees, including the M.B.A. It has the advantage of being situated in a city where major firms are headquartered, including Albertson's, Boise Cascade, Idaho Power, Ore-Ida, Simplot, Trus Joist, and the state's leading banks and insurance companies. Major manufacturing locations for Hewlett-Packard and Micron Technology are also located in Boise.

Applying

Applicants must possess a bachelor's degree from an accredited institution. Admission is based on the student's undergraduate record and a satisfactory score on the GMAT. Two letters of recommendation, a current professional resume, a writing sample, and official transcripts are also required. In addition, two years of significant work experience are required; this requirement can be waived based on a superior GMAT score. International students must also submit TOEFL scores, a statement of adequate funding, and certified English translations of transcripts.

Applicants for admission to the M.B.A. program must submit credentials by March 1 for the fall or summer semester and October 1 for the spring semester. The application fee is $20. Application forms for scholarships and loans may be obtained from the Financial Aid Office. Applications for financial aid must be submitted by March 1. The application deadline for assistantships is March 1; forms are available from the director of graduate studies.

Correspondence and Information

For more information:
Renée Anchustegui
Graduate Studies
College of Business and Economics B310
Boise State University
Boise, Idaho 83725-1600
Telephone: 208-385-1126
800-824-7017 Ext. 1126 (toll-free)
E-mail: abuanchu@bsu.idbsu.edu

International students should contact:
Brenda Ross
Foreign Admissions
Boise State University
Boise, Idaho 83725
Telephone: 800-824-7017 Ext. 1757 (toll-free)

Boise State University

THE FACULTY AND THEIR RESEARCH

Robert Anson, Professor of Computer Information Systems; Ph.D., Indiana, 1990. Management information systems, group decision support system technology.
Dwayne Barney, Professor of Finance; Ph.D., Texas A&M, 1984. Mathematical economics, risk and uncertainty.
Chris Baughn, Assistant Professor of Management; Ph.D., Wayne State, 1991. Work role transitions in organizational reentry.
John Bigelow, Professor of Management; Ph.D., Case Western Reserve, 1978. Organizational behavior.
Mike Bixby, Professor of Legal Environment; J.D., Michigan, 1968. Health care, technology and software legal issues.
Jerry Draayer, Professor of Economics; Ph.D., Ohio, 1970. Economic education, formation/student attitudes, economic justice.
Denise English, Associate Professor of Accounting; Ph.D., Indiana, 1987. Business process reengineering, enterprise-wide system implementation.
Thomas English, Professor of Accounting; Ph.D., Arizona State, 1987. Auditing.
Tom Foster, Associate Professor of Information Systems; Ph.D., Missouri–Columbia, 1993. Information systems.
Alan Frankle, Professor of Finance; Ph.D., Arizona, 1974. Finance.
Michael Fronmueller, Associate Professor of Management; Ph.D., Washington State, 1990. Strategic management.
Phillip Fry, Associate Professor of Decision Sciences; Ph.D., LSU, 1987. Multiobjective decision analysis.
Lyman Gallup, Associate Professor of Decision Sciences; Ph.D., Oregon, 1979. Decision analysis.
Roy Glen, Associate Professor of Management; Ph.D., Case Western Reserve, 1978. Organizational development and change.
Newell Gough, Associate Professor of Management; Ph.D., Utah, 1990. Strategy and policy, entrepreneurial management.
Gary Green, Professor of Computer Information Systems; Ph.D., Washington (Seattle), 1976. Management information systems, decision support systems.
David Groebner, Professor of Decision Sciences; Ph.D., Utah, 1974. Statistical decision theory.
Gundars Kaupins, Associate Professor of Management; Ph.D., Iowa, 1986. Human resource management.
David Koeppen, Associate Professor of Accounting; Ph.D., Wisconsin, 1983. Financial reporting.
Jerry LaCava, Professor of Decision Sciences; Ph.D., Kansas, 1971. Decision analysis, subjective assessment.
William Lathen, Professor of Accounting; D.B.A., Arizona State, 1982. Federal tax, estate and gift tax.
Kevin Learned, Associate Professor of Management; Ph.D., Texas Tech, 1995. Entrepreneurship and strategy.
Peter Lichtenstein, Professor of Economics; Ph.D., Colorado, 1974. International economics, economics of formerly socialist countries.
Mohan Limaye, Associate Professor; Ph.D., Wisconsin, 1977. Intercultural communication.
Doug Lincoln, Professor of Marketing; Ph.D., Virginia Tech, 1978. Marketing strategy and use, Internet marketing strategy.
Christine Loucks, Professor of Economics; Ph.D., Washington State, 1983. Money and banking, public choice economics.
Matthew Maher, Associate Professor of Finance; Ph.D., Illinois at Urbana-Champaign, 1989. Banking, money management performance evaluation.
Emerson Maxson, Associate Professor of Information Science; D.B.A., Texas Tech, 1978. Computer system design.
Gary McCain, Professor of Marketing; Ph.D., Oregon, 1977. Marketing research, services marketing, distance education.
John Medlin, Associate Professor of Accounting; M.B.A., Denver, 1965. Federal tax, social security legislation on tax laws.
Mike Merz, Professor of Accounting; D.B.A., USC, 1974. Advanced accounting systems.
Robert Minch, Associate Professor of Decision Sciences; D.B.A., Texas Tech, 1982. Management information systems, hypermedia business application of artificial intelligence.
Murli Nagasundaram, Assistant Professor of Computer Information Systems; Ph.D., Georgia, 1994. Creative group processes, group support systems, information technology.
Nancy Napier, Professor of Management; Ph.D., Ohio State, 1981. Ethnographic study of creation of business schools in a T economy, foreign women working in China and Turkey.
Dave Nix, Associate Professor of Accounting; Ph.D., Oklahoma State, 1974. Current changes in management accounting.
Shawn Novak, Associate Professor of Accounting; Ph.D., Houston, 1991. Taxation.
Richard Payne, Professor of Economics; Ph.D., USC, 1970. Public finance.
Ed Petkus, Associate Professor of Marketing; Ph.D., Tennessee, 1993. Customer value issues, nonprofit organization, detrimental effects of commercialism of American and global culture.
Gordon Pirrong, Professor of Accounting; D.B.A., Arizona State, 1972. International accounting, inflation and interest rates.
Richard Pompian, Assistant Professor; Ph.D., Texas at Austin, 1992. Written performance communications in business.
Arun Raha, Assistant Professor of Economics; Ph.D., Washington State, 1991. International open economics.
Nina Ray, Professor of Marketing; Ph.D., Texas Tech, 1985. Alienation in channels of distribution, nature and special interest tourism.
Larry Reynolds, Professor of Economics; Ph.D., Washington State, 1977. Applied economics; health, environment, and property rights.
William Ruud, Professor of Management; Ph.D., Nebraska, 1978. Organizational behavior, organizational management theory, small group communication.
Robert Sarikas, Associate Professor of Accounting; Ph.D., Illinois at Urbana-Champaign, 1992. Financial accounting, international accounting, petroleum accounting.
Diane Schooley, Associate Professor of Finance; D.B.A., Colorado, 1989. Individual investing, working capital management.
Patrick Shannon, Professor of Decision Sciences and Associate Dean; Ph.D., Oregon, 1975. Statistical analysis, quality management.
Charles Skoro, Professor of Economics; Ph.D., Columbia, 1977. Economic forecasting, labor marketing analysis.
Kirk Smith, Associate Professor of Marketing, Ph.D., Houston, 1993. Personal selling, sales management, pricing, business-to-business marketing.
Thomas E. Stitzel, Professor of Finance; Ph.D., Oregon, 1966. Corporate finance, hospital financing.
Charlotte Twight, Professor of Economics; Ph.D., Washington (Seattle), 1983. Public choice economics.
James Wanek, Assistant Professor of Management; Ph.D., Minnesota, 1995. Employment selection, training and development, ethics.
Harry White, Professor of Finance; Ph.D., Texas A&M, 1984. Corporate finance, cost of capital, international finance.
William Wines, Professor of Legal Environment; J.D., Michigan, 1974. Public-sector collective bargaining.
Greg Wojtkowski, Professor of Information Science; Ph.D., Case Western Reserve, 1973. Computer system design.
Wita Wojtkowski, Professor of Computer Information Systems; Ph.D., Case Western Reserve, 1975. Biomedical engineering, total quality management and information systems.

BOSTON COLLEGE

The Wallace E. Carroll Graduate School of Management

Programs of Study

The Wallace E. Carroll Graduate School of Management (CGSOM) is recognized for offering innovative programs uniquely suited to today's challenging management environment.

The School enrolls approximately 1,000 students in four highly regarded degree programs: the Master of Business Administration (M.B.A.), the Master of Science in Finance (M.S.F.), the Ph.D. in management with a concentration in finance, and the Ph.D. in management with a concentration in organization studies.

In conjunction with other Boston College graduate programs, CGSOM also offers the following dual degrees: the Master of Business Administration/Juris Doctor (M.B.A./J.D.), the Master of Business Administration/Master of Social Work (M.B.A./M.S.W.), the Master of Business Administration/Ph.D. in sociology (M.B.A./Ph.D. in sociology), and the Master of Business Administration/Master of Science in Nursing (M.B.A./M.S.N.). CGSOM also offers dual degrees with Boston College master's programs in mathematics, geology/geophysics, and biology (M.B.A./M.S. or M.A.).

The 55-credit, full-time and evening M.B.A. programs at Boston College are distinguished by their distinctive combination of classroom and applied learning. Students receive a thorough education in managerial concepts, which are complemented by extensive opportunities to utilize their management skills in actual business settings during the program. Global management issues and the role of technology in business are an integral part of the curriculum. Supplementing core study, the innovative management practice sequence provides training in the critical skills and issues in contemporary management, including communication, team building, and cross-functionality.

The Master of Science in Finance offers advanced financial training that builds on a foundation of business and quantitative skills. The program provides a strong conceptual understanding of finance and develops students' analytical abilities. The standard M.S.F. program of eight required courses and two electives may be completed in one year of full-time or two years of part-time study.

Research Facilities

The Boston College libraries offer a wealth of resources and services to support research, teaching, and learning. The book collections exceed 1.6 million volumes, and approximately 17,000 serial titles are currently received. The library holds 2.5 million microforms. Membership in the Boston Library Consortium and the Boston Theological Institute adds greater dimensions to the resources of the Boston College Libraries, providing graduate students with special research access to the millions of volumes and other services of the member institutions. Through membership in the New England Library Information Network (NELINET), there is online access to publishing, cataloging, and interlibrary loan locations from the OCLC, Inc., database, which contains more than 28 million records from the Library of Congress and from more than 17,000 contributing institutions worldwide. The libraries' Quest computer system provides instant access to information on library holdings, as well as supporting book circulation and acquisitions procedures. In addition, Boston College libraries provide access to more than 500 databases. Among these are the Dow Jones News Retrieval Service, Bloomberg Financial Services, LEXIS/NEXIS, ABI Inform, Compustat, CRSP, DRI Basic Economics, General Business File, and IMF.

Financial Aid

The Carroll School of Management offers a significant program of graduate assistantships and scholarships to full-time M.B.A. and M.S.F. classes. Awardees usually have two or more years of full-time work experience, 630 or above on the GMAT, 3.2 or above undergraduate GPA, and a strong set of application materials. Graduate assistantships involve research or administrative duties in exchange for tuition remission. A portion of assistantship awards is subject to tax. In addition to the assistantships and scholarships offered through the Carroll School, the University Financial Aid Office offers a variety of programs to help students finance their education.

Cost of Study

Tuition for the 1998–99 academic year for all graduate management programs is $714 per credit hour. Books, fees, and supplies average $966 per year, and medical insurance is $455.

Living and Housing Costs

Living expenses currently average $5662 per semester. Although graduate housing is not provided on campus, the Office of University Housing provides off-campus listings and suggestions for interested students.

Student Group

There are approximately 220 full-time and 550 evening M.B.A. students and 60 full-time and 115 part-time M.S.F. students. More than 30 percent in both full-time programs are international students. Approximately 30 percent of students in the M.B.A. program are women. Full-time M.B.A. students have an average of 3½ years of full-time work experience, while evening M.B.A. students have an average of 5.3 years. M.S.F. students average five years of full-time work experience.

Student Outcomes

Students who graduate with a Boston College M.B.A. or M.S.F. degree have a wide variety of career options open to them. A large number of students are employed in the finance, consulting, and marketing fields, but many also find work in operations, accounting, MIS, and general management. Recent employers include Fidelity Investments, Andersen Consulting, Ernst & Young, State Street Global Advisors, Harvard Pilgrim Health Care, Reebok International, Scudder Investor Services, and Johnson & Johnson. Students also benefit from the career advice and networking potential of the Boston College Alumni Association.

Location

Located on 185 acres in the Chestnut Hill section on the Boston/Newton line, Boston College is only 7 miles—just a short ride by car or subway—from downtown Boston, a world-renowned center of culture, learning, and industry.

The College

Boston College is a coeducational, two-campus university with four undergraduate schools and six graduate and professional schools. The university offers fourteen degree programs and two certificate programs and enrolls 8,900 full-time undergraduates and 4,600 graduate students. Established in 1863, Boston College is the largest Jesuit-affiliated university in the country. Committed to academic excellence and service to others, the university serves a diverse body of scholars from across the United States and more than ninety other countries.

Applying

The M.S.F. and evening M.B.A. programs admit students in September and January; the full-time M.B.A. and Ph.D. programs begin only in September. Admission to the graduate programs is open to qualified applicants with bachelor's (or graduate) degrees from accredited institutions. The GMAT is required for admission. Admission deadlines are April 1 for the full-time M.B.A., November 15 for January admission to the part-time M.B.A. and M.S.F. programs, July 1 for September admission to the evening M.B.A., and June 15 for September admission to the M.S.F. program. Deadlines for assistantships are outlined in the application. International students must have the equivalent of a U.S. bachelor's degree and a minimum score of 600 on the TOEFL.

Correspondence and Information

Director of Admissions
The Wallace E. Carroll Graduate School of Management
Fulton Hall, Room 315
Boston College
140 Commonwealth Avenue
Chestnut Hill, Massachusetts 02167-3808

M.B.A. Admissions: 617-552-3920
Graduate Finance Programs: 617-552-4488
Fax: 617-552-8078
World Wide Web: http://www.bc.edu/bc_org/avp/csom/

Boston College

THE FACULTY

ADMINISTRATION

John J. Neuhauser, Dean, Carroll School of Management and Professor of Computer Science; Ph.D., Rensselaer.
Hassell McClellan, Dean, Carroll Graduate School of Management and Associate Professor of Operations and Strategic Management; D.B.A., Harvard.
Richard C. Keeley, Associate Dean, Undergraduate Program; M.B.A., Boston College.

FULL-TIME FACULTY

Accounting

Steven Asare, Visiting Associate Professor; Ph.D., Arizona.
Jeffrey R. Cohen, Associate Professor and Chairperson of the Department; Ph.D., Massachusetts, Amherst.
Louis S. Corsini, Associate Professor; Ph.D., LSU.
Daniel Daly, S.J. Instructor; Ph.D. candidate, Michigan.
Theresa Davis Hammond, Associate Professor; Ph.D., Wisconsin.
Elaine M. Harwood, Assistant Professor; Ph.D., USC.
Ganesh Krishnamoorthy, Assistant Professor; Ph.D., USC.
Gil Manzon, Associate Professor; D.B.A., Boston University.
Ronald Pawliczek, Associate Professor; Ph.D., Massachusetts, Amherst.
Thomas Porter, Assistant Professor; Ph.D., Washington (Seattle).
Kenneth B. Schwartz, Associate Professor; Ph.D., Syracuse.
Louise Single, Assistant Professor; Ph.D., Florida.
Billy Soo, Associate Professor; Ph.D., Northwestern.
Gregory Trompeter, Associate Professor; Ph.D., Wisconsin.
Dorothy Lee Warren, Assistant Professor; Ph.D., Georgia.
G. Peter Wilson, Joseph L. Sweeney Professor; Ph.D., Carnegie-Mellon.
Arnold Wright, Arthur Andersen Professor; Ph.D., USC.

Business Law

Christine Neylon O'Brien, Associate Professor; J.D., Boston College.
Frank J. Parker, SJ, Professor; J.D., Fordham.
Alfred E. Sutherland, Associate Professor; J.D., Boston College.
David P. Twomey, Professor and Chairperson of the Department; J.D., Boston College.

Computer Science

William Ames, Lecturer; M.S., Michigan.
Margrit Betke, Assistant Professor; Ph.D., MIT.
Peter G. Clote, Professor; Ph.D., Duke; Paris VII.
James Gips, Professor; Ph.D., Stanford.
Peter Kugel, Associate Professor; Ph.D., Harvard.
Robert Muller, Assistant Professor; Ph.D., Boston University.
C. Peter Olivieri, Associate Professor; Ph.D., Columbia.
Edward Sciore, Associate Professor and Chairperson of the Department; Ph.D., Princeton.
Robert P. Signorile, Associate Professor; Ph.D., Polytechnic.
Howard Straubing, Professor; Ph.D., Berkeley.

Finance

George A. Aragon, Associate Professor; D.B.A., Harvard.
Elizabeth Strock Bagnani, Associate Professor; Ph.D., Massachusetts, Amherst.
Pierluigi Balduzzi, Assistant Professor; Ph.D., UCLA.
Michael Barry, Visiting Professor; Ph.D., Boston College.
Thomas J. Chemmanur, Assistant Professor; Ph.D., NYU.
Clifford G. Holderness, Associate Professor; M.Sc., London; J.D., Stanford.
Edith Hotchkiss, Assistant Professor, Ph.D., NYU.
Eric Jacquier, Assistant Professor; Ph.D., Chicago.
Edward J. Kane, Cleary Professor; Ph.D., MIT.
Alan Marcus, Professor and Chairperson of the Department; Ph.D., MIT.
Mya Maung, Professor; Ph.D., Catholic University.
Pegaret J. S. Pichler, Assistant Professor; Ph.D., Stanford.
John G. Preston, Associate Professor; D.B.A., Harvard.
Elliott Smith, Lecturer; M.S.F., Boston College.
Robert Taggart, Professor; Ph.D., MIT.
Hassan Tehranian, Professor and Director, Graduate Finance Programs; Ph.D., Alabama.
William J. Wilhelm, Associate Professor; Ph.D., LSU.

Marketing

Michael K. Brady, Assistant Professor; Ph.D., Florida State.
Victoria L. Crittenden, Associate Professor and Chairperson of the Department; D.B.A., Harvard.
John T. Hasenjaeger, Associate Professor; Ph.D., Syracuse.
George Jedras, Lecturer; Fulbright Scholar, Warsaw School of Economics.
Raymond F. Keyes, Associate Professor; M.B.A., Boston College.
Charles H. Noble, Assistant Professor; Ph.D., Arizona State.
Michael P. Peters, Associate Professor; Ph.D., Massachusetts, Amherst.
Maria Sannella, Lecturer; Ph.D. candidate, Boston College.
Gerald E. Smith, Associate Professor; D.B.A., Boston University.
Deborah Utter, Lecturer; M.B.A., Chicago.

Operations and Strategic Management

Catherine L. Bendheim, Assistant Professor; Ph.D., Massachusetts, Amherst.
Randolph H. Case, Assistant Professor; Ph.D., Pennsylvania.
Mary Cronin, Professor; Ph.D., Brown.
Charles E. Downing, Assistant Professor; Ph.D., Northwestern.
Joy M. Field, Assistant Professor; Ph.D., Minnesota.
Robert G. Fichman, Assistant Professor; Ph.D., MIT.
John M. Gallaugher, Assistant Professor; Ph.D., Syracuse.
Marta A. Geletkanycz, Assistant Professor; Ph.D., Columbia.
Samuel B. Graves, Associate Professor; D.B.A., George Washington.
Lawrence Halpern, Senior Lecturer; M.B.A., Columbia.
James Halpin, Lecturer and Assistant Dean for Academic Counseling; Th.D., Gregorian.
Debasish Mallick, Assistant Professor; Ph.D., Texas at Austin.
David McKenna, Lecturer; M.B.A., Boston College.
David C. Murphy, Associate Professor; D.B.A., Indiana.
Joseph A. Raelin, Professor; Ph.D., SUNY at Buffalo.
Jeffrey L. Ringuest, Professor; Ph.D., Clemson.
Larry P. Ritzman, Galligan Professor; D.B.A., Michigan State.
M. Hossein Safizadeh, Professor and Chairperson of the Department; Ph.D., Oklahoma State.
Sandra A. Waddock, Associate Professor; D.B.A., Boston University.

Organization Studies

Jean M. Bartunek, R.S.C.J., Professor; Ph.D., Illinois.
Stephen P. Borgatti, Associate Professor; Ph.D., California, Irvine.
Judith Clair, Assistant Professor; Ph.D., USC.
W. E. Douglas Creed, Assistant Professor; Ph.D., Berkeley.
Dalmar Fisher, Associate Professor; D.B.A., Harvard.
Judith R. Gordon, Associate Professor and Chairperson of the Department; Ph.D., MIT.
Candace Jones, Assistant Professor; Ph.D., Utah.
John W. Lewis III, Associate Professor; Ph.D., Case Western Reserve.
Richard P. Nielsen, Professor; Ph.D., Syracuse.
William Stevenson, Associate Professor; Ph.D., California, Riverside.
William R. Torbert, Professor; Ph.D., Yale.
Donald J. White, Distinguished Emeritus Professor; Ph.D., Harvard.

BRANDEIS UNIVERSITY

The Heller Graduate School
Master's Program

Programs of Study

The Master of Business Administration (M.B.A.) and the Master of Management (M.M.) degree programs at Brandeis University's Heller Graduate School are distinct from other degree programs because recipients are trained and educated for management careers in the context of health and human services. The M.B.A. (human services) prepares individuals to become managers in large, multisite health and human services corporate structures and develops future leaders who are trained to utilize large information systems and solve complex problems in an increasingly global environment. The M.M. degree is designed to meet the needs of individuals who are planning careers in community-based provider organizations, government agencies, think tanks, or foundations and prepares tomorrow's leaders to manage multiple aspects of an organization, from operations to marketing to financial control.

The context-specific curriculum at the core of both degrees is at the intersection of cutting-edge management and policy. It combines analytic and evaluation skills from classes such as financial accounting, managerial economics, statistics for managers, managerial accounting and control, operations management, marketing, leadership and organizational behavior, human resources, and strategic management. Study culminates with a Team Consulting Project, which allows students to apply their management and analytical skills to solve real organizational problems. Both degrees promote an awareness of how politics and markets work in the context of social policy. Students acquire a quantitative proficiency for use in problem solving, a mastery of organizational structures and process, skills in handling and communicating information, comprehension of and respect for strategy, and a working knowledge of financial and managerial accounting and control.

The master's degrees draw upon the rich offerings of the Heller School's doctoral program in social policy. Students augment their management training with policy courses in the areas of child, youth, and family services; health care; mental health; developmental disabilities; elder services; substance abuse; poverty; work-force and community development; violence; and social change and inequality. Master's students can declare management concentrations in health care; child, youth, and family services; or human services. In addition to full-time day study, there is an evening program for the M.M. degree only. Heller has joint-degree programs with Brandeis's Hornstein Program in Jewish communal services and with Tufts University's School of Medicine and Northeastern University's College of Business Administration.

Research Facilities

Students benefit from course offerings by and association with an expert research staff in six nationally recognized policy centers: the Institute for Health Policy, the Policy Center on Aging, the Center for Human Resources, the Family and Children's Policy Center, the Center for Social Change, and the Nathan and Toby Starr Center for Mental Retardation. Research is also conducted in mental health, substance abuse, work and inequality, and long-term care.

Financial Aid

The Heller School attempts to assist as many students as possible in securing financial aid. Candidates for admission are expected to explore a variety of outside funding sources such as private scholarships, G.I. bill benefits, and government loan programs. The School has a limited number of need-based scholarships and administrative fellowships. In order to be eligible for financial aid of any kind, a candidate must have both the Free Application for Federal Student Aid (FAFSA) and the CSS Profile Form on file at the School. Forms may be obtained from the Office of Admissions. Aid decisions are made on the combined basis of financial need and academic merit. Evening program students can apply for student loans by filing the FAFSA form.

Cost of Study

For 1998–99, the cost of study is $5600 per semester for the full-time, fifteen-month programs (four-semester programs). Part-time and evening study is $1940 per course.

Living and Housing Costs

In 1997–98, the cost of living for a single student was about $1300 a month. University housing at Brandeis University is limited; most students rent nearby apartments. Rents for a studio apartment are $500 to $650 per month; a one-bedroom apartment rents for $600 to $700 per month.

Student Group

The Master's Program, composed of both degree options, enrolls 35 to 40 full-time students per year. Full-time students complete the program in fifteen months (June through August of the following year), which is a considerable advantage in cost and time over equivalent two-year programs. Part-time students finish in two to three years. Evening students typically take two courses per semester and finish in four years. M.B.A. students must have an undergraduate degree and two or more years of work experience in health and human services (or extensive volunteer experience in health or human services). M.M. students must have an undergraduate degree and two or more years of work experience, although some applicants who have excellent academic records and evidence of leadership potential are accepted directly out of undergraduate programs.

Student Outcomes

The educational goal of the Master's Program is to develop outstanding leaders who are well prepared for managerial roles in health and human services organizations and responsible citizenship in the community. Heller's 25-year-old management program develops in graduates the capacity to frame, analyze, and solve managerial problems; make and execute effective decisions; and lead health and human services organizations through a complex and changing environment. Alumni have gone on to hold a variety of challenging positions in the not-for-profit, public, and for-profit sectors. From a recent survey, 71 percent are in management/administration and 29 percent are in research/policy analysis. For the new M.B.A. (human services) degree program, career placement is expected to be equally successful.

Location

Minutes from Boston, the Heller Graduate School is on Brandeis' picturesque 235-acre suburban campus in Waltham. Shuttle buses and the commuter train link the campus to the state capital, which is rich in history and offers many attractions and cultural resources and easy access to beaches and mountains.

The University

Founded in 1948, Brandeis has become one of the leading small private research universities in the United States, having earned recognition by Phi Beta Kappa only thirteen years after its founding—the youngest institution to be so honored in more than 100 years. In a national review, Brandeis was named the top rising research institution in the United States. The University has a student population of 3,800, almost 1,000 of whom are graduate students. Brandeis offers students a broad diversity of cultural events and opportunities. Student groups and clubs exist for a wide variety of academic and leisure activity. The Gosman Sports Center is a new facility with an indoor track, multipurpose courts, a swimming pool, and weight/fitness rooms.

Applying

Application forms and financial aid information can be obtained from the Office of Admissions. Students must submit a completed application, transcripts, two recommendations, writing samples, and test scores (GMAT required for the M.B.A. degree and preferred for the M.M. degree; however, the GRE may be substituted for M.M. candidates). The application fee is $50. M.B.A. and M.M. day program applicants must submit their materials by March 15 to begin in June, although review of applications begins in November; early application is encouraged. Applications for the M.M. evening program must be submitted by August 1 for fall admission and December 1 for spring admission. Prospective applicants are invited to attend information sessions.

Correspondence and Information

Office of Admissions
The Heller Graduate School, MS 035
Brandeis University
Waltham, Massachusetts 02454-9110

Telephone: 781-736-3820
Fax: 781-736-3881
E-mail: najarian@binah.cc.brandeis.edu
World Wide Web: http://www.brandeis.edu/heller

Brandeis University

THE FACULTY AND THEIR RESEARCH

Stuart H. Altman, Sol C. Chaikin Professor of National Health Policy; Ph.D., UCLA. Health-care policy.
Lawrence Neil Bailis, Associate Human Services Research Professor; Ph.D., Harvard. Youth development programs, welfare, poverty.
Dennis Beatrice, Human Serves Management Professor; M.P.A., Harvard. Health-care policy and management.
Sarita Bhalotra, Adjunct Lecturer; M.B.B.S., Delhi (India). Heath-care management, clinical information systems.
Christine Bishop, Research Professor; Ph.D., Harvard. Health and long-term care.
David Breakstone, Adjunct Lecturer; M.A., Harvard. Managerial communications.
James J. Callahan Jr., Research Professor and Director of the Policy Center on Aging; Ph.D., Brandeis. Aging, mental health, management.
John A. Capitman, Research Professor; Ph.D., Duke. Health policy and long-term care.
Susan Bryant Carnduff, Adjunct Lecturer; J.D., Suffolk. Negotiation, public-sector law, advocacy.
Jon A. Chilingerian, Associate Professor, Co-Director of the AHCPR Training Program, and Director of the Master's Program; Ph.D., MIT. Managerial accounting and behavior.
Susan P. Curnan, Associate Human Services Management Professor and Director of the Center for Human Resources; M.F.S., Yale. Employment and training.
Gunnar Dybwad, Professor Emeritus of Human Development; J.D., Halle (Germany); Graduate, New York School of Social Work. Developmental disabilities.
Stephen Fournier, Adjunct Lecturer; Ph.D., MIT. Computer applications to management and social science research.
John H. Friar, Adjunct Lecturer and Assistant Professor, Northeastern University; Ph.D., MIT. Strategic management, economics and marketing strategy.
Barry L. Friedman, Research Professor and Senior Research Associate; Ph.D., MIT. Labor and income maintenance, management.
Deborah Garnick, Research Professor; Sc.D., Johns Hopkins. Health policy.
Janet Z. Giele, Professor; Ph.D., Harvard. Child and family policy.
David G. Gil, Professor of Social Policy; D.S.W., Pennsylvania. Social welfare, inequality.
Andrew B. Hahn, Research Professor and Associate Dean for University Relations; Ph.D., Brandeis. Labor market studies.
William Harris, Visiting Professor; Ph.D., MIT. Child and family policy.
Dominic Hodgkin, Adjunct Lecturer; Ph.D., Boston University. Health economics, econometrics.
Constance Horgan, Research Professor and Deputy Director of Health Services Research; Sc.D., Johns Hopkins. Substance abuse policy, health policy and management.
Kenneth J. Jones, John Stein Professor of Human Rehabilitation; Ed.D., Harvard. Social model building.
Hilda Kahne, Professor and Senior Research Associate; Ph.D., Harvard. Labor economics, work and family-cycle issues.
Marty W. Krauss, Associate Professor and Director of the Nathan and Toby Starr Center for Mental Retardation; Ph.D., Brandeis. Developmental disabilities.
Norman R. Kurtz, Professor of Social Research; Ph.D., Colorado. Alcoholism, management.
Walter Leutz, Associate Research Professor; Ph.D., Brandeis. Managed care, long-term care.
Helen Levine, Associate Research Professor; Ph.D., Chicago. Health-care delivery systems.
Mary Ellen Marsden, Associate Research Professor; Ph.D., Chicago. Health policy, substance use and abuse.
Dennis McCarty, Research Professor; Ph.D., Kentucky. Substance abuse treatment and prevention services.
Thomas McGuire, Adjunct Professor; Ph.D., Yale. Mental health.
Robert Morris, Professor Emeritus; Ph.D., Columbia. Social planning.
Phyllis Mutschler, Lecturer and Senior Research Associate; Ph.D., Brandeis. Applied research in aging.
Robert Perlman, Professor Emeritus; Ph.D., Brandeis. Social planning.
Jeffrey M. Prottas, Research Professor and Executive Deputy Director of the Institute of Health Policy; Ph.D., MIT. Health policy.
Robert B. Reich, University Professor and Maurice B. Hexter Professor of Social and Economic Policy; J.D., Yale. Work and inequality.
Howard Rivenson, Adjunct Lecturer; M.B.A., NYU. Management and accounting.
David Rosenbloom, Adjunct Lecturer; Ph.D., MIT. Management theory, health-care management.
Carl Schulz, Adjunct Lecturer; Ed.D., Harvard. Operations management.
James H. Schulz, Meyer and Ida Kirstein Professor of Planning and Administration in Aging Policy; Ph.D., Yale. Economics of aging.
Mark Sciegaj, Adjunct Lecturer; Ph.D., Brandeis. Health care, ethics.
Donald Sloane Shepard, Research Professor; Ph.D., Harvard. Health financing, international systems.
David Sherman, Adjunct Lecturer; Ph.D., Harvard. Financial accounting.
Jack P. Shonkoff, Professor of Social Policy and Dean; M.D., NYU. Pediatrics, child and family policy.
Laurence R. Simon, Director of the Program on Sustainable International Development and Human Services Associate Research Professor; Ph.D., Clark. International development.
Carmen Sirianni, Associate Professor of Sociology; Ph.D., SUNY at Binghamton. Community development and organization.
Deborah A. Stone, David R. Pokross Professor of Law and Social Policy; Ph.D., MIT. Political science, law and social policy.
Christopher Tompkins, Associate Human Services Research Professor; Ph.D., Brandeis. Health-care financing and delivery systems.
Patricia E. VanLeuvan, Adjunct Lecturer; M.B.A., Northeastern. Human resource management.
Stanley S. Wallack, Research Professor and Director of the Institute of Health Policy; Ph.D., Washington (St. Louis). Health-care policy.
Constance Williams, Associate Professor and Director of the Ph.D. in Social Policy Program; Ph.D., Brandeis. Family and children, race, class, culture.

Joint Appointments

Shulamit Reinharz, Professor of Sociology and Director of the Women's Studies Program (also with Sociology); Ph.D., Brandeis. Women's issues.
Leonard Saxe, Adjunct Research Professor (also with Psychology); Ph.D., Pittsburgh. Mental health evaluation, interventions.

BRIGHAM YOUNG UNIVERSITY

Marriott School of Management

Programs of Study

The Marriott School of Management offers professional programs leading to the following degrees: Master of Business Administration, Master of Public Administration, Master of Accountancy, Master of Organizational Behavior, and Master of Information Systems Management.

The M.B.A. program emphasizes the integration of functional areas within a global environment as well as depth in selected areas of study. Emphasis on group interaction, case analysis, and field consulting projects develops management skills in communication, problem analysis, and decision making. Special emphasis is placed on the development of a global perspective, entrepreneurial skills, and values-based behavior.

The M.P.A. program prepares students for management careers in public-sector and not-for-profit organizations. Based on a broad core of courses in management and the social sciences, it allows students to concentrate in financial management, personnel administration, urban management, policy analysis, and program evaluation.

The M.Acc. program is designed for students desiring professional competence in one of two areas of accounting specialization (professional accounting and tax), along with substantial breadth in business-related subjects.

The M.O.B. program helps students develop skills in the management of organizational change in addition to the study of organizational dynamics such as culture, leadership, international organizational behavior, team effectiveness, worker vitality, strategy, and human resource management.

The M.I.S.M. program prepares students who want professional careers in information systems. Students seek employment with consulting firms, industrial organizations, and not-for-profit entities, performing a variety of services dealing with understanding the information needs of an organization; designing, developing, and implementing information systems to meet specified requirements; administering the information systems function; and formulating an information systems master plan to effectively utilize information technology throughout an organization.

These five degree programs are designed to prepare qualified students for careers in management. An emphasis on ethics is part of every class as well as the basis for a special ethics course. The programs are two years in length and are demanding in terms of time, intellectual activity, and the ability to deal with others. Other options include the following degrees: J.D./M.B.A., J.D./M.P.A., J.D./M.O.B., M.B.A./mechanical engineering, M.B.A./international relations, and M.O.B./international relations.

Research Facilities

The School is located in the N. Eldon Tanner Building. This facility provides a management library, expanded computer facilities, research areas, technology-enhanced learning environment (TELE) classrooms, and special graduate study rooms. Brigham Young University's Lee Library houses more than 3 million bound volumes and an extensive collection of pamphlets and titles on microfilm.

Financial Aid

The School provides financial assistance to qualified students through scholarship grants, teaching and research assistantships, and internships, as well as through loans (including Federal Stafford Student Loans) handled by the University's Financial Aid Department. Approximately 60 to 70 percent of the students in the School receive some financial assistance.

Cost of Study

In 1998–99, tuition is $2650 per semester for members of the Church of Jesus Christ of Latter-day Saints and $3975 per semester for nonmembers. Books and supplies average $700 per semester.

Living and Housing Costs

The University Housing Office assists all students in locating satisfactory accommodations on and off campus. Single students should budget $7200 for living costs for the 1998–99 academic year.

Student Group

Brigham Young University (BYU) has approximately 29,000 full-time students, including 900 graduate students in the Marriott School of Management. Students come from a variety of academic and ethnic backgrounds, fifty states, and nearly 100 countries. In the Marriott School, 20 percent of students are international, and 57 percent of the faculty and 80 percent of the students are bilingual.

Student Outcomes

Employers come to the Marriott School for candidates with diverse experiences in language and international living situations. Students are recruited into many industries by major public and private corporations, public accounting firms, public agencies, and governments. Students' quantitative and analytical skills, coupled with strong communications training, make them ideal employees.

Location

BYU's beautiful 600-acre campus is located in Provo, Utah, at the foot of the Wasatch Mountains. The University has excellent cultural programs and is near numerous outdoor recreational areas for skiing (snow and water), hiking, and camping. Salt Lake City, 45 miles north, offers the Utah Symphony, Ballet West, and Pioneer Theater, as well as professional basketball (Jazz), baseball, and hockey.

The University and The School

BYU is the largest privately owned university in the United States. It was established by the Church of Jesus Christ of Latter-day Saints in 1875 to promote high standards of scholarship and to develop religious faith, high moral character, and responsible citizenship. The Marriott School of Management's mission is to attract and develop men and women of faith, character, and professional ability who will become outstanding managers and leaders throughout the world. A Marriott School education is enhanced by three centers of excellence—the Center for the Study of Values in Organizations, the Center for Entrepreneurship, and the Center for International Business, Education and Research.

Applying

Admission to the Marriott School is contingent upon acceptance to one of the five degree programs. Criteria are established for each program; however, uniform emphasis is placed upon high academic achievement, the Graduate Management Admission Test, outstanding ability, and leadership potential. The deadline for admission applications is March 1. The deadline for the Executive M.B.A. and M.P.A. programs is May 1. International students must apply by January 15 and pass the Test of English as a Foreign Language (TOEFL) with a minimum score of 550.

Correspondence and Information

Marriott School of Management
Graduate Programs
730 Tanner Building
Brigham Young University
Provo, Utah 84602

Telephone: 801-378-4122
Fax: 801-378-4501
E-mail: msmonline@byu.edu
World Wide Web: http://msm.byu.edu

Brigham Young University

THE FACULTY AND THEIR RESEARCH

Professional Accounting:
W. Steve Albrecht, Professor and Chair, School of Accountancy and Information Systems; Ph.D., Wisconsin–Madison, 1976. Financial auditing. Dave Cottrell, Assistant Professor; Ph.D., Ohio State, 1992. Experimental markets. Berkeley L. Geddes, Visiting Instructor; B.S., Brigham Young, 1984. Accounting. Steven M. Glover, Assistant Professor; Ph.D., Washington (Seattle), 1994. Auditing. John W. Hardy, Professor; Ph.D., Texas at Austin, 1968. Managerial accounting. Keith R. Howe, Associate Professor; Ph.D., Arizona State, 1979. Operational, managerial, and not-for-profit accounting. Sharon Kay Hurley Johns, Assistant Professor; Ph.D., Texas A&M, 1997. Accounting. Donald H. Livingstone, Instructor and Director, Center for Entrepreneurship; B.S., Brigham Young, 1966. Finance. Richard E. McDermott, Visiting Professor; Ph.D., Oklahoma State, 1984. Accounting. Norman R. Nemrow, Instructor; M.Acc., Brigham Young, 1979. Finance. F. Grant Peterson, Assistant Professor; Ph.D., Utah, 1973. Quantitative methods. Douglas R. Prawitt, Assistant Professor; Ph.D., Arizona, 1992. Accounting. Lee H. Radebaugh, Professor and Director, Center for International Business; D.B.A., Indiana, 1973. International business. Financial accounting. K. Fred Skousen, Professor and Advancement Vice-President; Ph.D., Illinois at Urbana–Champaign, 1968. Financial accounting. James D. Stice, Assistant Professor; Ph.D., Washington (Seattle), 1989. Financial accounting. Kevin D. Stocks, Associate Professor; Ph.D., Oklahoma State, 1981. Managerial accounting. Monte Swain, Assistant Professor; Ph.D., Michigan State, 1992. Managerial systems. Leon W. Woodfield, Professor; D.B.A., Michigan State, 1965. Financial/managerial accounting.

Tax:
Richard S. Dalebout, Associate Professor; S.J.D., Utah, 1971. Business law. Robert L. Gardner, Professor; Ph.D., Texas at Austin, 1979. Taxation. Glen O. Palmer, Assistant Professor; M.Acc., Brigham Young, 1963; CPA. Taxation. Boyd C. Randall, Professor; Ph.D., Minnesota, 1972. Tax accounting. Brian C. Spilker, Assistant Professor; Ph.D., Texas at Austin, 1993. Tax. Dave N. Stewart, Professor; Ph.D., Florida, 1980. Taxation. G. Fred Streuling, Professor; Ph.D., Iowa, 1971. Tax accounting. Ronald G. Worsham, Assistant Professor; Ph.D., Florida, 1994. Tax.

Information Systems:
Glen L. Boyer, Associate Professor; Ph.D., North Dakota, 1972. Information systems. J. Owen Cherrington, Professor; Ph.D., Minnesota, 1972. Accounting, theory/systems. Eric L. Denna, Assistant Professor and Assistant Academic Vice-President, Computing; Ph.D., Michigan State, 1989. Information systems. Gary W. Hansen, Associate Professor; Ph.D., Indiana, 1974. Mathematics. James V. Hansen, Professor; Ph.D., Washington (Seattle), 1973. Information systems. Robert B. Jackson, Assistant Professor; Ph.D., Brigham Young, 1994. Information systems. Stephen W. Liddle, Assistant Professor; Ph.D., Brigham Young, 1995. Information systems. Lynn J. McKell, Professor; Ph.D., Purdue, 1973. Systems and controls. Rayman Meservy, Associate Professor; Ph.D., Minnesota, 1985. Accounting. Dallan Wendel Quass, Assistant Professor; Ph.D., Stanford, 1997. Computer science. Marshall B. Romney, Professor; Ph.D., Texas at Austin, 1977. Financial auditing.

Management–Finance:
Dwight M. Blood, Professor; Ph.D., Michigan, 1963. Micro and macro theory. Phillip J. Bryson, Professor; Ph.D., Ohio State, 1967. Comparative economic systems. Ivan T. Call, Professor; D.B.A., Indiana, 1969. Finance. Charles M. Cox, Associate Professor; Ph.D., Washington (Seattle), 1978. Finance. Robert G. Crawford, Associate Professor; Ph.D., Carnegie Mellon, 1976. Business economics. Hal B. Heaton, Professor; Ph.D., Stanford, 1983. Finance. Ned C. Hill, Professor and Assistant to the President for budgeting and planning; Ph.D., Cornell, 1976. Finance. Andrew L. Holmes, Assistant Professor; Ph.D., Houston, 1992. Corporate finance, financial institutions. William R. Lambert, Associate Professor; D.B.A., Indiana, 1968. Investments. W. Robert McConkie II, Visiting Professor; Ph.D., Florida State, 1995. Finance. Grant R. McQueen, Associate Professor; Ph.D., Washington (Seattle), 1989. Finance. Craig Merrill, Assistant Professor; Ph.D., Pennsylvania, 1994. Finance. Stephen D. Nadauld, Professor; Ph.D., Berkeley, 1978. Finance. Ray D. Nelson, Associate Professor; Ph.D., Berkeley, 1981. Futures market and price theory. Wayne Pearce, Instructor; M.B.A., Utah, 1961. Finance. J. Michael Pinegar, Professor; Ph.D., Utah, 1982. Finance. Bernell K. Stone, Professor; Ph.D., MIT, 1968. Financial systems. Steven R. Thorley, Professor; Ph.D., Washington (Seattle), 1991. Finance. Brent D. Wilson, Associate Professor; D.B.A., Harvard, 1979. Finance.

Marketing:
Roman Ray Andrus, Professor; Ph.D., Columbia, 1965. Marketing. Michael D. Geurts, Professor; Ph.D., Oregon, 1972. Marketing. H. Keith Hunt, Professor; Ph.D., Northwestern, 1972. Marketing. Gary F. McKinnon, Professor and Director, M.B.A. Program; Ph.D., Texas at Austin, 1968. Marketing. Gary K. Rhoads, Associate Professor; Ph.D., Texas Tech, 1988. Marketing. Ronald L. Schill, Professor; Ph.D., Oregon, 1971. Marketing. Scott M. Smith, Professor; Ph.D., Penn State, 1979. Marketing. Michael J. Swenson, Associate Professor; Ph.D., Oregon, 1989. Marketing. William R. Swinyard, Professor; Ph.D., Stanford, 1976. Marketing. Georgia White, Assistant Professor; Ph.D., Oregon, 1979. Marketing. David B. Whitlark, Assistant Professor; Ph.D., Virginia, 1990. Marketing science.

Operations:
Brent Barnett, Assistant Professor; Ph.D., MIT, 1983. Operations. Stanley E. Fawcett, Associate Professor; Ph.D., Arizona State, 1990. Logistic operations, international business. William C. Giauque, Professor; Ph.D., Harvard, 1972. Operations. Terry N. Lee, Associate Professor; Ph.D., Washington (Seattle), 1973. Quantitative analysis, operations. Scott E. Sampson, Assistant Professor; Ph.D., Virginia, 1993. Operations management. William J. Sawaya Jr., Associate Professor; Ph.D., Arizona State, 1971. Production management. Kristie W. Seawright, Assistant Professor; Ph.D., Utah, 1993. Operations.

Management Communication:
William H. Baker, Professor; Ed.D., Oklahoma State, 1974. Written, oral, and visual communication. Kristen Bell DeTienne, Professor; Ph.D., USC, 1991. Organizational communication. Garth A. Hanson, Associate Professor; Ph.D., Nebraska, 1983. Oral and written communication. Kaye T. Hanson, Assistant Lecturer; Ph.D., Brigham Young, 1983. Oral communication. Larry Hartman, Associate Professor; Ed.D., Oklahoma State, 1973. Written and oral communication. Janet M. Howard-Tuten, Assistant Professor; Ed.D., Brigham Young, 1985. Written and oral communication. Devern Perry, Professor; Ed.D., North Dakota, 1968. Written communication. Karl Smart, Assistant Professor; Ph.D., Florida, 1989. Written, oral, and visual communication. Ted D. Stoddard, Professor; Ed.D., Arizona State, 1967. Written communication. Michael P. Thompson, Associate Professor; Ph.D., Rensselaer, 1985. Rhetoric and communication. Paul R. Timm, Professor and Chair, Organizational Leadership and Strategy; Ph.D., Florida State, 1977. Communications.

Organizational Behavior/Human Resources:
Sheri Bischoff, Assistant Professor; Ph.D., Oregon, 1994. Organizational studies. Kim Cameron, Professor and Associate Dean, Marriott School of Management; Ph.D., Yale, 1978. Organizational change. David W. Cherrington, Professor; D.B.A., Indiana, 1970. Work values, motivation. W. Gibb Dyer, Professor and Director, M.O.B. program; Ph.D., MIT, 1984. Organizations and global leadership. Hal B. Gregersen, Assistant Professor; Ph.D., California, Irvine, 1989. Organizational behavior. Kate Kirkham, Associate Professor; Ph.D., Union (Ohio), 1977. Diversity, organizational change. Christopher B. Meek, Associate Professor; Ph.D., Cornell, 1983. Labor-management cooperation. Gordon E. Mills, Professor; Ph.D., Penn State, 1970. Analyst design, media development. Eric G. Stephan, Professor; Ph.D., Utah, 1966. Management, leadership, organization revitalization. David A. Whetten, Professor and Director, Center for Study of Values in Organizations; Ph.D., Cornell, 1974. Organizational values and change. Warner P. Woodworth, Professor; Ph.D., Michigan, 1974. Worker ownership, international development.

Strategy:
Darral G. Clarke, Professor; Ph.D., Purdue, 1972. Strategy, marketing research. Robert H. Daines, Professor; D.B.A., Indiana, 1966. Finance, strategy. Paul C. Godfrey, Assistant Professor; Ph.D., Washington (Seattle), 1994. Strategy. Mark H. Hansen, Assistant Professor; Ph.D., Texas A&M, 1996. Strategy. W. Burke Jackson, Associate Professor; Ph.D., Stanford, 1978. Strategy. Lee T. Perry, Professor; Ph.D., Yale, 1982. Organizational careers, corporate strategy. W. Gerard Sanders, Assistant Professor; Ph.D., Texas at Austin, 1996. Strategy.

Public Management:
Donald L. Adolphson, Professor; Ph.D., Wisconsin–Madison, 1973. Operations. F. Neil Brady, Professor; Ph.D., Texas at Austin, 1978. Management philosophy, ethics. Doyle W. Buckwalter, Associate Professor; Ph.D., Michigan, 1968. Public policy, state and local government. Gary C. Cornia, Professor and Associate Dean, Marriott School of Management; Ph.D., Ohio State, 1979. Public finance, budget. David Kirkwood Hart, Professor; Ph.D., Claremont, 1965. Business and government ethics. Lennis M. Knighton, Professor; Ph.D., Michigan State, 1966. Accounting and finance. Roland H. Koller II, Associate Professor; Ph.D., Wisconsin–Madison, 1969. Economics, industrial organization. Robert J. Parsons, Professor; Ph.D., California, Riverside, 1971. Finance and health economics. B. Michael Pritchett, Professor; Ph.D., Purdue, 1970. Quantitative methods, econometrics. J. Bonner Ritchie, Professor; Ph.D., Berkeley, 1968. Organization and leadership theory. Lawrence W. Walters, Associate Professor and Director, Institute of Public Management; Ph.D., Pennsylvania, 1987. Policy analysis, quantitative methods. Gloria E. Wheeler, Associate Professor; Ph.D., Michigan, 1972. Mathematics/quantitative methods. Gary M. Woller, Assistant Professor; Ph.D., Rochester, 1992. Public policy. N. Dale Wright, Professor; Ph.D., USC, 1972. Organizational behavior/theory, management strategy.

BRYANT COLLEGE

The Graduate School

Programs of Study

Students pursuing a graduate degree at Bryant College are learning at one of the nation's best business specialty schools. The academic programs are internationally ranked by AACSB–The International Association for Management Education. Bryant offers an M.B.A. with concentrations in accounting, computer information systems, finance, general business, health-care management, international business, management, marketing, and operations management; a Master of Science in Taxation (M.S.T.); a Master of Science in Accounting (M.S.A.); and a Certificate of Advanced Graduate Studies (C.A.G.S.).

Bryant's M.B.A. degree program can be pursued full- or part-time. Those who carry a full-time course load and have undergraduate degrees in business can achieve their degrees in as little as one year. Students pursuing study part-time set their own pace, taking up to six years to complete their degrees through evening study. Course work includes core courses, which provide in-depth study of key business disciplines; and the concentration and elective courses that allow students to specialize in an area of particular interest. Course work takes a practical approach that links theory to real life. Interactive teaching techniques include group projects, role-playing, case studies, and debates.

The M.S.A. degree program is designed to meet the needs of students from a variety of academic backgrounds. Students with an undergraduate degree in accounting may complete the program in one year of full-time study. Individuals who possess a bachelor's degree in another academic discipline can generally complete the program in two years, depending on the number of prerequisites that need to be met. The M.S.A. degree also may be completed on a part-time basis.

The M.S.T. is a part-time degree program designed for individuals who have a basic knowledge of tax codes and who seek advanced knowledge of federal and state laws and applications. This comprehensive program includes core tax courses in individuals, corporations, partnerships, trusts, and estates and electives in advanced areas of specialization.

The C.A.G.S. is for experienced professionals who have earned a master's degree but want to develop their knowledge in another field. C.A.G.S. is available in eight disciplines:accounting, computer information systems, finance, health-care management, management, marketing, operations management, and taxation.

Research Facilities

The Edith M. Hodgson Memorial Library occupies three levels in the Unistructure's academic wing. Containing more than 126,000 volumes, the library offers numerous reading tables, carrels, lounge areas, and group study rooms and one of the most technologically advanced library systems in New England. Newspaper and periodical databases (index/abstract and full-text) as well as corporate records are available at several compact-disk computer workstations. The library subscribes to a number of electronic resources. The LEXIS/NEXIS service provides access to more than 150 data libraries, providing information in business and finance, taxation, international trade, and many other subject specialties. The Dialog information retrieval system offers yet another 400 databases. Subscriptions to more than 1,300 American and European periodicals, journals, and annuals are maintained. Microfilm readers, printers, and photocopiers are available for graduate use. The library is linked by computer to other state and regional libraries.

The Koffler Technology Center houses 200 terminals, microcomputers, and workstations, as well as diverse software and desktop publishing packages with access to the Internet. Computers are also available elsewhere on campus, including the Davis Electronic Classroom and the Language and Learning Laboratory.

Financial Aid

Graduate students pursuing study on a full-time basis are eligible for merit-based graduate assistantships. Graduate assistants are expected to work about 15 hours a week for about forty-four weeks a year. Applicants must be graduates of an accredited college or university, have scored 500 or more on the GMAT, and have recommendations from 2 people who are not family members and who can attest to the applicant's business-education potential and overall qualifications.

Cost of Study

Tuition fees for the 1998–99 academic year for M.B.A. and M.S.A. courses are $1025 per course. For M.S.T. courses, tuition fees are $1350 per course, regardless of the number of courses taken.

Living and Housing Costs

There is on-campus housing available for graduate students in residence hall suites and in townhouse apartments. The College also has listings of housing available within a 10-mile radius of the campus.

Student Group

The graduate programs' enrollment for the 1997–98 academic year is approximately 53 full-time students and 487 part-time students. There are 224 women and 316 men.

Student Outcomes

Bryant graduates assume leadership positions in government, nonprofit organizations, and the private sector. Alumni include the auditor general for the state of Rhode Island, a senior financial analyst at Motorola, an account executive at the Rhode Island Economic Development Corporation, and the vice president of operations at The Stanley Works.

Location

Bryant College offers students the serenity of a 387-acre suburban campus in Smithfield, within a 15-minute drive of Providence and easily accessible to Rhode Island Route 146 and Interstates 95 and 295.

The College

Bryant College is more than a leader in business education; it is also renowned for practicing the principles it teaches. Through the College's outreach efforts, Bryant students and faculty and staff members form an important resource for the state's economic growth. Students are given the opportunity to get involved in international trade, telecommunications, management development, technology transfer, and small business development.

Applying

Entry requirements include a bachelor's degree from an accredited college and a strong score on the GMAT. For students for whom English is not their primary language, submission of a TOEFL score is required. Prospective students must also submit a resume, official transcripts, one letter of recommendation, and a 500-word statement of objectives. Degree program applications are accepted for the fall, spring, and summer terms. All correspondence should be directed to the address below.

Correspondence and Information

The Graduate School
Bryant College
1150 Douglas Pike
Smithfield, Rhode Island 02917-1284

Telephone: 401-232-6230
Fax: 401-232-6494
E-mail: gradprog@bryant.edu

Bryant College

THE FACULTY AND THEIR RESEARCH

Eugene A. Amelio, J.D., Boston College. Taxation.
Roger Anderson, Ph.D., Oregon. Management.
Laurie Bates, Ph.D., Connecticut. Economics.
David Beausejour, J.D., Suffolk (England). Accounting.
Robert Behling, Ph.D., Northern Colorado. Systems/management.
Frank Bingham, Ed.D., Massachusetts at Amherst. Marketing.
Dennis M. Bline, Ph.D., Arkansas. Accounting.
Joseph Bonnici, Ph.D., Arkansas. Marketing.
Michel Bougon, Ph.D., Cornell. Management.
Timothy C. Brown, Ph.D., Indiana. Management.
Kumar Chittipeddi, Ph.D., Penn State. Management.
Robert Conti, Ph.D., Lehigh. Management.
Charles Cullinan, Ph.D., Kentucky. Accounting.
Ron DiBattista, Ph.D., Arizona State. Management.
John R. Elder, Ph.D., Virginia. Economics.
Robert Farrar, Ph.D., Massachusetts at Amherst. Accounting.
Michael Filippelli, M.B.A., Rhode Island. Accounting.
Burton Fischman, Ph.D., Connecticut. Communications.
Kenneth F. Fougere, Ph.D., Boston College. Computer information systems.
Richard Glass, Ph.D., Concordia. Computer information systems.
Arthur C. Gudikinst, Ph.D., RPI. Finance.
Hsiang-Ling Han, A.B.D., Rochester. Economics.
Judith Harris, D.B.A., Boston University. Accounting.
Marcel G. Hebert, Ph.D., Texas Tech. Accounting.
Henry John Keigwin, M.B.A., Harvard. Entrepreneurship.
Kristin Kennedy, Ph.D., Rhode Island. Mathematics.
David Ketcham, Ph.D., Vermont. Finance.
Timothy Krumwiede, A.B.D., Texas Tech. Accounting.
Thomas Leonard, Ph.D., Illinois. Marketing.
Chantee Lewis, D.B.A., George Washington. Finance.
Hsi-Cheng Li, Ph.D., Massachusetts at Amherst. Finance.
David Louton, Ph.D., Michigan. Finance.
Dana Lowe, Ph.D., George Washington. Accounting.
Larry Lowe, Ph.D., Washington (Seattle). Marketing.
Harsh K. Luthar, Ph.D., Virginia Tech. Management.
Michael F. Lynch, J.D., New England Law. Accounting.
Hao Ma, Ph.D., Texas at Austin. Management.
Laurie MacDonald, Ph.D., Boston College. Computer information systems.
Thomas Malafronte, Ph.D., Brown. Mathematics.
Joseph McCarthy, D.B.A., Colorado. Finance.
Shirley-Jo Miller, Ph.D., Arkansas. Marketing.
Peter V. Mini, Ph.D., Tulane. Economics.
Sam Mirmirani, Ph.D., Clark. Economics.
Keith Murray, Ph.D., Arizona State. Marketing.
Margaret Noble, Ph.D., Indiana. Management.
R. D. Norton, Ph.D., Princeton. Economics.
Elaine Marie Notorantonio, Ph.D., Rhode Island. Marketing.
William T. O'Hara, L.H.D., Mount Saint Mary (New York). Management.
Alan Olinsky, Ph.D. candidate, Connecticut. Mathematics.
Chester Piascik, M.S., Rhode Island. Mathematics.
Hinda Pollard, J.D., California, Hastings Law. Management.
Thomas Powell, Ph.D., NYU. Management.
Charles J. Quigley Jr., Ph.D., Penn State. Marketing.
Harold Records, Ph.D., Cornell. Computer information systems.
Frederick Reinhardt Jr., M.S., Purdue. Mathematics.
Saeed Roohani, D.B.A., Mississippi State. Accounting.
Martin Rosenzweig, Ph.D., Iowa State. Mathematics.
J. Christopher Sandvig, Ph.D., Washington (Seattle). Management.
William Scheibal, Ph.D., Texas. Legal studies.
Phyllis Schumacher, Ph.D. candidate, Connecticut. Mathematics.
James Segovis, Ph.D., Texas. Management.
Joseph Shaanan, Ph.D., Cornell. Economics.
Kathleen A. Simons, D.B.A., Boston University. Accounting.
Janice A. Smith, Ph.D., LSU. Accounting.
John L. Swearingen Jr., D.B.A., Boston University. Computer information systems.
Shirley Wilson, D.B.A., Akron. Management.
Lawrence H. Witner, LL.M., George Washington. Taxation.
Wallace A. Wood, Ph.D., Boston College. Computer information systems.
Gail Wright, D.B.A., George Washington. Accounting.
Elizabeth Yobaccio, D.B.A., Boston University. Accounting.

CASE WESTERN RESERVE UNIVERSITY

Weatherhead School of Management

Programs of Study

The Weatherhead School of Management, which has been nationally recognized for innovation and excellence, offers a different philosophy and approach to M.B.A. education. The Management Assessment and Development Course, taken throughout the curriculum, helps students to evaluate their current management skills and knowledge and to develop an individualized learning plan. Business executives assist students in defining their career objectives through the Mentor Program. The Perspectives Courses encourage a liberalizing approach to problem solving and decision making. Students select six or more advanced elective courses (more than 120 are available) to develop breadth and depth within the management disciplines. Approximately 35 percent of these courses require field projects in area companies. A unifying theme, "creating economic, human, and intellectual value in organizations and society," permeates every course in the program. Weatherhead offers the M.B.A. in several formats. The two-year, 64-hour M.B.A. curriculum is directed at students from diverse undergraduate disciplines. The accelerated 48-hour M.B.A. curriculum is completed in eleven months, beginning in June, and is designed for students with recent undergraduate business degrees (although preference is given to applicants with work experience). Part-time (evening) M.B.A. students may pursue either option and can complete the program in three to four years. The Executive M.B.A. Program is a two-year, 45-hour program designed to prepare experienced managers for top-level management by providing them with a thorough grounding in analytical and decision-making frameworks. Weatherhead also offers the Master of Accountancy (M.Acct.), Master of Science in Management Science (M.S.M.S.), Master of Science in Organization Development and Analysis (M.S.O.D.A.), and a Master of Science in Management Information Systems. The Weatherhead School has joined with the American Graduate School of International Management (Thunderbird) to offer a joint M.B.A./Master of International Management degree program. The School also offers joint degree programs leading to the J.D./M.B.A., M.S.M.S./M.B.A., Master of Science in Nursing (M.S.N.)/M.B.A., and M.B.A./Master of Science in Management Information Systems, as well as Ph.D. programs in management, operations research, and organizational behavior. The Ph.D. programs, which generally require three to four years of study beyond the bachelor's degree, prepare students for careers as teachers, researchers, administrators, and managers in business and government.

Research Facilities

Resources include the Kelvin Smith Library, which provides access to one of the largest collections of electronic information in academic libraries in the world, and CWRUNET, the fiber-optic campus network. Many Weatherhead-affiliated centers and groups provide resources for applied research, field projects, and independent study as well as sources for information in cooperation with local business, industrial, and professional groups.

Financial Aid

Approximately 70 percent of Weatherhead M.B.A. students receive some form of financial aid. Options include scholarships (35 percent of full-time M.B.A. students receive these awards), minority scholarships and fellowships (10 percent), and need-based loans (70 percent). The Tuition Stabilization Plan allows students to borrow complete tuition costs from CWRU and repay them over five years.

Cost of Study

The 1997–98 tuition for Weatherhead School of Management was $838 per credit hour or $10,050 per semester for 12 or more hours. Tuition covers instructional costs and computer charges. Costs for books and supplies average $750 a year.

Living and Housing Costs

Room, board, and personal expenses are estimated at $9970 for the fall 1998 and spring 1999 semesters ($12,185 for the fall, spring, and summer semesters). A graduate single dormitory room at CWRU is $1850 a semester; the food plan is $945 a semester. Most Weatherhead students prefer apartment living, often in Cleveland Heights, a residential suburb within walking distance of the campus. The CWRU Off-Campus Housing Bureau maintains an extensive listing of apartments, rooms, and houses for sale or rent in the area.

Student Group

Weatherhead enrolls approximately 250 full-time, 690 part-time, and 80 executive M.B.A. students; 200 in other master's degree programs; and 100 in doctoral programs. The incoming class of full-time M.B.A. students typically consists of 32 percent women, 40 percent international students, and 10 percent U.S. members of minority groups. About 20 percent are business majors, 30 percent humanities and social sciences majors, and 28 percent engineering, math, and science majors. The average age is 28, and more than 80 percent have full-time work experience.

Student Outcomes

In 1997, 90 percent of the full-time M.B.A. graduates had job offers by commencement. Those that did averaged 2.3 offers each. The concentrations in most demand were marketing management, banking and finance, consulting, management information and decisions systems, and health systems management. Placement by industry was distributed approximately as follows: banking/finance, 23 percent; consulting, 38 percent; manufacturing, 24 percent; consumer products, 7 percent; other areas (including communications and health care), 8 percent.

Location

Cleveland is a preeminent center for academic and professional activity in the health-care industry, business, law, and social services. The city combines metropolitan life with comfortable suburban living. The CWRU campus is located 4 miles east of downtown Cleveland in University Circle, a 500-acre park-like area that contains the nation's largest concentration of cultural, educational, medical, religious, and social institutions.

The University and The School

Case Western Reserve University was created in 1967 through the federation of Western Reserve University (1826) and Case Institute of Technology (1880). Weatherhead, accredited by AACSB–The International Association for Management Education since 1958, is one of the University's six professional schools. Total CWRU enrollment is more than 9,900, with approximately 3,800 undergraduate and 6,100 graduate and professional students.

Applying

Applicants to the M.B.A., M.Acct., M.S. in Management Information Systems, and Ph.D. programs must submit GMAT results. Interviews are recommended for full-time M.B.A. program applicants. The application deadline is April 15 for both the 64-hour M.B.A. program and April 15 for the 48-hour program. Notification is done on a rolling basis. Application deadlines for the part-time (evening) M.B.A. program are set approximately six weeks in advance of the term.

Correspondence and Information

For the M.B.A. program:
M.B.A. Admissions Office
Weatherhead School of Management
Case Western Reserve University
Cleveland, Ohio 44106-7235
Telephone: 216-368-2030
800-723-0203 (toll-free)

For the Executive M.B.A. Program:
E.M.B.A. Program
Weatherhead School of Management
Case Western Reserve University
Cleveland, Ohio 44106-7166
Telephone: 216-368-2042

For all other programs:
Office of Graduate Studies—Admission
Case Western Reserve University
Cleveland, Ohio 44106-7027
Telephone: 216-368-4390

Case Western Reserve University

THE FACULTY

Jonlee Andrews, Assistant Professor of Marketing; Ph.D., Wisconsin–Madison. John D. Aram, Professor of Management Policy and Director, Executive Doctorate in Management Program; Ph.D., MIT. Darlyne Bailey, Associate Professor and Dean, Mandel School of Applied Social Sciences and Associate Professor of Organizational Behavior; Ph.D., Case Western Reserve. Robert N. Baird, Associate Professor of Economics; Ph.D., Kentucky. Ronald H. Ballou, Professor of Operations and Logistics Management; Ph.D., Ohio State. Diana Bilimoria, Associate Professor of Organizational Behavior; Ph.D., Michigan. William T. Bogart, Associate Professor of Economics; Ph.D., Princeton. Richard J. Boland Jr., Professor of Information Systems and of Accountancy and Chairman, Information Systems Department; Ph.D., Case Western Reserve. David A. Bowers, Professor of Banking and Finance and Chairman, Banking and Finance Department; Ph.D., SMU. Richard E. Boyatzis, Professor of Organizational Behavior; Chairman, Organizational Behavior Department; and Associate Dean for Executive Education; Ph.D., Harvard. Hilary Bradbury, Instructor of Organizational Behavior; Ph.D. candidate, Boston College. Robert J. Bricker, Associate Professor of Accountancy; Ph.D., Case Western Reserve. Anne M. Brumbaugh, Assistant Professor of Marketing; Ph.D., Duke. Apostolos N. Burnetas, Assistant Professor of Operations Research; Ph.D., Rutgers. David R. Campbell, Professor of Accountancy and Chairman, Accountancy Department; Ph.D., Georgia. Bo A. V. Carlsson, William E. Umstattd Professor of Industrial Economics and Associate Dean for Research and Graduate Programs; Ph.D., Stanford. Susan S. Case, Associate Professor of Organizational Behavior; Ph.D., SUNY at Buffalo. Sayan Chatterjee, Associate Professor of Management Policy; Ph.D., Michigan. Theodore E. Christensen, Assistant Professor of Accountancy; Ph.D., Georgia. Fred Collopy, Associate Professor of Information Systems; Ph.D., Pennsylvania. David L. Cooperrider, Associate Professor of Organizational Behavior; Ph.D., Case Western Reserve. Stanton G. Cort, Associate Professor of Marketing; D.B.A., Harvard. Scott S. Cowen, Professor of Accountancy and Albert J. Weatherhead III Professor and Dean of Management; D.B.A., George Washington. Eileen M. Doherty, Assistant Professor of Political Science, College of Arts and Sciences and of Marketing and Policy Studies; Ph.D., Berkeley. Avi Dor, Associate Professor of Economics and John R. Mannix Blue Cross and Blue Shield Associate Professor of Health Care Economics; Ph.D., CUNY Graduate Center. Vanessa Urch Druskat, Assistant Professor of Organizational Behavior; Ph.D., Boston. Robin A. Dubin, Associate Professor of Economics; Ph.D., Johns Hopkins. Hamilton Emmons, Professor of Operations Research and Chairman, Operations Research and Operations Management Department; Ph.D., Johns Hopkins. Asim Erdilek, Professor of Economics; Ph.D., Harvard. Steven P. Feldman, Associate Professor of Management Policy; Ph.D., Pennsylvania. A. Dale Flowers, Associate Professor of Operations Management; D.B.A., Indiana. Michael S. Fogarty, Professor of Economics, Ameritech Professor of Regional Economics, and Director, Center for Regional Economic Issues; Ph.D., Pittsburgh. Timothy J. Fogarty, Associate Professor of Accountancy; Ph.D., Penn State; J.D., SUNY at Buffalo. Ronald E. Fry, Associate Professor of Organizational Behavior and Director, Executive M.B.A. Program; Ph.D., MIT. Paul F. Gerhart, Professor of Labor and Human Resource Policy; Ph.D., Chicago. Stephen M. Gilbert, Associate Professor of Operations Management; Ph.D., MIT. Michael J. Ginzberg, Professor of Information Systems and Associate Dean for Professional and International Programs; Ph.D., MIT. Paul D. Gottlieb, Assistant Director, Center for Regional Economic Issues; Ph.D., Princeton. Julia E. S. Grant, Associate Professor of Accountancy; Ph.D., Cornell. Amresh D. Hanchate, Assistant Professor of Economics; Ph.D., Wisconsin–Madison. Susan R. Helper, Associate Professor of Economics; Ph.D., Harvard. Robert D. Hisrich, A. Malachi Mixon III Professor of Entrepreneurial Studies; Ph.D., Cincinnati. Ha Thi Hoang, Assistant Professor of Management Policy and Lewis-Progressive Assistant Professor of Management; Ph.D., Berkeley. Robert T. Kauer, Director, Information Technology and Strategic Planning, and Senior Lecturer of Banking and Finance; Ph.D., Case Western Reserve. Miles Kennedy, Associate Professor of Information Systems; Ph.D., London. David A. Kolb, Professor of Organizational Behavior; Ph.D., Harvard. Roberta E. Lamb, Assistant Professor of Information Systems; Ph.D., California, Irvine. Paul A. Laux, Associate Professor of Banking and Finance and Chair, M.B.A. Program; Ph.D., Vanderbilt. Inmoo Lee, Assistant Professor of Banking and Finance; Ph.D., Illinois at Urbana-Champaign. Laura B. Leete, Assistant Professor of Economics; Ph.D., Harvard. Bing Liang, Assistant Professor of Banking and Finance; Ph.D., Iowa. Christopher Lingle, Visiting Assistant Professor of Economics; Ph.D., Georgia. Thomas E. Love, Assistant Professor of Operations Research; Ph.D., Pennsylvania. James D. Ludema, Lecturer of Organizational Behavior and Executive Director, SIGMA Program; Ph.D., Case Western Reserve. Leonard H. Lynn, Professor of Management Policy and Chair, Marketing and Policy Studies Department; Ph.D., Michigan. Kamlesh Mathur, Associate Professor of Operations Research; Ph.D., Case Western Reserve. Poppy L. McLeod, Associate Professor of Organizational Behavior; Ph.D., Harvard. Andrew Morriss, Associate Professor of Economics and Associate Professor, School of Law; Ph.D., MIT. Thomas F. Morrissey, Professor of Banking and Finance; Ph.D., Syracuse. Ashok Mukherjee, Visiting Assistant Professor of Operations Management; Ph.D., Michigan. John P. Murry Jr., Assistant Professor of Marketing; Ph.D., Kansas. Ranga Narayanan, Assistant Professor of Banking and Finance; Ph.D., NYU. Eric H. Neilsen, Professor of Organizational Behavior and Director, MSODA Program; Ph.D., Harvard. Duncan vB. Neuhauser, Professor of Epidemiology and Biostatistics, School of Medicine, and of Organizational Behavior and Co-Director, Health Systems Management Center; Ph.D., Chicago. Richard L. Osborne, Professor for the Practice of Management and Director, George S. Dively Center for Management Development; M.S., Case Western Reserve. Larry M. Parker, Associate Professor of Accountancy and Director, Master of Accountancy Program; Ph.D., Houston. Richard J. Parkin, Assistant Professor of Economics; Ph.D., Cambridge. William S. Peirce, Professor of Economics and Chairman, Economics Department; Ph.D., Princeton. Sandy Kristin Piderit, Instructor of Organizational Behavior; B.A., Case Western Reserve; Ph.D. candidate, Michigan. Ernesto J. Poza, Professor for the Practice of Family Business and Associate Director, Partnership with Family Business; M.B.A., MIT. Gil Amitai Preuss, Assistant Professor of Labor and Human Resource Policy; Ph.D., MIT. Gary J. Previts, Professor of Accountancy and Associate Dean for Undergraduate Programs; Ph.D., Florida. Vaughan S. Radcliffe, Assistant Professor of Accountancy; Ph.D., Alberta (Canada). Vasudevan Ramanujam, Associate Professor of Management Policy; Ph.D., Pittsburgh. James B. Rebitzer, Frank Tracy Carlton Associate Professor of Economics; Ph.D., Massachusetts Amherst. N. Mohan Reddy, Associate Professor of Marketing and Nancy and Joseph Keithley Professor of Technology Management; Ph.D., Case Western Reserve. Kenneth S. Rhee, Lecturer of Organizational Behavior; Ph.D., Case Western Reserve. Peter H. Ritchken, Professor of Operations Research and of Banking and Finance; Ph.D., Case Western Reserve. Paul F. Salipante Jr., Professor of Labor and Human Resource Policy; Ph.D., Chicago. Harvey M. Salkin, Professor of Operations Research; Ph.D., Rensselaer. Richard A. Shatten, Professor for the Practice of Public Policy and Management and Interim Director, Center for Regional Economic Issues; M.B.A., Harvard. Ajai K. Singh, Visiting Associate Professor of Banking and Finance; Ph.D., Iowa. Gangaram Singh, Visiting Instructor of Labor and Human Resource Policy; M.B.A., MIR (Toronto). Jagdip Singh, Professor of Marketing; Ph.D., Texas Tech. Deepak Sirdeshmukh, Assistant Professor of Marketing; Ph.D., Ohio State. John Palmer Smith, Professor for the Practice of Nonprofit Management and Director, Mandel Center for Nonprofit Organizations; Ph.D., Columbia. Daniel Solow, Associate Professor of Operations Research; Ph.D., Stanford. Suresh Srivastva, Professor of Organizational Behavior; Ph.D., Michigan. Stephanie Watts Sussman, Instructor of Information Systems; Ph.D. candidate, Boston. Sam Thomas, Assistant Professor of Banking and Finance; Ph.D., Pennsylvania. George Vairaktarakis, Assistant Professor of Operations Management; Ph.D., Florida. Betty Vandenbosch, Assistant Professor of Information Systems; Ph.D., Western Ontario. Wendy E. Wagner, Associate Professor, School of Law, and of Marketing and Policy Studies; Ph.D., Western Ontario. Peter J. Whitehouse, Professor of Neurology, School of Medicine, and of Organizational Behavior; M.D., Ph.D., Johns Hopkins. Donald M. Wolfe, Professor of Organizational Behavior; Ph.D., Michigan. Margaret J. Wyszomirski, Professor of Political Science, College of Arts and Sciences, and Director, Arts Management Program; Ph.D., Cornell. Youngjin Yoo, Assistant Professor of Information Systems; Ph.D., Maryland College Park. Dennis R. Young, Professor, Mandel School of Applied Social Sciences, and of Economics; Ph.D., Stanford.

CLAREMONT GRADUATE UNIVERSITY

Peter F. Drucker Graduate School of Management

Programs of Study

At the Peter F. Drucker Graduate Management School, students develop mastery in applying integrative general management skills to capitalize on the challenges that face practicing executives. The School's mission is to study strategically important managerial issues and advance the theory and practice of management through teaching and field-based research that contribute to the betterment of society. This mission influences all aspects of the quantitatively and qualitatively balanced curriculum. The School's emphasis stresses the strategic dimension of each functional area and the role of executive leadership in outstanding organizational performance.

The two programs of the Peter F. Drucker Graduate Management School are differentiated by managerial experience. The Early Career Management Program is geared toward those in the first decade of their careers and offers the Drucker M.B.A., the 4+1 accelerated B.A./M.B.A., an M.S. in financial engineering, and an International Fellows Certificate Program in advanced English and cultural proficiency for management. The Executive Management Program is designed for the seasoned executive and offers M.A., Executive M.B.A., M.S. in advanced management, and Ph.D. degrees and certificates in strategy, leadership, and executive management.

The largest program of study at the Drucker School is the Drucker M.B.A. This world-class management program delivers marketable knowledge that goes beyond theory to enable early career students to assume leadership roles and execute strategic solutions to today's toughest business challenges. Through mentoring, workshops, and academic studies, students create a vision of leadership and obtain integrative strategic insight on an exceptional foundation of theoretical and practical know-how, skills, and tools. The Drucker M.B.A. includes "Drucker Signature Courses" in integrative leadership, strategy, and ethics and foundation courses in marketing, organizational behavior, finance, information management, operations, and managerial economics. In the early career program, concentrations are available in strategic management, marketing, and finance. In executive management, the curriculum delivers the most current thinking in critical areas of leadership, strategy, management of new ventures, technology, and international competitiveness.

The Claremont Colleges offer a variety of interdisciplinary programs and support customized business degrees in financial engineering, information sciences, human resources design, organizational design, management control systems, and many other specialties. Within these concentrations, students may choose to pursue a corporate, entrepreneurial, or not-for-profit track. In addition, students may pursue dual-degree options to combine early career management degrees with other Claremont Graduate University (CGU) master's and doctoral degree programs.

The Drucker School is accredited by AACSB–The International Association for Management Education, and Claremont Graduate University is accredited by the Western Association of Schools and Colleges (WASC).

Research Facilities

With the progressive curriculum, students have the opportunity to launch and manage strategic initiatives; participate in corporate, entrepreneurial, and not-for-profit practica; and conduct field studies. Resources available to students include the Claremont Colleges' state-of-the-art intercollegiate facilities, computer hardware and software, a 2-million-volume library system, and an exceptional senior faculty.

Financial Aid

A number of fellowships and assistantships are offered to Drucker M.B.A. students on the basis of merit and need. Loans and work-study opportunities are also available.

Cost of Study

Tuition for full-time students averages $20,250 for the 1998–99 academic year. For those who choose to take one or two courses per semester, the charge per unit is $913 for the Drucker M.B.A., 4+1 B.A./M.B.A., M.S. in financial engineering, and other early career programs and $1,020 for the executive programs.

Living and Housing Costs

The Claremont Graduate University operates residence halls that accommodate single students, couples, and couples with children. On-campus housing rents range from about $620 per month for single rooms to about $700 per month for two-bedroom apartments. Convenient off-campus housing is also available at varying prices. Further information on housing may be obtained from the Housing Office.

Student Group

The 425 students enrolled in the Drucker School are a diverse group selected for their strategic leadership potential, unique vision, and critical insight. Like today's workforce, they are a mix of nationalities and full- and part-timers. The full-time students support the social and intellectual functions of the residential campus, while the part-time (actively employed) students bring professionalism and real-world executive and professional challenges to the classroom. The majority of students complete several years of full-time work before entering the program, further encouraging relevant and insightful classroom discussion. Students come from across the United States and the continents, with a significant international group offering distinctive perspectives on strategic leadership challenges around the world. About 40 percent of the students are women. As suits future leaders, students create and run their own campus organizations. The Graduate Management Student Association, the International Business Association, the American Marketing Association, and the Finance Association provide additional activities for students.

Location

Claremont Graduate University is in Claremont, a peaceful residential community of 34,000 located 35 miles east of Los Angeles in southern California, close to skiing, the beach, the desert, and other recreational areas. This safe and pleasant college town is situated at an elevation of 1,150 feet in the foothills of the San Gabriel Mountains. Claremont is an attractive city with 225 acres of parks and tree-lined streets. The climate is sunny and warm most of the year.

The University

Founded in 1925, Claremont Graduate University is affiliated with a group of five prestigious undergraduate colleges (Pomona, Scripps, Claremont McKenna, Harvey Mudd, and Pitzer), which together form the Claremont Colleges. Their association is based on the Oxford Model, combining the strengths of a small college with those of a university. The small-college atmosphere at CGU offers the students closer relationships with faculty members and greater opportunities for individual development. At the same time, CGU cooperates with the other colleges to provide many facilities and services characteristic of a university. In keeping with the tradition of academic excellence at the Claremont Colleges, CGU offers both traditional academic curricula and professional programs with an interdisciplinary emphasis. It awards both master's and doctoral degrees. Enrollment is approximately 1,600, and the regular CGU faculty of more than 70 appointees is supplemented by approximately 200 faculty members from the undergraduate colleges in Claremont and other institutions.

Applying

Applications are accepted in the fall, spring, and summer semesters year-round. For the early career programs, applicants should submit a completed application form; transcripts of all college-level work, showing strong performance in support of a bachelor's degree; compelling GMAT scores (and TOEFL scores for international students); three or more letters of recommendation; a current resume; and a statement of purpose. Applications for fall fellowships need to be submitted by February 15. For the executive program, multiple entry points and application criteria apply. Interested executives may contact the Office of Educational Counseling and Recruiting.

Correspondence and Information

Office of Educational Counseling and Recruiting
Peter F. Drucker School of Graduate Management
Claremont Graduate University
1021 North Dartmouth Avenue
Claremont, California 91711-6184

Telephone: 909-607-7811
800-944-4312 (toll-free)
Fax: 909-607-9104
E-mail: mba@cgu.edu
emp@cgu.edu

Claremont Graduate University

THE FACULTY

The Drucker School is distinguished by academic rigor, exceptional teaching, personalized support, and monumental alumni success. The world-renowned management faculty is widely noted for its commitment to students, relevant research, global consulting, and top rankings in graduate business school reviews.

Dale E. Berger, Ph.D., UCLA.
Robin Cooper, D.B.A., Harvard.
Peter F. Drucker, Dr.Jur., Frankfurt.
Peter H. Farquhar, Ph.D., Cornell.
Paul Gray, Ph.D., Stanford.
Donald W. Griesinger, Ph.D., California, Santa Barbara.
Jean Lipman-Blumen, Ph.D., Harvard.
Joseph A. Maciariello, Ph.D., NYU.
M. Lynne Markus, Ph.D., Case Western Reserve.
Morcos F. Massoud, Ph.D., NYU.
James H. Myers, Ph.D., USC.
Kathy Pezdek, Ph.D., Massachusetts Amherst.
Vijay Sathe, Ph.D., Ohio State.
Richard L. Smith, Ph.D., UCLA.

Associate Professor

Richard R. Ellsworth, D.B.A., Harvard.

Visiting and Adjunct Professors

Nahum Biger, Ph.D., York.
Gary R. Evans, Ph.D., California, Riverside.
LeRoy Gilbertson, M.P.H., North Dakota.
Lady Hanson, Ph.D., Claremont.
Forrest E. Harding, Ph.D., Arizona State.
Richard Henage, Ph.D., Utah.
Lissa Petersen, M.A., Harvard.
Jay Prag, Ph.D., Rochester.
William Relf, Ph.D., Claremont.
Robert Sweitzer, Ph.D., Michigan State.

The Ron W. Burkle Family Building, the new home of the Peter F. Drucker Graduate School of Managament.

CLARKSON UNIVERSITY

School of Business

Programs of Study

Clarkson University, a leading professional and technical institution, offers graduate education leading to the Master of Business Administration (M.B.A.) and the Master of Science in Management Systems (M.S.M.S.). All programs are accredited by the American Assembly of Collegiate Schools of Business.

The M.B.A. program consists of foundation courses in nine areas and 32 credit hours of advanced graduate work. The foundation includes courses from computer and information systems, corporate finance, financial and managerial accounting, business law, organizational behavior, marketing, microeconomics and macroeconomics, operations/production management, and statistics. Students may receive credit for equivalent courses completed as undergraduates. Beyond the foundation, the M.B.A. program includes a 20-credit-hour integrated core and 12 credit hours of electives. The core consists of ten 2-credit interrelated modules that build upon one another to provide students with an integrated view of management. The core modules stress business functions and develop communication, interpersonal, technical, and management skills. Elective courses are available in accounting, economics, finance, human resource management, management information systems, marketing, and manufacturing management. All M.B.A. students participate in a leadership development program designed to assess and strengthen managerial skills. The School of Business provides opportunities for students to participate in consulting services, international programs, and/or corporate-sponsored partnership programs.

The M.S. in Management Systems is for students who desire specialized study in a particular field such as human resource management, manufacturing management, marketing, or management information systems. In addition to these specializations, students may design individualized programs to meet their personal career objectives. The foundation for the M.S.M.S. program includes a minimum of 24 credit hours of course work in the areas of accounting, computer information systems, economics, finance, marketing, organizational behavior, production, and statistics. Students may receive credit for equivalent courses completed as undergraduates. Beyond the foundation, the M.S.M.S. program consists of 30 credit hours. A special project/thesis and a course in strategic management and business environments are required.

The M.S.M.S. concentration in human resource management is designed for those interested in the strategic application of scientific principles and methods to the management and development of work behavior and performance. Course work includes the study of design and change, labor relations, organizational behavior, stress management, and training and development.

The M.S.M.S. concentration in marketing prepares managers who not only embrace customer orientation but make a commitment to customer satisfaction. Topics include marketing research, promotions and advertising, channel policy and management, and new product management.

The M.S.M.S. concentration in manufacturing management is designed for those who desire specialized study in the management of manufacturing and production systems. Course work includes the study of computer-integrated manufacturing, design of experiments, engineering economics and decision analysis, industrial and labor relations, management of technology, manufacturing planning and control, strategic operations management, systems control, and other related subjects.

The M.S.M.S. concentration in management information systems integrates the body of knowledge and skills in management with computer technology. Course work includes the study of analysis and design of computer-based information systems, database organization, development of decision support and expert systems, human factors in computing systems, structural analysis and design of software systems, and other related subjects.

The M.B.A. and M.S.M.S. can be earned through part-time studies.

Research Facilities

The School of Business provides a 30-seat graduate computer laboratory with full network/Internet support and printing capability. There is also a 16-seat Pentium multimedia laboratory/classroom available. Publishing capability exists in the School's desktop publishing lab, which has color scanning and printing devices. All School of Business computers are linked to the campuswide network for connection to all or any of the Novell, Microsoft, or UNIX servers as well as the Internet. There is also an IBM RS/6000 lab in the School of Business.

Financial Aid

Tuition assistantships are offered on a competitive basis, and approximately 75 percent of students receive partial or full tuition remission. Student Administrative Services helps candidates secure loans. International students must secure a guarantee of adequate financial support before arrival in Potsdam.

Cost of Study

Tuition for 1998–99 is $636 per credit. M.B.A. students who enroll in 32 credits per year are assessed $20,352 in tuition. M.S.M.S. students are assessed $19,080. Fees are $175, and books cost about $1100.

Living and Housing Costs

Living costs for one year of study are estimated at $6400, excluding tuition, but may be 20 percent more or less, depending on the choice of housing and on miscellaneous expenses.

Student Group

Current enrollment at Clarkson is about 2,200 at the undergraduate level and 400 at the graduate level. Graduate enrollment in the School of Business is 130, of whom 80 are full-time students.

Student Outcomes

Clarkson M.B.A./M.S. graduates enjoy favorable placement opportunities. Typically, more than 80 percent of the most recent graduates are employed in their chosen fields within three months of graduation. The most common job titles include consultant, analyst, system specialist, sales associate, supervisor, and manager. In addition to traditional on-campus recruiting, Clarkson M.B.A./M.S. graduates utilize an extensive alumni referral directory, specialized job placement workshops, and the Graduate Career Service.

Location

Potsdam is bounded on the northwest by the St. Lawrence River and on the southeast by Adirondack State Park. Skiing (downhill and cross-country), ice-skating, ice hockey, snowshoeing, hiking, canoeing, hunting, and fishing are some of the popular outdoor activities. In addition to the students at Clarkson University, about 3,200 students are enrolled at the State University of New York College at Potsdam. Ottawa and Montreal are both within two hours by car.

The University

Clarkson University was founded in 1896. About 60 percent of its student population is enrolled in the School of Engineering, and the remaining 40 percent is almost equally divided between the School of Science and the School of Business. The University's faculty of nearly 200 members promotes technical and professional competence, but also recognizes the need for an adequate liberal arts background.

Applying

Admission to the M.B.A. and M.S.M.S. programs is open to qualified students with a baccalaureate degree. The GMAT is required and should be taken as early as possible. Completed applications, transcripts, test scores, and references are reviewed after October 1 for January admission or after February 15 for summer or September admission. No deadlines are set, but early applicants are given preference. Applicants from non-English-speaking countries must submit scores on the TOEFL and a score from the Test of Spoken English (TSE).

Correspondence and Information

Director of Graduate Business Programs
School of Business
Clarkson University
Potsdam, New York 13699-5770

Telephone: 315-268-6613
Fax: 315-268-3810
E-mail: gradprog@icarus.som.clarkson.edu

Clarkson University

THE FACULTY AND THEIR RESEARCH

Jeffrey J. Archambault, Assistant Professor; Ph.D., Michigan State, 1992. Financial and managerial accounting.
Marie E. Archambault, Assistant Professor; Ph.D., Michigan State, 1992. Financial and managerial accounting.
H. Sonmez Atesoglu, Professor; Ph.D., Pittsburgh, 1972. Economics, monetary theory.
Michael R. W. Bommer, Professor; Ph.D., Pennsylvania, 1971. Management science, statistics.
Ronald W. Chorba, Associate Professor; Ph.D., Arizona, 1971. Management science, information systems.
Larry D. Compeau, Associate Professor; Ph.D., Virginia Tech, 1991. Marketing, statistics.
Mark Cornett, Instructor; M.B.A., Northeastern, 1988. Marketing.
Jefferson T. Davis, Assistant Professor; Ph.D., Tennessee, Knoxville, 1992. Accounting.
Vitaly J. Dubrovsky, Associate Professor; Ph.D., Moscow, 1972. Engineering psychology.
Michael Ensby, Instructor of Organization Studies; M.A., Webster, 1989; M.S., Clarkson, 1996.
Steven M. Farmer, Assistant Professor; Ph.D., Georgia Tech, 1993. Organizational behavior.
Mark R. Frascatore, Assistant Professor; Ph.D., Virginia Tech, 1994. Economics.
Ralph E. Janaro, Associate Professor; D.B.A., Florida State, 1982. Management science, computer science.
Eugene E. Kaczka, Professor; Ph.D., RPI, 1966. Management science, statistics.
John MacDonald, Assistant Professor; Ph.D., Virginia Tech, 1987. Finance.
Farzad Mahmoodi, Associate Professor; Ph.D., Michigan, 1989. Management.
Sanjay Menon, Assistant Professor; Ph.D., McGill, 1995. Organizational behavior.
Fredric Menz, Professor; Ph.D., Virginia, 1970. Environmental economics.
Charles T. Mosier, Professor; Ph.D., North Carolina at Chapel Hill, 1983. Operations management, statistics.
Kankana Mukherjee, Assistant Professor; Ph.D., Connecticut, 1997. Macroeconomics, banking.
John K. Mullen, Professor; Ph.D., SUNY at Binghamton, 1977. Economics, public finance.
Carolyn Y. Nicholson, Assistant Professor; Ph.D., Virginia Tech, 1993. Marketing communications.
Brian F. O'Neil, Professor; Ph.D., Purdue, 1971. Operations management, business logistics, operations research, quantitative methods.
Somendra Pant, Assistant Professor; Ph.D., Rensselaer, 1997. Management information systems.
Victor P. Pease, Professor and Dean; Ph.D., Arizona, 1970. Experimental-physiological psychology.
Rajesh Sethi, Assistant Professor; Ph.D., Pittsburgh, 1995. Marketing.
Gary Throop, Assistant Professor; Ph.D., Massachusetts at Amherst, 1993. Policy and strategic management.
Jon R. Vilasuso, Assistant Professor; Ph.D., Connecticut, 1994. Economics and finance.

The small size of the M.B.A. and M.S. programs enables students to have extensive personal attention and interaction with faculty.

M.B.A. students provide services to U.S. and Canadian businesses through participation in a consulting group which, along with Clarkson's Center for U.S.-Canadian Business Studies, adds an international dimension to the program.

CLARK UNIVERSITY

Graduate School of Management

Programs of Study

Clark University offers high-quality education to those interested in deepening their understanding of the corporate world and sharpening their expertise to become highly effective managers of people and resources.

To prepare leaders to meet the demands of the twenty-first century, Clark's Graduate School of Management encourages a global perspective. Both curriculum and faculty develop students to be insightful managers who understand the economic, technological, and political changes that are shaping the world's business communities. The program prepares managers not only to balance the complex and often conflicting demands of a changing work force but also to respond to a new mix of national and international competitors.

The Graduate School of Management offers an environment that features small classes, easy access to the faculty, and the stimulation that comes from exposure to a wide range of students from many different professional settings and levels of management experience.

The Graduate School of Management offers a Master of Business Administration (M.B.A.) and a Master of Science in Finance (M.S.F.). The M.B.A. is nationally accredited by AACSB–The International Association for Management Education. In the New Ventures Seminar, key regional entrepreneurs share their experiences with M.B.A. students. The M.S.F. program requires twenty courses, four of which are electives.

Through the Graduate School of Management's Business Development Center, located on campus, students and businesspeople extend their knowledge and skills in managing new businesses.

To accomodate the students' schedules, courses and seminars are held during the morning, afternoon, and evening. Evening classes are held in two locations, Worcester and Westboro.

Research Facilities

Personal computers, available exclusively for use by management students, are located in the MIS Laboratory in the Graduate School of Management. The Robert Hutchings Goddard Library houses 600,000 volumes as well as the Morton and Vivien Sigel Machine Readable Management Database in CD-ROM format. Extensive research facilities are also available through the ten other local colleges and universities.

Financial Aid

Graduate assistantships or scholarships are awarded to approximately one half of the entering full-time class. Graduate assistantships require research, teaching, or administrative duties in exchange for tuition remission. Both scholarship and assistantship awards are based on merit.

Cost of Study

For the 1998–99 academic year, graduate tuition is $1925 per course. Other charges are a $40 nonrefundable application fee, a $35 diploma fee, and an annual $50 student activities fee.

Living and Housing Costs

A limited number of University-owned apartments are available to graduate students through the Office of Housing and Residential Programs. Off-campus apartments are available in the immediate area at a cost of approximately $300 per person per month.

Student Group

The University has approximately 2,000 undergraduate and 700 graduate students. There are about 150 full-time and 250 part-time students enrolled in the M.B.A. program.

Student Outcomes

The class of 1997 found employment in the following functional areas: accounting (14 percent); advertising, marketing, and sales (21 percent); financial analysis and investments (19 percent); information systems (10 percent); management consulting and training (20 percent); human resources management (8 percent); and others (8 percent). Employers of program graduates include Allmerica Financial; Paine Webber, Inc.; Dun & Bradstreet Software; Fidelity Investments; Digital Equipment Corporation; and Bose Corporation.

Location

Worcester is the second-largest city in New England. It is located in central Massachusetts, New England's high-technology area, within an hour's drive of Boston and near the region's numerous recreational attractions. The city has diversified industry and is distinguished as an educational center. The ten institutions of higher education in the Worcester area, which have more than 15,000 students enrolled, have formed the Worcester Consortium for Higher Education. Students meet with area chief executive officers and senior executives through a variety of special programs.

The University and The School

Clark University is an urban, independent university that was founded in 1887 as a graduate institution. By design, the University has remained small in order to offer its students the educational experience of close personal relationships among the faculty members and students.

Applying

All undergraduate majors are given equal weight in the admission decision. The application deadline for students wishing to enroll full-time is June 1 for the fall semester and November 1 for the spring semester. After those dates, students are accepted on a space-available basis. The priority scholarship deadline is March 1 for fall and September 1 for spring. The deadline for students wishing to enroll part-time is July 31 for the fall semester, December 15 for the spring semester, and April 30 for the summer semester. Admission to the M.B.A. program is based on prior academic performance (transcripts are required), GMAT scores, extracurricular work and/or work experience, and letters of recommendation. Students interested in the program should request an application packet. Those wishing to apply should complete the application form and return it with the $40 application fee. When all supporting documents have been received, the application is considered by the Admissions Committee, which meets monthly throughout the academic year.

Correspondence and Information

Admissions Director
Graduate School of Management
Clark University
950 Main Street
Worcester, Massachusetts 01610

Telephone: 508-793-7406
Fax: 508-793-8822
E-mail: clarkmba@vax.clarku.edu
World Wide Web: http://www.mba.clarku.edu

Clark University

THE FACULTY

Maurry Tamarkin, Dean of the Graduate School of Management and Professor of Finance; Ph.D., Washington (St. Louis), 1979.

Margarete Arndt, Associate Professor of Health Administration; D.B.A., Boston University, 1991.
Subramanian Balachander, Assistant Professor of Marketing; Ph.D., Carnegie Mellon, 1991.
Sarita Bhalotra, Affiliate Instructor; Ph.D., Brandeis, 1995.
Barbara Bigelow, Associate Professor of Management; Ph.D., MIT, 1987.
Rockie Blunt, Lecturer in Communications; M.A., Clark, 1974.
Robert C. Bradbury, Director of the MHA Program and Professor of Health Administration; Ph.D., Ohio State, 1975.
Gary N. Chaison, Professor of Industrial Relations; Ph.D., SUNY at Buffalo, 1972.
Edson D. de Castro, Lecturer in New Venture Management; B.S., Massachusetts at Lowell, 1960.
Christian J. Delaunay, Visiting Lecturer; Ph.D., South Carolina, 1989.
Joan Cole Densberger, Affiliate Assistant Professor; J.D., Boston College, 1986.
Dileep G. Dhavale, Associate Professor of Accounting; Ph.D., Penn State, 1975; CPA, CPIM.
N. Lynn Eckhert, Affiliate Professor of Health Care; D.P.H., Johns Hopkins, 1980.
Priscilla Elsass, Assistant Professor of Organizational Behavior; Ph.D., Connecticut, 1992.
John H. Friar, Visiting Assistant Professor of Marketing; Ph.D., MIT, 1987.
Donald E. Fries, Lecturer in Management; LL.M., Boston University, 1990.
Joseph H. Golec, Associate Professor of Finance; Ph.D., Washington (St. Louis), 1986.
Laura M. Graves, Assistant Professor of Management; Ph.D., Connecticut, 1982.
Murray Hershman, Lecturer in Taxation and Business Law; J.D., Thomas M. Cooley Law, 1978.
Jane A. Kapral, Visiting Instructor of Accounting; M.S., Massachusetts at Amherst, 1989; CPA.
Robert E. Maher Jr., Lecturer in Health Care; M.H.A., Saint Louis, 1975.
Thomas P. Millott, Lecturer in Business Law; J.D., Boston College, 1980.
Kenneth A. Mundt, Affiliate Assistant Professor; Ph.D., North Carolina at Chapel Hill, 1990.
John T. O'Connor, Affiliate Professor of Management; Ph.D., Notre Dame, 1970.
Edward J. Ottensmeyer, Associate Professor of Management; Ph.D., Indiana, 1983.
Charlotte A. Pryor, Assistant Professor of Accounting; Ph.D., Penn State, 1996.
Joseph Sarkis, Associate Professor of Operations Management; Ph.D., SUNY at Buffalo, 1992.
Pamela D. Sherer, Affiliate Assistant Professor of Management; Ph.D., Massachusetts at Amherst, 1986.
Richard B. Spurgin, Assistant Professor of Finance; Ph.D. candidate, Massachusetts Amherst.
R. P. Sundarraj, Assistant Professor of Management; Ph.D., Tennessee, 1990.
Robert A. Ullrich, Professor of Management; D.B.A., Washington (St. Louis), 1968.
Daniel A. Verreault, Assistant Professor of Accounting; Ph.D., Texas A&M, 1984; CPA.
Rudolph C. Yaksick, Visiting Instructor of Economics; Ph.D. candidate, Pennsylvania.

Professor Laura Graves meets with M.B.A. students on the Wetzel Terrace in the new Higgins University Center.

Professor Ed Ottensmeyer assists M.B.A. students with their management consulting project.

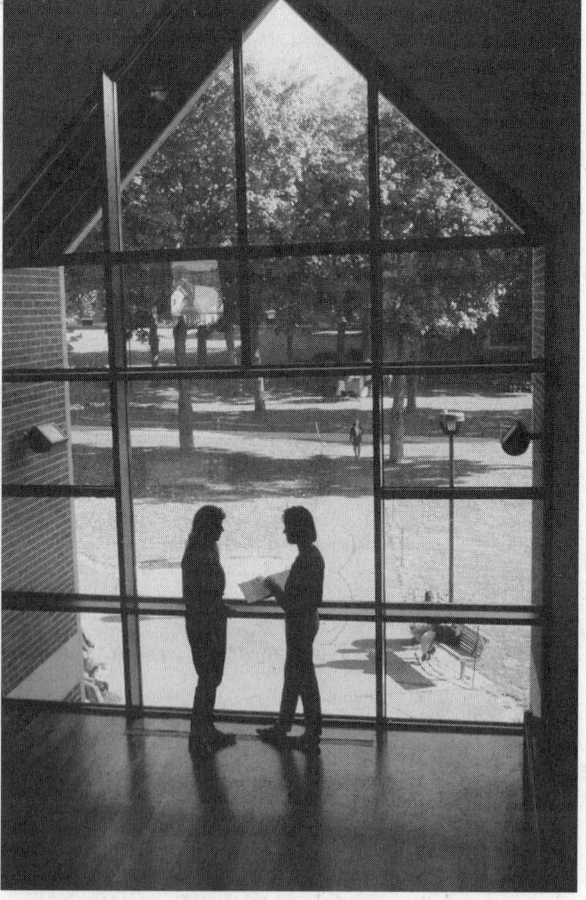

Clark University's tree-shaded campus is located in Worcester, New England's second-largest city and a center of high-technology, biotechnology, and financial services industries.

CLEMSON UNIVERSITY

College of Business and Public Affairs

Programs of Study

The College of Business and Public Affairs offers programs of study leading to the degree of Doctor of Philosophy (Ph.D.) in industrial management, applied economics, management science, and industrial/organizational psychology. In addition, the College offers the Master of Business Administration (M.B.A.); the Master of Arts (M.A.) in economics; the Master of Professional Accountancy (M.P.Acc.); the Master of Science (M.S.) in industrial management, applied psychology, and applied sociology; and the Master of Public Administration (M.P.A.). Graduate and undergraduate business programs are accredited by the AACSB–The International Association for Business Management.

The Ph.D. program in industrial management balances management theory, analytical techniques, and research methodology. The program develops a management scholar capable of applying the most advanced concepts and analytical methods to industrial management problems.

The Ph.D. program in management science targets individuals with a strong aptitude for qualitative analysis and a primary interest in scientific management research and practice. This degree is jointly offered by the College of Business and Public Affairs and the Department of Mathematical Sciences.

The Ph.D. program in industrial/organizational psychology and the M.S. program in applied psychology are designed to provide students with theoretical foundations, skills in quantitative techniques and research design, and practical problem-solving skills to address human problems related to work. The M.S. program offers concentrations in industrial/organizational psychology and human factors psychology.

The Master of Business Administration program enables individuals to study advanced concepts of business, industry, and government operations. The program targets active managers as well as recent graduates interested in advanced business studies. In addition to the full-time day program on the Clemson campus, two evening part-time programs are offered in Greenville and Greenwood, South Carolina. Also, a concentrated international program is offered in Asolo, Italy, and is intended for individuals interested in pursuing an M.B.A. degree in an international setting. Separate fee structures apply to the international program, the evening programs, and the Clemson campus.

The M.S. in industrial management (M.S.I.M.), taught in the evenings, focuses on management of operations and addresses systems, processes, and activities that produce the goods and services of an organization.

The Master of Public Administration (M.P.A.) examines historical developments in the field of public administration as well as current laws and practices as they relate to public policy, financial management, and government administration. This degree is jointly offered by the College of Business and Public Affairs and the Department of Government and International Relations at the University of South Carolina.

The M.S. in applied sociology emphasizes practical and theoretical knowledge in the areas of industrial and organizational sociology. The program focuses on the acquisition of social research skills, theory application, and practical field experience.

The Ph.D. in applied economics and the M.A. in economics focus on real-world problems and issues. Students can specialize in industrial organization or environmental, monetary, financial, public sector, or labor economics. Both programs require students to acquire technical research skills.

The M.P.Acc. program prepares students for professional accounting careers in the areas of industrial, commercial, governmental, financial, or public accounting. The program requires a minimum of 33 semester hours of graduate study. Undergraduate prerequisites are 18 credits of accounting and a 30-credit business core.

Research Facilities

All research facilities of the College are available to graduate students. These include access to the University's network of servers, mid-range, and mainframe computers, as well as Web access through multiple microcomputer laboratories. In addition, business classes frequently use in-class multimedia technologies. These capabilities offer exceptional opportunities to learn and experiment with some of the latest developments in computer technology. The main University library has approximately 1.6 million items.

Financial Aid

A number of assistantships and fellowships are available to entering graduate students. Stipends vary, depending on the type of aid and level of graduate work. Graduate assistants also receive special tuition rates.

Cost of Study

In-state graduate tuition for the 1997–98 academic year was $126 per semester hour. Out-of-state tuition was $252 per semester hour. For students enrolled in the M.B.A. program in Greenville, in-state tuition was $194 per semester hour, and out-of-state tuition was $388 per semester hour.

Living and Housing Costs

University dormitory rooms and apartments cost between $850 and $1350 per semester. Married student housing costs range from $320 to $400 per month. All meals are available from a variety of cafeterias on campus.

Student Group

There are approximately 16,500 students at the University, of whom 20 percent are graduate students. The College of Business and Public Affairs has a total enrollment of about 3,700 students, of whom 550 are graduate students.

Location

The town of Clemson, which has a population of 15,000, is a university and residential community with some industry in neighboring communities. The town and the University are on the shores of Lake Hartwell in the foothills of the Blue Ridge Mountains in western South Carolina. The climate is mild, with seasonal variation. Winter sports are enjoyed in the nearby mountains, even though Clemson is rarely inconvenienced by snow; summers are warm.

The University

Clemson is a land-grant university located on the plantation of John C. Calhoun, which was deeded to the state by his son-in-law, Thomas Clemson. The University has five colleges and offers seventy-three undergraduate and 109 graduate degree programs. The main campus is situated on a 1,400-acre site. In addition to its graduate programs, the College of Business and Public Affairs offers seven undergraduate degree programs in business.

Applying

All students applying for the M.S. in industrial management, the M.P.Acc., and the M.B.A. must submit adequate scores on the Graduate Management Admission Test. Students interested in any of the Ph.D. programs and the M.A. in economics program must submit scores on the General Test of the Graduate Record Examinations.

Correspondence and Information

Associate Dean
College of Business and Public Affairs
Clemson University
Clemson, South Carolina 29634-1315

Telephone: 864-656-3975
Fax: 864-656-0947
E-mail: mba@clemson.edu
World Wide Web: http://business.clemson.edu/

Clemson University

THE FACULTY

Accountancy

E. Lewis Bryan, Professor; D.B.A., George Washington, 1980; CPA. L. Stephen Cash, Associate Professor; J.D., Tennessee, 1980; LL.M., Washington (St. Louis), 1972; CPA. Sean S. Chen, Assistant Professor; Ph.D., Pittsburg, 1992. Lawrence S. Clark, Associate Professor; M.Acct., Georgia, 1970; CPA, CMA. James R. Davis, Professor; Ph.D., Georgia State, 1974; CMA. Thomas L. Dickens, Associate Professor; Ph.D., Texas A&M, 1983; CPA, CMA. Roger K. Doost, Associate Professor; D.P.A., Georgia, 1984; CPA, CMA. Alison C. Drews-Bryan, Associate Professor; Ph.D., Georgia, 1991; CPA. G. Thomas Friedlob, Professor; Ph.D., Mississippi, 1981; CPA, CMA. Joseph G. Louderback, Professor; Ph.D., Florida, 1970; CPA. Jeffrey McMillan, Associate Professor; Ph.D., South Carolina, 1990. Louis P. Ramsay, Associate Professor; D.B.A., Kent State, 1975; CPA. Lydia F. Schleifer, Associate Professor; Ph.D., Georgia, 1987. Jimmy D. Sheriff, Professor and Senior Associate Dean; Ph.D., Georgia, 1976. Jerry E. Trapnell, Professor and Dean; Ph.D., Georgia, 1977; CPA. Ralph E. Welton, Professor; Ph.D., LSU, 1982. Alan J. Winters, Professor and Director; Ph.D., Texas Tech, 1974; CPA.

Economics

Dan Benjamin, Professor; Ph.D., California, 1975. Dudley W. Blair, Professor, Director of M.B.A. Programs, and Acting Associate Dean; Ph.D., Texas A&M, 1975. William R. Dougan, Professor and Chair; Ph.D., Chicago, 1981. Gerald P. Dwyer Jr., Professor; Ph.D., Chicago, 1979. Ralph D. Elliott, Professor and Associate Dean for Executive Education and Development; Ph.D., North Carolina State, 1972. David B. Gordon, Associate Professor; Ph.D., Chicago. Cotton M. Lindsay, J. Wilson Newman Professor; Ph.D., Virginia, 1968. Michael T. Maloney, Professor; Ph.D., LSU, 1978. Robert E. McCormick, Professor; Ph.D., Texas A&M, 1978. Dennis L. Placone, Associate Professor; Ph.D., Pittsburgh, 1982. Raymond D. Sauer Jr., Associate Professor; Ph.D., Washington (Seattle), 1985. Curtis J. Simon, Associate Professor; Ph.D., SUNY at Binghamton, 1985. G. Richard Thompson, Professor; Ph.D., Virginia, 1972. Holley H. Ulbrich, Alumni Professor; Ph.D., Connecticut, 1968. Myles S. Wallace, Professor; Ph.D., Colorado, 1976. John T. Warner, Professor and Acting Head; Ph.D., North Carolina State, 1976.

Finance

John C. Alexander, Associate Professor; Ph.D., Florida State, 1990. Scott W. Barnhart, Associate Professor; Ph.D., Texas A&M, 1984. John M. Harris Jr., Associate Professor; Ph.D., South Carolina, 1980. Yong-Cheol Kim, Associate Professor; Ph.D., Ohio State, 1987. Richard H. Klein, Associate Professor; Ph.D., Texas, 1969. Robert B. McElreath Jr., Associate Professor and Chair; Ph.D., Georgia State, 1976. James Miller, Assistant Professor; Ph.D., Purdue, 1992. Michael F. Spivey, Professor; Ph.D., Tennessee, 1986. Neil G. Waller, Professor; Ph.D., Texas, 1986.

Legal Studies

Donald Boudreaux, Associate Professor; J.D., Virginia, 1992. Frances Edwards, Associate Professor; J.D., Kansas, 1981. Al Ringleb, Professor; J.D., Kansas State, 1981. T. Bruce Yandle Jr., Alumni Professor; Ph.D., Georgia State, 1970.

Management

Nagraj Balakrishnan, Associate Professor; Ph.D., Purdue, 1987. E. Earl Burch Jr., Professor; Ph.D., Clemson, 1970. John K. Butler Jr., Professor; D.B.A., Florida State, 1977. R. Stephen Cantrell, Professor; Ph.D., North Carolina State, 1982. Richard L. Clarke, Associate Professor; Ph.D., Texas, 1988. Michael D. Crino, Professor; Ph.D., Florida, 1978. John S. Davis, Professor; Ph.D., Georgia Tech, 1984. Lawrence Fredendall, Associate Professor; Ph.D., Michigan State, 1992. David Wayne Grigsby, Professor and Chair; Ph.D., North Carolina, 1980. John J. Kanet, Burlington Professor; Ph.D., Penn State, 1979. Robert Lawrence LaForge, Alumni Professor; Ph.D., Georgia, 1976. Terry L. Leap, Professor; Ph.D., Iowa, 1978. Mark A. McKnew, Professor; Ph.D., MIT, 1978. Janis Miller, Associate Professor; Ph.D., Missouri, 1990. J. Wayne Patterson, Associate Professor; Ph.D., Arkansas, 1977. Richard Pouder, Assistant Professor; Ph.D., Connecticut, 1991. Tina Robbins, Associate Professor; Ph.D., South Carolina, 1991. Phillip L. Roth, Associate Professor; Ph.D., Houston, 1988. Caron H. St. John, Associate Professor; Ph.D., Georgia, 1988. V. Sridharan, Professor; Ph.D., Iowa, 1987. Wayne H. Stewart, Assistant Professor; Ph.D., North Texas, 1995. Timothy Paul Summers, Associate Professor; Ph.D., South Carolina, 1986.

Marketing

Les Carlson, Associate Professor; Ph.D., Nebraska, 1985. Michael Dorsch, Associate Professor; Ph.D., Arkansas, 1987. Charles Duke, Associate Professor; Ph.D., Texas, 1988. Roger Gomes, Associate Professor; Ph.D., Virginia Tech, 1988. Stephen J. Grove, Associate Professor; Ph.D., Oklahoma State, 1979. Patricia A. Knowles, Associate Professor; Ph.D., Bowling Green State, 1987. Mary C. LaForge, Associate Professor; Ph.D., Georgia, 1980. John D. Mittlestaedt, Assistant Professor; Ph.D., Iowa, 1995. Jesse N. Moore, Assistant Professor; Ph.D., South Florida, 1997. Gregory M. Pickett, Associate Professor; Ph.D., Oklahoma State, 1985. Richard M. Reese, Professor and Chair; Ph.D., Texas, 1972.

Psychology

Thomas R. Alley, Professor; Ph.D., Connecticut, 1981. Edwin G. Brainerd Jr., Associate Professor; Ph.D., West Virginia, 1971. Robert L. Campbell, Associate Professor; Ph.D., Texas, 1986. Spurgeon Cole, Professor; Ph.D., Georgia, 1966. Patricia A. Comor-Greene, Professor; Ph.D., South Carolina, 1983. Eugene H. Galluscio, Professor; Ph.D., LSU, 1970. Mark Hallahan, Assistant Professor; Ph.D., Harvard, 1995. James A. McCubbin, Professor and Chair; Ph.D., North Carolina, 1980. DeWayne Moore, Professor; Ph.D., Hawaii, 1988. Ronald H. Nowaczyk, Professor; Ph.D., Miami (Ohio), 1977. Christopher Pagano, Assistant Professor; Ph.D., Connecticut, 1993. Lauretta I. Park, Associate Professor; Ph.D., Florida State, 1972. Richard Perlow, Assistant Professor; Ph.D., Houston, 1990. David J. Senn, Associate Professor; Ph.D., Massachusetts, 1967. Benjamin R. Stephens, Associate Professor; Ph.D., Texas, 1985. Fred S. Switzer III, Associate Professor; Ph.D., Illinois, 1988. Mary Anne Taylor-Carter, Associate Professor; Ph.D., Akron, 1990. Richard A. Tyrrell, Assistant Professor; Ph.D., Penn State, 1993. Janice G. Williams, Professor; Ph.D., Vanderbilt, 1985.

Sociology

John M. Coggeshall, Associate Professor; Ph.D., Southern Illinois at Carbondale, 1984. Kelly W. Crader, Professor; Ph.D., Emory, 1971. James E. Hawdon, Assistant Professor; Ph.D., Virginia, 1992. Catherine Mobley, Assistant Professor; Ph.D., Maryland, College Park, 1996. William Patterson, Assistant Professor; Ph.D., Cornell, 1984. Larry G. Peppers, Associate Professor; Ph.D., 1973. John Ryan, Professor; Ph.D., Vanderbilt, 1983. John P. Smith, Associate Professor; Ph.D., Missouri–Columbia, 1979. Linda Stephens, Assistant Professor; Ph.D., Washington (Seattle), 1996. Douglas K. Sturkie, Associate Professor; Ph.D., USC, 1979. Brenda J. Vander Mey, Associate Professor; Ph.D., Mississippi State, 1984. David Ward, Professor; Ph.D., Florida, 1975. William M. Wentworth, Professor; Ph.D., Virginia, 1978. Mervin F. White, Associate Professor; Ph.D., Kentucky, 1971.

CLEVELAND STATE UNIVERSITY

James J. Nance College of Business Administration

Programs of Study

The James J. Nance College of Business Administration offers a Doctor of Business Administration (D.B.A.) degree and several master's degree programs. The D.B.A. is designed to produce researchers who can advance business theory and practice and enhance the contributions that business can make to the larger community. Courses are offered evenings and weekends to serve both full- and part-time students. The curriculum includes majors in marketing, management, and operations management and a minor in global business.

The Master of Business Administration (M.B.A.) curriculum exposes students to the full range of business disciplines in both skill-building and integrative courses. It consists of three levels of course work: skill development, basic business knowledge, and required core courses. Courses in the first two levels may be waived based on prior course work. The M.B.A. is offered in a variety of programs: part-time and full-time weekday schedules, a weekend accelerated program for students with recent undergraduate business degrees, a weekend Executive M.B.A. program for persons with an established business career and a current position having managerial or senior professional responsibility, and a joint J.D./M.B.A. program in cooperation with Cleveland State's College of Law. An M.B.A. program with an emphasis in health administration is also offered. All M.B.A. programs are accredited by AACSB–The International Association for Management Education. The health administration specialization is accredited by the Accrediting Commission on Education for Health Services Administration (ACEHSA).

The College also offers other more specialized degree programs. The Master of Accountancy and Financial Information Systems (M.A.F.I.S.) aims to develop accountants who are knowledgeable in financial information systems and are able to provide and interpret sophisticated financial information; the Master of Computer Information Science (M.C.I.S.) combines an education in computer and information science with its application in business, engineering, and mathematics to qualify students as computer professionals; and the Master of Labor Relations and Human Resources (M.L.R.H.R.), which offers two tracks: (1) labor relations, dealing with unionized situations and (2) human resource development, presenting various personnel issues such as affirmative action, hiring, evaluation, and staff development.

Individuals with three-year bachelor's degrees who meet the regular admission standards of grade point average and GMAT/GRE and TOEFL scores can be admitted to an M.B.A. or M.C.I.S. bridge program that allows them to complete the entire master's degree program in two years on a full-time basis. The bridge program requires an additional 24 semester hours of credit before taking the core curriculum. Students admitted to either program are evaluated and given specific course assignments based on their backgrounds and levels of preparation.

Research Facilities

The resources of CSU's main library and Law Library and those of the Cleveland Public Library System are available to students. The College of Business Administration maintains computer laboratories that are open seven days a week and give graduate students access to the Internet and other online information sources and the use of most common business software packages. The business and health services sectors of greater Cleveland provide research topics, data, guest speakers, placements for internships, and cooperative work for students.

Financial Aid

Tuition grants are available for a limited number of the most highly qualified students in their first year of graduate work. Assistantships are normally reserved for second-year graduate students. Applications are available from the Graduate Business Programs Office.

Cost of Study

Graduate tuition for 1998–99 is $194.25 per credit hour or $2331 per semester for Ohio residents and $388.50 per credit hour or $4662 per semester for nonresidents. College of Business Administration courses carry an additional technology fee of $2.25 per credit hour. Books and supplies average $60–$95 per course. Tuition rates are subject to change without notice.

Living and Housing Costs

Limited dormitory space, ranging from $1505 to $2508 per semester (excluding meals), is available. Living and housing costs are subject to change without notice. Relatively low-cost rental housing is available in Cleveland and nearby suburbs; monthly rates range from $300 to $500.

Student Group

The total enrollment at the University is approximately 16,000, of whom one fourth are graduate students. Many are employed and enhance the classroom experience with their work experience. The student body is highly diversified, with representation from many Asian, African, European, and Latin American countries.

Location

The greater Cleveland area is headquarters for twenty-eight Fortune 500 corporations and home to the world-famous Cleveland Clinic and other major health-care institutions; the world-class Cleveland Orchestra; the Rock-and-Roll Hall of Fame; leading museums, including the Cleveland Museum of Art; major-league sports teams; the "Emerald Necklace" park system; a theater district; and restaurants and night clubs.

The University

CSU encompasses seven colleges offering twenty-seven degree programs at the master's level, six at the doctoral level, and sixty at the bachelor's level, as well as three advanced degrees in law.

Applying

Applicants must be admitted as degree-seeking graduate students by the College of Graduate Studies. Applications for admission must normally be received two months prior to the semester of desired entrance. Official copies of transcripts must be forwarded to CSU directly from all institutions previously attended. Applicants for the combined J.D./M.B.A. program must apply for admission to both the College of Graduate Studies and the College of Law. Application materials for the J.D. program may be obtained from Cleveland-Marshall College of Law, Room 115, Law Building, Cleveland, Ohio 44115.

Correspondence and Information

James J. Nance College of Business Administration
College of Business, Room 219
Cleveland State University
1860 East 18th Street
Cleveland, Ohio 44114

Telephone: 216-687-3730
Fax: 216-687-5311

Cleveland State University

THE FACULTY

Robert L. Minter, Dean; Ph.D., Purdue.
S. Ramagopala Rao, Executive Director; Ph.D., Arkansas.
Heidi H. Meier, D.B.A. Director; D.B.A., Kent State.
Allan D. Waren, Interim Associate Dean; Ph.D., Case Western Reserve.

Department of Accounting and Business Law

Jayne Fuglister, Associate Professor; D.B.A., George Washington.
Linda Garceau, Associate Professor and Chair; D.B.A., Boston University.
Lal C. Jagetia, Professor; Ph.D., Alabama.
Theresa Johnson Holt, Associate Professor; J.D., Georgia.
Lawrence A. Kreiser, Professor; Ph.D., Cincinnati.
Bruce W. McClain, Associate Professor; LL.M., NYU.
David T. Meeting, Associate Professor; D.B.A., Kent State.
Heidi H. Meier, Associate Professor; D.B.A., Kent State.
Peter Poznanski, Associate Professor; Ph.D., Texas Tech.
Etzmun S. Rozen, Associate Professor; Ph.D., NYU.
Abba V. Spero, Associate Professor; Ph.D., NYU.

Department of Computer and Information Science

Alan C. Benander, Associate Professor; Ph.D., Kent State.
Barbara A. Benander, Associate Professor; Ph.D., Kent State.
Ben A. Blake, Associate Professor; Ph.D., Ohio State.
Adam M. A. Fadlalla, Associate Professor; Ph.D., Cincinnati.
Donald G. Golden, Associate Professor and Chair; Ph.D., Case Western Reserve.
Paul J. Jalics, Professor; Ph.D., Case Western Reserve.
Chien-Hua Mike Lin, Associate Professor; Ph.D., Case Western Reserve.
Victor M. Matos, Associate Professor; Ph.D., Case Western Reserve.
David R. McIntyre, Associate Professor; Ph.D., Waterloo.
Santosh K. Misra, Associate Professor; D.B.A., Kent State.
Toshinori Munakata, Professor; Ph.D., Tokyo.
Michael A. Pechura, Associate Professor; Ph.D., Case Western Reserve.
Hao-Che Howard Pu, Associate Professor; Ph.D., Pittsburgh.
Janche Sang, Assistant Professor; Ph.D., Purdue.
James D. Schoeffler, Professor; D.Sc., MIT.

Department of Finance

Michael T. Bond, Associate Professor; Ph.D., Case Western Reserve.
Ravindra Kamath, Professor; Ph.D., Cincinnati.
F. C. Neil Myer, Associate Professor; Ph.D., Saint Louis.
Alan K. Reichert, Professor; Ph.D., Ohio State.
Jandhyala L. Sharma, Associate Professor; Ph.D., Arkansas.
James R. Webb, Professor; Ph.D., Illinois.

Department of Management and Labor Relations

Farrokh Alemi, Associate Professor; Ph.D., Wisconsin–Madison.
Charles H. Brooks, Professor; Ph.D., Michigan.
Tim R. V. Davis, Professor; Ph.D., Nebraska.
Kenneth J. Dunegan, Associate Professor; Ph.D., Cincinnati.
Brian P. Heshizer, Associate Professor; Ph.D., Wisconsin–Madison.
Mary Wilson Hrivnak, Associate Professor; Ph.D., Tennessee.
Augustine Lado, Associate Professor; Ph.D., Memphis State.
Brenda Stevenson Marshall, Associate Professor; Ph.D., Michigan.
Harry J. Martin, Associate Professor and Chair; Ph.D., Southern Illinois.
Robert L. Minter, Professor; Ph.D., Purdue.
Chul Moon, Assistant Professor; Ph.D., Maryland.
Nels E. Nelson, Associate Professor; Ph.D., Connecticut.
Lawrence R. Walker, Professor; Ph.D., Temple.

Department of Marketing

Margaret H. Bahniuk, Professor; Ed.D., Tennessee.
Bob D. Cutler, Associate Professor; Ph.D., North Texas.
Amit K. Ghosh, Associate Professor; Ph.D., Iowa.
Andrew C. Gross, Professor; Ph.D., Ohio State.
Rajshekhar G. Javalgi, Professor; Ph.D., Wisconsin–Milwaukee.
Rama K. Jayanti, Associate Professor; Ph.D., LSU.
W. Benoy Joseph, Associate Professor; Ph.D., Ohio State.
William J. Lundstrom, Professor; Ph.D., Colorado.
Kenneth R. Mayer, Associate Professor and Interim Chair; Ed.D., Temple.
Janet Y. Murray, Associate Professor; Ph.D., Missouri.
S. Ramagopala Rao, Associate Professor; Ph.D., Arkansas.
Edward G. Thomas, Professor; Ed.D., Kentucky.
Ivan R. Vernon, Associate Professor; D.B.A., Kent State.
Marion Webb, Associate Professor; Ph.D., Akron.
Thomas W. Whipple, Professor; Ph.D., SUNY at Buffalo.

Department of Operations Management and Business Statistics

Injazz Chen, Associate Professor; D.B.A., Kentucky.
Dalen T. Chiang, Associate Professor; Ph.D., Berkeley.
Chia-Shin Chung, Associate Professor; Ph.D., Berkeley.
Ronald L. Coccari, Associate Professor and Chair; Ph.D., West Virginia.
James O. Flynn, Professor; Ph.D., Berkeley.
Oya Icmeli Tukel, Associate Professor; Ph.D., Florida.
Walter O. Rom, Professor; Ph.D., Cornell.

COLORADO STATE UNIVERSITY

College of Business

Programs of Study

Diversity is a key word in the College of Business—diversity in programs and in the student body. The College, accredited by AACSB–The International Association for Management Education, employs a full range of programs to address the needs of the entire spectrum of students: domestic and international, part-time and full-time, and on-campus and off-campus distance learning. Students can obtain a general M.B.A. degree or an M.S. degree in business administration with a concentration. Students may complete the M.B.A. degree in one of four programs: the eleven-month Accelerated M.B.A. program, the Evening M.B.A. program, the Distance M.B.A. program, or the Executive M.B.A. program (Denver). The content of each program is integrative and has a strong emphasis on information technology, global issues, and teamwork. The Accelerated M.B.A. provides an opportunity to quickly supplement an undergraduate degree with a graduate business degree. It is also designed for those who wish to make a career change in the shortest period of time. This 36-credit program requires a full-time commitment and meets during the day Monday through Friday. The Evening M.B.A. is designed to serve the needs of working professionals. This 36-credit program takes twenty-two months to complete, including one summer session. All classes meet in the evening, Monday through Thursday, to minimize the impact on busy work schedules. The College is a nationally recognized leader in distance M.B.A. education. *Forbes Magazine* ranks the Colorado State University Network for Learning (CSUN) program among the nation's top twenty distance learning programs. Through the CSUN, the classroom is brought directly to the student via Internet and videotape. The Distance M.B.A. is designed to serve working professionals who need flexibility in schedule and location. There is no on-campus requirement; course work is completed entirely at a distance. This 36-credit program takes two to four years to complete and includes some summer classes. The Executive M.B.A. program is an accelerated program designed for students to complete their M.B.A. degree in twenty-one months. The schedule is sensitive to the needs of working professionals. Students attend classes two evenings per week. The program is offered in nine 8-week sessions, with a five-week winter break and a six-week summer break. The executive site is Colorado State University's Denver Center, which is located in downtown Denver, Colorado. The facility, including a computer center with multimedia instructional equipment, is specifically designed to support a state-of-the-art M.B.A. curriculum.

Research Facilities

The College of Business supports two fully accessible computer labs for the exclusive use of business students. The Hewlett-Packard Student Computer Laboratory is equipped with seventy-four Pentium-class computers, including Windows 95-based PCs and Macintoshes, seven networked laser printers and two color printers, a scanner, and more than sixty software packages. The computer teaching lab houses another thirty-three computers. All computers are connected to the Internet and have full Internet capabilities. The College uses a variety of CD-ROM databases, and several UNIX workstations are accessible from lab computers. Complementing the College resources, the University has provided an extensive set of UNIX and various Gopher and Web devices.

The University Libraries support the teaching and research activities of Colorado State's faculty and students by providing a diverse collection of approximately 4 million items. Library services include a comprehensive reserves and interlibrary loan service with electronic access. The central library houses the major part of the collection, which includes books, maps, journals, technical reports, archives, manuscripts, and the most recent issues of approximately 8,000 journal titles. The collection is enriched by a wide selection of CD-ROM databases and online services. The University is a member of the Association of Research Libraries (ARL), the Colorado Alliance of Research Libraries (CARL), and the Greater Midwest Research Library Consortium (GMRLC). Resource sharing is enhanced by participation in the Online Computer Library Center (OCLC), which supports electronic access to the holdings of more than 10 million libraries worldwide.

In addition to working on individual academic research projects, graduate students may participate in industrial and government research projects conducted by the faculty.

Financial Aid

The College offers several teaching and research assistantships in every business discipline. Forty-five percent of students receive institutionally administered aid in the form of fellowships, research assistantships, teaching assistantships, and work-study. Assistantships are not available for distance education students.

Cost of Study

In 1997–98, tuition for a Colorado resident for the eleven-month Accelerated M.B.A. program was $1638 per semester plus $516 for the summer session. Nonresident tuition for the Accelerated M.B.A. program was $5283 per semester plus $1732 for the summer session. Resident tuition for the Evening M.B.A. program was $1202 per semester plus $516 for the summer session. Nonresident tuition for the Evening M.B.A. program was $3634 per semester plus $1732 for the summer session. Tuition for the CSUN distance education program is assessed per credit hour of a course and is noted as student credit hour (SCH). Tuition includes delivery of the tapes to the student or to the site but does not include the cost of returning the tapes. Current rates are $328 per SCH to Colorado sites, $368 per SCH to non-Colorado sites, and $384 per SCH to individuals. These figures are based on the current published schedules and are subject to change without notice.

Living and Housing Costs

Graduate students have a number of housing options. Single students have a choice of University-owned apartments or dormitory housing. University-owned apartment housing, either furnished or unfurnished, is available to families. All University housing rent includes utilities, basic telephone service, and cable TV. In 1997–98, apartment housing rent for single students ranged from $320 per month per person for a two-bedroom shared apartment to $485 per month for a one-bedroom apartment. Rent for families ranged from $470 per month for a two-bedroom apartment to $580 per month for a three-bedroom apartment. The 1998–99 cost for dormitory housing ranges from $1116 per semester for a standard room to $1317 for a suite. The 1998–99 charge for meals is $1155 per semester for ten meals per week, $1275 per semester for fifteen meals per week, and $1395 per semester for unlimited meals per week. Meal plans are available to any Colorado State student. Married and single students can also find accommodations in numerous privately owned apartment buildings and residences surrounding the campus. For detailed information on current housing availability, students can contact the Office of Housing and Food Services (telephone: 970-491-6511).

Student Group

Approximately 22,000 students are enrolled at Colorado State University. Of these, about 24 percent are from outside of Colorado. The College of Business has about 1,600 undergraduate and 266 graduate students on campus, with an additional 500 distance education students.

Location

Fort Collins is located at the foot of the picturesque Rocky Mountains, 65 miles north of Denver. This city of about 100,000 people has numerous cultural and recreational activities. The climate is excellent, with more than 300 days of sunshine per year and generally pleasant temperatures. Skiing is a popular winter sport, while diverse summer activities can be enjoyed at nearby lakes and mountain areas.

The University

Colorado State University, founded in 1870, is the land-grant university of Colorado. There are three campuses: the main campus, covering more than 400 acres, about ½-mile south of the Fort Collins business district; the Foothills Research Campus of approximately 1,700 acres, located 3 miles west of the main campus; and the Pingree Park campus, located in the mountains, 54 miles west of Fort Collins.

Applying

The application deadline for financial aid is February 15. Requirements include a GMAT score, an application form, an application fee, a bachelor's degree, a minimum GPA, three letters of recommendation, a personal statement, college transcript(s), and a resume. The Evening M.B.A. and CSUN programs also require a minimum of four years of work experience. The Executive M.B.A. program requires a minimum of eight years of work experience.

Correspondence and Information

Associate Dean
College of Business
Colorado State University
Fort Collins, Colorado 80523

Telephone: 970-491-6471

Colorado State University

THE FACULTY AND THEIR RESEARCH

The faculty of the College of Business is composed of about 60 members who are actively engaged in teaching and research. Each program is supervised by a faculty member who is recognized as an outstanding authority in his or her field. Members of the graduate faculty are listed below.

Robert P. Allerheiligen, Assistant Professor; Ph.D., USC. Marketing.
Susan Athey, Associate Professor; Ph.D., Arizona. Computer information systems.
Vickie Bajtelsmit, Associate Professor; Ph.D., Pennsylvania. Finance and insurance.
Douglas A. Benton, Professor; D.B.A., Arizona State. Management.
Steven F. Bolander, Professor; D.B.A., Kent State. Management.
Charles W. Butler, Professor; Ph.D., Texas A&M. Computer information systems.
Joseph P. Cannon, Assistant Professor; Ph.D., North Carolina. Marketing.
Jon D. Clark, Professor and Associate Dean; Ph.D., Case Western Reserve. Management information decision systems.
Rick Edgeman, Professor; Ph.D., Wyoming. Statistics and operations research.
John W. Ellis, Associate Professor; Ph.D., Michigan State. Finance.
O. C. Ferrell, Professor; Ph.D., LSU. Marketing.
G. James Francis, Professor; Ph.D., Nebraska. Management.
Timothy J. Gallagher, Professor and Chairman of Finance and Real Estate; Ph.D., Illinois at Urbana-Champaign. Finance.
David I. Gilliland, Assistant Professor; Ph.D., Georgia State. Marketing.
Walter "Bud" Hivner, Associate Professor; Ph.D., California, Riverside. Management.
K. Douglas Hoffman, Associate Professor; Ph.D., Kentucky. Marketing.
Ray L. Hogler, Professor; Ph.D., J.D., Colorado. Management.
Willie Hopkins, Professor; Ph.D., Colorado. Management.
John Hoxmeier, Assistant Professor; Ph.D., Colorado. Computer information systems.
Myron Hulen, Associate Professor; Ph.D., Texas at Austin. Accounting and taxation.
Thomas N. Ingram, Professor and Chair of Marketing; Ph.D., Georgia State. Marketing.
Jackie Jankovich, Assistant Professor; Ph.D., Colorado State. Human resource development.
Laurence Johnson, Associate Professor; Ph.D., Texas Tech. Accounting.
Richard D. Johnson, Associate Professor; Ph.D., Oregon. Finance.
Vicki S. Kaman, Professor; Ph.D., Colorado State. Management.
Kathleen Kelly, Associate Professor; Ph.D., Colorado State. Marketing.
Terry L. Lantry, Professor; J.D., Valparaiso. Law and taxation.
Margarita Lenk, Associate Professor; Ph.D., South Carolina. Accounting.
Paul Mallette, Associate Professor; Ph.D., Nebraska. Management.
Ken Manning, Assistant Professor; Ph.D., South Carolina. Marketing.
Jim McCambridge, Associate Professor; Ph.D., Colorado State. Management.
Anne McCarthy, Assistant Professor; Ph.D., Purdue. Strategic management.
Ajay Menon, Associate Professor; Ph.D., North Texas. Marketing.
Dennis Middlemist, Professor; Ph.D., Washington (Seattle). Management.
Melanie R. Middlemist, Assistant Professor; Ph.D., Oklahoma State. Accounting.
Elaine Miller, Associate Professor; Ph.D., Michigan. Management.
William G. Mister, Professor; Ph.D., Berkeley. Accounting.
John Olienyk, Associate Professor; Ph.D., Colorado State. Economics.
Cherie J. O'Neil, Professor; Ph.D., Colorado. Accounting and taxation.
John Plotnicki, Associate Professor and Chairman of Computer Information Systems; Ph.D., Tennessee. Computer information systems.
Karen S. Powell, Associate Professor; D.A., Northern Colorado. Management.
Edward L. Prill, Assistant Professor; Ph.D., Illinois at Urbana-Champaign. Finance and real estate.
Robert A. Rademacher, Professor; Ph.D., Nebraska. Computer information systems.
John L. Roberts, Assistant Professor; J.D., Minnesota; M.S., Colorado State. Business law.
Norman O. Schultz, Associate Professor; Ph.D., Utah. Accounting.
Robert G. Schwebach, Assistant Professor; Ph.D., Nebraska. Finance.
Linda Stanley, Associate Professor; Ph.D., Wyoming. Marketing.
Ralph V. Switzer, Professor; J.D., Illinois at Urbana-Champaign. Law and taxation.
Billy M. Thornton, Professor; Ph.D., Texas A&M. Management.
Daniel E. Turk, Assistant Professor; Ph.D., Georgia. Computer information systems.
D. Michael Vaughan, Professor; D.B.A., Texas Tech. Accounting and taxation.
Frederick C. Weston Jr., Professor; D.B.A., Indiana. Computer information systems.
Joseph A. Williams, Associate Professor; Ph.D., Texas at Austin. Computer information systems.
Elaine Worzala, Associate Professor; Ph.D., Wisconsin–Madison. Finance and real estate.
Kent Zumwalt, Professor; Ph.D., Missouri. Finance.

DEPAUL UNIVERSITY

Charles H. Kellstadt Graduate School of Business

Programs of Study

The Graduate School of Business offers evening classes leading to the degrees of Master of Business Administration (M.B.A.), Master of Science in Accountancy (M.S.A.), Master of Accountancy (M.Acc.), Master of Science in Taxation (M.S.T.), Master of Science in Finance (M.S.F.), Master of Business Administration/Juris Doctor (M.B.A./J.D.), and Master of Science in Management Information Systems (M.S./M.I.S.). The programs are accredited by AACSB–The International Association for Management Education. The degrees may be pursued on a full-time or on a part-time basis. The curricular patterns are designed for carefully selected and properly qualified students. The content is intended to provide learning experiences that will deepen the basic knowledge and increase the functional skills essential for positions of responsible business leadership. In 1995, a full-time day M.B.A. program and a weekend program were inaugurated.

The emphasis of the M.B.A. program is on decision making as the characteristic function of business administration. It is the purpose of the program to integrate the several functional areas of business and the contributions they make to the development of administrative competence. The M.B.A. program is designed for students who have baccalaureate degrees in business or other disciplines. Neither a thesis nor a written or oral comprehensive examination is required. Approximately one fourth of the student's course work in the evening program may be taken in one of the following areas of specialization: management accounting, business economics, finance, international business, entrepreneurship, operations management, human resources management, marketing management, financial management and control, leadership/change management, and management information systems. The full-time day program has a concentration in international marketing and finance.

The M.S.A. program is meant to provide a formal integrated sequence of graduate courses emphasizing intensive study of topics relevant to the work of a professional accountant, as well as to allow ample opportunity to explore advanced topics of interest. It is expected that after completing the program the student will be well prepared for the CPA exam. The program is intended to serve the needs of holders of undergraduate liberal arts and science degrees or business degrees with nonaccounting backgrounds.

The M.Acc. program is for students who have an undergraduate background in accountancy.

Through its emphasis on planning and decision making as essential to the professional in taxation, it is the purpose of the M.S.T. program to integrate a sound technical competence with an awareness of other relevant functional areas of business and their contribution to professional competence.

The M.S.F. is an intensive program in advanced financial studies.

DePaul's College of Law and Graduate School of Business have designed a combined program of day law and evening business courses that permits a full-time law student to obtain the M.B.A. and J.D. degrees with a substantial reduction of time. A graduate of this program is prepared in each field and is competent to handle special problems that require an understanding of law as well as an understanding of business administration.

The School of Computer Science, Telecommunications and Information Systems and the Graduate School of Business have designed a joint program that combines computer science with management systems and leads to the degree of Master of Science in Management Information Systems.

The academic year consists of four quarters, commencing in September, January, March, and June. Class sizes range from 10 to 50.

Research Facilities

DePaul has a complete university library, and the Computer Center has facilities for class use and for research projects undertaken by graduate students and faculty. The University's ideal location in the heart of Chicago's business and financial district makes numerous facilities of business enterprises available.

Financial Aid

Each year a number of research assistantships are available in the Departments of Economics, Finance, Management, and Marketing and the School of Accountancy. Assistantship stipends range from $4000 to $4500 in 1998–99. Loans are available through several programs. Students may apply for these loans after being formally admitted to the Graduate School. Work-study program awards and outside employment opportunities are also available.

Cost of Study

Tuition for graduate study during 1998–99 is $2036 per course for the evening programs. A registration fee of $10 is charged each quarter.

Living and Housing Costs

The University aids the student in securing adequate quarters off campus. Accommodations of all types are available in the Chicago area.

Student Group

There are approximately 2,500 students in the Graduate School of Business, of whom 90 percent are usually part-time. About 65 percent have undergraduate degrees in business or economics, and 35 percent have undergraduate degrees in engineering, liberal arts, sciences, and other nonbusiness areas.

Location

DePaul's graduate programs in business are conducted in the DePaul Center in the heart of downtown Chicago. The best laboratory available—the dynamic commercial and financial center of Chicago—is just outside its doors. Lake Michigan, Grant Park, Orchestra Hall, and the Civic Opera House, Art Institute, Field Museum, Shedd Aquarium, and Adler Planetarium are within walking distance.

The University

DePaul University is a private coeducational institution that was founded in 1898. It has developed and widened its scope to embrace eight major academic divisions with approximately 17,000 students enrolled in day and evening programs. Classes are offered at two suburban locations as well.

Applying

Students may enter the evening M.B.A., M.S.A., M.Acc., M.S.T., M.S.F., or joint M.S./M.I.S. programs in any academic quarter. The application must be submitted with the $40 fee, official transcripts of all academic work, and a recent score on the GMAT. All required documents for admission in the autumn, winter, spring, and summer quarters are due about eight weeks prior to the beginning of that quarter. The full-time day M.B.A. program and the weekend program have entry in September only. Information on exact deadlines is included with the application form.

Correspondence and Information

Kellstadt Graduate School of Business
DePaul University
1 East Jackson Boulevard, Suite 7900
Chicago, Illinois 60604-2287
Telephone: 312-362-8810

DePaul University

THE FACULTY AND THEIR AREAS OF SPECIALIZATION

John T. Ahern, D.B.A., Kentucky; CPA (Illinois). Accountancy.
Adnan Almaney, Ph.D., Indiana. Management.
Abdul J. Alwan, Ph.D., Chicago. Management.
Linda F. Alwitt, Ph.D., Massachusetts at Amherst. Marketing.
Fred Arditti, Ph.D., MIT. Finance.
Roger Baran, Ph.D., Chicago. Marketing.
Bala Batavia, Ph.D., North Carolina State. Economics.
James A. Belohlav, Ph.D., Cincinnati. Management.
Thomas Berry, Ph.D., Missouri. Finance.
Steven Briggs, Ph.D., UCLA. Management.
Gabriella Bucci, Ph.D., Johns Hopkins. Economics.
Susanne Cannon, Ph.D., Texas at Austin. Finance.
Petr G. Chadraba, Chair of the Department of Marketing; Ph.D., Nebraska. Marketing.
Jin Choi, Ph.D., Iowa State. Economics.
James Ciecka, Ph.D., Purdue. Economics.
Edwin Cohen, Ph.D., Michigan State; CPA (Illinois). Accountancy.
Ray W. Coye, Ph.D., Oregon. Management.
Sasa Dekleva, Ph.D., Belgrade. Accountancy.
Alexander Devience, J.D., Loyola of Chicago. Management.
Floyd Dill, Ph.D., Cornell. Economics.
Thomas Donley, Ph.D., Wisconsin–Madison. Economics.
David E. Drehmer, Ph.D., IIT. Management.
Gail Eynon, Ph.D., Northwestern. Accountancy.
Edward Foth, Ph.D., Michigan State; CPA (Illinois). Accountancy.
Mark L. Frigo, Ph.D., Northern Illinois; CPA (Illinois); CMA. Accountancy.
Samuel Garber, J.D., Illinois at Urbana-Champaign. Management.
Richard Garrigan, Ph.D., Wisconsin–Madison. Finance.
Adam K. Gehr Jr., Ph.D., Ohio State. Finance.
Animesh Ghoshal, Ph.D., Michigan. Economics.
Lisa Gundry, Ph.D., Northwestern. Management.
Nancy Hill, Ph.D., Wisconsin–Madison. Accountancy.
Geoffrey Hirt, Ph.D., Illinois at Urbana-Champaign. Finance.
John Houston, Ph.D., Northwestern. Finance.
Keith M. Howe, Ph.D., Nebraska. Finance.
Joan Junkus, Chair of the Department of Finance; Ph.D., Illinois at Urbana-Champaign. Finance.
Howard Kanter, Ed.D., Northern Illinois; CPA (Illinois). Accountancy.
Glenda Kao, Ph.D., Illinois at Urbana-Champaign. Finance.
J. Steven Kelly, D.B.A., Kent State. Marketing.
Thomas J. Kewley, Ph.D., Michigan State. Finance.
Daniel J. Koys, Associate Dean of the College of Commerce; Ph.D., Cornell. Management.
Anthony Krautmann, Ph.D., Iowa. Economics.
Helen LaVan, Ph.D., Loyola of Chicago. Management.
Carl F. Luft, Ph.D., Georgia State. Finance.
Stanley C. Martens, Ph.D., Cornell; CPA (Illinois). Accountancy.
John N. Mathys, Ph.D., IIT. Finance.
Nicholas J. Mathys, Ph.D., IIT. Management.
Mark McCarthy, J.D., DePaul; CPA (Illinois), CMA. Accountancy.
John McEnroe, D.B.A., Kentucky; CPA (Illinois). Accountancy.
Michael S. Miller, Ph.D., Pittsburgh. Economics.
Thomas Mondschean, Ph.D., Wisconsin–Madison. Economics.
Michael A. Murray, Ph.D., Illinois at Urbana-Champaign. Management.
Belverd Needles Jr., Ph.D., Illinois at Urbana-Champaign; CPA (Texas, Illinois); CMA. Accountancy.
Bruce Newman, Ph.D., Illinois at Urbana-Champaign. Marketing.
Norman Nicholson, Ph.D., USC. Finance.
Denise Nitterhouse, D.B.A., Harvard; CPA (Illinois). Accountancy.
Robert O'Keefe, Ph.D., Northwestern. Marketing.
Margaret Oppenheimer, Chair of the Department of Economics; Ph.D., Northwestern. Economics.
Laura Owen, Ph.D., Yale. Economics.
Ronald J. Patten, Dean of the College of Commerce; Ph.D., Alabama. Accountancy.
Robert Peters, Associate Dean of the College of Commerce; Ph.D., Kentucky; CPA (Illinois). Accountancy.
Laura Pincus, J.D., IIT. Management.
Gerhard Plaschka, Chair of the Department of Management; Ph.D., Vienna. Management.
William M. Poppei, M.B.A., Chicago. Finance.
David J. Roberts, J.D., DePaul; CPA (Illinois). Accountancy.
Br. Leo V. Ryan, Ph.D., Saint Louis. Management.
William H. Sander, Ph.D., Cornell. Economics.
Donald Shannon, Ph.D., North Carolina at Chapel Hill; CPA (Illinois). Accountancy.
Frederic B. Shipley II, Ph.D., Northwestern. Finance.
Gary Siegel, Ph.D., Illinois at Urbana-Champaign; CPA (Illinois). Accountancy.
James Staruck, J.D., IIT. Management.
Kevin T. Stevens, D.B.A., Kentucky. Accountancy.
Owais Succari, Ph.D., Louvain (Belgium). Management.
Mark J. Sullivan, Ph.D., Wisconsin–Madison; CPA (Illinois). Accountancy.
Kenneth R. Thompson, Ph.D., Nebraska. Management.
Stephen Vogt, Ph.D., Washington (St. Louis). Finance.
Joseph Vu, Ph.D., Chicago. Finance.
Gemma L. Welsch, Ph.D., Northwestern; CPA (Illinois), CMA. Accountancy.
Harold Welsch, Ph.D., Northwestern. Management.
Joel Whalen, Ph.D., Florida State. Marketing.
Ray Whittington, Director of the School of Accountancy; Ph.D., Houston; CPA (California), CMA. Accountancy.
Richard Wiltgen, Ph.D., Illinois at Urbana-Champaign. Economics.

DOWLING COLLEGE

School of Business

Programs of Study

Dowling offers graduate students five M.B.A. degree programs to choose from, including general management, aviation management, banking and finance, public management, and total quality management.

The degree in general management provides a comprehensive foundation in various managerial disciplines and is ideal for students who did not specialize in business at the undergraduate level and managers in small to mid-size firms. The M.B.A. in aviation management is designated for aviation management professionals as well as individuals who aspire to land positions in the industry. Managers learn to run their divisions more efficiently and keep pace with the kinetic elements impacting the aviation industry today. This degree is applicable to professionals affiliated with air carriers, airport facilities, aerospace companies, and industry sectors such as manufacturers and the government. Banking and finance are among the most dynamic industries in the global economy. Due to the changing financial markets worldwide and the greater variety of financial instruments evolving, the information needed to thrive in this environment is expanding rapidly. Acquiring the skills necessary for not-for-profit institutions or government is key to Dowling's public management M.B.A. program. Courses on quantitative methods for public sector decision making, not-for-profit marketing, and public sector economics help focus the program on the specifics of this diverse field. The M.B.A. in total quality management (T.Q.M.) challenges students to meet customer needs in addition to traditional business operations. Students are taught T.Q.M. theories by faculty members who are leaders in quality management education.

The M.B.A. programs are recognized for addressing issues relative to the global economy, and the M.B.A. students develop a managerial view of the organization, planning, and leadership of a business enterprise. Additionally, students acquire key decision-making skills while applying classroom ideology to the professional work world. Dowling's management simulation capstone requirement places students in real-world situations. Students work in teams and must demonstrate the successful start-up of a business venture and direct its capital distribution, purchasing efforts, marketing campaigns, cash-flow logistics, and related responsibilities. Dowling also offers busy executives the opportunity to earn an M.B.A. in general management or banking and finance in a distinctive Saturdays-only structure. The Accelerated Saturday M.B.A. program enables students to complete their degrees in only three semesters by attending classes all day on Saturdays. It offers an innovative luncheon speakers series; a state-of-the-art notebook computer with word processing, spreadsheet, and presentation software; and all required textbooks. The speakers series features prominent local, national, and international business professionals and has included George Gallup of Gallup Poll International, Jerry Goodman of *Adam Smith's Money World*, Ben Cohen, cofounder of Ben & Jerry's Homemade Ice Cream, and Michael Moore, director of the documentary *Roger & Me*.

Research Facilities

The Nicholas and Constance Racanelli Center for Learning Resources houses Dowling's library and includes 182,661 volumes; 1,100 current periodicals; 577,097 microforms; 10,577 government documents; 2,721 videotapes; and 367 computer databases. A valuable research tool is the Online Computer Library Center (OCLC), used by Dowling's librarians to access the collections of thousands of libraries, universities, and research centers worldwide. The Academic Computing Center has three multimedia classrooms, three labs for individual use, and a faculty resource center and is available to students during extended day and evening hours. The College's membership in the New York State Education and Research Network (Nysernet) is a gateway to the Internet, a global network providing access to thousands of computers for research and communication.

Financial Aid

While numerous scholarship programs are available, various financing methods can be explored with a personal financial aid counselor. The College offers flexible payment options, such as tuition- and fee-deferred payment plans for each semester. Credit cards may also be used to pay tuition and fees. Additionally, new students may have their tuition charges frozen for two academic years at their entering semester's rate.

Cost of Study

Tuition is $440 per graduate credit and certain student fees are applicable.

Living and Housing Costs

On-campus housing is available in apartment-style suites for $3600 per semester, and there are ample off-campus apartments within a reasonable distance of the College.

Student Group

Dowling's diverse M.B.A. student population ranges from recent baccalaureate graduates and businesspeople to physicians and other professionals. The average age is 32 and graduate students comprise 37 percent of the student body. Dowling's international scope continues to grow with the addition of its National Aviation and Transportation Center®, a multidisciplinary facility—the first of its kind—dedicated to fufilling the promise of intermodal transportation planning, education, research, and training. Individualized tutorial programs are available to students who need help with the English language.

Location

Originated in 1955 as Suffolk County's first four-year college, Dowling's Oakdale campus is nestled on 52 acres along the picturesque banks of the Connetquot River on Long Island's south shore. Built at the turn of the century by industrial magnate William K. Vanderbilt, this exquisitely preserved mansion houses administrative and faculty offices, as well as ornately designed ceremonial rooms that are now used for meetings and lectures. Approximately 50 miles east of midtown Manhattan, it is within easy reach of New York's theaters and museums and just minutes from Long Island's beautiful beaches, parks, recreational facilities, and cultural attractions. Students at Dowling have the best of both worlds—city and country. The College also has centers in the World Trade Institute in Manhattan; in Riverhead, Long Island; and at the College of Aeronautics in Flushing, New York.

The College and The School

Dowling is known as The Personal College®, committed to a learning environment that encourages and provides for each individual's potential. Classes are small and the faculty is dedicated. For more than thirty years, Dowling's School of Business has been educating business leaders. Across Long Island, throughout the nation, and around the globe, Dowling's innovative partnerships with businesses have spawned numerous benefits for M.B.A. students including lectures, internships, and networking opportunities. Dowling's Board of Trustees and Advisory Council members, whose business expertise is vital to the College's exemplary leadership, serve as successful corporate examples. They are often on campus, where students can meet with them. The Office of Cooperative Education, Career Counseling, and Internship maintains a network of partnerships with businesses on Long Island, in New York, and across the nation. On-campus recruiters from respected companies are regularly scheduled, and Dowling's M.B.A. graduates maintain a high-visibility quotient. Students can also attend special lectures on resume writing, interviewing, and careerpathing. Students are encouraged to attend the varied networking activities that Dowling's alumni organization provides throughout the year.

Applying

Each candidate's academic record, required GMAT scores, and work experience are considered for admission. A GMAT score of 475 or higher and a minimum 2.8 GPA in undergraduate work are preferred. In addition to the minimum 36 credits of graduate work, each qualified applicant with a limited background in business administration must successfully complete certain preparatory courses such as accounting, economics, quantitative methods, computer science, and management. For students using English as a second language, a TOEFL score of 550 or better is required.

Correspondence and Information

Anthony F. Libertella, Ph.D., Dean
School of Business
Dowling College
Idle Hour Boulevard
Oakdale, Long Island, New York 11769-1999
Telephone: 516-244-3355; 800-DOWLING (toll-free)
Fax: 516-589-6644; 516-244-5098
World Wide Web: http://www.dowling.edu

Dowling College

THE FACULTY AND THEIR RESEARCH

Conducted within the personalized atmosphere of a small college, the graduate business program at Dowling has a faculty of highly qualified, experienced business professionals. Faculty members are noted for their presentations, scholarly works, expert testimonies, professional standings, and national conference participation.

Lawrence T. Bauer, Ph.D.; Assistant Professor of Management.
Reinaldo Blanco, M.S., CPA; Assistant Professor of Accounting.
Glen Brauchle, M.B.A, CPA; Assistant Professor of Accounting.
Gail Butler, J.D.; Assistant Professor of Aviation and Transportation.
Thomas Diamante, Ph.D.; Assistant Professor of Management.
Diane Fischer, Ph.D.; Associate Professor of Computer Information Systems.
George Foundotos, M.S., CPA; Professor of Accounting.
Thomas Frye, Ph.D.; Assistant Professor of Management.
Leo Giglio, Ph.D.; Assistant Professor of Management.
Bruce Haller, J.D.; Assistant Professor of Management.
Alan Hogenauer, Ph.D.; Associate Professor of Marketing.
Nicholas Mauro, Ph.D.; Associate Professor of Management.
Joseph Monahan, Ph.D.; Associate Professor of Finance.
Carol Okolica, Ph.D.; Associate Professor of Computer Information Systems.
Faith M. Pereira, D.P.S.; Associate Professor of Marketing.
Luis E. Rivera, Ph.D.; Assistant Professor of Finance.
Walter Rosenthal, Ph.D.; Associate Professor of Marketing.
Charles W. Rudiger, Ed.D.; Associate Professor of Management and Education.
Walter Schimpf, M.B.A., CPA; Assistant Professor of Accounting.
Michael Shapiro, Ph.D.; Assistant Professor of Marketing.
Caroline Spencer, Ph.D.; Assistant Professor of Finance.
Lori Kim Troboy, Ph.D.; Assistant Professor of Computer Information Systems.

The Racanelli Center is the College's learning resource facility.

A side view of Fortunoff Hall, which was once the summer home of William K. Vanderbilt and now serves as the administrative center of the College.

DREXEL UNIVERSITY

College of Business and Administration

Programs of Study

Cutting-edge preparation for the global future is provided by the College of Business and Administration, which offers curricula leading to the Master of Business Administration, Master of Science, and Doctor of Philosophy degrees. These curricula permit the student to choose among twenty-two areas of concentration and majors in the Departments of Accounting, Economics, Finance, Legal Studies, Management, Marketing, and Quantitative Methods. Degree programs are available for full- or part-time study. Classes are conducted in the day and evening hours as well as on Saturday mornings and afternoons. The variety of course offerings and the timing of classes are especially helpful to part-time students in arranging programs of study appropriate to their professional objectives and convenient to their business obligations.

The Co-op and Career Services Center coordinates Career Integrated Education (CIE), a program that offers graduate business students field experiences that complement their classroom training. Distinct from Drexel's traditional cooperative education program, CIE employment may be part-time or full-time, and it may begin on year-round dates mutually compatible with the employer's needs and the candidate's availability.

The M.B.A. program requires a minimum of 48 quarter hour credits and a maximum of 84 quarter hour credits. The exact number of credits required for the degree depends upon the student's prior academic experience; a full-time student with an undergraduate degree from an accredited business college can complete the M.B.A. program in one academic year (four quarters), while full-time students with degrees in other disciplines may require up to two years to complete the degree. The M.B.A. program combines a general management education with a limited specialization in one of fifteen functional areas of business study.

For students seeking a higher degree of specialization than that provided in the M.B.A. program, the College offers the Master of Science degree in accounting, decision sciences, finance, marketing, and taxation. The number of credits required varies with the academic experience of the student and the area of specialization, although the range of credits tends to match M.B.A. requirements.

The Ph.D. program prepares candidates for careers in university teaching, research positions in academic and nonacademic institutions, and administrative and decision-making positions in business, government, and not-for-profit institutions. Primary or secondary specializations are offered in accounting, decision sciences, economics, finance, marketing, organizational sciences, and strategic management. Secondary specializations are also offered in international business and statistics. The doctoral program strives to stimulate an intellectual curiosity that generates creative scholarship and research. To this end, the student must demonstrate a mastery of the literature appropriate to his or her discipline, an understanding of the issues and problems on the frontiers of that body of knowledge, and the ability to apply relevant tools and concepts leading to a significant advancement in professional knowledge.

The Ph.D. program admits students in alternating fall terms. No class will be admitted for fall 1999. Completed applications must be received by February 1.

The College offers advanced professional certificate programs for the holders of master's and doctoral degrees who seek specialized updating in a professional field or who wish to acquire a new skill.

Research Facilities

The College of Business and Administration houses such research institutes as the Center for Research on Technology and Strategy and the Center for Quality and Productivity. Computing services are provided by an IBM 9121-320 through remote-job-entry stations, three on-campus Prime superminicomputers (two of which are networked to support approximately 300 interactive terminals), and clusters of Apple Macintosh and IBM PC microcomputers. Also available for student use are computer data resources pertinent to research on business topics. All College programs emphasize hands-on experience with computer equipment that is integrated with course work.

Drexel's W. W. Hagerty Library houses 400,000 volumes, including a large collection in the fields of business and science. Reference assistance by specialist business librarians, an interlibrary loan program, use of modern audiovisual and duplicating equipment, and free computerized database searches are some of the special services available.

Financial Aid

Graduate teaching assistantships are available in the full-time M.B.A., M.S., and Ph.D. programs.

Cost of Study

Tuition is $494 per credit hour in 1998–99. The University fee is $121 per quarter for full-time students and $65 for part-time students.

Living and Housing Costs

Accommodations for single students are available in University residence halls. Ample housing is also available in the neighborhood bordering campus. For the nine-month academic year, transportation and living expenses for a single student are estimated at $11,450.

Student Group

The College of Business and Administration enrolls approximately 1,000 students in its master's and doctoral programs.

Location

Drexel is located in the University City area of Philadelphia, a complex comprising major universities, medical centers, and research institutes.

The University and The College

As a private university, Drexel builds on a century of experience in business-related education and on more than five decades of involvement in graduate business programs. Drexel gives its students the opportunity to combine graduate study with an atmosphere, a history, and a tradition of high-quality education and commitment to excellence.

The University Career Services Center offers career planning services to all students. Assistance is given in securing career information, writing resumes, interviewing, and planning job campaigns.

Graduate and undergraduate programs of the College of Business and Administration are fully accredited by the AACSB–The International Association for Management Education.

Applying

Students may receive a package with details on applying by writing to the Office of Graduate Admissions. The application fee is $35.

Correspondence and Information

Office of Graduate Admissions
Drexel University, Box P
Philadelphia, Pennsylvania 19104

Telephone: 215-895-6700
E-mail: admissions-grad@post.drexel.edu

Drexel University

THE FACULTY

Department of Accounting
Anthony Curatola, Ph.D., Joseph F. Ford Professor of Accounting and Department Head.
Henry R. Jaenicke, Ph.D., Professor; CPA.
Sung Soo Kwon, Ph.D., Assistant Professor.
Ramesh Narasimhan, Ph.D., Assistant Professor.
Gordian Ndubizu, Ph.D., Associate Professor.
William Stahlin, M.B.A., Instructor; CPA.
Michael G. Welker, M.B.A., Instructor; CPA.

Research interests include auditing standards, tax policy, capital markets, and management control systems.

Department of Economics
Mercia Grassi, M.B.A., Professor.
Shawkat Hammoudeh, Ph.D., Associate Professor.
Bang Nam Jeon, Ph.D., Assistant Professor.
Edward C. Koziara, Ph.D., Professor and Department Head.
Bijou Yang Lester, Ph.D., Assistant Professor.
Vibhas Madan, Ph.D., Assistant Professor.
Roger A. McCain, Ph.D., Professor.
Andrew G. Verzilli, Ph.D., Professor.
Chiou-Shuang Yan, Ph.D., Professor.

Research interests include relationships between world markets, price indices in developing countries, the relationship between economics and politics, and experimental economics.

Department of Finance
Thomas C. Chiang, Ph.D., Professor.
Michael Gombola, Ph.D., Professor and and Department Head.
George Higgins, Ph.D., Assistant Professor.
Thomas J. Hindelang, D.B.A., George B. Francis Professor and Associate Dean; CPA.
Samuel Szewczyk, Ph.D., Associate Professor.
George P. Tsetsekos, Ph.D., Associate Professor.

Research interests include stock volatilities, international investment decisions, plant closings, planning and control of capital expenditures, and multinational financing strategy.

Department of Legal Studies
Roger Collons, J.D., D.B.A., Professor.
Richard P. Freedman, J.D., LL.M., Assistant Professor and Department Coordinator.
Rosalie Kreider, J.D., Instructor.
Neal Orkin, J.D., Associate Professor.
Steven R. Sher, J.D., Associate Professor and Assistant Dean.

Department of Management
Orakwue Arinze, Ph.D., Associate Professor.
Avijit Banerjee, Ph.D., Professor.
An-Min Chung, Ph.D., Professor Emeritus.
Donna DeCarolis, Ph.D., Assistant Professor.
David Gefen, Ph.D.., Assistant Professor.
Jeffrey H. Greenhaus, Ph.D., Mackie Professor.
Robert Laessig, Ph.D., Professor.
Frank Linnehan, Ph.D., Assistant Professor.
Saroj Parasuraman, Ph.D., Professor.
Jason Shaw, Ph.D., Assistant Professor.
Sidney R. Siegel, Ph.D., Associate Professor.
Milton Silver, Ph.D., Professor and Department Head.
Joan L. Weiner, Ph.D., Associate Professor.
Thomas Wieckowski, Ph.D., Assistant Professor and Director of Master's Programs in Business.
D.J. Wu, Ph.D., Assistant Professor.

Research interests include career management, preretirement counseling, MIS design and implementation, artificial intelligence and expert systems, and strategy formation and implementation.

Department of Marketing
Rolph E. Anderson, Ph.D., Royal H. Gibson Sr. Professor.
Trina Larsen, Ph.D., Associate Professor and Department Head.
Jerold Muskin, Ph.D., Professor.
Bert Rosenbloom, Ph.D., G. Behrens Ulrich Professor.
Srinivasan Swaminathan, Ph.D., Assistant Professor.
Kevin L. Webb, Ph.D., Assistant Professor.

Research interests include marketing channels, international marketing, advertising clutter, buyer choice models, and shipper/ carrier partnerships.

Department of Decision Sciences
Lalit K. Aggarwal, Ph.D., Associate Professor.
Steve Bajgier, Ph.D., Associate Professor.
Jonathan S. Burton, Ph.D., Professor and Department Head.
Seung Lae Kim, Ph.D., Assistant Professor.
Hazem Maragah, Ph.D., Assistant Professor.
Fariborz Partovi, Ph.D., Associate Professor.

Research interests include statistical graphics, statistical quality control, total quality management, software reliability, environmetrics, and software development for statistical instruction.

EASTERN MICHIGAN UNIVERSITY

College of Business

Programs of Study

The College of Business offers four graduate programs: the Master of Business Administration (M.B.A.), the Master of Science in Accounting (M.S.A.), the Master of Science in Computer Based Information Systems (M.S.I.S.), and the Master of Science in Human Resource Management and Organizational Development (M.S.H.R./O.D.). All graduate programs in business are accredited by AACSB–The International Association for Management Education. The primary purpose of these programs is to provide the high-level professional education needed to enhance the career opportunities of men and women in business, industry, and public service positions. Courses are offered in the evenings and on weekends.

The objective of the M.B.A. degree is to provide students with a broad understanding of business functions, including the relationship of business to society as a whole, the impact of legal forces on business, and the internationalization of today's business climate. The program is designed to provide a general M.B.A. or a specialized M.B.A. in financial accounting, tax accounting, finance, international business, strategic quality management, human resource management, organizational development, marketing, information systems management, or production/operations management. The program requires 57 to 63 semester hours of graduate-level courses; however, students with undergraduate business degrees may need as few as 33 semester hours to complete the program.

The M.S.A. program is designed to provide a balanced education and an in-depth understanding of the theoretical and practical concepts of accounting. There are several areas of concentration available, and students are given the opportunity to relate accounting topics to other disciplines as they develop the broad base of knowledge necessary to create and use accounting skills.

The M.S.I.S. program is designed for students who are seeking a solid background in systems analysis and design, database management systems, expert systems, data communications, and software engineering. The emphasis is on the application of information systems in business.

The M.S.H.R./O.D. program is designed to prepare professionals who understand the relationship between organizational and human resource needs and are able to implement systems related to structure, process, and human resources.

Research Facilities

Research facilities for students in the College of Business include the main library; a new, modern, expanded facility will open in the winter of 1998. The Gary M. Owen College of Business building, completed in 1990, is a 122,000-square-foot, state-of-the-art facility. It includes classrooms, computer labs, seminar rooms, departmental and faculty offices, and behavioral labs that simulate a typical business environment. The College of Business has equipped its microcomputer laboratory with IBM PC-compatible and Macintosh microcomputers and laser printers. The lab also has Alpha terminals for accessing the University's mainframe. All faculty members are accessible through e-mail and linked to the Internet.

Financial Aid

The Office of Financial Aid provides students with information regarding sources of funds. A limited number of graduate assistantships are available through the College's four academic departments and in the Admissions/ Advising Office. Graduate assistantships are awarded competitively based on scholastic credentials, GMAT results, and experience. A personal interview is required. Stipends for 1997–98 averaged $5700 for nine-month appointments, in addition to an 18-credit-hour tuition waiver. Fellowships are also offered through the University Graduate School. In addition, loans and spring/summer work opportunities are available. Many students receive tuition reimbursement through employment.

Cost of Study

The tuition for fall 1997 was $145 per credit hour for Michigan residents and $339 for nonresidents. Tuition, fees, and books for full-time residents were approximately $6750 per year, and approximately $12,970 per year for nonresidents.

Living and Housing Costs

The University Housing/Dining Services Office provides information to assist students in locating on-campus housing. Double and single rooms in residence halls, as well as efficiency and one- and two-bedroom private apartments, are available on campus. A wide variety of off-campus housing is also available within walking distance of the University. On-campus housing costs $383–$478 per month for a one-bedroom apartment and $437–$521 per month for a two-bedroom apartment, including utilities.

Student Group

In fall 1997, 535 M.B.A. students, 139 M.S.I.S. students, 67 M.S.A. students, and 36 M.S.H.R./O.D. students were enrolled. The average age was 29. Fifty-two percent of the students were male. Seventy-five percent were enrolled part-time. Thirty-one percent were international students from thirty-two countries, with four countries (China, India, Taiwan, and Thailand) making up 65 percent of the international student total. The average class size is 22 students.

Location

The University is located approximately 40 miles west of Detroit, just off I-94 in the heart of the corporate and culturally rich region of southeastern Michigan. The University is a focal point of the historic city of Ypsilanti.

The University

Chartered in 1849, Eastern Michigan University is a coeducational institution with a student population of more than 23,000. The University offers instruction through five academic colleges. The school is located on 225 acres of lawn and wooded areas and 18 miles of walkways and jogging trails, making the campus a beautiful learning environment. A 188,000-square-foot recreation/intramural facility, the University-owned Corporate Education Center, and a championship golf course are among the many impressive University facilities.

Applying

A completed application for graduate admission, the $30 application fee, official transcripts from all collegiate institutions attended, and GMAT results are required. International students are required to submit TOEFL scores as well as a statement of financial responsibility. Admission is granted each semester, with semesters beginning in September, January, and May. All materials should be forwarded to the University Graduate School, Starkweather Hall.

Correspondence and Information

Graduate Business Programs
College of Business Office
Eastern Michigan University
401 Owen
Ypsilanti, Michigan 48197

Telephone: 734-487-4444
Fax: 734-480-0618
E-mail: bill.whitmire@emich.edu
World Wide Web:http://www.emich.edu

Eastern Michigan University

THE FACULTY

Department of Accounting
Linda J. Burilovich, Associate Professor; Ph.D., Michigan.
S. Thomas A. Cianciolo, Professor and Department Head; Ph.D., Michigan State; CPA (Michigan).
George S. Clark, Associate Professor; L.L.M., Wayne State; CPA (Michigan).
Elton A. Devine, Professor; Ph.D., LSU.
Wayne Ellis, Associate Professor; Ph.D.; Michigan.
Roger C. Gledhill, Associate Professor; Ph.D., Virginia Tech.
Susan C. Kattelus, Assistant Professor, Michigan State.
John W. Keros, Associate Professor; M.B.A., Michigan; CPA (Indiana).
Zafar U. Khan, Associate Professor; Ph.D., LSU; CIA.
Morrey Kramer, Associate Professor; Ph.D., Michigan.
Gary B. McCombs, Assistant Professor; M.B.A., Michigan.
D. Robert Okopny, Professor; Ph.D., Texas A&M; CMA, CIA.
Chandra P. Pathak, Professor; Ph.D., Tennessee; CPA (West Virginia).
Susan P. Ravenscroft, Associate Professor; Ph.D., Michigan State; CPA (Michigan).
Mohsen Sharifi, Professor; Ph.D., LSU; CMA.
Andrew G. Snyir, Associate Professor; Ph.D., Purdue.
Linda M. Woodland, Professor; Ph.D., Purdue.
Kenneth C. Young, Associate Professor; Ph.D., Purdue.

Department of Finance and Computer Information Systems
S. Imtiaz Ahmad, Professor; Ph.D., Ottawa.
Alahassane Diallo, Professor; Ph.D., Ohio State.
Juan C. Esteva, Associate Professor; Ph.D., Wayne State.
Badie N. Farah, Professor; Ph.D., Ohio State.
Ramesh C. Garg, Professor; D.B.A., Kent State.
Robert Hanson, Associate Professor; Ph.D., Utah.
Ronald E. Hutchins, Associate Professor; Ph.D., Missouri–Columbia.
Asad Khailany, Professor; D.Sc., Washington (St. Louis).
Wafa Khorshid, Associate Professor; Ph.D., Wayne State.
Roberdt M. Kiss, Associate Professor; Ph.D., Kent State.
Duncan Kretovich, Assistant Professor; Ph.D., Michigan State.
Michel Mitri, Associate Professor; Ph.D., Michigan State.
Susan E. Moeller, Associate Professor; Ph.D., Michigan State.
Stevan Mrdalj, Professor; Ph.D., Belgrade (Yugoslavia).
Mahmud Rahman, Assistant Professor; Ph.D., Texas at Arlington.
Pedro P. Sanchez, Professor; Ph.D., Michigan.
Charles S. Saxon, Professor; Ph.D., Michigan.
Fathi F. Sokkar, Professor; Ph.D., Illinois.
Asrat Tessema, Professor; Ph.D., Iowa.
V. M. Rao Tummala, Professor; Ph.D., Michigan State.
Reino Warren, Assistant Professor; Ph.D., IIT.
Nesa L.–J. Wu, Professor; Ph.D., Purdue.

Department of Management
P. Nick Blanchard, Professor; Ph.D., Wayne State.
Jean Bush-Bacelis, Associate Professor; Ph.D., Wayne State.
Richaurd R. Camp, Professor; Ph.D., Wayne State.
Pradeep Chowdhry, Associate Professor; Ph.D., Arkansas.
James H. Conley, Professor; Ph.D., Michigan State.
Robert P. Crowner, Professor; M.S., Butler.
Jagdish T. Danak, Associate Professor; Ph.D., Oklahoma.
Sahab Dayal, Professor and Department Head; Ph.D., Cornell.
Deborah Ettington, Assistant Professor; Ph.D., Michigan.
Lorraine U. Hendrickson, Professor; Ph.D., Michigan.
Mary E. Vielhaber Hermon, Professor; Ph.D., Michigan.
Raymond E. Hill, Professor; Ph.D., Purdue.
Denise T. Hoyer, Professor; Ph.D., Michigan.
Gregory E. Huszczo, Professor; Ph.D., Michigan State.
Stephanie Newell, Assistant Professor; Ph.D., Massachusetts Amherst.
Jean McEnery, Professor; Ph.D., Wayne State.
John P. Nightingale, Assistant Professor; M.A., North Dakota.
Floyd A. Patrick, Professor; Ph.D., Iowa.
Stewart L. Tubbs, Professor and Dean, College of Business; Ph.D., Kansas.
David A. Victor, Professor; Ph.D., Michigan.
Fraya W. Wagner-Marsh, Professor; D.B.A., Memphis State.
John L. Waltman, Professor; Ph.D., Texas.

Department of Marketing
Daryl L. Barton, Assistant Professor; J.D., Michigan.
Albert W. Belskus, Associate Professor; Ph.D., Michigan.
Joseph L. Braden, Professor; D.B.A., Indiana Bloomington.
Sandra J. Defebaugh, Associate Professor; J.D., Detroit Law.
H. Robert Dodge, Professor and Department Head; Ph.D., Ohio State.
Elizabeth A. Edwards, Assistant Professor; Ph.D., Michigan.
Judy Foster Davis, Professor; Ph.D., Michigan State.
Sammy D. Fullerton, Professor; Ph.D., Michigan State.
Tammy McCullough, Professor; Ph.D., Washington (Seattle).
Hugh B. McSurely, Professor; Ph.D., Syracuse.
G. Russell Merz, Professor; Ph.D., Michigan State.
Colin F. Neuhaus, Professor; Ph.D., Michigan.
Roger A. Peterson, Professor; D.B.A., Tennessee.
Harash Sachdev, Associate Professor; Ph.D., Georgia State.
Matthew H. Sauber, Professor; Ph.D., Texas.
Gary M. Victor, Professor; J.D., Toledo.
Patricia Weber, Professor; Ph.D., Indiana Bloomington.
Joel S. Welber, Assistant Professor; J.D., Wayne State.

ÉCOLE DES HAUTES ÉTUDES COMMERCIALES

affiliated with the Université de Montréal

Programs of Study

The Ph.D. program in administration is designed for the holder of a master's degree in administration or a closely related discipline who has pertinent work experience. It is intended mainly to train researchers and stimulate research on administration problems, particularly in the Québec and Canadian contexts, as well as prepare specialists qualified to join academic faculties and departments. The duration of the preparatory phase (Phase I) depends on the background of the applicant but may not exceed three years. Phase II (specialization) and Phase III (dissertation) require two years of full-time residential study. The Ph.D. program is offered jointly by HEC and the three other universities in the Montréal area.

The Master of Science in administration (M.Sc.) program is designed for the holder of a bachelor's degree in business administration or its equivalent. It aims to satisfy the growing need for specialized analysts and advisers. Students choose an option in applied economics, modelling and decision making, finance, financial engineering, management, management control, marketing, information systems, human resources management, international business, or production and operations management. The program totals 45 credits, including a minimum of 24 course credits. Applicants should expect to study full-time for two years or part-time for three years to complete this program. Some applicants may be required to take up to a year of preparatory courses. Committees composed of members of the teaching staff are assigned to advise students who are preparing theses or essays.

The aim of the Master in Business Administration (M.B.A.) program is to help students acquire professional know-how by mastering business fundamentals and leading-edge techniques of management through a multidisciplinary approach. Moreover, it strives to encourage students to develop a state of mind that will enable them to become managers who act as responsible agents of change, ethical and respectful of others, aware of society's problems and of the issues facing business. For full-time students, the intensive M.B.A. extends over fifty-four weeks, divided into four phases. A part-time option is also available for students who want to remain "in action" at their place of work. Both options include more than 800 hours of classes, guaranteeing a solid, comprehensive and in-depth M.B.A. education. The program totals 52 credits.

The Graduate Diploma, totaling 30 credits, is designed to train administrators for a specific sector in which the students are already involved. Diplomas are currently offered in management, energy sector management, management of cultural organizations, taxation, corporate finance, and professional accounting. All courses are given in French.

Research Facilities

HEC houses its own library in administration sciences and economics, with 320,000 bound volumes and 7,200 periodicals in French and English, microfilms, and newspapers, as well as a computer-assisted bibliographical research and interlibrary loan service with most libraries in Canada, the United States, and Europe. Information Technologies Services gives access to hundreds of applications through the network environment of the school. Software packages and access to databases such as ProQuest, FRI, and CANSIM are available. Many research and study centers, such as the Center for International Business Studies, the Study and Research Group on Decision-making, and the Maclean Hunter Chair of Entrepreneurship, offer facilities for research in their respective fields.

Financial Aid

For a catalog of the loans, grants, and stipends available, students should write to Service aux étudiants, Ecole des Hautes Etudes Commerciales, 3000, chemin de la Côte-Sainte-Catherine, Montréal (Québec) H3T 2A7. It is recommended that all inquiries be initiated at least a year in advance.

Cost of Study

Tuition varies depending on the program and the student's status. Specific information about tuition fees for Canadian and non-Canadian students may be obtained at the Bureau du registraire, Ecole des Hautes Etudes Commerciales, 3000, chemin de la Côte-Sainte-Catherine, Montréal (Québec) H3T 2A7.

Living and Housing Costs

The student services office maintains a listing of available off-campus housing and interested students should apply in person to the address given above. Information about dormitories on campus may be obtained from the Résidences du Campus, 2350, boul. Edouard-Montpetit, Montréal, Québec H3T 1J4.

Student Group

The total enrollment at HEC is 9,000, including about 1,000 graduate students. The School is located on the campus of the Université de Montréal, which has 45,000 students.

Location

Montréal is the second-largest French-speaking city in the world. A financial and commercial center, it is important for such industries as transportation, clothing, food, chemicals, and tourism.

The School

The first institution in Canada and the second in North America—after Wharton (Pennsylvania)—to teach business administration, HEC was founded in 1907. Wholly autonomous administratively and financially, HEC is affiliated academically with the Université de Montréal. HEC maintains ties with businesses, governments, and universities throughout the world, organizing seminars, exchanges, and meetings with their representatives.

Applying

Applications must be submitted on official forms of the School. Admission to all graduate programs is based on the excellence of academic records. The quality and pertinence of work experience are also considered in granting admission to some programs. GMAT scores are not essential except for the M.B.A. program. Candidates for that program must pass either the GMAT or the HEC M.B.A. Admission Test.

Correspondence and Information

For the Ph.D. program:

Secrétariat du programme de doctorat
Ecole des Hautes Etudes Commerciales
3000, chemin de la Côte-Sainte-Catherine
Montréal (Québec) H3T 2A7
Canada

Telephone: 514-340-6264

For the other programs:

Secrétariat des programmes d'études de deuxième cycle
Ecole des Hautes Etudes Commerciales
3000, chemin de la Côte-Sainte-Catherine
Montréal (Québec) H3T 2A7
Canada

Telephone: 514-340-6136
World Wide Web: http://www.hec.ca

École des Hautes Études Commerciales

THE FACULTY

Jean-Marie Toulouse, Director of the School; Post Doctorat Fellow (business administration), UCLA; Ph.D. (social psychology), Montréal.

Professors: O. Aktouf, M.B.A., Ph.D. (administration), HEC–Montréal. F. Amesse, M.B.A., Ph.D. (administration), HEC–Montréal. G. Archambault, M.S. (industrial relations), Montréal; M.B.E., Harvard. H. Barki, M.A. (operations research), Istanbul Technical; Ph.D. (information systems), Western Ontario. H. Boisvert, M.Sc. (operations research), Ph.D. (engineering economic systems), Stanford; CMA. M. Breton, Ph.D. (computer science), Montréal. A. Chanlat, D.B.A., George Washington. J.-F. Chanlat, Ph.D. (sociology), Montréal. J.-C. Chebat, M.B.A., Laval; Ph.D. (sociology), Montréal. F. Colbert, M.B.A., M.Sc. (management), HEC–Montréal. D. L. Dagenais, M.A. (social work), Connecticut; Ph.D. (economics), Montréal. J. David McNeil, D.Sc.écon., Paris. J. Desrosiers, M.Sc.stat., Ph.D. (mathematics), Montréal. G. Dionne, Ph.D. (economics science), Montréal. M. O. Diorio, M.Sc. (management), MIT; Sloan Fellow. C. R. Duguay, D.E.S.écon.appl., HEC–Montréal; M.Ph. (administration), Yale. L. J. Filion, M.A. (international relations), Ottawa; M.B.A., HEC–Montréal; Ph.D. (entrepreneurship), Lancaster. G. Gagné, L.Sc.comm., L.Sc.compt., HEC–Montréal; FCA. G. Gauthier, D.E.S. (applied economics), M.A. (economics), Pennsylvania. J.-C. Guérard, M.S. (statistics), North Carolina. M. Guindon, M.B.A., HEC–Montréal; Ph.D. (education), Montréal; FCGA. T. Hafsi, M.Sc. (management), MIT; D.B.A. (business policy), Harvard. P. Hansen, diplôme d'agrégation supérieur en math, Bruxelles. F. Harel Giasson, M.B.A., Ph.D. (administration), HEC–Montréal. J. Kélada, M.B.A., McGill. L. Lapierre, M.B.A., HEC–Montréal; Ph.D. (management), McGill. A. Lapointe, M.Sc. (economics), Laval; M.Sc. (economics), Harvard; D.Sc. (economics), Toulouse. G. Laporte, M.A. (operational research), Lancaster; Ph.D., London School of Economics. J.-P. Le Goff, Ph.D. (economics), Cornell. J.-Y. Le Louarn, M.S. (industrial relations), Montréal; Ph.D. (human resources management), Cornell. M. Lemelin, Ph.D. (industrial relations), UCLA. F. Leroux, M.B.A., HEC–Montréal; D.Sc.écon., Grenoble. M.-C. Malo, M.B.A., HEC–Montréal; Doctorat 3e cycle, Ecole des Hautes Etudes en Sciences Sociales (Paris). M. N. Marchon, Ph.D. (economics), Ohio State. J. Nantel, M.Sc. (management), HEC–Montréal; D.B.A. (marketing), Indiana. C. Nappi, Ph.D. (economics), McGill. A. Noël, M.B.A., HEC–Montréal; Ph.D. (management), McGill. J. Nollet, M.B.A., HEC–Montréal; Ph.D. (business administration), Western Ontario; CA, CGA, CMA. D. Racette, Ph.D. (economics), Toronto. J. Raynauld, Ph.D. (economics), Queen's at Kingston. S. Rivard, M.B.A., HEC–Montréal; Ph.D. (information systems), Western Ontario. A. Rondeau, D.Ps. (industrial psychology), Montréal. F. Séguin, Ph.D. (sociology), Harvard. L. Séguin Dulude, Ph.D. (economics), Montréal. G. K. Sletmo, Dipl.Adm., Bergen (Norway); Ph.D. (economics and transport), Columbia. Y. Stringer, D.E.S.(écon.appl.), HEC–Montréal; D.Phil. (economics), York (England). M. C. To, M.B.A., HEC–Montréal; Ph.D. (business administration), Concordia. A. Van Peeterssen, D.Sc.écon., Brussels. G. Zaccour, M.Sc. (management), Ph.D. (administration), HEC–Montréal.

Associate Professors: M. Allard, M.Sc.écon., Ph.D. (economics), Montréal. A. Ammara, Dipl., Institut d'Etudes du Développement Economique et Social (Paris); M.B.A., HEC–Montréal. D. Bélanger, M.A. (economics), Ph.D., (economics), Laval. C. Berneman, Ph.D. (marketing), York. J. M. Boisvert, M.Sc. (marketing), Sherbrooke; D.Sc. (applied economics), Louvain. J. Bourgeois, M.B.A., Western Ontario; D. gestion entreprises, Aix-Marseille. G. A. Brenner, Ph.D. (economics), Chicago. D. Chaput, M.A. (business and applied economics), Pennsylvania. M. Chokron, Ing. civil des télécommunications, E.N.S.T. (Paris); D.E.A.stat., Paris. C. Chriqui, Ph.D. (computer science), Montréal. D. Côté, M.A. (agribusiness), Ph.D. (economics), LSU. S. Dahan, D.E.A.stat., Paris. C. Demers, M.Sc. (communication), Montreal; Ph.D. (administration), HEC-Montréal. R. Déry, M.Sc.gestion, HEC–Montréal; Ph.D. (management), Laval. I. Deschamps, M.B.A., HEC–Montréal; D.B.A., Harvard. J.-G. Desforges, Ph.D. (public and international affairs), Pittsburgh. R. Desormeaux, Ph.D. (marketing), Concordia. R. Doucet, LL.M. (social law), Montréal. J. Drew, L.Sc.comm., L.Sc.compt., HEC–Montréal; CA. C. Duhaime, M.B.A., HEC–Montréal; Ph.D., (business administration), Western Ontario. R. Dupré, Ph.D. (economics), Toronto. J.-P. Dupuis, M.Sc. (sociology); Ph.D. (anthropology), Montréal. E. Etienne, Ph.D. (administration), Western Ontario. L. Fabien, M.Sc. (marketing), Sherbrooke; D.Sc. (applied economics), Louvain. V. Félix, L.Sc.comm., L.Sc.compt., HEC–Montréal; CA. M. Filion, M.B.A. (marketing, finance), Columbia. J. Fortin, M.B.A., HEC–Montréal; CA. J.-P. Frénois, L.Sc. (computer science and operational research), Lille; M.B.A., HEC–Montréal. R. Gagné, Ph.D. (economics), Montréal. B. P. Gauthier, M.Sc. (economics), Montréal; Ph.D. (applied economics and managerial sciences), Pennsylvania (Wharton); Post-doctoral Fellow, Washington (St. Louis). J. Gérin-Lajoie, M.A., Saint Louis; Ph.D. (economics), McGill. A. Girard, M.B.A., HEC–Montréal; Ph.D. (accounting), Tennessee; CA. A. Gosselin, Ph.D. (human resource management), Maryland. H. Goyette, C.Phil., UCLA. J. Guertin, D.B.A. Harvard. R. Handfield, M.S. (management), Cornell. J.-P. Hogue, Ph.D. (industrial psychology), Western Reserve. P. Hugron, M.B.A., HEC–Montréal. A. Joly, M.Sc. (gestion internationale), HEC–Montréal; Ph.D. (administration), Sao Paulo. J. Labrecque, M.B.A., Laval; Ph.D. (consumer economics), Cornell. R. Lachance, M.fisc., Sherbrooke; M.Sc. (economics), London School of Economics, CA. A. Lafortune, M.B.A. (information systems), Laval; CA. S. Lalancette, M.Sc. (finance), Sherbrooke; Ph.D. (finance), Concordia. S. Landry, M.Sc.A., Poly, Montréal; Ph.D. (production and operations management), HEC–Montréal; CFPIM. P. Langevin, D.E.S. (applied economics), M.Sc. (economics), Montréal; CMC, Adm.A., CA. P. Lanoie, M.Sc. (management), HEC–Montréal; Ph.D. (economics), Queen's at Kingston. C. Laroche, M.B.A., HEC–Montréal; CA. P. Laroche, Ph.D. (finance), Laval. R. Latour, D.E.S., I.S.U.P., Paris. Ph.D. (management), UCLA. J. D. Leck, M.B.A., Ph.D., McGill. J.-P. Lefebvre, B.Sc.comm., HEC–Montréal; CA. J.-F. L'Her, M.B.A., Ph.D. (finance), Laval. A. Mandron, Dipl.Man., McGill; M.A. (systems analysis), Sherbrooke; Ph.D. (administration), HEC–Montréal; CGA. L. Martel, M.Sc. (administration), HEC–Montréal, FCA. R. G. Martin, M.A., Montréal; Diploma (law), La Salle Extension University. G. Meloche, D.E.S. (administration law and economics), D.E.S. (international law), Ottawa. P. Mireault, M.Sc. (informatique), Montréal; Ph.D. (management science), MIT. E. Morin, M.Ps., Ph.D. (psychology), Montréal. M. Naud, M.fisc., Sherbrooke; CA. G. Paré, M.Sc. (management), HEC-Montréal; Ph.D. (administration), Florida International University. R. Ouellet, Ph.D. (mathematics), Montréal. G. Ouimet, M.Sc. (psychology), Ph.D. (politics), Montréal. R. Parent, M.Sc., Northern Arizona. M. Patry, M.Sc. (management), HEC–Montréal; Ph.D. (economics), British Columbia. T. C. Pauchant, Ph.D. (management), UCLA. A. Pérès, L.Sc.comm., L.Sc.compt., HEC–Montréal; CA. J.-M. Picard, M.S. (experimental statistics), North Carolina. P.-P. Pilon, M.Ph. (statistics), Yale. A. Pinsonneault, M.Sc. (information systems), HEC–Montréal; Ph.D. (administration), California. P. Pitcher, Ph.D. (management), McGill. S. Pozzebon, M.S. (labor economics), Ph.D. (industrial and labor relations), Cornell. M. Provost, M.A. (sociology), Montréal; M.B.A., HEC–Montréal. J. Roy, M.B.A., Laval; Ph.D. (finance), Pennsylvania (Wharton). L. Saint-Cyr, M.Sc. (gestion financière), HEC–Montréal; CA. S. St.-Onge, M.Sc., (management) HEC–Montréal; Ph.D. (organizational behavior and industrial relations), York. J. Talbot, M.B.A., HEC–Montréal; Doctorat (science in administration), Université de Montpellier II. V. The Nhut, M.B.A., HEC–Montréal; Ph.D. (accountancy), Illinois at Urbana–Champaign, CA. B. Tremblay, M.B.A., HEC–Montréal; Doctorat 3e cycle, Ecole des Hautes Etudes en Sciences Sociales (Paris). M. Tremblay, D.E.A., D.Sc. (management), Aix-Marseille. N. Turgeon, M.B.A., Laval; Ph.D. (marketing), Tennessee. L. Vallée, Ph.D. (economics), MIT. S. van Norden, Ph.D. (economics), MIT.

Assistant Professors: Paul André, M.Sc. (accounting), UQAM; Ph.D. (accounting), Waterloo. K. G. Assoé, M.B.A., UQAM; Ph.D. (finance), HEC–Montréal. B. A. Aubert, M.A.Sc. (information systems), Waterloo; Ph.D., HEC–Montréal. C. Bareil, M.Ps. (industrial psychology), Montréal. J.-P. Béchard, M.Ed., Montréal; Ph.D. (management), HEC-Montréal. M. Boyer, M.Sc. (economy), Montreal; M.A. (applied economics and management), Pennsylvania (Wharton). D. Bouteiller, M.Sc.; Ph.D. (industrial relations), Montréal. F. Chauny, M.Sc. (statistics), Montréal; Ph.D. (applied mathematics), Ecole Polytechnique. M. Coiteux, M.A. (economics), Queen's at Kingston; Ph.D. (political science), Institut Universitaire de Hautes Etudes Internationales, Genève. G. Corriveau, M.Sc. (rural economics), Laval. Y. Dufour, M.Sc. (health-care administration), Montréal; Ph.D. (industrial and business studies), Warwick. G. Gauthier, M.Sc. (mathematics), UQAM; Ph.D. (mathematics), Carleton (Canada). M.-H. Jobin, M.B.A. (production and operations management), Laval. V. Kisfalvi, M.A. (littérature anglaise), McGill; M.B.A., HEC–Montréal; Ph.D. (management), McGill. C. Lévesque, M.Sc. (industrial relations), Montréal; Ph.D. (industrial relations), Laval. A. Mersereau, D.E.A. (accounting), Paris IX (Dauphine); CMA. M. Morin, M.Sc. (management), HEC–Montréal; CA. R. Morissette, B.Sc. (accounting), UQTR; CA, CMA. F. Pasin, M.Ing., Polytechnique; Doctorat génie industriel, Ecole centrale de Paris. D. Paul, M. Sc. (management), HEC–Montréal; CA. L. Ricard, M.Sc., Sherbrooke; Ph.D. (marketing), UQAM. L. Rouleau, M.A. (sociology), Laval; Ph.D. (management), HEC–Montréal. J.-G. Simonato, M.Sc., HEC–Montréal; Ph.D. (finance), McGill. P. Soriano, M.Sc.A. (rehcerche opérationnelle), Polytechnique; Ph.D. (informatique et recherche opérationnelle), Montréal. J. Turbide, M.Sc. (management), HEC-Montréal; CA. D. Vencatachellum, Magistère (ing. écon), Université à Aix-Marseille II; Ph.D. (economics), Queen's. M. Vézina, M.Sc. (management), HEC–Montréal; D.Sc. (management), Université de Montpellier II; CA.

Lecturers: Y. Archer, D.E.A., Grenoble. L. Boily, M.B.A., HEC–Montréal. L. E. Péloquin, M.Sc. (management), HEC–Montréal.

EMPORIA STATE UNIVERSITY

School of Business

Programs of Study

The School of Business offers two graduate degrees: the Master of Science in business education and the Master of Business Administration.

The Master of Science in business education degree program requires 35 hours of graduate credit and is designed for teachers seeking advanced preparation in the areas of business, computers, and education. It consists of a core of courses that provide a broad perspective on business education and elective courses designed to meet individual needs.

The Master of Business Administration degree involves a 36-hour program of study. Each M.B.A. student must complete 21 hours of core courses and may select electives in areas such as finance, marketing, accounting, management, international business, or computer information systems. The M.B.A. degree with a concentration in accounting is also offered.

Research Facilities

The William Allen White Library, located near the School of Business, is a modern building with well-lighted study rooms, individual study carrels, and extensive research materials. A modern computer system is available to graduate students for research and course work.

Cremer Hall, which houses the School of Business, is a well-equipped five-story building with microcomputers and computer terminals available for use by graduate students. The School is the home of the Institute for Business and Economic Development, Center for Economic Education, Center for Insurance Education, and Small Business Development Center. These centers conduct research and provide a variety of services for businesses throughout the state and the region.

Financial Aid

The School of Business offers a number of graduate assistantships to qualified students. To qualify for an assistantship, an applicant must have a minimum overall grade point average of 2.5 for four years or 2.75 for the final two years of undergraduate study, based on a 4.0 system. Students who hold teaching assistantships may be eligible for fee reductions during each term in which they hold an assistantship. Nonresident full-time graduate assistants are assessed fees at the same rate as residents of Kansas.

Industries and businesses in the Emporia area are highly cooperative in offering employment to graduate students.

Cost of Study

Estimated fees for a full course load are $1150 per semester for state residents and $3006 per semester for nonresidents. For the 1998 summer session, resident fees were $99 per credit hour, and nonresident fees were $250 per credit hour.

Living and Housing Costs

Estimated cost of on-campus housing and meals is approximately $3600 per academic year. The University Housing Office maintains a list of off-campus rooms, apartments, and houses that may be rented by students. Also, housing is available at the University-owned Emporia State apartments.

Student Group

The total on-campus enrollment is 5,500, with approximately 350 enrolled as full-time and 1,000 as part-time graduate students. About 30 percent of the full-time graduate students receive financial assistance of some kind; 30 percent are international students. The School of Business has approximately 1,000 undergraduate and 80 graduate students.

Location

Emporia, with a population of more than 30,000, is an educational, industrial, trade, and medical center serving 60,000 people in east-central Kansas. It is situated on the eastern edge of the Bluestem region of the Flint Hills and is surrounded by numerous lakes and recreational facilities. The city is located on the Kansas Turnpike, Interstate 35, and the main line of the Santa Fe Railroad. Three major metropolitan areas of the state—Topeka, Kansas City, and Wichita—can be reached easily.

The University and The School

Emporia State University offers twenty-four different graduate degree programs in fifteen departments. "A place where people care about you" is how students describe Emporia State University. ESU is small enough to be comfortable, yet large enough to provide high-quality and comprehensive programs.

The Emporia State School of Business consists of the Division of Management, Marketing, Finance, and Economics; the Division of Accounting and Computer Information Systems; and the Division of Business Education and General Business. Many faculty members work actively as consultants to businesses, government agencies, and educational organizations. They conduct research, publish papers, and are leaders in many different professional organizations.

Applying

Application materials may be obtained from the School of Business. For admission as a master's degree student, an applicant must have a minimum grade point average of 2.5 for the last 60 hours of undergraduate credit. Applicants for the Master of Science program in business education must have a minimum total score of 1000 (verbal, quantitative, and analytical) on the General Test of the Graduate Record Examinations or an equivalent score on the Graduate Management Admission Test (GMAT). For unconditional admission to the M.B.A. program, applicants must submit an acceptable score on the GMAT. The GMAT score and transcripts of previous course work are used to determine admission status.

Correspondence and Information

For the Master of Science in business education:

Nancy Groneman
Chair, Business Education
School of Business
Emporia State University
Emporia, Kansas 66801
Telephone: 316-341-5345
Fax: 316-341-6345
E-mail: groneman@emporia.edu

For the Master of Business Administration:

Donald S. Miller
Director, M.B.A. Program
School of Business
Emporia State University
Emporia, Kansas 66801
Telephone: 316-341-5456
Fax: 316-341-6346
E-mail: millerdo@emporia.edu

Emporia State University

DIVISION CHAIRS

Accounting and Computer Information Systems: Nitham Hindi.
Business Education and General Business: Nancy Groneman.
Management, Marketing, Finance, and Economics: Varkey Titus.

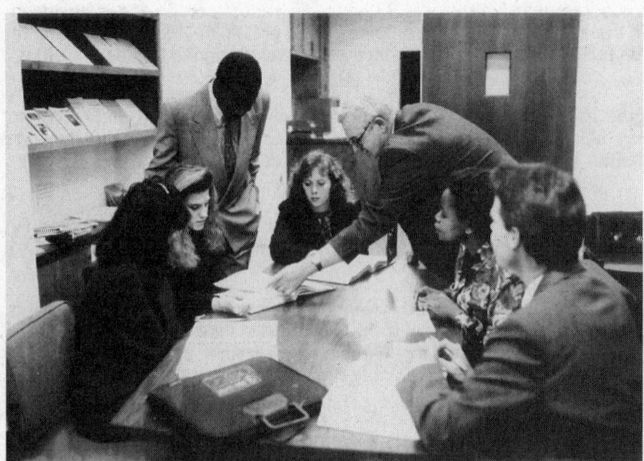

Teamwork and participation help graduate students prepare for professional careers in business.

The School of Business is located in Cremer Hall, a modern five-story building with excellent computer facilities.

Students have opportunities to discuss relevant business issues and develop interpersonal communication skills.

FAIRFIELD UNIVERSITY

School of Business

Programs of Study

The School of Business at Fairfield University is accredited by AACSB–The International Association for Management Education and offers three graduate programs: a Master of Business Administration, with specializations in finance, human resource management, marketing, international business, accounting and taxation, and information technology; a Master of Science in financial management; and a Certificate Program for Advanced Study in Finance or in the other specialization areas mentioned above.

The M.B.A. program is meant to be a generalist degree that covers all the relevant topical areas and gives a student the opportunity to specialize in a functional area of business. The M.B.A. program has three components: core courses, breadth courses, and specialization courses. The M.S. in financial management provides an opportunity for qualified, mature individuals to develop their managerial competence in the area of corporate financial management and focuses on the corporation's objectives and strategies in this area.

The Certificate Program for Advanced Study, a 15-credit program, is offered to provide an opportunity for qualified professionals to enhance their competence and update their skills in finance, human resource management, information technology, international business, marketing, accounting, or taxation. The program is pertinent to those who hold a graduate degree and seek more comprehensive knowledge in a business speciality.

Research Facilities

The Nyselius Library contains more than 325,000 volumes, 500,000 microforms, and 1,810 journals and newspapers, with extensive business collections, including Compact Disclosure (a CD-ROM database of 7,000 public companies), ABI Inform (a CD-ROM index to business periodicals), IAC's Business & Company Profiles (a campuswide network index to 1,000 business periodicals), Britannica Online, and LEXIS-NEXIS. Access to library facilities throughout the area is available. The Computer Center includes a DEC VAX 8600, with terminals throughout the campus; buildings on campus are equipped with fiber optics, and a campuswide network of microcomputers is in place.

Financial Aid

Scholarship aid is limited. Most students are employed and receive substantial financial support from their employers. Graduate research assistantships are also available in limited supply. Students may apply to the Dean for financial assistance after having been accepted into a program. Assistance is usually limited to U.S. citizens.

Cost of Study

Tuition is $450 per credit for part-time students or $7500 per semester for full-time students in 1998–99. The application fee is $40, and the registration fee is $20 per semester.

Living and Housing Costs

The large majority of graduate students live off campus in the surrounding communities. Housing costs in the area vary widely. There is a limited supply of on-campus housing available; single rooms with board are approximately $3600 per semester.

Student Group

Although some students in the program have only recently graduated from an undergraduate institution, most are employed full-time and have had several years of work experience. About 10 percent of the students attend classes full-time. There are an increasing number of international students in the programs, reflecting the desire to increase the international approach of the University. Since most students are employed full-time, most classes are held on evenings and weekends. The maturity and work experience of the students are reflected in the strong academic achievement and atmosphere within the programs.

Student Outcomes

Approximately 90 percent of the students in the M.B.A. and M.S. programs are employed full-time during their course of study and remain with their employers upon graduation. Full-time students usually have either received job offers by graduation or are fully employed within two months after graduation. Employment opportunities remain very good due to the large number of corporations operating in the Fairfield County region.

Location

Fairfield University is situated in a suburban area on the Connecticut shore of Long Island Sound, about 1 hour from New York City and 3 hours from Boston, in America's "academic corridor." This area contains the largest concentration of colleges and universities in the United States, along with the many cultural, recreational, and intellectual activities of such a region. The Fairfield County region is also the site of one of the largest concentrations of major corporate headquarters in the nation, permitting substantial cooperative activities with the business corporate sector and the School's programs.

The University

Fairfield University is a coeducational institution of higher learning founded by the Society of Jesus in 1942. It proudly aspires to the Jesuit tradition of developing the whole intellectual potential of students and creating the true sense of ethical and social responsibility within them.

The 200-acre campus is among the most beautiful in the country. The buildings are modern and well suited to the needs of the students.

In 1997, *U.S. News & World Report* rated Fairfield third in the top twenty-five comprehensive universities in the Northeast region.

Applying

Students who hold a bachelor's degree in any field or major from an accredited college or university and who have demonstrated their ability or potential to do high-quality academic work are encouraged to apply. The criteria for admission to the M.B.A. and M.S. programs are a strong undergraduate grade point average and an appropriate score on the Graduate Management Admission Test (GMAT). A formula score of at least 1100, derived by multiplying the grade point average by 200 and adding the GMAT score, is usually required for admission. Complete official transcripts of all undergraduate and graduate work, two letters of recommendation, and a letter of self-evaluation or work experience must be submitted. Students from non-English-speaking countries are required to submit a Test of English as a Foreign Language (TOEFL) score report with a score of 550 or better. Applicants to the certificate program are not required to submit GMAT scores.

Correspondence and Information

Graduate Admissions
School of Business
Fairfield University
Fairfield, Connecticut 06430

Telephone: 203-254-4070
E-mail: mba@fair1.fairfield.edu
World Wide Web: http://www.fairfield.edu

Fairfield University

THE GRADUATE FACULTY

Walter G. Ryba, Professor of Business Law and Dean; J.D., Connecticut.

Jeffrey B. Arthur, Assistant Professor of Management; Ph.D., Cornell.
Bharat B. Bhalla, Professor of Finance; Ph.D., Cornell.
Russell P. Boisjoly, Professor of Finance; D.B.A., Indiana.
Bruce Bradford, Associate Professor of Accounting; Ph.D., Memphis; CPA.
Paul Caster, Associate Professor of Accounting; Ph.D., North Texas.
Gerald O. Cavallo, Associate Professor of Marketing; Ph.D., CUNY Graduate Center.
J. Michael Cavanaugh, Assistant Professor of Management; Ph.D., Massachusetts.
Sharmila Chatterjee, Assistant Professor of Marketing; Ph.D., Pennsylvania (Wharton).
Arjun Chaudhuri, Associate Professor of Marketing; Ph.D., Connecticut.
Elia V. Chepaitis, Associate Professor of Information Systems; Ph.D., Connecticut.
Thomas E. Conine Jr., Professor of Finance; Ph.D., NYU.
Robert L. DeMichiell, Professor of Information Systems; Ph.D., Connecticut.
Sandra J. Ducoffe, Associate Professor of Marketing; Ph.D., Michigan State.
Walter F. Hlawitschka, Associate Professor of Finance; Ph.D., Virginia.
Christopher L. Huntley, Assistant Professor of Information Systems; Ph.D., Virginia.
Oscar W. Jensen, Professor of Quantitative Analysis; Ph.D., Connecticut.
Helene W. Johns, Assistant Professor of Accounting; LL.M., Florida; CPA.
Lucy V. Katz, Professor of Business Law; J.D., NYU.
Gregory D. Koutmos, Professor of Finance; Ph.D., CUNY Graduate Center.
Philip J. Lane, Associate Professor of Economics; Ph.D., Tufts.
Mark S. LeClair, Associate Professor of Economics; Ph.D., Rutgers.
Patrick S. Lee, Assistant Professor of Operations Management; Ph.D., Carnegie Mellon.
Lisa A. Mainiero, Professor of Management; Ph.D., Yale.
Anna D. Martin, Assistant Professor of Finance; Ph.D., Florida Atlantic.
R. Keith Martin, Professor of Information Systems; Ph.D., Washington (Seattle).
Dawn W. Massey, Assistant Professor of Accounting; Ph.D., Connecticut; CPA.
Sharlene McEvoy, Professor of Business Law; J.D., Connecticut; Ph.D., UCLA.
Krishna Mohan, Associate Professor of Marketing; Ph.D., Wisconsin–Madison.
Milo W. Peck Jr., Assistant Professor of Accounting and Acting Associate Dean; LL.M., Boston University; J.D., Suffolk; CPA.
Patricia M. Poli, Assistant Professor of Accounting; Ph.D., NYU; CPA.
Carl A. Scheraga, Associate Professor of International Business; Ph.D., Connecticut.
David P. Schmidt, Associate Professor of Business Ethics; Ph.D., Chicago.
Anna Tavis, Visiting PepsiCo Scholar; Ph.D., Princeton.
Cheryl L. Tromley, Associate Professor of Management; Ph.D., Yale.
Michael T. Tucker, Professor of Finance; D.B.A., Boston University.
Michael A. Zigarelli, Assistant Professor of Management; Ph.D., Rutgers.

FAIRLEIGH DICKINSON UNIVERSITY

Samuel J. Silberman College of Business Administration

Programs of Study

The Samuel J. Silberman College of Business Administration at Fairleigh Dickinson University (FDU) offers programs that lead to the degrees of Master of Business Administration, Master of Arts in financial economics, and Master of Science in Taxation. Courses for most M.B.A., M.A., and M.S.T. degrees are scheduled during the evenings and on Saturdays. Programs may be pursued either full-time or part-time. Students can complete a program in one calendar year and are required to finish in six calendar years.

The M.B.A. programs are cross-functional in nature and emphasize managerial skills, global-thinking strategy, and entrepreneurship. The traditional M.B.A. is offered in accounting (for nonaccountants), economics, entrepreneurial studies, finance, global management, human resource management, industrial and operations management, international business, management, marketing, pharmaceutical-chemical studies, and quantitative business analysis. All traditional M.B.A. programs require 60 credits. The number of total credits may be decreased to a minimum of 34½ through petition to waive core courses. The M.B.A. in management is offered with a concentration in information systems. The Executive M.B.A. and the Executive M.B.A. in health systems management each require completion of 48 credits, are offered in a Saturday format, and include a two-week seminar in international business that is held at Wroxton College, FDU's British campus. The M.S.T., designed for those who currently practice in the field, and the M.A. in financial economics require completion of 36 credits. The College also offers a 15-credit post-M.B.A. certificate in eleven different subject areas for individuals who already hold their M.B.A. but are interested in updating their business skills or in developing expertise in a particular area of study.

Research Facilities

The University maintains extensive library facilities at all locations, including numerous databases on CD-ROM. A business research library is located at the Teaneck-Hackensack campus. The library offers interlibrary capability to enable students to acquire material that is not available locally. The University also maintains computer laboratories at all locations, including the latest in personal computer technology and software as well as PRIME, Sun 4/490, and VAX 4000/5000 computers.

Financial Aid

Students can obtain loans through several national programs. Federal Work-Study Program awards are available for graduate students on a limited basis. The College of Business Administration offers a number of graduate fellowships on both campuses.

Cost of Study

Tuition for most programs is $522 per credit hour in 1998–99. The annual comprehensive fee is $302 for full-time study and $138 for part-time study. The program fee for the M.B.A. in global management is $25,000. For the Executive M.B.A. and the Executive M.B.A. in health systems management, the program fee for each is $38,856. Program fees for the M.B.A. in global management, the Executive M.B.A., and the Executive M.B.A. in health systems management include all books and materials, travel to the U.K. for the Seminar in International Business, room and board in the U.K., and all University fees.

Living and Housing Costs

Fairleigh Dickinson University makes available a limited amount of graduate housing. Housing in the community is readily available to students.

Student Group

The graduate enrollment at Fairleigh Dickinson University includes approximately 1,700 full- and part-time students at the Teaneck-Hackensack campus and approximately 1,180 at the Florham-Madison campus. The M.B.A. in global management, the Executive M.B.A., and the Executive M.B.A. in health systems management are offered only at the Teaneck-Hackensack campus.

Location

Fairleigh Dickinson University has two major campuses in northern New Jersey, both of which are located in attractive residential suburbs within easy reach of the cultural and social advantages of New York City. The University also operates an extension center in Eatontown, New Jersey, and Wroxton College, an overseas campus in England.

The University

Founded in 1942, Fairleigh Dickinson University today is one of the largest private universities in New Jersey, enrolling approximately 9,000 students. The Teaneck-Hackensack campus was opened in 1954, and the Florham-Madison campus became operational in 1958. Wroxton College, a center for graduate and undergraduate study, was opened in 1965 at historic Wroxton Abbey in England.

Applying

Applications should be filed during the semester preceding the one for which enrollment is sought. Applications are processed on a rolling basis, and early application is encouraged. Applicants for matriculation must hold a baccalaureate degree from a regionally accredited institution and must file the appropriate graduate studies application. The application and fee, official transcripts of all education beyond high school, and scores from the Graduate Management Admission Test (GMAT) should be forwarded to the admissions office.

Correspondence and Information

Graduate Admissions
Fairleigh Dickinson University
285 Madison Avenue—M103C
Madison, New Jersey 07940
Telephone: 943-443-8900

Graduate Admissions
Fairleigh Dickinson University
1000 River Road—T170A
Teaneck, New Jersey 07666
Telephone: 201-692-2551

Fairleigh Dickinson University

THE FACULTY

Administration

Paul Lerman, Professor of Business Administration and College Dean; Ph.D., NYU.
Robert S. Greenfield, Professor of Economics and Finance and Director of M.B.A. Programs, Florham-Madison; Ph.D., Rutgers.
Ronald Heim, Associate Professor of Marketing and Acting Associate Dean, Florham-Madison; Ph.D., Cornell.
Richard W. Kjetsaa, Associate Professor of Economics and Finance and M.B.A. Program Director, Teaneck-Hackensack; Ph.D., Fordham.
Govindasami Naadimuthu, Professor of Information Systems and Associate Dean, Teaneck-Hackensack; Ph.D., Kansas State.
Janette Shurdom, Director of Executive and Special Programs; M.B.A., Fairleigh Dickinson.
Walter Slegesky, Assistant Dean for Special and Off-Campus Programs and Director of the M.B.A. in Pharmaceutical-Chemical Studies; M.B.A., Fairleigh Dickinson.
Donald Zimmerman, Associate Professor of Management and Director of the Executive M.B.A. in Health Systems Management; Ph.D., SUNY at Stony Brook.

Department of Accounting, Taxation, Law, Economics, Finance and International Business

Virote Angkatavanich, Professor of Economics and Finance; Ph.D., New School. Thomas J. Beam, Professor of Accounting; Ph.D., NYU; CPA. John Paul Broussard, Assistant Professor of Finance; Ph.D., LSU. Frank Brunetti, Professor of Law and Taxation; LL.M., NYU. Matthew Calderisi, Associate Professor of Accounting; M.B.A., Iona; CPA. J. Richard Chaplin, Professor of Accounting; M.B.A., St. John's (New York); CPA. Theodore M. David, Associate Professor of Accounting; J.D., NYU. Robert A. DeFilippis, Associate Professor of Accounting; M.B.A., Rutgers; CPA. Evangelos S. Djimopoulos, Professor of Economics; Ph.D., Columbia. Amitabh S. Dutta, Associate Professor of Finance; Ph.D., Tennessee. Frederick Englander, Professor of Economics; Ph.D., Rutgers. Richard K. Ferguson, Associate Professor of Accounting; M.B.A., St. John's (New York); CPA. Henry L. Fuentes, Associate Professor of Accounting; M.B.A., Seton Hall; CPA. Patrick Gaughan, Associate Professor of Economics and Finance; Ph.D., CUNY Graduate Center. Kenneth R. Gillies, Associate Professor of Accounting; M.B.A., Rutgers; CPA. Claude Jonnard, Associate Professor of Economics and Finance; M.B.A., NYU. Adam Kessler, Associate Professor of Economics; Ph.D., NYU. Joseph J. Kiernan, Assistant Professor of Economics and Finance; Ph.D., Fordham. Roger Koppl, Professor of Economics and Finance; Ph.D., Auburn. Leon L. Kurland, Assistant Professor of Law; J.D., Seton Hall; CPA. Y. K. Lee, Professor of Economics; Ph.D., Columbia. Braimoh Oseghale, Associate Professor of Economics and Finance; Ph.D., Temple. Lance Rook, Associate Professor of Taxation; J.D., Columbia. Jonathan Schiff, Professor of Accounting; Ph.D., NYU. Frank L. Simonie, Associate Professor of Business Law; LL.B., Harvard. John H. Skarbnik, Associate Professor of Taxation; LL.M., NYU; CPA. Panadda Tantral, Assistant Professor of Accounting; Ph.D., NYU. Joseph Tramutola Jr., Professor of Business Law; J.D., Fordham. Rosemarie Twomey, Associate Professor of Business Law; J.D., West Virginia. Thomas Zullo, Associate Professor of Accounting and Law; J.D., Fordham; CPA.

Department of Management, Marketing, Information Systems and Sciences

Mary H. Beaven, Professor of Management; Ph.D., Northwestern. Gary J. Bronson, Professor of Information Systems; Ph.D., Stevens. Thomas Butler, Professor of Management; Ph.D., NYU. Rajesh Chandrashekaran, Assistant Professor of Marketing; Ph.D., Rutgers. Marlow A. Christensen, Assistant Professor of Entrepreneurial Studies; Ph.D., Brigham Young. Subahasish Dasgupta, Assistant Professor of Information Systems; Ph.D., CUNY, Baruch. Arthur Dolinsky, Associate Professor of Marketing; Ph.D., Pennsylvania (Wharton). Sandipa Dublish, Assistant Professor of Management; Ph.D., Florida International. Alan Fask, Associate Professor of Decision Systems; Ph.D., NYU. Joseph J. Fink, Associate Professor of Marketing; Ph.D., NYU. Mrudulla Gnanadesikan, Associate Professor of Systems; Ph.D, Purdue. Shanthi Gopalakrishnan, Assistant Professor of Management; Ph.D., Rutgers. Joel I. Harmon, Associate Professor of Management; Ph.D., SUNY at Albany. Drew Harris, Assistant Professor of Management; Ph.D., NYU. James Hutton, Assistant Professor of Management; Ph.D., Texas at Arlington. Gwen Jones, Assistant Professor of Management; Ph.D., SUNY at Albany. Yongbeom Kim, Assistant Professor of Information Systems; Ph.D., NYU. Ann F. Lucas, Professor of Management; Ph.D., Fordham. Gaston Mendoza, Associate Professor of Decision Sciences; Ph.D., Temple. Osita Nwachukwu, Associate Professor of Management; Ph.D., Mississippi. John F. O'Brien, Assistant Professor of Management; Ph.D., NYU. Richard Ottaway, Professor of Management; Ph.D., Manchester (England). Richard Panicucci, Professor of Quantitative Analysis; M.B.A., Fairleigh Dickinson. Manuel Pontes, Assistant Professor of Marketing; Ph.D., Florida. Dennis Scotti, Professor of Management and Public Administration; Ph.D., Temple. Sung Shim, Assistant Professor of Management; Ph.D., Rensselaer. Steven Smith, Assistant Professor of Management; Ph.D., Rutgers. Robert Stinerock, Assistant Professor of Marketing; Ph.D., Columbia. Srinivas Talluri, Assistant Professor of Management, Marketing, Information Systems and Sciences; Ph.D., Texas at Arlington. William L. Trombetta, Professor of Marketing; Ph.D., Ohio State. Daniel F. Twomey, Professor of Management; D.B.A., Kent State. Alkis Vazacopoulos, Instructor of Information Systems and Sciences; Ph.D., Carnegie Mellon. Zhaobo Wang, Assistant Professor of Production and Operations Management; Ph.D., Rutgers. Mahmoud Watad, Assistant Professor of Information Sciences; Ph.D., NYU. Peter Will, Assistant Professor of Pharmaceutical Chemistry and Management; Ph.D., Missouri. Kwangsun Paul Yoon, Professor of Information Systems and Sciences; Ph.D., Kansas State.

Pharmaceutical-Chemical Studies

Francis J. Honn, Professor of Pharmaceutical-Chemical Studies and Alfred E. Driscoll Chair Holder; Ph.D., Pittsburgh.

George Rothman Institute of Entrepreneurial Studies

James Almeida, Assistant Professor of Entrepreneurial Studies; M.B.A., Northeast Louisiana. Marlow A. Christensen, Associate Professor of Entrepreneurial Studies; Ph.D., Brigham Young. Thomas Kaplan, Assistant Professor of Entrepreneurial Studies; Ph.D., Virginia Commonwealth.

FLORIDA INSTITUTE OF TECHNOLOGY

School of Business

Programs of Study

The School of Business offers the Master of Business Administration (M.B.A.) degree on the Melbourne campus. The M.B.A. degree requires completion of 36 semester credits of core and elective courses. Requirements are identical for full-time and part-time students. The M.B.A. degree also requires completion of nine core courses and three elective courses. Electives can be taken with the faculty adviser's approval from other graduate-level course offerings.

Research Facilities

Academic and Research Computing Services (ARCS) provides graduate students with a wide range of computing resources for course work and research. These resources include a Sun Enterprise 3000 and several Sun SPARC Workstations. These machines are connected internally as part of the campus network and externally to the Internet. Many programs and departments have their own computing resources, which are also connected to the campus network. Access to these computing resources is available in computer labs and academic departments and through dial-up lines. Programming languages supported include C, Pascal, ADA, FORTRAN, and C++. A staff of professionals is available to assist users with consultation and documentation. In addition to these resources, ARCS maintains a large microcomputer center, located in the Library Pavilion.

Financial Aid

Each fall, assistantships are granted to full-time students for the duration of their degree work. Assistantships are merit based.

Cost of Study

Tuition is $550 per semester credit hour for graduate students in 1998–99. Book costs are estimated at $550 per year for a full-time student.

Living and Housing Costs

Room and board on campus cost approximately $2200 per semester in 1998–99. On-campus housing (dormitories and apartments) is available for full-time single and married graduate students, but priority for dormitory rooms is given to undergraduate students. Many apartment complexes and rental houses are available near the campus.

Student Group

Approximately 4,000 students are enrolled at the Melbourne campus. About 150 are enrolled in graduate study in business. About 35 percent of the students in graduate business programs are female.

Student Outcomes

School of Business graduates have been employed by such companies as Harris Corp., Northrop Grumman, United Technologies, First Union National Bank, Holmes Regional Medical Center, Johnson Controls World Services, McDonnell Douglas, Omni Corp., Dictaphone, Lockheed Martin, Rockwell International, Merrill Lynch, JC Penney, and Bell South.

Location

Melbourne is located within 3 miles of the Atlantic Ocean on the east coast of Florida, about midway between Jacksonville and Miami. It is approximately 30 miles from the Kennedy Space Center and 70 miles from Disney World. The area, especially known for its excellent beaches, has all of the outdoor recreational activities for which Florida is famous.

The Institute

Florida Institute of Technology was founded in 1958, primarily as a graduate school to provide advanced scientific education for the engineers and scientists at the Kennedy Space Center. It has developed rapidly into a residential university, providing both undergraduate and graduate education in the sciences, engineering, psychology, aviation, and business. It offers Ph.D. degrees in biology, electrical engineering, oceanography, physics, and science education, as well as M.S. degrees in applied mathematics, aviation, biology, computer science, electrical engineering, environmental engineering, environmental science, management, mechanical engineering, ocean engineering, oceanography, operations research, physics, and science education. The campus covers more than 180 acres and includes a beautiful botanical garden and an internationally known palm tree collection.

Applying

Forms and instructions for application may be obtained from the Office of Graduate Admissions. Students are evaluated for admissions purposes on the basis of their undergraduate records, with consideration given to work experience. The GMAT is required. Admissions are accepted for any semester, but for optimum scheduling application should be made for the fall term, which begins in late August.

Correspondence and Information

Graduate Admissions
Florida Institute of Technology
Melbourne, Florida 32901
Telephone: 407-674-8027
800-944-4398 (toll-free)
Fax: 407-723-9468
World Wide Web: http://www.fit.edu

Dr. David D. Hott, Associate Dean
School of Business
Florida Institute of Technology
Melbourne, Florida 32901
Telephone: 407-674-7392
E-mail: dhott@fit.edu

Florida Institute of Technology

THE FACULTY AND THEIR RESEARCH

A. T. Hollingsworth, Dean; Ph.D., Michigan State. Enhancement of creativity in organizations, relating pay to performance, small business development, ethical behavior in organizations.
Muzaffar A. Shaikh, Associate Dean; Ph.D., Illinois. Management science, production management, management information systems, decision support system models, systems/software engineering.

Gerald A. Cahill, Ph.D., NYU; PE. Corporate strategy and policy, financial management and planning, general corporate management.
John P. Callahan, Ed.D., Central Florida. Managerial psychology in work organizations, women's role in management, human resources, labor and industrial relations.
Karen Chambliss, Ph.D., Florida Atlantic. Finance, investments, mergers and acquisitions, international finance.
Lawrence B. Crowson, Alabama. Causal modeling and theory development in marketing, multivariate analysis, marketing strategy.
Carolyn J. Fausnaugh, Ph.D. candidate, Georgia. Policy and strategy, entrepreneurship, quality management in service organizations.
Gerald F. Goldberg, Ph.D., New School. Econometric modeling and forecasting, statistical analysis, operations research/management science applications for business decision making.
David Hott, Ph.D., Lehigh. Operations research, managerial decision making, business ethics, simulation.
T. Roger Manley, Ph.D., RIT. Behavior of individuals in work organizations, organizational effectiveness and productivity, work redesign, organizational change and development, measurement and management of work-related stress, measurement of organizational culture.
Michael H. Slotkin, Ph.D., North Carolina at Chapel Hill. Strategic trade policy, applied microeconomics, managerial economics, international business, macroeconomics.
John Snyder, Ph.D., South Carolina. Financial accounting, auditing, systems, health care accounting, behavioral aspects of accounting/auditing, expert systems, modeling.

All classes are conducive to interactive teaching methods.

High-tech computer lab located in the School of Business building is open throughout the day for students' use.

Student advisory committee on its way to a meeting.

FLORIDA INTERNATIONAL UNIVERSITY

College of Business Administration

Programs of Study

The College of Business Administration offers programs leading to the following degrees: Master of Accounting (M.Acc.), Master of Business Administration (M.B.A.), Master of Science in Finance (M.S.F.), and Master of Science in Taxation (M.S.T.). It also offers an Executive M.B.A. and an Executive M.S.T., as well as a doctoral program in business administration leading to the Doctor of Philosophy (Ph.D.).

The undergraduate and master's programs in business administration and accounting (including taxation) offered by the College of Business Administration at Florida International University are accredited by AACSB–The International Association for Management Education.

Research Facilities

The library collection comprises 1.25 million volumes, more than 8,800 serials, and a computerized catalog and bibliography searching capability. A DEC Alpha 7620 mainframe computer in the University Computing Center and several networked computer laboratories are available for business student use. Internet access is available.

Financial Aid

Tuition fee waivers and scholarships are available for all programs. A limited number of research and graduate assistantships are also available.

Cost of Study

Tuition for 1997–98 was $114.99 per credit hour for Florida residents and $385.73 per credit hour for nonresidents. This did not include the cost of books, supplies, and health, parking, and activity fees. An increase is anticipated for the 1998–99 academic year.

Living and Housing Costs

University housing is available in on-campus residence halls. On-campus housing fees range from $1345 to $2520 per semester, depending on the type of accommodation. Rents for private apartments in the area vary according to size and location.

Student Group

The College of Business Administration has an enrollment of more than 800 graduate students. Approximately 10 percent of those pursuing graduate degrees are international students. The University anticipates admitting students into the Ph.D. program every other year beginning in 1999–2000.

Location

The University is a multicampus institution. The University Park Campus is located approximately 10 miles west of downtown Miami on a 344-acre tract in west-central Dade County. The North Campus is located on Biscayne Bay in the city of North Miami. Selected doctoral seminars are offered at the University Tower in Fort Lauderdale. Because the University is located in the Miami area, it offers a dynamic metropolitan environment; a rich diversity of people, languages, and cultures; and an unusually good opportunity for students and faculty to explore and develop international emphases—both personally and professionally. Year-round activities include swimming, waterskiing, scuba diving, sailing, fishing, tennis, golf, and horseback riding. Students occasionally spend a weekend in the Florida Keys or the Bahamas.

The University

Florida International University, a member of the State University System of Florida, is recognized as one of the Southeast's leading centers of higher education, scholarly research, and technological activity. The University was founded in 1965 and opened for classes in 1972. The largest public university in South Florida, FIU was included in *U.S. News & World Report's Annual Guide to America's Best Colleges* from 1988 through 1994. *Money* magazine named FIU as one of the top ten public commuter colleges in the U.S. in its 1995 edition of "Money Guide". FIU was invited in 1992 to join the National Association of State Universities and Land-Grant Colleges (NASULGC), one of the nation's oldest and most prestigious higher education institutions. The University's student body numbers more than 30,000 enrolled in thirteen colleges and schools.

Applying

Students must hold a baccalaureate degree from an accredited college or university. Admission is based upon the undergraduate grade point average, Graduate Management Admission Test scores, and professional employment experience. International students must also submit TOEFL scores.

Correspondence and Information

For master's degree programs:
Graduate Counseling Office
College of Business Administration
Florida International University
University Park
Miami, Florida 33199
Telephone: 305-348-3256
Fax: 305-348-3278

For the doctoral degree program:
Director, Doctoral Program
College of Business Administration
Florida International University
University Park
Miami, Florida 33199
Telephone: 305-348-2751
Fax: 305-348-3278

Florida International University

THE FACULTY

Accounting

Rolf K. Auster, Professor; Ph.D., Northwestern, 1971. Amelia A. Baldwin, Associate Professor; Ph.D., Virginia Tech, 1991. Delano H. Berry, Assistant Professor; D.B.A., Kentucky, 1989. Doria Bonham-Yeaman, Associate Professor; J.D., Tennessee, 1957. Lewis F. Davidson, Professor; Ph.D., Penn State, 1974. Manuel Dieguez, Instructor; M.S.M., Florida International, 1976. Mortimer A. Dittenhofer, Professor; Ph.D., American, 1974. Donald W. Fair, Instructor and Associate Dean; M.Acc., Bowling Green State, 1971. Georgina M. Garcia, Instructor; M.S.M., Florida International, 1982. Rosalie C. Hallbauer, Associate Professor; Ph.D., Florida, 1973. Harvey S. Hendrickson, Professor; Ph.D., Minnesota, 1963. David Lavin, Associate Professor; Ph.D., Illinois at Urbana-Champaign, 1974. Myron S. Lubell, Associate Professor; D.B.A., Maryland, 1978. David Manry, Assistant Professor; Ph.D., Texas at Austin, 1994. Leandro S. Nunez, Instructor; J.D., Nova, 1982. Robert R. Oliva, Associate Professor; Ph.D., Florida International, 1995. Felix Pomeranz, Professor and Associate Director; Ph.D., Birmingham (England), 1992. Leonardo Rodriguez, Professor; D.B.A., Florida State, 1975. Ena Rose-Green, Assistant Professor; Ph.D., Florida State, 1994. James H. Scheiner, Professor and Director; Ph.D., Ohio State, 1975. Jerry Turner, Assistant Professor; Ph.D., Texas A&M, 1994. Clark Wheatley, Assistant Professor; Ph.D., Virginia Tech, 1994. Richard H. Wiskeman, Instructor; M.B.A., Miami (Florida), 1961. John A. Wrieden, Instructor; J.D., George Mason, 1980. Harold E. Wyman, Professor; Ph.D., Stanford, 1967.

Decision Sciences and Information Systems

Dinesh Batra, Associate Professor; Ph.D., Indiana, 1989. Joyce J. Elam, James L. Knight Professor and Dean; Ph.D., Texas at Austin, 1977. Sushil K. Gupta, Professor and Vice Provost; Ph.D., Delhi, 1979. Christos P. Koulamas, Professor and Chair; Ph.D., Texas Tech, 1990. Jerzy Kyparisis, Professor; D.S.C., George Washington, 1983. Tomislav Mandakovic, Professor; Ph.D., Pittsburgh, 1978. Kenneth Murphy, Assistant Professor; Ph.D., Carnegie Mellon, 1994. Rajiv Sabherwal, Associate Professor; Ph.D., Pittsburgh, 1989. Larry A. Smith, Associate Professor; Ph.D., SUNY at Buffalo, 1975. Steve H. Zanakis, Professor; Ph.D., Penn State, 1973. Peter J. Zegan, Instructor; M.S., Florida, 1970.

Finance

Gary A. Anderson, Associate Professor; Ph.D., Illinois at Urbana-Champaign, 1976. Joel R. Barber, Associate Professor; Ph.D., Arizona, 1989. Robert M. Bear, Professor; Ph.D., Iowa, 1970. Gerald Bierwag, Ryder System Professor; Ph.D., Northwestern, 1962. Chun-Hao Chang, Associate Professor; Ph.D., Northwestern, 1988. Robert T. Daigler, Associate Professor; Ph.D., Oklahoma, 1976. Krishnan Dandapani, Professor; Ph.D., Penn State, 1983. Maria E. DeBoyrie, Assistant Professor; Ph.D., Florida International, 1995. Shahid Hamid, Associate Professor; Ph.D., Maryland, 1988. James D. Keys, Instructor; M.B.A., Florida International, 1977. Raul Moncarz, Professor; Ph.D., Florida State, 1969. Simon J. Pak, Associate Professor; Ph.D., Berkeley, 1980. Ali M. Parhizgari, Professor and Director, M.B.A. Program; Ph.D., Maryland, 1976. Arun J. Prakash, Professor; Ph.D., Oregon, 1979. Emmanuel N. Roussakis, Professor; Ph.D., Louvain (Belgium), 1968. Michael A. Sullivan, Assistant Professor; Ph.D., Yale, 1989. William W. Welch, Associate Professor; Ph.D., Michigan, 1974. John S. Zdanowicz, Professor, Chair, and Director, Center for Banking and Finance; Ph.D., Michigan State, 1971.

Management and International Business

Mirtha Ansoleaga, Instructor; M.B.A., Florida International, 1996. Constance S. Bates, Associate Professor; D.B.A., Indiana, 1979. Maria Corrales, Instructor; M.B.A., Florida International, 1996. Larry Cox, Assistant Professor; Ph.D., Nebraska–Lincoln. Gary S. Dessler, Professor; Ph.D., CUNY, Baruch, 1972. Herman W. Dorsett, Associate Professor; Ed.D., Columbia, 1969. Dana L. Farrow, Professor and Associate Dean; Ph.D., Rochester, 1977. Earnest Friday, Assistant Professor; Ph.D., Miami (Florida), 1979. G. Ronald Gilbert, Associate Professor; Ph.D., USC, 1973. Joyce Harrigan, Instructor; M.B.A., Clark Atlanta, 1988. Richard M. Hodgetts, Professor; Ph.D., Oklahoma, 1968. K. Galen Kroeck, Associate Professor; Ph.D., Akron, 1981. Jan B. Luytjes, Professor; Ph.D., Pennsylvania, 1955. Karl O. Magnusen, Associate Professor and Chair; Ph.D., Wisconsin, 1970. Sherry Moss, Associate Professor; Ph.D., Florida State, 1991. Stephen L. Mueller, Assistant Professor; Ph.D., Texas at Dallas. Eleanor B. Polster, Instructor; M.B.A., Florida International, 1981. Kannan Ramaswamy, Associate Professor; Ph.D., Virginia Tech, 1990. Leonardo Rodriguez, Professor; D.B.A., Florida State, 1975. Donald Roomes, Instructor and Coordinator, Bachelor of Business Administration Weekend Program; M.B.A., Florida International, 1990. Ronnie Silverblatt, Associate Professor; Ph.D., Georgia State, 1982. George Sutija, Associate Professor; M.B.A., Columbia, 1961. Anisya S. Thomas, Associate Professor; Ph.D., Virginia Tech, 1990. Enzo R. Valenzi, Professor; Ph.D., Bowling Green State, 1970. Mary Ann Von Glinow, Professor; Ph.D., Ohio State, 1978.

Marketing and Business Environment

Mary Jane Burns, Assistant Professor; Ph.D., Tennessee, Knoxville, 1993. Deborah V. Cohen, Assistant Professor; Ph.D., Columbia, 1992. Dennis Gayle, Associate Professor; Ph.D., UCLA, 1982. Jonathan Goodrich, Professor; Ph.D., SUNY at Buffalo, 1977. Barnett Greenberg, Professor and Associate Dean; Ph.D., Colorado, 1971. Robert H. Hogner, Associate Professor; Ph.D., Pittsburgh, 1975. Carl J. Kranendonk, Instructor; M.B.A., Tulsa, 1969. Tiger Li, Assistant Professor; Ph.D., Michigan State, 1994. Paul Miniard, Professor; Ph.D., Florida, 1981. John A. F. Nicholls, Professor and Chair; D.B.A., Indiana, 1968. Marta Ortiz, Associate Professor; Ph.D., Miami (Florida), 1979. Karen Paul, Professor and Associate Dean; Ph.D., Emory, 1974. Lynda K. Raheem, Instructor and Assistant Dean; M.B.A., Miami (Florida), 1974. Bruce F. Seaton, Associate Professor; Ph.D., Washington (St. Louis), 1974. Philip L. Shepherd, Associate Professor; Ph.D., Vanderbilt, 1981. Kimberly A. Taylor, Assistant Professor; Ph.D., Pennsylvania, 1994. John Tsalikis, Associate Professor; Ph.D., Mississippi, 1987.

College of Business Administration Building.

FORDHAM UNIVERSITY

The Graduate School of Business Administration

Programs of Study

Fordham's Graduate School of Business Administration is committed to educating business professionals who can manage effectively at every level in any size company anywhere in the world. To fulfill its mission, Fordham takes full advantage of its location in New York City, the business capital of the world, to provide a "global gateway" for its students.

The Fordham M.B.A. is accredited by the American Assembly of Collegiate Schools of Business and can be earned in one of six areas of study, most of which require 60 credit hours for completion: accounting, communications and media management, finance, information and communication systems, management systems, and marketing.

Fordham's Graduate School of Business Administration also offers an eighteen-month Deming Scholars M.B.A. Program in Quality Management, a joint J.D./M.B.A. program with Fordham Law School, and an M.S. in taxation. There is also a Global Professional M.B.A. Program, which is designed to prepare business professionals for career opportunities in the international marketplace. A special 90-credit M.B.A. in taxation and accounting combines the M.B.A. in accounting and the M.S. in taxation. An international business designation can be added to any concentration. A new program, the Transnational M.B.A. (T.M.B.A), is geared toward students who typically have either ten or more years of business experience or are on a fast track to upper-level managerial positions. An M.B.A. upgrade is soon to be offered to provide the most current business education to individuals who completed their M.B.A. degrees ten or more years ago. A final offering is the Beijing M.B.A. Fordham's graduate school of business is serving as the lead school in a consortium of twenty-four U.S. Jesuit universities that offer an M.B.A. program in Beijing, China. Fordham will be the degree-granting institution in this program.

Throughout their course work, students are encouraged to take advantage of the access provided to corporate leaders and Wall Street executives. Fordham has two formal programs that provide networking opportunities. The Mentoring Program formally pairs an individual student with an executive or alumnus; the Field Study Program assigns student teams to consulting projects for corporations.

Fordham uses the trimester system, admitting students in September, January, and April. Classes are offered in the afternoons and evenings, Monday through Thursday, with some Saturday classes. Full-time students can complete their M.B.A.'s in twelve to eighteen months. Part-time students can schedule their classes to suit personal and professional needs.

Research Facilities

The Graduate School of Business Administration's Technology Center provides hardware and software for education projects, research, and experimentation. Students have access to LEXIS-NEXIS, Dow Jones News Retrieval, and Bloomberg Financial Markets online databases, in addition to word processing, spreadsheet, desktop publishing, and programming software. Students also have access to the University's Lincoln Center computer facility, which consists of a public-user terminal area and four supervised rooms of microcomputer equipment, including two VAX timesharing computers. All mainframe computers are inked via an internal DECNET network, which can be accessed through many microcomputers as well. The University offers students access to the Internet, along with an e-mail address, and terminals are located throughout the main academic hall. Fordham's library at Lincoln Center holds reference materials, books, and periodicals in the field of business. Ninety-five percent of the collection is accessible through the online catalog system. Through the in-depth search capabilities of the system, students can access more than 20 million records stored in more than 100 data files. The library also has CD-ROM workstations with business databases.

Financial Aid

Financial aid is available in the form of graduate assistantships, loan programs, scholarships, and fellowships. Graduate assistantships are awarded to full-time students for up to 12 credits in tuition per trimester for a maximum of three trimesters. Loan programs include the Fordham business school's loan program, which allows students registered for 6 or more credits to borrow up to $2500 per academic year; subsidized and unsubsidized Federal Stafford Loans, which provide up to $18,500 annually; M.B.A. Loans, a commercial loan program providing additional funds of up to $15,000 annually; and GradEXCEL Loans, an educational loan program offering students between $2000 and $20,000 annually. Scholarships/fellowships include the Alexis Welsh Memorial Scholarship, the Financial Women's Association Scholarship, the Global Fellowship Program, the Hitachi Fellowship, the Minority Business Students Alliance Scholarship, the National Black M.B.A. Association Scholarship, and the Xerox Fellowship.

Cost of Study

The annual tuition for 1998–99 is $1680 per 3-credit course ($560 per credit). Other fees include a nonrefundable $50 application fee, a $15 student activities fee per trimester, and an $8 insurance fee per trimester.

Living and Housing Costs

Off-campus housing is estimated to cost $11,000 per year.

Student Group

The Graduate School of Business Administration's student population is approximately 1,600, with 1,350 attending on a part-time/evening basis and 250 attending full-time. The average age is 28. International students comprise nearly 40 percent of the full-time student population and represent more than thirty countries. On average, students have had four years of work experience when they commence their M.B.A. studies.

Location

Fordham's business school is located in Manhattan at Lincoln Center on a campus that marks the southern border of the cultural heart of New York City. Fordham's 7-acre green campus includes the academic buildings and the residence hall, all of which are connected by a beautifully landscaped central plaza that serves as an island of calm in a city of skyscrapers. The campus is one block from Central Park, where 840 green acres provide a lush setting for a host of recreational activities, and Columbus Circle, a major transportation hub in midtown Manhattan.

Fordham also has a satellite campus in Tarrytown, New York, in the heart of suburban Westchester County. Students may take courses at both the Tarrytown and Lincoln Center locations.

The University and The School

Fordham was founded as a Jesuit institution in 1841 and formally organized as a university under a charter granted by the New York State Legislature in 1846. A 150-year heritage in New York City, a 450-year-old Jesuit tradition of quality education, and its diversity of academic specialties distinguishes Fordham from other universities. Fordham's Graduate School of Business Administration conferred its first M.B.A. degrees in 1971 at the school's then-new Lincoln Center campus in Manhattan. The School has adopted a new motto, "Urbi et Orbi"... For the City and the World, which illustrates a commitment to providing an international orientation for its students. The atmosphere of the School, however cosmopolitan, is friendly, open, and caring. Fordham's primary concern is each individual student's well-being and future success.

Applying

Admission to the M.B.A. program is open to all qualified women and men who hold a bachelor's degree from an accredited undergraduate institution. The Admissions Committee considers the applicant's academic background, GMAT results, and previous work experience, along with personal statements, a resume, and interviews. The TOEFL is required of all applicants whose native language is not English. The minimum TOEFL score that is accepted is 600.

Application deadlines are June 1 for the fall trimester beginning in September and November 1 for the winter trimester beginning in January. Decisions are made on a rolling basis, and notification is usually given within one month after an application is received.

Correspondence and Information

Dean of Admissions
Graduate School of Business Administration
Fordham University
113 West 60th Street, Suite 619
New York, New York 10023
Telephone: 212-636-6200
Fax: 212-636-7076
E-mail: admission@bschool.bnet.fordham.edu
World Wide Web: http://www.bnet.fordham.edu.

Fordham University

THE FACULTY

Ernest J. Scalberg, Dean of The Graduate School of Business Administration; Ph.D., UCLA, 1978. Janet R. Marks, Associate Professor and Associate Dean for Academic Affairs and Administration; Ph.D., NYU, 1988.

Accounting and Taxation

Paul M. Bochner, Visiting Assistant Professor; LL.M., NYU. Robert M. Halperin, Professor; Ph.D., Pennsylvania. John R. Hamilton, Visiting Assistant Professor; M.B.A., Harvard. Neal B. Hitzig, Associate Professor; Ph.D., CUNY. Bruce S. Koch, Visiting Professor; Ph.D., Ohio State. Paul S. Kushel, Visiting Associate Professor; Ph.D., Texas at Austin. Haim Mozes, Associate Professor; Ph.D., NYU. Harry A. Newman, Associate Professor; Ph.D., Northwestern. Walter F. O'Connor, Professor, Director of the Master's in Taxation and Area Chair of Accounting and Taxation; Ph.D., CUNY. Donna C. Rapaccioli, Assistant Professor; Ph.D., NYU. Allen I. Schiff, Professor of Accounting and Director of the Field Study Project; Ph.D., NYU. Patricia A. Williams, Assistant Professor; Ph.D., Boston University.

Communications and Media Management

Paul P. Baard, Associate Professor; Ph.D., Fordham. Katherine A. Combellick, Director, Undergraduate Business Communications; Ph.D., SUNY at Binghamton. Everette E. Dennis, Distinguished Visiting Professor and Area Chair; Ph.D., Minnesota. Albert N. Greco, Associate Professor; Ed.D., NYU. Sharon Livesey, Associate Professor; J.D., Northeastern. Marion K. Pinsdorf, Senior Fellow in Communications; Ph.D., NYU. John Polich, Assistant Professor; Ph.D., Stanford. Edmond H. Weiss, Associate Professor; Ph.D., Temple.

Finance and Business Economics

Christopher R. Blake, Assistant Professor; Ph.D., NYU. Victor M. Borun, Associate Professor and Area Chair of Finance and Business Economics; Ph.D., NYU. Sris Chatterjee, Associate Professor; Ph.D., Columbia. Robert Ferguson, Associate Professor; Ph.D., NYU. John D. Finnerty, Professor; Ph.D., Naval Postgraduate School. Robert G. George, Assistant Professor; Ph.D., Chicago. Gautam Goswami, Assistant Professor; Ph.D., Georgia State. Keith A. Heyen, Visiting Assistant Professor; Ph.D., Wisconsin. David T. Kleinman, Professor; Ph.D., Ohio State. Dean A. Leistikow, Associate Professor; Ph.D., Brown. James R. Lothian, Professor; Ph.D., Chicago. Katherin Marton, Professor; Ph.D., Vienna; Ph.D., NYU. Cornelia McCarthy, Visiting Assistant Professor; Ph.D., Columbia. Steven B. Raymar, Assistant Professor; Ph.D., Columbia. Leon Shilton, Associate Professor; Ph.D., Wisconsin. Yusif E. Simaan, Assistant Professor; Ph.D., CUNY, Baruch. Eric D. Stiles, Assistant Professor; Ph.D., NYU. David P. Stuhr, Associate Professor; Ph.D., NYU. Mingsung Tang, Assistant Professor; Ph.D., Yale. Thomas J. Urich, Visiting Associate Professor; Ph.D., NYU. Frank M. Werner, Associate Professor; Associate Dean, Tarrytown Campus; Ph.D., Columbia.

Information and Communications Systems

Christine V. Bullen, Visiting Assistant Instructor; M.S., MIT. Patrick J. Hynes, Visiting Associate Professor; M.B.A., Pennsylvania. Jaak Jurison, Assistant Professor and Area Chair; Ph.D., Claremont. Aditya N. Saharia, Associate Professor; Ph.D., Carnegie-Mellon. Kent M. Sandoe, Assistant Professor; Ph.D., Claremont. Dale H. Shao, Visiting Assistant Professor; Ph.D., Georgia State. Gregory E. Truman, Assistant Professor; Ph.D., NYU.

Management Systems

Eser U. Belding, Associate Professor; Ph.D., Michigan. William G. Egelhoff, Associate Professor; Ph.D., Columbia. Nicholas C. Georgantzas, Associate Professor; Ph.D., CUNY. Marek P. Hessel, Associate Professor; Ph.D., NYU. Frank M. Hull, Visiting Associate Professor; Ph.D., Columbia. Dorothy E. Klotz, Assistant Professor; Ph.D. Penn State. Vladimir L. Kvint, Visiting Professor; Ph.D., Moscow Institute of National Economy (Russia). Cornelia McCarthy, Visiting Assistant Professor; Ph.D., Columbia. Marta W. Mooney, Professor and Executive Director, Center for Advanced Management Studies (CAMS); Ph.D., UCLA. Joyce Nilsson Orsini, Associate Professor and Director, Deming Scholars Program and Associate Director for Education, Center for Advanced Management Studies; Ph.D., NYU. Paul Rackow, Associate Professor; Ph.D., NYU. Sumita Raghuram, Assistant Professor; Ph.D., Minnesota. Patricia P. Ramsey, Professor; Ph.D., Hofstra. Falguni K. Sen, Associate Professor; Ph.D., Northwestern. Sharon P. Smith, Professor and Dean, College of Business Administration; Ph.D., Rutgers. Esther E. Solomon, Associate Professor; Ph.D., Jerusalem. James E. Stoner, Professor; Ph.D., MIT. Robert M. Wharton, Professor and Area Chair of Management Systems; Ph.D. Temple. John Zhuang Yang, Assistant Professor; Ph.D., Columbia. Milan Zeleny, Professor; Ph.D., Rochester.

Marketing

Richard Colombo, Associate Professor; Ph.D., Columbia. Janet Dilorenzo-Aiss, Assistant Professor; Ed.D., Columbia. Hooman Estalami, Assistant Professor; Ph.D., Columbia. Marcia H. Flicker, Assistant Professor; Ph.D., Pennsylvania. Scott Hoenig, Assistant Professor; Ph.D., Columbia. Alfred C. Holden Jr., Associate Professor and Area Chair of Marketing; Ph.D., Syracuse. Robert F. Hurley, Assistant Professor; Ph.D., Columbia. Lawrence J. King, Assistant Professor; Ph.D., Michigan State. Arthur J. Kover, Professor; Ph.D., Yale. Jukka M. Laitamaki, Visiting Associate Professor and Director, Global Professional M.B.A. Program; Ph.D., Cornell. Sarah Maxwell, Assistant Professor; Ph.D., Florida International. Shahana Sen, Assistant Professor; Ph.D., NYU.

Legal and Ethical Studies

Miriam R. Albert, Assistant Professor; LL.M., NYU. Mark A. Conrad, Associate Professor and Area Chair; M.S., Columbia. Albert W. Cornachio, Associate Professor; J.D., Fordham. Kenneth R. Davis, Assistant Professor; J.D., Toledo. Kevin T. Jackson, Assistant Professor; Ph.D., Maryland. Mark Kreder, Assistant Professor; Assistant Dean, College of Business Administration; J.D., Catholic University.

GEORGETOWN UNIVERSITY

School of Business

Programs of Study The Georgetown program is a two-year, full-time, daytime, nonthesis M.B.A. program well-suited for the liberal arts, science, or technical graduate. The School seeks to enable its students to assume policymaking positions in business or government and to become leaders in society. Emphases are on acquiring a thorough knowledge of the skills traditional to business management and on integrating those skills with the social sciences, ethical, and philosophical systems. The Georgetown M.B.A. focuses on business knowledge applied in an international context. Through six team-based integrative experiences, a non-U.S. field-based global experience, thread courses in international business as well as in technology and knowledge management, an extensive selection of six- and twelve-week elective courses, career track options, and exchange program opportunities, Georgetown delivers an M.B.A. for the global marketplace. In conjunction with the Georgetown University Law Center and the School of Foreign Service, there is a four-year program leading to the J.D./M.B.A. degree and a three-year program leading to the M.B.A./M.S.F.S. degree, respectively. A three-year M.B.A./M.P.P. program and a five-year M.D./M.B.A. program are also offered.

Research Facilities The current holdings of all arts and sciences libraries include more than 2 million volumes, 2.6 million microforms, and approximately 450,000 government documents. Lauinger Library receives more than 26,000 current serials and has seating facilities for 1,350. The Washington, D.C., area offers excellent research facilities, including the Library of Congress, trade and professional organizations, agencies and departments of the federal government, foreign embassies, and regional, national, and international businesses. The School of Business Technology Center contains the Boland Information Systems Laboratory (BISL) and the Decision Support Center (DSC). These are computer classroom/laboratories for use by the students and faculty members of the business school. There are approximately 100 IBM-compatible computers, with an additional fifteen computers available to M.B.A. students in their lounge. Every unit is connected to a local area network that provides an extremely broad range of application software, access to laser printers, and connections to the University's data networks. Through these networks, users can work on a University minicomputer or mainframe computer, connect to other local area networks such as a library to access other forms of data such as CD-ROM, and connect to either BITNET or the Internet, as well as to external information services such as Dow Jones News/Retrieval Service, Lexis-Nexis, and Bloomberg. Students can also access the School network with a laptop computer through computer connections provided in the case-study classrooms and in the M.B.A. lounge. All M.B.A. students are required to own a personal computer and have Internet access from home. The Georgetown University Academic Computer Center provides additional computing resources. The Center for International Business, the Capital Markets Research Center, the Credit Research Center, the Connelly Program in Business Ethics, and the Global Entrepreneurship Program are research and program arms of the business school.

Financial Aid A majority of students receive aid from tuition scholarships and/or federal government programs. Research assistantships are available through the M.B.A. Scholars Program. Scholarship awards are based on merit. All admitted M.B.A. students are considered. M.B.A. Scholars assist faculty members on research projects or work in administrative offices within the School. Federal assistance, based on need, is available to U.S. citizens only and may include low-interest loans and work-study. Applicants are required to file the FAFSA and the Georgetown University Financial Aid Form.

Cost of Study Tuition for graduate students enrolled in the M.B.A. program at Georgetown University is $23,880 for the 1998–99 academic year. Approximately $1700 in required fees is charged to cover most of the cost of the integrative experiences, lab fees, and career management assessments.

Living and Housing Costs Health insurance, housing, books, supplies, transportation, and other personal expenses are additional to tuition charges. Academic-year costs are estimated at $10,000, excluding tuition. Off-campus housing is readily available. Students may seek assistance from the Office of Off-Campus Housing. Most graduate students live off-campus in adjacent neighborhoods. The campus and surrounding area are serviced by a convenient public transportation system.

Student Group The School enrolled 249 full-time M.B.A. students in fall 1997. Students have a wide variety of academic backgrounds and work experiences. All regions of the United States are represented. In the fall 1997 class, 35 percent of the students were non-U.S. citizens, the average age was 28, and 32 percent were women. Opportunities to participate in cocurricular activities that give students an active voice in the development of the M.B.A. program and School policy are numerous.

Location The historic Georgetown area of Washington, D.C., is only minutes from the White House and Capitol Hill. In addition to being the seat of the federal government, the District of Columbia contains the headquarters of many national and international corporations and organizations.

The University Georgetown is the oldest Jesuit institution of higher learning in the United States. Established in 1789 by Bishop John Carroll, the University is now known throughout the world for the superior quality of its programs. The main campus comprises six schools: the School of Business, the School of Liberal Arts and Sciences, the School of Foreign Service, the School of Nursing, the Graduate School, and the School of Continuing Education and Summer Programs, as well as the Faculty of Languages and Linguistics. Georgetown also has an outstanding medical school and law center.

Applying New students are admitted to the graduate business program in the fall semester of each year. Application forms must be supported by official transcripts of all previous undergraduate and graduate course work, two letters of recommendation, three essays, a current resume, the results of the GMAT, and the $75 application fee. Applicants whose native language is not English and who have not completed a degree at a university located in a country where English is the native language must submit a TOEFL score. Applications for fall 1999 should be submitted as early as possible in the 1998–99 academic year. International students and students seeking financial assistance are strongly encouraged to apply by February 1. Applicants to the M.B.A./M.S.F.S., M.B.A./M.P.P., and the M.D./M.B.A. joint programs must also meet a February 1 deadline. The final submission date for all 1999 application material is April 15.

Correspondence and Information

M.B.A. Admissions Office
105 Old North
Box 571148
Georgetown University
Washington, D.C. 20057-1148

Telephone: 202-687-4200
Fax: 202-687-7809 or 4031
E-mail: mba@gunet.georgetown.edu
World Wide Web: http://www.gsb.georgetown.edu

Georgetown University

THE FACULTY AND THEIR RESEARCH

Allyson Adrian, Assistant Professor; Ph.D., Maryland. Management communications.
Reena Aggarwal, Associate Professor; Ph.D., Maryland. Finance.
Paul Almeida, Assistant Professor; M.B.A., Ph.D., Pennsylvania (Wharton). Diffusion of technology.
Alan R. Andreasen, Professor; Ph.D., Columbia. Marketing.
James J. Angel, Associate Professor; Ph.D., Berkeley. Finance.
Robert J. Bies, Associate Professor; Ph.D., Stanford. Organizational behavior.
James N. Bodurtha Jr., Visiting Associate Professor; Ph.D., NYU. Finance, international business.
George G. Brenkert, Professor; Ph.D., Michigan. Management, business ethics.
Thomas L. Brewer, Associate Professor; Ph.D., Michigan. International business.
Ken Cavalluzzo, Assistant Professor; Ph.D., Pennsylvania. Accounting, business law.
Thomas Barry Cooke, Distinguished Teaching Professor; LL.M., M.L.T., Georgetown. Business law.
Duncan Copeland, Visiting Assistant Professor; D.B.A., Harvard. Management information systems.
Mary J. Culnan, Associate Professor; Ph.D., UCLA. Management information systems.
Michael R. Czinkota, Associate Professor; Ph.D., Ohio State. International marketing, distribution.
William G. Droms, John J. Powers, Jr., Professor of International Business and Finance; D.B.A., George Washington; CFA. Financial management, investments, personal finance.
Susan Dugan, Distinguished Teaching Professor; M.B.A., Michigan. Strategy, management.
Allan C. Eberhart, Associate Professor; Ph.D., South Carolina. Business finance and investments.
Ricardo Ernst, Associate Professor; Ph.D., Pennsylvania (Wharton). Operations management.
Patricia M. Fairfield, Associate Professor; Ph.D., Columbia. Accounting.
M. Ali Fekrat, Professor; Ph.D., Indiana. Managerial and international accounting.
Kasra Ferdows, Heisley Professor of Global Marketing; Ph.D., Wisconsin. Production and operations management.
Robert M. Grant, Professor; Ph.D., City (London). Strategic management.
Jose Luis Guerrero, Associate Professor; Ph.D., Illinois at Urbana-Champaign. Statistics.
Ken Homa, Distinguished Teaching Professor; M.B.A., Chicago. Marketing, new product development.
Charalambos L. Iacovou, Instructor; Ph.D. candidate, British Columbia. Management information systems.
Harvey J. Iglarsh, Associate Professor; Ph.D., Cornell. Management science.
Carla Inclan, Assistant Professor; Ph.D., Chicago. Statistics.
Johny K. Johansson, McCrane/Shaker Professor of International Business; Ph.D., Berkeley. International marketing.
Bardia Kamrad, Associate Professor; Ph.D., Case Western Reserve. Operations research.
Catherine Langlois, Associate Professor; Ph.D., Berkeley. Microeconomics, finance.
Michael B. Levy, Distinguished Teaching Professor; Ph.D., Rutgers. Political theory, policy sciences.
Ka Sing Man, Assistant Professor; M.B.A., Ph.D., Chicago. Econometrics/time series analysis, finance.
Alan P. Mayer-Sommer, Associate Professor; Ph.D., Georgia State. Accounting.
John N. Mayo, Professor; Ph.D., St. Louis. Management, public policy.
Daniel J. McAllister, Assistant Professor; Ph.D., California, Irvine. Organizational behavior.
Douglas M. McCabe, Professor; Ph.D., Cornell. Labor relations, human resources management.
William K. McHenry, Associate Professor; Ph.D., Arizona. Management information systems.
Marcia Miceli, Professor; M.B.A., Ph.D., Indiana. Management, business ethics.
Sandra J. Milberg, Assistant Professor; Ph.D., Pittsburgh. Marketing.
Dale Murphy, Assistant Professor; Ph.D., MIT. Management, international business diplomacy.
Karen N. Newman, Professor; Ph.D., Chicago. Organizational behavior.
Stanley D. Nollen, Professor; Ph.D., Chicago. Economics, management.
Robert S. Parker, Professor and Dean Emeritus; Ph.D., Pennsylvania (Wharton).
Christopher Puto, Professor and Dean; Ph.D., Duke. Marketing, strategic planning.
Dennis P. Quinn, Professor; Ph.D., Columbia. Public policy, business-government relations.
Lamar Reinsch, Associate Dean for Graduate Business Programs and Associate Professor; Ph.D., Kansas. Management communications, statistics.
Pietra Rivoli, Associate Professor; Ph.D., Florida. Financial management, international finance.
Elaine Romanelli, Associate Professor; Ph.D., Columbia. Business policy.
Ilkka A. Ronkainen, Associate Professor; Ph.D., South Carolina. Marketing, international business.
Srinivasan Sankaraguruswamy, Assistant Professor; Ph.D., Purdue. Trade behavior, capital asset pricing.
Glenn Schmidt, Assistant Professor; Ph.D., Stanford. Management.
Annette N. Shelby, Professor; Ph.D., LSU. Management communication.
Akhtar R. Siddique, Assistant Professor; Ph.D., Duke. Futures and options, financial econometrics.
Alexander Simonson, Assistant Professor; J.D., Ph.D., Columbia. Marketing public policy and ethics, legal aspects of marketing.
N. Craig Smith, Associate Professor; Ph.D., Cranfield School of Management (England). Marketing.
Richard J. Sweeney, Sullivan/Dean Professor of International Business; Ph.D., Princeton. Finance.
Robert J. Thomas, Professor; Ph.D., Pennsylvania (Wharton). Marketing research.
Catherine Honor Tinsley, Assistant Professor; Ph.D. candidate, Northwestern. Negotiations, conflict management.
Jeanine W. Turner, Assistant Professor; Ph.D., Ohio State. Management communications.
David A. Walker, Professor, John A. Largay Scholar, and Director, Center for Business-Government Relations; Ph.D., Iowa State. Economics, finance.
J. Scott Whisenant, Assistant Professor; Ph.D. candidate, Oklahoma; CPA, CMA. Financial analysis.
Rohan G. Williamson, Assistant Professor; Ph.D., Oklahoma; CPA, CMA. Finance.
Teri Lombardi Yohn, Associate Professor; Ph.D., Indiana. Accounting, finance.

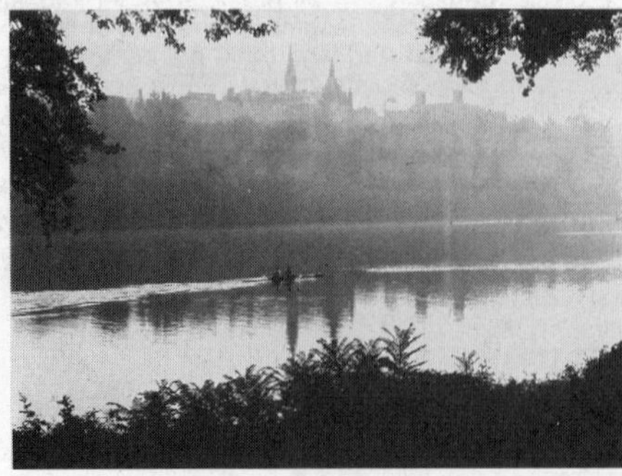

A view of Georgetown University, looking across the Potomac River.

THE GEORGE WASHINGTON UNIVERSITY

School of Business and Public Management

Programs of Study

The School of Business and Public Management (SBPM) offers the following master's degrees: Master of Accountancy (M.Accy.), Master of Business Administration (M.B.A.), Master of Taxation (M.Tax.), Master of Science in acquisition management, Master of Science in finance, Master of Science in Information Systems Technology (M.S.I.S.T.), Master of Public Administration (M.P.A.), Master of Science in project management, and Master of Tourism Administration (M.T.A.). In the post-master's degree programs, the Doctor of Philosophy (Ph.D.) is offered.

The Master of Business Administration program offers fields of instruction in accountancy; finance and investments; health services administration; human resources management; information systems management; international business; logistics, operations, and materials management; management of science, technology, and innovation; management decision making; marketing; organizational behavior and development; real estate and urban development; small business and entrepreneurship; strategic management and public policy; and tourism and hospitality management. The Master of Public Administration program has options in budget and public finance; federal policy, politics, and management; managing in public organizations; managing state and local governments; and policy analysis and evaluation. Students may also craft their own concentrations in the M.B.A. and M.P.A. programs.

The interdependence of government and business at both the national and the international levels has been recognized in the organization of these programs. Master's degrees are designed to meet the need for leaders who are familiar with new management techniques and concepts and who are alert to the changing philosophies of business and government. Doctoral programs are planned for those who expect to teach or pursue research-oriented careers in government or business.

Research Facilities

The School is ideally located for research. Students have access to the three University libraries, the Library of Congress, and the specialized libraries of the nearby Departments of Defense, State, Commerce, Agriculture, and the Interior; the Office of Personnel Management; and such government agencies as the Office of Management and Budget, the General Services Administration, and the National Bureau of Standards. In the international field, there are such agencies nearby as the International Monetary Fund, the World Bank, the Export-Import Bank, and the Latin American Development Bank, as well as the embassies and consulates of other countries. Because of its location, the University is able to invite leaders in industry and government to speak in its seminars and classes.

The Computer Information Resource Center (CIRC) provides computer facilities, technical assistance, and information on the use of computers and networks. CIRC supports IBM-PC, Apple Macintosh, UNIX, and IBM mainframe computers. CIRC facilities are available seven days a week, 24 hours a day.

Financial Aid

A number of fellowships are available each year through the School. Awards are made on the basis of a student's qualifications and academic achievement, and consideration is automatic. Departmental assistantships are also available. Other sources of aid may be coordinated through the Office of Student Financial Assistance and the Office of Fellowships at the University. International students are eligible for the bulk of School-authorized awards.

Cost of Study

Tuition is charged at the rate of $680 per credit hour in 1998–99 and is payable on a course-by-course basis. Additional fees include a University Center fee of $34.50 per credit hour.

Living and Housing Costs

Estimated costs for room, board, and miscellaneous personal expenses total about $11,000 per academic year. The majority of graduate students live off campus.

Student Group

The student body is characterized by diversity. Of the approximately 1,775 master's degree and 175 doctoral degree students, approximately 40 percent are women, 50 percent are non-U.S. citizens, and 50 percent are full-time. The average age is 31.

Location

The nation's capital, with its many cultural and educational attractions, is of considerable interest to students. The Washington area has the third-largest concentration of research and development activity in the country; more than 1,000 trade and professional associations have their headquarters in the city.

The University and The School

The School of Business and Public Management, established in 1928, is part of the George Washington University, a private, nonsectarian, coeducational university in downtown Washington, four blocks west of the White House. The University operates on a two-semester academic year; course work in basic and core courses is available in extended sessions during the summer months.

Applying

April 1 and October 1 are the completion dates for applications to ensure full consideration for the fall semester and spring semester, respectively. Doctoral applicants must submit applications by February 1 for the fall semester. Early application is recommended in all cases. Applicants who wish to be considered for graduate assistantships and fellowships should complete the admissions application process no later than February 1.

Correspondence and Information

Office of Graduate Admissions
School of Business and Public Management
The George Washington University
Washington, D.C. 20052
Telephone: 202-994-6584
Fax: 202-994-6382
E-mail: sbpmapp@gwu.edu
World Wide Web: http://www.sbpm.gwu.edu

The George Washington University

THE FACULTY

The School of Business and Public Management has a full-time faculty of approximately 125 members. Their activities, in addition to teaching, include research and publication, consulting for government and business, and participation in seminars and training programs dealing with current problems and developments. A part-time faculty of approximately 65 members is drawn from educationally qualified specialists associated with business in the area or with major departments and agencies of the federal government or international planning organizations.

Susan Phillips, Dean; Ph.D., LSU.
James E. Kee, Senior Associate Dean; M.P.A., J.D., NYU.
Joel Cook, Associate Dean for Undergraduate Programs; Ph.D., Indiana.
Michael M. Harmon, Director of Doctoral Programs; Ph.D., USC.

Accountancy

William Baber, Benjamin Franklin Professor; Ph.D., North Carolina at Chapel Hill; CPA. Michael G. Gallagher, Professor; LL.M., George Washington; CPA. Joseph Hilmy, Professor; Ph.D., Aberdeen. Krishna Kumar, Associate Professor; Ph.D., Columbia. Frederick W. Lindahl, Associate Professor; Ph.D., Chicago. Leo C. Moersen, Associate Professor; J.D., William and Mary; CPA. Chei-Min Paik, Professor; D.B.A., Harvard. Debra R. Sheldon, Professor; D.B.A., George Washington; CPA. Larry G. Singleton, Associate Professor; Ph.D., LSU. Keith E. Smith, Associate Professor; LL.M., Florida; CPA. Neil Tierney, Assistant Professor; M.S., Suffolk; D.B.A., Bryant. Gnankumar Visvanathan, Assistant Professor; Ph.D., NYU.

Finance

Frederick Amling, Professor; Ph.D., Pennsylvania. Isabelle G. Bajeux-Besnanou, Assistant Professor; Ph.D., Paris. Theodore Barnhill, Professor; Ph.D., Michigan. Neil Cohen, Associate Professor; D.B.A., Virginia. Mark J. Eppli, Assistant Professor; Ph.D., Wisconsin–Madison. William Handorf, Professor; Ph.D., Michigan State. George Jabbour, Associate Professor; Ph.D., George Washington. James V. Jordan, Associate Professor; Ph.D., North Carolina at Chapel Hill. Mark Klock, Associate Professor; Ph.D., Boston College; J.D., Maryland. Paul Peyser, Associate Professor; Ph.D., Wisconsin–Madison. J. Minor Sachlis, Associate Professor; D.B.A., Maryland. William Seale, Professor; Ph.D., Kentucky. Arthur Wilson, Assistant Professor; Ph.D., Chicago. William Wilson, Associate Professor; Ph.D., Indiana.

International Business

Hossein Askari, Professor; Ph.D., MIT. Reid Click, Assistant Professor; Ph.D., Chicago. Mary Lou Egan, Assistant Professor; Ph.D., George Washington. Peter Lauter, Professor; Ph.D., UCLA. Yoon Park, Professor; D.B.A., Harvard; Ph.D., George Washington. Scheherazade Rehman, Assistant Professor; Ph.D., George Washington. Fernando Robles, Associate Professor; Ph.D., Penn State. Douglas M. Sanford, Assistant Professor; Ph.D., Michigan. Liliana Schumacher, Assistant Professor; Ph.D., Chicago. Hildy Teegan, Assistant Professor; Ph.D., Texas at Austin. Robert J. Weiner, Associate Professor; Ph.D., Harvard. Jiawen Yang; Assistant Professor; Ph.D., NYU.

Management Science

Management Science encompasses entrepreneurship; human resources; information systems; logistics, operations, and materials management; organizational behavior; and project management.

John M. Artz, Assistant Professor; Ph.D., George Washington. Prabir K. Bagchi, Associate Professor; Ph.D., Tennessee. Laura M. Birou, Assistant Professor; Ph.D., Michigan State. Elias Carayannis, Assistant Professor; Ph.D., Rensselaer. John Carson, Professor; Ph.D., Lehigh. Edward J. Cherian, Professor; Ph.D., Rensselaer. Debra Cohen, Associate Professor; Ph.D., Ohio State. Zvi Covaliu, Assistant Professor; Ph.D., Berkeley. John P. Coyne, Associate Professor; Ph.D., Lehigh. Richard Donnelly, Associate Professor; Ph.D., MIT. Ernest H. Forman, Professor; D.Sc., George Washington. J. Davidson Frame, Professor; Ph.D., American. Lois Graff, Associate Professor; Ph.D., NYU. Mary Granger, Associate Professor; Ph.D., Cincinnati. William E. Halal, Professor; Ph.D., Berkeley. Jerry B. Harvey, Professor; Ph.D., Texas at Austin. Jay Liebowitz, Professor; D.Sc., George Washington. John F. Lobuts, Professor; Ed.D., George Washington. William Money, Assistant Professor; Ph.D., Northwestern. Thomas J. Nagy, Associate Professor; Ph.D., Texas at Austin. Srinivas Y. Prasad, Assistant Professor; Ph.D., SUNY at Buffalo. James H. Perry, Professor; Ph.D., Stanford. Pedro Sanchez, Associate Professor; Ph.D., Michigan. Stanley N. Sherman, Professor; D.B.A., Maryland. Refik Soyer, Associate Professor; D.Sc., George Washington. Paul Swiercz, Associate Professor; Ph.D., Virginia Tech. Charles Toftoy, Associate Professor; D.B.A. Nova. Stuart A. Umpleby, Professor; Ph.D., Illinois at Urbana-Champaign. William G. Wells, Associate Professor; D.B.A., George Washington. Erik K. Winslow, Professor (Behavioral Science); Ph.D., Case Western Reserve. Phillip W. Wirtz, Professor; Ph.D., George Washington. David L. Zalkind, Associate Professor; Ph.D., Johns Hopkins.

Marketing

Ravi Achrol, Professor; Ph.D., Northwestern. Salvatore Divita, Professor; D.B.A., Harvard. Robert Dyer, Professor; D.B.A., Maryland. Salah Hassan, Associate Professor; Ph.D., Ohio State. Marilyn Liebrenz-Himes, Associate Professor; Ph.D., Michigan State. Lynda Maddox, Associate Professor; Ph.D., Southern Illinois at Carbondale. Bernard Pitsvada, Professor; Ph.D., American. Amy Smith, Assistant Professor; Ph.D., Maryland.

Public Administration

William C. Adams, Professor; Ph.D., George Washington. Bayard L. Catron, Professor; Ph.D., Berkeley. Stephen R. Chitwood, Professor; Ph.D., USC; J.D., George Washington. Dwight Cropp, Associate Professor; Ed.D., George Washington. Michael M. Harmon, Professor; Ph.D., USC. Jill F. Kasle, Associate Professor; J.D., Boston University. James Edwin Kee, Professor; M.P.A., J.D., NYU. William Lucas, Visiting Professor; Ph.D., North Carolina at Chapel Hill. Cynthia McSwain, Associate Professor; Ph.D., North Carolina. Michele Moser, Assistant Professor; Ph.D., NYU. Kathryn Newcomer, Professor; Ph.D., Iowa. Susan J. Tolchin, Professor; Ph.D., NYU. Stephen J. Trachtenber, Professor and President of the University; J.D., Yale; M.P.A., Harvard.

Strategic Management and Public Policy

Howard Beales, Associate Professor; Ph.D., Chicago. William Becker, Professor; Ph.D., Johns Hopkins. Lee Burke, Associate Professor; Ph.D., Berkeley. Reba Anne Carruth, Associate Professor; Ph.D., Minnesota. Joel Cook, Associate Professor; Ph.D., Indiana. Herbert Davis, Professor; Ph.D., LSU. Ernest Englander, Associate Professor; Ph.D., Washington (Seattle). Jennifer Griffin, Assistant Professor; D.B.A., Boston University. Daniel Kane, Assistant Professor; LL.M., Georgetown. Hicheon Kim, Assistant Professor; Ph.D., Texas A&M. D. Jeffrey Lenn, Associate Professor; Ph.D., Boston College. Aseem Prakash, Assistant Professor; P.G.D.M., Indian Institute of Management. Mark Starik, Assistant Professor; Ph.D., Georgia. James Thurman, Associate Professor; Ph.D., Penn State.

Tourism Studies

Lisa A. Delpy, Assistant Professor; Ph.D., New Mexico. Douglas C. Frechtling, Associate Professor; Ph.D., George Washington. Joe Goldblatt, Assistant Professor; Ed.D., George Washington. Donald E. Hawkins, Professor; Ed.D., Lehigh. Sheryl M. Spivack, Instructor of Tourism Studies; M.A., George Washington. Liang Yu, Associate Professor; Ph.D., Oregon.

GOLDEN GATE UNIVERSITY

Graduate Programs

Programs of Study

The graduate programs of Golden Gate University lead to master's degrees, with concentrations in various specialties in private enterprise and public service management, and to doctoral degrees in business and public administration. The objective is to provide advanced instruction, blending theoretical principles of administration with tested practices in the management of business organizations and public agencies. The development of analytical thinking necessary for management decision making is stressed. Lectures, discussions, directed research, and the case method of study are employed. The graduate programs are offered through various professional schools. The School of Liberal Studies & Public Affairs offers the Master of Arts in applied psychology (with concentrations in counseling, industrial/organizational psychology, and marriage, family, and child counseling) and in liberal studies as well as an M.A. in arts administration and international relations, a joint M.A./J.D. in international relations, the Master of Healthcare Administration, the M.P.A. and Executive M.P.A. degrees, and a joint M.P.A./J.D. Programs leading to the D.B.A. and D.P.A. degrees are offered as well. The School of Business offers the Master of Accountancy, the Executive M.B.A., the M.B.A. (with concentrations in accounting, entrepreneurship, finance, human resource management, international business, management, marketing, operations management, and organizational behavior and development), a joint M.B.A./J.D. degree, the Master of International Business, and the M.S. degree in economics, finance, financial engineering, human resource management, manufacturing management, marketing, organizational behavior and development, procurement and logistics management, project and systems management, and public relations. The School of Taxation offers the M.S. degree in taxation. The School of Technology and Industry offers the M.B.A. (with concentrations in information systems and telecommunications) and the M.S. degree in hospitality administration and tourism, information systems, management of technology, software engineering, and telecommunications. Programs leading to the D.B.A. and D.P.A. degrees are offered as well. The School of Law offers the J.D. and LL.M. (taxation) degrees. The University operates on a trimester schedule, offering three 15-week terms yearly. Some programs are also offered in a five-, ten-, or twelve-week format. Graduate programs are offered through both day and evening classes. Students may enroll either full- or part-time.

Research Facilities

The General Library contains more than 300,000 volumes and more than 2,500 serials, including those located at off-campus sites. With a growth rate of some 3,500 volumes annually, it is one of the state's largest, most complete, and most current working collections of materials in business management, accounting, taxation, public administration, transportation, and related areas. The Law Library contains more than 200,000 volumes and more than 3,000 active serial subscriptions and offers online access to electronic legal databases.

Financial Aid

Financial assistance is available for qualified students who could not attend the University without it. Aid is provided through federal, state, and University loan, grant, and work-study programs. A limited number of scholarships are available. Students with Veterans Administration educational benefits may use them at the University. Many companies reimburse employees for the costs of graduate school.

Cost of Study

Tuition and fees are the same for California residents and nonresidents. Golden Gate University charges tuition by the course. The cost of each course varies by department and location. For 1998–99, graduate tuition ranges between $996 and $1567 per course. Books and supplies cost $300–$350 per trimester for full-time students.

Living and Housing Costs

Golden Gate University has no residence facilities for graduate students. Housing costs in the surrounding community vary widely.

Student Group

As of fall 1997, approximately 4,200 students were enrolled in the graduate programs. Approximately 48 percent of the graduate students are women. About two thirds of the graduate students are employed. Class discussions are enhanced by the maturity, motivation, and varied backgrounds and work experiences of students.

Location

Golden Gate University's San Francisco campus is situated in the downtown financial district of the city, close to rail and bus terminals, and is readily accessible by private transportation. The University has other campuses in California (Monterey, Sacramento, Silicon Valley, Sonoma County, Walnut Creek, Los Angeles, and Orange County) and in Seattle, Washington.

The University

Golden Gate is a private, nonprofit institution accredited by the Western Association of Schools and Colleges. Its combined day and evening enrollment of more than 7,000 students makes it one of California's largest independent accredited colleges and universities. It was formally founded in the mid-1800s, was incorporated in 1923, and became a university in 1972. Today, full- and part-time day and evening degree programs are offered in management, public service, liberal studies, technology, and law.

Applying

Applicants for master's programs must hold a bachelor's or higher degree from a regionally accredited institution and have a minimum GPA of 2.5. Individual programs may have special grade requirements. Conditional admission may be granted to applicants with a satisfactory GMAT or GRE score, depending on the student's choice of program. College graduates may enroll as nondegree students with the permission of the dean. Degree candidates must file a University application with a nonrefundable $55 fee ($70 for international applicants) and have official transcripts of all previous college-level work sent to the Admissions Office. New students must submit financial aid applications to the Financial Aid Office by March 2 to be considered for aid beginning in the fall.

Correspondence and Information

Enrollment Services
Golden Gate University
536 Mission Street
San Francisco, California 94105-2968
Telephone: 415-442-7800
800-448-4968 (toll-free)
Fax: 415-442-7807
E-mail: info@ggu.edu
World Wide Web: http://www.ggu.edu

Golden Gate University

THE FACULTY

The Golden Gate University faculty consists of a core of 91 full-time academic specialists and more than 500 part-time faculty members drawn from fields of professional activity that correspond to the University's curricular emphases. The part-time faculty members are practicing specialists in the subject areas in which they teach; they bring to the classroom a "real world" perspective on their fields of professional expertise.

Golden Gate University's San Francisco campus facility in the city's financial district.

An M.B.A. class in marketing.

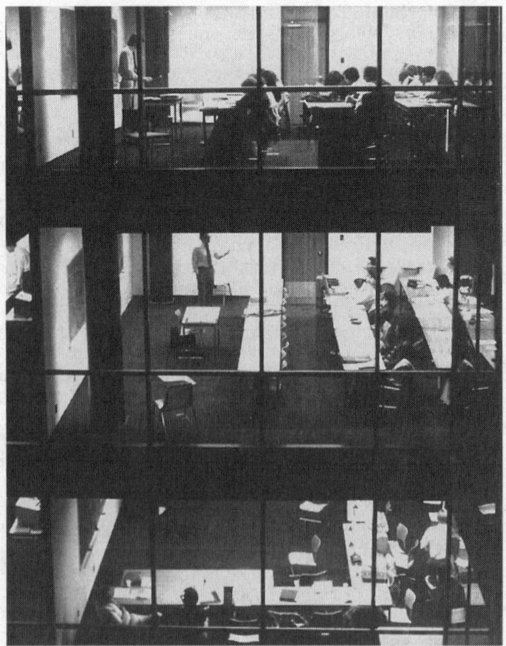

Day and evening classes are offered for the convenience of both full-time and part-time students. Evening classes are shown here.

HARVARD UNIVERSITY

Graduate School of Business Administration / Graduate School of Arts and Sciences Doctoral Programs in Management

Programs of Study

Harvard University's doctoral programs in management have consistently provided faculty members for prominent schools of management in the United States and abroad. The current high demand for such faculty members is demonstrated by the fact that attractive positions continue to be offered to graduates of the programs. Three doctoral programs in management are currently offered.

The Graduate School of Business Administration offers the degree of Doctor of Business Administration (D.B.A.). This degree is intended primarily for those who have already received an M.B.A. and who wish to study, at the doctoral level, administrative problems that do not fall neatly into a traditional academic discipline. The D.B.A. is offered with fields of specialization in business policy, accounting and control, management information systems, marketing, and technology and operations management.

The Graduate School of Arts and Sciences, in association with the Business School, offers two additional degrees: the Ph.D. in business economics and the Ph.D. in organizational behavior. Applicants with a bachelor's or a master's degree are eligible for these programs. The Ph.D. in business economics is intended for candidates who want to combine advanced formal training in modern economic analysis with advanced training in the realities of business operations and management. Fields of specialization are finance, industry and competitive analysis, international business, and most of the fields offered in the D.B.A. program. The Ph.D. in organizational behavior is offered to students who want to combine advanced formal training in sociology or psychology with empirical training in management and organizational behavior. Students select a program option based in the Business School and in either the Department of Sociology or the Department of Psychology.

Research Facilities

The Harry Elkins Widener Memorial Library is unrivaled, and the Baker Library at the Business School is the largest business library in the world. There are more than ninety other libraries at Harvard. Computer facilities at the Business School provide powerful computing and communications capabilities and include a student room equipped with IBM and Apple personal computers and laser printers. A full range of software packages is available, as well as access to a variety of databases. Other computing facilities are available at the Harvard Computing Center.

Financial Aid

Most incoming students receive a merit-based award regardless of need. This award includes funding for tuition, fees, and living expenses. Although no formal commitment is made, it is expected that this financial aid will be renewed up to a maximum of four years.

Cost of Study

For 1998–99, D.B.A. full-time tuition is $26,260 and required health fees are $1246; for the joint Ph.D. programs, full-time tuition and fees are $22,588.

Living and Housing Costs

For 1998–99, the twelve-month living expense budget for a single student may range from $16,000 to $22,000. Married students should add an additional $2000 to $7000 to these figures, and approximately $1000 should be added for each child. The Harvard University Housing Office administers the rental of University-owned apartments and maintains lists of off-campus housing accommodations.

Student Group

Current enrollment for the D.B.A. and joint Ph.D. programs is approximately 100 students. About 15 percent are women.

Student Outcomes

Approximately 85 percent of graduates secure academic positions. Recent graduates have been placed at Stanford University, Northwestern University, the University of Chicago, the University of Virginia, the University of Michigan, the University of Pennsylvania, and Harvard Business School.

Location

Cambridge and Boston offer varied opportunities for student enrichment and entertainment. There are more than forty colleges in the area. Boston, the capital of Massachusetts, offers a wealth of cultural resources. To the southeast are Cape Cod and the islands of Martha's Vineyard and Nantucket. All of New England presents attractions at every turn, including the Green Mountains of Vermont and the Berkshires of western Massachusetts.

The University

Harvard College was founded by a vote of the General Court of the Colony of Massachusetts Bay in 1636 and was granted a charter in 1650 under the corporate name "The President and Fellows of Harvard College." Today, Harvard University, operating under the Charter of 1650, is made up of a complex of enterprises engaged in virtually every form of scholarship, teaching, learning, and research known to humankind. Some 15,000 students are enrolled in degree programs and another 8,000 in nondegree programs. The faculty numbers more than 6,000 and the staff about another 5,000.

Applying

Admission to the programs is for the fall semester only. Application forms are available in September. The deadline for submission of a completed application is December 30 for all of the programs. All applicants must submit current GRE General Test or GMAT scores; three letters of recommendation; transcripts from undergraduate and, if applicable, graduate schools attended; and a completed application form. If an applicant's native language is not English, a current TOEFL score must also be submitted.

Correspondence and Information

For the D.B.A. program:
Doctoral Programs
Cotting House
Graduate School of Business Administration
Harvard University
Boston, Massachusetts 02163
Telephone: 617-495-6101
World Wide Web: http://www.hbs.edu

For the Ph.D. programs:
Admissions Office
Graduate School of Arts and Sciences
Byerly Hall, 2nd Floor
Harvard University
Cambridge, Massachusetts 02138
Telephone: 617-495-5315
World Wide Web: http://www-hugsas.harvard.edu

Harvard University

THE FACULTY

Graduate School of Business Administration Doctoral Programs
Jay W. Lorsch, Chairman.

Graduate School of Business Administration Doctoral Policy Committee
Jay W. Lorsch, Chairman.

Joseph L. Bower, Professor.
Adam M. Brandenburger, Professor.
Sanjiv R. Das, Professor.
Robert J. Dolan, Professor.
Pankaj Ghemawat, Professor.
Paul M. Healy, Professor.
Richard L. Nolan, Professor.
Gary P. Pisano, Associate Professor.
Howard H. Stevenson, Professor.

Graduate School of Business Administration Doctoral Program Coordinators
Sanjiv R. Das, Professor. Finance.
Paul M. Healy, Professor. Accounting and control.
Cynthia A. Montgomery, Professor. Industry and competitive analysis.
Richard L. Nolan, Professor. Management information systems.
Gary P. Pisano, Associate Professor. Technology and operations management.
Alvin J. Silk, Professor. Marketing.
Howard H. Stevenson, Professor. Business policy.

Standing Committee of the Faculty of Arts and Sciences on Higher Degrees in Business Studies
Pankaj Ghemawat, Chairman and Professor, Business School.
Theresa M. Amabile, Professor, Business School.
Stephen P. Bradley, Professor, Business School.
John Y. Campbell, Professor, Department of Economics.
Arthur P. Dempster, Professor, Department of Statistics.
J. Richard Hackman, Professor, Department of Psychology.
Yu-Chi Ho, Professor, Division of Applied Sciences.
Peter V. Marsden, Professor, Department of Sociology.
Nitin Nohria, Professor, Business School.
Michael E. Porter, Professor, Business School.
Peter P. Rogers, Professor, Division of Applied Sciences.
Aage B. Sørensen, Professor, Department of Sociology. (On leave 1997–98)
Jeffrey G. Williamson (Ex Officio), Professor, Department of Economics.

HAWAII PACIFIC UNIVERSITY

Business Administration Program

Programs of Study

Hawaii Pacific University, an established institution with leading programs in business administration, information systems, and management, offers a comprehensive Master of Business Administration (M.B.A.) degree program. This program—the fastest-growing graduate program in Hawaii—is noted for several distinctive features. First, it is pragmatic, emphasizing real-world applications, case studies, and specific skills and competences needed in contemporary business. Second, most courses include both an entrepreneurial and an international perspective. Third, computer applications are integrated into many of the M.B.A. courses. Fourth, interpersonal and communication skills are stressed throughout the curriculum. Fifth, as a major partner in the downtown business community, Hawaii Pacific University coordinates a large internship program that provides part-time and full-time managerial, technical, and professional positions in leading business firms. Through this internship program, M.B.A. candidates have the opportunity to supplement their income while earning academic credit.

The M.B.A. program at Hawaii Pacific University requires 45 semester hours of graduate work. Prerequisite courses in business subjects may be required. The curriculum is organized into nine core courses (27 semester hours), four elective courses tailored to the student's individual needs (12 semester hours), and a capstone sequence including a policy and strategy formulation course and professional paper (3 semester hours). Students may concentrate in any one of several business areas, including accounting, finance, human resource management, information systems, international business, management, marketing, not-for-profit management, and travel industry management. The University also offers an M.A. in management, which emphasizes the administrative/management function of the general business environment, and an M.A. in organizational change, which examines the models and strategies for leading change, organizational performance, and quality management. Courses include Comparative Management Systems, Managing Organizational Performance, Strategic Planning and Management, and Law for Managers. Some prerequisites may be required. Forty-two hours of graduate work are required to complete these programs.

Research Facilities

To support graduate studies, University libraries, with a collection exceeding 159,000 volumes, add an average of 2,500 volumes annually, 15 percent of which are on business topics. A significant number of business reference books, including national and international business directories, investment and financial services, accounting and tax information sources, and a collection of annual reports, are available. Periodical titles number more than 1,700, and 200,000 pieces of microfiche and 5,200 rolls of microfilm are maintained. Dial-up access to local area databases of public and state university library catalogs, legislative information, and business-oriented statistical data is available in the library. Other in-house, business-related, and commercially vendored databases support specialized information needs. The University's accessible on-campus computer center houses more than 100 IBM-compatible microcomputers with stand-alone and networked configurations that support the graduate program's integrated computer applications approach.

Financial Aid

The University participates in all federal financial aid programs designated for graduate students. These programs provide aid in the form of subsidized (need-based) and unsubsidized (non-need-based) Federal Stafford Student Loans. Through these loans, funds may be available to cover the student's entire cost of education. To apply for aid, students must submit the Free Application for Federal Student Aid (FAFSA) after January 1. Mailing of student award letters usually begins in April.

Cost of Study

For the 1998–99 academic year, tuition is $7920, and books cost approximately $700.

Living and Housing Costs

The University has both on-campus residence halls and off-campus university-leased apartments as well as an apartment referral service. Including tuition, books, housing, food, health insurance, and miscellaneous expenses, the cost of living for a typical single student for two semesters (nine months) is approximately $17,100.

Student Group

University enrollment currently stands at more than 8,000, including more than 1,100 graduate students. The largest number of students come from Hawaii; however, all fifty states and more than eighty countries are represented.

Location

The University has two campuses, 8 miles apart, connected by a shuttle system. The downtown Honolulu campus is situated within the center of the business and financial capital of the Pacific. The Hawaii Loa campus is located in a suburban, residential setting on 135 acres of green countryside.

The University

Hawaii Pacific University is the largest private postsecondary institution in the state of Hawaii. The University is coeducational, with a faculty of more than 300, a student-faculty ratio of 20:1, and an average class size of 24. A wide range of counseling and other student support services are available. There are some fifty-five student organizations on campus, including the Graduate Student Organization.

Applying

Hawaii Pacific University seeks students with academic promise, outstanding career potential, and high motivation. Applicants should complete and forward a graduate admissions application form, have official transcripts sent from all colleges or universities previously attended, and have two letters of recommendation forwarded. International applicants should submit results of the TOEFL. Admissions decisions are made on a rolling basis, and applicants are notified between one and two weeks after all documents have been submitted.

Correspondence and Information

Graduate Admissions
Hawaii Pacific University
1164 Bishop Street
Honolulu, Hawaii 96813
Telephone: 808-544-0279
800-669-4724 (toll-free)
Fax: 808-544-0280
E-mail: gradservctr@hpu.edu
World Wide Web: http://www.hpu.edu/

Hawaii Pacific University

THE FACULTY AND THEIR RESEARCH

Richard Chepkevich, M.S., USC. Information systems.
Larry Cross, Ph.D., Colorado. Economics.
Thomas Crowley, J.D., Hawaii. Law.
Cheryl Ann Crozier, M.B.A., Hawaii Pacific. Human resource management.
Patrick Doran, Ph.D., Georgia. Information systems.
Eric Drabkin, Ph.D., UCLA. Economics.
Peter Freeman, M.A., Florida. Communication arts.
Stanley Ghosh, Ph.D., Indiana. Strategic planning.
W. Gerald Glover, Ph.D., Florida. Quality assurance.
Randall Harakal, J.D., Widener. Law.
Bradford Harrison, M.B.A., Hawaii Pacific. Business administration.
Gordon L. Jones, Ph.D., New Mexico. Computer applications, information systems.
Thomas Kam, M.B.A., Hawaii. Business administration.
John Karbens, M.B.A., Ed.D., Hawaii; CPA, CMA, CIA. Accounting, finance.
John Kros, Ph.D., Virginia. Systems engineering.
Lola Lackey, M.B.A., Seattle. Marketing management.
David Lohmann, Ph.D., Arizona State. Marketing, management.
Ernesto Lucas, Ph.D., Hawaii. Agricultural economics.
Ward Mardfin, Ph.D., Hawaii. Economics.
Gunter Meissner, Ph.D., Kiel (Germany). Mathematics, derivatives.
Michael Miller, M.S., Hawaii Pacific. Information systems.
Wallace "John" Nabers, LL.B., Duke. Law.
Ronald Paglinawan, M.S., USC. EDP auditing.
Roy Reeber, M.B.A., Pepperdine; M.S., USC. International business management, systems management.
Rodney Roming, Ph.D., Nebraska. Economics.
Lawrence Rowland, M.S., USC. Systems management.
Michael Seiler, D.B.A., Cleveland. Finance.
Derek Shigesato, J.D., Georgetown. Law.
Ronald Slepecki, M.S.I.S., Hawaii Pacific. Information systems.
Mary Smith, M.S., Hawaii Pacific. Information systems.
Paul Stipek, M.S., Naval Postgraduate School. Information systems.
Bradley Tamm, J.D., Western State Law. Law.
Shue-Jane Thompson, M.S., Hawaii Pacific. Information systems.
Edwin Van Gorder, Ph.D., Stanford. Mathematics, management.
Phillip Viehl, M.B.A., Hawaii Pacific. Finance.
James Waddington, M.B.A., Hawaii; CPA. Accounting.
Richard Ward, Ed.D., USC. Human resource management, safety management.
Warren Wee, Ph.D., Washington (Seattle); M.B.A., Hawaii; CPA. Accounting.
Arthur Whatley, Ph.D., Texas. Management, economics.
Leslie Wiletzky, M.A., SUNY College at Buffalo; M.P.A., Penn State. Human resource management.
Alfred Zimermann, M.B.I.S., Georgia State. Business information systems.
Larry Zimmerman, M.S., USC. Systems management.

Graduation day.

HOFSTRA UNIVERSITY

Frank G. Zarb School of Business M.B.A. Program

Programs of Study

The M.B.A. Program was completely revised in 1995 to better reflect the actual environment in which contemporary managers must make decisions, often under conditions of uncertainty. Courses in the Zarb M.B.A. Program expose students to innovative strategies, group interaction, and simulated business situations. The curriculum emphasizes a cross-functional approach to teaching. Major areas of concentration include accounting, business computer information systems, banking and finance, marketing, management, international business, and taxation. The regular M.B.A. Program is two full academic years. A one-year program is available for students who hold a baccalaureate degree in business from an accredited institution. Classes may be attended in the day or evening, on either a full-time or a part-time basis.

A J.D./M.B.A. program is offered in conjunction with the Hofstra School of Law.

Research Facilities

The Hofstra University libraries contain more than 1.4 million volumes. The libraries are a depository for federal documents. They are fully computerized from acquisition to retrieval and feature LEXICAT, an online listing that includes records of books, periodicals, microforms, government documents, and media available through the libraries. Additional services available through the libraries include ABI/Inform, Business Periodicals on Disc, Compact D-SEC, Laser Disclosure, and Newspaper Abstracts on Disc.

Hofstra's computer facilities comprise several computer labs that are connected to the University's computer network to provide easy access to all systems from various locations on campus. Featured are a dedicated business student lab within the Zarb School, as well as the McGraw-Hill Technology Lab, which represents the only facility of its type at any university. All of the databases and software proprietary to the McGraw-Hill Companies are included in this facility, and it is extensively used by graduate business students. The lab was made possible through the generosity of Joseph Dionne, CEO of the McGraw-Hill Companies and an alumnus of the University. All M.B.A. students are automatically assigned e-mail accounts that provide them with Internet access at no charge.

The Merrill Lynch Center for the Study of International Financial Services and Markets at the Zarb School promotes and facilitates research and innovation in the field of international services and markets and is funded by Merrill Lynch.

Financial Aid

Academic scholarships, research assistantships, fellowships, and need-based awards are available to full-time and part-time students. Special scholarship programs are available for minority students. The Zarb School requires that all students applying for financial aid file the Free Application for Federal Student Aid (FAFSA).

Cost of Study

Graduate tuition is $457 per semester hour in 1998–99. University fees are $72 to $350 per semester, depending upon the number of credits taken.

Living and Housing Costs

Limited on-campus accommodations are available for graduate students. These accommodations include University-owned apartments as well as suites and conventional dormitories. The charges for these accommodations for 1997–98 were $2385 per semester for University apartments, $2640 for single-occupancy residence hall rooms, and $2215 per semester for double-occupancy suites. Meal plans are available at a range of costs.

The Office of Residence Life maintains listings of available accommodations for students who wish to live off campus.

Student Group

There are approximately 700 students currently enrolled in the M.B.A. Program. These students are drawn from ten states and twenty-eight countries. The ratio of women to men is 2:3. Students develop and manage their career and professional plans in conjunction with the M.B.A. placement coordinator. For the class of 1997, 93 percent of all students held jobs upon graduation, and the average starting salary was $53,388.

Location

Hofstra is located approximately 25 miles east of New York City, the world center of banking, finance, advertising, communications, transportation, fashion, and culture. The University's location in suburban Long Island provides students with an ideal, quiet academic retreat and a gateway to the wealth of professional, academic, and cultural opportunities that abound in Manhattan. Numerous cultural and sports activities, lecture series, and scholarly conferences are sponsored by the University each year.

The School

The Frank G. Zarb School of Business is a relatively young institution that offers graduate students a unique combination of small classes, proximity to Manhattan and its major business centers, and a campus-based program in a safe and hospitable environment among talented students and faculty members. Students at the Zarb School have a full complement of activities in which to become involved, including the M.B.A. Association, the Association for International Commerce (AISEC), the Minority Student Organization, Graduate Women in Business (GWIB), the Hofstra Consulting Group, and others. The M.B.A. program is fully accredited by AACSB–The International Association for Management Education.

Applying

Applicants for admission to the M.B.A. Program must hold a bachelor's degree from a regionally accredited institution. The School admits men and women who, through GMAT scores, overall undergraduate grade point average, letters of recommendation, and business experience, demonstrate considerable promise of success in graduate business studies. New students are admitted to the M.B.A. Program in the fall, spring, and summer semesters of each year. It is recommended that prospective students apply no later than May 1 for fall admission and by November 1 for spring admission.

Correspondence and Information

Office of Admissions
Hofstra University
Hempstead, New York 11549
Telephone: 516-463-6700
Fax: 516-560-7660
E-mail: hofstra@hofstra.edu

Susan M. McTiernan
Senior Assistant Dean and Director of Graduate Programs
Frank G. Zarb School of Business
Hofstra University
Hempstead, New York 11549
Telephone: 516-463-5683
Fax: 516-463-5268
E-mail: humba@hofstra.edu

Hofstra University

THE FACULTY

Ralph S. Polimeni, Chaykin Endowed Chair in Accounting and Dean; Ph.D., Arkansas; CPA, CCA.
Debra R. Comer, Associate Professor of Management and General Business and Associate Dean for Faculty Development; Ph.D., Yale.
Robert E. Brockway, Senior Executive-in-Residence in the Department of Marketing and International Business and Special Assistant to the Dean; B.S., Hofstra.
Susan M. McTiernan, Senior Assistant Dean for Graduate Programs and Special Adviser to the Dean; M.S.Ed., Hofstra.
Patricia E. Green, Senior Assistant Dean for Undergraduate Programs; M.B.A., C.A.S., Ed.D. candidate, Hofstra.
Rose Anne Manfredi, Senior Assistant Dean for Administration, Curriculum, and Personnel; M.A., Hofstra.
Esmeralda O. Lyn, Professor in the Department of Banking and Finance and Codirector of the Merrill Lynch Center for the Study of International Financial Services and Markets; Ph.D., CUNY, Baruch.
George J. Papaioannou, Professor in the Department of Banking and Finance and Codirector of the Merrill Lynch Center for the Study of International Financial Services and Markets; Ph.D., Penn State.

Accounting, Taxation, and Business Law
Lorinda P. Adair, Assistant Professor; Ph.D., Indiana; CPA. Anthony Basile, Instructor; M.S., LIU; CPA. Stuart L. Bass, Associate Professor; J.D., Hofstra. Jacqueline A. Burke, Instructor; M.B.A., Hofstra; CPA. Robert Fonfeder, Professor; Ph.D., CUNY, Baruch; CPA. Mark P. Holtzman, Assistant Professor; Ph.D., Texas; CPA. Richard C. Jones, Assistant Professor; B.S., Drexel; CPA. Robert Katz, Chaykin Distinguished Teaching Professor; LL.M., NYU. Cheryl R. Lehman, Professor; Ph.D., NYU. Eugene T. Maccarrone, Associate Professor; J.D., Hofstra; CPA. Sabir Manteen, Assistant Professor; J.D., CUNY, Queens. Dominic A. Marsicovetere, Assistant to the Chairperson; M.B.A., Pace. Susan L. Martin, Associate Professor; J.D., Hofstra. Linda J. Schain, Assistant Professor; M.B.A., Iona; CPA. Nathan S. Slavin, Associate Professor; Ph.D., CUNY, Baruch; CPA. Paul D. Warner, Professor and Chairperson; LL.M., Ph.D., NYU. Martha S. Weisel, Associate Professor; M.S., CUNY, Queens; J.D., St. John's (New York).

Business Computer Information Systems and Quantitative Methods
John F. Affisco, Professor; Ph.D., CUNY Graduate Center. Meral Binbasioglu, Associate Professor; Ph.D., NYU. Mahesh Chandra, Associate Professor; D.Sc., George Washington. Bernard H. Dickman, Associate Professor; Ph.D., NYU. Farrokh Guiahi, Associate Professor; Ph.D., Stanford. John A. Hardiman, Assistant Professor; Ph.D., St. John's (New York). Laura H. Lally, Associate Professor; Ph.D., NYU. Seung C. Lee, Special Assistant Professor; M.S., Georgia State. Farrokh Nasri, Associate Professor and Chairperson; Ph.D., CUNY, Baruch. M. Javad Paknejad, Associate Professor; Ph.D., CUNY Graduate Center. David N. Sessions, Associate Professor; Ph.D., NYU. Ashraf I. Shirani, Assistant Professor; M.B.A., Arkansas. Alvin M. Silver, Professor; Eng.Sc.D., Columbia. Nancy Stern, Brodlieb Distinguished Professor; Ph.D., SUNY at Stony Brook. Lonnie K. Stevans, Associate Professor; Ph.D., Oklahoma State. Mohammed H. Alai Tafti, Associate Professor; D.B.A., George Washington.

Finance
Troy A. Adair Jr., Assistant Professor; Ph.D., Indiana. Gioia P. Bales, Instructor; M.B.A., Hofstra. Rahul K. Bishnoi, Associate Professor; Ph.D., Massachusetts Amherst. Qi Huang, Assistant Professor; Ph.D., NYU. Nancy W. Huckins, Assistant Professor; Ph.D., CUNY Graduate Center. Steven B. Krull, Associate Professor; Ph.D., CUNY, Baruch. Susan L. Malley, Associate Professor; Ph.D., NYU. Sunil K. Mohanty, Assistant Professor; Ph.D., Cleveland State. Ehsan Nikbakht, Professor; D.B.A., George Washington. Anoop Rai, Associate Professor; Ph.D., Indiana. K. G. Viswanathan, Associate Professor; Ph.D., Tennessee. Edward J. Zychowicz, Associate Professor and Chairperson; Ph.D., SUNY at Binghamton.

Management and General Business
Mauritz D. Blonder, Associate Professor; Ph.D., CUNY, Baruch. Richard Buda, Assistant Professor; Ph.D., Stevens. Bruce H. Charnov, Associate Professor and Acting Chairperson; Ph.D., US International; J.D., Hofstra. Mamdouh I. Farid, Associate Professor; Ph.D., CUNY, Baruch. Lisa A. Ferguson, Assistant Professor; Ph.D., Arizona State. David M. Flynn, Associate Professor; Ph.D., Massachusetts Amherst. Li-Lian Gao, Associate Professor; Ph.D., Indiana. Harold Lazarus, Mel Weitz Distinguished Professor; Ph.D., Columbia. Patrick J. Montana, Professor; Ph.D., NYU. George S. Roukis, Professor; Ph.D., NYU. Charles H. Smith, Associate Professor; Ph.D., Syracuse. Matthew C. Sonfield, Dall Distinguished Professor; Ph.D., NYU. Mohamed A. Wahba, Associate Professor; Ph.D., Penn State.

Marketing and International Business
Benny Barak, Associate Professor and Chairperson; Ph.D., CUNY, Baruch. Barry Berman, Walter H. (Bud) Miller Distinguished Professor; Ph.D., CUNY Graduate Center. Dorothy Cohen, Distinguished Professor Emerita; Ph.D., Columbia. Joel R. Evans, RMI Distinguished Professor; Ph.D., CUNY, Baruch. Andrew M. Forman, Associate Professor; Ph.D., Tennessee. Tao Gao, Special Assistant Professor; M.E., Harbin Institute (China). Zhongjun Hao, C. V. Starr Chair in International Business and Associate Professor; Ph.D., Texas. William L. James, Professor; Ph.D., Purdue. Keun S. Lee, Assistant Professor; D.B.A., Kentucky. Anil Mathur, Associate Professor; Ph.D., Georgia State. Rusty M. Moore, Associate Professor; Ph.D., Tufts (Fletcher). James P. Neelankavil, Professor; Ph.D., NYU. Alexander P. Sharland, Assistant Professor; Ph.D., Florida State. Elaine Sherman, Professor; Ph.D., CUNY, Baruch. Gladys Torres-Baumgarten, Assistant Professor; M.B.A., Columbia. Yong Zhang, Assistant Professor; Ph.D., Houston.

ILLINOIS INSTITUTE OF TECHNOLOGY

Stuart School of Business

Programs of Study

The Stuart School of Business at the Illinois Institute of Technology (IIT) offers graduate programs leading to the Master of Business Administration, the Master of Science in financial markets and trading, the Master of Science in operations and technology management, the Master of Science in marketing communications, the Master of Science in environmental management, the Doctor of Philosophy in management science, and dual-degree programs, including the J.D./M.B.A. All Stuart graduate programs, including the Ph.D., offer evening or weekend courses and part-time enrollment at one or more campuses, including IIT's Downtown Chicago Campus and three suburban sites.

The M.B.A. program is designed to prepare business professionals for the age of technology and a global economy and is intended for liberal arts, social sciences, engineering, and other nonbusiness majors, as well as for business and economics majors. The M.B.A. program provides a thorough grounding in the core business and management disciplines and offers eleven specializations to suit a student's professional interests. The curriculum consists of twenty courses: eight core courses, eleven electives, and a capstone course in business policy. Some core courses may be waived for students who have taken undergraduate courses in economics or business, enabling the completion of the M.B.A. program in as few as sixteen courses. Specializations are offered in finance, financial risk management, information management, international business, management science, marketing, operations management, organization and management, quality management, strategic management, and telecommunications management. The program is offered at IIT's Downtown Campus in Chicago and at suburban locations in the evenings and on Saturdays.

The Master of Science in financial markets and trading degree program is a fourteen-course program taught by academics and industry experts that provides the theoretical background, quantitative skills, and practical knowledge needed to succeed in today's financial markets and related service industries.

The Master of Science in environmental management degree program is a fourteen-course, interdisciplinary program that integrates business, management, science, and law to provide the comprehensive perspective and broad skills needed by environmental professionals today.

The Master of Science in operations and technology management degree program is an eighteen-month (twelve courses) weekend program designed to advance the careers of experienced working engineers, scientists, and other technical professionals by applying business and management concepts directly to the areas of operations, manufacturing, R&D, new product development, MIS, logistics, and TQM.

The Master of Science in marketing communication degree program is a fourteen-course program, taught from a practical perspective that integrates advertising, public relations, database marketing, promotion, media planning, and other marketing tools within a strategy-driven approach.

The Doctor of Philosophy in management science may be completed on a full- or part-time basis and requires the completion of seventeen courses (quarter-length) and a dissertation. Two areas of study are available: operations and finance.

Research Facilities

IIT is a major university with extensive computer and library facilities. The Information Center at the Downtown Campus is an open-stack collection of more than 525,000 volumes, including the wide business holdings of the Stuart Business Library, the Chicago-Kent Law Library, and the Library of International Relations, which contains international materials in history, economics, political science, and law. The Downtown Campus Computer Lab provides access to a wide range of business tools and resources through a Microsoft Windows interface. Each of the lab's computers is directly connected to the Internet, allowing students access to Netscape and Usenet, the world's largest BBS.

Financial Aid

Financial support is made available to qualified full-time students through partial tuition scholarships and employment on campus. Loans may be arranged through the Financial Aid Office. IIT's personnel and career planning offices assist students in securing employment on campus or in the Chicago area.

Cost of Study

Tuition in 1998–99 is $1620 per course. All tuition rates are subject to change.

Living and Housing Costs

In comparison with costs in other major urban centers, living costs in Chicago are relatively reasonable. The university offers living quarters for graduate students on the main campus. A variety of other accommodations are available nearby.

Student Group

About 700 students are enrolled in the Stuart graduate programs. Approximately 80 percent are employed in local firms and study part-time in the evening, and 12 percent are international students.

Student Outcomes

Internships and networking often lead to employment for Stuart graduates. AT&T recently hired an M.B.A. marketing major who had completed an internship there while a student. Another M.B.A. graduate has joined GM Investment Management Company in New York City as a portfolio manager. Andersen Consulting hired a recent M.B.A. graduate as an information systems consultant. First Chicago/NBD hired several graduates of the M.S. in financial markets and trading degree program for foreign exchange trading positions. Other employers of recent Stuart graduates are AON Advisors (investment analysts), Northern Trust (financial analysts), Reuters (market data support specialists), and Alexander & Alexander (risk management specialists).

Location

The Chicago area has a great diversity of commercial, industrial, and financial institutions. It offers cultural and recreational facilities in a setting of architectural elegance served by a convenient mass-transit system. The local economy offers numerous employment opportunities to students and their spouses.

The University

Illinois Institute of Technology, an internationally respected, Ph.D.-granting university founded in 1890, offers graduate programs in business, engineering, science, architecture, psychology, design, and law. One of the seventeen institutions that comprise the Association of Independent Technological Universities (AITU), IIT offers exceptional preparation for professionals who require technological sophistication.

IIT's Stuart School of Business provides experienced working professionals and career-entry students from all countries with a range of intellectually challenging graduate-level business education programs, taught from a practical perspective, with an emphasis on analytic/quantitative skills and the relationship between business and technology. Faculty members and Ph.D. students conduct applied research in business and management.

The Stuart School of Business is located in downtown Chicago; the M.B.A. degree program is also offered at the Daniel F. and Ada L. Rice Campus in suburban Wheaton and at Motorola's Galvin Campus in Schaumburg.

Applying

Applications for admission are accepted throughout the year. Students may enter most programs at the beginning of any quarter, although new Ph.D. and M.S./OTM students enroll in fall quarter. The major factors used to determine admission are the applicant's grade point average and GMAT or GRE scores. Applicants from non-English-speaking countries are required to submit results of the TOEFL.

Correspondence and Information

Stuart School of Business
Illinois Institute of Technology
565 West Adams, Suite 430E
Chicago, Illinois 60661

Telephone: 312-906-6544
800-622-6398 (toll-free)
E-mail: degrees@stuart.iit.edu
World Wide Web: http://www.stuart.iit.edu

Illinois Institute of Technology

THE FACULTY AND THEIR RESEARCH

M. Zia Hassan, Dean and Professor; Ph.D., IIT. Effective organizations, strategic and quality issues in organizations.

Martin L. Bariff, Associate Professor; Ph.D., Illinois at Urbana-Champaign. The impact of information technology on business strategy, organizational structure, work group design, and human decision making.

Christopher M. Barlow, Assistant Professor; Ph.D., Case Western Reserve. Cross-functional teamwork with a particular emphasis on integrating technical and business perspectives.

John F. O. Bilson, Associate Professor; Ph.D., Chicago. Foreign exchange, the futures markets, and international economics.

Eve M. Caudill, Assistant Professor; Ph.D., Illinois at Urbana-Champaign. Consumer behavior.

Joseph S. Chung, Professor Emeritus; Ph.D., Wayne State. Asian economics, the economy of North and South Korea.

Martin E. Ginn, Associate Professor; Ph.D., Northwestern. Creativity management, new product development.

Joel Goldhar, Professor; D.B.A., George Washington. Computer-integrated manufacturing, the impacts of technology on business strategy.

Jon Michael Gorham, Lecturer; Ph.D., Wisconsin. Financial markets.

W. Clayton Hall, Associate Professor; Ph.D., Illinois at Urbana-Champaign. Public sector financial, economic, and industrial relations issues.

Charles T. Hamilton, Clinical Assistant Professor; Ph.D., Illinois at Urbana-Champaign. Accounting education, the behavioral factors that influence audit judgment.

Syed A. Imam, Assistant Professor; Ph.D., IIT. Design and management of manufacturing systems in domestic and international settings.

Kamyar Jabbari, Lecturer; M.B.A., Chicago. Project financing, international banking, independent power production.

Thomas W. Knowles, Professor; Ph.D., Chicago. Mathematical and computer modeling.

George D. Kraft, Associate Professor; Ph.D., Case Tech. Use of leading-edge technologies in enhancing the corporate information environment.

Michael L. Modica, Lecturer; Ph.D., Chicago. Quantitative methods for financial markets.

Paul R. Prabhaker, Associate Professor; Ph.D., Rochester. Advertising-price interaction.

David P. Quinn, Assistant Professor; Ph.D., Yale. Incentives for innovation, energy markets, bankruptcy in emerging markets, market microstructure, investments.

Spencer B. Smith, Professor Emeritus; Eng.Sc.D., Columbia. Computer-based production and inventory control.

Nick T. Thomopoulos, Professor; Ph.D., IIT. Forecasting, inventory, assembly-line systems.

Khairy A. Tourk, Associate Professor; Ph.D., Berkeley. Evolution of the Asian enterprise, economics of the newly industrializing Asia.

John R. Twombly, Clinical Assistant Professor; Ph.D., Chicago. Financial analysis.

The Stuart School of Business.

INDIANA UNIVERSITY BLOOMINGTON

Kelley School of Business
M.B.A. Program

Program of Study

The Indiana University Kelley School of Business offers study leading to the M.B.A. degree. Accredited by AACSB–The International Association for Management Education, the program takes two years and requires 54–60 credits. The Indiana M.B.A. curriculum reflects a new direction in graduate management education. The first year of the M.B.A. curriculum is designed to provide students with basic business principles and management tools. Students participate in a foundations and functional core that includes integrative teaching methods, group work, and consideration of the global economy. The critical issues of cultural diversity, ethics, and communication are among the topics addressed in an integrated form across the curriculum.

While the first year of the M.B.A. program is structured, the second year offers greater flexibility. In the second year, students choose from a wide variety of major courses and electives. Students also participate in the policy core, an integrated curriculum that includes business and government, strategy, international issues, law, and economics. In addition, computer literacy is a critical component of the program. Every M.B.A. student is required to own a personal computer and use technology to support their academic work.

Research Facilities

As a major research institution, Indiana University maintains an extensive computer network providing access to mainframe computers and numerous databases. M.B.A. students are actively involved with the e-mail system and the Internet, and they regularly use the Dow Jones News/Retrieval Service and other electronic resources, including INFOTRAC, DATEXT, and UMI INFORM. The library in the School of Business complex provides much computer access and also has more than 150,000 volumes of research materials. The main library is conveniently located across the street from the business school and is internationally known as one of the best university libraries.

Financial Aid

Approximately 35 percent of Bloomington M.B.A. students receive merit-based financial aid from the School of Business. Graduate assistantships are available; these provide a partial fee remission and stipend in return for a minimal work obligation with faculty members or within administrative departments in the School of Business. In addition, more than $200,000 in scholarship funds is awarded each year to M.B.A. students. The business school awards are based on merit, not need. The IU Office of Student Financial Assistance administers federal financial aid based on student need. (The cost of a personal computer is calculated into the student's financial aid budget.) Indiana University participates in the Consortium for Graduate Study in Management, which offers substantial support for candidates from minority groups.

Cost of Study

In the 1998–99 academic year, tuition and fees for Indiana residents are $8775. For out-of-state students, the charge is $17,013. Books and supplies cost approximately $1360 for the academic year.

Living and Housing Costs

Housing in Bloomington is very affordable. Off-campus housing is a popular option for M.B.A. students, with apartment rents ranging from $400 to $800 per month. Room and board in University housing for a single student total $6014 for the academic year.

Student Group

Indiana University is committed to maintaining a diverse student body. This commitment is apparent in the M.B.A. student population. Of the 600 students in the program, approximately 28 percent are women, 15 percent are members of minority groups, and 20 percent are international students. The average age of the M.B.A. students is 28; their average work experience prior to enrollment is four years.

Student Outcomes

M.B.A. students benefit from the activities of the Business Placement Office, which has been nationally recognized as one of the premier placement facilities in the country. It attracts more than 230 companies each year to interview M.B.A. candidates and invites more than 100 companies to interview summer intern candidates. Companies that recruit at IU represent geographical and functional diversity and include Procter & Gamble, Eli Lilly, Ernst & Young, Hewlett-Packard, Intel, Andersen Consulting, Ford Motor Company, and Price Waterhouse.

Location

Bloomington is located 50 miles southwest of the state capital, Indianapolis, and within a half-day's drive of Chicago, Cincinnati, and Louisville. Bloomington has a population of 60,000 and is surrounded by wooded hills and national forests. It is noted for its limestone industry, which has contributed to many of the buildings in the community.

Bloomington has many cosmopolitan features within a small-town setting. Ethnic restaurants and grocery stores, neighborhood boutiques, bookstores, and pubs provide constant variety and entertainment for Bloomington residents.

The University and The Program

Indiana University is a major research institution with more than 26,000 undergraduates and 8,000 graduate students. All fifty states and 117 other countries are represented within the student population. Numerous trees, an arboretum, and native limestone architecture beautify the 1,800-acre Bloomington campus.

The M.B.A. program is a small academic unit within the context of the larger University environment. The M.B.A. group is characterized by a collegial atmosphere of friendly competition, in which teamwork and cooperation predominate. The Indiana spirit is one that values hard work and community involvement and recognizes the worth of individual differences.

Applying

Admission application forms for the Indiana M.B.A. program are available from the address below. All applications must include a completed application form with essays, GMAT scores, official transcripts from undergraduate and graduate institutions, and two letters of recommendation. International students whose native language is not English are required to take the TOEFL. Application deadlines for fall admission are December 1, January 15, and March 1 for domestic students and permanent residents and December 1 and February 1 for international students. Applicants who meet the early deadlines are considered first.

Correspondence and Information

M.B.A. Program
Kelley School of Business
1309 East Tenth Street, Room 254
Indiana University
Bloomington, Indiana 47405-1701

Telephone: 812-855-8006
800-994-8622 (toll-free)
Fax: 812-855-9039
E-mail: mbaoffice@indiana.edu
World Wide Web: http://www.bus.indiana.edu/mba

Indiana University Bloomington

FACULTY HEADS AND RESEARCH AREAS

Administration

Dan R. Dalton, Dean and Samuel and Pauline Glaubinger Professor of Entrepreneurship; Ph.D., California, Irvine, 1979.

R. Jeffrey Green, Associate Dean, Research and Operations; Co-Director, Indiana Center for Econometric Model Research; and Professor of Business Economics and Public Policy; Ph.D., Illinois, 1967.

Bruce Jaffee, Associate Dean, Academics, and Professor of Business Economics and Public Policy; Ph.D., Johns Hopkins, 1971.

Daniel C. Smith, Chairperson of M.B.A. Program; Clair W. Barker Eminent Scholar in Marketing; and Professor of Marketing; Ph.D., Pittsburgh, 1988.

Chairpersons and Department Areas of Research

Franklin Acito, Chairperson and Professor of Marketing; Ph.D., SUNY at Buffalo, 1976. Department research: advertising and brand preference, managing product innovation and development, product design management, global marketing, industrial buyer behavior, U.S.-Chinese marketing.

Terry Morehead Dworkin, Chairperson of Business Law, Jack and Linda Gill Professor of Business Law, and Associate Director, Center for International Business Education and Research; J.D., Indiana, 1974. Department research: employment law, concentrating on whistle-blowing, harassment, privacy, and diversity.

Michele Fratianni, Chairperson and Professor of Business Economics and Public Policy; Ph.D., Ohio State, 1971. Department research: European integration, central bank independence, bank regulation.

W. Harvey Hegarty, Chairperson and Professor of Management; Ph.D., North Carolina, 1971. Department research: total quality management, diverse workforce issues, mergers and acquisitions

Robert Jennings, Chairperson and Professor of Finance; Ph.D., Texas, 1981. Department research: structuring takeover offers, market structure.

James H. Pratt, Chairperson and Professor of Accounting and Information Systems and Harry C. Sauvain Faculty Fellow; D.B.A., Indiana, 1978. Department research: behavioral issues in various accounting settings.

M. A. Venkataramanan, Chariperson and Associate Professor of Operations and Decision Technologies; Ph.D., Texas A&M, 1987. Department research: DSS for routing automated guided vehicle systems, artificial intelligent techniques in optimizing, parallel processing approaches to entropy models.

Directors of Centers and Institutes

Lawrence S. Davidson, Professor of Business Economics and Public Policy and Director, Indiana Center for Global Business; Ph.D., North Carolina, 1977.

Daniel W. DeHayes Jr., Professor of Business Administration, Entrepreneurship Academy Leader, and Director, Center for Entrepreneurship and Innovation; Ph.D., Ohio State, 1968.

Jeffrey D. Fisher, Associate Professor of Finance and Real Estate and Director, Center for Real Estate Studies; Ph.D., Ohio State, 1980.

Morton J. Marcus, Lecturer in Business Economics and Public Policy; Director, Indiana Business Research Center; and Co-Director, Indiana Center for Econometric Model Research; M.A., Washington (St. Louis), 1963.

Roger W. Schmenner, Professor of Operations and Decision Technologies and Director, Center for International Business Education and Research; Ph.D., Yale, 1973. Department research: manufacturing strategy and service operations.

George M. Smerk, Professor of Transportation and Director, Institute for Urban Transportation; D.B.A., Indiana, 1963.

Theresa Williams, Director, Center for Education and Research in Retailing; Ph.D., Tennessee, 1994.

IONA COLLEGE

Hagan Graduate School of Business

Programs of Study

The Hagan Graduate School of Business offers classes leading to the Master of Business Administration (M.B.A.) degree and to the Post Master's Certificate (P.M.C.) in business administration.

The programs are designed to meet the needs of both full-time and part-time students and are organized on a trimester basis during the academic year, September to June. Summer sessions are also available from early June through July.

The goal of the M.B.A. program is to prepare students for management careers in business and other organizations. Effective managers must know themselves, work in teams, lead organizational change, and understand the macro factors affecting the future. They must also appreciate the role of information technology, ethically and socially responsible decision making, and the globalization of business. The School's concentrations in financial management, human resource management, information and decision technology management, management, and marketing provide more knowledge in a specific functional area of business. Required course work consists of 27 credits in the core curriculum and 30 credits in the major and related fields. Students must complete at least 30 credits of graduate work at Iona. (Part-time students can complete the degree in four years.) The M.B.A. program is offered at the main campus at New Rochelle and at a branch campus in Orangeburg, New York. The program also offers a certificate in international business, which can be completed concurrently with the M.B.A. curriculum.

The Post Master's Certificate (P.M.C.) in business administration is designed to meet specific individual professional needs at the post-M.B.A. level through a program of advanced courses in a major field or in a highly specialized area of study. A minimum of 15 credits is required to earn the New York State–approved certificate.

Research Facilities

Academic computing is supported primarily by local area networks and the IBM 9121 under VM/ESA, VSE/ESA, and MUSIC/SP. Three hundred microcomputers (Pentiums, 486 systems, and 386 systems) are available for student use at the New Rochelle and Rockland campuses. There are six public terminal facilities on the New Rochelle campus, most available 24 hours a day, seven days a week. The Rockland campus supports public terminal facilities that provide access to the academic system six days a week. New Rochelle and Rockland campus facilities are connected via local area networks by high-speed T-1 data communication lines.

Financial Aid

Graduate assistantships are available to full-time and part-time students on the basis of academic qualifications. Loans are provided through the Federal Stafford Student Loan program. Employment opportunities are also available on campus and at local corporate businesses.

Cost of Study

Tuition is $473 per credit in 1998–99. The initial application fee is $50. A registration fee of $15 and a computing fee of $30 are charged each trimester and for the summer sessions. Other charges depend upon the course of study.

Living and Housing Costs

Rooms and apartments are available in the local community and the nearby metropolitan area for students attending Iona College.

Student Group

There are approximately 425 degree candidates attending classes; 95 percent are part-time students.

Location

The main campus is located in New Rochelle, a suburban community in Westchester County, near the northern perimeter of New York City. All degree programs are offered on this site. A branch campus is located in Rockland County. Major highways and public transportation connect both campuses with the cultural and business centers of the Greater New York metropolitan area.

The College

Founded in 1940, Iona is a private coeducational institution with a total enrollment of 6,100 students in both day and evening classes. The Hagan Graduate School of Business was instituted in 1965.

Applying

Candidates may enter the graduate program in the fall (September), winter (December), or spring (March) trimester and summer sessions. The completed application, with fee, must be supported by official transcripts from each institution of higher education attended, two letters of recommendation, and Graduate Management Admission Test (GMAT) scores. All required documents should be received no later than two weeks prior to the start of the trimester or summer session for which the candidate is applying.

Correspondence and Information

Director of Admissions
Hagan Graduate School of Business
Iona College
New Rochelle, New York 10801
Telephone: 914-633-2288
Fax: 914-633-2012

Iona College

THE FACULTY

Matthew A. Amat, Professor Emeritus; Ph.D., Columbia.
Marie-Louise Andersson, Assistant Professor; Ph.D., CUNY, Baruch.
George J. Barbero, Professor Emeritus; J.D., New York Law.
Nicholas J. Beutell, Professor and Dean; Ph.D., Stevens.
William Bottiglieri, Assistant Professor; J.D., New York Law.
Andrew W. Braunstein, Associate Professor; Ph.D., Rutgers.
Thomas J. Bryde, Associate Professor Emeritus; M.Litt., Pittsburgh.
Vincent J. Calluzzo, Associate Professor; Ph.D., Polytechnic.
Charles J. Cante, Assistant Professor; Ph.D., CUNY, City College.
Jill D'Aquila, Assistant Professor; Ph.D., NYU.
Charles Duffy, C.F.C., Associate Professor; Ed.D., Columbia Teachers College.
Robert A. Eberle, Associate Professor; M.B.A., NYU.
Kurt J. Engemann, Professor; Ph.D., NYU.
Everett Fergenson, Professor; Ph.D., Massachusetts.
Joseph Ford, Professor; Ph.D., Fordham.
Larry S. Goldstein, Associate Professor; Ph.D., CUNY, Baruch.
Donald Grunewald, Professor; D.B.A., Harvard.
William Gulotta, Adjunct Assistant Professor; M.B.A., Iona.
David Halpern, Associate Professor; Ph.D., NYU.
Irene M. Hammerbacher, Professor; Ph.D., NYU.
Daniel K. Kast, Professor Emeritus; J.D., New York Law; CPA.
Steven Kroleski, Assistant Professor; J.D., St. John's (New York).
Mitchel Langbert, Assistant Professor; Ph.D., Columbia.
Anthony Libertella, Associate Professor; Ph.D., Ohio State; J.D., St. John's (New York).
George A. Mangiero, Assistant Professor; Ph.D., NYU.
John Manley, Associate Professor; Ph.D., Rutgers.
Eleni Mariola, Assistant Professor; Ph.D., Rutgers.
Francis J. McGrath, Professor; Ph.D., Fordham.
LeRoy W. Mitchell, Associate Professor; D.P.A., NYU; CPA.
Donald R. Moscato, Professor; Ph.D., Columbia; CDP.
Jane-Louise Nasuti, Associate Professor; J.D., Boston University.
Samuel Natale, Professor; D.Phil., Oxford.
Charles F. O'Donnell, Professor; Ph.D., Fordham.
Thomas M. Pollina, Associate Professor; M.B.A., Iona; CPA.
George Priovolos, Assistant Professor; Ph.D., CUNY, Baruch.
Patrick J. Reville, Associate Professor; J.D., Fordham.
Robert J. Richardson, Associate Professor; Ph.D., Pittsburgh.
Susan Rozensher, Associate Professor; Ph.D., Columbia.
Fredrica Rudell, Associate Professor; Ph.D., Columbia.
Hulda Ryan, Associate Professor; Ph.D., Houston.
Theodore M. Schwartz, Professor; Ph.D., NYU.
Anand Shetty, Associate Professor; Ph.D., Pittsburgh.
Robert G. Strittmatter, Associate Professor; M.B.A., NYU; CPA.
John Tiglias, Adjunct Assistant Professor; M.S., Polytechnic.
Ursula K. Wittig-Berman, Associate Professor; Ph.D., CUNY, Baruch.
Ronald R. Yager, Professor; Ph.D., Polytechnic of Brooklyn.

IOWA STATE UNIVERSITY

College of Business

Programs of Study

The College of Business offers a variety of opportunities for graduate study in business to students with diverse academic backgrounds and work experiences. Students may pursue the Master of Business Administration (M.B.A.) either through the full-time program or, for those employed, through the part-time Saturday program. The 48-credit-hour M.B.A. consists of an integrated core curriculum and 24 credit hours of electives. Students may pursue a general management course of study or concentrate in various functional areas. Specializations are offered in accounting, agribusiness, finance, information systems, manufacturing and quality, and marketing.

Students with an undergraduate degree in business may wish to seek a specialized, research-oriented graduate degree. The Master of Science (M.S.) in business administrative sciences is designed to develop research skills and to advance one's knowledge in a functional area of business. The M.S. program, which can be completed with a minimum of 30 credit hours of study, includes a thesis requirement. In addition, the College coordinates an interdepartmental program leading to the M.S. in industrial relations. Both thesis and nonthesis options are available in this program.

Research Facilities

Research is supported by the Parks Library and the Durham Computation Center. The business collection includes 160,000 bound volumes and 400 periodical subscriptions. An online computerized catalog system provides easy access to research materials. The Durham Computation Center offers consultation services to graduate students, short courses in computer use, Internet services, and 24-hour microcomputer labs. There are more than 900 high-performance UNIX workstations across campus. The College of Business houses two state-of-the-art computer laboratories and supports such research centers as the Pappajohn Center for Entrepreneurship and the Murray G. Bacon Center for Ethics in Business. Other research opportunities are available through the College's close ties with the Center for Transportation Research and Education and the Iowa Small Business Development Center.

Financial Aid

Graduate assistantships are available to exceptional students. Graduate assistants in good academic standing earn a monthly stipend, receive a scholarship tuition credit, and pay resident tuition. Outstanding students may qualify for the Premium for Academic Excellence (PACE) program. PACE recipients generally have an undergraduate GPA of 3.5 or better or a GPA of 3.8 in previous graduate work. Some scholarship support is also available, including assistance to women and minority candidates. The Office of Minority Student Affairs provides financial support opportunities to minority graduate students. The Office of Student Financial Aid has information about financial assistance through low-interest loans and employment.

Cost of Study

Tuition for full-time graduate students for the 1998–99 academic year is $3166 for state residents and $9324 for nonresidents. The cost of the Saturday M.B.A. program is $230 per credit. Books and course-related materials are estimated at $700 per year. Other University fees are $208 per year.

Living and Housing Costs

Iowa State University has one residence hall designated for graduate students. Single- and double-occupancy room rates range from $240 to $312 per month. University apartments serve both singles and families with rates ranging from $359 to $406 per month. Privately owned apartments and houses are readily available at varying rates.

Student Group

The 220 graduate business students at Iowa State University represent a wide variety of educational, cultural, and professional backgrounds. Thirty percent of the students are women. Approximately 25 percent are international students representing eighteen countries. Undergraduate majors are divided among the sciences, liberal arts, business, engineering, and other technical disciplines. Most have at least three years of full-time work experience.

Student Outcomes

Students are actively recruited in all functional business areas by both national and international companies. Recent graduates have successfully secured employment in management consulting, financial services, marketing management, accounting, information systems, and transportation and logistics management. The Career Services Office provides comprehensive career development and placement programs and services, including job search workshops, individual career counseling, a career resource center, internship coordination, and campus interviews.

Location

Just thirty minutes north of Des Moines, the state capital, Iowa State University's scenic campus is a focal point of the Ames community. Ames is part of the national entertainment circuit, hosting national and international sporting events, concerts, and theater in the Iowa State Center and the C. Y. Stephens Auditorium. These resources create an ideal setting for academic and research pursuits.

The University

Established in 1858, Iowa State University became the nation's first land-grant college under the Morrill Land-Grant Act. Today, Iowa State University is a broad-based university of international stature. More than 25,000 students are enrolled in the University's nine colleges—Agriculture, Business, Design, Education, Engineering, Family and Consumer Sciences, Liberal Arts and Sciences, Veterinary Medicine, and the Graduate College.

Applying

The College of Business at Iowa State University seeks a diverse student body with varied academic backgrounds and work experiences. Careful review is made of the applicant's intellectual potential, academic achievements, work experiences, communication skills, goals, and motivation. Required application materials include a Graduate College application, official transcripts from all institutions attended, Graduate Management Admission Test (GMAT) scores, three letters of recommendation, a resume, and personal essays. Applications are accepted for fall admission only into the M.B.A. program. The M.S. program has both fall and spring admission. The deadlines for receipt of all application materials are May 1 for fall admission and November 1 for spring admission.

Correspondence and Information

Director of Graduate Admissions
College of Business
218 Carver Hall
Iowa State University
Ames, Iowa 50011-2063

Telephone: 515-294-8118
800-433-3452 (toll-free nationwide)
Fax: 515-294-2446
E-mail: busgrad@iastate.edu
World Wide Web: http://www.public.iastate.edu/~isubuscoll/homepage.html

Iowa State University

THE FACULTY AND THEIR RESEARCH

Benjamin J. Allen, Distinguished Professor and Dean; Ph.D., Illinois. Transport policy analysis, transportation management.

Department of Accounting

Marvin L. Bouillon, Associate Professor; Ph.D., Kansas. Management accounting and decision models.
Anne M. Clem, Assistant Professor; Ph.D., Texas. Capital market response to accounting information, accounting for employee stock options.
William N. Dilla, Associate Professor; Ph.D., Texas at Austin. Decision-making in auditing, risk analysis, group decision and negotiation issues in accounting and information systems.
B. Michael Doran, Associate Professor; Ph.D., Iowa. Financial accounting, reporting, and statement analysis; accounting education issues.
Labh S. Hira, Professor; Ph.D., Missouri. Taxation of employee benefits and insurance products.
Cynthia G. Jeffrey, Associate Professor; Ph.D., Minnesota. Auditor judgment and decision making, ethics, international accounting issues.
James M. Kurtenbach, Assistant Professor; Ph.D., Missouri. Government and nonprofit finance and financial reporting.
Gary L. Maydew, Associate Professor; Ph.D., Illinois. Agribusiness accounting, business and individual taxation.
Sue Ravenscroft, Associate Professor; Ph.D., Michigan State. Behavioral issues in managerial accounting, curricular reform, cooperative learning, ethics, gender issues.
Anne M. A. Sergeant, Assistant Professor; Arizona. Financial accounting, capital markets.
Robert D. Swanson, Associate Professor; Ph.D., Iowa. Tax planning, tax policy, estate and gift taxation, business valuation.
Timothy D. West, Assistant Professor; Ph.D., Tennessee. Managerial and cost accounting.

Department of Finance

Cynthia Campbell, Associate Professor; Ph.D., Michigan. Small business financing, security issuance, international security markets, executive compensation, corporate governance, capital structure.
Richard B. Carter, Associate Professor; Ph.D., Utah. Capital acquisition, investment banking, small business.
Arnold R. Cowan, Associate Professor; Ph.D., Iowa. Corporate finance, mergers and acquisitions, capital markets.
Frederick H. Dark, Associate Professor; Ph.D., Utah. Corporate finance and structure, capital markets and financial management.
Jann Howell, Assistant Professor; Ph.D., Georgia State. Financial institutions, mergers and acquisitions, corporate financing.
Gary D. Koppenhaver, Associate Professor; Ph.D., Iowa. Decision making with futures and options contracts, financial intermediation.
Michael Piwowar, Assistant Professor; Ph.D., Penn State. Market microstructure, international markets and institutions, corporate finance.
Mark L. Power, Associate Professor; Ph.D., Iowa. Impact of regulation and rating changes on insurance companies, insurance products, employee benefits.
August R. Ralston, Professor; Ph.D., Pennsylvania. Risk management, political risk, regulation.
Roger D. Stover, Professor; D.B.A., Virginia. Financial institutions, roles of capital markets, corporate finance.

Department of Logistics, Operations, and Management Information Systems

Chao-Hsien Chu, Associate Professor; Ph.D., Penn State. Intelligent manufacturing systems, cellular manufacturing, fuzzy and neural information systems, Japanese manufacturing management, strategic quality management.
Michael R. Crum, Associate Professor; D.B.A., Indiana. Economic analysis of freight and passenger transportation, transport policy analysis.
Thomas J. Goldsby, Assistant Professor; Ph.D., Michigan State. Logistics management and strategy, marketing and distribution channels, transportation and marketing principles.
Anthony R. Hendrickson, Assistant Professor; Ph.D., Arkansas. Measurement of behavioral IS constructs, object-oriented systems, virtual organizations.
Danny J. Johnson, Assistant Professor; Ph.D., Wisconsin. Cellular manufacturing/group technology, quick response manufacturing/time-based competition.
Sree Nilakanta, Associate Professor; Ph.D., Houston. Database management, adoption of information technology, innovation.
Daniel M. Norris, Associate Professor; Ph.D., Missouri. Auditing, fraud examination, accounting information systems.
Richard F. Poist Jr., Professor; Ph.D., Penn State. Logistics systems design, transportation purchase decisions, business-society issues related to transportation and logistics.
G. Premkumar, Associate Professor; Ph.D., Pittsburgh. Information systems planning and telecommunications.
Troy J. Strader, Assistant Professor; Ph.D., Illinois at Urbana-Champaign. Electronic commerce, strategic impacts of information technology, information economics, consumer behavior in online markets.
Yoshi Suzuki, Assistant Professor; Ph.D., Penn State. Losgistics and transportation decision analysis.
John G. Wacker, Professor; Ph.D., Wayne State. Resource requirements, operations research, production and inventory management.
Clyde K. Walter Jr., Associate Professor; Ph.D., Ohio State. Inventory management, truck driver issues.
Dan Zhu, Assistant Professor; Ph.D., Carnegie Mellon. Decision support systems, intelligent schedules, electronic commerce, data mining, knowledge discovery.

Department of Management

Gary L. Aitchison, Associate Professor; Ph.D., Iowa State. Entrepreneurship.
Virginia L. Blackburn, Associate Professor; D.B.A., Kentucky. Strategic management and competitive strategy.
Thomas I. Chacko, Professor; Ph.D., Iowa. Human resource management, pay and performance, union-management relations.
J. David Hunger, Professor; Ph.D., Ohio State. Strategic management, entrepreneurship.
W. Roy Johnson, Associate Professor; Ph.D., Bowling Green State. Industrial/organizational psychology, union attitudes, worker and supervisor behavioral issues.
James C. McElroy, Professor; Ph.D., Oklahoma State. Work commitment, attribution theory, leadership.
Paula C. Morrow, Professor; Ph.D., Iowa State. Work commitment, human resource management, employee relations.
C. Bradley Shrader, Professor; Ph.D., Indiana. Strategic planning and business ethics.
Howard E. Van Auken, Associate Professor; Ph.D., Oklahoma. Entrepreneurship, small-business finance, small business.
James D. Werbel, Associate Professor; Ph.D., Northwestern. Careers, employee selection.
Max S. Wortman Jr., Distinguished Professor and Pioneer Hi-Bred International Chair of Agribusiness; Ph.D., Minnesota. Agribusiness, family business, new ventures, entrepreneurship.

Department of Marketing

Sanjeev Agarwal, Associate Professor; Ph.D., Ohio State. International business and international marketing.
Michael J. Barone, Assistant Professor; Ph.D., South Carolina. Consumer behavior.
Thomas E. DeCarlo, Assistant Professor; Ph.D., Georgia. Sales, sales management, and consumer behavior.
DeAnna S. Kempf, Assistant Professor; Ph.D., Indiana. Product trial, advertising, brand attitudes.
Russell N. Laczniak, Associate Professor; Ph.D., Nebraska. Marketing communication, children's advertising and research methodology.
Kay M. Palan, Assistant Professor; Ph.D., Texas Tech. Consumer behavior, marketing strategy, services marketing.
Sridhar N. Ramaswami, Associate Professor; Ph.D., Texas at Austin. Sales management, marketing strategy, communication research, financial services.
R. Kenneth Teas, Distinguished Professor; Ph.D., Oklahoma. Marketing research methodology, sales force management, consumer behavior.
John K. F. Wong, Associate Professor; Ph.D., Alabama. Health-care markets, international marketing.

KENT STATE UNIVERSITY

Graduate School of Management

Programs of Study

The College of Business Administration and Graduate School of Management provide high-quality undergraduate, graduate, and executive programs, primarily to the citizens of northeastern Ohio. Programs are accredited by the AACSB–The International Association for Management Education.

The M.B.A. degree programs prepare students for management and staff positions in regional, national, and international organizations, with curricular emphases on ethical leadership, teamwork, creative problem solving, global perspectives, and skillful applications of information technology. The M.S. in accounting prepares students with diverse academic backgrounds for an accounting or auditing career in the public, private, government, or not-for-profit sectors by providing a strong foundation in accounting theory coupled with a thorough understanding of the practical applications of the discipline. The M.A. in economics provides rigorous training in economic analysis to prepare students for careers in the private and public sectors or for doctoral study. The Ph.D. program prepares graduates for careers in academia, industry, and government that involve education and scholarship for business.

Research Facilities

The Business Administration Building contains more than 300 microcomputers that are used extensively for instruction, research, and administration. These computers are connected via Ethernet hardware and Novell NetWare. About 100 computers are available to all students in the computer labs. The College of Business local area network supports e-mail, spreadsheet, graphics, word processing, and Internet access. University buildings are networked via a high-speed ATM backbone. The University's department of Academic Computing Technology supports computing on the IBM VM and UNIX environments. It offers statistical packages such as SAS and SPSS and datasets such as CRSP, Compustat, and ICPSR.

The University Libraries contain more than 1.8 million volumes, 1 million microforms, and extensive collections of other media. The Computerized Information Services provide access to remote computer-based data retrieval systems. Kent participates in the OhioLINK library network system, which allows students to access materials from other state universities, provides access to research databases, and acts as a gateway to the Internet.

Financial Aid

Financial assistance is available through a variety of sources. The University offers graduate assistantships for M.B.A. students as well as doctoral fellowships. The service commitment for a graduate assistantship entails assisting with instruction, research, or administrative duties. Doctoral fellows normally perform research and instruction-related duties. Both awards are merit based.

Cost of Study

As of summer 1998, the tuition and fees for an Ohio resident taking 11 to 18 graduate credits were $2376. For nonresidents, the tuition and fees were $4606. The individual credit hour fee was $216 for Ohio residents and $418.75 for nonresidents. Fees are subject to change consequent to actions taken by the University Board of Trustees.

Living and Housing Costs

The Department of Residence Services offers special housing for both single and married graduate students. Cost estimates for the academic year are $2632 for housing and $1704 for board. For those students who prefer to live off campus, there are numerous houses and apartment buildings in the Kent area.

Student Group

Each year the full-time M.B.A. program enrolls between 50 and 60 people. Approximately 38 percent of the students are women, 7 percent are members of minority groups, and 36 percent are international. The doctoral program enrolls between 10 and 15 new students per year.

The Graduate School and the Career Services Center sponsor several M.B.A. events each year; they also prepare a resume book for the class, provide on-campus interviews, and offer career counseling. The student-run Graduate Management Association sponsors a speaker series as well as other professional and social activities. The student-run Doctoral Student Management Association holds monthly lunch meetings with speakers and forum discussions.

Student Outcomes

Recent M.B.A. graduates have found positions in banking, accounting, consulting, marketing, sales, production, manufacturing, and small businesses. For example, one recent graduate with a finance background is employed as a management associate with a nationwide financial services provider headquartered in Cleveland, Ohio. Another, with a concentration in information systems, is working as a business systems analyst with an international manufacturing company based in New Jersey.

Location

The University is located in the city of Kent in northeastern Ohio. The surrounding cities of Akron, Canton, and Cleveland offer fine dining, entertainment, and cultural facilities such as symphony orchestras, art galleries, professional athletics, and an extensive parks system for recreation. The region is home to about 45 percent of the state's population.

The University

Kent State University, founded in 1910, is situated on a beautiful campus of more than 800 acres. Many of the older, traditional buildings are arranged on the rolling, tree-covered front campus; newer facilities are attractively landscaped to complement these structures. In fall 1997, student enrollment was more than 20,700, including a graduate enrollment of nearly 4,700.

Applying

The Graduate School of Management welcomes applications from students of all backgrounds. Admissions decisions are based on a combination of factors including evidence of scholarly achievement as shown by the undergraduate GPA, results from the GMAT, a resume, letters of recommendation, and a written response to an essay question. It is the policy of Kent State University to actively support equality of education and employment opportunity. The deadline to apply for graduate assistantships is April 1. For doctoral fellowships, it is February 1. For regular admission for the fall, the deadlines are July 1 for master's programs for domestic students and February 1 for international students.

Graduate students desiring financial assistance must complete the Free Application for Federal Student Aid (FAFSA). Graduate students applying for a Federal Direct Student Loan should do so through their local bank or credit union.

Correspondence and Information

The Graduate School of Management
A310 Business Administration Building
Kent State University
P.O. Box 5190
Kent, Ohio 44242-0001

Telephone: 330-672-2282 Ext. 235
Fax: 330-672-7303
E-mail: gradbus@bsa3.kent.edu
World Wide Web: http://business.kent.edu

Kent State University

THE FACULTY AND THEIR RESEARCH

Accounting

Anurag Agarwal, Assistant Professor; Ph.D., Ohio State. Management information systems.
Pervaiz Alam, Associate Professor; Ph.D., Houston. Financial reporting, auditing.
Mark Altieri, Assistant Professor; LL.M., NYU. Tax.
Ran Barniv, Associate Professor; Ph.D., Ohio State. Financial reporting, insurance and risk.
Richard E. Brown, Professor; D.P.A., Harvard. Governmental and nonprofit accounting, accounting history and regulation.
David F. Fetyko, Professor and Acting Chairperson; Ph.D., Michigan State. Financial reporting, accounting education.
Joanne P. Healy, Assistant Professor; Ph.D., SUNY at Buffalo. Cost managerial accounting.
Michael A. Pearson, Professor; D.B.A., Kent State. Auditing, accounting education, ethics.
Ray G. Stephens, KPMG Peat Marwick Professor; D.B.A., Harvard. SEC and international reporting, compilation and review practice.
Linda J. Zucca, Assistant Professor; Ph.D., Case Western Reserve. Financial reporting.

Administrative Sciences

William Acar, Associate Professor; Ph.D., Pennsylvania. Macro-organization theory, strategic information systems.
Catherine Bakes, Associate Professor; Ph.D., Penn State. Telecommunications, networks and services.
David E. Booth, Associate Professor; Ph.D., North Carolina. Operations management.
James Randall Brown, Professor; Ph.D., MIT. Operations research, scheduling theory.
Cathy L. DuBois, Assistant Professor; Ph.D., Minnesota. Human resource management and organizational behavior.
Nancy Duncan, Assistant Professor; Ph.D., Texas A&M. Information systems and competitive advantage.
Robert H. Faley, Associate Professor; Ph.D., Tennessee, Knoxville. Policy implications of EEO.
Geoffry Howard, Associate Professor; D.B.A., Kent State. Information systems, automated systems development.
Gregory Madey, Associate Professor; Ph.D., Case Western Reserve. Electronic commerce, information superhighway.
Aubrey L. Mendelow, Associate Professor; D.B.L., South Africa. Strategies for high-performance organizations and total quality management.
O. Felix Offodile, Associate Professor; Ph.D., Texas Tech. Operations management and quality control.
B. Eddy Patuwo, Associate Professor; Ph.D., Virginia Tech. Operations management, operations research and neural networks.
Murali S. Shanker, Assistant Professor; Ph.D., Minnesota, Twin Cities. Neural networks and optimization.
Robert D. Smith, Professor; Ph.D., Penn State. Leadership and total quality.
Geoffrey D. Steinberg, Assistant Professor; Ph.D., Temple. Human-computer natural-language dialogue.
George E. Stevens, Professor and Dean; D.B.A., Kent State. Human resource management, equal employment opportunity.
Glenn N. Thomas, Associate Professor; Ph.D., Washington (Seattle). Information systems and operations research.
Marvin D. Troutt, Professor; Ph.D., Illinois. Production and operations management, decision theory, MIS/DSS, MS/OR.
G. Jay Weinroth, Associate Professor and Chairperson; Ph.D., Union (Ohio). Information systems, simulation and total quality.

Economics

Cheryl A. Casper, Professor; Ph.D., Case Western Reserve. Applied microeconomics, economics of information.
Michael A. Ellis, Assistant Professor; Ph.D., Texas A&M. Monetary theory, international economics, macroeconomics
Richard J. Kent, Associate Professor and Chairperson of Economics, Chairperson of Finance; Ph.D., Berkeley. Macroeconomic theory, monetary theory, housing and mortgage markets.
David L. McKee, Professor; Ph.D., Notre Dame. Economics of development, regional economics, poverty.
Randall I. Mount, Professor; Ph.D, Purdue. Microeconomic theory, quantitative methods.
Min Qi, Assistant Professor; Ph.D., Ohio State. Applied econometrics, forecasting, neural networks.
Charles W. Upton, Professor; Ph.D., Carnegie Mellon. Macroeconomic theory, natural resource economics.
Donald R. Williams, Professor; Ph.D., Northwestern College. Labor economics, poverty and discrimination.
Kathryn Wilson, Assistant Professor; Ph.D., Wisconsin–Madison. Public economics, education, poverty, labor, disability.

Finance

James C. Baker, Professor and Director of Ph.D. Program; D.B.A., Indiana. International business, banking and financial institutions.
Lois Yoder Beier, Associate Professor; J.D., Akron. Business law, taxation.
James W. Boyd, Associate Professor; Ph.D., Arkansas. Real estate, corporate finance.
Richard J. Curcio, Professor; Ph.D., Penn State. Corporate finance, future markets.
Daniel C. Indro, Assistant Professor; Ph.D., Indiana. Corporate finance, banking, game theory.
Christine X. Jiang, Assistant Professor; Ph.D., Drexel. International asset pricing, market anomalies, time-series modeling.
Frederick W. Schroath, Associate Professor and Associate Dean; Ph.D., South Carolina. International business, risk and insurance.
Jacobus T. Severiens, Professor; Ph.D., Iowa. Corporate finance, banking and financial institutions, international business.

Marketing

Paul J. Albanese, Assistant Professor; Ph.D., Harvard. Personality and consumer behavior.
Eileen Bridges, Assistant Professor; Ph.D., Northwestern. Marketing of services and high-technology products.
Pamela Grimm, Assistant Professor; Ph.D., SUNY at Buffalo. Consumer behavior and advertising.
Michael Y. Hu, Professor; Ph.D., Minnesota. Marketing research.
Richard H. Kolbe, Assistant Professor; Ph.D., Cincinnati. Content analysis, public policy issues.
Robert F. Krampf, Associate Professor; Ph.D., Cincinnati. Health-care marketing, consumer satisfaction.
Lawrence J. Marks, Associate Professor and Associate Dean; Ph.D., Penn State. Consumer and marketing ethics, advertising effects.
Michael A. Mayo, Assistant Professor and Chairperson; Ph.D., Kent State. Consumer and marketing ethics, international marketing.
John K. Ryans Jr., Professor; D.B.A., Indiana. International marketing and business.
William L. Shanklin, Professor; D.B.A., Maryland College Park. Marketing strategy and entrepreneurship.

LESLEY COLLEGE

School of Management

Programs of Study

The School of Management at Lesley College offers master's in management programs in a number of delivery options, including semester-based specializations, accelerated programs, and intensive delivery models. Some courses and degree programs are offered both on and off campus.

Semester-based specialization programs include fund-raising management, general management, health services management, human resources management, and management of information technology.

The School of Management offers an accelerated Bachelor of Science in Management degree program (B.S.M.) and an accelerated Master of Science in Management (M.S.M.). Both programs are offered on campus and at off-site locations throughout Massachusetts and across the United States.

The intensive delivery format includes the Master of Science degree in training and development. This program prepares participants for the important job of planning, designing, and implementing training and development programs that match an organization's strategy and performance goals. In addition, the 18-credit, ten-month Certificate in Organizational Development prepares managers from all disciplines in change management skills. Students may also choose the 16-credit Certificate in Health Services Management.

Programs are designed to encourage students to apply theory to practice in the workplace. Core course work covers broad management competencies in organizational behavior and theory, finance, marketing, operations, and strategic management. Specialization course work focuses on the skills managers need to be successful in their professions. The student population is a diverse group of adult men and women who pursue degrees in a variety of options that allow them to continue to work full-time.

Research Facilities

The Ludcke Library maintains a working collection of books, periodicals, microfilm and microfiches, curriculum materials, nonprint materials, and software resources. The library provides Internet resources and database access to general and subject-specific resources appropriate to the subject focuses of the College. The Kresge Center for Teaching Resources provides instructional resources for individual and group instruction, and the Microcomputer Center houses the instructional computing activities of the College, including a collection of educational software. Through the Fenway Consortium, students can access thirteen other libraries in the Boston-Cambridge area.

Financial Aid

The Lesley College Financial Aid Office assists students as needed to obtain various types of educational assistance, including Federal Pell Grants, Federal Stafford Loans, and Federal Perkins Loans. The accelerated M.S.M. program qualifies as a full-time program for VA benefits. Many working adult students receive employer education assistance benefits.

Cost of Study

In 1998–99, the tuition for all M.S. programs is $425 per credit with various materials fees. Graduate degree requirements vary from 36 to 40 credits, depending upon the program.

Living and Housing Costs

Housing is not available on campus for graduate students. Information on local housing and assistance in obtaining housing are available upon request from the Residence Life Office.

Student Group

Approximately 700 graduate students are enrolled in School of Management classes. The population consists of women and men in their mid-twenties through early sixties. They represent a wide variety of managers, supervisors, teachers, and trainers employed in high-tech industries, manufacturing, banking and finance, health care, communications, education, the military, service industries, small business, and nonprofit organizations. Most have worked in the professional field of their choice and have returned to graduate school to learn new skills or change careers.

Location

Lesley College occupies a campus adjacent to Harvard Square in Cambridge, Massachusetts, and is easily accessible from downtown Boston by public transportation. The Boston area has one of the world's greatest concentrations of institutions of higher education and offers an unusual richness of cultural opportunities. Off-campus programs are available throughout Massachusetts and across the United States.

The College

Lesley College, founded in 1909 as a women's teaching college, continues its commitment to educating undergraduate women while also offering graduate and Ph.D. programs for women and men in the fields of education, human services, management, and the arts. With the next century's student in mind, Lesley College has successfully pioneered a wide variety of flexible programs for adult learners who share a commitment to quality, innovation, and the integration of theory with practice.

Lesley offers degree programs through four schools: the School of Undergraduate Studies, which includes the primarily residential Women's College, the coeducational Adult Baccalaureate College, and the Threshold Program; the Graduate School of Arts and Social Sciences; the School of Education; and the School of Management. The College also supports several centers and hosts a variety of academic and professional conferences and institutes. Lesley programs operate throughout Massachusetts and in fourteen other states, as well as at affiliated international sites.

Applying

Prospective students attend information seminars held at various geographically convenient locations and receive detailed information on degree options in management and in training and development. Student applications for admission are submitted to the Office of Admissions for Graduate and Adult Baccalaureate Programs.

It is recommended that students seeking admission to the School of Management have three years' work experience in a business, nonprofit, government, or comparable organizational setting. Candidates must complete an admissions application and submit a resume, official transcript from the regionally accredited institution that conferred their undergraduate degree, two letters of recommendation, and a written statement of goals and objectives. There is a nonrefundable application fee of $45.

Correspondence and Information

Office of Admissions
Graduate and Baccalaureate Programs
Lesley College
29 Everett Street
Cambridge, Massachusetts 02138-2790

Telephone: 617-349-8300
800-999-1959 Ext. 8300 (toll-free)
Fax: 617-349-8313
World Wide Web: http://www.lesley.edu

Lesley College

THE FACULTY

Earl Potter, Professor and Dean; Ph.D., Washington (Seattle).
Juan Evereteze, Assistant Professor and Assistant Dean; C.A.G.S., Boston State College.

Core Faculty

Nancy Alimansky, Associate Professor and Program Director/Management of Information Technology; M.B.A., Boston College.
Donald Boyle, Assistant Professor and Program Director/Warren AFB; M.B.A., Columbia.
Joan Dolamore, Assistant Professor and Assessment Center Coordinator; Ed.M., Harvard.
Ronald Fionte, Assistant Professor and Faculty Coordinator for Economics, Finance and Operations; M.B.A., Suffolk.
John Foran, Assistant Professor and Director of the Center for Management and Professional Development; M.B.A., Babson.
Richard Jette, Associate Professor and Program Director/Training and Development; Ph.D., NYU.
Barton Kunstler, Associate Professor and Program Director/General Education; Ph.D., Boston University.
Maria Mackavey, Associate Professor and Program Director/Human Resources Management; Ed.D., Boston University.
Leslie S. May, Assistant Professor and Faculty Coordinator for Research; Ed.D., Harvard.
Barry Sugarman, Professor and Faculty Coordinator for the Internship; Ph.D., Princeton.

Adjunct Faculty

R. Ann Abeille, M.Ed.
Donald J. Agostino, Ph.D.
Mildred Allen, M.Ed.
Nan Andrews Amish, M.B.A.
Daun Anderson, M.B.A.
Barbara Baig, M.A.
Steven Bardige, J.D.
Raymond Barnstone, M.Sc.
Kathryn Battillo, M.S.
John R. Bellenoit, M.B.A.
Peter Berkeley, Ed.M.
Bill Berkowitz, Ph.D.
John Bermingham, M.B.A.
Abigail E. Beutler, M.B.A.
Charles Blackburn, M.S.
Robert Blitz, Ph.D.
Peter Boland, M.B.A.
Arthur J. Bowes, M.B.A.
Cynthia Farr Brown, Ph.D.
David Brown, M.B.A.
Stephen Brown, Ed.D.
Mitchell J. Burek, Ph.D.
Sadie Burton-Goss, M.S.
Susan Caloggero, M.S.M.
Irene Burke Carew, Ed.D.
Lynette D. Carpenter, M.S.
Robert Caruso, M.B.A.
Margaret E. Catoline, M.B.A.
David Cavalier, M.H.A.
Marie Cedrone, M.Ed., M.A.
Charles S. Clayman, Ed.M.
Ronald L. Cobbett-Maribett, M.Ed.
Nancy Connery, M.S.
Judith A. Connolly, M.B.A.
James Conway, M.S.
Margaret Craven, M.B.A.
David Crimmin, M.S., M.A.
Joseph Dabek, M.B.A.
Lou Ann Daly, Ph.D.
Marian Darlington-Hope, M.C.P.
Catherine DeLorey, Dr.P.H.
Mark Deneen, M.B.A.
Bruce Desmond, M.B.A.
William F. Donovan, M.S.
W. Michael Donovan, M.B.A.
Lucinda Doran, Ph.D.
Cynthia Ebert, Ph.D.
Morton F. Elfenbein, Ph.D.
Carol V. Ewart, Ed.D.
Kathleen Ewing, M.S.
Brenda Fannon, M.Ed.
George L. Fearnley, M.B.A.
Jose Fernandez, M.A.
Jim Ferreira, M.B.A.
John Ferrie, Ph.D.
Nicholas A. Figurelli, M.S.
George Flavin, M.S.W., M.B.A.
Earle Flynn, M.S.
John Francis, M.B.A.
Paul Gilbert, M.Ed., M.S.W.
Joseph Gillen, Ph.D.
Leonard Glick, Ed.D.
Cynthia Goheen, Ph.D.
Arthur Granville, Ph.D.
Shelia Gray, M.B.A.
Harvey M. Greenberg, M.S.
Marsha Greenberg, M.Ed.
Patricia Griffin-Carty, M.A.
Raymond Guillette Jr., M.B.A.
Kimberly Hagenbach, M.S.
James Halpin, S.T.D.
David M. Harris, Ph.D.
Michael Harris, M.A.
Allan S. Hartman, Ed.D.
John V. Healy, M.B.A.
Charna Heiko, M.Ed.
Noel Herman-Gutierrez, M.S.W.
Darnley W. Howard, M.B.A.
Charles Hunt, M.B.A.
Diane Hunter, M.S.M.
Cynthia A. Ingols, Ed.D.
Jeffrey J. Isaacson, J.D.
Larry Israelite, Ph.D.
S. William Ives, Ph.D.
Richard J. Iwanicki, M.B.A.
Patricia M. Jerabek, M.A.
Laura Kangas, M.A.
Hilary Keane, M.B.A.
Ralph Kidder, M.B.A.
Linda Knight, M.S.
Annette Koren, Ph.D.
Daniel J. Kostreva, Ed.D.
Carole P. Kraus, M.P.A.
William Lamb, M.S.
Anne Lang, J.D.
Deborah Langstaff, Ed.D.
Joseph O. Lavoie Sr., M.B.A.
Doreen Lawrence, M.B.A.
Elaine Meyer Lee, M.A.
Pat Leonard, M.A.
Guy Lochiatto, M.B.A.
Sebastian Lockwood, M.A.
Dwight Lueth, M.A.
Bruce MacBain, Ph.D.
Steven MacIsaac, M.S.
Javad Maftoon, Ed.D.
William Mahoney, Ph.D.
Marianne Manzon-Winsser, M.B.A.
Edward Marakovitz, M.A.
Joseph Marrocco, M.B.A.
Thomas Martin, Ph.D.
David Maslen, J.D.
Willard L. Mason, Ed.D., M.P.A.
Thomas Matera, M.B.A.
Pamela Maus, M.Ed.
Donald Maynard, M.S.
Thomas McCarley, M.Ed.
Edward McGrath, M.B.A.
JoAnn D. McManamy, M.B.A.
Margaret Mello, M.S.
Elaine Meredith, M.B.A.
Kenneth Mermer, M.B.A.
Susan Milne, M.S.
Sitansu Mittra, Ph.D.
Samuel A. Modoono, Ph.D.
Steven Moe, M.S.
Russell Moore, M.B.A.
Patricia Mostue, Ph.D.
Charlene O'Brien, Ph.D.
Donald A. O'Neil, Ph.D.
Marsha Orr, M.S.
Linda Palmieri, M.S.
J. T. Perry, M.B.A.
Cheryl Bowser Petersen, Ph.D.
Leona Phillips, Ph.D.
Frank Picca, M.S.E.E.
Harry Piligian, M.B.A.
Lilly Platt, M.A.
John M. Poirier, M.B.A.
Matthew Puma, B.A.
Dennis Pyburn, M.S.
Richard S. Raben, M.Ed.
Michael A. Raphael, Ph.D.
Richard Record Jr., M.P.A.
Marianne Rigo-Shea, M.Ed.
Frederick Ritzau Jr., M.B.A.
Christine A. Rivers, Ph.D.
Rick H. Rogers, M.B.A.
Robert Rosenblum, Dr.P.H.
Houda Samaha, M.S.
Julia Santiago, Ed.D.
Dennis Santoro, M.A.
E. Allen Schenck, Ph.D.
Stephen Schuit, M.Ed., C.A.G.S.
John Scorzoni, M.Ed.
Jeffrey Seaman, Ph.D.
Raymond Sessler, M.S.
Joanne H. Shawcross, M.B.A.
Gail Sheffey, Ed.M.
Andrew Shulman, M.B.A.
S. Murray Simons, Ed.D.
Michael Sirota, M.A., M.F.A.
Jacqueline Sonnabend, M.B.A.
Michael J. Stacey, Ed.D.
Raymond F. Stanio, M.B.A.
Richard A. Stanton, Ed.M.
Ronald Stone, J.D.
Cynthia A. Soupis, M.B.A.
Sandra Terry, C.A.G.S.
Michael Tesler, M.B.A.
Janice Thibodeau, M.S.
David Thrope, M.B.A.
William Tiga Tita, Ph.D.
Francesco Tocci, M.B.A.
Peaco Todd, M.B.A.
Hallie Touger, Ph.D.
Mary Tzambazakis, M.B.A.
Judy Wallace, M.B.A.
Kathleen Walsh, M.B.A.
Ford Wheatley, J.D.
Gordon Kelvin White, M.S.
James Whitney, M.B.A., M.Ed.
James Withall, M.B.A.
Joan Wood, M.Ed.
Mary Barber Worthy, M.B.A.
Kathryn Yamartino, Ed.M.
Stephen Zammit, Ph.D.

LOYOLA COLLEGE

Joseph A. Sellinger, S.J. School of Business and Management

Programs of Study

The Sellinger School offers programs leading to the Master of Business Administration (M.B.A.) and the Master of Science in Finance (M.S.F.). All programs are accredited by AACSB–The International Association for Management Education and are designed to develop the analytical capabilities, breadth of understanding, strength of values, and strategic and global vision necessary for tomorrow's leaders. The M.B.A. is offered in three formats for traditional students, senior executives, and rising midlevel leaders.

The traditional M.B.A. offers a flexible curriculum on a part-time basis in the evening. Concentrations are offered in accounting, economics, finance, health-care management, information systems/decision sciences, international business, management, and marketing. Classes are offered at three graduate centers: the Baltimore, Timonium, and Columbia campuses. A fast-track option is offered, which allows completion of the program with as few as ten courses.

The Executive M.B.A. program offers advanced management studies for individuals who have already faced significant organizational responsibilities. Most students have eight to ten years of significant management experience. The Executive M.B.A. is a lockstep program meeting on alternating Fridays and Saturdays for two years.

The M.B.A. Fellows program, modeled after the Executive M.B.A., is for younger leaders who have been targeted for executive responsibilities. The M.B.A. Fellows program has a lockstep format with classes held every Saturday for three years.

The Master of Science in Finance (M.S.F.) is targeted for individuals in the financial services industry or who serve as financial decision makers. A flexible part-time format with evening classes allows students to design programs to meet their needs, including preparing for professional exams (CFA, CFP, CCM, and CBA).

Research Facilities

The College has a computer and telephone network that connects all classroom facilities, offices, the library, and laboratories to a digital and video network that is in turn linked to global and local data and communication systems. From the office or home, students may access this system for research, communication with instructors, or team projects. The library, linked to other libraries in the state of Maryland and outside the state, offers access to a vast array of information sources in computer, hard, and microform formats. The Sellinger School has a state-of-the-art MIS laboratory, and the College has state-of-the-art laboratories for IBM, Macintosh, and DEC midframe computing.

Financial Aid

Assistance is available to graduate students through the Federal Direct Stafford Student Loan program. The maximum amount available to students through the subsidized and unsubsidized direct loan programs is $18,500 per year. Resident assistantships are live-in, on-campus supervisory positions in undergraduate student housing. Assistantships are available on a limited basis with applications required; students should inquire about respective deadlines.

Cost of Study

The 1998–99 tuition rate for traditional, part-time, evening M.B.A./M.S.F. students is $365 per credit. Most courses are 3 credits each. Executive M.B.A. tuition for the entire program is $39,900, and M.B.A. Fellows tuition for the entire program is $37,900. The tuition figures for the Executive programs and M.B.A. Fellows cover all tuition fees, books, residency, and international field study.

Living and Housing Costs

There are many off-campus apartments available to graduate students. The Student Life Office maintains lists and will assist in finding married or single student housing. Public transportation to campus is convenient from surrounding areas.

Student Group

The Sellinger School enrolls about 900 part-time and 100 full-time traditional M.B.A. and M.S.F. students and approximately 175 in its Executive programs. The average age of entrants into the Executive M.B.A. is 40, the entering M.B.A. Fellows students average 32 years of age, and the entering M.B.A./M.S.F. traditional students average 28 years old. Five percent of the entering M.B.A./M.S.F. students are directly from college with no full-time work experience. The average GPA for incoming students in all programs is 3.2, and the average GMAT score is in the 67th percentile. About 200 CEOs in the area have graduate business degrees from Loyola College.

Location

Loyola is located in the northern residential section of Baltimore, Maryland. The Baltimore-Washington area is rich in cultural, sports, and recreational opportunities. Classes are also taught at two other graduate centers in Columbia and Timonium, Maryland.

The College and The School

Loyola College in Maryland, founded in 1852, is a comprehensive university founded in the Jesuit, liberal arts tradition. Graduate programs in the Joseph A. Sellinger, S.J. School of Business and Management are reflective of the traditions of global outlook, care for the individual, concern for values, and critical thinking, which define high-quality education and the foundations for leadership. Loyola's Executive M.B.A. program is one of the oldest and largest in the nation, serving corporate, state, federal, and other types of organizations in the mid-Atlantic region and beyond.

Applying

Admission to any of the graduate programs is based on performance in undergraduate and graduate studies (GPA), scores on the Graduate Management Admission Test (GMAT), and career progress. Each program puts a different emphasis on these criteria. Graduates from foreign undergraduate institutions must also have transcripts evaluated by a recognized service and must submit TOEFL scores. Traditional, part-time programs admit students for each term, and the Executive programs admit only for fall.

Correspondence and Information

Director of Graduate Admissions
Loyola College
4501 North Charles Street
Baltimore, Maryland 21210-2699

Telephone: 410-617-5067 (M.B.A. and M.S.F. programs)
410-617-5064 (Executive programs)
Fax: 410-617-2005
E-mail: mba@loyola.edu
World Wide Web: http://www.loyola.edu

Loyola College

THE FACULTY

Department of Accounting
William E. Blouch, Associate Professor; D.B.A., Kent State.
John P. Guercio, Associate Professor; M.B.A., Loyola (Baltimore).
Kermit O. Keeling, Associate Professor; LL.M., Houston.
Alfred R. Michenzi, Associate Professor; Ph.D., Case Western Reserve.
E. Barry Rice, Assistant Professor; M.B.A., Maryland.
Ali M. Sedaghat, Associate Professor; D.B.A., George Washington.
Jalal Soroosh, Professor and Chair; Ph.D., Mississippi.

Department of Economics
Arleigh T. Bell Jr., Associate Professor; Ph.D., New School.
Frederick W. Derrick, Professor; Ph.D., North Carolina State.
Thomas J. DiLorenzo, Professor; Ph.D., Virginia Tech.
Francis G. Hilton, S.J., Assistant Professor; Ph.D., Wisconsin.
John C. Larson, Professor and Chair; Ph.D., Minnesota.
Charles E. Scott, Professor; Ph.D., Vanderbilt.
Stephen J. K. Walters, Professor; Ph.D., UCLA.
Nancy A. Williams, Associate Professor; Ph.D., Berkeley.

Department of Finance
John S. Cotner, Associate Professor; Ph.D., Saint Louis.
Albert R. Eddy, Associate Professor; Ph.D., SUNY at Buffalo.
Lisa M. Fairchild, Assistant Professor; Ph.D., South Carolina.
Harold D. Fletcher, Professor and Chair; Ph.D., Illinois.
Walter R. Holman Jr., Associate Professor; Ph.D., Syracuse.
Joanne Li, Assistant Professor; Ph.D. candidate, Florida State.
Walter J. Reinhart, Associate Professor; Ph.D., North Carolina.
Thomas A. Ulrich, Professor; Ph.D., Michigan State.

Department of Information Systems and Decision Science
William L. Harris, Associate Professor and Chair; Sc.D., Johns Hopkins.
Ellen D. Hoadley, Associate Professor; Ph.D., Indiana.
Charles R. Margenthaler, Professor; Ph.D., Illinois.
John C. McFadden, Assistant Professor and Executive Director of Information Services; M.S.A., George Washington.
Phoebe C. Sharkey, Professor; Ph.D., Johns Hopkins.
A. Kimbrough Sherman, Associate Professor; Ph.D., Maryland.
Laurette P. Simmons, Associate Professor; Ph.D., North Texas.
LeRoy F. Simmons, Professor; Ph.D., Tennessee.
George M. Wright, Associate Professor; D.B.A., George Washington.

Department of Law and Social Responsibility
Timothy B. Brown, S.J., Associate Professor; J.D., George Mason.
Nan S. Ellis, Associate Professor and Chair; J.D., Ohio State.
Andrea Giampetro-Meyer, Associate Professor; J.D., William and Mary.
John A. Gray, Professor; J.D., Baltimore; S.T.D., Catholic University.
James B. O'Hara, Assistant Professor; J.D., Baltimore.

Department of Management and International Business
Ronald J. Anton, S.J., Assistant Professor; Ph.D., Northwestern.
Harsha B. Desai, Professor; Ph.D., Penn State.
Christy L. DeVader, Associate Professor; Ph.D., Akron.
Richard H. Franke, Professor; Ph.D., Rochester.
Raymond M. Jones, Assistant Professor; Ph.D., Maryland.
Roger Kashlak, Associate Professor; Ph.D., Temple.
Neng Liang, Associate Professor; Ph.D., Indiana.
Peter Lorenzi, Professor and Dean; Ph.D., Penn State.
Anthony J. Mento, Professor; Ph.D., Maryland.
Tagi Sagafi-nejad, Professor; Ph.D., Pennsylvania.

Department of Marketing
Gerard A. Athaide, Assistant Professor; Ph.D., Syracuse.
Ernest F. Cooke, Professor; Ph.D., Case Western Reserve.
Sandra K. S. Gooding, Assistant Professor; Ph.D., Illinois.
Darlene B. Smith, Associate Professor; Ph.D., Maryland.
Doris C. Van Doren, Professor; Ph.D., Maryland.

LOYOLA MARYMOUNT UNIVERSITY

College of Business Administration
Master of Business Administration Program

Programs of Study

Loyola Marymount University offers a Master of Business Administration (M.B.A.) Program that is aimed at serving both employed professionals in the southern California area and full-time students. The LMU M.B.A. Program is nationally accredited by AACSB–The International Association for Management Education.

The core curriculum of the M.B.A. Program consists of nine courses in ethics and the legal environment of business, management, business economics, financial management, accounting, statistics, marketing, management information systems, and operations analysis. Students who have recent bachelor's degrees in business administration may have some, or possibly all, core courses waived, or they may be given the opportunity to establish their competence through examination.

The advanced curriculum of the M.B.A. Program provides students with an opportunity to select a domestic or international track. Students who follow the domestic track take at least three courses in a major in one of the following eight fields: accounting, entrepreneurship, finance, human resource management, international business, management, management information systems and decision sciences, and marketing. To satisfy breadth requirements, students take at least five courses in three or more different fields outside of their major area. An integrative experience selected from one of three options provides the capstone learning experience. Students who choose the international track receive a regular M.B.A. degree plus a Graduate Certificate in International Business. The program's advanced curriculum is the same length as that of the domestic program. Students select a major from one of six fields, including accounting, finance, human resource management, management, management information systems, and marketing. One course in the major may be a corresponding international course. For example, finance majors may take international finance. The breadth requirement is met by taking an additional five international courses outside of the area of emphasis. The integrative requirement involves participation in the Comparative Management Systems course, which affords an opportunity to study the application of the student's area of emphasis within a given industry in at least five designated countries outside the U.S. (This course is also available to domestic-track students.)

Methods of instruction emphasize case analysis and discussion, role playing, computer games, problem seeking and solving, readings, reports, and other methods designed to bring about a positive transfer from the educational experience to the uncertainties of the real world. Particular focus is given to the manager's role in a world where scarcity of resources, allocations, and international, political, and governmental constraints loom large in planning and decision making.

During the fall and spring semesters, each 3-unit class meets once a week, usually in the late afternoon or evening hours. In the summer, classes meet twice a week. All students admitted to the M.B.A. Program must demonstrate proficiency in English composition, business mathematics, and computer applications.

A J.D./M.B.A. program is also available. Applicants must be admitted separately to both the J.D. and M.B.A. programs and then apply to the joint program. Students must be full-time. They spend their first year in the law school, their second year in the M.B.A. program, and their last two years in the law school. The number of students admitted to the joint program is limited to 12 per year.

Research Facilities

Graduate students have access to two computer facilities on campus: the University Computer Center and the College of Business Computer Lab. The Von der Ahe Library houses a large collection of current periodicals as well as an up-to-date instructional media center. Word processing units are also available in the library for student use.

Financial Aid

The University maintains an Office of Financial Aid with a full-time director and staff to assist students who require financial aid to pursue their education at Loyola Marymount University. Limited scholarship funds are available through the Graduate Division. M.B.A. assistantships are also available for academically qualified full-time students.

Cost of Study

The M.B.A. Program tuition for the 1998–99 academic year is $620 per unit. Each course is 3 semester units. The required fee for M.B.A. Student Association membership is $50 per semester.

Living and Housing Costs

On-campus housing is unavailable to graduate students; however, the University has an off-campus-housing office that assists students in finding nearby housing.

Student Group

Approximate enrollment in the LMU M.B.A. Program is 400 students. They enter the program from diverse educational and career backgrounds, creating a stimulating learning environment within the classroom.

Location

Loyola Marymount University is located in Westchester, a coastal suburb of Los Angeles, California. The city of Los Angeles as well as the University community provide a variety of cultural, social, spiritual, and athletic activities that can enhance students' learning experiences. The nearby Pacific Ocean provides an ideal smog-free climate year-round.

The University and The College

LMU developed from the merger of Loyola University of Los Angeles and Marymount College in 1973. Loyola Marymount University is a Catholic, coeducational, suburban university with concerns for academic excellence, for the total development of the student, and for the building of a more just society. College of Business Administration faculty members combine years of business or consulting experience with doctorates from the nation's leading Ph.D. and D.B.A. programs.

Applying

Admission to the M.B.A. Program is open to qualified individuals who hold bachelor's degrees in any field of study. Standards for acceptance are high and are aimed at determining the applicant's academic capability and his or her potential capacity as a manager. Primary consideration is given to the undergraduate grade point average and scores on the Graduate Management Admission Test. All international students, including those who have received their bachelor's degrees in the United States, must achieve a minimum score of 600 on the TOEFL. Letters of recommendation and work experience are also evaluated but are not weighted as heavily. All candidates for admission are encouraged to discuss their application with the associate dean. In addition, information seminars on the M.B.A. Program are held periodically. Students may begin the program in the fall, spring, or summer semester. The application fee is $35.

Correspondence and Information

M.B.A. Program
Loyola Marymount University
7900 Loyola Boulevard
Los Angeles, California 90045-8387

Telephone: 310-338-2848
Fax: 310-338-2899

Loyola Marymount University

THE FACULTY AND THEIR RESEARCH

John T. Wholihan, Dean of the College of Business Administration; Ph.D., American.
Rachelle Katz, Professor and Associate Dean of the M.B.A. Program; Ph.D., Stanford. Finance.
George L. Hess, Professor and Associate Dean of the College of Business Administration; D.B.A., Arizona State. Management.

Dolphy Abraham, Assistant Professor; Ph.D., Pittsburgh. Information systems.
Steven L. Beach, Assistant Professor; Ph.D., Washington State. Finance.
J. Ross Bengel, Professor; J.D., South Carolina. Accounting.
Benjamin F. Bobo, Professor; Ph.D., UCLA. Finance.
Alan A. Cherry, Professor; Ph.D., UCLA. Accounting.
Frank Daroca, Professor; Ph.D., Illinois. Accounting.
Patricia Douglas, Assistant Professor; Ph.D., Virginia Commonwealth. Accounting.
Ellen Ensher, Assistant Professor; Ph.D., Claremont. Management.
Kweku Ewusi-Mensah, Professor; Ph.D., UCLA. Information systems.
Renee Florsheim, Associate Professor; Ph.D., Northwestern. Marketing.
Jeffrey Gale, Professor; Ph.D., J.D., UCLA. Management.
Allen P. Gray, Associate Professor; Ph.D., California, Riverside. Information systems.
Edmund R. Gray, Professor; Ph.D., UCLA. Management.
Charles J. Higgins, Associate Professor; Ph.D., Claremont. Finance.
W. F. Kiesner, Professor; Ph.D., Claremont. Management.
Birgit Leisen, Assistant Professor; Ph.D., New Mexico State. Marketing.
Linda Leon, Associate Professor; Ph.D., UCLA. Operations management.
Christopher Manning, Professor; Ph.D., UCLA. Finance.
Christopher Manolis, Assistant Professor; Ph.D., Kentucky. Marketing.
David L. Mathison, Professor; Ph.D., Bowling Green State. Management.
Cathleen McGrath, Assistant Professor; Ph.D., Carnegie Mellon. Management.
Mahmoud Mehrdad Nourayi, Professor; Ph.D., USC. Accounting.
Yong Sun Paik, Assistant Professor; Ph.D., Washington (Seattle). Management.
Richard Perle, Professor; Ph.D., USC. Operations management.
Zbigniew Przasnyski, Professor; Ph.D., Sussex (England). Operations management.
Ralph L. Quinones, Associate Professor; J.D., NYU. Law.
Peter Smith Ring, Professor; Ph.D., California, Irvine; J.D., Northwestern. Management.
Raymond C. Rody, Assistant Professor; Ph.D., USC. Marketing.
Arthur Gross Schaefer, Associate Professor; J.D., Boston University. Law.
Kala Chand Seal, Associate Professor; Ph.D., Texas at Dallas. Operations management.
Gary P. Sibeck, Professor; Ph.D., USC. Law and marketing.
H. Daniel Stage, Professor; D.B.A., USC. Management.
Lawrence S. Tai, Professor; Ph.D., Georgia State. Finance.
Charles Vance, Professor; Ph.D., Syracuse. Management.
Robert D. Winsor, Associate Professor; Ph.D., USC. Marketing.
Anatoly Zhuplev, Assistant Professor; Ph.D., Moscow Management Institute. Management.

Loyola Marymount University Campus.

LOYOLA UNIVERSITY CHICAGO

Graduate School of Business

Programs of Study

The Graduate School of Business offers several programs leading to the degree of Master of Business Administration (M.B.A.), including joint M.B.A./law and joint M.B.A./nursing degrees, and master's programs in information systems management and accountancy. The school is fully accredited by AACSB–The International Association for Management Education. The school operates on the quarter system. Full-time students take three or four classes per quarter; part-time students take one or two classes.

The mission of the Loyola Graduate School of Business is to enable its graduates to be responsible executives, leaders, and policy makers. Therefore, the M.B.A. program emphasizes problem-solving skills and decision-making abilities. Reflecting its Jesuit heritage, Loyola's curriculum emphasizes ethical issues throughout the functional areas as well as in separate courses. Teaching excellence is an expectation of the school.

The curriculum is international in scope. All students are required to take at least one international elective and can earn an international business specialization. In addition to its innovative study-abroad programs in Bangkok and Athens, Loyola University Chicago uses its Rome, Italy, campus to teach an array of global business courses.

Students may opt to specialize in accounting, economics, finance, financial derivatives, health-care administration, international business, legal environment, management, management science and information systems, marketing, operations management, or strategic decision making.

Research Facilities

At the Graduate School of Business, research activity is considered essential. This activity is supported by state-of-the-art computing centers and Loyola's comprehensive library system, which offers access to more than 1 million books and 10,000 journals. In addition, Loyola's Water Tower Campus location in the heart of Chicago's business and financial district makes many off-campus research resources available.

Financial Aid

Tuition scholarships and monetary stipends are available through the Graduate Business Scholars Program. All full-time students are automatically considered for the program, which awards merit-based research assistantships and graduate assistantships. Long-term, low-interest loans are available to students regardless of financial need. Federally subsidized and other government-sponsored loans are administered through the Financial Aid Office.

Cost of Study

The tuition for the 1998–99 academic year is $1985 per course. Books and materials are estimated to be $75 per course.

Living and Housing Costs

A wide range of privately owned accommodations are available in the Chicago area within easy access of the Water Tower Campus. The University assists students in locating off-campus housing. University housing for graduate students is located on the Lake Shore Campus, which is 15 minutes away via a free University shuttle bus.

Student Group

There are approximately 1,000 students in the M.B.A. program. They come from more than 200 colleges and universities in the United States and abroad. International students represent more than forty different countries. Twenty percent of the M.B.A. students are full-time, 42 percent are women, 11 percent are members of minority groups, and 15 percent are international.

Student Outcomes

Placements by industry were evenly spread across the fields of consulting, manufacturing, health-care services, computers/computer-related services, investment banking/securities, diversified financial services, and telecommunications. Major employers included Andersen Consulting; Aon Corporation; Baxter Healthcare Corporation; Bricker & Associates, Inc.; Dean Witter; Deloitte & Touche; Ernst & Young, LLP; FBCP Corporation; KPMG Peat Marwick; Morgan Stanley; and Northern Trust Company.

Location

Loyola University's Graduate School of Business is located at the Water Tower Campus. Part of Chicago's "Magnificent Mile," this campus is named for the landmark Water Tower across the street. Adjacent to the campus are the city's most exclusive shops, restaurants, and housing. The campus is also just minutes from the center of the banking, communication, and commercial industries.

The University and The School

Loyola University Chicago, one of the most comprehensive of the Jesuit colleges in the United States, includes five higher education campuses (four in the Chicago area and one in Rome, Italy) and nine schools and colleges: arts and sciences, business administration, education, graduate studies, law, medicine, nursing, social work, and adult education and continuing studies. The Graduate School of Business is cited consistently in the top 10 percent of M.B.A. programs nationwide by *The Princeton Review Guide to the Best Business Schools.*

Applying

Applications to the Graduate School of Business are accepted for any of the four academic quarters. Prospective students should apply well in advance of the quarter in which they plan to enter.

Correspondence and Information

Graduate School of Business
Loyola University Chicago
820 North Michigan Avenue
Chicago, Illinois 60611
Telephone: 312-915-6120
Fax: 312-915-7207
E-mail: mba-loyola@luc.edu
World Wide Web: http://www.luc.edu/depts/mba

Loyola University Chicago

THE FACULTY AND THEIR RESEARCH

Accounting

Ellen L. Landgraf (Chairperson), Ph.D., Illinois; CPA. Corporate responsibility and executive compensation.
Harvey Boller, J.D., Cornell. Rights of individuals with disabilities, public and private law.
Barbara Brochie-Leonard, Ph.D., Oklahoma State. Executive compensation, employee benefits and social disclosure.
Charles Caufield, J.D., Loyola of Chicago; CPA. Federal and state taxation of income and estates.
Willard H. Galliart, Ph.D., Illinois; CPA. Not-for-profit entities, auditing.
John M. Janiga, J.D., Loyola of Chicago; LL.M., DePaul; CPA. Income and estate taxation.
John Kostolansky, Ph.D., Columbia; CPA. Financial statement analysis and accounting measurement.
Marc LeClere, Ph.D., Penn State. Corporate and individual tax policy, financial reporting, income taxes.
Lawrence Metzger, Ph.D., Illinois; CPA, CMA. Managerial accounting and systems.
John D. O'Malley, J.D., Loyola of Chicago. Officers' and directors' liability and negotiable instruments.
Gary Porter, Ph.D., Colorado; CPA. Corporate reporting and accounting education.
Brian Stanko, Ph.D., Kentucky; CPA. Industry-specific cash flow information and accounting ethics.
John Tabor, Ph.D., Northwestern; CPA. Auditing and managerial accounting.
Charles Werner, J.D., Chicago; CPA. Ethics, financial fraud, and legal liability issues for CPAs.
Thomas L. Zeller, Ph.D., Kent State; CPA. Quality management and activity-based costing.

Economics

Louis P. Cain (Chairperson), Ph.D., Northwestern. Economic and business history and urban economics.
E. Miné Cinar, Ph.D., Texas A&M. Economic development, applied econometrics, and international finance.
Paul Gabriel, Ph.D., Kentucky. Labor economics and microeconomics.
Roy T. Gobin, Ph.D., Illinois. Taxation, development finance, and demography.
Marc D. Hayford, Ph.D., Brown. Credit rationing and monetary policy and the effects of debt-financed fiscal policy.
A. G. Malliaris, The Walter F. Mullady Sr. Professor of Business Administration; Ph.D., Oklahoma. Application of stochastic and deterministic methods in international finance and financial derivatives.
David F. Merriman, Ph.D., Wisconsin. Regional economic growth in the U.S., Japan, and the Pacific Rim.
David B. Mirza, Ph.D., Northwestern. Commodity futures markets and international trade.
David Surdam, Ph.D., Chicago. Health economics.
Bruce S. Vanderporten, Ph.D., Wayne State. Macroeconomics, microeconomics, and real estate auction strategy.

Finance

William R. Bryan (Dean), Ph.D., Wisconsin. Financial institutions, banking, lifetime earnings measurement.
Vefa Tarhan (Chairperson), Ph.D., Berkeley. Mergers and acquisitions, monetary policy.
Jon Garfinkel, Ph.D., Florida. Earnings announcements, insider trading.
George Kaufman, The John F. Smith, Sr. Professor of Business Administration; Ph.D., Iowa. Banking, bond markets, financial regulation.
Nicholas A. Lash, Ph.D., Wayne State. Financial institutions, monetary policy.
Suk Hun Lee, Ph.D., USC. International finance, corporate finance.
Tom Nohel, Ph.D., Minnesota. Corporate finance, banking, dividend policy.
Jorge L. Urrutia, Ph.D., Texas at Austin. Investments, futures, options, international finance, corporate finance.

Management

Michael F. Keeley (Chairperson), Ph.D., Northwestern. Organizational effectiveness, business ethics.
Joseph A. Barney, Ph.D., Loyola of Chicago. Student attitudes and values, institutional accreditation.
Raymond Baumhart (Emeritus), S.J., S.T.L., D.B.A., Harvard. Business ethics and university administration.
John R. Boatright, The Raymond C. Baumhart, S.J. Professor of Business Ethics; Ph.D., Chicago. Business ethics.
Jill W. Graham, Ph.D., Northwestern. Organizational citizenship, loyalty and leadership.
Dawn Harris, Ph.D., Northwestern. Executive compensation and strategic change.
Eunice Jensen, D.B.A., Harvard. Reward distribution, organizational design.
Douglas P. Massengill, Ph.D., Tennessee. Employee selection, employment law.
Thomas M. McMahon, C.S.V., S.T.D., St. Thomas (Rome); M.B.A., George Washington. Business ethics.
Donald J. Peterson, Ph.D., IIT. Labor relations and arbitration.
Anne H. Reilly, Ph.D., Northwestern. Organizational change and crisis management, family issues.
Jasmine Tata, Ph.D., Syracuse. Organizational justice, rewards, quality management, international aspects of organizations.
John L. Ward, The Ralph Marotta Professor of Free Enterprise; Ph.D., Stanford. Strategy, family businesses.

Management Science and Information Systems

Enrique R. Venta (Chairperson), Ph.D., Northwestern. Operations management, location theory, production systems.
Frank G. Forst, Ph.D., Illinois. Operations management, quantitative methods.
Faruk Güder, Ph.D., Wisconsin. Operations management, quantitative methods.
Frederick Kaefer, Ph.D., Iowa. Informations systems, telecommunications.
Burak Kazaz, Ph.D., Purdue. Operations management, supply chain logistics.
Ronald J. Kizior, Ph.D., Notre Dame. Information systems.
Mary E. Malliaris, Ph.D., Loyola of Chicago. Information systems, database systems.
Gezinius Hidding, Ph.D., Carnegie Mellon. Strategic use of information technology, decision support systems, knowledge management.
George Nezlek, Ph.D., Wisconsin. Distributed and client-server system development, management of information technologies.
John M. Nicholas, Ph.D., Northwestern. Operations management, project management.
Francis J. Nourie, Ph.D., Chicago. Statistics, quantitative methods.
Samuel D. Ramenofsky, Ph.D., Oklahoma. Forecasting, statistics.
Linda M. Salchenberger, Ph.D., Northwestern. Information systems, decision support and expert systems.
James L. Zydiak, Ph.D., Northwestern. Operations management.

Marketing

Raymond Benton Jr. (Chairperson), Ph.D., Colorado State. Impact of natural and social environment on business, public policy.
Chaim M. Ehrman, Ph.D., Pennsylvania. Product planning and development, health-care marketing.
Ronald T. Lonsdale (Emeritus), Ph.D., Purdue. New product development and marketing in Latin America.
Mary Ann McGrath, Ph.D., Northwestern. Consumer and marketplace behavior.
Donald G. Meyer (Emeritus), Ph.D., Northwestern. Marketing and consumer welfare.
Paul S. Richardson, Ph.D., SUNY at Buffalo. Sales, international marketing and consumer behavior.
Stanley F. Stasch, The Charles H. Kellstadt Professor of Marketing, Ph.D., Northwestern. New product development, marketing planning and marketing strategy.
Frank J. Svestka, Ph.D., Wisconsin. Mass media marketing, statistical applications.

McGILL UNIVERSITY

Faculty of Management
M.B.A. Program

Programs of Study

The McGill M.B.A. is an internationally renowned graduate business program designed to provide students with a comprehensive understanding of the concepts of business, specialized knowledge in their chosen field, and the international perspective needed to meet the challenges of today's complex business environment.

Inside the classroom, the McGill M.B.A. builds on traditional strengths in functional areas and takes the learning experience one step further. Not only does it provide students with a strong foundation in the basic business disciplines, it also provides them with the intangible skills that are explicitly sought by employers today—the abilities to apply knowledge for the greatest benefit of the organization, make effective decisions, work in teams and lead others, and easily adapt to nonstructured situations.

Outside the classroom, the McGill M.B.A. offers additional value that is essential for tomorrow's managers. Students benefit from a host of networking opportunities, which include professional and social contacts, career development assistance, and real-life experience in a dynamic urban business setting. Upon graduation, alumni join a network of McGill M.B.A.'s around the world.

The McGill M.B.A. is a full-time, twenty-month program. In the first year (core year), students study the basic elements of management and gain exposure to the fundamental skills of business. In the second year, students choose a concentration in entrepreneurial studies, finance, international business, management for development, marketing, operations management, or strategic management or individually tailor a general management concentration. More than sixty support courses are offered as electives in the Faculty to supplement the six required courses within each concentration. Courses may also be taken from other graduate programs. Students can further expand on the international experiences provided through the program by participating in the Faculty's international exchange program, with world-renowned schools in more than twenty countries.

The joint M.B.A./Law is a four-year program offered with the Faculty of Law. This program permits a choice between two law options: the M.B.A./B.C.L. and M.B.A./LL.B. A joint M.Sc. (agricultural economics)/M.B.A. enables students to acquire expertise in agribusiness, environment, or natural resource economics.

The Joint M.B.A./Diploma in Management (Asian studies) permits candidates to develop expertise in the area of the Pacific Rim.

McGill's joint M.D./M.B.A. program is designed to graduate medical doctors with skills uniquely directed toward management in the health-care sector.

A twelve-month Master of Manufacturing Management (M.M.M.) is offered jointly with the Faculty of Engineering.

The post-M.B.A. graduate certificate in management is designed for managers already holding an M.B.A. or M.Sc. in administration and who wish to update their knowledge in a particular area. It requires completion of five second-year courses.

Research Facilities

The management library holds a collection of more than 600 journals and more than 100,000 publications. Electronic database searching services are also available. The Sandiford Computing Centre, also in the Bronfman Building, includes a large bank of microcomputers that are connected to the University network and the Bronfman Building's local area network, providing access to a variety of file servers and laser printers as well as the campus mainframes. Additional computer facilities are available for M.B.A. students in the M.B.A. Student Lounge area and the Acer Computer Lab.

Financial Aid

Entrance Fellowships are offered by the Faculty of Management and all accepted candidates are considered. Bilateral agreements exist with several nations to obtain an international fee waiver.

Cost of Study

Tuition fees for the 1998–99 academic year for international students are Can$16,000; for Quebec students, Can$2497; and for other Canadians, Can$3697.

Living and Housing Costs

Most students rent an apartment within walking distance of the campus. An excellent transportation system, consisting of a network of Metro (subway), buses, and trains, serves the McGill community. Cost of living for a single student for one year ranges from Can$8000 to Can$10,000.

Student Group

The Faculty welcomed 140 incoming M.B.A. students for the 1997–98 academic year. Currently, 156 students are completing their second year, and an additional 380 students attend the program on a part-time basis. International students from twenty-three different countries make up 54 percent of the incoming class.

Student Outcomes

The McGill Faculty of Management has approximately 14,000 alumni, including 3,000 M.B.A.'s. There are three main areas where graduates begin their careers—marketing, finance, and consulting.

Location

Montreal is a bilingual city situated in a multicultural environment with European charm. Head offices of many major Canadian corporations are located within walking distance of the campus. Because the city centre is residential as well as commercial, Montreal stays alive and vibrant long after business hours and on weekends.

The University

McGill is a world-renowned university, known for its high standards in teaching and research. The University, founded in 1821, today includes no less than fifty institutional buildings on 75 acres in downtown Montreal. Leading professional schools that are internationally renowned are the Faculties of Agriculture, Dentistry, Engineering, Law, Management, and Medicine.

Applying

Applications to the full-time program are accepted for September only. Admission is competitive, and decisions are based on many factors. Academic credentials, the GMAT score, TOEFL (if university education is not in the English language), work experience, leadership, and professional and extracurricular achievements will be considered. The application deadline is May 15 for Canadians and April 1 for international candidates.

Correspondence and Information

M.B.A. Admissions Office
Faculty of Management
McGill University
1001 Sherbrooke Street West
Montreal, Quebec H3A 1G5
Canada

Telephone: 514-398-4066
Fax: 514-398-2499
E-mail: mba@management.mcgill.ca
World Wide Web: http://www.management.mcgill.ca

McGill University

MEMBERS OF FACULTY

Accounting
B. Choi, M.B.A., Washington (Seattle); Ph.D., Iowa. A. J. Craighead, Ph.D., McGill. D. H. Drury, M.B.A., McMaster; Ph.D., Northwestern; RIA, CMA. J. A. Duff, M.A., Cambridge; CA, FCA. C. S. McWatters, M.B.A., Ph.D., Queen's at Kingston; CMA.

Finance
F. Carrieri, M.A., USC. J. Detemple, D.E.A., Paris IX (Dauphine); Ph.D., Pennsylvania (Wharton); Doctorat d'Etat, Institute of Louis Pasteur. V. R. Errunza, Ph.D., Berkeley. K. Jacobs, Ph.D., Pittsburgh. L. Rivera-Batiz, Ph.D., Chicago.

General Management
R. Brenner, Ph.D., Hebrew (Jerusalem). H. Etemad, M.B.A., Ph.D., Berkeley. T. Thomason, Ph.D., Cornell. R. W. Wright, D.B.A., Indiana.

Information Systems
L. Lapointe, M.Sc., (Montreal), Ph.D., (HEC) pending. A. Lee, Ph.D., MIT.

Management Science
W. B. Crowston, Ph.D., Carnegie Mellon. J. L. Goffin, Ph.D., Berkeley. S. Li, Ph.D., Texas. R. J. Loulou, Ph.D., Berkeley. V. Verter, Ph.D., Bilkent (Turkey). G. A. Whitmore, Ph.D., Minnesota. M. Yalovsky, Ph.D., McGill.

Marketing
S. K. Bandyopadhyay, M.B.A., Indian Institute of Management; Ph.D., Cincinnati. K. Basu, Ph.D., Florida. R. C. K. Bawa, Ph.D., Columbia. L. Dubé, M.B.A., HEC (France); Ph.D., Cornell. L. Gialloreto, M.B.A., L.L.M, McGill. A. T. Hale, M.B.A., Ph.D., Texas at Austin. A. Mukherjee, M.B.A., India. E. Sarigollu, M.B.A., Bogazici (Turkey); Ph.D., Pennsylvania.

Organizational Behavior
N. J. Adler, M.B.A., Ph.D., UCLA. M. L. Buck, Ph.D., Princeton. J. Hartwick, Ph.D., Illinois. A. M. Jaeger, M.B.A., Ph.D., Stanford. R. N. Kanungo, Ph.D., McGill. M. D. Lee, Ph.D., Yale. M. D. M. Saunders, Ph.D., Western Ontario.

Strategy and Organization
C. Hardy, Ph.D., Warwick (England). P. R. Johnson, B.A., Sir George Williams; CMC. J. Jorgensen, Ph.D., McGill. H. Mintzberg, Ph.D., MIT. N. Phillips, M.B.A., Calgary; Ph.D., Alberta. F. Westley, Ph.D., McGill.

Exchange Schools
Solvay Business School, Belgium; University of Louvain, Belgium; Getulio Vargas, Brazil; Manchester Business School, England; HEC, France; ISA, France; University of Cologne, Germany; Luigi Bocconi, Italy; ITAM, Mexico; ITESM, Mexico; Erasmus, Rotterdam, the Netherlands; Norwegian School of Economics, Norway; Asian Institute of Management, Philippines; ESADE, Spain; Stockholm School of Economics, Sweden; Thammasat University, Thailand; Bilkent University, Turkey; Bogazici University, Turkey; University of Texas at Austin, U.S.A.

International Advisory Board
Wallace Crowston, Dean, McGill Faculty of Management; David Culver, Chairman, CAI Capital Corporation; Jean-Claude Delorme, Consultant; Paul Desmarais, Jr., Chairman and Co-Chief Executive Officer; John Dobson, Chairman, Formula Growth; Paul Fribourg, President and Chief Officer, Continental Grain (USA); H. John Greeniaus, Chairman and Chief Executive Officer, Nabisco (USA); Pierre Haas, Senior Advisor, Parfinance, France; Marie Josée Kravis, Senior Fellow, Hudson Institute Inc. U.S.A.; Brian Levitt, President and Chief Executive Officer, IMASCO Ltd.; Patrick Odier, Managing Partner, Lombard Odier & Cie., Suisse; Yong H. Quek, President, Procter & Gamble (Canada); Raymond Royer, President and Chief Executive Officer, Domtar Inc.; Pierre Scohier, Chairman and CEO/COBEPA S.A./Brussels; Herschel Victor, Chairman and CEO, Jack Victor Ltd.

MIAMI UNIVERSITY

Richard T. Farmer School of Business Administration

Programs of Study

Miami University offers a full-time M.B.A. program with areas of concentration in finance, management information systems, marketing, quality and process improvement, and a self-designed option. The Richard T. Farmer School of Business Administration at Miami also offers a part-time M.B.A. in general management, a Master of Accountancy program, and a Master of Arts in Economics.

The full-time M.B.A. program requires twenty-one months to complete after prerequisite work in calculus, statistics, microeconomics, and macroeconomics that must be completed no later than the summer prior to enrollment. It is a five-semester program with a field study or internship during the summer between the first and second year. An accelerated curriculum designed for applicants who have recently completed the core requirements of an undergraduate business degree allows eligible students to waive up to 21 credit hours. The core courses are designed to develop analytical skills in accounting, behavioral science, business law, economics, finance, operations, and statistics and technical competence in management information systems. There are also courses in business presentation, team process, and negotiation. The concentration is taken in the second year.

Research Facilities

The School maintains a graduate student computer lab and two general-access labs. Network and dial-in access is provided to centralized University computer and Internet services. The range of application software includes simulation, database, and statistical analysis tools.

Miami University has one of the largest and oldest library collections in the Midwest.

Financial Aid

Numerous opportunities for financial assistance, both need- and merit-based, are available. Approximately half of the full-time students receive graduate assistantships that provided a stipend of approximately $3100 for the 1997–98 academic year and a $1600 summer scholarship, plus remission of the instructional and out-of-state tuition fees for one year. There are also special financial aid opportunities for minority students and international students. Loans are administered by the Office of Student Financial Aid.

Cost of Study

The tuition and general fee for the 1998–99 academic year is $2916 per semester for full-time in-state students. Out-of-state students pay $6131 per semester tuition. Books, supplies, and health insurance are additional. A personal computer is recommended but not required.

Living and Housing Costs

Estimated expenses for full-time graduate students over two semesters are $9580, including books, transportation, and living and personal expenses. Most graduate students live in private apartments located near campus. Housing costs start at approximately $350 per month, depending on the number of occupants. A limited number of spaces are available in graduate residence halls. Expenses vary according to individual needs.

Student Group

Approximately 60 students are enrolled in the full-time M.B.A. program each year. In a typical class, the average age is 26; 60 percent of the students have full-time work experience. Women make up 36 percent, international students 33 percent, and students from minority groups 12 percent of the enrollment. The program targets students from a diverse range of nonbusiness undergraduate backgrounds. Fourteen percent hold technical degrees (such as engineering or math), 5 percent humanities and social science degrees, 60 percent business degrees (including students in the accelerated program), and 21 percent other degrees.

Student Outcomes

Placement of graduates is nationwide, with the highest percentage of graduates joining consulting firms in operational or systems consulting and change management. Average starting salaries were $43,650 for the current year. A professional staff in Career Planning and Placement supports individual career-search efforts.

Location

Miami University is located in Oxford, a southwestern Ohio community of about 10,000 residents within an hour of much of the Midwest's commerce and industry. The town is located 35 miles north of Cincinnati and 46 miles southwest of Dayton. Miami's 1,100-acre campus is heavily wooded and accented with many historic landmarks.

The University and The School

Miami University, established in 1809, is renowned for its academic excellence and commitment to teaching. The University is often cited as one of the "Public Ivies." The Oxford campus enrolls 16,000 students. The School of Business Administration, founded in 1927, has held accreditation by the American Assembly of Collegiate Schools of Business at the undergraduate level since 1932 and at the graduate level since 1961. The Procter and Gamble Communication and Information Center includes classrooms with multimedia computer and audiovisual presentation facilities as well as videotaping and editing capabilities. The School is named after Richard T. Farmer, president and CEO of Cintas Corporation, who provides significant private support to business education at Miami.

Applying

Admission to the M.B.A. program is granted on the basis of undergraduate academic record, GMAT scores, TOEFL scores for international students, recommendation letters, work experience, and the quality of the essay. For full consideration for financial aid, applications should be completed by March 1. Applicants should submit a completed application form, an official copy of the GMAT score report, two copies of official transcripts of all previous undergraduate and graduate course work, required essays, and two letters of recommendation.

Correspondence and Information

For U.S. students:

Judy Barille
Director of Graduate Programs
School of Business Administration
Miami University
Oxford, Ohio 45056
Telephone: 513-529-6643
Fax: 513-529-2487

For international students:

Office of International Student Services
Langstroth House
Miami University
Oxford, Ohio 45056
Telephone: 513-529-2512
Fax: 513-529-7383

Miami University

SELECTED FACULTY AND THEIR RESEARCH

Accountancy

Barry P. Arlinghaus, Professor; Ph.D., Cincinnati. Taxation of corporations.
Robert J. Campbell, Professor; Ph.D., Indiana. Profit planning and information systems.
James D. Cashell, Professor; Ph.D., Cincinnati. Accounting and auditing.
Gyan Chandra, Professor; Ph.D., Ohio State. Accounting disclosure.
Philip G. Cottell Jr., Professor; D.B.A., Kentucky. Inventory accounting, ethics.
John Cumming, Professor and Chair; Ph.D., Illinois. Auditing.
Clayton A. Hock, Professor; Ph.D., Penn State. Financial accounting, theory, and disclosure.
Thomas M. Porcano, Professor; D.B.A., Indiana. Accounting taxation and information systems.
Marc A. Rubin, Professor; Ph.D., Texas. Governmental and nonprofit accounting.
W. Peter Salzarulo, Professor; D.B.A., Colorado. Federal income taxation.
Daniel G. Short, Professor and Dean; Ph.D., Michigan. Use of accounting information by decision makers.

Decision Sciences/Management Information

Bruce Lee Bowerman, Professor; Ph.D., Iowa State. Forecasting and applied statistics.
Michael S. Broida, Associate Professor; Ph.D., Ohio State. Economic development and small business.
Donald L. Dawley, Associate Professor; D.B.A., George Washington. Data processing and end-user computing.
John Marcus Jobe, Associate Professor; Ph.D., Iowa State. Linear programming and statistics.
Anne B. Koehler, Professor; Ph.D., Indiana. Multivariate data analysis and forecasting.
Timothy C. Krehbiel, Associate Professor; Ph.D., Wyoming. Experimental design, quality improvement.
Sooun Lee, Professor; Ph.D., Nebraska. Business data telecommunications, database design.
Neil Marks, Associate Professor; Ph.D., Ohio State. Simulation, queuing theory.
Richard H. McClure, Professor; Ph.D., Cincinnati. Quantitative methods.
Richard T. O'Connell, Senior Instructor; M.S., Northwestern. Statistical quality and process control.
Eleni Pratsini, Assistant Professor; Ph.D., Cincinnati. Mathematical programming models, environmental analysis.
T. M. Rajkumar, Associate Professor; Ph.D, Texas Tech. MIS, multimedia networking.
Chi-chung Yen, Professor and Chair; Ph.D., Nebraska. Artificial intelligence, database systems.

Economics

James Brock, Professor; Ph.D., Michigan State. Industrial organization and antitrust economics.
George K. Davis, Professor; Ph.D., SMU. Monetary theory.
O. Homer Erekson, Professor and Associate Dean; Ph.D., North Carolina. Public-sector economics, urban economics.
John D. Ferguson, Professor and Chair; Ph.D., Brown. Monetary theory and policy.
Gerald Granderson, Assistant Professor; Ph.D., North Carolina. Industrial organization and microeconomics.
Thomas E. Hall, Professor; Ph.D., California, Santa Barbara. Macroeconomics.
William K. Hutchinson, Professor; Ph.D., Iowa. Economic history, monetary theory.
Mark E. McBride, Professor; Ph.D., Washington (St. Louis). Industrial organization, production and cost.
Norman C. Miller, Professor; Ph.D., Pittsburgh. International economics.
Nicholas R. Noble, Professor; Ph.D., Cincinnati. Macroeconomics, econometrics.
Daniel A. Seiver, Professor; Ph.D., Yale. Demography, economic development.
Dennis H. Sullivan, Professor; Ph.D., Princeton. Public finance, urban economics.

Finance

Saul W. Adelman, Associate Professor and Chair; Ph.D., Georgia. Risk management and insurance.
Robert L. Conn, Professor; Ph.D., Houston. Corporate finance, international finance.
Mark L. Cross, Professor; Ph.D., Missouri. Risk management and insurance.
Raymond F. Gorman, Professor; D.B.A., Indiana. Financial aspects of regulated firms.
Daniel T. Herron, Associate Professor; J.D., Case Western. Employment relations, legal theory.
James B. Kehr, Associate Professor; Ph.D., Ohio State. Management of financial institutions.
David C. Leonard, Professor; Ph.D., Illinois. Financial markets and portfolio management.
Bruce H. Olson, Professor; D.B.A., Indiana. Investments, security markets.
Jeffrey G. Wyatt, Associate Professor; Ph.D., South Carolina. Investments, corporate control and governance.

Management

Kathy M. Adams, Assistant Professor; Ph.D., Michigan. Organizational behavior, human resource management.
David A. Cowan, Professor; Ph.D., Kansas. Cognition and decision making.
Charles R. Crain, Professor; Ph.D., Missouri. Purchasing and materials management.
Byron Finch, Professor; Ph.D., Georgia. Process-oriented manufacturing, spreadsheet applications.
Mark D. Hanna, Associate Professor; Ph.D., Clemson. Manufacturing strategy, productivity.
Joseph W. Leonard, Assistant Professor; Ph.D., Arkansas. Strategic management, international business.
Richard L. Luebbe, Professor; Ph.D., Nebraska. Quantitative techniques.
Rebecca A. Luzadis, Associate Professor; Ph.D., Cornell. Compensation, employee benefits.
John D. McNeill, Assistant Professor; D.B.A., Kentucky. Organizational culture, socialization, and stress.
William E. Newman Jr., Professor; Ph.D., Iowa. Computer-integrated manufacturing.
Joshua L. Schwarz, Professor and Chair; Ph.D., Cornell. Human resource management, collective bargaining.
B. Kay Snavely, Associate Professor; Ph.D., Cincinnati. Organizational behavior, leadership, power.
William B. Snavely, Associate Professor; Ph.D., Nebraska. Organizational behavior, communication.
Charles E. Watson, Professor; Ph.D., Illinois. Business policy, executive development.

Marketing

Thomas Boyd, Assistant Professor; Ph.D., North Carolina. Consumer innovativeness and adoption.
Charles T. Crespy, Professor and Chair; Ph.D., New Mexico. International marketing.
John B. Gifford, Professor; D.B.A., Colorado. Retailing, advertising.
Jack A. Lesser, Professor; Ph.D., Oklahoma. Behavioral theory in retailing, logistics.
Diane M. McConocha, Associate Professor; Ph.D., Michigan State. Consumer behavior, industrial marketing.
Kevin M. McNeilly, Professor; Ph.D., North Carolina. Sales management, international marketing.
Donald G. Norris, Associate Professor; Ph.D., Berkeley. Strategic marketing, consumer behavior.
David W. Rosenthal, Associate Professor; D.B.A., Virginia. Employment and career trends in marketing.
Thomas W. Speh, Professor; Ph.D., Michigan State. Warehouse management, logistics.
James M. Stearns, Associate Professor; Ph.D., Florida State. Consumer behavior, nonprofit marketing.
Lakshmi Thumuluri, Assistant Professor; Ph.D., Oklahoma. Services marketing.
Lynette S. Unger, Professor and Associate Dean; Ph.D., Cincinnati. Leisure marketing.
John R. Walton, Associate Professor; Ph.D., Ohio State. Strategy, retailing.

MISSISSIPPI STATE UNIVERSITY

College of Business and Industry

Programs of Study

The College of Business and Industry at Mississippi State University offers five accredited graduate degree programs.

The Master of Business Administration (M.B.A.) program, leading to an advanced professional degree in administration, is designed to provide a broad background in business and focuses on managerial decision making. Core requirements include accounting, economics, finance, management, marketing, and statistics, as well as business policy and strategy. Concentration in one of these areas or in information systems and quantitative decision making provides an opportunity for the student to develop specialized knowledge and skills. The M.B.A. program can be completed in one to two years, depending on the student's previous academic background.

The Master of Professional Accountancy (M.P.A.) program is structured for students who wish to concentrate in accounting. Core requirements of the program include courses in advanced accounting, accounting theory, and auditing. Concentration in information systems is available. The M.P.A. program can be completed in 1–2½ years, depending on the student's previous background in accounting.

The Master of Tax (MTX) program is designed to prepare students to enter the tax profession with competency in tax compliance and tax planning. The program requires completion of six tax courses, two accounting courses, and electives in two business or accounting courses. The MTX program can be completed in 1–2½ years, depending on the student's previous background in accounting.

The Master of Science in Business Administration (M.S.B.A.) program, with a concentration in business information systems, prepares students for careers in information systems design and management. Core courses in database management are augmented by courses in such areas as systems design, support systems, and quantitative problem solving. The M.S.B.A. program typically requires 1½ years to complete.

The Doctor of Business Administration (D.B.A.) program is designed to provide a broad background of interrelated concepts necessary for careers in teaching, academic research, and administration. Areas of specialization are accounting, business information systems, economics, finance, management, and marketing. In addition to developing a major and a minor area, students are required to demonstrate proficiency in research and quantitative analysis. The D.B.A. program typically requires four years to complete.

Research Facilities

Library and computer facilities at MSU provide excellent support for the graduate programs in business. The University library maintains a collection of more than 1.1 million volumes and currently subscribes to nearly 7,500 periodicals. Various retrieval search services are available.

Computer resources available for graduate study in business include clusters of Sun SPARCserver 690 machines, along with several microcomputer labs. A graduate-level microcomputer lab exists, along with two other microcomputer labs housing approximately fifty stations each. Popular software programs and remote access to the Sun servers are available from these labs, as well as other public-access computer labs on the MSU campus. Direct access is available to the Internet. Available databases include CRSP, CompuStat, and LEXIS/NEXIS.

Financial Aid

Assistantships are awarded on a competitive basis to exceptional students and may include a waiver of all tuition fees. Assistantships carried stipends in 1997–98 ranging from $5400 for master's students to $9300 (plus tuition remission) for doctoral students. Minority fellowships and assistantships are available through the Graduate School. The University Financial Aid Office offers additional sources of student aid.

Cost of Study

Full-time tuition and fees for two semesters in 1997–98 were $2731 for in-state graduate students and $5551 for out-of-state students. Part-time tuition and fees totaled $151.83 per hour for in-state students and $308.50 per hour for out-of-state students. Fees are subject to change.

Living and Housing Costs

The cost of living in the Mississippi State–Starkville area is low to moderate when compared to most of the United States. Living accommodations within a wide price range are available for single and married students. Moderately priced apartments can be found within walking distance of the campus.

Student Group

The master's programs enroll approximately 180 students and the doctoral program, nearly 70. Approximately 75 percent of the master's students are from the Southeast, 10 percent are from elsewhere in the United States, and 15 percent are from abroad. The master's programs attract students from diverse backgrounds, but predominantly engineering and business. Approximately 50 percent of the doctoral students are from outside of the Southeast, and 25 percent are from abroad.

Location

Starkville–Mississippi State, located in east-central Mississippi, has a population of approximately 20,000. Starkville is 23 miles west of Columbus, Mississippi, a city of 30,000, and 14 miles west of the Golden Triangle Regional Airport.

The University and The College

Mississippi State University was founded in 1878 as a land-grant college. The University has an enrollment of 14,000 students, including 2,000 students in graduate programs. The College of Business and Industry, with a total enrollment of 2,200, is one of six colleges within the University.

Applying

Application can be made for the fall, spring, or summer semester. Applicants for fall admission are urged to apply for financial assistance before February 1. Applicants for all programs must submit original transcripts of previous academic work, a Graduate Management Admission Test score, and the proper application forms to the University's Graduate Admissions Office, care of the College of Business and Industry. International applicants must also submit a TOEFL score and should apply at least three months before the semester in which they wish to begin study.

Correspondence and Information

Director, Graduate Studies in Business
College of Business and Industry
P.O. Drawer 5288
Mississippi State University
Mississippi State, Mississippi 39762
Telephone: 601-325-1891 or 8191
Fax: 601-325-8161
E-mail: gsb@cobilan.msstate.edu
World Wide Web: http://asgard:cbi.msstate.edu/cobi/gsb

Mississippi State University

THE GRADUATE FACULTY AND THEIR RESEARCH

Noel D. Addy, Associate Professor; Ph.D., Florida, 1985. Financial accounting.
Kirk P. Arnett, Professor; D.B.A., Mississippi State, 1984. Business information systems.
Robert Y. Awh, Professor; Ph.D., Florida, 1960. Microeconomics.
Habib H. Bazyari, Professor; D.B.A., Mississippi State, 1974. Economics.
Benjamin F. Blair, Assistant Professor; Ph.D., Florida, 1992. Economics.
James M. Bloodgood, Assistant Professor; Ph.D., South Carolina, 1997. Management.
Jeff P. Boone, Assistant Professor; Ph.D., North Texas, 1994. Accounting.
James A. Bryant, Professor; J.D., Mississippi, 1970. Law.
Charles A. Campbell, Professor; Ph.D., Tennessee, 1985. Economic models, regional economic growth.
Louis M. Capella, Professor; D.B.A., Kentucky, 1975. Consumer behavior, marketing theory.
Daniel S. Cochran, Professor; Ph.D., Arkansas, 1978. Organizational behavior, organizational communications.
Zoel W. Daughtrey, Professor; Ph.D., North Carolina State, 1970. Taxation, agricultural accounting.
Edwin H. Duett, Professor; Ph.D., Georgia, 1987. Portfolio management.
Brian T. Engelland, Assistant Professor; D.B.A., Southern Illinois, 1993. Marketing.
William D. Eshee, Professor; J.D., Mississippi, 1970. Law.
R H Gilmer Jr., Associate Professor; Ph.D., Illinois, 1982. Finance.
Paul W. Grimes, Professor; Ph.D., Oklahoma State, 1984. Labor economics.
Allison Harrison, Associate Professor; Ph.D., Auburn, 1993. Human resource management and organizational behavior.
C. E. Herring, Associate Professor; Ph.D., Alabama, 1988. Financial accounting.
Robert A. Hershbarger, Professor, Peter K. Lutken Chair of Insurance; Ph.D., Georgia, 1972. Insurance.
Mary C. Jones, Associate Professor; Ph.D., Oklahoma, 1990. Management and information systems.
G. Wayne Kelly, Associate Professor; Ph.D., Alabama, 1988. Finance.
Theodor Kohers, Professor; Ph.D., Oregon, 1971. Financial institutions.
Joseph Legoria Jr., Assistant Professor; Ph.D., Arkansas, 1997. Accounting.
Carol M. Lehman, Professor; Ed.D., Arkansas, 1984. Management.
Mark Lehman, Assistant Professor; Ph.D., Mississippi, 1995. Accounting.
Stephen A. LeMay, Professor; Ph.D., Tennessee, 1985. Transportation.
Kartono Liano, Associate Professor; Ph.D., Alabama, 1989. Finance.
Charles R. Litecky, Professor, Ph.D., Minnesota, 1974. Management information systems.
Frances M. McNair, Professor; Ph.D., Mississippi, 1987. Cost accounting and tax accounting.
Edward E. Milam, Professor; Ph.D., LSU, 1971. Tax accounting.
Jake L. Morrow, Assistant Professor; Ph.D., Texas A&M, 1995. Management.
Terry Obert, Associate Professor; Ph.D., Alabama, 1989. Quantitative analysis.
Ed O'Donnell, Assistant Professor; Ph.D., North Texas, 1995. Accounting.
Rodney A. Pearson, Professor; D.B.A., Harvard, 1984. Information systems development.
Joseph A. Peyrefitte, Assistant Professor; Ph.D., Florida Atlantic, 1996. Management.
John T. Rigsby, Associate Professor; Ph.D., Tennessee, 1986; CPA. Accounting and auditing.
Kevin E. Rogers, Assistant Professor; Ph.D., Georgia,, 1996. Economics.
William D. Salisbury, Assistant Professor; Ph.D., Calgary, 1996. Management.
Patricia L. Sanderson, Associate Professor; Ph.D., Oklahoma, 1977. Managerial economics.
Jung P. Shim, Professor; Ph.D., Nebraska, 1983. Research methods, management information systems.
Garry D. Smith, Professor; D.B.A., Louisiana Tech, 1976. Management strategy and policy, production management.
Barbara A. Spencer, Professor; Ph.D., Virginia Tech, 1985. Organization theory.
William W. Stammerjohan, Assistant Professor; Ph.D., Washington State, 1995. Accounting.
Joe H. Sullivan, Assistant Professor; Ph.D., Alabama, 1994. Applied statistics.
Alireza Tahai, Professor; Ph.D., Arizona State, 1987. Forecasting, statistics.
G. Stephen Taylor, Professor; Ph.D., Virginia Tech, 1985. Human resource management.
Ronald D. Taylor, Professor; Ph.D., North Texas State, 1978. Promotion, quantitative marketing.
Pierre L. Titard, Professor; Ph.D., LSU, 1970. Financial and managerial accounting.
George L. Verrall, Associate Professor; D.B.A., Mississippi State, 1972. Economics.
Cynthia Webster, Professor; Ph.D., North Texas State, 1984. Marketing, consumer behavior, marketing research.
Larry R. White, Associate Professor; Ph.D., Georgia, 1985. Finance, financial theory.
Linda Wright, Assistant Professor, Ph.D., Tennessee, 1994. Marketing.
Michael T. Young, Assistant Professor, Ph.D., Missouri, 1992. Finance, statistics, economics.

NEW HAMPSHIRE COLLEGE

Graduate School of Business

Programs of Study

The Graduate School of Business at New Hampshire College offers programs leading to the Master of Science degree in accounting, business education, community economic development, computer information systems, finance, and international business and to the Master of Business Administration degree in administration. The M.B.A. can be pursued in conjunction with a graduate certificate program in accounting, artificial intelligence, computer information systems, finance, health administration, human resource management, international business, marketing, operations management, public finance, school business administration, taxation, or training and development. It is also possible to earn a graduate certificate independent of a degree. The Graduate School also offers the Doctor of Business Administration (D.B.A.) in international business and the Doctor of Philosophy (Ph.D.) in community economic development.

Courses leading to the M.B.A. and selected certificates can be taken during the day at the main campus or in the evening at Concord, Laconia, Manchester, Nashua, Portsmouth, and Salem in New Hampshire; at the Brunswick Naval Air Station in Maine; at the Roosevelt Roads Naval Station in Puerto Rico; in Dubai, United Arab Emirates; and in Athens, Greece. Courses in the M.B.A. program are also offered through the Internet as part of the College's distance education program.

Research Facilities

New Hampshire College is served by the Shapiro Library, one of the most extensive business libraries in northern New England. Its constantly expanding collection contains approximately 79,000 volumes, 8,000 reels of periodicals and newspapers on microfilm, and more than 58,000 company financial reports on microfiche. The library receives more than 960 magazines and journals and subscribes to various business, tax, and financial services. It also serves as a depository for federal documents, particularly those issued by the Departments of Labor, Commerce, and the Treasury. These collections are supplemented by the holdings of an extensive audiovisual department.

Student research activities are aided by online connection between the College's IBM computer systems and remote terminal clusters at various on-campus and off-campus locations. Computational facilities also include Digital MicroVAX systems and IBM PCs. Access to the Internet and World Wide Web is available from all student computing laboratories and from the library. The Computer Center supports a variety of business-related languages, such as Visual Basic, Pascal, CICS, and assembler, as well as statistical and analytical packages, simulation and modeling software, and applications in such specialized areas as marketing, production management, and artificial intelligence. The Graduate School is the headquarters of the *Journal of Educational Computing Research.*

Financial Aid

Students accepted for enrollment in either day or evening graduate programs may be considered for several forms of institutional and federal financial aid. Scholarship and work programs are provided by the College; graduate students also have access to federal assistance programs, including the Federal Work-Study and Federal Stafford Student Loan programs.

Cost of Study

Tuition for the year 1998–99 for the day program is $17,044, with related fees of $530. There is an additional charge for any student who takes specified prerequisite courses at the College. Tuition for the evening graduate program is $945 per course, plus a yearly total of approximately $75 in fees.

Living and Housing Costs

Limited on-campus housing for single students is available at a cost of $2200 to $3000 for the 1998–99 year. A variety of off-campus options are available in the Manchester area.

Student Group

The evening graduate programs comprise a total enrollment of more than 1,700 students, predominantly individuals who are employed full-time in the private and public sectors and who have had several years of work experience. Most of the evening students live within commuting distance of the campus or center they attend. The day graduate programs, begun in 1982, have a total enrollment of approximately 350 students, including both recent graduates and those returning to graduate study with work experience. The day student body includes students from various parts of the United States and from several overseas locations.

Student Outcomes

Last year's graduates were hired for career positions in leading regional, national, and international business environments. Examples include consultant, KPMG Peat Marwick LLP; manager, product development, L. L. Bean, Inc.; retail sales engineer, Esso Columbiana Ltd.; supervisor, audit and analysis, Lockheed Martin Commercial Electronics; senior portfolio manager, Ram Trust Services; senior financial analyst, UNUM Corp.; client relations representative, The Boston Company; analyst programmer, MIT; and director of international sales, Eastern Air Devices.

Location

The College is an hour's drive from Boston and within easy traveling distance of the state's seacoast, lakes, and mountain recreational areas. The Graduate School offers uncrowded, aesthetically attractive surroundings and easy access to the cultural and other advantages of metropolitan and commercial centers.

The College and The School

New Hampshire College is a private, nonprofit, coeducational institution authorized by the state of New Hampshire to award undergraduate and graduate degrees. It is accredited by the New England Association of Schools and Colleges and by the Association of Collegiate Business Schools and Programs (ACBSP). The College was founded in 1932.

Since the start of the College's evening graduate program in 1974, the number of students enrolled has increased substantially with each successive year. Both day and evening students benefit from this growth, through the involvement of many students in activities and careers that add practical dimensions to classroom experience and through the breadth of contacts in the business community that offer opportunities for research, internships, and postgraduate employment.

Applying

Students may enter the day programs or the evening master's programs in September, December, March, or June. Applications are accepted on a rolling basis, and there is no application fee. Admission to all programs except the M.S. programs in business education and community economic development requires undergraduate preparation in accounting, economics, mathematics, business organization, computer systems, marketing, statistics, and business law or these courses will be added to the student's program.

Correspondence and Information

Dean, Graduate School of Business
New Hampshire College
2500 North River Road
Manchester, New Hampshire 03106-1045
Telephone: 603-644-3102

New Hampshire College

THE FACULTY

Jacqueline F. Mara, Dean of the Graduate School of Business and Professor of Education; Ed.D., Boston University.
Bryan O'Neil, Associate Dean of the Graduate School of Business; Ed.D., Nova.

Full-Time Graduate Faculty

Toscun Aricanli, Associate Professor of Community Economic Development; Ph.D., Harvard.
Christina Clamp, Associate Professor of Community Economic Development; Ph.D., Boston College.
Stephanie Collins, Assistant Professor of Computer Information Systems; Ph.D., Wisconsin.
Tej Dhakar, Assistant Professor of Production; Ph.D., Arkansas.
Euclid A. Dupuis, Professor and Chair of Accounting; M.S., Bentley; CPA.
Philip Fellman, Associate Professor of International Business; Ph.D., Cornell.
James Freiburger, Professor and Chair of Management; Ph.D., Connecticut.
Phillip H. Funk Jr., Associate Professor of Computer Information Systems; M.S., MIT.
Richard O. Hanson, Professor of Accounting; M.B.A., New Hampshire College; CPA, CMA.
Gerald I. Harel, Professor and Chair of Quantitative Analysis and Production ; Ph.D., Temple.
R. Larry Johnson, Professor of Economics and Finance; D.B.A., George Washington.
Burton S. Kaliski, Professor of Business Education; Ed.D., NYU.
Gerald E. Karush, Professor of Computer Information Systems; Ph.D., Pennsylvania.
G. David Miller, Associate Professor of Community Economic Development; M.S.W., Michigan.
Nicholas Nugent, Professor of Marketing and International Business; Ph.D., Florida State.
Marc A. Rubin, Assistant Professor and Chair of Marketing; M.B.A., Northeastern.
Massood V. Samii, Professor and Chair of Strategic Management and International Business; Ph.D., SUNY at Albany.
Paul Schneiderman, Professor and Chair of Finance and Economics; Ph.D., Clark.
Susan Schragle-Law, Associate Professor of Management; Ed.D., Massachusetts.
Robert H. Seidman, Professor and Chair of Computer Information Systems; Ph.D., Syracuse.
Michael Swack, Professor and Chair of Community Economic Development Program; Ph.D., Columbia.
Gary P. Tripp, Assistant Professor; Ph.D., Clark.

Adjunct Graduate Faculty

Dhar Baratula, Senior Industrial Engineer, Millipore Corporation; M.B.A., New Hampshire College.
*Frank J. Barnes, Assistant Professor of Computer Information Systems; M.B.A., New Hampshire.
George Carter, Instructor; Ed.D., Boston University.
Marcia Carter, Business Education Teacher, Trinity High School; Ed.D., Boston University.
Gary Driscoll, Financial Analyst, L. L. Bean, Inc.; M.B.A., William and Mary.
*Mahboudul Hassan, Associate Professor; M.A.P.E., Boston University.
*Ernest H. S. Holm, Professor of Government; Ph.D., Tufts.
Lundy Lewis, Research Engineer, Cabletron Systems; Ph.D., Virginia.
Leon-Charl Malan, Assistant Professor, Colby-Sawyer College; Ph.D., SUNY at Albany.
Keith Moon, Consultant; J.D., Franklin Pierce Law Center.
Steven Painchaud, D.Ed., Boston College.
Jonathan Posner, Manager, Employee Benefits, W. C. Grace; J.D., Suffolk.
Gordon D. Smith, Vice President, Eastern Air Systems; Ph.D., Penn State.
Maria del Pilar Torres-Delany, Professor; Ph.D., Bowling Green State.
*James D. Walter, Assistant Professor of Sociology; Ph.D., Ohio State.
*Charles V. A. White, Associate Professor of Economics; Ph.D., Ohio State.
Kathryn S. Williams, Attorney; M.B.A., Boston College, J.D., Suffolk.
John Wilson, Attorney; J.D., Franklin Pierce Law Center.

**Full-time faculty member of the New Hampshire College Undergraduate School of Business.*

NEW SCHOOL UNIVERSITY

Robert J. Milano Graduate School of Management and Urban Policy

Programs of Study

The Robert J. Milano Graduate School of Management and Urban Policy offers programs leading to the Master of Science degree in health services management and policy, human resources management, nonprofit management, and urban policy analysis and management. Students may earn a certificate, either as part of their master's degree program or independently, in the following areas: career planning and development, organization development, quantitative health studies, and training and development. Beginning in fall 1998, courses leading to the Ph.D. in public and urban policy will be offered.

The Robert J. Milano Graduate School's curriculum combines theory, practice, and a concern with social responsibility issues, enabling students to acquire an in-depth understanding of the managerial and analytical skills needed to become effective professionals. Required schoolwide courses are designed to provide a firm foundation for work in the degree programs. Each degree program also requires its students to complete a program core that focuses on the essential material to be mastered by professionals in that field. To round out their degree requirements, students choose elective courses from the array of course offerings in their specific program or from appropriate courses offered elsewhere in the Robert J. Milano Graduate School.

The master's degree program is highly flexible and generally can be completed within two years of full-time or three years of part-time study. Full-time students are encouraged to participate in a summer internship. Evening and weekend courses are offered to accommodate all students.

A laboratory course enables full-time students to learn policy analysis and decision-making skills. Students work in the laboratory in small teams under close faculty supervision, addressing real problems faced by public and private officials. Each lab team constructs alternative methods of solution and recommends appropriate action by the client.

The Placement Office assists students in locating internships and provides a full range of counseling and referral services.

New School University has branch campuses and satellite locations in the following areas: Syracuse/Utica, Middletown/Castle Point, Ballston Spa, Queens/Bronx, and Long Island. Special tuition rates apply. The New School also offers courses via the Internet each semester. These courses utilize the Dial Format and can be completed from the convenience of a student's home or office.

Research Facilities

The Raymond Fogelman Library, located in the Albert List Academic Center, contains more than 150,000 books and standard reference sources, a pamphlet collection, and periodicals essential to the programs of study offered at the Robert J. Milano Graduate School. Matriculated students may also use New York University's Elmer Holmes Bobst Library and the Cooper Union library, both of which are convenient to the New School. Students have access to two major computing facilities, both of which house open labs; one computing center contains several classrooms. Both facilities are fully networked with standard research and productivity software, including e-mail and Internet connectivity.

The Community Development Research Center conducts an active program of research and provides publications designed to expand the existing knowledge about community-based neighborhood revitalization and to assist public and private decision makers in their work.

The Leadership Center provides an innovative, intellectually stimulating environment in which organizations can learn and practice more effective techniques needed to face current workplace challenges.

The Health Policy Research Center (HPRC) investigates a broad spectrum of health improvement strategies for urban communities in the U.S. The HPRC incorporates theoretical disciplines of health policy research (such as anthropology and ethics) with the methods of health policy analysis (such as project evaluation, health services research, computer simulation, decision analysis, demography, epidemiology, and cost effectiveness analysis). The HPRC links state-of-the-art health research with real-world circumstances of patients, families, and communities in the analysis of the social and economic consequences of today's evolving health systems for vulnerable populations.

Financial Aid

The Robert J. Milano Graduate School participates in all federal financial aid programs. These include the Federal Work-Study Program and the Federal Perkins Loan Program. Fellowships, assistantships, merit scholarships, and need-based tuition remission are also available.

Cost of Study

Tuition in 1998–99 for the Robert J. Milano Graduate School of Management and Urban Policy is $622 per credit, payable at registration. A list of fees is included in the brochure describing the various programs.

Living and Housing Costs

The School maintains limited residence facilities for students. The cost of living in the New York metropolitan area varies according to location and the type of accommodations desired.

Student Group

The student body of the Robert J. Milano Graduate School consists of approximately 100 full-time students and 900 part-time evening students. The students represent highly diversified age groups and geographic backgrounds.

Location

New School University, located in Greenwich Village, is readily accessible from all parts of New York City. For those who wish to prepare for public service careers, New York is a valuable laboratory, the variety and scale of which are not to be found elsewhere.

The School

Established in 1919, New School University (formerly New School for Social Research) has exemplified a rare tradition of educational innovation. It offers a variety of day, evening, and weekend programs of undergraduate, graduate, and adult education.

Students in the Robert J. Milano Graduate School are welcome to participate in the many courses and cultural and art events sponsored by the seven divisions of the New School.

Applying

The admission decision is made after a careful examination of transcripts and letters of recommendation. An interview is required. There is no formal application deadline, but applicants requesting financial aid should apply by April 15. Students interested in applying should contact the Office of Admissions at the address below.

Correspondence and Information

Office of Admissions
Robert J. Milano Graduate School of Management and Urban Policy
New School University
66 Fifth Avenue
New York, New York 10011
Telephone: 212-229-5462

New School University

THE FACULTY

James Krauskopf, Professor and Dean; M.P.A., Princeton.
Warren Balinsky, Associate Professor; Ph.D., Case Western Reserve.
Robert A. Beauregard, Professor and Director of the Ph.D. in Public and Urban Policy Program; Ph.D., Cornell.
Howard S. Berliner, Associate Professor and Program Chair, Health Services Management and Policy; Sc.D., Johns Hopkins.
Anne-Emanuelle Birn, Assistant Professor; Sc.D., Johns Hopkins.
David W. Brown, Professor of Professional Practice; J.D., Harvard.
Henry Cohen, Professor Emeritus; M.C.P., MIT.
Hector R. Cordero-Guzmán, Assistant Professor; Ph.D., Chicago.
Dennis A. Derryck, Professor of Professional Practice; Ph.D., Fordham.
Heriberto Dixon, Associate Professor; Ph.D., Pittsburgh.
Marianne (Mimi) Fahs, Associate Professor and Director, Health Policy Research Center; Ph.D., Michigan
Alec I. Gershberg, Assistant Professor; Ph.D., Pennsylvania.
Fred Goldman, Associate Professor; Ph.D., CUNY Graduate Center.
Karla Hanson, Assistant Professor; Ph.D., NYU.
Bennett Harrison, Professor of Urban Political Economy; Ph.D., Pennsylvania.
David R. Howell, Associate Professor and Program Chair, Urban Policy Analysis and Management; Ph.D., New School.
Mark Lipton, Associate Professor and Program Chair, Human Resources Management; Ph.D., Massachusetts.
Lynn McCormick, Assistant Professor; Ph.D., MIT.
Bonnie McEwan, Acting Chair, Nonprofit Management; M.S., New School.
Edwin Melendez, Professor and Director of the Community Development Research Center; Ph.D., Massachusetts Amherst.
Elizabeth Mueller, Assistant Professor; Ph.D., Berkeley.
Christine Leiz Murray, Assistant Professor; Ph.D., Massachusetts.
Pier Camille Rogers, Assistant Professor; Ph.D., NYU.
Mary Bryna Sanger, Professor and Associate Dean; Ph.D., Brandeis.
Clyde Schechter, Research Professor and Director of the Program in Health, Technology, and Society; M.D., Columbia.
Alex F. Schwartz, Assistant Professor; Ph.D., Rutgers.
Kian Tajbakhsh, Assistant Professor; Ph.D., Columbia.

Adjunct Faculty

Adjunct faculty members include corporation executives, current and former government officials, and executives of nonprofit enterprises. Most are currently practicing their professions and are able to bring to their teaching firsthand experience and insights that make theory come alive. A complete list of the adjunct faculty members is available upon request.

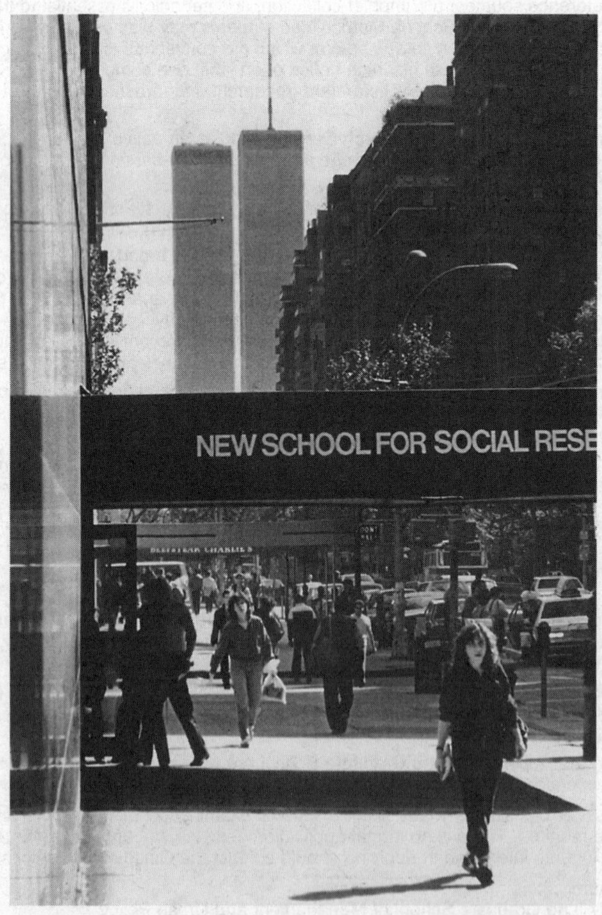

Classes for students in the Robert J. Milano Graduate School of Management and Urban Policy are held at the Greenwich Village campus.

NORTHEASTERN UNIVERSITY

College of Business Administration
Graduate School of Business Administration

Programs of Study Northeastern University is known for excellence in application, the integration of theory, and practice. In the two-year Full-Time M.B.A. program, students stay connected with the work force through relationships with executive mentors, with independent study, and with special team consulting projects. The Cooperative Education M.B.A. grows out of Northeastern's sustained success in combining work and study. After six intensive months of academics, Co-op M.B.A. students join the work force in paid positions appropriate to entry-level M.B.A.s; six months later they return to the classroom for another nine months of study and the team consulting project. In both programs, students master a general management curriculum and are welcome to tailor their electives to special interests, choosing from seventy to eighty course offerings within the College of Business Administration and abroad. Electives can also be taken within any of Northeastern's nine graduate and professional schools. Independent study projects can be designed for in-depth pursuit of a special competence. The Graduate School also offers part-time, high-technology, and executive M.B.A. programs and a Master of Science in finance program.

Research Facilities The Snell Library provides technologically sophisticated library services, including online catalog and circulation systems, an information gateway, and a seventeen-station network of CD-ROM optical disk databases. Graduate students also have access to other major research collections in the area through the Boston Library Consortium. Computing resources, provided by the Division of Academic Computing, are accessible from both on- and off-campus locations.

Financial Aid Northeastern awards need-based financial aid through Federal Perkins Loans, Federal Stafford Student Loans, and Federal Work-Study. In addition, M.B.A. students in the Cooperative Education Program can typically earn $19,000 during their six-month professional assignments. The Graduate School also offers a limited number of highly competitive merit-based assistantships that provide for partial or full tuition remission and may also include a quarterly stipend. Applicants interested in pursuing a graduate assistantship position in research, teaching, or administration are evaluated on the basis of academic credentials; certain positions may require an interview on campus. Both full-time and cooperative education applicants and students may be eligible for assistantship consideration. For more information on the assistantship program, including deadlines for application, students should contact the Admissions Office. International students must be prepared to fund their first year of study without assistantship support.

Cost of Study In 1998–99, comprehensive tuition costs for full-time and cooperative education M.B.A. study total $42,000 ($500 per quarter hour for a total of 84 quarter hours of course work). Students should also budget $900 for the annual Health Center fee, approximately $250 for additional activities fees, and $1000 annually for books and academic materials.

Living and Housing Costs On-campus living expenses are estimated at $750 per month, with limited on-campus housing available for graduate students. Boston and its surrounding areas offer a wide range of living environments; off-campus rental costs currently average $700 per month. An excellent public transportation system links the Northeastern community with the downtown and adjacent living areas. Living expenses are included in determining the need for financial aid support.

Student Group The Cooperative Education M.B.A. Program matriculates a class of about 35 students each June and January. The Full-Time M.B.A. Program matriculates about 100 students each September. A typical entering full-time class includes students from twenty-five or more countries other than the United States. Career goals can be equally diverse. About 90 percent have work experience, and 70 percent have earned their undergraduate degrees in areas other than business.

Student Outcomes Graduates of the two full-time programs pursue careers in every function and industry, private and not-for-profit, in the United States and abroad. Specific data change daily and can be obtained on request from the address below. A required course in career management ensures that graduates are adept both at securing their first jobs following the degree and advancing their careers in subsequent steps.

Location Northeastern is located in the heart of Boston, a city of history, culture, and cosmopolitan sophistication. From Northeastern, students can easily walk or take the "T" to the many famous sights and sports and cultural attractions of greater Boston.

The University and The College Founded in 1898, Northeastern University is a privately endowed nonsectarian institution of higher learning. The College of Business Administration was founded in 1922 and the Graduate School of Business in 1952. The College of Business Administration is accredited by the AACSB–The International Association for Management Education. The University operates nine undergraduate colleges and ten graduate and professional schools.

Applying The application deadline for the Cooperative Education M.B.A. Program is November 1 for a January start and April 15 for a June start. The deadline for the Full-Time Program, which begins once each year in September, is April 1; applicants for assistantship awards are encouraged to apply by February 15. The application fee is $50, and completed applications are reviewed on a rolling basis throughout the year. Successful applicants demonstrate academic excellence through undergraduate records and a (required) GMAT score. Motivation and maturity are communicated in essays, personal statements, and interviews with admissions personnel; interviews are required for the Cooperative Education Program. The Graduate School extends a welcome to students wishing to visit the campus, sit in on an M.B.A. class, or interact with faculty, current students, and alumni.

The equivalent of an American four-year bachelor's degree is required for international applicants. Transcripts from institutions outside the United States must be certified and translated with U.S. grade equivalencies. Candidates who completed their undergraduate work in a language other than English must submit a TOEFL score of 600 or higher.

Correspondence and Information

Graduate School of Business Administration
350 Dodge Hall
Northeastern University
360 Huntington Avenue
Boston, Massachusetts 02115

Telephone: 617-373-2714
Fax: 617-373-8564
E-mail: gsba@cba.neu.edu
World Wide Web: http://www.cba.neu.edu/gsba

Northeastern University

THE FACULTY

Accounting Group

Paul A. Janell, Professor and Group Coordinator; Ph.D., Michigan State; CPA. Jean C. Bedard, Associate Professor; Ph.D., Wisconsin–Madison; CPA. Sharon M. Bruns, Professor; Ph.D., Georgia State. Michael D. Cottrill, Lecturer; M.Acc., Virginia Tech; CPA. Hugh J. Crossland, Lecturer; LL.M., Yale, Boston University. Julie H. Hertenstein, Associate Professor; D.B.A., Harvard. Mario J. Maletta, Associate Professor; Ph.D., Massachusetts Amherst. Lynn W. Marples, Lecturer; M.B.A., Stanford. James J. Maroney, Assistant Professor; Ph.D., Connecticut. Peggy O'Kelly, Lecturer; M.B.A., Michigan. Marjorie Platt, Associate Professor; Ph.D., Michigan. Timothy J. Rupert, Assistant Professor; Ph.D., Penn State. H. David Sherman, Professor; D.B.A., Harvard. Ira R. Weiss, Professor and Dean; Ph.D., UCLA; CPA, CISA.

Finance and Insurance Group

Joseph W. Meador, Professor and Group Coordinator; Ph.D., Pennsylvania (Wharton). Paul J. Bolster, Associate Professor; Ph.D., Virginia Tech. Jeffery A. Born, Associate Professor; Ph.D., North Carolina. Cetin Ciner, Lecturer; Ph.D. candidate, LSU. Peggy L. Fletcher, Lecturer, M.B.A., Pittsburgh. Milton L. Glass, Adjunct Professor and Executive-in-Residence; M.B.A., Northeastern. Richard J. Goettle IV, Lecturer; Ph.D., Cincinnati. Shaikh A. Hamid, Visiting Assistant Professor; D.B.A., Boston University. Mark Kazarosian, Assistant Professor; Ph.D., Boston College. Steven R. Kursh, Academic Specialist; Ph.D., Pennsylvania. Donald G. Margotta, Associate Professor; Ph.D., North Carolina at Chapel Hill. Wesley W. Marple Jr., Professor; D.B.A., Harvard. Robert M. Mooradian, Assistant Professor; Ph.D., Pennsylvania. Harlan D. Platt, Professor; Ph.D., Michigan. Don R. Rich, Assistant Professor; Ph.D., Virginia Tech. Daniel A. Rogers, Lecturer; Ph.D. candidate, Utah. Richard Swasey, Lecturer; M.B.A., Virginia. Emery A. Trahan, Associate Professor; Ph.D., SUNY at Albany; CPA. Shiawee X. Yang, Assistant Professor; Ph.D., Penn State.

General Management Group

Ravi Sarathy, Professor and Group Coordinator; Ph.D., Michigan. F. Gerard Adams, Philip R. McDonald Visiting Professor; Ph.D., Michigan. Nicholas Athanassiou, Assistant Professor; Ph.D., South Carolina. Mary F. Costello, Lecturer; J.D., Boston College. William F. Crittenden, Associate Professor; Ph.D., Arkansas. Robert L. Goldberg, Lecturer; M.B.A., Boston University. Raymond M. Kinnunen, Associate Professor; D.B.A., LSU. Robert C. Lieb, Professor; D.B.A., Maryland. Daniel J. McCarthy, Professor; D.B.A., Harvard. Marc H. Meyer, Associate Professor; Ph.D., MIT. James F. Molloy Jr., Associate Professor; Ph.D., MIT. Carl W. Nelson, Associate Professor; Ph.D., Manchester (England). Richard P. Olsen, Lecturer; D.B.A., Harvard. Ravi Ramamurti, Professor; D.B.A., Harvard. Ronald Thomas, Lecturer; Ph.D., Harvard. Heidi Vernon, Professor; Ph.D., Boston University.

Human Resources Group

Francis C. Spital, Associate Professor and Group Coordinator; Ph.D., MIT. Rae Andre, Professor; Ph.D., Michigan. Brendan D. Bannister, Associate Professor and Associate Dean; D.B.A., Kent State. Thomas M. Begley, Associate Professor; Ph.D., Cornell. David P. Boyd, Professor; D.Phil., Oxford. Leonard J. Glick, Lecturer; Ed.D., Harvard. Ralph Katz, Professor; Ph.D., Pennsylvania (Wharton). Cynthia Lee, Associate Professor; Ph.D., Maryland. Edward F. McDonough III, Associate Professor; Ph.D., Massachusetts Amherst. Sheila M. Puffer, Associate Professor; Ph.D., Berkeley. Bert A. Spector, Associate Professor; Ph.D., Missouri. Judith Y. Weisinger, Assistant Professor; Ph.D., Case Western Reserve.

Management Science Group

Robert A. Parsons, Associate Professor and Group Coordinator; M.B.A., Northeastern. R. Balachandra, Associate Professor; Ph.D., Columbia. Richard J. Briotta, Lecturer; D.B.A., Boston University. Sangit Chatterjee, Professor; Ph.D., NYU. Michael J. Maggard, Professor; Ph.D., UCLA. Robert A. Millen, Professor; Ph.D., UCLA. Marius M. Solomon, Associate Professor; Ph.D., Pennsylvania. Eileen M. Trauth, Associate Professor; Ph.D., Pittsburgh. Merrill E. Warkentin, Associate Professor; Ph.D., Nebraska–Lincoln. Mustafa R. Yilmaz, Associate Professor; Ph.D., Johns Hopkins. Michael Zack, Assistant Professor; D.B.A., Harvard.

Marketing Group

Dan T. Dunn Jr., Associate Professor and Group Coordinator; D.B.A., Virginia. Gloria Barczak, Assistant Professor; Ph.D., Syracuse. Bruce H. Clark, Assistant Professor; Ph.D., Stanford. James A. Eckert, Lecturer; Ph.D. candidate, Michigan State. Jeffrey S. Hess, Assistant Professor; Ph.D. candidate, Colorado. Samuel Rabino, Professor; Ph.D., NYU. Fareena Sultan, Associate Professor; Ph.D., Columbia. Frederick Wiseman, Professor; Ph.D., Cornell. Robert F. Young, Associate Professor; D.B.A., Harvard.

NORTHERN ILLINOIS UNIVERSITY

College of Business
Graduate Studies in Business

Programs of Study

The College of Business offers the Master of Business Administration (M.B.A.) program in a part-time evening curriculum at campuses in Hoffman Estates, Rockford, and Naperville, with areas of study in finance, international business, management information systems, marketing, and strategic management in addition to the M.B.A. general area of study. The College also offers an Executive M.B.A. program in a twenty-one-month delivery format at the Hoffman Estates campus. The College also provides four specialized master's degree programs: the Master of Accounting Science (M.A.S.), encompassing the general area of study and a specialization in taxation and areas of study in public accounting, accounting information systems/information systems auditing, cost management, and governmental and not-for-profit accounting; the Master of Science in Taxation (M.S.T.); the Master of Science degree in finance (M.S.); and the Master of Science degree in management information systems (M.S.).

The primary mission of NIU's M.B.A. program is to serve business and other organizations by preparing students to be leaders. The themes of a global view of business, leadership, ethics, and communication are important and integral parts of the program. Students are encouraged to integrate these themes into term papers, case presentations, and classroom discussions.

The objective of the Master of Accounting Science program is to provide its graduates with technical expertise and competence for advancement in industrial, public accounting, government, and nonprofit organizations. The courses emphasize analysis of alternative theory structures and integrate practical problems, case studies, and studies of socioeconomic phenomena involving uncertainty.

The purpose of the M.S. in finance program is to provide preparation for careers in corporate financial management, investments, banking and other financial institutions, real estate, and insurance. In addition, the M.S. in finance might be chosen by those students interested in a career in teaching or pursuing a doctoral degree in finance.

The Master of Science program in management information systems combines the technical area of computer science with business administration. The purpose of this program is to prepare students to assume administrative and managerial roles in the field of management information systems.

Research Facilities

The University libraries contain nearly 1.5 million volumes, 16,000 current periodical titles, 2.6 million microform units, more than 215,000 maps, and more than 1.2 million government publications and hold membership in the Center for Research Libraries and the Illinet Online (IO) System. University computing resources consist of more than ninety Novell and UNIX file servers, an Amdahl 5890-300E mainframe running IBM MVS, and a number of midrange systems, all connected through a campuswide fiber-optic data network. This network supports approximately 100 subnets and more than 4,000 networked PCs and workstations and provides access to e-mail, library services, the Internet, and instruction- and research-related resources for faculty and staff members and all students.

Financial Aid

Need-based financial aid is administered by the University's Financial Aid Office. Full-time students are eligible to apply for graduate assistantships. In addition, a limited number of partial scholarships are available for M.B.A. students.

Cost of Study

Tuition and fees for DeKalb courses are approximately $145 per semester hour. Tuition and fees for courses at the other campuses are $266 per semester hour. These figures are subject to revision without notice.

Living and Housing Costs

The cost for housing on the DeKalb campus for 1997–98 varied from $1765 per semester for a fourteen-meal plan in a double room in one of the low-rise residence halls to $2350 for a single room with a twenty-one-meal plan in one of the high-rise residence halls. The University offers several residence hall options that may appeal to graduate students. Several floors are designated for students 21 years and older and graduate students. The University has a limited number of apartment units for married students and single parents. Accommodations are also available in the surrounding community. Students in the M.B.A. program commonly live in the Chicago suburban areas or in Rockford.

Student Group

The M.B.A. student profile for the 1997–98 academic year was as follows: average undergraduate GPA, 3.16/4.0; average GMAT score, 547; average age, 32; and average number of years' work experience, five to seven. Fifty-seven percent of the students had undergraduate degrees in business and economics, 18 percent in engineering, 10 percent in math and sciences, 6 percent in social sciences, 5 percent in the humanities, and 4 percent in other areas, including education. Approximately 70 percent of all graduate business students were enrolled in the M.B.A. program. At least 95 percent of all M.B.A. students were employed full-time when entering the program.

Student Outcomes

M.B.A. students are usually employed on a full-time basis when they enter the program. Graduates of the M.B.A. program are now managers and directors at many of the Fortune 500 companies whose offices are located in the Chicago area and around the world. The average starting salary for M.B.A. graduates was $66,069 in 1996. Similarly, graduates from the specialized master's programs are filling management-level positions in industry.

Location

The students engaged in M.B.A. course work at the Hoffman Estates and Naperville campuses live and work almost exclusively in the Chicago and suburban areas. The Chicago area is one of the most dynamic areas in the world for commerce and industry. Students at the DeKalb and Rockford campuses live and work primarily in the DeKalb and Rockford areas. DeKalb is a quiet, semirural town located 65 miles west of Chicago, and Rockford is a major manufacturing center in Illinois.

The University

Northern Illinois University is a comprehensive university, established in 1895 by an act of the Illinois General Assembly. The University currently offers graduate study in seventy-two academic majors in more than 120 areas of study. Currently, the Ph.D. is offered in nine academic departments, and the Ed.D. is offered in six academic majors. The University is fully accredited by the North Central Association of Colleges and Schools. The total student population at the University is 22,082. In the College of Business, the M.A.S., M.B.A., M.S. in finance, and M.S. in management information systems programs are accredited by the American Assembly of Collegiate Schools of Business. The College of Business' accountancy department is ranked by its peers as among the top twenty programs nationwide and consistently places among the top ten institutions on the CPA pass rate. The Department of Finance was recently placed by the prestigious *Journal of Finance* among the top 30 percent of all schools in terms of research productivity and influence for total articles published in the top sixteen finance journals. The M.S. in management information systems is ranked in the top twenty-five such programs nationwide. Total graduate enrollment in the College of Business is approximately 800.

Applying

Application materials may be obtained from the Director of Graduate Studies in Business and Research at the address below. There is a $30 nonrefundable application fee payable by money order or check drawn on a U.S. bank. For U.S. citizens, the completed application form and fee must be received by the Graduate School by June 1 for the fall semester, November 1 for the spring semester, or April 1 for the summer session. All remaining application materials must be received by August 1 for the fall semester, January 1 the for spring semester, or June 1 for the summer session. International students must have all application materials submitted prior to May 1 for consideration for admission for the fall semester or by October 1 for the spring semester.

Correspondence and Information

Director of Graduate Studies in Business and Research
College of Business
Northern Illinois University
DeKalb, Illinois 60115

Telephone: 815-753-1245
800-323-8714 (toll-free)
E-mail: ljacobs@niu.edu
World Wide Web: http://www.cob.niu.edu/grad/grad.html

Northern Illinois University

THE FACULTY AND THEIR RESEARCH

Accountancy: The faculty research areas focus primarily on auditing, activity-based costing, and taxation.
Patrick R. Delaney, Arthur Andersen & Co. Alumni Professor of Accountancy and Chair; Ph.D., Illinois.
Richard E. Baker, Ernst & Young Professor of Accountancy; Ph.D., Wisconsin.
Robert E. Bennet, Ph.D., Missouri.
Rodger A. Bolling, LL.M., Florida.
Gregory A. Carnes, Ph.D., Georgia.
C. William Cummings, Ph.D., Missouri.
John H. Engstrom, KPMG Peat Marwick Professor of Accountancy; D.B.A., Indiana.
James A. Hendricks, Square D Professor of Accountancy; Ph.D., Illinois.
Linda M. Johnson, Ph.D., Arizona State.
Van E. Johnson, Ph.D., Arizona State.
David E. Keys, Household International Professor of Accountancy; Ph.D., Illinois.
Curtis L. Norton, Deloitte and Touche Professor of Accountancy; Ph.D., Arizona State.
John R. Simon, Coopers and Lybrand Professor of Accountancy; Ph.D., Illinois.

Finance: Faculty research focuses on analysis of stock yields.
Robert E. Miller, Safety-Kleen Professor of Finance and Chair; Ph.D., Kansas.
W. Scott Bauman, D.B.A., Indiana.
William Chittenden, Ph.D., Texas Tech.
Richard J. Dowen, Ph.D., SUNY at Binghamton.
John J. Dran, D.B.A., Kent State.
Gerald R. Jensen, Ph.D., Nebraska.
James M. Johnson, Ph.D., Ohio State.
Donald E. Weiss, Ph.D., Wisconsin.

Management: Faculty members conduct research on organizational behavior, human relations, and strategic management.
Daniel R. Wunsch, Chair; Ph.D., UCLA.
Curtiss K. Behrens, LL.M., DePaul.
Terrence R. Bishop, Ph.D., Iowa.
Ralph F. Catalanello, Ph.D., Wisconsin.
Luis G. Flores, Ph.D., Texas Tech.
Charles R. Gowen, Ph.D., Ohio State.
Marvin F. Hill, Ph.D., Iowa.
Albert S. King, D.B.A., Texas Tech.
C. Lynn Neeley, Associate Dean of the College of Business; Ph.D., Tennessee.
Christine Scheck, Ph.D., Arizona State.
Betty L. Schroeder, Ph.D., Michigan State.
Christopher Shook, Ph.D., LSU.
David R. Wade, J.D., Iowa.
Joseph P. Yaney, Ph.D., Michigan.

Marketing: Faculty research is in the areas of international marketing, business-to-business marketing, and sales marketing.
Peter F. Kaminski, Chair; Ph.D., Penn State.
Douglas J. Ayers, Ph.D., Kentucky.
Carol De Moranville, Ph.D., Virginia Tech.
Geoffrey L. Gordon, Ph.D., Kentucky.
Askari H. Kizilbash, Ph.D., Nebraska.
Rick E. Ridnour, Ph.D., Iowa State.
Denise D. Schoenbachler, Ph.D., Kentucky.
Tanuja Srivastava, D.B.A., Southern Illinois.
Jay S. Wagle, Ph.D., Nebraska.
Dan C. Weilbaker, UARCO Professor of Sales; Ph.D., South Carolina.

Operations Management (OM) and Information Systems (IS): OM research focuses on labor and operations scheduling; IS research focuses on information technology.
William J. Tallon, Chair; Ph.D., Iowa.
Richard G. Born, Ph.D., IIT.
Wei-Chien Chang, Ph.D., Wisconsin.
Thomas M. Galvin, Ph.D., IIT.
David K. Graf, Dean of the College of Business; Ph.D., North Dakota.
Larry W. Jacobs, Director of Graduate Studies in Business and Research; Ph.D., Florida State.
Gyu Chan Kim, Ph.D., Nebraska.
Joachim A. Lauer, Ph.D., IIT.
Jack T. Marchewka, Ph.D., Georgia State.
Kathleen L. McFadden, Ph.D., Texas at Arlington.
Ahmed K. Rifai, Ph.D., Syracuse.
Nancy L. Russo, Ph.D., Georgia State.
Elizabeth R. Towell, Ph.D., Wisconsin.

NOVA SOUTHEASTERN UNIVERSITY

School of Business and Entrepreneurship

Programs of Study

The School of Business and Entrepreneurship (SBE) conducts graduate degree programs at the master's and doctoral levels. Degree programs offered on the master's level include the Master of Business Administration (M.B.A.); Master of Public Administration (M.P.A.); Master of Accounting (M.Acc.); Master of Science (M.S.) in human resource management or health services administration; and Master of International Business Administration (M.I.B.A.). Adult professionals attend classes on an alternate-weekend format. One-year master's degree programs are available on the Fort Lauderdale campus for graduate students without previous management experience. An online M.B.A. will also be available in summer 1998. Degree programs offered on the doctoral level include the Doctor of Business Administration (D.B.A.), Doctor of Public Administration (D.P.A.), and Doctor of International Business Administration (D.I.B.A.).

Not only is Nova Southeastern University committed to high-quality education programs designed specifically for adult professionals, but it has also developed and maintained field-based delivery systems for programs in the field of management (and education) enabling the programs in the School of Business and Entrepreneurship to be delivered nationwide. The University is licensed to operate one or more programs in more than thirty states of the United States and several other countries and maintains a fully operational chartered center for graduate and undergraduate programs in management in the Republic of Panama. In addition, through the accreditation process overseen by the Commission on Colleges of the Southern Association of Colleges and Schools, a sample of Nova Southeastern University programs operating in all other regions of the United States has been carefully checked to ensure that the program standards are met in field locations as well as on campus. A large number of these field locations are corporate-based clusters of students employed in leading business and industrial firms.

Beginning summer term 1998, the SBE will offer the virtual M.B.A., designed to be delivered on line. The virtual M.B.A. allows management professionals to interact and study together anywhere throughout the globe by utilizing the latest computer and Internet technologies, including chat rooms, synchronous and asynchronous dialogue, and electronic submission of assignments.

Research Facilities

The School's master's and doctoral programs utilize on-line telecommunication through the UNIX operating system to support research activities. Library and other media resources are available to field-based students through the School's SPARCstation 1000.

Financial Aid

Nova Southeastern University operates several programs that provide financial aid in order to help students to meet direct and indirect educational expenses. Financial aid may be obtained from federal, state, University, and private sources. Most students qualify for employer tuition assistance. Details regarding financial aid are available from the Office of Financial Aid. Students who are eligible for Veterans Administration benefits are invited to consult the Nova Southeastern VA adviser in the Office of Financial Aid; telephone: 800-522-3243 (toll-free).

Cost of Study

For the master's programs in 1998–99, tuition is $425 per credit, registration costs $20 per term, and there is a graduation fee of $65. For the doctoral programs, tuition is $550 per credit, registration is $25 per term, and the graduation fee is $65. Information about additional fees for workshops, computer time, and dissertation binding can be obtained from the program office.

Living and Housing Costs

Campus apartments are available but are reserved for students enrolled in full-time programs in law and psychology and for undergraduate students.

Student Group

The typical weekend graduate student in the School's programs is 30 to 35 years old in the master's programs and 35 to 40 years old in doctoral programs, is working as a full-time professional in the middle to upper levels of management, and is engaged in study for the purpose of professional development and advancement. The average age of full-time students is 23. A career resource center is available on campus.

Location

The main campus of Nova Southeastern University is located on a 232-acre campus in urban Broward County, Florida, and is part of the Fort Lauderdale–Hollywood–Miami metropolitan area. The area supports both high-tech manufacturing and recreational industries. Cultural attractions and sports are available throughout the metropolitan area.

The University

Nova Southeastern University is organized into a number of academic and professional centers in addition to the School of Business and Entrepreneurship. These centers provide an educational, training, and research support base for a full spectrum of activities in the fields of law, psychology, oceanographic research, education, computer science and computer-based learning, early childhood development, dentistry, and business. The graduate and professional centers support the activities of the undergraduate center known as Nova College.

Applying

Students are admitted on a year-round basis and may begin classes in any of four terms in the master's programs (January, April, July, and October) or any of three terms in the doctoral programs (January, May, and September). Application materials may be obtained by writing or calling the School office or by contacting a site coordinator for a field location (see reverse). The application fee is $50.

Correspondence and Information

School of Business and Entrepreneurship
Nova Southeastern University
3100 SW 9 Avenue
Fort Lauderdale, Florida 33315
Telephone: 800-672-7223 Ext. 5100 (toll-free)

Nova Southeastern University

LOCATIONS AND CONTACTS

Nova Southeastern University's graduate programs in business and public administration are administered through a number of field locations across the country. Listed below are the locations and site coordinators as of March 1, 1996; additional sites are possible, depending on student demand and licensing by appropriate state authorities.

Doctoral Programs (USA)

Atlanta, Georgia (D.B.A.): (under development) Julia Flint, 800-672-7223 Ext. 5100 (work) (toll-free) or 800-801-3344 (toll-free).
Austin, Texas (D.B.A.): Jack Fuller, 512-749-5041 (home).
Birmingham, Alabama (D.B.A., D.P.A.): Paul Doran, 205-856-7894 (office).
Brattleboro, Vermont (D.B.A.): Kristie Tetrault, 800-672-7223 Ext. 5036 (work) (toll-free).
Danville, Virginia: Al Bolton, 804-791-5605 (office).
Davenport, Iowa (D.B.A.): Robert Banash, 319-383-8953 (office) or 319-391-9592 (home).
Daytona Beach, Florida (D.B.A.): (under development) Jay Dittmer 904-788-4766 (home).
Denver, Colorado: Mellani Day, 800-522-7574 (work) (toll-free).
Fort Lauderdale, Florida (D.B.A., D.P.A., D.I.B.A.): Main Campus, 954-262-5100. Accounting, finance, health services, human resource management, information technology management, international management, and marketing specialty courses are only offered at main campus.
Little Rock, Arkansas (D.B.A.): Rick Casey, 501-979-1232 (office) or 501-885-3432 (home).
Los Angeles, California area (D.B.A.): Earl Richardson, 805-734-1085.
National cluster–Fort Lauderdale, Florida (D.B.A., D.P.A., D.I.B.A.): Marketing Department, 800-672-7223 Ext. 5100. (toll-free)
Orlando, Florida (D.B.A.): Jay Dittmer, 904-788-4766 (home).
Phoeniz, Arizona (D.B.A.): Gerry Bedore, 602-995-5999 (Western Program Office) or 602-439-3250 (home).
Seattle, Washington (D.B.A.): Rick Coffey, 206-266-4212.
Spartanburg, South Carolina (D.B.A.): Phil McGee, 803-474-2459 (home).
Vienna, Virginia–Washington, D.C., area (D.B.A., D.P.A.): David Morton, 301-953-7724 (home).
Whiting, Indiana–greater Chicago area (D.B.A.): Phil Kemp, 708-653-1647 (home).

Master's Programs (North America, Jamaica, and Bahamas)

Aiken, South Carolina (HRM): Vincent Grosso, 803-642-0525 (home).
Aiken, South Carolina (M.B.A.): Larry Adkinson, 706-855-2255 (home).
Atlanta, Georgia (M.B.A.): Paula Wellons-Larkin, 404-629-9303 (home).
Baton Rouge, Louisiana (M.B.A.): JoAnn Spurlock, 504-769-9413 (home).
Birmingham, Alabama (M.B.A.): Steven Fraas, 770-632-9777 (home).
Boca Raton, Florida (M.B.A.): Mungree Samlal, 954-746-2281; Bridget Dickinson, 954-345-1711 (Spanish River High School).
Calgary, Alberta, Canada (HRM, M.B.A.): Carey Clenchy, 403-238-2383 (home).
Cedar Rapids, Iowa (M.B.A.): Pam Meyer, 319-294-2258 (home).
Coral Springs, Florida (M.B.A.): Mungree Samlal, 954-746-2281.
Daytona Beach, Florida (M.B.A.): Jay Dittmer, 904-788-4766 (home).
Fort Lauderdale, Florida (ACC): East Campus, Carlo Palazzese, 954-262-5038.
Fort Lauderdale, Florida (MBA, HRM): East Campus, Carlo Palazzese, 954-262-5038.
Fort Lauderdale, Florida (HSA, M.P.A.): East Campus, Shane Strum, 954-262-5035.
Fort Lauderdale, Florida (M.I.B.A.): East Campus, Maria Luisa Garcia, 954-262-5048.
Fort Myers, Florida (M.B.A.): Ron Stephens, 941-437-0726 (home).
Fort Wayne, Indiana (under development) (M.B.A.): 800-672-7223 Ext. 5046 (office).
Gainesville, Florida (M.B.A.): Ed Dice, 352-378-2329 (home).
Huntsville, Alabama (M.B.A.): Mike Hodges, 205-587-6929 (home).
Jacksonville (American Transtech), Florida (M.B.A.): Twinkle Maloy, 904-751-0932 (home).
Jacksonville (Southern Bell), Florida (M.B.A.): Greg Harker, 904-262-5411 (home).
Jamaica, West Indies (M.B.A.): Keith Rowe, 809-973-3405 (home).
Largo, Florida (M.B.A.): Frank Nickels, 813-784-4951.
Miami, Florida (H.R.M.): Jorge Alfonso, 305-382-5973.
Nassau, Bahamas (M.B.A.): Alphanette King, 242-326-4033.
Northwest Miami, Florida (M.B.A.): Jorge Alfonso, 305-382-5973.
Orlando, Florida (HSA): Leslie Johnson, 407-299-3192 (home).
Orlando, Florida (M.B.A.): Jay Dittmer, 904-788-4766 (home).
Panama (M.B.A.): Noemi Castillo de Miranda, 011-507-272-2494.
Pompano (Southern Bell), Florida (M.B.A.): Bud Shafer, 954-474-2433 (home).
Sarasota, Florida (M.B.A.): Mary Jane Gullick, 941-966-0148 (home).
Shreveport, Louisiana (M.B.A.): Beverly Hendricks, 318-682-7474 (home).
South Miami, Florida (ACC): Jorge Blanco, 305-829-4650 (home).
South Miami, Florida (M.B.A.): Jorge Alfonso, 305-382-5973.
Tallahassee, Florida (M.B.A.): Phyllis Burkhart, 850-893-2218 (home).
Tampa, Florida (M.B.A.): Frank Nickels, 813-784-4951 (home).
Vancouver, Canada (M.B.A.): John Brownlee-Baker, 604-925-3571 (home) or 604-984-1742 (work).
West Palm Beach, Florida (M.B.A.): Sandi Bateman, 954-426-6971.

ACC = Master of Accounting Program.
HRM = M.S./Human Resource Management Program.
HSA = M.S./Health Services Administration Program.
M.B.A. = Master of Business Administration Program.
M.I.B.A. = Master of International Business Administration.
M.P.A. = Master of Public Administration Program.

THE OHIO STATE UNIVERSITY

Fisher College of Business

Programs of Study

The Fisher M.B.A. program is a two-year curriculum organized around a core of accounting, economics, statistics, and organizational behavior. In addition to the core are courses in the functional business areas of finance, marketing, operations, and human resource management. The final activities integrate theory and practice of disciplines within management science, providing the opportunity to identify policy issues and implement effective business strategies.

Major areas from which students choose include corporate financial management, investment management, marketing management, operations and logistics management, and consulting. Minor areas are available in accounting, consulting, finance, human resources management, international business, logistics, management information systems, marketing, operations, and real estate.

In addition to business course work, the M.B.A. curriculum includes activities designed to build teamwork and leadership skills. Students work together to solve problems for area corporations as part of a Business Solution Team. They are also given the opportunity to participate in the Student Investment Management (SIM) Program, where the students actually control $15 million of the University's portfolio and are expected to make savvy investment decisions.

Ohio State also offers an evening M.B.A. program designed for business professionals who live in the central Ohio area and wish to pursue an M.B.A. on a part-time basis.

Nearly 200 companies visit the campus each year to interview M.B.A. students. Students can send their resumes via fax or e-mail through the University's resume referral service. Other opportunities include job fairs, counseling, seminars, internships, and practical experience.

The Fisher Ph.D. program in business administration recruits students exhibiting exceptional potential for teaching and research. Major areas include business strategy, decision sciences, finance, industrial relations, insurance and risk management, international business, marketing, organizational behavior, production and operations management, real estate and urban analysis, and logistics. Ph.D. programs in accounting and management information systems, as well as labor and human resources, also are offered.

Research Facilities

The OSU Library system is among the most advanced in the nation. It includes more than 4.8 million volumes as well as a computer system that allows easy access to the State of Ohio Library. The Business Library contains nearly 200,000 volumes and offers loose-leaf services, specialized indexes, and annual reports, and many materials are available on CD-ROM.

College computer labs have state-of-the-art hardware and software. Each M.B.A. student has an e-mail account that allows access to commercial online database systems as well as to campus research collections and the Internet. Two tiered M.B.A. classrooms allow for laptop computers networked between students and faculty members and for multimedia presentations.

Financial Aid

Fellowships and graduate associateships are available based upon academic credentials. Fellowships provide a one-year full waiver of tuition and fees and a monthly stipend of $1000. There is no work commitment associated with fellowships. Students may apply by indicating an interest on the Graduate School application. Graduate associateships are also awarded on the basis of academic credentials and offer a 50 percent tuition waiver and a monthly stipend of $500. Graduate associates work 10 hours per week for the College.

Cost of Study

The 1998–99 graduate tuition for students who are in-state residents is $2086 per quarter. Nonresident students pay $4986 per quarter. All costs are subject to change.

Living and Housing Costs

Affordable housing is available both on and off campus. There are 1,259 rooms on campus to accommodate graduate students that cost an estimated $6520 per year for room and board. Off-campus housing is comparable and can be found in the campus area, as well as in suburbs and villages within an easy commute. Columbus offers a low cost of living and a diversified employment base.

Student Group

There are nearly 150 full-time students who come from all over the United States and several other countries. The majority of students hold undergraduate degrees in business, engineering, science, social science, and the humanities. On average, admitted students possess five years of full-time work experience. Twenty-four percent of the students are international, 11 percent are members of minority groups, and 31 percent are women. The average age is 27, and the student-faculty ratio is 6:1.

Location

The campus is located in Columbus, recognized as one of the top ten cities for entrepreneurial activity and home of several Fortune 500 corporate headquarters, including Borden, Inc.; The Limited, Inc.; Nationwide Insurance; and Wendy's International, Inc.

The University

The Ohio State University is a major center for graduate and professional education offering more than 114 fields of graduate study. Interdisciplinary opportunities and student organizations abound.

Applying

The M.B.A. program encourages applications from individuals with bachelor's degrees in all academic areas from all parts of the United States and from around the world. Recommended prerequisites for the full-time program are courses in accounting, calculus, statistics, probability, microeconomics, and macroeconomics. Factors considered in admission decisions include undergraduate grades (GPA), scores on the Graduate Management Admission Test (GMAT), nature and length of work experience, and evidence of maturity and motivation. Applications must be complete by January 15 for financial aid consideration.

Correspondence and Information

Fisher College of Business
Graduate Program Services
Gerlach Hall
University Building 250
The Ohio State University
2108 Neil Avenue
Columbus, Ohio 43210-1144
Telephone: 614-292-8511

The Ohio State University

THE FACULTY

CHAIRED OR DESIGNATED PROFESSORS

Accounting and Management Information Systems
Peter Easton, John J. Gerlach Chair in Accounting; Ph.D., Berkeley.
John Fellingham, H.P. Wolfe Chair in Accounting; Ph.D., UCLA.
Daniel L. Jensen, Deloitte & Touche Professor of Accounting; Ph.D., Ohio State.

Finance
Patric H. Hendershott, John W. Galbreath Chair in Real Estate; Ph.D., Purdue.
Rene M. Stulz, Everett D. Reese Chair of Banking and Monetary Economics; Ph.D., MIT.

Management and Human Resources
Jay Barney, Bank One Chair for Excellence in Corporate Strategy; Ph.D., Yale.
Jerald Greenberg, Irving Abramowitz Memorial Professorship in Business Ethics; Ph.D., Wayne State.
Edward H. Jennings, William H. Davis Chair in the American Free Enterprise System; Ph.D., Michigan.
Roy J. Lewicki, Dean's Distinguished Teaching Professor; Ph.D., Columbia.
Marcia Miceli, Hoyt Designated Professor of Management; D.B.A., Indiana.

Management Sciences
W. C. Benton, Dean's Distinguished Research Professor; D.B.A., Indiana.
William Berry, Richard M. Ross Chair in Management; Ph.D., Harvard.

Marketing
Greg Allenby, W. Arthur Cullman Professorship in Marketing; Ph.D., Chicago.
Douglas Lambert, Raymond E. Mason Sr. Professor of Transportation and Logistics; Ph.D., Ohio State.
Robert P. Leone, Berry Chair of New Technologies in Marketing; Ph.D., Purdue.

ACCOUNTING AND MANAGEMENT INFORMATION SYSTEMS
Lawrence A. Tomassini, Chair; Ph.D., UCLA.
Anil Arya, Ph.D., Iowa.
William F. Bentz, Ph.D., Ohio State.
John Butler, Ph.D., Texas at Austin.
Paicheng Chu, Ph.D., Texas at Austin.
Alicia Jackson, Ph.D., Texas at Austin.
Varghese S. Jacob, Ph.D., Purdue.
James C. Kinard, Ph.D., Stanford.
Raymond J. Krasniewski, Ph.D., Purdue.
Waleed A. Muhanna, Ph.D., Wisconsin–Madison.
Richard J. Murdock, Ph.D., Cornell.
Erik Rolland, Ph.D., Ohio State.
Douglas A. Schroeder, Ph.D., Kansas.
Eric E. Spires, Ph.D., Illinois.
David E. Wallin, Ph.D., Arizona.
David D. Williams, Ph.D., Penn State.
Richard A. Young, Ph.D., Ohio State.
Kristina Zvinakis, Ph.D., Texas.

FINANCE
Stephen A. Buser, Chair; Ph.D., Boston College.
Deborah A. Ballam, J.D., Ohio State.
John D. Blackburn, J.D., Cincinnati.
Kelly Brunarski, Ph.D., Ohio State.
Zhiw Chen, Ph.D., Yale.
Robert Goldstein, Ph.D., Berkeley; Ph.D., Illinois.
Jean Helwege, Ph.D., UCLA.
Andrew Karolyi, Ph.D., Chicago.
Elliot I. Klayman, LL.M., Harvard.
Anil Makhija, Ph.D., Wisconsin.
Bernadette Minton, Ph.D., Chicago.
Timothy Opler, Ph.D., UCLA.
John Persons, Ph.D., Chicago.
Paul Schultz, Ph.D., Chicago.
Michael L. Smith, Ph.D., Minnesota.
D. Deon Strickland, Ph.D., North Carolina at Chapel Hill.
Ralph W. Walkling, Ph.D., Maryland.
Paul Weinstock, J.D., Boston University.
Sony D. Williams-Stanton, Ph.D., Michigan.

MANAGEMENT AND HUMAN RESOURCES
David B. Greenberger, Chair; Ph.D., Wisconsin–Madison.
Joseph A. Alutto, Dean; Ph.D., Cornell.
Kathleen Conner, Ph.D., UCLA.
Jeffrey D. Ford, Ph.D., Ohio State.
Robert L. Heneman, Ph.D., Michigan State.
Stephen M. Hills, Ph.D., Wisconsin–Madison.
Jay S. Kim, Ph.D., Michigan State.
Howard Klein, Ph.D., Michigan State.
Michael Leiblein, Ph.D., Purdue.
Sven Lundstedt, Ph.D., Chicago.
Mona Makhija, Ph.D., Wisconsin.
Stephen L. Mangum, Ph.D., George Washington.
David Patton, M.A., Ohio State.
Mike Peng, Ph.D., Washington (Seattle).
Arnon E. Reichers, Ph.D., Michigan State.
Marcus H. Sandver, Ph.D., Wisconsin–Madison.
Oded Shenkar, Ph.D., Columbia.
William D. Todor, Ph.D., California, Irvine.
John P. Wanous, Ph.D., Yale.

MANAGEMENT SCIENCES
David A. Schilling, Chair; Ph.D., Johns Hopkins.
Tonya Boone, Ph.D., North Carolina at Chapel Hill.
Amelia Carr, Ph.D., Arizona State.
David A. Collier, Ph.D., Ohio State.
John R. Current, Ph.D., Johns Hopkins.
Nicholas Hall, Ph.D., Berkeley.
Keong Leong, Ph.D., South Carolina.
Glenn W. Milligan, Ph.D., Ohio State.
Paul C. Nutt, Ph.D., Wisconsin–Madison.
WanSoo T. Rhee, Ph.D., Kent State.
Peter T. Ward, D.B.A., Boston University.

MARKETING
Robert E. Burnkrant, Chair; Ph.D., Illinois.
Neelima Bendapudi, Ph.D., Kansas.
Roger D. Blackwell, Ph.D., Northwestern.
Martha C. Cooper, Ph.D., Ohio State.
Leslie M. Fine, Ph.D., Tennessee.
James L. Ginter, Ph.D., Purdue.
Curtis P. Haugtvedt, Ph.D., Missouri–Columbia.
H. Lee Mathews, Ph.D., Ohio State.
Mark Stiving, Ph.D., Berkeley.
H. Rao Unnava, Ph.D., Ohio State.
Patricia West, Ph.D., Chicago

OHIO UNIVERSITY

College of Business

Programs of Study

Ohio University's College of Business offers programs leading to the degrees of Master of Business Administration and Master of Science in Accountancy.

Built on the College's mission to provide a learning environment that enables individuals to develop the knowledge and skills needed for success in the complex global business community of the twenty-first century, the M.B.A. program offers a rigorous, innovative thirteen-month experience. The action-learning format places students into exactly the type of projects and work situations that they will face as future leaders of information-age organizations. Students learn basic business concepts in the context of their use, maximizing their ability to both recall and apply those concepts. The Joint Student Study Abroad Project enhances students' understanding of the complexities of international business. Comfort with information technology also increases dramatically as students collaborate electronically and develop professional-level computer-driven presentations. For high-potential, working individuals with a minimum of two to four years' experience, Ohio University's part-time program combines a series of short, high-intensity residencies and online education based on the OUMBA Intranet, a virtual learning community. Further information is available from the University's Web site at the address below.

Ohio University's Master of Science in Accountancy program provides strong students the opportunity to target public accounting or industry-specific careers in accounting, auditing, tax planning and compliance, or accounting information systems. The M.S.A. stresses development of specialized accounting and business knowledge with communication and teamwork skills necessary for success. The twelve-course individualized program of study, cooperatively developed by the student and faculty advisers, provides the depth and the breadth necessary for graduates to become leaders in the accounting profession. Required accounting courses include accounting theory, environment of the profession, and contemporary issues; three additional accounting courses are selected to target the student's chosen career path. Six business and nonbusiness courses are selected to complete a comprehensive career-oriented package.

Research Facilities

The physical and technological environments are designed to support the team-oriented, project-based nature of the learning process. A network of computers, each with access to the information superhighway, is available 24 hours a day. Students routinely seek information on the Internet and collaborate and submit work electronically, preparing them to participate productively in information-age organizations. Ohio University's Alden Library, a modern seven-story air-conditioned building, has well over a million bound volumes, including more than 50,000 documents on business topics. Alden is also a government document repository library.

Financial Aid

Graduate associateships provide stipends of about $8100, and tuition waivers are available. Special scholarship aid is offered to qualified applicants from minority groups. Awards of aid are generally announced in April.

Cost of Study

Tuition for a normal quarter's load (9–18 hours) was $1373 for Ohio residents and $2946 for nonresidents for 1997–98. Students paid a general fee of $335 quarterly. The M.B.A. program requires four quarters, with an additional fee of $4000 for the mandatory Joint Student Study Abroad Project.

Living and Housing Costs

Both University and private housing are available for single and married students. Housing costs vary from $400 to $600 per month, depending on accommodations and furnishings.

Student Group

With about 40 students in the full-time M.B.A. program, all regions of the United States and many other countries are represented. About half of the students have liberal arts or technical backgrounds. The M.S.A. program is limited to 30 strong students. All students possess undergraduate accounting degrees or will have completed the background necessary for such a degree before entering the final phase of the programs.

Location

Athens, a pleasant college town of 20,000, is located in the rolling, green hills of southeastern Ohio, the most scenic part of the state. There are ample facilities for fishing, boating, camping, swimming, biking, and hiking.

The University

Founded in 1804, Ohio University has grown from a single building to 108 principal buildings covering 623 acres. Full-time University enrollment was about 19,000 students in 1997–98, including about 2,800 in the Graduate College. Student facilities include a 165,000-square-foot recreation center, the aquatic center, an indoor ice-skating rink, a golf course, and basketball, tennis, and racquetball courts.

Applying

The deadline for the M.B.A. program is March 1. Late applications will be considered for admission, but applicants may not receive financial awards. Computer proficiency in spreadsheets and word processing is expected. M.S.A. applications for the fall quarter must be received by April 1. M.S.A. applicants are normally in the top half of their graduating class. GMAT scores of 500 or higher, a TOEFL score of 600 or higher (for international students only), and recommendations are considered in reviewing applications for both programs. The application fee is $30.

Correspondence and Information

Director of Graduate Programs
Copeland Hall
College of Business
Ohio University
Athens, Ohio 45701

Telephone: 614-593-2007
Fax: 614-593-9823
E-mail: rossj@ouvaxa.cats.ohiou.edu
World Wide Web: http://oumba.cob.ohiou.edu/~oumba/

Ohio University

THE FACULTY

Catherine N. Axinn, Associate Professor of Marketing; Ph.D., Michigan State.
Frank Barone, Associate Professor of Management and Associate Dean; Ph.D., Ohio State.
Bruce Berlin, Assistant Professor of Finance; Ph.D., Michigan State.
Elizabeth Blair, Associate Professor of Marketing; Ph.D., South Carolina.
Thomas W. Bolland, Professor of Quantitative Business Analysis; Ph.D., Chicago.
Gerard Carvalho, Associate Professor of Management; Ph.D., Michigan.
David S. Chappell, Assistant Professor of Management; Ph.D., Colorado at Boulder.
Yining Chen, Assistant Professor of Accountancy; Ph.D., South Carolina.
Natalie Chieffe, Assistant Professor of Finance; candidate, Mississippi State.
Ted Compton, Professor of Accountancy; Ph.D., Cincinnati; CMA, CSP.
Garth Coombs, Assistant Professor of Management; Ph.D., Colorado.
James Cox, Associate Professor of Accountancy; Ph.D., Pittsburgh; CPA.
Kenneth Cutright, Associate Professor of Management; Ph.D., West Virginia.
John Day, Professor and Chair, Management Information Systems; Ph.D., Ohio.
Barbara Dyer, Assistant Professor of Marketing; Ph.D., Tennessee.
Patricia C. Gunn, Associate Professor of Law; J.D., Boston College.
Ashok Gupta, Professor of Marketing and Chair, Department of Marketing; Ph.D., Syracuse.
Timothy P. Hartman, Associate Professor of Marketing; Ph.D., Ohio.
Carol Anne Hilton, Assistant Professor of Accountancy; Ph.D., Arkansas.
Joseph N. Hilton, Assistant Professor of Accountancy; Ph.D., Arkansas.
Ellsworth Holden, Assistant Professor of Management Information Systems; M.A., Harvard.
Leon Hoshower, Associate Professor of Accountancy; Ph.D., Michigan State; CPA.
Daniel Innis, Assistant Professor of Marketing; Ph.D., Ohio State.
Robert Jamison, Professor of Accountancy; Ph.D., Texas.
Mary Carter Keifer, Associate Professor of Law; J.D., Virginia.
David Kirch, Visiting Associate Professor of Accountancy; Ph.D., Penn State; CPA.
Manjulika Koshal, Professor of Business Administration; Ph.D., Patna (India).
Hao Lou, Assistant Professor of Management Information Systems; Ph.D., Houston.
Thomas G. Luce, Professor of Management Information Systems; Ph.D., Purdue.
Jeffrey A. Manzi, Assistant Professor of Finance; Ph.D., Kent State.
Arthur Marinelli, Professor of Law and Chair, Department of Management Systems; Ph.D., Ohio State.
Clarence Martin, Associate Professor of Management; Ph.D., Carnegie Mellon.
Anne H. McClanahan, Professor of Management Information Systems; Ph.D., Ohio.
E. James Meddaugh, Professor of Accountancy; Ph.D., Penn State.
Azmi Mikhail, Professor of Finance; Ph.D., Ohio State.
Richard Milter, Associate Professor of Management; Ph.D., SUNY at Albany.
Kahandas Nandola, Professor of Marketing; Ph.D., Pennsylvania.
James Perotti, Professor of Management Information Systems; Ph.D., Duquesne.
Valerie Perotti, Professor of Management; Ph.D., Ohio.
Dwight Pugh, Associate Professor of Finance; Ph.D., Ohio.
Ganas K. Rakes, O'Bleness Professor of Banking and Chair, Department of Finance; D.B.A., Washington (St. Louis).
Nanda Rangan, Visiting Bank One Professor of Financial Services; Ph.D., Texas A&M.
Bonnie Roach, Associate Professor of Human Resource Management; Ph.D., Ohio State.
Jessie C. Roberson Jr., Associate Professor of Law; J.D., Michigan.
Richard C. Scamehorn, Executive in Residence; M.B.A., Michigan.
John Schermerhorn, O'Bleness Professor of Management; Ph.D., Northwestern.
David Senteney, Assistant Professor of Accountancy; Ph.D., Illinois.
Florence Sharp, O'Bleness Professor of Accountancy; Ph.D., Illinois at Urbana–Champaign; CPA.
Robert Sharp, Associate Professor of Accountancy; Ph.D., Texas at Austin; CPA.
Hugh Sherman, Assistant Professor of Management; Ph.D., Temple.
Jane Sojka, Visiting Assistant Professor of Marketing; Ph.D., Vanderbilt.
Lucian Spataro, Professor of Management; Ph.D., Illinois.
John E. Stinson, Professor of Management; Ph.D., Ohio State.
David Sutherland, Assistant Professor of Management Information Systems; Ph.D., Kansas.
Rebecca Thacker, Assistant Professor of Human Resource Management; Ph.D., Texas A&M.
Lane Tracy, Professor of Management; Ph.D., Washington (Seattle).
Ed Yost, Associate Professor of Management; Ph.D., Ohio State.

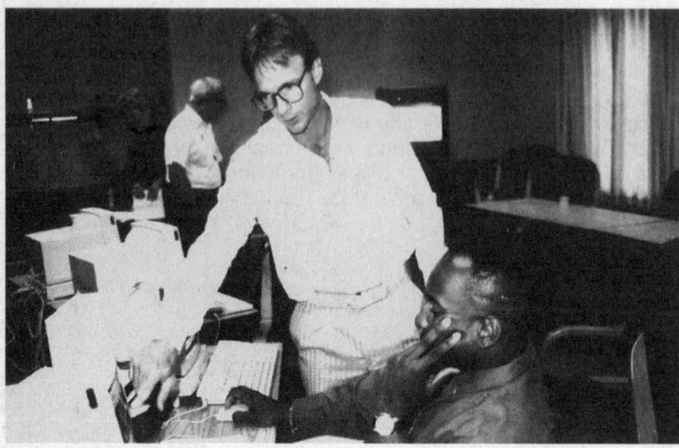

The M.B.A. program incorporates the latest in technology advancements.

M.B.A. students are continuously exposed to business executives.

OLD DOMINION UNIVERSITY

College of Business and Public Administration
Graduate Programs in Business and Public Administration

Programs of Study

The College of Business and Public Administration at Old Dominion University offers graduate programs of study leading to the degrees of Master of Arts in economics, Master of Business Administration, Master of Public Administration, Master of Science in accounting, Master of Science in computer science (information science option), Master of Taxation, Master of Urban Studies, and Doctor of Philosophy in business administration and in urban services.

The master's programs are designed to present broad but thorough insights into issues relevant to all effective managers. These programs are structured to provide students with the opportunity to design a program of study to meet their individual needs. Some students in the M.B.A. program may choose a program with a 12-hour concentration plus 6 hours of electives, while others may elect not to concentrate and develop general electives. Concentrations are available in each of the following disciplines: accounting, economics, finance, health-care management, human resource management, information systems, international business, marketing, port maritime management, public administration, service operations management, and urban services.

The Doctor of Philosophy program in business administration is a scholarly research-based and internationally focused program with a professional orientation. The objective of the program is to prepare men and women of superior promise and potential for careers in higher education, teaching, and research and for administrative and research careers in the private and public sectors. In addition to a strong international business orientation, including a foreign language requirement, the program is based on established business disciplines.

The Doctor of Philosophy in urban services is a multidisciplinary degree program designed to address the complex human, social, and technological problems of contemporary urban society. This program encompasses five main themes: urban studies, policy analysis and problem solving, administration and management, research, and an area of specialization.

Research Facilities

The University Library provides a full complement of services and materials, with approximately 1.5 million items, including monographs, government publications, periodicals and serials, microforms, scores, and recordings for student and faculty use. Computer-assisted searches of more than 200 indexing and abstracting services, in addition to instruction in the use of the library and its services and resources, are available in the reference department. The Computer Center offers services ranging from software development to professional consulting to training programming and analysis support, all of which are provided for users as diverse as faculty members, students, and administrators.

Financial Aid

Financial aid is available for graduate students in the form of University fellowships, doctoral fellowships, tuition grants, teaching or research assistantships, and doctoral teaching fellowships. In addition, graduate students in the College of Business and Public Administration may apply for the Theodore F. and Constance C. Constant Fellowship. Graduate students may also qualify for various University scholarships, such as the Alumni Association Outstanding Scholar Fellowship, the Meredith Construction Company Scholarship, the Herman E. Valentine Scholarship, and Special Part-Time Minority Tuition Grants.

Cost of Study

Fees in 1998–99 are $176 per credit hour for Virginia residents and $464 per credit hour for nonresidents.

Living and Housing Costs

A wide variety of housing is available for rent on campus and in the immediate community within walking, biking, or easy commuting distance.

Student Group

Currently, Old Dominion University has about 11,000 undergraduate students and 5,100 graduate students.

Location

Old Dominion University is located in Norfolk, Virginia, which is the center of a metropolitan area with a population of approximately 1.4 million. Norfolk is the hub of the world's largest natural harbor and is regarded as one of the nation's leading cities in business and industry. The area is a major recreational area known for its beach and historical landmarks. Norfolk also benefits from its heavy military concentration and its proximity to Washington, D.C., and the Outer Banks of North Carolina.

The University and The College

Old Dominion University interacts closely with a vigorous community at the heart of the seven-city Hampton Roads region. The University had its formal beginning in 1930 as a branch of the College of William and Mary, and by 1969, Old Dominion University was an independent institution with university status. At present, it has more than 16,000 students.

The College of Business and Public Administration is one of approximately 330 schools in the world to have achieved accreditation on the graduate and undergraduate levels by the AACSB–The International Association for Management Education. The College's highly productive faculty is dedicated to the intellectual development of students through a variety of course offerings enhanced by an impressive spectrum of research and service activities.

Applying

The College of Business and Public Administration welcomes applications from men and women who have earned a bachelor's degree from an accredited institution. Admission to the program is competitive and is granted only to those who show high ability and likely success in graduate study. To apply students must submit application forms for graduate study, official transcripts of all previous college work, one letter of recommendation, scores on the Graduate Management Admission Test or Graduate Record Examinations, and a goals and interest statement. Applicants whose native language is not English are also required to achieve an acceptable score on the Test of English as a Foreign Language (TOEFL).

Correspondence and Information

For program information:
Graduate Programs
College of Business and Public Administration
Old Dominion University
Norfolk, Virginia 23529
Telephone: 804-683-3520
Fax: 804-683-4076

For application forms:
Graduate Admissions
Old Dominion University
Norfolk, Virginia 23529
Telephone: 804-683-3637
800-348-7926 (toll free)

Old Dominion University

THE FACULTY

Department of Accounting

Abdel M. Agami, Professor; Ph.D., Illinois. Walter W. Berry, Senior Lecturer; M.B.A., Old Dominion. Patricia M. Doherty, Lecturer; M.B.A., Golden Gate. Ted D. Englebrecht, Professor; Ph.D., South Carolina. Laurie J. Henry, Assistant Professor; Ph.D., Mississippi. Michael S. Luehlfing, Assistant Professor; Ph.D., Georgia. Otto B. Martinson, Associate Professor; Ph.D., George Washington. Timothy McKee, Associate Professor; J.D., Indiana. Michael Mosebach, Assistant Professor; Ph.D., Oklahoma. Ula K. Motekat, Professor; D.B.A., Colorado. Richard Newmark, Assistant Professor; Ph.D., Miami. Douglas E. Ziegenfuss, Associate Professor; Ph.D., Virginia Commonwealth.

Department of Business Administration

Claire J. Anderson, Associate Professor; Ph.D., Massachusetts. Barbara R. Bartkus, Assistant Professor; Ph.D., Texas A&M. John C. Bratton, Assistant Professor; Ph.D., Florida State. Paul J. Champagne, Professor; Ph.D., Massachusetts. Kae H. Chung, Professor; Ph.D., LSU. Kathryn Coulter, Assistant Professor; Ph.D., Georgia. Jon R. Crunkleton, Associate Professor; Ph.D., South Carolina. Roy R. Cunningham, Instructor; M.S., Nebraska. Diana L. Deadrick, Associate Professor; Ph.D., Virginia Tech. John A. Doukas, Professor; Ph.D., NYU. Theresa B. Flaherty, Assistant Professor; Ph.D., Kentucky. John B. Ford, Professor; Ph.D., Georgia. Myron Glassman, Professor; Ph.D., Illinois. Earl D. Honeycutt Jr., Professor; Ph.D., Georgia. Sylvia C. Hudgins, Associate Professor; Ph.D., Virginia Tech. James Johnson, Assistant Professor; Ph.D., South Carolina. John F. Keeling, Instructor; M.B.A., Virginia Tech. Kiran Kirande, Assistant Professor; Ph.D., Houston. Steve Maurer, Associate Professor; Ph.D., Oregon. R. Bruce McAfee, Professor; Ph.D., Wayne State. Sara A. Morris, Associate Professor; Ph.D., Texas at Austin. Geoffrey A. Motte, Professor and Director; Ph.D., Union (Ohio). Anil Nair, Assistant Professor; Ph.D., NYU. Mohammad S. Najand, Associate Professor; Ph.D., Syracuse. Bruce L. Rubin, Associate Professor; Ph.D., Case Western Reserve. Bruce M. Seifert, Professor; Ph.D., Michigan. J. Taylor Sims, Professor and Dean; Ph.D., Illinois. Anusorn Singhapakdi, Associate Professor; Ph.D., Mississippi. Theodore F. Smith, Associate Professor; D.B.A., Indiana. Kenneth K. Yung, Associate Professor; Ph.D., Georgia. Michael T. Zugelder, Assistant Professor; J.D., Toledo.

Department of Economics

Vinod Agarwal, Professor; Ph.D., California, Santa Barbara. Eric E. Anderson, Associate Professor; Ph.D., Washington (Seattle). Christopher B. Colburn, Associate Professor; Ph.D., Texas A&M. Martha Hofler, Lecturer; M.A., Old Dominion. Gail E. Mullin, Professor; D.B.A., Indiana. Ann V. Schwarz-Miller, Associate Professor; Ph.D., Northwestern. Raymond S. Strangways, Professor; Ph.D., Tulane. Wayne K. Talley, Professor; Ph.D., Kentucky. Charlie G. Turner, Associate Professor; Ph.D., Harvard. Gilbert R. Yochum, Professor; Ph.D., West Virginia.

Department of Information Systems and Decision Sciences

Alireza Ardalan, Professor and Associate Dean; Ph.D., Arizona. Jimmie Carraway, Senior Lecturer; M.B.A., Old Dominion. David P. Cook, Assistant Professor; Ph.D., Kentucky. Samuel F. Coppage, Associate Professor; Ph.D., NYU. Edward M. Cross, Professor; D.B.A., George Washington. William H. Crouch, Associate Professor; Ph.D., Northern Colorado. Fred W. Granger Jr., Associate Professor; Ph.D., LSU. Joan Mann, Assistant Professor; Ph.D., Georgia. Carol A. Markowski, Professor; Ph.D., Penn State. Edward P. Markowski, Professor; Ph.D., Penn State. G. Steven Rhiel, Associate Professor; Ph.D., Northern Colorado. Mukesh Rohatgi, Assistant Professor; Ph.D., Texas Tech. Marek Wermus, Associate Professor; Ph.D., Wroclaw Technical (Poland).

Graduate Center for Urban Studies and Public Administration

Gail Johnson, Assistant Professor; Ph.D., Connecticut. William Leavitt, Assistant Professor; Ph.D., Colorado. Berhanu Mengistu, Associate Professor; Ph.D., Delaware. Wolfgang Pindur, Professor; Ph.D., Wayne State. Roger S. Richman, Professor; Ph.D., NYU. Leonard L. Ruchelman, Professor; Ph.D., Columbia.

Students on the campus of Old Dominion University.

The addition of azaleas and shrubs decorate the east side of Chandler Hall.

OREGON GRADUATE INSTITUTE OF SCIENCE & TECHNOLOGY

Department of Management in Science and Technology

Programs of Study

The Department of Management in Science and Technology (MST) offers graduate study leading to the degree of Master of Science in Management (nonthesis) or a six-course certificate program. Classes for working professionals are offered on an individual basis as a part-time degree study program, with most classes being offered on a Friday evening/Saturday day format for the convenience of working professionals. Taking two courses per quarter, four quarters per year, allows one to finish within two years. Up to four years are allowed for completion of the degree program, with a fifth year available upon petition to the EPC. Attendance may be waived for one or more terms, upon petition, to allow time for commitments at work, such as major business trips or new product line rollouts. Up to four courses may be taken on an individual basis before application for admission to the degree program must be made. A full-time program is being created for the convenience of international professionals who wish to study in this degree program and want to enter the U.S. on a student visa. Full-time study requires some travel to other locations for additional classes.

The department currently consists of 3 full-time faculty members and 12 adjunct faculty members. All faculty members have extensive industrial experience, as well as strong academic credentials.

Research Facilities

The Diack Library is located in the Administration Building on the Oregon Graduate Institute (OGI) campus. The collection includes approximately 11,000 books and more than 450 serial titles. The library's catalog, SADICAT (SAmuel DIack CAT), is available online. The library's Web pages are convenient links for locating books and journal articles and going to the Engineering Village or Environmental Routenet, among other functions. In addition, the Institute has CD-ROM databases available only on the library's computers. The library provides electronic access to many science, technology, and business-related databases through the Internet via PORTALS, FirstSearch, CSA/IDS, and other software providers. PORTALS is a cooperative endeavor in the Portland metropolitan area. Its purpose is to provide improved library and information services. As a member of PORTALS, the Diack Library has access to online library catalogs, online databases, gateways to the Internet, and rapid interlibrary loans.

Financial Aid

Because of the part-time nature of the program, there are few financial aid programs available to students. However, as most of the students in the program are already working, many have education benefits programs available to them. In view of this factor, OGI has established a deferred-payment plan, which consists of a promissory note due after the end of the term. The student pays a nominal fee of $75 per credit hour and signs a personal promissory note for the remainder of the tuition. This note is due thirty days after the issuance of grades for the term, thus ensuring that the student has sufficient time to turn in his or her grades and receive the reimbursement before the due date of the promissory note.

Full- or part-time M.S. or Ph.D. students who are U.S. citizens or permanent residents may apply for low-interest student loans. Full- or part-time M.S. or Ph.D. students who are U.S. citizens may apply for the Federal Work-Study Program. Application forms for Stafford Loans and information about Federal Work-Study may be obtained from the Office of Student Services.

Cost of Study

Tuition for 1998–99 for a part-time program is $425 per credit hour, or $4250 per academic quarter. A 3-credit class is $1275, and a 4-credit class is $1700 (9 or more credit hours are considered full-time).

Living and Housing Costs

Generally, MST students are already working in the area and have housing established. All graduate students live off campus, and monthly rent for apartments ranges from $550 to $800. More housing information is available from the Office of Student Services.

Student Group

Approximately 65 students are pursuing the M.S. in Management degree program, with another 60 taking individual courses or taking part in the certificate program. Almost 98 percent of MST students are currently working full-time, and 20 percent are women. The average age is 36, with approximately nine years of working experience. International students were first accepted into the MST program in fall 1997.

Location

The Oregon Graduate Institute is located in the beautiful Pacific Northwest, which provides a very enjoyable setting for study. OGI is 12 miles west of downtown Portland and just 60 miles from the famous Oregon coast or from excellent downhill and cross-country skiing on Mount Hood.

The Institute

The Oregon Graduate Institute is a private, graduate-only institute dedicated to contemporary scientific research and education and business education and research. Founded in 1963, OGI combines the vigorous research emphasis of a large university with the personal interaction and collaboration characteristics of a small research institute.

Applying

M.S. applications are accepted at any term of the year. Required admissions materials include three letters of recommendation and transcripts of all previous college work. An undergraduate degree is assumed. A GMAT score of 500 is required of anyone whose undergraduate GPA is less than 3.0. TOEFL results are required of those applicants whose native language is not English, who have not graduated from a school whose primary teaching language is English, or who have not worked for a company whose primary business language is English for at least two years. A minimum TOEFL score of 650 is required for admission into the program.

Correspondence and Information

Director of Admissions
Office of Academic and Student Services
Oregon Graduate Institute
P.O. Box 91000
Portland, Oregon 97291-1000
Telephone: 503-690-1027
800-685-2423 (toll-free)
E-mail: admissions@admin.ogi.edu
World Wide Web: http://www.ogi.edu

Victoria Anne Tyler
MST Department Administrator
Department of Management
Oregon Graduate Institute
P.O. Box 91000
Portland, Oregon 97291-1000
Telephone: 503-690-1335
E-mail: vtyler@admin.ogi.edu

Oregon Graduate Institute of Science & Technology

THE FACULTY AND THEIR RESEARCH

Fred Young Phillips, Professor and Department Head; Ph.D. (Management Science/Business Administration), Texas at Austin, 1978. Market research, marketing innovative and high-technology products, managing the new product development process, incubation and commercialization of new technologies, strategic and innovative business use of computers.

Brockett, P., et al. **(F. Phillips)**. Marketing research unification by information theoretic methods. *European J. Operations Res.* 84:310–29, 1995.

Thore, S., G. Kozmetsky, and **F. Phillips**. DEA of financial statements data: the U.S. computer industry. *J. Prod. Anal.* 5(3):229, 1994.

Phillips, F. Conditional information characterization of brand shifting in a hierarchical market structure. *J. Operational Res. Society.* 45(8):901, 1994.

Phillips, F., R. K. Srivastava, and R. S. Springer. Project valuation and scheduling with recourse. *Proceedings of PICMET 91,* the Portland International Conference on Management of Engineering and technology (IEEE Engineering Management Society) (October 1991).

Phillips, F., and B. Golany. A heuristic for estimating densities from data in histogram form. *Decis. Sci.* 21(4):862–81, 1990.

D. Lynne Persing, Assistant Research Professor of Management; Ph.D. (Management/Business Administration), Oregon, 1991. Management of innovation and technology, determinants and measures of high performance in intellectually intensive work in technology and science, effects of temporal structures on R & D performance.

Persing, D. L. Research scientists and the temporal parameters of intellectual work. *Conference of the Institute of Behavioral and Applied Management*. Denver, Colorado, 1993.

Persing, D. L. The effects of temporal allocation information on perceptions of software engineers and evaluations of their work. *Tech. Rept.* OGI CID-093–011 (1993).

Persing, D. L. The Pitfalls of Managing Intellectual Work in Engineering and Technology. *Portland International Conference on Management of Engineering and Technology*. Portland, Oregon, 1991.

Russell, J. S., **D. L. Persing**, J. A. Dunn, and R. J. Rankin. Focusing on the selection process: a field study of the measures that influence selection decisions. *Educ. Psych. Meas.* 50:901, 1990.

Nicole Steckler, Associate Professor; Ph.D. (Organizational Behavior), Harvard, 1990.

Steckler, N., and N. Fondas. Building team leader effectiveness: a diagnostic tool. *Org. Dynamics* 23(3):20–33, 1995.

White, J., et al. **(N. Steckler)**. You just don't understand: gendered interaction and the process of doing. *J. Manage. Inquiry* 4(4):370–9, 1995.

Steckler, N. A diagnostic tool for understanding and improving team leader effectiveness. *Proceedings of the Association for Quality and Participation's 18th Annual Spring Conference*. Portland, Oregon, 1996.

Alvin Tong, Professor; Ph.D. (Electrical Engineering), Minnesota, 1967. Extensive industrial background (more than twenty-five years): such positions as Executive Vice President and Chief Operating Officer, Acer, Inc., and the first Deputy Director General of SBIP, the Science-Based Industrial Park, in Hsin-Chu, Taiwan.

Adjunct Faculty

Julian Gresser, J.D. LogosNet Corporation.
Frederic Kropp, Ph.D., Oregon. Faculty member at Bond University (Australia).
Rita Laxton, Ph.D., Witwatersrand (South Africa). KPMG Peat Marwick LLP.
Earl Littrell, Ph.D., Oregon. Faculty member at Willamette University.
S. Manivannan, Ph.D., Penn State. Consolidated Freightways.
Lyle Ochs, M.S., Oregon.
LaVonne Reimer-Young, J.D., California, Hastings Law. amicus interactive, inc.
Leslie Smid, M.S., The Leadership Institute of Seattle. Leslie Smid & Associates.
Richard Teutsch, M.S., Oregon; CPA. Arcadia Financial Group.
J. Frederick Truitt, Ph.D., Indiana. Faculty member at Willamette University.
John Wallner, M.B.A., Wisconsin. Tektronix, Inc.
G. Dale Weight, Ph.D.
Eugene Weissman, Ph.D., Case Western Reserve. Weissman Associates.

The Cooley Science Center.

PACE UNIVERSITY

Lubin School of Business Graduate Programs

Programs of Study

The Lubin School of Business of Pace University offers graduate programs of study leading to master's and doctoral degrees. Degrees awarded at the New York City campus are the Master of Business Administration in accounting, business economics, financial management, health systems management, information systems, international business, management, management science, marketing, and taxation; the Master of Science in accounting, economics, investment management, and taxation; and the Doctor of Professional Studies. Degrees awarded at the Pleasantville/Briarcliff and White Plains campuses are the Master of Business Administration in accounting, financial management, information systems, international business, management, management science, marketing, and taxation and the Master of Science in accounting and taxation. For those holding master's degrees, an 18-credit Advanced Professional Certificate in business is available. In conjunction with Pace University's School of Law, located on the White Plains campus, the Lubin School of Business offers an M.B.A./J.D. program. Special M.B.A. programs include the Executive M.B.A. Program in management, the one-year M.B.A. in finance, the dual concentration M.B.A. program, international exchange programs with schools in Heidelberg, Paris, and Grenoble, and the new M.B.A. program in Milan, Italy.

The following degree requirements must be satisfied: for the M.B.A. degree, a 36- to 61-credit course requirement; for the M.S. degree, a 33- to 67-credit course requirement; and for the doctoral program, a 57-credit course requirement, two-field written and oral qualifying examinations, and a dissertation and defense. Each candidate for the M.B.A. degree must successfully complete a minimum of 30 credits in residence at the Lubin School of Business. All requirements for the M.B.A. or M.S. degree must be completed within five years of the date of initial enrollment. The programs of study are relatively flexible to allow an ample selection of courses in keeping with a student's professional goals. Part-time study is permitted in all departments.

Research Facilities

Pace University's totally integrated online library system holds approximately 825,000 volumes and subscribes to nearly 4,000 serial publications. Electronic access to internal and external information and knowledge sources, including locally mounted CD-ROM databases, online retrieval systems, and the Internet, is available. The Pace libraries annually contract with Dialog, BRS, LEXIS-NEXIS, and Dow Jones/News Retrieval to access statistical, bibliographic, directory, and full-text databases that cover all major subjects. The University computing network provides access to a range of both mainframe and microcomputing hardware and software. Currently, more than 250 computers are located in academic computing facilities. Pace University's wide-area network (Pace Net) can be accessed from labs, dormitory rooms, and offices. Computing facilities housed in the Chase Computer Center are for the exclusive use of Lubin students and faculty members. The Lubin School of Business's Center for Applied Research, Center for Global Financial Markets, Center for International Business Studies, and Center for Innovation and Entrepreneurship offer students opportunities for research.

Financial Aid

A number of graduate scholarships and assistantships are available. Awards are made on the basis of outstanding academic performance, as indicated by the applicant's previous college record and standardized test scores. Assistantships are available for full- and part-time students. Graduate assistants received stipends of up to $5300 per year for 1997–98 and tuition remission for up to 24 credits. For further information, prospective students should contact the Financial Aid Office at 78 North Broadway, White Plains, New York 10603 (telephone number: 914-422-4050) or at Pace Plaza, New York, New York 10038 (telephone number: 212-346-1300).

Cost of Study

Tuition in 1998–99 is $545 per credit. A variety of deferred payment and loan options are offered.

Living and Housing Costs

Dormitory rooms cost $4520 for the 1998–99 academic year; a wide variety of rooms and apartments are also available off campus.

Student Group

Total graduate enrollment in the Lubin School of Business is approximately 2,000 and includes students from more than 350 colleges and universities.

Location

Pace University has three campuses, one in New York City and two in Westchester County. The Civic Center campus, a self-contained educational complex in lower Manhattan at City Hall Park, serves the adjacent financial, business, and governmental community and provides access to the nation's most significant cultural resources. Pace's new state-of-the-art Midtown Center is located on Fifth Avenue, in proximity to Grand Central Station. The beautiful Pleasantville/Briarcliff campus is in a rural setting. The campus in White Plains is in a major metropolitan satellite area. The Graduate Center is located in the heart of the White Plains business district.

The University

Founded in 1906, Pace University is a private, nonsectarian, coeducational institution. In 1948, Pace Institute became Pace College; in 1973, the New York State Board of Regents approved a charter change to designate Pace a university. Founded in 1958, the Graduate School became a separate school in 1963 and was expanded to Pace in Pleasantville in 1968 and to the White Plains campus in 1975. In 1977, the Graduate School was reorganized to form the Graduate School of Business. In 1980, the Graduate School of Business and the Undergraduate School of Business merged to form the Lubin School of Business. The Lubin School of Business is accredited by AACSB–The International Association for Management Education. Pace University is chartered by the Board of Regents and accredited by the Middle States Association of Colleges and Schools and other academic and professional bodies.

Applying

Admission is open to qualified recipients of bachelor's degrees in any field from accredited undergraduate institutions. All applicants for the M.B.A., M.S., and doctoral programs are required to take the Graduate Management Admission Test. Evaluation of applicants is based upon capacity for scholarship as indicated by the undergraduate record, class rank, previous graduate study (if any), GMAT scores, letters of recommendation, career objectives, and other available information. The application fee is $60. Application deadlines are August 1 for fall, December 1 for spring, and May 1 for the summer session.

The Lubin School of Business welcomes applications from graduates of colleges or universities in other countries. Applicants whose native language is not English are required to submit TOEFL scores.

Correspondence and Information

New York City campus:
Office of Graduate Admission
Pace University
1 Pace Plaza
New York, New York 10038
Telephone: 212-346-1531
Fax: 212-346-1585
E-mail: gradnyc@ny2.pace.edu

White Plains campus:
Office of Graduate Admission
Pace University
1 Martine Avenue
White Plains, New York 10606
Telephone: 914-422-4283
Fax: 914-422-4287
E-mail: gradwp@ny2.pace.edu

Pace University

THE FACULTY

Basheer Ahmed, Professor Emeritus in Residence, Management Science; Ph.D., Texas A&M.
Peter Allan, Professor of Management; Ph.D., NYU.
Lewis Altfest, Associate Professor of Finance; Ph.D., CUNY Graduate Center.
Uzo Anakwe, Assistant Professor of Management; Ph.D., Drexel.
Walter Antognini, Associate Professor of Taxation; LL.M., NYU.
Verne S. Atwater, Professor Emeritus in Residence, Finance; Ph.D., NYU.
Vincent Barrella, Associate Professor of Taxation; LL.M., NYU.
Arnold Berman, Professor of Accounting; LL.M., NYU.
Elayn K. Bernay, Professor Emeritus in Residence, Marketing; Ph.D., CUNY Graduate Center.
Vasanthakumar Bhat, Associate Professor of Management Science; Ph.D., Yale.
Stephen Blank, Professor of International Business; Ph.D., Harvard.
Larry Bridwell, Associate Professor of Management; Ph.D., CUNY, Baruch.
Roberta Cable, Professor of Accounting; Ph.D., Columbia.
Robert Cangemi, Professor of Management; Ph.D., NYU.
John Carter, Professor of Management Science; Ph.D., Columbia.
Arthur L. Centonze, Associate Professor of Economics and Dean; Ph.D., NYU.
Kam C. Chan, Associate Professor of Accounting; Ph.D., South Carolina.
Navin Chopra, Associate Professor of Finance and Economics; Ph.D., Michigan.
William J. Coffey, Professor Emeritus in Residence, Accounting; Ph.D., NYU.
Robert Dennehy, Professor of Management; Ph.D., NYU.
Joseph C. DiBenedetto, Professor of Accounting; J.D., Brooklyn Law.
Bairj Donabedian, Associate Professor of Accounting; Ph.D., Columbia.
John Dory, Associate Professor of Management; D.B.A., Harvard.
Hubert J. Dwyer, Professor of Management Science; Ph.D., NYU.
Alan B. Eisner, Assistant Professor of Management; Ph.D., NYU.
Samir El-Gazzar, Professor of Accounting; Ph.D., CUNY, Baruch.
Ronald W. Filante, Associate Professor of Finance; Ph.D., Purdue.
Phillip Finn, Associate Professor of Accounting; M.S., Columbia.
John E. Flaherty, Professor Emeritus in Residence, Management; Ph.D., NYU.
Anne Marie Francesco, Associate Professor of Management; Ph.D., Ohio State.
William C. Freund, Professor of Economics; Ph.D., Columbia.
Rosario J. Girasa, Associate Professor of Law; Ph.D., Fordham.
Barry Gold, Associate Professor of Management; Ph.D., Columbia.
Pradeep Gopalakrishna, Associate Professor of Marketing; Ph.D., North Texas.
James Gould, Professor of Marketing; Ph.D., Cornell.
James Hall, Associate Professor of Management; Ph.D., Chicago.
P. F. Hayek, Associate Professor of International Business; Ph.D., Columbia.
Patricia Healy, Associate Professor of Accounting; M.B.A., Rutgers.
Peter Hoefer, Professor of Management Science and Associate Dean and Director of Graduate Programs; Ph.D., CUNY Graduate Center.
Robert Isaak, Professor of International Business; Ph.D., NYU.
Rudolph Jacob, Professor of Accounting; Ph.D., NYU.
Walter Joyce, Professor of Legal Studies; LL.M., Fordham.
Albert Kalter, Professor of Taxation; LL.M., NYU.
Surendra K. Kaushik, Professor of Finance; Ph.D., Boston University.
Sara L. Keck, Associate Professor of Management; Ph.D., Columbia.
Warren Keegan, Professor of International Business; D.B.A., Harvard.
Bertram Kessler, Associate Professor of Taxation; LL.M., NYU.
Eric Kessler, Assistant Professor of Management; Ph.D., Rutgers.
John D. Knopf, Assistant Professor of Finance; Ph.D., NYU.
Chua-hua Kuei, Associate Professor of Management Science; Ph.D., CUNY Baruch.
Maurice Larrain, Associate Professor of Finance; Ph.D., Columbia.
Louis Laucirica, Executive in Residence, Management; M.B.A., Pace.
John Lee, Schaeberle Professor of Accounting; Ph.D., LSU.
Wei-Lin Liu, Assistant Professor of Finance; Ph.D., Florida.
Raymond H. Lopez, Professor of Finance; Ph.D., NYU.
Christian Madu, Professor of Management Science; Ph.D., CUNY, Baruch.
Edmund Mantell, Professor of Finance; Ph.D., Pennsylvania.
Ira Morrow, Associate Professor of Management; Ph.D., NYU.
Bernard Newman, Professor of Accounting; Ph.D., NYU.
Lawrence Newman, Professor of Taxation; S.J.D., New York Law.
Susanne O'Callaghan, Assistant Professor of Accounting; Ph.D., Cincinnati.
Mary Ellen Oliverio, Professor of Accounting; Ph.D., Columbia.
Robert H. Parks, Professor of Finance; Ph.D., Pennsylvania.
J. Marion Posey, Professor of Accounting; Ph.D., Arkansas.
Allan M. Rabinowitz, Professor of Accounting; M.B.A., NYU.
Raymond Reisig, Assistant Professor of Accounting; M.B.A., Pace.
Menahem Rosenberg, Visiting Assistant Professor of Finance and Economics; Ph.D., CUNY Graduate Center.
James Russell, Professor of Management and Associate Dean and Director of Undergraduate Programs; Ph.D., NYU.
Joseph Salerno, Associate Professor of Economics; Ph.D., Rutgers.
Dennis Sandler, Associate Professor of Marketing; Ph.D., NYU.
Lewis Schier, Professor of Accounting; Ph.D., NYU.
Susan Schor, Associate Professor of Management; Ph.D., Massachusetts.
Lewis Seagull, Professor of Marketing; Ph.D., Chicago.
Barnard Seligman, Professor Emeritus in Residence, Finance; Ph.D., NYU.
Kaustav Sen, Assistant Professor of Accounting; Ph.D., Rutgers.
Fred Silverman, Professor of Management Science; Ph.D., Columbia.
Michael Szenberg, Professor of Economics; Ph.D., CUNY Graduate Center.
Charles Tang, Assistant Professor of Accounting; Ph.D., CUNY Baruch.
John L. B. Teall, Associate Professor of Finance; Ph.D., NYU.
Pelis Thottathil, Professor of Finance; Ph.D., Columbia.
Daniel Tinkelman, Assistant Professor of Accounting; Ph.D., NYU.
Martin Topol, Professor of Marketing; Ph.D., CUNY Graduate Center.
Alan Tucker, Associate Professor of Finance; Ph.D, Florida State.
Michael Ulinski, Assistant Professor of Accounting; Ph.D., NYU.
Robert Vambery, Professor of International Business; Ph.D., Columbia.
Andrew Varanelli, Professor of Management; Ph.D., Rutgers.
Terry Vavra, Associate Professor of Marketing; Ph.D., Illinois.
P. V. Viswanath, Associate Professor of Finance; Ph.D., Chicago.
Thomas Webster, Assistant Professor of Economics; Ph.D., CUNY Graduate Center.
Ellen S. Weisbord, Associate Professor of Management; Ph.D., CUNY Graduate Center.
William Welty, Professor of Management; Ph.D., NYU.
Janice Winch, Assistant Professor of Management Science; Ph.D., Rutgers.
Leon Winer, Professor of Marketing; Ph.D., Columbia.
Kathryn Winsted, Assistant Professor of Marketing; Ph.D., Colorado State.
Kevin Wynne, Associate Professor of Finance; Ph.D., Fordham.
Philip K. Y. Young, Professor of Economics; Ph.D., NYU.
Jack Yurkiewicz, Professor of Management Science; Ph.D., Yale.
Robert P. Zwicker, Assistant Professor of Accounting; Ed.D., Bridgeport.

PEPPERDINE UNIVERSITY

The George L. Graziadio School of Business and Management
Malibu Graduate Business Programs

Programs of Study

The George L. Graziadio School of Business and Management offers full-time programs leading to the degrees of Master of Business Administration (M.B.A.) and Master of International Business (M.I.B.). A joint program culminating in both the M.B.A. and Juris Doctor (J.D.) is also offered. Combined, these programs constitute the full-time Graduate Business Programs.

The M.B.A. is designed to provide students with a working knowledge of business administration and management. The one-year, 48-unit program is geared toward students who have completed the necessary business prerequisites and have a minimum of two years of professional work experience. The two-year, 60-unit program includes an opportunity for a summer internship, which is strongly encouraged, and/or the option to study abroad for a trimester. Both M.B.A. programs offer concentrations in marketing and finance.

Students in the M.I.B. program enter either the French, German, or Spanish track. The M.I.B. degree provides students with the management tools, cultural and global understanding, and language skills necessary for a successful international business career. The first year consists of an international business curriculum and intensive language study at the Malibu campus. During the second year, students travel to Montpellier, Frankfurt, or Monterrey to complete their course work and an internship.

Research Facilities

Students have access to a variety of library sources, including Payson Library and the School of Law Library at Malibu, Pepperdine University Library in Culver City, and reference centers throughout southern California. Several computer databases are available in the centers for researching journal articles and reference information. Library materials are listed in the online catalog that is accessible from home or office with appropriate equipment and software. E-mail and Internet access are also available for all students.

Financial Aid

Financial aid is available to qualified students enrolled in a program at the School. The Graziadio School offers financial aid through merit-based scholarships and graduate assistantships. Applicants are reviewed on the basis of academic and professional experience. The University participates in state and federal financial aid programs administered through the Financial Aid Office. In addition, limited loan funds are available through the School. Candidates are selected for these resources on the basis of academic achievement and financial need.

Cost of Study

Tuition is $11,025 per trimester for the 1998–99 academic year. The one-year M.B.A. program consists of a total of three consecutive trimesters. Both the two-year M.B.A. and the M.I.B. consist of two trimesters per year. A minitrimester should be added for the M.I.B. program at the end of the first year.

Living and Housing Costs

On-campus housing costs are $2500–$3600 per trimester for the 1998–99 academic year. Most students choose to live off campus in the surrounding areas, spending $400–$650 per person a month for rent. Additional costs include food, books, supplies, and insurance. M.I.B. students are also responsible for transportation costs to and from Europe or Mexico.

Student Group

Each year, the Malibu Graduate Business Programs enroll approximately 125 new students with diverse backgrounds from all regions of the world. About 75 students enroll in the two-year program, 20 in the one-year program, and 30 in the M.I.B. program. The average class size is 22 students.

Location

Nestled in the Santa Monica mountains and overlooking the Pacific Ocean in Malibu, Pepperdine's campus is located just 35 miles northwest of downtown Los Angeles. The economy of southern California is as varied as its population, thriving in the areas of banking, agribusiness, high technology, and entertainment. A primary focus of the School revolves around providing students with the chance to take advantage of the rich opportunities afforded by the area through practicum and internship experiences.

The University and The School

Founded in 1937, Pepperdine University presents a unique combination of academic excellence and a strong emphasis on values. It is an independent institution that enrolls 9,500 students in five schools. The business school was established in 1969, developing its hallmark by its practical approach of teaching students ethical business concepts that are applicable in the real world. Including all programs, the School is one of the largest in the country. It was endowed as The George L. Graziadio School of Business and Management in 1996.

Applying

Application deadlines are May 1 for the two-year M.B.A. and the M.I.B. programs (September admission) and February 15 for the one-year M.B.A. program (April admission). After the deadlines, applications are reviewed on a space-available basis. A completed application is composed of an application form, a $45 fee, three essays, two recommendations, a resume, a GMAT score, and college transcripts. A minimum TOEFL score of 550 is required for students whose first language is not English. Interviews are recommended but not required.

Correspondence and Information

Director of Admission
The Graziadio School of Business and Management
Pepperdine University
24255 Pacific Coast Highway
Malibu, California 90263-4858
Telephone: 310-456-4858
800-726-9283 (toll-free within the U.S.)
E-mail: gsbmadm@pepperdine.edu
World Wide Web: http://bschool.pepperdine.edu

Pepperdine University

THE FACULTY

Steven R. Ferraro, Assistant Professor of Finance; Ph.D., LSU.
Bruce J. Hanson, Assistant Professor of Management; Ph.D., Case Western Reserve.
Michael Magasin, Associate Professor of Business Law; J.D., UCLA.
Stanley K. Mann, Associate Professor of Business Law; J.D., Colorado.
James T. Martinoff, Professor of Finance; Ph.D., USC; Ph.D., Claremont; M.D., Bulgaria.
Bob Namvar, Assistant Professor of Economics; Ph.D., California, Riverside.
John D. Nicks Jr., Professor of Quantitative Methods; Ph.D., Oregon.
Fred A. Petro, Professor of Accounting; Ph.D., Arkansas; CMA.
Margaret E. Phillips, Assistant Professor of Organization and Management; Ph.D., UCLA.
Joanne C. Preston, Professor of Organization Development; Ph.D., LSU.
John E. Richardson, Associate Professor of Management; D.Min., Fuller Theological Seminary.
David M. Smith, Assistant Professor of Economics; Ph.D., Michigan State.
William Smith, Associate Professor of Marketing; Ph.D., North Carolina at Chapel Hill.
Darrol Stanley, Professor of Finance and Accounting; D.B.A., USC.
Wayne L. Strom, Professor of Behavioral Science; Ph.D., UCLA.
Nikolai Wasilewski, Associate Professor of Strategy; Ph.D., NYU.
W. Bradley Zehner, Assistant Professor of Business Strategy; Ph.D., Claremont.

The George L. Graziadio School of Business and Management, with a mountain landscape overlooking the Pacific Ocean, is located on the main campus of Pepperdine University in the coastal community of Malibu, California.

PLYMOUTH STATE COLLEGE

of the University System of New Hampshire

Master of Business Administration Degree Program

Program of Study

Plymouth State College offers Master of Business Administration program sequences for students whose undergraduate major was in business or another discipline. Building on a firm base of business knowledge, the master's degree program extends and refines a student's business proficiency through a series of theoretical and substantive courses. Working with faculty members who have had experience in business, industry, and government, students can tailor their own program by selecting courses from a wide variety of business and business-related electives.

There are seven M.B.A. centers (Plymouth, Conway, Hanover, Keene, Manchester, Portsmouth, and Rochester, New Hampshire) with coordinated schedules for part-time study on a quarter calendar. A student with an undergraduate degree in business may earn the 36-credit degree at the Plymouth center by attending three consecutive quarters (fall, winter, spring) full-time. Those who need preparatory work may require additional time to complete the program. All students, part-time and full-time, have six years in which to complete the degree.

Plymouth State College, through its Department of Business, is accredited by the Association of Collegiate Business Schools and Programs.

Research Facilities

Research in the field of business management is facilitated by the rapidly expanding holdings of the Lamson Library. In addition to 250,000 volumes and 475,000 units of filmed and recorded materials, the library houses a remote-access system for retrieval of appropriate audiovisual programs. Formal library support services are supplemented by a business department collection and by interlibrary agreements with other institutions. Computer resources available allow communication with other institutions throughout the country. In addition, there are microcomputers, which include IBM and Macintosh PCs, available in public clusters.

Financial Aid

Graduate scholarships and assistantships are reserved for full-time graduate students. Additional financial aid is offered in the form of tuition grants and loans; a work-study plan may be arranged. Resident hall positions are also available to graduate students.

Cost of Study

Tuition in 1998–99 for students at all centers is $819 per course for New Hampshire residents and $897 per course for nonresidents. This includes all fees.

Living and Housing Costs

Graduate students may live in single rooms at approximately $5000 per year in 1998–99 and double rooms at approximately $4800 per year in Plymouth State College dormitories, with meal service included. Apartments are available on campus for married and single students. Off-campus apartments vary widely in cost.

Student Group

Plymouth State College has a student population of about 4,200 undergraduate and about 50 full-time and 1,100 part-time graduate students in 1998–99. Approximately 45 percent of Plymouth's total student population comes from out of state. The M.B.A. program is expanding at both on-campus and off-campus centers. Students are mostly New Hampshire residents, although there is a small out-of-state and international representation.

Location

Plymouth is situated in the Lakes and White Mountains region of New Hampshire. The scenic beauty of the area is breathtaking, and the surrounding countryside is a center for extensive recreational activities during the summer and winter. The town of Plymouth has a year-round population of 6,000, with a seasonal increase of twice that number. Plymouth is approximately 2 hours north of Boston via Interstate 93 and only 40 minutes from the capital city of Concord.

The College

Plymouth State College is a unit of the University System of New Hampshire. Founded in 1871, the College has undergone many changes and has shifted its role from that of a normal school, and later a state teachers college, to that of a multipurpose institution. It offers the Master of Education and the Master of Business Administration, as well as associate and bachelor's degrees.

Applying

Applications for the M.B.A. program are accepted throughout the year. Applicants must have a bachelor's degree. Three letters of recommendation, official transcripts, and an acceptable GMAT score are also required. To be considered for a graduate scholarship or assistantship, students should submit all materials as early as possible. An interview with the M.B.A. program director is desirable.

Correspondence and Information

Colleen Brickley, M.B.A. Program Director
Karen Hammond, Assistant to the Director
Graduate Studies in Business
Plymouth State College
Plymouth, New Hampshire 03264
Telephone: 603-535-2826
800-FOR-GRAD (800-367-4723)(toll-free)
Fax: 603-535-2648
E-mail: khammond@mail.plymouth.edu
World Wide Web: http://www.plymouth.edu

Plymouth State College

THE FACULTY

Jane Babin, Associate Professor; M.B.A., Plymouth State, 1988; J.D., Franklin Pierce Law Center, 1989.
Roger Babin, Associate Professor; J.D., Boston College, 1977; M.S.T., Bentley, 1983.
Bonnie Bechard, Professor; Ed.D., Arizona State, 1987.
William Benoit, Professor; D.B.A., Nova Southeastern, 1989; CIRM.
Trent Boggess, Professor; Ph.D., Kansas, 1980.
Colleen Brickley, Instructor; M.A., New Hampshire, 1978, doctoral candidate, New Hampshire.
Paul Buck, Professor; M.S., Northeastern, 1970; CPA.
Mehmet Canlar, Professor; M.B.A., NYU, 1970; Ph.D., Hacettepe (Turkey), 1977.
Michael Couvillion, Associate Professor; M.B.A., 1975, Ph.D., 1982, Louisiana Tech.
Edward Harding, Associate Professor; M.B.A., Dartmouth, 1977; Ph.D., Massachusetts, 1989.
Soo Jang, Professor; M.B.A., Hawaii, 1970; Ph.D., Cincinnati, 1978.
David Kent, Professor; M.B.A., Northeastern, 1968; J.D., Boston College, 1971.
Frank Kopczynski, Associate Professor; M.B.A., Plymouth State, 1982; Ph.D., Union (Ohio), 1993; CPA, CMA.
David Leuser, Professor; Ph.D., New Hampshire, 1979.
Barton Macchiette, Professor; M.B.A., American, 1970; Ph.D., Union (Ohio), 1980.
Warren Mason Jr., Professor; Ed.D., Boston University, 1980.
Duncan McDougall, Professor; M.B.A., 1970, Ph.D., 1986, Harvard.
Daniel Moore, Associate Professor; M.B.A., Youngstown State, 1983; Ph.D., Drexel, 1992.
Terrence Murphy, Assistant Professor; M.B.A., Suffolk, 1969.
Abhijit Roy, Instructor; M.B.A., 1986, M.S., 1989, Arizona; doctoral candidate, Boston University.
Julian Shlager, Associate Professor; M.B.A., Babson, 1965; Ph.D., Boston College, 1972.
Richard Sparks, Associate Professor; Ph.D., Manchester (England), 1989.

Hyde Hall houses the business department.

PORTLAND STATE UNIVERSITY

School of Business Administration

Programs of Study

The M.B.A. program prepares individuals with the integrity and skills necessary to lead businesses into the future. Balancing pragmatism with theory, the M.B.A. curriculum emphasizes an integrated and systemic perspective of how business competitiveness is achieved. The themes of decision making, problem solving, managing innovation and change, quality management practices, and global competitiveness cut across the program. Careful attention is given to communication, leadership, teamwork skills, and close involvement with the business community.

The two-year, 72-quarter-credit-hour M.B.A. program is composed of five distinct elements that are designed to produce a systematic and integrated understanding of business operations. These elements are business perspective and foundation skills, business disciplines, integrated applications, a business project, and a specialization. Learning is facilitated by the use of team- and project-based learning, information and information technology, and continued exposure to the thinking and practices of world-class business firms and their leaders. The curriculum includes two 8-hour integrated courses, with each team taught by several faculty members. Students participate, individually or in teams, in an applied business project. Noncredit activities are available to help in career planning and development of computer skills.

The Master of International Management (M.I.M.) is an innovative twelve-month (August to August) full-time or two-year part-time program that places emphasis on the dynamic and rapidly growing Pacific Rim markets. The M.I.M. is a cohort program that requires 65 quarter credit hours of course work, Pacific Rim executive seminars, corporate field visits, tutorials, foreign language study, and a field study trip to China and Japan. The Master of International Management also offers a set of courses, which is designed for those with a limited academic business background, prior to entering the twelve-month program, The eight-week pre-M.I.M. program begins in late June and covers the fundamentals of business statistics, accounting, business finance, and economics.

The School of Business Administration participates in the systems science Ph.D. program, which combines the study of systems with the study of business. Students work closely with faculty members to design an individualized program of study that will give the student the needed foundation in systems, research, and two fields of business.

Research Facilities

The School of Business is located just a few minutes' walk from the downtown Portland business district. Students have access to the University's main library, which houses nearly 1 million volumes, including approximately 10,000 serial publications, a growing number of CD-ROM and online computer databases, and an extensive collection of government documents. The School of Business Administration has a special computer lab for graduate students, which is equipped with high-speed laser printers and more than twenty-five workstations. From the lab, students have access to the University's main computer, the Portland Area Library System (PORTALS), the Internet, and numerous other databases.

The Master of International Management program is located about 15 minutes from the main campus, in the midst of the "Silicon Forest." Surrounded by numerous high-technology firms and other graduate programs, students study at the Capital Center, a modern facility equipped with the latest teaching technology.

Financial Aid

The School of Business Administration offers assistance in the form of graduate assistantships and scholarships. Other forms of aid for students from the United States may be available through the University's Financial Aid Office.

Cost of Study

Tuition for 1998–99 for all full-time students enrolled in the M.B.A. program is estimated at $1956 per quarter for in-state students and $3362 for out-of-state students. Tuition for students enrolling in the full-time Master of International Management is $14,500. An additional fee is assessed for travel and other expenses incurred as part of the Asian field study.

Living and Housing Costs

Portland State University provides housing for its students through College Housing Northwest, Inc. (telephone: 800-547-8887 Ext. 4333, toll-free), a private nonprofit corporation located on the PSU campus. If students desire off-campus housing, there are many suitable residential apartments and homes within 10 minutes of the campus or the Capital Center.

Student Group

The University's total enrollment of nearly 15,000 includes about 450 students in the M.B.A. program. Approximately 25 percent of the M.B.A. students are full-time. The remaining 75 percent work in the Portland community and attend evening M.B.A. classes.

Student Outcomes

Graduates from the M.B.A. program typically pursue careers with private, public, or not-for-profit organizations. Currently, 75 percent of the M.B.A. students are enrolled in the part-time M.B.A. program; thus, they continue to work and/or reside in the Portland or southwest Washington areas. Approximately 90 percent of the graduating M.B.A. students take placement in the Pacific Northwest region of the United States.

Location

Portland State University is located at the center of a dynamic community. The Portland metropolitan area, home to approximately 1.5 million people, is ideally situated only 90 minutes from the ocean beaches and mountain slopes. With its excellent parks, cultural facilities, transportation systems, and cityscape, Portland is one of the finest cities in the United States.

The University

Founded in 1946, the PSU campus is a cityscape designed to meet students' needs. Occupying forty buildings in a 36-acre area, the campus is built around the Park Blocks, a greenway area reserved for pedestrians and bicyclists.

The University provides a large variety of activities, ranging from the many musical organizations, the University Theater, and the Multicultural Center to football, basketball, baseball, and track.

Applying

Application deadlines for the M.B.A. program for international students are March 1 for fall admission and July 1 for winter admission; for domestic students, the dates are April 1 for fall admission and August 1 for winter admission. The Master of International Management program has a deadline of April 1 for domestic students and March 1 for international students. The Graduate Management Admission Test (GMAT) is required for admission to the graduate program. International applicants must submit results from the Test of English as a Foreign Language (TOEFL).

Correspondence and Information

Ms. Kelly Diamond
Director of Student Services
School of Business Administration
Portland State University
P.O. Box 751
Portland, Oregon 97207-0751

Telephone: 503-725-3712
Fax: 503-725-5850
E-mail: kellyd@sba.pdx.edu
World Wide Web: http://www.capital.osshe.edu/ojpsb/
http://www.sba.pdx.edu/

Portland State University

THE FACULTY

Accounting
George Battistel, Ph.D., Oregon.
Darrell Brown, Ph.D., Utah.
Anne L. Christensen, Ph.D., Utah.
Michael C. Henton, M.B.A., Oregon; CPA.
H. Thomas Johnson, Ph.D., Wisconsin.
Raymond N. Johnson, Ph.D., Oregon; CPA.
William Kenny, M.S., Golden Gate; J.D., Gonzaga; CPA.
Donna R. Philbrick, Ph.D., Cornell.
Rodney Rogers, Ph.D., Case Western Reserve.
Richard Sapp, Ph.D., Houston; CPA.
Ellen Slapikas, M.B.A., Alaska; CPA, CMA.
Richard Visse, Ph.D., Arizona State; CPA.
Donald A. Watne, Ph.D., Berkeley; CPA.

Finance and Law
Roger S. Ahlbrandt, Dean, School of Business Administration; Ph.D., Washington (Seattle).
Leslie P. Anderson, Ph.D., Wisconsin.
Beverly Fuller, Ph.D., Virginia Tech.
Janet Hamilton, Ph.D., Michigan State.
Chi-Cheng Hsia, Ph.D., UCLA.
John Oh, Ph.D., Virginia.
Shafiqur Rahman, Ph.D., Illinois.
John W. Settle, Ph.D., Washington (Seattle).

Management and Information Systems
Hayward Andres, Ph.D., Florida State.
Talya N. Bauer, Ph.D., Purdue.
Steven N. Brenner, D.B.A., Harvard.
Leland Buddress, B.S., Berkeley.
Alan M. Cabelly, Ph.D., Washington (Seattle).
Henry D. Crockett, Ph.D., Texas.
Robert W. Eder, D.B.A., Colorado.
David Gerbing, Ph.D., Michigan State.
Lewis N. Goslin, Ph.D., Washington (Seattle).
William A. Manning, Ph.D., Oregon.
Earl A. Molander, Ph.D., Berkeley.
Alan R. Raedels, Ph.D., Purdue.
David Raffo, Ph.D., Carnegie Mellon.
Mary S. Taylor, Ph.D., Washington (Seattle).
Pamela Tierny, Ph.D., Cincinnati.
Ellen L. West, Associate Dean of Undergraduate Programs; Ph.D., Oregon State.

Marketing
Scott A. Dawson, Associate Dean of Graduate Programs; Ph.D., Arizona.
Thomas R. Gillpatrick, Ph.D., Oregon.
Edward L. Grubb, Ph.D., Washington (Seattle).
Robert R. Harmon, Ph.D., Arizona State.
Joanne M. Klebba, Ph.D., Minnesota.
Alan J. Resnik, Ph.D., Arizona State.
Bruce L. Stern, Ph.D., Arizona State.
L. P. Douglas Tseng, Ph.D., Texas.

Students can enjoy Portland's beautiful waterfront.

PROVIDENCE COLLEGE

Graduate Business Program

Program of Study

The Graduate Business Program offers a program of graduate study leading to a degree of Master of Business Administration (M.B.A.) that consists of practical courses useful in the workplace. Every course is planned so that it will be a meaningful learning experience beneficial to the individual in his or her career. Many of the courses have a quantitative emphasis with computer applications. Courses are held at night from Monday through Thursday. One or two electives are offered on Saturday mornings. While M.B.A. programs are often criticized for producing graduates who master technique but lack substance, the Providence College program gives due consideration to the social purpose and responsibilities as well as to the technical aspects of business. In short, Providence College recognizes the critically important challenge of "humanizing" business administration programs.

The Providence College M.B.A. Program fosters an interdisciplinary approach to the problems facing Rhode Island and American businesses. The faculty includes professors not only from the business department but also from the political science, sociology, psychology, and economics departments. In addition, about a third of the courses are taught by adjunct faculty members who bring to their classes a wealth of current, practical business experience.

The M.B.A. Program requires a total of twelve to nineteen courses, depending upon the student's undergraduate background. Theses, while not required, are encouraged; they may be purely academic, but practical, applied topics are also welcomed. The M.B.A. Program has links with local businesses and with the state government for the promotion of research projects and internships.

Research Facilities

M.B.A. students have access to numerous computers, including large mainframe IBM 370s via telecommunications links with Brown University and the University of Rhode Island, an IBM 4341, a microcomputer network consisting of 100 terminals linked to a dozen 40-megabyte CompuPro System 816s (CP/M 86 and CP/M 80), and about fifty IBM PCs and compatibles (MS-DOS). The College possesses the entire current public-domain software libraries for CP/M and MS-DOS.

The Phillips Memorial Library holds 280,000 volumes in open stacks and has seating accommodations for 1,000 students. The library is a member of the Consortium of Rhode Island Academic and Research Libraries (which includes the libraries of Brown University, the University of Rhode Island, and the Naval War College), making the resources of most of the libraries of the state available to Providence College students. The library is also a member of the New England Library Network (NELINET) and the Online Computer Library Center (OCLC), which has 3,800 member libraries and a database containing more than 10.6 million records. Through interlibrary loan, most of the resources of these libraries are available to Providence College students.

Financial Aid

Nearly all M.B.A. students have full-time employment, and about half receive financial aid from their employer. Work-study opportunities are available through the Office of Financial Aid.

Cost of Study

For the 1998–99 academic year, tuition is $729 per 3-credit course. The total tuition cost for the M.B.A. Program ranges from $8748 (for twelve courses) to $13,851 (for nineteen courses). The cost of books averages $85 per course. The graduation fee is $125.

Living and Housing Costs

No College housing is available for M.B.A. students, but there is an adequate supply of rental accommodations in the Providence College area. While prices vary widely depending upon quality, a two-bedroom apartment in the area rents for approximately $500 to $700 per month.

Student Group

Ninety percent of the 300 M.B.A. students work full-time. The 1998 graduating class of 56 students averaged 31 years of age and consisted of 34 men and 22 women. More than 90 percent of the entering students score above 1000 points on the AACSB–The International Association for Management Education criteria (200 times the undergraduate GPA plus the GMAT score). More than 90 percent of the students are from Rhode Island and nearby Massachusetts and Connecticut, but more and more students are being attracted from other regions of the United States and from other nations; in the past few years, students have been accepted from Canada, Ecuador, England, India, Indonesia, Ireland, Japan, Pakistan, the Panama Canal Zone, the People's Republic of China, Philippines, Spain, Sri Lanka, Switzerland, Thailand, and Turkey.

Location

Providence College's beautiful 105-acre campus is located about a mile from the state capitol and 3 miles from the center of Providence, Rhode Island. The College enjoys the advantages of an atmosphere far removed from the traffic and commerce of the metropolitan area, yet it provides easy access to the many cultural attractions of a city that is not only the capital of one of the original thirteen states but also the location of a variety of institutions of higher learning.

The College

Providence College is primarily a four-year college of the liberal arts and sciences with an undergraduate enrollment of approximately 3,600 men and women. It is conducted under the auspices of the Order of Preachers of the Province of St. Joseph, commonly known as the Dominicans. Founded in 1917 under an Act of Incorporation approved by the General Assembly of the State of Rhode Island, the College states in its charter: "No person shall be denied any of the privileges, honors or degrees of said college on account of the religious opinions he may entertain." Providence College is a coeducational, equal opportunity institution and is duly accredited by the New England Association of Schools and Colleges. It is also a member of AACSB–The International Association for Management Education and, wherever feasible, adheres to its principles.

Applying

Application materials may be obtained from the M.B.A. Program director. Applications are considered throughout the year, and students may enter the program in any semester. Full semesters start in September and January, and two 5-week semesters start in May and July. Detailed application instructions are contained in the Graduate School catalog. Students must submit the completed application form, the application fee ($40), two letters of reference (preferably one academic and one professional), and an official undergraduate transcript from a regionally accredited U.S. college or university (or, if a foreign institution, one recognized by the American Council on Education). Applicants are required to take the GMAT prior to admission to the M.B.A. Program. Applicants whose native language is not English are required to take the TOEFL.

Correspondence and Information

M.B.A. Office
Koffler Hall, Room 113
Providence College
Providence, Rhode Island 02918-0001
Telephone: 401-865-2333
Fax: 401-865-2978

Providence College

THE FACULTY AND THEIR RESEARCH

Deirdre Bird, Adjunct Professor; Ph.D., Purdue. International marketing.
Helen M. Caldwell, Assistant Professor; Ph.D., Connecticut. Advertising, international marketing, promotion strategy.
Ronald P. Cerwonka, Professor Emeritus; Ph.D., Missouri. Financial analysis, theory of finance.
Joseph M. D'Adamo, Assistant Professor; M.B.A., Indiana. Management accounting, financial accounting theory.
Clement DeMayo, Associate Professor; Ph.D., Clark. Statistical concepts.
Norman Desmarais, Associate Professor; M.B.A., Providence. Computer systems.
Francis A. Donahue, Adjunct Instructor; M.P.A., Rhode Island. Health-care delivery systems, seminar in health-care.
Cemal A. Ekin, Associate Professor; Ph.D., Academy of Economics and Commercial Sciences (Turkey). Marketing theory, management information systems.
Richard B. Goldstein, Professor; Ph.D., Brown. Statistics, management information systems.
Peter S. Goodrich, Associate Professor; Ph.D., Manchester; CMA. International accounting, the politics of information.
Carol A. Hartley, Assistant Professor; M.B.A., Rhode Island; CPA. EDP audit.
Linda F. Jamieson, Associate Professor; Ph.D., Texas. Research methodology.
John R. King, Associate Professor; M.A., Boston College. Statistics, management information systems.
Hugh F. Lena, Professor; Ph.D., Connecticut. Organizational behavior.
MaryJane Lenon, Assistant Professor; Ph.D., Connecticut. Urban economics, macroeconomic theory.
Stephen G. Misovich, Professor; Ph.D., Connecticut. Human resource management, personnel psychology.
Francine Newth, Assistant Professor; D.B.A., Nova Southeastern. Business policy, global strategic alliances, international business.
Francis T. O'Brien, Associate Professor; M.A., Boston College. Collective bargaining, labor relations.
Charlotte G. O'Kelly, Professor; Ph.D., Connecticut. Women and management, sociology and management.
Vivian Okere, Assistant Professor; Ph.D., Rhode Island. Econometrics, financial modeling, international finance.
George F. Sawdy, Associate Professor; Ph.D., Brown. Economics of the firm, economic theory.
John J. Shaw, Professor; D.B.A., Oklahoma. Consumer behavior, international marketing, marketing management.
Mark H. Stone, Adjunct Instructor; M.S., Boston University. Computer systems, advanced topics in MIS.
Harold B. Tamule, Assistant Professor; Ph.D., Massachusetts at Amherst. Corporate finance, capital structure.
Vincent C. Trofi, Assistant Professor; Ph.D., Detroit. Business communication.
William J. Waters, Adjunct Instructor; Ph.D., Ohio State. Managed health-care systems, strategic planning in health-care, seminar in health-care.
Katherine W. Wilkicki, Assistant Professor; Ph.D., Connecticut. Not-for-profit organization, financial reporting, health-care finance.
David A. Zalewski, Assistant Professor; Ph.D., Clark. Managerial economics, international finance.

Thomas Flaherty, Ph.D., Dean of the Graduate School.

Harkins Hall, built in 1917, is the main administration building.

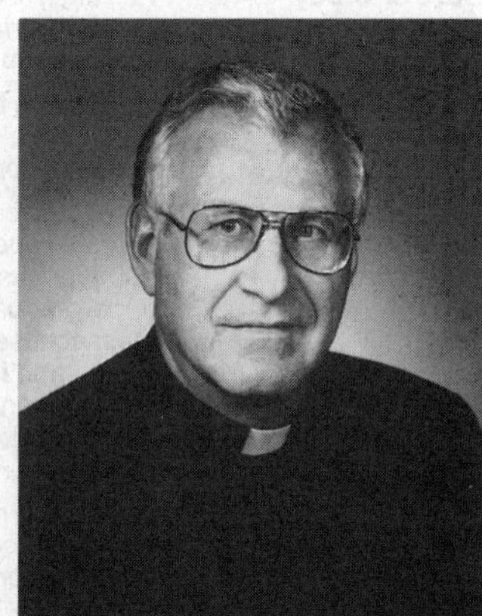

Philip A. Smith, O.P., President of Providence College.

PURDUE UNIVERSITY

Krannert Graduate School of Management

Programs of Study

The Krannert programs combine the "science"—management information systems, statistics, and organizational behavior—with the "art"—creative problem solving, presentation skills, and team building—of business management. What sets Krannert graduates apart is their ability to make data-driven business decisions, combined with leadership skills and a strong work ethic. Graduates of Krannert's three master's programs are sought by recruiters in the fields of operations, corporate finance, consulting, information systems, human resource management, and marketing.

The programs emphasize fundamental management theory, case studies, teamwork, and experiential learning opportunities, including computer simulations and consulting projects. Small class size allows frequent interaction with and personal attention from faculty members. Students also learn from each other in diverse, cross-disciplinary study teams. Complementing course work, student-run organizations provide leadership opportunities, networking with executives and recruiters, and personal and professional development.

The Master of Science in Management (M.S.M.) is a two-year residential program. Students select from options in accounting, finance, human resource management, management information systems, marketing, operations, strategic management, and three interdisciplinary options: general, international, or manufacturing management. The Master of Science in Human Resource Management (M.S.H.R.M.) is a two-year residential program that combines the best of human resource management with a strong business focus. The Master of Science in Industrial Administration (M.S.I.A.) is an eleven-month residential program that allows students to earn a management degree in a condensed time span. All three programs benefit from the global reputation of Purdue University.

Research Facilities

Students benefit from Krannert's exceptional information technology infrastructure. The computer laboratories have been developed in conjunction with corporate partners such as Ameritech, AT&T, Hewlett-Packard, IBM, Microsoft, PictureTel, and SAP America. The Enterprise Integration Lab runs SAP R/3 software using real company data. Students can analyze information from all areas of a company simultaneously and see how management decisions impact the various business functions of the enterprise. The Krannert Library, with extensive online resources, is conveniently located in the same complex students attend for classes. Students and faculty members are fully connected with Internet access and e-mail, which encourages them to communicate, exchange data, and conduct research.

Financial Aid

Cash graduate awards are based on academic merit and other criteria and typically range from $2000 to $8000. Graduate awards are restricted to U.S. citizens and permanent residents. Assistantships, awarded during the second year of study, provide a monthly stipend and a partial tuition and fee remission, ranging from $8600 to $18,000 a year. Residence hall counselorships provide for room and board, a stipend for books, and a partial tuition and fee remission. All students are eligible to apply for residence hall counselorships. Federal Stafford Student Loans are available to U.S. citizens and eligible noncitizens.

Cost of Study

Estimated 1998–99 academic-year tuition for the M.S.M. and M.S.H.R.M. programs is $7176 for Indiana residents and $15,424 for nonresidents. Estimated 1998–99 tuition for the eleven-month M.S.I.A. program is $9116 for Indiana residents and $19,679 for nonresidents.

Living and Housing Costs

Per-month rentals range from $260 to $520 at the full-service graduate halls connected to the Krannert complex. On-campus apartment housing for individuals and families ranges from $390 to $490 a month and includes utilities and local telephone service. Off-campus rooms, apartments, and houses are convenient and affordable.

Student Group

Krannert students come from a wide range of undergraduate disciplines, with engineering, science, and mathematics well represented. The average age at entry is 27. Twenty-seven percent of students are women, 9 percent are members of minority groups, and 30 percent are international. GMAT scores typically range from 590 to 690; the average GPA is 3.2. Four years of work experience is the average, but motivated students without on-the-job experience should still apply.

Student Outcomes

Major recruiters include AlliedSignal, Ernst & Young, Federal Express, Ford, General Motors, Hewlett-Packard, IBM, Intel, International Paper, Price Waterhouse, Procter & Gamble, and United Technologies. Operations, finance, and consulting are the top functions; consulting, computers, and automotive are the top industries. Forty-four percent of graduates find jobs in the Midwest, 19 percent in the West, and 5 percent internationally. Preliminary averages in 1998 are $67,000 in base salary and $84,000 in total compensation.

Location

Krannert is located in a friendly college town in the heartland of America. The area economy is strong, with many job opportunities for spouses. Local schools are top rated, and neighborhoods are safe and pleasant. Summers are warm and sunny, with some snow in winter. The major metropolitan areas of Chicago and Indianapolis are conveniently reached by car.

The University and The School

Purdue University, a world-class research and teaching institution, has 35,000 students and 2,200 faculty members at West Lafayette, Indiana. In addition to management, Purdue is known for its strengths in engineering, computer science, and agriculture. Krannert, with an enrollment of less than 500 master's students, takes pride in its affiliation with these University programs as well as its corporate partnerships in providing nationally ranked and accredited master's in management programs.

Applying

Applicants must submit academic records, GMAT scores, essays, recommendations, and resumes. Campus interviews are available after applications are submitted. TOEFL scores are required of applicants from non-English-speaking countries. Admission is on a rolling basis. Students who apply by November 1 receive a decision by December 15. The international application deadline is February 1. Late applications may be accepted through May. Those interested should contact the admissions office for preview days and tour arrangements. Purdue University is an Equal Access/Equal Opportunity university.

Correspondence and Information

Ward Snearly, Director of Admissions
1310 Krannert Center, Room 104
Krannert Graduate School of Management
Purdue University
West Lafayette, Indiana 47907-1310

Telephone: 765-494-4365
Fax: 765-494-9841
E-mail: krannert_ms@mgmt.purdue.edu
World Wide Web: http://www.mgmt.purdue.edu

Purdue University

THE FACULTY AND THEIR RESEARCH

Krannert has 80 full-time management and economics faculty members who specialize in the areas of accounting, business communication, business law, economics, finance, management information systems, marketing, operations management, organizational behavior and human resources, quantitative methods, and strategic management. Those interested in more information about faculty members and their research can visit Krannert's Web site (http://www.mgmt.purdue.edu).

Krannert graduates are sought by top corporations, especially in the consulting, computer, and automotive industries.

Information technology, such as SAP R/3 enterprise integration software, is a key component of Krannert's curricula.

Students work in teams inside and outside the classroom; an outdoor challenge course is one popular team-building event.

QUINNIPIAC COLLEGE

Master of Business Administration Program

Program of Study

The School of Business offers a Master of Business Administration (M.B.A.) program that has been carefully planned to help individuals develop not only today's required technical skills but also the knowledge and conceptual base needed to meet career challenges of the year 2000 and beyond. The program is designed to develop leaders who can capitalize on opportunities, take risks, and participate actively in teams. Apart from providing training for business careers, the M.B.A. degree earned at Quinnipiac can furnish opportunities to enter or advance in professional positions in government, education, health care, and a wide variety of social services.

The program is built on a broad-based foundation of business knowledge and includes the opportunity to gain expertise in a chosen area. This knowledge is relayed to students through distinct experiences inside and outside the classroom. An integrated approach to learning is used in which faculty members and students work in teams to solve problems and develop strategies in areas such as marketing, international business, finance, computer information systems, health services administration, and management. Quinnipiac M.B.A. students also have the opportunity to analyze global concerns through an optional three-week summer session that has taken M.B.A. students to such places as Europe, Latin America, and Asia. This intensive experience includes seminars, comprehensive studies, lectures from corporate executives, and meetings with government officials.

M.B.A. students are challenged to be creative and innovative in their approach to solving problems and making decisions. Exposure to sound ethical standards and skill development in the areas of negotiation, cooperation, and interpersonal relations are an integral part of the curriculum. Graduates are action oriented and can effectively demonstrate the competencies and insights acquired at Quinnipiac.

All M.B.A. students must complete a 30-hour core curriculum. A capstone course, the Integrative Management Seminar, is also part of the core. Students who enter the program without formal business training or academic experience may need to complete a series of introductory courses. Following completion of the core curriculum, students may opt for a 6-credit thesis program involving research with a faculty adviser. This option requires 36 credits for graduation. Those pursuing thesis research develop a concentration in accounting/taxation, computer information systems, economics, finance, health administration, international business, management, or marketing. In lieu of a thesis, students may choose to take three additional courses that build on core subjects. These courses may focus on a specific concentration or cover multiple disciplines. This option requires 39 credit hours for graduation.

Students may apply for acceptance to both the Law School and the M.B.A. program and, upon completion of both programs, receive a J.D./M.B.A. degree. This specialized joint program shortens the length of time necessary to receive the degrees.

Research Facilities

The main research facilities for the M.B.A. program are the Computer Laboratories, the Research Library, and the Lender School of Business Center. A large library of the latest version of software used by business and industry is available for student use. The Research Library provides M.B.A. students with access to such databases as ABI/INFORM, LEXIS-NEXIS, and the Business Periodicals Index through CD-ROM. Online access to the Dialog database, as well as a comprehensive collection of business holdings in hard copy, is provided.

Financial Aid

The Financial Aid Office offers all M.B.A. students assistance in obtaining publicly and privately funded loans and scholarships. Graduate assistantships are available for some M.B.A. students.

Cost of Study

In 1998–99, the tuition rate for all M.B.A. students is $395 per credit hour. The tuition cost for the program is approximately $15,500. Part-time students pay a $20 registration fee each semester. Full-time students are charged a student fee of $185 for access to the student health center and athletic facilities.

Living and Housing Costs

On-campus housing is available during the summer. Privately owned housing is available near the campus. For more information concerning off-campus housing, interested students should contact the Office of Residential Life at 203-281-8666.

Student Group

There are approximately 200 students enrolled in the program; 40 percent are women. The average age is 30 years. The students represent a rich mix of backgrounds and experiences, ranging from mid- and top-level managers, beginning and veteran entrepreneurs, family and small-business owner-operators, and accomplished professionals seeking to develop business leadership competencies to recent baccalaureate recipients preparing to enter the business world. There are a small but significant number of international students enrolled in the M.B.A. program, and the College has made a firm commitment to increase the diversity in the student body.

Student Outcomes

Quinnipiac M.B.A. graduates currently hold top positions in such companies as United Technologies, Bayer Corporation, Aetna, and General Electric. On-campus recruiters include four of the "big six" accounting firms, a division of NBC in New York, Pratt & Whitney, and other regional manufacturing firms, insurance companies, banks, pharmaceutical companies, health-care organizations, and state and federal government agencies. Most School of Business graduates find positions in their fields within three months of graduation.

Location

Quinnipiac is located on a beautiful campus in Hamden, Connecticut, a suburb of New Haven. It is 30 minutes from Hartford, 1½ hours from New York City, and 2 hours from Boston.

The College

Quinnipiac enrolls 3,310 full-time undergraduates and approximately 1,800 graduate and continuing education students. The College comprises the Schools of Health Sciences, Business, Law, and Liberal Arts and the College for Adults. A dean, reporting to the provost/vice president for academic affairs, heads each of these units, and a distinguished faculty of 170 full-time members and nearly 100 adjunct members provide instruction for the programs of the College.

Applying

Students with superior intellectual and interpersonal skills are admitted. Applications from men and women of diverse educational, social, and employment backgrounds are encouraged. Neither a particular undergraduate major nor prior course work in management is required for admission. Depending on their background, students may have to take some prerequisite courses. Admission to part-time and full-time programs is rolling. The GMAT is required of all applicants.

Correspondence and Information

Graduate Admissions
Quinnipiac College
Mount Carmel Avenue
Hamden, Connecticut 06518

Telephone: 203-281-8672
Fax: 203-287-5238
E-mail: qcgradadmi@quinnipiac.edu

Quinnipiac College

THE FACULTY AND THEIR RESEARCH

Janice Ammons, Associate Professor of Accounting; Ph.D., Michigan. Cost management practices, design of cost systems at universities, accounting education.

Frank P. Bellizzi, Professor of Management; Ed.D., Massachusetts. Self-management and entrepreneurship training.

Charles M. Brooks, Assistant Professor of Marketing; Ph.D., Georgia State. Geographic information systems, retail site selection modeling, sales force management, industrial buyer-seller relationships.

David T. Cadden, Associate Professor of Management and Director of Accreditation for the School of Business; M.B.A., Ph.D., CUNY, Baruch. Expert systems, neural networks, quality controls.

Ramon Castellblanch, Assistant Professor of Health Management; M.P.P., Harvard; Ph.D., Johns Hopkins. U.S. mental health policy, local opposition to health-care corporations, U.S. health insurance legislation.

Vincent R. Celeste, Professor of Computer Information Systems; Ph.D., Polytechnic of Brooklyn. Applications of information systems in professional service firms.

Dongsae Cho, Professor of Finance; M.A.S., Ph.D., Illinois at Urbana-Champaign. Cost of capital, capital budgeting, working capital management, life insurance products, risk management.

Earl Chrysler, Professor of Information Systems and Director of the M.B.A. Program; D.B.A., USC; CCP. Group decision support systems, measuring computer programmer productivity.

William C. Clyde, Associate Professor of Finance; Ph.D., Edinburgh. Global marketing for trading pollution emissions credits, foreign exchange rate models.

Vincent F. DeAndrea, Professor of Economics; M.B.A., Ph.D., Massachusetts. Economic history.

Marlin Dearden, Professor of Health Management; D.P.H., Yale. International health, public health epidemiology.

Vincent R. Driscoll, Professor of Finance and Economics and Chair of Finance; M.B.A., NYU; Ph.D., New School. Corporate finance, economic theory.

Michael J. Everett, Assistant Professor of Economics; Ph.D., Connecticut. Industrial organization, economic history, history of economic thought.

Phillip Frese, Associate Professor of Accounting and Dean of School of Business; M.B.A., Fairleigh Dickinson; Ph.D., Drexel. Accounting in Eastern Europe.

Martin L. Gosman, Professor of Accounting; M.B.A., Ph.D., Wisconsin–Madison. Effects of lease accounting on firms' reported debt levels, increased customer concentration: economic effects and adequacy of financial-reporting disclosures, segment reporting, bankers' use of cash flow statements.

Lawrence Harris, Professor of Marketing; Ph.D., NYU. Quantitative decision methods in business.

Xiaohong He, Associate Professor of International Business; Ph.D., Texas at Dallas. Foreign direct investment.

Donn M. Johnson, Assistant Professor of Economics; M.B.A., Washington State; Ph.D., Colorado State. Fisheries economics, valuing fishing and other forms of outdoor recreation using the travel cost and contingent valuation methods.

Patricia M. Kelly, Assistant Professor of Economics; Ph.D., Massachusetts. International trade and finance, economic growth, macroeconomic policy.

Osman Kilec, Assistant Professor of Finance; M.B.A., South Alabama; Ph.D., New Orleans. Financial markets and institutions, international finance.

Patrice Luoma, Assistant Professor of Management; M.B.A., St. Cloud State; Ph.D., Washington State. Corporate governance, corporate social performance, institutional effects on organizations, legal environment influences on company stucture and processes.

Ronald S. McMullen, Associate Professor of Management; Ed.D., Massachusetts. Achievement motivation and entrepreneurship, African Americans in American business.

Chadwick C. Nehrt, Associate Professor of International Business; M.B.A., Columbia; Ph.D., Michigan. International diversification, dual diversification, environmental strategies.

Mario Norbis, Associate Professor of Management; Ph.D., Massachusetts Amherst. Production scheduling, decision support systems, optimization methods.

Anne J. Rich, William S. Perlroth Professor and Chief of Accounting; M.B.A., Bridgeport; Ph.D., Massachusetts; CPA, CMA. Ethical issues, management accounting, financial statement analysis.

Shiv L. Sawhney, Professor and Chair of Management; M.B.A., Ph.D., NYU. Strategic management, entrepreneurship.

Michael J. Tucker, Professor of Accounting; M.B.A., J.D., NYU; Ph.D., Houston; LL.M., Georgetown; CPA. Taxes, entrepreneurship in the former Soviet Union.

RENSSELAER POLYTECHNIC INSTITUTE

Lally School of Management and Technology

Programs of Study

The Lally School of Management and Technology is focused on the intersection of management and technology and built upon the conviction that for all firms in all future markets, sustainable competitive advantage will be built upon a technological foundation. The School's mission is to educate a new breed of managers who are prepared to lead their companies in the effective and strategic use of technology. The Lally School offers M.B.A., M.S., and Ph.D. degree programs in management and has an Executive M.B.A. program and an international exchange program. The School's degree programs are accredited by AACSB–The International Association for Management Education.

The Management and Technology M.B.A. (M&T M.B.A.) Program is the flagship program of Rensselaer's Lally School of Management and Technology. Course modules are offered in a stream format that provides integration across disciplines and between traditional management and technical areas. The 60-credit-hour M&T M.B.A. is designed to achieve a dual purpose: the development of technical managers who understand and are able to perform effectively in general management functions, and the development of general managers who understand and are able to interact effectively within the technological environment. Approximately 20 percent of full-time students pursue a dual degree, linking their management studies with graduate work in technical fields and completing both degrees in a reduced amount of time. The Master of Science is a 30-credit-hour program leading to a specified degree in a field.

The M&T M.B.A. and M.S. programs are offered to both full-time and part-time students. All students are required to complete a core curriculum and may choose a concentration. Concentration areas include management information systems, manufacturing systems, manufacturing management, product development and management, technological entrepreneurship, research and development management, environmental management and policy, and financial technology.

The three-year Ph.D. program is designed for students with superior abilities and a technological orientation who wish to pursue careers as educators, researchers, or professional specialists. Interdisciplinary graduate programs include those leading to the Ph.D. degree in decision sciences and engineering systems and to M.S. degrees in operations research and statistics, manufacturing systems engineering, industrial and management engineering, and environmental management and policy. An M.B.A./J.D. program is also offered in cooperation with Albany Law School of Union University. A new, state-of-the-art facility in Troy, New York, serves as the home of the Lally School. This fully networked building contains computer-interactive, videoconferencing, and distance education classrooms. A second campus is located in Hartford, Connecticut. M.B.A. and M.S. degrees are offered at this campus.

Research Facilities

The Lally School of Management and Technology is linked with the Design and Manufacturing Institute (searches out solutions to productivity problems), the Center for Technological Entrepreneurship (provides focus for research in new ventures), the Center for Services Research and Education (applies information and decision technologies to improve productivity in the service sector), and the Center for the Study of Financial Technology (financial engineering, the impact of information technology on financial markets, and entrepreneurial finance). Research is supported by such state-of-the-art facilities as the Rensselaer Libraries, whose library systems allow access to collections, databases, and resources via the Internet. A computer network permeates the campus with a coherent array of advanced workstations, a shared toolkit of applications for interactive learning and research, and high-speed Internet connectivity. The Lally School also has its own microcomputer lab with extended user access hours.

Financial Aid

Most support is in the form of tuition scholarships and research or teaching assistantships. Outstanding students may qualify for Rensselaer Scholar Fellowships ($15,000 plus full waiver of tuition and fees) or other specially designated fellowships (stipends up to $10,000 plus tuition). Low-interest, deferred-repayment graduate loans are also available to U.S. citizens with demonstrated need.

Cost of Study

Tuition for 1998–99 is $630 per credit hour. Other fees amount to approximately $525 per semester. Books and supplies cost about $1600 per year.

Living and Housing Costs

The cost of a room for a single student in a residence hall or apartment ranges from $3150 to $5040 for the 1998–99 academic year. Family student housing, with a monthly rent of $592 to $720, is available. Local telephone service is included in all residences and apartments.

Student Group

Enrollment is about 4,000 undergraduates and 1,875 graduate students. The Lally School has approximately 400 master's and doctoral students with a wide range of academic and work backgrounds.

Student Outcomes

Ninety-eight percent of Rensselaer's M.B.A. graduate students were hired within three months of graduation, with starting salaries that averaged $51,500 for master's degree recipients.

Location

Troy, Albany, and Schenectady form an upstate metropolitan area with a population of approximately 750,000. The area is a major center of government, industrial, research, and academic activity. Within easy driving distance are the headquarters or major research centers of some of the world's largest technology-based firms.

The University

Rensselaer is eminently qualified to merge the disciplines of technology and management. One of America's first technological universities, Rensselaer was established in 1824. Rensselaer has five schools—Architecture, Engineering, Management, Science, and Humanities and Social Sciences—that offer a total of ninety-four graduate degrees in forty-six fields.

Applying

Online and paper applications should be received approximately three to six months before the start of the desired term. The application fee is $35. Students should contact the School for application deadlines for the Ph.D. and Executive M.B.A. programs. Admissions decisions are based on academic performance, GMAT scores, references, proven leadership qualities, and employment history. A good mathematics background and basic computer skills are helpful. Online applications are available via the School's Web site at the address below.

Correspondence and Information

For written information about graduate study:

Manager of Enrollment Services
Lally School of Management and Technology
Rensselaer Polytechnic Institute
110 8th Street
Troy, New York 12180-3590
Telephone: 518-276-4800
Fax: 518-276-8661
E-mail: management@rpi.edu
World Wide Web: http://lallyschool.rpi.edu

For applications and admissions information:

Director of Graduate Academic and Enrollment Services, Graduate Center
Rensselaer Polytechnic Institute
110 8th Street
Troy, New York 12180-3590
Telephone: 518-276-6789
E-mail: grad-services@rpi.edu
World Wide Web: http://www.rpi.edu

Rensselaer Polytechnic Institute

THE FACULTY AND THEIR RESEARCH

Joseph G. Ecker, Dean; Ph.D., Michigan. Mathematical programming, operations research.
Richard P. LeMay, Associate Dean; Ph.D., Iowa. Management engineering, production/operations management.
Gene R. Simons, Associate Dean; Ph.D., Rensselaer. Industrial and management engineering, production and operations management, project planning and control, manufacturing systems.
Mark Rice, Associate Dean; Ph.D. Rensselaer. Entrepreneurship, new ventures.

Professors—Troy
Robert A. Baron, Ph.D., Iowa. Organizational behavior, entrepreneurship.
Daniel Berg, Institute Professor of Science and Technology; Ph.D., Yale. Management of technological organizations, policy issues of research and development in the service sector.
G. Judd, Ph.D., Rensselaer. Management of higher education organizations, strategy and change.
J. R. Norsworthy, Ph.D., Virginia. Economics, business economics.
Albert S. Paulson, Frank and Lillian Gilbreth Professor in the Technologies of Management; Ph.D., Virginia Tech. Operations research and statistics, risk management and investment analysis.
Gene R. Simons, Ph.D., Rensselaer. Industrial and management engineering, production and operations management, project planning and control, manufacturing systems.

Clinical Professors—Troy
Pier A. Abetti, Ph.D., IIT; PE. Management of technology, international business development and strategic planning, entrepreneurship.
Michael M. Danchak, Ph.D., Rensselaer. Computer science.
William Stitt, M.B.A., Harvard. Entrepreneurship.
Shubo Xu, Director, Sino-U.S. Management and Technology M.B.A. Program; Ph.D., Tianjin (China). Decision sciences, quantitative methods.

Associate Professors—Troy
Wolfgang Bessler, Ph.D., Hamburg (Germany). Financial management and institutions, international finance.
Jeffrey F. Durgee, Ph.D., Pittsburgh. Marketing research and advertising.
David H. Goldenberg, Ph.D., Florida. Corporation finance and investments.
Jorgé Haddock, Ph.D., Purdue. Modeling of production and service systems, including simulation and optimization techniques.
Richard Leifer, Ph.D., Wisconsin. Organizational behavior and organizational design, management information systems.
Richard P. LeMay, Ph.D., Iowa. Management engineering, production/operations management.
Lois S. Peters, Ph.D., NYU. Science and technology policy.
Bruce Piasecki, Ph.D., Cornell. Environmental management and policy, hazardous-waste management, analysis of environmental executive decisions.
Susan S. Sanderson, Ph.D., Pittsburgh. International business, manufacturing policy, new product development.
Thomas T. Triscari, Ph.D., Rensselaer. Information systems.

Clinical Associate Professor—Troy
Ralph Miccio, J.D., Albany Law. Law, ethics.

Assistant Professors—Troy
Richard Burke, Ph.D., Massachusetts Amherst. Statistics, operations research, quality management.
David Hollingworth, Ph.D., Ohio State. Operations management.
Moren Levesque, Ph.D., British Columbia. Operations research, entrepreneurship.
Christopher McDermott, Ph.D., North Carolina at Chapel Hill. Manufacturing strategy, operations management.
Gina O'Connor, Ph.D., NYU. Marketing, product management.
Thiagarajan Ravichandran, Ph.D., Southern Illinois at Carbondale. Management information systems.
Mark P. Rice, Ph.D., Rensselaer. Entrepreneurship, new ventures.
Shikhar Sarin, Robert and Irene Bozzone Professorship of Management and Technology; Ph.D., Texas at Austin. New product development, high-technology marketing.
Dean Shepherd, Ph.D., Bond (Australia). Entrepreneurship.
Robert Veryzer, Ph.D., Florida. Marketing and consumer behavior.

Clinical Assistant Professors—Troy
Robert Boylan, Ph.D., Duke. Accounting and economics.
Irvin Morgan, M.B.A., Chicago. Finance.
William St. John, Ph.D., Rensselaer. Accounting, finance.
Robert Sands, M.B.A., SUNY at Albany. Organizational behavior and human resources management.
Kathy Silvester, Ph.D., Maryland. Accounting.

Adjunct Faculty—Troy
Judith A. Barnes, Ph.D., Rensselaer. Communication.
Zenas Block, B.S., CUNY, City College. Clinical professor of management at New York University, Stern School of Business; corporate entrepreneurship.
Glenn Doell, M.B.A., Rensselaer. Entrepreneurship.
Michael Hurley, Ph.D., Rensselaer. Human resource management, organizational behavior.
Jules Jacquin, M.B.A., Rensselaer. Accounting information systems, auditing.
Hugh Johnson, A.B., Dartmouth. Financial markets and analysis.
Jerry Mahone, B.A., Howard. Entrepreneurship.
K. Gary McClure, Ph.D., Central Florida. Finance.
James Murtagh, M.B.A., Northern Colorado. Finance.
Samuel Rabino, Ph.D., NYU. Marketing, international business.
Charles Rancourt, M.S., Rensselaer. Statistics.
Peter Skinner, M.E., Rensselaer. Management of environmental technology.
Steven Walsh, Ph.D., Rensselaer. Strategy, management of technology.
Frank Wright, M.S.E.E., Naval Postgraduate School. General management, manufacturing operations, international business.

RICE UNIVERSITY

Jesse H. Jones Graduate School of Management

Programs of Study

At the forefront of management education is the new Jones Graduate School curriculum leading to the Master of Business Administration (M.B.A.). The 60-credit-hour program requires two years of full-time study. In the first year, students participate in an innovative modular curriculum that provides a solid foundation in the core management subjects and includes instruction in ethics, information technology, communication skills, and the globalization of business. They also concentrate on developing their management and leadership skills. During the last part of the second semester, students engage in an Action Learning Project where they form teams to work full-time on-site at a company to solve a specific problem. In this project, they learn how to integrate the business disciplines they studied and how to turn that knowledge into action. The school also helps students find summer internships in fields relevant to their career interests.

In the second year, students take only two core courses: entrepreneurship and strategy. The entrepreneurship class is one of the few required courses of its kind in the nation. Students use the remaining 26 credit hours to customize a curriculum with electives from the Jones School's course offerings and/or upper level courses from other Rice University departments. The M.B.A. program offers electives that provide advanced perspectives in aspects of accounting, entrepreneurship, finance, international business, legal and government processes, management information systems, marketing, organizational behavior and human resource management, and strategy and operations management.

The Jones Graduate School and the George R. Brown School of Engineering offer a joint Master of Business Administration/Master of Engineering degree for students with the requisite background. Requiring 2½ academic years of full-time study, the program includes 24 hours of engineering and 49 hours of business administration.

Research Facilities

Students can access the Internet, exchange files, and send and receive e-mail from home or from various locations within the School. They also have access to the University's computer center, which houses DOS-compatible, UNIX, and Macintosh PCs. The School's Business Information Center contains management and accounting monographs and reference works as well as current periodicals. The center also has online capabilities and subscribes to several compact disk services that provide financial and bibliographic information.

Financial Aid

Student loans are readily available; submission of the Free Application for Financial Student Aid (FAFSA) is required. Approximately 65 percent of the student body receives some form of financial aid. In addition, approximately 50 percent of each class receives tuition waivers, up to full remission of tuition.

Cost of Study

Tuition for 1998–99 is $15,750; fees are $420. Students may provide their own health insurance or purchase it through the University for about $600 to $800, depending on the plan. Books for the year cost approximately $1100. Students are required to have a notebook computer and associated software; computer expenses are approximately $4000.

Living and Housing Costs

Houston's cost of living is considerably lower than that of other major metropolitan areas. Moderately priced apartments near the University may be rented for $500 to $650 per month. The Graduate House, operated by Rice, accommodates a limited number of single students; monthly rent is approximately $300.

Student Group

To keep class sizes small and promote class participation, the student body is limited to approximately 300. Students come from across the United States and several other countries. Thirty-four percent are women, 12 percent are international students, and 12 percent are members of a minority group. Eighty-eight percent have at least one year of full-time work experience.

Student Outcomes

The School's placement record is excellent for both full-time employment and summer internships. Organizations hiring recent graduates include American Airlines, Amoco, Arthur Andersen, Arthur D. Little, Bankers Trust, Booz Allen & Hamilton, Chase Manhattan Bank, Compaq, Deloitte & Touche, Enron, Exxon, FMC, Morgan Stanley, Oracle, and Shell Oil. Members of the class of 1997 accepted positions in the following fields: consulting (20 percent), finance (40 percent), marketing (20 percent), and operations (20 percent).

Location

Situated on a 300-acre tree-lined campus in one of the city's finest residential districts, Rice is just 3 miles from downtown Houston and adjacent to the renowned Texas Medical Center. Nearby Hermann Park features hundreds of acres of picnic grounds, a zoo, a golf course, and horseback riding facilities. Houston's symphony, ballet, grand opera, and repertory theater are nationally known performing arts organizations. Sports fans enjoy the professional baseball, basketball, and hockey clubs based in Houston. The nation's fourth-largest city, Houston is the headquarters of more than 2,000 major companies, both domestic and international, and is a major center of finance and agribusiness. It is the energy capital of the world and the home of NASA's Johnson Space Center.

The University

Rice University, a private, nonsectarian, coeducational institution, admitted its first students in 1912. The Jones Graduate School is one of the seven academic units offering undergraduate and graduate study in management, architecture, natural science, engineering, social science, music, and humanities. Rice, which has the tenth-largest endowment of any private university in the country, deliberately keeps its enrollment relatively small; the student body of 4,100 includes 1,400 graduate students. A low student-faculty ratio ensures that students receive individual attention from their professors.

Applying

Admission to the School is for the fall semester only. The School has four deadlines: December 1, January 15, March 1, and April 15. Applicants are advised to meet the December 1 or January 15 deadline in order to increase their chances of acceptance. Prospective students must submit a completed application, which includes essays, three letters of recommendation, and official transcripts from all universities attended. An applicant to the M.B.A. program must have a GMAT score sent to the School. If the applicant's native language is not English, a TOEFL score must be submitted, unless the applicant received an undergraduate degree from a U.S. university. An applicant to the joint Master of Business Administration/Master of Engineering program must submit a GRE rather than a GMAT score. June 1 is the deadline for financial aid applications, but earlier submission is encouraged.

Correspondence and Information

Jill L. Deutser, Director of Admissions and Marketing
Jesse H. Jones Graduate School of Management MS 531
Rice University
P.O. Box 1892
Houston, Texas 77251-1892
Telephone: 713-527-4918
Fax: 713-285-5251
E-mail: enterjgs@rice.edu
World Wide Web: http://www.rice.edu/jgs

Rice University

FULL-TIME FACULTY MEMBERS AND THEIR RESEARCH

Deborah J. Barrett, Instructor and Director of M.B.A. Communications; Ph.D., Rice, 1983. Strategic employee communications (models and best practices), computer technology and the teaching of managerial communications, change communication and management, ethos and argumentative appeals in business communications.
Richard R. Batsell, Associate Professor; Ph.D., Texas at Austin, 1976. Mathematical models of choice behavior, analytical approaches to marketing, human-computer interface.
Steven C. Currall, Assistant Professor; Ph.D., Cornell, 1990. Work relationships among organizational boundary role persons and the role of trust, group processes within corporate boards of directors, the effect of employee work attitudes on organizational effectiveness.
Michele J. Daley, Assistant Professor; Ph.D., Rochester, 1995. Association of earnings components with stock returns, economic determinants of financial accounting choices.
Bala H. Dharan, Professor; Ph.D., Carnegie Mellon, 1981. Earnings management, behavior of accounting accruals over time, stock market's and managers' use of financial analysts' earnings forecasts.
Jeff Fleming, Assistant Professor; Ph.D., Duke, 1993. Valuation and microstructure of financial futures and options, stock market volatility.
Gustavo Grullon, Assistant Professor; Ph.D., Cornell, 1998. Corporate finance, market microstructure, banking.
David Ikenberry, Associate Professor; Ph.D., Illinois, 1990. Empirical issues in capital markets and corporate finance.
Quintus R. Jett, Assistant Professor; Ph.D., Stanford, 1998. Strategic and organizational responses to highly competitive, dynamic industries.
George Kanatas, Professor; Ph.D., Johns Hopkins, 1978. Financial economics with an emphasis on financial institutions and corporate finance.
Trichy V. Krishnan, Assistant Professor; Ph.D., Texas at Dallas, 1994. Retailing, new product diffusion, international marketing, game theory, mathematical marketing.
Piyush Kumar, Assistant Professor; Ph.D., Purdue, 1996. Customer satisfaction, service quality, customer relationships, waiting time management.
E. Geoffrey Love, Assistant Professor; Ph.D., Harvard, 1997. Organizational change and transformation, with emphasis on downsizing and other types of restructuring.
Sharon F. Matusik, Assistant Professor; Ph.D., Washington (Seattle), 1998. Strategic management, organizational knowledge, international business, entrepreneurship.
H. Albert Napier, Associate Professor; Ph.D., Texas at Austin, 1971. Management information systems, computer-human interface.
Barbara Ostdiek, Assistant Professor; Ph.D., Duke, 1994. Financial market linkages, international asset pricing, risk management.
Sundaresh Ramnath, Assistant Professor; Ph.D., Penn State, 1996. Capital markets–based research in accounting.
Karen E. Schnietz, Assistant Professor; Ph.D., Berkeley, 1994. Political, legal, and regulatory environment of business; institutional origins of U.S. trade regulation; comparative business-government relations with emphasis on the United States, the European Union, and Japan.
Douglas A. Schuler, Assistant Professor; Ph.D., Minnesota, 1992. Business and public policy, political strategies of firms, U.S. trade policies.
Sanjay Sood, Assistant Professor; Ph.D., Stanford, 1997. Managerial decision making, behavioral decision theory, psychological issues relating to building, measuring, and leveraging brand equity.
Ronald N. Taylor, Professor; Ph.D., Minnesota, 1970. Decision making, strategic planning, managerial problem solving.
Wilfred C. Uecker, Professor; Ph.D., Texas at Austin, 1973. Empirical and applied research in managerial accounting and auditing.
Fu-Kuo Albert Wang, Assistant Professor; Ph.D., North Carolina at Chapel Hill, 1994. Market microstructure, asset pricing, behavioral finance.
Robert A. Westbrook, Professor; Ph.D., Michigan, 1975. Customer satisfaction, customer analysis, marketing research, marketing management.
Gilbert R. Whitaker Jr., Dean and Professor; Ph.D., Wisconsin, 1961. Managerial economics.
Edward E. Williams, Professor; Ph.D., Texas at Austin, 1968. Entrepreneurship, economics, mergers and acquisitions, business policy.
Duane Windsor, Professor; Ph.D., Harvard, 1978. Business-government relations, business strategy, public financial management.
Bennett C. K. Yim, Associate Professor; Ph.D., Purdue, 1989. Price expectations, pricing and promotion strategies, market structure, customer satisfaction model.
Stephen A. Zeff, Professor; Ph.D., Michigan, 1962. Comparative historical study of standard setting, accounting practice, and accounting thought.

Part-Time Faculty Members and Their Teaching Areas

W. Clifford Atherton Jr., Lecturer; Ph.D., Texas at Austin, 1983. Investment banking.
David M. Austgen, Lecturer; Ph.D., Texas at Austin, 1989. Management of technical innovation.
Lovett Baker, Lecturer; B.A., Princeton, 1952. Management strategy.
Stephen J. Banks, Adjunct Professor; M.B.A., Harvard, 1967. Venture capital.
Amir Barnea, Adjunct Professor; Ph.D., Cornell, 1972. Finance.
Donald D. Clayton, Lecturer; M.B.A., Rice, 1990. Systems analysis and design.
Caryn Crump, Lecturer; M.B.A., Chicago, 1977. Product management.
Robert N. Flatt, Adjunct Associate Professor; M.B.A., Harvard, 1973. Production and operations management.
John Hannan, Adjunct Associate Professor; J.D., South Texas Law, 1988. International business law.
Patricia R. Lawrence, Lecturer; M.B.A., Fordham, 1987. Product management.
James P. Mandel, Lecturer; Ph.D., Illinois, 1973. Financial and management accounting.
Edward D. McDonald, Adjunct Professor; M.S., Rice, 1964. Organizational computing.
Dennis E. Murphree, Lecturer; M.B.A., Pennsylvania, 1971. Entrepreneurship.
David Ross III, Adjunct Professor; M.B.A., Harvard, 1970. Corporate financial strategy.
V. Richard Viebig Jr., Lecturer; M.Acco., Rice, 1977. Federal taxation.
Alan Westheimer, Lecturer; M.B.A., Berkeley, 1966. Business strategy.
Donald L. Williams, Adjunct Associate Professor; M.S., Louisville, 1971. Real estate development.

ROLLINS COLLEGE

Crummer Graduate School of Business

Programs of Study

The Crummer Graduate School of Business offers four M.B.A. programs for motivated and talented individuals. The Accelerated M.B.A. (A.M.B.A.) Program is a one-year intensive full-time program designed for candidates with at least three years of significant work experience; one benefit of this program is that career interruption and income loss are less than one year. The Early Advantage M.B.A. (E.A.M.B.A.) Program is a two-year full-time program for students with little or no work experience who wish to pursue their degree before starting their careers; heavy emphasis is placed on career development. The Professional M.B.A. (P.M.B.A.) Program is a part-time evening program designed for working professionals; this thirty-two–month program allows students to apply course material directly to their jobs. The Executive M.B.A. (E.M.B.A.) Program is an eighteen-month program for professionals with eight to fifteen years of experience who have been targeted by their employers for career advancement. The mission of the Crummer M.B.A. programs is to teach students to apply the knowledge learned from their course work to real-world situations. Thus, learning textual material is not the goal but an intermediate step in the learning process. The case method is used extensively to apply the skills learned in the classroom to actual business issues, thereby preparing students for the many and varied challenges that face management professionals. The fully integrated curriculum is composed of core courses that provide students with a broad understanding of management; elective courses then allow students to concentrate in an area that suits their skills and career ambitions.

Research Facilities

The facilities of the School are designed for a state-of-the-art M.B.A. program and include modern executive classrooms, an 80-seat auditorium, an M.B.A. student lounge, and the Crummer Computer Center. The center is equipped with IBM and AT&T PCs that can run an extensive list of business-oriented applications software. Each executive classroom has a ceiling-mounted color video projection system that allows the use of spreadsheet and graphics software in the classroom. Students receive notebook computers when they first enroll in the M.B.A. program. Students use the computers in class as part of the process of analysis for management decision making. The Crummer library collection is housed in the Olin Library. The recently renovated Career Services offices offer recruiting rooms, a job search library, computer-network access, and video teleconferencing equipment.

Financial Aid

All A.M.B.A. and E.A.M.B.A. candidates are automatically considered for merit-based scholarship and graduate assistantship awards; there are no special application forms for these funds. These awards are based on the strength of the applicant and not on financial need. Merit-based aid is available to about one half of the entering class of full-time students. Scholarships cover 20 to 100 percent of the annual tuition. Graduate assistants are given both a tuition waiver and a monthly cash stipend for working for a professor or an administrative office. In addition, federally funded loan programs are available to all students according to federal guidelines.

Cost of Study

Tuition totals for the 1998–99 year are $32,000 for the A.M.B.A. Program, $40,800 for the E.A.M.B.A. Program, $31,360 for the P.M.B.A. Program, and $39,900 for the E.M.B.A. Program. Tuition includes a notebook computer and software with a retail value in excess of $2000. E.A.M.B.A. and E.M.B.A. tuition includes the cost of an international study trip, and E.M.B.A. tuition also covers books. Books (except for E.M.B.A. students), supplies, health insurance, and personal expenses are additional.

Living and Housing Costs

Estimated costs of room, board, personal items, books, and supplies total about $13,500 for the 1998–99 academic year for full-time students at the Crummer Graduate School of Business. All graduate students live off campus.

Student Group

The 1997 entering class represented twenty-six states and fifteen other countries. The average GMAT score for full-time students was 590, and the average undergraduate GPA was 3.22. Full-time M.B.A. program enrollment is approximately 180, and part-time enrollment approximately 220.

Student Outcomes

Crummer students accept positions in a wide variety of industries and functional areas; 25 percent are in finance/accounting, 27 percent in marketing, 33 percent in consulting, 27 percent in management, and 2 percent in operations. Of the class of 1997, 96 percent were employed three months after graduation. Companies hiring graduates include AAA, Andersen Consulting, KPMG Peat Marwick, Jimmy Dean Foods, Morgan Stanley, and Ernst and Young.

Location

The School is located on the Rollins campus on the shores of Lake Virginia. Rollins has been listed by *U.S. News & World Report* and *Time* magazine as one of "America's Best Colleges." Winter Park is a quaint and sophisticated city, well known as the cultural center of Florida. The campus is 5 miles from downtown Orlando yet has the highly desired small-town atmosphere. Many major corporations have their headquarters nearby. The College is a short drive from well-known attractions and the Atlantic and Gulf beaches.

The College and The School

Founded in 1885, Rollins is the oldest college in Florida and has developed a tradition of excellence in liberal arts education over the past 113 years. Rollins is a small college, with 1,400 undergraduate students equally divided between men and women. It is private and independent of both state and church. The student-faculty ratio is 12:1. The faculty members emphasize teaching as well as research, and all full-time faculty members hold doctorates and have published an average of 4 texts per person. The Crummer Graduate School of Business holds the distinction of belonging to a small, outstanding group of schools that specialize in graduate business education; of the 305 schools accredited by the AACSB–The International Association for Management Education, only twenty-one offer programs at the graduate level only, and the Crummer School is one of these prestigious schools. The *Gourman Report* ranked the Crummer School in the top 10 percent of all business schools. A *Wall Street Journal* article highlighted many of the School's newest and most innovative programs and achievements.

Applying

Admission to the Crummer School is selective and based upon academic potential as demonstrated by an interview, work experience, undergraduate records, and performance on the GMAT. Other information that would influence a positive decision includes recommendations, awards, and leadership positions held in social and school-related organizations. The Crummer School has a rolling admission process, and early application is encouraged. An interview is required of all applicants. If applicants are unable to visit the school, a phone or video teleconferencing interview can be scheduled. Late applicants are considered on a space-available basis. International applicants must also submit TOEFL scores.

Correspondence and Information

Director of Admissions
Crummer Graduate School of Business
Rollins College
1000 Holt Avenue-2722
Winter Park, Florida 32789-4499

Telephone: 407-646-2405
800-866-2405 Ext. 64 (toll-free)
Fax: 407-646-2402
World Wide Web: http://www.crummer.rollins.edu

Rollins College

THE FACULTY

The Crummer School has a nationally recognized faculty with an outstanding publication record and excellent teaching skills. Teaching performance is emphasized to such a degree that the School hires only those faculty members who have already established themselves as outstanding teachers at other schools.

The Crummer School is distinctive in that it encourages faculty members to write textbooks in addition to research articles published in refereed academic journals. Consequently, the teaching faculty of the School has authored a total of 85 textbooks, which is an average of 4 books per person. Besides writing and teaching, many Crummer faculty members also serve as consultants to companies in and outside the central Florida area.

Carol H. Anderson, Professor of Marketing; Ph.D., Texas A&M.
Charles H. Brandon, Professor of Accounting; Ph.D., Georgia.
Samuel C. Certo, Professor of Management; Ph.D., Ohio.
Michael A. Cipollaro, Executive-in-Residence; M.S., Johns Hopkins.
Ronnie Clayton, Associate Professor of Finance; Ph.D., Georgia.
David M. Currie, Associate Professor of Economics and Finance; Ph.D., USC.
Ralph Drtina, Professor of Accounting; Ph.D., Ohio State.
James P. Gilbert, Associate Professor of Operations Research; Ph.D., Nebraska–Lincoln.
Theodore Herbert, Professor of Management; D.B.A., Georgia State.
James M. Higgins, Professor of Management; Ph.D., Georgia State.
Mark W. Johnston, Professor of Marketing; Ph.D., Texas A&M.
Serge Matulich, Professor of Accounting; Ph.D., Berkeley.
Craig M. McAllaster, Director of the E.M.B.A. program; Ed.D., Columbia.
Edward A. Moses, Dean and Barnett Banks Professor of Finance; Ph.D., Georgia.
Christine Nielsen, Associate Professor of International Business; D.B.A., George Washington.
Donald R. Plane, Professor of Management Science; D.B.A., Indiana.
Barry Render, Professor of Operations Management; Ph.D., Cincinnati.
Max D. Richards, Distinguished Professor Emeritus of Management; Ph.D., Illinois.
Martin Schatz, Professor of Management and Dean Emeritus; Ph.D., NYU.
Martin K. Starr, Distinguished Professor of Operations Management; Ph.D., Columbia.
Jack W. Trifts, Professor of Finance; Ph.D., Florida.
E. Theodore Veit, Professor of Finance; Ph.D., Arkansas.
Julian W. Vincze, Professor of Marketing; Ph.D., Bradford (England).

Every student receives a notebook computer, which is used throughout the program.

Crummer School's world-renowned faculty members work closely with each student, often teaching materials from their own published textbooks.

The Crummer School is located in beautiful Winter Park, Florida, 5 miles from downtown Orlando.

SANTA CLARA UNIVERSITY

Leavey School of Business and Administration
Master of Business Administration Program

Program of Study

The Leavey School of Business and Administration seeks to develop men and women of competence, conscience, and compassion who can lead organizations to positions of competitive strength in the technologically advanced and rapidly changing global environments. The program combines tradition with innovation, excellence in research with excellence in teaching, and theory with practice, designed to develop leaders for the twenty-first century.

Santa Clara's M.B.A. program was among the first group of M.B.A. programs accredited by AACSB–The International Association for Management Education in 1961 and has consistently met the AACSB's high standards. The program is ideally suited for people who want to pursue their education while continuing in their current job positions. However, many students attend on a full-time basis, taking advantage of the flexible class scheduling and the opportunity to meet and study with employees from local companies. Most class sessions are held twice a week in the evenings.

The course of study at Santa Clara University primarily takes a generalist perspective, preparing students to be decision makers across the various functional fields rather than specialists or technocrats. A full range of electives does, however, allow in-depth concentration in selected areas. Depending on prior academic background, students take fifteen to twenty-four courses.

In addition to the regular M.B.A. program, the School offers a program leading to the M.B.A. in agribusiness and, in conjunction with the School of Law, a combined J.D./M.B.A. program.

Research Facilities

The Michel Orradre Library, which dates from the founding of Mission Santa Clara, contains more than 650,000 volumes and nearly 660,000 microforms. The library currently receives more than 4,900 serial subscriptions and is a depository for more than 545,000 U.S. and California government documents. In addition, the library provides access to many other information resources through the World Wide Web and other electronic services. OSCAR, the library's online catalog, is available in the library or via the campus network. Mainframe support and personal computing facilities are available to all graduate students. PCs are concentrated in two general-purpose laboratories containing 150 IBM machines, 20 Macs, and six workstations. Each PC can also function as a terminal to the VAX. Students may access an e-mail system through the University's mainframe, which offers an alternative communication channel for M.B.A. students.

Financial Aid

Awards of financial assistance are determined based on a combination of scholastic record and financial need. Most assistance funded by the School requires part-time work as an assistant on research or administrative projects. Application forms for scholarships funded by the School of Business and Administration may be obtained from the M.B.A. office. Financial aid is not available for noncitizens unless they reside in the U.S. permanently and have filed for citizenship.

Graduate students in business may qualify for the federal student loan programs on the same basis as other students at the University. Further information is available from the M.B.A. financial aid coordinator.

Cost of Study

Tuition in 1998–99 is $458 per quarter unit; tuition for agribusiness courses is $483 per quarter unit. All courses carry 3 units of credit. A $12 registration fee and a $10 Student Association fee are payable each quarter.

Living and Housing Costs

The University does not provide residential facilities for graduate students. Housing costs in the surrounding area vary. A typical budget (excluding tuition) for a student attending Santa Clara University and living off campus is about $9000 per year.

Student Group

Most of Santa Clara's 1,100 M.B.A. students have full-time jobs and attend class part-time. About 15 percent are enrolled full-time. The typical entering student has had five or more years of work experience. Ten percent hold graduate degrees in other fields. Undergraduate majors represented are humanities and social science, including economics (29 percent), engineering (43 percent), business (26 percent), and other disciplines (2 percent). More than 36 percent of the students are women. Eight percent of the students in the program are international.

Student Outcomes

Career Services offers complete career services for students and alumni, including counseling, on-campus recruiting, seminars, and workshops. They work closely with alumni and students coordinating networking opportunities. SCU alumni hold prominent positions in a wide variety of local and national companies, including Hewlett-Packard, Sun Microsystems, Applied Materials, Intel Corporation, IBM, Oracle, Cisco Systems, KLA Instruments, General Electric, and Wells Fargo Bank. In addition, many alumni have started successful entrepreneurial ventures.

Location

Santa Clara University is 46 miles from San Francisco, near the southern tip of the Bay. The campus is situated in Silicon Valley, in the midst of one of the nation's greatest concentrations of high-technology industry and professional and scientific activity. The cultural and entertainment centers of San Francisco, Berkeley, and Oakland can be reached within an hour by bus, train, or car. The Pacific beaches of Santa Cruz are about 30 minutes away, and the Monterey Peninsula and Carmel are 2 hours away. The University is accessible via San Jose, San Francisco, and Oakland international airports.

The University and The School

Founded in 1851 by missionaries of the Society of Jesus, Santa Clara University was the first institution of higher learning on the West Coast. The University consists of the College of Arts and Sciences; the Schools of Engineering, Law, and Business and Administration; and the Graduate Division of Counseling Psychology and Education. The University enrolls about 4,000 undergraduate and 3,700 graduate students.

The School of Business and Administration, established as part of the University in 1926, was named the Leavey School of Business and Administration in 1983 in recognition of Thomas and Dorothy Leavey, major benefactors of the University and the School. In addition to its undergraduate and M.B.A. programs, the School offers educational programs through the Executive Development Center.

Applying

Applicants must have a U.S. bachelor's degree or its equivalent from an accredited college or university. An application form, two confidential letters of recommendation, official transcripts, the GMAT score, and the TOEFL score (if applicable) should be on file with the M.B.A. Office by the application deadline. A $55 application fee ($75 for international applicants) is required. Applicants whose first language is not English must submit TOEFL/TWE scores; the minimum acceptable scores are 600 and 4.0, respectively. All application materials must be on file at the University before an application can be evaluated. Application deadlines are as follows: fall quarter, June 1; winter quarter, September 1; and spring quarter, December 1.

Correspondence and Information

M.B.A. Office
Leavey School of Business and Administration
Santa Clara University
Santa Clara, California 95053

Telephone: 408-554-4500
Fax: 408-554-4571
E-mail: mbaadmissions@scu.edu
World Wide Web: http://LSB.scu.edu

Santa Clara University

THE FACULTY

Dale D. Achabal, Professor; Director, Retail Studies; and Associate Dean, Research and Development; Ph.D., Texas at Austin, 1975.
Narendra Agrawal, Assistant Professor; Ph.D., Pennsylvania (Wharton), 1994.
Gregory A. Baker, Associate Professor; Ph.D., Purdue, 1982.
Mario L. Belotti, Professor; Ph.D., Texas at Austin, 1960.
Yaron Brook, Assistant Professor; Ph.D., Texas at Austin, 1994.
Albert V. Bruno, Professor; Ph.D., Purdue, 1971.
Thomas A. Burnham, Acting Assistant Professor; Ph.D., Texas at Austin, 1998.
David F. Caldwell, Professor; Ph.D., UCLA, 1978.
Martin Calkins, S.J., Assistant Professor; Ph.D., Virginia, 1998.
Sandra Chamberlain, Assistant Professor; Ph.D., Chicago, 1991.
Robert Collins, Professor; Ph.D., Missouri, 1975.
Jacques J. Delacroix, Professor; Ph.D., Stanford, 1974.
André Delbecq, Professor; D.B.A., Indiana, 1963.
Henry G. Demmert, Associate Professor and Chair, Department of Economics; Ph.D., Stanford, 1972.
William Donnelly, S.J., Professor; Ph.D., NYU, 1969.
Michael J. Eames, Assistant Professor; Ph.D., Washington (Seattle), 1995.
Charles D. Feinstein, Associate Professor; Ph.D., Stanford, 1980.
Alexander J. Field, Professor; Ph.D., Berkeley, 1974.
Karen F. A. Fox, Associate Professor; Ph.D., Stanford, 1973.
David Friedman, Professor; Ph.D., Chicago, 1971.
Manoochehr Ghiassi, Associate Professor and Chair, Department of Operations and Management Information Systems; Ph.D., Illinois at Urbana-Champaign, 1980.
James L. Hall, Associate Professor; Ph.D., Washington (Seattle), 1971.
John M. Heineke, Professor; Ph.D., Iowa, 1968.
Robert Hendershott, Assistant Professor; Ph.D., Ohio State, 1993.
Lawrence R. Iannaccone, Professor; Ph.D., Chicago, 1984.
Hoje Jo, Associate Professor; Ph.D., Florida, 1986.
Kirthi Kalyanam, Assistant Professor; Ph.D., Purdue, 1993.
Linda Kamas, Associate Professor; Ph.D., Berkeley, 1982.
Michael Kevane, Assistant Professor; Ph.D., Berkeley, 1993.
Chaiho Kim, Professor; Ph.D., Columbia, 1963.
Daniel B. Klein, Associate Professor; Ph.D., NYU, 1990.
James L. Koch, Professor and Director, Center for Science, Technology and Society; Ph.D., UCLA, 1972.
Michele LaPlante, Assistant Professor; Ph.D., Penn State, 1996.
Joel K. Leidecker, Associate Professor; Ph.D., Washington (Seattle), 1969.
Paul L. Locatelli, S.J., Professor and University President; D.B.A., USC, 1971.
Suzanne Luttman, Associate Professor; Ph.D., Illinois at Urbana-Champaign, 1988.
Shelby H. McIntyre, Professor; Ph.D., Stanford, 1979.
Edward F. McQuarrie, Associate Professor and Associate Dean, Graduate Studies; Ph.D., Cincinnati, 1985.
Dennis J. Moberg, Professor; D.B.A., USC, 1974.
Georg Muller, Acting Assistant Professor; Ph.D., Chicago, 1998.
J. Michael Munson, Associate Professor and Chair, Department of Marketing; Ph.D., Illinois at Urbana-Champaign, 1973.
Steven Nahmias, Professor; Ph.D., Northwestern, 1972.
Sarma R. Nidumolu, Assistant Professor; Ph.D., UCLA, 1991.
Jane Ou, Associate Professor; Ph.D., Berkeley, 1984.
David Palmer, Senior Lecturer; Ph.D., Berkeley, 1983.
Susan Parker, Assistant Professor; Ph.D., Oregon, 1997.
Helen Popper, Associate Professor; Ph.D., Berkeley, 1990.
Barry Z. Posner, Professor and Dean; Ph.D., Massachusetts, 1976.
Rhonda L. Righter, Associate Professor; Ph.D., Berkeley, 1986.
David Roth, Assistant Professor; Ph.D., Yale, 1993
Thomas R. Russell, Associate Professor; Ph.D., Cambridge, 1973.
Atulya Sarin, Associate Professor; Ph.D., Virginia Tech, 1992.
Shahrokh M. Saudagaran, Associate Professor; Ph.D., Washington (Seattle), 1986.
James F. Sepe, Associate Professor; Ph.D., Washington (Seattle), 1980.
Hersh M. Shefrin, Professor; Ph.D., London School of Economics, 1974.
Wesley Szu-Way Shu, Assistant Professor; Ph.D., Arizona, 1997.
Ranjan Sinha, Assistant Professor; Ph.D., Berkeley, 1993.
Stephen A. Smith, Professor; Ph.D., Stanford, 1982.
S. Andrew Starbird, Associate Professor and Director, Institute of Agribusiness; Ph.D., Cornell, 1987.
Meir Statman, Professor and Chair, Department of Finance; Ph.D., Columbia, 1978.
William A. Sundstrom, Associate Professor; Ph.D., Stanford, 1986.
Andy A. Tsay, Assistant Professor; Ph.D., Stanford, 1996.
Tyzoon T. Tyebjee, Professor; Ph.D., Berkeley, 1976.
Neal L. Ushman, Associate Professor and Chair, Department of Accounting; Ph.D., Cornell, 1983.
Manuel Velasquez, Professor and Chair, Department of Organizational Analysis and Management; Ph.D., Berkeley, 1975.
Thaddeus J. Whalen Jr., Professor and Associate Dean, Undergraduate Studies; Ph.D., Berkeley, 1964.
Lewis Winters, Executive Lecturer; Ph.D., Delaware, 1969.

SEATTLE PACIFIC UNIVERSITY

School of Business and Economics

Programs of Study

The Master of Business Administration (M.B.A.) and the Master of Science in Information Systems Management (M.S.I.S.M.) degrees offer the highest quality graduate management education informed by Christian faith and values. These two master's programs are offered in a convenient late afternoon/evening format with some Saturday morning classes available. Small classes allow dynamic interaction with professors and in student groups. Both programs may be pursued on either a full-time or part-time basis. Courses in the two programs are 3 quarter credits each and are scheduled to meet for one 3-hour session each week. A flexible schedule of summer classes is also offered.

The M.B.A. degree is intended primarily for working professionals who have achieved a meaningful level of career success. These individuals now seek to enhance their effectiveness in their current positions and to open opportunities for new responsibilities. The M.B.A. program consists of twenty-four courses divided among nine core, ten advanced, and five elective courses. The M.B.A. core courses are waivable based upon prior college course work. Students are encouraged to choose their M.B.A. electives to satisfy their own professional interests and goals. Current areas of emphasis include general management, human resource management, and information systems management. Other areas of emphasis within the M.B.A. program are also possible.

The M.S.I.S.M. degree seeks to prepare its graduates for positions in the planning, development, and management of information technology and systems in networked organizations. They learn to use information as a resource of strategic significance while studying in a collaborative, team-centered environment. The M.S.I.S.M. curriculum consists of twenty courses divided between five background business courses, ten core courses, and five elective courses. The five background courses are waivable based upon prior college course work.

Students in SPU's School of Business and Economics benefit from the School's strong ties with the business community. Regional executives network with students through participation in classes, advisory meetings with students, and company support of projects and internships.

Both degree programs seek to prepare students for significant levels of service in accordance with the School's mission: "We prepare students for service and leadership in business and society by developing their professional competence and integrity in the context of Christian faith and values. We are a learning community which prizes educational excellence and effective teaching, supported by scholarship and service."

Research Facilities

The campus library, a state-of-the-art facility, offers online access to a wide range of publications and research materials as well as traditional periodical and text sources. Three networked computer labs are available for student use.

Financial Aid

The majority of M.B.A. and M.S.I.S.M. students attending Seattle Pacific University are supported in their studies by their employers. A limited number of graduate assistantship positions are offered each year, and student loans are available for U.S. students taking at least two courses each term.

Cost of Study

Tuition for the 1998–99 academic year is $412 per quarter credit hour. One-time application ($35) and matriculation ($50) fees and a $200 advance tuition payment are charged.

Living and Housing Costs

Representative room and board costs for three quarters of study range from approximately $4500 in campus residence halls or University-owned, nontraditional housing to $6000 off campus.

Student Group

The average age of M.B.A. and M.S.I.S.M. students is 32. International students make up 15 percent of the M.B.A. program. Three quarters of the students work full-time. Forty-seven percent are women. An active student association plans activities between the students and faculty, and it represents student interests to the School.

Student Outcomes

Students in the evening programs designed for working professionals receive significant support from their employers. Upon completion of their studies, most obtain enhanced positions in their firms. Graduates of the M.S.I.S.M. program are in very high demand by Pacific Northwest manufacturing, high technology, and service industries. Large area employers such as The Boeing Company and Microsoft, Inc., employ a significant percentage of graduates.

Location

Seattle Pacific University is located on the north side of Queen Anne Hill, just north of downtown Seattle, Washington. The attractive campus borders the Lake Washington Ship Canal, which joins Lake Union with Puget Sound. Seattle is the premier business and trade center of the Pacific Northwest and is the U.S. gateway to the Pacific Rim. Bounded by the Cascade Mountains to the east, by the Olympic Mountains and Puget Sound to the west, and by Mount Rainier to the south, the region is a haven for all forms of outdoor recreation. Graduate business courses are also taught at a South King County classroom location.

The University and The School

Founded in 1891 as an outreach of the Free Methodist Church of North America, Seattle Pacific University has served the Seattle community through Christian higher education for more than 100 years. On-campus enrollment includes 2,400 undergraduate students and 1,200 graduate students, of whom approximately 200 are pursuing M.B.A. or M.S.I.S.M. degrees. The School of Business and Economics is one of three professional schools. The M.B.A. program started in 1983, followed by the M.S.I.S.M. program in 1985. The School seeks to balance learning with service—to educate people who will make a positive contribution to the world.

Applying

Applications are accepted for all quarters, including summer. Admission deadlines generally precede the quarter of admission by two months. Admission to the M.B.A. program requires successful completion of the GMAT exam; the GRE test is required for admission to the M.S.I.S.M. program. An essay and two recommendations are also required parts of the admission process. The application fee is $35. Applications are encouraged from students holding accredited bachelor's degrees from all disciplines. M.S.I.S.M. applicants should also be able to document experience with at least two programming languages.

Correspondence and Information

Assistant Graduate Director
School of Business and Economics
Seattle Pacific University
3307 Third Avenue, West
Seattle, Washington 98119

Telephone: 206-281-2753
Fax: 206-281-2733
E-mail: djwysom@spu.edu
World Wide Web: http://www.spu.edu/depts/sbe/

Seattle Pacific University

THE FACULTY

The faculty of the Seattle Pacific University School of Business and Economics is known for its high quality of instruction and broad experience in the marketplace. Additional faculty members in the M.S.I.S.M. program are drawn from the Department of Computer Science at SPU and from industry. An executive-in-residence and a small number of effective adjunct instructors complete the teaching faculty.

Denise Daniels, Ph.D. (management), Washington (Seattle), 1997. At SPU since 1996.
Jonathan C. Deming, Ph.D. (economics), Oregon, 1979. At SPU since 1977.
Douglas A. Downing, Ph.D. (economics and quantitative methods), Yale, 1987. At SPU since 1983.
Randal S. Franz, Ph.D. (management), Stanford, 1991. At SPU since 1991.
Loren T. Gustafson, Ph.D. (management and strategy), Arizona State, 1995. At SPU since 1995.
Dan W. Hess, M.B.A., Washington (Seattle), 1973; Ph.D. (finance), Arizona, 1982. At SPU since 1977.
Alexander D. Hill, Dean, School of Business and Economics; J.D. (business law and ethics), Washington (Seattle), 1980. At SPU since 1979.
Gary L. Karns, Joseph C. Hope Professor of Leadership and Ethics and Director of Graduate Studies; M.B.A., Oklahoma, 1977; Ph.D. (marketing), Washington (Seattle), 1987. At SPU since 1979.
Herbert E. Kierulff, Donald Snellman Professor of Entrepreneurship; D.B.A. (finance and entrepreneurship), USC, 1966. At SPU since 1980.
Kenneth E. Knight, Ph.D. (management), Carnegie-Mellon, 1963. At SPU since 1988.
Joanna Poznanska, Ph.D. (economics and international business), Warsaw Technical, 1976; Researcher, Woodrow Wilson School of Public and International Affairs, Princeton University. At SPU since 1988.
Regina P. Schlee, Ph.D. (marketing), Washington State, 1981. At SPU since 1984.
Gerhard H. Steinke, M.B.A., Ball State, 1984; Ph.D. (management and information systems), Passau (Germany), 1992. At SPU since 1992.
Ian C. Stewart, M.Com., Auckland, 1970; Ph.D. (accounting), New England, 1975; B.D., Melbourne College of Divinity, 1986. At SPU since 1991.
Ross E. Stewart, M.Com., Auckland, 1979; Dip.Cs., 1981, M.T.S., 1983, Regent College (Canada); Ph.D. (accounting), Glasgow (Scotland), 1986; Associate Chartered Accountant (New Zealand). At SPU since 1986.
Lisa K. Surdyk, Ph.D. (economics), Washington (Seattle), 1991. At SPU since 1991.
Kenman L. Wong, Ph.D. (social ethics), USC, 1997. At SPU since 1997.

Learning takes place in dynamic, small-group settings.

Seattle Pacific University has served the Pacific Northwest through Christian higher education for more than 100 years.

SEATTLE UNIVERSITY

Albers School of Business and Economics

Programs of Study

The Albers School offers six graduate programs, available on a full-time or part-time basis: the M.B.A., the Weekend M.B.A., the J.D./M.B.A., the Master of International Business (M.I.B.), the Master of Arts in Applied Economics (M.A.E.), and the Master of Science in Finance (M.S.F.). The Albers School is accredited by AACSB–The International Association for Management Education.

The M.B.A. is designed to develop leadership and analytical skills in students preparing for careers in management. Students have the opportunity for some specialization, with concentrations available in accounting, business law, economics, finance, human resource management, information systems, international business, management, marketing, operations, or quantitative and statistical methods. The Weekend M.B.A. program is similar, with the same faculty and curriculum, but is offered on Saturdays.

The Master of International Business (M.I.B.) allows students to specialize in global applications of business. Students must fulfill an international experience requirement and establish language proficiency prior to graduation. Students have the opportunity to travel on short international study tours with University faculty members.

The Master of Arts in Applied Economics (M.A.E.) develops the analytical and decision-making skills essential to sound management practices in both private businesses and public sector agencies. Students enter the program with a variety of interests, including forecasting, industry and market analysis, international economics, tax policy, and cost/benefit and impact analysis. The program also provides a stepping-stone to Ph.D. programs for some students.

The Master of Science in Finance (M.S.F.) provides in-depth treatment of three major areas—business finance, investments, and financial institutions and markets on both domestic and international fronts. It also includes course work in the corollary fields of accounting and economics and incorporates discussion of ethical issues in business and finance.

Classes are offered in the late afternoon, evening, and on Saturday and are available at two locations: Seattle and Bellevue. Students may enter any of four quarters and may complete their program in two to three years, depending on their previous course work in business. The programs are divided into waivable fundamentals, required, and elective courses. The Albers School offers more than fifty electives. A highlight of the Albers School is its Executive Mentor Program, matching senior executives from the Puget Sound area with graduate students. It offers opportunities to develop business contacts, access industry information, and gain valuable insights from experienced and successful professionals.

Certificate programs are also offered to graduates of these or comparable programs who wish to take additional classes at the graduate level. The School offers a Certificate of Post-M.B.A., Post-M.S.F., Post-M.I.B., and Post-M.A.E. studies, each requiring successful completion of six specified advanced graduate electives from the Albers School.

The Albers School is a participant in the Multilateral MBA Agreement, allowing eligible students to finish their degrees at another member school in case of relocation. Twenty-one Jesuit universities participate.

Research Facilities

The Lemieux Library at Seattle University has in excess of 200,000 volumes and more than 225 business periodicals. ABI, an electronic periodical database on CD-ROM with references to articles from more than 800 journals in business and economics, access to DIALOG databases, study lounges, and open stack privileges, is available to all students. The Albers School maintains Compustat PC Plus on a CD-ROM reader, as well as CITIBASE and CRSP business financial information databases. Student computing facilities include four networked microcomputer labs with IBM-PC compatibles and Apple Macintoshes. Word processing, spreadsheet, database, statistical analysis, and other software applications are available. Two 20-station computer classrooms are used for business courses. The Seattle University Information Services maintains a Sun Microsystems SPARCstation 10 Model UNIX computer with 24-hour student access terminals. The University's electronic mail system has access to a worldwide network of scholars through the Internet.

Financial Aid

Scholarships, student loans, and graduate assistantships based on both merit and need are available to both full-time and part-time domestic students. Students should contact the Seattle University Financial Aid Office, Broadway and Madison, Seattle, Washington 98122-4460 or call 206-296-5840.

Cost of Study

Tuition is charged on a per-class basis. The cost for graduate classes in the Albers School during the 1998–99 academic year is $1320 per 3-credit course. Books average $80 per course.

Living and Housing Costs

Limited on-campus room and board is available at a cost of $5493 for the 1998–99 academic year. Most graduate students live off campus in the Seattle area. One-bedroom apartments can generally be rented for $550 to $800 per month.

Student Group

As of fall 1997, there were 724 graduate students in the Albers School. Nineteen percent are full-time students, and the remaining 81 percent attend part-time while they continue in their careers. The average age of graduate students is 32, 40 percent are women, 13 percent are international students, and 10 percent are from minority groups. They represent a broad diversity of undergraduate and work experience.

Location

Seattle is one of America's most livable cities and an outstanding setting for educational growth. The University is located minutes from downtown Seattle, the business and cultural center of a five-state region. The city and surrounding ethnic neighborhoods provide a living laboratory for students. In addition, the Pacific Northwest offers a variety of recreational and sports opportunities.

The University

Seattle University, founded in 1891 by Jesuit priests, is dedicated to teaching and educating for leadership and service. While the University has grown to be the largest independent institution in the Pacific Northwest, students still enjoy a small-college atmosphere that balances academic challenges with personal, individual attention. The University offers a diverse and high-quality curriculum to students of every religion and culture, and faculty members are committed to a strong student-teacher relationship.

Applying

Students may apply to begin their program during the fall, winter, spring, or summer quarters. The Albers School looks for individuals who demonstrate aptitude, interest, and the ability to successfully complete a challenging academic program. Applicants must have a bachelor's degree from a regionally accredited institution but are not required to have had previous course work in business. Applicants should have at least one year of full-time work experience and must also submit scores from the Graduate Management Admission Test (GMAT). M.A.E. applicants may substitute GRE scores for the GMAT.

Correspondence and Information

Director of Admissions
Seattle University
900 Broadway
Seattle, Washington 98122-4460
Telephone: 206-296-5900
Fax: 206-296-5902
E-mail: grad-admissions@seattleu.edu
World Wide Web: http://www.seattleu.edu/asbe

Seattle University

THE FACULTY

Jan Warren Duggar, Dean of the Albers School of Business and Economics; Ph.D., Florida State.
C. Frederick DeKay, Associate Dean of the Albers School of Business and Economics; Ph.D., Johns Hopkins.

Al Ansari, Associate Professor of Operations; Ph.D., Nebraska.
David Arnesen, Associate Professor of Business Law; J.D., Puget Sound.
Vidya Awasthi, Assistant Professor of Accounting; Ph.D., Washington (Seattle).
Peter Brous, Associate Professor of Finance; Ph.D., Oregon.
Karen A. Brown, Chairperson of the Department of Management and Professor of Operations; Ph.D., Washington (Seattle).
Chauncey Burke, Assistant Professor of Marketing; Ph.D, Washington (Seattle).
Robert E. Callahan, Associate Professor of Management; Ph.D., Case Western Reserve.
Vinay Datar, Assistant Professor of Finance; Ph.D., Florida.
Suzanne Erickson, Associate Professor of Finance; Ph.D., Washington (Seattle).
C. Patrick Fleenor, Professor of Management; Ph.D., Washington (Seattle).
Sharon Galbraith, Assistant Professor of Marketing; Ph.D., Washington (Seattle).
Bridget Hiedemann, Assistant Professor of Economics; Ph.D., Duke.
Thomas J. Hofferd, Assistant Professor of Accounting; Ph.D., Central Florida.
Sharon Lobel, Associate Professor of Management; Ph.D., Harvard.
Diane L. Lockwood, Associate Professor of Information Systems; Ph.D., Nebraska.
Gregory Magnan, Assistant Professor of Operations; Ph.D. candidate, Michigan State.
Carl Obermiller, Associate Professor of Marketing; Ph.D., Ohio State.
Ayesegul Ozsomer, Assistant Professor of Marketing; Ph.D., Michigan State.
Barbara Parker, Associate Professor of Management; Ph.D., Colorado.
Russ Petersen, Thomas F. Gleed Professor of Business Administration; Ph.D., Washington (Seattle).
Dean Peterson, Assistant Professor of Economics; Ph.D., Illinois at Urbana-Champaign.
Gregory Prussia, Assistant Professor of Management; Ph.D., Arizona State.
Mary Jean Rivers, Associate Professor of Economics; Ph.D. Pittsburgh.
J. Fiona Robertson, Assistant Professor of Finance; Ph.D., Queen's.
Susan Shevlin, Associate Professor of Accounting; Ph.D., Rochester.
Timothy Sorenson, Assistant Professor of Economics; Ph.D., Harvard.
Harriet B. Stephenson, Professor of Management; Ph.D., Washington (Seattle).
David E. Tinius, Chairperson of the Department of Accounting and Professor of Accounting; Ph.D., Washington (Seattle).
Rex Swee-Kee Toh, Professor of Marketing; Ph. D., Minnesota.
Ruben Trevino, Associate Professor of Finance; Ph.D., Alabama.
Christian Weber, Assistant Professor of Economics; Ph.D., Duke.
Susan Weihrich, Assistant Professor of Accounting; Ph.D., Houston.
William L. Weis, Professor of Accounting; Ph.D., Washington (Seattle).
Peter Wilamoski, Assistant Professor of Economics; Ph.D., Oregon.
Geoff Willis, Assistant Professor of Operations; Ph.D., Texas Tech.
Barbara M. Yates, Chairperson of the Department of Economics and Finance and Professor of Economics; Ph.D., Michigan.

SETON HALL UNIVERSITY

W. Paul Stillman School of Business

Programs of Study

At the graduate program level, the W. Paul Stillman School of Business offers a Master of Business Administration (M.B.A.), a Master of Science (M.S.), joint degrees, and certificates. M.B.A. concentrations offered are in accounting, economics, finance, human resource management, management, management information systems, marketing, quantitative analysis, and sports management. Available M.S. programs are in accounting and professional accounting, human resource management, international business, information systems, and taxation.

Most M.B.A. and M.S. students are enrolled in the evening programs. Daytime programs include the Day M.B.A. Program (full-time, weekdays), M.S. in information systems (part-time, Saturdays), and full-time option toward completion of the M.S. in accounting (combination of weekdays and evenings). The evening M.B.A. requires 30–60 credits, depending on course waivers granted, while the Day M.B.A. Program, an innovative, sixteen-month experiential learning program, requires 48 credits, including built-in externship and skill-building phases. Minimum credit completion requirements for M.S. degrees begin at 30 (33 for international business), depending on the number of prerequisites needed for individual students.

In addition to the M.B.A. and M.S. programs, the W. Paul Stillman School of Business offers an international business certificate to M.B.A. students who enroll in additional course work, joint M.B.A./M.S. in international business, and J.D./M.B.A. degrees and post-M.B.A. and post-M.S. tax certificates. All degrees require completion within five years.

The School of Business programs are dedicated to the facilitation of lifelong professional learning. The M.B.A. curriculum provides a strong graduate-level foundation and encourages specialization in timely areas of employer need and personal interest in today's global and technological workforce. In contrast to the breadth provided in the M.B.A. programs, the focus of the M.S. degrees is depth of knowledge, skills, and competencies in a specific business area.

Research Facilities

In 1994, the Walsh Library opened its doors. This 155,000-square-foot research facility seats more than 1,100 students. Information technology available includes CD-ROM databases (both index and full-text), multimedia computer labs, audiovisual installations, an electronic visual aid (scanner-reader), and Setoncat, the online catalog of holdings accessible both on-site and via the campus network.

In addition to University facilities such as the library and University Computer Center, the School of Business' Andersen Planning Skills Center provides a computer lab and technical support services solely for/to business students. Extensive School of Business faculty research initiatives include the publishing of the *MidAtlantic Journal of Business* by the Division of Research.

Financial Aid

Graduate assistantships are awarded to selected full-time students. Admission to a full-time program is required prior to being considered for a position. For an application for Seton Hall funded aid (graduate assistantships), students should contact the University's Office of Graduate Services at 973-275-2036. For more information on federal financial aid and loans, students should contact Seton Hall's Financial Aid Office by mail or telephone (973-761-9350).

Cost of Study

Graduate business tuition for the 1998–99 academic year is $530 per credit. Additional fees include a $50 application fee, a per-semester registration fee ($85 for part-time and $105 for full-time fall/spring studies, $45 each for summers and winters), course materials/books, and living expenses. More detailed information about costs of study as well as University policies and procedures is published in the 1998–99 Seton Hall University *Graduate Bulletin.*

Living and Housing Costs

On- and off-campus housing in dormitories, apartments, and houses is available. Due to the large number of options and price ranges, it is best to contact Seton Hall's Department of Housing and Residence Life by mail or telephone (973-761-9172) for further information.

Student Group

Seton Hall's enrollment is approximately 10,000, almost half of whom are graduate students. Approximately 850 are pursuing M.B.A. and/or M.S. degrees in business, mostly on a part-time basis. Approximately 90 percent of School of Business graduate students are fully employed. Student groups, including the International Student Organization, provide social support and networking opportunities.

Location

Seton Hall's main campus, which houses the School of Business, is located on 58 acres in the suburban village of South Orange, New Jersey. The campus is located only 14 miles from New York City and less than ½ mile from the Midtown Direct train. It is easily accessible from most of the state's major highways, including the Garden State Parkway, New Jersey Turnpike, and Routes 78 and 280.

The University and The School

Seton Hall's School of Business was the first private school in New Jersey to earn accreditation by the AACSB–The International Association for Management Education. Founded in 1856, Seton Hall is the oldest and largest diocesan-affiliated Catholic University in the nation and maintains regional accreditation through the Middle States Association of Colleges and Schools. The School of Business' new state-of-the-art academic facility was completed in fall 1997.

Applying

For consideration, applicants must hold a baccalaureate degree from a regionally accredited college or university. Admissions decisions are based on the following submitted evidence of relevant professional and academic potential: work experience and credentials, personal statement, grade point averages, letters of academic and professional recommendation, and GMAT scores. A limited number of Master of Science (not M.B.A.) students with extensive, relevant professional experience and exemplary academic records are granted GMAT waivers. Additional application information is required from international applicants. Members of minority groups are encouraged to apply.

Correspondence and Information

W. Paul Stillman School of Business
Student Information Office (Room 536)
Seton Hall University
400 South Orange Avenue
South Orange, New Jersey 07079-2692

Telephone: 973-761-9222
Fax: 973-761-9217
E-mail: busgrad@shu.edu
World Wide Web: http://www.shu.edu:80/academic/business/mastoc.html

Seton Hall University

THE FACULTY

DEPARTMENT CHAIRS

Accounting and Taxation: James W. Greenspan, Assistant Professor; Ph.D., Texas A&M.

Computing and Decision Sciences: David Rosenthal, Associate Professor; Ph.D., Pennsylvania (acting).

Economics: John J. Dall Jr., Professor; Ph.D., Pennsylvania (Wharton) (acting).

Finance and Legal Studies: Philip R. Phillips, Professor of Finance; Ph.D., NYU.

Management: Leigh Stelzer, Professor; Ph.D., Michigan.

Marketing: Joseph Z. Wisenblit, Associate Professor; Ph.D., CUNY, Baruch.

FACULTY MEMBERS

Sheldon Epstein, Interim Dean; Ph.D., NYU.

Wagdy Abdallah, Associate Professor of Accounting; Ph.D., North Texas State.
Paula Becker Alexander, Associate Professor of Management; Ph.D., Rutgers; J.D., NYU.
Amar dev Amar, Professor of Management; Ph.D., CUNY, Baruch.
Henry J. Amoroso, Associate Professor of Legal Studies; J.D., Delaware.
A. J. G. Babu, Associate Professor of Computing and Decision Sciences; Ph.D., SMU.
Myron C. Bakun, Assistant Professor of Computing and Decision Sciences; Ph.D., CUNY, Baruch.
Karen E. Boroff, Associate Professor of Management; Ph.D., Columbia.
Joan H. Coll, Professor of Management; Ph.D., Fordham.
Reed Easton, Associate Professor of Accounting and Taxation; LL.M., NYU; J.D., William and Mary; CPA (New Jersey).
Paul Forbes, Faculty Associate of Management; B.S., Fordham.
David Gelb, Assistant Professor of Accounting; Ph.D., NYU.
Brian Greenstein, Associate Professor of Accounting; Ph.D., Houston.
John J. Harrington Jr., Professor of Finance; Ph.D., NYU.
Richard J. Hunter Jr., Professor of Business Law; J.D., Notre Dame.
Andrew Ikpoh, Associate Professor of Economics; Ph.D., Columbia.
Vasanti A. Jategaonkar, Associate Professor of Computing and Decision Sciences; Ph.D., Cornell.
W. John Jordan, Professor of Economics; Ph.D., SUNY at Albany.
Chander Kant, Associate Professor of Economics; Ph.D., SMU.
Frederick J. Kelly, Professor of Finance; Ph.D., Columbia.
Kusum Ketkar, Professor of Economics; Ph.D., Vanderbilt.
Anthony Loviscek, Assistant Professor of Economics; Ph.D., West Virginia.
Hector R. Lozada, Assistant Professor of Marketing; Ph.D., Kentucky.
Ann M. Mayo, Assistant Professor of Management; Ph.D., Ohio State.
Robert W. McGee, Associate Professor of Accounting; J.D., Cleveland State; Ph.D., Union (Ohio); Ph.D., Warwick (England); CPA (New Jersey).
Athar Murtuza, Associate Professor of Accounting; Ph.D., Washington State.
Agnes P. Olszewski, Associate Professor of Marketing and Director of the Institute for International Business; Ph.D., Warsaw.
Raghavan Parthasarthy, Assistant Professor of Management; Ph.D., CUNY, Baruch.
Stephen F. Pirog, Assistant Professor of Marketing; Ph.D., Temple.
Cecilia L. Ricci, Associate Professor of Finance; Ph.D., University of International Business and Economics (Beijing).
Robert E. Shapiro, Associate Professor of Taxation; LL.M. (taxation), NYU; J.D., Harvard; CPA (New Jersey).
William Stoever, Professor of Management; J.D., Harvard; Ph.D., NYU.
Joyce A. Strawser, Assistant Professor of Accounting; Ph.D., LSU.
Frank Tinari, Professor of Economics; Ph.D., Fordham.
George Tzannetakis, Professor of Economics; Ph.D., NYU.
Rob R. Weitz, Associate Professor of Computing and Decision Sciences; Ph.D., Massachusetts at Amherst.
Yonah Wilamowsky, Professor of Computing and Decision Sciences; Ph.D., NYU.
Baichun Xiao, Associate Professor of Computing and Decision Sciences; Ph.D., Pennsylvania (Wharton).
Jason Yin, Associate Professor of Management; Ph.D., NYU.
Yeomin Yoon, Associate Professor of Finance; Ph.D., Bryn Mawr.

SIMMONS COLLEGE

Graduate School of Management

Programs of Study

Simmons offers the only M.B.A. program designed to meet the needs of women. With work experience averaging ten years, compared to two or three years for most business schools, students come to Simmons knowing a great deal both about themselves and about what they want from their education. Students include women in the process of career change, women who have reached a career plateau, and women with substantial management experience who want to move ahead in their careers.

The Simmons M.B.A. program teaches quantitative skills in economics, accounting, finance, operations, and marketing. All are fundamental to management and are essentials learned at all highly respected business schools. The Simmons program then gives its students something no other M.B.A. program can: the ability to deal confidently with the issues women face on their way to management leadership. Cases featuring women managers are researched and written at Simmons to help students anticipate critical management choices. A market research project, a six-week internship, and an advanced elective in the last term of study offer each student three opportunities to specialize and to apply her new knowledge and skills.

A dedicated career services staff and a required course in career strategies ensure that students are synthesizing their academic learning and career aspirations as they progress through the program. The alumnae network is actively involved in many of the industry and function career panels that are offered throughout the year.

Simmons offers three options for earning the M.B.A. An accelerated one-year program allows a woman to take a sabbatical from her career to earn the degree, while the two- and three-year tracks make it possible to parallel work—and earnings—with learning. The same faculty members teach classes for full-time and part-time students. Students may begin in September or July.

Research Facilities

Students have access to a core collection in the Graduate School of Management (GSM) library as well as to computer searching, reserve collections, and interlibrary loans. The library offers course and career support, and its services are dedicated to management students. The Beatley Library of Simmons College and the facilities of an eleven-member college library consortium are also available.

Financial Aid

Merit scholarships are available, and applicants are automatically considered. The program participates in federal student loan plans and administers its own grant and loan funds. Counselors advise individuals on both conventional and creative means of financing graduate education.

Cost of Study

In 1998–99, total M.B.A. tuition is $26,820 ($596 per credit hour). A student activity fee of $25 per semester and an optional health fee of $200 per semester ($400 per year) are also charged. Students should allow $3000 for books and course materials for three semesters of study. These figures are estimated and subject to change.

Living and Housing Costs

A single student can expect to spend $1000 a month on housing. This figure may be cut by about 30 percent through several alternatives; graduate housing, including meals, was available for approximately $900 a month ($8070 for the academic year) in 1997–98, and many students share apartments in the area. Local alumnae often greet and help new international students learn about Boston and the school.

Student Group

The profile of a Simmons M.B.A. class differs from many other schools' in several respects. Entering students have, on average, eight to ten years of work experience. Total enrollment is about 250 students. A typical student, working individually and in group study projects, completes course work with a class of about 45 women. In recent years, new students have represented twenty countries.

Simmons students and more than 3000 alumnae form a tight-knit community embodying a culture that supports achievement. Alumnae have excelled in profit-making and not-for-profit ventures. Career services and the library are available to GSM alumnae for life.

Location

Located in Boston's Back Bay, a historic district of turn-of-the-century town houses, the Graduate School of Management consists of a classroom building, administrative building, and student services building containing the library, computer laboratory, study and meeting rooms—all within half of a city block. Public transportation is at the door. Boston offers a full spectrum of cultural resources that students can access with special discounts. A range of private and nonprofit enterprises provides choice internships and practical opportunities.

The College

Simmons College is a private, nonsectarian institution serving some 1,300 undergraduate women and 1,700 women and men in graduate and related studies. Since the early 1900s, society's attitudes toward women as well as women's perceptions of themselves and what they can contribute have changed dramatically. Simmons College has not only kept pace with these changes but has also helped to shape them in its classrooms.

Applying

Applicants must have at least two years of work experience and must show evidence of academic capability in analytic thinking and quantitative skills. A complete application includes transcripts of grades for all courses completed beyond high school, three essays, three recommendations, and a GMAT score (plus TOEFL for international students). Applications are evaluated on a rolling basis.

Correspondence and Information

Admissions Office
Graduate School of Management
Simmons College
409 Commonwealth Avenue
Boston, Massachusetts 02215
Telephone: 617-521-3840
800-597-1MBA (toll-free)
Fax: 617-521-3880
E-mail: gsmadm@simmons.edu

Simmons College

THE FACULTY

Patricia O'Brien, Dean; D.B.A., Harvard.

Faculty
Nicholas Amdur, M.B.A., Boston University.
Margarete Arndt, D.B.A., Boston University.
Annabel Beerel, M.B.A., Cranfield Institute of Technology; Ph.D. candidate, Boston University.
April Evans, M.B.A., Simmons.
Maurice Gervais, M.B.A., Boston University.
James Grant, Ph.D., Chicago.
Susan Hass, M.B.A., Harvard; CPA.
Mary Louise Hatten, Ph.D., Purdue.
Ben Hunt, Ph.D., Harvard.
Cynthia Ingols, Ed.D., Harvard.
Deborah Kolb, Ph.D., MIT.
Ann Lindsey, M.B.A., Simmons.
Deborah Marlino, Ph.D., UCLA.
David Novak, Ph.D., Washington State.
Barbara A. Sawtelle, Ph.D., MIT.
Mary Shapiro, M.B.A., Wright State.
Christine Sullivan, M.S., Fordham.

SOUTHERN ILLINOIS UNIVERSITY AT CARBONDALE

College of Business and Administration Graduate Programs

Programs of Study

Beginning in 1998, the College of Business and Administration offers incoming Master of Business Administration (M.B.A.) students three new options. Students may choose between the M.B.A. in International Business (IB), the M.B.A. in Management of Information (MOI), or the M.B.A. in general studies. Students in the general studies M.B.A. program may choose to specialize in a wide variety of areas within the College (including finance, management, and marketing) or outside the College (including agribusiness economics, industrial technology, workforce education, and computer science). The M.B.A. curriculum consists of 33 core credit hours, with additional foundation course requirements for students with non-business undergraduate degrees. The new M.B.A. program has expanded the elective options, allowing students greater latitude to customize their learning experience. Students are encouraged to take advantage of the accessibility of the graduate faculty members to complete an independent study or thesis in their chosen area of concentration. The M.B.A. program is accredited by AACSB–The International Association for Management Education.

The College of Business and Administration offers three concurrent degree programs. The School of Law (M.B.A./J.D.), the School of Mass Communication (M.B.A./M.A.), and the School of Agribusiness Economics (M.B.A./M.S.) work with the College to provide these unique educational choices. The College also offers students the opportunity to study in France through exchange agreements with GROUPE ESC Grenoble and GROUPE Sup de Co Montpellier.

Research Facilities

The University's Morris Library contains over 2 million volumes and subscribes to more than 11,000 current serials. Supplementing the resources of Morris Library is the Center for Research Libraries (Chicago), in which the University holds membership. Students also have access to ILLINET Online (IO), the statewide automated catalog, circulation, and interlibrary loan system. Online bibliographic search capability and CD-ROM workstations are also available. Computing Affairs operates a general purpose computing facility that provides related computer services and support to the University academic and research community. In addition, the College of Business and Administration houses a computer laboratory equipped with microcomputers and terminals for mainframe access. Internet and BITNET are also available to the students.

Financial Aid

Financial assistance is available to qualified students in several forms. Graduate Fellowships are awarded by the Graduate School and include a monthly stipend and tuition waiver. Graduate research assistantships are available within the College of Business and Administration and are awarded on the basis of student potential or academic performance in the program. Graduate assistants receive a salary and tuition scholarship. Students may also apply for assistantships in the Morris Library, the Student Center, and the Computer Center. Other sources of financial assistance in the form of fellowships and loans are available through the Financial Aid Office.

Cost of Study

Tuition and fees are established by the Board of Trustees and are subject to change without prior notification. In 1998–99, the tuition and fees for a student enrolled for 12 credit hours are $1702.50 per semester for Illinois residents and $4073.70 per semester for nonresidents. This includes a $221 charge per semester for student medical benefits, which may be waived for students carrying comparable coverage.

Living and Housing Costs

SIUC offers residence hall double and single occupancy housing for graduate students on a first-come, first-served basis. Efficiency apartments for single graduate students are also available. Family housing is available at two apartment complexes operated by SIUC. Many off-campus rental units are available within walking distance of the campus, including apartments, boarding houses, and mobile homes; costs vary. In 1998–99, residence hall rates are $1880 per semester for double occupancy with room and board and $2427 per semester for single occupancy, board optional. University apartments rent for $333 per month for an efficiency, utilities included, and $361 per month for one bedroom, utilities included. For further information, students should contact University Housing (telephone: 618-453-2301).

Student Group

The M.B.A. program enrolls approximately 120 students. Nearly 50 percent of the students are international, representing twenty different countries. The male-to-female ratio is nearly 50:50. Most students have had previous work experience and attend the program full-time.

Location

Carbondale, with a population of 20,000, is located approximately 100 miles southeast of St. Louis, Missouri. Immediately south of Carbondale are the "Illinois Ozarks," some of the most beautiful and rugged terrain in the state. Within 10 miles of campus are two state parks, four recreational lakes, and the 240,000-acre Shawnee National Forest. Camping, caving, rock climbing, boating, hunting, and fishing are just a few of the diversions that are easily accessible.

The University and The College

Southern Illinois University at Carbondale became a four-year, degree-granting institution in 1907. Graduate work was instituted in 1943, with the first doctoral degrees granted in 1959. Total enrollment today is approximately 20,000 undergraduates and 4,000 graduate students. SIUC has the eleventh largest international student population in the country, with students representing over 100 nations currently enrolled.

The College of Business and Administration was established in 1956 and was accredited six years later. The M.B.A. program was established in 1966. Offices for the College are located in Rehn Hall. Independently affiliated with the College is the Pontikes Center for Management of Information. Placement services are provided by University Career Services and by the College's H. Scott Hines Placement Center.

Applying

Applicants to the M.B.A. program are required to submit a Graduate School application, a College of Business and Administration application, official transcripts, three letters of recommendation, GMAT scores, brief essay responses, a description of previous work experience, and a nonrefundable $20 application fee. International students whose native language is not English are also required to submit TOEFL scores (minimum 550). Applications are considered on a case-by-case basis. Decisions are made based upon the entire application. There is no minimum GMAT score requirement.

Students may enter the program in August, January, May, or June. Individual programs of study are determined after consultation with the M.B.A. coordinator.

Correspondence and Information

Joe Pineau
M.B.A. Coordinator
College of Business and Administration
133 Rehn Hall
Mail Code 4625
Southern Illinois University at Carbondale
Carbondale, Illinois 62901-4625

Telephone: 618-453-3030
Fax: 618-453-7961
E-mail: mbagp@siu.edu

Southern Illinois University at Carbondale

THE FACULTY AND THEIR RESEARCH

School of Accountancy

Donald Gribbin, Associate Professor; Ph.D., Oklahoma State, 1989; CPA. Managerial and cost accounting.
Randall Hahn, Associate Professor; Ph.D., Kentucky, 1984, CPA. Taxation and auditing.
Allan Karnes, Professor and Director; M.A., J.D., Southern Illinois at Carbondale, 1986. CPA; Taxation and auditing.
James King, Associate Professor; Ph.D., Indiana, 1988; CPA. Behavioral auditing and financial accounting.
Michael M. Masoner, Associate Professor; Ph.D., Minnesota, 1975; CPA. Accounting systems and cost accounting.
Marcus Dean Odom, Assistant Professor; Ph.D., Oklahoma State, 1993; CPA. Accounting information systems.
Richard Rivers, Professor; D.B.A., Kent State, 1976; CPA. Quantitative decisions models, information systems and managerial accounting.
Julie Sobery, Associate Professor; Ph.D., Saint Louis, 1982; CPA. Financial accounting and accounting theory.
Raymond Wacker, Associate Professor; Ph.D., Houston, 1989; CPA. Taxation.
Robert B. Welker, Rehn Professor of Accountancy; Ph.D., Arizona State, 1977. Managerial accounting and accounting theory.

Department of Finance

Marcia M. Cornett, Professor; Ph.D., Indiana, 1983. Corporate finance, financial institutions and markets.
Peter DaDalt, Assistant Professor; Ph.D., Georgia State, 1998. Corporate and investment finance.
Wallace N. Davidson III, Rehn Professor of Finance; Ph.D., Ohio State, 1982. Corporate finance.
Hussein H. Elsaid, Professor and Chair; Ph.D., Illinois, 1968. International finance and financial management.
Iqbal Mathur, Professor; Ph.D., Cincinnati, 1974. Financial management, international finance.
James Musumeci, Assistant Professor; Ph.D., Texas, 1987. Investments and corporate finance.
Evren Orrs, Assistant Professor; Ph.D., Boston College, 1998. Financial Institutions.
Mark A. Peterson, Assistant Professor; Ph.D., Penn State, 1996. Investment and corporate finance.
Andrew C. Szakmary, Assistant Professor; Ph.D., New Orleans, 1989. International finance and investments.

Department of Management

Steven J. Karau, Assistant Professor; Ph.D., Purdue, 1993. Organizational behavior, human resource management.
William McKinley, Associate Professor; Ph.D., Columbia, 1983. Organization theory, organizational behavior and strategic management.
Arlyn J. Melcher, Professor; Ph.D., Chicago, 1964. Organization theory, strategic management and research methodology.
Michael Michalisin, Assistant Professor; Ph.D., Kent State, 1996. Strategic management, organization theory and international business.
Reed Nelson, Associate Professor; Ph.D., Cornell, 1983. Organizational behavior and theory.
Arkalgud Ramaprasad, Professor; Ph.D., Pittsburgh, 1980. Strategic management and management information systems.
Charles Stubbart, Associate Professor; Ph.D., Pittsburgh, 1983. Strategic management, international business and entrepreneurship.
Suresh K. Tadisina, Associate Professor; Ph.D., Cincinnati, 1987. Operations management and management sciences.
Gregory P. White, Associate Professor; Ph.D., Cincinnati, 1976. Production management and management sciences.

Department of Marketing

Siva K. Balasubramanian, Professor; Ph.D., SUNY at Buffalo, 1986. Advertising/promotional management, consumer behavior, new product diffusion models and measurement issues in marketing.
Gordon C. Bruner II, Associate Professor; Ph.D., North Texas, 1983. Consumer behavior, promotion management and scale compilation.
John P. Fraedrich, Associate Professor; Ph.D., Texas A&M, 1988. Ethics, international marketing and industrial sales.
Maryon F. King, Associate Professor; Ph.D., Indiana, 1989. Marketing management, consumer behavior and promotion management.
Anand Kumar, Assistant Professor; Ph.D., Indiana, 1996. Consumer behavior, customer delight, customer value, customer emotions, advertising effectiveness.
Zarrel V. Lambert, Professor and Chair; Ph.D., Penn State, 1966. Research methodology and statistics.
Lynette Mathur, Associate Professor; Ph.D., Ohio State, 1990. International business and marketing, marketing channels and physical distribution.
Donald L. Perry, Associate Professor; Ph.D., Illinois, 1966. Social marketing, management and sales management.
John H. Summey, Associate Professor; Ph.D., Arizona State, 1974. Marketing management, product strategy and marketing research.

SOUTHERN METHODIST UNIVERSITY

Edwin L. Cox School of Business

Programs of Study

The Edwin L. Cox School of Business offers three programs that lead to the degree of Master of Business Administration: a traditional two-year, full-time M.B.A. program; a ten-semester, three-year Professional M.B.A. Program for working professionals, and; a twenty-one-month Executive M.B.A. Program designed to enhance significant management experience with classroom and collaborative learning. Joint-degree programs are offered in conjunction with the law school for a Juris Doctor/M.B.A. (four years) and with the Meadows School of Arts for a Master of Arts Administration/M.B.A. (six semesters).

The M.B.A. program at the Edwin L. Cox School of Business is designed to provide students with a broad graduate management education, which supplements theoretical classroom learning with mentoring relationships and real business experiences. Classes are taught using a variety of both teaching styles to ensure that graduates not only master the basic tools of business but can also apply those tools in real-life experiences. The School's Business Leadership Center and M.B.A. Career Management Office have full-time staff members who assist students in the assessment and development of their classroom learning and enhance their success in their careers.

The full-time M.B.A. program requires four semesters with an intervening summer internship. The 60-hour program consists of required core courses in basic business analysis tools and management skills. Core courses are available in each of the traditional subject areas as well as in specialized areas such as strategic management, quality management, and business law. Electives cover a wide variety of subjects, with an emphasis on exposure to issues of global concern.

Students may choose to further their global business experience by participating in a study abroad opportunity. The Cox School has formal exchange arrangements with schools in Australia, Belgium, Brazil, Denmark, France, Great Britain, Japan, Mexico, Singapore, Spain, and Venezuela. Students may also participate in the prestigious M.B.A. Enterprise Corps, a program that sends graduates from the country's top M.B.A. programs to nations with emerging market economies.

The ten-semester, Professional M.B.A. Program is designed for students who wish to continue working while pursuing their M.B.A. degree. Classes meet on weekday evenings and Saturday mornings. The degree requirements are equivalent to those of the full-time program.

The Executive M.B.A. Program is specially designed for senior managers sponsored by their firms. Candidates must have a minimum of ten years of work experience with at least five years of significant management experience. Classes meet all day Friday and Saturday twice a month for five semesters; the program requires twenty-one months of study.

Cox School faculty members provide specialization in seven subject areas: accounting, business policy, finance and business economics, management information sciences, marketing, organizational behavior, and real estate and urban land economics. Each M.B.A. program emphasizes a broad-based education and offers students an opportunity to acquire job knowledge and skills for management positions. Additional courses are offered in entrepreneurship, international business, and other special areas of interest, such as the oil and gas industry.

Research Facilities

The 2-million-volume University Library System is available for advanced study by graduate students at the Cox School. The Cox School also has its own Business Information Center, a state-of-the-art library and computer facility that is designed to leverage technology and customize information resources to the student's benefit. Readily available information resources and software applications give M.B.A. students at Cox a competitive edge both inside and outside the classroom.

Financial Aid

Southern Methodist University is committed to making aid available to eligible students. The Cox School offers merit scholarships and graduate assistantships. Other forms of aid are available, including loans and Texas Equalization Grants. Information and application forms are available upon request.

Cost of Study

The cost of tuition in 1998–99 for either the full-time or the part-time program is $677 per credit hour, exclusive of fees, books, and supplies. The cost of the Executive M.B.A. Program is $40,000, including books and fees.

Living and Housing Costs

University housing is available for both single and married students. On-campus housing costs $3300 per year for a single student (double occupancy) and $3705 to $4415 per year for married student apartments. Off-campus housing ranges in cost from $550 to $1100 per month.

Student Group

The student population reflects a global diversity that is essential for the academic exploration and interaction that take place in the classroom. Nearly all students are returning to academics after a period of employment, and many enter with academic backgrounds in fields other than business administration.

Location

SMU is centrally located in Dallas, Texas. In addition to the advantages presented by the close ties of the Cox School to the Dallas business community, the metropolitan setting provides many other opportunities. Cultural events and sports activities are within a 20-minute drive of the campus, and many other opportunities are within walking distance. Dallas is a national and international business center, ranking third in the U.S. as a home to major corporate headquarters and sixth in the world for multinational corporate headquarters.

The University

A private university, SMU traditionally has attracted students from the entire country and not just the Southwest. SMU seeks to provide opportunities for interaction among students of varying cultural, economic, and social backgrounds. University governance and policy encourage the open exchange of ideas by the students, the faculty, and the administration.

Applying

Admission to the Cox School is highly selective. Applicants must submit an application with essays, transcripts from all colleges and universities attended, two letters of recommendation, GMAT scores (and TOEFL scores for international students), and a $50 application fee. Interviews are strongly recommended.

Students enter the full-time program in the fall semester. Application deadlines are as follows: early, November 30; first, February 15; second, April 15. After April 15, the University follows a rolling admissions policy. The Professional M.B.A. Program begins in fall (May 15 application deadline) and spring (November 1 application deadline). The Executive M.B.A. Program begins in the fall only (May 15 application deadline). SMU does not discriminate on the basis of race, color, national or ethnic origin, sex, age, or disability.

Correspondence and Information

Graduate Admissions Office
Edwin L. Cox School of Business
Southern Methodist University
P.O. Box 750333
Dallas, Texas 75275-0333

Telephone: 214-768-2630
800-472-3622 (toll-free)
Fax: 214-768-3956
E-mail: mbainfo@mail.cox.smu.edu
World Wide Web: http://www.cox.smu.edu/

Southern Methodist University

THE FACULTY

Ellen P. Allen, Lecturer in Management Information Sciences; Ph.D., SMU.
Jeffrey W. Allen, Assistant Professor of Finance; Ph.D., Purdue.
Uday Apte, Associate Professor of Management Information Sciences; Ph.D., Pennsylvania.
Thomas E. Barry, Professor of Marketing; Ph.D., North Texas.
Cynthia M. Beath, Associate Professor and Chair of Management Information Sciences; Ph.D., UCLA.
Randolph P. Beatty, Distinguished Professor of Accounting; Ph.D., Illinois.
Joan F. Brett, Assistant Professor of Organizational Behavior and Business Policy; Ph.D., NYU.
Steven P. Brown, Associate Professor of Marketing; Ph.D., Texas at Austin.
Brian R. Bruce, Lecturer in Finance; M.B.A., Chicago.
William B. Brueggeman, Clara R. and Leo F. Corrigan Sr. Professor of Real Estate; Ph.D., Ohio State.
Howard J. Bunsis, Assistant Professor of Accounting; Ph.D., Chicago.
Marvin L. Carlson, Professor of Accounting; Ph.D., Wisconsin.
Albert V. Casey, Executive in Residence in Organizational Behavior and Business Policy; M.B.A., Harvard.
Andrew H. Chen, Distinguished Professor of Finance; Ph.D., Berkeley.
James C. Collins Jr., Lecturer in Management Information Sciences; M.S.I.E., SMU.
Sue A. Conger, Associate Professor of Management Information Sciences; Ph.D., NYU.
William L. Cron, Marilyn and Leo F. Corrigan Endowment Professor of Marketing; D.B.A., Indiana.
Hemang A. Desai, Assistant Professor of Accounting; Ph.D., Tulane.
William R. Dillon, Herman W. Lay Professor of Marketing and Associate Dean of Academic Affairs; Ph.D., CUNY.
Venkat R. Eleswarapu, Assistant Professor of Finance; Ph.D., Iowa.
Judith H. Foxman, Lecturer in Marketing; M.B.A., SMU.
Elbert B. Greynolds Jr., Associate Professor of Accounting and Assistant Dean of Undergraduate Studies; Ph.D., Georgia State.
Richard J. Haayen, Executive in Residence in Finance; B.S., Ohio State.
Richard W. Hansen, Professor of Marketing; Ph.D., Minnesota.
George H. Hempel, Professor of Finance; Ph.D., Michigan.
Steven L. Henning, Assistant Professor of Accounting; Ph.D., Wisconsin–Madison.
David G. Hoopes, Assistant Professor of Organizational Behavior and Business Policy; Ph.D., UCLA.
Daniel J. Howard, Professor and Chair of Marketing; Ph.D., Ohio State.
Ellen F. Jackofsky, Associate Professor of Organizational Behavior and Business Policy and Associate Provost; Ph.D., Texas at Dallas.
Padmaja Kadiyala, Assistant Professor of Finance; Ph.D., Ohio State.
Roger A. Kerin, Harold C. Simmons Distinguished Professor of Marketing; Ph.D., Minnesota.
Barbara Kincaid, Lecturer in Business Law and Tax; J.D., SMU.
James T. Kindley, Lecturer in Marketing; M.B.A., Harvard.
Amna Kirmani, Assistant Professor of Marketing; Ph.D., Stanford.
Chun H. Lam, Associate Professor of Finance; Ph.D., Duke.
David T. Lei, Associate Professor of Organizational Behavior and Business Policy; Ph.D., Columbia.
James G. Livingston, Assistant Professor of Accounting and Business Law And Tax; Ph.D., Rochester.
Peter MacKay, Instructor of Finance; M.B.A., Laval (France).
Tammy Madsen, Assistant Professor of Organizational Behavior and Business Policy; Ph.D., UCLA.
Joseph Magliolo III, Professor and Chair of Accounting; Ph.D., Stanford.
Richard O. Mason, Carr P. Collins Jr. Distinguished Professor of Management Information Sciences; Ph.D., Berkeley.
Richard D. Metters, Assistant Professor of Management Information Sciences; Ph.D., North Carolina at Chapel Hill.
Sara B. Moeller, Instructor of Management Information Sciences; M.A., Ohio State.
C. Page Moreau, Instructor of Marketing; M.P., Columbia.
Gary T. Moskowitz, Instructor of Organizational Behavior and Business Policy; M.B.A., Dartmouth.
Albert W. Niemi Jr., Professor of Economics and Dean; Ph.D., Connecticut.
Mark John Nigrini, Visiting Assistant Professor of Accounting; Ph.D., Cincinnati.
Thomas R. Perkowski, Lecturer in Organizational Behavior and Business Policy; B.A., Penn State.
Robin L. Pinkley, Marilyn and Leo F. Corrigan Endowment Professor, Associate Professor, and Chair of Organizational Behavior and Business Policy; Ph.D., North Carolina.
Bobbette Pippenger, Visiting Assistant Professor of Finance; Ph.D., Maryland.
Catherine Elizabeth Plummer, Assistant Professor of Accounting; Ph.D., Texas at Austin.
Amy V. Puelz, Assistant Professor of Management Information Sciences; Ph.D., Nebraska.
Robert Puelz, Dexter Endowment Assistant Professor of Insurance and Financial Services; Ph.D., Georgia.
Madeleine E. Pullman, Assistant Professor of Management Information Sciences; Ph.D., Utah.
Neil C. Ramiller, Visiting Assistant Professor of Management Information Sciences; Ph.D., UCLA.
Robert W. Rasberry, Assistant Professor of Organizational Behavior and Business Policy; Ph.D., Kansas.
Marc R. Reinganum, Mary Jo Vaughn Rauscher Professor of Financial Investments; Ph.D., Chicago.
Lola Rhodes, Lecturer in Accounting; M.S., Texas at Arlington.
Susan M. Riffe, Assistant Professor of Accounting; Ph.D., USC.
Jennifer Roney, Assistant Professor of Organizational Behavior and Business Policy; Ph.D., Utah.
Ulrike Schultze, Assistant Professor of Management Information Sciences; Ph.D., Case Western Reserve.
John H. Semple, Assistant Professor of Management Information Sciences; Ph.D., Texas at Austin.
Raj Sethuraman, Assistant Professor of Marketing; Ph.D., Northwestern.
Wayne H. Shaw, Robert B. Cullum Professor in Accounting; Ph.D., Texas at Austin.
John W. Slocum Jr., O. Paul Corley Distinguished Professor of Organizational Behavior and Administration; Ph.D., Washington (Seattle).
James L. Smith, Cary M. Maguire Professor of Oil & Gas Management; Ph.D., Harvard.
Marion G. Sobol, Professor of Management Information Sciences; Ph.D., Michigan.
Jonathan S. Sokobin, Assistant Professor of Finance; Ph.D., Chicago.
John A. Stieber, Assistant Professor of Finance; M.A., SMU.
Kirk Lee Tennant, Lecturer in Accounting; M.S., Purdue.
Thomas G. Thibodeau, Professor of Finance and Senior Research Fellow; Ph.D., SUNY at Stony Brook.
Rex W. Thompson, James M. Collins Professor of Finance; Ph.D., Rochester.
Michael F. van Breda, Associate Professor of Accounting; Ph.D., Stanford.
Donald M. VandeWalle, Assistant Professor of Organizational Behavior and Business Policy; Ph.D., Minnesota.
Michael R. Vetsuypens, Professor of Finance; Ph.D., Rochester.
Gordon Walker, Marilyn and Leo F. Corrigan Endowment Professor of Organizational Behavior and Business Policy; Ph.D., Pennsylvania.
Rhonald D. Walker, Associate Professor of Accounting; J.D., SMU.
Catherine Weber, Lecturer in Business Law and Tax; J.D., SMU; LT.
Leland Michael Wooton, Associate Professor of Organizational Behavior and Business Policy; Ph.D., USC.

STANFORD UNIVERSITY

Graduate School of Business and School of Engineering Manufacturing Programs

Programs of Study

The Graduate School of Business and the School of Engineering, in partnership with Stanford Integrated Manufacturing Association (SIMA) companies, are committed to educating outstanding managers, engineers, and professors who will contribute creatively and substantively to meeting manufacturing challenges faced by industry in the twenty-first century.

The manufacturing systems engineering (MSE) master's degree program is jointly offered by the Departments of Mechanical Engineering and of Industrial Engineering and Engineering Management. The three-quarter curriculum integrates engineering design and management focused on manufacturing. Areas of emphasis include quality assurance, organizational behavior, analysis of production systems, manufacturing strategy, manufacturing systems design, supply chain management, design for manufacturability, robotics, smart product design, and integrated design for marketability and manufacture. Vigorous industrial interaction, team-based work, and an emphasis on product development distinguish this program.

The M.B.A./MSE dual-degree program combines study in manufacturing systems engineering with business management and leads to two master's degrees. This seven-quarter dual-degree program is offered jointly by the Schools of Engineering (MSE) and Business (M.B.A.). Students are admitted to and complete degree requirements for both schools.

The Future Professors of Manufacturing (FPM) Program is a special Ph.D. program designed for men and women with engineering and business backgrounds who are committed to conducting research and teaching on advanced manufacturing topics at U.S. universities. Students must first be admitted to an established Ph.D. degree program (see departmental descriptions) in business or engineering, then nominated for the FPM Program.

Research Facilities

The J. Hugh Jackson Library in Business offers an extensive collection of up-to-date research journals and other material, including electronic resources. The Terman Engineering Center houses a modern engineering research library with an extensive collection of professional journals. Other libraries on campus are also open to graduate students. Mainframe, workstation, and personal computers are widely available for course work and research. While numerous research facilities are involved in manufacturing-related research, five laboratories (Manufacturing Models, Product Realization, Rapid Prototyping, Smart Product Design, and Robotics) and two centers (Thornton Center for Engineering Management and Center for Design Research) specifically focus on manufacturing. Graduate students interact with manufacturing firms through course projects and research work and through SIMA, an industry-Stanford partnership.

Financial Aid

Manufacturing students may apply for financial aid through the Schools of Business and Engineering (students should refer to school and department listings). SIMA fellowships are available at the master's level. At the Ph.D. level, financial aid is offered through the Future Professors of Manufacturing Program.

Cost of Study

The 1998–99 nine-month academic year tuition for engineering is $23,595 and for business is $24,990, plus approximately $1850 for books, supplies, and fees.

Living and Housing Costs

The 1998–99 estimated cost of living for nine months is $10,332 for a single student living on campus, $15,567 for a single student living off campus, $19,977 for a married student living on campus, and $22,356 for a married student living off campus. Families with children should anticipate higher costs.

Student Group

The student body in the Schools of Business and Engineering represents a wide variety of nationalities and geographical areas. The Graduate School of Business Manufacturing Club and the Stanford Engineering Club for Automation and Manufacturing (SECAM) form an exceptionally strong community of manufacturing students at Stanford.

Student Outcomes

Graduates of the MSE and dual-degree master's programs typically return to industry in engineering and management positions in manufacturing (e.g., supply chain management, product management, product and process design, operations, quality, systems, and materials). Future Professors of Manufacturing Ph.D. graduates have obtained faculty positions at major U.S. universities, where they focus their teaching and research on manufacturing.

Location

Stanford University is located on an 8,200-acre campus, adjacent to the residential communities of Palo Alto and Menlo Park in the Santa Clara Valley and 35 miles south of San Francisco. The University is in the heart of Silicon Valley's high-technology manufacturing center. The climate is temperate, with rainfall normally occurring in the winter months. This climate encourages athletic activities, with opportunities for virtually all recreational pursuits.

The University and The Schools

Stanford University is a private university, founded in 1885. Enrollment is approximately 14,000. Forty-seven percent are undergraduates and 53 percent are graduate students. The Graduate School of Business offers courses in the areas of accounting, economic analysis and policy, finance, marketing, operations, information and technology, organizational behavior, and political economics. The School of Engineering includes the areas of aeronautics and astronautics, chemical engineering, civil and environmental engineering, computer science, electrical engineering, engineering–economic systems and operations research, industrial engineering and engineering management, materials science and engineering, and mechanical engineering. Cooperation among the faculty members of the different departments and schools makes it possible for students to pursue individual interests with the assistance of some of the most prominent educators and researchers in the world.

Applying

MSE program applicants request the mechanical engineering packet from the Graduate Admissions Office. Dual-M.B.A./MSE program applicants apply to both programs through the M.B.A. Admissions Office. Ph.D. applicants request materials for engineering from the Graduate Admissions Office and for business from the Doctoral Program Office. Students are admitted to begin study in the autumn quarter only. Application deadlines are as follows: for the MSE program, January 15, 1999; for the M.B.A./MSE program, November 4, 1998, and January 13, 1999; and for Ph.D. programs in business, January 4, 1999. For Ph.D. programs in engineering, applicants must contact the department. The GRE is required for the MSE program; the GMAT for the M.B.A./MSE program. The MSE program also requires an undergraduate degree in engineering or science. Applicants should contact individual departments for Ph.D. requirements and SIMA for the Future Professors of Manufacturing Program.

Correspondence and Information

Stanford Integrated Manufacturing Association (SIMA)
Stanford University, Building 02-530
Stanford, California 94305-3036

Telephone: 650-723-3016 (SIMA)
650-723-4291 (Graduate Admissions)
650-723-2766 (M.B.A. Admissions)
650-725-7462 (Doctoral Program Office—Business)

E-mail: sima-info@sima.stanford.edu
ck.gaa@forsythe.stanford.edu (Graduate Admissions)
mbainquiries@gsb.stanford.edu (M.B.A. Admissions)
phd_program_inquiries@gsb.stanford.edu (Doctoral Program Office—Business)

World Wide Web: http://www-sima.stanford.edu/

Stanford University

THE FACULTY AND THEIR RESEARCH

James L. Adams, Professor, Industrial Engineering and Engineering Management; Ph.D., Stanford, 1961. Creative problem solving and management of design in organizations.

Stephen R. Barley, Professor, Industrial Engineering and Engineering Management; Ph.D., MIT, 1994. Organizational theory; technical labor force; technological change; network analysis, ethnography, management of R&D operations.

David W. Beach, Professor, Mechanical Engineering; Stanford, 1961. Design and problem solving; linkage between design and manufacturing; computer-aided prototyping; integrated marketing, design and manufacturing.

Margaret L. Brandeau, Professor, Industrial Engineering and Engineering Management; Ph.D., Stanford, 1985. Analytical models of management problems in areas of manufacturing systems.

Robert C. Carlson, Professor, Industrial Engineering and Engineering Management, Graduate School of Business; Ph.D., Johns Hopkins, 1976. Manufacturing strategy, models of production scheduling and control systems, multiobjective decision systems.

Mark R. Cutkosky, Professor and Associate Chair for Design and Manufacturing, Mechanical Engineering; Ph.D., Carnegie Mellon, 1985. Mechanical design, computer-aided manufacturing and robotics.

George Foster, Paul L. and Phyllis Wattis Foundation Professor of Management and Co-Director of the Executive Program for Smaller Companies; Ph.D., Stanford, 1975. Cost accounting and cost management.

Peter W. Glynn, Professor, Engineering–Economic Systems and Operations Research; Ph.D., Stanford, 1982. Stochastic modeling and simulation; performance analysis for computer, telecommunications, and manufacturing systems; risk analysis in finance and engineering.

J. Michael Harrison, Professor, Operations Management, Graduate School of Business; Ph.D., Stanford, 1970. Production and operations management, with emphasis on time dimension of system performance.

Warren H. Hausman, Professor, Industrial Engineering and Engineering Management, Graduate School of Business; Ph.D., MIT, 1966. Operations management, planning and control; inventory control; supply chain management.

Charles A. Holloway, Kleiner, Perkins, Caufield and Byers Professor of Management, Graduate School of Business, and Founding Co-Chair of the Stanford Integrated Manufacturing Association; Ph.D., UCLA, 1969. Management of technology, manufacturing strategy, quantitative analysis.

Kosuke Ishii, Associate Professor, Mechanical Engineering; Ph.D., Stanford, 1987. Design for manufacturability, life-cycle quality of mechanical and electromechanical systems.

James V. Jucker, Professor, Industrial Engineering and Engineering Management; Ph.D., Stanford 1968. Design and organization of manufacturing systems, impact on workforce.

Sunil Kumar, Assistant Professor, Operations, Information, and Technology, Graduate School of Business; Ph.D., Illinois, 1996. Performance evaluation and dynamic control of manufacturing processes and communication systems using stochastic network models.

Rajiv Lal, Professor, Marketing and Management Science; Ph.D., Carnegie Mellon, 1983. Retailing and supply chain management.

Jean-Claude Latombe, Professor and Director of the Robotics Laboratory, Computer Science; Ph.D., Grenoble, 1977. Robotics and artificial intelligence.

Hau L. Lee, Professor, Industrial Engineering and Engineering Management, Graduate School of Business; Ph.D., Pennsylvania, 1983. Production and operations management, with emphasis on supply chain management, inventory planning, integrated design, and quality management.

Larry Leifer, Professor and Director of the Center for Design Research and the Design Affiliates Program, Mechanical Engineering; Ph.D., Stanford, 1969. Design methodology, rehabilitation engineering, and programmable electromechanical systems.

Haim Mendelson, James Irvin Miller Professor of Information Systems; Ph.D., Tel Aviv, 1979. Information systems.

James M. Patell, Hoover Professor of Public and Private Management, Graduate School of Business; Ph.D., Carnegie Mellon, 1974. Manufacturing systems and performance measurement.

Evan L. Porteus, Professor and Co-Director of the Product Development and Manufacturing Strategy Executive Program, Industrial Engineering and Engineering Management, Graduate School of Business; Ph.D., Case Tech, 1967. Operations research.

Friedrich B. Prinz, Rodney H. Adams Professor of Engineering, Departments of Mechanical Engineering and Material Science and Engineering; Ph.D., Vienna, 1975. Rapid part prototyping and rapid tool generation, geometric modeling and material processing for manufacturing and design.

William C. Reynolds, Professor, Mechanical Engineering; Ph.D., Stanford, 1958. Turbulence, thermodynamics, and computational fluid dynamics.

Krishna C. Saraswat, Professor, Electrical Engineering; Ph.D., Stanford, 1974. Fabrication processes, device structures, materials and equipment for VLSI and flat panel display manufacturing.

Sheri D. Sheppard, Associate Professor, Mechanical Engineering; Ph.D., Michigan, 1985. Finite-element analysis and fracture mechanics.

George S. Springer, Professor, Departmental Chair, and Director of the Structures and Composites Laboratory, Aeronautics and Astronautics; Ph.D., Yale, 1962. Manufacture, design, and environmental effects of fiber-reinforced composite materials.

V. "Seenu" Srinivasan, Ernest C. Arbuckle Professor of Marketing and Management Science; Ph.D., Carnegie Mellon, 1971. Market research for product development and pricing decisions.

Robert I. Sutton, Professor, Industrial Engineering and Engineering Management, Graduate School of Business; Ph.D., Michigan, 1984. Organizational decline and death; technology and work; innovation and the product design process, organizational performance.

Seungjin Whang, Associate Professor, Operations, Information, and Technology, Graduate School of Business; Ph.D., Rochester, 1988. Economic analysis of management information system, design of database management systems, performance evaluation of computer systems.

Samuel C. Wood, Assistant Professor, Manufacturing and Technology, Graduate School of Business; Ph.D., Stanford, 1992. Product and technology development, manufacturing technology, modeling and simulation of manufacturing systems.

STEVENS INSTITUTE OF TECHNOLOGY

Wesley J. Howe School of Technology Management

Programs of Study

Rapidly changing technologies, intensifying global competition, organizational re-engineering, and the increasing diversity of the workforce are creating new and demanding challenges for today's managers. More than ever, effective managers require a broad range of managerial and technical knowledge and skills to successfully lead their organizations into the twenty-first century. Standard graduate business programs do not address how the management of technologies supports business objectives. Stevens' School of Technology Management is at the forefront of management education, offering graduate certificate and degree programs that provide students with an innovative, integrated combination of business and technological issues. These programs are designed to help working professionals enhance their practice of management and to position them for career growth in a changing world.

Stevens offers several programs of study that lead to the Master of Science in Management (M.S.M.), the Master of Information Management (M.I.M.), the Master of Science in Information Systems (M.S.I.S.), the Master of Science (M.S.) in telecommunications management, and the Master of Technology Management (M.T.M.).

The Stevens degree of Master of Science in Management is a twelve-course, 30-credit graduate degree program. It provides students a rigorous grounding in the core disciplines (economics, accounting, organization behavior, and quantitative systems) that are necessary for the successful practice of management.

The M.I.M. twelve-course, 30-credit degree program is designed for midlevel and senior-level professionals responsible for information technologies (IT) within their organizations. The program's courses are taught at the Stevens campus and at selected corporate locations in New Jersey.

The M.S.I.S. degree program provides students with a rigorous background in the elements of computer science and information management that are necessary to design and manage sophisticated information technologies within organizations. It is a twelve-course, 30-credit interdisciplinary degree offered jointly by the School of Technology Management and the Department of Computer Science of the School of Applied Sciences and Liberal Arts. The program combines key management courses that are included in the M.I.M. degree with technical courses developed in Stevens' M.S. degree program in computer science.

The M.S. in telecommunications management degree program addresses a pressing need of the telecommunications industry for professionals possessing both technical expertise and business skills. It is a twelve-course, 30-credit interdisciplinary degree that combines advanced knowledge of applied telecommunications with management techniques.

The M.T.M. eleven-course, 32.5-credit degree program is designed for midlevel and senior-level professionals who have advanced technical degrees or extensive experience (at least five years) in R&D and engineering functions of their organizations. This innovative program was developed as part of the Stevens Alliance for Technology Management, a partnership between the School of Technology Management and sponsoring corporations in northern New Jersey.

The School of Technology Management offers the following minigraduate programs in specialized topics leading to a graduate certificate: engineering management, technology management, project management, information management, information systems, and telecommunications management. Each graduate certificate consists of four graduate courses, which may also be applied to the Master of Science degree programs.

The School of Technology Management offers doctoral programs designed for highly qualified students who are interested in careers in teaching and research or in industry. The Ph.D. requires 60 credits of course work beyond the bachelor's degree and 30 credits of original research.

The Ph.D. in information management program is built on the M.S. in Management concentration in information management. Students must pass qualifying examinations as well as complete an original dissertation to receive a degree.

The Ph.D. in technology management program is built on the M.S. in Management concentration in technology management and the Master of Technology Management degree program. Students must pass a preliminary examination covering master's-level course work and a qualifying examination on doctoral-level course work in specified areas of study as well as complete an original dissertation.

The Ph.D. in telecommunications management is an interdisciplinary program offered by the School of Technology Management and the Department of Electrical and Computer Engineering of the School of Engineering.

Research Facilities

The Wesley J. Howe School of Technology Management has developed industrial alliances with leading members of U.S. industry that strive to identify, in concert with these industrial leaders, relevant problems to which the School can identify solutions and research projects to improve productivity and competitiveness. In addition, modern techniques and facilities are available for information gathering in the age of ever-expanding information technology.

Financial Aid

Assistantships, fellowships, scholarships, loan and deferred-payment plans, work-study, and employer tuition benefits are available to qualified students. Assistantships include a minimum $9800 stipend for 1998–99 plus remission of tuition and fees; recipients devote 20 hours per week to teaching or research.

Cost of Study

Tuition is $675 per credit for the 1998–99 academic year. The fee for a typical 2½-credit graduate course is $1687.50.

Living and Housing Costs

Residence costs for 1998–99 range from $3030 to $5300 per academic year for an off-campus room to $5100 per academic year for on-campus married and graduate student apartments. Additional living expenses are approximately $4050 for thirty-eight weeks. Books and supplies cost about $500 per year.

Student Group

There is an exceptionally diverse group of about 2,000 graduate students at Stevens, nearly 65 percent of whom are enrolled part-time. More than 40 are enrolled at off-campus corporate sites.

Location

Stevens is located on the west bank of the Hudson River in Hoboken, New Jersey, a community that has undergone a remarkable renaissance and become a popular residential and cultural center. The campus is 15 minutes from the center of New York City. World-famous year-round resort areas and beaches are less than 2 hours away.

The Institute

Founded in 1870, Stevens is a pioneer in technical education and a highly regarded independent center of study and research, accredited by MSACS, ABET, and CSAB. Total enrollment is approximately 3,500, and there are 130 full-time faculty members, more than 90 percent of whom hold the doctorate. A leader in integrating computers into engineering education, Stevens was the first university in the country to require freshmen to purchase personal computers. A campuswide computer network greatly expands the capabilities of the entire university community.

Applying

An application, transcripts, two recommendations, and a $45 application fee should be filed with the dean's office two to four weeks before the beginning of a semester for domestic applicants and two to four months before for international applicants. The fall semester begins in late August and the spring semester in mid-January. Additional information on financial aid may be obtained from the financial aid office. Registration should be completed about a week before the term begins.

Working professionals are able to complete each of these programs and earn a degree in two to three years of part-time study. Admission to the programs requires a bachelor's degree with at least a B average from an accredited college or university and two letters of recommendation. At least one year of full-time work experience is preferred. International students must submit TOEFL scores and either GRE or GMAT scores.

Correspondence and Information

Dr. Charles Suffel, Dean of the Graduate School/G-2
Stevens Institute of Technology
Castle Point on Hudson
Hoboken, New Jersey 07030
Telephone: 201-216-5234
World Wide Web: http://www.stevens-tech.edu

Stevens Institute of Technology

PROGRAM DIRECTORS AND TOPICS OF STUDY

Master of Science in Management

General Management Concentration: C. Timothy Koeller (telephone: 201-216-5376).
Information Management Concentration: M. Peter Jurkat (telephone: 201-216-5371).
Technology Management Concentration: Donald N. Merino (telephone: 201-216-5504).
Management Planning Concentration: C. Timothy Koeller (telephone: 201-216-5376).
Project Management Concentration: Aaron Shenhar (telephone: 201-216-8024).

Master of Information Management: Jerry Luftman (telephone: 201-216-8255).
Graduates of the Master of Information Management program are equipped with the management, strategic, and technical skills necessary to effectively structure and manage information technologies to meet business challenges, including corporate reengineering, new competition, and rightsizing.

Master of Science in Information Systems: Jerry Luftman (telephone: 201-216-8255).
Concentrations in the Master of Science in Information Systems incorporate computer science topics that include programming and operating systems, data structures, and database management systems with management topics that include management information systems, managing information technology–based organizations, and the strategic management of information systems.

Master of Science in telecommunications management: Kazem Sohraby (telephone: 201-216-8902).
Concentrations in the program include telecommunications in probability and stochastic processes, information networks, regulation and telecommunications policy, traffic engineering, telecommunications switching, network management, and management topics that include accounting, organization theory, engineering economy, project management, and decision theory.

Master of Technology Management: Donald N. Merino (telephone: 201-216-5504).
The program's graduates are equipped to lead initiatives within their organizations to integrate strategic business goals with technological concerns about innovation, product development, process management, and emerging technologies.

Ph.D. in information management: M. Peter Jurkat (telephone: 201-216-5371).
Students in this program concentrate on information management, organization behavior and theory, and human factors.

Ph.D. in technology management: Donald N. Merino (telephone: 201-216-5504).
Students pursue course work in quantitative methods, management and organization behavior, and technology management.

Ph.D. in telecommunications management: Kazem Sohraby (telephone: 201-216-8902).
This program is interdisciplinary, combining concentrations from the School of Technology Management and the Department of Electrical and Computer Engineering of the School of Engineering.

THE FACULTY

Leonid Bazilevich, Visiting Professor; Ph.D., Moscow State, 1970. (telephone: 201-216-5271)
Edward A. Friedman, Professor; Ph.D., Columbia, 1963. (telephone: 201-216-5188)
Patricia J. Holahan, Associate Professor; Ph.D., Purdue, 1992. (telephone: 201-216-8991)
M. Peter Jurkat, Alexander Crombie Humphreys Professor; Ph.D., Stevens, 1973. (telephone: 201-216-5371)
C. Timothy Koeller, Associate Professor; Ph.D., Rutgers, 1979. (telephone: 201-216-5376)
Peter Koen, Associate Professor; Ph.D., Drexel, 1978. (telephone: 201-216-5406)
Hans J. Lang, Exemplary Service Professor; M.S., MIT, 1936. (telephone: 201-216-5377)
Jerome N. Luftman, Distinguished Service Professor; Ph.D., Stevens, 1991. (telephone: 201-216-8255)
Gary Lynn, Associate Professor; Ph.D., Rensselaer, 1993. (telephone: 201-216-8028)
Donald N. Merino, Professor; Ph.D., Stevens, 1975. (telephone: 201-216-5504)
John Mihalasky, Exemplary Service Professor; Ed.D., Columbia, 1973. (telephone: 201-216-5378)
Michael Poli, Senior Lecturer; M.S./M.O.T., Stevens, 1996. (telephone: 201-216-8289)
Richard R. Reilly, Professor; Ph.D., Tennessee, 1969. (telephone: 201-216-5383)
Ira H. Sack, Associate Professor; Ph.D., Stevens, 1976. (telephone: 201-216-8229)
Arthur Shapiro, Professor and Provost; Ph.D., Berkeley, 1956. (telephone: 201-216-5228)
Aaron Shenhar, Professor; Ph.D., Stanford, 1976. (telephone: 201-216-8024)
Richard B. Skov, Associate Professor; Ph.D., Indiana, 1982. (telephone: 201-216-5407)
James J. Tietjen, Professor and Dean; Ph.D., Penn State, 1963. (telephone: 201-216-5386)
Elizabeth Watson, Senior Lecturer; M.B.A., Fairleigh Dickinson, 1994. (telephone: 201-216-5081)

SUFFOLK UNIVERSITY

Sawyer School of Management

Programs of Study

Suffolk University's Sawyer School of Management offers programs leading to the M.B.A., M.B.A./Health, M.B.A./J.D., accelerated M.B.A. for attorneys, M.S.A., M.S. in Entrepreneurial Studies (M.S.E.S.), M.S.F., M.S. in Financial Services and Banking (M.S.F.S.B.), M.S.F./J.D., M.P.A., M.P.A./J.D., M.P.A./M.S. in mental health counseling, M.S.T., and M.H.A. degrees. A graduate diploma in professional accounting (G.D.P.A.), advanced (post-master's) certificate programs in management and in public administration, and a certificate program in finance are also offered. The M.B.A. program consists of twelve core courses and six electives. Students with extensive backgrounds in management may be able to accelerate the program to as few as 30 credits or ten courses through course waivers or competency exams. The Sawyer School also offers an Executive M.B.A. (Saturdays only) for students who have a minimum of five years of full-time managerial experience. Admission to this program is based on previous educational background and work experience. A sixteen-course program in entrepreneurial studies began in 1996. The M.S.A., M.S.F., M.S.F.S.B., and M.S.T. programs offer specialized study in accounting, finance, financial services and banking, and taxation. The Master of Public Administration (M.P.A.) offers students the option of a fifteen-course program in public administration or a seventeen-course program with a concentration in disability studies, finance and human resources, health, nonprofit management, or state and local government. These programs prepare students to perform managerial and administrative work at all levels of government or in public-service institutions. The Master of Health Administration (M.H.A.) is a specialized fifteen-course program for students pursuing a career in health administration. For the joint-degree programs with the Suffolk Law School (M.B.A./J.D., M.S.F./J.D., and M.P.A./J.D.), students must be admitted to both the Sawyer School of Management and the Suffolk Law School. For the M.P.A./M.S. and M.P.A./M.S.C.J. programs, students must be admitted to Suffolk's College of Liberal Arts and to the Sawyer School of Management. Most of the programs can be completed on a part-time or full-time basis. The Executive M.B.A., M.S.F., and M.S.F.S.B. programs operate on a quarter system, admitting students twice a year. Other programs admit students for fall, spring, or summer. Students with the appropriate background can complete many of the programs in one year of full-time study or two or more years of part-time evening work.

Research Facilities

Suffolk University's library is ranked among the top twenty university libraries in New England, with a permanent collection of 112,000 volumes, 1,300 current periodicals, and more than 177,000 microfilm and microfiche. Students may use the resources of all thirteen libraries in the Fenway Library Consortium, including the Kirstein Business branch of the Boston Public Library and the Massachusetts State Library.

Students may access the University's dedicated academic computing system seven days a week by terminal or by phone. There is a University-wide e-mail system and worldwide access through the Internet.

Financial Aid

Graduate students are eligible for financial assistance in the form of full and partial tuition graduate fellowships, Federal Work-Study employment, and loans. International students are eligible for institutional fellowships.

Cost of Study

The tuition for 1998–99 is as follows: M.B.A., M.S.E.S., G.D.P.A., and A.P.C. full-time, $17,490 per year and $1749 per course part-time; M.P.A., M.H.A., M.P.A./M.S., M.P.A./M.S.C.J., and C.A.S.P.A. full-time, $16,122 and $1611 per course part-time; M.S.A. and M.S.T. full-time, $18,300 and $1830 per course part-time; M.S.F., M.S.F.S.B., and finance certificate full-time, $19,212 and $1920 per course part-time; Executive M.B.A., $2169 per course; and J.D. joint programs, $20,250 per year full-time.

Living and Housing Costs

Suffolk University is an urban university, and many students choose to live in apartments near the campus. Additional information on housing can be obtained from the Office of Enrollment Management.

Student Group

In 1997–98, 106 full-time students and 540 part-time students were enrolled in the M.B.A. program. The M.P.A. program had 35 full-time students and 156 part-time students. The M.S.F. program had 73 students; the M.S.A. and M.S.T. programs had 27 and 37 students, respectively. The Executive M.B.A. program had 97 part-time students, and the M.H.A. program had 14.

Student Outcomes

Graduates of the Sawyer School hold responsible and influential positions in businesses and public service organizations throughout the nation and abroad. Ninety-five percent of last year's graduates are currently working full-time at salaries that are very competitive with the national average.

Location

Suffolk University's proximity to the downtown Boston business and financial district and the Route 128 industrial complex provides students with opportunities to observe actual businesses in a dynamic setting. For students whose interests lie in the area of government administration, Boston's Government Center and the Massachusetts State House are a 1-minute walk from the campus. The urban location provides a myriad of opportunities for part-time employment while in school as well as career placement upon graduation. Internships and co-op placement opportunities are also available.

The University and The School

Suffolk University is a private, urban, coeducational institution. It was founded in 1906 as a part-time evening law school. In 1934 the College of Liberal Arts first offered courses for undergraduates, and the College of Business Administration (now the Sawyer School of Management) was established in 1937. In that same year, the Law School and the Colleges were incorporated into Suffolk University by the Massachusetts legislature.

The Sawyer School is fully accredited by AACSB–The International Association for Management Education at both the undergraduate and graduate levels. The Public Administration Program is accredited by the National Association of Schools of Public Affairs and Administration (NASPAA).

Applying

To apply, candidates must hold a bachelor's degree from an accredited college or university. Applicants must submit, along with the application, a statement of professional goals, two letters of recommendation, transcripts of all previous academic work, and a resume. Applicants to the M.B.A., M.S.E.S., M.S.A., M.S.F., M.S.F.S.B., M.S.T., and Executive M.B.A. programs must submit official copies of their GMAT scores. Applicants to the joint M.B.A./J.D. and accelerated M.B.A. for attorneys may submit LSAT scores only. International students must achieve a TOEFL score of 550 or better and submit a statement of financial resources. Application deadlines are June 15 for fall (March 15 if applying for financial aid), November 15 for spring, and April 15 for summer. Applications for the Executive M.B.A. program are due February 15 for spring and August 15 for fall. Late applications are reviewed on a space-available basis until the beginning of the semester.

Correspondence and Information

Director of Graduate Admission
Suffolk University
8 Ashburton Place
Boston, Massachusetts 02108

Telephone: 617-573-8302 or 8337
Fax: 617-523-0116
E-mail: grad.admission@admin.suffolk.edu

Suffolk University

THE FACULTY

John Brennan, Dean; M.B.A., Harvard.
C. Richard Torrisi, Associate Dean; Ph.D., Syracuse.
Susan C. Atherton, Associate Dean; M.B.A., NYU.

Accounting Department
James Angelini, Associate Professor of Accounting and Taxation; M.B.A., Babson; Ph.D., Houston; CPA (Massachusetts).
Sudip Bhattacharjee, Assistant Professor of Accounting; M.B.A., Virginia Tech; Ph.D., Massachusetts at Amherst.
Bradley Childs, Assistant Professor of Accounting; Ph.D., Purdue; CPA (Ohio).
Ross Fuerman, Assistant Professor of Accounting; J.D., George Washington; Ph.D., Cincinnati.
Ruth Ann McEwan, Associate Professor of Accounting; Ph.D., Georgia Tech.
James Morrison McInnes, Professor of Accounting; D.B.A., Harvard.
Jane E. Morton, Assistant Professor of Accounting; Ph.D., Arizona; CPA (Arizona).
Laurie W. Pant, Professor of Accounting; M.Ed., Emory; M.B.A., D.B.A., Boston University; CMA.
Mawdudur Rahman, Professor of Accounting and Chair; Ph.D., Manchester (England); CMA.
Gail K. Sergenian, Assistant Professor of Accounting; M.B.A., Pace; Ph.D., Connecticut; CPA (New York).
Lewis Shaw, Instructor; M.S.F., Bentley.
Jeffrey F. Shields, Assistant Professor of Accounting; M.B.A., Ph.D., Pittsburgh.

Business Law Area
Mark S. Blodgett, Associate Professor; M.B.A., Georgia; J.D., Saint Louis.
Anthony Eonas, Associate Professor; M.B.A., Northeastern; J.D., Suffolk.
David Silverstein, Professor and Chair; J.D., Cornell; M.A.L.D., Ph.D., Tufts.

Computer Information Systems Department
Warren G. Briggs, Professor and Chair; M.B.A., Harvard; Ph.D., MIT.
Patricia J. Carlson, Associate Professor; M.B.A., Houston; Ph.D., Minnesota.
Nancy Croll, Instructor; M.S., Union.
Jonathan S. Frank, Associate Professor; Ph.D., Strathclyde (Scotland).
Beverly K. Kahn, Associate Professor; Ph.D., Michigan.
Denis M. S. Lee, Professor; Ph.D., MIT.
Mostapha Ziad, Assistant Professor; Ph.D., Boston University.

Finance Department
Lin Guo, Assistant Professor; Ph.D., Boston College.
Ki C. Han, Associate Professor, Chair, and Director of Graduate Programs in Finance; M.B.A., Texas at Arlington; Ph.D., Michigan State.
Mai Iskandar-Datta, Assistant Professor; Ph.D., Missouri.
Shahriar Khaksari, Professor; Ph.D., Saint Louis; CFA.
Robyn McLaughlin, Associate Professor; M.B.A., Michigan; Ph.D., MIT.
H. Thomas O'Hara, Associate Professor; Ph.D., Clark.
Alexandros P. Prezas, Associate Professor and Academic Director of Graduate Programs in Finance; Ph.D., Northwestern.
Carolyn Shellhorn, Visiting Assistant Professor; M.B.A., Ph.D., Texas.
Gopala Vasudevan, Assistant Professor; Ph.D. candidate, NYU.

Management Department
Michael B. Arthur, Professor; Ph.D., Cranfield School of Management (England).
Robert J. DeFillippi, Associate Professor; Ph.D., Yale.
Pierre Dujardin, Visiting Associate Professor; D.B.A., Harvard.
Colette Dumas, Associate Professor; Ph.D., Fielding Institute.
Sanjay Goel, Assistant Professor; Ph.D., Arizona State.
C. Gopinath, Associate Professor; Ph.D., Massachusetts at Amherst.
V. Daniel Guide, Assistant Professor; Ph.D., Georgia.
Neil Hunt, Visiting Assistant Professor; M.B.A., Suffolk.
A. Magid Mazen, Associate Professor; Ph.D., Purdue.
Teresa Nelson, Assistant Professor; M.B.A., Western Michigan.
Regina O'Neill, Assistant Professor; M.B.A., Dartmouth.
Suzyn Ornstein, Associate Professor; Ph.D., Ohio State.
Hakan Polotoglu, Assistant Professor; Ph.D. (I.E.), Bilkent (Turkey); Ph.D. (Man.Sci.), Wisconsin–Milwaukee.
Daniel Sankowsky, Professor and Chair; Ph.D., Berkeley.
Charles J. Shelley, Assistant Professor; Ph.D., Massachusetts at Amherst.
M. Murat Tarimcilar, Associate Professor; Ph.D., LSU.
Alberto Zanzi, Associate Professor; Ph.D., USC.

Marketing Department
Nizamettin Aydin, Associate Professor; Ph.D., Michigan.
David R. Lambert, Professor and Chair; Ph.D., Cincinnati.
John Newton, Assistant Professor and Executive-in-Residence; B.A., Massachusetts Amherst.
Rhonda Thomas, Assistant Professor; M.B.A., SMU; Ph.D., Texas at Arlington.
Joseph P. Vaccaro, Professor; M.B.A., J.D., Suffolk.
Meera Venkatraman, Associate Professor; Ph.D., Pittsburgh.
David R. Wheeler, Associate Professor; Ph.D., Texas Tech.

Public Management Department
Richard H. Beinecke, Assistant Professor of Health Administration; Ph.D., George Washington.
Frances Burke, Professor of Public Management; Ph.D., Boston University.
Terry Buss, Professor and Chair; Ph.D., Ohio State.
Clarence A. Cooper, Associate Professor of Management; M.A., Temple; M.P.A., Harvard.
Eric Fortess, Associate Professor of Health Administration; Sc.D., Harvard.
Michael Lavin, Associate Professor of Public Management; Ph.D., Tufts.
Sandra Matava, Program Coordinator; M.P.A., Suffolk.
Douglas Snow, Assistant Professor; M.P.A., Brigham Young; Ph.D., Northern Illinois.

SYRACUSE UNIVERSITY

School of Management

Programs of Study

The M.B.A. curriculum is designed to produce manager-leaders for business. Seven unifying themes are a foundation for the curriculum: Major Paradigms of Business, Managing Diversity, Managing in a Global Setting, Managing Total Quality, Critical Thinking and Problem Analysis, Ethics for Management, and Management and the Natural Environment. The heart of the curriculum is its highly integrated group of professional core courses required of every student. Seven elective courses are also integral to the program offering students the opportunity to tailor the program to their own professional and career interests. Concentrations are offered in nine areas: accounting, finance, general management, global entrepreneurship, innovation management, management of technology, marketing management, strategic management of human resources, and supply chain management. Elective courses may also be selected from other graduate programs in the university. Summer internship programs are available with companies in the United States, London, Singapore, and Hong Kong. Summer course work is offered in Shanghai, China. Part-time M.B.A. study includes evening programs in Syracuse and Corning, the Executive MBA Program, and an independent study program.

The Ph.D. program requires between 60 and 90 graduate credits beyond the baccalaureate degree, including transfer credit that forms an integral part of the candidate's program. The required credit hours include a dissertation demonstrating the candidate's ability to do original scholarly research. A candidate for the Ph.D. must spend at least two academic years in residence on campus at Syracuse University. Ample teaching opportunities are available to all candidates.

Additional graduate degree programs include the Master of Science (M.S.) in accounting, the M.S. in finance, Juris Doctor (J.D./M.B.A. and J.D./M.S. in accounting) in cooperation with the College of Law, and a Master of Professional Studies (M.P.S.) in media administration, offered jointly with the S. I. Newhouse School of Public Communications.

Research Facilities

The University libraries serve the informational and research needs of the entire Syracuse University community. The library system is one of the largest in the country and ranks in the top 2 percent of university libraries nationally. It contains more than 6 million books, periodicals, and pieces of microform information, housed in the main Ernest Stevenson Bird Library and five branch libraries. In addition, the University has reciprocal direct borrowing arrangements with neighboring university libraries; it is a member of the Center for Research Libraries in Chicago, which provides access to more than 3 million volumes of research material; and it is a participating member of the Archives and Manuscript Collections Program of the Research Libraries Group, Inc. Research centers within the School of Management offer graduate students the opportunity to work with faculty members on projects of mutual interest. For specific areas of faculty research, students can visit the School's Web site. The mainframe academic computing systems at Syracuse are interconnected by a data network to about 4000 public workstations located on the main campus. Also available are sixteen microcomputer clusters of twenty to fifty IBM and Macintosh personal computers, which are located at several campus locations, including two in the School of Management.

Financial Aid

Approximately 30 percent of the M.B.A. students receive merit-based assistance in the form of fellowships, assistantships, or scholarships. Fellowships include full remitted tuition plus a generous stipend. For 1998–99, scholarships include 10–30 credits of remitted tuition; and assistantships include a stipend of $1800 to $7200. Most graduate assistants also receive a scholarship. Nearly all Ph.D. students are funded with assistantships with competitive stipends or fellowships. Financial need-based programs include federal loan programs and Federal Work-Study employment. Applicants for those programs must submit the Free Application for Federal Student Aid.

Cost of Study

Tuition in 1998–99 is $555 per credit ($16,650 for an academic year of 30 credits). Books and other course materials are estimated at $1155 per academic year.

Living and Housing Costs

For 1998–99, living expenses are estimated at $10,336 for a single graduate student for nine months. University housing is available for single and married students. Off-campus housing is plentiful.

Student Group

There are approximately 225 full-time and 300 part-time M.B.A. students. Of the full-time students, 33 percent are women, 36 percent are international students, and approximately 90 percent have full-time work experience prior to enrollment. There are about 40 full-time Ph.D. students.

Location

Syracuse lies in the center of New York State, 265 miles northwest of New York City. Nearby are Lake Ontario, the Finger Lakes, the Thousand Islands, and the Adirondack Mountains. With a metropolitan population of 600,000, Syracuse is an important educational, commercial, medical, and cultural center.

The University

Founded in 1870, Syracuse University—a private, nonsectarian, liberal arts institution—is one of the largest and most comprehensive independent universities in the nation. The School of Management, in existence since 1919, has offered graduate programs since 1947.

Applying

Applications for admission to the full-time M.B.A. program should be submitted by May 1 for fall admission. M.B.A. applicants may apply on line (http://MBA.CollegeEdge.com). The deadline for Ph.D. applicants is March 1. Applicants must submit transcripts of all previous college work, their GMAT score, a completed application for admission, and one letter of recommendation, together with a $40 application fee. Prior work experience is strongly preferred, and personal interviews are encouraged.

Correspondence and Information

For the master's programs:

Paula A. Charland, Assistant Dean
M.B.A. and Master's Admission and
Financial Aid Office
Suite 100 School of Management
Syracuse University
Syracuse, New York 13244-2130

Telephone: 315-443-9214
Fax: 315-443-9517
E-mail: mbainfo@som.syr.edu
World Wide Web: http://sominfo.syr.edu

For the Ph.D. program:

Associate Dean S. P. Raj
Director, Ph.D. Program
Suite 200 School of Management
Syracuse University
Syracuse, New York 13244-2130

Telephone: 315-443-1001
Fax: 315-443-5389
E-mail: phd@som.syr.edu
World Wide Web: http://sominfo.syr.edu

Syracuse University

THE FACULTY AND THEIR RESEARCH

Abdul Ali, Ph.D., Purdue. Marketing research, new product management, marketing principles and organization.
John C. Anderson, Ph.D., Syracuse. Auditing, financial accounting theory, accounting information and capital markets, tax and incentive issues.
Kristin Anderson, Ph.D., Ohio State. Accounting.
Amiya K. Basu, Ph.D., Stanford. Marketing models and multivariate analysis, quantitative research.
Michel Benaroch, Ph.D. candidate, NYU. Management information systems, knowledge-based systems, application of new methods.
Paul M. Bobrowski, Ph.D., Indiana. Quantitative methods, job shop scheduling, project management, total quality management.
Elletta Sangrey Callahan, J.D., Syracuse. Employment law, education law, First Amendment, whistle blowing, law and society, work and family.
Chung Chen, Ph.D., Wisconsin. Time-series analysis, forecasting methods, quality control, neural network methods.
R. J. Chesser, Ph.D., Michigan State. Conflict management, leadership, information technology and job design.
Sherman Chottiner, Ph.D., NYU. Nonparametric statistics, estimating tax equalization rates, data analysis.
Patrick J. Cihon, LL.M., Yale. Comparable worth, labor and employment law, labor relations, employment discrimination law.
John W. Collins, J.D., Harvard. Business ethics, business and society.
Fernando Diz, Ph.D., Cornell. Financial theory, options, futures, mortgage instruments, market volatility, derivative securities.
Mildred Doering, Ph.D., Minnesota. Career decisions, expatriate spouses, international human resources.
D. Harold Doty, Ph.D., Texas. Strategic management, organizational behavior, organizational design.
Frederick Easton, Ph.D., Washington (Seattle). Scheduling in manufacturing and service organizations, capacity management issues.
Randal Elder, Ph.D., Michigan State. Audit theory and practice, small-business management.
Edwin Etter, Ph.D., Ohio. Transitional accounting information, financial accounting principles.
Richard Fenzl, Ph.D., California, Davis. Management information systems.
Thomas J. Finucane, Ph.D., Cornell. Capital markets, options and futures, corporate finance, market volatility.
E. Bruce Fredrikson, Ph.D., Columbia. Financial management and investments.
Dennis J. Gillen, Ph.D., Maryland. Strategy and leadership, transformational management, teamwork, organizational learning.
John Grabner, D.B.A., Indiana. Logistics, transportation distribution.
Leon J. Hanouille, Ph.D., Syracuse; CPA. Accounting information systems, educational development.
Kermith Harrington, Ph.D., Texas A&M. Organizational behavior and theory, computer anxiety, multicultural diversity, age disparity.
Sandra N. Hurd, J.D., Syracuse. Securities law, employment testing, international liability and safety.
Badr Ismail, Ph.D., Illinois. Measurement of product costs, cash flow variables, strategic cost management.
James P. Karp, J.D., Villanova. Land development law, environmental law, land-use planning, land stewardship, pollution prevention.
Moon K. Kim, Ph.D., Illinois. Capital market theory; inflation effects on finance; relationship among accounting, income statements, and securities prices.
Peter E. Koveos, Ph.D., Penn State. International finance, foreign exchange market behavior.
Alice C. Lee, Ph.D., Pennsylvania. Cost of capital, investments. (On leave)
Gerald J. Lobo, Ph.D., Michigan. Financial accounting, accounting information and security prices.
Susan B. Long, Ph.D., Washington (Seattle). Multivariate methods, causal modeling, measurement and evaluation methods, information technology.
Tridib Mazumdar, Ph.D., Virginia Tech. Pricing and product strategy, innovation management, marketing research.
Murray Millson, Ph.D., Syracuse. Marketing, new product development, proficiency and success.
Mohamed Onsi, Ph.D., Illinois. Trends in budgetary controls in the public sector, total quality management, accounting education.
S. P. Raj, Ph.D., Carnegie-Mellon. Promotional strategies, product development, marketing communications strategy, marketing research.
Susan R. Rhodes, Ph.D., Oregon. Worker ownership and control of organizations, age-related differences, career change, employee absenteeism.
Michael Schuster, J.D., Ph.D., Syracuse. Labor-management cooperation, employment discrimination, compensation strategy and reward systems.
Sung Shim, Ph.D., Rensselaer. Management information systems, financial expert systems, robotics industry.
Ravi Shukla, Ph.D., SUNY at Buffalo. Investments, asset pricing, methodological issues, derivative securities, international investments.
Kenneth Smith, Ph.D., Maryland. Strategy, role of teams, entrepreneurship, international business.
Clint B. Tankersley, Ph.D., Cincinnati. Marketing research, multivariate analysis, marketing strategy implementation, the mature customer.
Alex Thevaranjan, Ph.D., Minnesota. Empirical research in managerial and financial accounting, contractual arrangements.
Frances Gaither Tucker, Ph.D., Ohio State. Logistics, strategies, and service marketing, benchmarking.
James Vedder, Ph.D., Michigan. Decision theory, decision support, research methods, management planning, applied statistics.
Thomas J. Vogel, Ph.D., Penn State; CPA. Financial accounting, corporate control, corporate structure and financial performance.
Gisela M. von Dran, D.P.A., Arizona State. Organizational behavior, human resources, information resources management.
John H. Walker, Ph.D., Cornell. Data analysis, linear models, regression diagnostics, statistical computing.
Theodore O. Wallin, Ph.D., Cornell. Transportation and distribution management, public policy. (On leave)
Yu-Ming Wang, Ph.D., NYU. Information systems, economic theories to model and evaluate information technology.
Scott Webster, Ph.D., Indiana. Operations management.
Elizabeth C. Wesman, Ph.D., Cornell. International pay equity and labor relations, employment discrimination and procedural justice.
David Wilemon, Ph.D., Michigan State. Product, project, and new-venture management, managing teams and organizations, entrepreneurship.
Chunchi Wu, Ph.D., Illinois. Investments and corporate financial decisions, securities markets.
Allan Young, Ph.D., Columbia. Securities markets, investment techniques and models, privatization, capital and financial infrastructure.
Paul H. Zinszer, Ph.D., Ohio State. Market strategy, distribution management, customer segments.
Frances E. Zollers, J.D., Syracuse. Product liability and safety, administrative law, business-government relations.

TEMPLE UNIVERSITY

of the Commonwealth System of Higher Education

School of Business and Management

Programs of Study

Graduate students can earn a variety of degrees, including the M.B.A., Executive M.B.A., M.S.B.A., and Ph.D. in business administration; M.A. and Ph.D. in economics; M.S. and Ph.D. in statistics; and M.S. in actuarial science. Dual M.B.A. degrees include the M.B.A./M.S. in health administration/health-care financial management, M.B.A./J.D. (with the School of Law), M.B.A./M.S. in environmental health (with the College of Engineering), and D.M.D./M.B.A. (with the School of Dentistry). All programs are fully accredited by AACSB–The International Association for Management Education.

The M.B.A. program prepares students to respond to contemporary management challenges through the integration of current business practice with academic research. Students use theory to improve practice through case analyses and presentations, interaction with business practitioners, and team-based projects. The M.B.A. program comprises ten advanced courses and eight core courses; students with undergraduate degrees from AACSB schools can waive the entire core curriculum. Other students can waive individual courses through comparable undergraduate courses or by passing a waiver examination. Temple offers sixteen concentrations, including accounting, actuarial science, business administration, chemistry, computer and information sciences, economics, finance, general and strategic management, health administration, human resource administration, international business administration, management science/ operations management, marketing, physical distribution, real estate and urban land studies, and risk management and insurance. Full- and part-time evening programs are available.

The two-year Executive M.B.A. program is designed for experienced managers (ten or more years of work experience, including five in management) who are seeking top-level positions. Classes meet on alternate Fridays and Saturdays; this allows participants to complete their studies without career interruption.

The International M.B.A. Program, with study in France, the United States, and Japan, prepares students for global management. It is offered in collaboration with the IGS University in Lyon and Paris.

The Master of Science in Business Administration (M.S.B.A.) programs provide in-depth knowledge of one discipline and comprise ten courses. M.S. programs are offered in accounting, finance, health-care financial management, human resource administration, information technology, marketing, real estate, and risk management and insurance. Most students hold an undergraduate business degree; those who don't must take certain core courses. The Master of Science (M.S.) in actuarial science and statistics are professional research degrees; each comprises ten courses plus a comprehensive examination.

The doctoral programs in business administration, economics, and statistics equip candidates with the knowledge and skills to attain faculty positions at leading universities or to pursue research careers in the public or private sectors. Students are expected to have a general understanding of the management environment before beginning doctoral-level courses and must demonstrate competence in economic analysis, behavioral science, and research methodology. The Ph.D. in business administration program offers a choice of eight fields of study, including accounting, finance, general and strategic management, health administration, human resource administration, international business administration, marketing, and risk management. All doctoral candidates must demonstrate the ability to do independent research through a dissertation.

Research Facilities

As one of the nation's senior comprehensive research institutions, Temple University offers a wealth of resources for graduate study, including extensive library and state-of-the-art information technology facilities. Faculty members are actively engaged in a wide range of research activities and are readily accessible to students.

Financial Aid

Assistantships range from $8250 to $10,000 plus tuition. Assistantships are primarily awarded to doctoral students. Fellowships range from $12,000 to $16,000 plus tuition. University fellowships are rarely, if ever, awarded to master's-level students. Loan programs are available.

Cost of Study

Graduate tuition at Temple University is among the lowest of any university in Pennsylvania. Tuition for Pennsylvania residents was $308 per credit in 1997–98. Out-of-state tuition was $429 per credit. All tuition rates are subject to change.

Living and Housing Costs

The cost of living in Philadelphia is quite reasonable compared to other major urban centers. Graduate students can live on campus in apartments designated for them or off-campus in rooms, apartments, or houses easily accessible to the University via the city's mass-transit system.

Student Group

Temple University has more than 31,000 students; nearly 1,300 of these are graduate students at the School of Business and Management. These students bring an exciting array of talents, backgrounds, and goals to each program.

Student Outcomes

Students in all of the School's graduate programs graduate with the skills needed to succeed in middle and top management and the capacity to advance to leadership positions. The School is a primary provider of management talent to the Philadelphia region's business community.

Location

The quality of student life is rich and varied at Temple University. An international center of commerce, culture, and history, Philadelphia is the fifth-largest city in America. Center City, with hundreds of restaurants, historic sites, cultural attractions, and sporting events, is less than 2 miles from the Main Campus, a short drive or subway or bus ride away.

The University

The University enters its second century with more than 31,000 students. Part of Pennsylvania's Commonwealth System of Higher Education, the University offers more than eighty master's degrees and nearly sixty doctoral degrees.

The School of Business and Management is the largest business school in the region and the sixteenth-largest in the nation. A primary provider of management talent to the Philadelphia region's business community, the School has more than 33,000 graduates, most of whom live and work in the area. Graduate study in business (M.S. in statistics, M.S. in actuarial science, M.A. in economics, and all Ph.D. programs) is offered at the Main Campus, which is two miles north of Center City. Temple University Center City, which offers the M.B.A. and M.S.B.A. programs, is in the heart of the downtown business district. The Ambler Campus, which offers the M.B.A. and M.S.B.A. programs, is located in suburban Montgomery County. A general M.B.A. program is offered at the Harrisburg Campus. The Executive M.B.A. program is held at Eagle Lodge Conference Center in Lafayette Hill, Pennsylvania.

Applying

Application for admission can be made for the fall or spring semester, for the summer term (master's programs), or for fall only (for the doctoral programs). All applicants must have at least a bachelor's degree. Other requirements and deadlines vary according to the program.

Correspondence and Information

School of Business and Management
Speakman Hall, Room 5
Temple University
Philadelphia, Pennsylvania 19122
Telephone: 215-204-7678
Fax: 215-204-8300
E-mail: linda@sbm.temple.edu
World Wide Web: http://www.sbm.temple.edu

Temple University

THE FACULTY

Jonathan Scott, Acting Dean.

Accounting
Sharad Asthana, Assistant Professor; Ph.D., Texas at Austin. Stephen Balsalm, Associate Professor; Ph.D., CUNY, Baruch. James L. Cottrell, Associate Professor; Ph.D., Pennsylvania; CPA (Pennsylvania). Howard M. Felt, Associate Professor; D.B.A., USC; CPA (California). Stephen L. Fogg, Associate Professor and Chair; Ph.D., NYU; CPA (Pennsylvania). Mary Anne Gaffney, Associate Professor and Assistant Dean; Ph.D., Maryland. Ralph Greenberg, Associate Professor; Ph.D., Ohio State. Jagannathan Krishnan, Associate Professor; Ph.D., Ohio State. Roland Lipka, Professor; Ph.D., Rutgers; CPA (New Jersey). Janice Mereba, Assistant Professor; Ph.D., Penn State. Eric G. Press, Associate Professor; Ph.D., Oregon; CPA (Washington). David Ryan, Associate Professor; Ph.D., South Carolina. Heibatollah Sami, Professor; Ph.D., LSU.

Actuarial Science
Bonnie Averbach, Associate Professor; M.A., Temple; ASA. Michael R. Powers, Associate Professor; Ph.D., Harvard.

Economics
Vladimir N. Bandera, Professor; Ph.D., Berkeley. Richard E. Bernstein, Associate Professor; Ph.D., Brown. Erwin Blackstone, Professor; Ph.D., Michigan. Michael Bognanno, Assistant Professor; Ph.D., Cornell. Gary Bowman, Associate Professor; Ph.D., Carnegie-Mellon. Andrew Buck, Professor; Ph.D., Illinois. Dimitrios Diamantaras, Associate Professor; Ph.D., Rochester. William C. Dunkelberg, Professor; Ph.D., Michigan. Mohsen Fardmanesh, Associate Professor; Ph.D., Yale. Joseph Friedman, Professor; Ph.D., Berkeley. Michael Goetz, Associate Professor; Ph.D., Minnesota. Simon Hakim, Professor; Ph.D., Pennsylvania. William Holmes, Associate Professor; Ph.D., Illinois. Masaaki Kotabe, Professor; Ph.D., Michigan State. Benjamin Klotz, Associate Professor; Ph.D., Minnesota. Kenneth Kopecky, Associate Professor (joint with Finance) and Assistant Dean; Ph.D., Brown. Fyodor Kushnirsky, Professor; Ph.D., National Economy Institute (USSR). George Lady, Associate Professor; Ph.D., Johns Hopkins. Michael Leeds, Associate Professor; Ph.D., Princeton. Charlotte Phelps, Associate Professor; Ph.D., Yale. Arnold H. Raphaelson, Professor; Ph.D., Clark. Paul N. Rappoport, Associate Professor; Ph.D., Ohio State. Ingrid Rima, Professor; Ph.D., Pennsylvania. Daniel Ryan, Assistant Professor; Ph.D., Berkeley. Paul Seidenstat, Associate Professor; Ph.D., Northwestern. John Sorrentino, Associate Professor; Ph.D., Purdue. William Stull, Professor and Chair; Ph.D., MIT. Charles Swanson, Assistant Professor; Ph.D., Minnesota. Andrew Weintraub, Associate Professor; Ph.D., Rutgers. Merle Weiss, Associate Professor; Ph.D., Columbia. Jilleen Westbrook, Assistant Professor; Ph.D., Claremont. Susan Wolcott, Associate Professor; Ph.D., Stanford.

Finance
J. Jay Choi, Professor; Ph.D., NYU. Morris Danielson, Assistant Professor; Ph.D., Washington (Seattle). Elyas Elyasiani, Professor and Chair; Ph.D., Michigan State. Joseph Friedman, Professor; Ph.D., Berkelely. Manak C. Gupta, Professor; Ph.D., UCLA. Kenneth Kopecky, Professor; Ph.D., Brown. Herbert E. Phillips, Professor; Ph.D., Washington (Seattle). Trib Huvan Puri, Assistant Professor; Ph.D., Pennsylvania. John C. Ritchie Jr., Professor; Ph.D., Pennsylvania. Jonathan Scott, Associate Professor; Ph.D., Purdue. Anne-Marie Zissu, Associate Professor; Ph.D., CUNY.

General and Strategic Management
Paul Andrisani, Professor; Ph.D., Ohio State. Raj Chaganti, Professor; Ph.D., SUNY at Buffalo. Robert D. Hamilton III, Associate Professor; Ph.D., Northwestern. H. Donald Hopkins, Associate Professor; Ph.D., Penn State. Frances Katrishen, Assistant Professor; Ph.D., South Carolina. Harold E. Klein, Associate Professor; Ph.D., Columbia. Masaaki Kotabe, Professor; Ph.D., Michigan State. Arvind V. Phatak, Professor; Ph.D., UCLA. George J. Titus., Professor; Ph.D., Pennsylvania.

Health-Care Management
William E. Aaronson, Associate Professor; Ph.D., Temple. R. B. Drennan, Associate Professor; Ph.D., Pennsylvania. Thomas Getzen, Professor; Ph.D., Washington (Seattle). Charles P. Hall, Professor; Ph.D., Pennsylvania; CLU, CPCU, FACHE. David Barton Smith, Professor and Program Director; Ph.D., Michigan. Jack VanDerhei, Associate Professor; Ph.D., Pennsylvania. Jacqueline Zinn, Associate Professor; Ph.D., Pennsylvania.

Adjunct Faculty
H. Robert Cathcart, B.A., Iowa; FACHE. Peter Chodoff, M.P.H., M.D., Jefferson Medical College. Michael Dolfman, Ph.D., Pennsylvania. Judy B. Harrington, M.B.A., Temple. Harry L. Karpeles, Ph.D., Brandeis. Soon W. Lee, M.B.A., NYU; CPA. Robert M. Sigmond, M.A., Penn State. Joel Telles, Ph.D., Columbia. George Wan, Ph.D., St. Louis.

Human Resource Administration
Gary Blau, Professor; Ph.D., Cincinnati. Thomas Daymont, Associate Professor; Ph.D., Wisconsin–Madison. John R. Deckop, Associate Professor and Chair; Ph.D., Minnesota. Deanna Geddes, Associate Professor; Ph.D., Purdue. Arthur Hochner, Associate Professor; Ph.D., Harvard. Russell E. Johannesson, Associate Professor; Ph.D., Bowling Green State. Alison Konrad, Associate Professor; Ph.D., Claremont. Karen S. Koziara, Professor; Ph.D., Wisconsin–Madison. Robert Mangel, Assistant Professor; Ph.D., Pennsylvania. John A. McClendon, Associate Professor; Ph.D., South Carolina. James D. Portwood, Professor; Ph.D., Michigan. Stuart M. Schmidt, Professor; Ph.D., Wisconsin–Madison. Gerald Zeitz, Associate Professor; Ph.D., Wisconsin-Madison.

International Business Administration
Vladimir N. Bandera, Professor; Ph.D., Berkeley. Rajan Chandran, Professor and Associate Dean; Ph.D., Syracuse. J. Jay Choi, Associate Professor; Ph.D., NYU. C. Anthony DiBenedetto, Associate Professor; Ph.D., McGill. Mohsen Fardmanesh, Assistant Professor; Ph.D., Yale. Charles P. Hall, Professor; Ph.D., Pennsylvania. Frances Katrishen, Assistant Professor; Ph.D., South Carolina. Arvind V. Phatak, Professor; Ph.D., UCLA. M. Moshe Porat, Professor and Dean; Ph.D., Temple. James D. Portwood, Professor; Ph.D., Michigan. Trib Puri, Assistant Professor; Ph.D., Tennessee. Jack VanDerhei, Associate Professor; Ph.D., Pennsylvania. Mary Weiss, Associate Professor; Ph.D., Pennsylvania. Susan Wolcott, Associate Professor; Ph.D., Stanford.

Legal Studies
Paul Asabere, Professor; Ph.D., Illinois. Joseph Bongiovanni III, Assistant Professor; J.D., Temple. Terry Ann Halbert, Associate Professor; J.D., Rutgers. Samuel Hodge Jr., Professor and Chair; J.D., Temple. Forrest Huffman, Professor; Ph.D., South Carolina. Vanessa Lawrence, Assistant Professor; J.D., Pennsylvania. S. Jay Sklar, Assistant Professor; J.D., Temple. Michael Valenza, Assistant Professor; J.D., Temple.

Management Science/Operations Management
Mark E. Gershon, Professor and Chair; Ph.D., Arizona. Jugoslav Milutinovich, Associate Professor; Ph.D., NYU. Frederic H. Murphy, Professor; Ph.D., Yale. Edward C. Rosenthal, Associate Professor; Ph.D., Northwestern. Howard J. Weiss, Professor; Ph.D., Northwestern.

Marketing
Rajan Chandran, Professor and Associate Dean; Ph.D., Syracuse. Anthony DiBenedetto, Associate Professor and Chair; Ph.D., McGill. James Hunt, Associate Professor; Ph.D., Cincinnati. Masaaki Kotabe, Professor; Ph.D., Michigan State. Richard A. Lancioni, Professor; Ph.D., Ohio State. Leonard LoScuito, Professor; Ph.D., Purdue. Terrence Oliva, Professor; Ph.D., Alabama. William Ross, Associate Professor and Assistant Dean; Ph.D., Duke. Indrajit Sinha, Assistant Professor; Ph.D., Michigan. Michael Smith, Associate Professor; D.B.A., Indiana.

Real Estate and Urban Land Studies
Paul Asabere, Professor; Ph.D., Illinois. Samuel D. Hodge Jr., Professor and Chair; J.D., Temple. Forrest Huffman, Professor; Ph.D., South Carolina. Vanessa Lawrence, Assistant Professor; J.D., Pennsylvania. Michael Valenza, Assistant Professor; J.D., Temple.

Risk Management and Insurance
R. B. Drennan, Associate Professor; Ph.D., Pennsylvania. Charles P. Hall Jr, Professor; Ph.D., Pennsylvania; CLU; CPCU. M. Moshe Porat, Professor and Dean; Ph.D., Temple; CPCU. Michael R. Powers, Associate Professor and Chair; Ph.D., Harvard. Laureen Regan, Assistant Professor; Ph.D., Pennsylvania. Brenda A. Robinson, Assistant Professor; M.A., M.B.A., Pennsylvania. Jack VanDerhei, Associate Professor; Ph.D., Pennsylvania. Mary Weiss, Associate Professor; Ph.D., Pennsylvania.

Statistics
Luisa T. Fernholz, Associate Professor; Ph.D., Rutgers. Richard M. Heiberger, Professor; Ph.D., Harvard. Burt S. Holland, Professor; Ph.D., North Carolina State. Francis Hsuan, Associate Professor; Ph.D., Cornell. Boris Iglewicz, Professor; Ph.D., Virginia Tech. Alan Izenman, Professor; Ph.D., Berkeley. Dirk Moore, Associate Professor; Ph.D., Washington (Seattle). Milton N. Parnes, Associate Professor; Ph.D., Wayne State. Damaraju Raghavarao, Professor; Ph.D., Bombay. Sanat Sarkar, Professor; Ph.D., Calcutta. Jagbir Singh, Professor and Chair; Ph.D., Florida State. Woollcott K. Smith, Professor; Ph.D., Johns Hopkins. Marcus J. Sobel, Associate Professor; Ph.D., Berkeley. William W. S. Wei, Professor; Ph.D., Wisconsin–Madison

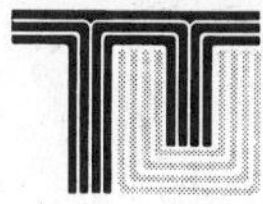

TENNESSEE TECHNOLOGICAL UNIVERSITY

College of Business Administration
Division of M.B.A. Studies

Program of Study

The College of Business Administration offers a program leading to the Master of Business Administration (M.B.A.) that is accredited by AACSB–The International Association for Management Education. Tennessee Tech is one of approximately 130 U.S. schools that have the additional accounting accreditation. The program offers professional preparation for high-level careers in business. Course material gives students an opportunity to develop managerial competence through extensive use of the case method and selected use of other pedagogical methods such as problem analysis, simulations, and research projects. Students interact with senior managers through the Executive Seminar Series.

The program is designed to meet the needs of students with business or nonbusiness undergraduate majors, as well as experienced managers. Students with business preparation must complete core courses and electives for a total of 36 semester hours. The program may be completed in three semesters of full-time work. Students with a nonbusiness undergraduate background are required to complete additional foundation courses. M.B.A. areas of concentration include accounting and management information systems. Other areas of interest can be selected through elective courses in any discipline.

Research Facilities

The College has excellent research and instructional facilities and is recognized for its leadership in information technology infrastructure and applications. The Research Resources Center and two computer centers, a business multimedia center, and a distance learning and telecommunications center are located within the College. All classrooms have multimedia presentation capabilities and Internet connectivity. Housed in the College are Chairs of Excellence in both Management Information Systems and Quality. The M.B.A. division participates in the State Center for Manufacturing Research at Tennessee Technological University. Research assistantships are available through the center.

Financial Aid

Sources of aid include scholarships, assistantships, and out-of-state tuition waivers. A number of whole and half-time assistantships are awarded to superior applicants. Graduate assistants receive a full tuition waiver and a monthly stipend; in-state tuition and monthly stipends are reduced by one half for the half-time assistants. Scholarships are available through the College of Business Administration Foundation; applications are accepted with admission applications.

Cost of Study

Information on tuition and fees for in-state and out-of-state residents may be found in the *Graduate Catalog*. In 1998–99, maintenance fees for all students are $138 per hour (up to $1480 per semester), and tuition, paid only by out-of-state students, is $211 per hour (up to $2413 per semester).

Living and Housing Costs

University housing includes both dormitories and apartments. Costs in 1998–99 are $850 to $950 per semester in residence halls and $210 to $250 per month in student apartments. Housing is also available in the community.

Student Group

The M.B.A. class in fall 1997 was composed of 123 students, of whom 49 percent were women. The mean GPA was 3.2, and the mean GMAT score was 523. Students enter the program with a variety of undergraduate degrees. About 50 percent have full-time work experience.

Location

Tennessee Tech is located in Cookeville, Tennessee, on Interstate 40 and 80 miles east of Nashville. Several state parks, golf courses, rivers, and beautiful lakes are within a few minutes' drive of the city. Cookeville, consistently listed by *USA Today* as one of "America's Most Affordable Cities," is the trade center of the 225,000 people who live in the Upper Cumberland region of middle Tennessee.

The University and The College

The University, founded in 1916, is a state-supported coeducational institution. The College is composed of the Department of Accounting and Business Law; the Department of Economics, Finance, and Marketing; the Department of Decision Sciences and Management; and the Division of M.B.A. Studies. Nonacademic units include the Institute for Business Development, the Business Media Training Center, the Distance Learning Center, the Small Business Development Center, the computer center, and Research Resources Center. The University enrolls about 8,000 students per semester; the College enrolls about 1,300 undergraduates and 140 graduate students, including a number who attend part-time while pursuing full-time careers.

Applying

Admission is open to qualified students with a bachelor's degree from an accredited institution. Previous business courses are not required. Qualification is determined by undergraduate grade point average and scores on the GMAT. Generally, students must have a score of 1000 points (200 x grade point average + GMAT score). Employment experience is also considered. Applications for admission should be received at least one month before the semester in which the student plans to enroll (six months for international students). Students can begin the program any semester in the year. Applications for assistantships and scholarships should be submitted by March 15 to be considered for fall semester support. Although assistantships may be available during the year, most appointments are made in the spring for the following academic year. International students must submit (directly from the testing agency) a minimum score of 550 on the TOEFL.

Correspondence and Information

Dr. Virginia M. Moore, Assistant Dean
College of Business Administration
Tennessee Technological University
P.O. Box 5023
Cookeville, Tennessee 38505
Telephone: 931-372-3600
Fax: 931-372-6249
E-mail: mbastudies@tntech.edu
World Wide Web: http://www.tntech.edu

Tennessee Technological University

THE FACULTY AND THEIR RESEARCH

Robert R. Bell, Ph.D., Florida, 1972. Human resources management, organizational behavior.
William H. Bonner, Ph.D., Ohio State, 1961. Communications in business.
Jon A. Booker, Ph.D., North Texas State, 1971. Accounting standards and financial reporting, microcomputer applications in accounting.
John M. Burnham, Ph.D., Texas at Austin, 1970. Operations management, manufacturing productivity.
Charles W. Caldwell, D.B.A., Florida State, 1979. Accounting.
Rodney L. Carlson, Ph.D., LSU, 1976. Quantitative modeling.
Whewon Cho, Ph.D., Vanderbilt, 1971. Demographic economics and applied economics in public finance, industrial organization, and business conditions analysis.
Robert C. Elmore, Ph.D., Mississippi, 1986. Managerial and cost accounting, tax.
Robert D. Fesler, D.B.A., Mississippi State, 1986. Managerial accounting.
Susan Coomer Galbreath, Ph.D., Tennessee, 1993. Auditing behavior.
Tor Guimaraes, Ph.D., Minnesota, 1981. Information systems.
Seisel N. Jonakin, Ph.D., Tennessee, 1992. Economics.
Russell C. Kick Jr., Ph.D., Alabama, 1975. Artificial intelligence and expert systems in accounting and finance, microcomputer applications in accounting.
Linda D. Lerner, Ph.D., Tennessee, 1990. Strategic management.
O. Karl Mann, Ph.D., Virginia Tech, 1985. Marketing, marketing research.
Lawrence D. Maples, D.B.A., Mississippi State, 1976. Taxation, accounting standards, financial reporting.
Deryl W. Martin, Ph.D., Texas A&M, 1984. Investment and options pricing.
Christine Miller, Ph.D., Houston, 1994. Management.
Virginia M. Moore, J.D., Tennessee, 1966. Business law.
Ramachandran Natarajan, Ph.D., Kansas, 1984. Operations management, productivity management.
Mary M. Pashley, D.B.A., Tennessee, 1986. Mergers and acquisitions, corporate divestitures.
Marijan R. Paskov, Ph.D., Illinois, 1974. Organizational communications.
Julie Moore Pharr, D.B.A., Mississippi State, 1987. Marketing, retailing.
Gary C. Pickett, D.B.A., Mississippi State, 1978. Computer resources management, information systems implementation.
Rodley Pineda, Ph.D., Texas Tech, 1994. Management.
Richard Rand, Ph.D., South Carolina, 1989. Accounting and international business.
Magadalena I. Rappl, Ph.D., South Carolina, 1985. Economics.
Mark Stephens, Ph.D., Tennessee, 1985. International trade and finance, development strategies for Third World economies.
G. A. Swanson, Ph.D., Georgia State, 1982. General systems theory, accounting history.
J. Donald Weinrauch, Ph.D., Arkansas, 1973. Small business/entrepreneurship, industrial marketing, marketing management.
F. Stuart Wells, D.B.A., Louisiana Tech, 1988. Management information systems, systems analysis.
Norman C. Williams, Ph.D., Arkansas, 1972. Modeling applications in litigation.
Bob G. Wood, Ph.D., LSU, 1994. Global finance.

TEXAS A&M UNIVERSITY

Lowry Mays Graduate School of Business

Programs of Study

The Lowry Mays Graduate School of Business is dedicated to developing in its students the core competencies needed to succeed in their fields of endeavor. The School offers the degrees of M.B.A., M.S. (in five academic fields), and a Ph.D. in business administration. The College is fully accredited by AACSB–The International Association for Management Education.

The M.S. programs are for students desiring in-depth knowledge in the fields of accounting, finance, human resource management, management information systems, marketing, or land economics and real estate. A minimum of 36 hours is required. If lacking certain business education fundamentals, a student may be required to complete certain foundation courses to complete the degree. A master's degree in life cycle engineering and operations management is also offered as a joint program with Texas A&M's College of Engineering.

The Ph.D. program prepares individuals to conduct research in business and other organizational environments, communicate research findings, and teach at the university level. This highly individualized program structure requires the designation of an area of specialization in business (accounting, information systems, production operations management, management science, finance, management, or marketing), but offers the student the freedom to use interdisciplinary course work in a supporting role.

The M.B.A. program is highly integrated and features a large variety of elective course work and specialized program options. Prestigious faculty members with extensive corporate contacts and experience comprise the core of the M.B.A. faculty group. The M.B.A. program is fully described in *Peterson's Guide to M.B.A. Programs*.

Research Facilities

The Lowry Mays Graduate School of Business is housed in the ultramodern E.L. Wehner Building. All classrooms are equipped with the latest in computing and communications technology, providing a dynamic and exceptional teaching and research environment. Master's program students have several computer labs available specifically for them within the college, as well as access to all student computer labs on the Texas A&M campus. The West Campus Library, adjacent to the Wehner Building, offers advanced electronic resources for accessing information worldwide.

Financial Aid

Graduate students compete for a wide variety of university, college, and departmental scholarships and fellowships, with awards ranging from $1000 to $12,000 per year. Students may hold graduate assistantships for 10 or 20 hours of work per week. Nonresident recipients of 20-hour graduate assistantships or competitive scholarships and fellowships are eligible for the resident tuition rate. Loans are also available through the Student Financial Aid Office (telephone: 409-845-3236).

Cost of Study

For 1998–99, a resident graduate student should expect to pay $1600 per semester for tuition and fees. Nonresident and international students pay approximately $4100 respectively for tuition and fees per semester.

Living and Housing Costs

Graduate students live off-campus in nearby residential neighborhoods, with extensive options in living accommodations and price ranges. Many are within walking or biking distance. For more information, students can contact Student Life's Off-Campus Housing at 409-845-1741.

Student Group

The graduate student body reflects diverse educational, cultural, and professional backgrounds. A typical class of entering master's students is composed of 68 percent men of 32 percent women. Forty-eight percent hold non-business undergraduate degrees, 19 percent are from out-of-state, 16 percent are international students, and 9 percent belong to a minority group. Total enrollment in the master's degree programs averages 600, and doctoral students number approximately 100.

Student Outcomes

Because of the combination of excellent foundational knowledge, cutting-edge research, exceptional resources, and advanced instructional technologies, the students of the Mays Graduate School of Business are highly sought in their respective fields. More than 150 companies recruit business graduate students, and 96 percent are employed within three months of graduation.

Location

Texas A&M University's 5,200-acre campus is located in College Station, which is convenient to three of the ten largest cities in the United States and the state capital. The small-town charm of College Station and its sister city, Bryan (combined population of 120,000) offers many cultural and recreational opportunities. Bryan/College Station is strategically positioned at the heart of the Texas Triangle, a dynamic and diverse region formed by the Dallas, Houston, and Austin metroplexes. Texas A&M's Easterwood Airport is serviced by Continental Express out of Houston's Intercontinental Airport, and by American Airlines out of the Dallas/Fort Worth International Airport.

The University

Texas A&M University, a land-grant, sea-grant, and space-grant institution, opened in 1876 and now has a student body of more than 41,000, including 6,775 graduate students. It consistently ranks among the top ten universities in attracting National Merit Scholars and total research dollars.

Applying

M.S. and Ph.D. applicants may submit GMAT scores or GRE General Test scores. Only GMAT scores are accepted for M.B.A. applicants. Priority deadlines for applications are February 1, for fall semester admission and September 1 for spring semester admission. M.B.A. admission is fall only. Meeting these deadlines insures full consideration for financial aid. International students should contact the International Admission Office at 409-845-1071 for international deadline dates.

Correspondence and Information

Lowry Mays Graduate School of Business
Texas A&M University
College Station, Texas 77843-4113
Telephone: 409-845-4711
Fax: 409-845-6639
World Wide Web: http://business.tamu.edu

Texas A&M University

THE FACULTY

Evan Anderson, Ph.D., Cornell, 1970. Managerial economics, management of technology.
Zoe Barsness, Ph.D., Northwestern, 1996. Group processes and work group effectiveness.
James J. Benjamin, D.B.A., Indiana, 1972. Financial accounting.
Leonard Berry, Ph.D., Arizona State, 1968. Services marketing, service quality, retailing.
Leonard Bierman, J.D., Pennsylvania, 1978. Law and economics, labor law.
Lorence L. Bravenec, LL.M., NYU, 1966. Federal taxation, business planning.
Kurt M. Bretthauer, Ph.D., Indiana, 1990. Integer and combinatorial optimization, nonconvex optimization.
Frank P. Buffa, Ph.D., LSU, 1971. Forecasting, inventory/transportation management, information systems in supply chains.
Paul S. Busch, Ph.D., Penn State, 1974. Product management, sales, sales management.
Albert A. Canella, Jr., Ph.D., Columbia, 1989. Executives and strategies.
Joobin Choobineh, Ph.D., Arizona, 1985. Information engineering analysis and design.
A. Benton Cocanougher, Ph.D., Texas at Austin, 1969. Strategic marketing planning.
Jeffrey S. Conant, Ph.D., Arizona State, 1986. Marketing strategy, mail survey design.
S. Kerry Cooper, Ph.D., Texas at Austin, 1971. International business, international finance.
James F. Courtney Jr., Ph.D., Texas at Austin, 1974. Management information systems, organizational learning, decision support systems.
William M. Cready, Ph.D., Ohio State, 1985. Role of costly information in security markets.
Peter A. Dacin, Ph.D., Toronto, 1989. Consumer judgment formation, memory and knowledge, brand equity/dilution.
Tina Dacin, Ph.D., Toronto, 1993. Organizational theory, organizational adaptation to institutional competitive pressures.
R. Austin Daily, Ph.D., North Carolina at Chapel Hill, 1970. Reporting forecasted information.
Robert A. Davis, Ph.D., South Carolina, 1982. Production/operations management.
John J. Dinkel, Ph.D., Northwestern, 1971. Management of information systems.
Lorraine Eden, Ph.D., Dalhousie, 1976. International business.
Maha El-Shinnaway, Ph.D., UCLA, 1993. Impacts of computer-mediated communication technologies.
Wayne E. Etter, Ph.D., Texas at Austin, 1968. Real estate investment, finance, and development.
Paige Fields, Ph.D., South Carolina, 1988. Corporate finance.
James C. Flagg, Ph.D., Texas A&M, 1988. Financial accounting, auditing for public accounting.
Benito E. Flores, Ph.D., Houston, 1969. Forecasting systems, operations strategy, international operations comparative studies.
Donald R. Fraser, Ph.D., Arizona, 1969. Financial institutions, financial market.
William L. Fuerst, Ph.D., Texas Tech, 1979. Emerging information technologies.
Charles M. Futrell, Ph.D., Arkansas, 1975. Sales training, marketing research.
Jennifer M. George, Ph.D., NYU 1987. Organizational behavior, job satisfaction.
Javier Gimeno, Ph.D., Purdue, 1994. Competitive strategy, strategic management.
Gary A. Giroux, D.B.A., Texas Tech, 1979. Government/non-profit, financial accounting.
Ricky W. Griffin, Ph.D., Houston, 1978. Human resource management, violence in the workplace.
John C. Groth, Ph.D., Purdue, 1976. Corporate finance, valuation, project evaluation.
Roberto Gutierrez, Ph.D., North Carolina, 1998. Investments.
Richard L. Haney Jr., D.B.A., Indiana, 1974. Appraisal methods used to estimate real estate values.
Jared E. Hazleton, Ph.D., Rice, 1965. Economics: antitrust/regulation, public policy.
Don Hellriegel, Ph.D., Washington (Seattle), 1969. Organizational environments, managerial cognitive style.
Richard T. Hise, D.B.A., Maryland, 1970. Commercial feasibility studies of new products.
Michael A. Hitt, Ph.D., Colorado, 1974. Corporate diversification, structure and performance.
Sarah A. Holmes, Ph,.D., North Texas, 1984. Governmental accounting, financial accounting.
Gareth R. Jones, Ph.D., Lancaster (England), 1978. Organization theory, design and environment.
Gerald D. Keim, Ph.D., Virginia Tech, 1975. International political economy, corporations.
David S. Kerr, Ph.D., Michigan State, 1989. Auditing.
Michael R. Kinney, Ph.D., Arizona, 1990. Income tax incentives, tax policy.
James W. Kolari, D.B.A., Arizona State, 1980. Financial markets, banking, international finance.
Dennis R. Lassila, Ph.D., Minnesota, 1981. Compensation and employees benefit plans taxation.
D. Scott Lee, Ph.D., Oregon, 1990. Corporate finance, corporate restructuring, corporate control.
James H. Leigh, Ph.D., Michigan, 1981. Consumer behavior, marketing research, advertising.
David Loree, Ph.D., Texas at Dallas, 1996. Organizational theory, organizational ecology and institutional theory, innovation and technology.
Martha L. Loudder, Ph.D., Arizona State, 1990. Financial accounting for public utilities.
Arvind Mahajan, Ph.D., Georgia State, 1980. International finance, corporate finance, exchange rate behavior, international corporate governance.
Stephen W. McDaniel, Ph.D., Arkansas, 1979. Marketing research, survey research.
Annie L. McGowan, Ph.D., North Texas. Cost/managerial accounting, control system design.
Raymond G. McLeod Jr., D.B.A., Colorado, 1975. Management information systems, executive/marketing/HR information systems, multimedia.
Rita C. McMillan, Ph.D., Florida, 1997. Customer satisfaction, services marketing.
James U. McNeal, Ph.D., Texas at Austin, 1964. Consumer behavior, marketing to children.
Uday S. Murthy, Ph.D., Indiana, 1989. Accounting information systems, database systems.
Clair J. Nixon, Ph.D., Texas A&M, 1980. Use of computer models to analyze the impact of tax laws.
David L. Olson, Ph.D., Nebraska, 1981. Mathematical and multiple objective programming, project management, multiple objective decision making.
Ramona L. Paetzold, J.D., Nebraska, 1990. Discrimination law, sexual harassment.
David B. Paradice, Ph.D., Texas Tech, 1986. Information systems design and development.
William M. Pride, Ph.D., LSU, 1972. Advertising, consumer research, promotion.
Michael W. Pustay, Ph.D., Yale, 1973. International trade relations, regional trading blocks.
R. Malcolm Richards, Ph.D., Michigan, 1974. Investments, corporate and personal finance.
Dan H. Robertson, Ph.D., Texas at Austin, 1971. Personal selling, sales management.
E. Powell Robinson Jr., Ph.D., Texas at Austin, 1985. Supply chain management, manufacturing/logistics information systems.
Peter S. Rose, Ph.D., Arizona, 1969. Planning for mergers and acquisitions.
Anthony Ross, Ph.D., Indiana, 1996. Decision support approaches.
Arun Sen, Ph.D., Penn State, 1979. Database management, expert systems, case-based reasoning, software reuse, program comprehension.
Ahmed Shabana, Ph.D., UCLA, 1995. Information technology–based organizational transformation.
Winston Shearon, D.B.A., Virginia 1974. Computerized information systems, systems analysis.
Bala Shetty, Ph.D., Southern Methodist, 1985. Mathematical programming, statistics.
L. Murphy Smith, D.B.A., Louisiana Tech, 1983. Auditing, accounting, information systems.
William E. Stein, Ph.D., North Carolina, 1975. Statistics, operations research, probabilistic decision models, efficient markets, option pricing.
Robert H. Strawser, D.B.A., Maryland, 1969. Auditing, financial accounting, managerial accounting.
Edward P. Swanson, Ph.D., Wisconsin, 1977. Market value accounting by financial institutions.
David M. Szymanski, Ph.D., Wisconsin-Madison, 1987. Personal selling/sales management, retailing, marketing strategy.
Marietta J. Tretter, Ph.D., Wisconsin, 1973. Applications of computers and statistics in business.
P. Rajan Varadarajan, Ph.D., Massachusetts, 1979. Marketing management, strategy and planning.
Dean W. Wichern, Ph.D., Wisconsin, 1969. Time series analysis and forecasting, multivariate analysis.
Casper Wiggins, D.B.A., Tennessee, Knoxville, 1982. Implications of object-oriented AIS, DBMS, and data modeling.
Christopher J. Wolfe, D.B.A., Kent State, 1984. Financial forecasting.
Richard W. Woodman, Ph.D., Purdue, 1978. Organizational behavior, change, development, and creativity.
Manjit Yadav, Ph.D., Virginia Tech, 1990. Price perception, pricing strategy, consumer and managerial decision making.
Asghar Zardkoohi, Ph.D., Virginia Tech, 1977. Public policy.
Jing Zhou, Ph.D., Illinois, 1996. Organizational behavior, organizational creativity and innovation, work environment design.

TEXAS TECH UNIVERSITY

College of Business Administration

Programs of Study

The College offers ten fully accredited graduate degree programs. The M.B.A. program is designed to provide a broad background in business administration, complemented by a well-developed managerial perspective and strong analytical skills. Core courses cover the financial, managerial, marketing, and analytical functions of the firm, as well as economics and business policy. Concentrations and electives offer the opportunity to develop the specialized knowledge and skills needed for various managerial careers. Students may expect to complete the M.B.A. in one to two years, depending on their background.

The Master of Business Administration/Master of Arts (foreign language) (M.B.A./M.A.) is offered in association with the College of Arts and Sciences. The Master of Business Administration/Master of Architecture (M.B.A./M.Arch.) is offered in association with the College of Architecture. The Master of Business Administration/Master of Science in Nursing (M.B.A./M.S.N.) is offered in association with the Texas Tech Health Sciences Center School of Nursing. The program enables students to obtain both degrees with certification in health organization management. The program is under accreditation review by the Accrediting Commission on Education for Health Services Administration (ACEHSA). Course credits of 21 hours are applied to both degree programs. An applicant must be approved by both programs. The M.B.A./M.D. is offered in association with the Texas Tech Health Sciences Center School of Medicine. Students interested in the M.B.A./M.D. program should contact the School of Medicine at the following address: Texas Tech University Health Sciences Center, School of Medicine, Office of Admissions—2B116, Attention: MD/MBA Program, Lubbock, Texas 79430. The Master of Business Administration degree with health organization management certification is offered through a joint program with Texas Tech Health Sciences Center. The program is accredited by ACEHSA. Those interested in this program can find more information in *Peterson's Guide to Graduate Programs in the Biological and Agricultural Sciences.*

The Master of Science in Business Administration (M.S.B.A.) degree program is designed to produce specialists in one of the following functions of business: finance, marketing, management information systems, business statistics, or management. M.S.B.A. students take the majority of their course work in their area of specialization. Required quantitative courses and electives compose the balance of their programs. The degree may be completed in one to two years, depending on the student's background. The Master of Science in Accounting (M.S.A.) degree is offered for students who wish to specialize in an area of accounting. Concentrations in taxation, professional accounting, and controllership are available. The programs may be completed in 1 to 2½ years of study, depending on the student's background. The M.S.A./J.D. is offered in association with the School of Law. Students earn both degrees in three to five years of full-time study, roughly one year less than it would take to complete the degrees separately.

The Ph.D. in business administration degree program prepares students for careers in teaching, scholarly research and publication, and service to the university and business communities. Areas of specialization are accounting, finance, management, marketing, business statistics, management information systems, and operations management. Doctoral students achieve high levels of expertise in their area of specialization.

Research Facilities

Graduate study in business at Texas Tech is supported by excellent library and computer resources. The University library collections include approximately 1.9 million volumes and 16,000 current serial titles. Scholarly and general business articles are readily referenced through the Business Index, a comprehensive, up-to-date microfilm service. An efficient interlibrary loan service provides materials not available on campus, and requests can be submitted by way of the campus VAX system. The Advanced Technology Learning Center (ATLC) provides state-of-the-art capabilities for computing and communications. The ATLC is a 25,000-square-foot facility with microcomputer labs, mainframe access, a reference room, and a help desk. Computer resources in the College include an internal VAX-11/750 system, microcomputer labs, and a remote-access center linked to the University's central computing facilities. More than seventy computer terminals access the large systems, and an extensive library of software packages is available.

Financial Aid

Teaching and research assistantships are awarded on a competitive basis to students with outstanding academic credentials. They carried stipends of $6000 for 1997–98 and a waiver of out-of-state tuition. Additional aid, primarily loan funds, is available through the University Student Financial Aid Office. Dean's scholarships are awarded to students with high GPAs and GMAT scores. In 1997–98, these provided a $1000 tuition credit and qualified the student for in-state tuition.

Cost of Study

Total tuition and fees in 1997–98 for Texas residents were $1600 per semester; non-Texas residents paid $4100 per semester. These fees were based on a 12-hour course load.

Living and Housing Costs

The overall cost of living in Lubbock is lower than in many other metropolitan areas in the United States. An ample supply of moderately priced apartments ranging from $250 to $400 per month is available for both single and married students off campus.

Student Group

The College of Business Administration enrolls about 350 master's and 90 doctoral students. Approximately 60 percent are from the Southwest; the remaining 40 percent come from other areas of the United States and several other countries. They bring to their graduate studies diverse backgrounds in the liberal arts, the sciences, and business administration. More than two thirds have previous work experience. Graduates of the master's programs are aggressively recruited by business and industry. Doctoral graduates are placed on the faculties of major universities across the United States.

Location

With a population of 250,000, Lubbock has the amenities of a major metropolitan area, and yet it maintains its small-town charm. Lubbock is a principal financial, trade, medical, and industrial center and a growing agricultural, petroleum, and ranching region. The city has a thriving cultural life, featuring a symphony orchestra, three internationally acclaimed wineries, and an annual three-day arts festival. As a member of the Big 12 Conference, Lubbock hosts a variety of intercollegiate sports events. Situated on the high plains of west Texas, Lubbock has a pleasant climate year-round, with about 265 days of sunshine annually.

The University

Founded in 1923, Texas Tech University is a major state-supported coeducational institution with an enrollment of 24,000 students. The University complex includes seven colleges; highly regarded schools of law, medicine, and health sciences; and the graduate school. Professional and graduate degrees are offered in ninety disciplines. A total of 4,000 students are currently enrolled for graduate work.

Applying

Application may be made for the fall, spring, or summer term. Applicants to the master's degree programs are required to submit official copies of all transcripts, scores on the Graduate Management Admission Test, a current resume, and application forms to the College of Business Administration and the University Graduate Admissions Office. Applicants to the M.S.A. program must have a minimum GPA of 3.0.

Correspondence and Information

Graduate Services Center, College of Business Administration
Texas Tech University
Lubbock, Texas 79409-2101

Telephone: 806-742-3184
800-882-6220 (toll-free)
Fax: 806-742-3958
E-mail: bagrad@coba2.ttu.edu
World Wide Web: http://www.ba.ttu.edu/www/grad/Index.htm

Texas Tech University

THE FACULTY AND THEIR RESEARCH

Lane K. Anderson, Professor and Ernst & Whinney Faculty Fellow in Accounting; Ph.D., Wisconsin–Madison, 1970; CPA, CMA. Cost/managerial accounting, oil and gas accounting, financial information systems, quantitative methods.
John D. Blair, Professor and Management Area Coordinator; Ph.D., Michigan, 1975. Organization theory, organizational behavior, health organization management.
Kimberly B. Boal, Associate Professor; Ph.D., Wisconsin–Madison, 1980. Organizational behavior, management theory.
Oswald D. Bowlin, Professor; Ph.D., Illinois, 1959. Capital budgeting, refunding decisions, financial futures.
Ralph R. Bravoco, Associate Professor; Ph.D., Massachusetts, 1971. Management of information systems, information systems engineering, computer-integrated manufacturing.
Ronald Bremer, Assistant Professor; Ph.D., Texas A&M, 1987. Linear statistical models.
Glenn Browne, Associate Professor; Ph.D., Minnesota, 1993. Information requirement determination and decision support principles.
James R. Burns, Professor and Area Coordinator of Information Systems and Quantitative Sciences; Ph.D., Purdue, 1973; PE. Computer science, management science, simulation.
Jane O. Burns, Professor and Frank M. Burke Chair in Taxation; Ph.D., Penn State, 1976; CPA. Taxation.
Mary F. Burns, Assistant Professor; Ph.D. candidate, South Florida. Data management, systems analysis and design, distributed information systems/business data communication.
Donald K. Clancy, Professor, Main Hurdman Faculty Fellow in Accounting, and Director of Accounting Programs; Ph.D., Penn State, 1976. Managerial accounting.
William J. Conover, Horn Professor; Ph.D., Catholic University, 1964. Nonparametric statistical analysis.
C. Dwayne Dowell, Price Waterhouse Teaching Excellence Professor of Accounting; Ph.D., Michigan State, 1974; CPA. Financial accounting.
Dale Duhan, Assistant Professor; Ph.D., Oregon, 1984. Marketing research, consumer behavior, promotions.
William P. Dukes, Professor; Ph.D., Cornell, 1968. Valuation, security options, required return for utilities, risk on equity securities.
Patrick M. Dunne, Associate Professor; Ph.D., Michigan State, 1972. Marketing cost analysis, new-product introductions, retailing.
John Durrett, Assistant Professor; Ph.D. candidate, Texas at Austin. Electronic commerce.
Don W. Finn, Professor; Ph.D., Arkansas, 1982. Cost, managerial, and behavioral accounting.
Robert J. Freeman, Distinguished Professor of Accounting; Ph.D., Arkansas, 1966; CPA. Governmental accounting.
Paul Goebel, Associate Professor; Ph.D., Georgia, 1980. Investment analysis, real estate.
David Hart, Visiting Assistant Professor; Ph.D., SUNY at Albany, 1997. Organization theory and management.
Scott E. Hein, Professor, First National Bank at Lubbock Distinguished Faculty Fellow in Banking, and Area Coordinator of Finance; Ph.D., Purdue, 1979. Monetary policy, financial institutions.
A. Kathleen Hennessey, Associate Professor; Ph.D., Lancaster (England), 1972. Computer science, systems design.
Roy D. Howell, Professor and Dean; Ph.D., Arkansas, 1979. Marketing models, quantitative methods, marketing strategic planning.
James G. Hunt, Horn Professor; Ph.D., Illinois at Urbana-Champaign, 1966. Leadership, organizational behavior, organization theory.
Shelby D. Hunt, Horn Professor; Ph.D., Michigan State, 1968. Macromarketing, marketing theory, franchising, ethics, philosophy of marketing science.
Dena Johnson, Assistant Professor; Ph.D., Texas A&M, 1996. Accounting systems.
James C. Lampe, Arthur Andersen Professor of Accounting; Ph.D., Michigan, 1970; CPA. EDP auditing, computer usage in accounting, financial accounting.
Deborah Laverie, Assistant Professor; Ph.D., Arizona State, 1995. Long-term consumption patterns, activity marketing, public policy.
Barry A. Macy, Professor; Ph.D., Ohio State, 1975. Organizational design and redesign systems and technological change, work innovation and organizational change.
David Malone, Visiting Associate Professor; Ph.D., Arkansas, 1987. Financial accounting.
M. Herschel Mann, Peat, Marwick, Mitchell & Co. Professor of Accounting; Ph.D., Alabama, 1971; CPA. Financial accounting.
Nirup Menon, Assistant Professor; Ph.D. candidate, Arizona. Telecommunication, IS strategy, modeling and simulation.
Linda M. Nichols, Assistant Professor; Ph.D., LSU, 1989; CPA. Financial accounting.
Richard L. Peterson, Professor and Briscoe Chair in Bank Management; Ph.D., Michigan, 1966. Financial institutions, consumer finance, economic theory.
Robert L. Phillips, Associate Professor; Ph.D., Ohio State, 1972. Leadership, strategic management, work-group behavior.
Paul H. Randolph, Professor; Ph.D., Minnesota, 1955. Management science, database management, statistical decision theory.
Ramesh Rao, Assistant Professor; Ph.D., Texas Tech, 1985. Corporate finance and investments.
Robert Ricketts, Assistant Professor; Ph.D., North Texas, 1988; CPA. Taxation.
Robert J. Ritchey, Associate Professor; Ph.D., Arizona, 1981. Securities markets, capital budgeting.
Grant T. Savage, Associate Professor and Director of the Graduate Program in Health Organization Management; Ph.D., Ohio State, 1983. Managerial, organizational, and small-group communication.
R. Steven Sears, Lubbock Bankers Association Professor and Area Coordinator of Finance and Director of the Institute for Banking and Financial Studies; Ph.D., North Carolina, 1980. Investments; options and futures; pricing of securities; marketing anomalies; normative portfolio management techniques, risk management techniques, and risk analysis.
Ritch Sorenson, Associate Professor; Ph.D., Purdue, 1979. Managerial communications.
Carl H. Stem, Professor; Ph.D., Harvard, 1969. Eurodollar banking, operation of the international monetary system.
Alex Stewart, Associate Professor; Ph.D., York, 1987. Strategic management, entrepreneurship, ethnography.
Dara Szyliowicz, Assistant Professor; Ph.D., Illinois, 1997. International entrepreneurship, organizational theory.
Peter H. Westfall, Associate Professor; Ph.D., California, Davis, 1983. Linear models, statistical resampling.
Gary E. White, Professor; Ph.D., Washington (Seattle), 1969; CPA. Accounting, taxation.
Carlton J. Whitehead, Professor and Associate Dean; Ph.D., LSU, 1964. Organization theory, environmental analysis.
James B. Wilcox, Professor and Area Coordinator of Marketing; D.B.A., Indiana, 1972. Research methodology, quantitative methods.
Robert E. Wilkes, Professor; Ph.D., Alabama, 1971. Consumer behavior, marketing strategy.
Surya B. Yadav, Professor and Area Coordinator of Information Systems and Quantitative Sciences; Ph.D., Georgia State, 1981. Expert systems for information systems requirement determination, adaptive knowledge-based systems, software engineering and design.

TULANE UNIVERSITY

A. B. Freeman School of Business

Programs of Study

To educate the well-rounded, balanced manager, the Freeman School stresses an interdisciplinary approach to general management education with a global perspective. A theoretical foundation is provided in all functional areas, and students learn to solve applied problems with an emphasis on analyzing these problems, developing solutions, and implementing plans. Teaching techniques include lecture, case analysis, group projects, simulation games, videotape sessions, and field assignments. State-of-the-art facilities allow considerable interaction between students and faculty and foster an atmosphere of professional support and cooperation among students. The 63-hour curriculum of the M.B.A. program is divided into focus modules, ten required core courses, and ten elective courses. First-year classes consist of study in human resources management, economics, statistics, operations, accounting, finance, marketing, communication, international business, and one elective. The second year includes a policy capstone course and nine electives appropriate to individual career interests. Students can choose to concentrate in a functional area or to pursue general studies while maintaining breadth. A summer-abroad program combines studies in Europe, Asia, and Latin America with international internships throughout the world. Tulane offers three joint-degree programs in the areas of law, health systems management, and Latin American studies. The evening professional M.B.A. program may be completed in three calendar years. A one-year Master of Accounting program is also available. The Ph.D. program offers concentrated study in accounting, finance, or organizational behavior.

Research Facilities

The School offers state-of-the-art information technologies, including schoolwide Novell network and several Windows NT servers running as application platforms. The Management Technology Center provides fifty Pentium-Pro microcomputers and access to Tulane's shared systems and the Internet. Two computer classrooms offer an additional sixty-six Pentium II–based computers with full network access. A small computer room features eighteen Pentium computers. All instructor workstations are Pentium-based. The Turchin Library is the area's most comprehensive business reference facility. The library offers more than 30,000 volumes, approximately 700 periodicals, and ten computer-based data systems. Many classrooms are equipped with projection equipment for video and computer instruction. The Management Communication Center offers skill-building resources, including professional writing instruction and assistance in developing business presentation skills.

Financial Aid

The Freeman School is strongly committed to making aid available to eligible students. Approximately half of the entering class receives merit-based fellowship awards, which range from partial to full tuition waivers, plus stipends. Many students work as teaching, research, or administrative assistants. Need-based work-study jobs and federal loans are also available. Students may be considered for all types of aid.

Cost of Study

The cost of tuition in the 1998–99 academic year, including University fees and student activity fees, is $23,304.

Living and Housing Costs

For the nine-month 1998–99 academic year, living expenses for a single student, including housing, food, transportation, medical, and miscellaneous expenses, average approximately $10,000. Books cost about $800 per year. Rent in the University area for one-bedroom apartments averages $400 to $500 a month, plus utilities.

Student Group

Freeman students come from all parts of the world and from varied academic and professional backgrounds. This diversity enlivens classroom discussion and enriches the quality of the graduate program. More than 90 percent of the class has full-time work experience.

Student Outcomes

Freeman students receive individual assistance in their professional development through an in-house placement office. At graduation, 89 percent of the class of 1997 accepted positions with investment and commercial banks, international consulting firms, "Big-Six" accounting firms, and oil, telecommunications, and manufacturing companies. A growing number of graduates began their own entrepreneurial ventures. The average starting salary for the class was $60,267.

Location

New Orleans, a cosmopolitan city founded by the French in 1717, is famous for its architecture, food, and music. The University's 110-acre campus sits in a 1900s residential area adjacent to the Audubon park and zoo. As the largest port in the nation, New Orleans maintains extensive contact with the international marketplace. Annual events such as Mardi Gras, the Sugar Bowl, and the Jazz and Heritage Festival make New Orleans an exciting tourist destination.

The University

Tulane, founded in 1834, is a private nonsectarian university that now has 11,500 students and 950 full-time faculty members in its eleven schools and colleges and a library with more than 2 million volumes. Tulane ranks among the top twenty-five private research institutions in the nation. The Freeman School, founded in 1914, is a founding member of AACSB–The International Association for Management Education.

Applying

Admission to the M.B.A. program is possible at two times during the academic year. The largest admission period is the fall semester, beginning in late August, at which time approximately 120 full-time and 30 evening students begin graduate studies. Because applications are considered on a rolling basis, early application is strongly recommended. Only evening students may be admitted for the spring semester, which starts in early January. A completed application package consists of one official transcript from each institution attended, two letters of recommendation, GMAT scores, the application form and response to the essay question, and a $40 application fee. International students must also submit a statement of adequate funding, certified English translations of transcripts, and TOEFL scores if their undergraduate education was not conducted in English. Interviews are required for applicants living in the United States and Canada.

Correspondence and Information

Office of Admissions
A. B. Freeman School of Business
Goldring/Woldenberg Hall
Tulane University
New Orleans, Louisiana 70118-5669

Telephone: 504-865-5410
800-223-5402 (toll-free)
Fax: 504-865-6770
E-mail: admissions@office.sob.tulane.edu
World Wide Web: http://freeman.tulane.edu

Tulane University

THE FACULTY AND THEIR RESEARCH

Yasemin Aksoy, Ph.D., Florida. Management science.
Larry R. Arnold, Ph.D., Johns Hopkins. Management science.
Jeffrey A. Barach, D.B.A., Harvard. Management.
Kenneth J. Boudreaux, Ph.D., Washington (Seattle). Economics and finance.
Arthur P. Brief, Lawrence Martin Professor of Business; Ph.D., Wisconsin–Madison. Human resources management.
Salvatore Cantale, Ph.D., INSEAD. Finance.
Amiya K. Chakravarty, Ph.D., London School of Economics. Management science.
N. K. Chidambaran, Ph.D., NYU. Finance.
Victor J. Cook Jr., Ph.D., Michigan. Marketing.
Scott S. Cowen, President; D.B.A., George Washington. Management and economics.
Stanislav D. Dobrev, Ph.D., Stanford. Organizational behavior.
Chitru Fernando, Ph.D., Pennsylvania. Finance.
Robert G. Folger, Ph.D., North Carolina at Chapel Hill. Human resources management.
Mahesh Gopinath, Ph.D., Michigan. Marketing.
David W. Harvey, Ph.D., Minnesota. Accounting.
Frances E. Hauge, Ph.D., Texas at Austin. Strategic management.
D. Lee Heavner, Ph.D., Chicago. Finance.
Prem Jain, Ph.D., Florida. Accounting.
Arnold Juster, Ph.D., Carnegie Mellon. Financial economics.
Mary Konovsky, Ph.D., Indiana. Human resources management.
Guiseppe Labianca, Ph.D., Pennsylvania. Organizational behavior.
Irving H. LaValle, Francis Martin Professor of Decision Theory; D.B.A., Harvard. Economic analysis.
C. Jevons Lee, Ph.D., Rochester. Accounting.
David Lesmond, Ph.D., SUNY at Buffalo. Accounting.
David A. Malueg, Ph.D., Northwestern. Economics.
James W. McFarland, Dean; Ph.D., Texas A&M. Management science and economics.
William A. Mindak, Ph.D., Illinois. Management.
Robert D. Nixon, Ph.D., Texas A&M. Management.
Thomas H. Noe, A. B. Freeman Professor of Finance; Ph.D., Texas at Austin. Finance.
Daniel Padgett, Ph.D., Pennsylvania. Marketing.
John R. Page, Ph.D., Tulane. Accounting.
Beauregard J. Parent, M.B.A., Loyola, New Orleans. Accounting.
Geoffrey Parker, Ph.D., MIT. Management.
Russell P. Robins, Associate Dean; Ph.D., California, San Diego. Economic analysis.
Joshua G. Rosett, Ph.D., Princeton. Accounting.
Willow Sheremata, Ph.D., NYU. Management.
Soliman Y. Soliman, Ph.D., Georgia. Accounting.
Paul A. Spindt, Keehn Berry Professor of Banking and Finance; Ph.D., California, Santa Barbara. Finance.
Edward C. Strong, Ph.D., Stanford. Marketing.
Venkat Subramaniam, Ph.D., Texas at Austin. Finance.
Sheri Tice, Ph.D., Michigan. Finance.
John M. Trapani III, Associate Dean; Ph.D., Tulane. Economics.
Gerard E. Watzke, Ph.D., Stanford. Management.
Robert Wiggins, Ph.D., Texas at Austin. Strategic management.
Arch G. Woodside, Malcolm S. Woldenberg Professor of Marketing; Ph.D., Penn State. Marketing.
Jianan Wu, Ph.D., Pennsylvania. Marketing.

Part-Time Faculty
Rodolfo J. Aguilar, Ph.D., North Carolina State. Finance.
Rafiq Ahmed, Ph.D., Mainz (Germany). Management.
Leslie Baker, M.A., Tulane. Management communication.
James H. Biteman, D.B.A., Harvard. Management.
Ernest Edmundson III, B.A., Harvard. Management.
John B. Elstrott Jr., Ph.D., Colorado. Management.
Melissa C. Fairbanks, M.A., South Florida. Management communication.
Michael H. Hogg, J.D., Tulane. Business law.
Frank Jaster, Ph.D., Tulane. Management communication.
Neal W. Kaye Jr., M.B.A., Tulane. Marketing.
Helen S. Kohlman, J.D., Loyola, New Orleans. Business law.
Gary Kuzina, Ph.D., Purdue. Management.
Francis Lobrano, LL.M., NYU. Taxation.
James C. Marvel, M.A., Pennsylvania. Management communication.
Jennie Phillips, M.A., Tulane. Management.
Peter F. Ricchiuti, M.B.A., New Orleans. Finance.
F. Kelleher Riess, LL.M., Boston University. Taxation.
Lucy T. Riess, M.B.A., Tulane. Accounting.
Sidney F. Rothschild, J.D., Tulane. Business law.
Ashton J. Ryan Jr., M.B.A., Tulane. Accounting.
John M. Shay, M.B.A., Tulane. Accounting.
James J. Sowers, Ph.D., Columbia. Management.
Matthew Wellman, J.D., LSU. Business law.

UNION COLLEGE

Graduate Management Institute

Programs of Study

The Master of Business Administration degree programs are designed for students with varied undergraduate backgrounds (e.g., natural and social sciences, humanities) who wish to prepare for managerial and administrative careers in government, industry, health organizations, and public accounting firms. The M.B.A. core curriculum provides a foundation in the essentials of management with a heavy emphasis on effective problem solving within a complex system. It is structured so that students can achieve a high level of understanding and proficiency with modern management concepts and techniques. Beyond the core, students concentrate in general management, health systems administration, accounting, or international management. The M.B.A. programs take approximately two years of full-time study, but can be completed in one calendar year by well-prepared students. Students with appropriate undergraduate backgrounds may waive up to four courses. The M.B.A. in health systems administration is fully accredited by ACEHSA, the Accrediting Commission on Education for Health Services Administration. The M.B.A. in accounting provides students enough credits to sit for the CPA examination. The M.B.A. in international management combines language requirements with international management to prepare students for careers in the global economy.

The combination M.B.A./J.D. degree may be earned in four years of study. A student must apply separately to the Albany Law School and the Graduate Management Institute and must meet the requirements of both. A minimum of one year of full-time study on each campus is generally required.

The Master of Science in Industrial Administration program is designed for students with a science or engineering background who want a thorough preparation in technical management. A Master of Science in Health Systems Management is offered as a joint program on a part-time basis with Albany Medical College and Albany College of Pharmacy for students with experience in the health professions. Students without such experience may pursue the M.B.A. in health systems administration, which offers a broad introduction to health services management. All Master of Science degrees can normally be completed in one calendar year of full-time study.

Union College's Department of Electrical Engineering and Computer Science and the Graduate Management Institute have agreed to offer an interdepartmental graduate degree program leading to a Master of Science in Computer Management Systems. This program is designed to meet the special needs of students who desire both a technical education in applied computer science and an understanding of the managerial processes involved in the successful operation of modern computer-based information systems.

All students are encouraged to participate in internship programs.

Research Facilities

Union College has a strong library and is also involved in an extensive interlibrary loan arrangement with thirty-five private and public libraries. Union operates a large computer center on campus with several time-sharing and batch-processing computers. Terminals are located within the Institute and throughout the campus. Software includes major statistical packages (SPSS, BMDP), and all major programming languages are used. The Institute participates in a number of research projects that offer opportunities for student participation every year.

Financial Aid

Scholarships, assistantships, and fellowships carrying various combinations of stipends and tuition waivers are awarded in accordance with academic promise. Stipends range from $1500 to $2700 for the 1998–99 year. Partial tuition waivers are awarded to students for merit and need.

Cost of Study

Tuition is $1432 per course in 1998–99. The cost of books and supplies is about $1000 per year. Full-time students pay a resource and facility fee of $200 per academic year.

Living and Housing Costs

Private off-campus room and apartment rents range from $300 to $500 per month, and furnished rooms are available for rents ranging from $60 to $75 per week. Off-campus housing is within walking distance of the College.

Student Group

Current enrollment is approximately 350 full-time and part-time students at the master's level. Graduates have obtained responsible management and research positions in public and private business and in educational and health organizations.

Location

Schenectady is part of New York's Capital District (Albany, Schenectady, and Troy). There are many opportunities for recreational activities, such as skiing, hiking, and water sports, in New York's Adirondack Forest Preserve and in nearby Vermont. New York City, Boston, and Montreal are all within a 3-hour drive. Tanglewood, Massachusetts, and Saratoga, New York, are close by. They are, respectively, the summer homes of the Boston Symphony and Philadelphia orchestras.

The College and The Institute

Union College is a member of Union University, which also includes Albany Medical College, Albany Law School, and Albany College of Pharmacy.

The Graduate Management Institute is part of Union College. Founded in 1795, Union has a tradition of leadership in innovative introductory programs in the liberal arts, science, and engineering. The Institute selects its faculty members on the basis of academic excellence and teaching ability. Senior managers and distinguished researchers from public and private organizations serve as visiting professors and help the Institute maintain close relations with the business world.

Applying

Union College operates on a trimester schedule and holds two summer sessions. Full-time students ordinarily are accepted for the fall term. The application fee is $35. Selection is based on academic ability and leadership potential. The admission requirements are superior scholarship, as demonstrated by undergraduate or graduate work, and a superior score on the GMAT. International students must also submit their scores on the Test of English as a Foreign Language (TOEFL).

Correspondence and Information

Joseph Zolner, Director
Graduate Management Institute
Union College
Schenectady, New York 12308
Telephone: 518-388-6235
World Wide Web: http://gmi.union.edu

Union College

THE FACULTY AND THEIR RESEARCH

Joseph Zolner, Director; Ed.D., Harvard. Management education.
Donald Arnold, Professor; Ph.D., SUNY at Buffalo. Accounting.
Thomas Ashman, Assistant Professor; Ph.D., SUNY at Buffalo. Finance and healthcare finance.
Robert Baker, Professor; Ph.D., Minnesota. Philosophy, ethics.
Theodore A. Bick, Professor; Ph.D., Rochester. Quantitative methods.
Alan Bowman, Associate Professor; Ph.D., Cornell. Operations research.
Todd A. Burgman, Assistant Professor; Ph.D., Nebraska–Lincoln. Finance, international finance.
Chandon DeSarkar, Visiting Assistant Professor; Ph.D., Southern Illinois. Marketing and strategic management.
James Lambrinos, Professor; Ph.D., Rutgers. Managerial and health economics.
Susan Lehrman, Associate Professor; Ph.D., Berkeley. Strategic planning, organization theory.
Bradley G. Lewis, Associate Professor; Ph.D., Chicago. Financial management.
Presha Neidermeyer, Assistant Professor; Ph.D., Virginia Commonwealth. Accounting.
Rudy Nydegger, Associate Professor; Ph.D., Washington (St. Louis). Organizational behavior.
Kimmo Rosenthal, Professor; Ph.D., SUNY at Buffalo. Quantitative methods.
Josef Schmee, Professor; Ph.D., Union (New York). Statistics.
Martin A. Strosberg, Professor; Ph.D., Syracuse. Health policy.

Adjunct Faculty

Alan T. Belasen, Ph.D., SUNY at Albany. Organizational theory.
Necip Doganaksoy, Ph.D., Union (New York). Statistics.
James D. Horwitz, J.D., Western New England. Health-care law.
Jane Openlander, Ph.D., Union (New York). Statistics.
Patricia Schaeffer, M.S., Union (New York). Computer management systems.

UNIVERSITY OF ARKANSAS

College of Business Administration
Graduate Studies

Program of Study

The University of Arkansas (UA) Master of Business Administration program is designed to produce graduates with a broad view of the issues confronting managers in cutting-edge organizations. In a departure from the traditional collection of 3-hour courses, the Arkansas M.B.A. program is organized around a collection of coordinated modules. UA M.B.A. students are involved in classes and projects that ensure students possess the following five competencies upon graduation: the skills, knowledge, and ability to lead change; the ability to approach problems from a managerial perspective; the ability to manage and work in teams; the ability to write and speak persuasively, based upon a comprehensive analysis of situations facing managers; and self-confidence grounded in one's ability.

Both the full-time and the managerial (part-time) programs comprise five primary blocks: preparatory work, foundations, core modules, a partnering project, and a concentration in one of five areas: strategic retail alliances, finance, entrepreneurship and strategic innovation, global business, or a customized concentration. The customized concentration is designed by the student and can be completed with either business administration courses and/or courses outside of the College. Joint-degree programs are available with several colleges at the University of Arkansas.

The UA M.B.A. program is a one-year program for all students, regardless of their undergraduate degree. Through extensive self-study with preparatory materials, participation in prematriculation workshops, and completion of the foundations module, all students should have sufficient background to pursue the rigorous 38-hour, lock-step curriculum. The managerial curriculum is a two-year (minimum) program. Initial matriculation for the full-time program is around July 1, and for the managerial program is around May 20.

Research Facilities

Computing facilities are updated each 12–24 month period. Currently, the College supplies 586-Pentium units for student use in its primary computer labs. A variety of software is available for students, including word processing, spread sheets, graphics, and analysis. Library support includes LEXIS-NEXIS, ABI Inform, and Wilson Business Abstracts. COMPUSTAT is also available for student access. Each of these support systems is provided within the framework of normal student fees. Twenty-four–hour access is available.

Financial Aid

Graduate assistantships are available on a competitive basis and provide stipends of $5200 for the academic year as well as a tuition waiver. Several scholarships are available that provide funding but do not include tuition waivers.

Cost of Study

Estimated full-time tuition fees for 1998–99 are $1932 per semester for residents of Arkansas and $4596 per semester for nonresidents. Students enrolled in 6 or more hours will be assessed an additional $175 to cover health, activity, and recreation facilities fees. International students must show proof of health insurance and are required to pay a Non-Immigrant Student Services Fee of $50 per semester.

Living and Housing Costs

Among American cities, Fayetteville, which has been selected as one of America's Top 15 Cities in Which to Live by *Money* magazine and other publications for the past five years, is a relatively low cost-of-living city. The twelve-month cost of living in Fayetteville is approximately $9000. This figure includes room and board, personal expenses, books and supplies, and equipment and enhancement fees.

Student Group

Diversity describes the composition of the Arkansas M.B.A. program. Students average 27 years of age and nearly three years of professional experience prior to joining the Arkansas M.B.A. program. Nearly 40 percent are women and approximately 10 percent are members of minority groups. Student enrollment reflects participants from twenty different states representing all regions of the country. The program's global focus is enhanced by the nearly 35 percent of students who represent eastern and western European, Asian, Chinese, Russian, and Central and South American cultures. Undergraduate majors of students reflect baccalaureate degrees in business, education, economics, engineering, psychology, and history.

Student Outcomes

Graduates of the M.B.A. program attain jobs within a diverse number of companies in a host of marketplaces. Most members of the 1997 class were employed within three months after graduation. Alumni hold positions in organizations such as Wal-Mart, Sara Lee, PEPSICO, Kraft, Tyson Foods, American Airlines, Phillips Petroleum, and Merck.

Location

Fayetteville is a community of 60,000 residents in Washington County and is situated in the northwestern corner of the state in the heart of the Ozark Mountains at an elevation of 1,400 feet. The surroundings are of great natural beauty and the climate of the region is pleasant in all seasons.

The University and The College

The University of Arkansas, Fayetteville, serves as the major center of liberal and professional education and as the primary land-grant campus in the state. The University offers graduate education leading to the master's degree in more than eighty fields and to the doctoral degree in thirty carefully selected areas. The University currently enrolls approximately 15,000 students who represent global demographics. The College of Business Administration is a professional learning community that seeks the discovery of knowledge and strives to produce graduates who are valued for their contributions to the marketplace and to society. In this way, the College contributes to the well-being of local, regional, national, and global economies. The College currently enrolls approximately 2,300 undergraduate and 300 graduate students.

Applying

Admission to the Master of Business Administration program requires a bachelor's degree from a recognized institution with a cumulative grade point average (CGPA) of 3.1 or above. Admission decisions are based upon acceptable Graduate Management Admission Test (GMAT) scores, acceptable cumulative grade point average, letters of recommendation, and experience. The application deadline for admission and financial aid is February 15.

Correspondence and Information

M.B.A. Director
Graduate Studies Office
College of Business Administration
CBA Suite 475
University of Arkansas
Fayetteville, Arkansas 72701

Telephone: 501-575-2851
Fax: 501-575-8721
E-mail: gso@comp.uark.edu
World Wide Web: http://www.uark.edu/depts/mba/public_html/

University of Arkansas

THE FACULTY AND THEIR RESEARCH

John Aloysius, Ph.D., Temple. Operations management.
Dub Ashton, Ph.D., Georgia. Marketing management.
Richard Barnett, Ph.D., Minnesota. Economics.
Ervan Black, Ph.D., Washington (Seattle). Financial accounting.
Marinus Bouwman, Ph.D., Carnegie-Mellon. Managerial accounting.
Charles Britton, Ph.D., Iowa. Economics.
Scot Burton, Ph.D., Houston. Consumer behavior.
Thomas Carnes, Ph.D., Florida State. Accounting.
Michael Carter, Ph.D., Texas A&M. Finance.
Rebecca Chaney, Ph.D., Louisiana Tech. Quantitative analysis.
Doris Cook, Ph.D., Arkansas. Accounting.
Elizabeth Creyer, Ph.D., Duke. Marketing.
Timothy Cronan, Ph.D., Louisiana Tech. Computer information systems.
William Curington, Ph.D., Syracuse. Labor economics.
Parshotam Dass, Ph.D., Michigan State. Management.
John Delery, Ph.D., Texas A&M. Human resources management.
F. Johnny Deng, Ph.D., Memphis. Managerial accounting.
John Dominick, Ph.D., Alabama. Finance and banking.
David Douglas, Ph.D., Arkansas. Computer information systems.
Yvonne Durham, Ph.D., Arizona. Experimental economics.
Gery Ferrier, Ph.D., North Carolina. Managerial economics.
Bruce Ferrin, Ph.D., Pennsylvania. Transportation and logistics.
Daniel Ganster, Ph.D., Purdue. Organizational behavior.
David Gay, Ph.D., Texas A&M. Economics.
Julie Gentry, Ph.D., Arizona State. Marketing.
William Glezen, Ph.D., Arkansas. Auditing.
Louis Glorfeld, Ph.D., Northern Colorado. Quantitative analysis.
Nina Gupta, Ph.D., Michigan. Human resources management.
Bill Hardgrave, Ph.D., Oklahoma State. Management information systems.
William Hardin, Ph.D., North Carolina. Financial policy.
Douglas Hearth, Ph.D., Iowa. Financial theory.
Ann Henry, J.D., Arkansas. Accounting.
Andrew Horowitz, Ph.D., Wisconsin–Madison. Development economics.
Thomas Jensen, Ph.D., Arkansas. Consumer behavior.
Jon Johnson, Ph.D., Indiana. Corporate governance.
Thomas Jones, Ph.D., Virginia Tech. Quantitative analysis.
Robert Kennedy, Ph.D., Texas. Investments.
Steven Kopp, Ph.D., Michigan State. Marketing strategy.
David Kurtz, Ph.D., Arkansas. Marketing management.
Charles Leflar, Ph.D., Mexico. Accounting.
Carl Linvill, Ph.D., North Carolina. Economics.
Pu Liu, Ph.D., Indiana. Financial theory.
Gene Lynch, Ph.D., Texas. Finance.
Donald Market, Ph.D., LSU. Economics.
Thomas McKinnon, Ph.D., Mississippi. Economics.
James Millar, Ph.D., Oklahoma. Financial theory.
Jeffrey Murray, Ph.D., Virginia Tech. Consumer behavior.
Tracy Murray, Ph.D., Michigan State. International economics.
John Norwood, J.D., Tulane. Legal environments.
Anne O'Leary-Kelly, Ph.D., Michigan State. Organizational behavior.
Scott O'Leary-Kelly, Ph.D., Texas A&M. Production operations management.
John Ozment, Ph.D., Minnesota. Logistics and transportation.
John Pendley, Ph.D., Georgia. Accounting.
Larry Perry, Ph.D., Louisiana Tech. Financial theory.
Karen Pincus, Ph.D., Maryland. Auditing.
Molly Rapert, Ph.D., Memphis. Marketing research.
Carol Reeves, Ph.D., Georgia. Management policy.
Janet Renwick, Ph.D., Indiana. Management information systems.
Cynthia Riemenschneider, Ph.D., Texas at Arlington. Computer information systems.
James Rimbey, Ph.D., Kentucky. Investments.
Craig Schulman, Ph.D., Texas A&M. Economic theory.
Keith Sellers, Ph.D., Memphis. Taxation.
Miles Sonstegaard, Ph.D., Oregon. Economics.
Robert Stapp, Ph.D., Oklahoma State. International economics.
Robert Stassen, Ph.D., Nebraska. Marketing channels.
Phillip Taylor, Ph.D., Arkansas. Quantitative analysis.
Deborah Thomas, M.S.A., Arkansas. Taxation.
John Todd, D.B.A., Harvard. Entrepreneurship.
Yien Tu, Ph.D., Iowa State. Economics.
Kent Walstrom, Ph.D., Oklahoma State. Quantitative analysis.
M. A. Waller, Ph.D., Penn State. Marketing.
Donald White, Ph.D., Nebraska. Organization behavior.
Doyle Williams, Ph.D., LSU. Accounting.
Lawrence Yarbrough, Ph.D., Arkansas. Marketing strategy.
Joseph Zeigler, Ph.D., Notre Dame. Resource economics.

UNIVERSITY OF BRIDGEPORT

School of Business
Master of Business Administration (M.B.A.) Program

Program of Study

The School of Business offers an M.B.A. degree program in general administration. It features a combination of courses, including accounting, finance, international business, management, marketing, and information systems. Degree completion normally requires two years of full-time or three to five years of part-time study. Accelerated study is available for qualified students who have recently completed a business degree from an accredited college. The accelerated weekend M.B.A. program is available at the University's Stamford campus on alternate weekends for twelve to eighteen months. The M.B.A. program begins with a focus on analysis and evaluation of the control of an organization and of the environment for leadership. Courses include accounting, decision theory, economics, the organization and management of finance, production, and marketing, and the sociocultural aspects of people in organizations. Advanced courses expand and integrate topics explored in foundation courses and provide a strong focus on the global perspective necessary for contemporary management. The School is nationally accredited by the Association of Collegiate Business Schools and Programs (ACBSP).

Research Facilities

The University's Wahlstrom Library contains approximately 275,000 bound volumes (including bound journals and indexes) and more than 1 million microforms and subscribes to more than 1,500 periodicals and other serials. Online database searching is available on the Internet, Dialog, FirstSearch, EBSCO's Academic Search Full Text 1,000, and LEXIS-NEXIS. CD-ROM databases include ERIC, Moody's Company Data, MEDLINE, reQuest, Books in Print Plus (BIP Plus), and the National Trade Data Bank. The Center for Academic Computing in Wahlstrom Library is available to students for word processing. The Trefz Center for Venture Management, the Bridgeport Foreign Trade Institute, the Business Development Institute, the Special Projects Unit, and the Urban Management Institute are affiliated with the School. An extension library is maintained at the Stamford campus with more than 500 titles, more than forty periodicals, and extensive electronic access.

Financial Aid

Financial aid is available to U.S. citizens in the form of Federal Stafford Student Loans and graduate assistantships. The University also hires graduate students as residence hall directors and assistant hall directors. Further information can be obtained from the Office of Financial Aid at 203-576-4568. International students must demonstrate that they have sufficient funds to finance their studies in the United States by completing the financial statement for international students included in the International Application for Admissions.

Cost of Study

In 1998–99, tuition is $350 per credit hour up to 12 credits per semester.

Living and Housing Costs

Graduate students may reside either in the University's on-campus residence halls or in off-campus apartments or rooms. The cost of off-campus living varies widely. Additional information related to on-campus residency can be obtained from the Office of Residence Life at 203-576-4461.

Student Group

The M.B.A. program maintains an enrollment of 150, of whom 75 are full time. Most part-time students work in local corporate headquarters in management positions. The University and the School maintain an international focus: international students make up 25 percent of the University student body, representing sixty countries. The average GMAT score of M.B.A. students is 500; the average quality point ratio is 3.2. Enrollment of women is 51 percent for the University and 32 percent for the M.B.A. program.

Location

The University of Bridgeport's 86-acre campus is situated on Long Island Sound. Sixty-five of Connecticut's largest corporations are located in Fairfield County; these companies provide students with excellent opportunities for jobs. Through the Trefz Center for Venture Management and the Urban Management Institute, University faculty members maintain close relationships with local corporations, school systems, and agencies.

The University and The School

Founded in 1927, the University is a private, nonsectarian, comprehensive, urban university of more than 2,600 students. Approximately half of the total student body is graduate. The University's campus is composed of ninety-one buildings of diverse architectural styles. The Bernhard Arts and Humanities Center is a cultural hub, and the Wheeler Recreation Center is a complete recreation and physical fitness facility. The University's Stamford campus is a convenient place for working professionals from southern Fairfield County and Westchester County, New York, and New Jersey.

In addition to the M.B.A., the School of Business offers the Bachelor of Science degree. An associate degree is available in paralegal/legal assistant studies.

Applying

Students are admitted to M.B.A. study from many undergraduate backgrounds. Introductory courses in computer science and calculus may be required for students with deficiencies in these areas. Undergraduate records (and/or those of previous graduate study), GMAT score, two letters of recommendation, and a personal statement are used to evaluate applicants. Provisional admission may be granted to a limited number of students pending GMAT scores, provided that the undergraduate records are exceptionally strong and the student has at least three years of management experience. If a student is admitted provisionally, the GMAT must be taken during the first semester of residency. For students whose native language is not English, a TOEFL score of 575 is required. The University has an intensive English program on campus for students who require additional English language study. Students may enter in the fall, spring, or summer. Applications must be submitted two months prior to the date of intended entry. Electronic applications are welcome through the University's Web site and Polaris.

Correspondence and Information

For an application:
Office of Admissions
University of Bridgeport
126 Park Avenue
Bridgeport, Connecticut 06601
Telephone: 203-576-4552
800-EXCEL-UB (392-3582)(toll-free)
Fax: 203-576-4941
E-mail: admit@cse.bridgeport.edu
World Wide Web: http://www.bridgeport.edu

For more information:
M.B.A. Program
School of Business
University of Bridgeport
230 Park Avenue
Bridgeport, Connecticut 06601
Telephone: 203-576-4363
Fax: 203-576-4388

University of Bridgeport

THE FACULTY AND THEIR RESEARCH

Glenn Bassett, Director; Ph.D., Yale. Organization and policy.
Kueun Choi, Ph.D., Florida. Operations research.
Biagio Coppolella, M.B.A., NYU. Accounting.
William Greenspan, LL.M., Suffolk. Law.
Gew-rae Kim, Ph.D., CUNY. Investment.
Robert Maine, Ph.D., Connecticut. Economics.
Frank Moriya, D.B.A., George Washington. International business, marketing.
Llewellyn Mullings, Director, M.B.A. program; Ph.D., Clark. Economics.
Robert Schaff, M.B.A., Northeastern. Marketing.
Stanley Schenkerman, Ph.D., Polytechnic of Brooklyn. Operations research.
Robert Todd, Ph.D., Connecticut. Management information systems.
Vincent Tong, Ph.D., Yale. Organization development.

UNIVERSITY OF CALGARY

Faculty of Management

Programs of Study

Dynamic, innovative, creative—the Faculty of Management, a leader in management education and research, is one of Canada's most progressive business schools. Graduate and undergraduate programs are accredited by AACSB–The International Association for Management Education. More than 80 full-time research-oriented faculty members plus part-time industry-based instructors deliver programs applicable to today's business contexts. Focused on the development of superior business leaders, the Faculty offers undergraduate (B.Comm.) and graduate (M.B.A., Ph.D.) programs. The Ph.D. program integrates teaching and research as basics. Students contribute to a dynamic community of faculty members and business people. They should have a strong, broadly based bachelor's degree or its equivalent plus an M.B.A. and several years of professional work experience. Programs are individualized and include a major, a minor, and two supporting areas of study; advanced courses taught outside the Faculty may be selected as supporting areas. Course work, including candidacy examinations, must be completed within twenty-eight months of registration; there is a six-year time limit to complete the degree. New Ph.D. initiatives include entrepreneurship, tourism, financial services management, energy resource management, international business, technology management, and family enterprise.

Research Facilities

The University library system contains more than 3 million volumes of books, journals, documents, and microforms, which are accessible via an online catalog (http://www.ucalgary.ca/library). The Faculty's Management Resource Centre's collection includes electronic resources (direct access to 2,600 full-text journals and newspapers and a wide-ranging collection of databases on CD-ROM and the Internet, including ProQuest Direct, IAC Insite, and Compact Disclosure Canada Compustat; Investext, Moody's Company Data, and Moody's International; and data and bibliographic resources for statistical services), corporate information (a wide range of company information on CD-ROM and the Internet, including annual reports; 10Ks; and prospectuses for Canadian, U.S., and international companies), journals (current subscriptions to more than 250 core business journals), and newspapers (current subscriptions to the *Calgary Herald, Globe and Mail, Wall Street Journal, Financial Post, Barron's Weekly, Nikkei Weekly,* and *Asian Wall Street Journal*). University Computing Services provides computer facilities with campuswide access. Within the Faculty, IBM microcomputers and software are available, and doctoral students have access to PCs in their designated office space. For research projects, there is a specialized Group Decision Support System (GDSS) facility.

Financial Aid

The Faculty of Graduate Studies offers assistance to full-time students in the Ph.D. program. These awards, fellowships, and teaching and research assistantships are based on academic standing. Government financial assistance is available to needy Canadian citizens or permanent residents of Canada. Visa students seeking graduate assistantships must obtain appropriate employment authorization visas.

Cost of Study

For an academic year (September through April), estimated tuition and fees for Canadian citizens total Can$3630 for the Ph.D. program. Visa students pay double.

Living and Housing Costs

Estimated living expenses for an academic year are Can$15,000. On-campus housing is available in University residences. The city of Calgary contains privately owned rental apartments and houses at varying costs. To obtain a visitor's visa with student authorization, international students must be able to finance their expenses, including tuition, living expenses, and transportation to and from Canada.

Student Group

Current enrollment in the Ph.D. program is 30 doctoral students. Students come from many countries and disciplines with several years of full-time work experience in a variety of industries, occupations, and professions.

Location

A cosmopolitan, forward-thinking community, Calgary, with a population of more than 750,000, is the energy and banking capital of Canada. It has the largest concentration of research facilities in Western Canada. Quality of life is unparalleled, as excellent cultural and recreational opportunities abound, including the nearby Rocky Mountains, with year-round recreational activities.

The University

The University of Calgary has sixteen faculties and more than sixty academic departments or major program areas. There are more than 25,000 students from more than eighty countries. Bachelor's, master's, doctoral, and professional degrees in traditional and interdisciplinary fields are offered. Home of excellent athletic facilities, the University also has museums, art galleries, a medical school, and an Environmental Sciences Centre. The Faculty of Management, established in 1967, is in Scurfield Hall, which features state-of-the-art technology in lecture theatres, laboratories, and conference rooms.

Applying

All applicants are required to provide three letters of recommendation, a statement of career and learning objectives, scores from the GMAT, and original transcripts. Scores from the TOEFL are required of applicants whose native language is not English. Completed applications must be received by March 1 for the Ph.D. program for September admission. The closing date for most applications for financial assistance in the Ph.D. program is February 1. Late applications may be considered.

Correspondence and Information

Ph.D. Program Admissions Office
Faculty of Management
University of Calgary
2500 University Drive NW
Calgary, Alberta, Canada T2N 1N4
Telephone: 403-220-3803
Fax: 403-282-0095

University of Calgary

THE FACULTY

P. Michael Maher, Professor and Dean; Ph.D., Northwestern.

Accounting

Philip Beaulieu, Associate Professor; Ph.D., Washington (Seattle). Murray Davis, Associate Professor and Assistant Dean, Special Projects; Ph.D., London School of Economics and Political Science. Duncan Green, Instructor; M.Sc., Saskatchewan. Irene Herremans, Associate Professor; Ph.D., Kent State. Stuart Jones, Senior Instructor; Ph.D., Wales. Dean Neu, Professor; Ph.D., Queen's at Kingston. Cynthia Simmons, Associate Professor; Ph.D., Houston. Michael Stein, Associate Professor; Ph.D., British Columbia. Rashmi Thakkar, Associate Professor; Ph.D., SUNY at Buffalo. Michael Wright, Associate Professor; Ph.D., Queen's at Kingston.

Finance

Mark Cassano, Associate Professor; Ph.D., Yale. Philip Chang, Associate Professor and Chair; Ph.D., Illinois at Urbana-Champaign. Jess Chua, Professor and Associate Dean (Academic); Ph.D., Michigan. Thomas Cottrell, Associate Professor; Ph.D., Berkeley. Mary Kelly, Assistant Professor; Ph.D., British Columbia. Anne Kleffner, Associate Professor; Ph.D., Pennsylvania (Wharton). Per Mokkelbost, Professor; Ph.D., Minnesota. Alli Nathan, Associate Professor; Ph.D., Queen's at Kingston. Norma Nielson, Professor and Chair, Risk and Insurance Management; Ph.D., Pennsylvania (Wharton). Michael Robinson, Associate Professor; Ph.D., Western Ontario. Gordon Sick, Professor; Ph.D., British Columbia. Larry Wood, Senior Instructor; M.B.A., Calgary.

Management Information Systems

Deborah Compeau, Associate Professor; Ph.D., Western Ontario. Abhijit Gopal, Associate Professor; Ph.D., Georgia. Paul Licker, Professor; Ph.D., Pennsylvania. Barbara Marcolin, Associate Professor; Ph.D., Western Ontario. Malcolm Munro, Professor and Associate Dean (Planning and Development); Ph.D., Minnesota. Ron Murch, Senior Instructor; M.B.A., Calgary. Peter Newsted, Professor and Chair; Ph.D., Carnegie Mellon.

Management of Organizations and Human Resources

Allan Cahoon, Professor; Ph.D., Syracuse. Sloane Dugan, Associate Professor; Ph.D., Syracuse. Loren Falkenberg, Associate Professor and Chair; Ph.D., Illinois. Michele Fraser, Senior Instructor; Ph.D., Minnesota. Ed McMullan, Professor; Ph.D., British Columbia. Amy Pablo, Associate Professor and Director, Enterprises M.B.A. Program; Ph.D., Texas at Austin. Allen Ponak, Professor; Ph.D., Wisconsin. Pushkala Prasad, Associate Professor; Ph.D., Massachusetts. Julie Rowney, Professor; Ph.D., Calgary. Daphne Taras, Associate Professor; Ph.D., Calgary. Janice Thomas, Assistant Professor; Ph.D. candidate, Alberta. Myron Weber, Associate Professor; Ph.D., Minnesota. Wilf Zerbe, Associate Professor and Director, Part-time M.B.A. Program; Ph.D., British Columbia.

Marketing

Debbie Andrus, Assistant Professor; Ph.D., Strathclyde (Scotland). Nicole Coviello, Associate Professor; Ph.D., Auckland (New Zealand). C. L. Hung, Associate Professor; Ph.D., British Columbia. Vernon Jones, Professor and Associate Dean (External); Ph.D., British Columbia. Ashwin Joshi, Associate Professor; Ph.D., Queen's (Northern Ireland). Alan Miciak, Associate Professor; Ph.D., Kent State. Doug Olsen, Associate Professor; Ph.D., Alberta. Stanley Paliwoda, Professor and Chair; Ph.D., Cranfield Institute of Technology (U.K.). Lynne Ricker, Instructor and Director of Undergraduate Programs; M.B.A., Calgary. J. R. Brent Ritchie, Professor and Chair, World Tourism Education and Research Centre; Ph.D., Western Ontario. Harrie Vredenburg, Professor; Ph.D., Western Ontario.

New Venture Development

James Chrisman, Professor, Associate Dean (Research), and Director, Ph.D. and M.B.A. Thesis Programs; Ph.D., Georgia. Leo Donlevy, Instructor and Co-Director, New Venture Development; M.B.A., Calgary. Ed McMullan, Professor; Ph.D., British Columbia. Peter Robinson, Associate Professor and Co-Director, New Venture Development; Ph.D., Brigham Young.

Operations Management

Jaydeep Balakrishnan, Associate Professor; Ph.D., Indiana Bloomington. Thomas Grossman Jr., Associate Professor; Ph.D., Stanford. Thomas Rohleder, Associate Professor; Ph.D., Minnesota. Randolph Russell, Associate Professor; Ph.D., Ohio State. Edward Silver, Professor and Carma Chair in Operations Management; Sc.D., MIT.

Policy and Environment

Peter Bowal, Associate Professor; LL.M., Cambridge. H. Allan Conway, Associate Professor; D.B.A., Harvard. Urs Daellenbach, Associate Professor; Ph.D., Purdue. Ashis Gupta, Professor; Ph.D., Boston University. Mansour Javidan, Professor; Ph.D., Minnesota. William Martello, Associate Professor; Ph.D., Pittsburgh. Terrance Rock, Assistant Professor; Ph.D. candidate, Texas Tech. Robert Schulz, Professor; Ph.D., Ohio State. Carol Stewart, Senior Instructor; M.B.A., Lancaster (England). Terry Ursacki, Associate Professor and Chair; Ph.D., British Columbia. Gerry Wilson, Senior Instructor; M.Div., Saskatchewan. Jaana Woiceshyn, Associate Professor; Ph.D., Pennsylvania (Wharton).

Tourism

Don Anderson, Senior Instructor; M.B.A., Michigan State. Donald Getz, Professor; Ph.D., Edinburgh. J. R. Brent Ritchie, Professor and Chair, World Tourism Education and Research Centre; Ph.D., Western Ontario.

UNIVERSITY OF CALIFORNIA, DAVIS

Graduate School of Management

Program of Study

The University of California, Davis, has an excellent M.B.A. program and is accredited by AACSB–The International Association for Management Education. The School offers joint degrees in law, engineering, medicine, and agricultural economics. Student are also able to select special concentrations in technology management, information technology, accounting, finance, marketing, and environmental and natural resource management. A student-faculty ratio of 10:1 gives students an exceptional opportunity to work closely with faculty members. This program is founded on a strong tradition of mutual support and teamwork among students, yet it allows students the flexibility to structure their degree program around their interests, skills, and capabilities. The School's Career Services Center coordinates an extensive internship program.

The program is full-time and takes two years to complete. Each student must successfully complete 72 hours of credit with a cumulative grade point average of 3.0 or better. The first year centers on a group of core courses that stress the fundamentals of business—accounting, economics, finance, marketing, organizational behavior, decision sciences, and information systems. The second year offers students flexibility to take courses in individually selected concentrations. In addition, each student participates in a strategic planning course, Management Policy and Strategy, which emphasizes decision making and problem solving on real-world management problems. Students work in teams with real client businesses and interact with top executives from these businesses.

In addition to the full-time program, the Graduate School of Management offers an evening/weekend program for working professionals.

Research Facilities

The UC Davis libraries serve as the principal information resource for the educational and research programs offered by the Graduate School of Management. Ranked among the top research libraries in North America, the libraries contain more than 2.3 million volumes, including extensive collections in business. The School provides an information systems laboratory, which is available to students 24 hours a day.

Financial Aid

The University of California offers a wide range of financial aid, including loans, grants, work-study, and fee deferments. For information regarding aid, students should contact the Financial Aid Office, Voorhies Hall (telephone: 530-752-9246). The University also offers scholarships for students based on academic achievement. For further information regarding scholarships, students should contact the Graduate School of Management Admissions Office (telephone: 530-752-7399).

Cost of Study

The 1998–99 estimated fees are $10,468 per year for California residents and $19,452 per year for nonresidents. These figures are subject to change. The University is on the quarter system.

Living and Housing Costs

Most M.B.A. students live off campus where they can take advantage of the many reasonably priced apartments within biking distance. Rents range from $553 for a one-bedroom to $700 for a two-bedroom apartment.

The University offers student family housing, with rents ranging from $427 per month to $559 per month. For additional information, students should contact the Student Housing Office (telephone: 530-752-2483).

Student Group

The School has an enrollment of approximately 125 full-time day students. Thirty-seven percent of the students are women, and the average age is 27. Thirty-three undergraduate institutions are represented, and students have an average of 4½ years' work experience.

Student Outcomes

Last year, 95 percent of the School's M.B.A. graduates were placed three months after graduation. Fifty-five percent of the School's graduates went into the high technology industry, while another 26 percent accepted job offers in the finance industry. More than 76 percent of the School's graduates stayed in the northern California region.

Location

The location of the University of California, Davis, offers some special benefits for students. The community of Davis has all the special attributes of a college-oriented town. The University has developed a special relationship with the community in which it resides, and that relationship provides an enhanced quality of life for all who attend UC Davis.

UC Davis is located just outside of Sacramento, which is fast becoming one of the nation's most vibrant and dynamic cities. Not far away lies the San Francisco Bay Area, with its strong corporate foundation and distinctive linkage to the international business arena. The School's location between these two economically powerful regions adds depth and diversity to its program.

The School

In 1998, the Graduate School of Management at UC Davis was listed among the top thirty-one business schools in the country by *U.S. News & World Report*. The ranking places the management school among the top thirteen public M.B.A. programs in the country, which makes the Graduate School of Management the youngest public school ever to be ranked. The Graduate School of Management educates outstanding men and women for positions of leadership in business. High academic standards, coupled with small classes, allow the faculty to create an exceptionally productive educational environment.

Applying

The program is open to eligible students from all undergraduate majors. Admission is for the fall quarter only. Application materials may be obtained from the Graduate School of Management and should be completed and returned with all supporting documents by February 1. A second deadline of April 1 is also available. Admission is based on several factors: performance in undergraduate course work, scores on the Graduate Management Admission Test (GMAT), letters of recommendation, and work experience. The deadline for financial aid applications is March 1. International students are required to earn a score of at least 600 on the Test of English as a Foreign Language (TOEFL) to be eligible for admission to the program.

Correspondence and Information

Graduate School of Management
University of California, Davis
One Shields Avenue
Davis, California 95616-8609

Telephone: 530-752-7399
E-mail: gsm@ucdavis.edu
World Wide Web: http://www.gsm.ucdavis.edu

University of California, Davis

THE FACULTY

Robert H. Smiley, Dean and Professor of Management; Ph.D., Stanford. Applied microeconomics and public policy, including energy economics, the economics of public utilities, antitrust policy, strategy, and public policy analysis.

Brad M. Barber, Associate Professor of Management; Ph.D., Chicago. Investments, options, corporate finance, statistics.

Nicole Woolsey Biggart, Professor of Management and Sociology; Ph.D., Berkeley. Structure and consequences of business networks in northeast Asian countries.

George Bittlingmayer, Professor of Management; Ph.D., Chicago. Industrial organization, law and economics, public policy.

Eyal Biyalogorsky, Assistant Professor of Marketing; Ph.D., Duke. Marketing, marketing strategy, pricing, new product development, managerial decision making.

David S. Bunch, Associate Professor of Management; Ph.D., Rice. Nonlinear optimization, statistical parameter estimation, discrete choice analysis.

Richard P. Castanias II, Associate Professor of Management; Ph.D., Carnegie Mellon. Corporate finance, security markets behavior, monetary and capital theory.

Peter K. Clark, Professor of Management; Ph.D., Harvard. Macroeconomics, investment theory, derivative securities analysis, international finance.

Masako Darrough, Associate Professor of Accounting; Ph.D., British Columbia. Finance and accounting, using agency theory, information economics, and other quantitative and analytical approaches; interorganizational and intraorganizational relations models.

Richard C. Dorf, Professor Emeritus of Electrical and Computer Engineering and of Management; US Naval Postgraduate School. Engineering management, innovative management, new venture management, strategic planning, automation, robotics and manufacturing, energy policy.

Kimberly Elsbach, Assistant Professor of Organizational Behavior; Ph.D., Stanford. Negotiations, symbolic processes, individual identification and trust processes, linking macrolevel and microlevel organizations.

Eitan Gerstner, Professor of Management; Ph.D., San Diego. Marketing, distribution channels, service marketing, sales promotion, pricing.

Paul A. Griffin, Professor of Management; Ph.D., Ohio State. Relationship between financial information and the behavior of investors, creditors, and others in securities markets.

Michael R. Hagerty, Associate Professor of Management; Ph.D., Illinois. Estimation of the effectiveness of pricing, advertising, sales force, and quality changes for firms and how these vary by industry.

John Lyon, Assistant Professor of Accounting; Ph.D., Ohio State. Financial accounting and auditing.

Michael W. Maher, Associate Dean and Professor of Management; Ph.D., Washington (Seattle). Management accountability and cost analysis in public- and private-sector organizations.

Prasad Naik, Assistant Professor of Management; Ph.D., Florida. Advertising strategy, consumer choice, behavior, sales forecasting, dynamic market response models.

Terrance Odean, Assistant Professor of Finance; Ph.D., Berkeley. Behavioral decision theory applied to finance, the effect of behavior-motivated decisions on asset prices and trading.

Donald A. Palmer, Associate Professor of Management; Ph.D., SUNY at Stony Brook. Organizational behavior.

Srinivasan Rangan, Assistant Professor of Accounting; Ph.D., Pennsylvania. Financial statement analysis, market efficiency, earning management, capital raising transactions.

David M. Rocke, Professor of Management; Ph.D., Illinois. Application of statistics and mathematical models to policy issues, quality and productivity improvement, statistical computing, robust statistical methods.

Jerome J. Suran, Senior Lecturer Emeritus in the Graduate School of Management and the Department of Electrical and Computer Engineering; B.S.E.E., Columbia. Solid-state technology.

Arand Swanminathan, Assistant Professor of Organizational Behavior; Ph.D., Berkeley. Organizational behavior.

Donald M. Topkis, Professor of Management; Ph.D., Stanford. Applications of mathematical programming in telecommunications and computer networks.

Chih-Ling Tsai, Professor of Management; Ph.D., Minnesota. Regression diagnostics, optimal design, application of geometry in statistics.

Gary M. Walton, Professor of Management; Ph.D., Washington (Seattle).

David L. Woodruff, Associate Professor of Management; Ph.D., Northwestern. Production and inventory control.

Visiting Faculty

John Chambers, Ph.D., Claremont. Health-care management.

Daniel Kennedy, M.A., Toronto. Current president and publisher of *Business Journal* in Sacramento, California.

Robert L. Lorber, Ph.D., Union (Ohio). President, chief executive officer, and founder of Lorber Kamai Associates, a management consulting firm.

Robert W. Medearis, B.S.C.E., Stanford; M.B.A., Harvard. Chairman of the Board of PAMA Corporation, Sacramento, California.

Richard Pashley, Ph.D., Caltech. Director of Engineering for Intel-Flashmemory Division.

Dennis Shimek, M.S., California State, San Francisco. Associate Vice Chancellor for Employee Relations at University of California, Davis.

Charles Soderquist, Ph.D., California, Davis. President of Technology Development Center and Director of CSLM Hayes Medical.

Sandra Stewart, Ph.D., Illinois. Project Manager for Student Information Systems at University of California, Davis.

John Troidl, M.B.A., UCLA. Adjunct faculty at California State University, San Francisco, and Lecturer at University of California, Davis.

Executive in Residence

John Collins, A.B., Dartmouth. Retired President and Chief Operating Officer of Clorox Company.

UNIVERSITY OF CALIFORNIA, IRVINE

Graduate School of Management

Programs of Study

The UCI Graduate School of Management (GSM) offers an innovative M.B.A. program with strategic emphases on information technology management and international management. These foci complement a challenging curriculum grounded in the core, functional areas of business: accounting, finance, information systems, marketing, organizational behavior, operations and decision technologies, public policy, and strategy. An emphasis in health-care management is offered, as well as a joint program with the College of Medicine. Irvine's new Information Technology Management (ITM) Track within the management M.B.A. program comprehensively integrates the teaching of information technology management into all facets of the M.B.A. curriculum. Participants in the ITM Track, comprised of students from all functional areas with a variety of backgrounds, learn how technology affects organizations and markets, and how to use information to create new strategic options and gain a lasting competitive advantage. This is all done in a state-of-the-art technological environment with electronic classrooms, a mandatory notebook computer program, and a top-ranked instructional computing facility.

In addition to the full-time program, the Graduate School of Management offers three other M.B.A. programs designed for working professionals: an Executive M.B.A. program, a Fully-Employed M.B.A. program, and a Health-Care Executive M.B.A. program. A Ph.D. program, designed to prepare individuals for teaching and scholarly research, is available on a full-time basis.

Research Facilities

The University of California, Irvine, is part of the extensive University of California library system, a resource with more than 26 million volumes. The ability to use and manage electronic resources plays an increasingly significant role in today's information age. Of special note is the GSM Computing Facility, which is dedicated entirely to GSM students and is consistently ranked as one of the top business school computing facilities in the country. All GSM students are connected to electronic mail, and every seat in GSM's largest classrooms has a network connection, enabling the student to maximize productivity within the classroom setting. Research units associated with the Graduate School of Management and its faculty include the Center for Research on Information Technology (CRITO), the only center in the country that is funded by the U.S. National Science Foundation to study the impact of technology on organizations and markets.

Financial Aid

Primary sources of financial aid for the full-time M.B.A. program include fellowships, grants, and loans. The School also has an on-site financial aid director to assist and guide students in this process. To be considered for the full range of financial aid programs, applicants are strongly encouraged to meet the institutional financial aid deadline. Financial aid is awarded only to citizens or permanent residents of the U.S. A variety of internship and part-time positions are also available through the School's on-site M.B.A. Career Services Office.

Cost of Study

The 1997–98 fees for the full-time M.B.A. program were $3670 per quarter for California residents (three academic quarters per year) and $6665 per quarter for non-California residents.

Living and Housing Costs

There is a variety of both on- and off-campus housing accommodations to suit student needs. The University has some residence hall facilities for single students that include meal plans as well as on-campus apartments for both married and unmarried students. Many students also live in adjacent off-campus areas. Costs for on-campus room and board range from $5382 to $7074; for off-campus, approximately $8485.

Student Group

Approximately 120 students enter each year into the full-time program, for a total population of 240 or more full-time students. Students in this program come not only from California but from many parts of the country and the world. Their backgrounds are varied, and the school makes special efforts to admit a culturally, professionally, and academically diverse group of students each year.

Location

The University of California, Irvine, located midway between Los Angeles and San Diego, is in the center of Orange County, one of the nation's fastest-growing regions. It is also one of the most prolific and dynamic seedbeds for entrepreneurial, high-growth, and high-technology companies. The area provides easy access to professional theater, first-run movies, and dance companies as well as a rich diversity of international cuisine at world-class restaurants. Other advantages include proximity to the mountains and beaches, which offer a variety of recreational opportunities such as water and snow skiing, hang gliding, bicycling, tennis, hiking, sailing, golf, and surfing on a year-round basis.

The University

The University emerged from what had been a 170,000-acre ranch whose origins lay in a Mexican land grant. James Irvine Jr. inherited the land from his father, and in 1947 the James Irvine Foundation came into control of the Irvine Company. The Foundation foresaw the need for housing to replace orange groves but was determined not to replicate the urban sprawl of Los Angeles. One of their first acts was to deed 1,000 acres of land to the state so that it could build a new University of California campus, which many feel is the most lovely of the nine UC campuses. The UCI campus incorporates significant amounts of open space, and the surrounding environment includes the San Joaquin Freshwater Marsh Reserve. The Graduate School of Management has experienced tremendous growth along with the University since their founding in 1965, and it continues to grow.

Applying

Admission for the M.B.A. program is offered each fall and is on a rolling basis. Deadline for the full-time program is May 1. Admissions decisions are based on an overall evaluation of undergraduate GPA, GMAT scores (required), letters of recommendation, statement of purpose, and work experience.

Correspondence and Information

MBA Admissions Office
Graduate School of Management
University of California, Irvine
200 GSM
Irvine, California 92697-3125

Telephone: 949-824-5232 (Full-time M.B.A. program; e-mail: gsm-mba@uci.edu)
949-824-8318 (Ph.D.)
949-824-5374 (Executive, Fully-Employed, and Health-Care Executive M.B.A. programs)
World Wide Web: http://www.gsm.uci.edu

University of California, Irvine

THE FACULTY AND THEIR RESEARCH

Dennis J. Aigner, Professor of Management and Economics; Ph.D., Berkeley. Applied econometrics, experimental design.
Yannis Bakos, Associate Professor of Management and of Information and Computer Science; Ph.D., MIT. Management information systems, strategic uses of information technology, economics of computing.
David H. Blake, Professor of Management and Dean of the Graduate School of Management; Ph.D., Rutgers. Multinational corporations and the international political economy, politics and power in the leadership of organizations, constituency management, management of universities.
George W. Brown, Professor Emeritus of Management; Ph.D., Princeton. Mathematical statistics; game theory; dynamic decision processes; operations research; computer design, operation, and application; information networks.
Thomas C. Buchmueller, Assistant Professor of Management and Economics; Ph.D., Wisconsin–Madison. Health economics, public finance, labor economics.
Nai-fu Chen, Professor of Management; Ph.D., UCLA; Ph.D., Berkeley. Financial investments, relation between real economy and financial markets, contingent claims.
Imran S. Currim, Professor of Management; Ph.D., Stanford. Marketing management, marketing research, marketing strategy, models of customer choice.
Marta M. Elvira, Assistant Professor of Management; Ph.D., Berkeley. Organizational reward structures, strategic human resources, international management, comparative institutional analysis, organizational diversity.
Paul J. Feldstein, Professor of Management and Economics and FHP Foundation Distinguished Chair in Health Care Management; Ph.D., Chicago. Economics of health care.
Mary C. Gilly, Associate Professor of Management and Associate Dean, Research and Graduate Studies; Ph.D., Houston. Marketing strategy, consumer behavior, services marketing.
Dan Givoly, Professor of Management; Ph.D., NYU. Financial accounting, financial reporting, corporate disclosure.
John L. Graham, Professor of Management; Ph.D., Berkeley. International marketing, management and strategy, international business negotiations, managing firms in volatile environments.
Vijay Gurbaxani, Professor of Management and Associate Dean, Academic Degree Programs; Ph.D., Rochester. Economics of information systems management, impact of information technology on organization and market structure.
Robert A. Haugen, Professor of Management; Ph.D., Illinois. Impact of agency problems, impact of taxes on security pricing and investment strategy, design and pricing of financial securities.
Joanna L. Ho, Associate Professor of Management; Ph.D., Texas at Austin. Human information processing systems, behavioral issues in auditing and accounting, decision making under uncertainty.
Philippe Jorion, Professor of Management; Ph.D., Chicago. International financial markets, exchange rate behavior, global fixed-income allocation, optimal diversification under uncertainty, management of global portfolios and integration of international financial markets.
L. Robin Keller, Associate Professor of Management; Ph.D., UCLA. Decision analysis, risk analysis, operations research.
John Leslie King, Professor of Management and of Information and Computer Science; Ph.D., California, Irvine. Computers and public policy, public management uses and impacts of information systems, economics and management of computing.
Kenneth L. Kramer, Professor of Management and Information and Computer Science, Associate Dean of Research, and Director, CRITO; Ph.D., USC. Public policy, information systems, social and managerial impacts of computing.
Newton Margulies, Professor Emeritus of Management; Ph.D., UCLA. Multiple impacts of organization culture on the individual and on subsequent behavior of the organization, organizational change.
Joseph W. McGuire, Professor Emeritus of Management; Ph.D., Columbia. Strategy, entrepreneurship, managerial economics, organizations and their environments.
Richard B. McKenzie, Professor of Management and Economics and Walter B. Gerken Distinguished Chair in Enterprise and Society; Ph.D., Virginia Tech. Public choice and public finance, applied microeconomics, policy issues.
Barrie R. Nault, Associate Professor of Management; Ph.D., British Columbia. Interorganizational information systems, incentives and investments in networks, centralization/decentralization, electronic data interchange, technology introduction and conversion, diffusion and critical-mass public policy and externalities, object-oriented systems.
Peter Navarro, Associate Professor of Management; Ph.D., Harvard. Applied microeconomics, comparative regulation and public policy, industrial organization, public finance.
Paul Olk, Assistant Professor of Management; Ph.D., Pennsylvania (Wharton). Research and development of consortium management, organization creation, strategic alliances, international management, CEO succession.
Jone L. Pearce, Professor of Management; Ph.D., Yale. Behavioral and interpersonal effects of various modes of compensation and related personnel practices.
Cornelia Pechmann, Assistant Professor of Management; Ph.D., Vanderbilt. Advertising strategy, consumer behavior, behavioral decision theory, marketing research, product management, health-care marketing, evaluation research, multivariate analysis, international marketing and advertising.
Lyman W. Porter, Professor Emeritus of Management and Psychology; Ph.D., Yale. Organizational behavior, management education and development.
Judy B. Rosener, Senior Lecturer in Management; Ph.D., Claremont. Political analysis, citizen participation, gender roles and management.
Claudia B. Schoonhoven, Ph.D., Stanford. Organizational theory, strategic management of innovation and technology, entrepreneurship.
Carlton H. Scott, Professor of Management; Ph.D., New South Wales (England). Operations research methodology, decision support systems, optimization theory, statistics and operations management.
Kut C. So, Professor of Management; Ph.D., Stanford. Design of production and inventory systems, optimization of queuing systems, operations research.
Jing-Sheng Song, Associate Professor of Management; Ph.D., Columbia. Operations research, operations management, stochastic modeling and optimization inventory control.
Neal M. Stoughton, Associate Professor of Management; Ph.D., Stanford. Corporate financial structure, security valuation methods, applications of game theory, optimal contracting.
Eli Talmor, Professor of Management; Ph.D., North Carolina at Chapel Hill. Corporate finance, taxation, financial markets.
Alladi Venkatesh, Professor of Management; Ph.D., Syracuse. Household consumption behavior, marketing theory, and macromarketing; postmodernism and consumer culture; cultural aspects of technology adoption and diffusion; technology and development.
Margarethe F. Wiersema, Associate Professor of Management; Ph.D., Michigan. Corporate strategy, corporate entrepreneurship, executive succession.
William F. Wright, Associate Professor of Management; Ph.D., Berkeley. Human information processing and auditing/accounting decisions, nature of expert judgments, microcomputer-based decision aids, artificial intelligence/expert systems.

UNIVERSITY OF CALIFORNIA, LOS ANGELES

The Anderson School at UCLA
Master of Business Administration Program

Programs of Study

Professional management education at The Anderson School requires rigorous study, creativity and imagination, analytical thinking, problem diagnosis and solution, and teamwork. The Anderson School M.B.A. program is designed for highly motivated, exceptional students and is structured to ensure that each graduate leaves with a leadership-level knowledge of all key management disciplines as well as the conceptual and analytical frameworks underlying those disciplines. Consisting of three components—the management core, advanced electives, and the management field study—the curriculum is regularly updated to address the evolving challenges today's business managers must meet.

The management core is a set of eight courses that provides the fundamental knowledge of the major functional fields of management and builds a foundation for advanced study in a variety of areas. The integrated and sequential nature of the management core courses ensures that each successive course builds upon the knowledge gained in prior courses.

Chosen from course offerings in nine curriculum areas and several interdisciplinary areas, advanced electives comprise about two thirds of the M.B.A. curriculum. The large number of advanced electives lends great flexibility and diversity to each student's program of study. Because of the program's general management focus, M.B.A. students are not required to declare a major or concentration. Traditional areas of study offered at The Anderson School are discipline-based. Students may tailor an individual M.B.A. program that reflects several interdisciplinary areas of study. These include arts management, entertainment management, entrepreneurial studies, international business and comparative management, public/not-for-profit management, and real estate.

Management field study is the capstone requirement of the M.B.A. program and is conducted during the second year of the program. In this project, students integrate and apply their knowledge and skills in a professional setting outside the classroom.

Research Facilities

The UCLA Library System is ranked in the top five among the nation's college and university libraries. While the resources of all UCLA libraries are available to Anderson School students, the collections, online systems, and services available in the School's Rosenfeld Library are of particular value. Holdings include 147,000 volumes; subscriptions to nearly 3,000 journals, periodicals, and newspapers; 445,000 items on microfilm and microfiche; and 85,000 pamphlets including annual reports and working papers from other schools. Research programs and study centers associated with the School and its faculty include the Price Center for Entrepreneurial Studies, the Center for International Business Education and Research, the Center for Real Estate, the Center for Technology Management, the Center for Corporate Renewal, and the Center for Public Policy.

Financial Aid

All applicants to The Anderson School interested in obtaining financial assistance must complete a Free Application for Federal Student Aid (FAFSA) by March 2, regardless of when they are admitted. The FAFSA may be accessed on the World Wide Web (http://www.ed.gov/offices/OPE/express.html) or by calling the Department of Education at 800-433-3243 (toll-free). Admitted applicants automatically receive additional information regarding the financial aid process two to three weeks after being offered admission. All admitted full-time students who are U.S. citizens or permanent residents may apply for need-based financial aid. A limited number of research and teaching assistantship positions are also available, and some fellowship support is available for exceptional applicants to the M.B.A. program. Merit-based fellowships and scholarships at The Anderson School are more commonly awarded to continuing students based on their academic performance and leadership activities during the first year of the M.B.A. program.

Cost of Study

For 1997–98, tuition and fees per academic year totaled $12,586 for California residents and $21,570 for nonresidents.

Living and Housing Costs

Room and board for the 1997–98 academic year were $8800. Books and supplies were $6793 (includes a laptop computer). Transportation, entertainment, and miscellaneous costs were $4284. These costs were for students living off campus in shared housing. Additional costs may include support of dependents, medical expenses, and travel. Married students should expect to budget about $3500 in additional costs.

Student Group

The Anderson School at UCLA has a vibrant student body whose extraordinary intellectual, cultural, social, and athletic energies spill out of the classroom into a plethora of nonacademic activities. The average student is 27 years old, with just more than four years of full-time work experience. Women comprise 26 percent of the student population, members of minority groups make up 24 percent, and international students make up 23 percent.

Location

Strolling to classes through the serene gardens on UCLA's campus, it is easy to forget that The Anderson School is located in the middle of the second-largest city in the U.S. and one of the most vital economic and cultural areas in the world. For Anderson students, Los Angeles offers the best of many worlds. Beach, mountain, and desert recreation areas are plentiful and easily accessible by car. Los Angeles museums house some of the finest art collections in the country, and theaters and the splendid Music Center offer some of the world's most acclaimed entertainment. Westwood Village, which adjoins the UCLA campus to the south, offers shopping, dining, and a wide range of services.

The School

The Anderson School's management education complex is a testament to the School's vision of the growing importance of superior management education. Continuing the School's reputation as a national leader in the use of computing in M.B.A. instruction, the eleven specially-designed case study rooms have data ports at each seating station to integrate the instructional program of each faculty member with the School's central computing facility in the Rosenfeld Library.

Applying

Applicants may apply for fall 1999 admission from October 1, 1998, through April 3, 1999. The Admissions Committee begins considering applications in December of each year.

Correspondence and Information

Ms. Linda Baldwin
Director of M.B.A. Admissions
The Anderson School at UCLA
110 Westwood Plaza, Suite B201
Box 951481
Los Angeles, California 90095-1481

Telephone: 310-825-6944
Fax: 310-825-8582
E-mail: mba.admissions@anderson.ucla.edu
World Wide Web: http://www.anderson.ucla.edu/

University of California, Los Angeles

THE FACULTY

John W. Mamer, Interim Dean of The Anderson School at UCLA; Ph.D., Berkeley.

Accounting

David Aboody, Assistant Professor; Ph.D., Berkeley. Schlomo Benartzi, Assistant Professor; Ph.D., Cornell. John W. Buckley, Ernst and Young Chair in Accounting, Vice Dean, and Professor; Ph.D., Washington (Seattle). Jack Farrell, Retired Adjunct Professor; CPA. Stephen C. Hansen, Assistant Professor; Ph.D., Carnegie Mellon. Carla Hayn, Associate Professor; Ph.D., Michigan. Patricia J. Hughes, Professor; Ph.D., British Columbia. John J. McDonough, Chairman, Vice Dean, and Professor; D.B.A., Harvard. Bruce L. Miller, Professor; Ph.D., Stanford. Michael Williams, Assistant Professor; Ph.D., Princeton and USC. Sung-Soo Yoon, Assistant Professor; Ph.D., Illinois at Urbana-Champaign.

Business Economics

Michael R. Darby, Warren C. Cordner Chair in Money and Financial Markets and Professor; Ph.D., Chicago. Sebastian Edwards, Henry Ford II Chair in International Management and Professor; Ph.D., Chicago. Larry J. Kimbell, Professor; Ph.D., Texas at Austin. Edward E. Leamer, Chauncey J. Medberry Chair in Management and Professor; Ph.D., Michigan. Alfred E. Osborne Jr., Associate Professor; Ph.D., Stanford. Victor Tabbush, Adjunct Professor; Ph.D., UCLA.

Decision Sciences

Sushil Bikhchandani, Associate Professor; Ph.D., Stanford. Donald Erlenkotter, Professor; Ph.D., Stanford. Arthur M. Geoffrion, Professor; Ph.D., Stanford. Glenn W. Graves, Professor Emeritus, Recalled; Ph.D., Michigan. Steven A. Lippman, Vice Dean and Professor; Ph.D., Stanford. James B. MacQueen, Professor; Ph.D., Oregon. John W. Mamer, Interim Dean and Professor; Ph.D., Berkeley. Christopher Tang, Professor; Ph.D., Yale.

Finance

Theodore A. Andersen, Professor Emeritus, Recalled; Ph.D., Wisconsin. Antonio E. Bernardo, Assistant Professor; Ph.D., Stanford. Michael J. Brennen, Goldyne and Irwin Hearsh Chair in Money and Banking and Professor; Ph.D., MIT. Bhagwan Chowdhry, Associate Professor; Ph.D., Chicago. William Cockrum, Adjunct Professor; M.B.A., Harvard. Bradford Cornell, Professor; Ph.D., Stanford. Robert L. Geske, Associate Professor; Ph.D., Berkeley. Mark S. Grinblatt, Associate Professor; Ph.D., Yale. Matthias Kahl, Assistant Professor; Ph.D. candidate, Pennsylvania. Olivier Ledoit, Assistant Professor, Ph.D., MIT. Francis Longstaff, Professor; Ph.D., Chicago. Richard W. Roll, The Allstate Chair in Finance and Insurance and Professor; Ph.D., Chicago. Pedro Santa-Clara, Assistant Professor; Ph.D., INSEAD. Eduardo S. Schwartz, California Chair in Real Estate and Land Economics and Professor; Ph.D., British Columbia. Avanidhar Subrahmanyam, Acting Associate Professor; Ph.D., UCLA. Walt Torous, Professor; Ph.D., Pennsylvania. Leonard Weil, Adjunct Assistant Professor; B.A., UCLA. Ivo I. Welch, Associate Professor; Ph.D., Chicago. J. Fred Weston, Professor Emeritus, Recalled; Ph.D., Chicago.

Human Resources and Organizational Behavior

Samuel A. Culbert, Professor; Ph.D., UCLA. Christopher L. Erickson, Associate Professor; Ph.D., MIT. Eric G. Flamholtz, Professor; Ph.D., Michigan. Connie J. G. Gersick, Associate Professor; Ph.D., Yale. Sanford M. Jacoby, Professor; Ph.D., Berkeley. Archie Kleingartner, Professor; Ph.D., Wisconsin. Barbara S. Lawrence, Associate Professor; Ph.D., MIT. David Lewin, Vice Dean and Professor; Ph.D., UCLA. John J. McDonough, Chairman, Vice Dean, and Professor; D.B.A., Harvard. Daniel J. B. Mitchell, Professor; Ph.D., MIT. David M. Porter Jr., Assistant Professor; Ph.D., Harvard. Karen Stephenson, Assistant Professor; Ph.D., Harvard.

Information Systems

Jason Frand, Assistant Dean and Director; Ph.D., UCLA. George Geis, Adjunct Professor; Ph.D., USC. Martin Greenberger, IBM Chair in Computers and Information Systems and Professor; Ph.D., Harvard. Bennet P. Lientz, Professor; Ph.D., Washington (Seattle). E. Burton Swanson, Professor; Ph.D., Berkeley.

Marketing

Jennifer L. Aaker, Assistant Professor; Ph.D., Stanford. David R. Bell, Assistant Professor; Ph.D., Stanford. Randolph E. Bucklin, Associate Professor; Ph.D., Stanford. Margaret C. Campbell, Assistant Professor; Ph.D., Stanford. Lee G. Cooper, Professor; Ph.D., Illinois. Aimee Drolet, Assistant Professor; Ph.D., Stanford. Gavan J. Fitzsimons, Assistant Professor; Ph.D., Columbia. Dominique M. Hanssens, Professor; Ph.D., Purdue. Deborah D. Heisley, Assistant Professor; Ph.D., Northwestern. Donald G. Morrison, William E. Leonhard Chair in Management and Professor; Ph.D., Stanford. Carol A. Scott, Professor; Ph.D., Northwestern. Atanu R. Sinha, Assistant Professor; Ph.D., NYU. Shi Zhang, Assistant Professor; Ph.D., Columbia.

Operations and Technology Management

Reza H. Ahmadi, Associate Professor; Ph.D., Texas at Austin. Robert B. Andrews, Professor, Recalled; Ph.D., UCLA. Charles Corbett, Assistant Professor; Ph.D., INSEAD. Donald Erlenkotter, Professor; Ph.D., Stanford. Robert Foster, Adjunct Assistant Professor; M.B.A., UCLA. Teck Ho, Assistant Professor; Ph.D., Pennsylvania. Uday S. Karmarkar, Times Mirror Chair in Management Strategy and Policy and Professor; Ph.D., MIT. William P. Pierskalla, Dean Emeritus; Ph.D., Stanford. Kumar Rajaram, Acting Assistant Professor; Ph.D. candidate; Pennsylvania. Rakesh K. Sarin, Paine Chair in Management and Professor; Ph.D., UCLA. Christopher S. Tang, Professor; Ph.D., Yale. William Yost, Adjunct Professor; D.B.A., Harvard.

Strategy and Organization

Eric D. Darr, Assistant Professor; Ph.D., Carnegie Mellon. José de la Torre, Professor; D.B.A., Harvard. Richard A. Goodman, Associate Professor; D.B.A., Washington (St. Louis). Barbara S. Lawrence, Associate Professor; Ph.D., MIT. Marvin B. Lieberman, Associate Professor; Ph.D., Harvard. Bill McKelvey, Professor; Ph.D., MIT. Elaine Mosakowski, Assistant Professor; Ph.D., Berkeley. William G. Ouchi, Professor; D.Litt., Williams; Ph.D., Chicago. Richard P. Rumelt, Harry and Elsa Kunin Professor of Business and Society; D.B.A., Harvard. Mariko Sakakibara, Assistant Professor; Ph.D., Harvard. Hans Schollhammer, Professor; D.B.A., Indiana. Sanford Sigoloff, Adjunct Professor; B.S., UCLA. James Q. Wilson, James A. Collins Chair in Management; Ph.D., Chicago. George Yip, Adjunct Professor; D.B.A., Harvard.

The Anderson School at UCLA.

UNIVERSITY OF CALIFORNIA, RIVERSIDE

The A. Gary Anderson Graduate School of Management

Program of Study

The A. Gary Anderson Graduate School of Management offers a professional program leading to the degree of Master of Business Administration (M.B.A.). The program is characterized by a tradition of academic excellence and an innovative student-centered curriculum. It provides a strong foundation in the common body of knowledge in the field of management—plus the opportunity for advanced elective course work in accounting, entrepreneurial management, finance, human resources management, international management, management information systems, management science, marketing, and production management.

The M.B.A. program is flexible in design in order to accommodate the requirements of both full-time students and career professionals studying part-time. In addition to regularly scheduled course work during the day, sufficient numbers of course sections are offered in the evenings to permit pursuit of the M.B.A. on a part-time basis.

The program, which can normally be finished in two years, requires the completion of twenty-three courses (92 quarter units). In the first year, all students take 48 units in a common body of knowledge consisting of courses in statistical methods for management, managerial economics, managerial accounting, organizational behavior, human resources management, management science, operations management, computer systems, financial analysis, marketing, business and society, and management synthesis. Thereafter, students take a minimum of 28 units selected from both general and specialized electives and complete a required internship, a capstone business strategy course, and a case analysis or a thesis. All students also complete a nondegree credit workshop in management communication.

Research Facilities

The University library has a collection of more than 1.8 million bound volumes, 13,300 serial subscriptions, and 1.5 million microforms. Extensive batch and interactive computer facilities are available on campus. In addition, the A. Gary Anderson Graduate School of Management has its own on-site computing lab and computer software libraries capable of supporting a wide variety of research and instruction in management.

Financial Aid

A variety of loans, grants, work-study credits, and fee deferments are available through the Financial Aid Office. The A. Gary Anderson Graduate School of Management also offers fellowships and numerous teaching assistantships to qualified students each year. Salaries for teaching assistants vary according to the type of appointment but can range up to $12,810 per academic year.

Cost of Study

Fees were $1622 per quarter for California residents in 1997–98. Tuition and fees for nonresident students were $4618 per quarter. In 1997–98, M.B.A. students also paid a $2500 per year professional school fee. Fees and tuition charges are subject to change.

Living and Housing Costs

The availability of reasonably priced housing is of particular importance to graduate students. The University of California at Riverside has two coeducational on-campus residence halls, which house about 1,200 students; a modern apartment complex; and the Canyon Crest complex, consisting of 268 houses available to married students. Student family housing costs $410 per month for unfurnished two-bedroom units. Off-campus housing rents range from $450 to $850 per month for one- and two-bedroom units.

Student Group

Enrollment at the School is 150 students. AGSM's students have a wide range of academic and professional backgrounds. More than 40 percent of the students are women, and the average age is 27.

Student Outcomes

The graduate school has its own M.B.A. Career Services Center in addition to the UC Riverside Career Services Center. The majority of M.B.A. students participate in the annual West Coast M.B.A. Consortium (a total of twelve universities), which sponsors a recruitment fair held in January of each year. In the January 1997 consortium, 85 percent of the students that attended received interviews for jobs in accounting, finance, marketing, sales, and consulting. The largest percentage of 1996–97 M.B.A. graduates accepted jobs in banking and finance, followed by accounting, marketing, and consulting. During interviews, M.B.A. students found that the diversity of their undergraduate studies provided a competitive edge.

Location

The 1,200-acre Riverside campus of the University of California is located about 50 miles east of Los Angeles, within easy driving distance of most of the major cultural and recreational offerings in southern California. The lights of Los Angeles, the beaches of Orange County, the desert area of Palm Springs, and the slopes of the San Bernardino and San Gabriel mountains are all about an hour's drive away.

The School

The educational philosophy of the A. Gary Anderson Graduate School of Management is founded on the premise that the ability to adapt to new conditions and realities is an essential requirement for effective and innovative management in an era of rapid technological and institutional change. The challenge of professional education in management is to provide a learning environment that not only encourages the development of the basic analytical, behavioral, and leadership skills for management but also enhances the student's potential for continuing growth under uncertain and changing conditions in an international marketplace. The curriculum of the M.B.A. program and the instructional process are designed to meet this challenge. Most classes are small and are structured to maximize both formal and informal learning experiences. Computers and software are used extensively both for teaching purposes and as tools for effective management decision making.

Applying

The program is open to eligible students from all undergraduate majors. New students are admitted in the fall, winter, and spring quarters. Applications from U.S. citizens for fall should be submitted by May 1, for winter by September 1, and for spring by December 1. Deadlines for international applicants are February 1 for fall, July 1 for winter, and October 1 for spring. Admission is based on several factors, including the quality of previous academic work, scores on the Graduate Management Admission Test (GMAT), letters of recommendation, and potential for success in the program. International applicants must submit scores on the Test of English as a Foreign Language (TOEFL). Work experience is not required for admission.

Correspondence and Information

The A. Gary Anderson Graduate School of Management
University of California
Riverside, California 92521-0203

Telephone: 909-787-4551
Fax: 909-787-3970
E-mail: agsmmba@ucrac1.ucr.edu
World Wide Web: http://www.agsm.ucr.edu

University of California, Riverside

THE FACULTY

K. Hung Chan, Ph.D. (accounting), Penn State, 1974.
Y. Peter Chung, Ph.D. (finance), Ohio State, 1989.
Bajis Dodin, Ph.D. (operations research), North Carolina State, 1981.
Sunil Erevelles, Ph.D. (marketing), Ohio State, 1992.
Mohsen El Hafsi, Ph.D. (operations research), Florida, 1995.
Carolyn Galantine, Ph.D. (accounting), USC, 1994.
Jerayr Haleblian, Ph.D. (business), USC, 1995.
E. Mark Hanson, Ph.D. (educational administration), New Mexico, 1968.
Walter Henry, Ph.D. (marketing), Claremont, 1973.
Herbert E. Johnson, Ph.D. (finance), UCLA, 1981.
Sarkis J. Khoury, Ph.D. (finance), Pennsylvania (Wharton), 1978.
Alan H. Lewis, M.B.A. (marketing), Pennsylvania (Wharton), 1967.
Woody M. Liao, Ph.D. (accounting), Florida, 1974.
Ray Maghroori, Ph.D. (political science), California, Riverside, 1978.
David Mayers, Ph.D. (finance), Rochester, 1972.
Kathleen Montgomery, Ph.D. (organizational behavior), NYU, 1987.
Janis Pasquali, Ph.D. (organizational behavior), California, Irvine, 1982.
Waymond Rodgers, Ph.D. (accounting), USC, 1984.
Erik Rolland, Ph.D. (management information systems), Ohio State, 1991.
Susan Sassalos, Ph.D. (organizational behavior), Berkeley, 1994.
Siegfried Schaible, Ph.D. (operations research), Cologne, 1971.
Andrew Spicer, Ph.D. (management), Pennsylvania (Wharton), 1998.
Shuba Srinivasan, Ph.D. (management science), Texas at Dallas, 1995.
Charlotte M. Weber, Ph.D. (public administration), Johns Hopkins, 1978.
G. Lawrence Zahn, Ph.D. (organizational behavior), Yale, 1971.
Chunsheng Zhou, Ph.D. (financial economics), Princeton, 1995.

The M.B.A. Career Services Coordinator provides students with information on career opportunities.

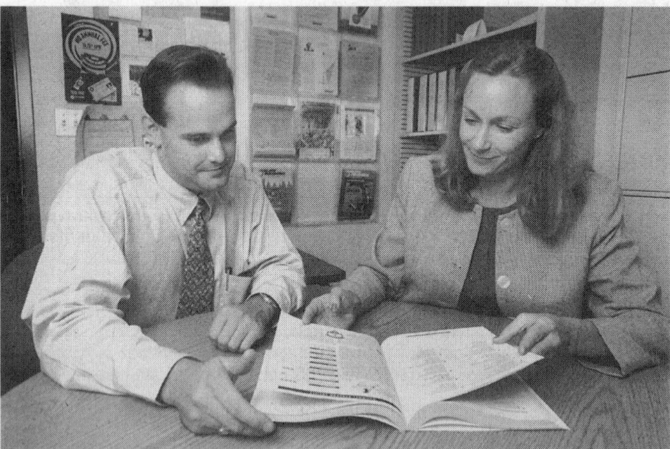

The Anderson Graduate School Placement Developer provides students with information on internships.

Anderson Hall is the home of the A. Gary Anderson Graduate School of Management.

UNIVERSITY OF CENTRAL FLORIDA

College of Business Administration

Programs of Study

The College of Business Administration offers five professional degree programs: the Master of Business Administration (M.B.A.), Master of Science in Accounting (M.S.A.), Master of Science in Taxation (M.S.T.), Master of Arts in Applied Economics (M.A.A.E.), and Ph.D. in business administration. UCF's graduate and undergraduate programs in business are accredited by the AACSB–the International Association for Management Education.

The M.B.A. program is designed to develop the student's analytical, decision-making, and problem-solving capabilities to meet the challenges of leadership in professional management positions at present and in the changing world of the future. The program has a broad-based administrative emphasis permitting a limited degree of specialization in a particular field of business. A thesis is not required. The program involves between 33 and 63 semester hours of course work, depending on the student's prior academic preparation, and can generally be completed in one to two years of full-time study. The M.B.A. program is open to students with baccalaureate degrees in nonbusiness or business fields and can be pursued on either a full-time or part-time basis.

The M.S.A. degree program stresses the development of advanced accounting skills to provide resources for decision making and problem solving in public, private, and government accounting. Course work is practice-oriented, emphasizing quantitative techniques and computer skills. There is considerable flexibility with regard to advanced accounting areas of concentration. The length of the program depends on the student's background in accounting and other business disciplines.

The M.S.T. degree program stresses the development of advanced knowledge of taxation for use in decision making and problem solving in public, private, and government accounting positions. Course work is practice-oriented, emphasizing quantitative techniques and the development of research skills. The length of the program depends on the student's background in accounting and other disciplines. For a student with no deficiencies, the program involves 18 semester hours of required tax courses and 12 hours of restricted electives.

The M.A.A.E. degree program, which requires 30 semester hours, provides specialization in economics for individuals desiring careers as economists in the academic, government, business, and financial communities.

The Ph.D. in business administration is designed to prepare students for academic careers in higher education and management careers in profit and nonprofit organizations. Success in the program is judged by the student's understanding of the issues and methodologies essential to the advancement of knowledge. Doctoral work is based on the achievement of academic and research competencies rather than a specific number of courses. The program requires students to have an M.B.A. or an equivalent degree. The Ph.D. program has been revised, and students are being accepted for the 1999 fall semester.

Research Facilities

Extensive computer facilities for batch and interactive modes are available both in the College of Business Administration and in the University Computer Center. Graduate business students have access to equipment that ranges from large mainframe computers to minicomputers and microcomputers. The University Library holdings include more than 300,000 books, 5,000 periodicals, 2,000 microforms, and other research materials necessary to support high-caliber graduate programs. The library also participates in online information searching through a variety of services.

Financial Aid

Limited financial aid is available in the form of graduate assistantships, out-of-state tuition waivers, and student loan programs. Most assistantship stipends range from $3400 to $4600 for the 1997–98 academic year and require 20 hours of service per week to the College of Business Administration.

Cost of Study

Tuition, which is subject to change, was $129.13 per semester hour for Florida residents and $434.52 per semester hour for out-of-state residents in 1997–98.

Living and Housing Costs

Off-campus living accommodations for graduate students are available throughout the Orlando area; some are within walking distance of the University.

Student Group

Enrollment on campus is more than 28,000, with 5,700 students in the College of Business Administration. Approximately 700 graduate students are pursuing degrees in the College; approximately half of them have undergraduate degrees in nonbusiness fields. Diverse geographical backgrounds and areas of professional experience are represented.

Location

Metropolitan Orlando is a growing, dynamic area of more than 2 million people. Cultural and recreational activities and facilities are abundant. Although best known for its various tourist attractions, Orlando also has an extremely broad industrial base. Central Florida has an ideal climate, with an average temperature of 72°F, which makes it possible to enjoy outdoor activities during the whole year. The Atlantic Ocean is an hour's drive east of campus.

The University

The University of Central Florida, formerly known as Florida Technological University, was founded in 1963. A youthful, dynamic institution, UCF is part of the State University System of Florida. The picturesque campus, located 13 miles east of downtown Orlando, consists of 1,227 acres. Baccalaureate, master's, and doctoral degrees are offered in a wide variety of fields.

Applying

Students may enter the M.B.A., M.S.A., M.S.T., and M.A.A.E. degree programs in the fall, spring, or summer semester. Applications should be made at least four months prior to the desired enrollment date. Admission is open to students showing high promise of success. A bachelor's degree from a regionally accredited college or university, submission of satisfactory scores on the Graduate Management Admission Test, an essay, and three recommendations are required for admission consideration.

Correspondence and Information

Coordinator of Graduate Programs
College of Business Administration, Suite 240
University of Central Florida
Orlando, Florida 32816-1400
Telephone: 407-823-2184

University of Central Florida

THE FACULTY

Rajshree Agarwal, Assistant Professor; Ph.D., Buffalo, 1994.
Jeff Allen, Assistant Professor of Marketing; D.B.A., Kentucky, 1987.
Henry R. Anderson, Professor of Accounting; Ph.D., Missouri–Columbia, 1971.
Stanley M. Atkinson, Associate Professor of Finance; D.B.A., Mississippi State, 1977.
Charles D. Bailey, Professor of Accounting; Ph.D., Georgia State, 1981.
D. Dale Bandy, Professor of Accounting; Ph.D., Texas at Austin, 1972.
Bruce Barringer, Assistant Professor; Ph.D., Missouri–Columbia, 1995.
Walter A. Bogumil, Associate Professor of Management; Ph.D., Georgia, 1972.
Bradley M. Braun, Associate Professor of Economics; Ph.D., Tulane, 1986.
Anthony K. Byrd, Assistant Professor of Finance; Ph.D., South Carolina, 1992.
William G. Callarman, Associate Professor of Management; D.B.A., Arizona State, 1973.
John M. Cheney, Associate Professor of Finance and Chair; D.B.A., Tennessee, 1977.
Duane L. Davis, Professor of Marketing; D.B.A., Kentucky, 1978.
A. Edward Day, Associate Professor of Economics; Ph.D., Purdue, 1976.
E. Taylor Ellis, Associate Professor of Hospitality Management; Ph.D., Texas A&M, 1976.
Thomas G. Evans, Professor of Accounting; Ph.D., Michigan State, 1969.
Lloyd W. Fernald Jr., Professor of Management; D.B.A., George Washington, 1981.
Cameron Ford, Associate Professor of Management; Ph.D., Penn State, 1997.
Robert C. Ford, Professor of Hospitality Management and Chair; Ph.D., Arizona State, 1972.
Donald A. Fuller, Associate Professor of Marketing; Ph.D., Georgia State, 1972.
Craig Gallet, Assistant Professor of Economics; Ph.D., Iowa State, 1996.
W. Ernest Gibbs, Associate Professor of Economics; Ph.D., Rutgers, 1987.
Peter L. Gillett, Professor of Marketing; Ph.D., Michigan State, 1969.
Paul Goldwater, Associate Professor of Accounting; Ph.D., LSU, 1989.
Stephen H. Goodman, Associate Professor of Management; Ph.D., Penn State, 1972.
Jeffrey S. Harrison, Associate Professor of Management; Ph.D., Utah, 1985.
Richard A. Hofler, Professor of Economics and Chair; Ph.D., North Carolina at Chapel Hill, 1982.
Djehane Hosni, Associate Professor of Economics; Ph.D., Arkansas, 1978.
Richard S. Huseman, Professor of Management; Ph.D., Illinois, 1965.
Walter L. Johnson, Associate Professor of Accounting; Ph.D., Texas at Austin, 1974; CPA.
Foard F. Jones, Assistant Professor of Management; Ph.D., Georgia, 1991.
Halsey R. Jones, Professor of Management and Interim Chair; Ph.D., Penn State, 1966.
Andrew Judd, Associate Professor of Accounting and Interim Chair; Ph.D., Florida, 1985.
Charles Kelliher, Associate Professor of Accounting; Ph.D., Texas A&M, 1990.
Thomas L. Keon, Dean and Professor of Management; Ph.D., Michigan State, 1979.
Stephen LeBruto, Associate Professor of Hospitality Management; Ed.D., Central Florida, 1992.
William E. Leigh, Professor of Management; Ph.D., Cincinnati, 1984.
John List, Assistant Professor of Economics; Ph.D., Wyoming, 1996.
Thomas L. Martin, Associate Professor of Economics; Ph.D., Rice, 1981.
Warren W. McHone, Professor of Economics; Ph.D., Pennsylvania, 1980.
Ron Michaels, Professor of Marketing, Chair, and Interim Associate Dean; Ph.D., Indiana, 1983.
Ady Milman, Associate Professor of Hospitality Management; Ph.D., Massachusetts, 1986.
Naval K. Modani, Associate Professor of Finance; Ph.D., South Carolina, 1980.
Hoon Park, Associate Professor of Finance; Ph.D., Georgia State, 1988.
Gordon W. Paul, Professor of Marketing; Ph.D., Michigan State, 1966.
Robert L. Pennington, Associate Professor of Economics, Associate Dean, and Director, M.B.A. Program; Ph.D., Texas A&M, 1977.
Thomas E. Phillips, Associate Professor of Accounting; Ph.D., Nebraska, 1974; CPA.
Abraham Pizam, Professor of Hospitality Management; Ph.D., Cornell, 1970.
Gary D. Porter, Assistant Professor of Finance; Ph.D., South Carolina, 1992.
James Potts, Professor of Accounting; Ph.D., Alabama, 1976.
Russel Purvis, Assistant Professor of Management; Ph.D., Florida State, 1994.
William J. Quain, Professor of Hospitality Management; Ph.D., New Orleans, 1982.
Frederick A. Raffa, Professor of Economics; Ph.D., Florida State, 1969.
Pamela B. Roush, Associate Professor of Accounting; Ph.D., Georgia State, 1989.
Ronald S. Rubin, Professor of Marketing; Ph.D., Massachusetts, 1973.
Brian A. Rungeling, Professor of Economics and Interim Chair; Ph.D., Kentucky, 1969.
John H. Salter, Professor of Accounting; Ph.D., LSU, 1975; CPA.
Linda J. Savage, Associate Professor of Accounting; Ph.D., Florida, 1976; CPA.
David F. Scott Jr., Professor of Finance and Phillips-Schenck Chair in American Private Enterprise; Ph.D., Florida, 1970.
Mark D. Soskin, Associate Professor of Economics; Ph.D., Penn State, 1979.
Mary Uhl-Bien, Associate Professor of Management; Ph.D., Cincinnati, 1996.
William C. Weaver, Associate Professor of Finance; Ph.D., Georgia State, 1983.
Judith K. Welch, Associate Professor of Accounting; Ph.D., Florida State, 1985.
Kenneth R. White, Associate Professor of Economics; Ph.D., Oklahoma, 1971.
James A. Xander, Associate Professor of Economics; Ph.D., Georgia, 1974.

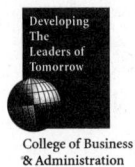

Developing The Leaders of Tomorrow

College of Business & Administration

UNIVERSITY OF COLORADO AT BOULDER

College of Business and Administration
Graduate School of Business Administration

Programs of Study

Developing people who are competitive in the global economy is the mission of the College of Business and Administration. Offering the Ph.D., M.S., and M.B.A. graduate degrees, the College prides itself on educating the leaders of the next millennium.

The College's strong Ph.D. program educates the nation's future professors. As the flagship program in the region, the University of Colorado (CU) provides doctoral students with a comprehensive background in their areas of study, a thorough understanding of another related discipline, and a strong research base. Students conduct research with the University's distinguished faculty and major in accounting, business strategy, finance, information systems, marketing, operations management and research, or organization management. The full-time program consists of at least 30 hours of course work and at least 30 hours of dissertation credit, in addition to significant research and teaching responsibilities.

Specialized graduate degrees are critical for highly motivated students pursuing the complex fields of accounting and taxation. The Master of Science in business administration degree offers in-depth programs in these fields and the opportunity to minor in a second field. Students complete 30 credits, pass their comprehensive examination in their final semester, and are not required to present a thesis.

Teamwork, management, and communication skills prepare graduates of the M.B.A. program for leadership positions within the international marketplace. Majoring in entrepreneurship, finance, marketing, organization management, real estate, or technology and innovation management, students graduate with the skills necessary to compete on a global level. A self-designed major, as well as the Juris Doctor/M.B.A. and the M.B.A./Master of Science in telecommunications dual-degree programs, give students specialization to supplement their management background. Students interested in a global focus can pursue a certificate in international business. All master's programs are available on a full- or part-time basis.

Research Facilities

The University of Colorado network system, which is a depository for U.S. government, international, and state documents, has nearly 200 million volumes, an equal number of microforms, and 13,000 periodicals. The College's White Library offers students financial reference works, directories, loose-leaf services, and corporate annual reports on microfiche for all companies on the New York and American stock exchanges. Company reports, available on Compact Disclosure, Compustat, and LEXIS/NEXIS, provide optimal services for research projects. Bibliographic information is available on ABI-Inform, InfoTrac, the Chinook system, and LEXIS/NEXIS. Subscriptions to more than 1,000 journals and access to an additional 400 are available in the business collection.

A technological focus is placed on projects, and the College houses eight technology team rooms to give students experience with the latest technological resources. The PepsiCo Case Room is equipped with laptop computer workstations and has multimedia and distance learning capabilities. As part of the White Library, the Buck Electronic Media Center provides access to CD-ROM and online information. Ph.D. students and faculty members also have access to the DEC Alpha 2000 computer system, which runs OSF 3.0. Data sets include CRSP, Compustat, Citibase, and TAQ, and available programs include SPSS, SAS, GAUSS, and matlab.

Financial Aid

Several types of financial support, including student loans, scholarships, grants, and work-study, are offered to students. Half of CU's students receive financial aid. Students should call 303-492-5091 for financial aid information.

Most doctoral students receive research and teaching assistantships or fellowships. In addition to a tuition waiver, Ph.D. students received a stipend of $12,798 for the 1997–98 academic year. Doctoral students should contact the Ph.D. adviser at 303-492-4984 for information regarding financial support.

Cost of Study

Tuition for full-time residents was $1774 for M.S. students and $1855 for M.B.A. students per semester in 1997–98. Full-time nonresident tuition cost $7200 for M.S. students and $7335 for M.B.A. students per semester. Ph.D. students should call 303-492-4984 for financial information.

Living and Housing Costs

In addition to dormitories for single students, housing is available for married couples and students with dependent children. Most graduate students live off campus in a variety of private housing options. Information is available by calling Off-Campus Housing at 303-492-7053 or Campus Housing at 303-492-6871.

Student Group

CU's students are an exciting group of high-achieving individuals. The M.S. class is composed of 37 percent women, 11 percent members of minority groups, and 5 percent international students. The doctoral student body is composed of 38 percent women, 5 percent members of minority groups, and 13 percent international students. The average M.B.A. student is 27 years old and has more than five years of work experience; 26 percent are women.

Student Outcomes

The strong research and teaching backgrounds of doctoral graduates prepare them for professorships at top universities. Graduates of the M.S. program are consistently placed in the Big Six public accounting firms and in technical industry positions. High-level management positions are often accepted by M.B.A. graduates in consulting, high-technology, biopharmaceutical, entrepreneurial, and venture capital firms.

Location

Home to many telecommunications, microelectronics, aerospace, computer peripheral, and biotechnology companies, Boulder holds a strong entrepreneurial concentration of technological research and development firms. The University of Colorado at Boulder, just 25 miles from downtown Denver, enjoys a close relationship with the businesses in the area, and many course projects and research are conducted in conjunction with local firms. Outdoor enthusiasts also find Boulder's recreational activities ideal. Biking, hiking, and skiing provide optimal study breaks for many graduate students at CU.

The College and The School

As a leader in higher education since it was founded in 1876, the University of Colorado at Boulder provides students with high-level skills for prominent business positions. CU ranks tenth among U.S. public universities and nineteenth overall in federal research support and is one of thirty public institutions belonging to the prestigious Association of American Universities. The College's nationally ranked entrepreneurship program provides valuable opportunities for those starting new ventures.

Applying

All College of Business and Administration programs begin in the fall semester. Individuals interested in the full-time master's programs are encouraged to submit their applications by March 15, and part-time applicants should submit their materials by June 1. Doctoral applicants should submit their materials by January 30.

Correspondence and Information

Director of Graduate Student Services
Graduate School of Business Administration
Campus Box 419
University of Colorado at Boulder
Boulder, Colorado 80309-0419

Telephone: 303-492-1831
Fax: 303-492-1727
E-mail: busgrad@spot.colorado.edu
World Wide Web: http://www-bus.colorado.edu/

University of Colorado at Boulder

THE FACULTY AND THEIR RESEARCH

Accounting and Information Systems

James Brancheau, Associate Professor of Information Systems; Ph.D., Minnesota. Implementing new IT, end-user computing, the Internet.
Thomas Buchman, Associate Professor of Accounting; Ph.D., Illinois. Financial reporting.
David Frederick, Associate Professor of Accounting; Ph.D., Michigan; CPA. The nature of expertise, influence of memory on judgment and decision making, economics of salary arbitration, goal setting and task performance.
Edward Gac, Associate Professor of Business Law; J.D., Illinois. Tax policy, legal environment of accounting.
Wayne Gazur, Associate Professor of Accounting; LL.M., Denver; CPA. Policy and application of the tax laws.
Betty Jackson, Professor of Accounting; Ph.D., Texas at Austin; CPA. Behavioral/cognitive analysis of judgments by tax professionals and taxpayer; identification and measurement of intangible assets.
Kenneth Kozar, Associate Professor of Information Systems; Ph.D., Minnesota. Linking IT to competitive strategy, enhancing team performance through IT, improving systems development through enhanced communication.
Akhil Kumar, Assistant Professor of Information Systems; Ph.D., Berkeley. Database systems, distributed information systems, expert systems, workflow management systems, knowledge of discovery in databases.
Barry Lewis, Professor of Accounting; Ph.D., Penn State; CPA. Behavioral/cognitive analysis of judgments by auditors and users of financial information, expert decision support systems in auditing, empirical links between economic theory and accounting practice.
David Monarchi, Professor of Information Systems; Ph.D., Arizona. Object-oriented systems: evaluative models, design metrics; database systems; conceptual modeling.
Ramiro Montealegre, Assistant Professor of Information Systems; D.B.A., Harvard. Introduction and assimilation of IT, organizational transformation through the implementation of information technology, transfer of technology to less-developed countries.
Frank Selto, Professor of Accounting; Ph.D., Washington (Seattle). Effects of accounting information on managerial decision making and organizational performance, implementation and effectiveness of activity-based management.
Toby Stock, Assistant Professor of Accounting; Ph.D., Indiana. Taxation effects on firm decision making, tax practitioners' effect on taxpayer compliance.
John Tracy, Professor of Accounting; Ph.D., Wisconsin; CPA. Financial reporting, management accounting.
Ilze Zigurs, Associate Professor of Information Systems; Ph.D., Minnesota. Group support systems, computer support of collaborative work, behavioral and managerial issues associated with development and implementation of IT, impact of IT on organizations.

Finance and Economics

Sanjai Bhagat, Professor of Finance; Ph.D., Washington (Seattle). Corporate restructuring and lawsuits, business valuation, institutional investors.
Francisco Delgado, Assistant Professor of Finance; Ph.D., Pennsylvania. International finance, derivatives, emerging markets.
David Ellsworth Frame, Assistant Professor of Finance and Real Estate; Ph.D., Carnegie Mellon. Real estate finance, urban economics, insurance.
Michael Goldstein, Assistant Professor of Finance; Ph.D., Pennsylvania. Market microstructure, real estate, corporate and international finance.
J. Chris Leach, Associate Professor of Finance; Ph.D., Cornell. Corporate and venture financing, mergers and acquisitions, securities markets.
P. John Lymberopoulos, Professor of Finance; Ph.D., Texas at Austin. International financial management, the European Community.
Ronald Melicher, Professor of Finance; D.B.A., Washington (St. Louis). Corporate mergers, bankruptcy, and other restructuring; asymmetric information and financial signaling topics as they relate to capital structure issues; public utility financing issues.
Michael Palmer, Professor of Finance and International Business; Ph.D., Washington (Seattle). International debt and sovereign debt rescheduling, management and assessment of country risk, foreign exchange markets, economic trading blocs.
David Rush, Professor of Finance; D.B.A., Indiana. Capital structure changes, IPOs, excess funded defined benefit pension programs.
Russell Wermers, Assistant Professor of Finance; Ph.D., UCLA. Investor behavior and performance measurement, efficiency of markets.
Daryl Norman Winn, Associate Professor of Business Economics; Ph.D., Michigan. Managerial economics, business and government (antitrust and regulation), contemporary public policies as they affect business.
Richard Wobbekind, Associate Professor of Business Economics; Ph.D., Colorado. Public policy, forecasting, development.

Marketing

Bridgette Braig, Assistant Professor of Marketing; Ph.D., Northwestern. Consumer information processing, types of cognitive elaboration and persuasion, judgment formation processes, experiential aspects of consumption.
Dipankar Chakravarti, Professor of Marketing and Ortloff Professor of Business; Ph.D., Carnegie Mellon. Consumer/managerial judgment and decision making in marketing contexts, new methodologies for consumer/market measurement, marketing in developing economies.
Calvin Duncan, Associate Professor of Marketing; D.B.A., Indiana. Marketing communications, advertising and sales promotion, marketing strategy.
Charles Goeldner, Professor of Marketing; Ph.D., Iowa. Travel, tourism, ski industry, market research, economic impact.
Paul Herr, Associate Professor of Marketing; Ph.D., Indiana. Consumer memory, attitude theory, decision making, brand management.
John Hess, Professor of Marketing; Ph.D., Stanford. Leadership style implications, socioeconomic policy, industry structure.
Donald Lichtenstein, Associate Professor of Marketing; Ph.D., South Carolina. Consumer perceptions, consumer marketplace attributions.
Patrick Long, Associate Professor of Tourism Management; Ed.D., Western Michigan. Tourism planning and development.
James Nelson, Associate Professor of Marketing; Ph.D., Minnesota. Marketing management, marketing strategy.
Lisa Peñaloza, Assistant Professor of Marketing; Ph.D., California, Irvine. Interrelationships between marketing and culture; postpositivistic philosophy of science and research methods; gender, race, and ethnic influences on marketing and consumer behavior.
Richard Perdue, Associate Professor of Tourism and Management; Ph.D., Texas A&M. Management in tourism settings, tourist behavior, international tourism.
Nancy Ridgway, Associate Professor of Marketing; Ph.D., Texas at Austin. Consumption behavior, consumer creativity, compulsive shopping.
Dilip Soman, Assistant Professor of Marketing; Ph.D., Chicago. Consumer decision making, sales promotions.
Robert Taylor, Professor of Marketing; D.B.A., Indiana. Total quality management, actuarial science, demographic trends, consumer satisfaction.

Management and Operations Management

Maureen Ambrose, Associate Professor of Management; Ph.D., Illinois. Organizational fairness, performance monitoring, cognitive processes.
David Balkin, Professor of Management; Ph.D., Minnesota. Relationship between pay policies and firm strategy, high-tech firms, firm innovations.
R. Wayne Boss, Professor of Management; D.P.A., Georgia. Organization effectiveness, behavior, and development; TQM.
Minnette Bumpus, Assistant Professor of Management; Ph.D., South Carolina. Leadership, ethics, motivation, workforce diversity.
Julio DeCastro, Associate Professor of Management; Ph.D., South Carolina. Strategy, price wars, entrepreneurship, transfer of technology to less-developed countries.
Jerry Foster, Associate Professor of Transportation Management; Ph.D., Syracuse. Deregulation, distribution service quality, international logistics.
Fred Glover, Professor of Management; Ph.D., Carnegie Tech. Applications of optimization models and methods, computer decision support systems, discrete and nonconvex programming networks, applied artificial intelligence, computer applications.
Kenneth R. Gordon, Senior Instructor of Management and International Business; Ph.D., Northwestern. International operations management; Japanese business: management, manufacturing, and marketing; doing business in southeast Asia; TQM and control; international productivity and competitiveness; international procurement and facility location; international finance (external indebtedness, country risk).
Anne Sigismund Huff, Professor of Management; Ph.D., Northwestern. Decision making, organizational politics, strategic renewal.
James Kelly, Assistant Professor of Management; Ph.D., Maryland. Combinatorial optimization, heuristic search, neural networks, artificial intelligence.
Christine Koberg, Associate Professor of Organization Management; Ph.D., Oregon. Organizational culture, high-technology organizations, mentor/protégé relationships, status of women.
Manuel Laguna, Assistant Professor of Management; Ph.D., Texas at Austin. Optimization problems in telecommunications, production and logistic problems in manufacturing systems, linkages between operations research and artificial intelligence, robust optimization.
Stephen Lawrence, Associate Professor of Management; Ph.D., Carnegie Mellon. International operations, capacity strategy and design, operations scheduling and strategy, environmental operations.
G. Dale Meyer, Professor of Management and Ted G. Anderson Professor of Entrepreneurial Development; Ph.D., Iowa. Entrepreneurship, choices of top management teams, competitive advantage, strategic management, qualitative research, privatization in Europe.
Joseph Rosse, Associate Professor of Management; Ph.D., Illinois. Human resource practices in small businesses, employee adaptation to stress and job dissatisfaction, workplace substance abuse.
Richard Spinetto, Associate Professor of Management; Ph.D., Cornell. Audit sampling, stochastic operations research models.

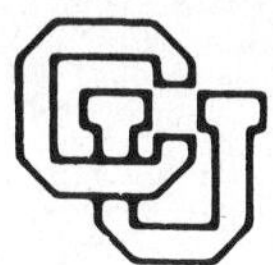

UNIVERSITY OF COLORADO AT DENVER

College of Business and Administration
Graduate School of Business Administration

Programs of Study

The M.B.A. and Master of Science (M.S.) degree programs at the University of Colorado at Denver (CU-Denver) are designed to develop analytical, team-building, and communication skills that are important for effective business management. Sixty-five full-time faculty members are committed to both teaching and research, and most bring professional experience in business to the classroom. International topics and issues are incorporated into all areas of the curriculum.

The sixteen-course (48-credit-hour) M.B.A. program provides an intensive, broad-based education in all areas of business management, with an emphasis on how these areas relate to organizational objectives and the broader societal environment. The breadth of education is achieved through a core of eleven courses in basic management and five elective courses, including one in international business. Oral, written, and computer communication skills; qualitative and quantitative analysis techniques; and decision-making skills are emphasized throughout the curriculum. The M.B.A. program is suitable for persons with or without an undergraduate business degree. No previous work experience is required.

New for the fall term 1998 is an eleven-month format for the M.B.A. program that enables a select group of students to complete the program in five 8-week sessions. Following the same M.B.A. curriculum as their colleagues in the regular program, students pursuing the M.B.A. in the eleven-month format begin the program in late August and complete the degree in mid-July of the following year. Admission to this program is competitive. Enrollment is limited to 40 students.

Master of Science programs are designed for those who want an academic program that is focused on the development of expertise in a particular business field. Specialization is available in accounting, finance, health administration, information systems, international business, marketing, and organization and management.

Dual-degree programs are available, which combine either the M.B.A. with a Master of Science degree in any field of study in business or two Master of Science degree plans. Interdepartmental dual-degree programs include the M.B.A. and Master of Arts in psychology, the M.B.A. and Master of Science in Nursing (in cooperation with the University of Colorado Health Sciences Center), the M.B.A. and Master of Science in architecture or urban planning, and the Master of Science in finance with the Master of Arts in economics. Through a special consortium agreement with Thunderbird, The American Graduate School of International Management in Glendale, Arizona, students admitted to both institutions may choose to complete both the M.B.A at CU-Denver and the Master of International Management at Thunderbird.

The Graduate School of Business now offers a selection of business courses through CU Online. CU Online is a virtual campus of the University of Colorado that offers interactive courses and student services via the World Wide Web. CU Online offers core curriculum and elective courses on a variety of topics for the same high-quality courses that are taught on the CU-Denver campus. Registration for CU Online courses is open to any graduate student in the College of Business.

Research Facilities

Students have access to four computer labs equipped with IBM-compatible machines that are part of a local area network (LAN) and linked to the Internet. One lab is reserved exclusively for business students. The Auraria Library owns more than 750,000 books, videos, government publications, and media items, and subscribes to more than 3,500 journals, magazines, and newspapers. In addition, hundreds of periodicals are accessible via the Auraria Online Information System. Within the library, students have access to more than 300 online and CD-ROM commercial databases and the Internet. Registered students and faculty and staff members may easily tap into many of these databases from home via their personal computers. The library is also a depository for Colorado and U.S. government publications.

Financial Aid

The University of Colorado at Denver participates in all forms of federally subsidized financial aid for degree-seeking students who are U.S. residents or citizens. Information on how and when to apply for financial aid through the University is included with the application for admission. Both domestic and international graduate students in business administration who have completed 12 hours of study may qualify for Dean's Scholarship funds, which are awarded annually for exceptional academic achievement. Other scholarships are available. Part-time assistantships, internships, and health management residencies may be available, but only after students enroll in the program.

Cost of Study

In 1997–98, Colorado state-resident tuition was $222 per credit hour. Full-time residents paid no more than $1853 per semester for up to 15 credit hours. Nonresident tuition was $752 per credit hour for up to a maximum of $6274 per semester.

Living and Housing Costs

Single students should budget approximately $1000 per month for housing, food, and moderate entertainment expenses. No on-campus housing is provided, but students can find reasonably priced accommodations in neighborhoods close to the campus or in the greater Denver area.

Student Group

The typical student in the Graduate School of Business Administration is 32 years of age and has a minimum of five years of work experience. More than 60 percent are employed full-time. Approximately 12 percent of the graduate student body are international students.

Location

The University of Colorado at Denver is one of three institutions of higher education in the Auraria Higher Education Consortium. The Auraria Campus is a safe, 171-acre campus located in booming downtown Denver, the heart of a five-county metropolitan area of more than 2 million residents. Colorado's mild climate and the city's proximity to the Rocky Mountains and some of the best skiing contribute to Denver's recognition as being one of the most rapidly growing cities in the country.

The School

The Graduate School of Business Administration is the largest graduate business program in Colorado. Its high quality is nationally certified by the AACSB–The International Association for Management Education, which granted the School additional, specialized accreditation in accounting in 1996. The health administration program is accredited by the Council for Higher Education Accreditation and the U.S. Office of Education for Health Administration Programs.

Applying

All degree programs may be commenced in January, June, or August, except for the eleven-month M.B.A., which begins in the fall term only. A two-part application form, resume (optional), personal essay, GMAT score (required), two original transcripts from each institution of higher education attended, and an application fee (M.B.A. or M.S. programs, $50; M.B.A./M.S. dual-degree applicants, $80; international students, $60) must be submitted by the published deadlines. International students whose native language is not English must submit TOEFL scores. Letters of recommendation are required for all international students and applicants for the M.S. in health administration program. Application forms may be downloaded from the Internet (address listed below) or obtained through the Graduate School of Business Administration.

Correspondence and Information

Graduate School of Business Administration
University of Colorado at Denver
P.O. Box 173364, Campus Box 165
Denver, Colorado 80217-3364

Telephone: 303-556-5900
Fax: 303-556-5904
E-mail: lori_cain@maroon.cudenver.edu
World Wide Web: http://www.cudenver.edu/public/business

University of Colorado at Denver

THE FACULTY

Yash P. Gupta, Dean and Professor of Management; Ph.D., Bradford (England).
Marlene A. Smith, Associate Dean and Associate Professor of Quantitative Methods; Ph.D., Florida.
Jean-Claude Bosch, Associate Dean and Professor of Finance; Ph.D., Washington (Seattle).

Marcelle V. Arak, Professor of Finance; Ph.D. MIT.
Heidi Boerstler, Professor of Health Administration and Management; Dr.P.H., Yale; J.D., Denver.
Peter G. Bryant, Professor of Management and Information Systems; Ph.D., Stanford.
Wayne F. Cascio, Professor of Management; Ph.D., Rochester.
Lawrence F. Cunningham, Professor of Marketing and Transportation; D.B.A., Tennessee.
E. Woodrow Eckard Jr., Professor of Business Economics; Ph.D., UCLA.
Jahangir Karimi, Professor of Information Systems and Director, Management Information Systems Program; Ph.D., Arizona.
Gary A. Kochenberger, Professor of Operations Management, Ph.D., Colorado at Boulder.
James O. Morris, Professor of Finance; Ph.D., Berkeley.
Dennis F. Murray, Professor of Accounting and Director of Accounting Program; Ph.D., Massachusetts.
Bruce R. Neumann, Professor of Accounting and Health Administration; Ph.D., Illinois.
Edward J. O'Connor, Professor of Management; Ph.D., Akron.
John C. Ruhnka, Professor of Management and Business Law; J.D., Yale, L.L.M., Cambridge.
Donald L. Stevens, Professor of Finance and Director, Center for International Business, Ph.D., Michigan State.
Dean G. Taylor, Professor of Finance and Director, Finance Program; Ph.D., Chicago.
Raymond F. Zammuto, Professor of Management; Ph.D., Illinois.
Kang Rae Cho, Associate Professor of Management and International Business; Ph.D., Washington.
Edward J. Conry, Associate Professor of Business Law and Ethics; J.D., California, Davis.
Elizabeth S. Cooperman, Associate Professor of Finance; Ph.D., Georgia.
C. Marlena Fiol, Associate Professor of Management; Ph.D., Illinois.
Richard W. Foster, Associate Professor of Finance and Health Administration; Ph.D., Chicago.
James H. Gerlach, Associate Professor of Information Systems; Ph.D., Purdue.
Susan M. Keaveney, Associate Professor of Marketing and Director, M.B.A. Program; Ph.D., Colorado at Boulder.
Fen Yang "Bob" Kuo, Associate Professor of Information Systems; Ph.D., Arizona.
Manuel Serapio Jr., Associate Professor of Management and International Business and Director, International Business Program; Ph.D., Illinois.
Clifford E. Young, Associate Professor of Marketing and Director, Marketing Program; Ph.D., Utah.
Ajeyo Banerjee, Assistant Professor of Finance; Ph.D., Massachusetts.
Kenneth L. Bettenhausen, Assistant Professor of Management; Ph.D., Illinois.
Anol Bhattacherjee, Assistant Professor of Information Systems; Ph.D., Houston.
John W. Byrd, Assistant Professor of Finance; Ph.D., Oregon.
Gary J. Colbert, Assistant Professor of Accounting; Ph.D., Oregon.
Richard E. Cook, Assistant Professor of Finance; Ph.D., Washington (St. Louis).
David A. Forlani, Assistant Professor of Marketing; Ph.D., Minnesota.
Blair D. Gifford, Assistant Professor of Management and Health Administration; Ph.D., Chicago.
John Jacob, Assistant Professor of Accounting; Ph.D., Northwestern.
Deborah L. Kellogg, Assistant Professor of Operations Management; Ph.D., USC.
Sara Kovoor-Misra, Assistant Professor of Management; Ph.D., USC.
Vickie Ratcliff Lane, Assistant Professor of Marketing; Ph.D., Washington.
Linda G. Levy, Assistant Professor of Accounting; Ph.D., Colorado at Boulder.
L. Ann Martin, Assistant Professor of Accounting; Ph.D., Minnesota.
Madhavan Parthasarathy, Assistant Professor of Marketing; Ph.D., Nebraska.
Michele L. Wingate, Assistant Professor of Accounting; Ph.D., Oregon.
Errol Biggs, Senior Instructor in Health Administration and Management and Director, Health Services Administration Program; Ph.D., Penn State.
Elizabeth S. Conner, Senior Instructor in Accounting; M.S., Colorado State.
Charles M. Franks, Senior Instructor in Quantitative Methods; Ph.D., Colorado at Boulder.
Gary Giese, Senior Instructor in Business Law and Director, Organization and Management Program; J.D., Nebraska.
Robert D. Hockenbury, Senior Instructor in Accounting; M.S., Houston.
Lawrence F. Johnston, Senior Instructor in Finance; Ph.D., Colorado at Boulder.
Paul J. Patinka, Senior Instructor in Management; Ph.D., Purdue.
Barbara A. Pelter, Senior Instructor in Finance; M.A., California, Davis.
Marianne Plunkert, Senior Instructor in Finance; M.B.A., Ohio State.
Eric J. Thompson, Senior Instructor in Information Systems; M.S., Colorado at Boulder.
John Turner, Senior Instructor in Finance; Ph.D., Saint Louis.
Michael D. Harper, Instructor in Operations Management; Ph.D., Rensselaer.
Chen Ji, Instructor in Finance; M.B.A., Denver; M.S., Colorado at Boulder.
Charles A. Rice, Instructor in Management; M.B.A., Denver.
Gary R. Schornack, Instructor in Marketing; Ed.D., Nova.
M. Catherine Volland, Instructor in Management; M.A., Colorado at Boulder.

CU-Denver's campus is adjacent to thriving downtown Denver.

UNIVERSITY OF CONNECTICUT

School of Business Administration
M.B.A. Program

Program of Study

The School of Business Administration offers programs leading to the Master's in Business Administration (M.B.A.) and the Doctor of Philosophy in business (Ph.D.). The School also offers dual degree programs: J.D./M.B.A. in cooperation with the School of Law; M.A./M.B.A. in International Studies in cooperation with the College of Liberal Arts and Sciences; and M.S.W./M.B.A. in cooperation with the School of Social Work. The educational focus of the M.B.A. program is managerial decision making in today's complex business environment. The program's overall objective is to develop the students' capacity to make well-informed, responsible decisions in preparation for business leadership. Classes emphasize the practical application of current business theory within a dynamic business setting. The new M.B.A. curriculum provides a balance of integrative cross-functional projects and functional courses. This contemporary curriculum is carefully designed to provide solid grounding in accounting, finance, law, economics, statistics, operations management, information systems, marketing, and managerial/organizational behavior. The capstone course requires students to synthesize previous course work into an integrated whole.

Faculty members have incorporated extensive international components in required and elective courses. One course's sole objective is to improve students' verbal and written communication skills. A laptop computer requirement and specialized courses in information technology ensure that the student learns about technology while using technology to learn. Several courses develop a working knowledge of information systems. Students are trained to develop an expertise in making short-term, day-to-day decisions with a full awareness of the long-term implications these decisions have on the organization. The program emphasizes interpersonal, team work, and leadership skills needed to deal effectively with individuals, small groups, and departments.

After completing the required courses, M.B.A. students select a concentration (accounting, finance, health-care management, human resources, international business, management, management science, marketing, or real estate) or a specialization (accounting or health-care management). The School of Business Administration conducts the full-time M.B.A. program during the day in Storrs, the part-time M.B.A. programs in the evening in Hartford and Stamford, and an Executive M.B.A. program in Farmington.

Research Facilities

The School of Business Microcomputer Laboratory, the Placement Office, the Small Business Institute, and the Centers for Real Estate and Urban Economic Studies, Health Systems Management, and Research in Financial Services provide specialized resources for students at the University of Connecticut. The Center for Transnational Accounting is the repository for one of the nation's largest collections of worldwide annual and 10K reports in paper form. The University Library, located directly across the street from the School of Business Administration, contains more than 2 million volumes, serials, periodicals, and pieces of microfilm, including annual reports and 10K reports. Academic computing service is available to students, faculty members, and staff.

Financial Aid

Financial aid is awarded on the basis of established need. Application forms are available from the Student Financial Aid Office, 233 Glenbrook Road, Box U-116, Storrs, Connecticut 06268. Tuition remission, Federal Stafford Student Loans, and Federal Work-Study are offered.

Some graduate assistantships are also available. Assistantships normally involve working with faculty members or departments in teaching, grading, or research activities. Appropriate background or expertise—such as research experience, an undergraduate major in a business subject, or computer ability—is generally needed to qualify.

Cost of Study

Beginning in September 1998, tuition and fees for the full-time M.B.A. program at Storrs are estimated to be $3115 per semester for Connecticut residents and $7327 per semester for out-of-state students. Books cost approximately $400 per semester, and students must have a notebook computer for use throughout the program.

Living and Housing Costs

For a nine-month academic year, the approximate cost of living, in addition to tuition and fees, is estimated to be $5850. Many single students reside in the Graduate Residence in single dormitory rooms. Specific information is available by contacting the Graduate Dormitory Assignments Office, 233 Glenbrook Road, Box U-22. A wide variety of off-campus housing is available to students. A visit to the area is recommended for all students interested in finding off-campus housing.

Student Group

M.B.A. students come to the School of Business Administration from a wide variety of undergraduate institutions, both domestic and international. Their undergraduate degrees represent majors in many diverse areas—from engineering to English, from natural sciences to fine arts, and, of course, business and economics. A typical class has 46 percent women, an average age of 26, and 30 to 45 percent international students.

Friendliness and informality characterize student life at the main campus. Social as well as professional organizations offer a variety of activities to satisfy the needs of students.

Student Outcomes

By the December following graduation, 90 to 95 percent of the M.B.A. graduates secure job placement. In 1996, the salary range began in the upper $30,000's and went as high as the mid $70,000's with the average salary between $40,000 and $50,000. Employers who hire the most University of Connecticut M.B.A. graduates include General Electric, "Big 6" accounting firms, CIGNA, AETNA, IBM, United Technologies Corp., Andersen Consulting, and American Management Systems.

Location

The University of Connecticut is located on about 1,900 acres in the Storrs section of the town of Mansfield in northeastern Connecticut. It is about 30 minutes from Hartford, the state capital and prominent insurance center. Boston is a 90-minute drive, while New York City is 3 hours away.

The University and The School

Seventeen schools and colleges constitute the University, which has a student population of approximately 18,000. There are about 250 students in the full-time program in Storrs, 450 in the part-time program in Stamford, 650 in the part-time program in Hartford, and 60 in the executive program in Farmington. The M.B.A. program is nationally accredited by AACSB–The International Association for Management Education. The School of Business is a member of the Graduate Management Admissions Council (GMAC) and the European Foundation for Management Development (EFMD).

Applying

Individuals holding degrees from accredited institutions are encouraged to apply. The admissions committee evaluates an individual on academic and professional accomplishments, potential for success, recommendations, information provided in the written application, and scores on the Graduate Management Admission Test. Students may enter the M.B.A. program at the Storrs campus only in the fall semester. The application and all accompanying materials should be received as early as possible, since admissions decisions are made on a rolling basis.

Correspondence and Information

For the master's program:
Full-Time M.B.A. Director, Storrs
School of Business Administration
University of Connecticut
368 Fairfield Road, U-41MBA
Storrs, Connecticut 06269-2041
Telephone: 860-486-2872
Fax: 860-486-5222
E-mail: pmason@sbaserv.sba.uconn.edu

For the Ph.D. program:
Ph.D. Director
School of Business Administration
University of Connecticut
368 Fairfield Road, U-41PHD
Storrs, Connecticut 06269-2041

University of Connecticut

THE FACULTY

Theophilus Lane Barrow, M.A., Harvard.
Barbara Beliveau, Ph.D., Yale.
Stanley F. Biggs, Ph.D., Minnesota.
Patricia Born, Ph.D., Duke.
Mary Ellen Brigham, M.A., Connecticut.
Bruce R. Buzby, Ph.D., Indiana.
Gerard M. Campbell, Ph.D., Indiana.
Kate Campbell, Ph.D., Washington (Seattle).
Wesley A. Cann Jr., J.D., Connecticut.
Vincent A. Carrafiello, J.D., Connecticut.
John M. Clapp, Ph.D., Columbia.
Robin Higie Coulter, Ph.D., Pittsburgh.
Kathleen Dechant, Ed.D., Columbia.
Moustapha Diaby, Ph.D., SUNY at Buffalo.
Richard N. Dino, Ph.D., SUNY at Buffalo.
Walter C. Dolde Jr., Ph.D., Yale.
Joseph A. Fields, Ph.D., Penn State.
Karen File, Ph.D., Temple.
Steven W. Floyd, Ph.D., Colorado.
Karla Fox, J.D., Duke.
Robert S. Garfinkel, Ph.D., Johns Hopkins.
Chinmoy Ghosh, Ph.D., Penn State.
Carmelo Giacotto, Ph.D., Kentucky.
John L. Glascock, Ph.D., North Texas.
Paulo B. Goes, Ph.D., Rochester.
Ram Gopal, Ph.D., SUNY at Buffalo.
Lawrence J. Gramling, D.B.A., Maryland; CPA.
David A. Guenther, Ph.D., Washington (Seattle).
Alok Gupta, Ph.D., Texas at Austin.
Thomas G. Gutteridge, Ph.D., Purdue.
John P. Harding, Ph.D., Berkeley.
Shantaram P. Hegde, Ph.D., Massachusetts.
James A. Heintz, D.B.A., Washington (St. Louis).
Robert E. Hoskin, Ph.D., Cornell.
Donald Huffmire, D.B.A., Georgia State.
Mohamed E. Hussein, Ph.D., Pittsburgh.
Subhash C. Jain, Ph.D., Oregon.
Harry M. Johnson, Ph.D., Pennsylvania; CLU, CPCU.
Deborah Kidder, Ph.D., Minnesota.
Linda Schmid Klein, Ph.D., Florida State.
Richard F. Kochanek, Ph.D., Missouri.
Jeffrey A. Kramer, Ph.D., Connecticut.
Peter J. LaPlaca, Ph.D., RPI.
Michael J. Lubatkin, D.B.A., Tennessee.
Gary Marchant, Ph.D., Michigan.
James Marsden, J.D., Kentucky; Ph.D., Purdue.
Luis Martins, Ph.D., NYU.
Paul Mason, M.B.A., Connecticut.
Frederick McKinney, Ph.D., Yale.
Norman H. Moore, Ph.D., Florida State.
Suresh K. Nair, Ph.D., Northwestern.
Minerva Heller Neidtz, Ph.D., Connecticut.
Kenneth P. Nunn Jr., Ph.D., Massachusetts.
Thomas J. O'Brien, Ph.D., Florida.
Paul A. Pacter, Ph.D., Michigan State.
David D. Palmer, Ph.D., SUNY at Buffalo.
Katherine A. Pancak, J.D., Boston College.
Stephen R. Peters, Ph.D., Indiana.
Gary N. Powell, Ph.D., Massachusetts.
Girish N. Punj, Ph.D., Carnegie Mellon.
David A. Ralston, D.B.A., Florida State.
Srinivasan Ratneshwar, Ph.D., Vanderbilt.
Andrew J. Rosman, Ph.D., North Carolina.
Jeffrey Rummel, Ph.D., Rochester.
William S. Schulze, Ph.D., Colorado at Boulder.
George M. Scott, Ph.D., Washington (Seattle); CPA.
Gim-Seong Seow, Ph.D., Oregon.
Murphy A. Sewall, Ph.D., Washington (St. Louis).
C. F. Sirmans, Ph.D., Georgia.
Susan Spiggle, Ph.D., Connecticut.
Narasimhan Srinivasan, Ph.D., SUNY at Buffalo.
Melissa Succi, Ph.D., Michigan.
Lakshman S. Thakur, Eng.Sc.D., Columbia.
Edwin W. Tucker, S.J.D., New York Law.
Yung-Chin Alex Tung, Ph.D., Kentucky.
John F. Veiga, D.B.A., Kent State.
Zhiping Walter, Ph.D., Rochester.
Michael Willenborg, Ph.D., Penn State.
John N. Yanouzas, Ph.D., Penn State.
Mark Youndt, Ph.D., Penn State.

The University of Connecticut's main campus in Storrs, Connecticut.

UConn provides state-of-the-art classrooms and education.

UNIVERSITY OF DALLAS

Graduate School of Management

Programs of Study

The Graduate School of Management (GSM) is a professional school whose primary purpose is to prepare its students to become competent, responsible practitioners of management and related professions. GSM's programs are designed for mature students and focus on the practical realities of managerial life. To support this practical focus, the faculty has extensive business experience, and many professors are actively engaged in business activities. The variety of programs provide detailed insights into the practical aspects of each specialization. GSM's distinctive project courses give students hands-on experience with real problems in marketing and strategic planning.

The Master of Business Administration (M.B.A.) degree is offered with concentrations in business, corporate finance, engineering, financial planning, health services, human resources, industrial, international, information systems, marketing, and telecommunications management. Additional specialization is available within each concentration. The M.B.A. program can be completed in three to four semesters of full-time study. Part-time students normally take 2½ to 3½ years to complete the M.B.A. program.

The Master of Management (M.M.) degree program allows graduates of an M.B.A. program to earn a second master's degree by completing 30 credit hours in any of the above concentrations.

The Pre-M.B.A. program is a noncredit M.B.A. preparatory program for international students. This thirteen-week intensive program is designed to enhance communication skills, improve GMAT scores, and teach fundamental business concepts. A full-time Intensive English program is also available.

The M.M. and M.B.A. degree programs may be pursued on a full- or part-time basis. A full schedule of evening and weekend courses is available. Classes are taught in several locations in Dallas–Fort Worth.

Research Facilities

The University of Dallas library has more than 280,000 volumes in book form, 75,000 volumes in microfilm, and 946 periodical titles. Faulkner's Communications Infodisk, Computer Select, the National Trade Data Base, EPIC, OCLC's First-Search, Compact Disclosure, and the ABI-Inform full text system are available to all students. Students also have access to the resources of many other libraries in north Texas through interlibrary loan agreements.

Computer facilities are available to all students. Open and staffed seven days a week, the Computer Center provides access to personal computers, the Internet, and the University's Prime superminicomputer.

Financial Aid

Financial aid is available in the form of competitive graduate assistantships, which are distributed according to students' academic records and the University's need for student assistance. Graduate students are also eligible to apply for federally funded student loans and grants.

Cost of Study

Graduate tuition is $380 per credit hour in 1998–99 for residents and nonresidents.

Living and Housing Costs

A wide variety of private, off-campus apartments are available, with monthly rents from $450 to $650. Limited dormitory facilities are also available on campus for graduate students.

Student Group

GSM attracts mature students with a wide variety of educational, cultural, and professional backgrounds. Forty-seven percent of GSM students hold degrees in business or economics, 19 percent in engineering, 16 percent in science, and 18 percent in liberal arts. The total M.B.A. enrollment is approximately 1,350, with 23 percent of the student body representing fifty-five countries. Sixty-four percent of the students are men, and 36 percent are women.

Location

The Dallas–Fort Worth metroplex has 3.4 million people and is one of the fastest-growing population centers in the country. Its diversified economy includes important industries in electronics, aerospace, insurance, and banking. The moderate climate and abundance of lakes and parks in the surrounding area offer numerous recreational opportunities. The metroplex also provides rich cultural and entertainment opportunities. The University of Dallas, located in the suburban community of Irving, is within 10 miles of downtown Dallas and the Dallas–Fort Worth International Airport and is directly adjacent to Texas Stadium, home of the Dallas Cowboys football team.

The University and The School

The University of Dallas, a Catholic university founded in 1956, is a selective, private, coeducational institution offering both undergraduate and graduate programs. The current total enrollment exceeds 3,000 students. The Graduate School of Management was founded in 1966 as an evening graduate school for individuals who were already employed in business and the professions. Over the years, the school's educational scope has broadened to serve a diverse student population, but serving the employed professional remains a primary emphasis.

Applying

Applicants must have a bachelor's degree from an accredited institution. Other admission criteria include an undergraduate grade point average of at least 3.0, a satisfactory score on the Graduate Management Admission Test, and a work history of effective managerial work experience. International students whose native language is not English must submit satisfactory TOEFL scores. Applications are accepted for the fall, spring, and summer trimester.

Correspondence and Information

Director of Admissions
Graduate School of Management
University of Dallas
1845 East Northgate Drive
Irving, Texas 75062

Telephone: 972-721-5174
Fax: 972-721-4009
E-mail: admiss@gsm.udallas.edu
World Wide Web: http://gsm.udallas.edu

University of Dallas

THE FACULTY

Resident Faculty
Paula Ann Hughes, Dean; Ph.D., North Texas.

Michael H. Cosgrove, Ph.D., Ohio State.
Bernard Cunningham, Ph.D., Texas at Dallas.
Robert H. Dunikoski, Ph.D., Texas Tech.
Bruce D. Evans, M.B.A., Michigan.
Lewis C. Gaspar, Ph.D., Duke.
Saul W. Gellerman, Ph.D., Pennsylvania.
David Gordon, D.Eng., Oklahoma.
Mary M. Graves, Ph.D., North Texas.
David P. Higgins, Ph.D., Texas at Austin.
Raymond F. Hopkins, Ph.D., Oklahoma State.
Joseph A. Kottukapalli, D.Sc.A., Montreal.
Stanley L. Kroder, Ph.D., Texas at Dallas.
John B. Kusewitt, Ph.D., Texas at Arlington.
Robert G. Lynch, M.B.A., Ohio State.
Samuel G. Oberstein, Ph.D., Minnesota.
Richard Peregoy, D.P.S., Pace.
Bill Shoemaker, M.B.A., Golden Gate; CPA.
Dennis D. Strouble, J.D., Ph.D., Texas Tech.

The symbol of the University of Dallas, the Braniff Memorial Tower, overlooks the campus and the Dallas skyline.

UNIVERSITY OF DELAWARE

College of Business and Economics
Master of Business Administration Programs

Programs of Study

The College of Business and Economics offers rigorous programs for superior students leading to the M.B.A. and the M.A./M.B.A. degrees. The combination of academically accomplished faculty members, highly qualified students, and ideal location—a small university town in the midst of a large eastern megalopolis—provides the necessary environment for an outstanding experience in graduate business education.

The Delaware M.B.A. program's revised curriculum includes courses that focus on capable leadership, effective team building, group decision making, strategic use of technology, power negotiating, creative problem-solving techniques, international concerns, coordinating an effective Total Quality Management process, and ethical considerations. The new courses complement traditional courses relating to accounting, economics, finance, operations, and marketing. Students who wish to pursue more in-depth course work are offered the option of concentrating in accounting, business economics, finance, information technology, international business, leadership and management of museums, management, operations, or technology and innovation management. Internships are also available to supplement the student's academic program.

The Delaware M.B.A. program is highly selective and comparatively small, allowing for a high level of student involvement. The combination of small classroom size, classroom theory, and students' practical experiences creates a stimulating environment for the analysis of today's business world.

The 48-credit M.B.A. can normally be completed in eighteen to twenty-one months. Up to 12 credits may be waived for students with prior instruction in accounting or business, making it possible for some individuals to complete the program in twelve months.

Research Facilities

The University library, a modern research facility with more than 2 million volumes, is a member of the Association of Research Libraries and is a depository for U.S. government documents and patents.

Mainframe computer facilities include an extensive array of both hardware and software. An IBM 3090-300E is used for research, course work, and text processing and operates under VM/CMS-XA. Sun workstations operating under UNIX are also available. Electronic mail and the World Wide Web provide an integral form of communication between administration, faculty, and students. The College has a computer laboratory that focuses on business applications, as well as a state-of-the-art local area network.

Financial Aid

Various financial aid packages are available to superior full-time M.B.A. students. These include corporate assistantships, fellowships, graduate assistantships, and tuition grants, which are awarded on a competitive basis. Awards to first-year students are based on prior academic performance, work experience, and test scores. Awards to second-year students are based on academic performance in the program.

A typical aid package may include a $4500-per-year stipend and/or a 50-percent waiver of tuition. A corporate assistant position provides full tuition remission and a $10,000 stipend per academic year. This requires that the student interns with the corporate partner. Members of minority groups may qualify for an additional fellowship program that includes a stipend and full tuition.

Cost of Study

The 1997–98 yearly tuition for full-time M.B.A. students was $5190 for Delaware residents and $11,750 for nonresidents. Part-time study was $288 per credit hour for Delaware residents and $653 per credit hour for nonresident students.

Living and Housing Costs

Rental costs for shared occupancy in a graduate student complex were $350 per month in 1997–98. University and privately owned apartments, furnished and unfurnished, were available at costs ranging from $325 to $900 per month.

Student Group

Delaware M.B.A. students are a highly accomplished group. For fall 1998, the mean GMAT score of entering students was 605, and the mean undergraduate GPA was 3.1. The average length of work experience for entering students was four years; the average age was 26. In 1998–99, approximately 550 students are enrolled in the M.B.A. programs, of whom 36 percent are women, 7 percent are members of minority groups, 7 percent are international students (25 percent of full-time students), and 9 percent hold additional graduate degrees.

Location

The University of Delaware is located in Newark, a suburban community of approximately 30,000. Newark is situated in the northwest corner of Delaware within 3 miles of the Pennsylvania and Maryland borders. It is located within easy driving distance of Philadelphia (45 miles), Baltimore (50 miles), Washington, D.C. (100 miles), and New York City (130 miles). Nearby Wilmington is a major center for credit banking and the chemical industry. More than fifty percent of all Fortune 500 companies are incorporated in Delaware. The College maintains strong ties with the corporate sector.

The University and The College

The University of Delaware, founded in 1743 as a small liberal arts school, was later moved to Newark, where it became both a land-grant and a sea-grant college. It now ranks among the finest of the nation's medium-sized universities, with approximately 14,000 undergraduate and 3,000 graduate students. Included in the College of Business and Economics are four departments: accounting, business administration, economics, and finance. All accounting and business programs are accredited by AACSB–The International Association for Management Education.

Applying

Applications for the fall semester will be processed from January 1 to May 1, depending on date of receipt. Students seeking financial aid should submit their application early. Applicants must take the Graduate Management Admission Test (GMAT). International students must take the Test of English as a Foreign Language (TOEFL). Qualified applicants are required to interview.

Correspondence and Information

Kathy Kuck, Admissions
M.B.A. Programs
College of Business and Economics
103 MBNA America Hall
University of Delaware
Newark, Delaware 19716

Telephone: 302-831-2221
Fax: 302-831-3329
E-mail: mba@udel.edu
World Wide Web: http://www.mba.udel.edu

University of Delaware

THE FACULTY AND ADMINISTRATION

Administration
Dana J. Johnson, Dean, College of Business and Economics, and Professor (finance); D.B.A., Kent State.
Helen M. Bowers, Associate Dean, College of Business and Economics, and Associate Professor (finance); Ph.D., South Carolina.
James L. Butkiewicz, Chairman and Professor (macroeconomics); Ph.D., Virginia.
Howard Garland, Chairman and Chaplin Tyler Professor of Business (business administration); Ph.D., Cornell.
Robert L. Schweitzer, Chairman and Professor (finance); Ph.D., Duke.
Kent St. Pierre, Chairman and Arthur Andersen Alumni Professor (accounting); Ph.D., Washington (St. Louis); CPA.
Robert B. Barker, Director, M.B.A. Programs (business administration); M.B.A./M.Ed., Delaware.
Peggy Bottorff, Director, Executive Programs; M.B.A., Delaware.
Alex L. Brown, Assistant Director, M.B.A. Programs; M.B.A., Delaware.

Business Administration
Rick L. Andrews, Assistant Professor (marketing); Ph.D., Virginia Tech.
John H. Antil, Associate Professor (marketing) and Head of Marketing Management Faculty; Ph.D., Penn State.
Thomas E. Becker, Assistant Professor (management); Ph.D., Ohio State.
S. Alexander Billon, Professor (management); Ph.D., Michigan State.
V. Carter Broach Jr., Instructor (marketing); Ph.D., Michigan State.
Donald E. Conlon, Associate Professor (management); Ph.D., Illinois.
Darwin Davis, Assistant Professor (operations); Ph.D., Indiana.
Ramarao Desiraju, Assistant Professor (marketing); Ph.D., Florida.
Diane L. Ferry, Associate Professor (management); Ph.D., Pennsylvania.
Meryl P. Gardner, Associate Professor (marketing); Ph.D., Carnegie Mellon.
William V. Gehrlein, Professor (operations); Ph.D., Penn State.
C. Gopinath, Assistant Professor (management); Ph.D., Massachusetts.
Mary C. Kernan, Associate Professor (management) and Head of Management Faculty; Ph.D., Akron.
John L. Kmetz, Associate Professor (management); D.B.A., Maryland.
James R. Krum, Professor (marketing); D.B.A., Michigan State.
Christine T. Kydd, Associate Professor (operations); Ph.D., Pennsylvania.
Ajay K. Manrai, Associate Professor (marketing); Ph.D., Northwestern.
Lalita A. Manrai, Associate Professor (marketing); Ph.D., Northwestern.
Sharon O'Donnell, Assistant Professor (management); Ph.D., South Carolina.
Michael F. Pohlen, Associate Professor (operations); Ph.D., Ohio State.
John F. Preble, Associate Professor (management); Ph.D., Massachusetts.
Erwin M. Saniga, Professor (operations) and Head of Operations Management Faculty; Ph.D., Penn State.
John E. Sawyer, Associate Professor (management); Ph.D., Illinois.
Stewart Shapiro, Assistant Professor (marketing); Ph.D., Arizona.
Arthur A. Sloane, Professor (management); D.B.A., Harvard.
Daniel P. Sullivan, Assistant Professor (management); Ph.D., South Carolina.
Bret J. Wagner, Assistant Professor (management); Ph.D., Michigan State.
Gary R. Weaver, Assistant Professor (management); Ph.D., Iowa; Ph.D., Penn State.
Richard M. Weiss, Associate Professor (management); Ph.D., Cornell.

Accounting
Dale A. Buckmaster, Professor (financial accounting); Ph.D., Penn State; CPA.
Lester W. Chadwick, Associate Professor (tax); Ph.D., Syracuse; CPA.
Araya Debessay, Professor (auditing and financial accounting); Ph.D., Syracuse; CPA, CMA.
Jackson F. Gillespie, Associate Professor (accounting); Ph.D., Virginia Tech.
Paul Hooper, Professor (managerial accounting); Ph.D., Tulane; CPA.
Scott K. Jones, Associate Professor (management control systems); Ph.D., Drexel.
Robert L. Paretta, Associate Professor (financial accounting); Ph.D., Syracuse; CPA.
Janis R. Reeder, Associate Professor (tax); Ph.D., South Carolina; CPA.
Frederic M. Stiner, Associate Professor (financial accounting systems); Ph.D., Nebraska; CPA.
Clinton E. White, Associate Professor (systems); D.B.A., Indiana.
John H. Wragge, Associate Professor (auditing systems); Ph.D., Houston; CPA.

Economics
Burton A. Abrams, Professor (public choice); Ph.D., Ohio State.
Richard J. Agnello, Associate Professor (econometrics); Ph.D., Johns Hopkins.
Michael A. Arnold, Assistant Professor (microeconomics); Ph.D., UCLA.
David E. Black, Associate Professor (microeconomics); Ph.D., MIT.
Eleanor D. Craig, Associate Professor and Associate Chair (public finance); M.A., Pennsylvania.
Joseph Daniel, Assistant Professor (industrial organization); Ph.D., Minnesota.
Lawrence P. Donnelley, Associate Professor (international economics) and Associate Provost, International Programs and Special Sessions; Ph.D., Brown.
Conrado M. Gempesaw II, Chairman and Professor (food and resource economics); Ph.D., Penn State.
Farley Grubb, Professor (economic history); Ph.D., Chicago.
Saul D. Hoffman, Professor (labor economics); Ph.D., Michigan.
Kenneth J. Koford, Professor (industrial organization) and Associate Professor of Political Science; Ph.D., UCLA.
William Latham III, Associate Professor (economics); Ph.D., Illinois.
Kenneth A. Lewis, Chaplin Tyler Professor of Business and Associate Chair (applied econometrics); Ph.D., Princeton.
Charles R. Link, Professor (labor economics); Ph.D., Wisconsin.
Jeffrey B. Miller, Professor (monetary economics); Ph.D., Pennsylvania.
James G. Mulligan, Professor (urban and regional economics); Ph.D., Minnesota.
James B. O'Neill, Professor (economic education); Ph.D., Purdue.
Laurence S. Seidman, Professor (macroeconomics); Ph.D., Berkeley.
Russell F. Settle, Professor (public finance); Ph.D., Wisconsin.
Pamela Smith, Assistant Professor (international economics); Ph.D., Wisconsin.
James R. Thornton, Associate Professor (comparative economic systems); Ph.D., Cornell.
Toni M. Whited, Associate Professor (econometrics); Ph.D., Princeton.
John S. Ying, Associate Professor (industrial organization); Ph.D., Berkeley.

Finance
Kenneth R. Biederman, Professor; Ph.D., Purdue.
Daniel Deli, Assistant Professor; Ph.D., Arizona State.
Rudolph E. D'Souza, Associate Professor; Ph.D., South Carolina.
M. Andrew Fields, Associate Professor; Ph.D., Virginia Tech.
Brian Hatch, Assistant Professor; Ph.D., Indiana.
Donald J. Puglisi, MBNA America Business Professor; D.B.A., Indiana.
Breck Robinson, Assistant Professor; Ph.D., Tennessee.
Janet M. Todd, Assistant Professor; Ph.D., Michigan State.
Raj Varma, Associate Professor; Ph.D., Penn State.

UNIVERSITY OF DENVER

Daniels College of Business
Graduate School

Programs of Study

The University of Denver Daniels College of Business graduate management programs reflect real-world decision making required of today's business leaders. Seven different programs are offered and focus on technical business tools, managerial excellence, and values in leadership. Also, M.B.A. and Master of International Management (M.I.M.) specializations are available in accounting, entrepreneurship, finance, management information systems, marketing, real estate finance, and real estate and construction management. Students may create a unique, individualized specialization, and may pursue programs either full- or part-time. All programs prepare qualified men and women for business leadership in a vast range of careers and industries. Distinct, cross-disciplinary core courses develop key technical tools and leadership and managerial skills. Students gain breadth of knowledge in the relationships and applications of primary business disciplines through team-teaching, study teams, case studies, and experiential leadership and team-building training through a unique outdoor leadership program.

The M.B.A. program expands on the integrated technical and managerial skills core with courses in international business, quality, and values. The curriculum addresses value-based decision making in current business environments, and a team field-study project provides the opportunity to work directly with businesses. Electives round out the program.

The M.I.M. (Master of International Management) program prepares students for international business management and leadership through a cross-disciplinary curriculum that combines the M.B.A. core with international law, political and economic systems, and international relations through the University of Denver School of Law and the Graduate School of International Studies. Proficiency in a second language is required.

The M.S.F. (Master of Science in Finance) Program prepares students for corporate finance and portfolio investment management through a finance intensive curriculum. The curriculum also provides value-based leadership and team-building training through M.B.A. core courses.

The M.Acc. (Master of Accounting) program is an accounting-intensive program that prepares students for accounting-specific careers. Additional leadership skills and disciplines are developed, including communication skills, information systems, and the social and ethical responsibilities of professional accountants.

The M.R.E.C.M. (Master of Real Estate and Construction Management) program prepares students for careers in the real estate and construction management arenas through an industry-specific curriculum. The curriculum also provides value-based leadership and team-building training through M.B.A. core courses.

The M.S.R.T.M. (Master of Science in Resort and Tourism Management) program develops professionals to manage the planning, development, and marketing of destination tourism areas through a cross-disciplinary curriculum that combines courses in general management, hospitality management and tourism, geography, and anthropology.

The M.S.M. (Master of Science in Management) program offers a joint program with engineering and communications, and emphases in education, health-care systems management, and sport management. Combining the core of the M.B.A. program with specific courses from other departments provides management expertise in specific industries.

Research Facilities

The Daniels College of Business has computer centers with IBM-compatible and Macintosh PCs; access to VAX mainframes; and specialized computer programs for construction management, accounting, and quantitative methods. The Center for Managerial Communications provides students with the facilities and equipment to help develop and refine their communication skills. Penrose Library houses more than 1 million items.

Financial Aid

Financial assistance is available through scholarships, Colorado resident grants, and work-study positions and through Federal Perkins and Federal Stafford student loans. Applicants must file a Free Application for Federal Student Aid (FAFSA), ideally by February 19. Minority scholarships for up to 50 percent of tuition are available. All scholarships are awarded on a merit and need basis. Assistantships are available and provide tuition credit and a stipend.

Cost of Study

Tuition for the 1998–99 academic year is $6072 per quarter for all full-time students and $506 per quarter hour for part-time students.

Living and Housing Costs

On-campus housing for graduate students is available for $500 to $700 per month. Students should contact the Department of Residence at 303-871-2246 for more information. Many students prefer to live off campus, as one-bedroom apartments near the University are available for as little as $500 per month.

Student Group

The Daniels Graduate School of Business enrolls approximately 650 full- and part-time students, of whom 24 percent are international and 36 percent are women. In the modular core, students are part of cohort groups of 35, and elective classes usually have class sizes of 25. The average age is 28, and 80 percent of the students have full-time work experience.

Student Outcomes

The employment situations of recent graduates of the Daniels College of Business are as diverse as the programs offered. M.B.A. graduates are employed in both the public and private sectors, including the positions of Business Manager for Denver Public Schools, and Senior Financial Analyst for Storage Technology. They are also heavily recruited by consulting firms including Andersen Consulting, Peat Marwick, and Ernst and Young. Recent M.I.M. graduates hold positions with an international focus, including International Business Planner for Texas Instruments, and Intercultural Services Program Manager for Prudential Relocation Services. Other graduates pursue not only corporate careers, but also entrepreneurial opportunities, as a recent graduate of the M.R.E.C.M. program is the owner of Historical Properties in Virginia.

Location

The University of Denver campus of 125 acres is in a residential area 7 miles south of downtown Denver. Denver is the commercial, cultural, and recreational center of the Rocky Mountain region and is key to a thriving regional economy. The 2.2 million residents enjoy a mild climate, with an average of 300 sunny days a year.

The College

Founded in 1908, the University of Denver Daniels College of Business is the eighth-oldest school of business in the United States and has been accredited by AACSB–The International Association for Management Education since 1923. Benefactor and businessman Bill Daniels is supporting real-world education program developments and a new building through gifts of $22 million. The Daniels College of Business's 75 full-time faculty members focus on teaching, and their involvement in national and international business environments as consultants and practitioners ensures relevant and current course work. The University of Denver enrolls approximately 8,700 students.

Applying

Admission to the Graduate School is on a rolling basis, with enrollment points at autumn and spring quarters. Candidates must submit a completed application form, essay question responses, two letters of recommendation, official transcripts of undergraduate and previous graduate work from regionally accredited or equivalent institutions, and GMAT or GRE scores. International students whose native language is not English must submit TOEFL scores. An application is available on diskette.

Correspondence and Information

Daniels College of Business
Graduate School
University of Denver
2020 South Race Street, BA-122
Denver, Colorado 80208

Telephone: 303-871-3416
800-622-4723 (toll-free)
Fax: 303-871-4466
E-mail: dcb@du.edu
World Wide Web: http://www.dcb.du.edu

University of Denver

FACULTY HEADS

James R. Griesemer, Dean; Ph.D., Colorado.
Glyn Hanbery, Associate Dean, Graduate Studies; Ph.D., Arizona State.

Schools and Departments

School of Accountancy: A. Ronald Kucic, Director; Ph.D., New Hampshire; CMA.
School of Hotel, Restaurant and Tourism Management: Robert M. O'Halloran, Acting Director; Ph.D., Michigan State.
Department of Business Law and Burns School of Real Estate and Construction Management: Mark L. Levine, Chairman/Director; J.D., Denver; LL.M., NYU; Ph.D., Century.
Department of Finance: Maclyn Clouse, Chairman; Ph.D., Washington (Seattle).
Department of Information Technology and Electronic Commerce: Donald McCubbrey, Chairman; M.B., Swinburne (Australia).
Department of Management: Robert McGowan, Chairman; Ph.D., Syracuse.
Department of Marketing: John Burnett, Chairman; D.B.A., Kentucky.
Department of Statistics and Operations Technology: Darl Bien, Chairman; Ph.D., Case Western Reserve.

Program Areas

Master of Business Administration: C. Thomas Howard, Director; Ph.D., Washington (Seattle).
Master of International Management: David M. Hopkins, Director; Ph.D., Syracuse.
Master of Accountancy: A. Ronald Kucic, Director; Ph.D., New Hampshire; CMA.
Master of Real Estate and Construction Management: Mark L. Levine, Director; J.D., Denver; LL.M., NYU; Ph.D., Century.
Master of Science in Resort and Tourism Management: Robert M. O'Halloran, Acting Director; Ph.D., Michigan State.
Master of Science in Management: Gordon Von Stroh, Director; Ph.D., Oklahoma.
Graduate Tax Program: Mark Vogel, Director; Ph.D., LL.M., Denver.
Executive and Mountain M.B.A.: Paul Stames, Director; M.A., Yale.

University Hall represents over a century of academic excellence.

The picturesque Rocky Mountains near Denver.

UNIVERSITY OF DETROIT MERCY

College of Business Administration
Graduate Business Programs

Programs of Study

The Graduate Business Programs at the University of Detroit Mercy are intended to provide education of high quality in the areas of business, computer information systems, and law. The M.B.A. program, fully accredited by the American Assembly of Collegiate Schools of Business, has one of the largest enrollments among the University's graduate and professional programs.

The M.B.A. program is designed to accommodate the career needs of professionals working in a wide variety of organizations, such as business, health care, industry, education, and government. The Master of Science degree in computer and information systems provides students with leading-edge knowledge in the rapidly expanding field of software engineering and software development. The joint J.D./M.B.A. program is offered to those who plan to pursue career avenues in business and law, including corporate and labor law, governmental agency work, or the management of specialized product firms.

Graduate business classes meet once a week during Terms I and II from 6:35 to 9:05 p.m., Monday through Thursday. Classes are also held on Saturday from 8:00 a.m. to 12:30 p.m. and 1:00 to 5:30 p.m. In addition, there are two 7-week sessions: Summer I, from early May to mid-June, and Summer II, from mid-June through July. Classes in these sessions typically meet for 2½ hours on two evenings per week. International study abroad is offered by the College each summer.

Through its Division of Professional Practice and Career Development, the University of Detroit Mercy offers a professional practice program for graduate students. After the successful completion of the appropriate credit hours in the graduate business program, students are eligible for career-related professional practice assignments. The professional practice model combines the success of the traditional co-op with the new demands for graduate student programming.

Research Facilities

The University libraries have large holdings in each area of graduate study, including more than 3,000 leading periodicals. Academic computing is supported by a Unisys A3K. The College of Business has two fully equipped networked computer labs. The University has a rich library of software packages available to students.

Financial Aid

Graduate research assistantships are available to full-time students and provide tuition remission for up to 9 credit hours per term in the College. The assistantships are offered competitively on a term-to-term basis for the two terms of the academic year. Federal Perkins Loans and graduate loans are available. Michigan residents may qualify for Michigan Tuition Grants. Information regarding federal and/or state financial aid programs may be obtained from the Financial Aid Office at 313-993-3350.

Cost of Study

Tuition in 1998–99 for the College of Business Administration is $448 per credit hour. Registration fees are $30 per term for part-time and $55 per term for full-time students; those who carry 9 credit hours or more per term are considered full-time students.

Living and Housing Costs

On- and off-campus housing is readily available. The typical dormitory rate is approximately $2400 for single and $1390 for double accommodations. The Student Life Office maintains lists of off-campus housing. Information on housing facilities may be obtained from the Residence Life Office at 313-993-1230.

Student Group

In the College of Business Administration, 634 students are enrolled in the M.B.A. and computer and information systems programs. The average age of those participating in the graduate business programs is 30 years. Approximately 90 percent are employed full-time and are pursuing their degrees on a part-time basis.

Location

The campus and the city offer a wide variety of cultural programs. The city has a world-renowned symphony orchestra, the Detroit Institute of Arts, excellent library facilities, and several resident theaters. The metropolitan area is dotted with lakes for swimming and waterskiing, and ski resorts are located within a half-hour drive. The city of Detroit is home to professional sports teams in baseball, basketball, football, and hockey.

The University

The University of Detroit Mercy is an independent, Catholic institution of higher education, sponsored by the Jesuits and Sisters of Mercy. The 70-acre McNichols campus is located in the College Park area, a residential section in northwest Detroit. The major degree-granting divisions of the University housed on the McNichols campus are the College of Business Administration, the College of Engineering and Science, the College of Liberal Arts, and the School of Architecture. The School of Law and the School of Dentistry are on two other campuses in downtown Detroit. The College of Education and Human Services and the College of Health Professions are housed on the Outer Drive campus. The College of Business Administration Saturday classes are offered on this campus. All campuses are within a few minutes' driving distance.

Applying

Applications for admission to graduate business programs should be completed at least six weeks before the beginning of a term. Applications for the M.B.A. program should include a completed application form, official GMAT scores, and official transcripts from all undergraduate and graduate programs previously attended. Although the GMAT is preferred for entrance into the computer and information systems program, it is not required. Persons who wish to enroll in the joint J.D./M.B.A. program must be accepted by both the School of Law and the College of Business Administration's M.B.A. program. In most cases, students apply to the M.B.A. program after the first year of law school. The application fee is $25.

Correspondence and Information

Graduate Business Programs Office
University of Detroit Mercy
P.O. Box 19900
Detroit, Michigan 48219-0900
Telephone: 313-993-1202/03
Fax: 313-993-1052
E-mail: mirshabb@udmercy.edu

University of Detroit Mercy

THE FACULTY

Michael D. Bernacchi, Professor of Marketing; Ph.D., Southern Illinois; J.D., Detroit.
Jacques G. Boettcher, Associate Professor of Business Law; J.D., Detroit.
Larry J. Bossman, Associate Professor of Management; Ph.D., Wisconsin.
Bruce M. Brorby, Assistant Professor of Economics and Associate Dean of Administrative Affairs; M.A., Detroit.
Gerald F. Cavanagh, S.J., Charles T. Fisher III Chair of Business Ethics and Chancellor; Ph.L., M.Ed., Saint Louis; S.T.L., Loyola Chicago; D.B.A., Michigan State.
Trevor F. Crick, Associate Professor of Finance; M.B.A., Northern Illinois; Ph.D., Iowa.
Jeanne M. David, Associate Professor of Accounting; M.B.A., Ph.D., Texas A&M.
Steven Freund, Assistant Professor of Finance; M.B.A., Connecticut; Ph.D., NYU.
Ira S. Greenberg, Professor of Accounting and Director of the School of Accountancy; M.Acc., Arizona; Ph.D., Missouri–Columbia; CPA.
Mary Ann Hazen, Associate Professor of Management; M.S.W., Michigan; Ph.D., Case Western Reserve.
Mary A. Higby, Associate Professor of Marketing; M.B.A., Ph.D., Michigan State.
Vladan Jovanovic, Associate Professor of Computer and Information Science; M.Sc., Ph.D., Belgrade.
Ram Kesavan, Professor of Marketing; M.B.A., Ph.D., Rochester.
Suk Hi Kim, Professor of Finance; Ph.D., Saint Louis.
Janice N. Kneale, Instructor of Computer and Information Systems; M.S., Michigan State.
Oswald A. J. Mascarenhas, S.J., Kellstadt Professor of Marketing; M.B.A., Ph.D., Pennsylvania (Wharton).
Thomas C. Mawhinney, Professor of Management; Ph.D., Ohio State.
Bahman Mirshab, Associate Professor of Industrial Management and Information Systems and Director of Graduate Business Programs and Acting Dean of the College of Business Administration; Ph.D., Wayne State.
Cyrus K. Motlagh, Associate Professor of Management Science; M.E., Detroit; M.B.A., Ph.D., Michigan; J.D., Wayne State.
Martha Soleau, Director of Undergraduate Day Programs, Assistant Professor of Finance; M.A., Wayne State.
George D. Schmelzle, Assistant Professor of Accounting; Ph.D., Mississippi; CPA.
Daniel P. Shoemaker, Associate Professor of Computer and Information Science; Ph.D., Michigan.
Carl B. Smalls, Instructor of Finance and Director of Evening and Weekend Undergraduate Programs; M.B.A., Atlanta.
Shahram Taj, Professor of Industrial Management and Information Systems; Ph.D., Massachusetts.
Gregory W. Ulferts, Professor of Industrial Management and Information Systems; D.B.A., Louisiana Tech.
Alice Hyland Walton, Associate Professor of Management; Ph.D., Iowa State.
Michael D. Whitty, Professor of Management and Industrial Relations; Ph.D., Syracuse.
Patrick T. Wirtz, Associate Professor of Accounting; M.B.A., Detroit; CPA.
Lawrence E. Zeff, Associate Professor of Management; M.B.A., Wayne State; Ph.D., Pittsburgh.
Christopher Zorski, Associate Professor of Accounting; M.B.A., Ph.D., Warsaw.

UNIVERSITY OF GEORGIA

Terry College of Business
Graduate School of Business Administration

Programs of Study

Seven graduate degree programs are offered: the Master of Business Administration, Master of Accountancy, Master of Marketing Research, Master of Arts in economics, and Doctor of Philosophy in business administration and in economics. The M.B.A., M.Acc., and M.M.R. degrees lead to professional and managerial careers. The M.A. programs can be used for intensive specialization or as paths to the Ph.D. The Ph.D. programs lead to research and/or teaching careers.

The College's M.B.A. program has been profiled as one of the nation's top programs by *Business Week, Forbes, U.S. News & World Report, Success, ARCO's Top Business Schools, the Ultimate Guide, Computer World,* and *Which MBA?* The program consists of both a one-year and a two-year tract. The one-year M.B.A. program begins in summer only and requires three semesters of study. Students with an undergraduate degree in business from an institution accredited by AACSB–The International Association for Management Education are eligible to apply. Business majors from institutions that are not accredited by AACSB–The International Association for Management Education are eligible to petition to be considered for the one-year program. The two-year M.B.A. program begins in the fall only and is for both business and nonbusiness baccalaureate degree holders. The first year exposes students to the various functional areas of business. The second year of the two-year program and the final two semesters of the one-year program are composed of course work in the student's area(s) of specialization and free electives. The M.Acc. is designed to prepare students for careers as professional accountants, whether as tax experts, members of management, computer systems specialists, or CPAs. The program consists of 30 credit hours beyond the business and accounting foundation courses. The M.M.R. program requires twelve months of intensive academic course work and six months of on-the-job research experience. After the internship, students present their research reports to the faculty and Board of Advisors. The M.A. in economics program is discussed as part of a separate listing in this guide.

The Ph.D. programs provide a background for careers in government, business, academia, and research organizations. Students in the business administration program develop a high level of competence in a major field of business, with a minor field in business or in a relevant discipline outside business. Each student also completes courses in research methodology and in differential and integral calculus. The major field is chosen from accounting, finance, human resource management and organizational behavior, management information systems, management science, marketing, operations management, real estate, risk management and insurance, and strategic management. The economics program consists of a calculus foundation, an economic theory core, two fields in economics, and electives.

Research Facilities

The University of Georgia libraries provide one of the largest academic resources for research and instructional support in the nation. In a recent ranking by the Association of Research Libraries, the University of Georgia libraries placed in the top twenty among the nation's best 106 university, government, and private research libraries. Standard works on all phases of business activity are available. The University has the largest academic computer center in the Southeast and one of the largest in the nation. Areas of excellence include large-scale systems research, library automation, and computer-based instruction. The Terry College of Business supports a network of microcomputers for classroom and lab use as well as a mainframe lab that provides access to the University's mainframe system.

Financial Aid

Graduate assistantships are awarded on the basis of merit at both the College and University levels. Stipends for one-third-time assistantships range from $4000 to $10,000 at the master's level and from $10,300 to $12,000 at the doctoral level. Merit-based scholarships ranging from $200 to $3000 are also awarded. Assistantships for members of minority groups are available at the College level. The Progressive Partners Program (M.B.A.) includes company-sponsored internships and scholarships for minority students. All need-based financial assistance is processed through the Student Financial Aid Office.

Cost of Study

Tuition and fees for Georgia residents for 1998–99 are $3290 per year; nonresident tuition and fees are $11,300 per year. Tuition and fees for students on an assistantship of one third time or greater are $670 for the academic year. These figures are subject to change.

Living and Housing Costs

On-campus housing is available. Room and board for students living on campus is approximately $4500 per year. Off-campus housing adds between $1500 and $2500 to a yearly budget.

Student Group

In 1998–99, 152 M.B.A., 80 M.Acc., 39 M.M.R., 19 M.A., and 90 Ph.D. students are enrolled. All M.M.R. and most Ph.D. students are awarded graduate assistantships. Approximately 50 percent of M.B.A. and M.Acc. students receive assistantships. One fourth of graduate business students are women and one fourth are international students. Ten percent of the M.B.A. class are members of minority groups.

Student Outcomes

Although placement is geographically disperse, the Southeast, especially the Atlanta area, is the number one preference of our students. Recent graduates can be found at various companies such as Andersen Consulting, BellSouth, Cintas, Dell Computers, Deloitte & Touche, Delta, EDS, FedEx, Ford, Goldman Sachs, Intel, International Paper, Kimberly-Clark, Lehman Brothers, Merck, Microsoft, NationsBank, Philip Morris, Price Waterhouse, Suntrust, Union Camp, UPS, Wachovia, and W. M. Mercer in positions such as senior consultant, financial analyst, marketing analyst, software development manager, senior project manager, international pricing analyst, and real estate analyst.

Location

Located about 1 hour northeast of Atlanta, Athens and the University of Georgia are nestled in north Georgia's rolling foothills. Georgia's 30,000 students enjoy the benefits of the cultural and social excitement of Atlanta, the solitude of the Appalachian Mountains, and the beauty and fun of the southeastern seacoast.

The University

Established in 1785, the University of Georgia is the state's largest and most comprehensive and diversified educational institution. Recent projects such as the biotechnology complex continue to set the pace for research and teaching excellence on the national level. Founded in 1912, the Terry College of Business is a fully accredited member of the AACSB–The International Association for Management Education . The College is devoted to providing leadership in the areas of instruction, research, and service.

Applying

Students in all degree programs other than the M.B.A. and M.M.R. programs may enter the year round. Applications should be filed at least six months prior to the intended semester of matriculation. The GMAT is required of M.B.A., M.Acc., and M.M.R. applicants. The GRE is required of Ph.D. and M.A. applicants. International applicants must also submit TOEFL scores. Application deadlines to be given priority consideration for University-wide and Terry College of Business assistantships are January 1 and February 1, respectively.

Correspondence and Information

Graduate Coordinator
Terry College of Business
Graduate School of Business Administration
350 Brooks Hall
University of Georgia
Athens, Georgia 30602-6264

Telephone: 706-542-5671
E-mail: ugamba@cba.uga.edu
World Wide Web: http://www.cba.uga.edu

University of Georgia

THE FACULTY

P. George Benson, Dean; Ph.D., Florida, 1977.
James S. Trieschmann, Associate Dean; D.B.A., Indiana Bloomington, 1970.

Accounting
Benjamin C. Ayers, Ph.D., Texas at Austin, 1996. E. Michael Bamber, Ph.D., Ohio State, 1980. Linda S. Bamber, Ph.D., Ohio State, 1983. Russell M. Barefield, Ph.D., Ohio State, 1969. John B. Barrack, Ph.D., Oklahoma State, 1974. Dennis R. Beresford, B.S., USC, 1961. Paul A. Copley, Ph.D., Alabama, 1987. Mark C. Dawkins, Ph.D., Florida State, 1994. Jennifer J. Gaver, Ph.D., Arizona, 1987. Kenneth M. Gaver, Ph.D., Carnegie Mellon, 1974. Gordon S. May, Ph.D., Michigan State, 1972. Gary F. Peters, Ph.D., Oregon, 1998. Randolph A. Shockley, Ph.D., North Carolina at Chapel Hill, 1979. E. Daniel Smith, Ph.D., Ohio State, 1974. Paul J. Streer, Ph.D., Illinois at Urbana-Champaign, 1978. Carl S. Warren, Ph.D., Michigan State, 1973.

Banking and Finance
Shane A. Corwin, Ph.D., Ohio State, 1996. Jimmy E. Hilliard, Ph.D., Tennessee, 1972. John B. Legler, Ph.D., Purdue, 1967. Marc L. Lipson, Ph.D., Michigan, 1994. William L. Megginson, Ph.D., Florida State, 1986. Jeffry M. Netter, Ph.D., Ohio State, 1980. Kathleen N. Petrie, Ph.D., Indiana Bloomington, 1997. Annette B. Poulsen, Ph.D., Ohio State, 1983. Joseph F. Sinkey Jr., Ph.D., Boston College, 1971. Christopher T. Stivers, Ph.D., North Carolina at Chapel Hill, 1998. James A. Verbrugge, Ph.D., Kentucky, 1968.

Economics
Michael Aarstol, Ph.D., Stanford, 1996. Scott E. Atkinson, Ph.D., Colorado, 1972. Fred Bateman, Ph.D., Tulane, 1965. Christopher M. Cornwell, Ph.D., Michigan State, 1985. Charles D. DeLorme Jr., Ph.D., LSU, 1966. Jill Ann Holman, Ph.D., Colorado, 1997. David R. Kamerschen, Ph.D., Michigan State, 1964. Donald C. Keenan, D.Sc., Washington (St. Louis), 1978. Peter Klein, Ph.D., Berkeley, 1995. William D. Lastrapes, Ph.D., North Carolina at Chapel Hill, 1986. Dwight R. Lee, Ph.D., California, San Diego, 1972. C. A. Knox Lovell, Ph.D., Duke, 1966. David B. Mustard, Ph.D., Chicago, 1997. Nadeem Naqvi, Ph.D., SMU, 1984. George A. Selgin, Ph.D., NYU, 1986. Arthur Snow, Ph.D., Wisconsin–Madison, 1979. Gregory A. Trandel, Ph.D., Princeton, 1992. Ronald S. Warren, Ph.D., North Carolina at Chapel Hill, 1976. Lawrence H. White, Ph.D., UCLA, 1982.

Insurance, Legal Studies, Real Estate, and Management Science
Dawn D. Bennett-Alexander, J.D., Howard, 1975. Robert G. Boehmer, J.D., Oregon, 1977. David Downs, Ph.D., North Carolina at Chapel Hill, 1995. Charles F. Floyd, Ph.D., North Carolina at Chapel Hill, 1966. Sandra G. Gustavson, Ph.D., Illinois at Urbana-Champaign, 1979. Jan W. Henkel, J.D., Loyola, New Orleans, 1971. Robert Hoyt, Ph.D., Pennsylvania, 1987. James B. Kau, Ph.D., Washington (Seattle), 1971. Jere Morehead, J.D., Georgia, 1980. Henry J. Munneke, Ph.D., Illinois at Urbana-Champaign, 1993. Steven Pottier, Ph.D., Texas at Austin, 1994. O. Lee Reed, J.D., Chicago, 1971. Andrew F. Seila, Ph.D., North Carolina at Chapel Hill, 1976. Peter J. Shedd, J.D., Georgia, 1977. David Sommer, Ph.D., Pennsylvania, 1994. Ralph E. Steuer, Ph.D., North Carolina at Chapel Hill, 1973. James S. Trieschmann, D.B.A., Indiana Bloomington, 1970. Betty J. Whitten, Ph.D., Georgia, 1972.

Management
Allen C. Amason, Ph.D., South Carolina, 1993. Jay E. Aronson, Ph.D., Carnegie Mellon, 1980. John H. Blackstone Jr., Ph.D., Texas A&M, 1979. Robert P. Bostrom, Ph.D., Minnesota, 1978. Ann K. Buchholtz, Ph.D., NYU, 1991. Archie B. Carroll, D.B.A., Florida State, 1972. James F. Cox III, Ph.D., Clemson, 1975. K. Roscoe Davis, Ph.D., North Texas State, 1972. Alan R. Dennis, Ph.D., Arizona, 1991. Robert D. Gatewood, Ph.D., Purdue, 1971. Dale L. Goodhue, Ph.D., MIT, 1988. Charles W. Hofer, D.B.A., Harvard, 1969. Asterios G. Kefalas, Ph.D., Iowa, 1971. James M. Lahiff, Ph.D., Penn State, 1969. James D. Ledvinka, Ph.D., Michigan, 1969. Patrick G. McKeown, Ph.D., North Carolina at Chapel Hill, 1973. Karen J. Napoleon, Ph.D., Georgia Tech, 1997. Christine M. Riordan, Ph.D., Georgia State, 1995. Lori V. Ryan, Ph.D., Washington (Seattle), 1994. Antonie Stam, Ph.D., Kansas, 1986. Robert J. Vandenberg, Ph.D., Georgia, 1982. Hugh J. Watson, D.B.A., Florida State, 1969. Richard T. Watson, Ph.D., Minnesota, 1987.

Marketing
Gail S. Ayala, Ph.D., Florida State, 1995. Barbara Carroll, Ph.D., Indiana Bloomington, 1986. Melvin R. Crask, D.B.A., Indiana Bloomington, 1975. Ellen Day, Ph.D., Indiana Bloomington, 1983. Richard J. Fox, Ph.D., Michigan State, 1968. Warren A. French, Ph.D., Penn State, 1970. Roberto Friedmann, Ph.D., Kansas, 1986. Rajiv Grover, Ph.D., Massachusetts at Amherst, 1983. Kay Keck, Ph.D., Texas at Dallas, 1988. Thomas W. Leigh, D.B.A., Indiana Bloomington, 1981. Srinivas K. Reddy, Ph.D., Columbia, 1983. Frederick Stephenson, Ph.D., Minnesota, 1975. Mary Zimmer, Ph.D., Texas at Austin, 1985. George M. Zinkhan, Ph.D., Michigan, 1981.

UNIVERSITY OF HOUSTON

College of Business Administration

Programs of Study

The intellectually challenging master's programs enhance students' knowledge, skills, and credentials, giving graduates an edge in today's competitive job market. Graduate students develop skills in managerial problem analysis, solution, and implementation. Each student is exposed to the major behavioral, economic, and quantitative concepts that underlie the administrative decision process.

Scheduling options allow all M.B.A. students to attend classes on a full- or part-time basis with day or evening classes. The College of Business Administration (CBA) offers the M.B.A., the Master of Science in Accountancy, the Master of Science in Administration, one- and two-year Executive M.B.A. programs, the three-year Professional M.B.A. program, and the Ph.D. program. All programs are accredited by AACSB–The International Association for Management Education. The CBA also offers joint M.B.A. degree options, including the M.B.A./J.D. degree with the University of Houston (UH) Law Center; the M.B.A./M.A. in Spanish with the UH College of Humanities, Fine Arts and Communications; the M.B.A./M.H.M. (Master of Hospitality) with the UH Conrad Hilton College of Hotel Restaurant Management; the M.B.A./M.I.E. (Master of Industrial Engineering) with UH Cullen College of Engineering; the M.B.A./M.I.M. (Master of International Management) in cooperation with the American Graduate School of International Management (Thunderbird in Glendale Arizona); and the M.B.A./M.S.W. (Master of Social Work) with the UH Graduate School of Social Work.

The 54-semester-hour M.B.A. program prepares students for management positions in modern enterprises. Admission is open to qualified holders of bachelor's degrees in fields other than business administration. The 36-hour M.B.A. program for applicants with a degree in business administration gives students the opportunity to earn an M.B.A. in a shorter amount of time. Areas of concentration are available in accountancy, finance, international business, management, management information systems, marketing, operations management, statistics and operations research, and taxation.

The Master of Science program in accountancy provides a well-rounded background in business administration, but the 36- to 60-hour curriculum is specifically designed for individuals who plan to specialize in financial, managerial, and tax accounting.

The Doctor of Philosophy in business administration is research oriented and directed toward the education of teacher-scholars. The program not only focuses on business and industry but also encompasses governmental, service, and social institutions. This full-time program can be tailored to the interests and background of the candidate through continuous consultation with his or her advisory committee. Areas of specialization are accountancy and taxation, finance, management, management information systems, marketing, operations management, and statistics and operations research.

Each of the graduate programs requires prerequisite course work in calculus, finite mathematics, and management information systems. All or part of these requirements may be waived upon entrance to the graduate programs if previous equivalent college courses have been completed in the respective areas.

Research Facilities

The CBA has a number of programs and institutes to support and promote research. These centers and institutes include the A. A. White Dispute Resolution Institute; the Center for Entrepreneurship and Innovation; the Center for Executive Development; the Center for Global Manufacturing; the Energy Institute; the Fixed Income Research Program; the Information Systems Research Center; the Institute for Business, Ethics, and Public Issues; the Institute for Corporate Environmental Management; the Institute for Diversity and Cross-Cultural Management; the Institute for Health Care Marketing; the Small Business Development Center; and the Southwest Center for International Business.

The CBA operates more than 150 IBM-compatible personal computers for student use in the Melcher Hall computer laboratories. Melcher Hall also houses multimedia equipment in the College's auditoria and multimedia lab.

Financial Aid

To help finance UH's reasonable tuition, business scholarships and fellowships, including funds specifically for study abroad, are available for graduate students. For scholarship information, call 713-743-4620. Teaching and research assistantships are available for doctoral candidates.

Cost of Study

Tuition and fees for the 1998–99 academic year are $2570 for Texas residents and $7200 for out-of-state and international students. Tuition is based on 12 hours for two semesters and is subject to change.

Living and Housing Costs

UH offers a full range of housing options for graduate and professional students, including those with families. On-campus room and board costs are approximately $4000 for the academic year and may be paid in full or in installments. Costs are subject to change. Students may also find an ideal home in one of the many apartments, condominiums, and duplexes located throughout the city.

Student Group

UH has an enrollment of approximately 31,000 students representing eighty countries around the world. Approximately 1,000 of the 5,000 students in the College of Business Administration are engaged in master's degree programs, and about 70 students are pursuing doctoral degrees.

Location

Houston is the fourth-largest city in the United States. Located approximately 50 miles from the Gulf of Mexico, Houston offers a full range of recreational activities and all the cultural advantages expected in a large metropolitan area. The city is a major international center for high-technology activities that involve the aerospace and petrochemical industries, oceanography, and medical research. The UH campus is located 3 miles from Houston's central business district.

The University

Founded in 1927 as a private institution, the University of Houston became part of the state system of higher education in 1963. The campus has 540 acres of parks, fountains, and plazas that surround ninety-four buildings. UH consists of fourteen colleges and schools, offering bachelor's degrees in 129 fields, master's degrees in 115 fields, and doctoral degrees in 53 fields. UH is one of the top eighty research universities in the country.

Applying

Applicants must provide a personal resume, a completed UH application, two official transcripts from all previously attended institutions, official GMAT scores, and a nonrefundable application fee of $50 ($125 for international applicants). Official TOEFL scores are required from students for whom English is not the primary language. Information is due by May 1 for the fall semester and by October 1 for the spring semester. All Ph.D. applicants are encouraged to submit applications and supporting materials, including a statement of research interests, at least two months prior to the stated deadline dates.

Correspondence and Information

Office of Student Services
College of Business Administration
University of Houston
Houston, Texas 77204-6282

Telephone: 713-743-4900
Fax: 713-743-4942
E-mail: oss1@cba.uh.edu
World Wide Web: http://www.cba.uh.edu

University of Houston

DEPARTMENT HEADS AND RESEARCH AREAS

The College's strong academic programs are enhanced by the enthusiasm and dedication of the faculty. There are 82 full-time tenure-track faculty members, 14 executive professors, 9 visiting professors, and adjunct lecturers. Ninety-eight percent hold doctoral degrees. All faculty members share the UH spirit of excellence in teaching, research, and service.

Accountancy and Taxation

Gary L. Schugart, Department Chair and Associate Professor; Ph.D., Kansas.

Research areas within the department include financial statement analysis, internal auditing, international accounting standards, corporation taxation, individual tax planning, basic concepts in estate planning, accounting in the petroleum industry, ethics and CPAs, management information systems in auditing, computer applications in accounting, federal income tax issues of entity formation, and issues in tax practice and procedure.

Decision and Information Sciences

Dennis A. Adams, Department Chair and Associate Professor; Ph.D., Texas Tech.

Areas of study are management information systems, operations management, and statistics and operations research. Research areas include information system auditing, cost control methods, high-technology system design and development, decision-making support systems, telecommunications management, technology innovation and diffusion, information systems effectiveness, production and inventory models, health operations research, Bayesian inference, outlier detection and identification, linear models, manufacturing and distribution planning, facilities location, and forecasting models.

Finance

Ronald F. Singer, Department Chair and Professor; Ph.D., Michigan State.

Areas of research include international and domestic financial institutions, corporate funding policies, small-business financial management, insurance, risk management, debt crises in less-developed countries, strategic behavior in mergers and acquisitions, consumer finance, investment characteristics of the world's stock markets, bankruptcy restructuring, security valuations, impact of government regulation on financial institutions, and regulation and management of financial institutions.

Management

Michael T. Matteson, Department Chair and Professor; Ph.D., Houston.

Areas of study within the department include cross-cultural communication and management, entrepreneurship, job loss, motivation, joint-venture management, international management, international strategy, corporate health promotion, business and public policy, corporate strategy, energy policy and history, strategies for managing human resources during mergers and acquisitions, stress management, the Type-A coronary behavior pattern, leadership, international differences in leadership styles, goal setting, and turnover predictors.

Marketing and Entrepreneurship

Edward A. Blair, Department Chair and Professor; Ph.D., Illinois.

Research areas within the department include customer satisfaction, strategic planning and marketing in nonprofit firms, health-care marketing, advertising and promotion, survey research methods, price information processing by consumers, network analysis, coalitions and influence in organizational buying, buyer-seller relationships, scarcity effects on perceived value, legal issues in marketing, business ethics, competitiveness in industries, foreign investment policies, marketing decision support systems, knowledge development, service priority in department stores, and cultural differences.

Melcher Hall, opened in 1986, houses the College of Business Administration.

UNIVERSITY OF ILLINOIS AT CHICAGO

Master of Business Administration Program

Program of Study

The University of Illinois at Chicago (UIC) offers an innovative full-time program for students who are preparing themselves for advanced managerial responsibility.

The full-time program is a comprehensive two-year program that begins with a year of core courses taught in integrated modules. Each week students attend the Professional Topics Sequence (PTS), a series of workshops, seminars, and lectures that focuses on areas of skill acquisition and managerial practice not covered in traditional academic courses. In addition, students have the option of studying abroad at partner institutions in Great Britain, France, or Austria. "Know Europe," an intensive, interactive course, is taught in Europe every summer by faculty members from around the world. For those students who want to gain international work experience, many opportunities exist for global internships with top multinational firms through the International Student Exchange Program.

In the second year of the full-time program, students complete at least six advanced elective courses offered in the following areas: accounting, economics, entrepreneurship, finance, health administration, human resource management, international business, management information systems, marketing, operations management, statistical methodology for business and industry, strategic management, and pharmacy administration. Students can also tailor their curriculum by taking courses through UIC's other graduate programs.

Convenience and flexibility are the hallmarks of the Professional Managers Program. This is UIC's evening M.B.A. program and is designed for working professionals who are preparing themselves to undertake increased managerial responsibility.

Joint degrees are offered together with master's degree programs in economics, public health, nursing, and accounting or through the Normandy Business School in France.

The UIC M.B.A. programs are fully accredited by AACSB–The International Association for Management Education.

Research Facilities

More than 1.5 million volumes are housed in the University's library and specialized collections. The library serves as a government depository, holding more than 800,000 items. It also provides computer search and interlibrary loan services. The computer center includes an IBM 3081 K64 mainframe and an IBM 3090/120E/Vector facility with remote terminals throughout campus, utilizing the most advanced software. The College of Business Administration maintains its own microcomputer laboratory. The College also supports the Center for Research in Information Management, the Center for Urban Business, the Small Business Development Center, the Office for Advanced Financial Research, the Office for Entrepreneurial Studies, and the Office for Governmental Accounting.

Financial Aid

The UIC M.B.A. programs award scholarships to outstanding domestic and international full-time students. In the second year of full-time study, students are eligible to apply for graduate assistantships. Need-based aid, through a variety of state, federal, private, and institutional programs, is administered by the University's Office of Financial Aid.

Cost of Study

Tuition and fees for the 1998–99 academic year are $10,576 for Illinois residents and $17,212 for nonresidents and international students in the full-time program. Evening program tuition and fees vary by the number of courses taken per semester. For Illinois residents, the costs are $1244 (one course) and $2173 (two courses); for nonresidents and international students, the costs are $2318 (one course) and $4321 (two courses). These figures are subject to revision without notice.

Living and Housing Costs

Students should budget at least $9826 for nine months of living expenses. UIC and the city of Chicago cater to a wide variety of housing preferences. Although most M.B.A. students seek off-campus housing, on-campus housing is available.

Student Group

The UIC M.B.A. programs have approximately 330 evening students and 100 full-time students. The full-time class of 1999 is 45 percent international, 10 percent minority, and 48 percent women. Undergraduate business majors comprise 27 percent of the class, with the rest of the class having diverse backgrounds. The median GPA is 3.2 on a 4.0 scale, and the mean GMAT is 560. The mean age of full-time students entering the program is 26.5, and they average four years of full-time work experience.

Student Outcomes

Reflecting the diversity of backgrounds and interests, UIC M.B.A. graduates work in all major functional areas of business, both domestically and internationally. Recent graduates have accepted positions at such firms as Abbott Laboratories, Baxter Healthcare, Lucent Technologies, and IBM in areas including marketing, finance, and management information systems. The UIC M.B.A. programs also place students in smaller, more entrepreneurial companies; government; and nonprofits, including Argonne National Laboratories and Illinois Development Finance Authority.

Location

The Chicago area is home to many Fortune 500 companies and thousands of small to mid-sized firms. UIC itself is located within the largest concentration of health-care facilities in the world. The Chicago Board of Trade, Mercantile Exchange, Sears Tower, Chicago Symphony Orchestra, Lyric Opera of Chicago, Art Institute, and major-league sports facilities are all just minutes from campus.

The University

UIC is an academic institution that commands international attention and is the largest institution of higher learning in the city of Chicago. In recognition of the depth and scope of the academic programs, UIC has been identified by the Carnegie Foundation for the Advancement of Teaching as a Research I university, indicating that UIC is one of the nation's eighty-eight leading research universities.

Applying

Applications are welcome from individuals holding a baccalaureate degree from accredited colleges and universities in all major fields of study. Full-time students are eligible to apply for the fall term. The deadline for application is March 21 for international applicants and June 16 for U.S. citizens and permanent residents, although earlier application is recommended; decisions are made on a rolling basis. Part-time students may begin during fall, spring, or summer terms. The Graduate Management Admission Test is required; no other test may substitute for the GMAT. International applicants whose native language is not English must also submit TOEFL scores; the minimum required score is 570.

Correspondence and Information

For M.B.A. application materials:

The M.B.A. Programs
College of Business Administration (M/C 077)
University of Illinois at Chicago
815 West Van Buren Street, Suite 220
Chicago, Illinois 60607-7025

Telephone: 312-996-4573
Fax: 312-413-0338
E-mail: mba@uic.edu
World Wide Web: http://www.uic.edu/cba/mba

For Ph.D. information:

Graduate Business Programs (M/C 075)
College of Business Administration
University of Illinois at Chicago
601 South Morgan Street, Room 2230 UH
Chicago, Illinois 60607-7122

Telephone: 312-996-4751

University of Illinois at Chicago

THE FACULTY

Lawrence H. Officer, Professor of Economics and Interim Dean, College of Business Administration; Ph.D., Harvard.
Robert Abrams, Professor of Information and Decision Sciences; Ph.D., Northwestern.
Sankar Acharya, Associate Professor of Finance; Ph.D., Northwestern.
Ali T. Akarca, Lecturer in Economics; M.S., Wisconsin–Madison.
Maryann H. Albrecht, Associate Professor of Management; Ph.D., Emory.
Eliezer B. Ayal, Associate Professor of Economics; Ph.D., Cornell.
Fred Balluff, Lecturer in Accounting; M.B.A., Tulane.
Darold T. Barnum, Professor of Management; Ph.D., Pennsylvania.
Hale C. Bartlett, Associate Professor of Management; Ph.D., Michigan.
Gilbert W. Bassett Jr., Professor of Economics; Ph.D., Michigan.
Ahmed Riahl-Belkaoui, Professor of Accounting; Ph.D., Syracuse.
John Binder, Associate Professor of Finance; Ph.D., Chicago.
Elmer H. Burack, Professor of Management; Ph.D., Northwestern.
Antonio Camacho, Professor of Economics; Ph.D., Minnesota.
Patrick Catania, Adjunct Professor of Finance and Vice President, Chicago Board of Trade; M.B.A., Western Illinois.
Peter Chalos, Associate Professor of Accounting; Ph.D., Illinois at Urbana-Champaign.
Frank J. Chaloupka, Professor of Economics; Ph.D., CUNY Graduate Center.
James L. Chan, Professor of Accounting; Ph.D., Illinois at Urbana-Champaign.
Joyce T. Chen, Associate Professor of Accounting; Ph.D., Illinois at Urbana-Champaign.
Joseph Cherian, Associate Professor of Marketing; Ph.D., Texas at Austin.
Barry R. Chiswick, Research Professor of Economics; Ph.D., Columbia.
Carmel U. Chiswick, Professor of Economics; Ph.D., Columbia.
Claude Cohen, Adjunct Professor of Information and Decision Sciences; Ph.D., Illinois at Urbana-Champaign.
Robert A. Cooke, Associate Professor of Management; Ph.D., Northwestern.
Laurence Feldman, Professor of Marketing; Ph.D., Minnesota.
Eugene Fregetto, Lecturer in Marketing; M.B.A., DePaul.
Owen K. Gregory, Associate Professor of Finance; Ph.D., Case Western Reserve.
Jane N. Hagstrom, Associate Professor of Information and Decision Sciences; Ph.D., Berkeley.
Gerald Hills, Denton Thorne Professor of Entrepreneurship and Smaller Enterprises; D.B.A., Indiana.
James Ho, Professor of Information and Decision Sciences; Ph.D., Stanford.
S. G. Huneryager, Professor of Management; Ph.D., Illinois at Urbana-Champaign.
Ralph Hybels, Assistant Professor of Management; Ph.D., Cornell.
Kathryn Ierulli, Assistant Professor of Economics; Ph.D., Chicago.
Ronald E. Jablonski, Associate Professor of Information and Decision Sciences; D.B.A., Harvard.
Georgios Karras, Associate Professor of Economics; Ph.D., Ohio State.
Charles King, Professor of Marketing; D.B.A., Harvard.
Richard F. Kosobud, Professor of Economics; Ph.D., Pennsylvania.
Thomas Lee, Associate Professor of Information and Decision Sciences; Ph.D., Yale.
Evelyn Lehrer, Professor of Economics; Ph.D., Northwestern.
Robert Liden, Professor of Management; Ph.D., Cincinnati.
Lon-Mu Liu, Professor of Information and Decision Sciences; Ph.D., Wisconsin–Madison.
King-Tim Mak, Associate Professor of Information and Decision Sciences; Ph.D., Berkeley.
Prashant Malaviya, Assistant Professor of Marketing; Ph.D., Northwestern.
John F. McDonald, Professor of Economics; Ph.D., Yale.
J. Fred McLimore, Associate Professor of Management; Ph.D., Purdue.
Harold Miller, Lecturer in Accounting; M.B.A., Michigan.
Oscar Miller, Professor of Economics; M.A., Chicago.
Edward Minieka, Professor of Information and Decision Sciences; Ph.D., Yale.
Ronald Moses, Assistant Professor of Economics; Ph.D., Chicago.
Chem Narayana, Professor of Marketing; Ph.D., Iowa.
M. Aris Ouksel, Associate Professor of Information and Decision Sciences; Ph.D., Northwestern.
Vesper Owei, Assistant Professor of Information and Decision Sciences; Ph.D., Georgia Tech.
Anthony M. Pagano, Associate Professor of Management; Ph.D., Penn State.
Albert Page, Professor of Marketing; Ph.D., Northwestern.
Barbara Peck, Adjunct Professor of Accounting; M.B.A., DePaul.
Richard M. Peck, Associate Professor of Economics; Ph.D., Princeton.
Joseph J. Persky, Professor of Economics; Ph.D., Harvard.
Ronald D. Picur, Professor of Accounting; Ph.D., Northwestern.
Paul Pieper, Associate Professor of Economics; Ph.D., Northwestern.
Stanley R. Pliska, Professor of Finance and of Information and Decision Sciences; Ph.D., Stanford.
Michael Popowits, Lecturer in Accounting; M.A.S., Illinois at Urbana-Champaign.
Ram T. S. Ramakrishnan, Ernst & Young Professor of Accounting; Ph.D., Northwestern.
Helen Roe, Lecturer in Accounting; J.D., DePaul.
Stanley L. Sclove, Professor of Information and Decision Sciences; Ph.D., Columbia.
Lois Shelton, Assistant Professor of Management; Ph.D., Harvard.
K. Sivakumar, Assistant Professor of Marketing; Ph.D., Syracuse.
William G. Stanford, Associate Professor of Economics; Ph.D., Northwestern.
Houston H. Stokes, Professor of Economics; Ph.D., Chicago.
Jaeyoung Sung, Assistant Professor of Finance; Ph.D., Washington (St. Louis).
Edward L. Suntrup, Associate Professor of Management; Ph.D., Minnesota.
Mo-Yin Tam, Professor of Economics; Ph.D., SUNY at Stony Brook.
Walter J. Wadycki, Associate Professor of Information and Decision Sciences; Ph.D., Northwestern.
Sandy J. Wayne, Professor of Management; Ph.D., Texas A&M.
Robert Weigand, Professor of Marketing; Ph.D., Illinois at Urbana-Champaign.

UNIVERSITY OF ILLINOIS AT URBANA-CHAMPAIGN

College of Commerce and Business Administration
Department of Business Administration
Executive Development Center

Program of Study

The Master of Science in Business Administration (M.S.B.A.) is an intensive twelve-month graduate degree program combined with an extensive executive education program. The program is designed for experienced international managers and administrators who want to earn an advanced degree in order to develop and sharpen skills needed in today's constantly changing global business environment. Whether a manager has five or fifteen years of experience, he or she will benefit from this program. The curriculum includes Managerial Economics, Analytical Problem Solving, Accounting Analysis, Financial Management, Human Resources, the International Economic Environment, Marketing, Operations Management, Business Strategy, and International Management.

The executive education portion of the M.S.B.A. includes visits to a variety of corporations and business institutions in Chicago, St. Louis, and during the week of spring break in New York City. The Executive-In-Residence program provides numerous opportunities throughout the fall and spring semesters for students to interact with high-level executives from major corporations.

Research Facilities

The University of Illinois at Urbana-Champaign (UIUC) is rich in research possibilities. UIUC is one of the premier public research institutions in the United States. The world-class library, with more than 15 million items, is the third largest library in the United States, the seventh largest in the world, and a leader in the evolving field of information technology. Research conducted at UIUC has resulted in 10 Nobel Prize winners. UIUC is home to one of two National Centers for Supercomputing Applications (NCSA). Funded on an ongoing basis by the National Science Foundation, NCSA seeks to forge partnerships between universities and industries through the use of computers.

Financial Aid

There are no fee or tuition waivers or other financial aid available for the M.S.B.A. program. The majority of students are sponsored either by the companies for which they work or by their governments, while others are self-sponsored.

Cost of Study

Tuition and fees for the M.S.B.A. program are currently $22,050 for the three-semester, twelve-month program. If a student needs more than twelve months to complete the degree, additional tuition and fees are charged for each additional summer or semester. Books cost approximately $1000.

Living and Housing Costs

The estimated expenses for a single individual for the twelve-month period are $12,120. Dependents are estimated to cost an additional $300 per month for a spouse and $240 per month per child. Purchase of health insurance for dependents costs $1134 per year for a spouse and $567 per year for each child. A contingency fund of $1000 to $1500 is strongly recommended.

Student Group

The majority of M.S.B.A. students are already well established in their careers and have an average of seven years of experience in a wide range of businesses. The average age of students is 28, and 40 percent of the class is women. Many are sponsored by their companies or their governments. Asians predominate, with other students coming from Eastern Europe and South America. Since the M.S.B.A. was established, more than forty nationalities have participated in the program. The desire to expand knowledge, the reputation of UIUC, and the opportunity to meet and interact with managers from other countries are the primary factors that led to students' selection of the M.S.B.A. program.

Student Outcomes

Upon completion of the M.S.B.A. program, most students return to their companies to continue their careers. Others go on to positions of greater responsibility or establish their own businesses.

Location

The University is situated in the heart of the United States in east-central Illinois. Secure in the Midwest, UIUC is surrounded by some of the world's richest farmland. The communities of Urbana-Champaign, with a population of about 100,000, are home to the University and its students. The two cities offer a variety of cultural and recreational opportunities. For those who want to visit a more urban environment, Chicago is a 2½-hour drive north, while Indianapolis and St. Louis can be reached within 2 and 3 hours, respectively.

The University

The UIUC business school was ranked fifth in the nation by *U.S. News & World Report*. The engineering school, ranked second in the nation, contains the Departments of Civil Engineering, ranked first in the U.S., and Environmental, Electrical, and Materials Engineering, all ranked second in the U.S. Overall, the National Research Council placed UIUC among the nation's top twenty universities that grant doctoral degrees.

Applying

The M.S.B.A. program begins in June of each year, although some students enter in August. June applications must be received by March 15 and August applications by June 15. University requirements state that international students must have a 550 or better TOEFL score. No GMAT score is required for entry into the program. Applicants must have a minimum of two years of work experience, although five years is preferred. Three letters of recommendation and a financial document proving amount and duration of funding to cover the course of study are required. Applicants must hold a degree equivalent to a U.S. bachelor's degree from an accredited university.

Correspondence and Information

Master of Science in Business Administration
University of Illinois at Urbana-Champaign
1407 West Gregory Drive, Room 205
Urbana, Illinois 61801

Telephone: 217-244-2571
Fax: 217-244-8537
E-mail: edc@uiuc.edu
World Wide Web: http://www.cba.uiuc.edu/edc

University of Illinois at Urbana-Champaign

THE FACULTY AND THEIR RESEARCH

Department of Business Administration

Charles E. Blair, Professor; Ph.D., Carnegie-Mellon. Management science, mathematics and operations research.
Franklin Carter, Assistant Professor; Ph.D., Carnegie-Mellon. Marketing.
Joseph Cheng, Professor; Ph.D., Michigan. Organizational studies and international management.
Dilip Chhajed, Associate Professor; Ph.D., Purdue. Operational management.
Susan I. Cohen, Associate Professor; Ph.D., Northwestern. Decision and information sciences.
Richard Englebrecht-Wiggans, Professor; Ph.D., Cornell. Game theory, computer simulation, and operations research.
Richard V. Evans, Professor; D.Engr., Johns Hopkins. Design and control of stochastic systems applied to inventory, data storage, and teaching.
David M. Gardner, Professor; Ph.D., Minnesota. Promotion management.
Abbie Griffin, Professor; Ph.D., MIT. Technology management/marketing.
Nile W. Hatch, Assistant Professor; Ph.D., Berkeley. Management of technology, innovation, manufacturing/operations strategy, service operations.
Jean-Francois Hennart, Professor; Ph.D., Maryland. Pricing and sales promotion, distribution channels.
James Hess, Professor; Ph.D., MIT. Analytic models and empirical validation of theories of brand managers' coupon decision, loss leader pricing.
Richard M. Hill, Professor; Ph.D., Columbia. Industrial marketing, buyer behavior, product innovation in high-technology companies.
Douglas Johnson, Assistant Professor; Ph.D., UCLA. Competitive strategy, industry dynamics, sources of competitive advantage.
John W. Kindt, Professor; LL.M., Virginia. Business law and legal environment of business.
Ruth King, Assistant Professor; Ph.D., Texas. Management information systems.
Matthew S. Kraatz, Assistant Professor; Ph.D., Northwestern. Antecedents and consequences of organizational adaptation and change.
Paul Lansing, Professor; J.D., Illinois at Urbana-Champaign. International business and international law.
Huseyin Leblebici, Professor; Ph.D., Illinois at Urbana-Champaign. Organizational decision making, interorganizational organizations, organizational design.
Ben S. Liu, Assistant Professor; Ph.D., SUNY at Buffalo. Industrial marketing.
Ravindranath Madhaven, Assistant Professor; Ph.D., Pittsburgh. Interorganizational networks, strategic alliances, organizational knowledge.
Joseph T. Mahoney, Associate Professor; Ph.D., Pennsylvania. Strategic management, business policy.
Steven Michael, Assistant Professor; Ph.D., Harvard. Entrepreneurship, strategy.
George E. Monahan, Professor; Ph.D., Northwestern. Decision making under uncertainty.
Kent B. Monroe, Professor and Head of the Department; D.B.A., Illinois at Urbana-Champaign. Marketing and pricing.
Elizabeth Moore-Shay, Assistant Professor; Ph.D., Florida. Promotion management, consumer behavior.
Carol M. Motley, Assistant Professor; Ph.D., Georgia. Consumer behavior, marketing strategy, retailing.
Sunder Narayanan, Assistant Professor; Ph.D., Columbia. Marketing, consumer learning and choice.
Gregory B. Northcraft, Professor; Ph.D., Stanford. Management and organizational behavior, behavioral aspects of decision making.
Greg R. Oldham, Professor; Ph.D., Yale. Organizational science, the effects of work and work environments on employee reactions.
Nicholas Petruzzi, Assistant Professor; Ph.D., Purdue. Decision making in the management of a firm's operations, forecasting systems.
Joseph E. Porac, Professor; Ph.D., Rochester. Organizational behavior, work motivation.
Michael Pratt, Assistant Professor; Ph.D., Michigan. Transformation of member ambivalence into intense organizational attachment.
William Qualls, Professor; Ph.D., Indiana. Industrial distribution, marketing.
Zvi Ritz, Associate Professor; Ph.D., Northwestern. Operations research.
Donald M. Roberts, Professor Emeritus; Ph.D., Stanford. Application of statistical principles to decision processes.
Thomas W. Roehl, Assistant Professor; Ph.D., Washington (Seattle). International business.
Jose A. Rosa, Assistant Professor; Ph.D., Michigan. Marketing and organizational psychology.
Mark E. Roszkowski, Professor; J.D., Illinois at Urbana-Champaign. Business law.
Anju Seth, Associate Professor; Ph.D., Michigan. Strategic management, international strategy, industry and competitive analysis.
Michael J. Shaw, Professor; Ph.D., Purdue. Artificial intelligence.
Riyaz Sikora, Assistant Professor; Ph.D., Illinois. Management information systems.
Devanathan Sudharshan, Professor; Ph.D., Pittsburgh. Marketing research.
Seymour Sudman, Professor; Ph.D., Chicago. Applied sampling.
Howard Thomas, Professor and Dean; Ph.D., Edinburgh. Decision and policy analysis.
Madhubalan Viswanathan, Assistant Professor; Ph.D., Minnesota. Marketing.
James Wade, Assistant Professor; Ph.D., Berkeley. Organizational design and environment.
Brian Wansink, Associate Professor; Ph.D., Stanford. Marketing.
Russell Wright, Assistant Professor; Ph.D., USC. Entrepreneurship, technology management, strategy.
Rachel Yang, Assistant Professor; Ph.D., UCLA. Market- and technology-driven strategies for manufacturers and service providers, multinational supply chain management.

UNIVERSITY OF ILLINOIS AT URBANA-CHAMPAIGN

College of Commerce and Business Administration
Illinois M.B.A.

Program of Study

For the first year of the Illinois M.B.A. program, students work in teams within four 7-week core course modules that guide them step-by-step through the process of establishing or managing a business. Faculty members also work in teams and present business problems from their own functional perspectives such as finance, accounting, and marketing. The faculty teams coordinate their assignments and case studies so that student teams can integrate the different perspectives and provide comprehensive solutions. The faculty and student teams remain in constant contact using First Class networking software.

In addition to the course modules, students participate in a weeklong Applying Business Perspectives seminar once every semester. Applying Business Perspectives seminars are in-depth computer simulations or case studies that require students to analyze and apply their functional knowledge, exercise leadership and motivational skills, and formulate effective solutions under tight time constraints. They must then present their results to a panel of judges selected from the world's leading firms.

During the second year of the Illinois M.B.A. program, each student focuses on a professional track that teaches skills specific to a student's chosen career. Students can select from 18 subtracks, which include entrepreneurship and new venture creation or technology systems management, or design one of their own. Alternately, they can enroll in a Joint Degree Program with any of several other programs at the University, including engineering, law, or medicine, to name just a few. A capstone course at the end of the second year pulls together all the lessons students have learned and provides them with an overview of contemporary business.

Research Facilities

Long heralded for its accomplishments in graduate education and research, the University of Illinois is home to national research centers for many disciplines, including supercomputing, engineering, education, and genetics. The Illinois M.B.A. program has formed strategic partnerships with these powerhouse programs through the Office for Strategic Business Initiatives (OSBI). These partnerships mean Illinois M.B.A. students have opportunities to work on technology transfer projects with researchers from the Beckman Institute, which brings together the biological and physical sciences to develop a better understanding of human and artificial intelligence. They can also get involved in managing start-up companies based on technologies straight out of the National Center for Supercomputing Applications, which established the University of Illinois as a world leader in supercomputing and changed the face of personal computing forever with the development of the NCSA Mosaic browser for the World Wide Web. These research facilities are all backed by the nation's third largest academic library, housing more than 15 million items.

Financial Aid

The Illinois M.B.A. offers a Student Management Leadership Grant program. The grants are based on merit, not financial need, and the application for admittance to the Illinois M.B.A. program is used in choosing recipients. During their second year of study, students receive grant assignments that allow them to assist in the management of this largely student-run program. Several other merit-based scholarships are available for first-year students, and the Federal Direct Student Loan Program provides need-based financial aid for U.S. citizens and permanent residents.

Cost of Study

Tuition and fees for Illinois residents enrolling in the fall of 1997 were $10,700 for the academic year. Nonresident tuition and fees were $16,500. Books for the academic year cost about $1500.

Living and Housing Costs

Students can expect to pay approximately $8000 for room and board and $2000 for personal expenses during the academic year. Students can choose single or double rooms in a graduate student dormitory, or rent a furnished or unfurnished apartment. Married students can obtain affordable housing through the Family Housing Office.

Student Group

Forty percent of Illinois M.B.A. students have technological backgrounds, and more than 50 percent have expressed interest in starting their own company after graduation. The Illinois M.B.A. class of 1999 is split almost evenly between U.S. citizens and international students; 31 percent are women, and twenty percent of the class are members of racial or ethnic minorities. The average student is 26 years old and brings nearly four years of work experience to the program.

Student Outcomes

Some of the major corporations recruiting graduates of the Illinois M.B.A. program are Ford Motor Company, Arthur Andersen, AlliedSignal, Citibank, Ernst & Young, Dow Chemical, Eaton Corp., and Pillsbury. Increasingly, Illinois M.B.A. graduates are forming their own companies, many based on cutting-edge technologies developed by the engineering and supercomputing programs at the University.

Location

Located on the Illinois prairie within a three-hour drive of Chicago, St. Louis, and Indianapolis, the University of Illinois and the twin cities of Urbana and Champaign form a thriving community rich in social, cultural, and recreational opportunities. This ideal location offers students easy access to the best of metropolitan life while providing the comfort and security of living in the heart of the Midwest.

The University and the Program

The University of Illinois at Urbana-Champaign is a world leader in applied and theoretical research in engineering, agriculture, supercomputing, life sciences, and business. The College of Commerce and Business Administration at the University has long been ranked as one of the best schools in the world for its programs in accounting, finance, and marketing; but, with a major new curriculum designed by faculty members and students in place, the Illinois M.B.A. program is quickly becoming its flagship program.

Applying

The application deadline is April 1. Admission is based on undergraduate GPA over the last 60 credit hours, GMAT results, communication skills demonstrated in essays and interviews, TOEFL and TSE for nonnative speakers of English, demonstrated leadership qualities, professional work experience, analytical ability, and letters of recommendation. Applicants should hold a bachelor's degree from an accredited U.S. college or university, or the equivalent from another country. Students should have a grade of B in at least one semester of calculus.

Correspondence and Information

Illinois M.B.A.
410 David Kinley Hall
1407 West Gregory Drive
University of Illinois at Urbana-Champaign
Urbana, Illinois 61801

Telephone: 800-MBA-UIUC (outside the U.S.: 217-244-7602)
Fax: 217-333-1156
E-mail: mba@uiuc.edu
World Wide Web: http://mba.cba.uiuc.edu.

University of Illinois at Urbana-Champaign

THE FACULTY AND THEIR RESEARCH

Department of Accountancy

J. Richard Dietrich, Professor; Ph.D., Carnegie Mellon, 1981. Financial reporting issues.
Thomas Finnegan, Lecturer; Ph.D., Illinois at Urbana-Champaign, 1993. Financial and managerial accounting.
Robert M. Halperin, Visiting Professor; Ph.D., Pennsylvania, 1977. Tax issues.
Frederick L. Neumann, Professor; Ph.D., Chicago, 1967. Auditing, education, ethics.
Theodore Sougiannis, Assistant Professor; Ph.D., Berkeley, 1990. Financial accounting, stock market valuations.
Eugene Willis, Professor and Head of the Department; Ph.D., Cincinnati, 1975. Taxpayer compliance, federal taxation.
David Ziebart, Professor; Ph.D., Michigan State, 1983. Not-for-profit, financial, and principles of accounting.
Richard E. Ziegler, Associate Professor; Ph.D., North Carolina, 1973. Auditing, financial accounting.

Department of Business Administration

Joseph Cheng, Professor; Ph.D., Michigan, 1977. Organizational studies, international management.
Dilip Chhajed, Associate Professor; Ph.D., Purdue, 1989. Operations management.
David M. Gardner, Professor; Ph.D., Minnesota, 1967. Promotion management.
Abbie Griffin, Professor; Ph.D., MIT, 1989. Measurement and improvement of new product development processes.
Nile W. Hatch, Assistant Professor; Ph.D., Berkeley, 1995. Management of technology, innovation, and manufacturing/operations strategy.
Jean-Francois Hennart, Professor; Ph.D., Maryland, 1977. International business.
James D. Hess, Professor; Ph.D., MIT, 1975. Pricing and sales promotion, distribution channels.
Douglas R. Johnson, Assistant Professor; Ph.D., UCLA, 1995. Strategic management, competitive strategy.
Jeffrey Kauffmann, Visiting Assistant Professor; Ph.D., North Carolina, 1997. Organizational behavior.
John W. Kindt, Professor; S.J.D., Virginia, 1981. Business law and legal environment of business.
Ruth C. King, Assistant Professor; Ph.D., Texas, 1987. Strategic management of information systems.
Don N. Kleinmuntz, Associate Professor; Ph.D. Chicago, 1982. Decision-making processes and models.
Matthew S. Kraatz, Assistant Professor; Ph.d., Northwestern, 1994. Antecedents and consequences of organizational adaptation and change.
Paul Lansing, Professor; J.D., Illinois at Urbana-Champaign, 1971; Graduate Diploma in International Legal Studies, Stockholm, 1973. International business and international law.
Huseyin Leblebici, Professor; Ph.D., Illinois at Urbana-Champaign, 1975. Organizational behavior and interorganizational relations.
Ben S. Liu, Assistant Professor; Ph.D., SUNY at Buffalo, 1991. Industrial marketing.
Ravi Madhavan, Assistant Professor; Ph.D., Pittsburgh, 1995. Strategic planning and management.
Joseph T. Mahoney, Associate Professor; Ph.D., Pennsylvania, 1989. Strategic management, business policy.
Steven C. Michael, Assistant Professor; Ph.D., Harvard, 1993. Interface of entrepreneurship, strategy, and economics.
Kent B. Monroe, Professor and Head of Department; D.B.A., Illinois at Urbana-Champaign, 1968. Marketing and pricing.
Elizabeth Moore-Shay, Assistant Professor; Ph.D., Florida, 1994. Promotion management, consumer behavior.
Carol M. Motley, Assistant Professor; Ph.D., Georgia, 1994. Consumer behavior, marketing strategy, retailing.
Sunder Narayanan, Assistant Professor; Ph.D., Columbia, 1990. Product management, marketing research, advertising media planning.
Gregory B. Northcraft, Professor; Ph.D., Stanford, 1981. Management and organizational behavior, behavioral aspects of decision-making.
Greg R. Oldham, Professor; Ph.D., Yale, 1974. Organizational science, the effects of work and work environments on employee reactions.
Nicholas Petruzzi, Assistant Professor; Ph.D., Purdue, 1995. Pricing models in operations management, distribution, logistics.
Joseph F. Porac, Professor; Ph.D., Rochester, 1979. Organizational behavior.
Michael G. Pratt, Assistant Professor; Ph.D., Michigan, 1994. Organizational culture and symbolism, management and consequences of conflicting ideologies and identities.
Zvi Ritz, Associate Professor; Ph.D., Northwestern, 1981. Operations research.
Donald M. Roberts, Professor Emeritus; Ph.D., Stanford, 1959. Application of statistical principles to decision processes.
Thomas W. Roehl, Assistant Professor; Ph.D., Washington, 1983. International business.
Mark E. Roszkowski, Professor; J.D., Illinois at Urbana-Champaign, 1975. Business law.
Anju Seth, Associate Professor; Ph.D., Michigan, 1988. Strategic management, international strategy, industry and competitive analysis.
Michael J. Shaw, Professor; Ph.D., Purdue, 1984. Artificial intelligence.
Riyaz T. Sikora, Assistant Professor; Ph.D., Illinois, 1994. Intelligent manufacturing, AI/expert systems.
Devanathan Sudharshan, Professor; Ph.D., Pittsburgh, 1982. Marketing research.
Seymour Sudman, Professor; Ph.D., Chicago, 1962. Applied sampling.
Howard Thomas, Professor and Dean; Ph.D., Edinburgh, 1970. Decision and policy analysis.
James Wade, Assistant Professor; Ph.D., Berkeley, 1993. Organizational design and environment.
Brian Wansink, Associate Professor; Ph.D., Stanford, 1990. Revitalization, management, and leveraging of mature brands.
Lillian Cheng Wright, Visiting Lecturer; Ph.D., USC, 1997. International business.
Russell Wright, Assistant Professor; Ph.D., Southern California, 1992. Entrepreneurship, technology management, strategy.
Rachel Yang, Assistant Professor; Ph.D., UCLA, 1996. Global supply chain management, design of production and distribution systems.

Department of Economics

Richard J. Arnould, Professor and Head of Department; Ph.D., Iowa State, 1968. Industrial organization, economics of regulation.
Lawrence DeBrock, Associate Professor; Ph.D., Cornell, 1980. Industrial organization, microeconomics.
Hadi Salehi Esfahani, Associate Professor; Ph.D., Berkeley, 1984. Developing economies.

Department of Finance

Roger E. Cannaday, Associate Professor; Ph.D., South Carolina, 1980. Real estate.
Louis Chan, Associate Professor; Ph.D., Rochester, 1984. Multinational business and investments.
Peter F. Colwell, Professor; Ph.D., Wayne State, 1973. Real estate and urban land economics.
Joseph E. Finnerty, Professor; Ph.D., Michigan, 1974. Investments, corporate finance.
Virginia France, Assistant Professor; Ph.D., Chicago, 1986. Portfolio management and derivatives, financial regulation.
James A. Gentry, Professor; D.B.A., Indiana, 1966. Corporate financial management.
Charles J. Hadlock, Assistant Professor; Ph.D., MIT, 1994. Issues related to raising capital, management incentives, CEO compensation, and ownership structure of public corporations.
Marasimhan Jegadeesh, Professor; Ph.D., Columbia, 1987. Investments, contingent claims pricing.
Charles M. Kahn, Professor; Ph.D., Harvard, 1981. Financial institutions, informations and uncertainty, game theory.
Josef Lakonishok, Professor; Ph.D., Cornell, 1976. Investments, mergers, acquisitions.
Charles M. Linke, Professor; D.B.A., Indiana, 1966. Business finance and investments.
David Lins, Adjunct Professor; Ph.D., Illinois, 1972. Financial management, investment analysis, agricultural finance.
Morgan J. Lynge, Professor and Chair of Department; Ph.D., Michigan, 1975. Credit and financial markets, management of financial institutions, and corporate finance.
Hun Park, Associate Professor; Ph.D., Ohio State, 1982. Speculative markets and investments.
Neil Pearson, Associate Professor; Ph.D., MIT, 1990. Options and futures, financial institutions, financial engineering.
George G. Pennacchi, Professor; Ph.D., MIT, 1984. Financial institutions.
David T. Whitford, Associate Professor; Ph.D., Georgia State, 1980. Corporate finance and investments.
Kent Zumwalt, Visiting Professor; Ph.D., Missouri, 1974. Corporate finance.

UNIVERSITY OF IOWA

School of Management

Programs of Study

The University of Iowa M.B.A. program provides students with a foundation for future growth and flexibility in business management. Students build broad-based personal portfolios of analytical skills, knowledge, and professional experiences. The curriculum is rigorous, yet learning takes place in a collaborative environment that builds teamwork skills and encourages independent problem solving. The M.B.A. requires 60 semester hours, including four courses in an area of concentration and six electives in business or in other academic areas of the University. Concentrations are available in accounting, entrepreneurship, finance, human resources/organizational performance, management information systems, marketing, operations management, and product development and management.

In addition to offering a nationally recognized M.B.A. program, the University of Iowa School of Management offers the Master of Arts (M.A.) degree in accounting and management information systems and Ph.D. programs in business administration and economics. Joint degree programs are available to M.B.A. students in hospital and health administration, nursing, library and information science, and law.

Research Facilities

The School of Management is housed in the $36-million John Pappajohn Business Administration Building. The facility includes a 16,000-square-foot Business Library and a Computer Lab of more than 5,500 square feet, offering more than 100 individual workstations, specialized equipment, and small-group study rooms with computer hook-ups. Students also make use of University-wide resources, including approximately 2.3 million volumes in the University Libraries System, and the Weeg Computing Center, with terminals accessing numerous mainframes. The College of Business Administration houses several research institutes, including the Institute for Economic Research, the Entrepreneurial Management Institute, the Financial Markets Institute, the Manufacturing Productivity Center, the Ira B. McGladrey Institute for Accounting Research, the Management Center, and the Small Business Development Center.

Financial Aid

Merit-based scholarships and fellowships are available to M.B.A. students. All applicants are considered for these competitive awards. Awards are based on information found within the application portfolio (including GMAT scores, GPA, and work experience). Students are also encouraged to apply for need-based financial assistance through the University Office of Student Financial Aid. Second-year students are eligible for research or teaching assistantships in the School of Management.

Cost of Study

Estimated tuition and fees for full-time study for the 1998–99 academic year are $4130 for state residents and $11,246 for out-of-state students.

Living and Housing Costs

The costs of living in Iowa City are quite reasonable. Estimates provided by the Office of Student Financial Aid suggest that M.B.A. students budget approximately $600 per month for room and board. The University offers Family Housing, as well as the Housing Clearinghouse, to help those interested in locating rental units in the area.

Student Group

M.B.A. students come from every region of the United States and countries throughout the world. They represent a variety of backgrounds, undergraduate majors, and prior professional experiences. The cooperative spirit that characterizes Iowa M.B.A. students enables each one to benefit from the diversity of experience found in the student body. During the 1997–98 academic year, approximately 200 full-time M.B.A. students were enrolled. Women constituted 34 percent of this group and students from minority groups, 9 percent. Students recently admitted to the program have GMAT scores above 600, TOEFL scores in excess of 600, an average undergraduate GPA of 3.21, and more than three years' full-time work experience.

Student Outcomes

The most recent graduating class had an average starting salary of $55,228 and an average sign-on bonus of $7750. M.B.A. graduates with job offers at graduation totaled 87 percent of the graduating class. For summer 1997, 100 percent of the first-year M.B.A. students held internships, consulting jobs, and international study assignments.

Location

Iowa City, with a population of 80,000 including students, offers a uniquely friendly yet cosmopolitan atmosphere. Big Ten athletics, world-class cultural events, and a downtown shopping area featuring one-of-a-kind shops and restaurants are all readily accessible. Situated along the banks of the Iowa River in the rolling hills of eastern Iowa, Iowa City and the surrounding area offer numerous recreational opportunities. Students are encouraged to visit Iowa City, tour the campus and community, and meet with faculty members and other students.

The University

Founded in 1847, the University of Iowa is the oldest of Iowa's three state universities. In addition to the College of Business Administration, the University includes the Colleges of Dentistry, Education, Engineering, Law, Liberal Arts, Medicine, Nursing, and Pharmacy. The University enrolls approximately 27,000 students, of whom 6,500 are graduate students.

Applying

The applicant's entire portfolio is considered. The admissions committee reviews each file individually and in full, looking for candidates who are a good match with the Iowa program. Students are asked to submit a completed application form, transcripts of all undergraduate and graduate work, a resume, responses to essay questions, GMAT scores, three references, and an application fee. Admission preference for the full-time program (fall entrance) will be given to those applications completed by April 15. Applications for the evening M.B.A. programs offered in Cedar Rapids, Newton, and the Quad Cities are accepted year-round.

Correspondence and Information

School of Management
The University of Iowa
108 Pappajohn Business Administration Building, Suite C140
Iowa City, Iowa 52242-1000

Telephone: 319-335-1039
800-622-4692 (toll-free)
Fax: 319-335-3604
E-mail: iowamba@uiowa.edu
World Wide Web: http://www.biz.uiowa.edu/mba

University of Iowa

THE FACULTY AND THEIR RESEARCH

Accounting. Joyce Berg, Ph.D., Minnesota: experimental methods in accounting. Thomas J. Carroll, Ph.D., Michigan: market-based accounting research. Daniel W. Collins, Ph.D., Iowa: agency theory, capital markets. Douglas DeJong, Ph.D., Michigan: accounting, experimental markets. Amy E. Dunbar, Ph.D., Texas at Austin: tax policy research. W. Bruce Johnson, Ph.D., Ohio State: corporate financial reporting. Valdean Lembke, Ph.D., Michigan: corporate financial accounting. Morton Pincus, Ph.D., Washington (St. Louis): financial reporting. Albert Schepanski, Ph.D., Illinois: managerial accounting, financial accounting. Richard M. Tubbs, Ph.D., Florida: cognitive accounting research. Gregory B. Waymire, Ph.D., Chicago: financial accounting.

Economics. William P. Albrecht, Ph.D., Yale: industrial organization, income distribution, regulation. Michael S. Balch, Ph.D., NYU: mathematical economics. Andreas Blume, Ph.D., California, San Diego: game theory and industrial organization. Dean Corbae, Ph.D., Yale: macroeconomics, international economics. Carol C. Fethke, Ph.D., Iowa: health economics, international marketing, microeconomics, family and personal financial management. Robert Forsythe, Ph.D., Carnegie Mellon: financial economics, public economics, general equilibrium theory. John W. Fuller, Ph.D., Washington State: transportation and public utilities, public finance. Joel L. Horowitz, Ph.D., Cornell: econometrics, transportation and environmental economics. Marlynne Beth Fisher Ingram, Ph.D., Minnesota: macroeconomics, econometrics. Hyman Joseph, Ph.D., Northwestern: health economics, applied microeconomics. Ignacio Lobato, Ph.D., London School of Economics: theoretical econometrics, applied economics. Dierdre McCloskey, Ph.D., Harvard: economic history, economic philosophy, applied microeconomics. Forrest D. Nelson, Ph.D., Rochester: econometrics, applied microeconomics. George Neumann, Ph.D., Northwestern: labor economics, applied econometrics. Harry Paarsch, Ph.D., Stanford: applied econometrics, industrial organization and labor economics. Scott Page, Ph.D., Northwestern: public economics, computational complexity, political science. Thomas F. Pogue, Ph.D., Yale: public finance, macroeconomics. B. Ravikumar, Ph.D., Iowa: economic development, macroeconomics, asset pricing, public finance. Raymond G. Riezman, Ph.D., Minnesota: international trade, microeconomic theory. N. Eugene Savin, Ph.D., Berkeley: econometrics. Calvin D. Siebert, Ph.D., Berkeley: monetary economics, macroeconomics. John L. Solow, Ph.D., Stanford: public finance, industrial organization. Ted Temzelides, Ph.D., Minnesota: monetary theory, economic theory, payment systems. Charles H. Whiteman, Ph.D., Minnesota: macroeconomics, time series analysis. Stephen Williamson, Ph.D., Wisconsin: monetary economics, macroeconomics.

Finance. David S. Bates, Ph.D., Princeton: international finance, futures and options, testing option pricing models, foreign currency futures options, futures market performance. Matthew T. Billett, Ph.D., Florida: corporate finance, financial institutions, financial management. F. Douglas Foster, Ph.D., Cornell: information economics, financial intermediation, underwriting syndication, market microstructure. Thomas George, Ph.D., Michigan: market microstructure, investments, information economics. Puneet Handa, Ph.D., Iowa: corporate finance, asset pricing, market microstructure. Timothy Loughran, Ph.D., Illinois: equity offerings, financial institutions. Thomas Rietz, Ph.D., Iowa: experimental economics, monetary and financial economics, asset pricing models. Jarjisu Sa-Aadu, Ph.D., Wisconsin: real estate investment analysis, mortgage markets and institutions, housing economics, public finance. G. Carl Schweser, Ph.D., Georgia: investment analysis, financial management, small-business financing, futures trading. John Spitzer, Ph.D., Duke: fixed income securities, financial institutions, credit and cash management, mortgage finance. Michael J. Stutzer, Ph.D., Minnesota: financial intermediation, asset pricing. Gerry L. Suchanek, Ph.D., Northwestern: financial economic theory, investments, experimental finance, economic history. Emmett J. Vaughan, Ph.D., Nebraska: risk management, property and liability insurance. Anand Vijh, Ph.D., Berkeley: dividends policy, restructurings, market volatility, options and derivatives. Paul Weller, Ph.D., Essex (England): international finance, futures and options. Benjamin Wilner, Ph.D., Northwestern: corporate finance, working capital management, cash management, trade credit.

Management and Organizations. Murray R. Barrick, Ph.D., Akron: personality and job performance, selection, compensation, utility analysis. Terry L. Boles, Ph.D., California, Santa Barbara: negotiation and conflict management, behavioral decision theory (in particular, the effects of reference points on choice), ethics. Jay Christensen-Szalanski, Ph.D., Washington (Seattle): behavioral decision theory, health policy. John T. Delaney, Ph.D., Illinois: effects of organizational rules on firm performance, industrial relations, ethics in business. Nancy R. Hauserman, J.D., Iowa: ethics, family law, diversity, sexual harassment. Timothy A. Judge, Ph.D., Illinois: personality measurement and prediction, staffing, job attitudes, careers. Amy Kristof-Brown, Ph.D., Maryland: person-environment fit in selection and socialization, impression management, goal setting, levels of analysis issues. Lola L. Lopes, Ph.D., California, San Diego: behavioral decision making, psychology of risk, rhetoric of inquiry. Michael K. Mount, Ph.D., Iowa State: personality and job performance, 360-degree feedback systems, staffing. Sara L. Rynes, Ph.D., Wisconsin: human resource management and strategies, total quality management, staffing, compensation. Frank L. Schmidt, Ph.D., Purdue: personnel testing, employment selection, validity generalization, meta-analysis, utility analysis. Jude P. West, Ph.D., Iowa: training and development, stress, personnel administration.

Management Sciences. Kurt M. Anstreicher, Ph.D., Stanford: mathematical programming, interior point methods. Warren J. Boe, Ph.D., Purdue: operations management—flexible manufacturing systems, group technology, database management systems. Renato de Matta, Ph.D., Pennsylvania: operations management, combinatorial optimization. Gary C. Fethke, Ph.D., Iowa: managerial economics, dynamic pricing models, macroeconomics, labor economics. Raj Jagannathan, Ph.D., Carnegie Mellon: stochastic modeling, production planning and control, mathematical programming. Philip C. Jones, Ph.D., Berkeley: manufacturing and logistics, management. Kenneth O. Kortanek, Ph.D., Northwestern: optimization, semi-infinite programming, applications. Johannes Ledolter, Ph.D., Wisconsin: statistical forecasting, time-series analysis, quality management. Timothy J. Lowe, Ph.D., Northwestern: production, logistics, mathematical programming. June Park, Ph.D., Ohio State: computer information systems, stochastic modeling and control, combinatorial optimization. Alberto Segre, Ph.D., Illinois: artificial intelligence, automated reasoning, distributed algorithms. Padmini Srinivasan, Ph.D., Syracuse: design of intelligent systems, temporal databases, medical databases. Rodney Traub, Ph.D., Purdue: operations management, scheduling, combinatorial optimization. Yinyu Ye, Ph.D., Stanford: mathematical programming, computational algorithms, complexity analysis. Dan Zhu, Ph.D., Carnegie Mellon: decision support systems, intelligent scheduling, financial information systems.

Marketing. Catherine A. Cole, Ph.D., Wisconsin: older consumer behavior and advertising effects. Carol C. Fethke, Ph.D., Iowa: international marketing, personal acquisitions, microeconomics. Gary Gaeth, Ph.D., Kansas State: consumer decision making, service marketing. Thomas S. Gruca, Ph.D., Illinois: marketing models, defensive marketing strategy, strategic management in the health-care sector. Wagner A. Kamakura, Ph.D., Texas: choice modeling, market segmentation, market structure analysis, diffusion of innovations. Peter C. Riesz, Ph.D., Columbia: global marketing management, industrial marketing, sales management, marketing management. Gary J. Russell, Ph.D., Chicago: choice models, brand price competition, market segmentation. Randall L. Schulz, Ph.D., Northwestern: market response models, systems implementation, forecasting strategy. Baba Shiv, Ph.D., Duke: marketing communication, consumer decision making. Doyle L. Weiss, Ph.D., Carnegie Tech: market response models, forecasting, marketing strategy.

UNIVERSITY OF KANSAS

Graduate School of Business

Programs of Study

The improved full-time M.B.A. program at KU's Lawrence campus retains the best of the traditional program—strong quantitative skills development; a solid base in marketing, finance, economics, and human resources core disciplines; and an outstanding spectrum of electives—with some striking innovations. Emphasis on team-building is integrated throughout the program; Immersion Weeks focus on critical new areas of business; and new concentrations include information technology, international business, and management of technology. The program accommodates students who were not business undergraduates; only about a third of the M.B.A. students have a background in business when they begin the program.

Top-notch faculty, an excellent placement record, actively supportive alumni, and the resources of a world-class university give the KU M.B.A. great value. This program is 60 credit hours long and takes two years to complete, full-time. Students are required to take an internship, study abroad, or participate in a similarly meaningful experience that complements first-year studies during the summer between the first and second years. Internships have been offered with such companies as Andersen Consulting, Koch Industries, Payless ShoeSource, and Sprint. Study-abroad opportunities include England, France, and Italy. The part-time M.B.A. program offers the same faculty and academic excellence as the full-time program and can be completed in three years (48 credit hours). At least two years of meaningful work experience is required for admission. This program, taught at the Regents Center in Overland Park, Kansas (near Kansas City), features an enriched classroom environment; students have an average of eight years of work experience.

The Master of Accounting and Information Systems (M.A.I.S.) prepares students for careers in taxation, auditing, or information systems. With an undergraduate degree in accounting, students can complete this program in one year (30 credit hours); otherwise, the degree requires two years. The doctoral (Ph.D.) program, designed for those interested in research and teaching careers, emphasizes basic knowledge in three core areas (behavioral sciences, economic theory, and probability and statistics) during the first year. Then students specialize in one of the following concentrations: accounting, finance, human resources, management science, marketing, organizational behavior, or strategic management.

Research Facilities

With more than thirty special research facilities, fourteen major academic divisions, and three major libraries containing more than 3 million volumes, research is integral to the University's mission. KU is one of only fifty-eight member schools in the prestigious American Association of Universities and is classified as a Research I institution by the Carnegie Foundation for the Advancement of Teaching.

Financial Aid

Some financial aid is available in the form of scholarships, fellowships, and graduate assistantships. Most aid is awarded competitively based on such factors as academic achievement and financial need.

Cost of Study

In-state tuition for the 1998–99 academic year is $100 per graduate credit hour; out-of-state tuition is $328.75 per graduate credit hour. There is a campus fee of $214 per semester. All students in the part-time M.B.A. program in Overland Park pay $196 per graduate business credit hour, including fees.

Living and Housing Costs

Housing costs vary widely. Residence hall rates are $3736 to $4860 per academic year and include nineteen meals per week. Apartments and married student housing are also available on campus. Off-campus housing ranges upward from $350 per month.

Student Group

Admissions to the M.B.A. or M.A.I.S. programs are carefully screened by Admissions Board faculty members whose decision is based on four factors: two letters of recommendation, work experience, undergraduate GPA, and GMAT score. The TOEFL is required for international students. The admission rate is approximately 50 percent. Thirty-five percent of full-time M.B.A. students are women, 7 percent are minorities, 19 percent are international students, and 50 percent have some work experience. The average age is 26.

Student Outcomes

More than 80 percent of the M.B.A. and M.A.I.S. graduates have positions within six weeks of graduation. The average annual starting salary was $44,518 in 1997. Top employers include Payless ShoeSource, Andersen Consulting, Sprint, Deloite & Touche, and Koch Industries.

Location

The main campus occupies 1,000 acres of forested, rolling hills on and around Mount Oread in the city of Lawrence, a growing community of 68,000. Located only 35 miles west of Kansas City, historic Lawrence combines the atmosphere of a small college town with the cosmopolitan flavor of a major city. Shopping areas, restaurants, entertainment, and recreational facilities are easily accessible from campus.

The University

The University of Kansas is a major educational and research institution with more than 27,000 students, including about 8,000 graduate students, and 1,900 faculty members. The School of Business is housed in Summerfield Hall, located in the heart of campus. Because classes are small (approximately 45 students in core courses and fewer than 25 in most electives), personal contact with professors is a reality. The KU M.B.A. program is a nationally recognized program, fully accredited by the American Association of Collegiate Schools of Business.

Applying

The following are required to be considered for admission: application for admission to the Graduate School, supplemental data sheet, $50 application fee (nonrefundable), official transcript of all undergraduate and graduate courses and degree(s) conferred, at least two letters of recommendation from professors or employers, and official Graduate Management Admissions Test (GMAT) score. An official TOEFL score report is required for international students. Deadline for application is May 1 to begin full-time M.B.A. study in Lawrence in August. M.A.I.S. and part-time M.B.A. program deadlines are May 1 (for fall), October 1 (for spring), and March 1 (for summer).

Correspondence and Information

For the master's and doctoral programs:

Director of Master's or Doctoral Programs
206 Summerfield Hall
University of Kansas
Lawrence, Kansas 66045

Telephone: 913-864-4254
Fax: 913-864-5328
E-mail: grad@bschool.wpo.ukans.edu
World Wide Web: http://www.bschool.ukans.edu/

University of Kansas

THE FACULTY AND THEIR RESEARCH

Accounting

Bruce Bublitz, Associate Professor and Associate Dean; Ph.D., Illinois at Urbana–Champaign, 1992. Current cost accounting.
Charles J. Coate, Assistant Professor; Ph.D., Maryland, 1992. Audit, managerial accounting.
Michael Ettredge, Associate Professor; Ph.D., Texas at Austin, 1982. Accounting profession economics, financial capital markets.
Allen Ford, Professor; Ph.D., Arkansas, 1970. Taxation.
Kay Nelson, Assistant Professor; Ph.D., Texas at Austin, 1995. Software system flexibility, structured methods.
David Paul, Assistant Professor; Ph.D., Texas at Austin, 1997. Health-care information systems, virtual organizations.
Vernon J. Richardson, Assistant Professor; Ph.D., Illinois at Urbana–Champaign, 1997. Empirical-capital markets, earning management, voluntary disclosures.
Susan Scholz, Assistant Professor; Ph.D., USC, 1996. Economic issues of the audit environment.
Timothy L. Shaftel, Professor; Ph.D., Carnegie Mellon, 1972. O.R. models in M.I.S. and accounting.
Rajendra P. Srivastava, Professor; Ph.D., Oklahoma, 1982. Auditing.
James F. Waegelein, Associate Professor; Ph.D., Penn State, 1982. Executive compensation on managerial decisions.
Beverly Wilson, Assistant Professor; Ph.D., Arizona, 1983. Optimal decision making.

Finance

William L. Beedles, Professor; Ph.D., Texas at Austin, 1975. Small business, finance for operating managers.
Henry N. Butler, Professor; Ph.D., Virginia Tech, 1982. Antitrust, corporate governance, economics of organizations.
Jack E. Gaumnitz, Professor; Ph.D., Stanford, 1967. Social security, portfolio management, real estate.
Mark Hirschey, Professor; Ph.D., Wisconsin at Madison, 1977. Intangible capital, valuation of corporate investments.
O. Maurice Joy, Professor; Ph.D., North Carolina, 1969. Securities analysis, valuation of company stock and assets.
Paul D. Koch, Professor; Ph.D., Michigan State, 1980. International finance, investments, options and futures markets, financial institutions.
Kelly D. Welch, Assistant Professor; Ph.D. candidate, Chicago. Institutional monitoring and corporate debt ownership.

Human Resources

Ronald Ash, Professor; Ph.D., South Florida, 1981. Human resources management, employment discrimination.
Kevin Chauvin, Associate Professor; Ph.D., Illinois at Urbana–Champaign, 1989. Gender-earnings differentials.
James P. Guthrie, Associate Professor; Ph.D., Maryland, 1989. Compensation management, strategic management.
Douglas A. Houston, Professor; D.B.A., Indiana, 1980. Electric power markets (economics and public policy).
Charles E. Krider, Professor; Ph.D., Chicago, 1976. State/community economic development strategy.
Anthony Redwood, Professor; Ph.D., Illinois at Urbana-Champaign, 1973. Regional economic development.
David E. Shulenberger, Professor; Ph.D., Illinois at Urbana–Champaign. Arbitration, factors determining wages.

Law

John W. Gergacz, Professor; J.D., Indiana, 1975. Attorney-corporate client privilege.
Murray S. Levin, Associate Professor; J.D., Kansas, 1977. Dispute resolution and negotiation, contract law.
Clyde D. Stoltenberg, Professor; J.D., Harvard, 1972. Trade/investment issues in China, Taiwan, and Korea.
Douglas F. Whitman, Professor; J.D., Missouri at Columbia, 1973. Professional advertising and advertising law.

Management Science

John M. Charnes, Associate Professor; Ph.D., Minnesota, 1989. Statistical process control, inventory models, production.
Steven C. Hillmer, Professor; Ph.D., Wisconsin–Madison, 1976. Total quality management.
Dennis F. Karney, Professor; Ph.D., Illinois at Urbana–Champaign, 1980. Total quality commitment.
Prakash P. Shenoy, Professor; Ph.D., Cornell, 1977. Expert systems, game theory, decision analysis.
Lawrence A. Sherr, Professor; Ph.D., Michigan, 1966. Total quality management, service organizations' management.
Po-Lung Yu, Professor; Ph.D., Johns Hopkins, 1969. Habitual domain theory, management science, operations research.

Marketing

Rohini Ahluwalia, Assistant Professor; Ph.D., Ohio State, 1996.
Kissan Joseph, Assistant Professor; Ph.D., Purdue, 1992. Sales compensation plans, sales force retention.
V. Parker Lessig, Professor; Ph.D., Kansas, 1970. Marketing strategy, market segmentation.
Sanjay Mishra, Associate Professor; Ph.D., Washington State, 1990. Consumer behavior, new product development.
Dennis L. Rosen, Associate Professor; Ph.D., Minnesota, 1977. Qualitative analysis, customer service.
Surendra Singh, Professor and Director of Research and Ph.D. Program; Ph.D., Wisconsin–Madison, 1982. Advertising, services marketing.

Organizational Behavior

Jill Kleinberg, Associate Professor; Ph.D., Michigan. Organizational culture, cross-cultural negotiation.
Kenneth D. Mackenzie, Professor; Ph.D., Berkeley, 1964. Organizational holograms and design.
Renate Mai-Dalton, Associate Professor; Ph.D., Washington (Seattle), 1978. Cultural diversity, leadership.
H. Joseph Reitz, Professor; Ph.D., MIT, 1969. Business ethics.
Catherine Schwoerer, Associate Professor; Ph.D., North Carolina at Chapel Hill, 1990. Career management, workplace rights.
Daniel G. Spencer, Associate Professor; Ph.D., Oregon, 1979. Individual/group critical thinking and creative problem solving.

Strategic Management

Barry Baysinger, Visiting Professor; Ph.D., Virginia Tech, 1978. Strategic management, organizational economics.
Melissa Birch, Associate Professor; Ph.D., Illinois, 1984. Latin American business.
Deepak K. Datta, Professor; Ph.D., Pittsburgh, 1986. Mergers and acquisitions, strategic planning systems.
H. Gordon Fitch, Professor; Ph.D., Purdue, 1969. Telecommunications, infomedia, aircraft manufacturing industries.
John Garland, Associate Professor; D.B.A., Indiana, 1982. Soviet and Eastern European economic trends.
V. K. Narayanan, Professor; Ph.D., Pittsburgh, 1979. Management of technology, competitor and environmental analysis.

UNIVERSITY OF KENTUCKY

Carol Martin Gatton College of Business and Economics

Programs of Study

The Carol Martin Gatton College of Business and Economics educates students at the master's and doctoral levels. Degree programs are offered in accounting (M.S.Acc.), business administration (M.B.A., Ph.D.), and economics (M.A., Ph.D.). Joint M.B.A./J.D. and M.B.A./B.S. in engineering degrees are also available.

The M.S.Acc. program requires a minimum of 30 semester hours at the graduate level and is designed to prepare students for responsible, professional positions in public accounting, industry, and government. Students have the opportunity to concentrate in selected areas of accounting. Students can also structure their course work in preparation for teaching at the community college level or to pursue further graduate study. The M.B.A. program offers two tracks, each requiring a minimum of 36 semester hours. Students without an undergraduate business degree acquire a broad-based management training; students with an undergraduate degree in business can choose a concentration from the following areas: accountancy and corporate finance; finance, real estate, and banking; international business; management information systems; marketing and distribution; and production and manufacturing systems. The M.A. in economics requires a minimum of 30 hours of graduate credit and prepares graduates for employment in universities, government, business, and other organizations. Specialization is offered in the areas of econometrics, international economics, labor and monetary economics, industrial organization, environmental and resource economics, and public, urban, and regional economics.

The Ph.D. program in business administration prepares students for careers in a university setting. A minimum of 39 credit hours of course work in core and major areas is followed by 18 residence credit hours upon successful completion of the qualifying examination. Oral defense of a dissertation is required. Major areas include accountancy, decision science information systems, finance, management, and marketing. The Ph.D. in economics prepares students for careers in university as well as business and government settings. A minimum of 48 hours of course work includes both theory and qualifying examinations. Specialization areas are similar to those of the M.A. degree. Oral defense of a dissertation is required.

Research Facilities

As a Carnegie Foundation Research I University, the University of Kentucky has excellent research facilities. The M. I. King Library contains more than 2.5 million volumes and receives more than 27,000 periodical and serial titles. The library's more than 5 million units of microform include 1 million technical reports from U.S. and foreign governments. Since 1907, the University has served as a depository for U.S. federal government publications as well as official publications from the United Nations, European Union, Great Britain, and Canada. The library is a member of the interlibrary loan system and the Center for Research Libraries in Chicago. The new $58-million W. T. Young Library opened in spring 1998. The University Computing Center has several high-level systems that support research and networking needs. At sites throughout the campus, computer workstations cater to all students. Within the Gatton College, the Business Information Center (BIC) provides state-of-the-art business database access for research and information. Gatton College's Center for Labor and Economic Research (CLEAR), Center for Business Development (CBD), Center for Business and Economic Research (CBER), Small Business Development Center (SBDC), Center for Real Estate Studies (CRES), and International Business and Management Center (IBMC) serve as resources to the local, state, national, and international communities.

Financial Aid

The College and Graduate School offer merit-based scholarships and fellowships. The College also awards teaching, research, and graduate assistantships to eligible students. Internship opportunities are also available. Other forms of financial aid are administered by the Student Financial Aid Office of the University.

Cost of Study

In 1998–99, full-time resident tuition and fees are $1638 per semester; full-time nonresident tuition and fees are $4578. Part-time resident students pay tuition and fees of $170 per credit hour; part-time nonresident tuition and fees are $496 per credit hour.

Living and Housing Costs

On-campus housing rents range from $318 to $540 per month. A single student living frugally needs approximately $5200 in housing and living expenses for an academic year.

Student Group

The Gatton College enrolls approximately 380 graduate students each year, of whom approximately 120 are doctoral students. The student body is diverse, with more than fifteen countries and several different ethnic origins represented. Most of the students, especially the doctoral students, have had substantial prior professional work experience.

Student Outcomes

Graduates of the M.B.A. program are employed in a number of specialties, including information systems, accounting, finance, and marketing. Recent employers include Andersen Consulting, Gillette Co., Procter & Gamble, Ford Motor Co., and Lexmark. Accounting graduates often find jobs with Big 5 accounting firms.

Recent graduates of the doctoral programs occupy tenure-track positions at universities and colleges in the U.S. and abroad as well as in government agencies and research institutes.

Location

Lexington is famed worldwide as the "Heart of the Bluegrass" and for its thoroughbred horse farms. With a population of 230,000, Lexington combines the amenities of a large city with the courtesies and charm of a small town; it lies within a 500-mile radius of nearly three fourths of the manufacturing, retail sales, and population of the United States. Today, there is a substantial international component to business interests in Lexington and the commonwealth of Kentucky.

The University and The College

Situated on an urban campus, the University of Kentucky was established in 1875 and currently enrolls more than 24,000 students, of whom 6,400 are graduate students. Founded in 1925 as the College of Commerce, the Carol Martin Gatton College occupies a modern building with all the facilities needed to fulfill the mission of excellence in teaching, research, and service. The College has three divisions: the School of Accountancy, the School of Management (incorporating the areas of finance, information systems, management, and marketing), and the Department of Economics. Seventy-five full-time faculty members teach, conduct research, and publish, as well as provide consulting services to government agencies and private institutions, both in the U.S. and abroad.

Applying

Students apply to both the Graduate School and their College program of choice. Admission deadlines for U.S. citizens are July 26 for fall admission and December 9 for spring admission. U.S. citizens applying to the M.B.A. program, however, should apply by July 1 for fall admission. Deadlines for international applicants are February 1 for fall admission and June 15 for spring admission. Not all programs offer spring admission. Students requesting any form of financial aid from the College or the Graduate School should apply by February 1.

Correspondence and Information

Ms. Donna Ballos
Graduate Center, 237
Carol Martin Gatton College of Business and Economics
University of Kentucky
Lexington, Kentucky 40506
Telephone: 606-257-3592
Fax: 606-257-3293
E-mail: drball01@pop.uky.edu

University of Kentucky

THE FACULTY

Richard Furst, Dean; D.B.A., Washington (St. Louis). Finance.
Michael Tearney, Associate Dean; Ph.D., Missouri. Accounting.

Endowed Chair Professors
Greg Dess, Ph.D., Washington (Seattle). Management.
Clyde Holsapple, Ph.D., Purdue. Management information systems.
Donald Mullineaux, Ph.D., Boston College. Banking, finance.

Named Professorships
Glenn Blomquist, Ph.D., Chicago. Economics.
James Donnelly, Ph.D., Maryland. Marketing.
James Gibson, Ph.D., Kentucky. Management.
Charles Haywood, Ph.D., Berkeley. Finance.
Charles Hultman, Ph.D., Iowa. International economics.
James Knoblett, Ph.D., Washington (Seattle). Accounting.
Donald Madden, Ph.D., Texas. Accounting.
Steven Skinner, D.B.A., Kentucky. Marketing.
Michael Tearney, Ph.D., Missouri. Accounting.

SCHOOL OF ACCOUNTANCY
Myrtle Clark, Ph.D., South Carolina.
Jean Cooper, Ph.D., North Carolina.
Daniel Fulks, Ph.D., Georgia State.
James Holmes, Ph.D., Missouri.
David Hulse, Ph.D., Penn State.
Stuart Keller, Ph.D., North Carolina.
Douglas Poe, Ph.D., Texas A&M.
Thomas Pope, D.B.A., Kentucky.
Robert Ramsey, Ph.D., Indiana.
Relmond Van Daniker, D.B.A., Maryland.
Ralph Viator, Ph.D., Texas A&M.
Jane Wells, M.S., Kentucky.

SCHOOL OF MANAGEMENT
Decision Science and Information Systems (DSIS):
Chen Chung, Ph.D., Ohio State.
Albert Lederer, Ph.D., Ohio State.
Krishnamurty Muralidhar, Ph.D., Texas A&M.
Ram Pakath, Ph.D., Purdue.
Anita Lee Post, Ph.D., Iowa.

Finance:
Michael Carpenter, Ph.D., Arizona State.
It-Keong Chew, Ph.D., South Carolina.
Paul Childs, Ph.D., Wisconsin.
Merl Hackbart, Ph.D., Kansas State.
Keith Johnson, Ph.D., Illinois.
Bradford Jordan, Ph.D., Florida.
Susan Jordan, Ph.D., Georgia.
Dennis Officer, Ph.D., Arkansas.
Steven Ott, Ph.D., Wisconsin.
Leonard Schneck, Ph.D., Carnegie Mellon.

Management:
Terry Amburgey, Ph.D., Stanford.
Phil Berger, Ph.D., Texas Christian.
Mark Davis, Ph.D., Virginia Tech.
Walter Ferrier, Ph.D., Maryland.
Timothy Folta, Ph.D., Purdue.
James Freeman, LL.M., Harvard.
Andrew Grimes, Ph.D., Minnesota.
Gordon Holbein, Ph.D., Penn State.
Nancy Johnson, Ph.D., Kansas.
Joan Phillips, Ph.D., Illinois.
Chamu Sundaramurthy, Ph.D., Illinois.
Bennett Tepper, Ph.D., Miami (Florida).

Marketing:
Robert Dahlstrom, Ph.D., Cincinnati.
Jule Gassenheimer, Ph.D., Alabama.
Diane Halstead, Ph.D., Michigan State.
William Keep, Ph.D., Michigan State.
Scott Kelley, D.B.A., Kentucky.
Fred Morgan, Ph.D., Michigan State.
Valerie Taylor, Ph.D., South Carolina.
Kelly Tepper, Ph.D., Georgia State.
Tommy Whittler, Ph.D., Purdue.

DEPARTMENT OF ECONOMICS
Mukhtar Ali, Ph.D., Wisconsin.
Dan Black, Ph.D., Purdue.
Stacy Dickert, Ph.D., Wisconsin.
James Fackler, Ph.D., Indiana.
Gail Hoyt, Ph.D., Kentucky.
William Hoyt, Ph.D., Wisconsin.
Richard Jensen, Ph.D., Northwestern.
Yoonbai Kim, Ph.D., Stanford.
Joseph Krislov, Ph.D., Wisconsin.
Randolph McGee, Ph.D., Tulane.
Frank Scott, Ph.D., Virginia.
William Stober, Ph.D., Duke.
James Stoker, Ph.D., Chicago.
Eugenia Toma, Ph.D., Virginia Tech.
Mark Toma, Ph.D., Virginia Tech.
Weiren Wang, Ph.D., USC.
Michael Webb, Ph.D., Illinois.

RESEARCH AND SERVICE CENTER HEADS
Mark Berger, Ph.D., Ohio State. Economics.
John Madden, Ph.D., Kansas. Economics.
Steven Ott, Ph.D., Wisconsin. Real estate.
Governor Martha Layne Collins.
Janet Holloway, M.S.W., SUNY at Stony Brook.

UNIVERSITY OF MAINE

The Maine Business School

Program of Study

The Maine Business School offers a nationally accredited program of study leading to the degree of Master of Business Administration. The M.B.A. program equips candidates with the concepts, analytical tools, and executive skills required for competent and responsible management. Built-in course and program flexibility enables the Business School to meet the needs of the individual student. Students have the opportunity to take up to 30 percent of their graduate course work in electives to meet their own career goals. Participants with full- or part-time jobs can complete their studies without interruption of their career responsibilities by enrolling in late afternoon, evening, and summer courses. Full-time students with an undergraduate degree in business administration can usually complete the 30-hour graduate program in one calendar year. Students with no business course work can complete requirements in two years of full-time study.

The Business School has 14 graduate faculty members and about 90 M.B.A. candidates. The relatively small size of graduate classes permits a one-on-one working relationship with the faculty.

Research Facilities

The Fogler Library houses more than 900,000 volumes, subscribes to more than 5,600 journals, and is a tristate regional federal depository for U.S. and Canadian government documents. The M.B.A. program exposes students to state-of-the-art systems for management decision support. Both mainframe and microcomputer facilities on the Orono campus are excellent. The central computing facility for the entire University of Maine system is located on the Orono campus. Centrally located public-access microcomputer clusters are available in the library and the Student Union. The Business School also supports two labs of networked 486 and Pentium-class microcomputers. Students have access to an extensive software library as well as full access to the Internet and Web, the library, and the mainframe.

Financial Aid

M.B.A. students are eligible for trustee tuition scholarships, international tuition waivers, and graduate assistantships; these are highly competitive and awarded on a University-wide basis. Information about loans and work-study positions can be obtained by contacting the Student Aid Office, Wingate Hall. The Free Application for Federal Student Aid (FAFSA) should be filed no later than March 1.

Cost of Study

Tuition in 1997–98 for state residents was $564 per course. Tuition for nonresidents was $1593 per course. These figures do not include the cost of books, supplies, or health and activity fees.

Living and Housing Costs

The University has a graduate dormitory for single students. A limited number of University apartments for married students are also available. Inquiries about these should be directed to Campus Living. Off-campus rental housing and other living expenses vary widely.

Student Group

Maine M.B.A. students come from a wide variety of backgrounds. More than 50 percent of the current class had undergraduate preparation in fields other than business administration. The average age of students is 28. Women comprise 30 percent of the enrollment. Students enter from all regions of the United States and from many countries. The total University enrollment is more than 9,000 students; more than 2,000 are graduate students.

Location

The Business School is located on the main campus of the University of Maine in Orono, an attractive town with a population of about 10,000. The extensive campus of more than 1,100 acres is about a mile from the Orono business section and approximately 8 miles from Bangor, Maine's third-largest city. M.B.A. students benefit from the advantages of both rural and urban environments. Located just a 1- to 2-hour drive from Mount Katahdin, state parks, ski slopes, and the Maine coast, the University is a 4-hour drive from Boston on Interstate 95. Bangor International Airport provides service to many major U.S. and international cities.

The Maine Center for the Arts provides cultural focus for the University campus, the communities of the region, and all the citizens of Maine. Music, dance, and theater performances, in addition to lectures given by distinguished speakers, are presented in the 1,628-seat Hutchins Concert Hall. The center also includes the Hudson Museum and Palmer Gallery.

The University

Founded in 1865, the University opened in 1868 as the land-grant university of the state of Maine. Today, the Orono campus is the site of a dynamic modern university, encompassing five colleges, various schools and academic programs, and a graduate school. Both the undergraduate and graduate programs in business administration are accredited by AACSB–The International Association for Management Education.

Applying

All applicants must hold a baccalaureate degree from a regionally accredited college or university. Consideration is given to an applicant's official transcript(s), Graduate Management Admission Test scores, three letters of recommendation, work experience, and potential for leadership in business. Applicants whose native language is not English must submit a minimum TOEFL score of 550. Applications should be submitted to the Graduate School, 2 Winslow Hall, six weeks prior to the start of the desired semester of enrollment. There is a $50 nonrefundable application fee. Students who are applying for financial aid should file the FAFSA no later than March 1.

Correspondence and Information

For program information:
Director of the Graduate Program
The Maine Business School
5723 Donald P. Corbett Business Building
University of Maine
Orono, Maine 04469-5723
Telephone: 207-581-1973
E-mail: mba@maine.maine.edu
WWW: http://www.maine.edu/~gibson/umocba.html

For application forms and catalogs:
Graduate School
2 Winslow Hall
University of Maine
Orono, Maine 04469-0163
Telephone: 207-581-3218
Fax: 207-581-3232
E-mail: graduate@maine.maine.edu

University of Maine

THE FACULTY AND THEIR RESEARCH

Darlene Bay, Assistant Professor of Accounting; Ph.D., Washington State, 1997. Accounting and business ethics, ethics education, accounting education, small business management and accounting.

Richard H. Borgman, Assistant Professor of Finance; Ph.D., Florida, 1994. Asset securitization and banking, security valuation, asset allocation and portfolio concentration, developing financial markets in Eastern Europe.

Steven C. Colburn, Associate Professor of Accounting; Ph.D., Georgia, 1989. Taxation of individuals, corporations, trusts, and estates, with emphasis on tax planning.

Harold Z. Daniel, Assistant Professor of Marketing; Ph.D., Connecticut, 1997. Organizational buying behavior and strategic acquisition, collaborative research and development, strategic management of technology, diffusion of innovations, customer satisfaction.

John Kingston Ford, Salgo Professor of Business Administration, Professor of Finance, and Director of the M.B.A. Program; D.B.A., Harvard, 1977. Diversification of bond and stock portfolios.

Virginia R. Gibson, Associate Professor of Management Information Systems and Dean; Ph.D., SUNY at Binghamton, 1986. Information systems for management decision support, business climate.

Carol B. Gilmore, Professor of Management; Ph.D., Massachusetts, 1979. Labor law, labor arbitration, public sector collective bargaining, personnel management, employee rights, employee relations law.

Diana R. Lawson, Associate Professor of Marketing; Ph.D., Kent State, 1993. International business and marketing strategy, international business education, economic integration, social responsibility of firms, wood products marketing.

Ivan M. Manev, Assistant Professor of Management; Ph.D., Boston College, 1997. Management of the multinational corporation, formation of strategy and competitive advantage in social networks, organizational change in post-Communist transition societies.

Kim K. R. McKeage, Assistant Professor of Marketing; Ph.D., Massachusetts, 1996. Retailing, customer service quality, relationship marketing, internal marketing, socially responsible marketing, marketing education.

Patrick R. McMullen, Assistant Professor of Management; Ph.D., Oregon, 1995. Assembly line design, computer simulation, applied optimization, production scheduling, Just-In-Time systems.

Judith G. Oakley, Assistant Professor of Management; Ph.D., Syracuse, 1995. Strategic alliances and partnerships, organizational change, strategic planning, managerial issues in virtual corporations, comparative analysis of Canadian and American businesses.

Robert A. Strong, Professor of Finance; Ph.D., Penn State, 1983. Divided growth rate implied in common stock beta, asset allocation and purchasing power risk, bond portfolio duration.

Gloria Vollmers, Associate Professor of Accounting; Ph.D., Texas at Dallas, 1993. History of accounting, ethics in accounting and business, business history, topics in practical taxation.

The Donald P. Corbett Business Building was completed in 1993 and provides state-of-the-art computing and instructional facilities that are unique in Maine and among the best in the nation.

UNIVERSITY OF MARYLAND, COLLEGE PARK

Robert H. Smith School of Business

Programs of Study

The Robert H. Smith School of Business has put together an exceptional combination of resources that provides students with an incomparable educational value. Three of the many strengths of the Robert H. Smith School of Business are its top-quality and cutting-edge programs, a location that is minutes from Washington, D.C., and Baltimore, and the fact that the costs of the programs are about half the cost of many other top business programs. Accredited by AACSB–The International Association for Management Education and a full member of the Graduate Management Admissions Council, the Robert H. Smith School of Business is a leader in the field of graduate management education.

The Master of Business Administration (M.B.A.) program has a fully integrated experience-based curriculum designed to create the type of graduate that business has long demanded. The first half of the curriculum is spent gaining the fundamental skills and judgment necessary to succeed in a contemporary management team. Learning Modules (LMs) and course work ensure that new skills are applied in and out of the classroom.

LMs are intensive experience-based courses that focus on specific topics such as interaction with the federal government in Washington, D.C.; an international business simulation; and leadership and the management of diversity. These courses provide the student with experience in areas often ignored by other programs.

The second year allows the student to specialize in a particular area of business and to participate in a group field project. Group field projects assign teams of students to work as consultants to an American organization for a semester. The teams address specific concerns within the organization and make recommendations regarding those concerns to the management staff of the client organization. This program is required of all second-year full-time students.

The Master of Science (M.S.) program requires a strong quantitative background. There are several areas of concentration available: information systems, operations research, statistics, logistics, transportation, and finance. The M.S. program can be completed in two to five semesters, depending on undergraduate preparation.

The doctoral (Ph.D.) program is designed to develop outstanding research scholars and teachers in the management-related disciplines. Specializations include accounting, finance, human resource management and labor relations, information systems, management science and statistics, management strategy and policy, marketing, organizational behavior, and transportation and logistics.

Research Facilities

Classified as a Research I facility (its highest ranking) by the Carnegie Foundation, the research facilities at the University of Maryland are among the best in the world. With the addition of the national archives facility, Maryland offers access to one of the world's most complete collections of research material right in College Park. The University proper offers an outstanding library collection of almost two million volumes, state-of-the-art laboratories, a network of campus research centers, and excellent microcomputing and mainframe computing facilities. Beyond the facilities at College Park, students have access, within minutes, to other world-class research facilities at sites such as the Library of Congress, the Smithsonian Institution, the Federal Reserve, and the National Libraries of Medicine and Agriculture, to name just a few.

Financial Aid

A limited amount of financial support is available in the form of teaching and graduate assistantships, fellowships, and scholarship monies. Most financial aid is awarded on a competitive basis.

Cost of Study

The low cost of the University of Maryland is a benefit to both in-state and out-of-state students. For the 1998–99 academic year, full-time tuition is $9,818 for in-state residents and $14,100 for out-of-state residents. Students may qualify for in-state status in the second year of study.

Living and Housing Costs

Expenses in the Washington, D.C., area are comparable to other metropolitan areas in the United States. Many housing choices are available for graduate students, who may live either on or off campus. Information about off-campus housing is available through the Office of Commuter Affairs.

Student Group

The graduate student population of the M.B.A. program consists of about 430 full-time M.B.A. students, 420 part-time M.B.A. students, 35 M.S. students, and 100 Ph.D. students. Of the incoming 1997 M.B.A. class, 39 percent were international students, 18 percent were members of minority groups, and about 30 percent were women.

Location

Nine miles from downtown Washington, D.C., the University of Maryland at College Park is located on a beautiful 1,300-acre campus. This location provides students with the benefits of living in a suburban setting while maintaining access to the cultural and employment advantages of the cities of Washington, D.C., and Baltimore. Not only is College Park around a national and global focal point, but Washington, D.C., has developed into a leading cultural center as well. An abundance of theaters, concert halls, art galleries, museums, sport facilities, and embassies are a short 15-minute ride from campus.

The University

The University of Maryland, College Park is the flagship institution of the University of Maryland system. The enrollment of approximately 34,000 students, of whom about 9,000 are graduate students, supports nearly 100 doctoral and master's programs. The University is a member of the prestigious 58-member Association of American Universities. The University of Maryland is further recognized as having more than a dozen programs rated among the ten best at public universities in the United States by the National Academy of Sciences and other prestigious organizations.

Applying

The decision to admit an applicant is based on a thorough evaluation of the candidate's potential for completing the program, the ability of the candidate to add to the perspective of the class, and the School's ability to accommodate a limited number of students. Admission to the master's programs is for fall only, and admission to the Ph.D. programs are for both fall and spring. Taken into consideration are the applicant's past academic achievement, test scores on the Graduate Management Admission Test (GMAT), work experience, essay statements, recommendation letters, and the candidate's fit to the program.

Correspondence and Information

For the master's programs:

Director of M.B.A./M.S. Admission
2308 Van Munching Hall
University of Maryland
College Park, Maryland 20742

Telephone: 301-405-2278
Fax: 301-314-9862
E-mail: mba_info@rhsmith.umd.edu
World Wide Web: http://www.rhsmith.umd.edu

For the doctoral program:

Director of Doctoral Studies
College of Business and Management
University of Maryland
College Park, Maryland 20742

Telephone: 301-405-2214
Fax: 301-314-9157

University of Maryland, College Park

CHAIRPERSONS AND DEPARTMENT AREAS OF RESEARCH

Accounting: Dr. James Bedingfield, Chair
Department research: Management accounting, accounting for regulated industries, government contract accounting, capital budgeting, decision support systems, financial accounting, accounting information systems, tax, auditing, accounting ethics.

Decision Information Technology: Dr. Michael Ball and Dr. Arjang Assad, Co-chairs.
Department research: Operations and quality management, network and combinatorial optimization, statistical quality control, mathematical programming, telecommunications, simulation, queuing theory, production/inventory control, neural networks, transportation science, end-user computing, information systems analysis and design, knowledge-based systems, expert systems, production management systems, parallel computing, database systems.

Finance: Dr. Lemma Senbet, Chair
Department research: Corporate finance, financial institutions, investments, futures and options contracts, investment analysis, portfolio management, capital asset pricing theory, international finance, portfolio analysis, capital market theory, commercial banking, financial theory, agency theory.

Logistics, Business, and Public Policy: Dr. Curtis Grim, Chair
Department research: Deregulation, international aviation, airline pricing and competition, carrier management, government policies toward business, international business regulation, global management strategies, international trade policies, international joint ventures, public utility pricing.

Management and Organization: Dr. Susan Taylor, Chair
Department research: Performance appraisal and compensation design, management by objectives systems, executive leadership, strategy implementation, labor relations, goal setting, employee motivation, organizational staffing, teamwork, organizational life cycles, competitive strategy.

Marketing: Dr. Richard Durand, Chair
Department research: New product development, marketing strategy, international marketing, business-to-business marketing, consumer behavior, advertising.

UNIVERSITY OF MARYLAND UNIVERSITY COLLEGE

Graduate School of Management & Technology

Programs of Study

Bringing together expertise in technology, international business, and management, the Graduate School of Management & Technology at University of Maryland University College (UMUC) offers eight 36-semester-hour degree programs with twenty-two specialty tracks and three executive programs. These programs include the Master of International Management (M.I.M.), with tracks in international commerce, international finance, and international marketing (this degree is also offered in an executive format); the Master of Science in Computer Systems Management (M.S.C.S.M.), with tracks in applied computer systems, database systems and security, information resources management, and software development management (this degree is also offered in an executive format); the Master of Science in Engineering Management (M.S.Eng.M.), with tracks in bioengineering management, environmental engineering management, manufacturing engineering management, systems engineering management, and traditional engineering management (this degree is offered jointly with University of Maryland Baltimore County); the Master of Science in Environmental Management (M.S.Env.M.); the Master of Science in Management (M.S.M.), with tracks in applied management, financial management, health-care administration, human resource management, management information systems, marketing, not-for-profit management, and procurement and contract management (an executive version of this degree allows students to attend classes as a cohort on Friday evenings and Saturdays and complete their program in eighteen months); the Master of Software Engineering (M.Sw.E.), which is offered jointly with the University of Maryland College Park (UMCP) Department of Computer, Math, and Physical Sciences; the Master of Science in Technology Management (M.S.T.M.), with tracks in biotechnology management and technology systems management (this degree is also offered in an executive format); and the Master of Science in Telecommunications Management (M.S.T.M.)(this degree is also offered in an executive format).

Among the Graduate School's many strengths are its impressive faculty members, who bring a wealth of professional and academic experience to the teaching/learning process; professionally developed syllabi that ensure consistency and quality across classes; an emphasis on effective communication and leadership skills as the keystones of effective organizational management; and a curriculum that blends theory with practice to ensure that students know how to apply what they have learned.

The Graduate School offers courses around the greater Washington, D.C., and Baltimore area while also serving students at a distance via the World Wide Web. The Graduate School offers four degree programs at a distance—the Master of International Management (M.I.M.) (three tracks), the Master of Science in Management (M.S.M.) (eight tracks), the Master of Science in Computer Systems Management (M.S.C.S.M.) (information resource management track), and the Master of Science in Technology Management (M.S.T.M.) (nontrack option). More information about these degree programs may be found on the Web site listed below.

Research Facilities

The Graduate School manages the Institute for Environmental Management and the Institute for Global Management, both of which help ensure a transfer of knowledge to organizations and communities represented by students. Four fully equipped computer laboratories serve students around the Washington region. Graduate students have borrowing privileges at all University System of Maryland (USM) libraries, including Morgan State University and St. Mary's College of Maryland. The USM online catalog, VICTOR, provides access to USM library resources and includes Business Index and ASAP, Company Profiles, Dialog Files, National Newspaper Index, Expanded Academic Index, and UNCOVER. Information about library services may be obtained at library@info.umuc.edu or http://www.umuc.edu/library or by calling 301-985-7209. In addition, students have easy access to a wide array of institutions in the greater Washington-Baltimore region, including the Library of Congress and the National Archives.

Financial Aid

Since approximately 92 percent of the Graduate School's students are employed, the primary source of financial aid is in the form of student loans for qualified applicants. Limited scholarship monies are available for students with strong academic records and for those meeting donor criteria.

Cost of Study

Tuition for regular-format degree programs in summer and fall 1998 and spring 1999 is $277 per semester hour for Maryland residents and $367 per semester hour for nonresidents. Tuition for the software engineering program is $385 per semester hour for core courses. For Maryland residents, the cost for UMUC elective courses is $277 per semester hour and for UMCP elective courses is $272 per semester hour. Nonresidents pay $367 per semester hour for UMUC elective courses and $400 for UMCP elective courses. Executive program tuitions are $4950 (9 semester hours) for the Executive Master of General Administration, $5900 (7.2 semester hours) for the Executive Master of International Management, and $4950 (9 semester hours) for the Executive Master of Science in Technology Management.

Living and Housing Costs

UMUC provides housing information for international students but does not directly provide housing facilities. Students can obtain this information by contacting the University at the address below.

Student Group

The Graduate School currently enrolls about 4,000 students each fall and spring semester, with a slightly smaller enrollment in the eight-week compressed summer semester. A richly diverse and mature student body (the average age is 36, 48 percent are women, and 33.8 percent represent minority groups) helps create a stimulating and supportive learning environment for working professionals. An active alumni association provides support and information for students and graduates.

Student Outcomes

The majority of enrolled students are already fully employed upon entrance.

Location

The administrative offices of UMUC are located just inside the Washington Beltway in College Park, Maryland, about 8 miles from downtown Washington and 25 miles from downtown Baltimore. UMUC offers courses to students around the globe via the World Wide Web as well as in the classroom. Courses are offered at College Park and at thirteen other locations around the region; they include Baltimore, Washington, and Annapolis.

The University

UMUC is one of the eleven degree-granting institutions of the University System of Maryland. The principal mission of UMUC is to serve adult, part-time students. UMUC is accredited by the Commission on Higher Education of the Middle States Association of Colleges and Schools.

Applying

Applications are received and admission decisions are made year-round. A $50 nonrefundable application fee is due at the time of application. The specific requirements for admission to each degree program may be found in the *1998/99 Catalog*. The only program that requires a GRE or GMAT score is the Master of Science in Engineering Management degree program. Details are available with the application materials. Internationally educated applicants seeking a Form I-20 must contact the Office of Graduate Admissions and Advising at 301-985-7155 (telephone) or gradinfo@nova.umuc.edu (e-mail) to arrange for individualized admissions assistance. For further information, students may contact the address below.

Correspondence and Information

Office of Graduate Admissions and Advising
Graduate School of Management & Technology
University of Maryland University College
University Boulevard at Adelphi Road
College Park, Maryland 20741-0869

Telephone: 301-985-4617
Fax: 301-985-4611
E-mail: gradschool@nova.umuc.edu
World Wide Web: http://www.umuc.edu

University of Maryland University College

THE FACULTY AND THEIR RESEARCH

Twenty-nine of the Graduate School's more than 250 faculty members work full-time for the University as academic administrators with teaching, program design and management, faculty supervision, and advising responsibilities.

John O. Aje, Director, Technology Management and Engineering Programs; D.Sc., George Washington, 1988.
Nicholas H. Allen, Dean, Graduate Studies; D.P.A., George Washington, 1986.
Glenda J. Barrett, Human Resource Management; Ph.D., George Washington, 1993.
Diane Bartoo, Health Care Administration; Ph.D., Southern Mississippi, 1985.
Robert G. Beauchamp, Environmental and Waste Management; Ph.D., Maryland College Park, 1988.
Alan D. Carswell, Management Information Systems; M.B.A., Harvard, 1982; Ph.D. candidate.
Bernard Anthony Carver, Applied Computer Systems; Ph.D., Maryland College Park, 1993.
David J. Cohen, Telecommunication Studies; Ph.D., Penn State, 1971.
Kathleen F. Edwards, Health Care Administration; Ph.D., Catholic University, 1981.
Michael Evanchik, Financial Management; Ph.D., Washington (Seattle), 1989.
Ted Field, Not-for-Profit Management; Ph.D., Cornell, 1988.
Emmett L. Fleming, Procurement and Contract Management; J.D., Maryland, Baltimore, 1976; Ph.D., Catholic University, 1977.
Michael S. Frank, Applied Management; Ph.D., Maryland College Park, 1981.
James P. Gelatt, General Management; Ph.D., USC, 1979.
Christina Hannah, Associate Dean, Academic Affairs; Ph.D., Carleton (Ottawa), 1989.
Robert Jerome, Director, Worldwide Programs; Ph.D., Geneva (Switzerland), 1981.
Joseph Kasser, Software Development Management, Database Systems and Security; D.Sc., George Washington, 1997.
Paul F. G. Keller, Computer Systems Management; Ph.D., Southern Illinois at Carbondale, 1977.
Judith B. Kirkhorn, Associate Dean, Graduate Outreach and Executive Management Programs; Ph.D., Wisconsin–Milwaukee, 1977.
Clarence J. Mann, Director, International Programs; LL.B., Yale, 1963; Dr.jur., Bonn (Germany), 1967.
Theresa Marron-Grodsky, Marketing; Ph.D., Maryland College Park, 1985.
Salvatore J. Monaco, Director, Executive Programs; Ph.D., Rensselaer, 1974.
Richard D. Neidig, Director, General Management Programs; Ph.D., Penn State, 1976.
Alfred S. Raider, International Management; J.D., Maryland, Baltimore, 1978; LL.M., Georgetown, 1987.
John M. Richardson, Director, Telecommunications Management; Ph.D., Harvard, 1951.
Claudine SchWeber, Director, Distance Learning and Instructional Technology; Ph.D., SUNY at Buffalo, 1978.
Edward Shafer, Director, Financial Management; D.B.A., George Washington, 1980.
Joyce T. Shirazi, Engineering Management; Ph.D., George Washington, 1994.
Stephen V. Versace, Executive Management Programs; Ph.D., Maryland College Park, 1978.

UNIVERSITY OF MEMPHIS

Fogelman College of Business and Economics

Programs of Study

The Fogelman College of Business and Economics offers AACSB–accredited programs leading to the Master of Business Administration (M.B.A.); the Master of Science (M.S.) in accounting with concentrations in accounting, accounting systems, and taxation; the Master of Science (M.S.) in business administration with concentrations in finance, management, management information systems, marketing, and real estate development; and the Master of Arts (M.A.) in economics. A joint M.B.A./J.D. program is offered in conjunction with the School of Law. An Executive M.B.A. program meets weekly on alternate Fridays and Saturdays over a twenty-two month period and allows successful managers to obtain the M.B.A. degree without interrupting their careers. An International M.B.A. program incorporates language, cultural, and geographic area studies with business instruction in a full-time twenty-two month program and offers rigorous, intensive, and challenging international business education to qualified students. The I.M.B.A. features a semester-long, University-arranged internship in the country of the student's language track, personalized faculty involvement, and scholarships or assistantships for superior applicants. The Ph.D. in business administration is offered with concentrations in accounting, economics, finance, management, management information systems and decision sciences, and marketing.

The M.B.A. program offers a flexible design to serve students who have a bachelor's degree in the arts and sciences, engineering, law, or other areas of study as well as business. M.B.A. areas of concentration include accounting, economics, finance, insurance, management, management information systems, management science, marketing, and real estate. A minimum of 33 credit hours of course work is required; students with a nonbusiness undergraduate background are required to complete certain foundation courses in addition to the minimum. The M.S. and M.A. programs have similar requirements. The Executive M.B.A. and International M.B.A. have prescribed sequences of courses over the twenty-two month period. The Ph.D. program normally requires at least three to four years of intensive study and research beyond the master's level. It is composed of a research core (12 credit hours), a concentration and a minor (30 credit hours), and a dissertation (18 credit hours).

Research Facilities

Fogelman College has up-to-date business research facilities. Several computer laboratories are devoted to microcomputer technology, and some classrooms have integrated video-computer facilities, enabling students and faculty members to develop state-of-the-art case presentations. The College is known for its information systems capability and its market research laboratory.

Financial Aid

A number of graduate research and teaching assistantships are available each year. These assistantships, which provide a monthly stipend, are granted on the basis of GMAT scores, GPA, and personal interviews. All recipients of assistantships are granted in-state tuition status. A student must be fully admitted to the M.B.A., M.S., or M.A. program by mid-July or to the I.M.B.A. or Ph.D. program by April to be considered for an assistantship. Other sources of aid may be coordinated through the Office of Student Aid at the University.

Cost of Study

The 1998–99 estimated tuition for students who are Tennessee residents is $131 per credit hour; tuition for out-of-state students is $321 per credit hour. All students must pay an activities fee of $34 per semester.

Living and Housing Costs

Rates for residence halls on campus in 1998–99 range from approximately $770 to $1435 per semester. The University has 126 apartments for student families on the South Campus, with some units constructed specifically for students with disabilities. Rates for these apartments range from $350 to $500 per month. Students are responsible for the cost of utilities. Numerous housing facilities are also available off campus.

Student Group

Students enter the Fogelman College graduate programs with a variety of undergraduate degrees. Nearly 200 students entered the M.B.A. or M.S. program in 1997–98. Their mean undergraduate GPA was 3.2, and their mean GMAT score was 530. The total number of master's students in the Fogelman College is approximately 700, and there are more than 100 students working toward the Ph.D. degree.

Location

With a population of a million, Memphis is one of the South's largest and most attractive cities. As a primary medical, communication, and transportation center, Memphis offers a full range of research opportunities and cultural experiences. The city, known for its musical heritage, has many fine restaurants, museums, and theaters. Built on a bluff that towers over the mighty Mississippi River, Memphis is devoted to preserving its heritage while it vigorously builds its future.

The College

As one of only twenty-six Centers of International Business Education and Research in the country, the College offers a strong emphasis on developing managers for the complex requirements of global business competition. The Fogelman College of Business and Economics is the largest of the colleges in the University, with an enrollment of about 2,800 and modern facilities on the northwest corner of the campus. The research faculty of more than 100 professors works closely with graduate students on teaching and research activities.

Applying

Applications may be obtained from the Office of Graduate Admissions or from the address below. Completed forms must be returned with a $5 nonrefundable application fee ($30 for international applicants). Application deadlines are August 1 for the fall semester, December 1 for the spring semester, and May 1 for the summer term. The International M.B.A. and Executive M.B.A. programs accept students only for fall semester, and the Ph.D. program generally accepts students for the fall semester. Applicants for these programs are encouraged to submit their materials in the preceding spring to ensure a place in the class. GMAT scores must be submitted for the M.B.A., M.S., and Ph.D. programs; GRE scores are acceptable only for the M.A. program in economics. All applicants who will be attending the University of Memphis on a student visa must supply a minimum score of 550 on the Test of English as a Foreign Language (TOEFL). All test scores must be sent directly from the testing agency to the University of Memphis, Office of Graduate Admissions, 216 Administration Building, Memphis, TN 38152.

Correspondence and Information

For further information on graduate business programs, interested students should write or call:

Office of Graduate Programs
Fogelman College of Business and Economics
Room 101
University of Memphis
Memphis, Tennessee 38152

Telephone: 901-678-3721
E-mail: fcbegp@cc.memphis.edu

University of Memphis

THE FACULTY

School of Accountancy

Surendra P. Agrawal, Ph.D., Florida. Larry DuCharme, Ph.D., Washington (Seattle). Ronald H. Eaton, Ph.D., Arkansas. Kenneth R. Lambert, Ph.D., Arkansas. Craig Langstraat, J.D., Arizona State. James Lukawitz, Ph.D., Florida State. John M. Malloy, Ph.D., LSU. Peter L. McMickle, Ph.D., Alabama. George S. Minmier, Ph.D., Arkansas. Patricia Myers, Ph.D., Arizona. J. David Spiceland, Ph.D., Arkansas. Kay Zekany, Ph.D., South Carolina.

Department of Decision Sciences

Mohammad Amini, Ph.D., SMU. Charles J. Campbell, Ph.D., Texas. Satish Mehra, Ph.D., Georgia. Ravinder Nath, Ph.D., Texas Tech. Ernest L. Nichols, Ph.D., Michigan State. Donna Retzlaff-Roberts, Ph.D., Cincinnati. Michael L. Vineyard, Ph.D., Cincinnati.

Department of Business Economics

Pinaki Bose, Ph.D., SUNY at Buffalo. Cyril Chang, Ph.D., Virginia. David H. Ciscel, Ph.D., Houston. Coldwell Daniel, Ph.D., Virginia. Thomas Depperschmidt, Ph.D., Texas. Richard Evans, Ph.D., Missouri. K. K. Fung, Ph.D., Harvard. John Gnuschke, Ph.D., Missouri. Michael Gootzeit, Ph.D., Purdue. Julia H. Heath, Ph.D., South Carolina. David Kemme, Ph.D., Ohio State. Albert A. Okunade, Ph.D., Arkansas. V. Lane Rawlins, Ph.D., Berkeley. John Joseph Reid, Ph.D., Virginia. Rose Rubin, Ph.D., Kansas State. William T. Smith, Ph.D., Virginia. Shelley White-Means, Ph.D., Northwestern.

Department of Finance

M. E. Bond, Ph.D., Iowa. Quentin C. Chu, Ph.D., Illinois. Kee H. Chung, Ph.D., Cincinnati. Thomas H. McInish, Ph.D., Pittsburgh. Stephen W. Pruitt, Ph.D., Florida State. C. S. Pyun, Ph.D., Georgia. L. S. Scruggs, Ph.D., Vanderbilt. Floyd N. Tyler, Ph.D., Florida State. Robert A. Wood, Ph.D., Pittsburgh.

Department of Insurance, Real Estate and Business Legal Studies

Sherman M. Franklin, J.D., Memphis. Gaylon E. Greer, Ph.D., Colorado. Phillip T. Kolbe, Ph.D., Arizona. Nancy Hisey Kratzke, J.D., Memphis. Michael J. McNamara, Ph.D., Nebraska. Larry Moore, J.D., Washington (St. Louis). Mars A. Pertl, Ph.D., Iowa. Irvin Tankersley, J.D., Tulane.

Department of Management

Rabi S. Bhagat, Ph.D., Illinois. Lillian H. Chaney, Ed.D., Tennessee, Knoxville. V. Carol Danehower, D.B.A., Kentucky. Barbara D. Davis, Ed.D., Memphis. Peter S. Davis, Ph.D., South Carolina. Irene M. Duhaime, Ph.D., Pittsburgh. John B. Gilmore, Ph.D., Oklahoma. Coy A. Jones, Ph.D., Oklahoma. Banwari Kedia, Ph.D., Case Western Reserve. Jeffrey Krug, Ph.D., Indiana. Thomas R. Miller, Ph.D., Ohio State. Binford H. Peeples, Ed.D., Kentucky. Donna M. Randall, Ph.D., Washington State. Robert W. Renn, Ph.D., Georgia State. Robert R. Taylor, Ph.D., LSU. Howard S. Tu, Ph.D., Massachusetts. Peter Wright, Ph.D., LSU.

Department of Management Information Systems

Lloyd D. Brooks, Ed.D., Tennessee. Judith Brown, M.S., Tennessee. Mark N. Frolick, Ph.D., Georgia. Mark L. Gillenson, Ph.D., Ohio State. Wade M. Jackson, Ph.D., Texas A&M. Brian S. Janz, Ph.D., Minnesota. Prashant Palvia, Ph.D., Minnesota. Judith C. Simon, Ed.D., Oklahoma State. James C. Wetherbe, Ph.D., Texas Tech. Steven M. Zeltmann, Ph.D., Florida State.

Department of Marketing

Emin Babakus, Ph.D., Alabama. Robert L. Berl, Ph.D., Georgia State. Gregory W. Boller, Ph.D., Penn State. Alan J. Bush, Ph.D., LSU. Robert P. Bush, Ph.D., LSU. T. Bettina Cornwell, Ph.D., Texas. O. C. Ferrell, Ph.D., LSU. John Pepin, Ph.D., Mississippi. James P. Rakowski, Ph.D., Columbia. Dan L. Sherrell, Ph.D., South Carolina. R. Neil Southern, Ph.D., Arizona State. Peter K. Tat, D.B.A., Mississippi State.

UNIVERSITY OF MIAMI

School of Business Administration

Programs of Study

The University of Miami School of Business Administration offers two tracks leading to the Master of Business Administration degree. Track I (36 credits) is the traditional program for the student who holds an undergraduate degree in business from an institution accredited by AACSB–The International Association for Management Education, enabling the student to complete all requirements for graduation in approximately one year. A student who did not major in business or who graduated from a foreign or other institution not accredited by AACSB–The International Association for Management Education follows Track II (58 credits), which may be completed in two years or less. Each track includes 24 elective credits. Students may choose from a list of 28 areas of specialization in accounting, computer information systems, economics, finance, international business, legal implications, management, management science, marketing, and political science.

The School offers the MIBS Program, which awards a Master in Business Administration (M.B.A.) degree with a certificate in international business. The program features University-arranged internships with firms operating in the international business arena, second language training, personalized faculty and corporate involvement, and fellowships for superior applicants. The School also offers the Master of Professional Accounting, M.S. in computer information systems, M.S. in operations research/statistics, M.S. in taxation, M.A. in economics, Master of Public Administration, Ph.D. in business administration, and Ph.D. in economics. Executives may earn an M.B.A. degree by attending Saturday classes in one the following programs: general management, health administration, international business, working professional, or Master of Business Administration/Master of Science in Industrial Engineering (M.B.A./M.S.I.E.). Off-campus M.B.A. programs are offered to residents of the Bahamas and at selected corporate locations.

The goal of the School is to provide a sound background in the functional areas of business. To this end, a variety of teaching methods are used: lecture, discussion, case method, and team projects. Classes are small to encourage exchange between teacher and student and among students.

Research Facilities

The School of Business Administration, which has a $3-million library endowment, and the University libraries, which can accommodate special requests from students conducting research, have combined holdings of 2.1 million volumes, 20,353 periodicals, and 3.1 million microforms (excluding government publications). The Ungar Computer Center houses an IBM 9672-R42 and two VAX 3000s. In addition, seventy-five Dell 486DX workstations networked to a Compaq Pentium file server are available in the School of Business Administration for student use.

Financial Aid

A limited number of graduate assistantships, available for outstanding students, usually include both a tuition scholarship and a monthly stipend. Graduate students are eligible to apply for student loans and work-study assistance through the University's Office of Financial Assistance Services.

Cost of Study

Graduate tuition for the 1998–99 academic year is $815 per credit. This does not include the cost of books, supplies, or miscellaneous fees and is subject to change.

Living and Housing Costs

Full-time students may live on campus in University residence halls. On-campus housing fees ranged from $2100 to $2700 per semester in 1997–98, depending on the type of accommodation. Rents for private apartments, available close to the University, vary according to the size and location of the apartment.

Student Group

As of fall 1997, the School of Business Administration had an enrollment of approximately 1,140 graduate students. Students come to the School from all parts of the continental United States as well as countries in Latin America, the Caribbean, Europe, the Middle East, and the Far East.

Location

The University is located in Coral Gables, a beautiful residential area 10 miles from downtown Miami. One of the stations for the modern 21-mile Metrorail rapid transit system is situated on the edge of campus. More than 100 multinational corporations have their Latin American headquarters in Miami. The city of Miami is known as a hemispheric banking center as well as a center for travel and tourism. The metropolitan area has about 2 million people, an international flavor, and a wide range of cultural resources and activities.

The University and The School

The University consists of fourteen colleges and schools on four campuses and enrolls approximately 13,700 students at the graduate and undergraduate levels. The School of Business Administration complex is composed of the George W. Jenkins Building, the Elsa and William Stubblefield Classroom Building, the James McLamore Executive Education Center, the Sanford L. Ziff Placement Center, the Carlos and Rosa de la Cruz Study Center, and Storer Auditorium. Faculty members of the School have been recruited from top-ranking universities. The faculty's diversity of backgrounds brings many perspectives and teaching methods to the campus. The School of Business Administration is the only private school in south Florida that is accredited by AACSB–The International Association for Management Education at both the undergraduate and graduate levels. In addition, the undergraduate accounting program, the Master of Professional Accounting program, and the M.S. in taxation program are accredited under the special Accounting Accreditation Standards of AACSB–The International Association for Management Education. Programs in health administration are also accredited by ACEHSA. The Sanford L. Ziff Placement Center provides state-of-the-art placement services for all graduate business students. Two recruitment seasons—fall and spring—are held so that students may interview with major national, international, and local firms. In addition, a resume book is compiled and distributed to corporations.

Applying

Applicants must hold a baccalaureate degree from an accredited college or university. Each applicant's GPA is evaluated on the basis of the rigor of the undergraduate major and the general reputation of the institution attended. Submission of the GMAT score and an official transcript of all undergraduate work is required. International students whose native language is not English must also submit TOEFL scores; a minimum score of 550 is required for admission. All international applicants must provide proof of financial support.

Correspondence and Information

Director, Graduate Business Recruiting and Admissions
School of Business Administration
University of Miami
P.O. Box 248505
Coral Gables, Florida 33124-6524

Telephone: 305-284-2510
Fax: 305-284-1878
E-mail: gba@sba.miami.edu
World Wide Web: http://www.bus.miami.edu/grad

University of Miami

THE FACULTY

Accounting

Paul Munter, Professor and Chairman; D.B.A., Colorado, 1978. Elizabeth Dreike Almer, Assistant Professor; Ph.D., Arizona State, 1976; CPA. Frank Collins, Professor; Ph.D., Houston, 1974; CPA. Shirley Dennis-Escoffier, Associate Professor; Ph.D., Miami (Florida), 1981; CPA. Mark E. Friedman, Associate Professor; Ph.D., NYU, 1978; CPA. Oscar J. Holzmann, Associate Professor; Ph.D., Penn State, 1974. Lawrence C. Phillips, Professor and Director of the M.S. in Taxation Program; Ph.D., Ohio State, 1966; CPA. Olga Quintana, Associate Professor; D.B.A., George Washington, 1975; CPA. Thomas R. Robinson, Assistant Professor; Ph.D., Case Western Reserve, 1992; CPA. Avi Rushinek, Associate Professor; Ph.D., Texas at Austin, 1979. Kay W. Tatum, Associate Professor and Director of the Master of Professional Accounting Program; Ph.D., Texas Tech, 1986; CPA.

Business Law

Rene Sacasas, Associate Professor and Chairman; J.D., Emory, 1975. Anita Cava, Associate Professor; J.D., NYU, 1978. Larry A. DiMatteo, Assistant Professor; J.D., Cornell, 1982.

Computer Information Systems

Joel D. Stutz, Professor and Chairman; Ph.D., Texas at Austin, 1971. Robert T. Grauer, Associate Professor; Ph.D., Polytechnic of Brooklyn, 1972. Robert T. Plant, Associate Professor; Ph.D., Liverpool, 1987. Sara F. Rushinek, Professor; Ph.D., Texas at Austin, 1979. John F. Stewart, Associate Professor; Ph.D., Columbia, 1974.

Economics

Philip K. Robins, Professor and Chairman; Ph.D., Wisconsin–Madison, 1972. Kevin Carey, Assistant Professor; Ph.D., Princeton, 1995. Michael B. Connolly, Professor; Ph.D., Chicago, 1969. Louis De Alessi, Professor; Ph.D., UCLA, 1961. John Devereux, Associate Professor; Ph.D., Chicago, 1989. Raymond P. H. Fishe, Professor; Ph.D., Florida, 1979. James W. Foley, Associate Professor and Associate Dean; Ph.D., Michigan State, 1969. A. G. Holtmann Jr., Professor; Ph.D., Washington (St. Louis), 1963. Luis Locay, Associate Professor; Ph.D., Chicago, 1983. Karen Lombard, Assistant Professor; M.A., Chicago, 1989. Hollis F. Price Jr., Associate Professor and Director of the M.A. and Ph.D. in Economics Program; Ph.D., Colorado, 1972. Lanny E. Streeter, Associate Professor; Ph.D., Illinois at Urbana-Champaign, 1970. Alexander Taber, Professor; Ph.D., Chicago, 1964.

Finance

Raymond P. H. Fishe, Professor and Chairman; Ph.D., Florida, 1979. W. Brian Barrett, Associate Professor; Ph.D., Georgia Tech, 1983. Thor W. Bruce Jr., Associate Professor; Ph.D., Washington (St. Louis), 1971. Timothy Burch, Assistant Professor; Ph.D., Michigan, 1997. Tina M. Galloway, Assistant Professor; Ph.D., Purdue, 1993. Lawrence G. Goldberg, Professor; Ph.D., Chicago, 1972. Andrea J. Heuson, Associate Professor; Ph.D., Illinois at Urbana-Champaign, 1982. William F. Landsea, Associate Professor; Ph.D., Illinois at Urbana-Champaign, 1966. Manfred H. Ledford, Associate Professor; Ph.D., Kentucky, 1973. David C. Mauer, Professor; Ph.D., Purdue, 1986. Michael A. Robe, Assistant Professor; Ph.D., Carnegie Mellon, 1995. Ricardo Rodriguez, Assistant Professor; Ph.D., Texas at Austin, 1986. Adam Schwartz, Assistant Professor; Ph.D., Georgia, 1995. Tie Su, Assistant Professor; Ph.D., Missouri, 1995.

Management

Linda L. Neider, Professor and Chair; Ph.D., SUNY at Buffalo, 1979. Harold W. Berkman, Professor and Vice Dean; Ph.D., St. John's, 1971. John W. Bradford, Associate Professor; Ph.D., Columbia, 1986. Kenneth H. Doerr, Assistant Professor; Ph.D., Washington (Seattle), 1994. Donald R. Hudson, Associate Professor; Ph.D., Georgia State, 1974. Jeffrey L. Kerr, Associate Professor; Ph.D., Penn State, 1983. Duane Kujawa, Professor; Ph.D., Michigan, 1970. Carl E. B. McKenry Jr., Professor; LL.M., NYU, 1965. Gina J. Medsker, Assistant Professor; Ph.D., Purdue, 1993. Thomas A. Natiello, Professor; Ph.D., Michigan State, 1966. Rajnandini K. Pillai, Assistant Professor; Ph.D., SUNY at Buffalo, 1994. Terri A. Scandura, Associate Professor; Ph.D., Cincinnati, 1988. Chester A. Schrleshelm, Distinguished Professor; Ph.D., Ohio State, 1978. Maurice E. Schweitzer, Assistant Professor; Ph.D., Pennsylvania, 1993. Thomas W. Sloan, Assistant Professor; Ph.D. candidate, Berkeley. Harold Strauss, Professor; Ph.D., Geneva (Switzerland), 1952. Steven G. Ullmann, Professor and Vice Provost; Ph.D., Michigan, 1980. William B. Werther Jr., Samuel N. Friedland Chair Professor; Ph.D., Florida, 1971.

Management Science

Edward K. Baker, Professor and Chairman; D.B.A., Maryland, 1979. Ronny Aboudi, Assistant Professor and Director of the M.S. in Management Science Program; Ph.D., Cornell, 1986. Moshe F. Friedman, Professor; Ph.D., Hebrew (Jerusalem), 1973. Howard S. Gitlow, Professor; Ph.D., NYU, 1974. Malcolm Golden, Professor; Ph.D., Claremont, 1966. Anito Joseph, Assistant Professor, Ph.D., Maryland, 1993. Charles N. Kurucz, Associate Professor; Ph.D., SUNY at Buffalo, 1969. Joseph J. Moder, Professor Emeritus; Ph.D., Northwestern, 1950. Paul K. Sugrue, Professor and Dean; Ph.D., Massachusetts at Amherst, 1977. Earl L. Wiener, Professor; Ph.D., Ohio State, 1961.

Marketing

Michael Levy, Professor and Chairman; Ph.D., Ohio State, 1978. Dhruv Grewal, Associate Professor; Ph.D., Virginia Tech, 1989. Howard Marmorstein, Associate Professor; Ph.D., Florida, 1989. A. Parasuraman, James W. McLamore Chair in Marketing; D.B.A., Indiana, 1975. Dan Sarel, Associate Professor; D.B.A., Harvard, 1978. Arun Sharma, Assistant Professor; Ph.D., Illinois, 1988. Michal Strahilevitz, Assistant Professor; Ph.D., Berkeley. Walter Zinn, Associate Professor; Ph.D., Michigan State, 1986.

Political Science

Jonathan P. West, Professor and Chairman; Ph.D., Northwestern, 1969. June T. Dreyer, Professor; Ph.D., Harvard, 1973. Thomas A. Koelble, Associate Professor; Ph.D., California, San Diego, 1988. Michael E. Milakovich, Associate Professor; Ph.D., Indiana, 1972. James P. Monroe, Assistant Professor; Ph.D., UCLA, 1994. Stuart Strelchler, Instructor; J.D., Michigan, 1982. Annette Steinacker, Assistant Professor; Ph.D., Rochester, 1995. Nathan Teske, Assistant Professor; Ph.D., Berkeley, 1994.

UNIVERSITY OF MISSOURI–COLUMBIA

College of Business and Public Administration

Programs of Study

The College of Business and Public Administration (B&PA) offers fully accredited programs of study leading to the degrees of Doctor of Philosophy (Ph.D.) in business administration or accountancy, Master of Business Administration (M.B.A.), Master of Accountancy (M.Acc.), and Master of Public Administration (M.P.A.).

The Ph.D. programs in business administration and accountancy prepare graduates for careers as effective university researchers and teachers or for senior research positions in business or government. Business administration students may concentrate study in finance, management, or marketing. The Ph.D. programs are residential and full-time only, normally requiring four years beyond the master's degree.

The M.B.A. program is flexible and individualized, designed to prepare superior graduate students for managerial careers in corporations or public organizations or as entrepreneurs. Course work may vary from 33 to 55 semester hours, depending on previous college work. Up to 9 hours of course work outside the College may be included, or students may develop individualized specialties. Dual-degree programs exist with health administration, industrial engineering, and law.

The M.Acc. program is a flexible program for superior graduate students interested in becoming high-level accounting professionals. It is a broadly based program that allows students to develop specialized expertise in financial accounting and auditing, managerial accounting and information systems, and taxation. Dual majors in related areas such as economics, law, computer science, finance, or management are encouraged.

The M.P.A. program offers full academic preparation for administrative careers in local, state, and national governments and other public and not-for-profit organizations. This two-year program consists of 39 hours of graduate work. A summer internship provides field learning and experience in public administration. Up to 9 hours of specialized course work may be taken, allowing students to develop their own emphasis area.

Research Facilities

Ellis Library houses more than 1.5 million volumes and nearly 18,000 serial titles. Friendly, professional staff members are available to answer questions, help solve research problems, and support online and CD-ROM databases. Middlebush Hall, which houses B&PA, contains computer labs with networked PCs providing access to the mainframe, the Internet, and a variety of up-to-date software. Online databases include the BRIDGE System for real-time stockmarket data, LEXIS/NEXIS, Dow Jones News Retrieval, ABI-Inform, Compact Disclosure SEC and Worldscope, Extell, and Compustat PC+. The B&PA Research Center also provides computer support services including Compustat, Census, CRSP, FDIC, and Citibank files.

Financial Aid

A large number of assistantships are available to qualified students. Master's assistantships involve 10 hours of work per week at a rate of $1924 per semester and may include a waiver of educational fees. Scholarships that may waive out-of-state tuition charges are also available. Scholarships, grants, and loans are available through the MU Financial Aid Office. International students enrolled at MU can apply for a Curator's Grant-in-Aid. Assistantships for Ph.D. students involve approximately 20 hours of work per week. Doctoral funding, including assistantships and scholarships, ranges from $10,695 to $13,695 annually, waives the educational fees, and continues for up to four years.

Cost of Study

For the academic year 1998–99, graduate students pay in-state or out-of-state educational fees of $162.60 or $489.10 per credit hour, respectively. Other miscellaneous fees of approximately $300 per semester are also assessed.

Living and Housing Costs

In addition to excellent residence halls, MU maintains more than 300 unfurnished University apartments for student families and graduate students. Plentiful off-campus housing is also readily available. Housing costs are so reasonable that some MU students own their own homes. Estimated living expenses per year include $7000 for room and board and $2500 for books, supplies, and miscellaneous items.

Student Group

Of MU's more than 22,500 students, nearly 4,000 are graduate students. During 1997–98, B&PA enrolled 240 master's candidates and 36 Ph.D. candidates. Students admitted to B&PA's graduate programs are committed to and capable of academic and professional success. Programs are kept small; the average class size is 20. B&PA graduate students represent colleges and universities in many U.S. states and a host of international countries.

Student Outcomes

Employment opportunities have been excellent for recent B&PA graduates. M.Acc. and M.B.A. graduates typically accept employment with Big 6 accounting and consulting firms, with medium-size and large firms based in the Midwest, or in entrepreneurial ventures. M.P.A. graduates enter government positions at both the state and national levels. In the last ten years, Ph.D. graduates in business and accountancy have all entered teaching/research positions at a variety of regional and national universities.

Location

Columbia, located midway between St. Louis and Kansas City, is a warm, friendly, cosmopolitan, and safe college community with a population of more than 75,000. The city's growing economy and low unemployment rate offer job opportunities for student family members. Sidewalk restaurants, pubs, and coffee houses and the quaint downtown shopping district are within three blocks of the campus and help make the community a pleasant place to live.

The University and The College

The University of Missouri is the oldest state university west of the Mississippi River. With nearly 250 degree programs, MU is one of the most comprehensive universities in the nation and is categorized as a Research I university. MU is listed as one of the nation's "best buys in college education" by Edward Fiske, former education editor of the *New York Times*. The College of B&PA was among the first in the nation to have accredited business programs. The College's 21,000 alumni can be found contributing their expertise to organizations in every state and in a multitude of international countries.

Applying

Applicants for graduate degree programs in accountancy or business administration are required to submit a score from the Graduate Management Admission Test (GMAT). M.P.A. applicants must submit a score from the GMAT, GRE, or MAT. Application deadlines and requirements vary by degree program.

Correspondence and Information

Director of the 150-Hour Accountancy Program (M.Acc.) or Director of Ph.D. in Accountancy
312 Middlebush Hall, Box P
College of Business and Public Administration
University of Missouri
Columbia, Missouri 65211
Telephone: 573-882-4463
E-mail: accountancy@bpa.missouri.edu

Graduate Studies in Business
303D Middlebush Hall, Box P
College of Business and Public Administration
University of Missouri
Columbia, Missouri 65211
Telephone: 573-882-2750
E-mail: grad@bpa.missouri.edu

Director of Graduate Studies in Public Administration
315 Middlebush Hall, Box P
College of Business and Public Administration
University of Missouri
Columbia, Missouri 65211
Telephone: 573-882-3304
E-mail: publicadmin@bpa.missouri.edu

University of Missouri–Columbia

THE FACULTY

Everette E. Adam Jr., Professor of Management; D.B.A., Indiana, 1970.
Guy B. Adams, Professor and Chair of Public Administration; D.P.A., George Washington, 1977.
Christopher W. Anderson, Assistant Professor of Finance; Ph.D., Iowa, 1995.
Vairam Arunachalam, Associate Professor of Accountancy; Ph.D., Illinois, 1991.
T. J. Atwood, Assistant Professor of Accountancy; Ph.D., Illinois, 1995.
Peter H. Bloch, Professor of Marketing; Ph.D., Texas at Austin, 1981.
Allen C. Bluedorn, Associate Professor of Management; Ph.D., Iowa, 1976.
Charles J. Corrado, Associate Professor of Finance; Ph.D., SUNY at Albany, 1985; Ph.D., Arizona, 1988.
Michael A. Diamond, Professor of Public Administration; Ph.D., Maryland, 1981.
Raymond C. Dockweiler, Joseph A. Silvoso Director of the 150-Hour Accountancy Program; Ph.D., Illinois, 1969.
Thomas W. Dougherty, Professor of Management; Ph.D., Houston, 1981.
Ronald J. Ebert, Professor of Management; D.B.A., Indiana, 1969.
Kenneth R. Evans, Professor of Marketing and Associate Dean; Ph.D., Colorado, 1980.
Stephen P. Ferris, Professor and Chair of Finance; Ph.D., Pittsburgh, 1984.
John P. Forrester, Associate Professor of Public Administration; D.P.A., Georgia, 1988.
Jere R. Francis, Arthur Andersen & Co./Joseph A. Silvoso Distinguished Professor of Accountancy; Ph.D., University of New England (Australia), 1982.
Charles R. Franz, Associate Professor of Management; Ph.D., Nebraska, 1979.
Lori S. Franz, Professor of Management, Associate Dean, and Director of Graduate Studies in Business; Ph.D., Nebraska, 1980.
Srinath Gopalakrishna, Assistant Professor of Marketing; Ph.D., Purdue, 1988.
Daniel W. Greening, Associate Professor of Management; Ph.D., Penn State, 1991.
John S. Howe, Professor of Finance; Ph.D., Purdue, 1981.
Arthur G. Jago, Professor and Chair of Management; Ph.D., Yale, 1977.
Richard A. Johnson, Associate Professor of Management; Ph.D., Texas A&M, 1992.
Inder K. Khurana, Associate Professor of Accountancy and Baird, Kurtz, and Dobson Faculty Fellow; Ph.D., Arizona State, 1989.
Elaine G. Mauldin, Assistant Professor of Accountancy; Ph.D., Nebraska, 1997.
Thomas W. Miller Jr., Associate Professor of Finance; Ph.D., Washington (Seattle), 1992.
Douglas D. Moesel, Assistant Professor of Management; Ph.D., Texas A&M, 1996.
Loren A. Nikolai, Ernst & Young Professor of Accountancy; Ph.D., Minnesota, 1973.
James E. Parker, Price Waterhouse/Joseph A. Silvoso Distinguished Professor of Accountancy; Ph.D., Michigan State, 1969.
Richard H. Pettway, Missouri Bankers Chair Professor of Finance and Director of Financial Research Institute; Ph.D., Texas at Austin, 1965.
Jenice P. Prather, Associate Professor of Accountancy; Ph.D., Alabama, 1985.
Marsha L. Richins, Professor of Marketing; Ph.D., Texas at Austin, 1979.
Lisa K. Scheer, Associate Professor of Marketing; Ph.D., Northwestern, 1990.
James C. Stallman, Professor of Accountancy; Ph.D., Illinois, 1969.
Clifford P. Stephens, Assistant Professor of Finance; Ph.D., Arizona, 1996.
John D. Stowe, Professor of Finance; Ph.D., Houston, 1974.
Scott L. Summers, Assistant Professor of Accountancy; Ph.D., Texas A&M, 1993.
John T. Sweeney, Assistant Professor of Accountancy; Ph.D., Missouri, 1992.
Daniel B. Turban, Associate Professor of Management; Ph.D., Houston, 1989.
William B. Wagner, Professor of Marketing; Ph.D., Ohio State, 1967.
Bruce J. Walker, Professor of Marketing and Dean of College of Business and Public Administration; Ph.D., Colorado, 1971.
James A. Wall Jr., Professor of Management; Ph.D., North Carolina, 1972.
Sheilah S. Watson, Associate Professor of Public Administration and Director of Graduate Studies in Public Administration; Ph.D., Oklahoma, 1988.
David A. West, Professor of Finance; Ph.D., Arkansas, 1961.
Albert R. Wildt, Bailey K. Howard World Book Professor of Marketing and Director of the M.B.A. Program; Ph.D., Purdue, 1972.
Earl R. Wilson, KPMG Peat Marwick/Joseph A. Silvoso Distinguished Professor of Accountancy and Director of the School of Accountancy; Ph.D., Missouri, 1982.
Lisa A. Zanetti, Assistant Professor of Public Administration; Ph.D., Tennessee, 1997.
Shaoming Zou, Assistant Professor of Marketing; Ph.D., Michigan State, 1994

THE UNIVERSITY OF MONTANA–MISSOULA

School of Business Administration

Programs of Study

The University of Montana offers two master's degrees in the School of Business Administration: the Master of Business Administration (M.B.A.) and the Master of Accountancy (M.Acct.). Both programs are open to graduates of any undergraduate degree program. A foundation program of 31 semester credits in the fundamentals of business administration is required. Mathematics equivalent to college algebra or precalculus and basic computer literacy are also required, but no business courses need be taken prior to beginning either of the programs. Previous course work can be applied to the foundation program. Graduates of AACSB–The International Association for Management Education-accredited schools are exempt from the foundation program.

The M.B.A. Professional Program consists of 30 semester credits beyond the foundation. Twenty-one credits are taken in seven required classes, and 9 credits are taken in elective classes. Six elective credits may be taken in internship or thesis work. Those who do not write a thesis must pass a comprehensive exam.

The M.Acct. Professional Program has the same foundation requirements as the M.B.A. Professional Program, plus 24 credits of undergraduate accounting fundamentals. Most undergraduate accounting majors have completed both the foundation and accounting fundamentals prior to entry. The M.Acct. Professional Program consists of 30 credits: 15 in advanced accounting classes, 6 in graduate management, and 9 in electives. Those who do not write a thesis must pass a comprehensive exam.

The M.B.A. or M.Acct. Professional Program can be completed in two semesters, but most students finish the program in two semesters plus a summer session or three semesters.

All undergraduate and graduate programs are fully accredited by the AACSB–The International Association for Management Education.

Research Facilities

The Maureen and Mike Mansfield Library, a five-level modern structure, holds some 700,000 volumes and 8,000 professional journal titles. It is a regional depository for all federal documents. The computer center has several VAX mainframe computers that support computer labs across campus. Each of the labs has terminals to the mainframe and also has microcomputers available for all students to use. The University adheres to a free-use policy. All registered students may use the computer facilities without limits or budget constraints. The School of Business Administration moved into its new state-of-the-art building in fall 1996.

Financial Aid

Several teaching or research assistantships are available to outstanding applicants in both programs. The assistantship stipend was $7463 plus most fees for the 1997–98 academic year. Applicants with strong research potential may be eligible for Bertha Morton scholarships of $2000 to $5000. Assistantships are normally awarded only to those who have completed the foundation program.

Cost of Study

Tuition and fees for 1998–99 are estimated at $1600 for Montana residents and $4300 for nonresidents for 12 to 18 credits per semester.

Living and Housing Costs

Campus dormitory and meal packages vary from $1850 to $2700 per semester. Families may apply to live in one of the University's apartments. These apartments, ranging from studio to four-bedroom, rent for $200 to $450 per month. Other privately owned rental apartments and houses are available in the city of Missoula.

Student Group

The University has about 11,500 students, including 1,700 graduate students. The School of Business Administration has limited its graduate enrollment to 80 in the M.B.A. program and 40 in the M.Acct. program. The student body represents a wide range of academic backgrounds from diverse locations. About three fourths are full-time students. Forty percent are women and 20 percent are international.

Student Outcomes

The Office of Career Services offers on-campus interviews with national and regional firms, directs workshops on employment skills, and coordinates the Ask-an-Alum program. Internships are readily available through the Cooperative Education Office. Public and private accounting firms, as well as nonprofit and government organizations, hire the School's M.Acct. students. M.B.A. graduates are employed across a broad diversity of businesses, ranging from small to large companies, including entrepreneurial firms.

Location

The University is located in a residential area of Missoula, a city of 80,000 situated midway between Yellowstone and Glacier national parks in the mountains and forests of western Montana. As a center of tourism, Missoula is served by an interstate highway and several major airlines, with direct connections to major cities in the West and Midwest. The average rainfall is 15 inches per year; daily high temperatures average 21 degrees in January and 84 degrees in July.

The University

The University of Montana, the state's first university, was established in 1893, just three years after Montana became a state. In addition to the College of Arts and Sciences, there are seven professional schools: Business Administration, Fine Arts, Education, Forestry, Journalism, Pharmacy and Allied Health Sciences, and Law. The University confers bachelor's degrees in fifty-five areas, master's degrees in forty-eight, and doctoral degrees in nine.

Applying

Students must have a better-than-average undergraduate grade point average and GMAT score for admission to the graduate business programs. International students should have a TOEFL score of 580 or higher. Students can begin their studies in the fall or spring semester or in the summer session. The application deadline for the fall semester and summer session is March 1; the spring semester deadline is September 1. Later applications may be reviewed on May 1 and November 1. Students may take undergraduate foundation or accounting fundamentals classes without formal admission to the graduate school, but they must be admitted to register for any graduate-level courses. Most scholarship applications are due by March 1.

Correspondence and Information

Director of Graduate Programs in Business
School of Business Administration
The University of Montana–Missoula
Missoula, Montana 59812

Telephone: 406-243-4983 or 6715
V/5136TT (TTY/TDD)
Fax: 406-243-2086
E-mail: spritzer@selway.umt.edu

The University of Montana–Missoula

THE FACULTY

Accounting

Paul R. Bahnson, Ph.D., Utah; CPA. Financial accounting, financial statement analysis.
Teresa K. Beed, Ph.D., Colorado; CPA. Financial accounting, accounting theory, television teaching.
Michael R. Brown, J.D., Montana; CPA. Income tax, accounting law and ethics.
Bruce P. Budge, Ph.D., Minnesota; CPA. Financial accounting, research methods, cash flows.
Patricia P. Douglas, Ph.D., Berkeley; CPA. Financial accounting, nonprofit communications, standard-setting in the public sector.
Terri L. Herron, Ph.D., Texas at Arlington; CPA. Accounting information systems, nonprofit accounting.
Stanley Jenne, Ph.D., Illinois; CPA. Auditing, accounting information systems, financial accounting.
Roy W. Regel, Ph.D., Colorado; CPA, CMA. Management accounting, financial accounting, operations control, international accounting.
Joseph A. Weber, Ph.D., Minnesota; CPA. Income taxation, financial accounting, capitalizing closely-held corporations.

Finance

Anthony J. Crawford, Ph.D., Penn State. Corporate finance, banking, investments, agency relations, financial markets.
Timothy A. Manuel, Ph.D., South Carolina. Markets and institutions, investments, international finance, corporate finance, capital structure, valuation, risk management.
Bruce D. Niendorf, Ph.D., Florida State. Financial management.

Information Systems and Operations Management

Gary L. Cleveland, Ph.D., Minnesota. Operations management, management science, operations strategy, total quality management.
Gerald E. Evans, Ph.D., Claremont. Research methods, small business information systems, statistics.
Larry D. Gianchetta, Ph.D., Texas A&M. Research methods, strategic management.
Thomas A. Ottaway, Ph.D., Texas Tech. Intelligent manufacturing systems, distributed artificial intelligence.
Charles A. P. Smith, Ph.D., Arizona. Management information systems, database design, networks, crisis management.
Lee Tangedahl, Ph.D., Colorado. Microcomputer applications, management game, management science, computer science.

Management/Marketing

Aaron Andreason, Ph.D., Brigham Young. International business, cross-cultural management, human resource management, changes in Japanese culture and business practices.
Carol L. Bruneau, Ph.D., Arizona. Marketing management.
Mary Ellen Campbell, M.A., Illinois. Management communications, marketing communications, nonprofit health care marketing.
Richard T. Dailey, Ph.D., Penn State. Business and society, ethics, policy, small business issues, international management, Pacific Rim economies.
Maureen J. Fleming, Ph.D., Southern Illinois. Organizational behavior, human resource management, cross-cultural management, internships, privatization of higher education.
Jerry L. Furniss, J.D., Idaho. Real estate law, employment law, corporate and business law, small claims courts, international law.
Robert W. Hollmann, Ph.D., Washington (Seattle). Human resource management, management.
Paul R. Larson, Ph.D., Utah. Entrepreneurship, small business management, strategic management, human resource management.
Jakki J. Mohr, Ph.D., Wisconsin–Madison. Marketing, marketing communications.
Jack K. Morton, J.D., Montana. Business law, real estate law.
Clyde W. Neu, Ph.D., Minnesota. Finance.
Paul E. Polzin, Ph.D., Michigan State. Economic analysis.
Nader N. Shooshtari, Ph.D., Arizona State. Marketing management, channels of distribution, international business, business curriculum internationalization, strategic marketing.
Thomas J. Steele, Ph.D., Penn State. Marketing research, marketing management.

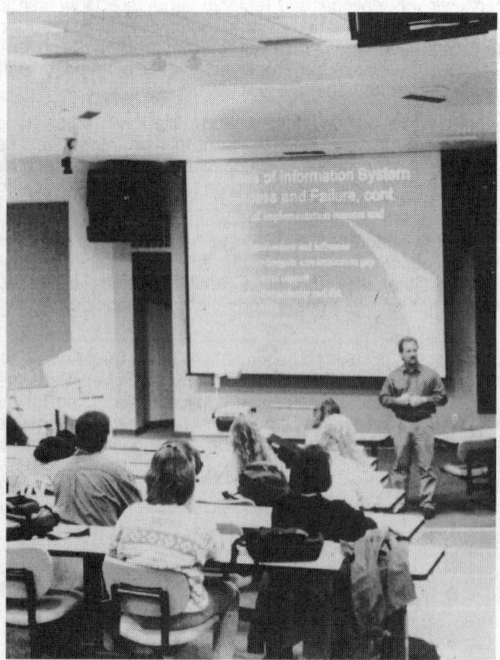

Learning in the business school's new building is enhanced by state-of-the-art technology.

The new William and Rosemary Gallagher Building for the School of Business Administration opened in 1996.

UNIVERSITY OF NEW HAMPSHIRE

Whittemore School of Business and Economics M.B.A. Programs

Programs of Study

The Whittemore School of Business and Economics offers three programs leading to an M.B.A. degree: a day program of full-time study, a part-time evening program, and a weekend executive program for experienced managers with significant work responsibilities. Program length varies from a minimum of 2 years to a maximum of 3½ years.

The day program, open to students with any undergraduate degree, consists of an integrated sequence of required and elective courses. The ten courses required in the first year have been designed to build a base of understanding and analytical competence. The common course format of the first year often resembles organization work requiring group activities and decisions; it also fosters class cohesiveness. The Whittemore faculty has more than 50 members, and the relatively small size of each M.B.A. class contributes to close, informal relationships among students and between students and faculty members. During the second year of the day M.B.A. program, students complete required courses and a complement of seven elective courses. Second-year required courses give special attention to the integration of first-year course material and the application of that material to the development of overall management policy. Choosing from electives, a student may pursue a second year of study to suit individual career goals. In addition to participating in advanced courses, independent study, and internships in various fields of business, students are encouraged to select electives from the economics curriculum and, where appropriate to their objectives, from graduate courses offered by other departments of the University.

The part-time evening M.B.A. program is open to individuals with above-average academic records and two to four years of work experience. Classes are held weekly over the duration of each trimester. It is expected that students complete six courses per year and take a minimum of 3⅓ years to complete the degree.

The Executive M.B.A. program develops management expertise without career interruption. This accelerated program, aimed at broad professional training rather than intensive specialization, begins each year in September with a full week of instruction. Thereafter, classes are held twice each month in full-day Friday and Saturday sessions.

Research Facilities

The University library houses more than 1 million volumes, 6,500 periodicals, and substantial microfilm and audiotape collections. Computer facilities for academic use include the VAX 8820 and 8650, VAX-interactive and graphics terminals, and many Macintosh and IBM PC machines. Graduate students may use the Interlibrary Loan System to supplement material available in the University library. The library is a U.S. government document depository, and there is a full-time documents librarian. Online database search services are offered at cost through the reference and branch departments.

Financial Aid

Day M.B.A. applicants with strong academic records may qualify for graduate assistantships. Graduate assistants receive a stipend of $5050 for the 1998–99 academic year, plus a half-tuition waiver. Full-tuition scholarships are also available.

Cost of Study

Yearly tuition for the day M.B.A. program in 1997–98 was $4900 for New Hampshire students. Nonresident tuition for that program was $13,760. Mandatory fees were $790. Yearly tuition for the executive program, including part-time room and board at the New England Center, was $15,950. Part-time study rates are $1050 per course for residents and $1275 for nonresidents. Costs are subject to change.

Living and Housing Costs

Babcock House, the graduate residence hall, provided single rooms at a cost of $2978 for the 1997–98 academic year. Students may remain in Babcock during the summer at reduced rates. Limited on-campus housing for married students is provided at Forest Park. Prices for efficiency and one- or two-bedroom apartments ranged from $352 to $468 per month. Optional meal contracts (nineteen meals per week) cost $1980 per academic year. Off-campus housing is available at a wide range of prices.

Student Group

Currently, there are 50 day M.B.A. students, almost equally divided between the first- and second-year classes, 75 part-time evening M.B.A. students, and 60 students in the executive program. The University has an enrollment of about 12,000 students, 1,550 of whom are graduate students; many are international students.

Location

Located 60 miles north of Boston, the University of New Hampshire occupies a picturesque 170-acre campus in the attractive New England town of Durham. It is only 10 miles from the Atlantic Ocean and 50 miles from the scenic lakes and mountains for which the state is well known.

The University and The School

The University of New Hampshire was founded in 1866. It serves as a cultural and scientific center for the area, with its New England Center for Continuing Education, Space Science Center, and Paul Arts Center. The Whittemore School of Business and Economics, established in 1962 and one of six schools and colleges of the University, offers undergraduate as well as graduate degrees.

Applying

All M.B.A. programs begin in the fall semester. An applicant for admission must submit the following materials directly to the Graduate School, Room 109, Thompson Hall, University of New Hampshire, in Durham: the official Graduate School application forms for admission to graduate study; two official transcripts showing the grades earned in all of the applicant's previous graduate and undergraduate academic work; three letters of recommendation, on Whittemore School recommendation forms, from persons in a position to judge the applicant's preparation for and ability to undertake graduate study (e.g., the applicant's previous instructors or coworkers); answers to specific M.B.A. essay questions; and GMAT scores. In addition, executive program applicants must submit a resume. The application deadline is July 1 for the full-time M.B.A. program and July 30 for the part-time and executive M.B.A. programs. The application deadline for international students is March 1.

Correspondence and Information

Director, Graduate and Executive Programs
McConnell Hall, Box PM
Whittemore School of Business and Economics
University of New Hampshire
15 College Road
Durham, New Hampshire 03824-3593
Telephone: 603-862-1367
Fax: 603-862-4468
E-mail: wsbe.grad.program@unh.edu

University of New Hampshire

THE FACULTY AND THEIR RESEARCH

Carole K. Barnett, Assistant Professor of Management; Ph.D., Michigan. Organizational change and transformation, organizational learning, continuous quality improvement, innovation.
Gene Boccialetti, Associate Professor of Organizational Behavior; Ph.D., Case Western Reserve. Authority relations in organizations, organizational change and large-scale system design, career and adult development, small-group and interpersonal analysis.
Karen M. Smith Conway, Associate Professor of Economics; Ph.D., North Carolina at Chapel Hill. Public economics, econometrics, labor supply.
Catherine Craycraft, Associate Professor of Accounting; Ph.D., Ohio State. Financial accounting, government and nonprofit accounting.
Joseph F. Durocher, Associate Professor of Hospitality Management; Ph.D., Cornell. Food service management, marketing, human resources, restaurant and hotel design, computers in management and training.
Bruce T. Elmslie, Associate Professor of Economics; Ph.D., Utah. International trade, history of economic thought, growth theory.
Richard W. England, Professor of Economics; Ph.D., Michigan. Environmental policy, ecological economics, environmental management.
Ahmad Etebari, Professor of Finance and Accounting; Ph.D., North Texas State. Investments, corporate finance.
L. Franklin Fant, Assistant Professor of Finance; Ph.D., Florida State. Corporate finance, investments, mutual funds.
Stephen L. Fink, Professor of Management; Ph.D., Case Western Reserve. Organizational change, crisis and stress management, total quality management.
John Freear, Professor of Accounting and Finance; M.A. (economics), Cambridge; M.A. (accounting), Kent; FCA, CPA. Accounting history, informal venture capital market, management accounting.
Ross Gittell, Associate Professor of Business Administration; Ph.D., Harvard. Business, government and competition, regional and urban development, public policy.
Michael Goldberg, Associate Professor of Economics; Ph.D., NYU. Macroeconomic theory, international finance, financial markets, expectations.
Raymond J. Goodman Jr., Professor of Hospitality Management; Ph.D., Cornell. Human resources management: training and performance evaluation; retirement facilities planning, design, marketing, management and operations; resort ownership development.
Roger Grinde, Assistant Professor of Management Science; Ph.D., Penn State. Operations research/management science; linear, nonlinear, and integer programming; mathematical modeling.
Charles W. Gross, Professor of Marketing; Ph.D., Colorado. International marketing, marketing planning and strategy, forecasting.
Flora Guidry, Assistant Professor of Accounting; Ph.D., Arizona. Financial accounting, managerial accounting, auditing.
Jonathan Gutman, Professor of Marketing; Ph.D., USC. Marketing research, advertising, consumer behavior, franchising.
Francine S. Hall, Professor of Organizational Behavior; Ph.D., Toronto. Organizational behavior, management, human resource management.
Lucy Henke, Associate Professor of Marketing; Ph.D., Massachusetts. Marketing, marketing communication, children and advertising, consumer behavior, new technologies, social marketing.
Marc W. Herold, Associate Professor of Economic Development; Ph.D., Berkeley. Third-world economic development, women and development, international studies, postmodernism, economic systems, political economy.
Manley R. Irwin, Professor Emeritus of Business Administration and Economics; Ph.D., Michigan State. Industrial organization, government regulation, communications industry.
Fred R. Kaen, Professor of Finance; Ph.D., Michigan. Financial management, international finance, corporate finance, corporate governance.
Marvin J. Karson, Professor of Statistics; Ph.D., North Carolina State. Statistical theory and methods.
Allen M. Kaufman, Professor of Business Administration; Ph.D., Rutgers. Business-government relations, corporate strategy, business history.
Walfried M. Lassar, Assistant Professor of Marketing; Ph.D., USC. Channel of distribution, strategic product management, business-to-business marketing, services marketing.
Michael J. Merenda, Professor of Business Administration; Ph.D., Massachusetts. Strategic planning and management, entrepreneurship, network strategies, SME competitiveness.
Joseph E. Michael Jr., Esq., Adjunct Professor in Law; J.D., Boston University. Business law.
Richard L. Mills, Associate Professor of Economics and Business Administration; Ph.D., Indiana. Applied microeconomics, energy economics, statistical methods.
William Naumes, Associate Professor of Management; Ph.D., Stanford. International business, strategic management, entrepreneurship.
Neil B. Niman, Associate Professor of Economics; Ph.D., Texas at Austin. History of economic thought, information systems, organizational economics.
R. Dan Reid, Associate Professor of Operations Management; Ph.D., Ohio State. Production/operations management, purchasing, business logistics.
Yae Sock Roh, Assistant Professor of Hospitality Management; Ph.D., Penn State. Hospitality franchising, hospitality real estate, hospitality valuation and appraisal, hospitality investment decision making.
Torsten Schmidt, Associate Professor of Economics; Ph.D., Florida. Industrial organization, microeconomic theory, economics of information and uncertainty, franchising, public choice, econometrics.
Christine Shea, Assistant Professor of Operations Management; Ph.D., Western Ontario. Production and operations management, technological innovation, continuous improvement.
Barry Shore, Professor of Information Systems and Associate Dean; Ph.D., Wisconsin. Information systems, international management.
Evangelos O. Simos, Professor of Economics; Ph.D., Northern Illinois. Macroeconomics, monetary theory and policy, modeling and forecasting, international trade and finance, econometrics, economic growth, international affairs.
Jeffrey E. Sohl, Professor of Management Science; Ph.D., Maryland. Early stage equity, financing of high-growth ventures, time series forecasting.
Linda G. Sprague, Professor of Operations Management; D.B.A., Harvard. Operations strategy, international manufacturing and distribution, operations scheduling and information systems, capacity management.
Doug Stevens, Assistant Professor of Accounting; Ph.D., Indiana. Budgeting, management control, experimental tests of price and trading volume theory.
Allen R. Thompson, Associate Professor of Economics and Business Administration; Ph.D., Texas at Austin. Banking, macroeconomics, public policy.
Emery Trowbridge, Associate Professor of Hospitality Management; Ed.D., Northern Arizona. Hospitality marketing and services management, casino management, resort and time-share management.
Angadipuram Venkatachalam, Associate Professor of Information Systems; Ph.D., Alabama. MIS, artificial intelligence in business, global information management, system analysis and design, electronic commerce.
Rita P. Weathersby, Associate Professor of Organizational Behavior; Ed.D., Harvard. Leadership, adult learning and management education, international management.
James R. Wible, Associate Professor of Economics; Ph.D., Penn State. Macroeconomics and monetary theory, economics of science and methodology, law and ethics.
Craig Wood, Associate Professor of Operations Management; Ph.D., Ohio State. Production and operations management, operations strategy, total quality management, technology management.

UNIVERSITY OF NORTH CAROLINA AT CHARLOTTE

The Belk College of Business Administration Master of Business Administration Program

Program of Study

The M.B.A. program, begun in 1970, is AACSB–accredited. The primary objective of the graduate program in business administration is to develop leaders for positions in the complex organizations of the future. Managerial strategies, procedures, and practices of today are subject to rapid change, and the program emphasizes a process of analyzing and solving administrative problems in an increasingly complex environment to address those changes. Organizations are analyzed as behavioral, financial, and technical units operating in an environment with a variety of regional, national, and international dimensions.

Courses are scheduled in the evening to accommodate part-time students. A part-time student can complete the program in three years. Full-time students can complete the program in two years. The curriculum stresses the universal characteristics of management and their applications in various types of organizations. Fundamental management problems are examined from economic, technological, and behavioral perspectives. Concentrations are offered in accounting, business finance, economics, financial institutions/commercial banking, information and technology management, management, and marketing. Students who do not choose one of the structured concentrations may propose a self-structured concentration in a significant area of interest. Prerequisites, determined at admission, include foundations in accounting, computers in business, economics, legal environment, and quantitative analysis.

The core consists of basic analysis and functional area requirements for all candidates. Courses in economic analysis and managerial accounting focus on financial performance and resource allocation, while the course in organizational behavior emphasizes the development of leadership skills and strategies. Courses in marketing management, financial management, and operations management provide exposure to the major functional areas in an organization. Electives provide additional depth in the functional areas and increased opportunities to develop analytical skills in the behavioral and quantitative aspects of decision making. Integrative courses are designed to integrate the concepts and methods of analysis developed throughout the program of study. Students are required to solve administrative problems that illustrate the integrative aspects of an executive role, taking into consideration the ethical and legal aspects of that role.

The M.B.A. Plus Certificate program is an opportunity for graduates of M.B.A. programs to broaden and update their business education. Participants take four graduate courses—three in a specified concentration, plus one additional graduate course. The College welcomes M.B.A. graduates to take courses either to apply toward the M.B.A. Plus Certificate or for enrichment.

Research Facilities

Facilities at UNC Charlotte include the J. Murrey Atkins Library and University Computing Services. The library contains more than 600,000 bound volumes and more than 1 million units in microform. It also houses a 6,000-volume rare book collection and an estimated 1.5 million documents in its manuscript collection. The library offers access to a growing array of electronic sources. Computing laboratories afford access to a variety of microcomputers and workstations. Access is provided to the University's mainframes and superminicomputers via a campus local area network.

Financial Aid

The College offers a limited number of graduate assistantships to full-time students. Applicants should have an excellent record and must have been unconditionally admitted to the program. In 1997–98, stipends were $6300 for the nine-month academic year.

Cost of Study

For 1997–98, tuition for full-time in-state graduate students was $890.50 per semester; $4454.50 per semester for full-time out-of-state students. Books and other fees are extra.

Living and Housing Costs

On-campus dormitory costs, including a campus meal plan, ranged from $1600 to $2000 per semester for the academic year 1997–98. Private apartments are also available near the University. Housing, food, and miscellaneous living expenses in the Charlotte area compare favorably with national averages.

Student Group

Enrollment in the program is 480: 179 women and 301 men. Approximately 10 percent are international students. About 20 students receive financial aid through graduate assistantships. Graduates of UNCC's M.B.A. program fill a variety of positions in service, banking, and manufacturing industries, including management trainee and analytical positions.

Student Outcomes

Graduates are employed in a variety of positions utilizing their specializations in accounting, banking, economics, finance, information and technology management, management, and marketing in the region's thriving economy. Major employers of the College's students include banks, consulting firms, manufacturers, retailers, health organizations, and a diversity of both private and public organizations.

Location

The University is located in a dynamic setting in the largest urban center in the Carolinas. UNC Charlotte is situated just inside the Charlotte city limits and within the Charlotte SMSA, with a population of 1.2 million. The city boasts a number of diverse cultural experiences including the Charlotte Symphony, Opera Carolina, the Oratorio Singers, the N.C. Dance Theatre, the Mint Museum of Art, and Spirit Square. Charlotte is home to a number of professional sports teams, including the Charlotte Hornets of the National Basketball Association and the Carolina Panthers of the National Football League. North Carolina ski resorts are within a 2-hour drive of Charlotte, and the beaches of North and South Carolina are easily accessible. The Charlotte-Douglas International Airport is served by all major airlines.

The University

The University of North Carolina at Charlotte is an accredited state university that offers the opportunities of a comprehensive university while maintaining the intimacy of a small school. Present enrollment is about 15,895.

Applying

Applications are reviewed on a continuous basis. Applications, accompanied by full credentials (transcripts of all colleges attended and references), should be filed at least sixty days in advance of the term for which admission is sought. The GMAT is also required for admission. For more information about applying to the University, students should contact the Graduate Admissions Office via e-mail at gradadm@email.uncc.edu. International students should contact the Office of International Admissions via e-mail at intnladm@email.uncc.edu.

Correspondence and Information

Dr. Virginia T. Geurin
Associate Dean for Graduate Studies and Research
The Belk College of Business Administration
University of North Carolina at Charlotte
9201 University City Boulevard
Charlotte, North Carolina 28223-0001

Telephone: 704-547-2569
Fax: 704-547-4014
World Wide Web: http://www.uncc.edu/colleges/business/mbaprog

University of North Carolina at Charlotte

THE FACULTY AND THEIR RESEARCH

Edward M. Mazze, Dean of the Belk College of Business Administration (Marketing); Ph.D., Penn State. International business.

Parvez Ahmed (IOM); Ph.D., Texas at Arlington. Global financial issues.
Haldun Aytug (IOM); Ph.D., Florida. Genetic algorithm development and artificial intelligence.
Christie H. Amato (Marketing); Ph.D., Alabama. Marketing research and strategy.
Ted Amato (Economics); Ph.D., South Carolina. Antitrust, industrial relations, retailing.
Joanna R. Baker (IOM); Ph.D., Clemson. Applied mathematical programming and optimization in public-sector decision making.
Frank C. Barnes (IOM); Ph.D., Georgia State. Synchronous manufacturing processes, computer-integrated manufacturing.
Joyce M. Beggs (Management); Ph.D., Tennessee, Knoxville. Strategic planning and management.
Elle E. Bell (Management); Ph.D., Case Western Reserve. Race relations, women in management, careers, group dynamics and organizational change.
Charles D. Bodkin (Marketing); Ph.D., Virginia Tech. Retail strategy, salesperson behavior and performance.
Rosemary Booth (Management); Ph.D., Kentucky. Gender and management communication and media relations.
Hughlene A. Burton (Accounting); Ph.D., San Jose State. Corporate integration, tax policy, corporate and international tax issues.
Gerald E. Calvasina (Management); Ph.D., Mississippi. Employment law, personnel, and human resource issues.
Claudio Carpano (Management); Ph.D., South Carolina. International strategy and competition.
Jack M. Cathey (Accounting); Ph.D., Virginia Tech; CPA. Microcomputers, EDI, internal control.
Richard M. Conboy (Management); Ph.D., Virginia Tech. Organizational structure and control, school finance, strategic planning.
John E. Connaughton (Economics); Ph.D., Northeastern. Forecasting.
W. Douglas Cooper (IOM); Ph.D., North Carolina State. Decision support systems, synchronous manufacturing systems.
Michael Cornick (Accounting); Ph.D., North Carolina at Chapel Hill. Managerial accounting, activity-based management.
Connie W. Crook (IOM); Ph.D., South Carolina. Telecommunications and office automation systems.
Kent E. Curran (Management); D.B.A., LSU. Strategic management.
W. Young Davis (Economics); Ph.D., Georgia. Labor relations.
Carol B. Dole (Economics); Ph.D., Florida. Business cycles, monetary policy.
Virginia T. Geurin (Management); Ph.D., Arkansas. Employee assistance programs, substance abuse policies.
Robert Giacalone (Management); Ph.D., SUNY at Albany. Ethics, employee sabotage, impression management, exit interviewing.
L. Howard Godfrey (Accounting); Ph.D., Alabama; CPA. Embezzlement control, tax research, tax planning.
Kent N. Gourdin (Marketing); D.B.A., Tennessee, Knoxville. Logistics systems, air transportation, EDI.
Mary A. Gowan (Management); Ph.D., Georgia. Career/diversity factors affecting employee success in the workplace, compensation and benefits, the effects of company closings and layoffs on individuals.
Dolan R. Hinson (Accounting); Ph.D., South Carolina; CMA. Activity-based management, personal financial planning.
Jack T. Hogue (IOM); Ph.D., Georgia. Decision support systems.
Robert W. Hornaday (Management); D.B.A., Florida State. Small business planning, strategic management.
I. Edward Jernigan III (Management); D.B.A., Memphis State. Employment training.
William F. Kennedy (Finance and Business Law); Ph.D., Virginia Tech. Commercial loans management, banking, capital budgeting.
Moutaz J. Khouja (IOM); Ph.D., Kent State. Materials management, computer integrated manufacturing.
Gary F. Kohut (Management); Ph.D., Southern Illinois. Strategic and corporate communication.
Ram L. Kumar (IOM); Ph.D., Maryland College Park. Management of information systems.
Reinhold P. Lamb (Finance and Business Law); Ph.D., Florida State. Insurance/risk, corporate finance.
Claude C. Lilly (Finance and Business Law); Ph.D., Georgia State. Insurance company operations, reinsurance, rate making, self-insurance.
Gaines H. Liner (Economics); Ph.D., Clemson. Employment and age discrimination, econometric analysis.
Ronald A. Madsen (Economics); D.B.A., Arizona State. Regional development and labor force demographics.
Mary C. Martin (Marketing); Ph.D., Nebraska. Advertising.
Rob Roy McGregor (Economics); Ph.D., South Carolina. Monetary policy.
Ellen M. Miller (Economics); Ph.D., Florida. Applied microeconomics, industrial organization.
Patricia G. Mynatt (Accounting); Ph.D., North Carolina at Chapel Hill; CPA. Accounting profession.
Stella M. Nkomo (Management); Ph.D., Massachusetts. Human resource management, women in management.
Bennie H. Nunnally Jr. (Finance and Business Law); D.B.A., Virginia. Small business finance and valuation.
Craig Pearce (Management); Ph.D., Maryland at College Park. Team-based management change.
Anthony Plath (Finance and Business Law); D.B.A., Kent State. Banking, corporate finance, lending.
John F. Repede (IOM); Ph.D., Kentucky. Decision support systems, health-care operations systems.
Stephanie S. Robbins (IOM); Ph.D., Alabama/LSU. MIS for marketing.
Benjamin Russo (Economics); Ph.D., Iowa. Fiscal policy, federal tax policy, interest rates and saving.
Cem A. Saydam (IOM); Ph.D., Clemson. Decision support systems and project management.
Richard G. Schroeder (Accounting); Ph.D., Arizona. Financial accounting, impact on behavior.
Peter M. Schwarz (Economics); Ph.D., Ohio State. Airline pricing/issues and privatization.
Calvin W. Sealey (Finance and Business Law); Ph.D., Montreal. Banking and financial services industry.
Alan T. Shao (Marketing); Ph.D., Alabama. International marketing and advertising.
Thomas H. Stevenson (Marketing); Ph.D., Case Western Reserve. Sales management issues.
Anthony C. Stylianou (IOM); Ph.D., Kent State. Expert systems.
Linda E. Swayne (Marketing); Ph.D., North Texas State. Strategic marketing and promotional strategies.
Louis A. Trosch (Finance and Business Law); J.D., West Virginia. Business, commercial law.
Hui-kuan "Alice" Tseng (Economics); Ph.D., Illinois at Urbana–Champaign. Economic impact studies, international finance.
Richard A. Zuber (Economics); Ph.D., Kentucky. Economics of sports and crime.

UNIVERSITY OF OKLAHOMA

Price College of Business

Programs of Study

The Price College of Business offers the following graduate programs: the Master of Business Administration (M.B.A.), the Master of Accountancy (M.Acc.), and the Doctor of Philosophy (Ph.D.). Dual-degree programs offered are the M.B.A./J.D., M.B.A./M.S. in mathematics, M.B.A./M.A. in language (French, German, Spanish), M.B.A./M.S. in construction science, M.B.A./M.S. in pharmacy administration, and M.B.A./Master of Public Health. For the dual-degree programs, applicants must apply and be admitted to each program separately. Programs in the Price College of Business are fully accredited by AACSB–The International Association for Management Education.

The full-time M.B.A. is a 53-credit-hour, twenty-one-month program. All courses are at the graduate level and are offered during the day. The part-time M.B.A. requires 42–54 credit hours, depending on the student's undergraduate background. All courses are at the graduate level and are offered in the evening. Both programs require that the student become familiar with the functional areas of business, the necessary tools for management decision making, and the environment in which business firms operate. Knowledge prerequisites include an introduction to calculus, matrix algebra, and linear programming; computer familiarity; and communication skills. Students from all undergraduate majors are encouraged to apply.

The M.Acc. is a 33-hour program for students with an undergraduate degree in accounting. Other students may enter this program, but they must take a minimum of 12 hours of undergraduate accounting courses as well as other core business courses. The core business courses are all graduate courses. The Master of Accountancy is a terminal professional degree.

The full-time Ph.D. program is small and research oriented. Eighteen hours of course work are stipulated; most degree requirements and major and supporting fields are determined on an individual basis. Close association with faculty, as well as early research involvement, is standard. Doctoral students normally receive financial aid. Doctoral degrees are available in accounting, finance, management, and marketing. A master's degree is not required to enter the doctoral program.

Research Facilities

Research facilities available to graduate students include an extensive University library, the Bass Business History Collection, the Oklahoma University Research Institute, the Center for Economic and Management Research, and extensive computer facilities.

Financial Aid

Graduate assistantships of up to $11,000 a year, special instructorships, fellowships and scholarships, and fee-waiver scholarships are available for qualified graduate students. Graduate assistantships may include a waiver of out-of-state fees.

Cost of Study

Tuition in 1997–98 for full-time state residents was $91.47 per credit hour ($2835.57 per year, based on 31 semester hours); nonresident students paid $265.58 per credit hour ($8232.98 per year, based on 31 semester hours). Books and supplies are estimated at $800 per academic year; other fees are $75 per semester.

Living and Housing Costs

Most graduate students live in off-campus housing, which is readily available. University housing is also available and varies in cost from $185 to $440 per month. There is a referral service to assist students in finding accommodations.

Student Group

Typically, 40 percent of an M.B.A. class consists of business majors, 25 percent engineering majors, and the remainder science and humanities majors. More than 60 percent have two years or more of work experience. The average age is 27, and approximately 42 percent are women. There are generally 300–325 graduate students in the College.

Location

Although part of the Oklahoma City metropolitan area, Norman began and continues as an independent community with a permanent population of nearly 80,000. It has extensive parks and recreation programs, a 10,000-acre lake and park area, a community theater, an art center and art league, and other amenities of a university town. Norman is minutes from downtown Oklahoma City and 3 hours from Dallas. Summers are hot with low humidity, and winters are mild to cold.

The University

Entering its second century, the University of Oklahoma, founded in 1890, is a comprehensive university offering 119 undergraduate degree programs, 128 master's-level programs, 89 doctoral programs, and 4 professional degrees. There are eleven colleges on the Norman campus, and six medical and health-related colleges are located on the Health Sciences Center campus in Oklahoma City and at the Tulsa Medical College.

Applying

There is a nonrefundable application processing fee of $25 for U.S. citizens and permanent residents and $50 for international applicants. Admission is open to qualified individuals holding a bachelor's degree from an accredited college or university who show high promise of success in graduate study. Applicants need not have undergraduate backgrounds in business. All applicants must submit satisfactory scores on the Graduate Management Admission Test (GMAT). International applicants must submit satisfactory scores on the Test of English as a Foreign Language (TOEFL). In addition, the Test of Spoken English (TSE) is required of international applicants to the Ph.D. program. Letters of recommendation are required for all applicants.

Students may enter the fall semester beginning late August, the spring semester beginning early January, or the eight-week summer session beginning early in June. Students may only enter the full-time M.B.A. program in the fall semester.

Correspondence and Information

Graduate Programs Office
Price College of Business
307 West Brooks, Room 105-K
University of Oklahoma
Norman, Oklahoma 73019-0450
Telephone: 405-325-4107
Fax: 405-325-1957

University of Oklahoma

THE FACULTY AND THEIR RESEARCH

Jeff Austin, Ph.D., Georgia. Individual and corporate tax.
Frances L. Ayres, Director, School of Accounting; Ph.D., Iowa. Financial accounting, tax policy.
Samir Barman, Ph.D., Clemson. Production/operations, management information systems.
Michael R. Buckley, Ph.D., Auburn. Human resource management, performance appraisal, interviewing.
Stephen A. Butler, Ph.D., Iowa. Cost and managerial accounting.
Richard A. Cosier, Dean and Fred E. Brown Chair; Ph.D., Iowa. Decision-making processes, conflict-handling behavior, effects of external forces on business.
Terry L. Crain, Director, Master of Accountancy Program; Ph.D., Texas Tech. Taxation.
Robert C. Dauffenbach, Director, Center for Economic and Management Research; Ph.D., Illinois at Urbana-Champaign. Regional economics and business.
Russell W. Driver, Ph.D., Georgia. Human resource management, organization communication.
Louis H. Ederington, Oklahoma Bankers' Chair in Finance; Ph.D., Washington (St. Louis). Financial markets and institutions, econometrics, securities, interest rates.
Gary W. Emery, Director, Division of Finance; Ph.D., Kansas. Corporate finance and investments.
Rodney E. Evans, Ph.D., Michigan State. Marketing management, sales management, marketing research.
Forrest L. Frueh, J.D., Oklahoma. Commercial law, taxation.
Dipankar Ghosh, Ph.D., Penn State. Agency theory, negotiation and conflict resolution, transfer pricing.
Willie E. Gist, Ph.D., Texas A&M. Auditing, marketing auditing in regard to marketing performance.
Michael G. Harvey, Director, Management Division and Puterbaugh Chair of Free Enterprise; Ph.D., Arizona. International business strategy, entrepreneurship.
James F. Horrell, Ph.D., Colorado State. Statistics, stochastic differential equations.
Jack J. Kasulis, Ph.D., Northwestern. Consumer research, retail patronage behavior, channels of distribution.
James M. Kenderdine, Director, Division of Marketing; D.B.A., Indiana. Channels of distribution, consumer research, small-business management.
M. Chris Knapp, Ph.D., Oklahoma. Cost and managerial accounting, auditing, financial accounting, banking industry.
Jae Lee, Ph.D., Indiana. Investments.
Scott Linn, Ph.D., Purdue. Corporate finance.
Robert F. Lusch, Helen Robson Walton Chair in Marketing; Ph.D., Wisconsin. Channels of distribution, marketing productivity and cost analysis, strategic market planning.
Roberto Mejias, Ph.D., Arizona. Information systems management, international application of information technology, cross-cultural application of GSS technology in developing countries.
Larry K. Michaelsen, Ph.D., Michigan. Organizational behavior, organizational theory.
Shane R. Moriarity, Associate Dean, College of Business Administration; Ph.D., Illinois at Urbana-Champaign. Managerial accounting, audit judgment.
James W. Mouser, J.D., Oklahoma. Commercial law.
Nandkumar Nayar, Ph.D., Iowa. Business finance, investments, financial institutions, signaling theory, capital acquisition processes, options.
R. Leon Price, D.B.A., Oklahoma. Management information systems, production/operations.
Nim Razook Jr., Director, M.B.A. Program; J.D., Oklahoma. Commercial law.
Terry D. Robertson, Ph.D., Georgia. Real estate, urban economics.
Drue Schuler, Ph.D., North Carolina. Health-care marketing, services marketing.
A. B. Schwarzkopf, Director, Division of Management; Ph.D., Virginia. Information systems management, quantitative methods.
Vijay Sethi, Ph.D., Pittsburgh. Management information systems.
Mark Sharfman, Ph.D., Arizona. Organizational-environmental interactions, organizational responses to environmental uncertainty, environment on strategic decision making, corporate social responsibility.
Bryan E. Stanhouse, Ph.D., Illinois at Urbana-Champaign. Corporate finance, financial institutions.
Duane R. Stock, Ph.D., Illinois at Urbana-Champaign. Money and banking.
Richard J. Tersine, Baldwin Professor of Management; D.B.A., Florida State. Production/operations management, materials management.
Richard Van Horn, Ph.D., Carnegie Mellon. Management information systems.
William T. Whitely, Ph.D., Minnesota. Staffing, training, compensation, organization design.
G. Lee Willinger, Director, Ph.D. Program; D.B.A., Florida State. Financial accounting.
Daniel A. Wren, David Ross Boyd Professor of Management and Curator, Harry W. Bass Business History Collection; Ph.D., Illinois at Urbana-Champaign. Development of management thought, environment for business, business policy.

UNIVERSITY OF PITTSBURGH

Joseph M. Katz Graduate School of Business
Full-Time M.B.A. Programs

Programs of Study

The Katz Graduate School of Business offers a unique eleven-month full-time program leading to the Master of Business Administration (M.B.A.). Dual-degree options that extend the eleven-month program are also available leading to the M.B.A. and Master of Science in the Management of Information Systems (M.B.A./M.S.–MoIS), M.B.A. and Master of International Business (M.B.A./M.I.B.), M.B.A. and Master of Public and International Affairs (M.B.A./ M.P.I.A.), M.B.A. and Master of Arts in Area Studies (M.B.A./M.A.), M.B.A. and Master of Health Administration (M.B.A./M.H.A.), M.B.A. and Juris Doctor (M.B.A./J.D.), and M.B.A. and Master of Divinity (M.B.A./M.Div.). All programs are accredited by the AACSB–The International Association for Management Education.

The M.B.A. curriculum includes student participation in team-building exercises, learning organizations, capability assessments, and career evaluations. The curriculum provides a global management perspective in every phase of the program; emphasizes interrelationships across business functions; incorporates continuous quality improvement in theory and methods; focuses on teamwork, interpersonal skills, and the empowerment process; and applies leading-edge management theory to real-world problems and issues by emphasizing today's set of challenges.

Seven concentrations, from accounting to strategic planning, are offered. Forty-four percent of the full-time M.B.A. program's credits are elective. In addition to traditional courses, students may also participate in project courses, internships, practicums, and independent studies.

The Center for Executive Education offers an Executive Master of Business Administration (E.M.B.A.) that is completed in two years. Classes are conducted on alternating Fridays and Saturdays. Also offered is the FLEX–M.B.A., which is completed in two years with only fourteen weeks of in-residence classes. Class experiences are divided into two 1-week sessions and six 2-week sessions over the two-year period.

Research Facilities

The facilities at the Joseph M. Katz Graduate School of Business center on a contemporary teaching and research complex, Mervis Hall. The complex includes a major business library, the Rockwell Computer Laboratory, and a multitude of microcomputers. It also enjoys preferred access to the University Computer Center. The School houses a variety of institutes, including the Institute for Industrial Competitiveness, the Center for Research on Contracts and the Structure of Enterprise, and the International Business Center. Students may participate in project courses in which they solve real-world corporate problems with the possibility of having their proposed solutions implemented by the companies. The University also maintains a network of seventeen libraries housing 3.5 million volumes.

Financial Aid

The primary source of financial assistance is tuition fellowships, which are awarded in various dollar amounts and applied against tuition charges. These fellowships are awarded primarily on the basis of academic merit, with financial need as a secondary consideration. Applicants applying for scholarship aid/financial assistance must submit the Katz School's Scholarship Aid Application with their M.B.A. application. Teaching fellowships and assistantships are not usually offered at the master's level due to the amount of course work students undertake. The Katz School provides detailed loan information to all incoming students who are U.S. citizens or U.S. permanent residents.

Cost of Study

In 1997–98, tuition and fees for the eleven-month full-time M.B.A. program were $17,540 for state residents and $28,354 for nonresidents.

Living and Housing Costs

Pittsburgh has some of the most reasonable rental fees of any major city in the United States. An enormous variety of apartments and homes are available in the University area. Living expenses (not including tuition and fees) generally average $11,000–$13,000 for the year of study.

Student Group

There are approximately 1,100 students enrolled in the various programs of the Joseph M. Katz Graduate School of Business. Students have completed their undergraduate studies at institutions throughout the United States and in many other countries. International students represent 41 percent of the full-time M.B.A. class.

Location

The city of Pittsburgh is the hub of the eastern business wheel, equidistant from the major economic centers of New York and Chicago and only an hour's plane ride from other primary business points like Philadelphia, Boston, Toronto, Montreal, Detroit, Atlanta, and Washington, D.C. Pittsburgh has a diverse economic base developed through both phases of its heralded renaissance, and it is a prominent transportation, technological, medical, commercial, and communications center, as well as an international industrial leader. It is one of the country's largest corporate headquarters. Pittsburgh is also one of the nation's most attractive cities, with a rich mixture of robust industry and colorful neighborhoods. This combination of vital business and comfortable living is unusually compelling. Pittsburgh is consistently ranked as one of the most livable cities in the United States.

The University

The Katz Graduate School of Business at the University of Pittsburgh is part of an academic community that provides approximately 35,000 students with a creative and exciting environment. In addition to the Katz Graduate School of Business, the University is made up of fifteen other schools, including the Schools of Law, Medicine, Dental Medicine, Public and International Affairs, Engineering, Public Health, and the Faculty of Arts and Sciences. The University is located in the Oakland district—the educational, medical, and cultural center of Pittsburgh.

Applying

The Katz Graduate School of Business has developed an application procedure managed by the applicant. Applicants should request an application package from the School's Office of Admissions. All applicants are required to have earned an undergraduate degree or, for international students, the equivalency of a U.S. bachelor's degree; to have taken the GMAT; and to have completed at least introductory college-level work in integral and differential calculus. The Test of English as a Foreign Language (TOEFL) is required if the applicant's native language is not English. Applicants who request financial aid should submit their applications before February 15. The deadline for international applications is February 15. The full-time eleven-month M.B.A. program begins in mid-July and concludes in mid-June.

Correspondence and Information

Director of Admissions
276 Mervis Hall
Joseph M. Katz Graduate School of Business
University of Pittsburgh
Pittsburgh, Pennsylvania 15260

Telephone: 412-648-1700
Fax: 412-648-1659
E-mail: mba-admissions@katz.business.pitt.edu
World Wide Web: http://www.pitt.edu/~business/

University of Pittsburgh

THE FACULTY AND THEIR RESEARCH

Bradley R. Agle, Ph.D., Washington (Seattle). Environmental studies.
Robert S. Atkin, Ph.D., Pittsburgh. Organizational studies, human resources.
Jacob G. Birnberg, Ph.D., Minnesota. Accounting, management information systems.
Andrew R. Blair, Ph.D., Fordham. Economics, international business.
John C. Camillus, D.B.A., Harvard. Strategic planning and policy, accounting.
Madeleine Carlin, M.B.A., Temple. Accounting.
Rabikar Chatterjee, Ph.D., Pennsylvania. Marketing.
Vivek Choudhury, Ph.D., UCLA. Information systems.
James A. Craft, Ph.D., Berkeley. Human resources management, strategic planning and policy.
John H. Evans III, Ph.D., Carnegie Mellon. Accounting.
Lawrence F. Feick, Ph.D., Penn State. Marketing.
Gary Florkowski, Ph.D., Syracuse. Human resources.
Daniel S. Fogel, Ph.D., Wisconsin. Organizational studies, international business.
Richard Franklin, M.S., Pittsburgh. Management information systems.
Dennis Galletta, Ph.D., Minnesota. Management information systems.
Esther Gal-Or, Ph.D., Northwestern. Economics.
Timothy B. Heath, Ph.D., Iowa. Marketing.
Gajanan Hegde, Ph.D., Rochester. Operations management.
Vicky B. Hoffman, Ph.D., Michigan. Accounting.
Kathleen Kahle, Ph.D., Ohio State. Finance.
Wagner A. Kamakura, Ph.D., Texas at Austin. Marketing.
Chris Kemerer, Ph.D., Carnegie Mellon. Management information systems.
Ralph H. Kilmann, Ph.D., UCLA. Organizational studies.
William R. King, Ph.D., Case Tech. Strategic planning and policy, management information systems.
Daria C. Kirby, Ph.D., Michigan. Organizational studies.
Laurie J. Kirsch, Ph.D., Minnesota. Management information systems.
Carrie R. Leana, Ph.D., Houston. Organizational studies.
Kenneth M. Lehn, Ph.D., Washington (St. Louis). Finance.
Allan MacQuarrie, Ph.D., Penn State. Accounting.
Anil Makhija, Ph.D., Wisconsin–Madison. Finance.
Mona Makhija, Ph.D., Wisconsin–Madison. International business.
Gershon Mandelker, Ph.D., Chicago. Finance.
Marick F. Masters, Ph.D., Illinois. Human resources management.
Jerrold H. May, Ph.D., Yale. Quantitative methods.
Franklin L. McCarthy, Ph.D., Minnesota. Accounting.
Susan K. McEvily, Ph.D., Minnesota. Strategic planning and policy.
Prakash Mirchandani, Ph.D., MIT. Operations research.
Barry M. Mitnick, Ph.D., Pennsylvania. Environmental studies.
Maureen Morrin, Ph.D., NYU. Marketing.
Donald V. Moser, Ph.D., Wisconsin–Madison. Accounting.
Audrey J. Murrell, Ph.D., Delaware. Organizational studies.
Robert Nachtmann, Ph.D., Indiana. Finance, international business.
Nandu Nagarajan, Ph.D., Northwestern. Accounting.
Raghu Nath, Ph.D., MIT. Organizational studies, international business.
Dung Nguyen, Ph.D., Maryland. Economics.
Josephine E. Olson, Ph.D., Brown. Economics, international business.
G. Richard Patton, Ph.D., Purdue. Strategic planning and policy.
James M. Patton, Ph.D., Washington (St. Louis). Accounting.
Frits K. Pil, Ph.D., Pennsylvania. Human resources management.
Prem Prakash, Ph.D., MIT. Accounting.
John E. Prescott, Ph.D., Penn State. Strategic planning and policy, organizational studies.
Thomas L. Saaty, Ph.D., Yale. Quantitative methods.
Shiou-Chen Shang, Ph.D., Texas at Austin. Quantitative methods.
Kuldeep Shastri, Ph.D., UCLA. Finance.
Dennis P. Slevin, Ph.D., Stanford. Organizational studies, management information systems.
Michael H. Spiro, Ph.D., MIT. Economics, finance.
Dhinu Srinivasan, Ph.D., Minnesota. Accounting.
Edward Sussna, Ph.D., Illinois. Economics, finance.
Pandu R. Tadikamalla, Ph.D., Iowa. Quantitative methods, management information systems.
Ben Tuchi, Ph.D., Saint Louis. Finance.
Luis Vargas, Ph.D., Pennsylvania. Quantitative methods.
R. Venkatesh, Ph.D., Texas at Austin. Marketing.
Richard E. Wendell, Ph.D., Northwestern. Quantitative methods.
Frederick W. Winter, Ph.D., Purdue. Marketing.
Donna Wood, Ph.D., Vanderbilt. Environmental studies.
H. J. Zoffer, Ph.D., Pittsburgh. Accounting.

UNIVERSITY OF RHODE ISLAND

College of Business Administration

Programs of Study

The College of Business Administration offers a course of study leading to the degree of Master of Business Administration in full-time day (one year), part-time evening, and executive (weekend) programs. The College prepares students for executive and administrative positions in business, government, and nonprofit organizations. Accredited by the AACSB, the program emphasizes a solid grounding in current business thought and the ability to thrive in an environment of rapid technological change.

The full-time M.B.A. program integrates course work, career planning and development, and work experience within a one-calendar-year period. It takes the traditional curriculum of 54 credits and integrates the material into modules. Students are exposed to modules in the functional areas of marketing, finance, accounting, operations, information systems, and human resources. The program is completed after the summer in which the student, in addition to taking classes, participates in a career-related internship. It is a program—not just a curriculum—that focuses on developing decision making, problem solving, team building, and presentation skills.

Part-time evening study is the answer for candidates who desire to pursue a graduate business degree while maintaining their personal and professional commitments. Classes meet Monday through Thursday evening at two locations: Kingston and the new Graduate Professional Center in Providence. The 54-credit program is structured so students can complete the program in two to five years. Specialties include finance, international business, management, management science, and marketing.

The College also offers the degree of Master of Science in accounting and a Ph.D. program.

Research Facilities

The College of Business Administration has a number of research facilities available to graduate students. The University libraries have a combined collection of about 1 million bound volumes and over 1 million volume-equivalent microforms. The Dennis Callaghan Microcomputer Laboratory provides access to PC and PS/2 microcomputers and a broad range of software. The Decision Support Lab provides access to the University's extensive mainframe computer and superminicomputer facilities. Three Macintosh labs are also available for students. The Research Center in Business and Economics initiates and conducts research activities in a number of areas. The center maintains a library of research materials that are available for graduate student use. In addition, the center conducts market surveys for area companies, nonprofit organizations, and government agencies. Other research projects in which M.B.A. students play active roles are the Pacific-Basin Capital Markets Research Project, the Institute for International Business, the Telecommunications Marketing Research Project, and the Telemarketing Study Project.

Financial Aid

Several forms of financial assistance are available to graduate students. A number of graduate assistantships are awarded throughout the academic year as they become available. Tuition scholarships, which cover tuition and the registration fee, are awarded by the Dean of the Graduate School from University funds. These scholarships are awarded to qualified students demonstrating need of financial assistance. Several Junior Achievement scholarships, in which students work with area schools, are available to full-time students each year. Additionally, students may apply for one or more of the federal student aid programs, details of which may be obtained from the Financial Aid Office (telephone: 401-874-2314).

Cost of Study

Tuition and fees in 1997–98 for full-time students were $2300 per semester for Rhode Island residents and $6700 for out-of-state residents. Part-time study costs were $187 per credit for in-state residents and $521 per credit for out-of-state residents.

Living and Housing Costs

In 1997–98, on-campus housing costs for graduate students ranged from $440 to $530 per month, and off-campus housing ranged from $300 to $600 per month. Board costs of the University's dining services program ranged from $720 to $850 per semester, depending upon the meal plan selected.

Student Group

Class size in the one-year full-time program is limited to 30 students each August; approximately 30 percent are international students. The average age of full-time students is 29, with four years of work experience. In 1997, more than 160 students were enrolled in the part-time program, with an average age of 32. Approximately 30 percent of the M.B.A. candidates hold degrees in engineering and science, 40 percent in business and economics, and 30 percent in social sciences.

Student Outcomes

Of the 1997 class, 90 percent of the full-time and 100 percent of the part-time students were employed within three months of graduation: 90 percent entered the service industry and 10 percent went to work in manufacturing. Median starting base salary was $50,000. Graduates obtained positions that included Vice President of Finance, Fleet Bank; Manufacturing Supervisor, Texas Instruments; Controller, Rhode Island Philharmonic; and Director of Clinical Engineering, Massachusetts Eye and Ear Infirmary.

Location

The University of Rhode Island's main campus and site of the full-time program is located in the southern part of the state, in the northeastern metropolitan corridor between New York and Boston, in close proximity to the ocean. Providence, the state capital, is 30 miles to the north. Part-time M.B.A. classes are held in both Kingston and the new Graduate Professional Center in Providence.

The University

The University of Rhode Island, a medium-sized state university, was founded as a land-grant college in 1892. The University emphasizes preparation for responsible citizenship, carries on research, and takes its expertise to the community through its extension programs. The University enrolls about 15,000 students, of whom 3,000 are pursuing master's and doctoral degrees. There are approximately 750 full-time faculty members.

Applying

All candidates for admission are required to provide a completed application form, a résumé, scores from the Graduate Management Admission Test (GMAT), a statement of purpose, two letters of recommendation, and all transcripts of previous undergraduate and postbaccalaureate work. Applicants for whom English is not the native language are expected to score 575 or above on the TOEFL.

Correspondence and Information

Assistant Director, M.B.A. Programs
College of Business Administration
7 Lippitt Road
Ballentine Hall, Room 210
University of Rhode Island
Kingston, Rhode Island 02881

Telephone: 401-874-5000
Fax: 401-874-4312
E-mail: hadz@uriacc.uri.edu

University of Rhode Island

THE FACULTY

Richard W. Scholl, Professor of Management and Director of Graduate Programs; Ph.D., California, Irvine, 1979.
Shaw K. Chen, Associate Professor of Management Science and Director of the Ph.D. Program; Ph.D., Michigan, 1988.
Laura Beauvais, Professor of Management and Director, Full-Time M.B.A. Program; Ph.D., Tennessee, 1987.
Lisa Hadzekyriakides, Assistant Director of Graduate Programs; M.B.A., Babson, 1994.
Charlotte Manni, Administrative Assistant

Accounting
Chairperson: Henry R. Schwarzbach, D.B.A., Colorado, 1976; CPA.
Judy K. Beckman, Ph.D., Texas Tech, 1991; CPA.
Edmund J. Boyle, Ph.D., Penn State, 1990; CPA.
Marshall A. Geiger, Ph.D., Penn State, 1988; CPA.
Alex Hazera, Ph.D., Kentucky, 1990; CPA.
Mark M. Higgins, Master of Science in Accounting Program Director; Ph.D., Tennessee, 1989; CPA.
Spencer J. Martin, Ph.D., Illinois, 1970; CPA.
Joseph P. Matoney Jr., Ph.D., Penn State, 1973; CPA.
Richard Vangermeersch, Ph.D., Florida, 1970; CPA; CMA.

Business Law
John Dunn, J.D., Boston College, 1977.
Charles Hickox, J.D., Washington (St. Louis), 1979.
Andrew Laviano, J.D., NYU, 1965.

Finance
Chairperson: Gene Lai, Ph.D., Texas at Austin, 1988.
Rosita P. Chang, Codirector, Center for Pacific-Basin Capital Markets Research; Ph.D., Pittsburgh, 1981; CFA.
Gordon H. Dash Jr., D.B.A., Colorado, 1978.
Yul Lee, Ph.D., Texas at Austin, 1986.
Blair M. Lord, Ph.D., California, Davis, 1975.
Dennis W. McLeavey, D.B.A., Indiana Bloomington, 1972; CFA.
Henry Oppenheimer, Ph.D., Purdue, 1979.
S. Ghon Rhee, Codirector, Center for Pacific-Basin Capital Markets Research; Ph.D., Ohio State, 1978.

Management
Chairperson: Sanjiv Dugal, Ph.D., Massachusetts, 1991.
Robert A. Comerford, Ph.D., Massachusetts, 1976.
Elizabeth Cooper, Ph.D., Akron, 1985.
George deLodzia, Ph.D., Syracuse, 1969.
Craig E. Overton, Ph.D., Massachusetts, 1971.
Linda M. Randall, Ph.D., Massachusetts, 1993.
Charles T. Schmidt Jr., Master of Science in Industrial and Labor Relations Program Director; Ph.D., Michigan State, 1968.
Clay V. Sink, Ph.D., Ohio State, 1968; CAM.

Management Science
Chairperson: Maling Ebrahimpour, Ph.D., Nebraska, 1986.
Roy Ageloff, Ph.D., Massachusetts, 1975.
Charles P. Armstrong, Ph.D., Arizona, 1973.
Frank S. Budnick, D.B.A., Maryland, 1973.
Shaw K. Chen, Ph.D., Michigan, 1988.
Alan B. Humphrey, Ph.D., North Carolina State, 1965.
Jeffrey Jarrett, Ph.D., NYU, 1967.
Chai Kim, Director, Institute for International Business; Ph.D., Pittsburgh, 1973.
Russell C. Koza, Ph.D., RPI, 1968.
Paul M. Mangiameli, Ph.D., Ohio State, 1979.
Richard Mojena, Ph.D., Cincinnati, 1971.
Seetharama Narasimhan, Ph.D., Ohio State, 1973.
Rohit Rampal, Ph.D. candidate, Oklahoma State.
Stuart Westin, Ph.D., Massachusetts, 1983.

Marketing
Chairperson: Albert J. Della Bitta, Ph.D., Massachusetts, 1971.
Nikhilesh Dholakia, Associate Director, Research Institute for Telecommunications and Information Marketing; Ph.D., Northwestern, 1975.
Ruby R. Dholakia, Director, Research Institute for Telecommunications and Information Marketing; Ph.D., Northwestern, 1976.
Bari Harlam, Ph.D., Pennsylvania, 1991.
Eugene M. Johnson, D.B.A., Washington (St. Louis), 1969.
Deborah Rosen, Ph.D., Tennessee, 1991.
Jonathan E. Schroeder, Ph.D., Berkeley, 1990.
Carol F. Surprenant, Ph.D., Wisconsin, 1981.
M. Venkatesan, Ph.D., Minnesota, 1965.

UNIVERSITY OF ROCHESTER

William E. Simon Graduate School of Business Administration

Programs of Study

The William E. Simon Graduate School of Business Administration offers programs leading to the degrees of Master of Business Administration (M.B.A.), Master of Science in business administration (M.S.), and Ph.D. in business administration. Joint programs with other schools of the University offer the M.B.A./M.D., the M.B.A./M.P.H. in public health, the M.B.A./M.S. in nursing, and the M.B.A./M.S. in microbiology and immunology. The Simon School's integrated, cross-functional approach to management is enhanced by the School's small size and significant international composition. The School uses the discipline of economics as both a framework and a common language of business.

The M.B.A. degree program requires 67 hours (twenty quarter courses) and can be completed in five or six quarters of full-time study. Five core courses are required in economics, applied statistics, accounting, and computers and information systems. One course must be taken in each of the functional areas of finance, marketing, operations management, and organization theory. A 2-credit course in business communications and a Practicum in Management capstone course are required of all full-time students. Ten elective courses are required, of which five or more may form a sequence of concentration. Although a concentration is not required for graduation, thirteen areas of concentration are offered: corporate accounting, public accounting, accounting and information systems, business environment and public policy, competitive and organizational strategy, computers and information systems, entrepreneurship, finance, health-care management, international management, marketing, services operations management, and manufacturing operations management. Double concentrations allow students to customize their M.B.A. degrees. The Simon School offers international exchange programs with eight well-regarded graduate business schools. The Ph.D. program requires 90 hours. Concentrations offered are as follows: accounting, competitive and organizational strategy, computers and information systems, finance, information systems economics, marketing, and operations management.

Research Facilities

The Management Library, housed in the main library of the University, contains extensive collections of reference, research, and reserve materials keyed to business and economic research. The School maintains its own Computing Center in Schlegel Hall. The modern facility supports student-accessible IBM-compatible and Macintosh personal computers linked for data sharing and laser printing via local area networks. Center staff also provide extensive consulting and reference documentation services for students, faculty, and staff. The center also offers access to several external data sources, such as Bloomberg, Business News, and Dow Jones as well as E-mail services in the Internet.

Financial Aid

For M.B.A. students, merit-based financial assistance is awarded by the School in the form of scholarships for both September and January entrance. Most admitted Ph.D. applicants receive a tuition scholarship and a fellowship. Graduate student loans are available through the Federal Ford Direct Loan Program and the GMAC-sponsored Tuition Loan Program. The Simon School is a member of the Consortium for Graduate Study in Management, through which financial aid is available to students from minority groups. Of the students who entered in fall 1997, 67 percent received merit-based awards.

Cost of Study

Tuition is $792 per credit hour or $26,136 per year in 1998–99. Costs of books and supplies average $1300 a year.

Living and Housing Costs

Living expenses are estimated at under $10,000 for the 1998–99 year. This includes rent, food, personal expenses, and health insurance.

Student Group

Enrollment in the M.B.A. program includes 420 full-time and 370 part-time students; about 50 are enrolled in the doctoral program for full-time study only. Full-time M.B.A. students' average age at entrance is 27. More than 90 percent enter the program with full-time work experience. Students have had a considerable variety of undergraduate majors that break down as follows: business administration, 30 percent; economics, 20 percent; engineering, science, and mathematics, 34 percent; and social sciences and humanities, 16 percent.

Location

Located on Lake Ontario, the Rochester area, with a population of nearly a million, is large enough to offer diverse opportunities for living, working, and enjoying recreation. Rochester and the surrounding metropolitan area gain much of their character and stability from industries that are, for the most part, highly technical. These industries, represented by such companies as Eastman Kodak and Bausch & Lomb, provide the Rochester-area labor force with a large percentage of skilled and professional employees.

The University

The University of Rochester, located in upstate New York, is coeducational, nonsectarian, independent, and privately endowed. Approximately 9,000 students are enrolled, 33 percent of whom are studying at the graduate level. Programs that range from the undergraduate through the postdoctoral levels are offered in some fifty major disciplines. The University is large enough to attract and retain a distinguished faculty and to offer all the other resources students require for graduate study. The Graduate School of Management, founded in 1958, was renamed the William E. Simon Graduate School of Business Administration in 1986. It is accredited by the American Assembly of Collegiate Schools of Business.

Applying

Each applicant is considered individually. Applicants for the M.B.A., M.S., and Ph.D. degree programs must take the Graduate Management Admission Test. The Graduate Record Examinations is an alternative for Ph.D. applicants only. This score, the undergraduate GPA, and work experience are important in the decision-making process; however, evidence of leadership, teamwork skills, and strong letters of recommendation also play key roles.

To be considered for admission in the fall quarter and for financial aid, M.B.A. applicants must send the completed forms and supporting data by March 1. If financial aid is not sought, application materials must be submitted by June 1. One third of the graduating class is admitted for the winter quarter and completes the six-quarter degree program eighteen months later in June; the application deadline for January entrance is November 15. The deadline for Ph.D. applicants is February 15.

Correspondence and Information

Admissions Office
William E. Simon Graduate School
of Business Administration
University of Rochester
Rochester, New York 14627

Telephone: 716-275-3533 (M.B.A. programs)
716-275-2959 (Ph.D. program)
Fax: 716-271-3907
E-mail: mbaadm@mail.ssb.rochester.edu
phdoffice@mail.ssb.rochester.edu
World Wide Web: http://www.ssb.rochester.edu

University of Rochester

THE FACULTY AND THEIR RESEARCH

Charles I. Plosser, Dean and Professor of Economics and Public Policy; Ph.D., Chicago.
Ronald W. Hansen, Associate Dean for Academic Affairs; Ph.D., Chicago.
Charles W. Miersch, Associate Dean for M.B.A. Programs and Development; M.B.A., Rochester.
Richard M. Popovic, Associate Dean for Executive Programs; M.B.A., Rochester.
Richard E. West, Associate Dean for Operations; M.B.A., Rochester.
Pamela Black-Colton, Assistant Dean for M.B.A. Admissions and Administration; M.B.A., Rochester.
Kevin Brennan, Assistant Dean for Information Technologies; M.B.A., Rochester.
Lee A. Junkans, Assistant Dean for Career Services; M.B.A., Baldwin-Wallace.
Stacey R. Kole, Assistant Dean for Academic Affairs and Assistant Professor of Economics and Management; Ph.D., Chicago.

Don B. Allen, Senior Lecturer in Business Administration and Business Law; J.D., Yale.
Ray Ball, Professor of Accounting; Ph.D., Chicago. Accounting, finance, economic analysis of organizations and markets.
Michael J. Barclay, Professor of Finance; Ph.D., Stanford. Empirical finance, economics of information.
Gregory H. Bauer, Assistant Professor of Finance; Ph.D., Pennsylvania (Wharton). International finance, investments, empirical asset pricing.
Patricia Bower-Cooley, Senior Lecturer in Management Communication; M.A., NYU.
James A. Brickley, Professor of Economics and Management; Ph.D., Oregon. Compensation contracts, corporate control, finance.
Thomas F. Cooley, Professor of Economics and Applied Statistics and Director, Bradley Policy Research Center; Ph.D., Pennsylvania. Microeconomic theory, econometrics.
Rajiv M. Dewan, Assistant Professor of Computers and Information Systems; Ph.D., Rochester. Decision support systems, financial information systems, management of information systems.
Gregory Dobson, Associate Professor of Operations Management and Operations Research; Ph.D., Stanford. Areas of operations management that deal with combinatorial problems of scheduling, routing, and location.
Marshall Freimer, Associate Professor of Applied Statistics, Operations Management, and Operations Research; Ph.D., Harvard. Statistical inferences.
Henri Groenevelt, Associate Professor of Operations Management; Ph.D., Columbia. Operations research and its applications, especially physical distribution and inventory models, stochastic systems, and dynamic programming; resource allocation.
Terrence J. Hendershott, Assistant Professor of Computers and Information Systems; Ph.D. candidate, Stanford. Electronic commerce, technology in financial markets, telecommunications, and software pricing.
Ludger Hentschel, Assistant Professor of Finance; Ph.D., Princeton. Financial economics, time-series econometrics, international finance.
Dan Horsky, Professor of Marketing; Ph.D., Purdue. Theoretical and empirical analysis of consumer and firm behavior.
Shailendra P. Jain, Assistant Professor of Marketing; Ph.D., NYU. Processing issues relating to comparative advertising, message framing and its influence on processing and judgments.
Gregg A. Jarrell, Professor of Economics and Finance; Ph.D., Chicago. Finance and securities markets.
Roy Jones, Assistant Professor of Computers and Information Systems; Ph.D. candidate, Stanford. Product and price competition for information goods.
A. Scott Keating, Assistant Professor of Accounting; D.B.A., Harvard. Management accounting and control, organization economics and the theory of the firm.
Melinda Knight, Professorial Lecturer in Management Communication; Ph.D., NYU. Contemporary rhetorical theory and practice, assessment, communication strategy, business history, and American studies.
S. P. Kothari, Professor of Accounting; Ph.D., Iowa. Capital structure, security price performance.
Phillip J. Lederer, Associate Professor of Operations Management; Ph.D., Northwestern. Theory and practice of management science and operations research as applied to economic problems.
Andrew J. Leone, Assistant Professor of Accounting; Ph.D., Pittsburgh. Management accounting, design of management control systems, and economic determinants of incentive compensation arrangements.
John B. Long Jr., Professor of Finance and Economics; Ph.D., Carnegie Mellon. Financial decision problems of firms.
Glenn M. MacDonald, Professor of Economics and Management; Ph.D., Rochester. Industry dynamics and technological change.
Leslie M. Marx, Assistant Professor of Economics and Management; Ph.D., Northwestern. Microeconomic theory, game theory, industrial organization.
Lawrence Matteson, Executive Professor of Business Administration; M.B.A., Rochester. Quality management.
K. Shridhar Moorthy, Associate Professor of Marketing; Ph.D., Stanford. Strategic decentralization and interaction in channels, product and price competition in a duopoly.
Paul E. Nelson, Associate Professor of Marketing; Ph.D., Rochester. Multiattribute models of consumer behavior, product positioning, and pricing segmentation.
Edieal Pinker, Assistant Professor of Computers and Information Systems; Ph.D., MIT. Modeling of flexible workforces and information technologies' effect on workforce management.
Steven S. Posavac, Assistant Professor of Marketing; Ph.D. candidate, Utah. Judgement and decision process, role of attitudes in consumer choice, and economic psychology.
Oliver M. Richard, Assistant Professor of Economics and Management; Ph.D., Northwestern. Empirical and industrial organization, with application to the airline industry.
Michael D. Ryall, Assistant Professor of Economics and Management; Ph.D., UCLA. Firm behavior in competitive markets, boundaries of the firm, internal organization.
Ronald M. Schmidt, Professorial Lecturer and Chairman, Faculty Committee on International Executive Programs; M.A., Ohio State. Price theory, marketing, labor economics, organization theory, theory of finance.
Paul J. Schweitzer, Professor of Operations Research and of Computers and Information Systems; Sc.D., MIT. Operations management, computer-integrated manufacturing, telecommunications.
G. William Schwert, Professor of Finance and Statistics; Ph.D., Chicago. Portfolio and capital market theory, econometrics and time-series analysis, effects of public regulation on business.
Abraham Seidmann, Professor of Computers and Information Systems and of Operations Management; Ph.D., Texas Tech. Robotic manufacturing systems design, evaluation of computer systems, manufacturing information systems.
Edna Seidmann, Senior Lecturer in Business Administration; M.A., Tel-Aviv. Accounting and finance.
Greg Shaffer, Assistant Professor of Marketing; Ph.D., Princeton. Pricing and promotions, vertical relations among firms, database marketing, and business law and competition policy.
Jay A. Shanken, Professor of Finance; Ph.D., Carnegie Mellon. Asset-pricing models, theory and testing; empirical work in finance and accounting, applied and theoretical econometrics.
Robert A. Shumsky, Assistant Professor of Operations Management; Ph.D., MIT. Stochastic modeling of components of U.S. air traffic system, forecasting.
Clifford W. Smith Jr., Professor of Finance and Economics; Ph.D., North Carolina at Chapel Hill. Option pricing, corporate financial policy, financial intermediation.
R. Lawrence Van Horn, Assistant Professor of Economics and Management; Ph.D., Pennsylvania. Agency relations in health care, dynamics of organizational response to competition, value of reputation in health-care markets.
Jerold B. Warner, Professor of Finance; Ph.D., Chicago. Portfolio theory, capital markets, corporate finance.
Ross L. Watts, Professor of Accounting and Finance; Ph.D., Chicago. Accounting, finance, economics.
Allan Wolk, Senior Lecturer in Business Law and Accounting; J.D., Syracuse. Federal and state taxation and corporate law.
Ronald N. Yeaple, Executive Professor in Marketing and Business Policy; Ph.D., Rochester. High-technology products and marketing.
Jerold L. Zimmerman, Professor of Accounting; Ph.D., Berkeley. Financial and managerial accounting.
Ellen Zuroski, Senior Lecturer in Management Communication; Ph.D. candidate, Rochester. Cross-cultural communication and second language acquisition.

UNIVERSITY OF ST. THOMAS

Graduate School of Business

Programs of Study

The Graduate School of Business (GSB) at the University of St. Thomas has more than 3,000 students in nine master's degree programs and is the fourth-largest graduate school of business in the United States. In addition, thirteen professional development centers and institutes serve more than 18,000 students annually. The mission of the GSB is to provide learning opportunities and services for individuals at various stages of development. The School seeks to enhance the knowledge, skills, and judgment required to perform effectively in a quality-conscious, global marketplace. The School pursues this mission to enrich the lives of individuals, enhance the effectiveness of organizations, and promote a more vital ethical community.

The Evening M.B.A. program provides working professionals with a comprehensive business management education, beginning with foundation and core courses tailored to students' individual needs. Students complete a minimum of four concentration courses, and the program culminates with one of four integrative capstone courses. St. Thomas' new program, the Day M.B.A., launched in fall 1997. Designed for recent college graduates and career changers, it provides students with the business knowledge and skills needed to get careers off to a strong start. Areas of concentration include accounting, environmental management, finance, financial services management, franchise management, health-care management, human resource management, information management, management, manufacturing systems, marketing, nonprofit management, real estate, risk and insurance management, sports and entertainment management, and venture management.

Other master's programs include the Accounting M.B.A., a full-time, fifteen-month program for recent liberal arts and sciences graduates and those seeking a career change to the accounting profession; the Executive M.B.A., with an integrative focus for experienced managers; the Master of Business Communication, for professional communicators who wish to broaden their business knowledge and enhance their technical skills; the Master of International Management, for managers wishing to develop or extend a career in international business; the M.B.A. in Human Resource Management, for human resource professionals or career-changers wishing to develop specific competencies; the M.B.A. in Medical Group Management, for health-care professionals and those wishing to develop a management career in that field; and the M.S. in Real Estate Appraisal, for real estate appraisers who are involved in complex appraisal assignments.

Research Facilities

The majority of programs at the UST Graduate School of Business take place at its downtown Minneapolis campus. This state-of-the-art facility offers comprehensive services and a dynamic educational environment. The Graduate School of Business also conducts classes and programs in St. Paul on the beautiful, 78-acre original campus. In addition, GSB courses take place in the surrounding Minnesota communities of Anoka, Chaska, Owatonna, and Rochester and at the Mall of America. Students have access to more than 150 computing stations, which provide access to the Internet, VAX network, e-mail system, electronic databases, and other library resources. Comprehensive library resources, with more than 300,000 volumes, are located on both the Minneapolis and St. Paul campuses. Distance-learning facilities also exist on most campuses.

Financial Aid

Financial aid is available through a variety of private, institutional, and federal programs on both a need and merit basis. For information on these programs, students should contact Student Financial Services at 612-962-6550. In addition, many employers will pay or subsidize their employees' tuition expenses.

Cost of Study

Tuition for 1998–99 is $416 per credit hour for all programs except the Executive M.B.A. program, which is $585 per credit hour. Book expenses vary by program and course. Nondegree professional development courses are also available at competitive rates for both employers and individuals.

Living and Housing Costs

On- and off-campus housing is available to graduate students. The University of St. Thomas Residence Life department will help students arrange for on-campus housing. Housing costs range from $1275 to $1870 per semester. For information on on-campus housing, students should call 612-962-6470. A number of services and publications in the Twin Cities area provide off-campus residential listings.

Student Group

Students in the GSB range from working professionals and recent college graduates to adults interested in changing career fields. The majority of students are employed full-time and are pursuing their degrees on a part-time basis.

Location

The Twin Cities of Minneapolis and St. Paul are among the country's most vibrant cultural centers. The business community features a number of Fortune 500 corporations. The Twin Cities are also home to two world-class symphonies and internationally acclaimed theaters and art museums. In addition, Minneapolis features many professional sports teams and provides a wide range of opportunities for recreational athletes. The Mall of America in Bloomington is within minutes of the St. Paul and Minneapolis campuses.

The University

The University of St. Thomas is a comprehensive, coeducational, Catholic university. Founded in 1885, St. Thomas is now the largest private university in Minnesota. It is dedicated to providing career-oriented, value-centered education in a dynamic, stimulating environment. St. Thomas welcomes students of any race, color, creed, and national or ethnic origin.

Applying

Admission requirements vary by degree program, especially with regard to previous work or managerial experience (many programs require at least two years of postundergraduate work experience), requirements for a personal essay, and letters of recommendation. In general, programs require GMAT scores above the fiftieth percentile and TOEFL scores of at least 550. The Executive M.B.A. program requires the Miller Analogies Test. The average undergraduate GPA of incoming students is 3.0, based upon receipt of official transcripts from applicants' schools.

Applications are considered on a rolling basis for most programs. Most programs adhere to a semester schedule, but cohort programs such as the Accounting M.B.A., Day M.B.A., Executive M.B.A., and M.B.A. in Medical Group Management may have different start times. For specific information and application materials, students should contact the Graduate School of Business at the address listed below.

Correspondence and Information

Graduate School of Business
University of St. Thomas
1000 LaSalle Avenue, MPL251
Minneapolis, Minnesota 55403-2005

Telephone: 612-962-4200
800-328-6819 Ext. 2-4200 (toll-free)
Fax: 612-962-4260
E-mail: mba@stthomas.edu
World Wide Web: http://www.gsb.stthomas.edu

University of St. Thomas

FACULTY

St. Thomas' full-time and adjunct faculty members, many of whom are leaders in their industries, bring a wealth of business and academic experience to the classroom. This unique mixture of expertise results in leading-edge curricula and the real-world applied approach that makes a University of St. Thomas degree so valued in the business community. Students benefit from this expertise through the accessibility that results from small class sizes and the advisory or mentoring roles assumed by many faculty members.

Deans and Directors of the Master's Programs
Jeanne Buckeye, Associate Dean, Graduate School of Business.
Theodore Fredrickson, Dean, Graduate School of Business.

Bill Davidson, Director, Accounting M.B.A. Program.
Mohammad Eftekhari, Director, Master of International Management Program.
Thomas Gilliam, Director, M.B.A. in Medical Group Management.
Nona Mason, Director, Master of Business Communication Program.
Bill Monson, Director, Executive M.B.A. Program.
Thomas Musil, Director, M.S. in Real Estate Appraisal Program.
R. Stanford Nyquist, Director, Day and Evening M.B.A. Programs.
Philip Schechter, Director, M.B.A. in Human Resource Management Program.

UNIVERSITY OF SAN DIEGO

School of Business Administration

Programs of Study

The Master of Business Administration (M.B.A.) and the Master of International Business (M.I.B.) programs are 60 units in length and are designed for students with no prior academic background in business. Students with prior course work in the core business subjects may waive up to 30 units. The cornerstone of the degree programs at the University of San Diego (USD) is flexibility. Students can begin their studies in fall, spring, or summer. They can also attend full-time or part-time and days or evenings. Students can choose from such fields as finance, management, marketing, international business, real estate, project management, supply management, or new venture management or can obtain a broad-based general M.B.A. or M.I.B. degree. They can also choose which elective courses to take and in which semester to take them. The School of Business Administration provides students with the choice to avail themselves of contact with local firms and well-placed alumni, to participate in internship programs here or abroad, or to experience other cultures through study-abroad opportunities.

To meet the challenges of a new century, the student in the M.B.A. and M.I.B. programs at the University of San Diego receives comprehensive training in theory and case analysis. This develops technical and financial skills, fosters global and strategic thinking, and provides a philosophy that stresses corporate responsibility and the interconnectedness among all the stakeholders of the business enterprise. These skills are reinforced through extensive team exercises and group projects in classes that average 25 students and through interaction with businesses and business leaders locally, nationally, and internationally.

Research Facilities

Copely Library features more than 360,000 books and 2,200 current journal subscriptions as well as newspapers, government documents, reference books, rare books, and access to many databases. The Media Center has an extensive AV collection. The Legal Research Center in the School of Law maintains a collection in excess of 375,000 volumes.

Funded by a $4.5 million grant from the Olin Foundation, Inc., Olin Hall is home to the School of Business Administration. It houses equipment and facilities that are on the cutting edge of business education.

Financial Aid

The University distributes financial aid in the form of fellowships, scholarships, grants, loans, student employment, and assistantships. To file for financial aid, students must complete the Free Application for Federal Student Aid (FAFSA) and the USD Financial Aid Application (USD FAA). Students should contact the Office of Financial Aid, Hughes Administration Center, University of San Diego, 5998 Alcala Park, San Diego, California 92110 or call 619-260-4514 or 800-248-4873 (toll-free) for application material. Students interested in applying for Graduate Fellowships should contact the School of Business Administration and for Graduate Assistantships, the Human Resources Office (619-260-4626).

Cost of Study

For the 1998–99 academic year, master's tuition costs are $585 per semester unit.

Living and Housing Costs

Information on graduate housing can be obtained by contacting the Housing Office, University of San Diego, Mission Crossroads, 5998 Alcala Park, San Diego, California 92110 or by calling 619-260-4622. Limited graduate housing is available in the one-bedroom Presidio Terrace Apartments. The University is surrounded by affordable off-campus apartments, condominiums, and homes. Many students reside in nearby Mission Beach.

Student Group

The University's student population in 1997–98 was 6,534, including 1,194 graduate students and 1,105 law students. Students come from all over the United States, and international students represent about 10 percent of the graduate enrollment.

Location

San Diego, a city of more than 1 million people, is the second-largest city in California. Just 30 minutes north of the border of Mexico, it offers spectacular views of the Pacific Ocean and the surrounding mountains. USD's 180-acre campus provides access to business, cultural, residential, and recreational areas with its proximity to air and rail terminals, city bus stops, and freeways.

The School

The USD School of Business Administration currently enrolls approximately 1,000 students in its undergraduate programs and 400 at the graduate level in its Master of Business Administration (M.B.A.), Master of International Business (M.I.B.), and joint M.B.A./J.D., M.I.B./J.D., and M.B.A./M.S.N. programs.

Applying

Application for admission is made to the Office of Graduate Admissions. All applicants must submit the application form, application fee, one official copy of all postsecondary transcripts, three letters of recommendation, a resume, and official GMAT scores. International applicants are advised to contact the Office of Graduate Admissions for specific directives. Application priority filing dates are May 1 for the fall semester, November 15 for the spring semester, and March 15 for the summer term.

Correspondence and Information

Office of Graduate Admissions
University of San Diego
5998 Alcala Park
San Diego, California 92110
Telephone: 619-260-4524
800-248-4873 (toll-free)
Fax: 619-260-4158
E-mail: grads@acusd.edu

University of San Diego

THE FACULTY

Curtis W. Cook, Dean and Professor of Management; D.B.A., USC.
Gary G. Whitney, Associate Dean and Professor of Management; Ph.D., Washington (Seattle).
Carmen M. Barcena, Assistant Dean; Ed.D., San Diego.
Charles J. Teplitz, Director of Graduate Business Programs and Professor of Operations and Project Management; D.B.A., Kent State.
Gregory M. Gazda, Director of the John Ahlers Center for International Business and Professor of Marketing; Ph.D., Arizona State.
Jane Usatin, Director of Undergraduate Programs; Ph.D., Texas at Austin.

Andrew T. Allen, Associate Professor of Economics; Ph.D., Illinois at Urbana-Champaign.
Jean-Pierre Amor, Associate Professor of Management Science; Ph.D., UCLA.
*Joan B. Anderson, Professor of Economics; Ph.D., California, San Diego.
E. Elizabeth Arnold, Professor of Business Law; J.D., San Diego, M.B.A., California State, Sacramento.
Craig B. Barkacs, Associate Professor of Business Law; J.D., M.B.A., San Diego.
Dennis R. Briscoe, Professor of Human Resource Management; Ph.D., Michigan State.
Mary E. Bullock, Assistant Professor of Business Law; J.D., M.B.A., San Diego.
James M. Burns, Professor of Management; D.B.A., Harvard.
David N. Burt, NAPM Professor of Supply Management; Ph.D., Stanford.
*James M. Caltrider, Associate Professor of Operations Management; Ph.D., Colorado School of Mines.
N. Ellen Cook, Professor of Accounting and International Business; Ph.D., UCLA.
Thomas M. Dalton, Associate Professor of Accounting; Ph.D., Houston; CPA.
Shreesh D. Deshpande, Associate Professor of Finance; Ph.D., Penn State.
*Denise E. Dimon, Professor of Economics; Ph.D., Illinois at Urbana-Champaign.
Kokila Doshi, Associate Professor of Economics; Ph.D., Rochester.
Seth Ellis, Associate Professor of Marketing; Ph.D., Arizona.
James W. Evans, Associate Professor of Business and Government; Ph.D., Claremont.
Alan Gin, Associate Professor of Economics; Ph.D., California, Santa Barbara.
Donald L. Helmich, Professor of Management Science; Ph.D., Oregon.
Charles F. Holt, Associate Professor of Economics; Ph.D., Purdue.
Johanna Steggert Hunsaker, Professor of Management and Education; Ph.D., Wisconsin–Milwaukee.
Phillip L. Hunsaker, Professor of Management; D.B.A., USC.
Robert R. Johnson, Professor of Economics; Ph.D., Oregon.
Ahmer S. Karim, Associate Professor of Computer Information Systems; Ph.D., Arizona State.
Timothy P. Kelley, Professor of Accounting; Ph.D., Houston; CPA.
Scott W. Kunkel, Associate Professor of Management; Ph.D., Georgia.
Marc Lampe, Associate Professor of Business Law and Social Responsibility; J.D., San Francisco; M.B.A., San Francisco State.
C. David Light, Associate Professor of Marketing; Ph.D., North Texas.
Don H. Mann, Associate Professor of Marketing; Ph.D., UCLA.
Loren L. Margheim, Professor of Accounting; Ph.D., Arizona State; CPA.
Thomas O. Morris, Professor of International Management; Ph.D., Denver.
Andrew Narwold, Associate Professor of Economics; Ph.D., California, Santa Barbara.
Arti Notani, Assistant Professor of Marketing; Ph.D., Cincinnati.
Robert F. O'Neil, Professor of Economics; Ph.D., Fordham.
Rosalie Liccardo Pacula, Assistant Professor of Economics; Ph.D., Duke.
Diane D. Pattison, Professor of Accounting; Ph.D., Washington (Seattle).
Cynthia Pavett, Professor of Management; Ph.D., Utah.
James T. Perry, Professor of Management Information Systems; Ph.D., Penn State.
Mario J. Picconi, Professor of Finance; Ph.D., Rutgers.
Darlene A. Pienta, Assistant Professor of Strategic Management; Ph.D., USC.
Manzur Rahman, Associate Professor of Finance; Ph.D., South Carolina.
Eugene J. Rathswohl, Professor of Information Management; Ph.D., Pittsburgh.
Mark J. Riedy, Ernest W. Hahn Professor of Real Estate Finance; Ph.D., Michigan.
Daniel A. Rivetti, Associate Professor of Finance; D.B.A., Kent State.
John R. Ronchetto Jr., Associate Professor of Marketing; Ph.D., Arizona State.
Miriam Rothman, Associate Professor of Human Resource Management; Ph.D., Washington (Seattle).
Jonathan Sandy, Professor of Economics; Ph.D., California, Santa Barbara.
Gary P. Schneider, Associate Professor of Accounting and Information Systems; Ph.D., Tennessee; CPA.
Tyagarajan N. Somasundaram, Associate Professor of Marketing; Ph.D., Wisconsin–Milwaukee.
William R. Soukup, Associate Professor of Management; Ph.D., Purdue.
Donn W. Vickrey, Associate Professor of Accounting; Ph.D., Oklahoma State; CPA.
Barbara Withers, Associate Professor of Management Science; Ph.D., Colorado.
Dirk S. Yandell, Professor of Economics; Ph.D., Purdue.
Dennis P. Zocco, Professor of Finance; Ph.D., Lehigh.

Denotes Fulbright scholar

UNIVERSITY OF SOUTH CAROLINA

College of Business Administration

Programs of Study

The College of Business Administration, accredited by the AACSB–The International Association for Management Education, offers programs of study leading to the degrees of Doctor of Philosophy (Ph.D.) in business administration, Master of Business Administration (M.B.A.), Master of Accountancy (M.Acc.), Master of Taxation (M.Tax.), Master of Human Resources (M.H.R.), Master of International Business Studies (M.I.B.S.), and International Master of Business Administration (I.M.B.A.). Joint-degree programs with the Law School are available. The program leading to the Ph.D. degree in business administration is designed for students of outstanding ability who wish to do advanced work in preparation for careers in university teaching and research, business, and government. Areas of concentration are accounting, finance, international business, international finance, management information systems, marketing, operations research, organizational behavior, probability and statistics, production/operations management, and strategic management/business policy. The M.B.A. program serves the needs of individuals wishing to pursue either full- or part-time advanced degree work in business administration. The program requires 60 semester hours of course work: thirteen core courses, five elective courses, and a summer field consulting project. The field consulting project gives the student practical business experience through an assigned group project with a participating company. For information about the M.I.B.S. program, interested students should refer to the M.I.B.S. entry in this publication. The I.M.B.A. is a 45-semester-hour program offered cooperatively with the University of Economics and Business in Vienna, Austria. Students study for approximately eight months in Vienna and seven months at USC. The M.Acc. program is designed to prepare students for careers in public, private, and governmental accounting. The program requires a minimum of 30 semester hours of graduate study for students with appropriate undergraduate backgrounds in accounting and business administration. The M.Tax. program is a professional-degree program that provides students with the knowledge and technical skills necessary for entry-level positions as tax accountants. Thirty-six semester hours are required to complete the program. The M.H.R. program is designed to train specialized professionals for careers in personnel and employment relations. The program requires 42 semester hours of course work consisting of eleven core courses, two elective courses, and a work internship.

Research Facilities

The modern nine-story facility that houses the College of Business Administration has one floor devoted to a computer and statistics center and one floor to a library for business administration. Facilities also include case rooms, a television center, and a behavioral learning laboratory. The College offers students access to more than 200 computer terminals. The Division of Information Resources operates a large open-systems network comprising multiple Novell and UNIX servers with 650 clients and 32 billion characters of online storage. The division also has access to the University's central computer facility, which features an IBM 3081 D24 using MVS/XA for batch support and IBM 3081 D24 using VM/CMS for interactive support. The University's main library, which can seat 2,500 users at one time, houses more than 6.3 million volumes, microform entries, manuscripts, and periodicals.

Financial Aid

A number of competitive assistantships and fellowships are available to entering graduate students. Assistantships carry stipends of $2000 to $5000 for the 1998–99 academic year for master's students and up to $9000 per academic year for doctoral students. Graduate assistants are charged a special tuition rate.

Cost of Study

Tuition for 1998–99 for all full-time students is estimated at $1862 per semester for in-state students and $3817 per semester for out-of-state students. There is a one-time, nonrefundable enrichment fee, which is $2900 for in-state students and $4400 for out-of-state students for all master's degree programs except M.I.B.S. The enrichment fee for M.I.B.S. students is estimated at $5000 for in-state students and $8800 for out-of-state students. Tuition and fees for the I.M.B.A. program are $25,000 with no enrichment fees. Tuition and fees are set by the Board of Trustees and are subject to change.

Living and Housing Costs

Information on University housing can be obtained by contacting the director of housing at the University of South Carolina (telephone: 803-777-4283). Students desiring off-campus housing should contact the Off-Campus Student Services Office (telephone: 803-777-4174).

Student Group

The University's total enrollment of more than 26,000 students at the Columbia campus includes more than 3,300 students in the College of Business Administration. More than 1,100 are enrolled in graduate business programs. Graduate students represent most areas of the United States and many countries and bring to the University diverse backgrounds from the liberal arts and sciences as well as from business administration.

Student Outcomes

Fortune 500 companies, other large national and multinational corporations, small- to medium-size companies, government agencies, and not-for-profit organizations actively recruit individuals from the College's graduate programs. Recent graduates have been employed by companies such as Andersen Consulting (management consulting), Nations Bank (investment banking), Pepsico (product management), Ernst & Young (accounting), Michelin (operations management), Continental Airlines (finance), and Datastream Systems (information systems).

Location

Serving a metropolitan area of approximately 472,000 people, the Columbia community offers a variety of cultural and religious activities. For recreation, there are a variety of city and state parks, the acclaimed Riverbanks Zoo, and Lake Murray. Within a few hours' time, one can reach varied activities ranging from the nightlife of Atlanta to Hilton Head and the coastal beaches to the ski resorts of North Carolina.

The University

Founded in 1801, the University is a state-supported coeducational institution. During the last decade, the University has manifested a strong commitment to graduate and professional education. With more than 9,000 students now enrolled in graduate work, a highly regarded Law School, and a School of Medicine, the University has assumed a place among the major graduate institutions in the nation.

Applying

Applications may be made for the M.Acc., M.Tax., M.H.R., and Ph.D. programs in the summer or fall. The I.M.B.A. and M.I.B.S. programs can be entered only in June. All M.B.A. students begin the core of their program in the fall term. All applications require submission of the Graduate Management Admission Test score. Assistantship and fellowship applications and the application package must be postmarked by February 1 for priority consideration.

Correspondence and Information

Graduate Division, PG98
College of Business Administration
University of South Carolina
Columbia, South Carolina 29208

Telephone: 803-777-4346
Fax: 803-777-0414
World Wide Web: http://www.business.sc.edu

University of South Carolina

THE FACULTY

Accounting

Garnett F. Beazley Jr., Professor; Ph.D., Pittsburgh, 1963. Eugene G. Chewning, Associate Professor; Ph.D., South Carolina, 1984. Maribeth Coller, Associate Professor; Ph.D., Indiana, 1991. Frank T. DeZoort, Assistant Professor; Ph.D., Alabama, 1995. Timothy S. Doupnik, Professor; Ph.D., Illinois at Urbana-Champaign, 1983. James B. Edwards, Professor; Ph.D., Georgia, 1973. Adrian M. Harrell, Professor; Ph.D., Texas at Austin, 1975. Paul D. Harrison, Associate Professor; Ph.D., Arizona State, 1982. Robert A. Leitch, Professor; Ph.D., Tennessee, 1973. Gary A. Luoma, Professor; D.B.A., Washington (St. Louis), 1966. Robert J. Rolfe, Professor; Ph.D., Oklahoma, 1983. Earl A. Spiller Jr., Professor; Ph.D., Michigan, 1960. Caroline D. Strobel, Professor; Ph.D., Georgia, 1978. Brad M. Tuttle, Associate Professor; Ph.D., Arizona State, 1991. Richard A. White, Professor; Ph.D., Arizona State, 1981.

Banking, Financial Management, Insurance, and Real Estate

LeRoy D. Brooks, Professor; Ph.D., Michigan State, 1971. Helen I. Doerpinghaus, Associate Professor; Ph.D., Pennsylvania, 1989. Scott E. Harrington, Professor; Ph.D., Illinois at Urbana-Champaign, 1979. Timothy W. Koch, Professor; Ph.D., Purdue, 1976. Steven V. Mann, Associate Professor; Ph.D., Nebraska, 1987. William T. Moore, Professor; Ph.D., Virginia Tech, 1982. Gregory R. Niehaus, Associate Professor; Ph.D., Washington (St. Louis), 1985. S. Travis Pritchett, Professor; D.B.A., Indiana, 1969. Pradipkumar Ramanlal, Assistant Professor; Ph.D., Michigan, 1987. Rodney L. Roenfeldt, Professor; D.B.A., Indiana, 1972. Ronald C. Rogers, Associate Professor; Ph.D., Ohio State, 1982. Neil W. Sicherman, Associate Professor; Ph.D., Florida, 1986.

International Business

Jeffrey S. Arpan, Professor; D.B.A., Indiana, 1971. W. Randolph Folks, Professor; D.B.A., Harvard, 1970. Kent W. Hargis, Assistant Professor; Ph.D., Illinois at Urbana-Champaign, 1995. Tatiana D. Kostova, Assistant Professor; Ph.D., Minnesota, 1996. James A. Kuhlman, Professor; Ph.D., Northwestern, 1971. Chun-Yau Kwok, Professor; Ph.D., Texas at Austin, 1984. R. Bruce Money, Assistant Professor; Ph.D., California, Irvine, 1995. Douglas W. Nigh, Associate Professor; Ph.D., UCLA, 1981. Kendall Roth, Professor; Ph.D., South Carolina, 1986. Martin A. Roth, Associate Professor; Ph.D., Pittsburgh, 1990.

Management

Alan D. Bauerschmidt, Professor; Ph.D., Florida, 1968. Daniel C. Feldman, Professor; Ph.D., Yale, 1976. Brian S. Klaas, Associate Professor; Ph.D., Wisconsin–Madison, 1987. M. Audrey Korsgaard, Associate Professor; Ph.D., NYU, 1990. Shirley Kuiper, Associate Professor; Ed.D., Indiana, 1976. Michael J. Leiblein, Assistant Professor; Ph.D., Purdue, 1996. John E. Logan, Associate Professor; Ph.D., Columbia, 1969. Bruce M. Meglino, Professor; Ph.D., Massachusetts, 1973. Elizabeth Ravlin, Associate Professor; Ph.D., Carnegie Mellon, 1986. Richard B. Robinson Jr., Professor; Ph.D., Georgia, 1980. William R. Sandberg, Associate Professor; Ph.D., Georgia, 1984. Harry Sapienza, Associate Professor; Ph.D., Maryland, 1989. David M. Schweiger, Professor; D.B.A., Maryland, 1980. Hoyt N. Wheeler, Professor; Ph.D., Wisconsin–Madison, 1974.

Management Science

Joan Donohue, Associate Professor; Ph.D., Virginia Tech, 1988. Kirk D. Fiedler, Associate Professor; Ph.D., Pittsburgh, 1991. Timothy D. Fry, Associate Professor; Ph.D., Georgia, 1984. J. Stanley Fryer, Professor; D.B.A., Indiana, 1971. Varun Grover, Associate Professor; Ph.D., Pittsburgh, 1990. Edgar P. Hickman, Professor; Ph.D., North Carolina at Chapel Hill, 1958. James G. Hilton, Professor; Ph.D., Iowa State, 1960. Kirk R. Karwan, Associate Professor; Ph.D., Carnegie Mellon, 1979. William J. Kettinger, Assistant Professor; Ph.D., South Carolina, 1992. Manoj K. Malhotra, Associate Professor; Ph.D., Ohio State, 1990. Robert E. Markland, Professor; D.B.A., Washington (St. Louis), 1969. Dennis H. Oberhelman, Associate Professor; Ph.D., Purdue, 1978. Patrick R. Philipoom, Associate Professor; Ph.D., Virginia Tech, 1986. Gary R. Reeves, Professor; D.S., Washington (St. Louis), 1973. J. Michael Ryan, Associate Professor; Ph.D., Missouri–Columbia, 1972. David L. Shrock, Professor; D.B.A., Indiana, 1973. Daniel C. Steele, Associate Professor; Ph.D., Iowa, 1992. James R. Sweigart, Associate Professor; Ph.D., Carnegie Mellon, 1976. James T. C. Teng, Associate Professor; Ph.D., Minnesota, 1980. Kathleen M. Whitcomb, Associate Professor; Ph.D., Minnesota, 1989.

Marketing

William O. Bearden, Professor; Ph.D., South Carolina, 1975. James F. Kane, Professor; D.B.A., Washington (St. Louis), 1964. Thomas J. Madden, Associate Professor; Ph.D., Massachusetts, 1982. Randall L. Rose, Associate Professor; Ph.D., Ohio State, 1986. Subhash Sharma, Professor; Ph.D., Texas at Austin, 1978. Terence A. Shimp, Professor; D.B.A., Maryland, 1974. F. Kelly Shuptrine, Associate Professor; Ph.D., Texas at Austin, 1971. Jesse E. Teel, Professor; Ph.D., North Carolina at Chapel Hill, 1976. John F. Willenborg, Professor; D.B.A., Washington (St. Louis), 1969.

UNIVERSITY OF TENNESSEE, KNOXVILLE

College of Business Administration

Programs of Study

The College of Business Administration offers AACSB–accredited programs leading to the Master of Business Administration (M.B.A.), the Executive Master of Business Administration (E.M.B.A.), the Master of Accountancy (M.Acc.), the Master of Science (M.S.) with concentrations in industrial/organizational psychology, management science, or statistics; the Master of Arts (M.A.) in economics; the Doctor of Philosophy (Ph.D.) in business administration with concentrations in accounting, finance, logistics and transportation, marketing, management science, statistics, and strategic management; and the Ph.D. with majors in economics, management science, and industrial/organizational psychology. The M.B.A. program, the centerpiece of graduate studies, encompasses the principles of creating consumer value, total quality management, cross-functional systems, integrated systems course work, just-in-time teaching, and leadership and interpersonal skills. Through an intensive first-year curriculum featuring a fully integrated yearlong case incorporating research, experiential learning, individual assessment, and team projects, a foundation is built for the second-year focus on areas of concentration. These areas include logistics/transportation, new-venture analysis, environmental management, and statistics, in addition to interdisciplinary and traditional fields of study. The M.B.A. program is available on a full-time basis only and requires 54 semester hours of course work and two years to complete. All students participate in a summer internship between their first and second years. A joint-degree Doctor of Jurisprudence (J.D.)/M.B.A. program is offered in conjunction with the College of Law, and a joint M.S./M.B.A. in manufacturing management and engineering is offered in conjunction with the College of Engineering. Placement assistance is provided by the College's business placement director. The E.M.B.A. program is a one-year accelerated program designed for experienced managers who will play a leadership role in their organizations. The program curriculum is unique in applying its principles to major products within the sponsoring organization during the year of study. The one-year format of six residence periods away from work (one is international), study, and applications on the job accommodates participants from around the country. The M.Acc. degree offers three tracks of specialization: tax, information systems, and auditing. The 30-semester-hour program is designed for students who have completed an accredited bachelor's degree program with a major in accounting. However, a student with a bachelor's degree in another area may receive the M.Acc. degree by doing additional course work in accounting. The M.S. and M.A. program requirements range from 30 to 38 semester hours of master's-level course work; the option of preparing a thesis for 6 hours of credit is available in all programs. The Ph.D. program normally requires at least three years of intensive study and research beyond the master's level, and it is designed for full-time students only. The first two years consist of course work, writing, and research. The following years focus on completion of the dissertation. Each doctoral student acts as a teaching or research assistant and receives financial support for these services from the College.

Research Facilities

The University's $27-million library is the largest in Tennessee. It is equipped with the latest in research-oriented computer technology and with study carrels set aside for graduate students. The College operates personal computer laboratories containing sixty PCs. A variety of business-oriented software, which has been fully integrated into the curriculum, is available to the students through these laboratories.

Financial Aid

Merit-based fellowships are awarded by the College. Teaching and research assistantships carrying a full tuition waiver and a monthly stipend are also granted. Other sources of aid may be coordinated through the Office of Financial Aid, 115 Student Services Building (telephone: 423-974-3131).

Cost of Study

The 1998–99 in-state tuition for full-time study is $3154 per year; out-of-state tuition is $8210 per year. All students must pay an activities fee of $222 per year.

Living and Housing Costs

Information about University-owned apartments for graduate students is available from the Office of Rental Properties, 474 South Stadium Hall (telephone: 423-974-3431). Information concerning Knoxville area housing is provided by the Off-Campus Housing Office, 336 University Center (telephone: 423-974-5276). Single, independent in-state students should plan a budget of approximately $11,000 to cover annual educational and living expenses. Out-of-state students should budget around $15,000.

Student Group

The entering M.B.A. class in fall 1997 was composed of 85 students, of whom 30 percent were women. Their mean GPA was 3.33, and the mean GMAT score was 610 (85th percentile). Thirty-seven percent of these students were business undergraduates, 38 percent earned liberal arts degrees, 12 percent earned degrees in engineering, and 13 percent earned their degrees in other areas. Ninety-two percent of the entering students had more than a year of full-time work experience. The total number of M.B.A. students is 181. There are about 95 M.Acc. students and a smaller number in each of the M.S., M.A., and Ph.D. programs. The College's placement record in the past few years has been excellent: 95 percent of the graduating classes obtained positions within forty-five days of graduation.

Student Outcomes

The placement rate for UTK M.B.A. graduates is high, with 90 percent typically placed by graduation and nearly all placed within three months of graduation. More than 416 companies recruit program graduates annually, and average salaries have increased steadily. Graduates take positions with some of the nation's leading businesses in such areas as consulting, marketing research, sales, health-care delivery, flexible manufacturing, and investment banking, among others. Alumni report challenging and rewarding careers.

Location

Knoxville lies within a metropolitan area of approximately 600,000 that houses major corporate headquarters and numerous industrial and commercial operations. Many cultural and entertainment activities are available year-round, and the nearby Great Smoky Mountains National Park offers summer and winter recreational opportunities. Knoxville is consistently rated as one of the top ten cities in the country in providing gracious amenities and a high quality of life.

The University and The College

The University of Tennessee, Knoxville, a federal land-grant institution, is one of the nation's twenty largest universities, enrolling approximately 25,000 students, including 6,500 graduate students. The College of Business Administration is the second-largest college of the University, enrolling 3,900 students.

Applying

The M.B.A. program application deadline (fall entrance only) for all students is March 1. The M.Acc. and Ph.D. program deadlines are also March 1. The deadline for University-wide sources of financial aid is March 1. College awards are usually granted by May 1. Application materials may be obtained from the Office of Graduate Business Programs.

Correspondence and Information

Director of Admissions
M.B.A. Program Office
College of Business Administration
527 Stokely Management Center
University of Tennessee
Knoxville, Tennessee 37996-0552
Telephone: 423-974-5033
Fax: 423-974-3826
World Wide Web: http://mba.bus.utk.edu

Office of Graduate Admissions and Records
218 Student Services Building
University of Tennessee
Knoxville, Tennessee 37996-0220
Telephone: 423-974-3251

University of Tennessee, Knoxville

THE FACULTY

Department of Accounting and Business Law

E. B. Anderson, Lecturer, M. Acc., Tennessee; CPA. K. E. Anderson, Associate Professor; Ph.D., Indiana; CPA. D. D. Bentley, Assistant Professor; J.D., Vanderbilt. A. Faye Borthick, Associate Professor; D.B.A., Tennessee; CPA, CMA, CISA. J. V. Carcello, Assistant Professor; Ph.D., Georgia State; CPA. N. E. Dittrich, Professor Emeritus; Ph.D., Ohio State; CPA. B. D. Fisher, Professor; LL.M., George Washington. A. W. Gatian, Assistant Professor; Ph.D., Virginia Tech. L. W. Hendrick, Lecturer; J.D., Houston; CPA. H. C. Herring III, Professor; Ph.D., Alabama; CPA. K. B. Hethcox, Assistant Professor; Ph.D., Oklahoma State. H. N. Hughes, Lecturer; B.S., Tennessee. C. D. Izard, Associate Professor; Ph.D., Mississippi, CPA. J. E. Kiger, Warren L. Slagle Professor of Accounting; Ph.D., Missouri; CPA. C. S. Massingale, Associate Professor; M.B.A., J.D., Tennessee. D. P. Murphy, Assistant Professor; Ph.D., North Carolina; CPA. I. A. Posey, Associate Professor; M.S., Tennessee; CPA, CMA. J. M. Reeve, Professor; Ph.D., Oklahoma State; CPA. H. P. Roth, Professor; Ph.D., Virginia Tech; CPA. M. D. Slaubaugh, Assistant Professor; Ph.D., Indiana. K. G. Stanga, Arthur Anderson Professor of Accounting and Department Head; Ph.D., LSU; CPA. R. L. Townsend, Associate Professor; Ph.D., Texas; CPA. J. R. Williams, Ernst & Young Professor of Accounting; Ph.D., Arkansas; CPA.

Department of Economics

R. A. Bohm, Professor; Ph.D., Washington (St. Louis). R. L. Bowlby, Professor; Ph.D., Texas. S. L. Carroll, Professor; Ph.D., Harvard. H. S. Chang, Professor; Ph.D., Vanderbilt. D. P. Clark, Professor; Ph.D., Michigan State. W. E. Cole, Professor; Ph.D., Texas. A. F. Curry, Assistant Professor; Ph. D., Duke. P. Davidson, Professor; Ph.D., Pennsylvania. W. F. Fox, Professor and Department Head; Ph.D., Ohio State. C. B. Garrison, Professor; Ph.D., Kentucky. J. A. Gauger, Associate Professor; Ph.D., Iowa. E. Glustoff, Associate Professor; Ph.D., Stanford. H. W. Herzog, Professor; Ph.D., Maryland. H. S. Jensen, Professor; Ph.D., Texas. J. Kahn, Associate Professor; Ph.D., Maryland. F. Y. Lee, Professor; Ph.D., Michigan State. D. M. Mandy, Associate Professor; Ph.D., Illinois. A. Mayhew, Professor; Ph.D., Texas. J. W. Mayo, Associate Professor; Ph.D., Washington (St. Louis). J. R. Moore, Professor; Ph.D., Cornell. M. N. Murray, Associate Professor; Ph.D., Syracuse. W. C. Neale, Professor; Ph.D., London. K. E. Phillips, Associate Professor; Ph.D., Washington (Seattle). J. Rubin, Assistant Professor; Ph.D., California, Davis.

M. Russell, Professor; Ph.D., Oklahoma. A. M. Schlottman, Professor; Ph.D., Washington (St. Louis). W. R. Schriver, Adjunct Professor; Ph.D., Tennessee. G. A. Spiva, Professor; Ph.D., Texas.

Department of Finance

A. L. Auxier, Associate Professor; Ph.D., Iowa. H. A. Black, Professor and Department Head; Ph.D., Ohio State. T. P. Boehm, Professor; Ph.D., Washington (St. Louis). M. C. Collins, Assistant Professor; Ph.D., Georgia. P. R. Daves, Assistant Professor; Ph.D., North Carolina at Chapel Hill. R. P. DeGennaro, Associate Professor; Ph.D., Ohio State. M. C. Ehrhardt, Associate Professor; Ph.D., Georgia Tech. D. L. Gunthorpe, Assistant Professor; Ph.D., Florida. G. C. Philippatos, Professor; Ph.D., NYU. R. E. Shrieves, Professor; Ph.D., UCLA. M. B. Stern, Assistant Professor; Ph.D., Virginia. J. M. Wachowicz Jr., Associate Professor; Ph.D., Illinois. J. W. Wansley, Professor; Ph.D., South Carolina.

Department of Management

M. R. Bowers, Assistant Professor; Ph.D., Clemson. I. J. Clelland, Assistant Professor; Ph.D., USC. T. J. Dean, Assistant Professor; Ph.D., Colorado. H. D. Dewhirst, Professor; Ph.D., Texas. G. H. Dobbins, Professor; Ph.D., Virginia Tech. C. P. Edirisinghe, Assistant Professor; Ph.D., British Columbia. O. S. Fowler, Associate Professor and Department Head; Ph.D., Georgia. G. E. Fryxell, Associate Professor; Ph.D., Indiana. K. C. Gilbert, Associate Professor; Ph.D., Tennessee. T. G. Greenwood, Assistant Professor; Ph.D., Tennessee. L. R. James, Professor; Ph.D., Utah. W. Q. Judge, Assistant Professor; Ph.D., North Carolina at Chapel Hill. R. T. Ladd, Associate Professor; Ph.D., Georgia. R. C. Maddox, Associate Professor; Ph.D., Texas. A. M. Miller, Associate Professor; Ph.D., Washington (Seattle). C. E. Noon, Associate Professor; Ph.D., Michigan. P. Postma, Director of E.M.B.A. Program; Ph.D., Tennessee. M. C. Rush, Professor; Ph.D., Akron. J. E. A. Russell, Associate Professor; Ph.D., Akron. M. M. Srinivasan, Associate Professor; Ph.D., Northwestern. M. J. Stahl, Professor; Ph.D., RPI.

Department of Marketing, Logistics, and Transportation

D. J. Barnaby, Professor; Ph.D., Purdue. E. R. Cadotte, Professor; Ph.D., Ohio State. P. A. Dabholkar, Assistant Professor; Ph.D., Georgia State. F. W. Davis Jr., Professor; Ph.D., Michigan State. G. N. Dicer, Professor; D.B.A., Indiana. J. H. Foggin, Associate Professor; D.B.A., Indiana. S. F. Gardial, Associate Professor; Ph.D., Houston. M. C. Holcomb, Assistant Professor; Ph.D., Tennessee. T. C. Johnston, Assistant Professor; Ph.D., Berkeley. C. J. Langley Jr., Professor; Ph.D., Penn State. B. Manrodt, Lecturer; Ph.D., Tennessee. J. T. Mentzer, Professor; Ph.D., Michigan State. M. A. Moon, Assistant Professor; Ph.D., North Carolina. R. A. Mundy, Professor; Ph.D., Penn State. E. P. Patton, Professor; Ph.D., North Carolina at Chapel Hill. R. C. Reizenstein, Associate Professor; Ph.D., Cornell. J. O. Rentz, Associate Professor; Ph.D., Georgia. D. W. Schumann, Associate Professor and Chair; Ph.D., Missouri. X. M. Song, Assistant Professor; Ph.D., Virginia. R. B. Woodruff, Professor; D.B.A., Indiana.

Department of Statistics

H. Bozdogan, Associate Professor; Ph.D., Chicago. D. Downing, Assistant Professor; Ph.D., Florida. F. M. Guess, Associate Professor; Ph.D., Florida State. M. G. Leitnaker, Associate Professor; Ph.D., Kentucky. R. V. Leon, Associate Professor; Ph.D., Florida State. D. K. J. Lin, Associate Professor; Ph.D., Wisconsin–Madison. S. A. McGuire, Associate Professor; Ph.D., Kansas State. R. A. McLean, Professor Emeritus; Ph.D., Purdue. R. W. Mee, Associate Professor; Ph.D., Iowa. W. Parr, Professor and Department Head; Ph.D., SMU. J. W. Philpot, Professor; Ph.D., Virginia Tech. G. B. Ranney, Associate Professor; Ph.D., North Carolina. R. D. Sanders, Professor; Ph.D., Texas. J. L. Schmidhammer, Lecturer; Ph.D., Pittsburgh. D. L. Sylwester, Professor; Ph.D., Stanford. C. C. Thigpen, Professor Emeritus; Ph.D., Virginia Tech. E. Walker, Associate Professor; Ph.D., Virginia Tech. T. Wright, Associate Professor; Ph.D., Ohio State. M. S. Younger, Associate Professor; Ph.D., Virginia Tech.

UNIVERSITY OF TEXAS AT ARLINGTON

College of Business Administration

Programs of Study

The College of Business Administration offers high-quality choices in ten graduate business programs accredited by AACSB–The International Association for Management Education. Students may begin their studies in any semester and complete those studies on either a part-time or full-time basis. Programs may require up to 30 hours of foundation work.

The Master of Professional Accounting is appropriate for students without significant prior study in business or accounting; it requires 39 semester hours in accounting. The M.S. in accounting (36 semester hours) is offered in accounting information systems, auditing, financial accounting, and managerial accounting. The M.S. in taxation (36 semester hours) is open to students with undergraduate degrees in accounting and covers accounting topics concerned with corporations, estates and gifts, extraction industries, individual taxation, partnerships, real estate transactions, and tax planning and research. The M.S. in information systems (30–33 semester hours) offers management- and technology-oriented courses to prepare students for careers in software and systems development and information systems management. The M.S. in marketing research (36 semester hours) prepares students for careers in marketing research, product/service management, and marketing planning. The M.S. in human resource management (36 semester hours) has courses in many areas of human resource management, including compensation administration, employee relations law, employee staffing, human resource planning and policy, industrial and labor relations, and performance management. The M.S. in real estate (36 semester hours) is a specialized degree in real estate decision making and focuses on real estate appraisal, architecture, investment analysis, land utilization, mortgage-backed securities, primary and secondary mortgage markets, real asset management, real property law, and urban and regional planning. The M.A. in economics (30–36 semester hours) prepares students for jobs in government, business, research, and teaching. Courses may be taken in econometrics and forecasting, global business, and the economics of business and strategy. The Ph.D. in business administration (67 semester hours) is a research-oriented program. Major fields of study are accounting, economics, finance, management, management information systems, management science, and marketing. The M.B.A. program includes an 18-hour core program for students with nonbusiness backgrounds as well as numerous choices in a 36-hour advanced program. Choices include a broad general management program of study or a concentration in accounting, economics, finance, information systems, management, management science, marketing, production and operations management, or real estate. The international business option provides extended coverage of the latest global trends and technologies and prepares students for international management careers.

Research Facilities

Teaching and research activities take place in a modern building with 120,000 square feet of space. The building contains a human behavior research laboratory suite, several personal computer laboratories and classrooms, and a remote computer center with equipment linked to IBM 4381 and Convex mainframes. The Center for Research on Organizational and Managerial Excellence, the Center for Research in Information Technology Management, the Center for Marketing Research, the Center for Accounting Software Evaluation, and the Ryan-Reilly Center for Urban Land Utilization provide research assistance to faculty members and graduate students.

Financial Aid

Approximately seventy-five assistantships are available to students on a competitive basis. For 1997–98, master's and doctoral stipends were $4680 and approximately $7500, respectively, for a nine-month period. Individuals desiring part-time work off campus are served by one of the nation's best student employment service centers. Students with excellent academic credentials may apply for scholarships.

Cost of Study

In 1998–99, tuition and fees for Texas residents are $1461 for 12 semester hours ($96 per semester hour), while nonresidents pay $4149 for the same course work. Students with assistantships or scholarships may qualify for resident tuition rates.

Living and Housing Costs

Information about University and off-campus housing can be obtained by contacting the housing office at 817-272-2706. An ample supply of moderately priced apartments is available for both single and married students.

Student Group

The College enrolls about 785 master's students and 67 doctoral students. These students come from a variety of academic backgrounds in over 200 universities in the United States and eleven other countries. Nearly 80 percent of the students have significant professional and technical work experience.

Location

Arlington, with a population of more than 300,000, is one of the fastest-growing cities in north Texas. It is located in the center of the vast Dallas–Fort Worth metroplex, which is a regional market and distribution center, a major convention site, a growing financial and cultural center, the tenth-largest market in the United States, and the home of the largest industrial district in the Southwest.

The University

The University of Texas at Arlington was founded in 1895 as a private liberal arts college called Arlington College. In recent years, it has grown significantly, becoming the second-largest institution in the University of Texas System (15,441 undergraduate and 4,631 graduate students). The University is composed of nine academic units, of which the College of Business Administration is one of the largest (4,631 students).

Applying

Application may be made for fall, spring, or summer semesters. U.S. students are encouraged to submit their applications and all related material prior to May 31 for the fall semester, September 30 for the spring semester, and March 1 for the summer semester. International students are encouraged to submit their applications by April 1, September 1, and January 1, respectively. Applications, official transcripts, scores on the GMAT, and three letters of recommendation are required. International students are required to provide a TOEFL score (and a TSE-A score if seeking graduate assistantships), financial statements, and statements of educational background.

Correspondence and Information

Assistant Director of Graduate Programs
College of Business Administration
UTA Box 19376
University of Texas at Arlington
Arlington, Texas 76019

Telephone: 817-272-3005
E-mail: admit@uta.edu
World Wide Web: http://www.uta.edu/gradbiz/gradweb.htm

University of Texas at Arlington

THE FACULTY AND THEIR RESEARCH

Ryan C. Amacher, Ph.D., Virginia, 1971. International economics, microeconomics, public finance.
Vincent Apilado, Ph.D., Michigan, 1970. Financial institutions and markets.
Julie Baker, Ph.D., Texas A&M, 1990. Marketing, services marketing.
R. C. Baker, Ph.D., Texas A&M, 1971. Management science and simulation.
John M. Beehler, Ph.D., Indiana, 1980. Financial accounting, taxation.
Myrtle Bell, Ph.D., Texas at Arlington, 1996. Human resource management.
Bijoy Bordoloi, Ph.D., Indiana, 1988. Information systems.
Indranil Bose, Ph.D., Purdue, 1997. Information systems.
Richard Buttimer, Ph.D., Georgia, 1993. Real estate economics.
Harley Courtney, Ph.D., Illinois, 1966. Accounting, information systems.
Christopher Craighead, Ph.D., Clemson, 1998. Operations management.
Bill Crowder, Ph.D., Arizona State, 1992. International money and finance.
Craig Depken, Ph.D., Georgia State, 1996. Industrial organization.
Roger Dickinson, Ph.D., Columbia, 1967. Marketing, retail management.
J. David Diltz, Ph.D., Illinois, 1980. Corporate finance, capital budgeting.
Mark Dunn, Ph.D., Florida, 1976. Financial accounting.
Mark Eakin, Ph.D., Texas A&M, 1980. Management science, statistics.
Regena Farnsworth, Ph.D., Texas A&M, 1993. Human resource management.
Roger Gates, Ph.D., Florida, 1973. Marketing, consumer research.
Edwin Gerloff, Ph.D., Texas at Austin, 1971. Management, organizational communication.
David Gray, Ph.D., Massachusetts, 1974. Management, industrial relations.
Philip Grossman, Ph.D., Virginia, 1984. Public finance, experimental economics.
Jan Guynes, Ph.D., North Texas State, 1984. Information systems.
Bethane Jo Pierce Hall, Ph.D., North Texas State, 1987. Accounting, taxation.
Thomas W. Hall, Ph.D., Oklahoma State, 1980. Financial accounting, auditing.
David Harrison, Ph.D., Illinois, 1988. Management, organizational behavior.
Paul Hayashi, Ph.D., SMU, 1969. Applied microeconomics.
Douglas Hensler, Ph.D., Washington (Seattle), 1989. Corporate finance and investments.
Debra Hill, Ph.D., Oklahoma State, 1980. Taxation.
Daniel Himarios, Ph.D., Virginia Tech, 1984. Macroeconomics.
Li Chin Ho, Ph.D., Texas at Austin, 1990. Managerial and financial accounting.
Faizul Huq, Ph.D., Kentucky, 1989. Production management, management science.
David C. Hyland, Ph.D., Ohio State, 1997. Corporate finance and investments.
Raja Iyer, Ph.D., Minnesota, 1984. Statistics, information systems.
Glen R. Jarboe, Ph.D., Purdue, 1981. Marketing research, new product development.
Eric N. Johnson, Ph.D., Arizona State, 1989. Accounting information systems, auditing, financial accounting.
Roberta Jones, Ph.D., Illinois, 1996. International accounting, accounting information systems.
Susan Kleiser, Ph.D., Cincinnati, 1996. Marketing, consumer decision making.
Patsy Lee, Ph.D., North Texas State, 1983. Financial accounting.
Radha Mahapatra, Ph.D., Texas A&M, 1994. Information systems.
Richard Mark, LL.M., Denver, 1977. Accounting, taxation.
John McCall, Ph.D., Oklahoma State, 1968. Macroeconomics, transportation.
Donald McConnell, Ph.D., North Texas State, 1981. Financial accounting and auditing.
Carl McDaniel, Ph.D., Arizona State, 1970. Marketing, global research.
Jeff McGee, Ph.D., Georgia, 1992. Venture development, small business management.
Gary McMahan, Ph.D., Texas A&M, 1993. Human resource management.
Roger Meiners, Ph.D., Virginia Tech, 1978. Law and economics.
J. D. Mosley-Matchett, Ph.D., Texas at Arlington, 1997. Marketing, Internet-based marketing, corporate communication.
Walter Mullendore, Ph.D., Iowa State, 1968. Microeconomics, regional analysis.
James Munch, Ph.D., Penn State, 1983. Consumer behavior, social influence, persuasion, consumer decision making.
Peter Mykytyn, Ph.D., Arizona State, 1985. Management information systems.
Don Panton, Ph.D., Arizona, 1972. Corporate finance, investments.
Russ Petersen, Ph.D., Washington (Seattle), 1971. Financial reporting, ethics in business, computer integration in accounting education.
Mark Peterson, Ph.D., Georgia Tech, 1994. Marketing, international marketing, and research methods.
Kenneth Price, Ph.D., Michigan State, 1973. Personnel, organizational behavior.
Richard Priem, Ph.D., Texas at Arlington, 1990. Management, business policy.
James C. Quick, Ph.D., Houston, 1977. Management, organizational behavior.
M. K. Raja, Ph.D., Texas Tech, 1971. Management information systems.
Abdul Rasheed, Ph.D., Pittsburgh, 1988. Management, business policy.
Nancy Sanchez, Ph.D., Texas A&M, 1998. Information systems.
Salil K. Sarkar, Ph.D., LSU, 1991. Corporate finance and investments.
Lawrence Schkade, Ph.D., LSU, 1961. Management science, information systems.
John Semple, Ph.D., Texas at Austin, 1990. Management science, optimization.
Chris Shook, Ph.D., LSU, 1997. Management, business strategy and firm performance.
Sumit Sircar, D.B.A., Harvard, 1976. Management information systems.
Craig Slinkman, Ph.D., Minnesota, 1982. Statistics, information systems.
Peggy Swanson, Ph.D., SMU, 1978. Corporate and international finance.
Steve Swidler, Ph.D., Brown, 1981. Investments, corporate finance.
Martin E. Taylor, Ph.D., Texas at Austin, 1974. Auditing.
Jeffrey Tsay, Ph.D., Missouri, 1973. Managerial accounting.
Judy Wagner, Ph.D., Virginia Tech, 1994. Sales and sales management.
Larry Walther, Ph.D., Oklahoma State, 1980. Financial accounting, auditing.
Kenneth Wheeler, Ph.D., Minnesota, 1978. Personnel and human resource management.
Mary Whiteside, Ph.D., Texas Tech, 1974. Statistics, management science.
Jerry Wofford, Ph.D., Baylor, 1962. Management, organizational behavior.
Dan Worrell, Ph.D., LSU, 1978. Management, business and society.

UNIVERSITY OF TEXAS AT DALLAS

School of Management

Programs of Study

The University of Texas at Dallas (UTD) School of Management offers the Master of Business Administration, the Master of Arts in International Management, the Master of Science in Accounting, and Master of Science degrees in various concentration areas. The part-time M.B.A. is the largest program in the School. In 1996 a lockstep day-format Cohort M.B.A. program was added to a part-time format, which is offered primarily in the evening and caters to full-time working students. Cohort students complete the program in three semesters.

Both the M.A. and M.S. programs require 36 hours of study, with classes offered on both a part-time and full-time basis. Classes, primarily at night, allow the student to specialize in accounting, international management, decision sciences, finance, managerial economics, marketing, and organization strategies. A Master of Arts in International Studies (M.I.M.S.) is offered in a distance learning format that requires 36 hours of study and a year to complete. Students earn the M.I.M.S. degree via the Internet, audio instruction, and campus retreats held three times a year.

A specialized M.B.A., the E.M.B.A., is offered in the Executive Education program. It focuses on management for change with a curriculum that stresses skills and perspectives needed for leadership in the twenty-first century. The E.M.B.A. is a lockstep, two-year weekend program for executives with at least ten years of managerial experience. Classes meet twice a month.

In addition to the E.M.B.A., the executive education programs include a certificate program in project/program management; this module leads to PMI certification and can become a master's degree track for 12 additional hours.

The Ph.D. Program is distinguished by its emphasis on interdisciplinary research. It provides a rigorous training in theoretical and empirical skills that are applied to problems faced by managers. Students work closely with internationally renowned faculty members to address questions at the leading edge of their field. Research supervision is available in the areas of accounting, finance and economics, information systems, marketing, operations management, operations research and organizations, and strategy and international management. Students entering the Ph.D. program are provided financial aid in the form of teaching or research assistantships.

Research Facilities

Academic Computer Services provides central computing facilities, workstations, microcomputer equipment, and network services for student, faculty, and staff use in instruction and research.

Complementing existing campus labs, the new School of Management Computer Lab, based on Windows-NT, is open primarily to management students. The Microcomputer Center, located in the McDermott Library building, provides a modern, fully networked personal computing environment with both IBM-compatible and Macintosh computers. The Computing Lab, located in the Jonsson Center building, is the focal point for student access to the University's extensive UNIX environment, which is based primarily on SUN servers accessed via X-Windows terminals. Dedicated servers support such functions as campus information services, programming instruction, applications instruction, research-related instruction, and computationally intense applications.

External network connections are extensive since UTD is the primary Dallas-Fort Worth hub for the worldwide Internet superhighway. Dial-in lines permit access to many of these resources from off campus.

Financial Aid

A variety of scholarships are awarded by the UTD Committee for Fellowships and Scholarships each fall. Applications are available from the Office of Financial Aid. UTD also participates in most federal and state aid programs. Short-term loans with a 12 percent rate of interest are also available. The full-time M.B.A. (Cohort) program offers scholarships to students in need of financial aid. As of fall 1997, part-time M.B.A. students can also apply for Dean's Excellence Scholarship funds given on a semester basis. For more information, students can consult the UTD School of Management's home page, listed below.

Cost of Study

Tuition and fees are billed per semester hour depending on course load. A full-time Texas resident student carrying 9 hours pays $1379; a non-Texas resident student pays $3305. Cohort M.B.A. students take 15 semester hours for a nonresident tuition fee of $5239. Additional hours exceeding 9 are charged $527 per course for Texas residents and $1169 per course for others. A minimum tuition of $120 per hour is charged for all students. Fees include advising, career-planning placement, and intern/co-op services.

Living and Housing Costs

UTD has many affordable housing options near its campus between the Dallas suburbs of Richardson and Plano. The Waterview Park Apartments, run by a private company, are available on campus and are approved student residences.

Student Group

Participants in the programs are full-time working students with a minimum of five years of managerial experience. About 90 percent are pursuing their degrees part-time. About 38 percent of master's students are women, 22 percent are members of minority groups, and 32.2 percent are international. Students range in age from 28 to more than 50. The Cohort M.B.A. program, however, draws a group that ranges in age from 22 to 30 and has less managerial experience.

Location

The University of Texas at Dallas is located just north of Dallas in a growing suburban area of almost 400,000 people.

The University

UTD was created in September 1969 by the Texas legislature after eight years as a privately sponsored teaching and research institution known as the Southwest Center for Advanced Studies that featured graduate studies. After UTD was established, undergraduates first attended in 1975. It is known for innovative educational programs. The School of Management was established in 1972 as an upper-level graduate institution.

Applying

All applicants must have obtained a bachelor's degree, not necessarily in business, from an accredited institution. Prerequisites include completion of an undergraduate calculus class, personal computer proficiency, and spreadsheet proficiency. Also required are scores on the GMAT and three letters of reference. A TOEFL score is required for applicants for whom English is not their native language. Applicants are evaluated based on their personal qualities and academic backgrounds following the admission formula guidelines as set forth by the AACSB. Personal interviews are not required. The application deadline for fall admission is July 15, spring admission is December 1, and summer admission is May 1. The deadline for the Cohort M.B.A. and specialized master's programs is July 4.

Correspondence and Information

Dr. Gary Horton
Manager of Administrative Services
School of Management-Advising Office
University of Texas at Dallas
P.O. Box 830688, JO53
Richardson, Texas 75083-0688
Telephone: 972-883-4079
Fax: 972-883-6425
E-mail: grad-admission@utdallas.edu
WWW: http://www.utdallas.edu/dept/mgmt

Dr. Gurumurthy Kalyanaram
Director of Academic Master's Program
School of Management
University of Texas at Dallas
P.O. Box 830688, JO51
Richardson, Texas 75083-0688
Telephone: 972-883-2834
Fax: 972-883-6727

Mr. David Ritchey
Director of Advising Services
School of Management
University of Texas at Dallas
P.O. Box 830688, JO53
Richardson, Texas 75083-0688
Telephone: 972-883-2701
Fax: 972-883-6425

University of Texas at Dallas

THE FACULTY AND THEIR RESEARCH

Mark Anderson, Assistant Professor in Accounting; Ph.D., Florida.
Rajiv Banker, Professor in Accounting; Ph.D., Harvard. Development of analytical methods for productivity and efficiency evaluation.
Roderick Barclay, Senior Lecturer in Accounting; Ph.D., Kent.
George Barnes, Senior Lecturer in OSIM/International Business Management; Ph.D., Tufts.
Frank Bass, Eugene McDermott Professor of Marketing; Ph.D., Illinois. Bass model of product diffusion, business systems marketing, marketing models, strategy.
Jack Brittain, Associate Professor of Organizational Behavior; Ph.D., Berkeley.
Mary Chaffin, Senior Lecturer in Finance; Ph.D., Texas at Dallas.
Ramaswamy Chandrasekaran, Professor of Decision Sciences; Ph.D., Berkeley. Operations research, robotics, combinatorics, discrete mathematics.
Reba Cunningham, Senior Lecturer in Accounting; Ph.D., North Texas.
Ted Day, Associate Professor of Finance; Ph.D., Stanford. Interest rate term structure, market microstructures in finance.
William Dent, Senior Lecturer in Accounting; Ph.D. candidate, Texas.
Adolf Enthoven, Professor of Accounting; Ph.D., Rotterdam.
Richard Fisher, Senior Lecturer in Decision Sciences; M.S., Texas at Dallas.
David Ford, Professor of Organizations, Strategy and International Management; Ph.D., Wisconsin–Madison. Group processes, leadership, managing change.
Paul Gaddis, Professor of Organization, Strategy and International Management; M.S., MIT. Strategic management of multinational corporations, role of U.S. private-sector corporations in U.S. society.
Tiffany Galvin, Assistant Professor in Organizations and Strategies.
Stephen Guisinger, Professor of International Management Studies; Ph.D., Harvard. International trade and development.
Richard Harrison, Associate Professor of International Management Studies; Ph.D., Berkeley. Corporate governance, management behavior, political processes in organizations.
Michael Intille, Senior Lecturer in Decision Sciences; Ph.D., Texas at Dallas.
Varghese Jacob, Professor in Decision Sciences; Ph.D., Purdue. Applications of neural networks and genetic algorithms, design of expert systems, group and organizational decision support systems.
Joakim Kalvanes, Assistant Professor in Decision Sciences; Ph.D., Vanderbilt.
Gurumurty Kalyanaram, Associate Professor of Marketing; Ph.D., MIT. Pioneering brands and first mover advantage.
Constantine Konstans, Professor of Accounting; Ph.D., Michigan State.
Jeho Lee, Visiting Assistant Professor in OSIM; Ph.D., Pennsylvania.
Stan Liebowitz, Professor of Managerial Economics and Associate Dean; Ph.D., UCLA. Creation and protection of standards, networks, and other intellectual properties.
Ray Lutz, Professor of Operations Management; Ph.D., Iowa State. Operations management and engineering economics.
Kevin Marshall, Senior Lecturer in OSIM; Ph.D., Texas at Dallas.
Diane McNulty, Associate Dean and Senior Lecturer in Business Policy; Ph.D., Texas at Dallas. Ethics and regulatory issues.
Larry Merville, Professor of Finance; Ph.D., Texas at Austin. Financial markets and structures.
B. P. S. Murthi, Assistant Professor of Marketing; Ph.D., Carnegie Mellon. Choice models, market structuring, segmentation, manufacturing-marketing interface issues.
Shun-Chen Niu, Professor of Decision Sciences; Ph.D., Berkeley. Probability models in operations research and computer simulation.
Gerardo Okhuysen, Assistant Professor of Organization, Strategy, and International Management; Ph.D., Stanford. Organizational theory.
Dale Osborne, Professor of Finance and Managerial Economics; Ph.D., Kentucky. Game theory, monetary theory.
Raymond Patterson, Assistant Professor in Accounting; Ph.D., Ohio State.
Carl Peters, Senior Lecturer in Decision Sciences; M.S., SMU.
Michael Pich, Assistant Professor of Decision Sciences; Ph.D., Stanford. Operations management, application of mathematics to management, transfer of technology with multinational firms.
Hasan Pirkul, Dean and Caruth Professor of Decision Sciences; Ph.D., Rochester. Information technologies in management.
Ram Rao, Founders Professor of Marketing; Ph.D., Carnegie Mellon. Competitive marketing strategies, competition among supermarkets and retailers; marketing on the Internet.
Sury Ravindran, Assistant Professor in Decision Sciences; Ph.D., Texas.
Young Ryu, Assistant Professor of Decision Sciences; Ph.D., Texas at Dallas. Artificial intelligence and expert systems in bureaucracy.
Peter Sattler, Visiting Assistant Professor in Marketing; Ph.D. candidate, Northwestern.
Gerald Scully, Professor of Managerial Economics; Ph.D., Rutgers. Sports economics, comparison of economic and social systems.
Suresh Sethi, Ashbell Smith Professor of Operations Management and Fellow of the Royal Society of Canada; Ph.D., Carnegie Mellon. Operations management.
John F. Sherman, Senior Lecturer in Accounting; Ph.D. candidate, North Texas.
Charles Solcher, Senior Lecturer in Accounting; J.D., South Texas Law.
David Springate, Associate Professor of Finance and Associate Dean; D.B.A., Harvard.
Suzanne Stout, Assistant Professor of Organizational Behavior; Ph.D., Stanford. Interorganizational actions, organizational learning, strategic decision making.
Anne Townsend, Senior Lecturer in Accounting; M.L., SMU.
Demetrios Vakratsas, Visiting Assistant Professor in Marketing; Ph.D., Texas at Dallas. Market response analysis, retailing, advertising, product innovation, econometrics.
John Wiorkowski, Professor of Mathematical Statistics; Ph.D., Chicago.
Habte Woldu, Senior Lecturer in OSIM/International Business Management; Ph.D., Poznan (Poland).
Yexiao Xu, Assistant Professor in Managerial Economics; Ph.D., Princeton.
Laurie Ziegler, Senior Lecturer in OSIM; Ph.D., Texas at Arlington.

THE UNIVERSITY OF TEXAS–PAN AMERICAN

College of Business Administration

Programs of Study

The College of Business Administration at the University of Texas (UT)–Pan American offers high-quality graduate business programs, including the M.B.A. and the Ph.D. in business administration with an emphasis in international business, which are designed to prepare students to meet the challenges of an ever-changing global business environment. The M.B.A. program is fully accredited by AACSB–The International Association for Management Education, and the new Ph.D. program will seek initial accreditation in 1999. The M.B.A. is a broad-based program requiring a minimum of 30 hours of graduate study and is generally completed within two academic years. A student may enter the program at the beginning of any semester or summer session. Courses are scheduled for evening hours or weekends. The Weekend M.B.A. Program accommodates those who wish to pursue a graduate business education while maintaining full-time employment. The twenty-four-month Saturday-only program consists of four sessions. Once admitted to the program, students must enroll for prescribed course work in each session. The M.B.A. for physicians is a Saturday-only program that focuses on health industry issues. This is a two-year program and is open to students with medical degrees in any area. The Ph.D. in business administration with an emphasis in international business is a minimum 66-hour, double-major degree program. Each student selects a functional area major from accounting/law, finance/economics, management, or marketing and in consultation with an advisory committee, chooses courses to create an individual degree program. All students are expected to complete a quantitative methods sequence and support field sequence, which are designed to provide an understanding of the cultural, political, and social implications of global business administration. Easy access to the maquiladoras and numerous exchange agreements make it possible for the student to complete an internship in an international business or to engage in joint research projects with an international university. After course work is completed, students take comprehensive examinations, which are followed by the writing and defending of the dissertation.

Research Facilities

The University Library contains approximately 300,000 catalogued volumes, more than 50,000 government documents, more than 2,000 periodical subscriptions, more than 900,000 units of microforms, more than 5,300 audiovisual items, and more than 18,000 graphic/cartographic materials. Business databases available include ABI Inform/BPO, F&S Index-United States, Wall Street Journal Index, Heck's Economic Literature Index, LEXIS-NEXIS, DataStream, Compact Disclosure, World Scope, Emerging Markets, Business Mexico Index, GPO, Social Sciences Index, and PIF International. The Internet linkage provided by Netscape accesses other library collections, and shared databases are made available by the University of Texas System and the Tex-Share Project. The University provides major computer support to serve the academic and research requirements of the College of Business Administration. Research at the College is conducted under the auspices of the Institute for International Business Research, the Center for International Studies, and the Center for Applied Research in Education.

Financial Aid

The College provides a limited number of teaching and research assistantships for qualified students as part of the education and professional preparation. Stipends for M.B.A. and Ph.D. students may vary according to the assignment and qualifications of the applicant. Applications for assistantships may be obtained by contacting the respective programs (M.B.A or Ph.D.). A limited number of Ph.D. fellowships are available annually. Student loans and campus employment are also available.

Cost of Study

In 1998–99, tuition for graduate students is about $56 per semester credit hour for Texas residents and $249 for nonresidents. With mandatory fees, a full-time graduate student enrolled for nine semester credit hours pays $820.40 if a resident of Texas and $2557.40 if a nonresident. Tuition and fees are subject to change.

Living and Housing Costs

Housing on campus is available for single students in the Women's Residence Hall and Troxel Hall for Men. Each residence hall houses almost 200 undergraduate and graduate students. The cost is about $1311 per semester in 1998–99. All fees are subject to change. For students who prefer off-campus living, there are many apartments available near the University.

Student Group

The 1997 enrollment for the College of Business Administration was more than 2,400, including 144 M.B.A. and 38 Ph.D. students. Of all M.B.A. students, 24 percent are female, 33 percent are American Hispanic, and 38 percent are international students from North and South America, East Asia, Central Asia, and Europe. The Ph.D. class is 33 percent female, 43 percent American Hispanic, and 23 percent international students. The Ph.D. program had representation from Bangladesh, Canada, Columbia, Ecuador, India, Mexico, Saudi Arabia, Spain, Thailand, and Turkey.

Student Outcomes

The majority of M.B.A. students are employed at graduation in the manufacturing, service, government, consulting, and nonprofit sectors. A small percentage are self-employed, and the remainder pursue doctoral or other graduate studies. The first Ph.D. degrees were awarded in 1998.

Location

UT–Pan American is located in Edinburg, Texas, close to the Mexican border and the Gulf of Mexico. Popular South Padre Island is only 75 miles away. The Rio Grande Valley, one of the nation's fastest growing areas, is semitropical and culturally diverse, with many people speaking both English and Spanish.

The University and The College

UT–Pan American is a comprehensive, public coeducational institution with about 13,000 students. Established in 1927, it joined the University of Texas System in 1989. About 85 percent of its students are Hispanic, reflecting the demographic characteristics of the area. The programs and curricula of the College of Business Administration, one of six academic colleges, take advantage of the University's location on the border of Mexico and opportunities provided by the North American Free Trade Agreement (NAFTA).

Applying

Applicants are encouraged to apply to the M.B.A. programs by May 1 for admission in the fall semester and by September 1 for admission in the spring semester. Scores on the GMAT are required of both master and doctoral program applicants. International applicants must provide official TOEFL scores. Individuals seeking admission to the Ph.D. program are encouraged to apply by April 1 for admission in the fall semester. By applying early, the applicant can ensure full consideration for financial aid. International applicants should contact International Admissions at the Office of Admissions and Records for application deadlines.

Correspondence and Information

College of Business Administration
The University of Texas–Pan American
1201 West University Drive
Edinburg, Texas 78539-2999

Telephone: 956-381-3311
Fax: 956-381-3312
E-mail: vhuerta@panam.edu
World Wide Web: http://www.coba.panam.edu

The University of Texas–Pan American

THE FACULTY AND THEIR RESEARCH

Linda McCallister, Professor and Dean, College of Business Administration; Ph.D., Purdue, 1981. Management.
Alberto Davila, Professor, Neuhaus Chair for Entrepreneurship, and Chair, Department of Economics and Finance; Ph.D., Iowa State, 1982. Economics.
Ercan Nasif, Associate Professor and Chair, Department of Management, Marketing, and International Business; Ph.D., North Texas, 1988. Management.
A. George Petrie, Associate Professor and Chair, Department of Accounting and Business Law; Ph.D., LSU, 1970. Accounting.
Lester M. Rydl, Associate Professor and Chair, Department of Computer Information Systems and Quantitative Methods; Ph.D., Texas A&M, 1978. Statistics.

Rubik Atamian, Assistant Professor; Ph.D., Texas at Austin, 1984. Accounting.
Angelica Cortez, Assistant Professor; Ph.D., Bradford, 1997. Business administration.
Nancy Davidson, Assistant Professor; Ph.D., Auburn, 1998. Information systems management.
Jeffery De Looze, Assistant Professor; Ph.D., Virginia Tech, 1998. Management science and information technology.
Gilberto de los Santos, Professor; Ph.D., Texas at Austin, 1972. Marketing.
Wig De Moville, Professor; Ph.D., Texas Tech, 1978. Accounting.
Charles Ellard, Professor; Ph.D., Houston, 1974. Economics.
Oscar Flores, Assistant Professor; Ph.D., North Texas, 1992. Business computer information systems.
Ellen Folk, Assistant Professor; J.D., Bridgepoint, 1989. Law.
Gouranga Ganguli, Professor; Ph.D., Mississippi, 1983. Accounting.
Walter E. Greene, Professor; Ph.D., Arkansas, 1976. Management.
DeWayne L. Hodges, Assistant Professor; Ph.D., Northern Colorado, 1984. Quantitative methods.
Evelyn O. Hume, Associate Professor; Ph.D., LSU, 1988. Accounting.
Susan Jarvis, Professor; J.D., Tulane, 1974. Business law.
Hale Kaynak, Assistant Professor; Ph.D., North Texas, 1996. Production operations management.
Shalini Kesar, Assistant Professor; Ph.D., De Monfort, 1998. Management information systems.
Eric Kirby, Assistant Professor; Ph.D., Kentucky, 1996. Strategy.
Susan Kirby, Assistant Professor; Ph.D., Kentucky, 1996. Organizational behavior, management.
Jane LeMaster, Assistant Professor; Ph.D., North Texas, 1994. Management.
Linda Matthews, Assistant Professor; Ph.D., Washington (Seattle), 1996. Organizational behavior, human resource management.
Timothy McCoy, Assistant Professor; Ph.D., Mississippi, 1994. Accounting.
Michael Minor, Associate Professor; Ph.D., Vanderbilt, 1987. Marketing, international business.
José A. Pagan, Assistant Professor; Ph.D., New Mexico at Albuquerque, 1995. Economics.
Jerry D. Prock, Professor; Ph.D., Arizona State, 1970. Finance.
John Sargent, Assistant Professor; Ph.D., Washington (Seattle), 1994. Organizational behavior.
Gocke Soydemir, Assistant Professor; Ph.D., Claremont, 1997. Economics.
David L. Sturges, Associate Professor; Ph.D., North Texas, 1988. Communications.
Paul M. Taube, Associate Professor; Ph.D., SUNY at Albany, 1986. Economics.
William Thompson, Professor; Ph.D., Arkansas, 1974. Marketing.
Arturo Vasquez-Parraga, Associate Professor; Ph.D., Texas Tech, 1990. International business.
Vern C. Vincent, Professor; Ph.D., Northern Colorado, 1972. Quantitative methods.

THE UNIVERSITY OF TOLEDO

College of Business Administration

Programs of Study

The College of Business Administration offers an M.B.A. program with areas of specialization in finance, international business, management, marketing, operations management, and information systems, as well as administration (general). In addition, the college offers a joint-degree program with the College of Law (J.D./M.B.A.), a Master of Science in Accounting, and a Master of Science and Ph.D. in Manufacturing Management. A unique fifteen-month Executive M.B.A. program is also offered for executives of midsized and growing firms.

Students with an undergraduate degree in business administration must complete a minimum of 30 graduate credit hours. Those with no undergraduate course work in business are required to complete additional prerequisite work. However, any or all prerequisite courses may be waived because of prior course work or through passing proficiency exams.

The University is on a semester system. UT offers day and evening classes; many students are studying part-time. The six required core courses are offered on a flexible schedule during the academic year.

Research Facilities

The College of Business Administration, including its graduate division, is located in Stranahan Hall. The University library is housed in the $8-million William S. Carlson Library building, the second-largest structure on campus. The library has holdings of more than 1.5 million volumes and more than 1.4 million physical units of microtext in all forms. It subscribes to approximately 5,000 current periodicals. For a nominal cost, graduate students can utilize a computerized bibliographic retrieval service that searches more than 200 recognized databases.

The University of Toledo Computer Center houses an IBM mainframe and a VAX 6420. Operating systems include OS/VS, VM, CMS, and CICS. Languages supported include BASIC, COBOL, FORTRAN, and Pascal. Software packages include BMDP, GPSS, IMSL, SAS, SPSSX, and Script. The College of Business Administration also houses four microcomputer laboratories with Pentium machines that are networked and have mainframe and Internet capabilities. There are more than 500 PCs for student use on the campus.

Financial Aid

Graduate assistantships are available on a competitive basis. The assistantships paid stipends ranging from $1800 to $3600 per semester in 1997–98 and provided fee payment for 6 to 12 credit hours of graduate course work. Two types of scholarships are available on a competitive basis. The Board of Trustees Scholarships pay tuition fees, and the Clement O. Miniger Scholarship and the Bostleman Scholarship are cash awards.

Cost of Study

In 1997–98, full-time tuition and fees were $2788 per semester for residents; nonresidents paid $5752 per semester.

Living and Housing Costs

Apartments and rooms for graduate students are available near the University. Listings of apartments and rooms available may be obtained by contacting the Coordinator of Off-Campus Housing, 100 Dowd Hall. Housing costs range from $150 to $200 a month for rooms and upward from $250 for apartments, depending on the number of occupants. Balanced meals are served daily in the cafeteria, and several restaurants are within a few minutes' walk. Board is available; in 1997–98, costs ranged from $475 to $675 per quarter.

Student Group

The graduate programs in business at UT admit approximately 150 students per year. More than one third of them are women. Of those admitted, about 50 percent have undergraduate degrees in business administration. Others have backgrounds in the social sciences, engineering, or the natural sciences. The University supports an active M.B.A. Association for currently enrolled students.

Location

The community provides a broad range of cultural resources to complement academic life. The Toledo Museum of Art is widely known for its antiquities and collections of paintings, sculpture, glass, and decorative arts. Its distinctive Peristyle is the site of performances by the Toledo Symphony Orchestra and the Toledo Choral Society and other concerts given by visiting orchestras and noted performing artists. The Toledo Zoological Park has an extensive zoological collection and includes the Museum of Science and Natural History, an amphitheater (where free concerts are offered during the summer months), a botanical center, and a large freshwater aquarium. Since Toledo is a port city, boating and water sports are available in the warmer months.

The University

The University originated in 1872 with a gift of 160 acres of farmland, contributed by Jesup W. Scott. This area is now known as Scott Park, the site of the University's Community and Technical College campus. The main campus began its period of greatest growth in 1931. It has since expanded to encompass more than a score of collegiate buildings in a picturesque 200-acre campus in one of the most pleasant residential settings in the metropolitan area. The campus is close to shopping, restaurants, and entertainment.

Applying

To be admitted to the M.B.A. or M.S.A. program at the University, a student must hold a bachelor's degree from an accredited college or university and must have earned a minimum GPA of 2.7 and a minimum GMAT score of 450. Admission is based on the GMAT score; the undergraduate grade point average; three letters of recommendation, either academic or professional; work experience; and the student's career objectives. International students whose native language is not English must have a score of at least 550 on the TOEFL. Admission requirements for the manufacturing management program include a GMAT score of at least 525 for the M.S. program and 575 for the Ph.D. program. Application material is due in the Graduate School office at least eight weeks prior to the opening of registration for the semester that the student wishes to enter.

Correspondence and Information

College of Business Administration
The University of Toledo
Toledo, Ohio 43606-3390
Telephone: 419-530-2775

The University of Toledo

THE FACULTY AND THEIR RESEARCH

Accounting

Philip Fink, J.D., Ohio Northern: partnership tax, taxation of small businesses. Diana Franz, Ph.D., Texas Tech: auditing and financial accounting. Dennis Gaffney, Ph.D., Illinois: tax effects of property transactions. Brian Laverty, Ph.D., Michigan State: tax policy, capital recovery, corporate transactions. Bhanu Raghunathan, Ph.D., Pittsburgh: auditing and information systems. Donald Saftner, Ph.D., Penn State: accounting systems. Nicholas Schroeder, D.B.A., Colorado: managerial accounting.

Finance

Linda Bowyer, Ph.D., Iowa State: banking and financial markets. Robert Deans, Ph.D., Pittsburgh: international finance. Greg Filbeck, Ph.D., Kentucky: corporate finance. Bruce Kuhlman, Ph.D., Florida: M.B.A. Director. David Lindsley, Ph.D., Michigan: factors leading to the enactment of rent control. Gary Moore, Ph.D., Arizona State: banking and financial markets. Michael Sherman, Ph.D., Washington (St. Louis): small-business finance. Gerald Smolen, Ph.D., Tennessee: banking. Sue Visscher, Ph.D., Indiana: manufacturing management finance. Herb Weinraub, Ph.D., Michigan State: working capital management. Glenn Wolfe, Ph.D., Virginia Tech: financial management.

Information Systems and Operations Management

Mesbah Ahmed, Ph.D., Texas Tech: information systems development and expert systems. Terence Barron, Ph.D., Washington (Seattle): information systems. William Clegg, Ed.D., Toledo: manufacturing management. Jerzy Kamburowski, Ph.D., Wroclaw Technical (Poland): project planning. Anand Kunnathur, Ph.D., Tennessee: computer application and management science. Douglas Lind, Ph.D., Toledo: use of subjective probability in forecasting. William Marchal, D.Sc., George Washington: waiting-line theory and its applications to flexible manufacturing systems. Udayan Nandkeolyar, Ph.D., Penn State: design analysis and justification of advanced manufacturing technologies. Ram Rachamadugu, Ph.D., Carnegie Mellon: assembly design and production scheduling. T. S. Ranghunathan, Ph.D., Pittsburgh: information systems. Subba Rao, Ph.D., Delhi: manufacturing management and operations research. Cynthia Ruppel, Ph.D., Kent State: information systems. Joseph Scazzero, Ph.D., Penn State: statistical quality control and linear models. Arthur Smith, Ph.D., Oklahoma: production planning and control. P. S. Sundararaghavan, Ph.D., Tennessee: inventory control and production scheduling in the chemical industry. Mark Vonderembse, Ph.D., Michigan: computer-integrated manufacturing as a competitive weapon.

Management

Sonny Ariss, Ph.D., Ohio State: strategic planning, finance, small business management. Don Beeman, D.B.A., Indiana: analysis of direct investment by U.S. manufacturing firms in other countries. Rebecca Bennett, Ph.D., Northwestern: motivation, punishment, negotiation. Bhal Bhatt, Ph.D., Wisconsin: aspects of international corporate strategy and policy in the auto and glass industries. William Doll, D.B.A., Kent State: computer-integrated manufacturing as a competitive weapon. Deborah Dwyer, Ph.D., Nebraska: organizational behavior. Larry Fink, Ph.D., Purdue: performance evaluation. Ken Kim, D.B.A., Indiana: comparative organization theory. Clint Longenecker, Ph.D., Penn State: performance appraisal. Dean Ludwig, Ph.D., Pennsylvania: product management, social issues in business. Nick Nykodym, Ph.D., Nebraska: transactional analysis and organizational communication. Fred Post, J.D., Toledo: labor arbitration. Robert Schwartz, Ph.D., Michigan: organization theory and health-care management. Thomas Sharkey, Ph.D., Indiana: international management and business. Jack Simonetti, D.B.A., Kent State: micro and macro human resource values. Steve Spirn, Ph.D., Illinois at Urbana-Champaign: labor management cooperation, comparable worth. Sherm Timmins, Ph.D., Penn State: small-business management, reward systems. Donald Wedding, J.D., Toledo: patent law.

Marketing

Richard Boden, Ph.D., Maryland College Park: labor economics. William Darley, Ph.D., Indiana: consumer behavior and research methods. J. Marc DeKorte, Ph.D., Wisconsin: marketing and the arts. Alan Flaschner, Ph.D., North Carolina at Chapel Hill: power in channels of distribution. Anthony Koh, Ph.D., Alabama: retailing. Paul Kozlowski, Ph.D., Connecticut: business conditions analysis, regional economic development. Jeen Lim, Ph.D., Indiana: buyer behavior and marketing research. Susan Mantell, Ph.D., Cincinnati: consumer behavior and marketing strategy. Sam Okoroafo, Ph.D., Michigan State: international business and trade. Ellen Pullins, Ph.D., Ohio State: sales/consumer behavior. David Reid, Ph.D., SUNY at Binghamton: industrial marketing and sales. Andrew Solocha, Ph.D., Michigan State: international finance, business economics. Le Thuong, Ph.D., Michigan State: international transportation and marketing. Ronald Zallocco, D.B.A., Kent State: health-care marketing.

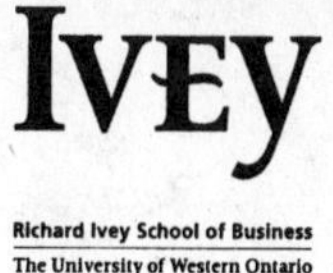

UNIVERSITY OF WESTERN ONTARIO

Ivey Business School

Programs of Study

The Ivey M.B.A. has long been regarded as one of the leading M.B.A. programs in the world. The Ivey program is highly integrated and focuses on the leadership skills and perspectives essential for success in a global marketplace. The faculty members are dedicated to teaching and creating an intense and "real world" learning environment. As the second-largest producer of teaching cases in the world, Ivey utilizes a variety of interactive and experiential learning methods that capitalize on the rich base of experience in the class. The general management focus and global perspective have led Ivey to be ranked repeatedly as the best business school in Canada by *Canadian Business,* and among the top in the world by *Business Week, The Economist Intelligence Unit, Asian Business,* and *Asia, Inc.*

Ivey helps develop a global perspective that transcends national boundaries. A multinational student body, faculty members with international experience as consultants and teachers, specialized international courses, integration of global issues in all core courses, and a large exchange program with leading schools in Europe, Asia, and the Americas contribute to this perspective.

The M.B.A. program is two years in length. The first year is the same for all students, while the second year allows students to choose from an array of options. In addition, teamwork is an essential part of Ivey's learning process.

Ivey also offers undergraduate business, LL.B./M.B.A., Executive M.B.A., Videoconferencing E.M.B.A., and Ph.D. programs.

Research Facilities

Students have access to all University libraries, including a specialized and well-stocked business library. The School operates its own computer facility and student laboratories. The National Centre for Management Research and Development undertakes full-time research on major challenges facing management today.

Financial Aid

Well-qualified students are automatically considered for scholarships and awards. International students should contact the Canadian Embassy or Consulate in their country regarding scholarship programs in Canada and their own university about private funding available for overseas study. Employment for students and spouses is also possible at the University and in the community.

Cost of Study

The tuition fee for 1998–99 for Canadian citizens is approximately Can$12,000 and for international students, Can$14,000. The application fee is Can$100.

Living and Housing Costs

Costs of housing, food, transportation, and personal items add Can$13,000 to Can$18,000 for single students and Can$20,000 to Can$25,000 for a family of 4. The cost of books and supplies ranges from Can$1500 to Can$2000 per year. Reasonably priced on- and off-campus housing is available through the University Housing Office.

Student Group

The students are distinguished by the diversity of their educational and professional backgrounds and their history of outstanding achievement. On average they are 28 years of age with four years of full-time work experience. They come from more than twenty countries worldwide. About 40 percent have substantial work or educational experience outside Canada, and about one third speak at least two languages.

Student Outcomes

In 1997, 91 percent of the M.B.A. graduates who were seeking employment found jobs in consulting, financial services, general management, marketing, manufacturing, and many other fields. More than 1,000 of the 11,000 graduates are presidents and CEOs of companies around the world. Each fall, career services sends résumé books that contain profiles of second-year M.B.A. students to hundreds of employers who then come to interview students.

Location

London is called the Forest City in recognition of the many trees that line the streets and grace its parks. With a population of 320,000, London is a university city as well as a center of services, light industry, and commerce. It takes just 2 hours by car or train to reach Toronto or Detroit.

The University and The School

Since it was founded in 1878, the University of Western Ontario has established a tradition of excellence in teaching and research. One of Canada's oldest and largest universities, Western consists of seventeen faculties in the sciences, arts, social sciences, and professions, serving a student body of more than 22,000. The University is particularly well known nationally and internationally for its professional schools, which include Business, Dentistry, Law, and Medicine.

Applying

For admission to the M.B.A. program, a candidate must usually hold an undergraduate degree with high academic standing from an accredited university. The Admissions Committee looks at leadership skills, achievements, undergraduate grades, GMAT score, full-time work experience, and extracurricular involvement. Admission may be offered to candidates without an undergraduate degree who have at least seven years of challenging work experience, some university courses with high academic standing, and other strong management qualities.

Correspondence and Information

Larysa Gamula
Admissions Director
Ivey Business School
University of Western Ontario
London, Ontario N6A 3K7
Canada

Telephone: 519-661-3212
Fax: 519-661-3431
E-mail: admiss@ivey.uwo.ca
World Wide Web: http://www.ivey.uwo.ca

University of Western Ontario

THE FACULTY

Entrepreneurship

K. Cumberland, B.A., Western Ontario.
J. H. Eggers, Ph.D., California State.
M. J. Grant, B.A., Western Ontario.
J. E. Hatch, M.B.A., McMaster; Ph.D., Michigan.
D. C. Shaw, M.B.A., Ph.D., Pennsylvania; CA (Nova Scotia).
L. Smith, M.A., Western Ontario.

Finance-Economics

P. M. Bishop, D.B.A., Harvard.
C. Dunbar, Ph.D., Rochester.
S. R. Foerster, Ph.D., Pennsylvania.
J. E. Hatch, M.B.A., McMaster; Ph.D., Michigan.
D. Heike, M.B.A., British Columbia.
G. A. Karolyi, Ph.D., Chicago.
R. W. White, M.B.A., British Columbia; Ph.D., MIT.
R. G. Wirick, Ph.D., Western Ontario.
L. Wynant, D.B.A., Harvard.

General Management

J. Banks, Ph.D., York.
P. W. Beamish, Ph.D., Western Ontario.
M. M. Crossan, M.B.A., Ph.D., Western Ontario.
T. Frost, M.Sc., Ph.D., MIT.
J. N. Fry, M.B.A., Western Ontario; Ph.D., Stanford.
J. G. McLeod, LL.M., London School of Economics.
B. Pierce, M.S.W., Toronto.
R. E. White, D.B.A., Harvard.

Global Environment of Business

D. Conklin, Ph.D., Toronto.
A. Ferreria, M.B.A., Philippines.
T. Frost, M.Sc., Ph.D., MIT.
J. Gandz, M.B.A., Ph.D., York.
J. Gutierrez-Vilarreal, Ph.D., North Carolina State.
T. Tsai, Ph.D., Cambridge.
C. Xiaoyue, Ph.D., Tsinghua.

Management Communications

A. Hurst, M.A., Western Ontario.
C. Reddin, Ph.D., Dalhousie.
K. E. Slaughter, B.A., Western Ontario.

Management Science and Information Systems

P. C. Bell, M.B.A., Ph.D., Chicago.
C. A. Higgins, Ph.D., Waterloo.
S. L. Huff, M.B.A., Queen's at Kingston; Ph.D., MIT.
E. F. P. Newson, M.B.A., Western Ontario; Ph.D., MIT.
M. Parent, M.B.A., Ph.D., Queen's at Kingston.

Managerial Accounting and Control

T. R. Archibald, Ph.D., Chicago; FCA (Ontario).
M. Bryant, Ph.D., Cincinnati; CA.
R. P. Kudar, M.B.A., Ph.D., Western Ontario; CMA (Ontario).
C. P. Lanfranconi, M.B.A., McMaster; Ph.D., Western Ontario; CA (Ontario and Quebec).
S. C. Mavrinac, M.Sc., London School of Economics.
D. A. Robertson, M.B.A., Ph.D., Western Ontario; CA (Ontario).
B. Sainty, Ph.D., Ohio.
D. J. Sharp, M.A., Oxford; M.Sc., Manchester; Ph.D., MIT.

Marketing

D. W. Barclay, M.B.A., McMaster; Ph.D., Michigan.
N. Dawar, Ph.D., Penn State.
T. H. Deutscher, M.B.A., Ph.D., Stanford.
K. G. Hardy, M.B.A., Ph.D., Michigan.
J. S. Hulland, M.B.A., Queen's at Kingston; Ph.D., MIT.
R. A. More, M.B.A., Ph.D., Western Ontario.
M. R. Pearce, D.B.A., Harvard.
A. B. Ryans, M.B.A., Ph.D., Stanford.
M. Vandenbosch, Ph.D., British Columbia.

Operations Management

J. A. Erskine, D.B.A., Indiana.
J. S. Haywood-Farmer, Ph.D., British Columbia; M.B.A., Western Ontario.
N. Jones, D.B.A., Harvard.
R. Klassen, M.B.A., Ph.D., North Carolina.
M. R. Leenders, D.B.A., Harvard.
C. J. Piper, M.B.A., Western Ontario; Ph.D., Carnegie Mellon.
L. Purdy, Ph.D., Waterloo.

Organizational Behaviour

J. J. DiStefano, M.B.A, Harvard; Ph.D., Cornell.
A. Frost, M.Sc., Ph.D., MIT.
B. R. Golden, Ph.D., Northwestern.
J. M. Howell, Ph.D., British Columbia.
H. W. Lane, D.B.A., Harvard.
M. Mayo, Ph.D., SUNY at Buffalo.
A. Mikalachki, M.B.A., Ph.D., Western Ontario.
L. Purdy, Ph.D., Waterloo.
M. C. Rothstein, Ph.D., Western Ontario.
S. Safran, M.B.A., Western Ontario.

VIRGINIA POLYTECHNIC INSTITUTE AND STATE UNIVERSITY

Pamplin College of Business Graduate Programs in Business

Programs of Study

The Departments of Finance, Insurance, and Business Law; Management; Management Science; and Marketing at Virginia Polytechnic Institute and State University offer graduate programs of study leading to the degrees of Master of Business Administration and Doctor of Philosophy.

The Master of Business Administration degree is a professional degree designed to provide the student seeking a career in industry with advanced educational experience in business administration. This is a nonthesis degree designed to intensify and enlarge the scope of the student's decision-making capacity, thereby increasing his or her career opportunities. The degree consists of 48 semester hours, which includes 12 hours of electives. Economics and calculus must be completed before entering the program. Most students take four semesters to complete the program. Extensive placement support is offered.

The Doctor of Philosophy in business is designed to enable students with outstanding ability to do advanced work in preparation for careers in college and university teaching and research, in industry, and in public service. The student is required to take one major field, one minor field, and 9 semester hours of research methodology courses. In addition to completing the course work, students must pass field examinations and complete an acceptable dissertation under the guidance of a faculty committee.

Graduate programs in accounting are listed separately.

Research Facilities

The Pamplin College of Business is committed to providing its students with the best educational experience possible. Pamplin has two computer labs equipped with Pentium PCs and Power Macs. The labs also make available some of the latest peripherals, such as flatbed color scanners, laser printers, and multimedia equipment. Students have unlimited access to the Internet. This virtual connection with business programs allows students to download full-text articles from the library, register for classes, and download assignments. These and other time-saving activities allow students to focus more time on their studies. Blacksburg and Virginia Tech are also the home of Blacksburg Electronic Village (BEV), the oldest and most connected Internet community in the world. With the growing importance of information and computer technologies in mind, the programs in business prepare students for a competitive and changing world.

Carol M. Newman Library houses more than 1.7 million volumes and 13,000 periodicals and has seating facilities for 3,000 students. The standard works on all phases of business activity, including all major business journals and periodicals, are available for reference and circulation.

Financial Aid

Financial aid is available for graduate students in the form of fellowships, fee waivers, and graduate assistantships. Stipends for graduate assistantships in 1998–99 are normally $542.50 per month for M.B.A. and M.S. students and range from $1155 to $1190 per month for Ph.D. students. The amount of the stipend is based upon the student's experience and academic achievement. Assistantships require from 10 to 20 hours of duty per week and permit holders to register for 12 credit hours each term.

Cost of Study

Tuition in 1998–99 for full-time graduate study are $4927 per year for Virginia residents and $7537 for out-of-state residents.

Living and Housing Costs

Attractive housing for graduate students is available at reasonable cost in Blacksburg and the surrounding area. Graduate students may use the off-campus-housing services of Virginia Tech, or they may make their own arrangements for room and board.

Student Group

Currently, Virginia Tech has about 19,400 undergraduate students and 4,100 graduate students in more than sixty departments. There are approximately 220 students in the Blacksburg M.B.A. program, permitting much individual attention and supervision. The College also enrolls about 325 part-time students in its off-campus programs. M.S. and Ph.D. students together number about 170.

Location

Blacksburg is located between the Allegheny and Blue Ridge mountains at an altitude of 2,100 feet. The area is regarded as one of the most scenic in the country. Adjacent recreational areas provide opportunities for camping, fishing, golfing, boating, hiking, and horseback riding. The climate is ideal for summer study.

The University and The College

Virginia Polytechnic Institute and State University, founded in 1872, is Virginia's land-grant university. Its recent history is one of rapid, well-planned growth. Virginia Tech is the largest university in the state in terms of full-time enrollment.

The Pamplin College of Business has AACSB–The International Association for Management Education accreditation at both the undergraduate and graduate levels. The young, dynamic faculty has distinguished itself by its research endeavors, its participation in professional organizations, and its service to the business community.

Applying

The M.B.A. program is open to students who hold a bachelor's degree from an accredited institution and who present evidence of their ability to do graduate work. In most cases, an applicant for the Ph.D. program should have completed some graduate work. All applicants must submit satisfactory scores on the Graduate Management Admission Test (GMAT). A completed application form, letters of recommendation, and transcripts are also required.

Applications for financial aid should be submitted prior to February 15. Applications for admission may be accepted at any time. Application materials may be obtained from the associate dean at the address below.

Correspondence and Information

Associate Dean for Graduate Programs
Pamplin College of Business
Virginia Polytechnic Institute and State University
Blacksburg, Virginia 24061-0209
Telephone: 540-231-6152
E-mail: mbainfo@vt.edu

Virginia Polytechnic Institute and State University

THE FACULTY

Department of Finance, Insurance, and Business Law
Randall S. Billingsley, Associate Professor; Ph.D., Texas A&M. Vittorio A. Bonomo, Associate Professor; Ph.D., Brown. Don M. Chance, Professor; Ph.D., LSU. John C. Easterwood, Associate Professor; Ph.D., Texas at Austin. Robert S. Hansen, Professor; Ph.D., Florida. Janine S. Hiller, Associate Professor; J.D., Richmond. Walter E. Jensen Jr., Professor; Ph.D., Duke. Gregory Kadlec, Associate Professor; Ph.D., Purdue. Arthur J. Keown, R. B. Pamplin Professor; D.B.A., Indiana. Raman Kumar, Associate Professor; Ph.D., Pittsburgh. George E. Morgan, Professor; Ph.D., North Carolina. Abon Mozumdar, Assistant Professor; Ph.D., NYU. Douglas M. Patterson, Associate Professor; Ph.D., Wisconsin. John M. Pinkerton, CRESTAR Professor of Banking; Ph.D., Florida. M. I. Schneller, Professor; Ph.D., NYU. Dilip K. Shome, Associate Professor; Ph.D., Florida. Vijay Singal, Associate Professor; Ph.D., Michigan. Andrew C. Thompson, Assistant Professor; Ph.D., Washington (Seattle). G. Rodney Thompson, Professor; Ph.D., Florida.

Department of Management
Larry D. Alexander, Associate Professor; Ph.D., UCLA. Michael K. Badawy, Professor; Ph.D., NYU. J. M. Barringer, Professor Emeritus; M.S., Virginia. T. W. Bonham, Professor and Associate Dean; Ph.D., South Carolina. Kevin D. Carlson, Assistant Professor; Ph.D., Iowa. Anthony T. Cobb, Associate Professor; Ph.D., California, Irvine. Mary Connerley, Assistant Professor; Ph.D., Iowa. J. Lawrence French, Associate Professor; Ph.D., Cornell. Devi R. Gnyawali, Assistant Professor; Ph.D., Pittsburgh. Donald Hatfield, Assistant Professor; Ph.D., UCLA. James R. Lang, Professor; Ph.D., Massachusetts. Robert M. Madigan, Associate Professor; Ph.D., Michigan State. Steven E. Markham, Professor; Ph.D., SUNY at Buffalo. Kent F. Murrmann, Associate Professor; Ph.D., Michigan State. Christopher P. Neck, Assistant Professor; Ph.D., Arizona State. Laura Poppo, Assistant Professor; Ph.D., Pennsylvania. Jerald F. Robinson, Professor; Ph.D., Illinois. Martin C. Schnitzer, Professor Emeritus; Ph.D., Florida. Jon M. Shepard, Pamplin Professor; Ph.D., Michigan State. Wanda J. Smith, Assistant Professor; Ph.D., North Carolina at Chapell Hill. Carroll U. Stephens, Assistant Professor; Ph.D., Duke. Linda F. Tegarden, Assistant Professor; Ph.D., Colorado at Boulder. Richard E. Wokutch, Pamplin Professor; Ph.D., Pittsburgh.

Department of Management Science
Ralph D. Badinelli, Associate Professor; Ph.D., Purdue. Edward R. Clayton, Lenz Professor; Ph.D., Clemson. Deborah Cook, Associate Professor; Ph.D., Texas A&M. Parviz Ghandforoush, Professor; Ph.D., Texas Tech. Barbara J. Hoopes, Assistant Professor; Ph.D., North Carolina at Chapell Hill. Ernest C. Houck, Pamplin Professor; Ph.D., Alabama. Philip Y. Huang, Professor; Ph.D., Penn State. Raymond L. Major, Assistant Professor; Ph.D., Florida. Lance A. Matheson, Associate Professor; Ph.D., Washington (Seattle). Laurence J. Moore, Bell Atlantic Professor; Ph.D., Arizona State. Quniton J. Nottingham, Assistant Professor; Ph.D., Virginia Tech. Cliff T. Ragsdale, Associate Professor; Ph.D., Georgia. Terry R. Rakes, Professor; Ph.D., Virginia Tech. Loren P. Rees, Arthur Andersen Professor; Ph.D., Georgia Tech. Richard E. Sorensen, Professor and Dean of the Pamplin College of Business; Ph.D., NYU. Robert T. Sumichrast, Professor; Ph.D., Clemson. Bernard W. Taylor III, Pamplin Professor and Head of Management Science and Information Technology; Ph.D., Georgia Tech. Roberta Russell Tillar, Professor; Ph.D., Virginia Tech.

Department of Marketing
Neeraj Arora, Assistant Professor; Ph.D., Ohio State. Monroe Murphy Bird, Purchasing Management Association of the Carolinas–Virginia Professor of Purchasing; Ph.D., Arkansas. David Brinberg, Robert O. Goodykoontz Professor and Department Head; Ph.D., Illinois. James R. Brown, Associate Professor; D.B.A., Indiana. Eloise Coupey, Assistant Professor; Ph.D., Duke. Corinne Faure, Assistant Professor; Ph.D., Florida. Edward F. Fern, Associate Professor; Ph.D., Ohio State. Shankar Ganesan, Assistant Professor; Ph.D., Florida. Janet E. Keith, Associate Professor; Ph.D., Arizona State. Noreen M. Klein, Associate Professor; Ph.D., Penn State. James E. Littlefield, Professor; Ph.D., Wisconsin. Meg Meloy, Assistant Professor; Ph.D., Cornell. Kent Nakamoto, R. B. Pamplin Professor of Marketing; Ph.D., Stanford. Julie L. Ozanne, Associate Professor; Ph.D., North Carolina. M. Joseph Sirgy, Professor; Ph.D., Massachusetts. Ruth A. Smith, Associate Professor; Ph.D., Wisconsin.

Pamplin Hall Atrium, the Pamplin College of Business.

Pamplin Hall, the Pamplin College of Business.

WAYNE STATE UNIVERSITY

School of Business Administration

Programs of Study

The Master of Business Administration (M.B.A.) program is intended to prepare men and women for leadership and management careers in business, government, and other types of organizations. With six electives among the twelve courses (36 semester hours) required, students have the flexibility to pursue graduate programs that meet their particular objectives and requirements. Students may choose electives from a wide variety of courses in accounting, business economics, entrepreneurship, finance, industrial relations, information systems management, international business, management and organizational behavior, marketing, personnel/human resources management, quality management, and taxation. All applicants must also meet foundation requirements in accounting, computing, economics, finance, management, marketing, production management, business writing, and statistics. Applicants with a baccalaureate degree in business administration usually meet all of these requirements. Applicants who must meet some or all of these foundation requirements enroll in special accelerated foundation courses as needed. The M.B.A. program is accredited by the AACSB–The International Association for Management Education.

The Master of Science in Taxation (M.S.T.) is designed to prepare students for entry into professional tax practice in both the public and private sectors. Through the interdisciplinary nature of the program, students learn the accounting, legal, and public policy aspects of taxation. The core, concentration, elective, and capstone requirements for the program consist of 33 semester hours (eleven courses). Students with a bachelor's degree in accounting usually meet all of the program's foundation requirements. Applicants with a baccalaureate degree in a field other than accounting may have to complete foundation courses in the areas of accounting, business law, management information systems, and statistics. Concentration areas consist of accounting and taxation, public finance, and public administration.

The academic year has two 15-week semesters. The spring-summer semester is divided into two terms. A full schedule of graduate courses is offered each term, both on campus and at two suburban locations. All M.B.A. requirements can be completed on Saturdays at the Oakland Center.

Research Facilities

Wayne State, with four mainframe computers, operates one of the largest computing centers in the Detroit area. Links with MichNet provide users with access to the Internet (NSFNET), SprintNet, AutoNet, and Datapac networks. The University is also linked to the BITNET academic network. The total system is available 24 hours a day.

Currently, 300 terminals and 128 dial-up lines are available for student use. Students use terminals and microcomputers in the School's six microcomputer classrooms and laboratories as an integral part of many graduate courses.

Wayne State University is the host institution for DALNET, Detroit Area Library Network, made up of twelve local libraries. Through computer terminals in the libraries, users can access more than 7.8 million volumes, representing the majority of holdings in the area's educational institutions.

Financial Aid

The Office of Scholarships and Financial Aid provides students with information regarding sources of funds. Graduate teaching and research assistantships are offered through the School's four academic departments and its Bureau of Business Research. Stipends for 1997–98 averaged $10,030, plus tuition and benefits, for nine-month appointments. The University offers graduate and professional scholarships to both full- and part-time graduate students.

Cost of Study

Tuition per semester in 1998–99 for Michigan residents is $159 per credit hour. Non-Michigan residents pay $341 per credit hour.

Living and Housing Costs

The University Housing Office provides information to assist students in locating on-campus housing. Double and single rooms in residence halls as well as efficiency and one- and two-bedroom modern private apartments are available on campus. There are 120 apartments specially equipped for handicapped students. Apartment rental rates for 1998–99 range from $236 to $721 per month.

Student Group

The School of Business Administration has approximately 200 full-time and 2,000 part-time M.B.A. students enrolled. More than one third are women, and approximately 93 percent are employed either full- or part-time. Half of the M.B.A. students hold supervisory positions. Classes average 35 students. Almost 5 percent are international students.

Student Outcomes

Most students pursuing a master's degree in business administration or taxation have already made impressive starts to their careers. An advanced degree can be a vehicle to broaden one's expertise, enhance one's opportunities for advancement, and increase one's earning potential. While more than 30 percent of the graduate students work for the major automotive companies, the majority work in nonautomotive settings that include health care, accounting, government, banking and finance, and a host of other industries. Several students have initiated successful businesses of their own.

Location

The modern University campus is a distinctive element in Detroit's expansive cultural center, which includes Orchestra Hall; the Museum of African-American History; the Fisher Theatre; the Detroit Institute of Arts, Historical Museum, Science Center, and the Main Public Library; and four University theaters. Also near the campus are The Detroit Medical Center, the Merrill Palmer Institute, and the world headquarters of General Motors.

The University

Tracing its origins to 1868, Wayne State occupies a 185-acre campus that is graced by open courtyards and malls and whose 105 buildings represent a blend of traditional and ultramodern architecture. The 2,600 University faculty members continue to distinguish the University through their dedication to teaching, scholarly activity, and service.

Applying

The M.B.A. and M.S.T. programs are open to students who hold bachelor's degrees from regionally accredited institutions and who demonstrate considerable promise of success in pursuing graduate study. A completed application for graduate admission, the $20 application fee, official transcripts from all collegiate institutions attended, and GMAT results are required. Admission is granted each semester. The application and other required documents are due by August 1 for fall semester admission, December 1 for winter semester admission, and April 1 for spring-summer semester admission. International students must provide required materials four months prior to the beginning of the term. Semesters begin in September, January, and May.

Correspondence and Information

Office of Student Services
School of Business Administration
Wayne State University
Detroit, Michigan 48202

Telephone: 313-577-4510
800-910-EARN (toll-free)
Fax: 313-577-5299
World Wide Web: http://www.busadm.wayne.edu

Wayne State University

THE FACULTY

Richard A. Ajayi, Associate Professor of Finance and Business Economics; Ph.D., Temple.
Sadhana Alangar, Senior Lecturer in Finance and Business Economics; Ph.D., Texas Tech.
Mark E. Bayless, Associate Professor of Finance and Business Economics; Ph.D., Washington (St. Louis).
John D. Beard, Associate Professor of Business Communication; D.A., Michigan.
Richard F. Beltramini, Professor of Marketing; Ph.D., Texas at Austin.
B. Anthony Billings, Professor of Accounting; Ph.D., Texas A&M.
Kenneth A. Borokhovich, Visiting Assistant Professor of Finance and Business Economics; Ph.D., Ohio State.
Robert C. Bushnell, Associate Professor of Finance and Business Economics; Ph.D., Princeton.
Timothy W. Butler, Associate Professor of Finance and Business Economics; Ph.D., South Carolina.
Hugh M. Cannon, Professor and Adcraft/Simons-Michelson Professor in Advertising; Ph.D., NYU.
Yitzhak Fried, Associate Professor and Interim Chair of Management and Organization Sciences; Ph.D., Illinois.
Sue D. Garr, Senior Lecturer in Accounting; M.B.A., Detroit; CPA.
James L. Hamilton, Professor of Finance and Business Economics; Ph.D., Duke.
Melvin Houston, Lecturer in Business Law and Accounting; J.D., Wayne State.
Angela Hwang, Assistant Professor of Accounting; Ph.D., Houston.
George C. Jackson, Associate Professor and Interim Chair of Marketing; Ph.D., Ohio State.
Deborah Jones, Assistant Professor of Accounting and Taxation; Ph.D., Kent State.
Harvey Kahalas, Dean and Professor; Ph.D., Massachusetts.
J. Patrick Kelly, Professor and Kmart Endowed Chair of Marketing; Ph.D., Illinois.
Catherine Kirchmeyer, Associate Professor of Management and Organization Sciences; Ph.D., York.
K. S. Krishnan, Associate Professor of Management and Organization Sciences; Ph.D., Pennsylvania.
Ariel Levi, Senior Lecturer in Management and Organization Sciences; Ph.D., Yale.
James T. Low, Associate Professor of Marketing; Ph.D., Michigan.
James E. Martin, Professor of Management and Industrial Relations; Ph.D., Washington (St. Louis).
Mbodja Mougoue, Associate Professor of Finance and Business Economics; Ph.D., New Orleans.
Peter E. Mudrack, Assistant Professor of Management and Organization Sciences; Ph.D., Toronto.
Anuradha Nagarajan, Senior Lecturer in Management and Organization Sciences; Ph.D., Michigan.
Thomas J. Naughton, Associate Professor of Management and Organization Sciences; Ph.D., SUNY at Buffalo.
Klara Nelson, Assistant Professor of Management Information Systems; Ph.D., Florida State.
Harvey Nussbaum, Associate Professor of Management and Organization Sciences; Ph.D., Wayne State.
Richard N. Osborn, Professor of Management and Organization Sciences; D.B.A., Kent State.
Barbara Price, Associate Professor of Finance and Business Economics and Associate Dean; Ph.D., Utah.
Kelly R. Price, Associate Professor of Finance and Business Economics; Ph.D., Michigan.
Arik Ragowsky, Assistant Professor of Management Information Systems; Ph.D., Tel Aviv.
Sabine Reddy, Assistant Professor of Management and Organization Sciences; Ph.D., Illinois.
Irvin D. Reid, University President and Professor of Management and Organization Sciences and Marketing; Ph.D., Pennsylvania.
Alan Reinstein, Professor of Accounting; D.B.A., Kentucky; CPA.
Edward A. Riordan, Professor of Marketing; D.B.A., Kentucky.
Jone M. Rymer, Professor of Business Communication; Ph.D., SUNY at Buffalo.
Jack D. Schroeder, Assistant Professor of Accounting; M.B.A., Wayne State; Ph.D., Michigan State; CPA.
Margaret Smoller, Assistant Professor of Finance and Business Economics; Ph.D., Florida.
Charles A. Soberman, Senior Lecturer in Management and Organizational Behavior; M.B.A., Michigan State; J.D., Harvard.
Toni M. Somers, Associate Professor and Interim Chair of Finance and Business Economics; Ph.D., Toledo.
Albert D. Spalding Jr., Associate Professor of Business Law and Taxation and Interim Chair of Accounting; J.D., M.B.A., George Washington; CPA.
Myles S. Stern, Associate Professor of Accounting; Ph.D., Michigan State; CMA.
Jeffrey J. Stoltman, Associate Professor of Marketing; Ph.D., Syracuse.
Audrey G. Taylor, Lecturer in Accounting; M.B.A., Tennessee; CPA.
John C. Taylor, Assistant Professor of Marketing; Ph.D., Michigan State.
Harish L. Verma, Associate Professor of Management and Organization Sciences; Ph.D., Michigan State.
David L. Verway, Associate Professor of Finance and Business Economics; Ph.D., Michigan State.
William H. Volz, Professor of Business Law and Interim Chair of Accounting; J.D., Wayne State; M.B.A., Harvard.
John D. Wagster, Associate Professor of Finance and Business Economics; Ph.D., Texas A&M.
Antonie Walsh, Lecturer in Accounting; M.L.T., Florida; J.D., Wayne State.
David L. Williams, Associate Professor of Marketing; Ph.D., Wayne State.
Attila Yaprak, Professor of Marketing and Associate Dean; Ph.D., Georgia State.

WESTERN NEW MEXICO UNIVERSITY

Department of Business Administration and Economics

Program of Study

The Department of Business Administration and Economics at Western New Mexico University offers a program leading to the Master of Business Administration degree. The program is designed to prepare students for professional careers in management. Western's M.B.A. program spans 60 credit hours. Twenty-four of the 60 hours consist of prerequisites for the graduate courses and may be waived if certain undergraduate courses have been taken. Two 4-hour survey courses may be taken in lieu of the 24 hours of prerequisites. The remaining 36 credit hours are made up of 30 credit hours of specifically required graduate courses and 6 hours of electives. Required courses are normally offered in the fall, spring, and summer semesters, while electives are offered during the two 5-week summer sessions. Through the use of independent studies, faculty members attempt to accommodate individual students' areas of interest in the elective courses.

Graduate courses usually are offered in the late afternoon and evening for the convenience of part-time and working students. No thesis is required.

Research Facilities

The Miller Library contains approximately 112,000 bound volumes and 44,000 microform titles. ACCESS, a fully automated system that provides computer access to the library's book holdings, is also available to users, both on and off campus. Computer workstations are also available for accessing information on compact disc. Periodical indexes, government publications, and encyclopedias are available in this format. Electronic online search facilities may also be accessed, as well as the Internet. Through membership in the Online Computer Library, the library has online access to more than 23 million records in more than 12,000 libraries throughout the world. Materials unavailable at Miller Library can usually be obtained through the interlibrary loan department.

Computer needs are met by a variety of technologies. A well-equipped computer laboratory contains 110 microcomputers in addition to twelve VAX workstations, fifteen VAX terminals, and two UNIX workstations. The Central Campus Computer Network is connected to the NSFnet national network (the Internet) to provide means of exchanging information, electronic mail, and communication with other universities.

Financial Aid

A limited number of graduate assistantships are available. These are offered in two categories: academic (nine-month contracts usually beginning in the fall semester) and administrative (twelve-month contracts running from the beginning of the fall or spring semester). Graduate assistants normally enroll for 9 graduate credit hours and may not take more than 12 or fewer than 6 credit hours per semester. There are also part-time employment opportunities available within the University, as well as internships. Inquiries should be made to the Financial Aid Office.

Cost of Study

Tuition for the 1997–98 academic year for full-time graduate students was $1370 (9 credit hours) for New Mexico state residents and $4436 (9 credit hours) for nonresidents. No out-of-state tuition is charged during the summer sessions. The admission application fee is $10, and there is a one-time matriculation fee of $5. Students who are required to use the computer lab are subject to a per-semester computer lab fee of $10. The cost of books is approximately $400 per semester. Tuition and fees are subject to change.

Living and Housing Costs

The housing office of Western New Mexico University provides living accommodations for University students who desire campus housing. For 1997–98, dormitory rooms rented for $595 per semester for double occupancy and $676 per semester for single occupancy. (A $75 deposit is required.) Apartments are also available. Monthly costs for 1997–98 were $264 for one bedroom and $298 for two bedrooms. Utilities are included, and a $150 deposit is necessary. The charge for board ranged from $794 to $848. Off-campus housing is also available, but the rent is generally higher.

Student Group

The total enrollment of the University is approximately 2,600 students. Of these, almost 600 are involved in various graduate programs. The M.B.A. program is relatively small, ensuring personalized attention. Students in Western's M.B.A. program bring a wide variety of work experience, educational backgrounds, and interests to the program. The enrollment is made up of both full- and part-time students. Numerous states are represented, as are a number of other countries. There is an active association of M.B.A. students.

Location

Silver City, a delightful town of about 15,000, was founded as a Spanish community in 1872. Located midway between Tucson and El Paso in the foothills of the beautiful and rugged Black Range and Mogollon Mountains, at an elevation of 5,900 feet, Silver City has a climate that is dry, mild, and invigorating. The Gila National Forest and the Gila Wilderness Area, minutes away by car, provide an attractive setting for backpacking, camping, picnicking, hunting, and fishing. Numerous hiking trails and the Gila Cliff Dwellings National Monument offer recreational and education opportunities in the immediate area. National parks, including the Carlsbad Caverns, the Grand Canyon, and the Painted Desert, are easily accessible, as are the vast New Mexico and Arizona Indian lands. Mexico is 1¼ hours away by car.

The University and The Program

Western New Mexico University was founded in 1893 as a state coeducational institution of higher learning. It has a small, attractive campus where students get to know their professors and each other on an individual basis. Major efforts are made to accommodate students' interests and lifestyles.

Because the M.B.A. program is still relatively small, there is more latitude and informality than in the rigid structure of many larger programs. Students are encouraged to explore individual areas of interest through their choices of electives and independent or directed studies.

Applying

Application forms may be requested by writing to the Office of Admissions. Applicants must submit GMAT scores. International students whose native language is not English must earn a minimum score of 550 on the TOEFL.

Correspondence and Information

M.B.A. Director
Department of Business Administration and Economics
Western New Mexico University
P.O. Box 680
Silver City, New Mexico 88062
E-mail: strangc@wnmu.edu

Office of Admissions
Western New Mexico University
P.O. Box 680
Silver City, New Mexico 88062
Telephone: 800-872-9668 (toll-free in-state)
800-222-9668 (toll-free out-of-state)

Western New Mexico University

THE FACULTY

All of the graduate faculty members in the Department of Business Administration and Economics hold terminal degrees in their respective fields. Emphasis is placed on teaching excellence, and the majority of the faculty members bring business-world experience to the classroom. A student-faculty ratio of 8:1 in the M.B.A. program ensures small classes and easy access to individual faculty members. Research interests include international trade and countertrade, entrepreneurship, economic development, ethics, and fraud auditing.

WILLAMETTE UNIVERSITY

Geo. H. Atkinson Graduate School of Management

Program of Study

The Geo. H. Atkinson Graduate School of Management offers the Master of Management (M.M.) degree and prepares students for careers in business, government, and not-for-profit organizations. The Atkinson School M.M. is the first and only management degree in the U.S. to achieve dual accreditation for business administration (AACSB–The International Association for Management Education) and public administration (NASPAA).

The Atkinson School's primary objective is to help students develop the analytical and qualitative skills necessary to manage effectively in corporate, small business, entrepreneurial, federal, state, municipal, and not-for-profit organizations. Atkinson School alumni are employed as managers in a wide range of industries (e.g., high technology, manufacturing, financial services, consulting, human services) and perform a diverse set of job functions (e.g., finance, accounting, marketing, information management, human resources).

The Atkinson School offers a highly interactive and supportive learning environment. During their first year, Atkinson students complete the required core curriculum and the cocurriculum, which include the study and application of economics, finance, quantitative methods, computing, accounting, management information systems, organizational behavior, marketing, human resources, government, international issues, negotiation, ethics, legal issues, communication, and strategic career management. Most students undertake a paid internship during the summer following completion of the core courses. The second year of study is entirely self-selected; classes are chosen according to the student's career goals. Elective courses support eight areas of career interest, including accounting, finance, human resources, international management, marketing, general management, public management, and management science.

Research Facilities

The Atkinson School's primary research holdings are located at the Mark O. Hatfield Library, which includes more than 220,000 volumes and 1,300 current journal subscriptions; another 100,000 volumes are at the Truman Wesley Collins Legal Center, also on campus. University library resources also include specialized computerized information databases of specific interest to management students. The Atkinson School houses its own personal computer laboratory. Students have 24-hour-a-day access to Macintosh and IBM-compatible computers. A local network provides all standard word processing, spreadsheet, and graphics applications. The Internet provides access to worldwide information services and electronic mail.

Financial Aid

Loans, scholarships, research assistantships, and work-study are available. Financial aid is awarded on the basis of the student's qualifications and financial need. Students seeking need-based financial aid must submit the Free Application for Federal Student Aid (FAFSA). In 1997–98, 50 percent of Atkinson students received merit scholarship assistance.

Cost of Study

Tuition for the 1998–99 academic year is $15,450 for full-time students. Additional fees are approximately $250 per year. Books and supplies cost an average of $1000 per year.

Living and Housing Costs

Housing is readily available in the Salem area. Single students should budget about $800 per month for expenses, exclusive of tuition; married students should budget $1000 per month.

Student Group

Each year, approximately 65 full-time students and 5 part-time students enter the M.M. program. The average age is 26; 75 percent have at least one year of full-time work experience. Thirty percent of the class are women, 10 percent are multicultural, and 25 percent are international. Approximately 70 percent plan careers in the private sector and 30 percent in the public and not-for-profit sectors.

Student Outcomes

Seventy percent of Atkinson graduates live and work in the Northwest. Thirty percent are located throughout the United States and the world. A sample of employers and position titles of recent graduates includes manager, IBM Corporation; consultant, Deloitte & Touche Ltd. and Andersen Consulting; general account manager, Synektron; channel support specialist, Tektronix Inc.; information system analyst, FHP Health Care; human resource manager, Corvallis School District; market development analyst, Kaiser Permanente Health Care; financial consultant, Merrill Lynch; international inside sales representative, Esco Corporation; marketing manager, Nike; and program evaluator, Oregon Youth Authority.

Location

Willamette University is located in Salem, Oregon, 45 miles south of Portland, the Northwest's second-largest city. Salem, the state capital, is situated in the beautiful Willamette Valley between the Cascade Range and the Oregon coast. Rated one of the most livable cities in the United States, Salem provides easy access to Oregon's scenic, recreational, cultural, and professional opportunities.

The University and The School

Willamette University, founded in 1842, is an independent coeducational university. The University has been named the best smaller comprehensive university west of the Mississippi River and is recognized for excellence and innovation in professional education. The University consists of the College of Liberal Arts, the College of Law, the Atkinson Graduate School of Management, and the School of Education.

The Atkinson School, established in 1974, provides managers the skills for private and public enterprise. The School's Master of Management degree is the only management program in the U.S. professionally accredited for both business administration and public affairs and administration. The Atkinson School experience is characterized by a high degree of student-faculty interaction, teamwork, practical application, and contact with external organizations. The rigorous program demands the best efforts of students and faculty.

Applying

Admission decisions consider important variables reflecting academic ability, motivation, and leadership. Applicants are evaluated on the basis of their overall academic record, including transcripts, GMAT or GRE scores, letters of recommendation, a personal statement, and work experience. Applications should be received by March 31 for maximum consideration for admission and scholarship assistance. Later applications are also considered for admission.

Correspondence and Information

Director of Admission
Geo. H. Atkinson Graduate School of Management
Willamette University
Salem, Oregon 97301

Telephone: 503-370-6167
Fax: 503-370-3011
E-mail: agsm-admission@willamette.edu
World Wide Web: http://www.willamette.edu/agsm

Willamette University

THE FACULTY

G. Marc Choate, Professor of Finance and Business Economics; Ph.D., Washington (Seattle).
Patrick E. Connor, Professor of Organization Theory and Behavior; Ph.D., Washington (Seattle).
Michael U. Dothan, Guy F. Atkinson Professor of Economics and Finance; Ph.D., Harvard.
Alan L. Eliason, Professor of Management Information Technology; Ph.D., Minnesota.
Bruce L. Gates, Professor of Quantitative Methods and Public Management; Ph.D., Pittsburgh.
Michael L. Hand, Professor of Applied Statistics and Information Systems; Ph.D., Iowa State.
Earl K. Littrell, Professor of Accounting and Information Sciences; Ph.D., Oregon.
Steven M. Maser, Interim Dean and Professor of Public Management and Public Policy; Ph.D., Rochester.
Kathleen J. Powers, Associate Professor of Human Resource Management; Ph.D., Florida.
Debra J. Ringold, Professor of Marketing; Ph.D., Maryland.
Fred G. Thompson, Elmer and Grace Goudy Professor of Public Policy and Management; Ph.D., Claremont.
J. Frederick Truitt, Helen Simpson Jackson Professor of International Management; D.B.A., Indiana.

The Atkinson Graduate School of Management is part of Willamette University.

Atkinson students concentrate on a case discussion.

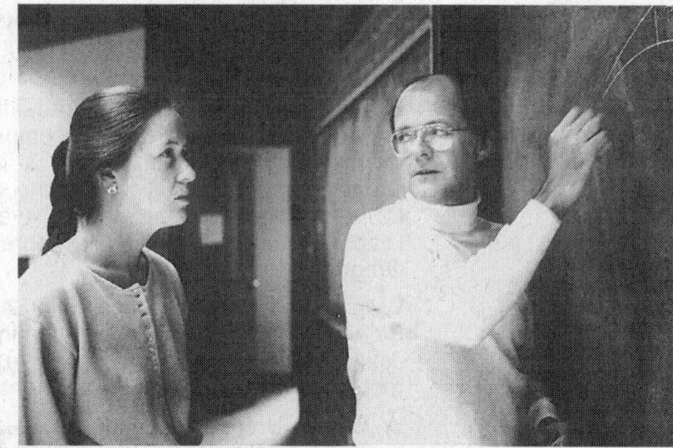

Professor Marc Choate delves into finance with a first-year student.

WOODBURY UNIVERSITY

Master of Business Administration Program

Program of Study

The high quality of course work in Woodbury University's M.B.A. Program is affirmed by the school's accreditation by the Association of Collegiate Business Schools and Programs (ACBSP). All of the courses in accounting, computer information systems, finance, international business, management, and marketing emphasize teamwork and presentation skills. Designed primarily for those fully employed, classes are scheduled on weekends and evenings. More than 30 percent of the M.B.A. students are international and attend Woodbury's M.B.A. Program full-time.

Candidates for the degree must complete 36 units or a total of twelve 3-unit courses. Students who hold undergraduate degrees in a discipline other than business may have to complete additional preparatory courses called the Common Professional Component, which may be waived through testing or work experience or may be taken as electives. Up to 6 graduate semester units may be transferred from another accredited institution.

Woodbury University's professors have excellent academic credentials. The majority have current corporate executive and management experience, which strengthens the ties between Woodbury's M.B.A. Program and the southern California business community. Other distinctive features of the M.B.A. Program are small classes, an intensive and responsive academic environment, and individual attention to the special needs of each graduate student. The dean, academic advisers, and professors are readily available to assist students with their studies, projects, and progress in the program. Methods of instruction include seminars, small-group discussions, case-study analysis, individual and group projects, problem solving, simulation and modeling, and the application of theory to challenges encountered by students in the business world. Computer technology is integrated into the core of this program, keeping students abreast of contemporary business practices.

The M.B.A. curriculum has a comprehensive management core that provides the basic foundation for understanding the various business disciplines and prepares the student for further study in general or specific interest areas. Areas of emphasis allow students to study more intensively according to their goals. Accounting covers major areas required for the CPA examination. Computer information systems includes systems design and development, communication networks, and Internet and Web design. Finance includes financial institutions, corporate finance, mergers and acquisitions, investment analysis, and capital markets. International business includes finance, economics, marketing, world business area studies, and comparative management. Management includes organizational behavior–human relations, policy studies, organizational theory, management systems, strategic planning, entrepreneurship, and strategy formulation. Marketing includes international marketing, advertising, contemporary marketing problems, and market research.

Research Facilities

Woodbury's Los Angeles Times Library provides a valuable resource for M.B.A. students, who can study either on campus or via their personal computers. Multiple databases are accessible over the Internet (with a student password) and offer access to more than 6,000 journals through online subscriptions, including LEXIS-NEXIS and Proquest Direct. Particularly strong in business and historical materials, the library houses a comprehensive collection of books, periodicals, CD-ROMs, and technical and year-end reports that are selected to meet the curricular needs of the students. Woodbury also provides a modern online computer resource center that features sixty Windows PC and Macintosh computers with the latest in business and graphics software plus printers and scanners.

Financial Aid

Federal and state loans and fellowships are awarded on the basis of financial need and qualifications.

Cost of Study

Tuition for the academic year 1998–99 is $550 per unit; the tuition for the twelve-course M.B.A. Program is $19,800. Each semester, the University charges a services fee of $150, and the M.B.A. Association Fee is $30 per semester.

Living and Housing Costs

Woodbury has two residence halls that accommodate 189 men and women. There is plenty of off-campus housing available near the campus. The University uses the California Student Aid Commission estimate of at least $9144 for two semesters for food, housing, transportation, books, and miscellaneous expenses.

Student Group

The program has been designed to enable the working adult as well as the full-time student to pursue the M.B.A. degree. International students in the program provide a wider and more comprehensive view of the business world. An active M.B.A. Association gives extensive opportunities for professional, educational, and social development.

Location

Situated in the hills of Burbank, the northern most suburb of Los Angeles and media capital of the world, Woodbury offers students easy access to beaches, mountains, and deserts; it is within a 20-minute drive from downtown Los Angeles. Art, history, and science museums; professional sports events; and world-class entertainment are readily accessible to Woodbury students.

One of the largest cities in the United States, Los Angeles serves as a worldwide business and financial center. The University is linked to the business, financial, design, entertainment, and commercial communities, providing networking and career development opportunities for students who choose to take advantage of the wealth of business opportunities in southern California.

The University

Woodbury was founded in 1884. The University is an independent, nonprofit institution whose primary mission is to provide, through undergraduate and graduate programs, the background needed for success in varied fields, including business, professional design (animation arts, fashion, graphic and interior design, and multimedia), architecture, and computer information systems. The principal emphasis is on instruction, but supporting programs offer opportunities for applied research and community service.

Applying

M.B.A. study at Woodbury may begin during any term. A bachelor's degree from an accredited institution and a minimum GPA of 2.5 are required for admission (international applicants are required to achieve a minimum GPA of 2.75). The completed application should be submitted with a $35 fee ($50 for international applicants), transcripts from all colleges attended, TOEFL scores (international applicants), and two letters of recommendation from employers or professors. The GMAT must be taken within the first two terms at Woodbury, but it is not required for admission.

Correspondence and Information

Master of Business Administration Program
Woodbury University
7500 Glenoaks Boulevard
Burbank, California 91510-7846

Telephone: 818-767-0888 Ext. 261
Fax: 818-767-0032
E-mail: mba@vaxb.woodbury.edu
World Wide Web: http://www.woodburyu.edu

Woodbury University

THE FACULTY

Woodbury's faculty members bring into the classroom not only educational credentials and experience but also the practical side of the business world. All faculty members can refer to and draw on firsthand knowledge of their respective fields.

Tahmoures A. Afshar, (Economics, Finance); Ph.D., Indiana.
Joseph L. Beachboard (Management); J.D., Vanderbilt.
Frank Benson (Accounting); Ph.D., Claremont; CPA, CIA, CMA, CFP.
David R. Black (Computer Information Systems); M.B.A., Pepperdine.
Joan Branin (Finance, Management); Ph.D., Claremont.
Ray Briant (Computer Information Systems); M.A., Pepperdine.
John Charnay (Management, Marketing); M.S., Columbia; J.D., Southwestern Law; Advanced Studies, Pennsylvania (Wharton).
Inoh Choi (Economics); Ph.D., USC.
Satinder Dhiman (Accounting, Management), Chair of Business; Ed.D., Pepperdine.
Eugene B. Gendel (Economics); Ph.D., Boston University.
John Gleiter (Management, Marketing); California State, Northridge.
Cassandra Hart-Franklin (Business Law); J.D., Harvard.
Judith Heineman (Human Resources Development); M.H.R.O., San Francisco.
Norman Kaderlan (Management); Ph.D., Wisconsin.
Karen Kaigler-Walker (Marketing); Ph.D., Ohio State.
Rauf Kahn (Management, Organizational Behavior); D.B.A., USC; Postgraduate Diploma, Institute of Social Studies (Netherlands).
Peter Kutzer (Strategic Management); M.B.A., Harvard.
William Lieberman (Management Information Systems, Artificial Intelligence); Ph.D., Washington (St. Louis).
Horst J. Liebl (Finance); Ph.D., Bonn.
Kenneth H. Marcus (International Business, Management); Ph.D., Cambridge.
Dennis McGuckian (Computer Information Systems); M.B.A., Dartmouth.
Sheila J. Moore (Finance); Ph.D., Arizona.
Gwynda J. Myers (Management, Computer Information Systems); Ph.D., Claremont.
Jon W. Myers (Accounting); M.B.A., Berkeley; CPA
Paul O'Reilly (Marketing); M.B.A., Clark.
James Orcutt (Computer Information Systems); J.D., UCLA.
J. U. Overall IV (Quantitative Methods, Management); Ph.D., UCLA.
Marvin J. Richman (Management, Finance); M.U.P., NYU; M.B.A., Chicago.
Alexandra Saba (International Business, Management); Ph.D., Stanford.
Kailas C. Sahu (Management); Ph.D., Institute of Technology (India).
Mohammad A. Sangeladji (Accounting); Ph.D., Oklahoma; CPA, CMA, CCA.
Robert A. Schultz (Computer Information Systems); Ph.D., Harvard.
Sameer Shah (International Business, Management); M.I.M., American Graduate School of International Management.
Xiaochuan Song (Economics, Finance); Ph.D. candidate, USC.
Craig Stern (Management, Marketing); Ph.D., USC.
Hamid Taheri (Accounting); M.B.A., Illinois State; CPA
Vivian A. Terr (Law); J.D., Columbia.
Ravi Tripuraneni (Marketing, Management); Ph.D., Drexel.
E. Bud Walker (Management); M.A., Hawaii.
Stephen A. Wilburn (Management); M.B.A., UCLA.

Woodbury University Los Angeles Times Library.

WRIGHT STATE UNIVERSITY

College of Business and Administration

Programs of Study

Wright State University offers graduate business education through the Master of Business Administration, the Master of Accountancy, the Master of Science in logistics management, and the Master of Science in social and applied economics programs. All programs emphasize broad concepts and analytical tools and provide the student with the opportunity to develop competence in a specialized field. The M.B.A. program is accredited by the American Assembly of Collegiate Schools of Business.

Students in the M.B.A. program may need to complete foundation courses, including accounting, business law, algebra and calculus, statistics, economics, finance, management, marketing, computers, and information systems. Foundation courses may be waived based on undergraduate courses or by passing a proficiency test.

The M.B.A. program requires a minimum of 51 quarter hours. The curriculum consists of required courses (39 hours) and an area of concentration (12 to 18 hours). Areas of concentration include business economics, finance, financial administration, health-care management, international business, logistics management, management, management information systems, marketing, operations management, and project management.

Research Facilities

Wright State University's IBM 3090-1505 and VAX 6340 computers are accessed by 150 terminals, including approximately 25 in the College. BASIC, COBOL, FORTRAN, and other programming languages are available, as are a variety of software packages, including SPSS and SAS, and peripheral equipment. Microcomputers are available for student use. The University library has a collection of more than 360,000 volumes, plus 6,700 periodicals, microtext, and government documents. Additional materials are available through interlibrary loan from other units of the state's higher education system.

Financial Aid

More than forty graduate assistantships are granted by the College each year. The assistantships carry a stipend of about $4000 for three quarters and a complete tuition waiver. The College also can award about twenty Graduate Tuition Fellowships per year to full-time students. These carry a tuition waiver only. Through the University's financial aid office, federal loans, University short-term loans, and other types of aid are available.

Cost of Study

Tuition for Ohio residents for 1997–98 was $148 per credit hour for part-time study and $1563 per quarter for full-time study. Tuition for nonresidents was $263 per credit hour for part-time study and $2799 per quarter for full-time study. Fees, books, and supplies are estimated to cost $1000 per year.

Living and Housing Costs

Limited on-campus housing is available. On-campus room and board cost approximately $1500 per year. Off-campus accommodations are readily available in the area for graduate students attending Wright State University.

Student Group

Current enrollment at Wright State is 16,033 students, of whom 4,156 are graduate students. The student body is drawn from across the country and the world. Graduate enrollment in the College of Business and Administration is approximately 585 students, of whom 172 are full-time. Students enter with a variety of undergraduate degrees. The average age of the graduate students is about 30. Approximately 40 percent are women, 8 percent are members of minority groups, and 16 percent are from other countries.

Location

Dayton is located in southwestern Ohio, 60 miles north of Cincinnati and 60 miles southwest of Columbus. It is the fastest-growing labor market in the Midwest and has the highest concentration of scientists and engineers. Wright-Patterson Air Force Base, the air force's research and development center, is located in Dayton, an important factor in the city's attraction of technology industries. Very few cities of Dayton's size have so many excellent performing arts activities; the arts are widely supported. Dayton's location makes it an important interchange in the movement of people and goods: it is the nation's largest 90-minute air-travel market and tenth-largest 90-minute over-the-road market (more than 4.1 million people).

The University and The College

Wright State, one of Ohio's newest and most exciting centers of learning, was accredited as an independent university in 1967. Today, it offers nine different baccalaureate degrees and thirty programs of graduate and professional study. Located on more than 500 acres northeast of Dayton, the University enjoys both the stimulation of a metropolitan area and the atmosphere of a rural setting. The University's chief purposes are to achieve excellence in teaching, substantial contributions to human knowledge, and major service to humanity and to maintain a free and cosmopolitan environment in which people may work toward such achievements. The College of Business and Administration has gained prominence in the last ten years. Its faculty members represent diverse backgrounds and are dedicated to excellence in teaching and high quality in research. Class sizes are kept small to encourage development of close personal relationships between students and faculty members.

Applying

Admission to the graduate business programs is open to qualified students with a regionally accredited baccalaureate degree. The GMAT is required for the M.B.A., the Master of Accountancy, and the M.S. in logistics management programs. The GRE General Test is required for the M.S. in social and applied economics program. Applicants from non-English-speaking countries must submit TOEFL scores. No deadlines are set, but the completed application, application fee, official transcripts, and test scores should be submitted as early as possible.

Correspondence and Information

For information on the M.S. in social and applied economics program, please contact:

Director of M.S. in social and applied economics
College of Business and Administration
Wright State University
Dayton, Ohio 45435
Telephone: 937-775-2437
Fax: 937-775-3545
E-mail: rsylvester@desire.wright.edu

For information on all other programs, please contact:

Director of Graduate Programs in Business
and Logistics Management
College of Business and Administration
Wright State University
Dayton, Ohio 45435
Telephone: 937-775-2437
Fax: 937-775-3545
E-mail: jcrawford@desire.wright.edu
World Wide Web: http://www.coba.wright.edu

Wright State University

THE FACULTY AND THEIR RESEARCH

Rishi Kumar, Professor and Dean of the College of Business and Administration; Ph.D., Wayne State, 1972. International economics, economic development, comparative economic systems, economic theory.
Robert F. Scherer, Professor and Associate Dean for Community Relations; Ph.D., Mississippi, 1987. Organizational behavior, human resources, labor relations, organization development, statistics/research methods.
Richard Williams, Associate Professor and Associate Dean of Academic Programs; Ph.D., Michigan State, 1975. Financial management, investments, estate planning.
Roger Sylvester, Director of M.S. in Social and Applied Economics; M.S., Wright State, 1987.
James Crawford, Director of Graduate Programs in Business and Logistics Management; M.S., Dayton, 1976.
Khurshid Ahmad, Associate Professor; Ph.D., Pennsylvania, 1970. Insurance, real estate, personal finance.
M. Fall Ainina, Associate Professor; Ph.D., Arizona State, 1986. Financial management and investments.
Peter Bacon, Professor; D.B.A., Indiana, 1967. Financial management.
Francis J. Baker, Assistant Professor; Ph.D., Claremont, 1984. Project management, organizational behavior, strategic management.
John Blair, Professor; Ph.D., West Virginia, 1974. Urban and regional economics, public finance.
Sonia Brecha, Assistant Professor; D.B.A., Kent State, 1983. International accounting, accounting systems.
Greg Bushong, Assistant Professor; Ph.D., LSU, 1989. Financial accounting, small business.
Frank Carmone, Professor; Ph.D., Waterloo, 1971. Quantitative techniques in marketing, models of choice behavior.
Peter Carusone, Professor; Ph.D., Ohio State, 1969. Contemporary marketing issues, entrepreneurship, marketing strategy.
Joseph Castellano, Professor; Ph.D., Saint Louis, 1971. Financial and managerial accounting.
Joseph W. Coleman, Associate Professor; Ph.D., Arizona State, 1982. Statistical analysis, simulation, management information systems.
Jeanette Davy, Assistant Professor; Ph.D., Arizona, 1986. Organizational behavior, organization development, compensation, human resource strategy.
W. Steven Demmy, Professor; Ph.D., Ohio State, 1971. Management information systems, logistics, production and inventory management.
Thomas Dovel, Associate Professor; M.B.A., Miami (Ohio), 1961. Marketing policy, marketing research.
Tran Dung, Assistant Professor; Ph.D., Syracuse, 1978. Microeconomics, international economics, physical economics.
Rudy Fichtenbaum, Associate Professor; Ph.D., Missouri, 1980. Macroeconomics, labor economics, health economics.
Waldemar M. Goulet, Professor; Ph.D., Michigan State, 1973. Financial management, real estate.
Nicolas Gressis, Professor; Ph.D., Penn State, 1975. Investments, financial management.
Charles Gulas, Assistant Professor; Ph.D., Massachusetts at Amherst, 1994. Advertising, consumer behavior, marketing management.
Charles Hartmann, Professor; J.D., Missouri, 1966. Legal environment of business, government regulation, economic analysis of law.
Russell H. Hereth, Associate Professor; M.B.A., Miami (Ohio), 1965. Taxation.
Jon Hobbs, Associate Professor; Ph.D., Stanford, 1972. Logistics modeling, simulation, reliability, management information systems.
Inder Khera, Professor; Ph.D., Iowa, 1968. Marketing strategy, consumer behavior, marketing communications, international marketing.
Rebecca Koop, Assistant Professor; Ph.D., Cincinnati, 1994. Management information systems.
James E. Larsen, Assistant Professor, Ph.D., Nebraska, 1987. Real estate and financial institutions.
Susan Lightle, Assistant Professor; Ph.D., Cincinnati, 1991. Auditing, financial.
Paulette I. Olson, Associate Professor; Ph.D., Utah, 1989. Labor economics, history of economic thought, methodology, economics of gender.
Crystal L. Owen, Assistant Professor; Ph.D., Ohio State, 1987. Organizational behavior, organizational theory.
Joseph A. Petrick, Associate Professor; Ph.D., Penn State, 1972. Management, international management, business ethics, quality management, leadership studies.
Robert Ping, Assistant Professor; Ph.D., Cincinnati, 1990. Psychometrics, political economy of distribution channels.
George G. Polak, Associate Professor; Ph.D., Carnegie Mellon, 1983. Network optimization, queuing theory, simulation.
Robert Premus, Professor; Ph.D., Lehigh, 1974. Regional and urban economics, public finance, economic theory, monetary economics.
Stephen Renas, Professor; Ph.D., Georgia State, 1971. Macroeconomics, monetary theory, financial institutions, environmental economics, cost-benefit analysis.
Nada R. Sanders, Assistant Professor; Ph.D., Ohio State, 1987. Forecasting, decision theory, expert systems, materials management.
Paula M. Saunders, Associate Professor; Ph.D., Miami (Ohio), 1979. Marketing strategy, service marketing and direct marketing.
G. Thomas Sav, Professor; Ph.D., George Washington, 1981. Energy economics, economics of higher education, microeconomics, engineering economics.
William M. Slonaker, Associate Professor; J.D., Ohio State, 1972. Legal environment of business, legal aspects of business organizations, legal aspects of commercial transactions, labor law.
Hans-Dieter Sprohge, Professor; Ph.D., SUNY at Buffalo, 1974. Financial accounting and taxation.
Frank Stickney, Professor; Ph.D., Ohio State, 1969. Strategic management, systems management, business policy, organizational behavior.
James Swaney, Professor; Ph.D., Colorado State, 1979. History of economic thought, methodology, resource and environmental economics.
Robert J. Sweeney, Associate Professor; Ph.D., South Carolina, 1985. Financial management.
John Talbott, Professor; D.B.A., Kentucky, 1974. Taxes, managerial accounting.
Thomas L. Traynor, Associate Professor; Ph.D., Purdue, 1988. Forecasting, econometrics, industrial organization, microeconomics.
Ann C. Wendt, Associate Professor; Ph.D., Utah, 1987. Industrial relations, labor relations, human resource management.
Li D. Xu, Assistant Professor; Ph.D., Portland State, 1986. Systems theory, integrated information systems, artificial intelligence.
Vincent Yen, Associate Professor; Ph.D., Ohio State, 1975. Operation research, statistics and MIS.

YALE UNIVERSITY

Schools of Arts and Sciences and of Management
Ph.D. Program in Management

Program of Study

The Ph.D. Program in Management prepares students with strong quantitative backgrounds for careers in research and teaching in management. Students first acquire a strong methodological foundation in areas such as economics, statistics, and operations research. They then apply this knowledge to the study of a specific field of management. Currently specialization is offered in the management fields of accounting, financial economics, and marketing.

Students take two years of course work. A set of core courses (designed to provide a broad basis that is common across the three specializations) is followed by courses in the social sciences (e.g., economics, psychology), empirical methods (e.g., statistics, econometrics), and a depth area designed to focus the students on a particular research paradigm. Each student has to pass a qualifying examination in his or her chosen field of specialization at the end of the second year. In addition, students have to write a research paper in the first summer of the program and another paper in their second year of residence. Students who have passed the qualifying examination, satisfied the two paper requirements, met all of the program's course requirements, and have been judged by the faculty to be able to satisfactorily complete a dissertation are admitted to Ph.D. candidacy. Students normally complete all requirements for the Ph.D. degree in four years. Students are eligible for an M.A. degree after satisfactory completion of two years of course work, for an M.Phil. degree upon admission to Ph.D. candidacy, and for the Ph.D. degree upon the submission and defense of an acceptable dissertation.

Research Facilities

Students can take advantage of the outstanding Yale University Library, including special collections in the mathematics and statistics departments; the Social Science Library; the Medical School; the Seeley G. Mudd Library for Government Documents; and the Cowles Foundation for Research in Economics. Students have access to a wide range of computing resources. They may use the School of Management's Sun minicomputer or one of its many IBM personal computers, which are linked by a network. The larger mainframe computers of the Yale University Computer Center are also accessible to students.

Financial Aid

All students admitted to the program receive a tuition waiver and a stipend (which consists of a combination of fellowship, research assistantship, and teaching assistantship) for four years as long as they are making suitable progress. The amount of the stipend is comparable to the stipends provided by other major schools of management.

Cost of Study

The tuition for full-time graduate study during the academic year 1998–99 is $21,760.

Living and Housing Costs

The 1998–99 estimated expense for housing, food, and moderate entertainment is $12,560 for a single student and $19,490 for a married student. The Housing Office provides information and help to students seeking off-campus housing.

Student Group

Approximately 5 students enter the program each fall. For the academic year 1998–99, 16 students are in residence, including 2 women. Graduates have usually taken academic positions, many having been placed at the best universities in the United States and abroad. A few have taken research positions in government, business, or nonprofit organizations.

Location

Yale University is located in downtown New Haven, Connecticut, a small New England city of 126,000 situated on Long Island Sound. New Haven is a harbor city with a proud history, an energetic civil life, and challenging urban plans. It is a short walk from the campus to the historic New Haven Green. The city is a major center for theater and music, including the nationally acclaimed Long Wharf and Yale Repertory theaters. The Connecticut countryside is easily accessible, and there are delightful opportunities for bicycling, hiking, sailing, and swimming.

The University and The Program

Yale began to offer graduate education in 1847, and in 1861 conferred the first Ph.D. degree awarded in North America. With the appointment of a dean in 1892, the Graduate School was formally established. The School of Management is Yale's newest professional school; it granted its first degrees in 1978.

The opportunities presented by the Ph.D. Program in Management reflect its organization within the University. While it is a program of Yale's Graduate School of Arts and Science, its faculty members hold primary appointments in the Yale School of Management, many with joint appointments in various departments of the Graduate School. Students also take courses offered by other educational units at Yale, such as the departments of the Graduate School (e.g., Computer Science, Economics, Mathematics, Statistics) and the other professional schools (e.g., Law, Forestry and Environmental Studies). Other distinguishing features in the program are an excellent research faculty, small classes, and an extensive amount of faculty-student interaction.

Applying

Applications should be initiated in the fall of the academic year preceding the one in which the individual proposes to register. Application materials may be secured by writing to Graduate School Admissions, Yale University, P.O. Box 1504A Yale Station, New Haven, Connecticut 06520-7368 (telephone: 203-432-2770). When writing, students must state their interest in the Ph.D. Program in Management. Application files should be complete by January 2. Applicants are notified of action concerning admission by April 15.

Applicants are judged on the basis of scholastic record, letters of recommendation, and scores on the Graduate Record Examinations (GRE) or the Graduate Management Admission Test (GMAT). The GRE scores are preferred.

Correspondence and Information

Director of Graduate Studies
Ph.D. Program in Management
Yale School of Management
135 Prospect Street
New Haven, Connecticut 06511
Telephone: 203-432-6050
Fax: 203-432-6974

Yale University

THE FACULTY

Rick Antle, Professor of Accounting; Ph.D., Stanford.
Ramesh Arjunji, Assistant Professor of Marketing; Ph.D., Texas at Dallas.
Sigal Barsade, Associate Professor of Organizational Behavior; Ph.D., Berkeley.
Andrew Bernard, Associate Professor of Economics; Ph.D., Stanford.
Paul Bracken, Professor of International Business and of Political Science; Ph.D., Yale.
Arturo Bris, Assistant Professor of Finance; Ph.D., INSEAD.
Meghan Busse, Assistant Professor of Economics; Ph.D., MIT.
Ravi Dhar, Associate Professor of Marketing; Ph.D., Berkeley.
Jonathan S. Feinstein, Professor of Economics; Ph.D., MIT.
Oren Fuerst, Assistant Professor of Accounting; Ph.D., Columbia.
Stanley J. Garstka, Professor in the Practice of Management; Ph.D., Carnegie Mellon.
Jeffrey E. Garten, Dean and William S. Beinecke Professor in the Practice of International Trade and Finance; Ph.D., Johns Hopkins.
Donald Gibson, Assistant Professor of Organizational Behavior; Ph.D., UCLA.
William Goetzmann, Professor of Finance; Ph.D., Yale.
Albert Y. Ha, Associate Professor of Production Management; Ph.D., Stanford.
Roger G. Ibbotson, Professor in the Practice of Finance; Ph.D., Chicago.
Jonathan E. Ingersoll Jr., Adrian C. Israel Professor of International Trade and Finance; Ph.D., MIT.
Andrew Jeffrey, Assistant Professor of Finance; Ph.D., New South Wales.
Edward H. Kaplan, Professor of Management Sciences and of Medicine; Ph.D., MIT.
Lode Li, Professor of Production Management; Ph.D., Northwestern.
Paul W. MacAvoy, Williams Brothers Professor of Management Studies; Ph.D., Yale.
Theodore R. Marmor, Professor of Public Policy and Management and of Political Science; Ph.D., Harvard.
Mark Mason, Associate Professor of Management; Ph.D., Harvard.
Christopher McCusker, Associate Professor of Organizational Behavior; Ph.D., Illinois.
Barry Nalebuff, Milton Steinbach Professor of Management; D.Phil., Oxford.
Katherine M. O'Regan, Associate Professor of Economics and Public Policy; Ph.D., Berkeley.
Sharon M. Oster, Frederic D. Wolfe Professor of Management and Entrepreneurship; Ph.D., Harvard.
James A. Phills Jr., Assistant Professor of Organizational Behavior and Management; Ph.D., Harvard.
Nagpurnanand Prabhala, Assistant Professor of Finance; Ph.D., NYU.
Douglas W. Rae, Richard Ely Professor of Public Management; Ph.D., Wisconsin.
K. Geert Rouwenhorst, Associate Professor of Finance; Ph.D., Rochester.
Subrata K. Sen, Joseph F. Cullman 3rd Professor of Organization, Management and Marketing; Ph.D., Carnegie Mellon.
Martin S. Shubik, Seymour H. Knox Professor of Mathematical Institutional Economics; Ph.D., Princeton.
Arthur J. Swersey, Professor of Operations Research; D.Eng.Sci., Columbia.
Victor H. Vroom, John G. Searle Professor of Organization and Management and Professor of Psychology; Ph.D., Michigan.
Klaus Wertenbroch, Assistant Professor of Marketing; Ph.D., Chicago.
Dick R. Wittink, General George Rogers Clark Professor of Marketing and Management; Ph.D., Purdue.

Recent Ph.D. Dissertations

Student's affiliation upon leaving the program is in parentheses.
"The Entropy Pricing Theory," Boleslav Gulko, 1998. (General Reinsurance Corporation)
"Essays on Swap Markets," Haitao Li, 1998. (Cornell University)
"Two Essays in Direct Marketing," Sridhar Balasubramanian, 1997. (University of Texas at Austin)
"Corporate Long Term Dividend Policy and Dynamic Capital Structure Policy Under the Danger of Corporate Takeovers," Mingsung Tang, 1996. (Fordham University)
"Strategic Market Games and the Capital Asset Pricing Model," Jingxi Liu, 1996. (Capital Market Risk Advisors, New York)
"Collusion: Effects on Internal Control," Bente Villadsen, 1993. (Washington University in St. Louis)
"Three Essays in Financial Economics," Kyle Kashima, 1993. (Cornerstone Research, San Francisco)
"Pricing of Foreign Currency Options," Hans-Jurgen Knoch, 1992. (J. P. Morgan)
"A Theory of Optimal Ownership Structure and Sharing Rules," Steven Huddart, 1991. (Stanford University)
"Three Essays in Asset Pricing Theories: A General Equilibrium with Incomplete Asset Markets Approach," Gyutaeg Oh, 1991. (University of Iowa)
"Concave Production Technology and the Term Structure of Interest Rates," Michael Sullivan, 1991. (Florida International University)
"Bootstrapping and Simulation Tests of Long-Term Patterns in Stock Market Behavior," William Goetzmann, 1990. (Columbia University)
"The Timing of Information, a Test of Rationality, and the Behavior of Long Rates: A New Perspective on Each," Jonathan Berk, 1990. (University of British Columbia)
"Changing Tastes and Asset Pricing in Multiperiod Economies," Zhiwu Chen, 1990. (University of Wisconsin–Madison)
"A Theoretical and Empirical Investigation of the Black-Scholes Implied Volatility," Steven Feinstein, 1989. (Boston University)
"Three Essays on the Federal Funds Market and Development and Evaluation of Testing Procedures for Unit Roots," Buhmsoo Choi, 1988. (Korea Development Institute, South Korea)
"Asymmetric Information in Financial Markets." Jaime Zender, 1988. (University of Utah)
"Essays in Financial Economics," Yashushi Hamao, 1987. (University of California, San Diego)
"Essays in Valuation," Jonathan Tiemann, 1986. (Harvard University)

YORK UNIVERSITY

Schulich School of Business

Programs of Study

Established in 1966, the Schulich School of Business (formerly the Faculty of Administrative Studies) at York University is Canada's largest graduate school of management. Schulich programs emphasize relevance to real-world contexts, an applied focus, globalization, a broad frame of reference, and critical skills such as group, negotiation, and presentation skills. In addition to becoming strong generalists, students have exceptional opportunities for multiple specializations. Areas of study and specialization include management functions (finance, marketing, human resource management, strategic management, accounting, applied economics, operations management, and information systems), industry sectors (financial services, arts and media, and real property), and special areas (international business, entrepreneurism, financial engineering, business and the environment, public management, nonprofit management, and business ethics).

Schulich has become a global business school, with strategic alliances in more than forty-five countries around the world, including academic exchange agreements with twenty-nine leading international management schools.

At the master's level, Schulich offers three degrees: the M.B.A., the International M.B.A. (I.M.B.A.), and the Master of Public Administration (M.P.A.). M.B.A. and M.P.A. students can study on a full-time and/or a part-time basis three semesters a year. Admission is in September or January. Schulich also offers a joint M.B.A./LL.B. degree with Osgoode Hall Law School at York, a joint M.B.A./M.F.A. degree with the Faculty of Fine Arts at York, and a joint M.B.A. degree with Laval University in Quebec.

The I.M.B.A. is a twenty-four-month (six-semester) full-time program that admits 60 students each September. In addition to taking foundations of management and international business courses, students develop specialized region and country expertise, master a foreign language, and spend up to six months working and studying abroad.

The Ph.D. in administration program exposes students to quantitative and qualitative research methods and techniques through core and elective courses. Students may tailor specializations to individual needs in either management functions or thematic issues such as international business and change management.

Research Facilities

York University houses five libraries with considerable resources, including a book collection of nearly 2 million volumes, 13,000 serials (including periodicals, magazines, reports and digests, collections of microfiches, maps, videos, films, sound recordings, compact discs, and databases in CD-ROM and diskette to which the students have access). In addition, the University has one of the best business reference collections in metropolitan Toronto.

Financial Aid

Entrance scholarships are offered to a limited number of students each fall. Students may also apply for graduate assistantships and teaching assistantships throughout their stay at York University.

Cost of Study

At the master's level, based on an academic year of 30 semester credits, the 1998–99 tuition for Canadian students is approximately Can$4400 and for international students, approximately Can$18,000.

Living and Housing Costs

On-campus housing is available at reasonable rates. Travel and personal expenses vary with each student; a single student should anticipate a budget between Can$6000 and Can$8000 per semester.

Student Group

Students admitted to the School are expected to be of the highest calibre, with demonstrated leadership qualities and experience to build on. At any one time, there are approximately 450 full-time and 700 part-time master's students enrolled in the School. With two entry points per year and a large mix of full and part-time students in the elective classes, the experience is a rich and rewarding one.

Location

Toronto is Canada's industrial, commercial, and financial heartland and the capital of Ontario. Canada offers all business students the advantage of its traditional role as a major international trading nation with a balanced perspective on global issues. Transportation to the main campus from the downtown area takes approximately 50 minutes by public transit or 30 minutes by car, depending on traffic. The majority of the School's students commute.

The University

Founded in 1959, York University soon achieved an international reputation for excellence in teaching, research, and scholarship in both undergraduate and graduate studies. Today, York is the third-largest university in Canada and is similar to other large urban North American commuter universities.

Applying

Decisions on admission are made after a thorough review of the applicant's file. In addition to previous academic performance and the GMAT score, the applicant's work experience, demonstrated leadership qualities, and communication skills, as well as apparent creativity and innovation, are taken into consideration. Further, previous managerial experience, volunteer and extracurricular activity (particularly in a leadership capacity), and evidence of writing ability and interpersonal skills are examined. Work experience may be a significant factor for candidates whose applications are not consistently strong in all areas.

Admission may be offered to some applicants without an undergraduate degree under the nonbaccalaureate category. Applicants in this group must present several years of management-level working experience and acceptable GMAT results.

Correspondence and Information

Division of Student Affairs
Schulich School of Business
York University
4700 Keele Street
Toronto, Ontario M3J 1P3
Canada

Telephone: 416-736-5060
Fax: 416-736-5687
E-mail: admissions@bus.yorku.ca
World Wide Web: http://www.bus.yorku.ca

York University

THE FACULTY

Dezsö J. Horváth, Professor of Policy, Dean, and Tanna H. Schulich Chair in Strategic Management; Ph.D., UMEA (Sweden).

Accounting

Thomas H. Beechy, Professor; D.B.A., Washington (St. Louis); CPA, Illinois. John Friedlan, Associate Professor; Ph.D., Washington (Seattle). Patricia C. O'Brien, Associate Professor; Ph.D., Chicago. L. S. Rosen, Professor; Ph.D., Washington (Seattle). Paul Roy, Associate Professor; Ph.D., Iowa. Linda Thorne, Assistant Professor; Ph.D., McGill. Brenda Zimmerman, Associate Professor; Ph.D., York.

Economics

A. Bhanich Supapol, Associate Professor; Ph.D., Carleton (Ottawa). Donald J. Daly, Senior Scholar; Ph.D., Chicago. Irene Henriques, Associate Professor; Ph.D., Queen's at Kingston. Fred Lazar, Associate Professor; Ph.D., Harvard. Perry A. Sadorsky, Assistant Professor; Ph.D., Queen's at Kingston. John N. Smithin, Professor; Ph.D., McMaster. Klaus Weiermair, Professor Emeritus; Ph.D., Vienna. Bernard M. Wolf, Professor; Ph.D., Yale. Uri Zohar, Professor; Ph.D., Claremont.

Finance

Dawson E. Brewer, Associate Professor; Ph.D., Northwestern. David J. Fowler, Associate Professor Emeritus; Ph.D., Toronto. Elizabeth M. Maynes, Associate Professor; Ph.D., Queen's at Kingston. Sumon Mazumdar, Associate Professor; Ph.D., SMU. Moshe Milevsky, Assistant Professor; Ph.D., York. Eliezer Prisman, Professor and Nigel Martin Chair in Finance; D.Sc., Technion (Israel). Gordon Roberts, Professor; Ph.D., Boston College. Christopher M. Robinson, Associate Professor; Ph.D., Toronto.

Management Science

W. Russell Blackmore, Professor Emeritus; Ph.D., MIT. John Buzacott, Professor; Ph.D., Birmingham (England). Wade D. Cook, Professor; Ph.D., Dalhousie. Richard H. Irving, Associate Professor; Ph.D., Waterloo. David Johnston, Associate Professor; Ph.D., Western Ontario. Ronald J. McClean, Assistant Professor; Ph.D., Waterloo. Gordon C. Shaw, Professor Emeritus; Ph.D., Toronto. Daniele Thomassin-Singh, Assistant Professor; Ph.D., Case Western Reserve. Peter Tryfos, Professor; Ph.D., Berkeley. J. Scott Yeomans, Associate Professor; Ph.D., McMaster.

Marketing

Alexandra Campbell, Associate Professor; Ph.D., Toronto. Ian D. Fenwick, Professor; Ph.D., London. Eileen Fischer, Associate Professor; Ph.D., Queen's at Kingston. Brenda Gainer, Associate Professor; Ph.D., York. Roger M. Heeler, Professor; Ph.D., Stanford. Charles S. Mayer, Professor Emeritus; Ph.D., Michigan. Melvin S. Moyer, Professor Emeritus; Ph.D., Columbia. Marshall D. Rice, Associate Professor; Ph.D., Illinois. Ajay K. Sirsi, Assistant Professor; Ph.D., Arizona. Donald N. Thompson, Nabisco Brands Professor of Marketing; Ph.D., Berkeley.

Organizational Behavior and Industrial Relations

Patricia Bradshaw, Associate Professor; Ph.D., York. Ronald J. Burke, Professor; Ph.D., Michigan. David E. Dimick, Associate Professor; Ph.D., Minnesota. Rekha Karambayya, Associate Professor; Ph.D., Northwestern. Robert G. Lucas, Associate Professor; Ph.D., Cornell. Graeme H. McKechnie, Associate Professor; Ph.D., Wisconsin. Gareth Morgan, Distinguished Research Professor; Ph.D., Lancaster (England). Christine Oliver, Professor; Ph.D., Toronto. Hazel Rosin, Associate Professor; Ph.D, Yale.

Policy/Strategic Management

Ellen Auster, Associate Professor; Ph.D., Cornell. Wesley Cragg, George R. Gardiner Professor of Business Ethics; D.Phil., Oxford. Robert Cuff, Professor; Ph.D., Princeton. James L. Darroch, Associate Professor; Ph.D., York. Jerry D. Dermer, Professor; Ph.D., Illinois. James M. Gillies, Professor Emeritus; Ph.D., Indiana. Joseph G. Green, Professor Emeritus; Ph.D., Indiana. I. A. Litvak, Pierre Lassonde Chair in International Business; Ph.D., Columbia. H. Ian Macdonald, Professor and President Emeritus; M.A., Oxford; Hon.LL.D., Toronto. Charles J. McMillan, Professor; Ph.D., Bradford (England). Theodore Peridis, Associate Professor; Ph.D., NYU. Rein Peterson, Professor; Ph.D., Cornell. Phillip Phan, Associate Professor; Ph.D., Washington (Seattle). Stephen Weiss, Associate Professor; Ph.D., Pennsylvania. Tom Wesson, Assistant Professor; Ph.D., Harvard. H. Thomas Wilson, Professor; Ph.D., Rutgers. Joyce Zemans, University Professor; D.F.A., Nova Scotia College of Art and Design.

The Schulich School of Business, Main Campus.

Graduate housing on Passy Gardens, Main Campus.

Student Commons on graduation day, Main Campus.

Section 2
Accounting and Finance

This section contains directories of institutions offering graduate work in accounting, finance and banking, and taxation, followed by in-depth entries submitted by institutions that chose to prepare detailed program descriptions. Additional information about programs listed in the directories but not augmented by an in-depth entry may be obtained by writing directly to the dean of a graduate school or chair of a department at the address given in the directory.

For programs offering related work, see also in this book Business Administration and Management, International Business, and Nonprofit Management. In Book 2, Economics and Home Economics and Family Studies (Consumer Economics). In Book 4, see Mathematical Sciences; and in Book 5, Computer Science and Information Technology.

CONTENTS

Accounting

Abilene Christian University, College of Business Administration, Program in Accountancy, Abilene, TX 79699-9100. Awards M Acc. Faculty: 6 part-time (1 woman). Students: 0. *Degree requirements:* Comprehensive exam required, foreign language and thesis not required. *Entrance requirements:* GMAT or GRE General Test. Application deadline: 4/1 (priority date; rolling processing; 11/1 for spring admission). Application fee: $25 ($45 for international students). *Expenses:* Tuition $308 per credit hour. Fees $430 per year full-time, $85 per semester (minimum) part-time. *Financial aid:* Application deadline 4/1. • Bill Fowler, Department Chair, 915-674-2080. Application contact: Dr. Carley Dodd, Graduate Dean, 915-674-2354. Fax: 915-674-6717. E-mail: gradinfo@nicanor.acu.edu.

Adelphi University, School of Management and Business, Department of Accounting and Law, Garden City, NY 11530. Awards MS Acct. Part-time and evening/weekend programs available. Faculty: 6 full-time (1 woman), 7 part-time (0 women). Students: 6 full-time (3 women), 4 part-time (2 women). Average age 30. In 1997, 2 degrees awarded. *Degree requirements:* Computer language required, foreign language and thesis not required. *Average time to degree:* master's–3 years full-time, 5 years part-time. *Entrance requirements:* GMAT (minimum score 450), TOEFL (minimum score 550), bachelor's degree in accounting. Application deadline: 8/15 (priority date; rolling processing; 12/15 for spring admission). Application fee: $50. *Expenses:* Tuition $16,000 per year full-time, $485 per credit part-time. Fees $500 per year full-time, $150 per semester part-time. *Financial aid:* Career-related internships or fieldwork available. Financial aid application deadline: 3/1. • Grace M. Conway, Chairperson, 516-877-4620. Application contact: Jennifer Spiegel, Associate Director of Admissions, 516-877-3055.

Alabama State University, School of Graduate Studies, College of Business Administration, Department of Accounting and Finance, Program in Accountancy, Montgomery, AL 36101-0271. Awards MS. Program new for fall 1998. *Application deadline:* 7/15 (rolling processing; 12/15 for spring admission). *Application fee:* $10. *Expenses:* Tuition $85 per credit hour for state residents; $170 per credit hour for nonresidents. Fees $486 per year. • Dr. Jean Crawford, Chair, Department of Accounting and Finance, 334-229-4134.

American University, Kogod College of Business Administration, Department of Accounting, Program in Accounting, Washington, DC 20016-8001. Awards MBA, MS. Part-time and evening/weekend programs available. Faculty: 13 full-time (3 women), 2 part-time (0 women). Students: 17 full-time (8 women), 20 part-time (8 women); includes 6 minority (3 African Americans, 3 Asian Americans), 17 international. 47 applicants, 81% accepted. In 1997, 19 degrees awarded. *Entrance requirements:* GMAT. Application deadline: 2/1 (priority date; 10/1 for spring admission). Application fee: $50. *Expenses:* Tuition $19,080 per year full-time, $687 per credit hour (minimum) part-time. Fees $180 per year full-time, $110 per year part-time. *Financial aid:* Fellowships, research assistantships, Federal Work-Study, institutionally sponsored loans, and career-related internships or fieldwork available. Aid available to part-time students. Financial aid application deadline: 2/1. • Dr. Nancy A. Bagranoff, Chair, Department of Accounting, 202-885-1930. Fax: 202-885-1992.

Angelo State University, College of Professional Studies, Department of Accounting, Economics, and Finance, San Angelo, TX 76909. Offers program in accounting (MBA). Part-time and evening/weekend programs available. Faculty: 8 full-time (1 woman). Students: 13 full-time (10 women), 9 part-time (5 women); includes 3 minority (all Hispanics). Average age 36. 12 applicants, 75% accepted. In 1997, 8 degrees awarded. *Degree requirements:* Comprehensive exam required, thesis optional, foreign language not required. *Entrance requirements:* GMAT, minimum GPA of 2.5. Application deadline: 8/7 (priority date; rolling processing; 1/2 for spring admission). Application fee: $25 ($50 for international students). *Expenses:* Tuition $1022 per year full-time, $36 per semester hour part-time for state residents; $7382 per year full-time, $246 per semester hour part-time for nonresidents. Fees $1140 per year full-time, $165 per semester (minimum) part-time. *Financial aid:* In 1997–98, 10 fellowships were awarded; teaching assistantships, graduate assistantships, partial tuition waivers, Federal Work-Study also available. Aid available to part-time students. Financial aid application deadline: 8/1. • Dr. Andrew Dane, Head, 915-942-2046.

Appalachian State University, John A. Walker College of Business, Department of Accounting, Boone, NC 28608. Awards MS. Part-time programs available. Faculty: 10 full-time (1 woman). Students: 29 full-time (13 women), 4 part-time (all women); includes 1 minority (African American). 37 applicants, 92% accepted. In 1997, 8 degrees awarded. *Degree requirements:* Thesis or alternative, comprehensive exam required, foreign language not required. *Entrance requirements:* GMAT. Application deadline: 7/31 (priority date). Application fee: $35. *Tuition:* $1811 per year full-time, $354 per semester (minimum) part-time for state residents; $9081 per year full-time, $2171 per semester (minimum) part-time for nonresidents. *Financial aid:* In 1997–98, 13 assistantships were awarded; fellowships, research assistantships, teaching assistantships also available. *Faculty research:* Audit assurance risk, state taxation, financial accounting inconsistencies, management information systems, charitable contribution taxation. • Dr. Randy Edwards, Chairman, 704-262-2036. Fax: 704-262-2094. Application contact: Dr. Phil Witmer, Graduate Adviser, 704-262-6232.

Arizona State University, College of Business, Program in Business Administration, Tempe, AZ 85287. Offerings include accountancy (PhD). Program faculty: 93 full-time (21 women), 10 part-time (1 woman). *Degree requirements:* Dissertation. *Application fee:* $45. *Expenses:* Tuition $2088 per year full-time, $110 per hour part-time for state residents; $9040 per year full-time, $377 per hour part-time for nonresidents. Fees $72 per year full-time, $18 per semester (minimum) part-time. • Dr. Lee R. McPheters, Associate Dean, 602-965-9377. Fax: 602-965-3368. Application contact: Judy Heilala, Director of MBA, 602-965-3331.

Arizona State University, College of Business, School of Accountancy and Information Management, Tempe, AZ 85287. Offers programs in accountancy (M Accy), information management (MS), taxation (M Tax). Faculty: 47 full-time (11 women). Students: 102 full-time (43 women), 29 part-time (10 women); includes 18 minority (4 African Americans, 8 Asian Americans, 5 Hispanics, 1 Native American), 30 international. Average age 30. 65 applicants, 72% accepted. In 1997, 93 degrees awarded. *Degree requirements:* Thesis optional. *Entrance requirements:* GMAT. Application fee: $45. *Expenses:* Tuition $2088 per year full-time, $110 per hour part-time for state residents; $9040 per year full-time, $377 per hour part-time for nonresidents. Fees $72 per year full-time, $18 per semester (minimum) part-time. *Faculty research:* Business law, management communication, purchasing and logistics management, real estate, computer information systems, management science, operations management, statistics. • Dr. M. J. Philip Reckers, Director, 602-965-3631.

Arizona State University West, School of Management, Program in Accountancy, Phoenix, AZ 85069-7100. Awards Certificate. *Expenses:* Tuition $2088 per year full-time, $330 per course part-time for state residents; $9040 per year full-time, $1131 per course part-time for nonresidents. Fees $10 per year (minimum). • Dr. Abagail McWilliams, MBA Programs Director, School of Management, 602-543-6223. Application contact: Jon Delany, Academic Adviser, 602-543-6123. Fax: 602-543-6220.

Armstrong University, Graduate School of Business Administration, Program in Finance and Accounting, Oakland, CA 94612. Offers accounting (MBA), finance (MBA). *Degree requirements:* Thesis required, foreign language not required. *Entrance requirements:* Minimum GPA of 2.5. Application deadline: 8/15 (priority date; rolling processing; 1/1 for spring admission). Application fee: $50. • Prof. Thomas Smith, Director, 510-835-7900. E-mail: info@armstrong-u.edu. Application contact: Judy Battle, Director of Admissions, 510-835-7900. Fax: 510-835-8935. E-mail: info@armstrong-u.edu.

Auburn University, College of Business, School of Accountancy, Auburn University, AL 36849-0001. Awards M Acc. Part-time programs available. Faculty: 14 full-time (2 women). Students: 45 full-time (18 women), 4 part-time (1 woman); includes 2 minority (1 Asian American, 1 Hispanic), 1 international. 49 applicants, 71% accepted. In 1997, 37 degrees awarded. *Entrance requirements:* GMAT, GRE General Test, TOEFL. Application deadline: 9/1 (rolling processing; 3/1 for spring admission). Application fee: $25 ($50 for international students). *Expenses:* Tuition $2760 per year full-time, $76 per credit hour part-time for state residents; $8280 per year full-time, $228 per credit hour part-time for nonresidents. Fees $30 per year full-time, $160 per quarter part-time for state residents; $30 per year full-time, $480 per quarter part-time for nonresidents. *Financial aid:* Teaching assistantships, Federal Work-Study available. Aid available to part-time students. Financial aid application deadline: 3/15. • Dr. Ronald L. Clark, Director, 334-844-5340. Application contact: Dr. John F. Pritchett, Dean of the Graduate School, 334-844-4700.

Ball State University, College of Business, Department of Accounting, 2000 University Avenue, Muncie, IN 47306-1099. Awards MS. Admissions temporarily suspended. Faculty: 7. Students: 0. *Expenses:* Tuition $3454 per year full-time, $518 per semester (minimum) part-time for state residents; $9316 per year full-time, $1221 per semester (minimum) part-time for nonresidents. Fees $242 per year full-time, $18 per semester (minimum) part-time. • Dr. Paul Parkison, Head, 765-285-5100.

Baruch College of the City University of New York, School of Business, Department of Accounting, Program in Accounting, 17 Lexington Avenue, New York, NY 10010-5585. Awards MBA, MS, PhD. PhD offered jointly with the Graduate School and University Center of the City University of New York. Part-time and evening/weekend programs available. Faculty: 10 full-time (0 women), 2 part-time (1 woman). Students: 131 full-time (89 women), 54 part-time (33 women). In 1997, 83 master's awarded. Terminal master's awarded for partial completion of doctoral program. *Degree requirements:* For master's, computer language required, foreign language not required; for doctorate, computer language, dissertation required, foreign language not required. *Entrance requirements:* For master's, GMAT, TOEFL (minimum score 570), TWE (minimum score 4.5); for doctorate, GMAT. Application deadline: 6/15 (11/1 for spring admission). Application fee: $40. *Expenses:* Tuition $4350 per year full-time, $185 per credit part-time for state residents; $7600 per year full-time, $320 per credit part-time for nonresidents. Fees $53 per year. *Financial aid:* Research assistantships, Federal Work-Study, and career-related internships or fieldwork available. Aid available to part-time students. Financial aid application deadline: 5/3; applicants required to submit FAFSA. • Application contact: Michael S. Wynne, Office of Graduate Admissions, 212-802-2330. Fax: 212-802-2335. E-mail: graduate_admissions@baruch.cuny.edu.

Baylor University, Hankamer School of Business, Department of Accounting, Waco, TX 76798. Awards M Acc, MT, JD/MT. Part-time programs available. Faculty: 11 full-time (2 women). Students: 6 full-time (2 women), 1 part-time (0 women); includes 2 minority (1 Asian American, 1 Hispanic). In 1997, 8 degrees awarded. *Entrance requirements:* GMAT (minimum score 500). Application deadline: 8/1 (rolling processing; 12/1 for spring admission). Application fee: $25. *Expenses:* Tuition $7392 per year full-time, $308 per semester hour part-time. Fees $1024 per year. *Financial aid:* Research assistantships, Federal Work-Study, institutionally sponsored loans, and career-related internships or fieldwork available. *Faculty research:* Continuing professional education (CPE), accounting education, retirement plans. • Dr. Dan Hollingsworth, Chair, 254-710-3536. Application contact: Dr. Charles Davis, Director, 254-710-3536.

Bentley College, Graduate School of Business, Program in Accounting, 175 Forest Street, Waltham, MA 02154-4705. Awards MSA, Certificate. Part-time and evening/weekend programs available. Faculty: 22 full-time (6 women), 6 part-time (0 women). Students: 31 full-time (23 women), 85 part-time (39 women); includes 9 minority (2 African Americans, 6 Asian Americans, 1 Hispanic), 13 international. Average age 30. 69 applicants, 68% accepted. In 1997, 51 master's awarded (100% found work related to degree). *Degree requirements:* For master's, computer language required, foreign language and thesis not required. *Entrance requirements:* For master's, GMAT (average 540), TOEFL (minimum score 580). Application deadline: 6/1 (priority date; rolling processing; 11/1 for spring admission). Application fee: $50. *Expenses:* Tuition $20,500 per year full-time, $2050 per course part-time. Fees $65 per year full-time, $15 per semester part-time. *Financial aid:* In 1997–98, 27 students received aid, including 8 research assistantships (3 to first-year students) averaging $500 per month, 3 departmental assistantships; Federal Work-Study and career-related internships or fieldwork also available. Aid available to part-time students. Financial aid application deadline: 4/15; applicants required to submit CSS PROFILE or FAFSA. *Faculty research:* Audit risk assessment, ethics in accounting, corporate governance, accounting information systems and management control. • David Schwarzkopf, Director, 781-891-2783. Application contact: Holly Chase, Associate Director, 781-891-2108. Fax: 781-891-2464. E-mail: hchase@bentley.edu.

Announcement: Bentley College offers the Master of Science in Accountancy (MSA) degree and the MBA with a concentration in accountancy and advanced accountancy. The MSA is flexibly designed to provide a strong accounting foundation for those with little prior accounting course work or to provide in-depth, advanced courses for those wishing to build on an accounting undergraduate degree to expand their knowledge and meet certification requirements. The College also offers a 7-course graduate certificate in accountancy.

Bentley College, Graduate School of Business, Program in Accounting Information Systems, 175 Forest Street, Waltham, MA 02154-4705. Awards MSAIS. Program new for fall 1998. *Degree requirements:* Computer language required, foreign language and thesis not required. *Entrance requirements:* TOEFL (minimum score 580). Application deadline: 6/1 (priority date; rolling processing; 11/1 for spring admission). Application fee: $50. *Expenses:* Tuition $20,500 per year full-time, $2050 per course part-time. Fees $65 per year full-time, $15 per semester part-time. *Financial aid:* Application deadline 4/15; applicants required to submit CSS PROFILE. • David Schwarzkopf, Director, 781-891-2783. Application contact: Holly Chase, Associate Director, 781-891-2108. Fax: 781-891-2464. E-mail: hchase@bentley.edu.

Bentley College, Graduate School of Business, Self-paced MBA Program, 175 Forest Street, Waltham, MA 02154-4705. Offerings include accountancy (MBA), advanced accountancy (MBA). Program faculty: 70 full-time (21 women), 22 part-time (8 women). *Degree requirements:* Computer language required, foreign language and thesis not required. *Entrance requirements:* GMAT (average 540), TOEFL (minimum score 580). Application deadline: 6/1 (priority date; rolling processing; 11/1 for spring admission). Application fee: $50. *Expenses:* Tuition $20,500 per year full-time, $2050 per course part-time. Fees $65 per year full-time, $15 per semester part-time. • Dr. Judith B. Kamm, Director, 781-891-3433. Application contact: Holly Chase, Associate Director, 781-891-2108. Fax: 781-891-2464. E-mail: hchase@bentley.edu.

Birmingham–Southern College, Program in Accounting, Birmingham, AL 35254. Awards M Ac. Part-time and evening/weekend programs available. Faculty: 2 full-time (0 women). Students: 11 full-time (all women). Average age 27. 3 applicants, 100% accepted. In 1997, 2 degrees awarded. *Degree requirements:* Thesis optional, foreign language not required. *Entrance requirements:* GMAT (minimum score 500). Application deadline: 8/1 (rolling processing; 2/3 for spring admission). Application fee: $25. *Expenses:* Tuition $900 per course. Fees $16 per course. *Financial aid:* Scholarships available. Aid available to part-time students. • Dr. E. Byron Chew, Dean-Partner, 205-226-4892. Fax: 205-226-4843.

Bloomsburg University of Pennsylvania, School of Graduate Studies, College of Business, Department of Accounting, Bloomsburg, PA 17815-1905. Awards MS. Students: 3 full-time (all women), 3 part-time (1 woman); includes 1 minority (African American). Average age 27. 5 applicants, 100% accepted. *Entrance requirements:* GMAT or GRE, minimum QPA of 2.5. Application deadline: rolling. Application fee: $25. *Expenses:* Tuition $3468 per year full-time, $193 per credit part-time for state residents; $6236 per year full-time, $346 per credit part-time for nonresidents. Fees $748 per year full-time, $166 per semester (minimum) part-time. • Coordinator, 717-389-4125. Fax: 717-389-3892.

Boise State University, College of Business and Economics, Program in Accountancy, Boise, ID 83725-0399. Awards MS. Part-time programs available. Faculty: 10 full-time (1 woman), 1 part-time (0 women). Students: 3 full-time (2 women), 9 part-time (5 women). Average age 36. 9 applicants, 67% accepted. *Entrance requirements:* GMAT (minimum score 500), TOEFL (minimum score 550), minimum GPA of 3.0. Application deadline: 7/26 (priority date; rolling processing; 11/29 for spring admission). Application fee: $20 ($30 for international students). Electronic applications accepted. *Tuition:* $3020 per year full-time, $135 per credit part-time for state residents; $8900 per year full-time, $135 per credit part-time for nonresidents. *Financial aid:* In 1997–98, 2 students received aid, including 1 graduate assistantship; Federal Work-Study, institutionally sponsored loans, and career-related internships or fieldwork also available. Aid available to part-time students. Financial aid application deadline: 3/1. • Dr. Harry White, Coordinator, 208-385-1126. Application contact: J. Renee Anchustegui, Adviser, 208-385-1126. Fax: 208-385-1135.

Boston College, Wallace E. Carroll Graduate School of Management, Department of Accounting, Chestnut Hill, MA 02167-9991. Awards MBA. Part-time and evening/weekend programs available. *Entrance requirements:* GMAT (average 610), TOEFL (minimum score 600; average 630). Application deadline: 4/1 (priority date; rolling processing; 11/15 for spring admission). Application fee: $45. *Expenses:* Tuition $22,134 per year full-time, $714 per semester hour part-time. Fees $80 per year (minimum) full-time, $30 per semester part-time. *Financial aid:* Fellowships, research assistantships, teaching assistantships, administrative assistantships, Federal Work-Study, and career-related internships or fieldwork available. Financial aid application deadline: 3/1. *Faculty research:* Management control. • Dr. Jeffrey Cohen, Chairperson, 617-552-3165. Application contact: Simone Marthers, Director of Admissions, 617-552-3920. Fax: 617-552-8078.

Boston University, School of Management, Boston, MA 02215. Offerings include accounting (DBA). School faculty: 110 full-time, 54 part-time. *Degree requirements:* Dissertation required, foreign language not required. *Entrance requirements:* GMAT or GRE General Test. Application deadline: 5/1 (rolling processing). Application fee: $50. Electronic applications accepted. *Expenses:* Tuition $22,830 per year full-time, $713 per credit part-time. Fees $218 per year full-time, $40 per semester part-time. • Therese M. Hofmann, Assistant Dean, 617-353-2673. Application contact: Peter G. Kelly, Director of Admissions and Financial Aid, 617-353-2670. Fax: 617-353-7368. E-mail: mba@bu.edu.

Bowling Green State University, College of Business Administration, Program in Accountancy, Bowling Green, OH 43403. Awards M Acc. Faculty: 13 full-time (2 women). Students: 6 full-time (1 woman), 2 part-time (0 women); includes 1 minority (Asian American), 4 international. 15 applicants, 40% accepted. *Entrance requirements:* GMAT, TOEFL. Application fee: $30. Electronic applications accepted. *Tuition:* $6070 per year full-time, $284 per credit hour part-time for state residents; $11,358 per year full-time, $536 per credit hour part-time for nonresidents. *Financial aid:* Assistantships, Federal Work-Study available. Financial aid application deadline: 2/15; applicants required to submit FAFSA. • Dr. Mark Asman, Chair, 419-372-2767. Application contact: Dr. David Albrecht, Graduate Coordinator, 419-372-8016.

Bradley University, College of Business Administration, Program in Accounting, Peoria, IL 61625-0002. Awards MS. *Degree requirements:* Comprehensive exam required, foreign language and thesis not required. *Entrance requirements:* GMAT (minimum score 500), TOEFL (minimum score 500), minimum undergraduate GPA of 2.75 in major. Application deadline: 7/1 (priority date; rolling processing; 11/1 for spring admission). Application fee: $35. *Tuition:* $13,240 per year full-time, $359 per semester hour (minimum) part-time.

Brigham Young University, Marriott School of Management, School of Accountancy and Information Systems, Provo, UT 84602-1001. Awards M Acc, MISM. Faculty: 36 full-time (1 woman). Students: 155 full-time (41 women); includes 7 minority (all Asian Americans), 6 international. Average age 25. 239 applicants, 65% accepted. In 1997, 180 degrees awarded. *Average time to degree:* master's–1.5 years full-time. *Entrance requirements:* GMAT (minimum score 500), TOEFL (minimum score 575), minimum GPA of 3.0 in last 60 hours. Application deadline: 3/1. Application fee: $30. *Financial aid:* In 1997–98, scholarships totaling $168,100 were awarded; research assistantships, teaching assistantships, institutionally sponsored loans, and career-related internships or fieldwork also available. Financial aid application deadline: 3/1. *Faculty research:* Quality processing–management approach, fraudulent activities, database languages, electronic data exchange, knowledge-based systems. • Dr. W. Steve Albrecht, Director, 801-378-4195. Application contact: Kathy O'Brien, Academic Adviser, 801-378-3951. Fax: 801-378-5933. E-mail: kathy_obrien@byu.edu.

Brooklyn College of the City University of New York, Department of Economics, 2900 Bedford Avenue, Brooklyn, NY 11210-2889. Offerings include accounting (MA). Department faculty: 29 full-time, 17 part-time, 37.5 FTE. *Application deadline:* 3/1 (11/1 for spring admission). *Application fee:* $40. *Expenses:* Tuition $4350 per year full-time, $185 per credit part-time for state residents; $7600 per year full-time, $320 per credit part-time for nonresidents. Fees $500 per year for state residents; $806 per year for nonresidents. • Dr. Patricia F. Bowers, Chairperson, 718-951-5317. Application contact: Dr. Paul Goldberg, Graduate Deputy Chairperson, 718-951-5101.

Bryant College, College of Business Administration, Program in Accounting, Smithfield, RI 02917-1284. Awards MBA, MSA, CAGS. Part-time and evening/weekend programs available. Faculty: 7 full-time (1 woman), 2 part-time (0 women). Students: 10 full-time (6 women), 56 part-time (22 women); includes 1 minority (Native American), 3 international. Average age 32. 21 applicants, 67% accepted. In 1997, 14 master's, 2 CAGSs awarded. *Entrance requirements:* For master's, GMAT (minimum score 480; average 520). Application deadline: 7/1 (priority date; rolling processing; 11/15 for spring admission). Application fee: $55 ($70 for international students). *Tuition:* $1025 per course. *Financial aid:* In 1997–98, 2 research assistantships were awarded; graduate assistantships and career-related internships or fieldwork also available. Aid available to part-time students. Financial aid applicants required to submit FAFSA. • Michael Lynch, Coordinator of MBA, 401-232-6230. Fax: 401-232-6494. E-mail: gradprog@bryant.edu.

Bucknell University, College of Arts and Sciences, Department of Management, Lewisburg, PA 17837. Offerings include accounting (MSBA). Department faculty: 12 full-time. *Degree requirements:* Thesis required, foreign language not required. *Entrance requirements:* GMAT, TOEFL (minimum score 550), minimum GPA of 2.8. Application deadline: 6/1 (priority date; rolling processing; 12/1 for spring admission). Application fee: $25. *Tuition:* $2410 per course. • Dr. Mark Bettner, Head, 717-524-1306.

Caldwell College, Graduate Studies, Program in Accounting, Caldwell, NJ 07006-6195. Awards MS. Program new for fall 1998. *Application deadline:* rolling. *Application fee:* $25. *Tuition:* $365 per credit. • Alvin Neiman, Coordinator, 973-228-4424 Ext. 255. Fax: 973-783-7037. Application contact: Dr. Rina Spano, Director of Graduate Studies, 973-228-4424 Ext. 408. Fax: 973-364-7618. E-mail: rspano@caldwell.edu.

California State University, Chico, College of Business, Program in Accountancy, Chico, CA 95929-0041. Awards MSA. Faculty: 11 full-time (1 woman). Students: 10 full-time (2 women), 5 part-time (2 women); includes 1 minority (Asian American), 3 international. Average age 32. 15 applicants, 33% accepted. In 1997, 4 degrees awarded. *Degree requirements:* Thesis or alternative. *Entrance requirements:* GMAT (minimum score 500). Application deadline: 4/1 (rolling processing). Application fee: $55. *Expenses:* Tuition $0 for state residents; $246 per unit for nonresidents. Fees $2108 per year full-time, $1442 per year part-time. *Financial aid:* Federal Work-Study and career-related internships or fieldwork available. Financial aid applicants required to submit FAFSA. • Graduate Coordinator, 530-898-4425. Fax: 530-898-4584.

California State University, Fullerton, School of Business Administration and Economics, Department of Accounting, PO Box 34080, Fullerton, CA 92834-9480. Offers programs in accounting (MBA, MS), taxation (MS). Part-time and evening/weekend programs available. Faculty: 18 full-time (4 women), 9 part-time, 20 FTE. Students: 12 full-time (8 women), 54 part-time (32 women); includes 26 minority (2 African Americans, 20 Asian Americans, 4 Hispanics), 8 international. Average age 31. 62 applicants, 55% accepted. In 1997, 10 degrees awarded. *Degree requirements:* Computer language, thesis or alternative, project required, foreign language not required. *Entrance requirements:* GMAT (minimum score 950), minimum AACSB index of 950. Application fee: $55. *Expenses:* Tuition $0 for state residents; $246 per unit for nonresidents. Fees $1947 per year full-time, $1281 per year part-time. *Financial aid:* Teaching assistantships, state grants, Federal Work-Study, institutionally sponsored loans available. Aid available to part-time students. Financial aid application deadline: 3/1. • Dr. Robert McCabe, Chair, 714-278-2225.

California State University, Hayward, School of Business and Economics, Department of Accounting and Computer Information Systems, Option in Accounting, Hayward, CA 94542-3000. Awards MBA. Faculty: 17 full-time (4 women). *Degree requirements:* Comprehensive exam or thesis required, foreign language not required. *Entrance requirements:* GMAT, minimum GPA of 2.75. Application deadline: 4/19 (priority date; rolling processing; 1/5 for spring admission). Application fee: $55. *Expenses:* Tuition $0 for state residents; $164 per unit for nonresidents. Fees $1827 per year full-time, $1161 per year part-time. *Financial aid:* Federal Work-Study, institutionally sponsored loans, and career-related internships or fieldwork available. Aid available to part-time students. Financial aid application deadline: 3/1. • Dr. Charlene Abendroth, Coordinator, 510-885-3298. Application contact: Dr. Donna L. Wiley, Director of Graduate Programs, 510-885-3964.

California State University, Los Angeles, School of Business and Economics, Department of Accounting, Los Angeles, CA 90032-8530. Offers programs in accountancy (MS), including business taxation, financial accounting, information systems, management accounting; accounting (MBA). Part-time and evening/weekend programs available. Faculty: 16 full-time, 8 part-time. Students: 16 full-time (11 women), 28 part-time (10 women); includes 21 minority (20 Asian Americans, 1 Hispanic), 13 international. In 1997, 14 degrees awarded. *Degree requirements:* Computer language, comprehensive exam (MBA), thesis (MS) required, foreign language not required. *Entrance requirements:* GMAT, TOEFL (minimum score 550), minimum GPA of 2.5 during previous 2 years. Application deadline: 6/30 (rolling processing; 11/30 for spring admission). Application fee: $55. *Expenses:* Tuition $0 for state residents; $164 per unit for nonresidents. Fees $1763 per year full-time, $1097 per year part-time. *Financial aid:* 9 students received aid; Federal Work-Study and career-related internships or fieldwork available. Aid available to part-time students. Financial aid application deadline: 3/1. • Dr. Ralph Spanswick, Chair, 213-343-2830.

California State University, Northridge, College of Business Administration and Economics, Department of Accounting and Management Information Systems, Program in Accounting, Northridge, CA 91330. Awards MS. Students: 9 full-time (5 women), 12 part-time (7 women); includes 7 minority (6 Asian Americans, 1 Hispanic), 2 international. Average age 31. 48 applicants, 67% accepted. *Degree requirements:* Thesis or alternative required, foreign language not required. *Entrance requirements:* GMAT (score in 50th percentile or higher), TOEFL, minimum GPA of 3.0 in last 60 units. Application deadline: 11/30. Application fee: $55. *Expenses:* Tuition $0 for state residents; $246 per unit for nonresidents. Fees $1970 per year full-time, $1304 per year part-time. *Financial aid:* Application deadline 3/1. • Application contact: Dr. Richard Moore, Director of Graduate Programs, 818-677-2467.

California State University, Sacramento, School of Business Administration, Department of Accountancy, Sacramento, CA 95819-6048. Awards MS. Part-time and evening/weekend programs available. *Degree requirements:* Thesis or alternative, writing proficiency exam required, foreign language not required. *Entrance requirements:* GMAT, TOEFL (minimum score 550). Application deadline: 4/15 (11/1 for spring admission). Application fee: $55. *Expenses:* Tuition $0 for state residents; $246 per unit for nonresidents. Fees $2012 per year full-time, $1346 per year part-time. *Financial aid:* Research assistantships, teaching assistantships, Federal Work-Study, and career-related internships or fieldwork available. Aid available to part-time students. Financial aid application deadline: 3/1. • Dr. Eugene Sauls, Chair, 916-278-7124.

Canisius College, Wehle School of Business, Program in Professional Accounting, Buffalo, NY 14208-1098. Awards MBA. Faculty: 4 full-time (0 women). Students: 3 full-time (0 women), 36 part-time (11 women); includes 8 international. Average age 30. 12 applicants, 75% accepted. *Degree requirements:* Computer language required, foreign language and thesis not required. *Entrance requirements:* GMAT. Application deadline: 7/1 (priority date; rolling processing; 11/1 for spring admission). Application fee: $20. *Expenses:* Tuition $499 per credit hour. Fees $10 per credit hour. *Financial aid:* Graduate assistantships available. Financial aid application deadline: 6/15. • Edward Gress, Chair, 716-888-2865.

Carnegie Mellon University, Graduate School of Industrial Administration, Program in Accounting, Pittsburgh, PA 15213-3891. Awards PhD. Faculty: 5 full-time (0 women). *Degree requirements:* Dissertation required, foreign language not required. *Entrance requirements:* GRE. Application deadline: 2/1. Application fee: $50. *Financial aid:* Fellowships, teaching assistantships available. Financial aid application deadline: 5/1. • Application contact: Jackie Cavendish, Administrative Assistant, 412-268-2301.

Case Western Reserve University, Weatherhead School of Management, Department of Accountancy, Cleveland, OH 44106. Awards M Acc, PhD. PhD offered through the School of Graduate Studies. Evening/weekend programs available. Faculty: 10 full-time (1 woman), 3 part-time (1 woman), 11.5 FTE. Students: 30 full-time (13 women), 8 part-time (4 women); includes 1 minority (African American), 24 international. In 1997, 17 master's, 1 doctorate awarded. *Degree requirements:* For doctorate, dissertation required, foreign language not required. *Entrance requirements:* For master's, GMAT (average 603); for doctorate, GMAT. Application deadline: 4/15 (priority date; rolling processing). Application fee: $35. *Tuition:* $20,900 per year full-time, $871 per credit hour part-time. *Financial aid:* Full and partial tuition waivers, Federal Work-Study, institutionally sponsored loans, and career-related internships or fieldwork available. Financial aid application deadline: 5/1. *Faculty research:* Behavior issues in decision making, financial reporting, regulation and analysis of corporate disclosure, accounting history. • David R. Campbell, Chairman, 216-368-2073. Fax: 216-368-4776. Application contact: Linda S. Gaston, Director of Marketing and Admissions, 216-368-2030. Fax: 216-368-5548. E-mail: lxg10@po.cwru.edu.

The Catholic University of America, School of Arts and Sciences, Department of Economics and Business, Program in Accounting, Washington, DC 20064. Awards MA, JD/MA. Part-time and evening/weekend programs available. Students: 2 full-time (both women), 1 (woman) part-time; includes 2 international. Average age 26. 3 applicants, 33% accepted. In 1997, 5 degrees awarded (100% found work related to degree). *Degree requirements:* Computer language, comprehensive exam required, foreign language and thesis not required. *Entrance requirements:* GRE General Test, TOEFL. Application deadline: 8/1 (priority date; rolling processing; 12/1 for spring admission). Application fee: $50. *Expenses:* Tuition $17,325 per year full-time, $668 per credit hour part-time. Fees $680 per year full-time, $360 per year part-time. *Financial aid:* Teaching assistantships, full and partial tuition waivers, Federal Work-Study, institutionally sponsored loans, and career-related internships or fieldwork available. Aid available to part-time students. Financial aid application deadline: 2/1. *Faculty research:* Cost accounting, public versus private, nonprofit organization. • Dr. Ernest M. Zampelli, Chair, Department of Economics and Business, 202-319-6683. Fax: 202-319-4426. E-mail: zampelli@cua.edu.

Centenary College, Program in Professional Accounting, 400 Jefferson Street, Hackettstown, NJ 07840-2100. Awards MS. Program new for fall 1998. Faculty: 2 full-time. *Application*

Directory: Accounting

Centenary College (continued)

deadline: 8/15 (rolling processing). *Application fee:* $30. *Tuition:* $355 per credit. • Dr. Thomas A. Brunner, Director of Graduate Studies, 908-852-1400 Ext. 2299.

Central Michigan University, College of Business Administration, Department of Accounting, Mount Pleasant, MI 48859. Awards MBA. Faculty: 11 full-time (1 woman). Students: 35 full-time (15 women), 114 part-time (47 women); includes 11 minority (3 African Americans, 6 Asian Americans, 2 Native Americans), 30 international. Average age 31. In 1997, 66 degrees awarded. *Entrance requirements:* GMAT. Application deadline: 3/1 (priority date; rolling processing). Application fee: $30. *Expenses:* Tuition $139 per credit hour (minimum) for state residents; $276 per credit hour (minimum) for nonresidents. Fees $260 per year full-time, $150 per semester part-time. *Financial aid:* In 1997–98, 2 research assistantships (both to first-year students) were awarded; teaching assistantships, Federal Work-Study, and career-related internships or fieldwork also available. Financial aid application deadline: 3/7. *Faculty research:* Accounting and financial reporting for local government, tax accounting for partnerships and small corporations, accounting for employee stock ownership plans. • Dr. Edward B. Grant, Chairperson, 517-774-3796. Fax: 517-774-2372. E-mail: edward.b.grant@cmich.edu.

Central Missouri State University, Harmon College of Business Administration, Department of Accounting, Warrensburg, MO 64093. Awards MA. Part-time programs available. Faculty: 11 full-time. Students: 1 (woman) full-time. *Entrance requirements:* GMAT, TOEFL (minimum score 550), minimum GPA of 2.5. Application deadline: 6/30 (priority date; rolling processing). Application fee: $25 ($50 for international students). *Tuition:* $3288 per year full-time, $137 per credit hour part-time for state residents; $5928 per year full-time, $274 per credit hour part-time for nonresidents. *Financial aid:* In 1997–98, 1 research assistantship was awarded; teaching assistantships, Federal Work-Study also available. Aid available to part-time students. Financial aid application deadline: 3/1; applicants required to submit FAFSA. • Dr. John Elfrink, Chair, 660-543-4245. Fax: 660-543-8885. E-mail: elfrink@cmsu1.cmsu.edu.

Charleston Southern University, Program in Business, Charleston, SC 29423-8087. Offerings include accounting (MBA). Program faculty: 8 full-time (0 women), 1 (woman) part-time, 8.33 FTE. *Entrance requirements:* GMAT. Application deadline: rolling. Application fee: $25. *Tuition:* $9821 per year full-time, $173 per hour (minimum) part-time. • Dr. Al Parish, MBA Director, 803-863-7904. Fax: 803-863-7919. E-mail: aparish@awdd.com. Application contact: Terri Jordan, MBA Coordinator, 803-863-7955. Fax: 803-863-7922.

Claremont Graduate University, Peter F. Drucker Graduate Management Center, Program in Management, Claremont, CA 91711-6163. Offerings include finance (MBA), with option in accounting control. *Entrance requirements:* GMAT, TOEFL. Application deadline: 2/15 (priority date; rolling processing). Application fee: $40. Electronic applications accepted. *Expenses:* Tuition $20,250 per year full-time, $913 per unit part-time. Fees $130 per year. • Dr. Jeffrey Decker, Director, 909-621-8073. Fax: 909-621-8390. E-mail: jeff.decker@cgu.edu. Application contact: Kathy Hubener, Admissions Coordinator, 909-621-8073. Fax: 909-621-8543. E-mail: mba@cgu.edu.

Clemson University, College of Business and Public Affairs, School of Accountancy and Legal Studies, Clemson, SC 29634. Awards MP Acc. Part-time programs available. Students: 15 full-time (11 women), 13 part-time (9 women); includes 2 international. Average age 30. 38 applicants, 37% accepted. In 1997, 19 degrees awarded (100% found work related to degree). *Degree requirements:* Oral final exam required, foreign language and thesis not required. *Average time to degree:* master's–1 year full-time, 3 years part-time. *Entrance requirements:* GMAT (minimum score 500; average 547), TOEFL, BS in accounting or equivalent, minimum GPA of 3.0. Application deadline: 5/1 (priority date; rolling processing; 10/1 for spring admission). Application fee: $35. *Expenses:* Tuition $3154 per year full-time, $130 per credit hour part-time for state residents; $6452 per year full-time, $264 per credit hour part-time for nonresidents. Fees $190 per year. *Financial aid:* Research assistantships available. • Dr. Alan J. Winters, Director, 864-656-3265. E-mail: awinter@clemson.edu. Application contact: Dr. Ralph E. Welton Jr., Program Coordinator, 864-656-4881. Fax: 864-656-4892. E-mail: edwisur@clemson.edu.

Cleveland State University, James J. Nance College of Business Administration, Program in Accounting and Financial Information Systems, Cleveland, OH 44115-2440. Awards MAFIS. Part-time programs available. Faculty: 10 full-time (3 women). Students: 35 full-time (17 women), 51 part-time (23 women); includes 13 minority (8 African Americans, 4 Asian Americans, 1 Hispanic), 34 international. Average age 30. 55 applicants, 64% accepted. In 1997, 35 degrees awarded (100% found work related to degree). *Degree requirements:* Computer language required, foreign language and thesis not required. *Entrance requirements:* GMAT, minimum GPA of 2.75. Application deadline: 9/1 (priority date; rolling processing). Application fee: $25. *Expenses:* Tuition $5252 per year full-time, $202 per credit hour part-time for state residents; $10,504 per year full-time, $404 per credit hour part-time for nonresidents. Fees $2.25 per credit hour (minimum). *Financial aid:* In 1997–98, 1 research assistantship, 2 administrative assistantships were awarded; Federal Work-Study and career-related internships or fieldwork also available. *Faculty research:* Internal auditing, computer auditing, taxation, accounting education. • Dr. Linda Garceau, Chair, 216-687-4723. Fax: 216-687-9212. E-mail: l.garceau@csuohio.edu.

The College of Saint Rose, School of Business, Accounting Department, Albany, NY 12203-1419. Awards MS. Part-time and evening/weekend programs available. Faculty: 3 full-time (1 woman), 1 part-time (0 women). Students: 13 part-time (8 women); includes 3 minority (all Asian Americans). Average age 32. In 1997, 6 degrees awarded. *Entrance requirements:* GMAT or graduate degree, minimum undergraduate GPA of 3.0. Application deadline: 7/15 (priority date; rolling processing; 12/1 for spring admission). Application fee: $30. *Expenses:* Tuition $338 per credit. Fees $60 per year. *Financial aid:* Research assistantships, partial tuition waivers available. Aid available to part-time students. Financial aid application deadline: 3/1; applicants required to submit FAFSA. • Barry Hughes, Head, 518-458-5466. Application contact: Graduate Office, 518-454-5136. Fax: 518-458-5479. E-mail: ace@rosnet.strose.edu.

Colorado State University, College of Business, Department of Accounting and Taxation, Fort Collins, CO 80523-0015. Offers programs in accounting (MBA, MS), taxation (MBA, MS). Part-time programs available. Faculty: 14 full-time (4 women). Students: 17 full-time (10 women), 22 part-time (12 women); includes 4 minority (2 Asian Americans, 2 Native Americans), 1 international. 20 applicants, 80% accepted. In 1997, 13 degrees awarded. *Degree requirements:* Thesis optional, foreign language not required. *Entrance requirements:* GMAT, TOEFL, minimum GPA of 3.0. Application deadline: 2/1 (priority date; rolling processing). Application fee: $30. Electronic applications accepted. *Tuition:* $2920 per year (minimum) full-time, $328 per credit hour (minimum) part-time for state residents; $9000 per year (minimum) full-time, $368 per credit hour (minimum) part-time for nonresidents. *Financial aid:* In 1997–98, 18 teaching assistantships were awarded; fellowships, traineeships, Federal Work-Study, and career-related internships or fieldwork also available. Financial aid application deadline: 2/1. *Faculty research:* Business law, malpractice/ethics of CPA's, managerial accountancy, cost accountancy, systems accountancy, governmental accountancy, audit accountancy. • Application contact: Dr. Jon Clark, Interim Chair, 970-491-5102. Fax: 970-491-2676.

Columbia University, Graduate School of Business, Doctoral Program in Business, New York, NY 10027. Offerings include business (PhD), with options in accounting (PhD), finance and economics (PhD), management of organizations (PhD), management science/operations research (PhD), marketing (PhD). Program faculty: 105 full-time (15 women), 86 part-time (15 women). *Degree requirements:* Dissertation, teacher training seminars, research paper, oral exam required, foreign language not required. *Average time to degree:* doctorate–4 years full-time. *Entrance requirements:* GMAT or GRE, TOEFL or TSE. Application deadline: 2/1. Application fee: $50. *Expenses:* Tuition is $26,520 per year, fees of 1,250 per year, and students receive tuition and fee exemptions for a maximum of 12 terms. • Application contact: Elizabeth Elam, Administrative Director, 212-854-2836. Fax: 212-932-2359.

Columbia University, Graduate School of Business, MBA Program, New York, NY 10027. Offerings include accounting (MBA). Program faculty: 105 full-time (15 women), 86 part-time (15 women). *Entrance requirements:* GMAT, TOEFL (minimum score 610). Application deadline: 4/20 (rolling processing; 11/1 for spring admission). Application fee: $125 ($150 for international students). *Expenses:* Tuition $26,520 per year. Fees $1250 per year. • Prof. Safwan Masri, Vice Dean of Students and the MBA Program, 212-854-8716. Fax: 212-854-0545. E-mail: smm1@columbia.edu. Application contact: Linda Meehan, Assistant Dean and Executive Director of Admissions and Financial Aid, 212-854-1961. Fax: 212-662-6754. E-mail: gohermes@claven.gsb.columbia.edu.

Concordia University, Faculty of Commerce and Administration, Montréal, PQ H3G 1M8, Canada. Offerings include accounting (Diploma), with options in institutional administration, sports administration; management accounting (Certificate). *Application fee:* $30. *Expenses:* Tuition $56 per credit (minimum) for Canadian residents; $249 per credit (minimum) for nonresidents. Fees $152 per year full-time, $111 per year (minimum) part-time. • Dr. M. Anvari, Dean, 514-848-2700. Fax: 514-848-4502. Application contact: Dale Doreen, Director, 514-848-2958. Fax: 514-848-4208.

Cornell University, Graduate Field of Management, Ithaca, NY 14853-0001. Offerings include accounting (PhD). Terminal master's awarded for partial completion of doctoral program. Faculty: 43 full-time. *Degree requirements:* Dissertation required, foreign language not required. *Entrance requirements:* GMAT or GRE General Test, TOEFL. Application deadline: 1/10 (priority date). Application fee: $65. *Expenses:* Tuition $24,300 per year. Fees $48 per year. • Director of Graduate Studies, 607-255-3669. Application contact: Graduate Field Assistant, 607-255-3669. Fax: 607-254-4590. E-mail: maria@johnson.cornell.edu.

Dallas Baptist University, College of Business, Business Administration Program, Dallas, TX 75211-9299. Offerings include accounting (MBA). Program faculty: 15 full-time (4 women), 26 part-time (5 women). *Entrance requirements:* GMAT, TOEFL (minimum score 550). Application deadline: rolling. Application fee: $25. *Tuition:* $285 per hour. • Annette Hoffman, Director of Graduate Business Programs, 214-333-5280. Application contact: Travis Bundrick, Director of Graduate Programs, 214-333-5243. Fax: 214-333-5579. E-mail: graduate@dbu.edu.

Delta State University, School of Business, Department of Accounting, Cleveland, MS 38733-0001. Awards MPA. Part-time and evening/weekend programs available. Faculty: 5 full-time (1 woman). Students: 8 full-time (6 women), 14 part-time (10 women); includes 8 minority (6 African Americans, 2 Asian Americans). Average age 30. 8 applicants, 100% accepted. In 1997, 8 degrees awarded. *Degree requirements:* Thesis or alternative required, foreign language not required. *Entrance requirements:* GMAT (minimum score 380). Application deadline: 8/1 (priority date; rolling processing). Application fee: $0. *Tuition:* $2596 per year full-time, $121 per semester hour part-time for state residents; $5546 per year full-time, $285 per semester hour part-time for nonresidents. *Financial aid:* Research assistantships, Federal Work-Study, institutionally sponsored loans, and career-related internships or fieldwork available. Aid available to part-time students. Financial aid application deadline: 6/1. • Dr. Rita Jones, Chair, 601-846-4182. Application contact: Dr. John Thornell, Dean of Graduate Studies and Continuing Education, 601-846-4310. Fax: 601-846-4016.

DePaul University, Charles H. Kellstadt Graduate School of Business, School of Accountancy, Program in Accounting, Chicago, IL 60604-2287. Awards PMSA, M Acc, MBA, MSA. Part-time and evening/weekend programs available. Students: 66 full-time (24 women), 58 part-time (26 women); includes 24 minority (5 African Americans, 15 Asian Americans, 4 Hispanics), 3 international. Average age 30. 62 applicants, 65% accepted. In 1997, 55 master's awarded. *Entrance requirements:* For master's, GMAT. Application deadline: 8/1 (rolling processing; 3/1 for spring admission). Application fee: $40. *Expenses:* Tuition $1593 per course. Fees $30 per year. *Financial aid:* Application deadline 4/30. • Application contact: Christine Munoz, Director of Admissions, 312-362-8810. Fax: 312-362-6677. E-mail: mbainfo@wppost.depaul.edu.

Detroit College of Business, Graduate Studies Division, 4801 Oakman Boulevard, Dearborn, MI 48126-3799. Offerings include accounting (MBA). Postbaccalaureate distance learning degree programs offered. Division faculty: 5 full-time (2 women), 28 part-time (4 women). *Entrance requirements:* Minimum GPA of 2.7, previous course work in accounting and statistics. Application deadline: 8/12 (priority date; rolling processing; 4/17 for spring admission). Application fee: $50. • Dr. James J. Krolik, Dean, 313-581-4400 Ext. 372. E-mail: dbjkrol@dcb.edu. Application contact: Ofelia Tabarez, Graduate Admissions Representative, 313-581-4400 Ext. 3781. Fax: 313-581-6822. E-mail: dbaotabarez@dcb.edu.

Dominican University, Graduate School of Business, River Forest, IL 60305-1099. Offerings include accounting (MSA). School faculty: 52 (15 women). *Application deadline:* 8/1 (priority date; rolling processing). *Application fee:* $25. • Dr. Molly Burke, Dean, 708-524-6810. E-mail: burkemg@email.dom.edu. Application contact: Dr. Dan Condon, Director Admissions and Advising, 708-524-6223. Fax: 708-366-5360. E-mail: condond@email.dom.edu.

Drexel University, College of Business and Administration, Program in Business Administration, 3141 Chestnut Street, Philadelphia, PA 19104-2875. Offerings include business administration (MBA, PhD, APC), with options in accounting (MBA, PhD), decision sciences (PhD), economics (MBA, PhD), finance (MBA, PhD), legal studies (MBA), management (MBA), marketing (MBA, PhD), organizational sciences (PhD), quantitative methods (MBA), strategic management (PhD). Terminal master's awarded for partial completion of doctoral program. *Degree requirements:* For doctorate, computer language required, foreign language and dissertation not required. *Entrance requirements:* For doctorate, GMAT, TOEFL (minimum score 570). Application deadline: 8/21 (rolling processing; 3/5 for spring admission). Application fee: $35. *Expenses:* Tuition $494 per credit hour. Fees $121 per quarter full-time, $65 per quarter part-time. • Dr. Jerold B. Muskin, Director of Master's Programs in Business, 215-895-2115. Application contact: Denise Bigham, Director of Admissions, 215-895-6700. Fax: 215-895-5969.

Drexel University, College of Business and Administration, Department of Accounting, Program in Accounting, 3141 Chestnut Street, Philadelphia, PA 19104-2875. Awards MS. Students: 13 full-time (8 women), 16 part-time (8 women); includes 3 minority (1 African American, 2 Asian Americans), 10 international. Average age 31. 31 applicants, 42% accepted. In 1997, 6 degrees awarded. *Degree requirements:* Computer language required, foreign language and thesis not required. *Entrance requirements:* GMAT (minimum score 500), TOEFL (minimum score 570), minimum GPA of 2.75. Application deadline: 8/21. Application fee: $35. *Expenses:* Tuition $494 per credit hour. Fees $121 per quarter full-time, $65 per quarter part-time. *Financial aid:* Teaching assistantships available. Financial aid application deadline: 2/1. • Application contact: Denise Bigham, Director of Admissions, 215-895-6700. Fax: 215-895-5969.

East Carolina University, School of Business, Greenville, NC 27858-4353. Offerings include accounting (MSA). School faculty: 39 full-time (4 women). *Application deadline:* 6/1 (priority date; rolling processing). *Application fee:* $40. *Tuition:* $1886 per year full-time, $472 per semester (minimum) part-time for state residents; $9156 per year full-time, $2289 per semester (minimum) part-time for nonresidents. • Donald B. Boldt, Director of Graduate Studies, 252-328-6970. Fax: 252-328-6664. E-mail: boldtd@mail.ecu.edu. Application contact: Dr. Paul D. Tschetter, Associate Dean, 252-328-6012. Fax: 252-328-6071. E-mail: grad@mail.ecu.edu.

Eastern College, Graduate Business Programs, St. Davids, PA 19087-3696. Offerings include business administration (MBA), with options in accounting, economics, finance, management, marketing. M Div/MS and M Div/MBA offered jointly with Eastern Baptist Theological Seminary. Faculty: 32 full-time (18 women), 14 part-time (12 women). *Application deadline:* rolling. *Application fee:* $35. • Dr. John Stapleford, Chair, 610-341-5848. Application contact: Megan Miscioscia, Graduate Admissions Representative, 610-341-5972. Fax: 610-341-1466.

Eastern Michigan University, College of Business, Department of Accounting, Ypsilanti, MI 48197. Offers programs in accounting (MSA); accounting and taxation (MBA); accounting, financial, and operational control (MBA). Faculty: 16 full-time (3 women). 33 applicants, 70%

accepted. In 1997, 25 degrees awarded. *Entrance requirements:* GMAT (minimum score 500), TOEFL (minimum score 550). Application deadline: 5/15 (rolling processing; 3/15 for spring admission). Application fee: $30. *Expenses:* Tuition $2691 per year full-time, $150 per credit hour part-time for state residents; $6300 per year full-time, $350 per credit hour part-time for nonresidents. Fees $368 per year full-time, $88 per semester (minimum) part-time. *Financial aid:* Fellowships, teaching assistantships available. Aid available to part-time students. Financial aid application deadline: 3/15; applicants required to submit FAFSA. • Dr. Thomas Cianciolo, Head, 734-487-3320.

East Tennessee State University, College of Business, Department of Accountancy, Johnson City, TN 37614-0734. Awards M Acc. Part-time and evening/weekend programs available. Faculty: 11 full-time (1 woman). Students: 19 full-time (10 women), 17 part-time (10 women); includes 4 minority (1 African American, 3 Asian Americans), 5 international. Average age 31. 29 applicants, 72% accepted. In 1997, 14 degrees awarded. *Degree requirements:* Comprehensive exam required, foreign language and thesis not required. *Entrance requirements:* GMAT (minimum score 450), TOEFL (minimum score 550), minimum GPA of 2.5. Application deadline: 7/1 (priority date; rolling processing; 12/1 for spring admission). Application fee: $25 ($35 for international students). *Tuition:* $2944 per year full-time, $158 per credit hour part-time for state residents; $7770 per year full-time, $369 per credit hour part-time for nonresidents. *Financial aid:* In 1997–98, 5 research assistantships (3 to first-year students) were awarded. Financial aid application deadline: 8/15. *Faculty research:* Financial accounting, taxation, auditing, management accounting. • Dr. Thomas E. McKee, Chair, 423-439-4432. E-mail: temckee@etsu-tn.edu. Application contact: Dr. John Nash, Director of Graduate Business Studies, 423-439-5314. Fax: 423-439-5274. E-mail: nashj@etsu-tn.edu.

École des Hautes Études Commerciales, Program in Controllership, Montréal, PQ H3T 2A7, Canada. Awards M Sc. Most courses are given in French. Part-time programs available. *Degree requirements:* 1 foreign language, thesis. *Application deadline:* 3/15. *Application fee:* $40. *Financial aid:* Fellowships, research assistantships, teaching assistantships available. • Dr. Jean-Yves Le Louarn, Director, 514-340-6295. E-mail: jean-yves.lelouarn@hec.ca. Application contact: Nicole Rivet, Registrar, 514-340-6110. Fax: 514-340-5640. E-mail: nicole.rivet@hec.ca.

École des Hautes Études Commerciales, Program in Public Accounting, Montréal, PQ H3T 2A7, Canada. Awards Diploma. Most courses are given in French. *Degree requirements:* 1 foreign language required, thesis not required. *Application fee:* $40. *Financial aid:* Fellowships available. • Dr. Jean-Pierre Le Goff, Director, 514-340-6441. Application contact: Nicole Rivet, Registrar, 514-340-6110. Fax: 514-340-5640. E-mail: nicole.rivet@hec.ca.

Fairfield University, School of Business, Fairfield, CT 06430-5195. Offerings include accounting (MBA, CAS). School faculty: 36 full-time (12 women), 4 part-time (2 women), 37.3 FTE. *Average time to degree:* master's–2 years full-time, 3.5 years part-time. *Application deadline:* 8/1 (priority date; rolling processing; 12/1 for spring admission). *Application fee:* $40. *Expenses:* Tuition $15,000 per year full-time, $450 per credit hour part-time. Fees $40 per year. • Dr. Walter G. Ryba Jr., Acting Dean, 203-254-4070. Application contact: Cynthia S. Chegwidden, Director of Graduate Programs, 203-254-4070. Fax: 203-254-4105. E-mail: cchegwidden@fairl.fairfield.edu.

Fairleigh Dickinson University, Florham–Madison Campus, Samuel J. Silberman College of Business Administration, Program in Accounting, 285 Madison Avenue, Madison, NJ 07940-1099. Awards MBA. Part-time and evening/weekend programs available. Faculty: 11 full-time (0 women), 7 part-time (2 women). Students: 12 full-time (8 women), 84 part-time (36 women); includes 7 minority (3 African Americans, 4 Asian Americans), 3 international. Average age 30. 48 applicants, 67% accepted. In 1997, 24 degrees awarded. *Degree requirements:* Thesis optional, foreign language not required. *Entrance requirements:* GMAT. Application deadline: rolling. Application fee: $35. *Expenses:* Tuition $522 per credit. Fees $302 per year full-time, $138 per year part-time. *Financial aid:* Fellowships, research assistantships, teaching assistantships available. • Prof. Claude Jonnard, Chairperson, 973-443-8810.

Fairleigh Dickinson University, Teaneck–Hackensack Campus, Samuel J. Silberman College of Business Administration, Department of Accounting, Taxation, Law, Economics, and Finance, Program in Accounting, 1000 River Road, Teaneck, NJ 07666-1914. Awards MBA, MS. Faculty: 11 full-time, 7 part-time. Students: 9 full-time (5 women), 26 part-time (15 women); includes 3 minority (1 African American, 1 Asian American, 1 Hispanic), 3 international. Average age 32. In 1997, 20 degrees awarded. *Degree requirements:* Computer language required, thesis optional, foreign language not required. *Entrance requirements:* GMAT. Application deadline: rolling. Application fee: $35. *Expenses:* Tuition $522 per credit. Fees $302 per year full-time, $138 per year part-time. *Financial aid:* Fellowships available. *Faculty research:* Corporate accounting, legal issues. • Dr. Virote Angkatavanich, Chair, Department of Accounting, Taxation, Law, Economics, and Finance, 201-692-7221.

Florida Agricultural and Mechanical University, Division of Graduate Studies, Research, and Continuing Education, School of Business and Industry, Tallahassee, FL 32307-3200. Offerings include accounting (MBA). *Entrance requirements:* GRE General Test (minimum combined score of 1000), minimum GPA of 3.0. Application deadline: 5/13. Application fee: $20. *Expenses:* Tuition $140 per credit hour for state residents; $484 per credit hour for nonresidents. Fees $130 per year. • Dr. Sybil Mobley, Dean, 850-599-3565.

Florida Atlantic University, College of Business, School of Accounting, Boca Raton, FL 33431-0991. Awards M Ac, M Tax. Part-time and evening/weekend programs available. Faculty: 26 full-time (9 women), 1 part-time (0 women). Students: 6 full-time (3 women), 49 part-time (29 women); includes 11 minority (6 African Americans, 1 Asian American, 4 Hispanics). Average age 25. 29 applicants, 52% accepted. In 1997, 33 degrees awarded (100% found work related to degree). *Degree requirements:* Communications program required, foreign language and thesis not required. *Average time to degree:* master's–1 year full-time, 3 years part-time. *Entrance requirements:* GMAT (minimum score 450), BS in accounting or equivalent, minimum GPA of 3.0 in accounting. Application deadline: 6/1 (rolling processing; 10/1 for spring admission). Application fee: $20. *Expenses:* Tuition $2520 per year full-time, $140 per credit hour part-time for state residents; $8712 per year full-time, $484 per credit hour part-time for nonresidents. Fees $5 per year (minimum). *Financial aid:* In 1997–98, 12 students received aid, including 1 research assistantship; fellowships, teaching assistantships, partial tuition waivers, Federal Work-Study, institutionally sponsored loans, and career-related internships or fieldwork also available. Aid available to part-time students. Financial aid application deadline: 3/1. *Faculty research:* Systems and computer applications, accounting theory, information systems. • Dr. Kenneth Wiant, Director, 954-762-5233. Fax: 954-762-5245. E-mail: wiant@acc.fau.edu. Application contact: Ella Smith, Graduate Adviser, 561-297-3650. Fax: 561-297-3978. E-mail: smith@acc.fau.edu.

Florida International University, College of Business Administration, School of Accounting, Program in Accounting, Miami, FL 33199. Awards M Acc, PhD. Part-time and evening/weekend programs available. Students: 31 full-time (17 women), 164 part-time (79 women); includes 115 minority (12 African Americans, 18 Asian Americans, 85 Hispanics), 14 international. Average age 36. 87 applicants, 69% accepted. In 1997, 92 master's awarded. *Degree requirements:* For master's, computer language required, foreign language and thesis not required; for doctorate, computer language, dissertation. *Entrance requirements:* For master's, GMAT, minimum AACSB index of 1000, minimum GPA of 3.0; for doctorate, GMAT (minimum score 560), minimum GPA of 3.0. Application deadline: 4/1 (priority date; rolling processing; 10/1 for spring admission). Application fee: $20. *Expenses:* Tuition $138 per credit hour for state residents; $482 per credit hour for nonresidents. Fees $46 per semester. *Faculty research:* Financial and managerial accounting. • Dr. James Scheiner, Director, School of Accounting, 305-348-2581. E-mail: scheiner@fiu.edu.

Florida Metropolitan University–Orlando College, North, Division of Business Administration, 5421 Diplomat Circle, Orlando, FL 32810-5674. Offerings include accounting (MBA). Division faculty: 7. *Degree requirements:* Thesis or alternative. *Application deadline:* rolling. *Application fee:* $25. *Tuition:* $263 per credit hour. • Director of Graduate Studies, 407-851-2525. Application contact: Annette Gallina, Director of Admissions, 407-851-2525 Ext. 30. Fax: 407-851-1477.

Florida Southern College, Program in Business Administration, Lakeland, FL 33801-5698. Offerings include accounting (MBA). College faculty: 13 full-time (2 women), 10 part-time (3 women). *Average time to degree:* master's–3 years part-time. *Entrance requirements:* GMAT (minimum score 450) or GRE General Test (minimum combined score of 850), minimum GPA of 2.75. Application deadline: 8/1 (rolling processing; 12/1 for spring admission). Application fee: $30. Electronic applications accepted. *Tuition:* $280 per credit hour. • Dr. Lawrence Ross, Head, 941-680-4285. Fax: 941-680-4355. E-mail: lross@flsouthern.edu. Application contact: Bill Walker, Coordinator of External Programs, 941-680-4205. Fax: 941-680-3088. E-mail: hwalker@flsouthern.edu.

Florida State University, College of Business, Tallahassee, FL 32306. Offerings include accounting (M Acc). College faculty: 85 full-time. *Average time to degree:* master's–1 year full-time, 2.5 years part-time; doctorate–4.5 years full-time. *Application deadline:* rolling. *Application fee:* $20. *Tuition:* $139 per credit hour for state residents; $482 per credit hour for nonresidents. • Dr. Pamela L. Perrewé, Associate Dean for Graduate Studies, 850-644-3090. Application contact: Scheri L. Martin, Coordinator of Graduate Programs, 850-644-6458. E-mail: smartin@cob.fsu.edu.

Fordham University, Graduate School of Business Administration, New York, NY 10023. Offerings include accounting (GPMBA, MBA). School faculty: 85 full-time (22 women), 95 part-time (12 women). *Average time to degree:* master's–2 years full-time, 3 years part-time. *Application deadline:* 6/1 (priority date; rolling processing; 11/1 for spring admission). *Application fee:* $50. • Dr. Ernest J. Scalberg, Dean, 212-636-6111. Fax: 212-307-1779. Application contact: Kathy Pattison, Assistant Dean of Admission, 212-636-6200. Fax: 212-636-7076. E-mail: admission@bschool.bnet.fordham.edu.

Fort Hays State University, College of Business, Department of Business Administration, Hays, KS 67601-4099. Offerings include accounting (MBA). Department faculty: 14 full-time (2 women). *Degree requirements:* Thesis optional, foreign language not required. *Entrance requirements:* GMAT. Application deadline: 7/1 (priority date; rolling processing). Application fee: $25 ($35 for international students). *Tuition:* $94 per credit hour for state residents; $249 per credit hour for nonresidents. • Dr. Dale McKemey, Acting Director, 785-628-4201.

Gannon University, School of Graduate Studies, College of Humanities, Business, and Education, School of Business, Program in Accounting, Erie, PA 16541. Awards Certificate. Part-time and evening/weekend programs available. Students: 0. 0 applicants. *Entrance requirements:* GMAT, TOEFL. Application deadline: rolling. Application fee: $25. *Expenses:* Tuition $405 per credit. Fees $200 per year full-time, $8 per credit part-time. *Financial aid:* Application deadline 3/1; applicants required to submit FAFSA. • Application contact: Beth Nemenz, Director of Admissions, 814-871-7240. Fax: 814-871-5803. E-mail: admissions@gannon.edu.

George Mason University, School of Management, Program in Accounting, Fairfax, VA 22030-4444. Awards MS. Part-time and evening/weekend programs available. Faculty: 67 full-time (15 women), 29 part-time (8 women), 76.5 FTE. Students: 12 full-time (all women), 40 part-time (18 women); includes 10 minority (1 African American, 8 Asian Americans, 1 Native American), 4 international. Average age 35. 44 applicants, 84% accepted. In 1997, 25 degrees awarded. *Entrance requirements:* GMAT (minimum score 500; average 555), TOEFL (minimum score 575), minimum GPA of 3.0 in last 60 hours. Application deadline: 5/1 (11/1 for spring admission). Application fee: $30. Electronic applications accepted. *Tuition:* $4344 per year full-time, $181 per credit hour part-time for state residents; $12,504 per year full-time, $521 per credit hour part-time for nonresidents. *Financial aid:* In 1997–98, 4 research assistantships (2 to first-year students) were awarded; fellowships, teaching assistantships also available. Aid available to part-time students. Financial aid application deadline: 3/1; applicants required to submit FAFSA. *Faculty research:* EDP audit, accounting information systems, financial accounting standards. • Teresa Domzal, Associate Dean, 703-993-1807. Fax: 703-993-1867. Application contact: Sandy Mitchell, Director of Graduate Admissions, 703-993-2136. Fax: 703-993-1886.

The George Washington University, School of Business and Public Management, Department of Accountancy, Washington, DC 20052. Offers programs in accountancy (M Accy, PhD), taxation (M Tax). Part-time and evening/weekend programs available. Faculty: 9 full-time (1 woman), 9 part-time (1 woman), 11 FTE. Students: 47 full-time (23 women), 49 part-time (26 women); includes 20 minority (7 African Americans, 11 Asian Americans, 2 Hispanics), 36 international. Average age 31. 91 applicants, 85% accepted. In 1997, 38 master's, 1 doctorate awarded. *Degree requirements:* For master's, computer language required, foreign language and thesis not required; for doctorate, dissertation required, foreign language not required. *Entrance requirements:* For master's, GMAT, TOEFL (minimum score 550); for doctorate, GMAT or GRE, TOEFL (minimum score 550). Application deadline: 4/1 (priority date; rolling processing; 10/1 for spring admission). Application fee: $50. *Expenses:* Tuition $680 per semester hour. Fees $35 per semester hour. *Financial aid:* Fellowships, teaching assistantships, Federal Work-Study, institutionally sponsored loans, and career-related internships or fieldwork available. Financial aid application deadline: 4/1. *Faculty research:* Management accounting and capital markets, financial accounting and the analytic hierarchy process, ethics and accounting, accounting information systems. • Dr. Debra Sheldon, Chair, 202-994-6825. Application contact: Lilly Hastings, Graduate Admissions, 202-994-6584. Fax: 202-994-6382.

Georgia Southern University, College of Business, Department of Accounting, Statesboro, GA 30460-8126. Awards M Acc. Part-time and evening/weekend programs available. Faculty: 13 full-time (4 women). Students: 2 full-time (both women), 1 (woman) part-time; includes 1 international. 4 applicants, 75% accepted. *Degree requirements:* Computer language, terminal exams required, foreign language and thesis not required. *Entrance requirements:* GMAT. Application deadline: 7/15 (priority date; rolling processing; 11/15 for spring admission). *Tuition:* $2619 per year full-time, $287 per semester (minimum) part-time for state residents; $8619 per year full-time, $1037 per semester (minimum) part-time for nonresidents. *Financial aid:* Teaching assistantships available. Financial aid application deadline: 4/15. • Dr. Ralph Byington, Chair, 912-681-5061. Fax: 912-681-0105. E-mail: byington@gasou.edu.

Georgia State University, College of Business Administration, School of Accountancy, Atlanta, GA 30303-3083. Awards MBA, MPA, MTX, PhD. Part-time and evening/weekend programs available. Faculty: 26 full-time, 3 part-time. Students: 87 full-time (44 women), 91 part-time (50 women); includes 22 minority (10 African Americans, 10 Asian Americans, 2 Hispanics), 38 international. Average age 30. In 1997, 79 master's, 2 doctorates awarded. Terminal master's awarded for partial completion of doctoral program. *Degree requirements:* For doctorate, dissertation required, foreign language not required. *Entrance requirements:* For master's, GMAT (average 566), TOEFL; for doctorate, GMAT (average 670), TOEFL. Application deadline: 5/1 (rolling processing; 10/1 for spring admission). Application fee: $25. *Expenses:* Tuition $2673 per year full-time, $99 per semester hour part-time for state residents; $10,692 per year full-time, $396 per semester hour part-time for nonresidents. Fees $228 per year. *Financial aid:* Fellowships, research assistantships, teaching assistantships, partial tuition waivers, and career-related internships or fieldwork available. Aid available to part-time students. Financial aid applicants required to submit FAFSA. • Dr. Fenwick Huss, Director, 404-651-2611. Fax: 404-651-1033. Application contact: Office of Academic Assistance and Master's Admissions, 404-651-1913. Fax: 404-651-0219.

Golden Gate University, School of Business, San Francisco, CA 94105-2968. Offerings include accounting (M Ac, MBA). MBA (telecommunications, management information systems) offered jointly with the School of Technology and Industry. *Average time to degree:* master's–2.5 years full-time. *Application deadline:* 7/1 (priority date; rolling processing). *Application fee:*

Directory: Accounting

Golden Gate University (continued)

$55 ($70 for international students). *Tuition:* $996 per course (minimum). • Dr. Hamid Shomali, Dean, 415-442-6500. Fax: 415-442-6579. Application contact: Enrollment Services, 415-442-7800. Fax: 415-442-7807. E-mail: info@ggu.edu.

Goldey–Beacom College, MBA Program, 4701 Limestone Road, Wilmington, DE 19808-1999. Offerings include accounting (MBA). MBA (accounting) new for fall 1998. College faculty: 6 full-time (3 women), 4 part-time (1 woman). *Average time to degree:* master's–2 years full-time, 3 years part-time. *Entrance requirements:* GMAT (minimum score 450; average 507), TOEFL (minimum score 525), minimum GPA of 3.0. Application deadline: 8/20 (rolling processing; 5/15 for spring admission). Application fee: $30. Electronic applications accepted. *Expenses:* Tuition $6030 per year full-time, $335 per credit hour part-time. Fees $5 per credit hour. • Bruce D. Marsland, Director, 302-998-8814 Ext. 276. Fax: 302-998-8631. E-mail: graduate@goldey.gbc.edu.

Gonzaga University, Graduate School, School of Business Administration, Program in Accounting, Spokane, WA 99258-0001. Awards M Acc, JD/M Acc. *Entrance requirements:* GMAT (minimum score 450), TOEFL (minimum score 550). Application deadline: 7/20 (priority date; rolling processing; 11/1 for spring admission). Application fee: $40. *Tuition:* $7380 per year (minimum) full-time, $410 per credit (minimum) part-time. *Financial aid:* Application deadline 3/1. • Application contact: Dr. Larry Lewis, Assistant Dean, 509-328-4220 Ext. 3430.

Governors State University, College of Business and Public Administration, Program in Accounting, University Park, IL 60466. Awards MS. In 1997, 3 degrees awarded. *Entrance requirements:* GMAT. Application deadline: 7/15 (priority date; rolling processing; 11/10 for spring admission). Application fee: $0. *Expenses:* Tuition $1140 per trimester full-time, $95 per credit hour part-time for state residents; $3420 per trimester full-time, $285 per credit hour part-time for nonresidents. Fees $95 per trimester. *Financial aid:* Application deadline 5/1. • Dr. Anthony Jackson, Head, 708-534-4936. Application contact: Michael Witak, Adviser, 708-534-4395.

Graduate School and University Center of the City University of New York, Program in Business, New York, NY 10036-8099. Offerings include accounting (PhD). Terminal master's awarded for partial completion of doctoral program. Program faculty: 66 full-time (5 women). *Degree requirements:* Dissertation required, foreign language not required. *Entrance requirements:* GMAT. Application deadline: 3/1. Application fee: $40. *Expenses:* Tuition $4350 per year full-time, $185 per credit (minimum) part-time for state residents; $7600 per year full-time, $320 per credit (minimum) part-time for nonresidents. Fees $69 per year. • Dr. Gloria Thomas, Executive Officer, 212-802-6580.

Grove City College, Program in Accounting, Grove City, PA 16127-2104. Awards MS. Faculty: 4 full-time, 1 part-time. Students: 4 full-time (3 women), 21 part-time (8 women). *Tuition:* $266 per credit hour. • Dr. Jeff Patterson, Head, 724-458-3861. Application contact: Admissions Office, 724-458-2000.

Hawaii Pacific University, School of Business Administration, 1166 Fort Street, Honolulu, HI 96813-2785. Offerings include accounting (MBA). School faculty: 30 full-time (3 women), 12 part-time (1 woman), 38 FTE. *Average time to degree:* master's–2 years full-time, 4 years part-time. *Application deadline:* rolling. *Application fee:* $50. Electronic applications accepted. *Tuition:* $7920 per year full-time, $330 per credit part-time. • Dr. Richard Ward, Dean for Graduate Management Studies, 808-544-0279. Application contact: Leina Danao, Admissions Coordinator, 808-544-1120. Fax: 808-544-0280. E-mail: gradservctr@hpu.edu.

Hofstra University, Frank G. Zarb School of Business, Department of Accounting and Business Law, Program in Accounting, Hempstead, NY 11549. Awards MBA. Part-time and evening/weekend programs available. Faculty: 24 full-time (12 women), 8 part-time (4 women). Students: 18 full-time (10 women), 37 part-time (11 women); includes 4 minority (2 Asian Americans, 2 Hispanics), 4 international. Average age 29. 35 applicants, 60% accepted. In 1997, 21 degrees awarded. *Degree requirements:* Computer language, thesis or alternative required, foreign language not required. *Entrance requirements:* GMAT (average 580). Application deadline: rolling. Application fee: $40 ($75 for international students). *Expenses:* Tuition $10,968 per year full-time, $457 per credit hour part-time. Fees $670 per year full-time, $112 per semester (minimum) part-time. *Financial aid:* Fellowships, research assistantships, Federal Work-Study, and career-related internships or fieldwork available. Financial aid application deadline: 4/1. • Application contact: Susan McTiernan, Senior Assistant Dean, 516-463-5683. Fax: 516-463-5268.

Houston Baptist University, College of Business and Economics, Program in Management, Houston, TX 77074-3298. Offerings include accounting (MBA). Program faculty: 9 full-time (1 woman), 7 part-time (1 woman). *Entrance requirements:* GMAT (minimum score 450), minimum GPA of 2.5, work experience. Application deadline: 6/1 (priority date; rolling processing; 1/1 for spring admission). Application fee: $25 ($85 for international students). *Expenses:* Tuition $300 per semester hour. Fees $235 per quarter. • Dr. Carter L. Franklin II, Associate Dean, College of Business and Economics, 281-649-3429. Application contact: Karen Murray, Program Assistant, 281-649-3306.

Illinois State University, College of Business, Department of Accounting, Normal, IL 61790-2200. Awards MS. Faculty: 14 full-time (5 women). Students: 18 full-time (11 women), 19 part-time (14 women); includes 1 minority (Asian American), 2 international. 18 applicants, 83% accepted. In 1997, 10 degrees awarded. *Degree requirements:* Comprehensive exam required, thesis not required. *Entrance requirements:* GMAT, TOEFL (minimum score 600), minimum GPA of 2.75 in last 60 hours. Application deadline: rolling. Application fee: $0. *Expenses:* Tuition $2454 per year full-time, $102 per hour part-time for state residents; $7362 per year full-time, $307 per hour part-time for nonresidents. Fees $1048 per year full-time, $44 per hour part-time. *Financial aid:* In 1997–98, 11 research assistantships averaging $524 per month, 5 teaching assistantships were awarded; full tuition waivers, Federal Work-Study, institutionally sponsored loans also available. Financial aid application deadline: 4/1. • Dr. James Moon, Chairperson, 309-438-7651.

Indiana University Bloomington, School of Business, Doctoral Programs in Business, Bloomington, IN 47405. Offerings include accounting (DBA, PhD). PhD offered through the University Graduate School. *Degree requirements:* Computer language, dissertation required, foreign language not required. *Entrance requirements:* GMAT (minimum score 600), GRE General Test. Application deadline: 3/1. Application fee: $35. *Expenses:* Tuition $261 per credit hour for state residents; $523 per credit hour for nonresidents. Fees $343 per year. • Dr. Janet Near, Chairperson, 812-855-3476. Application contact: Barbara Clark, Program Secretary and Assistant to Chairperson, 812-855-3476. Fax: 812-855-8679. E-mail: bclark@ucs.indiana.edu.

Indiana University Northwest, Division of Business and Economics, Gary, IN 46408-1197. Offerings include accountancy (M Acc), accounting (Certificate). M Acc offered jointly with Purdue University. Division faculty: 19 full-time (2 women), 3 part-time (1 woman), 20 FTE. *Average time to degree:* master's–2 years full-time, 4 years part-time. *Application deadline:* 7/15 (priority date; rolling processing; 11/15 for spring admission). *Application fee:* $25 ($40 for international students). • Dr. Donald Coffin, Dean, 219-980-6633. Fax: 219-980-6579. Application contact: Kathryn M. Lantz, Director of Graduate Programs, 219-980-6635. Fax: 219-980-6916.

Indiana University South Bend, Division of Business and Economics, Program in Accounting, South Bend, IN 46634-7111. Awards MS. Faculty: 6 full-time (1 woman), 1 (woman) part-time, 6.3 FTE. Students: 60; includes 21 minority (19 Asian Americans, 2 Hispanics), 9 international. Average age 29. 64 applicants, 94% accepted. *Entrance requirements:* GMAT (minimum score 450), TOEFL (minimum score 550). Application deadline: 7/1 (priority date; rolling processing; 11/1 for spring admission). Application fee: $35 ($40 for international students). *Expenses:* Tuition $3648 per year full-time, $152 per credit hour part-time for state residents; $8640 per year full-time, $360 per credit hour part-time for nonresidents. Fees $222 per year full-time, $34 per semester (minimum) part-time. *Financial aid:* Application deadline 3/1. • Application contact: Graduate Director, 219-237-4183. Fax: 219-237-6549.

Inter American University of Puerto Rico, Metropolitan Campus, Division of Economics and Business Administration, Program in Accounting, San Juan, PR 00919-1293. Awards MBA. Faculty: 2 full-time, 3 part-time. Students: 49 full-time (22 women), 73 part-time (34 women); includes 122 minority (all Hispanics). *Degree requirements:* Comprehensive exam required, foreign language and thesis not required. *Entrance requirements:* GRE or PAEG, interview. Application deadline: 5/15 (priority date; rolling processing; 11/15 for spring admission). Application fee: $31. Electronic applications accepted. *Expenses:* Tuition $3272 per year full-time, $1740 per year part-time. Fees $328 per year full-time, $176 per year part-time. *Financial aid:* Federal Work-Study available. • Application contact: Dr. Antonio Llorens, Director, 787-250-1912 Ext. 2320. Fax: 787-250-0361.

Inter American University of Puerto Rico, San Germán Campus, Department of Business Administration, Program in Business Administration, San Germán, PR 00683-5008. Offerings include accounting (MBA). *Degree requirements:* Comprehensive exam required, foreign language and thesis not required. *Entrance requirements:* Minimum GPA of 3.0, GRE General Test, or PAEG. Application deadline: 4/30 (priority date; rolling processing; 11/15 for spring admission). Application fee: $31. *Expenses:* Tuition $150 per credit. Fees $177 per semester. • Application contact: Mildred Camacho, Admissions Director, 787-892-3090. Fax: 787-892-6350.

Iona College, Hagan Graduate School of Business, Program in Accounting, 715 North Avenue, New Rochelle, NY 10801-1890. Awards MBA. Admissions temporarily suspended. Students: 0. *Degree requirements:* Computer language required, foreign language and thesis not required. *Expenses:* Tuition $480 per credit hour. Fees $25 per semester. • Dr. Donald Moscato, Chairman, 914-633-2555.

Jackson State University, School of Business, Department of Accounting, Jackson, MS 39217. Awards MPA, PhD. PhD new for fall 1998. Part-time and evening/weekend programs available. Faculty: 4 full-time (0 women). Students: 6 full-time (3 women), 8 part-time (6 women); includes 10 minority (all African Americans), 3 international. 11 applicants, 64% accepted. In 1997, 5 master's awarded. *Degree requirements:* For master's, written comprehensive exam required, thesis not required. *Entrance requirements:* For master's, GRE General Test (minimum combined score of 1000), TOEFL (minimum score 550); for doctorate, MAT (minimum score 45). Application deadline: 3/1 (priority date; rolling processing; 10/1 for spring admission). Application fee: $20. *Tuition:* $2688 per year (minimum) full-time, $150 per semester hour part-time for state residents; $5546 per year (minimum) full-time, $309 per semester hour part-time for nonresidents. *Financial aid:* Full and partial tuition waivers, Federal Work-Study, and career-related internships or fieldwork available. Aid available to part-time students. Financial aid application deadline: 3/1. • Dr. Jessie C. Pennington, Director, 601-982-6315. Fax: 601-982-6124. Application contact: Mae Robinson, Admissions Coordinator, 601-968-2455. Fax: 601-968-8246. E-mail: mrobinson@ccaix.jsums.edu.

James Madison University, College of Business, School of Accounting, Harrisonburg, VA 22807. Awards MS. Part-time and evening/weekend programs available. Faculty: 5 full-time (3 women). Students: 10 full-time (5 women), 9 part-time (4 women); includes 1 minority (Asian American), 2 international. Average age 30. In 1997, 6 degrees awarded. *Entrance requirements:* GMAT. Application deadline: 7/1 (priority date; rolling processing). Application fee: $50. *Tuition:* $134 per credit hour for state residents; $404 per credit hour for nonresidents. *Financial aid:* In 1997–98, 2 teaching assistantships totaling $18,810, 4 assistantships totaling $34,560 were awarded; fellowships, Federal Work-Study also available. Financial aid application deadline: 2/15; applicants required to submit FAFSA. *Faculty research:* Controllership, government accounting. • Dr. Alexander Gabbin, Director, 540-568-3084.

Johnson & Wales University, Graduate School, Program in Accounting, 8 Abbott Park Place, Providence, RI 02903-3703. Awards MBA, MS. MS being phased out; applicants no longer accepted. Part-time and evening/weekend programs available. Faculty: 3 full-time (0 women), 4 part-time (1 woman). Students: 12 full-time (4 women), 25 part-time (7 women); includes 5 minority (3 African Americans, 2 Hispanics), 4 international. Average age 26. 36 applicants, 67% accepted. In 1997, 31 degrees awarded. *Average time to degree:* master's–1.5 years full-time, 2.5 years part-time. *Entrance requirements:* Minimum GPA of 2.75. Application deadline: 8/21 (priority date; rolling processing). Application fee: $0. *Expenses:* Tuition $194 per quarter hour (minimum). Fees $477 per year. *Financial aid:* In 1997–98, 11 students received aid, including 5 graduate assistantships (2 to first-year students) averaging $735 per month. Financial aid application deadline: 5/1. *Faculty research:* Applying new technology. • Application contact: Dr. Allan G. Freedman, Director of Graduate Admissions, 401-598-1015. Fax: 401-598-4773. E-mail: clifb@jwu.edu.

Kansas State University, College of Business Administration, Department of Accounting, Manhattan, KS 66506. Awards M Acc. Faculty: 8 full-time (0 women). Students: 38 full-time (28 women), 7 part-time (4 women); includes 7 minority (1 African American, 6 Asian Americans). Average age 25. 23 applicants, 96% accepted. In 1997, 34 degrees awarded. *Degree requirements:* Comprehensive exam required, foreign language not required. *Entrance requirements:* GMAT (minimum score 500; average 547), minimum undergraduate GPA of 3.0. Application deadline: 6/1 (rolling processing; 11/1 for spring admission). Application fee: $45. *Tuition:* $2218 per year full-time, $401 per semester (minimum) part-time for state residents; $6336 per year full-time, $1087 per semester (minimum) part-time for nonresidents. *Faculty research:* Theory, history, taxation, ethics, value of accounting information. • Cynthia S. McCahon, Director, 785-532-7190. Fax: 785-532-7216. E-mail: cmccahon@business.cba.ksu.edu.

Keller Graduate School of Management, 1 Tower Lane, Oak Brook Terrace, IL 60181. Offerings include accounting and financial management (MAFM). School faculty: 604. *Average time to degree:* master's–3 years part-time. *Application deadline:* rolling. *Application fee:* $0. *Tuition:* $1235 per course. • Dr. Sherrill Hole, Director, Academic Affairs, 630-574-1894. Application contact: Michael J. Alexander, Director, Central Services, 630-574-1957. Fax: 630-574-1969.

Kennesaw State University, Michael J. Coles College of Business, Program in Business Administration, Kennesaw, GA 30144-5591. Offerings include accounting (M Acc, MBA). Program faculty: 54 full-time (18 women), 5 part-time (0 women). *Application deadline:* 7/1 (rolling processing; 2/20 for spring admission). *Application fee:* $20. *Expenses:* Tuition $2398 per year full-time, $83 per credit hour part-time for state residents; $8398 per year full-time, $333 per credit hour part-time for nonresidents. Fees $338 per year. • Dr. Rodney Alsup, Assistant Dean, 770-423-6087. Fax: 770-423-6141. E-mail: ralsup@ksumail.kennesaw.edu. Application contact: Susan N. Barrett, Administrative Specialist, Admissions, 770-423-6500. Fax: 770-423-6541. E-mail: sbarrett@ksumail.kennesaw.edu.

Kent State University, Graduate School of Management, Doctoral Program in Accounting, Kent, OH 44242-0001. Awards PhD. Faculty: 9 full-time (2 women), 1 part-time (0 women). Students: 12 full-time (2 women), 2 part-time (1 woman); includes 1 minority (African American), 5 international. 5 applicants, 0% accepted. In 1997, 1 degree awarded. *Degree requirements:* Dissertation, comprehensive exams, oral defense required, foreign language not required. *Entrance requirements:* GMAT. Application deadline: 2/1. Application fee: $30. *Tuition:* $4752 per year full-time, $216 per credit hour part-time for state residents; $9213 per year full-time, $419 per credit hour part-time for nonresidents. *Financial aid:* In 1997–98, 8 teaching assistantships averaging $1,000 per month were awarded; Federal Work-Study also available. Financial aid application deadline: 2/1; applicants required to submit FAFSA. *Faculty research:* Information economics, capital management, use of accounting information, curriculum design. • David F. Fetyko, Acting Chair, 330-672-2545 Ext. 371. Fax: 330-672-2448. E-mail: dfetyko@bsa3.kent.edu. Application contact: Dr. James C. Baker, Doctoral Director, 330-672-2282 Ext. 235. Fax: 330-672-7303. E-mail: jbaker@bsa3.kent.edu.

Kent State University, Graduate School of Management, Master's Program in Accounting, Kent, OH 44242-0001. Awards MS. Part-time programs available. Faculty: 9 full-time (2 women), 1 part-time (0 women). Students: 16 full-time (11 women), 13 part-time (7 women); includes 1 minority (African American), 6 international. 34 applicants, 53% accepted. In 1997, 9 degrees awarded. *Degree requirements:* Internship required, foreign language and thesis not required. *Entrance requirements:* GMAT, minimum GPA of 2.75. Application deadline: 5/1 (rolling processing; 12/15 for spring admission). Application fee: $30. *Tuition:* $4752 per year full-time, $216 per credit hour part-time for state residents; $9213 per year full-time, $419 per credit hour part-time for nonresidents. *Financial aid:* In 1997–98, 7 students received aid, including 5 research assistantships (3 to first-year students) averaging $500 per month; Federal Work-Study also available. Financial aid application deadline: 4/1; applicants required to submit FAFSA. *Faculty research:* Financial accounting, managerial accounting, auditing, systems, nonprofit. • David F. Fetyko, Acting Chair, 330-672-2545 Ext. 371. Fax: 330-672-2448. E-mail: dfetyko@bsa3.kent.edu. Application contact: Louise M. Ditchey, Associate Director, 330-672-2282 Ext. 235. Fax: 330-672-7303. E-mail: gradbus@bsa3.kent.edu.

King's College, William G. McGowan School of Business, Wilkes-Barre, PA 18711-0801. Offerings include finance (MS), with options in accounting/taxation, finance. School faculty: 7 full-time (1 woman), 3 part-time (0 women). *Average time to degree:* master's–2.5 years part-time. *Entrance requirements:* GMAT. Application deadline: 7/31 (priority date; rolling processing; 12/1 for spring admission). Application fee: $35. *Tuition:* $460 per credit. • Dr. Edward J. Schoen, Dean, 717-208-5932. Fax: 717-826-5989. E-mail: ejschoen@rs01.kings.edu. Application contact: Dr. Elizabeth S. Lott, Director of Graduate Programs, 717-208-5991. Fax: 717-825-9049. E-mail: eslott@rs02.kings.edu.

Lehman College of the City University of New York, Division of Natural and Social Sciences, Department of Economics and Accounting, 250 Bedford Park Boulevard West, Bronx, NY 10468-1589. Offers program in accounting (MS). Faculty: 3 full-time (2 women), 4 part-time (0 women). Students: 3 full-time (1 woman), 16 part-time (4 women). *Entrance requirements:* GMAT. Application deadline: 4/1 (rolling processing; 11/1 for spring admission). Application fee: $40. *Expenses:* Tuition $4350 per year full-time, $185 per credit part-time for state residents; $7600 per year full-time, $320 per credit part-time for nonresidents. Fees $120 per year full-time, $80 per year part-time. *Financial aid:* Full and partial tuition waivers, Federal Work-Study available. Aid available to part-time students. Financial aid application deadline: 5/15; applicants required to submit FAFSA. • Chanoch Shreiber, Chairperson, 718-960-8297. Application contact: Itzhak Sharav, Adviser, 718-960-8297.

Long Island University, Brooklyn Campus, School of Business and Public Administration, Program in Accountancy, Taxation and Law, Brooklyn, NY 11201-8423. Offers accounting (MS), taxation (MS). Part-time and evening/weekend programs available. Faculty: 8 full-time (1 woman). Students: 16 full-time (10 women), 25 part-time (9 women); includes 29 minority (22 African Americans, 6 Asian Americans, 1 Hispanic). 27 applicants, 74% accepted. In 1997, 14 degrees awarded. *Entrance requirements:* GMAT or GRE General Test. Application deadline: rolling. Application fee: $30. Electronic applications accepted. *Expenses:* Tuition $480 per credit. Fees $415 per year full-time, $73 per semester (minimum) part-time. *Financial aid:* Career-related internships or fieldwork available. • Dr. Myrna Fischman, Director, 718-488-1070. Application contact: Bernard W. Sullivan, Associate Director of Admissions, 718-488-1011.

Long Island University, C.W. Post Campus, College of Management, School of Professional Accountancy, Brookville, NY 11548-1300. Offers programs in accounting (MS), accounting/taxation (CAS), strategic management accounting (MS), taxation (MS). Part-time and evening/weekend programs available. Faculty: 10 full-time (2 women), 7 part-time (2 women). Students: 43 full-time (21 women), 154 part-time (71 women). 78 applicants, 91% accepted. In 1997, 50 master's awarded. *Entrance requirements:* GMAT, minimum GPA of 2.7. Application deadline: rolling. Application fee: $30. Electronic applications accepted. *Expenses:* Tuition $480 per credit. Fees $316 per year full-time, $71 per semester (minimum) part-time. *Financial aid:* In 1997–98, 4 graduate assistantships (1 to a first-year student) were awarded; Federal Work-Study, institutionally sponsored loans, and career-related internships or fieldwork also available. Aid available to part-time students. Financial aid application deadline: 5/15; applicants required to submit FAFSA. *Faculty research:* International taxation. • Dr. Philip H. Siegel, Director, 516-299-2366. Fax: 516-299-3221. E-mail: psiegel@tital.liu.edu. Application contact: Fred Tobias, Adviser, 516-299-2098.

Louisiana State University and Agricultural and Mechanical College, College of Business Administration, Department of Accounting, Baton Rouge, LA 70803. Awards MS, PhD. Faculty: 11 full-time (3 women), 1 part-time (0 women). Students: 21 full-time (3 women), 4 part-time (2 women). Average age 27. 42 applicants, 31% accepted. In 1997, 10 master's, 1 doctorate awarded. *Degree requirements:* For doctorate, dissertation required, foreign language not required. *Entrance requirements:* For master's, GMAT, TOEFL (minimum score 600), minimum GPA of 3.2; for doctorate, GMAT, TOEFL (minimum score 600), minimum GPA of 3.4. Application deadline: 1/25 (priority date; rolling processing). Application fee: $25. *Tuition:* $2736 per year full-time, $285 per semester (minimum) part-time for state residents; $6636 per year full-time, $460 per semester (minimum) part-time for nonresidents. *Financial aid:* In 1997–98, 1 fellowship, 3 teaching assistantships, 12 service assistantships (2 to first-year students) were awarded; research assistantships, Federal Work-Study also available. Financial aid application deadline: 4/15. • Dr. Lamar Jones, Chair, 504-388-6210. Application contact: Dr. Nick Apostolou, Director, 504-388-6211. Fax: 504-388-6201.

Louisiana Tech University, College of Administration and Business, School of Professional Accountancy, Ruston, LA 71272. Awards MBA, MPA, DBA. Part-time programs available. Faculty: 7 full-time (0 women). Students: 21 full-time (9 women), 14 part-time (6 women); includes 2 minority (both African Americans), 5 international. Average age 27. In 1997, 11 master's, 2 doctorates awarded. *Degree requirements:* For master's, computer language required, foreign language and thesis not required; for doctorate, computer language, dissertation required, foreign language not required. *Entrance requirements:* GMAT. Application deadline: 7/29 (2/3 for spring admission). Application fee: $20 ($30 for international students). *Tuition:* $2382 per year full-time, $223 per quarter (minimum) part-time for state residents; $5307 per year full-time, $223 per quarter (minimum) part-time for nonresidents. *Financial aid:* Fellowships, research assistantships, teaching assistantships available. Financial aid application deadline: 2/1. • Dr. Tommy Phillips, Director, 318-257-2822.

Loyola University Chicago, Graduate School of Business, 820 North Michigan Avenue, Chicago, IL 60611-2196. Offerings include accountancy (MS). School faculty: 68 full-time (9 women), 3 part-time (1 woman). *Average time to degree:* master's–1.2 years full-time, 4 years part-time. *Application deadline:* 6/31 (rolling processing; 11/30 for spring admission). *Application fee:* $35. *Tuition:* $1985 per course. • Paul Davidovitch, Director, MBA Program, 312-915-6120. Application contact: Carmen Santiago, Admissions Coordinator, 312-915-6120.

Manchester College, Department of Accounting, North Manchester, IN 46962-1225. Awards M Acc. Faculty: 9 full-time (2 women). Students: 11 full-time (3 women); includes 2 international. Average age 22. 13 applicants, 85% accepted. In 1997, 19 degrees awarded. *Average time to degree:* master's–1 year full-time. *Entrance requirements:* GMAT, TOEFL (minimum score 500; average 550), minimum GPA of 2.75. Application deadline: 5/1 (priority date; rolling processing). Application fee: $20. *Expenses:* Tuition $13,030 per year full-time, $440 per semester hour part-time. Fees $150 per year full-time. *Financial aid:* In 1997–98, 11 students received aid, including 4 graduate assistantships averaging $277 per month and totaling $10,000; teaching assistantships and career-related internships or fieldwork also available. Financial aid application deadline: 5/1; applicants required to submit FAFSA. • Janis Fahs, Coordinator, 219-982-5000. Fax: 219-982-5043.

Manhattan College, Program in Business Administration, Riverdale, NY 10471. Offerings include accounting (MBA). Program faculty: 18 full-time (3 women), 8 part-time (0 women). *Degree requirements:* Computer language, thesis or alternative. *Entrance requirements:* GMAT, minimum GPA of 2.8. Application deadline: 8/10 (priority date; rolling processing; 1/7 for spring admission). Application fee: $50. *Expenses:* Tuition $440 per credit. Fees $100 per year. • Dr. Charles E. Brunner, Director, 718-862-7222. Fax: 718-862-8023. Application contact: William J. Bisset Jr., Dean of Admissions/Financial Aid, 718-862-7200. Fax: 718-863-8019. E-mail: admit@manhattan.edu.

Miami University, Richard T. Farmer School of Business Administration, Department of Accountancy, Oxford, OH 45056. Awards M Acct. Part-time programs available. Faculty: 16. Students: 8 full-time (7 women), 2 part-time (1 woman); includes 1 minority (Asian American), 3 international. 21 applicants, 81% accepted. In 1997, 9 degrees awarded. *Degree requirements:* Final exam required, foreign language and thesis not required. *Entrance requirements:* GMAT (minimum score 475), minimum undergraduate GPA of 3.0 during previous 2 years or 2.75 overall. Application deadline: 3/1 (priority date; rolling processing). Application fee: $35. *Tuition:* $5932 per year full-time, $255 per credit hour part-time for state residents; $12,392 per year full-time, $524 per credit hour part-time for nonresidents. *Financial aid:* Research assistantships, full tuition waivers, Federal Work-Study available. Financial aid application deadline: 3/1. • Dr. Philip B. Cottell Jr., Director of Graduate Studies, 513-529-6214. Application contact: Judy Barille, Director of Graduate Study, 513-529-6643.

Michigan State University, Eli Broad Graduate School of Management, Department of Accounting, East Lansing, MI 48824-1020. Offers programs in accounting (PhD), professional accounting (MBA). Faculty: 23 (4 women). Students: 69 (31 women); includes 6 minority (4 African Americans, 1 Asian American, 1 Hispanic), 5 international. In 1997, 37 master's, 4 doctorates awarded. *Degree requirements:* For doctorate, dissertation required, foreign language not required. *Entrance requirements:* For master's, GMAT (minimum score 500); for doctorate, GMAT. Application deadline: rolling. Application fee: $30 ($40 for international students). *Expenses:* Tuition $4609 per year full-time, $223 per credit hour (minimum) part-time for state residents; $8704 per year full-time, $450 per credit hour (minimum) part-time for nonresidents. Fees $576 per year full-time, $476 per year part-time. *Financial aid:* Research assistantships, teaching assistantships available. • Dr. Frederic Jacobs, Acting Chairperson, 517-355-3388.

Middle Tennessee State University, College of Business, Department of Accounting, Murfreesboro, TN 37132. Offers programs in accounting (MS), information systems (MS). Faculty: 11 full-time (2 women). Students: 6 full-time (3 women), 33 part-time (24 women); includes 3 minority (2 African Americans, 1 Hispanic), 3 international. Average age 32. 53 applicants, 34% accepted. In 1997, 4 degrees awarded. *Degree requirements:* Comprehensive exams required, foreign language and thesis not required. *Entrance requirements:* GMAT. Application deadline: 8/1 (priority date). Application fee: $5. *Expenses:* Tuition $2560 per year full-time, $129 per semester hour part-time for state residents; $7386 per year full-time, $340 per semester hour part-time for nonresidents. Fees $486 per year full-time, $17 per semester (minimum) part-time. *Financial aid:* Teaching assistantships, institutionally sponsored loans available. Aid available to part-time students. Financial aid application deadline: 5/1; applicants required to submit FAFSA. • Dr. William Grasty, Chair, 615-898-2558. Fax: 615-898-5045. E-mail: wgrasty@mtsu.edu.

Millsaps College, School of Management, Jackson, MS 39210-0001. Offerings include accounting (M Acc). School faculty: 21 full-time (4 women), 5 part-time (1 woman). *Average time to degree:* master's–1.2 years full-time, 3.2 years part-time. *Application deadline:* 7/1 (priority date; rolling processing; 11/15 for spring admission). *Application fee:* $25. *Tuition:* $540 per semester hour. • Dr. Walter Neely, Acting Dean, 601-974-1250. Application contact: Bart Herridge, Director of Graduate Business Admissions, 601-974-1253. Fax: 601-974-1260.

Mississippi College, School of Business Administration, Department of Accounting, Clinton, MS 39058. Awards MBA. *Degree requirements:* Oral and written comprehensive exams required, foreign language and thesis not required. *Entrance requirements:* GMAT, minimum GPA of 2.5, 24 hours of undergraduate course work in business. Application deadline: 8/15 (priority date; rolling processing). Application fee: $25 ($75 for international students). *Expenses:* Tuition $6624 per year full-time, $276 per hour part-time. Fees $230 per year full-time, $35 per semester (minimum) part-time. *Financial aid:* Application deadline 4/1. • Dr. Sharon Seay, Chair, 601-925-3412.

Mississippi State University, College of Business and Industry, School of Accountancy, Mississippi State, MS 39762. Awards MPA, MTX. Part-time programs available. Faculty: 12 full-time (1 woman). Students: 24 full-time (13 women), 7 part-time (2 women); includes 2 minority (both African Americans). Average age 24. In 1997, 38 degrees awarded. *Degree requirements:* Comprehensive oral exam required, foreign language not required. *Entrance requirements:* GMAT (minimum score 500), minimum QPA of 2.75 in accountancy, 3.0 in last 60 hours. Application deadline: rolling. Application fee: $0 ($25 for international students). *Tuition:* $3017 per year full-time, $168 per credit hour part-time for state residents; $6119 per year full-time, $340 per credit hour part-time for nonresidents. *Financial aid:* Research assistantships, teaching assistantships, Federal Work-Study, institutionally sponsored loans available. Aid available to part-time students. Financial aid application deadline: 3/15. *Faculty research:* Income tax, financial accounting system, managerial accounting, auditing. • Dr. Pierre L. Titard, Director, 601-325-3710. Fax: 601-325-1646. Application contact: Dr. Barbara A. Spencer, Acting Head, Department of Management and Information Systems, 601-325-1891. Fax: 601-325-8161. E-mail: gsb@cobilan.msstate.edu.

Montana State University–Bozeman, College of Business, 211 Montana Hall, Bozeman, MT 59717. Offers programs in business education (MS), professional accountancy (MPA). MS offered during summer only. Part-time programs available. Faculty: 21 full-time (3 women), 2 part-time (both women). Students: 14 full-time (7 women), 7 part-time (all women); includes 2 minority (both Asian Americans). Average age 34. 11 applicants, 100% accepted. In 1997, 9 degrees awarded. *Degree requirements:* Thesis or alternative required, foreign language not required. *Entrance requirements:* GRE General Test, TOEFL (minimum score 550). Application deadline: 6/1 (priority date; rolling processing; 11/1 for spring admission). Application fee: $50. *Tuition:* $3994 per year full-time, $367 per semester (minimum) part-time for state residents; $9507 per year full-time, $957 per semester (minimum) part-time for nonresidents. *Financial aid:* In 1997–98, 5 teaching assistantships (all to first-year students) averaging $587 per month and totaling $13,200 were awarded; research assistantships also available. Financial aid application deadline: 3/1. *Faculty research:* Small business, innovative teaching, technology transfer, tourism, leadership, student outcome assessment, investment analysis, human resources. Total annual research expenditures: $50,565. • Michael Owen, Dean, 406-994-4421. Fax: 406-994-6206. E-mail: busgrad@montana.edu.

Montclair State University, School of Business, Department of Accounting, Upper Montclair, NJ 07043-1624. Awards MS. Part-time and evening/weekend programs available. *Entrance requirements:* GMAT, minimum GPA of 3.0. Application deadline: 4/1 (rolling processing; 11/1 for spring admission). Application fee: $40. *Expenses:* Tuition $201 per credit for state residents; $257 per credit for nonresidents. Fees $22.05 per credit. *Financial aid:* Available to part-time students. Financial aid application deadline: 3/1; applicants required to submit FAFSA. • Frank Aquilino, Chairperson.

Montclair State University, School of Business, Program in Business Administration, Concentration in Accounting, Upper Montclair, NJ 07043-1624. Awards MBA. Part-time and evening/weekend programs available. Faculty: 13 full-time. Students: 6 full-time (4 women), 13 part-time (8 women). *Entrance requirements:* GMAT. Application deadline: 4/1 (rolling processing; 11/1 for spring admission). Application fee: $40. *Expenses:* Tuition $201 per credit for state residents; $257 per credit for nonresidents. Fees $22.05 per credit. *Financial aid:* Research assistantships available. Aid available to part-time students. Financial aid application deadline: 3/1; applicants required to submit FAFSA. • Application contact: Dr. Eileen Kaplan, Adviser, 973-655-4306.

New Hampshire College, Graduate School of Business, Program in Accounting, Manchester, NH 03106-1045. Awards MS. Part-time and evening/weekend programs available. Faculty: 3

Directory: Accounting

New Hampshire College (continued)
full-time (1 woman), 8 part-time (1 woman), 7 FTE. Students: 10 full-time (4 women), 79 part-time (36 women); includes 8 international. Average age 30. In 1997, 21 degrees awarded. *Degree requirements:* Thesis or alternative required, foreign language not required. *Average time to degree:* master's–1.5 years full-time, 3.5 years part-time. *Entrance requirements:* Minimum GPA of 2.5. Application deadline: rolling. Application fee: $0. *Expenses:* Tuition $17,044 per year full-time, $945 per course part-time. Fees $530 per year full-time, $80 per year part-time. *Financial aid:* In 1997–98, 2 research assistantships (both to first-year students) were awarded; Federal Work-Study, institutionally sponsored loans, and career-related internships or fieldwork also available. Aid available to part-time students. • Dr. Paul Schneiderman, Acting Dean, Graduate School of Business, 603-644-3102. Fax: 603-644-3150.

New Hampshire College, Graduate School of Business, Program in Business Administration, Manchester, NH 03106-1045. Offerings include accounting (Certificate). Program faculty: 7 full-time (1 woman), 66 part-time (11 women), 47 FTE. *Average time to degree:* master's–1.5 years full-time, 4.5 years part-time. *Application deadline:* rolling. *Application fee:* $0. *Expenses:* Tuition $17,044 per year full-time, $945 per course part-time. Fees $530 per year full-time, $80 per year part-time. • Dr. Paul Schneiderman, Acting Dean, Graduate School of Business, 603-644-3102. Fax: 603-644-3150.

New Mexico State University, College of Business Administration and Economics, Department of Accounting and Business Computer Systems, Las Cruces, NM 88003-8001. Awards M Acct. Part-time programs available. Faculty: 13 full-time (2 women). Students: 18 full-time (11 women), 8 part-time (7 women); includes 8 minority (2 Asian Americans, 5 Hispanics, 1 Native American), 6 international. Average age 30. 13 applicants, 92% accepted. In 1997, 8 degrees awarded. *Degree requirements:* Thesis optional, foreign language not required. *Entrance requirements:* GMAT, TOEFL, minimum undergraduate GPA of 3.0. Application deadline: 7/1 (priority date; rolling processing; 11/1 for spring admission). Application fee: $15 ($35 for international students). Electronic applications accepted. *Tuition:* $2514 per year full-time, $105 per credit hour part-time for state residents; $7848 per year full-time, $327 per credit hour part-time for nonresidents. *Financial aid:* Fellowships, research assistantships, teaching assistantships, Federal Work-Study, and career-related internships or fieldwork available. Aid available to part-time students. Financial aid application deadline: 3/1. *Faculty research:* Taxation, financial accounting, managerial accounting, accounting systems, accounting education. • Dr. Manson P. Dillaway, Head, 505-646-4901. Fax: 505-646-1552. E-mail: mdillowa@nmsu.edu.

New York University, Leonard N. Stern School of Business, Department of Accounting, Program in Accounting, New York, NY 10012-1019. Awards MBA, PhD, APC. *Degree requirements:* For master's, computer language required, foreign language and thesis not required; for doctorate, computer language, dissertation required, foreign language not required. *Entrance requirements:* For master's, GMAT, TOEFL (minimum score 600); for doctorate, GMAT. Application deadline: 3/15 (rolling processing). Application fee: $75. *Financial aid:* Application deadline 1/15. • Application contact: Mary Miller, Director, Graduate Admissions, 212-998-0600. Fax: 212-995-4231. E-mail: sternmba@stern.nyu.edu.

Nichols College, Graduate Program in Business Administration, Dudley, MA 01571. Offerings include accounting (MBA). College faculty: 21 full-time (3 women), 6 part-time (2 women). *Degree requirements:* Computer language required, foreign language and thesis not required. *Entrance requirements:* GMAT, TOEFL, minimum AACSB index of 950. Application deadline: rolling. Application fee: $25. *Tuition:* $1050 per course. • William F. Keith, Director, 508-213-2207. E-mail: keithwf@nichols.edu.

North Carolina State University, College of Management, Department of Accounting, Raleigh, NC 27695. Awards MAC. Faculty: 16 full-time (5 women). Students: 56 full-time (24 women), 10 part-time (5 women); includes 7 minority (3 African Americans, 4 Asian Americans), 3 international. Average age 29. 102 applicants, 66% accepted. In 1997, 9 degrees awarded. *Entrance requirements:* GRE General Test (for aid only), TOEFL (minimum score 550). Application deadline: rolling. Application fee: $45. *Tuition:* $2370 per year full-time, $517 per semester (minimum) part-time for state residents; $11,536 per year full-time, $2809 per semester (minimum) part-time for nonresidents. *Financial aid:* In 1997–98, 1 fellowship (to a first-year student) totaling $986, 16 teaching assistantships (13 to first-year students) totaling $10,890 were awarded. *Faculty research:* Financial reporting issues using positive economic models and empirical studies of human behavior related to accounting decisions. Total annual research expenditures: $3551. • Dr. Carl J. Messere, Head, 919-515-2256. E-mail: carl_messere@ncsu.edu. Application contact: Dr. Robert L. Peace, Director of Graduate Programs, 919-515-4434. Fax: 919-515-4446. E-mail: bob_peace@ncsu.edu.

Northeastern Illinois University, College of Business and Management, Chicago, IL 60625-4699. Offerings include accounting (MBA). College faculty: 26 full-time (3 women), 14 part-time (6 women). *Degree requirements:* Thesis optional, foreign language not required. *Entrance requirements:* GMAT (minimum score 450), TOEFL (minimum score 550), minimum GPA of 2.75. Application deadline: 3/18 (priority date; rolling processing; 9/30 for spring admission). Application fee: $0. *Expenses:* Tuition $2226 per year full-time, $93 per credit hour part-time for state residents; $6678 per year full-time, $278 per credit hour part-time for nonresidents. Fees $358 per year full-time, $14.90 per credit hour part-time. • Dr. Charles Falk, Dean, 773-583-4050 Ext. 5247. Application contact: Dr. Kathleen Carlson, Coordinator, 773-583-4050.

Northeastern University, Graduate School of Business Administration, Graduate School of Professional Accounting, Boston, MA 02115-5096. Awards MST, CAS, JD/MS/MBA, MS/MBA. Part-time and evening/weekend programs available. Faculty: 17 full-time. Students: 61 full-time (27 women), 104 part-time (42 women). Average age 25. 45% of applicants accepted. In 1997, 71 master's awarded. *Degree requirements:* For master's, computer language, internship required, foreign language and thesis not required. *Entrance requirements:* For master's, GMAT, interview. Application deadline: 5/1 (priority date; rolling processing). Application fee: $50. *Expenses:* Tuition $22,590 per year. Fees $675 per year. *Financial aid:* In 1997–98, 30 fellowships (all to first-year students) were awarded; research assistantships, teaching assistantships, Federal Work-Study, institutionally sponsored loans, and career-related internships or fieldwork also available. Aid available to part-time students. Financial aid applicants required to submit FAFSA. • William I. Kelly, Interim Dean of Graduate Programs, Graduate School of Business Administration, 617-373-2714. E-mail: gsba@neu.edu. Application contact: Program Director, 617-373-2714. Fax: 617-373-8564. E-mail: gsba@neu.edu.

See in-depth description on page 451.

Northern Illinois University, College of Business, Department of Accountancy, De Kalb, IL 60115-2854. Awards MAS, MST. Part-time and evening/weekend programs available. Faculty: 14 full-time (2 women). Students: 21 full-time (12 women), 54 part-time (34 women); includes 7 minority (5 Asian Americans, 2 Hispanics), 12 international. Average age 34. 82 applicants, 62% accepted. In 1997, 30 degrees awarded. *Entrance requirements:* GMAT, TOEFL (minimum score 550), minimum GPA of 2.75. Application deadline: 6/1 (rolling processing; 11/1 for spring admission). Application fee: $30. *Tuition:* $3984 per year full-time, $154 per credit hour part-time for state residents; $8160 per year full-time, $328 per credit hour part-time for nonresidents. *Financial aid:* In 1997–98, 7 research assistantships, 6 teaching assistantships, 2 staff assistantships were awarded; fellowships, full tuition waivers, Federal Work-Study, and career-related internships or fieldwork also available. Aid available to part-time students. • Dr. Patrick Delaney, Chair, 815-753-1250. Application contact: Dr. John Simon, Graduate Adviser, 815-753-6203.

Northwestern University, J. L. Kellogg Graduate School of Management, Department of Accounting and Information Systems, Evanston, IL 60208. Offers program in accounting (PhD). Admissions and degree offered through The Graduate School. Faculty: 13 full-time (2 women), 3 part-time (0 women). Students: 8 full-time (0 women); includes 1 minority (Asian American), 5 international. 39 applicants, 10% accepted. In 1997, 1 degree awarded. *Degree requirements:* Computer language, dissertation required, foreign language not required. *Entrance requirements:* GMAT or GRE General Test. Application deadline: 1/15. Application fee: $50 ($55 for international students). *Tuition:* $25,872 per year. *Financial aid:* In 1997–98, 4 students received aid, including fellowships averaging $1,256 per month, research assistantships averaging $1,592 per month; institutionally sponsored loans and career-related internships or fieldwork also available. Financial aid application deadline: 1/15; applicants required to submit FAFSA. *Faculty research:* Managerial and financial accounting theory, financial accounting/theory, managerial accounting and performance measurement, international accounting, joint cost allocation. • Ronald A. Dye, Chair, 847-491-2663. Application contact: Lucy Vandenburgh, Admission Contact, 847-491-3400. Fax: 847-491-5071. E-mail: l-vandenburgh@nwu.edu.

Northwest Missouri State University, College of Professional and Applied Studies, Program in Accounting, 800 University Drive, Maryville, MO 64468-6001. Awards MBA. Faculty: 3 full-time (1 woman). Students: 2 full-time (1 woman), 6 part-time (4 women). 5 applicants, 100% accepted. In 1997, 7 degrees awarded. *Degree requirements:* Comprehensive exam required, foreign language and thesis not required. *Entrance requirements:* GMAT, TOEFL (minimum score 550), minimum GPA of 2.5. Application deadline: 7/1 (rolling processing; 12/1 for spring admission). Application fee: $0 ($50 for international students). *Expenses:* Tuition $113 per credit hour for state residents; $197 per credit hour for nonresidents. Fees $3 per credit hour. *Financial aid:* Application deadline 3/1. • Application contact: Dr. Frances Shipley, Dean of Graduate School, 816-562-1145. E-mail: gradsch@acad.nwmissouri.edu.

Nova Southeastern University, School of Business and Entrepreneurship, Program in Accounting, Fort Lauderdale, FL 33314-7721. Awards M Acc. Part-time and evening/weekend programs available. Students: 8 full-time (5 women), 93 part-time (48 women); includes 38 minority (13 African Americans, 3 Asian Americans, 22 Hispanics), 6 international. In 1997, 37 degrees awarded. *Degree requirements:* Computer language, thesis or alternative required, foreign language not required. *Entrance requirements:* GMAT (minimum score 450), GRE General Test (minimum combined score of 1000), undergraduate degree in accounting, work experience. Application deadline: rolling. Application fee: $50. *Tuition:* $270 per credit hour (minimum). • Dr. Preston Jones, Director, 954-262-5127. Application contact: Carlo A. Palazzese, Marketing Manager, 954-262-5038. E-mail: carlop@sbe.nova.edu.

Oakland University, School of Business Administration, Rochester, MI 48309-4401. Offerings include accounting (M Acc). School faculty: 47 full-time. *Application deadline:* 7/15 (3/15 for spring admission). *Application fee:* $30. *Expenses:* Tuition $3852 per year full-time, $214 per credit hour part-time for state residents; $8532 per year full-time, $474 per credit hour part-time for nonresidents. Fees $420 per year. • Dr. John Gardner, Dean, 248-370-3286. Application contact: Sheryl Clark, Coordinator, 248-370-3287.

The Ohio State University, Max M. Fisher College of Business, Department of Accounting and Management Information Systems, Columbus, OH 43210. Awards MA, PhD. Faculty: 20. Students: 11 full-time (3 women); includes 5 international. 44 applicants, 16% accepted. In 1997, 5 master's, 4 doctorates awarded. Terminal master's awarded for partial completion of doctoral program. *Degree requirements:* For doctorate, dissertation required, foreign language not required. *Entrance requirements:* For master's, GMAT, TOEFL (minimum score 575); for doctorate, GMAT, TOEFL. Application deadline: 8/15 (rolling processing). Application fee: $30 ($40 for international students). *Tuition:* $6018 per year full-time, $635 per quarter (minimum) part-time for state residents; $14,835 per year full-time, $1514 per quarter (minimum) part-time for nonresidents. *Financial aid:* Fellowships, research assistantships, teaching assistantships, Federal Work-Study, institutionally sponsored loans, and career-related internships or fieldwork available. Aid available to part-time students. *Faculty research:* Artificial intelligence, protocol analysis, database design in decision-supporting systems. • Lawrence Tomassini, Chairman, 614-292-9368. Fax: 614-292-2118. E-mail: tomassini.1@osu.edu.

Ohio University, Graduate Studies, College of Business, School of Accountancy, Athens, OH 45701-2979. Offers program in accounting (MS). Part-time programs available. Faculty: 11 full-time (3 women), 2 part-time (0 women). Students: 12 full-time (9 women), 2 part-time (0 women); includes 6 international. 23 applicants, 52% accepted. In 1997, 10 degrees awarded. *Entrance requirements:* GMAT (minimum score 500), minimum GPA of 3.0. Application deadline: 4/1 (priority date). Application fee: $30. *Tuition:* $5430 per year full-time, $216 per quarter hour part-time for state residents; $10,431 per year full-time, $423 per quarter hour part-time for nonresidents. *Financial aid:* In 1997–98, 10 associateships were awarded; full and partial tuition waivers, Federal Work-Study, institutionally sponsored loans, and career-related internships or fieldwork also available. Financial aid application deadline: 4/1. • Dr. Robert Jamison, Director, 740-593-2020. Application contact: Jan Ross, Graduate Services Coordinator, 740-593-2007. Fax: 740-593-9823. E-mail: rossj@ouvaxa.cats.ohiou.edu.

Oklahoma City University, School of Management and Business Sciences, Program in Accounting, Oklahoma City, OK 73106-1402. Awards MSA. Part-time and evening/weekend programs available. Faculty: 5 full-time (3 women). Students: 18 full-time (10 women), 3 part-time (1 woman); includes 2 minority (both African Americans), 16 international. Average age 30. In 1997, 7 degrees awarded. *Degree requirements:* Comprehensive exam required, foreign language and thesis not required. *Entrance requirements:* TOEFL, minimum GPA of 2.75. Application deadline: 8/25 (priority date; rolling processing; 1/15 for spring admission). Application fee: $35 ($55 for international students). *Expenses:* Tuition $350 per hour. Fees $124 per year. *Financial aid:* Fellowships, partial tuition waivers, Federal Work-Study, institutionally sponsored loans, and career-related internships or fieldwork available. Aid available to part-time students. Financial aid application deadline: 8/1; applicants required to submit FAFSA. • Jim Thompson, Head, 405-521-5486. Application contact: Laura L. Rahhal, Director of Graduate Admissions, 800-633-7242 Ext. 2. Fax: 405-521-5356. E-mail: lrahhal1@frodo.okcu.edu.

Oklahoma State University, College of Business Administration, School of Accounting, Stillwater, OK 74078. Awards MS, PhD. Faculty: 15 full-time (5 women), 1 part-time (0 women), 15.5 FTE. Students: 44 full-time (26 women), 12 part-time (8 women); includes 4 minority (2 African Americans, 2 Native Americans), 3 international. Average age 26. In 1997, 35 master's awarded. *Degree requirements:* For doctorate, dissertation required, foreign language not required. *Entrance requirements:* For master's, GMAT, TOEFL (minimum score 550); for doctorate, TOEFL (minimum score 550). Application deadline: 7/1 (priority date). Application fee: $25. *Financial aid:* In 1997–98, 22 students received aid, including 22 teaching assistantships (10 to first-year students) totaling $191,400; partial tuition waivers, Federal Work-Study, and career-related internships or fieldwork also available. Aid available to part-time students. Financial aid application deadline: 3/1. • Lanny Chasteen, Head, 405-744-5123.

Old Dominion University, College of Business and Public Administration, Department of Accounting, Program in Accounting, Norfolk, VA 23529. Awards MS. Part-time and evening/weekend programs available. Postbaccalaureate distance learning degree programs offered (no on-campus study). Students: 16 full-time (10 women), 19 part-time (12 women); includes 7 minority (6 African Americans, 1 Asian American), 5 international. In 1997, 7 degrees awarded. *Entrance requirements:* GMAT (minimum score 470), minimum GPA of 2.75 in accounting, 2.5 overall. Application deadline: 7/1 (rolling processing; 10/1 for spring admission). Application fee: $30. *Expenses:* Tuition $180 per credit hour for state residents; $477 per credit hour for nonresidents. Fees $140 per year full-time, $32 per semester part-time. *Financial aid:* In 1997–98, 11 students received aid, including 4 research assistantships (1 to a first-year student) totaling $26,564; partial tuition waivers and career-related internships or fieldwork also available. Aid available to part-time students. Financial aid application deadline: 2/15; applicants required to submit FAFSA. • Application contact: Dr. Douglas Ziegenfuss, Graduate Director, 757-683-3514. Fax: 757-683-5639. E-mail: dziegenf@odu.edu.

Oral Roberts University, School of Business, Tulsa, OK 74171-0001. Offerings include accounting (MBA). *Degree requirements:* Computer language required, thesis optional, foreign language not required. *Entrance requirements:* GMAT (minimum score 400; average 500).

Application deadline: 7/31 (priority date; rolling processing; 12/31 for spring admission). Application fee: $35. Electronic applications accepted.

Pace University, Lubin School of Business, Accounting Program, New York, NY 10038. Offers managerial accounting (MBA), public accounting (MBA, MS). Part-time and evening/weekend programs available. *Degree requirements:* Computer language required, foreign language and thesis not required. *Entrance requirements:* GMAT. Application deadline: 7/31 (priority date; rolling processing; 11/30 for spring admission). Application fee: $60. *Expenses:* Tuition $545 per credit. Fees $360 per year full-time, $53 per semester (minimum) part-time.

Pennsylvania State University University Park Campus, The Mary Jean and Frank P. Smeal College of Business Administration, MS Programs in Business Administration, Department of Accounting, University Park, PA 16802-1503. Awards MS. *Degree requirements:* Paper or thesis required, foreign language not required. *Entrance requirements:* GMAT. Application fee: $40. *Expenses:* Tuition $6534 per year full-time, $276 per credit part-time for state residents; $13,460 per year full-time, $561 per credit part-time for nonresidents. Fees $252 per year (minimum) full-time, $43 per semester (minimum) part-time. • Dr. Charles Smith, Chair, 814-865-0041.

Pennsylvania State University University Park Campus, The Mary Jean and Frank P. Smeal College of Business Administration, PhD Programs in Business Administration, Program in Accounting, University Park, PA 16802-1503. Awards PhD. *Degree requirements:* Dissertation. *Entrance requirements:* GMAT. Application fee: $40. *Expenses:* Tuition $6534 per year full-time, $276 per credit part-time for state residents; $13,460 per year full-time, $561 per credit part-time for nonresidents. Fees $252 per year (minimum) full-time, $43 per semester (minimum) part-time. • Dr. Jane F. Mutchler, Field Adviser, 814-863-3569.

Philadelphia College of Textiles and Science, School of Business, Program in Business, Philadelphia, PA 19144-5497. Offerings include accounting (MBA). *Entrance requirements:* GMAT, minimum GPA of 2.85. Application deadline: rolling. Application fee: $35. *Tuition:* $448 per credit hour. • Rita Powell, Director, 215-951-2950. Fax: 215-951-2652. E-mail: powellr@phila.col.edu. Application contact: Robert J. Reed, Director of Graduate Admissions, 215-951-2943. Fax: 215-951-2907. E-mail: gradadm@phila.col.edu.

Pittsburg State University, Gladys A. Kelce School of Business and Economics, Department of Accounting, Pittsburg, KS 66762-5880. Awards MBA. Faculty: 5 full-time (0 women). *Degree requirements:* Thesis or alternative required, foreign language not required. *Entrance requirements:* GMAT. Application deadline: 7/1. Application fee: $40. *Tuition:* $2418 per year full-time, $103 per credit hour part-time for state residents; $6130 per year full-time, $258 per credit hour part-time for nonresidents. *Financial aid:* Research assistantships, teaching assistantships, Federal Work-Study, and career-related internships or fieldwork available. Financial aid application deadline: 3/1. *Faculty research:* Accountant's legal liability, computer audit. • Dr. Guy Owings, Chairperson, 316-235-4561.

Purdue University, Krannert Graduate School of Management, Department of Management, West Lafayette, IN 47907. Offerings include accounting (MS, PhD). Department faculty: 51 full-time (5 women). *Degree requirements:* For doctorate, dissertation required, foreign language not required. *Average time to degree:* doctorate–4 years full-time. *Entrance requirements:* For doctorate, GMAT, TOEFL (minimum score 575). Application fee: $30. Electronic applications accepted. *Tuition:* $3500 per year full-time, $126 per credit hour part-time for state residents; $11,720 per year full-time, $387 per credit hour part-time for nonresidents. • Dr. J. J. McConnell, Director of Doctoral Programs, 765-494-4375. Application contact: Kelly Felty, Assistant Director of Administration for Doctoral Programs, 765-494-4375. Fax: 765-494-1526. E-mail: feltyk@mgmt.purdue.edu.

Quinnipiac College, School of Business, Program in Business Administration, Hamden, CT 06518-1904. Offerings include accounting (MBA). Program faculty: 17 full-time (2 women), 4 part-time (1 woman). *Degree requirements:* Thesis optional, foreign language not required. *Average time to degree:* master's–2 years full-time, 4 years part-time. *Entrance requirements:* GMAT (minimum score 400; average 470), interview, minimum GPA of 2.5. Application deadline: 8/1 (priority date; rolling processing). Application fee: $45. Electronic applications accepted. *Expenses:* Tuition $395 per credit hour. Fees $380 per year full-time. • Dr. Earl Chrysler, Director, 203-281-8799. Fax: 203-281-8664. E-mail: chrysler@quinnipiac.edu. Application contact: Scott Farber, Director of Graduate Admissions, 203-281-8795. Fax: 203-287-5238. E-mail: qcgradadmi@quinnipiac.edu.

Rensselaer Polytechnic Institute, Lally School of Management and Technology, Troy, NY 12180-3590. Offerings include accounting/finance (PhD); business administration (MBA, PhD), with options in finance and accounting (MBA), information systems management (MBA), management (PhD), management of technology and entrepreneurships (MBA), manufacturing management (MBA), marketing management (MBA), operations research (MBA), organizational behavior and human resource management (MBA), statistical methods for management (MBA). Postbaccalaureate distance learning degree programs offered (no on-campus study). School faculty: 36 full-time (5 women), 6 part-time (0 women). *Degree requirements:* For doctorate, computer language, dissertation required, foreign language not required. *Entrance requirements:* For doctorate, GMAT or GRE General Test, TOEFL (minimum score 570). Application deadline: 2/1 (priority date; rolling processing). Application fee: $35. *Expenses:* Tuition $630 per credit hour. Fees $1000 per year. • Dr. Joseph G. Ecker, Dean, 518-276-6802. Application contact: Michele Martens, Manager of Enrollment Services, 518-276-4800. Fax: 518-276-8661.

Rhodes College, Department of Economics/Business Administration, Memphis, TN 38112-1690. Offers program in accounting (MS). Part-time programs available. Faculty: 4 full-time, 4 part-time. Students: 12 full-time (5 women); includes 1 African American. Average age 22. 8 applicants, 75% accepted. In 1997, 6 degrees awarded. *Entrance requirements:* GMAT. Application deadline: 3/1. Application fee: $25. *Expenses:* Tuition $18,038 per year full-time, $700 per credit hour part-time. Fees $158 per year. *Financial aid:* 11 students received aid; grants, Federal Work-Study, and career-related internships or fieldwork available. Aid available to part-time students. Financial aid application deadline: 3/1; applicants required to submit FAFSA. • Pam Church, Director of Accounting Program, 901-843-3863. Fax: 901-843-3798. E-mail: church@rhodes.edu.

Robert Morris College, Program in Business Administration, 881 Narrows Run Road, Moon Township, PA 15108-1189. Offerings include accounting (MBA, MS). Only part-time programs offered. Program faculty: 35 full-time (6 women), 35 part-time (5 women). *Entrance requirements:* GMAT (minimum score 450), minimum GPA of 2.5. Application deadline: 8/1 (priority date; rolling processing; 11/30 for spring admission). Application fee: $25 ($35 for international students). *Expenses:* Tuition $328 per credit. Fees $15 per credit. • Dr. Joseph F. Constable, Dean, School of Management, 412-262-8451. Fax: 412-262-8494. E-mail: constabl@robert-morris.edu. Application contact: Vincent J. Kane, Recruiting Coordinator, 412-262-8535. Fax: 412-299-2425.

Rochester Institute of Technology, College of Business, Department of Business Administration, Program in Accounting, Rochester, NY 14623-5604. Awards MBA, MS. Students: 3 full-time (2 women), 6 part-time (5 women). 0 applicants. In 1997, 4 degrees awarded. *Entrance requirements:* GMAT, minimum GPA of 2.5. Application deadline: 3/1 (priority date; rolling processing). Application fee: $40. *Expenses:* Tuition $18,765 per year full-time, $527 per credit hour part-time. Fees $126 per year full-time. *Financial aid:* Research assistantships and career-related internships or fieldwork available. • Patricia Sorce, Associate Dean, Department of Business Administration, 716-475-2313.

Roosevelt University, Walter E. Heller College of Business Administration, Program in Accounting, Chicago, IL 60605-1394. Awards MSA. Part-time and evening/weekend programs available. Faculty: 7 full-time (2 women), 7 part-time (0 women). Students: 7 full-time (2 women), 39 part-time (20 women); includes 14 minority (7 African Americans, 4 Asian Americans, 3 Hispanics), 5 international. In 1997, 6 degrees awarded. *Degree requirements:* Computer language required, foreign language and thesis not required. *Entrance requirements:* GMAT. Application deadline: 6/1 (priority date; rolling processing). Application fee: $25 ($35 for international students). *Expenses:* Tuition $445 per credit hour. Fees $100 per year. *Financial aid:* Application deadline 2/15. • Deborah Pavelka, Graduate Adviser, 312-341-3851. Application contact: Joanne Canyon-Heller, Coordinator of Graduate Admissions, 312-341-3612.

Rutgers, The State University of New Jersey, Newark, Department of Management, Newark, NJ 07102-3192. Offerings include accounting (PhD), accounting information systems (PhD). Offered jointly with New Jersey Institute of Technology. Terminal master's awarded for partial completion of doctoral program. Department faculty: 113 full-time (13 women), 3 part-time (1 woman). *Degree requirements:* Dissertation, cumulative exams required, foreign language not required. *Average time to degree:* doctorate–5 years full-time, 7 years part-time. *Entrance requirements:* GMAT or GRE, minimum undergraduate B average. Application deadline: 4/1 (rolling processing; 11/1 for spring admission). Application fee: $40. *Expenses:* Tuition $6248 per year full-time, $257 per credit part-time for state residents; $9160 per year full-time, $380 per credit part-time for nonresidents. Fees $738 per year full-time, $107 per semester (minimum) part-time. • Glenn R. Shafer, Director, 973-353-1604. E-mail: gshafer@andromeda.rutgers.edu. Application contact: Ana Gonzalez, Program Secretary, 973-353-5371. Fax: 973-353-5691. E-mail: anag@gsmack.rutgers.edu.

Rutgers, The State University of New Jersey, Newark, Graduate School of Management, Department of Accounting and Information Systems, Newark, NJ 07102-3192. Offers program in professional accounting (MBA). *Degree requirements:* Computer language required, thesis not required. *Entrance requirements:* GMAT, TOEFL. Application deadline: 6/1 (rolling processing). Application fee: $40. *Financial aid:* Federal Work-Study, institutionally sponsored loans, and career-related internships or fieldwork available. Financial aid application deadline: 3/15; applicants required to submit FAFSA. • Dr. Dan Palmon, Chairman, 973-353-5472. Fax: 973-353-1283. E-mail: dpalmon@ardromeda.rutgers.edu. Application contact: Director of Admissions, 973-353-1234. Fax: 973-353-1592. E-mail: admit@gsmack.rutgers.edu.

St. Ambrose University, College of Business, Program in Accounting, Davenport, IA 52803-2898. Awards M Ac. Part-time and evening/weekend programs available. *Degree requirements:* Capstone Seminar required, foreign language and thesis not required. *Entrance requirements:* GMAT. Application deadline: 8/15 (priority date; rolling processing). Application fee: $25. Electronic applications accepted.

St. Bonaventure University, School of Business Administration, St. Bonaventure, NY 14778-2284. Offerings include accounting and finance (MBA). School faculty: 19 full-time (2 women), 3 part-time (0 women). *Average time to degree:* master's–1.5 years full-time, 3 years part-time. *Entrance requirements:* GMAT (minimum score 400), TOEFL (minimum score 600). Application deadline: 8/1 (rolling processing). Application fee: $35. *Tuition:* $8100 per year full-time, $450 per credit hour part-time. • Dr. Michael Fischer, Dean, 716-375-2200. Application contact: Brian C. McAllister, MBA Director, 716-375-2098. Fax: 716-375-2191. E-mail: bmac@sbu.edu.

St. Cloud State University, College of Business, Department of Accounting, St. Cloud, MN 56301-4498. Awards MS. Part-time programs available. Faculty: 13 full-time (2 women). Students: 3 full-time (2 women), 2 part-time (1 woman). *Degree requirements:* Comprehensive exam required, foreign language and thesis not required. *Entrance requirements:* GMAT (minimum score 470), minimum GPA of 2.75. Application fee: $20 ($100 for international students). *Expenses:* Tuition $128 per credit for state residents; $203 per credit for nonresidents. Fees $16.32 per credit. *Financial aid:* In 1997–98, 3 graduate assistantships were awarded; Federal Work-Study also available. Financial aid application deadline: 3/1. • Dr. Kate Mooney, Chairperson, 320-255-3038. Application contact: Ann Anderson, Graduate Studies Office, 320-255-2113. Fax: 320-654-5371. E-mail: anna@grad.stcloud.msus.edu.

St. Edward's University, School of Business Administration, Austin, TX 78704-6489. Offerings include accounting (Certificate). School faculty: 13 full-time (3 women), 12 part-time (1 woman). *Average time to degree:* master's–1.5 years full-time, 2.7 years part-time. *Application deadline:* 8/1 (priority date; rolling processing; 12/1 for spring admission). *Application fee:* $25. • Dr. David Kendall, Dean, 512-448-8696. E-mail: davidk@admin.stedwards.edu. Application contact: Tom Evans, Director of Graduate Admissions, 512-448-8600. Fax: 512-448-8492. E-mail: seu.grad@admin.stedwards.edu.

St. John's University, College of Business Administration, Department of Accounting and Taxation, Program in Accounting, Jamaica, NY 11439. Awards MBA, Adv C. Part-time and evening/weekend programs available. Students: 24 full-time (12 women), 81 part-time (36 women); includes 27 minority (8 African Americans, 12 Asian Americans, 6 Hispanics, 1 Native American), 19 international. Average age 30. 68 applicants, 65% accepted. In 1997, 38 master's awarded. *Degree requirements:* For master's, thesis optional, foreign language not required. *Entrance requirements:* For master's, GMAT. Application deadline: 6/1 (rolling processing; 10/1 for spring admission). Application fee: $40. *Expenses:* Tuition $600 per credit. Fees $150 per year. *Financial aid:* Federal Work-Study available. Aid available to part-time students. Financial aid application deadline: 3/1; applicants required to submit FAFSA. • Application contact: Shamus J. McGrenra, TOR, Associate Director, Graduate Admissions, 718-990-6107. Fax: 718-990-5736. E-mail: mcgrenrs@stjohns.edu.

Saint Joseph's University, Erivan K. Haub School of Business, Programs in Graduate Business, Program in Accounting, Philadelphia, PA 19131-1395. Awards MBA. Evening/weekend programs available. Students: 54 (18 women). In 1997, 16 degrees awarded. *Entrance requirements:* GMAT, TOEFL. Application deadline: 7/15 (priority date; rolling processing; 11/15 for spring admission). Application fee: $35. *Tuition:* $510 per credit hour. *Financial aid:* Graduate assistantships available. Financial aid application deadline: 5/1. • Adele C. Foley, Associate Dean, Programs in Graduate Business, 610-660-1690. Fax: 610-660-1599. E-mail: afoley@sju.edu.

Saint Louis University, School of Business and Administration, Department of Accounting, 3674 Lindell Boulevard, St. Louis, MO 63108. Awards M Acct, MBA, PhD. Part-time and evening/weekend programs available. Faculty: 9 full-time (3 women). Students: 2 full-time (1 woman), 5 part-time (2 women). Average age 25. 3 applicants, 33% accepted. In 1997, 1 master's awarded. *Degree requirements:* For master's, oral exam required, thesis not required; for doctorate, dissertation. *Average time to degree:* master's–1.5 years full-time, 3 years part-time; doctorate–5 years full-time, 6 years part-time. *Entrance requirements:* For master's, GMAT, TOEFL; for doctorate, GMAT. Application deadline: 7/15 (rolling processing; 11/15 for spring admission). Application fee: $40. *Financial aid:* Fellowships, research assistantships, teaching assistantships, Federal Work-Study available. Aid available to part-time students. • Dr. James Jennings, Chairman, 314-977-3828.

Saint Peter's College, Program in Accountancy, 2641 Kennedy Boulevard, Jersey City, NJ 07306-5997. Awards MS, Certificate, MBA/MS. Part-time and evening/weekend programs available. Faculty: 11 full-time (0 women), 8 part-time (3 women). Students: 5 full-time (2 women), 23 part-time (10 women); includes 8 minority (4 African Americans, 2 Asian Americans, 2 Hispanics), 2 international. Average age 32. 31 applicants, 81% accepted. In 1997, 10 master's awarded. *Entrance requirements:* For master's, GMAT (400) or MAT (minimum score 40). Application deadline: 8/1 (priority date; rolling processing). Application fee: $20. *Tuition:* $516 per credit. *Faculty research:* Taxation, international business and finance, decision support and expert systems. • Sr. Jeanne Gilligan, Associate Vice President for Academic Affairs, 201-915-7252. Fax: 201-946-7528. E-mail: gillganj@spcvxa.spc.edu. Application contact: Nancy P. Campbell, Associate Vice President for Enrollment, 201-915-9213. Fax: 201-432-5860. E-mail: admissions@spcvxa.spc.edu.

St. Thomas University, School of Graduate Studies, Department of Professional Management, Miami, FL 33054-6459. Offerings include accounting (MBA). *Average time to degree:* master's–1 year full-time. *Application deadline:* rolling. *Application fee:* $30. *Tuition:* $410 per credit.

Directory: Accounting

Salve Regina University, Program in Accounting, Newport, RI 02840-4192. Awards MS. Part-time and evening/weekend programs available. Faculty: 3 part-time (1 woman), 1.25 FTE. Students: 1 (woman) full-time, 9 part-time (6 women). Average age 37. 1 applicant, 0% accepted. In 1997, 6 degrees awarded. *Average time to degree:* master's–2 years full-time, 3 years part-time. *Entrance requirements:* GMAT, GRE General Test, or MAT. Application deadline: rolling. Application fee: $35. *Expenses:* Tuition $275 per credit hour. Fees $70 per year. *Financial aid:* Federal Work-Study and career-related internships or fieldwork available. Aid available to part-time students. Financial aid application deadline: 3/1. • Terrence Gavan, Director, 401-847-6650 Ext. 3123. Application contact: Laura E. McPhie, Dean of Enrollment Services, 401-847-6650 Ext. 2908. Fax: 401-848-2823. E-mail: sruadmis@salve.edu.

San Diego State University, Graduate School of Business, School of Accountancy, San Diego, CA 92182. Awards MBA, MS. Students: 42 full-time (19 women), 53 part-time (25 women); includes 25 minority (3 African Americans, 20 Asian Americans, 2 Hispanics), 9 international. Average age 30. In 1997, 48 degrees awarded. *Degree requirements:* Computer language, thesis or alternative required, foreign language not required. *Entrance requirements:* GMAT (minimum score 570), TOEFL (minimum score 570). Application deadline: 4/15 (priority date; rolling processing; 11/1 for spring admission). Application fee: $55. *Expenses:* Tuition $0 for state residents; $246 per unit for nonresidents. Fees $1932 per year full-time, $1266 per year part-time. • Andrew Barnett, Director, 619-594-5070. E-mail: abarnett@mail.sdsu.edu.

San Jose State University, College of Business, Program in Accountancy, San Jose, CA 95192-0001. Awards MS. Students: 21 full-time (12 women); includes 6 minority (5 Asian Americans, 1 Hispanic). Average age 27. 57 applicants, 47% accepted. In 1997, 18 degrees awarded. *Degree requirements:* Computer language, thesis or alternative, comprehensive exam required, foreign language not required. *Entrance requirements:* GMAT, minimum GPA of 3.0. Application deadline: 6/1 (rolling processing). Application fee: $59. *Expenses:* Tuition $0 for state residents; $246 per unit for nonresidents. Fees $2017 per year full-time, $1351 per year part-time. • Dr. Joseph Mori, Head, 408-924-3460.

Seton Hall University, W. Paul Stillman School of Business, Department of Accounting and Taxation, South Orange, NJ 07079-2692. Awards MBA, MS, Certificate, MBA/MS. Programs in accounting (MBA, MS), professional accounting (MS), taxation (MS, Certificate). Part-time programs available. Postbaccalaureate distance learning degree programs offered (no on-campus study). Faculty: 11 full-time (1 woman), 8 part-time (1 woman). *Degree requirements:* For master's, thesis optional, foreign language not required. *Entrance requirements:* For master's, GMAT (minimum score 500), TOEFL (minimum score 550); for Certificate, MS in taxation. Application deadline: 6/1 (priority date; rolling processing). Application fee: $50. *Expenses:* Tuition $538 per credit. Fees $185 per semester. *Financial aid:* Research assistantships and career-related internships or fieldwork available. Aid available to part-time students. Financial aid applicants required to submit FAFSA. • Dr. James Greenspan, Chairperson, 973-761-9647. E-mail: greensja@shu.edu. Application contact: Student Information Office, 973-761-9222. Fax: 973-761-9217. E-mail: busgrad@shu.edu.

Siena College, Business Division, Loudonville, NY 12211-1462. Offers program in professional accountancy (MBA). Part-time and evening/weekend programs available. Faculty: 10 part-time (3 women). Students: 3 full-time (2 women), 36 part-time (22 women); includes 1 minority (Asian American). Average age 32. 15 applicants, 93% accepted. *Degree requirements:* Community service, minimum GPA of 3.0 required, foreign language and thesis not required. *Entrance requirements:* GMAT, previous course work in accounting, economics, finance, business law, business statistics. Application deadline: 6/15 (priority date; rolling processing; 12/15 for spring admission). Application fee: $50. *Faculty research:* Valuation of businesses, management of family owned businesses, ethical issues in business. Total annual research expenditures: $8000. • Leonard Stokes, Director, MBA Program, 518-786-5015. E-mail: stokes@siena.edu. Application contact: Allison Hastings, Assistant Director, MBA Program, 518-786-5015. Fax: 518-786-5040. E-mail: hastings@siena.edu.

Simon Fraser University, Faculty of Business Administration, Burnaby, BC V5A 1S6, Canada. Offerings include accounting (MBA). Faculty: 48 full-time (12 women). *Application fee:* $55. *Expenses:* Tuition $2400 per year (minimum). Fees $207 per year. • S. McShane, Director, 604-291-3639. Application contact: Program Assistant, 604-291-3047. Fax: 604-291-3404. E-mail: mba@sfu.ca.

Slippery Rock University of Pennsylvania, College of Information Science and Business Administration, Department of Accounting, Slippery Rock, PA 16057. Awards MS. *Entrance requirements:* GMAT or GRE, CPA certificate. Application deadline: 7/1 (11/1 for spring admission). Application fee: $25. *Tuition:* $4484 per year full-time, $247 per credit part-time for state residents; $7667 per year full-time, $423 per credit part-time for nonresidents.

Southeastern University, Program in Accounting, Washington, DC 20024-2788. Awards MBA. Part-time and evening/weekend programs available. Faculty: 3 full-time (0 women), 11 part-time (1 woman), 7 FTE. Students: 9 full-time (3 women), 14 part-time (8 women); includes 10 minority (all African Americans), 13 international. Average age 35. 4 applicants, 50% accepted. In 1997, 20 degrees awarded. *Degree requirements:* Computer language required, foreign language and thesis not required. *Entrance requirements:* TOEFL. Application deadline: rolling. Application fee: $45. *Expenses:* Tuition $228 per credit hour. Fees $175 per quarter. *Financial aid:* Federal Work-Study and career-related internships or fieldwork available. Aid available to part-time students. Financial aid application deadline: 8/21; applicants required to submit FAFSA. • James McCarthy, Head, 202-488-8162. Application contact: Jack Flinter, Director of Admissions, 202-265-5343. Fax: 202-488-8093.

Southern Illinois University at Carbondale, College of Business and Administration, School of Accountancy, Carbondale, IL 62901-6806. Awards M Acc, DBA, JD/M Acc. Part-time programs available. Faculty: 10 full-time (1 woman). Students: 32 full-time (15 women), 6 part-time (4 women); includes 2 minority (1 African American, 1 Native American), 14 international. 31 applicants, 61% accepted. In 1997, 18 master's awarded. *Degree requirements:* For master's, computer language required, foreign language and thesis not required; for doctorate, computer language, dissertation required, foreign language not required. *Entrance requirements:* For master's, GMAT, TOEFL (minimum score 550), minimum GPA of 2.7; for doctorate, GMAT, TOEFL (minimum score 550), minimum graduate GPA of 3.25. Application deadline: 6/15 (priority date; rolling processing). Application fee: $20. *Expenses:* Tuition $2964 per year full-time, $99 per semester hour part-time for state residents; $8892 per year full-time, $270 per semester hour part-time for nonresidents. Fees $1034 per year full-time, $298 per semester (minimum) part-time. *Financial aid:* In 1997–98, 6 research assistantships, 6 teaching assistantships were awarded; fellowships, Federal Work-Study, institutionally sponsored loans also available. Aid available to part-time students. Financial aid application deadline: 4/1. *Faculty research:* Not-for-profit accounting, SEC regulations, computers and accounting education, taxation. • Dr. Raymond Wacker, Director, 618-453-2287.

Southern Illinois University at Edwardsville, School of Business, Department of Accountancy, Edwardsville, IL 62026-0001. Awards MSA. Students: 8 full-time (6 women), 5 part-time (2 women); includes 1 minority (African American), 3 international. 10 applicants, 70% accepted. In 1997, 1 degree awarded. *Entrance requirements:* GMAT. Application deadline: 7/24. Application fee: $25. *Expenses:* Tuition $1716 per year full-time, $95 per credit hour part-time for state residents; $5149 per year full-time, $286 per credit hour part-time for nonresidents. Fees $463 per year full-time, $433 per year part-time. *Financial aid:* In 1997–98, 3 assistantships were awarded; fellowships, research assistantships, teaching assistantships, Federal Work-Study, institutionally sponsored loans also available. Aid available to part-time students. • Michael Costigan, Chairperson, 618-692-2633.

Southern University and Agricultural and Mechanical College, College of Business, Baton Rouge, LA 70813. Offerings include professional accountancy (MPA). College faculty: 1 (woman) full-time, 1 (woman) part-time. *Degree requirements:* Thesis optional. *Entrance requirements:* GMAT or GRE General Test, TOEFL. Application deadline: 6/1 (priority date; rolling processing; 11/1 for spring admission). Application fee: $5. *Tuition:* $2226 per year full-time, $267 per semester (minimum) part-time for state residents; $6262 per year full-time, $267 per semester (minimum) part-time for nonresidents. • Dr. Brenda Birkett, Dean, 504-771-5640. Fax: 504-771-5262.

Southern Utah University, School of Business, Cedar City, UT 84720-2498. Awards M Acc. Part-time programs available. Faculty: 6 full-time (0 women). Students: 33 full-time (11 women), 8 part-time (3 women); includes 2 minority (1 Asian American, 1 Native American). Average age 26. 47 applicants, 87% accepted. In 1997, 23 degrees awarded. *Degree requirements:* Computer language required, foreign language and thesis not required. *Entrance requirements:* GMAT, bachelor's degree in accounting or business. Application deadline: 9/1 (priority date; rolling processing). Application fee: $30. *Financial aid:* In 1997–98, 5 research assistantships were awarded; assistantships, full and partial tuition waivers, institutionally sponsored loans, and career-related internships or fieldwork also available. • Carl Templin, Dean, 435-586-5401. E-mail: templin@suu.edu. Application contact: Paula Alger, Curriculum Coordinator/Adviser, 435-865-8157. Fax: 435-586-5493. E-mail: alger@suu.edu.

Southwest Baptist University, School of Graduate Studies, School of Business, 1600 University Avenue, Bolivar, MO 65613-2597. Offerings include administration (MS), with options in accounting, business administration, health services. School faculty: 11 part-time (3 women). *Average time to degree:* master's–1.2 years full-time. *Entrance requirements:* Interviews, minimum GPA of 2.75. Application deadline: rolling. Application fee: $25. *Tuition:* $145 per credit hour. • Dr. Michael Awad, Interim Dean, 417-326-1751. Fax: 417-326-1887. E-mail: business@sbuniv.edu. Application contact: Dr. Rodney Oglesby, Director of Graduate Studies, 417-326-1756.

Southwestern Adventist University, Program in Business Administration, Keene, TX 76059. Offers accounting (MBA). Part-time and evening/weekend programs available. Faculty: 3 full-time (0 women), 3 part-time (0 women), 5 FTE. Students: 7 full-time (3 women), 12 part-time (6 women); includes 8 minority (3 African Americans, 4 Hispanics, 1 Native American), 3 international. Average age 28. 40 applicants, 75% accepted. *Degree requirements:* Capstone Course required, thesis not required. *Entrance requirements:* GMAT (minimum score 400), GRE General Test (minimum combined score of 850). Application deadline: 8/24 (priority date; rolling processing; 12/28 for spring admission). Application fee: $0. *Tuition:* $3300 per year full-time, $275 per hour part-time. • Dr. José Goris, Director, 817-645-3921 Ext. 226. Application contact: Dr. Marie Redwine, Graduate Dean, 817-645-3921 Ext. 211. Fax: 817-556-4744. E-mail: redwinem@swau.edu.

Southwest Missouri State University, College of Business Administration, Department of Accountancy, Springfield, MO 65804-0094. Awards M Acc. Part-time and evening/weekend programs available. Faculty: 15 full-time (2 women), 1 part-time (0 women). Students: 6 full-time (1 woman), 11 part-time (5 women); includes 1 minority (Hispanic), 4 international. In 1997, 6 degrees awarded (100% found work related to degree). *Degree requirements:* Thesis or alternative, comprehensive exam required, foreign language not required. *Entrance requirements:* GMAT (minimum score 450), minimum GPA of 2.75. Application deadline: 8/6 (priority date; rolling processing; 1/4 for spring admission). Application fee: $25. *Expenses:* Tuition $1980 per year full-time, $110 per credit hour part-time for state residents; $3960 per year full-time, $220 per credit hour part-time for nonresidents. Fees $274 per year full-time, $73 per semester part-time. *Financial aid:* In 1997–98, 5 graduate assistantships averaging $583 per month and totaling $21,000 were awarded; research assistantships, Federal Work-Study, and career-related internships or fieldwork also available. Aid available to part-time students. *Faculty research:* Financial, managerial, tax, and systems accounting; auditing; accounting education. • Application contact: Dr. David Byrd, Program Coordinator, 417-836-5414. Fax: 417-836-6337. E-mail: dbb414f@wpgate.smsu.edu.

Southwest Texas State University, School of Business, Program in Accounting, San Marcos, TX 78666. Awards M Acy. Part-time programs available. Faculty: 6 full-time (2 women). Students: 15 full-time (10 women), 37 part-time (21 women); includes 10 minority (2 African Americans, 5 Asian Americans, 3 Hispanics), 5 international. Average age 32. In 1997, 11 degrees awarded. *Degree requirements:* Comprehensive exam required, foreign language and thesis not required. *Entrance requirements:* GMAT (minimum score 400), TOEFL (minimum score 550), TSE (minimum score 220). Application deadline: 7/15 (priority date; rolling processing; 11/15 for spring admission). Application fee: $25 ($50 for international students). *Expenses:* Tuition $648 per year full-time, $120 per semester (minimum) part-time for state residents; $4500 per year full-time, $750 per semester (minimum) part-time for nonresidents. Fees $1264 per year full-time, $314 per semester (minimum) part-time. *Financial aid:* Federal Work-Study, institutionally sponsored loans available. Aid available to part-time students. Financial aid application deadline: 4/1; applicants required to submit FAFSA. *Faculty research:* Tax and estate planning, foreign exchange risk. • Dr. Robert J. Olney, Associate Dean, 512-245-3591. Fax: 512-245-8375. E-mail: ro02@swt.edu.

State University of New York at Albany, School of Business, Department of Accounting, Albany, NY 12222-0001. Offers programs in accounting (MS), taxation (MS). Faculty: 15 full-time (5 women), 2 part-time (0 women). Students: 32 full-time (21 women), 19 part-time (10 women); includes 3 minority (2 African Americans, 1 Asian American), 11 international. 69 applicants, 57% accepted. In 1997, 35 degrees awarded. *Degree requirements:* Research project. *Entrance requirements:* GMAT. Application deadline: 7/1 (priority date; rolling processing). Application fee: $50. *Expenses:* Tuition $5100 per year full-time, $213 per credit hour part-time for state residents; $8416 per year full-time, $351 per credit hour part-time for nonresidents. Fees $705 per year full-time, $26.85 per credit hour part-time. *Financial aid:* Application deadline 4/1. *Faculty research:* Professional ethics, statistical analysis, cost management systems, accounting theory. • Daniel Marcinko, Chair, 518-442-4978. Application contact: Jeffrey Collins, Assistant Director, Graduate Admissions, 518-442-3980.

State University of New York at Binghamton, School of Management, Program in Accounting, Binghamton, NY 13902-6000. Awards MS, PhD. Evening/weekend programs available. In 1997, 42 master's awarded. *Degree requirements:* For master's, computer language required, thesis not required; for doctorate, dissertation. *Entrance requirements:* GMAT, TOEFL. Application deadline: 4/15 (priority date; rolling processing; 11/1 for spring admission). Application fee: $50. Electronic applications accepted. *Expenses:* Tuition $5100 per year full-time, $213 per credit hour part-time for state residents; $8416 per year full-time, $351 per credit hour part-time for nonresidents. Fees $654 per year full-time, $75 per semester (minimum) part-time. *Financial aid:* In 1997–98, 4 students received aid, including 2 teaching assistantships (1 to a first-year student) averaging $550 per month and totaling $8,250, 2 graduate assistantships averaging $550 per month and totaling $11,000; fellowships, research assistantships, Federal Work-Study, institutionally sponsored loans, and career-related internships or fieldwork also available. Aid available to part-time students. Financial aid application deadline: 2/15. • Dr. Martin Freedman, Professor, 607-777-2306.

State University of New York Institute of Technology at Utica/Rome, School of Business, Program in Accountancy, PO Box 3050, Utica, NY 13504-3050. Awards MS. Part-time and evening/weekend programs available. Faculty: 13 full-time (2 women), 2 part-time (0 women). Students: 8 full-time (5 women), 14 part-time (6 women). Average age 35. 10 applicants, 90% accepted. *Degree requirements:* Comprehensive exam required, foreign language and thesis not required. *Entrance requirements:* GMAT, TOEFL (minimum score 550), minimum GPA of 3.0. Application deadline: 6/15 (priority date; rolling processing). Application fee: $50. *Expenses:* Tuition $5100 per year full-time, $213 per credit hour part-time for state residents; $8416 per year full-time, $351 per credit hour part-time for nonresidents. Fees $570 per year full-time, $17.60 per credit hour part-time. *Financial aid:* 14 students received aid; fellowships, research assistantships, Federal Work-Study, and career-related internships or fieldwork available. Aid available to part-time students. Financial aid applicants required to submit FAFSA. *Faculty research:* Ethics in business and accounting, capital structure and firm performance, federal taxation, health and aging related processes, decision and accounting information systems. Total annual research expenditures: $10,000. • Thomas Tribunella, Chair, 315-792-7126. Fax:

315-792-7429. E-mail: ftjt@sunyit.edu. Application contact: Marybeth Lyons, Director of Admissions, 315-792-7500. Fax: 315-792-7837. E-mail: smbl@sunyit.edu.

State University of West Georgia, College of Business, Department of Accounting, Carrollton, GA 30118. Awards MP Acc. Part-time and evening/weekend programs available. Faculty: 8 full-time (0 women). Students: 12 full-time (6 women), 1 part-time (0 women); includes 1 minority (African American), 8 international. Average age 30. In 1997, 10 degrees awarded (100% found work related to degree). *Degree requirements:* Comprehensive exam required, foreign language and thesis not required. *Average time to degree:* master's–1 year full-time, 2 years part-time. *Entrance requirements:* GMAT, minimum GPA of 2.5. Application deadline: 8/30 (rolling processing). Application fee: $15. *Expenses:* Tuition $2428 per year full-time, $83 per semester hour part-time for state residents; $8428 per year full-time, $250 per semester hour part-time for nonresidents. Fees $428 per year. *Financial aid:* Research assistantships available. Financial aid applicants required to submit FAFSA. *Faculty research:* Impact of distance learning, bank management, taxation, inventory systems. Total annual research expenditures: $5500. • Dr. Ara G. Volkan, Chairman, 770-836-6469. Fax: 770-836-6774. E-mail: avolkan@sbf.bus.westga.edu. Application contact: Dr. Jack O. Jenkins, Dean, Graduate School, 770-836-6419. Fax: 770-836-2301. E-mail: jjenkins@cob.as.westga.edu.

Stephen F. Austin State University, College of Business, Program in Professional Accountancy, Nacogdoches, TX 75962. Awards MPA. Students admitted at the undergraduate level. Students: 2 full-time (1 woman); includes 1 minority (African American). 11 applicants, 18% accepted. In 1997, 1 degree awarded. *Degree requirements:* Computer language, comprehensive exam required, foreign language and thesis not required. *Entrance requirements:* GMAT. Application deadline: 8/1 (priority date; rolling processing; 12/15 for spring admission). Application fee: $0 ($25 for international students). *Tuition:* $1465 per year full-time, $263 per semester (minimum) part-time for state residents; $5299 per year full-time, $890 per semester (minimum) part-time for nonresidents. *Financial aid:* In 1997–98, 1 teaching assistantship totaling $5,600 was awarded. Financial aid application deadline: 3/1. • Dr. Jack Ethridge, Chair, 409-468-3105.

Stetson University, School of Business Administration, Program in Accounting, 421 North Woodland Boulevard, DeLand, FL 32720-3781. Awards M Acc. Part-time programs available. Students: 13 full-time (8 women); includes 1 international. Average age 22. 13 applicants, 100% accepted. In 1997, 8 degrees awarded. *Degree requirements:* Computer language required, foreign language and thesis not required. *Entrance requirements:* GMAT. Application deadline: 7/1. Application fee: $25. *Tuition:* $370 per credit hour. *Financial aid:* In 1997–98, 3 research assistantships (all to first-year students) were awarded; Federal Work-Study, institutionally sponsored loans also available. Aid available to part-time students. Financial aid application deadline: 3/15. • Dr. William Jens, Director, 904-822-7415.

Strayer University, Graduate School, 1025 15th Street, NW, Washington, DC 20005-2603. Offerings include professional accounting (MS). Postbaccalaureate distance learning degree programs offered (minimal on-campus study). School faculty: 76 full-time (3 women), 49 part-time (10 women). *Degree requirements:* Thesis required, foreign language not required. *Entrance requirements:* GMAT (minimum score 450), GRE General Test (minimum combined score of 1000), minimum GPA of 2.75. Application deadline: 9/28 (priority date; rolling processing; 4/6 for spring admission). Application fee: $25. Electronic applications accepted. *Tuition:* $6750 per year full-time, $250 per credit hour part-time. • Dr. Samad Hafazi, Director of Graduate Studies, 202-408-2400. Application contact: Michael Williams, Campus Coordinator, 202-408-2400. Fax: 202-289-1831.

Suffolk University, Sawyer School of Management, Department of Accounting, Boston, MA 02108-2770. Offers programs in accounting (MSA, GDPA), taxation (MST). Part-time and evening/weekend programs available. Faculty: 11 full-time (3 women), 6 part-time (1 woman). Students: 5 full-time (3 women), 88 part-time (37 women); includes 4 minority (all Asian Americans), 5 international. Average age 30. 48 applicants, 77% accepted. In 1997, 32 master's awarded. *Entrance requirements:* For master's, GMAT (average 500). Application deadline: 6/15 (priority date; rolling processing; 11/15 for spring admission). Application fee: $50. *Expenses:* Tuition $18,300 per year full-time, $1830 per course part-time. Fees $50 per year full-time, $20 per year part-time. *Financial aid:* In 1997–98, 14 students received aid, including 7 fellowships; Federal Work-Study, institutionally sponsored loans, and career-related internships or fieldwork also available. Aid available to part-time students. Financial aid application deadline: 4/1; applicants required to submit CSS PROFILE. *Faculty research:* Tax policy, tax research, decision making in accounting, accounting information systems, capital markets and strategic planning. • Laurie Pant, Chair, 617-573-8394. E-mail: lpant@acad.suffolk.edu. Application contact: Judy Reynolds, Acting Director of Graduate Admissions, 617-573-8302. Fax: 617-523-0116. E-mail: grad.admission@admin.suffolk.edu.

Announcement: The Department of Accounting and Taxation offers courses of study leading to a Master of Science in Accounting, a Master of Science in Taxation, a 9-course graduate diploma in accounting, and a 5-course advanced certificate in taxation. Specializations are offered in public, international, and forensic accounting; public and private controllerships; and international and estate taxation. Course waivers are offered for appropriate educational and professional experience. Suffolk Accounting and Taxation programs prepare professionals for the global financial market in an era of changing technology and increasing economic complexity. For information and an application, contact the Office of Graduate Admissions (telephone: 617-573-8302; fax: 617-523-0116; e-mail: grad.admission@admin.suffolk.edu).

Syracuse University, School of Management, PhD Program in Business Administration, Syracuse, NY 13244-0003. Offerings include accounting (PhD). Program faculty: 75. *Entrance requirements:* GMAT (minimum score 600). Application deadline: 2/1. Application fee: $40. *Tuition:* $13,320 per year full-time, $555 per credit hour part-time. • S. P. Raj, Associate Dean. Application contact: Barbara Buske, Secretary, 315-443-1001.

Syracuse University, School of Management, Program in Accounting, Syracuse, NY 13244-0003. Awards MBA, MS Acct, JD/MS Acct. Faculty: 12. Students: 8 full-time (6 women), 18 part-time (9 women); includes 1 minority (Asian American), 7 international. 52 applicants, 46% accepted. In 1997, 11 degrees awarded. *Entrance requirements:* GMAT. Application deadline: 2/1 (rolling processing). Application fee: $40. *Tuition:* $13,320 per year full-time, $555 per credit hour part-time. *Financial aid:* Fellowships, research assistantships, teaching assistantships, partial tuition waivers, Federal Work-Study available. Financial aid application deadline: 3/1. • John Anderson, Chair. Application contact: Associate Dean, 315-443-3850.

Temple University, School of Business and Management, Doctoral Program in Business Administration, Philadelphia, PA 19122-6096. Offerings include accounting (PhD). *Degree requirements:* Dissertation, preliminary exams required, foreign language not required. *Entrance requirements:* GMAT, TOEFL (minimum score 600), master's degree, minimum GPA of 3.5. Application deadline: 1/15 (rolling processing). Application fee: $40. *Expenses:* Tuition $323 per semester hour for state residents; $444 per semester hour for nonresidents. Fees $170 per year full-time, $28 per semester (minimum) part-time. • Dr. Roland Lipka, Director, 215-204-8125. Fax: 215-204-5574. Application contact: Linda Whelan, Director, 215-204-7678. Fax: 215-204-8300.

Temple University, School of Business and Management, Master's Program in Business Administration, Philadelphia, PA 19122-6096. Offerings include accounting (MBA, MS). Program faculty: 72 full-time (13 women). *Entrance requirements:* GMAT (average 540), TOEFL (minimum score 575). Application fee: $40. *Expenses:* Tuition $323 per semester hour for state residents; $444 per semester hour for nonresidents. Fees $170 per year full-time, $28 per semester (minimum) part-time. • Application contact: Linda Whelan, Director, 215-204-7678. Fax: 215-204-8300. E-mail: linda@astro.ocis.temple.edu.

Texas A&M International University, Division of Business Administration, Program in Professional Accountancy, 5201 University Boulevard, Laredo, TX 78041-1900. Awards MP Acc. *Entrance requirements:* GMAT or GRE General Test. Application deadline: 7/15 (priority date; rolling processing; 11/12 for spring admission). Application fee: $0.

Announcement: The Graduate School of International Trade and Business Administration's Master of Professional Accountancy is designed to provide graduate-level education to prepare students for careers in accounting requiring higher levels of technical and professional competence. This professional program provides students trained in accounting with problem-solving and managerial skills needed in the practice of accountancy. These skills include the ability to research complex business problems, with special emphasis on the tax implications, and to present the findings in a professional manner. In addition, students gain additional understanding concerning the management of a professional accounting firm or department. Job opportunities include management positions within the accounting, auditing, or treasury functions of a business, governmental agency, or public accounting firm.

Texas A&M University, Lowry Mays Graduate School of Business, Department of Accounting, College Station, TX 77843-4113. Awards MS, PhD. Faculty: 36 full-time (12 women), 1 (woman) part-time. Students: 150 full-time (79 women). Average age 27. 200 applicants, 63% accepted. In 1997, 60 master's, 6 doctorates awarded. Terminal master's awarded for partial completion of doctoral program. *Degree requirements:* For master's, oral comprehensive exam required, foreign language and thesis not required; for doctorate, dissertation required, foreign language not required. *Average time to degree:* master's–1.5 years full-time; doctorate–4 years full-time. *Entrance requirements:* For master's, GMAT, TOEFL (minimum score 600); for doctorate, GMAT or GRE General Test, TOEFL. Application deadline: 3/1 (priority date; rolling processing; 8/1 for spring admission). Application fee: $35 ($75 for international students). *Financial aid:* 100 students received aid; fellowships, research assistantships, teaching assistantships, institutionally sponsored loans, and career-related internships or fieldwork available. Financial aid application deadline: 2/1. *Faculty research:* Financial reporting, taxation management, decision making, accounting information systems, government accounting. • Dr. James J. Benjamin, Head, 409-845-5014. Application contact: Dr. Casper E. Wiggins Jr., Adviser, 409-845-3784. Fax: 409-845-0028. E-mail: casper@tamu.edu.

Texas A&M University–Corpus Christi, College of Business Administration, Corpus Christi, TX 78412-5503. Offerings include accounting (M Acc). *Application deadline:* 7/15 (priority date; rolling processing; 11/15 for spring admission). *Application fee:* $10 ($30 for international students). *Expenses:* Tuition $648 per year full-time, $120 per semester (minimum) part-time for state residents; $4482 per year full-time, $747 per semester (minimum) part-time for nonresidents. Fees $1010 per year full-time, $205 per semester part-time. • Dr. Moustafa H. Abdelsamad, Dean, 512-994-2655. E-mail: addba001@tamucc.edu. Application contact: Mary Margaret Dechant, Director of Admissions, 512-994-2624. Fax: 512-994-5887.

Texas Christian University, M. J. Neeley School of Business, Program in Accounting, Fort Worth, TX 76129-0002. Awards M Ac. Students: 7 (5 women). *Entrance requirements:* GMAT, TOEFL (minimum score 550), 6 hours in economics, 3 hours in college algebra. Application deadline: 4/30 (priority date; rolling processing). Application fee: $50. *Expenses:* Tuition $10,350 per year full-time, $345 per credit hour part-time. Fees $1240 per year full-time, $50 per credit hour part-time. *Financial aid:* Application deadline 5/1. • Application contact: Peggy Conway, Director, MBA Admissions, 817-257-7531. Fax: 817-257-7227. E-mail: p.conway@tcu.edu.

Texas Tech University, Graduate School, College of Business Administration, Program in Accounting, Lubbock, TX 79409. Offers accounting (PhD), controllership (MSA), professional accounting (MSA), taxation (MSA). Part-time programs available. Faculty: 11 full-time (3 women). Students: 60 full-time (31 women), 9 part-time (5 women); includes 4 minority (2 Asian Americans, 2 Hispanics), 1 international. Average age 27. 40 applicants, 90% accepted. In 1997, 36 master's awarded (100% found work related to degree); 2 doctorates awarded (100% entered university research/teaching). *Degree requirements:* For master's, computer language, comprehensive exam required, foreign language and thesis not required; for doctorate, computer language, dissertation, qualifying exams required, foreign language not required. *Entrance requirements:* For master's, GMAT (minimum score 500; average 560), minimum GPA of 3.0; for doctorate, GMAT (minimum score 580; average 620), minimum GPA of 3.0. Application deadline: 4/15 (priority date; rolling processing; 9/30 for spring admission). Application fee: $25 ($50 for international students). *Expenses:* Tuition $864 per year full-time, $120 per semester (minimum) part-time for state residents; $5976 per year full-time, $747 per semester (minimum) part-time for nonresidents. Fees $2321 per year full-time, $302 per semester (minimum) part-time. *Financial aid:* Fellowships, teaching assistantships, scholarships, Federal Work-Study, and career-related internships or fieldwork available. Financial aid applicants required to submit FAFSA. *Faculty research:* Governmental and nonprofit accounting, managerial and financial accounting. • Dr. Dwayne Dowell, Director, 806-742-3181. Application contact: Nancy Dodge, Director, 806-742-3184. Fax: 806-742-3958.

Towson University, Program in Accountancy, Towson, MD 21252-0001. Awards MS. Program new for fall 1998. *Application deadline:* 3/1 (priority date; rolling processing; 10/1 for spring admission). *Application fee:* $40. *Expenses:* Tuition $187 per credit hour for state residents; $364 per credit hour for nonresidents. Fees $40 per credit hour. *Financial aid:* Application deadline 4/1. • Dr. Charles Martin, Director, 410-830-2064. E-mail: chmartin@towson.edu. Application contact: Fran Musotto, Office Manager, 410-830-2501. Fax: 410-830-4675. E-mail: fmusotto@towson.edu.

Trinity University, Division of Behavioral and Administrative Studies, Department of Business Administration, San Antonio, TX 78212-7200. Offers program in accounting (MS). Part-time programs available. Faculty: 8 full-time (3 women). Students: 21 full-time (10 women); includes 5 minority (1 African American, 2 Asian Americans, 2 Hispanics). Average age 22. 35 applicants, 66% accepted. *Entrance requirements:* GMAT, minimum GPA of 3.0, previous course work in accounting, business law. Application deadline: 2/1 (priority date). Application fee: $25. *Expenses:* Tuition $14,580 per year full-time, $608 per hour part-time. Fees $18 per year full-time, $6 per hour part-time. *Financial aid:* In 1997–98, 12 research assistantships (all to first-year students) were awarded. • Dr. Petrea K. Sandlin, Director of the Accounting Program, 210-736-7296. E-mail: psandlin@trinity.edu.

Troy State University Dothan, School of Business, Department of Accounting and Business Law, Dothan, AL 36304-0368. Offers programs in accounting (MS), business law (MS). *Entrance requirements:* GMAT, GRE General Test, or MAT, minimum GPA of 2.5. Application deadline: rolling. Application fee: $20. *Expenses:* Tuition $68 per credit hour for state residents; $140 per credit hour for nonresidents. Fees $2 per credit hour. • Dr. Khamus Bilbeisi, Chair. Application contact: Reta Cordell, Director of Admissions and Records, 334-983-6556. Fax: 334-983-6322. E-mail: rcordell@tsud.edu.

Troy State University Dothan, School of Business, Department of Management and Marketing, Dothan, AL 36304-0368. Offerings include accounting (MBA). *Application deadline:* rolling. *Application fee:* $20. *Expenses:* Tuition $68 per credit hour for state residents; $140 per credit hour for nonresidents. Fees $2 per credit hour. • Dr. Darryel Roberds, Chair. Application contact: Reta Cordell, Director of Admissions and Records, 334-983-6556. Fax: 334-983-6322. E-mail: rcordell@tsud.edu.

Truman State University, Division of Business and Accountancy, Kirksville, MO 63501-4221. Offers program in accounting (M Ac). *Degree requirements:* Comprehensive exams required, foreign language and thesis not required. *Entrance requirements:* GMAT, minimum GPA of 3.0. Application deadline: 6/15 (priority date; rolling processing; 11/1 for spring admission). Application fee: $0 ($25 for international students). *Tuition:* $2718 per year full-time, $151 per credit part-time for state residents; $4824 per year full-time, $268 per credit part-time for nonresidents.

Union College, Graduate and Continuing Studies, Graduate Management Institute, Program in Accounting, Schenectady, NY 12308-2311. Awards MBA. Part-time and evening/weekend programs available. Students: 11 full-time (9 women), 4 part-time (3 women); includes 1 minority (Asian American), 2 international. 1 applicant, 100% accepted. In 1997, 13 degrees

Directory: Accounting

Union College (continued)

awarded. *Degree requirements:* Computer language, comprehensive exam required, foreign language and thesis not required. *Entrance requirements:* GMAT. Application deadline: 5/15 (rolling processing). Application fee: $35. *Tuition:* $1434 per course. *Financial aid:* Research assistantships, full and partial tuition waivers, and career-related internships or fieldwork available. Financial aid application deadline: 5/15. • Dr. Donald F. Arnold, Director, 518-388-6302. Application contact: Carolyn Micklas, Recruiting and Admissions Coordinator, 518-388-6239.

Universidad del Turabo, Programs in Business Administration, Program in Accounting, Gurabo, PR 00778-3030. Awards MBA. Part-time and evening/weekend programs available. *Entrance requirements:* GRE, PAEG, interview. Application deadline: 8/5. Application fee: $25.

Universidad Metropolitana, School of Business Administration, Río Piedras, PR 00928-1150. Offerings include accounting (MBA). School faculty: 4 full-time (2 women), 24 part-time (10 women). *Average time to degree:* master's–1.5 years full-time, 3 years part-time. *Entrance requirements:* GMAT (score in 70th percentile or higher), PAEG (score in 60th percentile or higher). Application deadline: 8/31 (priority date; rolling processing; 1/15 for spring admission). Application fee: $0. • Pedro Hernández, Dean, 787-766-1717 Ext. 6255.

Université de Sherbrooke, Faculty of Administration, Program in Accounting, Sherbrooke, PQ J1K 2R1, Canada. Awards M Sc. *Application deadline:* 5/31. *Application fee:* $15.

Université du Québec à Montréal, Program in Accounting, Montréal, PQ H3C 3P8, Canada. Awards MPA, M Sc, Diploma. Part-time programs available. *Degree requirements:* For master's, thesis required (for some programs), foreign language not required. *Entrance requirements:* For master's, appropriate bachelor's degree or equivalent and proficiency in French. Application deadline: 6/1. Application fee: $50.

Université du Québec à Trois-Rivières, Program in Accounting Science, Trois-Rivières, PQ G9A 5H7, Canada. Awards DESS. Program new for fall 1998. *Application deadline:* 2/1 (rolling processing). *Application fee:* $30. • Jocelyne Josselin, Director, 819-376-5034 Ext. 3111. Fax: 819-376-5180. Application contact: Suzanne Camirand, Admissions Officer, 819-376-5045 Ext. 2591. Fax: 819-376-5210. E-mail: suzanne_camirand@uqtr.uquebec.ca.

The University of Akron, College of Business Administration, School of Accountancy, Akron, OH 44325-0001. Awards MBA, MS, MT, JD/MT. Programs in accountancy (MS), accounting (MBA), taxation (MT). Part-time and evening/weekend programs available. Students: 24 full-time (16 women), 96 part-time (35 women); includes 8 minority (3 African Americans, 2 Asian Americans, 2 Hispanics, 1 Native American), 16 international. Average age 32. 30 applicants, 93% accepted. In 1997, 45 degrees awarded. *Entrance requirements:* GMAT (minimum score 450), minimum GPA of 2.75. Application deadline: 8/15 (rolling processing). Application fee: $25 ($50 for international students). *Expenses:* Tuition $178 per credit hour for state residents; $333 per credit hour for nonresidents. Fees $145 per year full-time, $32 per semester (minimum) part-time. *Financial aid:* In 1997–98, 11 students received aid, including 7 research assistantships, 1 administrative assistantship; teaching assistantships, partial tuition waivers, Federal Work-Study, and career-related internships or fieldwork also available. Financial aid application deadline: 4/30. *Faculty research:* Auditing, municipal bond reporting. • Dr. Mostafa Sarhan, Chair, 330-972-7588. E-mail: msarhan@uakron.edu. Application contact: Dr. J. Daniel Williams, Director of Graduate Business Programs, 330-972-7043. E-mail: jwilliams@uakron.edu.

The University of Alabama, The Manderson Graduate School of Business, Culverhouse School of Accountancy, Program in Accounting, Tuscaloosa, AL 35487. Awards M Acc, PhD. Students: 38 full-time (27 women); includes 5 minority (3 African Americans, 1 Asian American, 1 Hispanic), 3 international. Average age 28. In 1997, 44 master's awarded; 2 doctorates awarded (100% entered university research/teaching). *Degree requirements:* For doctorate, dissertation, comprehensive exam. *Average time to degree:* doctorate–4 years full-time. *Entrance requirements:* For master's, GMAT (minimum score 500; average 580), TOEFL (minimum score 550), minimum GPA of 3.0; for doctorate, GMAT, TOEFL (minimum score 600), minimum GPA of 3.0. Application deadline: 7/6 (rolling processing). Application fee: $25. *Tuition:* $2684 per year full-time, $594 per semester (minimum) part-time for state residents; $7216 per year full-time, $1248 per semester (minimum) part-time for nonresidents. *Financial aid:* In 1997–98, 2 fellowships, 7 research assistantships, 15 teaching assistantships were awarded. Financial aid application deadline: 3/31. • Dr. Thomas Howard, Director, Culverhouse School of Accountancy, 205-348-2907.

The University of Alabama in Huntsville, College of Administrative Science, Huntsville, AL 35899. Offerings include accountancy (M Acc). M Acc new for fall 1998. College faculty: 24 full-time (3 women), 7 part-time (1 woman), 25.75 FTE. *Application deadline:* 7/24 (priority date; rolling processing; 11/15 for spring admission). *Application fee:* $20. Electronic applications accepted. *Tuition:* $2886 per year full-time, $540 per semester (minimum) part-time for state residents; $5298 per year full-time, $1098 per semester (minimum) part-time for nonresidents. • Dr. C. David Billings, Dean, 205-890-6735. Fax: 205-890-6328. E-mail: billind@email.uah.edu.

University of Alberta, Faculty of Graduate Studies and Research, Doctoral Program in Business, Edmonton, AB T6G 2E1, Canada. Offerings include accounting (PhD). Terminal master's awarded for partial completion of doctoral program. Program faculty: 34 full-time (5 women). *Degree requirements:* Dissertation required, foreign language not required. *Average time to degree:* doctorate–6 years full-time, 8.5 years part-time. *Entrance requirements:* GMAT (average 675), TOEFL (minimum score 600; average 627). Application deadline: 3/1 (priority date). Application fee: $60. *Expenses:* Tuition $390 per course for Canadian residents; $781 per course for nonresidents. Fees $500 per year full-time, $184 per year part-time. • Dr. Michael Gibbins, Director, 403-492-2361. Application contact: Jeanette Gosine, Department Office, 403-492-2361. Fax: 403-492-3325. E-mail: jgosine@gpu.srv.ualberta.ca.

The University of Arizona, College of Business and Public Administration, Karl Eller Graduate School of Management, Department of Accounting, Tucson, AZ 85721. Awards M Ac. *Entrance requirements:* GMAT (minimum score 550), GRE General Test, TOEFL (minimum score 550), minimum GPA of 3.0. Application fee: $35. *Tuition:* $2162 per year full-time, $337 per semester (minimum) part-time for state residents; $6860 per year full-time, $1138 per semester (minimum) part-time for nonresidents. *Faculty research:* Auditing, financial reporting and financial markets, taxation policy and markets, behavioral research in accounting.

University of Arkansas, College of Business Administration, Department of Accounting, Fayetteville, AR 72701-1201. Awards M Acc. Faculty: 14 full-time (2 women). Students: 1 (woman) full-time. 10 applicants, 0% accepted. In 1997, 6 degrees awarded. *Entrance requirements:* GMAT. Application fee: $25 ($35 for international students). *Tuition:* $3144 per year full-time, $173 per credit hour part-time for state residents; $7140 per year full-time, $395 per credit hour part-time for nonresidents. *Financial aid:* Research assistantships, Federal Work-Study, and career-related internships or fieldwork available. Aid available to part-time students. Financial aid application deadline: 4/1; applicants required to submit FAFSA. • Dr. Karen Pincus, Chair, 501-575-4051.

University of Baltimore, School of Business, Department of Accounting, Baltimore, MD 21201-5779. Awards MS. Part-time and evening/weekend programs available. Faculty: 12 full-time (4 women), 1 (woman) part-time. Students: 9 full-time (8 women), 23 part-time (14 women); includes 11 minority (6 African Americans, 5 Asian Americans), 3 international. Average age 32. 24 applicants, 67% accepted. In 1997, 7 degrees awarded. *Entrance requirements:* GMAT. Application deadline: 7/15 (priority date; rolling processing; 11/15 for spring admission). Application fee: $30. *Expenses:* Tuition $5736 per year full-time, $239 per credit part-time for state residents; $8544 per year full-time, $356 per credit part-time for nonresidents. Fees $550 per year full-time, $208 per semester (minimum) part-time. *Financial aid:* Federal Work-Study and career-related internships or fieldwork available. Aid available to part-time students. Financial aid application deadline: 4/1; applicants required to submit FAFSA. *Faculty research:* Health care, accounting and administration, managerial accounting, financial accounting theory, accounting information. Total annual research expenditures: $5000. • Application contact: Tracey Jamison, Assistant Director of Admissions, 410-837-4809. Fax: 410-837-4793. E-mail: admissions@ubmail.ubalt.edu.

University of British Columbia, Faculty of Commerce and Business Administration, Doctoral Program in Commerce and Business Administration, Vancouver, BC V6T 1Z2, Canada. Offerings include accounting (PhD). *Degree requirements:* Dissertation required, foreign language not required. *Entrance requirements:* GMAT or GRE, TOEFL. Application deadline: 12/31 (priority date; rolling processing). Application fee: $60.

University of California, Berkeley, Haas School of Business, Doctoral Program in Business, Berkeley, CA 94720-1500. Offerings include accounting (PhD). Program faculty: 64 full-time (11 women). *Degree requirements:* Dissertation, oral exam, written preliminary exams required, foreign language not required. *Entrance requirements:* GMAT or GRE, TOEFL, minimum GPA of 3.0. Application deadline: 2/10. Application fee: $40. *Expenses:* Tuition $0 for state residents; $9384 per year for nonresidents. Fees $4409 per year. • Dr. David C. Mowery, Director, 510-643-9992. E-mail: jan@haas.berkeley.edu. Application contact: Jan Price Greenough, Coordinator, 510-642-1409. Fax: 510-643-6659. E-mail: jan@haas.berkeley.edu.

University of Central Florida, College of Business Administration, Program in Accounting, Orlando, FL 32816. Awards MSA. Part-time and evening/weekend programs available. Faculty: 24. Students: 45 full-time (26 women), 43 part-time (19 women); includes 9 minority (1 African American, 3 Asian Americans, 5 Hispanics), 6 international. Average age 30. 52 applicants, 65% accepted. In 1997, 24 degrees awarded. *Degree requirements:* Thesis or alternative required, foreign language not required. *Entrance requirements:* GMAT. Application deadline: 6/15 (rolling processing; 11/1 for spring admission). Application fee: $20. *Expenses:* Tuition $3288 per year full-time, $137 per credit hour part-time for state residents; $11,520 per year full-time, $480 per credit hour part-time for nonresidents. Fees $105 per year. *Financial aid:* Assistantships, Federal Work-Study, institutionally sponsored loans, and career-related internships or fieldwork available. Aid available to part-time students. • Dr. Andrew J. Judd, Director, 407-823-2876. E-mail: judd@pegasus.cc.ucf.edu. Application contact: Dr. L. Savage, Graduate Adviser, 407-823-5661. E-mail: savage@pegasus.cc.ucf.edu.

University of Charleston, South Carolina, School of Business and Economics, Department of Accounting and Legal Studies, Charleston, SC 29424-0001. Offers program in accountancy (MS). Faculty: 9 full-time (3 women). Students: 16 full-time (10 women), 17 part-time (11 women); includes 1 minority (African American), 1 international. Average age 34. 21 applicants, 81% accepted. In 1997, 13 degrees awarded. *Entrance requirements:* GMAT (minimum score 500), minimum GPA of 3.0 in last 60 hours of undergraduate course work; 24 hours of accounting course work with 6 hours of elementary accounting, 6 hours of intermediate accounting, 3 hours of cost accounting, 3 hours of individual taxation accounting, 3 hours o. Application deadline: rolling. Application fee: $35. *Expenses:* Tuition $2568 per year full-time, $438 per semester (minimum) part-time for state residents; $4596 per year full-time, $876 per semester (minimum) part-time for nonresidents. Fees $51 per year full-time, $21 per semester (minimum) part-time. *Financial aid:* In 1997–98, 2 research assistantships (1 to a first-year student) totaling $7,100 were awarded. Aid available to part-time students. Financial aid applicants required to submit FAFSA. • Dr. Linda Bradley, Program Director, 843-953-8039. Fax: 843-953-5697. Application contact: Laura H. Hines, Graduate School Coordinator, 843-953-5614. Fax: 843-953-1434. E-mail: hinesl@cofc.edu.

University of Chicago, Graduate School of Business, Chicago, IL 60637-1513. Offerings include accounting (MBA). IEMBA offered through the University of Chicago at Barcelona, Spain. School faculty: 114 full-time (17 women), 48 part-time (6 women). *Average time to degree:* master's–2 years full-time, 5 years part-time; doctorate–5.5 years full-time. *Application deadline:* 3/17 (priority date; rolling processing). *Application fee:* $125. • Robert S. Hamada, Dean, 773-702-7121. Application contact: Donald Martin, Director of Admissions and Financial Aid, 773-702-7369. Fax: 773-702-9085.

University of Cincinnati, College of Business Administration, Department of Accounting and Information Systems, Cincinnati, OH 45221. Offers programs in accounting (MBA, PhD), information systems (MBA, PhD). MBA (accounting) offered to full-time students only. Part-time and evening/weekend programs available. Faculty: 4 full-time. Students: 5 full-time (2 women), 23 part-time (9 women); includes 3 minority (all Asian Americans), 4 international. 15 applicants, 20% accepted. In 1997, 10 master's, 3 doctorates awarded. *Degree requirements:* For doctorate, computer language, dissertation. *Average time to degree:* master's–1.3 years full-time; doctorate–6.3 years full-time. *Entrance requirements:* GMAT. Application deadline: 3/1. Application fee: $30. *Tuition:* $7228 per year full-time, $185 per credit hour part-time for state residents; $13,812 per year full-time, $352 per credit hour part-time for nonresidents. *Financial aid:* Graduate assistantships, full tuition waivers available. Aid available to part-time students. Financial aid application deadline: 2/15. • J. Timothy Sale, Head, 513-556-7062. Application contact: James Bast, Assistant Dean, Graduate Programs, 513-556-7020. Fax: 513-556-4891. E-mail: james.bast@uc.edu.

University of Colorado at Boulder, Graduate School of Business Administration, Division of Accounting, Boulder, CO 80309. Awards MS. Students: 19 full-time (11 women), 3 part-time (2 women); includes 1 minority (Asian American), 2 international. Average age 30. 25 applicants, 68% accepted. In 1997, 4 degrees awarded. *Degree requirements:* Computer language required, foreign language and thesis not required. *Entrance requirements:* GMAT. Application deadline: 3/1 (priority date; rolling processing). Application fee: $40 ($60 for international students). *Expenses:* Tuition $3594 per year (minimum) full-time, $597 per semester (minimum) part-time for state residents; $14,868 per year (minimum) full-time, $2478 per semester (minimum) part-time for nonresidents. Fees $667 per year full-time, $130 per semester (minimum) part-time. *Financial aid:* Application deadline 3/1; applicants required to submit FAFSA. • Frank Selto, Chair, 303-492-4271. Fax: 303-492-5962. E-mail: frank.selto@colorado.edu. Application contact: Diana Marinaro, Graduate Student Admissions, 303-492-1831. Fax: 303-492-1727. E-mail: busgrad@spot.colorado.edu.

University of Colorado at Colorado Springs, Graduate School of Business Administration, Colorado Springs, CO 80933-7150. Offerings include accounting (MBA). School faculty: 24 full-time (4 women). *Entrance requirements:* GMAT. Application deadline: 6/1 (priority date; 11/1 for spring admission). Application fee: $50. *Expenses:* Tuition $2860 per year full-time, $121 per credit hour part-time for state residents; $10,254 per year full-time, $420 per credit hour part-time for nonresidents. Fees $399 per year (minimum) full-time, $106 per year (minimum) part-time. • Dr. Richard Dicenza, Dean, 719-262-3113. E-mail: rdicenz@mail.uccs.edu. Application contact: Diane Belger, Adviser, 719-262-3408. Fax: 719-262-3494. E-mail: dbelger@mail.uccs.edu.

University of Colorado at Denver, Graduate School of Business Administration, Division of Accounting, Denver, CO 80217-3364. Awards MS, MBA/MS. Part-time and evening/weekend programs available. Faculty: 8 full-time. Students: 139. In 1997, 31 degrees awarded. *Entrance requirements:* GMAT (minimum score 400; average 520), TOEFL (minimum score 525; average 560). Application deadline: 7/1 (priority date; rolling processing; 11/1 for spring admission). Application fee: $50 ($60 for international students). *Expenses:* Tuition $3754 per year full-time, $225 per semester hour part-time for state residents; $12,962 per year full-time, $777 per semester hour part-time for nonresidents. Fees $252 per year. *Financial aid:* Application deadline 4/1. *Faculty research:* Transfer pricing, behavioral accounting, environmental accounting, health services, international auditing. • Dennis Murray, Director, 303-556-5891. Fax: 303-556-5899. Application contact: Lori Cain, Graduate Business Admissions Office, 303-556-5900. Fax: 303-556-5904. E-mail: lori_cain@maroon.cudenver.edu.

University of Connecticut, School of Business Administration, Storrs, CT 06269. Offerings include accounting (MBA, PhD). School faculty: 63. *Degree requirements:* For doctorate, dissertation. *Entrance requirements:* For master's, GMAT; for doctorate, GMAT, TOEFL. Application deadline: 6/1 (priority date; rolling processing; 11/1 for spring admission). Application fee: $40 ($45 for international students). *Expenses:* Tuition $5272 per year full-time, $293 per credit part-time for state residents; $13,696 per year full-time, $761 per credit part-time for nonresidents. Fees $948 per year full-time, $640 per year part-time. • Thomas G. Gutteridge, Dean, 860-486-3096. Application contact: David W. Palmer, Chairperson, 860-486-3096.

University of Delaware, College of Business and Economics, Department of Accounting, Newark, DE 19716. Awards MS. Part-time and evening/weekend programs available. Faculty: 12 full-time (1 woman). Students: 8 full-time (6 women), 7 part-time (4 women); includes 1 minority (Asian American), 5 international. Average age 32. 17 applicants, 71% accepted. In 1997, 4 degrees awarded. *Degree requirements:* Thesis optional, foreign language not required. *Entrance requirements:* GMAT (minimum score 500), TOEFL (minimum score 600). Application deadline: 7/1 (rolling processing; 12/1 for spring admission). Application fee: $45. Electronic applications accepted. *Expenses:* Tuition $4250 per year full-time, $236 per credit hour part-time for state residents; $12,250 per year full-time, $681 per credit hour part-time for nonresidents. Fees $466 per year full-time, $15 per semester (minimum) part-time. *Financial aid:* In 1997–98, 3 research assistantships, 3 scholarships (all to first-year students) were awarded; fellowships and career-related internships or fieldwork also available. Financial aid application deadline: 4/1. *Faculty research:* External reporting, managerial accounting, auditing information systems, taxation. • Dr. Kent St. Pierre, Chairman, 302-831-2961.

University of Denver, Daniels College of Business, School of Accountancy, Denver, CO 80208. Offers programs in accountancy (M Acc), accounting (MBA). Part-time and evening/weekend programs available. Faculty: 14 full-time (3 women). Students: 23 full-time (13 women), 7 part-time (2 women); includes 11 international. Average age 30. 43 applicants, 88% accepted. In 1997, 23 degrees awarded. *Entrance requirements:* GMAT (average 545). Application deadline: 5/1 (priority date; rolling processing; 1/1 for spring admission). Application fee: $50. *Expenses:* Tuition $18,216 per year full-time, $506 per credit hour part-time. Fees $159 per year. *Financial aid:* In 1997–98, 14 students received aid, including 6 teaching assistantships averaging $555 per month and totaling $29,967, 6 grants, scholarships totaling $6,550; research assistantships, Federal Work-Study, institutionally sponsored loans, and career-related internships or fieldwork also available. Aid available to part-time students. Financial aid application deadline: 2/15; applicants required to submit FAFSA. *Faculty research:* Management accounting, activity-based management, benchmarking, financial management and human services, derivatives. • Dr. Ronald Kucic, Director, 303-871-3337. Application contact: Jan Johnson, Executive Director, Student Services, 303-871-3416. Fax: 303-871-4466. E-mail: dcb@du.edu.

University of Florida, College of Business Administration, Fisher School of Accounting, Gainesville, FL 32611. Awards M Acc, PhD, JD/M Acc. Part-time programs available. Faculty: 14 full-time (1 woman). Students: 176 full-time (73 women), 67 part-time (36 women); includes 36 minority (2 African Americans, 13 Asian Americans, 21 Hispanics), 12 international. 133 applicants, 64% accepted. In 1997, 106 master's awarded; 3 doctorates awarded (100% entered university research/teaching). Terminal master's awarded for partial completion of doctoral program. *Degree requirements:* For doctorate, computer language, dissertation required, foreign language not required. *Average time to degree:* doctorate–5 years full-time. *Entrance requirements:* For master's, GMAT (minimum score 550) or GRE General Test (minimum combined score of 1200), minimum GPA of 3.0; for doctorate, GRE General Test, minimum GPA of 3.0. Application deadline: 6/5 (rolling processing). Application fee: $20. *Tuition:* $138 per credit hour for state residents; $481 per credit hour for nonresidents. *Financial aid:* In 1997–98, 43 students received aid, including 23 fellowships averaging $430 per month, 19 teaching assistantships averaging $500 per month, 1 graduate assistantship averaging $320 per month; research assistantships, Federal Work-Study also available. Aid available to part-time students. *Faculty research:* Auditing/financial accounting, accounting systems, taxation. • Dr. Douglas Snowball, Director, 352-392-0155. E-mail: snowbal@nervm.nerdc.ufl.edu. Application contact: Dominique Santiago, Graduate Coordinator, 352-392-0155. Fax: 352-392-7962. E-mail: desantda@dale.cba.ufl.edu.

University of Georgia, Terry College of Business, J. M. Tull School of Accounting, Athens, GA 30602. Awards M Acc, JD/M Acc. Faculty: 10 full-time (2 women). Students: 36 full-time, 3 part-time (all women); includes 1 minority (African American), 10 international. 38 applicants, 47% accepted. In 1997, 29 degrees awarded. *Entrance requirements:* GMAT. Application deadline: 7/1 (priority date; 11/15 for spring admission). Application fee: $30. Electronic applications accepted. *Tuition:* $3290 per year full-time, $643 per semester (minimum) part-time for state residents; $11,300 per year full-time, $1645 per semester (minimum) part-time for nonresidents. *Financial aid:* Fellowships, research assistantships, teaching assistantships, assistantships available. • Dr. Russell M. Barefield Jr., Director, 706-542-4234. E-mail: rbarefield@cba.uga.edu. Application contact: Dr. Jennifer J. Gaver, Graduate Coordinator, 706-542-3600. Fax: 706-542-7196. E-mail: phoyt@cba.uga.edu.

University of Hartford, Barney School of Business and Public Administration, Program in Business Administration, West Hartford, CT 06117-1599. Offerings include accounting (MBA). Program faculty: 24 full-time (4 women), 15 part-time (1 woman). *Average time to degree:* master's–1.5 years full-time, 3 years part-time. *Entrance requirements:* GMAT, TOEFL. Application deadline: 7/1 (priority date; rolling processing; 12/1 for spring admission). Application fee: $35 ($50 for international students). Electronic applications accepted. • Christopher Galligan, Director, 860-768-4390. Application contact: Claire Silverstein, Assistant Director, 860-768-4900. Fax: 860-768-4821. E-mail: silverste@unavax.hartford.edu.

University of Hartford, Barney School of Business and Public Administration, Department of Accounting, Program in Accounting, West Hartford, CT 06117-1599. Awards MSPA. Part-time and evening/weekend programs available. Faculty: 6 full-time (2 women), 2 part-time (0 women). Students: 26 full-time, 27 part-time; includes 8 international. Average age 28. 18 applicants, 83% accepted. In 1997, 25 degrees awarded. *Average time to degree:* master's–1.5 years full-time, 3 years part-time. *Entrance requirements:* GMAT, TOEFL. Application deadline: 7/1 (priority date; rolling processing; 12/1 for spring admission). Application fee: $35 ($50 for international students). Electronic applications accepted. *Financial aid:* Research assistantships, institutionally sponsored loans, and career-related internships or fieldwork available. Financial aid application deadline: 5/1. • Application contact: Claire Silverstein, Assistant Director, 860-768-4900. Fax: 860-768-4821. E-mail: silverste@unavax.hartford.edu.

University of Hawaii at Manoa, College of Business Administration, School of Accountancy, Honolulu, HI 96822. Awards M Acc. Part-time programs available. Faculty: 11 full-time (3 women). Students: 8 full-time (2 women), 7 part-time (5 women); includes 6 international. Average age 29. 22 applicants, 27% accepted. In 1997, 12 degrees awarded. *Average time to degree:* master's–1.5 years full-time, 3 years part-time. *Entrance requirements:* GMAT (minimum score 500; average 550), bachelor's degree in accounting, minimum GPA of 3.0. Application deadline: 3/1. Application fee: $25 ($50 for international students). *Tuition:* $4029 per year full-time, $214 per credit hour part-time for state residents; $9957 per year full-time, $461 per credit hour part-time for nonresidents. *Financial aid:* Full tuition waivers, Federal Work-Study, and career-related internships or fieldwork available. *Faculty research:* International accounting, current tax topics, insurance industry financial reporting, behavioral accounting, auditing. Total annual research expenditures: $15,000. • Dr. David Yang, Director, 808-956-6975. Fax: 808-956-9888. E-mail: soa@busadm.cba.hawaii.edu. Application contact: Student Academic Services, 808-956-8266. Fax: 808-956-9890.

University of Houston, College of Business Administration, Department of Accountancy and Taxation, 4800 Calhoun, Houston, TX 77204-2163. Offers programs in accountancy (MS Accy), accounting (MBA, PhD), taxation (MBA). Part-time and evening/weekend programs available. Faculty: 22 full-time (7 women), 3 part-time (1 woman). Students: 38 full-time (17 women), 44 part-time (21 women); includes 21 minority (6 African Americans, 12 Asian Americans, 2 Hispanics, 1 Native American), 11 international. Average age 32. In 1997, 39 master's awarded. *Degree requirements:* For master's, computer language required, foreign language and thesis not required; for doctorate, computer language, dissertation, comprehensive exam required, foreign language not required. *Average time to degree:* master's–2 years full-time, 3.5 years part-time; doctorate–4.5 years full-time. *Entrance requirements:* For master's, GMAT (average 575), TOEFL (minimum score 620); for doctorate, GMAT or GRE. Application deadline: 5/1 (rolling processing; 10/1 for spring admission). Application fee: $50 ($125 for international students). *Expenses:* Tuition $1152 per year full-time, $120 per semester (minimum) part-time for state residents; $4482 per year full-time, $249 per credit hour part-time for nonresidents. Fees $977 per year full-time, $119 per semester (minimum) part-time. *Financial aid:* Research assistantships, teaching assistantships, Federal Work-Study, and career-related internships or fieldwork available. Aid available to part-time students. Financial aid application deadline: 3/1; applicants required to submit FAFSA. • Dr. Gary Schugart, Chairperson, 713-743-4820. Fax: 713-743-4828. Application contact: Office of Student Services, 713-743-4900. Fax: 713-743-4942. E-mail: oss@cba.uh.edu.

University of Houston–Clear Lake, School of Business and Public Administration, Program in Accounting, Houston, TX 77058-1098. Awards MS. Faculty: 6. Students: 48 full-time, 38 part-time; includes 22 minority (3 African Americans, 16 Asian Americans, 3 Hispanics), 19 international. Average age 32. 35 applicants, 89% accepted. In 1997, 17 degrees awarded. *Degree requirements:* Thesis optional, foreign language not required. *Entrance requirements:* GMAT (average 510). Application deadline: 8/1 (rolling processing; 12/1 for spring admission). Application fee: $30 ($60 for international students). *Tuition:* $207 per credit hour for state residents; $336 per credit hour for nonresidents. *Financial aid:* Teaching assistantships available. Financial aid application deadline: 5/1. • Dr. Joan Bruno, Chair, 281-283-3107. Application contact: Dr. Sue Neeley, Associate Dean, 281-283-3110.

University of Idaho, College of Graduate Studies, College of Business and Economics, Department of Accounting, Moscow, ID 83844-4140. Awards M Acct. Faculty: 8 full-time (3 women). Students: 5 full-time (2 women), 6 part-time (2 women); includes 1 minority (African American), 3 international. In 1997, 1 degree awarded. *Degree requirements:* Comprehensive exam required, foreign language not required. *Entrance requirements:* Minimum GPA of 3.0. Application deadline: 8/1 (12/15 for spring admission). Application fee: $35 ($45 for international students). *Expenses:* Tuition $0 for state residents; $6000 per year full-time, $95 per credit part-time for nonresidents. Fees $2676 per year full-time, $134 per credit part-time. *Financial aid:* In 1997–98, 1 teaching assistantship (to a first-year student) averaging $1,556 per month and totaling $14,007 was awarded. Financial aid application deadline: 2/15. • Marcia Niles, Head, 208-885-7238. Fax: 208-885-8939. E-mail: marcian@novell.widaho.edu.

University of Illinois at Chicago, College of Business Administration, Department of Accounting, Chicago, IL 60607-7128. Awards MS, MBA/MS. Part-time programs available. Faculty: 10 full-time (2 women). Students: 36 full-time (21 women), 29 part-time (11 women); includes 10 minority (3 African Americans, 4 Asian Americans, 3 Hispanics), 29 international. Average age 29. 43 applicants, 42% accepted. In 1997, 23 degrees awarded. *Degree requirements:* Computer language required, foreign language and thesis not required. *Entrance requirements:* GMAT, TOEFL (minimum score 570), minimum GPA of 3.75 on a 5.0 scale. Application deadline: 7/3 (11/8 for spring admission). Application fee: $30 ($40 for international students). *Financial aid:* In 1997–98, 13 research assistantships, 2 teaching assistantships were awarded; fellowships, full tuition waivers, Federal Work-Study, institutionally sponsored loans, and career-related internships or fieldwork also available. Aid available to part-time students. Financial aid application deadline: 2/15. *Faculty research:* Governmental accounting, managerial accounting, auditing. • Ahmed Riahi-Belkaoui, Director of Graduate Studies, 312-996-2869. Application contact: Ann Rosi, Graduate Business Programs, 312-996-4751.

University of Illinois at Springfield, School of Business and Management, Program in Accountancy, Springfield, IL 62794-9243. Awards MA. Part-time and evening/weekend programs available. Faculty: 6 full-time (1 woman), 5 part-time (1 woman), 7.25 FTE. Students: 9 full-time (6 women), 46 part-time (24 women); includes 5 minority (3 African Americans, 2 Asian Americans), 2 international. Average age 35. 19 applicants, 79% accepted. In 1997, 3 degrees awarded. *Degree requirements:* Thesis or alternative required, foreign language not required. *Application deadline:* rolling. *Application fee:* $0. *Expenses:* Tuition $99 per credit hour for state residents; $296 per credit hour for nonresidents. Fees $242 per year full-time, $63 per semester (minimum) part-time. *Financial aid:* In 1997–98, 15 students received aid, including 1 assistantship averaging $606 per month; research assistantships, partial tuition waivers, Federal Work-Study, and career-related internships or fieldwork also available. Aid available to part-time students. Financial aid application deadline: 6/1; applicants required to submit FAFSA. *Faculty research:* Capital gains taxation, international accounting, tax equity, accounting disclosures on annual reports. • Leonard Branson, Chair, 217-786-6305.

University of Illinois at Urbana–Champaign, College of Commerce and Business Administration, Department of Accountancy, Urbana, IL 61801. Awards MAS, MS, PhD. Faculty: 25 full-time (5 women). Students: 107 full-time (51 women); includes 16 minority (3 African Americans, 13 Asian Americans), 44 international. 158 applicants, 55% accepted. In 1997, 57 master's, 3 doctorates awarded. *Degree requirements:* For doctorate, dissertation required, foreign language not required. *Entrance requirements:* For master's, GMAT (minimum score 540; average 595), TSE; for doctorate, GMAT (minimum score 620; average 681), TSE. Application deadline: rolling. Application fee: $40 ($50 for international students). *Financial aid:* In 1997–98, 3 fellowships, 3 research assistantships, 40 teaching assistantships were awarded; full and partial tuition waivers also available. Financial aid application deadline: 2/15. • Eugene Willis, Head, 217-333-2451.

See in-depth description on page 455.

University of Indianapolis, Graduate Business Programs, Indianapolis, IN 46227-3697. Offerings include accounting (M Acc). *Average time to degree:* master's–2 years full-time, 4 years part-time. *Application deadline:* rolling. *Application fee:* $30.

The University of Iowa, College of Business Administration, Department of Accounting, Iowa City, IA 52242-1316. Awards M Ac, PhD, JD/MBA, JD/M Ac. Programs in accountancy (M Ac), business administration (PhD). Part-time programs available. Faculty: 13 full-time (2 women), 2 part-time (1 woman), 14 FTE. Students: 39 full-time (18 women), 2 part-time (both women); includes 3 minority (1 African American, 1 Asian American, 1 Hispanic), 10 international. Average age 27. 78 applicants, 44% accepted. In 1997, 10 master's awarded; 1 doctorate awarded (100% entered university research/teaching). Terminal master's awarded for partial completion of doctoral program. *Degree requirements:* For master's, comprehensive exam required, foreign language and thesis not required; for doctorate, dissertation, thesis defense required, foreign language not required. *Average time to degree:* master's–1.5 years full-time, 3 years part-time; doctorate–5 years full-time. *Entrance requirements:* For master's, GMAT (minimum score 550), TOEFL (minimum score 600), minimum GPA of 3.0; for doctorate, GMAT (minimum score 600), TOEFL (minimum score 600). Application deadline: 7/15 (priority date; rolling processing; 12/1 for spring admission). Application fee: $30 ($50 for international students). *Expenses:* Tuition $3166 per year full-time, $176 per semester hour part-time for state residents; $10,202 per year full-time, $176 per semester hour part-time for nonresidents. Fees $202 per year full-time, $52 per year (minimum) part-time. *Financial aid:* In 1997–98, 32 students received aid, including 3 fellowships (all to first-year students), 3 research assistantships totaling $11,500, 23 teaching assistantships (4 to first-year students); Federal Work-Study and career-related internships or fieldwork also available. Financial aid applicants required to submit FAFSA. *Faculty research:* Capital markets, experimental economics, behavioral decision making, managerial and modeling. Total annual research expenditures: $70,000. • Daniel W. Collins, Chair, 319-335-0910. E-mail: daniel-collins@uiowa.edu. Application contact: Steve Reimer, Lecturer/Adviser, 319-335-0918. Fax: 319-335-1956. E-mail: steven-reimer@uiowa.edu.

University of Kansas, School of Business, Program in Accounting, Lawrence, KS 66045. Awards MAIS, PhD. Students: 49 full-time (28 women), 5 part-time (4 women); includes 6 minority (1 African American, 4 Asian Americans, 1 Hispanic), 12 international. In 1997, 35

Directory: Accounting

University of Kansas (continued)

master's awarded. *Degree requirements:* For doctorate, dissertation, departmental qualifying exam required, foreign language not required. *Entrance requirements:* For master's, GMAT (minimum score 580); for doctorate, GMAT (minimum score 650). Application deadline: 5/1 (priority date; rolling processing). Application fee: $50. *Expenses:* Tuition $2400 per year full-time, $100 per credit hour part-time for state residents; $7890 per year full-time, $329 per credit hour part-time for nonresidents. Fees $428 per year full-time, $31 per credit hour part-time. *Financial aid:* Fellowships, research assistantships, teaching assistantships available. *Faculty research:* Audit; artificial intelligence; agency theory; compensation; production, regulation, and use of accounting information. • Beverly Wilson, Director, Accounting Division, 785-864-4500. E-mail: grad@bschool.wpo.ukans.edu. Application contact: David Collins, Associate Director, Master's Program, 785-864-4254. Fax: 785-864-5328. E-mail: grad@bschool.wpo.ukans.edu.

University of Kentucky, Graduate School Programs from the College of Business and Economics, Program in Accounting, Lexington, KY 40506-0032. Awards MSACC. Faculty: 18 full-time (4 women). Students: 15 full-time (11 women), 5 part-time (3 women); includes 1 minority (Asian American), 3 international. 32 applicants, 50% accepted. In 1997, 15 degrees awarded. *Degree requirements:* Comprehensive exam required, foreign language and thesis not required. *Entrance requirements:* GMAT (minimum score 550), minimum undergraduate GPA of 3.0. Application deadline: 7/19 (rolling processing). Application fee: $30 ($35 for international students). *Financial aid:* Fellowships, Federal Work-Study, institutionally sponsored loans, and career-related internships or fieldwork available. Aid available to part-time students. *Faculty research:* Taxation, financial accounting and auditing, managerial accounting, not-for-profit accounting. • Dr. James A. Knoblett, Director of Graduate Studies, 606-257-1763. Fax: 606-323-3654. Application contact: Dr. Constance L. Wood, Associate Dean, 606-257-4613. Fax: 606-323-1928.

University of Manitoba, Faculty of Management, Department of Accounting and Finance, Program in Accounting, Winnipeg, MB R3T 2N2, Canada. Awards MBA. *Degree requirements:* Thesis or alternative.

The University of Memphis, Fogelman College of Business and Economics, Accountancy Area, Memphis, TN 38152. Offers programs in accounting (MS), accounting systems (MS), taxation (MS). Faculty: 12 full-time (1 woman). Students: 8 full-time (4 women), 31 part-time (23 women); includes 3 minority (all African Americans), 6 international. Average age 31. 22 applicants, 82% accepted. In 1997, 31 degrees awarded. *Degree requirements:* Comprehensive exams required, thesis not required. *Entrance requirements:* GMAT. Application deadline: 8/1 (12/1 for spring admission). Application fee: $25 ($50 for international students). *Tuition:* $2862 per year full-time, $166 per credit hour part-time for state residents; $6696 per year full-time, $379 per credit hour part-time for nonresidents. *Financial aid:* In 1997–98, 8 research assistantships totaling $32,500, 9 teaching assistantships totaling $74,500 were awarded. *Faculty research:* Financial accounting, bartering, EDP auditing, evolution of system analysis, product life cycle costing. • Application contact: Dr. Ravinder Nath, Associate Dean of Academic Programs, 901-678-3721. Fax: 901-678-4705. E-mail: fcbegp@memphis.edu.

The University of Memphis, Fogelman College of Business and Economics, Program in Business Administration, Memphis, TN 38152. Offerings include accounting (MBA, PhD). Program faculty: 92 full-time (15 women), 2 part-time (0 women). *Degree requirements:* For doctorate, dissertation, comprehensive exams. *Entrance requirements:* For doctorate, GMAT (average 633), interview, minimum GPA of 3.4. Application deadline: 8/1 (12/1 for spring admission). Application fee: $25 ($50 for international students). *Tuition:* $2862 per year full-time, $166 per credit hour part-time for state residents; $6696 per year full-time, $379 per credit hour part-time for nonresidents. • Application contact: Dr. Ravinder Nath, Associate Dean of Academic Programs, 901-678-3721. Fax: 901-678-4705. E-mail: fcbegp@memphis.edu.

University of Miami, School of Business Administration, Department of Accounting, Coral Gables, FL 33124. Offers programs in accounting (MBA), professional accounting (MP Acc), taxation (MS Tax). Part-time and evening/weekend programs available. Faculty: 11 full-time (4 women), 2 part-time (0 women). Students: 46 full-time (14 women), 25 part-time (10 women); includes 39 minority (3 African Americans, 8 Asian Americans, 28 Hispanics), 8 international. Average age 24. 52 applicants, 65% accepted. In 1997, 28 degrees awarded. *Degree requirements:* Computer language required, foreign language and thesis not required. *Average time to degree:* master's–1.2 years full-time, 2.1 years part-time. *Entrance requirements:* GMAT (minimum score 500; average 580) or CPA exam, TOEFL (minimum score 550; average 650). Application deadline: 7/30 (priority date; rolling processing; 11/30 for spring admission). Application fee: $35. *Expenses:* Tuition $815 per credit hour. Fees $174 per year. *Financial aid:* 20 students received aid; scholarships, Federal Work-Study, institutionally sponsored loans, and career-related internships or fieldwork available. Aid available to part-time students. Financial aid application deadline: 3/1. *Faculty research:* Behavioral research in accounting, financial reporting, audit risk, public policy and taxation issues, government accounting and public choice. • Dr. Paul Munter, Chairman, 305-284-5492. Fax: 305-284-5737.

University of Minnesota, Twin Cities Campus, Carlson School of Management, Department of Accounting, Minneapolis, MN 55455-0213. Awards MBA, PhD. MBA offered jointly with the Master's Program in Business Administration; PhD offered jointly with the Doctoral Program in Business Administration. *Degree requirements:* For doctorate, dissertation required, foreign language not required. *Entrance requirements:* GMAT. *Faculty research:* Experimental markets, information economics, behavioral sciences, audit.

University of Mississippi, Graduate School, School of Accountancy, University, MS 38677-9702. Offers programs in accountancy (M Acc, PhD), taxation accounting (M Tax). Faculty: 11 full-time (3 women). Students: 83 full-time (31 women), 21 part-time (9 women); includes 10 minority (8 African Americans, 1 Hispanic, 1 Native American), 2 international. In 1997, 50 master's, 1 doctorate awarded. *Degree requirements:* For doctorate, dissertation. *Entrance requirements:* For master's, GMAT, TOEFL, minimum GPA of 3.0; for doctorate, GMAT, TOEFL. Application deadline: 8/1 (rolling processing). Application fee: $0 ($25 for international students). *Financial aid:* Application deadline 3/1. • Dr. James W. Davis, Dean, 601-232-7468.

University of Missouri–Columbia, College of Business and Public Administration, School of Accountancy, Columbia, MO 65211. Awards MA, M Acc, MS, PhD. Part-time programs available. Faculty: 14 full-time (4 women). Students: 14 full-time (12 women), 7 part-time (3 women); includes 1 minority (Native American), 1 international. In 1997, 10 master's, 2 doctorates awarded. *Degree requirements:* For master's, thesis or alternative required, foreign language not required; for doctorate, dissertation required, foreign language not required. *Entrance requirements:* For master's, GMAT, minimum GPA of 3.0; for doctorate, minimum GPA of 3.0. Application deadline: 2/15 (priority date; rolling processing). Application fee: $25 ($50 for international students). *Expenses:* Tuition $3240 per year full-time, $180 per credit hour part-time for state residents; $9108 per year full-time, $506 per credit hour part-time for nonresidents. Fees $55 per year full-time. *Financial aid:* Fellowships, Federal Work-Study available. Aid available to part-time students. • Dr. Raymond Dockweiler, Director of Graduate Studies, 573-882-3478.

University of Missouri–Kansas City, School of Business and Public Administration, Division of Accountancy, Kansas City, MO 64110-2499. Offers program in accounting (MS). Part-time and evening/weekend programs available. Faculty: 9 full-time (2 women), 6 part-time (2 women), 12 FTE. Students: 52 full-time (33 women), 82 part-time (43 women); includes 14 minority (2 African Americans, 11 Asian Americans, 1 Hispanic), 28 international. Average age 30. 73 applicants, 70% accepted. In 1997, 52 degrees awarded. *Degree requirements:* Computer language required, foreign language and thesis not required. *Entrance requirements:* GMAT (minimum score 450; average 536), minimum GPA of 2.5. Application deadline: 5/1 (priority date; rolling processing; 10/1 for spring admission). Application fee: $25. *Expenses:* Tuition $182 per credit hour for state residents; $508 per credit hour for nonresidents. Fees $60 per year. *Financial aid:* Fellowships, research assistantships, teaching assistantships, full and partial tuition waivers, Federal Work-Study, institutionally sponsored loans, and career-related internships or fieldwork available. Aid available to part-time students. Financial aid applicants required to submit FAFSA. *Faculty research:* Taxation, auditing, information systems, international accounting. Total annual research expenditures: $15,000. • Dr. L. E. Krueger, Director, 816-235-2218. Application contact: Admissions Office, 816-235-1111.

University of Missouri–St. Louis, School of Business Administration, Program in Accounting, St. Louis, MO 63121-4499. Awards M Acc. Part-time and evening/weekend programs available. Faculty: 10 (4 women). Students: 1 (woman) full-time, 28 part-time (14 women); includes 2 minority (both Asian Americans). 15 applicants, 47% accepted. In 1997, 8 degrees awarded. *Entrance requirements:* GMAT (minimum score 500; average 580). Application deadline: 7/1 (rolling processing; 11/1 for spring admission). Application fee: $0. Electronic applications accepted. *Expenses:* Tuition $3903 per year full-time, $167 per credit hour part-time for state residents; $11,745 per year full-time, $489 per credit hour part-time for nonresidents. Fees $816 per year full-time, $34 per credit hour part-time. *Financial aid:* In 1997–98, 11 research assistantships, 2 teaching assistantships were awarded; Federal Work-Study, institutionally sponsored loans, and career-related internships or fieldwork also available. Aid available to part-time students. Financial aid application deadline: 4/1; applicants required to submit FAFSA. *Faculty research:* Auditor judgement, decision support in accounting research. • Application contact: Graduate Admissions, 314-516-5458. Fax: 314-516-6759. E-mail: gradadm@umslvma.umsl.edu.

University of Missouri–St. Louis, School of Business Administration, Program in Business Administration, St. Louis, MO 63121-4499. Offerings include accounting (MBA). Program faculty: 19 (3 women). *Entrance requirements:* GMAT (minimum score 500; average 554). Application deadline: 7/1 (rolling processing; 11/1 for spring admission). Application fee: $0. Electronic applications accepted. *Expenses:* Tuition $3903 per year full-time, $167 per credit hour part-time for state residents; $11,745 per year full-time, $489 per credit hour part-time for nonresidents. Fees $816 per year full-time, $34 per credit hour part-time. • Application contact: Graduate Admissions, 314-516-5458. Fax: 314-516-6759. E-mail: gradadm@umslvma.umsl.edu.

The University of Montana–Missoula, School of Business Administration, Department of Accounting and Finance, Missoula, MT 59812-0002. Awards M Acct. Faculty: 10 full-time (1 woman). Students: 21 full-time (8 women); includes 3 minority (all Asian Americans), 7 international. Average age 30. 25 applicants, 84% accepted. In 1997, 20 degrees awarded. *Degree requirements:* Thesis optional, foreign language not required. *Average time to degree:* master's–1 year full-time. *Entrance requirements:* GMAT (average 545), TOEFL (minimum score 580). Application deadline: 3/1 (priority date; 9/1 for spring admission). Application fee: $30. *Tuition:* $2499 per year (minimum) full-time, $376 per semester (minimum) part-time for state residents; $6528 per year (minimum) full-time, $1048 per semester (minimum) part-time for nonresidents. *Financial aid:* In 1997–98, 3 teaching assistantships (all to first-year students) averaging $736 per month and totaling $22,080 were awarded; fellowships, research assistantships, Federal Work-Study, institutionally sponsored loans, and career-related internships or fieldwork also available. Aid available to part-time students. Financial aid application deadline: 3/1. *Faculty research:* Income tax, financial markets, nonprofit accounting, accounting information systems, auditing. • Dr. Bruce Budge, Chair, 406-243-2233. Application contact: Dr. Teresa K. Beed, Director of Graduate Programs, 406-243-4983. Fax: 406-243-2086.

University of Nebraska at Omaha, College of Business Administration, Program in Accounting, Omaha, NE 68182. Awards MPA. Part-time and evening/weekend programs available. Faculty: 7 full-time (0 women). Students: 1 part-time (0 women). Average age 34. 10 applicants, 60% accepted. In 1997, 7 degrees awarded. *Degree requirements:* Comprehensive exam required, foreign language and thesis not required. *Entrance requirements:* GMAT (minimum score 500), GRE General Test, minimum GPA of 3.0. Application deadline: 7/1 (priority date; rolling processing; 12/1 for spring admission). Application fee: $35. *Expenses:* Tuition $1670 per year full-time, $94 per credit hour part-time for state residents; $4082 per year full-time, $227 per credit hour part-time for nonresidents. Fees $302 per year full-time, $108 per semester (minimum) part-time. *Financial aid:* Research assistantships, full tuition waivers, institutionally sponsored loans available. Aid available to part-time students. Financial aid application deadline: 3/1; applicants required to submit FAFSA. • Dr. H. P. Garsombke, Chairperson, 402-554-2744. Application contact: Dr. Richard Ortman, Adviser, 402-554-3650.

University of Nebraska–Lincoln, College of Business Administration, Interdepartmental Area of Business, Lincoln, NE 68588. Offerings include accountancy (PhD). Faculty: 26 full-time (2 women), 2 part-time (0 women), 27.05 FTE. *Degree requirements:* Dissertation, comprehensive exams required, foreign language not required. *Average time to degree:* doctorate–5.2 years full-time. *Entrance requirements:* GMAT, TOEFL (minimum score 500). Application deadline: 5/15 (10/15 for spring admission). Application fee: $35. Electronic applications accepted. *Expenses:* Tuition $110 per credit hour for state residents; $270 per credit hour for nonresidents. Fees $480 per year full-time, $110 per semester part-time. • Dr. Gordon Karels, Graduate Committee Chair, 402-472-9500. Fax: 402-472-5180. E-mail: gradadv@cbamail.unl.edu.

University of Nebraska–Lincoln, College of Business Administration, School of Accountancy, Lincoln, NE 68588. Awards MPA, PhD, JD/MPA. Faculty: 8 full-time (2 women). Students: 18 full-time (15 women), 9 part-time (7 women); includes 1 minority (Asian American), 2 international. Average age 30. 20 applicants, 40% accepted. In 1997, 15 master's awarded. *Entrance requirements:* For master's, GMAT, TOEFL (minimum score 550). Application deadline: 6/15 (11/15 for spring admission). Application fee: $35. Electronic applications accepted. *Expenses:* Tuition $110 per credit hour for state residents; $270 per credit hour for nonresidents. Fees $480 per year full-time, $110 per semester part-time. *Financial aid:* In 1997–98, 9 teaching assistantships totaling $94,650 were awarded; fellowships, research assistantships, Federal Work-Study also available. Aid available to part-time students. Financial aid application deadline: 2/15. *Faculty research:* Auditing, financial accounting, managerial accounting, capital markets, tax accounting. • Dr. Thomas D. Hubbard, Director, 402-472-2337.

University of Nevada, Las Vegas, College of Business, Department of Accounting, Las Vegas, NV 89154-9900. Awards MS. Part-time and evening/weekend programs available. Faculty: 17 full-time (3 women). Students: 4 full-time (3 women), 16 part-time (9 women); includes 2 minority (both Asian Americans), 2 international. 18 applicants, 61% accepted. In 1997, 3 degrees awarded. *Degree requirements:* Comprehensive exam required, thesis optional, foreign language not required. *Entrance requirements:* GMAT, minimum GPA of 2.75. Application deadline: 6/15 (priority date; rolling processing; 11/15 for spring admission). Application fee: $40 ($95 for international students). *Expenses:* Tuition $93 per credit for state residents; $93 per credit full-time, $190 per credit part-time for nonresidents. Fees $5570 per year full-time for nonresidents. *Financial aid:* In 1997–98, 4 teaching assistantships were awarded. Financial aid application deadline: 3/1. • Dr. James Swayze, Chairman, 702-895-1559. Application contact: Graduate College Admissions Evaluator, 702-895-3320.

University of Nevada, Reno, College of Business Administration, Department of Accountancy, Reno, NV 89557. Awards M Acc. Program new for fall 1998. *Entrance requirements:* GMAT, TOEFL (minimum score 500), minimum GPA of 2.75. Application fee: $40. *Expenses:* Tuition $0 for state residents; $5770 per year full-time, $200 per credit part-time for nonresidents. Fees $93 per credit. • Dr. H. Michael Reed, Dean, College of Business Administration, 702-784-4912. Application contact: Dr. Brent Bowman, Associate Dean, 702-784-4912. E-mail: bowman@unr.edu.

University of New Haven, School of Business, Program in Accounting, West Haven, CT 06516-1916. Offers financial accounting (MS), managerial accounting (MS), taxation (MS). Students: 6 full-time (2 women), 41 part-time (20 women); includes 6 minority (2 African Americans, 3 Asian Americans, 1 Hispanic), 15 international. 12 applicants, 67% accepted. *Degree requirements:* Thesis required, foreign language not required. *Application deadline:*

rolling. *Application fee:* $50. *Expenses:* Tuition $1125 per course. Fees $13 per trimester. *Financial aid:* Federal Work-Study available. Aid available to part-time students. Financial aid application deadline: 5/1; applicants required to submit FAFSA. • Robert G. McDonald, Coordinator, 203-932-7127.

University of New Haven, School of Business, Program in Business Administration, West Haven, CT 06516-1916. Offerings include accounting (MBA). *Degree requirements:* Thesis or alternative required, foreign language not required. *Application deadline:* rolling. *Application fee:* $50. *Expenses:* Tuition $1125 per course. Fees $13 per trimester. • Dr. Omid Nodoushani, Coordinator, 203-932-7123.

University of New Mexico, Robert O. Anderson Graduate School of Management, Program in Accounting, Albuquerque, NM 87131-1221. Awards M Acc, MBA. Faculty: 11 full-time (4 women), 4 part-time (2 women), 12 FTE. *Degree requirements:* Computer language required, foreign language and thesis not required. *Entrance requirements:* GMAT (minimum score 540), TOEFL (minimum score 550). Application deadline: 7/1 (priority date; rolling processing; 11/15 for spring admission). Application fee: $25. *Expenses:* Tuition $2442 per year full-time, $103 per credit hour part-time for state residents; $8691 per year full-time, $103 per credit hour (minimum) part-time for nonresidents. Fees $32 per year. *Financial aid:* Fellowships, research assistantships available. *Faculty research:* Critical accounting, accounting pedagogy, theory, taxation. • Jesse Dillard, Department Chair, 505-277-3207. Fax: 505-277-7108. E-mail: dillard@unm.edu. Application contact: Sue Podeyn, MBA Program Director, 505-277-3147. Fax: 505-277-9356.

University of New Orleans, College of Business Administration, Department of Accounting, Program in Accounting, New Orleans, LA 70148. Awards MS. Part-time and evening/weekend programs available. Faculty: 6 full-time (1 woman), 2 part-time (0 women). Students: 18 full-time (13 women), 56 part-time (27 women); includes 11 minority (2 African Americans, 3 Asian Americans, 6 Hispanics), 7 international. Average age 32. 50 applicants, 72% accepted. In 1997, 5 degrees awarded. *Entrance requirements:* GMAT. Application deadline: 7/1 (priority date; rolling processing). Application fee: $20. *Expenses:* Tuition $2362 per year full-time, $373 per semester (minimum) part-time for state residents; $7888 per year full-time, $1423 per semester (minimum) part-time for nonresidents. Fees $170 per year full-time, $25 per semester (minimum) part-time. *Financial aid:* Research assistantships, Federal Work-Study available. • Application contact: Gordon Hosch, Graduate Coordinator, 504-280-6438. Fax: 504-280-5430. E-mail: gahac@uno.edu.

The University of North Carolina at Chapel Hill, Kenan-Flagler Business School, Doctoral Program in Business Administration, Chapel Hill, NC 27599. Offerings include accounting (PhD). Program faculty: 79 full-time (15 women), 29 part-time (6 women). *Degree requirements:* Dissertation required, foreign language not required. *Average time to degree:* doctorate–4 years full-time. *Entrance requirements:* GMAT (average 657) or GRE General Test (minimum combined score of 1350). Application deadline: 1/1 (priority date; rolling processing). Application fee: $55. Electronic applications accepted. *Expenses:* Tuition $1428 per year for state residents; $10,414 per year for nonresidents. Fees $787 per year. • Ann Marucheck, Associate Dean for PhD Programs, 919-962-3193. Application contact: Liz Griffin, Director, 919-962-1657. E-mail: kfphd_app@unc.edu.

The University of North Carolina at Chapel Hill, Kenan-Flagler Business School, Program in Accounting, Chapel Hill, NC 27599. Awards MAC. Faculty: 23 full-time (7 women), 9 part-time (3 women). Students: 81 full-time (43 women); includes 7 minority (1 African American, 5 Asian Americans, 1 Hispanic), 1 international. Average age 23. 111 applicants, 76% accepted. In 1997, 82 degrees awarded (100% found work related to degree). *Average time to degree:* master's–1 year full-time. *Entrance requirements:* GMAT (average 622), TOEFL (minimum score 600). Application deadline: 3/1 (rolling processing). Application fee: $55. *Expenses:* Tuition $2248 per year for state residents; $14,304 per year for nonresidents. Fees $2187 per year. *Financial aid:* In 1997–98, 26 fellowships (all to first-year students) totaling $119,000, 1 research assistantship (to a first-year student) totaling $8,500, 5 teaching assistantships (all to first-year students) were awarded; institutionally sponsored loans also available. Financial aid application deadline: 3/1. *Faculty research:* Mandated financial disclosure, employee stock options. • Winnie Fowler, Director, 919-962-1643. Application contact: Philip Bues, Assistant Director, Admissions, 919-962-3186. Fax: 919-962-6964. E-mail: mac_info@unc.edu.

University of North Carolina at Charlotte, College of Business Administration, Department of Accounting, Charlotte, NC 28223-0001. Awards M Acc. Faculty: 10 full-time (2 women). Students: 1 full-time (0 women), 17 part-time (12 women); includes 1 international. Average age 29. 27 applicants, 93% accepted. *Entrance requirements:* Minimum GPA of 3.0 in undergraduate major, 2.8 overall. Application deadline: 7/1. Application fee: $35. *Tuition:* $1786 per year full-time, $339 per semester (minimum) part-time for state residents; $8914 per year full-time, $2121 per semester (minimum) part-time for nonresidents. *Financial aid:* In 1997–98, 1 research assistantship averaging $788 per month, 2 teaching assistantships averaging $788 per month were awarded. Financial aid application deadline: 4/1. • Dr. Howard L. Godfrey, Chair, 704-547-2445. Application contact: Kathy Barringer, Assistant Director of Graduate Admissions, 704-547-3366. Fax: 704-547-3279. E-mail: gradadm@email.uncc.edu.

University of North Carolina at Greensboro, Joseph M. Bryan School of Business and Economics, Department of Accounting, Greensboro, NC 27412-0001. Awards MS. Faculty: 8 full-time (2 women). Students: 42 full-time (25 women), 15 part-time (7 women); includes 4 minority (3 African Americans, 1 Asian American), 3 international. 32 applicants, 75% accepted. In 1997, 33 degrees awarded. *Average time to degree:* master's–1.5 years full-time. *Entrance requirements:* GMAT, previous course work in accounting and business. Application deadline: 7/1 (priority date; rolling processing; 11/1 for spring admission). Application fee: $35. *Expenses:* Tuition $1842 per year full-time, $370 per semester (minimum) part-time for state residents; $10,296 per year full-time, $2484 per semester (minimum) part-time for nonresidents. Fees $806 per year full-time, $111 per semester (minimum) part-time. *Financial aid:* In 1997–98, 17 students received aid, including 2 fellowships totaling $12,000, 11 research assistantships totaling $35,937; Federal Work-Study also available. • Dr. Charles Mecimore, Head, 336-334-5647.

University of North Carolina at Wilmington, School of Business, Program in Accountancy, Wilmington, NC 28403-3201. Awards MS. Faculty: 3 full-time (2 women). Students: 39 full-time (21 women), 1 part-time (0 women); includes 3 minority (2 African Americans, 1 Asian American). 69 applicants, 72% accepted. In 1997, 23 degrees awarded. *Degree requirements:* Comprehensive exam required, thesis not required. *Entrance requirements:* GMAT, 1 year of appropriate work experience. Application deadline: 7/1 (rolling processing). Application fee: $35. *Tuition:* $1748 per year full-time, $270 per semester (minimum) part-time for state residents; $8882 per year full-time, $2058 per semester (minimum) part-time for nonresidents. *Financial aid:* In 1997–98, 10 teaching assistantships were awarded; Federal Work-Study and career-related internships or fieldwork also available. Aid available to part-time students. Financial aid application deadline: 3/15. • John A. Marts, Chair, 910-962-3509. Application contact: Neil F. Hadley, Dean, Graduate School, 910-962-4117.

University of North Florida, College of Business Administration, Department of Accounting, Jacksonville, FL 32224-2645. Awards M Acct. Faculty: 10 full-time (1 woman). Students: 21 full-time (6 women), 53 part-time (30 women); includes 9 minority (2 African Americans, 6 Asian Americans, 1 Hispanic), 4 international. Average age 30. 20 applicants, 80% accepted. In 1997, 17 degrees awarded. *Degree requirements:* Computer language required, thesis not required. *Entrance requirements:* GMAT, minimum GPA of 3.0. Application deadline: rolling. Application fee: $20. *Tuition:* $3388 per year full-time, $141 per credit hour part-time for state residents; $11,634 per year full-time, $485 per credit hour part-time for nonresidents. *Financial aid:* Fellowships and career-related internships or fieldwork available. • Dr. John MacArthur, Chair, 904-646-2630.

University of North Texas, College of Business Administration, Department of Accounting, Denton, TX 76203-6737. Awards MS, PhD. Part-time programs available. Faculty: 16 full-time (3 women), 2 part-time (0 women). Students: 69 full-time (34 women), 73 part-time (37 women); includes 13 minority (4 African Americans, 5 Asian Americans, 4 Hispanics), 14 international. Average age 28. In 1997, 60 master's awarded (100% found work related to degree); 5 doctorates awarded (100% entered university research/teaching). *Degree requirements:* For master's, computer language required, foreign language and thesis not required; for doctorate, computer language, dissertation required, foreign language not required. *Entrance requirements:* For master's, GMAT, TOEFL; for doctorate, GMAT or GRE General Test, TOEFL. Application deadline: 7/17 (rolling processing; 12/1 for spring admission). Application fee: $25 ($50 for international students). *Tuition:* $2063 per year full-time, $815 per year part-time for state residents; $5897 per year full-time, $2100 per year part-time for nonresidents. *Financial aid:* Teaching assistantships, Federal Work-Study, institutionally sponsored loans, and career-related internships or fieldwork available. Financial aid application deadline: 2/1. *Faculty research:* Taxation and accounting problems of extractive industries, problems and issues in public interest areas, public sector empirical studies, historical perspective for accounting issues, behavioral issues in taxation and auditing. • Dr. John Ellis Price, Chair, 940-565-3092.

University of Notre Dame, College of Business Administration, Program in Accountacy, Notre Dame, IN 46556. Awards MS. Faculty: 24 full-time (4 women), 1 (woman) part-time. *Entrance requirements:* GMAT. Application fee: $50. • Dr. Thomas Frecka, Department Chair, 219-631-8395. E-mail: frecka.1@nd.edu. Application contact: Margot O'Brien, MS in Accountancy Program Administrator and Adjunct Instructor, 219-631-9732. Fax: 219-631-5255. E-mail: msacct.1@nd.edu.

University of Oklahoma, College of Business Administration, School of Accounting, Norman, OK 73019-0390. Awards M Acc. Part-time programs available. Faculty: 12 full-time (3 women), 2 part-time (1 woman). Students: 28 full-time (20 women), 13 part-time (8 women); includes 2 minority (1 African American, 1 Asian American), 16 international. Average age 30. 83 applicants, 20% accepted. In 1997, 25 degrees awarded. *Degree requirements:* Comprehensive exam required, foreign language and thesis not required. *Entrance requirements:* GMAT (minimum score 550), TOEFL (minimum score 550), minimum GPA of 3.0 in last 60 hours. Application deadline: 4/1 (priority date; rolling processing; 11/1 for spring admission). Application fee: $25. *Expenses:* Tuition $1920 per year full-time, $80 per credit hour part-time for state residents; $6108 per year full-time, $255 per credit hour part-time for nonresidents. Fees $468 per year full-time, $12 per semester (minimum) part-time. *Financial aid:* In 1997–98, 16 students received aid, including 3 research assistantships, 2 teaching assistantships; fellowships, partial tuition waivers, Federal Work-Study, and career-related internships or fieldwork also available. Financial aid application deadline: 4/1. *Faculty research:* Cost allocations, tax compliance, behavioral accounting, tax planning, financial accounting. • Fran Ayres, Director, 405-325-4221.

University of Oregon, Graduate School, Charles H. Lundquist College of Business, Department of Accounting, Eugene, OR 97403. Awards PhD. Part-time programs available. Faculty: 9 full-time (1 woman). Students: 9 full-time (2 women), 1 (woman) part-time; includes 1 minority (Asian American), 3 international. 10 applicants, 20% accepted. Terminal master's awarded for partial completion of doctoral program. *Degree requirements:* For doctorate, computer language, dissertation, 2 comprehensive exams required, foreign language not required. *Entrance requirements:* For doctorate, GMAT, TOEFL (minimum score 600). Application deadline: 3/1. Application fee: $50. *Tuition:* $6429 per year full-time, $873 per quarter (minimum) part-time for state residents; $10,857 per year full-time, $1360 per quarter (minimum) part-time for nonresidents. *Financial aid:* In 1997–98, 9 teaching assistantships (2 to first-year students) were awarded; Federal Work-Study and career-related internships or fieldwork also available. *Faculty research:* Empirical financial accounting, effects of regulation on accounting standards, use of protocol analysis as a research methodology in accounting. • Helen Gernon, Head, 541-346-3305. Application contact: Linda Johnson, Graduate Secretary, 541-346-3306.

University of Pennsylvania, Wharton School, Accounting Department, Philadelphia, PA 19104. Awards MBA, PhD. Faculty: 15 full-time (2 women), 2 part-time (0 women). Students: 2 full-time (1 woman), 2 part-time (1 woman); includes 2 minority (both Asian Americans). Terminal master's awarded for partial completion of doctoral program. *Degree requirements:* For doctorate, dissertation required, foreign language not required. *Entrance requirements:* For master's, GMAT; for doctorate, GMAT or GRE. Application fee: $125. *Faculty research:* Financial reporting, information disclosure, performance measurement, executive compensation. • Dr. Stanley Baiman, Chairperson, 215-898-1290. Fax: 215-573-2054. Application contact: Robert Alig, Director of Admissions, 215-898-3430. Fax: 215-898-0120.

University of Rhode Island, College of Business Administration, Department of Accounting, Kingston, RI 02881. Awards MS. *Application deadline:* 4/15 (priority date; rolling processing). *Application fee:* $35. *Expenses:* Tuition $3446 per year full-time, $191 per credit part-time for state residents; $9850 per year full-time, $547 per credit part-time for nonresidents. Fees $1276 per year full-time, $135 per semester (minimum) part-time.

University of St. Thomas, Graduate School of Business, Day MBA Program, St. Paul, MN 55105-1096. Offerings include accounting (MBA). Program faculty: 13 part-time. *Degree requirements:* Computer language required, foreign language and thesis not required. *Entrance requirements:* GMAT (score in 50th percentile or higher). Application deadline: 5/1 (priority date; rolling processing). Application fee: $30. *Tuition:* $473 per credit hour. • Application contact: Jim O'Connor, Student Adviser, 612-962-4233. Fax: 612-962-4260.

University of St. Thomas, Graduate School of Business, Evening MBA Program, St. Paul, MN 55105-1096. Offerings include accounting (MBA, Certificate). Program faculty: 16 full-time (2 women), 89 part-time (17 women). *Degree requirements:* For master's, computer language required, foreign language and thesis not required. *Entrance requirements:* For master's, GMAT (score in 50th percentile or higher). Application deadline: 8/1 (priority date; rolling processing; 12/1 for spring admission). Application fee: $30. *Tuition:* $416 per credit hour. • Dr. Stanford Nyquist, MBA Director, 612-962-4242. Application contact: Martha Ballard, Director of Student Services, 612-962-4226. Fax: 612-962-4260.

University of St. Thomas, Graduate School of Business, Program in Accounting, St. Paul, MN 55105-1096. Awards MBA. Faculty: 3 part-time (0 women). Students: 19 full-time (9 women); includes 3 international. Average age 28. In 1997, 11 degrees awarded (100% found work related to degree). *Average time to degree:* master's–1.2 years full-time. *Entrance requirements:* GMAT (score in 50th percentile or higher). Application deadline: 6/1 (rolling processing). Application fee: $30. *Tuition:* $416 per credit hour. *Financial aid:* In 1997–98, 4 grants (all to first-year students) totaling $2,308 were awarded; career-related internships or fieldwork also available. Financial aid application deadline: 4/1; applicants required to submit FAFSA. • Bill Davidson, Director, 612-962-4271. E-mail: amba@stthomas.edu. Application contact: Laurel Baughn, Program Services Manager, 612-962-4270. Fax: 612-962-4710. E-mail: amba@stthomas.edu.

University of Saskatchewan, College of Commerce, Department of Accounting, Saskatoon, SK S7N 5A2, Canada. Awards M Sc. Part-time programs available. *Degree requirements:* Thesis. *Entrance requirements:* GMAT, TOEFL. Application deadline: 7/1 (priority date; rolling processing). Application fee: $0.

University of Scranton, Program in Business Administration, Scranton, PA 18510-4622. Offerings include accounting (MBA). Program faculty: 39 full-time (9 women), 1 part-time (0 women). *Entrance requirements:* GMAT, TOEFL (minimum score 500), minimum GPA of 2.75. Application deadline: rolling. Application fee: $35. *Expenses:* Tuition $465 per credit. Fees $25 per semester. • Dr. Wayne H. J. Cunningam, Director, 717-941-4043. Fax: 717-941-4342. E-mail: cunninghamw1@uofs.edu.

Directory: Accounting

University of South Alabama, College of Business and Management Studies, Program in Accounting, Mobile, AL 36688-0002. Awards M Acct. Part-time and evening/weekend programs available. Faculty: 8 full-time (2 women). Students: 15 full-time (12 women), 7 part-time (4 women); includes 2 minority (1 Asian American, 1 Hispanic), 3 international. 19 applicants, 53% accepted. In 1997, 7 degrees awarded. *Degree requirements:* Oral comprehensive exams required, foreign language and thesis not required. *Entrance requirements:* GMAT, minimum undergraduate GPA of 3.0. Application deadline: 9/1 (priority date; rolling processing). Application fee: $25. *Financial aid:* Available to part-time students. Financial aid application deadline: 4/1. • Dr. Frank Urbanic, Chairman, 334-460-6144.

University of South Carolina, Graduate School, College of Business Administration, Program in Accounting, Columbia, SC 29208. Awards M Acc, JD/M Acc. Part-time programs available. Faculty: 20 full-time (3 women). Students: 35 full-time (22 women), 6 part-time (3 women); includes 4 minority (2 African Americans, 1 Asian American, 1 Hispanic), 13 international. Average age 26. 83 applicants, 53% accepted. In 1997, 17 degrees awarded (100% found work related to degree). *Entrance requirements:* GMAT (minimum score 550; average 580), minimum GPA of 3.0. Application deadline: 2/1 (priority date; rolling processing; 12/1 for spring admission). Application fee: $35. Electronic applications accepted. *Financial aid:* In 1997–98, 5 fellowships (all to first-year students), 10 research assistantships (all to first-year students) were awarded; teaching assistantships, Federal Work-Study, institutionally sponsored loans also available. Financial aid application deadline: 2/1. *Faculty research:* Judgment modeling, international accounting, accounting information systems, behavioral accounting, cost/management accounting. Total annual research expenditures: $10,000. • James L. Burkett, Managing Director, 803-777-6412. Fax: 803-777-6876. E-mail: burkett@darla.badm.sc.edu. Application contact: Carol Williams, Director of Admissions, 803-777-6749. Fax: 803-777-0414. E-mail: carol@darla.badm.sc.edu.

University of South Dakota, School of Business, Department of Accounting, Vermillion, SD 57069-2390. Awards MP Acc, JD/MA, JD/MP Acc. Faculty: 5 full-time (1 woman), 2 part-time (1 woman). Students: 30 full-time (15 women), 2 part-time (both women). 8 applicants, 75% accepted. In 1997, 12 degrees awarded. *Entrance requirements:* GMAT. Application deadline: rolling. Application fee: $15. *Expenses:* Tuition $1530 per year full-time, $85 per credit hour part-time for state residents; $4518 per year full-time, $251 per credit hour part-time for nonresidents. Fees $792 per year full-time, $44 per credit hour part-time. *Financial aid:* Federal Work-Study available. • Dr. Richard Metcalf, Director of Graduate Studies, 605-677-5232.

University of Southern California, Graduate School, Marshall School of Business, Leventhal School of Accounting, Program in Accounting, Los Angeles, CA 90089. Awards M Acc. Students: 53 full-time (29 women), 2 part-time (1 woman); includes 12 minority (11 Asian Americans, 1 Hispanic), 17 international. Average age 27. 80 applicants, 44% accepted. In 1997, 54 degrees awarded. *Entrance requirements:* GMAT. Application fee: $55. *Expenses:* Tuition $16,944 per year full-time, $706 per unit part-time. Fees $414 per year full-time, $32 per year part-time. *Financial aid:* In 1997–98, 12 fellowships, 1 teaching assistantship, 7 scholarships were awarded; research assistantships, Federal Work-Study, institutionally sponsored loans also available. Aid available to part-time students. Financial aid application deadline: 2/15; applicants required to submit FAFSA. • Leslie R. Porter, Director.

University of Southern Indiana, Graduate Studies, School of Business, Program in Accountancy, Evansville, IN 47712-3590. Awards MSA. Students: 1 (woman) part-time. 3 applicants, 33% accepted. *Application fee:* $25. *Tuition:* $129 per credit hour for state residents; $260 per credit hour for nonresidents. • Dr. Daniel Wade, Associate Dean, 812-464-1796. Fax: 812-464-1956. E-mail: dwade.ucs.@smtp.usi.edu.

University of Southern Mississippi, College of Business Administration, School of Professional Accountancy, Hattiesburg, MS 39406-5167. Awards MPA. Part-time and evening/weekend programs available. Faculty: 10 full-time (1 woman), 1 part-time (0 women). Students: 25 full-time (14 women), 6 part-time (5 women); includes 4 minority (2 African Americans, 2 Asian Americans), 2 international. Average age 27. 26 applicants, 62% accepted. In 1997, 20 degrees awarded. *Entrance requirements:* GMAT, TOEFL (minimum score 550), minimum GPA of 2.75. Application deadline: 8/9 (priority date; rolling processing). Application fee: $0 ($25 for international students). *Tuition:* $2870 per year full-time, $137 per credit hour part-time for state residents; $5972 per year full-time, $172 per credit hour part-time for nonresidents. *Financial aid:* Research assistantships, Federal Work-Study, institutionally sponsored loans available. Aid available to part-time students. Financial aid application deadline: 3/15. *Faculty research:* Bank liquidity, subchapter S corporations, internal auditing, governmental accounting, inflation accounting. Total annual research expenditures: $1000. • Dr. Paul Torres, Interim Chair, 601-266-4641. Application contact: Mary Schlottman, Manager of Graduate Business Programs, 601-266-4664. Fax: 601-266-5814.

University of South Florida, College of Business Administration, School of Accounting, Tampa, FL 33620-9951. Awards M Acc. Part-time and evening/weekend programs available. Faculty: 11 full-time (2 women). Students: 47 full-time (26 women), 85 part-time (43 women); includes 19 minority (4 African Americans, 5 Asian Americans, 9 Hispanics, 1 Native American), 3 international. Average age 28. 69 applicants, 64% accepted. In 1997, 45 degrees awarded. *Degree requirements:* Comprehensive exam required, foreign language and thesis not required. *Entrance requirements:* GMAT (minimum score 500), minimum AACSB index of 1100, minimum GPA of 3.0. Application deadline: 5/15 (10/15 for spring admission). Application fee: $20. Electronic applications accepted. *Tuition:* $142 per credit hour for state residents; $486 per credit hour for nonresidents. *Financial aid:* In 1997–98, 9 students received aid, including 2 fellowships averaging $567 per month and totaling $10,200, 5 teaching assistantships (4 to first-year students) averaging $708 per month, 2 graduate assistantships averaging $708 per month; Federal Work-Study, institutionally sponsored loans also available. Aid available to part-time students. Financial aid applicants required to submit FAFSA. *Faculty research:* Financial accountancy theory, auditing, taxes, managerial accounting, computer information systems. • Robert Keith, Director, 813-974-6516. E-mail: rkeith@bsn01.bsn.usf.edu. Application contact: Theresa Price, Adviser, 813-974-6578. Fax: 813-974-6528. E-mail: tprice@bsn01.bsn.usf.edu.

University of Tennessee at Chattanooga, School of Business Administration, Program in Accountancy, Chattanooga, TN 37403-2598. Awards M Acc. Part-time and evening/weekend programs available. Students: 5 full-time (3 women), 18 part-time (13 women); includes 3 minority (1 African American, 1 Asian American, 1 Hispanic). Average age 33. 11 applicants, 73% accepted. In 1997, 7 degrees awarded. *Entrance requirements:* GMAT (average 482). Application deadline: rolling. Application fee: $25. *Tuition:* $2864 per year full-time, $160 per credit hour part-time for state residents; $6806 per year full-time, $379 per credit hour part-time for nonresidents. *Financial aid:* Fellowships, research assistantships, Federal Work-Study, institutionally sponsored loans available. Aid available to part-time students. Financial aid application deadline: 4/1. • Dr. John Fulmer, Head, 423-755-4101. Fax: 423-755-5255. E-mail: john-fulmer@utc.edu. Application contact: Dr. Deborah Arfken, Assistant Provost for Graduate Studies, 423-755-4667. Fax: 423-755-4478.

The University of Tennessee at Martin, School of Business Administration, Program in Accounting, Martin, TN 38238-1000. Awards M Ac. Part-time and evening/weekend programs available. Postbaccalaureate distance learning degree programs offered (no on-campus study). Students: 7 full-time (5 women), 17 part-time (12 women). 12 applicants, 75% accepted. In 1997, 6 degrees awarded. *Degree requirements:* Computer language required, foreign language and thesis not required. *Entrance requirements:* GMAT (minimum score 400), minimum GPA of 2.5. Application deadline: rolling. Application fee: $25 ($50 for international students). *Tuition:* $2962 per year full-time, $165 per semester hour part-time for state residents; $7788 per year full-time, $434 per semester hour part-time for nonresidents. *Financial aid:* In 1997–98, 4 students received aid, including 2 research assistantships averaging $324 per month and totaling $6,075, 1 graduate assistantship (to a first-year student) averaging $550 per month and totaling $5,746; fellowships, teaching assistantships, partial tuition waivers also available. Financial aid application deadline: 3/1. *Faculty research:* Managerial, financial, tax, nonprofit, and systems accounting; auditing. • Dr. Richard Griffin, Coordinator, 901-587-7308. Fax: 901-587-7241. E-mail: bagrad@utm.edu.

University of Tennessee, Knoxville, College of Business Administration, Department of Accounting and Business Law, Knoxville, TN 37996. Offers programs in accounting (M Acc), including financial auditing; systems (M Acc); taxation (M Acc). Faculty: 17 full-time (5 women). Students: 78 full-time (34 women), 6 part-time (5 women); includes 5 international. 136 applicants, 71% accepted. In 1997, 69 degrees awarded. *Degree requirements:* Thesis or alternative required, foreign language not required. *Entrance requirements:* GMAT, TOEFL (minimum score 550), minimum GPA of 2.7. Application deadline: 2/1 (priority date; rolling processing). Application fee: $35. Electronic applications accepted. *Tuition:* $3354 per year full-time, $181 per semester hour part-time for state residents; $8410 per year full-time, $462 per semester hour part-time for nonresidents. *Financial aid:* In 1997–98, 10 fellowships, 6 research assistantships, 76 teaching assistantships were awarded; Federal Work-Study, institutionally sponsored loans also available. Financial aid application deadline: 2/1. • Dr. Keith Stanga, Head, 423-974-1750. Fax: 423-974-4631. E-mail: kstanga@utk.edu.

University of Tennessee, Knoxville, College of Business Administration, Program in Business Administration, Knoxville, TN 37996. Offerings include accounting (PhD). Postbaccalaureate distance learning degree programs offered. Program faculty: 51 full-time (6 women). *Degree requirements:* Computer language, dissertation required, foreign language not required. *Entrance requirements:* GMAT, TOEFL (minimum score 550), minimum GPA of 2.7. Application deadline: 2/1 (priority date). Application fee: $35. Electronic applications accepted. *Tuition:* $3354 per year full-time, $181 per semester hour part-time for state residents; $8410 per year full-time, $462 per semester hour part-time for nonresidents. • Dr. Gary Dicer, Director, 423-974-5033. E-mail: gdicer@utk.edu. Application contact: Donald Potts, Graduate Representative, 423-974-5033. Fax: 423-974-3826. E-mail: dpotts@utk.edu.

The University of Texas at Arlington, College of Business Administration, Department of Accounting, Program in Accounting, Arlington, TX 76019-0407. Awards MBA, MPA, MS. Students: 36 full-time (23 women), 39 part-time (27 women); includes 19 minority (6 African Americans, 10 Asian Americans, 3 Hispanics), 21 international. In 1997, 34 degrees awarded. *Degree requirements:* Thesis optional, foreign language not required. *Entrance requirements:* GMAT, TOEFL (minimum score 550). Application deadline: rolling. Application fee: $25 ($50 for international students). *Tuition:* $3206 per year full-time, $468 per semester (minimum) part-time for state residents; $8612 per year full-time, $1137 per semester (minimum) part-time for nonresidents. • Application contact: Dr. James E. Walther, Graduate Adviser, 817-272-3004. Fax: 817-794-5799.

The University of Texas at Austin, Graduate School, College of Business Administration, Department of Accounting, Austin, TX 78712. Awards MPA, PhD. Students: 250 full-time (110 women); includes 1 minority (African American), 1 international. *Entrance requirements:* GMAT. Application fee: $75 ($100 for international students). *Expenses:* Tuition $2592 per year full-time, $324 per semester (minimum) part-time for state residents; $7704 per year full-time, $963 per semester (minimum) part-time for nonresidents. Fees $778 per year full-time, $161 per semester (minimum) part-time. *Financial aid:* Fellowships, teaching assistantships available. Financial aid application deadline: 2/1. • Dr. Stephen T. Limberg, Chairman, 512-471-1251. E-mail: acc-chair@bus.utexas.edu. Application contact: Ross Jennings, Graduate Adviser, 512-471-5340.

The University of Texas at El Paso, College of Business Administration, Department of Accounting, 500 West University Avenue, El Paso, TX 79968-0001. Awards MACY. Part-time and evening/weekend programs available. *Entrance requirements:* GMAT (minimum score 450), TOEFL (minimum score 550), minimum GPA of 2.7. Application deadline: 7/1 (priority date; rolling processing; 11/1 for spring admission). Application fee: $15 ($65 for international students). Electronic applications accepted. *Tuition:* $2063 per year full-time, $284 per credit hour part-time for state residents; $5753 per year full-time, $425 per credit hour part-time for nonresidents. *Faculty research:* International accounting, tax, not-for-profit accounting.

The University of Texas at San Antonio, College of Business, San Antonio, TX 78249-0617. Offerings include accounting (MP Acct). College faculty: 72 full-time (18 women), 40 part-time (9 women). *Application deadline:* 7/1 (rolling processing). *Application fee:* $20. *Expenses:* Tuition $2476 per year full-time, $309 per semester (minimum) part-time for state residents; $7584 per year full-time, $948 per semester (minimum) part-time for nonresidents. Fees $361 per year full-time, $133 per semester (minimum) part-time. • James F. Gaertner, Dean, 210-458-4313. Application contact: Dr. John H. Brown, Director of Admissions and Registrar, 210-458-4530.

The University of Texas of the Permian Basin, Graduate School, School of Business, Program in Accountancy, Odessa, TX 79762-0001. Awards MPA. *Degree requirements:* Thesis required, foreign language not required. *Entrance requirements:* GMAT. *Expenses:* Tuition $1314 per year full-time, $73 per hour part-time for state residents; $4896 per year full-time, $272 per hour part-time for nonresidents. Fees $383 per year full-time, $111 per semester (minimum) part-time.

University of Toledo, Graduate School of Business, Department of Accounting, Program in Accounting, Toledo, OH 43606-3398. Awards MBA, MS Acct. Faculty: 6 full-time (2 women). Students: 5 full-time (4 women), 22 part-time (18 women); includes 2 minority (1 Asian American, 1 Hispanic). Average age 29. 37 applicants, 57% accepted. In 1997, 13 degrees awarded. *Entrance requirements:* GMAT (minimum score 450), TOEFL (minimum score 550). Application deadline: 8/1 (priority date; rolling processing). Application fee: $30. *Tuition:* $5907 per year full-time, $246 per hour part-time for state residents; $11,835 per year full-time, $493 per hour part-time for nonresidents. *Financial aid:* Application deadline 4/1. • Dr. Philip Fink, Chair, Department of Accounting, 419-530-2277. Fax: 419-530-7744. E-mail: pfink2@uoft02.utoledo.edu.

University of Toronto, School of Graduate Studies, Social Sciences Division, Faculty of Management, Toronto, ON M5S 1A1, Canada. Awards MBA, MMPA, PhD, LL B/MBA, MBA/MA. Part-time and evening/weekend programs available. Faculty: 50. Students: 368 full-time (147 women), 315 part-time (87 women); includes 66 international. 1,114 applicants, 37% accepted. In 1997, 259 master's, 8 doctorates awarded. *Degree requirements:* For doctorate, dissertation. *Application fee:* $100. *Expenses:* Tuition $4070 per year for Canadian residents; $7870 per year for nonresidents. Fees $628 per year. *Financial aid:* Fellowships, research assistantships, teaching assistantships, and career-related internships or fieldwork available. *Faculty research:* Natural resources, organizational behavior, finance. • P. J. Halpern, Interim Dean, 416-978-3422. Application contact: Secretary, 416-978-3499. Fax: 416-978-5812. E-mail: mba.prog@fmgmt.mgmt.utoronto.ca.

University of Tulsa, College of Business Administration, Program in Accounting, Tulsa, OK 74104-3189. Awards M Acct, JD/M Acct. Part-time and evening/weekend programs available. Faculty: 7 full-time (2 women). Students: 1 (woman) full-time, 5 part-time (3 women); includes 1 minority (Asian American). Average age 29. 7 applicants, 100% accepted. In 1997, 2 degrees awarded. *Entrance requirements:* GMAT, TOEFL (minimum score 575). Application deadline: rolling. Application fee: $0. Electronic applications accepted. *Expenses:* Tuition $480 per credit hour. Fees $2 per credit hour. *Financial aid:* In 1997–98, 1 student received aid, including 1 teaching assistantship averaging $575 per month and totaling $6,908; fellowships, research assistantships also available. Aid available to part-time students. Financial aid application deadline: 2/1; applicants required to submit FAFSA. *Faculty research:* Capital markets, financial reporting, innovation in accounting. • Dr. Patrick A. Hennessee, Chairperson, 918-631-2794. Application contact: Dr. Richard C. Burgess, Assistant Dean/Director of Graduate Business Studies, 918-631-2242. Fax: 918-631-2142.

University of Tulsa, College of Business Administration, Program in Accounting and Information Systems, Tulsa, OK 74104-3189. Awards MAIS. Program new for fall 1998. *Entrance* *requirements:* TOEFL (minimum score 575). Application deadline: rolling. Application fee: $30. *Expenses:* Tuition $480 per credit hour. Fees $2 per credit hour. *Financial aid:* Application deadline 2/1. • Dr. Patrick A. Hennessee, Chairperson, 918-631-2794. Fax: 918-631-2164. Application contact: Dr. Richard C. Burgess, Assistant Dean/Director of Graduate Business Studies, 918-631-2242. Fax: 918-631-2142.

University of Utah, Graduate School of Business, Department of Accounting, Salt Lake City, UT 84112-1107. Awards MBA, M Pr A, PhD. Faculty: 16 full-time (2 women), 3 part-time (1 woman). Students: 31 full-time (14 women), 12 part-time (9 women); includes 3 minority (2 Asian Americans, 1 Hispanic), 1 international. Average age 28. In 1997, 32 master's awarded. *Degree requirements:* For master's, computer language required, foreign language not required; for doctorate, computer language, dissertation, oral qualifying exams, written qualifying exams required, foreign language not required. *Entrance requirements:* GMAT, TSE, TOEFL (minimum score 500). Application deadline: 2/15. Application fee: $30 ($50 for international students). *Tuition:* $2045 per year full-time, $562 per semester (minimum) part-time for state residents; $6129 per year full-time, $1607 per semester (minimum) part-time for nonresidents. *Financial aid:* In 1997–98, 6 teaching assistantships were awarded; fellowships, Federal Work-Study also available. *Faculty research:* Auditing, taxation, information systems, financial accounting, accounting theory. • Martha Eining, Director, 801-581-7798. Fax: 801-581-7214.

University of Virginia, Graduate School of Arts and Sciences, McIntire School of Commerce, Program in Accounting, Charlottesville, VA 22903. Awards MS, JD/MS. Faculty: 52 full-time (12 women), 7 part-time (3 women), 54 FTE. Students: 32 full-time (14 women), 4 part-time (3 women); includes 7 minority (2 African Americans, 4 Asian Americans, 1 Hispanic), 1 international. Average age 25. 48 applicants, 71% accepted. In 1997, 25 degrees awarded. *Entrance requirements:* GMAT, TOEFL. Application deadline: 7/15 (rolling processing; 12/1 for spring admission). Application fee: $40. *Tuition:* $4876 per year for state residents; $15,824 per year for nonresidents. *Financial aid:* Fellowships, Federal Work-Study available. • Application contact: Duane J. Osheim, Associate Dean, 804-924-7184.

See in-depth description on page 591.

University of Waterloo, Faculty of Arts, School of Accountancy, Waterloo, ON N2L 3G1, Canada. Offers programs in accounting (M Acc, PhD), finance (M Acc), taxation (M Tax). Faculty: 18 full-time (2 women), 6 part-time (1 woman). Students: 96 full-time (50 women). In 1997, 83 master's, 1 doctorate awarded. *Degree requirements:* For master's, thesis or alternative; for doctorate, dissertation. *Entrance requirements:* For master's, TOEFL (minimum score 600), honors degree, minimum B average; for doctorate, GMAT, TOEFL (minimum score 600), master's degree. Application fee: $50. *Tuition:* $5046 per year. *Faculty research:* Auditing, management accounting, financial accounting, taxation. • Dr. Morley Lemon, Director, 519-888-4567 Ext. 3732. Application contact: Dr. G. Richardson, Graduate Officer, 519-888-4567 Ext. 6549. Fax: 519-888-7562.

University of West Florida, College of Business, Department of Accounting, Pensacola, FL 32514-5750. Awards MA. Part-time programs available. Students: 31 full-time (18 women), 43 part-time (30 women); includes 11 minority (2 African Americans, 4 Asian Americans, 4 Hispanics, 1 Native American), 2 international. Average age 33. 29 applicants, 97% accepted. In 1997, 26 degrees awarded. *Degree requirements:* Computer language required, thesis not required. *Entrance requirements:* GMAT (minimum score 450; average 550). Application deadline: 7/1 (priority date; 11/1 for spring admission). Application fee: $20. *Tuition:* $131 per credit hour (minimum) for state residents; $436 per credit hour (minimum) for nonresidents. *Financial aid:* Fellowships, Federal Work-Study available. Aid available to part-time students. Financial aid application deadline: 4/1; applicants required to submit FAFSA. *Faculty research:* Audit risk, tax legislation, product costing, bank core deposit intangibles, financial reporting. • Dr. Richard V. Calvasina, Chairperson, 850-474-2717.

University of Wisconsin–Madison, School of Business, Program in Accounting, Madison, WI 53706-1380. Awards M Acc, MBA, MS, PhD. *Degree requirements:* For doctorate, dissertation. *Entrance requirements:* GMAT. Application deadline: 6/1 (rolling processing; 10/1 for spring admission). Application fee: $38. *Tuition:* $5950 per year full-time, $1118 per semester (minimum) part-time for state residents; $16,230 per year full-time, $3044 per semester (minimum) part-time for nonresidents. *Faculty research:* Accounting standards, security valuation, accounting for derivatives, international accounting standards.

University of Wisconsin–Whitewater, College of Business and Economics, Department of Accounting, Whitewater, WI 53190-1790. Awards MPA. Part-time and evening/weekend programs available. *Degree requirements:* Computer language required, foreign language and thesis not required. *Entrance requirements:* GMAT, minimum AACSB index of 1000, minimum GPA of 2.75. Application deadline: rolling. Application fee: $38.

Utah State University, College of Business, School of Accountancy, Logan, UT 84322. Awards M Acc. Faculty: 9 full-time (1 woman), 2 part-time (0 women). Students: 51 full-time (24 women), 6 part-time (2 women). Average age 28. 30 applicants, 77% accepted. In 1997, 52 degrees awarded. *Degree requirements:* Computer language required, foreign language not required. *Entrance requirements:* GMAT (score in 40th percentile or higher), TOEFL (minimum score 550), minimum GPA of 3.0. Application deadline: 6/15 (priority date; rolling processing; 10/15 for spring admission). Application fee: $40. *Expenses:* Tuition $1448 per year full-time, $624 per year part-time for state residents; $5082 per year full-time, $2192 per year part-time for nonresidents. Fees $421 per year full-time, $165 per year part-time. *Financial aid:* In 1997–98, 16 fellowships, 14 graduate assistantships were awarded; full tuition waivers and career-related internships or fieldwork also available. Financial aid application deadline: 3/15. • Clifford R. Skousen, Head, 435-797-2340. E-mail: cskousen@b202.usu.edu. Application contact: James Brackner, Graduate Program Director, 435-797-2330. Fax: 435-797-1475. E-mail: jbracknr@b202.usu.edu.

Virginia Commonwealth University, School of Business, Program in Accountancy, Richmond, VA 23284-9005. Offers accounting/taxation (PhD). Faculty: 21. Students: 16 full-time (9 women), 19 part-time (8 women); includes 3 minority (2 African Americans, 1 Asian American), 4 international. Average age 42. 47 applicants, 32% accepted. *Degree requirements:* Dissertation. *Entrance requirements:* GMAT. Application deadline: rolling. Application fee: $30 ($0 for international students). *Tuition:* $4960 per year full-time, $257 per credit part-time for state residents; $12,652 per year full-time, $684 per credit part-time for nonresidents. *Financial aid:* Fellowships, research assistantships, teaching assistantships, full and partial tuition waivers, Federal Work-Study, institutionally sponsored loans available. Financial aid application deadline: 3/15. • Dr. Ruth W. Epps, Chair, 804-828-1608. Fax: 804-828-1719. E-mail: rwepps@vcu.edu. Application contact: Dr. Edward L. Millner, Associate Dean of Graduate Studies, 804-828-1741. Fax: 804-828-7174.

Virginia Polytechnic Institute and State University, Pamplin College of Business, Department of Accounting, Blacksburg, VA 24061. Awards M Acct, PhD. Faculty: 22 full-time (4 women). Students: 60 full-time (31 women), 13 part-time (6 women); includes 14 minority (7 African Americans, 5 Asian Americans, 2 Hispanics), 13 international. 80 applicants, 61% accepted. In 1997, 35 master's, 3 doctorates awarded. *Degree requirements:* For doctorate, dissertation required, foreign language not required. *Entrance requirements:* GMAT, TOEFL (minimum score 600). Application deadline: 12/1 (priority date; rolling processing). Application fee: $25. *Tuition:* $4927 per year full-time, $792 per semester (minimum) part-time for state residents; $7537 per year full-time, $1227 per semester (minimum) part-time for nonresidents. *Financial aid:* In 1997–98, 18 teaching assistantships, 23 assistantships were awarded; fellowships also available. Financial aid application deadline: 4/1. *Faculty research:* Financial accounting, international accounting, information systems, management accounting. • Dr. Wayne E. Leininger, Head, 540-231-6591.

See in-depth description on page 459.

Wake Forest University, Department of Accountancy, Winston-Salem, NC 27109. Awards MSA. Faculty: 8 full-time (0 women). Students: 66 full-time (26 women), 1 part-time (0 women); includes 4 minority (3 African Americans, 1 Asian American). 40 applicants, 93% accepted. In 1997, 34 degrees awarded. *Degree requirements:* 1 foreign language required (computer language can substitute), thesis not required. *Entrance requirements:* GMAT. Application deadline: 2/15. Application fee: $25. *Tuition:* $17,150 per year full-time, $550 per hour part-time. *Financial aid:* In 1997–98, 31 students received aid, including 9 teaching assistantships totaling $146,700, 22 scholarships (3 to first-year students) totaling $358,600. Financial aid application deadline: 2/15; applicants required to submit FAFSA. • Dr. Paul Juras, Director, 336-758-4836. E-mail: juras@wfu.edu.

Walsh College of Accountancy and Business Administration, Program in Accountancy, Troy, MI 48007-7006. Awards MSPA. Part-time and evening/weekend programs available. Faculty: 4 full-time (1 woman), 11 part-time (3 women). *Degree requirements:* Computer language required, thesis optional, foreign language not required. *Entrance requirements:* TOEFL (minimum score 550), minimum GPA of 2.75, previous course work in business. Application deadline: rolling. Application fee: $25. *Expenses:* Tuition $273 per credit hour. Fees $75 per semester. *Financial aid:* Federal Work-Study available. Aid available to part-time students. • Robert Shanahan, Interim Chairman, 248-689-8282. Fax: 248-689-9066. Application contact: Sherree Hyde, Director, Enrollment Services, 248-689-8282 Ext. 215. Fax: 248-524-2520.

Washington State University, College of Business and Economics, Programs in Business, Department of Accounting and Business Law, Pullman, WA 99164-1610. Awards M Acc. Faculty: 10. Students: 15 full-time (11 women), 3 part-time (2 women); includes 2 minority (1 African American, 1 Asian American), 7 international. In 1997, 8 degrees awarded. *Degree requirements:* Oral exam, research paper required, thesis not required. *Average time to degree:* master's–1.5 years full-time. *Entrance requirements:* GMAT (minimum score 550), TOEFL (minimum score 580), minimum GPA of 3.0. Application deadline: 3/1 (priority date; rolling processing). Application fee: $35. *Tuition:* $5334 per year full-time, $267 per credit hour part-time for state residents; $13,380 per year full-time, $677 per credit hour part-time for nonresidents. *Financial aid:* Research assistantships, teaching assistantships, teaching associateships, partial tuition waivers, Federal Work-Study, institutionally sponsored loans available. Financial aid application deadline: 4/1. • Dr. Glenn Johnson, Chairman, 509-335-8541. Fax: 509-335-4275. E-mail: arndtm@wsu.edu.

Weber State University, College of Business and Economics, School of Accountancy, Ogden, UT 84408-3803. Awards MP Acc. Part-time programs available. Faculty: 11 full-time (2 women). Students: 40 full-time (19 women), 20 part-time (10 women); includes 3 minority (2 Asian Americans, 1 Hispanic), 5 international. Average age 31. 44 applicants, 89% accepted. In 1997, 35 degrees awarded. *Average time to degree:* master's–1 year full-time, 3 years part-time. *Entrance requirements:* GMAT (minimum AACSB index of 1050). Application deadline: 3/1 (priority date; rolling processing). Application fee: $30 ($35 for international students). *Financial aid:* 13 students received aid; research assistantships, teaching assistantships, scholarships, full and partial tuition waivers, Federal Work-Study, institutionally sponsored loans available. Financial aid application deadline: 3/1. *Faculty research:* Taxation, financial accounting, auditing, managerial accounting, accounting education. • Dr. James G. Swearingen, Coordinator, 801-626-6897.

Western Carolina University, College of Business, Program in Accountancy, Cullowhee, NC 28723. Awards M Ac. *Degree requirements:* Comprehensive exam required, foreign language and thesis not required. *Entrance requirements:* GRE General Test. Application deadline: rolling. Application fee: $35. *Tuition:* $1799 per year full-time, $144 per credit hour (minimum) part-time for state residents; $9069 per year full-time, $1053 per credit hour (minimum) part-time for nonresidents. *Financial aid:* Fellowships, research assistantships, teaching assistantships available. Financial aid application deadline: 3/15. • Gary A. Williams, Director, 828-227-7401. Application contact: Kathleen Owen, Assistant to the Dean, 828-227-7398. Fax: 828-227-7480.

Western Illinois University, College of Business and Technology, Department of Accountancy, Macomb, IL 61455-1390. Awards M Acct. Part-time programs available. Faculty: 9 full-time (4 women). Students: 9 full-time (6 women), 1 (woman) part-time; includes 6 international. Average age 27. 9 applicants, 67% accepted. In 1997, 2 degrees awarded. *Degree requirements:* Thesis or alternative required, foreign language not required. *Entrance requirements:* GMAT (score in 50th percentile or higher), minimum GPA of 2.75. Application deadline: rolling. Application fee: $0 ($25 for international students). *Expenses:* Tuition $2304 per year full-time, $96 per semester hour part-time for state residents; $6912 per year full-time, $288 per semester hour part-time for nonresidents. Fees $944 per year full-time, $33 per semester hour part-time. *Financial aid:* In 1997–98, 5 students received aid, including 5 research assistantships averaging $610 per month; full tuition waivers also available. Financial aid applicants required to submit FAFSA. *Faculty research:* International business. • Dr. Penelope Yunker, Chairperson, 309-298-1152. Application contact: Barbara Baily, Director of Graduate Studies, 309-298-1806. Fax: 309-298-2245. E-mail: barb_baily@ccmail.wiu.edu.

Western International University, Program in Accounting, 9215 North Black Canyon Highway, Phoenix, AZ 85021-2718. Awards MS. Evening/weekend programs available. *Degree requirements:* Thesis, research project required, foreign language not required. *Entrance requirements:* GMAT (strongly recommended), minimum GPA of 2.75. Application deadline: rolling. Application fee: $50 ($100 for international students). • Janice Washington, Chair, 602-943-2311. Application contact: Enrollment Department, 602-943-2311. Fax: 602-371-8637.

Western Kentucky University, College of Business Administration, Department of Accounting, Bowling Green, KY 42101-3576. Awards MPA. Part-time and evening/weekend programs available. Faculty: 12 full-time (2 women). Students: 6 full-time (3 women), 1 (woman) part-time; includes 2 minority (1 African American, 1 Asian American). Average age 25. 3 applicants, 100% accepted. In 1997, 7 degrees awarded. *Entrance requirements:* GMAT, minimum GPA of 2.5. Application deadline: 8/1 (priority date; rolling processing; 12/1 for spring admission). Application fee: $20. *Tuition:* $2460 per year full-time, $133 per credit hour part-time for state residents; $6700 per year full-time, $369 per credit hour part-time for nonresidents. *Financial aid:* In 1997–98, service awards averaging $421 per month and totaling $9,000 were awarded; Federal Work-Study, institutionally sponsored loans also available. Aid available to part-time students. Financial aid application deadline: 4/1; applicants required to submit FAFSA. • Dr. Jack O. Hall, Head, 502-745-3895. Fax: 502-745-3893.

Western Michigan University, Haworth College of Business, Department of Accountancy, Kalamazoo, MI 49008. Awards MSA. Students: 9 full-time (5 women), 21 part-time (13 women); includes 1 minority (African American), 3 international. 17 applicants, 71% accepted. In 1997, 18 degrees awarded. *Degree requirements:* Computer language required, thesis not required. *Entrance requirements:* GMAT. Application deadline: 2/15 (priority date; rolling processing). Application fee: $25. *Expenses:* Tuition $154 per credit hour for state residents; $372 per credit hour for nonresidents. Fees $602 per year full-time, $132 per semester part-time. *Financial aid:* Fellowships, research assistantships, teaching assistantships, Federal Work-Study available. Financial aid application deadline: 2/15; applicants required to submit FAFSA. • Dr. Jack Ruhl, Chairperson, 616-387-5120. Application contact: Paula J. Boodt, Coordinator, Graduate Admissions and Recruitment, 616-387-2000. E-mail: paulaboodt@wmich.edu.

Western New England College, School of Business, Program in Accounting, Springfield, MA 01119-2654. Awards MBA, MSA. *Application deadline:* rolling. *Application fee:* $30. *Expenses:* Tuition $353 per credit hour. Fees $44 per semester (minimum). *Financial aid:* Application deadline 4/1. • Application contact: Rod Pease, Director of Student Administrative Services, 413-796-2080.

Directories: Accounting; Finance and Banking

West Texas A&M University, T. Boone Pickens College of Business, Department of Accounting, Economics, and Finance, Program in Accounting, Canyon, TX 79016-0001. Awards MP Acc. Part-time and evening/weekend programs available. Postbaccalaureate distance learning degree programs offered (minimal on-campus study). Faculty: 8 full-time (0 women). Students: 9 full-time (4 women), 4 part-time (2 women); includes 2 minority (both Asian Americans), 2 international. Average age 34. 3 applicants, 100% accepted. In 1997, 3 degrees awarded. *Degree requirements:* Comprehensive exam required, thesis optional, foreign language not required. *Average time to degree:* master's–3 years full-time, 6 years part-time. *Entrance requirements:* GMAT (minimum score 450; average 530), minimum GPA of 2.75. Application deadline: rolling. Application fee: $0 ($50 for international students). Electronic applications accepted. *Expenses:* Tuition $46 per semester hour for state residents; $259 per semester hour for nonresidents. Fees $156 per semester (minimum). *Financial aid:* Partial tuition waivers, Federal Work-Study, institutionally sponsored loans available. Aid available to part-time students. Financial aid applicants required to submit FAFSA. • Application contact: Dr. Darlene Smith, Graduate Adviser, 806-651-2521. Fax: 806-651-2514. E-mail: darlene.smith@wtamu.edu.

West Virginia University, College of Business and Economics, Program in Professional Accountancy, Morgantown, WV 26506. Awards MPA. Part-time programs available. Faculty: 12 full-time (2 women), 3 part-time (all women). Students: 20 full-time (10 women), 4 part-time (2 women); includes 1 minority (Asian American), 4 international. Average age 24. 35 applicants, 57% accepted. In 1997, 13 degrees awarded (100% found work related to degree). *Entrance requirements:* GMAT (minimum score 500), TOEFL (minimum score 580), BS in accounting or equivalent, minimum GPA of 3.0. Application deadline: 6/30 (priority date; rolling processing; 11/15 for spring admission). Application fee: $45. *Tuition:* $3130 per year for state residents; $8554 per year for nonresidents. *Financial aid:* Federal Work-Study, institutionally sponsored loans available. Financial aid application deadline: 2/1; applicants required to submit FAFSA. *Faculty research:* Accounting for libraries, auditing, microcomputers in accounting. • Robert Maust, Chair, 304-293-7840. E-mail: maust@wvube1.be.wvu.edu. Application contact: Dr. Paul J. Speaker, Director of Graduate Programs, 304-293-5408. Fax: 304-293-7061. E-mail: thomas@wvube1.be.wvu.edu.

Wheeling Jesuit University, Graduate Business Program, Wheeling, WV 26003-6295. Offerings include accounting (MS). Program faculty: 10 full-time (1 woman), 8 part-time (1 woman), 13.5 FTE. *Average time to degree:* master's–2 years full-time, 4 years part-time. *Application deadline:* 8/1 (priority date; rolling processing; 12/15 for spring admission). *Application fee:* $25. *Tuition:* $360 per credit hour. • Dr. Edward W. Younkins, Director, 304-243-2255. Fax: 304-243-2243. Application contact: Carol Carroll, Graduate Secretary, 304-243-2344. Fax: 304-243-4441.

Wichita State University, W. Frank Barton School of Business, School of Accountancy, Wichita, KS 67260. Offers program in professional accountancy (MPA). Part-time and evening/weekend programs available. Faculty: 8 full-time (3 women). Students: 19 full-time (11 women), 30 part-time (19 women); includes 1 minority (African American), 8 international. Average age 34. 14 applicants, 36% accepted. In 1997, 10 degrees awarded. *Degree requirements:* Computer language required, foreign language and thesis not required. *Entrance requirements:* GMAT, TOEFL (minimum score 550), minimum AACSB index of 1100, minimum GPA of 2.75. Application deadline: 7/1 (priority date; rolling processing; 1/1 for spring admission). Application fee: $25 ($40 for international students). Electronic applications accepted. *Expenses:* Tuition $2303 per year full-time, $96 per credit hour part-time for state residents; $7691 per year full-time, $321 per credit hour part-time for nonresidents. Fees $490 per year full-time, $75 per semester (minimum) part-time. *Financial aid:* In 1997–98, 6 teaching assistantships averaging $533 per month and totaling $21,875, 1 graduate assistantship averaging $886 per month and totaling $5,318 were awarded; institutionally sponsored loans also available. Aid available to part-time students. Financial aid application deadline: 4/1; applicants required to submit FAFSA. *Faculty research:* Professional standards, behavioral issues, social accounting, taxation, auditing issues. • Dr. James W. Deskins, Director, 316-978-3215. E-mail: deskins@twsuvm.uc.twsu.edu. Application contact: Graduate Coordinator, 316-978-3215. Fax: 316-978-3845.

Widener University, School of Business Administration, Program in Accounting, Chester, PA 19013-5792. Awards MS. Part-time and evening/weekend programs available. Faculty: 6 full-time (2 women), 3 part-time (0 women). Students: 3 full-time, 16 part-time; includes 5 international. Average age 27. 9 applicants, 89% accepted. In 1997, 9 degrees awarded. *Average time to degree:* master's–2 years full-time, 4 years part-time. *Entrance requirements:* Certified Management Accountant Exam, Certified Public Accountant Exam, or GMAT (minimum score 450). Application deadline: 8/1 (priority date; rolling processing; 12/1 for spring admission). Application fee: $25 ($300 for international students). *Tuition:* $455 per credit. • Lisa Bussom Jr., Director, Graduate Programs in Business, School of Business Administration, 610-499-4305. Fax: 610-499-4615. E-mail: gradbus.advise@widener.edu.

Wilkes University, Programs in Business Administration, Wilkes-Barre, PA 18766-0002. Offerings include accounting (MBA). MBA (management, management information systems) being phased out; applicants no longer accepted. Faculty: 11 full-time, 2 part-time. *Entrance requirements:* GMAT. Application deadline: rolling. Application fee: $30. *Expenses:* Tuition $12,552 per year full-time, $523 per credit hour part-time. Fees $240 per year full-time, $10 per credit hour part-time. • Dr. Robert Seeley, Director, 717-408-4717.

Wright State University, College of Business and Administration, Department of Accountancy, Dayton, OH 45435. Awards M Acc. Program new for fall 1998. *Entrance requirements:* GMAT, TOEFL (minimum score 550), minimum AACSB index of 1000. Application fee: $25. *Tuition:* $5109 per year full-time, $161 per credit hour part-time for state residents; $9039 per year full-time, $282 per credit hour part-time for nonresidents. *Financial aid:* In 1997–98, 4 graduate assistantships were awarded. • Dr. Susan Lightle, Chair, 937-775-2377. Application contact: Dr. Hans Dieter Sprohge, Graduate Adviser, 937-775-2365.

Yale University, School of Management and Graduate School of Arts and Sciences, Doctoral Program in Management, New Haven, CT 06520. Offerings include accounting (PhD). Terminal master's awarded for partial completion of doctoral program. Program faculty: 36 full-time (4 women). *Degree requirements:* Dissertation required, foreign language not required. *Average time to degree:* doctorate–5 years full-time. *Entrance requirements:* GMAT or GRE General Test (GRE preferred). Application deadline: 1/2. Application fee: $65. *Expenses:* Tuition waived upon acceptance into program. • Application contact: Subrata Sen, Director of Graduate Studies, 203-432-6028. Fax: 203-432-6974. E-mail: subrata.sen@yale.edu.

Youngstown State University, Warren P. Williamson Jr. College of Business Administration, Department of Accounting and Finance, Youngstown, OH 44555-0002. Offers programs in accounting (MBA), finance (MBA). Part-time and evening/weekend programs available. Faculty: 10 full-time (2 women). Students: 10 full-time (5 women), 14 part-time (4 women); includes 3 international. 8 applicants, 100% accepted. In 1997, 6 degrees awarded. *Degree requirements:* Computer language required, thesis optional, foreign language not required. *Entrance requirements:* GMAT (minimum score 450), TOEFL (minimum score 550), minimum GPA of 2.7. Application deadline: 8/15 (priority date; rolling processing; 2/15 for spring admission). Application fee: $30 ($75 for international students). *Expenses:* Tuition $90 per credit hour for state residents; $144 per credit hour (minimum) for nonresidents. Fees $528 per year full-time, $244 per year (minimum) part-time. *Financial aid:* In 1997–98, 6 students received aid, including 3 research assistantships averaging $666 per month and totaling $25,560, 3 scholarships totaling $2,752; fellowships, teaching assistantships, Federal Work-Study, institutionally sponsored loans also available. Aid available to part-time students. Financial aid application deadline: 3/1. *Faculty research:* Taxation and compliance, capital markets, accounting information systems, accounting theory, tax and government accounting. • Dr. James A. Tackett, Chair, 330-742-3084. Application contact: Dr. Peter J. Kasvinsky, Dean of Graduate Studies, 330-742-3091. Fax: 330-742-1580. E-mail: amgrad03@ysub.ysu.edu.

Finance and Banking

Adelphi University, School of Management and Business, Certificate Programs in Management, Garden City, NY 11530. Offerings include banking (Certificate). *Average time to degree:* other advanced degree–2 years full-time, 2.5 years part-time. *Application deadline:* 8/15 (priority date; rolling processing; 12/15 for spring admission). *Application fee:* $50. *Expenses:* Tuition $16,000 per year full-time, $485 per credit part-time. Fees $500 per year full-time, $150 per semester part-time. • Application contact: Jennifer Spiegel, Associate Director of Admissions, 516-877-3055.

Adelphi University, School of Management and Business, Department of Banking, Economics, and Finance, Garden City, NY 11530. Offers program in finance and banking (MS). Part-time and evening/weekend programs available. Faculty: 6 full-time (0 women). Students: 7 full-time (2 women), 3 part-time (1 woman). Average age 28. In 1997, 7 degrees awarded. *Average time to degree:* master's–2.5 years full-time, 3.5 years part-time. *Entrance requirements:* GMAT (minimum score 450), TOEFL (minimum score 550). Application deadline: 8/15 (priority date; rolling processing; 12/15 for spring admission). Application fee: $50. *Expenses:* Tuition $16,000 per year full-time, $485 per credit part-time. Fees $500 per year full-time, $150 per semester part-time. *Financial aid:* Application deadline 3/1. • Dr. Robert Felheim, Chairperson, 516-877-4660. Application contact: Jennifer Spiegel, Associate Director of Admissions, 516-877-3055.

Alabama Agricultural and Mechanical University, School of Business, Department of Economics and Finance, PO Box 1357, Normal, AL 35762-1357. Awards MS. Evening/weekend programs available. Faculty: 8 full-time (0 women), 1 part-time (0 women). Students: 1 (woman) full-time, 18 part-time (12 women); includes 2 minority (both African Americans), 6 international. Average age 28. *Degree requirements:* Comprehensive exam required, foreign language and thesis not required. *Entrance requirements:* GRE General Test, TOEFL (minimum score 500), minimum undergraduate GPA of 2.5. Application deadline: 5/1 (rolling processing). Application fee: $15 ($20 for international students). *Expenses:* Tuition $2782 per year full-time, $565 per semester (minimum) part-time for state residents; $5164 per year full-time, $1015 per semester (minimum) part-time for nonresidents. Fees $560 per year full-time, $390 per year part-time. *Financial aid:* Teaching assistantships and career-related internships or fieldwork available. Financial aid application deadline: 4/1. *Faculty research:* Energy, banking, financial management, agricultural economics, sports economics. • Dr. Eric Rahimian, Chair, 205-851-5294. Fax: 205-851-5874.

American College, Graduate School of Financial Sciences, Bryn Mawr, PA 19010-2105. Awards MSFS. Part-time and evening/weekend programs available. Postbaccalaureate distance learning degree programs offered (minimal on-campus study). Faculty: 27 full-time (3 women), 8 part-time (0 women). Students: 1,500 part-time. *Degree requirements:* Thesis required, foreign language not required. *Application deadline:* rolling. *Application fee:* $275. *Tuition:* $490 per course. *Faculty research:* Retirement counseling, social security, aging, family composition, inflation. • M. Donald Wright, Director, 610-526-1365. Application contact: Joanne F. Patterson, Associate Director of Graduate Administration, 610-526-1366. Fax: 610-526-1310. E-mail: joannep@amercoll.edu.

American University, College of Arts and Sciences, Department of Economics, Program in Development Banking, Washington, DC 20016-8001. Awards MA. Part-time and evening/weekend programs available. Faculty: 22 full-time (4 women), 5 part-time (0 women). Students: 9 full-time (1 woman), 2 part-time (0 women); includes 1 minority (Hispanic), 6 international. 14 applicants, 71% accepted. In 1997, 15 degrees awarded. *Degree requirements:* Comprehensive exams required, foreign language and thesis not required. *Average time to degree:* master's–2 years full-time, 3 years part-time. *Entrance requirements:* TOEFL (minimum score 550). Application deadline: 6/1 (priority date; rolling processing; 10/1 for spring admission). Application fee: $50. *Expenses:* Tuition $687 per credit hour. Fees $180 per year full-time, $110 per year part-time. *Financial aid:* Federal Work-Study, institutionally sponsored loans, and career-related internships or fieldwork available. Financial aid application deadline: 2/1. • Application contact: Larry Sawers, Adviser, 202-885-3766. Fax: 202-885-3790. E-mail: sawer@american.edu.

American University, Kogod College of Business Administration, Department of Finance, Program in Finance, Washington, DC 20016-8001. Awards MBA, MS. Part-time and evening/weekend programs available. Faculty: 9 full-time (1 woman), 4 part-time (3 women). Students: 65 full-time (20 women), 67 part-time (22 women); includes 22 minority (11 African Americans, 9 Asian Americans, 2 Hispanics), 49 international. 151 applicants, 83% accepted. In 1997, 57 degrees awarded. *Entrance requirements:* GMAT. Application deadline: 2/1 (priority date; 10/1 for spring admission). Application fee: $50. *Expenses:* Tuition $19,080 per year full-time, $687 per credit hour (minimum) part-time. Fees $180 per year full-time, $110 per year part-time. *Financial aid:* Fellowships, research assistantships, Federal Work-Study, institutionally sponsored loans, and career-related internships or fieldwork available. Aid available to part-time students. Financial aid application deadline: 2/1. • Dr. Robert L. Losey, Chair, Department of Finance, 202-885-1941. Fax: 202-885-1946.

Arizona State University, College of Business, Program in Business Administration, Tempe, AZ 85287. Offerings include finance (PhD). Program faculty: 93 full-time (21 women), 10 part-time (1 woman). *Degree requirements:* Dissertation. *Application fee:* $45. *Expenses:* Tuition $2088 per year full-time, $110 per hour part-time for state residents; $9040 per year full-time, $377 per hour part-time for nonresidents. Fees $72 per year full-time, $18 per semester (minimum) part-time. • Dr. Lee R. McPheters, Associate Dean, 602-965-9377. Fax: 602-965-3368. Application contact: Judy Heilala, Director of MBA, 602-965-3331.

Armstrong University, Graduate School of Business Administration, Program in Finance and Accounting, Oakland, CA 94612. Offers accounting (MBA), finance (MBA). *Degree requirements:* Thesis required, foreign language not required. *Entrance requirements:* Minimum GPA of 2.5. Application deadline: 8/15 (priority date; rolling processing; 1/1 for spring admission). Application fee: $50. • Prof. Thomas Smith, Director, 510-835-7900. E-mail: info@armstrong-u.edu. Application contact: Judy Battle, Director of Admissions, 510-835-7900. Fax: 510-835-8935. E-mail: info@armstrong-u.edu.

Baruch College of the City University of New York, School of Business, Department of Economics and Finance, Program in Finance, 17 Lexington Avenue, New York, NY 10010-5585. Awards MBA, MS, PhD. PhD offered jointly with the Graduate School and University Center of the City University of New York. Part-time and evening/weekend programs available. Faculty: 23 full-time (3 women), 2 part-time (0 women). Students: 281 full-time (104 women),

294 part-time (75 women). In 1997, 170 master's awarded. Terminal master's awarded for partial completion of doctoral program. *Degree requirements:* For master's, computer language required, foreign language not required; for doctorate, computer language, dissertation required, foreign language not required. *Average time to degree:* master's–2 years full-time, 4 years part-time. *Entrance requirements:* For master's, GMAT, TOEFL (minimum score 570), TWE (minimum score 4.5); for doctorate, GMAT. Application deadline: 6/15 (11/1 for spring admission). Application fee: $40. *Expenses:* Tuition $4350 per year full-time, $185 per credit part-time for state residents; $7600 per year full-time, $320 per credit part-time for nonresidents. Fees $53 per year. *Financial aid:* Research assistantships, Federal Work-Study, and career-related internships or fieldwork available. Aid available to part-time students. Financial aid application deadline: 5/3; applicants required to submit FAFSA. • Application contact: Michael S. Wynne, Office of Graduate Admissions, 212-802-2330. Fax: 212-802-2335. E-mail: graduate_admissions@baruch.cuny.edu.

Bentley College, Graduate School of Business, Program in Finance, 175 Forest Street, Waltham, MA 02154-4705. Awards MSF. Part-time and evening/weekend programs available. Faculty: 16 full-time (2 women), 7 part-time (0 women). Students: 16 full-time (4 women), 109 part-time (36 women); includes 3 minority (1 African American, 1 Asian American, 1 Hispanic), 12 international. Average age 29. 103 applicants, 68% accepted. In 1997, 43 degrees awarded (100% found work related to degree). *Degree requirements:* Computer language required, foreign language and thesis not required. *Entrance requirements:* GMAT (average 540), TOEFL (minimum score 580). Application deadline: 6/1 (priority date; rolling processing; 11/1 for spring admission). Application fee: $50. *Expenses:* Tuition $20,500 per year full-time, $2050 per course part-time. Fees $65 per year full-time, $15 per semester part-time. *Financial aid:* In 1997–98, 27 students received aid, including 5 research assistantships (2 to first-year students) averaging $416 per month, 1 departmental assistantship; Federal Work-Study and career-related internships or fieldwork also available. Aid available to part-time students. Financial aid application deadline: 4/15; applicants required to submit CSS PROFILE or FAFSA. *Faculty research:* Corporate finance, international finance, capital markets, trading rooms. • David Milton, Director, 781-891-2734. Fax: 781-891-2896. Application contact: Holly Chase, Associate Director, 781-891-2108. Fax: 781-891-2464. E-mail: hchase@bentley.edu.

Announcement: Bentley College Graduate School of Business offers the Master of Science in Finance (MSF) degree and the MBA with a concentration in finance. Those wanting to specialize within a specific area of finance (e.g., financial services or investments) may do so through their elective courses. Classroom learning is supported by extensive use of an on-site trading room facility.

Bentley College, Graduate School of Business, Program in Personal Financial Planning, 175 Forest Street, Waltham, MA 02154-4705. Awards MSPFP. Part-time and evening/weekend programs available. Faculty: 4 full-time (0 women), 14 part-time (2 women). Students: 8 full-time (0 women), 57 part-time (13 women); includes 7 minority (1 African American, 5 Asian Americans, 1 Hispanic). Average age 41. 55 applicants, 93% accepted. *Degree requirements:* Computer language required, foreign language and thesis not required. *Entrance requirements:* TOEFL (minimum score 580). Application deadline: 6/1 (priority date; rolling processing; 11/1 for spring admission). Application fee: $50. *Expenses:* Tuition $20,500 per year full-time, $2050 per course part-time. Fees $65 per year full-time, $15 per semester part-time. *Financial aid:* In 1997–98, 12 students received aid, including 1 research assistantship (to a first-year student) totaling $19,800; Federal Work-Study and career-related internships or fieldwork also available. Aid available to part-time students. Financial aid application deadline: 4/15; applicants required to submit CSS PROFILE or FAFSA. • Glenn Frank, Director, 781-891-2771. Application contact: Holly Chase, Associate Director, 781-891-2108. Fax: 781-891-2464. E-mail: hchase@bentley.edu.

Bentley College, Graduate School of Business, Self-paced MBA Program, 175 Forest Street, Waltham, MA 02154-4705. Offerings include finance (MBA). Program faculty: 70 full-time (21 women), 22 part-time (8 women). *Degree requirements:* Computer language required, foreign language and thesis not required. *Entrance requirements:* GMAT (average 540), TOEFL (minimum score 580). Application deadline: 6/1 (priority date; rolling processing; 11/1 for spring admission). Application fee: $50. *Expenses:* Tuition $20,500 per year full-time, $2050 per course part-time. Fees $65 per year full-time, $15 per semester part-time. • Dr. Judith B. Kamm, Director, 781-891-3433. Application contact: Holly Chase, Associate Director, 781-891-2108. Fax: 781-891-2464. E-mail: hchase@bentley.edu.

Boston College, Wallace E. Carroll Graduate School of Management, Department of Finance, Chestnut Hill, MA 02167-9991. Awards MBA, MSF, PhD, MBA/MSF. Program in). Part-time and evening/weekend programs available. *Degree requirements:* For doctorate, dissertation required, foreign language not required. *Entrance requirements:* For master's, GMAT (average 610), TOEFL (minimum score 600; average 630). Application deadline: 4/1 (priority date; rolling processing; 11/15 for spring admission). Application fee: $45. *Expenses:* Tuition $22,134 per year full-time, $714 per semester hour part-time. Fees $80 per year (minimum) full-time, $30 per semester part-time. *Financial aid:* Fellowships, research assistantships, teaching assistantships, administrative assistantships, Federal Work-Study, institutionally sponsored loans available. Financial aid application deadline: 3/1; applicants required to submit FAFSA. *Faculty research:* Capital structure, compensation, options, valuation, corporate takeovers. • Dr. Alan Marcus, Chairman, 617-552-2767. Application contact: Simone Marthers, Director of Admissions, 617-552-3920. Fax: 617-552-8078.

Boston University, School of Law, Boston, MA 02215. Offerings include American banking law (LL M), international banking law (LL M). School faculty: 60 full-time (20 women), 75 part-time (21 women). *Average time to degree:* master's–1 year full-time; first professional–3 years full-time. *Entrance requirements:* JD, ranking in the top half of law school class. Application deadline: 3/1 (rolling processing). Application fee: $50. *Expenses:* Tuition $22,830 per year full-time, $713 per credit part-time. Fees $218 per year full-time, $40 per semester part-time. • Ronald A. Cass, Dean, 617-353-3112. Application contact: Barbara J. Selmo, Director of Admissions and Financial Aid, 617-353-3100. E-mail: bulawadm@bu.edu.

Boston University, School of Management, Boston, MA 02215. Offerings include finance (DBA). School faculty: 110 full-time, 54 part-time. *Degree requirements:* Dissertation required, foreign language not required. *Entrance requirements:* GMAT or GRE General Test. Application deadline: 5/1 (rolling processing). Application fee: $50. Electronic applications accepted. *Expenses:* Tuition $22,830 per year full-time, $713 per credit part-time. Fees $218 per year full-time, $40 per semester part-time. • Therese M. Hofmann, Assistant Dean, 617-353-2673. Application contact: Peter G. Kelly, Director of Admissions and Financial Aid, 617-353-2670. Fax: 617-353-7368. E-mail: mba@bu.edu.

Boston University, Metropolitan College, Program in Administrative Studies, Boston, MA 02215. Offerings include financial economics (MSAS). Program faculty: 7 full-time (2 women), 25 part-time (5 women). *Degree requirements:* Thesis optional, foreign language not required. *Average time to degree:* master's–1 year full-time, 2 years part-time. *Entrance requirements:* TOEFL (minimum score 550). Application deadline: rolling. Application fee: $50. *Expenses:* Tuition $15,488 per year full-time, $484 per credit part-time. Fees $218 per year full-time, $40 per semester part-time. • Dr. Kip Becker, Chairman. E-mail: adminsc@bu.edu. Application contact: Department of Administrative Sciences, 617-353-3016. Fax: 617-353-6840. E-mail: adminsc@bu.edu.

See in-depth description on page 537.

Brandeis University, Graduate School of International Economics and Finance, MS-32, PO Box 9110, Waltham, MA 02254-9110. Offers programs in finance (MSF), international business (MBAi), international economics and finance (MA, PhD). Faculty: 24 (4 women). Students: 122 full-time (41 women), 25 part-time (11 women); includes 81 international. Average age 26. 334 applicants, 43% accepted. In 1997, 30 master's, 2 doctorates awarded. Terminal master's awarded for partial completion of doctoral program. *Degree requirements:* For master's, 1 foreign language, semester abroad; for doctorate, dissertation. *Entrance requirements:* For master's, GMAT or GRE General Test (MA), GMAT (MBAi), TOEFL (minimum score 600); for doctorate, GRE General Test, GRE Subject Test, TOEFL (minimum score 600). Application deadline: 2/15 (priority date). Application fee: $50. *Expenses:* Tuition $23,360 per year full-time, $2960 per course part-time. Fees $45 per year. *Financial aid:* 76 students received aid; assistantships, scholarships, institutionally sponsored loans available. Financial aid application deadline: 2/15; applicants required to submit FAFSA. *Faculty research:* International finance and business, trade policy, macroeconomics, Asian economic issues, developmental economics. • Dr. Peter Petri, Dean, 781-736-4817. Application contact: Marsha Ginn, Associate Dean, 781-736-4829.

Announcement: The new 10-course, fast-track Master of Science in Finance Program is offered part-time for working professionals. Five core courses include Analysis of Financial Institutions, Capital Market Finance, International Economic Environment, Risk Management, and Quantitative Methods. Five elective courses may be chosen from a menu of more than 20 offerings, including International Banking, Fixed Income, Managing Portfolio Risk, Financial Modeling, Options and Derivatives, Venture Business Plans, Bond Portfolio Management, Financial Strategies, and a weeklong international field study in a major financial center such as London, Hong Kong, Singapore, and New York. Admission requirements include a BA or equivalent, 2 letters of recommendation, a resume, a goal statement, an application, official transcripts, and at least 2–3 years of professional experience. The GMAT is recommended.

See in-depth description on page 539.

Briercrest Biblical Seminary, Program in Leadership and Management, Caronport, SK S0H 0S0, Canada. Offerings include financial leadership (MA). *Degree requirements:* Thesis optional, foreign language not required. *Application fee:* $25. *Tuition:* $471 per course. • Application contact: Michael Penner, Enrollment Management Officer, 306-756-3200. Fax: 306-756-7366.

Bryant College, College of Business Administration, Program in Finance, Smithfield, RI 02917-1284. Awards MBA, CAGS. Part-time and evening/weekend programs available. Faculty: 8 full-time (1 woman), 1 part-time (0 women). Students: 8 full-time (4 women), 92 part-time (26 women); includes 2 minority (both Asian Americans), 3 international. Average age 31. 45 applicants, 60% accepted. In 1997, 29 master's, 2 CAGSs awarded. *Entrance requirements:* For master's, GMAT (minimum score 480; average 520). Application deadline: 7/1 (priority date; rolling processing; 11/15 for spring admission). Application fee: $55 ($70 for international students). *Tuition:* $1025 per course. *Financial aid:* In 1997–98, 3 research assistantships were awarded; graduate assistantships and career-related internships or fieldwork also available. Aid available to part-time students. Financial aid applicants required to submit FAFSA. • Cathy Lalli, Assistant Director of Graduate Programs, Graduate School, 401-232-6230. Fax: 401-232-6494. E-mail: gradprog@bryant.edu.

Bucknell University, College of Arts and Sciences, Department of Management, Lewisburg, PA 17837. Offerings include managerial finance and economics (MSBA). Department faculty: 12 full-time. *Degree requirements:* Thesis required, foreign language not required. *Entrance requirements:* GMAT, TOEFL (minimum score 550), minimum GPA of 2.8. Application deadline: 6/1 (priority date; rolling processing; 12/1 for spring admission). Application fee: $25. *Tuition:* $2410 per course. • Dr. Mark Bettner, Head, 717-524-1306.

California Lutheran University, School of Business Administration, Thousand Oaks, CA 91360-2787. Offerings include finance (MBA). School faculty: 8 full-time (3 women), 29 part-time (4 women). *Entrance requirements:* GMAT, minimum GPA of 3.0, interview. Application deadline: 8/1 (priority date; rolling processing). Application fee: $50. *Tuition:* $395 per unit. • Dr. Ronald Hagler, Director, 805-493-3371.

California State University, Fullerton, School of Business Administration and Economics, Department of Finance, PO Box 34080, Fullerton, CA 92834-9480. Awards MBA. Part-time and evening/weekend programs available. Faculty: 18 full-time (3 women), 13 part-time, 21.6 FTE. Students: 7 full-time (5 women), 87 part-time (26 women); includes 27 minority (1 African American, 25 Asian Americans, 1 Hispanic), 36 international. Average age 29. 73 applicants, 49% accepted. In 1997, 35 degrees awarded. *Degree requirements:* Computer language, project or thesis required, foreign language not required. *Entrance requirements:* GMAT (minimum score 950), minimum AACSB index of 950. Application fee: $55. *Expenses:* Tuition $0 for state residents; $246 per unit for nonresidents. Fees $1947 per year full-time, $1281 per year part-time. *Financial aid:* Teaching assistantships, state grants, Federal Work-Study, institutionally sponsored loans available. Aid available to part-time students. Financial aid application deadline: 3/1. • Dr. John Erickson, Chair, 714-278-2217. Application contact: Robert Miyake, Assistant Dean, 714-278-2211.

California State University, Hayward, School of Business and Economics, Department of Management and Finance, Option in Finance, Hayward, CA 94542-3000. Awards MBA. Part-time and evening/weekend programs available. *Degree requirements:* Comprehensive exam or thesis required, foreign language not required. *Entrance requirements:* GMAT, minimum GPA of 2.75. Application deadline: 4/19 (priority date; rolling processing; 1/5 for spring admission). Application fee: $55. *Expenses:* Tuition $0 for state residents; $164 per unit for nonresidents. Fees $1827 per year full-time, $1161 per year part-time. *Financial aid:* Federal Work-Study, institutionally sponsored loans, and career-related internships or fieldwork available. Aid available to part-time students. Financial aid application deadline: 3/1. • Dr. Sam N. Basu, Coordinator, 510-885-3556. Application contact: Dr. Donna L. Wiley, Director of Graduate Programs, 510-885-3964.

California State University, Los Angeles, School of Business and Economics, Major in Business Administration, Department of Finance and Law, Los Angeles, CA 90032-8530. Offers program in finance and banking (MBA, MS). Part-time and evening/weekend programs available. Faculty: 9 full-time, 5 part-time. *Degree requirements:* Computer language, comprehensive exam (MBA), thesis (MS) required, foreign language not required. *Entrance requirements:* GMAT, TOEFL (minimum score 550), minimum GPA of 2.5 during previous 2 years. Application deadline: 6/30 (rolling processing; 11/30 for spring admission). Application fee: $55. *Expenses:* Tuition $0 for state residents; $164 per unit for nonresidents. Fees $1763 per year full-time, $1097 per year part-time. *Financial aid:* Federal Work-Study and career-related internships or fieldwork available. Aid available to part-time students. Financial aid application deadline: 3/1. • Dr. Jean Loo, Chair, 213-343-2870.

California State University, Northridge, College of Business Administration and Economics, Department of Finance, Real Estate and Insurance, Northridge, CA 91330. Awards MBA. Faculty: 13 full-time, 5 part-time. 4 applicants, 50% accepted. *Degree requirements:* Thesis or alternative required, foreign language not required. *Entrance requirements:* GMAT (score in 50th percentile or higher), TOEFL, minimum GPA of 3.0 in last 60 units. Application deadline: 11/30. Application fee: $55. *Expenses:* Tuition $0 for state residents; $246 per unit for nonresidents. Fees $1970 per year full-time, $1304 per year part-time. *Financial aid:* Application deadline 3/1. *Faculty research:* Real estate education improvement. • Dr. William Jennings, Chair, 818-677-2459. Application contact: Dr. Richard Moore, Director of Graduate Programs, 818-677-2467.

Carnegie Mellon University, Graduate School of Industrial Administration, Program in Finance, Pittsburgh, PA 15213-3891. Awards PhD. Faculty: 9 full-time (0 women). *Degree requirements:* Dissertation required, foreign language not required. *Entrance requirements:* GRE General Test. Application deadline: 2/1. Application fee: $50. *Financial aid:* Fellowships available. Financial aid application deadline: 5/1. • Application contact: Jackie Cavendish, Administrative Assistant, 412-268-2301.

Carnegie Mellon University, Mellon College of Science, Department of Mathematical Sciences, Pittsburgh, PA 15213-3891. Offerings include mathematical finance (PhD). PhD (algorithms, combinatorics, & optimization) offered jointly with Sch of Computer Science & Grad Sch of Industrial Administration. PhD (pure & applied logic) with Sch of Computer

Directory: Finance and Banking

Carnegie Mellon University (continued)
Science & Dept of Philosophy. PhD (mathematical finance) with Dept of Statistics & Grad Sch of Industrial Administration. Terminal master's awarded for partial completion of doctoral program. Department faculty: 33 full-time (5 women). *Average time to degree:* master's–2 years full-time; doctorate–6 years full-time. *Application deadline:* 1/15 (priority date). *Application fee:* $0. *Expenses:* Tuition $21,275 per year full-time, $295 per unit part-time. Fees $130 per year. • James Greenberg, Head, 412-268-2545. E-mail: greenber@andrew.cmu.edu. Application contact: Stella P. Andreoletti, Graduate Coordinator, 412-268-2545. Fax: 412-268-6380. E-mail: sd2e@andrew.cmu.edu.

Case Western Reserve University, Weatherhead School of Management, Department of Banking and Finance, Cleveland, OH 44106. Awards MBA, PhD. PhD offered through the School of Graduate Studies. Faculty: 10 full-time (0 women), 2 part-time (0 women), 11 FTE. Students: 180 full-time (54 women), 236 part-time (75 women); includes 19 minority (14 African Americans, 4 Asian Americans, 1 Hispanic), 84 international. In 1997, 106 master's, 2 doctorates awarded. *Degree requirements:* For doctorate, dissertation required, foreign language not required. *Entrance requirements:* For master's, GMAT (average 603); for doctorate, GMAT. Application fee: $50. *Tuition:* $20,900 per year full-time, $871 per credit hour part-time. *Faculty research:* Monetary and fiscal policy, corporate finance, future markets, derivative pricing, capital market efficiency. • David Bowers, Chair, 216-368-2165. Application contact: Linda S. Gaston, Director of Marketing and Admissions, 216-368-2030. Fax: 216-368-5548. E-mail: lxg10@po.cwru.edu.

Case Western Reserve University, Weatherhead School of Management, Department of Operations Research and Operations Management, Cleveland, OH 44106. Offerings include management science (MS), with options in finance, information systems, marketing, operations management, operations research, quality management. MS and PhD offered through the School of Graduate Studies. Department faculty: 12 full-time (0 women). *Average time to degree:* doctorate–4 years full-time. *Application deadline:* 4/15 (priority date; rolling processing). *Application fee:* $50. *Tuition:* $20,900 per year full-time, $871 per credit hour part-time. • Hamilton Emmons, Chairman, 216-368-3841. Application contact: Linda S. Gaston, Director of Marketing and Admissions, 216-368-2030. Fax: 216-368-5548. E-mail: lxg10@po.cwru.edu.

The Catholic University of America, School of Arts and Sciences, Department of Economics and Business, Program in Financial Management, Washington, DC 20064. Awards MA, JD/MA. Evening/weekend programs available. Students: 3 full-time (1 woman), 3 part-time (1 woman); includes 2 minority (1 African American, 1 Asian American), 4 international. Average age 31. 6 applicants, 67% accepted. In 1997, 1 degree awarded. *Degree requirements:* Computer language, comprehensive exam required, foreign language and thesis not required. *Entrance requirements:* GRE General Test, TOEFL. Application deadline: 8/1 (priority date; rolling processing; 12/1 for spring admission). Application fee: $50. *Expenses:* Tuition $17,325 per year full-time, $668 per credit hour part-time. Fees $680 per year full-time, $360 per year part-time. *Financial aid:* Teaching assistantships, full and partial tuition waivers, Federal Work-Study, institutionally sponsored loans, and career-related internships or fieldwork available. Aid available to part-time students. Financial aid application deadline: 2/1. *Faculty research:* Management for nonprofit organizations, incentives, efficiency and effectiveness of management for large organizations. • Dr. Ernest M. Zampelli, Chair, Department of Economics and Business, 202-319-6683. Fax: 202-319-4426. E-mail: zampelli@cua.edu.

Central Michigan University, College of Business Administration, Department of Finance, Mount Pleasant, MI 48859. Awards MBA. Faculty: 9 full-time (2 women). *Entrance requirements:* GMAT. Application deadline: 3/1 (priority date; rolling processing). Application fee: $30. *Expenses:* Tuition $139 per credit hour (minimum) for state residents; $276 per credit hour (minimum) for nonresidents. Fees $260 per year full-time, $150 per semester part-time. *Financial aid:* In 1997–98, 2 research assistantships were awarded. Financial aid application deadline: 3/7. *Faculty research:* Investments, commercial banking, financial management. • Dr. R. Gene Stout, Chairperson, 517-774-3362. Fax: 517-774-6456. E-mail: 376tt32@cmich.edu.

Charleston Southern University, Program in Business, Charleston, SC 29423-8087. Offerings include finance (MBA). Program faculty: 8 full-time (0 women), 1 (woman) part-time, 8.33 FTE. *Entrance requirements:* GMAT. Application deadline: rolling. Application fee: $25. *Tuition:* $9821 per year full-time, $173 per hour (minimum) part-time. • Dr. Al Parish, MBA Director, 803-863-7904. Fax: 803-863-7919. E-mail: aparish@awdd.com. Application contact: Terri Jordan, MBA Coordinator, 803-863-7955. Fax: 803-863-7922.

City University, School of Business and Management Professions, Bellevue, WA 98004-6442. Offerings include financial management (MBA, Certificate). Postbaccalaureate distance learning degree programs offered (no on-campus study). School faculty: 14 full-time (6 women), 689 part-time (247 women). *Application deadline:* rolling. *Application fee:* $75 ($175 for international students). Electronic applications accepted. *Tuition:* $280 per credit hour. • Dr. Roman Borboa, Dean, 425-637-1010 Ext. 3759. Fax: 425-277-2439. E-mail: rborboa@cityu.edu. Application contact: Nabil El-Khatib, Vice President, Admissions, 800-426-5596. Fax: 425-277-2437. E-mail: nel-khatib@cityu.edu.

Claremont Graduate University, Department of Mathematics, Claremont, CA 91711-6163. Offerings include financial engineering (MS). PhD (engineering mathematics) offered jointly with California State University, Long Beach. MA (mathematics education) offered jointly with the Department of Education. MS (financial engineering) offered jointly with the Peter F. Drucker Graduate Management Center. Department faculty: 5 full-time (0 women), 2 part-time (0 women). *Application deadline:* 2/15 (priority date; rolling processing). *Application fee:* $40. Electronic applications accepted. *Expenses:* Tuition $20,250 per year full-time, $913 per unit part-time. Fees $130 per year. • Robert Williamson, Chair, 909-621-8080. Application contact: Mary Solberg, Program Secretary, 909-621-8080. Fax: 909-621-8390. E-mail: math@cgu.edu.

Claremont Graduate University, Peter F. Drucker Graduate Management Center, Program in Management, Claremont, CA 91711-6163. Offerings include finance (MBA), with option in accounting control. *Entrance requirements:* GMAT, TOEFL. Application deadline: 2/15 (priority date; rolling processing). Application fee: $40. Electronic applications accepted. *Expenses:* Tuition $20,250 per year full-time, $913 per unit part-time. Fees $130 per year. • Dr. Jeffrey Decker, Director, 909-621-8073. Fax: 909-621-8390. E-mail: jeff.decker@cgu.edu. Application contact: Kathy Hubener, Admissions Coordinator, 909-621-8073. Fax: 909-621-8543. E-mail: mba@cgu.edu.

Clark Atlanta University, School of Business Administration, Department of Finance, Atlanta, GA 30314. Awards MBA. Part-time programs available. Students: 33 full-time (15 women), 2 part-time (1 woman); includes 33 minority (all African Americans), 2 international. In 1997, 24 degrees awarded. *Entrance requirements:* GMAT. Application deadline: 4/1 (rolling processing; 11/1 for spring admission). Application fee: $40. *Expenses:* Tuition $9672 per year full-time, $403 per credit hour part-time. Fees $200 per year. *Financial aid:* Application deadline 4/30. • Dr. Kasim Alli, Chairperson, 404-880-6413. Application contact: Michelle Clark-Davis, Graduate Program Assistant, 404-880-8709.

Clark University, Graduate School of Management, Program in Finance, Worcester, MA 01610-1477. Awards MSF. Students: 1 full-time. *Degree requirements:* Computer language required, foreign language not required. *Application deadline:* 7/31 (priority date; rolling processing). *Application fee:* $40. *Financial aid:* Application deadline 5/31. • Application contact: Admissions Director, 508-793-7406.

College for Financial Planning, Program in Financial Planning, Denver, CO 80237-3403. Offers program in personal financial planning (MS). Part-time and evening/weekend programs available. Faculty: 11 full-time. Students: 1,033 part-time; includes 3 international. Average age 44. 227 applicants, 65% accepted. In 1997, 357 degrees awarded. *Degree requirements:* Thesis. *Average time to degree:* master's–5 years part-time. *Entrance requirements:* Minimum GPA of 2.5. Application deadline: 10/15 (rolling processing; 2/15 for spring admission). Application fee: $225 ($275 for international students). *Tuition:* $600 per course. • Jeffrey Mershon, Director of Academic Programs, 303-220-4828. Application contact: Glen Steelman, Registrar, 303-220-4861. Fax: 303-220-5146.

College of Insurance, Graduate Programs, Program in Business Administration, New York, NY 10007-2165. Offerings include financial management (MBA). Program faculty: 12 full-time (1 woman), 12 part-time (1 woman). *Degree requirements:* Computer language required, thesis optional, foreign language not required. *Entrance requirements:* GMAT (minimum score 500), TOEFL (minimum score 550). Application deadline: 7/15 (priority date; rolling processing; 11/1 for spring admission). Application fee: $30 ($50 for international students). *Expenses:* Tuition $554 per credit. Fees $15 per credit. • Application contact: Theresa C. Marro, Director of Admissions, 212-815-9232. Fax: 212-964-3381. E-mail: admissions@tci.edu.

See in-depth description on page 523.

Colorado State University, College of Business, Department of Finance and Real Estate, Fort Collins, CO 80523-0015. Awards MBA. Part-time programs available. Faculty: 8 full-time (1 woman). Students: 5 full-time (0 women), 10 part-time (6 women); includes 4 international. 12 applicants, 83% accepted. In 1997, 2 degrees awarded. *Degree requirements:* Thesis optional, foreign language not required. *Entrance requirements:* GMAT, TOEFL, minimum GPA of 3.0. Application deadline: 2/1 (priority date; rolling processing). Application fee: $30. Electronic applications accepted. *Tuition:* $2920 per year (minimum) full-time, $328 per credit hour (minimum) part-time for state residents; $9000 per year (minimum) full-time, $368 per credit hour (minimum) part-time for nonresidents. *Financial aid:* In 1997–98, 6 research assistantships were awarded; fellowships, teaching assistantships, traineeships, Federal Work-Study, and career-related internships or fieldwork also available. Financial aid application deadline: 2/1. *Faculty research:* Mutual funds, exchange rates, risk analysis, neural networks. • Application contact: Dr. Kent Zumwalt, Chair, 970-491-5062.

Columbia University, Graduate School of Business, Doctoral Program in Business, New York, NY 10027. Offerings include business (PhD), with options in accounting (PhD), finance and economics (PhD), management of organizations (PhD), management science/operations research (PhD), marketing (PhD). Program faculty: 105 full-time (15 women), 86 part-time (15 women). *Degree requirements:* Dissertation, teacher training seminars, research paper, oral exam required, foreign language not required. *Average time to degree:* doctorate–4 years full-time. *Entrance requirements:* GMAT or GRE, TOEFL or TSE. Application deadline: 2/1. Application fee: $50. *Expenses:* Tuition is $26,520 per year, fees of 1,250 per year, and students receive tuition and fee exemptions for a maximum of 12 terms. • Application contact: Elizabeth Elam, Administrative Director, 212-854-2836. Fax: 212-932-2359.

Columbia University, Graduate School of Business, MBA Program, New York, NY 10027. Offerings include finance and economics (MBA). Program faculty: 105 full-time (15 women), 86 part-time (15 women). *Entrance requirements:* GMAT, TOEFL (minimum score 610). Application deadline: 4/20 (rolling processing; 11/1 for spring admission). Application fee: $125 ($150 for international students). *Expenses:* Tuition $26,520 per year. Fees $1250 per year. • Prof. Safwan Masri, Vice Dean of Students and the MBA Program, 212-854-8716. Fax: 212-854-0545. E-mail: smm1@columbia.edu. Application contact: Linda Meehan, Assistant Dean and Executive Director of Admissions and Financial Aid, 212-854-1961. Fax: 212-662-6754. E-mail: gohermes@claven.gsb.columbia.edu.

Concordia University Wisconsin, Division of Graduate Studies, MBA Program, Mequon, WI 53097-2402. Offerings include finance (MBA). Postbaccalaureate distance learning degree programs offered (minimal on-campus study). *Degree requirements:* Thesis or alternative, comprehensive exam. *Average time to degree:* master's–2 years part-time. *Entrance requirements:* TOEFL (minimum score 550). Application deadline: 8/1 (priority date; rolling processing; 1/15 for spring admission). Application fee: $50. *Tuition:* $300 per credit. • David Borst, Director, 414-243-4298. Fax: 414-243-4428. E-mail: dborst@bach.cuw.edu.

Cornell University, Graduate Field of Management, Ithaca, NY 14853-0001. Offerings include finance (PhD). Terminal master's awarded for partial completion of doctoral program. Faculty: 43 full-time. *Degree requirements:* Dissertation required, foreign language not required. *Entrance requirements:* GMAT or GRE General Test, TOEFL. Application deadline: 1/10 (priority date). Application fee: $65. *Expenses:* Tuition $24,300 per year. Fees $48 per year. • Director of Graduate Studies, 607-255-3669. Application contact: Graduate Field Assistant, 607-255-3669. Fax: 607-254-4590. E-mail: maria@johnson.cornell.edu.

Cornell University, Graduate Fields of Arts and Sciences, Field of Economics, Ithaca, NY 14853-0001. Offerings include public finance (PhD). Terminal master's awarded for partial completion of doctoral program. Faculty: 44 full-time. *Degree requirements:* Dissertation required, foreign language not required. *Entrance requirements:* GRE General Test, TOEFL. Application deadline: 1/15. Application fee: $65. Electronic applications accepted. *Expenses:* Tuition $22,780 per year. Fees $48 per year. • Director of Graduate Studies, 607-255-4893. Application contact: Graduate Field Assistant, 607-255-4893. Fax: 607-255-2818. E-mail: econ_phd@cornell.edu.

Dallas Baptist University, College of Business, Business Administration Program, Dallas, TX 75211-9299. Offerings include finance (MBA). Program faculty: 15 full-time (4 women), 26 part-time (5 women). *Entrance requirements:* GMAT, TOEFL (minimum score 550). Application deadline: rolling. Application fee: $25. *Tuition:* $285 per hour. • Annette Hoffman, Director of Graduate Business Programs, 214-333-5280. Application contact: Travis Bundrick, Director of Graduate Programs, 214-333-5243. Fax: 214-333-5579. E-mail: graduate@dbu.edu.

DePaul University, Charles H. Kellstadt Graduate School of Business, Department of Finance, Chicago, IL 60604-2287. Awards MBA, MSF. Faculty: 20 full-time (4 women), 14 part-time (3 women). Students: 318 full-time (73 women), 308 part-time (91 women); includes 73 minority (29 African Americans, 29 Asian Americans, 15 Hispanics), 15 international. Average age 29. 209 applicants, 68% accepted. In 1997, 223 degrees awarded. *Degree requirements:* Computer language required, foreign language and thesis not required. *Entrance requirements:* GMAT. Application deadline: 8/1 (rolling processing; 3/1 for spring admission). Application fee: $40. *Expenses:* Tuition $1593 per course. Fees $30 per year. *Financial aid:* In 1997–98, 9 students received aid, including 5 research assistantships averaging $450 per month. Aid available to part-time students. Financial aid application deadline: 4/30. *Faculty research:* Derivatives, valuation, international finance, real estate. • Dr. Joan Junkus, Chair, 312-362-8826. Application contact: Dr. Carl Luft, Program Administrator, 312-362-8428. Fax: 312-362-6566.

DePaul University, College of Liberal Arts and Sciences, Programs in Public Services, Chicago, IL 60604-2287. Offerings include financial administration management (Certificate). Faculty: 7 full-time (4 women), 18 part-time (7 women). *Application deadline:* 7/1 (priority date; rolling processing; 1/20 for spring admission). *Application fee:* $25. *Expenses:* Tuition $320 per credit hour. Fees $30 per year. • Dr. J. Patrick Murphy, Director, 312-362-8441. Fax: 312-362-5506. E-mail: jpmurphy@wppost.depaul.edu. Application contact: Graduate Information, 312-362-5367. Fax: 312-362-5749.

See in-depth description on page 619.

Dowling College, School of Business, Oakdale, NY 11769-1999. Offerings include banking and finance (MBA, Certificate). School faculty: 17 full-time, 75 part-time. *Degree requirements:* For master's, thesis optional, foreign language not required. *Entrance requirements:* For master's, GMAT, TOEFL. Application deadline: rolling. Application fee: $0. Electronic applications accepted. • Dr. Anthony F. Libertella, Interim Dean, 516-244-3355. Fax: 516-589-6644. Application contact: Kate Rowe, Director of Admissions, 516-244-3030. Fax: 516-563-3827. E-mail: rowek@dowling.edu.

Drexel University, College of Business and Administration, Department of Finance, 3141 Chestnut Street, Philadelphia, PA 19104-2875. Awards MS. Faculty: 12 full-time, 4 part-time, 13.3 FTE. Students: 9 full-time (2 women), 24 part-time (9 women); includes 3 minority (1

African American, 2 Asian Americans), 13 international. Average age 30. 43 applicants, 70% accepted. In 1997, 18 degrees awarded. *Degree requirements:* Computer language, seminar paper required, foreign language and thesis not required. *Entrance requirements:* GMAT (minimum score 450), TOEFL (minimum score 570), minimum GPA of 2.75. Application deadline: 8/21 (rolling processing). Application fee: $35. *Expenses:* Tuition $494 per credit hour. Fees $121 per quarter full-time, $65 per quarter part-time. *Financial aid:* In 1997–98, 6 teaching assistantships, 1 graduate assistantship were awarded; research assistantships and career-related internships or fieldwork also available. Financial aid application deadline: 2/1. *Faculty research:* Investment analysis, portfolio mix, capital budgeting, banking and financial institutions, international finance. • Dr. Michael J. Gombola, Head, 215-895-1741. Application contact: Denise Bigham, Director of Admissions, 215-895-6700. Fax: 215-895-5969.

Drexel University, College of Business and Administration, Program in Business Administration, 3141 Chestnut Street, Philadelphia, PA 19104-2875. Offerings include business administration (MBA, PhD, APC), with options in accounting (MBA, PhD), decision sciences (PhD), economics (MBA, PhD), finance (MBA, PhD), legal studies (MBA), management (MBA), marketing (MBA, PhD), organizational sciences (PhD), quantitative methods (MBA), strategic management (PhD). Terminal master's awarded for partial completion of doctoral program. *Degree requirements:* For doctorate, computer language required, foreign language and dissertation not required. *Entrance requirements:* For doctorate, GMAT, TOEFL (minimum score 570). Application deadline: 8/21 (rolling processing; 3/5 for spring admission). Application fee: $35. *Expenses:* Tuition $494 per credit hour. Fees $121 per quarter full-time, $65 per quarter part-time. • Dr. Jerold B. Muskin, Director of Master's Programs in Business, 215-895-2115. Application contact: Denise Bigham, Director of Admissions, 215-895-6700. Fax: 215-895-5969.

East Carolina University, School of Business, Greenville, NC 27858-4353. Offerings include finance (MBA). School faculty: 39 full-time (4 women). *Application deadline:* 6/1 (priority date; rolling processing). *Application fee:* $40. *Tuition:* $1886 per year full-time, $472 per semester (minimum) part-time for state residents; $9156 per year full-time, $2289 per semester (minimum) part-time for nonresidents. • Donald B. Boldt, Director of Graduate Studies, 252-328-6970. Fax: 252-328-6664. E-mail: boldtd@mail.ecu.edu. Application contact: Dr. Paul D. Tschetter, Associate Dean, 252-328-6012. Fax: 252-328-6071. E-mail: grad@mail.ecu.edu.

Eastern College, Graduate Business Programs, St. Davids, PA 19087-3696. Offerings include business administration (MBA), with options in accounting, economics, finance, management, marketing. M Div/MS and M Div/MBA offered jointly with Eastern Baptist Theological Seminary. Faculty: 32 full-time (18 women), 14 part-time (12 women). *Application deadline:* rolling. *Application fee:* $35. • Dr. John Stapleford, Chair, 610-341-5848. Application contact: Megan Miscioscia, Graduate Admissions Representative, 610-341-5972. Fax: 610-341-1466.

Eastern Michigan University, College of Business, Department of Finance and Computer Information Systems, Ypsilanti, MI 48197. Offerings include finance (MBA). Department faculty: 19 full-time (1 woman). *Application deadline:* 5/15 (rolling processing; 3/15 for spring admission). *Application fee:* $30. *Expenses:* Tuition $2691 per year full-time, $150 per credit hour part-time for state residents; $6300 per year full-time, $350 per credit hour part-time for nonresidents. Fees $368 per year full-time, $88 per semester (minimum) part-time. • Dr. Alahassana Diallo, Interim Head, 734-487-2454. Application contact: Dr. Wafa Korshid, Coordinator, 734-487-2454.

École des Hautes Études Commerciales, Program in Finance, Montréal, PQ H3T 2A7, Canada. Awards M Sc, Diploma. Most courses are given in French. Diploma offered jointly with Télé-université. Part-time programs available. *Degree requirements:* For master's, 1 foreign language, thesis (for some programs); for Diploma, 1 foreign language required, thesis not required. *Application deadline:* 3/15. *Application fee:* $40. *Financial aid:* Fellowships, research assistantships, teaching assistantships available. • Dr. Jacques Nantel, Director, 514-340-6421. Application contact: Nicole Rivet, Registrar, 514-340-6110. Fax: 514-340-5640. E-mail: nicole.rivet@hec.ca.

École des Hautes Études Commerciales, Program in Financial Engineering, Montréal, PQ H3T 2A7, Canada. Awards M Sc. Most courses are given in French. Part-time programs available. *Degree requirements:* 1 foreign language, thesis. *Application deadline:* 3/15. *Application fee:* $40. *Financial aid:* Fellowships, research assistantships, teaching assistantships available. • Dr. Jean-Yves Le Louarn, Director, 514-340-6295. E-mail: jean-yves.lelouarn@hec.ca. Application contact: Nicole Rivet, Registrar, 514-340-6110. Fax: 514-340-5640. E-mail: nicole.rivet@hec.ca.

Emporia State University, School of Graduate Studies, School of Business, Division of Management, Marketing, Finance and Economics, Emporia, KS 66801-5087. Awards MBA. Faculty: 12 full-time (1 woman), 1 part-time (0 women). Students: 36 full-time (9 women), 23 part-time (10 women); includes 3 minority (2 African Americans, 1 Asian American), 19 international. 25 applicants, 88% accepted. In 1997, 23 degrees awarded. *Degree requirements:* Comprehensive exam required, foreign language not required. *Entrance requirements:* GMAT, TOEFL (minimum score 550). Application deadline: 8/15 (priority date; rolling processing). Application fee: $30 ($75 for international students). Electronic applications accepted. *Tuition:* $2300 per year full-time, $103 per credit hour part-time for state residents; $6012 per year full-time, $258 per credit hour part-time for nonresidents. *Financial aid:* In 1997–98, 2 fellowships averaging $667 per month, 2 research assistantships averaging $558 per month, 3 teaching assistantships averaging $522 per month were awarded; Federal Work-Study, institutionally sponsored loans, and career-related internships or fieldwork also available. Financial aid application deadline: 3/15; applicants required to submit FAFSA. • Dr. Varkey Titus, Chair, 316-341-5347. E-mail: titusvar@emporia.edu. Application contact: Dr. Donald Miller, Director, 316-341-5456. E-mail: millerdo@emporia.edu.

Fairfield University, School of Business, Fairfield, CT 06430-5195. Offerings include finance (MBA, CAS), financial management (MSFM). School faculty: 36 full-time (12 women), 4 part-time (2 women), 37.3 FTE. *Degree requirements:* For master's, thesis or alternative required, foreign language not required. *Average time to degree:* master's–2 years full-time, 3.5 years part-time. *Entrance requirements:* For master's, GMAT (minimum score 500), TOEFL (minimum score 550). Application deadline: 8/1 (priority date; rolling processing; 12/1 for spring admission). Application fee: $40. *Expenses:* Tuition $15,000 per year full-time, $450 per credit hour part-time. Fees $40 per year. • Dr. Walter G. Ryba Jr., Acting Dean, 203-254-4070. Application contact: Cynthia S. Chegwidden, Director of Graduate Programs, 203-254-4070. Fax: 203-254-4105. E-mail: cchegwidden@fairl.fairfield.edu.

Fairleigh Dickinson University, Florham–Madison Campus, Samuel J. Silberman College of Business Administration, Program in Finance, 285 Madison Avenue, Madison, NJ 07940-1099. Awards MBA. Part-time and evening/weekend programs available. Faculty: 12 full-time (1 woman), 12 part-time (2 women). Students: 25 full-time (8 women), 251 part-time (100 women); includes 14 minority (5 African Americans, 6 Asian Americans, 1 Hispanic, 2 Native Americans), 3 international. Average age 30. 77 applicants, 82% accepted. In 1997, 71 degrees awarded. *Degree requirements:* Thesis optional, foreign language not required. *Entrance requirements:* GMAT. Application deadline: rolling. Application fee: $35. *Expenses:* Tuition $522 per credit. Fees $302 per year full-time, $138 per year part-time. *Financial aid:* Fellowships available. • Prof. Claude Jonnard, Chairperson, 973-443-8810.

Fairleigh Dickinson University, Teaneck–Hackensack Campus, Samuel J. Silberman College of Business Administration, Department of Accounting, Taxation, Law, Economics, and Finance, Program in Finance, 1000 River Road, Teaneck, NJ 07666-1914. Awards MBA. Students: 31 full-time (8 women), 106 part-time (33 women); includes 19 minority (5 African Americans, 8 Asian Americans, 5 Hispanics, 1 Native American), 21 international. Average age 31. In 1997, 67 degrees awarded. *Degree requirements:* Computer language required, thesis optional, foreign language not required. *Entrance requirements:* GMAT. Application deadline: rolling. Application fee: $35. *Expenses:* Tuition $522 per credit. Fees $302 per year full-time, $138 per year part-time. *Financial aid:* Fellowships, research assistantships available. *Faculty research:* Financial planning. • Dr. Virote Angkatavanich, Chair, Department of Accounting, Taxation, Law, Economics, and Finance, 201-692-7221.

Florida Agricultural and Mechanical University, Division of Graduate Studies, Research, and Continuing Education, School of Business and Industry, Tallahassee, FL 32307-3200. Offerings include finance (MBA). *Entrance requirements:* GRE General Test (minimum combined score of 1000), minimum GPA of 3.0. Application deadline: 5/13. Application fee: $20. *Expenses:* Tuition $140 per credit hour for state residents; $484 per credit hour for nonresidents. Fees $130 per year. • Dr. Sybil Mobley, Dean, 850-599-3565.

Florida International University, College of Business Administration, Department of Finance, Miami, FL 33199. Awards MSF, PhD. Part-time and evening/weekend programs available. Faculty: 15 full-time (1 woman), 1 part-time (0 women), 15.5 FTE. Students: 42 full-time (18 women), 54 part-time (17 women); includes 38 minority (4 African Americans, 4 Asian Americans, 30 Hispanics), 35 international. Average age 29. 69 applicants, 48% accepted. In 1997, 10 master's awarded. *Degree requirements:* For master's, computer language required, foreign language and thesis not required; for doctorate, computer language, dissertation required, foreign language not required. *Entrance requirements:* For master's, GMAT, minimum AACSB index of 1000, minimum GPA of 3.0; for doctorate, GMAT (minimum score 560), minimum GPA of 3.0. Application deadline: 4/1 (priority date; rolling processing; 10/1 for spring admission). Application fee: $20. *Expenses:* Tuition $138 per credit hour for state residents; $482 per credit hour for nonresidents. Fees $46 per semester. • Dr. John Zdanowicz, Chairperson, 305-348-2771. Fax: 305-348-4182. E-mail: zdanowicz@fiu.edu.

Fordham University, Graduate School of Business Administration, New York, NY 10023. Offerings include finance (GPMBA, MBA). School faculty: 85 full-time (22 women), 95 part-time (12 women). *Average time to degree:* master's–2 years full-time, 3 years part-time. *Application deadline:* 6/1 (priority date; rolling processing; 11/1 for spring admission). *Application fee:* $50. • Dr. Ernest J. Scalberg, Dean, 212-636-6111. Fax: 212-307-1779. Application contact: Kathy Pattison, Assistant Dean of Admission, 212-636-6200. Fax: 212-636-7076. E-mail: admission@bschool.bnet.fordham.edu.

Fort Hays State University, College of Business, Department of Business Administration, Hays, KS 67601-4099. Offerings include finance (MBA). Department faculty: 14 full-time (2 women). *Degree requirements:* Thesis optional, foreign language not required. *Entrance requirements:* GMAT. Application deadline: 7/1 (priority date; rolling processing). Application fee: $25 ($35 for international students). *Tuition:* $94 per credit hour for state residents; $249 per credit hour for nonresidents. • Dr. Dale McKemey, Acting Director, 785-628-4201.

Gannon University, School of Graduate Studies, College of Humanities, Business, and Education, School of Business, Program in Finance, Erie, PA 16541. Awards Certificate. Part-time and evening/weekend programs available. Students: 0. 0 applicants. *Entrance requirements:* GMAT, TOEFL. Application deadline: rolling. Application fee: $25. *Expenses:* Tuition $405 per credit. Fees $200 per year full-time, $8 per credit part-time. *Financial aid:* Career-related internships or fieldwork available. Financial aid application deadline: 3/1; applicants required to submit FAFSA. • Application contact: Beth Nemenz, Director of Admissions, 814-871-7240. Fax: 814-871-5803. E-mail: admissions@gannon.edu.

The George Washington University, School of Business and Public Management, Department of Finance, Washington, DC 20052. Offers programs in finance (MSF), finance and investments (MBA, PhD), real estate development (MBA). Part-time and evening/weekend programs available. Faculty: 10 full-time (0 women), 5 part-time (0 women), 11 FTE. Students: 168 full-time (62 women), 196 part-time (71 women); includes 42 minority (12 African Americans, 20 Asian Americans, 10 Hispanics), 146 international. Average age 28. 521 applicants, 71% accepted. In 1997, 216 master's awarded. *Degree requirements:* For master's, computer language required, foreign language and thesis not required; for doctorate, dissertation required, foreign language not required. *Entrance requirements:* For master's, GMAT, TOEFL (minimum score 550); for doctorate, GMAT or GRE, TOEFL (minimum score 550). Application deadline: 4/1 (priority date; rolling processing; 10/1 for spring admission). Application fee: $50. *Expenses:* Tuition $680 per semester hour. Fees $35 per semester hour. *Financial aid:* Fellowships, teaching assistantships, Federal Work-Study, institutionally sponsored loans, and career-related internships or fieldwork available. Financial aid application deadline: 4/1. • Dr. James Jordan, Chair, 202-994-5996. Application contact: Lilly Hastings, Graduate Admissions, 202-994-6584. Fax: 202-994-6382.

See in-depth description on page 447.

The George Washington University, School of Business and Public Management, Department of Public Administration, Program in Budget and Public Finance, Washington, DC 20052. Awards MPA. Part-time and evening/weekend programs available. Faculty: 2 full-time (0 women). Students: 4 full-time (3 women), 5 part-time (2 women); includes 2 minority (both Hispanics), 1 international. Average age 31. 9 applicants, 89% accepted. In 1997, 3 degrees awarded. *Entrance requirements:* GRE General Test, TOEFL (minimum score 550). Application deadline: 4/1 (priority date; rolling processing; 10/1 for spring admission). Application fee: $45. *Expenses:* Tuition $680 per semester hour. Fees $35 per semester hour. *Financial aid:* Fellowships, teaching assistantships, Federal Work-Study, institutionally sponsored loans, and career-related internships or fieldwork available. Financial aid application deadline: 4/1. • Dr. Kathryn Newcomer, Chair, Department of Public Administration, 202-994-6295.

Georgia State University, College of Business Administration, Department of Finance, Atlanta, GA 30303-3083. Awards MBA, MS, PhD. Part-time and evening/weekend programs available. Faculty: 20 full-time, 1 part-time. Students: 250 full-time (60 women), 167 part-time (51 women); includes 31 minority (19 African Americans, 9 Asian Americans, 2 Hispanics, 1 Native American), 75 international. Average age 32. In 1997, 72 master's, 5 doctorates awarded. Terminal master's awarded for partial completion of doctoral program. *Degree requirements:* For doctorate, dissertation required, foreign language not required. *Entrance requirements:* For master's, GMAT (average 566), TOEFL; for doctorate, GMAT (average 670), TOEFL. Application deadline: 5/1 (rolling processing; 10/1 for spring admission). Application fee: $25. *Expenses:* Tuition $2673 per year full-time, $99 per semester hour part-time for state residents; $10,692 per year full-time, $396 per semester hour part-time for nonresidents. Fees $228 per year. *Financial aid:* Fellowships, research assistantships, teaching assistantships, partial tuition waivers, and career-related internships or fieldwork available. Aid available to part-time students. Financial aid applicants required to submit FAFSA. • Dr. Gerald D. Gay, Chair, 404-651-2628. Fax: 404-651-2630. Application contact: Office of Academic Assistance and Master's Admissions, 404-651-1913. Fax: 404-651-0219.

Golden Gate University, School of Business, San Francisco, CA 94105-2968. Offerings include finance (MBA, MS), financial engineering (MS), financial planning (Certificate). MBA (telecommunications, management information systems) offered jointly with the School of Technology and Industry. *Average time to degree:* master's–2.5 years full-time. *Application deadline:* 7/1 (priority date; rolling processing). *Application fee:* $55 ($70 for international students). *Tuition:* $996 per course (minimum). • Dr. Hamid Shomali, Dean, 415-442-6500. Fax: 415-442-6579. Application contact: Enrollment Services, 415-442-7800. Fax: 415-442-7807. E-mail: info@ggu.edu.

Goldey–Beacom College, MBA Program, 4701 Limestone Road, Wilmington, DE 19808-1999. Offerings include financial management (MBA). MBA (accounting) new for fall 1998. College faculty: 6 full-time (3 women), 4 part-time (1 woman). *Average time to degree:* master's–2 years full-time, 3 years part-time. *Entrance requirements:* GMAT (minimum score 450; average 507), TOEFL (minimum score 525), minimum GPA of 3.0. Application deadline: 8/20 (rolling processing; 5/15 for spring admission). Application fee: $30. Electronic applications accepted. *Expenses:* Tuition $6030 per year full-time, $335 per credit hour part-time. Fees $5 per credit hour. • Bruce D. Marsland, Director, 302-998-8814 Ext. 276. Fax: 302-998-8631. E-mail: graduate@goldey.gbc.edu.

Directory: Finance and Banking

Graduate School and University Center of the City University of New York, Program in Business, New York, NY 10036-8099. Offerings include finance (PhD). Terminal master's awarded for partial completion of doctoral program. Program faculty: 66 full-time (5 women). *Degree requirements:* Dissertation required, foreign language not required. *Entrance requirements:* GMAT. Application deadline: 3/1. Application fee: $40. *Expenses:* Tuition $4350 per year full-time, $185 per credit (minimum) part-time for state residents; $7600 per year full-time, $320 per credit (minimum) part-time for nonresidents. Fees $69 per year. • Dr. Gloria Thomas, Executive Officer, 212-802-6580.

Hawaii Pacific University, School of Business Administration, 1166 Fort Street, Honolulu, HI 96813-2785. Offerings include finance (MBA). School faculty: 30 full-time (3 women), 12 part-time (1 woman), 38 FTE. *Average time to degree:* master's–2 years full-time, 4 years part-time. *Application deadline:* rolling. *Application fee:* $50. Electronic applications accepted. *Tuition:* $7920 per year full-time, $330 per credit part-time. • Dr. Richard Ward, Dean for Graduate Management Studies, 808-544-0279. Application contact: Leina Danao, Admissions Coordinator, 808-544-1120. Fax: 808-544-0280. E-mail: gradservctr@hpu.edu.

Hofstra University, Frank G. Zarb School of Business, Department of Finance and Banking, Hempstead, NY 11549. Awards MBA. Part-time and evening/weekend programs available. Postbaccalaureate distance learning degree programs offered (no on-campus study). Faculty: 13 full-time (4 women), 3 part-time (0 women). Students: 53 full-time (14 women), 227 part-time (64 women); includes 14 minority (3 African Americans, 3 Asian Americans, 8 Hispanics), 27 international. Average age 29. 132 applicants, 58% accepted. In 1997, 99 degrees awarded. *Degree requirements:* Computer language, thesis or alternative required, foreign language not required. *Entrance requirements:* GMAT (average 580). Application deadline: rolling. Application fee: $40 ($75 for international students). *Expenses:* Tuition $10,968 per year full-time, $457 per credit hour part-time. Fees $670 per year full-time, $112 per semester (minimum) part-time. *Financial aid:* 22 students received aid; Federal Work-Study and career-related internships or fieldwork available. Financial aid application deadline: 4/1; applicants required to submit FAFSA. *Faculty research:* Future markets, foreign investment, securities markets, international finance, portfolio theory, corporate finance. • Dr. Esmeralda Lyn, Chairperson, 516-463-5698. Fax: 516-463-4834. E-mail: fineol@hofstra.edu. Application contact: Susan McTiernan, Senior Assistant Dean, 516-463-5683. Fax: 516-463-5268. E-mail: bizsmm@hofstra.edu.

Houston Baptist University, College of Business and Economics, Program in Management, Houston, TX 77074-3298. Offerings include finance (MBA). Program faculty: 9 full-time (1 woman), 7 part-time (1 woman). *Entrance requirements:* GMAT (minimum score 450), minimum GPA of 2.5, work experience. Application deadline: 6/1 (priority date; rolling processing; 1/1 for spring admission). Application fee: $25 ($85 for international students). *Expenses:* Tuition $300 per semester hour. Fees $235 per quarter. • Dr. Carter L. Franklin II, Associate Dean, College of Business and Economics, 281-649-3429. Application contact: Karen Murray, Program Assistant, 281-649-3306.

Illinois Institute of Technology, Stuart School of Business, Program in Financial Markets and Trading, Chicago, IL 60616-3793. Awards MS, JD/MS, MBA/MS. Part-time and evening/weekend programs available. *Degree requirements:* Comprehensive exam required, foreign language and thesis not required. *Entrance requirements:* GMAT, TOEFL (minimum score 550). Application deadline: 8/1 (rolling processing; 4/15 for spring admission). Application fee: $30. *Tuition:* $1620 per course. *Financial aid:* Application deadline 3/1. • John F. O. Bilson, Director. Application contact: Lynn Miller, Director, Admission, 312-906-6544. Fax: 312-906-6549. E-mail: degrees@stuart.iit.edu.

See in-depth description on page 449.

Indiana University Bloomington, School of Business, Doctoral Programs in Business, Bloomington, IN 47405. Offerings include finance (DBA, PhD). PhD offered through the University Graduate School. *Degree requirements:* Computer language, dissertation required, foreign language not required. *Entrance requirements:* GMAT (minimum score 600), GRE General Test. Application deadline: 3/1. Application fee: $35. *Expenses:* Tuition $261 per credit hour for state residents; $523 per credit hour for nonresidents. Fees $343 per year. • Dr. Janet Near, Chairperson, 812-855-3476. Application contact: Barbara Clark, Program Secretary and Assistant to Chairperson, 812-855-3476. Fax: 812-855-8679. E-mail: bclark@ucs.indiana.edu.

Indiana University Bloomington, School of Business, Program in Business Administration, Bloomington, IN 47405. Offerings include finance (MBA). Self-designed programs available. *Entrance requirements:* GMAT, TOEFL (minimum score 580). Application deadline: 3/1. Application fee: $50 ($65 for international students). *Expenses:* Tuition $8232 per year for state residents; $16,470 per year for nonresidents. Fees $343 per year. • Dr. George Hettenhouse, Chair, 812-855-8006. Application contact: Dr. James J. Holmen, Director of Admissions and Financial Aid, 812-855-8006. Fax: 812-855-9039.

Instituto Tecnológico y de Estudios Superiores de Monterrey, Graduate School of Management and Leadership, Program in Business Administration, Monterrey, Nuevo León 64849, Mexico. Offerings include finance (M Sc). *Application deadline:* 4/30 (priority date).

Instituto Tecnológico y de Estudios Superiores de Monterrey, Ciudad de México Campus, Graduate Programs, Calle del Puente Num 222, Tlalpan, Ciudad de Mexico, D.F. 14380, Mexico. Offerings include administration/finance/economy (MBA). EMBA jointly offered with The University of Texas at Austin. *Average time to degree:* master's–3 years part-time; doctorate–2 years full-time, 3.3 years part-time. *Application deadline:* 10/13 (4/5 for spring admission). *Application fee:* $65.

Instituto Tecnológico y de Estudios Superiores de Monterrey, Estado de México Campus, Graduate Division, Atizapán de Zaragoza 52926, Mexico. Offerings include finance (MAF). Postbaccalaureate distance learning degree programs offered (minimal on-campus study). Institute faculty: 19 full-time (3 women), 32 part-time (3 women). *Average time to degree:* master's–2 years full-time, 3.3 years part-time. *Application deadline:* 1/12 (priority date; rolling processing; 4/4 for spring admission). *Application fee:* $72. • Emilio Alvarado Badillo, Headmaster, 5-326-5500. Fax: 5-326-5507. E-mail: ealvarad@campus.cem.itesm.mx. Application contact: Lourdes Turrubiates, Admissions Officer, 5-326-5776. E-mail: lturrubi@campus.cem.itesm.mx.

Instituto Tecnológico y de Estudios Superiores de Monterrey, Guadalajara Campus, Program in Finance, Zapopan, Jalisco 44100, Mexico. Awards MA. Faculty: 9 full-time (2 women), 23 part-time (2 women). Students: 40. Average age 30. *Degree requirements:* 1 foreign language, thesis. *Average time to degree:* master's–1.5 years full-time, 2.5 years part-time. *Entrance requirements:* ITESM admission test. Application deadline: 8/1 (rolling processing; 3/1 for spring admission). Application fee: $40. *Financial aid:* Fellowships, Federal Work-Study, institutionally sponsored loans, and career-related internships or fieldwork available. Financial aid application deadline: 8/1. • Jaime Navarro, Director, 3-669-3099. E-mail: jnavarro@campus.gda.itesm.mx. Application contact: Marcela Tapia, Administrative Coordinator, MBA Program, 3-669-3095. Fax: 3-669-3093. E-mail: mtapia@campus.gda.itesm.mx.

Instituto Tecnológico y de Estudios Superiores de Monterrey, Morelos Campus, Programs in Business Administration, Cuernavaca, Morelos 62589, Mexico. Offerings include finance (MA).

Inter American University of Puerto Rico, Metropolitan Campus, Division of Economics and Business Administration, Programs in Finance, San Juan, PR 00919-1293. Awards MBA. Faculty: 4 full-time, 8 part-time. Students: 101 full-time (64 women), 299 part-time (149 women); includes 400 minority (all Hispanics). *Degree requirements:* Comprehensive exam required, foreign language and thesis not required. *Entrance requirements:* GRE or PAEG, interview. Application deadline: 5/15 (priority date; rolling processing; 11/15 for spring admission). Application fee: $31. Electronic applications accepted. *Expenses:* Tuition $3272 per year full-time, $1740 per year part-time. Fees $328 per year full-time, $176 per year part-time. *Financial aid:* Federal Work-Study available. • Application contact: Dr. Antonio Llorens, Director, 787-250-1912 Ext. 2320. Fax: 787-250-0361.

Inter American University of Puerto Rico, San Germán Campus, Department of Business Administration, Program in Business Administration, San Germán, PR 00683-5008. Offerings include finance (MBA). *Degree requirements:* Comprehensive exam required, foreign language and thesis not required. *Entrance requirements:* Minimum GPA of 3.0, GRE General Test, or PAEG. Application deadline: 4/30 (priority date; rolling processing; 11/15 for spring admission). Application fee: $31. *Expenses:* Tuition $150 per credit. Fees $177 per semester. • Application contact: Mildred Camacho, Admissions Director, 787-892-3090. Fax: 787-892-6350.

Iona College, Hagan Graduate School of Business, Department of Finance and Business Economics, 715 North Avenue, New Rochelle, NY 10801-1890. Offers program in financial management (MBA, PMC). Part-time and evening/weekend programs available. Faculty: 10 full-time (1 woman). Students: 10 full-time (4 women), 93 part-time (40 women); includes 5 minority (2 African Americans, 2 Asian Americans, 1 Hispanic). Average age 31. In 1997, 47 master's, 1 PMC awarded. *Degree requirements:* For master's, computer language required, foreign language and thesis not required. *Entrance requirements:* For master's, GMAT (minimum score 450; average 498). Application deadline: rolling. Application fee: $50. *Expenses:* Tuition $480 per credit hour. Fees $25 per semester. *Financial aid:* Graduate assistantships, partial tuition waivers available. Aid available to part-time students. *Faculty research:* Options, insurance financing, asset depreciation ranges, international finance, emerging markets. • Dr. Francis J. McGrath, Chairman, 914-633-2269. Application contact: Carol Shea, Director of MBA Admissions, 914-633-2288.

Johns Hopkins University, School of Continuing Studies, Division of Business and Management, Baltimore, MD 21218-2699. Offerings include investments (Certificate). Division faculty: 12 full-time, 190 part-time. *Application deadline:* rolling. *Application fee:* $50. • Dr. Jon Heggan, Director, 410-516-0755. Application contact: Lenora Henry, Admissions Coordinator, 410-872-1234. Fax: 410-872-1251. E-mail: adv_mail@jhuvms.hcf.jhu.edu.

Keller Graduate School of Management, 1 Tower Lane, Oak Brook Terrace, IL 60181. Offerings include accounting and financial management (MAFM). School faculty: 604. *Average time to degree:* master's–3 years part-time. *Application deadline:* rolling. *Application fee:* $0. *Tuition:* $1235 per course. • Dr. Sherrill Hole, Director, Academic Affairs, 630-574-1894. Application contact: Michael J. Alexander, Director, Central Services, 630-574-1957. Fax: 630-574-1969.

Kennesaw State University, Michael J. Coles College of Business, Program in Business Administration, Kennesaw, GA 30144-5591. Offerings include finance (MBA). Program faculty: 54 full-time (18 women), 5 part-time (0 women). *Application deadline:* 7/1 (rolling processing; 2/20 for spring admission). *Application fee:* $20. *Expenses:* Tuition $2398 per year full-time, $83 per credit hour part-time for state residents; $8398 per year full-time, $333 per credit hour part-time for nonresidents. Fees $338 per year. • Dr. Rodney Alsup, Assistant Dean, 770-423-6087. Fax: 770-423-6141. E-mail: ralsup@ksumail.kennesaw.edu. Application contact: Susan N. Barrett, Administrative Specialist, Admissions, 770-423-6500. Fax: 770-423-6541. E-mail: sbarrett@ksumail.kennesaw.edu.

Kent State University, Graduate School of Management, Doctoral Program in Finance, Kent, OH 44242-0001. Awards PhD. Faculty: 8 full-time (2 women). Students: 7 full-time (2 women), 5 part-time (0 women); includes 5 international. 14 applicants, 21% accepted. In 1997, 5 degrees awarded. *Degree requirements:* Dissertation, comprehensive exams, oral defense required, foreign language not required. *Entrance requirements:* GMAT. Application deadline: 2/1. Application fee: $30. *Tuition:* $4752 per year full-time, $216 per credit hour part-time for state residents; $9213 per year full-time, $419 per credit hour part-time for nonresidents. *Financial aid:* In 1997–98, 5 teaching assistantships (1 to a first-year student) averaging $1,000 per month were awarded; Federal Work-Study also available. Financial aid application deadline: 2/1; applicants required to submit FAFSA. *Faculty research:* Corporate finance, investments, international finance, futures and options, risk and insurance. • Richard J. Kent, Chair, 330-672-2366 Ext. 221. E-mail: rkent@bsa3.kent.edu. Application contact: Dr. James C. Baker, Doctoral Director, 330-672-2282 Ext. 235. Fax: 330-672-2448. E-mail: jbaker@bsa3.kent.edu.

King's College, William G. McGowan School of Business, Wilkes-Barre, PA 18711-0801. Offerings include finance (MS), with options in accounting/taxation, finance. School faculty: 7 full-time (1 woman), 3 part-time (0 women). *Average time to degree:* master's–2.5 years part-time. *Entrance requirements:* GMAT. Application deadline: 7/31 (priority date; rolling processing; 12/1 for spring admission). Application fee: $35. *Tuition:* $460 per credit. • Dr. Edward J. Schoen, Dean, 717-208-5932. Fax: 717-826-5989. E-mail: ejschoen@rs01.kings.edu. Application contact: Dr. Elizabeth S. Lott, Director of Graduate Programs, 717-208-5991. Fax: 717-825-9049. E-mail: eslott@rs02.kings.edu.

Long Island University, C.W. Post Campus, College of Management, School of Business, Department of Finance, Brookville, NY 11548-1300. Awards MBA, CAS. Part-time and evening/weekend programs available. Faculty: 8 full-time (1 woman), 11 part-time (4 women). Students: 19 full-time (4 women), 59 part-time (19 women). 44 applicants, 70% accepted. In 1997, 43 master's awarded. *Degree requirements:* For master's, computer language required, thesis not required. *Entrance requirements:* For master's, GMAT; for CAS, MBA. Application deadline: 8/15 (priority date; rolling processing; 12/15 for spring admission). Application fee: $30. Electronic applications accepted. *Expenses:* Tuition $480 per credit. Fees $316 per year full-time, $71 per semester (minimum) part-time. *Financial aid:* Graduate assistantships, partial tuition waivers available. Aid available to part-time students. Financial aid application deadline: 5/15; applicants required to submit FAFSA. • Owen T. Smith, Chair, 516-299-2308. E-mail: osmith@titan.liunet.edu. Application contact: Sally Luzader, Associate Director of Graduate Admissions, 516-299-2417. Fax: 516-299-2137. E-mail: admissions@collegehall.liunet.edu.

Louisiana State University and Agricultural and Mechanical College, College of Business Administration, Department of Finance, Baton Rouge, LA 70803. Offers programs in business administration (PhD), including finance; finance (MS). Faculty: 8 full-time (1 woman), 1 part-time (0 women). Students: 28 full-time (6 women), 8 part-time (4 women); includes 4 minority (1 African American, 1 Asian American, 1 Hispanic, 1 Native American), 13 international. Average age 27. 67 applicants, 22% accepted. In 1997, 13 master's, 3 doctorates awarded. *Degree requirements:* For master's, thesis or alternative required, foreign language not required; for doctorate, computer language, dissertation required, foreign language not required. *Entrance requirements:* GMAT, TOEFL. Application deadline: 1/25 (priority date; rolling processing). Application fee: $25. *Tuition:* $2736 per year full-time, $285 per semester (minimum) part-time for state residents; $6636 per year full-time, $460 per semester (minimum) part-time for nonresidents. *Financial aid:* In 1997–98, 8 research assistantships (2 to first-year students), 1 teaching assistantship were awarded; fellowships, service assistantships, and career-related internships or fieldwork also available. Financial aid application deadline: 4/1. *Faculty research:* Dividend policy, mergers and corporate control, financial markets and institutions, investment theory, option pricing models. • Dr. Gary C. Sanger, Chair, 504-388-6291. Application contact: Dr. William Lane, Graduate Adviser, 504-388-6291.

Louisiana Tech University, College of Administration and Business, Department of Finance and Economics, Ruston, LA 71272. Offers programs in business economics (MBA, DBA), finance (MBA, DBA). Part-time programs available. Faculty: 11 full-time (0 women). Students: 27 full-time (7 women), 10 part-time (0 women); includes 2 minority (1 Asian American, 1 Hispanic), 16 international. In 1997, 23 master's, 3 doctorates awarded. *Degree requirements:* For master's, computer language required, foreign language and thesis not required; for doctorate, computer language, dissertation required, foreign language not required. *Entrance requirements:* GMAT. Application deadline: 7/29 (2/3 for spring admission). Application fee: $20 ($30 for international students). *Tuition:* $2382 per year full-time, $223 per quarter (minimum) part-time for state residents; $5307 per year full-time, $223 per quarter (minimum) part-time for nonresidents. *Financial aid:* Fellowships, research assistantships, teaching assistantships available. Financial aid application deadline: 2/1. • Dr. Dwight Anderson, Head, 318-257-4149.

Loyola College, Sellinger School of Business and Management, Program in Finance, Baltimore, MD 21210-2699. Awards MSF. Part-time and evening/weekend programs available. Students: 6 full-time (1 woman), 71 part-time (14 women); includes 3 minority (2 African Americans, 1 Hispanic), 2 international. In 1997, 22 degrees awarded. *Entrance requirements:* GMAT, TOEFL. Application deadline: 7/20 (11/20 for spring admission). Application fee: $35. *Tuition:* $365 per credit. • Dr. Harold Fletcher, Chairman, 410-617-2750.

Loyola College, Sellinger School of Business and Management, Programs in Business Administration, Baltimore, MD 21210-2699. Offerings include finance (MBA). *Application deadline:* 7/20 (11/20 for spring admission). *Application fee:* $35. *Tuition:* $365 per credit. • Dr. Peter Lorenzi, Dean, Sellinger School of Business and Management, 410-617-2301.

Manhattan College, Program in Business Administration, Riverdale, NY 10471. Offerings include finance (MBA). Program faculty: 18 full-time (3 women), 8 part-time (0 women). *Degree requirements:* Computer language, thesis or alternative. *Entrance requirements:* GMAT, minimum GPA of 2.8. Application deadline: 8/10 (priority date; rolling processing; 1/7 for spring admission). Application fee: $50. *Expenses:* Tuition $440 per credit. Fees $100 per year. • Dr. Charles E. Brunner, Director, 718-862-7222. Fax: 718-862-8023. Application contact: William J. Bisset Jr., Dean of Admissions/Financial Aid, 718-862-7200. Fax: 718-863-8019. E-mail: admit@manhattan.edu.

Marywood University, Graduate School of Arts and Sciences, Department of Business and Managerial Science, Program in Finance and Investments, Scranton, PA 18509-1598. Awards MBA. Students: 5 full-time (3 women), 46 part-time (22 women); includes 1 minority (African American). Average age 33. 6 applicants, 83% accepted. In 1997, 26 degrees awarded. *Degree requirements:* Computer language, comprehensive exam required, foreign language and thesis not required. *Entrance requirements:* GMAT, TOEFL (minimum score 550; average 590). Application deadline: 7/15 (priority date; rolling processing; 12/1 for spring admission). Application fee: $20. *Expenses:* Tuition $449 per credit hour. Fees $530 per year full-time, $180 per year part-time. *Financial aid:* Research assistantships, scholarships/tuition reductions, partial tuition waivers, and career-related internships or fieldwork available. Aid available to part-time students. Financial aid application deadline: 2/15; applicants required to submit FAFSA. *Faculty research:* Accountant/auditor liability, corporate finance acquisitions and mergers, corporate bankruptcy. • Application contact: Deborah M. Flynn, Coordinator of Admissions, 717-340-6002. Fax: 717-961-4745.

Mercy College, Department of Business, Concentration in Banking, Dobbs Ferry, NY 10522-1189. Awards MS. Offered jointly with the American Institute of Banking. *Entrance requirements:* Interview, minimum GPA of 3.0. Application fee: $60. *Tuition:* $390 per credit. • Application contact: Admissons Office, 800-MERCY-NY. Fax: 914-674-7382. E-mail: admission@merlin.mercynet.edu.

Metropolitan State University, Management and Administration Program, St. Paul, MN 55106-5000. Offerings include finance (MBA). Program faculty: 17 full-time (5 women), 150 part-time. *Application deadline:* rolling. *Application fee:* $20. *Tuition:* $133 per credit for state residents; $208 per credit for nonresidents. • Gary Seiler, Graduate Coordinator, 612-373-2754. E-mail: seiler@msus1.msus.edu. Application contact: Gloria Marcus, Recruiter/Admissions Adviser, 612-373-2724. Fax: 612-373-2888. E-mail: marcusg@msus1.msus.edu.

Miami University, Richard T. Farmer School of Business Administration, Oxford, OH 45056. Offerings include finance (MBA). School faculty: 50. *Application deadline:* 3/1 (priority date; rolling processing). *Application fee:* $35. *Tuition:* $5932 per year full-time, $255 per credit hour part-time for state residents; $12,392 per year full-time, $524 per credit hour part-time for nonresidents. • Judy Barille, Director of Graduate Programs, 513-529-6643.

Michigan State University, Eli Broad Graduate School of Management, Department of Finance, East Lansing, MI 48824-1020. Awards MBA, PhD. Faculty: 14 (2 women). Students: 135 (37 women); includes 7 minority (1 African American, 5 Asian Americans, 1 Hispanic), 67 international. Average age 27. In 1997, 43 master's, 3 doctorates awarded. *Degree requirements:* For doctorate, dissertation required, foreign language not required. *Entrance requirements:* For master's, GMAT (minimum score 575); for doctorate, GMAT (minimum score 600). Application deadline: rolling. Application fee: $30 ($40 for international students). *Expenses:* Tuition $4609 per year full-time, $223 per credit hour (minimum) part-time for state residents; $8704 per year full-time, $450 per credit hour (minimum) part-time for nonresidents. Fees $576 per year full-time, $476 per year part-time. *Financial aid:* In 1997–98, 5 research assistantships, 10 teaching assistantships were awarded. *Faculty research:* Corporate governance, capital structure, investment performance, options and futures, valuation. • Dr. Richard Simonds, Chairperson, 517-353-1745.

Middle Tennessee State University, College of Business, Department of Economics and Finance, Murfreesboro, TN 37132. Offers programs in economics (MA, DA), finance (MBA), industrial relations (MA). Faculty: 17 full-time (2 women). Students: 15 full-time (8 women), 18 part-time (5 women); includes 1 minority (Hispanic), 12 international. Average age 35. 26 applicants, 38% accepted. In 1997, 1 master's awarded. *Degree requirements:* For master's, comprehensive exams; for doctorate, dissertation, comprehensive exams required, foreign language not required. *Entrance requirements:* For master's, GMAT. Application deadline: 8/1 (priority date). Application fee: $5. *Expenses:* Tuition $2560 per year full-time, $129 per semester hour part-time for state residents; $7386 per year full-time, $340 per semester hour part-time for nonresidents. Fees $486 per year full-time, $17 per semester (minimum) part-time. *Financial aid:* Teaching assistantships, institutionally sponsored loans available. Aid available to part-time students. Financial aid application deadline: 5/1; applicants required to submit FAFSA. • Dr. John Lee, Chair, 615-898-2520. Fax: 615-898-5596. E-mail: jlee@mtsu.edu.

Montclair State University, School of Business, Department of Economics and Finance, Upper Montclair, NJ 07043-1624. Awards MA. Part-time and evening/weekend programs available. Faculty: 15 full-time. Students: 6 full-time (4 women), 13 part-time (8 women). *Degree requirements:* Comprehensive exam required, foreign language and thesis not required. *Entrance requirements:* GRE General Test. Application deadline: 4/1 (rolling processing; 11/1 for spring admission). Application fee: $40. *Expenses:* Tuition $201 per credit for state residents; $257 per credit for nonresidents. Fees $22.05 per credit. *Financial aid:* Research assistantships available. Aid available to part-time students. Financial aid application deadline: 3/1; applicants required to submit FAFSA. • Dr. Serpil Leveen, Chair, 973-655-5255. Application contact: Dr. Harold Flint, Adviser, 973-655-5255.

Montclair State University, School of Business, Program in Business Administration, Upper Montclair, NJ 07043-1624. Offerings include finance (MBA). Program faculty: 57 full-time. *Entrance requirements:* GMAT. Application deadline: 4/1 (rolling processing; 11/1 for spring admission). Application fee: $40. *Expenses:* Tuition $201 per credit for state residents; $257 per credit for nonresidents. Fees $22.05 per credit. • Dr. Eileen Kaplan, Director, 973-655-4306.

New Hampshire College, Graduate School of Business, Program in Business Administration, Manchester, NH 03106-1045. Offerings include finance (Certificate). Program faculty: 7 full-time (1 woman), 66 part-time (11 women), 47 FTE. *Average time to degree:* master's–1.5 years full-time, 4.5 years part-time. *Application deadline:* rolling. *Application fee:* $0. *Expenses:* Tuition $17,044 per year full-time, $945 per course part-time. Fees $530 per year full-time, $80 per year part-time. • Dr. Paul Schneiderman, Acting Dean, Graduate School of Business, 603-644-3102. Fax: 603-644-3150.

New Hampshire College, Graduate School of Business, Program in Finance, Manchester, NH 03106-1045. Awards MS. Part-time and evening/weekend programs available. Faculty: 3 full-time (1 woman), 6 part-time (2 women), 4 FTE. Students: 9 full-time (3 women), 12 part-time (4 women); includes 7 international. Average age 28. In 1997, 3 degrees awarded. *Degree requirements:* Thesis or alternative required, foreign language not required. *Average time to degree:* master's–1.5 years full-time, 3.5 years part-time. *Entrance requirements:* Minimum GPA of 2.5. Application deadline: rolling. Application fee: $0. *Expenses:* Tuition $17,044 per year full-time, $945 per course part-time. Fees $530 per year full-time, $80 per year part-time. *Financial aid:* Partial tuition waivers, Federal Work-Study, and career-related internships or fieldwork available. • Dr. Paul Schneiderman, Acting Dean, Graduate School of Business, 603-644-3102. Fax: 603-644-3150.

New York University, Leonard N. Stern School of Business, Department of Finance, New York, NY 10006. Awards MBA, PhD, APC. Faculty: 46 full-time (4 women), 33 part-time (3 women). Students: 877 full-time, 1,584 part-time. In 1997, 940 master's, 5 doctorates, 4 APCs awarded. *Degree requirements:* For master's, computer language required, foreign language and thesis not required; for doctorate, computer language, dissertation required, foreign language not required. *Entrance requirements:* For master's, GMAT, TOEFL (minimum score 600); for doctorate, GMAT. Application deadline: 3/15 (rolling processing). Application fee: $75. *Financial aid:* Federal Work-Study available. Financial aid application deadline: 1/15; applicants required to submit FAFSA. *Faculty research:* Corporate decision making, portfolio management, derivatives, mutual funds, corporate distress. • Anthony Saunders, Chairman, 212-998-0300. Application contact: Mary Miller, Director, Graduate Admissions, 212-998-0600. Fax: 212-995-4231. E-mail: sternmba@stern.nyu.edu.

New York University, Robert F. Wagner Graduate School of Public Service, Program in Public Administration, New York, NY 10012-1019. Offerings include financial management and public finance (MPA, APC). Program faculty: 14 full-time (6 women), 49 part-time (21 women), 23 FTE. *Degree requirements:* For master's, thesis or alternative. *Average time to degree:* master's–2 years full-time, 4 years part-time; doctorate–5 years full-time, 7 years part-time; other advanced degree–1 year full-time. *Entrance requirements:* For master's, minimum undergraduate GPA of 3.0. Application deadline: 8/1 (rolling processing; 1/1 for spring admission). Application fee: $50 ($70 for international students). • Leanna Stiefel, Director, 212-998-7400. Application contact: Hedy Flanders, Director, Admissions and Financial Aid, 212-998-7414. Fax: 212-995-4164. E-mail: wagner.admissions@nyu.edu.

Nichols College, Graduate Program in Business Administration, Dudley, MA 01571. Offerings include finance (MBA). College faculty: 21 full-time (3 women), 6 part-time (2 women). *Degree requirements:* Computer language required, foreign language and thesis not required. *Entrance requirements:* GMAT, TOEFL, minimum AACSB index of 950. Application deadline: rolling. Application fee: $25. *Tuition:* $1050 per course. • William F. Keith, Director, 508-213-2207. E-mail: keithwf@nichols.edu.

Northeastern Illinois University, College of Business and Management, Chicago, IL 60625-4699. Offerings include finance (MBA). College faculty: 26 full-time (3 women), 14 part-time (6 women). *Degree requirements:* Thesis optional, foreign language not required. *Entrance requirements:* GMAT (minimum score 450), TOEFL (minimum score 550), minimum GPA of 2.75. Application deadline: 3/18 (priority date; rolling processing; 9/30 for spring admission). Application fee: $0. *Expenses:* Tuition $2226 per year full-time, $93 per credit hour part-time for state residents; $6678 per year full-time, $278 per credit hour part-time for nonresidents. Fees $358 per year full-time, $14.90 per credit hour part-time. • Dr. Charles Falk, Dean, 773-583-4050 Ext. 5247. Application contact: Dr. Kathleen Carlson, Coordinator, 773-583-4050.

Northeastern University, Graduate School of Business Administration, Program in Finance, Boston, MA 02115-5096. Awards MSF. Part-time and evening/weekend programs available. Faculty: 21 full-time (4 women), 7 part-time (1 woman). Students: 61 part-time (18 women). 45 applicants, 69% accepted. In 1997, 2 degrees awarded (100% found work related to degree). *Average time to degree:* master's–2 years part-time. *Entrance requirements:* GMAT, bachelor's degree in business. Application deadline: 8/1 (priority date; rolling processing). Application fee: $50. *Expenses:* Tuition $500 per credit hour. Fees $55 per quarter full-time, $13.25 per quarter part-time. *Financial aid:* Institutionally sponsored loans available. *Faculty research:* Mergers and acquisitions, corporate bankruptcy, crisis management, risk management, financial markets, intermediation. • Application contact: Market Center Representative, 617-373-2714. Fax: 617-373-8564. E-mail: gsba@neu.edu.

Northern Illinois University, College of Business, Department of Finance, De Kalb, IL 60115-2854. Awards MS. Part-time programs available. Faculty: 9 full-time (0 women). Students: 11 full-time (3 women), 15 part-time (4 women); includes 2 minority (1 African American, 1 Asian American), 2 international. Average age 32. 44 applicants, 41% accepted. In 1997, 10 degrees awarded. *Degree requirements:* Thesis optional, foreign language not required. *Entrance requirements:* GMAT, TOEFL (minimum score 550), minimum GPA of 2.75. Application deadline: 6/1 (rolling processing; 11/1 for spring admission). Application fee: $30. *Tuition:* $3984 per year full-time, $154 per credit hour part-time for state residents; $8160 per year full-time, $328 per credit hour part-time for nonresidents. *Financial aid:* In 1997–98, 7 research assistantships were awarded; fellowships, teaching assistantships, staff assistantships, full tuition waivers, Federal Work-Study, and career-related internships or fieldwork also available. Aid available to part-time students. • Dr. Robert E. Miller, Chair, 815-753-1114. Application contact: Dr. Richard J. Dowen, Faculty Adviser, 815-753-6394.

Northwestern University, J. L. Kellogg Graduate School of Management, Department of Finance, Evanston, IL 60208. Awards PhD. Admissions and degree offered through The Graduate School. Faculty: 19 full-time (2 women). Students: 17 full-time (3 women); includes 11 international. 134 applicants, 9% accepted. In 1997, 3 degrees awarded. *Degree requirements:* Computer language, dissertation required, foreign language not required. *Entrance requirements:* GMAT or GRE General Test, 2 years of undergraduate mathematics. Application deadline: 1/15. Application fee: $50 ($55 for international students). *Tuition:* $25,872 per year. *Financial aid:* In 1997–98, 3 students received aid, including fellowships averaging $1,256 per month, research assistantships averaging $1,592 per month; institutionally sponsored loans and career-related internships or fieldwork also available. Financial aid application deadline: 1/15; applicants required to submit FAFSA. *Faculty research:* Corporate finance, asset pricing, international finance, micro-structure, empirical finance. • Deborah Lucas, Chair, 847-491-8333. Application contact: Lucy Vandenburgh, Admission Contact, 847-491-3400. Fax: 847-491-5071. E-mail: l-vandenburgh@nwu.edu.

Oklahoma City University, School of Management and Business Sciences, Program in Business Administration, Oklahoma City, OK 73106-1402. Offerings include finance (MBA). *Degree requirements:* Comprehensive exam required, foreign language and thesis not required. *Entrance requirements:* TOEFL, minimum GPA of 2.5. Application deadline: rolling. Application fee: $35 ($55 for international students). *Expenses:* Tuition $350 per hour. Fees $124 per year. • Application contact: Laura L. Rahhal, Director of Graduate Admissions, 800-633-7242 Ext. 2. Fax: 405-521-5356. E-mail: lrahhal1@frodo.okcu.edu.

Oklahoma State University, College of Business Administration, Department of Finance, Stillwater, OK 74078. Awards MBA, PhD. *Degree requirements:* For doctorate, dissertation required, foreign language not required. *Entrance requirements:* For doctorate, TOEFL (minimum score 550). Application deadline: 7/1 (priority date). Application fee: $25. *Financial aid:* Partial tuition waivers, Federal Work-Study, and career-related internships or fieldwork available. Aid available to part-time students. Financial aid application deadline: 3/1. • Janice Jadlow, Head, 405-624-5192.

Oral Roberts University, School of Business, Tulsa, OK 74171-0001. Offerings include finance (MBA). *Degree requirements:* Computer language required, thesis optional, foreign language not required. *Entrance requirements:* GMAT (minimum score 400; average 500).

Directory: Finance and Banking

Oral Roberts University (continued)
Application deadline: 7/31 (priority date; rolling processing; 12/31 for spring admission). Application fee: $35. Electronic applications accepted.

Our Lady of the Lake University of San Antonio, School of Business and Public Administration, 411 Southwest 24th Street, San Antonio, TX 78207-4689. Offerings include general (MBA), with options in finance, international business, management. School faculty: 15 full-time (2 women), 15 part-time (2 women). *Degree requirements:* Thesis optional. *Entrance requirements:* GMAT, GRE General Test, or MAT. Application deadline: rolling. Application fee: $15. *Expenses:* Tuition $371 per credit hour. Fees $57 per semester full-time, $32 per semester part-time. • Dr. W. Earl Walker, Dean, 210-434-6711 Ext. 281. Application contact: Quentin W. Korte, MBA Adviser, 210-434-6711 Ext. 491. Fax: 210-434-0821.

Pace University, Lubin School of Business, Financial Management Program, New York, NY 10038. Offers banking and finance (MBA), corporate financial management (MBA), financial management (MBA), investment management (MBA, MS). Part-time and evening/weekend programs available. *Degree requirements:* Computer language required, foreign language and thesis not required. *Entrance requirements:* GMAT. Application deadline: 7/31 (priority date; rolling processing; 11/30 for spring admission). Application fee: $60. *Expenses:* Tuition $545 per credit. Fees $360 per year full-time, $53 per semester (minimum) part-time.

Pacific States University, College of Business, Los Angeles, CA 90006. Offerings include finance (MBA). *Entrance requirements:* TOEFL (minimum score 450), minimum undergraduate GPA of 2.5 during last 90 hours. Application deadline: 6/15 (12/15 for spring admission). Application fee: $100. *Tuition:* $200 per unit. • Dr. Kamol Somvichian, Director, 888-200-0383.

Pennsylvania State University University Park Campus, The Mary Jean and Frank P. Smeal College of Business Administration, MS Programs in Business Administration, Department of Finance, University Park, PA 16802-1503. Awards MS. *Degree requirements:* Paper or thesis required, foreign language not required. *Entrance requirements:* GMAT. Application fee: $40. *Expenses:* Tuition $6534 per year full-time, $276 per credit part-time for state residents; $13,460 per year full-time, $561 per credit part-time for nonresidents. Fees $252 per year (minimum) full-time, $43 per semester (minimum) part-time. • Dr. William A. Kracaw, Chair, 814-863-0486.

Pennsylvania State University University Park Campus, The Mary Jean and Frank P. Smeal College of Business Administration, PhD Programs in Business Administration, Program in Finance/Insurance and Real Estate, University Park, PA 16802-1503. Awards PhD. *Degree requirements:* Dissertation. *Entrance requirements:* GMAT. Application fee: $40. *Expenses:* Tuition $6534 per year full-time, $276 per credit part-time for state residents; $13,460 per year full-time, $561 per credit part-time for nonresidents. Fees $252 per year (minimum) full-time, $43 per semester (minimum) part-time. • Dr. Dennis P. Sheehan, Field Adviser, 814-863-8512.

Philadelphia College of Textiles and Science, School of Business, Program in Business, Philadelphia, PA 19144-5497. Offerings include finance (MBA). *Entrance requirements:* GMAT, minimum GPA of 2.85. Application deadline: rolling. Application fee: $35. *Tuition:* $448 per credit hour. • Rita Powell, Director, 215-951-2950. Fax: 215-951-2652. E-mail: powellr@phila.col.edu. Application contact: Robert J. Reed, Director of Graduate Admissions, 215-951-2943. Fax: 215-951-2907. E-mail: gradadm@phila.col.edu.

Polytechnic University, Brooklyn Campus, Department of Management, Major in Financial Engineering, Six Metrotech Center, Brooklyn, NY 11201-2990. Awards MS. Students: 44. 48 applicants, 75% accepted. In 1997, 6 degrees awarded. *Degree requirements:* Thesis or alternative. *Entrance requirements:* GMAT, minimum B average in undergraduate course work. Application deadline: rolling. Application fee: $45. Electronic applications accepted. *Expenses:* Tuition $19,530 per year full-time, $675 per credit part-time. Fees $600 per year full-time, $135 per semester part-time. • Frederick Novomestky, Academic Director, 718-260-3436. Fax: 718-260-3874. E-mail: fnovomes@poly.edu. Application contact: John S. Kerge, Dean of Admissions, 718-260-3200. Fax: 718-260-3446. E-mail: admitme@poly.edu.

Polytechnic University, Farmingdale Campus, Graduate Programs, Department of Management, Major in Financial Engineering, Route 110, Farmingdale, NY 11735-3995. Awards MS. Students: 0. 2 applicants, 50% accepted. *Application fee:* $45. *Expenses:* Tuition $19,530 per year full-time, $675 per credit part-time. Fees $600 per year full-time, $135 per semester part-time. *Financial aid:* Institutionally sponsored loans available. Aid available to part-time students. Financial aid applicants required to submit FAFSA. • Frederick Novomestky, Director, 718-260-3436. Fax: 718-260-3874. E-mail: fnovomes@poly.edu. Application contact: John S. Kerge, Dean of Admissions, 718-260-3200. Fax: 718-260-3446. E-mail: admitme@poly.edu.

Polytechnic University, Westchester Graduate Center, Division of Management, Major in Financial Engineering, Hawthorne, NY 10532-1507. Awards MS. Students: 1 (woman) part-time. 1 applicant, 100% accepted. *Degree requirements:* Computer language. *Application deadline:* rolling. *Application fee:* $45. Electronic applications accepted. *Expenses:* Tuition $19,530 per year full-time, $675 per credit part-time. Fees $600 per year full-time, $135 per semester part-time. • Frederick Novomestky, Director, 718-260-3436. Fax: 718-260-3874. E-mail: fnovomes@poly.edu. Application contact: John S. Kerge, Dean of Admissions, 718-260-3200. Fax: 718-260-3446. E-mail: admitme@poly.edu.

Purdue University, Krannert Graduate School of Management, Department of Management, West Lafayette, IN 47907. Offerings include finance (MSM, PhD). Department faculty: 51 full-time (5 women). *Degree requirements:* For doctorate, dissertation required, foreign language not required. *Average time to degree:* doctorate–4 years full-time. *Entrance requirements:* For doctorate, GMAT, TOEFL (minimum score 575). Application fee: $30. Electronic applications accepted. *Tuition:* $3500 per year full-time, $126 per credit hour part-time for state residents; $11,720 per year full-time, $387 per credit hour part-time for nonresidents. • Dr. J. J. McConnell, Director of Doctoral Programs, 765-494-4375. Application contact: Kelly Felty, Assistant Director of Administration for Doctoral Programs, 765-494-4375. Fax: 765-494-1526. E-mail: feltyk@mgmt.purdue.edu.

Quinnipiac College, School of Business, Program in Business Administration, Hamden, CT 06518-1904. Offerings include finance (MBA). Program faculty: 17 full-time (2 women), 4 part-time (1 woman). *Degree requirements:* Thesis optional, foreign language not required. *Average time to degree:* master's–2 years full-time, 4 years part-time. *Entrance requirements:* GMAT (minimum score 400; average 470), interview, minimum GPA of 2.5. Application deadline: 8/1 (priority date; rolling processing). Application fee: $45. Electronic applications accepted. *Expenses:* Tuition $395 per credit hour. Fees $380 per year full-time. • Dr. Earl Chrysler, Director, 203-281-8799. Fax: 203-281-8664. E-mail: chrysler@quinnipiac.edu. Application contact: Scott Farber, Director of Graduate Admissions, 203-281-8795. Fax: 203-287-5238. E-mail: qcgradadmi@quinnipiac.edu.

Rensselaer Polytechnic Institute, Lally School of Management and Technology, Troy, NY 12180-3590. Offerings include accounting/finance (PhD); business administration (MBA, PhD), with options in finance and accounting (MBA), information systems management (MBA), management (PhD), management of technology and entrepreneurships (MBA), manufacturing management (MBA), marketing management (MBA), operations research (MBA), organizational behavior and human resource management (MBA), statistical methods for management (MBA). Postbaccalaureate distance learning degree programs offered (no on-campus study). School faculty: 36 full-time (5 women), 6 part-time (0 women). *Degree requirements:* For doctorate, computer language, dissertation required, foreign language not required. *Entrance requirements:* For doctorate, GMAT or GRE General Test, TOEFL (minimum score 570). Application deadline: 2/1 (priority date; rolling processing). Application fee: $35. *Expenses:* Tuition $630 per credit hour. Fees $1000 per year. • Dr. Joseph G. Ecker, Dean, 518-276-6802. Application contact: Michele Martens, Manager of Enrollment Services, 518-276-4800. Fax: 518-276-8661.

Robert Morris College, Program in Business Administration, 881 Narrows Run Road, Moon Township, PA 15108-1189. Offerings include finance (MBA, MS). Only part-time programs offered. Program faculty: 35 full-time (6 women), 35 part-time (5 women). *Entrance requirements:* GMAT (minimum score 450), minimum GPA of 2.5. Application deadline: 8/1 (priority date; rolling processing; 11/30 for spring admission). Application fee: $25 ($35 for international students). *Expenses:* Tuition $328 per credit. Fees $15 per credit. • Dr. Joseph F. Constable, Dean, School of Management, 412-262-8451. Fax: 412-262-8494. E-mail: constabl@robert-morris.edu. Application contact: Vincent J. Kane, Recruiting Coordinator, 412-262-8535. Fax: 412-299-2425.

Rochester Institute of Technology, College of Business, Department of Business Administration, Program in Finance, Rochester, NY 14623-5604. Awards MS. Students: 11 full-time (5 women), 9 part-time (3 women); includes 2 minority (1 African American, 1 Asian American), 4 international. 18 applicants, 67% accepted. In 1997, 7 degrees awarded. *Entrance requirements:* GMAT, minimum GPA of 2.5. Application deadline: 3/1 (priority date; rolling processing). Application fee: $40. *Expenses:* Tuition $18,765 per year full-time, $527 per credit hour part-time. Fees $126 per year full-time. • Patricia Sorce, Associate Dean, Department of Business Administration, 716-475-2313.

Rutgers, The State University of New Jersey, Newark, Department of Management, Newark, NJ 07102-3192. Offerings include finance (PhD). Offered jointly with New Jersey Institute of Technology. Terminal master's awarded for partial completion of doctoral program. Department faculty: 113 full-time (13 women), 3 part-time (1 woman). *Degree requirements:* Dissertation, cumulative exams required, foreign language not required. *Average time to degree:* doctorate–5 years full-time, 7 years part-time. *Entrance requirements:* GMAT or GRE, minimum undergraduate B average. Application deadline: 4/1 (rolling processing; 11/1 for spring admission). Application fee: $40. *Expenses:* Tuition $6248 per year full-time, $257 per credit part-time for state residents; $9160 per year full-time, $380 per credit part-time for nonresidents. Fees $738 per year full-time, $107 per semester (minimum) part-time. • Glenn R. Shafer, Director, 973-353-1604. E-mail: gshafer@andromeda.rutgers.edu. Application contact: Ana Gonzalez, Program Secretary, 973-353-5371. Fax: 973-353-5691. E-mail: anag@gsmack.rutgers.edu.

Rutgers, The State University of New Jersey, Newark, Graduate School of Management, Department of Finance and Economics, Newark, NJ 07102-3192. Awards MBA. *Degree requirements:* Computer language required, thesis not required. *Entrance requirements:* GMAT, TOEFL. Application deadline: 6/1 (rolling processing). Application fee: $40. *Financial aid:* Federal Work-Study, institutionally sponsored loans, and career-related internships or fieldwork available. Financial aid application deadline: 3/15; applicants required to submit FAFSA. • Dr. Ivan Brick, Chairman, 973-353-5155. Fax: 973-353-1233. E-mail: ibrick@gsmack.rutgers.edu. Application contact: Director of Admissions, 973-353-1234. Fax: 973-353-1592. E-mail: admit@gsmack.rutgers.edu.

Sage Graduate School, Graduate School, Division of Management Studies, Program in Business Administration, Troy, NY 12180-4115. Offerings include finance (MBA). MBA/JD offered jointly with Albany Law School of Union University. Program faculty: 1 full-time (0 women), 10 part-time (1 woman). *Entrance requirements:* Minimum GPA of 2.75. Application fee: $25. *Expenses:* Tuition $360 per credit hour. Fees $50 per semester. • Application contact: Melissa Robertson, Associate Director of Admissions, 518-244-6878. Fax: 518-244-6880. E-mail: sgsadm@sage.edu.

St. Bonaventure University, School of Business Administration, St. Bonaventure, NY 14778-2284. Offerings include accounting and finance (MBA). School faculty: 19 full-time (2 women), 3 part-time (0 women). *Average time to degree:* master's–1.5 years full-time, 3 years part-time. *Entrance requirements:* GMAT (minimum score 400), TOEFL (minimum score 600). Application deadline: 8/1 (rolling processing). Application fee: $35. *Tuition:* $8100 per year full-time, $450 per credit hour part-time. • Dr. Michael Fischer, Dean, 716-375-2200. Application contact: Brian C. McAllister, MBA Director, 716-375-2098. Fax: 716-375-2191. E-mail: bmac@sbu.edu.

St. Cloud State University, College of Business, Department of Management and Finance, St. Cloud, MN 56301-4498. Offers program in finance (MBA). Part-time programs available. Faculty: 19 full-time (5 women), 1 part-time (0 women). *Degree requirements:* Comprehensive exam required, foreign language and thesis not required. *Entrance requirements:* GMAT (minimum score 470), minimum GPA of 2.75. Application fee: $20 ($100 for international students). *Expenses:* Tuition $128 per credit for state residents; $203 per credit for nonresidents. Fees $16.32 per credit. *Financial aid:* Graduate assistantships, Federal Work-Study available. Financial aid application deadline: 3/1. • Application contact: Ann Anderson, Graduate Studies Office, 320-255-2113. Fax: 320-654-5371. E-mail: anna@grad.stcloud.msus.edu.

St. John's University, College of Business Administration, Department of Economics and Finance, Program in Finance, Jamaica, NY 11439. Awards MBA, Adv C. Part-time and evening/weekend programs available. Students: 58 full-time (17 women), 418 part-time (157 women); includes 100 minority (36 African Americans, 35 Asian Americans, 27 Hispanics, 2 Native Americans), 55 international. Average age 29. 229 applicants, 75% accepted. In 1997, 163 master's, 1 Adv C awarded. *Degree requirements:* For master's, thesis optional, foreign language not required. *Entrance requirements:* For master's, GMAT. Application deadline: 6/1 (rolling processing; 10/1 for spring admission). Application fee: $40. *Expenses:* Tuition $600 per credit. Fees $150 per year. *Financial aid:* Federal Work-Study available. Aid available to part-time students. Financial aid application deadline: 3/1; applicants required to submit FAFSA. • Application contact: Shamus J. McGrenra, TOR, Associate Director, Graduate Admissions, 718-990-6107. Fax: 718-990-5736. E-mail: mcgrenrs@stjohns.edu.

Saint Joseph's University, Ervian K. Haub School of Business, Programs in Graduate Business, Program in Finance, Philadelphia, PA 19131-1395. Awards MBA. Evening/weekend programs available. Students: 198 (43 women). In 1997, 85 degrees awarded. *Entrance requirements:* GMAT, TOEFL. Application deadline: 7/15 (priority date; rolling processing; 11/15 for spring admission). Application fee: $35. *Tuition:* $510 per credit hour. *Financial aid:* Graduate assistantships available. Financial aid application deadline: 5/1. • Adele C. Foley, Associate Dean, Programs in Graduate Business, 610-660-1690. Fax: 610-660-1599. E-mail: afoley@sju.edu.

Saint Louis University, School of Business and Administration, Department of Finance, 3674 Lindell Boulevard, St. Louis, MO 63108. Awards MBA, M Fin, PhD. Part-time programs available. Faculty: 10 full-time (0 women), 2 part-time (0 women). Students: 30 full-time (21 women), 42 part-time (10 women); includes 31 international. Average age 26. 26 applicants, 73% accepted. In 1997, 54 master's, 1 doctorate awarded. *Degree requirements:* For doctorate, dissertation. *Average time to degree:* master's–1.5 years full-time, 3 years part-time; doctorate–5 years full-time. *Entrance requirements:* For master's, GMAT, TOEFL; for doctorate, GMAT. Application deadline: 7/15 (rolling processing; 11/15 for spring admission). Application fee: $40. Electronic applications accepted. *Financial aid:* Fellowships, research assistantships, teaching assistantships, Federal Work-Study, and career-related internships or fieldwork available. Aid available to part-time students. • Dr. Frederick C. Yeager, Chairman, 314-977-3858.

St. Thomas Aquinas College, Division of Business Administration, Sparkill, NY 10976. Offerings include finance (MBA). Division faculty: 7 full-time (2 women), 8 part-time (0 women). *Entrance requirements:* GMAT. Application deadline: rolling. Application fee: $35. Electronic applications accepted. *Expenses:* Tuition $390 per credit. Fees $10 per year. • Barbara Donn, Chairperson, 914-398-4113. Fax: 914-359-8136. Application contact: Joseph L. Chillo, Executive Director of Enrollment Services, 914-398-4100. Fax: 914-398-4224. E-mail: joestacenroll@rockland.net.

Saint Xavier University, Graham School of Management, Chicago, IL 60655-3105. Offerings include certified financial planner (MBA, Certificate), finance (MBA), financial trading and practice (MBA, Certificate). School faculty: 15 full-time (2 women), 6 part-time (3 women). *Entrance requirements:* For master's, GMAT, minimum GPA of 3.0, 2 years of work experience. Application deadline: 8/15. Application fee: $35. *Expenses:* Tuition $455 per hour. Fees $50 per year. • Dr. John Eber, Dean, 773-298-3601. Fax: 773-298-3610. E-mail: eber@sxu.edu. Application contact: Sr. Evelyn McKenna, Vice President of Enrollment Management, 773-298-3050. Fax: 773-298-3076. E-mail: mckenna@sxu.edu.

San Diego State University, Graduate School of Business, Department of Finance, San Diego, CA 92182. Awards MBA, MS. Part-time and evening/weekend programs available. Students: 40 full-time (15 women), 84 part-time (21 women); includes 25 minority (3 African Americans, 11 Asian Americans, 11 Hispanics), 12 international. Average age 29. *Degree requirements:* Thesis or alternative required, foreign language not required. *Average time to degree:* master's–2 years full-time, 3.5 years part-time. *Entrance requirements:* GMAT (minimum score 550), TOEFL (minimum score 570). Application deadline: 4/15 (priority date; rolling processing; 11/1 for spring admission). Application fee: $55. Electronic applications accepted. *Expenses:* Tuition $0 for state residents; $246 per unit for nonresidents. Fees $1932 per year full-time, $1266 per year part-time. *Financial aid:* Fellowships, research assistantships, teaching assistantships, Federal Work-Study available. • Nikhil P. Varaiya, Chair, 619-594-5323. Fax: 616-594-1573. E-mail: nvaraiya@sciences.sdsu.edu. Application contact: Patricia Martin, Director of Admissions, 619-594-5217. Fax: 619-594-1863. E-mail: sdsumba@mail.sdsu.edu.

Seattle University, Albers School of Business and Economics, Program in Finance, Seattle, WA 98122. Awards MSF, Certificate, JD/MSF. Certificate and JD/MSF new for fall 1998. Part-time and evening/weekend programs available. Faculty: 7 full-time (3 women). Students: 14 full-time (3 women), 67 part-time (23 women); includes 6 minority (4 Asian Americans, 2 Native Americans), 11 international. Average age 31. 34 applicants, 65% accepted. In 1997, 28 master's awarded. *Entrance requirements:* For master's, GMAT (minimum score 500; average 560), TOEFL (minimum score 580), minimum GPA of 3.0, 1 year of related work experience. Application deadline: 8/20 (priority date; rolling processing; 2/20 for spring admission). Application fee: $55. *Expenses:* Tuition $440 per credit hour. Fees $70 per year. *Financial aid:* Federal Work-Study and career-related internships or fieldwork available. Aid available to part-time students. Financial aid applicants required to submit FAFSA. • Dr. Barbara Yates, Chairperson, 206-296-5700. Fax: 206-296-5795. E-mail: bmyates@seattleu.edu. Application contact: Michael McKeon, Dean of Admissions, 206-296-5900. Fax: 206-296-5656. E-mail: admissions@seattleu.edu.

Seton Hall University, W. Paul Stillman School of Business, Department of Finance and Legal Studies, South Orange, NJ 07079-2692. Offers program in finance (MBA). Part-time and evening/weekend programs available. Faculty: 11 full-time (2 women), 2 part-time (0 women). *Degree requirements:* Thesis optional, foreign language not required. *Entrance requirements:* GMAT (minimum score 500), TOEFL (minimum score 550). Application deadline: 6/1 (priority date; rolling processing). Application fee: $50. *Expenses:* Tuition $538 per credit. Fees $185 per semester. *Financial aid:* Research assistantships and career-related internships or fieldwork available. Financial aid applicants required to submit FAFSA. • Dr. Philip Phillips, Chairperson, 973-761-9505. E-mail: philliph@shu.edu. Application contact: Student Information Office, 973-761-9222. Fax: 973-761-9217. E-mail: busgrad@shu.edu.

Simon Fraser University, Faculty of Business Administration, Burnaby, BC V5A 1S6, Canada. Offerings include finance (MBA). Faculty: 48 full-time (12 women). *Application fee:* $55. *Expenses:* Tuition $2400 per year (minimum). Fees $207 per year. • S. McShane, Director, 604-291-3639. Application contact: Program Assistant, 604-291-3047. Fax: 604-291-3404. E-mail: mba@sfu.ca.

Southeastern University, Program in Financial Management, Washington, DC 20024-2788. Awards MBA. Part-time and evening/weekend programs available. Faculty: 4 full-time (1 woman), 5 part-time (0 women), 8 FTE. Students: 33 full-time (16 women), 20 part-time (13 women); includes 11 minority (all African Americans), 42 international. Average age 31. 4 applicants, 100% accepted. In 1997, 32 degrees awarded. *Degree requirements:* Computer language required, foreign language not required. *Entrance requirements:* TOEFL. Application deadline: rolling. Application fee: $45. *Expenses:* Tuition $228 per credit hour. Fees $175 per quarter. *Financial aid:* Federal Work-Study and career-related internships or fieldwork available. Aid available to part-time students. • Dr. Mohammed Safa, Head, 202-488-8162. Application contact: Jack Flinter, Director of Admissions, 202-265-5343. Fax: 202-488-8093.

State University of New York at Albany, School of Business, Department of Finance, Albany, NY 12222-0001. Awards MBA. Faculty: 5 full-time (1 woman), 2 part-time (0 women). Students: 6 full-time (0 women); includes 1 minority (African American), 2 international. *Degree requirements:* Field study project. *Entrance requirements:* GMAT. Application deadline: 7/1 (priority date; rolling processing). Application fee: $50. *Expenses:* Tuition $5100 per year full-time, $213 per credit hour part-time for state residents; $8416 per year full-time, $351 per credit hour part-time for nonresidents. Fees $705 per year full-time, $26.85 per credit hour part-time. *Financial aid:* Application deadline 4/1. *Faculty research:* Tax-exempt securities, public finance, financial engineering, international finance, investments management. • Hany Shawky, Chair, 518-442-4915. Application contact: Jeffrey Collins, Assistant Director, Graduate Admissions, 518-442-3980.

State University of New York at Binghamton, School of Arts and Sciences, Department of Economics, Binghamton, NY 13902-6000. Offerings include economics and finance (MA, PhD). Terminal master's awarded for partial completion of doctoral program. Department faculty: 16 full-time, 4 part-time. *Degree requirements:* For doctorate, dissertation. *Entrance requirements:* GRE General Test, TOEFL. Application deadline: 8/15 (priority date; rolling processing; 11/1 for spring admission). Application fee: $50. Electronic applications accepted. *Expenses:* Tuition $5100 per year full-time, $213 per credit hour part-time for state residents; $8416 per year full-time, $351 per credit hour part-time for nonresidents. Fees $654 per year full-time, $75 per semester (minimum) part-time. • Dr. Edward Kokkelenberg, Chairperson, 607-777-2573.

Suffolk University, Sawyer School of Management, Department of Finance, Boston, MA 02108-2770. Awards MS, MSF, JD/MSF. Programs in banking and financial services (MS), finance (MSF). Part-time programs available. Faculty: 9 full-time (3 women), 3 part-time (0 women). Students: 72 part-time (19 women). Average age 30. 71 applicants, 55% accepted. In 1997, 29 degrees awarded. *Entrance requirements:* GMAT (average 550), interview, minimum GPA of 2.39. Application deadline: 6/15 (priority date; rolling processing; 11/15 for spring admission). Application fee: $50. *Expenses:* Tuition $19,212 per year full-time, $1920 per course part-time. Fees $50 per year full-time, $20 per year part-time. *Financial aid:* In 1997–98, 18 students received aid, including 12 fellowships; Federal Work-Study, institutionally sponsored loans, and career-related internships or fieldwork also available. Aid available to part-time students. Financial aid application deadline: 4/1; applicants required to submit FAFSA. *Faculty research:* Financial institutions, corporate finance, ownership structure, dividend policy, corporate restructuring, security issues. • Ki Han, Chair, 617-573-8561. Application contact: Judy Reynolds, Acting Director of Graduate Admissions, 617-573-8302. Fax: 617-523-0116. E-mail: grad.admission@admin.suffolk.edu.

Announcement: The graduate programs in finance are fast-paced, highly specialized programs that prepare graduates with the tools to meet the challenges of today's highly competitive financial industry. The Master of Science in Finance (MSF) program is geared toward successful performance in areas such as corporate finance, investment banking, portfolio management, international finance, and financial institutions management. The Master of Science in Financial Services and Banking (MSFSB) prepares its graduates to perform successfully in areas such as commercial banking, cash management, international banking, and asset securitization. The Juris Doctor/Master of Science in Finance (JD/MSF) program recognizes the need in today's market for professionals to be educated in both law and finance. Graduates are prepared for careers in areas such as banking, securities, insurance, and corporate finance. For more information, contact the Office of Graduate Admission (telephone: 617-573-8302; fax: 617-523-0116; e-mail: grad.admission@admin.suffolk.edu).

Suffolk University, Sawyer School of Management, Department of Public Management, Boston, MA 02108-2770. Offerings include public finance and human resources (MPA). MPA/MS offered jointly with Department of Education and Human Services. Department faculty: 7 full-time (2 women), 20 part-time (12 women). *Application deadline:* 6/15 (priority date; rolling processing; 11/15 for spring admission). *Application fee:* $50. *Expenses:* Tuition $16,122 per year full-time, $1611 per course part-time. Fees $50 per year full-time, $20 per year part-time. • Michael Lavin, Chair, 617-573-8317. Fax: 617-573-8345. E-mail: mlavin@acad.suffolk.edu. Application contact: Judy Reynolds, Acting Director of Graduate Admissions, 617-573-8302. Fax: 617-523-0116. E-mail: grad.admission@admin.suffolk.edu.

Syracuse University, School of Management, PhD Program in Business Administration, Syracuse, NY 13244-0003. Offerings include finance (PhD). Program faculty: 75. *Entrance requirements:* GMAT (minimum score 600). Application deadline: 2/1. Application fee: $40. *Tuition:* $13,320 per year full-time, $555 per credit hour part-time. • S. P. Raj, Associate Dean. Application contact: Barbara Buske, Secretary, 315-443-1001.

Syracuse University, School of Management, Program in Finance, Syracuse, NY 13244-0003. Awards MBA. Faculty: 10. Students: 39 full-time (12 women), 42 part-time (11 women); includes 10 minority (3 African Americans, 4 Asian Americans, 1 Hispanic, 2 Native Americans), 34 international. 183 applicants, 51% accepted. In 1997, 35 degrees awarded. *Entrance requirements:* GMAT. Application deadline: 2/1 (rolling processing). Application fee: $40. *Tuition:* $13,320 per year full-time, $555 per credit hour part-time. *Financial aid:* Partial tuition waivers, Federal Work-Study available. Financial aid application deadline: 3/1. • Peter K. Koveos, Chair, 315-443-1040. Application contact: Associate Dean, 315-443-3850.

Temple University, School of Business and Management, Doctoral Program in Business Administration, Philadelphia, PA 19122-6096. Offerings include finance (PhD). *Degree requirements:* Dissertation, preliminary exams required, foreign language not required. *Entrance requirements:* GMAT, TOEFL (minimum score 600), master's degree, minimum GPA of 3.5. Application deadline: 1/15 (rolling processing). Application fee: $40. *Expenses:* Tuition $323 per semester hour for state residents; $444 per semester hour for nonresidents. Fees $170 per year full-time, $28 per semester (minimum) part-time. • Dr. Roland Lipka, Director, 215-204-8125. Fax: 215-204-5574. Application contact: Linda Whelan, Director, 215-204-7678. Fax: 215-204-8300.

Temple University, School of Business and Management, Master's Program in Business Administration, Philadelphia, PA 19122-6096. Offerings include finance (MBA, MS). Program faculty: 72 full-time (13 women). *Entrance requirements:* GMAT (average 540), TOEFL (minimum score 575). Application fee: $40. *Expenses:* Tuition $323 per semester hour for state residents; $444 per semester hour for nonresidents. Fees $170 per year full-time, $28 per semester (minimum) part-time. • Application contact: Linda Whelan, Director, 215-204-7678. Fax: 215-204-8300. E-mail: linda@astro.ocis.temple.edu.

Texas A&M International University, Division of Business Administration, Program in International Banking, 5201 University Boulevard, Laredo, TX 78041-1900. Awards MBA. Part-time and evening/weekend programs available. *Entrance requirements:* GMAT or GRE General Test. Application deadline: 7/15 (priority date; rolling processing; 11/12 for spring admission). Application fee: $0.

Announcement: The Graduate School of International Trade and Business Administration's MBA in International Banking prepares a cadre of global business leaders with a mastery of the various activities of international banking and a thorough knowledge of the different functions performed by banks competing in a globalized economy. Because of the University's unique location on the border of Mexico, it serves as a laboratory for the study of international banking and finance. The program includes a capstone seminar that combines preceding course work and individual experiences into meaningful practical exercises and simulations. Student exchange programs that allow students to study abroad while earning credit toward their degree are available at universities in many countries.

Texas A&M University, Lowry Mays Graduate School of Business, Department of Finance, College Station, TX 77843-4113. Awards MS, PhD. Faculty: 22 full-time (3 women), 1 (woman) part-time. Students: 66 full-time (12 women); includes 20 international. Average age 27. 110 applicants, 33% accepted. In 1997, 32 master's, 2 doctorates awarded. Terminal master's awarded for partial completion of doctoral program. *Degree requirements:* For master's, oral comprehensive exam required, foreign language and thesis not required; for doctorate, dissertation required, foreign language not required. *Average time to degree:* master's–1.5 years full-time; doctorate–4 years full-time. *Entrance requirements:* For master's, GMAT, TOEFL (minimum score 600); for doctorate, GMAT or GRE General Test, TOEFL. Application deadline: 3/1 (priority date; rolling processing; 8/1 for spring admission). Application fee: $35 ($75 for international students). *Financial aid:* 30 students received aid; fellowships, research assistantships, teaching assistantships, institutionally sponsored loans, and career-related internships or fieldwork available. Financial aid application deadline: 2/1. • Dr. Donald R. Fraser, Head, 409-845-3514. Application contact: Scott Lee, Adviser, 409-845-4840. Fax: 409-845-3884. E-mail: slee@tamu.edu.

Texas Tech University, Graduate School, College of Business Administration, Program in Finance, Lubbock, TX 79409. Awards MSBA, PhD. Part-time programs available. Faculty: 8 full-time (0 women). Students: 26 full-time (6 women), 5 part-time (1 woman); includes 13 international. Average age 29. 25 applicants, 52% accepted. In 1997, 5 master's awarded (100% found work related to degree); 3 doctorates awarded (100% entered university research/teaching). *Degree requirements:* For master's, computer language, comprehensive exam required, foreign language and thesis not required; for doctorate, computer language, dissertation, qualifying exams required, foreign language not required. *Entrance requirements:* For master's, GMAT (minimum score 500; average 560); for doctorate, GMAT (minimum score 580; average 620). Application deadline: 4/15 (priority date; rolling processing; 9/30 for spring admission). Application fee: $25 ($50 for international students). *Expenses:* Tuition $864 per year full-time, $120 per semester (minimum) part-time for state residents; $5976 per year full-time, $747 per semester (minimum) part-time for nonresidents. Fees $2321 per year full-time, $302 per semester (minimum) part-time. *Financial aid:* Research assistantships, Federal Work-Study available. Aid available to part-time students. Financial aid applicants required to submit FAFSA. *Faculty research:* Portfolio theory, banking and financial institutions, corporate finance, securities and options futures. • Dr. R. Stephen Sears, Coordinator, 806-742-3196. Fax: 806-742-2099. Application contact: Nancy Dodge, Director, 806-742-3184. Fax: 806-742-3958.

Troy State University Dothan, School of Business, Department of Finance and Quantitative Methods, Dothan, AL 36304-0368. Offers programs in finance (MS), quantitative methods (MS). *Entrance requirements:* GMAT, GRE General Test, or MAT, minimum GPA of 2.5. Application deadline: rolling. Application fee: $20. *Expenses:* Tuition $68 per credit hour for state residents; $140 per credit hour for nonresidents. Fees $2 per credit hour. • Dr. Adair Gilbert, Chair. Application contact: Reta Cordell, Director of Admissions and Records, 334-983-6556. Fax: 334-983-6322. E-mail: rcordell@tsud.edu.

United States International University, College of Business Administration, San Diego, CA 92131-1799. Offerings include international business (MIBA, DBA), with options in finance (DBA), marketing (DBA). Terminal master's awarded for partial completion of doctoral program. College faculty: 13 full-time (4 women), 14 part-time (6 women), 20 FTE. *Degree requirements:* Computer language, dissertation required, foreign language not required. *Average time to degree:* master's–1.5 years full-time, 2.5 years part-time; doctorate–3 years full-time, 5 years part-time. *Entrance requirements:* GMAT (minimum score 490; average 560), minimum GPA of 3.3. Application deadline: rolling. Application fee: $40. Electronic applications accepted. *Expenses:* Tuition $360 per unit. Fees $120 per year. • Dr. Mink H. Stavenga, Dean, 619-635-

Directory: Finance and Banking

United States International University (continued)

4695. Fax: 619-635-4528. E-mail: mstaveng@usiu.edu. Application contact: Susan Topham, Assistant Director of Admissions, 619-635-4885. Fax: 619-635-4739. E-mail: admissions@usiu.edu.

United States International University–Africa, College of Business Administration, PO Box 14634, Nairobi, Kenya. Offerings include finance (MBA, MIBA). College faculty: 15 full-time (2 women), 50 part-time (5 women). *Application deadline:* (2/8 for spring admission). *Application fee:* $55. • Application contact: Office of Admissions, 254-2-802532. Fax: 254-2-803764. E-mail: usiu_adm@usiu.edu.

Universidad de las Américas–Puebla, Division of Graduate Studies, School of Social Sciences, Program in Economics, Cholula 72820, Mexico. Offerings include finance (M Adm). Program faculty: 9 full-time (1 woman), 4 part-time (2 women). *Average time to degree:* master's–2.5 years full-time, 3.5 years part-time. *Application deadline:* 7/18 (rolling processing). *Application fee:* $0. *Expenses:* Tuition $5400 per year full-time, $113 per year part-time. Fees $361 per year. • Mariano Rojos, Chair, 22-29-20-64. Fax: 22-29-26-35. E-mail: mrojas@mail.udlap.mx. Application contact: Mauricio Villegas, Chair of Admissions Office, 22-29-20-17. Fax: 22-29-20-18. E-mail: admision@mail.udlap.mx.

Université de Sherbrooke, Faculty of Administration, Program in Finance, Sherbrooke, PQ J1K 2R1, Canada. Awards M Sc. *Application deadline:* 5/31. *Application fee:* $15.

Université du Québec à Montréal, Program in Finance, Montréal, PQ H3C 3P8, Canada. Awards Diploma. Part-time programs available. *Entrance requirements:* Appropriate bachelor's degree or equivalent and proficiency in French. Application deadline: 6/15. Application fee: $50.

Université du Québec à Trois-Rivières, Program in Finance, Trois-Rivières, PQ G9A 5H7, Canada. Awards DESS. Students: 4 full-time (3 women), 20 part-time (4 women). 28 applicants, 96% accepted. *Application deadline:* 2/1. *Application fee:* $30. • Dr. Claude Mathiew, Director, 819-376-5080. Application contact: Suzanne Camirand, Admissions Officer, 819-376-5045 Ext. 2591. Fax: 819-376-5210. E-mail: suzanne_camirand@uqtr.uquebec.ca.

The University of Akron, College of Business Administration, Department of Finance, Akron, OH 44325-0001. Awards MBA, JD/MBA. Part-time and evening/weekend programs available. Students: 16 full-time (8 women), 62 part-time (17 women); includes 6 minority (4 African Americans, 2 Asian Americans), 10 international. Average age 30. In 1997, 40 degrees awarded. *Entrance requirements:* GMAT (minimum score 450), minimum GPA of 2.75. Application deadline: 8/15 (rolling processing). Application fee: $25 ($50 for international students). *Expenses:* Tuition $178 per credit hour for state residents; $333 per credit hour for nonresidents. Fees $145 per year full-time, $32 per semester (minimum) part-time. *Financial aid:* In 1997–98, 7 students received aid, including 6 research assistantships; teaching assistantships, partial tuition waivers also available. Financial aid application deadline: 4/30. *Faculty research:* Real estate, financial planning, investment analysis. • David A. Redle, Chair, 330-972-6329. E-mail: dredle@uakron.edu. Application contact: Dr. J. Daniel Williams, Director of Graduate Business Programs, 330-972-7043. E-mail: jwilliams@uakron.edu.

The University of Alabama, The Manderson Graduate School of Business, Economics, Finance and Legal Studies Department, Program in Banking and Finance, Tuscaloosa, AL 35487. Awards MA, MSC, PhD. Faculty: 13 full-time (2 women). Students: 34 full-time (6 women), 2 part-time (both women); includes 2 minority (both African Americans), 10 international. Average age 25. 45 applicants, 71% accepted. In 1997, 14 master's awarded (93% found work related to degree, 7% continued full-time study); 1 doctorate awarded (100% entered university research/teaching). *Degree requirements:* For master's, comprehensive exam (MA), thesis (MSC) required, foreign language not required; for doctorate, dissertation, comprehensive exam required, foreign language not required. *Entrance requirements:* For master's, GMAT (minimum score 550; average 580) or GRE General Test (minimum combined score of 1000), TOEFL (minimum score 525), minimum GPA of 3.0; for doctorate, GMAT (minimum score 500) or GRE General Test (minimum combined score of 1000), TOEFL (minimum score 525), minimum GPA of 3.0. Application deadline: 7/1 (rolling processing; 11/1 for spring admission). Application fee: $25. Electronic applications accepted. *Tuition:* $2684 per year full-time, $594 per semester (minimum) part-time for state residents; $7216 per year full-time, $1248 per semester (minimum) part-time for nonresidents. *Financial aid:* In 1997–98, 21 students received aid, including 9 research assistantships (1 to a first-year student) averaging $845 per month and totaling $57,000, 12 teaching assistantships (4 to first-year students) averaging $845 per month and totaling $83,600; fellowships, Federal Work-Study, institutionally sponsored loans also available. Financial aid application deadline: 6/15. *Faculty research:* Commodity prices, decision models, demand for residential mortgages, efficiency of bank share prices, investment analysis. • Dr. Billy Helms, Chairman, Economics, Finance and Legal Studies Department, 205-348-7842. Fax: 205-348-0590. E-mail: bhelms@alston.cba.ua.edu.

University of Alberta, Faculty of Graduate Studies and Research, Department of Economics, Edmonton, AB T6G 2E1, Canada. Offerings include economics and finance (MA). Department faculty: 28 full-time (2 women), 1 part-time (0 women). *Entrance requirements:* GRE, TOEFL (minimum score 550). Application deadline: 6/15 (rolling processing). Application fee: $60. *Expenses:* Tuition $390 per course for Canadian residents; $781 per course for nonresidents. Fees $500 per year full-time, $184 per year part-time. • Dr. K. H. Norrie, Chair, 403-492-7634. Application contact: Leslie Wayne, Graduate Program Office, 403-492-7634. Fax: 403-492-3300. E-mail: lwayne@econ.ualberta.ca.

University of Alberta, Faculty of Graduate Studies and Research, Doctoral Program in Business, Edmonton, AB T6G 2E1, Canada. Offerings include finance (PhD). Terminal master's awarded for partial completion of doctoral program. Program faculty: 34 full-time (5 women). *Degree requirements:* Dissertation required, foreign language not required. *Average time to degree:* doctorate–6 years full-time, 8.5 years part-time. *Entrance requirements:* GMAT (average 675), TOEFL (minimum score 600; average 627). Application deadline: 3/1 (priority date). Application fee: $60. *Expenses:* Tuition $390 per course for Canadian residents; $781 per course for nonresidents. Fees $500 per year full-time, $184 per year part-time. • Dr. Michael Gibbins, Director, 403-492-2361. Application contact: Jeanette Gosine, Department Office, 403-492-2361. Fax: 403-492-3325. E-mail: jgosine@gpu.srv.ualberta.ca.

The University of Arizona, College of Business and Public Administration, Karl Eller Graduate School of Management, Department of Finance, Tucson, AZ 85721. Awards MS. *Degree requirements:* Thesis required, foreign language not required. *Entrance requirements:* GMAT, GRE General Test, TOEFL (minimum score 550), minimum GPA of 3.0. Application deadline: 3/15 (rolling processing). Application fee: $35. *Tuition:* $2162 per year full-time, $337 per semester (minimum) part-time for state residents; $6860 per year full-time, $1138 per semester (minimum) part-time for nonresidents. *Faculty research:* Corporate finance, banking, investments, stock market.

University of Baltimore, School of Business, Department of Economics and Finance, Baltimore, MD 21201-5779. Offers program in finance (MS). Part-time and evening/weekend programs available. Faculty: 15 full-time (1 woman), 2 part-time (0 women). Students: 12 full-time (4 women), 34 part-time (13 women); includes 4 minority (2 African Americans, 2 Asian Americans), 13 international. Average age 29. 23 applicants, 96% accepted. In 1997, 24 degrees awarded. *Entrance requirements:* GMAT. Application deadline: 7/15 (priority date; rolling processing; 11/15 for spring admission). Application fee: $30. *Expenses:* Tuition $5736 per year full-time, $239 per credit part-time for state residents; $8544 per year full-time, $356 per credit part-time for nonresidents. Fees $550 per year full-time, $208 per semester (minimum) part-time. *Financial aid:* In 1997–98, 3 research assistantships were awarded; fellowships, Federal Work-Study, and career-related internships or fieldwork also available. Aid available to part-time students. Financial aid application deadline: 4/1; applicants required to submit FAFSA. *Faculty research:* International finance, corporate finance, health care, regional economics, small business. Total annual research expenditures: $1.864 million. • Application contact: Tracey Jamison, Assistant Director of Admissions, 410-837-4809. Fax: 410-837-4793. E-mail: admissions@ubmail.ubalt.edu.

University of British Columbia, Faculty of Commerce and Business Administration, Doctoral Program in Commerce and Business Administration, Vancouver, BC V6T 1Z2, Canada. Offerings include finance (PhD). *Degree requirements:* Dissertation required, foreign language not required. *Entrance requirements:* GMAT or GRE, TOEFL. Application deadline: 12/31 (priority date; rolling processing). Application fee: $60.

University of British Columbia, Faculty of Commerce and Business Administration, Program in Business Administration, Vancouver, BC V6T 1Z2, Canada. Offerings include finance (M Sc). *Degree requirements:* Thesis required (for some programs), foreign language not required. *Average time to degree:* master's–2 years full-time. *Entrance requirements:* GMAT (average 620), TOEFL (minimum score 600). Application fee: $100.

University of California, Berkeley, Haas School of Business, Doctoral Program in Business, Berkeley, CA 94720-1500. Offerings include finance (PhD). Program faculty: 64 full-time (11 women). *Degree requirements:* Dissertation, oral exam, written preliminary exams required, foreign language not required. *Entrance requirements:* GMAT or GRE, TOEFL, minimum GPA of 3.0. Application deadline: 2/10. Application fee: $40. *Expenses:* Tuition $0 for state residents; $9384 per year for nonresidents. Fees $4409 per year. • Dr. David C. Mowery, Director, 510-643-9992. E-mail: jan@haas.berkeley.edu. Application contact: Jan Price Greenough, Coordinator, 510-642-1409. Fax: 510-643-6659. E-mail: jan@haas.berkeley.edu.

University of Central Florida, College of Business Administration, Program in Business Administration, Orlando, FL 32816. Offerings include finance (PhD). Program faculty: 61. *Degree requirements:* Dissertation, departmental candidacy exam. *Entrance requirements:* GMAT. Application deadline: 6/15 (rolling processing; 11/1 for spring admission). Application fee: $20. *Expenses:* Tuition $3288 per year full-time, $137 per credit hour part-time for state residents; $11,520 per year full-time, $480 per credit hour part-time for nonresidents. Fees $105 per year. • Application contact: Dr. Robert L. Pennington, Graduate Coordinator, 407-823-3922.

University of Chicago, Division of the Physical Sciences, Department of Mathematics, Program in Financial Mathematics, Chicago, IL 60637-1513. Awards MS. Part-time and evening/weekend programs available. Faculty: Students: 20 full-time (3 women), 22 part-time (1 woman); includes 15 international. Average age 30. 92 applicants, 51% accepted. In 1997, 17 degrees awarded. *Average time to degree:* master's–1 year full-time. *Entrance requirements:* GRE General Test, GRE Subject Test, TOEFL. Application deadline: 1/5 (priority date). Application fee: $50 ($55 for international students). *Expenses:* Tuition $23,616 per year full-time, $3258 per course part-time. Fees $378 per year. *Financial aid:* Institutionally sponsored loans and career-related internships or fieldwork available. Aid available to part-time students. Financial aid applicants required to submit FAFSA. • Niels Nygaard, Director, 773-702-7391. Fax: 773-702-9787. E-mail: niels@math.uchicato.edu. Application contact: Alice Brugman, Program Assistant, 312-464-8658. Fax: 312-464-8656. E-mail: alice@math.uchicago.edu.

University of Cincinnati, College of Business Administration, Department of Finance, Cincinnati, OH 45221. Offers programs in finance (MBA, PhD), real estate (MBA). Part-time and evening/weekend programs available. Faculty: 9 full-time. Students: 22 full-time (6 women), 79 part-time (26 women); includes 11 minority (4 African Americans, 6 Asian Americans, 1 Hispanic), 6 international. 41 applicants, 39% accepted. In 1997, 42 master's, 3 doctorates awarded. *Degree requirements:* For master's, thesis or alternative; for doctorate, computer language, dissertation. *Average time to degree:* master's–2.7 years full-time; doctorate–5.8 years full-time. *Entrance requirements:* GMAT. Application fee: $30. *Tuition:* $7228 per year full-time, $185 per credit hour part-time for state residents; $13,812 per year full-time, $352 per credit hour part-time for nonresidents. *Financial aid:* Fellowships, graduate assistantships, full tuition waivers available. Aid available to part-time students. Financial aid application deadline: 2/15. • Dr. Michael C. Walker, Head, 513-556-7078. Application contact: Glenn V. Henderson Jr., Graduate Program Director, 513-556-7079. Fax: 513-556-4891.

University of Colorado at Boulder, Graduate School of Business Administration, Division of Finance, Boulder, CO 80309. Awards MBA, PhD. Students: 63 full-time (18 women), 1 (woman) part-time; includes 7 minority (4 Asian Americans, 2 Hispanics, 1 Native American), 4 international. Average age 29. 106 applicants, 39% accepted. *Degree requirements:* For master's, computer language required, foreign language and thesis not required; for doctorate, dissertation, research internship. *Entrance requirements:* GMAT. Application deadline: 3/1 (priority date; rolling processing). Application fee: $40 ($60 for international students). *Expenses:* Tuition $3594 per year (minimum) full-time, $597 per semester (minimum) part-time for state residents; $14,868 per year (minimum) full-time, $2478 per semester (minimum) part-time for nonresidents. Fees $667 per year full-time, $130 per semester (minimum) part-time. *Financial aid:* Application deadline 3/1. • Ronald Melicher, Chair, 303-492-8468. Fax: 303-492-5962. E-mail: ronald.melicher@colorado.edu. Application contact: Diana Marinaro, Graduate Student Admissions, 303-492-1831. Fax: 303-492-1727. E-mail: busgrad@spot.colorado.edu.

University of Colorado at Colorado Springs, Graduate School of Business Administration, Colorado Springs, CO 80933-7150. Offerings include finance (MBA). School faculty: 24 full-time (4 women). *Entrance requirements:* GMAT. Application deadline: 6/1 (priority date; 11/1 for spring admission). Application fee: $50. *Expenses:* Tuition $2860 per year full-time, $121 per credit hour part-time for state residents; $10,254 per year full-time, $420 per credit hour part-time for nonresidents. Fees $399 per year (minimum) full-time, $106 per year (minimum) part-time. • Dr. Richard Dicenza, Dean, 719-262-3113. E-mail: rdicenz@mail.uccs.edu. Application contact: Diane Belger, Adviser, 719-262-3408. Fax: 719-262-3494. E-mail: dbelger@mail.uccs.edu.

University of Colorado at Denver, Graduate School of Business Administration, Division of Finance, Denver, CO 80217-3364. Awards MS, MBA/MS. Part-time and evening/weekend programs available. Faculty: 9 full-time. Students: 180. In 1997, 81 degrees awarded. *Entrance requirements:* GMAT (minimum score 400; average 570), TOEFL (minimum score 525; average 560). Application deadline: 7/1 (priority date; rolling processing; 11/1 for spring admission). Application fee: $50 ($60 for international students). *Expenses:* Tuition $3754 per year full-time, $225 per semester hour part-time for state residents; $12,962 per year full-time, $777 per semester hour part-time for nonresidents. Fees $252 per year. *Financial aid:* Application deadline 4/1. *Faculty research:* Corporate governance, debt maturity policies, regulation and financial markets, option management strategies. • Dean Taylor Jr., Director, 303-556-5888. Fax: 303-556-5899. Application contact: Lori Cain, Graduate Business Admissions Office, 303-556-5900. Fax: 303-556-5904. E-mail: lori_cain@maroon.cudenver.edu.

University of Connecticut, School of Business Administration, Storrs, CT 06269. Offerings include finance (PhD). School faculty: 63. *Degree requirements:* Dissertation. *Entrance requirements:* GMAT, TOEFL. Application deadline: 6/1 (priority date; rolling processing; 11/1 for spring admission). Application fee: $40 ($45 for international students). *Expenses:* Tuition $5272 per year full-time, $293 per credit part-time for state residents; $13,696 per year full-time, $761 per credit part-time for nonresidents. Fees $948 per year full-time, $640 per year part-time. • Thomas G. Gutteridge, Dean, 860-486-3096. Application contact: David W. Palmer, Chairperson, 860-486-3096.

University of Dallas, Graduate School of Management, Program in Corporate Finance, Irving, TX 75062-4799. Awards MBA, MM. Part-time programs available. Students: 178 (68 women). In 1997, 93 degrees awarded. *Average time to degree:* master's–1.3 years full-time, 2.5 years part-time. *Entrance requirements:* GMAT (minimum score 400), TOEFL (average 520), minimum GPA of 3.0. Application deadline: 8/6 (priority date; rolling processing; 12/8 for spring admission). Application fee: $25 ($50 for international students). *Expenses:* Tuition $380 per credit hour. Fees $125 per year. *Financial aid:* Application deadline 2/15. • Dr. David

P. Higgins, Director, 972-721-5304. Fax: 972-721-5130. Application contact: Roxanne Del Rio, Director of Admissions, 972-721-5174. Fax: 972-721-4009. E-mail: admiss@gsm.udallas.edu.

University of Dallas, Graduate School of Management, Program in Financial Planning Services, Irving, TX 75062-4799. Awards MBA, MM. Part-time programs available. Students: 36 (11 women). In 1997, 19 degrees awarded. *Average time to degree:* master's–1.3 years full-time, 2.5 years part-time. *Entrance requirements:* GMAT (minimum score 400), TOEFL (average 520), minimum GPA of 3.0. Application deadline: 8/6 (priority date; rolling processing; 12/8 for spring admission). Application fee: $25 ($50 for international students). *Expenses:* Tuition $380 per credit hour. Fees $125 per year. *Financial aid:* Application deadline 2/15. • Alan Goldfarb, Director, 972-721-5063. Fax: 972-721-5130. Application contact: Roxanne Del Rio, Director of Admissions, 972-721-5174. Fax: 972-721-4009. E-mail: admiss@gsm.udallas.edu.

University of Denver, Daniels College of Business, Department of Finance, Denver, CO 80208. Offers programs in finance (MBA, MS, MSF), finance/real estate (MBA). MSF new for fall 1998. Part-time and evening/weekend programs available. Faculty: 10 full-time (3 women). Students: 137 full-time (38 women), 27 part-time (6 women); includes 15 minority (1 African American, 4 Asian Americans, 8 Hispanics, 2 Native Americans), 45 international. Average age 27. 128 applicants, 83% accepted. In 1997, 67 degrees awarded. *Entrance requirements:* GMAT (average 545). Application deadline: 5/1 (priority date; rolling processing; 1/1 for spring admission). Application fee: $50. *Expenses:* Tuition $18,216 per year full-time, $506 per credit hour part-time. Fees $159 per year. *Financial aid:* In 1997–98, 68 students received aid, including 10 teaching assistantships averaging $390 per month and totaling $33,722, 33 grants, scholarships totaling $35,859; research assistantships, Federal Work-Study, institutionally sponsored loans, and career-related internships or fieldwork also available. Aid available to part-time students. Financial aid application deadline: 2/15; applicants required to submit FAFSA. • Dr. Maclyn Clouse, Chairman, 303-871-3320. Application contact: Jan Johnson, Executive Director, Student Services, 303-871-3416. Fax: 303-871-4466. E-mail: dcb@du.edu.

The University of Findlay, College of Professional Studies, MBA Program, 1000 North Main Street, Findlay, OH 45840-3653. Offerings include financial management (MBA). Postbaccalaureate distance learning degree programs offered (minimal on-campus study). Program faculty: 9 full-time (0 women), 6 part-time (0 women), 11 FTE. *Degree requirements:* Cumulative project. *Average time to degree:* master's–1.5 years full-time, 2.5 years part-time. *Entrance requirements:* GMAT, TOEFL. Application deadline: 8/15 (rolling processing; 12/15 for spring admission). Application fee: $25. *Tuition:* $299 per semester hour. • Dr. Theodore C. Alex, Director, 419-424-4704. Fax: 419-424-4822.

University of Florida, College of Business Administration, Department of Finance, Insurance and Real Estate, Gainesville, FL 32611. Offers programs in finance (PhD), real estate and urban analysis (MA, PhD). Faculty: 20. Students: 22 full-time (3 women), 5 part-time (0 women); includes 2 minority (both Asian Americans), 5 international. 113 applicants, 23% accepted. In 1997, 11 master's, 2 doctorates awarded. *Degree requirements:* Thesis/dissertation required, foreign language not required. *Entrance requirements:* GMAT or GRE General Test, minimum GPA of 3.0. Application deadline: 2/16 (rolling processing). Application fee: $20. *Tuition:* $138 per credit hour for state residents; $481 per credit hour for nonresidents. *Financial aid:* In 1997–98, 21 students received aid, including 5 fellowships averaging $1,962 per month, 12 research assistantships averaging $560 per month, 2 teaching assistantships averaging $1,746 per month, 2 graduate assistantships averaging $320 per month; career-related internships or fieldwork also available. *Faculty research:* Financial management, financial markets and institutions, investments, risk and insurance, real estate development. • Dr. David Brown, Chair, 352-392-0153. E-mail: dbrown@dale.cba.ufl.edu. Application contact: Dr. Michael Ryngaert, Graduate Coordinator, 352-392-3184. Fax: 352-392-0301. E-mail: ryngaert@dale.cba.ufl.edu.

University of Hartford, Barney School of Business and Public Administration, Program in Business Administration, West Hartford, CT 06117-1599. Offerings include finance (MBA). Program faculty: 24 full-time (4 women), 15 part-time (1 woman). *Average time to degree:* master's–1.5 years full-time, 3 years part-time. *Entrance requirements:* GMAT, TOEFL. Application deadline: 7/1 (priority date; rolling processing; 12/1 for spring admission). Application fee: $35 ($50 for international students). Electronic applications accepted. • Christopher Galligan, Director, 860-768-4390. Application contact: Claire Silverstein, Assistant Director, 860-768-4900. Fax: 860-768-4821. E-mail: silverste@unavax.hartford.edu.

University of Houston, College of Business Administration, Department of Finance, 4800 Calhoun, Houston, TX 77204-2163. Awards MBA, PhD. Part-time and evening/weekend programs available. Faculty: 13 full-time (1 woman), 5 part-time (0 women). Students: 105 full-time (34 women), 112 part-time (30 women); includes 32 minority (5 African Americans, 19 Asian Americans, 7 Hispanics, 1 Native American), 46 international. Average age 30. In 1997, 80 master's awarded. *Degree requirements:* For master's, computer language required, foreign language and thesis not required; for doctorate, computer language, dissertation, comprehensive exam required, foreign language not required. *Average time to degree:* master's–2 years full-time, 3.5 years part-time; doctorate–4.5 years full-time. *Entrance requirements:* For master's, GMAT (average 590), TOEFL (minimum score 620); for doctorate, GMAT or GRE. Application deadline: 5/1 (rolling processing; 10/1 for spring admission). Application fee: $50 ($125 for international students). *Expenses:* Tuition $1152 per year full-time, $120 per semester (minimum) part-time for state residents; $4482 per year full-time, $249 per credit hour part-time for nonresidents. Fees $977 per year full-time, $119 per semester (minimum) part-time. *Financial aid:* Research assistantships, teaching assistantships, Federal Work-Study, and career-related internships or fieldwork available. Aid available to part-time students. Financial aid application deadline: 3/1; applicants required to submit FAFSA. • Dr. Ron Singer, Chair, 713-743-4755. Application contact: Office of Student Services, 713-743-4900. Fax: 713-743-4942. E-mail: oss@cba.uh.edu.

University of Houston–Clear Lake, School of Business and Public Administration, Program in Finance, Houston, TX 77058-1098. Awards MS. Faculty: 6. Students: 26 full-time, 39 part-time; includes 3 minority (2 Asian Americans, 1 Hispanic), 19 international. Average age 32. 36 applicants, 75% accepted. In 1997, 26 degrees awarded. *Degree requirements:* Thesis optional, foreign language not required. *Entrance requirements:* GMAT (average 510). Application deadline: 8/1 (rolling processing; 12/1 for spring admission). Application fee: $30 ($60 for international students). *Tuition:* $207 per credit hour for state residents; $336 per credit hour for nonresidents. *Financial aid:* Federal Work-Study, institutionally sponsored loans, and career-related internships or fieldwork available. Financial aid application deadline: 5/1. • Dr. Grady Perdue, Chair, 281-283-3213. Application contact: Dr. Sue Neeley, Associate Dean, 281-283-3110.

University of Illinois at Chicago, College of Business Administration, Department of Finance, Chicago, IL 60607-7128. Awards PhD. Faculty: 7 full-time (0 women). Students: 1 full-time (0 women), 1 part-time (0 women); includes 1 international. Average age 32. 0 applicants. In 1997, 1 degree awarded. *Degree requirements:* Dissertation required, foreign language not required. *Entrance requirements:* GMAT or GRE General Test, TOEFL (minimum score 550), minimum GPA of 3.75 on a 5.0 scale. Application deadline: 5/1. Application fee: $40 ($50 for international students). *Financial aid:* In 1997–98, 1 research assistantship was awarded; fellowships, teaching assistantships also available. • John Binder, Director of Graduate Studies, 312-996-0821. Application contact: Ann Rosi, 312-996-4751.

University of Illinois at Urbana–Champaign, College of Commerce and Business Administration, Department of Finance, Urbana, IL 61801. Awards MS, PhD. Faculty: 17 full-time (1 woman). Students: 54 full-time (16 women); includes 3 minority (2 Asian Americans, 1 Native American), 40 international. 55 applicants, 7% accepted. In 1997, 23 master's, 6 doctorates awarded. *Degree requirements:* For doctorate, dissertation required, foreign language not required. *Entrance requirements:* GMAT, GRE General Test. Application deadline: rolling. Application fee: $40 ($50 for international students). *Financial aid:* In 1997–98, 3 fellowships, 15 research assistantships, 5 teaching assistantships were awarded; full and partial tuition waivers also available. Financial aid application deadline: 2/15. • Morgan J. Lynge, Chair, 217-244-9416. Application contact: Graduate Coordinator, 217-333-2110.

See in-depth description on page 457.

The University of Iowa, College of Business Administration, Department of Finance, Iowa City, IA 52242-1316. Awards PhD. Faculty: 10 full-time (0 women), 2 part-time (0 women). Students: 10 full-time (1 woman); includes 6 international. Average age 26. 70 applicants, 4% accepted. In 1997, 2 degrees awarded (100% entered university research/teaching). *Degree requirements:* Dissertation required, foreign language not required. *Average time to degree:* doctorate–5 years full-time. *Entrance requirements:* GMAT (minimum score 620; average 700), TOEFL (minimum score 600; average 650). Application deadline: 1/31 (priority date; rolling processing). Application fee: $30 ($50 for international students). *Expenses:* Tuition $3166 per year full-time, $176 per semester hour part-time for state residents; $10,202 per year full-time, $176 per semester hour part-time for nonresidents. Fees $202 per year full-time, $52 per year (minimum) part-time. *Financial aid:* In 1997–98, 1 fellowship averaging $1,570 per month and totaling $18,820, research assistantships averaging $1,300 per month and totaling $15,600, teaching assistantships averaging $950 per month and totaling $15,600 was awarded. Financial aid application deadline: 1/31; applicants required to submit FAFSA. *Faculty research:* Market microstructure, international finance, real estate finance, empirical corporate finance, asset pricing theory, derivatives. • Jarjisu Sa-Aadu, Chairman, 319-335-0929. Application contact: Paul Weller, Director of PhD Program, 319-335-1017. Fax: 319-335-3690.

University of Kansas, School of Business, Program in Finance, Lawrence, KS 66045. Awards PhD. *Degree requirements:* Dissertation, departmental qualifying exam required, foreign language not required. *Entrance requirements:* GMAT. Application deadline: 1/15. Application fee: $50. *Expenses:* Tuition $2400 per year full-time, $100 per credit hour part-time for state residents; $7890 per year full-time, $329 per credit hour part-time for nonresidents. Fees $428 per year full-time, $31 per credit hour part-time. *Financial aid:* Fellowships, research assistantships, teaching assistantships available. *Faculty research:* Valuation, corporate restructuring, international finance, investments, option and futures markets. • Paul Koch, Director, 785-864-3841. Application contact: Student Advising Center, 785-864-4254. Fax: 785-864-5328. E-mail: grad@bschool.ukans.edu.

University of Manitoba, Faculty of Management, Department of Accounting and Finance, Program in Finance, Winnipeg, MB R3T 2N2, Canada. Awards MBA. *Degree requirements:* Thesis or alternative.

The University of Memphis, Fogelman College of Business and Economics, Program in Business Administration, Memphis, TN 38152. Offerings include finance (PhD); finance, insurance, and real estate (MBA, MS). Program faculty: 92 full-time (15 women), 2 part-time (0 women). *Degree requirements:* For master's, comprehensive exams required, thesis not required; for doctorate, dissertation, comprehensive exams. *Entrance requirements:* For master's, GMAT (minimum score 430; average 535), GRE General Test; for doctorate, GMAT (average 633), interview, minimum GPA of 3.4. Application deadline: 8/1 (12/1 for spring admission). Application fee: $25 ($50 for international students). *Tuition:* $2862 per year full-time, $166 per credit hour part-time for state residents; $6696 per year full-time, $379 per credit hour part-time for nonresidents. • Application contact: Dr. Ravinder Nath, Associate Dean of Academic Programs, 901-678-3721. Fax: 901-678-4705. E-mail: fcbegp@memphis.edu.

University of Michigan, College of Engineering, Program in Financial Engineering, Ann Arbor, MI 48109. Awards MS. *Application fee:* $55. • Application contact: John R. Birge, Program Office, 734-764-6315. Fax: 734-764-3451.

University of Minnesota, Twin Cities Campus, Carlson School of Management, Department of Finance, Minneapolis, MN 55455-0213. Awards MBA, PhD. MBA offered jointly with the Master's Program in Business Administration; PhD offered jointly with the Doctoral Program in Business Administration. *Degree requirements:* For doctorate, dissertation required, foreign language not required. *Entrance requirements:* GMAT. *Faculty research:* Financial management, financial institutions, banking, financial intermediation, investments, corporate finance.

University of Missouri–St. Louis, School of Business Administration, Program in Business Administration, St. Louis, MO 63121-4499. Offerings include finance (MBA). Program faculty: 19 (3 women). *Entrance requirements:* GMAT (minimum score 500; average 554). Application deadline: 7/1 (rolling processing; 11/1 for spring admission). Application fee: $0. Electronic applications accepted. *Expenses:* Tuition $3903 per year full-time, $167 per credit hour part-time for state residents; $11,745 per year full-time, $489 per credit hour part-time for nonresidents. Fees $816 per year full-time, $34 per credit hour part-time. • Application contact: Graduate Admissions, 314-516-5458. Fax: 314-516-6759. E-mail: gradadm@umslvma.umsl.edu.

University of Nebraska–Lincoln, College of Business Administration, Interdepartmental Area of Business, Department of Finance, Lincoln, NE 68588. Offers program in business (MA, PhD). Faculty: 8 full-time (1 woman). *Degree requirements:* For doctorate, dissertation, comprehensive exams required, foreign language not required. *Entrance requirements:* GMAT, TOEFL (minimum score 500). Application deadline: 5/15 (10/15 for spring admission). Application fee: $35. Electronic applications accepted. *Expenses:* Tuition $110 per credit hour for state residents; $270 per credit hour for nonresidents. Fees $480 per year full-time, $110 per semester part-time. *Financial aid:* In 1997–98, 1 research assistantship totaling $2,520, 8 teaching assistantships totaling $56,260 were awarded; fellowships also available. Financial aid application deadline: 2/15. *Faculty research:* Banking, investments, international finance, insurance, corporate finance. • Dr. Manferd Peterson, Chair, 402-472-2330. E-mail: gradadv@cbamail.unl.edu.

University of New Haven, School of Business, Program in Business Administration, West Haven, CT 06516-1916. Offerings include finance (MBA). *Degree requirements:* Thesis or alternative required, foreign language not required. *Application deadline:* rolling. *Application fee:* $50. *Expenses:* Tuition $1125 per course. Fees $13 per trimester. • Dr. Omid Nodoushani, Coordinator, 203-932-7123.

University of New Haven, School of Business, Program in Finance and Financial Services, West Haven, CT 06516-1916. Awards MS. Students: 20 full-time (6 women), 22 part-time (7 women); includes 3 minority (2 African Americans, 1 Asian American), 24 international. 17 applicants, 65% accepted. *Application deadline:* rolling. *Application fee:* $50. *Expenses:* Tuition $1125 per course. Fees $13 per trimester. *Financial aid:* Federal Work-Study and career-related internships or fieldwork available. Financial aid application deadline: 5/1; applicants required to submit FAFSA. • Dr. Robert Rainish, Coordinator, 203-932-7363.

University of New Mexico, Robert O. Anderson Graduate School of Management, Program in Financial Management, Albuquerque, NM 87131-1221. Awards MBA. Part-time and evening/weekend programs available. Faculty: 5 full-time (0 women), 1 part-time (0 women). *Degree requirements:* Computer language required, foreign language and thesis not required. *Entrance requirements:* GMAT (minimum score 540), TOEFL (minimum score 550). Application deadline: 7/1 (priority date; rolling processing; 11/15 for spring admission). Application fee: $25. *Expenses:* Tuition $2442 per year full-time, $103 per credit hour part-time for state residents; $8691 per year full-time, $103 per credit hour (minimum) part-time for nonresidents. Fees $32 per year. *Financial aid:* Fellowships, research assistantships, teaching assistantships, Federal Work-Study, and career-related internships or fieldwork available. *Faculty research:* Corporation finance, investments, applied macroeconomics, risk management and banking, international finance, option pricing. • Dr. Suleiman Kassicieh, Head, 505-277-9870. Fax: 505-277-7108. E-mail: kasicieh@unm.edu. Application contact: Sue Podeyn, MBA Program Director, 505-277-3147. Fax: 505-277-9356.

Directory: Finance and Banking

The University of North Carolina at Chapel Hill, Kenan-Flagler Business School, Doctoral Program in Business Administration, Chapel Hill, NC 27599. Offerings include finance (PhD). Program faculty: 79 full-time (15 women), 29 part-time (6 women). *Degree requirements:* Dissertation required, foreign language not required. *Average time to degree:* doctorate–4 years full-time. *Entrance requirements:* GMAT (average 657) or GRE General Test (minimum combined score of 1350). Application deadline: 1/1 (priority date; rolling processing). Application fee: $55. Electronic applications accepted. *Expenses:* Tuition $1428 per year for state residents; $10,414 per year for nonresidents. Fees $787 per year. • Ann Marucheck, Associate Dean for PhD Programs, 919-962-3193. Application contact: Liz Griffin, Director, 919-962-1657. E-mail: kfphd_app@unc.edu.

University of North Texas, College of Business Administration, Department of Finance, Insurance, Real Estate, and Law, Denton, TX 76203-6737. Offers programs in banking (MBA, PhD), finance (MBA, PhD), insurance (MBA), real estate (MBA). Part-time programs available. Faculty: 22 full-time (3 women), 4 part-time (0 women). Students: 40 full-time (18 women), 138 part-time (47 women); includes 12 minority (4 African Americans, 5 Asian Americans, 3 Hispanics), 29 international. In 1997, 38 master's, 1 doctorate awarded. *Degree requirements:* For master's, computer language required, foreign language and thesis not required; for doctorate, computer language, dissertation required, foreign language not required. *Entrance requirements:* For master's, GMAT, TOEFL; for doctorate, GMAT or GRE General Test, TOEFL. Application deadline: 7/17. Application fee: $25 ($50 for international students). *Tuition:* $2063 per year full-time, $815 per year part-time for state residents; $5897 per year full-time, $2100 per year part-time for nonresidents. *Financial aid:* Fellowships, research assistantships, teaching assistantships, and career-related internships or fieldwork available. Financial aid application deadline: 4/1. *Faculty research:* Financial impact of regulation, risk management, financial instrument rating changes, taxes and valuation, bankruptcy. • Dr. Imre Karafiath, Chair, 940-565-3050.

University of Oregon, Graduate School, Charles H. Lundquist College of Business, Department of Finance, Eugene, OR 97403. Awards MA, MS, PhD. Part-time programs available. Faculty: 7 full-time (2 women), 3 part-time (1 woman), 7.76 FTE. Students: 6 full-time (0 women), 1 part-time (0 women); includes 2 international. 20 applicants, 20% accepted. In 1997, 1 doctorate awarded (100% entered university research/teaching). Terminal master's awarded for partial completion of doctoral program. *Degree requirements:* For doctorate, computer language, dissertation, 2 comprehensive exams required, foreign language not required. *Average time to degree:* doctorate–6 years full-time. *Entrance requirements:* For doctorate, GMAT, TOEFL (minimum score 600). Application deadline: 3/1. Application fee: $50. *Tuition:* $6429 per year full-time, $873 per quarter (minimum) part-time for state residents; $10,857 per year full-time, $1360 per quarter (minimum) part-time for nonresidents. *Financial aid:* In 1997–98, 6 teaching assistantships (2 to first-year students) were awarded; Federal Work-Study and career-related internships or fieldwork also available. *Faculty research:* Changes in firm value in response to corporate takeovers and defenses, capital structure, regulatory changes, financial intermediaries. • Megan Partch, Co-Head, 541-346-3353. Application contact: Linda Johnson, Graduate Secretary, 541-346-3306.

University of Pennsylvania, Wharton School, Doctoral Program in Finance, Philadelphia, PA 19104. Awards PhD. Faculty: 17 full-time (1 woman). Students: 25 full-time (2 women), 2 part-time (0 women); includes 1 minority (Asian American), 17 international. Average age 28. 200 applicants, 6% accepted. In 1997, 1 doctorate awarded (100% found work related to degree). Terminal master's awarded for partial completion of doctoral program. *Degree requirements:* For doctorate, computer language, dissertation required, foreign language not required. *Average time to degree:* doctorate–4 years full-time. *Entrance requirements:* For doctorate, GMAT or GRE. Application deadline: 2/1. Application fee: $125. *Financial aid:* In 1997–98, 23 students received aid, including fellowships averaging $1,250 per month and totaling $750,000, 17 teaching assistantships averaging $1,193 per month and totaling $220,000. Financial aid application deadline: 2/1. *Faculty research:* Corporate finance, investments, macroeconomics, international finance. • Dr. Andrew Abel, Coordinator. Application contact: Wharton Doctoral Program Office, 215-898-4877.

University of Rhode Island, College of Business Administration, Kingston, RI 02881. Offerings include finance (MBA). *Application deadline:* 4/15 (priority date; rolling processing). *Application fee:* $35. *Expenses:* Tuition $3446 per year full-time, $191 per credit part-time for state residents; $9850 per year full-time, $547 per credit part-time for nonresidents. Fees $1276 per year full-time, $135 per semester (minimum) part-time.

University of St. Thomas, Graduate School of Business, Day MBA Program, St. Paul, MN 55105-1096. Offerings include finance (MBA), financial services management (MBA). Program faculty: 13 part-time. *Degree requirements:* Computer language required, foreign language and thesis not required. *Entrance requirements:* GMAT (score in 50th percentile or higher). Application deadline: 5/1 (priority date; rolling processing). Application fee: $30. *Tuition:* $473 per credit hour. • Application contact: Jim O'Connor, Student Adviser, 612-962-4233. Fax: 612-962-4260.

University of St. Thomas, Graduate School of Business, Evening MBA Program, St. Paul, MN 55105-1096. Offerings include finance (MBA), financial services management (MBA). Program faculty: 16 full-time (2 women), 89 part-time (17 women). *Degree requirements:* Computer language required, foreign language and thesis not required. *Entrance requirements:* GMAT (score in 50th percentile or higher). Application deadline: 8/1 (priority date; rolling processing; 12/1 for spring admission). Application fee: $30. *Tuition:* $416 per credit hour. • Dr. Stanford Nyquist, MBA Director, 612-962-4242. Application contact: Martha Ballard, Director of Student Services, 612-962-4226. Fax: 612-962-4260.

University of St. Thomas, Graduate School of Business, Program in International Management, St. Paul, MN 55105-1096. Offerings include international finance (MIM, Certificate). Program faculty: 1 full-time (0 women), 18 part-time (6 women). *Degree requirements:* For master's, 1 foreign language, computer language required, thesis not required. *Entrance requirements:* For master's, GMAT. Application deadline: 7/1 (priority date; rolling processing; 12/1 for spring admission). Application fee: $30. *Tuition:* $416 per credit hour. • Dr. Mohammed Eftekhari, Director, 612-962-4840. Application contact: Wendy Williams, Student Services Manager, 612-962-4847. Fax: 612-962-4129.

University of San Francisco, McLaren School of Business, Program in Business Administration, San Francisco, CA 94117-1080. Offerings include finance and banking (MBA). Program faculty: 33 full-time (7 women), 27 part-time (3 women). *Entrance requirements:* GMAT (average 540), TOEFL (minimum score 600), minimum undergraduate GPA of 3.2. Application deadline: 7/1 (priority date; rolling processing; 11/30 for spring admission). Application fee: $40 ($50 for international students). *Tuition:* $658 per unit (minimum). • Cathy Fusco, Director, 415-422-6314. Fax: 415-422-2502. E-mail: mbausf@usfca.edu.

University of Saskatchewan, College of Commerce, Department of Finance and Management Science, Saskatoon, SK S7N 5A2, Canada. Awards M Sc. Part-time programs available. *Degree requirements:* Thesis. *Entrance requirements:* GMAT, TOEFL. Application deadline: 7/1 (priority date; rolling processing). Application fee: $0.

University of Scranton, Program in Business Administration, Scranton, PA 18510-4622. Offerings include finance (MBA). Program faculty: 39 full-time (9 women), 1 part-time (0 women). *Entrance requirements:* GMAT, TOEFL (minimum score 500), minimum GPA of 2.75. Application deadline: rolling. Application fee: $35. *Expenses:* Tuition $465 per credit. Fees $25 per semester. • Dr. Wayne H. J. Cunningam, Director, 717-941-4043. Fax: 717-941-4342. E-mail: cunninghamw1@uofs.edu.

University of Southern California, Graduate School, Marshall School of Business, Department of Finance and Business Economics, Los Angeles, CA 90089. Awards MBA. *Entrance requirements:* GMAT. *Expenses:* Tuition $730 per unit. Fees $414 per year full-time, $32 per year part-time. *Financial aid:* Fellowships, research assistantships, teaching assistantships, Federal Work-Study, institutionally sponsored loans available. Aid available to part-time students. Financial aid application deadline: 2/15; applicants required to submit FAFSA. • Anthony Marino, Chair.

University of Tennessee at Chattanooga, School of Business Administration, Program in Business Administration, Chattanooga, TN 37403-2598. Offerings include finance (MBA). *Entrance requirements:* GMAT (average 527). Application deadline: rolling. Application fee: $25. *Tuition:* $2864 per year full-time, $160 per credit hour part-time for state residents; $6806 per year full-time, $379 per credit hour part-time for nonresidents. • Ashley Williams, Director, 423-755-4169. Fax: 423-755-5255. Application contact: Dr. Deborah Arfken, Assistant Provost for Graduate Studies, 423-755-4667. Fax: 423-755-4478.

University of Tennessee, Knoxville, College of Business Administration, Program in Business Administration, Knoxville, TN 37996. Offerings include finance (MBA, PhD). MS/MBA offered jointly with the College of Engineering. Postbaccalaureate distance learning degree programs offered. Program faculty: 51 full-time (6 women). *Degree requirements:* For doctorate, computer language, dissertation required, foreign language not required. *Entrance requirements:* For doctorate, GMAT, TOEFL (minimum score 550), minimum GPA of 2.7. Application deadline: 2/1 (priority date). Application fee: $35. Electronic applications accepted. *Tuition:* $3354 per year full-time, $181 per semester hour part-time for state residents; $8410 per year full-time, $462 per semester hour part-time for nonresidents. • Dr. Gary Dicer, Director, 423-974-5033. E-mail: gdicer@utk.edu. Application contact: Donald Potts, Graduate Representative, 423-974-5033. Fax: 423-974-3826. E-mail: dpotts@utk.edu.

The University of Texas at Arlington, College of Business Administration, Program in Business Administration, Concentration in Finance, Arlington, TX 76019-0407. Awards MBA. Faculty: 8 full-time (1 woman). Students: 0. 0 applicants. *Degree requirements:* Computer language required, foreign language and thesis not required. *Entrance requirements:* GMAT (minimum score 480), minimum GPA of 2.9. Application deadline: rolling. Application fee: $25 ($50 for international students). *Tuition:* $3206 per year full-time, $468 per semester (minimum) part-time for state residents; $8612 per year full-time, $1137 per semester (minimum) part-time for nonresidents. *Financial aid:* Research assistantships, teaching assistantships, and career-related internships or fieldwork available. • Dr. Peggy Swanson, Chair, 817-272-3705. Application contact: Richard Buttimer, Graduate Adviser, 817-272-3705.

The University of Texas at Austin, Graduate School, College of Business Administration, Department of Finance, Austin, TX 78712. Awards PhD. Students: 22 (3 women); includes 2 minority (1 Asian American, 1 Hispanic), 12 international. 62 applicants, 15% accepted. In 1997, 2 degrees awarded. *Entrance requirements:* GMAT or GRE. Application fee: $50 ($75 for international students). *Expenses:* Tuition $2592 per year full-time, $324 per semester (minimum) part-time for state residents; $7704 per year full-time, $963 per semester (minimum) part-time for nonresidents. Fees $778 per year full-time, $161 per semester (minimum) part-time. *Financial aid:* Fellowships available. Financial aid application deadline: 2/1. • George W. Gau, Chairman, 512-471-6612. E-mail: gaug@cbacc.bus.utexas.edu. Application contact: Ramesh Rao, Graduate Adviser, 512-471-5840.

University of Toledo, Graduate School of Business, Department of Finance, Toledo, OH 43606-3398. Awards MBA. Evening/weekend programs available. Faculty: 5 full-time (2 women). Students: 14 full-time (2 women), 37 part-time (12 women); includes 1 minority (African American), 30 international. Average age 28. 78 applicants, 60% accepted. In 1997, 29 degrees awarded. *Degree requirements:* Thesis or alternative required, foreign language not required. *Entrance requirements:* GMAT (minimum score 450), TOEFL (minimum score 550). Application deadline: 8/1 (priority date; rolling processing). Application fee: $30. *Tuition:* $5907 per year full-time, $246 per hour part-time for state residents; $11,835 per year full-time, $493 per hour part-time for nonresidents. *Financial aid:* Research assistantships, administrative assistantships, tuition scholarships, full tuition waivers, Federal Work-Study, institutionally sponsored loans, and career-related internships or fieldwork available. Aid available to part-time students. Financial aid application deadline: 4/1; applicants required to submit FAFSA. *Faculty research:* Financial management, banking, international finance, investments. • Dr. Herbert Weinraub, Chair, 419-530-2436. Application contact: Dr. Bruce Kuhlman, MBA Director, 419-530-2774. Fax: 419-530-7260. E-mail: mba0001@uoft01.utoledo.edu.

University of Utah, Graduate School of Business, Department of Finance, Salt Lake City, UT 84112-1107. Awards MBA, MS, PhD. Faculty: 15 full-time (1 woman), 7 part-time (0 women). Students: 1 part-time (0 women). Average age 47. *Degree requirements:* For master's, computer language, thesis (MS) required, foreign language not required; for doctorate, computer language, dissertation, oral qualifying exams, written qualifying exams required, foreign language not required. *Entrance requirements:* GMAT, TSE, TOEFL (minimum score 500). Application deadline: 2/15. Application fee: $30 ($50 for international students). *Tuition:* $2045 per year full-time, $562 per semester (minimum) part-time for state residents; $6129 per year full-time, $1607 per semester (minimum) part-time for nonresidents. *Financial aid:* Fellowships, teaching assistantships available. *Faculty research:* Investment, managerial finance, corporate finance, capital budgeting, risk management. • Dr. Calvin M. Boardman, Chairperson, 801-581-7463. Fax: 801-585-5257.

University of Victoria, Faculty of Human and Social Development, School of Public Administration, Victoria, BC V8W 2Y2, Canada. Offerings include financial analysis (MPA). School faculty: 14 full-time (1 woman), 13 part-time (6 women), 18 FTE. *Degree requirements:* Report required, foreign language and thesis not required. *Average time to degree:* master's–4 years full-time. *Entrance requirements:* GMAT or GRE General Test, TOEFL (minimum score 550). Application deadline: 5/1 (rolling processing; 10/15 for spring admission). Application fee: $50. *Tuition:* $2080 per year full-time, $557 per semester part-time. • Dr. B. Wharf, Acting Director, 250-721-8054. Application contact: Dr. B. Bish, Graduate Adviser, 250-721-8065.

University of Waterloo, Faculty of Arts, School of Accountancy, Waterloo, ON N2L 3G1, Canada. Offerings include finance (M Acc). School faculty: 18 full-time (2 women), 6 part-time (1 woman). *Application fee:* $50. *Tuition:* $5046 per year. • Dr. Morley Lemon, Director, 519-888-4567 Ext. 3732. Application contact: Dr. G. Richardson, Graduate Officer, 519-888-4567 Ext. 6549. Fax: 519-888-7562.

University of Wisconsin–Madison, School of Business, Program in Finance, Investment, and Banking, Madison, WI 53706-1380. Awards MBA, MS, PhD. Evening/weekend programs available. Faculty: 12 full-time (2 women). Students: 132. In 1997, 99 master's awarded. Terminal master's awarded for partial completion of doctoral program. *Degree requirements:* For master's, computer language required, foreign language and thesis not required; for doctorate, computer language, dissertation required, foreign language not required. *Entrance requirements:* GMAT. Application deadline: 6/1 (rolling processing; 10/1 for spring admission). Application fee: $45. *Tuition:* $5950 per year full-time, $1118 per semester (minimum) part-time for state residents; $16,230 per year full-time, $3044 per semester (minimum) part-time for nonresidents. *Financial aid:* Fellowships, research assistantships, teaching assistantships, project assistantships, and career-related internships or fieldwork available. *Faculty research:* Psychology of financial markets, banking and financial institutions, business cycles, deficit and monetary policy. • Howard E. Thompson, Chair, 608-262-1991. Application contact: Lisa Urban, Director of Master's Marketing and Recruiting, 608-262-4610. Fax: 608-265-4192.

University of Wyoming, College of Business, Department of Economics and Finance, Program in Finance, Laramie, WY 82071. Awards MS. Part-time programs available. Faculty: 5 (0 women). Students: 12 full-time (5 women), 4 part-time (2 women); includes 5 international. 16 applicants, 56% accepted. In 1997, 8 degrees awarded (100% found work related to degree). *Entrance requirements:* GMAT, minimum GPA of 3.0. Application deadline: 3/1 (rolling processing; 10/1 for spring admission). Application fee: $40. *Expenses:* Tuition $2430 per year full-time, $135 per credit hour part-time for state residents; $7518 per year full-time, $418 per credit hour part-time for nonresidents. Fees $386 per year full-time, $9.25 per credit hour part-time. *Financial aid:* In 1997–98, 3 research assistantships, 3 teaching assistantships were awarded. Financial aid application deadline: 3/1. *Faculty research:* Banking. • Dr. Shelby Gerking, Chairperson, Department of Economics and Finance, 307-766-2178. E-mail: gerking@uwyo.edu. Application contact: Dr. William E. Morgan, Director of Graduate Studies, 307-766-2178. Fax: 307-766-5090. E-mail: wemorgan@uwyo.edu.

Vanderbilt University, Owen Graduate School of Management and Graduate School, Program in Management, Nashville, TN 37240-1001. Offerings include finance (PhD). PhD offered through the Graduate School. *Degree requirements:* Dissertation required, foreign language not required. *Entrance requirements:* GMAT (minimum score 650), GRE, TOEFL (minimum score 600). Application deadline: 1/15. Application fee: $50. *Tuition:* $871 per semester hour. • Bruce Barry, Director, 615-322-3489. Application contact: Maureen Writesman, 615-343-1989. Fax: 615-343-7177. E-mail: owenphd@ctrvax.vanderbilt.edu.

Virginia Commonwealth University, College of Humanities and Sciences, Department of Political Science and Public Administration, Richmond, VA 23284-9005. Offerings include public finance (MPA). Department faculty: 8 full-time. *Entrance requirements:* GMAT, GRE General Test (minimum combined score of 1000), LSAT, or MAT, interview. Application fee: $30 ($0 for international students). *Tuition:* $4960 per year full-time, $257 per credit part-time for state residents; $12,652 per year full-time, $684 per credit part-time for nonresidents. • Dr. Scott Keeter, Chair, 804-828-1575. E-mail: skeeter@vcu.edu. Application contact: Dr. Ralph S. Hambrick, Graduate Program Director, 804-828-1046. Fax: 804-828-7463. E-mail: rhambric@vcu.edu.

Virginia Commonwealth University, School of Business, Program in Finance, Richmond, VA 23284-9005. Awards MS, PhD. *Degree requirements:* For doctorate, dissertation. *Entrance requirements:* GMAT. Application deadline: rolling. Application fee: $30 ($0 for international students). *Tuition:* $4960 per year full-time, $257 per credit part-time for state residents; $12,652 per year full-time, $684 per credit part-time for nonresidents. *Financial aid:* Fellowships, research assistantships, teaching assistantships, full and partial tuition waivers, Federal Work-Study, institutionally sponsored loans available. Financial aid application deadline: 3/15. • Dr. Neil B. Murphy, Chair, 804-828-1620. Fax: 804-828-3972. E-mail: nbmurphy@vcu.edu. Application contact: Dr. Edward L. Millner, Associate Dean of Graduate Studies, 804-828-1741. Fax: 804-828-7174.

Virginia Polytechnic Institute and State University, Pamplin College of Business, Department of Finance, Insurance, and Business Law, Blacksburg, VA 24061. Offers program in business administration/finance (PhD). Students: 9 full-time (3 women), 1 (woman) part-time; includes 1 minority (Asian American), 6 international. 23 applicants, 9% accepted. In 1997, 2 degrees awarded (100% entered university research/teaching). *Degree requirements:* Dissertation, comprehensive exams required, foreign language not required. *Entrance requirements:* GMAT (minimum score 580), TOEFL (minimum score 600). Application deadline: 12/1 (priority date; rolling processing). Application fee: $25. *Tuition:* $4927 per year full-time, $792 per semester (minimum) part-time for state residents; $7537 per year full-time, $1227 per semester (minimum) part-time for nonresidents. *Financial aid:* In 1997–98, 1 teaching assistantship was awarded; assistantships also available. Financial aid application deadline: 4/1. *Faculty research:* Options and futures, banking regulation, bond yield differentials, dividend policy, agency theory of capital structure. • Dr. Arthur J. Keown, Head, 540-231-5904.

Virginia State University, School of Business, Department of Economics and Finance, 1 Hayden Drive, Petersburg, VA 23806-2096. Awards MA. Faculty: 6 full-time (0 women). In 1997, 8 degrees awarded. *Entrance requirements:* GRE General Test. Application deadline: 8/15 (rolling processing). Application fee: $25. *Tuition:* $3739 per year full-time, $133 per credit hour part-time for state residents; $9056 per year full-time, $364 per credit hour part-time for nonresidents. *Financial aid:* 1 student received aid. Financial aid application deadline: 5/1. • Dr. Yaw Badu, Chair, 804-524-5363. Application contact: Dr. Wayne F. Virag, Dean, Graduate Studies and Continuing Education, 804-524-5985. Fax: 804-524-5104. E-mail: wvirag@vsu.edu.

Wagner College, Department of Business Administration, Program in Finance and Banking, Staten Island, NY 10301. Awards MBA. Part-time and evening/weekend programs available. Faculty: 4 full-time (2 women), 2 part-time (1 woman). Students: 11 full-time (3 women), 26 part-time (10 women); includes 8 minority (3 African Americans, 3 Asian Americans, 2 Hispanics). 16 applicants, 94% accepted. In 1997, 7 degrees awarded. *Degree requirements:* Thesis optional, foreign language not required. *Entrance requirements:* Minimum GPA of 2.6. Application deadline: 8/1 (priority date; rolling processing; 12/10 for spring admission). Application fee: $50 ($65 for international students). *Tuition:* $580 per credit. *Financial aid:* In 1997–98, 5 alumni fellowships (3 to first-year students) were awarded; teaching assistantships, partial tuition waivers also available. • Application contact: Admissions Office, 718-390-3411.

Walsh College of Accountancy and Business Administration, Program in Finance, Troy, MI 48007-7006. Awards MSF. Part-time and evening/weekend programs available. Faculty: 4 full-time (0 women), 24 part-time (2 women). *Degree requirements:* Computer language required, foreign language and thesis not required. *Entrance requirements:* TOEFL (minimum score 550), minimum GPA of 2.75, previous course work in business. Application deadline: rolling. Application fee: $25. *Expenses:* Tuition $273 per credit hour. Fees $75 per semester. *Financial aid:* Federal Work-Study available. Aid available to part-time students. • Joe Drolshagen, Director, 248-689-8282. Fax: 248-689-9066. Application contact: Sherree Hyde, Director, Enrollment Services, 248-689-8282 Ext. 215. Fax: 248-524-2520.

Webster University, School of Business and Technology, Department of Business, St. Louis, MO 63119-3194. Offerings include finance (MA, MBA). Department faculty: 5 full-time (1 woman). *Application deadline:* rolling. *Application fee:* $25 ($50 for international students). *Tuition:* $350 per credit hour. • Lucille Berry, Chair, 314-968-7022. Fax: 314-968-7077. E-mail: berrylm@webster.edu. Application contact: Beth Russell, Director of Graduate Admissions, 314-968-7089. Fax: 314-968-7166. E-mail: russellmb@webster.edu.

West Chester University of Pennsylvania, School of Business and Public Affairs, Program in Business Administration, West Chester, PA 19383. Offerings include economics/finance (MBA). Program faculty: 2 part-time. *Degree requirements:* Comprehensive exam required, thesis optional, foreign language not required. *Entrance requirements:* GMAT, interview, minimum GPA of 3.0. Application deadline: 4/15 (priority date; rolling processing; 10/15 for spring admission). Application fee: $25. *Expenses:* Tuition $3468 per year full-time, $193 per credit part-time for state residents; $6236 per year full-time, $346 per credit part-time for nonresidents. Fees $660 per year full-time, $38 per credit part-time. • Dr. Jim Hamilton, Graduate Coordinator, 610-436-2608.

Western International University, Program in Finance, 9215 North Black Canyon Highway, Phoenix, AZ 85021-2718. Awards MBA. Evening/weekend programs available. *Degree requirements:* Thesis, research project. *Entrance requirements:* GMAT (strongly recommended), minimum GPA of 2.75. Application deadline: rolling. Application fee: $50 ($100 for international students). • Dr. Innocent Abiaka, Chair, 602-943-2311. Application contact: Enrollment Department, 602-943-2311. Fax: 602-371-8637.

Western New England College, School of Business, Program in Finance, Springfield, MA 01119-2654. Awards MBA. *Application deadline:* rolling. *Application fee:* $30. *Expenses:* Tuition $353 per credit hour. Fees $44 per semester (minimum). *Financial aid:* Application deadline 4/1. • Application contact: Rod Pease, Director of Student Administrative Services, 413-796-2080.

West Texas A&M University, T. Boone Pickens College of Business, Department of Accounting, Economics, and Finance, Program in Finance and Economics, Canyon, TX 79016-0001. Awards MS. Part-time and evening/weekend programs available. Postbaccalaureate distance learning degree programs offered (minimal on-campus study). Faculty: 8 full-time (0 women). Students: 4 full-time (2 women), 6 part-time (1 woman); includes 3 international. Average age 34. 5 applicants, 100% accepted. In 1997, 4 degrees awarded. *Degree requirements:* Thesis or alternative, comprehensive exam required, foreign language not required. *Average time to degree:* master's–3 years full-time, 6 years part-time. *Entrance requirements:* GMAT (minimum score 450; average 530), minimum GPA of 2.75. Application deadline: rolling. Application fee: $0 ($50 for international students). Electronic applications accepted. *Expenses:* Tuition $46 per semester hour for state residents; $259 per semester hour for nonresidents. Fees $156 per semester (minimum). *Financial aid:* Partial tuition waivers, Federal Work-Study, institutionally sponsored loans available. Aid available to part-time students. Financial aid applicants required to submit CSS PROFILE or FAFSA. • Application contact: Dr. Ron Hiner, Graduate Adviser, 806-651-2517. Fax: 806-651-2927. E-mail: ron.hiner@wtamu.edu.

Wilkes University, Programs in Business Administration, Wilkes-Barre, PA 18766-0002. Offerings include finance (MBA). MBA (management, management information systems) being phased out; applicants no longer accepted. Faculty: 11 full-time, 2 part-time. *Entrance requirements:* GMAT. Application deadline: rolling. Application fee: $30. *Expenses:* Tuition $12,552 per year full-time, $523 per credit hour part-time. Fees $240 per year full-time, $10 per credit hour part-time. • Dr. Robert Seeley, Director, 717-408-4717.

Wright State University, College of Business and Administration, Department of Finance, Insurance, and Real Estate, Dayton, OH 45435. Offers program in finance and financial administration (MBA). Students: 32 full-time (12 women), 69 part-time (27 women); includes 15 minority (11 African Americans, 2 Asian Americans, 2 Hispanics), 19 international. Average age 31. 56 applicants, 59% accepted. In 1997, 53 degrees awarded. *Degree requirements:* Computer language required, foreign language and thesis not required. *Entrance requirements:* GMAT, TOEFL (minimum score 550), minimum AACSB index of 1000. Application fee: $25. *Tuition:* $5109 per year full-time, $161 per credit hour part-time for state residents; $9039 per year full-time, $282 per credit hour part-time for nonresidents. *Financial aid:* In 1997–98, 10 fellowships (all to first-year students), 1 teaching assistantship, 4 graduate assistantships were awarded; research assistantships also available. Aid available to part-time students. Financial aid applicants required to submit FAFSA. • Dr. Robert J. Sweeney, Chair, 937-775-3175. Application contact: James Crawford, Director of Graduate Programs, 937-775-2437. Fax: 937-775-3301.

Yale University, School of Management and Graduate School of Arts and Sciences, Doctoral Program in Management, New Haven, CT 06520. Offerings include financial economics (PhD). Terminal master's awarded for partial completion of doctoral program. Program faculty: 36 full-time (4 women). *Degree requirements:* Dissertation required, foreign language not required. *Average time to degree:* doctorate–5 years full-time. *Entrance requirements:* GMAT or GRE General Test (GRE preferred). Application deadline: 1/2. Application fee: $65. *Expenses:* Tuition waived upon acceptance into program. • Application contact: Subrata Sen, Director of Graduate Studies, 203-432-6028. Fax: 203-432-6974. E-mail: subrata.sen@yale.edu.

Youngstown State University, Warren P. Williamson Jr. College of Business Administration, Department of Accounting and Finance, Youngstown, OH 44555-0002. Offers programs in accounting (MBA), finance (MBA). Part-time and evening/weekend programs available. Faculty: 10 full-time (2 women). Students: 10 full-time (5 women), 14 part-time (4 women); includes 3 international. 8 applicants, 100% accepted. In 1997, 6 degrees awarded. *Degree requirements:* Computer language required, thesis optional, foreign language not required. *Entrance requirements:* GMAT (minimum score 450), TOEFL (minimum score 550), minimum GPA of 2.7. Application deadline: 8/15 (priority date; rolling processing; 2/15 for spring admission). Application fee: $30 ($75 for international students). *Expenses:* Tuition $90 per credit hour for state residents; $144 per credit hour (minimum) for nonresidents. Fees $528 per year full-time, $244 per year (minimum) part-time. *Financial aid:* In 1997–98, 6 students received aid, including 3 research assistantships averaging $666 per month and totaling $25,560, 3 scholarships totaling $2,752; fellowships, teaching assistantships, Federal Work-Study, institutionally sponsored loans also available. Aid available to part-time students. Financial aid application deadline: 3/1. *Faculty research:* Taxation and compliance, capital markets, accounting information systems, accounting theory, tax and government accounting. • Dr. James A. Tackett, Chair, 330-742-3084. Application contact: Dr. Peter J. Kasvinsky, Dean of Graduate Studies, 330-742-3091. Fax: 330-742-1580. E-mail: amgrad03@ysub.ysu.edu.

Taxation

American University, Kogod College of Business Administration, Department of Accounting, Program in Taxation, Washington, DC 20016-8001. Awards MS. Part-time and evening/weekend programs available. Faculty: 13 full-time (3 women), 2 part-time (0 women). Students: 1 (woman) full-time, 45 part-time (21 women); includes 8 minority (4 African Americans, 4 Asian Americans). 18 applicants, 89% accepted. In 1997, 19 degrees awarded. *Entrance requirements:* GMAT. Application deadline: 2/1 (priority date; 10/1 for spring admission). Application fee: $50. *Expenses:* Tuition $19,080 per year full-time, $687 per credit hour (minimum) part-time. Fees $180 per year full-time, $110 per year part-time. *Financial aid:* Fellowships, Federal Work-Study, institutionally sponsored loans, and career-related internships or fieldwork available. Aid available to part-time students. Financial aid application deadline: 2/1. • Dr. Nancy A. Bagranoff, Chair, Department of Accounting, 202-885-1930. Fax: 202-885-1992.

Arizona State University, College of Business, School of Accountancy and Information Management, Tempe, AZ 85287. Offerings include taxation (M Tax). School faculty: 47 full-time (11 women). *Application fee:* $45. *Expenses:* Tuition $2088 per year full-time, $110 per hour part-time for state residents; $9040 per year full-time, $377 per hour part-time for nonresidents. Fees $72 per year full-time, $18 per semester (minimum) part-time. • Dr. M. J. Philip Reckers, Director, 602-965-3631.

Baruch College of the City University of New York, School of Business, Department of Accounting, Program in Taxation, 17 Lexington Avenue, New York, NY 10010-5585. Awards MBA, MS. Part-time and evening/weekend programs available. Faculty: 4 full-time (0 women), 5 part-time (1 woman). Students: 3 full-time (1 woman), 73 part-time (36 women). In 1997, 32 degrees awarded. *Degree requirements:* Computer language required, foreign language not required. *Average time to degree:* master's–2 years full-time. *Entrance requirements:* GMAT, TOEFL (minimum score 570), TWE (minimum score 4.5). Application deadline: 6/15 (11/1 for spring admission). Application fee: $40. *Expenses:* Tuition $4350 per year full-time, $185 per credit part-time for state residents; $7600 per year full-time, $320 per credit part-time for nonresidents. Fees $53 per year. *Financial aid:* Research assistantships, Federal Work-Study, and career-related internships or fieldwork available. Aid available to part-time students. Financial aid application deadline: 5/3; applicants required to submit FAFSA. • Application

Directory: Taxation

Baruch College of the City University of New York (continued)
contact: Michael S. Wynne, Office of Graduate Admissions, 212-802-2330. Fax: 212-802-2335. E-mail: graduate_admissions@baruch.cuny.edu.

Bentley College, Graduate School of Business, Program in Taxation, 175 Forest Street, Waltham, MA 02154-4705. Awards MST. Part-time and evening/weekend programs available. Faculty: 4 full-time (0 women), 14 part-time (2 women). Students: 12 full-time (5 women), 274 part-time (137 women); includes 13 minority (11 Asian Americans, 1 Hispanic, 1 Native American), 4 international. Average age 36. 88 applicants, 84% accepted. In 1997, 118 degrees awarded (100% found work related to degree). *Degree requirements:* Computer language required, foreign language and thesis not required. *Entrance requirements:* GMAT (not required for students with CPA or master's degree in business), TOEFL (minimum score 580). Application deadline: 6/1 (priority date; rolling processing; 11/1 for spring admission). Application fee: $50. *Expenses:* Tuition $20,500 per year full-time, $2050 per course part-time. Fees $65 per year full-time, $15 per semester part-time. *Financial aid:* In 1997–98, 24 students received aid, including 2 research assistantships (both to first-year students) totaling $23,760; departmental assistantships, Federal Work-Study, and career-related internships or fieldwork also available. Aid available to part-time students. Financial aid application deadline: 4/15; applicants required to submit CSS PROFILE or FAFSA. *Faculty research:* Individual and corporate tax planning and advocacy, estate and financial planning techniques. • Frank Wolpe, Director, 781-891-2117. Application contact: Holly Chase, Associate Director, 781-891-2108. Fax: 781-891-2464. E-mail: hchase@bentley.edu.

Announcement: Bentley College Graduate School of Business offers the Master of Science in Taxation (MST) degree and the MBA with a concentration in taxation. The MST is designed to meet the needs of people with taxation, accounting, or legal experience who want to specialize in taxation careers. Many practicing tax professionals enroll to enhance their careers. The College also offers an advanced professional certificate in taxation.

Bentley College, Graduate School of Business, Self-paced MBA Program, 175 Forest Street, Waltham, MA 02154-4705. Offerings include taxation (MBA). Program faculty: 70 full-time (21 women), 22 part-time (8 women). *Degree requirements:* Computer language required, foreign language and thesis not required. *Entrance requirements:* GMAT (average 540), TOEFL (minimum score 580). Application deadline: 6/1 (priority date; rolling processing; 11/1 for spring admission). Application fee: $50. *Expenses:* Tuition $20,500 per year full-time, $2050 per course part-time. Fees $65 per year full-time, $15 per semester part-time. • Dr. Judith B. Kamm, Director, 781-891-3433. Application contact: Holly Chase, Associate Director, 781-891-2108. Fax: 781-891-2464. E-mail: hchase@bentley.edu.

Boston University, School of Law, Boston, MA 02215. Offerings include taxation (LL M). School faculty: 60 full-time (20 women), 75 part-time (21 women). *Average time to degree:* master's–1 year full-time; first professional–3 years full-time. *Entrance requirements:* JD, ranking in the top half of law school class. Application deadline: 3/1 (rolling processing). Application fee: $50. *Expenses:* Tuition $22,830 per year full-time, $713 per credit part-time. Fees $218 per year full-time, $40 per semester part-time. • Ronald A. Cass, Dean, 617-353-3112. Application contact: Barbara J. Selmo, Director of Admissions and Financial Aid, 617-353-3100. E-mail: bulawadm@bu.edu.

Bryant College, College of Business Administration, Program in Taxation, Smithfield, RI 02917-1284. Awards MST, CAGS. Part-time and evening/weekend programs available. Faculty: 3 full-time (0 women), 16 part-time (1 woman). Students: 68 part-time (31 women); includes 1 minority (Asian American). Average age 37. 16 applicants, 88% accepted. In 1997, 20 master's awarded. *Entrance requirements:* For master's, GMAT (minimum score 480; average 520). Application deadline: 7/1 (priority date; rolling processing; 11/15 for spring admission). Application fee: $55 ($70 for international students). *Tuition:* $1350 per course. *Financial aid:* Research assistantships, graduate assistantships, and career-related internships or fieldwork available. Aid available to part-time students. Financial aid applicants required to submit FAFSA. • Eugene A. Amelio, Coordinator of MST Program, 401-232-6230.

California State University, Fullerton, School of Business Administration and Economics, Department of Accounting, PO Box 34080, Fullerton, CA 92834-9480. Offerings include taxation (MS). Department faculty: 18 full-time (4 women), 9 part-time, 20 FTE. *Application fee:* $55. *Expenses:* Tuition $0 for state residents; $246 per unit for nonresidents. Fees $1947 per year full-time, $1281 per year part-time. • Dr. Robert McCabe, Chair, 714-278-2225.

California State University, Hayward, School of Business and Economics, Department of Accounting and Computer Information Systems, Option in Taxation, Hayward, CA 94542-3000. Awards MBA, MS. Part-time and evening/weekend programs available. Students: 1 (woman) full-time, 19 part-time (11 women); includes 1 minority (Asian American). 5 applicants, 60% accepted. In 1997, 11 degrees awarded. *Degree requirements:* Comprehensive exam or thesis required, foreign language not required. *Entrance requirements:* GMAT, minimum GPA of 2.75. Application deadline: 4/19 (priority date; rolling processing; 1/5 for spring admission). Application fee: $55. *Expenses:* Tuition $0 for state residents; $164 per unit for nonresidents. Fees $1827 per year full-time, $1161 per year part-time. *Financial aid:* Federal Work-Study, institutionally sponsored loans, and career-related internships or fieldwork available. Aid available to part-time students. Financial aid application deadline: 3/1. • Dr. Gary McBride, Coordinator, 510-885-3097. Application contact: Dr. Donna L. Wiley, Director of Graduate Programs, 510-885-3964.

California State University, Los Angeles, School of Business and Economics, Department of Accounting, Los Angeles, CA 90032-8530. Offerings include accountancy (MS), with options in business taxation, financial accounting, information systems, management accounting. Department faculty: 16 full-time, 8 part-time. *Application deadline:* 6/30 (rolling processing; 11/30 for spring admission). *Application fee:* $55. *Expenses:* Tuition $0 for state residents; $164 per unit for nonresidents. Fees $1763 per year full-time, $1097 per year part-time. • Dr. Ralph Spanswick, Chair, 213-343-2830.

California State University, Northridge, College of Business Administration and Economics, Department of Accounting and Management Information Systems, Program in Taxation, Northridge, CA 91330. Awards MS. Part-time programs available. Students: 4 full-time (all women), 9 part-time (4 women); includes 2 minority (both Asian Americans). Average age 37. 6 applicants, 67% accepted. *Degree requirements:* Thesis or alternative required, foreign language not required. *Entrance requirements:* GMAT (score in 50th percentile or higher), TOEFL, minimum GPA of 3.0 in last 60 units. Application deadline: 11/30. Application fee: $55. *Expenses:* Tuition $0 for state residents; $246 per unit for nonresidents. Fees $1970 per year full-time, $1304 per year part-time. *Financial aid:* Application deadline 3/1. • Application contact: Dr. Richard Moore, Director of Graduate Programs, 818-677-2467.

Capital University, Law School, Program in Taxation, Columbus, OH 43209-2394. Awards LL M, MT. Part-time and evening/weekend programs available. Faculty: 5 full-time (2 women), 14 part-time (0 women). Students: 10 full-time (4 women), 67 part-time (30 women); includes 6 minority (3 African Americans, 2 Asian Americans, 1 Hispanic). Average age 32. 26 applicants, 77% accepted. In 1997, 23 degrees awarded. *Degree requirements:* Thesis or alternative required, foreign language not required. *Entrance requirements:* Previous course work in accounting, business law, and taxation. Application deadline: 8/15 (priority date; rolling processing; 1/1 for spring admission). Application fee: $25. *Tuition:* $635 per credit hour. *Financial aid:* Fellowships, teaching assistantships, scholarships, Federal Work-Study available. Aid available to part-time students. Financial aid applicants required to submit FAFSA. • Carole Berry, Director, 614-236-6402. E-mail: gradtx@law.capital.edu. Application contact: Sharon Jacks, Coordinator, 614-236-6444. Fax: 614-236-6972. E-mail: gradtax@law.capital.edu.

Case Western Reserve University, School of Law, Cleveland, OH 44106. Offerings include taxation (LL M). School faculty: 41 full-time (10 women), 59 part-time (13 women). *Entrance requirements:* TOEFL. Application deadline: 4/1 (priority date; rolling processing). Application fee: $40. *Expenses:* Tuition $20,500 per year full-time, $854 per credit hour part-time. Fees $600 per year. • Gerald Korngold, Dean, 216-368-3283. Application contact: Barbara F. Andelman, Assistant Dean for Admissions and Financial Aid, 216-368-3600. Fax: 216-368-6144. E-mail: lawadmissions@po.cwru.edu.

Colorado State University, College of Business, Department of Accounting and Taxation, Fort Collins, CO 80523-0015. Offers programs in accounting (MBA, MS), taxation (MBA, MS). Part-time programs available. Faculty: 14 full-time (4 women). Students: 17 full-time (10 women), 22 part-time (12 women); includes 4 minority (2 Asian Americans, 2 Native Americans), 1 international. 20 applicants, 80% accepted. In 1997, 13 degrees awarded. *Degree requirements:* Thesis optional, foreign language not required. *Entrance requirements:* GMAT, TOEFL, minimum GPA of 3.0. Application deadline: 2/1 (priority date; rolling processing). Application fee: $30. Electronic applications accepted. *Tuition:* $2920 per year (minimum) full-time, $328 per credit hour (minimum) part-time for state residents; $9000 per year (minimum) full-time, $368 per credit hour (minimum) part-time for nonresidents. *Financial aid:* In 1997–98, 18 teaching assistantships were awarded; fellowships, traineeships, Federal Work-Study, and career-related internships or fieldwork also available. Financial aid application deadline: 2/1. *Faculty research:* Business law, malpractice/ethics of CPA's, managerial accountancy, cost accountancy, systems accountancy, governmental accountancy, audit accountancy. • Application contact: Dr. Jon Clark, Interim Chair, 970-491-5102. Fax: 970-491-2676.

DePaul University, Charles H. Kellstadt Graduate School of Business, School of Accountancy, Program in Taxation, Chicago, IL 60604-2287. Awards MST. Part-time and evening/weekend programs available. Students: 47 full-time (28 women), 153 part-time (61 women); includes 23 minority (4 African Americans, 13 Asian Americans, 5 Hispanics, 1 Native American), 1 international. Average age 30. 48 applicants, 79% accepted. In 1997, 74 degrees awarded. *Entrance requirements:* GMAT. Application deadline: 8/1 (rolling processing; 3/1 for spring admission). Application fee: $40. *Expenses:* Tuition $1593 per course. Fees $30 per year. *Financial aid:* Application deadline 4/30. • Dr. Edward Foth, Coordinator, 312-362-8770. Fax: 312-362-6208. Application contact: Christine Munoz, Director of Admissions, 312-362-8810. Fax: 312-362-6677. E-mail: mbainfo@wppost.depaul.edu.

Drexel University, College of Business and Administration, Department of Accounting, Program in Taxation, 3141 Chestnut Street, Philadelphia, PA 19104-2875. Awards MS. Part-time and evening/weekend programs available. Students: 4 full-time (2 women), 7 part-time (1 woman). Average age 33. 8 applicants, 50% accepted. In 1997, 5 degrees awarded. *Degree requirements:* Computer language required, foreign language and thesis not required. *Entrance requirements:* GMAT (minimum score 500), TOEFL (minimum score 570), minimum GPA of 2.75. Application deadline: 8/21 (rolling processing). Application fee: $35. *Expenses:* Tuition $494 per credit hour. Fees $121 per quarter full-time, $65 per quarter part-time. *Financial aid:* Research assistantships, teaching assistantships, graduate assistantships available. Financial aid application deadline: 2/1. *Faculty research:* Individual retirement accounts, state taxation, fiscal planning. • Application contact: Denise Bigham, Director of Admissions, 215-895-6700. Fax: 215-895-5969.

Duquesne University, Graduate School of Business Administration, Pittsburgh, PA 15282-0001. Offerings include taxation (MS). School faculty: 28 full-time (2 women), 14 part-time (2 women), 32 FTE. *Average time to degree:* master's–2 years full-time, 3.5 years part-time. *Application deadline:* 6/1 (priority date; rolling processing; 11/1 for spring admission). *Application fee:* $40. *Expenses:* Tuition $481 per credit. Fees $39 per credit. • Thomas J. Murrin, Dean, 412-396-5157. Application contact: Dr. William Presutti, Associate Dean and Director, 412-396-6269. Fax: 412-396-5304.

École des Hautes Études Commerciales, Program in Taxation, Montréal, PQ H3T 2A7, Canada. Awards Diploma. Most courses are given in French. Part-time programs available. *Degree requirements:* 1 foreign language required, thesis not required. *Application deadline:* 5/15. *Application fee:* $40. *Financial aid:* Fellowships available. • Dr. Jean-Pierre Le Goff, Director, 514-340-5670. Application contact: Nicole Rivet, Registrar, 514-340-6110. Fax: 514-340-5640. E-mail: nicole.rivet@hec.ca.

Fairfield University, School of Business, Fairfield, CT 06430-5195. Offerings include taxation (MBA, CAS). School faculty: 36 full-time (12 women), 4 part-time (2 women), 37.3 FTE. *Average time to degree:* master's–2 years full-time, 3.5 years part-time. *Application deadline:* 8/1 (priority date; rolling processing; 12/1 for spring admission). *Application fee:* $40. *Expenses:* Tuition $15,000 per year full-time, $450 per credit hour part-time. Fees $40 per year. • Dr. Walter G. Ryba Jr., Acting Dean, 203-254-4070. Application contact: Cynthia S. Chegwidden, Director of Graduate Programs, 203-254-4070. Fax: 203-254-4105. E-mail: cchegwidden@fairl.fairfield.edu.

Fairleigh Dickinson University, Florham–Madison Campus, Samuel J. Silberman College of Business Administration, Program in Taxation, 285 Madison Avenue, Madison, NJ 07940-1099. Awards MS. Part-time and evening/weekend programs available. Faculty: 2 full-time (0 women), 3 part-time (0 women). Students: 3 full-time (0 women), 100 part-time (42 women); includes 3 minority (1 African American, 2 Asian Americans). Average age 35. 23 applicants, 91% accepted. In 1997, 23 degrees awarded. *Degree requirements:* Thesis optional, foreign language not required. *Entrance requirements:* GMAT or LSAT. Application deadline: rolling. Application fee: $35. *Expenses:* Tuition $522 per credit. Fees $302 per year full-time, $138 per year part-time. • Frank Brunetti, Director, 973-443-8845.

Fairleigh Dickinson University, Teaneck–Hackensack Campus, Samuel J. Silberman College of Business Administration, Department of Accounting, Taxation, Law, Economics, and Finance, Program in Taxation, 1000 River Road, Teaneck, NJ 07666-1914. Awards MS. Students: 34 part-time (20 women); includes 3 minority (2 Asian Americans, 1 Hispanic), 1 international. Average age 38. In 1997, 12 degrees awarded. *Degree requirements:* Computer language required, thesis optional, foreign language not required. *Entrance requirements:* GMAT, LSAT. Application deadline: rolling. Application fee: $35. *Expenses:* Tuition $522 per credit. Fees $302 per year full-time, $138 per year part-time. *Financial aid:* Fellowships, research assistantships available. *Faculty research:* Liability, law. • Frank Brunetti, Director, 201-692-7240. Fax: 201-692-7219.

Florida Atlantic University, College of Business, School of Accounting, Boca Raton, FL 33431-0991. Awards M Ac, M Tax. Part-time and evening/weekend programs available. Faculty: 26 full-time (9 women), 1 part-time (0 women). Students: 6 full-time (3 women), 49 part-time (29 women); includes 11 minority (6 African Americans, 1 Asian American, 4 Hispanics). Average age 25. 29 applicants, 52% accepted. In 1997, 33 degrees awarded (100% found work related to degree). *Degree requirements:* Communications program required, foreign language and thesis not required. *Average time to degree:* master's–1 year full-time, 3 years part-time. *Entrance requirements:* GMAT (minimum score 450), BS in accounting or equivalent, minimum GPA of 3.0 in accounting. Application deadline: 6/1 (rolling processing; 10/1 for spring admission). Application fee: $20. *Expenses:* Tuition $2520 per year full-time, $140 per credit hour part-time for state residents; $8712 per year full-time, $484 per credit hour part-time for nonresidents. Fees $5 per year (minimum). *Financial aid:* In 1997–98, 12 students received aid, including 1 research assistantship; fellowships, teaching assistantships, partial tuition waivers, Federal Work-Study, institutionally sponsored loans, and career-related internships or fieldwork also available. Aid available to part-time students. Financial aid application deadline: 3/1. *Faculty research:* Systems and computer applications, accounting theory, information systems. • Dr. Kenneth Wiant, Director, 954-762-5233. Fax: 954-762-5245. E-mail: wiant@acc.fau.edu. Application contact: Ella Smith, Graduate Adviser, 561-297-3650. Fax: 561-297-3978. E-mail: smith@acc.fau.edu.

Florida International University, College of Business Administration, School of Accounting, Program in Taxation, Miami, FL 33199. Awards MST, PhD. Part-time and evening/weekend programs available. Students: 24 full-time (11 women), 74 part-time (26 women); includes 52 minority (4 African Americans, 3 Asian Americans, 45 Hispanics), 3 international. Average age 31. 27 applicants, 56% accepted. In 1997, 33 master's awarded. *Degree requirements:* For master's, computer language required, foreign language and thesis not required; for doctorate, computer language, dissertation. *Entrance requirements:* For master's, GMAT, minimum AACSB index of 1000, minimum GPA of 3.0; for doctorate, GMAT (minimum score 560), minimum GPA of 3.0. Application deadline: 4/1 (priority date; rolling processing; 10/1 for spring admission). Application fee: $20. *Expenses:* Tuition $138 per credit hour for state residents; $482 per credit hour for nonresidents. Fees $46 per semester. • Dr. James Scheiner, Director, School of Accounting, 305-348-2581. E-mail: scheiner@fiu.edu.

Fontbonne College, Department of Business Administration, Program in Taxation, St. Louis, MO 63105-3098. Awards MST. Part-time and evening/weekend programs available. Faculty: 2 part-time (0 women). Students: 1 full-time (0 women), 21 part-time (15 women); includes 2 minority (1 African American, 1 Asian American). Average age 37. In 1997, 9 degrees awarded. *Degree requirements:* Computer language, thesis required, foreign language not required. *Application deadline:* 8/1 (priority date; rolling processing). *Application fee:* $20. *Expenses:* Tuition $10,650 per year full-time, $346 per credit hour part-time. Fees $160 per year full-time, $7 per credit hour part-time. • Dr. Hans Helbling, Chairperson, Department of Business Administration, 314-889-4520. Fax: 314-889-1451. E-mail: hhelblin@fontbonne.edu.

Fordham University, Graduate School of Business Administration, New York, NY 10023. Offerings include taxation (MS). School faculty: 85 full-time (22 women), 95 part-time (12 women). *Average time to degree:* master's–2 years full-time, 3 years part-time. *Application deadline:* 6/1 (priority date; rolling processing; 11/1 for spring admission). *Application fee:* $50. • Dr. Ernest J. Scalberg, Dean, 212-636-6111. Fax: 212-307-1779. Application contact: Kathy Pattison, Assistant Dean of Admission, 212-636-6200. Fax: 212-636-7076. E-mail: admission@bschool.bnet.fordham.edu.

George Mason University, School of Management, Program in Taxation, Fairfax, VA 22030-4444. Awards MS. Part-time and evening/weekend programs available. Faculty: 67 full-time (15 women), 29 part-time (8 women), 76.5 FTE. Students: 39 part-time (21 women); includes 10 minority (1 African American, 6 Asian Americans, 3 Hispanics). Average age 36. 21 applicants, 86% accepted. In 1997, 15 degrees awarded. *Entrance requirements:* GMAT (minimum score 500; average 565), TOEFL (minimum score 575), minimum GPA of 3.0 in last 60 hours. Application deadline: 5/1 (11/1 for spring admission). Application fee: $30. Electronic applications accepted. *Tuition:* $4344 per year full-time, $181 per credit hour part-time for state residents; $12,504 per year full-time, $521 per credit hour part-time for nonresidents. *Financial aid:* Available to part-time students. Financial aid application deadline: 3/1; applicants required to submit FAFSA. *Faculty research:* Tax simplification, taxpayer compliance enhancement. • Robert Johnson, Director, 703-993-3725. Fax: 703-993-1870. Application contact: Sandy Mitchell, Director of Graduate Admissions, 703-993-2136. Fax: 703-993-1886.

Georgetown University, Law Center, Washington, DC 20001. Offerings include taxation (LL M). *Degree requirements:* Thesis required, foreign language not required. *Average time to degree:* master's–1 year full-time, 3 years part-time; first professional–3 years full-time, 4 years part-time. *Entrance requirements:* TOEFL (average 600), JD, LL B, or first law degree earned in country of origin. Application deadline: 2/1 (rolling processing). Application fee: $60. *Expenses:* Tuition $24,530 per year full-time, $855 per credit part-time. Fees $99 (one-time charge).

The George Washington University, School of Business and Public Management, Department of Accountancy, Program in Taxation, Washington, DC 20052. Awards M Tax. Part-time and evening/weekend programs available. Faculty: 2 full-time (0 women), 1 part-time (0 women). Students: 14 full-time (7 women), 16 part-time (9 women); includes 10 minority (2 African Americans, 7 Asian Americans, 1 Hispanic), 5 international. Average age 31. 19 applicants, 84% accepted. In 1997, 30 degrees awarded. *Degree requirements:* Computer language required, foreign language and thesis not required. *Entrance requirements:* GMAT, TOEFL (minimum score 550). Application deadline: 4/1 (priority date; rolling processing; 10/1 for spring admission). Application fee: $50. *Expenses:* Tuition $680 per semester hour. Fees $35 per semester hour. *Financial aid:* Fellowships, teaching assistantships, Federal Work-Study, institutionally sponsored loans, and career-related internships or fieldwork available. Financial aid application deadline: 4/1. • Application contact: Lilly Hastings, Graduate Admissions, 202-994-6584. Fax: 202-994-6382.

Georgia State University, College of Business Administration, School of Accountancy, Program in Taxation, Atlanta, GA 30303-3083. Awards MTX. Part-time and evening/weekend programs available. Students: 33 full-time (15 women), 40 part-time (16 women); includes 6 minority (3 African Americans, 3 Asian Americans), 7 international. Average age 31. In 1997, 33 degrees awarded. *Entrance requirements:* GMAT (average 566), TOEFL. Application deadline: 5/1 (rolling processing; 10/1 for spring admission). Application fee: $25. *Expenses:* Tuition $2673 per year full-time, $99 per semester hour part-time for state residents; $10,692 per year full-time, $396 per semester hour part-time for nonresidents. Fees $228 per year. *Financial aid:* Research assistantships, partial tuition waivers, and career-related internships or fieldwork available. Aid available to part-time students. Financial aid application deadline: 5/1; applicants required to submit FAFSA. • Ernest R. Larkins, Faculty Coordinator/Adviser, 404-651-2611. Fax: 404-651-1033. Application contact: Office of Academic Assistance and Master's Admissions, 404-651-1913. Fax: 404-651-0219.

Golden Gate University, School of Law, San Francisco, CA 94105-2968. Offerings include taxation (LL M). School faculty: 35 full-time (13 women), 89 part-time (37 women). *Average time to degree:* first professional–3 years full-time, 4 years part-time. *Application deadline:* 4/15 (priority date; rolling processing; 11/15 for spring admission). *Application fee:* $40. *Expenses:* Tuition $19,981 per year full-time, $13,780 per year part-time. Fees $224 per year. • Anthony J. Pagano, Dean, 415-442-6600. Fax: 415-442-6609. Application contact: Cherie Scricca, Assistant Dean of Admissions, 415-442-6630. Fax: 415-442-6631. E-mail: lawadmit@ggu.edu.

See in-depth description on page 1583.

Golden Gate University, School of Taxation, San Francisco, CA 94105-2968. Awards MS, Certificate. Part-time and evening/weekend programs available. Students: 15 full-time (6 women), 570 part-time (285 women); includes 133 minority (12 African Americans, 97 Asian Americans, 23 Hispanics, 1 Native American), 30 international. Average age 36. 142 applicants, 82% accepted. In 1997, 217 master's awarded. *Average time to degree:* master's–2.5 years full-time. *Entrance requirements:* For master's, TOEFL (minimum score 550), minimum GPA of 3.0. Application deadline: 7/1 (priority date; rolling processing). Application fee: $55 ($70 for international students). *Tuition:* $1494 per course. *Financial aid:* Federal Work-Study, institutionally sponsored loans, and career-related internships or fieldwork available. Aid available to part-time students. Financial aid applicants required to submit FAFSA. • Barbara Karlin, Dean, 415-442-7885. Fax: 415-543-2607. Application contact: Enrollment Services, 415-442-7800. Fax: 415-442-7807. E-mail: info@ggu.edu.

Grand Valley State University, Seidman School of Business, Program in Taxation, Allendale, MI 49401-9403. Awards MST. Part-time and evening/weekend programs available. Faculty: 3 full-time (1 woman), 1 part-time (0 women). Students: 3 full-time (0 women), 42 part-time (18 women); includes 1 minority (Native American). Average age 33. 10 applicants, 100% accepted. In 1997, 11 degrees awarded (100% found work related to degree). *Entrance requirements:* GMAT (minimum score 450), minimum AACSB index of 1000. Application deadline: 6/1 (priority date; rolling processing; 12/1 for spring admission). Application fee: $20. *Financial aid:* In 1997–98, 5 students received aid, including 1 research assistantship (to a first-year student) totaling $6,500; Federal Work-Study, institutionally sponsored loans also available. Financial aid application deadline: 4/1. • Dr. Richard Harris, Director, 616-771-6687. Fax: 616-771-6515.

Hofstra University, Frank G. Zarb School of Business, Department of Accounting and Business Law, Program in Taxation, Hempstead, NY 11549. Awards MBA. Part-time and evening/weekend programs available. Faculty: 24 full-time (12 women), 8 part-time (4 women). Students: 3 full-time (1 woman), 12 part-time (8 women); includes 1 minority (African American). Average age 29. 2 applicants, 100% accepted. In 1997, 6 degrees awarded. *Degree requirements:* Computer language, thesis or alternative required, foreign language not required. *Entrance requirements:* GMAT (average 580). Application deadline: rolling. Application fee: $40 ($75 for international students). *Expenses:* Tuition $10,968 per year full-time, $457 per credit hour part-time. Fees $670 per year full-time, $112 per semester (minimum) part-time. *Financial aid:* 5 students received aid; fellowships, research assistantships, Federal Work-Study, and career-related internships or fieldwork available. Financial aid application deadline: 4/1. *Faculty research:* Individual taxation, corporate taxation, estates and trusts. • Application contact: Susan McTiernan, Senior Assistant Dean, 516-463-5683. Fax: 516-463-5268. E-mail: bizsmm@hofstra.edu.

John Marshall Law School, Chicago, IL 60604-3968. Offerings include taxation (LL M). School faculty: 52 full-time (14 women), 230 part-time (43 women). *Average time to degree:* master's–1.5 years full-time, 2 years part-time; first professional–3 years full-time, 4 years part-time. *Application deadline:* 3/1 (priority date; rolling processing; 10/1 for spring admission). *Application fee:* $50 ($60 for international students). *Expenses:* Tuition $675 per credit (minimum). Fees $40 per semester. • Robert Gilbert Johnson, Dean, 312-427-2737. Application contact: William B. Powers, Dean of Admission and Student Affairs, 312-987-1403. Fax: 312-427-5136. E-mail: 6alonzo@jmls.edu.

King's College, William G. McGowan School of Business, Wilkes-Barre, PA 18711-0801. Offerings include finance (MS), with options in accounting/taxation, finance. School faculty: 7 full-time (1 woman), 3 part-time (0 women). *Average time to degree:* master's–2.5 years part-time. *Entrance requirements:* GMAT. Application deadline: 7/31 (priority date; rolling processing; 12/1 for spring admission). Application fee: $35. *Tuition:* $460 per credit. • Dr. Edward J. Schoen, Dean, 717-208-5932. Fax: 717-826-5989. E-mail: ejschoen@rs01.kings.edu. Application contact: Dr. Elizabeth S. Lott, Director of Graduate Programs, 717-208-5991. Fax: 717-825-9049. E-mail: eslott@rs02.kings.edu.

Long Island University, Brooklyn Campus, School of Business and Public Administration, Program in Accountancy, Taxation and Law, Brooklyn, NY 11201-8423. Offers accounting (MS), taxation (MS). Part-time and evening/weekend programs available. Faculty: 8 full-time (1 woman). Students: 16 full-time (10 women), 25 part-time (9 women); includes 29 minority (22 African Americans, 6 Asian Americans, 1 Hispanic). 27 applicants, 74% accepted. In 1997, 14 degrees awarded. *Entrance requirements:* GMAT or GRE General Test. Application deadline: rolling. Application fee: $30. Electronic applications accepted. *Expenses:* Tuition $480 per credit. Fees $415 per year full-time, $73 per semester (minimum) part-time. *Financial aid:* Career-related internships or fieldwork available. • Dr. Myrna Fischman, Director, 718-488-1070. Application contact: Bernard W. Sullivan, Associate Director of Admissions, 718-488-1011.

Long Island University, C.W. Post Campus, College of Management, School of Professional Accountancy, Program in Taxation, Brookville, NY 11548-1300. Awards MS. Students: 11 full-time (0 women), 63 part-time (23 women). 23 applicants, 100% accepted. In 1997, 16 degrees awarded. *Entrance requirements:* GMAT, minimum GPA of 2.7. Application deadline: rolling. Application fee: $30. Electronic applications accepted. *Expenses:* Tuition $480 per credit. Fees $316 per year full-time, $71 per semester (minimum) part-time. *Financial aid:* Graduate assistantships, Federal Work-Study, institutionally sponsored loans, and career-related internships or fieldwork available. Aid available to part-time students. Financial aid application deadline: 5/15; applicants required to submit FAFSA. *Faculty research:* Reporting methods, specialized tax rules and regulations. • Application contact: Fred Tobias, Adviser, 516-299-2098.

Mississippi State University, College of Business and Industry, School of Accountancy, Mississippi State, MS 39762. Awards MPA, MTX. Part-time programs available. Faculty: 12 full-time (1 woman). Students: 24 full-time (13 women), 7 part-time (2 women); includes 2 minority (both African Americans). Average age 24. In 1997, 38 degrees awarded. *Degree requirements:* Comprehensive oral exam required, foreign language not required. *Entrance requirements:* GMAT (minimum score 500), minimum QPA of 2.75 in accountancy, 3.0 in last 60 hours. Application deadline: rolling. Application fee: $0 ($25 for international students). *Tuition:* $3017 per year full-time, $168 per credit hour part-time for state residents; $6119 per year full-time, $340 per credit hour part-time for nonresidents. *Financial aid:* Research assistantships, teaching assistantships, Federal Work-Study, institutionally sponsored loans available. Aid available to part-time students. Financial aid application deadline: 3/15. *Faculty research:* Income tax, financial accounting system, managerial accounting, auditing. • Dr. Pierre L. Titard, Director, 601-325-3710. Fax: 601-325-1646. Application contact: Dr. Barbara A. Spencer, Acting Head, Department of Management and Information Systems, 601-325-1891. Fax: 601-325-8161. E-mail: gsb@cobilan.msstate.edu.

New Hampshire College, Graduate School of Business, Program in Business Administration, Manchester, NH 03106-1045. Offerings include taxation (Certificate). Program faculty: 7 full-time (1 woman), 66 part-time (11 women), 47 FTE. *Average time to degree:* master's–1.5 years full-time, 4.5 years part-time. *Application deadline:* rolling. *Application fee:* $0. *Expenses:* Tuition $17,044 per year full-time, $945 per course part-time. Fees $530 per year full-time, $80 per year part-time. • Dr. Paul Schneiderman, Acting Dean, Graduate School of Business, 603-644-3102. Fax: 603-644-3150.

New York University, Leonard N. Stern School of Business, Department of Accounting, Program in Taxation, New York, NY 10006. Awards MBA, PhD, APC. Faculty: 25 full-time (4 women), 10 part-time (2 women). Students: 6 full-time, 28 part-time. In 1997, 12 master's, 1 APC awarded. *Degree requirements:* For master's, computer language required, foreign language and thesis not required; for doctorate, computer language, dissertation required, foreign language not required. *Entrance requirements:* For master's, GMAT, TOEFL (minimum score 600); for doctorate, GMAT. Application deadline: 3/15 (rolling processing). Application fee: $75. *Financial aid:* Federal Work-Study available. Financial aid application deadline: 1/15; applicants required to submit FAFSA. *Faculty research:* Case studies for individual and corporate taxes. • Joseph Rebovich, Head, 212-998-0050. Application contact: Mary Miller, Director, Graduate Admissions, 212-998-0600. Fax: 212-995-4231. E-mail: sternmba@stern.nyu.edu.

Northeastern University, Graduate School of Business Administration, Graduate School of Professional Accounting, Program in Taxation, Boston, MA 02115-5096. Awards MST, CAS. Part-time and evening/weekend programs available. Faculty: 3 full-time, 21 part-time. Students: 104 part-time (42 women). 50 applicants, 88% accepted. *Degree requirements:* For master's, computer language, internship required, foreign language and thesis not required. *Entrance requirements:* For master's, GMAT or CPA exam, interview, undergraduate business degree. Application deadline: 8/15 (priority date; rolling processing; 3/1 for spring admission). Application fee: $50. *Expenses:* Tuition $500 per credit hour. Fees $55 per quarter full-time, $13.25 per quarter part-time. *Financial aid:* 3 students received aid; fellowships, research assistantships, teaching assistantships, institutionally sponsored loans, and career-related internships or fieldwork available. Financial aid application deadline: 3/1; applicants required to submit FAFSA. *Faculty research:* Estate planning, taxpayer compliance. • Thomas Flannagan, Director, 617-373-4621. Fax: 617-373-8890.

Announcement: The Northeastern University Master of Science in Taxation (MST) Program is the quality leader in graduate tax education. The MST Program is selective, the classes are highly interactive, and the administration is involved in the professional development of each student. The program is postprofessional in nature and is designed for the practicing tax or financial planning professional. Research is emphasized in every course to enhance a student's ability to spot issues and apply the tax law. The majority of faculty members are either tax partners or managers with large, international accounting firms or tax executives with leading

Directory: Taxation

Northeastern University (continued)

Boston-area corporations and financial services firms. Concentrations in corporate taxation or financial planning are available.

Northern Illinois University, College of Business, Department of Accountancy, De Kalb, IL 60115-2854. Awards MAS, MST. Part-time and evening/weekend programs available. Faculty: 14 full-time (2 women). Students: 21 full-time (12 women), 54 part-time (34 women); includes 7 minority (5 Asian Americans, 2 Hispanics), 12 international. Average age 34. 82 applicants, 62% accepted. In 1997, 30 degrees awarded. *Entrance requirements:* GMAT, TOEFL (minimum score 550), minimum GPA of 2.75. Application deadline: 6/1 (rolling processing; 11/1 for spring admission). Application fee: $30. *Tuition:* $3984 per year full-time, $154 per credit hour part-time for state residents; $8160 per year full-time, $328 per credit hour part-time for nonresidents. *Financial aid:* In 1997–98, 7 research assistantships, 6 teaching assistantships, 2 staff assistantships were awarded; fellowships, full tuition waivers, Federal Work-Study, and career-related internships or fieldwork also available. Aid available to part-time students. • Dr. Patrick Delaney, Chair, 815-753-1250. Application contact: Dr. John Simon, Graduate Adviser, 815-753-6203.

Old Dominion University, College of Business and Public Administration, Department of Accounting, Program in Taxation, Norfolk, VA 23529. Awards MTX. Postbaccalaureate distance learning degree programs offered (no on-campus study). Students: 1 (woman) full-time, 5 part-time (0 women). Average age 37. *Entrance requirements:* GMAT (minimum score 470), minimum GPA of 2.75 in accounting, 2.5 overall. Application deadline: 7/1 (rolling processing; 10/1 for spring admission). Application fee: $30. *Expenses:* Tuition $180 per credit hour for state residents; $477 per credit hour for nonresidents. Fees $140 per year full-time, $32 per semester part-time. *Financial aid:* Application deadline 2/15. • Application contact: Dr. Douglas Ziegenfuss, Graduate Director, 757-683-3514. Fax: 757-683-5639. E-mail: dziegenf@odu.edu.

Pace University, Lubin School of Business, Taxation Program, New York, NY 10038. Awards MBA, MS. Part-time and evening/weekend programs available. *Entrance requirements:* GMAT. Application deadline: 7/31 (priority date; rolling processing; 11/30 for spring admission). Application fee: $60. *Expenses:* Tuition $545 per credit. Fees $360 per year full-time, $53 per semester (minimum) part-time.

Philadelphia College of Textiles and Science, School of Business, Program in Taxation, Philadelphia, PA 19144-5497. Awards MBA, MS, MBA/MS. Part-time and evening/weekend programs available. *Entrance requirements:* GMAT, minimum GPA of 2.85. Application deadline: rolling. Application fee: $35. *Tuition:* $448 per credit hour. *Financial aid:* Research assistantships, graduate assistantships, residential assistantships, Federal Work-Study, and career-related internships or fieldwork available. Financial aid applicants required to submit FAFSA. • Al Brindisi, Director, 215-951-2560. Fax: 215-951-2652. E-mail: brindisia@phila.col.edu. Application contact: Robert J. Reed, Director of Graduate Admissions, 215-951-2943. Fax: 215-951-2907. E-mail: gradadm@phila.col.edu.

Portland State University, School of Business Administration, Program in Taxation, Portland, OR 97207-0751. Awards M Tax. Part-time and evening/weekend programs available. Faculty: 57 full-time (17 women), 34 part-time (9 women), 60 FTE. Students: 23 part-time (12 women); includes 2 minority (1 African American, 1 Asian American). Average age 35. 2 applicants, 50% accepted. *Entrance requirements:* GMAT, TOEFL (minimum score 550), minimum GPA of 3.0 in upper-division course work or 2.75 overall. Application deadline: 4/1 (priority date). Application fee: $50. *Tuition:* $6101 per year full-time, $689 per semester (minimum) part-time for state residents; $10,445 per year full-time, $689 per semester (minimum) part-time for nonresidents. *Financial aid:* Research assistantships, teaching assistantships, Federal Work-Study, institutionally sponsored loans, and career-related internships or fieldwork available. Aid available to part-time students. Financial aid application deadline: 3/1; applicants required to submit FAFSA. *Faculty research:* Taxpayer behavior and tax fairness issues, international tax matters, tax education issues, individual tax issues. • Dr. William Kenny, Associate Dean, 503-725-3721. Fax: 503-725-5850. E-mail: billk@sba.pdx.edu.

Robert Morris College, Program in Taxation, 881 Narrows Run Road, Moon Township, PA 15108-1189. Awards MS. Only part-time programs offered. Part-time and evening/weekend programs available. Faculty: 35 full-time (6 women), 35 part-time (5 women). Students: 111 part-time. Average age 34. In 1997, 41 degrees awarded. *Entrance requirements:* MAT (minimum score 42), minimum GPA of 2.5. Application deadline: 8/1 (priority date; rolling processing; 11/30 for spring admission). Application fee: $25 ($35 for international students). *Expenses:* Tuition $343 per credit. Fees $25 per credit. *Financial aid:* Assistantships available. Aid available to part-time students. Financial aid application deadline: 5/1; applicants required to submit FAFSA. • Dr. William G. Brucker, Director, Graduate Taxation, 412-227-6874. Fax: 412-227-4083. Application contact: Vincent J. Kane, Recruiting Coordinator, 412-262-8535. Fax: 412-299-2425.

St. John's University, College of Business Administration, Department of Accounting and Taxation, Program in Taxation, Jamaica, NY 11439. Awards MBA, Adv C. Part-time and evening/weekend programs available. Students: 1 full-time (0 women), 45 part-time (20 women); includes 13 minority (9 African Americans, 2 Asian Americans, 2 Hispanics), 1 international. Average age 31. 13 applicants, 62% accepted. In 1997, 9 master's, 1 Adv C awarded. *Degree requirements:* For master's, thesis optional, foreign language not required. *Entrance requirements:* For master's, GMAT. Application deadline: 6/1 (rolling processing; 10/1 for spring admission). Application fee: $40. *Expenses:* Tuition $600 per credit. Fees $150 per year. *Financial aid:* Federal Work-Study available. Aid available to part-time students. Financial aid application deadline: 3/1; applicants required to submit FAFSA. • Application contact: Shamus J. McGrenra, TOR, Associate Director, Graduate Admissions, 718-990-6107. Fax: 718-990-5736. E-mail: mcgrenrs@stjohns.edu.

Saint Xavier University, Graham School of Management, Chicago, IL 60655-3105. Offerings include taxation (MBA, Certificate). School faculty: 15 full-time (2 women), 6 part-time (3 women). *Entrance requirements:* For master's, GMAT, minimum GPA of 3.0, 2 years of work experience. Application deadline: 8/15. Application fee: $35. *Expenses:* Tuition $455 per hour. Fees $50 per year. • Dr. John Eber, Dean, 773-298-3601. Fax: 773-298-3610. E-mail: eber@sxu.edu. Application contact: Sr. Evelyn McKenna, Vice President of Enrollment Management, 773-298-3050. Fax: 773-298-3076. E-mail: mckenna@sxu.edu.

San Francisco State University, College of Business, Program in Taxation, San Francisco, CA 94132-1722. Awards MS. Part-time programs available. *Degree requirements:* Computer language, thesis, essay test required, foreign language not required. *Entrance requirements:* GMAT (minimum score 470; average 530), minimum GPA of 2.5 in last 60 units. Application deadline: 6/1 (priority date; rolling processing; 11/30 for spring admission). Application fee: $55. *Expenses:* Tuition $0 for state residents; $246 per unit for nonresidents. Fees $1982 per year full-time, $1316 per year part-time.

San Joaquin College of Law, Taxation Program, 901 5th Street, Clovis, CA 93612-1312. Awards MS. Part-time and evening/weekend programs available. Faculty: 7 part-time (1 woman). Students: 14 part-time (5 women). *Average time to degree:* master's–4 years part-time. *Entrance requirements:* 30 undergraduate credits in accounting. Application deadline: rolling. Application fee: $25. *Expenses:* Tuition $375 per unit. Fees $40 per semester. • Sally Ann Perring, Professor of Law, 209-323-2100. Application contact: Joyce Morodomi, Registrar/Admissions Officer, 209-323-2100. Fax: 209-323-5566.

San Jose State University, College of Business, Program in Taxation, San Jose, CA 95192-0001. Awards MS. Students: 1 full-time (0 women), 5 part-time (3 women); includes 3 minority (all Asian Americans), 3 international. Average age 29. 27 applicants, 74% accepted. In 1997, 20 degrees awarded. *Degree requirements:* Computer language, thesis or alternative, comprehensive exam required, foreign language not required. *Entrance requirements:* GMAT, minimum GPA of 3.0. Application deadline: 6/1 (rolling processing). Application fee: $59. *Expenses:* Tuition $0 for state residents; $246 per unit for nonresidents. Fees $2017 per year full-time, $1351 per year part-time. • Dr. Stewart Karlinsky, Director, 408-924-3482.

Seton Hall University, W. Paul Stillman School of Business, Department of Accounting and Taxation, Program in Taxation, South Orange, NJ 07079-2692. Awards MS, Certificate, MBA/MS. Part-time programs available. *Degree requirements:* For master's, thesis optional, foreign language not required. *Entrance requirements:* For master's, GMAT (minimum score 500), TOEFL (minimum score 550); for Certificate, MS in taxation. Application deadline: 6/1 (priority date; rolling processing). Application fee: $50. *Expenses:* Tuition $538 per credit. Fees $185 per semester. *Financial aid:* Research assistantships and career-related internships or fieldwork available. Aid available to part-time students. Financial aid applicants required to submit FAFSA. • Dr. Brian Greenstein, Director, 973-761-9428. E-mail: greensbr@shu.edu. Application contact: Student Information Office, 973-761-9222. Fax: 973-761-9217. E-mail: busgrad@shu.edu.

Southeastern University, Program in Taxation, Washington, DC 20024-2788. Awards MS. Part-time and evening/weekend programs available. Faculty: 3 full-time (0 women), 11 part-time (1 woman), 5 FTE. Students: 1 (woman) full-time, 3 part-time (2 women); includes 4 minority (all African Americans). Average age 36. In 1997, 8 degrees awarded. *Degree requirements:* Computer language required, foreign language not required. *Entrance requirements:* TOEFL. Application deadline: rolling. Application fee: $45. *Expenses:* Tuition $228 per credit hour. Fees $175 per quarter. *Financial aid:* Federal Work-Study and career-related internships or fieldwork available. Aid available to part-time students. Financial aid applicants required to submit FAFSA. • James McCarthy, Head, 202-488-8162. Application contact: Jack Flinter, Director of Admissions, 202-265-5343. Fax: 202-488-8093.

Southern Methodist University, School of Law, Dallas, TX 75275. Offerings include taxation (LL M). School faculty: 42 full-time (10 women), 95 part-time (20 women). *Degree requirements:* Thesis optional. *Entrance requirements:* TOEFL (minimum score 575), JD (LL M in law, taxation), foreign law degree (LL M in comparative and international law). Application deadline: 2/1 (priority date; rolling processing). Application fee: $45. • Dr. Harvey Wingo, Interim Dean, 214-768-2620. Application contact: Lynn Switzer, Director of Admissions, 214-768-2550. Fax: 214-768-2549.

State University of New York at Albany, School of Business, Department of Accounting, Albany, NY 12222-0001. Offerings include taxation (MS). Department faculty: 15 full-time (5 women), 2 part-time (0 women). *Degree requirements:* Research project. *Entrance requirements:* GMAT. Application deadline: 7/1 (priority date; rolling processing). Application fee: $50. *Expenses:* Tuition $5100 per year full-time, $213 per credit hour part-time for state residents; $8416 per year full-time, $351 per credit hour part-time for nonresidents. Fees $705 per year full-time, $26.85 per credit hour part-time. • Daniel Marcinko, Chair, 518-442-4978. Application contact: Jeffrey Collins, Assistant Director, Graduate Admissions, 518-442-3980.

Suffolk University, Sawyer School of Management, Department of Accounting, Boston, MA 02108-2770. Offerings include taxation (MST). Department faculty: 11 full-time (3 women), 6 part-time (1 woman). *Application deadline:* 6/15 (priority date; rolling processing; 11/15 for spring admission). *Application fee:* $50. *Expenses:* Tuition $18,300 per year full-time, $1830 per course part-time. Fees $50 per year full-time, $20 per year part-time. • Laurie Pant, Chair, 617-573-8394. E-mail: lpant@acad.suffolk.edu. Application contact: Judy Reynolds, Acting Director of Graduate Admissions, 617-573-8302. Fax: 617-523-0116. E-mail: grad.admission@admin.suffolk.edu.

Temple University, School of Law, Philadelphia, PA 19140. Offerings include taxation (LL M). School faculty: 55 full-time (17 women), 171 part-time (53 women). *Application deadline:* rolling. *Application fee:* $50. • Robert J. Reinstein, Dean, 215-204-7863. Application contact: Marylouise C. Esten, Assistant Dean for Admissions, Financial Aid, and Student Affairs, 800-560-1428. Fax: 215-204-1185. E-mail: law@astro.ocis.temple.edu.

See in-depth description on page 1603.

Texas Tech University, Graduate School, College of Business Administration, Program in Accounting, Lubbock, TX 79409. Offerings include taxation (MSA). Program faculty: 11 full-time (3 women). *Degree requirements:* Computer language, comprehensive exam required, foreign language and thesis not required. *Entrance requirements:* GMAT (minimum score 500; average 560), minimum GPA of 3.0. Application deadline: 4/15 (priority date; rolling processing; 9/30 for spring admission). Application fee: $25 ($50 for international students). *Expenses:* Tuition $864 per year full-time, $120 per semester (minimum) part-time for state residents; $5976 per year full-time, $747 per semester (minimum) part-time for nonresidents. Fees $2321 per year full-time, $302 per semester (minimum) part-time. • Dr. Dwayne Dowell, Director, 806-742-3181. Application contact: Nancy Dodge, Director, 806-742-3184. Fax: 806-742-3958.

Université de Sherbrooke, Faculty of Administration, Program in Taxation, Sherbrooke, PQ J1K 2R1, Canada. Awards M Tax, Diploma. *Application fee:* $15.

The University of Akron, College of Business Administration, School of Accountancy, Program in Taxation, Akron, OH 44325-0001. Awards MT. Students: 6 full-time (2 women), 69 part-time (20 women); includes 6 minority (2 African Americans, 2 Asian Americans, 1 Hispanic, 1 Native American), 3 international. Average age 32. In 1997, 16 degrees awarded. *Entrance requirements:* GMAT (minimum score 450), minimum GPA of 2.75. Application deadline: 8/15 (rolling processing). Application fee: $25 ($50 for international students). *Expenses:* Tuition $178 per credit hour for state residents; $333 per credit hour for nonresidents. Fees $145 per year full-time, $32 per semester (minimum) part-time. *Financial aid:* Application deadline 4/30. • Application contact: Dr. J. Daniel Williams, Director of Graduate Business Programs, 330-972-7043. E-mail: jwilliams@uakron.edu.

The University of Alabama, The Manderson Graduate School of Business, Culverhouse School of Accountancy, Program in Tax Accounting, Tuscaloosa, AL 35487. Awards MTA. Students: 16 full-time (6 women). Average age 27. In 1997, 19 degrees awarded. *Entrance requirements:* GMAT (minimum score 500; average 580), TOEFL (minimum score 550), minimum GPA of 3.0. Application deadline: 7/6 (rolling processing). Application fee: $25. *Tuition:* $2684 per year full-time, $594 per semester (minimum) part-time for state residents; $7216 per year full-time, $1248 per semester (minimum) part-time for nonresidents. *Financial aid:* In 1997–98, 3 fellowships (all to first-year students), 6 research assistantships (3 to first-year students), 5 teaching assistantships were awarded; Federal Work-Study, institutionally sponsored loans, and career-related internships or fieldwork also available. Financial aid application deadline: 3/31. • Dr. Edward Schnee, Coordinator, 205-348-6131.

University of Baltimore, School of Law, Baltimore, MD 21201-5779. Offerings include taxation (LL M). School faculty: 41 full-time (16 women), 60 part-time (17 women). *Average time to degree:* first professional–3 years full-time, 4.5 years part-time. *Application deadline:* 4/1 (priority date; rolling processing). *Application fee:* $35. *Expenses:* Tuition $8376 per year full-time, $349 per credit part-time for state residents; $14,136 per year full-time, $589 per credit part-time for nonresidents. Fees $550 per year full-time, $208 per semester (minimum) part-time. • John Sebert, Dean, 410-837-4458. Application contact: Claire Valentine, Assistant Director of Law Admissions, 410-837-4459. Fax: 410-837-4450. E-mail: cvalentine@ubmail.ubalt.edu.

University of Baltimore, School of Business, Program in Taxation, Baltimore, MD 21201-5779. Awards MS. Part-time and evening/weekend programs available. Faculty: 12 full-time (4 women), 1 part-time (0 women). Students: 46 part-time (20 women); includes 8 minority (5 African Americans, 3 Asian Americans). Average age 34. 15 applicants, 93% accepted. In 1997, 17 degrees awarded. *Average time to degree:* master's–2 years full-time. *Entrance* *requirements:* GMAT, minimum GPA of 3.0. Application deadline: 7/15 (priority date; rolling processing; 11/15 for spring admission). Application fee: $30. *Expenses:* Tuition $9528 per year full-time, $397 per credit part-time for state residents; $14,808 per year full-time, $617 per credit part-time for nonresidents. Fees $550 per year full-time, $208 per semester (minimum) part-time. *Financial aid:* Fellowships, research assistantships, Federal Work-Study, and career-related internships or fieldwork available. Aid available to part-time students. Financial aid application deadline: 4/1; applicants required to submit FAFSA. *Faculty research:* Taxation of not-for-profit entities. • Dr. Walter Schwidetsky, Chair, 410-837-4470. Application contact: Judy Sabalauskas, Graduate Adviser, 410-837-4944.

University of Central Florida, College of Business Administration, Program in Taxation, Orlando, FL 32816. Awards MST. Students: 31 full-time (16 women), 18 part-time (7 women); includes 2 minority (both Asian Americans). Average age 34. 14 applicants, 64% accepted. In 1997, 22 degrees awarded. *Entrance requirements:* GMAT. Application deadline: 6/15 (rolling processing; 11/1 for spring admission). Application fee: $20. *Expenses:* Tuition $3288 per year full-time, $137 per credit hour part-time for state residents; $11,520 per year full-time, $480 per credit hour part-time for nonresidents. Fees $105 per year. • Dr. Andrew J. Judd, Director, 407-823-2876. Application contact: Dr. Dale Bandy, Coordinator, 407-823-2964. E-mail: dbandy@pegasus.cc.ucf.edu.

University of Colorado at Boulder, Graduate School of Business Administration, Boulder, CO 80309. Offerings include taxation (MS). School faculty: 66 full-time (12 women). *Application deadline:* 3/1 (priority date; rolling processing). *Application fee:* $40 ($60 for international students). *Expenses:* Tuition $3594 per year (minimum) full-time, $597 per semester (minimum) part-time for state residents; $14,868 per year (minimum) full-time, $2478 per semester (minimum) part-time for nonresidents. Fees $667 per year full-time, $130 per semester (minimum) part-time. • Larry Singell, Dean, 303-492-1809. Fax: 303-492-7676. E-mail: larry.singell@colorado.edu. Application contact: Diana Marinaro, Graduate Student Admissions, 303-492-1831. Fax: 303-492-1727. E-mail: busgrad@spot.colorado.edu.

University of Denver, College of Law, Taxation Program, Denver, CO 80208. Awards LL M, MT. Part-time and evening/weekend programs available. Faculty: 7 full-time (0 women). Students: 77 full-time (28 women), 79 part-time (32 women); includes 19 minority (5 African Americans, 8 Asian Americans, 6 Hispanics). 130 applicants, 90% accepted. In 1997, 100 degrees awarded. *Entrance requirements:* GMAT (MT), JD from an ABA approved institution (LL M). Application deadline: 5/1 (priority date; rolling processing). Application fee: $25. *Tuition:* $418 per credit hour. *Financial aid:* In 1997–98, 123 students received aid, including 67 scholarships totaling $624,230; Federal Work-Study, institutionally sponsored loans also available. Aid available to part-time students. Financial aid application deadline: 6/1; applicants required to submit FAFSA. • Dr. Mark Vogel, Director, 303-871-6239. Application contact: Robin Ricker, Coordinator, 303-871-6209. Fax: 303-871-6358.

See in-depth description on page 453.

University of Florida, College of Law and Graduate School, Program in Taxation, Gainesville, FL 32611. Awards LL M T. Part-time programs available. Faculty: 11 full-time (2 women), 1 part-time (0 women). Students: 39 full-time (10 women), 39 part-time (8 women); includes 5 minority (3 African Americans, 2 Hispanics). Average age 29. 205 applicants, 53% accepted. In 1997, 68 degrees awarded. *Degree requirements:* Thesis or alternative required, foreign language not required. *Entrance requirements:* LSAT, TOEFL. Application deadline: 6/2. Application fee: $20. *Tuition:* $154 per credit hour for state residents; $512 per credit hour for nonresidents. *Financial aid:* In 1997–98, 31 students received aid, including 1 fellowship averaging $1,140 per month, 30 research assistantships averaging $320 per month; full and partial tuition waivers, Federal Work-Study, institutionally sponsored loans also available. Financial aid application deadline: 5/1. • Application contact: Dr. Michael Friel, Director, 352-392-1081. Fax: 352-392-7647. E-mail: friel@law.ufl.edu.

University of Hartford, Barney School of Business and Public Administration, Department of Accounting, Program in Taxation, West Hartford, CT 06117-1599. Awards MST. Part-time and evening/weekend programs available. Faculty: 2 full-time (1 woman), 5 part-time (0 women). Students: 2 full-time, 40 part-time. Average age 33. 12 applicants, 100% accepted. In 1997, 19 degrees awarded. *Average time to degree:* master's–1.5 years full-time, 3 years part-time. *Entrance requirements:* GMAT, TOEFL. Application deadline: 7/1 (priority date; rolling processing; 12/1 for spring admission). Application fee: $35 ($50 for international students). Electronic applications accepted. *Financial aid:* Research assistantships, institutionally sponsored loans, and career-related internships or fieldwork available. Financial aid application deadline: 5/1. • Patricia Nodoushani, Director, 860-768-4346. Fax: 860-768-4398. E-mail: nodoushan@uhavax.hartford.edu. Application contact: Claire Silverstein, Assistant Director, 860-768-4900. Fax: 860-768-4821. E-mail: silverste@unavax.hartford.edu.

University of Houston, College of Business Administration, Department of Accountancy and Taxation, 4800 Calhoun, Houston, TX 77204-2163. Offers programs in accountancy (MS Accy), accounting (MBA, PhD), taxation (MBA). Part-time and evening/weekend programs available. Faculty: 22 full-time (7 women), 3 part-time (1 woman). Students: 38 full-time (17 women), 44 part-time (21 women); includes 21 minority (6 African Americans, 12 Asian Americans, 2 Hispanics, 1 Native American), 11 international. Average age 32. In 1997, 39 master's awarded. *Degree requirements:* For master's, computer language required, foreign language and thesis not required; for doctorate, computer language, dissertation, comprehensive exam required, foreign language not required. *Average time to degree:* master's–2 years full-time, 3.5 years part-time; doctorate–4.5 years full-time. *Entrance requirements:* For master's, GMAT (average 575), TOEFL (minimum score 620); for doctorate, GMAT or GRE. Application deadline: 5/1 (rolling processing; 10/1 for spring admission). Application fee: $50 ($125 for international students). *Expenses:* Tuition $1152 per year full-time, $120 per semester (minimum) part-time for state residents; $4482 per year full-time, $249 per credit hour part-time for nonresidents. Fees $977 per year full-time, $119 per semester (minimum) part-time. *Financial aid:* Research assistantships, teaching assistantships, Federal Work-Study, and career-related internships or fieldwork available. Aid available to part-time students. Financial aid application deadline: 3/1; applicants required to submit FAFSA. • Dr. Gary Schugart, Chairperson, 713-743-4820. Fax: 713-743-4828. Application contact: Office of Student Services, 713-743-4900. Fax: 713-743-4942. E-mail: oss@cba.uh.edu.

The University of Memphis, Fogelman College of Business and Economics, Accountancy Area, Memphis, TN 38152. Offerings include taxation (MS). Faculty: 12 full-time (1 woman). *Degree requirements:* Comprehensive exams required, thesis not required. *Entrance requirements:* GMAT. Application deadline: 8/1 (12/1 for spring admission). Application fee: $25 ($50 for international students). *Tuition:* $2862 per year full-time, $166 per credit hour part-time for state residents; $6696 per year full-time, $379 per credit hour part-time for nonresidents. • Application contact: Dr. Ravinder Nath, Associate Dean of Academic Programs, 901-678-3721. Fax: 901-678-4705. E-mail: fcbegp@memphis.edu.

University of Miami, School of Business Administration, Department of Accounting, Coral Gables, FL 33124. Offerings include taxation (MS Tax). Department faculty: 11 full-time (4 women), 2 part-time (0 women). *Average time to degree:* master's–1.2 years full-time, 2.1 years part-time. *Application deadline:* 7/30 (priority date; rolling processing; 11/30 for spring admission). *Application fee:* $35. *Expenses:* Tuition $815 per credit hour. Fees $174 per year. • Dr. Paul Munter, Chairman, 305-284-5492. Fax: 305-284-5737.

University of Minnesota, Twin Cities Campus, Carlson School of Management, Master's Program in Business Taxation, Minneapolis, MN 55455-0213. Awards MBT. Part-time and evening/weekend programs available. *Entrance requirements:* GMAT. *Faculty research:* Partnership taxation, tax theory, corporate taxation.

University of Mississippi, Graduate School, School of Accountancy, University, MS 38677-9702. Offerings include taxation accounting (M Tax). School faculty: 11 full-time (3 women). *Application deadline:* 8/1 (rolling processing). *Application fee:* $0 ($25 for international students). • Dr. James W. Davis, Dean, 601-232-7468.

University of Missouri–Kansas City, School of Law, Graduate Programs in Law, Kansas City, MO 64110-2499. Offerings include taxation (LL M). Faculty: 6 full-time (2 women), 3 part-time (1 woman), 7.5 FTE. *Degree requirements:* Thesis (general) required, foreign language not required. *Average time to degree:* master's–1 year full-time, 3 years part-time. *Entrance requirements:* Minimum GPA of 3.0 in law (general), 2.7 (tax). Application deadline: 4/1 (rolling processing). Application fee: $25. *Expenses:* Tuition $345 per credit hour for state residents; $689 per credit hour for nonresidents. Fees $326 per year. • Dr. Burnele Powell, Dean, School of Law, 816-235-1672.

University of Missouri–St. Louis, School of Business Administration, Program in Taxation, St. Louis, MO 63121-4499. Awards Certificate. *Application deadline:* 7/1 (rolling processing; 11/1 for spring admission). *Application fee:* $0. *Expenses:* Tuition $3903 per year full-time, $167 per credit hour part-time for state residents; $11,745 per year full-time, $489 per credit hour part-time for nonresidents. Fees $816 per year full-time, $34 per credit hour part-time. *Financial aid:* Application deadline 4/1. • Application contact: Graduate Admissions, 314-516-5458. Fax: 314-516-6759. E-mail: gradadm@umslvma.umsl.edu.

University of New Haven, School of Business, Program in Accounting, West Haven, CT 06516-1916. Offerings include taxation (MS). *Degree requirements:* Thesis required, foreign language not required. *Application deadline:* rolling. *Application fee:* $50. *Expenses:* Tuition $1125 per course. Fees $13 per trimester. • Robert G. McDonald, Coordinator, 203-932-7127.

University of New Haven, School of Business, Program in Taxation, West Haven, CT 06516-1916. Offers corporate taxation (MS), public taxation (MS). Part-time and evening/weekend programs available. Students: 52 part-time (24 women); includes 2 minority (both Hispanics). 13 applicants, 54% accepted. *Degree requirements:* Thesis or alternative required, foreign language not required. *Application deadline:* rolling. *Application fee:* $50. *Expenses:* Tuition $1125 per course. Fees $13 per trimester. *Financial aid:* Federal Work-Study available. Aid available to part-time students. Financial aid application deadline: 5/1; applicants required to submit FAFSA. • Robert Wnek, Coordinator, 203-932-7111.

University of New Mexico, Robert O. Anderson Graduate School of Management, Albuquerque, NM 87131-1221. Offerings include tax accounting (MBA). School faculty: 50 full-time (11 women). *Application deadline:* 7/1 (priority date; rolling processing; 11/15 for spring admission). *Application fee:* $25. *Expenses:* Tuition $2442 per year full-time, $103 per credit hour part-time for state residents; $8691 per year full-time, $103 per credit hour (minimum) part-time for nonresidents. Fees $32 per year. • Howard L. Smith, Dean, 505-277-6471. Fax: 505-277-7108. Application contact: Sue Podeyn, MBA Program Director, 505-277-3147. Fax: 505-277-9356. E-mail: podeyn@unm.edu.

University of New Orleans, College of Business Administration, Department of Accounting, Program in Taxation, New Orleans, LA 70148. Awards MS. Part-time and evening/weekend programs available. Faculty: 3 full-time (0 women), 3 part-time (0 women). Students: 5 full-time (4 women), 22 part-time (16 women); includes 3 minority (all African Americans), 2 international. Average age 33. 12 applicants, 67% accepted. In 1997, 10 degrees awarded. *Entrance requirements:* GMAT. Application deadline: 7/1 (priority date; rolling processing). Application fee: $20. *Expenses:* Tuition $2362 per year full-time, $373 per semester (minimum) part-time for state residents; $7888 per year full-time, $1423 per semester (minimum) part-time for nonresidents. Fees $170 per year full-time, $25 per semester (minimum) part-time. *Financial aid:* Research assistantships, Federal Work-Study available. • Application contact: Gordon Hosch, Graduate Coordinator, 504-280-6438. Fax: 504-280-5430. E-mail: gahac@uno.edu.

University of San Diego, School of Law, San Diego, CA 92110-2492. Offerings include taxation (LL M, Diploma). School faculty: 50 full-time (16 women), 34 part-time (13 women), 55.1 FTE. *Application deadline:* 3/1. *Application fee:* $40. *Expenses:* Tuition $20,980 per year full-time, $710 per unit part-time. Fees $50 per year full-time, $40 per year part-time. • Kristine Strachan, Dean, 619-260-4527. Application contact: Carl Eging, Director of Admissions, 619-260-4528.

University of South Carolina, Graduate School, College of Business Administration, Program in Taxation, Columbia, SC 29208. Awards M Tax. Students: 10 full-time (5 women), 4 part-time (3 women). Average age 26. In 1997, 11 degrees awarded. *Application fee:* $35. Electronic applications accepted. • Application contact: Carol Williams, Director of Admissions, 803-777-6749. Fax: 803-777-0414. E-mail: carol@darla.badm.sc.edu.

University of Southern California, Graduate School, Marshall School of Business, Leventhal School of Accounting, Program in Business Taxation, Los Angeles, CA 90089. Awards MBT, JD/MBT. Students: 50 full-time (24 women), 99 part-time (48 women); includes 73 minority (3 African Americans, 55 Asian Americans, 14 Hispanics, 1 Native American), 15 international. Average age 29. 70 applicants, 76% accepted. In 1997, 68 degrees awarded. *Entrance requirements:* GMAT. Application fee: $55. *Expenses:* Tuition $16,944 per year full-time, $706 per unit part-time. Fees $414 per year full-time, $32 per year part-time. *Financial aid:* In 1997–98, 17 fellowships, 8 scholarships were awarded; research assistantships, teaching assistantships, Federal Work-Study, institutionally sponsored loans also available. Aid available to part-time students. Financial aid application deadline: 2/15; applicants required to submit FAFSA. • Dr. Kenneth A. Merchant, Dean, Leventhal School of Accounting, 213-740-4841.

The University of Texas at Arlington, College of Business Administration, Department of Accounting, Program in Taxation, Arlington, TX 76019-0407. Awards MS. Faculty: 4 full-time (2 women), 1 part-time (0 women). Students: 2 full-time (0 women), 20 part-time (8 women); includes 1 minority (Asian American). 8 applicants, 75% accepted. In 1997, 7 degrees awarded. *Degree requirements:* Thesis optional, foreign language not required. *Entrance requirements:* GMAT, TOEFL (minimum score 550). Application deadline: rolling. Application fee: $25 ($50 for international students). *Tuition:* $3206 per year full-time, $468 per semester (minimum) part-time for state residents; $8612 per year full-time, $1137 per semester (minimum) part-time for nonresidents. *Financial aid:* In 1997–98, 5 research assistantships (2 to first-year students) averaging $520 per month, 3 teaching assistantships (all to first-year students) averaging $800 per month, 1 scholarship were awarded; career-related internships or fieldwork also available. • Application contact: Dr. James E. Walther, Graduate Adviser, 817-272-3004. Fax: 817-794-5799.

The University of Texas at San Antonio, College of Business, San Antonio, TX 78249-0617. Offerings include taxation (MT). College faculty: 72 full-time (18 women), 40 part-time (9 women). *Application deadline:* 7/1 (rolling processing). *Application fee:* $20. *Expenses:* Tuition $2476 per year full-time, $309 per semester (minimum) part-time for state residents; $7584 per year full-time, $948 per semester (minimum) part-time for nonresidents. Fees $361 per year full-time, $133 per semester (minimum) part-time. • James F. Gaertner, Dean, 210-458-4313. Application contact: Dr. John H. Brown, Director of Admissions and Registrar, 210-458-4530.

University of the Sacred Heart, Graduate Programs, Department of Business Administration, Program in Taxation, San Juan, PR 00914-0383. Awards MBA. Part-time and evening/weekend programs available. Faculty: 6 full-time (3 women), 11 part-time (1 woman), 9.67 FTE. Students: 2 full-time (1 woman), 24 part-time (10 women). 25 applicants, 64% accepted. *Degree requirements:* Computer language, thesis. *Entrance requirements:* PAEG, minimum undergraduate GPA of 2.5. Application deadline: 5/15. Application fee: $25. *Expenses:* Tuition $150 per credit. Fees $240 per credit. • Prof. Pedro Fraile, Coordinator, 787-728-1515 Ext. 2436. Fax: 787-728-1515 Ext. 2273. E-mail: p_fraile@uscac1.usc.clu.edu. Application contact: Dr. Blanca Villamil, Acting Director, Admissions Office, 787-728-1515 Ext. 3237. Fax: 787-728-2066. E-mail: b_villami@uscsi.usc.clu.edu.

Directory: Taxation; Cross-Discipline Announcements

University of Tulsa, College of Business Administration, Program in Taxation, Tulsa, OK 74104-3189. Awards M Tax, JD/M Tax. Part-time and evening/weekend programs available. Students: 3 full-time (0 women), 20 part-time (9 women); includes 1 minority (Hispanic), 1 international. Average age 32. 12 applicants, 100% accepted. In 1997, 6 degrees awarded. *Entrance requirements:* GMAT, TOEFL (minimum score 575). Application deadline: rolling. Application fee: $30. Electronic applications accepted. *Expenses:* Tuition $480 per credit hour. Fees $2 per credit hour. *Financial aid:* Research assistantships, teaching assistantships available. Financial aid application deadline: 2/1; applicants required to submit FAFSA. *Faculty research:* Oil and gas taxation, estates and trusts, personal service corporations, federal taxation and financial reporting issues. • Dr. Patrick A. Hennessee, Chairperson, 918-631-2794. Application contact: Dr. Richard C. Burgess, Assistant Dean/Director of Graduate Business Studies, 918-631-2242. Fax: 918-631-2142.

University of Washington, School of Law, Seattle, WA 98105. Offerings include taxation (LL M). School faculty: 47 full-time (19 women), 46 part-time (14 women). *Degree requirements:* Thesis required, foreign language not required. *Average time to degree:* master's–1 year full-time, 2 years part-time; first professional–3 years full-time. *Entrance requirements:* TOEFL (minimum score 580), language proficiency (LL M in Asian law). Application deadline: 1/15. Application fee: $50. *Tuition:* $5763 per year for state residents; $14,169 per year for nonresidents. • Roland L. Hjorth, Dean, 206-543-9476. Fax: 206-616-5305. E-mail: hjorth@u.washington.edu. Application contact: Sandra Madrid, Assistant Dean, 206-543-0199. Fax: 206-543-5671. E-mail: smadrid@u.washington.edu.

University of Waterloo, Faculty of Arts, School of Accountancy, Waterloo, ON N2L 3G1, Canada. Offerings include taxation (M Tax). School faculty: 18 full-time (2 women), 6 part-time (1 woman). *Application fee:* $50. *Tuition:* $5046 per year. • Dr. Morley Lemon, Director, 519-888-4567 Ext. 3732. Application contact: Dr. G. Richardson, Graduate Officer, 519-888-4567 Ext. 6549. Fax: 519-888-7562.

Villanova University, College of Commerce and Finance, Graduate Taxation Program, Villanova, PA 19085-1699. Awards LL M in Tax, MT. LL M in Tax offered jointly with the School of Law. Part-time and evening/weekend programs available. Faculty: 8 full-time (1 woman), 34 part-time (7 women). Students: 29 full-time (12 women), 161 part-time (57 women); includes 14 minority (5 African Americans, 8 Asian Americans, 1 Hispanic). Average age 27. 79 applicants, 97% accepted. In 1997, 59 degrees awarded (100% found work related to degree). *Average time to degree:* master's–1.5 years full-time, 3 years part-time. *Entrance requirements:* GMAT (average 520). Application deadline: 6/30 (rolling processing; 11/15 for spring admission). Application fee: $25. *Financial aid:* Available to part-time students. Financial aid application deadline: 3/15. *Faculty research:* Estate planning, corporate tax planning, international taxation. • Michael Mulroney, Director, 610-519-7043.

Virginia Commonwealth University, School of Business, Program in Taxation, Richmond, VA 23284-9005. Offers accounting/taxation (PhD), taxation (M Tax). Students: 2 full-time (both women), 28 part-time (12 women); includes 2 minority (1 African American, 1 Asian American). Average age 33. 15 applicants, 87% accepted. In 1997, 11 master's awarded. *Degree requirements:* For doctorate, dissertation. *Entrance requirements:* GMAT. Application deadline: rolling. Application fee: $30 ($0 for international students). *Tuition:* $4960 per year full-time, $257 per credit part-time for state residents; $12,652 per year full-time, $684 per credit part-time for nonresidents. *Financial aid:* Fellowships, research assistantships, teaching assistantships, full and partial tuition waivers, Federal Work-Study, institutionally sponsored loans available. Financial aid application deadline: 3/15. • Dr. Bill N. Schwartz, Chair, 804-828-1608. Application contact: Dr. Edward L. Millner, Associate Dean of Graduate Studies, 804-828-1741. Fax: 804-828-7174.

Walsh College of Accountancy and Business Administration, Program in Taxation, Troy, MI 48007-7006. Awards MST. Part-time and evening/weekend programs available. Faculty: 1 full-time (0 women), 12 part-time (0 women). *Entrance requirements:* TOEFL (minimum score 550), minimum GPA of 2.75, previous course work in individual income taxation and business. Application deadline: rolling. Application fee: $25. *Expenses:* Tuition $273 per credit hour. Fees $75 per semester. *Financial aid:* Federal Work-Study available. Aid available to part-time students. • Mark R. Solomon, Chairman, 248-689-8282. Fax: 248-689-9066. Application contact: Sherree Hyde, Director, Enrollment Services, 248-689-8282 Ext. 215. Fax: 248-524-2520.

Wayne State University, School of Business Administration, Detroit, MI 48202. Offerings include taxation (MS). School faculty: 117. *Application deadline:* 8/1 (4/1 for spring admission). *Application fee:* $20 ($30 for international students). *Expenses:* Tuition $163 per credit hour for state residents; $355 per credit hour for nonresidents. Fees $498 per year full-time, $114 per semester (minimum) part-time. • Dr. Harvey Kahalos, Dean, 313-577-4500. Fax: 313-577-4557. Application contact: Linda S. Zaddach, Assistant Dean, 313-577-4510. Fax: 313-577-5299. E-mail: lzaddach@cms.cc.wayne.edu.

Widener University, School of Business Administration, Program in Taxation, Chester, PA 19013-5792. Awards MS. Part-time and evening/weekend programs available. Faculty: 4 full-time (1 woman), 16 part-time (4 women). Students: 3 full-time, 69 part-time; includes 3 international. 33 applicants, 94% accepted. In 1997, 31 degrees awarded. *Average time to degree:* master's–2 years full-time, 4 years part-time. *Entrance requirements:* Certified Public Accountant Exam or GMAT (minimum score 450). Application deadline: 8/1 (priority date; rolling processing; 12/1 for spring admission). Application fee: $25 ($300 for international students). *Tuition:* $455 per credit. *Financial aid:* Available to part-time students. *Faculty research:* Financial planning, taxation fraud. • Lisa Bussom Jr., Director, Graduate Programs in Business, School of Business Administration, 610-499-4305. Fax: 610-499-4615. E-mail: gradbus.advise@widener.edu.

Cross-Discipline Announcements

Bentley College, Graduate School of Business, Program in Accounting Information Systems, 175 Forest Street, Waltham, MA 02154-4705.

The Bentley College Graduate School of Business offers a Master of Science in Accounting Information Systems (MSAIS) for students with backgrounds in accounting or computer information systems. The program covers information technologies that firms use in their financial and accounting decision-making processes. Included are assurance services and an understanding of electronic commerce and Web-based applications.

Rensselaer Polytechnic Institute, Lally School of Management and Technology, Troy, NY 12180-3590.

The Lally Financial Technology Program offers graduate education in the emerging field of applied finance in that it combines the discipline of finance with information technology, modeling, and entrepreneurship. The emphasis in the program is on application of mathematical and statistical modeling in finance, the impact of information technology on the financial services industry, and the financing of new technological ventures and high-technology firms.

Texas A&M University, College of Science, Department of Mathematics, College Station, TX 77843.

Business/Financial/Industrial Mathematics Option is a nonthesis degree plan that emphasizes essential advanced mathematics for business, finance, and manufacturing. Core courses include probability, optimization, and mathematical modeling as well as essential elements of statistics, computer science, and operations research. Students may choose electives from a group of analytically oriented business, finance, economics, and industrial engineering courses. See in-depth description in Book 4, section 7.

THE GEORGE WASHINGTON UNIVERSITY

School of Business and Public Management
Department of Finance
Master of Science in Finance Program

Program of Study

The School of Business and Public Management (SBPM) offers a Master of Science in Finance (M.S.F.) degree. This intensive program is for individuals with a career focus in finance, and provides advanced education for those with specific career interests in areas of financial management and research. It builds upon a bachelor's or master's degree in business administration, economics, and other quantitative disciplines. The degree emphasizes the theoretical foundations and quantitative methods in financial management. Students will be engaged in applied research and modeling, using a variety of data sets and computer software packages. The international and regulatory dimensions of finance are also explored in depth. Compared to the M.B.A., the M.S.F. provides a broader and deeper exposure to finance with more limited work on general management topics. The M.S.F. is a specialized degree preparing graduates for positions in a wide variety of private and public organizations requiring highly trained finance professionals.

The M.S.F. Program is designed to be completed in twelve months of full-time study, including a summer session, or twenty-four months of part-time study, including two summer sessions. Because the program is designed to accommodate working professionals, classes are conveniently scheduled on Thursday and Friday evenings after 6 p.m. and on Saturdays.

The M.S.F. Program at the George Washington University is regarded in the industry as the quality leader in the field of financial education, enabling students to fully prepare for careers as financial experts.

Research Facilities

A new, spacious computer laboratory, exclusively available to M.S.F. degree candidates, contains extensive database collections and software to support graduate studies. The four gigabytes of data span the full range of financial and economic data, from trade-by-trade option prices to developed and emerging market countries' macroeconomics performance. M.S.F. students have full remote and on-campus access to these databases on the George Washington University's central computers as well as access to other major research collections in the area through the GW consortium. The M.S.F. lab is connected via the Internet to resources around the world. Lab technicians and teaching assistants are available to maintain the lab and assist students with computer assignments.

The University is ideal for research, located next door to the World Bank and International Monetary Fund, and a short walk from the Federal Reserve, the Federal Deposit Insurance Corporation, and the U.S. Treasury Department. Because of the University's location, M.S.F. students have benefited on a regular basis from lectures by leaders in industry and government.

Financial Aid

A select number of graduate scholarships and assistantships are available each year through the program. Awards are merit based and made on the basis of a student's qualifications and academic achievement. Need-based and other loan programs are available to graduate students through the Office of Student Financial Assistance at the University.

Cost of Study

In 1998–99, tuition for the Master of Science in Finance is $655 per credit hour, or $31,440 for the entire program. In addition, students should also budget approximately $2800 annually for books and University fees. A $200 nonrefundable tuition deposit is required upon acceptance.

Living and Housing Costs

On-campus housing is not available to graduate students. Off-campus living expenses near the University are estimated at $920 per month. An excellent public transportation system of subways and buses serves the District of Columbia and the states of Maryland and Virginia. The Foggy Bottom campus is easily accessible by metro.

Student Group

The student body of the M.S.F. Program is a cosmopolitan one and includes students who are graduates from Harvard, Stanford, MIT, Cornell, Columbia, NYU, and the University of Pennsylvania. The 1997 entering class included students from twenty-four countries; students with an average of approximately eight years of work experience; a male-female ratio of 57:43; and 46 percent of the class already holding a master's or Ph.D. degree. All students have very strong quantitative backgrounds. Approximately 25–35 students per section are selected each year.

Student Outcomes

Graduates from the M.S.F. Program are employed by insurance companies, investment houses, international and government agencies, and the banking industry. Some of these companies include the International Finance Corporation, Freddie Mac, Bankers Trust, Signet Banking Corp., Prudential Securities Inc., Money Store, and Citibank.

Location

The nation's capital, with its many cultural and educational offerings, is a great attraction to students. The M.S.F. Program is located at the main campus of the George Washington University in the Foggy Bottom area of Washington's northwest quadrant.

Located at the center of it all, the University is four blocks from the White House and within walking distance to most capital monuments, museums, and theaters.

The University and The School

The George Washington University was created by an Act of Congress in 1821. Today, GW is the largest institution of higher education in the nation's capital. The School of Business and Public Management was established in 1928 and has been accredited by the AACSB–The International Association for Management Education since 1981. The M.S.F. Program, which is part of the School, was established in 1993 and has earned a reputation of producing leaders in the field of finance.

Applying

The program operates on a rolling admission basis; action follows immediately upon the receipt of a completed file. All applicants must furnish original transcripts from their undergraduate and graduate (if applicable) institutions. Scores from the GMAT or other graduate level exams (GRE or LSAT) are also required. International students are required to take the TOEFL exam. In addition, three letters of recommendation and a statement of purpose must be provided. Students should apply as early as possible to identify what prerequisites, if any, are required, and because enrollment is limited. The application fee is $50.

Correspondence and Information

George Jabbour, M.S.F. Program Director
Valeria Bellagamba, M.S.F. Program Associate Director
Master of Science in Finance Program
The George Washington University
School of Business and Public Management
Lisner Hall, Suite 535
2023 G Street, N.W.
Washington, D.C. 20052

Telephone: 202-994-1576
Fax: 202-994-8926
E-mail: msfinan@gwu.edu
World Wide Web: http://www.gwu.edu/~msf

The George Washington University

THE FACULTY AND THEIR RESEARCH

Fred Amling, Professor of Finance; Ph.D., Pennsylvania. Investments, portfolio management, forecasting.
Hossein G. Askari, Professor of International Finance; Ph.D., MIT. International finance, international trade, Islamic finance.
Isabelle G. Bajeux-Besnainou, Associate Professor of Finance; Ph.D., Paris. Investments, portfolio management, derivatives security pricing, continuous time finance.
Theodore Barnhill, Professor of Finance; Ph.D., Michigan. Futures, options, modeling, and risk management.
Neil Cohen, Associate Professor of Finance; D.B.A., Virginia. Corporate financial management, investment/portfolio management, personal financial advising.
Mark J. Eppli, Assistant Professor of Finance; Ph.D., Wisconsin-Madison. Real estate finance, real estate valuation, and capital budgeting.
Theresa A. Gabaldon, Professor of Law; J.D., Harvard. Corporate and securities law, contract law, professional responsibility.
William Handorf, Professor of Finance; Ph.D., Michigan State. Banking and real estate.
George Jabbour, Associate Professor of Finance; Ph.D., George Washington. Investments, options, financial engineering.
James V. Jordan, Professor of Finance; Ph.D., North Carolina at Chapel Hill. Financial markets and institutions, fixed income securities, derivatives.
Frederick L. Joutz, Associate Professor of Economics; Ph.D., Washington (Seattle). Macroeconomics, econometrics, forecasting economic time series.
Mark Klock, Professor of Finance; Ph.D., Boston College; J.D. Maryland. Investment analysis and portfolio management, corporate finance, econometrics, securities regulation.
Yoon S. Park, Professor of International Banking and Finance; D.B.A., Harvard. International banking, international financial markets.
Paul Peyser, Associate Professor of Finance; Ph.D., Wisconsin-Madison. Corporate finance, financial theory, interaction of finance, microeconomics.
Scheherazade S. Rehman, Assistant Professor of International Business and Finance; Ph.D., George Washington. International finance, central banks, European union, central and Eastern Europe.
J. Minor Sachlis, Associate Professor of Finance; D.B.A., Maryland. Business finance, computer modeling of valuation theory, business simulation.
William Seale, Professor of Finance; Ph.D., Kentucky. Corporate finance, derivatives securities, regulatory environment of financial markets.
Keith Smith, Associate Professor of Accountancy; LL.M., Florida. Federal taxation, financial accounting.
Refik Soyer, Professor of Management Science; D.Sc., George Washington. Bayesian statistics, reliability modeling and analysis, quality control, time series analysis, forecasting, decisions analysis.
Arthur Wilson, Assistant Professor of Finance; Ph.D., Chicago. Finance.
William Wilson, Assistant Professor of Finance; Ph.D., Indiana. Socially responsible investments, corporate finance.
Jiawen Yang, Assistant Professor of International Business; Ph.D., NYU. International finance, and international trade theory and policy.

ILLINOIS INSTITUTE OF TECHNOLOGY

Stuart School of Business
Financial Markets and Trading Program

Program of Study

The Stuart School of Business offers an M.S. in financial markets and trading (FM&T). The Ph.D. in management science, with a focus on finance, and a four-course certificate program are also offered. Dual degrees include an M.B.A./M.S. in FM&T and a J.D./M.S. in FM&T offered with IIT's Chicago-Kent College of Law.

The M.S. FM&T program provides the theoretical background, quantitative skills, and practical market knowledge needed to achieve success in today's financial markets and related financial services industries. The program provides an intellectual framework for understanding how financial markets are structured, regulated, and interconnected in the U.S. and globally, along with a practitioner's perspective concerning the economics and mathematics of both traditional and new financial products and their global markets. Faculty members include about 30 academically qualified industry practitioners who share their professional expertise and give students a user-oriented grounding. The program is supported by the latest technology, including real-time data, software currently used in the industry, and a simulated trading environment.

The M.S. curriculum consists of fourteen to eighteen quarter courses, including ten required core courses, four elective courses, and four courses that may be required, depending on knowledge of mathematics or basic accounting. The degree can be completed in as few as five to six quarters, depending on starting date and prerequisite knowledge. Students may take up to six years to complete the program. Courses are offered once a week in the evenings at IIT's Downtown Chicago Campus. Some late afternoon classes are also offered.

Research Facilities

Stuart's Quantitative Research Lab (QRL) provides an interactive computer-based learning environment featuring simulated trading, investment analysis, and industry databases and programs. Popular programs include the FAST Simulation package, the Zero Base Foreign Exchange Market Simulator, and Barra on Campus. The QRL has a number of programs for Monte Carlo simulation, including Crystal Ball and @Risk. The QRL also features real-time and delayed market data feeds from Knight-Ridder and Instinet. The Knight-Ridder feed supports the Aspen Graphics analysis package for charting and price evaluation. Historical data are available from a number of CD-ROM databases, including Knight Ridder, International Financial Statistics, Standard & Poor's, and Investext.

The Downtown Campus Information Center is an open-stack collection of more than 500,000 volumes, including the business holdings of the Stuart Business Library and the Chicago-Kent Law Library. Stuart students have access to IIT's full library system and, using the Illinet Online library catalog, can access materials and books in hundreds of Illinois libraries.

Financial Aid

Partial tuition scholarships of 25 to 50 percent are offered on a merit basis to full-time students. A variety of government-supported loans are available for qualified U.S. residents enrolled in at least two courses per quarter. IIT alumni receive a one-third reduction in tuition in one course per quarter. A tuition installment plan is available and, for students whose employers offer tuition reimbursement, a tuition deferment plan is available.

Cost of Study

Tuition for 1998–99 is $1620 per course.

Living and Housing Costs

Housing is available in apartments at discounted student rates just one block from the campus. Full-time students may also live in apartment housing on IIT's Main Campus. Room and board ranges from $4860 to $6485, depending on occupancy arrangements and meal plans.

Student Group

In 1997, nearly 700 students were enrolled in Stuart School programs. Of these, 30 percent were enrolled in the FM&T program. More than 90 percent of FM&T students are working professionals, with 80 percent already employed in the financial industry. Approximately 25 percent of Stuart students are female, 15 percent are Asian American, 6 percent are African American, 3 percent are Hispanic, and 12 percent are international.

Student Outcomes

Currently, 270 graduates are employed in the financial industry. Recent graduates have obtained positions at AON Advisors, Arthur Andersen Consulting, Central Bank of China, Chicago Board of Trade, Chicago Board Options Exchange, Chicago Mercantile Exchange, Citibank, Dean Witter, Ernst & Young LLP, First Chicago NBD, First Options Corporation, Lehman Brothers, Merrill Lynch, Morgan Stanley, NationsBanc-CRT, New York Stock Exchange, Paine Webber, Reuters, and Republic Bank of New York.

Location

The Stuart School of Business is located in IIT's state-of-the-art Downtown Chicago Campus, just blocks from the major exchanges and Chicago's financial and business center. Stuart's downtown Chicago location makes it easily accessible by public transportation from most locations in the metropolitan area. Chicago offers a rich variety of recreation and culture ranging from professional basketball to the Lyric Opera. The shoreline of Lake Michigan features beaches, parks, and splendid scenery.

The University and The School

Illinois Institute of Technology, established in 1890, is a private university. IIT's Stuart School of Business has focused on unique industry-responsive master's programs. The FM&T program was established in 1992, with the assistance of leaders in Chicago's financial industry, and continues to be guided by an advisory board composed of 40 leaders in Chicago's financial markets. Stuart also offers M.S. degrees in environmental management, operations and technology management, and marketing communication, along with the M.B.A. and Ph.D. in management science.

Applying

Admission to the FM&T program is based on a profile combination of GPA, GMAT or GRE test scores, professional goals, work experience, and letters of recommendation. Applicants from non-English-speaking countries must also submit TOEFL scores. Applications are accepted throughout the year and students may enter the program any quarter. Stuart follows an academic calendar of four quarters, beginning in August, November, February, and May. To ensure full consideration, early submission of applications is encouraged.

Correspondence and Information

Stuart School of Business
Illinois Institute of Technology
565 West Adams Street
Chicago, Illinois 60661

Telephone: 312-906-6506
Fax: 312-906-6511
E-mail: degrees@stuart.iit.edu
World Wide Web: http://www.stuart.iit.edu/fmt

Illinois Institute of Technology

THE FACULTY AND THEIR RESEARCH

John F. O. Bilson, Associate Professor and Program Director; Ph.D., Chicago. Investments, foreign exchange, and capital markets.
James B. Bittman, Adjunct Professor; M.B.A., Harvard. Commodity Options Member, Chicago Board of Trade.
Keith Black, Adjunct Professor; Ph.D. candidate, IIT. Quantitative Analyst, Chicago Investment Analytics.
Thomas A. Bond, Adjunct Professor; M.S., Purdue. Member, Director, Market Maker, and Former Vice Chairman, Chicago Board Options Exchange.
Brian K. Boonstra, Adjunct Professor; Ph.D., Michigan. Mathematical Modeler, the Helios Group, LLC.
Deborah Cernauskas, Adjunct Professor; Ph.D. candidate, IIT. Director, Financial Planning and Analysis, Ameritech.
Edward B. Chez, Adjunct Professor; J.D., Northwestern; M.S., Pennsylvania (Wharton). Managing Partner, Schultz, Chez, and Jesser, CPAs.
Joel C. Gibbons, Senior Lecturer; Ph.D., Chicago; Ph.D., Northwestern. President, Logistic Research and Trading.
Eric Goodbar, Adjunct Professor; M.B.A., Chicago. Executive Vice President, Fund Management Research, New Century Investment Research and Management, Inc.
Lawrence E. Harb, Adjunct Professor; M.M., Northwestern. President and CEO, AON Securities Corporation.
Dennis Lee Heskel, Adjunct Professor; Ph.D., Harvard. Executive Vice President, Refco Portfolio Management.
Timothy F. Hinkes, Adjunct Professor; M.A., DePaul. Vice President and Chief Economist, Options Clearing Corporation.
Samuel D. Kahan, Adjunct Professor; Ph.M., Columbia. President, A.S.K. Financial Research.
Anthony L. Karydakis, Adjunct Professor; Ph.D., Paris IV (Sorbonne). Senior Financial Economist and Director, First Chicago Capital Markets.
Anlong Li, Adjunct Professor, Ph.D.; Case Western Reserve. Vice President, Structured Products, ABN/AMRO.
Steven D. Moffitt, Adjunct Professor; Ph.D., Texas at Houston. President, Dynamic Trading Systems.
Michael Modica, Lecturer; Ph.D., Chicago. Author of four mathematics books, including *Day of the Quants*.
James T. Moser, Adjunct Professor; Ph.D., Ohio State. Senior Director, Financial Product Research, Chicago Mercantile Exchange.
Michael Ong, Adjunct Professor; Ph.D., SUNY at Stony Brook. Senior Vice President, Treasury Business Research, ABN/AMRO, and Chair, Global Risk Management Research Council.
Bjorn Petterson, Adjunct Professor; M.I.M., American Graduate School of International Management. Director, Financial Risk Strategy, KPMG Peat Marwick.
David Quinn, Assistant Professor; Ph.D., Yale. Rational expectation in markets with diverse opinions, the pricing and risk management of derivative securities, the analysis of trader behavior.
John B. Rowsell, Adjunct Professor; Ph.D., Virginia Tech. Director of Research, Carr Asset Management.
Howard L. Simons, Adjunct Professor; M.B.A., Chicago. Director, Quantitative Research, FIMAT USA, Inc.
John Stochetti, Adjunct Professor; M.B.A., Chicago. Senior Vice President, Interest Rate Operations, NationsBank, and Chief Operating Officer, NationsBanc Financial Products.
Ralph Collins Walter III, Adjunct Professor; Ph.D., California Coast. Chief Administrative Officer, ABN/AMRO Chicago Corporation.
Harvey Zabinsky, Adjunct Professor; Ph.D., Rochester. Director, Research Group, First Chicago NBD Corp.

NORTHEASTERN UNIVERSITY

Graduate School of Professional Accounting
M.S. / M.B.A. Program (Joint Degree)

Program of Study

The Graduate School of Professional Accounting offers an unusual fifteen-month joint degree M.S./M.B.A. program in accounting, specifically designed for students with backgrounds in the arts and sciences who are interested in a business career. The program is comprehensive and condensed and includes a paid internship.

The first half of the program (June–December) is directed toward ensuring success during the internship period. From January through March, students are assigned to leading accounting firms as paid interns. During this time, they participate in three to five different audit, tax, and consulting engagements. Students return to school in April; a comprehensive core of M.B.A. courses, including marketing, operations, finance, and strategy, replaces accounting as the main focus, but there are still several accounting courses in the second half. The program is generally completed in September.

The internship enables students uninitiated in business to experience a wide variety of industries, companies of all sizes, and profit and nonprofit entities before making a permanent commitment in any direction. The program is regarded as one of the best executive development tracks by academicians and industry leaders alike.

Research Facilities

A large, technologically sophisticated central library contains extensive print, database, and media collections supporting graduate studies. Graduate students also have access to other major research collections in the area through the Boston Library Consortium. A high-speed data network links users and facilities on the central campus and on three satellite campuses. The campus network is also connected via the global Internet to computing resources around the world. At the University, students have access to Digital VAX systems, labs of microcomputers, a computer mail-and-conferencing system, and an array of specialized computing equipment. The College of Business Administration has its own terminals.

Financial Aid

The three-month internship is paid; students earn an average of $8000–$12,000. In addition, all students are eligible for merit-based scholarships awarded by the program to the top 25 percent of the class each quarter; the awards range from $500 to $1000 per quarter. Northeastern awards need-based financial aid to graduate students through the Federal Perkins Loan, Federal Work-Study, and Federal Stafford Student Loan programs. The University also offers a limited number of minority fellowships and Martin Luther King Jr. Scholarships. The graduate schools offer financial assistance through teaching, research, and administrative assistantship awards that provide partial or full tuition remission and require a maximum of 10 hours of work per week.

Cost of Study

Tuition in the Graduate School of Professional Accounting for the academic year beginning in June 1999 is $7530 per quarter, or $30,120 for the entire program. In addition, there is a nominal fee to cover use of library, computer, and athletic facilities. The application fee is $50, and students are required to pay a $100 tuition deposit upon acceptance.

Living and Housing Costs

On-campus housing is available to newly accepted students; on-campus living expenses for graduate students in the School are estimated at $720 per month. The School offers a small off-campus referral service for students looking for a roommate within the program. Off-campus living expenses are estimated at $800 per month. An excellent public transportation system of subways and buses serves the Greater Boston area and the University. Living expenses are included in determining the need for financial aid.

Student Group

In fall 1997, about 30,000 students were enrolled at Northeastern University, representing a wide variety of academic, professional, geographic, and cultural backgrounds. Each year, the Graduate School of Professional Accounting admits 65–70 students on a full-time basis. The program draws students nationwide, but 80 percent come from prestigious and competitive arts and sciences programs in the Northeast. The majority of the students have little or no professional experience. Almost all join major accounting firms upon graduation. Approximately 95 percent are offered positions as a result of their internships.

Location

The Graduate School of Professional Accounting is located at the main campus of Northeastern University, in the Back Bay section of Boston. Back Bay is notable for its academic life, as the site for eleven colleges and universities; for its cultural life, as the home of several major museums and the Boston Symphony Orchestra; and for its role as the most visible manifestation of inner-city gentrification and redevelopment.

The University and The College

Founded in 1898, Northeastern University is a privately endowed nonsectarian institution of higher learning and one of the largest private universities in the country. Today, Northeastern has nine undergraduate colleges, ten graduate and professional schools, two undergraduate divisions offering part-time study, a number of continuing and special education programs and institutes, several suburban campuses, and an extensive research division.

The College of Business Administration was founded in 1922. The Graduate School of Professional Accounting, which is a part of the College, was established in 1965 and has earned a reputation as the premier educational resource to the accounting profession in New England. The College of Business Administration is fully accredited by the American Assembly of Collegiate Schools of Business.

Applying

The program operates on a rolling admissions basis; action follows immediately upon receipt of a completed file. All applicants must furnish original transcripts from their undergraduate institution, showing ability to succeed in graduate school; three recommendations; and scores on the GMAT. In addition, all applicants must be interviewed by the director and at least one member of the Advisory Council whose firms underwrite the internships. All factors are considered in concert, with no single factor disproportionately weighted. Because of the internship, students with no work experience are encouraged to apply. Applications are due not later than May 1 for the program that begins in June.

Students should apply as early as possible, since enrollment is limited and the program is substantially filled prior to the filing deadline. A select number of applications are accepted on a deferred basis, due primarily to lateness of application or a perceived need for further personal development prior to matriculation.

Correspondence and Information

William I. Kelly, Director
Graduate School of Professional Accounting
412 Dodge Hall
Northeastern University
360 Huntington Avenue
Boston, Massachusetts 02115
Telephone: 617-373-3244

Northeastern University

THE FACULTY

Accounting Group

Paul A. Janell, Professor and Group Coordinator; Ph.D., Michigan State; CPA. Brenda H. Anderson, Assistant Professor; Ph.D., Massachusetts at Amherst. Jean C. Bedard, Associate Professor; Ph.D., Wisconsin–Madison; CPA. Sharon M. Bruns, Professor; Ph.D., Georgia State. Michael D. Cottrill, Lecturer; M.Acc., Virginia Tech; CPA. Hugh J. Crossland, Lecturer; LL.M., Yale, Boston University. Amitabh Dugar, Assistant Professor; Ph.D., Northwestern. Julie H. Hertenstein, Associate Professor; D.B.A., Harvard. James J. Maroney, Assistant Professor; Ph.D., Connecticut. Lynn W. Marples, Lecturer; M.B.A., Stanford. Peggy O'Kelly, Lecturer; M.B.A., Michigan. Thomas C. Omer, Associate Professor; Ph.D., Iowa. Marjorie Platt, Associate Professor; Ph.D., Michigan. Timothy J. Rupert, Assistant Professor; Ph.D., Penn State. Marjorie K. Shelley, Assistant Professor; Ph.D., Texas at Austin. H. David Sherman, Professor; D.B.A., Harvard. Ira R. Weiss, Professor and Dean; Ph.D., UCLA; CPA, CISA.

Finance and Insurance Group

Joseph W. Meador, Professor and Group Coordinator; Ph.D., Pennsylvania (Wharton). Alan D. Alford, Assistant Professor; Ph.D., South Carolina. Paul J. Bolster, Associate Professor; Ph.D., Virginia Tech. Jeffery A. Born, Associate Professor; Ph.D., North Carolina. Peggy L. Fletcher, Lecturer, Ph.D. candidate, Pittsburgh. Milton L. Glass, Adjunct Professor and Executive-in-Residence; M.B.A., Northeastern. Richard J. Goettle IV, Lecturer; Ph.D., Cincinnati. Vahan Jangigian, Assistant Professor; Ph.D., Virginia Tech. Mark Kazarosian, Assistant Professor; Ph.D., Boston College. Steven R. Kursh, Visiting Assistant Professor; Ph.D., Pennsylvania. Donald G. Margotta, Associate Professor; Ph.D., North Carolina at Chapel Hill. Wesley W. Marple Jr., Professor; D.B.A., Harvard. Robert M. Mooradian, Assistant Professor; Ph.D., Pennsylvania. Coleen C. Pantalone, Associate Professor and Associate Dean; Ph.D., Iowa State. Harlan D. Platt, Professor; Ph.D., Michigan. Don R. Rich, Assistant Professor; Ph.D., Virginia Tech. Harley E. Ryan Jr., Assistant Professor; Ph.D., Georgia State. Carolin Schellhorn, Assistant Professor; Ph.D., Texas at Austin. Emery A. Trahan, Associate Professor; Ph.D., SUNY at Albany; CPA. Shiawee X. Yang, Assistant Professor; Ph.D., Penn State.

General Management Group

James F. Molloy Jr., Associate Professor and Group Coordinator; Ph.D., MIT. Nicholas Athanassiou, Assistant Professor; Ph.D., South Carolina. Roger M. Atherton Jr., Professor and Senior Associate Dean; Ph.D., Michigan. Charles D. Baker, Professor; M.B.A., Harvard. Stanley R. Berkowitz, Lecturer; J.D., Boston College. James S. Cook, Lecturer and Executive-In-Residence; A.B., Brown. Mary F. Costello, Lecturer; J.D., Boston College. William F. Crittenden, Associate Professor and Associate Dean; Ph.D., Arkansas. Robert L. Goldberg, Lecturer; M.B.A., Boston University. Raymond M. Kinnunen, Associate Professor; D.B.A., LSU. Robert C. Lieb, Professor; D.B.A., Maryland. Daniel J. McCarthy, Professor; D.B.A., Harvard. Marc H. Meyer, Associate Professor; Ph.D., MIT. Carl W. Nelson, Associate Professor; Ph.D., Manchester (England). Richard P. Olsen, Lecturer; D.B.A., Harvard. Ravi Ramamurti, Associate Professor; D.B.A., Harvard. Ravi Sarathy, Professor; Ph.D., Michigan. Ronald Thomas, Lecturer; Ph.D., Harvard. Heidi Vernon-Wortzel, Professor; Ph.D., Boston University.

Human Resources Group

Brendan D. Bannister, Associate Professor and Group Coordinator; D.B.A., Kent State. Rae Andre, Professor; Ph.D., Michigan. Thomas M. Begley, Associate Professor; Ph.D., Cornell. David P. Boyd, Professor; D.Phil., Oxford. Leonard J. Glick, Lecturer; Ed.D., Harvard. Kim R. Kanaga, Lecturer; Ph.D., Pennsylvania. Ralph Katz, Professor; Ph.D., Pennsylvania (Wharton). Cynthia Lee, Associate Professor; Ph.D., Maryland. Edward F. McDonough III, Associate Professor, Ph.D., Massachusetts at Amherst. Sheila M. Puffer, Associate Professor; Ph.D., Berkeley. Bert A. Spector, Associate Professor, Ph.D., Missouri. Francis C. Spital, Associate Professor; Ph.D., MIT. Judith Y. Weisinger, Assistant Professor; Ph.D., Case Western Reserve.

Management Science Group

Michael J. Maggard, Professor and Group Coordinator; Ph.D., UCLA. R. Balachandra, Associate Professor; Ph.D., Columbia. Richard J. Briotta, Lecturer; D.B.A., Boston University. Sangit Chatterjee, Professor; Ph.D., NYU. Kathleen Foley Curley, Associate Professor; D.B.A., Harvard. Victor B. Godin, Associate Professor; D.B.A., Harvard. Robert A. Millen, Professor; Ph.D., UCLA. Robert A. Parsons, Associate Professor; M.B.A., Northeastern. Marius M. Solomon, Associate Professor, Ph.D., Pennsylvania. Eileen M. Trauth, Associate Professor, Ph.D., Pittsburgh. Merrill E. Warkentin, Associate Professor; Ph.D., Nebraska–Lincoln. Mustafa R. Yilmaz, Associate Professor, Ph.D., Johns Hopkins. Michael Zack, Assistant Professor; D.B.A., Harvard.

Marketing Group

Robert F. Young, Associate Professor and Group Coordinator; D.B.A., Harvard. Gloria Barczak, Assistant Professor; Ph.D., Syracuse. Bruce H. Clark, Assistant Professor; Ph.D., Stanford. Dan T. Dunn Jr., Associate Professor; D.B.A., Virginia. Samuel Rabino, Professor; Ph.D., NYU. E. Craig Stacey, Assistant Professor; Ph.D., Alabama. Fareena Sultan, Associate Professor; Ph.D., Columbia. Frederick Wiseman, Professor; Ph.D., Cornell.

UNIVERSITY OF DENVER

Graduate Tax Program

Program of Study

The Graduate Tax Program prepares students for entry into professional tax practice in both the public and private sectors. The interdisciplinary nature of the program fosters a knowledge of the accounting aspects of tax practice in the law graduate and an understanding of the legal process in the accounting graduate. Graduates of accredited law schools who successfully complete the program receive the Master of Laws in Taxation (LL.M.) degree; all other candidates receive the Master of Taxation degree (M.T.).

Research Facilities

The Graduate Tax Program is located in the Lowell Thomas Law Building on the 33-acre Law Center campus. The Law Center houses exceptional classroom, library, and student facilities that are configured to provide state-of-the-art information processing and computer research technology for faculty members, students, and practitioners. The entire Law Center complex is designed to utilize existing and future high-technology systems for voice, data, and audiovisual communications. The 55,000-square-foot Westminster Law Library consists of two levels with a capacity for up to 300,000 volumes and seating for 543 patrons. The library's collection comprises more than 196,000 volumes, including some 6,700 volumes on taxation in the United States and abroad. In addition to traditional library services, the library offers WESTLAW, LEXIS, CCH-ACCESS, and other computer research services. It also contains a state-of-the-art computer lab, with Internet and World Wide Web access available to students.

Financial Aid

Admission decisions are made without regard to financial need. Financial aid is available upon completion of the first quarter of study to any qualified student with demonstrated academic ability and financial need. Aid takes the form of the Boetcher Scholarship Fund, the Schramm Foundation Scholarship, the Debra Schliem Cameron/Lehman Butterwick Scholarship Fund, and student loans. Interested students should make application to the Director of the Graduate Tax Program and submit this statement with their application materials.

In addition to aid available from the program, subsidized and unsubsidized Federal Stafford Student Loans, subsidized and unsubsidized Stafford/Ford Federal Direct Loans, and Federal Work-Study programs are administered by the Office of Financial Aid. All questions regarding these programs should be directed to the address listed below.

Cost of Study

Tuition for the 1998–99 academic year is $418 per quarter hour. Tuition increases are normally effective beginning with the fall quarter of each year and accrue at the rate of approximately 4 percent per year.

Living and Housing Costs

The facilities at the Law Center include residence halls and apartments for students. Any student interested in living in an on-campus residence hall should contact the DU/CWC Conference Office, #214 Foote Hall, 7150 Montview Boulevard, Denver, Colorado 80220 (telephone: 303-871-6830). For those students not interested in University housing, suitable housing can generally be found close to the Law Center campus after the student arrives in Denver.

Student Group

In fall 1997, 175 students were enrolled in the Graduate Tax Program. Approximately 35 percent were women and 65 percent were men. The number of students attending on a full- or part-time basis is about equal.

Student Outcomes

The Graduate Tax Program has distinguished itself in the Arthur Andersen Tax Challenge, a national competition to determine the best undergraduate/graduate team in federal tax knowledge. Over the last six years, the Graduate Tax Program has won three national championships and two silver medals.

Every Big Six accounting firm and many other national, regional, and local firms interview applicants on campus each year. The national firms are represented by their national or regional partners in charge of recruiting tax personnel. In addition, an extensive informal placement procedure is available for those students with more specialized interests. In recent years, virtually every recipient of an LL.M. or M.T. degree has secured employment as a tax professional within six months of graduation.

Location

Colorado is one of the most beautiful states in the country; Denver, the gateway to the Rocky Mountains, is one of the country's most dynamic metropolitan cities. Denver is the capital of the state, the industrial and manufacturing center of the region, and the site of the headquarters of a large number of major businesses, many of which are associated with energy development and high technology. Although Colorado is famous for its winter recreational activities, the city of Denver is located east of a high mountain barrier in a precipitation shield that makes it almost a desert. The city receives only 15 inches of precipitation a year, and the sun shines an average of 70 percent of the time; Denver logs more annual hours of sunshine than San Diego or Miami Beach. A true four-season haven for the sports-minded, Colorado's advantages include what some consider to be the world's finest skiing, mountaineering, fishing, and camping. Sites for many of these activities are located within a 1- to 2-hour drive of Denver and include such world-famous resorts as Vail, Aspen, and Steamboat.

The University

The University of Denver is an accredited, independent, coeducational institution of national reputation. Founded in 1864 by John Evans (second Governor of the Colorado Territory and founder of Northwestern University) and other pioneer citizens, the University was originally chartered as Colorado Seminary by an act of the territory. The seminary was reorganized in 1880, with the University of Denver established as the degree-granting body and Colorado Seminary as the property-holding corporation.

Applying

Since the number of applications received by the program exceeds the number of students admitted, the Admissions Committee only admits those students whose previous academic performance and/or work experience indicate a desire and an ability to excel. While test scores and records of academic performance are evaluated individually, the applicant's personal qualifications and accomplishments are of equal consideration in the application process. Admission to the Graduate Tax Program requires either the J.D. degree or its equivalent from a college of law approved by the American Bar Association or a baccalaureate degree from an accredited university and a satisfactory score on the Graduate Management Admission Test (GMAT). The GPAs and GMAT scores of applicants with baccalaureate degrees are indexed as follows during the application process: 2 x GPA + GMAT = scoring index. A minimum scoring index of 1050 is required for admission to the Graduate Tax Program. The baccalaureate program must satisfy the requirements of the common body of knowledge for undergraduate business education, as currently defined by AACSB–The International Association for Management Education. Master of Taxation candidates admitted without having satisfied this requirement are required to make up any deficiencies before graduation. To be considered for admission to the Graduate Tax Program, all applicants must submit an application for admission; official transcripts of all college credits, both undergraduate and graduate, which must be sent directly by the registrar from the college or university where the credit was earned; and GMAT scores (or LSAT scores if they are not recorded on a law school transcript). A $25 application charge is assessed if the applicant has never been registered at the University of Denver as a degree candidate and must be remitted in the form of a check or money order that accompanies the application. The University of Denver operates on the quarter system. The Graduate Tax Program follows a rolling admissions system, and applications are received and reviewed throughout the year. Applications should be completed at least two weeks prior to the expected date of registration.

Correspondence and Information

Graduate Tax Program
University of Denver
1900 Olive Street #F-102
Denver, Colorado 80220

Telephone: 303-871-6239
Fax: 303-871-6358
E-mail: rricker@du.edu
World Wide Web: http://www.law.du.edu/gtp

University of Denver

THE FACULTY

Full-Time Faculty Members

Jerome Borison, Associate Professor of Law; LL.M., NYU, 1982; CPA.
Richard S. Leaman, Assistant Professor of Accounting; M.B.A., Stanford, 1978; J.D., Chicago, 1979; CPA.
Rex Logemann, Visiting Professor of Taxation; LL.M., NYU, 1979; LL.M., Denver, 1996.
Kevin O'Brien, Associate Professor of Accounting; LL.M., NYU, 1980; CPA.
Edward J. Roche Jr., Professor of Law; J.D., Chicago, 1976; CPA.
Robert B. Smith, Associate Professor of Law; LL.M., Florida, 1987.
John C. Tripp, Professor of Accounting; M.S.B.A., 1975, M.T., 1976, Denver; Ph.D., Houston, 1980.
Mark A. Vogel, Associate Professor of Taxation and Director, Graduate Program in Taxation; LL.M., Denver, 1976; CPA.

Part-Time Faculty Members

Frederic Bender, Adjunct Professor of Taxation; J.D., Boston University, 1968.
Rick Budd, Adjunct Professor of Taxation; LL.M., Denver, 1978.
Richard D. D'Estrada, Adjunct Professor of Taxation; J.D., Marquette, 1971.
William T. Diss, Adjunct Professor of Law; J.D., Denver, 1959; CPA.
Stephen W. Forbes, Adjunct Professor of Taxation; LL.M., George Washington, 1987.
Theodore Z. Gelt, Adjunct Professor of Taxation; LL.M., NYU, 1976.
Mark A. Kozik, Adjunct Professor of Taxation; LL.M., Miami (Florida), 1981.
David L. Lockwood, Adjunct Professor of Taxation; LL.M., NYU, 1978.
Richard B. Robinson, Adjunct Professor of Taxation; LL.M., NYU, 1975.
Gordon E. Schieman, Adjunct Professor of Taxation; LL.M., Denver, 1979.
Sheldon H. Smith, Adjunct Professor of Taxation; LL.M., Denver, 1980.
Joseph H. Thibodeau, Adjunct Professor of Taxation; J.D., Detroit, 1966.
Sal L. Tripodi, Adjunct Professor of Taxation; LL.M., Georgetown, 1983.

UNIVERSITY OF ILLINOIS AT URBANA-CHAMPAIGN

College of Commerce and Business Administration
Department of Accountancy
The Executive Development Center

Program of Study

The Master of Science in Accountancy (M.S.A.) is an intensive twelve-month graduate degree program combined with an extensive executive education program. The program is designed to meet the professional accounting career development needs of individuals engaged in international business. Core courses include financial, managerial, and tax accounting and auditing. Faculty advisers also work with each student to identify courses that meet his or her special needs and interests. The M.S.A. provides the academic prerequisites for candidates who wish to take the United States Uniform Certified Public Accountant (CPA) examination.

The executive education portion of the M.S.A. includes visits to major accounting firms in Chicago and, during the week of spring break, in New York City. The Executive-In-Residence Program provides numerous opportunities throughout the fall and spring semesters for students to interact with high-level executives from major corporations. Ranked by *U.S. News & World Report* as the number one accountancy department in the United States, the Department of Accountancy enjoys close and long-standing relationships with the major U.S. accounting firms.

Research Facilities

The University of Illinois at Urbana-Champaign (UIUC) is rich in research possibilities. UIUC is one of the premier public research institutions in the United States. The world-class library, with more than 15 million items, is the third-largest library in the United States and the seventh-largest in the world and a leader in the evolving field of information technology. Research conducted at UIUC has resulted in 10 Nobel Prize winners. UIUC is home to one of two National Centers for Supercomputing Applications (NCSA). Funded on an ongoing basis by the National Science Foundation, NCSA seeks to forge partnerships between universities and industries through the use of computers.

Financial Aid

There are no fee or tuition waivers or other financial aid available for the M.S.A. program. The majority of students are sponsored either by the companies for which they work or by their governments. Others are self-sponsored.

Cost of Study

Tuition and fees for the M.S.A. program are currently $22,982 for the twelve-month program. If a student needs more than twelve months to complete the degree, additional tuition and fees are charged for each additional summer or semester. Books cost approximately $1000.

Living and Housing Costs

The estimated living expenses for a single individual for the twelve-month period are $12,120. Dependents are estimated to cost an additional $300 per month for a spouse and $240 per month per child. Purchase of health insurance for dependents costs $1134 per year for a spouse and $567 annually for each child. A contingency fund of $1000–$1500 is strongly recommended.

Student Group

The majority of M.S.A. students are already established in their careers and have experience in some aspect of accounting, taxation, or auditing. Of the current class, 79 percent are company sponsored and 21 percent are self sponsored. Men comprise 61 percent of the class. The average age is 28. The majority of students come from Asia (61 percent), while 32 percent are from the Middle East and 7 percent are from Europe and Latin America.

Student Outcomes

M.S.A. graduates have had notable success in passing the CPA exam as well as the Certified Management Accountant exam and the Certified Internal Auditor exam. While most of the students return to the companies and governments that sponsored them, the larger international firms show interest in M.S.A. graduates as well.

Location

The University is situated in the heart of the United States in east-central Illinois. Secure in the Midwest, UIUC is surrounded by some of the world's richest farmland. The communities of Urbana-Champaign, with a combined population of about 100,000, are home to the University and its students. The two cities offer a variety of cultural and recreational opportunities. Chicago is a 2½ hour drive north, while St. Louis and Indianapolis can be reached within 3 and 2 hours, respectively.

The University and The Department

The UIUC Department of Accountancy is ranked number one in the U.S. The UIUC business school is ranked fifth by *U.S. News & World Report*. The engineering school, ranked second in the nation, contains the departments of civil engineering (ranked first in the U.S.) and environmental, electrical, and materials engineering (all ranked second in the U.S.). Overall, the National Research Council placed UIUC among the nation's top twenty universities that grant doctoral degrees.

Applying

The M.S.A. program begins in June or August each year. Applicants who have previously taken Principles of Accounting and Intermediate Financial Accounting or their equivalent may enter in the fall. Those with no accounting background must enter in June. Applications for June must be received no later than March 15, while August applications have a June 15 deadline. University requirements state that international students must have a TOEFL score of 550 or better. No GMAT score is required for entry into the program. Applicants must submit three letters of recommendation and a financial document proving amount and duration of funding to cover the cost of study. Applicants must hold a degree equivalent to a U.S. bachelor's degree from an accredited university.

Correspondence and Information

Master of Science in Accountancy
University of Illinois at Urbana-Champaign
1407 West Gregory Drive, Room 205
Urbana, Illinois 61801

Telephone: 217-333-2571
Fax: 217-244-8537
E-mail: edc@uiuc.edu
World Wide Web: http://www.cba.uiuc.edu/edc

University of Illinois at Urbana-Champaign

THE FACULTY AND THEIR RESEARCH

Department of Accountancy

Andrew D. Bailey Jr., Professor; Ph.D., Ohio State, 1971. Auditing.
Paul Beck, Professor; Ph.D., Texas, 1977. Auditing, tax.
Clifton E. Brown, Professor; Ph.D., Florida, 1978. Behavioral, cost, and managerial accounting.
John S. Chandler, Associate Professor; Ph.D., Ohio State, 1977. Management information and control systems.
John Davis, Associate Professor; Ph.D., Arizona, 1987. Tax accounting.
J. Richard Dietrich, Professor; Ph.D., Carnegie-Mellon, 1981. Financial reporting issues.
Thomas Finnegan, Visiting Assistant Professor; Ph.D., Illinois at Urbana-Champaign, 1993. Financial and managerial accounting.
Robert Halperin, Visiting Professor; Ph.D., Pennsylvania, 1977. Financial and tax accounting.
Van Johnson, Visiting Associate Professor; Ph.D., Arizona State, 1992. Auditing.
Karen Hrcha Molloy, Associate Professor; Ph.D., Virginia Tech, 1980. Tax research, estate planning, effective corporate tax rates.
Frederick L. Neumann, Professor; Ph.D., Chicago, 1967. Auditing, education, ethics.
Sridhar Ramamoorti, Visiting Assistant Professor; Ph.D., Ohio State, 1995. Human judgment/reasoning processes, expert and decision support systems, internal auditing, international accounting.
Peter Silhan, Associate Professor; D.B.A., Tennessee, 1980. Managerial and systems accounting.
Ira Solomon, Professor; Ph.D., Texas at Austin, 1979. Attestation and auditing.
Theodore Sougiannis, Assistant Professor; Ph.D., Berkeley, 1990. Financial accounting, stock market valuations.
Thomas J. Sternburg, Lecturer; Ph.D., Arizona State, 1993. Tax accounting.
Dan N. Stone, Associate Professor; Ph.D., Texas, 1987. Accounting systems design, decision making, information systems.
Eugene Willis, Professor and Head; Ph.D., Cincinnati, 1975. Federal taxation accounting, taxpayer compliance.
Arthur Wyatt, Adjunct Professor; Ph.D., Illinois at Urbana-Champaign, 1953. Financial accounting.
David Ziebart, Associate Professor; Ph.D., Michigan State, 1983. Not-for-profit and financial accounting, principles of accounting.
Richard E. Ziegler, Associate Professor; Ph.D., North Carolina, 1973. Auditing, financial accounting.

UNIVERSITY OF ILLINOIS AT URBANA-CHAMPAIGN

College of Commerce and Business Administration
Department of Finance
The Executive Development Center

Program of Study

The Master of Science in Finance (M.S.F.) is an intensive twelve-month graduate degree program combined with an extensive executive education program. The program is designed to address the needs of experienced financial professionals who work with financial assets in the constantly changing global economy and who wish to acquire a more in-depth understanding of financial markets and the financial function of firms. Some of the courses included in the program are financial management, corporate finance, investments, banking, economic theory, and quantitative methods. Students may take two electives in the area of their choice. The most popular electives have been courses related to financial derivatives.

The executive education portion of the M.S.F. includes visits to a variety of corporations and financial institutions in Chicago, St. Louis, and, during the week of spring break, New York City. The Executive-In-Residence Program provides numerous opportunities throughout the fall and spring semesters for students to interact with high-level executives from major corporations.

Research Facilities

The University of Illinois at Urbana-Champaign (UIUC) is rich in research possibilities. UIUC is one of the premier public research institutions in the United States. The world-class library, with more than 15 million items, is the third-largest library in the United States and the seventh-largest in the world and a leader in the evolving field of information technology. Research conducted at UIUC has resulted in ten Nobel Prize winners. UIUC is home to one of two National Centers for Supercomputing Applications (NCSA). Funded on an ongoing basis by the National Science Foundation, NCSA seeks to forge partnerships between universities and industries through the use of computers.

Financial Aid

There are no fee or tuition waivers or other financial aid available for the M.S.F. program. Currently, most M.S.F. students are sponsored by the companies for which they work or by their governments. Self-sponsored students are also admitted.

Cost of Study

Tuition and fees for the M.S.F. program are currently $23,000 for the three-semester, twelve-month program. If a student needs more than twelve months to complete the degree, additional tuition and fees are charged for each additional summer or semester. Books cost approximately $1000.

Living and Housing Costs

The estimated living expenses for a single individual for the twelve-month period are $12,120. Dependents are estimated to cost an additional $300 per month for a spouse and $240 per month per child. Purchase of health insurance for dependents costs $1134 a year for a spouse and $567 annually for each child. A contingency fund of $1000–$1500 is strongly recommended.

Student Group

The majority of M.S.F. students are already well established in their careers, with an average of six years' work experience. The average age is 30. Women comprise one third of the current M.S.F. class. Most are sponsored by their companies or their governments. The majority of students come from Asia, with others from the Middle East, Mexico, and Europe.

Student Outcomes

Upon completion of the M.S.F. program, most students return to their companies to continue their careers. Some immediately advance to positions of greater responsibility.

Location

The University is situated in the heart of the United States in east-central Illinois. Secure in the Midwest, UIUC is surrounded by some of the world's richest farmland. The communities of Urbana-Champaign, with a combined population of about 100,000, are home to the University and its students. The two cities offer a variety of cultural and recreational opportunities. Chicago is a 2½ hour drive north, while St. Louis and Indianapolis can be reached within 3 and 2 hours, respectively.

The University

The UIUC business school was ranked fifth by *U.S. News & World Report*. The engineering school, ranked second in the nation, contains the departments of civil engineering (ranked first in the U.S.) and environmental, electrical, and materials engineering (all ranked second in the U.S.). Overall, the National Research Council placed UIUC among the nation's top twenty universities that grant doctoral degrees.

Applying

The M.S.F. program begins in June of each year. The admission process begins in January, and applications are reviewed upon receipt. It is recommended that applications be sent no later than mid-March. University requirements state that international students must have a TOEFL score of 550 or better. No GMAT score is required for entry into the program. Five years' working experience is preferred, but a minimum of two years is required. The application requires three letters of recommendation and a financial document proving amount and duration of funding to cover the cost of study. Applicants must hold a degree equivalent to a U.S. bachelor's degree from an accredited university.

Correspondence and Information

Master of Science in Finance
University of Illinois at Urbana-Champaign
1407 West Gregory Drive, Room 205
Urbana, Illinois 61801
Telephone: 217-333-2571
Fax: 217-244-8537
E-mail: edc@uiuc.edu
World Wide Web: http://www.cba.uiuc.edu/edc

University of Illinois at Urbana-Champaign

THE FACULTY AND THEIR RESEARCH

Department of Finance

Andres Almazan, Assistant Professor; Ph.D., MIT, 1996. Corporate finance and contract theory.
Roger E. Cannaday, Associate Professor; Ph.D., South Carolina, 1980. Real estate.
Louis K. C. Chan, Associate Professor; Ph.D., Rochester, 1984. Investments, international investment and international finance.
Peter F. Colwell, Professor; Ph.D., Wayne State, 1973. Real estate and urban land economics.
Stephen P. D'Arcy, Professor; Ph.D., Illinois, 1982. Insurance and risk management.
Joseph E. Finnerty, Professor; Ph.D., Michigan, 1974. Investments, corporate finance.
Virginia France, Associate Professor; Ph.D., Chicago, 1986. Portfolio management and derivative financial regulation.
James A. Gentry, Professor; D.B.A., Indiana, 1966. Corporate financial management.
Charles J. Hadlock, Assistant Professor; Ph.D., MIT, 1994. Corporate finance.
Josef Lakonishok, Professor; Ph.D., Cornell, 1976. Investments, mergers, acquisitions.
Narasimhan Jegadeesh, Professor; Ph.D., Columbia, 1987. Portfolio management.
Charles Kahn, Professor; Ph.D., Harvard, 1981. Economics of information and uncertainty.
Charles M. Linke, Professor; D.B.A., Indiana, 1966. Business finance and investments.
Morgan J. Lynge, Professor and Chair; Ph.D., Michigan, 1975. Credit and financial markets, management of financial institutions, corporate finance.
Hun Park, Associate Professor; Ph.D., Ohio State, 1982. Speculative markets and investments.
Neil D. Pearson, Associate Professor; Ph.D., MIT, 1990. Speculative markets and investments.
George G. Pennacchi, Associate Professor; Ph.D., MIT, 1984. Financial institutions.
David T. Whitford, Associate Professor; Ph.D., Georgia State, 1980. Corporate finance and investments.

VIRGINIA POLYTECHNIC INSTITUTE AND STATE UNIVERSITY

Department of Accounting

Programs of Study

The Department of Accounting offers graduate programs leading to the Master of Accountancy and Doctor of Philosophy degrees. The Master of Accountancy program is open to qualified students with a bachelor's degree in any discipline. Students without prior collegiate studies in accounting and business administration should expect to spend at least two years in the program. For those who have fulfilled the background requirements, the program consists of 30 semester hours (ten courses) and is usually completed in about fifteen months. All master's students must take courses in accounting theory, advanced managerial accounting, and management of information systems. The remaining courses are dependent upon whether the student selects the professional accounting, accounting information systems, or tax accounting option. Students choosing the professional accounting option take classes in tax impact on management decisions, auditing theory, multinational accounting, and either advanced auditing practice or information systems development, as well as two non-accounting electives and a free elective. Students choosing the option in accounting information systems take advanced database management systems, information systems development, information center functions, and applied software development classes, as well as two non-accounting electives and a free elective. Students choosing the tax accounting option take classes in tax planning and research, tax concepts, partnership/corporate tax, advanced corporate tax, and family tax planning, as well as two non-accounting electives. Students with background deficiencies may use two of the 5000-level background business courses to meet the non-accounting electives course requirements.

The Ph.D. program in accounting at Virginia Tech provides advanced graduate studies as preparation for a career in university teaching and research. The program's basic requirements call for course work in accounting and statistics, courses related to a student's primary research area, and a supporting minor. The remainder of the student's time is devoted to the dissertation. There is no foreign language requirement.

Research Facilities

The Department of Accounting is housed in Pamplin Hall, a modern building located near the center of the campus. Graduate students have access to the University Computing Center, one of the largest in the United States. The center houses an IBM 3090 mainframe computer with 64 megabytes of memory used for VM/CMS, an IBM 3084 with 64 megabytes of memory used for MVS/IMS and VM/CMS, an IBM 4341, and three DEC VAX-11/780s and a VAX-11/785 with 8 megabytes of memory each. A wide variety of software is used in course work, including various programming, statistical, and generalized audit software as well as simulation and database management system packages. Various research databases, such as the Compustat and CRSP files, are also accessible. Three computer laboratories containing twenty IBM Personal Computers each are available for classroom and student use in the Pamplin College of Business. In addition, the Department of Accounting has its own personal-computer laboratory available for faculty and graduate students.

The Carol M. Newman Library contains more than 1.7 million volumes, 4 million microforms, special collections, an online catalog system, and 18,000 periodicals, including in-depth holdings in accounting and other business fields. It also offers access to major online databases.

Financial Aid

The department offers graduate assistantships that carry stipends of $525 to $1240 per month in 1998–99. The stipend permits the student to carry 12 hours of course work. Additional grants and scholarships are awarded by the department, including fellowships from industrial and public accounting firms and Virginia state scholarships. A limited number of instructorships are available for doctoral students. Financial support is awarded on the basis of the applicant's grade record, GMAT scores, and letters of recommendation. Job opportunities for students' spouses are available in the community.

Cost of Study

Student fees in 1998–99 are $2463.50 per semester. Out-of-state graduate students who do not have an assistantship are required to pay an additional $1305 tuition fee per semester. Book costs average $500 per year.

Living and Housing Costs

A wide variety of housing for graduate students is available at reasonable cost in Blacksburg and the surrounding area. In general, the cost of living in Blacksburg is less than the national average. Limited on-campus housing is also available.

Student Group

Currently, there are approximately 22,500 students enrolled at VPI&SU, of whom 4,000 are graduate students and 9,000 are women. Virginia Tech offers master's programs in eighty-one areas and doctoral work in seventy-four fields. There are approximately 75 students in the Master of Accountancy program and 12 students in the doctoral program in accounting.

Location

Virginia Tech is located in Blacksburg, Virginia, a rapidly growing town with a population of almost 30,000. The campus is nestled on a plain in the Appalachians, 2,100 feet above sea level. The area around Blacksburg offers numerous recreational opportunities for those who like such outdoor activities as hiking, fishing, boating, camping, sightseeing, and mountain climbing.

The University

Virginia Polytechnic Institute and State University, Virginia's land-grant university, has grown since its founding in 1872 into the largest university in the state. Its recent history is one of rapid, well-planned growth in size and quality of programs. The programs of the College of Business, of which the Department of Accounting is an integral part, are fully accredited by AACSB–The International Association for Management Education. In addition, both the undergraduate and master's degree programs in accounting have separate AACSB accounting accreditation.

The University provides a large variety of activities, ranging from the University Theater, glee club, orchestra, and Lecture-Concert Series to football, basketball, and baseball. An extensive visiting-scholar program brings many outstanding people to the campus.

Applying

Applications for admission to the Master of Accountancy program and the doctoral program in accounting can be made at any time. Applications for financial aid should be submitted prior to April 1. Application materials should be obtained from the dean of the Graduate School. The Graduate Management Admission Test (GMAT) is required for admission to the graduate programs in accounting.

Correspondence and Information

Master's and Ph.D. Committee
Department of Accounting
3007 Pamplin Hall (0101)
Pamplin College of Business
Virginia Polytechnic Institute and State University
Blacksburg, Virginia 24061
Telephone: 540-231-6591

Virginia Polytechnic Institute and State University

THE FACULTY AND THEIR RESEARCH

John C. Anderson, Ph.D., Tennessee, 1987. Information systems.
Reza Barkhi, Ph.D., Ohio State, 1995. Information systems.
Floyd A. Beams, Ph.D., Illinois at Urbana-Champaign, 1968. Financial accounting, accounting theory, governmental accounting.
France Belanger, Ph.D., South Florida, 1997. Information systems.
Robert M. Brown, Ph.D., Georgia State, 1977. Information systems, managerial accounting.
John A. Brozovsky, Ph.D., Colorado, 1990. Financial accounting, managerial accounting.
Debra S. Callihan, Ph.D., South Carolina, 1993. Income tax.
Cintia M. Easterwood, Ph.D., Houston, 1992. Financial accounting, auditing.
Christine M. Haynes, Ph.D., Texas, 1992. Managerial accounting.
James O. Hicks Jr., Ph.D., Georgia State, 1976. Information systems, managerial accounting.
Sam A. Hicks, Ph.D., Wisconsin, 1976. Income tax, information systems.
Larry N. Killough, Ph.D., Missouri–Columbia, 1969. Managerial accounting.
Konrad W. Kubin, Ph.D., Washington (Seattle), 1972. Auditing, international accounting, financial accounting.
Wayne E. Leininger, Ph.D., Massachusetts Amherst, 1971. Managerial accounting.
D. Jordan Lowe, Ph.D., Arizona, 1992. Auditing.
John J. Maher, Ph.D., Penn State, 1985. Information systems, financial accounting.
Kimberly K. Moreno, Ph.D., Massachusetts Amherst, 1998. Financial accounting.
Ernest J. Pavlock, Ph.D., Michigan, 1965. Financial accounting, management control, auditing.
Frederick M. Richardson, Ph.D., North Carolina, 1980. Financial accounting, accounting theory.
W. Eugene Seago, J.D., Ph.D., Georgia, 1970. Income tax.
Tarun K. Sen, Ph.D., Iowa, 1985. Information systems.
Steven D. Sheetz, Ph.D., Colorado, 1996. Information systems.
Craig D. Shoulders, Ph.D., Texas Tech, 1982. Governmental accounting, financial accounting.
David P. Tegarden, Ph.D., Colorado, 1991. Information systems.
Valaria P. Vendrzyk, Ph.D., Texas A&M, 1993. Financial accounting, managerial accounting, information systems.
James A. Yardley, Ph.D., Illinois at Urbana-Champaign, 1986. Auditing.

An aerial view of the campus.

Section 3
Advertising and Public Relations

This section contains a directory of institutions offering graduate work in advertising and public relations, followed by in-depth entries submitted by institutions that chose to prepare detailed program descriptions. Additional information about programs listed in the directory but not augmented by an in-depth entry may be obtained by writing directly to the dean of a graduate school or chair of a department at the address given in the directory.

For programs offering related work, see also in this book Business Administration and Management and Marketing. In Book 2, Communication and Media.

CONTENTS

Program Directory

Announcement

In-Depth Description

See:

Advertising and Public Relations

Austin Peay State University, College of Arts and Sciences, Department of Speech, Communication and Theatre, Clarksville, TN 37044-0001. Offerings include communication arts (MA), with options in corporate communication, journalism, public relations, radio, television, speech, theatre. *Entrance requirements:* GRE General Test. Application deadline: 7/31 (priority date; rolling processing; 12/4 for spring admission). Application fee: $15. *Expenses:* Tuition $2438 per year full-time, $123 per semester hour part-time for state residents; $7034 per year full-time, $324 per semester hour part-time for nonresidents. Fees $484 per year (minimum) full-time, $154 per semester (minimum) part-time. • Mike Gotcher, Chair, 931-648-7378. E-mail: gotcherm@apsu.edu. Application contact: Dr. Reece Elliott, Director of Graduate Program, 931-648-7244. Fax: 931-648-5992. E-mail: elliottr@apsu.edu.

Ball State University, College of Communication, Information, and Media, Department of Journalism, 2000 University Avenue, Muncie, IN 47306-1099. Offerings include public relations (MA). Accredited by ACEJMC. Department faculty: 14. *Application fee:* $15 ($25 for international students). *Expenses:* Tuition $3454 per year full-time, $518 per semester (minimum) part-time for state residents; $9316 per year full-time, $1221 per semester (minimum) part-time for nonresidents. Fees $242 per year full-time, $18 per semester (minimum) part-time. • Marilyn Weaver, Acting Chairperson, 765-285-8200.

Barry University, School of Arts and Sciences, Department of Communication, Miami Shores, FL 33161-6695. Offerings include public relations (MA). Department faculty: 6 full-time (3 women). *Application deadline:* rolling. *Application fee:* $30. Electronic applications accepted. *Tuition:* $450 per credit (minimum). • Dr. Kathy J. Wahlers, Chair, 305-899-3456. Fax: 305-899-3451. E-mail: wahlers@aquinas.barry.edu. Application contact: Angela Scott, Enrollment Services, Assistant Dean, 305-899-3112. Fax: 305-899-3149. E-mail: ascott@jeanne.barry.edu.

Boston University, College of Communication, Department of Mass Communication, Advertising, and Public Relations, Boston, MA 02215. Awards MS, JD/MS. Programs in mass communication (MS), public relations (MS). Faculty: 58 full-time, 61 part-time. Students: 110 full-time (82 women), 47 part-time (41 women); includes 13 minority (2 African Americans, 8 Asian Americans, 3 Hispanics), 41 international. Average age 26. In 1997, 52 degrees awarded. *Degree requirements:* Thesis required, foreign language not required. *Entrance requirements:* GRE General Test or MAT, TOEFL, LSAT (JD/MS), samples of written work. Application deadline: 2/1. Application fee: $45. *Expenses:* Tuition $22,830 per year full-time, $713 per credit part-time. Fees $218 per year full-time, $40 per semester part-time. *Financial aid:* Fellowships, research assistantships, teaching assistantships, Federal Work-Study, institutionally sponsored loans, and career-related internships or fieldwork available. Financial aid application deadline: 4/1. • Dr. Melvin DeFleur, Chairman, 617-353-3482.

California State University, Fullerton, School of Communications, Department of Communications, PO Box 34080, Fullerton, CA 92834-9480. Offerings include advertising (MA), public relations (MA). Department faculty: 24 full-time (10 women), 22 part-time, 33 FTE. *Degree requirements:* Project or thesis required, foreign language not required. *Entrance requirements:* GRE General Test. Application fee: $55. *Expenses:* Tuition $0 for state residents; $246 per unit for nonresidents. Fees $1947 per year full-time, $1281 per year part-time. • Dr. Wendell Crow, Chair, 714-278-3517. Application contact: Coordinator, 714-278-3832.

Colorado State University, College of Liberal Arts, Department of Journalism and Technical Communication, Fort Collins, CO 80523-0015. Offers program in technical communication (MS). Faculty: 9 full-time (4 women). Students: 20 full-time (12 women), 14 part-time (10 women); includes 5 minority (1 African American, 2 Asian Americans, 2 Hispanics), 2 international. Average age 31. 57 applicants, 51% accepted. In 1997, 3 degrees awarded. *Degree requirements:* Thesis required (for some programs), foreign language not required. *Entrance requirements:* GRE General Test, TOEFL, samples of written work. Application deadline: 2/1 (priority date; rolling processing). Application fee: $30. Electronic applications accepted. *Expenses:* Tuition $2632 per year full-time, $109 per credit hour part-time for state residents; $10,216 per year full-time, $425 per credit hour part-time for nonresidents. Fees $708 per year full-time, $32 per semester (minimum) part-time. *Financial aid:* In 1997–98, research assistantships averaging $921 per month, 10 teaching assistantships (5 to first-year students) averaging $921 per month were awarded; fellowships, traineeships, Federal Work-Study, institutionally sponsored loans, and career-related internships or fieldwork also available. Aid available to part-time students. Financial aid application deadline: 4/1. *Faculty research:* Science communication, health communication, public relations, new media technologies, communication campaigns, document usability. Total annual research expenditures: $120,000. • Donna Rouner, Coordinator, 970-491-5556. Fax: 970-491-2908. E-mail: drouner@vines.colostate.edu.

Announcement: The MS emphasizes communication management training in public relations, new communication technologies, public information, and technical, scientific, and health communication. Teaching and research assistantships include special opportunities for minority students. Students from most Western states pay only Colorado in-state tuition, as this is a Western Regional Graduate Program.

Emerson College, School of Communication, Management, and Public Policy, Department of Communication, Program in Global Marketing Communication and Advertising, Boston, MA 02116-1511. Awards MA. Students: 42 full-time (32 women); includes 3 minority (1 African American, 2 Hispanics), 8 international. Average age 26. 45 applicants, 89% accepted. In 1997, 22 degrees awarded. *Average time to degree:* master's–1 year full-time. *Entrance requirements:* GMAT or GRE General Test, minimum GPA of 3.0. Application deadline: 7/1 (rolling processing; 12/1 for spring admission). Application fee: $45 ($75 for international students). *Expenses:* Tuition $566 per credit. Fees $30 per semester (minimum). *Financial aid:* Divisional/administrative assistantships available. Financial aid application deadline: 2/15; applicants required to submit FAFSA. • Theodore O'Hearn, Graduate Coordinator, 617-824-8737. Application contact: Lynn Terrell, Director of Graduate Admissions, 617-824-8610. Fax: 617-824-8614. E-mail: gradapp@emerson.edu.

Emerson College, School of Communication, Management, and Public Policy, Department of Communication, Program in Integrated Marketing Communication, Boston, MA 02116-1511. Awards MA. Part-time programs available. Students: 107 full-time (69 women), 37 part-time (28 women); includes 5 minority (1 Asian American, 4 Hispanics). Average age 26. 133 applicants, 87% accepted. *Entrance requirements:* GMAT or GRE General Test, minimum GPA of 3.0. Application deadline: 7/1 (priority date; rolling processing; 12/1 for spring admission). Application fee: $45 ($75 for international students). *Expenses:* Tuition $566 per credit. Fees $30 per semester (minimum). *Financial aid:* Fellowships, research assistantships, teaching assistantships, divisional/administrative assistantships, and career-related internships or fieldwork available. Aid available to part-time students. Financial aid application deadline: 2/15; applicants required to submit FAFSA. • Dr. Mary Joyce, Graduate Coordinator, 617-824-8737. Application contact: Lynn Terrell, Director of Graduate Admissions, 617-824-8610. Fax: 617-824-8614. E-mail: gradapp@emerson.edu.

Golden Gate University, School of Business, San Francisco, CA 94105-2968. Offerings include public relations (MS, Certificate). *Average time to degree:* master's–2.5 years full-time. *Application deadline:* 7/1 (priority date; rolling processing). *Application fee:* $55 ($70 for international students). *Tuition:* $996 per course (minimum). • Dr. Hamid Shomali, Dean, 415-442-6500. Fax: 415-442-6579. Application contact: Enrollment Services, 415-442-7800. Fax: 415-442-7807. E-mail: info@ggu.edu.

Iona College, School of Arts and Science, Program in Communication Arts, 715 North Avenue, New Rochelle, NY 10801-1890. Offerings include public relations (MS). Program faculty: 2 full-time (0 women), 4 part-time (1 woman). *Degree requirements:* Comprehensive exam or thesis. *Entrance requirements:* GRE General Test, minimum GPA of 3.0. Application deadline: rolling. Application fee: $25. *Expenses:* Tuition $410 per credit hour. Fees $25 per semester. • Dr. Raymond Smith, Chair, 914-633-2230. Application contact: Arlene Melillo, Director of Graduate Recruitment, 914-633-2328. Fax: 914-633-2023.

Marquette University, College of Communication, Program in Advertising and Public Relations, Milwaukee, WI 53201-1881. Offers advertising (MA), public relations (MA). Accredited by ACEJMC. Part-time and evening/weekend programs available. Faculty: 5 full-time (2 women). Students: 10 full-time, 25 part-time; includes 16 international. Average age 28. 29 applicants, 83% accepted. In 1997, 9 degrees awarded. *Degree requirements:* Thesis, comprehensive exam required, foreign language not required. *Entrance requirements:* GRE General Test, TOEFL (minimum score 550). Application fee: $40. *Tuition:* $490 per credit. *Financial aid:* Research assistantships, teaching assistantships, scholarships, full and partial tuition waivers, Federal Work-Study, institutionally sponsored loans available. Aid available to part-time students. Financial aid application deadline: 2/15. *Faculty research:* First Amendment rights, couponing, sports marketing, advertising effects, public relations history. • John H. Crowley, Chair, 414-288-7291. Fax: 414-288-3099.

Michigan State University, College of Communication Arts and Sciences, Department of Advertising, East Lansing, MI 48824-1020. Offers programs in advertising (MA), public relations (MA). Part-time and evening/weekend programs available. Postbaccalaureate distance learning degree programs offered (no on-campus study). Faculty: 8 (3 women). Students: 94 (62 women); includes 11 minority (6 African Americans, 3 Asian Americans, 1 Hispanic, 1 Native American), 42 international. In 1997, 38 degrees awarded. *Degree requirements:* Thesis optional. *Application deadline:* 3/1 (priority date; rolling processing). *Application fee:* $30 ($40 for international students). *Expenses:* Tuition $4609 per year full-time, $223 per credit hour (minimum) part-time for state residents; $8704 per year full-time, $450 per credit hour (minimum) part-time for nonresidents. Fees $576 per year full-time, $476 per year part-time. *Financial aid:* Fellowships, teaching assistantships, and career-related internships or fieldwork available. *Faculty research:* International advertising, political advertising, consumer behavior, inoculation theory. • Dr. Bonnie Reece, Chairperson, 517-353-9317. Application contact: Dr. Gordon E. Miracle, Director of Graduate Studies, 517-353-3862. Fax: 517-432-2584. E-mail: miracle@pilot.msu.edu.

Monmouth University, Department of Communication, West Long Branch, NJ 07764-1898. Offerings include public relations (Certificate). Department faculty: 3 full-time (2 women). *Application deadline:* 8/1 (rolling processing; 12/1 for spring admission). *Application fee:* $35. *Expenses:* Tuition $459 per credit. Fees $274 per semester full-time, $137 per semester part-time. • Dr. Don R. Swanson, Chair, 732-571-3449. Fax: 732-571-5120. E-mail: dswanson@mondec.monmouth.edu. Application contact: Office of Graduate Admissions, 732-571-3452. Fax: 732-571-5123.

Northwestern University, Medill School of Journalism, Program in Integrated Marketing Communications, Evanston, IL 60208. Offerings include advertising/sales promotion (MSIMC), public relations (MSIMC). Program faculty: 15 full-time, 12 part-time. *Entrance requirements:* GRE General Test or GMAT, TOEFL (minimum score 625), full-time work experience (preferred). Application deadline: 3/1. Application fee: $50. *Tuition:* $24,112 per year. • Application contact: Office of Graduate Admissions and Financial Aid, 847-491-5228. Fax: 847-467-7342. E-mail: medill-admis@nwu.edu.

See in-depth description on page 611.

Oklahoma City University, School of Management and Business Sciences, Program in Business Administration, Oklahoma City, OK 73106-1402. Offerings include marketing and advertising (MBA). *Degree requirements:* Comprehensive exam required, foreign language and thesis not required. *Entrance requirements:* TOEFL, minimum GPA of 2.5. Application deadline: rolling. Application fee: $35 ($55 for international students). *Expenses:* Tuition $350 per hour. Fees $124 per year. • Application contact: Laura L. Rahhal, Director of Graduate Admissions, 800-633-7242 Ext. 2. Fax: 405-521-5356. E-mail: lrahhal1@frodo.okcu.edu.

Rowan University, College of Communication, Glassboro, NJ 08028-1701. Offers program in public relations (MA). Part-time and evening/weekend programs available. Students: 55 (35 women); includes 11 minority (7 African Americans, 1 Asian American, 3 Hispanics). 26 applicants, 42% accepted. In 1997, 19 degrees awarded. *Degree requirements:* Thesis, comprehensive exam required, foreign language not required. *Entrance requirements:* GRE General Test (minimum combined score of 800), interview, minimum GPA of 2.8. Application deadline: 11/1 (priority date; rolling processing; 4/1 for spring admission). Application fee: $50. *Tuition:* $5728 per year full-time, $258 per credit hour part-time for state residents; $8968 per year full-time, $393 per credit hour part-time for nonresidents. *Financial aid:* Career-related internships or fieldwork available. Aid available to part-time students. *Faculty research:* Public school communications, public school public relations, corporate public relations. • Dr. Antoinette Libro, Dean, 609-256-4290. Application contact: Dr. Suzanne Sparks, Adviser, 609-256-4265.

San Diego State University, College of Professional Studies and Fine Arts, School of Communication, Programs in Communication, San Diego, CA 92182. Offerings include advertising and public relations (MA). *Entrance requirements:* GRE General Test (minimum combined score of 950), TOEFL (minimum score 550). Application deadline: 6/1 (priority date; rolling processing; 11/1 for spring admission). Application fee: $55. *Expenses:* Tuition $0 for state residents; $246 per unit for nonresidents. Fees $1932 per year full-time, $1266 per year part-time. • Application contact: Joel Davis, Graduate Coordinator, 619-594-6714. Fax: 619-594-6246. E-mail: jdavis@mail.sdsu.edu.

Syracuse University, S. I. Newhouse School of Public Communications, Department of Advertising, Syracuse, NY 13244-0003. Awards MA, MS. Accredited by ACEJMC. Faculty: 3. Students: 29 full-time (21 women), 17 part-time (12 women); includes 5 minority (all African Americans), 17 international. 64 applicants, 5% accepted. In 1997, 6 degrees awarded. *Entrance requirements:* GRE General Test. Application deadline: rolling. Application fee: $40. *Tuition:* $13,320 per year full-time, $555 per credit hour part-time. *Financial aid:* Fellowships, research assistantships, teaching assistantships, partial tuition waivers, Federal Work-Study available. Financial aid application deadline: 3/1. • Carla Lloyd, Chair. Application contact: Graduate Admissions, 315-443-4039.

The University of Alabama, College of Communication, Department of Advertising and Public Relations, Tuscaloosa, AL 35487. Awards MA, PhD. Accredited by ACEJMC. Faculty: 7 full-time (3 women). Students: 25 full-time (19 women); includes 4 minority (all Asian Americans), 2 international. Average age 22. In 1997, 16 master's awarded. *Degree requirements:* For master's, thesis or alternative required, foreign language not required; for doctorate, 1 foreign language (computer language can substitute), dissertation. *Entrance requirements:* For master's, GRE General Test; for doctorate, GRE. Application deadline: 2/15 (priority date; rolling processing; 11/1 for spring admission). Application fee: $25. Electronic applications accepted. *Tuition:* $2684 per year full-time, $594 per semester (minimum) part-time for state residents; $7216 per year full-time, $1248 per semester (minimum) part-time for nonresidents. *Financial aid:* In 1997–98, 2 research assistantships, 2 teaching assistantships were awarded; Federal Work-Study, institutionally sponsored loans, and career-related internships or fieldwork also available. Financial aid application deadline: 2/15. *Faculty research:* Advertising and public relations management, public opinion, political communication, advertising media, international communication. • William Gonzenbach, Chair, 205-348-7158. E-mail: gonzenbach@apr.ua.edu. Application contact: Yorgo Pasadeos, Graduate Coordinator, 205-348-8641. Fax: 205-348-2401. E-mail: pasadeos@apr.ua.edu.

University of Denver, Graduate Studies, School of Communication, Department of Mass Communications, Denver, CO 80208. Offerings include advertising management (MS), public relations (MS). Department faculty: 12 full-time (5 women). *Application deadline:* 3/15 (priority date; rolling processing). *Application fee:* $40 ($45 for international students). *Expenses:* Tuition $18,216 per year full-time, $506 per credit hour part-time. Fees $159 per year. • Dr. Michael Wirth, Chairperson, 303-871-2166. Application contact: Dr. Rodney Buxton, Director of Graduate Studies, 303-871-2166.

University of Florida, College of Journalism and Communications, Specialization in Advertising, Gainesville, FL 32611. Awards MAMC, PhD. One or more programs accredited by ACEJMC. *Degree requirements:* For master's, thesis optional, foreign language not required; for doctorate, dissertation. *Entrance requirements:* GRE General Test (minimum combined score of 1000), minimum GPA of 3.0. Application deadline: 6/5 (priority date; rolling processing). Application fee: $20. *Tuition:* $138 per credit hour for state residents; $481 per credit hour for nonresidents. • Dr. Joseph R. Pisani, Chair, 352-392-4046. E-mail: jpisani@jou.ufl.edu. Application contact: Dr. John Sutherland, Graduate Coordinator, 352-392-9172. Fax: 352-392-3919. E-mail: jsuther@jou.ufl.edu.

University of Florida, College of Journalism and Communications, Specialization in Public Relations, Gainesville, FL 32611. Awards MAMC, PhD. One or more programs accredited by ACEJMC. *Degree requirements:* For master's, thesis optional, foreign language not required; for doctorate, dissertation. *Entrance requirements:* GRE General Test (minimum combined score of 1000), minimum GPA of 3.0. Application deadline: 6/5 (priority date; rolling processing). Application fee: $20. *Tuition:* $138 per credit hour for state residents; $481 per credit hour for nonresidents. • Dr. Gail Baker Woods, Chair, 352-392-1686. E-mail: gbwoods@jou.ufl.edu. Application contact: Dr. Robert Kendall, Graduate Coordinator, 352-392-0427. Fax: 352-392-3919. E-mail: rkendall@jou.ufl.edu.

University of Houston, College of Humanities, Fine Arts and Communication, School of Communication, Program in Public Relations Studies, 4800 Calhoun, Houston, TX 77204-2163. Awards MA. Part-time and evening/weekend programs available. Faculty: 9 full-time (2 women), 1 part-time (0 women). Students: 10 full-time (8 women), 28 part-time (21 women); includes 5 African Americans, 2 Asian Americans, 2 Hispanics, 3 international. Average age 29. *Entrance requirements:* GRE General Test (minimum score 450 on each section), minimum GPA of 3.0 in last 60 hours. Application deadline: 7/3 (priority date; rolling processing). Application fee: $25 ($75 for international students). *Expenses:* Tuition $1152 per year full-time, $120 per semester (minimum) part-time for state residents; $4482 per year full-time, $249 per credit hour part-time for nonresidents. Fees $977 per year full-time, $119 per semester (minimum) part-time. *Financial aid:* Teaching assistantships available. Financial aid application deadline: 7/15. • William Douglas, Director of Graduate Studies, 713-743-2877. Application contact: Anna Marchese, Graduate Coordinator, 713-743-2873. Fax: 713-743-2876.

University of Illinois at Urbana–Champaign, College of Communications, Department of Advertising, Urbana, IL 61801. Awards MS. Accredited by ACEJMC. Faculty: 7 full-time (3 women). Students: 30 full-time (20 women); includes 1 minority (African American), 14 international. 76 applicants, 18% accepted. In 1997, 9 degrees awarded. *Entrance requirements:* GMAT or GRE General Test, minimum GPA of 4.0 on a 5.0 scale. Application deadline: rolling. Application fee: $40 ($50 for international students). *Financial aid:* In 1997–98, 2 fellowships, 17 research assistantships were awarded; teaching assistantships, full and partial tuition waivers also available. Financial aid application deadline: 2/15. *Faculty research:* Consumer behavior, persuasive communication. • James E. Haefner, Head, 217-333-1602. Application contact: Cinda Cornstubble, Secretary, 217-333-1602. Fax: 217-244-5348.

University of Maryland, College Park, College of Journalism, College Park, MD 20742-5045. Offerings include advertising (MA, PhD), public relations (MA, PhD). College faculty: 20 full-time (8 women), 20 part-time (10 women). *Degree requirements:* For master's, thesis or alternative required, foreign language not required; for doctorate, dissertation. *Entrance requirements:* For master's, GRE General Test, minimum GPA of 3.0. Application deadline: rolling. Application fee: $50 ($70 for international students). *Expenses:* Tuition $272 per credit hour for state residents; $400 per credit hour for nonresidents. Fees $564 per year full-time, $342 per year part-time. • Dr. Reese Cleghorn, Dean, 301-405-2383. Fax: 301-314-1978. Application contact: John Mollish, Director, Graduate Admissions and Records, 301-405-4198. Fax: 301-314-9305.

University of Miami, School of Communication, Coral Gables, FL 33124. Offerings include public relations (MA). School faculty: 43 (13 women). *Application fee:* $35. *Expenses:* Tuition $815 per credit hour. Fees $174 per year. • Edward J. Pfister, Dean, 305-284-2265. Application contact: Dr. Stanley Harrison, Director of Graduate Studies, 305-284-2265. Fax: 305-284-3648. E-mail: sumiller@miami.edu.

University of New Haven, School of Business, Program in Business Administration, West Haven, CT 06516-1916. Offerings include public relations (MBA). *Degree requirements:* Thesis or alternative required, foreign language not required. *Application deadline:* rolling. *Application fee:* $50. *Expenses:* Tuition $1125 per course. Fees $13 per trimester. • Dr. Omid Nodoushani, Coordinator, 203-932-7123.

University of Oklahoma, College of Arts and Sciences, School of Journalism and Mass Communication, Norman, OK 73019-0390. Offerings include advertising (MA), public relations (MA). School faculty: 21 full-time (8 women), 3 part-time (1 woman). *Degree requirements:* Thesis. *Entrance requirements:* GRE General Test, TOEFL (minimum score 550), TWE (minimum score 5), minimum GPA of 3.2, 12 hours of course work in journalism. Application deadline: 3/1 (11/1 for spring admission). Application fee: $25. *Expenses:* Tuition $1920 per year full-time, $80 per credit hour part-time for state residents; $6108 per year full-time, $255 per credit hour part-time for nonresidents. Fees $468 per year full-time, $12 per semester (minimum) part-time. • David Dary, Director, 405-325-2721. Application contact: Dr. Tim Hudson, Graduate Liaison, 405-325-2721. Fax: 405-325-7565.

University of St. Thomas, Graduate School of Business, Program in Business Communication, St. Paul, MN 55105-1096. Offerings include public relations (Certificate). Program faculty: 1 full-time (0 women), 13 part-time (2 women). *Application deadline:* 8/1 (priority date; rolling processing; 12/1 for spring admission). *Application fee:* $30. *Tuition:* $416 per credit hour. • Dr. Nona Mason, Director, 612-962-4382. Application contact: Coordinator, 612-962-4383. Fax: 612-962-4710.

University of Southern California, Graduate School, Annenberg School for Communication, School of Journalism, Program in Public Relations, Los Angeles, CA 90089. Awards MA. *Entrance requirements:* GRE General Test. Application deadline: 4/1 (priority date). Application fee: $55. *Expenses:* Tuition $16,944 per year full-time, $706 per unit part-time. Fees $414 per year full-time, $32 per year part-time.

University of Southern Mississippi, College of Liberal Arts, School of Communication, Hattiesburg, MS 39406-5167. Offerings include public relations (MS). School faculty: 18 full-time (4 women), 2 part-time (0 women). *Application deadline:* 8/9 (priority date; rolling processing). *Application fee:* $0 ($25 for international students). *Tuition:* $2870 per year full-time, $137 per credit hour part-time for state residents; $5972 per year full-time, $172 per credit hour part-time for nonresidents. • Robert G. Wiggins, Director, 601-266-5650. Application contact: Mazharal Haque, Director of Graduate Studies, 601-266-5650. Fax: 601-266-4263.

University of Tennessee, Knoxville, College of Communications, Knoxville, TN 37996. Offerings include advertising (MS, PhD), public relations (MS, PhD). One or more programs accredited by ACEJMC. Postbaccalaureate distance learning degree programs offered (no on-campus study). College faculty: 25 full-time (8 women). *Degree requirements:* For master's, thesis or alternative required, foreign language not required; for doctorate, dissertation required, foreign language not required. *Entrance requirements:* GRE General Test, TOEFL (minimum score 550), minimum GPA of 2.7. Application deadline: 2/1 (priority date; rolling processing). Application fee: $35. Electronic applications accepted. *Tuition:* $3354 per year full-time, $181 per semester hour part-time for state residents; $8410 per year full-time, $462 per semester hour part-time for nonresidents. • Dr. Dwight Teeter, Dean, 423-974-3031. Application contact: Dr. Herbert Howard, Program Head, 423-974-6651. Fax: 423-974-3896. E-mail: hhoward@utk.edu.

The University of Texas at Austin, Graduate School, College of Communication, Department of Advertising, Austin, TX 78712. Awards MA, PhD. Faculty: 10 full-time (6 women), 2 part-time (both women). Students: 86 full-time (46 women); includes 14 minority (5 African Americans, 4 Asian Americans, 5 Hispanics), 41 international. 159 applicants, 43% accepted. In 1997, 16 master's, 3 doctorates awarded. *Entrance requirements:* GRE General Test. Application deadline: 2/1 (priority date). Application fee: $50 ($75 for international students). Electronic applications accepted. *Expenses:* Tuition $2592 per year full-time, $324 per semester (minimum) part-time for state residents; $7704 per year full-time, $963 per semester (minimum) part-time for nonresidents. Fees $778 per year full-time, $161 per semester (minimum) part-time. *Financial aid:* Fellowships, teaching assistantships available. Financial aid application deadline: 2/1. • Dr. Gary Wilcox, Chairman, 512-471-1101. Application contact: Jef Richards, Graduate Adviser, 512-471-1101.

University of the Sacred Heart, Graduate Programs, Department of Communication, Program in Public Relations, San Juan, PR 00914-0383. Awards MA. Part-time and evening/weekend programs available. Faculty: 7 full-time (5 women), 3 part-time (1 woman), 8 FTE. Students: 9 full-time (6 women), 88 part-time (68 women). 50 applicants, 66% accepted. In 1997, 10 degrees awarded. *Degree requirements:* Computer language, thesis. *Entrance requirements:* PAEG, minimum undergraduate GPA of 2.5. Application deadline: 5/15. Application fee: $25. *Expenses:* Tuition $150 per credit. Fees $240 per credit. • Prof. Yaritza Medina, Coordinator, 787-728-1515 Ext. 2326. Fax: 787-728-1515 Ext. 2359. Application contact: Dr. Blanca Villamil, Acting Director, Admissions Office, 787-728-1515 Ext. 3237. Fax: 787-728-2066. E-mail: b_villami@uscsi.usc.clu.edu.

University of Wisconsin–Stevens Point, College of Fine Arts and Communication, Division of Communication, Stevens Point, WI 54481-3897. Offerings include public relations (MA). Division faculty: 16 (2 women). *Degree requirements:* Thesis required, foreign language not required. *Entrance requirements:* GRE. Application deadline: 3/1 (priority date; rolling processing). Application fee: $38. *Tuition:* $3702 per year full-time, $664 per semester (minimum) part-time for state residents; $11,346 per year full-time, $1938 per semester (minimum) part-time for nonresidents. • Dr. Chris Sadler, Graduate Coordinator, 715-346-3898.

Virginia Commonwealth University, College of Humanities and Sciences, School of Mass Communications, Adcenter, Richmond, VA 23284-9005. Offers programs in account management (MS), art direction (MS), copywriting (MS). Students: 98 full-time (41 women); includes 21 minority (12 African Americans, 2 Asian Americans, 4 Hispanics, 3 Native Americans), 1 international. Average age 25. 73 applicants, 84% accepted. *Degree requirements:* Thesis or alternative, comprehensive exams required, foreign language not required. *Entrance requirements:* GRE General Test, interview, portfolio, screening test. Application deadline: 7/1. Application fee: $30 ($0 for international students). *Tuition:* $4960 per year full-time, $257 per credit part-time for state residents; $12,652 per year full-time, $684 per credit part-time for nonresidents. *Financial aid:* Federal Work-Study and career-related internships or fieldwork available. Aid available to part-time students. • Dr. Diane Cook-Tench, Director, 804-828-8384. Fax: 804-828-9175. E-mail: dmcookte@vcu.edu.

Wayne State University, College of Fine, Performing and Communication Arts, Department of Communication, Detroit, MI 48202. Offerings include public relations and organizational communication (MA). Department faculty: 36. *Degree requirements:* Thesis or alternative, thesis, essay or comprehensive exam required, foreign language not required. *Entrance requirements:* Minimum GPA of 3.0. Application deadline: 4/1. Application fee: $20 ($30 for international students). *Expenses:* Tuition $163 per credit hour for state residents; $355 per credit hour for nonresidents. Fees $498 per year full-time, $114 per semester (minimum) part-time. • Dr. Edward Pappas, Interim Chairperson, 313-577-2943. E-mail: jkay@cms.cc.wayne.edu. Application contact: Dr. Matthew Seeger, Graduate Committee Chair, 313-577-2945. Fax: 313-577-6300. E-mail: mseeger@cms.cc.wayne.edu.

Section 4
Entrepreneurship

This section contains a directory of institutions offering graduate work in entrepreneurship, followed by in-depth entries submitted by institutions that chose to prepare detailed program descriptions. Additional information about programs listed in the directory but not augmented by an in-depth entry may be obtained by writing directly to the dean of a graduate school or chair of a department at the address given in the directory.

For programs offering related work, see also in this book Business Administration and Management, International Business, and Education (Business Education).

CONTENTS

Program Directory

Announcement

Entrepreneurship

American University, Kogod College of Business Administration, Department of Management, Program in Entrepreneurship and Management, Washington, DC 20016-8001. Awards MBA. Faculty: 17 full-time (5 women), 6 part-time (1 woman). Students: 3 full-time (0 women), 15 part-time (6 women); includes 4 minority (3 African Americans, 1 Native American), 2 international. 53 applicants, 75% accepted. In 1997, 3 degrees awarded. *Entrance requirements:* GMAT. Application deadline: 2/1 (priority date; 10/1 for spring admission). Application fee: $50. *Expenses:* Tuition $19,080 per year full-time, $687 per credit hour (minimum) part-time. Fees $180 per year full-time, $110 per year part-time. *Financial aid:* Fellowships, research assistantships available. Financial aid application deadline: 2/1. • Dr. Edward A. Wasil Jr., Chair, Department of Management, 202-885-1915. Fax: 202-885-1916.

Antioch Southern California/Los Angeles, Program in Organizational Management, 13274 Fiji Way, Marina del Rey, CA 90292-7090. Offerings include entrepreneurship (MA). Program faculty: 2 full-time (1 woman), 5 part-time (3 women). *Degree requirements:* Computer language, thesis required, foreign language not required. *Entrance requirements:* TOEFL (minimum score 600), interview. Application deadline: 8/8 (priority date; 2/6 for spring admission). Application fee: $50. • Scott Schroeder, Chair, 310-578-1080. Fax: 310-822-4824. E-mail: scott_schroeder@antiochla.edu. Application contact: MeHee Hyun, Director of Admissions, 310-578-1090. Fax: 310-822-4842. E-mail: mehee_hyun@antiochla.edu.

Bentley College, Graduate School of Business, Self-paced MBA Program, 175 Forest Street, Waltham, MA 02154-4705. Offerings include entrepreneurial studies (MBA). Program faculty: 70 full-time (21 women), 22 part-time (8 women). *Degree requirements:* Computer language required, foreign language and thesis not required. *Entrance requirements:* GMAT (average 540), TOEFL (minimum score 580). Application deadline: 6/1 (priority date; rolling processing; 11/1 for spring admission). Application fee: $50. *Expenses:* Tuition $20,500 per year full-time, $2050 per course part-time. Fees $65 per year full-time, $15 per semester part-time. • Dr. Judith B. Kamm, Director, 781-891-3433. Application contact: Holly Chase, Associate Director, 781-891-2108. Fax: 781-891-2464. E-mail: hchase@bentley.edu.

California Lutheran University, School of Business Administration, Thousand Oaks, CA 91360-2787. Offerings include small business/entrepreneurship (MBA). School faculty: 8 full-time (3 women), 29 part-time (4 women). *Entrance requirements:* GMAT, minimum GPA of 3.0, interview. Application deadline: 8/1 (priority date; rolling processing). Application fee: $50. *Tuition:* $395 per unit. • Dr. Ronald Hagler, Director, 805-493-3371.

California State University, Hayward, School of Business and Economics, Department of Marketing, Option in New Ventures/Small Business Management, Hayward, CA 94542-3000. Awards MBA. *Degree requirements:* Comprehensive exam or thesis required, foreign language not required. *Entrance requirements:* GMAT, minimum GPA of 2.75. Application deadline: 4/19 (priority date; rolling processing; 1/5 for spring admission). Application fee: $55. *Expenses:* Tuition $0 for state residents; $164 per unit for nonresidents. Fees $1827 per year full-time, $1161 per year part-time. *Financial aid:* Application deadline 3/1. • Dr. Ricardo Singson, Coordinator, 510-885-3557. Application contact: Dr. Donna L. Wiley, Director of Graduate Programs, 510-885-3964.

Columbia University, Graduate School of Business, MBA Program, New York, NY 10027. Offerings include entrepreneurship (MBA). Program faculty: 105 full-time (15 women), 86 part-time (15 women). *Entrance requirements:* GMAT, TOEFL (minimum score 610). Application deadline: 4/20 (rolling processing; 11/1 for spring admission). Application fee: $125 ($150 for international students). *Expenses:* Tuition $26,520 per year. Fees $1250 per year. • Prof. Safwan Masri, Vice Dean of Students and the MBA Program, 212-854-8716. Fax: 212-854-0545. E-mail: smm1@columbia.edu. Application contact: Linda Meehan, Assistant Dean and Executive Director of Admissions and Financial Aid, 212-854-1961. Fax: 212-662-6754. E-mail: gohermes@claven.gsb.columbia.edu.

DePaul University, Charles H. Kellstadt Graduate School of Business, Department of Management, Program in Entrepreneurship, Chicago, IL 60604-2287. Awards MBA. Students: 58 full-time (19 women), 51 part-time (12 women); includes 15 minority (3 African Americans, 9 Asian Americans, 3 Hispanics), 1 international. Average age 30. 42 applicants, 64% accepted. In 1997, 43 degrees awarded. *Entrance requirements:* GMAT (minimum score 480; average 550), TOEFL. Application deadline: 8/1 (rolling processing; 3/1 for spring admission). Application fee: $40. *Expenses:* Tuition $1593 per course. Fees $30 per year. *Financial aid:* In 1997–98, research assistantships averaging $400 per month were awarded. Financial aid application deadline: 4/1. • Application contact: Christine Munoz, Director of Admissions, 312-362-8810. Fax: 312-362-6677. E-mail: mbainfo@wppost.depaul.edu.

Golden Gate University, School of Business, San Francisco, CA 94105-2968. Offerings include entrepreneurship (MBA). MBA (telecommunications, management information systems) offered jointly with the School of Technology and Industry. *Average time to degree:* master's–2.5 years full-time. *Application deadline:* 7/1 (priority date; rolling processing). *Application fee:* $55 ($70 for international students). *Tuition:* $996 per course (minimum). • Dr. Hamid Shomali, Dean, 415-442-6500. Fax: 415-442-6579. Application contact: Enrollment Services, 415-442-7800. Fax: 415-442-7807. E-mail: info@ggu.edu.

Indiana University Bloomington, School of Business, Program in Business Administration, Bloomington, IN 47405. Offerings include entrepreneurship (MBA). Self-designed programs available. *Entrance requirements:* GMAT, TOEFL (minimum score 580). Application deadline: 3/1. Application fee: $50 ($65 for international students). *Expenses:* Tuition $8232 per year for state residents; $16,470 per year for nonresidents. Fees $343 per year. • Dr. George Hettenhouse, Chair, 812-855-8006. Application contact: Dr. James J. Holmen, Director of Admissions and Financial Aid, 812-855-8006. Fax: 812-855-9039.

Kennesaw State University, Michael J. Coles College of Business, Program in Business Administration, Kennesaw, GA 30144-5591. Offerings include entrepreneurship (MBA). Program faculty: 54 full-time (18 women), 5 part-time (0 women). *Application deadline:* 7/1 (rolling processing; 2/20 for spring admission). *Application fee:* $20. *Expenses:* Tuition $2398 per year full-time, $83 per credit hour part-time for state residents; $8398 per year full-time, $333 per credit hour part-time for nonresidents. Fees $338 per year. • Dr. Rodney Alsup, Assistant Dean, 770-423-6087. Fax: 770-423-6141. E-mail: ralsup@ksumail.kennesaw.edu. Application contact: Susan N. Barrett, Administrative Specialist, Admissions, 770-423-6500. Fax: 770-423-6541. E-mail: sbarrett@ksumail.kennesaw.edu.

Rensselaer Polytechnic Institute, Lally School of Management and Technology, Troy, NY 12180-3590. Offerings include business administration (MBA, PhD), with options in finance and accounting (MBA), information systems management (MBA), management (PhD), management of technology and entrepreneurships (MBA), manufacturing management (MBA), marketing management (MBA), operations research (MBA), organizational behavior and human resource management (MBA), statistical methods for management (MBA). Postbaccalaureate distance learning degree programs offered (no on-campus study). School faculty: 36 full-time (5 women), 6 part-time (0 women). *Application deadline:* 2/1 (priority date; rolling processing). *Application fee:* $35. *Expenses:* Tuition $630 per credit hour. Fees $1000 per year. • Dr. Joseph G. Ecker, Dean, 518-276-6802. Application contact: Michele Martens, Manager of Enrollment Services, 518-276-4800. Fax: 518-276-8661.

Suffolk University, Sawyer School of Management, Program in Entrepreneurial Studies, Boston, MA 02108-2770. Awards MS. Part-time programs available. Students: 2 full-time (1 woman), 7 part-time (3 women); includes 1 international. 6 applicants, 100% accepted. *Entrance requirements:* GMAT (average 500). Application deadline: 6/15 (priority date; rolling processing; 11/15 for spring admission). Application fee: $50. *Expenses:* Tuition $17,490 per year full-time, $1749 per course part-time. Fees $50 per year full-time, $20 per year part-time. *Financial aid:* In 1997–98, 4 students received aid, including 2 fellowships; Federal Work-Study, institutionally sponsored loans, and career-related internships or fieldwork also available. Aid available to part-time students. Financial aid application deadline: 4/1; applicants required to submit FAFSA. • Robert DeFillippi, Director, 617-573-8243. E-mail: rdefillipi@acad.suffolk.edu. Application contact: Judy Reynolds, Acting Director of Graduate Admissions, 617-573-8302. Fax: 617-523-0116. E-mail: grad.admission@admin.suffolk.edu.

Announcement: The Master of Science in entrepreneurial studies program is designed for students with a special interest in creating or joining a new venture, for those wishing to join an innovative growth company, and for post-MBAs eager to embrace a more entrepreneurial career. The curriculum includes 10 core courses that provide a general business background and 6 specialized entrepreneurial studies courses. With the appropriate background, some core courses can be waived. For MBAs, the program may be completed in 1 calendar year. The program directors are Robert DeFillippi (617-573-8243) and Charles Shelley (617-573-8377). For an application and information, students should contact the Office of Graduate Admission, 617-573-8302, fax: 617-523-0116, e-mail: grad.admission@admin.suffolk.edu

Trinity College, School of Professional Studies, Programs in Administration, Washington, DC 20017-1094. Offerings include human resources (MSA), with options in entrepreneurial development, human resource development, human resource management. Faculty: 4 full-time (1 woman), 4 part-time (all women). *Application deadline:* rolling. *Application fee:* $35. *Tuition:* $460 per credit hour. • Dr. Sheri Levin, Division Chair, Human Services, 202-884-9553. Application contact: Karen Goodwin, Director of Graduate Admissions, 202-884-9400. Fax: 202-884-9229.

Université du Québec à Trois-Rivières, Program in Management of Small and Medium-Sized Enterprises and Their Environment, Trois-Rivières, PQ G9A 5H7, Canada. Awards M Sc. Part-time programs available. Students: 23 full-time (9 women), 5 part-time (3 women). 97 applicants, 77% accepted. *Degree requirements:* Research report required, thesis not required. *Entrance requirements:* Appropriate bachelor's degree, proficiency in French. Application deadline: 2/1. Application fee: $30. *Financial aid:* Fellowships, research assistantships, teaching assistantships available. • Yvon Bigras, Director, 819-376-5080 Ext. 3127. Fax: 819-376-5012. E-mail: yvon_bigras@uqtr.uquebec.ca. Application contact: Suzanne Camirand, Admissions Officer, 819-376-5045 Ext. 2591. Fax: 819-376-5210. E-mail: suzanne_camirand@uqtr.uquebec.ca.

University of Colorado at Boulder, Graduate School of Business Administration, Boulder, CO 80309. Offerings include technology and innovation management (MBA). School faculty: 66 full-time (12 women). *Application deadline:* 3/1 (priority date; rolling processing). *Application fee:* $40 ($60 for international students). *Expenses:* Tuition $3594 per year (minimum) full-time, $597 per semester (minimum) part-time for state residents; $14,868 per year (minimum) full-time, $2478 per semester (minimum) part-time for nonresidents. Fees $667 per year full-time, $130 per semester (minimum) part-time. • Larry Singell, Dean, 303-492-1809. Fax: 303-492-7676. E-mail: larry.singell@colorado.edu. Application contact: Diana Marinaro, Graduate Student Admissions, 303-492-1831. Fax: 303-492-1727. E-mail: busgrad@spot.colorado.edu.

University of Houston, College of Business Administration, Department of Marketing and Entrepreneurship, 4800 Calhoun, Houston, TX 77204-2163. Awards MBA, PhD. Part-time and evening/weekend programs available. Faculty: 9 full-time (3 women), 11 part-time (2 women). Students: 40 full-time (22 women), 35 part-time (13 women); includes 16 minority (6 African Americans, 6 Asian Americans, 4 Hispanics), 14 international. Average age 30. In 1997, 14 master's awarded. *Degree requirements:* For master's, computer language required, foreign language and thesis not required; for doctorate, computer language, dissertation, comprehensive exam required, foreign language not required. *Average time to degree:* master's–2 years full-time, 3.5 years part-time; doctorate–4.5 years full-time. *Entrance requirements:* For master's, GMAT (average 590), TOEFL (minimum score 620); for doctorate, GMAT or GRE. Application deadline: 5/1 (rolling processing; 10/1 for spring admission). Application fee: $50 ($125 for international students). *Expenses:* Tuition $1152 per year full-time, $120 per semester (minimum) part-time for state residents; $4482 per year full-time, $249 per credit hour part-time for nonresidents. Fees $977 per year full-time, $119 per semester (minimum) part-time. *Financial aid:* Research assistantships, teaching assistantships, and career-related internships or fieldwork available. Aid available to part-time students. Financial aid application deadline: 3/1; applicants required to submit FAFSA. • Dr. Ed Blair, Chair, 713-743-4646. Application contact: Office of Student Services, 713-743-4900. Fax: 713-743-4942. E-mail: oss@cba.uh.edu.

University of Tennessee, Knoxville, College of Business Administration, Program in Business Administration, Knoxville, TN 37996. Offerings include entrepreneurship/new venture analysis (MBA). MS/MBA offered jointly with the College of Engineering. Postbaccalaureate distance learning degree programs offered. Program faculty: 51 full-time (6 women). *Application deadline:* 2/1 (priority date). *Application fee:* $35. Electronic applications accepted. *Tuition:* $3354 per year full-time, $181 per semester hour part-time for state residents; $8410 per year full-time, $462 per semester hour part-time for nonresidents. • Dr. Gary Dicer, Director, 423-974-5033. E-mail: gdicer@utk.edu. Application contact: Donald Potts, Graduate Representative, 423-974-5033. Fax: 423-974-3826. E-mail: dpotts@utk.edu.

Section 5
Facilities Management

This section contains a directory of institutions offering graduate work in facilities management, followed by in-depth entries submitted by institutions that chose to prepare detailed program descriptions. Additional information about programs listed in the directory but not augmented by an in-depth entry may be obtained by writing directly to the dean of a graduate school or chair of a department at the address given in the directory.

For programs offering related work, see also in this book Business Administration and Management.

CONTENTS

Program Directory

Facilities Management

Cornell University, Graduate Fields of Human Ecology, Field of Design and Environmental Analysis, Ithaca, NY 14853-0001. Offerings include facilities planning and management (MS). Faculty: 11 full-time. *Application deadline:* 2/1. *Application fee:* $65. Electronic applications accepted. • Director of Graduate Studies, 607-255-2168. Application contact: Graduate Field Assistant, 607-255-2168. Fax: 607-255-0305. E-mail: dea_grad@cornell.edu.

Indiana State University, School of Health and Human Performance, Department of Health and Safety, Terre Haute, IN 47809-1401. Offerings include health program and facility administration (MA, MS). Department faculty: 11 full-time (4 women). *Application deadline:* rolling. *Application fee:* $20. *Tuition:* $143 per credit hour for state residents; $325 per credit hour for nonresidents. • Dr. Portia Plummer, Chairperson, 812-237-3071. Application contact: Dr. Richard Spear, Graduate Adviser, 812-237-3107.

Indiana University of Pennsylvania, College of Health and Human Services, Department of Health and Physical Education, Indiana, PA 15705-1087. Offerings include aquatics administration and facilities management (MS). *Degree requirements:* Thesis optional, foreign language not required. *Entrance requirements:* TOEFL (minimum score 500). Application deadline: 7/1 (priority date; rolling processing; 11/1 for spring admission). Application fee: $30. *Expenses:* Tuition $3468 per year full-time, $193 per credit part-time for state residents; $6236 per year full-time, $346 per credit part-time for nonresidents. Fees $313 per year (minimum) full-time, $84 per year part-time. • Dr. James Mill, Chairperson and Graduate Coordinator, 724-357-2770. E-mail: jimmill@grove.iup.edu.

Michigan State University, College of Human Ecology, Department of Human Environment and Design, East Lansing, MI 48824-1020. Offerings include interior design and facilities management (MA). Department faculty: 12 (9 women). *Application deadline:* 11/15 (rolling processing). *Application fee:* $30 ($40 for international students). *Expenses:* Tuition $4609 per year full-time, $223 per credit hour (minimum) part-time for state residents; $8704 per year full-time, $450 per credit hour (minimum) part-time for nonresidents. Fees $576 per year full-time, $476 per year part-time. • Dr. Dana Stewart, Acting Chairperson, 517-355-7712.

Pratt Institute, School of Architecture, Program in Facilities Management, Brooklyn, NY 11205-3899. Awards MS. *Degree requirements:* Thesis required, foreign language not required. *Entrance requirements:* TOEFL (minimum score 550), writing sample. Application deadline: 3/1 (priority date; rolling processing). Application fee: $35 ($80 for international students). *Expenses:* Tuition $15,288 per year full-time, $637 per credit part-time. Fees $480 per year. *Faculty research:* Benchmarking, organizational studies, resource planning and management, computer-aided facilities management, value analysis.

University of North Texas, School of Community Service, Department of Applied Gerontology, Denton, TX 76203-6737. Offerings include administration of retirement facilities (MA, MS). Department faculty: 4 full-time (0 women). *Degree requirements:* Thesis, internship required, foreign language not required. *Entrance requirements:* GRE General Test (minimum combined score of 800). Application deadline: 7/17 (rolling processing; 12/1 for spring admission). Application fee: $25 ($50 for international students). *Tuition:* $2063 per year full-time, $815 per year part-time for state residents; $5897 per year full-time, $2100 per year part-time for nonresidents. • Dr. Richard A. Lusky, Director, 940-565-2765. Application contact: Phyllis Eccleston, Academic Program Coordinator, 940-565-3449. Fax: 940-565-4370.

Section 6
Hospitality Management

This section contains directories of institutions offering graduate work in hospitality management and travel and tourism, followed by in-depth entries submitted by institutions that chose to prepare detailed program descriptions. Additional information about programs listed in the directories but not augmented by an in-depth entry may be obtained by writing directly to the dean of a graduate school or chair of a department at the address given in the directory.

For programs offering related work, see also in this book Business Administration and Management, Advertising and Public Relations, and Health Services. In Book 2, see Home Economics and Family Studies. In Book 4, see Agricultural and Food Sciences (Food Science and Technology).

CONTENTS

Program Directories

Announcements

Cross-Discipline Announcement

In-Depth Descriptions

See also:

Hospitality Management

Black Hills State University, College of Business and Technology, Spearfish, SD 57799-9502. Offers program in tourism and hospitality management (MS). Program new for fall 1998. Part-time programs available. Faculty: 16 full-time (7 women). *Degree requirements:* Thesis required (for some programs), foreign language not required. *Entrance requirements:* TOEFL (minimum score 550), bachelor's degree in related field. Application deadline: 8/1 (priority date; rolling processing). Application fee: $15. *Expenses:* Tuition $85 per credit hour for state residents; $251 per credit hour for nonresidents. Fees $41 per credit hour. *Financial aid:* Research assistantships, partial tuition waivers, Federal Work-Study, and career-related internships or fieldwork available. Aid available to part-time students. *Faculty research:* Tourism in western South Dakota, marketing. Total annual research expenditures: $30,000. • Tom Hills, Dean, 605-642-6212. Fax: 605-642-6273.

Central Michigan University, College of Business Administration, Department of Marketing and Hospitality Services Administration, Mount Pleasant, MI 48859. Awards MBA. Faculty: 9 full-time (1 woman). *Entrance requirements:* GMAT. Application deadline: 3/1 (priority date; rolling processing). Application fee: $30. *Expenses:* Tuition $139 per credit hour (minimum) for state residents; $276 per credit hour (minimum) for nonresidents. Fees $260 per year full-time, $150 per semester part-time. *Financial aid:* Fellowships, research assistantships, teaching assistantships available. Financial aid application deadline: 3/7. • Dr. Robert Welsh, Chairperson, 517-774-3701. Fax: 517-774-7713. E-mail: robert.s.welsh@cmich.edu.

Cornell University, Field of Hotel Administration, Ithaca, NY 14853-0001. Awards MMH, MS, PhD. Faculty: 37 full-time. Students: 128 full-time (51 women). 267 applicants, 27% accepted. In 1997, 57 master's, 2 doctorates awarded. *Degree requirements:* For master's, thesis (MS); for doctorate, dissertation. *Entrance requirements:* GMAT, TOEFL (minimum score 600), interview. Application deadline: 2/1. Application fee: $65. *Expenses:* Tuition $22,780 per year. Fees $48 per year. *Financial aid:* In 1997–98, 11 students received aid, including 3 fellowships (all to first-year students), 8 teaching assistantships (1 to a first-year student); research assistantships, full and partial tuition waivers, institutionally sponsored loans also available. Financial aid applicants required to submit FAFSA. *Faculty research:* Hospitality finance, properties, and real estate; management and human resources; organizational communication and behavior; food and beverage management; hospitality marketing management. • Director of Graduate Studies, 607-255-7245. Application contact: Graduate Field Assistant, 607-255-7245. Fax: 607-255-4179. E-mail: eh23@cornell.edu.

Announcement: The Master of Management in Hospitality (MMH) program in hotel administration provides a complete graduate management curriculum in hospitality and services fields for students with a bachelor's degree in any academic area. Additional electives enable students to specialize in management areas of their choice, including real estate, properties, operations, food and beverage, finance, human resources, organizational behavior, marketing, computer information systems, and entrepreneurship.

See in-depth description on page 475.

Florida International University, School of Hospitality Management, North Miami, FL 33181. Offers program in hotel and food service management (MS). Faculty: 24 full-time (5 women), 2 part-time (0 women), 25 FTE. Students: 124 full-time (68 women), 43 part-time (25 women); includes 29 minority (9 African Americans, 5 Asian Americans, 15 Hispanics), 111 international. Average age 28. 159 applicants, 46% accepted. In 1997, 92 degrees awarded. *Entrance requirements:* GMAT (minimum score 450) or GRE General Test (minimum combined score of 1000), TOEFL, minimum GPA of 3.0. Application fee: $20. *Expenses:* Tuition $138 per credit hour for state residents; $482 per credit hour for nonresidents. Fees $46 per semester. • Dr. Anthony G. Marshall, Dean, 305-919-4500. Fax: 305-919-4555. E-mail: marshall@fiu.edu.

The George Washington University, School of Business and Public Management, Department of Tourism Studies, Washington, DC 20052. Offerings include tourism and hospitality management (MBA). Department faculty: 1 full-time (0 women), 3 part-time (2 women), 2 FTE. *Application deadline:* 4/1 (priority date; rolling processing; 10/1 for spring admission). *Application fee:* $50. *Expenses:* Tuition $680 per semester hour. Fees $35 per semester hour. • Dr. Douglas Frechtling, Program Director, 202-994-6280. Fax: 202-994-1420.

Golden Gate University, School of Technology and Industry, San Francisco, CA 94105-2968. Offerings include hospitality administration and tourism (MS). MS (hospitality administration and tourism) new for fall 1998. *Degree requirements:* Computer language required, foreign language and thesis not required. *Average time to degree:* master's–2.5 years full-time. *Entrance requirements:* GMAT (MBA), TOEFL (minimum score 550), minimum GPA of 2.5. Application deadline: 7/1 (priority date; rolling processing). Application fee: $55 ($70 for international students). *Tuition:* $996 per course (minimum). • James Koerlin, Dean, 415-442-6540. Fax: 415-442-7049. Application contact: Enrollment Services, 415-442-7800. Fax: 415-442-7807. E-mail: info@ggu.edu.

Iowa State University of Science and Technology, College of Family and Consumer Sciences, Department of Hotel, Restaurant and Institution Management, Ames, IA 50011. Awards MFCS, MS, PhD. Faculty: 10 full-time. Students: 11 full-time (8 women), 8 part-time (7 women); includes 1 minority (African American), 13 international. 35 applicants, 43% accepted. In 1997, 7 master's awarded. *Degree requirements:* For master's, thesis or alternative; for doctorate, dissertation. *Entrance requirements:* GRE General Test or GMAT, TOEFL. Application fee: $20 ($30 for international students). *Expenses:* Tuition $3166 per year full-time, $176 per credit part-time for state residents; $9324 per year full-time, $518 per credit part-time for nonresidents. Fees $200 per year. *Financial aid:* In 1997–98, 5 research assistantships (2 to first-year students), 2 scholarships (both to first-year students) were awarded; teaching assistantships also available. • Dr. Donna L. Cowan, Interim Head, 515-294-1730. E-mail: dlcowan@iastate.edu. Application contact: Nancy E. Brown, Director of Graduate Education, 515-294-8474. E-mail: hrim@iastate.edu.

Johnson & Wales University, Graduate School, Program in Hospitality Administration, 8 Abbott Park Place, Providence, RI 02903-3703. Awards MBA. Part-time and evening/weekend programs available. Faculty: 4 full-time (3 women), 3 part-time (1 woman). Students: 157 full-time (71 women), 73 part-time (31 women); includes 23 minority (14 African Americans, 3 Asian Americans, 6 Hispanics), 135 international. Average age 25. 98 applicants, 68% accepted. In 1997, 61 degrees awarded (5% found work related to degree, 3% continued full-time study). *Degree requirements:* Thesis optional. *Average time to degree:* master's–1.5 years full-time, 2.7 years part-time. *Entrance requirements:* Minimum GPA of 2.75. Application deadline: 8/21 (priority date; rolling processing). Application fee: $0. *Expenses:* Tuition $194 per quarter hour (minimum). Fees $477 per year. *Financial aid:* In 1997–98, 22 graduate assistantships (6 to first-year students) averaging $735 per month were awarded; partial tuition waivers also available. Aid available to part-time students. Financial aid application deadline: 5/1. *Faculty research:* Trade and tourism, hotel marketing, personal budget assessments, international ventures. • Application contact: Dr. Allan G. Freedman, Director of Graduate Admissions, 401-598-1015. Fax: 401-598-4773. E-mail: clifb@jwu.edu.

Kansas State University, College of Human Ecology, Department of Hotel, Restaurant, Institutional Management, and Dietetics, Manhattan, KS 66506. Offers programs in dietetics (MS), food service and hospitality management (MS, PhD), human ecology (PhD). Part-time programs available. Faculty: 6 full-time (5 women). Students: 28 full-time (23 women), 4 part-time (3 women); includes 21 minority (1 African American, 20 Hispanics), 11 international. 25 applicants, 80% accepted. In 1997, 3 master's awarded (100% found work related to degree); 1 doctorate awarded (100% entered university research/teaching). *Degree requirements:* For master's, thesis or alternative required, foreign language not required. *Average time to degree:* master's–2 years full-time, 3 years part-time; doctorate–3 years full-time, 5 years part-time. *Entrance requirements:* For master's, GMAT, GRE, TOEFL (minimum score 570), minimum GPA of 3.0, industry experience; for doctorate, GMAT, GRE, TOEFL (minimum score 600), minimum GPA of 3.5, industry experience. Application deadline: 3/1 (priority date; rolling processing; 11/1 for spring admission). Application fee: $0 ($25 for international students). Electronic applications accepted. *Tuition:* $2218 per year full-time, $401 per semester (minimum) part-time for state residents; $6336 per year full-time, $1087 per semester (minimum) part-time for nonresidents. *Financial aid:* In 1997–98, 14 students received aid, including 9 research assistantships, 5 teaching assistantships. *Faculty research:* Food safety, environmental issues, forecasting, tourism, hospitality administration. • Judith L. Miller, Head, 785-532-5521. Application contact: Carol Shanklin, Graduate Coordinator, 785-532-2206.

Lynn University, School of Graduate Studies, School of Hospitality Administration, Boca Raton, FL 33431-5598. Offers programs in hospitality administration (MS), sports and athletics administration (MS). Part-time and evening/weekend programs available. Faculty: 5 full-time (1 woman), 2 part-time (1 woman). Students: 19 full-time (8 women), 4 part-time (2 women); includes 2 international. 20 applicants, 75% accepted. In 1997, 6 degrees awarded. *Degree requirements:* Computer language, project required, foreign language not required. *Average time to degree:* master's–1.6 years full-time, 3.6 years part-time. *Entrance requirements:* GMAT, minimum undergraduate GPA of 3.0. Application deadline: rolling. Application fee: $50. Electronic applications accepted. *Expenses:* Tuition $375 per credit hour. Fees $60 per year. *Financial aid:* In 1997–98, 16 students received aid, including 3 graduate assistantships (all to first-year students); partial tuition waivers and career-related internships or fieldwork also available. Financial aid application deadline: 6/15; applicants required to submit FAFSA. *Faculty research:* Labor relations, virtual reality, computer technology applications, dynamic balance in leisure-time skills, ethics in athletics. • Dr. Linsley DeVeau, Dean, 561-994-0770 Ext. 260. Fax: 561-997-9541. E-mail: admission@lynn.edu. Application contact: Peter Gallo, Graduate Admissions Counselor, 800-544-8035. Fax: 561-241-3552. E-mail: admission@lynn.edu.

Michigan State University, Eli Broad Graduate School of Management, The School of Hospitality Business, East Lansing, MI 48824-1020. Offers programs in food service management (MS), hospitality (MBA). Part-time programs available. Faculty: 9 (1 woman). Students: 10 (3 women); includes 1 minority (Hispanic), 2 international. In 1997, 2 degrees awarded. *Entrance requirements:* GMAT (minimum score 500 required for MBA), GRE General Test (MS). Application deadline: rolling. Application fee: $30 ($40 for international students). *Expenses:* Tuition $4609 per year full-time, $223 per credit hour (minimum) part-time for state residents; $8704 per year full-time, $450 per credit hour (minimum) part-time for nonresidents. Fees $576 per year full-time, $476 per year part-time. *Financial aid:* Fellowships, research assistantships, teaching assistantships, scholarships, Federal Work-Study, and career-related internships or fieldwork available. Aid available to part-time students. *Faculty research:* Hospitality accounting and finance, information systems, human resources management, marketing, and leadership. • Dr. Ronald F. Cichy, Director, 517-355-5080. Fax: 517-432-1170. E-mail: cichy@pilot.msu.edu.

New York University, School of Continuing Education, Center for Hospitality, Tourism and Travel Administration, Program in Hospitality Industries Studies, New York, NY 10012-1019. Awards MS. Part-time and evening/weekend programs available. Faculty: 20 (4 women). Students: 12 full-time (10 women), 40 part-time (27 women); includes 29 minority (4 African Americans, 23 Asian Americans, 2 Hispanics). Average age 28. 76 applicants, 55% accepted. In 1997, 27 degrees awarded. *Average time to degree:* master's–1.5 years full-time, 2.5 years part-time. *Entrance requirements:* GMAT (minimum score 650) or GRE General Test (minimum combined score of 1000), 1 year of work experience. Application deadline: 5/15 (priority date; rolling processing; 10/15 for spring admission). Application fee: $50. *Financial aid:* In 1997–98, 1 research assistantship averaging $700 per month was awarded; scholarships, Federal Work-Study, institutionally sponsored loans, and career-related internships or fieldwork also available. Aid available to part-time students. Financial aid application deadline: 3/1; applicants required to submit FAFSA. *Faculty research:* Financial and market analysis, asset management, feasibility, valuation, investment. • Dr. Mark M. Warner, Graduate Director, 212-998-9107. Fax: 212-995-4676. E-mail: mmw4@is4.nyu.edu.

See in-depth description on page 477.

New York University, School of Education, Department of Nutrition and Food Studies, Program in Food and Food Management, New York, NY 10012-1019. Offers food and food management (PhD), food management (MA), food studies (MA). Faculty: 8 full-time, 46 part-time. Students: 11 full-time, 29 part-time. 31 applicants, 58% accepted. In 1997, 22 master's, 1 doctorate awarded. *Degree requirements:* For master's, thesis required (for some programs), foreign language not required; for doctorate, dissertation. *Entrance requirements:* For master's, TOEFL; for doctorate, GRE General Test, TOEFL, interview. Application deadline: 2/1 (priority date; rolling processing; 12/1 for spring admission). Application fee: $40 ($60 for international students). *Financial aid:* Partial tuition waivers, Federal Work-Study, institutionally sponsored loans, and career-related internships or fieldwork available. Financial aid application deadline: 3/1; applicants required to submit FAFSA. • Application contact: Office of Graduate Admissions, 212-998-5030. Fax: 212-995-4328.

The Ohio State University, College of Human Ecology, Department of Human Nutrition and Food Management, Columbus, OH 43210-1295. Offerings include food service management (MS, PhD), foods (MS, PhD). Department faculty: 10. *Degree requirements:* For master's, thesis optional, foreign language not required; for doctorate, dissertation required, foreign language not required. *Entrance requirements:* GRE General Test. Application deadline: 4/1 (rolling processing). Application fee: $30 ($40 for international students). *Tuition:* $5472 per year full-time, $554 per quarter (minimum) part-time for state residents; $14,172 per year full-time, $1424 per quarter (minimum) part-time for nonresidents. • Tammy Bray, Chair, 614-292-4485. Fax: 614-292-8880. E-mail: bray.21@osu.edu.

Oklahoma State University, College of Human Environmental Sciences, Program in Human Environmental Sciences, Stillwater, OK 74078. Offerings include hotel and restaurant administration (PhD). *Degree requirements:* Dissertation required, foreign language not required. *Entrance requirements:* TOEFL (minimum score 550). Application deadline: 7/1 (priority date). Application fee: $25. • Dr. Patricia Knaub, Dean, College of Human Environmental Sciences, 405-744-5053.

Oklahoma State University, College of Human Environmental Sciences, School of Hotel and Restaurant Administration, Stillwater, OK 74078. Awards MS. Faculty: 6 full-time (2 women). Students: 10 full-time (6 women), 11 part-time (4 women); includes 1 minority (African American), 9 international. Average age 32. In 1997, 3 degrees awarded. *Degree requirements:* Thesis required, foreign language not required. *Entrance requirements:* TOEFL (minimum score 550). Application deadline: 7/1 (priority date). Application fee: $25. *Financial aid:* In 1997–98, 12 students received aid, including 8 research assistantships totaling $71,550, 4 teaching assistantships totaling $40,068; partial tuition waivers, Federal Work-Study, and career-related internships or fieldwork also available. Aid available to part-time students. Financial aid application deadline: 3/1. • Dr. Bill Ryan, Director, 405-744-8486.

Pennsylvania State University University Park Campus, College of Health and Human Development, School of Hotel, Restaurant, and Recreation Management, Program in Hotel, Restaurant, and Institutional Management, University Park, PA 16802-1503. Awards MHRIM. Students: 10 full-time (4 women), 1 part-time (0 women). In 1997, 2 degrees awarded. *Entrance requirements:* GRE General Test. Application fee: $40. *Expenses:* Tuition $6534 per year full-time, $276 per credit part-time for state residents; $13,460 per year full-time, $561 per credit part-time for nonresidents. Fees $252 per year (minimum) full-time, $43 per semester (minimum) part-time. • Dr. William P. Andrew, Professor in Charge, 814-865-1851.

See in-depth description on page 1317.

Purdue University, School of Consumer and Family Sciences, Department of Restaurant, Hotel, and Institutional and Tourism Management, West Lafayette, IN 47907. Awards MS. Faculty: 17 full-time, 2 part-time. Students: 44 full-time (30 women), 8 part-time (4 women); includes 32 minority (1 African American, 29 Asian Americans, 2 Hispanics). 80 applicants, 31% accepted. In 1997, 16 degrees awarded. *Degree requirements:* Thesis optional, foreign language not required. *Average time to degree:* master's–2 years full-time, 3.5 years part-time. *Entrance requirements:* GMAT (minimum score 550) or GRE General Test (minimum combined score of 1000), TOEFL (minimum score 550), minimum GPA of 3.0. Application fee: $30. Electronic applications accepted. *Tuition:* $3500 per year full-time, $126 per credit hour part-time for state residents; $11,720 per year full-time, $387 per credit hour part-time for nonresidents. *Financial aid:* In 1997–98, 4 research assistantships, 14 teaching assistantships (6 to first-year students) averaging $950 per month were awarded; career-related internships or fieldwork also available. Aid available to part-time students. Financial aid applicants required to submit FAFSA. *Faculty research:* Human resources, marketing, hotel and restaurant operations, food product and equipment development, tourism. • Dr. R. R. Kavanaugh, Head, 765-494-4643. Application contact: Dr. T. E. Pearson, Coordinator of Graduate Programs, 765-494-4733.

Announcement: The graduate program is designed for students who identify a need for concentrated study in a hospitality industry specialization or academic area. Typical students have management experience or a strong undergraduate experience and a well-developed specialized career orientation. The 5 program options have a limited management core requirement and allow the greatest possible flexibility in choosing courses and research projects that will lead to the student's desired level of specialized skill. Students with other academic backgrounds may be admitted with special provisions.

Rochester Institute of Technology, College of Applied Science and Technology, Department of Food, Hotel, and Travel Management, Program in Hospitality-Tourism Management, Rochester, NY 14623-5604. Awards MS. Students: 17 full-time (9 women), 2 part-time (both women); includes 1 minority (Asian American), 9 international. 40 applicants, 90% accepted. In 1997, 16 degrees awarded. *Entrance requirements:* Minimum GPA of 3.0. Application deadline: 3/1 (priority date; rolling processing). Application fee: $40. *Expenses:* Tuition $18,765 per year full-time, $527 per credit hour part-time. Fees $126 per year full-time. • Dr. Richard Marecki, Graduate Programs Chairperson, Department of Food, Hotel, and Travel Management, 716-475-6017.

Rochester Institute of Technology, College of Applied Science and Technology, Department of Food, Hotel, and Travel Management, Program in Service Management, Rochester, NY 14623-5604. Awards MS. Students: 10 full-time (6 women), 5 part-time (4 women); includes 1 minority (African American), 7 international. 6 applicants, 83% accepted. In 1997, 13 degrees awarded. *Entrance requirements:* Minimum GPA of 3.0. Application deadline: 3/1 (priority date; rolling processing). Application fee: $40. *Expenses:* Tuition $18,765 per year full-time, $527 per credit hour part-time. Fees $126 per year full-time. • Dr. Richard Marecki, Graduate Programs Chairperson, Department of Food, Hotel, and Travel Management, 716-475-6017.

Roosevelt University, Evelyn T. Stone University College, Program in Hospitality Management, Chicago, IL 60605-1394. Awards MS. *Degree requirements:* Thesis required, foreign language not required. *Entrance requirements:* Minimum GPA of 2.75, previous work experience. Application deadline: 6/1 (priority date; rolling processing). Application fee: $25 ($35 for international students). *Expenses:* Tuition $445 per credit hour. Fees $100 per year. *Financial aid:* Application deadline 2/15. • Application contact: Joanne Canyon-Heller, Coordinator of Graduate Admissions, 312-341-3612.

Schiller International University, MBA Programs, Program in International Hotel and Tourism Management, 453 Edgewater Drive, Dunedin, FL 34698-7532. Awards MBA. *Degree requirements:* Thesis optional, foreign language not required. *Entrance requirements:* GMAT, bachelor's degree or equivalent. Application deadline: rolling. Application fee: $35. *Expenses:* Tuition $11,800 per year. Fees $210 per year. *Financial aid:* Available to part-time students. Financial aid application deadline: 3/30. • Application contact: Muriel Jault, Admissions Representative, 813-736-5082. Fax: 813-734-0359. E-mail: siuadmis@aol.com.

See in-depth description on page 479.

Schiller International University, Graduate Programs, Program in International Hotel and Tourism Management, 51-55 Waterloo Road, London SE1 8TX, United Kingdom. Awards MA, MBA. *Degree requirements:* Thesis optional, foreign language not required. *Entrance requirements:* GMAT. Application deadline: 8/1 (priority date; rolling processing; 12/1 for spring admission). Application fee: $35. *Expenses:* Tuition $12,800 per year. Fees $210 per year. *Financial aid:* Scholarships available. Aid available to part-time students. Financial aid application deadline: 4/30. • Application contact: Muriel Jault, Admissions Representative, 813-736-5082. Fax: 813-734-0359. E-mail: siuadmis@aol.com.

See in-depth description on page 479.

Temple University, School of Tourism and Hospitality, Department of Sport Management and Leisure Studies, Program in Tourism and Hospitality Management, Philadelphia, PA 19122-6096. Awards MTHM. Program new for fall 1998. Part-time and evening/weekend programs available. *Degree requirements:* Computer language required, foreign language and thesis not required. *Entrance requirements:* GRE General Test or MAT, minimum undergraduate GPA of 2.8. Application deadline: 6/1 (priority date; 10/1 for spring admission). Application fee: $40. *Expenses:* Tuition $323 per semester hour for state residents; $444 per semester hour for nonresidents. Fees $170 per year full-time, $28 per semester (minimum) part-time. *Financial aid:* Teaching assistantships available. • Application contact: Dr. Elizabeth Barber, Graduate Coordinator, 215-204-8706. Fax: 215-204-1455. E-mail: betsyb@astro.temple.edu.

See in-depth description on page 1903.

Texas Tech University, Graduate School, College of Human Sciences, Department of Education, Nutrition, and Restaurant/Hotel Management, Program in Restaurant, Hotel, and Institutional Management, Lubbock, TX 79409. Awards MS. Part-time programs available. Postbaccalaureate distance learning degree programs offered (minimal on-campus study). Faculty: 6 full-time (3 women), 1 part-time (0 women), 6.5 FTE. Students: 14 full-time (8 women), 8 part-time (6 women); includes 2 minority (both Hispanics), 12 international. Average age 30. 30 applicants, 67% accepted. In 1997, 8 degrees awarded (50% found work related to degree, 50% continued full-time study). *Degree requirements:* Thesis optional, foreign language not required. *Average time to degree:* master's–2 years full-time, 4 years part-time. *Entrance requirements:* GMAT (minimum score 500) or GRE General Test (minimum combined score of 900). Application deadline: rolling. Application fee: $25 ($50 for international students). Electronic applications accepted. *Expenses:* Tuition $864 per year full-time, $120 per semester (minimum) part-time for state residents; $5976 per year full-time, $747 per semester (minimum) part-time for nonresidents. Fees $2321 per year full-time, $302 per semester (minimum) part-time. *Financial aid:* In 1997–98, 17 students received aid, including 2 research assistantships (1 to a first-year student) averaging $611 per month and totaling $11,000, 10 teaching assistantships (5 to first-year students) averaging $611 per month and totaling $55,000; fellowships, Federal Work-Study, institutionally sponsored loans, and career-related internships or fieldwork also available. Financial aid application deadline: 2/1. *Faculty research:* Nontraditional work force, wine marketing, operations management, consumer issues, hospitality education and training, distance/extended learning, food service, tourism, educational technology. Total annual research expenditures: $75,000. • Dr. Tim Dodd, Graduate Adviser, 806-742-3077. Fax: 806-742-0125. E-mail: tdodd@ttu.edu.

Texas Woman's University, College of Health Sciences, Department of Nutrition and Food Sciences, Denton, TX 76204. Offerings include institutional administration (MS). Department faculty: 14 full-time (11 women), 4 part-time (all women). *Degree requirements:* Thesis required (for some programs), foreign language not required. *Entrance requirements:* GRE General Test (minimum combined score of 700), minimum GPA of 3.0. Application deadline: rolling. Application fee: $25. • Dr. Carolyn Bednar, Chair, 940-898-2636. Fax: 940-898-2634.

The University of Alabama, College of Human Environmental Sciences, Department of Human Nutrition and Hospitality Management, Tuscaloosa, AL 35487. Awards MSHES. Part-time programs available. Faculty: 5 full-time (4 women). Students: 12 full-time (11 women), 1 (woman) part-time; includes 2 minority (both Asian Americans). In 1997, 4 degrees awarded (100% found work related to degree). *Degree requirements:* Thesis required, foreign language not required. *Entrance requirements:* GRE General Test or MAT, minimum GPA of 3.0. Application deadline: 7/6 (rolling processing). Application fee: $25. *Tuition:* $2684 per year full-time, $594 per semester (minimum) part-time for state residents; $7216 per year full-time, $1248 per semester (minimum) part-time for nonresidents. *Financial aid:* In 1997–98, 4 students received aid, including 2 research assistantships (both to first-year students), 2 teaching assistantships; career-related internships or fieldwork also available. Financial aid application deadline: 3/15. *Faculty research:* Fat determination of low-fat foods, maternal and child nutrition, obesity and eating disorders, community nutrition interventions. • Dr. Judy L. Bonner, Head, 205-348-6157.

University of Denver, Daniels College of Business, Department of Hotel, Restaurant, and Tourism Management, Denver, CO 80208. Offers program in resort and tourism management (MS, MSRTM). MSRTM new for fall 1998. Part-time and evening/weekend programs available. Faculty: 4 full-time (0 women). Students: 19 full-time (13 women), 3 part-time (all women); includes 1 minority (Asian American), 9 international. 24 applicants, 83% accepted. In 1997, 1 degree awarded. *Entrance requirements:* GMAT (average 545). Application deadline: 5/1 (priority date; rolling processing; 1/1 for spring admission). Application fee: $50. *Expenses:* Tuition $18,216 per year full-time, $506 per credit hour part-time. Fees $159 per year. *Financial aid:* In 1997–98, 11 students received aid, including 1 teaching assistantship averaging $517 per month and totaling $4,650, 7 grants, scholarships totaling $5,065; research assistantships, Federal Work-Study, institutionally sponsored loans, and career-related internships or fieldwork also available. Financial aid application deadline: 2/15; applicants required to submit FAFSA. *Faculty research:* Resort and tourism planning and development, public policy, menu development, hotel feasibility, resort and tourism marketing. • Dr. Robert O'Halloran, Chair, 303-871-2322. Fax: 303-871-4260. Application contact: Jan Johnson, Executive Director, Student Services, 303-871-3416. Fax: 303-871-4466. E-mail: dcb@du.edu.

University of Guelph, College of Social and Applied Human Sciences, Department of Hotel and Food Administration, Guelph, ON N1G 2W1, Canada. Offers program in management studies (MMS). Faculty: 12 full-time (3 women), 2 part-time (0 women). Students: 15 full-time (9 women); includes 2 international. 18 applicants, 67% accepted. In 1997, 5 degrees awarded (100% found work related to degree). *Degree requirements:* Thesis (for some programs). *Average time to degree:* master's–2.5 years full-time. *Entrance requirements:* GMAT (minimum score 575), minimum B- average during previous 2 years. Application deadline: 5/1 (priority date; rolling processing; 12/1 for spring admission). Application fee: $60. *Expenses:* Tuition $4725 per year full-time, $3165 per year part-time for Canadian residents; $6999 per year for nonresidents. Fees $612 per year full-time, $38 per year (minimum) part-time for Canadian residents; $612 per year for nonresidents. *Financial aid:* In 1997–98, 13 students received aid, including 12 teaching assistantships (7 to first-year students) averaging $1,000 per month and totaling $72,000. *Faculty research:* Hospitality management, hospitality marketing and tourism, organizational behavior. • Dr. J. Walsh, Acting Director, 519-824-4120 Ext. 3703. Application contact: Dr. M. Shaw, Graduate Coordinator, 519-824-4120 Ext. 8552. Fax: 519-823-5512. E-mail: hafamms@uoguelph.ca.

University of Hawaii at Manoa, School of Travel Industry Management, Honolulu, HI 96822. Awards MPS. Part-time programs available. *Degree requirements:* Thesis or alternative required, foreign language not required. *Average time to degree:* master's–2.5 years full-time. *Entrance requirements:* GMAT (minimum score 500; average 560) or GRE General Test (minimum combined score of 1800 on three sections; average 1844); TOEFL (minimum score 560; average 618), minimum GPA of 3.0. Application deadline: 3/1 (rolling processing; 9/1 for spring admission). Application fee: $0. *Tuition:* $4029 per year full-time, $214 per credit hour part-time for state residents; $9957 per year full-time, $461 per credit hour part-time for nonresidents. *Faculty research:* Tourism economics, transportation, hospitality management, ecotourism.

University of Houston, Conrad N. Hilton College of Hotel and Restaurant Management, 4800 Calhoun, Houston, TX 77204-2163. Awards MHM. Part-time and evening/weekend programs available. Postbaccalaureate distance learning degree programs offered (minimal on-campus study). Faculty: 11 full-time (4 women), 6 part-time (1 woman), 13.33 FTE. Students: 53 full-time (27 women), 14 part-time (9 women); includes 11 minority (1 African American, 5 Asian Americans, 5 Hispanics), 29 international. Average age 30. 111 applicants, 32% accepted. In 1997, 19 degrees awarded. *Degree requirements:* Computer language, thesis, practical experience required, foreign language not required. *Average time to degree:* master's–1.7 years full-time, 3.5 years part-time. *Entrance requirements:* GMAT (average 550) or GRE General Test (minimum combined score of 1100), TOEFL (minimum score 600; average 610), current resume. Application deadline: 5/1 (rolling processing; 10/1 for spring admission). Application fee: $25 ($75 for international students). *Expenses:* Tuition $1152 per year full-time, $120 per semester (minimum) part-time for state residents; $4482 per year full-time, $249 per credit hour part-time for nonresidents. Fees $977 per year full-time, $119 per semester (minimum) part-time. *Financial aid:* In 1997–98, 4 research assistantships (3 to first-year students) averaging $680 per month, 16 teaching assistantships (8 to first-year students) averaging $680 per month were awarded; partial tuition waivers, Federal Work-Study, institutionally sponsored loans, and career-related internships or fieldwork also available. Aid available to part-time students. *Faculty research:* Catering, tourism, hospitality marketing, security and risk management, purchasing and financial information usage. Total annual research expenditures: $36,000. • Alan T. Stutts, Dean, 713-743-2550. E-mail: astutts@uh.edu. Application contact: Lillian Sutawan-Binns, Academic Adviser, Graduate Studies, 713-743-2457. Fax: 713-743-2498. E-mail: lbinns@uh.edu.

See in-depth description on page 481.

University of Massachusetts Amherst, College of Food and Natural Resources, Department of Hotel, Restaurant, and Travel Administration, Amherst, MA 01003-0001. Awards MS. Part-time programs available. Faculty: 10 full-time (3 women). Students: 29 full-time (18 women), 2 part-time (both women); includes 1 minority (Hispanic), 18 international. Average age 27. 59 applicants, 58% accepted. In 1997, 18 degrees awarded. *Degree requirements:* Thesis optional, foreign language not required. *Entrance requirements:* GMAT. Application deadline: 3/1 (priority date; rolling processing; 10/1 for spring admission). Application fee: $40. *Expenses:* Tuition $2640 per year full-time, $110 per credit part-time for state residents; $3690 per year (minimum) full-time, $165 per credit (minimum) part-time for nonresidents. Fees $2856 per year full-time, $422 per semester part-time for state residents; $3204 per year full-time, $480 per semester part-time for nonresidents. *Financial aid:* In 1997–98, 2 research assistantships, 25 teaching assistantships were awarded; fellowships also available. Aid available to part-time students. Financial aid application deadline: 3/1. • Dr. Frank Lattuca, Director, 413-545-1389. Fax: 413-545-1235. E-mail: lattuca@hrta.umass.edu.

University of Missouri–Columbia, College of Human Environmental Science, Department of Human Nutrition, Foods, and Food System Management, Columbia, MO 65211. Offerings include foods and food systems management (MS). Offered jointly with the Department of Food Science. Department faculty: 11 full-time (5 women). *Application deadline:* rolling. *Application fee:* $25 ($50 for international students). *Expenses:* Tuition $3240 per year full-time, $180 per credit hour part-time for state residents; $9108 per year full-time, $506 per credit hour part-time for nonresidents. Fees $55 per year full-time. • Dr. Richard Dowdy, Director of Graduate Studies, 573-882-7014.

University of Nevada, Las Vegas, William F. Harrah College of Hotel Administration, Program in Hotel Administration, Las Vegas, NV 89154-9900. Offers hospitality administration (PhD),

Directories: Hospitality Management; Travel and Tourism

University of Nevada, Las Vegas (continued)
hotel administration (MS). Part-time programs available. Faculty: 25 full-time (8 women). Students: 34 full-time (13 women), 38 part-time (15 women); includes 9 minority (1 African American, 5 Asian Americans, 2 Hispanics, 1 Native American), 22 international. 119 applicants, 34% accepted. In 1997, 11 master's awarded. *Degree requirements:* For master's, comprehensive exam required, thesis optional, foreign language not required; for doctorate, dissertation defense, seminar. *Entrance requirements:* For master's, GMAT or GRE, minimum GPA of 2.75; for doctorate, GMAT (minimum score 550), minimum graduate GPA of 3.0. Application deadline: 6/15 (priority date; rolling processing; 11/15 for spring admission). Application fee: $40 ($95 for international students). *Expenses:* Tuition $93 per credit for state residents; $93 per credit full-time, $190 per credit part-time for nonresidents. Fees $5570 per year full-time for nonresidents. *Financial aid:* In 1997–98, 10 research assistantships, 3 teaching assistantships were awarded. Financial aid application deadline: 3/1. • Dr. John Bowen, Director, 702-895-0876.

See in-depth description on page 483.

University of New Haven, School of Business, Program in Business Administration, West Haven, CT 06516-1916. Offerings include hotel and restaurant management (MBA). *Degree requirements:* Thesis or alternative required, foreign language not required. *Application deadline:* rolling. *Application fee:* $50. *Expenses:* Tuition $1125 per course. Fees $13 per trimester. • Dr. Omid Nodoushani, Coordinator, 203-932-7123.

University of New Haven, College of Arts and Sciences, School of Hotel, Restaurant, Tourism and Dietetics Administration, Program in Hospitality and Tourism, West Haven, CT 06516-1916. Awards MS. Students: 7 full-time (6 women), 3 part-time (1 woman); includes 1 minority (African American), 6 international. 17 applicants, 65% accepted. In 1997, 15 degrees awarded. *Application deadline:* rolling. *Application fee:* $50. *Expenses:* Tuition $1125 per course. Fees $13 per trimester. *Financial aid:* Application deadline 5/1; applicants required to submit FAFSA. • Sherie Brezina, Coordinator, 203-932-7359.

University of North Carolina at Greensboro, School of Human Environmental Sciences, Department of Nutrition and Foodservice Systems, Greensboro, NC 27412-5001. Offers programs in food service management (M Ed, MS), human nutrition (M Ed, MS, PhD). Faculty: 10 full-time (6 women). Students: 36 full-time (28 women), 3 part-time (2 women); includes 4 minority (1 African American, 3 Asian Americans), 6 international. 53 applicants, 47% accepted. In 1997, 8 master's, 1 doctorate awarded. *Degree requirements:* Thesis/dissertation. *Entrance requirements:* GRE General Test, TOEFL. Application deadline: 3/1 (11/1 for spring admission). Application fee: $35. *Financial aid:* In 1997–98, 2 fellowships totaling $8,000, 18 assistantships totaling $156,149 were awarded; research assistantships, teaching assistantships also available. • Dr. Mark Failla, Chair, 336-334-5313. Fax: 336-334-4129. E-mail: mlfailla@erickson.uncg.edu.

University of North Texas, School of Merchandising and Hospitality Management, Denton, TX 76203-6737. Offers programs in hotel/restaurant management (MS), merchandising and fabric analytics (MS). Part-time programs available. Faculty: 12 full-time (9 women). Students: 14 full-time (9 women), 17 part-time (9 women); includes 4 minority (3 Asian Americans, 1 Hispanic), 17 international. In 1997, 11 degrees awarded. *Degree requirements:* Thesis or alternative, comprehensive exam required, foreign language not required. *Entrance requirements:* GRE General Test (minimum score 400 on verbal section, 800 combined), minimum GPA of 2.8, previous course work in major area. Application deadline: 7/17. Application fee: $25 ($50 for international students). *Tuition:* $2063 per year full-time, $815 per year part-time for state residents; $5897 per year full-time, $2100 per year part-time for nonresidents. *Financial aid:* Fellowships, research assistantships, teaching assistantships, Federal Work-Study, institutionally sponsored loans, and career-related internships or fieldwork available. Financial aid application deadline: 4/1. *Faculty research:* Employee imaging, western wear, diversity in the workplace, leadership development, quality assessment. • Dr. Suzanne V. LaBrecque, Dean, 940-565-2436. Fax: 940-565-4348.

University of South Carolina, Graduate School, College of Applied Professions Sciences, School of Hotel, Restaurant and Tourism Administration, Columbia, SC 29208. Awards MHRTA. Faculty: 6 full-time (2 women). Students: 25 full-time (10 women), 3 part-time (1 woman); includes 2 minority (1 Asian American, 1 Hispanic), 8 international. Average age 29. In 1997, 16 degrees awarded. *Entrance requirements:* GMAT (minimum score 500) or GRE General Test (minimum combined score of 1000), minimum GPA of 3.0, 1 year of management experience. Application deadline: 8/1 (rolling processing; 11/15 for spring admission). Application fee: $35. Electronic applications accepted. *Expenses:* Tuition $3894 per year full-time, $193 per credit hour part-time for state residents; $8114 per year full-time, $404 per credit hour part-time for nonresidents. Fees $125 per year full-time, $37 per semester (minimum) part-time. *Faculty research:* Quality management, conference and meeting management, multicultural dimensions, international tourism development. • Dr. Sandra K. Strick, Interim Chair, 803-777-7684. Fax: 803-777-6427.

University of Tennessee, Knoxville, College of Human Ecology, Department of Consumer and Industry Services Management, Program in Recreation, Tourism, and Hospitality Management, Knoxville, TN 37996. Offers hospitality management (MS), recreation administration (MS), therapeutic recreation (MS), tourism (MS). Part-time programs available. Students: 11 full-time (6 women), 11 part-time (10 women); includes 1 minority (Asian American), 1 international. Average age 24. 13 applicants, 85% accepted. In 1997, 16 degrees awarded. *Degree requirements:* Thesis or alternative required, foreign language not required. *Entrance requirements:* TOEFL (minimum score 550), GRE General Test, minimum GPA of 2.7. Application deadline: 2/1 (priority date; rolling processing). Application fee: $35. Electronic applications accepted. *Tuition:* $3354 per year full-time, $181 per semester hour part-time for state residents; $8410 per year full-time, $462 per semester hour part-time for nonresidents. *Financial aid:* Career-related internships or fieldwork available. Financial aid application deadline: 2/1. • Dr. Nancy B. Fair, Head, Department of Consumer and Industry Services Management, 423-974-2141. Fax: 423-974-5236. E-mail: nbfair@utk.edu.

See in-depth description on page 1857.

University of Wisconsin–Stout, College of Human Development, Program in Hospitality and Tourism, Menomonie, WI 54751. Awards MS. Part-time programs available. Students: 26 full-time (17 women), 6 part-time (5 women); includes 1 minority (Hispanic), 18 international. 31 applicants, 71% accepted. In 1997, 11 degrees awarded. *Degree requirements:* Thesis required, foreign language not required. *Application deadline:* 5/1 (10/1 for spring admission). *Application fee:* $45. *Tuition:* $3284 per year full-time, $183 per credit hour part-time for state residents; $7644 per year full-time, $425 per credit hour part-time for nonresidents. *Financial aid:* In 1997–98, 4 research assistantships were awarded; teaching assistantships, full and partial tuition waivers, Federal Work-Study also available. Aid available to part-time students. Financial aid application deadline: 4/1; applicants required to submit FAFSA. • Dr. Randall Upchurch, Director, 715-232-1407.

Virginia Polytechnic Institute and State University, College of Human Resources and Education, Department of Hospitality and Tourism Management, Blacksburg, VA 24061. Awards MS, PhD. Students: 35 full-time (11 women), 3 part-time (2 women); includes 5 minority (2 African Americans, 2 Asian Americans, 1 Hispanic), 20 international. 55 applicants, 38% accepted. In 1997, 2 master's, 8 doctorates awarded. *Degree requirements:* Thesis/dissertation. *Entrance requirements:* For master's, GRE, TOEFL (minimum score 600); for doctorate, GRE, TOEFL. Application deadline: 12/1 (priority date; rolling processing). Application fee: $25. *Tuition:* $4927 per year full-time, $792 per semester (minimum) part-time for state residents; $7537 per year full-time, $1227 per semester (minimum) part-time for nonresidents. *Financial aid:* Research assistantships, teaching assistantships, assistantships available. Financial aid application deadline: 4/1. • Dr. Mahmood Khan, Head, 540-231-5515. E-mail: mahmood@vt.edu.

Travel and Tourism

Black Hills State University, College of Business and Technology, Spearfish, SD 57799-9502. Offers program in tourism and hospitality management (MS). Program new for fall 1998. Part-time programs available. Faculty: 16 full-time (7 women). *Degree requirements:* Thesis required (for some programs), foreign language not required. *Entrance requirements:* TOEFL (minimum score 550), bachelor's degree in related field. Application deadline: 8/1 (priority date; rolling processing). Application fee: $15. *Expenses:* Tuition $85 per credit hour for state residents; $251 per credit hour for nonresidents. Fees $41 per credit hour. *Financial aid:* Research assistantships, partial tuition waivers, Federal Work-Study, and career-related internships or fieldwork available. Aid available to part-time students. *Faculty research:* Tourism in western South Dakota, marketing. Total annual research expenditures: $30,000. • Tom Hills, Dean, 605-642-6212. Fax: 605-642-6273.

Clemson University, College of Health, Education, and Human Development, Department of Parks, Recreation, and Tourism Management, Clemson, SC 29634. Awards MPRTM, MS, PhD. Part-time programs available. Students: 33 full-time (17 women), 25 part-time (16 women); includes 3 minority (1 African American, 2 Hispanics), 10 international. Average age 25. 49 applicants, 49% accepted. In 1997, 5 master's, 4 doctorates awarded. *Degree requirements:* For master's, thesis required (for some programs), foreign language not required; for doctorate, dissertation required, foreign language not required. *Entrance requirements:* For master's, GRE General Test, TOEFL, minimum undergraduate GPA of 3.0; for doctorate, GRE General Test, TOEFL, minimum graduate GPA of 3.0. Application deadline: 5/1 (priority date; 10/1 for spring admission). Application fee: $35. *Expenses:* Tuition $3154 per year full-time, $130 per credit hour part-time for state residents; $6452 per year full-time, $264 per credit hour part-time for nonresidents. Fees $190 per year. *Financial aid:* Fellowships, research assistantships, teaching assistantships, assistantships, partial tuition waivers, and career-related internships or fieldwork available. Financial aid application deadline: 4/15. *Faculty research:* Recreation resource management, leisure behavior, therapeutic recreation, community leisure services. • Dr. Ann James, Chair, 864-656-3400. E-mail: ajms@clemson.edu. Application contact: Dr. Fran McGuire, Graduate Coordinator, 864-656-2183. Fax: 864-656-2226. E-mail: lefty@clemson.edu.

The George Washington University, School of Business and Public Management, Department of Tourism Studies, Washington, DC 20052. Offers programs in destination management (MTA), event management (MTA), sport management (MTA), tourism administration (MTA), tourism and hospitality management (MBA), travel marketing (MTA). Part-time programs available. Faculty: 1 full-time (0 women), 3 part-time (2 women), 2 FTE. Students: 37 full-time (28 women), 23 part-time (11 women); includes 7 minority (6 African Americans, 1 Asian American), 13 international. Average age 29. 58 applicants, 76% accepted. In 1997, 22 degrees awarded. *Degree requirements:* Thesis, comprehensive exam required, foreign language not required. *Entrance requirements:* GRE General Test, TOEFL (minimum score 550). Application deadline: 4/1 (priority date; rolling processing; 10/1 for spring admission). Application fee: $50. *Expenses:* Tuition $680 per semester hour. Fees $35 per semester hour. *Financial aid:* Fellowships, teaching assistantships, partial tuition waivers, Federal Work-Study, institutionally sponsored loans, and career-related internships or fieldwork available. Financial aid application deadline: 4/1. *Faculty research:* Tourism policy, tourism impact forecasting, geotourism. • Dr. Douglas Frechtling, Program Director, 202-994-6280. Fax: 202-994-1420.

Golden Gate University, School of Technology and Industry, San Francisco, CA 94105-2968. Offerings include hospitality administration and tourism (MS). MS (hospitality administration and tourism) new for fall 1998. *Degree requirements:* Computer language required, foreign language and thesis not required. *Average time to degree:* master's–2.5 years full-time. *Entrance requirements:* GMAT (MBA), TOEFL (minimum score 550), minimum GPA of 2.5. Application deadline: 7/1 (priority date; rolling processing). Application fee: $55 ($70 for international students). *Tuition:* $996 per course (minimum). • James Koerlin, Dean, 415-442-6540. Fax: 415-442-7049. Application contact: Enrollment Services, 415-442-7800. Fax: 415-442-7807. E-mail: info@ggu.edu.

Michigan State University, College of Agriculture and Natural Resources, Department of Park, Recreation and Tourism Resources, East Lansing, MI 48824-1020. Offers program in park, recreation and tourism resources (MS, PhD). Part-time and evening/weekend programs available. Faculty: 11 (2 women). Students: 64 (27 women); includes 5 minority (2 African Americans, 2 Asian Americans, 1 Hispanic), 26 international. In 1997, 9 master's, 1 doctorate awarded. *Degree requirements:* For master's, thesis or alternative, final exam; for doctorate, dissertation, qualifying exam. *Entrance requirements:* GRE General Test (minimum combined score of 1000; average 1100). Application deadline: 1/15 (priority date; rolling processing). Application fee: $30 ($40 for international students). *Expenses:* Tuition $4609 per year full-time, $223 per credit hour (minimum) part-time for state residents; $8704 per year full-time, $450 per credit hour (minimum) part-time for nonresidents. Fees $576 per year full-time, $476 per year part-time. *Financial aid:* In 1997–98, 25 students received aid, including 5 fellowships, 16 research assistantships, 4 teaching assistantships; Federal Work-Study also available. *Faculty research:* Tourism behavior and economics, economic inputs of recreation and tourism, park and recreation policy management, visitor management, input/output modeling. • Dr. Joseph D. Fridgen, Chairperson, 517-353-5190. Fax: 517-432-3597. E-mail: jfridgen@pilot.msu.edu.

New York University, School of Continuing Education, Center for Hospitality, Tourism and Travel Administration, Program in Tourism and Travel Management, New York, NY 10012-1019. Awards MS. Part-time and evening/weekend programs available. Faculty: 4 full-time (3 women), 20 part-time (5 women). Students: 10 full-time (8 women), 33 part-time (24 women); includes 21 minority (4 African Americans, 11 Asian Americans, 6 Hispanics). Average age 27. 64 applicants, 36% accepted. In 1997, 24 degrees awarded. *Average time to degree:* master's–1.5 years full-time, 2.5 years part-time. *Entrance requirements:* GMAT (minimum score 650) or GRE General Test (minimum combined score of 1000), 1 year of work experience. Application deadline: 5/15 (priority date; rolling processing; 10/15 for spring admission). Application fee: $50. *Financial aid:* In 1997–98, 1 research assistantship averaging $700 per month was awarded; scholarships, Federal Work-Study, institutionally sponsored loans, and career-related internships or fieldwork also available. Aid available to part-time students. Financial aid application deadline: 3/1; applicants required to submit FAFSA. *Faculty research:* Destination, management, and marketing technology. • Dr. Mark M. Warner, Graduate Director, 212-998-9107. Fax: 212-995-4676. E-mail: mmw4@is4.nyu.edu.

See in-depth description on page 477.

North Carolina State University, College of Forest Resources, Department of Parks, Recreation and Tourism Management, Raleigh, NC 27695. Offers programs in geographic information systems (MS), maintenance management (MRRA, MS), recreation planning (MRRA, MS), recreation resources administration/public administration (MRRA), recreation/park management (MRRA, MS), sports management (MRRA, MS), travel and tourism management (MS). Faculty: 15 full-time (5 women), 7 part-time (0 women). Students: 29 full-time (15 women), 33 part-time (15 women); includes 6 minority (3 African Americans, 2 Asian Americans, 1 Hispanic), 2 international. Average age 29. 42 applicants, 45% accepted. In 1997, 23 degrees awarded. *Degree requirements:* Thesis required (for some programs), foreign language not required. *Entrance requirements:* GRE General Test, TOEFL (minimum score 550). Application deadline: 6/25 (11/25 for spring admission). Application fee: $45. *Tuition:* $2370 per year full-time, $517 per semester (minimum) part-time for state residents; $11,536 per year full-time, $2809 per semester (minimum) part-time for nonresidents. *Financial aid:* In 1997–98, 21 research assistantships (3 to first-year students) averaging $654 per month and totaling $61,815, 6 teaching assistantships totaling $18,099 were awarded; fellowships, institutionally sponsored loans, and career-related internships or fieldwork also available. Financial aid application deadline: 4/1. *Faculty research:* Park and recreation management, tourism policy and development, spatial information systems, natural resource recreation management, recreational sports management. Total annual research expenditures: $740,100. • Dr. Philip S. Rea, Head, 919-515-3675. E-mail: phil_rea@ncsu.edu. Application contact: Dr. Beth E. Wilson, Director of Graduate Programs, 919-515-3665. Fax: 919-515-3687. E-mail: beth_wilson@ncsu.edu.

Purdue University, School of Consumer and Family Sciences, Department of Restaurant, Hotel, and Institutional and Tourism Management, West Lafayette, IN 47907. Awards MS. Faculty: 17 full-time, 2 part-time. Students: 44 full-time (30 women), 8 part-time (4 women); includes 32 minority (1 African American, 29 Asian Americans, 2 Hispanics). 80 applicants, 31% accepted. In 1997, 16 degrees awarded. *Degree requirements:* Thesis optional, foreign language not required. *Average time to degree:* master's–2 years full-time, 3.5 years part-time. *Entrance requirements:* GMAT (minimum score 550) or GRE General Test (minimum combined score of 1000), TOEFL (minimum score 550), minimum GPA of 3.0. Application fee: $30. Electronic applications accepted. *Tuition:* $3500 per year full-time, $126 per credit hour part-time for state residents; $11,720 per year full-time, $387 per credit hour part-time for nonresidents. *Financial aid:* In 1997–98, 4 research assistantships, 14 teaching assistantships (6 to first-year students) averaging $950 per month were awarded; career-related internships or fieldwork also available. Aid available to part-time students. Financial aid applicants required to submit FAFSA. *Faculty research:* Human resources, marketing, hotel and restaurant operations, food product and equipment development, tourism. • Dr. R. R. Kavanaugh, Head, 765-494-4643. Application contact: Dr. T. E. Pearson, Coordinator of Graduate Programs, 765-494-4733.

Rochester Institute of Technology, College of Applied Science and Technology, Department of Food, Hotel, and Travel Management, Program in Hospitality-Tourism Management, Rochester, NY 14623-5604. Awards MS. Students: 17 full-time (9 women), 2 part-time (both women); includes 1 minority (Asian American), 9 international. 40 applicants, 90% accepted. In 1997, 16 degrees awarded. *Entrance requirements:* Minimum GPA of 3.0. Application deadline: 3/1 (priority date; rolling processing). Application fee: $40. *Expenses:* Tuition $18,765 per year full-time, $527 per credit hour part-time. Fees $126 per year full-time. • Dr. Richard Marecki, Graduate Programs Chairperson, Department of Food, Hotel, and Travel Management, 716-475-6017.

Rochester Institute of Technology, College of Applied Science and Technology, Department of Food, Hotel, and Travel Management, Program in Service Management, Rochester, NY 14623-5604. Awards MS. Students: 10 full-time (6 women), 5 part-time (4 women); includes 1 minority (African American), 7 international. 6 applicants, 83% accepted. In 1997, 13 degrees awarded. *Entrance requirements:* Minimum GPA of 3.0. Application deadline: 3/1 (priority date; rolling processing). Application fee: $40. *Expenses:* Tuition $18,765 per year full-time, $527 per credit hour part-time. Fees $126 per year full-time. • Dr. Richard Marecki, Graduate Programs Chairperson, Department of Food, Hotel, and Travel Management, 716-475-6017.

Schiller International University, MBA Programs, Program in International Hotel and Tourism Management, 453 Edgewater Drive, Dunedin, FL 34698-7532. Awards MBA. *Degree requirements:* Thesis optional, foreign language not required. *Entrance requirements:* GMAT, bachelor's degree or equivalent. Application deadline: rolling. Application fee: $35. *Expenses:* Tuition $11,800 per year. Fees $210 per year. *Financial aid:* Available to part-time students. Financial aid application deadline: 3/30. • Application contact: Muriel Jault, Admissions Representative, 813-736-5082. Fax: 813-734-0359. E-mail: siuadmis@aol.com.

See in-depth description on page 479.

Schiller International University, Graduate Programs, Program in International Hotel and Tourism Management, 51-55 Waterloo Road, London SE1 8TX, United Kingdom. Awards MA, MBA. *Degree requirements:* Thesis optional, foreign language not required. *Entrance requirements:* GMAT. Application deadline: 8/1 (priority date; rolling processing; 12/1 for spring admission). Application fee: $35. *Expenses:* Tuition $12,800 per year. Fees $210 per year. *Financial aid:* Scholarships available. Aid available to part-time students. Financial aid application deadline: 4/30. • Application contact: Muriel Jault, Admissions Representative, 813-736-5082. Fax: 813-734-0359. E-mail: siuadmis@aol.com.

See in-depth description on page 479.

Temple University, School of Tourism and Hospitality, Department of Sport Management and Leisure Studies, Program in Tourism and Hospitality Management, Philadelphia, PA 19122-6096. Awards MTHM. Program new for fall 1998. Part-time and evening/weekend programs available. *Degree requirements:* Computer language required, foreign language and thesis not required. *Entrance requirements:* GRE General Test or MAT, minimum undergraduate GPA of 2.8. Application deadline: 6/1 (priority date; 10/1 for spring admission). Application fee: $40. *Expenses:* Tuition $323 per semester hour for state residents; $444 per semester hour for nonresidents. Fees $170 per year full-time, $28 per semester (minimum) part-time. *Financial aid:* Teaching assistantships available. • Application contact: Dr. Elizabeth Barber, Graduate Coordinator, 215-204-8706. Fax: 215-204-1455. E-mail: betsyb@astro.temple.edu.

See in-depth description on page 1903.

University of Denver, Daniels College of Business, Department of Hotel, Restaurant, and Tourism Management, Denver, CO 80208. Offers program in resort and tourism management (MS, MSRTM). MSRTM new for fall 1998. Part-time and evening/weekend programs available. Faculty: 4 full-time (0 women). Students: 19 full-time (13 women), 3 part-time (all women); includes 1 minority (Asian American), 9 international. 24 applicants, 83% accepted. In 1997, 1 degree awarded. *Entrance requirements:* GMAT (average 545). Application deadline: 5/1 (priority date; rolling processing; 1/1 for spring admission). Application fee: $50. *Expenses:* Tuition $18,216 per year full-time, $506 per credit hour part-time. Fees $159 per year. *Financial aid:* In 1997–98, 11 students received aid, including 1 teaching assistantship averaging $517 per month and totaling $4,650, 7 grants, scholarships totaling $5,065; research assistantships, Federal Work-Study, institutionally sponsored loans, and career-related internships or fieldwork also available. Financial aid application deadline: 2/15; applicants required to submit FAFSA. *Faculty research:* Resort and tourism planning and development, public policy, menu development, hotel feasibility, resort and tourism marketing. • Dr. Robert O'Halloran, Chair, 303-871-2322. Fax: 303-871-4260. Application contact: Jan Johnson, Executive Director, Student Services, 303-871-3416. Fax: 303-871-4466. E-mail: dcb@du.edu.

University of Hawaii at Manoa, School of Travel Industry Management, Honolulu, HI 96822. Awards MPS. Part-time programs available. *Degree requirements:* Thesis or alternative required, foreign language not required. *Average time to degree:* master's–2.5 years full-time. *Entrance requirements:* GMAT (minimum score 500; average 560) or GRE General Test (minimum combined score of 1800 on three sections; average 1844); TOEFL (minimum score 560; average 618), minimum GPA of 3.0. Application deadline: 3/1 (rolling processing; 9/1 for spring admission). Application fee: $0. *Tuition:* $4029 per year full-time, $214 per credit hour part-time for state residents; $9957 per year full-time, $461 per credit hour part-time for nonresidents. *Faculty research:* Tourism economics, transportation, hospitality management, ecotourism.

University of Massachusetts Amherst, College of Food and Natural Resources, Department of Hotel, Restaurant, and Travel Administration, Amherst, MA 01003-0001. Awards MS. Part-time programs available. Faculty: 10 full-time (3 women). Students: 29 full-time (18 women), 2 part-time (both women); includes 1 minority (Hispanic), 18 international. Average age 27. 59 applicants, 58% accepted. In 1997, 18 degrees awarded. *Degree requirements:* Thesis optional, foreign language not required. *Entrance requirements:* GMAT. Application deadline: 3/1 (priority date; rolling processing; 10/1 for spring admission). Application fee: $40. *Expenses:* Tuition $2640 per year full-time, $110 per credit part-time for state residents; $3690 per year (minimum) full-time, $165 per credit (minimum) part-time for nonresidents. Fees $2856 per year full-time, $422 per semester part-time for state residents; $3204 per year full-time, $480 per semester part-time for nonresidents. *Financial aid:* In 1997–98, 2 research assistantships, 25 teaching assistantships were awarded; fellowships also available. Aid available to part-time students. Financial aid application deadline: 3/1. • Dr. Frank Lattuca, Director, 413-545-1389. Fax: 413-545-1235. E-mail: lattuca@hrta.umass.edu.

University of New Haven, School of Business, Program in Business Administration, West Haven, CT 06516-1916. Offerings include travel and tourism administration (MBA). *Degree requirements:* Thesis or alternative required, foreign language not required. *Application deadline:* rolling. *Application fee:* $50. *Expenses:* Tuition $1125 per course. Fees $13 per trimester. • Dr. Omid Nodoushani, Coordinator, 203-932-7123.

University of New Haven, College of Arts and Sciences, School of Hotel, Restaurant, Tourism and Dietetics Administration, Program in Hospitality and Tourism, West Haven, CT 06516-1916. Awards MS. Students: 7 full-time (6 women), 3 part-time (1 woman); includes 1 minority (African American), 6 international. 17 applicants, 65% accepted. In 1997, 15 degrees awarded. *Application deadline:* rolling. *Application fee:* $50. *Expenses:* Tuition $1125 per course. Fees $13 per trimester. *Financial aid:* Application deadline 5/1; applicants required to submit FAFSA. • Sherie Brezina, Coordinator, 203-932-7359.

University of South Carolina, Graduate School, College of Applied Professions Sciences, School of Hotel, Restaurant and Tourism Administration, Columbia, SC 29208. Awards MHRTA. Faculty: 6 full-time (2 women). Students: 25 full-time (10 women), 3 part-time (1 woman); includes 2 minority (1 Asian American, 1 Hispanic), 8 international. Average age 29. In 1997, 16 degrees awarded. *Entrance requirements:* GMAT (minimum score 500) or GRE General Test (minimum combined score of 1000), minimum GPA of 3.0, 1 year of management experience. Application deadline: 8/1 (rolling processing; 11/15 for spring admission). Application fee: $35. Electronic applications accepted. *Expenses:* Tuition $3894 per year full-time, $193 per credit hour part-time for state residents; $8114 per year full-time, $404 per credit hour part-time for nonresidents. Fees $125 per year full-time, $37 per semester (minimum) part-time. *Faculty research:* Quality management, conference and meeting management, multicultural dimensions, international tourism development. • Dr. Sandra K. Strick, Interim Chair, 803-777-7684. Fax: 803-777-6427.

University of Tennessee, Knoxville, College of Human Ecology, Department of Consumer and Industry Services Management, Program in Recreation, Tourism, and Hospitality Management, Knoxville, TN 37996. Offers hospitality management (MS), recreation administration (MS), therapeutic recreation (MS), tourism (MS). Part-time programs available. Students: 11 full-time (6 women), 11 part-time (10 women); includes 1 minority (Asian American), 1 international. Average age 24. 13 applicants, 85% accepted. In 1997, 16 degrees awarded. *Degree requirements:* Thesis or alternative required, foreign language not required. *Entrance requirements:* TOEFL (minimum score 550), GRE General Test, minimum GPA of 2.7. Application deadline: 2/1 (priority date; rolling processing). Application fee: $35. Electronic applications accepted. *Tuition:* $3354 per year full-time, $181 per semester hour part-time for state residents; $8410 per year full-time, $462 per semester hour part-time for nonresidents. *Financial aid:* Career-related internships or fieldwork available. Financial aid application deadline: 2/1. • Dr. Nancy B. Fair, Head, Department of Consumer and Industry Services Management, 423-974-2141. Fax: 423-974-5236. E-mail: nbfair@utk.edu.

See in-depth description on page 1857.

University of Wisconsin–Stout, College of Human Development, Program in Hospitality and Tourism, Menomonie, WI 54751. Awards MS. Part-time programs available. Students: 26 full-time (17 women), 6 part-time (5 women); includes 1 minority (Hispanic), 18 international. 31 applicants, 71% accepted. In 1997, 11 degrees awarded. *Degree requirements:* Thesis required, foreign language not required. *Application deadline:* 5/1 (10/1 for spring admission). *Application fee:* $45. *Tuition:* $3284 per year full-time, $183 per credit hour part-time for state residents; $7644 per year full-time, $425 per credit hour part-time for nonresidents. *Financial aid:* In 1997–98, 4 research assistantships were awarded; teaching assistantships, full and partial tuition waivers, Federal Work-Study also available. Aid available to part-time students. Financial aid application deadline: 4/1; applicants required to submit FAFSA. • Dr. Randall Upchurch, Director, 715-232-1407.

Western Illinois University, College of Education and Human Services, Department of Recreation, Park, and Tourism Administration, Macomb, IL 61455-1390. Awards MS. Part-time programs available. Faculty: 12 full-time (2 women). Students: 28 full-time (11 women), 5 part-time (1 woman); includes 2 minority (1 African American, 1 Native American), 6 international. Average age 28. 28 applicants, 64% accepted. In 1997, 21 degrees awarded. *Degree requirements:* Thesis or alternative required, foreign language not required. *Application deadline:* rolling. *Application fee:* $0 ($25 for international students). *Expenses:* Tuition $2304 per year full-time, $96 per semester hour part-time for state residents; $6912 per year full-time, $288 per semester hour part-time for nonresidents. Fees $944 per year full-time, $33 per semester hour part-time. *Financial aid:* In 1997–98, 23 students received aid, including 23 research assistantships averaging $610 per month; full tuition waivers and career-related internships or fieldwork also available. Financial aid applicants required to submit FAFSA. *Faculty research:* Park district services, disability rehabilitation. • Dr. B. Nicholas DiGrino, Chairperson, 309-298-1967. Application contact: Barbara Baily, Director of Graduate Studies, 309-298-1806. Fax: 309-298-2245. E-mail: barb_baily@ccmail.wiu.edu.

Cross-Discipline Announcement

University of Tennessee, Knoxville, College of Human Ecology, Department of Nutrition, Knoxville, TN 37996.

The Department of Nutrition offers graduate programs leading to MS and PhD degrees. Students choose a research specialization in one of 3 areas: experimental nutritional biochemistry and metabolism, public health nutrition, or sociocultural nutrition. Students are provided with core course work to address competencies expected of nutrition graduate students.

CORNELL UNIVERSITY

School of Hotel Administration

Programs of Study

The School of Hotel Administration (SHA) at Cornell University offers a program leading to the degree of Master of Management in Hospitality (M.M.H.), for which students with bachelor's degrees in all academic areas, including hotel administration, may apply. The School also has programs of study leading to the Master of Science and Doctor of Philosophy degrees for exceptional students who plan to teach at the college level or conduct research in the area of hotel administration.

There is a continuing need in the hospitality industry for persons with a wide variety of professional and graduate management skills at both the corporate and operational levels. Through its M.M.H. program, the School of Hotel Administration seeks to prepare students with diverse undergraduate backgrounds to meet this need. The M.M.H. program provides extensive professional training in disciplines pertinent to the hospitality industry. The curriculum includes courses in administration and management, entrepreneurship, financial management, food and beverage management, human resources, management information systems, marketing, real estate, communications, and properties management. Students work with a faculty member to develop an individual program of study. Applicants to the M.M.H. program must already have at least two years of full-time hospitality-related work experience. The program is a two-year, four-semester program.

Research Facilities

Statler Hall is an unusual educational facility designed expressly to meet the needs of the faculty and students of the School of Hotel Administration. The building has two parts: a classroom section and a full-service hotel and conference center. This provides the School with classrooms, lecture rooms, laboratories, a library, and a video and computer center for instruction and research in hospitality administration. Statler Hall's facilities have periodically been upgraded to reflect technological advances and changes in the industry. Now, some forty-seven years after the building was constructed, Statler Hall has been renovated and expanded to support the School's teaching and research activities and the hotel's many functions.

The School's library provides an extensive collection of publications (more than 25,000 volumes) on hospitality administration and related subjects. The University libraries, containing well over 5 million volumes and subscribing to 60,000 periodicals, provide excellent resources for research and study. The School's Binenkorb Computer Center facilitates student training in computing. IBM and Apple Macintosh computer labs are used extensively, and the Computer Center benefits from more than $600,000 worth of donated hospitality-systems hardware and software.

Financial Aid

Financial assistance is available to students enrolled in the Master of Management program, but scholarship funds are limited. To be eligible for a scholarship, a student must be a U.S. citizen or a permanent resident and demonstrate financial need. Some graduate assistantships are available to qualified students in the M.S. and Ph.D. programs and in the second year for M.M.H. students. These assistantships are awarded on the basis of educational achievements, independent of need.

Cost of Study

Full-time estimated tuition and fees for 1998–99 are $21,840. The estimated cost of books and materials is $700.

Living and Housing Costs

The estimated cost of room and board for a single student for the 1998–99 academic year is $9000. Personal expenses are about $2400. Married students should add $5900 for their spouse and $3800 for each child.

Student Group

Cornell University administers graduate programs in eighty-five fields of study, encompassing approximately 4,600 students and a graduate faculty numbering 1,600. The M.M.H. program enrollment is 115 students, about half men and half women; generally, 33 percent are international students.

Student Outcomes

Students obtain positions in consulting, hotel management, restaurant management, real estate, finance, air lines, cruise lines, tourism, and other areas of services management. Students take positions such as vice president of operations, consultant, hotel marketing director, restaurant developer, controller, systems-planning manager, entrepreneur, and real estate developer in locations around the world. For the class of 1997, with 70 percent of students reporting, the mean salary was $47,863, the median was $47,000, and the range was $24,000–$90,000.

Location

Situated in the scenic Finger Lakes region of central New York State and surrounded by spectacular gorges and waterfalls, Cornell's campus is renowned for its natural beauty. The Ithaca area is distinctly rural—a lovely blend of farms, quiet and expansive parks, and some light industry. State parks, minutes away, offer extensive facilities for swimming, fishing, boating, hiking, camping, and picnicking. Within an hour are the New York wine district, the Corning Glass Center, Watkins Glen, and centers for the performing arts.

The University and The School

Since its founding in 1865, Cornell University has been a training ground for technologies and sciences as well as for the classics. More than 16,000 students are enrolled in this independent Ivy League institution, and its fourteen colleges and schools provide great diversity. Founded in 1922, the School of Hotel Administration was the first institution with a degree program in hotel studies. Cornell supports one of the largest intercollegiate athletic programs in the country and is host to many cultural activities.

Applying

Admission to the M.M.H. program is granted for the fall semester only. Applications must be filed by February 1. The deadline for submitting all supporting documents (i.e., academic transcripts, two letters of recommendation, and scores on the Graduate Management Admission Test) and fulfilling the personal interview requirement is February 20. M.S. and Ph.D. applicants may apply for admission for the fall semester; the deadline is February 1 for applications and March 1 for all supporting documentation. Applicants are required to have had full-time practical experience in the hospitality field.

Correspondence and Information

For SHA graduate programs:

Master of Management in Hospitality Program
School of Hotel Administration
Statler Hall
Cornell University
Ithaca, New York 14853

Telephone: 607-255-7245
Fax: 607-255-4179
E-mail: master_mgmt_hosp@cornell.edu

Cornell University

THE FACULTY

David A. Dittman, Ph.D., Dean.
Judi L. Brownell, Ph.D., Professor and Richard J. and Monene P. Bradley Director for Graduate Studies.

Communications, Information Technologies, Law, and Quantitative Methods
Judi L. Brownell, Ph.D., Professor.
Elizabeth M. Huettman, Ph.D., Assistant Professor.
Daphne A. Jameson, Ph.D., Associate Professor.
Sheryl E. Kimes, Ph.D., Associate Professor.
Richard G. Moore, M.E.E., M.B.A., Associate Professor.
John E. H. Sherry, J.D., LL.M., Professor Emeritus.
Elizabeth Stevens, Ph.D., Assistant Professor.
Gary Thompson, Ph.D., Associate Professor.

Financial Management
Avner Arbel, Ph.D., Professor.
Linda Canina, Ph.D., Assistant Professor.
Stephen A. Carvell, Ph.D., Associate Professor.
James J. Eyster, Ph.D., Professor.
Dennis H. Ferguson, Ph.D., Associate Professor.
A. Neal Geller, Ph.D., Professor.
Gordon S. Potter, Ph.D., Associate Professor.

Food and Beverage Management
Christopher C. Muller, Ph.D., Assistant Professor.
Stephen Mutkoski, Ph.D., Professor.
Peter Rainsford, Ph.D., Associate Professor.
Mary H. Tabacchi, Ph.D., Associate Professor.

Management: Organizations and Human Resources
Florence C. Berger, Ph.D., Professor.
Thomas P. Cullen, Ph.D., Associate Professor.
Cathy A. Enz, Ph.D., Associate Professor.
Timothy R. Hinkin, Ph.D., Associate Professor.
Craig C. Lundberg, Ph.D., Professor.
Tony L. Simons, Ph.D., Assistant Professor.
J. Bruce Tracey, Ph.D., Assistant Professor.

Marketing and Tourism
Chekitan S. Dev, Ph.D., Associate Professor.
Michael Lynn, Ph.D., Associate Professor.
Leo M. Renaghan, Ph.D., Associate Professor.

Properties Management
John J. Clark Jr., Ph.D., Professor.
John B. Corgel, Ph.D., Associate Professor.
Jan deRoos, Ph.D., Assistant Professor.
Richard H. Penner, M.S.Arch., Professor.
Michael H. Redlin, Ph.D., Professor.

RESEARCH ACTIVITIES

Sponsored by private foundations, industry groups, the University, and the School, faculty members and graduate students undertake research on topics relevant to the hospitality field. Projects of a theoretical nature, as well as those with practical applications, are pursued. One of the important thrusts of current research is the development of advanced decision support models for the hospitality industry, using new quantitative techniques and the computer. Examples are forecasting models, optimizing the pricing of hotel rooms, and capital budgeting. Research in and discovery of the "neglected firm effect" in the stock market have led to the publication of a well-received book and to several articles. Topics of other recently published books have been law, hotel planning and design, hotel engineering, and negotiations of management contracts.

A group of diverse projects continues exploring topics such as creative leadership in the hospitality industry, analysis of restaurant failure, pricing models for hotels, and the importance of end-user computing in strategic planning for the hotel industry. Research that is now beginning includes identifying restaurant capacity utilization, identifying critical success factors in the restaurant business, creating valuation systems for hospitality profit units, and studying the patterns and costs of water consumption in the lodging industry.

The School of Hotel Administration has the advantage of being able to tap the resources of the hospitality industry and combine them with the fine research facilities available at Cornell, including the computing, scientific, and engineering equipment and one of the finest collegiate libraries in the world.

A view of the west campus and McGraw Tower—a landmark of the University, overlooking Cayuga Lake.

M.M.H. students present the results of their team's study of an actual development project.

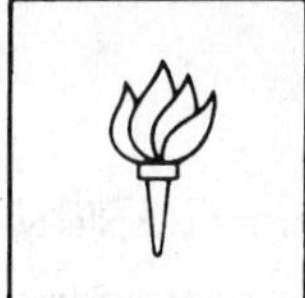

NEW YORK UNIVERSITY

School of Continuing and Professional Studies
Center for Hospitality, Tourism, and Travel Administration

Program of Study

The Center for Hospitality, Tourism, and Travel Administration at New York University (NYU) offers two master of science degree programs: an M.S. in hospitality industry studies and an M.S. in tourism and travel management. As a result of the increased complexities and burgeoning growth of the fields of hospitality and tourism, the demand for professionals with advanced degrees is accelerating. The graduate programs at NYU feature the advanced knowledge and skills necessary to successfully compete in either global industry.

The graduate programs feature a multilayered learning environment that combines applied research, team projects, lectures by leading industry professionals, and conferences. The blending of classroom learning with a series of professional and business activities ensures an integrated educational experience. In concert with the unique location, the city is the classroom and the faculty members are professionals from all aspects of the industry.

The Master of Science in hospitality industry studies is a 39-credit program with a unique focus on asset management and product development. Students gain competence in the areas of finance and investment analysis, hotel feasibility and valuation, and technology and product development.

The Master of Science in tourism and travel management is a 39-credit program. Specialized areas of study include destination management and strategic marketing systems. Students gain competence in the areas of tourism planning and development; specialized tourism, such as ecotourism and cultural heritage tourism; and tourism impacts and trends.

Research Facilities

NYU's Elmer Holmes Bobst Library and Study Center, one of the largest open-stack research libraries in the world, houses more than 2.5 million volumes. Bobst is one of seven NYU libraries.

The Academic Computing Facility has four instructional computer labs with more than 340 Apple and IBM-compatible computers. All are linked to NYU-NET, the campus data network, and are connected to Novell-based file servers and printers. A collection of more than 100 software packages is available.

Financial Aid

The Center for Hospitality, Tourism, and Travel Administration offers financial aid in the form of scholarships to new and continuing domestic and international students. NYU's centralized Office of Financial Aid assists students with loan packages, and the NYU monthly payment plan enables students to spread out their tuition payments.

Cost of Study

Tuition for the 1998–99 academic year is $570 per credit. Additional nonrefundable fees are charged on a per-credit basis: registration and service fees are charged on the first credit, and registration fees are charged on each additional credit. The fee structure by semester is as follows: for fall 1998, $148 on the first credit, $40 on each additional credit; for spring 1999, $162 on the first credit, $40 on each additional credit; and for summer 1999, $89 on the first credit, $40 on each additional credit. Full-time status is 12 or more credits; part-time status is fewer than 12 credits.

Living and Housing Costs

Most graduate student housing is located within walking distance of the Washington Square campus and provides separate kitchen and bathroom facilities and laundry rooms. A free NYU shuttle bus links housing and academic facilities. An off-campus housing office is also available to assist students. Room rates for the academic year (fall and spring) range from $5775 to $10,350, with available meal plans ranging from $1485 to $3625.

Student Group

In spring 1998, there were 91 students enrolled in the master's programs, 56 in the M.S. in hospitality industry studies and 35 in the M.S. in tourism and travel management. Overall, approximately 20 percent were full-time students and 80 percent were part-time. The student population is representative of the global nature of the industry, with individuals from Europe, Asia, Africa, South America, and the Caribbean as well as the United States.

Location

New York University is located in the heart of Manhattan, surrounded by major attractions, accommodations, and entertainment. The center's programs are ideally situated in New York City, which is universally recognized as the hospitality and tourism capital of the world.

The University

NYU is a private university composed of thirteen schools, colleges, and divisions. The University was founded in 1831, and the School of Continuing and Professional Studies (formerly the School of Continuing Education) was founded in 1934. The Center for Hospitality, Tourism, and Travel Administration, which offers the master's degrees, two undergraduate degrees, summer intensive programs, and noncredit professional development courses, was established in 1992.

Application

Students may apply for fall, spring, or summer admission. Application packages must include official transcripts, results of the GMAT or GRE (and TOEFL, for students whose native language is not English), résumés or professional summaries, two or more letters of recommendation, and a statement of purpose.

Correspondence and Information

Department of Graduate Studies
Center for Hospitality, Tourism, and Travel Administration
School of Continuing and Professional Studies
New York University
7 East 12th Street, 11th Floor
New York, New York 10003-4475
Telephone: 212-998-9100
Fax: 212-995-3656
E-mail: sce.hospitality@nyu.edu

New York University

THE FACULTY

Full-Time Faculty

Ruthe Davis, M.S., M.B.A., Clinical Assistant Professor of Hospitality and Director of Professional Development, Center for Hospitality, Tourism, and Travel Administration.

Sharr Prohaska, M.A., Clinical Assistant Professor of Tourism and Travel and Director of Undergraduate Programs, Center for Hospitality, Tourism, and Travel Administration.

Lalia Rach, Ed.D., Associate Dean, Clinical Professor, and Director, Center for Hospitality, Tourism, and Travel Administration.

Adjunct Faculty

Lawrence Adams, B.Arch., Principal, Adams, Rosenberg, Kolb Architects.
Kurt Barkley, M.B.A., Vice President/Manager–Public Finance Department, Kredietbank.
Paul S. Biederman, Ph.D., Associate Professor.
Barry A. N. Bloom, B.S., Vice President, Tischman Hotel Corporation.
Cheryl Boyer, B.S., Director, Hotel Partners, Inc.
George Buckley, Ph.D., Adjunct Assistant Professor of Management, Stern School of Business.
Gail Butler, M.B.A., J.D., Associate Professor, Dowling College.
Salvatore Castelli, M.S.M.E., Project Manager, Goldman Capeland Assoc.
Roger Deitz, Esq., J.D., The Law Office of Roger Deitz, Esq.
Lisa J. Don, M.S., M.B.A., Account Executive, United Airlines.
David Edgell Sr., Ph.D., Executive Director, Tourism Division of Ruf Strategic Solutions.
Steven Eichberg, B.S., B.A., Director–Operations, Tishman Hotel Corporation.
Jeffrey French, M.S., Senior Vice President–Sales and Marketing, Marriott's Frenchman's Reef.
Tom Gallagher, M.B.A., Managing Director, CIBC WoodGundy Securities Corp.
Donald S. Garvett, M.S., M.B.A., Vice President, SH&E Inc.
Greg Gilstrap, B.A., Managing Director, Young Nichols Gilstrap, Inc.
Bernard Goldberg, J.D., Principal, Gotham Hotel Group.
Eric Goldberg, J.D., Partner, Baer, Marks & Upham.
Bunny Grossinger, Ph.D. (hon.), Bunny Grossinger Enterprises.
Stan E. Hannibal, Electronic Engineer, LaGuardia Marriott Hotel.
Bjorn Hanson, Ph.D., Industry Chairman–Hospitality, Coopers & Lybrand.
Susan Heinbuch, Ph.D., Adjunct Assistant Professor of Management, Stern School of Business.
Mark Kahan, J.D., Vice Chairman, Executive Vice President, and General Counsel, Spirit Airlines, Inc.
Martin Keller, M.B.A., Manager–Operational Control, Swissair.
Andrew Levy, J.D., Partner, Schulte Roth & Zabel.
Frank Lewis, M.S., Consultant, MTI.
Sarah Graham Mann, B.A., Managing Director, Discover New England.
Stephanie Meth, M.B.A., Adjunct Assistant Professor.
Sandra Momjian, B.S., Assistant Manager, Union Club.
Daniel Neumann, B.S., CPA, Manager, Pannell Kerr Forster.
George Ntim, B.A., Guest Relations/Manager on Duty, New York Marriott Marquis Hotel.
Niels Olsen, M.B.A., Director–New Jersey State Accounts, Hilton Hotels Corporation.
George Papagapatos, M.B.A., President, Travel Dynamics.
Rick Rogovin, B.T., Senior Investment Analyst, TIAA/CREF.
Joel R. Ross, M.B.A., President/Chief Executive Officer, Ross Properties, Inc.
Iris W. Schiffman, M.B.A., Resident Manager, LaGuardia Marriott Hotel.
David Smith, M.B.A., Chairman, David A. Smith Company.
Michael Taylor, M.S., Director, AT&T/Benchmark Hospitality.
Allen Toman, M.P.A., Managing Director, Hotel Partners Capital Group.
Judith Trent, M.B.A., Managing Director, Global Aviation Associations, Ltd.
Rob Whalen, M.A., Athletic Director, Downtown Athletic Club.
Philip Wolf, M.B.A., Chairman, PhoCusWright, Inc.
Doug Young, M.A., M.B.A., Managing Director, Young Nichols Gilstrap, Inc.

SCHILLER INTERNATIONAL UNIVERSITY

Programs in Hotel Management and Business Administration

Programs of Study

Apart from the Master of Business Administration (M.B.A.) in hotel and tourism management and the M.B.A. in international business, Schiller International University (SIU) also offers the Master of Arts (M.A.) in international hotel and tourism management, the M.A. in international relations and diplomacy, and the Master of International Management (M.I.M.) in international management.

The M.A. in international hotel and tourism management is intended for those wishing to better their chances for advancement in their present occupation or to shift their interest to this expanding field. It is designed specifically for students who have already completed a course of study in fields both related and unrelated to hotel management. This M.A. degree may be completed during one academic year (two semesters and a summer session). The M.A. in international hotel and tourism management builds upon the previous studies in hotel and tourism management, gastronomy, hotel corporate finance and control, tourism planning and marketing, and other areas. Students from the international hotel and tourism management program are well equipped to take on a management role within a hotel or travel organization in any country.

The M.A. in international relations and diplomacy is a professional program that prepares students for careers in international affairs with their own governments or with international organizations, in journalism, or in business. It combines a traditional theoretical approach to the study of international relations, contemporary diplomacy, and international negotiation. Central to the program is a two-semester laboratory course in diplomacy that introduces students to the structure and functions of diplomatic missions and trains them in the skills of diplomacy. This M.A. program may be completed in two semesters of full-time study. By completing three additional graduate courses in European studies or international business, students may also specialize their international and diplomacy degree in either field. Students in Schiller International University's graduate program in international relations and diplomacy may gain employment with the government in their home countries or with international organizations such as Amnesty International and UNESCO. Schiller International University offers the M.A. in international relations and diplomacy at their London and Paris campuses.

The M.I.M. program has been designed to prepare students who have already completed a course of study in a nonbusiness field specifically for positions in international management. The 45-semester-credit program leading to the M.I.M. degree may be completed during one academic year (two semesters and a summer session). Course work includes business administration, economics, and international relations.

Research Facilities

All Schiller International University campuses are equipped with libraries and computer laboratories. There are also agreements with the major libraries in the cities where the campuses are located, which gives the students at Schiller full access to their facilities. In London there are also agreements with the London School of Economics, Company House (which has information about all businesses registered in the U.K.), and City Library.

Financial Aid

Schiller International University is an independent institution with limited funds for financial aid. Students are encouraged to seek assistance through private or governmental loans and scholarship programs before applying to the University. Students wishing to apply for financial assistance from IS should request a scholarship application form when applying for admission. Schiller International University is approved for Title IV U.S. federal funds.

Cost of Study

Graduate fees for a one-year program (two semesters and a summer session) are as follows: fifteen courses, $14,850; activity fee, $360; thesis fee, $250; and liability deposit, $120. The liability deposit is refundable. Books cost between $250 and $500, depending on whether they are new or used.

Living and Housing Costs

The Florida, London, Heidelberg, and Strasbourg campuses have on-campus housing facilities. Room and board are $2250 per semester and $950 for the summer session. At the other Schiller campuses, Paris and Madrid, the campus staff assists the students in finding housing in apartments, rooms, or with host families. The prices for rent vary quite a lot between the different countries. Campus staff members are happy to answer any questions about living costs.

Student Group

The student body at Schiller International University represents many cultures. Students come from more than 100 nations. The total number of students in fall 1996 was 1,433. Fifty-seven percent were men, and 90 percent were full-time students. Of the students, 232 came from the United States, and the rest are from all over the world. Most students return to their home countries after completing their degree, but some stay on in the country of study to do internships in order to be more competitive in the job market in their home countries.

Student Outcomes

Many students in Schiller International University's graduate program in International Relations and Diplomacy find employment with the government in their home countries, or with international organizations such as Amnesty International and UNESCO. Students from the International Hotel and Tourism Management program are well equipped to take on a management role within a hotel or travel organization in any country.

Location

Schiller International University offers the M.A. in international relations and diplomacy at its London and Paris campuses. The London campus is located in the center of London, just opposite the Waterloo station. This location gives easy access not only to the whole underground network of London, but also to the rest of England, and now also Paris and Brussels via the Eurostar trains. The Paris campus is located in the center of Paris close to the Montparnasse Tower and Montparnasse train station.

The University

Schiller International University was established in 1964, laying the foundation of what was to become a small, independent university offering its students an education of high quality. During the 1960s, when many large universities emerged as mass institutions in which the individual student often felt lost in a crowd, the founding of Schiller was a conscious departure from the growing anonymity of such institutions. With alumni from more than 130 countries and with men and women from more than 100 nations currently enrolled, SIU offers students the unique opportunity to gain an American education in an international setting. English is the language of instruction at all of SIU's ten campuses in six countries where students are prepared for careers in academic institutions, business and management, governmental agencies, multinational organizations, and social services or for further education in their chosen field. Through enrollment in both practical and theoretical courses and through discussions in small classes with instructors and classmates of multicultural backgrounds, students gain firsthand knowledge of business and cultural relations among the peoples of the world. SIU students have the unique opportunity to transfer among SIU's campuses without losing any credits while continuing their chosen program of study.

Applying

Schiller International University has rolling admissions procedures. The financial aid deadline each year is April 30. The admissions requirement for the international hotel and tourism management program is a bachelor's degree or its equivalent. No particular field of undergraduate specialization is required, but a year of undergraduate mathematics is strongly advised. For the M.A. in international relations and diplomacy, the requirements are as follows: a bachelor of arts degree or its equivalent, with a major concentration in either political science or international relations and diplomacy; one year of undergraduate economics; and at least the intermediate level of one foreign language.

Correspondence and Information

Mr. Christoph Leibrecht
Director of Admissions
Schiller International University
435 Edgewater Drive
Dunedin, Florida 34698-7532

Telephone: 800-336-4133 (toll-free)
Fax: 813-734-0359
World Wide Web: http://www.schiller.edu

Schiller International University

FACULTY

Andreas Backhouse, Dr.Ing., Karlsruhe (Germany).
Scott Blair, Ph.D., Paris IV (Sorbonne).
Jale Bradley, Ph.D., South Bank (England).
Charles Carattini, Ph.D., Boston University.
Roger Cox, M.A., London.
Richard de Metz, M.Sc., Cambridge.
Kevin Dodrill, M.Sc., Surrey (England).
Salim El Sayegh, Ph.D., Paris IV (Sorbonne).
Susanne Fawssett, Ph.D., London.
Michael Flagg, M.A., Polytechnic (London).
Terrance Fox, M.A., Connecticut.
Jesus Galvan, Ph.D., Escuela Técnica Superior de Ingenieros de Telecommunicación (Spain).
Mahkameh Ghanei, M.Sc., Hull (England).
Gail Hamilton, M.B.A., Institute Européen d'Adminstration des Affaires (France).
Else Hassing, M.A., Boston University.
Arthur Hoffman, Ph.D., Institut Universitaire de Hautes Etudes (Switzerland).
Graham J. Hollister-Short, Ph.D., London.
Martin Huck, Ph.D., Karlsruhe (Germany).
Wilfried Iskat, Ph.D., NYU.
Judith Jaffe, M.B.A., Institute Européen d'Adminstration des Affaires (France).
Clare Kelliher, Ph.D., London Business School.
Richard Kotas, Professor Emeritus; M.Phil, Surrey (England).
George Lambrakis, Ph.D., George Washington.
John A. R. Lee, Ph.D., Minnesota.
Nicolle Macho, Ph.D., South Carolina.
Hassan Mansoor, Ph.D., London.
Beatriz Margolis, Ph.D., Maryland.
Samuel Nonju, Ph.D., Nanterre (France).
Sharon Nuskey, M.B.A., Columbia.
Wordsworth Price, Ph.D., London.
Ali Shamsavari, Ph.D., Vanderbilt.
Parisima Shamsavari, Ph.D., London.
Kadom Shubber, Ph.D., Loughborough (England).
Howard Turner, Ph.D., Aberdeen (Scotland).

UNIVERSITY OF HOUSTON

Conrad N. Hilton College of Hotel and Restaurant Management

Program of Study

The Conrad N. Hilton College of Hotel and Restaurant Management, regularly rated among the world's premier hospitality education programs, offers a graduate program leading to a Master of Hospitality Management (M.H.M.) degree, for which students with an equivalent of a U.S. four-year bachelor's degree in any discipline, including hotel and restaurant management, are eligible to apply; students with three-year bachelor's or diploma degrees are ineligible to apply. The M.H.M. program can be pursued on either a full-time or part-time basis. The two-year M.H.M. study program requires 55 credit hours composed of 13 hours of prerequisite courses; 27 hours of core courses, including a 3-hour professional paper; and 15 hours of elective courses. In addition, the Conrad N. Hilton College has implemented the PlusOne program for students with a bachelor's degree in hospitality management from a selected list of hospitality programs and colleges in the U.S. This program waives 19 of the 55 hours required for the M.H.M. degree. This allows the student to earn the M.H.M. degree in only one year of full-time enrollment. Furthermore, the M.H.M. candidate may specialize in either lodging administration, food service administration, or hospitality administration. Hospitality industry experience is preferred for admission into the graduate program. The Conrad N. Hilton College of Hotel and Restaurant Management and the College of Business of Administration also offer a concurrent degree program that enables students to prepare for careers in which business and hospitality complement each other. By pursuing both the M.H.M. and the Master of Business Administration (M.B.A.) degrees concurrently, students can complete both degrees in a shorter time period than if they were to pursue the two independently, for a total of 84 semester hours.

Research Facilities

The University of Houston and the Conrad N. Hilton College have some of the most advanced research facilities in the United States. The University of Houston libraries provide more than 2 million volumes of books and research materials, including subscriptions to more than 15,000 research journals, full text of database research journals, and extensive CD-ROM access to research information. The Conrad N. Hilton College maintains one of the largest hospitality industry libraries and archives in the world. The library includes an extensive collection of periodicals, volumes of hospitality related texts, more than 7,000 international and regional cookbooks, and access to electronic reference materials. The Hospitality Industry Archives focus strongly on Hilton Hotels Corporation and its founder, Conrad N. Hilton. In addition, the Archives collects historically significant business records, films, videos, blueprints, and transcribed oral history interviews with hospitality leaders, generated by industry leaders and employees who have contributed greatly to the success of the industry. The Archives is also the official repository for memorabilia from Hall of Honor inductees, the AH&MA's Audiovisual Collection, and out-of-print trade publications.

Financial Aid

Graduate assistantships are awarded based on academic performance, qualification, and work experience in areas such as culinary/food service, human resources, lodging, accounting/finance, and computer systems. Tuition waivers and stipends are available to graduate students with teaching and research assistantship positions. Scholarships and other financial aid are available through the College and the University of Houston, respectively. For further information, students should contact the Office of Scholarships and Financial Aid, University of Houston, Houston, Texas 77203-2160.

Cost of Study

Graduate tuition for the 1998–99 academic year is $180 per three-credit hour for Texas residents or $747 per three-credit hour for non-resident or international students. In addition, the University charges approximately $394 in fees for student services, computer use, the health center, the library, and international education.

Living and Housing Costs

On- and off-campus housing is available to graduate students. Cougar Place, an on-campus garden-apartment complex, and Cambridge Oaks, a privately owned and operated apartment facility located adjacent to campus, are reserved for graduate students. An ample supply of apartments is located close to campus. A typical dorm room with double occupancy and 19 meals per week is estimated at $4200 per academic year.

Student Group

There are about 90 students enrolled in the M.H.M. program; 55 percent are women. About 60 percent attend full time and 40 percent are international students. Students are encouraged to join the Graduate Student Association, which provides opportunities for student interaction and a forum for dealing with issues specific to graduate study.

Student Outcomes

Career guidance and assistance are available to the students of the Conrad N. Hilton College through the College's placement office and biennial career fair. The career fair allows students to establish contacts with representatives from hotels, restaurants, caterers, theme parks, resorts, and gaming properties. These representatives continue their association with the placement office throughout the year. As a result, graduates of the Conrad N. Hilton College are serving in responsible positions worldwide with the finest firms in the hospitality industry, including Bristols Hotels and Resort, Caesar's World, Hilton Hotels Corporation, Four Seasons Hotels, Holiday Inn Hotels, Hyatt Hotels and Resorts, Marriott Hotels, Mirage Resorts, Omni Hotels, Radisson Hotels, Regents International Hotels, Stouffer Hotels and Resorts, Westin Hotels, and Wyndham Hotels.

Location

The parklike campus of the University of Houston is situated just 3 miles from downtown Houston. The nation's fourth-largest city offers a wide choice of cultural and entertainment activities, including a major symphony orchestra, internationally acclaimed ballet and opera companies, music and comedy clubs, and professional sports events, as well as superb shopping. The diverse ethnic population provides restaurants to suit any taste.

The University and The College

The University of Houston ranks among the nation's leading research and teaching institutions. Its position is on the cutting edge of higher education, and its work receives accolades from around the world. The broad mix of cultural backgrounds in a student population drawn from more than 100 countries, combined with the benefits and opportunities offered by the city of Houston, greatly enhances the richness of the academic experience at the University of Houston. One of the University's world-renowned assets is the Conrad N. Hilton College, with its incomparable facilities, distinguished faculty impressively blending strong academic credentials and corporate experience, comprehensive curriculum, first-rate students, and close ties to leading corporations and executives in the hospitality industry. The Conrad N. Hilton College strives to provide its students with ample opportunities and ideas to enrich the education they receive, including two lecture series, the Dean's Distinguished Lecture Series and the Curt Strand Lecture Series. These lectures enable noted hospitality industry leaders to visit the College and speak with faculty members and students. The College also initiated in 1966 the first International Conference on Graduate Education and Graduate Student Research in Hospitality and Tourism, which is held at the University of Houston campus biennially. The Conrad N. Hilton College's Hall of Honor for the hotel, restaurant, and hospitality industry recognizes industry founders and leaders whose immense contributions to the industry and society serve as a powerful inspiration to all; inductees include Walt Disney, J. W. Marriott, J. W. Marriott Jr., William Barron Hilton, Lord Charles Forte, Curtis Leroy Carlson, Ray Kroc, Ellsworth Statler, Kemmons Wilson, and Vernon Stouffer.

Applying

Application deadlines are July 7 for the fall semester and December 1 for the spring semester. International applications must be filed by May 1 for the fall semester and October 1 for the spring semester. Applicants must also submit two sets of academic transcripts and GRE or GMAT test scores. International applicants must also submit TOEFL scores.

Correspondence and Information

Office of Graduate Affairs
Conrad N. Hilton College
University of Houston
Houston, Texas 77204-3902

Telephone: 713-743-2457
Fax: 713-743-2498
E-mail: lbinns@uh.edu
World Wide Web: http://www.hrm.uh.edu

University of Houston

THE FACULTY, CENTERS, INSTITUTES, PROGRAMS, AND RESEARCH

Faculty members possess strong academic credentials and industry experience, have received awards for teaching excellence, and have the competence and expertise that are important to the operational element of the hotel, restaurant, and hospitality industry.

Alan T. Stutts, Dean, Professor; Ph.D., Illinois. Hotel operations, casino management, restaurant management, hotel design and engineering.
JeAnna L. Abbott, Associate Professor; M.H.M., J.D., Houston; CHE. Hospitality industry law, catering and convention management.
Stephen C. Barth, Associate Professor; J.D., Texas Tech; CHE. Hotel and restaurant management, hospitality industry law, social and legal environments.
Frank Borsenik, Visiting Professor; Ph.D., Michigan State. Gaming and facilities management.
William N. Chernish, Assistant Professor; Ph.D., Pennsylvania; CHE. Diversity, human resources, management, strategic planning.
Kye-Sung (Kaye) Chon, Professor; Ph.D., Virginia Tech; CHE. Hospitality marketing, tourism, research methods.
Agnes L. DeFranco, Assistant Professor; M.B.A., Ed.D., Houston; CHE. Hospitality industry finance and accounting.
Nancy S. Graves, Associate Professor and Registered Dietitian; Ed.D., Houston. Applied nutrition for hospitality management, quantity food production, kitchen layout and design.
Connie Mok, Associate Professor; Ph.D., Murdoch (Australia); CHE. Method of research in hospitality industry, service marketing, consumer behavior, tourism.
Ron Nykiel, Adjunct Professor and Conrad N. Hilton Distinguished Chair; Ph.D., Walden; CHA, CHE. Marketing, strategic planning, hospitality management, lodging operations.
Clinton L. Rappole, Professor and Eric Hilton Distinguished Chair; Ph.D., Cornell; CHE. Food service systems and restaurant management, management of public health and safety, hotel and motel management.
Karl Titz, Assistant Professor; Ph.D., Kansas State. Food and beverage management, casino resort and hotel management and marketing.

Centers, Institutes, and Programs

NACE Catering Research Institute: Dr. JeAnna Abbott, Director
Continuing Education and Executive Development: Jeff Graves, Director.
Hospitality Industry Diversity Institute (HIDI): Dr. Ronald Nykiel, Chairman.
Hospitality Industry Hall of Honor: Dr. Ronald Nykiel, Chairman.
Loss Prevention Management Institute (LPMI): Raymond Ellis Jr., Director.
Management Training Work Experience Program (MTWEP): Mary Douglas, Director of Placement.
Office of Gaming Education and Research Institute (GERI): James Wortman, Director.
Technology Research and Education Center (TREC): Mark E. Hamilton, Director.
The Tourism Industry Institute: Dr. Kye-Sung (Kaye) Chon, Director.

Research Activities

The Conrad N. Hilton College has initiated several innovative research programs demonstrating its determination to serve the hospitality industry and society as a whole in meaningful ways relevant to current developments. The Catering Research Institute was established as joint project between the Foundation of the National Association of Catering Executives (NACE) and the Conrad N. Hilton College of Hotel and Restaurant Management to provide a research vehicle for catering professionals and to provide a comprehensive curriculum for individuals who wish to pursue catering and convention services as a career. The Technology Research and Education Center (TREC) at the Conrad N. Hilton College of Hotel and Restaurant Management was conceived to provide a base of collection, study, analysis, and research in those technologies that most directly affect the hospitality industry. It further pursues the effective integration of technology in every segment of the curricula. TREC envisions the preparation of the student to carry this knowledge of technology to the workplace. The Loss Prevention Management Institute (LPMI) furnishes a forum for studying risk demands affecting the hospitality industry in the areas of insurance, safety, security, fire protection, and emergency planning. The Gaming Education and Research Institute (GERI) provides public and private policymakers with current information to assist them in gauging the social, economic, and regulatory impacts of gaming activity.

Selected Graduate Student Research

A Feasibility Study of an On-Premise Catering Facility with an Off-Premise Catering Capability
A Model for Ecotourism Development: A Case of Alaska
An Analysis of the Origins, Development and Current Issues of Ecotourism
An Analysis of Hotel Company Programs Designed to Assist and Attract International Guests
An Analysis of Tourist Expenditures by Houston Visitors: Characteristics and Economic Impact
Casino on the Internet
Convention and Visitor Bureaus on the World Wide Web
Child Care in the Hospitality Industry: An Incentive for Employees
Front Office and Concierge Employee Training Regarding the Americans with Disabilities Act
Restaurant Concept: Trends as Identified by Content Analysis

UNIVERSITY OF NEVADA, LAS VEGAS

The William F. Harrah College of Hotel Administration

Programs of Study

The William F. Harrah College of Hotel Administration, known for its tradition of offering world-class programs in hospitality administration, offers graduate programs that lead to the Master of Science degree in hotel administration, the Master of Science degree in leisure studies, and the Doctor of Philosophy degree in hospitality administration. The Ph.D in hospitality administration is supported by the ACE Denken Co. Ltd. Endowment. The M.S. programs are available on either a full-time or a part-time basis. The Ph.D. program is designed for full-time students.

The M.S. programs require 36 credit hours, which include a 6-credit-hour thesis or a 3-credit-hour professional paper. The programs are designed to meet the needs of managers/consultants in the hospitality industry. Students can pursue a program emphasis in food service administration, hotel administration, casino and gaming operations, leisure studies, or hospitality education. One year of full-time managerial/administrative experience in the hospitality industry is required before admission to the M.S. program in hotel administration. There is no work experience requirement for the M.S. program in leisure studies.

The Ph.D. program is a research-based degree program designed to produce top-quality hospitality educators and researchers. The Ph.D. program builds research and teaching skills. All students are required to teach a course under the supervision of a professor. Most full-time students receive research assistantships and conduct research and publish with professors. The program requires a minimum of 60 hours of approved credits beyond a master's degree. The Ph.D. applicant must hold a master's degree and achieve a minimum GMAT score of 550.

Research Facilities

For students interested in research activities, the Hospitality Research and Development Center and the UNLV International Gaming Institute, both within the College of Hotel Administration, have an excellent track record of serving the industry through a commitment to research. The breadth of research conducted through the College reflects the diversity of its faculty, which numbers more than 40. Past research projects have included industry-wide management assistance programs, food equipment and kitchen design, tourism development, market studies, hotel information systems, casino operations, and profiles of various managerial occupations and their implications for management development.

Financial Aid

Graduate assistantships, Barrick Fellowships, and alumni scholarships are a few of the types of assistance available through the Graduate College. In addition, a limited number of extramurally funded graduate assistantships are offered in the College of Hotel Administration. Interested students should contact the Graduate College for additional information. The Ph.D. program offers a limited number of ACE Denken Doctoral Fellowships. Information on grants, loans, and employment opportunities may be obtained from Student Financial Services at 702-895-3424.

Cost of Study

Tuition for the 1998–99 academic year is $93 per credit hour for Nevada residents. Nonresident tuition is $2885 for 7 or more credits or $93 plus $97 per credit, up to 6 credits. These fees are subject to change.

Living and Housing Costs

On-campus and off-campus housing is available to graduate students of the College; numerous apartments are located close to campus.

Student Group

There are approximately 85 students in the M.S. programs and 10 students in the Ph.D. program. Approximately 70 percent of the students are full-time students, and 25 percent are international students. Undergraduate backgrounds of M.S. students include hospitality administration, tourism, business, recreation, liberal arts, engineering, and education. Ph.D. students currently in the program hold their master's degrees in business administration, travel industry management, hospitality management, and nutrition and foods. Students are invited to join the Graduate Hotel Association (GHA). The GHA provides opportunities for graduate students to interact socially and academically and provides a forum for dealing with problems specific to graduate student life. There are also student chapters of various professional organizations that allow students to interact with industry professionals.

Student Outcomes

The management experience that students come into the programs with has an influence on the jobs they receive after graduation. Thus, there is a great deal of variance in the jobs that students receive upon graduation. Recent graduates include the vice president of Hospitality Media Solutions, a consultant with KPMG in Los Angeles, and the senior vice president of Human Resources and Administration with MGM Grand. Each year, several graduates go on to get a doctorate and then go into teaching.

Location

Location is another excellent feature of the program. UNLV is in one of the most picturesque areas of the entire Southwest. Its location on a 335-acre campus in Las Vegas makes it an ideal place to study the hotel, restaurant, resort, and convention business. The student is immersed in a hotel and tourism environment through the cooperation of the individual hoteliers, travel and tourism organizations, restaurants, and trade associations. Las Vegas has many attractions. Like any other large metropolitan area, the city has fine libraries, museums, community theater, art galleries, and parks, which are enjoyed and supported by more than 1 million local residents. As one of the fastest-growing metropolitan areas in the United States, southern Nevada is an example of modern urban living for families and individuals. Waterskiing on Lake Mead and snowskiing on Mount Charleston are both about an hour's drive from the campus.

The University and The College

UNLV is an institution striving to become one of the nation's leading urban universities by providing students with an excellent education at a reasonable cost. UNLV has been described as a "rising star in American higher education" in *U.S. News & World Report's College Guide,* which listed UNLV as an "up and coming" university for four straight years. Located in one of the most pleasant areas of Las Vegas, UNLV has a beautiful campus with an extensive library and residential facilities connected by spacious lawns and tree-shaded walkways and complemented by desert foliage. Just outside the campus are apartments, restaurants, shopping centers, libraries, hospitals, and all the other hallmarks of a modern urban area. The University is integral to the cultural environment of a city that bills itself as the "Entertainment Capital of the World." The Master Series features world-class artists and performers, while the Barrick Lecture Series brings some of the foremost thinkers of our time to the campus.

Applying

Applications are accepted for the fall and spring semesters. Current deadlines for all application materials are June 15 and November 15 for fall and spring semesters, respectively. For international students, the application deadlines are May 1 and October 1 for fall and spring semesters, respectively. All application materials must be in by these dates. The deadlines for the Ph.D. program are April 1 and October 1 for fall and spring semesters, respectively.

Correspondence and Information

John Bowen, Director of Graduate Studies and Research
William F. Harrah College
Mail Code 6013
University of Nevada, Las Vegas
Las Vegas, Nevada 89154-6013
Telephone: 702-895-0876
Fax: 702-895-4870
E-mail: bowen@ccmail.nevada.edu

University of Nevada, Las Vegas

THE FACULTY

James R. Abbey, Professor; Ph.D., Utah State. Convention management, hospitality marketing.
Donald Bell, Professor; Ph.D., Michigan State. Food service systems and management.
Seyhmus Bolaglu, Assistant Professor; Ph.D., Virginia Tech. Hospitality marketing, tourism marketing.
Frank Borsenik, Professor Emeritus; Ph.D., Michigan State. Operational analysis, hospitality engineering.
Robert Bosselman, Professor and Associate Director of Graduate Studies and Research; Ph.D., Oklahoma State. Food service systems and management.
John Bowen, Professor and Director of Graduate Studies and Research; Ph.D., Texas A&M. Hospitality marketing, casino marketing, services management.
Kathleen Pearl Brewer, Associate Professor; Ph.D., Purdue. Human resources, information systems.
James A. Busser, Associate Professor; Ph.D., Illinois at Urbana-Champaign. Sport and leisure studies.
Shannon Bybee, Associate Professor and Rose Chair Professor; J.D., Utah. Gaming.
Cynthia P. Carruthers, Associate Professor; Ph.D., Illinois at Urbana-Champaign. Sport and leisure studies.
David J. Christianson, Dean; Ph.D., Texas A&M. Travel and tourism, hospitality education.
Leslie E. Cummings, Professor; D.P.A., Arizona State. Information technologies, hospitality environmental policies.
Bernard Fried, Assistant Professor; Ed.D., La Verne. Financial management, accounting.
Jolie Gaston, Assistant Professor; J.D., Tennessee. Hospitality and travel law, ethics.
Gerald Goll, Associate Professor; D.B.A., US International. Human resources, organizational behavior.
John R. Goodwin, Professor Emeritus; J.D., West Virginia. Hospitality law.
Zheng Gu, Assistant Professor; Ph.D., Central Florida. Financial management.
David L. Holmes, Professor; Ph.D., Utah. Sport and leisure studies.
Susan Ivancevich, Assistant Professor; Ph.D., Texas A&M. Accounting, financial management.
Thomas Jones, Assistant Professor; Ed.D., Arizona State. Lodging management, hospitality education.
Audrey McCool, Professor; Ed.D., Texas Tech. Food service systems and management.
Rhonda Montgomery, Assistant Professor; Ph.D., South Carolina. Club management, convention management, resort management.
Michael Petrillose, Assistant Professor; Ph.D., Kansas State. Human resource management, hotel operations, service management.
Wesley Roehl, Associate Professor; Ph.D., Texas A&M. Travel and tourism, research methods.
Gail Sammons, Assistant Professor; Ph.D., Penn State. Human resources, information systems.
Stowe Shoemaker, Assistant Professor; Ph.D., Cornell. Strategic management, consumer behavior, services management, casino marketing, research methods.
John M. Stefanelli, Professor and Associate Dean; Ph.D., Denver. Food service systems and management.
Skip Swerdlow, Associate Professor; Ph.D., Arizona State. Franchising management, lodging management.
Jerome Vallen, Professor Emeritus; Ph.D., Cornell. Lodging management, hospitality education.

Class size is limited to 15 students, ensuring good classroom discussions and allowing for project-oriented assignments.

The Stan Fulton Building, housing the College's International Gaming Institute, is scheduled to open in 1999.

There are a number of recreation areas near UNLV, including Mount Charleston.

Section 7
Human Resources

This section contains directories of institutions offering graduate work in human resources development and human resources management, followed by in-depth entries submitted by institutions that chose to prepare detailed program descriptions. Additional information about programs listed in the directories but not augmented by an in-depth entry may be obtained by writing directly to the dean of a graduate school or chair of a department at the address given in the directory.

For programs offering related work, see also in this book Business Administration and Management, Advertising and Public Relations, Hospitality Management, Industrial and Manufacturing Management, and Organizational Behavior. In Book 2, see Public, Regional, and Industrial Affairs (Industrial and Labor Relations).

CONTENTS

Human Resources Development

Abilene Christian University, Program in Organizational and Human Resource Development, Abilene, TX 79699-9100. Awards MS. Part-time and evening/weekend programs available. Faculty: 9 full-time (0 women). Students: 23 full-time (14 women), 20 part-time (7 women); includes 11 minority (9 African Americans, 2 Native Americans), 2 international. 32 applicants, 72% accepted. In 1997, 14 degrees awarded. *Degree requirements:* Comprehensive exam required, foreign language and thesis not required. *Entrance requirements:* GMAT, GRE General Test, or MAT. Application deadline: 4/1 (priority date; rolling processing; 11/1 for spring admission). Application fee: $25 ($45 for international students). *Expenses:* Tuition $308 per credit hour. Fees $430 per year full-time, $85 per semester (minimum) part-time. *Financial aid:* Federal Work-Study available. Aid available to part-time students. Financial aid application deadline: 4/1. • Lynda Thornton, Graduate Adviser, 915-674-2562. Application contact: Dr. Carley Dodd, Graduate Dean, 915-674-2354. Fax: 915-674-6717. E-mail: gradinfo@nicanor.acu.edu.

Amber University, Graduate School, Program in Human Relations and Business, Garland, TX 75041-5595. Awards MA, MS. Students: 100 full-time (50 women), 100 part-time (50 women); includes 75 minority (50 African Americans, 5 Asian Americans, 15 Hispanics, 5 Native Americans). Average age 35. In 1997, 100 degrees awarded. *Entrance requirements:* Minimum GPA of 3.0. Application fee: $25 ($100 for international students). *Expenses:* Tuition $150 per semester hour. Fees $25 per year. • Dr. Algia Allen, Academic Dean, Graduate School, 972-279-6511 Ext. 135. Fax: 972-279-9773.

American International College, School of Continuing Education and Graduate Studies, School of Psychology and Education, Center for Human Resource Development, Springfield, MA 01109-3189. Awards MA, CAGS. Part-time programs available. Faculty: 2 full-time (1 woman), 3 part-time (all women). Students: 15 full-time (12 women), 1 part-time (0 women); includes 3 minority (2 African Americans, 1 Hispanic), 2 international. 80% of applicants accepted. In 1997, 11 master's, 3 CAGSs awarded. *Degree requirements:* For master's, practicum required, foreign language and thesis not required. *Entrance requirements:* For master's, minimum C average in undergraduate course work. Application fee: $15 ($25 for international students). *Expenses:* Tuition $363 per credit hour. Fees $25 per semester. *Financial aid:* Federal Work-Study available. • Dr. Debra Anderson, Director, 413-747-6372.

Antioch Southern California/Los Angeles, Program in Organizational Management, 13274 Fiji Way, Marina del Rey, CA 90292-7090. Offerings include human resource development (MA). Program faculty: 2 full-time (1 woman), 5 part-time (3 women). *Degree requirements:* Computer language, thesis required, foreign language not required. *Entrance requirements:* TOEFL (minimum score 600), interview. Application deadline: 8/8 (priority date; 2/6 for spring admission). Application fee: $50. • Scott Schroeder, Chair, 310-578-1080. Fax: 310-822-4824. E-mail: scott_schroeder@antiochla.edu. Application contact: MeHee Hyun, Director of Admissions, 310-578-1090. Fax: 310-822-4842. E-mail: mehee_hyun@antiochla.edu.

Azusa Pacific University, School of Business and Management, Program in Human Resource Development, Azusa, CA 91702-7000. Awards MHRD. Part-time and evening/weekend programs available. Faculty: 4 part-time (1 woman). Students: 7. In 1997, 5 degrees awarded. *Degree requirements:* Comprehensive exam, final project required, foreign language and thesis not required. *Average time to degree:* master's–1 year full-time, 3 years part-time. *Entrance requirements:* Minimum GPA of 3.0. Application fee: $45 ($65 for international students). *Expenses:* Tuition $405 per unit. Fees $57 per year. • Dr. Phillip Lewis, Dean, School of Business and Management, 626-812-3090. Application contact: Kim Gara, Academic Adviser, 626-812-3818. Fax: 626-815-3802.

Barry University, School of Education, Program in Human Resource Development, Miami Shores, FL 33161-6695. Awards MS. Part-time and evening/weekend programs available. Faculty: 2 full-time (both women), 1 (woman) part-time. Students: 7 full-time (all women), 101 part-time (63 women); includes 41 minority (28 African Americans, 13 Hispanics), 2 international. Average age 41. In 1997, 24 degrees awarded. *Degree requirements:* Practicum, written comprehensive exam required, foreign language and thesis not required. *Entrance requirements:* GRE General Test or MAT, minimum GPA of 3.0. Application deadline: 5/1 (priority date; rolling processing). Application fee: $30. Electronic applications accepted. *Tuition:* $450 per credit (minimum). *Financial aid:* Partial tuition waivers and career-related internships or fieldwork available. Aid available to part-time students. Financial aid application deadline: 5/1; applicants required to submit FAFSA. • Dr. Toni Powell, Director, 305-899-3708. Fax: 305-899-3630. E-mail: powell@aquinas.barry.edu. Application contact: Angela Scott, Enrollment Services, Assistant Dean, 305-899-3112. Fax: 305-899-3149. E-mail: ascott@jeanne.barry.edu.

Barry University, School of Education, Program in Leadership and Education, Miami Shores, FL 33161-6695. Offerings include human resource development (PhD). Program faculty: 1 full-time (0 women), 2 part-time (1 woman), 2 FTE. *Degree requirements:* Dissertation. *Entrance requirements:* GRE General Test, minimum GPA of 3.25. Application deadline: 5/1 (priority date; rolling processing). Application fee: $30. Electronic applications accepted. *Tuition:* $450 per credit (minimum). • Dr. Jack Dezek, Chair, 305-899-3700. Fax: 305-899-3630. E-mail: dezek@aquinas.barry.edu. Application contact: Angela Scott, Enrollment Services, Assistant Dean, 305-899-3112. Fax: 305-899-3149. E-mail: ascott@jeanne.barry.edu.

Bowie State University, Program in Human Resource Development, 14000 Jericho Park Road, Bowie, MD 20715. Awards MA. *Degree requirements:* Research paper, written comprehensive exam required, thesis optional. *Application deadline:* 8/16 (rolling processing). *Application fee:* $30. *Expenses:* Tuition $169 per credit hour for state residents; $304 per credit hour for nonresidents. Fees $171 per year.

California State University, Sacramento, School of Business Administration, Program in Business Administration, Sacramento, CA 95819-6048. Offerings include human resources (MBA). *Degree requirements:* Thesis or alternative, writing proficiency exam required, foreign language not required. *Entrance requirements:* GMAT, TOEFL (minimum score 550). Application deadline: 4/15 (11/1 for spring admission). Application fee: $55. *Expenses:* Tuition $0 for state residents; $246 per unit for nonresidents. Fees $2012 per year full-time, $1346 per year part-time. • Application contact: Dr. Herbert Blake, Graduate Adviser, 916-278-6771.

Carlow College, Division of Professional Leadership, Pittsburgh, PA 15213-3165. Offerings include training and development (MS). Division faculty: 2 full-time (both women), 16 part-time (14 women). *Degree requirements:* Thesis or alternative required, foreign language not required. *Average time to degree:* master's–2 years part-time. *Entrance requirements:* Interview, minimum GPA of 3.0. Application deadline: 6/1 (priority date; 11/1 for spring admission). Application fee: $35. • Dr. M. Sandie Turner, Director, 412-578-6669. Application contact: Bonnie Potthoff, Office Manager, Graduate Studies, 412-578-8764. Fax: 412-578-8822.

Chapman University, Professional Studies, Orange, CA 92866. Offerings include human resources (MS). Faculty: 3 full-time (2 women). *Application deadline:* rolling. *Application fee:* $40. • Harry J. Schuler, Vice Provost, 714-997-6730.

Chapman University, Program in Human Resources, Orange, CA 92866. Awards MSHR. Part-time and evening/weekend programs available. Faculty: 3 full-time (2 women). In 1997, 51 degrees awarded. *Degree requirements:* Comprehensive exam, internship required, thesis not required. *Entrance requirements:* GRE General Test (minimum combined score of 900) or MAT (minimum score 52), minimum GPA of 3.0, previous course work in statistics. Application deadline: rolling. Application fee: $40. *Tuition:* $7020 per year full-time, $390 per credit part-time. *Financial aid:* Career-related internships or fieldwork available. Financial aid application deadline: 3/1. • Cris Giannantonio, Chair, 714-744-1945. Application contact: Martha McDonald, Coordinator, 714-744-0641.

City University, School of Human Services and Applied Behavioral Sciences, Bellevue, WA 98004-6442. Offerings include organizational and human systems design (XMA). Postbaccalaureate distance learning degree programs offered (no on-campus study). School faculty: 6 full-time (2 women), 59 part-time (38 women). *Application deadline:* rolling. *Application fee:* $75 ($175 for international students). Electronic applications accepted. *Tuition:* $280 per credit hour. • Dr. Roman Borboa, Dean, 425-637-1010 Ext. 3759. Fax: 425-277-2439. E-mail: rborboa@cityu.edu. Application contact: Nabil El-Khatib, Vice President, Admissions, 800-426-5596. Fax: 425-277-2437. E-mail: nel-khatib@cityu.edu.

Clemson University, College of Health, Education, and Human Development, Department of Technology and Human Resource Development, Program in Human Resource Development, Clemson, SC 29634. Awards MHRD. Part-time programs available. Students: 27 full-time (19 women), 120 part-time (85 women); includes 39 minority (37 African Americans, 2 Hispanics), 2 international. 66 applicants, 83% accepted. In 1997, 52 degrees awarded. *Entrance requirements:* TOEFL. Application deadline: 6/1 (10/1 for spring admission). Application fee: $45. Electronic applications accepted. *Expenses:* Tuition $3154 per year full-time, $130 per credit hour part-time for state residents; $6452 per year full-time, $264 per credit hour part-time for nonresidents. Fees $190 per year. • Dr. Gerald Lovedahl, Chair, Department of Technology and Human Resource Development, 864-656-3447. Fax: 864-656-4808. E-mail: march21@clemson.edu.

College of New Rochelle, Division of Human Services, Program in Career Development, New Rochelle, NY 10805-2308. Awards MS, Certificate. Part-time programs available. Faculty: 6 part-time (5 women), 2 FTE. Students: 1 (woman) full-time, 29 part-time (26 women); includes 10 minority (8 African Americans, 2 Hispanics). 3 applicants, 100% accepted. In 1997, 3 master's awarded. *Degree requirements:* For master's, fieldwork, internship required, foreign language not required. *Average time to degree:* master's–1.5 years full-time, 3 years part-time. *Entrance requirements:* For master's, interview, minimum GPA of 3.0, sample of written work. Application deadline: 8/1 (priority date; rolling processing). Application fee: $35. *Tuition:* $329 per credit. *Financial aid:* In 1997–98, 9 students received aid, including 1 assistantship totaling $948; research assistantships also available. *Faculty research:* Technology. • Dr. Jerri Frantzve, Division Head, Division of Human Services, 914-654-5561.

Florida International University, College of Education, Department of Educational Leadership and Policy Studies, Program in Human Resource Development, Miami, FL 33199. Awards MS. Part-time and evening/weekend programs available. Students: 8 full-time (5 women), 25 part-time (23 women); includes 18 minority (7 African Americans, 11 Hispanics), 3 international. Average age 45. 22 applicants, 59% accepted. In 1997, 10 degrees awarded. *Entrance requirements:* GRE General Test (minimum combined score of 1000) or minimum GPA of 3.0. Application deadline: 4/1 (priority date; rolling processing; 10/1 for spring admission). Application fee: $20. *Expenses:* Tuition $138 per credit hour for state residents; $482 per credit hour for nonresidents. Fees $46 per semester. *Financial aid:* In 1997–98, 3 teaching assistantships were awarded; research assistantships also available. • Dr. Kingsley Banya, Chairperson, Department of Educational Leadership and Policy Studies, 305-348-2724. Fax: 305-348-2081. E-mail: banyak@fiu.edu.

Friends University, Graduate Programs, College of Continuing Education, Program in Human Resource Development/Occupational Development, Wichita, KS 67213. Awards MHRDOD. Evening/weekend programs available. Students: 27. *Application deadline:* 8/15 (priority date; rolling processing). *Application fee:* $45. *Expenses:* Tuition $326 per credit hour (minimum). Fees $215 per year. • Dr. Graydon Dawson, Director, 800-794-6945 Ext. 5526. Application contact: Director of Graduate Admissions, 800-794-6945 Ext. 5300.

The George Washington University, Graduate School of Education and Human Development, Department of Counseling, Human and Organizational Services, Program in Human Resource Development, Washington, DC 20052. Offers executive leadership (Ed D), human resource development (MA Ed, Ed S). Faculty: 6 full-time (2 women), 2 part-time (0 women), 7 FTE. Students: 55 full-time (25 women), 194 part-time (124 women); includes 51 minority (29 African Americans, 20 Asian Americans, 2 Hispanics), 11 international. Average age 40. 131 applicants, 89% accepted. In 1997, 45 master's, 7 doctorates, 1 Ed S awarded. *Degree requirements:* For master's, comprehensive exam required, foreign language and thesis not required; for doctorate, dissertation, comprehensive exam required, foreign language not required; for Ed S, comprehensive exam required, thesis not required. *Entrance requirements:* For master's, GRE General Test or MAT, minimum GPA of 2.75; for doctorate, GRE General Test or MAT, interview, minimum GPA of 3.3; for Ed S, GRE General Test or MAT, minimum GPA of 3.3. Application deadline: 3/1 (priority date; rolling processing; 10/1 for spring admission). Application fee: $45. *Expenses:* Tuition $680 per semester hour. Fees $35 per semester hour. *Financial aid:* Fellowships, research assistantships, partial tuition waivers, Federal Work-Study, and career-related internships or fieldwork available. Financial aid applicants required to submit FAFSA. *Faculty research:* Organizational learning, program evaluation. • Dr. Neal Chalofsky, Faculty Coordinator, 202-994-0829.

Georgia State University, School of Policy Studies, Department of Public Administration and Urban Studies, Atlanta, GA 30303-3083. Offerings include human resource development (MS); urban studies (MS), with options in gerontology, human resources, nonprofit administration, planning and economic development, transportation. Department faculty: 18 full-time (7 women), 2 part-time (1 woman). *Average time to degree:* master's–2 years full-time, 3 years part-time. *Application deadline:* 7/1 (rolling processing; 11/1 for spring admission). *Application fee:* $25. *Expenses:* Tuition $2673 per year full-time, $99 per semester hour part-time for state residents; $10,692 per year full-time, $396 per semester hour part-time for nonresidents. Fees $228 per year. • Dr. John Thomas, Chair, 404-651-4591. Application contact: Sue Fagan, Director, 404-651-3504.

Georgia State University, School of Policy Studies, Program in Human Resource Development, Atlanta, GA 30303-3083. Awards MS, PhD. Part-time and evening/weekend programs available. Students: 0. *Degree requirements:* For master's, comprehensive exam; for doctorate, dissertation, comprehensive exam. *Application deadline:* 7/1 (rolling processing; 11/1 for spring admission). *Application fee:* $25. *Expenses:* Tuition $2673 per year full-time, $99 per semester hour part-time for state residents; $10,692 per year full-time, $396 per semester hour part-time for nonresidents. Fees $228 per year. *Financial aid:* Research assistantships, teaching assistantships available. *Faculty research:* Human resource management, corporate-scholastic partnerships, human resource development consulting. • Verna J. Willis, Coordinator, 404-651-2500.

Heritage College, Graduate Program in Education, Program in Community and Human Resource Development, Toppenish, WA 98948-9599. Awards M Ed. *Degree requirements:* Comprehensive exam required, thesis optional, foreign language not required. *Application deadline:* rolling. *Application fee:* $35 ($75 for international students). *Tuition:* $270 per credit. • Application contact: Dr. David Zufelt, Adviser, 509-865-2244.

Illinois Institute of Technology, Institute of Psychology, Chicago, IL 60616-3793. Offerings include personnel/human resource development (MS). Institute faculty: 17 full-time (7 women), 2 part-time (both women), 18 FTE. *Degree requirements:* Thesis (for some programs), comprehensive exam required, foreign language not required. *Entrance requirements:* GRE General Test, TOEFL (minimum score 550), minimum GPA of 3.2. Application deadline: 1/15 (priority date; rolling processing; 11/1 for spring admission). Application fee: $30. Electronic applications accepted. *Expenses:* Tuition $17,250 per year full-time, $575 per credit hour part-time. Fees $60 per year full-time, $1.50 per credit hour part-time. • Dr. M. Ellen Mitchell, Chairman, 312-567-3362. Fax: 312-567-3493. E-mail: mitchell@charlie.acc.iit.edu. Application contact: Graduate College, 312-567-3024. Fax: 312-567-7517. E-mail: grad@minna.cns.iit.edu.

Directory: Human Resources Development

Indiana State University, School of Technology, Department of Industrial Technology Education, Terre Haute, IN 47809-1401. Offerings include human resource development (MS). Department faculty: 8 full-time (1 woman). *Application deadline:* rolling. *Application fee:* $20. *Tuition:* $143 per credit hour for state residents; $325 per credit hour for nonresidents. • Dr. Anthony Gilberti, Chairperson, 812-237-2640.

Indiana University Bloomington, School of Business, Program in Business Administration, Bloomington, IN 47405. Offerings include human resources (MBA). Self-designed programs available. *Entrance requirements:* GMAT, TOEFL (minimum score 580). Application deadline: 3/1. Application fee: $50 ($65 for international students). *Expenses:* Tuition $8232 per year for state residents; $16,470 per year for nonresidents. Fees $343 per year. • Dr. George Hettenhouse, Chair, 812-855-8006. Application contact: Dr. James J. Holmen, Director of Admissions and Financial Aid, 812-855-8006. Fax: 812-855-9039.

Inter American University of Puerto Rico, Metropolitan Campus, Division of Economics and Business Administration, Program in Human Resources, San Juan, PR 00919-1293. Awards MBA. Faculty: 2 full-time, 5 part-time. Students: 86 full-time (60 women), 127 part-time (89 women); includes 213 minority (all Hispanics). In 1997, 5 degrees awarded. *Degree requirements:* Comprehensive exam required, foreign language and thesis not required. *Entrance requirements:* GRE or PAEG, interview. Application deadline: 5/15 (priority date; rolling processing; 11/15 for spring admission). Application fee: $31. Electronic applications accepted. *Expenses:* Tuition $3272 per year full-time, $1740 per year part-time. Fees $328 per year full-time, $176 per year part-time. *Financial aid:* Federal Work-Study available. • Application contact: Dr. Antonio Llorens, Director, 787-250-1912 Ext. 2320. Fax: 787-250-0361.

Inter American University of Puerto Rico, San Germán Campus, Department of Business Administration, Program in Business Administration, San Germán, PR 00683-5008. Offerings include human resources (MBA). *Degree requirements:* Comprehensive exam required, foreign language and thesis not required. *Entrance requirements:* Minimum GPA of 3.0, GRE General Test, or PAEG. Application deadline: 4/30 (priority date; rolling processing; 11/15 for spring admission). Application fee: $31. *Expenses:* Tuition $150 per credit. Fees $177 per semester. • Application contact: Mildred Camacho, Admissions Director, 787-892-3090. Fax: 787-892-6350.

John F. Kennedy University, School of Management, Program in Career Development, Orinda, CA 94563-2689. Awards MA, Certificate. Part-time and evening/weekend programs available. Students: 3 full-time (2 women), 37 part-time (31 women); includes 6 minority (1 African American, 2 Asian Americans, 3 Hispanics). Average age 41. 6 applicants, 100% accepted. In 1997, 14 master's, 1 Certificate awarded. *Degree requirements:* For master's, thesis or alternative. *Entrance requirements:* For master's, TOEFL (minimum score 550), interview. Application deadline: rolling. Application fee: $50. *Expenses:* Tuition $316 per unit. Fees $9 per quarter. *Financial aid:* Application deadline 3/2. • Susan Aiken, Chair, 925-295-0600. Application contact: Ellena Bloedorn, Director of Admissions, 925-258-2213. Fax: 925-254-6964.

Johns Hopkins University, School of Continuing Studies, Division of Business and Management, Baltimore, MD 21218-2699. Offerings include organizational development and human resources (MS). Division faculty: 12 full-time, 190 part-time. *Degree requirements:* Project required, foreign language and thesis not required. *Entrance requirements:* Minimum GPA of 3.0. Application deadline: rolling. Application fee: $50. • Dr. Jon Heggan, Director, 410-516-0755. Application contact: Lenora Henry, Admissions Coordinator, 410-872-1234. Fax: 410-872-1251. E-mail: adv_mail@jhuvms.hcf.jhu.edu.

Kennesaw State University, Michael J. Coles College of Business, Program in Business Administration, Kennesaw, GA 30144-5591. Offerings include human resources management and development (MBA). Program faculty: 54 full-time (18 women), 5 part-time (0 women). *Application deadline:* 7/1 (rolling processing; 2/20 for spring admission). *Application fee:* $20. *Expenses:* Tuition $2398 per year full-time, $83 per credit hour part-time for state residents; $8398 per year full-time, $333 per credit hour part-time for nonresidents. Fees $338 per year. • Dr. Rodney Alsup, Assistant Dean, 770-423-6087. Fax: 770-423-6141. E-mail: ralsup@ksumail.kennesaw.edu. Application contact: Susan N. Barrett, Administrative Specialist, Admissions, 770-423-6500. Fax: 770-423-6541. E-mail: sbarrett@ksumail.kennesaw.edu.

Lesley College, School of Management, Cambridge, MA 02138-2790. Offerings include training and development (MS). Postbaccalaureate distance learning degree programs offered (no on-campus study). School faculty: 10 full-time (4 women), 204 part-time (78 women). *Application deadline:* rolling. *Application fee:* $45. *Tuition:* $425 per credit. • Dr. Earl Potter, Dean, 617-349-8682. Fax: 617-349-8678. Application contact: Marilyn Gove, Associate Director, 617-349-8690. Fax: 617-349-8313. E-mail: mgove@mail.lesley.edu.

Loyola University Chicago, Graduate School, Program in Training and Development, 820 North Michigan Avenue, Chicago, IL 60611-2196. Awards MSTD, MSHR/MSTD, MSIR/MSTD, MSOD/MSTD. Students: 3 full-time (all women), 28 part-time (21 women); includes 3 minority (2 African Americans, 1 Hispanic). In 1997, 9 degrees awarded. *Entrance requirements:* GMAT (minimum score 500) or GRE General Test (minimum combined score of 1550 on three sections). Application deadline: rolling. Application fee: $35. *Tuition:* $1665 per course. *Financial aid:* Federal Work-Study, institutionally sponsored loans, and career-related internships or fieldwork available. Aid available to part-time students. Financial aid applicants required to submit FAFSA. *Faculty research:* Global employee development, teams. • Dr. Linda K. Stroh, Director, 312-915-6595. Fax: 312-915-6231. E-mail: lstroh@luc.edu.

Manhattanville College, Humanities and Social Sciences Programs, Program in Organization Management and Human Resources Development, Purchase, NY 10577-2132. Awards MS. Part-time and evening/weekend programs available. Students: 170. *Degree requirements:* Thesis required, foreign language not required. *Application deadline:* 9/1 (priority date; rolling processing; 3/1 for spring admission). *Application fee:* $45. *Expenses:* Tuition $410 per credit (minimum). Fees $25 per semester. • Application contact: Donald J. Richards, Associate Dean, 914-694-3425. Fax: 914-694-3488. E-mail: drichard@mville.edu.

Marquette University, College of Business Administration, Program in Human Resources, Milwaukee, WI 53201-1881. Awards MSHR. Part-time and evening/weekend programs available. Faculty: 42 full-time (7 women), 3 part-time (0 women). Students: 16 full-time (12 women), 48 part-time (34 women); includes 1 international. Average age 34. 23 applicants, 91% accepted. In 1997, 1 degree awarded. *Entrance requirements:* GMAT or GRE General Test, TOEFL (minimum score 550). Application fee: $40. *Tuition:* $510 per credit. *Financial aid:* Research assistantships, teaching assistantships, full and partial tuition waivers, Federal Work-Study, institutionally sponsored loans available. Aid available to part-time students. Financial aid application deadline: 2/15. *Faculty research:* Diversity, mentoring. • Dr. Timothy Keaveny, Management Chair, 414-288-3643. Application contact: Joseph P. Fox, Director of Graduate Programs, 414-288-7145. Fax: 414-288-1660.

National-Louis University, College of Management and Business, Program in Human Resource Management and Development, 2840 Sheridan Road, Evanston, IL 60201-1730. Awards MS. Part-time programs available. Students: 95 full-time (66 women), 7 part-time (3 women); includes 63 minority (52 African Americans, 5 Asian Americans, 6 Hispanics), 1 international. Average age 40. In 1997, 95 degrees awarded. *Degree requirements:* Thesis required, foreign language not required. *Entrance requirements:* GRE, MAT, or Watson-Glaser Critical Thinking Appraisal, minimum GPA of 3.0. Application deadline: rolling. *Financial aid:* Available to part-time students. Financial aid applicants required to submit FAFSA. • Dr. Larry Ryley, Coordinator, 813-286-8087. Application contact: Dr. David McCulloch, Vice President for University Services, 800-443-5522 Ext. 5127. Fax: 847-465-0593. E-mail: dmcc@wheeling1.nl.edu.

New School University, Robert J. Milano Graduate School of Management and Urban Policy, Program in Human Resources Management, New York, NY 10011-8603. Offerings include organization development (Adv C), training (Adv C). Program faculty: 3 full-time (0 women), 37 part-time (16 women). *Average time to degree:* master's–1.5 years full-time, 3 years part-time. *Application deadline:* 9/1 (priority date; rolling processing). *Application fee:* $30. *Tuition:* $622 per credit. • Dr. Mark Lipton, Chair, 212-229-8969. E-mail: mlipton@newschool.edu. Application contact: Susan Morris, Assistant Dean, 212-229-5388. Fax: 212-229-8935. E-mail: smorris@newschool.edu.

North Carolina Agricultural and Technical State University, Graduate School, School of Education, Department of Human Development and Services, Greensboro, NC 27411. Offerings include human resources (MS). Department faculty: 7 full-time (3 women). *Degree requirements:* Thesis, comprehensive exam, qualifying exam required, foreign language not required. *Entrance requirements:* GRE General Test, minimum GPA of 3.0. Application deadline: 6/1 (priority date; rolling processing; 12/1 for spring admission). Application fee: $35. *Tuition:* $1662 per year full-time, $272 per semester (minimum) part-time for state residents; $8790 per year full-time, $2054 per semester (minimum) part-time for nonresidents. • Dr. Wyatt Kirk, Chairperson, 336-334-7916. Fax: 336-334-7280. E-mail: kirkw@aurora.ncat.edu.

Northeastern Illinois University, College of Education, Department of Educational Leadership and Development, Program in Human Resource Development, Chicago, IL 60625-4699. Awards MA. Part-time and evening/weekend programs available. Faculty: 4 part-time (3 women). Students: 4 full-time (3 women), 54 part-time (46 women); includes 19 minority (11 African Americans, 4 Asian Americans, 4 Hispanics), 1 international. Average age 38. 36 applicants, 42% accepted. In 1997, 17 degrees awarded. *Degree requirements:* Comprehensive exam, comprehensive papers required, foreign language not required. *Entrance requirements:* Minimum GPA of 2.75, BA in human resource development. Application deadline: 3/18 (priority date; rolling processing; 9/30 for spring admission). Application fee: $0. *Expenses:* Tuition $2226 per year full-time, $93 per credit hour part-time for state residents; $6678 per year full-time, $278 per credit hour part-time for nonresidents. Fees $358 per year full-time, $14.90 per credit hour part-time. *Financial aid:* 14 students received aid; full and partial tuition waivers, Federal Work-Study, institutionally sponsored loans, and career-related internships or fieldwork available. Aid available to part-time students. • Dr. Diane Ehrlich, Coordinator, 773-794-2779. Application contact: Dr. Mohan K. Sood, Dean of Graduate College, 773-583-4050 Ext. 6143. Fax: 773-794-6670.

Oakland University, School of Education and Human Services, Program in Training and Development, Rochester, MI 48309-4401. Awards MTD. *Entrance requirements:* Minimum GPA of 3.0 for unconditional admission. Application fee: $30. *Expenses:* Tuition $3852 per year full-time, $214 per credit hour part-time for state residents; $8532 per year full-time, $474 per credit hour part-time for nonresidents. Fees $420 per year. • Dr. James Quinn, Coordinator, 248-370-4109.

Ottawa University, Department of Human Resources, Ottawa, KS 66067-3399. Awards MA. Offered at both the Arizona and Kansas campuses. Part-time and evening/weekend programs available. Postbaccalaureate distance learning degree programs offered (minimal on-campus study). Faculty: 1 full-time (0 women), 16 part-time (8 women). Students: 64 part-time (38 women). 44 applicants, 100% accepted. In 1997, 16 degrees awarded. *Degree requirements:* Thesis optional, foreign language not required. *Application deadline:* rolling. *Application fee:* $50. *Tuition:* $275 per hour. *Financial aid:* Available to part-time students. • Dr. W. A. Breytspraak, Director of Graduate Studies, 913-451-1431. Application contact: David Leiter, Admissions Officer, 913-451-1431.

Palm Beach Atlantic College, MacArthur School of Continuing Education, West Palm Beach, FL 33416-4708. Offers program in human resource development (MS). Faculty: 6 full-time (1 woman). Students: 46 full-time (32 women), 6 part-time (5 women); includes 10 minority (7 African Americans, 3 Hispanics), 1 international. Average age 39. 25 applicants, 88% accepted. In 1997, 31 degrees awarded. *Degree requirements:* Thesis optional. *Entrance requirements:* GRE. Application deadline: 9/6 (priority date; rolling processing). Application fee: $35. *Tuition:* $280 per credit hour. • Dr. Elizabeth Hirst, Dean, 561-803-2317. Fax: 561-803-2306. Application contact: Carolanne M. Brown, Director of Graduate Admissions, 800-281-3466. Fax: 561-803-2115. E-mail: grad@pbac.edu.

Pennsylvania State University University Park Campus, College of Liberal Arts, Department of Labor and Industrial Relations, University Park, PA 16802-1503. Offers program in industrial relations and human resources (MS). Students: 8 full-time (5 women), 1 part-time (0 women). *Entrance requirements:* GRE General Test. Application fee: $40. *Expenses:* Tuition $6534 per year full-time, $276 per credit part-time for state residents; $13,460 per year full-time, $561 per credit part-time for nonresidents. Fees $252 per year (minimum) full-time, $43 per semester (minimum) part-time. • Dr. Mark Wardell, Head, 814-865-5425.

Pittsburg State University, School of Technology, Department of Technical Education, Program in Human Resource Development, Pittsburg, KS 66762-5880. Awards MS. Faculty: 3 full-time (0 women), 3 part-time (1 woman). Students: 35 full-time (15 women), 32 part-time (14 women); includes 2 minority (1 Hispanic, 1 Native American), 23 international. In 1997, 30 degrees awarded. *Degree requirements:* Thesis or alternative required, foreign language not required. *Application fee:* $40. *Tuition:* $2418 per year full-time, $103 per credit hour part-time for state residents; $6130 per year full-time, $258 per credit hour part-time for nonresidents. *Financial aid:* Teaching assistantships, Federal Work-Study, and career-related internships or fieldwork available. • Dr. Mark Johnson, Chairperson, Department of Technical Education, 316-235-4631.

Rensselaer Polytechnic Institute, Lally School of Management and Technology, Troy, NY 12180-3590. Offerings include human resource (PhD). Postbaccalaureate distance learning degree programs offered (no on-campus study). School faculty: 36 full-time (5 women), 6 part-time (0 women). *Degree requirements:* Computer language, dissertation required, foreign language not required. *Entrance requirements:* GMAT or GRE General Test, TOEFL (minimum score 570). Application deadline: 2/1 (priority date; rolling processing). Application fee: $35. *Expenses:* Tuition $630 per credit hour. Fees $1000 per year. • Dr. Joseph G. Ecker, Dean, 518-276-6802. Application contact: Michele Martens, Manager of Enrollment Services, 518-276-4800. Fax: 518-276-8661.

Rochester Institute of Technology, College of Applied Science and Technology, Department of Food, Hotel, and Travel Management, Program in Career and Human Resource Development, Rochester, NY 14623-5604. Awards MS. Students: 9 full-time (8 women), 26 part-time (20 women); includes 4 minority (all African Americans), 3 international. 14 applicants, 86% accepted. In 1997, 33 degrees awarded. *Entrance requirements:* Minimum GPA of 3.0. Application deadline: 3/1 (priority date; rolling processing). Application fee: $40. *Expenses:* Tuition $18,765 per year full-time, $527 per credit hour part-time. Fees $126 per year full-time. • Stanley Bissell, Human Resources Coordinator, 716-475-5069.

Rollins College, Program in Human Resources, Winter Park, FL 32789-4499. Awards MA. Part-time and evening/weekend programs available. Faculty: 4 full-time (3 women). Students: 48 part-time (37 women); includes 2 minority (1 African American, 1 Hispanic). Average age 30. 67 applicants, 66% accepted. In 1997, 31 degrees awarded. *Degree requirements:* Thesis optional, foreign language not required. *Entrance requirements:* GMAT, GRE, or MAT, interview. Application deadline: 4/1. Application fee: $50. *Tuition:* $258 per hour. *Financial aid:* 7 students received aid. Financial aid application deadline: 3/23. • Dr. Donald Rogers, Director, 407-646-2348. Application contact: Laura Pfister, Coordinator of Records and Registration, 407-646-2416. Fax: 407-646-1551.

St. John Fisher College, School of Adult and Graduate Education, Human Resources Development Program, Rochester, NY 14618-3597. Awards MS. Part-time and evening/weekend programs available. Faculty: 1 (woman) full-time. Students: 14 part-time (10 women); includes 1 minority (African American). Average age 35. 10 applicants, 80% accepted. *Degree requirements:* Computer language required, thesis not required. *Application deadline:* 8/1 (priority date; rolling processing; 1/1 for spring admission). *Application fee:* $30. *Tuition:*

Directory: Human Resources Development

St. John Fisher College (continued)

$13,500 per year full-time, $375 per credit hour part-time. • Dr. Marilynn Butler, Graduate Director, 716-385-8157. E-mail: mbutler@sjfc.edu. Application contact: Steven T. Hoskins, Director, Graduate Admissions, 716-385-8161. Fax: 716-385-8344. E-mail: hoskins@sjfc.edu.

Siena Heights University, Program in Human Resource Development, Adrian, MI 49221-1796. Awards MA. Part-time and evening/weekend programs available. *Degree requirements:* Computer language, thesis, internship, presentation, project required, foreign language not required. *Entrance requirements:* Minimum GPA of 3.0, interview. Application deadline: 8/24 (priority date; rolling processing; 4/30 for spring admission). Application fee: $25.

Suffolk University, College of Liberal Arts and Sciences, Department of Education and Human Services, Program in Counseling and Human Relations, Program in Human Resource Development, Boston, MA 02108-2770. Awards MS, CAGS. Part-time and evening/weekend programs available. Faculty: 2 full-time (both women), 4 part-time (3 women). *Entrance requirements:* For master's, GRE General Test (average 500 on each section) or MAT (average 50). Application deadline: 6/15 (priority date; rolling processing; 11/15 for spring admission). Application fee: $50. *Expenses:* Tuition $14,544 per year full-time, $1452 per course part-time. Fees $20 per year full-time, $10 per year part-time. *Financial aid:* Fellowships, Federal Work-Study, institutionally sponsored loans, and career-related internships or fieldwork available. Aid available to part-time students. Financial aid application deadline: 4/1; applicants required to submit FAFSA. • Application contact: Judy Reynolds, Acting Director of Graduate Admissions, 617-573-8302. Fax: 617-523-0116. E-mail: grad.admission@admin.suffolk.edu.

Texas A&M University, College of Education, Department of Educational Human Resource Development, College Station, TX 77843. Offers programs in adult education (M Ed, MS, Ed D, PhD), educational human resource development (M Ed, MS, Ed D, PhD), industrial education (M Ed, MS, Ed D, PhD). Faculty: 14 full-time (5 women). Students: 46 full-time (26 women), 77 part-time (42 women); includes 17 minority (5 African Americans, 3 Asian Americans, 9 Hispanics), 6 international. Average age 37. 75 applicants, 63% accepted. In 1997, 13 master's, 19 doctorates awarded. *Degree requirements:* For doctorate, dissertation required, foreign language not required. *Entrance requirements:* GRE General Test, TOEFL. Application fee: $35 ($75 for international students). *Financial aid:* Fellowships, research assistantships, teaching assistantships, and career-related internships or fieldwork available. *Faculty research:* Adult and family literacy, distance education, adult learning and development, training and development. • Lloyd Korhonan, Head, 409-845-3016. E-mail: lloyd@summa.tamu.edu. Application contact: Anne Koppa, Graduate Admissions Supervisor, 409-862-4154. Fax: 409-845-0409. E-mail: cak5866@zeys.tamu.edu.

Towson University, Program in Human Resource Development, Towson, MD 21252-0001. Awards MS. Part-time and evening/weekend programs available. Faculty: 10 full-time (5 women). Students: 23 full-time (19 women), 109 part-time (94 women); includes 28 minority (27 African Americans, 1 Native American), 7 international. In 1997, 42 degrees awarded. *Degree requirements:* Exam required, foreign language and thesis not required. *Application deadline:* 3/1 (priority date; rolling processing; 10/1 for spring admission). *Application fee:* $40. *Expenses:* Tuition $187 per credit hour for state residents; $364 per credit hour for nonresidents. Fees $40 per credit hour. *Financial aid:* Assistantships, Federal Work-Study, and career-related internships or fieldwork available. Financial aid application deadline: 4/1; applicants required to submit FAFSA. *Faculty research:* Workforce training and development. • Dr. Lawrence Froman, Director, 410-830-2678. Fax: 410-830-3434. E-mail: lfroman@towson.edu. Application contact: Fran Musotto, Office Manager, 410-830-2501. Fax: 410-830-4675. E-mail: fmusotto@towson.edu.

Trinity College, School of Professional Studies, Programs in Administration, Washington, DC 20017-1094. Offerings include human resources (MSA), with options in entrepreneurial development, human resource development, human resource management. Faculty: 4 full-time (1 woman), 4 part-time (all women). *Application deadline:* rolling. *Application fee:* $35. *Tuition:* $460 per credit hour. • Dr. Sheri Levin, Division Chair, Human Services, 202-884-9553. Application contact: Karen Goodwin, Director of Graduate Admissions, 202-884-9400. Fax: 202-884-9229.

Universidad del Turabo, Programs in Business Administration, Program in Human Resources, Gurabo, PR 00778-3030. Awards MBA. *Entrance requirements:* GRE, PAEG, interview. Application deadline: 8/5. Application fee: $25.

University of Bridgeport, College of Graduate and Undergraduate Studies, School of Education and Human Resources, Division of Counseling and Human Resources, 380 University Avenue, Bridgeport, CT 06601. Offers programs in community agency counseling (MS), human resource development and counseling (MS). MS (human resource development and counseling) offered jointly with the School of Business. Part-time and evening/weekend programs available. Faculty: 3 full-time (1 woman), 9 part-time (4 women), 6 FTE. Students: 11 full-time (9 women), 82 part-time (62 women); includes 19 minority (13 African Americans, 6 Hispanics), 6 international. Average age 49. 80 applicants, 46% accepted. In 1997, 26 degrees awarded. *Application deadline:* rolling. *Application fee:* $35 ($50 for international students). *Tuition:* $340 per credit. *Financial aid:* In 1997–98, 46 students received aid, including 8 teaching assistantships; fellowships, research assistantships, Federal Work-Study, institutionally sponsored loans, and career-related internships or fieldwork also available. Aid available to part-time students. Financial aid application deadline: 6/1; applicants required to submit FAFSA. *Faculty research:* Corporate elder care programs. • Dr. Joseph E. Nechasek, Director, 203-576-4175.

See in-depth description on page 501.

University of Georgia, College of Education, Department of Adult Education, Program in Human Resource and Organization Development, Athens, GA 30602. Awards M Ed. Faculty: 9 full-time (4 women). Students: 6 full-time, 6 part-time (5 women); includes 2 minority (1 African American, 1 Hispanic). 9 applicants, 67% accepted. In 1997, 3 degrees awarded. *Entrance requirements:* GRE General Test or MAT. Application deadline: 7/1 (priority date; 11/15 for spring admission). Application fee: $30. Electronic applications accepted. *Tuition:* $3290 per year full-time, $643 per semester (minimum) part-time for state residents; $11,300 per year full-time, $1645 per semester (minimum) part-time for nonresidents. • Dr. Ronald M. Cervero, Graduate Coordinator, Department of Adult Education, 706-542-4011. Fax: 706-542-4204.

Announcement: The Master of Education in human resource and organization development is a multidisciplinary program that emphasizes individual and organizational learning, technology, and adult education. It prepares students for careers in training, management development, and organizational consultation. Program features applied field experiences and innovative course delivery. For application, contact Department of Adult Education, 410 River's Crossing, University of Georgia, Athens, GA 30602; e-mail: kwatkins@uga.cc.uga.edu; World Wide Web: http://www.coe.uga.edu/adulted

University of Oregon, Graduate School, Charles H. Lundquist College of Business, Program in Human Resources and Industrial Relations, Eugene, OR 97403. Awards MHRIR. Part-time programs available. Students: 4 full-time (3 women), 3 part-time (all women); includes 2 international. 6 applicants, 0% accepted. In 1997, 14 degrees awarded (100% found work related to degree). *Degree requirements:* Computer language required, foreign language not required. *Entrance requirements:* GMAT or GRE General Test. Application deadline: 3/1. Application fee: $50. *Tuition:* $6429 per year full-time, $873 per quarter (minimum) part-time for state residents; $10,857 per year full-time, $1360 per quarter (minimum) part-time for nonresidents. *Financial aid:* In 1997–98, 1 teaching assistantship was awarded; Federal Work-Study and career-related internships or fieldwork also available. • Dan Poston, Director, 541-346-3251. E-mail: mohoric@oregon.uoregon.edu. Application contact: Linda Johnson, Graduate Secretary, 541-346-3306.

University of San Francisco, College of Professional Studies, Department of Organizational Studies, Program in Human Resources and Organization Development, San Francisco, CA 94117-1080. Awards MHROD. Part-time and evening/weekend programs available. Faculty: 5 full-time (4 women), 44 part-time (12 women). Students: 296 full-time (225 women); includes 72 minority (28 African Americans, 18 Asian Americans, 24 Hispanics, 2 Native Americans). Average age 39. 136 applicants, 82% accepted. In 1997, 104 degrees awarded. *Degree requirements:* Thesis required, foreign language not required. *Average time to degree:* master's–3 years full-time. *Entrance requirements:* Minimum GPA of 3.0. Application fee: $35. *Financial aid:* 87 students received aid. Financial aid application deadline: 3/2. • Application contact: Advising Office, 415-422-6000.

University of Scranton, Department of Health Administration and Human Resources, Program in Human Resources Administration, Scranton, PA 18510-4622. Offerings include human resources development (MS). *Degree requirements:* Comprehensive exam required, foreign language and thesis not required. *Entrance requirements:* TOEFL (minimum score 575), minimum GPA of 2.75. Application deadline: rolling. Application fee: $35. *Expenses:* Tuition $465 per credit. Fees $25 per semester. • Dr. Daniel J. West, Chair, Department of Health Administration and Human Resources, 717-941-4126. Fax: 717-941-4201. E-mail: westd1@uofs.edu.

University of Tennessee, Knoxville, College of Human Ecology, Department of Human Resource Development, Knoxville, TN 37996. Offers program in training and development (MS). Part-time programs available. Faculty: 15 full-time (2 women). Students: 28 full-time (13 women), 97 part-time (60 women); includes 16 minority (15 African Americans, 1 Hispanic). 48 applicants, 35% accepted. In 1997, 44 degrees awarded. *Degree requirements:* Thesis optional, foreign language not required. *Entrance requirements:* GRE General Test (minimum score 550), minimum GPA of 2.7. Application deadline: 2/1. Application fee: $35. Electronic applications accepted. *Tuition:* $3354 per year full-time, $181 per semester hour part-time for state residents; $8410 per year full-time, $462 per semester hour part-time for nonresidents. *Financial aid:* In 1997–98, 10 teaching assistantships were awarded; fellowships, research assistantships, graduate assistantships, Federal Work-Study, institutionally sponsored loans, and career-related internships or fieldwork also available. • Dr. Greg Petty, Head, 423-974-2574. Fax: 423-974-2048. E-mail: gpetty@utk.edu. Application contact: Dr. Ernest Brewer, Graduate Representative, 423-974-2574. E-mail: ebrewer1@utk.edu.

See in-depth description on page 507.

University of Tennessee, Knoxville, College of Human Ecology, Program in Human Ecology, Knoxville, TN 37996. Offerings include human resource development (PhD). *Degree requirements:* Dissertation required, foreign language not required. *Entrance requirements:* GRE General Test, TOEFL (minimum score 550), minimum GPA of 2.7. Application deadline: 2/1 (priority date; rolling processing). Application fee: $35. Electronic applications accepted. *Tuition:* $3354 per year full-time, $181 per semester hour part-time for state residents; $8410 per year full-time, $462 per semester hour part-time for nonresidents. • Dr. James D. Moran III, Chair, 423-974-5224. Fax: 423-974-2617. E-mail: jmoran@utk.edu.

University of Wisconsin–Stout, College of Technology, Engineering, and Management, Program in Training and Development, Menomonie, WI 54751. Awards MS. Part-time programs available. Students: 22 full-time (11 women), 36 part-time (24 women); includes 7 minority (5 African Americans, 1 Asian American, 1 Native American), 2 international. 26 applicants, 100% accepted. In 1997, 22 degrees awarded. *Degree requirements:* Thesis required, foreign language not required. *Application deadline:* rolling. *Application fee:* $45. *Tuition:* $3284 per year full-time, $183 per credit hour part-time for state residents; $7644 per year full-time, $425 per credit hour part-time for nonresidents. *Financial aid:* In 1997–98, 8 research assistantships were awarded; teaching assistantships, full and partial tuition waivers, Federal Work-Study also available. Aid available to part-time students. Financial aid application deadline: 4/1; applicants required to submit FAFSA. • Dr. Joseph Benkowski, Director, 715-232-5266.

Vanderbilt University, Peabody College, Department of Human Resources, Nashville, TN 37240-1001. Offerings include human resource development (M Ed, Ed D). *Entrance requirements:* For doctorate, GRE General Test, MAT. Application deadline: 3/1 (priority date; rolling processing). Application fee: $35. • Robert B. Innes, Acting Chair, 615-322-6881.

Villanova University, Graduate School of Liberal Arts and Sciences, Program in Human Organization Science, Human Resource Development Option, Villanova, PA 19085-1699. Awards MS. Part-time programs available. Students: 16 full-time (12 women), 25 part-time (19 women); includes 3 minority (all African Americans), 2 international. Average age 30. 19 applicants, 84% accepted. *Degree requirements:* Comprehensive exam required, foreign language and thesis not required. *Entrance requirements:* GRE General Test, minimum GPA of 3.0. Application deadline: 8/1 (priority date; 12/1 for spring admission). Application fee: $40. *Expenses:* Tuition $400 per credit. Fees $60 per year. *Financial aid:* Federal Work-Study and career-related internships or fieldwork available. Financial aid application deadline: 4/1. • Dr. David F. Bush, Coordinator, 610-519-4746.

Virginia Polytechnic Institute and State University, College of Human Resources and Education, Department of Family and Child Development, Program in Adult Learning and Human Resource Development, Blacksburg, VA 24061. Awards MS, PhD. Offered jointly with Northern Virginia campus. *Degree requirements:* Thesis/dissertation required, foreign language not required. *Entrance requirements:* For master's, GRE General Test (minimum combined score of 900), TOEFL (minimum score 600), minimum GPA of 3.0; for doctorate, GRE General Test (minimum combined score of 900), TOEFL (minimum score 600), minimum GPA of 3.5. Application deadline: 12/1 (priority date; rolling processing). Application fee: $25. *Tuition:* $4927 per year full-time, $792 per semester (minimum) part-time for state residents; $7537 per year full-time, $1227 per semester (minimum) part-time for nonresidents. *Financial aid:* Application deadline 4/1. • Dr. Michael Sporakowski, Head, Department of Family and Child Development, 540-231-4794. E-mail: fed@vt.edu.

Webster University, School of Business and Technology, Department of Business, St. Louis, MO 63119-3194. Offerings include human resources development (MA, MBA). Department faculty: 5 full-time (1 woman). *Application deadline:* rolling. *Application fee:* $25 ($50 for international students). *Tuition:* $350 per credit hour. • Lucille Berry, Chair, 314-968-7022. Fax: 314-968-7077. E-mail: berrylm@webster.edu. Application contact: Beth Russell, Director of Graduate Admissions, 314-968-7089. Fax: 314-968-7166. E-mail: russellmb@webster.edu.

Western Carolina University, College of Education and Allied Professions, Department of Human Services, Program in Human Resource Development, Cullowhee, NC 28723. Awards MS. Part-time and evening/weekend programs available. Students: 8 full-time (2 women), 32 part-time (24 women); includes 2 minority (1 African American, 1 Native American), 2 international. 30 applicants, 63% accepted. In 1997, 12 degrees awarded. *Degree requirements:* Comprehensive exam required, foreign language and thesis not required. *Entrance requirements:* GRE General Test. Application deadline: rolling. Application fee: $35. *Tuition:* $1799 per year full-time, $144 per credit hour (minimum) part-time for state residents; $9069 per year full-time, $1053 per credit hour (minimum) part-time for nonresidents. *Financial aid:* In 1997–98, 5 students received aid, including 4 research assistantships (2 to first-year students) totaling $11,976, 1 teaching assistantship (to a first-year student) totaling $4,000; fellowships, Federal Work-Study also available. Financial aid application deadline: 3/15. • Application contact: Kathleen Owen, Assistant to the Dean, 828-227-7398. Fax: 828-227-7480.

Western New England College, School of Business, Program in Human Resources, Springfield, MA 01119-2654. Awards MBA. *Application deadline:* rolling. *Application fee:* $30. *Expenses:* Tuition $353 per credit hour. Fees $44 per semester (minimum). *Financial aid:* Application deadline 4/1. • Application contact: Rod Pease, Director of Student Administrative Services, 413-796-2080.

Xavier University, College of Social Sciences, Department of Education, Program in Human Resource Development, Cincinnati, OH 45207-2111. Awards M Ed. Part-time and evening/weekend programs available. Faculty: 2 full-time (both women), 4 part-time (1 woman), 3 FTE. Students: 31 full-time (22 women), 27 part-time (18 women); includes 8 minority (all African Americans). Average age 37. 53 applicants, 58% accepted. In 1997, 33 degrees awarded (100% found work related to degree). *Average time to degree:* master's–2 years part-time. *Entrance requirements:* GRE or MAT (minimum score 35; average 50), minimum GPA of 2.8, resume. Application deadline: 12/28 (priority date). Application fee: $25. *Tuition:* $430 per credit hour. *Financial aid:* In 1997–98, 8 students received aid, including 8 scholarships (4 to first-year students). Aid available to part-time students. Financial aid application deadline: 5/15. *Faculty research:* Teams, needs assessment, evaluation, college teaching, instructional design. • Dr. Brenda Gardner, Director, 513-745-4287. E-mail: gardner@xavier.xu.edu. Application contact: Sheila Speth, Director of Graduate Services, 513-745-3360. Fax: 513-745-1048. E-mail: xugrad@admin.xu.edu.

Human Resources Management

Adelphi University, School of Management and Business, Certificate Programs in Management, Garden City, NY 11530. Offerings include human resource management (Certificate). *Average time to degree:* other advanced degree–2 years full-time, 2.5 years part-time. *Application deadline:* 8/15 (priority date; rolling processing; 12/15 for spring admission). *Application fee:* $50. *Expenses:* Tuition $16,000 per year full-time, $485 per credit part-time. Fees $500 per year full-time, $150 per semester part-time. • Application contact: Jennifer Spiegel, Associate Director of Admissions, 516-877-3055.

Alabama Agricultural and Mechanical University, School of Education, Department of Counseling and Special Education, Area in Psychology and Counseling, PO Box 1357, Normal, AL 35762-1357. Offerings include personnel management (MS). Faculty: 7 full-time (3 women), 1 part-time (0 women). *Degree requirements:* Thesis or alternative, comprehensive exam required, foreign language not required. *Entrance requirements:* GRE General Test. Application deadline: 5/1. Application fee: $15 ($20 for international students). *Expenses:* Tuition $2782 per year full-time, $565 per semester (minimum) part-time for state residents; $5164 per year full-time, $1015 per semester (minimum) part-time for nonresidents. Fees $560 per year full-time, $390 per year part-time. • Dr. Annie Grace Robinson, Chair, Department of Counseling and Special Education, 205-851-5533.

Albany State University, School of Arts and Sciences, Department of History and Political Science, Albany, GA 31705-2717. Offerings include human resources management (MPA). Department faculty: 3 full-time (2 women), 4 part-time (0 women). *Degree requirements:* Thesis, comprehensive exam. *Entrance requirements:* GRE General Test (minimum combined score of 800), minimum GPA of 2.5. Application deadline: 9/1. Application fee: $10. • Dr. Veula J. Rhodes, Chairperson, 912-430-4870. E-mail: vrhodes@fld94.alsnet.peachnet.edu. Application contact: Dr. Lois B. Hollis, Program Coordinator, 912-430-4873. Fax: 912-430-7895. E-mail: lhollis@fld94.alsnet.peachnet.edu.

Amber University, Graduate School, Program in Human Relations and Business, Garland, TX 75041-5595. Awards MA, MS. Students: 100 full-time (50 women), 100 part-time (50 women); includes 75 minority (50 African Americans, 5 Asian Americans, 15 Hispanics, 5 Native Americans). Average age 35. In 1997, 100 degrees awarded. *Entrance requirements:* Minimum GPA of 3.0. Application fee: $25 ($100 for international students). *Expenses:* Tuition $150 per semester hour. Fees $25 per year. • Dr. Algia Allen, Academic Dean, Graduate School, 972-279-6511 Ext. 135. Fax: 972-279-9773.

American University, Kogod College of Business Administration, Department of Management, Program in Human Resource Management, Washington, DC 20016-8001. Awards MBA. Part-time and evening/weekend programs available. Faculty: 17 full-time (5 women), 6 part-time (1 woman). Students: 4 full-time (2 women), 2 part-time (both women); includes 1 international. 26 applicants, 69% accepted. In 1997, 11 degrees awarded. *Entrance requirements:* GMAT. Application deadline: 2/1 (priority date; 10/1 for spring admission). Application fee: $50. *Expenses:* Tuition $19,080 per year full-time, $687 per credit hour (minimum) part-time. Fees $180 per year full-time, $110 per year part-time. *Financial aid:* Fellowships, research assistantships, Federal Work-Study, institutionally sponsored loans, and career-related internships or fieldwork available. Aid available to part-time students. Financial aid application deadline: 2/1. • Application contact: Dr. David Martin, Director, 202-885-1922. Fax: 202-885-1992.

American University, School of Public Affairs, Department of Public Administration, Program in Personnel and Human Resource Management, Washington, DC 20016-8001. Awards MS. Faculty: 17 full-time (3 women), 18 part-time (8 women). Students: 34 full-time (29 women), 19 part-time (17 women); includes 20 minority (16 African Americans, 3 Asian Americans, 1 Native American), 5 international. 88 applicants, 40% accepted. *Application deadline:* 2/1 (10/1 for spring admission). *Application fee:* $50. *Expenses:* Tuition $687 per credit hour. Fees $180 per year full-time, $110 per year part-time. *Financial aid:* Application deadline 2/1. • Application contact: Academic Adviser, 202-885-1994.

Appalachian State University, John A. Walker College of Business, Program in Business Administration, Boone, NC 28608. Offerings include industrial organization/human resource management (MA). Program faculty: 15 full-time (5 women), 1 part-time (0 women). *Application deadline:* 5/31 (priority date; rolling processing). *Application fee:* $35. *Tuition:* $1811 per year full-time, $354 per semester (minimum) part-time for state residents; $9081 per year full-time, $2171 per semester (minimum) part-time for nonresidents. • Dr. Rickey C. Kirkpatrick, Assistant Dean for Graduate and External Programs, 704-262-6127. Fax: 704-262-2925. E-mail: kirkprc@appstate.edu.

Auburn University, College of Business, Department of Management, Auburn University, AL 36849-0001. Offerings include human relations management (PhD). Department faculty: 25 full-time (3 women). *Degree requirements:* Dissertation. *Entrance requirements:* GMAT, GRE General Test, TOEFL. Application deadline: 9/1 (rolling processing; 3/1 for spring admission). Application fee: $25 ($50 for international students). *Expenses:* Tuition $2760 per year full-time, $76 per credit hour part-time for state residents; $8280 per year full-time, $228 per credit hour part-time for nonresidents. Fees $30 per year full-time, $160 per quarter part-time for state residents; $30 per year full-time, $480 per quarter part-time for nonresidents. • Dr. Robert E. Niebuhr, Head, 334-844-4071. Application contact: Dr. John F. Pritchett, Dean of the Graduate School, 334-844-4700.

See in-depth description on page 143.

Baker College Center for Graduate Studies, Programs in Business, Flint, MI 48507. Offerings include human resource management (EMBA, MBA). MBA (health and recreation services management) enrollment limited to international students. Faculty: 8 full-time, 73 part-time. *Degree requirements:* Portfolio required, foreign language not required. *Entrance requirements:* 3 years of work experience, minimum undergraduate GPA of 2.5, writing sample. Application deadline: rolling. Application fee: $25. *Tuition:* $215 per quarter hour. • Dr. Michael Heberling, President, 800-469-3165. Application contact: Chuck Gurden, Director of Admissions, 800-469-3165. Fax: 810-766-4399.

Baruch College of the City University of New York, School of Business, Department of Management, 17 Lexington Avenue, New York, NY 10010-5585. Offerings include human resources management (MBA). Department faculty: 33 full-time (6 women), 15 part-time (0 women). *Degree requirements:* Computer language required, foreign language not required. *Average time to degree:* master's–2 years full-time, 4 years part-time. *Entrance requirements:* GMAT, TOEFL (minimum score 570), TWE (minimum score 4.5). Application deadline: 6/15 (11/1 for spring admission). Application fee: $40. *Expenses:* Tuition $4350 per year full-time, $185 per credit part-time for state residents; $7600 per year full-time, $320 per credit part-time for nonresidents. Fees $53 per year. • Harry M. Rosen, Chairman, 212-802-6870. Application contact: Michael S. Wynne, Office of Graduate Admissions, 212-802-2330. Fax: 212-802-2335. E-mail: graduate_admissions@baruch.cuny.edu.

Baruch College of the City University of New York, School of Public Affairs, Program in Industrial and Labor Relations, 17 Lexington Avenue, New York, NY 10010. Offerings include personnel and human resources management (EMSILR). *Degree requirements:* Thesis or alternative required, foreign language not required. *Entrance requirements:* GMAT or GRE General Test, relevant work experience. Application deadline: 9/1 (rolling processing). Application fee: $40. *Expenses:* Tuition $4350 per year full-time, $185 per credit part-time for state residents; $7600 per year full-time, $320 per credit part-time for nonresidents. Fees $53 per year. • Barbara Fife, Director, 212-802-5900. Fax: 212-802-5903.

Boston College, Wallace E. Carroll Graduate School of Management, Department of Organization Studies/Human Resources Management, Chestnut Hill, MA 02167-9991. Awards MBA, PhD. Part-time and evening/weekend programs available. *Degree requirements:* For doctorate, dissertation required, foreign language not required. *Entrance requirements:* For master's, GMAT (average 610), TOEFL (minimum score 600; average 630). Application deadline: 4/1 (priority date; rolling processing; 11/15 for spring admission). Application fee: $45. *Expenses:* Tuition $22,134 per year full-time, $714 per semester hour part-time. Fees $80 per year (minimum) full-time, $30 per semester part-time. *Financial aid:* Fellowships, research assistantships, teaching assistantships, administrative assistantships, full and partial tuition waivers, Federal Work-Study, and career-related internships or fieldwork available. Financial aid application deadline: 3/1; applicants required to submit FAFSA. *Faculty research:* Organizational transformation, mergers and acquisitions, managerial effectiveness, organizational change, organizational structure. • Dr. Judy Gordon, Chairperson, 617-552-0454. Application contact: Simone Marthers, Director of Admissions, 617-552-3920. Fax: 617-552-8078.

See in-depth description on page 629.

Boston University, School of Education, Department of Administration, Training, and Policy Studies, Program in Human Resource Education, Boston, MA 02215. Awards Ed M, Ed D, CAGS. Students: 8 full-time (5 women), 22 part-time (15 women); includes 4 minority (1 African American, 2 Asian Americans, 1 Native American). Average age 40. In 1997, 15 master's, 2 doctorates awarded. *Degree requirements:* For doctorate, dissertation, comprehensive exam required, foreign language not required; for CAGS, comprehensive exam required, foreign language and thesis not required. *Entrance requirements:* GRE or MAT, TOEFL. Application deadline: 2/15 (priority date; rolling processing). Application fee: $50. *Expenses:* Tuition $22,830 per year full-time, $713 per credit part-time. Fees $218 per year full-time, $40 per semester part-time. *Financial aid:* Application deadline 3/30. • Dr. Alan Gaynor, Coordinator, 617-353-3307. E-mail: agaynor@bu.edu.

Briercrest Biblical Seminary, Program in Leadership and Management, Caronport, SK S0H 0S0, Canada. Offerings include human resource management (MA). *Degree requirements:* Thesis optional, foreign language not required. *Application fee:* $25. *Tuition:* $471 per course. • Application contact: Michael Penner, Enrollment Management Officer, 306-756-3200. Fax: 306-756-7366.

California State University, Hayward, School of Business and Economics, Department of Management and Finance, Option in Human Resources Management, Hayward, CA 94542-3000. Awards MBA. Part-time and evening/weekend programs available. Average age 32. *Degree requirements:* Comprehensive exam or thesis required, foreign language not required. *Entrance requirements:* GMAT, minimum GPA of 2.75. Application deadline: 4/19 (priority date; rolling processing; 1/5 for spring admission). Application fee: $55. *Expenses:* Tuition $0 for state residents; $164 per unit for nonresidents. Fees $1827 per year full-time, $1161 per year part-time. *Financial aid:* Application deadline 3/1. • Dr. Donna L. Wiley, Coordinator, 510-885-3964.

California State University, Sacramento, School of Business Administration, Program in Business Administration, Sacramento, CA 95819-6048. Offerings include human resources (MBA). *Degree requirements:* Thesis or alternative, writing proficiency exam required, foreign language not required. *Entrance requirements:* GMAT, TOEFL (minimum score 550). Application deadline: 4/15 (11/1 for spring admission). Application fee: $55. *Expenses:* Tuition $0 for state residents; $246 per unit for nonresidents. Fees $2012 per year full-time, $1346 per year part-time. • Application contact: Dr. Herbert Blake, Graduate Adviser, 916-278-6771.

Case Western Reserve University, Weatherhead School of Management, Department of Marketing and Policy Studies, Division of Labor and Human Resource Policy, Cleveland, OH 44106. Awards MBA, PhD. PhD offered through the School of Graduate Studies. Part-time and evening/weekend programs available. Faculty: 4 full-time (0 women), 2 part-time (0 women), 5 FTE. Students: 23 full-time (16 women), 19 part-time (13 women); includes 7 minority (5 African Americans, 2 Asian Americans), 4 international. Average age 28. In 1997, 8 master's awarded. *Degree requirements:* For doctorate, dissertation required, foreign language not required. *Entrance requirements:* For master's, GMAT (average 603); for doctorate, GMAT. Application deadline: 4/15 (priority date; rolling processing). Application fee: $50. *Tuition:* $20,900 per year full-time, $871 per credit hour part-time. *Financial aid:* Full and partial tuition waivers, Federal Work-Study, institutionally sponsored loans, and career-related internships or fieldwork available. Financial aid application deadline: 5/1. *Faculty research:* Grievance and conflict resolution, employee participation, strategic human resource management, negotiation. • Paul F. Gerhart, Head, 216-368-2045. Application contact: Linda S. Gaston, Director of Marketing and Admissions, 216-368-2030. Fax: 216-368-5548. E-mail: lxg10@po.cwru.edu.

The Catholic University of America, School of Arts and Sciences, Department of Economics and Business, Program in Human Resource Management, Washington, DC 20064. Awards MA, JD/MA. Evening/weekend programs available. Students: 1 (woman) full-time, 1 (woman) part-time. Average age 30. 1 applicant, 100% accepted. In 1997, 1 degree awarded. *Degree requirements:* Computer language, comprehensive exam required, foreign language and thesis not required. *Entrance requirements:* GRE General Test, TOEFL. Application deadline: 8/1 (priority date; rolling processing; 12/1 for spring admission). Application fee: $50. *Expenses:* Tuition $17,325 per year full-time, $668 per credit hour part-time. Fees $680 per year full-time, $360 per year part-time. *Financial aid:* Teaching assistantships, full and partial tuition waivers, Federal Work-Study, institutionally sponsored loans, and career-related internships or fieldwork available. Financial aid application deadline: 2/1; applicants required to submit FAFSA. *Faculty research:* Management for nonprofit organizations, incentives, efficiency and effectiveness of

Directory: Human Resources Management

The Catholic University of America (continued)
management for large organizations. • Dr. Ernest M. Zampelli, Chair, Department of Economics and Business, 202-319-6683. Fax: 202-319-4426. E-mail: zampelli@cua.edu.

Central Michigan University, College of Extended Learning, Program in Administration, Mount Pleasant, MI 48859. Offerings include human resources administration (MSA, Certificate). Postbaccalaureate distance learning degree programs offered. *Entrance requirements:* For master's, minimum GPA of 2.5 in major. Application fee: $50. *Tuition:* $211 per credit hour. • Dr. Susan Smith, Director, 517-774-4373. Application contact: Marketing Office, 800-950-1144. Fax: 517-774-2461.

Chapman University, Professional Studies, Orange, CA 92866. Offerings include human resources (MS). Faculty: 3 full-time (2 women). *Application deadline:* rolling. *Application fee:* $40. • Harry J. Schuler, Vice Provost, 714-997-6730.

Chapman University, Program in Human Resources, Orange, CA 92866. Awards MSHR. Part-time and evening/weekend programs available. Faculty: 3 full-time (2 women). In 1997, 51 degrees awarded. *Degree requirements:* Comprehensive exam, internship required, thesis not required. *Entrance requirements:* GRE General Test (minimum combined score of 900) or MAT (minimum score 52), minimum GPA of 3.0, previous course work in statistics. Application deadline: rolling. Application fee: $40. *Tuition:* $7020 per year full-time, $390 per credit part-time. *Financial aid:* Career-related internships or fieldwork available. Financial aid application deadline: 3/1. • Cris Giannantonio, Chair, 714-744-1945. Application contact: Martha McDonald, Coordinator, 714-744-0641.

Claremont Graduate University, Department of Human Resources Design, Claremont, CA 91711-6163. Awards MS. Part-time programs available. Students: 1 full-time (0 women), 29 part-time (21 women); includes 11 minority (2 African Americans, 5 Asian Americans, 4 Hispanics), 1 international. Average age 34. In 1997, 13 degrees awarded. *Entrance requirements:* GMAT or GRE General Test. Application deadline: 2/15 (priority date; 11/15 for spring admission). Application fee: $40. Electronic applications accepted. *Expenses:* Tuition $20,250 per year full-time, $913 per unit part-time. Fees $130 per year. *Financial aid:* In 1997–98, 14 fellowships totaling $37,000 were awarded; Federal Work-Study, institutionally sponsored loans, and career-related internships or fieldwork also available. Aid available to part-time students. Financial aid application deadline: 2/15; applicants required to submit FAFSA. • Program Administrator, 909-607-3286. E-mail: hrd@cgu.edu. Application contact: Gloria Leffer, Secretary, 909-621-8084. Fax: 909-621-8905.

Announcement: The Master of Science in Human Resources Design (MSHRD) prepares graduates to participate in strategic decisions involving their organizations' most important assets, their human resources. Courses emphasize HR management in contexts of global environment, changing technology, diversity, and change management. The MSHRD requires 36 units and can be completed in less than 2 years.

Clarkson University, School of Business, Program in Management Systems, Concentration in Human Resource Management, Potsdam, NY 13699. Awards MS. *Degree requirements:* Project or thesis required, foreign language not required. *Entrance requirements:* GMAT, GRE General Test (highly recommended), TOEFL. Application deadline: rolling. Application fee: $25 ($35 for international students). *Expenses:* Tuition $19,075 per year full-time, $635 per credit hour part-time. Fees $178 per year. • Application contact: Dr. Fredric C. Menz, Director, Graduate Program, 315-268-6427. Fax: 315-268-3810. E-mail: menzf@icarus.som.clarkson.edu.

Announcement: Either the MBA or MS may be completed in 1 year by students with course work equivalent to 1st-year requirements. The more specialized MS program allows for focused course work and research in human resource management. Class size averages 20–30 students and allows for strong interaction between faculty members and students.

Cleveland State University, James J. Nance College of Business Administration, Program in Labor Relations and Human Resources, Cleveland, OH 44115-2440. Awards MLRHR. Part-time programs available. Faculty: 16 full-time (3 women). Students: 13 full-time (8 women), 39 part-time (23 women); includes 7 minority (6 African Americans, 1 Asian American). Average age 31. 23 applicants, 43% accepted. In 1997, 12 degrees awarded. *Degree requirements:* Computer language required, foreign language and thesis not required. *Entrance requirements:* GMAT. Application deadline: 9/1 (priority date; rolling processing). Application fee: $25. *Expenses:* Tuition $5252 per year full-time, $202 per credit hour part-time for state residents; $10,504 per year full-time, $404 per credit hour part-time for nonresidents. Fees $2.25 per credit hour (minimum). *Financial aid:* Research assistantships, administrative assistantships available. • Dr. Harry J. Martin, Chairperson, 216-687-3790. Fax: 216-687-9354. E-mail: h.martin@csuohio.edu.

Colorado Technical University, Graduate Studies, Program in Management, 4435 North Chestnut Street, Colorado Springs, CO 80907-3896. Offerings include human resources management (MSM). Program faculty: 8 full-time (2 women), 8 part-time (1 woman), 12 FTE. *Average time to degree:* master's–2 years full-time. *Application deadline:* 10/4 (rolling processing; 4/5 for spring admission). *Application fee:* $100. *Expenses:* Tuition $230 per quarter hour. Fees $6 per quarter. • Dr. Mark Pieffer, Dean, 719-590-6765. Application contact: Judy Galante, Graduate Admissions, 719-590-6720. Fax: 719-598-3740.

Columbia University, Graduate School of Business, MBA Program, New York, NY 10027. Offerings include human resource management (MBA). Program faculty: 105 full-time (15 women), 86 part-time (15 women). *Entrance requirements:* GMAT, TOEFL (minimum score 610). Application deadline: 4/20 (rolling processing; 11/1 for spring admission). Application fee: $125 ($150 for international students). *Expenses:* Tuition $26,520 per year. Fees $1250 per year. • Prof. Safwan Masri, Vice Dean of Students and the MBA Program, 212-854-8716. Fax: 212-854-0545. E-mail: smm1@columbia.edu. Application contact: Linda Meehan, Assistant Dean and Executive Director of Admissions and Financial Aid, 212-854-1961. Fax: 212-662-6754. E-mail: gohermes@claven.gsb.columbia.edu.

Concordia University Wisconsin, Division of Graduate Studies, MBA Program, Mequon, WI 53097-2402. Offerings include human resource management (MBA). Postbaccalaureate distance learning degree programs offered (minimal on-campus study). *Degree requirements:* Thesis or alternative, comprehensive exam. *Average time to degree:* master's–2 years part-time. *Entrance requirements:* TOEFL (minimum score 550). Application deadline: 8/1 (priority date; rolling processing; 1/15 for spring admission). Application fee: $50. *Tuition:* $300 per credit. • David Borst, Director, 414-243-4298. Fax: 414-243-4428. E-mail: dborst@bach.cuw.edu.

Cornell University, Graduate Fields of Industrial and Labor Relations, Ithaca, NY 14853-0001. Offerings include human resource studies (MILR, MPS, MS, PhD). Faculty: 48 full-time. *Degree requirements:* For master's, thesis (for some programs); for doctorate, dissertation. *Entrance requirements:* GRE General Test, TOEFL. Application deadline: 2/15. Application fee: $65. • Director of Graduate Studies, 607-255-1522. Application contact: Graduate Field Assistant, 607-255-1522. Fax: 607-255-7774. E-mail: ilrgrad@cornell.edu.

Cumberland University, Division of Graduate Studies, Program in Human Relations Management, Lebanon, TN 37087-3554. Awards MS. Part-time and evening/weekend programs available. Faculty: 8 part-time (3 women). Students: 31 part-time; includes 4 minority (2 African Americans, 2 Hispanics). In 1997, 4 degrees awarded. *Average time to degree:* master's–2 years part-time. *Entrance requirements:* GMAT, GRE, or MAT. Application fee: $50. *Tuition:* $375 per semester hour. *Financial aid:* Institutionally sponsored loans and career-related internships or fieldwork available. Aid available to part-time students. Financial aid application deadline: 8/1; applicants required to submit FAFSA. • Dr. Charlene Kozy, Head, 615-444-2562 Ext. 1243. Application contact: Stephanie Walker, Director of Admissions, 615-444-2562 Ext. 1120. Fax: 615-444-2569. E-mail: swalker@cumberland.edu.

Dallas Baptist University, College of Business, Organizational Management Program, Dallas, TX 75211-9299. Offerings include human resource management (MA). Program faculty: 15 full-time (4 women), 26 part-time (5 women). *Entrance requirements:* TOEFL (minimum score 550). Application deadline: rolling. Application fee: $25. *Tuition:* $285 per hour. • Annette Hoffman, Director of Graduate Business Programs, 214-333-5280. Application contact: Travis Bundrick, Director of Graduate Programs, 214-333-5243. Fax: 214-333-5579. E-mail: graduate@dbu.edu.

DePaul University, Charles H. Kellstadt Graduate School of Business, Department of Management, Program in Human Resource Management, Chicago, IL 60604-2287. Awards MBA. Students: 40 full-time (31 women), 44 part-time (37 women); includes 9 minority (5 African Americans, 2 Asian Americans, 2 Hispanics). Average age 29. 31 applicants, 58% accepted. In 1997, 39 degrees awarded. *Entrance requirements:* GMAT, TOEFL. Application deadline: 8/1 (rolling processing; 3/1 for spring admission). Application fee: $40. *Expenses:* Tuition $1593 per course. Fees $30 per year. *Financial aid:* Application deadline 4/1. • Application contact: Christine Munoz, Director of Admissions, 312-362-8810. Fax: 312-362-6677. E-mail: mbainfo@wppost.depaul.edu.

East Central University, Department of Human Resources, Ada, OK 74820-6899. Offers programs in administration (MSHR), counseling (MSHR), criminal justice (MSHR), rehabilitation counseling (MSHR). Part-time and evening/weekend programs available. Faculty: 7 part-time (3 women). Students: 68 full-time (48 women), 101 part-time (76 women); includes 36 minority (11 African Americans, 3 Hispanics, 22 Native Americans), 1 international. Average age 37. 125 applicants, 90% accepted. In 1997, 67 degrees awarded. *Degree requirements:* Thesis optional, foreign language not required. *Entrance requirements:* GRE General Test, MAT, minimum GPA of 2.5. Application deadline: rolling. Application fee: $0 ($50 for international students). *Expenses:* Tuition $75 per semester hour for state residents; $177 per semester hour for nonresidents. Fees $39 per year full-time, $31 per year part-time. *Financial aid:* In 1997–98, 1 teaching assistantship (to a first-year student) was awarded. • Dr. Richard Baumgartner, Chairman, 405-332-8000.

Eastern Michigan University, College of Business, Department of Management, Program in Human Resources Management and Organizational Development, Ypsilanti, MI 48197. Awards MSHROD. *Degree requirements:* Thesis optional, foreign language not required. *Entrance requirements:* GMAT (minimum score 450), TOEFL (minimum score 550). Application deadline: 5/15 (rolling processing; 3/15 for spring admission). Application fee: $30. *Expenses:* Tuition $2691 per year full-time, $150 per credit hour part-time for state residents; $6300 per year full-time, $350 per credit hour part-time for nonresidents. Fees $368 per year full-time, $88 per semester (minimum) part-time. *Financial aid:* Application deadline 3/15. • Dr. Mary Herman, Coordinator, 734-487-3240.

École des Hautes Études Commerciales, Program in Human Resources Management, Montréal, PQ H3T 2A7, Canada. Awards M Sc. Most courses are given in French. Part-time programs available. *Degree requirements:* 1 foreign language, thesis. *Application deadline:* 3/15. *Application fee:* $40. *Financial aid:* Fellowships, research assistantships, teaching assistantships available. • Dr. Jean-Yves Le Louarn, Director, 514-340-6295. E-mail: jean-yves.lelouarn@hec.ca. Application contact: Nicole Rivet, Registrar, 514-340-6110. Fax: 514-340-5640. E-mail: nicole.rivet@hec.ca.

Emmanuel College, Program in Human Resource Management, Boston, MA 02115. Awards MA. Part-time and evening/weekend programs available. *Degree requirements:* Computer language, thesis, internship required, foreign language not required. *Entrance requirements:* GRE General Test or MAT, interview. Application deadline: 9/7 (priority date; rolling processing). Application fee: $50. *Financial aid:* Federal Work-Study and career-related internships or fieldwork available. Aid available to part-time students. • Audrey Ashton-Savage, Director, 617-735-9844. Fax: 617-735-9877. Application contact: Lorene Ashton-Reed, Graduate Program Assistant, 617-735-9844.

Fairfield University, School of Business, Fairfield, CT 06430-5195. Offerings include human resource management (MBA, CAS). School faculty: 36 full-time (12 women), 4 part-time (2 women), 37.3 FTE. *Average time to degree:* master's–2 years full-time, 3.5 years part-time. *Application deadline:* 8/1 (priority date; rolling processing; 12/1 for spring admission). *Application fee:* $40. *Expenses:* Tuition $15,000 per year full-time, $450 per credit hour part-time. Fees $40 per year. • Dr. Walter G. Ryba Jr., Acting Dean, 203-254-4070. Application contact: Cynthia S. Chegwidden, Director of Graduate Programs, 203-254-4070. Fax: 203-254-4105. E-mail: cchegwidden@fair1.fairfield.edu.

Fairleigh Dickinson University, Florham–Madison Campus, Samuel J. Silberman College of Business Administration, Program in Human Resource Management, 285 Madison Avenue, Madison, NJ 07940-1099. Awards MBA. Part-time and evening/weekend programs available. Faculty: 7 full-time (1 woman), 17 part-time (3 women). Students: 10 full-time (5 women), 46 part-time (37 women); includes 2 minority (1 African American, 1 Hispanic), 1 international. Average age 30. 25 applicants, 56% accepted. In 1997, 12 degrees awarded. *Degree requirements:* Thesis optional, foreign language not required. *Entrance requirements:* GMAT. Application deadline: rolling. Application fee: $35. *Expenses:* Tuition $522 per credit. Fees $302 per year full-time, $138 per year part-time. • Dr. Daniel Twomey, Director, 973-443-8802.

Announcement: FDU offers one of the largest human resource management/MBA programs in the US. Full-time students are eligible for graduate assistant (GA) positions in the Center for Human Resource Management Studies (CHRMS). GAs receive a $2000 per semester stipend from a CHRMS business partner and full tuition from FDU. GAs assist faculty members with applied research and work with top-level executives and faculty members on several projects. The program's strong relationship with the human resource (HR) community provides exceptional learning, networking, and career opportunities. The curriculum, which was developed with top HR executives, emphasizes the strategic orientation of HR executives and focuses on preparing HR generalists.

Fairleigh Dickinson University, Teaneck–Hackensack Campus, Samuel J. Silberman College of Business Administration, Department of Management, Marketing, and Information Systems and Sciences, Program in Human Resource Administration, 1000 River Road, Teaneck, NJ 07666-1914. Awards MBA. Students: 5 full-time (4 women), 15 part-time (11 women); includes 4 minority (1 Asian American, 3 Hispanics), 2 international. Average age 29. In 1997, 4 degrees awarded. *Degree requirements:* Computer language required, thesis optional, foreign language not required. *Entrance requirements:* GMAT. Application deadline: rolling. Application fee: $35. *Expenses:* Tuition $522 per credit. Fees $302 per year full-time, $138 per year part-time. *Financial aid:* Fellowships, research assistantships, and career-related internships or fieldwork available. *Faculty research:* Human resource management, organizational behavior. • Dr. Daniel Twomey, Director, 973-443-8802.

Florida Institute of Technology, School of Extended Graduate Studies, Program in Management, Melbourne, FL 32901-6975. Offerings include human resources management (MS, PMBA). *Entrance requirements:* GMAT (minimum score 425), minimum GPA of 2.75. Application fee: $50. *Tuition:* $550 per credit hour. • Application contact: Carolyn P. Farrior, Associate Dean of Graduate Admissions, 407-674-7118. Fax: 407-723-9468. E-mail: cfarrior@fit.edu.

Florida Metropolitan University–Tampa College, Department of Business Administration, 3319 West Hillsborough Avenue, Tampa, FL 33614-5899. Offerings include human resources (MBA). College faculty: 1 full-time, 5 part-time. *Degree requirements:* Thesis optional, foreign language not required. *Entrance requirements:* GMAT (minimum score 470) or GRE, minimum GPA of 3.0. Application deadline: rolling. Application fee: $25. *Expenses:* Tuition $250 per credit hour. Fees $100 per year. • Daniel Palladino, Director of Graduate Studies, 813-879-

6000 Ext. 51. Application contact: Foster Thomas, Director of Admissions, 813-879-6000 Ext. 36. Fax: 813-871-2483.

Fordham University, Graduate School of Education, Division of Administration, Policy, and Urban Education, New York, NY 10023. Offerings include human resource program administration (MS). Division faculty: 11 full-time, 7 part-time. *Application fee:* $50. • Dr. Barbara Jackson, Chairperson, 212-636-6430.

Framingham State College, Graduate Programs, Program in Human Resources Administration, Framingham, MA 01701-9101. Awards MA. Part-time and evening/weekend programs available. Faculty: 2 full-time, 3 part-time. Students: 37 part-time. In 1997, 11 degrees awarded. *Tuition:* $4184 per year full-time, $523 per course part-time for state residents; $4848 per year full-time, $606 per course part-time for nonresidents. • Dr. Charles White, Adviser, 508-626-4892. Application contact: Graduate Office, 508-626-4550.

Gannon University, School of Graduate Studies, College of Humanities, Business, and Education, School of Business, Program in Human Resources Management, Erie, PA 16541. Awards Certificate. Part-time and evening/weekend programs available. Students: 2 full-time (both women). Average age 44. 0 applicants. *Entrance requirements:* GMAT, TOEFL. Application deadline: rolling. Application fee: $25. *Expenses:* Tuition $405 per credit. Fees $200 per year full-time, $8 per credit part-time. *Financial aid:* Application deadline 3/1; applicants required to submit FAFSA. • Application contact: Beth Nemenz, Director of Admissions, 814-871-7240. Fax: 814-871-5803. E-mail: admissions@gannon.edu.

George Mason University, College of Arts and Sciences, Department of Social and Organizational Learning, Fairfax, VA 22030-4444. Awards MA. Faculty: 7 full-time (2 women), 1 part-time (0 women), 7.25 FTE. Students: 6 full-time (2 women), 38 part-time (24 women); includes 7 minority (5 African Americans, 2 Asian Americans), 4 international. *Application fee:* $30. *Tuition:* $4344 per year full-time, $181 per credit hour part-time for state residents; $12,504 per year full-time, $521 per credit hour part-time for nonresidents. *Financial aid:* Application deadline 3/1. • Ann C. Baker, Director, 703-993-3813. E-mail: psol@gmu.edu.

The George Washington University, Columbian School of Arts and Sciences, Program in Administrative Sciences, Washington, DC 20052. Offerings include human resource management (MA). Program faculty: 3 part-time (0 women), 1 FTE. *Degree requirements:* Comprehensive exam required, thesis not required. *Entrance requirements:* GRE General Test, minimum GPA of 3.0. Application deadline: 5/1. Application fee: $50. *Expenses:* Tuition $680 per semester hour. Fees $35 per semester hour. • Dr. Joseph Zeidner, Director, 202-496-8380.

The George Washington University, School of Business and Public Management, Department of Management Science, Washington, DC 20052. Offerings include human resources management (MBA). Department faculty: 29 full-time (3 women), 23 part-time (5 women), 35 FTE. *Application deadline:* 4/1 (priority date; rolling processing; 10/1 for spring admission). *Application fee:* $50. *Expenses:* Tuition $680 per semester hour. Fees $35 per semester hour. • Dr. Erik K. Winslow, Chair, 202-994-7375. Application contact: Lilly Hastings, Graduate Admissions, 202-994-6584. Fax: 202-994-6382.

Georgia State University, College of Business Administration, W. T. Beebe Institute of Personnel and Employment Relations, Atlanta, GA 30303-3083. Awards MBA, MS, PhD. Part-time and evening/weekend programs available. Students: 32 full-time (18 women), 18 part-time (17 women); includes 8 minority (all African Americans), 7 international. Average age 32. In 1997, 10 master's, 2 doctorates awarded. Terminal master's awarded for partial completion of doctoral program. *Degree requirements:* For doctorate, dissertation required, foreign language not required. *Entrance requirements:* For master's, GMAT (average 566), TOEFL; for doctorate, GMAT (average 670), TOEFL. Application deadline: 5/1 (rolling processing; 10/1 for spring admission). Application fee: $25. *Expenses:* Tuition $2673 per year full-time, $99 per semester hour part-time for state residents; $10,692 per year full-time, $396 per semester hour part-time for nonresidents. Fees $228 per year. *Financial aid:* Fellowships, research assistantships, teaching assistantships, partial tuition waivers, and career-related internships or fieldwork available. Aid available to part-time students. Financial aid applicants required to submit FAFSA. • Dr. Michael J. Jedel, Director, 404-651-3596. Fax: 404-651-1700. Application contact: Office of Academic Assistance and Master's Admissions, 404-651-1913. Fax: 404-651-0219.

Announcement: The Beebe Institute offers one of the most comprehensive graduate programs in human resources management in the southern United States. Program strengths include large faculty, multidisciplinary course work, emphasis on progressive employment relations practices, generous financial aid, practitioner-relevant orientation, location in Atlanta. Both master's and PhD degree programs are available. Write to Dr. Michael Jay Jedel, Institute Director, for additional information.

Georgia State University, School of Policy Studies, Department of Public Administration and Urban Studies, Atlanta, GA 30303-3083. Offerings include urban studies (MS), with options in gerontology, human resources, nonprofit administration, planning and economic development, transportation. Department faculty: 18 full-time (7 women), 2 part-time (1 woman). *Average time to degree:* master's–2 years full-time, 3 years part-time. *Application deadline:* 7/1 (rolling processing; 11/1 for spring admission). *Application fee:* $25. *Expenses:* Tuition $2673 per year full-time, $99 per semester hour part-time for state residents; $10,692 per year full-time, $396 per semester hour part-time for nonresidents. Fees $228 per year. • Dr. John Thomas, Chair, 404-651-4591. Application contact: Sue Fagan, Director, 404-651-3504.

Golden Gate University, School of Business, San Francisco, CA 94105-2968. Offerings include human resource management (MBA, MS), human resources management (Certificate). MBA (telecommunications, management information systems) offered jointly with the School of Technology and Industry. *Average time to degree:* master's–2.5 years full-time. *Application deadline:* 7/1 (priority date; rolling processing). *Application fee:* $55 ($70 for international students). *Tuition:* $996 per course (minimum). • Dr. Hamid Shomali, Dean, 415-442-6500. Fax: 415-442-6579. Application contact: Enrollment Services, 415-442-7800. Fax: 415-442-7807. E-mail: info@ggu.edu.

Goldey–Beacom College, MBA Program, 4701 Limestone Road, Wilmington, DE 19808-1999. Offerings include human resource management (MBA). MBA (accounting) new for fall 1998. College faculty: 6 full-time (3 women), 4 part-time (1 woman). *Average time to degree:* master's–2 years full-time, 3 years part-time. *Entrance requirements:* GMAT (minimum score 450; average 507), TOEFL (minimum score 525), minimum GPA of 3.0. Application deadline: 8/20 (rolling processing; 5/15 for spring admission). Application fee: $30. Electronic applications accepted. *Expenses:* Tuition $6030 per year full-time, $335 per credit hour part-time. Fees $5 per credit hour. • Bruce D. Marsland, Director, 302-998-8814 Ext. 276. Fax: 302-998-8631. E-mail: graduate@goldey.gbc.edu.

Hawaii Pacific University, School of Business Administration, 1166 Fort Street, Honolulu, HI 96813-2785. Offerings include human resource management (MA, MBA). School faculty: 30 full-time (3 women), 12 part-time (1 woman), 38 FTE. *Average time to degree:* master's–2 years full-time, 4 years part-time. *Application deadline:* rolling. *Application fee:* $50. Electronic applications accepted. *Tuition:* $7920 per year full-time, $330 per credit part-time. • Dr. Richard Ward, Dean for Graduate Management Studies, 808-544-0279. Application contact: Leina Danao, Admissions Coordinator, 808-544-1120. Fax: 808-544-0280. E-mail: gradservctr@hpu.edu.

Houston Baptist University, College of Business and Economics, Program in Human Resources Management, Houston, TX 77074-3298. Awards MSHRM. Part-time and evening/weekend programs available. Faculty: 4 full-time (1 woman), 10 part-time (2 women). Students: 18 full-time (16 women), 21 part-time (14 women); includes 11 minority (8 African Americans, 1 Asian American, 2 Hispanics), 1 international. In 1997, 20 degrees awarded (100% found work related to degree). *Entrance requirements:* GMAT (minimum score 450), GRE General Test (minimum combined score of 900), minimum GPA of 2.5, work experience. Application deadline: 7/1 (priority date; rolling processing; 1/1 for spring admission). Application fee: $25 ($85 for international students). *Expenses:* Tuition $300 per semester hour. Fees $235 per quarter. *Financial aid:* Federal Work-Study available. Financial aid application deadline: 6/1. • Application contact: Suzanne Sullivan, Program Assistant, 281-649-3265.

Indiana University Bloomington, School of Business, Program in Business Administration, Bloomington, IN 47405. Offerings include human resources (MBA). Self-designed programs available. *Entrance requirements:* GMAT, TOEFL (minimum score 580). Application deadline: 3/1. Application fee: $50 ($65 for international students). *Expenses:* Tuition $8232 per year for state residents; $16,470 per year for nonresidents. Fees $343 per year. • Dr. George Hettenhouse, Chair, 812-855-8006. Application contact: Dr. James J. Holmen, Director of Admissions and Financial Aid, 812-855-8006. Fax: 812-855-9039.

Instituto Tecnológico y de Estudios Superiores de Monterrey, Morelos Campus, Programs in Business Administration, Cuernavaca, Morelos 62589, Mexico. Offerings include human resources management (MA).

Inter American University of Puerto Rico, Metropolitan Campus, Division of Economics and Business Administration, Program in Human Resources, San Juan, PR 00919-1293. Awards MBA. Faculty: 2 full-time, 5 part-time. Students: 86 full-time (60 women), 127 part-time (89 women); includes 213 minority (all Hispanics). In 1997, 5 degrees awarded. *Degree requirements:* Comprehensive exam required, foreign language and thesis not required. *Entrance requirements:* GRE or PAEG, interview. Application deadline: 5/15 (priority date; rolling processing; 11/15 for spring admission). Application fee: $31. Electronic applications accepted. *Expenses:* Tuition $3272 per year full-time, $1740 per year part-time. Fees $328 per year full-time, $176 per year part-time. *Financial aid:* Federal Work-Study available. • Application contact: Dr. Antonio Llorens, Director, 787-250-1912 Ext. 2320. Fax: 787-250-0361.

Inter American University of Puerto Rico, San Germán Campus, Department of Business Administration, Program in Business Administration, San Germán, PR 00683-5008. Offerings include human resources (MBA). *Degree requirements:* Comprehensive exam required, foreign language and thesis not required. *Entrance requirements:* Minimum GPA of 3.0, GRE General Test, or PAEG. Application deadline: 4/30 (priority date; rolling processing; 11/15 for spring admission). Application fee: $31. *Expenses:* Tuition $150 per credit. Fees $177 per semester. • Application contact: Mildred Camacho, Admissions Director, 787-892-3090. Fax: 787-892-6350.

Iona College, Hagan Graduate School of Business, Department of Management, 715 North Avenue, New Rochelle, NY 10801-1890. Offerings include human resource management (MBA, PMC). Department faculty: 11 full-time (2 women), 1 (woman) part-time. *Degree requirements:* For master's, computer language required, foreign language and thesis not required. *Entrance requirements:* For master's, GMAT (minimum score 450); for PMC, GMAT. Application deadline: rolling. Application fee: $50. *Expenses:* Tuition $480 per credit hour. Fees $25 per semester. • Dr. Ursula Witting–Berman, Chair, 914-633-2588. Application contact: Carol Shea, Director of MBA Admissions, 914-633-2288.

Keller Graduate School of Management, 1 Tower Lane, Oak Brook Terrace, IL 60181. Offerings include human resources management (MHRM). School faculty: 604. *Average time to degree:* master's–3 years part-time. *Application deadline:* rolling. *Application fee:* $0. *Tuition:* $1235 per course. • Dr. Sherrill Hole, Director, Academic Affairs, 630-574-1894. Application contact: Michael J. Alexander, Director, Central Services, 630-574-1957. Fax: 630-574-1969.

Kennesaw State University, Michael J. Coles College of Business, Program in Business Administration, Kennesaw, GA 30144-5591. Offerings include human resources management and development (MBA). Program faculty: 54 full-time (18 women), 5 part-time (0 women). *Application deadline:* 7/1 (rolling processing; 2/20 for spring admission). *Application fee:* $20. *Expenses:* Tuition $2398 per year full-time, $83 per credit hour part-time for state residents; $8398 per year full-time, $333 per credit hour part-time for nonresidents. Fees $338 per year. • Dr. Rodney Alsup, Assistant Dean, 770-423-6087. Fax: 770-423-6141. E-mail: ralsup@ksumail.kennesaw.edu. Application contact: Susan N. Barrett, Administrative Specialist, Admissions, 770-423-6500. Fax: 770-423-6541. E-mail: sbarrett@ksumail.kennesaw.edu.

La Roche College, Program in Human Resources Management, Pittsburgh, PA 15237-5898. Awards MS. Part-time and evening/weekend programs available. Faculty: 5 full-time (1 woman), 16 part-time (4 women). Students: 123. *Entrance requirements:* GMAT (minimum score 420), GRE General Test (minimum combined score of 1200), MAT (minimum score 50), TOEFL (minimum score 500), minimum GPA of 3.0 during previous 2 years. Application deadline: rolling. Application fee: $25. *Tuition:* $385 per credit. *Financial aid:* Graduate assistantships and career-related internships or fieldwork available. Aid available to part-time students. Financial aid applicants required to submit FAFSA. *Faculty research:* Personnel administration, human resources development. • Dr. Astrid Kersten, Coordinator, 412-536-1192. Application contact: Roland Gagne, Director of Graduate Studies, 412-536-1265. Fax: 412-536-1283.

Lesley College, Graduate School of Arts and Social Sciences, Cambridge, MA 02138-2790. Offerings include intercultural relations (MA, CAGS), with options in development project administration (MA), individually designed (MA), intercultural conflict resolution (MA), intercultural health and human services (MA), intercultural training and consulting (MA), international education exchange (MA), international student advising (MA), managing culturally diverse human resources (MA), multicultural education (MA). Postbaccalaureate distance learning degree programs offered (minimal on-campus study). School faculty: 24 full-time (14 women), 344 part-time (225 women). *Application deadline:* rolling. *Application fee:* $45. *Tuition:* $425 per credit. • Dr. Martha B. McKenna, Dean, 617-349-8467. Application contact: Graduate Admissions, 617-349-8300. Fax: 617-349-8366.

Lesley College, School of Management, Cambridge, MA 02138-2790. Offerings include human resources management (MSM). Postbaccalaureate distance learning degree programs offered (no on-campus study). School faculty: 10 full-time (4 women), 204 part-time (78 women). *Application deadline:* rolling. *Application fee:* $45. *Tuition:* $425 per credit. • Dr. Earl Potter, Dean, 617-349-8682. Fax: 617-349-8678. Application contact: Marilyn Gove, Associate Director, 617-349-8690. Fax: 617-349-8313. E-mail: mgove@mail.lesley.edu.

Lindenwood University, Programs in Individualized Education, St. Charles, MO 63301-1695. Offerings include human resource management (MS). Faculty: 10 full-time (7 women), 23 part-time (6 women). *Application deadline:* 6/30 (priority date; rolling processing; 12/1 for spring admission). *Application fee:* $25. *Tuition:* $5880 per year full-time, $245 per credit hour part-time. • Dr. Dan Kemper, Dean, 314-916-9125. Application contact: John Guffey, Director of Graduate Admissions, 314-949-4933. Fax: 314-949-4910.

Long Island University, C.W. Post Campus, College of Management, School of Business, Department of Management, Brookville, NY 11548-1300. Offerings include human resource management (MBA). MBA (international business) offered jointly with Franklin College Switzerland. JD/MBA offered jointly with Touro College. Department faculty: 8 full-time (4 women), 13 part-time (2 women). *Entrance requirements:* GMAT. Application deadline: 8/15 (priority date; rolling processing; 12/15 for spring admission). Application fee: $30. Electronic applications accepted. *Expenses:* Tuition $480 per credit. Fees $316 per year full-time, $71 per semester (minimum) part-time. • Dr. Anthony M. Akel, Chairman, 516-299-2360. E-mail: aakel@eagle.liunet.edu. Application contact: Sally Luzader, Associate Director of Graduate Admissions, 516-299-2417. Fax: 516-299-2137. E-mail: admissions@collegehall.liunet.edu.

Loyola University Chicago, Graduate School, Institute of Human Resources and Industrial Relations, 820 North Michigan Avenue, Chicago, IL 60611-2196. Awards MSHR, MSIR, JD/MSIR, MSHR/MSOD, MSHR/MSTD, MSIR/MSOD, MSIR/MSTD. Part-time programs available. Faculty: 8 full-time, 10 part-time. Students: 23 full-time (18 women), 185 part-time (143 women); includes 48 minority (30 African Americans, 10 Asian Americans, 8 Hispanics), 2 international.

Directory: Human Resources Management

Loyola University Chicago (continued)

Average age 29. 58 applicants, 88% accepted. In 1997, 116 degrees awarded. *Entrance requirements:* GMAT (minimum score 500) or GRE General Test (minimum combined score of 1550 on three sections). Application deadline: rolling. Application fee: $35. *Tuition:* $1665 per course. *Financial aid:* In 1997–98, 3 research assistantships (all to first-year students) averaging $600 per month were awarded; Federal Work-Study and career-related internships or fieldwork also available. Aid available to part-time students. Financial aid applicants required to submit FAFSA. *Faculty research:* Human resource management, labor relations, global human resource management, organizational development, compensation. • Dr. Linda K. Stroh, Director, 312-915-6595. E-mail: lstroh@luc.edu. Application contact: Dr. Fran Daly, Associate Director, 312-915-6595. Fax: 312-915-6231.

Lynchburg College, School of Business, Lynchburg, VA 24501-3199. Offerings include administration (M Ad), with options in industrial management, personnel management. *Application fee:* $20.

Marquette University, College of Business Administration, Program in Human Resources, Milwaukee, WI 53201-1881. Awards MSHR. Part-time and evening/weekend programs available. Faculty: 42 full-time (7 women), 3 part-time (0 women). Students: 16 full-time (12 women), 48 part-time (34 women); includes 1 international. Average age 34. 23 applicants, 91% accepted. In 1997, 1 degree awarded. *Entrance requirements:* GMAT or GRE General Test, TOEFL (minimum score 550). Application fee: $40. *Tuition:* $510 per credit. *Financial aid:* Research assistantships, teaching assistantships, full and partial tuition waivers, Federal Work-Study, institutionally sponsored loans available. Aid available to part-time students. Financial aid application deadline: 2/15. *Faculty research:* Diversity, mentoring. • Dr. Timothy Keaveny, Management Chair, 414-288-3643. Application contact: Joseph P. Fox, Director of Graduate Programs, 414-288-7145. Fax: 414-288-1660.

Marshall University, Graduate School of Management, Program in Employee Relations, South Charleston, WV 25303-1600. Awards MSM. Part-time and evening/weekend programs available. Faculty: 1 full-time (0 women). Students: 5 part-time (4 women); includes 1 minority (African American). Average age 37. *Degree requirements:* Comprehensive exam required, foreign language and thesis not required. *Entrance requirements:* GMAT (minimum score 450) or GRE General Test (minimum combined score of 1000), minimum GPA of 2.5. Application deadline: 8/1 (priority date; rolling processing). Application fee: $0. *Financial aid:* Full tuition waivers available. Aid available to part-time students. Financial aid applicants required to submit FAFSA. • Dr. Kurt Olmosk, Associate Dean, Graduate School of Management, 304-746-1958. Fax: 304-746-2503.

Marygrove College, Department of Administration, Detroit, MI 48221-2599. Offerings include human resources management (MA). *Degree requirements:* Research project required, foreign language and thesis not required. *Average time to degree:* master's–2 years full-time, 3.5 years part-time. *Entrance requirements:* MAT, interview, minimum undergraduate GPA of 3.0. Application deadline: 8/15 (rolling processing). Application fee: $25.

Marymount University, School of Business Administration, Program in Human Performance Systems, Arlington, VA 22207-4299. Awards MA. Part-time and evening/weekend programs available. Students: 54. In 1997, 12 degrees awarded. *Degree requirements:* Thesis or alternative required, foreign language not required. *Entrance requirements:* GMAT or GRE General Test, interview. Application deadline: rolling. Application fee: $35. *Expenses:* Tuition $465 per credit hour. Fees $120 per year full-time, $5 per credit hour part-time. *Financial aid:* Career-related internships or fieldwork available. Aid available to part-time students. Financial aid applicants required to submit FAFSA. *Faculty research:* Total quality management concepts in human environments. • Dr. Karen Medsker, Chair, 703-284-5959. Fax: 703-527-3815. E-mail: karen.medsker@marymount.edu.

Marymount University, School of Business Administration, Program in Human Resources Management, Arlington, VA 22207-4299. Awards MA. Part-time and evening/weekend programs available. Students: 111. In 1997, 30 degrees awarded. *Degree requirements:* Thesis or alternative required, foreign language not required. *Entrance requirements:* GMAT or GRE General Test, interview. Application deadline: rolling. Application fee: $35. *Expenses:* Tuition $465 per credit hour. Fees $120 per year full-time, $5 per credit hour part-time. *Financial aid:* Career-related internships or fieldwork available. Aid available to part-time students. Financial aid applicants required to submit FAFSA. • Dr. Karen Medsker, Chair, 703-284-1622. Fax: 703-527-3815. E-mail: karen.medsker@marymount.edu.

McMaster University, Faculty of Business, Program in Human Resources/Labor Relations, Hamilton, ON L8S 4M2, Canada. Awards MBA, PhD. Part-time and evening/weekend programs available. *Degree requirements:* For doctorate, computer language, dissertation, comprehensive exam required, foreign language not required. *Entrance requirements:* For master's, GMAT; for doctorate, GMAT or GRE, master's degree. Application deadline: 6/1. Application fee: $50. *Expenses:* Tuition $4422 per year full-time, $1590 per year part-time for Canadian residents; $12,000 per year full-time, $6165 per year part-time for nonresidents. Fees $257 per year full-time, $188 per year part-time. *Financial aid:* Teaching assistantships available. • Dr. W. Wiesner, Coordinator, 905-525-9140 Ext. 23958.

Mercy College, Program in Human Resource Management, Dobbs Ferry, NY 10522-1189. Awards MS. Part-time and evening/weekend programs available. Students: 142 (105 women). *Degree requirements:* Thesis required, foreign language not required. *Average time to degree:* master's–1 year full-time, 2.5 years part-time. *Entrance requirements:* GMAT. Application deadline: 8/15 (priority date; rolling processing; 2/15 for spring admission). Application fee: $35. *Tuition:* $390 per credit. *Financial aid:* Research assistantships, Federal Work-Study, and career-related internships or fieldwork available. Aid available to part-time students. *Faculty research:* Team building, motivation, leadership, training. • Linda Jerris, Director, 914-674-9331 Ext. 500. Application contact: Admissions Office, 800-MERCY-NY. Fax: 914-674-7382. E-mail: admission@merlin.mercynet.edu.

Metropolitan State University, Management and Administration Program, St. Paul, MN 55106-5000. Offerings include human resource management (MBA), manpower administration (MMA). MMA (law enforcement) new for fall 1998. Program faculty: 17 full-time (5 women), 150 part-time. *Degree requirements:* Thesis required, foreign language not required. *Entrance requirements:* GMAT. Application deadline: rolling. Application fee: $20. *Tuition:* $133 per credit for state residents; $208 per credit for nonresidents. • Gary Seiler, Graduate Coordinator, 612-373-2754. E-mail: seiler@msus1.msus.edu. Application contact: Gloria Marcus, Recruiter/Admissions Adviser, 612-373-2724. Fax: 612-373-2888. E-mail: marcusg@msus1.msus.edu.

Michigan State University, College of Social Science, School of Labor and Industrial Relations, East Lansing, MI 48824-1020. Offers programs in labor relations and human resources (MLRHR), labor relations and human resources-urban studies (MLRHR). Part-time and evening/weekend programs available. Faculty: 16 (5 women). Students: 117 (72 women); includes 21 minority (9 African Americans, 5 Asian Americans, 5 Hispanics, 2 Native Americans), 20 international. In 1997, 50 degrees awarded. *Degree requirements:* Thesis optional, foreign language not required. *Entrance requirements:* GRE General Test. Application deadline: rolling. Application fee: $30 ($40 for international students). *Expenses:* Tuition $4609 per year full-time, $223 per credit hour (minimum) part-time for state residents; $8704 per year full-time, $450 per credit hour (minimum) part-time for nonresidents. Fees $576 per year full-time, $476 per year part-time. *Financial aid:* In 1997–98, 41 fellowships, 20 research assistantships were awarded; institutionally sponsored loans and career-related internships or fieldwork also available. *Faculty research:* Human resource management, compensation systems, organizational change, conflict resolution. • Dr. Michael L. Moore, Director, 517-355-1801. Application contact: Dr. Ed Montemayor, Associate Director, 517-355-3285. Fax: 517-355-7656. E-mail: ed.montemayor@ssc.msu.edu.

Michigan State University, Eli Broad Graduate School of Management, Department of Management, East Lansing, MI 48824-1020. Offerings include human resources management (MBA), organizational behavior-personnel (PhD). Department faculty: 12 (5 women). *Degree requirements:* For doctorate, dissertation required, foreign language not required. *Entrance requirements:* For master's, GMAT (minimum score 500); for doctorate, GMAT (score in 90th percentile or higher). Application deadline: rolling. Application fee: $30 ($40 for international students). *Expenses:* Tuition $4609 per year full-time, $223 per credit hour (minimum) part-time for state residents; $8704 per year full-time, $450 per credit hour (minimum) part-time for nonresidents. Fees $576 per year full-time, $476 per year part-time. • Dr. John Wagner III, Acting Chairperson, 517-355-1878. Fax: 517-432-1111. E-mail: wagner@pilot.msu.edu.

National–Louis University, College of Management and Business, Program in Human Resource Management and Development, 2840 Sheridan Road, Evanston, IL 60201-1730. Awards MS. Part-time programs available. Students: 95 full-time (66 women), 7 part-time (3 women); includes 63 minority (52 African Americans, 5 Asian Americans, 6 Hispanics), 1 international. Average age 40. In 1997, 95 degrees awarded. *Degree requirements:* Thesis required, foreign language not required. *Entrance requirements:* GRE, MAT, or Watson-Glaser Critical Thinking Appraisal, minimum GPA of 3.0. Application deadline: rolling. *Financial aid:* Available to part-time students. Financial aid applicants required to submit FAFSA. • Dr. Larry Ryley, Coordinator, 813-286-8087. Application contact: Dr. David McCulloch, Vice President for University Services, 800-443-5522 Ext. 5127. Fax: 847-465-0593. E-mail: dmcc@wheeling1.nl.edu.

National University, School of Management and Technology, Department of Professional Studies, Program in Human Resource Management, La Jolla, CA 92037-1011. Awards MA. Students: 45 full-time (25 women), 16 part-time (5 women); includes 34 minority (11 African Americans, 7 Asian Americans, 15 Hispanics, 1 Native American), 1 international. Average age 34. In 1997, 44 degrees awarded. *Entrance requirements:* Interview, minimum GPA of 2.5. Application deadline: rolling. Application fee: $60 ($100 for international students). *Tuition:* $7830 per year full-time, $870 per course part-time. *Financial aid:* Application deadline 5/1. • Carla Anthony, Head, 619-642-8192. Application contact: Nancy Rohland, Director of Enrollment Management, 619-563-7100. Fax: 619-563-7393.

New England College, Program in Organizational Management, 7 Main Street, Henniker, NH 03242-3293. Offerings include human resource management (Certificate). College faculty: 7 full-time, 13 part-time. *Application deadline:* rolling. *Application fee:* $25. *Expenses:* Tuition $175 per credit. Fees $20 per semester. • Dr. Patricia Prinz, Director of Graduate and Continuing Studies, 603-428-2252. Fax: 603-428-2266. Application contact: Robert Godard, Associate Director, 603-428-2483.

New Hampshire College, Graduate School of Business, Program in Business Administration, Manchester, NH 03106-1045. Offerings include human resource management (Certificate). Program faculty: 7 full-time (1 woman), 66 part-time (11 women), 47 FTE. *Average time to degree:* master's–1.5 years full-time, 4.5 years part-time. *Application deadline:* rolling. *Application fee:* $0. *Expenses:* Tuition $17,044 per year full-time, $945 per course part-time. Fees $530 per year full-time, $80 per year part-time. • Dr. Paul Schneiderman, Acting Dean, Graduate School of Business, 603-644-3102. Fax: 603-644-3150.

New School University, Robert J. Milano Graduate School of Management and Urban Policy, Program in Human Resources Management, New York, NY 10011-8603. Offers human resources management (MS), labor relations (Adv C), organization development (Adv C), training (Adv C). Part-time and evening/weekend programs available. Faculty: 3 full-time (0 women), 37 part-time (16 women). Students: 53 full-time (all women), 249 part-time (213 women); includes 128 minority (88 African Americans, 7 Asian Americans, 33 Hispanics), 8 international. Average age 31. In 1997, 64 master's awarded. *Degree requirements:* For master's, computer language, thesis required, foreign language not required. *Average time to degree:* master's–1.5 years full-time, 3 years part-time. *Entrance requirements:* For master's, interview. Application deadline: 9/1 (priority date; rolling processing). Application fee: $30. *Tuition:* $622 per credit. *Financial aid:* In 1997–98, 39 students received aid, including 39 scholarships (12 to first-year students) totaling $157,800; teaching assistantships, full and partial tuition waivers, Federal Work-Study, and career-related internships or fieldwork also available. Aid available to part-time students. Financial aid application deadline: 3/1; applicants required to submit FAFSA. *Faculty research:* Organization, management, leadership development, training and development. • Dr. Mark Lipton, Chair, 212-229-8969. E-mail: mlipton@newschool.edu. Application contact: Susan Morris, Assistant Dean, 212-229-5388. Fax: 212-229-8935. E-mail: smorris@newschool.edu.

New York Institute of Technology, School of Management, Program in Human Resources Management and Labor Relations, Old Westbury, NY 11568-8000. Awards MS, Certificate. Part-time and evening/weekend programs available. Faculty: 4 full-time (0 women), 10 part-time (4 women). Students: 32 full-time (16 women), 110 part-time (86 women); includes 38 minority (28 African Americans, 4 Asian Americans, 3 Hispanics, 3 Native Americans), 17 international. Average age 32. 76 applicants, 86% accepted. In 1997, 31 master's awarded. *Degree requirements:* For master's, comprehensive exam required, thesis optional, foreign language not required. *Average time to degree:* master's–2 years full-time, 3 years part-time. *Entrance requirements:* For master's, GMAT (minimum score 400; average 550), GRE General Test, TOEFL (minimum score 550), minimum QPA of 2.85. Application deadline: rolling. Application fee: $50. *Tuition:* $413 per credit. *Financial aid:* In 1997–98, 25 students received aid, including 7 research assistantships (1 to a first-year student); fellowships, full and partial tuition waivers, institutionally sponsored loans, and career-related internships or fieldwork also available. Aid available to part-time students. *Faculty research:* Ethics in industrial relations, employee relations, public sector labor relations, benefits. • Dr. Richard Dibble, Chair, 516-686-7722. Application contact: Glenn Berman, Executive Director of Admissions, 516-686-7519. Fax: 516-626-0419. E-mail: gberman@iris.nyit.edu.

New York University, Robert F. Wagner Graduate School of Public Service, Program in Public Administration, New York, NY 10012-1019. Offerings include human resources management (MPA, APC). Program faculty: 14 full-time (6 women), 49 part-time (21 women), 23 FTE. *Degree requirements:* For master's, thesis or alternative. *Average time to degree:* master's–2 years full-time, 4 years part-time; doctorate–5 years full-time, 7 years part-time; other advanced degree–1 year full-time. *Entrance requirements:* For master's, minimum undergraduate GPA of 3.0. Application deadline: 8/1 (rolling processing; 1/1 for spring admission). Application fee: $50 ($70 for international students). • Leanna Stiefel, Director, 212-998-7400. Application contact: Hedy Flanders, Director, Admissions and Financial Aid, 212-998-7414. Fax: 212-995-4164. E-mail: wagner.admissions@nyu.edu.

North Carolina Agricultural and Technical State University, Graduate School, School of Education, Department of Human Development and Services, Greensboro, NC 27411. Offerings include human resources (MS). Department faculty: 7 full-time (3 women). *Degree requirements:* Thesis, comprehensive exam, qualifying exam required, foreign language not required. *Entrance requirements:* GRE General Test, minimum GPA of 3.0. Application deadline: 6/1 (priority date; rolling processing; 12/1 for spring admission). Application fee: $35. *Tuition:* $1662 per year full-time, $272 per semester (minimum) part-time for state residents; $8790 per year full-time, $2054 per semester (minimum) part-time for nonresidents. • Dr. Wyatt Kirk, Chairperson, 336-334-7916. Fax: 336-334-7280. E-mail: kirkw@aurora.ncat.edu.

Nova Southeastern University, School of Business and Entrepreneurship, Program in Human Resources Management, Fort Lauderdale, FL 33314-7721. Awards MSHRM. Part-time and evening/weekend programs available. Students: 2 full-time (both women), 70 part-time (53 women); includes 28 minority (18 African Americans, 9 Hispanics, 1 Native American), 6 international. In 1997, 44 degrees awarded. *Degree requirements:* Thesis or alternative. *Entrance requirements:* GMAT (minimum score 450), GRE General Test (minimum combined score of 1000), work experience. Application deadline: 8/15 (rolling processing; 2/10 for spring admission). Application fee: $50. *Tuition:* $270 per credit hour (minimum). • Dr. Preston Jones,

Director, 954-262-5127. Application contact: Carlo Palazzese, Marketing Manager, 954-262-5038. E-mail: carlop@sbe.nova.edu.

The Ohio State University, Max M. Fisher College of Business, Program in Labor and Human Resources, Columbus, OH 43210. Awards MLHR, PhD. Faculty: 23. Students: 46 full-time (31 women), 23 part-time (13 women); includes 11 minority (10 African Americans, 1 Asian American), 12 international. 125 applicants, 38% accepted. In 1997, 38 master's awarded. *Degree requirements:* For master's, thesis optional, foreign language not required; for doctorate, dissertation required, foreign language not required. *Entrance requirements:* For master's, GRE General Test, TOEFL (minimum score 575); for doctorate, GRE General Test, TOEFL. Application deadline: rolling. Application fee: $30 ($40 for international students). *Tuition:* $6018 per year full-time, $635 per quarter (minimum) part-time for state residents; $14,835 per year full-time, $1514 per quarter (minimum) part-time for nonresidents. *Financial aid:* Fellowships, research assistantships, teaching assistantships, Federal Work-Study, institutionally sponsored loans available. Aid available to part-time students. • Dr. Robert L. Heneman, Graduate Studies Committee Chair, 614-292-8532. Fax: 614-292-7062. E-mail: heneman.1@osu.edu.

Ottawa University, Department of Human Resources, Ottawa, KS 66067-3399. Awards MA. Offered at both the Arizona and Kansas campuses. Part-time and evening/weekend programs available. Postbaccalaureate distance learning degree programs offered (minimal on-campus study). Faculty: 1 full-time (0 women), 16 part-time (8 women). Students: 64 part-time (38 women). 44 applicants, 100% accepted. In 1997, 16 degrees awarded. *Degree requirements:* Thesis optional, foreign language not required. *Application deadline:* rolling. *Application fee:* $50. *Tuition:* $275 per hour. *Financial aid:* Available to part-time students. • Dr. W. A. Breytspraak, Director of Graduate Studies, 913-451-1431. Application contact: David Leiter, Admissions Officer, 913-451-1431.

Purdue University, Krannert Graduate School of Management, Department of Organizational Behavior and Human Resource Management, West Lafayette, IN 47907. Offers programs in human resource management (MS), organizational behavior and human resource management (PhD). Faculty: 10 full-time (2 women). Students: 52 full-time (34 women), 2 part-time (1 woman); includes 14 minority (7 African Americans, 3 Asian Americans, 4 Hispanics), 11 international. Average age 28. 109 applicants, 36% accepted. In 1997, 19 master's, 2 doctorates awarded. *Degree requirements:* For doctorate, dissertation required, foreign language not required. *Average time to degree:* doctorate–4 years full-time. *Entrance requirements:* For master's, GMAT, TOEFL (minimum score 575); for doctorate, GMAT or GRE General Test, TOEFL (minimum score 575). Application fee: $30. Electronic applications accepted. *Tuition:* $3500 per year full-time, $126 per credit hour part-time for state residents; $11,720 per year full-time, $387 per credit hour part-time for nonresidents. *Financial aid:* In 1997–98, 3 fellowships averaging $960 per month, 10 research assistantships (1 to a first-year student) averaging $960 per month, 5 teaching assistantships averaging $960 per month were awarded; career-related internships or fieldwork also available. Aid available to part-time students. Financial aid applicants required to submit FAFSA. *Faculty research:* Leadership, staff management and selection, teams, human resource information systems. • Dr. J. J. McConnell, Director of Doctoral Programs, 765-494-4375. Application contact: Kelly Felty, Assistant Director of Administration for Doctoral Programs, 765-494-4375. Fax: 765-494-1526. E-mail: feltyk@mgmt.purdue.edu.

Rensselaer Polytechnic Institute, Lally School of Management and Technology, Troy, NY 12180-3590. Offerings include business administration (MBA, PhD), with options in finance and accounting (MBA), information systems management (MBA), management (PhD), management of technology and entrepreneurships (MBA), manufacturing management (MBA), marketing management (MBA), operations research (MBA), organizational behavior and human resource management (MBA), statistical methods for management (MBA); human resource (PhD). Postbaccalaureate distance learning degree programs offered (no on-campus study). School faculty: 36 full-time (5 women), 6 part-time (0 women). *Degree requirements:* For doctorate, computer language, dissertation required, foreign language not required. *Entrance requirements:* For doctorate, GMAT or GRE General Test, TOEFL (minimum score 570). Application deadline: 2/1 (priority date; rolling processing). Application fee: $35. *Expenses:* Tuition $630 per credit hour. Fees $1000 per year. • Dr. Joseph G. Ecker, Dean, 518-276-6802. Application contact: Michele Martens, Manager of Enrollment Services, 518-276-4800. Fax: 518-276-8661.

Rivier College, Department of Business Administration, Nashua, NH 03060-5086. Offerings include employee relations (MBA), human resources management (MBA, MS). *Entrance requirements:* GMAT. Application deadline: rolling. Application fee: $25.

Rollins College, Program in Human Resources, Winter Park, FL 32789-4499. Awards MA. Part-time and evening/weekend programs available. Faculty: 4 full-time (3 women). Students: 48 part-time (37 women); includes 2 minority (1 African American, 1 Hispanic). Average age 30. 67 applicants, 66% accepted. In 1997, 31 degrees awarded. *Degree requirements:* Thesis optional, foreign language not required. *Entrance requirements:* GMAT, GRE, or MAT, interview. Application deadline: 4/1. Application fee: $50. *Tuition:* $258 per hour. *Financial aid:* 7 students received aid. Financial aid application deadline: 3/23. • Dr. Donald Rogers, Director, 407-646-2348. Application contact: Laura Pfister, Coordinator of Records and Registration, 407-646-2416. Fax: 407-646-1551.

Rutgers, The State University of New Jersey, Newark, Department of Public Administration, Newark, NJ 07102-3192. Offerings include human resources administration (MPA). Department faculty: 11 full-time (3 women), 6 part-time (1 woman), 12 FTE. *Degree requirements:* Thesis or alternative, comprehensive exam. *Average time to degree:* master's–2 years full-time, 3 years part-time. *Entrance requirements:* GRE, minimum undergraduate B average. Application deadline: 7/1 (priority date; rolling processing; 12/1 for spring admission). Application fee: $40. *Expenses:* Tuition $6248 per year full-time, $257 per credit part-time for state residents; $9160 per year full-time, $380 per credit part-time for nonresidents. Fees $738 per year full-time, $107 per semester (minimum) part-time. • Dr. Marcia Whicker, Director, 973-353-5093. E-mail: whicker@andromeda.rutgers.edu.

Rutgers, The State University of New Jersey, New Brunswick, School of Management and Labor Relations, Program in Human Resource Management, New Brunswick, NJ 08903. Awards MHRM. Also available at Singapore and Indonesian campuses. Part-time programs available. Faculty: 15 full-time (3 women), 2 part-time (0 women). Students: 40 full-time (27 women), 147 part-time (111 women); includes 21 minority (8 African Americans, 6 Asian Americans, 7 Hispanics), 65 international. Average age 31. 150 applicants, 84% accepted. In 1997, 68 degrees awarded (83% found work related to degree). *Average time to degree:* master's–2 years full-time, 5 years part-time. *Entrance requirements:* GMAT or GRE General Test. Application deadline: 5/1 (priority date; rolling processing; 11/1 for spring admission). Application fee: $40. *Expenses:* Tuition $6492 per year full-time, $268 per credit part-time for state residents; $9520 per year full-time, $395 per credit part-time for nonresidents. Fees $208 per year (minimum). *Financial aid:* In 1997–98, 8 fellowships (5 to first-year students) totaling $74,179, 1 research assistantship (to a first-year student) averaging $1,108 per month and totaling $11,086 were awarded; teaching assistantships, full and partial tuition waivers, and career-related internships or fieldwork also available. Financial aid application deadline: 3/1. *Faculty research:* Human resource policy and planning, employee ownership and profit sharing, compensation and appraisal of performance, law and public policy, computers and decision making. • Dr. Charles Fay, Director, 732-445-5831. Application contact: Judy von Loewe, Graduate Program Coordinator, 732-445-5973.

See in-depth description on page 497.

Rutgers, The State University of New Jersey, New Brunswick, School of Management and Labor Relations, Program in Industrial Relations and Human Resources, New Brunswick, NJ 08903. Awards PhD. Faculty: 15 full-time (2 women). Students: 13 full-time (6 women); includes 1 minority (African American), 3 international. Average age 31. 25 applicants, 16% accepted. Terminal master's awarded for partial completion of doctoral program. *Degree requirements:* For doctorate, dissertation required, foreign language not required. *Average time to degree:* doctorate–4.5 years full-time. *Application deadline:* 3/1. *Application fee:* $40. *Expenses:* Tuition $6492 per year full-time, $268 per credit part-time for state residents; $9520 per year full-time, $395 per credit part-time for nonresidents. Fees $208 per year (minimum). *Financial aid:* In 1997–98, 12 students received aid, including 2 fellowships (1 to a first-year student) totaling $31,739, 10 teaching assistantships (2 to first-year students) totaling $154,350; research assistantships, full and partial tuition waivers, and career-related internships or fieldwork also available. Financial aid application deadline: 3/1. *Faculty research:* Compensation and appraisal of performance, law and public policy, computers and decision making, collective bargaining, technology and work. • Dr. Jeffrey Keefe, Director, 732-932-1749. Application contact: Judy von Loewe, Graduate Program Coordinator, 732-445-5973.

See in-depth description on page 497.

Sage Graduate School, Graduate School, Division of Management Studies, Program in Business Administration, Troy, NY 12180-4115. Offerings include human resources management (MBA). MBA/JD offered jointly with Albany Law School of Union University. Program faculty: 1 full-time (0 women), 10 part-time (1 woman). *Entrance requirements:* Minimum GPA of 2.75. Application fee: $25. *Expenses:* Tuition $360 per credit hour. Fees $50 per semester. • Application contact: Melissa Robertson, Associate Director of Admissions, 518-244-6878. Fax: 518-244-6880. E-mail: sgsadm@sage.edu.

Saint Francis College, Graduate School of Human Resource Management and Industrial Relations, Loretto, PA 15940-0600. Awards MA. Part-time and evening/weekend programs available. Faculty: 1 full-time (0 women), 27 part-time (7 women). Students: 2 full-time (1 woman), 123 part-time (85 women); includes 7 minority (all African Americans). Average age 30. In 1997, 43 degrees awarded. *Degree requirements:* Research paper required, foreign language and thesis not required. *Average time to degree:* master's–1.5 years full-time, 2.5 years part-time. *Entrance requirements:* Minimum GPA of 2.5 or 3.0 depending on experience. Application deadline: 8/1 (priority date; rolling processing; 12/1 for spring admission). Application fee: $15. *Financial aid:* In 1997–98, 7 students received aid, including 1 fellowship (to a first-year student); Federal Work-Study also available. Aid available to part-time students. • Dr. Philip Benham, Director, 814-472-3026. E-mail: pbenham@sfcpa.edu. Application contact: Judith McMullen, Assistant to the Director, 814-472-3026. Fax: 814-472-3369. E-mail: hrir@sfcpa.edu.

See in-depth description on page 499.

St. Thomas University, School of Graduate Studies, Department of Professional Management, Specialization in Human Resource Management, Miami, FL 33054-6459. Awards MSM, Certificate. Part-time and evening/weekend programs available. *Degree requirements:* For master's, comprehensive exam required, foreign language and thesis not required. *Average time to degree:* master's–1 year full-time. *Entrance requirements:* For master's, TOEFL (minimum score 550), interview, minimum GPA of 3.0 or GMAT. Application deadline: 6/15 (priority date; rolling processing; 11/15 for spring admission). Application fee: $30. *Tuition:* $410 per credit.

Salve Regina University, Program in Human Resources Management, Newport, RI 02840-4192. Awards MA, MS. Part-time and evening/weekend programs available. Postbaccalaureate distance learning degree programs offered (no on-campus study). Faculty: 1 (woman) full-time, 4 part-time (0 women), 2.25 FTE. Students: 13 full-time (8 women), 102 part-time (34 women). Average age 35. 40 applicants, 78% accepted. In 1997, 19 degrees awarded. *Average time to degree:* master's–2 years full-time, 3 years part-time. *Entrance requirements:* GMAT, GRE General Test, or MAT. Application deadline: rolling. Application fee: $35. *Expenses:* Tuition $275 per credit hour. Fees $70 per year. *Financial aid:* Federal Work-Study and career-related internships or fieldwork available. Aid available to part-time students. Financial aid application deadline: 3/1. • Dr. John W. Britton, Director, 401-847-6650 Ext. 3140. Fax: 401-847-0372. Application contact: Laura E. McPhie, Dean of Enrollment Services, 401-847-6650 Ext. 2908. Fax: 401-848-2823. E-mail: sruadmis@salve.edu.

Seton Hall University, W. Paul Stillman School of Business, Department of Management, South Orange, NJ 07079-2692. Offerings include human resource management (MBA, MS). Department faculty: 9 full-time (3 women), 1 part-time (0 women). *Degree requirements:* Thesis optional, foreign language not required. *Entrance requirements:* GMAT (minimum score 500), TOEFL (minimum score 550). Application deadline: 6/1 (priority date; rolling processing). Application fee: $50. *Expenses:* Tuition $538 per credit. Fees $185 per semester. • Dr. Leigh Stelzer, Chairperson, 973-761-9218. E-mail: stelzele@shu.edu. Application contact: Student Information Office, 973-761-9222. Fax: 973-761-9217. E-mail: busgrad@shu.edu.

Southeast Missouri State University, Program in Administrative Science, Cape Girardeau, MO 63701-4799. Offerings include human resources administration (MSA). *Degree requirements:* Thesis or alternative required, foreign language not required. *Entrance requirements:* Minimum GPA of 2.5. Application deadline: 4/1 (priority date; rolling processing; 11/21 for spring admission). Application fee: $20 ($100 for international students). *Tuition:* $2034 per year full-time, $113 per credit hour part-time for state residents; $3672 per year full-time, $204 per credit hour part-time for nonresidents. • Application contact: Office of Graduate Studies, 573-651-2192.

State University of New York at Albany, School of Business, Department of Management, Albany, NY 12222-0001. Offers program in human resource systems (MBA). Faculty: 10 full-time (3 women), 1 (woman) part-time. Students: 19 full-time (11 women). *Degree requirements:* Field study project. *Entrance requirements:* GMAT. Application deadline: 7/1 (priority date; rolling processing). Application fee: $50. *Expenses:* Tuition $5100 per year full-time, $213 per credit hour part-time for state residents; $8416 per year full-time, $351 per credit hour part-time for nonresidents. Fees $705 per year full-time, $26.85 per credit hour part-time. *Financial aid:* Application deadline 4/1. *Faculty research:* Leadership, strategic management, performance appraisal, franchising, job satisfaction. • Hal Gueutal, Chair, 518-442-4966. Application contact: Jeffrey Collins, Assistant Director, Graduate Admissions, 518-442-3980.

Suffolk University, Sawyer School of Management, Department of Public Management, Boston, MA 02108-2770. Offerings include public finance and human resources (MPA). MPA/MS offered jointly with Department of Education and Human Services. Department faculty: 7 full-time (2 women), 20 part-time (12 women). *Application deadline:* 6/15 (priority date; rolling processing; 11/15 for spring admission). *Application fee:* $50. *Expenses:* Tuition $16,122 per year full-time, $1611 per course part-time. Fees $50 per year full-time, $20 per year part-time. • Michael Lavin, Chair, 617-573-8317. Fax: 617-573-8345. E-mail: mlavin@acad.suffolk.edu. Application contact: Judy Reynolds, Acting Director of Graduate Admissions, 617-573-8302. Fax: 617-523-0116. E-mail: grad.admission@admin.suffolk.edu.

Syracuse University, School of Management, Program in Human Resource Management, Syracuse, NY 13244-0003. Awards MBA. Faculty: 5. Students: 12 full-time (3 women), 12 part-time (8 women); includes 4 minority (1 African American, 1 Asian American, 2 Hispanics), 1 international. 23 applicants, 57% accepted. In 1997, 9 degrees awarded. *Entrance requirements:* GMAT. Application deadline: 2/1. Application fee: $40. *Tuition:* $13,320 per year full-time, $555 per credit hour part-time. *Financial aid:* Application deadline 3/1. • R. J. Chesser, Chairman, 315-443-2804. Application contact: Associate Dean, 315-443-3850.

Temple University, School of Business and Management, Doctoral Program in Business Administration, Philadelphia, PA 19122-6096. Offerings include human resource administration (PhD). *Degree requirements:* Dissertation, preliminary exams required, foreign language not required. *Entrance requirements:* GMAT, TOEFL (minimum score 600), master's degree, minimum GPA of 3.5. Application deadline: 1/15 (rolling processing). Application fee: $40. *Expenses:* Tuition $323 per semester hour for state residents; $444 per semester hour for nonresidents. Fees $170 per year full-time, $28 per semester (minimum) part-time. • Dr.

Directory: Human Resources Management

Temple University (continued)

Roland Lipka, Director, 215-204-8125. Fax: 215-204-5574. Application contact: Linda Whelan, Director, 215-204-7678. Fax: 215-204-8300.

Temple University, School of Business and Management, Master's Program in Business Administration, Philadelphia, PA 19122-6096. Offerings include human resource administration (MBA, MS). Program faculty: 72 full-time (13 women). *Entrance requirements:* GMAT (average 540), TOEFL (minimum score 575). Application fee: $40. *Expenses:* Tuition $323 per semester hour for state residents; $444 per semester hour for nonresidents. Fees $170 per year full-time, $28 per semester (minimum) part-time. • Application contact: Linda Whelan, Director, 215-204-7678. Fax: 215-204-8300. E-mail: linda@astro.ocis.temple.edu.

Trinity College, School of Professional Studies, Programs in Administration, Washington, DC 20017-1094. Offerings include human resources (MSA), with options in entrepreneurial development, human resource development, human resource management. Faculty: 4 full-time (1 woman), 4 part-time (all women). *Application deadline:* rolling. *Application fee:* $35. *Tuition:* $460 per credit hour. • Dr. Sheri Levin, Division Chair, Human Services, 202-884-9553. Application contact: Karen Goodwin, Director of Graduate Admissions, 202-884-9400. Fax: 202-884-9229.

Troy State University, Graduate School, University College, Sorrell College of Business and Commerce, Troy, AL 36082. Offerings include personnel management (MS). *Application deadline:* rolling. *Application fee:* $20. Electronic applications accepted. *Expenses:* Tuition $2040 per year full-time, $68 per hour part-time for state residents; $4200 per year full-time, $140 per hour part-time for nonresidents. Fees $240 per year full-time, $27 per quarter (minimum) part-time. • Dr. Thomas Ratcliffe, Dean, 334-670-3299. Fax: 334-670-3592. Application contact: Dr. Rodney Cox, Dean, University College, 334-670-3457. Fax: 334-670-3770. E-mail: rcox@trojan.troyst.edu.

Troy State University Dothan, School of Business, Department of Management and Marketing, Dothan, AL 36304-0368. Offerings include human resource management (MBA, MS). *Entrance requirements:* GMAT (MBA); GMAT, GRE General Test, or MAT (MS), minimum GPA of 2.5. Application deadline: rolling. Application fee: $20. *Expenses:* Tuition $68 per credit hour for state residents; $140 per credit hour for nonresidents. Fees $2 per credit hour. • Dr. Darryel Roberds, Chair. Application contact: Reta Cordell, Director of Admissions and Records, 334-983-6556. Fax: 334-983-6322. E-mail: rcordell@tsud.edu.

Troy State University Montgomery, Division of Business, Program in Human Resources Management, PO Drawer 4419, Montgomery, AL 36103-4419. Awards MS. Part-time and evening/weekend programs available. In 1997, 45 degrees awarded. *Degree requirements:* Thesis or alternative. *Entrance requirements:* GMAT, GRE, or MAT; TOEFL. Application deadline: rolling. Application fee: $20. *Expenses:* Tuition $52 per quarter hour for state residents; $104 per quarter hour for nonresidents. Fees $30 per year. • Dr. Freda Hartman, Dean, Division of Business, 334-241-9597. Fax: 334-241-9734. E-mail: fhartman@tsum.edu.

Universidad del Turabo, Programs in Business Administration, Program in Human Resources, Gurabo, PR 00778-3030. Awards MBA. *Entrance requirements:* GRE, PAEG, interview. Application deadline: 8/5. Application fee: $25.

Université de Sherbrooke, Faculty of Administration, Program in Management of Human Productivity, Sherbrooke, PQ J1K 2R1, Canada. Awards M Sc. *Application deadline:* 5/31. *Application fee:* $15.

The University of Akron, College of Business Administration, Department of Management, Program in Management-Human Resources, Akron, OH 44325-0001. Awards MSM. Students: 4 full-time (all women), 8 part-time (5 women); includes 1 international. In 1997, 1 degree awarded. *Entrance requirements:* GMAT (minimum score 450), minimum GPA of 2.75. Application deadline: 8/15 (rolling processing). Application fee: $25 ($50 for international students). *Expenses:* Tuition $178 per credit hour for state residents; $333 per credit hour for nonresidents. Fees $145 per year full-time, $32 per semester (minimum) part-time. *Financial aid:* Application deadline 4/30. • Dr. Kenneth Dunning, Acting Chair, Department of Management, 330-972-7037. E-mail: kdunning@uakron.edu. Application contact: Dr. J. Daniel Williams, Director of Graduate Business Programs, 330-972-7043. E-mail: jwilliams@uakron.edu.

University of Charleston, Jones-Benedum Division of Business, Program in Human Resource Management, Charleston, WV 25304-1099. Awards MHRM. Part-time and evening/weekend programs available. Faculty: 7. Students: 22 part-time (15 women). *Degree requirements:* Thesis required, foreign language not required. *Entrance requirements:* GRE General Test or MAT, 3 years of related experience. Application deadline: 8/1 (priority date; rolling processing; 12/15 for spring admission). Application fee: $40. *Tuition:* $365 per credit hour. *Financial aid:* Available to part-time students. • Dr. Mary Ellen Molinaro, Director, 304-357-4818. Application contact: Lynn Jackson, Director of Admissions, 304-357-4750. Fax: 304-357-4715.

University of Connecticut, School of Business Administration, Storrs, CT 06269. Offerings include human resources management (MBA). School faculty: 63. *Entrance requirements:* GMAT. Application deadline: 6/1 (priority date; rolling processing; 11/1 for spring admission). Application fee: $40 ($45 for international students). *Expenses:* Tuition $5272 per year full-time, $293 per credit part-time for state residents; $13,696 per year full-time, $761 per credit part-time for nonresidents. Fees $948 per year full-time, $640 per year part-time. • Thomas G. Gutteridge, Dean, 860-486-3096. Application contact: David W. Palmer, Chairperson, 860-486-3096.

University of Dallas, Graduate School of Management, Program in Human Resources Management, Irving, TX 75062-4799. Awards MBA, MM. Part-time programs available. Students: 49 (37 women). In 1997, 24 degrees awarded. *Average time to degree:* master's–1.3 years full-time, 2.5 years part-time. *Entrance requirements:* GMAT (minimum score 400), TOEFL (average 520), minimum GPA of 3.0. Application deadline: 8/6 (priority date; rolling processing; 12/8 for spring admission). Application fee: $25 ($50 for international students). *Expenses:* Tuition $380 per credit hour. Fees $125 per year. *Financial aid:* Application deadline 2/15. • Rosemary Maellaro, Director, 972-721-5277. Fax: 972-721-5130. Application contact: Roxanne Del Rio, Director of Admissions, 972-721-5174. Fax: 972-721-4009. E-mail: admiss@gsm.udallas.edu.

The University of Findlay, College of Professional Studies, MBA Program, 1000 North Main Street, Findlay, OH 45840-3653. Offerings include human resource management (MBA). Postbaccalaureate distance learning degree programs offered (minimal on-campus study). Program faculty: 9 full-time (0 women), 6 part-time (0 women), 11 FTE. *Degree requirements:* Cumulative project. *Average time to degree:* master's–1.5 years full-time, 2.5 years part-time. *Entrance requirements:* GMAT, TOEFL. Application deadline: 8/15 (rolling processing; 12/15 for spring admission). Application fee: $25. *Tuition:* $299 per semester hour. • Dr. Theodore C. Alex, Director, 419-424-4704. Fax: 419-424-4822.

University of Florida, College of Business Administration, Department of Management, Gainesville, FL 32611. Offerings include human resources management (PhD). Department faculty: 8. *Degree requirements:* Dissertation required, foreign language not required. *Entrance requirements:* GMAT or GRE General Test, minimum GPA of 3.0. Application deadline: 2/16 (rolling processing). Application fee: $20. *Tuition:* $138 per credit hour for state residents; $481 per credit hour for nonresidents. • Dr. Virginia Maurer, Chair, 352-392-0163. E-mail: maurer@dale.cba.ufl.edu. Application contact: Dr. Henry Tosi, Graduate Coordinator, 352-392-6147. Fax: 352-392-6020. E-mail: tosi@nervm.nerdc.ufl.edu.

University of Hartford, Barney School of Business and Public Administration, Program in Business Administration, West Hartford, CT 06117-1599. Offerings include human resource management (MBA). Program faculty: 24 full-time (4 women), 15 part-time (1 woman). *Average time to degree:* master's–1.5 years full-time, 3 years part-time. *Entrance requirements:* GMAT, TOEFL. Application deadline: 7/1 (priority date; rolling processing; 12/1 for spring admission). Application fee: $35 ($50 for international students). Electronic applications accepted. • Christopher Galligan, Director, 860-768-4390. Application contact: Claire Silverstein, Assistant Director, 860-768-4900. Fax: 860-768-4821. E-mail: silverste@unavax.hartford.edu.

University of Hartford, Barney School of Business and Public Administration, Department of Management/Marketing, Program in Organizational Behavior, West Hartford, CT 06117-1599. Offerings include human resource management (MSOB). Program faculty: 5 full-time (2 women), 2 part-time (1 woman). *Average time to degree:* master's–1.5 years full-time, 3 years part-time. *Entrance requirements:* GMAT, GRE, TOEFL. Application deadline: 7/1 (priority date; rolling processing; 12/1 for spring admission). Application fee: $35 ($50 for international students). Electronic applications accepted. • Dr. Sandra Morgan, Director, 860-768-4974. Fax: 860-768-4198. E-mail: morgan@uhavax.hartford.edu. Application contact: Claire Silverstein, Assistant Director, 860-768-4900. Fax: 860-768-4821. E-mail: silverste@unavax.hartford.edu.

University of Houston–Clear Lake, School of Business and Public Administration, Program in Public Affairs, Houston, TX 77058-1098. Offerings include human resource management (MA). Program faculty: 15. *Application deadline:* 8/1 (rolling processing; 12/1 for spring admission). *Application fee:* $30 ($60 for international students). *Tuition:* $207 per credit hour for state residents; $336 per credit hour for nonresidents. • Dr. Richard Allison, Chair, 281-283-3251. Application contact: Dr. Sue Neeley, Associate Dean, 281-283-3110.

University of Illinois at Chicago, College of Business Administration, Department of Human Resources Management, Chicago, IL 60607-7128. Awards PhD. Faculty: 14 full-time (3 women). Students: 6 full-time (3 women), 10 part-time (4 women); includes 2 minority (1 Asian American, 1 Hispanic), 1 international. Average age 41. 11 applicants, 18% accepted. In 1997, 2 degrees awarded. *Degree requirements:* Dissertation required, foreign language not required. *Entrance requirements:* GMAT, TOEFL (minimum score 550), minimum GPA of 3.75 on a 5.0 scale. Application deadline: 5/1. Application fee: $40 ($50 for international students). *Financial aid:* In 1997–98, 1 fellowship, 3 research assistantships were awarded; teaching assistantships also available. • Robert Liden, Director of Graduate Studies, 312-996-4480. Application contact: Ann Rosi, 312-996-4751.

University of Illinois at Urbana–Champaign, Institute of Labor and Industrial Relations, Program in Human Resources, Urbana, IL 61801. Awards AM, PhD. *Degree requirements:* For doctorate, dissertation required, foreign language not required. *Entrance requirements:* For master's, GRE, minimum GPA of 4.0 on a 5.0 scale; for doctorate, GRE, research experience. Application deadline: rolling. Application fee: $40 ($50 for international students). • Peter Feuille, Director, Institute of Labor and Industrial Relations, 217-333-1480. Fax: 217-244-9290.

See in-depth description on page 503.

The University of Iowa, College of Business Administration, Department of Management and Organizations, Iowa City, IA 52242-1316. Offers program in business administration (PhD). Faculty: 11 full-time (3 women), 4 part-time (2 women). Students: 12 full-time (4 women), 2 part-time (1 woman); includes 1 minority (African American), 2 international. Average age 37. 32 applicants, 16% accepted. In 1997, 2 doctorates awarded (50% entered university research/teaching, 50% found other work related to degree). Terminal master's awarded for partial completion of doctoral program. *Degree requirements:* For doctorate, computer language, dissertation required, foreign language not required. *Average time to degree:* doctorate–4 years full-time, 5 years part-time. *Entrance requirements:* For doctorate, GMAT (minimum score 600; average 650). Application deadline: 3/1. Application fee: $30 ($50 for international students). *Expenses:* Tuition $3166 per year full-time, $176 per semester hour part-time for state residents; $10,202 per year full-time, $176 per semester hour part-time for nonresidents. Fees $202 per year full-time, $52 per year (minimum) part-time. *Financial aid:* In 1997–98, 13 students received aid, including 1 fellowship totaling $3,200, 7 research assistantships averaging $1,278 per month and totaling $32,884, 10 teaching assistantships averaging $1,278 per month and totaling $76,019, 9 summer research grants, tuition grants (1 to a first-year student) totaling $27,456; Federal Work-Study and career-related internships or fieldwork also available. Financial aid application deadline: 3/1; applicants required to submit FAFSA. *Faculty research:* Personality and job performance, behavioral decision making, employment selection, negotiation and conflict management, ethics. • Michael Mount, Chair, 319-335-0927. E-mail: michael-mount@uiowa.edu. Application contact: Murray Barrick, Associate Professor, 319-335-0924. Fax: 319-335-1956. E-mail: mbarrick@uiowa.edu.

The University of Memphis, College of Arts and Sciences, Department of Political Science, Program in Public Administration, Memphis, TN 38152. Offerings include human resources administration (MPA). *Degree requirements:* Thesis or alternative, comprehensive exam, internship. *Entrance requirements:* GRE General Test (minimum combined score of 1000) or GMAT (minimum score 500), minimum GPA of 3.0. Application deadline: 8/1 (rolling processing; 12/1 for spring admission). Application fee: $25 ($50 for international students). *Tuition:* $2862 per year full-time, $166 per credit hour part-time for state residents; $6696 per year full-time, $379 per credit hour part-time for nonresidents. • Dr. Dorothy Norris-Tirrell, Coordinator, 901-678-3360. E-mail: dnrrstrr@memphis.edu. Application contact: James R. Carruth, Coordinator of Graduate Studies, 901-678-3360. Fax: 901-678-2983. E-mail: jrcarrth@memphis.edu.

University of Minnesota, Twin Cities Campus, Carlson School of Management, Program in Human Resources and Industrial Relations, 321 19th Avenue South, Minneapolis, MN 55455-0213. Awards MA, PhD. Part-time and evening/weekend programs available. Faculty: 25 full-time (5 women), 4 part-time (1 woman). Terminal master's awarded for partial completion of doctoral program. *Degree requirements:* For master's, thesis optional, foreign language not required; for doctorate, dissertation required, foreign language not required. *Entrance requirements:* GRE General Test. *Financial aid:* Full and partial tuition waivers, Federal Work-Study, institutionally sponsored loans, and career-related internships or fieldwork available. Aid available to part-time students. Financial aid application deadline: 2/1. *Faculty research:* Staffing, training, and development; compensation and benefits; organization theory; collective bargaining. • Avner Ben-Ner, Chair, 612-624-2500. Application contact: Lyn Birkholz, Principal Secretary, 612-624-5704. E-mail: mbirkholz@csom.umn.edu.

See in-depth description on page 505.

University of Missouri–St. Louis, School of Business Administration, Program in Human Resource Management, St. Louis, MO 63121-4499. Awards Certificate. *Application deadline:* 7/1 (rolling processing; 11/1 for spring admission). *Application fee:* $0. *Expenses:* Tuition $3903 per year full-time, $167 per credit hour part-time for state residents; $11,745 per year full-time, $489 per credit hour part-time for nonresidents. Fees $816 per year full-time, $34 per credit hour part-time. *Financial aid:* Application deadline 4/1. • Application contact: Graduate Admissions, 314-516-5458. Fax: 314-516-6759. E-mail: gradadm@umslvma.umsl.edu.

University of New Haven, School of Business, Program in Business Administration, West Haven, CT 06516-1916. Offerings include human resources management (MBA). *Degree requirements:* Thesis or alternative required, foreign language not required. *Application deadline:* rolling. *Application fee:* $50. *Expenses:* Tuition $1125 per course. Fees $13 per trimester. • Dr. Omid Nodoushani, Coordinator, 203-932-7123.

University of New Haven, School of Business, Program in Public Administration, West Haven, CT 06516-1916. Offerings include personnel and labor relations (MPA). *Degree requirements:* Thesis or alternative required, foreign language not required. *Application deadline:* rolling. *Application fee:* $50. *Expenses:* Tuition $1125 per course. Fees $13 per trimester. • Charles Coleman, Chairman, 203-932-7375.

University of New Mexico, Robert O. Anderson Graduate School of Management, Albuquerque, NM 87131-1221. Offerings include human resources management (MBA). School faculty: 50 full-time (11 women). *Application deadline:* 7/1 (priority date; rolling processing; 11/15 for spring admission). *Application fee:* $25. *Expenses:* Tuition $2442 per year full-time, $103 per credit hour part-time for state residents; $8691 per year full-time, $103 per credit hour (minimum) part-time for nonresidents. Fees $32 per year. • Howard L. Smith, Dean, 505-277-6471. Fax: 505-277-7108. Application contact: Sue Podeyn, MBA Program Director, 505-277-3147. Fax: 505-277-9356. E-mail: podeyn@unm.edu.

University of North Florida, College of Business Administration, Department of Management, Marketing, and Logistics, Jacksonville, FL 32224-2645. Offerings include personnel management (MHRM). Department faculty: 33 full-time (4 women). *Application deadline:* rolling. *Application fee:* $20. *Tuition:* $3388 per year full-time, $141 per credit hour part-time for state residents; $11,634 per year full-time, $485 per credit hour part-time for nonresidents. • Dr. Robert Pickhardt, Chair, 904-646-2780.

University of North Florida, College of Business Administration, Program in Human Resource Management, Jacksonville, FL 32224-2645. Awards MHRM. *Degree requirements:* Computer language required, thesis not required. *Entrance requirements:* GMAT, minimum GPA of 3.0. Application deadline: rolling. Application fee: $20. *Tuition:* $3388 per year full-time, $141 per credit hour part-time for state residents; $11,634 per year full-time, $485 per credit hour part-time for nonresidents. • Application contact: Dr. Don Graham, Director of Graduate Advising, 904-646-2575.

University of Oregon, Graduate School, Charles H. Lundquist College of Business, Program in Human Resources and Industrial Relations, Eugene, OR 97403. Awards MHRIR. Part-time programs available. Students: 4 full-time (3 women), 3 part-time (all women); includes 2 international. 6 applicants, 0% accepted. In 1997, 14 degrees awarded (100% found work related to degree). *Degree requirements:* Computer language required, foreign language not required. *Entrance requirements:* GMAT or GRE General Test. Application deadline: 3/1. Application fee: $50. *Tuition:* $6429 per year full-time, $873 per quarter (minimum) part-time for state residents; $10,857 per year full-time, $1360 per quarter (minimum) part-time for nonresidents. *Financial aid:* In 1997–98, 1 teaching assistantship was awarded; Federal Work-Study and career-related internships or fieldwork also available. • Dan Poston, Director, 541-346-3251. E-mail: mohoric@oregon.uoregon.edu. Application contact: Linda Johnson, Graduate Secretary, 541-346-3306.

University of St. Thomas, Graduate School of Business, Day MBA Program, St. Paul, MN 55105-1096. Offerings include human resource management (MBA). Program faculty: 13 part-time. *Degree requirements:* Computer language required, foreign language and thesis not required. *Entrance requirements:* GMAT (score in 50th percentile or higher). Application deadline: 5/1 (priority date; rolling processing). Application fee: $30. *Tuition:* $473 per credit hour. • Application contact: Jim O'Connor, Student Adviser, 612-962-4233. Fax: 612-962-4260.

University of St. Thomas, Graduate School of Business, Evening MBA Program, St. Paul, MN 55105-1096. Offerings include human resource management (MBA, Certificate). Program faculty: 16 full-time (2 women), 89 part-time (17 women). *Degree requirements:* For master's, computer language required, foreign language and thesis not required. *Entrance requirements:* For master's, GMAT (score in 50th percentile or higher). Application deadline: 8/1 (priority date; rolling processing; 12/1 for spring admission). Application fee: $30. *Tuition:* $416 per credit hour. • Dr. Stanford Nyquist, MBA Director, 612-962-4242. Application contact: Martha Ballard, Director of Student Services, 612-962-4226. Fax: 612-962-4260.

University of St. Thomas, Graduate School of Business, Program in Human Resource Management, St. Paul, MN 55105-1096. Offers human resource management (MBA), human resource management–compensation (Certificate), human resource management–employee benefits (Certificate), human resource management–generalist (Certificate), human resource management–law (Certificate), international human resource management (Certificate). Part-time and evening/weekend programs available. Faculty: 1 full-time, 29 part-time. Students: 5 full-time (4 women), 103 part-time (76 women); includes 7 minority (3 African Americans, 4 Asian Americans), 1 international. Average age 32. 32 applicants, 91% accepted. In 1997, 12 master's, 12 Certificates awarded. *Entrance requirements:* For master's, GMAT (score in 50th percentile or higher). Application deadline: 8/1 (priority date; rolling processing; 12/1 for spring admission). Application fee: $30. *Tuition:* $416 per credit hour. *Financial aid:* In 1997–98, 2 grants totaling $2,218 were awarded; career-related internships or fieldwork also available. Aid available to part-time students. Financial aid application deadline: 4/1; applicants required to submit FAFSA. • Phil Schecter, Director, 612-962-4245. Application contact: David Baker, Student Adviser, 612-962-4228. Fax: 612-962-4260.

University of St. Thomas, Graduate School of Business, Program in International Management, St. Paul, MN 55105-1096. Offerings include international human resources (MIM, Certificate). Program faculty: 1 full-time (0 women), 18 part-time (6 women). *Degree requirements:* For master's, 1 foreign language, computer language required, thesis not required. *Entrance requirements:* For master's, GMAT. Application deadline: 7/1 (priority date; rolling processing; 12/1 for spring admission). Application fee: $30. *Tuition:* $416 per credit hour. • Dr. Mohammed Eftekhari, Director, 612-962-4840. Application contact: Wendy Williams, Student Services Manager, 612-962-4847. Fax: 612-962-4129.

University of Scranton, Program in Business Administration, Scranton, PA 18510-4622. Offerings include personnel/labor (MBA). Program faculty: 39 full-time (9 women), 1 part-time (0 women). *Entrance requirements:* GMAT, TOEFL (minimum score 500), minimum GPA of 2.75. Application deadline: rolling. Application fee: $35. *Expenses:* Tuition $465 per credit. Fees $25 per semester. • Dr. Wayne H. J. Cunningam, Director, 717-941-4043. Fax: 717-941-4342. E-mail: cunninghamw1@uofs.edu.

University of Scranton, Department of Health Administration and Human Resources, Program in Human Resources Administration, Scranton, PA 18510-4622. Offers human resources (MS), human resources development (MS), organizational leadership (MS). Part-time and evening/weekend programs available. Students: 7 full-time (6 women), 53 part-time (38 women); includes 2 minority (1 African American, 1 Hispanic), 3 international. Average age 33. 46 applicants, 83% accepted. In 1997, 35 degrees awarded. *Degree requirements:* Comprehensive exam required, foreign language and thesis not required. *Entrance requirements:* TOEFL (minimum score 575), minimum GPA of 2.75. Application deadline: rolling. Application fee: $35. *Expenses:* Tuition $465 per credit. Fees $25 per semester. *Financial aid:* Teaching assistantships, teaching fellowships, Federal Work-Study, and career-related internships or fieldwork available. Aid available to part-time students. Financial aid application deadline: 3/1. • Dr. Daniel J. West, Chair, Department of Health Administration and Human Resources, 717-941-4126. Fax: 717-941-4201. E-mail: westd1@uofs.edu.

University of South Carolina, Graduate School, College of Business Administration, Program in Human Resources, Columbia, SC 29208. Awards MHR, JD/MHR. Part-time programs available. Faculty: 16 full-time (3 women). Students: 48 full-time (37 women), 4 part-time (3 women); includes 4 minority (3 African Americans, 1 Hispanic). Average age 25. 88 applicants, 34% accepted. In 1997, 24 degrees awarded (100% found work related to degree). *Degree requirements:* Internship required, thesis optional, foreign language not required. *Entrance requirements:* GMAT (minimum score 550; average 570), minimum GPA of 3.0. Application deadline: 2/1 (priority date). Application fee: $35. Electronic applications accepted. *Financial aid:* In 1997–98, 32 students received aid, including 12 fellowships (10 to first-year students), 10 research assistantships (all to first-year students); Federal Work-Study, institutionally sponsored loans, and career-related internships or fieldwork also available. Financial aid application deadline: 2/1. *Faculty research:* Performance appraisal, work values, grievance systems, union formation, group behavior. Total annual research expenditures: $20,000. • Jane Wills, Managing Director, 803-777-4393. E-mail: jane@darla.badm.sc.edu. Application contact: Carol Williams, Director of Admissions, 803-777-6749. Fax: 803-777-0414. E-mail: carol@darla.badm.sc.edu.

The University of Texas at Arlington, College of Business Administration, Department of Management, Arlington, TX 76019-0407. Offers program in personnel and human resources management (MS). Students: 5 full-time (3 women), 11 part-time (10 women); includes 1 minority (Hispanic). 16 applicants, 31% accepted. In 1997, 7 degrees awarded. *Degree requirements:* Thesis optional. *Entrance requirements:* GMAT (minimum score 480; average 533). Application deadline: rolling. Application fee: $25 ($50 for international students). *Tuition:* $3206 per year full-time, $468 per semester (minimum) part-time for state residents; $8612 per year full-time, $1137 per semester (minimum) part-time for nonresidents. *Financial aid:* Career-related internships or fieldwork available. • Dr. Abdul Rasheed, Chair, 817-272-3166. Application contact: Dr. Kenneth Wheeler, Graduate Adviser, 817-272-3166.

University of the Sacred Heart, Graduate Programs, Department of Business Administration, Program in Human Resource Management, San Juan, PR 00914-0383. Awards MBA. Part-time and evening/weekend programs available. Faculty: 6 full-time (3 women), 11 part-time (1 woman), 9.67 FTE. Students: 1 (woman) full-time, 20 part-time (12 women). 13 applicants, 46% accepted. *Degree requirements:* Computer language, thesis. *Entrance requirements:* PAEG, minimum undergraduate GPA of 2.5. Application deadline: 5/15. Application fee: $25. *Expenses:* Tuition $150 per credit. Fees $240 per credit. • Prof. Pedro Fraile, Coordinator, 787-728-1515 Ext. 2436. Fax: 787-728-1515 Ext. 2273. E-mail: p_fraile@uscac1.usc.clu.edu. Application contact: Dr. Blanca Villamil, Acting Director, Admissions Office, 787-728-1515 Ext. 3237. Fax: 787-728-2066. E-mail: b_villami@uscsi.usc.clu.edu.

University of Utah, Graduate School of Business, Department of Management, Salt Lake City, UT 84112-1107. Offerings include human resources management (MHRM). Department faculty: 20 full-time (6 women), 11 part-time (1 woman). *Application deadline:* 2/15. *Application fee:* $30 ($50 for international students). *Tuition:* $2045 per year full-time, $562 per semester (minimum) part-time for state residents; $6129 per year full-time, $1607 per semester (minimum) part-time for nonresidents. • William Hesterly, Chair, 801-581-7415. Fax: 801-581-7214.

University of Wisconsin–Madison, School of Business, Program in Management and Human Resources, Madison, WI 53706-1380. Awards MBA, MS. *Entrance requirements:* GMAT. Application deadline: 6/1 (rolling processing; 10/1 for spring admission). Application fee: $38. *Tuition:* $5950 per year full-time, $1118 per semester (minimum) part-time for state residents; $16,230 per year full-time, $3044 per semester (minimum) part-time for nonresidents. *Faculty research:* Employee compensation, performance for work groups, small business management, venture financing, arts industry.

Upper Iowa University, Program in Business Leadership, Fayette, IA 52142-1857. Offerings include human resource management (MA). Also available at Des Moines, Iowa campus; Madison, Wisconsin campus; and Waterloo, Iowa campus. Postbaccalaureate distance learning degree programs offered (no on-campus study). Program faculty: 40. *Degree requirements:* Thesis optional, foreign language not required. *Entrance requirements:* GMAT, GRE, or minimum GPA of 2.5 during last 60 hours. Application deadline: 8/26 (rolling processing). Application fee: $50. *Tuition:* $200 per credit. • Dr. Patrick Langan, Director, 800-773-9298. Fax: 319-425-5383.

Utah State University, College of Business, Program in Human Resource Management, Logan, UT 84322. Awards MSS. Faculty: 15 full-time (3 women). Students: 31 full-time (14 women), 19 part-time (8 women). 31 applicants, 58% accepted. In 1997, 27 degrees awarded. *Degree requirements:* Computer language required, foreign language not required. *Average time to degree:* master's–1.5 years full-time, 2 years part-time. *Entrance requirements:* GMAT (score in 40th percentile or higher), TOEFL (minimum score 550), minimum GPA of 3.0. Application deadline: 6/15 (rolling processing; 10/15 for spring admission). Application fee: $40. *Expenses:* Tuition $1448 per year full-time, $624 per year part-time for state residents; $5082 per year full-time, $2192 per year part-time for nonresidents. Fees $421 per year full-time, $165 per year part-time. *Financial aid:* Fellowships, research assistantships, partial tuition waivers, Federal Work-Study, and career-related internships or fieldwork available. Financial aid application deadline: 4/1. *Faculty research:* International human resources, aging workforce. • Dr. John R. Cragun, Head, 435-797-2271. E-mail: cragun@cc.usu.edu. Application contact: Shari Tarnutzer, Graduate Program Adviser, 435-797-3736. Fax: 435-797-1091. E-mail: starnut@b202.usu.edu.

Virginia Commonwealth University, College of Humanities and Sciences, Department of Political Science and Public Administration, Richmond, VA 23284-9005. Offerings include human resources management (MPA), public personnel (MPA). Department faculty: 8 full-time. *Entrance requirements:* GMAT, GRE General Test (minimum combined score of 1000), LSAT, or MAT, interview. Application fee: $30 ($0 for international students). *Tuition:* $4960 per year full-time, $257 per credit part-time for state residents; $12,652 per year full-time, $684 per credit part-time for nonresidents. • Dr. Scott Keeter, Chair, 804-828-1575. E-mail: skeeter@vcu.edu. Application contact: Dr. Ralph S. Hambrick, Graduate Program Director, 804-828-1046. Fax: 804-828-7463. E-mail: rhambric@vcu.edu.

Virginia Commonwealth University, School of Business, Program in Human Resources Management and Industrial Relations, Richmond, VA 23284-9005. Awards MS. *Entrance requirements:* GMAT. Application deadline: rolling. Application fee: $30 ($0 for international students). *Tuition:* $4960 per year full-time, $257 per credit part-time for state residents; $12,652 per year full-time, $684 per credit part-time for nonresidents. *Financial aid:* Fellowships, research assistantships, teaching assistantships, full and partial tuition waivers, Federal Work-Study, institutionally sponsored loans available. Financial aid application deadline: 3/15. • Darrel R. Brown, Chair, 804-828-6468. Fax: 804-828-1600. E-mail: drbrown@vcu.edu. Application contact: Dr. Edward L. Millner, Associate Dean of Graduate Studies, 804-828-1741. Fax: 804-828-7174.

Webster University, School of Business and Technology, Department of Business, St. Louis, MO 63119-3194. Offerings include human resources management (MA). Department faculty: 5 full-time (1 woman). *Application deadline:* rolling. *Application fee:* $25 ($50 for international students). *Tuition:* $350 per credit hour. • Lucille Berry, Chair, 314-968-7022. Fax: 314-968-7077. E-mail: berrylm@webster.edu. Application contact: Beth Russell, Director of Graduate Admissions, 314-968-7089. Fax: 314-968-7166. E-mail: russellmb@webster.edu.

Western New England College, School of Business, Program in Human Resources, Springfield, MA 01119-2654. Awards MBA. *Application deadline:* rolling. *Application fee:* $30. *Expenses:* Tuition $353 per credit hour. Fees $44 per semester (minimum). *Financial aid:* Application deadline 4/1. • Application contact: Rod Pease, Director of Student Administrative Services, 413-796-2080.

Widener University, School of Business Administration, Program in Human Resource Management, Chester, PA 19013-5792. Awards MS. Part-time and evening/weekend programs available. Faculty: 5 full-time (1 woman), 5 part-time (3 women). Students: 4 full-time, 74 part-time; includes 3 international. Average age 34. 37 applicants, 84% accepted. In 1997, 21 degrees awarded. *Average time to degree:* master's–2 years full-time, 4 years part-time. *Entrance requirements:* GMAT, GRE, or MAT. Application deadline: 8/1 (priority date; rolling processing; 12/1 for spring admission). Application fee: $25 ($300 for international students). *Tuition:* $455 per credit. *Financial aid:* Research assistantships, Federal Work-Study available. Aid available to part-time students. *Faculty research:* Training and development, collective bargaining and arbitration, business communication. • Lisa Bussom Jr., Director, Graduate Programs in Business, School of Business Administration, 610-499-4305. Fax: 610-499-4615. E-mail: gradbus.advise@widener.edu.

Wilkes University, Programs in Business Administration, Wilkes-Barre, PA 18766-0002. Offerings include human resource management (MBA). MBA (management, management informa-

Directory: Human Resources Management; Cross-Discipline Announcement

Wilkes University (continued)

tion systems) being phased out; applicants no longer accepted. Faculty: 11 full-time, 2 part-time. *Entrance requirements:* GMAT. Application deadline: rolling. Application fee: $30. *Expenses:* Tuition $12,552 per year full-time, $523 per credit hour part-time. Fees $240 per year full-time, $10 per credit hour part-time. • Dr. Robert Seeley, Director, 717-408-4717.

Wilmington College, Division of Business, New Castle, DE 19720-6491. Offerings include human resource management (MS). *Average time to degree:* master's–3 years part-time. *Application deadline:* rolling. *Application fee:* $25. *Expenses:* Tuition $4410 per year full-time, $735 per course part-time. Fees $50 per year. • Dr. John Camp, Chair, 302-328-9401. Application contact: Michael Lee, Director of Admissions and Financial Aid, 302-328-9401 Ext. 102.

Cross-Discipline Announcement

Illinois Institute of Technology, Institute of Psychology, Chicago, IL 60616-3793.

The Institute of Psychology at IIT offers the master's degree in personnel and human resource development (PHRD) and the master's and PhD degrees in industrial/organizational (I/O) psychology. The I/O program prepares students for academic, consulting, or human resource management and organizational development careers.

RUTGERS, THE STATE UNIVERSITY OF NEW JERSEY, NEW BRUNSWICK

Graduate Programs in Human Resource Management, Labor and Industrial Relations

Programs of Study

The School of Management and Labor Relations (SMLR) offers a Ph.D. in industrial relations and human resources, a Master of Human Resources Management (M.H.R.M.), and a Master of Labor and Industrial Relations (M.L.I.R.).

The Ph.D. program is designed to prepare students for academic positions in colleges and universities. It consists of 58 credit hours of course work and 24 credit hours of dissertation study. All students take seven courses to fulfill their interdisciplinary distributional requirements, including a minimum of three statistics and research methods courses, two Ph.D. seminars, the Pro-Seminar, and six electives. The Ph.D. program requires full-time study.

The M.H.R.M. degree, which requires 48 credits of course work, focuses on the strategic role of HRM in shaping and supporting the organization's business plan. It is a professional program integrating theory and practice, training students to become internal consultants and business partners. Students are accepted into the program on a full-time or part-time basis, and courses are scheduled in the late afternoon and evening for the convenience of working adults. The proximity of a wide variety of the nation's leading businesses provides excellent opportunities for internships, research, and eventual job placement. The program is also offered in Singapore, Indonesia, and off-site in New Jersey at firms such as AT&T and Prudential.

The M.L.I.R. program, which requires 39 credits of course work, affords students the opportunity to explore the causes and consequences of changes in labor relations as well as to develop the professional skills necessary to function in their chosen fields. The program combines professional education in the discipline of labor relations with a broader approach to the study of work and work-related issues. Students prepare to pursue careers in the labor movement, in labor relations for private and public sector employers, or in government agencies that regulate employment.

Research Facilities

The School of Management and Labor Relations conducts programs of graduate instruction, research, and continuing professional education for both management and labor to further their understanding of human resources management, the process of industrial relations, and public employment and training policy.

SMLR has a specialized library within the 3 million–volume University library system. The SMLR library provides access to leading journals, reporting services, and databases in industrial relations and human resources. Graduate students have access to the school's thirty-five–station state-of-the-art computer laboratory and Rutgers' Center for Computer and Information Services, which contains some of the most powerful and innovative computer equipment in the country. Students are encouraged to develop computer skills through courses that rely heavily on the computer and its application to human resource issues.

Financial Aid

Research and teaching assistantships are available on a competitive basis. There are also opportunities for paid employment and paid or unpaid internships in the New Jersey–New York–Pennsylvania area. Rutgers is a member of the Industrial Relations Council of GOALS, a nationwide coalition of industrial relations graduate schools and departments joined in a comprehensive campaign to recruit minority students. Work-study programs and Federal Stafford Student Loans are offered by the Financial Aid Office. The University offers Graduate Scholar Awards, Garden State Fellowships, Ralph J. Bunche Fellowships, and tuition awards.

Cost of Study

State residents pursuing graduate full-time study without financial assistance from the University paid tuition and student fees totaling $6700 for the 1997–98 academic year. Nonresidents and international students paid $9528.

Living and Housing Costs

Dormitory housing for the 1997–98 academic year ranged from $4102 to $4682. A full meal plan for the academic year cost $2202. Off-campus housing is generally more costly.

Student Group

One to 7 students are admitted to the Ph.D. program each fall, about 150 students are enrolled in the M.H.R.M. program, and 40 are enrolled in the M.L.I.R. program. Two thirds are women. The average age is 30.

Student Outcomes

Because the programs provide students with a broad theoretical foundation and an impressive array of professional skills, graduates have consistently obtained excellent positions in a variety of organizations. Recent placements of SMLR students include IBM, AT&T, Merck, Schering-Plough, GE, Merrill Lynch, Allied Signal, CWA, and SEIU.

Location

New Brunswick, with a population of about 42,000, is located in central New Jersey at Exit 9 of the New Jersey Turnpike and along the New York–Philadelphia railroad line. It is approximately 35 miles from New York City. To the south lie Princeton, 16 miles away; Philadelphia, about 60 miles; and Washington, D.C., under 200 miles. The many educational, cultural, and recreational resources of the New York–Philadelphia region are easily accessible to the interested student, and Rutgers attracts many distinguished visitors, lecturers, and performing artists not always available to less favorably situated institutions.

The University

As a university strongly committed to graduate education and research, Rutgers, The State University of New Jersey, provides graduate programs of exceptional academic quality taught by a distinguished faculty. Chartered in 1766, Rutgers is now one of the nation's largest state university systems; enrollment at the New Brunswick, Newark, and Camden campuses is approximately 48,000 students.

Applying

The M.H.R.M. and M.L.I.R. program application deadlines are March 1 for the summer session, May 1 (M.H.R.M.) and July 1 (M.L.I.R.) for the fall semester, and November 1 (M.H.R.M.) and December 1 (M.L.I.R.) for the spring semester. The Ph.D. program deadline is March 1 for fall admission. The Graduate Record Examinations General Test or the Graduate Management Admissions Test is required. The M.H.R.M. and M.L.I.R. programs have a rolling admission policy. Admission decisions are made by judgment, not formula, but successful applicants are expected to achieve competitive grades and scores and provide letters of recommendation that indicate potential for graduate study.

Correspondence and Information

Director
Graduate Programs in HRM and IRHR
Janice H. Levin Building
Rutgers, The State University of New Jersey
Rockafeller Road
New Brunswick, New Jersey 08903-5062
Telephone: 908-445-5973
E-mail: mhrm@rci.rutgers.edu

Director
Graduate Program in Labor and Industrial Relations
Labor Education Center
Rutgers, The State University of New Jersey
Ryders Lane
P.O. Box 231
New Brunswick, New Jersey 08903
Telephone: 908-932-8559
E-mail: mlir@rci.rutgers.edu

Rutgers, The State University of New Jersey, New Brunswick

THE FACULTY AND THEIR RESEARCH

John R. Aiello, Ph.D., Michigan State. Industrial and organizational psychology, environmental stress, nonverbal communications.
Clayton Alderfer, Ph.D., Yale. Organizational behavior and organizational change.
Richard W. Beatty, Ph.D., Washington (St. Louis). Performance management, compensation, strategic human resource management.
David Bensman, Ph.D., Columbia. American labor history, contemporary collective bargaining, international labor issues.
Joseph Blasi, Ed.D., Harvard. Employee ownership, management stock ownership, profit sharing, corporate governance, privatization in transitional and stable economies.
John Burton, Ph.D., LL.D., Michigan. Workers' compensation and occupational safety and health law, other types of social insurance programs.
Cary Cherniss, Ph.D., Yale. Job stress and burnout, careers, organizational change, supervision.
Dorothy Sue Cobble, Ph.D., Stanford. History of work and of labor-management relations, impact of the service workforce.
Steven M. Director, Ph.D., Northwestern. Interaction between public and private employment policy.
Adrienne Eaton, Ph.D., Wisconsin. Labor-management cooperation and employee involvement programs with a particular focus on union roles in these programs.
Charles H. Fay, Ph.D., Washington (Seattle). Compensation, performance management, work redesign, and the use of human resource decision support systems.
Stanley M. Gully, Ph.D., Michigan State. Training, teams, leadership, motivation, multilevel phenomena.
Charles Heckscher, Ph.D., Harvard. Changing roles and attitudes of managers and professionals concerning corporate change, emerging forms of corporate organizations, effectiveness of "mutual gains" bargaining, the relation of organized labor to employment-rights movements.
Mark Huselid, Ph.D., SUNY at Buffalo. Linkages between human resource management systems, corporate strategy, and firm performance.
Susan E. Jackson, Ph.D., Berkeley. Teamwork, workforce diversity, strategically aligned human resource management systems.
Jeffrey H. Keefe, Ph.D., Cornell. Collective bargaining, technological and organizational change in unionized settings.
Marlene Kim, Ph.D., Berkeley. Compensation, discrimination, pay equity, and the working poor.
Douglas L. Kruse, Ph.D., Harvard. Profit sharing, employee ownership, worker displacement, wage differentials.
Barbara A. Lee, Ph.D., Ohio State; J.D., Georgetown. Impact of legislation and judicial decisions on employment relations policy and practices in academic and business organizations in the U.S. and Western Europe.
Claudia G. Meer, Ed.D., Rutgers. Training and development and adult learning.
Charles A. Nanry, Ph.D., Rutgers. Training policy, public personnel management, training and program evaluation.
Jean M. Phillips, Ph.D., Michigan State. Teams and leadership, motivation, recruitment, socialization.
Saul Rubenstein, Ph.D., MIT. New forms of firm governance and work organizations.
Randall S. Schuler, Ph.D., Michigan State. Strategic human resource management, international human resource management.
Susan Schurman, Ph.D., Michigan. Labor, workers, and the work environment.
Ryan A. Smith, Ph.D., UCLA. Social stratification, managing workplace diversity and race and ethnic relations.
Kirsten Wever, Ph.D., MIT. International and comparative political economy and labor/business/government relations, gender and economic development.
John D. Worrall, Ph.D., Rutgers. Workers' compensation, property-casualty insurance, labor economics.

SAINT FRANCIS COLLEGE

Graduate School of Human Resource Management and Industrial Relations

Program of Study

The Graduate School of Human Resource Management and Industrial Relations offers a ten-course (30-credit) program leading to the Master of Arts (M.A.) degree in human resource management and industrial relations. The program is accredited by the Middle States Association of Colleges and Schools.

Classes are offered at three sites: Loretto, Harrisburg, and Pittsburgh. Students can take all courses required for the degree in any of the three sites. Three courses are offered each semester (fall, spring, and summer).

The Graduate School of Human Resource Management and Industrial Relations offers a program for working professionals and new career entrants. The program is designed to accommodate the needs of working professionals by offering evening courses at all three locations. Full-time students can complement their evening courses with part-time internships and strengthen their credentials for entering the human resources field.

Students may begin the program in any semester; however, full-time students are encouraged to start in the fall. It is recommended that working professionals enroll for no more than two courses per semester. Part-time students usually graduate in two to three years; full-time students graduate in 1½ years. Students have five years to complete all degree requirements.

Students benefit from real-world practical applications in classes taught by faculty members who are experienced in human resource management and industrial relations issues.

Upon completing the ten-course program with a minimum GPA of 3.0, students sit for the Professional in Human Resources (PHR) or Senior Professional in Human Resources (SPHR) examination administered by the Society for Human Resource Management to complete the requirements for graduation.

Research Facilities

The Pasquarilla Library at Saint Francis College is available to all students; it can also be accessed on the College's Web site. Articles from 1,000 periodicals can be accessed and sent to a student's e-mail through the INNVIEW database on line, and research titles can be accessed through the online database FRANCIS. Students can borrow College holdings by either visiting the library or by contacting library staff.

The Pasquarilla Library has also made arrangements with local libraries in the Pittsburgh and Harrisburg areas to meet the research needs of students in these areas.

Financial Aid

Full-time students may apply to individual departments on campus for graduate assistantships. Assistantships in the form of tuition remission are awarded for one academic year and cover about 60 percent of total tuition for the degree. The awards are based on academic merit and personal interviews. Partial tuition remission grants of $200 to $400 per semester are available in all locations. Awards are based on academic merit and need. Subsidized, deferred-payment Federal Stafford Student Loans are available to students taking at least two courses (6 credits or more) who meet eligibility requirements.

Cost of Study

Tuition for the academic year 1998–99 is $420 per credit; all courses are 3 credits. There are no fees except for the graduation fee of $125. The cost of books varies with each course.

Living and Housing Costs

Dormitory facilities are available only in Loretto. Students who are interested in reserving rooms should contact the Residence Life Office by April 15. Costs are approximately $3340 per semester for room and board (the exact amount depends upon the plan chosen). Students in the Pittsburgh and Harrisburg centers interested in housing should contact rental agencies in those areas.

Student Group

The student population totals 125 students in three centers, 35 percent men and 65 percent women. There are 123 students enrolled in the program part-time; 2 students are enrolled full-time. Enrollments at each campus are as follows: Loretto, 35; Pittsburgh, 56; and Harrisburg, 34. Students range in age from 22 to 55 years; the average age is 33. Most students enter the program after having established their careers. Admissions decisions are based on undergraduate GPA, personal recommendations, and working experience in the field.

Student Outcomes

According to the most recent survey, 95 of the graduates who responded are employed. They hold such position titles as Vice President/Manager of Personnel, Director of Human Resources, Senior Human Resources Consultant, Employee Relations Manager, Benefits Specialist, and Human Resources Coordinator. Graduates are also employed in variety of other administrative positions.

Location

Class sites are located in Loretto, Pittsburgh, and Harrisburg, Pennsylvania. The main campus is located in Loretto, a rural area 25 miles east of Johnstown and 20 miles west of Altoona. Downtown Pittsburgh classes are held in the Union Trust Building at 501 Grant Street, and Harrisburg classes are held at the Harrisburg Area Community College Wildwood Campus.

The College and The School

Saint Francis College was founded in 1847 under the tradition of the Franciscan Friars of the Third Order Regular. The College's philosophy of education emphasizes two values: instruction of high quality and respect for the student as an individual. Total enrollment is 1,886 students.

Saint Francis College acknowledges the growing importance of graduate education and fully supports the M.A. in human resource management/industrial relations program. The Graduate School of Human Resource Management and Industrial Relations was established by Saint Francis College in 1961, with centers established in Harrisburg in 1971 and in Pittsburgh in 1976. A new curriculum implemented in the fall of 1997 was modeled after the certification standards set by the Society for Human Resource Management.

Applying

Applications for the Graduate School of Human Resource Management and Industrial Relations are accepted on a rolling basis up to three weeks prior to the semester in which the student wishes to enroll. Applicants must provide a completed application form, a fee of $15, an official transcript from their undergraduate college certifying a bachelor's degree, and three recommendation forms. No graduate testing is required. An admissions decision is made within two weeks after all materials have been received.

Correspondence and Information

Philip Benham, Ph.D., SPHR
Director
Graduate School of Human Resource Management and Industrial Relations
Saint Francis College
Loretto, Pennsylvania 15940-0600

Telephone: 814-472-3026 (direct number)
800-457-6300 Ext. 3026 (toll-free in Pennsylvania)
Fax: 814-472-3369
E-mail: hrir@sfcpa.edu
World Wide Web: http://www.sfcpa.edu (click on Academic Programs, Graduate Programs, and then HRM/IR)

Saint Francis College

THE FACULTY AND THEIR RESEARCH

Loretto Campus

David Andrews, Adjunct Professor of Employment and Labor Law and Managing Partner, law firm of Andrews and Wagner; J.D., Dickinson Law, 1977. Labor law, alternative dispute resolution, Family and Medical Leave Act.

Carl Beard, Adjunct Assistant Professor of Employment and Labor Law and Partner, law firm of Andrews and Wagner; J.D., Ohio Northern, 1980. Collective bargaining.

Philip Benham, Associate Professor and Director of the Graduate School of Human Resource Management and Industrial Relations; Ph.D., Colorado, 1980; SPHR. Performance management, management development.

James Lakso, Adjunct Professor of Human Resource Management and Acting Provost/Professor of Economics at Juniata College; Ph.D., Maryland, 1973. Compensation.

Christina Gatehouse Long, Adjunct Instructor in Human Resource Management and Human Resources Specialist at Memorial Medical Center; M.A., Saint Francis (Pennsylvania), 1997. Benefits.

Deirdre Moloney, Adjunct Assistant Professor of Labor History and Assistant Professor of History/Political Science at Saint Francis College; Ph.D., Wisconsin, 1995. History of American labor.

Bradley Reist, Adjunct Instructor in Human Resource Management and Human Resources Manager at Appleton Papers Inc; M.A., Saint Francis (Pennsylvania), 1989; SPHR. Human resource management.

John Showalter, Adjunct Instructor in Human Resource Management and Mill Manager at Appleton Papers Inc; M.S., Ohio, 1975. Health and safety.

Christine Smith, Adjunct Instructor in Human Resource Management and Vice President of Human Resources at Allegheny Lutheran Social Ministries; M.A., Saint Francis College, 1990; SPHR. Diversity and changing work practices.

Michael Wagner, Adjunct Assistant Professor of Employment and Labor Law and Partner, law firm of Andrews and Wagner; J.D., Dickinson Law, 1983. Employment law, employment discrimination law.

Pittsburgh Center

Walter Bleil, Adjunct Professor of Employment and Labor Law and Partner, law firm of Deopken, Keevican and Weiss; J.D., Harvard, 1975. Alternative dispute resolution.

David Borrebach, Adjunct Associate Professor of Human Resource Management and Senior Consultant and Associate in the Pittsburgh office of William M. Mercer, Inc; Ph.D., George Peabody, 1977. Compensation.

Ruth Carosone, Adjunct Instructor in Human Resource Management and Human Resource Manager, Travelers Aetna Property Casualty Corporation; M.A., Saint Francis (Pennsylvania), 1993; SPHR. Performance management.

Eugene Connors, Adjunct Professor of Employment and Labor Law and Partner, law firm of Reed, Smith, Shaw and McClay; J.D., Columbia, 1971. Alternative dispute resolution.

Charles Frame, Adjunct Instructor in Human Resource Management and Director of Employee Services at the U.S. Steel Group of the USX Corporation; M.A., Saint Francis (Pennsylvania), 1984. Human resource management.

Nicholas Kachur, Adjunct Instructor in Human Resource Management and Director of Safety and Security, Neville Chemical Company; M.S., Indiana of Pennsylvania, 1996. Health and safety.

Albert Lee, Adjunct Assistant Professor of Employment and Labor Law and Partner, law firm of Bechtol, Lee, and Eberhard Associates; J.D., Pittsburgh, 1991. Employment law.

Mark McColloch, Adjunct Professor of Labor History and Chairperson of Behavioral Sciences Division and Associate Professor of History at the University of Pittsburgh at Greensburg; Ph.D., Pittsburgh, 1975. History of American labor.

Samuel Pasquarelli, Adjunct Associate Professor of Employment and Labor Law and Partner, law firm of Sherrard, German, and Kelly; J.D., Duquesne, 1967. Labor law, collective bargaining.

Harrisburg Center

Vincent Candiello, Adjunct Assistant Professor of Employment and Labor Law and of counsel, law firm of Morgan, Lewis and Bockius; J.D., Detroit, 1978. Alternative dispute resolution.

Jennifer Cooney, Adjunct Instructor in Human Resource Management and President, Employment Dispute Resolutions, Inc.; M.A., Saint Francis (Pennsylvania), 1994; SPHR, CEBS. Compensation.

Kurt Decker, Adjunct Professor of Employment and Labor Law and Partner, law firm of Stevens and Lee; J.D., Vanderbilt, 1976. Labor law and employment law.

Janet McNally, Adjunct Instructor in Human Resource Management and Manager of Professional Staffing at AMP, Inc; M.A., Saint Francis (Pennsylvania), 1980. Performance management.

Ferdinand Molz, Adjunct Professor of Human Resource Management and Professor of Business Administration, Millersville University; Ph.D., Catholic University, 1968. Collective bargaining.

Bruce Nilson, Adjunct Instructor in Human Resource Management and Certified Management Consultant and President, Bruce Nilson Associates, Inc.; M.S., Penn State, 1981; CMC. Leadership.

Ronald Schaible, Adjunct Instructor in Human Resource Management and Consultant, Schaible Associates; M.S., West Chester, 1990; CSP, CIH. Health and safety.

Evening classes, such as this Performance Management class taught by the Director, Dr. Philip Benham, allow the student to study for a Master of Arts degree while holding a full-time position during the day.

Small classes provide the opportunity for faculty members to give individual attention to the students. Attorney Samuel Pasquarelli assists students in this Labor Law class.

UNIVERSITY OF BRIDGEPORT

School of Education and Human Resources
Division of Counseling and Human Resources
Master of Science in Counseling

Program of Study

The Division of Counseling and Human Resources offers a Master of Science degree with specializations in community agency counseling and human resource development and counseling.

The community agency counseling program emphasizes academic courses and field experiences, which prepare students to provide counseling services in public or private agencies that offer services to a variety of human services clients. Selected courses in counseling the aged are available.

The human resource development and counseling program is offered in conjunction with the School of Business. Professional development is attained by studying both management and counseling, enabling students to develop their communication, organizational, and management skills.

All programs are community oriented and provide a wide range of experiences in community, agency, or business settings. Community agency students have access to practicums in diverse agencies; human resource students have internships in corporate and public settings.

Research Facilities

The University's Wahlstrom Library contains approximately 275,000 bound volumes (including bound journals and indexes) and more than 1 million microforms and subscribes to more than 1,500 periodicals and other serials. Online database searching is available on the Internet, Dialog, FirstSearch, EBSCO's Academic Search Full Text 1,000, and LEXIS-NEXIS. CD-ROM databases include ERIC, Moody's Company Data, MEDLINE, reQuest, Books in Print Plus (BIP Plus), and the National Trade Data Bank. An extension library is maintained at the Stamford Campus, with more than 500 titles, more than forty periodicals, and extensive electronic access. All students have access to e-mail, Netscape, and word processing. Residence halls are prewired for individual computer hookups.

Financial Aid

Financial aid is available to U.S. citizens in the form of endowed scholarships, Federal Stafford Student Loans, graduate assistantships, and internships. The University also hires graduate students as residence hall directors and assistant hall directors. Further information can be obtained from the Office of Financial Aid at 203-576-4568. International students must demonstrate that they have sufficient funds to finance their studies in the United States. They must complete the financial aid statement for international students that is included in the International Application for Admissions.

Cost of Study

In 1998–99, tuition is $340 per credit hour for up to 12 credit hours per semester.

Living and Housing Costs

Graduate students may reside either in the University's on-campus residence halls or in off-campus apartments or rooms. The cost of off-campus living varies widely. Additional information related to on-campus residency can be obtained from the Office of Residence Life (203-576-4461). A number of counseling students also serve as Residential Directors, who receive a stipend and tuition benefits.

Student Group

The average enrollment in the master's program is 110 students, evenly split between the community agency and human resource specializations. Most community agency students are part-time, employed in the region, and taking evening and weekend courses. More than 90 percent of human resource majors pursue the degree on weekends over a twenty-two-month period at the Stamford Campus.

Location

The University of Bridgeport's 86-acre campus is situated on Long Island Sound. The University's Stamford Campus is a convenient location for counseling and human resource students from Connecticut as well as Westchester County, New York, and New Jersey.

The University

Founded in 1927, the University is a private, nonsectarian, comprehensive, urban university of more than 2,600 students. Approximately half of the total student body are graduate students. The University's campus is composed of ninety-one buildings with diverse architectural styles. The Bernhard Arts and Humanities Center is a cultural hub, and the Wheeler Recreation Center is a complete recreation and physical fitness facility.

Applying

Students are admitted to the programs from various undergraduate backgrounds. Undergraduate records, work experience, a personal statement of professional goals, and two letters of recommendation are used to evaluate applicants. TOEFL scores are required for students whose primary language is not English. The University has an intensive English program on campus for students who require additional English language study. Students may enter in the fall or spring semester. Electronic applications are welcome through the University's Web site and Polaris.

Correspondence and Information

Office of Admissions
University of Bridgeport
126 Park Avenue
Bridgeport, Connecticut 06601
Telephone: 203-576-4552
800-EXCEL-UB (392-3582)
Fax: 203-576-4941
E-mail: admit@cse.bridgeport.edu
World Wide Web: http://www.bridgeport.edu

Division of Counseling and Human Resources
Carlson Hall
University of Bridgeport
Bridgeport, Connecticut 06601
Telephone: 203-576-4175
Fax: 203-576-4200

University of Bridgeport

THE FACULTY AND THEIR RESEARCH

Dorothy Hurley, Ed.D., Temple. Organization development.
John E. Lewison, M.B.A., NYU. Management.
Joan O'Connell, M.S., Bridgeport. Group process.
Joseph Onofrio II, M.S., Bridgeport. Youth, family therapy.
Joseph Nechasek, Ph.D., SUNY at Buffalo. Health policy and benefits.
Phanos Patelis, Ph.D., Fordham. Research methods, statistics.
Larry Phillips, Ed.D., Ball State. Community and college counseling.
Gerald Seen, Ed.D., SUNY at Albany. Counseling theory.
Michael J. Stacey, Ed.D., Massachusetts. Management of human resources.

UNIVERSITY OF ILLINOIS AT URBANA–CHAMPAIGN

Institute of Labor and Industrial Relations

Programs of Study

The Institute of Labor and Industrial Relations is a graduate program offering both the Master of Human Resources and Industrial Relations (M.H.R.I.R.) and the Doctor of Philosophy (Ph.D.) in human resources and industrial relations. Graduate work for the master's degree program includes twelve courses and usually takes three semesters to complete. Required courses in the master's program include human resources/industrial relations systems, quantitative methods, and research/analytical methods. Students have a choice among the following three subject distributions as areas of concentration: human resource management and organizational behavior, labor markets and employment, and unions, management, and labor relations policy. Career opportunities in business firms include human resource generalist, labor relations specialist, compensation and benefits analyst, training and development specialist, labor relations administrator, and other human resource functions. Employment opportunities with government agencies, educational institutions, municipalities, and union organizations offer other career alternatives.

Graduate work at the Ph.D. level leads primarily to academic research and teaching careers in management or industrial relations departments in business schools. The program can be completed in three to four years beyond the master's degree. The doctoral degree requires 24 units of course work, including a thesis.

Research Facilities

The University's library has the third-largest collection among academic libraries in the United States. The Institute's departmental library, housed in its own building, has an extensive labor and human resource collection with a full-time librarian and a responsive and informed staff. The computer laboratory is equipped with state-of-the-art personal computers, networked for worldwide access by scholars and practitioners in the field, that operate current software packages used in organizations.

Financial Aid

Extremely competitive financial aid awards are available from the Institute. Award recipients are selected on the basis of academic excellence. Fellowships that include a tuition and service-fee waiver and research assistantships are available to highly qualified students. Some fellowships sponsored by various organizations, corporations, and alumni funds are designated for students in a particular area of interest or from a minority group. There is no separate form on which to apply for financial aid. For information on loans, grants, and need-based aid from the government or other University sources, students should contact the Student Financial Aid Office, Turner Student Services Building, 610 East John Street, Champaign, Illinois 61820 (telephone: 217-333-0100).

Cost of Study

Tuition and fees are approximately $4990 for state residents and $11,860 for nonresidents for the 1998–99 academic year. Textbook expenses range from $500 to $800 per year.

Living and Housing Costs

University housing is available for single and married graduate students. Privately owned housing is abundant near campus, and monthly rent for an unfurnished two-bedroom apartment ranges from $300 to $500. Students should contact the University Housing Office (telephone: 217-333-1752 or e-mail: famhouse@uiuc.edu) for more complete information.

Student Group

The Institute strives to maintain a student body balanced in geographic, gender, and ethnic composition. Students from every region of the United States and the world are actively recruited and offered financial aid packages. With a student population of about 120, a multiplicity of perspectives and experience characterize the student population. The Institute fosters racial, ethnic, and international diversity to accurately reflect the complexity of today's workplace.

Location

The University of Illinois is located in the twin cities of Champaign and Urbana, with a combined population of about 110,000. The University enhances the community through a large variety of performing arts and entertainment bookings, in addition to various museums and intramural and intercollegiate athletic facilities. Champaign-Urbana is near the center of the state at the crossroads of two major interstate highways that lead to three regional metropolitan centers. Chicago is 130 miles to the north, St. Louis is 150 miles to the south, and Indianapolis is 110 miles to the east. Excellent park facilities for hiking, camping, and other outdoor activities are nearby.

The University and The Institute

The University of Illinois at Urbana-Champaign, founded in 1867 as one of the original thirty-seven public land-grant institutions, today ranks among the world's great universities. It offers more than 150 fields of study for its 26,000 undergraduates and more than 100 disciplines for nearly 10,000 graduate and professional students. The Institute's size, with approximately 100 students, provides fertile ground for learning, research, and close interaction with those at the vanguard of workplace issues from management and labor sectors. The Institute's faculty members represent a variety of disciplines and workplace perspectives.

Applying

Students enter the Institute with a wide range of social science backgrounds. Psychology, business administration, history, economics, political science, and communication are typical undergraduate areas of study. Admission to the master's program is made for fall and spring semesters. The application deadline for the fall semester is February 1; for the spring semester, it is November 1. Admission to the doctoral program is made for the fall semester only. The General Test of the Graduate Record Examinations (GRE) is required for both programs. The GMAT is also acceptable. The Graduate College application and three letter of reference are also required.

Correspondence and Information

Institute of Labor and Industrial Relations
University of Illinois at Urbana-Champaign
504 East Armory Avenue
Champaign, Illinois 61820
Telephone: 217-333-1480
Fax: 217-244-9290
World Wide Web: http://www.ilir.uiuc.edu

University of Illinois at Urbana-Champaign

THE FACULTY AND THEIR RESEARCH

Robert Bruno, Assistant Professor of Labor and Industrial Relations, Chicago Labor Education Program; Ph.D. (political theory/American politics), NYU. Working-class culture, social context of welfare reform, class consciousness and political theory.

Peter J. Carnevale, Associate Professor of Psychology and of Labor and Industrial Relations; Ph.D. (psychology), SUNY at Buffalo. Negotiation, mediation, and dispute resolution processes in organizations.

Fritz Drasgow, Professor of Psychology and of Labor and Industrial Relations; Ph.D. (psychology), Illinois at Urbana-Champaign. Psychological testing and issues related to fairness in hiring and merit promotion, test bias, mismeasurement, and evaluation in human resource decision making.

Helen Elkiss, Associate Professor of Labor and Industrial Relations, Chicago Labor Education Program; M.L.I.R. (labor and industrial relations), Michigan State. Women's leadership in trade unions, occupational health and safety, labor and technological change.

Gerald Ferris, Professor of Labor and Industrial Relations, Business Administration, and Psychology; Ph.D. (human resource management/organizational behavior), Illinois at Urbana-Champaign. Political behavior and influence in organizations, performance evaluation, human resources strategy.

Peter Feuille, Professor of Labor and Industrial Relations and Director of the Institute; Ph.D. (industrial relations/organizational behavior), Berkeley. Consequences of appealed grievance arbitration awards, nonunion grievance procedures, public sector collective bargaining, political influence and government decision making.

Matthew W. Finkin, Professor of Law and of Labor and Industrial Relations; LL.M., Yale. Employee privacy issues, labor law, arbitral and judicial treatment of conflict of interest issues in the employment relationship.

Kevin F. Hallock, Assistant Professor of Economics and of Labor and Industrial Relations; Ph.D. (economics), Princeton. Executive pay, corporate performance and interlocking directorates, welfare, labor economics and discrimination.

Wallace E. Hendricks, Professor of Economics and of Labor and Industrial Relations; Ph.D. (economics), Berkeley. Graduation rates and career choices for university athletes, labor market returns to education, labor relations in deregulated industries.

Charles L. Hulin, Professor of Psychology and of Labor and Industrial Relations; Ph.D. (psychology), Cornell. Cross-cultural measurement equivalence, organizational response to changes in labor markets and technology.

Michelle Kaminski, Assistant Professor of Labor and Industrial Relations, Labor Education Program; Ph.D. (organizational psychology), Michigan. Union-management transformation partnerships, high-performance work organizations, union-based health and safety committees and training outcomes.

John J. Lawler, Associate Professor of Labor and Industrial Relations; Ph.D. (industrial relations/organizational behavior), Berkeley. Computer applications in human resource management, international human resource practices, and labor-management relations.

Michael H. LeRoy, Associate Professor of Labor and Industrial Relations, Labor Education Program; J.D., North Carolina. Striker replacements and public policy, labor-management cooperation and government employment regulation.

Joseph J. Martocchio, Associate Professor of Labor and Industrial Relations; Ph.D. (human resource management), Michigan State. Self-regulatory processes in employee training, compensation systems, self-efficacy, computer technology in training, disciplinary decisions, and absenteeism.

Gregory B. Northcraft, Professor of Business Administration and of Labor and Industrial Relations; Ph.D. (social psychology/organizational behavior), Stanford. Social dilemmas in managing the diverse organization, bargaining and negotiation in the human resource context.

Greg R. Oldham, Professor of Labor and Industrial Relations and C. Clinton Spivey Professor of Business Administration; Ph.D. (organizational behavior), Yale. Office environment, job design and productivity, work redesign, and the psychological well-being of employees.

Elissa L. Perry, Assistant Professor of Labor and Industrial Relations and of Business Administration; Ph.D. (organizational behavior and theory), Carnegie Mellon. Bias in human resource management decision making, sexual harassment and individual differences in the training process.

Ronald J. Peters, Professor of Labor and Industrial Relations and Head of Labor Education Program; Ph.D. (education and continuing education), Michigan State. Collective bargaining in public employment, labor relations in health care, and unions in academe.

Koji Taira, Professor of Economics and of Labor and Industrial Relations; Ph.D. (economics), Stanford. Convergence of industrial relations systems between the United States and Japan, technological progress and global challenges.

David T. Whitford, Associate Professor of Finance and of Labor and Industrial Relations; Ph.D. (finance), Georgia State. Corporate cash flow and equity valuation, executive compensation, capital market efficiency and resource allocation for nonprofit organizations.

UNIVERSITY OF MINNESOTA

Industrial Relations Center

Programs of Study

The University of Minnesota offers both the Master of Arts (M.A.) and the Doctor of Philosophy (Ph.D.) degrees in human resources and industrial relations through the Industrial Relations Center (IRC). The M.A. degree may be completed through either the day or evening program. The course of study focuses on five areas: collective bargaining and labor relations; compensation and benefits; labor market analysis; organization behavior and theory; and staffing, training, and development. Doctoral students are trained to enter the academic world. Master's students usually are hired by major corporations, public sector agencies, and unions for human resource management development programs or as compensation analysts, staffing managers, or human resource representatives.

Full-time day students usually need two years to complete the M.A., while evening students average about 3½ years of part-time study. Both thesis and nonthesis options are offered. The thesis option calls for twelve courses and a thesis. The nonthesis option requires sixteen courses and three papers of thesis quality.

After taking core classes in human resources and industrial relations, the doctoral student completes specialized course work and takes written preliminary examinations in research methodology and in two areas of concentration. Following the oral preliminary exam and the completion of the dissertation, the Ph.D. degree is awarded.

Basic research is conducted on topics that expand current knowledge in human resources and industrial relations. Examples include psychological responses to unemployment, the role of emotionality in the work place, predictors of the use of worker's compensation and unemployment insurance, and the effect of human resource management on firm performance.

Research Facilities

The Industrial Relations Center recently moved to a new state-of-the-art business school facility. Classrooms and laboratories are equipped with the latest hardware and software. The Industrial Relations Center's Reference Room, staffed by librarians knowledgeable in the field, maintains an up-to-date collection of journals, books, reporting services, and other human resources and industrial relations research materials. The University's O. Meredith Wilson Library offers a first-rate collection of social science and business periodicals and books. The Carlson School of Management provides e-mail accounts for all graduate students in the school. Mainframe resources are available on the school's Sun servers. All major statistical software packages are available on these systems. In addition, students may apply for accounts on the University's supercomputers. The school's networked desktops provide access to business software, laser and color printing, and the resources of the Internet.

Financial Aid

Graduate assistantships, fellowships, scholarships, and grants are available. Generally, graduate assistantships and fellowships are allocated for the academic year beginning with the fall quarter, but occasionally money is available at other times during the year. Ph.D. students may be awarded up to four years of annually renewable financial aid.

Cost of Study

During the academic year 1997–98, tuition for full-time day students (12–19 credits) was $1636 per quarter for Minnesota residents and $3287 for nonresidents. Evening students paid $235.70 per credit hour (for 11 or fewer credits) regardless of residency.

Living and Housing Costs

The University has housing for married students and families, including accommodations for single parent families. There is usually a waiting list, but its length fluctuates during the year. The University Housing Office in Comstock Hall, bulletin boards on the West Bank campus, and the *Minnesota Daily* (the student newspaper) list housing opportunities.

Student Group

The University of Minnesota's human resource and industrial relations graduate programs attract students from all over the United States as well as from other countries. More than 10 percent of the students currently come from countries outside of North America, including China, Colombia, Ghana, Hungary, Korea, Taiwan, and Turkey. There are 100 full-time and 110 part-time students in the master's program and 18 students in the Ph.D. program. Master's program graduates take jobs in major corporations and in the public sector throughout the United States. Ph.D. students have accepted academic positions with colleges and universities in the United States, Canada, Indonesia, Israel, Japan, and Korea.

Location

Minneapolis and St. Paul—known as the Twin Cities—are clean and safe, and housing is affordable. The Twin Cities are home to the nationally renowned Guthrie Theater, Walker Art Center, Minneapolis Institute of Arts, historic Fort Snelling, and professional sports teams, the Minnesota Twins, Vikings, and Timberwolves. More than 900 lakes, 500 parks, and 3 rivers are located within the metropolitan region.

The University and The Center

The University of Minnesota, the state's major university, offers graduate students a comprehensive range of programs, collaboration with faculty members in pacesetting research, and an international learning environment. The Industrial Relations Center traces its roots back to the Depression. In 1936, the University established the Employment Stabilization Research Institute (ESRI), which focused on effectively matching individuals to jobs. The ESRI's research strongly influenced U.S. Employment Service testing and job placement programs. A grant from the Rockefeller Foundation established the creation of the Industrial Relations Center in 1945. In 1953, the Master of Arts program was created, and a decade later, the Ph.D. program accepted its first students.

Applying

M.A. students may enter in the fall or spring quarters. Ph.D. students may enroll in any quarter, but most choose to enter in the fall. Students seeking admission for the fall quarter should apply by July 15 and for the spring quarter, by December 15. Students must apply by February 1 for financial aid beginning in the subsequent fall term. Each applicant must take the GRE General Test; no Subject Test is required. The IRC accepts students with bachelor's degrees in a wide variety of majors. Interviews are not required.

Correspondence and Information

Director of Graduate Studies
Industrial Relations Center
3-300 Carlson School of Management
University of Minnesota
321 19th Avenue, South
Minneapolis, Minnesota 55455-0231

Telephone: 612-624-5704
Fax: 612-624-8360
E-mail: mbirkholz@csom.umn.edu
World Wide Web: http://www.irc.csom.umn.edu

University of Minnesota

THE FACULTY AND THEIR RESEARCH

Dennis A. Ahlburg, Professor; Ph.D. (economics), Pennsylvania. Economic-demographic linkages in models of developed and developing nations, impact of voter abstention on the outcome of union representation elections, retraining of displaced workers and their subsequent labor market behavior, cohort size effects on behavior, aging.
Richard D. Arvey, Professor; Ph.D. (industrial/organizational psychology), Minnesota. Sex bias in job evaluation methods, sex-based wage discrimination, improvement of the predictive accuracy of employment tests, perception of organizational justice and discipline among employees.
Ross E. Azevedo, Associate Professor; Ph.D. (industrial and labor relations), Cornell. Labor mobility, compensation of special groups, human resource planning, equity theory, sex difference effects in collective bargaining outcomes.
Avner Ben-Ner, Professor and Director of the Industrial Relations Center; Ph.D. (economics), SUNY at Stony Brook. Applied microeconomics, organizational theory of employee-owned firms and nonprofit organizations, organizational life cycles, bargaining and union effects on productivity, comparative economics, organization of firms in different systems and cultures.
Mario F. Bognanno, Professor; Ph.D. (economics), Iowa. Bargaining theory and collective bargaining, labor-management cooperation, employee pay and job evaluation, economics of arbitration, employment policy and labor demand analysis.
John W. Budd, Associate Professor and Director of Graduate Studies; Ph.D. (economics), Princeton. Collective bargaining: labor union bargaining goals, international unions in Canada, and labor union jurisdictional disputes; labor economics: job evaluations programs and labor markets; bargaining goals of the UAW and the role of U.S.–based unions in Canadian collective bargaining.
Richard J. Butler, Professor; Ph.D. (economics), Chicago. Moral hazard effects, low back claims in workers' compensation, interactive effects of various forms of compensation, experience rating in workers' compensation.
John A. Fossum, Professor; Ph.D. (labor and industrial relations), Michigan State. Factors associated with managerial decision making in employee compensation, causes and consequences of skills obsolescence, perceived effects of union and employer organizing election campaign practices on employee voting behavior.
Theresa Glomb, Assistant Professor; Ph.D. (industrial/organizational psychology), Illinois. Emotionality in the work place, sexual harassment.
Brian P. McCall, Associate Professor; Ph.D. (economics), Princeton. Models of job matching, occupational choice, and job search; incentive mechanism design in union rank-and-file negotiator and employer-employee relations; econometric issues that arise when analyzing duration data.
John Remington, Professor; Ph.D. (administrative science), Michigan. Structure, organization, and employment in the building and construction trades; correlation of labor management cooperative programs.
Paul R. Sackett, Professor; Ph.D. (industrial/organizational psychology), Ohio State. Human judgment processes in personnel decision making, methodological issues in personnel selection research, managerial assessment, employee theft.
James G. Scoville, Professor; Ph.D. (economics), Harvard. Labor market studies in developing countries, especially studies of traditional industrial and craft employments; comparative studies of international and national industrial conflict and worker participation; wage-wage linkages between industry and construction.
Connie R. Wanberg, Assistant Professor; Ph.D. (industrial/organizational psychology), Iowa State. Predictors of mental health and reemployment among individuals without jobs, perceived fairness of layoff experiences.
Yijiang Wang, Associate Professor; Ph.D. (economics), Harvard. Organization theory and theory of the firm, industrial organization economics, comparative economics, monetary economics, Chinese economy and Socialist economic reform, Japanese management system, internal organization of the firm and its productivity implication, intrafirm relationship and incentive design, innovation as an organization issue.
Andrew F. Whitman, Professor; Ph.D. (business administration), Wisconsin; J.D. (law), Minnesota. Agents'/brokers' duties, workers' compensation funding, liability risk management, employee health benefit options.
Mahmood A. Zaidi, Professor; Ph.D. (economics), Berkeley. Labor market analysis, public policy, human capital in multinational corporations, wage determination, income policies, unemployment-inflation productivity relationships, international human resource management.

Faculty Members with Primary Appointments Elsewhere in the University
Hyman Berman, Professor of History; Ph.D. (history), Columbia.
John P. Campbell, Professor of Psychology; Ph.D. (psychology), Minnesota.
Marvin D. Dunnette, Professor of Psychology; Ph.D. (psychology), Minnesota.
Jo-Ida Hansen, Professor of Psychology; Ph.D. (psychology), Minnesota.
Michael P. Keane, Professor of Economics; Ph.D. (economics), Brown.
Morris M. Kleiner, Professor of Public Affairs; Ph.D. (economics), Illinois.
Jeylan T. Mortimer, Professor of Sociology; Ph.D. (sociology), Michigan.
Deniz Ones, Assistant Professor of Psychology; Ph.D. (business administration), Iowa.

THE UNIVERSITY OF TENNESSEE, KNOXVILLE

College of Human Ecology
Department of Human Resource Development

Programs of Study

The Department of Human Resource Development offers M.S. and Ph.D. programs in the integrated use of training and development, organization development, and career development to improve individual, group, and organizational effectiveness.

Graduate programs lead to the Master of Science (M.S.) degree in human resource development (HRD), with concentrations in training and development and teacher licensure. The teacher licensure concentration is specifically for students who seek initial teacher licensure in family and consumer sciences education, business and marketing education, and technology education.

The training and development concentration is designed to meet the needs of professionals who work in programs encompassing all areas of human resource development in business and industry as well as the teaching areas of business/marketing education, family and consumer sciences education, health science and technology education, technology education, and occupational studies education.

Doctoral study is for graduate students who seek careers in higher education or as managers/administrators of HRD; its goal is to prepare students to be facilitators of growth in institutions, to develop professional practices and attitudes, and to become agents of organizational change.

Research Facilities

The John C. Hodges Library provides valuable study and research space for students and faculty members. The library is conveniently located at the center of the campus; nearly 90 percent of the almost 2 million volumes are housed in a beautiful six-story (350,000 square feet) building. The library has available 18,825 serial titles and 164,295 audiovisual items. There are terminals for an online catalog, copy machines, telephones, typing rooms, a microcomputer lab that helps accommodate the word processing needs of students and faculty members, and a CD-ROM facility.

Financial Aid

Research and teaching assistantships are provided for approximately 10 graduate students. Half-time assistantships range from $7900 to $10,500, depending on the source of the assistantship and on the competence of the applicant. In addition, assistantships provide waiver of tuition and fees in the amount of $3993 per year (fall, spring, and summer terms) for in-state students and $11,016 per year for out-of-state students.

Cost of Study

For 1998, all fees, except a $140 per semester program and services fee, are waived for students supported by graduate assistantships. For those not supported by assistantships, there is an additional maintenance fee of $1232 per semester for in-state students and $3400 per semester for out-of-state students. A technology fee of $100 has been added for all students.

Living and Housing Costs

Modern University apartments are available for both single and married graduate students with or without families. Private apartments, within a wide price range, are also available in the campus area.

Student Group

As of the fall term of 1997, there were approximately 700 students pursuing a degree with a major in human resource development. Almost half of these students (350) were seeking a baccalaureate degree. There were about the same number in the master's program, and the remaining 35 were in the Ph.D. program. Many master's degree students were employed full-time and were pursuing their degree on a part-time, evening school basis.

Location

Knoxville lies between the Cumberland and the Great Smoky Mountains, close to hiking trails, white-water rivers, and Tennessee Valley Authority (TVA) lakes. Knoxville has a population of approximately 175,000, while the metropolitan area has a population of about 400,000. The area offers an exceptionally high quality of life, a mild climate year-round, low-cost housing, and easy access to major cities in the Southeast and on the Atlantic seaboard. The numerous scenic and recreation opportunities lure millions of visitors to the Great Smoky Mountains National Park, making it the most visited national park in the United States.

The University

The University of Tennessee, Knoxville, founded in 1794, is a comprehensive state research university with a strong commitment to graduate research and training. The University has several campuses across the state. The main campus, the agricultural campus, the School of Veterinary Medicine, and a graduate medical campus are located in Knoxville. The medical school is located in Memphis. The total enrollment is approximately 26,000 students, about 20 percent of whom are graduate students.

Applying

Applications are considered three times per year, on February 1, June 1, and November 1. Applications must be complete, including a statement of the student's potential applied and/or research interests and long-term professional goals, three recommendations (five for Ph.D. students), and GRE scores (master's students may submit MAT scores). All applicants are required to be interviewed by the department admissions board. TOEFL scores are required of students whose primary language is not English.

Correspondence and Information

Department of Human Resource Development
The University of Tennessee, Knoxville
Knoxville, Tennessee 37996-1900
Telephone: 423-974-2574
Fax: 423-974-2048
E-mail: hrd@utk.edu
World Wide Web: http://hrd.he.utk.edu

The University of Tennessee, Knoxville

THE FACULTY AND THEIR RESEARCH

Ernest Brewer, Professor; Ed.D., Tennessee, 1977. Human resource management, self-directed work teams, employee empowerment, worker compensation, research methods, program evaluation. Editor of *Journal of Educational Opportunity*.

Clifton Campbell, Professor; Ed.D., Maryland, 1971. Performance-based education and training, international workforce development policy, apprenticeships. *Workforce Requirements: The Basis for Relevant Occupational Training* (Monograph No. 21/8). Bradford, West Yorkshire, England: MCB University Press Limited, 1997.

Gerald Cheek, Professor Emeritus; Ph.D., Kansas State, 1972. Corporate workforce training, school-to-work, total quality management, international. Adopting a continuous improvement training model. *Maintenance Technology*, June 1997.

Allen Chesney, Adjunct Associate Professor; Ph.D., Case Western Reserve, 1971. Executive Director of Human Resource Management.

Carroll Coakley, Professor Emeritus; Ph.D., Wisconsin, 1968. Marketing education, manpower training and development, computer software. *Pathways to Excellence: Shaping the Future of Development Disabilities* (1995).

David Craig, Professor Emeritus; Ed.D., Cornell, 1967. Technology education, computer-based training.

Peter J. Dean II, Associate Professor; Ph.D., Iowa, 1986. Performance improvement, business ethics, originating learning systems, organizational change and development. Editor of *Performance Improvement Quarterly* and *Performance Engineering at Work*. Coeditor of *Performance Improvememt Pathfinders* and *Performance Improvement Interventions*.

Jacky DeJonge, Dean; Ph.D., Iowa State, 1976. New models of leadership, organizational change, human resource development, issues and trends.

Robert Hanson, Associate Professor; Ph.D., Purdue, 1970. Technology education, hands-on learning. High school to employment transition: Contemporary issues. In *The At-Risk Student and Vocational Education,* ed. A. Pautler. Ann Arbor, Mich.: Prakken Publications, Inc., 1994 (with DeRidder). *Communications and Media Technology High School Curriculum Guide*. Tennessee State Department of Education, 1994.

Roger Haskell, Professor Emeritus; Ph.D., Purdue, 1969. Industry and education partnerships, school-to-work transition. The dual system: Admission criteria, progression, and evaluation. In *Workforce Development in the Federal Republic of Germany,* eds. C. P. Campbell and R. B. Armstrong Jr. Pittsburg, Kans.: Press International, 1993.

Connie Hollingsworth, Adjunct Assistant Professor; Ph.D., Tennessee, 1995. Disadvantaged and underserved populations; educational instructional technology; secondary education, including school-to-work and grantwriting.

Virginia W. Kupritz, Assistant Professor; Ph.D., Virginia Tech, 1990. Privacy management in work organizations; organizational culture; changing nature of the workforce; diversity in the workforce, including intergenerational perspectives.

Jackie H. McInnis, Associate Dean; Ph.D., Florida State, 1972. Home economics education.

Susan Mettlen, Adjunct Associate Professor; Ed.D., Missouri–Columbia, 1989. Vice Chancellor for Information Infrastructure.

Cheryl A. Mimbs, Assistant Professor; Ph.D., Virginia Tech, 1996. Reform in teacher education, critical thinking in curriculum development, family and consumer sciences education.

Dulcie Peccolo, Adjunct Assistant Professor; Ph.D., Tennessee, 1982. Career development, needs assessment, total quality management, curriculum development, DACUM job analysis.

Debra Martin Petty, Adjunct Assistant Professor; Ed.D., Tennessee, 1987. Organizational change, leadership, personal empowerment, community inclusion of people with disabilities.

Gregory Petty, Professor and Head; Ph.D., Missouri–Columbia, 1978. Occupational work ethic, motivation, program evaluation, adults with disabilities.

Randal Pierce, Assistant Professor; Ph.D., Ohio State, 1981. Vocational-technical education, industrial training. Vocational education in the 1990s II: A source book for strategies, methods and materials. In *Developing Audiovisual Media,* eds. C. Anderson and L. C. Rampp. Ann Arbor, Mich.: Prakken Publications, Inc., 1993 (with Cameron).

Vickie Johnson Stout, Associate Professor; Ed.D., Tennessee, 1980. Business education, teacher education, learning how to learn, learning as a technology, interpersonal and organizational communications, diversified instructional modalities.

Constance Thomas, Adjunct Assistant Professor; Ph.D., Tennessee, 1997. Total quality management, technical training, career development, needs assessment, curriculum development, DACUM job analysis.

Section 8
Industrial and Manufacturing Management

This section contains a directory of institutions offering graduate work in industrial and manufacturing management, followed by in-depth entries submitted by institutions that chose to prepare detailed program descriptions. Additional information about programs listed in the directory but not augmented by an in-depth entry may be obtained by writing directly to the dean of a graduate school or chair of a department at the address given in the directory.

For programs offering related work, see also in this book Business Administration and Management and Human Resources. In Book 2, see Public, Regional, and Industrial Affairs (Industrial and Labor Relations).

CONTENTS

Program Directory

Cross-Discipline Announcements

In-Depth Descriptions

Industrial and Manufacturing Management

Baker College Center for Graduate Studies, Programs in Business, Flint, MI 48507. Offerings include industrial management (EMBA, MBA). MBA (health and recreation services management) enrollment limited to international students. Faculty: 8 full-time, 73 part-time. *Degree requirements:* Portfolio required, foreign language not required. *Entrance requirements:* 3 years of work experience, minimum undergraduate GPA of 2.5, writing sample. Application deadline: rolling. Application fee: $25. *Tuition:* $215 per quarter hour. • Dr. Michael Heberling, President, 800-469-3165. Application contact: Chuck Gurden, Director of Admissions, 800-469-3165. Fax: 810-766-4399.

Baruch College of the City University of New York, School of Business, Department of Management, 17 Lexington Avenue, New York, NY 10010-5585. Offerings include industrial and service management (MBA). Department faculty: 33 full-time (6 women), 15 part-time (0 women). *Degree requirements:* Computer language required, foreign language not required. *Average time to degree:* master's–2 years full-time, 4 years part-time. *Entrance requirements:* GMAT, TOEFL (minimum score 570), TWE (minimum score 4.5). Application deadline: 6/15 (11/1 for spring admission). Application fee: $40. *Expenses:* Tuition $4350 per year full-time, $185 per credit part-time for state residents; $7600 per year full-time, $320 per credit part-time for nonresidents. Fees $53 per year. • Harry M. Rosen, Chairman, 212-802-6870. Application contact: Michael S. Wynne, Office of Graduate Admissions, 212-802-2330. Fax: 212-802-2335. E-mail: graduate_admissions@baruch.cuny.edu.

Bentley College, Graduate School of Business, Self-paced MBA Program, 175 Forest Street, Waltham, MA 02154-4705. Offerings include operations management (MBA). Program faculty: 70 full-time (21 women), 22 part-time (8 women). *Degree requirements:* Computer language required, foreign language and thesis not required. *Entrance requirements:* GMAT (average 540), TOEFL (minimum score 580). Application deadline: 6/1 (priority date; rolling processing; 11/1 for spring admission). Application fee: $50. *Expenses:* Tuition $20,500 per year full-time, $2050 per course part-time. Fees $65 per year full-time, $15 per semester part-time. • Dr. Judith B. Kamm, Director, 781-891-3433. Application contact: Holly Chase, Associate Director, 781-891-2108. Fax: 781-891-2464. E-mail: hchase@bentley.edu.

Boston University, School of Management, Boston, MA 02215. Offerings include operations management (DBA). School faculty: 110 full-time, 54 part-time. *Degree requirements:* Dissertation required, foreign language not required. *Entrance requirements:* GMAT or GRE General Test. Application deadline: 5/1 (rolling processing). Application fee: $50. Electronic applications accepted. *Expenses:* Tuition $22,830 per year full-time, $713 per credit part-time. Fees $218 per year full-time, $40 per semester part-time. • Therese M. Hofmann, Assistant Dean, 617-353-2673. Application contact: Peter G. Kelly, Director of Admissions and Financial Aid, 617-353-2670. Fax: 617-353-7368. E-mail: mba@bu.edu.

Bryant College, College of Business Administration, Program in Operations Management, Smithfield, RI 02917-1284. Awards MBA, CAGS. Part-time and evening/weekend programs available. Faculty: 8 full-time (2 women), 9 part-time (1 woman). Students: 3 full-time (1 woman), 48 part-time (9 women); includes 3 minority (2 Asian Americans, 1 Hispanic), 1 international. Average age 34. 15 applicants, 93% accepted. In 1997, 10 master's awarded. *Entrance requirements:* For master's, GMAT (minimum score 480; average 520). Application deadline: 7/1 (priority date; rolling processing; 11/15 for spring admission). Application fee: $55 ($70 for international students). *Tuition:* $1025 per course. *Financial aid:* In 1997–98, 1 research assistantship was awarded; graduate assistantships and career-related internships or fieldwork also available. Aid available to part-time students. Financial aid applicants required to submit FAFSA. • Cathy Lalli, Assistant Director of Graduate Programs, Graduate School, 401-232-6230. Fax: 401-232-6494. E-mail: gradprog@bryant.edu.

Bucknell University, College of Arts and Sciences, Department of Management, Lewisburg, PA 17837. Offerings include quantitative methods and operations management (MSBA). Department faculty: 12 full-time. *Degree requirements:* Thesis required, foreign language not required. *Entrance requirements:* GMAT, TOEFL (minimum score 550), minimum GPA of 2.8. Application deadline: 6/1 (priority date; rolling processing; 12/1 for spring admission). Application fee: $25. *Tuition:* $2410 per course. • Dr. Mark Bettner, Head, 717-524-1306.

California Polytechnic State University, San Luis Obispo, College of Business, Department of Industrial Technology, San Luis Obispo, CA 93407. Offers program in industrial and technical studies (MA). Faculty: 9 full-time (2 women). Students: 14 full-time (0 women), 12 part-time. Average age 29. 14 applicants, 93% accepted. In 1997, 8 degrees awarded. *Degree requirements:* Thesis or alternative required, foreign language not required. *Entrance requirements:* GRE, minimum GPA of 2.8 in last 60 semester units. Application deadline: 7/1 (priority date; rolling processing). Application fee: $55. *Expenses:* Tuition $0 for state residents; $164 per unit for nonresidents. Fees $2102 per year full-time, $1632 per year part-time. *Financial aid:* Federal Work-Study, institutionally sponsored loans, and career-related internships or fieldwork available. Aid available to part-time students. Financial aid application deadline: 5/15. • Gerald E. Cunico, Coordinator, 805-756-2676. Application contact: Dr. Anthony Randazzo, Coordinator, 805-756-1618.

Carnegie Mellon University, Graduate School of Industrial Administration, Pittsburgh, PA 15213-3891. Offerings include industrial administration (MSIA), with option in administration and public management; manufacturing and operating systems (PhD), with option in industrial administration. JD/MSIA offered jointly with University of Pittsburgh. MOM, MS with Carnegie Inst of Tech. PhD (robotics) with Carnegie Inst of Tech & Sch of Computer Sci. MIS, MS, JD/MS, M Div/MS with H. John Heinz III Sch of Public Policy & Mgmt. PhD (mathematical finance) with Departments of Mathematical Sciences an. Terminal master's awarded for partial completion of doctoral program. School faculty: 86 full-time (15 women), 12 part-time (2 women). *Degree requirements:* For doctorate, dissertation required, foreign language not required. *Average time to degree:* master's–2 years full-time, 2.7 years part-time. *Application fee:* $50. • Douglas Dunn, Dean, 412-268-2265. Application contact: Director of Admissions, 412-268-2272.

The Catholic University of America, School of Arts and Sciences, Department of Economics and Business, Washington, DC 20064. Offerings include industrial organization (PhD). PhD admissions temporarily suspended. Terminal master's awarded for partial completion of doctoral program. Department faculty: 11 full-time (4 women), 5 part-time (2 women), 13 FTE. *Degree requirements:* 2 foreign languages, computer language, dissertation, comprehensive exam. *Application deadline:* 8/1 (priority date; rolling processing; 12/1 for spring admission). *Application fee:* $50. *Expenses:* Tuition $17,325 per year full-time, $668 per credit hour part-time. Fees $680 per year full-time, $360 per year part-time. • Dr. Ernest M. Zampelli, Chair, 202-319-6683. Fax: 202-319-4426. E-mail: zampelli@cua.edu.

Central Connecticut State University, School of Technology, Program in Industrial (Technical) Management, New Britain, CT 06050-4010. Awards MS. Part-time and evening/weekend programs available. Students: 4 full-time (0 women), 47 part-time (5 women); includes 4 minority (1 Asian American, 2 Hispanics, 1 Native American), 1 international. Average age 37. 45 applicants, 29% accepted. In 1997, 12 degrees awarded. *Degree requirements:* Comprehensive exam required, foreign language and thesis not required. *Entrance requirements:* TOEFL (minimum score 550), minimum GPA of 2.7. Application deadline: 6/1 (priority date; rolling processing; 12/1 for spring admission). Application fee: $40. *Expenses:* Tuition $4458 per year full-time, $175 per credit hour part-time for state residents; $9943 per year full-time, $175 per credit hour part-time for nonresidents. Fees $45 per semester. *Financial aid:* Research assistantships, Federal Work-Study available. Financial aid application deadline: 3/15; applicants required to submit FAFSA. *Faculty research:* All aspects of middle management, technical supervision in the workplace. • Dr. William Davison, Coordinator, 860-832-1831.

Central Michigan University, College of Science and Technology, Department of Industrial and Engineering Technology, Mount Pleasant, MI 48859. Offers programs in industrial education (MA), industrial education administration (MAV Ed), industrial management and technology (MA). MAV Ed being phased out; applicants no longer accepted. Faculty: 16 full-time (3 women). Students: 7 full-time (2 women), 9 part-time (2 women); includes 8 international. Average age 28. In 1997, 9 degrees awarded. *Entrance requirements:* 2 years of teaching experience, undergraduate major/minor in industrial engineering or related field. Application deadline: 3/1 (priority date; rolling processing). Application fee: $30. *Expenses:* Tuition $139 per credit hour (minimum) for state residents; $276 per credit hour (minimum) for nonresidents. Fees $260 per year full-time, $150 per semester part-time. *Financial aid:* In 1997–98, 4 teaching assistantships (3 to first-year students) were awarded; fellowships, research assistantships, Federal Work-Study, and career-related internships or fieldwork also available. Financial aid application deadline: 3/7. *Faculty research:* Computer applications, manufacturing process control, automation, industrial activities. • Dr. Larry Fryda, Chairperson, 517-774-3033. Fax: 517-774-4700. E-mail: 3z3iihn@cmich.edu.

Central Missouri State University, College of Applied Sciences and Technology, Department of Manufacturing and Construction, Warrensburg, MO 64093. Offerings include industrial management (MS). Department faculty: 10 full-time. *Degree requirements:* Comprehensive exam required, thesis not required. *Entrance requirements:* Minimum GPA of 2.5; previous course work in mathematics, science, and technology. Application deadline: 6/30 (priority date; rolling processing). Application fee: $25 ($50 for international students). *Tuition:* $3288 per year full-time, $137 per credit hour part-time for state residents; $5928 per year full-time, $274 per credit hour part-time for nonresidents. • Dr. John Sutton, Chair, 660-543-4439. Fax: 660-543-4578.

Clarkson University, Interdisciplinary Studies, Potsdam, NY 13699. Offers program in engineering and manufacturing management (MS). Part-time and evening/weekend programs available. Faculty: 2 full-time (0 women). Students: 4 part-time (1 woman). Average age 34. 6 applicants, 33% accepted. In 1997, 15 degrees awarded. *Application deadline:* rolling. *Application fee:* $25 ($35 for international students). *Expenses:* Tuition $19,075 per year full-time, $635 per credit hour part-time. Fees $178 per year. *Financial aid:* Fellowships, research assistantships, teaching assistantships available. • Dr. Michael Bommer, Director, 315-268-6456.

Clarkson University, School of Business, Program in Management Systems, Concentration in Manufacturing Management, Potsdam, NY 13699. Awards MS. *Degree requirements:* Project or thesis required, foreign language not required. *Entrance requirements:* GMAT, GRE General Test (highly recommended), TOEFL. Application deadline: rolling. Application fee: $25 ($35 for international students). *Expenses:* Tuition $19,075 per year full-time, $635 per credit hour part-time. Fees $178 per year. • Application contact: Dr. Fredric C. Menz, Director, Graduate Program, 315-268-6427. Fax: 315-268-3810. E-mail: menzf@icarus.som.clarkson.edu.

Clemson University, College of Business and Public Affairs, Department of Management, Program in Industrial Management, Clemson, SC 29634. Awards MS, PhD. Students: 22 full-time (8 women), 7 part-time (2 women); includes 4 minority (all African Americans), 9 international. Average age 25. 23 applicants, 35% accepted. In 1997, 8 master's, 3 doctorates awarded. *Degree requirements:* For doctorate, dissertation required, foreign language not required. *Entrance requirements:* For master's, GMAT, GRE General Test, TOEFL, minimum GPA of 3.0; for doctorate, GRE General Test, TOEFL, minimum GPA of 3.5. Application deadline: 2/1 (10/1 for spring admission). Application fee: $35. *Expenses:* Tuition $3154 per year full-time, $130 per credit hour part-time for state residents; $6452 per year full-time, $264 per credit hour part-time for nonresidents. Fees $190 per year. • Application contact: Dr. R. L. LaForge, Graduate Coordinator, 864-656-2011. Fax: 864-656-2015.

See in-depth description on page 515.

DePaul University, Charles H. Kellstadt Graduate School of Business, Department of Management, Program in Operations Management, Chicago, IL 60604-2287. Awards MBA. Students: 67 full-time (19 women), 74 part-time (11 women); includes 21 minority (10 African Americans, 9 Asian Americans, 2 Hispanics), 1 international. Average age 30. 39 applicants, 82% accepted. In 1997, 40 degrees awarded. *Entrance requirements:* GMAT, TOEFL. Application deadline: 8/1 (rolling processing; 3/1 for spring admission). Application fee: $40. *Expenses:* Tuition $1593 per course. Fees $30 per year. *Financial aid:* Application deadline 4/1. • Application contact: Christine Munoz, Director of Admissions, 312-362-8810. Fax: 312-362-6677. E-mail: mbainfo@wppost.depaul.edu.

Eastern Michigan University, College of Business, Department of Management, Ypsilanti, MI 48197. Offerings include production and operations management (MBA). Department faculty: 20 full-time (8 women). *Application deadline:* 5/15 (rolling processing; 3/15 for spring admission). *Application fee:* $30. *Expenses:* Tuition $2691 per year full-time, $150 per credit hour part-time for state residents; $6300 per year full-time, $350 per credit hour part-time for nonresidents. Fees $368 per year full-time, $88 per semester (minimum) part-time. • Dr. Sahab Dayal, Head, 734-487-3240. Application contact: Dr. William Whitmire, Coordinator, 734-487-3240.

École des Hautes Études Commerciales, Program in Production and Operations Management, Montréal, PQ H3T 2A7, Canada. Awards M Sc. Most courses are given in French. *Degree requirements:* 1 foreign language, thesis. *Application deadline:* 3/15. *Application fee:* $40. *Financial aid:* Fellowships, research assistantships, teaching assistantships available. • Dr. Jean-Yves Le Louarn, Director, 514-340-6295. E-mail: jean-yves.lelouarn@hec.ca. Application contact: Nicole Rivet, Registrar, 514-340-6110. Fax: 514-340-5640. E-mail: nicole.rivet@hec.ca.

Fairleigh Dickinson University, Florham–Madison Campus, Samuel J. Silberman College of Business Administration, Program in Industrial Management, 285 Madison Avenue, Madison, NJ 07940-1099. Awards MBA. Part-time and evening/weekend programs available. Faculty: 7 full-time (0 women), 9 part-time (2 women). Students: 1 full-time (0 women), 6 part-time (2 women). Average age 32. 4 applicants, 25% accepted. In 1997, 3 degrees awarded. *Degree requirements:* Thesis optional, foreign language not required. *Entrance requirements:* GMAT. Application deadline: rolling. Application fee: $35. *Expenses:* Tuition $522 per credit. Fees $302 per year full-time, $138 per year part-time. *Financial aid:* Fellowships available. • Dr. Joel Harmon, Chairman, 973-443-8850.

Fairleigh Dickinson University, Teaneck–Hackensack Campus, Samuel J. Silberman College of Business Administration, Department of Management, Marketing, and Information Systems and Sciences, Program in Industrial Management, 1000 River Road, Teaneck, NJ 07666-1914. Awards MBA. Students: 4 part-time (2 women); includes 4 minority (1 African American, 3 Hispanics). Average age 45. In 1997, 1 degree awarded. *Degree requirements:* Computer language required, thesis optional, foreign language not required. *Entrance requirements:* GMAT. Application deadline: rolling. Application fee: $35. *Expenses:* Tuition $522 per credit. Fees $302 per year full-time, $138 per year part-time. *Financial aid:* Fellowships, research assistantships available. *Faculty research:* Production. • Paul Yoon, Chair, Department of Management, Marketing, and Information Systems and Sciences, 201-692-7223.

The George Washington University, School of Business and Public Management, Department of Management Science, Program in Logistics, Operations, and Materials Management, Washington, DC 20052. Awards MBA, MPA. Part-time and evening/weekend programs available. 28 applicants, 89% accepted. In 1997, 8 degrees awarded. *Degree requirements:* Computer language required, foreign language and thesis not required. *Entrance requirements:* GMAT, TOEFL (minimum score 550). Application deadline: 4/1 (priority date; rolling processing; 10/1 for spring admission). Application fee: $45. *Expenses:* Tuition $680 per semester hour. Fees $35 per semester hour. *Financial aid:* Application deadline 4/1. • Dr. Erik K. Winslow, Chair,

Directory: Industrial and Manufacturing Management

Department of Management Science, 202-994-7375. Application contact: Lilly Hastings, Graduate Admissions, 202-994-6584. Fax: 202-994-6382.

GMI Engineering & Management Institute, see Kettering University.

Golden Gate University, School of Business, San Francisco, CA 94105-2968. Offerings include manufacturing management (MS, Certificate), operations management (MBA). MBA (telecommunications, management information systems) offered jointly with the School of Technology and Industry. *Average time to degree:* master's–2.5 years full-time. *Application deadline:* 7/1 (priority date; rolling processing). *Application fee:* $55 ($70 for international students). *Tuition:* $996 per course (minimum). • Dr. Hamid Shomali, Dean, 415-442-6500. Fax: 415-442-6579. Application contact: Enrollment Services, 415-442-7800. Fax: 415-442-7807. E-mail: info@ggu.edu.

Illinois Institute of Technology, Stuart School of Business, Chicago, IL 60661-3691. Offerings include operations and technology management (MS). School faculty: 21 full-time (1 woman), 49 part-time (6 women). *Application deadline:* 8/1 (rolling processing; 4/15 for spring admission). *Application fee:* $30. Electronic applications accepted. *Tuition:* $1620 per course. • Dr. M. Zia Hassan, Dean, 312-906-6515. E-mail: hassan@stuart.iit.edu. Application contact: Lynn Miller, Director, Admission, 312-906-6544. Fax: 312-906-6549. E-mail: degrees@stuart.iit.edu.

Inter American University of Puerto Rico, Metropolitan Campus, Division of Economics and Business Administration, Program in Industrial Management, San Juan, PR 00919-1293. Awards MBA. Faculty: 3 part-time (0 women). Students: 47 full-time (22 women), 71 part-time (34 women); includes 118 minority (all Hispanics). *Degree requirements:* Comprehensive exam required, foreign language and thesis not required. *Entrance requirements:* GRE or PAEG, interview. Application deadline: 5/15 (priority date; rolling processing; 11/15 for spring admission). Application fee: $31. Electronic applications accepted. *Expenses:* Tuition $3272 per year full-time, $1740 per year part-time. Fees $328 per year full-time, $176 per year part-time. *Financial aid:* Federal Work-Study available. • Application contact: Dr. Antonio Llorens, Director, 787-250-1912 Ext. 2320. Fax: 787-250-0361.

Iona College, Hagan Graduate School of Business, Department of Information and Technology Management, 715 North Avenue, New Rochelle, NY 10801-1890. Offerings include production and operations management (MBA, PMC). Department faculty: 6 full-time (0 women), 3 part-time (0 women). *Degree requirements:* For master's, computer language required, foreign language and thesis not required. *Entrance requirements:* For master's, GMAT (minimum score 425; average 510); for PMC, GMAT. Application deadline: rolling. Application fee: $50. *Expenses:* Tuition $480 per credit hour. Fees $25 per semester. • Dr. Donald Moscato, Chairman, 914-633-2555. Application contact: Carol Shea, Director of MBA Admissions, 914-633-2288.

Kettering University, Management Department, Flint, MI 48504-4898. Offers program in manufacturing management (MSMM). *Entrance requirements:* GMAT. Application deadline: 7/15 (rolling processing). Application fee: $0. *Financial aid:* Institutionally sponsored loans available. Aid available to part-time students. • Dr. Joseph Zima, Head, 810-762-7959.

Lawrence Technological University, College of Management, 21000 West Ten Mile Road, Southfield, MI 48075-1058. Offerings include industrial operations (MS). College faculty: 7 full-time (2 women), 22 part-time (5 women), 17 FTE. *Average time to degree:* master's–3 years part-time. *Application deadline:* 8/1 (priority date; rolling processing; 1/1 for spring admission). *Application fee:* $50. Electronic applications accepted. *Expenses:* Tuition $11,400 per year full-time, $380 per credit hour part-time. Fees $100 per year. • Dr. Lou DeGennaro, Dean, 248-204-3050. E-mail: degennaro@ltu.edu. Application contact: Paul Kinder, Director of Admissions, 248-204-3160. Fax: 248-204-3188. E-mail: admissions@ltu.edu.

Lynchburg College, School of Business, Lynchburg, VA 24501-3199. Offerings include administration (M Ad), with options in industrial management, personnel management. *Application fee:* $20.

Massachusetts Institute of Technology, School of Engineering, Leaders for Manufacturing Program, Cambridge, MA 02139-4307. Offers engineering (SM), management (MBA, SM). Offered in cooperation with the Sloan School of Management. *Degree requirements:* Thesis. *Entrance requirements:* GMAT or GRE General Test, 2 years of work experience. Application deadline: 1/15. Application fee: $55. *Tuition:* $24,050 per year. *Financial aid:* In 1997–98, 90 students received aid, including 90 fellowships (42 to first-year students) totaling $1.98 million; institutionally sponsored loans and career-related internships or fieldwork also available. Financial aid application deadline: 1/15. *Faculty research:* Scheduling logistics, product life cycle, variation reduction, product development, manufacturing operations. • Don Rosenfield, Director, 617-253-1064. Application contact: Bettina von Akerman, Recruiting and Admissions Coordinator, 617-253-1055. E-mail: lfm@mit.edu.

McGill University, Faculty of Graduate Studies and Research, Faculty of Engineering, Department of Mechanical Engineering, Program in Manufacturing Management, Montréal, PQ H3A 2T5, Canada. Awards MMM. Offered jointly with the Faculty of Management. *Degree requirements:* Thesis. *Entrance requirements:* TOEFL (minimum score 550), B Eng or equivalent, minimum GPA of 3.0. Application deadline: 2/1 (rolling processing). Application fee: $60. *Expenses:* Tuition $1668 per year for Canadian residents; $8268 per year for nonresidents. Fees $828 per year for Canadian residents; $1216 per year for nonresidents. *Financial aid:* Application deadline 2/1. • N. Hori, Graduate Program Coordinator, Department of Mechanical Engineering, 514-398-6282. E-mail: hori@mecheng.lan.mcgill.ca. Application contact: A. Cianci, Graduate Secretary, 514-398-6281. Fax: 514-398-7365. E-mail: annac@mecheng.lan.mcgill.ca.

Michigan State University, Eli Broad Graduate School of Management, Department of Management, East Lansing, MI 48824-1020. Offerings include materials and logistics management-operations management (MBA), materials and logistics management-purchasing management (MBA), production and operations management (PhD). Department faculty: 12 (5 women). *Degree requirements:* For doctorate, dissertation required, foreign language not required. *Entrance requirements:* For master's, GMAT (minimum score 500); for doctorate, GMAT (score in 90th percentile or higher). Application deadline: rolling. Application fee: $30 ($40 for international students). *Expenses:* Tuition $4609 per year full-time, $223 per credit hour (minimum) part-time for state residents; $8704 per year full-time, $450 per credit hour (minimum) part-time for nonresidents. Fees $576 per year full-time, $476 per year part-time. • Dr. John Wagner III, Acting Chairperson, 517-355-1878. Fax: 517-432-1111. E-mail: wagner@pilot.msu.edu.

Michigan Technological University, School of Business and Economics, Program in Operations Management, Houghton, MI 49931-1295. Awards MS. Program being phased out; applicants no longer accepted. Part-time programs available. Faculty: 8 full-time (1 woman). Students: 2 full-time (0 women). Average age 35. 0 applicants. In 1997, 5 degrees awarded. *Degree requirements:* Thesis required, foreign language not required. *Expenses:* Tuition $3867 per year full-time, $216 per credit hour part-time for state residents; $8307 per year full-time, $462 per credit hour part-time for nonresidents. Fees $360 per year (minimum) full-time, $120 per quarter (minimum) part-time. *Financial aid:* Federal Work-Study and career-related internships or fieldwork available. Aid available to part-time students. *Faculty research:* Production management, operations research, quality management, system thinking and technology management. Total annual research expenditures: $20,162. • Dr. R. Eugene Klippel, Dean, School of Business and Economics, 906-487-2669. Fax: 906-487-2944. E-mail: reklippe@mtu.edu. Application contact: Dr. Terry Monson, Associate Dean, 906-487-3174. Fax: 906-487-1863. E-mail: tmonson@mtu.edu.

New Jersey Institute of Technology, School of Management, Newark, NJ 07102-1982. Awards MS, PhD, M Arch/MS. PhD offered jointly with Rutgers, The State University of New Jersey, Newark. Part-time and evening/weekend programs available. Faculty: 27 full-time (3 women), 5 part-time (0 women), 28 FTE. Students: 65 full-time (26 women), 346 part-time (130 women); includes 105 minority (38 African Americans, 42 Asian Americans, 24 Hispanics, 1 Native American), 50 international. Average age 30. 284 applicants, 73% accepted. In 1997, 192 master's awarded. Terminal master's awarded for partial completion of doctoral program. *Degree requirements:* For master's, thesis optional, foreign language not required; for doctorate, dissertation, residency required, foreign language not required. *Entrance requirements:* For master's, GRE General Test (minimum score 450 on verbal section, 600 on quantitative, 550 on analytical); for doctorate, GRE General Test (minimum score 450 on verbal section, 600 on quantitative, 550 on analytical), minimum graduate GPA of 3.5. Application deadline: 6/5 (priority date; rolling processing; 10/15 for spring admission). Application fee: $50. Electronic applications accepted. *Expenses:* Tuition $6952 per year full-time, $1104 per semester (minimum) part-time for state residents; $9770 per year full-time, $1527 per semester (minimum) part-time for nonresidents. Fees $938 per year full-time, $196 per semester (minimum) part-time. *Financial aid:* Fellowships, research assistantships, teaching assistantships, assistantships, Federal Work-Study, institutionally sponsored loans, and career-related internships or fieldwork available. Financial aid application deadline: 3/15. *Faculty research:* Management of new technologies, information systems management, operations management systems, marketing management, human resource management. Total annual research expenditures: $232,000. • Dr. Alok Chakrabarti, Dean, 973-596-3256. E-mail: chakrabart@admin.njit.edu. Application contact: Kathy Kelly, Director of Admissions, 973-596-3300. Fax: 973-596-3461. E-mail: admissions@njit.edu.

See in-depth description on page 517.

New York University, Leonard N. Stern School of Business, Operations Management Area, New York, NY 10012-1019. Awards MBA. Faculty: 10 full-time (2 women), 1 part-time (0 women). Students: 21 full-time, 31 part-time. In 1997, 29 degrees awarded. *Degree requirements:* Computer language required, foreign language and thesis not required. *Entrance requirements:* GMAT, TOEFL (minimum score 600). Application deadline: 3/15 (rolling processing). Application fee: $75. *Financial aid:* Application deadline 1/15. *Faculty research:* Supply and recovery chain management, business process improvement, service quality, corporate and operation strategy. • Eitan Zemel, Chairman, 212-998-0280. Application contact: Mary Miller, Director, Graduate Admissions, 212-998-0600. Fax: 212-995-4231. E-mail: sternmba@stern.nyu.edu.

Northeastern State University, College of Business and Industry, Department of Technology, Tahlequah, OK 74464-2399. Offers program in industrial management (MS). Part-time and evening/weekend programs available. Faculty: 5 part-time (0 women). Students: 61 (16 women); includes 3 international. In 1997, 13 degrees awarded. *Degree requirements:* Thesis or alternative required, foreign language not required. *Entrance requirements:* GRE General Test (minimum combined score of 900) or MAT (minimum score 33), minimum GPA of 2.5. Application deadline: 6/1 (priority date; rolling processing). Application fee: $0. *Expenses:* Tuition $74 per credit hour for state residents; $176 per credit hour for nonresidents. Fees $30 per year. *Financial aid:* Teaching assistantships, Federal Work-Study available. Financial aid application deadline: 3/1. • Dr. Don Ruby, Head, 918-456-5511 Ext. 2964. Application contact: Graduate College, 918-456-5511.

Northern Illinois University, College of Engineering and Engineering Technology, Department of Technology, De Kalb, IL 60115-2854. Offers program in industrial management (MS). Part-time and evening/weekend programs available. Faculty: 10 full-time (1 woman), 1 part-time (0 women). Students: 16 full-time (1 woman), 40 part-time (4 women); includes 3 minority (1 African American, 1 Asian American, 1 Native American), 9 international. Average age 33. 26 applicants, 73% accepted. In 1997, 31 degrees awarded. *Degree requirements:* Comprehensive exam required, thesis optional, foreign language not required. *Entrance requirements:* GRE General Test, TOEFL (minimum score 550), minimum GPA of 2.75. Application deadline: 6/1 (rolling processing; 11/1 for spring admission). Application fee: $30. *Tuition:* $3984 per year full-time, $154 per credit hour part-time for state residents; $8160 per year full-time, $328 per credit hour part-time for nonresidents. *Financial aid:* In 1997–98, 2 teaching assistantships, 7 staff assistantships were awarded; fellowships, research assistantships, full tuition waivers, Federal Work-Study, and career-related internships or fieldwork also available. Aid available to part-time students. • Dennis Stoia, Chair, 815-753-1349.

Northwestern University, J. L. Kellogg Graduate School of Management, Programs in Management, Evanston, IL 60208. Offerings include manufacturing management (MMM). MMM offered jointly with the Robert R. McCormick School of Engineering and Applied Science; MMM/MSN offered jointly with Rush Presbyterian Hospital. Faculty: 129 full-time (24 women), 89 part-time (15 women). *Application deadline:* 3/16. *Application fee:* $125. *Tuition:* $25,872 per year. • Michele Rogers, Assistant Dean of Admissions and Financial Aid, 847-491-3308. Fax: 847-491-4960.

Pennsylvania State University University Park Campus, Intercollege Graduate Programs, Intercollege Program in Quality and Manufacturing Management, University Park, PA 16802-1503. Awards MMM. Students: 27 full-time (10 women), 6 part-time (2 women). *Entrance requirements:* GRE or GMAT. Application fee: $40. *Expenses:* Tuition $6534 per year full-time, $276 per credit part-time for state residents; $13,460 per year full-time, $561 per credit part-time for nonresidents. Fees $252 per year (minimum) full-time, $43 per semester (minimum) part-time. • Dr. M. P. Hottenstein, Co-Director, 814-863-5802.

Pennsylvania State University University Park Campus, The Mary Jean and Frank P. Smeal College of Business Administration, PhD Programs in Business Administration, Program in Management Science/Operations/Logistics, University Park, PA 16802-1503. Awards PhD. *Degree requirements:* Dissertation. *Entrance requirements:* GMAT. Application fee: $40. *Expenses:* Tuition $6534 per year full-time, $276 per credit part-time for state residents; $13,460 per year full-time, $561 per credit part-time for nonresidents. Fees $252 per year (minimum) full-time, $43 per semester (minimum) part-time. • Dr. Jack C. Hayya, Field Adviser, 814-865-1461.

Polytechnic University, Brooklyn Campus, Department of Management, Major in Operations Management, Six Metrotech Center, Brooklyn, NY 11201-2990. Awards MS. Students: 3 part-time (0 women). *Degree requirements:* Thesis or alternative. *Entrance requirements:* GMAT, minimum B average in undergraduate course work. Application deadline: rolling. Application fee: $45. Electronic applications accepted. *Expenses:* Tuition $19,530 per year full-time, $675 per credit part-time. Fees $600 per year full-time, $135 per semester part-time. • Application contact: John S. Kerge, Dean of Admissions, 718-260-3200. Fax: 718-260-3446. E-mail: admitme@poly.edu.

Polytechnic University, Farmingdale Campus, Graduate Programs, Department of Management, Major in Operations Management, Route 110, Farmingdale, NY 11735-3995. Awards MS. Students: 2 part-time (1 woman). 0 applicants. In 1997, 2 degrees awarded. *Application fee:* $45. *Expenses:* Tuition $19,530 per year full-time, $675 per credit part-time. Fees $600 per year full-time, $135 per semester part-time. *Financial aid:* Institutionally sponsored loans available. Aid available to part-time students. Financial aid applicants required to submit FAFSA. • Application contact: John S. Kerge, Dean of Admissions, 718-260-3200. Fax: 718-260-3446. E-mail: admitme@poly.edu.

Polytechnic University, Westchester Graduate Center, Division of Management, Major in Operations Management, Hawthorne, NY 10532-1507. Awards MS. Students: 2 part-time (0 women). 1 applicant, 100% accepted. *Degree requirements:* Computer language. *Application deadline:* rolling. *Application fee:* $45. Electronic applications accepted. *Expenses:* Tuition $19,530 per year full-time, $675 per credit part-time. Fees $600 per year full-time, $135 per semester part-time. • Application contact: John S. Kerge, Dean of Admissions, 718-260-3200. Fax: 718-260-3446. E-mail: admitme@poly.edu.

Purdue University, Krannert Graduate School of Management, Department of Management, West Lafayette, IN 47907. Offerings include industrial administration (MSIA), manufacturing

Directory: Industrial and Manufacturing Management

Purdue University (continued)
management (MSM). Department faculty: 51 full-time (5 women). *Average time to degree:* doctorate–4 years full-time. *Application fee:* $30. Electronic applications accepted. *Tuition:* $3500 per year full-time, $126 per credit hour part-time for state residents; $11,720 per year full-time, $387 per credit hour part-time for nonresidents. • Dr. J. J. McConnell, Director of Doctoral Programs, 765-494-4375. Application contact: Kelly Felty, Assistant Director of Administration for Doctoral Programs, 765-494-4375. Fax: 765-494-1526. E-mail: feltyk@mgmt.purdue.edu.

Rensselaer Polytechnic Institute, Lally School of Management and Technology, Troy, NY 12180-3590. Offerings include business administration (MBA, PhD), with options in finance and accounting (MBA), information systems management (MBA), management (PhD), management of technology and entrepreneurships (MBA), manufacturing management (MBA), marketing management (MBA), operations research (MBA), organizational behavior and human resource management (MBA), statistical methods for management (MBA); manufacturing (PhD). Postbaccalaureate distance learning degree programs offered (no on-campus study). School faculty: 36 full-time (5 women), 6 part-time (0 women). *Degree requirements:* For doctorate, computer language, dissertation required, foreign language not required. *Entrance requirements:* For doctorate, GMAT or GRE General Test, TOEFL (minimum score 570). Application deadline: 2/1 (priority date; rolling processing). Application fee: $35. *Expenses:* Tuition $630 per credit hour. Fees $1000 per year. • Dr. Joseph G. Ecker, Dean, 518-276-6802. Application contact: Michele Martens, Manager of Enrollment Services, 518-276-4800. Fax: 518-276-8661.

Rochester Institute of Technology, College of Business, Department of Business Administration, Program in Manufacturing Management and Leadership, Rochester, NY 14623-5604. Awards MS. Students: 1 full-time (0 women), 31 part-time (4 women). 32 applicants, 59% accepted. In 1997, 19 degrees awarded. *Entrance requirements:* GMAT, minimum GPA of 2.5. Application deadline: 3/1 (priority date; rolling processing). Application fee: $40. *Expenses:* Tuition $18,765 per year full-time, $527 per credit hour part-time. Fees $126 per year full-time. • Patricia Sorce, Associate Dean, Department of Business Administration, 716-475-2313.

Southeastern Oklahoma State University, School of Science and Technology, Durant, OK 74701-0609. Offers program in technology (MT). Part-time and evening/weekend programs available. Faculty: 6 full-time (0 women). Students: 6 full-time (1 woman), 6 part-time (4 women); includes 1 minority (Native American). Average age 35. 7 applicants, 57% accepted. In 1997, 7 degrees awarded. *Degree requirements:* Computer language required, thesis optional, foreign language not required. *Entrance requirements:* Minimum GPA of 3.0 in last 60 hours or 2.75 overall. Application deadline: 8/1. *Tuition:* $76 per credit hour for state residents; $178 per credit hour for nonresidents. *Financial aid:* 8 students received aid; Federal Work-Study, institutionally sponsored loans available. Aid available to part-time students. Financial aid application deadline: 6/15. • Dean, 580-924-0121 Ext. 2533.

Stevens Institute of Technology, Wesley J. Howe School of Technology Management, Program in Concurrent Design Management, Hoboken, NJ 07030. Awards M Eng. Offered in cooperation with the Department of Mechanical Engineering. 13 applicants, 92% accepted. *Degree requirements:* Computer language required, thesis optional, foreign language not required. *Entrance requirements:* GMAT, GRE, TOEFL. Application deadline: rolling. Application fee: $45. Electronic applications accepted. *Expenses:* Tuition $13,500 per year full-time, $675 per credit part-time. Fees $160 per year. • J. Cordes, Head, 201-216-8258.

Stevens Institute of Technology, Wesley J. Howe School of Technology Management, Program in Design and Production Management, Hoboken, NJ 07030. Awards MS, Certificate. Offered in cooperation with the Department of Mechanical Engineering. 2 applicants, 0% accepted. *Degree requirements:* For master's, computer language required, thesis optional, foreign language not required; for Certificate, computer language required, foreign language not required. *Entrance requirements:* For master's, GMAT, GRE, TOEFL. Application deadline: rolling. Application fee: $45. Electronic applications accepted. *Expenses:* Tuition $13,500 per year full-time, $675 per credit part-time. Fees $160 per year. • Dr. James Teitjen, Head, Wesley J. Howe School of Technology Management, 201-216-5384. Fax: 201-216-5385.

Syracuse University, School of Management, PhD Program in Business Administration, Syracuse, NY 13244-0003. Offerings include operations management (PhD). Program faculty: 75. *Entrance requirements:* GMAT (minimum score 600). Application deadline: 2/1. Application fee: $40. *Tuition:* $13,320 per year full-time, $555 per credit hour part-time. • S. P. Raj, Associate Dean. Application contact: Barbara Buske, Secretary, 315-443-1001.

Syracuse University, School of Management, Program in Operations Management, Syracuse, NY 13244-0003. Awards MBA. Faculty: 4. Students: 5 full-time (2 women), 20 part-time (1 woman); includes 2 minority (both Asian Americans), 1 international. 18 applicants, 72% accepted. In 1997, 5 degrees awarded. *Entrance requirements:* GMAT. Application deadline: 2/1. Application fee: $40. *Tuition:* $13,320 per year full-time, $555 per credit hour part-time. *Financial aid:* Application deadline 3/1. • Frederick Easton, Coordinator, 315-443-3463. Application contact: Associate Dean, 315-443-3850.

Texas Tech University, Graduate School, College of Business Administration, Program in Information Systems and Quantitative Sciences, Lubbock, TX 79409. Offerings include operations management (PhD). Program faculty: 11 full-time (1 woman). *Degree requirements:* Computer language, dissertation, qualifying exams required, foreign language not required. *Entrance requirements:* GMAT (minimum score 580; average 620). Application deadline: 4/15 (priority date; rolling processing; 9/30 for spring admission). Application fee: $25 ($50 for international students). *Expenses:* Tuition $864 per year full-time, $120 per semester (minimum) part-time for state residents; $5976 per year full-time, $747 per semester (minimum) part-time for nonresidents. Fees $2321 per year full-time, $302 per semester (minimum) part-time. • Dr. Surya Yadav, Coordinator, 806-742-3192. E-mail: odsby@ttacs.ttu.edu. Application contact: Nancy Dodge, Director, 806-742-3184. Fax: 806-742-3958.

Towson University, Program in Information Technology Management, Towson, MD 21252-0001. Offerings include operations management (MS). Offered jointly with the University of Baltimore. *Application deadline:* rolling. *Application fee:* $40. *Expenses:* Tuition $187 per credit hour for state residents; $364 per credit hour for nonresidents. Fees $40 per credit hour. • Dr. Tom Basuray, Director, 410-830-2124. Fax: 410-830-6091. E-mail: tbasuray@towson.edu. Application contact: Fran Musotto, Office Manager, 410-830-2501. Fax: 410-830-4675. E-mail: fmusotto@towson.edu.

Union College, Graduate and Continuing Studies, Graduate Management Institute, Program in Industrial Administration, Schenectady, NY 12308-2311. Awards MS. Part-time and evening/weekend programs available. Students: 1 full-time (0 women), 4 part-time (1 woman). 2 applicants, 100% accepted. In 1997, 4 degrees awarded. *Degree requirements:* Computer language, comprehensive exam required, foreign language and thesis not required. *Entrance requirements:* GMAT. Application deadline: 5/15 (rolling processing). Application fee: $35. *Tuition:* $1434 per course. *Financial aid:* Research assistantships, partial tuition waivers available. Financial aid application deadline: 5/15. • Application contact: Carolyn Micklas, Recruiting and Admissions Coordinator, 518-388-6239.

The University of Alabama, The Manderson Graduate School of Business, Department of Management Science, Management Science Program, Tuscaloosa, AL 35487. Offers management science (MA, MBA, PhD), manufacturing management (MA, MBA, PhD), production management (MA, MBA, PhD). Faculty: 9 full-time (1 woman). Students: 6 full-time (0 women), 4 part-time (1 woman); includes 6 international. Average age 27. 10 applicants, 50% accepted. In 1997, 1 master's, 5 doctorates awarded. Terminal master's awarded for partial completion of doctoral program. *Degree requirements:* For master's, comprehensive exam required, thesis optional, foreign language not required; for doctorate, 1 foreign language (computer language can substitute), dissertation, comprehensive exam. *Average time to degree:* master's–2 years full-time; doctorate–5 years full-time. *Entrance requirements:* For master's, GMAT (average 625), TOEFL (minimum score 550); for doctorate, TOEFL. Application deadline: 7/6 (rolling processing). Application fee: $25. *Tuition:* $2684 per year full-time, $594 per semester (minimum) part-time for state residents; $7216 per year full-time, $1248 per semester (minimum) part-time for nonresidents. *Financial aid:* In 1997–98, 2 teaching assistantships averaging $845 per month and totaling $15,210 were awarded; fellowships, research assistantships, and career-related internships or fieldwork also available. *Faculty research:* Supply chain management, production and inventory modeling, scheduling. • Dr. Charles P. Schmidt, Coordinator, 205-348-8914. Fax: 205-348-0560. E-mail: cschmidt@cba.ua.edu.

University of Cincinnati, College of Business Administration, Department of Quantitative Analysis and Operations Management, Cincinnati, OH 45221. Offers programs in operations management (MBA, PhD), quantitative analysis (MBA, MS, PhD). Part-time and evening/weekend programs available. Faculty: 11 full-time. Students: 30 full-time (13 women), 51 part-time (13 women). 47 applicants, 36% accepted. In 1997, 17 master's, 2 doctorates awarded. *Degree requirements:* For doctorate, computer language, dissertation. *Average time to degree:* master's–2.9 years full-time; doctorate–6.3 years full-time. *Entrance requirements:* GMAT. Application fee: $30. *Tuition:* $7228 per year full-time, $185 per credit hour part-time for state residents; $13,812 per year full-time, $352 per credit hour part-time for nonresidents. *Financial aid:* Fellowships, graduate assistantships available. Financial aid application deadline: 2/15. • Jeffrey D. Camm, Head, 513-556-7140. Fax: 513-556-5499.

University of Colorado at Colorado Springs, Graduate School of Business Administration, Colorado Springs, CO 80933-7150. Offerings include production management (MBA). School faculty: 24 full-time (4 women). *Entrance requirements:* GMAT. Application deadline: 6/1 (priority date; 11/1 for spring admission). Application fee: $50. *Expenses:* Tuition $2860 per year full-time, $121 per credit hour part-time for state residents; $10,254 per year full-time, $420 per credit hour part-time for nonresidents. Fees $399 per year (minimum) full-time, $106 per year (minimum) part-time. • Dr. Richard Dicenza, Dean, 719-262-3113. E-mail: rdicenz@mail.uccs.edu. Application contact: Diane Belger, Adviser, 719-262-3408. Fax: 719-262-3494. E-mail: dbelger@mail.uccs.edu.

University of Dallas, Graduate School of Management, Program in Industrial Management, Irving, TX 75062-4799. Awards MBA, MM. Part-time programs available. Students: 45 (12 women). In 1997, 21 degrees awarded. *Average time to degree:* master's–1.3 years full-time, 2.3 years part-time. *Entrance requirements:* GMAT (minimum score 400), TOEFL (average 520), minimum GPA of 3.0. Application deadline: 8/6 (priority date; rolling processing; 12/8 for spring admission). Application fee: $25 ($50 for international students). *Expenses:* Tuition $380 per credit hour. Fees $125 per year. *Financial aid:* Application deadline 2/15. • Dr. David Gordon, Director, 972-721-5354. Fax: 972-721-5130. Application contact: Roxanne Del Rio, Director of Admissions, 972-721-5174. Fax: 972-721-4009. E-mail: admiss@gsm.udallas.edu.

University of Hartford, Barney School of Business and Public Administration, Program in Business Administration, West Hartford, CT 06117-1599. Offerings include operations management (MBA). Program faculty: 24 full-time (4 women), 15 part-time (1 woman). *Average time to degree:* master's–1.5 years full-time, 3 years part-time. *Entrance requirements:* GMAT, TOEFL. Application deadline: 7/1 (priority date; rolling processing; 12/1 for spring admission). Application fee: $35 ($50 for international students). Electronic applications accepted. • Christopher Galligan, Director, 860-768-4390. Application contact: Claire Silverstein, Assistant Director, 860-768-4900. Fax: 860-768-4821. E-mail: silverste@unavax.hartford.edu.

University of Houston, College of Business Administration, Program in Operations Management, 4800 Calhoun, Houston, TX 77204-2163. Awards MBA, PhD. Part-time and evening/weekend programs available. Faculty: 6 full-time (2 women). Students: 8 full-time (2 women), 16 part-time (1 woman); includes 2 Asian Americans, 1 Hispanic, 2 international. Average age 34. In 1997, 20 master's awarded. *Degree requirements:* For master's, computer language required, foreign language and thesis not required; for doctorate, computer language, dissertation, comprehensive exam required, foreign language not required. *Average time to degree:* master's–2 years full-time, 3.5 years part-time; doctorate–4 years full-time. *Entrance requirements:* For master's, GMAT (average 590), TOEFL (minimum score 620); for doctorate, GMAT or GRE. Application deadline: 5/1 (rolling processing; 10/1 for spring admission). Application fee: $50 ($125 for international students). *Expenses:* Tuition $1152 per year full-time, $120 per semester (minimum) part-time for state residents; $4482 per year full-time, $249 per credit hour part-time for nonresidents. Fees $977 per year full-time, $119 per semester (minimum) part-time. *Financial aid:* Research assistantships, teaching assistantships, Federal Work-Study, and career-related internships or fieldwork available. Aid available to part-time students. Financial aid application deadline: 3/1; applicants required to submit FAFSA. • Dr. Dennis Adams, Chair, 713-743-4747. Application contact: Office of Student Services, 713-743-4900. Fax: 713-743-4942. E-mail: oss@cba.uh.edu.

University of La Verne, School of Business and Economics, La Verne, CA 91750-4443. Offerings include operations management (MS). *Application fee:* $25. *Expenses:* Tuition $335 per unit. Fees $60 per year.

University of Massachusetts Lowell, College of Management, Program in Manufacturing Management, 1 University Avenue, Lowell, MA 01854-2881. Awards MMS. Part-time and evening/weekend programs available. Students: 13 full-time (3 women), 27 part-time (3 women); includes 2 minority (both Asian Americans), 1 international. In 1997, 35 degrees awarded. *Degree requirements:* Computer language required, foreign language and thesis not required. *Entrance requirements:* GMAT. Application deadline: 4/1 (priority date; rolling processing; 10/1 for spring admission). Application fee: $20 ($35 for international students). *Tuition:* $4867 per year full-time, $618 per semester (minimum) part-time for state residents; $10,276 per year full-time, $1294 per semester (minimum) part-time for nonresidents. *Financial aid:* Fellowships, research assistantships, teaching assistantships, Federal Work-Study, institutionally sponsored loans, and career-related internships or fieldwork available. Aid available to part-time students. Financial aid application deadline: 4/1. • Dr. Kathryn Verreault, Dean, College of Management, 978-934-2740. Application contact: Dr. Norma Powell, Coordinator, 978-934-2848. E-mail: norma_powell@woods.uml.edu.

University of Minnesota, Twin Cities Campus, Carlson School of Management, Department of Operations and Management Science, Minneapolis, MN 55455-0213. Awards MBA, PhD. MBA offered jointly with the Master's Program in Business Administration; PhD offered jointly with the Doctoral Program in Business Administration. *Degree requirements:* For doctorate, dissertation required, foreign language not required. *Entrance requirements:* GMAT. *Faculty research:* Applied statistics, operations strategy, technology management, quality management, simulation, scheduling.

University of North Dakota, College of Business and Public Administration, Department of Industrial Technology, Grand Forks, ND 58202. Awards MS. Admissions temporarily suspended. Faculty: 5 full-time (1 woman). Students: 7 full-time (2 women), 5 part-time (3 women). 1 applicant, 100% accepted. In 1997, 4 degrees awarded. *Degree requirements:* Thesis or alternative. *Financial aid:* In 1997–98, 4 students received aid, including 3 teaching assistantships totaling $14,500, 1 assistantship totaling $3,625; fellowships, research assistantships, partial tuition waivers also available. • Dr. James Navara, Chairperson, 701-777-2249. Fax: 701-777-4320. E-mail: undgrad@mail.und.nodak.edu.

University of North Texas, College of Business Administration, Department of Management, Denton, TX 76203-6737. Offerings include production/operations management (MBA, PhD). Department faculty: 16 full-time (3 women), 5 part-time (3 women). *Degree requirements:* For master's, computer language required, foreign language and thesis not required; for doctorate, computer language, dissertation required, foreign language not required. *Entrance requirements:* For master's, GMAT, TOEFL, work experience; for doctorate, GMAT or GRE General Test, TOEFL, work experience. Application deadline: 7/17. Application fee: $25 ($50 for international students). *Tuition:* $2063 per year full-time, $815 per year part-time for state residents; $5897 per year full-time, $2100 per year part-time for nonresidents. • Dr. Lewis A. Taylor, Chair, 940-565-3140. Application contact: Dr. J. Lyn Johnson, Graduate Adviser, 940-565-3147. Fax: 940-565-4394.

University of Rhode Island, College of Business Administration, Kingston, RI 02881. Offerings include management science (MBA), with options in management information systems, manufacturing. *Application deadline:* 4/15 (priority date; rolling processing). *Application fee:* $35. *Expenses:* Tuition $3446 per year full-time, $191 per credit part-time for state residents; $9850 per year full-time, $547 per credit part-time for nonresidents. Fees $1276 per year full-time, $135 per semester (minimum) part-time.

University of St. Thomas, Graduate School of Business, Day MBA Program, St. Paul, MN 55105-1096. Offerings include manufacturing systems (MBA). Program faculty: 13 part-time. *Degree requirements:* Computer language required, foreign language and thesis not required. *Entrance requirements:* GMAT (score in 50th percentile or higher). Application deadline: 5/1 (priority date; rolling processing). Application fee: $30. *Tuition:* $473 per credit hour. • Application contact: Jim O'Connor, Student Adviser, 612-962-4233. Fax: 612-962-4260.

University of St. Thomas, Graduate School of Business, Evening MBA Program, St. Paul, MN 55105-1096. Offerings include manufacturing systems (MBA). Program faculty: 16 full-time (2 women), 89 part-time (17 women). *Degree requirements:* Computer language required, foreign language and thesis not required. *Entrance requirements:* GMAT (score in 50th percentile or higher). Application deadline: 8/1 (priority date; rolling processing; 12/1 for spring admission). Application fee: $30. *Tuition:* $416 per credit hour. • Dr. Stanford Nyquist, MBA Director, 612-962-4242. Application contact: Martha Ballard, Director of Student Services, 612-962-4226. Fax: 612-962-4260.

University of Southern Indiana, Graduate Studies, School of Science and Engineering Technology, Program in Industrial Management, Evansville, IN 47712-3590. Awards MS. Part-time and evening/weekend programs available. Faculty: 5 full-time (0 women). Students: 10 part-time (1 woman). Average age 38. 2 applicants, 100% accepted. In 1997, 1 degree awarded. *Degree requirements:* Project required, foreign language and thesis not required. *Entrance requirements:* Minimum GPA of 2.5, BS in engineering or engineering technology. Application deadline: rolling. Application fee: $25. *Tuition:* $129 per credit hour for state residents; $260 per credit hour for nonresidents. • Larry Goss, Director, 812-465-1087. E-mail: lgoss.ucs@smtp.usi.edu.

University of Southern Maine, School of Applied Science, Program in Manufacturing Management, Portland, ME 04104-9300. Awards MS. Part-time and evening/weekend programs available. Faculty: 6 full-time (0 women), 2 part-time (0 women). Students: 6 part-time (0 women). Average age 31. 0 applicants. *Average time to degree:* master's–2 years full-time. *Entrance requirements:* GMAT (minimum score 500; average 570), minimum GPA of 3.0. Application fee: $25. *Expenses:* Tuition $178 per credit hour for state residents; $267 per credit hour (minimum) for nonresidents. Fees $282 per year full-time, $83 per semester (minimum) part-time. *Financial aid:* Federal Work-Study available. Aid available to part-time students. Financial aid application deadline: 4/1. *Faculty research:* Resource allocation, organizational creativity, simulation, process optimization. • James W. Smith, Director, 207-780-5584. Fax: 207-780-5129. Application contact: Mary Sloan, Assistant Director of Graduate Studies, 207-780-4386. Fax: 207-780-4969. E-mail: msloan@usm.maine.edu.

University of Tennessee at Chattanooga, School of Business Administration, Program in Business Administration, Chattanooga, TN 37403-2598. Offerings include operations/production (MBA). *Entrance requirements:* GMAT (average 527). Application deadline: rolling. Application fee: $25. *Tuition:* $2864 per year full-time, $160 per credit hour part-time for state residents; $6806 per year full-time, $379 per credit hour part-time for nonresidents. • Ashley Williams, Director, 423-755-4169. Fax: 423-755-5255. Application contact: Dr. Deborah Arfken, Assistant Provost for Graduate Studies, 423-755-4667. Fax: 423-755-4478.

University of Tennessee, Knoxville, College of Business Administration, Program in Business Administration, Knoxville, TN 37996. Offerings include manufacturing management (MBA). MS/MBA offered jointly with the College of Engineering. Postbaccalaureate distance learning degree programs offered. Program faculty: 51 full-time (6 women). *Application deadline:* 2/1 (priority date). *Application fee:* $35. Electronic applications accepted. *Tuition:* $3354 per year full-time, $181 per semester hour part-time for state residents; $8410 per year full-time, $462 per semester hour part-time for nonresidents. • Dr. Gary Dicer, Director, 423-974-5033. E-mail: gdicer@utk.edu. Application contact: Donald Potts, Graduate Representative, 423-974-5033. Fax: 423-974-3826. E-mail: dpotts@utk.edu.

University of Toledo, Graduate School of Business, Department of Information Systems and Operations Management, Program in Manufacturing Management, Toledo, OH 43606-3398. Awards MS, PhD. Students: 49 full-time (8 women), 33 part-time (10 women); includes 1 minority (African American), 60 international. Average age 30. 48 applicants, 75% accepted. In 1997, 6 master's, 1 doctorate awarded. *Degree requirements:* For doctorate, dissertation. *Entrance requirements:* For master's, GMAT (minimum score 525), TOEFL (minimum score 550), minimum GPA of 2.7; for doctorate, GMAT (minimum score 575), TOEFL (minimum score 550). Application deadline: 8/1 (priority date; rolling processing). Application fee: $30. *Tuition:* $5907 per year full-time, $246 per hour part-time for state residents; $11,835 per year full-time, $493 per hour part-time for nonresidents. *Financial aid:* Application deadline 4/1. • Dr. Mark Vonderembse, Director, 419-530-2067. Fax: 419-530-8497.

University of Victoria, Faculty of Human and Social Development, School of Public Administration, Victoria, BC V8W 2Y2, Canada. Offerings include personnel and industrial relations (MPA). School faculty: 14 full-time (1 woman), 13 part-time (6 women), 18 FTE. *Degree requirements:* Report required, foreign language and thesis not required. *Average time to degree:* master's–4 years full-time. *Entrance requirements:* GMAT or GRE General Test, TOEFL (minimum score 550). Application deadline: 5/1 (rolling processing; 10/15 for spring admission). Application fee: $50. *Tuition:* $2080 per year full-time, $557 per semester part-time. • Dr. B. Wharf, Acting Director, 250-721-8054. Application contact: Dr. B. Bish, Graduate Adviser, 250-721-8065.

University of Wisconsin–Madison, School of Business, Program in Manufacturing and Technology Management, Madison, WI 53706-1380. Awards MS. Part-time programs available. *Average time to degree:* master's–2 years full-time. *Entrance requirements:* GMAT (minimum score 580; average 630), minimum GPA of 3.0, 2 years of work experience. Application deadline: 6/1 (priority date; rolling processing; 10/1 for spring admission). Application fee: $38. Electronic applications accepted. *Tuition:* $5950 per year full-time, $1118 per semester (minimum) part-time for state residents; $16,230 per year full-time, $3044 per semester (minimum) part-time for nonresidents. *Faculty research:* Analysis, design, evaluation, implementation and operation of manufacturing systems, management of technological change.

University of Wisconsin–Madison, School of Business, Program in Operations and Information Management, Madison, WI 53706-1380. Awards MBA, MS, PhD. Part-time programs available. Faculty: Students: 22 full-time (8 women), 7 part-time (2 women); includes 3 minority (2 African Americans, 1 Asian American), 5 international. Average age 27. 22 applicants, 45% accepted. In 1997, 12 master's awarded. Terminal master's awarded for partial completion of doctoral program. *Degree requirements:* For doctorate, dissertation. *Entrance requirements:* For master's, GMAT (minimum score 580; average 600), minimum GPA of 3.0. Application deadline: 6/1 (priority date; rolling processing; 10/1 for spring admission). Application fee: $45. Electronic applications accepted. *Tuition:* $5950 per year full-time, $1118 per semester (minimum) part-time for state residents; $16,230 per year full-time, $3044 per semester (minimum) part-time for nonresidents. *Financial aid:* In 1997–98, 3 students received aid, including 3 teaching assistantships; fellowships, research assistantships, project assistantships, Federal Work-Study, institutionally sponsored loans, and career-related internships or fieldwork also available. Aid available to part-time students. Financial aid application deadline: 2/15. *Faculty research:* Cost improvement, productivity improvement, transportation economics, financial signalling, optimization models, distribution system design. • James G. Morris, Chair, 608-262-1284. Fax: 608-263-3142. E-mail: jmorris@bus.wisc.edu. Application contact: Lisa Urban, Director of Master's Marketing and Recruiting, 608-262-4610. Fax: 608-265-4192.

University of Wisconsin–Platteville, College of Business, Industry, Life Science, and Agriculture, Program in Industrial Technology Management, Platteville, WI 53818-3099. Awards MS. Part-time programs available. Faculty: 6 part-time (0 women). Students: 4 full-time (0 women), 10 part-time (2 women). 10 applicants, 60% accepted. In 1997, 5 degrees awarded. *Degree requirements:* Thesis or alternative, comprehensive exam required, foreign language not required. *Entrance requirements:* TOEFL (minimum score 500). Application deadline: 7/1 (priority date; rolling processing; 11/1 for spring admission). Application fee: $45. *Financial aid:* In 1997–98, 4 assistantships (3 to first-year students) were awarded; Federal Work-Study, institutionally sponsored loans, and career-related internships or fieldwork also available. Aid available to part-time students. • Dr. Joe Thomas, Chair, Department of Industrial Studies, 608-342-1246. Fax: 608-342-1246. E-mail: thomas@uwplatt.edu.

Vanderbilt University, Owen Graduate School of Management and Graduate School, Program in Management, Nashville, TN 37240-1001. Offerings include operations management (PhD). PhD offered through the Graduate School. *Degree requirements:* Dissertation required, foreign language not required. *Entrance requirements:* GMAT (minimum score 650), GRE, TOEFL (minimum score 600). Application deadline: 1/15. Application fee: $50. *Tuition:* $871 per semester hour. • Bruce Barry, Director, 615-322-3489. Application contact: Maureen Writesman, 615-343-1989. Fax: 615-343-7177. E-mail: owenphd@ctrvax.vanderbilt.edu.

Worcester Polytechnic Institute, Department of Management, Worcester, MA 01609-2280. Offerings include manufacturing management (MS). MBA, MSM (administration and management, engineering management), MS (manufacturing management) being phased out; applicants no longer accepted. Department faculty: 15 full-time (4 women), 7 part-time (1 woman). *Application deadline:* 2/15 (priority date; rolling processing; 10/15 for spring admission). *Application fee:* $50. Electronic applications accepted. *Tuition:* $636 per credit hour. • Dr. McRae Banks, Head, 508-831-5218. E-mail: macb@wpi.edu. Application contact: Norm Wilkinson, Director, 508-831-5218. Fax: 508-831-5720. E-mail: nwilkins@wpi.edu.

Wright State University, College of Business and Administration, Department of Management Science and Information Systems, Dayton, OH 45435. Offerings include operations management (MBA). *Application fee:* $25. *Tuition:* $5109 per year full-time, $161 per credit hour part-time for state residents; $9039 per year full-time, $282 per credit hour part-time for nonresidents. • Dr. Barbara Denison, Chair, 937-775-2895. Application contact: James Crawford, Director of Graduate Programs, 937-775-2437. Fax: 937-775-3301.

Cross-Discipline Announcements

Clarkson University, Interdisciplinary Studies, Potsdam, NY 13699.

Clarkson University offers an interdisciplinary Master of Science degree in engineering and manufacturing management (EMM) that provides a background in manufacturing engineering, quality control, and management. There are two ways that this degree can be obtained: through a regular academic-year program or through a summer program. Details can be found on the Web (http://www.clarkson.edu/~grad/gs/message.html) or by contacting Professor F. Mahmoodi (telephone: 315-268-3998; e-mail: mahmoodi@icarus.som.clarkson.edu).

Rensselaer Polytechnic Institute, Lally School of Management and Technology, Troy, NY 12180-3590.

The Lally Entrepreneurship Program offers world-class graduate programs, research, and out-of-the-classroom interaction opportunities with Rensselaer's highly regarded Incubator Program, Technology Park, Venture Affiliates of RPI, Office of Technology Commercialization, and extensive networks of successful entrepreneurs. The Center for Technological Entrepreneurship hosts a general and student business plan competition each year that features cash awards and seed capital.

CLEMSON UNIVERSITY

College of Business and Public Affairs
Department of Management

Programs of Study

The department awards M.S. and Ph.D. degrees in industrial management. Industrial management, also known as operations management, is concerned with the systems, processes, and activities that produce the goods and services of an organization.

The Master of Science in Industrial Management (M.S.I.M.) program is designed to provide a comprehensive education to current and future managers of manufacturing and service operations as well as students interested in further study at the doctoral level. The M.S.I.M. focuses on the capabilities and resources of operations and the role of operations in the formulation and implementation of organization strategies. The program requires 15 semester hours of core courses, 15 semester hours of focus electives beyond the program corequisites, and a final examination. Full-time students may complete the M.S.I.M. program in one calendar year, including summer school. Part-time students may complete the program in two calendar years. Distinguishing features of the M.S.I.M. program include its emphasis on operations management and opportunities for field projects and international study.

The Ph.D. program in industrial management is designed to produce operations management scholars who are capable of contributing to the body of knowledge through research and teaching. The program requires 42 semester hours of course work, a comprehensive examination, and successful completion of the dissertation. Full-time students may complete the program in four calendar years. Faculty members are actively involved in guiding student research, which covers a wide spectrum of operations management issues that focus on operations strategy, planning and control systems, information systems, and management science modeling.

Research Facilities

Students have access to campus PC laboratories that contain various application software packages and provide access to the MVS main frame computer, several UNIX servers, the Internet, and the World Wide Web. Sirrine Hall, which houses the industrial management programs, has forty-four networked PCs in student laboratories in addition to several computer-equipped classrooms. The department also has access to industrial manufacturing resource planning software, which is often used for experimental research. Students have access to the main library, which holds more than 1.6 million items (books, periodicals, microforms, government publications, and electronic materials). Access to the library's collections is provided through the Online Libraries Catalog, a part of the Library's CU Explorer system. To assist in finding journal and newspaper articles, the library provides access to a number of electronic indexes, several of which give access to full-text journals on line. CU Explorer is accessible from most computers on campus as well as through dial-in access.

Financial Aid

The department offers financial assistance packages comparable to peer graduate programs. Assistantships include significant tuition reduction and a graduate stipend. Full-time M.S.I.M. students are eligible for graduate assistantships for a maximum period of eighteen months. Ph.D. students may be offered teaching or research assistantships, which are typically renewable for up to four years, pending satisfactory progress. In addition to regular departmental assistantships, the Liberty Fellowship pays $6000 (nonrenewable) and the Graduate School awards numerous University-wide fellowships of $5000 each for the academic year. South Carolina Graduate Incentive Fellowships of $5000 for master's students and $10,000 for doctoral students are available to members of minority groups.

Cost of Study

For 1997–98, graduate assistants paid a flat tuition fee of $480 per semester and $160 for each summer session. Full-time graduate students not on assistantship paid semester tuition fees of $1531 (South Carolina residents) or $3702 (nonresidents). Part-time graduate students paid $126 (South Carolina residents) or $252 (nonresidents) per semester hour. These figures are subject to change for 1998–99.

Living and Housing Costs

For 1997–98, living and housing costs are estimated to be $9000 per calendar year. In addition, each student is expected to pay a medical fee of $258 per year. Health insurance is estimated to cost $549 annually. Limited on-campus apartment-style housing is available for both single and married graduate students. Plenty of reasonably priced apartment-style housing is available off campus.

Student Group

Graduate students in industrial management are a diverse and highly motivated group. Students from Brazil, Bulgaria, China, France, Germany, India, Portugal, Taiwan, and Turkey make up approximately 50 percent of the student body. This diversity significantly enriches the learning environment. One third of the students are women. Approximately 75 percent of the students receive financial assistance. Many industrial management graduate students have professional work experience, and all have serious interests in operations management.

Student Outcomes

Graduates of the M.S.I.M. program are operations analysts, managers, and consultants in a variety of organizations, including Federal Express, Ford Motor Company, Sonoco Products, Andersen Consulting, and the Greenville Hospital System. Ph.D. graduates serve on the business school faculty at regional, national, and international universities, including the University of Houston, the Air Force Institute of Technology, James Madison University, the University of Oklahoma, Howard University, and the University of Coimbra, Portugal.

Location

Clemson University is approximately 2½ hours from Atlanta, Georgia; Columbia, South Carolina; and Charlotte, North Carolina and less than an hour west of Greenville, South Carolina. Clemson University's 1,400-acre main campus, located in the city of Clemson in the northwestern corner of South Carolina, is surrounded by 17,000 acres of University farms and woodlands that are devoted to research.

The University and The Department

Clemson University was founded in 1889 as a land-grant institution of South Carolina. Clemson's Department of Management has developed an outstanding reputation for its broad-based programs in industrial management. The department consists of 25 full-time faculty members whose teaching and research interests include operations management, organizational behavior, human resource management, logistics, management science, strategic management, management information systems, and international business management. The industrial management programs address significant issues related to these disciplines.

Applying

Students are admitted in both the fall and spring semesters. M.S.I.M. applications must be received at least five weeks prior to registration. International students must apply by April 15 for the fall semester or September 15 for the spring semester. Ph.D. applications must be received by February 1 for the fall semester or October 1 for the spring semester.

All completed application materials are submitted to the Graduate School, Clemson University, Clemson, South Carolina 29634-5120 (telephone: 864-656-3195). Online applications and information are available at http://www.grad.clemson.edu.

Correspondence and Information

Col. Ben Huneycutt
Department of Management
Clemson University
Clemson, South Carolina 29634-1305
Telephone: 864-656-1333
Fax: 864-656-2015
E-mail: tben@clemson.edu
World Wide Web: http://www.clemson.edu/management

Clemson University

THE FACULTY AND THEIR RESEARCH

Nagraj Balakrishnan, Associate Professor (management science, statistics, and operations management); Ph.D., Purdue, 1987. Job and tool scheduling on flexible machines, capacity allocation models, interface between manufacturing and marketing, transportation planning.
John Butler, Professor (organizational behavior); D.B.A., Florida State, 1977. Conflict management and negotiation, building trust, leadership, informal organization.
Stephen Cantrell, Professor (statistics); Ph.D., North Carolina State, 1982. Applied statistical analysis.
Richard Clarke, Associate Professor (transportation and logistics); Ph.D., Texas, 1988. Productivity assessment in nonprofit organizations, international transportation.
Michael Crino, Professor (organizational behavior and human resource management); Ph.D., Florida, 1978. Personnel management.
J. Steve Davis, Professor (management information systems); Ph.D., Georgia Tech, 1984. Decision support systems, human factors in computer systems, supply chain management.
Larry Fredendall, Associate Professor (operations management); Ph.D., Michigan State, 1990. Implementing theory of constraints, implementing quality management.
David Grigsby, Professor (strategy and international management) and Department Chair; Ph.D., North Carolina, 1980. International strategic management.
Ben Huneycutt, Lecturer (operations management); M.S., Air Force Tech, 1973.
John J. Kanet, Burlington Professor (operations management); Ph.D., Penn State, 1979. Manufacturing logistics planning.
R. Lawrence LaForge, Alumni Distinguished Professor (operations management); Ph.D., Georgia, 1976. Manufacturing planning, control systems.
Terry Leap, Professor (organizational behavior, human resource management, and business strategy); Ph.D., Iowa, 1978. Human resource management issues in mergers and acquisitions, employment discrimination, employee problem behaviors in the workplace.
Judith McKnew, Lecturer (management science and statistics); Ph.D., Clemson, 1994.
Mark McKnew, Professor (management science); Ph.D., MIT, 1978. Management science modeling.
Janis Miller, Associate Professor (management science and statistics); Ph.D., Missouri, 1990. Application of management science techniques, service recovery.
Gary Newkirk, Lecturer (management science and operations management); Ph.D., Clemson University, 1992.
J. Wayne Patterson, Associate Professor (management science, operations management, and statistics); Ph.D., Arkansas, 1977. Operations management, with emphasis on the theory of constraints; capacity management; quality management and maintenance.
Richard Pouder, Assistant Professor (strategy); Ph.D., Connecticut, 1993. Application of strategic, institutional, and cognitive perspectives to such areas as innovation, downsizing, and governance.
Tina Robbins, Associate Professor (organizational behavior and human resource management); Ph.D., South Carolina, 1991. Employee empowerment, organizational justice.
Phil Roth, Professor (organizational behavior and human resource management); Ph.D., Houston, 1988. Personnel selection, cognitive ability tests, interviewing, utility analysis, missing data.
Caron St. John, Associate Professor (strategy and operations management); Ph.D., Georgia State, 1988. Competitive, technology, and operations strategies of business, specifically the role of geographical clustering in high-technology industries and its effects on strategies, innovation, and competitiveness over time.
V. Sridharan, Professor (operations management and management science); Ph.D., Iowa, 1987. Manufacturing planning control systems, artificial intelligence applications, capacity and demand management.
Wayne H. Stewart Jr., Assistant Professor (strategy and entrepreneurship); Ph.D., North Texas, 1995. Individual determinants of new venture creation and performance, including cross-cultural considerations; strategy and human resource issues in the Russian Federation.
Timothy Summers, Associate Professor (organizational behavior and human resource management); Ph.D., South Carolina, 1986. Organizational justice, particularly perceptions of procedural and distributive justice and their effects; linking corporate strategy to human resources strategy.

NEW JERSEY INSTITUTE OF TECHNOLOGY

School of Management

Program of Study

The management programs place particular emphasis on how technology and information management relate to human resources, the environment, marketing, operations management, finance, international business auditing, and transportation. The School of Management (SOM), fully accredited by AACSB–The International Association for Management Education, offers a variety of program opportunities leading to the Master of Science degree in management.

The basic program is a minimum of 30 credits, including a thesis option. The specialization in environmental management is 48 credits. There is an intensive, accelerated Executive Program, which focuses on global competitiveness, total quality, and environmental and ethical issues in business.

There is close academic collaboration with neighboring Rutgers University through cross-registration and a Ph.D. program in management offered at the Newark campus of Rutgers University. NJIT faculty are responsible for several specialized areas within the Ph.D. program. The School of Management operates courses for the Master of Science programs at off-campus locations throughout the state. Dual degree program options exist at NJIT between the School of Management and the NJIT School of Architecture and also with the manufacturing engineering program.

Research Facilities

Graduate students are an integral part of all research at NJIT. The University is recognized nationally and internationally for its innovative research in environmental science and engineering, hazardous-waste management, advanced manufacturing, microelectronics and communications, the management of technology, biomedical engineering, architectural building science, and transportation. The Hazardous Substance Management Research Center is the nation's largest industry/university cooperative research program devoted to hazardous substance management and is internationally recognized. There are also leading research centers on information technologies, robotics, communications, signal processing, microelectronics, applied mathematics, and transportation. The Microelectronics Research Center is a facility (featuring a class 10 clean room) devoted to the design and testing of silicon-based microelectronic and optoelectronics control devices and the development of electronic imaging systems and microwave and lightwave devices and systems. NJIT has centralized its computing services through a number of powerful systems. A fiber-optic spine connects nearly 2,000 campus locations and beyond.

Financial Aid

Support is available to full-time students in the form of teaching, graduate, and research assistantships. Support for summer research is available. Tuition remission is often included in assistantships. Securing financial support is highly competitive, so early application is strongly recommended.

Cost of Study

Tuition for part-time students in 1997–98 was $346 per credit for residents of New Jersey and $479 for nonresidents. Full-time tuition (12 to 19 credits) was $3330 per semester for residents and $4739 for nonresidents. The tuition costs cited do not include student fees.

Living and Housing Costs

A limited amount of on-campus housing, the cost of which averages $4490 annually, is available for graduate students. Average room and board total $6382 per academic year. The Office of Residence Life assists in finding off-campus housing in Newark and surrounding communities.

Student Group

Of the 8,133 students enrolled at New Jersey Institute of Technology, 3,138 are either full- or part-time graduate students.

Location

NJIT's 45-acre campus is located in the University Heights section of New Jersey's largest city, Newark. Its location offers many activities. It is home to the New Jersey Performing Arts Center, the New Jersey Symphony, and the Newark Museum. Branch Brook Park is just minutes from the campus, New York City is 10 miles away, and blocks away are campuses of Rutgers University, the University of Medicine and Dentistry of New Jersey, Seton Hall Law School, and Essex County College. Many programs operate collaboratively with these institutions. Public transportation is available, and the New Jersey shore is close by.

The University

New Jersey Institute of Technology is the state's public technological research university. Founded in 1881, NJIT has maintained close ties with industry by preparing generations of students to assume leadership roles in an increasingly technological society. The university's first and largest school is Newark College of Engineering, which was established in 1919 to reflect the institution's evolution into a four-year college. When the School of Architecture was established in 1973, a name change to New Jersey Institute of Technology reflected a broadened mission. The College of Science and Liberal Arts, founded in 1982; the School of Management, founded in 1988; and the Albert Dorman Honors College, founded in 1993, round out the university's educational offerings.

Applying

Applicants should contact the Office of University Admissions for admission instructions and forms. Completed applications must be received before June 5 for fall admission and October 15 for spring admission. Students can also apply on line via the World Wide Web. January 15 is the deadline for applying for financial support for the following fall.

GMAT scores are required for admission to the master's degree programs in management. Transcripts, letters of recommendation, and a $50 nonrefundable application fee are required. International students must provide TOEFL scores as well as equivalent academic credentials from their countries of origin.

Correspondence and Information

Office of University Admissions
New Jersey Institute of Technology
University Heights
Newark, New Jersey 07102-1982
Telephone: 973-596-3300
Fax: 973-596-3461
World Wide Web: http://www.njit.edu

New Jersey Institute of Technology

THE FACULTY

Alok Chakrabarti, Ph.D.; Dean and Sponsored Chair in Management of Technology.

Distinguished Professors
Alok Chakrabarti, Ph.D., Northwestern.
Bruce Kirchhoff, Ph.D., Utah.
Murray Turoff, Ph.D., Brandeis.

Professors
Iftekhar Hasan, Ph.D., Houston.
David Hawk, Ph.D., Pennsylvania.
Kenneth Lawrence, Ph.D., Rutgers.
Naomi Rotter, Ph.D., NYU.
Hindy Schachter, Ph.D., Columbia.

Associate Professors
Homer Bonitsis, Ph.D., CUNY, City College.
Rene Cordero, Ph.D., Rutgers.
William Havlena, Ph.D., Columbia.
Mark Somers, Ph.D., CUNY, City College.
Lazar Spasovic, Ph.D., Pennsylvania.
Cheickna Sylla, Ph.D., SUNY at Buffalo.

Assistant Professors
Asokan Anandarajan, Ph.D., Drexel.
C. Lenard Anyanwu, Ph.D., Texas.
Jerry Fjermestad, Ph.D., Rutgers.
Gertrude Heller, Ph.D., Pennsylvania.
Gary Kleinman, Ph.D., Rutgers; CPA.
Roswell Mathis, Ph.D., Florida Tech.
Steven Walsh, Ph.D., Rensselaer.
Joseph Wen, Ph.D., Virginia Commonwealth.

Special Lecturers
Paul Dine, Ph.D., Gregorian (Rome).
David P. Wachspress, Ph.D., NYU.
Malcolm Worrell, Ph.D., Rutgers.

Visiting Faculty
Ranjit Sau, Ph.D., Wayne State.

RESEARCH AREAS

International Business. Government regulation of international firms with production facilities in many countries, public policy in the People's Republic of China, human resource considerations in investing in Eastern European countries, multinational strategy in international competition. Dine, Hawk.

Economics. Gender discrimination in labor markets, labor markets in developing countries, foreign exchange exposure and management, art as investment. Bonitsis, Hasan, Mathis.

Operations Management. Operations research techniques in manufacturing quality assurance systems, modeling of training systems, Japanese just-in-time inventory. Cordero, Lawrence, Sylla.

Organizational Behavior. Links among aspects of nonverbal behavior, gender differences, and personality variables; training needs assessment in technical organizations; adjustment process and how it is affected by expectations associated with career and occupational identities; commitment development. Heller, Rotter, Somers.

Marketing. Productivity and compensation of industrial salespersons. Havlena, Lawrence.

Management of Technology. Defense technology and its impact on the civilian sector, interaction between technology and human resources, international competitiveness of the U.S. economy. Chakrabarti, Hawk, Walsh.

Public Management. Frederick Taylor and the public administration community. Schachter.

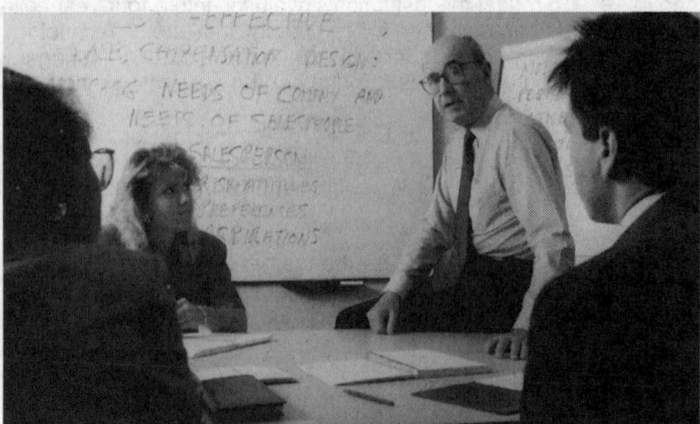

Researchers at NJIT's School of Management focus on the utilization of new technologies to develop creative new approaches to business concerns such as organizational behavior, manufacturing productivity, international competitiveness, and the role of small businesses in the economy.

Section 9
Insurance and Actuarial Science

This section contains directories of institutions offering graduate work in actuarial science and insurance, followed by in-depth entries submitted by institutions that chose to prepare detailed program descriptions. Additional information about programs listed in the directories but not augmented by an in-depth entry may be obtained by writing directly to the dean of a graduate school or chair of a department at the address given in the directory.

For programs offering related work, see also in this book Business Administration and Management.

CONTENTS

Program Directories

Announcement

In-Depth Description

Actuarial Science

Ball State University, College of Sciences and Humanities, Department of Mathematical Sciences, Program in Actuarial Science, 2000 University Avenue, Muncie, IN 47306-1099. Awards MA. Students: 12 full-time (3 women); includes 2 minority (1 African American, 1 Hispanic), 5 international. Average age 24. 16 applicants, 81% accepted. In 1997, 7 degrees awarded. *Entrance requirements:* GMAT. Application fee: $15 ($25 for international students). *Expenses:* Tuition $3454 per year full-time, $518 per semester (minimum) part-time for state residents; $9316 per year full-time, $1221 per semester (minimum) part-time for nonresidents. Fees $242 per year full-time, $18 per semester (minimum) part-time. *Financial aid:* Research assistantships available. • William Frye, Director, 765-285-8659.

Boston University, Metropolitan College, Program in Actuarial Science, Boston, MA 02215. Awards MS. Part-time and evening/weekend programs available. Students: 53 full-time (29 women), 21 part-time (9 women); includes 4 minority (all Asian Americans), 39 international. Average age 26. In 1997, 21 degrees awarded. *Degree requirements:* Computer language required, foreign language and thesis not required. *Entrance requirements:* TOEFL (minimum score 550). Application deadline: rolling. Application fee: $45. *Expenses:* Tuition $15,488 per year full-time, $484 per credit part-time. Fees $218 per year full-time, $40 per semester part-time. *Financial aid:* Federal Work-Study, institutionally sponsored loans, and career-related internships or fieldwork available. *Faculty research:* Survival models, life contingencies, numerical analysis, operations research. • Dr. Austin Lee, Director, 617-353-9553. Fax: 617-353-8100. E-mail: fong@math.bu.edu.

College of Insurance, Graduate Programs, Program in Business Administration, New York, NY 10007-2165. Offerings include actuarial science (MBA). Program faculty: 12 full-time (1 woman), 12 part-time (1 woman). *Degree requirements:* Computer language required, thesis optional, foreign language not required. *Entrance requirements:* GMAT (minimum score 500), TOEFL (minimum score 550). Application deadline: 7/15 (priority date; rolling processing; 11/1 for spring admission). Application fee: $30 ($50 for international students). *Expenses:* Tuition $554 per credit. Fees $15 per credit. • Application contact: Theresa C. Marro, Director of Admissions, 212-815-9232. Fax: 212-964-3381. E-mail: admissions@tci.edu.

See in-depth description on page 523.

Georgia State University, College of Business Administration, Department of Risk Management and Insurance, Atlanta, GA 30303-3083. Offerings include actuarial science (MAS). Department faculty: 21 full-time, 1 part-time. *Application deadline:* 5/1 (rolling processing; 10/1 for spring admission). *Application fee:* $25. *Expenses:* Tuition $2673 per year full-time, $99 per semester hour part-time for state residents; $10,692 per year full-time, $396 per semester hour part-time for nonresidents. Fees $228 per year. • Bruce A. Palmer, Chair, 404-651-2725. Fax: 404-651-4219. Application contact: Office of Academic Assistance and Master's Admissions, 404-651-1913. Fax: 404-651-0219.

Roosevelt University, College of Arts and Sciences, School of Science and Mathematics, Program in Mathematics, Chicago, IL 60605-1394. Offerings include mathematical sciences (MS), with option in actuarial science. Program faculty: 6 full-time (0 women). *Application deadline:* 6/1 (priority date; rolling processing). *Application fee:* $25 ($35 for international students). *Expenses:* Tuition $445 per credit hour. Fees $100 per year. • John Currano, Graduate Adviser, 312-341-3773. Application contact: Joanne Canyon-Heller, Coordinator of Graduate Admissions, 312-341-3612.

Temple University, School of Business and Management, Master's Program in Business Administration, Philadelphia, PA 19122-6096. Offerings include actuarial science (MBA). Program faculty: 72 full-time (13 women). *Application fee:* $40. *Expenses:* Tuition $323 per semester hour for state residents; $444 per semester hour for nonresidents. Fees $170 per year full-time, $28 per semester (minimum) part-time. • Application contact: Linda Whelan, Director, 215-204-7678. Fax: 215-204-8300. E-mail: linda@astro.ocis.temple.edu.

Temple University, School of Business and Management, Program in Actuarial Science, Philadelphia, PA 19122-6096. Awards MS. Evening/weekend programs available. Students: 20 (5 women); includes 2 minority (1 African American, 1 Asian American), 7 international. Average age 27. 43 applicants, 56% accepted. In 1997, 10 degrees awarded. *Entrance requirements:* GMAT (minimum score 500) or GRE General Test (minimum combined score of 1000), TOEFL (minimum score 575), minimum GPA of 3.0 during previous 2 years, 2.8 overall. Application deadline: 4/15 (priority date; rolling processing; 12/15 for spring admission). Application fee: $40. *Expenses:* Tuition $323 per semester hour for state residents; $444 per semester hour for nonresidents. Fees $170 per year full-time, $28 per semester (minimum) part-time. *Financial aid:* Institutionally sponsored loans available. *Faculty research:* Insurance regulation. • Dr. Michael Powers, Director, 215-204-7293. Fax: 215-204-5698.

Université du Québec à Montréal, Program in Actuarial Sciences, Montréal, PQ H3C 3P8, Canada. Awards Diploma. Offered jointly with the Univerité du Québec à Chicoutimi, the Université du Québec à Hull, the Université du Québec en Abitibi-Témiscamingue, the Université du Québec à Trois-Riviéres, and the Université du Québec à Chicoutimi. Part-time programs available. *Entrance requirements:* Appropriate bachelor's degree or equivalent and proficiency in French. Application deadline: 5/1. Application fee: $50.

University of Manitoba, Faculty of Management, Department of Actuarial and Management Sciences, Winnipeg, MB R3T 2N2, Canada. Offers program in actuarial mathematics and operational research (MA, M Sc). *Degree requirements:* Thesis or alternative.

University of Nebraska–Lincoln, College of Business Administration, Interdepartmental Area of Actuarial Science, Lincoln, NE 68588. Awards MS. Students: 9 full-time (1 woman); includes 5 international. Average age 28. 14 applicants, 64% accepted. In 1997, 3 degrees awarded. *Degree requirements:* Computer language required, foreign language and thesis not required. *Entrance requirements:* Survey of Actuaries (minimum score 100), TOEFL (minimum score 550). Application deadline: 3/1 (10/1 for spring admission). Application fee: $35. Electronic applications accepted. *Expenses:* Tuition $110 per credit hour for state residents; $270 per credit hour for nonresidents. Fees $480 per year full-time, $110 per semester part-time. *Financial aid:* Fellowships, teaching assistantships, Federal Work-Study available. Aid available to part-time students. Financial aid application deadline: 2/15. *Faculty research:* Risk theory, pensions, actuarial finance, decision theory, stochastic calculus. • Dr. Colin Ramsay, Director, 402-472-2698. E-mail: actusci@unlinfo.unl.edu.

University of Waterloo, Faculty of Mathematics, Department of Statistics and Actuarial Science, Waterloo, ON N2L 3G1, Canada. Awards M Math, PhD. Faculty: 29 full-time (6 women), 15 part-time (1 woman). Students: 44 full-time (20 women), 3 part-time (1 woman). 100 applicants, 47% accepted. In 1997, 24 master's, 5 doctorates awarded. *Degree requirements:* For master's, essay or thesis required, foreign language not required; for doctorate, dissertation required, foreign language not required. *Entrance requirements:* For master's, TOEFL (minimum score 580), honors degree in field, minimum B average; for doctorate, TOEFL (minimum score 580), master's degree. Application deadline: 3/31 (rolling processing; 12/31 for spring admission). Application fee: $50. *Tuition:* $3220 per year. *Financial aid:* Research assistantships, teaching assistantships, scholarships, and career-related internships or fieldwork available. Financial aid application deadline: 2/28. *Faculty research:* Biometry, multivariate analysis, risk theory, inference, stochastic processes, quantitative finance. • Dr. M. E. Thompson, Chair, 519-888-4567 Ext. 5543. Application contact: Dr. C. G. Small, Graduate Officer, 519-888-4567 Ext. 5541. Fax: 519-746-1875. E-mail: sasgrad@math.uwaterloo.ca.

University of Wisconsin–Madison, School of Business, Program in Actuarial Science, Madison, WI 53706-1380. Awards MS, PhD. Terminal master's awarded for partial completion of doctoral program. *Entrance requirements:* For master's, GMAT or GRE. Application deadline: 6/1 (rolling processing; 10/1 for spring admission). Application fee: $38. *Tuition:* $5950 per year full-time, $1118 per semester (minimum) part-time for state residents; $16,230 per year full-time, $3044 per semester (minimum) part-time for nonresidents. *Faculty research:* Fuzzy logic, business forecasting, health insurance, international insurance.

Insurance

California State University, Northridge, College of Business Administration and Economics, Department of Finance, Real Estate and Insurance, Northridge, CA 91330. Awards MBA. Faculty: 13 full-time, 5 part-time. 4 applicants, 50% accepted. *Degree requirements:* Thesis or alternative required, foreign language not required. *Entrance requirements:* GMAT (score in 50th percentile or higher), TOEFL, minimum GPA of 3.0 in last 60 units. Application deadline: 11/30. Application fee: $55. *Expenses:* Tuition $0 for state residents; $246 per unit for nonresidents. Fees $1970 per year full-time, $1304 per year part-time. *Financial aid:* Application deadline 3/1. *Faculty research:* Real estate education improvement. • Dr. William Jennings, Chair, 818-677-2459. Application contact: Dr. Richard Moore, Director of Graduate Programs, 818-677-2467.

College of Insurance, Graduate Programs, Program in Business Administration, New York, NY 10007-2165. Offers actuarial science (MBA), financial management (MBA), financial management of risk (MBA), insurance (MBA), risk management (MBA). Part-time and evening/weekend programs available. Faculty: 12 full-time (1 woman), 12 part-time (1 woman). Students: 43 full-time (19 women), 56 part-time (22 women); includes 24 minority (9 African Americans, 9 Asian Americans, 6 Hispanics), 33 international. Average age 28. 87 applicants, 62% accepted. In 1997, 51 degrees awarded. *Degree requirements:* Computer language required, thesis optional, foreign language not required. *Entrance requirements:* GMAT (minimum score 500), TOEFL (minimum score 550). Application deadline: 7/15 (priority date; rolling processing; 11/1 for spring admission). Application fee: $30 ($50 for international students). *Expenses:* Tuition $554 per credit. Fees $15 per credit. *Financial aid:* Graduate assistantships, Federal Work-Study, and career-related internships or fieldwork available. Aid available to part-time students. Financial aid application deadline: 5/15. • Application contact: Theresa C. Marro, Director of Admissions, 212-815-9232. Fax: 212-964-3381. E-mail: admissions@tci.edu.

Announcement: The College of Insurance was established and is supported by the insurance and financial services industry. This accredited educational institution offers an MBA with concentrations in insurance, financial management, risk management, financial management of risk, and actuarial science and an MS with a concentration in risk management. The graduate programs exemplify the strong commitment to meet the changing needs of students and the industry.

See in-depth description on page 523.

College of Insurance, Graduate Programs, Program in Risk and Insurance, New York, NY 10007-2165. Awards MS. Program new for fall 1998. *Degree requirements:* Thesis optional, foreign language not required. *Entrance requirements:* GMAT (minimum score 500), TOEFL (minimum score 550). *Expenses:* Tuition $554 per credit. Fees $15 per credit. *Financial aid:* Graduate assistantships, Federal Work-Study, and career-related internships or fieldwork available. Aid available to part-time students. Financial aid application deadline: 5/15. • Application contact: Theresa C. Marro, Director of Admissions, 212-815-9232. Fax: 212-964-3381. E-mail: admissions@tci.edu.

Georgia State University, College of Business Administration, Department of Risk Management and Insurance, Atlanta, GA 30303-3083. Offers programs in actuarial science (MAS), personal financial planning (MS), risk management and insurance (MBA, MS, PhD). Part-time and evening/weekend programs available. Faculty: 21 full-time, 1 part-time. Students: 63 full-time (26 women), 44 part-time (10 women); includes 11 minority (6 African Americans, 3 Asian Americans, 2 Hispanics), 29 international. Average age 28. In 1997, 37 master's awarded. Terminal master's awarded for partial completion of doctoral program. *Degree requirements:* For doctorate, dissertation required, foreign language not required. *Entrance requirements:* For master's, GMAT (average 566), TOEFL; for doctorate, GMAT (average 670), TOEFL. Application deadline: 5/1 (rolling processing; 10/1 for spring admission). Application fee: $25. *Expenses:* Tuition $2673 per year full-time, $99 per semester hour part-time for state residents; $10,692 per year full-time, $396 per semester hour part-time for nonresidents. Fees $228 per year. *Financial aid:* Fellowships, research assistantships, teaching assistantships, partial tuition waivers, and career-related internships or fieldwork available. Financial aid applicants required to submit FAFSA. • Bruce A. Palmer, Chair, 404-651-2725. Fax: 404-651-4219. Application contact: Office of Academic Assistance and Master's Admissions, 404-651-1913. Fax: 404-651-0219.

Pennsylvania State University University Park Campus, The Mary Jean and Frank P. Smeal College of Business Administration, MS Programs in Business Administration, Department of Insurance, University Park, PA 16802-1503. Awards MS. *Degree requirements:* Thesis or alternative required, foreign language not required. *Entrance requirements:* GMAT. Application fee: $40. *Expenses:* Tuition $6534 per year full-time, $276 per credit part-time for state residents; $13,460 per year full-time, $561 per credit part-time for nonresidents. Fees $252 per year (minimum) full-time, $43 per semester (minimum) part-time. • Kenneth M. Lusht, Chair, 814-865-1190.

Pennsylvania State University University Park Campus, The Mary Jean and Frank P. Smeal College of Business Administration, PhD Programs in Business Administration, Program in Finance/Insurance and Real Estate, University Park, PA 16802-1503. Awards PhD. *Degree requirements:* Dissertation. *Entrance requirements:* GMAT. Application fee: $40. *Expenses:* Tuition $6534 per year full-time, $276 per credit part-time for state residents; $13,460 per year full-time, $561 per credit part-time for nonresidents. Fees $252 per year (minimum) full-time, $43 per semester (minimum) part-time. • Dr. Dennis P. Sheehan, Field Adviser, 814-863-8512.

Temple University, School of Business and Management, Master's Program in Business Administration, Philadelphia, PA 19122-6096. Offerings include risk management insurance (MBA, MS). Program faculty: 72 full-time (13 women). *Entrance requirements:* GMAT (average 540), TOEFL (minimum score 575). Application fee: $40. *Expenses:* Tuition $323 per semester hour for state residents; $444 per semester hour for nonresidents. Fees $170 per year full-time, $28 per semester (minimum) part-time. • Application contact: Linda Whelan, Director, 215-204-7678. Fax: 215-204-8300. E-mail: linda@astro.ocis.temple.edu.

University of Hartford, Barney School of Business and Public Administration, Program in Business Administration, West Hartford, CT 06117-1599. Offerings include insurance (MBA). Program faculty: 24 full-time (4 women), 15 part-time (1 woman). *Average time to degree:* master's–1.5 years full-time, 3 years part-time. *Entrance requirements:* GMAT, TOEFL. Application deadline: 7/1 (priority date; rolling processing; 12/1 for spring admission). Application fee: $35 ($50 for international students). Electronic applications accepted. • Christopher Galligan, Director, 860-768-4390. Application contact: Claire Silverstein, Assistant Director, 860-768-4900. Fax: 860-768-4821. E-mail: silverste@unavax.hartford.edu.

University of Hartford, Barney School of Business and Public Administration, Department of Economics/Finance/Insurance, Program in Insurance, West Hartford, CT 06117-1599. Offers life insurance (MSI), property and casualty insurance (MSI). Part-time and evening/weekend programs available. Faculty: 3 full-time (1 woman), 1 part-time (0 women). Students: 14 full-time, 4 part-time; includes 14 international. Average age 26. 17 applicants, 59% accepted. In 1997, 9 degrees awarded. *Average time to degree:* master's–1 year full-time, 3 years part-time. *Entrance requirements:* GMAT, TOEFL. Application deadline: 7/1 (priority date; rolling processing; 12/1 for spring admission). Application fee: $35 ($50 for international students). Electronic applications accepted. *Financial aid:* Research assistantships, institutionally sponsored loans, and career-related internships or fieldwork available. Financial aid application deadline: 5/1. • Thomas Dooley, Director, 860-768-4828. Fax: 860-768-4911. Application contact: Claire Silverstein, Assistant Director, 860-768-4900. Fax: 860-768-4821. E-mail: silverste@unavax.hartford.edu.

University of North Texas, College of Business Administration, Department of Finance, Insurance, Real Estate, and Law, Denton, TX 76203-6737. Offers programs in banking (MBA, PhD), finance (MBA, PhD), insurance (MBA), real estate (MBA). Part-time programs available. Faculty: 22 full-time (3 women), 4 part-time (0 women). Students: 40 full-time (18 women), 138 part-time (47 women); includes 12 minority (4 African Americans, 5 Asian Americans, 3 Hispanics), 29 international. In 1997, 38 master's, 1 doctorate awarded. *Degree requirements:* For master's, computer language required, foreign language and thesis not required; for doctorate, computer language, dissertation required, foreign language not required. *Entrance requirements:* For master's, GMAT, TOEFL; for doctorate, GMAT or GRE General Test, TOEFL. Application deadline: 7/17. Application fee: $25 ($50 for international students). *Tuition:* $2063 per year full-time, $815 per year part-time for state residents; $5897 per year full-time, $2100 per year part-time for nonresidents. *Financial aid:* Fellowships, research assistantships, teaching assistantships, and career-related internships or fieldwork available. Financial aid application deadline: 4/1. *Faculty research:* Financial impact of regulation, risk management, financial instrument rating changes, taxes and valuation, bankruptcy. • Dr. Imre Karafiath, Chair, 940-565-3050.

University of Pennsylvania, Wharton School, Graduate Group in Insurance and Risk Management, Philadelphia, PA 19104. Awards MBA, PhD. Faculty: 7 full-time (2 women), 2 part-time (0 women). Students: 17 full-time (7 women); includes 2 African Americans, 5 international. Average age 26. 50 applicants, 10% accepted. In 1997, 2 master's awarded (100% found work related to degree); 4 doctorates awarded (100% entered university research/teaching). *Degree requirements:* For doctorate, dissertation. *Entrance requirements:* For master's, GMAT; for doctorate, GMAT or GRE. Application deadline: 2/15. Application fee: $125. *Financial aid:* 12 students received aid; fellowships, Federal Work-Study, institutionally sponsored loans available. Financial aid application deadline: 2/15. *Faculty research:* Fair rate of return in insurance economics of pension plans, insurance regulation, malpractice insurance, actuarial science. • Dr. Jean H. Lemaire, Chairperson, 215-898-7765. Application contact: Michelle Henry, Administrative Assistant, 215-898-7761. Fax: 215-898-0310. E-mail: henrym@wharton.upenn.edu.

University of St. Thomas, Graduate School of Business, Day MBA Program, St. Paul, MN 55105-1096. Offerings include insurance and risk management (MBA). Program faculty: 13 part-time. *Degree requirements:* Computer language required, foreign language and thesis not required. *Entrance requirements:* GMAT (score in 50th percentile or higher). Application deadline: 5/1 (priority date; rolling processing). Application fee: $30. *Tuition:* $473 per credit hour. • Application contact: Jim O'Connor, Student Adviser, 612-962-4233. Fax: 612-962-4260.

University of St. Thomas, Graduate School of Business, Evening MBA Program, St. Paul, MN 55105-1096. Offerings include insurance and risk management (MBA). Program faculty: 16 full-time (2 women), 89 part-time (17 women). *Degree requirements:* Computer language required, foreign language and thesis not required. *Entrance requirements:* GMAT (score in 50th percentile or higher). Application deadline: 8/1 (priority date; rolling processing; 12/1 for spring admission). Application fee: $30. *Tuition:* $416 per credit hour. • Dr. Stanford Nyquist, MBA Director, 612-962-4242. Application contact: Martha Ballard, Director of Student Services, 612-962-4226. Fax: 612-962-4260.

University of Wisconsin–Madison, School of Business, Program in Risk Management and Insurance, Madison, WI 53706-1380. Awards MBA, MS, PhD. Terminal master's awarded for partial completion of doctoral program. *Entrance requirements:* For master's, GMAT. Application deadline: 6/1 (rolling processing; 10/1 for spring admission). Application fee: $38. *Tuition:* $5950 per year full-time, $1118 per semester (minimum) part-time for state residents; $16,230 per year full-time, $3044 per semester (minimum) part-time for nonresidents. *Faculty research:* Superfund, health insurance, workers co mpensation, employee benefits, fuzzy logic, hazardous waste.

Virginia Commonwealth University, School of Business, Program in Risk Management and Insurance, Richmond, VA 23284-9005. Awards MS. *Entrance requirements:* GMAT. Application deadline: rolling. Application fee: $30 ($0 for international students). *Tuition:* $4960 per year full-time, $257 per credit part-time for state residents; $12,652 per year full-time, $684 per credit part-time for nonresidents. *Financial aid:* Fellowships, research assistantships, teaching assistantships, full and partial tuition waivers, Federal Work-Study, institutionally sponsored loans available. Financial aid application deadline: 3/15. • Application contact: Dr. Edward L. Millner, Associate Dean of Graduate Studies, 804-828-1741. Fax: 804-828-7174.

COLLEGE OF INSURANCE

Master of Business Administration and Master of Science Degree Programs

Program of Study

The College of Insurance offers a program leading to the Master of Business Administration (M.B.A.) degree with concentrations available in financial management, financial management of risk, insurance, risk management, and actuarial science and a program leading to the Master of Science (M.S.) in risk management. The College follows the curriculum guidelines of the AACSB–The International Association for Management Education. A common body of knowledge is incorporated into the core. Elective courses provide breadth to the program. Computers are integrated as tools and a worldwide dimension is stressed. Although a full-time status exists, the programs are primarily designed for professionals who wish to pursue their degree on a part-time basis. Classes are offered in the evening and on Saturdays and meet once a week. The programs of study are designed to prepare students for leadership positions in the financial services industry. The M.B.A. program with a concentration in actuarial science allows the student to receive the Master of Business Administration degree while preparing for up to five actuarial examinations. The program is specifically designed for highly motivated individuals who seek a graduate management degree as well as solid credentials in actuarial science.

A large percentage of the students entering the M.B.A. program have undergraduate degrees in areas other than business. The program requires the completion of 17 courses totaling 51 credit hours. The core courses provide a broad foundation for future managerial assignments; concentrations in financial management, financial management of risk, insurance, and risk management require 27 credits in core courses, and the concentration in actuarial science requires 24 credits. The major area requires 9 credit hours for financial management, financial management of risk, insurance, and risk management and 15 credit hours for actuarial science. The major area (finance or insurance) comprises 9 credit hours. Electives (12 credits for insurance, financial management, financial management of risk, and risk management and 9 credits for actuarial science) are chosen from among insurance, finance, international business, ethics, personnel administration, and other related business topics. Business Policy, the 3-credit capstone course integrating the lessons from earlier courses, is taken in the last semester of the program. The College may waive courses for students with undergraduate degrees in business administration or with specific courses matching the core. Such students complete the program in fewer than 51 credit hours.

The Master of Science curriculum totals 36 credits and is structured around three components: the common body of knowledge, designated electives, and a thesis or comprehensive final examination. Students, in consultation with their individual advisers, will devise a Plan of Study that details the students' program track and identifies the risk management topic in which they will specialize. The curriculum provides students with the knowledge and practical skills necessary to work effectively in the global risk and insurance industry. Students in the M.S. program may choose either full- or part-time study.

Research Facilities

The Kathryn and Shelby Cullom Davis Library of the College of Insurance is an outstanding research facility for students, scholars, researchers, and the insurance industry as a whole. Recognized internationally as the largest and most comprehensive insurance library in the world, it houses more than 98,000 bound volumes, subject files, pamphlets, periodicals, and other pieces of informational material plus numerous microform items. The library is divided into the Insurance Society Collection and the Frederick W. Ecker Collection, the latter housing material on liberal arts and business subjects. In addition to the insurance laws and regulations of the fifty states, the library contains information on the insurance laws of many countries and the proceedings and reports of most large insurance organizations. The library has historical as well as contemporary collections, with the oldest volume dating back to 1569, and extensive collections of old insurance policies and documents tracing the development of insurance terminology and contracts since 1665.

Financial Aid

The College of Insurance has graduate scholarships available as well as on-campus employment. Additional funds may be obtained through commercial or government loan programs.

Cost of Study

For graduate students employed by organizations that sponsor the College (by contributing a yearly membership fee), tuition is $518 per credit in 1998–99. For all other students, tuition is $535 per credit. Each term, a registration fee of $15 per credit, not to exceed $180, is assessed. The estimated cost of books and supplies is $650 per year.

Living and Housing Costs

The College has dormitory rooms available for 120 undergraduate and graduate students. The housing fees per four-month term range in 1998–99 from $3550 to $4647, depending on whether accommodations are for single or double occupancy and on the number of meals eaten on the premises. Some students rent apartments singly or with fellow students. However, a high proportion of M.B.A. degree candidates work in the New York–New Jersey–Connecticut area and already live in the College's vicinity.

Student Group

In 1997–98, students enrolled in the Graduate Division for an M.B.A. degree included 41 women and 58 men, of whom 31 were international students. Their average age was 28, about half of them were married, and many were employed in the areas of management and insurance. Most of the students work in the financial services industry during the day and attend classes at night. They find the combination of work and study—with the opportunity to utilize newly acquired classroom knowledge in genuine work situations—to be beneficial.

Location

The College of Insurance is located in the heart of New York City's downtown financial and insurance district, within walking distance of the New York Stock Exchange, South Street Seaport, the World Trade Center, and the Staten Island Ferry. Conveniently located near public transportation, the College is just a short ride away from the Broadway and Lincoln Center theaters, Greenwich Village, Chinatown, SoHo, and the uptown department stores, boutiques, restaurants, and museums.

The College and The Program

The College of Insurance traces its beginnings to the founding of its parent organization, the Insurance Society of New York, in 1901. Informal learning sessions developed into classroom situations, and the School of Insurance was founded in 1946. In 1962, it became the College of Insurance—the only undergraduate degree-granting institution in the United States established by, and supported by, a particular segment of the business world. In 1984, the College moved to a new ten-story building, where it enjoys greatly expanded classroom, office, and conference room space; additional facilities for the College library; and dormitory space.

The graduate program has an especially well qualified faculty whose members are chosen for their knowledge, both theoretical and practical, of all aspects of the insurance and business worlds.

Applying

Application deadlines are July 15 for the fall term and November 1 for the spring term. The minimum requirements for admission to the program are a bachelor's degree with grades of B or better, a satisfactory score on the Graduate Management Admission Test (GMAT), and a personal interview. There is a one-time $30 application fee. International students must take the TOEFL and submit a notarized certificate of finance and a $50 application fee.

Correspondence and Information

Office of Admissions
College of Insurance
101 Murray Street
New York, New York 10007
Telephone: 212-815-9232
800-242-9548 (toll-free)
E-mail: admissions@tci.edu
World Wide Web: http://www.tci.edu

College of Insurance

THE FACULTY AND THEIR RESEARCH

James T. Barrese, Associate Professor; Ph.D., Rutgers. Economics and quantitative analysis.
Robert Beiber, Adjunct Assistant Professor; B.B.A., College of Insurance; M.A., NYU. Risk management.
Robert Benjes, Adjunct Assistant Professor; M.Ed., Columbia. Management information systems.
Richard Bennett, Associate Professor; M.B.A., College of Insurance; M.A., CUNY, Queens. Insurance and management.
Frank Bensics, Associate Professor; Ph.D., Pennsylvania; FSA. Insurance and actuarial science.
Kenneth Bigel, Adjunct Assistant Professor; Ph.D. candidate, NYU; M.B.A., NYU. Finance.
Laurie Bilik, Associate Professor; M.Phil., NYU; Dip. in Risk and Insurance, College of Insurance. Organizational theory.
Jeff Carr, Adjunct Assistant Professor; B.A., Wright State. Marketing.
Thomas Collimore, Adjunct Assistant Professor; M.B.A., NYU. Finance.
Charles D. Edinger, Associate Professor; M.Div., Princeton; M.B.A., Seton Hall. Marketing.
George M. Gottheimer Jr., Adjunct Associate Professor; M.B.A., College of Insurance. Strategy for reinsurance management (with research grant from Chartered Property-Casualty Underwriters [CPCU]–Harry J. Loman Foundation).
Brian Jones, Adjunct Assistant Professor; J.D., NYU; M.A., Oxford. Law and actuarial science.
Seymour D. Mintz, Associate Professor; M.B.A., CUNY, Baruch; J.D., Touro; CPA (New York). Accounting and taxation.
Jack M. Nelson, Chief Academic Officer; Ph.D., Pennsylvania. Insurance.
Thomas Nowak, Adjunct Assistant Professor; M.B.A., Pace. Finance.
Anthony V. Pucciarelli, Adjunct Assistant Professor; M.B.A., Saint John's (New York). Business management.
Srinivasa Ramanujam, Associate Professor; Ph.D., Brown. Actuarial science.
Thomas Schwartz, Adjunct Assistant Professor; Ph.D., UCLA. Human resources.
Nicos Scordis, Associate Professor; Ph.D., South Carolina. Insurance and finance.
William Simon, Adjunct Assistant Professor; Ph.D., CUNY Graduate Center; M.S.A., George Washington. International business and insurance.
James Smith, Adjunct Assistant Professor; M.A., Montclair State. Insurance.
Karen Wells, Adjunct Assistant Professor; B.S., Columbia. Finance.

This ten-story building near the World Trade Center is the College's home.

A residence hall room at the College of Insurance.

Section 10
International Business

This section contains a directory of institutions offering graduate work in international business, followed by in-depth entries submitted by institutions that chose to prepare detailed program descriptions. Additional information about programs listed in the directory but not augmented by an in-depth entry may be obtained by writing directly to the dean of a graduate school or chair of a department at the address given in the directory.

For programs offering related work, see also in this book Business Administration and Management, Entrepreneurship, Industrial and Manufacturing Management, and Organizational Behavior. In Book 2, Political Science and International Affairs and Public, Regional, and Industrial Affairs.

CONTENTS

International Business

American InterContinental University, Program in International Business, 1651 Westwood Boulevard, Los Angeles, CA 90024-5603. Awards MBA. Program new for fall 1998. Faculty: 4 full-time (0 women). *Application deadline:* rolling. *Application fee:* $50. • John Rooney, Dean of School of Business, 800-333-2652. Application contact: Allan Gueco, Director of Admissions, 800-333-2652. Fax: 310-477-8640.

American InterContinental University, Program in International Business, 3330 Peachtree Road, NE, Atlanta, GA 30326-1019. Awards MBA. Program new for fall 1998. Part-time programs available. Faculty: 4 full-time (0 women). *Entrance requirements:* Computer Programmer Aptitude Battery Exam, interview. Application deadline: rolling. Application fee: $50. • Dr. Derrick Moore, Chair, 404-812-9000. Fax: 404-812-1062. Application contact: Jeff Bostic, Vice President of Admissions, 404-812-7400. Fax: 404-812-7499. E-mail: acatt@ix.netcom.com.

American InterContinental University, Program in Business Administration, London W1M 3DB, United Kingdom. Offers international business (MBA). Faculty: 4 full-time (2 women). Students: 50 full-time, 10 part-time. Average age 24. *Entrance requirements:* GMAT or interview. Application fee: $35. *Financial aid:* Fellowships, research assistantships, teaching assistantships available. • Dr. Andrew Hageman, Dean, School of Business. Application contact: Study Abroad Office, 800-255-6839.

American University, Kogod College of Business Administration, Department of International Business, Washington, DC 20016-8001. Awards MBA. Part-time and evening/weekend programs available. Faculty: 9 full-time (2 women), 1 (woman) part-time. Students: 45 full-time (25 women), 30 part-time (16 women); includes 19 minority (4 African Americans, 8 Asian Americans, 7 Hispanics), 22 international. 188 applicants, 77% accepted. In 1997, 50 degrees awarded. *Entrance requirements:* GMAT. Application deadline: 2/1 (priority date; 10/1 for spring admission). Application fee: $50. *Expenses:* Tuition $19,080 per year full-time, $687 per credit hour (minimum) part-time. Fees $180 per year full-time, $110 per year part-time. *Financial aid:* Fellowships, research assistantships, Federal Work-Study, institutionally sponsored loans, and career-related internships or fieldwork available. Aid available to part-time students. Financial aid application deadline: 2/1. • Dr. Anne Perry, Chair, 202-885-1960. Fax: 202-885-1992.

Armstrong University, Graduate School of Business Administration, Program in International Business, Oakland, CA 94612. Awards MBA. *Degree requirements:* Thesis required, foreign language not required. *Entrance requirements:* Minimum GPA of 2.5. Application deadline: 8/15 (priority date; rolling processing; 1/1 for spring admission). Application fee: $50. • Application contact: Judy Battle, Director of Admissions, 510-835-7900. Fax: 510-835-8935. E-mail: info@armstrong-u.edu.

Azusa Pacific University, School of Business and Management, Azusa, CA 91702-7000. Offerings include international business (MBA). School faculty: 11 full-time (2 women), 6 part-time (1 woman). *Average time to degree:* master's–1 year full-time, 3 years part-time. *Application deadline:* 8/15 (priority date; rolling processing). *Application fee:* $45 ($65 for international students). *Expenses:* Tuition $405 per unit. Fees $57 per year. • Dr. Phillip Lewis, Dean, 626-812-3090. Application contact: Kim Gara, Academic Adviser, 626-812-3818. Fax: 626-815-3802.

Babson College, F. W. Olin Graduate School of Business, Babson Park, MA 02157-0310. Offerings include international business (MBA). School faculty: 151 full-time (42 women), 53 part-time (24 women). *Entrance requirements:* GMAT, TOEFL, 2 years of work experience, resume. Application deadline: rolling. Application fee: $50. Electronic applications accepted. *Expenses:* Tuition $21,940 per year full-time, $2046 per course part-time. Fees $660 per year. • Thomas Moore, Dean, 781-239-4542. Application contact: Rita S. Edmunds, Director of Graduate Admissions, 781-239-5591. Fax: 781-239-4194. E-mail: edmundsr@babson.edu.

Baker College Center for Graduate Studies, Programs in Business, Flint, MI 48507. Offerings include international business (EMBA, MBA). MBA (health and recreation services management) enrollment limited to international students. Faculty: 8 full-time, 73 part-time. *Degree requirements:* Portfolio required, foreign language not required. *Entrance requirements:* 3 years of work experience, minimum undergraduate GPA of 2.5, writing sample. Application deadline: rolling. Application fee: $25. *Tuition:* $215 per quarter hour. • Dr. Michael Heberling, President, 800-469-3165. Application contact: Chuck Gurden, Director of Admissions, 800-469-3165. Fax: 810-766-4399.

Baldwin-Wallace College, Division of Business Administration, Program in International Management, Berea, OH 44017-2088. Awards MBA. Part-time and evening/weekend programs available. Faculty: 14 full-time (1 woman), 6 part-time (1 woman). Students: 26 full-time (11 women), 65 part-time (34 women); includes 46 international. Average age 27. 56 applicants, 68% accepted. In 1997, 61 degrees awarded. *Degree requirements:* 1 foreign language required, thesis not required. *Average time to degree:* master's–1.5 years full-time, 2 years part-time. *Entrance requirements:* GMAT (minimum score 500), TOEFL (minimum score 500), interview, work experience. Application deadline: 7/1 (priority date; rolling processing; 3/1 for spring admission). Application fee: $15. Electronic applications accepted. *Financial aid:* Career-related internships or fieldwork available. Aid available to part-time students. Financial aid applicants required to submit FAFSA. *Faculty research:* International finance, systems approach, international marketing. • Application contact: Peggy Shepard, Graduate Coordinator, 440-826-2196. Fax: 440-826-3868. E-mail: pshepard@bw.edu.

See in-depth description on page 535.

Baruch College of the City University of New York, School of Business, International Business Program, 17 Lexington Avenue, New York, NY 10010-5585. Awards MBA. Part-time and evening/weekend programs available. Faculty: 4 full-time (0 women). Students: 54 full-time (23 women), 62 part-time (20 women). In 1997, 28 degrees awarded. *Degree requirements:* Computer language, thesis or alternative required, foreign language not required. *Average time to degree:* master's–2 years full-time, 4 years part-time. *Entrance requirements:* GMAT, TOEFL (minimum score 570), TWE (minimum score 4.5). Application deadline: 6/15 (11/1 for spring admission). Application fee: $40. *Expenses:* Tuition $4350 per year full-time, $185 per credit part-time for state residents; $7600 per year full-time, $320 per credit part-time for nonresidents. Fees $53 per year. *Financial aid:* Research assistantships, Federal Work-Study, and career-related internships or fieldwork available. Aid available to part-time students. Financial aid application deadline: 5/3; applicants required to submit FAFSA. • Jean J. Boddewyn, Coordinator, 212-802-6480. Application contact: Michael S. Wynne, Office of Graduate Admissions, 212-802-2330. Fax: 212-802-2335. E-mail: graduate_admissions@baruch.cuny.edu.

Baylor University, College of Arts and Sciences, Programs in Economics, Waco, TX 76798. Offerings include international economics (MA, MIE, MS). MIE new for fall 1998. *Entrance requirements:* GRE General Test. Application deadline: rolling. Application fee: $25. *Expenses:* Tuition $7392 per year full-time, $308 per semester hour part-time. Fees $1024 per year. • Dr. W. James Truitt, Chair, 254-710-1213.

Baylor University, Hankamer School of Business, Interdisciplinary Program in International Management, Waco, TX 76798. Awards MIM, MBA/MIM. Part-time programs available. Students: 9 full-time (7 women), 1 part-time (0 women); includes 1 minority (Asian American), 4 international. In 1997, 5 degrees awarded. *Entrance requirements:* GRE General Test (minimum combined score of 1050) or GMAT (minimum score 450). Application deadline: 8/1 (rolling processing; 12/1 for spring admission). Application fee: $25. *Expenses:* Tuition $7392 per year full-time, $308 per semester hour part-time. Fees $1024 per year. *Financial aid:* Research assistantships, Federal Work-Study, institutionally sponsored loans, and career-related internships or fieldwork available. • Dr. Donald F. Cunningham, Co-Director, 254-710-3718.

Bentley College, Graduate School of Business, Self-paced MBA Program, 175 Forest Street, Waltham, MA 02154-4705. Offerings include international business (MBA). Program faculty: 70 full-time (21 women), 22 part-time (8 women). *Degree requirements:* Computer language required, foreign language and thesis not required. *Entrance requirements:* GMAT (average 540), TOEFL (minimum score 580). Application deadline: 6/1 (priority date; rolling processing; 11/1 for spring admission). Application fee: $50. *Expenses:* Tuition $20,500 per year full-time, $2050 per course part-time. Fees $65 per year full-time, $15 per semester part-time. • Dr. Judith B. Kamm, Director, 781-891-3433. Application contact: Holly Chase, Associate Director, 781-891-2108. Fax: 781-891-2464. E-mail: hchase@bentley.edu.

Boston University, Metropolitan College, Program in Administrative Studies, Boston, MA 02215. Offers financial economics (MSAS), innovation and technology (MSAS), multinational commerce (MSAS), organizational policy (MSAS). Part-time and evening/weekend programs available. Faculty: 7 full-time (2 women), 25 part-time (5 women). Students: 126 full-time (66 women), 164 part-time (83 women); includes 33 minority (3 African Americans, 20 Asian Americans, 9 Hispanics, 1 Native American), 141 international. Average age 28. 60% of applicants accepted. In 1997, 60 degrees awarded (2% entered university research/teaching, 88% found other work related to degree, 10% continued full-time study). *Degree requirements:* Thesis optional, foreign language not required. *Average time to degree:* master's–1 year full-time, 2 years part-time. *Entrance requirements:* TOEFL (minimum score 550). Application deadline: rolling. Application fee: $50. *Expenses:* Tuition $15,488 per year full-time, $484 per credit part-time. Fees $218 per year full-time, $40 per semester part-time. *Financial aid:* In 1997–98, 5 students received aid, including 5 research assistantships; Federal Work-Study and career-related internships or fieldwork also available. *Faculty research:* International business, innovative process. • Dr. Kip Becker, Chairman. E-mail: adminsc@bu.edu. Application contact: Department of Administrative Sciences, 617-353-3016. Fax: 617-353-6840. E-mail: adminsc@bu.edu.

See in-depth description on page 537.

Brandeis University, Graduate School of International Economics and Finance, MS-32, PO Box 9110, Waltham, MA 02254-9110. Offers programs in finance (MSF), international business (MBAi), international economics and finance (MA, PhD). Faculty: 24 (4 women). Students: 122 full-time (41 women), 25 part-time (11 women); includes 81 international. Average age 26. 334 applicants, 43% accepted. In 1997, 30 master's, 2 doctorates awarded. Terminal master's awarded for partial completion of doctoral program. *Degree requirements:* For master's, 1 foreign language, semester abroad; for doctorate, dissertation. *Entrance requirements:* For master's, GMAT or GRE General Test (MA), GMAT (MBAi), TOEFL (minimum score 600); for doctorate, GRE General Test, GRE Subject Test, TOEFL (minimum score 600). Application deadline: 2/15 (priority date). Application fee: $50. *Expenses:* Tuition $23,360 per year full-time, $2960 per course part-time. Fees $45 per year. *Financial aid:* 76 students received aid; assistantships, scholarships, institutionally sponsored loans available. Financial aid application deadline: 2/15; applicants required to submit FAFSA. *Faculty research:* International finance and business, trade policy, macroeconomics, Asian economic issues, developmental economics. • Dr. Peter Petri, Dean, 781-736-4817. Application contact: Marsha Ginn, Associate Dean, 781-736-4829.

See in-depth description on page 539.

Bryant College, College of Business Administration, Program in International Business, Smithfield, RI 02917-1284. Awards MBA. Part-time and evening/weekend programs available. Students: 1 full-time (0 women), 11 part-time (7 women). Average age 32. 21 applicants, 33% accepted. In 1997, 3 degrees awarded. *Entrance requirements:* GMAT (minimum score 480; average 520). Application deadline: 7/1 (priority date; rolling processing; 11/15 for spring admission). Application fee: $55 ($70 for international students). *Tuition:* $1025 per course. *Financial aid:* Research assistantships, graduate assistantships, and career-related internships or fieldwork available. Aid available to part-time students. Financial aid applicants required to submit FAFSA. • Cathy Lalli, Assistant Director of Graduate Programs, Graduate School, 401-232-6230. Fax: 401-232-6494. E-mail: gradprog@bryant.edu.

California Lutheran University, School of Business Administration, Thousand Oaks, CA 91360-2787. Offerings include international business (MBA). School faculty: 8 full-time (3 women), 29 part-time (4 women). *Entrance requirements:* GMAT, minimum GPA of 3.0, interview. Application deadline: 8/1 (priority date; rolling processing). Application fee: $50. *Tuition:* $395 per unit. • Dr. Ronald Hagler, Director, 805-493-3371.

California State University, Fullerton, School of Business Administration and Economics, Department of Marketing, PO Box 34080, Fullerton, CA 92834-9480. Offerings include international business (MBA). Department faculty: 11 full-time (3 women), 14 part-time, 14 FTE. *Degree requirements:* Computer language, project or thesis required, foreign language not required. *Entrance requirements:* GMAT (minimum score 950), minimum AACSB index of 950. Application fee: $55. *Expenses:* Tuition $0 for state residents; $246 per unit for nonresidents. Fees $1947 per year full-time, $1281 per year part-time. • Dr. Irene Lange, Chair, 714-278-2223. Application contact: Robert Miyake, Assistant Dean, 714-278-2211.

California State University, Hayward, School of Business and Economics, Department of Management and Finance, Option in International Business, Hayward, CA 94542-3000. Awards MBA. Part-time and evening/weekend programs available. *Degree requirements:* Comprehensive exam or thesis required, foreign language not required. *Entrance requirements:* GMAT, minimum GPA of 2.75. Application deadline: 4/19 (priority date; rolling processing; 1/5 for spring admission). Application fee: $55. *Expenses:* Tuition $0 for state residents; $164 per unit for nonresidents. Fees $1827 per year full-time, $1161 per year part-time. *Financial aid:* Federal Work-Study, institutionally sponsored loans, and career-related internships or fieldwork available. Aid available to part-time students. Financial aid application deadline: 3/1. • Dr. Loretta Breuning, Coordinator, 510-885-4277. Application contact: Dr. Donna L. Wiley, Director of Graduate Programs, 510-885-3964.

California State University, Los Angeles, School of Business and Economics, Major in Business Administration, Department of Marketing, Los Angeles, CA 90032-8530. Offerings include international business (MBA, MS). Department faculty: 8 full-time, 5 part-time. *Degree requirements:* Computer language, comprehensive exam (MBA), thesis (MS) required, foreign language not required. *Entrance requirements:* GMAT, TOEFL (minimum score 550), minimum GPA of 2.5 during previous 2 years. Application deadline: 6/30 (rolling processing; 11/30 for spring admission). Application fee: $55. *Expenses:* Tuition $0 for state residents; $164 per unit for nonresidents. Fees $1763 per year full-time, $1097 per year part-time. • Dr. Shirley Stretch, Chair, 213-343-2960.

Cardinal Stritch University, College of Business and Management, Programs in Management for Adults, Milwaukee, WI 53217-3985. Offerings include international business (MBA). *Application deadline:* 4/1 (priority date; rolling processing). *Application fee:* $20. *Expenses:* Tuition $338 per credit. Fees $25 per semester. • Application contact: Shirley Hansen, Director of Marketing, 414-410-4315.

Central Connecticut State University, School of Business, Program in International Business Administration, New Britain, CT 06050-4010. Awards MBA. Part-time and evening/weekend programs available. Students: 18 full-time (4 women), 23 part-time (13 women); includes 4 minority (1 African American, 3 Asian Americans), 15 international. Average age 31. 56 applicants, 55% accepted. In 1997, 12 degrees awarded. *Degree requirements:* 1 foreign language, thesis or alternative, special project. *Entrance requirements:* GMAT, TOEFL (minimum score 550), minimum GPA of 2.7. Application deadline: 6/1 (priority date; rolling processing; 12/1 for spring admission). Application fee: $40. *Expenses:* Tuition $4458 per year full-time, $175 per credit hour part-time for state residents; $9943 per year full-time, $175 per credit hour part-time for nonresidents. Fees $45 per semester. *Financial aid:* Federal Work-Study available. Financial aid application deadline: 3/15; applicants required to submit FAFSA. *Faculty research:* Contemporary issues in international business and global perspectives, international markets and market planning. • Dr. George Claffey, Coordinator, 860-832-3210.

Chaminade University of Honolulu, Program in Japanese Business Studies, Honolulu, HI 96816-1578. Awards MSJBS, MBA/MSJBS. Faculty: 4 full-time (1 woman), 4 part-time (1 woman). Students: 18 full-time (8 women), 4 part-time (2 women); includes 3 minority (1 African American, 1 Asian American, 1 Hispanic), 9 international. Average age 29. 100 applicants, 32% accepted. In 1997, 12 degrees awarded (100% found work related to degree). *Degree requirements:* 1 foreign language, thesis, summer internship in Japan. *Entrance requirements:* GMAT (minimum score 400), TOEFL (minimum score 550), minimum GPA of 3.0. Application deadline: 9/15 (priority date; rolling processing; 3/1 for spring admission). Application fee: $50. *Financial aid:* 3 students received aid; career-related internships or fieldwork available. Aid available to part-time students. Financial aid application deadline: 3/1. • Dr. Caryn Callahan, Director, 808-739-4689. Fax: 808-735-4734.

Claremont Graduate University, Peter F. Drucker Graduate Management Center, Program in Management, Claremont, CA 91711-6163. Offerings include international business (MBA). *Entrance requirements:* GMAT, TOEFL. Application deadline: 2/15 (priority date; rolling processing). Application fee: $40. Electronic applications accepted. *Expenses:* Tuition $20,250 per year full-time, $913 per unit part-time. Fees $130 per year. • Dr. Jeffrey Decker, Director, 909-621-8073. Fax: 909-621-8390. E-mail: jeff.decker@cgu.edu. Application contact: Kathy Hubener, Admissions Coordinator, 909-621-8073. Fax: 909-621-8543. E-mail: mba@cgu.edu.

Clark Atlanta University, School of International Affairs and Development, Atlanta, GA 30314. Offerings include international business and development (MA). *Degree requirements:* 1 foreign language (computer language can substitute), thesis. *Entrance requirements:* GRE General Test, minimum GPA of 2.5. Application deadline: 4/1 (rolling processing; 11/1 for spring admission). Application fee: $40. *Expenses:* Tuition $9672 per year full-time, $403 per credit hour part-time. Fees $200 per year. • Dr. Herschelle Challenor, Dean, 404-880-8337. Application contact: Michelle Clark-Davis, Graduate Program Assistant, 404-880-8709.

Columbia University, Graduate School of Business, MBA Program, New York, NY 10027. Offerings include international business (MBA). Program faculty: 105 full-time (15 women), 86 part-time (15 women). *Entrance requirements:* GMAT, TOEFL (minimum score 610). Application deadline: 4/20 (rolling processing; 11/1 for spring admission). Application fee: $125 ($150 for international students). *Expenses:* Tuition $26,520 per year. Fees $1250 per year. • Prof. Safwan Masri, Vice Dean of Students and the MBA Program, 212-854-8716. Fax: 212-854-0545. E-mail: smm1@columbia.edu. Application contact: Linda Meehan, Assistant Dean and Executive Director of Admissions and Financial Aid, 212-854-1961. Fax: 212-662-6754. E-mail: gohermes@claven.gsb.columbia.edu.

Concordia University Wisconsin, Division of Graduate Studies, MBA Program, Mequon, WI 53097-2402. Offerings include international business (MBA). Postbaccalaureate distance learning degree programs offered (minimal on-campus study). *Degree requirements:* Thesis or alternative, comprehensive exam. *Average time to degree:* master's–2 years part-time. *Entrance requirements:* TOEFL (minimum score 550). Application deadline: 8/1 (priority date; rolling processing; 1/15 for spring admission). Application fee: $50. *Tuition:* $300 per credit. • David Borst, Director, 414-243-4298. Fax: 414-243-4428. E-mail: dborst@bach.cuw.edu.

Dallas Baptist University, College of Business, Business Administration Program, Dallas, TX 75211-9299. Offerings include international business (MBA). Program faculty: 15 full-time (4 women), 26 part-time (5 women). *Entrance requirements:* GMAT, TOEFL (minimum score 550). Application deadline: rolling. Application fee: $25. *Tuition:* $285 per hour. • Annette Hoffman, Director of Graduate Business Programs, 214-333-5280. Application contact: Travis Bundrick, Director of Graduate Programs, 214-333-5243. Fax: 214-333-5579. E-mail: graduate@dbu.edu.

DePaul University, Charles H. Kellstadt Graduate School of Business, Department of International Business, Chicago, IL 60604-2287. Awards MBA. Students: 72 full-time (32 women), 61 part-time (30 women); includes 31 minority (2 African Americans, 23 Asian Americans, 6 Hispanics), 6 international. Average age 29. 68 applicants, 53% accepted. In 1997, 44 degrees awarded. *Degree requirements:* 1 foreign language required, thesis not required. *Entrance requirements:* GMAT. Application deadline: 8/1 (rolling processing; 3/1 for spring admission). Application fee: $40. Electronic applications accepted. *Expenses:* Tuition $1593 per course. Fees $30 per year. *Financial aid:* Application deadline 4/30. • Dr. Ashok Batavia, Director, 312-362-5010. Application contact: Christine Munoz, Director of Admissions, 312-362-8810. Fax: 312-362-6677. E-mail: mbainfo@wppost.depaul.edu.

DePaul University, Charles H. Kellstadt Graduate School of Business, Program in International Marketing and Finance, Chicago, IL 60604-2287. Awards MBA. Students: 57 full-time (25 women); includes 6 minority (5 Asian Americans, 1 Hispanic), 6 international. Average age 28. 124 applicants, 57% accepted. In 1997, 26 degrees awarded. *Degree requirements:* 1 foreign language, computer language, thesis or alternative, foreign study tour, internship. *Entrance requirements:* GMAT (average 590), interview. Application deadline: 5/30 (priority date; rolling processing). Application fee: $40. Electronic applications accepted. *Expenses:* Tuition $1593 per course. Fees $30 per year. *Financial aid:* Research assistantships, full and partial tuition waivers, Federal Work-Study, and career-related internships or fieldwork available. Financial aid application deadline: 4/30. • Dr. Ashok Batavia, Executive Director, 312-362-8811. E-mail: mbaimf@wppost.depaul.edu. Application contact: Dee Dee Wolff, Administrative Director, 312-362-8810. Fax: 312-362-6677. E-mail: mbaimf@wppost.depaul.edu.

See in-depth description on page 541.

Dominican College of San Rafael, School of Business and International Studies, Program in International Business, Pacific Basin, San Rafael, CA 94901-2298. Awards MBA. In 1997, 11 degrees awarded (100% found work related to degree). *Average time to degree:* master's–2 years full-time, 4 years part-time. *Entrance requirements:* TOEFL (minimum score 600), minimum GPA of 3.0, previous course work in macroeconomics, microeconomics, statistics, managerial finance, managerial accounting. Application deadline: 3/2 (12/1 for spring admission). Application fee: $50. *Expenses:* Tuition $12,816 per year full-time, $534 per unit part-time. Fees $320 per year full-time. *Financial aid:* Fellowships available. • Dr. Françoise O. Lepage, Director, 415-485-3284. Application contact: Signe Sugiyama, Director of Admissions, 415-257-1359. Fax: 415-459-3206. E-mail: pbsadm@dominican.edu.

See in-depth description on page 543.

Drury College, Breech School of Business Administration, Program in Business and International Management, Springfield, MO 65802-3791. Awards MBA, MBA/MIM. MBA/MIM offered jointly with Thunderbird, The American Graduate School of International Management. Students: 2 full-time (1 woman). Average age 27. *Entrance requirements:* GMAT, TOEFL. Application deadline: rolling. Application fee: $25. *Expenses:* Tuition $242 per credit hour. Fees $190 per year. *Financial aid:* Career-related internships or fieldwork available. • Dr. Tom Zimmerer, Director, Breech School of Business Administration, 417-873-7241. Fax: 417-873-7537. E-mail: tzimmere@lib.drury.edu.

D'Youville College, Division of Business, Buffalo, NY 14201-1084. Offerings include international business (MS). MS (international business) new for fall 1998. Division faculty: 3 full-time (all women), 9 part-time (3 women). *Degree requirements:* Computer language, thesis required, foreign language not required. *Entrance requirements:* Minimum GPA of 3.0 in major. Application deadline: rolling. Application fee: $25. *Expenses:* Tuition $357 per credit hour. Fees $350 per year. • Dr. Jayanti Sen, Interim Director, 716-881-3200. Application contact: Joseph Syracuse, Graduate Admissions Director, 716-881-7676. Fax: 716-881-7790.

Eastern Michigan University, College of Business, Program in Business Administration, Ypsilanti, MI 48197. Offerings include international business (MBA). *Entrance requirements:* GMAT (minimum score 450), TOEFL (minimum score 550). Application deadline: 5/15 (rolling processing; 3/15 for spring admission). Application fee: $30. *Expenses:* Tuition $2691 per year full-time, $150 per credit hour part-time for state residents; $6300 per year full-time, $350 per credit hour part-time for nonresidents. Fees $368 per year full-time, $88 per semester (minimum) part-time. • Dr. William Whitmire, Coordinator, 734-487-4444.

Eastern Michigan University, College of Arts and Sciences, Department of Foreign Languages and Bilingual Studies, Program in Language and International Trade, Ypsilanti, MI 48197. Awards MA. Evening/weekend programs available. In 1997, 11 degrees awarded. *Degree requirements:* 1 foreign language required, thesis not required. *Entrance requirements:* TOEFL (minimum score 500). Application deadline: 5/15 (rolling processing; 3/15 for spring admission). Application fee: $30. *Expenses:* Tuition $2691 per year full-time, $150 per credit hour part-time for state residents; $6300 per year full-time, $350 per credit hour part-time for nonresidents. Fees $368 per year full-time, $88 per semester (minimum) part-time. *Financial aid:* Fellowships, teaching assistantships, and career-related internships or fieldwork available. Aid available to part-time students. Financial aid application deadline: 3/15; applicants required to submit FAFSA. • William Cline, Coordinator, 734-487-2283.

École des Hautes Études Commerciales, Program in International Business, Montréal, PQ H3T 2A7, Canada. Awards M Sc. Most courses are given in French. Part-time programs available. *Degree requirements:* 1 foreign language, thesis. *Application deadline:* 3/15. *Application fee:* $40. *Financial aid:* Fellowships, research assistantships, teaching assistantships available. • Dr. Jean-Yves Le Louarn, Director, 514-340-6295. E-mail: jean-yves.lelouarn@hec.ca. Application contact: Nicole Rivet, Registrar, 514-340-6110. Fax: 514-340-5640. E-mail: nicole.rivet@hec.ca.

Fairfield University, School of Business, Fairfield, CT 06430-5195. Offerings include international business (MBA, CAS). School faculty: 36 full-time (12 women), 4 part-time (2 women), 37.3 FTE. *Average time to degree:* master's–2 years full-time, 3.5 years part-time. *Application deadline:* 8/1 (priority date; rolling processing; 12/1 for spring admission). *Application fee:* $40. *Expenses:* Tuition $15,000 per year full-time, $450 per credit hour part-time. Fees $40 per year. • Dr. Walter G. Ryba Jr., Acting Dean, 203-254-4070. Application contact: Cynthia S. Chegwidden, Director of Graduate Programs, 203-254-4070. Fax: 203-254-4105. E-mail: cchegwidden@fair1.fairfield.edu.

Fairleigh Dickinson University, Florham–Madison Campus, Samuel J. Silberman College of Business Administration, Program in International Business, 285 Madison Avenue, Madison, NJ 07940-1099. Awards MBA. Part-time and evening/weekend programs available. Faculty: 1 full-time (0 women), 6 part-time (1 woman). Students: 11 full-time (8 women), 81 part-time (31 women); includes 7 minority (5 Asian Americans, 2 Native Americans), 3 international. Average age 30. 36 applicants, 56% accepted. In 1997, 37 degrees awarded. *Degree requirements:* Thesis optional, foreign language not required. *Entrance requirements:* GMAT. Application deadline: rolling. Application fee: $35. *Expenses:* Tuition $522 per credit. Fees $302 per year full-time, $138 per year part-time. • Prof. Claude Jonnard, Director, 973-443-8810.

Fairleigh Dickinson University, Teaneck–Hackensack Campus, Samuel J. Silberman College of Business Administration, Department of Accounting, Taxation, Law, Economics, and Finance, International Business Programs, 1000 River Road, Teaneck, NJ 07666-1914. Awards MBA. Students: 8 full-time (3 women), 23 part-time (10 women); includes 5 minority (1 African American, 2 Asian Americans, 2 Hispanics), 11 international. Average age 31. In 1997, 18 degrees awarded. *Degree requirements:* Computer language required, thesis optional, foreign language not required. *Entrance requirements:* GMAT. Application deadline: rolling. Application fee: $35. *Expenses:* Tuition $522 per credit. Fees $302 per year full-time, $138 per year part-time. *Financial aid:* Fellowships, research assistantships available. *Faculty research:* Global management, trade. • Application contact: Richard Panicucci, Director of Recruiting, 201-692-2426. Fax: 201-692-7249.

Florida Institute of Technology, School of Extended Graduate Studies, Program in Management, Melbourne, FL 32901-6975. Offerings include global management (PMBA). *Application fee:* $50. *Tuition:* $550 per credit hour. • Application contact: Carolyn P. Farrior, Associate Dean of Graduate Admissions, 407-674-7118. Fax: 407-723-9468. E-mail: cfarrior@fit.edu.

Florida International University, College of Business Administration, Department of Management and International Business, Program in International Business, Miami, FL 33199. Awards MIB, PhD. Part-time and evening/weekend programs available. Students: 20 full-time (9 women), 44 part-time (22 women); includes 40 minority (5 African Americans, 1 Asian American, 34 Hispanics), 10 international. Average age 33. 102 applicants, 42% accepted. In 1997, 12 master's, 1 doctorate awarded. *Degree requirements:* For master's, computer language required, foreign language and thesis not required; for doctorate, computer language, dissertation. *Entrance requirements:* For master's, GMAT, minimum AACSB index of 1000, minimum GPA of 3.0; for doctorate, GMAT (minimum score 560), minimum GPA of 3.0. Application deadline: 4/1 (priority date; rolling processing; 10/1 for spring admission). Application fee: $20. *Expenses:* Tuition $138 per credit hour for state residents; $482 per credit hour for nonresidents. Fees $46 per semester. *Financial aid:* Research assistantships, teaching assistantships available. • Dr. Gary Dessler, Chairperson, 305-348-3300. E-mail: dessleg@fiu.edu.

Florida Metropolitan University–Orlando College, North, Division of Business Administration, 5421 Diplomat Circle, Orlando, FL 32810-5674. Offerings include international business (MBA). Division faculty: 7. *Degree requirements:* Thesis or alternative. *Application deadline:* rolling. *Application fee:* $25. *Tuition:* $263 per credit hour. • Director of Graduate Studies, 407-851-2525. Application contact: Annette Gallina, Director of Admissions, 407-851-2525 Ext. 30. Fax: 407-851-1477.

Florida Metropolitan University–Tampa College, Department of Business Administration, 3319 West Hillsborough Avenue, Tampa, FL 33614-5899. Offerings include international business (MBA). College faculty: 1 full-time, 5 part-time. *Degree requirements:* Thesis optional, foreign language not required. *Entrance requirements:* GMAT (minimum score 470) or GRE, minimum GPA of 3.0. Application deadline: rolling. Application fee: $25. *Expenses:* Tuition $250 per credit hour. Fees $100 per year. • Daniel Palladino, Director of Graduate Studies, 813-879-6000 Ext. 51. Application contact: Foster Thomas, Director of Admissions, 813-879-6000 Ext. 36. Fax: 813-871-2483.

The George Washington University, School of Business and Public Management, Department of International Business, Washington, DC 20052. Awards MBA, PhD, MBA/MA. Part-time and evening/weekend programs available. Faculty: 12 full-time (3 women), 3 part-time (1 woman), 13 FTE. Students: 133 full-time (44 women), 105 part-time (48 women); includes 29 minority (4 African Americans, 18 Asian Americans, 6 Hispanics, 1 Native American), 99 international. Average age 29. 343 applicants, 67% accepted. In 1997, 173 master's awarded. *Degree requirements:* For master's, computer language required, foreign language and thesis not required; for doctorate, dissertation required, foreign language not required. *Entrance requirements:* For master's, GMAT, TOEFL (minimum score 550); for doctorate, GMAT or GRE, TOEFL (minimum score 550). Application deadline: 4/1 (priority date; rolling processing; 10/1 for spring admission). Application fee: $50. *Expenses:* Tuition $680 per semester hour. Fees $35 per semester hour. *Financial aid:* Fellowships, teaching assistantships, Federal Work-Study, institutionally sponsored loans, and career-related internships or fieldwork available. Financial aid application deadline: 4/1. *Faculty research:* International trade, competitiveness, business management. • Dr. Peter Lauter, Chair, 202-994-6892. Application contact: Lilly Hastings, Graduate Admissions, 202-994-6584. Fax: 202-994-6382.

Georgia State University, College of Business Administration, Institute of International Business, Atlanta, GA 30303-3083. Awards MBA, MIB. Part-time and evening/weekend programs available. Students: 74 full-time (32 women), 59 part-time (28 women); includes 14 minority (4 African Americans, 6 Asian Americans, 4 Hispanics), 24 international. Average age 29. In

Directory: International Business

Georgia State University (continued)

1997, 13 degrees awarded. *Entrance requirements:* GMAT (average 566), TOEFL. Application deadline: 5/1 (rolling processing; 10/1 for spring admission). Application fee: $25. *Expenses:* Tuition $2673 per year full-time, $99 per semester hour part-time for state residents; $10,692 per year full-time, $396 per semester hour part-time for nonresidents. Fees $228 per year. *Financial aid:* Fellowships, research assistantships, teaching assistantships, partial tuition waivers, and career-related internships or fieldwork available. Aid available to part-time students. Financial aid application deadline: 5/1; applicants required to submit FAFSA. • Kamal M. El-sheshai, Acting Director, 404-651-4068. Fax: 404-651-2804. Application contact: Office of Academic Assistance and Master's Admissions, 404-651-1913. Fax: 404-651-0219.

Golden Gate University, School of Business, San Francisco, CA 94105-2968. Offerings include international business (MBA), professional export management (Certificate). MBA (telecommunications, management information systems) offered jointly with the School of Technology and Industry. *Average time to degree:* master's–2.5 years full-time. *Application deadline:* 7/1 (priority date; rolling processing). *Application fee:* $55 ($70 for international students). *Tuition:* $996 per course (minimum). • Dr. Hamid Shomali, Dean, 415-442-6500. Fax: 415-442-6579. Application contact: Enrollment Services, 415-442-7800. Fax: 415-442-7807. E-mail: info@ggu.edu.

Hawaii Pacific University, School of Business Administration, 1166 Fort Street, Honolulu, HI 96813-2785. Offerings include international business (MBA). School faculty: 30 full-time (3 women), 12 part-time (1 woman), 38 FTE. *Average time to degree:* master's–2 years full-time, 4 years part-time. *Application deadline:* rolling. *Application fee:* $50. Electronic applications accepted. *Tuition:* $7920 per year full-time, $330 per credit part-time. • Dr. Richard Ward, Dean for Graduate Management Studies, 808-544-0279. Application contact: Leina Danao, Admissions Coordinator, 808-544-1120. Fax: 808-544-0280. E-mail: gradservctr@hpu.edu.

High Point University, Graduate Studies, University Station, Montlieu Avenue, High Point, NC 27262-3598. Offerings include international management (MS). Faculty: 11 full-time (1 woman). *Average time to degree:* master's–2 years full-time. *Application deadline:* 4/1 (priority date; 10/1 for spring admission). *Application fee:* $35 ($50 for international students). *Tuition:* $849 per course. • Dr. Alberta Herron, Dean, 336-841-9198. Fax: 336-841-4599. E-mail: aherron@acme.highpoint.edu.

Hofstra University, Frank G. Zarb School of Business, Department of Marketing and International Business, Program in International Business, Hempstead, NY 11549. Awards MBA. Part-time and evening/weekend programs available. Faculty: 4 full-time (1 woman). Students: 14 full-time (6 women), 21 part-time (12 women); includes 3 minority (1 African American, 1 Asian American, 1 Hispanic), 9 international. Average age 29. 27 applicants, 44% accepted. In 1997, 14 degrees awarded. *Degree requirements:* Computer language, thesis or alternative required, foreign language not required. *Entrance requirements:* GMAT (average 580). Application deadline: rolling. Application fee: $40 ($75 for international students). *Expenses:* Tuition $10,968 per year full-time, $457 per credit hour part-time. Fees $670 per year full-time, $112 per semester (minimum) part-time. *Financial aid:* 5 students received aid; fellowships, research assistantships, Federal Work-Study, and career-related internships or fieldwork available. Financial aid application deadline: 4/1; applicants required to submit FAFSA. *Faculty research:* International management, international consumer behavior, international finance, cross-cultural research, strategic policy. • Application contact: Susan McTiernan, Senior Assistant Dean, 516-463-5683. Fax: 516-463-5268. E-mail: bizsmm@hofstra.edu.

Hope International University, Graduate Studies, MBA Program, Fullerton, CA 92831-3138. Offerings include international development (MS); management (MBA), with options in international development, non-profit organizations management. Program faculty: 2 full-time (0 women), 23 part-time (4 women). *Average time to degree:* master's–1.5 years full-time, 2 years part-time. *Application deadline:* rolling. *Application fee:* $100. Electronic applications accepted. • Dr. Raj Singh, Director, 800-762-1294 Ext. 633. Application contact: Connie Born, Director of Admissions, 800-762-1294 Ext. 626. Fax: 714-738-4564. E-mail: cborn@pacificcc.edu.

Indiana University Bloomington, School of Business, Program in Business Administration, Bloomington, IN 47405. Offerings include international business (MBA). Self-designed programs available. *Entrance requirements:* GMAT, TOEFL (minimum score 580). Application deadline: 3/1. Application fee: $50 ($65 for international students). *Expenses:* Tuition $8232 per year for state residents; $16,470 per year for nonresidents. Fees $343 per year. • Dr. George Hettenhouse, Chair, 812-855-8006. Application contact: Dr. James J. Holmen, Director of Admissions and Financial Aid, 812-855-8006. Fax: 812-855-9039.

Instituto Tecnológico y de Estudios Superiores de Monterrey, Graduate School of Management and Leadership, Program in Business Administration, Monterrey, Nuevo León 64849, Mexico. Offerings include international business (M Sc). *Application deadline:* 4/30 (priority date).

Instituto Tecnológico y de Estudios Superiores de Monterrey, Chihuahua Campus, Graduate Programs, Chihuahua, Chihuahua 31110, Mexico. Offerings include international trade (MIT).

Instituto Tecnológico y de Estudios Superiores de Monterrey, Morelos Campus, Programs in Business Administration, Cuernavaca, Morelos 62589, Mexico. Offerings include international business (MA).

Iona College, Hagan Graduate School of Business, Department of Management, 715 North Avenue, New Rochelle, NY 10801-1890. Offerings include international business (MBA, PMC). Department faculty: 11 full-time (2 women), 1 (woman) part-time. *Degree requirements:* For master's, computer language required, foreign language and thesis not required. *Entrance requirements:* For master's, GMAT (minimum score 450); for PMC, GMAT. Application deadline: rolling. Application fee: $50. *Expenses:* Tuition $480 per credit hour. Fees $25 per semester. • Dr. Ursula Witting–Berman, Chair, 914-633-2588. Application contact: Carol Shea, Director of MBA Admissions, 914-633-2288.

John Marshall Law School, Chicago, IL 60604-3968. Offerings include international business and trade (LL M). School faculty: 52 full-time (14 women), 230 part-time (43 women). *Average time to degree:* master's–1.5 years full-time, 2 years part-time; first professional–3 years full-time, 4 years part-time. *Application deadline:* 3/1 (priority date; rolling processing; 10/1 for spring admission). *Application fee:* $50 ($60 for international students). *Expenses:* Tuition $675 per credit (minimum). Fees $40 per semester. • Robert Gilbert Johnson, Dean, 312-427-2737. Application contact: William B. Powers, Dean of Admission and Student Affairs, 312-987-1403. Fax: 312-427-5136. E-mail: 6alonzo@jmls.edu.

Johnson & Wales University, Graduate School, Program in International Business, 8 Abbott Park Place, Providence, RI 02903-3703. Awards MBA. Part-time and evening/weekend programs available. Faculty: 4 full-time (1 woman), 5 part-time (1 woman). Students: 147 full-time (56 women), 74 part-time (28 women). Average age 25. 149 applicants, 71% accepted. In 1997, 78 degrees awarded (5% continued full-time study). *Average time to degree:* master's–1.5 years full-time, 2.7 years part-time. *Entrance requirements:* Minimum GPA of 2.75. Application deadline: 8/21 (priority date; rolling processing). Application fee: $0. *Expenses:* Tuition $194 per quarter hour (minimum). Fees $477 per year. *Financial aid:* In 1997–98, 18 graduate assistantships (4 to first-year students) averaging $735 per month were awarded; partial tuition waivers also available. Aid available to part-time students. Financial aid application deadline: 5/1. *Faculty research:* International banking, global economy, international trade, cultural differences. • Application contact: Dr. Allan G. Freedman, Director of Graduate Admissions, 401-598-1015. Fax: 401-598-4773. E-mail: clifb@jwu.edu.

Long Island University, C.W. Post Campus, College of Management, School of Business, Department of Management, Brookville, NY 11548-1300. Offerings include international business (MBA). MBA (international business) offered jointly with Franklin College Switzerland. JD/MBA offered jointly with Touro College. Department faculty: 8 full-time (4 women), 13 part-time (2 women). *Entrance requirements:* GMAT. Application deadline: 8/15 (priority date; rolling processing; 12/15 for spring admission). Application fee: $30. Electronic applications accepted. *Expenses:* Tuition $480 per credit. Fees $316 per year full-time, $71 per semester (minimum) part-time. • Dr. Anthony M. Akel, Chairman, 516-299-2360. E-mail: aakel@eagle.liunet.edu. Application contact: Sally Luzader, Associate Director of Graduate Admissions, 516-299-2417. Fax: 516-299-2137. E-mail: admissions@collegehall.liunet.edu.

Loyola College, Sellinger School of Business and Management, Programs in Business Administration, Baltimore, MD 21210-2699. Offerings include international business (MIB). *Application deadline:* 7/20 (11/20 for spring admission). *Application fee:* $35. *Tuition:* $365 per credit. • Dr. Peter Lorenzi, Dean, Sellinger School of Business and Management, 410-617-2301.

Lynn University, School of Graduate Studies, School of Business, Boca Raton, FL 33431-5598. Offers program in international management (MBA). Part-time and evening/weekend programs available. Faculty: 5 full-time (0 women), 2 part-time (1 woman). Students: 29 full-time (16 women), 21 part-time (11 women); includes 6 international. 53 applicants, 74% accepted. In 1997, 5 degrees awarded. *Average time to degree:* master's–1.9 years full-time, 2.8 years part-time. *Entrance requirements:* GMAT (minimum score 400 required, 4.0 on written portion), minimum undergraduate GPA of 3.0. Application deadline: rolling. Application fee: $50. Electronic applications accepted. *Expenses:* Tuition $375 per credit hour. Fees $60 per year. *Financial aid:* In 1997–98, 18 students received aid, including 3 graduate assistantships (all to first-year students); partial tuition waivers and career-related internships or fieldwork also available. Financial aid application deadline: 6/15; applicants required to submit FAFSA. *Faculty research:* Total quality management, international capital markets, motivation, entrepreneurship. • Dr. James P. Miller, Dean, 561-994-0770 Ext. 250. Application contact: Peter Gallo, Graduate Admissions Counselor, 800-544-8035. Fax: 561-241-3552. E-mail: admission@lynn.edu.

Madonna University, Program in Business Administration, Livonia, MI 48150-1173. Offerings include international business (MSBA). Postbaccalaureate distance learning degree programs offered (minimal on-campus study). Program faculty: 8 full-time (2 women), 13 part-time (2 women). *Degree requirements:* Thesis required (for some programs), foreign language not required. *Entrance requirements:* GMAT, GRE General Test, minimum GPA of 3.0. Application deadline: 8/1 (priority date; rolling processing; 4/1 for spring admission). *Expenses:* Tuition $260 per credit hour (minimum). Fees $50 per semester. • Dr. Stuart Arends, Dean of Business School, 734-432-5366. Fax: 734-432-5364. E-mail: arends@smtp.munet.edu. Application contact: Sandra Kellums, Coordinator of Graduate Admissions, 734-432-5666. Fax: 734-432-5393. E-mail: kellums@smtp.munet.edu.

Manhattan College, Program in Business Administration, Riverdale, NY 10471. Offerings include international business (MBA). Program faculty: 18 full-time (3 women), 8 part-time (0 women). *Degree requirements:* Computer language, thesis or alternative. *Entrance requirements:* GMAT, minimum GPA of 2.8. Application deadline: 8/10 (priority date; rolling processing; 1/7 for spring admission). Application fee: $50. *Expenses:* Tuition $440 per credit. Fees $100 per year. • Dr. Charles E. Brunner, Director, 718-862-7222. Fax: 718-862-8023. Application contact: William J. Bisset Jr., Dean of Admissions/Financial Aid, 718-862-7200. Fax: 718-863-8019. E-mail: admit@manhattan.edu.

Metropolitan State University, Management and Administration Program, St. Paul, MN 55106-5000. Offerings include international business (MBA). Program faculty: 17 full-time (5 women), 150 part-time. *Application deadline:* rolling. *Application fee:* $20. *Tuition:* $133 per credit for state residents; $208 per credit for nonresidents. • Gary Seiler, Graduate Coordinator, 612-373-2754. E-mail: seiler@msus1.msus.edu. Application contact: Gloria Marcus, Recruiter/Admissions Adviser, 612-373-2724. Fax: 612-373-2888. E-mail: marcusg@msus1.msus.edu.

Montclair State University, School of Business, Program in Business Administration, Upper Montclair, NJ 07043-1624. Offerings include international business (MBA). Program faculty: 57 full-time. *Entrance requirements:* GMAT. Application deadline: 4/1 (rolling processing; 11/1 for spring admission). Application fee: $40. *Expenses:* Tuition $201 per credit for state residents; $257 per credit for nonresidents. Fees $22.05 per credit. • Dr. Eileen Kaplan, Director, 973-655-4306.

Monterey Institute of International Studies, Fisher Graduate School of International Business, 425 Van Buren Street, Monterey, CA 93940-2691. Awards MBA. Faculty: 10 full-time (1 woman), 11 part-time (2 women), 14 FTE. Students: 114 full-time (48 women), 4 part-time (2 women); includes 17 Asian Americans, 4 Hispanics, 51 international. Average age 26. 183 applicants, 79% accepted. In 1997, 67 degrees awarded. *Degree requirements:* 1 foreign language, thesis. *Average time to degree:* master's–2 years full-time. *Entrance requirements:* GMAT, TOEFL (minimum score 550), minimum GPA of 3.0, proficiency in a foreign language. Application deadline: 6/1 (priority date; rolling processing). Application fee: $50. *Expenses:* Tuition $18,200 per year full-time, $760 per semester hour part-time. Fees $45 per year. *Financial aid:* Federal Work-Study, institutionally sponsored loans, and career-related internships or fieldwork available. Financial aid application deadline: 3/15; applicants required to submit FAFSA. *Faculty research:* International trade, organizational behavior, international marketing. • Dr. William Pendergast, Dean, 408-647-4140. Fax: 408-647-6506. Application contact: Admissions Office, 408-647-4123. Fax: 408-647-6405. E-mail: admit@miis.edu.

See in-depth description on page 547.

Monterey Institute of International Studies, Graduate School of International Policy Studies, Program in Commercial Diplomacy, 425 Van Buren Street, Monterey, CA 93940-2691. Awards MA. Faculty: 15 full-time (7 women), 22 part-time (7 women), 22 FTE. Students: 33 full-time (13 women); includes 2 minority (both Hispanics), 9 international. Average age 26. 23 applicants, 83% accepted. *Degree requirements:* 1 foreign language. *Entrance requirements:* TOEFL (minimum score 550), minimum GPA of 3.0, proficiency in a foreign language. Application deadline: 8/1 (priority date; rolling processing; 12/1 for spring admission). Application fee: $50. *Expenses:* Tuition $18,200 per year full-time, $760 per semester hour part-time. Fees $45 per year. *Financial aid:* Application deadline 3/15. • Dr. Geza Feketekuty, Head, 408-647-6424. Application contact: Admissions Office, 408-647-4123. Fax: 408-647-6405. E-mail: admit@miis.edu.

See in-depth description on page 545.

National Technological University, Program in International Business Administration, Fort Collins, CO 80526-1842. Awards IMBA. Program new for spring 1998. *Entrance requirements:* GMAT, minimum GPA of 2.9, 2 years of managerial experience. Application deadline: rolling. Application fee: $50. *Tuition:* $585 per credit (minimum). • Greg Mosier, Chair, 405-744-5118.

National University, School of Management and Technology, Department of Business Studies, La Jolla, CA 92037-1011. Offerings include international business (MA). *Application deadline:* rolling. *Application fee:* $60 ($100 for international students). *Tuition:* $7830 per year full-time, $870 per course part-time. • Donald Schwartz, Chair, 619-642-8420. Application contact: Nancy Rohland, Director of Enrollment Management, 619-563-7100. Fax: 619-563-7393.

New Hampshire College, Graduate School of Business, Program in Business Administration, Manchester, NH 03106-1045. Offerings include international business (Certificate). Program faculty: 7 full-time (1 woman), 66 part-time (11 women), 47 FTE. *Average time to degree:* master's–1.5 years full-time, 4.5 years part-time. *Application deadline:* rolling. *Application fee:* $0. *Expenses:* Tuition $17,044 per year full-time, $945 per course part-time. Fees $530 per year full-time, $80 per year part-time. • Dr. Paul Schneiderman, Acting Dean, Graduate School of Business, 603-644-3102. Fax: 603-644-3150.

Directory: International Business

New Hampshire College, Graduate School of Business, Program in International Business, Manchester, NH 03106-1045. Awards MS, DBA, Certificate. Part-time and evening/weekend programs available. Faculty: 2 full-time (0 women), 6 part-time (0 women), 3 FTE. Students: 15 full-time (6 women), 16 part-time (6 women); includes 12 international. Average age 28. In 1997, 21 master's awarded. *Degree requirements:* For master's, thesis or alternative required, foreign language not required. *Average time to degree:* master's–1.5 years full-time, 3.5 years part-time. *Entrance requirements:* For master's, minimum GPA of 2.5. Application deadline: rolling. Application fee: $0. *Expenses:* Tuition $17,044 per year full-time, $945 per course part-time. Fees $530 per year full-time, $80 per year part-time. *Financial aid:* Federal Work-Study, institutionally sponsored loans, and career-related internships or fieldwork available. • Dr. Paul Schneiderman, Acting Dean, Graduate School of Business, 603-644-3102. Fax: 603-644-3150.

New York University, Graduate School of Arts and Science, Department of Politics, New York, NY 10012-1019. Offerings include international politics and international business (MA). Department faculty: 26 full-time (4 women), 7 part-time. *Degree requirements:* 1 foreign language, thesis or alternative. *Entrance requirements:* GRE General Test, TOEFL. Application deadline: 1/4 (priority date). Application fee: $60. *Expenses:* Tuition $715 per credit. Fees $1048 per year full-time, $229 per semester (minimum) part-time. • Russell Hardin, Chair, 212-998-8500. Application contact: Steven Brams, Director of Graduate Studies, 212-998-8500. Fax: 212-995-4184. E-mail: politics.program@nyu.edu.

New York University, Leonard N. Stern School of Business, International Business Area, New York, NY 10006. Awards MBA, PhD, APC. Faculty: 24 part-time (3 women). Students: 144 full-time, 315 part-time. In 1997, 344 master's, 2 doctorates awarded. *Degree requirements:* For master's, computer language required, foreign language and thesis not required; for doctorate, computer language, dissertation required, foreign language not required. *Entrance requirements:* For master's, GMAT, TOEFL (minimum score 600); for doctorate, GMAT. Application deadline: 3/15 (rolling processing). Application fee: $75. *Financial aid:* Federal Work-Study available. Financial aid application deadline: 1/15; applicants required to submit FAFSA. *Faculty research:* International finance, macroeconomics, and trade; global banking; cross-cultural; international expansion and competition; global business and marketing strategy. • Tom Pugel, Chairman, 212-998-0400. Application contact: Mary Miller, Director, Graduate Admissions, 212-998-0600. Fax: 212-995-4231. E-mail: sternmba@stern.nyu.edu.

Nichols College, Graduate Program in Business Administration, Dudley, MA 01571. Offerings include international business (MBA). College faculty: 21 full-time (3 women), 6 part-time (2 women). *Degree requirements:* Computer language required, foreign language and thesis not required. *Entrance requirements:* GMAT, TOEFL, minimum AACSB index of 950. Application deadline: rolling. Application fee: $25. *Tuition:* $1050 per course. • William F. Keith, Director, 508-213-2207. E-mail: keithwf@nichols.edu.

Nova Southeastern University, School of Business and Entrepreneurship, Program in International Business Administration, Fort Lauderdale, FL 33314-7721. Awards MIBA, DIBA. Part-time and evening/weekend programs available. Students: 10 full-time (5 women), 182 part-time (60 women); includes 53 minority (24 African Americans, 3 Asian Americans, 26 Hispanics), 39 international. In 1997, 42 master's, 9 doctorates awarded. *Degree requirements:* Field experience or internship. *Entrance requirements:* GMAT, TOEFL, Michigan English Language Assessment Battery. Application deadline: rolling. Application fee: $50. *Tuition:* $270 per credit hour (minimum). • Dr. J. Preston Jones, Director, 954-262-5127. Application contact: Maria-Luisa Garcia, 954-262-5048. E-mail: garciaml@sbe.nova.edu.

Oklahoma City University, School of Management and Business Sciences, Program in Business Administration, Oklahoma City, OK 73106-1402. Offerings include international business (MBA). *Degree requirements:* Comprehensive exam required, foreign language and thesis not required. *Entrance requirements:* TOEFL, minimum GPA of 2.5. Application deadline: rolling. Application fee: $35 ($55 for international students). *Expenses:* Tuition $350 per hour. Fees $124 per year. • Application contact: Laura L. Rahhal, Director of Graduate Admissions, 800-633-7242 Ext. 2. Fax: 405-521-5356. E-mail: lrahhal1@frodo.okcu.edu.

Oral Roberts University, School of Business, Tulsa, OK 74171-0001. Offerings include international business (MBA). *Degree requirements:* Computer language required, thesis optional, foreign language not required. *Entrance requirements:* GMAT (minimum score 400; average 500). Application deadline: 7/31 (priority date; rolling processing; 12/31 for spring admission). Application fee: $35. Electronic applications accepted.

Our Lady of the Lake University of San Antonio, School of Business and Public Administration, 411 Southwest 24th Street, San Antonio, TX 78207-4689. Offerings include general (MBA), with options in finance, international business, management. School faculty: 15 full-time (2 women), 15 part-time (2 women). *Degree requirements:* Thesis optional. *Entrance requirements:* GMAT, GRE General Test, or MAT. Application deadline: rolling. Application fee: $15. *Expenses:* Tuition $371 per credit hour. Fees $57 per semester full-time, $32 per semester part-time. • Dr. W. Earl Walker, Dean, 210-434-6711 Ext. 281. Application contact: Quentin W. Korte, MBA Adviser, 210-434-6711 Ext. 491. Fax: 210-434-0821.

Pace University, Lubin School of Business, International Business Program, New York, NY 10038. Awards MBA. Part-time and evening/weekend programs available. *Degree requirements:* Computer language required, foreign language not required. *Entrance requirements:* GMAT. Application deadline: 7/31 (priority date; rolling processing; 11/30 for spring admission). Application fee: $60. *Expenses:* Tuition $545 per credit. Fees $360 per year full-time, $53 per semester (minimum) part-time.

Pace University, Lubin School of Business, Program in Business Economics, New York, NY 10038. Offerings include international economics (MBA). *Application deadline:* 7/31 (priority date; rolling processing; 11/30 for spring admission). *Application fee:* $60. *Expenses:* Tuition $545 per credit. Fees $360 per year full-time, $53 per semester (minimum) part-time.

Pacific States University, College of Business, Los Angeles, CA 90006. Offerings include international business (MBA). *Entrance requirements:* TOEFL (minimum score 450), minimum undergraduate GPA of 2.5 during last 90 hours. Application deadline: 6/15 (12/15 for spring admission). Application fee: $100. *Tuition:* $200 per unit. • Dr. Kamol Somvichian, Director, 888-200-0383.

Pepperdine University, School of Business and Management, Culver City, CA 90230-7615. Offerings include business (MBA, MIB), with options in business administration (MBA), international business (MIB). School faculty: 72 full-time (10 women), 38 part-time (5 women). *Application deadline:* 5/1. *Application fee:* $45. • Dr. Otis Baskin, Dean, 310-568-5500. Application contact: Dianna Sadlouskos, Director of Career Development and Student Recruitment.

Pepperdine University, Malibu Graduate Business Programs, Malibu, CA 90263-0001. Offerings include international business (MIB). MBA and MIB offered jointly with the School of Business and Management at the Culver City campus. *Application deadline:* 5/1 (rolling processing). *Application fee:* $45. • Dr. James A. Goodrich, Associate Dean, 310-456-4100. Application contact: Dianna Sadlouskos, Director of Career Development and Student Recruitment, 310-456-4044. Fax: 310-456-4126.

Philadelphia College of Textiles and Science, School of Business, Program in Business, Philadelphia, PA 19144-5497. Offerings include international business (MBA). *Entrance requirements:* GMAT, minimum GPA of 2.85. Application deadline: rolling. Application fee: $35. *Tuition:* $448 per credit hour. • Rita Powell, Director, 215-951-2950. Fax: 215-951-2652. E-mail: powellr@phila.col.edu. Application contact: Robert J. Reed, Director of Graduate Admissions, 215-951-2943. Fax: 215-951-2907. E-mail: gradadm@phila.col.edu.

Philadelphia College of Textiles and Science, School of Textiles and Materials Science, Program in Global Textile Marketing, Philadelphia, PA 19144-5497. Awards MS. MS offered jointly with Reuttinger University, Germany and Shenkar College of Israel. Part-time and evening/weekend programs available. *Entrance requirements:* GMAT, GRE, or MAT, minimum GPA of 2.75. Application deadline: rolling. Application fee: $35. *Tuition:* $448 per credit hour. *Financial aid:* Research assistantships, graduate assistantships, residential assistantships, Federal Work-Study, and career-related internships or fieldwork available. Financial aid applicants required to submit FAFSA. • Dr. Jacob Gargir, Director, 215-951-2762. Fax: 215-951-2651. E-mail: gargirj@phila.col.edu. Application contact: Robert J. Reed, Director of Graduate Admissions, 215-951-2943. Fax: 215-951-2907. E-mail: gradadm@phila.col.edu.

Point Park College, Department of Business, Accounting, and Computer Science, International MBA Program, Pittsburgh, PA 15222-1984. Awards MBA. Part-time and evening/weekend programs available. Faculty: 2 full-time (0 women), 8 part-time (1 woman). Students: 51. *Degree requirements:* 1 foreign language. *Average time to degree:* master's–2.3 years full-time, 3.3 years part-time. *Entrance requirements:* GMAT (average 560), TOEFL (minimum score 500; average 525). Application deadline: rolling. Application fee: $30. *Financial aid:* Research assistantships, Federal Work-Study, institutionally sponsored loans, and career-related internships or fieldwork available. Aid available to part-time students. Financial aid application deadline: 5/1; applicants required to submit FAFSA. *Faculty research:* International organizations/administrations, multinational corporate issues, international investment issues. • Application contact: Cathy Ballis, Assistant to the Director, 412-392-3812. Fax: 412-391-7510.

See in-depth description on page 549.

Portland State University, School of Business Administration, Concentration in International Business, Portland, OR 97207-0751. Awards MBA. Part-time and evening/weekend programs available. Faculty: 57 full-time (17 women), 34 part-time (9 women), 60 FTE. Students: 1 part-time (0 women). 0 applicants. *Degree requirements:* 1 foreign language, project required, thesis not required. *Entrance requirements:* GMAT (minimum score 450), TOEFL (minimum score 550), minimum GPA of 3.0 in upper-division course work. Application deadline: 4/1 (priority date; rolling processing). Application fee: $50. *Tuition:* $6101 per year full-time, $689 per semester (minimum) part-time for state residents; $10,445 per year full-time, $689 per semester (minimum) part-time for nonresidents. *Financial aid:* Research assistantships, teaching assistantships, Federal Work-Study, institutionally sponsored loans, and career-related internships or fieldwork available. Aid available to part-time students. Financial aid application deadline: 3/1; applicants required to submit FAFSA. *Faculty research:* Quality management and organizational excellence, performance measurement, customer satisfaction, values, technology management and technology transfer. Total annual research expenditures: $75,000. • Dr. Scott Dawson, Head, 503-725-3721. E-mail: scott@sba.pdx.edu. Application contact: Pam Mitchell, 503-725-3730. Fax: 503-725-5850. E-mail: pamm@sba.pdx.edu.

Portland State University, School of Business Administration, Program in International Management, Beaverton, OR 97006. Awards MIM. Part-time and evening/weekend programs available. Faculty: 57 full-time (17 women), 34 part-time (9 women), 60 FTE. Students: 35 full-time (8 women), 2 part-time (1 woman); includes 18 minority (1 African American, 15 Asian Americans, 1 Hispanic, 1 Native American), 12 international. Average age 34. 93 applicants, 61% accepted. *Degree requirements:* Field study trip to China and Japan required, thesis not required. *Entrance requirements:* GMAT (minimum score 500), TOEFL (minimum score 550), minimum GPA of 2.75, resumé. Application deadline: 3/1 (priority date; rolling processing). Application fee: $50. *Expenses:* Tuition $16,500 per year. Fees $3850 per year. *Financial aid:* Research assistantships, teaching assistantships, Federal Work-Study, institutionally sponsored loans, and career-related internships or fieldwork available. Aid available to part-time students. Financial aid application deadline: 3/1; applicants required to submit FAFSA. • Dr. John Oh, Director, 503-725-3703. E-mail: ohj@capital.osshe.edu. Application contact: Andrew Wong, Coordinator, 503-725-5995. Fax: 503-725-2290. E-mail: andreww@sbamail.sba..pdx.edu.

See in-depth description on page 551.

Quinnipiac College, School of Business, Program in Business Administration, Hamden, CT 06518-1904. Offerings include international business (MBA). Program faculty: 17 full-time (2 women), 4 part-time (1 woman). *Degree requirements:* Thesis optional, foreign language not required. *Average time to degree:* master's–2 years full-time, 4 years part-time. *Entrance requirements:* GMAT (minimum score 400; average 470), interview, minimum GPA of 2.5. Application deadline: 8/1 (priority date; rolling processing). Application fee: $45. Electronic applications accepted. *Expenses:* Tuition $395 per credit hour. Fees $380 per year full-time. • Dr. Earl Chrysler, Director, 203-281-8799. Fax: 203-281-8664. E-mail: chrysler@quinnipiac.edu. Application contact: Scott Farber, Director of Graduate Admissions, 203-281-8795. Fax: 203-287-5238. E-mail: qcgradadmi@quinnipiac.edu.

Rochester Institute of Technology, College of Business, Department of Business Administration, Program in International Business, Rochester, NY 14623-5604. Awards MS. Students: 2 full-time (both women), 3 part-time (1 woman); includes 2 international. 14 applicants, 36% accepted. In 1997, 3 degrees awarded. *Entrance requirements:* GMAT, minimum GPA of 2.5. Application deadline: 3/1 (priority date; rolling processing). Application fee: $40. *Expenses:* Tuition $18,765 per year full-time, $527 per credit hour part-time. Fees $126 per year full-time. • Patricia Sorce, Associate Dean, Department of Business Administration, 716-475-2313.

Roosevelt University, Walter E. Heller College of Business Administration, Program in International Business, Chicago, IL 60605-1394. Awards MSIB. Part-time and evening/weekend programs available. Students: 33 (22 women); includes 5 minority (1 African American, 1 Asian American, 2 Hispanics, 1 Native American), 7 international. In 1997, 9 degrees awarded. *Degree requirements:* 1 foreign language required, thesis not required. *Entrance requirements:* GMAT. Application deadline: 6/1 (priority date; rolling processing). Application fee: $25 ($35 for international students). *Expenses:* Tuition $445 per credit hour. Fees $100 per year. *Financial aid:* Partial tuition waivers, Federal Work-Study, and career-related internships or fieldwork available. Financial aid application deadline: 2/15. • Dr. Alan G. Krabbenhoft, Director, 312-341-3846. E-mail: akrabben@acfsysv.roosevelt.edu. Application contact: Joanne Canyon-Heller, Coordinator of Graduate Admissions, 312-341-3612.

Rutgers, The State University of New Jersey, Newark, Department of Management, Newark, NJ 07102-3192. Offerings include international business (PhD). Offered jointly with New Jersey Institute of Technology. Terminal master's awarded for partial completion of doctoral program. Department faculty: 113 full-time (13 women), 3 part-time (1 woman). *Degree requirements:* Dissertation, cumulative exams required, foreign language not required. *Average time to degree:* doctorate–5 years full-time, 7 years part-time. *Entrance requirements:* GMAT or GRE, minimum undergraduate B average. Application deadline: 4/1 (rolling processing; 11/1 for spring admission). Application fee: $40. *Expenses:* Tuition $6248 per year full-time, $257 per credit part-time for state residents; $9160 per year full-time, $380 per credit part-time for nonresidents. Fees $738 per year full-time, $107 per semester (minimum) part-time. • Glenn R. Shafer, Director, 973-353-1604. E-mail: gshafer@andromeda.rutgers.edu. Application contact: Ana Gonzalez, Program Secretary, 973-353-5371. Fax: 973-353-5691. E-mail: anag@gsmack.rutgers.edu.

Rutgers, The State University of New Jersey, Newark, Graduate School of Management, Department of International Business, Newark, NJ 07102-3192. Awards MBA. *Degree requirements:* Computer language required, thesis not required. *Entrance requirements:* GMAT, TOEFL. Application deadline: 6/1 (rolling processing). Application fee: $40. *Financial aid:* Federal Work-Study, institutionally sponsored loans, and career-related internships or fieldwork available. Financial aid application deadline: 3/15; applicants required to submit FAFSA. • Dr. Jerry Rosenberg, Chair, 973-353-5812. Fax: 973-353-1273. E-mail: rosenbrg@ardromeda.rutgers.edu. Application contact: Director of Admissions, 973-353-1234. Fax: 973-353-1592. E-mail: admit@gsmack.rutgers.edu.

Saint Joseph's University, Erivan K. Haub School of Business, Department of Food Marketing, Program in International Marketing, Philadelphia, PA 19131-1395. Awards MS. Part-time and evening/weekend programs available. Faculty: 5 full-time (2 women), 1 part-time (0

Directory: International Business

Saint Joseph's University (continued)

women). Students: 21 full-time (12 women). Average age 24. In 1997, 10 degrees awarded (100% found work related to degree). *Degree requirements:* Thesis optional, foreign language not required. *Average time to degree:* master's–1.2 years full-time, 1.9 years part-time. *Entrance requirements:* GMAT, TOEFL. Application deadline: 4/7 (priority date; rolling processing). Application fee: $0. *Tuition:* $470 per credit hour. *Financial aid:* In 1997–98, 4 students received aid, including 4 research assistantships averaging $300 per month and totaling $4,000; Federal Work-Study, institutionally sponsored loans, and career-related internships or fieldwork also available. Financial aid application deadline: 5/15; applicants required to submit FAFSA. *Faculty research:* Export marketing, international marketing research, global marketing. • Dr. Alphonso O. Ogbuehi, Director, 610-660-1105. Fax: 610-660-1604. E-mail: ogbuehi@sju.edu.

Saint Joseph's University, Erivan K. Haub School of Business, Programs in Graduate Business, Program in International Business, Philadelphia, PA 19131-1395. Awards MBA. Students: 37 (13 women). In 1997, 18 degrees awarded. *Entrance requirements:* GMAT, TOEFL. Application deadline: 7/15 (priority date; rolling processing; 11/15 for spring admission). Application fee: $35. *Tuition:* $510 per credit hour. *Financial aid:* Graduate assistantships available. Financial aid application deadline: 5/1. • Adele C. Foley, Associate Dean, Programs in Graduate Business, 610-660-1690. Fax: 610-660-1599. E-mail: afoley@sju.edu.

Saint Joseph's University, Erivan K. Haub School of Business, Programs in Graduate Business, Program in International Marketing, Philadelphia, PA 19131-1395. Awards MBA. Students: 15 (5 women). In 1997, 5 degrees awarded. *Entrance requirements:* GMAT, TOEFL. Application deadline: 7/15 (priority date; rolling processing; 11/15 for spring admission). Application fee: $35. *Tuition:* $510 per credit hour. *Financial aid:* Graduate assistantships available. Financial aid application deadline: 5/1. • Adele C. Foley, Associate Dean, Programs in Graduate Business, 610-660-1690. Fax: 610-660-1599. E-mail: afoley@sju.edu.

Saint Louis University, School of Business and Administration, Program in International Business, 3674 Lindell Boulevard, St. Louis, MO 63108. Awards MBA, PhD. Part-time programs available. *Degree requirements:* For doctorate, dissertation. *Entrance requirements:* For master's, GMAT, TOEFL; for doctorate, GMAT. Application deadline: 7/15 (rolling processing; 11/15 for spring admission). Application fee: $30. *Financial aid:* Fellowships, research assistantships, teaching assistantships, Federal Work-Study available. Aid available to part-time students. • Dr. Seung H. Kim, Director, 314-977-3898. Fax: 314-977-7188.

Saint Louis University, School of Business and Administration, Institute of International Business, Executive Master of International Business Program, St. Louis, MO 63103-2097. Awards EMIB. Part-time and evening/weekend programs available. Faculty: 11 full-time (0 women), 9 part-time (2 women). Students: 48 part-time (20 women); includes 9 minority (3 African Americans, 1 Asian American, 5 Hispanics). 26 applicants, 100% accepted. In 1997, 27 degrees awarded. *Degree requirements:* Project report required, foreign language and thesis not required. *Entrance requirements:* GMAT, TOEFL. Application deadline: 4/30 (priority date; rolling processing). Application fee: $50. *Tuition:* $13,500 per year (minimum). *Financial aid:* Available to part-time students. • Application contact: J. Patrick Dugan, Program Coordinator, 314-977-3898. Fax: 314-977-7188. E-mail: iib@slu.edu.

Announcement: The School of Business and Administration's Institute of International Business offers several international business degrees. The Executive Master of International Business is a 2-year, part-time program that combines international business with culture. A 2-week study-abroad session and project report are required. The full-time Master of International Business program can be completed in 1 or 2 years. It provides a strong academic foundation in international business. Internships and/or team projects are required. In both programs, participants advance concurrently, sharing work experiences and case studies in team environments. Classes begin each fall. Application requirements: professional experience, excellent academic background, 2 letters of recommendation, and GMAT scores. Application deadline: April 30 (space available thereafter). Ph.D. and undergraduate degrees in international business are also available. For more information, contact 314-977-3898 (fax: 314-977-7188; e-mail: iib@slu.edu; World Wide Web: http://www.slu.edu/centers/iib).

Saint Louis University, School of Business and Administration, Institute of International Business, Master of International Business Program, St. Louis, MO 63103-2097. Awards MIB. Faculty: 9 full-time (1 woman), 5 part-time (0 women). Students: 19 full-time (12 women); includes 14 minority (13 Asian Americans, 1 Hispanic). 33 applicants, 58% accepted. *Degree requirements:* Internship required, foreign language and thesis not required. *Entrance requirements:* GMAT, TOEFL. Application deadline: 2/28 (priority date; rolling processing). Application fee: $40. *Tuition:* $26,110 per year full-time, $15,110 per year part-time. *Financial aid:* Federal Work-Study and career-related internships or fieldwork available. • Application contact: Dena McCaffrey, Program Coordinator, 314-977-3602. Fax: 314-977-7188. E-mail: iib@slu.edu.

Saint Mary's College of California, School of Economics and Business Administration, International Business Program, Moraga, CA 94575. Awards MBAIB. Faculty: 5 full-time (0 women), 10 part-time (2 women). Students: 4 full-time (1 woman); includes 2 international. Average age 33. 34 applicants, 47% accepted. In 1997, 16 degrees awarded (100% found work related to degree). *Average time to degree:* master's–1.1 years full-time. *Entrance requirements:* GMAT (minimum score 500), TOEFL (minimum score 550). Application deadline: rolling. Application fee: $40. *Tuition:* $5700 per quarter. *Financial aid:* Career-related internships or fieldwork available. Aid available to part-time students. Financial aid application deadline: 3/2; applicants required to submit FAFSA. • Nelson Shelton, Director of Graduate Business Programs, 925-631-4500. Application contact: Tracey Fanelli, Director of Admissions, 925-631-4504. Fax: 925-376-6521. E-mail: smcmba@stmarys-ca.edu.

Saint Peter's College, MBA Programs, 2641 Kennedy Boulevard, Jersey City, NJ 07306-5997. Offerings include international business (MBA). Faculty: 15 full-time (0 women), 16 part-time (5 women). *Degree requirements:* Exit presentation. *Entrance requirements:* GMAT (minimum score 400) or MAT (minimum score 40). Application deadline: 8/1 (priority date; rolling processing). Application fee: $20. *Tuition:* $516 per credit. • Sr. Jeanne Gilligan, Associate Vice President for Academic Affairs, 201-915-7252. Fax: 201-946-7528. E-mail: gilliganj@spcvxa.spc.edu. Application contact: Nancy P. Campbell, Associate Vice President for Enrollment, 201-915-9213. Fax: 201-432-5860. E-mail: amissions@spcvxa.spc.edu.

St. Thomas University, School of Graduate Studies, Department of Professional Management, Specialization in International Business, Miami, FL 33054-6459. Awards MBA, MSM, Certificate. Part-time and evening/weekend programs available. *Degree requirements:* For master's, comprehensive exam required, foreign language and thesis not required. *Average time to degree:* master's–1 year full-time. *Entrance requirements:* For master's, TOEFL (minimum score 550), interview, minimum GPA of 3.0 or GMAT. Application deadline: 6/15 (priority date; rolling processing; 11/15 for spring admission). Application fee: $30. *Tuition:* $410 per credit.

San Diego State University, Graduate School of Business, Program in International Business, San Diego, CA 92182. Awards MBA, MS. Evening/weekend programs available. Students: 6 full-time (4 women), 21 part-time (7 women); includes 6 minority (5 Asian Americans, 1 Hispanic), 3 international. Average age 29. In 1997, 28 degrees awarded. *Degree requirements:* Thesis or alternative required, foreign language not required. *Average time to degree:* master's–2 years full-time, 3.5 years part-time. *Entrance requirements:* GMAT (minimum score 550), TOEFL (minimum score 570). Application deadline: 4/15 (priority date; rolling processing; 11/1 for spring admission). Application fee: $55. Electronic applications accepted. *Expenses:* Tuition $0 for state residents; $246 per unit for nonresidents. Fees $1932 per year full-time, $1266 per year part-time. *Financial aid:* Career-related internships or fieldwork available. *Faculty research:* International management. • Jill Acevedo, Head, 619-594-4188. Application contact: Patricia Martin, Director of Admissions, 619-594-5217. Fax: 619-594-1863. E-mail: sdsumba@mail.sdsu.edu.

Schiller International University, MBA Programs, Program in International Business, 453 Edgewater Drive, Dunedin, FL 34698-7532. Awards MBA. *Degree requirements:* Thesis optional, foreign language not required. *Entrance requirements:* GMAT, bachelor's degree or equivalent. Application deadline: rolling. Application fee: $35. *Expenses:* Tuition $11,800 per year. Fees $210 per year. *Financial aid:* Available to part-time students. Financial aid application deadline: 3/30. • Application contact: Muriel Jault, Admissions Representative, 813-736-5082. Fax: 813-734-0359. E-mail: siuadmis@aol.com.

See in-depth description on page 479.

Schiller International University, MBA Program, 32 Boulevard de Vaugirard, Paris 75015, France. Offerings include international business (MBA). Bilingual French/English MBA available for native French speakers. Faculty: 5 full-time (1 woman), 10 part-time (5 women). *Application deadline:* 8/1 (priority date; rolling processing; 12/1 for spring admission). *Application fee:* $35. *Expenses:* Tuition $12,800 per year. Fees $210 per year. • John Lynch, Adviser, 1-4538-5601. Application contact: Muriel Jault, Admissions Representative, 813-736-5082. Fax: 813-734-0359. E-mail: siuadmis@aol.com.

Schiller International University, MBA Program, Chateau Pourtales, 161 rue Melanie, Strasbourg 6700, France. Offerings include international business (MBA). Faculty: 2 full-time (0 women), 5 part-time (1 woman). *Degree requirements:* Thesis optional, foreign language not required. *Entrance requirements:* GMAT, bachelor's degree or equivalent. Application deadline: 8/1 (priority date; rolling processing; 12/1 for spring admission). Application fee: $35. *Expenses:* Tuition $12,800 per year. Fees $210 per year. • Hanns Blasius, Adviser, 94-43-43. Fax: 94-22-55. Application contact: Muriel Jault, Admissions Representative, 813-736-5082. Fax: 813-734-0359. E-mail: siuadmis@aol.com.

Schiller International University, MBA Program, Bergstrasse 106, Heidelberg 69121, Germany. Offerings include international business (MBA, MIM). Faculty: 10 full-time (6 women), 13 part-time (4 women), 13 FTE. *Degree requirements:* Thesis optional, foreign language not required. *Entrance requirements:* GMAT, bachelor's degree or equivalent. Application deadline: 8/1 (priority date; rolling processing; 12/1 for spring admission). Application fee: $35. *Expenses:* Tuition $12,800 per year. Fees $210 per year. • Lisa Evans, Director, 49-6221-49159. Application contact: Muriel Jault, Admissions Representative, 813-736-5082. Fax: 813-734-0359. E-mail: siuadmis@aol.com.

Schiller International University, MBA Program, San Bernardo 97-99, Edif. Colomina, Madrid 28015, Spain. Offerings include international business (MBA). Faculty: 6 full-time, 4 part-time. *Degree requirements:* Thesis optional, foreign language not required. *Entrance requirements:* GMAT, bachelor's degree or equivalent. Application deadline: 8/1 (priority date; rolling processing; 12/1 for spring admission). Application fee: $35. *Expenses:* Tuition $12,800 per year. Fees $210 per year. • Terrance Reynolds, Adviser, 1-446-2349. Fax: 341-593-4446. Application contact: Muriel Jault, Admissions Representative, 813-736-5082. Fax: 813-734-0359. E-mail: siuadmis@aol.com.

Schiller International University, Graduate Programs, Program in International Business, 51-55 Waterloo Road, London SE1 8TX, United Kingdom. Awards MBA. *Degree requirements:* Thesis optional, foreign language not required. *Entrance requirements:* GMAT. Application deadline: 8/1 (priority date; rolling processing; 12/1 for spring admission). Application fee: $35. *Expenses:* Tuition $12,800 per year. Fees $210 per year. *Financial aid:* Application deadline 3/30. • Application contact: Muriel Jault, Admissions Representative, 813-736-5082. Fax: 813-734-0359. E-mail: siuadmis@aol.com.

See in-depth description on page 479.

Schiller International University, Graduate Programs, Program in International Management, 51-55 Waterloo Road, London SE1 8TX, United Kingdom. Awards MIM. *Degree requirements:* Thesis optional, foreign language not required. *Application deadline:* 8/1 (priority date; rolling processing; 12/1 for spring admission). *Application fee:* $35. *Expenses:* Tuition $12,800 per year. Fees $210 per year. *Financial aid:* Application deadline 3/30. • Application contact: Muriel Jault, Admissions Representative, 813-736-5082. Fax: 813-734-0359. E-mail: siuadmis@aol.com.

See in-depth description on page 479.

Schiller International University, American College of Switzerland, MBA Program, CH-1854 Leysin, Switzerland. Offers program in international business (MBA). *Degree requirements:* Thesis or alternative, comprehensive exams required, foreign language not required. *Entrance requirements:* GMAT. Application deadline: rolling. Application fee: $50.

School for International Training, Program in International and Intercultural Management, Brattleboro, VT 05302-0676. Awards MIIM. Faculty: 8 full-time (6 women), 12 part-time (5 women). Students: 95 full-time (62 women), 91 part-time (75 women). Average age 28. 258 applicants, 80% accepted. In 1997, 90 degrees awarded. *Degree requirements:* 1 foreign language, thesis. *Entrance requirements:* TOEFL (minimum score 550). Application deadline: rolling. Application fee: $45. *Expenses:* Tuition $18,000 per year (minimum). Fees $1283 per year (minimum). *Financial aid:* In 1997–98, 58 students received aid, including 51 grants, scholarships (all to first-year students); Federal Work-Study, institutionally sponsored loans, and career-related internships or fieldwork also available. Financial aid application deadline: 4/1; applicants required to submit FAFSA. *Faculty research:* Intercultural communication, conflict resolution, advising and training, world issues, international business. • Karen Blanchard, Program Chair, 802-257-7751 Ext. 3322. Application contact: Marshall Brewer, Admissions Counselor, 802-258-3265. Fax: 802-258-3500.

Seattle University, Albers School of Business and Economics, Program in International Business, Seattle, WA 98122. Awards MIB, Certificate, JD/MIB. Certificate and JD/MIB new for fall 1998. Part-time and evening/weekend programs available. Students: 8 full-time (6 women), 31 part-time (12 women); includes 5 minority (all Asian Americans), 7 international. Average age 32. 17 applicants, 29% accepted. In 1997, 3 master's awarded. *Degree requirements:* For master's, 1 foreign language, international experience required, thesis not required. *Entrance requirements:* For master's, GMAT (minimum score 500; average 560), TOEFL (minimum score 580), minimum GPA of 3.0, 1 year of related work experience. Application deadline: 8/20 (rolling processing; 2/20 for spring admission). Application fee: $55. *Expenses:* Tuition $440 per credit hour. Fees $70 per year. *Financial aid:* Federal Work-Study and career-related internships or fieldwork available. Aid available to part-time students. Financial aid applicants required to submit FAFSA. • David Arnesen, Director, 206-296-5700. Fax: 206-296-5795. E-mail: arnesen@seattleu.edu. Application contact: Michael McKeon, Dean of Admissions, 206-296-5900. Fax: 206-296-5656. E-mail: admissions@seattleu.edu.

Seton Hall University, W. Paul Stillman School of Business, Program in International Business, South Orange, NJ 07079-2692. Awards MS, Certificate, MBA/MS. Part-time and evening/weekend programs available. *Degree requirements:* For master's, thesis optional, foreign language not required. *Entrance requirements:* For master's, GMAT (minimum score 500), TOEFL (minimum score 550); for Certificate, master's degree. Application deadline: 6/1 (priority date; rolling processing). Application fee: $50. *Expenses:* Tuition $538 per credit. Fees $185 per semester. *Financial aid:* Research assistantships available. Aid available to part-time students. Financial aid applicants required to submit FAFSA. • Dr. Agnes Olszewski, Director, 973-761-9240. E-mail: olszewag@shu.edu. Application contact: Student Information Office, 973-761-9222. Fax: 973-761-9217. E-mail: busgrad@shu.edu.

Simon Fraser University, Faculty of Business Administration, Burnaby, BC V5A 1S6, Canada. Offerings include international business (MBA). Faculty: 48 full-time (12 women). *Application* *fee:* $55. *Expenses:* Tuition $2400 per year (minimum). Fees $207 per year. • S. McShane, Director, 604-291-3639. Application contact: Program Assistant, 604-291-3047. Fax: 604-291-3404. E-mail: mba@sfu.ca.

Southeastern University, Program in Business Management, Washington, DC 20024-2788. Offerings include international management (MBA). Program faculty: 4 full-time (1 woman), 17 part-time (1 woman). *Degree requirements:* Computer language required, thesis optional, foreign language not required. *Entrance requirements:* TOEFL. Application deadline: rolling. Application fee: $45. *Expenses:* Tuition $228 per credit hour. Fees $175 per quarter. • Dr. Mohammed Safa, Head, 202-488-8162. Application contact: Jack Flinter, Director of Admissions, 202-265-5343. Fax: 202-488-8093.

Suffolk University, College of Liberal Arts and Sciences, Department of Economics, Boston, MA 02108-2770. Awards MSIE, JD/MSIE. Program in international economics (MSIE). Part-time and evening/weekend programs available. Faculty: 7 full-time (2 women). Students: 4 full-time (3 women), 11 part-time (3 women). Average age 30. 27 applicants, 52% accepted. In 1997, 3 degrees awarded. *Degree requirements:* Thesis required, foreign language not required. *Entrance requirements:* GRE General Test (average 500 on each section) or MAT (average 50), minimum GPA of 2.5. Application deadline: 6/15 (priority date; rolling processing; 11/15 for spring admission). Application fee: $50. *Expenses:* Tuition $15,042 per year full-time, $1503 per course part-time. Fees $20 per year full-time, $10 per year part-time. *Financial aid:* In 1997–98, 5 students received aid, including 2 fellowships; Federal Work-Study, institutionally sponsored loans, and career-related internships or fieldwork also available. Aid available to part-time students. Financial aid application deadline: 4/1; applicants required to submit FAFSA. *Faculty research:* International trade, international finance, economic forecasting, country risk analysis, econometrics. • Dr. Shahruz Mohtadi, Director, 617-573-8670. Fax: 617-720-4272. E-mail: smohtadi@acad.suffolk.edu. Application contact: Judy Reynolds, Acting Director of Graduate Admissions, 617-573-8302. Fax: 617-523-0116. E-mail: grad.admission@admin.suffolk.edu.

Announcement: The Master of Science in International Economics degree is designed to prepare students for careers in international business and government as analysts and consultants and for study at the doctoral level. The program provides a solid foundation in economic theory and quantitative methods to study international economic trends and issues and to analyze economic data for estimation and forecasting. The program requires the successful completion of twelve 3-credit courses, which includes writing a thesis. Full-time students with appropriate backgrounds who enter in the fall semester can complete the program in 1 calendar year. For an application and information, contact the Office of Graduate Admission (telephone: 617-573-8302; fax: 617-523-0116; e-mail: grad.admission@admin.suffolk.edu).

Sul Ross State University, Department of Business Administration, Alpine, TX 79832. Offerings include international trade (MBA). Department faculty: 4 full-time (0 women), 2 part-time (0 women). *Degree requirements:* Thesis optional, foreign language not required. *Entrance requirements:* GMAT (minimum score 400) or GRE General Test (minimum combined score of 850), minimum GPA of 2.5 in last 60 hours of undergraduate work. Application deadline: rolling. Application fee: $0 ($50 for international students). *Expenses:* Tuition $864 per year full-time, $120 per semester (minimum) part-time for state residents; $5976 per year full-time, $747 per semester (minimum) part-time for nonresidents. Fees $754 per year full-time, $105 per semester (minimum) part-time. • William G. Green, Chair, 915-837-8066. Fax: 915-837-8003.

Syracuse University, School of Management, Program in International Business, Syracuse, NY 13244-0003. Awards MBA. Students: 18 full-time (6 women), 12 part-time (5 women); includes 2 minority (1 Hispanic, 1 Native American), 11 international. 90 applicants, 50% accepted. In 1997, 7 degrees awarded. *Entrance requirements:* GMAT. Application deadline: 2/1. Application fee: $40. *Tuition:* $13,320 per year full-time, $555 per credit hour part-time. *Financial aid:* Application deadline 3/1. • Peter K. Koveos, Chairman, 315-443-1040. Application contact: Associate Dean, 315-443-3850.

Temple University, School of Business and Management, Master's Program in Business Administration, Philadelphia, PA 19122-6096. Offerings include international business (MS), international business administration (MBA). Program faculty: 72 full-time (13 women). *Application fee:* $40. *Expenses:* Tuition $323 per semester hour for state residents; $444 per semester hour for nonresidents. Fees $170 per year full-time, $28 per semester (minimum) part-time. • Application contact: Linda Whelan, Director, 215-204-7678. Fax: 215-204-8300. E-mail: linda@astro.ocis.temple.edu.

Texas A&M International University, Division of Business Administration, Program in International Logistics, 5201 University Boulevard, Laredo, TX 78041-1900. Awards MSIL. Part-time and evening/weekend programs available. *Entrance requirements:* GMAT or GRE General Test. Application deadline: 7/15 (priority date; rolling processing; 11/12 for spring admission). Application fee: $0.

Texas A&M International University, Division of Business Administration, Program in International Trade, 5201 University Boulevard, Laredo, TX 78041-1900. Awards MBA. Part-time and evening/weekend programs available. *Degree requirements:* International trade simulation required, foreign language and thesis not required. *Entrance requirements:* GMAT or GRE General Test. Application deadline: 7/15 (priority date; rolling processing; 11/12 for spring admission). Application fee: $0.

Announcement: The Graduate School of International Trade and Business Administration's MBA in International Trade prepares a cadre of international business leaders who understand the complexities of trade in the global economy. Because of the University's unique location on the border of Mexico, it serves as a perfect laboratory for the study of international trade. Laredo is the country's largest commercial inland port of trade, and its air cargo service into Latin America is one of the top 10 cargo handling centers in the US. Student exchange programs that allow students to study in other countries while earning credit are also available with France, Germany, Mexico, and Costa Rica.

See in-depth description on page 553.

Thunderbird, The American Graduate School of International Management, Graduate Programs, Glendale, AZ 85306-3236. Awards MIHM, MIM, MIMLA, MIMOT, MIM/MBA. MIM/MBA offered jointly with Arizona State University, Arizona State University West, Case Western Reserve University, Drury College, University of Arizona, University of Colorado at Denver, University of Florida, University of Houston, University of Texas at Arlington, and ESADE in Barcelona, Spain. Faculty: 103 full-time (22 women), 19 part-time (12 women). Students: 1,508 full-time (528 women); includes 117 minority (16 African Americans, 40 Asian Americans, 56 Hispanics, 5 Native Americans), 670 international. Average age 28. 1,333 applicants, 56% accepted. In 1997, 928 degrees awarded. *Degree requirements:* 1 foreign language. *Average time to degree:* master's–1.5 years full-time. *Entrance requirements:* GMAT (minimum score 500; average 590), TOEFL (average 610). Application fee: $50. Electronic applications accepted. *Expenses:* Tuition $21,000 per year full-time, $1000 per credit hour part-time. Fees $200 per year. *Financial aid:* In 1997–98, 1,156 students received aid, including 23 fellowships (14 to first-year students) totaling $175,394, 582 merit scholarships, grants (165 to first-year students); partial tuition waivers, Federal Work-Study, and career-related internships or fieldwork also available. Aid available to part-time students. Financial aid application deadline: 4/1; applicants required to submit FAFSA. *Faculty research:* Management of global firms, government-business relationships, environmental technology firms and NAFTA, dispute resolutions, international financial management, business in Latin America. Total annual research expenditures: $3.903 million. • Dr. Melvyn R. Copen, Senior Vice President for Academic Affairs, 602-978-7250. Fax: 602-547-1356. E-mail: copenm@t-bird.edu. Application contact: Judy Johnson, Director of Admissions, 602-978-7100. Fax: 602-439-5432. E-mail: johnsonj@t-bird.edu.

See in-depth description on page 555.

Union College, Graduate and Continuing Studies, Graduate Management Institute, Program in International Management, Schenectady, NY 12308-2311. Awards MBA. Students: 8 full-time (2 women), 3 part-time (0 women); includes 5 international. 4 applicants, 100% accepted. In 1997, 3 degrees awarded. *Degree requirements:* 1 foreign language, computer language, comprehensive exam, internship required, thesis not required. *Entrance requirements:* GMAT. Application deadline: 5/15 (rolling processing). Application fee: $35. *Tuition:* $1434 per course. *Financial aid:* Application deadline 5/15. • Application contact: Carolyn Micklas, Recruiting and Admissions Coordinator, 518-388-6239.

United States International University, College of Business Administration, San Diego, CA 92131-1799. Offerings include international business (MIBA, DBA), with options in finance (DBA), marketing (DBA). Terminal master's awarded for partial completion of doctoral program. College faculty: 13 full-time (4 women), 14 part-time (6 women), 20 FTE. *Degree requirements:* For doctorate, computer language, dissertation required, foreign language not required. *Average time to degree:* master's–1.5 years full-time, 2.5 years part-time; doctorate–3 years full-time, 5 years part-time. *Entrance requirements:* For doctorate, GMAT (minimum score 490; average 560), minimum GPA of 3.3. Application deadline: rolling. Application fee: $40. Electronic applications accepted. *Expenses:* Tuition $360 per unit. Fees $120 per year. • Dr. Mink H. Stavenga, Dean, 619-635-4695. Fax: 619-635-4528. E-mail: mstaveng@usiu.edu. Application contact: Susan Topham, Assistant Director of Admissions, 619-635-4885. Fax: 619-635-4739. E-mail: admissions@usiu.edu.

United States International University–Mexico, Programs in Business, Alvaro Obregon #110, Colonia Roma, Mexico City CP06700, Mexico. Offerings include international business administration (MIBA). Faculty: 1 full-time (0 women), 11 part-time (3 women). *Application deadline:* 8/15 (priority date; rolling processing). *Application fee:* $35. • Application contact: Clarisa Desouches, Admissions Officer, 525-264-2187. Fax: 525-264-2188. E-mail: cristina@intmex.com.

Université du Québec, École nationale d'administration publique, Program in International Administration, Ste-Foy, PQ G1V 3J9, Canada. Awards Diploma. Part-time programs available. Students: 7 full-time (4 women), 39 part-time (21 women); includes 7 international. 81 applicants, 78% accepted. In 1997, 33 degrees awarded. *Entrance requirements:* Appropriate bachelor's degree, proficiency in French. Application deadline: 4/1. Application fee: $30. *Financial aid:* Fellowships, research assistantships, teaching assistantships available. • Application contact: Jean-Marc Alain, Registrar, 418-657-2485 Ext. 2267. Fax: 418-657-2620.

The University of Akron, College of Business Administration, Department of Marketing, Akron, OH 44325-0001. Offerings include international business (MBA). *Entrance requirements:* GMAT (minimum score 450), minimum GPA of 2.75. Application deadline: 8/15 (rolling processing). Application fee: $25 ($50 for international students). *Expenses:* Tuition $178 per credit hour for state residents; $333 per credit hour for nonresidents. Fees $145 per year full-time, $32 per semester (minimum) part-time. • Dr. Dale M. Lewison, Chair, 330-972-6306. E-mail: dlewison@uakron.edu. Application contact: Dr. J. Daniel Williams, Director of Graduate Business Programs, 330-972-7043. E-mail: jwilliams@uakron.edu.

The University of Akron, College of Business Administration, Program in International Business, Akron, OH 44325-0001. Awards MBA, JD/MBA. Part-time and evening/weekend programs available. Students: 28 full-time (10 women), 11 part-time (4 women); includes 3 minority (2 African Americans, 1 Asian American), 23 international. Average age 28. In 1997, 5 degrees awarded. *Entrance requirements:* GMAT (minimum score 450), minimum GPA of 2.75. Application deadline: 8/15 (rolling processing). Application fee: $25 ($50 for international students). *Expenses:* Tuition $178 per credit hour for state residents; $333 per credit hour for nonresidents. Fees $145 per year full-time, $32 per semester (minimum) part-time. *Financial aid:* In 1997–98, 3 students received aid, including 1 research assistantship, 1 administrative assistantship; partial tuition waivers also available. Financial aid application deadline: 4/30. • Application contact: Dr. J. Daniel Williams, Director of Graduate Business Programs, 330-972-7043. E-mail: jwilliams@uakron.edu.

University of Alberta, Faculty of Graduate Studies and Research, Program in Business Administration, Edmonton, AB T6G 2E1, Canada. Offerings include international business (MBA). *Degree requirements:* Thesis or alternative required, foreign language not required. *Entrance requirements:* GMAT, TOEFL. Application deadline: 5/31 (priority date; rolling processing). Application fee: $60. *Expenses:* Tuition $390 per course for Canadian residents; $781 per course for nonresidents. Fees $500 per year full-time, $184 per year part-time. • Dr. Kay Devine, Associate Dean, 403-492-3946. E-mail: kay.devine@ualberta.ca. Application contact: Darren Bondar, Assistant Director, 403-492-3946. Fax: 403-492-7825. E-mail: darren.bondar@ualberta.ca.

University of Chicago, Graduate School of Business, Chicago, IL 60637-1513. Offerings include international business administration (IEMBA, IMBA). IEMBA offered through the University of Chicago at Barcelona, Spain. School faculty: 114 full-time (17 women), 48 part-time (6 women). *Average time to degree:* master's–2 years full-time, 5 years part-time; doctorate–5.5 years full-time. *Application deadline:* 3/17 (priority date; rolling processing). *Application fee:* $125. • Robert S. Hamada, Dean, 773-702-7121. Application contact: Donald Martin, Director of Admissions and Financial Aid, 773-702-7369. Fax: 773-702-9085.

University of Cincinnati, College of Business Administration, Department of Management, Program in International Business, Cincinnati, OH 45221. Awards MBA. Part-time and evening/weekend programs available. Students: 5 full-time (2 women), 12 part-time (3 women); includes 2 minority (both Asian Americans), 1 international. 14 applicants, 57% accepted. In 1997, 3 degrees awarded. *Average time to degree:* master's–1.9 years full-time. *Entrance requirements:* GMAT. Application deadline: 5/30. Application fee: $30. *Tuition:* $7228 per year full-time, $185 per credit hour part-time for state residents; $13,812 per year full-time, $352 per credit hour part-time for nonresidents. *Financial aid:* Fellowships, graduate assistantships, full tuition waivers available. Aid available to part-time students. Financial aid application deadline: 2/15. • Dr. Sidney L. Barton, Head, Department of Management, 513-556-7126. Fax: 513-556-4891.

University of Colorado at Denver, Graduate School of Business Administration, Program in International Business, Denver, CO 80217-3364. Awards MS, MBA/MS. Part-time and evening/weekend programs available. Faculty: 2 full-time. Students: 44. In 1997, 6 degrees awarded. *Degree requirements:* 1 foreign language. *Entrance requirements:* GMAT (minimum score 400; average 570), TOEFL (minimum score 525; average 560). Application deadline: 7/1 (priority date; rolling processing; 11/1 for spring admission). Application fee: $50 ($60 for international students). *Expenses:* Tuition $3754 per year full-time, $225 per semester hour part-time for state residents; $12,962 per year full-time, $777 per semester hour part-time for nonresidents. Fees $252 per year. *Financial aid:* Application deadline 4/1. • Manuel Serapio, Director, 303-556-5832. Fax: 303-556-5899. Application contact: Lori Cain, Graduate Business Admissions Office, 303-556-5900. Fax: 303-556-5904. E-mail: lori_cain@maroon.cudenver.edu.

University of Connecticut, College of Liberal Arts and Sciences and School of Business Administration, Field of International Studies and Business Administration, Storrs, CT 06269. Awards MA/MBA. Faculty: 8. Students: 8 full-time (3 women); includes 2 minority (both Hispanics), 1 international. Average age 27. 5 applicants, 100% accepted. *Application deadline:* 4/15 (priority date; rolling processing; 11/1 for spring admission). *Application fee:* $40 ($45 for international students). *Expenses:* Tuition $5272 per year full-time, $293 per credit part-time for state residents; $13,696 per year full-time, $761 per credit part-time for nonresidents. Fees $948 per year full-time, $640 per year part-time. *Financial aid:* In 1997–98, 3 research assistantships (1 to a first-year student) totaling $21,967, 1 teaching assistantship totaling

Directory: International Business

University of Connecticut (continued)

$6,413 were awarded. Financial aid application deadline: 2/15. • Boris E. Bravo-Ureta, Chairperson, 860-486-2740.

University of Dallas, Graduate School of Management, Program in International Management, Irving, TX 75062-4799. Awards MBA, MM. Part-time programs available. Students: 119 (52 women). In 1997, 65 degrees awarded. *Average time to degree:* master's–1.3 years full-time, 2.5 years part-time. *Entrance requirements:* GMAT (minimum score 400), TOEFL (average 520), minimum GPA of 3.0. Application deadline: 8/6 (priority date; rolling processing; 12/8 for spring admission). Application fee: $25 ($50 for international students). *Expenses:* Tuition $380 per credit hour. Fees $125 per year. *Financial aid:* Application deadline 2/15. • Richard Peregoy, Director, 972-721-5326. Fax: 972-721-5130. Application contact: Roxanne Del Rio, Director of Admissions, 972-721-5174. Fax: 972-721-4009. E-mail: admiss@gsm.udallas.edu.

The University of Findlay, College of Professional Studies, MBA Program, 1000 North Main Street, Findlay, OH 45840-3653. Offerings include international management (MBA). Postbaccalaureate distance learning degree programs offered (minimal on-campus study). Program faculty: 9 full-time (0 women), 6 part-time (0 women), 11 FTE. *Degree requirements:* Cumulative project. *Average time to degree:* master's–1.5 years full-time, 2.5 years part-time. *Entrance requirements:* GMAT, TOEFL. Application deadline: 8/15 (rolling processing; 12/15 for spring admission). Application fee: $25. *Tuition:* $299 per semester hour. • Dr. Theodore C. Alex, Director, 419-424-4704. Fax: 419-424-4822.

University of Hartford, Barney School of Business and Public Administration, Program in Business Administration, West Hartford, CT 06117-1599. Offerings include international business (MBA). Program faculty: 24 full-time (4 women), 15 part-time (1 woman). *Average time to degree:* master's–1.5 years full-time, 3 years part-time. *Entrance requirements:* GMAT, TOEFL. Application deadline: 7/1 (priority date; rolling processing; 12/1 for spring admission). Application fee: $35 ($50 for international students). Electronic applications accepted. • Christopher Galligan, Director, 860-768-4390. Application contact: Claire Silverstein, Assistant Director, 860-768-4900. Fax: 860-768-4821. E-mail: silverste@unavax.hartford.edu.

University of Hawaii at Manoa, College of Business Administration, Program in International Management, Honolulu, HI 96822. Awards PhD. Program new for fall 1998. *Degree requirements:* 1 foreign language, dissertation. *Entrance requirements:* GMAT or GRE, minimum GPA of 3.0. Application fee: $25 ($50 for international students). *Tuition:* $4029 per year full-time, $214 per credit hour part-time for state residents; $9957 per year full-time, $461 per credit hour part-time for nonresidents. • Dr. Richard W. Brislin, Director.

University of Houston, College of Business Administration, Program in International Business, 4800 Calhoun, Houston, TX 77204-2163. Awards MBA. Students: 39 full-time (21 women), 56 part-time (20 women); includes 20 minority (12 Asian Americans, 8 Hispanics), 24 international. Average age 31. In 1997, 7 degrees awarded. *Degree requirements:* Computer language required, foreign language and thesis not required. *Entrance requirements:* GMAT (average 590), TOEFL (minimum score 620). Application deadline: 5/1 (rolling processing; 10/1 for spring admission). Application fee: $50 ($125 for international students). *Expenses:* Tuition $1152 per year full-time, $120 per semester (minimum) part-time for state residents; $4482 per year full-time, $249 per credit hour part-time for nonresidents. Fees $977 per year full-time, $119 per semester (minimum) part-time. *Financial aid:* Research assistantships, teaching assistantships, Federal Work-Study, and career-related internships or fieldwork available. Aid available to part-time students. Financial aid application deadline: 3/1; applicants required to submit FAFSA. • Application contact: Office of Student Services, 713-743-4900. Fax: 713-743-4942. E-mail: oss@cba.uh.edu.

University of Kentucky, Patterson School of Diplomacy and International Commerce, Lexington, KY 40506. Awards MA. Faculty: 3 full-time (0 women). Students: 39 full-time (18 women), 8 part-time (2 women); includes 4 minority (2 African Americans, 1 Asian American, 1 Hispanic), 8 international. 67 applicants, 42% accepted. In 1997, 20 degrees awarded. *Degree requirements:* 1 foreign language, comprehensive exam required, thesis optional. *Entrance requirements:* GRE General Test, minimum undergraduate GPA of 3.0. Application deadline: 2/1. Application fee: $30 ($35 for international students). *Financial aid:* In 1997–98, 11 fellowships were awarded; research assistantships, graduate assistantships, Federal Work-Study, institutionally sponsored loans also available. *Faculty research:* International relations, foreign and defense policy, cross-cultural negotiation, international science and technology, diplomacy. Total annual research expenditures: $26,000. • Dr. John D. Stempel, Director of Graduate Studies, 606-257-4666. Fax: 606-257-4676. E-mail: psdstem@ukcc.uky.edu. Application contact: Dr. Constance L. Wood, Associate Dean, 606-257-4613. Fax: 606-323-1928.

University of Maryland University College, Graduate School of Management and Technology, Program in International Management, College Park, MD 20742-1600. Awards Exec MIM, MIM. Offered evenings and weekends only. Part-time and evening/weekend programs available. Students: 26 full-time (15 women), 254 part-time (109 women); includes 101 minority (66 African Americans, 21 Asian Americans, 14 Hispanics), 42 international. 81 applicants, 95% accepted. In 1997, 81 degrees awarded. *Degree requirements:* Thesis or alternative. *Application deadline:* rolling. *Application fee:* $50. Electronic applications accepted. *Tuition:* $277 per semester hour for state residents; $367 per semester hour for nonresidents. *Financial aid:* Grants, scholarships, Federal Work-Study available. Aid available to part-time students. Financial aid application deadline: 5/1; applicants required to submit FAFSA. • Clarence Mann, Director, 301-985-7200. Fax: 301-985-4611. E-mail: clarence_mann%hpdesk@umuc.umd.edu. Application contact: Director of Graduate Admissions, 301-985-7155. Fax: 301-985-7175. E-mail: gradschool@europa.umuc.edu.

The University of Memphis, Fogelman College of Business and Economics, Program in Business Administration, International Master of Business Administration Program, Memphis, TN 38152. Awards MBA. *Entrance requirements:* GMAT (minimum score 430; average 535), GRE General Test. *Tuition:* $2862 per year full-time, $166 per credit hour part-time for state residents; $6696 per year full-time, $379 per credit hour part-time for nonresidents. • Application contact: Coordinator, 901-678-2038. Fax: 901-678-3678.

See in-depth description on page 557.

University of Miami, School of Business Administration, Program in International Business, Coral Gables, FL 33124. Awards MBA, MIBS. *Entrance requirements:* GMAT (minimum score 500), TOEFL (minimum score 550). Application deadline: 6/30 (priority date; rolling processing; 10/31 for spring admission). Application fee: $35. *Expenses:* Tuition $815 per credit hour. Fees $174 per year. *Financial aid:* Application deadline 3/1. • Dr. Harold W. Berkman, Vice Dean, School of Business Administration, 305-284-2510. Fax: 305-284-5905. Application contact: Dierdre Lacativa, Director of Admissions, 305-284-4607. Fax: 305-284-1878.

University of New Brunswick, Faculty of Business, Saint John, NB E2L 4L5, Canada. Offerings include international business (MBA). Faculty: 19 full-time (4 women). *Degree requirements:* Thesis optional. *Entrance requirements:* GMAT. Application deadline: 3/15. Application fee: $100. *Expenses:* Tuition $18,000 per year. Fees $50 per year full-time, $15 per year part-time. • Dr. John Chalykoff, Dean, 506-648-5571. Application contact: Dr. Robert Chanteloup, Associate Dean of Graduate Studies, 506-648-5673. Fax: 506-648-5528. E-mail: graduate@unbsj.ca.

University of New Haven, School of Business, Program in Business Administration, West Haven, CT 06516-1916. Offerings include international business logistics (MBA). *Degree requirements:* Thesis or alternative required, foreign language not required. *Application deadline:* rolling. *Application fee:* $50. *Expenses:* Tuition $1125 per course. Fees $13 per trimester. • Dr. Omid Nodoushani, Coordinator, 203-932-7123.

University of New Mexico, Robert O. Anderson Graduate School of Management, Albuquerque, NM 87131-1221. Offerings include international management (MBA), international management in Latin America (MBA). School faculty: 50 full-time (11 women). *Application deadline:* 7/1 (priority date; rolling processing; 11/15 for spring admission). *Application fee:* $25. *Expenses:* Tuition $2442 per year full-time, $103 per credit hour part-time for state residents; $8691 per year full-time, $103 per credit hour (minimum) part-time for nonresidents. Fees $32 per year. • Howard L. Smith, Dean, 505-277-6471. Fax: 505-277-7108. Application contact: Sue Podeyn, MBA Program Director, 505-277-3147. Fax: 505-277-9356. E-mail: podeyn@unm.edu.

University of North Carolina at Greensboro, Joseph M. Bryan School of Business and Economics, Program in Business Administration, Greensboro, NC 27412-0001. Offerings include international business administration (Certificate). *Application deadline:* 7/1 (priority date; rolling processing; 11/1 for spring admission). *Application fee:* $35. *Expenses:* Tuition $1842 per year full-time, $370 per semester (minimum) part-time for state residents; $10,296 per year full-time, $2484 per semester (minimum) part-time for nonresidents. Fees $806 per year full-time, $111 per semester (minimum) part-time. • Dr. Richard Ehrhardt, Director, 336-334-5390.

University of Ottawa, Faculty of Administration, Program in International Management, Ottawa, ON K1N 6N5, Canada. Awards IMBA. Faculty: 14 full-time. Students: 41 full-time (21 women); includes 9 international. Average age 28. In 1997, 24 degrees awarded. *Entrance requirements:* Bachelor's degree or equivalent, minimum B average. Application deadline: 4/15. Application fee: $60. *Expenses:* Tuition $4677 per year for Canadian residents; $9900 per year for nonresidents. Fees $230 per year. *Financial aid:* Full tuition waivers, Federal Work-Study, and career-related internships or fieldwork available. • Georges Hénault, Director, 613-562-5800 Ext. 4700. Application contact: Sylvie Séguin-Jak, Administrator, 613-562-5821. Fax: 613-562-5167.

University of Pennsylvania, School of Arts and Sciences and Wharton School, Joseph H. Lauder Institute of Management and International Studies, Philadelphia, PA 19104. Awards MA, MBA, MBA/MA. Program in international studies (MA). Applications made concurrently and separately to Lauder Institute and Wharton MBA program. Students: 115 full-time (35 women); includes 13 minority (2 African Americans, 4 Asian Americans, 7 Hispanics), 33 international. Average age 26. 300 applicants, 23% accepted. In 1997, 55 degrees awarded. *Degree requirements:* 1 foreign language, thesis. *Average time to degree:* master's–2 years full-time. *Entrance requirements:* GMAT, TOEFL, advanced proficiency in a non-native language. Application deadline: 2/6 (rolling processing). Application fee: $50. *Tuition:* $12,000 per year. *Financial aid:* Fellowships and career-related internships or fieldwork available. Financial aid application deadline: 2/6. *Faculty research:* Finance, marketing, strategy, operations management, multinational management. • Dr. Stephen Kobrin, Director, 215-898-1215. Application contact: Natacha Davis Keramidas, Assistant Director for Admissions, 215-898-1215. Fax: 215-898-2067. E-mail: lauderinfo@wharton.upenn.edu.

University of Phoenix, Graduate Programs, Business Administration and Management Programs, Program in Global Management, 4615 East Elwood St, PO Box 52069, Phoenix, AZ 85072-2069. Awards MBA. Programs offered online and at the Center for Distance Education. Postbaccalaureate distance learning degree programs offered (no on-campus study). Students: 619 full-time (326 women); includes 190 minority (95 African Americans, 41 Asian Americans, 45 Hispanics, 9 Native Americans). *Degree requirements:* Thesis or alternative required, foreign language not required. *Entrance requirements:* TOEFL (minimum score 520), minimum undergraduate GPA of 2.5, 3 years of work experience, comprehensive cognitive assessment (COCA). Application deadline: rolling. Application fee: $50. *Tuition:* $248 per credit hour. • Application contact: Campus Information Center, 602-966-9577.

University of Pittsburgh, Joseph M. Katz Graduate School of Business, Program in International Business, Pittsburgh, PA 15260. Awards MBA/MIB. Part-time programs available. Students: 9 full-time (5 women). 34 applicants, 50% accepted. *Average time to degree:* master's–2 years full-time, 5 years part-time. *Application deadline:* 5/1 (priority date; rolling processing). *Application fee:* $50. *Expenses:* Tuition $463 per credit for state residents; $867 per credit for nonresidents. Fees $480 per year full-time, $180 per year part-time. *Financial aid:* In 1997–98, 3 students received aid, including 3 fellowships (all to first-year students) totaling $27,000; partial tuition waivers, Federal Work-Study, institutionally sponsored loans, and career-related internships or fieldwork also available. Financial aid application deadline: 3/15; applicants required to submit FAFSA. *Faculty research:* Foreign exchange risk management and trade flow pattern emergence post-NAFTA, equity market performance in emerging markets and international variation in compensation/incentive plans, comparative corporate guidance and financial disclosure practices in emerging markets. Total annual research expenditures: $2.1 million. • Application contact: Amy J. Ruffenbach, Coordinator, 412-383-8835. Fax: 412-648-1693. E-mail: aruffen@katz.business.pitt.edu.

University of Rhode Island, College of Business Administration, Kingston, RI 02881. Offerings include international business (MBA). *Application deadline:* 4/15 (priority date; rolling processing). *Application fee:* $35. *Expenses:* Tuition $3446 per year full-time, $191 per credit part-time for state residents; $9850 per year full-time, $547 per credit part-time for nonresidents. Fees $1276 per year full-time, $135 per semester (minimum) part-time.

University of St. Thomas, Graduate School of Business, Program in International Management, St. Paul, MN 55105-1096. Offers international finance (MIM, Certificate), international human resources (MIM, Certificate), international managerial communication (MIM, Certificate), international marketing (MIM, Certificate), self-designed (MIM). Part-time and evening/weekend programs available. Faculty: 1 full-time (0 women), 18 part-time (6 women). Students: 19 full-time (11 women), 244 part-time (128 women); includes 41 minority (10 African Americans, 15 Asian Americans, 13 Hispanics, 3 Native Americans), 33 international. Average age 30. 80 applicants, 94% accepted. In 1997, 90 master's awarded. *Degree requirements:* For master's, 1 foreign language, computer language required, thesis not required. *Entrance requirements:* For master's, GMAT. Application deadline: 7/1 (priority date; rolling processing; 12/1 for spring admission). Application fee: $30. *Tuition:* $416 per credit hour. *Financial aid:* In 1997–98, 27 grants (11 to first-year students) totaling $60,643 were awarded; career-related internships or fieldwork also available. Aid available to part-time students. Financial aid application deadline: 4/1; applicants required to submit FAFSA. • Dr. Mohammed Eftekhari, Director, 612-962-4840. Application contact: Wendy Williams, Student Services Manager, 612-962-4847. Fax: 612-962-4129.

University of San Francisco, McLaren School of Business, Program in Business Administration, San Francisco, CA 94117-1080. Offerings include international business (MBA). Program faculty: 33 full-time (7 women), 27 part-time (3 women). *Entrance requirements:* GMAT (average 540), TOEFL (minimum score 600), minimum undergraduate GPA of 3.2. Application deadline: 7/1 (priority date; rolling processing; 11/30 for spring admission). Application fee: $40 ($50 for international students). *Tuition:* $658 per unit (minimum). • Cathy Fusco, Director, 415-422-6314. Fax: 415-422-2502. E-mail: mbausf@usfca.edu.

University of Scranton, Program in Business Administration, Scranton, PA 18510-4622. Offerings include international business (MBA). Program faculty: 39 full-time (9 women), 1 part-time (0 women). *Entrance requirements:* GMAT, TOEFL (minimum score 500), minimum GPA of 2.75. Application deadline: rolling. Application fee: $35. *Expenses:* Tuition $465 per credit. Fees $25 per semester. • Dr. Wayne H. J. Cunningam, Director, 717-941-4043. Fax: 717-941-4342. E-mail: cunninghamw1@uofs.edu.

University of South Carolina, Graduate School, College of Business Administration, Program in International Business Studies, Columbia, SC 29208. Awards MIBS, JD/MIBS. Faculty: 29 full-time (3 women). Students: 336 full-time (110 women), 14 part-time (2 women); includes 24 minority (2 African Americans, 13 Asian Americans, 9 Hispanics), 77 international. Average age 27. 770 applicants, 44% accepted. In 1997, 195 degrees awarded (100% found work related to degree). *Degree requirements:* 1 foreign language, internship required, thesis not required. *Entrance requirements:* GMAT (minimum score 550; average 612), minimum GPA of 3.0. Application deadline: 2/1 (priority date). Application fee: $35. Electronic applications accepted. *Financial aid:* In 1997–98, 312 students received aid, including 13 fellowships (all to first-year students), 45 research assistantships (all to first-year students); Federal Work-Study, institutionally sponsored loans, and career-related internships or fieldwork also available. Financial aid application deadline: 2/1. *Faculty research:* International competitiveness of U.S. textiles, international compensation, exchange rates, international finance. Total annual research expenditures: $300,000. • Brian Ewing, Managing Director, 803-777-6788. E-mail: ewing@darla.badm.sc.edu. Application contact: Allyson Hearn, Coordinator, 803-777-4344. Fax: 803-777-0414. E-mail: allyson@darla.badm.sc.edu.

See in-depth description on page 559.

University of Southern California, Graduate School, Marshall School of Business, International Business Education and Research (IBEAR) Program, Los Angeles, CA 90089-1421. Offers international business (MBA). Faculty: 19 full-time. Students: 48 full-time (9 women). Average age 33. 161 applicants, 56% accepted. In 1997, 48 degrees awarded. *Degree requirements:* Computer language, foreign language recommended required, thesis not required. *Entrance requirements:* GMAT, TOEFL. Application deadline: 4/1 (rolling processing). Application fee: $125. *Expenses:* Total cost of $42,550 in tuition and fees for complete one-year program. *Financial aid:* In 1997–98, 19 scholarships were awarded. *Faculty research:* Pacific Rim trade, international trade, international finance, international strategy. • Dr. Jack G. Lewis, Director. Application contact: Fujiko Terayama, Director, Admissions, 213-740-7140. Fax: 213-740-7559. E-mail: ibear@usc.edu.

See in-depth description on page 561.

University of Tennessee, Knoxville, College of Business Administration, Program in Business Administration, Knoxville, TN 37996. Offerings include global business (MBA). MS/MBA offered jointly with the College of Engineering. Postbaccalaureate distance learning degree programs offered. Program faculty: 51 full-time (6 women). *Application deadline:* 2/1 (priority date). *Application fee:* $35. Electronic applications accepted. *Tuition:* $3354 per year full-time, $181 per semester hour part-time for state residents; $8410 per year full-time, $462 per semester hour part-time for nonresidents. • Dr. Gary Dicer, Director, 423-974-5033. E-mail: gdicer@utk.edu. Application contact: Donald Potts, Graduate Representative, 423-974-5033. Fax: 423-974-3826. E-mail: dpotts@utk.edu.

The University of Texas at Dallas, School of Management, Program in International Management Studies, Richardson, TX 75083-0688. Awards MA, PhD. Part-time and evening/weekend programs available. Faculty: 15 full-time (5 women), 5 part-time (1 woman). Students: 22 full-time (6 women), 31 part-time (12 women); includes 9 minority (1 African American, 6 Asian Americans, 2 Hispanics), 10 international. Average age 32. 21 applicants, 71% accepted. In 1997, 9 master's awarded. *Degree requirements:* For master's, minimum GPA of 3.0 required, foreign language and thesis not required; for doctorate, dissertation, minimum GPA of 3.0 required, foreign language not required. *Entrance requirements:* GMAT (minimum AACSB index of 1100), TOEFL (minimum score 550). Application deadline: 7/15 (rolling processing; 11/15 for spring admission). Application fee: $25 ($75 for international students). *Financial aid:* Research assistantships, teaching assistantships, Federal Work-Study available. Aid available to part-time students. Financial aid application deadline: 11/1. *Faculty research:* International accounting, international trade and finance, economic development, international economics. • Dr. Stephen Guisinger, Head, 972-883-2033. Fax: 972-883-2799. E-mail: steveg@utdallas.edu.

University of the Incarnate Word, School of Graduate Studies, College of Professional Studies, Programs in Administration, San Antonio, TX 78209-6397. Offerings include international administration (MAA). *Entrance requirements:* GMAT, GRE, MAT, TOEFL (minimum score 550). Application deadline: 8/15 (priority date; rolling processing; 12/31 for spring admission). Application fee: $20. *Expenses:* Tuition $350 per semester hour. Fees $180 per year full-time, $111 per semester (minimum) part-time. • Victor Prosper, Coordinator, 210-829-3185. Fax: 210-829-3169. Application contact: Brian F. Dalton, Dean of Enrollment Services, 210-829-6005. Fax: 210-829-3921. E-mail: briand@the-college.iwctx.edu.

University of Toledo, Graduate School of Business, Department of Marketing, Program in International Business, Toledo, OH 43606-3398. Awards MBA. Evening/weekend programs available. Students: 6 full-time (3 women), 12 part-time (6 women); includes 11 international. Average age 27. 49 applicants, 33% accepted. In 1997, 11 degrees awarded. *Degree requirements:* Computer language required, foreign language and thesis not required. *Entrance requirements:* GMAT, TOEFL (minimum score 550), minimum GPA of 2.7. Application deadline: 8/1 (priority date; rolling processing). Application fee: $30. Electronic applications accepted. *Tuition:* $5907 per year full-time, $246 per hour part-time for state residents; $11,835 per year full-time, $493 per hour part-time for nonresidents. *Financial aid:* Full tuition waivers and career-related internships or fieldwork available. Financial aid application deadline: 4/1. • Dr. Ronald Zallocco, Chair, Department of Marketing, 419-530-2098. Application contact: Dr. Bruce Kuhlman, MBA Director, 419-530-2774. Fax: 419-530-7260. E-mail: mba0001@uoft01.utoledo.edu.

University of Wisconsin–Madison, School of Business, Program in International Business, Madison, WI 53706-1380. Awards MBA, MS. *Entrance requirements:* GMAT. Application deadline: 6/1 (rolling processing; 10/1 for spring admission). Application fee: $38. *Tuition:* $5950 per year full-time, $1118 per semester (minimum) part-time for state residents; $16,230 per year full-time, $3044 per semester (minimum) part-time for nonresidents.

Vanderbilt University, Owen Graduate School of Management, International Executive Business Administration Program, Nashville, TN 37240-1001. Awards MBA. Students: 16 full-time (3 women); includes 3 minority (all Hispanics), 6 international. *Degree requirements:* 1 foreign language required, thesis not required. *Entrance requirements:* GMAT, interview. Application deadline: 2/15 (rolling processing). Application fee: $50. *Tuition:* $52,000 per year. • Lorraine Sciadini, Director, 615-343-4087. Fax: 615-343-2293. E-mail: lori.sciadini@owen.vanderbilt.edu. Application contact: Coordinator, 305-448-5660. Fax: 305-448-5620. E-mail: iemba@worldnet.att.net.

Virginia Commonwealth University, School of Business, Richmond, VA 23284-9005. Offerings include international business (PhD). School faculty: 114 (16 women). *Degree requirements:* Dissertation. *Entrance requirements:* GMAT. Application deadline: rolling. Application fee: $30 ($0 for international students). *Tuition:* $4960 per year full-time, $257 per credit part-time for state residents; $12,652 per year full-time, $684 per credit part-time for nonresidents. • Dr. Howard P. Tuckman, Dean, 804-828-1595. E-mail: hptuckma@busnet.bus.vcu.edu. Application contact: Dr. Edward L. Millner, Associate Dean of Graduate Studies, 804-828-1741. Fax: 804-828-7174. E-mail: gsib@vcu.edu.

Wagner College, Department of Business Administration, Program in International Business, Staten Island, NY 10301. Awards MBA. Part-time and evening/weekend programs available. Faculty: 3 full-time (1 woman), 1 part-time (0 women). Students: 8 full-time (2 women), 5 part-time (3 women); includes 4 minority (all Asian Americans). 3 applicants, 67% accepted. In 1997, 1 degree awarded. *Degree requirements:* Thesis optional, foreign language not required. *Entrance requirements:* Minimum GPA of 2.6. Application deadline: 8/1 (priority date; rolling processing; 12/10 for spring admission). Application fee: $50 ($65 for international students). *Tuition:* $580 per credit. *Financial aid:* In 1997–98, 1 alumni fellowship was awarded; teaching assistantships, partial tuition waivers also available. • Application contact: Admissions Office, 718-390-3411.

Webster University, School of Business and Technology, Department of Business, St. Louis, MO 63119-3194. Offerings include international business (MA, MBA). Department faculty: 5 full-time (1 woman). *Application deadline:* rolling. *Application fee:* $25 ($50 for international students). *Tuition:* $350 per credit hour. • Lucille Berry, Chair, 314-968-7022. Fax: 314-968-7077. E-mail: berrylm@webster.edu. Application contact: Beth Russell, Director of Graduate Admissions, 314-968-7089. Fax: 314-968-7166. E-mail: russellmb@webster.edu.

Western International University, Program in International Business, 9215 North Black Canyon Highway, Phoenix, AZ 85021-2718. Awards MBA. Evening/weekend programs available. *Degree requirements:* Thesis, research project. *Entrance requirements:* GMAT (strongly recommended), minimum GPA of 2.75. Application deadline: rolling. Application fee: $50 ($100 for international students). • Dr. Sabrina Sabet, Chair, 602-943-2311. Application contact: Enrollment Department, 602-943-2311. Fax: 602-371-8637.

Western New England College, School of Business, Program in International Business, Springfield, MA 01119-2654. Awards MBA. *Application deadline:* rolling. *Application fee:* $30. *Expenses:* Tuition $353 per credit hour. Fees $44 per semester (minimum). *Financial aid:* Application deadline 4/1. • Application contact: Rod Pease, Director of Student Administrative Services, 413-796-2080.

Whitworth College, Department of International Management, Spokane, WA 99251-2704. Awards MIM. Part-time and evening/weekend programs available. Faculty: 4 full-time (1 woman), 14 part-time (5 women), 4.8 FTE. Students: 46 full-time (18 women); includes 16 minority (1 African American, 13 Asian Americans, 2 Hispanics), 3 international. Average age 32. 40 applicants, 75% accepted. In 1997, 24 degrees awarded (4% entered university research/teaching, 92% found other work related to degree, 4% continued full-time study). *Degree requirements:* 1 foreign language, practicum required, thesis not required. *Average time to degree:* master's–1.2 years full-time, 2 years part-time. *Entrance requirements:* GMAT or GRE, TOEFL (minimum score 550), TWE (minimum score 4), minimum GPA of 3.0. Application deadline: 3/1 (11/1 for spring admission). Application fee: $35. *Financial aid:* 11 students received aid; grants, merit scholarships and career-related internships or fieldwork available. Financial aid application deadline: 4/1. *Faculty research:* International business finance, risk management, strategic planning, cross-cultural management. Total annual research expenditures: $25,000. • Dr. Dan Sanford, Director, 509-777-3742. E-mail: dsanford@whitworth.edu. Application contact: Michelle-Lynn Morimoto, Assistant Director, 509-777-3742. Fax: 509-777-3723. E-mail: mmorimoto@whitworth.edu.

Wilkes University, Programs in Business Administration, Wilkes-Barre, PA 18766-0002. Offerings include international business (MBA). MBA (management, management information systems) being phased out; applicants no longer accepted. Faculty: 11 full-time, 2 part-time. *Entrance requirements:* GMAT. Application deadline: rolling. Application fee: $30. *Expenses:* Tuition $12,552 per year full-time, $523 per credit hour part-time. Fees $240 per year full-time, $10 per credit hour part-time. • Dr. Robert Seeley, Director, 717-408-4717.

Wright State University, College of Business and Administration, Department of Management, Dayton, OH 45435. Offerings include international business (MBA). *Entrance requirements:* GMAT, TOEFL (minimum score 550), minimum AACSB index of 1000. Application fee: $25. *Tuition:* $5109 per year full-time, $161 per credit hour part-time for state residents; $9039 per year full-time, $282 per credit hour part-time for nonresidents. • Dr. Crystal Owen, Chair, 937-775-2290. Application contact: James Crawford, Director of Graduate Programs, 937-775-2437. Fax: 937-775-3301.

Cross-Discipline Announcement

George Mason University, Institute of Public Policy, Program in International Commerce and Policy, Fairfax, VA 22030-4444.

The Master of Arts in International Commerce and Policy (MAICP) degree is an innovative, 42-credit professional graduate program providing practical skills to compete in the global marketplace. The program focuses on trade, economics, and cultural components to understand the context of international commerce rather than simply the tools of business.

BALDWIN–WALLACE COLLEGE

Division of Business Administration
M.B.A. in International Management Program

Program of Study

The M.B.A. in international management is offered through both full-time and part-time programs. It is designed to meet the needs of individuals who seek significant career advancement or the education necessary to become managers in a global setting. Full-time students can complete the program in as few as 16 months. Students who are currently employed in international management positions can complete the program part-time in two years. The part-time evening program is designed to meet the needs of individuals who work in such areas as accounting, data processing, engineering, marketing, and management.

The program has a sequential format requiring class attendance 3 hours per evening, two or three evenings per week. Students are required to take seminars on a variety of current business topics, along with twelve core courses to complete the degree.

Research Facilities

Academic computer resources available to Baldwin-Wallace students consist of several computers, supporting up to 100 concurrent users with Internet capability. Workstations are available in several attractive labs, and modems allow students remote access from their offices and homes. A large and expanding library of sophisticated, user-friendly programs is maintained for student and faculty use. Workstation areas are open evenings and weekends.

The modern library houses nearly 200,000 volumes and a wide selection of periodicals. There are facilities for viewing microfilms and listening to records as well as exhibit areas, lounges, a conference room, and computer facilities.

Financial Aid

No financial aid is currently available. However, graduate students are eligible for Federal Stafford Student Loans through local banks.

Cost of Study

Tuition for 1998–99 is $1512 for each foundation and core course and $504 for each seminar course. The cost of books is approximately $85 per course. All students are entitled to admittance to Baldwin-Wallace College home athletic and cultural events and access to recreation, health, and library facilities without the payment of additional fees.

Living and Housing Costs

Off-campus housing is available in the immediate area. The Office of Residential Life maintains a list of off-campus rooms, apartments, and houses that may be rented by students. Apartment rents start at $400 per month. An on-campus board plan is offered at $798 per semester. On-campus housing is available to graduate students.

Student Group

Of the 100 students currently enrolled in the program, approximately 25 percent are women and 45 percent are international students representing twenty-five countries on five continents. Approximately 50 percent of currently enrolled students are full-time. These students are encouraged to work with the part-time students, most of whom are employed full-time by Cleveland area businesses.

Location

The Baldwin-Wallace College campus is located in a picturesque residential suburb of Cleveland, Ohio. It is easily accessible from Cleveland Hopkins International Airport, which is 2 miles away, and interstate highways I-71, I-80, and I-480. Cleveland is the headquarters city of eighty-three major corporations with annual sales exceeding $100 million—a concentration of corporate headquarters larger than that of Los Angeles, Boston, or Atlanta. Cleveland is also the country's twelfth-largest consumer market, eighth-largest industrial market, and twelfth-largest retail market.

The College and The Division

Baldwin-Wallace is a liberal arts college, founded in 1845 in Berea, Ohio, a southwestern suburb of Cleveland. Today the College serves approximately 4,800 students: 1,450 part-time day and evening students, 2,300 full-time undergraduate students, and 650 graduate students in business administration and education. The scenic 56-acre campus includes more than forty buildings. The Division of Business Administration with more than 60 faculty members, its undergraduate program, and three M.B.A. programs, including the M.B.A. in International Management, is located in Jacob O. Kamm Hall.

The College maintains twenty-seven academic areas within seven divisions: Humanities, Business Administration, Health and Physical Education, Education, Music, Science and Mathematics, and Social Science. Baldwin-Wallace is affiliated with the United Methodist Church.

Applying

The requirements for admission to the M.B.A. in International Management Program include a bachelor's degree in any field from an accredited institution, the Graduate Management Admission Test (GMAT) score, two letters of recommendation, a resume, and a sufficient background in accounting, finance, quantitative analysis, and economics. Foundation courses make it possible for students with little or no undergraduate business education to successfully participate in the program. These courses are 3 credit hours, but they do not count toward the degree requirements. Other factors involved in the admission decision include the candidate's professional attainment and potential for growth and his or her cumulative grade point average in undergraduate studies.

To satisfy the requirements for admission, international students must also prove their English proficiency by obtaining a score of at least 523 on the Test of English as a Foreign Language (TOEFL) or by obtaining a GMAT score of 500 or better and a writing score of at least 4.5. International students who have either not taken the TOEFL or had insufficient English training to obtain the required TOEFL score may be eligible for a conditional letter of admission. Special programs, offered in cooperation with the American Language Academy (ALA), located on the Baldwin-Wallace College campus, are available for such students. These programs are designed to improve language proficiency and TOEFL results.

Correspondence and Information

Dr. Thomas A. Riemenschneider, Director
Graduate Business Programs
Baldwin-Wallace College
Berea, Ohio 44017-2088
Telephone: 440-826-2196
Fax: 440-826-3868
E-mail: pshepard@bw.edu

Baldwin-Wallace College

THE FACULTY AND THEIR RESEARCH

Gerald H. Anderson, Professor of Economics; Ph.D., Indiana. International economics.
Eugene R. Beem, Professor of Managerial Ethics; Ph.D., Pennsylvania. Corporate and management ethics.
Harry J. Bury, Professor of Management; Ph.D., Case Western Reserve. Organizational behavior.
Yu Da, Assistant Professor of Management; Ph.D., Connecticut. International management.
Pierre A. David, Assistant Professor of Marketing; Ph.D., Kent State. International marketing.
Susan Deville, Associate Professor of Business Administration; Ph.D., Case Western Reserve. International economics.
Robert R. Ebert, Buckhorn Professor of Economics; Ph.D., Case Western Reserve. International economics.
Ronald L. Ehresman, Professor of Finance; M.S., Case Tech. Finance.
Douglas Fryatt, Lecturer; M.B.A., Northland Open. International marketing.
Sylwia Gornik, Lecturer; Ph.D., Cleveland State. Information systems.
Stephen Hollender, Assistant Professor of German; Ph.D., Iowa. German.
Tony Khuri, Lecturer; Ph.D., Case Western Reserve. International management.
David Krueger, Spahr Professor of Managerial Ethics; Ph.D., Chicago. Corporate and management ethics.
Judy Krutky, Associate Professor of Political Science; Ph.D., Columbia. Political science.
James McInerney, Assistant Professor of Finance; M.B.A., Case Western Reserve. International finance.
Dennis Miller, Assistant Professor of Economics; Ph.D., Colorado. Macroeconomics.
Earl M. Peck, Professor of Finance; Ph.D., Colorado. International finance.
Lee Pickler, Associate Professor of Marketing; D.B.A., Nova. Marketing.
Peter Rea, Professor of Marketing and Chairman of the Division of Business Administration; Ph.D., Akron. Marketing.
Timothy Riggle, Professor of Mathematics and Computer Science; Ph.D., Ohio State. MIS.
Malcolm Watson, Assistant Professor and Director of the American Language Academy; M.A., Emory. Intercultural communications.
Ivan Winfield, Associate Professor; B.B.A., Pittsburgh. Management.

IMBA classes are taught in Jacob O. Kamm Hall.

The Cleveland city skyline can be seen from the Baldwin-Wallace College campus.

Baldwin-Wallace College includes forty-six buildings on 56 tree-shaded acres.

BOSTON UNIVERSITY

International Graduate Centers Graduate Programs in Management and Administrative Studies

Programs of Study

Since 1972, Boston University has offered graduate degree programs to the international community in Europe. The Master of Science in Management (M.S.M.), offered by Boston University's Metropolitan College, is a twelve-course program with an emphasis on international management. It is offered in Beer Sheva and Tel Aviv, Israel; Brussels, Belgium; and London, England. The Master of Science in Administration (M.S. Admin.) is available in Brussels and London. The option of transferring between locations (or to the Boston campus) is also available. The language of instruction at all locations is English. Students desiring an opportunity to earn an American graduate degree abroad will find this to be an outstanding experience.

These programs emphasize the American educational approach in an international setting. Courses are offered evenings and weekends. Both full- and part-time study are available. Completion of the program can take from one to two years, depending on the number of courses taken each semester.

Boston University faculty members possess high academic credentials and diverse international experience. Their American and international educational backgrounds and their wealth of practical experience provide a source for enriching class discussions of international issues. They use their skills in seminar discussions and other participation-oriented teaching methods to promote the understanding of concepts relevant to the international environment.

Research Facilities

Each graduate center has developed its own core library and also has cooperative relations with local institutions. For example, students in Brussels have access to the libraries of the Free University of Brussels. In Israel, where the M.S.M. program is offered, students have access to the libraries of Ben-Gurion University of the Negev.

Financial Aid

Internships may serve as a source of financial assistance as well as an opportunity for work experience. In Israel, many students receive funding from the joint scholarship program supported by Boston University and the World Zionist Organization. In addition, U.S. citizens and permanent residents of the United States may apply for certain loans through Boston University's Office of Financial Aid.

Cost of Study

Tuition and fees for each program vary according to the location and are quoted in local currency at all sites, except Israel. Israel program costs are quoted in U.S. dollars.

Living and Housing Costs

Costs vary greatly according to the particular country and the exchange rate, as well as the lifestyle individual students are anticipating in the international community.

Student Group

Students come from around the world to participate in these programs. The diversity of nationalities, educational backgrounds, and work experience of Boston University students enriches the learning experience. Students hold degrees in the sciences, social science, humanities and literature, engineering, economics, and other fields. Work experience ranges from only a few months to the senior level in major multinational corporations. Ages may range from the early twenties through the mid-fifties.

Locations

In Brussels, the program is offered jointly with the Vrije Universiteit Brussels. In Israel, the program is on the campus of Ben-Gurion University of the Negev in Beer Sheva and in the business district of Tel Aviv.

The University

Boston University is a private institution that traces its founding to 1839. It has grown to become the fourth-largest private university in the United States. It has more than 29,000 students and approximately 2,500 faculty members. More than 193,000 alumni have distinguished themselves in all walks of life.

Applying

Students may begin their studies in September, January, or April of each year. Admission is on a rolling basis, and each complete application package is reviewed within a few weeks of receipt. In addition to the application form and fee, the following must be provided: official results of the GMAT or GRE, official transcripts of all previous undergraduate and graduate work, and three letters of reference. TOEFL scores are required of students whose native language is not English. Applications and all supporting materials should be sent directly to the Graduate Center where admission is desired.

Correspondence and Information

Information and applications are available from any of the Overseas Graduate Centers or from the office on the Boston campus.

Boston University
43 Harrington Gardens
London, SW7 4JU, England
Telephone: 441-71-373-6262
Fax: 441-71-373-9430

Boston University
International Graduate Centers
Metropolitan College
755 Commonwealth Avenue
Boston, Massachusetts 02215
Telephone: 617-353-6000
Fax: 617-353-6633

Boston University
Ben-Gurion University of the Negev
P.O. Box 653
Beer Sheva 84105, Israel
Telephone: 972-76-481333
Fax: 972-76-481670

Boston University
Bd. du Triomphe 39
1160 Brussels, Belgium
Telephone: 32-2-640 7474
Fax: 32-2-640 6515

Boston University

THE FACULTY

Cecilia Andersen, Ph.D., Leiden (Netherlands).
John Archer, M.B.A., Harvard.
Jalal Ashayeri, Ph.D., Leuven (Belgium).
Michael Ashkenazi, Ph.D., Yale.
Zachary Barneis, Ph.D., South Carolina.
Ran Bar-Niv, Ph.D., Ohio State.
Luciano P. Battelli, Dr.Eng., Genoa; M.B.A., Harvard.
John Beasley, Ph.D., Imperial College (London).
George J. Beck, J.D., Brooklyn Law; CPA.
Kip Becker, M.B.A., Wilmington (Delaware); Ph.D., Florida State.
Remi Boelaert, Ph.D., Wisconsin.
Richard Boncy, LL.M., Brussels.
Hans Bottenberg, Ph.D., Darmstadt Technical (Germany).
Reba Anne Carruth, Ph.D., Minnesota.
David Chaffetz, Ph.D., Columbia.
Luc Chalmet, Ph.D., Leuven (Belgium).
Harold Chee, M.Sc., London.
Cynthia S. Chegwidden, M.B.A., Pittsburgh.
Robert Christofferson, M.B.A., Barcelona; IESE.
Roland Corluy, Ph.D., Free University (Brussels).
Caroline Daniels, Ph.D., London Business School.
Giovanni De Angelis, Dr.Eng., Naples.
Guy de Muyser, LL.D., Miami.
Walter Dermul, Special License, Ghent (Belgium).
Bruno DeVuyst, LL.M., Columbia.
Angel Diez Rubio, M.B.A., Escuela Superior de Administración y Dirección de Empresas.
Lee E. Duffer, Ph.D., Rochester.
Rik Duyck, Special License, Ghent (Belgium).
Lawrence H. Eaker Jr., LL.M., Miami (Florida).
Yizhar Eylon, Ph.D., Alberta.
Geoff Gibas, M.B.A., Warwick (England).
Georges Gillet, M.B.A., Chicago; CPA.
John Gregory, Ph.D., Washington (Seattle).
Michel Grisar, M.B.A., Lehigh.
Barry Harper, M.A., London School of Economics.
Angela Hatton, P.G.Dip.M., Surrey (England); MCIM.
Joseph J. Heinlein Jr., Ph.D., American.
Katherine B. Ideus, Ed.D., USC.
Francis Jacobs, M.A., Cambridge; M.A., Johns Hopkins.
Judith Jaffe, M.S., Saint Louis; M.B.A., INSEAD.
Ludo Janssens, Ph.D., Leuven (Belgium).
Manoj Juneja, M.Sc., London School of Economics.
Moshe Justman, Ph.D., Harvard.
Shlomo Kalish, Ph.D., MIT.
Meir Karlinsky, Ph.D., Berkeley.
Michel Karma, Dipl.Eng., Ecole Centrale des Arts et Manufactures; M.S., MIT.
Moshe Kaspi, Ph.D., Technion (Israel).
Philippe Kirsch, Civ.Eng., Liège (Belgium).
Anthony F. Kleitz, Ph.D., Tufts.
Paul A. Langley, M.B.A., London Business School.
Charles Olson Lerche III, Ph.D., Ibaden (Nigeria).
Enrique Llorente Gomez, M.B.A., USC.
Aroop Mahanty, Ph.D., Colorado State.
John Mark, M.A., Cambridge; M.Sc., University College (London).
Robert McGeehan, LL.B., Fordham; Ph.D., Columbia.
Sam Mendlinger, Ph.D., Hebrew (Jerusalem).
Karen L. K. Miller, J.D., Harvard.
Zlatibar Milovanovic, Doctorat en Droit, Nancy (France); Ph.D., Temple.
Hossein Mohsenzadeh, M.S., Boston University; M.S., MIT.
Laurens Narraina, Drs., Leiden (Netherlands).
Mia Nysmans, Ph.D., London School of Economics.
Aldo Patania, Dr.Pol.Sc., Catania (Italy).
Robert Peirce, License, Louvain (Belgium).
Joseph Pliskin, Ph.D., Harvard.
Nava Pliskin, Ph.D., Harvard.
Gad Rabinowitz, Ph.D., Case Western Reserve.
Arie Reichel, Ph.D., Massachusetts.
Andrea Ricci, Dr.Eng., Ecole Centrale de Paris.
Ahron Rosenfeld, Ph.D., Rochester.
Deniz Saral, M.B.A., Pittsburgh; Ph.D., Texas at Austin.
Willem Selen, Ph.D., South Carolina.
Stanley W. Shelton, M.P.A., Georgia; M.S., Boston College; CFA.
Shahin Shojai, M.B.A., City University Business School (London).
Peretz Shoval, Ph.D., Pittsburgh.
Victor Shtern, M.B.A., Boston University; Ph.D., Leningrad Aluminium Institute.
Romualdas Skvarcius, Ph.D., Vanderbilt.
Stuart Smith, Ph.D., Yale.
David Spence, Dipl., Nice; Dipl., Paris.
James J. Stewart, D.S., George Washington.
Mitchell P. Strohl, Ph.D., Tufts.
Michael Sutton, Ph.D., London School of Economics.
Michael Talalay, Ph.D., University College (London).
Eli Talmor, Ph.D., North Carolina at Chapel Hill.
Jacques J. Tortoroli, B.S., St. Francis (New York); CPA.
Patrick Uyttendaele, Ph.D., Free University (Brussels).
Paul Van den Noord, Ph.D., Amsterdam.
Eddy Vandijck, Ph.D., Free University (Brussels).
Leon Vanryckeghem, D.Phil, Oxford.
John H. Van Vliet, M.A., Georgetown; M.B.A., Georgia State.
Rona Votava, M.A., American (Beirut); M.A., UCLA.
Shinichi Watanabe, Ph.D., Louvain (Belgium).
Jacob Weber, Ph.D., USC.
Jimmy Weinblatt, Ph.D., Hebrew (Jerusalem).

BRANDEIS UNIVERSITY

Graduate School of International Economics and Finance

Programs of Study

The Graduate School offers innovative master's and Ph.D. programs for students preparing for careers in international finance, economics, or business. The School offers three unique master's programs: the Lemberg M.A. in international economics and finance (MAief), a new international M.B.A. (MBAi) and a part-time M.S. in Finance (M.S.F.) program. Candidates with significant professional experience may qualify for the eleven-month Mid-Career Track in the Lemberg M.A. The Lemberg MAief features concentrations in international finance and international economic policy. The MBAi curriculum combines parts of the Lemberg curriculum with specific course work in international business focusing on global markets. Students may choose to specialize in international finance.

Combining aspects of M.B.A. and international affairs degrees, the master's programs prepare students for careers in the global economy through developing practical and technical skills in international finance, accounting, marketing, and strategy and through systematic analysis of global trade, investment, and technology relationships. Classes are small and stress analytical, presentation, and quantitative skills; the case method is often used. The internationally known faculty is composed of a dynamic teaching and research team that works closely with students in course work as well as on projects outside the classroom. A unique feature of the programs is a semester-abroad exchange program with twenty of the best professional schools in Europe, the Far East, and Latin America. Nearly all master's students spend a semester abroad, and visiting students from international partners help to make the School's atmosphere lively, diverse, and truly international.

The two-year Lemberg M.A. and MBAi degrees require twelve courses at Brandeis, a semester abroad, and reasonable proficiency in a modern foreign language. The eleven-month intensive Mid-Career Track runs from September to August and does not require a semester abroad. MBAi candidates must have a minimum of two to three years professional work experience.

The part-time M.S.F. is a ten-course program for working professionals. The program consists of five required courses and five electives. Electives may include one-week field study courses given on location in major international financial markets.

Research Facilities

Both master's and Ph.D. students frequently participate in faculty research and in seminars and discussions with visiting scholars and practitioners. Officially designated as one of thirteen U.S. APEC Study Centers, the School provides special opportunities for those interested in Asian economics and business. There is also a strong faculty group specializing in Latin American economies.

The School operates its own IBM-compatible computer network and maintains major databases of U.S. and international statistics. The network is connected to several Brandeis mainframe computers and the Internet. Brandeis libraries hold a basic collection in the School's fields; specialized material is available from other local libraries through the Boston Library Consortium.

Financial Aid

Candidates for the M.A. and MBAi programs may apply for tuition scholarships, assistantships, and loans. Aid is based on merit and need and is open to both U.S. and international students. Special scholarships are also available for U.S. students considering careers in international business and finance. Special funds make possible more generous aid to Ph.D. candidates. U.S. applicants for financial aid must file a Free Application for Federal Student Aid (FAFSA) form.

Cost of Study

Tuition for 1998–99 is $23,360 per year for full-time programs, $35,040 for the three-semester Mid-Career Track, and $2100 per course for the part-time M.S.F. program. During their semester abroad, master's students continue to pay tuition to Brandeis and are awarded travel grants toward the cost of airfare.

Living and Housing Costs

The minimum yearly cost of living is estimated at $8500. Limited graduate housing is available on campus; rents for a one-bedroom apartment nearby range from $400 to $700 a month.

Student Group

The School's graduate programs emphasize close student-faculty interaction in teaching and research; admission is limited to approximately 7 Ph.D. students and 55 master's students each year. The student body is talented and diverse; half of the master's candidates are international, and one third are women. Social and extracurricular activities are organized by the Lemberg Student Association and the Lemberg Alumni Association.

Student Outcomes

Virtually all graduates are employed in positions utilizing their economic, financial, and international training. Approximately one third are overseas with both financial and nonfinancial companies. Leading employers include Citibank, Morgan Stanley, and the U.S. Federal Reserve Banks. Graduates from recent classes have also received offers from consulting firms such as the Boston Consulting Group and McKinsey & Co. and from corporations such as AT&T, Microsoft, and Stride-Rite that are searching for international management talent.

Location

Brandeis is located 10 miles west of Boston and Cambridge on a parklike, 250-acre campus. The School is located in a wooded corner of the campus in the Sachar International Center. The urban and educational amenities of Boston and Cambridge are easily reached by public transportation.

The University

Founded in 1948, Brandeis is one of the leading private research universities in the United States, with approximately 2,900 undergraduates and 1,000 graduate students. The University has excellent sports facilities and frequently brings distinguished lecturers, artists, and musical and theatrical performances to the campus.

Applying

Master's program applications are reviewed twice each year, February 15 and April 15. The Ph.D. application deadline is February 15. To maximize chances for admission and financial aid, students are urged to apply by February 15. An interview is recommended but not required. All applications must include official transcripts, test scores, three letters of recommendation, a resume, and a goal statement. The M.A. program will accept either GRE or GMAT testing. The MBAi and M.S.F. require the GMAT. Ph.D. students are required to take the both General Test and the economics Subject Test of the GRE. All international applicants must submit TOEFL scores.

Prior preparation for the master's programs should include at least two undergraduate semester courses in economics and some background in a major modern foreign language. Some prior work experience is recommended for applicants to the MBAi program, and two to three years of experience are required for the M.S.F. program. Applicants to the intensive eleven-month track will need to demonstrate significant international and work experience. Prior preparation for the Ph.D. program should include courses in statistics, intermediate microeconomics and macroeconomics, and some exposure to differential, integral, and multivariate calculus and linear algebra.

Correspondence and Information

Associate Dean for Admissions
Graduate School of International Economics and Finance
Sachar International Center
Brandeis University
Waltham, Massachusetts 02454-9110
Telephone: 781-736-2252
800-878-8866 (toll-free, United States only, for catalog and application)
Fax: 781-736-2263
E-mail: admission@lemberg.brandeis.edu
World Wide Web: http://www.brandeis.edu/ief/

Brandeis University

THE FACULTY AND THEIR TEACHING AND RESEARCH AREAS

Christopher Alt, Adjunct Assistant Professor; Ph.D., MIT. Corporate finance.
John W. Ballantine Jr., Adjunct Professor; Ph.D., NYU. Finance.
Anne P. Carter, Professor; Ph.D., Harvard. Technical progress, technology transfer, input-output.
Atreya Chakroborty, Assistant Professor; Ph.D., Boston College. Finance and mergers and acquisitions.
F. Trenery Dolbear Jr., Professor and Chair; Ph.D., Yale. Macroeconomics, theory, computer simulation.
Ron D'Vari, Adjunct Professor; Ph.D., UCLA. Portfolio management.
Frank Estrada, Adjunct Professor; Ph.D., London Institute. International marketing, trade and business development.
Richard F. Garbaccio, Visiting Assistant Professor; Ph.D., Berkeley. Development, resource, and environmental economics.
Benjamin Gomes-Casseres, Associate Professor; D.B.A., Harvard. International business.
Martin J. Gross, Adjunct Professor; J.D., Chicago. Hedge fund management.
Paul Harrison, Assistant Professor; Ph.D., Duke. Finance, econometrics, economic history.
Jane Hughes, Adjunct Professor; M.B.A., NYU. Domestic and international cash management.
Adam B. Jaffe, Associate Professor; Ph.D., Harvard. Industrial organization, technology, microeconomics.
Gary H. Jefferson, Professor; Ph.D., Yale. Chinese economy, technical progress, open-economy macroeconomics.
Sunghyun Henry Kim, Assistant Professor; Ph.D., Yale. International finance and macroeconomics.
M. Ayhan Kose, Assistant Professor; Ph.D., Iowa. Macroeconomics, international economics, and time series analysis.
Blake LeBaron, Professor; Ph.D., Chicago. Foreign exchange rates, time-seris models, simulated stock markets.
Rachel McCulloch, Professor; Ph.D., Chicago. International trade, trade policy, macroeconomic coordination.
Guive Mirfendereski, Adjunct Professor; Ph.D., Tufts (Fletcher). International corporate and business law.
Elliot R. Morss, Adjunct Professor; Ph.D., Johns Hopkins. International economic development and finance.
Julie Nelson, Associate Professor; Ph.D., Wisconsin. Microeconomics, public policy.
Peter A. Petri, Professor; Ph.D., Harvard. International trade, development, Japanese economy, East Asian NICs.
Michael Plummer, Associate Professor; Ph.D., Michigan State. European and East Asian economics, regional integration and trade.
Dianne S. Poulous, Adjunct Professor; M.B.A., Babson. Managerial accounting.
Charles Reed Jr., Adjunct Professor; M.B.A., Harvard. Entrepreneurship.
Lynne M. H. Rosansky, Adjunct Professor; Ph.D., Boston University. Negotiation, management development, organizational behavior.
Makino D. Ruth, Adjunct Professor; M.A.L.D., Tufts (Fletcher). International business and marketing.
Barney K. Schwalberg, Professor; Ph.D., Harvard. Soviet economy, labor, education.
David P. Simon, Associate Professor; Ph.D., Columbia. Fixed income securities, financial markets and institutions.
Christopher B. Steward, Adjunct Professor; M.A., Cambridge. Bond and corporate management.

BOARD OF OVERSEERS

Charles B. Housen, Chair; Chairman, Erving Industries, Inc.
Kemal Dervis, Vice President, Middle East and North Africa Region, The World Bank.
Donald G. Drapkin '68, Vice Chairman and Director, Revlon Group Incorporated.
Irving Epstein, Ph.D., Provost, Brandeis University.
Eugene M. Freedman, Managing Director, Monitor Clipper Partners.
Paul Fruitt, Vice President of Corporate Planning (retired), The Gillette Corporation.
Barry Kaplan '77, Partner, Goldman, Sachs & Company.
Suk-Won Kim '70, Chairman, Ssangyong Business Group, Korea.
Yotaro Kobayashi, Chairman, Fuji Xerox Co., Ltd., Japan.
John H. McArthur, Dean Emeritus, Harvard Business School.
Charles Miller Smith, Chief Executive, Imperial Chemical Industries, PLC.
Theodor Schmidt-Scheuber, Chairman, North Hampton Partners, LP.
Michael P. Schulhof, Ph.D. '70.
Ira S. Shapiro '69, Partner, Collier, Shannon, Rill & Scott, PLLC.
Malcolm L. Sherman, Chairman of the Board, EKCO Group.
Paula Spencer '91, Alumni Representative, Compliance Officer, State Street Global Advisors.
Irma Mann Stearns, Chairman, Irma S. Mann, Strategic Marketing, Inc.
Shinichiro Torii, President, Suntory Limited, Japan.
Stanley B. Tulin, Executive Vice President & CFO, Equitable Life Assurance Society.
Adam Usdan, General Partner, Trellus Management Company, LLC.
John Usdan, President, Midwood Management Corporation.
Lewis M. Weston, Limited Partner, Goldman, Sachs & Co.

AFFILIATED FOREIGN UNIVERSITIES

Catholic University of Louvain, Belgium.
Copenhagen School of Economics and Business Administration, Denmark.
Erasmus University, The Netherlands.
ESADE International Management Program, Spain.
ESSEC Graduate School of Management, France.
Fundaçao Getulio Vargas, Brazil.
Hong Kong University, Hong Kong.
Instituto Tecnológico Autónomo de México, Mexico.
International University, Japan.
Keio University, Japan.
Koblenz School of Corporate Management, Germany.
Luigi Bocconi University, Italy.
National University of Singapore.
Sophia University, Japan.
Sup de Co Rouen, France.
Tel Aviv University, Israel.
Universiteit Maastricht, The Netherlands.
University of International Business and Economics, Beijing, China.
University of Paris IX (Dauphine), France.
Yonsei University, Korea.

DEPAUL UNIVERSITY

Kellstadt Graduate School of Business
M.B.A. in International Marketing and Finance

Program of Study

DePaul University's M.B.A. in International Marketing and Finance (MBA/IMF) is the only program in the U.S. that integrates intensive cross-cultural training in marketing and financial decision making with a pragmatic international business orientation. The eighteen-month curriculum has been designed in response to the business world's demand for M.B.A. graduates with the ability to understand and manage complex business processes in a global environment. The MBA/IMF prepares students for constant changes in the international marketplace.

Today, international business is shaped by rapid political and economic change, shifting geographic boundaries, emerging economies, new strategic alliances, and an emphasis on global markets. This business evolution requires new skills and innovative approaches. The MBA/IMF curriculum is designed to develop those skills.

International experience is a vital component of the MBA/IMF curriculum. Students from the United States will have a practicum with a multinational corporation abroad or a tailored program at a partner university abroad. Students from other countries will have a practicum with a multinational corporation in Chicago. DePaul University's partnerships with the international business community provide a wide range of opportunities for these experiences. For the past twenty-five years, the college has sponsored a series of International Business Seminars in Europe and the Far East; since 1991, USIA has funded DePaul's management development programs for managers and educators in central Europe.

Central to the curriculum is the International Marketing and Finance Problems and Practice Series, which runs throughout the program. This series emphasizes case study and is designed to educate students in the most current international finance and marketing managerial techniques. Each course is team taught by faculty members from the Departments of Marketing and Finance and brings key international business executives into the classroom as a basis for incorporating real-world international business expertise.

Research Facilities

State-of-the-art resources support the MBA/IMF curriculum. The DePaul Center with its library, extensive computer labs, the Kellstadt Center for Marketing Analysis and Planning, and the Richard H. Driehaus Center for International Business are examples of the latest technological resources available to students and faculty for research.

Financial Aid

Each year, competitive research assistantships are awarded by DePaul's Kellstadt Graduate School of Business. In addition, several loan programs are available. Students may apply for assistantships and loans after admission to the MBA/IMF program.

Cost of Study

The cost of the MBA/IMF program during 1998–99 is $560 per credit hour.

Living and Housing Costs

Off-campus housing is available in the downtown and Lincoln Park areas. Housing in Chicago is considered to be among the most affordable of the country's major cities.

Student Group

The Kellstadt Graduate School of Business enrolls more than 2,500 students. A maximum of 60 students in the MBA/IMF program come from all over the world, about equally divided between the United States and other countries. Students will have undergraduate degrees in a wide range of fields in the liberal arts, technology, and business, and most already have significant work experience.

Location

The resources of Chicago are a major benefit for DePaul students. The city is the nation's third largest and is a financial and cultural center. The Kellstadt Graduate School of Business is right in the heart of the financial district, and cultural attractions and Lake Michigan are within walking distance.

The University

De Paul University is nearing its 100th anniversary. More than 16,500 students are enrolled in 200 undergraduate and graduate programs. About 70,000 alumni provide a powerful network of support for DePaul students. The University's leadership and extraordinary connections with organizations and businesses in Chicago are additional resources of immeasurable value.

Applying

Admission to the MBA/IMF program is competitive and is limited to the fall quarter. Admission decisions will be based on an evaluation of all prior academic work, scores on the GMAT, prior work experience, and an admission interview; for applicants from areas outside Illinois, admission interviews may be accommodated by telephone. All admission documents must be received by May 1.

Correspondence and Information

Dee Dee Wolff, Administrative Director, MBA/IMF
Charles H. Kellstadt Graduate School of Business
DePaul University
1 East Jackson Boulevard
Chicago, Illinois 60604
Telephone: 312-362-8811
Fax: 312-362-8828
E-mail: mbaimf@wppost.depaul.edu
World Wide Web: http://www.depaul.edu/~mbaimf

DePaul University

THE FACULTY AND THEIR TEACHING SPECIALTIES

It is Kellstadt's 114 full-time faculty members who account for the strengths of its programs. All are committed to teaching and scholarship, and many have received national recognition. The business community consistently uses them as a resource because they are at the cutting edge of current business practices. The following faculty members represent the core faculty in the MBA/IMF, each selected for their expertise and international experiences.

Mark Frigo, Ph.D. Management and cost accounting, applied econometrics and forecasting.
Animesh Ghoshal, Ph.D. International and managerial economics, regional trading blocks and policy coordination in the European Community.
Geoffry Hirt, Ph.D. Investments and managerial finance, U.S. and international capital markets.
Joan Junkus, Ph.D. Futures, international and corporate finance, microstructure of non-U.S. futures and options markets.
Michael Miller, Ph.D. Business conditions analysis, money and banking.
Michael Murray, J.D., Ph.D. Business law, public administration, urban problems and policy, organizational behavior.
Belverd Needles Jr., Ph.D. International accounting and auditing, international accounting education.
Norman Nicholson, Ph.D. International financial markets, economic and financial developments in Eastern Europe.
Robert Peters, Ph.D. Financial accounting.
William Poppei, M.B.A. Corporate finance, investments, demographics, human genome project, technology, nanomanufacturing.
Steven Vogt, Ph.D. Corporate finance, commercial banking, macroeconomics and monetary policy, corporate investment behavior.
Joel Whalen, Ph.D. Business communication, advertising and sales, memory and information processing, persuasion psychology.

Ronald J. Patten, Dean of the Kellstadt Graduate School of Business.

The state-of-the-art DePaul Center.

A graduate business seminar.

DOMINICAN COLLEGE OF SAN RAFAEL

Graduate Program in Pacific Basin Studies

Program of Study

The Graduate School in Pacific Basin Studies offers interdisciplinary M.B.A. and M.A. degrees for students preparing for careers in international finance, economics, business, or relations, with a focus on the Asia-Pacific region. Students learn and benefit from the dynamic curriculum and practical training through internship and corporate research programs in the international environment of the San Francisco Bay Area.

The M.B.A. program typically takes two years to complete and includes 55 academic units, an internship, and direct involvement in corporate research projects for companies such as Bank of America, Tandem Computers, and Sun Microsystems. The M.A. program usually takes eighteen months to complete and consists of 42 academic units, an internship, and social science research projects. Both programs require reasonable proficiency in a modern foreign language, preferably one from the Asia-Pacific region.

Upon graduation, students in both programs have firm backgrounds in cross-cultural communication and management, finance, economics, and Asia-Pacific area studies, as well as direct experience functioning in an international business or nonprofit environment. Internships are a required component of the program and are available in the U.S. and various international locations.

Research Facilities

The Alemany Library contains 97,000 volumes and microfilm reels and receives 500 periodicals. The Fletcher Jones Computer Center provides IBM PCs and Macintoshes, Sun Microsystems workstations, Internet access and database searches, workshops, and personalized assistance. Corporate and nonprofit research opportunities are available.

Financial Aid

The department offers a limited number of fellowships each year. Students may apply for loans under the Federal Stafford Student Loan program.

Cost of Study

Graduate tuition for 1998–99 is $12,816 per academic year.

Living and Housing Costs

A limited number of residence hall rooms are available for single graduate students. Housing for single and married students is available in the immediate area at varying costs; total housing and living expenses are estimated to be $6750 for the academic year.

Student Group

The program is limited to 70 students. The student profile is diverse; 38 percent are women. U.S. students comprise 56 percent of the student body, while 44 percent of students are non-U.S. nationals. International students represent countries such as Japan, China, Thailand, Taiwan, Spain, Germany, Australia, Guatemala, Turkey, Morocco, and Brazil. In addition to recent college graduates, the student body includes executives seeking career changes or advancement. Alumni make professional and social contacts through a world-wide network.

Student Outcomes

Alumni have found rewarding positions in international, corporate, and nonprofit sectors. A partial list of organizations who have hired or made offers to alumni includes Andersen Consulting, Bank of America, Charles Schwab, Davy McKee, Ernst & Young, Hewlett Packard, Hitachi Ltd., Johnson & Johnson, Merrill Lynch, Montgomery Securities, Oracle Software, Republic National Bank, U.S. Department of Energy, United Airlines, University of Maryland, Unocal, Volunteers in Technical Assistance, Warner Brothers, and Westdeutsches Landesbank.

Location

Nestled among tree-covered hills overlooking San Francisco Bay, San Rafael and the surrounding area offer an exciting array of cultural and recreational activities. Marin County is the home of an active artistic community and supports theater groups, museums, a symphony orchestra, and an opera company. Students have easy access to the educational, cultural, and social opportunities of cosmopolitan San Francisco, 11 miles to the south.

The College and the Program

Dominican College was chartered in 1890, and in 1986 became the first institution of higher learning in the United States to offer a graduate degree in Pacific Basin Studies. Dominican remains the only liberal arts college to incorporate relevant components—business, economics, culture, politics, and Pacific Basin case studies—within one uniquely integrated curriculum leading to a M.B.A or M.A.

Applying

M.A. and M.B.A. applicants should already have taken macroeconomics, microeconomics, and statistics. In addition, M.B.A. students should already have taken managerial accounting and college algebra. Any deficiencies in this background must be made up before the beginning of the third semester of graduate study.

Priority admission deadlines are March 2 for the fall and December 1 for the spring. Applicants must have a baccalaureate degree or equivalent from an accredited college or university. Qualifications considered by the Admissions Committee include undergraduate academic performance, professional experience, letters of reference, foreign language proficiency, and personal motivation.

Correspondence and Information

Ms. Signe Sugiyama
Director of PBS Admissions
Dominican College of San Rafael
50 Acacia Avenue
San Rafael, California 94901
Telephone: 415-257-1359
Fax: 415-459-3206
E-mail: pbsadm@dominican,edu
World Wide Web: http://www.dominican.edu/Schools/BIS/PBS

Dominican College of San Rafael

THE FACULTY AND THEIR RESEARCH

Francoise O. Lepage, Dean of Business and International Studies and Director of the Graduate Program in Pacific Basin Studies; Ph.D., Catholic University. Economic and political development of Asia-Pacific.
Asayehgn Desta, Professor; Ph.D., Stanford. Environmental degradation and sustainable development.
Arnon Hadar, Professor and Director, Corporate Research Program; Ph.D., NYU. International economics and business.
Frances Feng-Wai Lai, Associate Professor and Executive Director, Institute for Pacific Basin Affairs; Ph.D., Hawaii. Japanese politics and research methodology.
Wesley R. Young, Assistant Professor and Coordinator, Internship Program; Ph.D., Berkeley. International political economy of Northeast Asia.

Adjunct Faculty

Mark Cohen, M.S., Boston University. International corporate finance.
Armand Gilinsky, Ph.D., London. International management and finance.
Lawrence Lien, M.B.A., Golden Gate. Technology transfer and commercialization.
Ann Mannheimer, M.B.A., Harvard. International marketing.
Alister Milroy, M.A., Oxford. International management.
Alfred Siu, D.B.A., Golden Gate. International accounting, marketing and strategy formulation.

Pacific Basin Council Members

The Pacific Basin Council assists in the development and promotion of the graduate program, ensuring the program's quality and relevance while developing job placement and internship opportunities for students.

Andrew Barowsky, President, Lepage Bakeries, Auburn, Maine.
Michael Bianco, Chairman and CEO, Asia Pacific Capital Corporation, San Francisco, California.
Dr. Oleg Bogomolov, Director, Institute for International Economic and Political Studies, USSR Academy of Sciences, Moscow, Russia.
Mark Borthwick, Executive Director, United States Committee for Pacific Economic Cooperation, Washington, D.C.
Phil Brown, former President, Otis Elevator Inc., San Francisco, California.
Dr. Karen N. Brutents, Advisor to the President, International Foundation for Socio-Economic and Political Studies (The Gorbachev Foundation), Moscow, Russia.
Sandra Chin, Asian Art Historian, Tiburon, California.
Olga Dollar, founder and Academic Chair in Pacific Basin Studies, Kentfield, California.
Michael Emmons, Senior Partner, Arthur Andersen and Company, Walnut Creek, California.
Dr. William P. Fuller, President, The Asia Foundation, San Francisco, California.
Cordell Hull, Vice Chairman, Bechtel Enterprises, Inc., San Francisco, California.
Richard Jackson, former President, Wells Fargo Foundation, San Francisco, California.
Dr. Chalmers Johnson, President, Japan Policy Research Institute, Santa Barbara, California.
Lynne Joiner, Public Relations Representative, Port of Oakland, Oakland, California.
Mikio Kato, Associate Managing Director, The International House of Japan, Inc., Tokyo, Japan.
William Kimball, President, Kimball and Co., San Francisco, California.
Ken Miki, CEO, Jackson and Miki, Inc., Osaka, Japan.
Dr. Theodore H. Moran, Landegger Professor and Director, Karl F. Landegger Program in International Business Diplomacy, Georgetown University, Washington, D.C.
Dr. Kong Dan Oh-Hassig, Principal, Oh & Hassig Pacific Rim Consulting, Falls Church, Virginia.
Janet Owen, Vice President and Manager of Investments and Water Utility Business, Bechtel Enterprises, Inc., San Francisco, California.
Humphrey Polanen, General Manager, Internet Commerce Group, Sun Microsystems, Mountain View, California.
Kent Price, General Manager, Banking, Finance, and Securities Industries, IBM Asia Pacific Services Corporation, Singapore.
Mim Ryan, Managing Director, Asia Pacific Region, Landor Associates, San Francisco, California.
Federico Sacasa, Group Executive Vice President and Division Manager, International Trade Banking, Bank of America, San Francisco, California.
Dr. Robert A. Scalapino, Robson Research Professor of Government (Emeritus), Institute of East Asian Studies, University of California at Berkeley.
Jack Schafer, President, Jack Schafer and Associates, San Francisco, California.
Trevor Schultz, Vice President and Chief Operating Officer, Pegasus Gold Corporation, Spokane, Washington.
Francis So, General Manager, Fond Express (SFO), Inc., South San Francisco, California.
Ann Stephens, Trustee, Compton Foundation, Menlo Park, California.
Dr. Ross Terrill, Associate in Research, John King Fairbank Center for East Asian Research, Harvard University, Cambridge, Massachusetts.
Colburn Wilbur, Executive Director, The David and Lucile Packard Foundation, Los Altos, California.

Students on the campus of Dominican College.

Fanjeaux, a residence hall.

The Golden Gate Bridge, with San Francisco in the background.

MONTEREY INSTITUTE OF INTERNATIONAL STUDIES

Master of Arts in Commercial Diplomacy

Programs of Study

The Master of Arts in Commercial Diplomacy (M.A.C.D.), offered by the Institute's Graduate School of International Policy Studies, breaks new ground in providing professional training for commercial diplomacy. The M.A.C.D. program focuses on the management of complex issues and relationships related to international commerce between and among global corporations and governments and on the development of advanced language capability. The program of study brings together and integrates a number of diverse fields of knowledge and skills, including economics, politics, policy analysis, trade law, public advocacy techniques, negotiating strategy and tactics, foreign languages, and other cultures, which are used by professionals in government, nongovernmental organizations, and corporations to develop and negotiate international commercial agreements. The program seeks to give students a hands-on, operational command of the required knowledge and skills through the extensive use of case studies and simulations, many of which use different world languages. The program is partially organized on a modular basis to allow the participation of working professionals who are unable to fit a conventional academic term into their schedules.

Classes are taught by instructors with widely diverse backgrounds and many years of experience working on trade issues in academe, government, and business. In addition to offering the graduate program in commercial diplomacy, the M.A.C.D. staff is actively involved in the development of training materials in commercial diplomacy and offers customized training programs in the field. Staff members also organize and conduct cutting-edge research in new and emerging trade policy issues. These broader activities associated with the related Center for Trade and Commercial Diplomacy (CTCD), combined with the extensive network of government, business, and academic contacts, ensure that instruction in based on timely and relevant information and analyses and that the M.A.C.D. staff has ready access to information about internship and job opportunities.

Reports and studies produced by CTCD and its associates are designed to take account of the practical economic and political contexts in which government policymakers and corporate executives operate. CTCD thus seeks to support business executives and policymakers in framing the issues, in choosing from among competing options, and in developing effective negotiating solutions to complex commercial problems.

The M.A.C.D. staff works with local, national, and international partners to promote the field of commercial diplomacy and to achieve understanding of international trade and investment issues and their impact on economic welfare.

Research Facilities

The Monterey Institute's specialized international library has a collection of 68,000 carefully selected volumes and 550 periodical titles, about one third in languages other than English, and offers CD-ROM workstations. DOS-based and Macintosh microcomputer laboratories are available for course-related computing; they also offer workshops and individualized assistance.

Internships and research opportunities are available through the Institute's centers for Russian and Eurasian studies, for nonproliferation studies, for East Asian studies, and for trade and commercial diplomacy. Internships and advanced language study are also available through the Institute's summer programs in China, France, Germany, Mexico, and Russia.

Financial Aid

The Institute makes every effort to provide need-based, federally funded financial aid to U.S. citizens and eligible noncitizens. Approximately three quarters of the students receive some form of aid, usually a combination of grants, loans, and work opportunities. In addition, the Institute awards competitive merit-based scholarships to both U.S. citizens and international students. Scholarships are awarded to former participants of university-accredited study abroad programs, overseas volunteer programs, high school exchange programs, Concordia Language Villages, the Japanese Exchange and Teaching (JET) program, and the U.S. Peace Corps. Scholarships are also awarded in recognition of the academic achievements of international students, international employment experience, and Phi Beta Kappa membership. Minority scholarships are available to U.S. citizens.

Cost of Study

Fees for 1998–99 are $9100 per semester (two semesters per academic year).

Living and Housing Costs

In 1997–98, the average amount paid for off-campus housing was $450 per month, typically in a room in a nearby private house or a shared apartment. Total housing and living expenses are estimated at $7500 for the nine-month academic year.

Student Group

About half of the Institute's 800 students represent more than fifty countries outside the U.S., and almost all U.S. students have lived, worked, or studied abroad. Students share a multidisciplinary experience in course work and social activities. Monterey alumni form a worldwide network for professional and social contacts.

Location

The Monterey Institute is situated in one of the most spectacular natural environments in the world. The Monterey Peninsula is 130 miles south of San Francisco on California's central coast, surrounded by ocean and mountains; it has a population of 100,000. The area combines a variety of rich cultural resources and recreational activities.

The Institute

Founded in 1955, the Monterey Institute has maintained its character as a tightly knit cosmopolitan community. Its relatively small size creates a sense of intimacy and cohesion between students and faculty members, who encourage lively classroom interaction. The Institute is accredited by the Western Association of Schools and Colleges.

Applying

Applicants to the master's programs in the Graduate School of International Policy Studies must have a U.S. bachelor's degree or the equivalent, with a minimum grade point average of 3.0 on a 4.0 scale. Application may be made at any time, provided it is received at least one month prior to the applicant's proposed semester of enrollment, or three months in advance for international students residing in their home countries. There is no application deadline for most forms of financial aid; however, applications for California grants and fellowships (residents only) or for Monterey Institute scholarships must be submitted by the published February deadline. Nonnative English speakers must submit a minimum TOEFL score of 550 or enhance their language skills at the Institute's Intensive English as a Second Language Program. Other entering students ordinarily must have completed a minimum of two years of recent university courses in their second language to meet the Institute's entrance requirements. Students may develop or enhance language skills at the Institute's Summer Intensive Language Program.

Correspondence and Information

Admissions Office
Monterey Institute of International Studies
425 Van Buren Street
Monterey, California 93940

Telephone: 408-647-4123
800-824-7235 (toll-free within the United States)
Fax: 408-647-6405
E-mail: admit@miis.edu
World Wide Web: http://www.miis.edu

Monterey Institute of International Studies

THE FACULTY AND THEIR RESEARCH

E. Philip Morgan, Dean, International Policy Studies; Ph.D. (political science), Syracuse. Dean Morgan was a faculty member and the Director of Undergraduate Programs in the School of Public and Environmental Affairs at Indiana University. He served as Associate Dean of Indiana University's international programs and was Director of Indiana University Overseas Study. He was a Fulbright Lecturer at the Institute of Development Management at the University of Botswana. In 1992–93, he was coordinator of the World Bank's Regional Research Program on Indigenous Institutions and Management Practices in Africa. Dean Morgan has published widely in the areas of program and project management, comparative civil service systems and reforms, and the linkages between development policy formation and the instruments of policy action. He serves on the editorial advisory boards of several journals, including *Public Administration and Development* (U.K.) and the *Journal of African Public Policy,* and on the boards of publishing firms that specialize in international development policy and management. (E-mail: pmorgan@miis.edu)

Tsuneo Akaha, Professor and Director, Center for East Asian Studies; Ph.D. (political science), USC. A native of Japan, Dr. Akaha has undergraduate degrees from Oregon State University and Waseda University in Tokyo. He has been a professor in the Department of Political Science at Bowling Green State University, where he was Director of the Asian Studies Program. He was also a Senior Fulbright Fellow at Seikei University in Tokyo and Tokyo University.

Jan Knippers Black, Associate Professor; Ph.D. (international studies), American. Dr. Black was previously a research professor in the Division of Public Administration, University of New Mexico. She has held visiting positions with George Mason University and with the University of Pittsburgh's Semester-at-Sea Program.

Jackson Davis, Professor; Ph.D. (biology), Oregon. Dr. Davis holds a joint appointment at the Monterey Institute and as professor of biology and environmental studies, University of California, Santa Cruz. He has held postdoctoral appointments in neuroscience at the University of Oregon, Stanford, and the National Institutes of Health, and he is the author of dozens of scientific works on marine biology. For more than a decade, Dr. Davis has been an adviser to governments of Pacific island nations on international marine policy issues. He is currently Scientific Advisor and Delegate of the Republic of Nauru to the London Dumping Convention, U.N. Maritime Organization, London; South Pacific Forum, U.N. Alliance of Small Island States; U.N. Group of 77; and Framework Convention on Climate Change. He is the director of the Monterey Institute's Project Oceans, a computerized policy and scientific data bank on the state of the marine environment.

Geza Feketekuty, Research Professor and Director, Center for Trade and Commercial Diplomacy; M.A. (economics), Princeton. Professor Feketekuty came to the CTCD with twenty-seven years' experience in international economic policy making in the Executive Office of the President, twenty-one years of which were in senior policy development and negotiating positions in the Office of the United States Trade Representative. He served as Senior Assistant U.S. Trade Representative and chaired the OECD Trade Committee for several years. He was also a senior staff person on the Council of Economic Advisors and in the Office of Management and Budget. He was a Scholar in Residence at the International Trade Commission and taught economics at Princeton, Cornell, and Johns Hopkins. He has written numerous articles and books on trade policy issues, including *International Trade in Services: An Overview and Blueprint for Negotiations* and *The New Trade Agenda.*

Stephen Garrett, Professor; Ph.D. (political science), Virginia. Dr. Garrett has previously taught at the University of Virginia and the American University of Beirut. He spent academic year 1978–79 in Bangkok, Thailand, as a senior lecturer on a Fulbright Fellowship and was appointed to the Gordon Paul Smith Chair of International Policy Studies in 1988–89.

Gil Gunderson, Associate Professor; Ph.D., Berkeley. Dr. Gunderson has taught at California State University at Northridge, the University of Guam, Boston University (in Germany), and the American University of Beirut. He served as a Peace Corps volunteer in Nigeria. He did field research for his dissertation in Botswana and has served as a consultant to the governments of Northern Nigeria and Qatar.

Michael Hart, Visiting Professor; M.A. (history), Toronto. After twenty-one years as a trade policy official with the government of Canada, Professor Hart retired in 1995 to become a professor in the Norman Paterson School of International Affairs at Carleton University in Ottawa, Canada. Before joining the government, he taught European history at a number of Canadian universities. He is the author, editor, or coeditor of nineteen books and numerous articles and chapters on international trade issues, including *Decision at Midnight: Inside the Canada–U.S. Free Trade Negotiations, What's Next: Canada, The Global Economy and the New Trade Policy,* and *Multilateral Negotiations: Lessons from Arms Control, Trade and the Environment.*

Nuket Kardam, Associate Professor and M.P.A. Program Head; Ph.D. (political science), Michigan State. Dr. Kardam previously taught at Pomona College. She has served as a consultant to the UN office in Vienna, Division for Advancement of Women; for UNICEF on projects on women's education and employment in Turkey; and for the World Bank.

Edward J. Laurance, Professor and Associate Director, Program for Nonproliferation Studies; Ph.D. (international relations), Pennsylvania. Dr. Laurance taught at the Naval Postgraduate School and was a visiting professor at the University of California, Davis. He has served as a special assistant to the Chief, Arms Transfer Division, the U.S. Arms Control and Disarmament Agency and has testified twice before Congress on U.S. arms transfer policy. He was the study director for the Rockefeller Foundation's Arms Trade Project and is a consultant to the United Nation's Department of Disarmament Affairs. He is codirector of the Institute's International Missile Proliferation Project.

Beryl Levinger, Distinguished Professor of Nonprofit Management; Ph.D. (educational planning), Alabama. Dr. Levinger did her undergraduate studies at Cornell University, and she has previously taught at Teachers College, Columbia University. Until 1992, Dr. Levinger was president of AFS Intercultural Programs, the world's largest private educational exchange program. Before going to AFS, she served as the deputy executive director of CARE, the world's largest private international relief and development organization. Dr. Levinger has served on U.S. delegations to the Organization of Economic Cooperation and Development and has undertaken studies for UNESCO and USAID.

Robert McCleery, Professor; Ph.D. (economics), Stanford. Professor McCleery's international experiences include consulting for the Institute for Developing Economies in Tokyo, the International Center for Economic Growth in Osaka, and USAID in Jakarta. Before coming to Monterey Institute, Professor McCleery was a Visiting Associate Professor at Claremont McKenna and an Associate Professor at Kobe University's Research Institute for Economics and Business Administration. In addition, he has served as a postdoctoral researcher at Stanford and as a Research Associate for the East-West Center Development Policy Program. Among his many published articles, he has authored *The Dynamics of Integration in the Americas: A Look at the Political Economy of NAFTA Expansion, Relevance of Asian Development Experiences to African Development Problems, Economic Policy Reform: A Latin American Perspective,* and *On Continuing Economic Growth in Developing Asia: Is Human Resource Development the Key to the "Pacific Century?".*

William Monning, Senior Associate and Assistant Director, Graduate Programs; J.D., San Francisco. Professor Monning teaches courses on negotiations, mediation, and conflict resolution. He served as the Executive Director of the International Physicians for the Prevention of Nuclear War, the organizational recipient of the 1985 Nobel Peace Prize. He is an attorney and has served as an Adjunct Professor of Law at the Monterey College of Law. He has also published books on litigation practice with the Matthew Bender Company.

William Potter, Professor and Director, Center for Russian and Eurasian Studies and the Center for Nonproliferation Studies; Ph.D. (political science), Michigan. Dr. Potter has worked for the Center of International and Strategic Affairs at UCLA.

Andrew Procassini, Senior Associate; D.B.A., Nova Southeastern. Andrew Procassini recently retired as President of the Semiconductor Industry Association (SIA), where he was instrumental in forging a trade agreement with Japan and in the formation of SEMATECH, the industry's manufacturing development arm. Prior to heading the SIA, he held high-level executive management positions in a number of high-tech firms in the U.S., Europe, and Japan. He is active in university life in the San Francisco Bay area and is the author of *Competitors in Alliance: Industry Associations, Global Rivalries and Business-Government Relations.*

Moyara de Moraes Ruehsen, Assistant Professor; Ph.D. (international economics and Middle Eastern studies), Johns Hopkins. Dr. Ruehsen has taught at the University of California, Berkeley, University of San Francisco, Johns Hopkins University, and the Foreign Service Institute. She was a Fulbright scholar in Bahrain.

Laura Strohm, Assistant Professor; Ph.D. (international environmental policy), Tufts (Fletcher). Dr. Strohm has taught at the School of Public and Environmental Affairs, Indiana University. She has worked for the U.S. Soil Conservation Service and was a researcher for the International Union for the Conservation of Nature in Geneva, Switzerland.

Gale Summerfield, Associate Professor; Ph.D. (economics), Michigan. Dr. Summerfield also completed an M.A. in Asian studies at Michigan. She has taught at the University of Michigan and at California State University, Hayward. While at Michigan, she worked on the Chinese economics project with the Center for Chinese Studies.

Glynn Wood, Professor and Academic Dean; Ph.D. (political science), MIT. Dr. Wood has an M.A. in journalism from Stanford, was previously on the faculty of American University in Washington, D.C., and for two years was Dean of the School of Government and Public Administration there. He has been actively involved with the South Asia Division of the State Department's Foreign Service Institute as consultant and lecturer. He served with USIA as a cultural affairs officer with postings to Beirut, Kabul, and Bangalore, India. His primary research interests have focused on South Asia.

MONTEREY INSTITUTE OF INTERNATIONAL STUDIES

Fisher Graduate School of International Business

Programs of Study

The Monterey Institute offers a two-year M.B.A. and a ten-month advanced entry M.B.A. for students with previous formal undergraduate business education. All programs feature the key dimensions of the Monterey M.B.A.: international content, advanced language study, multicultural teamwork, and an international business plan. The international business plan integrates the functional disciplines of management for a sponsoring company. It exposes students to the unique aspects of international business environments, hones communication and presentation skills, and develops a strong entrepreneurial orientation. Plans are accomplished in close consultation with a team of experienced faculty members.

Optional concentrations of elective courses are offered in international trade management, entrepreneurial management, regional business environments, international marketing, international economics and finance, decision sciences, international human resources management, environmental studies, nonprofit management, and global business. The Fisher School is a member of AACSB–The International Association for Management Education and a candidate for AACSB accreditation.

The full-time programs include an advanced foreign language component, with special emphasis on the cultural context of the student's second language. While the base language of instruction at the Institute is English, management and elective courses are offered in other languages whenever staffing permits. Languages offered for nonnative speakers are Arabic, English, French, German, Japanese, Mandarin, Russian, and Spanish.

Most students at the Institute have studied, worked, or lived abroad. Selected full-time M.B.A. students may integrate a period of overseas study into their programs and are also encouraged to participate in internships at one of the Institute's research centers or to work with the Career Development Office (CDO) to obtain a relevant summer internship.

The Monterey Institute is a leader in integrating advanced foreign language education into the professional programs offered by the Graduate School of International Management and into the graduate programs in international policy studies, international public administration, and international environmental policy. For students with near-native language proficiency, the Monterey Institute also offers M.A. degrees in teaching English to speakers of other languages, teaching foreign language, and translation and interpretation.

Research Facilities

The Monterey Institute's specialized international library has a collection of 68,000 carefully selected volumes and 550 periodical titles, about one third of which are in languages other than English. The library also offers CD-ROM workstations. DOS-based and Macintosh microcomputer laboratories are available for course-related computing; they also offer workshops, individualized assistance, and free Internet access.

Internships and research opportunities are available through the Institute's Business and Economic Development Center, the Small Business Institute, the International Trade Research Center, and the Center for Trade and Commercial Diplomacy. Internships and advanced language study are also available through the Institute's summer programs in China, France, Germany, Japan, Mexico, and Russia.

Financial Aid

The Institute makes every effort to provide need-based, federally funded financial aid to U.S. citizens and eligible noncitizens; approximately three quarters of the students receive some form of aid, usually awarded as a combination of grants, loans, and work opportunities. In addition, the Institute awards competitive merit-based scholarships to both U.S. citizens and international students. Scholarships are awarded to former participants of university-accredited study-abroad programs, overseas volunteer programs, high school exchange programs, Concordia Language Villages, the Japanese Exchange and Teaching (JET) program, and the U.S. Peace Corps. Scholarships are also awarded in recognition of the academic achievements of international students, international employment experience, and Phi Beta Kappa membership. Minority scholarships are available to U.S. citizens.

Cost of Study

Fees for 1998–99 are $9100 per semester (two semesters per academic year).

Living and Housing Costs

In 1997–98, the average amount paid for off-campus housing was $450 per month, typically in a room in a nearby private house or a shared apartment. Total housing and living expenses are estimated at $7500 for the nine-month academic year.

Student Group

About one third of the Institute's 800 students represent more than fifty countries, and almost all U.S. students have lived, worked, or studied abroad. Forty-three percent of the M.B.A. students are from other countries, and half are women. Institute students share a multidisciplinary experience in course work and social activities. Monterey alumni form a worldwide network for professional and social contacts.

Location

The Monterey Institute is situated in one of the most spectacular natural environments in the world. The Monterey Peninsula is 120 miles south of San Francisco on California's central coast, surrounded by ocean and mountains; it has a population of 100,000. The area combines a variety of rich cultural resources and recreational activities.

The Institute

Founded in 1955, the Monterey Institute has maintained its character as a tightly knit cosmopolitan community. Its relatively small size creates a sense of intimacy and cohesion between students and faculty members, who encourage lively classroom interaction. The Institute is accredited by the Western Association of Schools and Colleges.

Applying

Applicants to the M.B.A. programs must have a U.S. bachelor's degree or the equivalent, with a minimum grade point average of 3.0 on a 4.0 scale. All applicants must submit the GMAT score report and demonstrate advanced foreign language proficiency or extend their program with summer language study. Nonnative English speakers must submit a minimum TOEFL score of 550 for the two-year M.B.A. and 600 for the advanced entry M.B.A. or enhance their language skills in the Institute's Intensive English as Second Language Program. Other entering students ordinarily must have completed a minimum of two years of recent university courses in their second language to meet the Institute's entrance requirements. Students may develop or enhance their language skills in the Institute's Summer Intensive Language Program. Preference is given to applicants with prior business experience. Application should be made at least three months prior to the proposed semester of enrollment. There is no application deadline for most forms of financial aid; however, applications for California grants and fellowships (residents only) or for Monterey Institute scholarships must be submitted by the published February deadline.

Correspondence and Information

Admissions Office
Monterey Institute of International Studies
425 Van Buren Street
Monterey, California 93940
Telephone: 408-647-4123
800-824-7235 (toll-free, United States only)
Fax: 408-647-6405
E-mail: admit@miis.edu
World Wide Web: http://www.miis.edu

Monterey Institute of International Studies

THE FACULTY

Fisher Graduate School of International Business
William R. Pendergast, Dean and Professor; Ph.D., Columbia.

Richard Cherry, Professor; Ph.D., Oregon State.
Lisbeth M. Claus, Associate Professor; Ph.D., Saint Louis.
Victor Cordell, Associate Professor; Ph.D., Houston.
Eddine Dahel, Associate Professor; Ph.D., IIT.
Juan R. España, Assistant Professor; Ph.D., California, Santa Barbara.
Charles V. Fishel, Senior Lecturer; J.D., Kansas.
Attila A. Freska, Associate Professor; Ph.D., Budapest School of Economic Sciences.
John Jenkins, Professor; D.Phil., Oxford, D.B.A., Harvard.
David Roberts, Professor; Ph.D., USC.
Len Trevino, Associate Professor; Ph.D., Indiana.
Beiming Wang, Assistant Professor; M.B.A., Monterey Institute.
Leslie Zambo, Professor; Ph.D., Texas at Austin.

Kip Becker, Adjunct Professor; Ph.D., Delaware.
Alan Bird, Adjunct Professor; Ph.D., Oregon.
Gene Bucciarelli, Adjunct Professor; M.B.A., Golden Gate; CPA.
Henry Calero, Adjunct Professor; M.B.A., UCLA.
Luis Calingo, Adjunct Professor; Ph.D., Pittsburgh.
Paul Fields, Adjunct Professor; Ph.D., Penn State.
Morton Galper, Adjunct Professor; D.B.A., Harvard.
J. Michael Geringer, Adjunct Professor; Ph.D., Washington (Seattle).
William MacPhee, Adjunct Professor; M.B.A., Vanderbilt.
Thomas Moore, Adjunct Professor; Ph.D., Virginia Tech.
Norman C. Parrish, Adjunct Professor; M.S., USC.
Ronald Schill, Adjunct Professor; Ph.D., Oregon.
Luc Soenen, Adjunct Professor; D.B.A., Harvard.
Katsuaki Terosawa, Adjunct Professor; Ph.D., Kansas.

Graduate School of International Policy Studies
E. Philip Morgan, Dean and Professor; Ph.D., Syracuse.

Tsuneo Akaha, Professor; Ph.D., USC.
Steven J. Baker, Provost and Associate Professor; Ph.D., UCLA.
Jan Knippers Black, Associate Professor; Ph.D., American.
Jackson Davis, Professor; Ph.D., Oregon.
Leslie Eliason, Associate Professor; Ph.D., Stanford.
Geza Feketekuty, Research Professor and Director, CTCD; M.A., Princeton.
Stephen Garrett, Professor; Ph.D., Virginia.
Gil Gunderson, Associate Professor; Ph.D., Berkeley.
Nuket Kardam, Assistant Professor; Ph.D., Michigan State.
Edward J. Laurance, Professor; Ph.D., Pennsylvania.
Beryl Levinger, Distinguished Professor; Ph.D., Alabama.
Robert McCleary, Professor; Ph.D., Stanford.
William Monning, Senior Associate and Assistant Director, CTCD; J.D., San Francisco.
William Potter, Professor; Ph.D., Michigan.
Andrew Procassini, Senior Associate; D.B.A., Nova Southeastern.
Moyara de Moraes Ruehsen, Assistant Professor; Ph.D., Johns Hopkins.
Laura Strohm, Assistant Professor; Ph.D., Tufts (Fletcher).
Gale Summerfield, Associate Professor; Ph.D., Michigan.
Glynn Wood, Professor; Ph.D., MIT.

Graduate School of Language and Educational Linguistics
Ruth Larimer, Dean and Professor; Ph.D., Berkeley.
Andreas Winkler, Professor and Associate Dean; D.Phil., Phillips (Germany).

Ovidio Casado-Fuente, Professor of Spanish; Th.D., Pontifical Gregorian University (Rome).
Rafael Gomez, Associate Professor; Ph.D., Indiana.
Michel Gueldry, Assistant Professor of French; Ph.D., Toulouse (France).
John Hedgcock, Associate Professor; Ph.D., USC.
Jiaying Zhuang Howard, Associate Professor of Chinese; Ph.D., California, Santa Barbara.
Gisele Kapscinski, Associate Professor of French; Ph.D., Columbia.
Natalie Lovick, Assistant Professor of Russian; M.A., Monterey Institute.
Naoko Matsuo, Instructor; M.A., Monterey Institute.
Anna Scherbakova, Professor of Russian; Ph.D., Russian Diplomatic Academy.
Nobuko Sugamoto, Assistant Professor; Ph.D., UCLA.
Leo van Lier, Professor; Ph.D., Lancaster.

Kawther Hakim, Adjunct Professor of Arabic; Ed.D., San Francisco.

POINT PARK COLLEGE

International Master of Business Administration Program

Program of Study

Point Park College offers a graduate program in international business leading to the International Master of Business Administration (M.B.A.) degree. The program admits students with a variety of undergraduate backgrounds. Its major goal is to prepare students to become effective managers in the complex environment of international business and multinational enterprises. While the emphasis is on business management, the program also prepares graduates for positions in international institutions and government agencies.

The program requires a minimum of 39 semester credits for the degree. Full-time students may complete the program in four semesters, or sixteen months, including a summer term. For part-time students, the program may take seven or more terms to complete. For students with no undergraduate training in business, prerequisite courses may be taken concurrently with the graduate curriculum. The 39-credit program consists of 21 credits of international business core courses, 12 credits of international business electives, and 6 credits of international studies. Electives include independent research and internship.

Students whose first language is not English are tested for language placement. Students who have completed graduate courses at another institution may be able to transfer up to 9 credits (three courses) toward the M.B.A. degree, leaving 30 credits to be completed.

Research Facilities

The Library Center is the product of a unique public/private partnership between Point Park College and the Carnegie Library of Pittsburgh. The Library Center combines Point Park's 110,000-volume collection with the extensive collection of the Downtown and Business Information Center of the Carnegie Library. The combined collection includes more than 10,000 reference works, subscriptions to about 600 current periodicals and newspapers, a 15,000-volume Library of American Civilization on microfiche, and a selection of videocassettes, CDs, and tapes. The online catalog, CAROLINE, a DRA product, and printers are readily available throughout the building at workstations, which also access the Internet and various databases. The library holds membership in PALINET, a consortium of more than 600 libraries in the Middle Atlantic region and also holds agreements with several area institutions allowing graduate students to borrow resources. In addition, the library has an International Master of Business Administration library collection, which specializes in regional and country-specific books, national reports and publications, research reports, and reference studios.

Financial Aid

Students may apply for financial aid, which is granted on the basis of need, and for various state and federal loans. International applicants may seek loans and scholarships from a number of home-country and international agencies.

A limited number of graduate assistantships are awarded each academic year. Graduate assistants receive pay for their services to defray tuition costs. United States citizens and international students are eligible to apply.

Cost of Study

Tuition is $337 per credit hour in 1998–99. The cost of books and supplies averages $250 per term. Certain computer-based courses carry a supplemental lab fee of $65.

Living and Housing Costs

Housing is available in the College's residence halls. The cost in 1997–98 was typically $2536 per term. Apartments are available to students within a short travel distance on Pittsburgh's effective mass transit system. A variety of meal plans are available at the campus student cafeteria.

Student Group

Enrollment in the M.B.A. program in fall 1997 was 51. With the addition of the College's accelerated M.B.A. program anticipated for fall 1998, enrollment is expected to reach more than 100 students over the next three years. About 50 percent are part-time and 50 percent full-time. Many part-time students hold internationally oriented jobs, adding a realistic dimension to the classroom experience. International students represent more than a dozen countries.

Location

Pittsburgh is the thirteenth-largest metropolitan area in the United States. The industrial, technological, and service base of Pittsburgh has developed far beyond the steel industry. There are nine universities and colleges in the immediate area and many more in surrounding counties. Moreover, Pittsburgh is a city with many major multinational corporate headquarters. In addition to being prominent in business and education, it is a major cultural, medical, and entertainment center.

The College

Point Park College, located in the Golden Triangle of downtown Pittsburgh, was founded in 1960. Although it is a young institution, its reputation as a pioneer in educational innovation is firmly established. The College is a member of the Academy of International Business, the District Export Council, the Pittsburgh Council on Higher Education, and other organizations. It is accredited by the Middle States Association of Colleges and Schools.

Applying

Applicants for the M.B.A. program must take the GMAT. Those whose first language is not English must take the TOEFL. Students may be admitted for the fall, spring, or summer term.

Correspondence and Information

For further information and for application forms:

Office of Part-Time and Accelerated Programs
Point Park College
201 Wood Street
Pittsburgh, Pennsylvania 15222-1984

Telephone: 412-392-3808
800-321-0129 (toll-free)
Fax: 412-392-6164
E-mail: ptaccel@ppc.edu
World Wide Web: http://www.ppc.edu

Point Park College

THE FACULTY

Below is a list of the program's full-time faculty members. In addition, a number of senior executives from multinational corporations in the area also function as adjunct instructors.

Dimitris J. Kraniou, Director; Ph.D., Pittsburgh.

Sumanta Banerjee, International M.B.A., Point Park.
William H. Breslove, Ph.D., Carnegie Mellon.
James H. Cook Jr., M.B.A., Pittsburgh.
Clifford T. Early, J.D., Pittsburgh.
Sharon L. Linhart, M.B.A., Point Park.
George C. Mitchell, Ph.D., Paris.

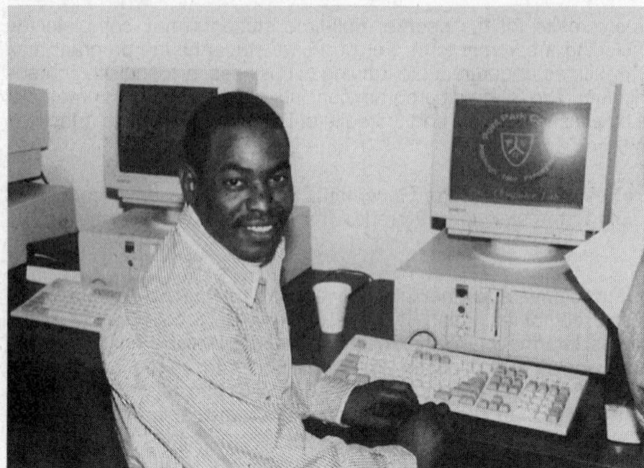

Point Park College recruits students from around the globe to provide technical business skills.

Computer facilities for students are readily available.

Students from Latin America, the Caribbean, and Asia develop the skills necessary to function in an international environment.

PORTLAND STATE UNIVERSITY

Oregon Joint Professional Schools of Business Master of International Management (M.I.M.)

Program of Study

Students complete the full-time Master of International Management (M.I.M.) course work in just twelve months (six 8-week terms) through a program sponsored by the Oregon Joint Professional Schools of Business (OJPSB). OJPSB is a cooperative venture between the graduate business schools in Portland State University (accredited by AACSB and the M.I.M. degree-granting institution), the University of Oregon, Oregon State University, and Southern Oregon University. Part-time course work is completed in two years. The M.I.M. program is specifically tailored to address the challenges created by evolving cultural mores, transforming social and political systems, and technological developments that have an impact on international business. The curriculum combines an in-depth exploration of innovative business practices and their relationship to contemporary world affairs with mandatory language study (either Chinese or Japanese), executive seminars, corporate visits, and a three-week field study trip to China and Japan. The program provides a stimulating and exciting learning environment by utilizing advanced technology, implementing an interactive/team-based teaching methodology, and capitalizing on the Just-in-Time learning approach. Each of the program's six terms is carefully structured to form an integrated package. For example, while studying contemporary global marketing, students participate in executive seminars and corporate field visits, enabling them to incorporate classroom learning into a real-world environment. Students receive feedback from world-renowned scholars, corporate executives, and government officials who are actively involved in the day-to-day workings of global business management.

The M.I.M. program concentrates on application-oriented knowledge and practical skills that can be applied globally through the exploration of business practices and their relationship to contemporary world affairs. Moreover, students have the opportunity to specifically focus on the Pacific Rim, as the curriculum's objective-oriented learning incorporates courses in cross-cultural communication and differences and foreign language study (either Chinese or Japanese). The language component of the program is designed to prepare the participant for the international Asian business environment. With attendant focus on relevant vocabulary, the content of the language courses is concentrated on business and social situations. The skills emphasized are listening, speaking, reading, and writing. During the final term of the program, students travel throughout China and Japan to visit companies, meet with international business executives, and truly experience these cultures. This capstone expedition presents students with an opportunity to compile firsthand information for their final exit project, practice the language they have been studying, and indulge themselves in the cultures and lifestyles of two very different countries. The M.I.M. program begins with a three-day outdoor field excursion.

In addition to the required 65 quarter credit hours, students have the option to participate in tutorials, which are minicourses designed to help students prepare for a future activity in the program. The M.I.M. core courses (listed here with the number of credits in parentheses) include Pacific Rim economies, trade and financial markets (3); contemporary global marketing (4); contemporary Pacific Rim and world affairs (3); accounting for global enterprises (4); managing multinational organizations (3); government regulations, ethics and multinational transactions (4); comparative operations management (4); international trade practices (4); managing information technology globally (4); global human resource management (3); international corporate finance and investment (4); marketing in Asia and the Pacific Rim (4); advanced cross-cultural communications (4); international business negotiations (4); global business strategy (4); special topics (e.g., Age of the Pacific Seminar Series) (4); and field study to China and Japan and project presentations (5).

The M.I.M. is a cohort program. Students enter and continue through the entire curriculum with their fellow classmates. This enables the student to establish a global network of friends and business contacts.

The pre-M.I.M. program has been developed to assure academic success for those incoming students who have either no academic business background or a limited one. The eight-week pre-M.I.M. program begins in late June and covers the fundamentals of business statistics, financial accounting, business finance, and economics (micro and macro). The admissions committee evaluates each student's application packet and determines which pre-M.I.M. courses are required. All international students must participate in the pre-M.I.M. These courses must be successfully completed prior to enrolling in the M.I.M. program in August.

Research Facilities

Classroom facilities are located in the CAPITAL Center in Beaverton, Oregon, 20 minutes from downtown Portland and the Portland State University campus. This modern facility hosts a state-of-the-art computer and language lab, a high-tech presentation classroom, an executive-style conference room, and a comfortable student reading room, which shelves the latest periodicals and other materials relevant to international business management and the Pacific Rim. In addition, students have on-line access to the campus libraries of Portland State University, the University of Oregon, Oregon State University, and Southern Oregon University and to the other library facilities in Portland.

Financial Aid

Federal assistance is available for U.S. graduate students in the form of grants, loans, and work-study employment. The Student Financial Aid Office can provide information on the types of loans available and can supply the necessary application forms. Some scholarships and fellowships are available through Portland State University. Students may contact the Office of Academic Affairs for more information.

Cost of Study

Tuition for students enrolling in the 1999–2000 M.I.M. program is $18,500 per year. An additional fee is assessed for travel and other expenses incurred as part of the required Asian field study.

Living and Housing Costs

Many suitable residential areas with apartments and homes exist within 5 to 10 minutes of the CAPITAL Center. The M.I.M. staff is available to assist new students in locating housing.

Student Group

The M.I.M. program enrolls up to 40 full-time and 40 part-time students. The class of 1997–98 was composed of 29 full-time and 27 part-time students. The average age for students in the 1997–98 class was 31, with approximately seven years of work and international experience. The academic experience is augmented by the cultural diversity represented in a student body in which international students represent 51 percent of the total enrollment.

Location

The Portland metropolitan area, home to approximately 1.5 million people, is surrounded on all four points of the compass by natural beauty: Mount Hood and the Cascade Range to the east, the Pacific coastline to the west, wine country to the south, and the Columbia River and Mount St. Helens to the north. With its excellent parks, cultural facilities, transportation systems, and cityscape, Portland is one of the finest cities in the United States. The CAPITAL Center is located in the midst of the "Silicon Forest", which is surrounded by numerous high-technology firms and other graduate programs. Students study in a modern facility equipped with the latest teaching technology at the center of a dynamic community.

The University

Founded in 1946, the PSU campus is a cityscape designed to meet students' needs. Occupying forty buildings in a 36-acre area, the campus is built around the Park Blocks, a greenway area reserved for pedestrians and bicyclists. The University provides a large variety of activities, ranging from the wide variety of musical organizations, the University Theater, and the Multicultural Center to football, basketball, baseball, and track.

Applying

Application deadlines for the M.I.M. program are March 1 for domestic students and February 1 for international students. The Graduate Management Admission Test (GMAT) or an acceptable GRE score is required for admission to the graduate program. International applicants must submit results from the Test of English as a Foreign Language (TOEFL).

Correspondence and Information

M.I.M. Marketing and Recruiting/OJPSB
18640 N.W. Walker Road, #1066
Portland State University
Beaverton, Oregon 97006-1975
Telephone: 503-725-2275
800-879-5088 (toll-free)
Fax: 503-725-2290
E-mail: mim@capital.osshe.edu
World Wide Web: http://www.capital.osshe.edu/ojpsb/

Portland State University

THE FACULTY

College of Business
Leland Buddress, Ph.D., Michigan State.
Alan Eliason, Ph.D., Minnesota, Twin Cities.
H. Thomas Johnson, Ph.D., Wisconsin; M.B.A., Rutgers.
Georgine Kryda, Ph.D., Illinois at Urbana-Champaign.
Steve Lawton, M.B.A., Cornell.
Chandrasekhar (Chandra) Mishra, Ph.D., Texas at Dallas.
Earl A. Molander, Ph.D., Berkeley.
John S. Oh, Director, M.I.M. Program; Ph.D., Virginia.
Yigang Pan, Ph.D., Columbia.
Candice Petersen, Ph.D., Portland State.
Alan Raedels, Ph.D., Purdue; CPM.
James E. Reinmuth, Ph.D., Oregon State.
Richard Sapp, Ph.D., Houston; CPA.
Sully Taylor, Ph.D., Washington (Seattle).
L. P. Douglas Tseng, Ph.D., Texas at Arlington.
Gerardo R. Ungson, Ph.D., Penn State.
Donald A. Watne, Ph.D., Berkeley.

Adjunct Business Faculty
Gareth C. C. Chang, M.B.A., Pepperdine; M.A. (engineering), USC; President of Hughes International and Corporate Senior Vice President Marketing, Hughes Electronics Corporation.
Ray Derrick, M.B.A., City (Seattle).
Margot C. Everett, M.S., California, Santa Cruz.
Joseph M. Ha, Ph.D., Columbia; Vice President, NIKE, Inc.
Haiou He, M.B.A., Portland State.
Atusi Kageyama, M.B.A., Oregon; M.A., Doshisha (Japan).
Mike Lawrence, M.B.A., Oregon; CPA.
Junichiro Nakane, Ph.D., Waseda (Tokyo); Professor, System Science Institute at Waseda University, Tokyo, Japan; President of the Japan Production and Inventory Control Society.
Martin Schmidt, Ph.D., Colorado State.
Masahide Shibusawa, B.A., Tokyo (Japan).
Linda Wanacott, M.B.A., Portland State; CPA.

Foreign Language Studies
Nobuko Murakami-Chalfen, Instructor (Japanese); B.A., Portland State; Certificate (teaching Japanese as a second language).
Meiru Liu, Instructor (Chinese); Ph.D., Portland State.

Department of Geography and International Studies
Gerald Fry, Ph.D., Stanford.
Mel Gurtov, Director, Asia Programs; Ph.D., UCLA.
Gil Latz, Ph.D., Chicago.
Devorah Lieberman, Ph.D., Florida.
Nancy Rosenberger, Ph.D., Michigan.
John Young, Ph.D., Stanford.

M.I.M. classroom.

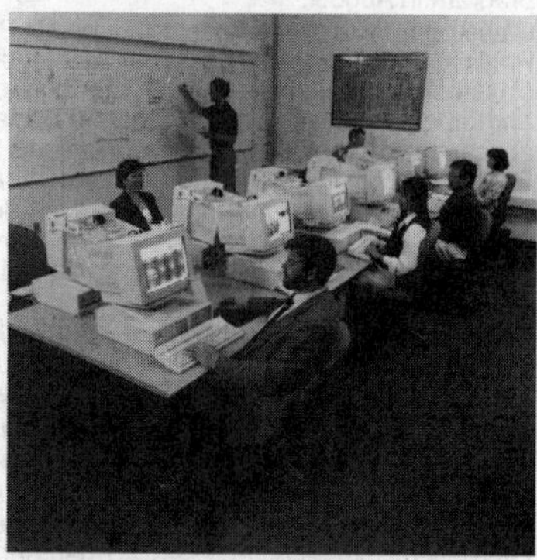

Computer lab for M.I.M. students.

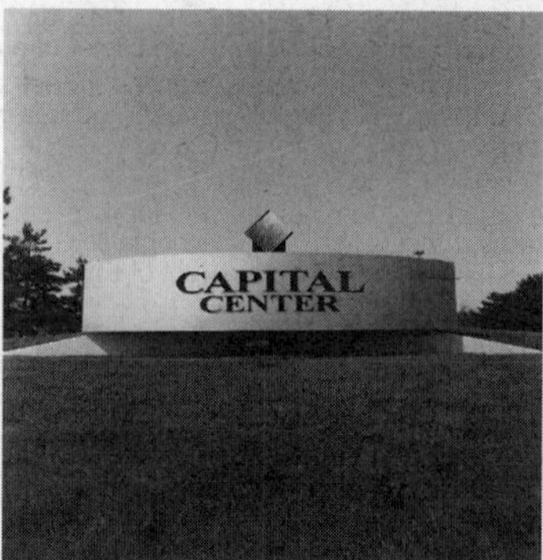

Location of the M.I.M. program.

TEXAS A&M INTERNATIONAL UNIVERSITY

Graduate School of International Trade and Business Administration

Programs of Study

Texas A&M International University has been a pioneer in the teaching of international business programs, offering the country's only M.B.A. in international trade or international banking and an M.S. in international logistics. These programs prepare students from a broad spectrum of experiences, cultures, and academic disciplines with skills to assume leadership roles in the international business community. Through the use of special lectures, attendance at various international trade–related conferences, guest speakers, workshops, and case studies, students gain a practical background and the competencies necessary for organizing, conducting, and evaluating international business operations. The M.B.A. in international banking program incorporates the study of the general theoretical framework of international banking, methods of measuring and attenuating bank counterparty risk, applications of computer analysis of bank portfolios, and other bank-related studies, all emphasized with practical applications in the field. The M.S. in international logistics emphasizes electronic data interchange (EDI) and international transportation. In addition to the international programs, Texas A&M International University also offers a general M.B.A., taught in either English or Spanish; an M.S. in information systems; and a Master of Professional Accountancy degree. All graduate programs consist of 36 graduate hours (twelve courses), with the total core courses and electives varying with each program. Students from a wide range of academic disciplines are accepted. Non–business majors may be required to complete up to seven preparatory courses before beginning study in a graduate program.

Research Facilities

The Killam Library currently holds 123,000 book volumes, approximately 1,000 journals in current print and microform subscription, and an additional 1,000 journals in electronic format. Special funds from the Texas state legislature will increase these collections by approximately 80 percent during the next three years. Business research, particularly international trade research, is emphasized. Of the eighty bibliographic and full-text databases available (not including KR/Dialog or World Wide Web sites), twelve are business related. The library is also in the process of acquiring all of the titles in the Harvard Baker Core Collection. Active interlibrary loan and document delivery services provide items not currently in the library at no extra charge to students. The library is an official selective depository of U.S. federal and Texas state documents.

The Office for the Study of U.S.–Mexico Trade Relations (NAFTA Information Center) compiles data from journals, newspapers, magazines, and other published sources into a comprehensive, electronic text database concerning all aspects of NAFTA. It is continually updated and currently consists of more than 55,000 listings from U.S., Canadian, Mexican, and other international sources.

The Texas Center for Border Economic and Enterprise Development, through its *Border Business Indicators* magazine, workshops, seminars, and conferences, provides public officials with timely economic development information. The Texas Center also publishes its top twenty-five products imported and exported through all U.S.–Mexico border ports by five-digit SITC and dollar value.

Financial Aid

Texas A&M International University's financial assistance is available in a combination of scholarships, grants, loans, and work-study employment. Of particular interest are the Graduate Business Fellowships offered by the Graduate School of International Trade and Business Administration. All students enrolled in one of the graduate business programs are eligible to apply for the fellowships. The fellowships are competitive and awarded according to merit criteria. All recipients receive a stipend; in addition, out-of-state and international students pay in-state tuition.

Cost of Study

Tuition and fees for 1998–99 are $925.16 for a 12-semester-hour load for Texas residents and $3481.16 for non-Texas residents and international students.

Living and Housing Costs

Brand-new one-, two-, and four-bedroom garden-style apartments are available on campus. The apartments have a fully equipped kitchen and private or semiprivate bathrooms. The two- and four-bedroom apartments are fully furnished with living room, dining room, and bedroom furniture. There are also a community center, swimming pool, sundeck, volleyball court, TV theater, and a barbecue area. The price for a full year ranges from $3658 to $6160 for room only.

Student Group

Approximately 300 students are enrolled in the Graduate School of International Trade and Business Administration. There are both full- and part-time students in the programs, with a cross-section of U.S. students representing near and distant states and international students representing about twenty countries. Since the programs' inception, international students representing fifty-two countries have graduated. The diverse professional, cultural, and educational backgrounds of these students create a stimulating international learning environment within the classroom and enhance the total educational experience at the University.

Student Outcomes

Depending on the individual courses of study, graduates of the international business programs are qualified to seek positions in manufacturing, importing, exporting, transportation, warehousing, insurance, custom brokerage, freight forwarding, banking, finance, and marketing.

Location

As the major inland port for trade between the United States and Mexico, the city of Laredo provides an outstanding laboratory for firsthand study of international logistics, trade, and banking activities. Located in the southern part of Texas on the Rio Grande, Laredo is 150 miles south of San Antonio, 150 miles west of Corpus Christi, and 150 miles north of Monterrey, Mexico.

The University

Texas A&M International University has been a pioneer in the teaching of international business programs. For twenty years, it has offered the country's only M.B.A. in international trade. In 1990, the University centralized the international trade program by establishing the Graduate School of International Trade and Business Administration and added the M.B.A. in international banking program. The University is located at an important gateway between the United States and Latin America, and through its educational programs it strives to prepare a cadre of leaders to serve in various fields of international importance.

In fall 1995, Texas A&M International University moved into a brand-new state-of-the-art campus in northeast Laredo. Phases I and II of construction include a joint library and administration building; business administration, science, arts and humanities, and all-purpose classroom buildings; and a kinesiology building.

Texas A&M International University is accredited by the Southern Association of Colleges and Schools and the Texas Education Agency. It is a member of the American Association of State Colleges and is an associate member of the AACSB–The International Association for Management Education.

Applying

Students from a wide range of academic disciplines are accepted. Full graduate standing is granted to applicants whose undergraduate GPA in all upper-division course work is at least 3.2 (4.0 scale). Applicants who do not meet this requirement must submit GMAT or GRE scores. Conditional admission may be granted in certain cases. International students whose native language is not English must earn a minimum score of 550 on the TOEFL. Applications are accepted for any semester, and admission is granted on a rolling basis.

Correspondence and Information

Ray Ortegon
Director of Graduate Student Services
Texas A&M International University
5201 University Boulevard
Laredo, Texas 78041-1900

Telephone: 956-326-2770
Fax: 956-326-2769
E-mail: coba@tamiu.edu
World Wide Web: http://www.tamiu.edu

Texas A&M International University

THE FACULTY AND THEIR RESEARCH

The faculty members of the Graduate School of International Trade and Business Administration have a very diverse and international background. Approximately 84 percent have extensive international business experience or are foreign nationals. Faculty members collectively possess functional literacy in twenty different languages and have living and/or working experience in Africa, Europe, the Middle East, South and Central America, and Asia.

William Larry Boyd, Professor of Finance and Provost and Vice President for Academic Affairs; Ph.D., Texas A&M, 1978. Corporate finance.
Martin Broin, Assistant Professor of Operations Management; Ph.D., Purdue, 1989. Location theory.
Willie Newton Cargill, Associate Professor of Accounting; Ph.D., Missouri–Columbia, 1986. Accounting.
Barry Carr, Assistant Professor of Economics; Ph.D., Oklahoma State, 1971. Agricultural economics.
Jim Qingjun Chen, Assistant Professor of Computer Information Systems; Ph.D., Nebraska–Lincoln, 1995. System design, computer-aided software engineering.
Kamal Fatehi, Professor of Management and Chair of the Department of Management and Marketing; Ph.D., LSU, 1972. International management.
Khosrow Fatemi, Professor of International Trade and Dean of the College of Business Administration; Ph.D., USC, 1972.
Alain D. Genestre, Assistant Professor of Marketing; Ph.D., Indiana, 1968; D.B.A., Memphis State, 1984. (French) Marketing management, distribution, international marketing.
James Giermanski, Professor of International Trade; D.A., Miami (Florida), 1975.
Cindy Houser, Assistant Professor of Economics; Ph.D., Florida, 1995. International economics, economic development.
Pedro S. Hurtado, Associate Professor of Business Administration; Ph.D., Maryland, 1978. Transportation.
Muhammad Mazharul Islam, Associate Professor of International Trade; Ph.D., Vanderbilt, 1987. Domestic and international finance, investment banking, financial institutions.
Kurt R. Jesswein, Associate Professor of International Banking; Ph.D., South Carolina, 1992. International banking and finance, exchange risk management, new banking products and techniques.
Leland G. Jordan, Associate Professor of Accounting; D.B.A., George Washington, 1985. Managerial accounting, financial accounting.
George Kostopoulos, Visiting Professor of Information Systems; Ph.D., Arizona State, 1971. Information systems, computer engineering.
Michael Landeck, Professor of Marketing and International Business; Ph.D., North Texas State, 1988. International marketing, North American Free Trade Agreement.
Stephen Lunce, Associate Professor of Computer Information Systems; Ph.D., Texas at Arlington, 1994. Systems analysis and design, decision support systems, knowledge-based systems.
Jacqueline Rowley Mayfield, Assistant Professor of Management and Business Communications; Ph.D., Alabama, 1993. Management, communications.
Milton Mayfield, Assistant Professor of Management and Research Methodology; Ph.D., Alabama, 1994. Management, statistics.
Thomas McGhee, Associate Professor of Accounting; Ph.D., South Carolina, 1989. International accounting.
Stephen McNett, Associate Professor of Accounting and Chair of the Department of Accounting and Information Systems; Ph.D., Missouri–Columbia, 1987. Accounting.
Sridhar P. Nerur, Assistant Professor of Information Systems; Ph.D., Texas at Arlington, 1994. Database, artificial intelligence application.
Kamal D. Parhizgar, Professor of Business Administration; Ph.D., Northwestern, 1972. Strategic management, organizational behavior, management theory, multinational business.
J. Michael Patrick, Professor of Economics and Chair of the Department of Economics and Finance; Ph.D., Michigan State, 1977.
Jacqueline Lou Power, Assistant Professor of Accounting; Ph.D., Texas A&M, 1993. International accounting standards, accounting systems for small businesses, capital markets, professional ethics.
David Norton Roberts, Assistant Professor of Accounting and Business Law; J.D., Texas at Austin, 1980. Commercial law.
Antonio J. Rodriguez, Associate Professor of Business Administration and Economics; Ph.D., Alabama, 1985. Treasury bills, futures trading.
Betty S. Rogers, Assistant Professor of Business; Ph.D., Oklahoma, 1983. Business education.
Henry Smith, Assistant Professor of Accounting; Ph.D., Virginia Commonwealth, 1994. Managerial accounting.
Stephanie Smith, Assistant Professor of Finance; Ph.D., Virginia Commonwealth, 1993. Corporate finance.
Edward N. Willman, Associate Professor of Business; Ph.D., North Texas State, 1981. Computer programming, decision sciences.
Rama Yelkur, Assistant Professor of Marketing; Ph.D., Mississippi State, 1995. International marketing, strategic alliance.

THUNDERBIRD, THE AMERICAN GRADUATE SCHOOL OF INTERNATIONAL MANAGEMENT

Master's Program in International Management

Program of Study

The American Graduate School of International Management ("Thunderbird") provides preparation for international management careers. The Master of International Management (M.I.M.) is awarded upon successful completion of prescribed courses, requirements, and electives. Entering students who speak a second language and who have some undergraduate business preparation are able to complete the minimum 42-hour plan in twelve to eighteen months.

Instruction is in three interrelated areas: world business, international studies, and modern languages. The curriculum provides a practical knowledge of business management skills and concepts; an understanding of the social, political, historical, and cultural natures of various parts of the world; and a basic proficiency in a second language—Arabic, English as a second language, French, German, Italian, Japanese, Chinese, Portuguese, Spanish, or Russian.

Dual degrees are offered with Arizona State University, the University of Arizona, the University of Colorado at Denver, Drury College, Case Western Reserve University, the University of Florida, the University of Houston, and ESADE in Barcelona, Spain. Study-abroad programs are offered in Europe, Asia, and Latin America. A Japan Center is located in Tokyo and a European campus is in Archamps, France, 10 kilometers from Geneva.

Research Facilities

Library and research facilities are centralized in the Merle A. Hinrichs International Business Information Centre, a 31,000-square-foot building housing library collections, multimedia facilities, extensive video and teleconferencing capabilities, and multiple online resources (the CARL System, CD-ROM databases, and online retrieval systems).

Two new research centers add to the resources available to students. The Barton Kyle Yount Centre is a high-tech communications center, complete with multimedia classrooms, distance learning facilities, and video production studios. In addition, the Thunderbird International Trade and Finance Center provides education, training, consulting, and research in trade and finance for banks, governments, and international organizations engaged in global trade.

The Joan and David Lincoln Computer Services Center supports both academic and administrative requirements. The student computing laboratories allow access to a wide range of applications, ranging from sophisticated models of futures trading and international banking to word processing and spreadsheet/database development.

Financial Aid

The Office of Financial Aid manages financial assistance for qualified persons in the following areas: processing federal loan funds for students; placing a limited number of students and spouses in part-time campus employment; and assisting in off-campus employment placement.

Scholarships, fellowships, and assistantships based on merit are available to new students. Grants based on a combination of need and merit are available to continuing students.

Cost of Study

Full-time tuition and fees for 1998–99 are $20,700. For the summer term, tuition and fees are $7240. Books and instructional materials should not exceed $500 per semester.

Living and Housing Costs

In 1998–99, on-campus room and board costs for a single person, single occupancy, total $5380. Total room and board costs for the summer term are $4235. Off-campus costs were slightly higher.

Student Group

The current enrollment is approximately 1,400. The average age of students is 27, with most having significant work and international exposure. Students hold degrees in more than 130 undergraduate majors from 594 colleges and universities worldwide.

The academic experience is enhanced by the cultural diversity represented in a student body where seventy-five countries are represented. Forty-five percent of the students are international students; 35 percent are women.

Student Outcomes

Thunderbird graduates are placed in jobs throughout the world. They typically choose careers in finance, marketing, or international trade in such industrial sectors as financial services, manufacturing, and consulting. Top employers include Citicorp, General Motors, Intel, EDS, and Chiquita.

Location

Thunderbird is located in the cosmopolitan area of Phoenix, Arizona, where the superb weather draws visitors from all over the world to enjoy outdoor recreational activities. The Grand Canyon is 5 hours north by car; Mexico is 4 hours south.

The School

Thunderbird, The American Graduate School of International Management, is accredited by the North Central Association of Colleges and Schools and by the AACSB–The International Association for Management Education. A private, nonprofit institution, it is the oldest graduate management school in the United States devoted exclusively to the education of college graduates for international careers.

Applying

Students may enter in the summer, fall, winterim, or spring terms. Complete application files include GMAT scores, TOEFL scores from non-native English speakers, official transcripts from undergraduate and graduate institutions, a personal essay, and three letters of reference; all documents must be received for review six months before the desired entrance date. The minimum TOEFL score for consideration is 500.

Correspondence and Information

Director of Admissions
Thunderbird, The American Graduate School of
International Management
15249 North 59th Avenue
Glendale, Arizona 85306
Telephone: 602-978-7100
Fax: 602-439-5432
E-mail: tbird@t-bird.edu

Thunderbird, The American Graduate School of International Management

THE FACULTY

International Studies

Glenn R. Fong, Associate Professor of International Studies; Ph.D., Cornell. Ameritech Research Fellow, University of Illinois Institute of Government and Public Affairs; Advanced International Research Fellow, Social Science Research Council and American Council of Learned Societies; Consultant, U.S. Congress, Office of Technology Assessment; Post-Doctoral Research Fellow, Graduate School of Business Administration, Harvard University; Author, *Export Dependence Versus the New Protectionism: Trade Policy in the Industrial World, Federal Support for Industrial Technology: Lessons from the VHSIC and VLSI Programs*; Articles in *The Political Economy of Defense: Issues & Implications* and *Comparative Politics*.

Llewellyn D. Howell, Professor and Department Chairman; Ph.D., Syracuse. Fulbright Scholar, National Institute of Public Administration, Malaysia; International Affairs Editor, *USA Today Magazine;* Coeditor, *International Education: The Unfinished Agenda* and *Malaysian Foreign Policy: Issues and Perspectives;* Editor, *International Studies Notes;* Author, *Papers on Political Risk Analysis;* articles in *International Organization, International Studies Quarterly, Asian Studies, Journal of Southeast Asian Studies, International Interactions,* and others.

Robert T. Moran, Professor; Ph.D., Minnesota. Coauthor, *Managing Cultural Differences, Managing Cultural Synergy,* and *Dynamics of Successful International Business Negotiations;* Author, *So You're Going Abroad; Are You Prepared?, Getting Your Yen's Worth: How to Negotiate with Japan, Inc., Venturing Abroad in Asia,* and *International Management's Cultural Guide to Europe;* Senior Editor, *Global Business Management for the 1990's.*

Karen S. Walch, Assistant Professor; Ph.D., Wisconsin. Senior Researcher and Writer for UW-Madison International Studies and Programs' Studies in Conflict Resolution Series; Author, "International Approaches to Dispute Resolution in International Business" in *Global Business Management in the 1990s;* "Caribbean Basin/U.S. Public and Private Sector Dialogue and Problem Solving Processes" in *Caribbean Affairs;* and "In Search of Caribbean Basin 'Sociocentric' Self Interest" in *Caribbean Basin New Pathways;* Editor, "International Conflict Cases in Central America" in *Community and Change.*

Yahia H. Zoubir, Associate Professor of International Studies; Ph.D., American. Former Assistant Professor, The American University, The American College of Switzerland, and the American Graduate School of Business; Coeditor and main contributor, *International Dimensions of the Western Sahara Conflict*; Articles in *Journal of Third World Studies, Canadian Journal of History, The Middle East Journal, Arab Studies Quarterly,* and others.

Modern Languages

Andrew C. Chang, Professor of Chinese and Japanese; M.A., Seton Hall. Master translator, Taiwan Telecommunications Administration; Specialist, Tourism Council, Republic of China; Author, *A Handbook of Business Writings in Japanese* and *A Thesaurus of Japanese Mimesis and Onomatopoeia.*

Christine Uber Grosse, Professor of Spanish; Ph.D., North Carolina. Coauthor, *Business Communication and Culture, Directory of Foreign Language Teacher Preparation Programs in the U.S.; BSOL Strategies for Content Area Teaching: Study Guide for the Telecourse; Case Studies in International Business.* Author of numerous book chapters, articles, and papers. Editorial Board Member, *College BSL.*

Leon F. Kenman, Associate Professor of English as a Second Language; Ph.D., USC. Acting Head of the Department of Slavonic and Oriental Studies, University of Victoria, Canada; Author, *Oral English Lessons for Lao Speakers: Dialogs and Drills*; Coauthor, *English for Lao Speakers; Vocabulary, Conversational and Written English.*

Kay Lewis Mittnik, Assistant Professor of German; Ph.D., Rice. Conference translator for Austrian Ministries of Finance and Education, IAEA, UNIDO, and other UN organizations; Austrian government grantee.

J. Donovan Penrose, Associate Professor of German; M.B.A., Washington (Seattle); Ph.D., Stanford. Training Instructor of German, Defense Language Institute. Instructor, Universität Tübingen (Germany).

Walter Vladimir Tuman, Associate Professor of Russian; Ph.D., Georgetown. Director, Foreign Language Laboratory, Louisiana State University; Education Specialist, Defense Language Institute; Coeditor, *Computer-Aided Language Learning Bibliography..*

Jorge Valdivieso, Professor of Spanish; Ph.D., Arizona State. Legal Advisor, Government of Ecuador; Consul of Ecuador for Arizona; Coauthor, *Negocios y communicaciones,* Studia Hispanico Medievalia.

Carmen Vega-Carney, Associate Professor of Spanish; Ph.D., Iowa; postdoctoral fellow, Harvard, Oxford; NEH postdoctoral fellowships, Yale, Texas at Austin, Arizona State.

World Business

M. Edgar Barrett, Distinguished Professor of Policy and Control and Vice President for Executive Education; Ph.D., Stanford. Editor, Financial Reporting Section and Small Sample Studies Section, *The Accounting Review;* Editorial Board Member, *Journal of International Business Studies* and *Petroleum Management;* Author, *Management Strategy in the Oil and Gas Industry—Cases and Readings;* Editor, *Case Problems in Management Accounting* (first and second editions).

Kenneth R. Ferris, Distinguished Professor of World Business; Ph.D., Ohio State. Editor, *Behavioral Research in Accounting Journal* and *How to Understand Financial Statements.* Author, *Financial Accounting and Corporate Reporting: A Casebook;* Coauthor, *Corporate Financial Reporting and Financial Accounting and Reporting.*

Robert E. Grosse, Professor of International Business and Department Chairman; Ph.D., North Carolina. Author, *Foreign Exchange Black Markets in Latin America; Technology Transfer in Services to Latin America; Multinationals in Latin America;* Editor and Coauthor, *Private Sector Solutions to the Latin American Debt Crises.*

Roy A. Herberger Jr., Professor and President; Ph.D., Colorado. Chairman, Arizona Joint Legislative Study Committee on International Trade; Chairman, International Committee, Greater Phoenix Economic Council; Member, American Management Association International Council; Member, Board of Directors, International Affairs Committee, and Strategic Issues Committee, American Assembly of Collegiate Schools of Business.

Robert A. Howell, Clinical Professor of Management Accounting; D.B.A., Harvard. Clinical Professor of Management and Accounting, New York University; Assistant Professor, Harvard Business School; Senior Vice President and CFO, Schick, Inc.; Vice President, Treasurer, and CFO, General Housewares Corp.; Manager, Business Controls, RCA; President, Howell Management Corporation; Coauthor, *Cost Management for Tomorrow, Management Accounting in the New Manufacturing Environment.*

Taeho Kim, Professor of World Business; Ph.D., Colorado. Editorial Board, The International Executive. Author, *International Money and Banking* (1st and 2nd editions).

F. John Mathis, Professor and Director of Thunderbird International Banking Institute; Ph.D., Iowa. Director, First Arizona Savings and Loan; Senior Portfolio Officer, International Finance Corporation; Senior Financial Policy Analyst, the World Bank; Chief International Economist, Continental Illinois National Bank; Vice President and International Economist, Chase Manhattan Bank; Author, *Offshore Lending by U.S. Commercial Banks;* Coauthor, *Prime Cash: First Steps in Treasury Management.*

John O'Connell, C. V. Starr Professor of Insurance; Ph.D., Ohio State. Commercial Multiline Underwriter, Unigard Insurance Group; CPCU-Charter Property and Casualty Underwriter; ARM-Associate in Risk Management; AAI-accredited Advisor in Insurance.

David Ricks, Professor; Ph.D., Indiana. Former Editor-in-Chief, *Journal of International Business Studies;* Member, National Committee on International Business Education; Author, *Blunders in International Business;* Coauthor, *International Business: An Introduction* and *Directory of Foreign Manufacturers in the United States.*

Bodo B. Schlegelmilch, Professor of World Business; Ph.D., Manchester Institute of Science and Technology. Author, *Advances in Business Marketing, Export Development and Promotion: The Role of Public Organizations,* and *New Perspectives on International Marketing.*

Michael W. Woolverton, Continental Grain Professor of Agribusiness; Ph.D., Missouri. Venture and Acquisition Analyst, Cargill, Inc.; Field Sales Representative, Geigy Agricultural Chemical Company; Author, *Marketing in Agribusiness, Cases in Agribusiness Management,* and *Computer Concepts for Agribusiness;* Managing Editor, *Agribusiness: An International Journal.*

THE UNIVERSITY OF MEMPHIS

Fogelman College of Business and Economics
International Master of Business Administration

Program of Study

The International Master of Business Administration (IMBA) Program at the University of Memphis is designed to prepare future managers to meet the challenges of working in a global environment. The IMBA program involves two years of continuous study that provide students with training in business administration while they gain proficiency in a second language. In the case of non-U.S. citizens, English is considered the second language. The program enables students to acquire sensitivity to cultural differences and knowledge of geographic area studies (culture, history, geography, and politics of Asia, Europe, and North and Latin America) via a summer or semester of study abroad (for U.S. citizens). Non-U.S. citizens take similar courses at the University of Memphis. All students may select from among a variety of electives that allow them to develop a functional specialization in business administration.

In addition to course work, IMBA students complete an internship with a company located in a country corresponding to their second language. The duration of this full-time internship is about four months. Students return in the spring to complete a final semester of studies and receive their degree. Students who are U.S. citizens work abroad in Chinese-, Japanese-, French-, German-, or Spanish-speaking countries. Non-U.S. citizens intern in the U.S.

Research Facilities

The IMBA program's offices are located in the Wang Center for International Business on the main campus of the University of Memphis in Memphis, Tennessee. A new IMBA classroom facility is wired to the Internet, allowing for real-time case research, and is equipped for multimedia instruction and presentations. Student computer laboratories support a broad range of research applications in business and international studies.

Financial Aid

Students admitted to the IMBA program may apply for a research assistantship that provides a monthly stipend and a waiver of tuition during the fall and spring semesters. All students pay regular tuition during the summer semester. Assistantships are granted on the basis of program need and student merit. Other sources of aid are coordinated through the Office of Students Aid at the University.

Cost of Study

The 1998–99 tuition is estimated at $1529 for in-state residents and $3942 for out-of-state students. Tuition and fees are set by the Tennessee Board of Regents and are subject to change. A nonrefundable program fee of $3000 per year is required to be paid at the beginning of the first and second years of study by all IMBA students.

Living and Housing Costs

In addition to living expenses while attending the University of Memphis, IMBA students are responsible for all costs during their internship, including domestic and international travel. The internship company may help defray some of the student's internship expenses.

Student Group

Admission to the IMBA program is limited and selective. A typical student is in his or her mid- to late twenties, is bilingual, is an experienced international traveler, and has two to five years of business or professional experience. While the number varies from year to year, about 60 percent of IMBA students are U.S. citizens. Of the international students, about half are from Asia and the Middle East, one fourth are from Europe, and one fourth are from Latin America.

Location

The University of Memphis is located in the heart of Memphis, Tennessee, a cosmopolitan city of more than 1 million. Situated on the Mississippi River, Memphis is home to many international corporations, including Federal Express and International Paper. With the largest cargo airport in the world, Memphis is known as "America's Distribution Center".

The University

The Wang Center for International Business at the University of Memphis is one of only twenty-five locations designated by the U.S. Department of Education as Centers of International Business Education and Research (CIBER). The purpose of the CIBER at the University of Memphis is to offer programs and services to help business personnel face the challenges of international business. The IMBA program helps fulfill this mission by providing a specialized program of international business education, foreign language training, and geographic area studies.

Applying

Applicants to the IMBA program must have a bachelor's degree from a U.S. university or equivalent from an international institution, a satisfactory GPA, an admissible score on the Graduate Management Admission Test (GMAT), and the equivalence of junior-level college proficiency in their chosen foreign language. Non-U.S. citizens must provide an acceptable score on the TOEFL. Although a business degree is not required, certain background courses in business and statistics are required.

Correspondence and Information

IMBA Program Coordinator
Wang Center for International Business
Fogelman Executive Center, Suite 220
The University of Memphis
Memphis, Tennessee 38152-6482
Telephone: 901-678-2038
Fax: 901-678-3678
E-mail: ptaylor@cc.memphis.edu
World Wide Web: http://imba.memphis.edu

The University of Memphis

THE FACULTY

School of Accountancy
Surendra Agrawal, Ph.D., Florida; Kenneth Lambert, Ph.D., Arkansas; Craig Langstraat, LL.M., San Diego; James Lukawitz, Ph.D., Florida State; John Malloy, Ph.D., LSU; Peter McMickle, Ph.D., Alabama; Michael Shields, Ph.D., Pittsburgh; David Spiceland, Ph.D., Arkansas.

Economics
Pinaki Bose, Ph.D., SUNY at Buffalo; Cyril Chang, Ph.D., Virginia; David Ciscel, Ph.D., Houston; Coldwell Daniel III, Ph.D., Virginia; Thomas Depperschmidt, Ph.D., Texas at Austin; Richard Evans, Ph.D., Missouri; Kwok-Kwan Fung, Ph.D., Harvard; John Gnuschke, Ph.D., Missouri; Michael Gootzeit, Ph.D., Purdue; Julia Heath, Ph.D., South Carolina; David Kemme, Ph.D., Ohio State; Albert Okunade, Ph.D., Arkansas; Rose Rubin, Ph.D., Kansas State; William Smith, Ph.D., Virginia; Donald Wells, Ph.D., USC; Shelley White-Means, Ph.D., Northwestern.

Finance, Insurance and Real Estate
Quentin Chu, Ph.D., Illinois; Kee Chung, Ph.D., Cincinnati; Gaylon Grer, Ph.D., Colorado; Phillip Kolbe, Ph.D., Arizona; Thomas McInish, Ph.D., Pittsburgh; Michael McNamara, Ph.D., Nebraska; Larry Moore, J.D., Washington (St. Louis); Stephen Pruitt, Ph.D., Florida State; C. S. Pyun, Ph.D., Georgia; Yiuman Tse, Ph.D., LSU; Robert Wood, Ph.D., Pittsburgh.

Management
Rabi Bhagat, Ph.D., Illinois; Lillian Chaney, Ed.D., Tennessee; Carol Danehower, D.B.A., Kentucky; Peter Davis, Ph.D., South Carolina; Irene Duhaime, Ph.D., Pittsburgh; John Gilmore, Ph.D., Oklahoma; Coy Jones, Ph.D., Oklahoma; Banwari Kedia, Ph.D., Case Western Reserve; Thomas Miller, Ph.D., Ohio State; Robert Renn, Ph.D., Georgia State; Robert Taylor, Ph.D., LSU; Howard Tu, Ph.D., Massachusetts; Peter Wright, Ph.D., LSU.

Management Information Systems and Decision Sciences
Mohammad Amini, Ph.D., SMU; Lloyd Brooks, Ed.D., Tennessee; Charles Campbell, Ph.D., Texas at Austin; Mark Frolick, Ph.D., Georgia; Mark Gillenson, Ph.D., Ohio State; Wade Jackson, Ph.D., Texas A&M; Brian Janz, Ph.D., Minnesota; Satish Mehra, Ph.D., Georgia; Ravinder Nath, Ph.D., Texas Tech; Ernest Nichols, Ph.D., Michigan State; Prashant Palvia, Ph.D., Minnesota; Donna Retzlaff-Roberts, Ph.D., Cincinnati; Judith Simon, Ed.D., Oklahoma State; Michael Vineyard, Ph.D., Cincinnati; James Wetherbe, Ph.D., Texas Tech; Ronald Wilkes, Ph.D., Minnesota; Steven Zeltmann, Ph.D., Florida State.

Marketing
C. L. Abercrombie, Ph.D., Illinois; Emin Babakus, Ph.D., Alabama; Robert Berl, Ph.D., Georgia State; Gregory Boller, Ph.D., Penn State; Alan Bush, Ph.D., LSU; Robert Bush, Ph.D., LSU; Bettina Cornwell, Ph.D., Texas at Austin; O. C. Ferrell, Ph.D., LSU; Thomas Ingram, Ph.D., Georgia State; George Lucas, Ph.D., Missouri; James Rakowski, Ph.D., Columbia; Patrick Schul, Ph.D., Texas A&M; Daniel Sherrell, Ph.D., South Carolina.

Department of Foreign Languages and Literature
Ralph Albanese, Ph.D., Yale; Fernando Burgos, Ph.D., Florida; Jeffrey Burkhart, Ph.D., Wisconsin–Madison; Stephane Charitos, Ph.D., North Carolina; Leo Connolly, Ph.D., NYU; Martine Danan, Ph.D., Michigan Tech; Mary Fenwick, Ph.D., Minnesota; Jose Freire, Ph.D., Michigan; Sharon Harwood-Gordon, Ph.D., Tulane; Susan Johnson, Ph.D., Indiana; Dragan Kujundzic, Ph.D., USC; Felipe Lapuente, Ph.D., St. Louis; Monika Nenon, Ph.D., Freiburg (Germany); David Patterson, Ph.D., Cornell; Nicholas Rokas, Ph.D., Missouri; William Thompson, Ph.D., Cornell; Antonio Torres-Alcala, Ph.D., Catholic University; Francisco Vivar, Ph.D., UCLA.

Department of English
Mary Battle, Ed.D., Memphis State; Theron Britt, Ph.D., California, Irvine; Thomas Carlson, Ph.D., Rutgers; Barbara Ching, Ph.D., Duke; Marvin Ching, Ph.D., Florida State; Patricia Connors, Ph.D., Detroit; John Duvall, Ph.D., Illinois; Charles Hall, Ph.D., Florida; Mary MacNealy, Ph.D., Carnegie Mellon; Catherine Martin, Ph.D., California, Santa Cruz; Reginald Martin, Ph.D., Tulsa; Bruce Maylath, Ph.D., Minnesota; Christina Murphy, Ph.D., Connecticut; William O'Donnell, Ph.D., Princeton; Gordon Osing, M.F.A., Arkansas; Gene Plunka, Ph.D., Maryland; Thomas Russell, Ph.D., Kansas; Naseeb Shaheen, Ph.D., UCLA; Brett Singer, M.A., Stanford; Bruce Speck, Ph.D., Nebraska–Lincoln; Emily Thrush, Ph.D., Georgia State; Cynthia Tucker, Ph.D., Iowa; Jennifer Wagner, Ph.D., Yale; Daniel Willbanks, Ph.D., Texas at Austin; Helen Wussow, Ph.D., Oxford.

Department of Geography
Devlin Fung, Ph.D., Georgia; Scott Kirsch, Ph.D., Illinois; Hsiang-te Kung, Ph.D., Tennessee; John Kupfer, Ph.D., Iowa.

Department of Political Science
Glen Chafetz, Ph.D., Virginia; Joy Clay, Ph.D., Virginia Tech; David Cox, Ph.D., Indiana; Greer Gay, Ph.D., South Carolina; Paul Hagner, Ph.D., Indiana; Kenneth Holland, Ph.D., Chicago; William Marty, Ph.D., Duke; Thomas Mason, Ph.D., Georgia; Dorothy Norris-Tirrell, Ph.D., Florida International; Robin Quinn, Ph.D., Memphis State; Winsor Schmidt, LL.M., Virginia.

UNIVERSITY OF SOUTH CAROLINA

College of Business Administration
Master of International Business Studies Program

Program of Study

The Master of International Business Studies (M.I.B.S.) program at the University of South Carolina prepares men and women for positions with multinational companies and organizations. The M.I.B.S. program offers a truly international curriculum in business administration. The development of foreign language skills and cultural sensitivity necessary for international business careers is an essential and required portion of the program. In addition, all students complete a five- to six-month corporate internship assignment in a location other than their native country. The M.I.B.S. program may be taken on a full-time basis only, with classes beginning each May.

Except for the three-year specializations in Chinese and Japanese, the M.I.B.S. program involves two years of continuous study divided into six phases, taken in the following sequence: intensive language training in French, German, Italian, Portuguese, Russian, or Spanish; integrated courses in business fundamentals and their international dimensions, designed specifically for the program; area studies course work; business language training at the University of South Carolina and at an overseas institute; an overseas internship; and an integrative course in strategic management of the multinational firm, emphasizing policy formulation and corporate planning; elective specialization courses are also taken.

The internship phase of the M.I.B.S. program occurs in the second year of study and allows students to apply their business and language skills to real-life situations. U.S. citizens intern in a country that uses the foreign language they have studied. Internships are currently offered in Belgium, Brazil, China, France, Germany, Italy, Japan, Russia, Switzerland, Spain, and several Spanish-speaking countries in Latin America. Non-U.S. citizens follow essentially the same six phases of study except for the following: In the first summer, students take either business courses or supplemental English-language courses. In the second summer, non-U.S. citizens take a specialty course on U.S. government and geography and have an opportunity to take additional courses in business before beginning their internships in the United States.

The M.I.B.S. program also offers specializations in Chinese and Japanese for U.S. citizens. All are full-time programs that normally require three years to complete. Students spend about half their time abroad polishing their business language skills; taking courses in government, history, and culture; and completing their internship. Because of the special nature of the Chinese and Japanese tracks, applicants should contact the M.I.B.S. office for specific details.

Research Facilities

The program's offices and classrooms are located on the Columbia campus. The complex offers the most modern environment for intensive course work and research. The College has a large open-systems network comprising multiple Novell and UNIX servers with 650 clients and 32 billion characters of online storage.

Financial Aid

M.I.B.S. students are eligible to apply for graduate assistantships, which pay a minimum of $2000 for one academic year only and lead to a special tuition rate. Awards require 10 hours of work per week. M.I.B.S. students are also eligible for a number of fellowships.

Cost of Study

In 1998–99, tuition is $1862 per semester for in-state students and $3817 per semester for out-of-state students. M.I.B.S. students must also pay a nonrefundable program fee in the first year of $5000 for in-state students and $8800 for out-of-state students. Tuition and fees are set by the Board of Trustees and subject to change.

Living and Housing Costs

In addition to living expenses while attending USC, students are responsible for all internship costs, including domestic and international travel. The internship company may make a contribution toward defraying the student's living expenses abroad.

Student Group

Total program enrollment is approximately 318. M.I.B.S. students come from throughout the United States and many other countries. Approximately one fifth of each class is composed of international students. The average GMAT score of U.S. nationals in the M.I.B.S. class of 1997 was 611; the average undergraduate GPA was 3.3.

Student Outcomes

Fortune 500 companies, other large national and multinational corporations, small- to medium-size companies, government agencies, and not-for-profit organizations actively recruit graduates from the College's M.I.B.S. program. Recent M.I.B.S. graduates have been employed by companies such as Andersen Consulting (management consulting), BMW (operations management), Credit Suisse (investment banking), Eli Lilly (marketing), General Electric (product management), Policy Management Systems (information systems), Robert Bosch (manufacturing), and Coca-Cola (finance).

Location

Serving a metropolitan area of approximately 472,000 people, the Columbia community offers a variety of cultural and religious activities. For recreation, there are a variety of city and state parks, the acclaimed Riverbanks Zoo, and Lake Murray. Within a few hours' time, one can reach varied activities ranging from the nightlife of Atlanta to Hilton Head and the coastal beaches to the ski resorts of North Carolina.

The University

Founded in 1801, the University is a state-supported coeducational institution. During the last several decades, the University has manifested a strong commitment to graduate and professional education. With more than 9,000 students now enrolled in graduate work, a highly regarded Law School, and a School of Medicine, the University has assumed a place among the major graduate institutions in the nation.

Applying

To be considered for the M.I.B.S. program, candidates must have graduated from a four-year college or university and must submit application forms, two letters of recommendation, and Graduate Management Admission Test scores. No specific prior course work or major is required for admission, although course work in languages, business, and economics is helpful as is work experience. International students must submit TOEFL scores of 550 or better. Entry into the program is based on each individual's background. Two years of work experience is preferred but not required. Entry in January is not permitted. Applications for assistantships and fellowships must be postmarked by February 1 for prime consideration.

Correspondence and Information

Graduate Division, PG98
College of Business Administration
University of South Carolina
Columbia, South Carolina 29208

Telephone: 803-777-4346
Fax: 803-777-0414
E-mail: mibs@darla.badm.sc.edu
World Wide Web: http://www.business.sc.edu

University of South Carolina

THE FACULTY

College of Business Administration
Jeffrey S. Arpan, Professor; D.B.A., Indiana, 1971.
Timothy S. Doupnik, Professor; Ph.D., Illinois, 1983.
Kirk D. Fiedler, Associate Professor; Ph.D., Pittsburgh, 1991.
William R. Folks Jr., Professor; D.B.A., Harvard, 1970.
Kent W. Hargis, Assistant Professor; Ph.D., Illinois at Urbana-Champaign, 1995.
Kirk R. Karwan, Associate Professor; Ph.D., Carnegie Mellon, 1979.
William J. Kettinger, Assistant Professor; Ph.D., South Carolina, 1992.
B. F. Kiker, Professor; Ph.D., Tulane, 1965.
Tatiana Kostova, Assistant Professor; Ph.D., Minnesota, 1996.
James A. Kuhlman, Professor; Ph.D., Northwestern, 1971.
Chun-Yau Kwok, Professor; Ph.D., Texas at Austin, 1984.
Gary A. Luoma, Professor; D.B.A., Washington (St. Louis), 1966.
Thomas J. Madden, Associate Professor; Ph.D., Massachusetts, 1982.
Manoj K. Malhotra, Associate Professor; Ph.D., Ohio State, 1990.
Steven V. Mann, Associate Professor; Ph.D., Nebraska, 1987.
John H. McDermott, Associate Professor; Ph.D., Brown, 1979.
R. Bruce Money, Assistant Professor; Ph.D., California, Irvine, 1995.
William T. Moore, Professor; Ph.D., Virginia Tech, 1982.
Douglas W. Nigh, Associate Professor; Ph.D., UCLA, 1981.
Dennis H. Oberhelman, Associate Professor; Ph.D., Purdue, 1978.
Richard B. Robinson, Professor; Ph.D., Georgia, 1980.
Robert J. Rolfe, Professor; Ph.D., Oklahoma, 1983.
Kendall Roth, Professor; Ph.D., South Carolina, 1966.
Martin S. Roth, Associate Professor; Ph.D., Pittsburgh, 1990.
E. Elisabet Rutstrom, Associate Professor; Ph.D., Stockholm School of Economics (Sweden), 1990.
David Schweiger, Professor; Ph.D., Maryland, 1980.
Terence A. Shimp, Professor; D.B.A., Maryland, 1974.
James T. C. Teng, Associate Professor; Ph.D., Minnesota, 1980.
Hoyt N. Wheeler, Professor; Ph.D., Wisconsin–Madison, 1974.

Foreign Language Studies
Charles J. Alber, Associate Professor; Ph.D., Indiana, 1971.
Alfredo Alsiando Bernal, Associate Professor; Ph.D., Indiana, 1964.
William F. Edmiston, Professor; Ph.D., Indiana, 1978.
Charlotte Elfe, Instructor; M.A., Massachusetts Amherst, 1966.
Wolfgang D. Elfe, Professor; Ph.D., Massachusetts, 1970.
Ursula Engelbrecht, Instructor; M.A., South Carolina, 1991.
T. Bruce Fryer, Professor; Ph.D., Texas at Austin, 1970.
Rita M. Gardiol, Professor; Ph.D., Indiana, 1968.
Antonio Di Giacomantonio, Senior Instructor; M.A., Rutgers, 1969.
Carla Grimes, Senior Instructor; M.A., South Carolina, 1989.
Ramona Lagos, Associate Professor; Ph.D., Arizona, 1982.
M. Angelica Gulmaraes Lopes, Associate Professor; Ph.D., Wisconsin–Madison, 1980.
Celso de Oliveira, Professor; Ph.D., South Carolina, 1976.
Faust Pauluzzi, Assistant Professor; Ph.D., Rutgers, 1980.
Margit Resch, Professor; Ph.D., Illinois, 1974.
Yoshitaka Sakakibara, Associate Professor; Ph.D., USC, 1984.
Elena Schmitt, Instructor; M.A., West Virginia, 1993.
Wiebke Strehl, Assistant Professor; Ph.D., Penn State, 1982.
Graciela Tissera, Assistant Professor; Ph.D., Pennsylvania, 1992.
Tan Ye, Assistant Professor; Ph.D., Washington (St. Louis), 1991.

Department of Geography
Patricia P. Gilmartin, Professor; Ph.D., Kansas, 1980.
Robert L. Janiskee, Associate Professor; Ph.D., Illinois, 1972.
Julian V. Minghi, Professor; Ph.D., Washington (Seattle), 1962.

Department of Government and International Studies
Kristia M. Finnigan, Research Assistant Professor; Ph.D., Georgetown, 1991.
D. Bruce Marshall, Professor; Ph.D., Yale, 1966.
Jerel Rosati, Associate Professor; Ph.D., American, 1982.
Gordon B. Smith, Professor; Ph.D., Indiana, 1976.

UNIVERSITY OF SOUTHERN CALIFORNIA

Marshall School of Business
IBEAR MBA Program

Program of Study

With emphasis on global business and the Pacific Rim, USC's Marshall School of Business offers an intensive, AACSB–The International Association for Management Education-accredited M.B.A. program for mid-managers pursuing international or Pacific Rim–related business careers. The wealth of experience that participants bring to the program, its practical rather than theoretical focus, and the strength and high quality of its alumni network make the International Business Education and Research (IBEAR) Program unique in the world of M.B.A. training.

Participants in the IBEAR MBA Program complete the equivalent of two years of M.B.A. course work in just twelve months. The year begins in mid-August with a three-week transition program in microcomputing and business communication, followed by four 11-week terms of M.B.A. classes. All courses, including Management in a Global Economy, Global Marketing Strategies, International Financial Management, Global Strategic Planning, International Trade, The National and International Economy, and Business Environment and Management Practices in the Pacific Rim, emphasize international business issues.

IBEAR MBA Program participants must complete an international consulting assignment for a major global firm. They work intensely in multicultural, multispecialty teams to provide professional results for the companies that sponsor their projects. These consulting projects, combined with the teamwork required to complete many other class projects, hone not only business practice skills but also critical skills in cross-cultural communication and negotiation.

Research Facilities

USC's Crocker Business Library houses more than 100,000 volumes and 1,400 periodicals, and the main University library houses an additional 2.4 million volumes, including 18,000 serial publications. The Crocker Library offers electronic access to LEXIS/NEXIS, the major research depositories of the world, and more than 150 informational databases.

Within the business school, the Keck Management Science Center and the Instructional Services Center have more than 280 IBM PC microcomputers and computer terminals in labs and libraries. Another 75 PCs are located in classrooms. The Experiential Learning Center uses state-of-the-art video and multimedia equipment in five simulation rooms designed to improve skills in business management communication and cross-cultural negotiations. IBEAR participants and faculty members are linked at home and in the classroom by a sophisticated e-mail and Internet system that permits virtual group work and Internet communication worldwide and supports IBEAR's commitment to interactive, team-based learning.

Financial Aid

Scholarships of $10,000 to $20,000 are available to high-potential U.S. and international applicants

Cost of Study

In 1998–99, the total educational fee for the IBEAR MBA Program is $42,550. This includes $33,050 in University tuition for 56 units (nineteen courses) and $9500 for the IBEAR professional program fee. The program fee supports the orientation and transition programs; a package of preparatory material; tutorial assistance; communication consulting; special seminars and workshops; guest executive lunches; faculty research and development; dissemination of research and program news; a participant-managed social fund for participants and their families; off-campus organization business lunches, dinners, and seminars; a team-building retreat; and job search services for self-sponsored participants.

Living and Housing Costs

For a single participant, living expenses range from $1250 to $2000 per month, depending on choice of housing and transportation. Most participants live off campus in apartments. Rent for a studio, one-bedroom, or two-bedroom unfurnished apartment averages $650, $850, and $1100, respectively. IBEAR assists participants in resolving their housing needs.

Student Group

Enrollment in the IBEAR MBA Program is limited to 48 outstanding men and women interested in pursuing careers in varied aspects of international business. Participants average 33 years of age and ten years of work experience, with ages ranging from 26 to the mid-40s. Fourteen or more countries are represented in the program each year. Current participants come from Argentina, Australia, Brazil, Canada, China, Colombia, France, India, Indonesia, Japan, Korea, Peru, Singapore, Switzerland, Taiwan, and the United States. In its twenty years, IBEAR has served 734 participants from forty-six countries.

Location

The IBEAR MBA Program is housed on USC's 150-acre main campus, 3 miles south of Los Angeles' downtown business center. Los Angeles is strategically located as an American gateway to the Pacific Basin. With a population of more than 7 million and manufacturing, trade, telecommunications, and financial activities to rival many countries in both diversity and volume, the city provides an excellent venue for managers who wish to expand their international horizons.

The University and The Program

Founded in 1880, USC is the oldest and largest private university in the western United States. USC offers degrees in 204 fields of study and has eighteen professional schools. Its 28,000 students come from all fifty states and 115 countries. Current enrollment in the Marshall School of Business includes 2,700 undergraduates and 1,300 graduate students. The business school has 170 full-time faculty members.

The IBEAR MBA Program supports a University-wide strategic initiative to strengthen USC's international ties, particularly with the countries in Asia and Latin America. It serves as a focal point for the promotion of teaching and research in international business. In addition to the MBA Program, IBEAR sponsors faculty research on international business and trade and provides a variety of nondegree executive education programs at USC and abroad. IBEAR also helps coordinate the business school's relationships with international businesses, governments, and academic institutions.

Applying

Applicants must have completed their undergraduate studies and five or more years of full-time work and/or military experience. All applicants must submit official GMAT results. International applicants must also submit official TOEFL scores. Admission decisions begin in October. IBEAR follows a rolling admission procedure and reviews application files when all application materials are received. If space is available, applications are considered until June 1.

Correspondence and Information

Admissions
IBEAR MBA Program
Marshall School of Business
University of Southern California
Los Angeles, California 90089-1421

Telephone: 213-740-7140
Fax: 213-740-7559
E-mail: ibear@usc.edu

University of Southern California

THE FACULTY AND THEIR RESEARCH

Listed below are selected USC international business faculty members, many of whom teach in the IBEAR MBA Program.

Paul S. Adler, Associate Professor; Ph.D., Picardie (France). Business management and organization.
Arvind Bhambri, Associate Professor; D.B.A., Harvard. Strategy development and international technology transfer.
Philip H. Birnbaum-More, Professor; Ph.D., Washington (Seattle). Global competition, competitive strategy formulation and implementation in technology-driven markets, management of research and development.
William H. Davidson, Associate Professor; D.B.A., Harvard. High technology and international management, international business (China and Japan), management of emerging businesses.
Richard H. Dekmejian, Professor; Ph.D., Columbia. U.S. foreign policy, risk assessment, corporate leadership and multinational corporations in the Islamic world and the Pacific Rim.
J. Kimball Dietrich, Associate Professor; Ph.D., Michigan. Financial institutions and markets, corporate financial theory, value production.
Richard L. Drobnick, Associate Professor, University Vice Provost for International Affairs, and Director, Center for International Business Education and Research; Ph.D., USC. U.S. and Pacific Rim trade and economic issues.
Sam Hariharan, Assistant Professor; Ph.D., Michigan. International management and organization.
Ayse Imrohoroglu, Associate Professor; Ph.D., Minnesota. Macroeconomics and monetary economics and international trade.
Douglas H. Joines, Associate Professor; Ph.D., Chicago. International monetary economics, macroeconomics and forecasting.
Michael A. Kamins, Associate Professor; Ph.D., NYU. International advertising strategy and consumer behavior.
Edward Lawler, Professor and Director of the Center for Effective Organizations; Ph.D., Berkeley. Industrialization, productivity, and work motivation; competitive advantage of organizational structure and strategy.
Jack G. Lewis, Associate Professor and IBEAR Program Director; Ph.D., Stanford. Social and political environment of business in Asia, patterns of management training and development for international executives.
Thomas W. Lin, Professor; Ph.D., Ohio State. Management accounting controls, computer auditing and information systems.
Anthony Marino, Professor and Director, Marshall School of Business Ph.D. Program; Ph.D., California, Santa Barbara. Applied microeconomics theory, economics of regulation and industrial organization.
Morgan W. McCall, Associate Professor and Faculty Director of the USC Executive Program; Ph.D., Cornell. Leadership in organizations, international executive development, identification of high-potential managers.
Aris Protopapadakis, Professor; Ph.D., Chicago. Monetary theory and policy and international finance.
Sampath Rajagopalan, Associate Professor; Ph.D., Carnegie Mellon. Operations management.
Kathleen K. Reardon, Associate Professor; Ph.D., Massachusetts. Cross-cultural negotiation and persuasion, interpersonal communication.
Naufel J. Vilcassim, Associate Professor; Ph.D., Cornell. Quantitative approaches to marketing, consumer choice, and price promotions.
Randolph W. Westerfield, Robert Dockson Professor and Dean, Marshall School of Business; Ph.D., UCLA. Former Chairman of the University of Pennsylvania (Wharton) Department of Finance. Mergers and acquisitions, investment management and analysis.

Professor Jim Gosline, an authority on business communication, provides feedback to the participants on their management communication presentations in the Marshall School of Business Experiential Learning Center.

IBEAR MBA participants take a break on the campus of the University of Southern California.

Participants stretch their limits during IBEAR's annual team-building retreat in the mountains above Malibu.

Section 11
Logistics and Transportation Management

This section contains directories of institutions offering graduate work in logistics and transportation management, followed by in-depth entries submitted by institutions that chose to prepare detailed program descriptions. Additional information about programs listed in the directories but not augmented by an in-depth entry may be obtained by writing directly to the dean of a graduate school or chair of a department at the address given in the directory.

For programs offering related work, see also in this book Business Administration and Management.

CONTENTS

Program Directories

Announcement

Logistics

Air Force Institute of Technology, School of Systems and Logistics, Department of Logistics Management, Wright-Patterson AFB, OH 45433-7765. Awards MS. Faculty: 15 full-time (1 woman). Students: 32 full-time (7 women); includes 3 minority (2 African Americans, 1 Hispanic), 1 international. Average age 29. In 1997, 32 degrees awarded (100% found work related to degree). *Degree requirements:* Computer language, thesis required, foreign language not required. *Average time to degree:* master's–1.3 years full-time. *Entrance requirements:* GMAT (minimum score 500), minimum GPA of 2.5, must be military officer or DOD civilian. Application fee: $0. *Tuition:* $0. • Dr. Craig M. Brandt, Head, 937-255-7777 Ext. 3329. Application contact: M. Sgt. James W. Johnson, Graduate Programs Administrator, 937-255-7777 Ext. 3308.

Arizona State University, College of Business, Program in Business Administration, Tempe, AZ 85287. Offerings include supply chain management (PhD). Program faculty: 93 full-time (21 women), 10 part-time (1 woman). *Degree requirements:* Dissertation. *Application fee:* $45. *Expenses:* Tuition $2088 per year full-time, $110 per hour part-time for state residents; $9040 per year full-time, $377 per hour part-time for nonresidents. Fees $72 per year full-time, $18 per semester (minimum) part-time. • Dr. Lee R. McPheters, Associate Dean, 602-965-9377. Fax: 602-965-3368. Application contact: Judy Heilala, Director of MBA, 602-965-3331.

Colorado Technical University, Graduate Studies, Program in Management, 4435 North Chestnut Street, Colorado Springs, CO 80907-3896. Offerings include logistics management (MSM). Program faculty: 8 full-time (2 women), 8 part-time (1 woman), 12 FTE. *Average time to degree:* master's–2 years full-time. *Application deadline:* 10/4 (rolling processing; 4/5 for spring admission). *Application fee:* $100. *Expenses:* Tuition $230 per quarter hour. Fees $6 per quarter. • Dr. Mark Pieffer, Dean, 719-590-6765. Application contact: Judy Galante, Graduate Admissions, 719-590-6720. Fax: 719-598-3740.

Florida Institute of Technology, School of Extended Graduate Studies, Program in Management, Melbourne, FL 32901-6975. Offerings include logistics management (MS). *Application fee:* $50. *Tuition:* $550 per credit hour. • Application contact: Carolyn P. Farrior, Associate Dean of Graduate Admissions, 407-674-7118. Fax: 407-723-9468. E-mail: cfarrior@fit.edu.

The George Washington University, School of Business and Public Management, Department of Management Science, Program in Logistics, Operations, and Materials Management, Washington, DC 20052. Awards MBA, MPA. Part-time and evening/weekend programs available. 28 applicants, 89% accepted. In 1997, 8 degrees awarded. *Degree requirements:* Computer language required, foreign language and thesis not required. *Entrance requirements:* GMAT, TOEFL (minimum score 550). Application deadline: 4/1 (priority date; rolling processing; 10/1 for spring admission). Application fee: $45. *Expenses:* Tuition $680 per semester hour. Fees $35 per semester hour. *Financial aid:* Application deadline 4/1. • Dr. Erik K. Winslow, Chair, Department of Management Science, 202-994-7375. Application contact: Lilly Hastings, Graduate Admissions, 202-994-6584. Fax: 202-994-6382.

Georgia College and State University, College of Arts and Sciences, Department of Government and Sociology, Logistics Education Center, Milledgeville, GA 31061. Offers programs in logistics management (MSA), logistics systems (MSLS). Students: 32 full-time (5 women), 34 part-time (16 women); includes 12 minority (10 African Americans, 2 Hispanics). Average age 36. In 1997, 50 degrees awarded. *Entrance requirements:* GMAT, GRE General Test, or LSAT. Application deadline: 7/31 (priority date; rolling processing). Application fee: $10. *Financial aid:* Application deadline 4/15. • Bobby Graham, Director of External Degree Programs, 912-926-6544.

Golden Gate University, School of Business, San Francisco, CA 94105-2968. Offerings include procurement and logistics management (MS, Certificate). *Average time to degree:* master's–2.5 years full-time. *Application deadline:* 7/1 (priority date; rolling processing). *Application fee:* $55 ($70 for international students). *Tuition:* $996 per course (minimum). • Dr. Hamid Shomali, Dean, 415-442-6500. Fax: 415-442-6579. Application contact: Enrollment Services, 415-442-7800. Fax: 415-442-7807. E-mail: info@ggu.edu.

Maine Maritime Academy, Department of Graduate Studies, Program in Logistics Management, Castine, ME 04420. Awards MS, Certificate, Diploma. Part-time programs available. Faculty: 5 full-time (2 women), 11 part-time (0 women). *Degree requirements:* For master's, computer language required, thesis optional. *Entrance requirements:* For master's, GMAT or GRE General Test, TOEFL. Application deadline: rolling. Application fee: $40. Electronic applications accepted. *Expenses:* Tuition $15,750 per year. Fees $360 per year. *Financial aid:* Teaching assistantships, Federal Work-Study, institutionally sponsored loans, and career-related internships or fieldwork available. Aid available to part-time students. Financial aid applicants required to submit FAFSA. • Application contact: Carolyn J. Ulrich, Administrative Assistant, 207-326-2485. Fax: 207-326-2411. E-mail: cjulrich@bell.mma.edu.

Maine Maritime Academy, Department of Graduate Studies, Program in Maritime Management, Castine, ME 04420. Awards MS, Certificate, Diploma. Part-time programs available. Faculty: 5 full-time (2 women), 11 part-time (0 women). Students: 38; includes 14 international. Average age 30. 18 applicants, 61% accepted. In 1997, 6 master's awarded (100% found work related to degree). *Degree requirements:* For master's, computer language required, thesis optional. *Average time to degree:* master's–1 year full-time, 3 years part-time. *Entrance requirements:* For master's, GMAT or GRE General Test, TOEFL. Application deadline: rolling. Application fee: $40. *Expenses:* Tuition $15,750 per year. Fees $360 per year. *Financial aid:* 1 student received aid; teaching assistantships, Federal Work-Study, institutionally sponsored loans, and career-related internships or fieldwork available. Aid available to part-time students. Financial aid applicants required to submit FAFSA. *Faculty research:* Human resources in maritime environment, management of organization change, economic analysis and maritime law. • Application contact: Carolyn J. Ulrich, Administrative Assistant, 207-326-2485. Fax: 207-326-2411. E-mail: cjulrich@bell.mma.edu.

Maine Maritime Academy, Department of Graduate Studies, Program in Port Management, Castine, ME 04420. Awards MS, Certificate, Diploma. Part-time programs available. Faculty: 5 full-time (2 women), 11 part-time (0 women). Students: 3 full-time (0 women); includes 1 international. Average age 30. 5 applicants, 60% accepted. In 1997, 1 master's awarded. *Degree requirements:* For master's, computer language required, thesis optional. *Average time to degree:* master's–1 year full-time. *Entrance requirements:* For master's, GMAT or GRE General Test, TOEFL. Application deadline: rolling. Application fee: $40. Electronic applications accepted. *Expenses:* Tuition $15,750 per year. Fees $360 per year. *Financial aid:* 1 student received aid; teaching assistantships, Federal Work-Study, institutionally sponsored loans, and career-related internships or fieldwork available. Financial aid applicants required to submit FAFSA. • Application contact: Carolyn J. Ulrich, Administrative Assistant, 207-326-2485. Fax: 207-326-2411. E-mail: cjulrich@bell.mma.edu.

Massachusetts Institute of Technology, School of Engineering, Center for Transportation Studies, Cambridge, MA 02139-4307. Offerings include logistics (MLOG). MLOG new for fall 1998. *Application deadline:* 1/15. *Application fee:* $55. *Tuition:* $24,050 per year. • Yossi Sheffi, Director, 617-253-5316. E-mail: sheffi@mit.edu. Application contact: Sydney Miller, Student Coordinator, 617-253-8069. Fax: 617-253-4560. E-mail: tec@mit.edu.

Michigan State University, Eli Broad Graduate School of Management, Department of Management, East Lansing, MI 48824-1020. Offerings include materials and logistics management-operations management (MBA), materials and logistics management-purchasing management (MBA). Department faculty: 12 (5 women). *Entrance requirements:* GMAT (minimum score 500). Application deadline: rolling. Application fee: $30 ($40 for international students). *Expenses:* Tuition $4609 per year full-time, $223 per credit hour (minimum) part-time for state residents; $8704 per year full-time, $450 per credit hour (minimum) part-time for nonresidents. Fees $576 per year full-time, $476 per year part-time. • Dr. John Wagner III, Acting Chairperson, 517-355-1878. Fax: 517-432-1111. E-mail: wagner@pilot.msu.edu.

Michigan State University, Eli Broad Graduate School of Management, Department of Marketing and Supply Chain Management, East Lansing, MI 48824-1020. Offerings include materials and logistics management-logistics (MBA). Department faculty: 28 (2 women). *Entrance requirements:* GMAT (minimum score 530). Application deadline: 3/31 (priority date; rolling processing; 11/1 for spring admission). Application fee: $30 ($40 for international students). Electronic applications accepted. *Expenses:* Tuition $4609 per year full-time, $223 per credit hour (minimum) part-time for state residents; $8704 per year full-time, $450 per credit hour (minimum) part-time for nonresidents. Fees $576 per year full-time, $476 per year part-time. • Dr. Robert Nason, Chairperson, 517-355-2240.

Northwestern University, Division of Interdepartmental Programs, Program in Transportation, Evanston, IL 60208. Offerings include logistics and operations (MS). Admissions and degrees offered through The Graduate School. *Degree requirements:* Course-based paper required, thesis not required. *Entrance requirements:* GRE General Test, TOEFL (minimum score 550). Application deadline: 8/30 (rolling processing). Application fee: $50 ($55 for international students). *Tuition:* $20,430 per year full-time, $2424 per course part-time. • Frank S. Koppelman, Director, 847-491-2276. Application contact: Jennifer Marx-Hohmeier, Secretary, 847-491-2276. Fax: 847-491-3090. E-mail: j-marx@nwu.edu.

Pennsylvania State University University Park Campus, The Mary Jean and Frank P. Smeal College of Business Administration, MS Programs in Business Administration, Department of Business Logistics, University Park, PA 16802-1503. Awards MS. *Degree requirements:* Thesis or alternative required, foreign language not required. *Entrance requirements:* GMAT. Application fee: $40. *Expenses:* Tuition $6534 per year full-time, $276 per credit part-time for state residents; $13,460 per year full-time, $561 per credit part-time for nonresidents. Fees $252 per year (minimum) full-time, $43 per semester (minimum) part-time. • Dr. John J. Spychalski, Chairman, 814-865-1866. Application contact: Dr. Alan J. Stenger, Associate Professor, 814-865-3923.

Pennsylvania State University University Park Campus, The Mary Jean and Frank P. Smeal College of Business Administration, PhD Programs in Business Administration, Program in Management Science/Operations/Logistics, University Park, PA 16802-1503. Awards PhD. *Degree requirements:* Dissertation. *Entrance requirements:* GMAT. Application fee: $40. *Expenses:* Tuition $6534 per year full-time, $276 per credit part-time for state residents; $13,460 per year full-time, $561 per credit part-time for nonresidents. Fees $252 per year (minimum) full-time, $43 per semester (minimum) part-time. • Dr. Jack C. Hayya, Field Adviser, 814-865-1461.

Syracuse University, School of Management, Program in Transportation and Distribution Management, Syracuse, NY 13244-0003. Awards MBA. Faculty: 2. Students: 1 full-time (0 women), 3 part-time (0 women); includes 2 international. 3 applicants, 33% accepted. In 1997, 1 degree awarded. *Entrance requirements:* GMAT. Application deadline: 2/1 (rolling processing). Application fee: $40. *Tuition:* $13,320 per year full-time, $555 per credit hour part-time. *Financial aid:* Fellowships, research assistantships, teaching assistantships, partial tuition waivers, Federal Work-Study available. Financial aid application deadline: 3/1. • Frances Tucker, Director, 315-443-3523. Application contact: Associate Dean, 315-443-3850.

Texas A&M International University, Division of Business Administration, Program in International Logistics, 5201 University Boulevard, Laredo, TX 78041-1900. Awards MSIL. Part-time and evening/weekend programs available. *Entrance requirements:* GMAT or GRE General Test. Application deadline: 7/15 (priority date; rolling processing; 11/12 for spring admission). Application fee: $0.

Announcement: The Graduate School of International Trade and Business Administration's MS in International Logistics prepares a cadre of international business leaders who understand the complexities of trade and the physical movement of cargo in the global economy. Because of the University's unique location on the border of Mexico, it serves as a perfect laboratory for the study of international trade and commerce. Laredo is the country's largest commercial inland port of trade, which makes it an intermodal transportation and distribution zenith. Its air cargo service into Latin America is one of the top 10 cargo handling centers in the US. Student exchange programs that allow students to study in other countries while earning credit are also available with France, Germany, Mexico, and Costa Rica.

Universidad del Turabo, Programs in Business Administration, Program in Logistics and Materials Management, Gurabo, PR 00778-3030. Awards MBA. Part-time and evening/weekend programs available. *Entrance requirements:* GRE, PAEG, interview. Application deadline: 8/5. Application fee: $25.

University of Arkansas, College of Business Administration, Department of Transportation and Logistics Management, Fayetteville, AR 72701-1201. Awards MTLM. Program new for fall 1998. *Tuition:* $3144 per year full-time, $173 per credit hour part-time for state residents; $7140 per year full-time, $395 per credit hour part-time for nonresidents. • Dr. Tom Jensen, Chair, 501-575-4055.

University of British Columbia, Faculty of Commerce and Business Administration, Program in Business Administration, Vancouver, BC V6T 1Z2, Canada. Offerings include transport and logistics (M Sc). *Degree requirements:* Thesis required (for some programs), foreign language not required. *Average time to degree:* master's–2 years full-time. *Entrance requirements:* GMAT (average 620), TOEFL (minimum score 600). Application fee: $100.

University of Minnesota, Twin Cities Campus, Carlson School of Management, Department of Marketing and Logistics Management, Minneapolis, MN 55455-0213. Awards MBA, PhD. MBA offered jointly with the Master's Program in Business Administration; PhD offered jointly with the Doctoral Program in Business Administration. *Degree requirements:* For doctorate, dissertation required, foreign language not required. *Entrance requirements:* GMAT. *Faculty research:* Consumer behavior, new product development, supply chain management, brand management.

University of New Haven, School of Business, Program in Business Administration, West Haven, CT 06516-1916. Offerings include international business logistics (MBA). *Degree requirements:* Thesis or alternative required, foreign language not required. *Application deadline:* rolling. *Application fee:* $50. *Expenses:* Tuition $1125 per course. Fees $13 per trimester. • Dr. Omid Nodoushani, Coordinator, 203-932-7123.

University of New Haven, School of Engineering and Applied Science, Program in Industrial Engineering, West Haven, CT 06516-1916. Offerings include logistics (Certificate). *Application deadline:* rolling. *Application fee:* $50. *Expenses:* Tuition $1125 per course. Fees $13 per trimester. • Dr. Ali Montazer, Coordinator, 203-932-7050.

University of Tennessee, Knoxville, College of Business Administration, Program in Business Administration, Knoxville, TN 37996. Offerings include logistics and transportation (MBA, PhD). MS/MBA offered jointly with the College of Engineering. Postbaccalaureate distance learning degree programs offered. Program faculty: 51 full-time (6 women). *Degree requirements:* For doctorate, computer language, dissertation required, foreign language not required. *Entrance requirements:* For doctorate, GMAT, TOEFL (minimum score 550), minimum GPA of 2.7. Application deadline: 2/1 (priority date). Application fee: $35. Electronic applications accepted. *Tuition:* $3354 per year full-time, $181 per semester hour part-time for state residents; $8410 per year full-time, $462 per semester hour part-time for nonresidents. • Dr. Gary Dicer,

Director, 423-974-5033. E-mail: gdicer@utk.edu. Application contact: Donald Potts, Graduate Representative, 423-974-5033. Fax: 423-974-3826. E-mail: dpotts@utk.edu.

University of Wisconsin–Madison, School of Business, Program in Distribution Management, Madison, WI 53706-1380. Awards MBA, MS. Part-time programs available. Faculty: 13 full-time (3 women). Students: 21 full-time (3 women); includes 1 minority (African American), 1 international. Average age 28. 25 applicants, 52% accepted. In 1997, 12 degrees awarded. *Average time to degree:* master's–2 years full-time. *Entrance requirements:* GMAT (minimum score 600; average 650), 3 years of work experience, minimum GPA of 3.0. Application deadline: 6/1 (rolling processing; 10/1 for spring admission). Application fee: $45. *Tuition:* $5950 per year full-time, $1118 per semester (minimum) part-time for state residents; $16,230 per year full-time, $3044 per semester (minimum) part-time for nonresidents. *Financial aid:* In 1997–98, 18 students received aid, including 7 fellowships (4 to first-year students) averaging $700 per month and totaling $45,000; research assistantships, teaching assistantships, project assistantships, Federal Work-Study, institutionally sponsored loans, and career-related internships or fieldwork also available. Aid available to part-time students. *Faculty research:* Franchises, strategic marketing management, channels of distribution, legal aspects of marketing. • Dr. John R. Nevin, Director, 608-262-8912. Fax: 608-263-0477. E-mail: jnevin@bus.wisc.edu. Application contact: Lisa Urban, Director of Master's Marketing and Recruiting, 608-262-4610. Fax: 608-265-4192.

Wright State University, College of Business and Administration, Department of Management Science and Information Systems, Dayton, OH 45435. Offerings include logistics management (MBA, MS). *Degree requirements:* Computer language required, foreign language and thesis not required. *Entrance requirements:* GMAT, TOEFL (minimum score 550), minimum AACSB index of 1000. Application fee: $25. *Tuition:* $5109 per year full-time, $161 per credit hour part-time for state residents; $9039 per year full-time, $282 per credit hour part-time for nonresidents. • Dr. Barbara Denison, Chair, 937-775-2895. Application contact: James Crawford, Director of Graduate Programs, 937-775-2437. Fax: 937-775-3301.

Transportation Management

Arizona State University, Interdisciplinary Program in Transportation Systems, Tempe, AZ 85287. Awards Certificate. Students must be enrolled in an appropriate degree program. Program new for fall 1998. *Application fee:* $45. *Expenses:* Tuition $2088 per year full-time, $110 per hour part-time for state residents; $9040 per year full-time, $377 per hour part-time for nonresidents. Fees $72 per year full-time, $18 per semester (minimum) part-time. • Dr. Mary Kihl, Director, 602-965-6693.

Arizona State University East, College of Technology and Applied Sciences, Department of Aeronautical Management Technology, Mesa, AZ 85206-0903. Awards MT. Part-time and evening/weekend programs available. Faculty: 4 full-time (0 women), 4 part-time (1 woman). Students: 3 full-time (1 woman), 4 part-time (1 woman); includes 1 minority (Hispanic), 3 international. Average age 30. 6 applicants, 83% accepted. *Degree requirements:* Applied project. *Application deadline:* rolling. *Application fee:* $45. *Expenses:* Tuition $110 per credit hour for state residents; $377 per credit hour for nonresidents. Fees $72 per year. *Financial aid:* In 1997–98, 6 students received aid, including 3 research assistantships averaging $930 per month, 3 graduate assistantships averaging $930 per month; full and partial tuition waivers, Federal Work-Study, and career-related internships or fieldwork also available. Financial aid applicants required to submit FAFSA. *Faculty research:* Approach lighting, cooperative and collaborative learning, distance education, human factors, situation awareness. Total annual research expenditures: $425,000. • Dr. William K. McCurry, Chair, 602-727-1998. Fax: 602-727-1730. E-mail: mccurry@asu.edu. Application contact: C. Vinette Cowart, Director of Academic Services, 602-727-1028. Fax: 602-727-1876. E-mail: asueast@asu.edu.

Concordia University, Faculty of Commerce and Administration, Montréal, PQ H3G 1M8, Canada. Offerings include business administration (Aviation MBA), with option in airline and aviation. *Application fee:* $30. *Expenses:* Tuition $56 per credit (minimum) for Canadian residents; $249 per credit (minimum) for nonresidents. Fees $152 per year full-time, $111 per year (minimum) part-time. • Dr. M. Anvari, Dean, 514-848-2700. Fax: 514-848-4502. Application contact: Dale Doreen, Director, 514-848-2958. Fax: 514-848-4208.

Delta State University, School of Business, Department of Commercial Aviation, Cleveland, MS 38733-0001. Awards MCA. Part-time programs available. Faculty: 3 full-time (0 women), 1 part-time (0 women), 3.75 FTE. Students: 4 full-time (1 woman), 1 part-time (0 women); includes 2 minority (1 African American, 1 Hispanic). Average age 29. 2 applicants, 100% accepted. In 1997, 2 degrees awarded. *Degree requirements:* Thesis or alternative required, foreign language not required. *Entrance requirements:* GMAT (minimum score 380). Application deadline: 8/1 (priority date; rolling processing). Application fee: $0. *Tuition:* $2596 per year full-time, $121 per semester hour part-time for state residents; $5546 per year full-time, $285 per semester hour part-time for nonresidents. *Financial aid:* Research assistantships, Federal Work-Study, institutionally sponsored loans, and career-related internships or fieldwork available. Aid available to part-time students. Financial aid application deadline: 6/1. • Tommy Sledge, Chairperson, 601-846-4205. Application contact: Dr. John Thornell, Dean of Graduate Studies and Continuing Education, 601-846-4310. Fax: 601-846-4016.

Dowling College, School of Business, Oakdale, NY 11769-1999. Offerings include aviation management (MBA, Certificate). School faculty: 17 full-time, 75 part-time. *Degree requirements:* For master's, thesis optional, foreign language not required. *Entrance requirements:* For master's, GMAT, TOEFL. Application deadline: rolling. Application fee: $0. Electronic applications accepted. • Dr. Anthony F. Libertella, Interim Dean, 516-244-3355. Fax: 516-589-6644. Application contact: Kate Rowe, Director of Admissions, 516-244-3030. Fax: 516-563-3827. E-mail: rowek@dowling.edu.

Embry–Riddle Aeronautical University, Department of Business Administration, Daytona Beach, FL 32114-3900. Offers program in business administration in aviation (MBAA). Part-time and evening/weekend programs available. Faculty: 13 full-time (2 women), 1 part-time (0 women). Students: 51 full-time (8 women), 37 part-time (9 women); includes 5 minority (1 African American, 3 Asian Americans, 1 Hispanic), 37 international. Average age 28. 54 applicants, 80% accepted. In 1997, 21 degrees awarded. *Degree requirements:* Thesis or alternative required, foreign language not required. *Entrance requirements:* GRE General Test (minimum combined score of 1000), TOEFL (minimum score 550), minimum GPA of 2.5. Application deadline: rolling. Application fee: $30 ($50 for international students). *Expenses:* Tuition $425 per credit hour. Fees $290 per year. *Financial aid:* In 1997–98, 1 fellowship, 9 research assistantships averaging $950 per month, 7 teaching assistantships averaging $950 per month, 1 administrative assistantship averaging $950 per month were awarded; Federal Work-Study and career-related internships or fieldwork also available. Aid available to part-time students. Financial aid application deadline: 4/15; applicants required to submit FAFSA. *Faculty research:* NASA joint venture in space, human factors considerations in air traffic management. Total annual research expenditures: $271,000. • Dr. Bijah Vasigh, Program Chair, 904-226-6722. Fax: 904-226-6696. E-mail: vasighb@cts.db.erau.edu. Application contact: Ginny Tait, Graduate Admissions Specialist, 904-226-6115. Fax: 904-226-6299. E-mail: taitg@cts.db.erau.edu.

Embry–Riddle Aeronautical University, Extended Campus, Department of Business Administration, Daytona Beach, FL 32114-3900. Offerings include aviation administration and management (MBAA). Postbaccalaureate distance learning degree programs offered (minimal on-campus study). *Application deadline:* rolling. *Application fee:* $30 ($50 for international students). Electronic applications accepted. *Tuition:* $220 per credit hour. • Dr. Vance Mitchell, Chair, 360-375-1986. E-mail: mitchelv@cts.db.erau.edu. Application contact: Pam Thomas, Director of Admissions and Records, 904-226-6910. Fax: 904-226-6984. E-mail: ecinfo@ec.db.erau.edu.

Georgia State University, School of Policy Studies, Department of Public Administration and Urban Studies, Atlanta, GA 30303-3083. Offerings include urban studies (MS), with options in gerontology, human resources, nonprofit administration, planning and economic development, transportation. Department faculty: 18 full-time (7 women), 2 part-time (1 woman). *Average time to degree:* master's–2 years full-time, 3 years part-time. *Application deadline:* 7/1 (rolling processing; 11/1 for spring admission). *Application fee:* $25. *Expenses:* Tuition $2673 per year full-time, $99 per semester hour part-time for state residents; $10,692 per year full-time, $396 per semester hour part-time for nonresidents. Fees $228 per year. • Dr. John Thomas, Chair, 404-651-4591. Application contact: Sue Fagan, Director, 404-651-3504.

Iowa State University of Science and Technology, College of Design, Department of Community and Regional Planning, Ames, IA 50011. Offerings include transportation (MS). MS offered in cooperation with the Program in Transportation. Department faculty: 8 full-time (2 women), 6 part-time (0 women), 10.5 FTE. *Average time to degree:* master's–2.5 years full-time. *Application deadline:* 3/1 (priority date; rolling processing). *Application fee:* $20 ($30 for international students). *Expenses:* Tuition $3166 per year full-time, $176 per credit part-time for state residents; $9324 per year full-time, $518 per credit part-time for nonresidents. Fees $200 per year. • Riad Mahayni, Chair, 515-294-8958. Fax: 515-294-4015. E-mail: rmahayni@iastate.edu.

Iowa State University of Science and Technology, Interdisciplinary Programs, Program in Transportation, Ames, IA 50011. Awards MS. 1 applicant, 0% accepted. *Degree requirements:* Thesis. *Entrance requirements:* TOEFL. Application fee: $20 ($30 for international students). *Expenses:* Tuition $3166 per year full-time, $176 per credit part-time for state residents; $9324 per year full-time, $518 per credit part-time for nonresidents. Fees $200 per year. • Dr. Thomas H. Maze, Supervisory Committee Chair, 515-294-8103. E-mail: tom@ctre.iastate.edu.

Maine Maritime Academy, Department of Graduate Studies, Program in Maritime Management, Castine, ME 04420. Awards MS, Certificate, Diploma. Part-time programs available. Faculty: 5 full-time (2 women), 11 part-time (0 women). Students: 38; includes 14 international. Average age 30. 18 applicants, 61% accepted. In 1997, 6 master's awarded (100% found work related to degree). *Degree requirements:* For master's, computer language required, thesis optional. *Average time to degree:* master's–1 year full-time, 3 years part-time. *Entrance requirements:* For master's, GMAT or GRE General Test, TOEFL. Application deadline: rolling. Application fee: $40. *Expenses:* Tuition $15,750 per year. Fees $360 per year. *Financial aid:* 1 student received aid; teaching assistantships, Federal Work-Study, institutionally sponsored loans, and career-related internships or fieldwork available. Aid available to part-time students. Financial aid applicants required to submit FAFSA. *Faculty research:* Human resources in maritime environment, management of organization change, economic analysis and maritime law. • Application contact: Carolyn J. Ulrich, Administrative Assistant, 207-326-2485. Fax: 207-326-2411. E-mail: cjulrich@bell.mma.edu.

Maine Maritime Academy, Department of Graduate Studies, Program in Port Management, Castine, ME 04420. Awards MS, Certificate, Diploma. Part-time programs available. Faculty: 5 full-time (2 women), 11 part-time (0 women). Students: 3 full-time (0 women); includes 1 international. Average age 30. 5 applicants, 60% accepted. In 1997, 1 master's awarded. *Degree requirements:* For master's, computer language required, thesis optional. *Average time to degree:* master's–1 year full-time. *Entrance requirements:* For master's, GMAT or GRE General Test, TOEFL. Application deadline: rolling. Application fee: $40. Electronic applications accepted. *Expenses:* Tuition $15,750 per year. Fees $360 per year. *Financial aid:* 1 student received aid; teaching assistantships, Federal Work-Study, institutionally sponsored loans, and career-related internships or fieldwork available. Financial aid applicants required to submit FAFSA. • Application contact: Carolyn J. Ulrich, Administrative Assistant, 207-326-2485. Fax: 207-326-2411. E-mail: cjulrich@bell.mma.edu.

Massachusetts Institute of Technology, School of Engineering, Center for Transportation Studies, Cambridge, MA 02139-4307. Offers programs in logistics (MLOG), transportation (MST, PhD). MLOG new for fall 1998. 58 applicants, 34% accepted. *Application deadline:* 1/15. *Application fee:* $55. *Tuition:* $24,050 per year. • Yossi Sheffi, Director, 617-253-5316. E-mail: sheffi@mit.edu. Application contact: Sydney Miller, Student Coordinator, 617-253-8069. Fax: 617-253-4560. E-mail: tec@mit.edu.

McGill University, Faculty of Graduate Studies and Research, Faculty of Engineering, School of Urban Planning, Montréal, PQ H3A 2T5, Canada. Offerings include transportation (MUP). School faculty: 4 full-time (1 woman), 3 part-time (1 woman). *Degree requirements:* Thesis. *Entrance requirements:* TOEFL (minimum score 550), minimum GPA of 3.0. Application deadline: 3/1. Application fee: $60. *Expenses:* Tuition $1668 per year for Canadian residents; $8268 per year for nonresidents. Fees $828 per year for Canadian residents; $1216 per year for nonresidents. • Jeanne M. Wolfe, Director, 514-398-4077. E-mail: jeannew@urbarc.lan.mcgill.ca. Application contact: Elvira Evangelista, Admissions Secretary, 514-398-4075. Fax: 514-398-8376. E-mail: elvirae@urbare.lan.mcgill.ca.

Michigan State University, Eli Broad Graduate School of Management, Department of Marketing and Supply Chain Management, East Lansing, MI 48824-1020. Offerings include transportation-distribution (PhD). Terminal master's awarded for partial completion of doctoral program. Department faculty: 28 (2 women). *Degree requirements:* Dissertation required, foreign language not required. *Entrance requirements:* GMAT (minimum score 600; average 660). Application deadline: 3/31 (priority date; rolling processing; 11/1 for spring admission). Application fee: $30 ($40 for international students). Electronic applications accepted. *Expenses:* Tuition $4609 per year full-time, $223 per credit hour (minimum) part-time for state residents; $8704 per year full-time, $450 per credit hour (minimum) part-time for nonresidents. Fees $576 per year full-time, $476 per year part-time. • Dr. Robert Nason, Chairperson, 517-355-2240.

Middle Tennessee State University, College of Basic and Applied Sciences, Department of Aerospace, Murfreesboro, TN 37132. Offerings include airport/airline management (MS). MS new for fall 1998. Department faculty: 3 full-time (0 women), 2 part-time (0 women). *Application deadline:* 8/1 (priority date). *Application fee:* $5. *Expenses:* Tuition $2560 per year full-time, $129 per semester hour part-time for state residents; $7386 per year full-time, $340 per semester hour part-time for nonresidents. Fees $486 per year full-time, $17 per semester (minimum) part-time. • Ronald J. Ferrara, Chair, 615-898-3515. E-mail: rferrara@frank.mtsu.edu.

Morgan State University, School of Education and Urban Studies, Department of Transportation, Baltimore, MD 21251. Awards MS. Part-time and evening/weekend programs available.

Directory: Transportation Management

Morgan State University (continued)

Faculty: 3 full-time (0 women). Students: 16 full-time (9 women), 7 part-time (4 women); includes 17 minority (all African Americans), 3 international. In 1997, 10 degrees awarded. *Degree requirements:* Comprehensive exams required, thesis optional, foreign language not required. *Entrance requirements:* Minimum undergraduate GPA of 2.5. Application deadline: 7/1 (rolling processing; 11/1 for spring admission). Application fee: $0. *Expenses:* Tuition $160 per credit hour for state residents; $286 per credit hour for nonresidents. Fees $326 per year. *Financial aid:* Fellowships, research assistantships, Federal Work-Study, and career-related internships or fieldwork available. Financial aid application deadline: 4/1. *Faculty research:* Distributional impacts of congestion, pricing education and training for intelligent vehicle highway systems. Total annual research expenditures: $100,000. • Andrew Farkas, Acting Director, 410-319-3348. Fax: 410-319-3224. E-mail: zfarkas@moac.morgan.edu. Application contact: James E. Waller, Admissions and Programs Officer, 410-319-3186. Fax: 410-319-3837.

New Jersey Institute of Technology, Department of Civil and Environmental Engineering, Interdisciplinary Program in Transportation, Newark, NJ 07102-1982. Awards MS, PhD. Part-time and evening/weekend programs available. Faculty: 2 full-time (0 women). Students: 30 full-time (12 women), 23 part-time (10 women); includes 10 minority (8 African Americans, 1 Asian American, 1 Hispanic), 20 international. Average age 30. 60 applicants, 77% accepted. In 1997, 12 master's awarded. Terminal master's awarded for partial completion of doctoral program. *Degree requirements:* For master's, thesis or alternative required, foreign language not required; for doctorate, dissertation, residency required, foreign language not required. *Entrance requirements:* For master's, GRE General Test (minimum score 450 on verbal section, 600 on quantitative, 550 on analytical); for doctorate, GRE General Test (minimum score 450 on verbal section, 600 on quantitative, 550 on analytical), minimum graduate GPA of 3.5. Application deadline: 6/5 (priority date; rolling processing; 10/15 for spring admission). Application fee: $50. Electronic applications accepted. *Expenses:* Tuition $6952 per year full-time, $1104 per semester (minimum) part-time for state residents; $9770 per year full-time, $1527 per semester (minimum) part-time for nonresidents. Fees $938 per year full-time, $196 per semester (minimum) part-time. *Financial aid:* Fellowships, research assistantships, teaching assistantships, assistantships, Federal Work-Study, institutionally sponsored loans, and career-related internships or fieldwork available. Financial aid application deadline: 3/15. *Faculty research:* Transportation planning, administration, and policy; intelligent vehicle highway systems; bridge maintenance. Total annual research expenditures: $4.8 million. • Dr. Lou Pignataro, Director, 973-596-3355. Fax: 973-596-2316. E-mail: pignataro@admin1.njit.edu. Application contact: Kathy Kelly, Director of Admissions, 973-596-3300. Fax: 973-596-3461. E-mail: admissions@njit.edu.

Northwestern University, Division of Interdepartmental Programs, Program in Transportation, Evanston, IL 60208. Offers analytical methods (MS), environment and natural resources (MS), international issues (MS), logistics and operations (MS), private sector management and decision making (MS), public transportation systems and analysis (MS). Admissions and degrees offered through The Graduate School. Part-time programs available. Students: 10 full-time (1 woman), 2 part-time (0 women); includes 1 minority (Asian American), 5 international. 14 applicants, 71% accepted. In 1997, 7 degrees awarded. *Degree requirements:* Course-based paper required, thesis not required. *Entrance requirements:* GRE General Test, TOEFL (minimum score 550). Application deadline: 8/30 (rolling processing). Application fee: $50 ($55 for international students). *Tuition:* $20,430 per year full-time, $2424 per course part-time. *Financial aid:* Research assistantships, institutionally sponsored loans, and career-related internships or fieldwork available. Financial aid application deadline: 1/15; applicants required to submit FAFSA. *Faculty research:* Economics of transportation, deregulation, transportation safety, logistics, transportation management. • Frank S. Koppelman, Director, 847-491-2276. Application contact: Jennifer Marx-Hohmeier, Secretary, 847-491-2276. Fax: 847-491-3090. E-mail: j-marx@nwu.edu.

Northwestern University, J. L. Kellogg Graduate School of Management, Programs in Management, Evanston, IL 60208. Offerings include transportation management (MM). MMM offered jointly with the Robert R. McCormick School of Engineering and Applied Science; MM/MSN offered jointly with Rush Presbyterian Hospital. Faculty: 129 full-time (24 women), 89 part-time (15 women). *Application deadline:* 3/16. *Application fee:* $125. *Tuition:* $25,872 per year. • Michele Rogers, Assistant Dean of Admissions and Financial Aid, 847-491-3308. Fax: 847-491-4960.

Polytechnic University, Brooklyn Campus, Department of Civil and Environmental Engineering, Major in Transportation Management, Six Metrotech Center, Brooklyn, NY 11201-2990. Awards MS. Part-time and evening/weekend programs available. Students: 15. 16 applicants, 81% accepted. In 1997, 5 degrees awarded. *Degree requirements:* Thesis or alternative. *Application deadline:* rolling. *Application fee:* $45. Electronic applications accepted. *Expenses:* Tuition $19,530 per year full-time, $675 per credit part-time. Fees $600 per year full-time, $135 per semester part-time. *Financial aid:* Fellowships, research assistantships, teaching assistantships, institutionally sponsored loans available. Aid available to part-time students. Financial aid applicants required to submit FAFSA. • Application contact: John S. Kerge, Dean of Admissions, 718-260-3200. Fax: 718-260-3446. E-mail: admitme@poly.edu.

Polytechnic University, Westchester Graduate Center, Department of Civil and Environmental Engineering, Major in Transportation Management, Hawthorne, NY 10532-1507. Awards MS. Students: 1 part-time (0 women). 0 applicants. *Degree requirements:* Computer language, thesis or alternative. *Application deadline:* rolling. *Application fee:* $45. Electronic applications accepted. *Expenses:* Tuition $19,530 per year full-time, $675 per credit part-time. Fees $600 per year full-time, $135 per semester part-time. • Application contact: John S. Kerge, Dean of Admissions, 718-260-3200. Fax: 718-260-3446. E-mail: admitme@poly.edu.

San Jose State University, College of Business, Program in Transportation Management, San Jose, CA 95192-0001. Awards MS. Part-time and evening/weekend programs available. Postbaccalaureate distance learning degree programs offered (minimal on-campus study). Students: 28. *Degree requirements:* Computer language, thesis or alternative, comprehensive exam required, foreign language not required. *Entrance requirements:* GMAT, minimum GPA of 3.0. Application deadline: 6/1 (priority date; rolling processing). Application fee: $59. *Expenses:* Tuition $0 for state residents; $246 per unit for nonresidents. Fees $2017 per year full-time, $1351 per year part-time. *Faculty research:* Surface inter-modal transportation, economics, security. Total annual research expenditures: $100,000. • Rob Vitale, Director, 408-924-3400.

State University of New York Maritime College, Program in Transportation Management, Throgs Neck, NY 10465-4198. Awards MS. Part-time and evening/weekend programs available. Faculty: 7 full-time, 12 part-time. Students: 187 (17 women); includes 81 international. Average age 30. 84 applicants, 45% accepted. In 1997, 18 degrees awarded. *Degree requirements:* Thesis. *Entrance requirements:* TOEFL (minimum score 500), minimum GPA of 2.5. Application fee: $40. *Tuition:* $5124 per year full-time, $214 per credit part-time for state residents; $8442 per year full-time, $352 per credit part-time for nonresidents. *Financial aid:* In 1997–98, 25 students received aid, including 3 fellowships (all to first-year students) averaging $1,000 per month and totaling $30,000, 2 research assistantships averaging $1,000 per month, 3 scholarships averaging $1,000 per month and totaling $14,000; partial tuition waivers, Federal Work-Study, and career-related internships or fieldwork also available. Aid available to part-time students. Financial aid application deadline: 4/1; applicants required to submit FAFSA. *Faculty research:* Ports, intermodal, shipping, logistics, port tax. Total annual research expenditures: $50,000. • Dr. Shmuel Yahalom, Director, 718-409-7285. E-mail: yahaloms@aol.com. Application contact: Pam Dettmer, Assistant Administrator, 718-409-7285. Fax: 718-409-7359.

Syracuse University, School of Management, Program in Transportation and Distribution Management, Syracuse, NY 13244-0003. Awards MBA. Faculty: 2. Students: 1 full-time (0 women), 3 part-time (0 women); includes 2 international. 3 applicants, 33% accepted. In 1997, 1 degree awarded. *Entrance requirements:* GMAT. Application deadline: 2/1 (rolling processing). Application fee: $40. *Tuition:* $13,320 per year full-time, $555 per credit hour part-time. *Financial aid:* Fellowships, research assistantships, teaching assistantships, partial tuition waivers, Federal Work-Study available. Financial aid application deadline: 3/1. • Frances Tucker, Director, 315-443-3523. Application contact: Associate Dean, 315-443-3850.

University of Arkansas, College of Business Administration, Department of Transportation and Logistics Management, Fayetteville, AR 72701-1201. Awards MTLM. Program new for fall 1998. *Tuition:* $3144 per year full-time, $173 per credit hour part-time for state residents; $7140 per year full-time, $395 per credit hour part-time for nonresidents. • Dr. Tom Jensen, Chair, 501-575-4055.

University of British Columbia, Faculty of Commerce and Business Administration, Program in Business Administration, Vancouver, BC V6T 1Z2, Canada. Offerings include transport and logistics (M Sc). *Degree requirements:* Thesis required (for some programs), foreign language not required. *Average time to degree:* master's–2 years full-time. *Entrance requirements:* GMAT (average 620), TOEFL (minimum score 600). Application fee: $100.

University of California, Davis, Program in Transportation Technology and Policy, Davis, CA 95616. Awards MS, PhD. *Entrance requirements:* For master's, GRE General Test; for doctorate, GRE General Test, minimum GPA of 3.5. *Expenses:* Tuition $0 for state residents; $9384 per year for nonresidents. Fees $4466 per year full-time, $2923 per year part-time. *Financial aid:* Fellowships, research assistantships, teaching assistantships available. • Patricia Makhtarian, Head.

University of Dubuque, Program in Business Administration, 2000 University Avenue, Dubuque, IA 52001-5050. Offerings include aviation management (MBA). Program faculty: 10 full-time (6 women), 18 part-time (2 women). *Degree requirements:* Computer language required, foreign language and thesis not required. *Average time to degree:* master's–1.5 years full-time, 3 years part-time. *Entrance requirements:* GMAT, TOEFL (minimum score 550). Application deadline: 8/15 (priority date; rolling processing). Application fee: $25. • John Wiemers, Director, 319-589-3300. Fax: 319-589-3184. E-mail: mbaprogm@univ.dbq.edu.

University of Tennessee, Knoxville, College of Architecture and Planning, School of Planning, Knoxville, TN 37996. Offerings include transportation planning (MSP). School faculty: 3 full-time (0 women), 3 part-time (2 women). *Degree requirements:* Thesis or alternative required, foreign language not required. *Entrance requirements:* GRE General Test, TOEFL (minimum score 550), minimum GPA of 2.7. Application deadline: 2/1 (priority date; rolling processing). Application fee: $35. Electronic applications accepted. *Tuition:* $3354 per year full-time, $181 per semester hour part-time for state residents; $8410 per year full-time, $462 per semester hour part-time for nonresidents. • Dr. David Patterson, Interim Director, 423-974-5227. Fax: 423-974-5229. E-mail: dap@utk.edu. Application contact: James Spencer, Graduate Representative. E-mail: spencerj@utk.edu.

University of Tennessee, Knoxville, College of Business Administration, Program in Business Administration, Knoxville, TN 37996. Offerings include logistics and transportation (MBA, PhD). MS/MBA offered jointly with the College of Engineering. Postbaccalaureate distance learning degree programs offered. Program faculty: 51 full-time (6 women). *Degree requirements:* For doctorate, computer language, dissertation required, foreign language not required. *Entrance requirements:* For doctorate, GMAT, TOEFL (minimum score 550), minimum GPA of 2.7. Application deadline: 2/1 (priority date). Application fee: $35. Electronic applications accepted. *Tuition:* $3354 per year full-time, $181 per semester hour part-time for state residents; $8410 per year full-time, $462 per semester hour part-time for nonresidents. • Dr. Gary Dicer, Director, 423-974-5033. E-mail: gdicer@utk.edu. Application contact: Donald Potts, Graduate Representative, 423-974-5033. Fax: 423-974-3826. E-mail: dpotts@utk.edu.

University of Virginia, School of Engineering and Applied Science, Department of Civil Engineering, Program in Transportation Engineering and Management, Charlottesville, VA 22903. Awards ME, MS, PhD. Part-time programs available. Faculty: 3 full-time (0 women). Students: 16 full-time (4 women); includes 3 international. Average age 27. 12 applicants, 83% accepted. In 1997, 5 master's awarded (100% found work related to degree). Terminal master's awarded for partial completion of doctoral program. *Degree requirements:* For master's, thesis required (for some programs), foreign language not required; for doctorate, dissertation, comprehensive exam required, foreign language not required. *Average time to degree:* master's–1.7 years full-time. *Entrance requirements:* GRE General Test. Application deadline: 2/1 (priority date; rolling processing). Application fee: $40. *Tuition:* $4876 per year full-time, $944 per semester (minimum) part-time for state residents; $15,824 per year full-time, $2748 per semester (minimum) part-time for nonresidents. *Financial aid:* In 1997–98, 16 students received aid, including 16 research assistantships (6 to first-year students) averaging $1,200 per month; fellowships, teaching assistantships also available. Financial aid application deadline: 2/1. *Faculty research:* Intermodal freight planning, highway safety, land use/air quality, intelligent transportation systems, artificial intelligence applications. Total annual research expenditures: $500,000. • Dr. Nicholas J. Garber, Chairman, Department of Civil Engineering, 804-924-7464. Fax: 804-982-2951. E-mail: njg@virginia.edu.

Webb Institute, Department of Ocean Technology and Commerce, Glen Cove, NY 11542-1398. Awards MS. Faculty: 5 full-time (1 woman), 2 part-time (0 women). Students: 0. Average age 23. 0 applicants. In 1997, 8 degrees awarded (100% found work related to degree). *Degree requirements:* Thesis. *Average time to degree:* master's–1 year full-time. *Entrance requirements:* GRE General Test (minimum combined score of 1200; average 1300). Application deadline: 1/15 (priority date; rolling processing). Application fee: $50. *Tuition:* $21,000 per year. *Financial aid:* Full tuition scholarships and career-related internships or fieldwork available. Financial aid application deadline: 7/1; applicants required to submit FAFSA. • Dr. Roger Compton, Dean, 516-671-2215. Application contact: William Murray, Director of Admissions, 516-671-2213. Fax: 516-674-9838. E-mail: admissions@webb.institute.edu.

Section 12
Management Information Systems

This section contains a directory of institutions offering graduate work in management information systems, followed by in-depth entries submitted by institutions that chose to prepare detailed program descriptions. Additional information about programs listed in the directory but not augmented by an in-depth entry may be obtained by writing directly to the dean of a graduate school or chair of a department at the address given in the directory.

For programs offering related work, see also in this book Business Administration and Management. In Book 5, see Computer Science and Information Technology and Management of Engineering and Technology.

CONTENTS

Program Directory

Announcements

Cross-Discipline Announcements

In-Depth Descriptions

See also:

Management Information Systems

Air Force Institute of Technology, School of Systems and Logistics, Department of System Acquisition Management, Wright-Patterson AFB, OH 45433-7765. Awards MS. Faculty: 13 full-time (1 woman). Students: 33 full-time (5 women); includes 1 minority (Hispanic), 7 international. Average age 29. In 1997, 41 degrees awarded (100% found work related to degree). *Degree requirements:* Computer language, thesis required, foreign language not required. *Average time to degree:* master's–1.5 years full-time. *Entrance requirements:* GMAT (minimum score 500), minimum GPA of 2.5, must be military officer or DOD civilian. Application fee: $0. *Tuition:* $0. • Dr. Roland D. Kankey, Head, 937-255-7777 Ext. 3382. Application contact: M. Sgt. James W. Johnson, Graduate Programs Administrator, 937-255-7777 Ext. 3308.

American InterContinental University, Graduate School of Information Technology, 1651 Westwood Boulevard, Los Angeles, CA 90024-5603. Awards MIT. Program new for fall 1998. *Entrance requirements:* Computer Programmer Aptitude Battery Exam, interview. Application deadline: rolling. Application fee: $50. • Kevin Martin, President, 800-333-2652. Fax: 310-477-8640.

American InterContinental University, Graduate School of Information Technology, 3330 Peachtree Road, NE, Atlanta, GA 30326-1019. Awards MIT. Part-time programs available. Students: 200. *Entrance requirements:* Computer Programmer Aptitude Battery Exam, interview. Application deadline: rolling. Application fee: $50. • Heather Mugg, Director, 404-812-8254. Application contact: Jeff Bostic, Vice President of Admissions, 404-812-7400. Fax: 404-812-7499.

American University, Kogod College of Business Administration, Department of Management, Program in Management of Global Technology, Washington, DC 20016-8001. Awards MBA. Part-time and evening/weekend programs available. Faculty: 17 full-time (5 women), 6 part-time (1 woman). Students: 83 full-time (37 women), 66 part-time (26 women); includes 26 minority (14 African Americans, 6 Asian Americans, 6 Hispanics), 38 international. 48 applicants, 85% accepted. In 1997, 24 degrees awarded. *Entrance requirements:* GMAT. Application deadline: 2/1 (priority date; 10/1 for spring admission). Application fee: $50. *Expenses:* Tuition $19,080 per year full-time, $687 per credit hour (minimum) part-time. Fees $180 per year full-time, $110 per year part-time. *Financial aid:* Fellowships, research assistantships, Federal Work-Study, institutionally sponsored loans, and career-related internships or fieldwork available. Aid available to part-time students. Financial aid application deadline: 2/1. • Dr. Edward A. Wasil Jr., Chair, Department of Management, 202-885-1915. Fax: 202-885-1916.

Andrews University, School of Graduate Studies, School of Business, Department of Information and Computer Science, Berrien Springs, MI 49104. Awards MBA, MS. Faculty: 6 full-time. *Degree requirements:* Computer language required, foreign language and thesis not required. *Entrance requirements:* GMAT (minimum score 400), TOEFL (minimum score 550), minimum GPA of 2.6. Application deadline: 8/15 (rolling processing). Application fee: $30. *Expenses:* Tuition $290 per quarter hour (minimum). Fees $75 per quarter. • Chairman, 616-471-3516.

Arizona State University, College of Business, Program in Business Administration, Tempe, AZ 85287. Offerings include information management (PhD). Program faculty: 93 full-time (21 women), 10 part-time (1 woman). *Degree requirements:* Dissertation. *Application fee:* $45. *Expenses:* Tuition $2088 per year full-time, $110 per hour part-time for state residents; $9040 per year full-time, $377 per hour part-time for nonresidents. Fees $72 per year full-time, $18 per semester (minimum) part-time. • Dr. Lee R. McPheters, Associate Dean, 602-965-9377. Fax: 602-965-3368. Application contact: Judy Heilala, Director of MBA, 602-965-3331.

Arizona State University, College of Business, School of Accountancy and Information Management, Tempe, AZ 85287. Offers programs in accountancy (M Accy), information management (MS), taxation (M Tax). Faculty: 47 full-time (11 women). Students: 102 full-time (43 women), 29 part-time (10 women); includes 18 minority (4 African Americans, 8 Asian Americans, 5 Hispanics, 1 Native American), 30 international. Average age 30. 65 applicants, 72% accepted. In 1997, 93 degrees awarded. *Degree requirements:* Thesis optional. *Entrance requirements:* GMAT. Application fee: $45. *Expenses:* Tuition $2088 per year full-time, $110 per hour part-time for state residents; $9040 per year full-time, $377 per hour part-time for nonresidents. Fees $72 per year full-time, $18 per semester (minimum) part-time. *Faculty research:* Business law, management communication, purchasing and logistics management, real estate, computer information systems, management science, operations management, statistics. • Dr. M. J. Philip Reckers, Director, 602-965-3631.

Arizona State University East, College of Technology and Applied Sciences, Department of Information and Management Technology, Mesa, AZ 85206-0903. Awards MT. Part-time and evening/weekend programs available. Faculty: 17 full-time (3 women), 10 part-time (2 women). Students: 23 full-time (7 women), 64 part-time (21 women); includes 19 minority (16 Asian Americans, 2 Hispanics, 1 Native American), 1 international. Average age 33. 30 applicants, 80% accepted. In 1997, 19 degrees awarded. *Average time to degree:* master's–2 years full-time, 5 years part-time. *Application deadline:* rolling. *Application fee:* $45. *Expenses:* Tuition $110 per credit hour for state residents; $377 per credit hour for nonresidents. Fees $72 per year. *Financial aid:* In 1997–98, 14 students received aid, including 1 teaching assistantship (to a first-year student) averaging $1,400 per month, 2 graduate assistantships averaging $1,400 per month; full and partial tuition waivers, Federal Work-Study, and career-related internships or fieldwork also available. Aid available to part-time students. Financial aid applicants required to submit FAFSA. *Faculty research:* Environmental technology management, digital imaging and publications, web development, interactive multimedia, high performance project management. Total annual research expenditures: $28,000. • Dr. Thomas Schildgen, Chair, 602-727-1005. Fax: 602-727-1684. E-mail: ts@asu.edu. Application contact: C. Vinette Cowart, Director of Academic Services, 602-727-1028. Fax: 602-727-1876. E-mail: asueast@asu.edu.

Auburn University, College of Business, Department of Management, Auburn University, AL 36849-0001. Offerings include management information systems (MMIS, PhD). Department faculty: 25 full-time (3 women). *Degree requirements:* For doctorate, dissertation. *Entrance requirements:* For doctorate, GMAT, GRE General Test, TOEFL. Application deadline: 9/1 (rolling processing; 3/1 for spring admission). Application fee: $25 ($50 for international students). *Expenses:* Tuition $2760 per year full-time, $76 per credit hour part-time for state residents; $8280 per year full-time, $228 per credit hour part-time for nonresidents. Fees $30 per year full-time, $160 per quarter part-time for state residents; $30 per year full-time, $480 per quarter part-time for nonresidents. • Dr. Robert E. Niebuhr, Head, 334-844-4071. Application contact: Dr. John F. Pritchett, Dean of the Graduate School, 334-844-4700.

See in-depth description on page 143.

Baruch College of the City University of New York, School of Business, Department of Statistics and Computer Information Systems, Program in Computer Information Systems, 17 Lexington Avenue, New York, NY 10010-5585. Awards MBA, MS. Part-time and evening/weekend programs available. Faculty: 19 full-time (5 women), 13 part-time (1 woman). Students: 105 full-time (40 women), 171 part-time (67 women). In 1997, 45 degrees awarded. *Degree requirements:* Computer language, thesis or alternative required, foreign language not required. *Average time to degree:* master's–2 years full-time, 4 years part-time. *Entrance requirements:* GMAT, GRE General Test (MS), TOEFL (minimum score 570), TWE (minimum score 4.5). Application deadline: 6/15 (11/1 for spring admission). Application fee: $40. *Expenses:* Tuition $4350 per year full-time, $185 per credit part-time for state residents; $7600 per year full-time, $320 per credit part-time for nonresidents. Fees $53 per year. *Financial aid:* Research assistantships, Federal Work-Study, and career-related internships or fieldwork available. Aid available to part-time students. Financial aid application deadline: 5/3; applicants required to submit FAFSA. • Application contact: Michael S. Wynne, Office of Graduate Admissions, 212-802-2330. Fax: 212-802-2335. E-mail: graduate_admissions@baruch.cuny.edu.

Baylor University, Hankamer School of Business, Department of Information Systems, Waco, TX 76798. Offers programs in information systems (MSIS), information systems management (MBA). Faculty: 12 full-time (4 women). Students: 15 full-time (4 women); includes 2 minority (1 Hispanic, 1 Native American), 7 international. In 1997, 15 degrees awarded. *Entrance requirements:* GMAT (minimum score 450), TOEFL (minimum score 600). Application deadline: 8/1 (rolling processing; 12/1 for spring admission). Application fee: $25. *Expenses:* Tuition $7392 per year full-time, $308 per semester hour part-time. Fees $1024 per year. *Financial aid:* Research assistantships, Federal Work-Study, and career-related internships or fieldwork available. *Faculty research:* Computer personnel, group systems, information technology standards and infrastructure, international information systems, technology and the learning environment. • Jonathan Trower, Adviser, 254-710-4754. Fax: 254-710-1091. E-mail: jonathan_trower@baylor.edu.

Bellevue University, Graduate School, Bellevue, NE 68005-3098. Offerings include computer information systems (MS). Postbaccalaureate distance learning degree programs offered (no on-campus study). School faculty: 22 full-time (9 women), 13 part-time (5 women). *Average time to degree:* master's–2 years full-time, 3 years part-time. *Application deadline:* 7/15 (priority date; rolling processing; 11/15 for spring admission). *Application fee:* $50. • Dr. Douglas Frost, Dean, 402-293-2025. E-mail: frostd@scholars.bellevue.edu. Application contact: Elizabeth Wall, Director of Marketing and Enrollment, 402-293-3702. Fax: 402-293-3730. E-mail: eaw@scholars.bellevue.edu.

Benedictine University, Program in Management Information Systems, Lisle, IL 60532-0900. Awards MS, MBA/MS, MPH/MS. Part-time programs available. Faculty: 1 (woman) full-time, 12 part-time (2 women). Students: 60 (29 women). *Degree requirements:* Computer language required, foreign language and thesis not required. *Entrance requirements:* GMAT. Application fee: $30. • Dr. Barbara T. Grabowski, Director, 630-829-6215. Fax: 630-829-6226. E-mail: bgrabowski@ben.edu.

Bentley College, Graduate School of Business, Program in Accounting Information Systems, 175 Forest Street, Waltham, MA 02154-4705. Awards MSAIS. Program new for fall 1998. *Degree requirements:* Computer language required, foreign language and thesis not required. *Entrance requirements:* TOEFL (minimum score 580). Application deadline: 6/1 (priority date; rolling processing; 11/1 for spring admission). Application fee: $50. *Expenses:* Tuition $20,500 per year full-time, $2050 per course part-time. Fees $65 per year full-time, $15 per semester part-time. *Financial aid:* Application deadline 4/15; applicants required to submit CSS PROFILE. • David Schwarzkopf, Director, 781-891-2783. Application contact: Holly Chase, Associate Director, 781-891-2108. Fax: 781-891-2464. E-mail: hchase@bentley.edu.

Bentley College, Graduate School of Business, Program in Computer Information Systems, 175 Forest Street, Waltham, MA 02154-4705. Offers management information systems (MSCIS). Part-time and evening/weekend programs available. Faculty: 13 full-time (2 women), 1 part-time (0 women). Students: 24 full-time (10 women), 114 part-time (44 women); includes 10 minority (2 African Americans, 6 Asian Americans, 2 Hispanics), 11 international. Average age 32. 103 applicants, 70% accepted. In 1997, 57 degrees awarded (100% found work related to degree). *Degree requirements:* Computer language required, foreign language and thesis not required. *Entrance requirements:* GMAT (average 540) or GRE General Test, TOEFL (minimum score 580). Application deadline: 6/1 (priority date; rolling processing; 11/1 for spring admission). Application fee: $50. *Expenses:* Tuition $20,500 per year full-time, $2050 per course part-time. Fees $65 per year full-time, $15 per semester part-time. *Financial aid:* In 1997–98, 23 students received aid, including 4 research assistantships (2 to first-year students) averaging $167 per month, 8 departmental assistantships; Federal Work-Study and career-related internships or fieldwork also available. Aid available to part-time students. Financial aid application deadline: 4/15; applicants required to submit CSS PROFILE or FAFSA. *Faculty research:* Electronic commerce, advanced systems analysis, data communication issues and impacts, 0-0 modeling and design, groupware, database integration. • Dr. Jay G. Cooprider, Director, 781-891-2952. Application contact: Holly Chase, Associate Director, 781-891-2108. Fax: 781-891-2464. E-mail: hchase@bentley.edu.

Bentley College, Graduate School of Business, Self-paced MBA Program, 175 Forest Street, Waltham, MA 02154-4705. Offerings include management information systems (MBA). Program faculty: 70 full-time (21 women), 22 part-time (8 women). *Degree requirements:* Computer language required, foreign language and thesis not required. *Entrance requirements:* GMAT (average 540), TOEFL (minimum score 580). Application deadline: 6/1 (priority date; rolling processing; 11/1 for spring admission). Application fee: $50. *Expenses:* Tuition $20,500 per year full-time, $2050 per course part-time. Fees $65 per year full-time, $15 per semester part-time. • Dr. Judith B. Kamm, Director, 781-891-3433. Application contact: Holly Chase, Associate Director, 781-891-2108. Fax: 781-891-2464. E-mail: hchase@bentley.edu.

Boise State University, College of Business and Economics, Program in Management Information Systems, Boise, ID 83725-0399. Awards MS. Part-time programs available. Faculty: 14 full-time (2 women). Students: 9 part-time (6 women); includes 1 minority (Native American), 3 international. Average age 33. 15 applicants, 100% accepted. *Entrance requirements:* GMAT or GRE, minimum GPA of 3.0. Application deadline: 7/26 (priority date; rolling processing; 11/29 for spring admission). Application fee: $20 ($30 for international students). Electronic applications accepted. *Tuition:* $3020 per year full-time, $135 per credit part-time for state residents; $8900 per year full-time, $135 per credit part-time for nonresidents. *Financial aid:* Graduate assistantships, Federal Work-Study, institutionally sponsored loans, and career-related internships or fieldwork available. Aid available to part-time students. Financial aid application deadline: 3/1. • Dr. Harry White, Coordinator, 208-385-1126. Application contact: J. Renee Anchustegui, Adviser, 208-385-1126. Fax: 208-385-1135.

Boston College, Wallace E. Carroll Graduate School of Management, Department of Computer Science, Chestnut Hill, MA 02167-9991. Awards MBA. Part-time and evening/weekend programs available. *Degree requirements:* Computer language required, foreign language and thesis not required. *Entrance requirements:* GMAT (average 610), TOEFL (minimum score 600; average 630). Application deadline: 4/1 (priority date; rolling processing; 11/15 for spring admission). Application fee: $45. *Expenses:* Tuition $22,134 per year full-time, $714 per semester hour part-time. Fees $80 per year (minimum) full-time, $30 per semester part-time. *Financial aid:* Fellowships, research assistantships, teaching assistantships, administrative assistantships, Federal Work-Study, and career-related internships or fieldwork available. Financial aid application deadline: 3/1. *Faculty research:* Artificial intelligence, robotics, operating systems, complexity theory, finite automation. • Dr. Edward Sciore, Chairman, 617-552-3928. Application contact: Simone Marthers, Director of Admissions, 617-552-3920. Fax: 617-552-8078.

Boston University, School of Management, Program in Management Information Systems, Boston, MA 02215. Awards MSMIS, DBA, MBA/MSMIS. Faculty: 8 full-time (2 women), 12 part-time (2 women). Students: 23 full-time (10 women), 3 part-time (1 woman); includes 2 minority (1 African American, 1 Asian American), 8 international. Average age 29. 45 applicants, 80% accepted. In 1997, 29 master's awarded. *Degree requirements:* For master's, internship required, foreign language and thesis not required; for doctorate, dissertation required, foreign language not required. *Average time to degree:* master's–1 year full-time. *Entrance requirements:* For master's, GMAT; for doctorate, GMAT or GRE General Test. Application fee: $50. *Expenses:* Tuition $22,830 per year full-time, $713 per credit part-time. Fees $218 per year full-time, $40 per semester part-time. *Financial aid:* Federal Work-Study, institutionally sponsored loans, and career-related internships or fieldwork available. Aid available to part-time students. Financial aid applicants required to submit FAFSA. • Dr. John Storck, Director, 617-353-3522. E-mail:

ms.mis@bu.edu. Application contact: Maxine Milstein, Assistant Director, 617-353-3522. Fax: 617-353-9498. E-mail: ms-mis@bu.edu.

See in-depth description on page 581.

Bowie State University, Program in Management Information Systems, 14000 Jericho Park Road, Bowie, MD 20715. Offers information systems analyst (Certificate), management information systems (MS). Part-time and evening/weekend programs available. *Degree requirements:* For master's, research paper, written comprehensive exam required, thesis optional. *Application deadline:* 8/16 (priority date; rolling processing). *Application fee:* $30. *Expenses:* Tuition $169 per credit hour for state residents; $304 per credit hour for nonresidents. Fees $171 per year.

Brigham Young University, Marriott School of Management, School of Accountancy and Information Systems, Provo, UT 84602-1001. Awards M Acc, MISM. Faculty: 36 full-time (1 woman). Students: 155 full-time (41 women); includes 7 minority (all Asian Americans), 6 international. Average age 25. 239 applicants, 65% accepted. In 1997, 180 degrees awarded. *Average time to degree:* master's–1.5 years full-time. *Entrance requirements:* GMAT (minimum score 500), TOEFL (minimum score 575), minimum GPA of 3.0 in last 60 hours. Application deadline: 3/1. Application fee: $30. *Financial aid:* In 1997–98, scholarships totaling $168,100 were awarded; research assistantships, teaching assistantships, institutionally sponsored loans, and career-related internships or fieldwork also available. Financial aid application deadline: 3/1. *Faculty research:* Quality processing–management approach, fraudulent activities, database languages, electronic data exchange, knowledge-based systems. • Dr. W. Steve Albrecht, Director, 801-378-4195. Application contact: Kathy O'Brien, Academic Adviser, 801-378-3951. Fax: 801-378-5933. E-mail: kathy_obrien@byu.edu.

Bryant College, College of Business Administration, Program in Computer Information Systems, Smithfield, RI 02917-1284. Awards MBA, CAGS. Part-time and evening/weekend programs available. Faculty: 7 full-time (0 women), 3 part-time (0 women). Students: 13 full-time (8 women), 43 part-time (21 women); includes 6 minority (1 African American, 5 Asian Americans), 3 international. Average age 33. 11 applicants, 64% accepted. In 1997, 8 master's, 3 CAGSs awarded. *Entrance requirements:* For master's, GMAT (minimum score 480; average 520). Application deadline: 7/1 (priority date; rolling processing; 11/15 for spring admission). Application fee: $55 ($70 for international students). *Tuition:* $1025 per course. *Financial aid:* In 1997–98, 4 research assistantships were awarded; graduate assistantships and career-related internships or fieldwork also available. Aid available to part-time students. Financial aid applicants required to submit FAFSA. • Cathy Lalli, Assistant Director of Graduate Programs, Graduate School, 401-232-6230. Fax: 401-232-6494. E-mail: gradprog@bryant.edu.

California Lutheran University, School of Business Administration, Thousand Oaks, CA 91360-2787. Offerings include management information systems (MBA). School faculty: 8 full-time (3 women), 29 part-time (4 women). *Entrance requirements:* GMAT, minimum GPA of 3.0, interview. Application deadline: 8/1 (priority date; rolling processing). Application fee: $50. *Tuition:* $395 per unit. • Dr. Ronald Hagler, Director, 805-493-3371.

California State University, Dominguez Hills, School of Management, Program in Business Administration, Carson, CA 90747-0001. Offerings include computer information systems (MBA). Program faculty: 21 full-time (2 women), 1 part-time (0 women). *Degree requirements:* Computer language required, foreign language and thesis not required. *Entrance requirements:* GMAT (minimum score 450), minimum GPA of 2.75. Application deadline: 6/1. Application fee: $55. *Expenses:* Tuition $0 for state residents; $246 per unit for nonresidents. Fees $1896 per year full-time, $1230 per year part-time. • Dr. Robert Dowling, Coordinator, 310-243-3465.

California State University, Fullerton, School of Business Administration and Economics, Department of Management Science, PO Box 34080, Fullerton, CA 92834-9480. Offers programs in management information systems (MS), management science (MBA, MS), operations research (MS), statistics (MS). Part-time and evening/weekend programs available. Faculty: 22 full-time (3 women), 13 part-time, 27 FTE. Students: 11 full-time (7 women), 44 part-time (16 women); includes 17 minority (1 African American, 15 Asian Americans, 1 Hispanic), 19 international. Average age 29. 36 applicants, 61% accepted. In 1997, 15 degrees awarded. *Degree requirements:* Computer language, project or thesis required, foreign language not required. *Entrance requirements:* GMAT (minimum score 950), minimum AACSB index of 950. Application fee: $55. *Expenses:* Tuition $0 for state residents; $246 per unit for nonresidents. Fees $1947 per year full-time, $1281 per year part-time. *Financial aid:* Teaching assistantships, state grants, Federal Work-Study, institutionally sponsored loans available. Aid available to part-time students. Financial aid application deadline: 3/1. • Dr. Barry Pasternack, Chair, 714-278-2221.

California State University, Hayward, School of Business and Economics, Department of Accounting and Computer Information Systems, Option in Computer Information Systems, Hayward, CA 94542-3000. Awards MBA. Part-time and evening/weekend programs available. *Degree requirements:* Computer language, comprehensive exam or thesis required, foreign language not required. *Entrance requirements:* GMAT, minimum GPA of 2.75. Application deadline: 4/19 (priority date; rolling processing; 1/5 for spring admission). Application fee: $55. *Expenses:* Tuition $0 for state residents; $164 per unit for nonresidents. Fees $1827 per year full-time, $1161 per year part-time. *Financial aid:* Federal Work-Study, institutionally sponsored loans, and career-related internships or fieldwork available. Aid available to part-time students. Financial aid application deadline: 3/1. • Dr. Franklin Lowenthal, Coordinator, 510-885-3417. Application contact: Dr. Donna L. Wiley, Director of Graduate Programs, 510-885-3964.

California State University, Los Angeles, School of Business and Economics, Major in Business Administration, Department of Information Systems, Los Angeles, CA 90032-8530. Offers programs in business information systems (MBA), management (MS), management information systems (MS), office management (MBA). Part-time and evening/weekend programs available. Faculty: 12 full-time, 7 part-time. *Degree requirements:* Computer language, comprehensive exam (MBA), thesis (MS) required, foreign language not required. *Entrance requirements:* GMAT, TOEFL (minimum score 550), minimum GPA of 2.5 during previous 2 years. Application deadline: 6/30 (rolling processing; 11/30 for spring admission). Application fee: $55. *Expenses:* Tuition $0 for state residents; $164 per unit for nonresidents. Fees $1763 per year full-time, $1097 per year part-time. *Financial aid:* Federal Work-Study and career-related internships or fieldwork available. Aid available to part-time students. Financial aid application deadline: 3/1. • Dr. David Liu, Chair, 213-343-2983.

California State University, Sacramento, School of Business Administration, Department of Management Information Science, Sacramento, CA 95819-6048. Awards MS. Part-time and evening/weekend programs available. *Degree requirements:* Computer language, thesis or alternative, writing proficiency exam required, foreign language not required. *Entrance requirements:* GMAT, TOEFL (minimum score 550). Application deadline: 4/15 (11/1 for spring admission). Application fee: $55. *Expenses:* Tuition $0 for state residents; $246 per unit for nonresidents. Fees $2012 per year full-time, $1346 per year part-time. *Financial aid:* Research assistantships, teaching assistantships, Federal Work-Study, and career-related internships or fieldwork available. Aid available to part-time students. Financial aid application deadline: 3/1. • Dr. Thomas Sandman, Chair, 916-278-6536.

Capitol College, Graduate School, Laurel, MD 20708-9759. Offerings include systems management (MS). School faculty: 1 full-time (0 women), 24 part-time (4 women). *Average time to degree:* master's–1 year full-time, 2.5 years part-time. *Entrance requirements:* GRE General Test (minimum score 500 on each section), minimum GPA of 3.0. Application deadline: 7/1 (priority date; rolling processing). Application fee: $25 ($100 for international students). *Tuition:* $367 per credit. • Dr. Joe Goldsmith, Dean of Graduate Studies, 301-369-2800. Fax: 301-953-3876. Application contact: Sandy Perriello, Coordinator of Graduate Administration, 703-998-5503. Fax: 703-379-8239. E-mail: gradschool@capitol-college.edu.

Case Western Reserve University, Weatherhead School of Management, Department of Management Information and Decision Systems, Cleveland, OH 44106. Awards MBA, MSM, PhD, MBA/MSM. PhD offered through the School of Graduate Studies. Part-time and evening/weekend programs available. Faculty: 8 full-time (2 women), 3 part-time (0 women), 9 FTE. Students: 67 full-time (23 women), 58 part-time (22 women); includes 14 minority (5 African Americans, 9 Asian Americans), 27 international. Average age 28. In 1997, 32 master's, 3 doctorates awarded. *Degree requirements:* For doctorate, dissertation required, foreign language not required. *Entrance requirements:* For master's, GMAT (average 603); for doctorate, GMAT. Application deadline: 4/15 (priority date; rolling processing). Application fee: $50. *Tuition:* $20,900 per year full-time, $871 per credit hour part-time. *Financial aid:* Full and partial tuition waivers, Federal Work-Study, institutionally sponsored loans, and career-related internships or fieldwork available. Financial aid application deadline: 5/1. *Faculty research:* Decision support, business forecasting systems, design and use of information systems, artificial intelligence, executive information systems. • Richard J. Boland Jr., Chairman, 216-368-6022. Fax: 216-368-4785. Application contact: Linda S. Gaston, Director of Marketing and Admissions, 216-368-2030. Fax: 216-368-5548. E-mail: lxg10@po.cwru.edu.

See in-depth description on page 583.

Case Western Reserve University, Weatherhead School of Management, Department of Operations Research and Operations Management, Cleveland, OH 44106. Offerings include management science (MS), with options in finance, information systems, marketing, operations management, operations research, quality management. MS and PhD offered through the School of Graduate Studies. Department faculty: 12 full-time (0 women). *Average time to degree:* doctorate–4 years full-time. *Application deadline:* 4/15 (priority date; rolling processing). *Application fee:* $50. *Tuition:* $20,900 per year full-time, $871 per credit hour part-time. • Hamilton Emmons, Chairman, 216-368-3841. Application contact: Linda S. Gaston, Director of Marketing and Admissions, 216-368-2030. Fax: 216-368-5548. E-mail: lxg10@po.cwru.edu.

Central Michigan University, College of Extended Learning, Program in Administration, Mount Pleasant, MI 48859. Offerings include information resource management (MSA, Certificate). Postbaccalaureate distance learning degree programs offered. *Entrance requirements:* For master's, minimum GPA of 2.5 in major. Application fee: $50. *Tuition:* $211 per credit hour. • Dr. Susan Smith, Director, 517-774-4373. Application contact: Marketing Office, 800-950-1144. Fax: 517-774-2461.

Christian Brothers University, Graduate Programs, School of Business, Memphis, TN 38104-5581. Offerings include telecommunications and information systems management (MS). School faculty: 11 full-time (2 women), 5 part-time (2 women). *Application deadline:* rolling. *Application fee:* $25. *Expenses:* Tuition $325 per hour. Fees $30 per semester. • Dr. Ray S. House, Dean, 901-321-3316. Application contact: Michael T. Smith, Director, MBA Program, 901-321-3317. Fax: 901-321-3494.

City University, School of Business and Management Professions, Bellevue, WA 98004-6442. Offerings include computer systems (MS), information systems (MBA, Certificate). Postbaccalaureate distance learning degree programs offered (no on-campus study). School faculty: 14 full-time (6 women), 689 part-time (247 women). *Application deadline:* rolling. *Application fee:* $75 ($175 for international students). Electronic applications accepted. *Tuition:* $280 per credit hour. • Dr. Roman Borboa, Dean, 425-637-1010 Ext. 3759. Fax: 425-277-2439. E-mail: rborboa@cityu.edu. Application contact: Nabil El-Khatib, Vice President, Admissions, 800-426-5596. Fax: 425-277-2437. E-mail: nel-khatib@cityu.edu.

Claremont Graduate University, Department of Information Sciences, Claremont, CA 91711-6163. Offerings include management of information systems (MSMIS, PhD). Terminal master's awarded for partial completion of doctoral program. Department faculty: 5 full-time (0 women), 3 part-time (0 women). *Degree requirements:* For doctorate, computer language, dissertation. *Entrance requirements:* For doctorate, GMAT, GRE General Test. Application deadline: 2/15 (priority date; rolling processing). Application fee: $40. Electronic applications accepted. *Expenses:* Tuition $20,250 per year full-time, $913 per unit part-time. Fees $130 per year. • Lorne Olfman, Chair, 909-621-8209. E-mail: lorne.olfman@cgu.edu. Application contact: Nancy Back, Program Coordinator, 909-621-8209. Fax: 909-621-8390. E-mail: infosci@cgu.edu.

Claremont Graduate University, Peter F. Drucker Graduate Management Center, Program in Management, Claremont, CA 91711-6163. Offerings include information systems (MBA). *Entrance requirements:* GMAT, TOEFL. Application deadline: 2/15 (priority date; rolling processing). Application fee: $40. Electronic applications accepted. *Expenses:* Tuition $20,250 per year full-time, $913 per unit part-time. Fees $130 per year. • Dr. Jeffrey Decker, Director, 909-621-8073. Fax: 909-621-8390. E-mail: jeff.decker@cgu.edu. Application contact: Kathy Hubener, Admissions Coordinator, 909-621-8073. Fax: 909-621-8543. E-mail: mba@cgu.edu.

Clarkson University, School of Business, Program in Management Systems, Concentration in Management Information Systems, Potsdam, NY 13699. Awards MS. *Degree requirements:* Project or thesis required, foreign language not required. *Entrance requirements:* GMAT, GRE General Test (highly recommended), TOEFL. Application deadline: rolling. Application fee: $25 ($35 for international students). *Expenses:* Tuition $19,075 per year full-time, $635 per credit hour part-time. Fees $178 per year. • Application contact: Dr. Fredric C. Menz, Director, Graduate Program, 315-268-6427. Fax: 315-268-3810. E-mail: menzf@icarus.som.clarkson.edu.

Announcement: Either the MBA or MS may be completed in 1 year by students with course work equivalent to 1st-year requirements. The more specialized MS program allows for focused course work and research in information systems. Class size averages 20–30 students and allows for strong interaction between faculty members and students.

Cleveland State University, James J. Nance College of Business Administration, Department of Computer and Information Science, Cleveland, OH 44115-2440. Offers programs in information systems (DBA), management and organization analysis (MCIS), systems programming (MCIS). Part-time and evening/weekend programs available. Faculty: 16 full-time (1 woman). Students: 80 full-time (35 women), 158 part-time (50 women); includes 30 minority (5 African Americans, 23 Asian Americans, 2 Native Americans), 103 international. Average age 31. 206 applicants, 55% accepted. In 1997, 57 master's awarded. *Degree requirements:* For master's, computer language required, foreign language and thesis not required; for doctorate, computer language, dissertation required, foreign language not required. *Entrance requirements:* For master's, GMAT or GRE, minimum GPA of 2.9; for doctorate, GMAT (score in 75th percentile or higher), minimum GPA of 3.5. Application deadline: 9/1 (priority date; rolling processing). Application fee: $25. *Expenses:* Tuition $5252 per year full-time, $202 per credit hour part-time for state residents; $10,504 per year full-time, $404 per credit hour part-time for nonresidents. Fees $2.25 per credit hour (minimum). *Financial aid:* In 1997–98, 2 research assistantships were awarded; administrative assistantships and career-related internships or fieldwork also available. • Dr. Chien-Hua Lin, Chairperson, 216-687-4760. Fax: 216-687-5448. E-mail: lin@cis.csuohio.edu.

Cleveland State University, James J. Nance College of Business Administration, Program in Accounting and Financial Information Systems, Cleveland, OH 44115-2440. Awards MAFIS. Part-time programs available. Faculty: 10 full-time (3 women). Students: 35 full-time (17 women), 51 part-time (23 women); includes 13 minority (8 African Americans, 4 Asian Americans, 1 Hispanic), 34 international. Average age 30. 55 applicants, 64% accepted. In 1997, 35 degrees awarded (100% found work related to degree). *Degree requirements:* Computer language required, foreign language and thesis not required. *Entrance requirements:* GMAT, minimum GPA of 2.75. Application deadline: 9/1 (priority date; rolling processing). Application fee: $25. *Expenses:* Tuition $5252 per year full-time, $202 per credit hour part-time for state residents; $10,504 per year full-time, $404 per credit hour part-time for nonresidents. Fees $2.25 per credit hour (minimum). *Financial aid:* In 1997–98, 1 research assistantship, 2 administrative assistantships were awarded; Federal Work-Study and career-related intern-

Directory: Management Information Systems

Cleveland State University (continued)

ships or fieldwork also available. *Faculty research:* Internal auditing, computer auditing, taxation, accounting education. • Dr. Linda Garceau, Chair, 216-687-4723. Fax: 216-687-9212. E-mail: l.garceau@csuohio.edu.

College of Notre Dame, Department of Systems Management, Belmont, CA 94002-1997. Awards MSSM. Part-time and evening/weekend programs available. Faculty: 1 full-time, 13 part-time. Students: 6 full-time (3 women), 44 part-time (23 women); includes 12 minority (3 African Americans, 3 Asian Americans, 6 Hispanics), 1 international. Average age 36. 30 applicants, 63% accepted. In 1997, 17 degrees awarded. *Entrance requirements:* TOEFL (minimum score 550), minimum GPA of 2.5. Application deadline: rolling. Application fee: $50 ($500 for international students). *Tuition:* $460 per unit. • Dr. Sylvia Shafto, Chair, 650-508-3724.

Colorado State University, College of Business, Department of Computer Information Systems, Fort Collins, CO 80523-0015. Awards MBA, MS. Part-time programs available. Faculty: 9 full-time (1 woman). Students: 41 full-time (13 women), 20 part-time (11 women); includes 8 minority (2 African Americans, 4 Asian Americans, 1 Hispanic, 1 Native American), 8 international. 57 applicants, 60% accepted. In 1997, 22 degrees awarded. *Degree requirements:* Thesis optional, foreign language not required. *Entrance requirements:* GMAT, TOEFL, minimum GPA of 3.0. Application deadline: 2/1 (priority date; rolling processing). Application fee: $30. Electronic applications accepted. *Tuition:* $2920 per year (minimum) full-time, $328 per credit hour (minimum) part-time for state residents; $9000 per year (minimum) full-time, $368 per credit hour (minimum) part-time for nonresidents. *Financial aid:* Fellowships, teaching assistantships, traineeships, Federal Work-Study, and career-related internships or fieldwork available. Financial aid application deadline: 2/1. *Faculty research:* Quality improvement, metrics, re-engineering, computer-integrated manufacturing, computer-aided software engineering. • Application contact: Dr. John Plotnicki, Chair, 970-491-6203.

Colorado Technical University, Graduate Studies, Program in Management, 4435 North Chestnut Street, Colorado Springs, CO 80907-3896. Offerings include management information systems (MSM), systems management (MSM). Program faculty: 8 full-time (2 women), 8 part-time (1 woman), 12 FTE. *Average time to degree:* master's–2 years full-time. *Application deadline:* 10/4 (rolling processing; 4/5 for spring admission). *Application fee:* $100. *Expenses:* Tuition $230 per quarter hour. Fees $6 per quarter. • Dr. Mark Pieffer, Dean, 719-590-6765. Application contact: Judy Galante, Graduate Admissions, 719-590-6720. Fax: 719-598-3740.

Concordia University Wisconsin, Division of Graduate Studies, MBA Program, Mequon, WI 53097-2402. Offerings include management information services (MBA). Postbaccalaureate distance learning degree programs offered (minimal on-campus study). *Degree requirements:* Thesis or alternative, comprehensive exam. *Average time to degree:* master's–2 years part-time. *Entrance requirements:* TOEFL (minimum score 550). Application deadline: 8/1 (priority date; rolling processing; 1/15 for spring admission). Application fee: $50. *Tuition:* $300 per credit. • David Borst, Director, 414-243-4298. Fax: 414-243-4428. E-mail: dborst@bach.cuw.edu.

Cornell University, Graduate Field of Management, Ithaca, NY 14853-0001. Offerings include management information systems (PhD). Terminal master's awarded for partial completion of doctoral program. Faculty: 43 full-time. *Degree requirements:* Dissertation required, foreign language not required. *Entrance requirements:* GMAT or GRE General Test, TOEFL. Application deadline: 1/10 (priority date). Application fee: $65. *Expenses:* Tuition $24,300 per year. Fees $48 per year. • Director of Graduate Studies, 607-255-3669. Application contact: Graduate Field Assistant, 607-255-3669. Fax: 607-254-4590. E-mail: maria@johnson.cornell.edu.

Dallas Baptist University, College of Business, Business Administration Program, Dallas, TX 75211-9299. Offerings include management information systems (MBA). Program faculty: 15 full-time (4 women), 26 part-time (5 women). *Entrance requirements:* GMAT, TOEFL (minimum score 550). Application deadline: rolling. Application fee: $25. *Tuition:* $285 per hour. • Annette Hoffman, Director of Graduate Business Programs, 214-333-5280. Application contact: Travis Bundrick, Director of Graduate Programs, 214-333-5243. Fax: 214-333-5579. E-mail: graduate@dbu.edu.

DePaul University, Schools of Accountancy and Computer Science, Telecommunications, and Information Systems, Program in Management Information Systems, Chicago, IL 60604-2287. Awards MBA, MSMIS. Part-time and evening/weekend programs available. Students: 21 full-time (7 women), 28 part-time (10 women); includes 8 minority (1 African American, 6 Asian Americans, 1 Hispanic), 1 international. Average age 31. 26 applicants, 77% accepted. In 1997, 11 degrees awarded. *Entrance requirements:* GMAT. Application deadline: 8/1 (rolling processing; 3/1 for spring admission). Application fee: $40. *Expenses:* Tuition $1593 per course. Fees $30 per year. *Financial aid:* Application deadline 4/30. *Faculty research:* Electronic commerce, data warehousing, distributed computing, business value of information technology. • Dr. Sasa DeKleva, Co-Administrator, 312-362-6789. Fax: 312-362-6208. E-mail: sdekleva@condor.depaul.edu.

DePaul University, Charles H. Kellstadt Graduate School of Business, School of Accountancy, Program in Systems, Chicago, IL 60604-2287. Awards MBA. Students: 65 full-time (25 women), 74 part-time (14 women); includes 28 minority (11 African Americans, 14 Asian Americans, 3 Hispanics), 3 international. Average age 30. 69 applicants, 68% accepted. In 1997, 28 degrees awarded. *Degree requirements:* Computer language required, foreign language and thesis not required. *Entrance requirements:* GMAT. Application deadline: 5/30 (priority date; rolling processing). Application fee: $40. Electronic applications accepted. *Expenses:* Tuition $1593 per course. Fees $30 per year. *Financial aid:* Application deadline 4/30. • Dr. Sasa DeKleva, Coordinator, 312-362-8770. Fax: 312-362-6208. Application contact: Christine Munoz, Director of Admissions, 312-362-8810. Fax: 312-362-6677. E-mail: mbainfo@wppost.depaul.edu.

Dominican University, Graduate School of Library and Information Science and Graduate School of Business, Interdisciplinary Program in Management Information Systems, River Forest, IL 60305-1099. Awards MSMIS. Part-time programs available. Faculty: 36 (12 women). Students: 6 full-time (2 women), 18 part-time (7 women); includes 4 minority (1 African American, 3 Asian Americans), 15 international. Average age 31. *Degree requirements:* Computer language required, foreign language and thesis not required. *Entrance requirements:* GMAT (minimum score 400; average 500), TOEFL (minimum score 600), minimum GPA of 3.0 or GRE General Test (minimum score 550 required on 2 out of 3 sections). Application deadline: 8/22 (priority date; rolling processing; 12/19 for spring admission). Application fee: $25. *Financial aid:* Student assistantships and career-related internships or fieldwork available. Financial aid application deadline: 4/15. • Prudence Dalrymple, Dean, Graduate School of Library and Information Science, 708-524-6472. Fax: 708-524-6657.

Duquesne University, Graduate School of Business Administration, Pittsburgh, PA 15282-0001. Offerings include information systems management (MS). School faculty: 28 full-time (2 women), 14 part-time (2 women), 32 FTE. *Average time to degree:* master's–2 years full-time, 3.5 years part-time. *Application deadline:* 6/1 (priority date; rolling processing; 11/1 for spring admission). *Application fee:* $40. *Expenses:* Tuition $481 per credit. Fees $39 per credit. • Thomas J. Murrin, Dean, 412-396-5157. Application contact: Dr. William Presutti, Associate Dean and Director, 412-396-6269. Fax: 412-396-5304.

Eastern Michigan University, College of Business, Department of Finance and Computer Information Systems, Ypsilanti, MI 48197. Offers programs in computer information systems (MBA), computer-based information systems (MSIS), finance (MBA). Evening/weekend programs available. Faculty: 19 full-time (1 woman). 93 applicants, 70% accepted. In 1997, 42 degrees awarded. *Degree requirements:* Computer language required, foreign language and thesis not required. *Entrance requirements:* GMAT (minimum score 450), TOEFL (minimum score 550). Application deadline: 5/15 (rolling processing; 3/15 for spring admission). Application fee: $30. *Expenses:* Tuition $2691 per year full-time, $150 per credit hour part-time for state residents; $6300 per year full-time, $350 per credit hour part-time for nonresidents. Fees $368 per year full-time, $88 per semester (minimum) part-time. *Financial aid:* Fellowships, teaching assistantships available. Aid available to part-time students. Financial aid application deadline: 3/15; applicants required to submit FAFSA. • Dr. Alahassana Diallo, Interim Head, 734-487-2454. Application contact: Dr. Wafa Korshid, Coordinator, 734-487-2454.

École des Hautes Études Commerciales, Program in Information Systems, Montréal, PQ H3T 2A7, Canada. Awards M Sc. Most courses are given in French. Part-time programs available. *Degree requirements:* 1 foreign language, thesis. *Application deadline:* 3/15. *Application fee:* $40. *Financial aid:* Fellowships, research assistantships, teaching assistantships available. • Dr. Jean-Yves Le Louarn, Director, 514-340-6295. E-mail: jean-yves.lelouarn@hec.ca. Application contact: Nicole Rivet, Registrar, 514-340-6110. Fax: 514-340-5640. E-mail: nicole.rivet@hec.ca.

Fairleigh Dickinson University, Teaneck–Hackensack Campus, University College: Arts, Sciences, and Professional Studies, School of Computer Science and Information Systems, Program in Management Information Systems, 1000 River Road, Teaneck, NJ 07666-1914. Awards MS. Faculty: 12 full-time (3 women), 21 part-time (7 women), 18.5 FTE. Students: 66 full-time (25 women), 32 part-time (13 women); includes 15 minority (3 African Americans, 10 Asian Americans, 2 Hispanics), 70 international. Average age 29. In 1997, 30 degrees awarded. *Degree requirements:* Computer language required, foreign language and thesis not required. *Entrance requirements:* GRE General Test. Application deadline: rolling. Application fee: $35. *Expenses:* Tuition $522 per credit. Fees $302 per year full-time, $138 per year part-time. *Faculty research:* Real time computer systems, software design modeling and simulation, parallel processing, pattern recognition, image processing. • Dr. Gilbert Steiner, Director, School of Computer Science and Information Systems, 201-692-2260. Fax: 201-692-2773. E-mail: steiner@alpha.fdu.edu.

Ferris State University, College of Business, Department of Accountancy/Computer Information Systems, Computer Information Systems Program, Big Rapids, MI 49307-2742. Offers information systems management (MS). Part-time and evening/weekend programs available. Faculty: 3 full-time (0 women), 4 part-time (0 women). Students: 55 full-time (17 women), 57 part-time (24 women); includes 10 minority (9 African Americans, 1 Hispanic), 31 international. In 1997, 58 degrees awarded (10% entered university research/teaching, 90% found other work related to degree). *Degree requirements:* Thesis or alternative required, foreign language not required. *Entrance requirements:* Minimum GPA of 3.0 in CIS and business core, 2.75 overall; writing sample. Application deadline: 8/1. Application fee: $20. *Expenses:* Tuition $220 per credit hour for state residents; $450 per credit hour for nonresidents. Fees $100 per year. *Financial aid:* In 1997–98, 50 research assistantships (32 to first-year students) averaging $495 per month were awarded; career-related internships or fieldwork also available. Aid available to part-time students. *Faculty research:* Health systems CQI, quality improvement, client/server end-user computing, information management and policy, learning space/Lotus Notes. • Clyoe Hardman, Coordinator, 616-592-2168. Fax: 616-592-3521. E-mail: jperrin@pada.ferris.edu.

Florida Agricultural and Mechanical University, Division of Graduate Studies, Research, and Continuing Education, School of Business and Industry, Tallahassee, FL 32307-3200. Offerings include management information systems (MBA). *Entrance requirements:* GRE General Test (minimum combined score of 1000), minimum GPA of 3.0. Application deadline: 5/13. Application fee: $20. *Expenses:* Tuition $140 per credit hour for state residents; $484 per credit hour for nonresidents. Fees $130 per year. • Dr. Sybil Mobley, Dean, 850-599-3565.

Florida Institute of Technology, School of Extended Graduate Studies, Program in Management, Melbourne, FL 32901-6975. Offerings include information systems (PMBA). *Application fee:* $50. *Tuition:* $550 per credit hour. • Application contact: Carolyn P. Farrior, Associate Dean of Graduate Admissions, 407-674-7118. Fax: 407-723-9468. E-mail: cfarrior@fit.edu.

Florida International University, College of Business Administration, Department of Decision Sciences and Information Systems, Miami, FL 33199. Offers program in management information systems (MS). Part-time and evening/weekend programs available. Faculty: 8 full-time (0 women), 1 part-time (0 women), 8.5 FTE. Students: 1 (woman) full-time, 2 part-time (0 women); includes 2 international. Average age 40. 0 applicants. *Degree requirements:* Computer language required, foreign language and thesis not required. *Entrance requirements:* GMAT, minimum AACSB index of 1000, minimum GPA of 3.0. Application deadline: 4/1 (priority date; rolling processing; 10/1 for spring admission). Application fee: $20. *Expenses:* Tuition $138 per credit hour for state residents; $482 per credit hour for nonresidents. Fees $46 per semester. • Dr. Christos Koulamas, Chairperson, 305-348-2830. Fax: 305-348-3278. E-mail: koulamas@fiu.edu.

Florida Metropolitan University–Orlando College, North, Division of Business Administration, 5421 Diplomat Circle, Orlando, FL 32810-5674. Offerings include information systems (MBA). Division faculty: 7. *Degree requirements:* Thesis or alternative. *Application deadline:* rolling. *Application fee:* $25. *Tuition:* $263 per credit hour. • Director of Graduate Studies, 407-851-2525. Application contact: Annette Gallina, Director of Admissions, 407-851-2525 Ext. 30. Fax: 407-851-1477.

Fordham University, Graduate School of Business Administration, New York, NY 10023. Offerings include information and communication systems (GPMBA, MBA), management systems (GPMBA). School faculty: 85 full-time (22 women), 95 part-time (12 women). *Average time to degree:* master's–2 years full-time, 3 years part-time. *Application deadline:* 6/1 (priority date; rolling processing; 11/1 for spring admission). *Application fee:* $50. • Dr. Ernest J. Scalberg, Dean, 212-636-6111. Fax: 212-307-1779. Application contact: Kathy Pattison, Assistant Dean of Admission, 212-636-6200. Fax: 212-636-7076. E-mail: admission@bschool.bnet.fordham.edu.

Fort Hays State University, College of Business, Department of Business Administration, Hays, KS 67601-4099. Offerings include computer information systems (MBA). Department faculty: 14 full-time (2 women). *Degree requirements:* Thesis optional, foreign language not required. *Entrance requirements:* GMAT. Application deadline: 7/1 (priority date; rolling processing). Application fee: $25 ($35 for international students). *Tuition:* $94 per credit hour for state residents; $249 per credit hour for nonresidents. • Dr. Dale McKemey, Acting Director, 785-628-4201.

Friends University, Graduate Programs, College of Business, Program in Management Information Systems, Wichita, KS 67213. Awards MS. Evening/weekend programs available. Students: 122. *Application deadline:* 8/15 (priority date; rolling processing). *Application fee:* $125. *Expenses:* Tuition $326 per credit hour (minimum). Fees $215 per year. • Dr. Al Saber, Director, 800-794-6945 Ext. 5685. Application contact: Director of Graduate Admissions, 800-794-6945 Ext. 5685.

Friends University, Graduate Programs, College of Continuing Education, Program in Quality Systems Management, Wichita, KS 67213. Awards MSQSM. Evening/weekend programs available. Faculty: 1 full-time (0 women), 4 part-time (0 women). Students: 44. *Application deadline:* rolling. *Application fee:* $45. *Expenses:* Tuition $326 per credit hour (minimum). Fees $215 per year. • Dr. Graydon Dawson, Director, 800-794-6945 Ext. 5526. Application contact: Director of Graduate Admissions, 800-794-6945 Ext. 5300.

The George Washington University, Columbian School of Arts and Sciences, Program in Administrative Sciences, Washington, DC 20052. Offerings include management information systems (MA). Program faculty: 3 part-time (0 women), 1 FTE. *Degree requirements:* Comprehensive exam required, thesis not required. *Entrance requirements:* GRE General Test, minimum GPA of 3.0. Application deadline: 5/1. Application fee: $50. *Expenses:* Tuition $680 per semester hour. Fees $35 per semester hour. • Dr. Joseph Zeidner, Director, 202-496-8380.

Directory: Management Information Systems

The George Washington University, School of Business and Public Management, Department of Management Science, Program in Information Systems, Washington, DC 20052. Awards MSIS. Part-time and evening/weekend programs available. Faculty: 3 full-time (0 women), 1 part-time (0 women). Students: 22 full-time (4 women), 64 part-time (25 women); includes 27 minority (14 African Americans, 9 Asian Americans, 3 Hispanics, 1 Native American), 27 international. Average age 32. 90 applicants, 80% accepted. In 1997, 31 degrees awarded. *Degree requirements:* Computer language required, foreign language and thesis not required. *Entrance requirements:* GMAT, TOEFL (minimum score 550). Application deadline: 4/1 (priority date; rolling processing; 10/1 for spring admission). Application fee: $45. *Expenses:* Tuition $680 per semester hour. Fees $35 per semester hour. *Financial aid:* Fellowships, teaching assistantships, Federal Work-Study, institutionally sponsored loans, and career-related internships or fieldwork available. Financial aid application deadline: 4/1. *Faculty research:* Expert systems, decision support systems. • Dr. John Carson, Director, 202-994-7375. Application contact: Lilly Hastings, Graduate Admissions, 202-994-6584. Fax: 202-994-6382.

Georgia Southwestern State University, School of Business, Americus, GA 31709-4693. Offerings include computer information systems (MSA). *Entrance requirements:* GMAT (minimum score 500) or GRE General Test (minimum score 400 on each section), minimum GPA of 2.5. Application deadline: 9/1 (rolling processing; 3/15 for spring admission). Application fee: $10. • Dr. John Bates, Acting Chair, 912-931-2090. Application contact: Chris Laney, Graduate Admissions Specialist, 912-931-2027. Fax: 912-931-2059. E-mail: claney@gsw1500.gsw.peachnet.edu.

Georgia State University, College of Business Administration, Department of Computer Information Systems, Atlanta, GA 30303-3083. Awards MBA, MS, PhD. Part-time and evening/weekend programs available. Faculty: 30 full-time, 7 part-time. Students: 347 full-time (118 women), 203 part-time (59 women); includes 65 minority (28 African Americans, 31 Asian Americans, 6 Hispanics), 142 international. Average age 29. In 1997, 77 master's, 1 doctorate awarded. Terminal master's awarded for partial completion of doctoral program. *Degree requirements:* For doctorate, dissertation required, foreign language not required. *Entrance requirements:* For master's, GMAT (average 566), TOEFL; for doctorate, GMAT (average 670), TOEFL. Application deadline: 5/1 (rolling processing; 10/1 for spring admission). Application fee: $25. *Expenses:* Tuition $2673 per year full-time, $99 per semester hour part-time for state residents; $10,692 per year full-time, $396 per semester hour part-time for nonresidents. Fees $228 per year. *Financial aid:* Fellowships, research assistantships, teaching assistantships, partial tuition waivers, and career-related internships or fieldwork available. Aid available to part-time students. Financial aid applicants required to submit FAFSA. • Dr. Richard Welke, Chair, 404-651-3885. Fax: 404-651-2804. Application contact: Office of Academic Assistance and Master's Admissions, 404-651-1913. Fax: 404-651-0219.

Golden Gate University, School of Business, San Francisco, CA 94105-2968. Offerings include information systems (MBA), project and systems management (MS, Certificate). MBA (telecommunications, management information systems) offered jointly with the School of Technology and Industry. *Average time to degree:* master's–2.5 years full-time. *Application deadline:* 7/1 (priority date; rolling processing). *Application fee:* $55 ($70 for international students). *Tuition:* $996 per course (minimum). • Dr. Hamid Shomali, Dean, 415-442-6500. Fax: 415-442-6579. Application contact: Enrollment Services, 415-442-7800. Fax: 415-442-7807. E-mail: info@ggu.edu.

Golden Gate University, School of Technology and Industry, San Francisco, CA 94105-2968. Offerings include information systems (MS, Certificate). MS (hospitality administration and tourism) new for fall 1998. *Degree requirements:* Computer language required, foreign language and thesis not required. *Average time to degree:* master's–2.5 years full-time. *Entrance requirements:* For master's, GMAT (MBA), TOEFL (minimum score 550), minimum GPA of 2.5. Application deadline: 7/1 (priority date; rolling processing). Application fee: $55 ($70 for international students). *Tuition:* $996 per course (minimum). • James Koerlin, Dean, 415-442-6540. Fax: 415-442-7049. Application contact: Enrollment Services, 415-442-7800. Fax: 415-442-7807. E-mail: info@ggu.edu.

Graduate School and University Center of the City University of New York, Program in Business, New York, NY 10036-8099. Offerings include management planning systems (PhD). Terminal master's awarded for partial completion of doctoral program. Program faculty: 66 full-time (5 women). *Degree requirements:* Dissertation required, foreign language not required. *Entrance requirements:* GMAT. Application deadline: 3/1. Application fee: $40. *Expenses:* Tuition $4350 per year full-time, $185 per credit (minimum) part-time for state residents; $7600 per year full-time, $320 per credit (minimum) part-time for nonresidents. Fees $69 per year. • Dr. Gloria Thomas, Executive Officer, 212-802-6580.

Hawaii Pacific University, School of Business Administration, 1166 Fort Street, Honolulu, HI 96813-2785. Offerings include information systems management (MSIS), information systems technology (MSIS). School faculty: 30 full-time (3 women), 12 part-time (1 woman), 38 FTE. *Average time to degree:* master's–2 years full-time, 4 years part-time. *Application deadline:* rolling. *Application fee:* $50. Electronic applications accepted. *Tuition:* $7920 per year full-time, $330 per credit part-time. • Dr. Richard Ward, Dean for Graduate Management Studies, 808-544-0279. Application contact: Leina Danao, Admissions Coordinator, 808-544-1120. Fax: 808-544-0280. E-mail: gradservctr@hpu.edu.

Hofstra University, Frank G. Zarb School of Business, Department of Business Computer Information Systems/Quantitative Methods, Hempstead, NY 11549. Awards MBA. Part-time and evening/weekend programs available. Faculty: 15 full-time (2 women), 1 part-time (0 women). Students: 11 full-time (4 women), 59 part-time (18 women); includes 6 minority (2 African Americans, 3 Asian Americans, 1 Hispanic), 5 international. Average age 30. 24 applicants, 71% accepted. In 1997, 23 degrees awarded. *Degree requirements:* Computer language, thesis (for some programs) required, foreign language not required. *Entrance requirements:* GMAT (average 580). Application deadline: rolling. Application fee: $40 ($75 for international students). *Expenses:* Tuition $10,968 per year full-time, $457 per credit hour part-time. Fees $670 per year full-time, $112 per semester (minimum) part-time. *Financial aid:* 10 students received aid; fellowships, research assistantships, Federal Work-Study, and career-related internships or fieldwork available. Financial aid application deadline: 4/1. *Faculty research:* Analysis of industrial performance, adaptation of new computer systems, history of computers, manufacturing and operating strategy, expert systems. • Dr. Farrokh Nasri, Chairperson, 516-463-5716. Fax: 516-463-4834. E-mail: acsfzn@hofstra.edu. Application contact: Susan McTiernan, Senior Assistant Dean, 516-463-5683. Fax: 516-463-5268. E-mail: bizsmm@hofstra.edu.

Houston Baptist University, College of Business and Economics, Program in Management, Computing and Systems, Houston, TX 77074-3298. Awards MSMCS. Part-time and evening/weekend programs available. Faculty: 5 full-time (1 woman), 4 part-time (0 women). Students: 28 full-time (14 women), 1 part-time (0 women); includes 14 minority (8 African Americans, 4 Asian Americans, 2 Hispanics), 1 international. 14 applicants, 79% accepted. In 1997, 13 degrees awarded (100% found work related to degree). *Degree requirements:* Computer language required, foreign language and thesis not required. *Entrance requirements:* GMAT (minimum score 450), GRE General Test (minimum combined score of 900), minimum GPA of 2.5, work experience. Application deadline: 7/1 (priority date; rolling processing; 1/1 for spring admission). Application fee: $25 ($85 for international students). *Expenses:* Tuition $9800 per year. Fees $705 per year. *Financial aid:* Federal Work-Study available. Financial aid application deadline: 6/1; applicants required to submit FAFSA. • Dr. Michael Bourke, Head, 281-649-3312. Application contact: Laurel Motal, Program Assistant, 281-649-3322.

Indiana University Bloomington, School of Business, Doctoral Programs in Business, Bloomington, IN 47405. Offerings include information and decision systems (DBA, PhD). PhD offered through the University Graduate School. *Degree requirements:* Computer language, dissertation required, foreign language not required. *Entrance requirements:* GMAT (minimum score 600), GRE General Test. Application deadline: 3/1. Application fee: $35. *Expenses:* Tuition $261 per credit hour for state residents; $523 per credit hour for nonresidents. Fees $343 per year. • Dr. Janet Near, Chairperson, 812-855-3476. Application contact: Barbara Clark, Program Secretary and Assistant to Chairperson, 812-855-3476. Fax: 812-855-8679. E-mail: bclark@ucs.indiana.edu.

Indiana University Bloomington, School of Business, Program in Business Administration, Bloomington, IN 47405. Offerings include management information systems (MBA). Self-designed programs available. *Entrance requirements:* GMAT, TOEFL (minimum score 580). Application deadline: 3/1. Application fee: $50 ($65 for international students). *Expenses:* Tuition $8232 per year for state residents; $16,470 per year for nonresidents. Fees $343 per year. • Dr. George Hettenhouse, Chair, 812-855-8006. Application contact: Dr. James J. Holmen, Director of Admissions and Financial Aid, 812-855-8006. Fax: 812-855-9039.

Instituto Tecnológico y de Estudios Superiores de Monterrey, Estado de México Campus, Graduate Division, Atizapán de Zaragoza 52926, Mexico. Offerings include information technology administration (MITA). Postbaccalaureate distance learning degree programs offered (minimal on-campus study). Institute faculty: 19 full-time (3 women), 32 part-time (3 women). *Average time to degree:* master's–2 years full-time, 3.3 years part-time. *Application deadline:* 1/12 (priority date; rolling processing; 4/4 for spring admission). *Application fee:* $72. • Emilio Alvarado Badillo, Headmaster, 5-326-5500. Fax: 5-326-5507. E-mail: ealvarad@campus.cem.itesm.mx. Application contact: Lourdes Turrubiates, Admissions Officer, 5-326-5776. E-mail: lturrubi@campus.cem.itesm.mx.

Instituto Tecnológico y de Estudios Superiores de Monterrey, Laguna Campus, Graduate School, Torreón, Coahuila 32583, Mexico. Offers programs in business administration (MBA), industrial engineering (MIE), management information systems (MS). Part-time programs available. *Degree requirements:* Computer language required, foreign language and thesis not required. *Entrance requirements:* GMAT (minimum score 450). Application deadline: 7/31 (priority date). Application fee: $0. *Faculty research:* Computer communications from home to the University.

Iona College, Hagan Graduate School of Business, Department of Information and Technology Management, 715 North Avenue, New Rochelle, NY 10801-1890. Offers programs in management information systems (MBA, PMC), management science (MBA, PMC), production and operations management (MBA, PMC). Part-time and evening/weekend programs available. Faculty: 6 full-time (0 women), 3 part-time (0 women). Students: 3 full-time (2 women), 26 part-time (9 women); includes 3 minority (1 African American, 1 Asian American, 1 Hispanic). Average age 29. In 1997, 17 master's, 1 PMC awarded. *Degree requirements:* For master's, computer language required, foreign language and thesis not required. *Entrance requirements:* For master's, GMAT (minimum score 425; average 510); for PMC, GMAT. Application deadline: rolling. Application fee: $50. *Expenses:* Tuition $480 per credit hour. Fees $25 per semester. *Financial aid:* Graduate assistantships, partial tuition waivers available. Aid available to part-time students. *Faculty research:* Fuzzy sets, risk management, computer security, competence set analysis, investment strategies. • Dr. Donald Moscato, Chairman, 914-633-2555. Application contact: Carol Shea, Director of MBA Admissions, 914-633-2288.

ISIM University, Programs in Information Management, Denver, CO 80246. Offerings in business administration (MBA), including business administration, health care management; information management (MS). Part-time and evening/weekend programs available. Postbaccalaureate distance learning degree programs offered (no on-campus study). Faculty: 1 full-time (0 women), 13 part-time (5 women). Students: 153 part-time (33 women); includes 29 international. Average age 37. *Application deadline:* rolling. *Application fee:* $50. Electronic applications accepted. • Tina Parscal, Director of Education, 800-441-4746. E-mail: tparscal@isim.edu. Application contact: Kristine Larson, Registrar, 303-333-4224. Fax: 303-336-1144. E-mail: klarson@isimu.edu.

Jackson State University, School of Business, Program in Systems Management, Jackson, MS 39217. Awards MSSM. *Degree requirements:* Comprehensive exam. *Entrance requirements:* GRE General Test (minimum combined score of 1000), TOEFL (minimum score 550). Application deadline: 3/1 (10/1 for spring admission). *Tuition:* $2688 per year (minimum) full-time, $150 per semester hour part-time for state residents; $5546 per year (minimum) full-time, $309 per semester hour part-time for nonresidents. • Dr. Jessie C. Pennington, Director, 601-982-6315. Fax: 601-982-6124. Application contact: Mae Robinson, Admissions Coordinator, 601-968-2455. Fax: 601-968-8246. E-mail: mrobinson@ccaix.jsums.edu.

John Marshall Law School, Chicago, IL 60604-3968. Offerings include information technology (LL M, MS). School faculty: 52 full-time (14 women), 230 part-time (43 women). *Average time to degree:* master's–1.5 years full-time, 2 years part-time; first professional–3 years full-time, 4 years part-time. *Entrance requirements:* TOEFL (minimum score 600), TWE (minimum score 415), JD. Application deadline: 3/1 (priority date; rolling processing; 10/1 for spring admission). Application fee: $50 ($60 for international students). *Expenses:* Tuition $675 per credit (minimum). Fees $40 per semester. • Robert Gilbert Johnson, Dean, 312-427-2737. Application contact: William B. Powers, Dean of Admission and Student Affairs, 312-987-1403. Fax: 312-427-5136. E-mail: 6alonzo@jmls.edu.

Johns Hopkins University, School of Continuing Studies, Division of Business and Management, Baltimore, MD 21218-2699. Offerings include information and telecommunication systems for business (MS, Certificate). Division faculty: 12 full-time, 190 part-time. *Degree requirements:* For master's, project required, foreign language and thesis not required. *Entrance requirements:* For master's, minimum GPA of 3.0. Application deadline: rolling. Application fee: $50. • Dr. Jon Heggan, Director, 410-516-0755. Application contact: Lenora Henry, Admissions Coordinator, 410-872-1234. Fax: 410-872-1251. E-mail: adv_mail@jhuvms.hcf.jhu.edu.

Kean University, School of Business, Government, and Technology, Department of Management Science, Union, NJ 07083. Offers program in management systems analysis (MSMSA). Part-time and evening/weekend programs available. Students: 14 full-time (5 women), 64 part-time (22 women); includes 31 minority (9 African Americans, 19 Asian Americans, 3 Hispanics). Average age 33. In 1997, 18 degrees awarded. *Degree requirements:* Computer language required, foreign language and thesis not required. *Entrance requirements:* GMAT or GRE General Test. Application deadline: 6/15 (11/15 for spring admission). Application fee: $35. *Tuition:* $5926 per year full-time, $248 per credit part-time for state residents; $7312 per year full-time, $304 per credit part-time for nonresidents. *Financial aid:* Graduate assistantships available. • Jack Ryder, Coordinator, 908-527-2637. Application contact: Joanne Morris, Director of Graduate Admissions, 908-527-2665. Fax: 908-527-2286. E-mail: grad_adm@turbo.kean.edu.

Keller Graduate School of Management, 1 Tower Lane, Oak Brook Terrace, IL 60181. Offerings include information systems management (MISM). School faculty: 604. *Average time to degree:* master's–3 years part-time. *Application deadline:* rolling. *Application fee:* $0. *Tuition:* $1235 per course. • Dr. Sherrill Hole, Director, Academic Affairs, 630-574-1894. Application contact: Michael J. Alexander, Director, Central Services, 630-574-1957. Fax: 630-574-1969.

Kennesaw State University, Michael J. Coles College of Business, Program in Business Administration, Kennesaw, GA 30144-5591. Offerings include business information systems management (MBA). Program faculty: 54 full-time (18 women), 5 part-time (0 women). *Application deadline:* 7/1 (rolling processing; 2/20 for spring admission). *Application fee:* $20. *Expenses:* Tuition $2398 per year full-time, $83 per credit hour part-time for state residents; $8398 per year full-time, $333 per credit hour part-time for nonresidents. Fees $338 per year. • Dr. Rodney Alsup, Assistant Dean, 770-423-6087. Fax: 770-423-6141. E-mail: ralsup@ksumail.kennesaw.edu. Application contact: Susan N. Barrett, Administrative Specialist, Admissions, 770-423-6500. Fax: 770-423-6541. E-mail: sbarrett@ksumail.kennesaw.edu.

Kent State University, Graduate School of Management, Doctoral Program in Management Systems, Kent, OH 44242-0001. Awards PhD. Faculty: 17 full-time (2 women), 2 part-time (0 women). Students: 18 full-time (2 women), 13 part-time (3 women); includes 4 minority (1

Directory: Management Information Systems

Kent State University (continued)
African American, 3 Asian Americans), 8 international. 11 applicants, 36% accepted. In 1997, 8 degrees awarded. *Degree requirements:* Dissertation, comprehensive exams, oral defense required, foreign language not required. *Entrance requirements:* GMAT. Application deadline: 2/1. Application fee: $30. *Tuition:* $4752 per year full-time, $216 per credit hour part-time for state residents; $9213 per year full-time, $419 per credit hour part-time for nonresidents. *Financial aid:* In 1997–98, 8 teaching assistantships (3 to first-year students) averaging $1,000 per month were awarded; fellowships, Federal Work-Study also available. Financial aid application deadline: 2/1; applicants required to submit FAFSA. • G. Jay Weinroth, Chair, 330-672-2750 Ext. 341. Fax: 330-672-2448. E-mail: jweinrot@bsa3.kent.edu. Application contact: Dr. James C. Baker, Doctoral Director, 330-672-2282 Ext. 235. Fax: 330-672-7303. E-mail: jbaker@bsa3.kent.edu.

Knowledge Systems Institute, Program in Computer and Information Sciences, Skokie, IL 60076. Offerings include management information systems (MS). Institute faculty: 4 full-time (0 women), 23 part-time (3 women), 10 FTE. *Application fee:* $40. *Tuition:* $6600 per year full-time, $715 per course part-time. • Judy Pan, Executive Director, 847-679-3135. Fax: 847-679-3166. E-mail: judy@ksi.edu.

Lawrence Technological University, College of Management, 21000 West Ten Mile Road, Southfield, MI 48075-1058. Offerings include information systems (MS). College faculty: 7 full-time (2 women), 22 part-time (5 women), 17 FTE. *Average time to degree:* master's–3 years part-time. *Application deadline:* 8/1 (priority date; rolling processing; 1/1 for spring admission). *Application fee:* $50. Electronic applications accepted. *Expenses:* Tuition $11,400 per year full-time, $380 per credit hour part-time. Fees $100 per year. • Dr. Lou DeGennaro, Dean, 248-204-3050. E-mail: degennaro@ltu.edu. Application contact: Paul Kinder, Director of Admissions, 248-204-3160. Fax: 248-204-3188. E-mail: admissions@ltu.edu.

The Leadership Institute of Seattle, School of Applied Behavioral Science, Systems Counseling Track, Bellevue, WA 98004-6934. Awards MAABS. Offered jointly with Bastyr University. Faculty: 6 full-time (2 women), 1 (woman) part-time. Students: 121 full-time (93 women), 8 part-time (7 women); includes 8 minority (1 African American, 1 Asian American, 1 Hispanic, 5 Native Americans), 15 international. Average age 41. *Degree requirements:* Thesis or alternative, oral exams required, foreign language not required. *Average time to degree:* master's–2.5 years full-time. *Application deadline:* 8/1 (priority date; rolling processing). *Application fee:* $65. *Tuition:* $359 per unit. *Financial aid:* Scholarships available. Financial aid applicants required to submit FAFSA. *Faculty research:* Family systems theory, marriage and family therapy, systems consultation, family and culture of origin, personal authority. • Dr. Timothy Weber, Head, 425-635-1187. E-mail: lios@cyberspace.com. Application contact: Lynn Morrison, Admissions Director, 425-635-1187 Ext. 253. Fax: 425-635-1188.

Lesley College, School of Management, Cambridge, MA 02138-2790. Offerings include management of information technology (MSM). Postbaccalaureate distance learning degree programs offered (no on-campus study). School faculty: 10 full-time (4 women), 204 part-time (78 women). *Application deadline:* rolling. *Application fee:* $45. *Tuition:* $425 per credit. • Dr. Earl Potter, Dean, 617-349-8682. Fax: 617-349-8678. Application contact: Marilyn Gove, Associate Director, 617-349-8690. Fax: 617-349-8313. E-mail: mgove@mail.lesley.edu.

Long Island University, C.W. Post Campus, College of Management, School of Business, Department of Management, Brookville, NY 11548-1300. Offerings include management information systems (MBA). MBA (international business) offered jointly with Franklin College Switzerland. JD/MBA offered jointly with Touro College. Department faculty: 8 full-time (4 women), 13 part-time (2 women). *Entrance requirements:* GMAT. Application deadline: 8/15 (priority date; rolling processing; 12/15 for spring admission). Application fee: $30. Electronic applications accepted. *Expenses:* Tuition $480 per credit. Fees $316 per year full-time, $71 per semester (minimum) part-time. • Dr. Anthony M. Akel, Chairman, 516-299-2360. E-mail: aakel@eagle.liunet.edu. Application contact: Sally Luzader, Associate Director of Graduate Admissions, 516-299-2417. Fax: 516-299-2137. E-mail: admissions@collegehall.liunet.edu.

Louisiana State University and Agricultural and Mechanical College, College of Business Administration, Department of Information Systems and Decision Sciences, Baton Rouge, LA 70803. Offers programs in business administration (PhD), including information systems and decision sciences; information systems and decision sciences (MS). Faculty: 9 full-time (1 woman). Students: 85; includes 11 minority (5 African Americans, 5 Asian Americans, 1 Hispanic), 35 international. Average age 30. 46 applicants, 43% accepted. In 1997, 17 master's, 3 doctorates awarded. Terminal master's awarded for partial completion of doctoral program. *Degree requirements:* For master's, computer language required, thesis optional, foreign language not required; for doctorate, computer language, dissertation required, foreign language not required. *Entrance requirements:* For master's, GMAT or GRE General Test. Application deadline: 1/25 (priority date; rolling processing). Application fee: $25. *Tuition:* $2736 per year full-time, $285 per semester (minimum) part-time for state residents; $6636 per year full-time, $460 per semester (minimum) part-time for nonresidents. *Financial aid:* In 1997–98, 11 research assistantships (2 to first-year students), 6 teaching assistantships, 13 service assistantships were awarded; fellowships also available. *Faculty research:* Management information systems, production/operations management, quality control. • Helmut Schneider, Chair, 504-388-2126.

Loyola University Chicago, Graduate School of Business, 820 North Michigan Avenue, Chicago, IL 60611-2196. Offerings include information systems management (MS). School faculty: 68 full-time (9 women), 3 part-time (1 woman). *Average time to degree:* master's–1.2 years full-time, 4 years part-time. *Application deadline:* 6/31 (rolling processing; 11/30 for spring admission). *Application fee:* $35. *Tuition:* $1985 per course. • Paul Davidovitch, Director, MBA Program, 312-915-6120. Application contact: Carmen Santiago, Admissions Coordinator, 312-915-6120.

Manhattan College, Program in Business Administration, Riverdale, NY 10471. Offerings include management information systems (MBA). Program faculty: 18 full-time (3 women), 8 part-time (0 women). *Degree requirements:* Computer language, thesis or alternative. *Entrance requirements:* GMAT, minimum GPA of 2.8. Application deadline: 8/10 (priority date; rolling processing; 1/7 for spring admission). Application fee: $50. *Expenses:* Tuition $440 per credit. Fees $100 per year. • Dr. Charles E. Brunner, Director, 718-862-7222. Fax: 718-862-8023. Application contact: William J. Bisset Jr., Dean of Admissions/Financial Aid, 718-862-7200. Fax: 718-863-8019. E-mail: admit@manhattan.edu.

Marymount University, School of Business Administration, Program in Information Management, Arlington, VA 22207-4299. Awards MS. Part-time and evening/weekend programs available. Students: 113. In 1997, 41 degrees awarded. *Degree requirements:* Thesis optional, foreign language not required. *Entrance requirements:* GMAT or GRE General Test, interview. Application deadline: rolling. Application fee: $35. *Expenses:* Tuition $465 per credit hour. Fees $120 per year full-time, $5 per credit hour part-time. *Financial aid:* Career-related internships or fieldwork available. Aid available to part-time students. Financial aid applicants required to submit FAFSA. • Dr. Barry Landson, Chair, 703-284-5910. Fax: 703-527-3815. E-mail: barry.landson@marymount.edu.

Marywood University, Graduate School of Arts and Sciences, Department of Business and Managerial Science, Program in Management Information Systems, Scranton, PA 18509-1598. Awards MBA, MS. Students: 1 full-time (0 women), 2 part-time (1 woman). Average age 32. 7 applicants, 57% accepted. In 1997, 2 degrees awarded. *Degree requirements:* Computer language, comprehensive exam required, foreign language and thesis not required. *Entrance requirements:* GMAT, TOEFL (minimum score 550; average 590). Application deadline: 7/15 (priority date; rolling processing; 12/1 for spring admission). Application fee: $20. *Expenses:* Tuition $449 per credit hour. Fees $530 per year full-time, $180 per year part-time. *Financial aid:* Research assistantships, scholarships/tuition reductions, partial tuition waivers, and career-related internships or fieldwork available. Aid available to part-time students. Financial aid application deadline: 2/15; applicants required to submit FAFSA. *Faculty research:* Systems design. • Application contact: Deborah M. Flynn, Coordinator of Admissions, 717-340-6002. Fax: 717-961-4745.

McMaster University, Faculty of Business, Program in Management Science/Systems, Hamilton, ON L8S 4M2, Canada. Awards PhD. Part-time and evening/weekend programs available. Faculty: 49 full-time, 2 part-time. *Degree requirements:* Computer language, dissertation, comprehensive exam required, foreign language not required. *Entrance requirements:* GMAT or GRE, master's degree. Application deadline: 6/1. Application fee: $50. *Expenses:* Tuition $4422 per year full-time, $1590 per year part-time for Canadian residents; $12,000 per year full-time, $6165 per year part-time for nonresidents. Fees $257 per year full-time, $188 per year part-time. *Financial aid:* Fellowships, research assistantships, teaching assistantships available. *Faculty research:* Information systems, operations management. • Dr. M. Parlar, Coordinator, 905-525-9140 Ext. 23858.

Metropolitan State University, Management and Administration Program, St. Paul, MN 55106-5000. Offerings include management information systems (MBA). Program faculty: 17 full-time (5 women), 150 part-time. *Application deadline:* rolling. *Application fee:* $20. *Tuition:* $133 per credit for state residents; $208 per credit for nonresidents. • Gary Seiler, Graduate Coordinator, 612-373-2754. E-mail: seiler@msus1.msus.edu. Application contact: Gloria Marcus, Recruiter/Admissions Adviser, 612-373-2724. Fax: 612-373-2888. E-mail: marcusg@msus1.msus.edu.

Miami University, Richard T. Farmer School of Business Administration, Oxford, OH 45056. Offerings include decision sciences (MBA), management information systems (MBA). School faculty: 50. *Application deadline:* 3/1 (priority date; rolling processing). *Application fee:* $35. *Tuition:* $5932 per year full-time, $255 per credit hour part-time for state residents; $12,392 per year full-time, $524 per credit hour part-time for nonresidents. • Judy Barille, Director of Graduate Programs, 513-529-6643.

Middle Tennessee State University, College of Business, Department of Accounting, Murfreesboro, TN 37132. Offerings include information systems (MS). Department faculty: 11 full-time (2 women). *Degree requirements:* Comprehensive exams required, foreign language and thesis not required. *Entrance requirements:* GMAT. Application deadline: 8/1 (priority date). Application fee: $5. *Expenses:* Tuition $2560 per year full-time, $129 per semester hour part-time for state residents; $7386 per year full-time, $340 per semester hour part-time for nonresidents. Fees $486 per year full-time, $17 per semester (minimum) part-time. • Dr. William Grasty, Chair, 615-898-2558. Fax: 615-898-5045. E-mail: wgrasty@mtsu.edu.

Middle Tennessee State University, College of Business, Department of Computer Information Systems, Murfreesboro, TN 37132. Awards MS. Faculty: 12 full-time (2 women). Students: 21 full-time (6 women), 30 part-time (9 women); includes 6 minority (5 African Americans, 1 Asian American), 15 international. Average age 32. In 1997, 22 degrees awarded. *Degree requirements:* Comprehensive exams required, foreign language and thesis not required. *Entrance requirements:* GMAT. Application deadline: 8/1 (priority date). Application fee: $5. *Expenses:* Tuition $2560 per year full-time, $129 per semester hour part-time for state residents; $7386 per year full-time, $340 per semester hour part-time for nonresidents. Fees $486 per year full-time, $17 per semester (minimum) part-time. *Financial aid:* Teaching assistantships, institutionally sponsored loans available. Aid available to part-time students. Financial aid application deadline: 5/1; applicants required to submit FAFSA. • Dr. Michael Gibson, Chair, 615-898-2362. Fax: 615-898-5045.

Mississippi State University, College of Business and Industry, Department of Management and Information Systems, Mississippi State, MS 39762. Offers programs in information systems (MSBA), systems management (MSSM). Part-time programs available. Faculty: 13 full-time. Students: 22 full-time (8 women), 9 part-time (1 woman); includes 2 minority (both African Americans), 6 international. Average age 25. 14 applicants, 93% accepted. In 1997, 20 degrees awarded. *Degree requirements:* Thesis (for some programs), comprehensive oral or written exam required, foreign language not required. *Entrance requirements:* GMAT (minimum score 450), TOEFL (minimum score 575), minimum QPA 4.0 in last 60 hours, 2.75 overall. Application deadline: 7/1 (priority date; rolling processing; 11/1 for spring admission). Application fee: $0 ($25 for international students). *Tuition:* $3017 per year full-time, $168 per credit hour part-time for state residents; $6119 per year full-time, $340 per credit hour part-time for nonresidents. *Financial aid:* In 1997–98, 12 research assistantships, 8 assistantships were awarded; teaching assistantships, Federal Work-Study also available. Financial aid application deadline: 3/15. • Dr. Barbara A. Spencer, Acting Head, 601-325-3928.

Naval Postgraduate School, Department of Systems Management, Monterey, CA 93943. Awards MS, PhD. Program only open to commissioned officers of the United States and friendly nations and selected United States federal civilian employees. Students: 381 full-time; includes 29 international. In 1997, 138 master's awarded. *Degree requirements:* For master's, computer language, thesis required, foreign language not required; for doctorate, 1 foreign language, computer language, dissertation. *Tuition:* $0. • Dr. Reuben T. Harris, Chairman, 831-656-2161. Application contact: Theodore H. Calhoon, Director of Admissions, 831-656-3093. Fax: 831-656-2891. E-mail: tcalhoon@nps.navy.mil.

New Hampshire College, Graduate School of Business, Program in Computer Information Systems, Manchester, NH 03106-1045. Awards MS, Certificate. Part-time and evening/weekend programs available. Faculty: 3 full-time (0 women), 6 part-time (0 women), 4 FTE. Students: 17 full-time (6 women), 53 part-time (20 women); includes 14 international. Average age 31. In 1997, 27 master's awarded. *Degree requirements:* For master's, computer language, thesis or alternative required, foreign language not required. *Average time to degree:* master's–1.5 years full-time, 4 years part-time. *Entrance requirements:* For master's, minimum GPA of 2.7 during previous 2 years, 2.5 overall. Application deadline: rolling. Application fee: $0. *Expenses:* Tuition $17,044 per year full-time, $945 per course part-time. Fees $530 per year full-time, $80 per year part-time. *Financial aid:* In 1997–98, 2 research assistantships (both to first-year students) were awarded; Federal Work-Study, institutionally sponsored loans, and career-related internships or fieldwork also available. Aid available to part-time students. • Dr. Paul Schneiderman, Acting Dean, Graduate School of Business, 603-644-3102. Fax: 603-644-3150.

New York University, Leonard N. Stern School of Business, Department of Information Systems, New York, NY 10006. Awards MBA, MS, PhD, APC. Faculty: 17 full-time (0 women), 16 part-time (2 women). Students: 70 full-time, 235 part-time. In 1997, 107 master's, 2 doctorates, 2 APCs awarded. *Degree requirements:* For master's, computer language required, foreign language and thesis not required; for doctorate, computer language, dissertation required, foreign language not required. *Entrance requirements:* For master's, GMAT, TOEFL (minimum score 600); for doctorate, GMAT. Application deadline: 3/15 (rolling processing). Application fee: $75. *Financial aid:* Federal Work-Study available. Financial aid application deadline: 1/15; applicants required to submit FAFSA. *Faculty research:* Electronic markets, knowledge management, financial engineering, information technology and service industry organization, information technology impact on organization firms and industry performance. Total annual research expenditures: $200,000. • Myron Uretsky, Chairman, 212-998-0800. Fax: 212-995-4228. E-mail: muretsky@stern.nyu.edu. Application contact: Mary Miller, Director, Graduate Admissions, 212-998-0600. Fax: 212-995-4231. E-mail: sternmba@stern.nyu.edu.

New York University, School of Continuing Education, Program in Information Systems Auditing, New York, NY 10012-1019. Awards APC. Faculty: 1 full-time (0 women), 4 part-time (2 women). Students: 24 part-time (9 women); includes 6 minority (2 African Americans, 2 Asian Americans, 2 Hispanics). Average age 35. 23 applicants, 78% accepted. In 1997, 9 degrees awarded (100% found work related to degree). *Entrance requirements:* Work related experience. Application deadline: 5/15 (priority date). Application fee: $25. *Financial aid:* Available to part-time students. Financial aid application deadline: 3/1. • Richard Vigilante, Director, 212-998-7199. Fax: 212-995-3550. E-mail: vigilant@is2.nyu.edu.

New York University, School of Continuing Education, The Virtual College, New York, NY 10012-1019. Offers programs in information technology (APC), management control and systems (MS). Part-time and evening/weekend programs available. Postbaccalaureate distance learning degree programs offered (no on-campus study). Students: 2 part-time (0 women). Average age 31. 5 applicants, 40% accepted. *Degree requirements:* For master's, project required, foreign language not required. *Entrance requirements:* For master's, GMAT, TOEFL, work experience; for APC, work related experience. Application deadline: 7/31 (priority date; rolling processing; 11/30 for spring admission). Application fee: $50. • Richard Vigilante, Senior Director, Information Technologies Institute, 212-998-7199. E-mail: vigilant@is2.nyu.edu. Application contact: Christina Camus, Administrative Aide, 212-998-9112. Fax: 212-995-3550. E-mail: cjci@is6.nyu.edu.

See in-depth description on page 585.

North Carolina State University, College of Management, Program in Management, Raleigh, NC 27695. Offerings include management information systems (MS). Program faculty: 53 full-time (7 women), 3 part-time (0 women). *Degree requirements:* Computer language required, foreign language and thesis not required. *Entrance requirements:* GRE or GMAT, TOEFL (minimum score 550), minimum undergraduate GPA of 3.0. Application deadline: 6/25 (rolling processing; 11/25 for spring admission). Application fee: $45. *Tuition:* $2370 per year full-time, $517 per semester (minimum) part-time for state residents; $11,536 per year full-time, $2809 per semester (minimum) part-time for nonresidents. • Dr. Jack W. Wilson, Director of Graduate Programs, 919-515-4327. Fax: 919-515-6943. E-mail: jack_wilson@ncsu.edu. Application contact: Dr. Steven G. Allen, Director of Graduate Programs, 919-515-6941. Fax: 919-515-5073. E-mail: steve_allen@ncsu.edu.

North Central College, Graduate Programs, Department of Business Administration, Department of Management Information Systems, Naperville, IL 60566-7063. Awards MS. Faculty: 12. Students: 25. In 1997, 11 degrees awarded. *Degree requirements:* Project required, thesis not required. *Entrance requirements:* GMAT or GRE General Test, minimum GPA of 2.75. Application deadline: 8/15 (rolling processing). Application fee: $25. *Financial aid:* Available to part-time students. • Judy Walters, Coordinator, 630-637-5840.

Northern Arizona University, College of Business Administration, Program in Management Information Systems, Flagstaff, AZ 86011. Awards MBA. Part-time programs available. *Degree requirements:* Computer language required, foreign language and thesis not required. *Entrance requirements:* GMAT. Application deadline: 3/1 (priority date; rolling processing; 10/15 for spring admission). Application fee: $45. *Expenses:* Tuition $2088 per year full-time, $330 per semester (minimum) part-time for state residents; $8004 per year full-time, $1002 per semester (minimum) part-time for nonresidents. Fees $72 per year full-time, $18 per semester (minimum) part-time. *Financial aid:* Research assistantships, full and partial tuition waivers, Federal Work-Study, institutionally sponsored loans available. • Dr. Mason Gerety, MBA Director, 520-523-7342.

Northern Illinois University, College of Business, Department of Operations Management and Information Systems, De Kalb, IL 60115-2854. Offers program in management information systems (MS). Part-time programs available. Faculty: 11 full-time (3 women), 2 part-time (0 women). Students: 41 full-time (14 women), 65 part-time (23 women); includes 13 minority (3 African Americans, 8 Asian Americans, 2 Hispanics), 22 international. Average age 31. 110 applicants, 49% accepted. In 1997, 33 degrees awarded. *Degree requirements:* Computer language required, foreign language and thesis not required. *Entrance requirements:* GMAT, TOEFL (minimum score 550), minimum GPA of 2.75. Application deadline: 6/1 (rolling processing; 11/1 for spring admission). Application fee: $30. *Tuition:* $3984 per year full-time, $154 per credit hour part-time for state residents; $8160 per year full-time, $328 per credit hour part-time for nonresidents. *Financial aid:* In 1997–98, 15 research assistantships, 1 staff assistantship were awarded; fellowships, teaching assistantships, full tuition waivers, Federal Work-Study, and career-related internships or fieldwork also available. Aid available to part-time students. • Dr. William Tallon, Chair, 815-753-1185.

Northwestern University, School of Speech, Department of Communication Studies, Communication Systems Program, Evanston, IL 60208. Awards MSC. Part-time programs available. Faculty: 8 full-time (0 women), 5 part-time (1 woman). Students: 43 part-time (14 women); includes 6 minority (4 African Americans, 1 Asian American, 1 Hispanic). Average age 34. 29 applicants, 76% accepted. In 1997, 19 degrees awarded. *Application deadline:* 6/30 (priority date; rolling processing). *Application fee:* $30. Electronic applications accepted. *Tuition:* $20,430 per year full-time, $2424 per course part-time. *Financial aid:* Institutionally sponsored loans available. Financial aid application deadline: 6/30; applicants required to submit FAFSA. • Donna Weirich, Director of Admissions, 847-491-3848. E-mail: comsystems@nwu.edu.

See in-depth description on page 587.

Nova Southeastern University, School of Computer and Information Sciences, Fort Lauderdale, FL 33314-7721. Offerings include information systems (PhD), management information systems (MS). Terminal master's awarded for partial completion of doctoral program. Postbaccalaureate distance learning degree programs offered. School faculty: 15 full-time (4 women), 8 part-time (2 women). *Degree requirements:* For master's, computer language required, thesis optional. *Average time to degree:* doctorate–4 years full-time. *Entrance requirements:* For master's, GRE or portfolio. Application deadline: 6/1 (priority date; rolling processing; 1/1 for spring admission). Application fee: $50. *Tuition:* $357 per credit hour (minimum). • Dr. Edward Lieblein, Dean. Application contact: Kimberly Jaggers, Marketing Assistant, 800-986-2247 Ext. 2000. Fax: 954-262-3872. E-mail: scisinfo@scis.nova.edu.

Nova Southeastern University, School of Computer and Information Sciences, Program in Management Information Systems, Fort Lauderdale, FL 33314-7721. Awards MS. Students: 53 full-time (20 women), 42 part-time (16 women); includes 3 African Americans, 3 Asian Americans, 6 Hispanics, 14 international. In 1997, 34 degrees awarded. *Degree requirements:* Computer language required, thesis optional. *Entrance requirements:* GRE or portfolio. Application deadline: 6/1 (priority date; rolling processing; 1/1 for spring admission). Application fee: $50. *Tuition:* $357 per credit hour (minimum). *Financial aid:* Application deadline 5/1. • Application contact: Liz Gawalek, Program Representative, 800-986-2247 Ext. 2000. Fax: 954-262-3915. E-mail: scisinfo@scis.nova.edu.

Announcement: MS and PhD degrees are available in management information systems. These programs focus on the application of information system concepts to the collection, retention, and dissemination of information for management planning and decision making. The formats, on campus or on line, offer the opportunity to earn the MS in 18 months and the PhD in 3 years.

The Ohio State University, Max M. Fisher College of Business, Department of Accounting and Management Information Systems, Columbus, OH 43210. Awards MA, PhD. Faculty: 20. Students: 11 full-time (3 women); includes 5 international. 44 applicants, 16% accepted. In 1997, 5 master's, 4 doctorates awarded. Terminal master's awarded for partial completion of doctoral program. *Degree requirements:* For doctorate, dissertation required, foreign language not required. *Entrance requirements:* For master's, GMAT, TOEFL (minimum score 575); for doctorate, GMAT, TOEFL. Application deadline: 8/15 (rolling processing). Application fee: $30 ($40 for international students). *Tuition:* $6018 per year full-time, $635 per quarter (minimum) part-time for state residents; $14,835 per year full-time, $1514 per quarter (minimum) part-time for nonresidents. *Financial aid:* Fellowships, research assistantships, teaching assistantships, Federal Work-Study, institutionally sponsored loans, and career-related internships or fieldwork available. Aid available to part-time students. *Faculty research:* Artificial intelligence, protocol analysis, database design in decision-supporting systems. • Lawrence Tomassini, Chairman, 614-292-9368. Fax: 614-292-2118. E-mail: tomassini.1@osu.edu.

Oklahoma City University, School of Management and Business Sciences, Program in Business Administration, Oklahoma City, OK 73106-1402. Offerings include information systems management (MBA). *Degree requirements:* Comprehensive exam required, foreign language and thesis not required. *Entrance requirements:* TOEFL, minimum GPA of 2.5. Application deadline: rolling. Application fee: $35 ($55 for international students). *Expenses:* Tuition $350 per hour. Fees $124 per year. • Application contact: Laura L. Rahhal, Director of Graduate Admissions, 800-633-7242 Ext. 2. Fax: 405-521-5356. E-mail: lrahhal1@frodo.okcu.edu.

Pace University, Lubin School of Business, Information Systems Program, New York, NY 10038. Awards MBA. Part-time and evening/weekend programs available. *Degree requirements:* Computer language required, foreign language not required. *Entrance requirements:* GMAT. Application deadline: 7/31 (priority date; rolling processing; 11/30 for spring admission). Application fee: $60. *Expenses:* Tuition $545 per credit. Fees $360 per year full-time, $53 per semester (minimum) part-time.

Pennsylvania State University Harrisburg Campus of the Capital College, School of Business Administration, Program in Information Systems, Middletown, PA 17057-4898. Awards MS. Students: 8 full-time (4 women), 67 part-time (22 women). Average age 33. In 1997, 11 degrees awarded. *Entrance requirements:* GMAT, TOEFL (minimum score 550). Application deadline: 7/26. Application fee: $40. *Expenses:* Tuition $6534 per year full-time, $276 per credit part-time for state residents; $12,516 per year full-time, $523 per credit part-time for nonresidents. Fees $232 per year (minimum) full-time, $40 per semester (minimum) part-time. • Dr. Gayle Yaverbaum, Director of Graduate Studies, 717-948-6140.

Pennsylvania State University University Park Campus, The Mary Jean and Frank P. Smeal College of Business Administration, MS Programs in Business Administration, Department of Management Science and Information Systems, University Park, PA 16802-1503. Awards MS. *Degree requirements:* Thesis or alternative required, foreign language not required. *Entrance requirements:* GMAT. Application fee: $40. *Expenses:* Tuition $6534 per year full-time, $276 per credit part-time for state residents; $13,460 per year full-time, $561 per credit part-time for nonresidents. Fees $252 per year (minimum) full-time, $43 per semester (minimum) part-time. • Dr. J. Keith Ord, Chair, 814-865-0073.

Philadelphia College of Textiles and Science, School of Science and Health, Program in Instructional Technology, Philadelphia, PA 19144-5497. Awards MS, MBA/MS. Part-time and evening/weekend programs available. *Entrance requirements:* GRE or MAT, minimum GPA of 2.85. Application deadline: rolling. Application fee: $35. *Tuition:* $427 per credit hour. *Financial aid:* Research assistantships, graduate assistantships, residential assistantships, Federal Work-Study, and career-related internships or fieldwork available. Financial aid applicants required to submit FAFSA. • Dr. Terry Olivier, Director, 215-951-2872. Fax: 215-951-2615. E-mail: oliviert@phila.col.com. Application contact: Robert J. Reed, Director of Graduate Admissions, 215-951-2943. Fax: 215-951-2907. E-mail: gradadm@phila.col.edu.

Purdue University, Krannert Graduate School of Management, Department of Management, West Lafayette, IN 47907. Offerings include management information systems (MSM, PhD). Department faculty: 51 full-time (5 women). *Degree requirements:* For doctorate, dissertation required, foreign language not required. *Average time to degree:* doctorate–4 years full-time. *Entrance requirements:* For doctorate, GMAT, TOEFL (minimum score 575). Application fee: $30. Electronic applications accepted. *Tuition:* $3500 per year full-time, $126 per credit hour part-time for state residents; $11,720 per year full-time, $387 per credit hour part-time for nonresidents. • Dr. J. J. McConnell, Director of Doctoral Programs, 765-494-4375. Application contact: Kelly Felty, Assistant Director of Administration for Doctoral Programs, 765-494-4375. Fax: 765-494-1526. E-mail: feltyk@mgmt.purdue.edu.

Quinnipiac College, School of Business, Program in Business Administration, Hamden, CT 06518-1904. Offerings include computer information systems (MBA). Program faculty: 17 full-time (2 women), 4 part-time (1 woman). *Degree requirements:* Thesis optional, foreign language not required. *Average time to degree:* master's–2 years full-time, 4 years part-time. *Entrance requirements:* GMAT (minimum score 400; average 470), interview, minimum GPA of 2.5. Application deadline: 8/1 (priority date; rolling processing). Application fee: $45. Electronic applications accepted. *Expenses:* Tuition $395 per credit hour. Fees $380 per year full-time. • Dr. Earl Chrysler, Director, 203-281-8799. Fax: 203-281-8664. E-mail: chrysler@quinnipiac.edu. Application contact: Scott Farber, Director of Graduate Admissions, 203-281-8795. Fax: 203-287-5238. E-mail: qcgradadmi@quinnipiac.edu.

Regis University, Program in Computer Information Systems, Denver, CO 80221-1099. Awards MSCIS. Offered at Boulder Campus, Northwest Denver Campus, Southeast Denver Campus, Fort Collins Campus, and Colorado Springs Campus. Part-time and evening/weekend programs available. Students: 236 full-time, 155 part-time; includes 47 minority (17 African Americans, 12 Asian Americans, 15 Hispanics, 3 Native Americans), 25 international. Average age 36. In 1997, 45 degrees awarded. *Degree requirements:* Computer language, final research project required, foreign language and thesis not required. *Average time to degree:* master's–2 years full-time, 3 years part-time. *Entrance requirements:* 3 years of related experience. Application deadline: rolling. Application fee: $75. Electronic applications accepted. *Tuition:* $275 per semester hour. *Financial aid:* Federal Work-Study available. Aid available to part-time students. Financial aid applicants required to submit FAFSA. *Faculty research:* Application of computer techniques to solving organizational problems, networking, object-oriented programs, multi-media technologies, data base technologies. • Don Archer, Chair, 303-458-4302. Application contact: Richard Boorom, Director of Marketing and Admissions, 800-677-9270. Fax: 303-964-5538. E-mail: admarg@regis.edu.

Rensselaer Polytechnic Institute, Lally School of Management and Technology, Troy, NY 12180-3590. Offerings include business administration (MBA, PhD), with options in finance and accounting (MBA), information systems management (MBA), management (PhD), management of technology and entrepreneurships (MBA), manufacturing management (MBA), marketing management (MBA), operations research (MBA), organizational behavior and human resource management (MBA), statistical methods for management (MBA); management information systems (PhD). Postbaccalaureate distance learning degree programs offered (no on-campus study). School faculty: 36 full-time (5 women), 6 part-time (0 women). *Degree requirements:* For doctorate, computer language, dissertation required, foreign language not required. *Entrance requirements:* For doctorate, GMAT or GRE General Test, TOEFL (minimum score 570). Application deadline: 2/1 (priority date; rolling processing). Application fee: $35. *Expenses:* Tuition $630 per credit hour. Fees $1000 per year. • Dr. Joseph G. Ecker, Dean, 518-276-6802. Application contact: Michele Martens, Manager of Enrollment Services, 518-276-4800. Fax: 518-276-8661.

Richmond, The American International University in London, Program in Systems Engineering and Management, Richmond, Surrey TW10 6JP, United Kingdom. Awards MS. Part-time and evening/weekend programs available. Faculty: 7 full-time (2 women), 7 part-time (0 women), 10.5 FTE. Students: 10 full-time (7 women), 6 part-time (3 women); includes 9 minority (4 African Americans, 4 Asian Americans, 1 Hispanic). Average age 26. 31 applicants, 29% accepted. *Average time to degree:* master's–1.5 years full-time, 3 years part-time. *Application deadline:* 9/1 (priority date; rolling processing; 1/26 for spring admission). *Application fee:* $58. *Expenses:* Tuition $23,257 per year. Fees $1485 per year. *Financial aid:* In 1997–98, 4 merit scholarships totaling $6,600 were awarded; partial tuition waivers and career-related internships or fieldwork also available. Aid available to part-time students. *Faculty research:* Critical systems safety, parallel processing systems, models and measures, software engineering, MIS. Total annual research expenditures: $20,000. • Dr. John Dwyer, Director, 171-368-8488. E-mail: mssem@richmond.ac.uk. Application contact: Catherine Byrne, Assistant Dean of Graduate Admissions, 171-368-8475. Fax: 171-376-0836. E-mail: grad@richmond.ac.uk.

Robert Morris College, Program in Business Administration, 881 Narrows Run Road, Moon Township, PA 15108-1189. Offerings include computer information systems (MBA, MS). Only part-time programs offered. Program faculty: 35 full-time (6 women), 35 part-time (5 women). *Entrance requirements:* GMAT (minimum score 450), minimum GPA of 2.5. Application deadline:

Directory: Management Information Systems

Robert Morris College (continued)

8/1 (priority date; rolling processing; 11/30 for spring admission). Application fee: $25 ($35 for international students). *Expenses:* Tuition $328 per credit. Fees $15 per credit. • Dr. Joseph F. Constable, Dean, School of Management, 412-262-8451. Fax: 412-262-8494. E-mail: constabl@robert-morris.edu. Application contact: Vincent J. Kane, Recruiting Coordinator, 412-262-8535. Fax: 412-299-2425.

Robert Morris College, Program in Communications and Information Systems, 881 Narrows Run Road, Moon Township, PA 15108-1189. Awards MS. Only part-time programs offered. Faculty: 35 full-time (6 women), 35 part-time (5 women). Students: 55 part-time. In 1997, 14 degrees awarded. *Entrance requirements:* Minimum GPA of 2.5. Application deadline: 8/1 (priority date; rolling processing; 11/30 for spring admission). Application fee: $25 ($35 for international students). *Expenses:* Tuition $328 per credit. Fees $15 per credit. *Financial aid:* Available to part-time students. Financial aid application deadline: 5/1; applicants required to submit FAFSA. • Dr. William L. Sipple, Dean, School of Communications and Information Systems, 412-262-8376. Fax: 412-262-4049. Application contact: Vincent J. Kane, Recruiting Coordinator, 412-262-8535. Fax: 412-299-2425.

Roosevelt University, Walter E. Heller College of Business Administration, Program in Information Systems, Chicago, IL 60605-1394. Awards MSIS. Part-time and evening/weekend programs available. Students: 73 (37 women); includes 18 minority (10 African Americans, 7 Asian Americans, 1 Hispanic), 11 international. In 1997, 16 degrees awarded. *Entrance requirements:* GMAT. Application deadline: 6/1 (priority date; rolling processing). Application fee: $25 ($35 for international students). *Expenses:* Tuition $445 per credit hour. Fees $100 per year. *Financial aid:* Application deadline 2/15. • Dr. Jennifer Wagner, Graduate Adviser, 312-341-3820. Fax: 312-341-3827. E-mail: jwagner@acfsysv.roosevelt.edu. Application contact: Joanne Canyon-Heller, Coordinator of Graduate Admissions, 312-341-3612.

Rutgers, The State University of New Jersey, Newark, Department of Management, Newark, NJ 07102-3192. Offerings include computer information systems (PhD), information technology (PhD). Offered jointly with New Jersey Institute of Technology. Terminal master's awarded for partial completion of doctoral program. Department faculty: 113 full-time (13 women), 3 part-time (1 woman). *Degree requirements:* Dissertation, cumulative exams required, foreign language not required. *Average time to degree:* doctorate–5 years full-time, 7 years part-time. *Entrance requirements:* GMAT or GRE, minimum undergraduate B average. Application deadline: 4/1 (rolling processing; 11/1 for spring admission). Application fee: $40. *Expenses:* Tuition $6248 per year full-time, $257 per credit part-time for state residents; $9160 per year full-time, $380 per credit part-time for nonresidents. Fees $738 per year full-time, $107 per semester (minimum) part-time. • Glenn R. Shafer, Director, 973-353-1604. E-mail: gshafer@andromeda.rutgers.edu. Application contact: Ana Gonzalez, Program Secretary, 973-353-5371. Fax: 973-353-5691. E-mail: anag@gsmack.rutgers.edu.

Rutgers, The State University of New Jersey, Newark, Graduate School of Management, Department of Management Science/Computer Information Systems, Newark, NJ 07102-3192. Awards MBA. *Degree requirements:* Computer language required, thesis not required. *Entrance requirements:* GMAT, TOEFL. Application deadline: 6/1 (rolling processing). Application fee: $40. *Financial aid:* Federal Work-Study, institutionally sponsored loans, and career-related internships or fieldwork available. Financial aid application deadline: 3/15; applicants required to submit FAFSA. • Dr. Ronald Armstrong, Chair, 973-353-5682. Fax: 973-353-5003. E-mail: rarmstrong@andromeda.rutgers.edu. Application contact: Director of Admissions, 973-353-1234. Fax: 973-353-1592. E-mail: admit@gsmack.rutgers.edu.

St. John's University, College of Business Administration, Department of Computer Information Systems and Decision Sciences, Jamaica, NY 11439. Awards MBA, Adv C. Part-time and evening/weekend programs available. Faculty: 16 full-time (0 women), 1 part-time (0 women). Students: 10 full-time (5 women), 76 part-time (22 women); includes 16 minority (5 African Americans, 8 Asian Americans, 3 Hispanics), 17 international. Average age 29. 49 applicants, 61% accepted. In 1997, 38 master's awarded. *Degree requirements:* For master's, thesis optional, foreign language not required. *Entrance requirements:* For master's, GMAT. Application deadline: 6/1 (rolling processing; 10/1 for spring admission). Application fee: $40. *Expenses:* Tuition $600 per credit. Fees $150 per year. *Financial aid:* In 1997–98, 5 research assistantships (1 to a first-year student) averaging $667 per month were awarded; Federal Work-Study also available. Aid available to part-time students. Financial aid application deadline: 3/1; applicants required to submit FAFSA. • Dr. Andrew Rasselkoff, Chair, 718-990-6338. Application contact: Shamus J. McGrenra, TOR, Associate Director, Graduate Admissions, 718-990-6107. Fax: 718-990-5736. E-mail: mcgrenrs@stjohns.edu.

Saint Joseph's University, Ervian K. Haub School of Business, Programs in Graduate Business, Program in Information Systems, Philadelphia, PA 19131-1395. Awards MBA. Evening/weekend programs available. Students: 87 (29 women). In 1997, 35 degrees awarded. *Entrance requirements:* GMAT, TOEFL. Application deadline: 7/15 (priority date; rolling processing; 11/15 for spring admission). Application fee: $35. *Tuition:* $510 per credit hour. *Financial aid:* Graduate assistantships available. Financial aid application deadline: 5/1. • Adele C. Foley, Associate Dean, Programs in Graduate Business, 610-660-1690. Fax: 610-660-1599. E-mail: afoley@sju.edu.

Saint Louis University, School of Business and Administration, Department of Decision Sciences and Management Information Systems, 3674 Lindell Boulevard, St. Louis, MO 63108. Offers programs in decision sciences (MBA, M Dec S, PhD), information systems management (MBA), management information systems (MMIS). Part-time programs available. Faculty: 10 full-time (0 women). Students: 3 full-time (1 woman), 11 part-time (2 women); includes 1 minority (Asian American), 2 international. Average age 26. 16 applicants, 44% accepted. In 1997, 2 doctorates awarded. *Degree requirements:* For master's, oral exam required, thesis not required; for doctorate, dissertation. *Average time to degree:* master's–1.5 years full-time, 3 years part-time. *Entrance requirements:* For master's, GMAT, TOEFL; for doctorate, GMAT. Application deadline: 7/15 (rolling processing; 11/15 for spring admission). Application fee: $40. Electronic applications accepted. *Financial aid:* Fellowships, research assistantships, teaching assistantships, Federal Work-Study available. Aid available to part-time students. • Dr. Mark E. Ferris, Chairman, 314-977-3878.

St. Mary's University of San Antonio, Program in Systems Administration, San Antonio, TX 78228-8507. Awards MS. Part-time and evening/weekend programs available. *Degree requirements:* Computer language required, foreign language and thesis not required. *Entrance requirements:* GMAT or GRE General Test. Application deadline: 8/1 (priority date; rolling processing). Application fee: $15. *Expenses:* Tuition $383 per credit hour (minimum). Fees $217 per year full-time, $58 per semester part-time. *Faculty research:* International operations, job satisfaction, total quality management, taxation, stress management.

Saint Peter's College, MBA Programs, 2641 Kennedy Boulevard, Jersey City, NJ 07306-5997. Offerings include management information systems (MBA). Faculty: 15 full-time (0 women), 16 part-time (5 women). *Degree requirements:* Exit presentation. *Entrance requirements:* GMAT (minimum score 400) or MAT (minimum score 40). Application deadline: 8/1 (priority date; rolling processing). Application fee: $20. *Tuition:* $516 per credit. • Sr. Jeanne Gilligan, Associate Vice President for Academic Affairs, 201-915-7252. Fax: 201-946-7528. E-mail: gilliganj@spcvxa.spc.edu. Application contact: Nancy P. Campbell, Associate Vice President for Enrollment, 201-915-9213. Fax: 201-432-5860. E-mail: amissions@spcvxa.spc.edu.

San Diego State University, Graduate School of Business, Department of Information and Decision Systems, San Diego, CA 92182. Awards MBA, MS. Evening/weekend programs available. Students: 23 full-time (10 women), 33 part-time (9 women); includes 9 minority (1 African American, 6 Asian Americans, 2 Hispanics), 8 international. Average age 29. In 1997, 24 degrees awarded. *Degree requirements:* Computer language, thesis or alternative required, foreign language not required. *Entrance requirements:* GMAT (minimum score 550), TOEFL (minimum score 570). Application deadline: 4/15 (priority date; rolling processing; 11/1 for spring admission). Application fee: $55. *Expenses:* Tuition $0 for state residents; $246 per unit for nonresidents. Fees $1932 per year full-time, $1266 per year part-time. *Financial aid:* Fellowships, research assistantships, teaching assistantships available. • John Penrose, Chair, 619-594-4759. Fax: 619-594-3675. E-mail: john.penrose@sdsu.edu. Application contact: Patricia Martin, Director of Admissions, 619-594-5217. Fax: 619-594-1863. E-mail: sdsumba@mail.sdsu.edu.

Seattle Pacific University, School of Business and Economics, Seattle, WA 98119-1997. Offerings include information systems management (MS). School faculty: 17 full-time (4 women), 12 part-time (3 women). *Average time to degree:* master's–2 years full-time, 4 years part-time. *Application deadline:* 8/1 (priority date; rolling processing; 2/1 for spring admission). *Application fee:* $35. *Tuition:* $412 per credit. • Gary Karns, Associate Dean, 206-281-2948. Application contact: Debbie Wysomierski, Admissions Coordinator, 206-281-2753. Fax: 206-281-2733. E-mail: mba@spu.edu.

Seton Hall University, W. Paul Stillman School of Business, Department of Computer and Decision Sciences, South Orange, NJ 07079-2692. Offers programs in information systems (MBA, MS), quantitative analysis (MBA). Part-time and evening/weekend programs available. Faculty: 9 full-time (1 woman), 3 part-time (0 women). *Degree requirements:* Thesis optional, foreign language not required. *Entrance requirements:* GMAT (minimum score 500), TOEFL (minimum score 550). Application deadline: 6/1 (priority date; rolling processing). Application fee: $50. *Expenses:* Tuition $538 per credit. Fees $185 per semester. *Financial aid:* Research assistantships and career-related internships or fieldwork available. Aid available to part-time students. Financial aid applicants required to submit FAFSA. • Dr. David Rosenthal, Acting Chairperson, 973-761-9250. E-mail: rosentdv@shu.edu. Application contact: Student Information Office, 973-761-9222. Fax: 973-761-9217. E-mail: busgrad@shu.edu.

Simon Fraser University, Faculty of Business Administration, Burnaby, BC V5A 1S6, Canada. Offerings include decision support systems (MBA). Faculty: 48 full-time (12 women). *Application fee:* $55. *Expenses:* Tuition $2400 per year (minimum). Fees $207 per year. • S. McShane, Director, 604-291-3639. Application contact: Program Assistant, 604-291-3047. Fax: 604-291-3404. E-mail: mba@sfu.ca.

Southeastern University, Program in Management Information Systems, Washington, DC 20024-2788. Awards MBA. Part-time and evening/weekend programs available. Faculty: 1 full-time (0 women), 14 part-time (1 woman), 5 FTE. Students: 18 full-time (8 women), 13 part-time (8 women). Average age 33. 13 applicants, 85% accepted. In 1997, 10 degrees awarded. *Degree requirements:* Computer language required, foreign language not required. *Entrance requirements:* TOEFL. Application deadline: rolling. Application fee: $45. *Expenses:* Tuition $228 per credit hour. Fees $175 per quarter. *Financial aid:* Federal Work-Study and career-related internships or fieldwork available. Aid available to part-time students. Financial aid applicants required to submit CSS PROFILE. • Dr. Paul Darling, Acting Head, Department of Computer Science, Information Systems and Mathematics, 202-488-8162 Ext. 254. Application contact: Jack Flinter, Director of Admissions, 202-265-5343. Fax: 202-488-8093.

Southern Illinois University at Edwardsville, School of Business, Program in Business Administration, Specialization in Management Information Systems, Edwardsville, IL 62026-0001. Awards MBA. Part-time programs available. Students: 11 full-time (4 women), 6 part-time (1 woman); includes 1 minority (Asian American), 6 international. 9 applicants, 67% accepted. In 1997, 2 degrees awarded. *Degree requirements:* Computer language, final exam, project required, foreign language and thesis not required. *Entrance requirements:* GMAT. Application deadline: 7/24. Application fee: $25. *Expenses:* Tuition $1716 per year full-time, $95 per credit hour part-time for state residents; $5149 per year full-time, $286 per credit hour part-time for nonresidents. Fees $463 per year full-time, $433 per year part-time. *Financial aid:* Fellowships, research assistantships, teaching assistantships, assistantships, Federal Work-Study, institutionally sponsored loans available. Aid available to part-time students. • Dr. Robert W. Klepper, Chairperson, 618-692-2504. Application contact: John Schrage, Adviser, 618-692-2504.

Southwest Missouri State University, College of Business Administration, Program in Computer Information Systems, Springfield, MO 65804-0094. Awards MS. Part-time and evening/weekend programs available. Students: 30 full-time (10 women); includes 3 minority (2 African Americans, 1 Asian American), 1 international. *Degree requirements:* Comprehensive exam required, foreign language not required. *Entrance requirements:* GMAT (minimum score 450), minimum GPA of 2.75. Application deadline: 8/6 (priority date; rolling processing; 1/4 for spring admission). Application fee: $25. *Tuition:* $295 per credit hour for state residents; $395 per credit hour for nonresidents. • Dr. Jerry Chin, Head, 417-836-4131. Fax: 417-836-6907. E-mail: jmc808f@vma.smsu.edu.

State University of New York at Albany, School of Business, Department of Management Science and Information Systems, Albany, NY 12222-0001. Awards MBA. Faculty: 12 full-time (3 women). Students: 19 full-time (5 women); includes 4 minority (3 Asian Americans, 1 Hispanic), 4 international. *Degree requirements:* Field study project. *Entrance requirements:* GMAT. Application deadline: 7/1 (priority date; rolling processing). Application fee: $50. *Expenses:* Tuition $5100 per year full-time, $213 per credit hour part-time for state residents; $8416 per year full-time, $351 per credit hour part-time for nonresidents. Fees $705 per year full-time, $26.85 per credit hour part-time. *Financial aid:* Application deadline 4/1. *Faculty research:* Data quality, expert systems, collaborative technology, expert information systems. • Peter Duchessi, Chair, 518-442-4916. Application contact: Jeffrey Collins, Assistant Director, Graduate Admissions, 518-442-3980.

Stevens Institute of Technology, Wesley J. Howe School of Technology Management, Program in Information Management, Hoboken, NJ 07030. Awards MIM, MS, PhD, Certificate. Part-time and evening/weekend programs available. Postbaccalaureate distance learning degree programs offered (no on-campus study). 135 applicants, 87% accepted. Terminal master's awarded for partial completion of doctoral program. *Degree requirements:* For master's, computer language required, thesis optional, foreign language not required; for doctorate, computer language, dissertation; for Certificate, computer language required, foreign language not required. *Entrance requirements:* For master's and doctorate, GMAT, GRE, TOEFL. Application deadline: rolling. Application fee: $45. Electronic applications accepted. *Expenses:* Tuition $13,500 per year full-time, $675 per credit part-time. Fees $160 per year. *Faculty research:* Strategic management, use of computers in education. • Dr. James Teitjen, Head, Wesley J. Howe School of Technology Management, 201-216-5384. Fax: 201-216-5385.

Strayer University, Graduate School, 1025 15th Street, NW, Washington, DC 20005-2603. Offerings include information systems (MS). Postbaccalaureate distance learning degree programs offered (minimal on-campus study). School faculty: 76 full-time (3 women), 49 part-time (10 women). *Degree requirements:* Thesis required, foreign language not required. *Entrance requirements:* GMAT (minimum score 450), GRE General Test (minimum combined score of 1000), minimum GPA of 2.75. Application deadline: 9/28 (priority date; rolling processing; 4/6 for spring admission). Application fee: $25. Electronic applications accepted. *Tuition:* $6750 per year full-time, $250 per credit hour part-time. • Dr. Samad Hafazi, Director of Graduate Studies, 202-408-2400. Application contact: Michael Williams, Campus Coordinator, 202-408-2400. Fax: 202-289-1831.

Syracuse University, School of Information Studies, Information Resources Management Program, Syracuse, NY 13244-0003. Awards MS, JD/MS. Students: 33 full-time (14 women), 120 part-time (52 women); includes 9 minority (7 African Americans, 1 Asian American, 1 Hispanic), 55 international. 68 applicants, 87% accepted. In 1997, 31 degrees awarded. *Entrance requirements:* GRE General Test (minimum combined score of 1000). Application fee: $40. *Tuition:* $13,320 per year full-time, $555 per credit hour part-time. *Financial aid:*

Application deadline 3/1. • Ralf T. Wigand, Director. Application contact: Barbara Settel, Assistant Dean, 315-443-2911.

See in-depth descriptions on pages 589 and 1647.

Syracuse University, School of Management, PhD Program in Business Administration, Syracuse, NY 13244-0003. Offerings include management information systems (PhD). Program faculty: 75. *Entrance requirements:* GMAT (minimum score 600). Application deadline: 2/1. Application fee: $40. *Tuition:* $13,320 per year full-time, $555 per credit hour part-time. • S. P. Raj, Associate Dean. Application contact: Barbara Buske, Secretary, 315-443-1001.

Syracuse University, School of Management, Program in Management Information Systems, Syracuse, NY 13244-0003. Awards MBA. Faculty: 4. Students: 11 full-time (5 women), 9 part-time (2 women); includes 4 minority (1 African American, 2 Asian Americans, 1 Hispanic), 6 international. 44 applicants, 50% accepted. In 1997, 4 degrees awarded. *Entrance requirements:* GMAT. Application deadline: 2/1 (rolling processing). Application fee: $40. *Tuition:* $13,320 per year full-time, $555 per credit hour part-time. *Financial aid:* Fellowships, research assistantships, teaching assistantships, partial tuition waivers, Federal Work-Study available. Financial aid application deadline: 3/1. • Mohan Tannieu, Coordinator, 315-443-3747. Application contact: Associate Dean, 315-443-3850.

Temple University, School of Business and Management, Master's Program in Business Administration, Philadelphia, PA 19122-6096. Offerings include computer and information sciences (MBA, MS). Program faculty: 72 full-time (13 women). *Entrance requirements:* GMAT (average 540), TOEFL (minimum score 575). Application fee: $40. *Expenses:* Tuition $323 per semester hour for state residents; $444 per semester hour for nonresidents. Fees $170 per year full-time, $28 per semester (minimum) part-time. • Application contact: Linda Whelan, Director, 215-204-7678. Fax: 215-204-8300. E-mail: linda@astro.ocis.temple.edu.

Texas A&M International University, Division of Business Administration, Program in Information Systems, 5201 University Boulevard, Laredo, TX 78041-1900. Awards MSIS. *Entrance requirements:* GMAT or GRE General Test. Application deadline: 7/15 (priority date; rolling processing; 11/12 for spring admission). Application fee: $0.

Announcement: The Graduate School of International Trade and Business Administration's MS in Information Systems is patterned after AITP and ACM curriculum recommendations and is designed to prepare the graduate to understand the complexities and the realities of the Information Age. Required courses include principles of information systems, database management, systems analysis and design, telecommunications and networks, conceptual issues, and international information systems issues. Elective courses may be selected from decision support systems, artificial intelligence, advanced software development methods, and general systems theory. The University's unique location on the border of Mexico provides a laboratory for the study of local, international, and multinational computer-based information systems. The program has both thesis and nonthesis options.

Texas A&M University, Lowry Mays Graduate School of Business, Department of Information and Operations Management, College Station, TX 77843-4113. Offers program in management information systems (MS, PhD). Faculty: 28 full-time (2 women), 4 part-time (all women). Students: 107 full-time (40 women), 16 part-time (4 women). Average age 31. 112 applicants, 50% accepted. In 1997, 32 master's, 1 doctorate awarded. Terminal master's awarded for partial completion of doctoral program. *Degree requirements:* For master's, computer language, oral comprehensive exam required, foreign language and thesis not required; for doctorate, computer language, dissertation required, foreign language not required. *Average time to degree:* master's–1.5 years full-time; doctorate–4 years full-time. *Entrance requirements:* For master's, GMAT, TOEFL (minimum score 600); for doctorate, GMAT or GRE General Test, TOEFL. Application deadline: 3/1 (priority date; rolling processing; 8/1 for spring admission). Application fee: $35 ($75 for international students). *Financial aid:* 51 students received aid; fellowships, research assistantships, teaching assistantships, Federal Work-Study, institutionally sponsored loans, and career-related internships or fieldwork available. Financial aid application deadline: 2/1. • Evan Anderson, Head, 409-845-1616. Application contact: Dr. Joobin Choobineh, Adviser, 409-845-4048. E-mail: joobin@sigma.tamu.edu.

Texas Tech University, Graduate School, College of Business Administration, Program in Information Systems and Quantitative Sciences, Lubbock, TX 79409. Offers business statistics (MSBA, PhD), management information systems (MSBA, PhD), operations management (PhD). Part-time programs available. Faculty: 11 full-time (1 woman). Students: 61 full-time (13 women), 7 part-time (2 women); includes 7 minority (1 African American, 6 Hispanics), 33 international. Average age 33. 33 applicants, 55% accepted. In 1997, 21 master's awarded; 3 doctorates awarded (100% entered university research/teaching). *Degree requirements:* For master's, computer language, comprehensive exam required, foreign language and thesis not required; for doctorate, computer language, dissertation, qualifying exams required, foreign language not required. *Entrance requirements:* For master's, GMAT (minimum score 500; average 560); for doctorate, GMAT (minimum score 580; average 620). Application deadline: 4/15 (priority date; rolling processing; 9/30 for spring admission). Application fee: $25 ($50 for international students). *Expenses:* Tuition $864 per year full-time, $120 per semester (minimum) part-time for state residents; $5976 per year full-time, $747 per semester (minimum) part-time for nonresidents. Fees $2321 per year full-time, $302 per semester (minimum) part-time. *Financial aid:* Teaching assistantships, Federal Work-Study available. *Faculty research:* Database management systems, systems management and engineering, expert systems and adaptive knowledge-based sciences, statistical analysis and design. • Dr. Surya Yadav, Coordinator, 806-742-3192. E-mail: odsby@ttacs.ttu.edu. Application contact: Nancy Dodge, Director, 806-742-3184. Fax: 806-742-3958.

Towson University, Program in Information Technology Management, Towson, MD 21252-0001. Offers information systems project management (MS), information technology (MS), operations management (MS). Offered jointly with the University of Baltimore. Students: 2 part-time (0 women). *Application deadline:* rolling. *Application fee:* $40. *Expenses:* Tuition $187 per credit hour for state residents; $364 per credit hour for nonresidents. Fees $40 per credit hour. *Financial aid:* Application deadline 4/1. • Dr. Tom Basuray, Director, 410-830-2124. Fax: 410-830-6091. E-mail: tbasuray@towson.edu. Application contact: Fran Musotto, Office Manager, 410-830-2501. Fax: 410-830-4675. E-mail: fmusotto@towson.edu.

Troy State University Dothan, School of Business, Department of Computer Information Systems and Business Education, Dothan, AL 36304-0368. Offers programs in business education (MS), computer information systems (MS). *Entrance requirements:* GMAT, GRE General Test, or MAT, minimum GPA of 2.5. Application deadline: rolling. Application fee: $20. *Expenses:* Tuition $68 per credit hour for state residents; $140 per credit hour for nonresidents. Fees $2 per credit hour. • Dr. Gary Buchanan, Chair. Application contact: Reta Cordell, Director of Admissions and Records, 334-983-6556. Fax: 334-983-6322. E-mail: rcordell@tsud.edu.

Troy State University Montgomery, Division of Business, Program in Computer and Information Science, PO Drawer 4419, Montgomery, AL 36103-4419. Awards MS. Part-time and evening/weekend programs available. In 1997, 17 degrees awarded. *Degree requirements:* Thesis or alternative. *Entrance requirements:* GRE, TOEFL, BS in computer science. Application deadline: rolling. Application fee: $20. Electronic applications accepted. *Expenses:* Tuition $52 per quarter hour for state residents; $104 per quarter hour for nonresidents. Fees $30 per year. • Dr. Freda Hartman, Dean, Division of Business, 334-241-9597. Fax: 334-241-9734. E-mail: fhartman@tsum.edu.

Union College, Department of Electrical Engineering and Computer Science and Graduate Management Institute, Program in Computer Management Systems, Schenectady, NY 12308-2311. Awards MS. Students: 1 full-time (0 women), 3 part-time (1 woman); includes 1 international. 1 applicant, 100% accepted. In 1997, 4 degrees awarded. *Degree requirements:* Computer language required, foreign language not required. *Entrance requirements:* Minimum GPA of 3.0. Application deadline: rolling. Application fee: $35. *Tuition:* $1714 per course. • Dr. George H. Williams, Chair, 518-388-6273.

Université de Sherbrooke, Faculty of Administration, Program in Management Information Systems, Sherbrooke, PQ J1K 2R1, Canada. Awards M Sc. *Application deadline:* 5/31. *Application fee:* $15.

Université du Québec à Montréal, Program in Management Information Systems, Montréal, PQ H3C 3P8, Canada. Awards M Sc, M Sc A. Part-time programs available. *Entrance requirements:* Appropriate bachelor's degree or equivalent and proficiency in French. Application deadline: 5/1. Application fee: $50.

The University of Akron, College of Business Administration, Department of Management, Program in Management-Information Systems, Akron, OH 44325-0001. Awards MSM. Students: 17 full-time (6 women), 16 part-time (4 women); includes 16 international. Average age 28. In 1997, 3 degrees awarded. *Entrance requirements:* GMAT (minimum score 450), minimum GPA of 2.75. Application deadline: 8/15 (rolling processing). Application fee: $25 ($50 for international students). *Expenses:* Tuition $178 per credit hour for state residents; $333 per credit hour for nonresidents. Fees $145 per year full-time, $32 per semester (minimum) part-time. *Financial aid:* Application deadline 4/30. • Dr. Kenneth Dunning, Acting Chair, Department of Management, 330-972-7037. E-mail: kdunning@uakron.edu. Application contact: Dr. J. Daniel Williams, Director of Graduate Business Programs, 330-972-7043. E-mail: jwilliams@uakron.edu.

The University of Arizona, College of Business and Public Administration, Karl Eller Graduate School of Management, Department of Management Information Systems, Tucson, AZ 85721. Awards MS. *Degree requirements:* Thesis or alternative required, foreign language not required. *Entrance requirements:* GMAT, GRE General Test, TOEFL (minimum score 550), TSE (minimum score 50), minimum GPA of 3.0. Application deadline: 4/1 (rolling processing). Application fee: $35. *Tuition:* $2162 per year full-time, $337 per semester (minimum) part-time for state residents; $6860 per year full-time, $1138 per semester (minimum) part-time for nonresidents. *Faculty research:* Group decision support systems, domestic and international computing issues, expert systems, data management and structures.

University of Arkansas, College of Business Administration, Department of Computer Information Systems and Quantitative Analysis, Fayetteville, AR 72701-1201. Awards MIS. Students: 4 full-time (1 woman), 1 part-time (0 women). 10 applicants, 90% accepted. *Entrance requirements:* GMAT. Application fee: $25 ($35 for international students). *Tuition:* $3144 per year full-time, $173 per credit hour part-time for state residents; $7140 per year full-time, $395 per credit hour part-time for nonresidents. *Financial aid:* Application deadline 4/1. • David Douglas, Chair, 501-575-4500. Application contact: T. P. Cronan, Graduate Coordinator.

University of Baltimore, School of Business, Department of Information and Quantitative Sciences, Baltimore, MD 21201-5779. Offers program in business/management information systems (MS). Part-time and evening/weekend programs available. Faculty: 13 full-time (3 women), 2 part-time (1 woman). Students: 19 full-time (8 women), 40 part-time (15 women); includes 11 minority (7 African Americans, 3 Asian Americans, 1 Hispanic), 17 international. Average age 32. 48 applicants, 81% accepted. In 1997, 24 degrees awarded. *Degree requirements:* Computer language required, foreign language and thesis not required. *Average time to degree:* master's–2 years full-time. *Entrance requirements:* GMAT. Application deadline: 7/15 (priority date; rolling processing; 11/15 for spring admission). Application fee: $30. *Expenses:* Tuition $5736 per year full-time, $239 per credit part-time for state residents; $8544 per year full-time, $356 per credit part-time for nonresidents. Fees $550 per year full-time, $208 per semester (minimum) part-time. *Financial aid:* In 1997–98, 3 research assistantships (1 to a first-year student) were awarded; fellowships, Federal Work-Study, and career-related internships or fieldwork also available. Aid available to part-time students. Financial aid application deadline: 4/1; applicants required to submit FAFSA. *Faculty research:* Simulation and mathematical programming, health care information systems, Internet/World Wide Web, group decision making. Total annual research expenditures: $2350. • Application contact: Tracey Jamison, Assistant Director of Admissions, 410-837-4809. Fax: 410-837-4793. E-mail: admissions@ubmail.ubalt.edu.

University of British Columbia, Faculty of Commerce and Business Administration, Doctoral Program in Commerce and Business Administration, Vancouver, BC V6T 1Z2, Canada. Offerings include management information systems (PhD). *Degree requirements:* Dissertation required, foreign language not required. *Entrance requirements:* GMAT or GRE, TOEFL. Application deadline: 12/31 (priority date; rolling processing). Application fee: $60.

University of British Columbia, Faculty of Commerce and Business Administration, Program in Business Administration, Vancouver, BC V6T 1Z2, Canada. Offerings include management information systems (M Sc). *Degree requirements:* Thesis required (for some programs), foreign language not required. *Average time to degree:* master's–2 years full-time. *Entrance requirements:* GMAT (average 620), TOEFL (minimum score 600). Application fee: $100.

University of Cincinnati, College of Business Administration, Department of Accounting and Information Systems, Cincinnati, OH 45221. Offers programs in accounting (MBA, PhD), information systems (MBA, PhD). MBA (accounting) offered to full-time students only. Part-time and evening/weekend programs available. Faculty: 4 full-time. Students: 5 full-time (2 women), 23 part-time (9 women); includes 3 minority (all Asian Americans), 4 international. 15 applicants, 20% accepted. In 1997, 10 master's, 3 doctorates awarded. *Degree requirements:* For doctorate, computer language, dissertation. *Average time to degree:* master's–1.3 years full-time; doctorate–6.3 years full-time. *Entrance requirements:* GMAT. Application deadline: 3/1. Application fee: $30. *Tuition:* $7228 per year full-time, $185 per credit hour part-time for state residents; $13,812 per year full-time, $352 per credit hour part-time for nonresidents. *Financial aid:* Graduate assistantships, full tuition waivers available. Aid available to part-time students. Financial aid application deadline: 2/15. • J. Timothy Sale, Head, 513-556-7062. Application contact: James Bast, Assistant Dean, Graduate Programs, 513-556-7020. Fax: 513-556-4891. E-mail: james.bast@uc.edu.

University of Colorado at Colorado Springs, Graduate School of Business Administration, Colorado Springs, CO 80933-7150. Offerings include information systems (MBA). School faculty: 24 full-time (4 women). *Entrance requirements:* GMAT. Application deadline: 6/1 (priority date; 11/1 for spring admission). Application fee: $50. *Expenses:* Tuition $2860 per year full-time, $121 per credit hour part-time for state residents; $10,254 per year full-time, $420 per credit hour part-time for nonresidents. Fees $399 per year (minimum) full-time, $106 per year (minimum) part-time. • Dr. Richard Dicenza, Dean, 719-262-3113. E-mail: rdicenz@mail.uccs.edu. Application contact: Diane Belger, Adviser, 719-262-3408. Fax: 719-262-3494. E-mail: dbelger@mail.uccs.edu.

University of Colorado at Denver, Graduate School of Business Administration, Division of Information Systems Management, Denver, CO 80217-3364. Awards MS, MBA/MS. Part-time and evening/weekend programs available. Faculty: 8 full-time. Students: 226. In 1997, 48 degrees awarded. *Degree requirements:* Computer language required, foreign language and thesis not required. *Entrance requirements:* GMAT (minimum score 400; average 540), TOEFL (minimum score 525; average 560). Application deadline: 7/1 (priority date; rolling processing; 11/1 for spring admission). Application fee: $50 ($60 for international students). *Expenses:* Tuition $3754 per year full-time, $225 per semester hour part-time for state residents; $12,962 per year full-time, $777 per semester hour part-time for nonresidents. Fees $252 per year. *Financial aid:* Application deadline 4/1. *Faculty research:* Human-computer interaction, expert systems, database management, electronic commerce, object-oriented software development. • Jahangir Karimi, Director, 303-556-5881. Fax: 303-556-5899. Application contact: Lori Cain, Graduate Business Admissions Office, 303-556-5900. Fax: 303-556-5904. E-mail: lori_cain@maroon.cudenver.edu.

Directory: Management Information Systems

University of Dallas, Graduate School of Management, Program in Management Information Systems, Irving, TX 75062-4799. Awards MBA, MM. Part-time programs available. Students: 169 (65 women). In 1997, 52 degrees awarded. *Average time to degree:* master's–1.3 years full-time, 2.5 years part-time. *Entrance requirements:* GMAT (minimum score 400), TOEFL (average 520), minimum GPA of 3.0. Application deadline: 8/6 (priority date; rolling processing; 12/8 for spring admission). Application fee: $25 ($50 for international students). *Expenses:* Tuition $380 per credit hour. Fees $125 per year. *Financial aid:* Application deadline 2/15. • Dr. Robert Dunikoski, Director, 972-721-5352. Fax: 972-721-5130. Application contact: Roxanne Del Rio, Director of Admissions, 972-721-5174. Fax: 972-721-4009. E-mail: admiss@gsm.udallas.edu.

University of Denver, Daniels College of Business, Department of Information Technology and Electronic Commerce, Denver, CO 80208. Awards MBA, MIM. Part-time and evening/weekend programs available. Faculty: 4 full-time (1 woman). Students: 31 full-time (10 women), 3 part-time (1 woman); includes 3 minority (2 Asian Americans, 1 Hispanic), 9 international. Average age 28. 37 applicants, 95% accepted. In 1997, 20 degrees awarded. *Entrance requirements:* GMAT (average 545). Application deadline: 5/1 (priority date; rolling processing; 1/1 for spring admission). Application fee: $50. *Expenses:* Tuition $18,216 per year full-time, $506 per credit hour part-time. Fees $159 per year. *Financial aid:* In 1997–98, 23 students received aid, including 5 teaching assistantships averaging $305 per month and totaling $14,850, 16 grants, scholarships totaling $21,696; research assistantships, Federal Work-Study, institutionally sponsored loans, and career-related internships or fieldwork also available. Aid available to part-time students. Financial aid application deadline: 2/15. *Faculty research:* Cross-cultural research in information systems, electronic commerce, distributed project management, strategic information systems, management of emerging technologies. • Don McCubbrey, Chair, 303-871-3695. Application contact: Jan Johnson, Executive Director, Student Services, 303-871-3416. Fax: 303-871-4466. E-mail: dcb@du.edu.

University of Detroit Mercy, College of Business Administration, Program in Computer Information Systems, Detroit, MI 48219-0900. Awards MS. Part-time and evening/weekend programs available. *Degree requirements:* Thesis or alternative required, foreign language not required. *Entrance requirements:* Minimum GPA of 3.75. Application deadline: 8/1 (priority date; rolling processing). Application fee: $25 ($35 for international students).

University of Florida, College of Business Administration, Department of Decision and Information Sciences, Gainesville, FL 32611. Awards MA, PhD. Faculty: 10. Students: 33 full-time (12 women), 17 part-time (5 women); includes 6 minority (4 Asian Americans, 2 Hispanics), 13 international. 60 applicants, 60% accepted. In 1997, 8 master's awarded. Terminal master's awarded for partial completion of doctoral program. *Degree requirements:* For master's, computer language required, foreign language and thesis not required; for doctorate, computer language, dissertation required, foreign language not required. *Entrance requirements:* GMAT or GRE General Test, minimum GPA of 3.0. Application deadline: 2/16 (priority date; rolling processing). Application fee: $20. *Tuition:* $138 per credit hour for state residents; $481 per credit hour for nonresidents. *Financial aid:* In 1997–98, 20 students received aid, including 3 fellowships averaging $522 per month, 2 research assistantships averaging $542 per month, 2 teaching assistantships averaging $912 per month, 13 graduate assistantships averaging $588 per month. *Faculty research:* Expert systems, nonconvex optimization, manufacturing management, production and operation management, teleco mmunication. • Dr. Selcvk Erenguc, Chair, 352-392-9600. E-mail: erenguc@nervm.nerdc.ufl.edu. Application contact: Dr. Gary Koehler, Graduate Coordinator, 352-392-0134. Fax: 352-392-5438. E-mail: koehler@nervm.nerdc.ufl.edu.

University of Hartford, Barney School of Business and Public Administration, Program in Business Administration, West Hartford, CT 06117-1599. Offerings include management information systems (MBA). Program faculty: 24 full-time (4 women), 15 part-time (1 woman). *Average time to degree:* master's–1.5 years full-time, 3 years part-time. *Entrance requirements:* GMAT, TOEFL. Application deadline: 7/1 (priority date; rolling processing; 12/1 for spring admission). Application fee: $35 ($50 for international students). Electronic applications accepted. • Christopher Galligan, Director, 860-768-4390. Application contact: Claire Silverstein, Assistant Director, 860-768-4900. Fax: 860-768-4821. E-mail: silverste@unavax.hartford.edu.

University of Houston, College of Business Administration, Program in Management Information Systems, 4800 Calhoun, Houston, TX 77204-2163. Awards MBA, PhD. Part-time and evening/weekend programs available. Faculty: 7 full-time (2 women), 3 part-time (0 women). Students: 39 full-time (17 women), 52 part-time (17 women); includes 22 minority (3 African Americans, 16 Asian Americans, 3 Hispanics), 24 international. Average age 29. In 1997, 10 master's awarded. *Degree requirements:* For master's, computer language required, foreign language and thesis not required; for doctorate, computer language, dissertation, comprehensive exam required, foreign language not required. *Average time to degree:* master's–2 years full-time, 3.5 years part-time; doctorate–4.5 years full-time. *Entrance requirements:* For master's, GMAT (average 590), TOEFL (minimum score 620); for doctorate, GMAT or GRE. Application deadline: 5/1 (rolling processing; 10/1 for spring admission). Application fee: $50 ($125 for international students). *Expenses:* Tuition $1152 per year full-time, $120 per semester (minimum) part-time for state residents; $4482 per year full-time, $249 per credit hour part-time for nonresidents. Fees $977 per year full-time, $119 per semester (minimum) part-time. *Financial aid:* Research assistantships, teaching assistantships, Federal Work-Study, and career-related internships or fieldwork available. Aid available to part-time students. Financial aid application deadline: 3/1; applicants required to submit FAFSA. • Dr. Dennis Adams, Chair, 713-743-4747. Application contact: Office of Student Services, 713-743-4900. Fax: 713-743-4942. E-mail: oss@cba.uh.edu.

University of Illinois at Chicago, College of Business Administration, Department of Information and Decision Sciences, Chicago, IL 60607-7128. Offers program in management information systems (MS, PhD). Faculty: 14 full-time (1 woman). Students: 24 full-time (11 women), 15 part-time (5 women); includes 10 minority (5 African Americans, 5 Asian Americans), 20 international. 60 applicants, 47% accepted. In 1997, 1 doctorate awarded. *Degree requirements:* For doctorate, dissertation required, foreign language not required. *Entrance requirements:* For doctorate, GMAT, TOEFL (minimum score 550), minimum GPA of 3.75 on a 5.0 scale. Application deadline: 5/1. Application fee: $40 ($50 for international students). *Financial aid:* In 1997–98, 4 research assistantships, 12 teaching assistantships were awarded; fellowships also available. • Aris Ouksel, Director of Graduate Studies, 312-996-8094. Application contact: Ann Rosi, 312-996-4751.

University of Illinois at Springfield, School of Business and Management, Department of Management Information Systems, Springfield, IL 62794-9243. Awards MA. Part-time and evening/weekend programs available. Faculty: 4 full-time (1 woman). Students: 33 full-time (9 women), 112 part-time (45 women); includes 23 minority (17 African Americans, 5 Asian Americans, 1 Hispanic), 22 international. Average age 35. 57 applicants, 86% accepted. In 1997, 9 degrees awarded. *Degree requirements:* Computer language, thesis or alternative required, foreign language not required. *Application deadline:* rolling. *Application fee:* $0. *Expenses:* Tuition $99 per credit hour for state residents; $296 per credit hour for nonresidents. Fees $242 per year full-time, $63 per semester (minimum) part-time. *Financial aid:* In 1997–98, 57 students received aid, including 10 assistantships averaging $606 per month; research assistantships, partial tuition waivers, Federal Work-Study, and career-related internships or fieldwork also available. Aid available to part-time students. Financial aid application deadline: 6/1; applicants required to submit FAFSA. *Faculty research:* Electronic data interchange, electronic commerce, expert systems strategic decision support systems, management of end user computing. • Rassule Hadidi, Chairperson, 217-786-6067.

The University of Iowa, College of Business Administration, Department of Management Sciences, Program in Management Information Systems, Iowa City, IA 52242-1316. Awards MA. Faculty: 11 full-time (1 woman), 4 part-time (1 woman). Students: 33 full-time (16 women); includes 2 minority (both African Americans), 20 international. Average age 40. 39 applicants, 72% accepted. In 1997, 4 degrees awarded (100% found work related to degree). *Degree requirements:* Computer language required, foreign language and thesis not required. *Average time to degree:* master's–2 years full-time. *Entrance requirements:* GMAT (minimum score 560), GRE General Test (minimum combined score of 1230 required, 1130 for international students), minimum GPA of 2.5. Application deadline: 7/1 (rolling processing; 11/15 for spring admission). Application fee: $30 ($50 for international students). *Expenses:* Tuition $3166 per year full-time, $176 per semester hour part-time for state residents; $10,202 per year full-time, $176 per semester hour part-time for nonresidents. Fees $202 per year full-time, $52 per year (minimum) part-time. *Financial aid:* In 1997–98, 11 students received aid, including 1 teaching assistantship averaging $1,278 per month; research assistantships and career-related internships or fieldwork also available. Financial aid application deadline: 3/1. • Philip C. Jones, Chair, 319-335-0859. Fax: 319-335-1956. E-mail: philip-c-jones@uiowa.edu. Application contact: Judy Putney, Graduate Secretary, 319-335-0858. Fax: 319-335-0297. E-mail: judy-putney@uiowa.edu.

University of Maryland University College, Graduate School of Management and Technology, Program in Computer Systems Management, College Park, MD 20742-1600. Awards MS. Offered evenings and weekends only. Part-time and evening/weekend programs available. Postbaccalaureate distance learning degree programs offered (no on-campus study). Students: 23 full-time (13 women), 676 part-time (279 women); includes 278 minority (162 African Americans, 93 Asian Americans, 23 Hispanics), 30 international. 179 applicants, 97% accepted. In 1997, 104 degrees awarded. *Degree requirements:* Thesis or alternative. *Application deadline:* rolling. *Application fee:* $50. Electronic applications accepted. *Tuition:* $277 per semester hour for state residents; $367 per semester hour for nonresidents. *Financial aid:* Grants, scholarships, Federal Work-Study available. Aid available to part-time students. Financial aid application deadline: 5/1; applicants required to submit FAFSA. • John Richardson, Director, 301-985-7200. Fax: 301-985-4611. E-mail: jrichard@ucsfs1.umd.edu. Application contact: Director of Graduate Admissions, 301-985-7155. Fax: 301-985-7175. E-mail: gradschool@europa.umuc.edu.

The University of Memphis, Fogelman College of Business and Economics, Program in Business Administration, Memphis, TN 38152. Offerings include management information systems (MBA, MS), management information systems and decision sciences (PhD). Program faculty: 92 full-time (15 women), 2 part-time (0 women). *Degree requirements:* For master's, comprehensive exams required, thesis not required; for doctorate, dissertation, comprehensive exams. *Entrance requirements:* For master's, GMAT (minimum score 430; average 535), GRE General Test; for doctorate, GMAT (average 633), interview, minimum GPA of 3.4. Application deadline: 8/1 (12/1 for spring admission). Application fee: $25 ($50 for international students). *Tuition:* $2862 per year full-time, $166 per credit hour part-time for state residents; $6696 per year full-time, $379 per credit hour part-time for nonresidents. • Application contact: Dr. Ravinder Nath, Associate Dean of Academic Programs, 901-678-3721. Fax: 901-678-4705. E-mail: fcbegp@memphis.edu.

University of Miami, School of Business Administration, Department of Computer Information Systems/Telecommunications, Coral Gables, FL 33124. Offers programs in computer information systems (MS), telecommunications management (Certificate). Certificate offered jointly with MBA or MS program, or as a 15 credit hour program for applicants with an undergraduate or master's degree. Part-time and evening/weekend programs available. Faculty: 7 full-time (1 woman), 7 part-time (3 women). Students: 31 full-time (9 women), 35 part-time (15 women); includes 31 minority (5 African Americans, 14 Asian Americans, 12 Hispanics), 15 international. Average age 28. In 1997, 35 master's, 14 Certificates awarded. *Entrance requirements:* For master's, GMAT (minimum score 400) or GRE, TOEFL (minimum score 550); for Certificate, TOEFL (minimum score 550). Application deadline: 6/30 (priority date; rolling processing; 10/31 for spring admission). Application fee: $35. *Expenses:* Tuition $815 per credit hour. Fees $174 per year. *Financial aid:* In 1997–98, 5 research assistantships (3 to first-year students) were awarded; scholarships, Federal Work-Study, institutionally sponsored loans, and career-related internships or fieldwork also available. Financial aid application deadline: 3/1. *Faculty research:* Database management, expert systems, systems analysis and design, software engineering, information systems and strategic management. • Dr. Joel Stutz, Chairman, 305-284-6294. Fax: 305-284-5161. E-mail: jstutz@miami.edu.

University of Minnesota, Twin Cities Campus, Carlson School of Management, Department of Information and Decision Sciences, Minneapolis, MN 55455-0213. Awards MBA, PhD. MBA offered jointly with the Master's Program in Business Administration; PhD offered jointly with the Doctoral Program in Business Administration. *Degree requirements:* For doctorate, dissertation required, foreign language not required. *Entrance requirements:* GMAT. *Faculty research:* Group decision making, expert systems, information systems management, problem formulation, database design.

University of Mississippi, Graduate School, School of Business Administration, Program in Systems Management, University, MS 38677-9702. Awards MS. *Entrance requirements:* GMAT, TOEFL, 2 years of work experience, minimum GPA of 3.0. Application deadline: 8/1 (rolling processing). Application fee: $0 ($25 for international students). *Financial aid:* Application deadline 3/1. • Dr. D. Hawley, Associate Dean of Business, 601-232-5820.

University of Missouri–St. Louis, School of Business Administration, Program in Business Administration, St. Louis, MO 63121-4499. Offerings include management information science (MBA). Program faculty: 19 (3 women). *Entrance requirements:* GMAT (minimum score 500; average 554). Application deadline: 7/1 (rolling processing; 11/1 for spring admission). Application fee: $0. Electronic applications accepted. *Expenses:* Tuition $3903 per year full-time, $167 per credit hour part-time for state residents; $11,745 per year full-time, $489 per credit hour part-time for nonresidents. Fees $816 per year full-time, $34 per credit hour part-time. • Application contact: Graduate Admissions, 314-516-5458. Fax: 314-516-6759. E-mail: gradadm@umslvma.umsl.edu.

University of Missouri–St. Louis, School of Business Administration, Program in Management Information Systems, St. Louis, MO 63121-4499. Awards MSMIS. Part-time and evening/weekend programs available. Faculty: 12 (3 women). Students: 14 full-time (7 women), 55 part-time (21 women); includes 14 minority (5 African Americans, 8 Asian Americans, 1 Hispanic), 11 international. 46 applicants, 72% accepted. In 1997, 10 degrees awarded. *Entrance requirements:* GMAT (minimum score 500; average 565). Application deadline: 7/1 (rolling processing; 11/1 for spring admission). Application fee: $0. Electronic applications accepted. *Expenses:* Tuition $3903 per year full-time, $167 per credit hour part-time for state residents; $11,745 per year full-time, $489 per credit hour part-time for nonresidents. Fees $816 per year full-time, $34 per credit hour part-time. *Financial aid:* Research assistantships, teaching assistantships, Federal Work-Study, institutionally sponsored loans, and career-related internships or fieldwork available. Aid available to part-time students. Financial aid application deadline: 4/1; applicants required to submit FAFSA. *Faculty research:* International information systems, operations management. • Application contact: Graduate Admissions, 314-516-5458. Fax: 314-516-6759. E-mail: gradadm@umslvma.umsl.edu.

University of New Haven, School of Business, Program in Business Administration, West Haven, CT 06516-1916. Offerings include computer and information science (MBA). *Degree requirements:* Thesis or alternative required, foreign language not required. *Application deadline:* rolling. *Application fee:* $50. *Expenses:* Tuition $1125 per course. Fees $13 per trimester. • Dr. Omid Nodoushani, Coordinator, 203-932-7123.

University of New Haven, School of Business, Program in Management Systems, West Haven, CT 06516-1916. Awards Sc D. Part-time and evening/weekend programs available. Students: 37 part-time (10 women); includes 2 minority (both Asian Americans), 6 international. *Degree requirements:* Dissertation. *Entrance requirements:* GMAT, master's degree or equivalent. Application deadline: rolling. Application fee: $50. *Expenses:* Tuition $1125 per course. Fees $13 per trimester. *Financial aid:* Federal Work-Study available. Financial aid application deadline: 5/1; applicants required to submit FAFSA. • Dr. Omid Nodoushani, Director, 203-932-7123. Application contact: Graduate Admissions Office, 203-932-7133.

Directory: Management Information Systems

University of New Haven, School of Engineering and Applied Science, Program in Computer and Information Science, West Haven, CT 06516-1916. Offerings include management information systems (MS). *Degree requirements:* Thesis or alternative required, foreign language not required. *Application deadline:* rolling. *Application fee:* $50. *Expenses:* Tuition $1125 per course. Fees $13 per trimester. • Dr. Tahany Fergany, Coordinator, 203-932-7067.

University of New Mexico, Robert O. Anderson Graduate School of Management, Albuquerque, NM 87131-1221. Offerings include management information systems (MBA). School faculty: 50 full-time (11 women). *Application deadline:* 7/1 (priority date; rolling processing; 11/15 for spring admission). *Application fee:* $25. *Expenses:* Tuition $2442 per year full-time, $103 per credit hour part-time for state residents; $8691 per year full-time, $103 per credit hour (minimum) part-time for nonresidents. Fees $32 per year. • Howard L. Smith, Dean, 505-277-6471. Fax: 505-277-7108. Application contact: Sue Podeyn, MBA Program Director, 505-277-3147. Fax: 505-277-9356. E-mail: podeyn@unm.edu.

The University of North Carolina at Chapel Hill, Kenan-Flagler Business School, Doctoral Program in Business Administration, Chapel Hill, NC 27599. Offerings include operations management/quantitative methods (PhD). Program faculty: 79 full-time (15 women), 29 part-time (6 women). *Degree requirements:* Dissertation required, foreign language not required. *Average time to degree:* doctorate–4 years full-time. *Entrance requirements:* GMAT (average 657) or GRE General Test (minimum combined score of 1350). Application deadline: 1/1 (priority date; rolling processing). Application fee: $55. Electronic applications accepted. *Expenses:* Tuition $1428 per year for state residents; $10,414 per year for nonresidents. Fees $787 per year. • Ann Marucheck, Associate Dean for PhD Programs, 919-962-3193. Application contact: Liz Griffin, Director, 919-962-1657. E-mail: kfphd_app@unc.edu.

University of North Carolina at Greensboro, Joseph M. Bryan School of Business and Economics, Department of Information Systems and Operations Management, Greensboro, NC 27412-0001. Awards MS. *Application deadline:* 7/1 (priority date; rolling processing; 11/1 for spring admission). *Application fee:* $35. *Expenses:* Tuition $1842 per year full-time, $370 per semester (minimum) part-time for state residents; $10,296 per year full-time, $2484 per semester (minimum) part-time for nonresidents. Fees $806 per year full-time, $111 per semester (minimum) part-time. • Dr. Gerald Hershey, Head, 336-334-5666.

University of North Texas, College of Business Administration, Department of Business Computer Information Systems, Denton, TX 76203-6737. Offers programs in information systems (MBA, PhD), management science (MBA, PhD). Part-time and evening/weekend programs available. Faculty: 18 full-time (0 women). Students: 62 full-time (18 women), 55 part-time (17 women); includes 23 minority (7 African Americans, 8 Asian Americans, 6 Hispanics, 2 Native Americans), 32 international. Average age 24. In 1997, 12 master's awarded. *Degree requirements:* For master's, computer language required, foreign language and thesis not required; for doctorate, computer language, dissertation required, foreign language not required. *Entrance requirements:* For master's, GMAT (minimum score 450), TOEFL, minimum GPA of 2.8; for doctorate, GMAT (minimum score 600) or GRE General Test, TOEFL, minimum GPA of 3.0. Application deadline: 7/17. Application fee: $25 ($50 for international students). *Tuition:* $2063 per year full-time, $815 per year part-time for state residents; $5897 per year full-time, $2100 per year part-time for nonresidents. *Financial aid:* Fellowships, research assistantships, teaching assistantships, Federal Work-Study, and career-related internships or fieldwork available. Financial aid application deadline: 4/1. *Faculty research:* Databases, systems design, expert systems, applied statistics, quality and reliability management. • Dr. John Windsor, Chair, 940-565-3110. Application contact: Dr. J. Wayne Spence, Doctoral Coordinator, 940-565-3116. Fax: 940-565-4835. E-mail: spence@cobaf.unt.edu.

University of Oregon, Graduate School, Charles H. Lundquist College of Business, Program in Applied Information Management, Eugene, OR 97403. Awards MS. Part-time and evening/weekend programs available. Students: 1 (woman) full-time, 37 part-time (13 women); includes 3 minority (1 African American, 1 Asian American, 1 Hispanic). 18 applicants, 56% accepted. In 1997, 17 degrees awarded (100% found work related to degree). *Degree requirements:* Thesis or alternative, project required, foreign language not required. *Average time to degree:* master's–2.5 years part-time. *Entrance requirements:* GMAT (average 593), GRE General Test (combined average 1370), TOEFL (minimum score 575). Application deadline: 5/15 (11/1 for spring admission). Application fee: $50. *Tuition:* $6429 per year full-time, $873 per quarter (minimum) part-time for state residents; $10,857 per year full-time, $1360 per quarter (minimum) part-time for nonresidents. *Financial aid:* Institutionally sponsored loans available. Aid available to part-time students. Financial aid application deadline: 2/1. *Faculty research:* Business management, information design. • Linda Ettinger, Academic Director, 541-346-1452. E-mail: lindae@oregon.uoregon.edu. Application contact: Janet Cormack, Coordinator, 541-725-2289. Fax: 541-725-2199. E-mail: jcormack@continue.uoregon.edu.

University of Pennsylvania, Wharton School, Operations and Information Management Department, Philadelphia, PA 19104. Awards MBA, PhD. Terminal master's awarded for partial completion of doctoral program. *Entrance requirements:* For master's, GMAT; for doctorate, GRE. Application fee: $125. • Dr. Patrick T. Harker, Chairman, 215-898-5041. Fax: 215-898-3664. E-mail: harker@opim.wharton.upenn.edu.

University of Pittsburgh, Graduate School of Public and International Affairs, Program in Public Management and Policy, Pittsburgh, PA 15260. Offerings include information services management (Certificate). Program faculty: 35 full-time (5 women), 24 part-time (6 women). *Average time to degree:* master's–1.5 years full-time, 4 years part-time. *Application deadline:* 3/1 (priority date; rolling processing; 12/1 for spring admission). *Application fee:* $30 ($40 for international students). *Expenses:* Tuition $8018 per year full-time, $329 per credit part-time for state residents; $16,508 per year full-time, $680 per credit part-time for nonresidents. Fees $480 per year full-time, $180 per year part-time. • Application contact: Barbara Porter, Assistant Dean, 412-648-7632. Fax: 412-648-7641. E-mail: barb+@pitt.edu.

University of Pittsburgh, Joseph M. Katz Graduate School of Business, Program in Management of Information Systems, Pittsburgh, PA 15260. Awards MS, MBA/MS. Part-time and evening/weekend programs available. Students: 30 full-time (8 women), 11 part-time (5 women); includes 4 minority (1 African American, 3 Asian Americans), 14 international. 70 applicants, 74% accepted. In 1997, 21 degrees awarded. *Degree requirements:* Computer language, thesis, internship, practicum required, foreign language not required. *Average time to degree:* master's–2 years full-time, 4 years part-time. *Entrance requirements:* GMAT, TOEFL (minimum score 600), experience with computers, previous course work in calculus. Application deadline: 5/1 (priority date; rolling processing). Application fee: $50. *Expenses:* Tuition $463 per credit for state residents; $867 per credit for nonresidents. Fees $480 per year full-time, $180 per year part-time. *Financial aid:* In 1997–98, 11 students received aid, including 11 fellowships (9 to first-year students) totaling $129,354; partial tuition waivers, Federal Work-Study, institutionally sponsored loans, and career-related internships or fieldwork also available. Financial aid application deadline: 3/15; applicants required to submit FAFSA. *Faculty research:* Case technologies, international information systems, system re-engineering, decision support systems, human-computer interaction. • Application contact: Enrique Mu, Coordinator, 412-648-2268. Fax: 412-648-1693. E-mail: enmu@katz.business.pitt.edu.

University of Redlands, Alfred North Whitehead College for Lifelong Learning, Program in Adult Education, PO Box 3080, Redlands, CA 92373-0999. Offerings include information systems (MBA). *Application deadline:* 9/1 (priority date; rolling processing; 3/1 for spring admission). *Application fee:* $40. Electronic applications accepted. • Dr. Hubbard Segur, Head, 909-793-2121 Ext. 4143.

University of Rhode Island, College of Business Administration, Kingston, RI 02881. Offerings include management science (MBA), with options in management information systems, manufacturing. *Application deadline:* 4/15 (priority date; rolling processing). *Application fee:* $35. *Expenses:* Tuition $3446 per year full-time, $191 per credit part-time for state residents; $9850 per year full-time, $547 per credit part-time for nonresidents. Fees $1276 per year full-time, $135 per semester (minimum) part-time.

University of St. Thomas, Graduate School of Business, Day MBA Program, St. Paul, MN 55105-1096. Offerings include information management (MBA). Program faculty: 13 part-time. *Degree requirements:* Computer language required, foreign language and thesis not required. *Entrance requirements:* GMAT (score in 50th percentile or higher). Application deadline: 5/1 (priority date; rolling processing). Application fee: $30. *Tuition:* $473 per credit hour. • Application contact: Jim O'Connor, Student Adviser, 612-962-4233. Fax: 612-962-4260.

University of St. Thomas, Graduate School of Business, Evening MBA Program, St. Paul, MN 55105-1096. Offerings include information management (MBA). Program faculty: 16 full-time (2 women), 89 part-time (17 women). *Degree requirements:* Computer language required, foreign language and thesis not required. *Entrance requirements:* GMAT (score in 50th percentile or higher). Application deadline: 8/1 (priority date; rolling processing; 12/1 for spring admission). Application fee: $30. *Tuition:* $416 per credit hour. • Dr. Stanford Nyquist, MBA Director, 612-962-4242. Application contact: Martha Ballard, Director of Student Services, 612-962-4226. Fax: 612-962-4260.

University of Southern California, Graduate School, Marshall School of Business, Department of Information and Operations Management, Los Angeles, CA 90089. Awards MS. Students: 9 full-time (2 women), 8 part-time (2 women); includes 2 minority (both Asian Americans), 7 international. Average age 30. 11 applicants, 64% accepted. In 1997, 9 degrees awarded. *Entrance requirements:* GMAT. *Expenses:* Tuition $16,944 per year full-time, $706 per unit part-time. Fees $414 per year full-time, $32 per year part-time. *Financial aid:* In 1997–98, 1 scholarship was awarded; fellowships, research assistantships, teaching assistantships, Federal Work-Study, institutionally sponsored loans also available. Aid available to part-time students. Financial aid application deadline: 2/15; applicants required to submit FAFSA. • Dr. Randolph Westerfield, Chair.

University of South Florida, College of Business Administration, Program in Management Information Systems, Tampa, FL 33620-9951. Awards MS. Students: 18 full-time (4 women), 41 part-time (30 women); includes 7 minority (1 African American, 6 Asian Americans), 10 international. 68 applicants, 57% accepted. In 1997, 7 degrees awarded. *Degree requirements:* Computer language required, foreign language and thesis not required. *Entrance requirements:* GMAT (minimum score 500), GRE General Test (minimum combined score of 1050). Application deadline: 5/15 (rolling processing). Application fee: $20. *Tuition:* $142 per credit hour for state residents; $486 per credit hour for nonresidents. *Financial aid:* In 1997–98, 1 fellowship (to a first-year student) totaling $7,000, 1 teaching assistantship averaging $708 per month were awarded; research assistantships also available. • Stan Birkin, Chairperson, 813-974-6763. E-mail: sbirkin@coba.usf.edu. Application contact: Alan Hevner, Director, 813-974-6753. Fax: 813-974-3030. E-mail: ahevner@coba.usf.edu.

The University of Texas at Arlington, College of Business Administration, Department of Information Systems and Management Science, Arlington, TX 76019-0407. Offers program in information systems (MS, PhD). Faculty: 12 full-time (1 woman), 1 part-time (0 women). Students: 59 full-time (26 women), 68 part-time (20 women); includes 18 minority (2 African Americans, 14 Asian Americans, 1 Hispanic, 1 Native American), 55 international. 79 applicants, 46% accepted. In 1997, 31 master's awarded; 2 doctorates awarded (100% entered university research/teaching). Terminal master's awarded for partial completion of doctoral program. *Degree requirements:* For master's, thesis optional; for doctorate, computer language, dissertation. *Entrance requirements:* For master's, GMAT (minimum score 480), minimum GPA of 3.0; for doctorate, GMAT (average 581), minimum GPA of 3.25. Application deadline: rolling. Application fee: $25 ($50 for international students). *Tuition:* $3206 per year full-time, $468 per semester (minimum) part-time for state residents; $8612 per year full-time, $1137 per semester (minimum) part-time for nonresidents. *Financial aid:* Research assistantships, teaching assistantships, and career-related internships or fieldwork available. *Faculty research:* Database modeling, strategic issues in information systems, simulations, production operations management. • Dr. Mary Whiteside, Chair, 817-272-3502. Application contact: Dr. Bijoy Bordoloi, Graduate Adviser, 817-272-3004.

The University of Texas at Arlington, College of Business Administration, Program in Business Administration, Arlington, TX 76019-0407. Offerings include information systems (MBA). *Degree requirements:* Computer language required, foreign language not required. *Entrance requirements:* GMAT (minimum score 480; average 550), minimum GPA of 2.9. Application deadline: rolling. Application fee: $25 ($50 for international students). *Tuition:* $3206 per year full-time, $468 per semester (minimum) part-time for state residents; $8612 per year full-time, $1137 per semester (minimum) part-time for nonresidents. • Application contact: Dr. James E. Walther, Graduate Adviser, 817-272-3004. Fax: 817-794-5799.

The University of Texas at Austin, Graduate School, College of Business Administration, Department of Management Sciences and Information Systems, Austin, TX 78712. Awards PhD. Faculty: 32 full-time (6 women). Students: 50 full-time (12 women); includes 30 international. 62 applicants, 23% accepted. *Average time to degree:* doctorate–4 years full-time. *Entrance requirements:* GMAT or GRE. Application deadline: 12/1. Application fee: $50 ($75 for international students). Electronic applications accepted. *Expenses:* Tuition $2592 per year full-time, $324 per semester (minimum) part-time for state residents; $7704 per year full-time, $963 per semester (minimum) part-time for nonresidents. Fees $778 per year full-time, $161 per semester (minimum) part-time. *Financial aid:* In 1997–98, 15 students received aid, including 15 teaching assistantships (5 to first-year students) averaging $944 per month; Federal Work-Study, institutionally sponsored loans also available. *Total annual research expenditures:* $405,708. • Dr. Patrick Jaillet, Chairman, 512-471-9447. E-mail: jaillet@athena.bus.utexas.edu. Application contact: Joyce Moyer, Graduate Coordinator, 512-471-8048. Fax: 512-471-0587. E-mail: moyerj@mail.utexas.edu.

University of the Sacred Heart, Graduate Programs, Department of Business Administration, Program in Management Information Systems, San Juan, PR 00914-0383. Awards MBA. Part-time and evening/weekend programs available. Faculty: 6 full-time (3 women), 11 part-time (1 woman), 9.67 FTE. Students: 3 full-time (2 women), 143 part-time (58 women). 38 applicants, 55% accepted. In 1997, 6 degrees awarded. *Degree requirements:* Computer language, thesis. *Entrance requirements:* PAEG, minimum undergraduate GPA of 2.5. Application deadline: 5/15. Application fee: $25. *Expenses:* Tuition $150 per credit. Fees $240 per credit. • Prof. Pedro Fraile, Coordinator, 787-728-1515 Ext. 2436. Fax: 787-728-1515 Ext. 2273. E-mail: p_faile@uscac1.usc.clu.edu. Application contact: Dr. Blanca Villamil, Acting Director, Admissions Office, 787-728-1515 Ext. 3237. Fax: 787-728-2066. E-mail: b_villami@uscsi.usc.clu.edu.

University of Toledo, Graduate School of Business, Department of Information Systems and Operations Management, Toledo, OH 43606-3398. Offers programs in decision sciences (MBA), information systems (MBA), manufacturing management (MS, PhD), operations management (MBA). Faculty: 16 full-time (2 women). Students: 53 full-time (9 women), 67 part-time (22 women); includes 2 minority (both African Americans), 76 international. Average age 29. 94 applicants, 60% accepted. In 1997, 11 master's, 1 doctorate awarded. *Degree requirements:* For doctorate, dissertation. *Entrance requirements:* For master's, GMAT, TOEFL (minimum score 550), minimum GPA of 2.7; for doctorate, GMAT, TOEFL (minimum score 550). Application deadline: 8/1 (priority date; rolling processing). Application fee: $37. *Tuition:* $5907 per year full-time, $246 per hour part-time for state residents; $11,835 per year full-time, $493 per hour part-time for nonresidents. *Financial aid:* In 1997–98, 26 research assistantships, 2 teaching assistantships were awarded; administrative assistantships, tuition scholarships, full tuition waivers, Federal Work-Study, institutionally sponsored loans, and career-related internships or fieldwork also available. Aid available to part-time students. Financial aid application deadline: 4/1; applicants required to submit FAFSA. • Dr. Arthur Smith, Chair, 419-530-2420. Application contact: Dr. Bruce Kuhlman, MBA Director, 419-530-2774. Fax: 419-530-7260. E-mail: mba0001@uoft01.utoledo.edu.

Directory: Management Information Systems

University of Tulsa, College of Business Administration, Program in Accounting and Information Systems, Tulsa, OK 74104-3189. Awards MAIS. Program new for fall 1998. *Entrance requirements:* TOEFL (minimum score 575). Application deadline: rolling. Application fee: $30. *Expenses:* Tuition $480 per credit hour. Fees $2 per credit hour. *Financial aid:* Application deadline 2/1. • Dr. Patrick A. Hennessee, Chairperson, 918-631-2794. Fax: 918-631-2164. Application contact: Dr. Richard C. Burgess, Assistant Dean/Director of Graduate Business Studies, 918-631-2242. Fax: 918-631-2142.

University of Virginia, Graduate School of Arts and Sciences, McIntire School of Commerce, Program in Management Information Systems, Charlottesville, VA 22903. Awards MS. Faculty: 52 full-time (12 women), 7 part-time (3 women), 54 FTE. Students: 16 full-time (4 women); includes 1 minority (African American), 4 international. Average age 29. 31 applicants, 58% accepted. In 1997, 18 degrees awarded. *Entrance requirements:* GMAT, TOEFL. Application deadline: 7/15 (rolling processing; 12/1 for spring admission). Application fee: $40. *Tuition:* $4876 per year for state residents; $15,824 per year for nonresidents. *Financial aid:* Fellowships, Federal Work-Study available. • Application contact: Duane J. Osheim, Associate Dean, 804-924-7184.

See in-depth description on page 591.

University of Waterloo, Faculty of Engineering, Department of Management Sciences, Waterloo, ON N2L 3G1, Canada. Offerings include management sciences (MA Sc, PhD), with options in information systems, management of technology. Postbaccalaureate distance learning degree programs offered (no on-campus study). Department faculty: 14 full-time (2 women), 12 part-time (3 women). *Degree requirements:* For master's, project or thesis required, foreign language not required; for doctorate, dissertation, comprehensive exam required, foreign language not required. *Entrance requirements:* For master's, TOEFL (minimum score 550), honors degree, minimum B average; for doctorate, TOEFL (minimum score 550), master's degree. Application deadline: rolling. Application fee: $50. *Tuition:* $3220 per year. • Dr. J. D. Fuller, Chair, 519-888-4567 Ext. 2683. Application contact: Dr. J. Webster, Graduate Officer, 519-888-4567 Ext. 5683. Fax: 519-746-7252. E-mail: jwebster@mansci2.watstar.uwaterloo.ca.

University of Wisconsin–Madison, School of Business, Program in Information Systems Analysis and Design, Madison, WI 53706-1380. Awards MBA, MS, PhD. PhD admissions temporarily suspended. Faculty: 2 full-time (0 women), 2 part-time (1 woman), 3.2 FTE. Students: In 1997, 18 master's awarded. *Degree requirements:* For doctorate, dissertation. *Entrance requirements:* For master's, GMAT. Application deadline: 6/1 (rolling processing; 10/1 for spring admission). Application fee: $45. *Tuition:* $5950 per year full-time, $1118 per semester (minimum) part-time for state residents; $16,230 per year full-time, $3044 per semester (minimum) part-time for nonresidents. *Financial aid:* In 1997–98, 4 teaching assistantships were awarded; fellowships, research assistantships, project assistantships also available. *Faculty research:* Operations management, just-in-time systems, total quality management, flexible manufacturing systems, optimization models. • James G. Morris, Chair, 608-262-1284. Fax: 608-263-3142. E-mail: jmorris@bus.wisc.edu. Application contact: Lisa Urban, Director of Master's Marketing and Recruiting, 608-262-4610. Fax: 608-265-4192.

University of Wisconsin–Madison, School of Business, Program in Operations and Information Management, Madison, WI 53706-1380. Awards MBA, MS, PhD. Part-time programs available. Faculty: Students: 22 full-time (8 women), 7 part-time (2 women); includes 3 minority (2 African Americans, 1 Asian American), 5 international. Average age 27. 22 applicants, 45% accepted. In 1997, 12 master's awarded. Terminal master's awarded for partial completion of doctoral program. *Degree requirements:* For doctorate, dissertation. *Entrance requirements:* For master's, GMAT (minimum score 580; average 600), minimum GPA of 3.0. Application deadline: 6/1 (priority date; rolling processing; 10/1 for spring admission). Application fee: $45. Electronic applications accepted. *Tuition:* $5950 per year full-time, $1118 per semester (minimum) part-time for state residents; $16,230 per year full-time, $3044 per semester (minimum) part-time for nonresidents. *Financial aid:* In 1997–98, 3 students received aid, including 3 teaching assistantships; fellowships, research assistantships, project assistantships, Federal Work-Study, institutionally sponsored loans, and career-related internships or fieldwork also available. Aid available to part-time students. Financial aid application deadline: 2/15. *Faculty research:* Cost improvement, productivity improvement, transportation economics, financial signalling, optimization models, distribution system design. • James G. Morris, Chair, 608-262-1284. Fax: 608-263-3142. E-mail: jmorris@bus.wisc.edu. Application contact: Lisa Urban, Director of Master's Marketing and Recruiting, 608-262-4610. Fax: 608-265-4192.

Utah State University, College of Business, Department of Business Information Systems and Education, Logan, UT 84322. Offers programs in business education (MS), business information systems (MS, Ed D, PhD), marketing education (MS), training and development (MS). Part-time and evening/weekend programs available. Postbaccalaureate distance learning degree programs offered (no on-campus study). Faculty: 10 full-time (0 women). Students: 53 full-time (26 women), 12 part-time (4 women). Average age 30. 27 applicants, 67% accepted. In 1997, 28 master's awarded. Terminal master's awarded for partial completion of doctoral program. *Degree requirements:* For master's, computer language required, thesis optional, foreign language not required; for doctorate, computer language, dissertation required, foreign language not required. *Entrance requirements:* For master's, GMAT (score in 40th percentile or higher), TOEFL (minimum score 550), minimum GPA of 3.0; for doctorate, GRE General Test (score in 40th percentile or higher), TOEFL (minimum score 550), minimum GPA of 3.0. Application deadline: 6/15 (priority date; rolling processing; 10/15 for spring admission). Application fee: $40. *Expenses:* Tuition $1448 per year full-time, $624 per year part-time for state residents; $5082 per year full-time, $2192 per year part-time for nonresidents. Fees $421 per year full-time, $165 per year part-time. *Financial aid:* Fellowships, research assistantships, teaching assistantships, Federal Work-Study, and career-related internships or fieldwork available. Financial aid application deadline: 3/1. *Faculty research:* Oral and written communication, methods of teaching, CASE tools, object-oriented programming, decision support systems, reengineering. • Dr. Lloyd Bartholome, Head, 435-797-2341. E-mail: lbart@b202.usu.edu. Application contact: Dr. Thomas Hilton, Graduate Adviser, 435-797-2353. Fax: 435-797-2351. E-mail: hilton@cc.usu.edu.

Villa Julie College, Department of Advanced Information Technologies, Stevenson, MD 21153. Awards MS. Part-time and evening/weekend programs available. Faculty: 7 part-time (1 woman). Students: 80 part-time (16 women). *Degree requirements:* Computer language, thesis required, foreign language not required. *Entrance requirements:* GRE General Test. Application deadline: 8/1 (rolling processing; 12/31 for spring admission). Application fee: $25. *Expenses:* Tuition $335 per credit. Fees $25 per semester. • Dr. Dean Cook, Director, 410-653-6400. E-mail: masters@vjc.edu. Application contact: Judy Snyder, Registrar, 410-653-6400. Fax: 410-653-6405. E-mail: masters@vjc.edu.

Virginia Commonwealth University, School of Business, Program in Information Systems, Richmond, VA 23284-9005. Awards MS, PhD, Certificate. *Degree requirements:* For master's, computer language required, foreign language and thesis not required; for doctorate, dissertation. *Entrance requirements:* For master's and doctorate, GMAT. Application deadline: rolling. Application fee: $30 ($0 for international students). *Tuition:* $4960 per year full-time, $257 per credit part-time for state residents; $12,652 per year full-time, $684 per credit part-time for nonresidents. *Financial aid:* Fellowships, research assistantships, teaching assistantships, full and partial tuition waivers, Federal Work-Study, institutionally sponsored loans available. Financial aid application deadline: 3/15. • Dr. George M. Kasper, Chair, 804-828-1737. Fax: 804-828-3972. E-mail: gmkasper@vcu.edu. Application contact: Dr. Edward L. Millner, Associate Dean of Graduate Studies, 804-828-1741. Fax: 804-828-7174.

Walsh College of Accountancy and Business Administration, Program in Information Management and Communication, Troy, MI 48007-7006. Awards MSIMC. Part-time and evening/weekend programs available. Faculty: 3. *Entrance requirements:* TOEFL (minimum score 550), minimum GPA of 2.75, previous course work in business. Application deadline: rolling. Application fee: $25. *Expenses:* Tuition $273 per credit hour. Fees $75 per semester. *Financial aid:* Federal Work-Study available. Aid available to part-time students. • Application contact: Sherree Hyde, Director, Enrollment Services, 248-689-8282 Ext. 215. Fax: 248-524-2520.

Webster University, School of Business and Technology, Department of Business, St. Louis, MO 63119-3194. Offerings include computer resources and information management (MA, MBA), computer science/distributed systems (MS). Department faculty: 5 full-time (1 woman). *Application deadline:* rolling. *Application fee:* $25 ($50 for international students). *Tuition:* $350 per credit hour. • Lucille Berry, Chair, 314-968-7022. Fax: 314-968-7077. E-mail: berrylm@webster.edu. Application contact: Beth Russell, Director of Graduate Admissions, 314-968-7089. Fax: 314-968-7166. E-mail: russellmb@webster.edu.

Western International University, Program in Information Systems, 9215 North Black Canyon Highway, Phoenix, AZ 85021-2718. Awards MS. Evening/weekend programs available. *Degree requirements:* Computer language, thesis, research project required, foreign language not required. *Entrance requirements:* GMAT (strongly recommended), minimum GPA of 2.75. Application deadline: rolling. Application fee: $50 ($100 for international students). • Bill Akins, Chair, 602-943-2311. Application contact: Enrollment Department, 602-943-2311. Fax: 602-371-8637.

Western International University, Program in Management Information Systems, 9215 North Black Canyon Highway, Phoenix, AZ 85021-2718. Awards MBA. Evening/weekend programs available. *Degree requirements:* Thesis, research project. *Entrance requirements:* GMAT (strongly recommended), minimum GPA of 2.75. Application deadline: rolling. Application fee: $50 ($100 for international students). • Bill Akins, Chair, 602-943-2311. Application contact: Enrollment Department, 602-943-2311. Fax: 602-371-8637.

Western New England College, School of Business, Program in Information Systems, Springfield, MA 01119-2654. Awards MSIS. *Application deadline:* rolling. *Application fee:* $30. *Expenses:* Tuition $353 per credit hour. Fees $44 per semester (minimum). *Financial aid:* Application deadline 4/1. • Application contact: Rod Pease, Director of Student Administrative Services, 413-796-2080.

Western New England College, School of Business, Program in Management Information Systems, Springfield, MA 01119-2654. Awards MBA. *Application deadline:* rolling. *Application fee:* $30. *Expenses:* Tuition $353 per credit hour. Fees $44 per semester (minimum). *Financial aid:* Application deadline 4/1. • Application contact: Rod Pease, Director of Student Administrative Services, 413-796-2080.

Wilkes University, Programs in Business Administration, Wilkes-Barre, PA 18766-0002. Offerings include management information systems (MBA). MBA (management, management information systems) being phased out; applicants no longer accepted. Faculty: 11 full-time, 2 part-time. *Entrance requirements:* GMAT. Application deadline: rolling. Application fee: $30. *Expenses:* Tuition $12,552 per year full-time, $523 per credit hour part-time. Fees $240 per year full-time, $10 per credit hour part-time. • Dr. Robert Seeley, Director, 717-408-4717.

Worcester Polytechnic Institute, Department of Management, Worcester, MA 01609-2280. Offerings include operations and information technology (MS). MBA, MSM (administration and management, engineering management), MS (manufacturing management) being phased out; applicants no longer accepted. Department faculty: 15 full-time (4 women), 7 part-time (1 woman). *Application deadline:* 2/15 (priority date; rolling processing; 10/15 for spring admission). *Application fee:* $50. Electronic applications accepted. *Tuition:* $636 per credit hour. • Dr. McRae Banks, Head, 508-831-5218. E-mail: macb@wpi.edu. Application contact: Norm Wilkinson, Director, 508-831-5218. Fax: 508-831-5720. E-mail: nwilkins@wpi.edu.

Wright State University, College of Business and Administration, Department of Management Science and Information Systems, Dayton, OH 45435. Offers programs in logistics management (MBA, MS), management information systems (MBA), operations management (MBA). Students: 38 full-time (19 women), 86 part-time (29 women); includes 16 minority (6 African Americans, 8 Asian Americans, 2 Hispanics), 13 international. Average age 32. 69 applicants, 67% accepted. In 1997, 44 degrees awarded. *Degree requirements:* Computer language required, foreign language and thesis not required. *Entrance requirements:* GMAT, TOEFL (minimum score 550), minimum AACSB index of 1000. Application fee: $25. *Tuition:* $5109 per year full-time, $161 per credit hour part-time for state residents; $9039 per year full-time, $282 per credit hour part-time for nonresidents. *Financial aid:* In 1997–98, 6 fellowships (all to first-year students), 2 teaching assistantships, 10 graduate assistantships were awarded; research assistantships also available. Aid available to part-time students. Financial aid applicants required to submit FAFSA. • Dr. Barbara Denison, Chair, 937-775-2895. Application contact: James Crawford, Director of Graduate Programs, 937-775-2437. Fax: 937-775-3301.

Cross-Discipline Announcements

Bentley College, Graduate School of Business, Program in Accounting Information Systems, 175 Forest Street, Waltham, MA 02154-4705.

The Bentley College Graduate School of Business offers a Master of Science in Accounting Information Systems (MSAIS) for students with backgrounds in accounting or computer information systems. The program covers information technologies that firms use in their financial and accounting decision-making processes. Included are assurance services and an understanding of electronic commerce and Web-based applications.

Rensselaer Polytechnic Institute, Lally School of Management and Technology, Troy, NY 12180-3590.

Management information systems (MIS) have been defined as "the development and use of effective information systems in organizations." Practitioners need to combine the worlds of technology and business. Information systems consist of hardware and software, but they must also deal with people and business processes. The two worlds are joined by data—the lifeblood of the business. The MIS concentration in the Lally School addresses the needs of both worlds and prepares students to accept responsible roles working with mid- to large-sized corporations in the development and use of information.

BOSTON UNIVERSITY

School of Management
Programs in Management Information Systems

Programs of Study

The Master of Science in Management Information Systems (M.S./M.I.S.) program at the Boston University School of Management develops the technical and managerial skills essential for effective use of information technology. This twelve-month, full-time program prepares students to meet the immediate challenges of implementing systems through course work that explores the fundamental concepts of management and technology. The M.S./M.I.S. curriculum consists of a rigorous series of twelve courses that provide the essential technical foundations of an M.I.S. education while emphasizing the strategic issues of information technology in a business environment. A seven-month internship project with a Boston-area company combines practical hands-on experience with classroom support and critique. For those interested in a broader-based management education, a dual-degree program is also available. The dual-degree program enables students to obtain both the M.B.A. degree and the M.S./M.I.S. degree in less than two calendar years of full-time study. M.S./M.I.S. students benefit from a variety of opportunities to meet and learn from practicing professionals. In addition to the internship, the program organizes a regular series of guest speakers who provide information on M.I.S. and management careers, the future of technology, and trends within the industry. Field trips to computer vendors and user organizations and presentations by alumni working in a variety of fields further enrich the classroom experience.

Research Facilities

The Boston University School of Management opened the nation's most technologically advanced building for management education in early 1997. Designed specifically for teaching management as an integrated system and built to accommodate team learning, the Rafik B. Hariri Building employs leading-edge technology throughout. The building features classrooms with computer ports and plugs for all students, instructional workstations with Internet access, and advanced audiovisual capabilities for slide, videotape, and computer-generated presentations. In addition, the management library houses more than 90,000 books, periodicals, and journals as well as the latest technology for information retrieval. The Advanced Technology Lab at Boston University School of Management has the most advanced computers available and is principally dedicated to the M.S./M.I.S. program. The Advanced Technology Lab will undergo regular updating of this technology platform so that future M.S./M.I.S. classes can expect to be working with the most current equipment.

The Boston University School of Management has a wealth of research centers and institutes, each of which addresses issues that extend beyond the boundaries of traditional functions. These organizations have become magnets for faculty members from other schools and colleges at Boston University and for top-level managers from around the world, who come together and share their understanding of contemporary management challenges. The research centers and institutes and the School's executive training programs offer significant advantages to students seeking leadership roles in major organizations. Through an industrial network that extends around the globe, faculty members maintain contact and exchange data with colleagues in universities and business firms. This real-world involvement brings exciting results to the classroom—timely and topical material for case studies and a steady stream of high-level managers from a variety of firms. The M.S./M.I.S. program benefits from an affiliation with the Systems Research Center, where member companies and M.I.S. faculty members work together to study a wide range of M.I.S. issues.

Financial Aid

The M.S./M.I.S. program offers scholarship and loan programs to students who are citizens or permanent residents of the United States. In general, financial aid is not available to international students.

Cost of Study

Tuition for 1998–99 is $33,822 for three semesters (twelve months) of study. Fees are approximately $300 for the entire program; medical insurance is available for $785 (covers summer, spring, and fall semesters; insurance is required of all international students); and books and other course materials are estimated at $1000. It is required that M.S./M.I.S. students bring or purchase a laptop computer.

Living and Housing Costs

Single students living off campus should anticipate living costs for twelve months of approximately $15,000. The costs for married students are estimated at $19,000. Most students live in apartments in nearby neighborhoods, easily accessible from the School by public transportation.

Student Group

The M.S./M.I.S. program admits about 55 students each year to its program. Students come from diverse cultural, work, and educational backgrounds with previous degrees in literature, education, health care, history, education, and psychology as well as management and computer science.

Student Outcomes

Graduates of the M.S./M.I.S. and dual-degree program embark on successful careers as information systems professionals, consultants, and general managers. Information technology opportunities are plentiful in all fields, including finance, accounting, health care, and government. The School of Management's Career Center takes an active role in helping students make informed career and life decisions. Through comprehensive career education programming, job development services, and individualized career counseling, the center collaborates with students in developing and managing careers at both the entry and experienced level. Ninety-five percent of 1997 graduates were employed at graduation, with an average starting salary of $65,500.

Location

Boston is a beautiful and historic city with vast business and technological resources. Cultural, educational, and sports activities abound. For music lovers, there is always an evening's entertainment at historic Symphony Hall, home of the Boston Pops Orchestra. The Huntington Theatre, in residence at Boston University Theater, features classical plays, popular musicals, and contemporary premiers each season. With numerous major universities in the area, Boston offers a wealth of lecture and seminar opportunities. Sports fans can see the Red Sox battle American League foes at Fenway Park (just around the corner from the new School of Management building), while the Celtics and Bruins play at the new Fleet Center.

The University

The fourth-largest private university in the nation, Boston University is situated at the 86-acre Charles River Campus and Boston University's Medical Center in the city's South End. The School of Management was established as the College of Business Administration in 1913 and is located on the Charles River Campus.

Applying

The M.S./M.I.S. program and the M.S./M.I.S. portion of the dual-degree program start at the end of May. The suggested application deadline for domestic and international students is March 1. A bachelor's degree from an accredited college or university is required for admission to the M.S./M.I.S. program. A previous degree in management or computer science is not required; however, applicants are expected to have a combination of work experience and course work that enables them to benefit from the program. The M.S./M.I.S. program requires Graduate Management Admissions Test (GMAT) scores. International students must also submit International Student Data Forms and documentation of financial support. The TOEFL is required of all international applicants who did not receive a previous degree from an institution where English was the language of instruction.

Correspondence and Information

M.S./M.I.S. Program Office
School of Management
Boston University
595 Commonwealth Avenue
Boston, Massachusetts 02215

Telephone: 617-353-3522
E-mail: ms-mis@bu.edu
World Wide Web: http://management.bu.edu/program/ms-mis

Boston University

THE FACULTY AND THEIR RESEARCH

The Department of Information Systems at Boston University School of Management conducts research in the following areas: competing in the knowledge economy, the impact of information technology on organizational capabilities and structures, how technology affects people and their work environment, and managing knowledge for strategic success.

P. R. Balasubramanian, Assistant Professor of Management Information Systems; Ph.D., NYU. Knowledge management, workflow management, hypermedia design and model management.

Thomas H. Davenport, Professor of Management Information Systems; Ph.D., Harvard. Knowledge management, the business implications of enterprise systems, management approaches in the information industry.

John C. Henderson, Professor of Management Information Systems; Chairman, Department of Information Systems; and Director, Systems Research Center; Ph.D., Texas at Austin. Alignment of business and information technology strategy, managing strategic partnerships, managing the value of I/T investments.

C. Suzanne Iacono, Assistant Professor of Management Information Systems; Ph.D., Arizona. Social dynamics of electronics interactions, the management of relationships in distributed work settings, the rise of social identity and the mobilization of interest in electronic groups.

Michael E. Lawson, Associate Professor of Economics and Associate Dean; Ph.D., Iowa. Health economics and industrial organizations, impact of end-user computing on business productivity.

G. Shankaranarayanan, Assistant Professor of Management Information Systems; Ph.D., Arizona. Schema evolution in databases, heterogeneous and distributed databases, genetic algorithms and visual interfaces and their applications in information retrieval.

Lee S. Sproull, Professor of Management; Ph.D., Stanford. Innovations in electronic communications (e-mail, electronic bulletin boards, and video conferences) and their impact on work life and organizations.

John S. Storck, Assistant Professor of Management Information Systems and Director, M.S./M.I.S. Program; D.B.A., Boston University. Social and commercial implications of advanced communications technologies, including videoconferencing and online services.

N. Venkatraman, Professor of Management; Ph.D., Pittsburgh. The role of information technology in creating new organizational capabilities, development of the concept of a corporation as a "portfolio of capabilities and relationships" that leverages the power of information technology to exploit different sources and types of expertise in the business network.

Richard Y. Wang, Associate Professor of Management Information Systems; Ph.D., MIT. Information quality: developing technical solutions and organizational processes that are fundamental to the long-term improvement of organizational information quality.

Boston University School of Management's Systems Research Center

The M.S./M.I.S. curriculum is enhanced by its affiliation with the Systems Research Center, where member companies and the Department of Information Systems faculty work together to study a wide range of MIS issues. The Systems Research Center's mission is to enhance both theory and practice related to the effective use of information technologies and systems in organizations. This mission is achieved through the development of active, ongoing partnerships between the research community and leading-edge organizations. The primary focus of the center's research activities is how information technologies and systems influence the effectiveness of organizations. Research themes supported by the center include emerging organizational forms: governance, alliances, and relationships; leveraging expertise through effective knowledge management; maximizing the value of investments in strategic capabilities; and IT and the nature of work relationships. Corporate members participate in theme-oriented working groups that meet periodically to exchange experiences, help structure the research projects, and disseminate research findings. The research methodologies employed by the faculty members range from single, in-depth case studies to large, cross-industry survey research. Common to all projects, however, is the goal of conducting both relevant and rigorous research.

CASE WESTERN RESERVE UNIVERSITY

Weatherhead School of Management
Department of Information Systems

Programs of Study

The Department offers an M.S. and a Ph.D. degree. The Master of Science in Management in Information Systems (M.S.M.I.S.) is an intensive eleven-month program that begins the first week of June. It prepares graduates for a leadership career in information systems consulting. The Ph.D. in management prepares graduates for a career in research and teaching. Both programs emphasize field work in organizations and a balanced search for human, intellectual, and economic value with information technology.

The M.S.M.I.S. combines business knowledge, consultancy skills, and experience in system development. Students work on project teams in a collaborative learning environment. Some unique features of the fourteen-course M.S.M.I.S. curriculum include three models of management courses that are team-taught by faculty members from accounting, marketing, finance, strategy, and operations management. Students apply the core knowledge of these disciplines to diagnosing organizational problems, analyzing alternatives, and designing solutions from a management perspective. Three consulting skills courses that develop students' abilities to communicate and negotiate, to manage large-scale change projects, and to approach their work with a professional and ethical vision are also available. In addition, students can take four technology skills courses that provide substantial experience in developing object-oriented, client-server applications. Four technology management courses are also offered that prepare graduates to be leaders of technology deployment over the coming decades.

The Ph.D. in management in information systems enables students to develop a unique program of study geared to their own research interests. The Ph.D. requires 36 hours of course work, successful completion of a comprehensive qualifying examination, and a dissertation that makes an original contribution to subject knowledge.

Research Facilities

Weatherhead was the first management school to develop a fully integrated network of personal computers for instruction and research. It is continuously updated and houses IBM-compatible and Macintosh, Sun, and DEC workstations. The network makes available a wide variety of software and special devices and Internet access.

Students in the M.S.M.I.S. program also have a small laboratory with servers and workstations that allow them to experiment with system development software, groupware, and networking. Faculty members have developed several software tools that are actively used in research programs, including cause mapping tools, rule-based forecasting tools, and tools for construct visualization.

University computing resources include CWRUnet, a fiber-optic network that links more than eighty-five campus buildings and provides access to a wide range of information resources and networks, including a multimedia laboratory.

The University libraries contain all major journals in information systems and related areas of management as well as a wide variety of electronic media in the University's growing digital library.

Financial Aid

Numerous assistance packages are available for M.S.M.I.S. program students, including merit scholarships, graduate assistantships, and an Express Financial Aid Service that helps students locate and qualify for available loan programs. For the Ph.D. program, teaching or research assistantships that cover full tuition and a monthly stipend are generally available to all incoming students.

Cost of Study

Tuition and fees for 1998–99 are $10,450 per semester. The M.S.M.I.S. program begins in June each year and includes three semesters of course work between June and the following May. Books and supplies are estimated at $750 per semester. The estimate for room and board is $4985 per semester.

Living and Housing Costs

A variety of on-campus and off-campus housing is available. On-campus housing includes graduate residential dorms. A large selection of off-campus housing is available throughout the University area. Information on housing is sent upon request.

Student Group

Graduate students at the Weatherhead School of Management represent a diversity of academic, professional, and cultural backgrounds. In the M.S.M.I.S. program, it is preferred that students in each class have a wide variety of undergraduate backgrounds and work experiences, including economics, social sciences, humanities, natural sciences, business, and engineering. The only background requirement for M.S.M.I.S. students is experience with a procedural programming language and a commitment to making effective use of information technology in the world.

Student Outcomes

The M.S.M.I.S. prepares students for careers as internal consultants with industrial or governmental organizations, external consultants with independent consulting firms, or entrepreneurs who are starting their own firms. Leading industrial and consulting companies serve as program affiliates and provide close links with prospective employers, sites for field projects, and guest presentations in class.

Graduates of the Ph.D. program currently hold faculty positions at leading research universities as well as top management positions in industry.

Location

Case Western Reserve University is in a park-like campus 4 miles east of downtown Cleveland in University Circle. Campus neighbors include the Botanical Garden, the Cleveland Orchestra, and the Cleveland Art Museum. The University Circle area has perhaps the most extensive concentration of educational, scientific, artistic, social, and cultural institutions in the United States.

The University and The School

Case Western Reserve University is an independent research university with programs in arts and sciences, engineering, management, law, medicine, nursing, and applied social sciences. Founded in 1826, the University has approximately 3,000 undergraduate and 6,000 graduate students. The University has more than 2,000 funded faculty research projects that total more than $100 million annually.

The Weatherhead School of Management has 82 faculty members and features research centers in technology management, health care, regional economics, nonprofit organizations, and arts management.

Applying

Applicants are admitted on the basis of academic and professional accomplishments, performance on the GMAT and GRE, written recommendations, and responses to interview and application essay questions. The application deadline is February 15 for June 1999 admission to the M.S.M.I.S., and March 31 for fall 1999 admission to the Ph.D. program. Late applications are accepted on a space available basis.

Correspondence and Information

Colleen Gepperth, Department Administrator
Information Systems
Weatherhead School of Management
Case Western Reserve University
Cleveland, Ohio 44106-7235
Telephone: 216-368-2144
800-689-2144 (toll-free)
Fax: 216-368-4776
E-mail: cam4@po.cwru.edu
World Wide Web: http://weatherhead.cwru.edu

Case Western Reserve University

THE FACULTY AND THEIR RESEARCH

Richard J. Boland Jr., Professor of Accountancy and Professor and Chairman of Information Systems; Ph.D., Case Western Reserve. Qualitative analysis of the design and use of information systems, organization and human consequences of information technologies, cause mapping and distributed cognition, collaboration technologies.

Fred Collopy, Associate Professor; Ph.D., Pennsylvania. Business forecasting, objective setting in organizations, and organizational impacts of information systems; methods for combining human judgment and machine intelligence; construct visualization.

Alan F. Dowling Jr., Adjunct Professor of Management Information and Decision Systems; Ph.D., MIT. Health-care information systems, system design and implementation, information system planning.

Michael J. Ginzberg, Professor; Associate Dean for Professional and International Programs; Ph.D., MIT. Managing information service activities, development of decision support systems, implementing new information systems and organizational arrangements, management of technical professionals, international deployment of information technology.

Miles H. Kennedy, Associate Professor; Ph.D., London School of Economics. Use of artificial intelligence, database, and networking technologies to improve organizational effectiveness; use of object-oriented techniques for improving systems and development of curricula and courses in the field of MIS.

Roberta Lamb, Assistant Professor; Ph.D., California. Social networks and online technologies; organizational impacts; technology and innovation.

Kai H. Lim, Assistant Professor; Ph.D., British Columbia. Managerial and behavioral aspects of information systems/technology; multimedia in organizations; electronic commerce; human-computer interaction and computer learning in organizational contexts; cross-cultural issues in information systems.

Betty Vandenbosch, Assistant Professor; Ph.D., Western Ontario. Impact of executive information systems, microcomputer tools and communication technologies on individual and organizational performance, relation of information sources and interactions on the development and change of managers' mental models.

Stephanie Watts Sussman, Assistant Professor; Ph.D., Boston University. Telecommunications and computer-mediated communication; management of IS and knowledge management; global information technology.

Youngjin Yoo, Assistant Professor; Ph.D., Maryland. Collaborative technology; role of information technology in learning; virtual team management; information technology and organizational transformation.

RECENT FACULTY PUBLICATIONS

Boland, R. J., and U. Schultze. From work to activity: Technology and the narrative of progress. In *Information Technology and the Transformation of Work*, pp. 308–24, eds. W. Orlikowski, G. Walsham, and M. Jones. Elsevier: Amsterdam, 1996.

Boland, R. J., and R. V. Tenkasi. Perspective making and perspective taking in communities of knowing. *Organ. Sci.* August:350–72, 1995.

Boland, R. J., R. V. Tenkasi, and D. Te'eni. Designing information technology to support distributed cognition. *Organ. Sci.* August:456–75, 1994.

Boland, R. J. Accounting and the interpretive act. *Accounting Organizations Soc.*, pp. 125–46, 1993.

Collopy, F. Bias in retrospective self-reports of time use: An empirical study of computer uses. *Manage. Sci.* 42:758–67, 1996.

Armstrong, J. S., and **F. Collopy.** Competitor orientation: Effects of objectives and information on managerial decision and profitability. *J. Marketing Res.* 33:188–99, 1996.

Adya, M., and **F. Collopy.** Does AI research aid prediction? A review and evaluation. In *Proceedings of the International Conference on Information Systems,* pp. 123–40, 1995.

Collopy, F., M. Adya, and J. S. Armstrong. Principles for examining predictive validity: The case of information systems spending forecasts. *Information Systems Res.* 5:170–9, 1994.

Dowling, A. F. Community health information networks. In *Community Health Information Networks,* chapter 2, eds. P. Brennan, S. Schneider, and E. Tomquist, 1996.

Dowling, A. F. The emerging healthcare environment. In *Proceedings of TDS Executive Seminar, Physician-Hospital Integration: A Strategic Imperative,* 1994.

Dowling, A. F. The information management implications of federal health care reform. *Healthcare Information Management,* Winter 1994.

Payton, F. C., F. Brennan, and **M. J. Ginzberg.** Needs determination for a community approach to health care delivery. *Int. J. Technol. Management, Special Publication on the Role of Management of Technology in Clinical and Administrative Health-Care Delivery,* pp. 157–74, 1995.

Ginzberg, M. J. Decision support systems. In *Macmillan Encyclopedia of Computers,* pp. 287–92, eds. G. G. Bitter et al. New York: Macmillan Publishing Company, 1992.

Lucas, H. C., **M. J. Ginzberg,** and R. L. Schultz. *IS Implementation: Testing a Structural Model.* Norwood, NJ: Ablex Publishing Corporation, 1990.

Lamb, R. After scholarship: Making information actionable. *Can. J. Commun.* 22(3–4), December 1997.

Lamb, R. Corporate use of information: How and why do firms differ? *Center Res. Information Technol. Organ. Newsletter* 6(1):Fall/Winter 1997–98.

Lamb, R. Who uses information resources? Interorganizational incentives for gathering data and going online. *SIGCAS Newsletter,* 1997.

Lamb, R. Bits of cities: How utopian visions structure social power in physical space and cyberspace. In *Urban Powers and Utopias of the World,* ed. E. Eveno. Presses Universitaires du Mirail, 1998.

Lim, K. H., L. M. Ward, and I. Benbasat. An empirical study of mental models and computer system learning. *Information Syst. Res.* September:254–72, 1997.

Lim, K. H., I. Benbasat, and P. Todd. an experimental investigation of the cognitive processing effort involved in direct manipulation and menu interfaces. *ACM Trans. Comput. Hum. Interact.* March:1–37, 1996.

Lim, K. H., and S. R. Swenseth. An iterative procedure for reducing problem size in large scale AHP problems. *Euro. J. Operational Res.* May:64–74, 1993.

Swenseth, S. R., and **K. H. Lim.** Facility location planning with multiple tangible and intangible objectives. In *Proceedings of the Decision Science Institute National Conference,* 1991.

Vandenbosch, B. An empirical analysis of the association between the use of executive support systems and perceived organizational competitiveness. *Accounting Organ. Soc.*, in press.

Vandenbosch, B., and **S. Huff.** Executive support system scanning: Influences and consequences. *MIS Q.* 21(1):81–107, 1997

Vandenbosch, B., and C. Higgins. Information acquisition and mental models: An investigation into the relationship between behaviour and learning. *Information Syst. Res.* 7(2):198–214, 1996.

Vandenbosch, B., and **M. J. Ginzberg.** Lotus notes and collaboration: Le plus ça change... *J. Manage. Information Syst.* 13(3)65–81, 1997.

Baid, L., J. C. Henderson, and **S. Watts Sussman.** Learning networks: An analysis of the center for army learned. *Hum. Resource Manage. J.*, in press.

Watts Sussman, S., and P. J. Guinan. Software development under conditions of high task complexity and ambiguity. In *Proceedings HICSS,* 1997.

Gosman, M. L., J. L. Ammons, M. G., Murphy, and **S. Watts Sussman.** Fraudulent reporting at Leslie Fay: Lessons learned. *Commercial Lending Rev.* 11(4):23–38, 1996.

Farrago, S., P. Fairy, and **S. Watts Sussman.** *Software Measurement Handbook: Measures and Metrics.* Seattle, WA: The Boeing Company Publications, 1995.

Yoo, Y. Predicting groupware acceptance. In *Proceedings HICSS,* in press.

Yoo, Y. Effects of electronic communication technology on top management teams' structures and decision-making process and outcomes. In *Proceedings ICIS,* 235–48, 1997.

Alavi, M., **Y. Yoo,** and D. Vogel. Using information technology to add value to management education. *Acad. Manage. J.* 40:6, 1997.

Yoo, Y., and M. Alavi. Emergence of leadership and its impact on group performance in virtual team environments: A longitudinal field study. In *Proceedings ICIS,* 1996.

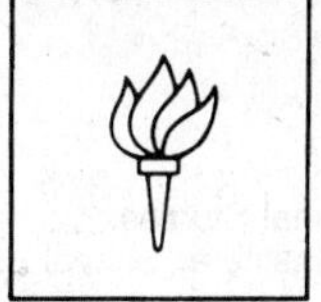

NEW YORK UNIVERSITY

School of Continuing and Professional Studies
The Virtual College

Programs of Study

The spread of computers and telecommunications and the rise of global markets is dramatically changing today's organizations. Increasingly, product and service production is becoming an information-based activity. In the near future, businesses will be organized around knowledge, not specific products, and employees will need skills in developing, managing, and controlling information resources for decision making at all stages of the production process.

The Master of Science in Management and Systems is designed to prepare midcareer nontechnical professionals wishing to assume management responsibilities within their departments or organizations. The degree requires the completion of 36 credits of graduate education, selected from required core courses, a group of electives, and a final master's project. The program can typically be completed in two to three years of part-time study.

In addition to the Master of Science degree, the Virtual College teleprogram offers an advanced professional certificate (APC) in information technology. This 16-credit graduate program is intended for nontechnical generalists faced with the need to analyze and develop information systems for their own organizations, manage projects and lead teams working within networked environments, and audit the processing, control, and management functions of computer and communications systems.

During each Virtual College telecourse, students and faculty members collaborate on line to analyze and implement case study management and information systems using advanced applications software packages. By the second or third week of each course, students are divided into groups of 4 to 5 participants to work asynchronously on various phases of business project development. Functioning as members of their virtual project teams, students establish guidelines, conduct studies, and manage online project responsibilities. During a typical telecourse, each student creates about 100 discussion, analysis, and assignment documents—a level of participation that is rare in most on-campus courses.

Research Facilities

The Virtual College uses a national digital network to provide students and faculty members with an electronic environment for undertaking courses and research using networked PCs. The teleprogram delivers to distance learners the same level of dynamic, hands-on instruction that characterizes the best on-campus lectures, seminars, and laboratories. All telecourses employ such advanced technologies as interactive multimedia, online laboratories, and hypertext readings. The Virtual College is a unique distance education program in which all instructional materials, including video, simulations, laboratories, and readings, are digital and interactively accessible through one common user interface.

Financial Aid

NYU's Office of Financial Aid assists students with loan packages, and NYU's monthly payment plan enables students to spread out their tuition payments.

Cost of Study

Tuition for the 1998–99 academic year is $570 per credit. Additional nonrefundable fees are charged on a per-credit basis: registration and service fees are charged on the first credit; registration fees are charged on each additional credit. The fee structure by semester is as follows: for fall 1998, $148 on the first credit, $40 on each additional credit; for spring 1999, $162 and $40; and for summer 1999, $89 and $40. Full-time status is 12 or more credits; part-time status is fewer than 12 credits.

Living and Housing Costs

As a distance education program delivered to students' home PCs, the Virtual College teleprograms impose no additional living, housing, or transportation costs. Students are expected to have an Integrated Services Digital Network (ISDN) phone line at home (one-time residential installation costs average $100–$250).

Virtual College students must have a Pentium PC with 16 MB RAM, 100 MB available hard disk space, Windows 95, and a 16-bit SoundBlaster or compatible audio board.

Student Group

During the first two years of this master's program, the student body numbered approximately 100 graduate students. Previous Virtual College students ranged in age from 25 to 50 (with a mean age of 35), and 35 percent were women. Most students were employed as full-time managers or professionals in finance, accounting, and marketing and studied on a part-time basis.

Location

While the offices of the School of Continuing and Professional Studies' Virtual College are located on NYU's Greenwich Village campus, all course work is conducted from the student's home or notebook PC; there are no on-campus sessions. Students complete courses largely at their own convenience and from practically anywhere in the United States.

The University and The College

NYU is a private university composed of thirteen schools, colleges, and divisions. The University was founded in 1831 and the School of Continuing and Professional Studies in 1934. The Virtual College, which offers the master's degree and the graduate-level advanced professional certificate, was created in 1992.

Applying

Admission to the M.S. in Management and Systems is open to qualified individuals who hold a bachelor's degree from an accredited undergraduate institution. Factors considered in evaluating applications include academic achievement in previous degree course work, scores on the GMAT, TOEFL scores (for international students), the nature and extent of previous work experience, a personal essay, and two letters of recommendation.

Correspondence and Information

For more information and an application package, students should contact the office listed below.

Master of Science Teleprogram
The Virtual College
School of Continuing and Professional Studies
New York University
7 East 12th Street, 11th Floor
New York, New York 10003-4475
Telephone: 212-998-9112
Fax: 212-995-3656
E-mail: sce.virtual@nyu.edu

New York University

ADMINISTRATION

Gerald A. Heeger, Ph.D., Dean, School of Continuing and Professional Studies.
Aaron Feinsot, Ph.D., Divisional Dean, Division of Professional and Industry Studies, School of Continuing and Professional Studies.
Richard Vigilante, Ph.D., Clinical Professor of Information Technology and Senior Director, Information Technologies Institute, School of Continuing and Professional Studies.
Howard Deckelbaum, M.A., Director, Information Technologies Institute, School of Continuing and Professional Studies.
Annie Stanton, B.A., Assistant Director, Information Technologies Institute, School of Continuing and Professional Studies.

NORTHWESTERN UNIVERSITY

School of Speech
Communication Systems Program

Program of Study

The Communication Systems Program offers an interdisciplinary course of study leading to a Master of Science in Communication degree. The Communication Systems Program is designed to provide graduate training for working professionals whose effective use of information technology is critical to organizational performance. The program originated in 1994.

Instruction focuses on user and organizational needs. While covering the basic principles of information technology, the program stresses the larger managerial perspectives required to develop information products and services and to manage information systems within organizations. The program emphasizes what might be called the "new perspective" on communication technologies, which sees these technologies as fundamental building blocks in the design of effective organizations.

The two-year curriculum, which has been designed to carry students through a logical learning progression of related skills, simultaneously addresses the key factors of technology, systems, and management. The first year introduces disciplines such as human factors engineering, basic technical terms, principles and procedures, and management and general applications of communication and technology and information systems. The second year extends this interdisciplinary groundwork into such areas as network management, systems design and analysis, statistical methods, competitive strategies, and legal and political ramifications.

Students enter the program in September and attend a full day of classes once a week on alternating Fridays and Saturdays throughout the academic year (fall through spring), a scheduling practice common to executive management programs. Recognizing that its students' time is valuable and limited, the Communication Systems Program provides a variety of services designed to minimize the time students must spend with the noncurricular aspects of university training.

Research Facilities

The Northwestern University Library and the Science, Engineering, Law, Medical, and Dental Libraries contain close to 4 million volumes in world-renowned collections and more than 28,000 current periodical subscriptions. Access is provided to online bibliographic retrieval services. The second floor of the Joseph Schaffner Library on the Chicago campus houses instructional programs and allows free access to computer databases. Materials can be accessed through interlibrary loan, which provides a daily delivery of books and materials to Northwestern's Chicago campus and allows Communication Systems Program students who work in that area to pick up materials at their convenience. A CD-ROM player is available for graduate student use.

Financial Aid

A loan program is available for all U.S. graduate students. No grants, scholarships, fellowships, assistantships, or deferred-payment plans are available.

Cost of Study

The fee for the academic year 1998–99 is $20,304. The all-inclusive fee covers tuition, the orientation session, books, software, a parking sticker, and weekly lunches with classmates and professors. Fee payments are due the first week of September, January, and April.

Living and Housing Costs

All students live off campus.

Student Group

Students are working professionals with at least three years of work experience. The current enrollment is 48 students. Ages range from 26 to 48 years. Eighty percent have nontechnical undergraduate degrees. Eighty percent receive some tuition reimbursement from their employers, and 30 percent participate in the student loan program.

Location

Northwestern University has lakefront campuses in Chicago and Evanston, a suburban residential community north of Chicago. All classes in the Communication Systems Program meet in Evanston.

The University and The School

Northwestern University is one of the most distinguished private universities in the United States. The University has a full- and part-time faculty of more than 2,500 members. Enrollment on the Evanston and Chicago campuses is about 14,000. The School of Speech awards the Master of Science in Communication degree.

Applying

Applicants must have earned a bachelor's degree or its equivalent from an accredited college or university. Applicants should send transcripts of undergraduate work from each college or university attended, GRE scores (GMAT and LSAT considered), three letters of recommendation, a completed application, a current résumé, and a $30 application fee to the address listed below. No engineering background is required. Applicants should schedule an interview with the Administrative Director of Admissions (847-491-3848). The application deadline is June 30.

Correspondence and Information

Donna Weirich, Administrative Director of Admissions
Communication Systems Program
Harris Hall
Northwestern University
1881 Sheridan Road
Evanston, Illinois 60208
Telephone: 847-467-3668
E-mail: comsystems@nwu.edu
World Wide Web: http://nuinfo.nwu.edu/mscs/

Northwestern University

THE FACULTY

Barbara A. Cherry, Adjunct Professor of Communication Systems Program and Director, Issues Analysis, Ameritech; J.D., Harvard, Ph.D., Northwestern.
James S. Ettema, Associate Professor and Chair of Communication Studies; Ph.D., Michigan.
Donald N. Frey, Professor of Industrial Engineering and Management Science; Ph.D., Michigan.
Gerald M. Hoffman, Adjunct Professor of Industrial Engineering and Management Science, Research Area Director, Center for Information and Telecommunications Technology, Northwestern University, and President, The Gerald Hoffman Company; Ph.D., Northwestern.
Srikanta P. R. Kumar, Associate Professor of Electrical and Computer Engineering; Ph.D., Yale.
Chung-Chieh Lee, Professor of Electrical and Computer Engineering; Ph.D., Princeton.
Brian Nielsen, Adjunct Professor and Manager, Learning Technologies Support, IT; Ph.D., North Carolina at Chapel Hill.
Michael E. Roloff, Professor of Communication Studies; Ph.D., Michigan State.
Ajit C. Tamhane, Professor of Industrial Engineering and Management Science; Ph.D., Cornell.
Paul Wang, Associate Professor of Integrated Marketing Communication; Ph.D., Northwestern.
Steven S. Wildman, Associate Professor of Communication Studies and Director, Program in Telecommunications Science, Management, and Policy; Ph.D., Stanford.

SYRACUSE UNIVERSITY

School of Information Studies
Master's Program in Information Resources Management

Programs of Study

The School of Information Studies offers a Master of Science in information resources management to prepare students for a growing number of dynamic careers that deal with the management and use of information, computers, and telecommunications technologies. Graduates of the program work in a broad range of managerial and technical positions in business, government, education, health care, and other fields.

The M.S. in information resources management requires the completion of 42 credit hours. Each student completes a 9-credit core, 24 credits in three secondary core tracks—management approaches and strategies, user information needs, and technological infrastructures—and 9 credits of electives and internship. The program provides an integrated approach to the effective management and use of information and communication technologies within organizations. Prior work experience and a familiarity with computers are desirable but not required. The M.S. may also be taken in a distance learning format requiring brief residencies in Syracuse. In this format, course work is completed mainly through home study with the use of the Internet. Courses are also offered in Washington, D.C.

Research Facilities

Access to computer facilities at Syracuse University and within the School is excellent. All students have access to data networks connecting the University's mainframe computer (an IBM 3090 and a Sun 6/670) as well as client-server environments. Students have access to more than 150 terminals and 160 microcomputers in public clusters throughout the University. All students are provided with free computer accounts and unlimited access to the Internet. The School is located in the Center for Science and Technology, the University's most sophisticated facility for teaching and research in the areas of information science, computing, and information technology. Faculty members and students work with two research centers in the building, the Center for Advanced Technology in Computer Applications and Software Engineering (CASE) and the Northeast Parallel Architectures Center (NPAC).

Financial Aid

Fellowships, scholarships, and assistantships are available to full-time students. Most prestigious and competitive are Syracuse University graduate fellowships, which include a 30-credit scholarship and a stipend of $10,894 for the 1998–99 academic year. University scholarships provide 24 credit hours of tuition, and graduate assistantships provide tuition and a stipend of $8000 per academic year. Tuition scholarships funded by the Gaylord Trust endowment and other small scholarships are available to part-time students.

Loans are available through the Financial Aid Office (200 Archbold). For Federal Work-Study contracts, students work through the University Student Employment Office. These kinds of assistance are awarded according to federal financial-need guidelines.

Cost of Study

Tuition for 1998–99 is $556 per graduate credit hour, or $1668 per 3-credit course. Fees are approximately $350 for one year of full-time study.

Living and Housing Costs

Academic-year living expenses are about $8000 for single students. The University has residence hall rooms and on-campus apartments for single and married graduate students. Many also live off campus.

Student Group

Syracuse University has about 15,000 students, including about 5,000 graduate students. Approximately 450 graduate students are enrolled in the School of Information Studies, many of them attending part-time. Ten percent are international students, with the remainder coming from all parts of the United States. Students have diverse backgrounds, with undergraduate majors in the liberal arts, business administration, computer science, and engineering.

Student Outcomes

Career opportunities for graduates of the program are excellent. Approximately 95 percent find professional positions within six months of graduation, which reflects the demand for graduates with this background. Many have taken positions in a wide variety of organizations with responsibilities ranging from information systems analysis to database design and software evaluation. Others are employed by major information processing corporations such as AT&T, DEC, and IBM. Other positions include staff consultant, networking technical consultant, systems manager, networking manager, customer support consultant, and operations research analyst/acquisitions specialist.

Location

Syracuse, a city of 500,000, is set at the transportation crossroads of central New York State and is the commercial, industrial, medical, and cultural center for a wide area. Downtown Syracuse is only a 20-minute walk from the University, yet the campus is spacious and attractive. Winters are snowy and summers are pleasant. Lake Ontario, the Finger Lakes, and the Adirondack and Catskill Mountains are nearby. Boston, Toronto, New York, and Philadelphia are within a day's drive.

The School

The School of Information Studies is a leading center for innovative graduate programs in information management, and it stands out from other institutions that offer computer science, management, and related programs. The School focuses on information users and understanding user information needs. The interdisciplinary faculty combines expertise in information science, telecommunications, public administration, business management and management information systems, linguistics, computer science, library science, and communication. The School offers a unique undergraduate degree program in information management and technology as well as professional graduate programs in information resources management, telecommunications, and library science. A Ph.D. in information transfer is also offered. Students benefit from close interaction with faculty.

Applying

Students are encouraged to apply for the fall semester, although admission is possible in the fall, spring, or summer semesters. Students applying for the master's-level program must have a bachelor's degree from an accredited undergraduate institution and an academic record satisfactory for admission to the graduate school. They must also supply three letters of recommendation and an essay on their academic plans and professional goals and have earned a combined score of at least 1000 on the verbal and quantitative sections of the GRE General Test. Whenever possible, an interview is recommended. International students should plan to take the Test of English as a Foreign Language (TOEFL); a score of at least 550 is expected. Students interested in University fellowships must apply by January 10. Other financial aid applicants must submit all materials by March 15.

Correspondence and Information

School of Information Studies
Syracuse University
4-206 Center for Science and Technology
Syracuse, New York 13244-4100

Telephone: 315-443-2911
E-mail:ist@syr.edu
World Wide Web: http://istweb.syr.edu

Syracuse University

THE FACULTY AND THEIR RESEARCH

Robert Benjamin, Professor; B.S. (economics), Pennsylvania (Wharton), 1948. Strategic applications of information technology, managing information technology–enabled change.

Susan Bonzi, Associate Professor; Ph.D. (library and information science), Illinois, 1983. Image retrieval systems. Received the first Information Science Doctoral Dissertation award from American Society for Information Science (ASIS), 1982.

Kevin Crowston, Assistant Professor; Ph.D. (information technologies), MIT, 1991. Organizational implications of technology, coordination-intensive processes in human organizations.

Marta Dosa, Professor Emerita; Ph.D. (library science), Michigan, 1971. Environmental and health information, information planning in developing countries, international information policies. Funded research includes: Health Information Sharing Project (National Institutes of Health/National Library of Medicine), International Clearinghouse on Information Education (UNECLO), and International Federation for Documentation (FID). Received 1986 American Society for Information Science (ASIS) Outstanding Information Science Teacher Award.

Michael B. Eisenberg, Professor; Ph.D. (information transfer), Syracuse, 1986. Information and technology literacy, development and management of Internet services and resources. Director, Information Institute of Syracuse, including the ERIC Clearinghouse on Information and Technology, AskERIC. Coauthor, *Helping with Homework: A Parent's Guide to Information Problem-Solving*; *Curriculum Initiative*; and *Information Problem-Solving*. Dissertation received national awards from the American Society for Information Science (ASIS) and Association for Library and Information Science Education (ALISE), 1986.

Robert Heckman, Assistant Professor; Ph.D. (information systems), Pittsburgh, 1993. Vendor-provided information systems, user satisfaction, end-user computing.

Jeffrey Katzer, Professor; Ph.D. (communication), Michigan State, 1970. The information environment of managers; information behavior; organizational, economic, and social implications of the information age. Funded research has included: representation of overlaps in computerized information retrieval systems (National Science Foundation), impact of anaphoric resolution in retrieval performance (National Science Foundation). Author and coauthor of *Free Association Behavior and Human Language Processing, Evaluating Information.*

Barbara Kwasnik, Associate Professor; Ph.D. (library and information studies), Rutgers, 1989. Classification research, knowledge representation and organization, research methods. Dissertation received 1989 best dissertation awards from the American Society for Information Science (ASIS) and from the Association for Library and Information Science Education (ALISE). Fulbright Visiting Scholar grantee (Royal School of Librarianship), Copenhagen, Denmark, 1996.

Antje B. Lemke, Professor Emerita; M.S.L.S., Syracuse, 1956. Study of the development of European libraries from the Age of Enlightenment to World War II; biography of Jacob and Wilhelm Grimm, with special emphasis on their contributions to librarianship and bibliography. Translator, *Out of My Life and Thought: An Autobiography of Albert Schweitzer.* Funded research: the Church and universities in Germany in the years of national socialism (Deutsche Forschungsgemeinschaft, Bonn). Awarded Syracuse University's Chancellor's Citation for Exceptional Academic Achievement, 1981.

Elizabeth Liddy, Professor; Ph.D. (information transfer), Syracuse, 1988. Indexing, data-mining, natural-language processing, information retrieval. Received ASIS Doctoral Dissertation Award and ALISE Doctoral Dissertation Award, 1988. Funded research: document retrieval using linguistic knowledge (DARPA) for development of DR-LINK.

Thomas H. Martin, Associate Professor; Ph.D. (communications), Stanford, 1974. Information policy, system design, human interaction with computers, human information processing, organizational communication and the foundations of information science. Assisted in the design of the Stanford Public Information Retrieval System (SPIRES).

Charles McClure, Distinguished Professor; Ph.D. (library and information studies), Rutgers, 1977. Management, planning, and evaluation of information services, federal information policy. Associate Editor, *Government Information Quarterly,* and coauthor, *Federal Information Policies in the 1990s*. Funded research: impacts and uses of national and statewide networks, electronic records management, and access to U.S. federal information.

Milton L. Mueller, Associate Professor; Ph.D. (telecommunication), Pennsylvania, 1989. Telecommunication policy and deregulation; universal service.

Michael Nilan, Associate Professor; Ph.D. (communication research), Washington (Seattle), 1985. Employing user behaviors for the design of collaborative work environments in a global electronic network environment, user-based system design.

Steve Sawyer, Assistant Professor; D.B.A. (management information systems), Boston University, 1995. Work group performance and work group use of information technology, social and behavioral aspects of information technology, software development and software development management.

Barbara Settel, Associate Dean; M.L.S., Syracuse, 1976. Design and use of online retrieval systems, training end users, augmenting subject access to books in online catalogs.

Ruth V. Small, Associate Professor; Ph.D. (instructional design, development, and evaluation), Syracuse, 1986. Motivational aspects of information literacy, design and use of information and information technologies in education.

Stuart Sutton, Associate Professor; Ph.D. (library and information studies), Berkeley, 1991. Organization of information and database systems; information retrieval theory; interactive media, including information design, the structuring of interaction, and presentation design; intellectual property issues.

Zixiang (Alex) Tan, Assistant Professor; Ph.D. (telecommunications management and policy), Rutgers, 1996. Telecommunications policy and regulations, economic and social impacts of new technology, standardization policy, telecommunications in Asia.

Robert S. Taylor, Professor Emeritus; M.S. (library science), Columbia, 1950. Descriptions of organizational information environments and information-seeking behavior, definition of the information profession. Funded research: value-added processes in the information life cycle (National Science Foundation). Author, *Value Added Processes in Information Systems.*

Murali Venkatesh, Associate Professor; Ph.D. (management), Indiana, 1991. Group-based decision support systems, human-computer interaction, telecommunications.

Raymond F. von Dran, Professor and Dean; Ph.D. (library and information science), Wisconsin, 1976. Leadership and change in the management of communication and information technology; technology convergence and organizational change; competencies, curriculum, and organization structures in information education; effectiveness of modes of delivery in information education.

Rolf T. Wigand, Professor; Ph.D. (communication), Michigan State, 1975. Electronic commerce, information management, organizational communication, telecommunications policy, technology transfer. Author, *Organizations and Information Management,* Associate Editor, *The Information Society,* and Editor, *Communications.*

Ping Zhang, Assistant Professor; Ph. D. (information systems), Texas at Austin, 1995. Computer technology, information visualization for decision making, human-computer interaction.

Cooperating Adjunct Faculty

John Beyers, Branch System Manager, AT&T, Syracuse, New York. Telecommunications systems.

Bruce Derr, Senior Program Analyst, Academic Computing Services, Syracuse University. Microcomputers and information management.

Patricia T. Fletcher, Assistant Professor, Department of Information Systems, University of Maryland. Strategic information systems, business process redesign, organizational restructuring.

William Gibbons, Vice President of the Central New York Communications Association. Former Associate Director of Marketing and Customer Network Design, NYNEX; doctoral candidate in the information transfer program, Syracuse University.

David Molta, Director, Network Systems, Syracuse University, Syracuse, New York. Local area networks.

Norman Shaw, Communications Engineer, N.Y.S. Electric & Gas Corp., Binghamton, New York. Telecommunications systems.

Ruth Stanat, President, Strategic Information Systems, New York City. Business information and strategic intelligence.

Theodora K. Watts, Program Manager, Business Transaction Services, InfoPro Inc., Washington, D.C. Strategic planning, information resources management.

Mary Frances Yafchak, Network Project Coordinator, NYSERNET, Inc., Syracuse, New York. Information networking.

UNIVERSITY OF VIRGINIA

McIntire School of Commerce Graduate Programs in Management Information Systems and Accounting

Programs of Study

The McIntire School of Commerce offers a master's degree in both management information systems (MIS) and accounting. Both programs are nationally recognized for excellence. Both programs require 30 semester hours of credit and are designed to be completed in one year. Faculty members work with students on an individualized level to build the skills and insights that will enable the students to enter organizations at a higher level and to interact and communicate with subordinates and executives on a wide variety of technical and managerial problems.

The MIS program provides education in database management, telecommunications, systems design, and the management of information resources. Graduates are actively recruited and typically accept offers with CPA or other consulting firms or in systems management with corporations such as IBM, DuPont, Mobil, and Aetna.

The accounting program allows students to select tracks in taxation, financial accounting and auditing, financial management, or management information systems. In addition, electives are available in such areas as professional services marketing, financial analysis, and professional practices management. Graduates are actively recruited and accept offers in taxation, auditing, and consulting with CPA firms; financial/accounting management with major corporations; and government.

Research Facilities

The McIntire School of Commerce offers state-of-the-art technology to its faculty members and students. The School has a Novell Netware network of personal computers available for both student and faculty member use. All faculty members are equipped with either Pentium or 486 PCs. Students have available for their use 110 personal computers, of which approximately half are Pentium-based; the other half are 486-based. Thirty-seven of these PCs are housed in a computer classroom, which allows for hands-on instruction in software applications. The School's network provides access to an in-house IBM RS/6000 as well as to all other mainframe computers on campus. The School's network also provides access to the Internet and the World Wide Web.

All classrooms are supported by state-of-the-art technology for instructional purposes. Personal computers are available for each classroom so that multimedia-based presentations that include sound, video, and graphics are available to every instructor.

The software platform for the School is Windows 3.1. A range of applications is available to students, including WordPerfect for Windows, Microsoft Office Suite, SPSS for Windows, and the Oracle Relational Database System.

There are also numerous financial systems available for use in faculty research and student assignments. Two on-line Bloomberg terminals are available, along with a Telerate financial system, which includes a satellite link, the Compact Disclosure financial database, and the PC Compustat financial database.

Financial Aid

Teaching assistantships offering tuition remission and stipends are awarded based on academic achievement and background in the field of study. Graduate assistantships are available for faculty research at an hourly rate. Government loans are available to students, as are fellowships and scholarships.

Cost of Study

The 1997–98 tuition and fees per academic year were $4790 for state residents and $15,034 for nonresidents. Rates are subject to change.

Living and Housing Costs

Dormitory facilities are available to single students for $1934 to $2320 per semester; these rates are subject to change. On-campus family housing is available for $408 to $505 per month; these rates are subject to change. The University Housing Office maintains up-to-date listings of unfurnished and furnished apartments, rooms, and houses available in Charlottesville. The cost of living is comparable to most medium to large cities in the U.S.

Student Group

There are more than 18,000 students at the University, more than 7,000 of them graduate students. The McIntire School of Commerce enrolls approximately 70 students for both programs. The School features traditional and nontraditional students. The male to female ratio is nearly even. Many students come directly from the University's undergraduate program, while others have spent years in business and return, offering others in the School a diverse mix of experiences. The McIntire Graduate Student Association consists of graduate students who serve to increase the social aspect of student life at McIntire and create a camaraderie among faculty members and students.

Location

Charlottesville is located approximately 110 miles south of Washington, D.C. The city sits at the base of the Blue Ridge Mountains and offers exciting trails in the Shenandoah National Forest for biking, backpacking, and hiking. Local ski resorts offer winter activities, and many historical sites are available for tours, such as Monticello, Montpelier, and Ash Lawn, which are the homes of past presidents Jefferson, Madison, and Monroe. The climate is mild and is ideal for year-round activities to suit most everyone's pleasures. Charlottesville offers a hometown image with many cultural features such as symphonies, art museums, and many local wineries.

The University

The University was founded in 1819 by Thomas Jefferson, who was the architect for its original buildings. The vast, beautiful grounds cover 1,500 acres, which are often referred to as Mr. Jefferson's "academical village." The center of this village is the Rotunda and Lawn, which are flanked by rows of columned rooms and pavilions. The Rotunda is modeled after the Roman Pantheon and is used today for presidential visits, lectures, ceremonial events, and important meetings.

Applying

The master's programs are open to students who have earned a bachelor's degree with a successful GPA from an accredited institution, who have successfully completed the GMAT, and who show high promise of success at the graduate level. Offers of admission are based on a competitive process. Ideally, students should have all prerequisite courses completed prior to entering the program. (The Management Information Systems Institute offers a six-week summer program to students lacking background in information systems, database management, and systems analysis.) The deadline for applications is March 1 of each year.

Correspondence and Information

Application materials may be obtained by writing or calling:

Director of Graduate Studies
McIntire School of Commerce
204 Monroe Hall
University of Virginia
Charlottesville, Virginia 22903

Telephone: 804-924-3571
E-mail: mcintiregrad@forbes.comm.virginia.edu
World Wide Web: http://www.commerce.virginia.edu/

University of Virginia

THE FACULTY AND THEIR RESEARCH

Professors

Elias M. Awad, Virginia Bankers Professor of Bank Management; D.B.A., Kentucky.
O. Whitfield Broome Jr., Frank S. Kaulback Jr. Professor of Commerce; Ph.D., Illinois; CPA.
Richard F. DeMong, Virginia Bankers Professor of Bank Management; Ph.D., Colorado; CFA, CCA.
Raymond M. Haas, University Professor of Commerce; D.B.A., Indiana.
Sally M. Jones, KPMG Peat Marwick Chair of Professional Accounting; Ph.D., Houston.
William J. Kehoe, William F. O'Dell Professor of Commerce; D.B.A., Kentucky.
Robert S. Kemp, D.B.A., Florida State; CPA.
John H. Lindgren Jr., Consumer Bankers Association Professor of Retail Banking; D.B.A., Kent State.
David Maloney, Ph.D., Illinois; CPA.
Bernard A. Morin, Robert Hill Carter Professor of Commerce; Ph.D., Duke.
Laurence Pettit Jr., D.B.A., Virginia.
Andrew C. Ruppel, Ph.D., North Carolina.
Sandra Schmidt, Ph.D., Cincinnati.
Charlotte H. Scott, University Professor of Commerce and Education; LL.D., Allegheny.
Richard A. Scott, Arthur Andersen and Co. Alumni Professor of Commerce; Ph.D., American; CPA.
William G. Shenkir, William Stamps Farish Professor of Free Enterprise; Ph.D., Texas; CPA.
David G. Smith, D.B.A., Maryland.
Neil H. Snyder, Ralph A. Beeton Professor of Free Enterprise; Ph.D., Georgia.
Robert H. Trent, Chesapeake and Potomac Telephone Company Professor of Commerce; Ph.D., North Carolina at Chapel Hill.

Associate Professors

Gib Akin, Ph.D., UCLA.
Michael D. Atchison, Ph.D., Michigan State; CPA.
Robert B. Brown, Ph.D., Washington (Seattle).
William K. Carter, Ph.D., Oklahoma State; CPA.
David B. Croll, Ph.D., Penn State.
John M. Gwin, Ph.D., North Carolina at Chapel Hill.
David W. LaRue, Ph.D., Houston.
Malcolm H. Lathan Jr., Ph.D., North Carolina at Chapel Hill; CPA.
Stewart C. Malone, Ph.D., Temple.
Felicia C. Marston, Ph.D., North Carolina at Chapel Hill.
R. Ryan Nelson, Ph.D., Georgia.
George A. Overstreet Jr., Ph.D., Alabama.
Susan E. Perry, Ph.D., Wisconsin; CPA, CMA.
Mark A. White, Ph.D., Michigan State.
Ellen M. Whitener, Ph.D., Michigan State.
William R. Wilkerson, Ph.D., Virginia.

Assistant Professors

Anthony H. Catanach Jr., Ph.D., Arizona State.
Katherine M. Chudoba, Ph.D., Arizona.
Leslie K. Cole, Ph.D., Louisiana State.
Patrick J. Dennis, Ph.D., North Carolina at Chapel Hill.
Gayle R. Erwin, Ph.D., Purdue.
William T. Faranda, Ph.D., Arizona State.
Adelaide Wilcox King, Ph.D., North Carolina at Chapel Hill.
John P. Leschke, Ph.D., Virginia.
Martha Maznevski, Ph.D., Western Ontario.
Vonda Powell, Ph.D., Illinois.
Paul L. Walker, Ph.D., Colorado.
John O. Wheeler, J.D., Virginia.

Section 13
Management Strategy and Policy

This section contains a directory of institutions offering graduate work in management strategy and policy, followed by in-depth entries submitted by institutions that chose to prepare detailed program descriptions. Additional information about programs listed in the directory but not augmented by an in-depth entry may be obtained by writing directly to the dean of a graduate school or chair of a department at the address given in the directory.

For programs offering related work, see also in this book Business Administration and Management. In Book 2, see Public, Regional, and Industrial Affairs (Public Policy and Administration).

CONTENTS

Program Directory

Cross-Discipline Announcement

In-Depth Description

See:

Management Strategy and Policy

Azusa Pacific University, School of Business and Management, Azusa, CA 91702-7000. Offerings include strategic management (MBA). School faculty: 11 full-time (2 women), 6 part-time (1 woman). *Average time to degree:* master's–1 year full-time, 3 years part-time. *Application deadline:* 8/15 (priority date; rolling processing). *Application fee:* $45 ($65 for international students). *Expenses:* Tuition $405 per unit. Fees $57 per year. • Dr. Phillip Lewis, Dean, 626-812-3090. Application contact: Kim Gara, Academic Adviser, 626-812-3818. Fax: 626-815-3802.

Baruch College of the City University of New York, School of Business, Department of Management, 17 Lexington Avenue, New York, NY 10010-5585. Offerings include general management and policy (MBA), organization and policy studies (PhD). PhD offered jointly with the Graduate School and University Center of the City University of New York. Department faculty: 33 full-time (6 women), 15 part-time (0 women). *Degree requirements:* For master's, computer language required, foreign language not required; for doctorate, computer language, dissertation required, foreign language not required. *Average time to degree:* master's–2 years full-time, 4 years part-time. *Entrance requirements:* For master's, GMAT, TOEFL (minimum score 570), TWE (minimum score 4.5); for doctorate, GMAT or GRE General Test. Application deadline: 6/15 (11/1 for spring admission). Application fee: $40. *Expenses:* Tuition $4350 per year full-time, $185 per credit part-time for state residents; $7600 per year full-time, $320 per credit part-time for nonresidents. Fees $53 per year. • Harry M. Rosen, Chairman, 212-802-6870. Application contact: Michael S. Wynne, Office of Graduate Admissions, 212-802-2330. Fax: 212-802-2335. E-mail: graduate_admissions@baruch.cuny.edu.

Boston College, Wallace E. Carroll Graduate School of Management, Department of Operations and Strategic Management, Chestnut Hill, MA 02167-9991. Awards MBA. Part-time and evening/weekend programs available. *Entrance requirements:* GMAT (average 610), TOEFL (minimum score 600; average 630). Application deadline: 4/1 (priority date; rolling processing; 11/15 for spring admission). Application fee: $45. *Expenses:* Tuition $22,134 per year full-time, $714 per semester hour part-time. Fees $80 per year (minimum) full-time, $30 per semester part-time. *Financial aid:* Fellowships, research assistantships, teaching assistantships, administrative assistantships, Federal Work-Study, and career-related internships or fieldwork available. Financial aid application deadline: 3/1; applicants required to submit FAFSA. *Faculty research:* Approaches for improved decision making, funding of research and development, partnerships, measures of industrial concentrations. • Dr. Hossein Safizadeh, Chairman, 617-552-0476. Application contact: Simone Marthers, Director of Admissions, 617-552-3920. Fax: 617-552-8078.

Boston University, Metropolitan College, Program in Administrative Studies, Boston, MA 02215. Offerings include organizational policy (MSAS). Program faculty: 7 full-time (2 women), 25 part-time (5 women). *Degree requirements:* Thesis optional, foreign language not required. *Average time to degree:* master's–1 year full-time, 2 years part-time. *Entrance requirements:* TOEFL (minimum score 550). Application deadline: rolling. Application fee: $50. *Expenses:* Tuition $15,488 per year full-time, $484 per credit part-time. Fees $218 per year full-time, $40 per semester part-time. • Dr. Kip Becker, Chairman. E-mail: adminsc@bu.edu. Application contact: Department of Administrative Sciences, 617-353-3016. Fax: 617-353-6840. E-mail: adminsc@bu.edu.

See in-depth description on page 537.

Case Western Reserve University, Weatherhead School of Management, Department of Marketing and Policy Studies, Division of Management Policy, Cleveland, OH 44106. Awards MBA, PhD. PhD offered through the School of Graduate Studies. Part-time and evening/weekend programs available. Faculty: 8 full-time (1 woman), 4 part-time (0 women), 10 FTE. Students: 25 full-time (8 women), 17 part-time (5 women); includes 5 minority (3 African Americans, 2 Asian Americans), 3 international. Average age 28. In 1997, 12 master's awarded (100% found work related to degree). *Degree requirements:* For doctorate, dissertation required, foreign language not required. *Entrance requirements:* For master's, GMAT (average 603); for doctorate, GMAT. Application deadline: 4/15 (priority date; rolling processing). Application fee: $50. *Tuition:* $20,900 per year full-time, $871 per credit hour part-time. *Financial aid:* Full and partial tuition waivers, Federal Work-Study, institutionally sponsored loans, and career-related internships or fieldwork available. Financial aid application deadline: 5/1. *Faculty research:* Corporate strategies, innovation management, mergers and acquisitions, entrepreneurship, corporate culture. • Robert D. Hisrich, Head, 216-368-5239. Fax: 216-368-4785. Application contact: Linda S. Gaston, Director of Marketing and Admissions, 216-368-2030. Fax: 216-368-5548. E-mail: lxg10@po.cwru.edu.

Claremont Graduate University, Peter F. Drucker Graduate Management Center, Program in Management, Claremont, CA 91711-6163. Offerings include strategic management (MBA). *Entrance requirements:* GMAT, TOEFL. Application deadline: 2/15 (priority date; rolling processing). Application fee: $40. Electronic applications accepted. *Expenses:* Tuition $20,250 per year full-time, $913 per unit part-time. Fees $130 per year. • Dr. Jeffrey Decker, Director, 909-621-8073. Fax: 909-621-8390. E-mail: jeff.decker@cgu.edu. Application contact: Kathy Hubener, Admissions Coordinator, 909-621-8073. Fax: 909-621-8543. E-mail: mba@cgu.edu.

DePaul University, Charles H. Kellstadt Graduate School of Business, Program in Management Planning and Strategy, Chicago, IL 60604-2287. Awards MBA. Part-time and evening/weekend programs available. Students: 61 full-time (17 women), 7 part-time (3 women); includes 10 minority (6 African Americans, 2 Asian Americans, 1 Hispanic, 1 Native American), 1 international. Average age 32. 54 applicants, 69% accepted. In 1997, 15 degrees awarded. *Entrance requirements:* GMAT. Application deadline: 8/1 (rolling processing). Application fee: $40. Electronic applications accepted. *Expenses:* Tuition $1593 per course. Fees $30 per year. • Ty Kahdman, Program Administrator, 312-362-5287. E-mail: tkahdema@wppost.depaul.edu. Application contact: Christine Munoz, Director of Admissions, 312-362-8810. Fax: 312-362-6677. E-mail: mbainfo@wppost.depaul.edu.

Dominican College of San Rafael, School of Liberal and Professional Studies, Program in Strategic Leadership, San Rafael, CA 94901-2298. Awards MBA. Faculty: 1 full-time (0 women), 3 part-time (1 woman), 1.75 FTE. Students: 32 part-time (16 women); includes 4 minority (2 African Americans, 2 Asian Americans). 26 applicants, 85% accepted. *Degree requirements:* Thesis or alternative, practicum required, foreign language not required. *Entrance requirements:* Minimum GPA of 3.0. Application fee: $25. *Financial aid:* Application deadline 3/2. • Alister Milroy, Co-Chair, 415-257-0191. Fax: 415-485-3214.

Drexel University, College of Business and Administration, Program in Business Administration, 3141 Chestnut Street, Philadelphia, PA 19104-2875. Offerings include business administration (MBA, PhD, APC), with options in accounting (MBA, PhD), decision sciences (PhD), economics (MBA, PhD), finance (MBA, PhD), legal studies (MBA), management (MBA), marketing (MBA, PhD), organizational sciences (PhD), quantitative methods (MBA), strategic management (PhD). Terminal master's awarded for partial completion of doctoral program. *Degree requirements:* Computer language required, foreign language and dissertation not required. *Entrance requirements:* GMAT, TOEFL (minimum score 570). Application deadline: 8/21 (rolling processing; 3/5 for spring admission). Application fee: $35. *Expenses:* Tuition $494 per credit hour. Fees $121 per quarter full-time, $65 per quarter part-time. • Dr. Jerold B. Muskin, Director of Master's Programs in Business, 215-895-2115. Application contact: Denise Bigham, Director of Admissions, 215-895-6700. Fax: 215-895-5969.

École des Hautes Études Commerciales, Program in Decision and Model-making, Montréal, PQ H3T 2A7, Canada. Awards M Sc. Most courses are given in French. Part-time programs available. *Degree requirements:* 1 foreign language, thesis. *Application deadline:* 3/15. *Application fee:* $40. *Financial aid:* Fellowships, research assistantships, teaching assistantships available. • Dr. Jean-Yves Le Louarn, Director, 514-340-6295. E-mail: jean-yves.lelouarn@hec.ca. Application contact: Nicole Rivet, Registrar, 514-340-6110. Fax: 514-340-5640. E-mail: nicole.rivet@hec.ca.

The George Washington University, School of Business and Public Management, Department of Strategic Management and Public Policy, Washington, DC 20052. Offers program in business economics and public policy (MBA). Part-time and evening/weekend programs available. Faculty: 11 full-time (2 women), 6 part-time (0 women), 13 FTE. Students: 157 full-time (50 women), 17 part-time (8 women); includes 16 minority (8 African Americans, 5 Asian Americans, 3 Hispanics), 6 international. Average age 34. 150 applicants, 85% accepted. In 1997, 56 degrees awarded. *Entrance requirements:* GMAT, TOEFL (minimum score 550). Application deadline: 4/1 (priority date; rolling processing; 10/1 for spring admission). Application fee: $50. *Expenses:* Tuition $680 per semester hour. Fees $35 per semester hour. *Financial aid:* Fellowships, teaching assistantships, Federal Work-Study, institutionally sponsored loans, and career-related internships or fieldwork available. Financial aid application deadline: 4/1. • Dr. Ernest Englander, Chair, 202-994-4988. Application contact: Lilly Hastings, Graduate Admissions, 202-994-6584. Fax: 202-994-6382.

The George Washington University, School of Business and Public Management, Department of Management Science, Program in Management Decision Making, Washington, DC 20052. Awards MBA, PhD. Part-time and evening/weekend programs available. Faculty: 3 full-time (1 woman), 1 part-time (0 women). Students: 24 (10 women); includes 4 minority (1 African American, 1 Asian American, 2 Hispanics), 10 international. Average age 29. 17 applicants, 82% accepted. In 1997, 3 master's awarded. *Degree requirements:* For master's, computer language required, foreign language and thesis not required; for doctorate, computer language, dissertation required, foreign language not required. *Entrance requirements:* For master's, GMAT, TOEFL (minimum score 550); for doctorate, GMAT or GRE, TOEFL (minimum score 550). Application deadline: 4/1 (priority date; rolling processing; 10/1 for spring admission). Application fee: $45. *Expenses:* Tuition $680 per semester hour. Fees $35 per semester hour. *Financial aid:* Fellowships, teaching assistantships available. Financial aid application deadline: 4/1. • Application contact: Lilly Hastings, Graduate Admissions, 202-994-6584. Fax: 202-994-6382.

Manhattanville College, Humanities and Social Sciences Programs, Program in Leadership and Strategic Management, Purchase, NY 10577-2132. Awards MS. Part-time and evening/weekend programs available. Students: 65. *Degree requirements:* Thesis required, foreign language not required. *Application deadline:* 9/1 (priority date; rolling processing; 3/1 for spring admission). *Application fee:* $45. *Expenses:* Tuition $410 per credit (minimum). Fees $25 per semester. • Application contact: Donald J. Richards, Associate Dean, 914-694-3425. Fax: 914-694-3488. E-mail: drichard@mville.edu.

Michigan State University, Eli Broad Graduate School of Management, Department of Management, East Lansing, MI 48824-1020. Offerings include management policy and strategy (PhD). Department faculty: 12 (5 women). *Degree requirements:* Dissertation required, foreign language not required. *Entrance requirements:* GMAT (score in 90th percentile or higher). Application deadline: rolling. Application fee: $30 ($40 for international students). *Expenses:* Tuition $4609 per year full-time, $223 per credit hour (minimum) part-time for state residents; $8704 per year full-time, $450 per credit hour (minimum) part-time for nonresidents. Fees $576 per year full-time, $476 per year part-time. • Dr. John Wagner III, Acting Chairperson, 517-355-1878. Fax: 517-432-1111. E-mail: wagner@pilot.msu.edu.

Northwestern University, J. L. Kellogg Graduate School of Management, Program in Managerial Economics and Strategy, Evanston, IL 60208. Awards PhD. Admissions and degree offered through The Graduate School. Faculty: 21 full-time (3 women). Students: 11 full-time (3 women); includes 1 minority (Asian American), 6 international. 60 applicants, 22% accepted. *Degree requirements:* Computer language, dissertation required, foreign language not required. *Entrance requirements:* GMAT or GRE General Test. Application fee: $50 ($55 for international students). *Tuition:* $25,872 per year. *Financial aid:* In 1997–98, fellowships averaging $1,256 per month, research assistantships averaging $1,592 per month were awarded; institutionally sponsored loans also available. Financial aid applicants required to submit FAFSA. *Faculty research:* Competitive strategy and organization, managerial economics, operations management, decision sciences, game theory. • James Dana, Co-Director, 847-491-9904. Application contact: Lucy Vandenburgh, Admission Contact, 847-491-3400. Fax: 847-491-5071. E-mail: l-vandenburgh@nwu.edu.

Purdue University, Krannert Graduate School of Management, Department of Management, West Lafayette, IN 47907. Offerings include strategic management (MSM, PhD). Department faculty: 51 full-time (5 women). *Degree requirements:* For doctorate, dissertation required, foreign language not required. *Average time to degree:* doctorate–4 years full-time. *Entrance requirements:* For doctorate, GMAT, TOEFL (minimum score 575). Application fee: $30. Electronic applications accepted. *Tuition:* $3500 per year full-time, $126 per credit hour part-time for state residents; $11,720 per year full-time, $387 per credit hour part-time for nonresidents. • Dr. J. J. McConnell, Director of Doctoral Programs, 765-494-4375. Application contact: Kelly Felty, Assistant Director of Administration for Doctoral Programs, 765-494-4375. Fax: 765-494-1526. E-mail: feltyk@mgmt.purdue.edu.

Rensselaer Polytechnic Institute, Lally School of Management and Technology, Troy, NY 12180-3590. Offerings include business policy and strategy (PhD). Postbaccalaureate distance learning degree programs offered (no on-campus study). School faculty: 36 full-time (5 women), 6 part-time (0 women). *Degree requirements:* Computer language, dissertation required, foreign language not required. *Entrance requirements:* GMAT or GRE General Test, TOEFL (minimum score 570). Application deadline: 2/1 (priority date; rolling processing). Application fee: $35. *Expenses:* Tuition $630 per credit hour. Fees $1000 per year. • Dr. Joseph G. Ecker, Dean, 518-276-6802. Application contact: Michele Martens, Manager of Enrollment Services, 518-276-4800. Fax: 518-276-8661.

Simon Fraser University, Faculty of Business Administration, Burnaby, BC V5A 1S6, Canada. Offerings include policy analysis (MBA). Faculty: 48 full-time (12 women). *Application fee:* $55. *Expenses:* Tuition $2400 per year (minimum). Fees $207 per year. • S. McShane, Director, 604-291-3639. Application contact: Program Assistant, 604-291-3047. Fax: 604-291-3404. E-mail: mba@sfu.ca.

Stevens Institute of Technology, Wesley J. Howe School of Technology Management, Program in Management Planning, Hoboken, NJ 07030. Awards MS. Part-time programs available. 1 applicant, 100% accepted. *Degree requirements:* Thesis optional, foreign language not required. *Entrance requirements:* GMAT, GRE, TOEFL. Application deadline: rolling. Application fee: $45. Electronic applications accepted. *Expenses:* Tuition $13,500 per year full-time, $675 per credit part-time. Fees $160 per year. *Financial aid:* In 1997–98, 1 assistantship was awarded. *Faculty research:* Industrial economics. • C. Timothy Koeller, Director, 201-216-5376. Fax: 201-216-5385.

Syracuse University, School of Management, PhD Program in Business Administration, Syracuse, NY 13244-0003. Offerings include strategy (PhD). Program faculty: 75. *Entrance requirements:* GMAT (minimum score 600). Application deadline: 2/1. Application fee: $40. *Tuition:* $13,320 per year full-time, $555 per credit hour part-time. • S. P. Raj, Associate Dean. Application contact: Barbara Buske, Secretary, 315-443-1001.

Temple University, School of Business and Management, Doctoral Program in Business Administration, Philadelphia, PA 19122-6096. Offerings include general and strategic management (PhD). *Degree requirements:* Dissertation, preliminary exams required, foreign language not required. *Entrance requirements:* GMAT, TOEFL (minimum score 600), master's degree, minimum GPA of 3.5. Application deadline: 1/15 (rolling processing). Application fee: $40. *Expenses:* Tuition $323 per semester hour for state residents; $444 per semester hour for nonresidents. Fees $170 per year full-time, $28 per semester (minimum) part-time. • Dr. Roland Lipka, Director, 215-204-8125. Fax: 215-204-5574. Application contact: Linda Whelan, Director, 215-204-7678. Fax: 215-204-8300.

Temple University, School of Business and Management, Master's Program in Business Administration, Philadelphia, PA 19122-6096. Offerings include general and strategic management (MBA). Program faculty: 72 full-time (13 women). *Application fee:* $40. *Expenses:* Tuition $323 per semester hour for state residents; $444 per semester hour for nonresidents. Fees $170 per year full-time, $28 per semester (minimum) part-time. • Application contact: Linda Whelan, Director, 215-204-7678. Fax: 215-204-8300. E-mail: linda@astro.ocis.temple.edu.

United States International University, College of Business Administration, San Diego, CA 92131-1799. Offerings include strategic business (DBA). Terminal master's awarded for partial completion of doctoral program. College faculty: 13 full-time (4 women), 14 part-time (6 women), 20 FTE. *Degree requirements:* Computer language, dissertation required, foreign language not required. *Average time to degree:* master's–1.5 years full-time, 2.5 years part-time; doctorate–3 years full-time, 5 years part-time. *Entrance requirements:* GMAT (minimum score 490; average 560), minimum GPA of 3.3. Application deadline: rolling. Application fee: $40. Electronic applications accepted. *Expenses:* Tuition $360 per unit. Fees $120 per year. • Dr. Mink H. Stavenga, Dean, 619-635-4695. Fax: 619-635-4528. E-mail: mstaveng@usiu.edu. Application contact: Susan Topham, Assistant Director of Admissions, 619-635-4885. Fax: 619-635-4739. E-mail: admissions@usiu.edu.

The University of Arizona, College of Business and Public Administration, Karl Eller Graduate School of Management, Department of Management and Policy, Tucson, AZ 85721. Awards MS. Evening/weekend programs available. *Degree requirements:* Thesis or alternative required, foreign language not required. *Entrance requirements:* GMAT, GRE General Test, TOEFL (minimum score 550), minimum GPA of 3.0. Application fee: $35. *Tuition:* $2162 per year full-time, $337 per semester (minimum) part-time for state residents; $6860 per year full-time, $1138 per semester (minimum) part-time for nonresidents. *Faculty research:* Organizational behavior, human resources, decision making, health economics and finance, immigration.

University of British Columbia, Faculty of Commerce and Business Administration, Doctoral Program in Commerce and Business Administration, Vancouver, BC V6T 1Z2, Canada. Offerings include policy analysis and strategy (PhD). *Degree requirements:* Dissertation required, foreign language not required. *Entrance requirements:* GMAT or GRE, TOEFL. Application deadline: 12/31 (priority date; rolling processing). Application fee: $60.

University of Florida, College of Business Administration, Department of Management, Gainesville, FL 32611. Offerings include strategy (PhD). Department faculty: 8. *Degree requirements:* Dissertation required, foreign language not required. *Entrance requirements:* GMAT or GRE General Test, minimum GPA of 3.0. Application deadline: 2/16 (rolling processing). Application fee: $20. *Tuition:* $138 per credit hour for state residents; $481 per credit hour for nonresidents. • Dr. Virginia Maurer, Chair, 352-392-0163. E-mail: maurer@dale.cba.ufl.edu. Application contact: Dr. Henry Tosi, Graduate Coordinator, 352-392-6147. Fax: 352-392-6020. E-mail: tosi@nervm.nerdc.ufl.edu.

University of Hartford, Barney School of Business and Public Administration, Program in Business Administration, West Hartford, CT 06117-1599. Offerings include strategy and policy (MBA). Program faculty: 24 full-time (4 women), 15 part-time (1 woman). *Average time to degree:* master's–1.5 years full-time, 3 years part-time. *Entrance requirements:* GMAT, TOEFL. Application deadline: 7/1 (priority date; rolling processing; 12/1 for spring admission). Application fee: $35 ($50 for international students). Electronic applications accepted. • Christopher Galligan, Director, 860-768-4390. Application contact: Claire Silverstein, Assistant Director, 860-768-4900. Fax: 860-768-4821. E-mail: silverste@unavax.hartford.edu.

University of Minnesota, Twin Cities Campus, Carlson School of Management, Department of Strategic Management and Organization, Minneapolis, MN 55455-0213. Awards MBA, PhD. MBA offered jointly with the Master's Program in Business Administration; PhD offered jointly with the Doctoral Program in Business Administration. *Degree requirements:* For doctorate, dissertation required, foreign language not required. *Entrance requirements:* GMAT. *Faculty research:* Organizational behavior, business ethics, international business, government policy.

University of New Haven, School of Business, Program in Business Administration, West Haven, CT 06516-1916. Offerings include business policy and strategy (MBA). *Degree requirements:* Thesis or alternative required, foreign language not required. *Application deadline:* rolling. *Application fee:* $50. *Expenses:* Tuition $1125 per course. Fees $13 per trimester. • Dr. Omid Nodoushani, Coordinator, 203-932-7123.

The University of North Carolina at Chapel Hill, Kenan-Flagler Business School, Doctoral Program in Business Administration, Chapel Hill, NC 27599. Offerings include business policy/strategy (PhD). Program faculty: 79 full-time (15 women), 29 part-time (6 women). *Degree requirements:* Dissertation required, foreign language not required. *Average time to degree:* doctorate–4 years full-time. *Entrance requirements:* GMAT (average 657) or GRE General Test (minimum combined score of 1350). Application deadline: 1/1 (priority date; rolling processing). Application fee: $55. Electronic applications accepted. *Expenses:* Tuition $1428 per year for state residents; $10,414 per year for nonresidents. Fees $787 per year. • Ann Marucheck, Associate Dean for PhD Programs, 919-962-3193. Application contact: Liz Griffin, Director, 919-962-1657. E-mail: kfphd_app@unc.edu.

Cross-Discipline Announcement

University of Southern California, Graduate School, Annenberg School for Communication, School of Communication, Program in Communication Management, Los Angeles, CA 90089.

The master's in communication management has concentrations in strategic and corporate communication management, marketing communication, entertainment management, communication and information technologies, and communication law and policy. The PhD program in communication has concentrations in mass communication, technology and public policy, organizational communication, interpersonal and social dynamics, and rhetorical and cultural studies. The Annenberg School is a partner in USC's Integrated Media Systems Center, the nation's only university-based multimedia research center, funded by the National Science Foundation.

Section 14
Marketing

This section contains directories of institutions offering graduate work in marketing and marketing research, followed by in-depth entries submitted by institutions that chose to prepare detailed program descriptions. Additional information about programs listed in the directories but not augmented by an in-depth entry may be obtained by writing directly to the dean of a graduate school or chair of a department at the address given in the directory.

For programs offering related work, see also in this book Advertising and Public Relations, Business Administration and Management, and Hospitality Management. In Book 2, see Communication and Media and Public, Regional, and Industrial Affairs.

CONTENTS

Program Directories

Cross-Discipline Announcements

In-Depth Descriptions

Marketing

Alabama Agricultural and Mechanical University, School of Business, Department of Management and Marketing, PO Box 1357, Normal, AL 35762-1357. Awards MBA. Part-time and evening/weekend programs available. Faculty: 13 full-time (2 women), 4 part-time (0 women). Students: 34 full-time (18 women), 74 part-time (47 women); includes 68 minority (64 African Americans, 4 Asian Americans), 17 international. Average age 28. In 1997, 37 degrees awarded. *Degree requirements:* Comprehensive exam required, thesis optional, foreign language not required. *Entrance requirements:* GMAT, TOEFL (minimum score 500), minimum undergraduate GPA of 2.5. Application deadline: 5/1 (priority date; rolling processing). Application fee: $15 ($20 for international students). *Expenses:* Tuition $2782 per year full-time, $565 per semester (minimum) part-time for state residents; $5164 per year full-time, $1015 per semester (minimum) part-time for nonresidents. Fees $560 per year full-time, $390 per year part-time. *Financial aid:* Research assistantships, Federal Work-Study, institutionally sponsored loans, and career-related internships or fieldwork available. Financial aid application deadline: 4/1. *Faculty research:* Consumer behavior of blacks, small business marketing, economics of education, China in transition, international economics, intergenerational economics/eco-demographics. • Dr. Herman Mixon, Chair, 205-851-5088. Application contact: Dr. Marsha D. Griffin, Coordinator, 205-851-5494.

American University, Kogod College of Business Administration, Department of Marketing, Washington, DC 20016-8001. Awards MBA. Part-time and evening/weekend programs available. Faculty: 9 full-time (2 women), 2 part-time (0 women). Students: 9 full-time (5 women), 16 part-time (11 women); includes 2 minority (1 African American, 1 Asian American), 5 international. 82 applicants, 76% accepted. In 1997, 24 degrees awarded. *Entrance requirements:* GMAT. Application deadline: 2/1 (priority date; 10/1 for spring admission). Application fee: $50. *Expenses:* Tuition $19,080 per year full-time, $687 per credit hour (minimum) part-time. Fees $180 per year full-time, $110 per year part-time. *Financial aid:* Fellowships, Federal Work-Study, institutionally sponsored loans, and career-related internships or fieldwork available. Aid available to part-time students. Financial aid application deadline: 2/1. • Dr. John L. Swasy, Chair, 202-885-1970.

Andrews University, School of Graduate Studies, School of Business, Department of Management and Marketing, Berrien Springs, MI 49104. Awards MBA, MSA. *Degree requirements:* Computer language required, foreign language and thesis not required. *Entrance requirements:* GMAT (minimum score 400), TOEFL (minimum score 550). Application deadline: 8/15 (rolling processing). Application fee: $30. *Expenses:* Tuition $290 per quarter hour (minimum). Fees $75 per quarter. • Dr. Allen Stembridge, Chair, 616-471-3339.

Arizona State University, College of Business, Program in Business Administration, Tempe, AZ 85287. Offerings include marketing (PhD). Program faculty: 93 full-time (21 women), 10 part-time (1 woman). *Degree requirements:* Dissertation. *Application fee:* $45. *Expenses:* Tuition $2088 per year full-time, $110 per hour part-time for state residents; $9040 per year full-time, $377 per hour part-time for nonresidents. Fees $72 per year full-time, $18 per semester (minimum) part-time. • Dr. Lee R. McPheters, Associate Dean, 602-965-9377. Fax: 602-965-3368. Application contact: Judy Heilala, Director of MBA, 602-965-3331.

Armstrong University, Graduate School of Business Administration, Program in Marketing and Management, Oakland, CA 94612. Offers management (MBA), marketing (MBA). *Degree requirements:* Thesis required, foreign language not required. *Entrance requirements:* Minimum GPA of 2.5. Application deadline: 8/15 (priority date; rolling processing; 1/1 for spring admission). Application fee: $50. • Application contact: Judy Battle, Director of Admissions, 510-835-7900. Fax: 510-835-8935. E-mail: info@armstrong-u.edu.

Baruch College of the City University of New York, School of Business, Department of Marketing, 17 Lexington Avenue, New York, NY 10010-5585. Awards MBA, MS, PhD. PhD offered jointly with the Graduate School and University Center of the City University of New York. Part-time and evening/weekend programs available. Faculty: 14 full-time (5 women), 15 part-time (3 women). Students: 79 full-time (45 women), 96 part-time (54 women). In 1997, 70 master's awarded. *Degree requirements:* For master's, computer language required, foreign language not required; for doctorate, computer language, dissertation required, foreign language not required. *Average time to degree:* master's–2 years full-time, 4 years part-time. *Entrance requirements:* For master's, GMAT, TOEFL (minimum score 570), TWE (minimum score 4.5). Application deadline: 6/15 (11/1 for spring admission). Application fee: $40. *Expenses:* Tuition $4350 per year full-time, $185 per credit part-time for state residents; $7600 per year full-time, $320 per credit part-time for nonresidents. Fees $53 per year. *Financial aid:* Research assistantships, Federal Work-Study, and career-related internships or fieldwork available. Aid available to part-time students. Financial aid application deadline: 5/3; applicants required to submit FAFSA. • Gary Soldow, Chairman, 212-802-6480. Application contact: Michael S. Wynne, Office of Graduate Admissions, 212-802-2330. Fax: 212-802-2335. E-mail: graduate_admissions@baruch.cuny.edu.

Bentley College, Graduate School of Business, Self-paced MBA Program, 175 Forest Street, Waltham, MA 02154-4705. Offerings include marketing (MBA). Program faculty: 70 full-time (21 women), 22 part-time (8 women). *Degree requirements:* Computer language required, foreign language and thesis not required. *Entrance requirements:* GMAT (average 540), TOEFL (minimum score 580). Application deadline: 6/1 (priority date; rolling processing; 11/1 for spring admission). Application fee: $50. *Expenses:* Tuition $20,500 per year full-time, $2050 per course part-time. Fees $65 per year full-time, $15 per semester part-time. • Dr. Judith B. Kamm, Director, 781-891-3433. Application contact: Holly Chase, Associate Director, 781-891-2108. Fax: 781-891-2464. E-mail: hchase@bentley.edu.

Boston College, Wallace E. Carroll Graduate School of Management, Department of Marketing, Chestnut Hill, MA 02167-9991. Awards MBA. Part-time and evening/weekend programs available. *Entrance requirements:* GMAT (average 610), TOEFL (minimum score 600; average 630). Application deadline: 4/1 (priority date; rolling processing; 11/15 for spring admission). Application fee: $45. *Expenses:* Tuition $22,134 per year full-time, $714 per semester hour part-time. Fees $80 per year (minimum) full-time, $30 per semester part-time. *Financial aid:* Fellowships, research assistantships, teaching assistantships, administrative assistantships available. Financial aid application deadline: 3/1; applicants required to submit FAFSA. *Faculty research:* Marketing management, product management, retailing, consumer behavior, advertising evaluation. • Dr. Victoria L. Crittenden, Chairperson, 617-552-0430. Application contact: Simone Marthers, Director of Admissions, 617-552-3920. Fax: 617-552-8078.

Boston University, School of Management, Boston, MA 02215. Offerings include marketing (DBA). School faculty: 110 full-time, 54 part-time. *Degree requirements:* Dissertation required, foreign language not required. *Entrance requirements:* GMAT or GRE General Test. Application deadline: 5/1 (rolling processing). Application fee: $50. Electronic applications accepted. *Expenses:* Tuition $22,830 per year full-time, $713 per credit part-time. Fees $218 per year full-time, $40 per semester part-time. • Therese M. Hofmann, Assistant Dean, 617-353-2673. Application contact: Peter G. Kelly, Director of Admissions and Financial Aid, 617-353-2670. Fax: 617-353-7368. E-mail: mba@bu.edu.

Bryant College, College of Business Administration, Program in Marketing, Smithfield, RI 02917-1284. Awards MBA, CAGS. Part-time and evening/weekend programs available. Faculty: 6 full-time (2 women), 5 part-time (4 women). Students: 7 full-time (4 women), 44 part-time (20 women); includes 2 minority (1 Asian American, 1 Hispanic), 5 international. Average age 31. 17 applicants, 71% accepted. In 1997, 19 master's, 2 CAGSs awarded. *Entrance requirements:* For master's, GMAT (minimum score 480; average 520). Application deadline: 7/1 (priority date; rolling processing; 11/15 for spring admission). Application fee: $55 ($70 for international students). *Tuition:* $1025 per course. *Financial aid:* In 1997–98, 1 research assistantship was awarded; graduate assistantships and career-related internships or fieldwork also available. Aid available to part-time students. Financial aid applicants required to submit FAFSA. • Cathy Lalli, Assistant Director of Graduate Programs, Graduate School, 401-232-6230. Fax: 401-232-6494. E-mail: gradprog@bryant.edu.

Bucknell University, College of Arts and Sciences, Department of Management, Lewisburg, PA 17837. Offerings include marketing (MSBA). Department faculty: 12 full-time. *Degree requirements:* Thesis required, foreign language not required. *Entrance requirements:* GMAT, TOEFL (minimum score 550), minimum GPA of 2.8. Application deadline: 6/1 (priority date; rolling processing; 12/1 for spring admission). Application fee: $25. *Tuition:* $2410 per course. • Dr. Mark Bettner, Head, 717-524-1306.

California Lutheran University, School of Business Administration, Thousand Oaks, CA 91360-2787. Offerings include marketing (MBA). School faculty: 8 full-time (3 women), 29 part-time (4 women). *Entrance requirements:* GMAT, minimum GPA of 3.0, interview. Application deadline: 8/1 (priority date; rolling processing). Application fee: $50. *Tuition:* $395 per unit. • Dr. Ronald Hagler, Director, 805-493-3371.

California State University, Fullerton, School of Business Administration and Economics, Department of Marketing, PO Box 34080, Fullerton, CA 92834-9480. Offers programs in international business (MBA), marketing (MBA). Part-time and evening/weekend programs available. Faculty: 11 full-time (3 women), 14 part-time, 14 FTE. Students: 5 full-time (4 women), 30 part-time (17 women); includes 4 minority (all Asian Americans), 14 international. Average age 29. 46 applicants, 35% accepted. In 1997, 12 degrees awarded. *Degree requirements:* Computer language, project or thesis required, foreign language not required. *Entrance requirements:* GMAT (minimum score 950), minimum AACSB index of 950. Application fee: $55. *Expenses:* Tuition $0 for state residents; $246 per unit for nonresidents. Fees $1947 per year full-time, $1281 per year part-time. *Financial aid:* Teaching assistantships, state grants, Federal Work-Study, institutionally sponsored loans available. Aid available to part-time students. Financial aid application deadline: 3/1. • Dr. Irene Lange, Chair, 714-278-2223. Application contact: Robert Miyake, Assistant Dean, 714-278-2211.

California State University, Hayward, School of Business and Economics, Department of Marketing, Option in Marketing Management, Hayward, CA 94542-3000. Awards MBA. Faculty: 9 full-time (2 women). *Degree requirements:* Comprehensive exam or thesis required, foreign language not required. *Entrance requirements:* GMAT, minimum GPA of 2.75. Application deadline: 4/19 (priority date; rolling processing; 1/5 for spring admission). Application fee: $55. *Expenses:* Tuition $0 for state residents; $164 per unit for nonresidents. Fees $1827 per year full-time, $1161 per year part-time. *Financial aid:* Application deadline 3/1. • Application contact: Dr. Donna L. Wiley, Director of Graduate Programs, 510-885-3964.

California State University, Los Angeles, School of Business and Economics, Major in Business Administration, Department of Marketing, Los Angeles, CA 90032-8530. Offers programs in international business (MBA, MS), marketing (MBA, MS). Part-time and evening/weekend programs available. Faculty: 8 full-time, 5 part-time. *Degree requirements:* Computer language, comprehensive exam (MBA), thesis (MS) required, foreign language not required. *Entrance requirements:* GMAT, TOEFL (minimum score 550), minimum GPA of 2.5 during previous 2 years. Application deadline: 6/30 (rolling processing; 11/30 for spring admission). Application fee: $55. *Expenses:* Tuition $0 for state residents; $164 per unit for nonresidents. Fees $1763 per year full-time, $1097 per year part-time. *Financial aid:* Federal Work-Study and career-related internships or fieldwork available. Aid available to part-time students. Financial aid application deadline: 3/1. • Dr. Shirley Stretch, Chair, 213-343-2960.

California State University, Northridge, College of Business Administration and Economics, Department of Marketing, Northridge, CA 91330. Awards MBA. Part-time programs available. Faculty: 11 full-time, 3 part-time. 6 applicants, 50% accepted. *Degree requirements:* Thesis or alternative required, foreign language not required. *Entrance requirements:* GMAT (score in 50th percentile or higher), TOEFL, minimum GPA of 3.0 in last 60 units. Application deadline: 11/30. Application fee: $55. *Expenses:* Tuition $0 for state residents; $246 per unit for nonresidents. Fees $1970 per year full-time, $1304 per year part-time. *Financial aid:* Application deadline 3/1. • Dr. Judith Hennessy, Chair, 818-677-2458. Application contact: Dr. Richard Moore, Director of Graduate Programs, 818-677-2467.

Carnegie Mellon University, Graduate School of Industrial Administration, Program in Marketing, Pittsburgh, PA 15213-3891. Awards PhD. Faculty: 4 full-time (1 woman). *Degree requirements:* Dissertation required, foreign language not required. *Application deadline:* 2/1. *Application fee:* $50. *Financial aid:* Fellowships, teaching assistantships available. Financial aid application deadline: 5/1. • Application contact: Jackie Cavendish, Administrative Assistant, 412-268-2301.

Case Western Reserve University, Weatherhead School of Management, Department of Operations Research and Operations Management, Cleveland, OH 44106. Offerings include management science (MS), with options in finance, information systems, marketing, operations management, operations research, quality management. MS and PhD offered through the School of Graduate Studies. Department faculty: 12 full-time (0 women). *Average time to degree:* doctorate–4 years full-time. *Application deadline:* 4/15 (priority date; rolling processing). *Application fee:* $50. *Tuition:* $20,900 per year full-time, $871 per credit hour part-time. • Hamilton Emmons, Chairman, 216-368-3841. Application contact: Linda S. Gaston, Director of Marketing and Admissions, 216-368-2030. Fax: 216-368-5548. E-mail: lxg10@po.cwru.edu.

Case Western Reserve University, Weatherhead School of Management, Department of Marketing and Policy Studies, Division of Marketing, Cleveland, OH 44106. Awards MBA, PhD. Faculty: 7 full-time (2 women), 2 part-time (both women), 8 FTE. Students: 117 full-time (49 women), 105 part-time (47 women); includes 25 minority (14 African Americans, 10 Asian Americans, 1 Native American), 43 international. Average age 28. In 1997, 55 master's, 1 doctorate awarded. *Degree requirements:* For doctorate, dissertation required, foreign language not required. *Entrance requirements:* For master's, GMAT (average 603); for doctorate, GMAT. Application fee: $50. *Tuition:* $20,900 per year full-time, $871 per credit hour part-time. *Financial aid:* Application deadline 5/1. *Faculty research:* Consumer decision making, international marketing, marketing channels, product management/brand equity, industrial marketing and technology. • Stanton Cort, Head, 216-368-2064. Application contact: Linda S. Gaston, Director of Marketing and Admissions, 216-368-2030. Fax: 216-368-5548. E-mail: lxg10@po.cwru.edu.

Central Michigan University, College of Business Administration, Department of Marketing and Hospitality Services Administration, Mount Pleasant, MI 48859. Awards MBA. Faculty: 9 full-time (1 woman). *Entrance requirements:* GMAT. Application deadline: 3/1 (priority date; rolling processing). Application fee: $30. *Expenses:* Tuition $139 per credit hour (minimum) for state residents; $276 per credit hour (minimum) for nonresidents. Fees $260 per year full-time, $150 per semester part-time. *Financial aid:* Fellowships, research assistantships, teaching assistantships available. Financial aid application deadline: 3/7. • Dr. Robert Welsh, Chairperson, 517-774-3701. Fax: 517-774-7713. E-mail: robert.s.welsh@cmich.edu.

Charleston Southern University, Program in Business, Charleston, SC 29423-8087. Offerings include marketing (MBA). Program faculty: 8 full-time (0 women), 1 (woman) part-time, 8.33 FTE. *Entrance requirements:* GMAT. Application deadline: rolling. Application fee: $25. *Tuition:* $9821 per year full-time, $173 per hour (minimum) part-time. • Dr. Al Parish, MBA Director, 803-863-7904. Fax: 803-863-7919. E-mail: aparish@awdd.com. Application contact: Terri Jordan, MBA Coordinator, 803-863-7955. Fax: 803-863-7922.

City University, School of Business and Management Professions, Bellevue, WA 98004-6442. Offerings include marketing (MBA, Certificate). Postbaccalaureate distance learning degree programs offered (no on-campus study). School faculty: 14 full-time (6 women), 689 part-time (247 women). *Application deadline:* rolling. *Application fee:* $75 ($175 for international students). Electronic applications accepted. *Tuition:* $280 per credit hour. • Dr. Roman Borboa, Dean, 425-637-1010 Ext. 3759. Fax: 425-277-2439. E-mail: rborboa@cityu.edu. Application contact: Nabil El-Khatib, Vice President, Admissions, 800-426-5596. Fax: 425-277-2437. E-mail: nel-khatib@cityu.edu.

Claremont Graduate University, Peter F. Drucker Graduate Management Center, Program in Management, Claremont, CA 91711-6163. Offerings include marketing (MBA). *Entrance requirements:* GMAT, TOEFL. Application deadline: 2/15 (priority date; rolling processing). Application fee: $40. Electronic applications accepted. *Expenses:* Tuition $20,250 per year full-time, $913 per unit part-time. Fees $130 per year. • Dr. Jeffrey Decker, Director, 909-621-8073. Fax: 909-621-8390. E-mail: jeff.decker@cgu.edu. Application contact: Kathy Hubener, Admissions Coordinator, 909-621-8073. Fax: 909-621-8543. E-mail: mba@cgu.edu.

Clark Atlanta University, School of Business Administration, Department of Marketing, Atlanta, GA 30314. Awards MBA. Part-time programs available. Students: 34 full-time (22 women), 2 part-time (both women); includes 36 minority (35 African Americans, 1 Hispanic). In 1997, 28 degrees awarded. *Entrance requirements:* GMAT. Application deadline: 4/1 (rolling processing; 11/1 for spring admission). Application fee: $40. *Expenses:* Tuition $9672 per year full-time, $403 per credit hour part-time. Fees $200 per year. *Financial aid:* Application deadline 4/30. • Dr. Lydia McKinley-Floyd, Chairperson, 404-880-8385. Application contact: Michelle Clark-Davis, Graduate Program Assistant, 404-880-8709.

Colorado State University, College of Business, Department of Marketing, Fort Collins, CO 80523-0015. Awards MBA, MS. Part-time programs available. Faculty: 9 full-time (2 women). Students: 3 full-time (2 women), 5 part-time (3 women); includes 1 international. 8 applicants, 75% accepted. In 1997, 5 degrees awarded. *Degree requirements:* Thesis optional, foreign language not required. *Entrance requirements:* GMAT, TOEFL, minimum GPA of 3.0. Application deadline: 2/1 (priority date; rolling processing). Application fee: $30. Electronic applications accepted. *Tuition:* $2920 per year (minimum) full-time, $328 per credit hour (minimum) part-time for state residents; $9000 per year (minimum) full-time, $368 per credit hour (minimum) part-time for nonresidents. *Financial aid:* In 1997–98, 4 research assistantships were awarded; fellowships, traineeships, Federal Work-Study, and career-related internships or fieldwork also available. Financial aid application deadline: 2/1. *Faculty research:* Artificial intelligence, strategic marketing, green marketing, alcohol/drug prevention, marketing to elderly. • Application contact: Dr. Thomas Ingram, Chair, 970-491-5063. E-mail: tingram@vines.colostate.edu.

Columbia University, Graduate School of Business, Doctoral Program in Business, New York, NY 10027. Offerings include business (PhD), with options in accounting (PhD), finance and economics (PhD), management of organizations (PhD), management science/operations research (PhD), marketing (PhD). Program faculty: 105 full-time (15 women), 86 part-time (15 women). *Degree requirements:* Dissertation, teacher training seminars, research paper, oral exam required, foreign language not required. *Average time to degree:* doctorate–4 years full-time. *Entrance requirements:* GMAT or GRE, TOEFL or TSE. Application deadline: 2/1. Application fee: $50. *Expenses:* Tuition is $26,520 per year, fees of 1,250 per year, and students receive tuition and fee exemptions for a maximum of 12 terms. • Application contact: Elizabeth Elam, Administrative Director, 212-854-2836. Fax: 212-932-2359.

Columbia University, Graduate School of Business, MBA Program, New York, NY 10027. Offerings include marketing (MBA). Program faculty: 105 full-time (15 women), 86 part-time (15 women). *Entrance requirements:* GMAT, TOEFL (minimum score 610). Application deadline: 4/20 (rolling processing; 11/1 for spring admission). Application fee: $125 ($150 for international students). *Expenses:* Tuition $26,520 per year. Fees $1250 per year. • Prof. Safwan Masri, Vice Dean of Students and the MBA Program, 212-854-8716. Fax: 212-854-0545. E-mail: smm1@columbia.edu. Application contact: Linda Meehan, Assistant Dean and Executive Director of Admissions and Financial Aid, 212-854-1961. Fax: 212-662-6754. E-mail: gohermes@claven.gsb.columbia.edu.

Concordia University Wisconsin, Division of Graduate Studies, MBA Program, Mequon, WI 53097-2402. Offerings include marketing (MBA). Postbaccalaureate distance learning degree programs offered (minimal on-campus study). *Degree requirements:* Thesis or alternative, comprehensive exam. *Average time to degree:* master's–2 years part-time. *Entrance requirements:* TOEFL (minimum score 550). Application deadline: 8/1 (priority date; rolling processing; 1/15 for spring admission). Application fee: $50. *Tuition:* $300 per credit. • David Borst, Director, 414-243-4298. Fax: 414-243-4428. E-mail: dborst@bach.cuw.edu.

Cornell University, Graduate Field of Management, Ithaca, NY 14853-0001. Offerings include marketing (PhD). Terminal master's awarded for partial completion of doctoral program. Faculty: 43 full-time. *Degree requirements:* Dissertation required, foreign language not required. *Entrance requirements:* GMAT or GRE General Test, TOEFL. Application deadline: 1/10 (priority date). Application fee: $65. *Expenses:* Tuition $24,300 per year. Fees $48 per year. • Director of Graduate Studies, 607-255-3669. Application contact: Graduate Field Assistant, 607-255-3669. Fax: 607-254-4590. E-mail: maria@johnson.cornell.edu.

Dallas Baptist University, College of Business, Business Administration Program, Dallas, TX 75211-9299. Offerings include marketing (MBA). Program faculty: 15 full-time (4 women), 26 part-time (5 women). *Entrance requirements:* GMAT, TOEFL (minimum score 550). Application deadline: rolling. Application fee: $25. *Tuition:* $285 per hour. • Annette Hoffman, Director of Graduate Business Programs, 214-333-5280. Application contact: Travis Bundrick, Director of Graduate Programs, 214-333-5243. Fax: 214-333-5579. E-mail: graduate@dbu.edu.

Delta State University, School of Business, Department of Management and Marketing, Cleveland, MS 38733-0001. Awards MBA. Part-time and evening/weekend programs available. Faculty: 6 full-time (1 woman), 1 part-time (0 women), 6.75 FTE. Students: 28 full-time (10 women), 73 part-time (35 women); includes 25 minority (20 African Americans, 5 Asian Americans). Average age 31. 53 applicants, 98% accepted. In 1997, 11 degrees awarded. *Entrance requirements:* GMAT (minimum score 380). Application deadline: 8/1 (priority date; rolling processing; 8/1 for spring admission). Application fee: $0. *Tuition:* $2596 per year full-time, $121 per semester hour part-time for state residents; $5546 per year full-time, $285 per semester hour part-time for nonresidents. *Financial aid:* Research assistantships, Federal Work-Study, institutionally sponsored loans, and career-related internships or fieldwork available. Aid available to part-time students. Financial aid application deadline: 6/1. • Cooper Johnson, Chair, 601-846-4237. Application contact: Dr. Jerry Williams, Graduate Coordinator, 601-846-4210. E-mail: jwillms@dsu.deltast.edu.

DePaul University, Charles H. Kellstadt Graduate School of Business, Department of Marketing, Program in Marketing, Chicago, IL 60604-2287. Awards MBA. Part-time and evening/weekend programs available. Faculty: 15 full-time (3 women), 14 part-time (4 women). Students: 155 full-time (74 women), 180 part-time (76 women); includes 44 minority (16 African Americans, 15 Asian Americans, 12 Hispanics, 1 Native American), 4 international. Average age 30. 134 applicants, 60% accepted. In 1997, 104 degrees awarded. *Entrance requirements:* GMAT. Application deadline: 8/1 (rolling processing; 3/1 for spring admission). Application fee: $40. *Expenses:* Tuition $1593 per course. Fees $30 per year. *Financial aid:* Application deadline 4/30. • Application contact: Christine Munoz, Director of Admissions, 312-362-8810. Fax: 312-362-6677. E-mail: mbainfo@wppost.depaul.edu.

Drexel University, College of Business and Administration, Department of Marketing, 3141 Chestnut Street, Philadelphia, PA 19104-2875. Awards MS. Part-time and evening/weekend programs available. Faculty: 10 full-time, 2 part-time, 10.6 FTE. Students: 6 full-time (4 women), 6 part-time (2 women); includes 5 international. Average age 28. 27 applicants, 44% accepted. In 1997, 4 degrees awarded. *Degree requirements:* Computer language required, foreign language and thesis not required. *Entrance requirements:* GMAT, TOEFL (minimum score 570), minimum GPA of 2.75. Application deadline: 8/21 (rolling processing). Application fee: $35. *Expenses:* Tuition $494 per credit hour. Fees $121 per quarter full-time, $65 per quarter part-time. *Financial aid:* In 1997–98, 5 teaching assistantships were awarded; research assistantships, graduate assistantships, and career-related internships or fieldwork also available. Financial aid application deadline: 2/1. *Faculty research:* Multivariate analysis, new product development, marketing research, strategic planning, professional personal selling and sales management. • Dr. Rolph E. Anderson, Head, 215-895-2145. Application contact: Denise Bigham, Director of Admissions, 215-895-6700. Fax: 215-895-5969.

Drexel University, College of Business and Administration, Program in Business Administration, 3141 Chestnut Street, Philadelphia, PA 19104-2875. Offerings include business administration (MBA, PhD, APC), with options in accounting (MBA, PhD), decision sciences (PhD), economics (MBA, PhD), finance (MBA, PhD), legal studies (MBA), management (MBA), marketing (MBA, PhD), organizational sciences (PhD), quantitative methods (MBA), strategic management (PhD). Terminal master's awarded for partial completion of doctoral program. *Degree requirements:* For doctorate, computer language required, foreign language and dissertation not required. *Entrance requirements:* For doctorate, GMAT, TOEFL (minimum score 570). Application deadline: 8/21 (rolling processing; 3/5 for spring admission). Application fee: $35. *Expenses:* Tuition $494 per credit hour. Fees $121 per quarter full-time, $65 per quarter part-time. • Dr. Jerold B. Muskin, Director of Master's Programs in Business, 215-895-2115. Application contact: Denise Bigham, Director of Admissions, 215-895-6700. Fax: 215-895-5969.

East Carolina University, School of Business, Greenville, NC 27858-4353. Offerings include marketing (MBA). School faculty: 39 full-time (4 women). *Application deadline:* 6/1 (priority date; rolling processing). *Application fee:* $40. *Tuition:* $1886 per year full-time, $472 per semester (minimum) part-time for state residents; $9156 per year full-time, $2289 per semester (minimum) part-time for nonresidents. • Donald B. Boldt, Director of Graduate Studies, 252-328-6970. Fax: 252-328-6664. E-mail: boldtd@mail.ecu.edu. Application contact: Dr. Paul D. Tschetter, Associate Dean, 252-328-6012. Fax: 252-328-6071. E-mail: grad@mail.ecu.edu.

Eastern College, Graduate Business Programs, St. Davids, PA 19087-3696. Offerings include business administration (MBA), with options in accounting, economics, finance, management, marketing. M Div/MS and M Div/MBA offered jointly with Eastern Baptist Theological Seminary. Faculty: 32 full-time (18 women), 14 part-time (12 women). *Application deadline:* rolling. *Application fee:* $35. • Dr. John Stapleford, Chair, 610-341-5848. Application contact: Megan Miscioscia, Graduate Admissions Representative, 610-341-5972. Fax: 610-341-1466.

Eastern Michigan University, College of Business, Department of Marketing, Ypsilanti, MI 48197. Awards MBA. Faculty: 17 full-time (6 women). *Entrance requirements:* GMAT (minimum score 500), TOEFL (minimum score 550). Application deadline: 5/15 (rolling processing; 3/15 for spring admission). Application fee: $30. *Expenses:* Tuition $2691 per year full-time, $150 per credit hour part-time for state residents; $6300 per year full-time, $350 per credit hour part-time for nonresidents. Fees $368 per year full-time, $88 per semester (minimum) part-time. *Financial aid:* Application deadline 3/15; applicants required to submit FAFSA. • Dr. H. Robert Dodge, Head, 734-487-3323.

École des Hautes Études Commerciales, Program in Marketing, Montréal, PQ H3T 2A7, Canada. Awards M Sc. Most courses are given in French. Part-time programs available. *Degree requirements:* 1 foreign language, thesis. *Application deadline:* 3/15. *Application fee:* $40. *Financial aid:* Fellowships, research assistantships, teaching assistantships available. • Dr. Jean-Yves Le Louarn, Director, 514-340-6295. E-mail: jean-yves.lelouarn@hec.ca. Application contact: Nicole Rivet, Registrar, 514-340-6110. Fax: 514-340-5640. E-mail: nicole.rivet@hec.ca.

Emporia State University, School of Graduate Studies, School of Business, Division of Management, Marketing, Finance and Economics, Emporia, KS 66801-5087. Awards MBA. Faculty: 12 full-time (1 woman), 1 part-time (0 women). Students: 36 full-time (9 women), 23 part-time (10 women); includes 3 minority (2 African Americans, 1 Asian American), 19 international. 25 applicants, 88% accepted. In 1997, 23 degrees awarded. *Degree requirements:* Comprehensive exam required, foreign language not required. *Entrance requirements:* GMAT, TOEFL (minimum score 550). Application deadline: 8/15 (priority date; rolling processing). Application fee: $30 ($75 for international students). Electronic applications accepted. *Tuition:* $2300 per year full-time, $103 per credit hour part-time for state residents; $6012 per year full-time, $258 per credit hour part-time for nonresidents. *Financial aid:* In 1997–98, 2 fellowships averaging $667 per month, 2 research assistantships averaging $558 per month, 3 teaching assistantships averaging $522 per month were awarded; Federal Work-Study, institutionally sponsored loans, and career-related internships or fieldwork also available. Financial aid application deadline: 3/15; applicants required to submit FAFSA. • Dr. Varkey Titus, Chair, 316-341-5347. E-mail: titusvar@emporia.edu. Application contact: Dr. Donald Miller, Director, 316-341-5456. E-mail: millerdo@emporia.edu.

Fairfield University, School of Business, Fairfield, CT 06430-5195. Offerings include marketing (MBA, CAS). School faculty: 36 full-time (12 women), 4 part-time (2 women), 37.3 FTE. *Average time to degree:* master's–2 years full-time, 3.5 years part-time. *Application deadline:* 8/1 (priority date; rolling processing; 12/1 for spring admission). *Application fee:* $40. *Expenses:* Tuition $15,000 per year full-time, $450 per credit hour part-time. Fees $40 per year. • Dr. Walter G. Ryba Jr., Acting Dean, 203-254-4070. Application contact: Cynthia S. Chegwidden, Director of Graduate Programs, 203-254-4070. Fax: 203-254-4105. E-mail: cchegwidden@fairl.fairfield.edu.

Fairleigh Dickinson University, Florham–Madison Campus, Samuel J. Silberman College of Business Administration, Program in Marketing, 285 Madison Avenue, Madison, NJ 07940-1099. Awards MBA. Part-time and evening/weekend programs available. Faculty: 5 full-time (0 women), 13 part-time (2 women). Students: 10 full-time (8 women), 152 part-time (83 women); includes 6 minority (1 African American, 3 Asian Americans, 2 Hispanics), 3 international. Average age 29. 44 applicants, 68% accepted. In 1997, 47 degrees awarded. *Degree requirements:* Thesis optional, foreign language not required. *Entrance requirements:* GMAT. Application deadline: rolling. Application fee: $35. *Expenses:* Tuition $522 per credit. Fees $302 per year full-time, $138 per year part-time. • Dr. Joel Harmon, Chairperson, 973-443-8850.

Fairleigh Dickinson University, Teaneck–Hackensack Campus, Samuel J. Silberman College of Business Administration, Department of Management, Marketing, and Information Systems and Sciences, Program in Marketing, 1000 River Road, Teaneck, NJ 07666-1914. Awards MBA. Students: 16 full-time (8 women), 56 part-time (37 women); includes 6 minority (4 African Americans, 1 Asian American, 1 Hispanic), 11 international. Average age 31. In 1997, 21 degrees awarded. *Degree requirements:* Computer language required, thesis optional, foreign language not required. *Entrance requirements:* GMAT. Application deadline: rolling. Application fee: $35. *Expenses:* Tuition $522 per credit. Fees $302 per year full-time, $138 per year part-time. *Financial aid:* Fellowships, research assistantships available. *Faculty research:* Consumer behavior, relationship selling. • Dr. Ronald Heim, Assistant Dean, 973-443-8864.

Florida Agricultural and Mechanical University, Division of Graduate Studies, Research, and Continuing Education, School of Business and Industry, Tallahassee, FL 32307-3200. Offerings include marketing (MBA). *Entrance requirements:* GRE General Test (minimum combined score of 1000), minimum GPA of 3.0. Application deadline: 5/13. Application fee: $20. *Expenses:* Tuition $140 per credit hour for state residents; $484 per credit hour for nonresidents. Fees $130 per year. • Dr. Sybil Mobley, Dean, 850-599-3565.

Florida International University, College of Business Administration, Department of Marketing and Business Environment, Miami, FL 33199. Awards MBA, PhD. Faculty: 16 full-time (4 women), 2 part-time (0 women), 16.62 FTE. Students: 145 full-time (43 women), 224 part-time (87 women); includes 224 minority (22 African Americans, 24 Asian Americans, 178 Hispanics), 42 international. 338 applicants, 36% accepted. In 1997, 127 master's, 1 doctorate awarded. *Degree requirements:* For master's, computer language required, thesis not required; for doctorate, computer language, dissertation. *Entrance requirements:* For master's, GMAT, minimum AACSB index of 1000, minimum GPA of 3.0; for doctorate, GMAT (minimum score 560), minimum GPA of 3.0. Application fee: $20. *Expenses:* Tuition $138 per credit hour for

Directory: Marketing

Florida International University (continued)
state residents; $482 per credit hour for nonresidents. Fees $46 per semester. • Dr. John A. Nicholls, Chairperson, 305-348-2571. Fax: 305-348-3792. E-mail: nicholls@fiu.edu.

Florida Metropolitan University–Orlando College, North, Division of Business Administration, 5421 Diplomat Circle, Orlando, FL 32810-5674. Offerings include marketing analysis (MBA). Division faculty: 7. *Degree requirements:* Thesis or alternative. *Application deadline:* rolling. *Application fee:* $25. *Tuition:* $263 per credit hour. • Director of Graduate Studies, 407-851-2525. Application contact: Annette Gallina, Director of Admissions, 407-851-2525 Ext. 30. Fax: 407-851-1477.

Fordham University, Graduate School of Business Administration, New York, NY 10023. Offerings include marketing (GPMBA, MBA). School faculty: 85 full-time (22 women), 95 part-time (12 women). *Average time to degree:* master's–2 years full-time, 3 years part-time. *Application deadline:* 6/1 (priority date; rolling processing; 11/1 for spring admission). *Application fee:* $50. • Dr. Ernest J. Scalberg, Dean, 212-636-6111. Fax: 212-307-1779. Application contact: Kathy Pattison, Assistant Dean of Admission, 212-636-6200. Fax: 212-636-7076. E-mail: admission@bschool.bnet.fordham.edu.

Franklin University, Department of Marketing and Communications, Columbus, OH 43215-5399. Awards MS. Program new for fall 1998. *Application deadline:* 7/15 (priority date; rolling processing). *Application fee:* $30 ($40 for international students). *Expenses:* Tuition $280 per credit hour. Fees $25 per trimester. *Financial aid:* Application deadline 6/30. • Application contact: MBA Associate, 614-341-6387. Fax: 614-221-7723.

The George Washington University, School of Business and Public Management, Department of Marketing, Washington, DC 20052. Awards MBA, PhD. Part-time and evening/weekend programs available. Faculty: 12 full-time (3 women), 2 part-time (0 women), 13 FTE. Students: 66 full-time (33 women), 67 part-time (38 women); includes 15 minority (12 African Americans, 3 Asian Americans), 43 international. Average age 27. 203 applicants, 66% accepted. In 1997, 73 master's, 1 doctorate awarded. *Degree requirements:* For master's, computer language required, foreign language and thesis not required; for doctorate, dissertation required, foreign language not required. *Entrance requirements:* For master's, GMAT, TOEFL (minimum score 550); for doctorate, GMAT or GRE, TOEFL (minimum score 550). Application deadline: 4/1 (priority date; rolling processing; 10/1 for spring admission). Application fee: $50. *Expenses:* Tuition $680 per semester hour. Fees $35 per semester hour. *Financial aid:* Fellowships, teaching assistantships, Federal Work-Study, institutionally sponsored loans, and career-related internships or fieldwork available. Financial aid application deadline: 4/1. *Faculty research:* Strategic marketing, marketing and public policy, marketing management. • Dr. Pradeep Rau, Chair, 202-994-8200. Application contact: Lilly Hastings, Graduate Admissions, 202-994-6584. Fax: 202-994-6382.

Georgia State University, College of Business Administration, Department of Marketing, Atlanta, GA 30303-3083. Awards MBA, MS, PhD. Part-time and evening/weekend programs available. Faculty: 19 full-time, 4 part-time. Students: 118 full-time (57 women), 105 part-time (49 women); includes 24 minority (14 African Americans, 3 Asian Americans, 6 Hispanics, 1 Native American), 22 international. Average age 32. In 1997, 34 master's, 2 doctorates awarded. Terminal master's awarded for partial completion of doctoral program. *Degree requirements:* For doctorate, dissertation required, foreign language not required. *Entrance requirements:* For master's, GMAT (average 566), TOEFL; for doctorate, GMAT (average 670), TOEFL. Application deadline: 5/1 (rolling processing; 10/1 for spring admission). Application fee: $25. *Expenses:* Tuition $2673 per year full-time, $99 per semester hour part-time for state residents; $10,692 per year full-time, $396 per semester hour part-time for nonresidents. Fees $228 per year. *Financial aid:* Fellowships, research assistantships, teaching assistantships, partial tuition waivers, and career-related internships or fieldwork available. Aid available to part-time students. Financial aid applicants required to submit FAFSA. • Dr. Danny Bellenger, Chair, 404-651-1979. Fax: 404-651-2804. Application contact: Office of Academic Assistance and Master's Admissions, 404-651-1913. Fax: 404-651-0219.

Golden Gate University, School of Business, San Francisco, CA 94105-2968. Offerings include marketing (MBA, MS). MBA (telecommunications, management information systems) offered jointly with the School of Technology and Industry. *Average time to degree:* master's–2.5 years full-time. *Application deadline:* 7/1 (priority date; rolling processing). *Application fee:* $55 ($70 for international students). *Tuition:* $996 per course (minimum). • Dr. Hamid Shomali, Dean, 415-442-6500. Fax: 415-442-6579. Application contact: Enrollment Services, 415-442-7800. Fax: 415-442-7807. E-mail: info@ggu.edu.

Hawaii Pacific University, School of Business Administration, 1166 Fort Street, Honolulu, HI 96813-2785. Offerings include marketing (MBA). School faculty: 30 full-time (3 women), 12 part-time (1 woman), 38 FTE. *Average time to degree:* master's–2 years full-time, 4 years part-time. *Application deadline:* rolling. *Application fee:* $50. Electronic applications accepted. *Tuition:* $7920 per year full-time, $330 per credit part-time. • Dr. Richard Ward, Dean for Graduate Management Studies, 808-544-0279. Application contact: Leina Danao, Admissions Coordinator, 808-544-1120. Fax: 808-544-0280. E-mail: gradservctr@hpu.edu.

Hofstra University, Frank G. Zarb School of Business, Department of Marketing and International Business, Program in Marketing, Hempstead, NY 11549. Awards MBA. Part-time and evening/weekend programs available. Faculty: 8 full-time (2 women), 2 part-time (1 woman). Students: 18 full-time (10 women), 81 part-time (52 women); includes 6 minority (2 African Americans, 3 Asian Americans, 1 Hispanic), 5 international. Average age 29. 54 applicants, 67% accepted. In 1997, 30 degrees awarded. *Degree requirements:* Computer language, thesis or alternative required, foreign language not required. *Entrance requirements:* GMAT (average 580). Application deadline: rolling. Application fee: $40 ($75 for international students). *Expenses:* Tuition $10,968 per year full-time, $457 per credit hour part-time. Fees $670 per year full-time, $112 per semester (minimum) part-time. *Financial aid:* 19 students received aid; fellowships, research assistantships, Federal Work-Study, and career-related internships or fieldwork available. Financial aid application deadline: 4/1; applicants required to submit FAFSA. *Faculty research:* Consumer behavior, product planning, marketing management, cross-cultural research, retail, strategic planning. • Application contact: Susan McTiernan, Senior Assistant Dean, 516-463-5683. Fax: 516-463-5268. E-mail: bizsmm@hofstra.edu.

Houston Baptist University, College of Business and Economics, Program in Management, Houston, TX 77074-3298. Offerings include marketing (MBA). Program faculty: 9 full-time (1 woman), 7 part-time (1 woman). *Entrance requirements:* GMAT (minimum score 450), minimum GPA of 2.5, work experience. Application deadline: 6/1 (priority date; rolling processing; 1/1 for spring admission). Application fee: $25 ($85 for international students). *Expenses:* Tuition $300 per semester hour. Fees $235 per quarter. • Dr. Carter L. Franklin II, Associate Dean, College of Business and Economics, 281-649-3429. Application contact: Karen Murray, Program Assistant, 281-649-3306.

Illinois Institute of Technology, Stuart School of Business, Program in Marketing Communication, Chicago, IL 60616-3793. Awards MS. *Tuition:* $1620 per course. • Dr. John Tarini, Director. Application contact: Lynn Miller, Director, Admission, 312-906-6544. Fax: 312-906-6549. E-mail: degrees@stuart.iit.edu.

See in-depth description on page 607.

Indiana University Bloomington, School of Business, Doctoral Programs in Business, Bloomington, IN 47405. Offerings include marketing (DBA, PhD). PhD offered through the University Graduate School. *Degree requirements:* Computer language, dissertation required, foreign language not required. *Entrance requirements:* GMAT (minimum score 600), GRE General Test. Application deadline: 3/1. Application fee: $35. *Expenses:* Tuition $261 per credit hour for state residents; $523 per credit hour for nonresidents. Fees $343 per year. • Dr. Janet Near, Chairperson, 812-855-3476. Application contact: Barbara Clark, Program Secretary and Assistant to Chairperson, 812-855-3476. Fax: 812-855-8679. E-mail: bclark@ucs.indiana.edu.

Indiana University Bloomington, School of Business, Program in Business Administration, Bloomington, IN 47405. Offerings include marketing (MBA). Self-designed programs available. *Entrance requirements:* GMAT, TOEFL (minimum score 580). Application deadline: 3/1. Application fee: $50 ($65 for international students). *Expenses:* Tuition $8232 per year for state residents; $16,470 per year for nonresidents. Fees $343 per year. • Dr. George Hettenhouse, Chair, 812-855-8006. Application contact: Dr. James J. Holmen, Director of Admissions and Financial Aid, 812-855-8006. Fax: 812-855-9039.

Instituto Tecnológico y de Estudios Superiores de Monterrey, Graduate School of Management and Leadership, Program in Business Administration, Monterrey, Nuevo León 64849, Mexico. Offerings include marketing (M Sc). *Application deadline:* 4/30 (priority date).

Instituto Tecnológico y de Estudios Superiores de Monterrey, Estado de México Campus, Graduate Division, Atizapán de Zaragoza 52926, Mexico. Offerings include marketing (MEM). Postbaccalaureate distance learning degree programs offered (minimal on-campus study). Institute faculty: 19 full-time (3 women), 32 part-time (3 women). *Average time to degree:* master's–2 years full-time, 3.3 years part-time. *Application deadline:* 1/12 (priority date; rolling processing; 4/4 for spring admission). *Application fee:* $72. • Emilio Alvarado Badillo, Headmaster, 5-326-5500. Fax: 5-326-5507. E-mail: ealvarad@campus.cem.itesm.mx. Application contact: Lourdes Turrubiates, Admissions Officer, 5-326-5776. E-mail: lturrubi@campus.cem.itesm.mx.

Instituto Tecnológico y de Estudios Superiores de Monterrey, Morelos Campus, Programs in Business Administration, Cuernavaca, Morelos 62589, Mexico. Offerings include marketing (MA).

Inter American University of Puerto Rico, Metropolitan Campus, Division of Economics and Business Administration, Program in Marketing, San Juan, PR 00919-1293. Awards MBA. Faculty: 3 full-time, 6 part-time. Students: 86 full-time (52 women), 135 part-time (80 women); includes 221 minority (all Hispanics). *Degree requirements:* Comprehensive exam required, foreign language and thesis not required. *Entrance requirements:* GRE or PAEG, interview. Application deadline: 5/15 (priority date; rolling processing; 11/15 for spring admission). Application fee: $31. Electronic applications accepted. *Expenses:* Tuition $3272 per year full-time, $1740 per year part-time. Fees $328 per year full-time, $176 per year part-time. *Financial aid:* Federal Work-Study available. • Application contact: Dr. Antonio Llorens, Director, 787-250-1912 Ext. 2320. Fax: 787-250-0361.

Inter American University of Puerto Rico, San Germán Campus, Department of Business Administration, Program in Business Administration, San Germán, PR 00683-5008. Offerings include marketing (MBA). *Degree requirements:* Comprehensive exam required, foreign language and thesis not required. *Entrance requirements:* Minimum GPA of 3.0, GRE General Test, or PAEG. Application deadline: 4/30 (priority date; rolling processing; 11/15 for spring admission). Application fee: $31. *Expenses:* Tuition $150 per credit. Fees $177 per semester. • Application contact: Mildred Camacho, Admissions Director, 787-892-3090. Fax: 787-892-6350.

Iona College, Hagan Graduate School of Business, Department of Marketing, 715 North Avenue, New Rochelle, NY 10801-1890. Awards MBA, PMC. Part-time and evening/weekend programs available. Faculty: 5 full-time (2 women), 4 part-time (0 women). Students: 4 full-time (3 women), 28 part-time (16 women); includes 1 minority (Asian American). Average age 30. In 1997, 16 master's awarded. *Degree requirements:* For master's, computer language required, foreign language and thesis not required. *Entrance requirements:* For master's, GMAT (minimum score 425; average 480); for PMC, GMAT. Application deadline: rolling. Application fee: $50. *Expenses:* Tuition $480 per credit hour. Fees $25 per semester. *Financial aid:* In 1997–98, 3 graduate assistantships were awarded; partial tuition waivers also available. Aid available to part-time students. *Faculty research:* Business ethics, international retailing, mega-marketing, consumer behavior and consumer confidence. Total annual research expenditures: $20,000. • Dr. Frederica Rudell, Chair, 914-633-2422. Application contact: Carol Shea, Director of MBA Admissions, 914-633-2288.

Johns Hopkins University, School of Continuing Studies, Division of Business and Management, Baltimore, MD 21218-2699. Offerings include marketing (MS). Division faculty: 12 full-time, 190 part-time. *Degree requirements:* Project required, foreign language and thesis not required. *Entrance requirements:* Minimum GPA of 3.0. Application deadline: rolling. Application fee: $50. • Dr. Jon Heggan, Director, 410-516-0755. Application contact: Lenora Henry, Admissions Coordinator, 410-872-1234. Fax: 410-872-1251. E-mail: adv_mail@jhuvms.hcf.jhu.edu.

Kennesaw State University, Michael J. Coles College of Business, Program in Business Administration, Kennesaw, GA 30144-5591. Offerings include marketing (MBA). Program faculty: 54 full-time (18 women), 5 part-time (0 women). *Application deadline:* 7/1 (rolling processing; 2/20 for spring admission). *Application fee:* $20. *Expenses:* Tuition $2398 per year full-time, $83 per credit hour part-time for state residents; $8398 per year full-time, $333 per credit hour part-time for nonresidents. Fees $338 per year. • Dr. Rodney Alsup, Assistant Dean, 770-423-6087. Fax: 770-423-6141. E-mail: ralsup@ksumail.kennesaw.edu. Application contact: Susan N. Barrett, Administrative Specialist, Admissions, 770-423-6500. Fax: 770-423-6541. E-mail: sbarrett@ksumail.kennesaw.edu.

Kent State University, Graduate School of Management, Doctoral Program in Marketing, Kent, OH 44242-0001. Awards PhD. Faculty: 9 full-time (2 women). Students: 4 full-time (2 women), 3 part-time (1 woman); includes 1 minority (African American), 1 international. 9 applicants, 22% accepted. In 1997, 3 degrees awarded. *Degree requirements:* Dissertation, comprehensive exams, oral defense required, foreign language not required. *Entrance requirements:* GMAT. Application deadline: 2/1. Application fee: $30. *Tuition:* $4752 per year full-time, $216 per credit hour part-time for state residents; $9213 per year full-time, $419 per credit hour part-time for nonresidents. *Financial aid:* In 1997–98, 3 teaching assistantships (1 to a first-year student) averaging $1,000 per month were awarded; Federal Work-Study also available. Financial aid application deadline: 2/1; applicants required to submit FAFSA. *Faculty research:* Advertising effects, satisfaction, international marketing, high-tech marketing, personality and consumer behavior. • Michael Mayo, Chair, 330-672-2170 Ext. 331. E-mail: mmayo@bsa3.kent.edu. Application contact: Dr. James C. Baker, Doctoral Director, 330-672-2282 Ext. 235. Fax: 330-672-2448. E-mail: jbaker@bsa3.kent.edu.

Lindenwood University, Programs in Individualized Education, St. Charles, MO 63301-1695. Offerings include marketing (MSA). Faculty: 10 full-time (7 women), 23 part-time (6 women). *Application deadline:* 6/30 (priority date; rolling processing; 12/1 for spring admission). *Application fee:* $25. *Tuition:* $5880 per year full-time, $245 per credit hour part-time. • Dr. Dan Kemper, Dean, 314-916-9125. Application contact: John Guffey, Director of Graduate Admissions, 314-949-4933. Fax: 314-949-4910.

Long Island University, C.W. Post Campus, College of Management, School of Business, Department of Marketing, Brookville, NY 11548-1300. Awards MBA. Part-time and evening/weekend programs available. Faculty: 4 full-time (0 women), 9 part-time (3 women). Students: 100 full-time (40 women), 188 part-time (88 women). 16 applicants, 69% accepted. In 1997, 10 degrees awarded. *Entrance requirements:* GMAT. Application deadline: 8/15 (priority date; rolling processing; 12/15 for spring admission). Application fee: $30. Electronic applications accepted. *Expenses:* Tuition $480 per credit. Fees $316 per year full-time, $71 per semester (minimum) part-time. *Financial aid:* Graduate assistantships, partial tuition waivers available. Aid available to part-time students. Financial aid application deadline: 5/15; applicants required to submit FAFSA. *Faculty research:* Direct marketing, intellectual property, packaging, retailing innovation, marketing strategy, technology impact on business processes. • Dr. Srikumar Rao, Chairman, 516-299-2143. Application contact: Sally Luzader, Associate Director of Graduate Admissions, 516-299-2417. Fax: 516-299-2137. E-mail: admissions@collegehall.liunet.edu.

Louisiana State University and Agricultural and Mechanical College, College of Business Administration, Department of Marketing, Baton Rouge, LA 70803. Offers programs in business administration (PhD), including marketing; marketing (MS). Part-time programs available. Faculty: 9 full-time (3 women). Students: 20 full-time (8 women), 9 part-time (6 women); includes 2 minority (1 African American, 1 Hispanic), 10 international. Average age 30. 41 applicants, 20% accepted. In 1997, 8 master's, 2 doctorates awarded. *Degree requirements:* For master's, thesis or alternative required, foreign language not required; for doctorate, dissertation required, foreign language not required. *Entrance requirements:* For master's, GMAT, TOEFL, minimum GPA of 3.0. Application deadline: 1/25 (priority date; rolling processing). Application fee: $25. *Tuition:* $2736 per year full-time, $285 per semester (minimum) part-time for state residents; $6636 per year full-time, $460 per semester (minimum) part-time for nonresidents. *Financial aid:* In 1997–98, 1 fellowship, 6 research assistantships, 7 service assistantships (2 to first-year students) were awarded; teaching assistantships and career-related internships or fieldwork also available. *Faculty research:* Consumer behavior, marketing research, promotion, marketing strategy, international marketing. • Dr. Alvin Burns, Chair, 504-388-8684. Application contact: Dr. Rick Netemeyer, Graduate Adviser, 504-388-8684.

Louisiana Tech University, College of Administration and Business, Department of Management and Marketing, Ruston, LA 71272. Offers programs in management (MBA, DBA), marketing (MBA, DBA). Part-time programs available. Faculty: 13 full-time (1 woman). Students: 29 full-time (5 women), 16 part-time (6 women); includes 3 minority (all African Americans), 4 international. Average age 27. In 1997, 10 master's, 5 doctorates awarded. *Degree requirements:* For master's, computer language required, foreign language and thesis not required; for doctorate, computer language, dissertation required, foreign language not required. *Entrance requirements:* GMAT. Application deadline: 7/29 (2/3 for spring admission). Application fee: $20 ($30 for international students). *Tuition:* $2382 per year full-time, $223 per quarter (minimum) part-time for state residents; $5307 per year full-time, $223 per quarter (minimum) part-time for nonresidents. *Financial aid:* Fellowships, research assistantships, teaching assistantships available. Financial aid application deadline: 2/1. • Dr. Gene Brown, Head, 318-257-4012.

Loyola College, Sellinger School of Business and Management, Programs in Business Administration, Baltimore, MD 21210-2699. Offerings include marketing/management (MBA). *Application deadline:* 7/20 (11/20 for spring admission). *Application fee:* $35. *Tuition:* $365 per credit. • Dr. Peter Lorenzi, Dean, Sellinger School of Business and Management, 410-617-2301.

Manhattan College, Program in Business Administration, Riverdale, NY 10471. Offerings include marketing (MBA). Program faculty: 18 full-time (3 women), 8 part-time (0 women). *Degree requirements:* Computer language, thesis or alternative. *Entrance requirements:* GMAT, minimum GPA of 2.8. Application deadline: 8/10 (priority date; rolling processing; 1/7 for spring admission). Application fee: $50. *Expenses:* Tuition $440 per credit. Fees $100 per year. • Dr. Charles E. Brunner, Director, 718-862-7222. Fax: 718-862-8023. Application contact: William J. Bisset Jr., Dean of Admissions/Financial Aid, 718-862-7200. Fax: 718-863-8019. E-mail: admit@manhattan.edu.

Metropolitan State University, Management and Administration Program, St. Paul, MN 55106-5000. Offerings include marketing (MBA). Program faculty: 17 full-time (5 women), 150 part-time. *Application deadline:* rolling. *Application fee:* $20. *Tuition:* $133 per credit for state residents; $208 per credit for nonresidents. • Gary Seiler, Graduate Coordinator, 612-373-2754. E-mail: seiler@msus1.msus.edu. Application contact: Gloria Marcus, Recruiter/Admissions Adviser, 612-373-2724. Fax: 612-373-2888. E-mail: marcusg@msus1.msus.edu.

Miami University, Richard T. Farmer School of Business Administration, Oxford, OH 45056. Offerings include marketing (MBA). School faculty: 50. *Application deadline:* 3/1 (priority date; rolling processing). *Application fee:* $35. *Tuition:* $5932 per year full-time, $255 per credit hour part-time for state residents; $12,392 per year full-time, $524 per credit hour part-time for nonresidents. • Judy Barille, Director of Graduate Programs, 513-529-6643.

Michigan State University, Eli Broad Graduate School of Management, Department of Marketing and Supply Chain Management, East Lansing, MI 48824-1020. Offers programs in marketing (MBA, PhD), materials and logistics management-logistics (MBA), transportation-distribution (PhD). Evening/weekend programs available. Faculty: 28 (2 women). Students: 72 (27 women); includes 13 minority (5 African Americans, 2 Asian Americans, 6 Hispanics), 18 international. In 1997, 33 master's, 4 doctorates awarded. Terminal master's awarded for partial completion of doctoral program. *Degree requirements:* For doctorate, dissertation required, foreign language not required. *Entrance requirements:* For master's, GMAT (minimum score 530); for doctorate, GMAT (minimum score 600; average 660). Application deadline: 3/31 (priority date; rolling processing; 11/1 for spring admission). Application fee: $30 ($40 for international students). Electronic applications accepted. *Expenses:* Tuition $4609 per year full-time, $223 per credit hour (minimum) part-time for state residents; $8704 per year full-time, $450 per credit hour (minimum) part-time for nonresidents. Fees $576 per year full-time, $476 per year part-time. *Financial aid:* Research assistantships, teaching assistantships, Federal Work-Study, and career-related internships or fieldwork available. *Faculty research:* International marketing, new product development, innovation management, logistics distribution, food and packaged goods. Total annual research expenditures: $500,000. • Dr. Robert Nason, Chairperson, 517-355-2240.

Montclair State University, School of Business, Program in Business Administration, Concentration in Marketing, Upper Montclair, NJ 07043-1624. Awards MBA. Part-time and evening/weekend programs available. Faculty: 9 full-time. Students: 3 full-time (1 woman), 12 part-time (6 women). *Entrance requirements:* GMAT. Application deadline: 4/1 (rolling processing; 11/1 for spring admission). Application fee: $40. *Expenses:* Tuition $201 per credit for state residents; $257 per credit for nonresidents. Fees $22.05 per credit. *Financial aid:* Research assistantships available. Aid available to part-time students. Financial aid application deadline: 3/1; applicants required to submit FAFSA. • Application contact: Dr. Eileen Kaplan, Adviser, 973-655-4306.

New York University, Leonard N. Stern School of Business, Department of Marketing, New York, NY 10006. Awards MBA, PhD, APC. Faculty: 24 full-time (7 women), 12 part-time (2 women), 28 FTE. Students: 179 full-time, 390 part-time. In 1997, 228 master's, 2 doctorates awarded. *Degree requirements:* For master's, computer language required, foreign language and thesis not required; for doctorate, computer language, dissertation required, foreign language not required. *Entrance requirements:* For master's, GMAT, TOEFL (minimum score 600); for doctorate, GMAT. Application deadline: 3/15 (rolling processing). Application fee: $75. *Financial aid:* Federal Work-Study available. Financial aid application deadline: 1/15; applicants required to submit FAFSA. *Faculty research:* Consumer information processing, international marketing, stochastic consumer choice models, marketing strategy, sales promotion. • Samuel Craig, Chairman, 212-998-0500. Application contact: Mary Miller, Director, Graduate Admissions, 212-998-0600. Fax: 212-995-4231. E-mail: sternmba@stern.nyu.edu.

New York University, School of Continuing Education, Center for Direct Marketing, New York, NY 10012-1019. Offers program in direct marketing communications (MS). Faculty: 13 part-time (3 women). Students: 7 full-time (4 women), 61 part-time (37 women); includes 17 minority (5 African Americans, 8 Asian Americans, 4 Hispanics), 6 international. Average age 30. 56 applicants, 86% accepted. *Entrance requirements:* GMAT, work experience. Application deadline: 6/30 (priority date; rolling processing; 11/30 for spring admission). Application fee: $50. *Financial aid:* 18 students received aid; career-related internships or fieldwork available. Aid available to part-time students. • Pierre Passavant, Director, 212-998-7221. Application contact: Alice Chin, Assistant Director, 212-998-7219. Fax: 212-995-4138. E-mail: chin@is3.nyu.edu.

See in-depth description on page 609.

Nichols College, Graduate Program in Business Administration, Dudley, MA 01571. Offerings include marketing (MBA). College faculty: 21 full-time (3 women), 6 part-time (2 women). *Degree requirements:* Computer language required, foreign language and thesis not required. *Entrance requirements:* GMAT, TOEFL, minimum AACSB index of 950. Application deadline: rolling. Application fee: $25. *Tuition:* $1050 per course. • William F. Keith, Director, 508-213-2207. E-mail: keithwf@nichols.edu.

Northeastern Illinois University, College of Business and Management, Chicago, IL 60625-4699. Offerings include marketing (MBA). College faculty: 26 full-time (3 women), 14 part-time (6 women). *Degree requirements:* Thesis optional, foreign language not required. *Entrance requirements:* GMAT (minimum score 450), TOEFL (minimum score 550), minimum GPA of 2.75. Application deadline: 3/18 (priority date; rolling processing; 9/30 for spring admission). Application fee: $0. *Expenses:* Tuition $2226 per year full-time, $93 per credit hour part-time for state residents; $6678 per year full-time, $278 per credit hour part-time for nonresidents. Fees $358 per year full-time, $14.90 per credit hour part-time. • Dr. Charles Falk, Dean, 773-583-4050 Ext. 5247. Application contact: Dr. Kathleen Carlson, Coordinator, 773-583-4050.

Northwestern University, Medill School of Journalism, Program in Integrated Marketing Communications, Evanston, IL 60208. Offers advertising/sales promotion (MSIMC), direct marketing (MSIMC), general studies (MSIMC), public relations (MSIMC). Faculty: 15 full-time, 12 part-time. Students: 85 full-time (45 women). Average age 26. In 1997, 89 degrees awarded. *Entrance requirements:* GRE General Test or GMAT, TOEFL (minimum score 625), full-time work experience (preferred). Application deadline: 3/1. Application fee: $50. *Tuition:* $24,112 per year. *Financial aid:* Grants, loans, Federal Work-Study, institutionally sponsored loans, and career-related internships or fieldwork available. Financial aid applicants required to submit FAFSA. *Faculty research:* Database marketing, business to business marketing, values in advertising, political advertising. • Application contact: Office of Graduate Admissions and Financial Aid, 847-491-5228. Fax: 847-467-7342. E-mail: medill-admis@nwu.edu.

See in-depth description on page 611.

Northwestern University, J. L. Kellogg Graduate School of Management, Department of Marketing, Evanston, IL 60208. Awards PhD. Admissions and degree offered through The Graduate School. Faculty: 21 full-time (5 women), 15 part-time (3 women). Students: 14 full-time (8 women); includes 3 minority (1 African American, 1 Asian American, 1 Hispanic), 7 international. 54 applicants, 19% accepted. In 1997, 4 degrees awarded. *Degree requirements:* Computer language, dissertation required, foreign language not required. *Entrance requirements:* GRE General Test or GMAT. Application deadline: 1/15. Application fee: $50 ($55 for international students). *Tuition:* $25,872 per year. *Financial aid:* In 1997–98, fellowships averaging $1,256 per month were awarded; institutionally sponsored loans and career-related internships or fieldwork also available. Financial aid application deadline: 1/15; applicants required to submit FAFSA. *Faculty research:* Choice models, database and high-tech marketing, consumer information processing, ethnographic analysis of consumption, psychometric analysis of consumer behavior. Total annual research expenditures: $100,000. • Lakshman Krishnamurthi, Chair, 847-467-1286. Application contact: Lucy Vandenburgh, Admission Contact, 847-491-3400. Fax: 847-491-5071. E-mail: l-vandenburgh@nwu.edu.

Oklahoma City University, School of Management and Business Sciences, Program in Business Administration, Oklahoma City, OK 73106-1402. Offerings include marketing and advertising (MBA). *Degree requirements:* Comprehensive exam required, foreign language and thesis not required. *Entrance requirements:* TOEFL, minimum GPA of 2.5. Application deadline: rolling. Application fee: $35 ($55 for international students). *Expenses:* Tuition $350 per hour. Fees $124 per year. • Application contact: Laura L. Rahhal, Director of Graduate Admissions, 800-633-7242 Ext. 2. Fax: 405-521-5356. E-mail: lrahhal1@frodo.okcu.edu.

Oklahoma State University, College of Business Administration, Department of Marketing, Stillwater, OK 74078. Awards MBA, PhD. Faculty: 11 full-time (1 woman), 1 part-time (0 women), 11.5 FTE. Students: 3 part-time (all women). Average age 47. *Degree requirements:* For doctorate, dissertation required, foreign language not required. *Entrance requirements:* GMAT, TOEFL (minimum score 550). Application deadline: 7/1 (priority date). Application fee: $25. *Financial aid:* Research assistantships, teaching assistantships, partial tuition waivers, Federal Work-Study, and career-related internships or fieldwork available. Aid available to part-time students. Financial aid application deadline: 3/1. • Dr. L. Lee Manzer, Head, 405-744-5202.

Oral Roberts University, School of Business, Tulsa, OK 74171-0001. Offerings include marketing (MBA). *Degree requirements:* Computer language required, thesis optional, foreign language not required. *Entrance requirements:* GMAT (minimum score 400; average 500). Application deadline: 7/31 (priority date; rolling processing; 12/31 for spring admission). Application fee: $35. Electronic applications accepted.

Pace University, Lubin School of Business, Marketing Program, New York, NY 10038. Offers marketing management (MBA), marketing research (MBA). Part-time and evening/weekend programs available. *Degree requirements:* Computer language required, foreign language not required. *Entrance requirements:* GMAT. Application deadline: 7/31 (priority date; rolling processing; 11/30 for spring admission). Application fee: $60. *Expenses:* Tuition $545 per credit. Fees $360 per year full-time, $53 per semester (minimum) part-time.

Pennsylvania State University University Park Campus, The Mary Jean and Frank P. Smeal College of Business Administration, MS Programs in Business Administration, Department of Marketing, University Park, PA 16802-1503. Awards MS. *Degree requirements:* Paper or thesis required, foreign language not required. *Entrance requirements:* GMAT. Application fee: $40. *Expenses:* Tuition $6534 per year full-time, $276 per credit part-time for state residents; $13,460 per year full-time, $561 per credit part-time for nonresidents. Fees $252 per year (minimum) full-time, $43 per semester (minimum) part-time. • Dr. Jerry C. Olson, Chairman, 814-865-6250.

Pennsylvania State University University Park Campus, The Mary Jean and Frank P. Smeal College of Business Administration, PhD Programs in Business Administration, Program in Marketing and Distribution, University Park, PA 16802-1503. Awards PhD. *Degree requirements:* Dissertation. *Entrance requirements:* GMAT. Application fee: $40. *Expenses:* Tuition $6534 per year full-time, $276 per credit part-time for state residents; $13,460 per year full-time, $561 per credit part-time for nonresidents. Fees $252 per year (minimum) full-time, $43 per semester (minimum) part-time. • Dr. Johann Baumgartner, Field Adviser, 814-863-3559.

Philadelphia College of Textiles and Science, School of Business, Program in Business, Philadelphia, PA 19144-5497. Offerings include marketing (MBA). *Entrance requirements:* GMAT, minimum GPA of 2.85. Application deadline: rolling. Application fee: $35. *Tuition:* $448 per credit hour. • Rita Powell, Director, 215-951-2950. Fax: 215-951-2652. E-mail: powellr@phila.col.edu. Application contact: Robert J. Reed, Director of Graduate Admissions, 215-951-2943. Fax: 215-951-2907. E-mail: gradadm@phila.col.edu.

Philadelphia College of Textiles and Science, School of Textiles and Materials Science, Program in Textile Marketing, Philadelphia, PA 19144-5497. Awards MS, MBA/MS. Part-time and evening/weekend programs available. *Entrance requirements:* GMAT, GRE, or MAT, minimum GPA of 2.75. Application deadline: rolling. Application fee: $35. *Tuition:* $448 per credit hour. *Financial aid:* Research assistantships, graduate assistantships, residential assistantships, Federal Work-Study, and career-related internships or fieldwork available. Financial aid applicants required to submit FAFSA. • Dr. Muthu Govindaraj, Director, 215-951-2684. Fax: 215-951-2651. E-mail: govindarajm@phila.col.edu. Application contact: Robert J. Reed, Director of Graduate Admissions, 215-951-2943. Fax: 215-951-2907. E-mail: gradadm@phila.col.edu.

Purdue University, Krannert Graduate School of Management, Department of Management, West Lafayette, IN 47907. Offerings include marketing (MSM, PhD). Department faculty: 51 full-time (5 women). *Degree requirements:* For doctorate, dissertation required, foreign language not required. *Average time to degree:* doctorate–4 years full-time. *Entrance requirements:* For

Directory: Marketing

Purdue University (continued)

doctorate, GMAT, TOEFL (minimum score 575). Application fee: $30. Electronic applications accepted. *Tuition:* $3500 per year full-time, $126 per credit hour part-time for state residents; $11,720 per year full-time, $387 per credit hour part-time for nonresidents. • Dr. J. J. McConnell, Director of Doctoral Programs, 765-494-4375. Application contact: Kelly Felty, Assistant Director of Administration for Doctoral Programs, 765-494-4375. Fax: 765-494-1526. E-mail: feltyk@mgmt.purdue.edu.

Quinnipiac College, School of Business, Program in Business Administration, Hamden, CT 06518-1904. Offerings include marketing (MBA). Program faculty: 17 full-time (2 women), 4 part-time (1 woman). *Degree requirements:* Thesis optional, foreign language not required. *Average time to degree:* master's–2 years full-time, 4 years part-time. *Entrance requirements:* GMAT (minimum score 400; average 470), interview, minimum GPA of 2.5. Application deadline: 8/1 (priority date; rolling processing). Application fee: $45. Electronic applications accepted. *Expenses:* Tuition $395 per credit hour. Fees $380 per year full-time. • Dr. Earl Chrysler, Director, 203-281-8799. Fax: 203-281-8664. E-mail: chrysler@quinnipiac.edu. Application contact: Scott Farber, Director of Graduate Admissions, 203-281-8795. Fax: 203-287-5238. E-mail: qcgradadmi@quinnipiac.edu.

Rensselaer Polytechnic Institute, Lally School of Management and Technology, Troy, NY 12180-3590. Offerings include business administration (MBA, PhD), with options in finance and accounting (MBA), information systems management (MBA), management (PhD), management of technology and entrepreneurships (MBA), manufacturing management (MBA), marketing management (MBA), operations research (MBA), organizational behavior and human resource management (MBA), statistical methods for management (MBA). Postbaccalaureate distance learning degree programs offered (no on-campus study). School faculty: 36 full-time (5 women), 6 part-time (0 women). *Application deadline:* 2/1 (priority date; rolling processing). *Application fee:* $35. *Expenses:* Tuition $630 per credit hour. Fees $1000 per year. • Dr. Joseph G. Ecker, Dean, 518-276-6802. Application contact: Michele Martens, Manager of Enrollment Services, 518-276-4800. Fax: 518-276-8661.

Robert Morris College, Program in Business Administration, 881 Narrows Run Road, Moon Township, PA 15108-1189. Offerings include marketing (MBA, MS). Only part-time programs offered. Program faculty: 35 full-time (6 women), 35 part-time (5 women). *Entrance requirements:* GMAT (minimum score 450), minimum GPA of 2.5. Application deadline: 8/1 (priority date; rolling processing; 11/30 for spring admission). Application fee: $25 ($35 for international students). *Expenses:* Tuition $328 per credit. Fees $15 per credit. • Dr. Joseph F. Constable, Dean, School of Management, 412-262-8451. Fax: 412-262-8494. E-mail: constabl@robert-morris.edu. Application contact: Vincent J. Kane, Recruiting Coordinator, 412-262-8535. Fax: 412-299-2425.

Rutgers, The State University of New Jersey, Newark, Department of Management, Newark, NJ 07102-3192. Offerings include marketing (PhD). Offered jointly with New Jersey Institute of Technology. Terminal master's awarded for partial completion of doctoral program. Department faculty: 113 full-time (13 women), 3 part-time (1 woman). *Degree requirements:* Dissertation, cumulative exams required, foreign language not required. *Average time to degree:* doctorate–5 years full-time, 7 years part-time. *Entrance requirements:* GMAT or GRE, minimum undergraduate B average. Application deadline: 4/1 (rolling processing; 11/1 for spring admission). Application fee: $40. *Expenses:* Tuition $6248 per year full-time, $257 per credit part-time for state residents; $9160 per year full-time, $380 per credit part-time for nonresidents. Fees $738 per year full-time, $107 per semester (minimum) part-time. • Glenn R. Shafer, Director, 973-353-1604. E-mail: gshafer@andromeda.rutgers.edu. Application contact: Ana Gonzalez, Program Secretary, 973-353-5371. Fax: 973-353-5691. E-mail: anag@gsmack.rutgers.edu.

Rutgers, The State University of New Jersey, Newark, Graduate School of Management, Department of Marketing, Newark, NJ 07102-3192. Awards MBA. *Degree requirements:* Computer language required, thesis not required. *Entrance requirements:* GMAT, TOEFL. Application deadline: 6/1 (rolling processing). Application fee: $40. *Financial aid:* Federal Work-Study, institutionally sponsored loans, and career-related internships or fieldwork available. Financial aid application deadline: 3/15; applicants required to submit FAFSA. • Dr. Elizabeth Hirschman, Chairman, 732-445-3525. Fax: 732-445-3236. E-mail: hirschma@everest.rutgers.edu. Application contact: Director of Admissions, 973-353-1234. Fax: 973-353-1592. E-mail: admit@gsmack.rutgers.edu.

Sage Graduate School, Graduate School, Division of Management Studies, Program in Business Administration, Troy, NY 12180-4115. Offerings include marketing (MBA). MBA/JD offered jointly with Albany Law School of Union University. Program faculty: 1 full-time (0 women), 10 part-time (1 woman). *Entrance requirements:* Minimum GPA of 2.75. Application fee: $25. *Expenses:* Tuition $360 per credit hour. Fees $50 per semester. • Application contact: Melissa Robertson, Associate Director of Admissions, 518-244-6878. Fax: 518-244-6880. E-mail: sgsadm@sage.edu.

St. Bonaventure University, School of Business Administration, St. Bonaventure, NY 14778-2284. Offerings include management and marketing (MBA). School faculty: 19 full-time (2 women), 3 part-time (0 women). *Average time to degree:* master's–1.5 years full-time, 3 years part-time. *Entrance requirements:* GMAT (minimum score 400), TOEFL (minimum score 600). Application deadline: 8/1 (rolling processing). Application fee: $35. *Tuition:* $8100 per year full-time, $450 per credit hour part-time. • Dr. Michael Fischer, Dean, 716-375-2200. Application contact: Brian C. McAllister, MBA Director, 716-375-2098. Fax: 716-375-2191. E-mail: bmac@sbu.edu.

St. Cloud State University, College of Business, Department of Marketing and General Business, St. Cloud, MN 56301-4498. Offers program in marketing (MBA). Part-time programs available. Faculty: 12 full-time (4 women). *Degree requirements:* Comprehensive exam required, foreign language and thesis not required. *Entrance requirements:* GMAT (minimum score 470), minimum GPA of 2.75. Application fee: $20 ($100 for international students). *Expenses:* Tuition $128 per credit for state residents; $203 per credit for nonresidents. Fees $16.32 per credit. *Financial aid:* Graduate assistantships, Federal Work-Study available. Financial aid application deadline: 3/1. • Application contact: Ann Anderson, Graduate Studies Office, 320-255-2113. Fax: 320-654-5371. E-mail: anna@grad.stcloud.msus.edu.

St. John's University, College of Business Administration, Department of Marketing, Jamaica, NY 11439. Awards MBA, Adv C. Part-time and evening/weekend programs available. Faculty: 10 full-time (1 woman), 3 part-time (0 women). Students: 18 full-time (7 women), 108 part-time (58 women); includes 20 minority (8 African Americans, 4 Asian Americans, 8 Hispanics), 14 international. Average age 28. 112 applicants, 71% accepted. In 1997, 42 master's awarded. *Degree requirements:* For master's, thesis optional, foreign language not required. *Entrance requirements:* For master's, GMAT. Application deadline: 6/1 (rolling processing; 10/1 for spring admission). Application fee: $40. *Expenses:* Tuition $600 per credit. Fees $150 per year. *Financial aid:* In 1997–98, 4 research assistantships (1 to a first-year student) averaging $667 per month were awarded; Federal Work-Study also available. Aid available to part-time students. Financial aid application deadline: 3/1; applicants required to submit FAFSA. • Dr. Herbert Katzenstein, Chair, 718-990-6391. Application contact: Shamus J. McGrenra, TOR, Associate Director, Graduate Admissions, 718-990-6107. Fax: 718-990-5736. E-mail: mcgrenrs@stjohns.edu.

Saint Joseph's University, Erivan K. Haub School of Business, Executive Program in Pharmaceutical Marketing, Philadelphia, PA 19131-1395. Awards MBA. Students: 112 part-time (55 women). In 1997, 33 degrees awarded. *Entrance requirements:* GMAT, TOEFL, 5 years of industry experience. Application deadline: rolling. Application fee: $0. Electronic applications accepted. *Tuition:* $470 per credit hour. • Dr. Gregory G. Dell'Omo, Dean, Erivan K. Haub School of Business, 610-660-1645. Fax: 610-660-1649. E-mail: gdellomo@sju.edu. Application contact: Adele C. Foley, Associate Dean, 610-660-1690. Fax: 610-660-1599. E-mail: afoley@sju.edu.

Saint Joseph's University, Erivan K. Haub School of Business, Department of Food Marketing, Executive Program in Food Marketing, Philadelphia, PA 19131-1395. Awards MS. Part-time and evening/weekend programs available. Students: 87 part-time (26 women). In 1997, 15 degrees awarded. *Entrance requirements:* GMAT or GRE, TOEFL, 5 years of industry experience. Application deadline: rolling. Application fee: $0. Electronic applications accepted. *Tuition:* $470 per credit hour. *Financial aid:* Research assistantships, Federal Work-Study, institutionally sponsored loans, and career-related internships or fieldwork available. Financial aid applicants required to submit FAFSA. • Joseph T. Lawlor, Administrator, 610-660-3152. Fax: 610-660-3160.

Saint Joseph's University, Erivan K. Haub School of Business, Programs in Graduate Business, Program in Marketing, Philadelphia, PA 19131-1395. Awards MBA. Evening/weekend programs available. Students: 121 (62 women). In 1997, 43 degrees awarded. *Entrance requirements:* GMAT, TOEFL. Application deadline: 7/15 (priority date; rolling processing; 11/15 for spring admission). Application fee: $35. *Tuition:* $510 per credit hour. *Financial aid:* Graduate assistantships available. Financial aid application deadline: 5/1. • Adele C. Foley, Associate Dean, Programs in Graduate Business, 610-660-1690. Fax: 610-660-1599. E-mail: afoley@sju.edu.

Saint Louis University, School of Business and Administration, Department of Marketing, 3674 Lindell Boulevard, St. Louis, MO 63108. Awards MBA, PhD. Part-time programs available. Faculty: 9 full-time (1 woman), 1 part-time (0 women). In 1997, 1 doctorate awarded. *Degree requirements:* For doctorate, dissertation. *Average time to degree:* doctorate–5 years full-time, 6 years part-time. *Entrance requirements:* For master's, GMAT, TOEFL; for doctorate, GMAT. Application deadline: 7/15 (rolling processing; 11/15 for spring admission). Application fee: $40. *Financial aid:* Fellowships, research assistantships, teaching assistantships, Federal Work-Study available. Aid available to part-time students. • Dr. Paul D. Boughton, Chairman, 314-977-3868.

St. Thomas Aquinas College, Division of Business Administration, Sparkill, NY 10976. Offerings include marketing (MBA). Division faculty: 7 full-time (2 women), 8 part-time (0 women). *Entrance requirements:* GMAT. Application deadline: rolling. Application fee: $35. Electronic applications accepted. *Expenses:* Tuition $390 per credit. Fees $10 per year. • Barbara Donn, Chairperson, 914-398-4113. Fax: 914-359-8136. Application contact: Joseph L. Chillo, Executive Director of Enrollment Services, 914-398-4100. Fax: 914-398-4224. E-mail: joestacenroll@rockland.net.

Saint Xavier University, Graham School of Management, Chicago, IL 60655-3105. Offerings include marketing (MBA). School faculty: 15 full-time (2 women), 6 part-time (3 women). *Entrance requirements:* GMAT, minimum GPA of 3.0, 2 years of work experience. Application deadline: 8/15. Application fee: $35. *Expenses:* Tuition $455 per hour. Fees $50 per year. • Dr. John Eber, Dean, 773-298-3601. Fax: 773-298-3610. E-mail: eber@sxu.edu. Application contact: Sr. Evelyn McKenna, Vice President of Enrollment Management, 773-298-3050. Fax: 773-298-3076. E-mail: mckenna@sxu.edu.

San Diego State University, Graduate School of Business, Department of Marketing, San Diego, CA 92182. Awards MBA, MS. Part-time and evening/weekend programs available. Students: 12 full-time (5 women), 43 part-time (26 women); includes 8 minority (2 African Americans, 3 Asian Americans, 3 Hispanics), 8 international. Average age 30. *Degree requirements:* Thesis or alternative required, foreign language not required. *Average time to degree:* master's–2 years full-time, 3.5 years part-time. *Entrance requirements:* GMAT (minimum score 550), TOEFL (minimum score 570). Application deadline: 4/15 (priority date; rolling processing; 11/1 for spring admission). Application fee: $55. Electronic applications accepted. *Expenses:* Tuition $0 for state residents; $246 per unit for nonresidents. Fees $1932 per year full-time, $1266 per year part-time. *Financial aid:* Fellowships, research assistantships, teaching assistantships, and career-related internships or fieldwork available. • George E. Belch, Chair, 619-594-5317. Fax: 619-594-1573. E-mail: gbelch@mail.sdsu.edu. Application contact: Patricia Martin, Director of Admissions, 619-594-5217. Fax: 619-594-1863. E-mail: sdsumba@mail.sdsu.edu.

Seton Hall University, W. Paul Stillman School of Business, Department of Marketing, South Orange, NJ 07079-2692. Awards MBA. Part-time and evening/weekend programs available. Faculty: 6 full-time (1 woman), 3 part-time (0 women). *Degree requirements:* Thesis optional, foreign language not required. *Entrance requirements:* GMAT (minimum score 500), TOEFL (minimum score 550). Application deadline: 6/1 (priority date; rolling processing). Application fee: $50. *Expenses:* Tuition $538 per credit. Fees $185 per semester. *Financial aid:* Research assistantships and career-related internships or fieldwork available. Aid available to part-time students. Financial aid applicants required to submit FAFSA. • Dr. Joseph Wisenblit, Chairperson, 973-761-9242. E-mail: wisenbjo@shu.edu. Application contact: Student Information Office, 973-761-9222. Fax: 973-761-9217. E-mail: busgrad@shu.edu.

Simon Fraser University, Faculty of Business Administration, Burnaby, BC V5A 1S6, Canada. Offerings include marketing (MBA). Faculty: 48 full-time (12 women). *Application fee:* $55. *Expenses:* Tuition $2400 per year (minimum). Fees $207 per year. • S. McShane, Director, 604-291-3639. Application contact: Program Assistant, 604-291-3047. Fax: 604-291-3404. E-mail: mba@sfu.ca.

Southeastern University, Program in Marketing, Washington, DC 20024-2788. Awards MBA. Part-time and evening/weekend programs available. Faculty: 4 full-time (1 woman), 17 part-time (1 woman), 8 FTE. Students: 10 full-time (6 women), 8 part-time (3 women); includes 10 minority (all African Americans), 8 international. Average age 29. 8 applicants, 63% accepted. In 1997, 11 degrees awarded. *Degree requirements:* Computer language. *Entrance requirements:* TOEFL. Application deadline: rolling. Application fee: $45. *Expenses:* Tuition $228 per credit hour. Fees $175 per quarter. *Financial aid:* Federal Work-Study and career-related internships or fieldwork available. Aid available to part-time students. Financial aid applicants required to submit FAFSA. • Dr. Mohammed Safa, Head, 202-488-8162. Application contact: Jack Flinter, Director of Admissions, 202-265-5343. Fax: 202-488-8093.

State University of New York at Albany, School of Business, Department of Marketing, Albany, NY 12222-0001. Awards MBA. Faculty: 6 full-time (0 women), 1 (woman) part-time. Students: 9 full-time (4 women); includes 2 international. *Degree requirements:* Field study project. *Entrance requirements:* GMAT. Application deadline: 7/1 (priority date; rolling processing). Application fee: $50. *Expenses:* Tuition $5100 per year full-time, $213 per credit hour part-time for state residents; $8416 per year full-time, $351 per credit hour part-time for nonresidents. Fees $705 per year full-time, $26.85 per credit hour part-time. *Financial aid:* Application deadline 4/1. *Faculty research:* Sales management, buyer-seller interaction, family decision making, sociological influence on consumption, health promotion. • W. Christian Buss, Chair, 518-442-4965. Application contact: Jeffrey Collins, Assistant Director, Graduate Admissions, 518-442-3980.

Stephen F. Austin State University, College of Business, Program in Business Administration, Nacogdoches, TX 75962. Offerings include management and marketing (MBA). Program faculty: 23 full-time (5 women). *Degree requirements:* Computer language, comprehensive exam required, foreign language and thesis not required. *Entrance requirements:* GMAT, minimum AACSB index of 1000. Application deadline: 7/15 (rolling processing; 11/15 for spring admission). Application fee: $0 ($25 for international students). *Tuition:* $1465 per year full-time, $263 per semester (minimum) part-time for state residents; $5299 per year full-time, $890 per semester (minimum) part-time for nonresidents. • Dr. Warren Fisher, Graduate Director, 409-468-3101.

Syracuse University, School of Management, PhD Program in Business Administration, Syracuse, NY 13244-0003. Offerings include marketing (PhD). Program faculty: 75. *Entrance requirements:* GMAT (minimum score 600). Application deadline: 2/1. Application fee: $40. *Tuition:* $13,320 per year full-time, $555 per credit hour part-time. • S. P. Raj, Associate Dean. Application contact: Barbara Buske, Secretary, 315-443-1001.

Syracuse University, School of Management, Program in Marketing, Syracuse, NY 13244-0003. Awards MBA. Students: 17 full-time (6 women), 27 part-time (9 women); includes 5 minority (2 African Americans, 1 Asian American, 2 Hispanics), 14 international. 104 applicants, 44% accepted. In 1997, 18 degrees awarded. *Entrance requirements:* GMAT. Application deadline: 2/1. Application fee: $40. *Tuition:* $13,320 per year full-time, $555 per credit hour part-time. *Financial aid:* Fellowships, research assistantships, teaching assistantships, partial tuition waivers, Federal Work-Study available. Financial aid application deadline: 3/1. • Frances Tucker, Chair, 315-443-2691. Application contact: Associate Dean, 315-443-3850.

Temple University, School of Business and Management, Doctoral Program in Business Administration, Philadelphia, PA 19122-6096. Offerings include marketing (PhD). *Degree requirements:* Dissertation, preliminary exams required, foreign language not required. *Entrance requirements:* GMAT, TOEFL (minimum score 600), master's degree, minimum GPA of 3.5. Application deadline: 1/15 (rolling processing). Application fee: $40. *Expenses:* Tuition $323 per semester hour for state residents; $444 per semester hour for nonresidents. Fees $170 per year full-time, $28 per semester (minimum) part-time. • Dr. Roland Lipka, Director, 215-204-8125. Fax: 215-204-5574. Application contact: Linda Whelan, Director, 215-204-7678. Fax: 215-204-8300.

Temple University, School of Business and Management, Master's Program in Business Administration, Philadelphia, PA 19122-6096. Offerings include marketing (MBA, MS). Program faculty: 72 full-time (13 women). *Entrance requirements:* GMAT (average 540), TOEFL (minimum score 575). Application fee: $40. *Expenses:* Tuition $323 per semester hour for state residents; $444 per semester hour for nonresidents. Fees $170 per year full-time, $28 per semester (minimum) part-time. • Application contact: Linda Whelan, Director, 215-204-7678. Fax: 215-204-8300. E-mail: linda@astro.ocis.temple.edu.

Texas A&M University, Lowry Mays Graduate School of Business, Department of Marketing, College Station, TX 77843-4113. Awards MS, PhD. Faculty: 18 full-time (1 woman). Students: 27 full-time (16 women). Average age 30. 53 applicants, 25% accepted. In 1997, 7 master's, 3 doctorates awarded. Terminal master's awarded for partial completion of doctoral program. *Degree requirements:* For master's, oral comprehensive exam required, foreign language and thesis not required; for doctorate, dissertation required, foreign language not required. *Average time to degree:* master's–1.5 years full-time; doctorate–4 years full-time. *Entrance requirements:* For master's, GMAT, TOEFL (minimum score 600); for doctorate, GMAT or GRE General Test, TOEFL. Application deadline: 3/1 (priority date; rolling processing; 8/1 for spring admission). Application fee: $35 ($75 for international students). *Financial aid:* 16 students received aid; fellowships, research assistantships, teaching assistantships, institutionally sponsored loans, and career-related internships or fieldwork available. Financial aid application deadline: 2/1. *Faculty research:* Consumer behavior, innovation and product management, international marketing, marketing management and strategy, services marketing, customer satisfaction. • P. Rajan Varadarajan, Head, 409-845-5861. Application contact: Samuel M. Gillespie, Adviser, 409-847-8876. Fax: 409-862-2811. E-mail: smgillespie@tamu.edu.

Texas Tech University, Graduate School, College of Business Administration, Program in Marketing, Lubbock, TX 79409. Awards MSBA, PhD. Part-time programs available. Faculty: 8 full-time (1 woman). Students: 8 full-time (2 women); includes 3 international. Average age 27. 14 applicants, 43% accepted. In 1997, 3 doctorates awarded (100% entered university research/teaching). *Degree requirements:* For master's, computer language, comprehensive exam required, foreign language and thesis not required; for doctorate, computer language, dissertation, qualifying exams required, foreign language not required. *Entrance requirements:* For master's, GMAT (minimum score 500; average 580); for doctorate, GMAT (minimum score 580; average 620). Application deadline: 4/15 (priority date; rolling processing; 9/30 for spring admission). Application fee: $25 ($50 for international students). *Expenses:* Tuition $864 per year full-time, $120 per semester (minimum) part-time for state residents; $5976 per year full-time, $747 per semester (minimum) part-time for nonresidents. Fees $2321 per year full-time, $302 per semester (minimum) part-time. *Financial aid:* Federal Work-Study available. *Faculty research:* Consumer behavior, macromarketing, marketing strategy and strategic planning. • Dr. James B. Wilcox, Interim Coordinator, 806-742-3162. Fax: 806-742-2099. Application contact: Nancy Dodge, Director, 806-742-3184. Fax: 806-742-3958.

United States International University, College of Business Administration, San Diego, CA 92131-1799. Offerings include international business (MIBA, DBA), with options in finance (DBA), marketing (DBA). Terminal master's awarded for partial completion of doctoral program. College faculty: 13 full-time (4 women), 14 part-time (6 women), 20 FTE. *Degree requirements:* Computer language, dissertation required, foreign language not required. *Average time to degree:* master's–1.5 years full-time, 2.5 years part-time; doctorate–3 years full-time, 5 years part-time. *Entrance requirements:* GMAT (minimum score 490; average 560), minimum GPA of 3.3. Application deadline: rolling. Application fee: $40. Electronic applications accepted. *Expenses:* Tuition $360 per unit. Fees $120 per year. • Dr. Mink H. Stavenga, Dean, 619-635-4695. Fax: 619-635-4528. E-mail: mstaveng@usiu.edu. Application contact: Susan Topham, Assistant Director of Admissions, 619-635-4885. Fax: 619-635-4739. E-mail: admissions@usiu.edu.

United States International University–Africa, College of Business Administration, PO Box 14634, Nairobi, Kenya. Offerings include marketing (MBA, MIBA). College faculty: 15 full-time (2 women), 50 part-time (5 women). *Application deadline:* (2/8 for spring admission). *Application fee:* $55. • Application contact: Office of Admissions, 254-2-802532. Fax: 254-2-803764. E-mail: usiu_adm@usiu.edu.

Universidad del Turabo, Programs in Business Administration, Program in Marketing, Gurabo, PR 00778-3030. Awards MBA. Part-time and evening/weekend programs available. *Entrance requirements:* GRE, PAEG, interview. Application deadline: 8/5. Application fee: $25.

Universidad Metropolitana, School of Business Administration, Río Piedras, PR 00928-1150. Offerings include marketing (MBA). School faculty: 4 full-time (2 women), 24 part-time (10 women). *Average time to degree:* master's–1.5 years full-time, 3 years part-time. *Entrance requirements:* GMAT (score in 70th percentile or higher), PAEG (score in 60th percentile or higher). Application deadline: 8/31 (priority date; rolling processing; 1/15 for spring admission). Application fee: $0. • Pedro Hernández, Dean, 787-766-1717 Ext. 6255.

Université de Sherbrooke, Faculty of Administration, Program in Marketing, Sherbrooke, PQ J1K 2R1, Canada. Awards M Sc. *Application deadline:* 5/31. *Application fee:* $15.

The University of Akron, College of Business Administration, Department of Marketing, Akron, OH 44325-0001. Awards MBA, JD/MBA. Programs in international business (MBA), marketing (MBA). Part-time and evening/weekend programs available. Students: 23 full-time (10 women), 36 part-time (16 women); includes 2 minority (both Asian Americans), 15 international. Average age 30. In 1997, 17 degrees awarded. *Entrance requirements:* GMAT (minimum score 450), minimum GPA of 2.75. Application deadline: 8/15 (rolling processing). Application fee: $25 ($50 for international students). *Expenses:* Tuition $178 per credit hour for state residents; $333 per credit hour for nonresidents. Fees $145 per year full-time, $32 per semester (minimum) part-time. *Financial aid:* In 1997–98, 8 students received aid, including 5 research assistantships; teaching assistantships, partial tuition waivers also available. Financial aid application deadline: 4/30. *Faculty research:* Retailing, branding, international marketing. • Dr. Dale M. Lewison, Chair, 330-972-6306. E-mail: dlewison@uakron.edu. Application contact: Dr. J. Daniel Williams, Director of Graduate Business Programs, 330-972-7043. E-mail: jwilliams@uakron.edu.

The University of Alabama, The Manderson Graduate School of Business, Department of Marketing and Management, Tuscaloosa, AL 35487. Awards MA, MSC, PhD. Faculty: 27 full-time (4 women). Students: 32 full-time (12 women), 25 part-time (10 women); includes 6 minority (2 African Americans, 4 Asian Americans). Average age 33. 34 applicants, 53% accepted. In 1997, 8 master's awarded; 3 doctorates awarded (100% entered university research/teaching). Terminal master's awarded for partial completion of doctoral program. *Degree requirements:* For master's, comprehensive exam (MA), thesis (MSC) required, foreign language not required; for doctorate, 1 foreign language (computer language can substitute), dissertation, comprehensive exam. *Average time to degree:* master's–1 year full-time, 2.5 years part-time; doctorate–5 years full-time. *Entrance requirements:* For master's, GMAT (minimum score 550), TOEFL (minimum score 500), minimum GPA of 2.75; for doctorate, GMAT (average 630), TOEFL (minimum score 550), minimum GPA of 2.75. Application deadline: 7/6 (rolling processing). Application fee: $25. *Tuition:* $2684 per year full-time, $594 per semester (minimum) part-time for state residents; $7216 per year full-time, $1248 per semester (minimum) part-time for nonresidents. *Financial aid:* In 1997–98, 31 students received aid, including 2 fellowships (1 to a first-year student) averaging $750 per month and totaling $10,000, 12 research assistantships (6 to first-year students) averaging $750 per month, 14 teaching assistantships averaging $750 per month. • Dr. Ron Dulek, Chairman, 205-348-8930.

University of Alberta, Faculty of Graduate Studies and Research, Doctoral Program in Business, Edmonton, AB T6G 2E1, Canada. Offerings include marketing (PhD). Terminal master's awarded for partial completion of doctoral program. Program faculty: 34 full-time (5 women). *Degree requirements:* Dissertation required, foreign language not required. *Average time to degree:* doctorate–6 years full-time, 8.5 years part-time. *Entrance requirements:* GMAT (average 675), TOEFL (minimum score 600; average 627). Application deadline: 3/1 (priority date). Application fee: $60. *Expenses:* Tuition $390 per course for Canadian residents; $781 per course for nonresidents. Fees $500 per year full-time, $184 per year part-time. • Dr. Michael Gibbins, Director, 403-492-2361. Application contact: Jeanette Gosine, Department Office, 403-492-2361. Fax: 403-492-3325. E-mail: jgosine@gpu.srv.ualberta.ca.

The University of Arizona, College of Business and Public Administration, Karl Eller Graduate School of Management, Department of Marketing, Tucson, AZ 85721. Awards MS. *Entrance requirements:* GMAT, GRE General Test, TOEFL (minimum score 550), TSE, minimum GPA of 3.0. Application deadline: 7/1 (rolling processing). Application fee: $35. *Tuition:* $2162 per year full-time, $337 per semester (minimum) part-time for state residents; $6860 per year full-time, $1138 per semester (minimum) part-time for nonresidents. *Faculty research:* Buyer behavior, marketing and economic development, marketing management.

University of British Columbia, Faculty of Commerce and Business Administration, Doctoral Program in Commerce and Business Administration, Vancouver, BC V6T 1Z2, Canada. Offerings include marketing (PhD). *Degree requirements:* Dissertation required, foreign language not required. *Entrance requirements:* GMAT or GRE, TOEFL. Application deadline: 12/31 (priority date; rolling processing). Application fee: $60.

University of California, Berkeley, Haas School of Business, Doctoral Program in Business, Berkeley, CA 94720-1500. Offerings include marketing (PhD). Program faculty: 64 full-time (11 women). *Degree requirements:* Dissertation, oral exam, written preliminary exams required, foreign language not required. *Entrance requirements:* GMAT or GRE, TOEFL, minimum GPA of 3.0. Application deadline: 2/10. Application fee: $40. *Expenses:* Tuition $0 for state residents; $9384 per year for nonresidents. Fees $4409 per year. • Dr. David C. Mowery, Director, 510-643-9992. E-mail: jan@haas.berkeley.edu. Application contact: Jan Price Greenough, Coordinator, 510-642-1409. Fax: 510-643-6659. E-mail: jan@haas.berkeley.edu.

University of Cincinnati, College of Business Administration, Department of Marketing, Cincinnati, OH 45221. Awards MBA, PhD. Part-time and evening/weekend programs available. Faculty: 11 full-time. Students: 19 full-time (9 women), 46 part-time (13 women); includes 7 minority (4 African Americans, 3 Asian Americans), 8 international. 37 applicants, 35% accepted. In 1997, 20 master's, 5 doctorates awarded. *Degree requirements:* For doctorate, computer language, dissertation. *Average time to degree:* master's–1.9 years full-time; doctorate–5.1 years full-time. *Entrance requirements:* GMAT. Application fee: $30. *Tuition:* $7228 per year full-time, $185 per credit hour part-time for state residents; $13,812 per year full-time, $352 per credit hour part-time for nonresidents. *Financial aid:* Fellowships, graduate assistantships, full tuition waivers available. Aid available to part-time students. Financial aid application deadline: 2/15. *Faculty research:* Advertising, consumer behavior, marketing channels, sales management. • Dr. F. Robert Dwyer, Head, 513-556-7103. Application contact: Chris Allen, Graduate Program Director, 513-556-7100. Fax: 513-556-4891.

University of Colorado at Boulder, Graduate School of Business Administration, Division of Marketing, Boulder, CO 80309. Awards MBA, PhD. Students: 40 full-time (18 women); includes 4 minority (1 African American, 2 Asian Americans, 1 Hispanic), 5 international. Average age 29. 100 applicants, 37% accepted. *Degree requirements:* For master's, computer language required, foreign language and thesis not required; for doctorate, dissertation, research internship. *Entrance requirements:* GMAT. Application deadline: 3/1 (priority date; rolling processing). Application fee: $40 ($60 for international students). *Expenses:* Tuition $3594 per year (minimum) full-time, $597 per semester (minimum) part-time for state residents; $14,868 per year (minimum) full-time, $2478 per semester (minimum) part-time for nonresidents. Fees $667 per year full-time, $130 per semester (minimum) part-time. *Financial aid:* Application deadline 3/1. • Charles Goeldner, Chair, 303-492-3650. Fax: 303-492-5962. E-mail: charles.goeldner@colorado.edu. Application contact: Diana Marinaro, Graduate Student Admissions, 303-492-1831. Fax: 303-492-1727. E-mail: busgrad@spot.colorado.edu.

University of Colorado at Colorado Springs, Graduate School of Business Administration, Colorado Springs, CO 80933-7150. Offerings include marketing (MBA). School faculty: 24 full-time (4 women). *Entrance requirements:* GMAT. Application deadline: 6/1 (priority date; 11/1 for spring admission). Application fee: $50. *Expenses:* Tuition $2860 per year full-time, $121 per credit hour part-time for state residents; $10,254 per year full-time, $420 per credit hour part-time for nonresidents. Fees $399 per year (minimum) full-time, $106 per year (minimum) part-time. • Dr. Richard Dicenza, Dean, 719-262-3113. E-mail: rdicenz@mail.uccs.edu. Application contact: Diane Belger, Adviser, 719-262-3408. Fax: 719-262-3494. E-mail: dbelger@mail.uccs.edu.

University of Colorado at Denver, Graduate School of Business Administration, Division of Marketing, Denver, CO 80217-3364. Awards MS, MBA/MS. Part-time and evening/weekend programs available. Faculty: 8 full-time. Students: 64. In 1997, 21 degrees awarded. *Entrance requirements:* GMAT (minimum score 400; average 520), TOEFL (minimum score 525; average 560). Application deadline: 7/1 (priority date; rolling processing; 11/1 for spring admission). Application fee: $50 ($60 for international students). *Expenses:* Tuition $3754 per year full-time, $225 per semester hour part-time for state residents; $12,962 per year full-time, $777 per semester hour part-time for nonresidents. Fees $252 per year. *Financial aid:* Application deadline 4/1. • Clifford E. Young, Director, 303-556-5816. Fax: 303-556-5899. Application contact: Lori Cain, Graduate Business Admissions Office, 303-556-5900. Fax: 303-556-5904. E-mail: lori_cain@maroon.cudenver.edu.

University of Connecticut, School of Business Administration, Storrs, CT 06269. Offerings include marketing (MBA, PhD). School faculty: 63. *Degree requirements:* For doctorate, dissertation. *Entrance requirements:* For master's, GMAT; for doctorate, GMAT, TOEFL. Application deadline: 6/1 (priority date; rolling processing; 11/1 for spring admission). Application fee: $40 ($45 for international students). *Expenses:* Tuition $5272 per year full-time, $293 per credit part-time for state residents; $13,696 per year full-time, $761 per credit part-time for nonresidents. Fees $948 per year full-time, $640 per year part-time. • Thomas G. Gutteridge, Dean, 860-486-3096. Application contact: David W. Palmer, Chairperson, 860-486-3096.

University of Dallas, Graduate School of Management, Program in Marketing, Irving, TX 75062-4799. Awards MBA, MM. Part-time programs available. Students: 74 (41 women). In 1997, 31 degrees awarded. *Average time to degree:* master's–1.3 years full-time, 2.5 years part-time. *Entrance requirements:* GMAT (minimum score 400), TOEFL (average 520), minimum GPA of 3.0. Application deadline: 8/6 (priority date; rolling processing; 12/8 for spring admission). Application fee: $25 ($50 for international students). *Expenses:* Tuition $380 per credit hour. Fees $125 per year. *Financial aid:* Application deadline 2/15. • Dr. Bernie Cunningham,

Directory: Marketing

University of Dallas (continued)

Director, 972-721-5034. Fax: 972-721-5130. Application contact: Roxanne Del Rio, Director of Admissions, 972-721-5174. Fax: 972-721-4009. E-mail: admiss@gsm.udallas.edu.

University of Denver, Daniels College of Business, Department of Marketing, Denver, CO 80208. Awards MBA, MIM. Part-time and evening/weekend programs available. Faculty: 10 full-time (1 woman). Students: 50 full-time (31 women), 6 part-time (4 women); includes 2 minority (1 Asian American, 1 Hispanic), 17 international. 70 applicants, 91% accepted. In 1997, 4 degrees awarded. *Entrance requirements:* GMAT (average 545). Application deadline: 5/1 (priority date; rolling processing; 1/1 for spring admission). Application fee: $50. *Expenses:* Tuition $18,216 per year full-time, $506 per credit hour part-time. Fees $159 per year. *Financial aid:* In 1997–98, 17 students received aid, including 2 teaching assistantships averaging $619 per month and totaling $12,067, 8 grants, scholarships totaling $6,560; research assistantships, Federal Work-Study, institutionally sponsored loans, and career-related internships or fieldwork also available. Aid available to part-time students. Financial aid application deadline: 2/15; applicants required to submit FAFSA. *Faculty research:* Social policy issues in marketing, price bundling, marketing to the disabled, marketing to the elderly, international marketing and logistics. • Dr. John Burnett, Chair, 303-871-3317. Application contact: Jan Johnson, Executive Director, Student Services, 303-871-3416. Fax: 303-871-4466. E-mail: dcb@du.edu.

The University of Findlay, College of Professional Studies, MBA Program, 1000 North Main Street, Findlay, OH 45840-3653. Offerings include marketing (MBA). Postbaccalaureate distance learning degree programs offered (minimal on-campus study). Program faculty: 9 full-time (0 women), 6 part-time (0 women), 11 FTE. *Degree requirements:* Cumulative project. *Average time to degree:* master's–1.5 years full-time, 2.5 years part-time. *Entrance requirements:* GMAT, TOEFL. Application deadline: 8/15 (rolling processing; 12/15 for spring admission). Application fee: $25. *Tuition:* $299 per semester hour. • Dr. Theodore C. Alex, Director, 419-424-4704. Fax: 419-424-4822.

University of Florida, College of Business Administration, Department of Marketing, Gainesville, FL 32611. Awards MA, PhD. Faculty: 18. Students: 8 full-time (3 women), 7 part-time (2 women); includes 3 minority (2 African Americans, 1 Hispanic), 7 international. 36 applicants, 6% accepted. In 1997, 1 master's, 2 doctorates awarded. Terminal master's awarded for partial completion of doctoral program. *Degree requirements:* For master's, thesis optional, foreign language not required; for doctorate, dissertation required, foreign language not required. *Entrance requirements:* For master's, GMAT or GRE General Test, minimum GPA of 3.0; for doctorate, GMAT (minimum score 600) or GRE General Test (minimum combined score of 1250), minimum GPA of 3.0. Application deadline: 2/16 (rolling processing). Application fee: $20. *Tuition:* $138 per credit hour for state residents; $481 per credit hour for nonresidents. *Financial aid:* In 1997–98, 8 fellowships averaging $1,688 per month, 8 research assistantships averaging $652 per month were awarded; teaching assistantships, graduate assistantships, institutionally sponsored loans, and career-related internships or fieldwork also available. Financial aid application deadline: 2/10. *Faculty research:* Consumer behavior, advertising and sales promotion, sales management, pricing and retailing, mathematical models of marketing phenomena. • Dr. Bart Weitz, Chair, 352-392-8436 Ext. 1238. E-mail: bweitz@dale.cba.ufl. Application contact: Dr. Chris Janiszewski, Graduate Coordinator, 352-392-8436 Ext. 1240. Fax: 352-392-6250. E-mail: chrisj@dale.cba.ufl.edu.

University of Hartford, Barney School of Business and Public Administration, Program in Business Administration, West Hartford, CT 06117-1599. Offerings include marketing (MBA). Program faculty: 24 full-time (4 women), 15 part-time (1 woman). *Average time to degree:* master's–1.5 years full-time, 3 years part-time. *Entrance requirements:* GMAT, TOEFL. Application deadline: 7/1 (priority date; rolling processing; 12/1 for spring admission). Application fee: $35 ($50 for international students). Electronic applications accepted. • Christopher Galligan, Director, 860-768-4390. Application contact: Claire Silverstein, Assistant Director, 860-768-4900. Fax: 860-768-4821. E-mail: silverste@unavax.hartford.edu.

University of Houston, College of Business Administration, Department of Marketing and Entrepreneurship, 4800 Calhoun, Houston, TX 77204-2163. Awards MBA, PhD. Part-time and evening/weekend programs available. Faculty: 9 full-time (3 women), 11 part-time (2 women). Students: 40 full-time (22 women), 35 part-time (13 women); includes 16 minority (6 African Americans, 6 Asian Americans, 4 Hispanics), 14 international. Average age 30. In 1997, 14 master's awarded. *Degree requirements:* For master's, computer language required, foreign language and thesis not required; for doctorate, computer language, dissertation, comprehensive exam required, foreign language not required. *Average time to degree:* master's–2 years full-time, 3.5 years part-time; doctorate–4.5 years full-time. *Entrance requirements:* For master's, GMAT (average 590), TOEFL (minimum score 620); for doctorate, GMAT or GRE. Application deadline: 5/1 (rolling processing; 10/1 for spring admission). Application fee: $50 ($125 for international students). *Expenses:* Tuition $1152 per year full-time, $120 per semester (minimum) part-time for state residents; $4482 per year full-time, $249 per credit hour part-time for nonresidents. Fees $977 per year full-time, $119 per semester (minimum) part-time. *Financial aid:* Research assistantships, teaching assistantships, and career-related internships or fieldwork available. Aid available to part-time students. Financial aid application deadline: 3/1; applicants required to submit FAFSA. • Dr. Ed Blair, Chair, 713-743-4646. Application contact: Office of Student Services, 713-743-4900. Fax: 713-743-4942. E-mail: oss@cba.uh.edu.

University of Illinois at Chicago, College of Business Administration, Department of Marketing, Chicago, IL 60607-7128. Awards PhD. Faculty: 9 full-time (0 women). Students: 8 full-time (1 woman), 3 part-time (1 woman); includes 3 minority (1 African American, 1 Asian American, 1 Hispanic), 4 international. Average age 39. 21 applicants, 10% accepted. *Degree requirements:* Dissertation required, foreign language not required. *Entrance requirements:* GMAT, TOEFL (minimum score 550), minimum GPA of 3.75 on a 5.0 scale. Application deadline: 5/1. Application fee: $40 ($50 for international students). *Financial aid:* In 1997–98, 3 research assistantships, 6 teaching assistantships were awarded; fellowships also available. • Robert Weigard, Director of Graduate Studies, 312-996-4361. Application contact: Ann Rosi, 312-996-4751.

The University of Iowa, College of Business Administration, Department of Marketing, Iowa City, IA 52242-1316. Awards PhD. Faculty: 8 full-time (1 woman), 1 (woman) part-time, 8.5 FTE. Students: 8 full-time (3 women), 3 part-time (2 women); includes 1 minority (African American), 4 international. Average age 35. 47 applicants, 6% accepted. In 1997, 1 degree awarded (100% entered university research/teaching). *Degree requirements:* Dissertation required, foreign language not required. *Average time to degree:* doctorate–5 years full-time. *Entrance requirements:* GMAT (minimum score 600; average 630), TOEFL (minimum score 600). Application deadline: 1/15 (priority date). Application fee: $30 ($50 for international students). *Expenses:* Tuition $3166 per year full-time, $176 per semester hour part-time for state residents; $10,202 per year full-time, $176 per semester hour part-time for nonresidents. Fees $202 per year full-time, $52 per year (minimum) part-time. *Financial aid:* In 1997–98, 8 fellowships (2 to first-year students) averaging $1,413 per month, 2 research assistantships, 5 teaching assistantships averaging $1,413 per month and totaling $59,793 were awarded; full and partial tuition waivers also available. Financial aid application deadline: 2/1. *Faculty research:* Marketing decision making, marketing response, category management. • John Delaney, Chair, 319-335-1013. Application contact: Catherine Till, Graduate Secretary, 319-335-1013. Fax: 319-335-3690. E-mail: catherine-till@uiowa.edu.

University of Kansas, School of Business, Program in Marketing, Lawrence, KS 66045. Awards PhD. *Degree requirements:* Dissertation, departmental qualifying exam required, foreign language not required. *Application deadline:* 1/15. *Application fee:* $50. *Expenses:* Tuition $2400 per year full-time, $100 per credit hour part-time for state residents; $7890 per year full-time, $329 per credit hour part-time for nonresidents. Fees $428 per year full-time, $31 per credit hour part-time. *Financial aid:* Fellowships, research assistantships, teaching assistantships available. *Faculty research:* Choice modeling, product management, salesforce management. • Application contact: Student Advising Center, 785-864-4254. Fax: 785-864-5328. E-mail: grad@bschool.ukans.edu.

University of Manitoba, Faculty of Management, Department of Business Administration, Program in Marketing, Winnipeg, MB R3T 2N2, Canada. Awards MBA. *Degree requirements:* Thesis or alternative. *Application deadline:* 5/1.

The University of Memphis, Fogelman College of Business and Economics, Program in Business Administration, Memphis, TN 38152. Offerings include marketing (MBA, MS, PhD). Program faculty: 92 full-time (15 women), 2 part-time (0 women). *Degree requirements:* For master's, comprehensive exams required, thesis not required; for doctorate, dissertation, comprehensive exams. *Entrance requirements:* For master's, GMAT (minimum score 430; average 535), GRE General Test; for doctorate, GMAT (average 633), interview, minimum GPA of 3.4. Application deadline: 8/1 (12/1 for spring admission). Application fee: $25 ($50 for international students). *Tuition:* $2862 per year full-time, $166 per credit hour part-time for state residents; $6696 per year full-time, $379 per credit hour part-time for nonresidents. • Application contact: Dr. Ravinder Nath, Associate Dean of Academic Programs, 901-678-3721. Fax: 901-678-4705. E-mail: fcbegp@memphis.edu.

University of Minnesota, Twin Cities Campus, Carlson School of Management, Department of Marketing and Logistics Management, Minneapolis, MN 55455-0213. Awards MBA, PhD. MBA offered jointly with the Master's Program in Business Administration; PhD offered jointly with the Doctoral Program in Business Administration. *Degree requirements:* For doctorate, dissertation required, foreign language not required. *Entrance requirements:* GMAT. *Faculty research:* Consumer behavior, new product development, supply chain management, brand management.

University of Missouri–St. Louis, School of Business Administration, Program in Business Administration, St. Louis, MO 63121-4499. Offerings include marketing (MBA). Program faculty: 19 (3 women). *Entrance requirements:* GMAT (minimum score 500; average 554). Application deadline: 7/1 (rolling processing; 11/1 for spring admission). Application fee: $0. Electronic applications accepted. *Expenses:* Tuition $3903 per year full-time, $167 per credit hour part-time for state residents; $11,745 per year full-time, $489 per credit hour part-time for nonresidents. Fees $816 per year full-time, $34 per credit hour part-time. • Application contact: Graduate Admissions, 314-516-5458. Fax: 314-516-6759. E-mail: gradadm@umslvma.umsl.edu.

University of Missouri–St. Louis, School of Business Administration, Program in Marketing, St. Louis, MO 63121-4499. Awards Certificate. *Application deadline:* 7/1 (rolling processing; 11/1 for spring admission). *Application fee:* $0. *Expenses:* Tuition $3903 per year full-time, $167 per credit hour part-time for state residents; $11,745 per year full-time, $489 per credit hour part-time for nonresidents. Fees $816 per year full-time, $34 per credit hour part-time. *Financial aid:* Application deadline 4/1. • Application contact: Graduate Admissions, 314-516-5489. Fax: 314-516-6759. E-mail: gradadm@umslvma.umsl.edu.

University of Nebraska–Lincoln, College of Business Administration, Interdepartmental Area of Business, Department of Marketing, Lincoln, NE 68588. Offers program in business (MA, PhD). Faculty: 7 full-time (1 woman). *Degree requirements:* For doctorate, dissertation, comprehensive exams required, foreign language not required. *Entrance requirements:* GMAT, TOEFL (minimum score 500). Application deadline: 5/15 (10/15 for spring admission). Application fee: $35. Electronic applications accepted. *Expenses:* Tuition $110 per credit hour for state residents; $270 per credit hour for nonresidents. Fees $480 per year full-time, $110 per semester part-time. *Financial aid:* In 1997–98, 9 teaching assistantships totaling $74,640 were awarded; fellowships, research assistantships also available. Financial aid application deadline: 2/15. *Faculty research:* Channel information, marketing research methodology, sales management, cross-cultural marketing, impact of new technology. • Dr. Sanford Grossbart, Chair, 402-472-2316. E-mail: gradadv@cbamail.unl.edu.

University of New Haven, School of Business, Program in Business Administration, West Haven, CT 06516-1916. Offerings include health care marketing (MBA), marketing (MBA). *Degree requirements:* Thesis or alternative required, foreign language not required. *Application deadline:* rolling. *Application fee:* $50. *Expenses:* Tuition $1125 per course. Fees $13 per trimester. • Dr. Omid Nodoushani, Coordinator, 203-932-7123.

University of New Mexico, Robert O. Anderson Graduate School of Management, Program in Marketing Management, Albuquerque, NM 87131-1221. Awards MBA. Part-time programs available. Faculty: 4 full-time (0 women). *Degree requirements:* Computer language required, foreign language and thesis not required. *Entrance requirements:* GMAT (minimum score 540), TOEFL (minimum score 550). Application deadline: 7/1 (priority date; rolling processing; 11/15 for spring admission). Application fee: $25. *Expenses:* Tuition $2442 per year full-time, $103 per credit hour part-time for state residents; $8691 per year full-time, $103 per credit hour (minimum) part-time for nonresidents. Fees $32 per year. *Financial aid:* Fellowships, research assistantships, teaching assistantships available. *Faculty research:* Technology commercialization, research methodology, marketing of services, international marketing, sales management, industrial marketing. • Dr. George C. Hozier Jr., Head, 505-277-6169. Fax: 505-277-9222. E-mail: hozier@anderson.unm.edu. Application contact: Sue Podeyn, MBA Program Director, 505-277-3147. Fax: 505-277-9356. E-mail: podeyn@unm.edu.

The University of North Carolina at Chapel Hill, Kenan-Flagler Business School, Doctoral Program in Business Administration, Chapel Hill, NC 27599. Offerings include marketing (PhD). Program faculty: 79 full-time (15 women), 29 part-time (6 women). *Degree requirements:* Dissertation required, foreign language not required. *Average time to degree:* doctorate–4 years full-time. *Entrance requirements:* GMAT (average 657) or GRE General Test (minimum combined score of 1350). Application deadline: 1/1 (priority date; rolling processing). Application fee: $55. Electronic applications accepted. *Expenses:* Tuition $1428 per year for state residents; $10,414 per year for nonresidents. Fees $787 per year. • Ann Marucheck, Associate Dean for PhD Programs, 919-962-3193. Application contact: Liz Griffin, Director, 919-962-1657. E-mail: kfphd_app@unc.edu.

University of North Carolina at Greensboro, School of Human Environmental Sciences, Department of Textile Products Design and Marketing, Greensboro, NC 27412-0001. Awards M Ed, MS, PhD. Faculty: 7 full-time (5 women). Students: 8 full-time (7 women), 2 part-time (both women); includes 2 international. 12 applicants, 50% accepted. In 1997, 2 master's awarded. *Degree requirements:* For master's, 1 foreign language; for doctorate, 1 foreign language, dissertation. *Entrance requirements:* For master's, GRE General Test, TOEFL. Application deadline: 7/1 (priority date; rolling processing; 11/1 for spring admission). Application fee: $35. *Expenses:* Tuition $1842 per year full-time, $370 per semester (minimum) part-time for state residents; $10,296 per year full-time, $2484 per semester (minimum) part-time for nonresidents. Fees $806 per year full-time, $111 per semester (minimum) part-time. *Financial aid:* In 1997–98, 6 students received aid, including 6 research assistantships totaling $41,500. *Faculty research:* Impact of phosphate removal, protective clothing for pesticide workers, fabric hand: subjective and objective measurements. • Dr. Betty L. Feathers, Chair, 336-334-5250.

University of North Texas, College of Business Administration, Department of Marketing, Denton, TX 76203-6737. Awards MBA, PhD. Part-time programs available. Faculty: 13 full-time (4 women), 2 part-time (0 women). Students: 16 full-time (8 women), 43 part-time (20 women); includes 7 minority (3 African Americans, 1 Asian American, 2 Hispanics, 1 Native American), 8 international. Average age 26. In 1997, 17 master's awarded. *Degree requirements:* For master's, computer language required, foreign language and thesis not required; for doctorate, computer language, dissertation required, foreign language not required. *Entrance requirements:* For master's, GMAT (minimum score 450), TOEFL; for doctorate, GMAT (minimum score 575) or GRE General Test (minimum combined score of 1250), TOEFL (minimum score 600). Application deadline: 7/17 (priority date; rolling processing; 10/15 for spring admission). Application fee: $25 ($50 for international students). *Tuition:* $2063 per year full-time, $815 per year part-time for state residents; $5897 per year full-time, $2100 per year part-time for nonresidents. *Financial aid:* Fellowships, teaching assistantships, Federal Work-Study, institutionally sponsored loans, and career-related internships or fieldwork available. Financial aid application deadline: 4/1. *Faculty research:* Promotion, distribution channels, international distribution, sales management, consumer behavior. • Dr. Ron Hasty, Chair, 940-565-3120. Fax: 940-565-3837.

University of Oregon, Graduate School, Charles H. Lundquist College of Business, Department of Marketing, Eugene, OR 97403. Awards MA, MS, PhD. Part-time programs available. Faculty: 8 full-time (1 woman), 1 part-time (0 women), 8.87 FTE. Students: 9 full-time (1 woman); includes 2 international. 16 applicants, 25% accepted. In 1997, 1 doctorate awarded (100% entered university research/teaching). Terminal master's awarded for partial completion of doctoral program. *Degree requirements:* For master's, computer language required, foreign language and thesis not required; for doctorate, computer language, dissertation, 2 comprehensive exams required, foreign language not required. *Average time to degree:* doctorate–4 years full-time. *Entrance requirements:* GMAT. Application deadline: 3/1. Application fee: $50. *Tuition:* $6429 per year full-time, $873 per quarter (minimum) part-time for state residents; $10,857 per year full-time, $1360 per quarter (minimum) part-time for nonresidents. *Financial aid:* In 1997–98, 8 teaching assistantships (3 to first-year students) were awarded; Federal Work-Study and career-related internships or fieldwork also available. *Faculty research:* Consumer behavior, marketing research, international marketing, marketing management, price quality. • David Boush, Head, 541-346-3345. Application contact: Linda Johnson, Graduate Secretary, 541-346-3306.

University of Pennsylvania, Wharton School, Marketing Department, Philadelphia, PA 19104. Awards PhD. Faculty: 23 full-time (3 women). Students: 15 full-time (7 women); includes 1 minority (African American), 4 international. Average age 25. *Degree requirements:* Dissertation required, foreign language not required. *Entrance requirements:* GMAT or GRE. Application deadline: 4/15. Application fee: $125. *Financial aid:* 15 students received aid; institutionally sponsored loans available. Financial aid application deadline: 4/15. *Faculty research:* Scanner data, consumer preferences, decision-making theory, modeling for marketing. • Dr. David C. Schmittlein, Chairman, 215-898-8248. E-mail: schmittlein@wharton.upenn.edu. Application contact: Dr. Stephen J. Hoch, Coordinator, 215-898-0233. Fax: 215-898-2534. E-mail: hochs@wharton.upenn.edu.

University of Rhode Island, College of Business Administration, Kingston, RI 02881. Offerings include marketing (MBA). *Application deadline:* 4/15 (priority date; rolling processing). *Application fee:* $35. *Expenses:* Tuition $3446 per year full-time, $191 per credit part-time for state residents; $9850 per year full-time, $547 per credit part-time for nonresidents. Fees $1276 per year full-time, $135 per semester (minimum) part-time.

University of St. Thomas, Graduate School of Business, Day MBA Program, St. Paul, MN 55105-1096. Offerings include marketing (MBA). Program faculty: 13 part-time. *Degree requirements:* Computer language required, foreign language and thesis not required. *Entrance requirements:* GMAT (score in 50th percentile or higher). Application deadline: 5/1 (priority date; rolling processing). Application fee: $30. *Tuition:* $473 per credit hour. • Application contact: Jim O'Connor, Student Adviser, 612-962-4233. Fax: 612-962-4260.

University of St. Thomas, Graduate School of Business, Evening MBA Program, St. Paul, MN 55105-1096. Offerings include marketing (MBA). Program faculty: 16 full-time (2 women), 89 part-time (17 women). *Degree requirements:* Computer language required, foreign language and thesis not required. *Entrance requirements:* GMAT (score in 50th percentile or higher). Application deadline: 8/1 (priority date; rolling processing; 12/1 for spring admission). Application fee: $30. *Tuition:* $416 per credit hour. • Dr. Stanford Nyquist, MBA Director, 612-962-4242. Application contact: Martha Ballard, Director of Student Services, 612-962-4226. Fax: 612-962-4260.

University of St. Thomas, Graduate School of Business, Program in Business Communication, St. Paul, MN 55105-1096. Offerings include marketing (Certificate). Program faculty: 1 full-time (0 women), 13 part-time (2 women). *Application deadline:* 8/1 (priority date; rolling processing; 12/1 for spring admission). *Application fee:* $30. *Tuition:* $416 per credit hour. • Dr. Nona Mason, Director, 612-962-4382. Application contact: Coordinator, 612-962-4383. Fax: 612-962-4710.

University of St. Thomas, Graduate School of Business, Program in International Management, St. Paul, MN 55105-1096. Offerings include international marketing (MIM, Certificate). Program faculty: 1 full-time (0 women), 18 part-time (6 women). *Degree requirements:* For master's, 1 foreign language, computer language required, thesis not required. *Entrance requirements:* For master's, GMAT. Application deadline: 7/1 (priority date; rolling processing; 12/1 for spring admission). Application fee: $30. *Tuition:* $416 per credit hour. • Dr. Mohammed Eftekhari, Director, 612-962-4840. Application contact: Wendy Williams, Student Services Manager, 612-962-4847. Fax: 612-962-4129.

University of San Francisco, McLaren School of Business, Program in Business Administration, San Francisco, CA 94117-1080. Offerings include marketing (MBA). Program faculty: 33 full-time (7 women), 27 part-time (3 women). *Entrance requirements:* GMAT (average 540), TOEFL (minimum score 600), minimum undergraduate GPA of 3.2. Application deadline: 7/1 (priority date; rolling processing; 11/30 for spring admission). Application fee: $40 ($50 for international students). *Tuition:* $658 per unit (minimum). • Cathy Fusco, Director, 415-422-6314. Fax: 415-422-2502. E-mail: mbausf@usfca.edu.

University of Saskatchewan, College of Commerce, Department of Management and Marketing, Saskatoon, SK S7N 5A2, Canada. Awards M Sc. Part-time programs available. *Degree requirements:* Thesis. *Entrance requirements:* GMAT, TOEFL. Application deadline: 7/1 (priority date; rolling processing). Application fee: $0.

University of Scranton, Program in Business Administration, Scranton, PA 18510-4622. Offerings include marketing (MBA). Program faculty: 39 full-time (9 women), 1 part-time (0 women). *Entrance requirements:* GMAT, TOEFL (minimum score 500), minimum GPA of 2.75. Application deadline: rolling. Application fee: $35. *Expenses:* Tuition $465 per credit. Fees $25 per semester. • Dr. Wayne H. J. Cunningam, Director, 717-941-4043. Fax: 717-941-4342. E-mail: cunninghamw1@uofs.edu.

University of Tennessee at Chattanooga, School of Business Administration, Program in Business Administration, Chattanooga, TN 37403-2598. Offerings include marketing (MBA). *Entrance requirements:* GMAT (average 527). Application deadline: rolling. Application fee: $25. *Tuition:* $2864 per year full-time, $160 per credit hour part-time for state residents; $6806 per year full-time, $379 per credit hour part-time for nonresidents. • Ashley Williams, Director, 423-755-4169. Fax: 423-755-5255. Application contact: Dr. Deborah Arfken, Assistant Provost for Graduate Studies, 423-755-4667. Fax: 423-755-4478.

University of Tennessee, Knoxville, College of Business Administration, Program in Business Administration, Knoxville, TN 37996. Offerings include marketing (MBA, PhD). MS/MBA offered jointly with the College of Engineering. Postbaccalaureate distance learning degree programs offered. Program faculty: 51 full-time (6 women). *Degree requirements:* For doctorate, computer language, dissertation required, foreign language not required. *Entrance requirements:* For doctorate, GMAT, TOEFL (minimum score 550), minimum GPA of 2.7. Application deadline: 2/1 (priority date). Application fee: $35. Electronic applications accepted. *Tuition:* $3354 per year full-time, $181 per semester hour part-time for state residents; $8410 per year full-time, $462 per semester hour part-time for nonresidents. • Dr. Gary Dicer, Director, 423-974-5033. E-mail: gdicer@utk.edu. Application contact: Donald Potts, Graduate Representative, 423-974-5033. Fax: 423-974-3826. E-mail: dpotts@utk.edu.

The University of Texas at Arlington, College of Business Administration, Program in Business Administration, Concentration in Marketing, Arlington, TX 76019-0407. Awards MBA. Faculty: 10 full-time (4 women). Students: 16 full-time (9 women), 6 part-time (3 women); includes 1 minority (Asian American), 9 international. 19 applicants, 47% accepted. In 1997, 8 degrees awarded. *Degree requirements:* Computer language required, foreign language and thesis not required. *Entrance requirements:* GMAT (minimum score 480), minimum GPA of 2.9. Application deadline: rolling. Application fee: $25 ($50 for international students). *Tuition:* $3206 per year full-time, $468 per semester (minimum) part-time for state residents; $8612 per year full-time, $1137 per semester (minimum) part-time for nonresidents. • Carl McDaniel, Chair, 817-272-2876. Application contact: Glen R. Jarboe, Graduate Adviser, 817-272-3004.

The University of Texas at Austin, Graduate School, College of Business Administration, Department of Marketing Administration, Austin, TX 78712. Awards PhD. Students: 10 (1 woman); includes 5 international. 22 applicants, 5% accepted. In 1997, 2 degrees awarded. *Entrance requirements:* GMAT or GRE. Application deadline: 2/1. Application fee: $60 ($75 for international students). *Expenses:* Tuition $2592 per year full-time, $324 per semester (minimum) part-time for state residents; $7704 per year full-time, $963 per semester (minimum) part-time for nonresidents. Fees $778 per year full-time, $161 per semester (minimum) part-time. *Financial aid:* Fellowships, teaching assistantships available. Financial aid application deadline: 2/1. • Dr. Linda Golden, Chairman, 512-471-5439. Application contact: Robert Peterson, Graduate Adviser, 512-471-5439.

University of the Sacred Heart, Graduate Programs, Department of Business Administration, Program in Marketing, San Juan, PR 00914-0383. Awards MBA. Part-time and evening/weekend programs available. Faculty: 6 full-time (3 women), 11 part-time (1 woman), 9.67 FTE. Students: 13 part-time (10 women). 16 applicants, 38% accepted. *Degree requirements:* Computer language, thesis. *Entrance requirements:* PAEG, minimum undergraduate GPA of 2.5. Application deadline: 5/15. Application fee: $25. *Expenses:* Tuition $150 per credit. Fees $240 per credit. • Prof. Pedro Fraile, Coordinator, 787-728-1515 Ext. 2436. Fax: 787-728-1515 Ext. 2273. E-mail: p_fraile@uscac1.usc.clu.edu. Application contact: Dr. Blanca Villamil, Acting Director, Admissions Office, 787-728-1515 Ext. 3237. Fax: 787-728-2066. E-mail: b_villami@uscsi.usc.clu.edu.

University of Toledo, Graduate School of Business, Department of Marketing, Program in Marketing, Toledo, OH 43606-3398. Awards MBA. Students: 9 full-time (1 woman), 12 part-time (4 women); includes 2 minority (1 African American, 1 Hispanic), 12 international. 45 applicants, 44% accepted. In 1997, 8 degrees awarded. *Entrance requirements:* GMAT, TOEFL (minimum score 550), minimum GPA of 2.7. Application deadline: 8/1 (priority date; rolling processing). Application fee: $30. Electronic applications accepted. *Tuition:* $5907 per year full-time, $246 per hour part-time for state residents; $11,835 per year full-time, $493 per hour part-time for nonresidents. *Financial aid:* Application deadline 4/1. • Application contact: Dr. Bruce Kuhlman, MBA Director, 419-530-2774. Fax: 419-530-7260. E-mail: mba0001@uoft01.utoledo.edu.

University of Utah, Graduate School of Business, Department of Marketing, Salt Lake City, UT 84112-1107. Awards MBA, PhD. Faculty: 9 full-time (3 women), 3 part-time (2 women). Students: 0. *Degree requirements:* For master's, computer language required, foreign language not required; for doctorate, computer language, dissertation, oral qualifying exams, written qualifying exams required, foreign language not required. *Entrance requirements:* GMAT, TSE, TOEFL (minimum score 500). Application deadline: 2/15. Application fee: $30 ($50 for international students). *Tuition:* $2045 per year full-time, $562 per semester (minimum) part-time for state residents; $6129 per year full-time, $1607 per semester (minimum) part-time for nonresidents. *Faculty research:* Marketing management, buyer behavior, marketing research. • Teresa A. Pavia, Acting Chair, 801-581-8696. Fax: 801-581-7214.

University of Wisconsin–Madison, School of Business, Program in Marketing, Madison, WI 53706-1380. Awards MBA. *Entrance requirements:* GMAT. Application deadline: 6/1 (rolling processing; 10/1 for spring admission). Application fee: $38. *Tuition:* $5950 per year full-time, $1118 per semester (minimum) part-time for state residents; $16,230 per year full-time, $3044 per semester (minimum) part-time for nonresidents. *Faculty research:* Marketing strategy, consumer behavior, channels of distribution, advertising, price promotions, public service advertising, public health issues.

Vanderbilt University, Owen Graduate School of Management and Graduate School, Program in Management, Nashville, TN 37240-1001. Offerings include marketing (PhD). PhD offered through the Graduate School. *Degree requirements:* Dissertation required, foreign language not required. *Entrance requirements:* GMAT (minimum score 650), GRE, TOEFL (minimum score 600). Application deadline: 1/15. Application fee: $50. *Tuition:* $871 per semester hour. • Bruce Barry, Director, 615-322-3489. Application contact: Maureen Writesman, 615-343-1989. Fax: 615-343-7177. E-mail: owenphd@ctrvax.vanderbilt.edu.

Virginia Commonwealth University, School of Business, Program in Marketing and Business Law, Richmond, VA 23284-9005. Awards MS, PhD. *Degree requirements:* For doctorate, dissertation. *Entrance requirements:* GMAT. Application deadline: rolling. Application fee: $30 ($0 for international students). *Tuition:* $4960 per year full-time, $257 per credit part-time for state residents; $12,652 per year full-time, $684 per credit part-time for nonresidents. *Financial aid:* Fellowships, research assistantships, teaching assistantships, full and partial tuition waivers, Federal Work-Study, institutionally sponsored loans available. Financial aid application deadline: 3/15. • Dr. Pamela Kiecker, Chair, 804-828-1618. Fax: 804-828-1602. E-mail: pkiecker@vcu.edu. Application contact: Dr. Edward L. Millner, Associate Dean of Graduate Studies, 804-828-1741. Fax: 804-828-7174.

Virginia Polytechnic Institute and State University, Pamplin College of Business, Department of Marketing, Blacksburg, VA 24061. Offers program in business administration/marketing (PhD). Faculty: 15 full-time (4 women). Students: 9 full-time (2 women); includes 4 international. 17 applicants, 0% accepted. In 1997, 5 degrees awarded (100% entered university research/teaching). *Degree requirements:* Dissertation, comprehensive exams required, foreign language not required. *Entrance requirements:* GMAT, TOEFL (minimum score 600). Application deadline: 12/1 (priority date; rolling processing). Application fee: $25. *Tuition:* $4927 per year full-time, $792 per semester (minimum) part-time for state residents; $7537 per year full-time, $1227 per semester (minimum) part-time for nonresidents. *Financial aid:* Fellowships, research assistantships, teaching assistantships, assistantships available. Financial aid application deadline: 4/1. *Faculty research:* Consumer behavior, pricing, sales management, channels of distribution, advertising. • Dr. James E. Littlefield, Head, 540-231-6949. Application contact: Dr. Ronald D. Johnson, Director, MBA Program, 540-231-6152.

Wagner College, Department of Business Administration, Program in Marketing, Staten Island, NY 10301. Awards MBA. Part-time and evening/weekend programs available. Faculty: 2 full-time (0 women), 1 part-time (0 women). Students: 7 full-time (4 women), 12 part-time (5 women); includes 6 minority (all Asian Americans). 8 applicants, 100% accepted. In 1997, 5 degrees awarded. *Degree requirements:* Thesis optional, foreign language not required. *Entrance requirements:* Minimum GPA of 2.6. Application deadline: 8/1 (priority date; rolling processing; 12/10 for spring admission). Application fee: $50 ($65 for international students). *Tuition:* $580 per credit. *Financial aid:* In 1997–98, 1 alumni fellowship was awarded; teaching assistantships, partial tuition waivers also available. • Application contact: Admissions Office, 718-390-3411.

Webster University, School of Business and Technology, Department of Business, St. Louis, MO 63119-3194. Offerings include marketing (MA, MBA). Department faculty: 5 full-time (1 woman). *Application deadline:* rolling. *Application fee:* $25 ($50 for international students). *Tuition:* $350 per credit hour. • Lucille Berry, Chair, 314-968-7022. Fax: 314-968-7077. E-mail: berrylm@webster.edu. Application contact: Beth Russell, Director of Graduate Admissions, 314-968-7089. Fax: 314-968-7166. E-mail: russellmb@webster.edu.

Western International University, Program in Marketing, 9215 North Black Canyon Highway, Phoenix, AZ 85021-2718. Awards MBA. Evening/weekend programs available. *Degree requirements:* Thesis, research project. *Entrance requirements:* GMAT (strongly recom-

Directories: Marketing; Marketing Research; Cross-Discipline Announcements

Western International University (continued)

mended), minimum GPA of 2.75. Application deadline: rolling. Application fee: $50 ($100 for international students). • Dr. Tony Muscia, Chair, 602-943-2311. Application contact: Enrollment Department, 602-943-2311. Fax: 602-371-8637.

Western Kentucky University, College of Business Administration, Department of Economics and Marketing, Bowling Green, KY 42101-3576. Awards MA. Part-time and evening/weekend programs available. Faculty: 23 full-time (2 women). Students: 4 full-time (2 women), 1 part-time (0 women); includes 1 minority (Asian American). Average age 34. 20 applicants, 80% accepted. In 1997, 4 degrees awarded. *Degree requirements:* Thesis or alternative required, foreign language not required. *Average time to degree:* master's–2 years full-time. *Application deadline:* 8/1 (priority date; rolling processing; 12/1 for spring admission). *Application fee:* $20. *Tuition:* $2460 per year full-time, $133 per credit hour part-time for state residents; $6700 per year full-time, $369 per credit hour part-time for nonresidents. *Financial aid:* In 1997–98, 3 service awards (all to first-year students) averaging $435 per month and totaling $12,000 were awarded; Federal Work-Study, institutionally sponsored loans also available. Aid available to part-time students. Financial aid application deadline: 4/1; applicants required to submit FAFSA. *Faculty research:* Economics of aging, human resource economics, economics of education, global economics. • Dr. John Wassom, Head, 502-745-2249. Fax: 502-745-3190.

Western New England College, School of Business, Program in Marketing, Springfield, MA 01119-2654. Awards MBA. *Application deadline:* rolling. *Application fee:* $30. *Expenses:* Tuition $353 per credit hour. Fees $44 per semester (minimum). *Financial aid:* Application deadline 4/1. • Application contact: Rod Pease, Director of Student Administrative Services, 413-796-2080.

Wilkes University, Programs in Business Administration, Wilkes-Barre, PA 18766-0002. Offerings include marketing (MBA). MBA (management, management information systems) being phased out; applicants no longer accepted. Faculty: 11 full-time, 2 part-time. *Entrance requirements:* GMAT. Application deadline: rolling. Application fee: $30. *Expenses:* Tuition $12,552 per year full-time, $523 per credit hour part-time. Fees $240 per year full-time, $10 per credit hour part-time. • Dr. Robert Seeley, Director, 717-408-4717.

Worcester Polytechnic Institute, Department of Management, Worcester, MA 01609-2280. Offerings include marketing and technological innovation (MS). MBA, MSM (administration and management, engineering management), MS (manufacturing management) being phased out; applicants no longer accepted. Department faculty: 15 full-time (4 women), 7 part-time (1 woman). *Application deadline:* 2/15 (priority date; rolling processing; 10/15 for spring admission). *Application fee:* $50. Electronic applications accepted. *Tuition:* $636 per credit hour. • Dr. McRae Banks, Head, 508-831-5218. E-mail: macb@wpi.edu. Application contact: Norm Wilkinson, Director, 508-831-5218. Fax: 508-831-5720. E-mail: nwilkins@wpi.edu.

Wright State University, College of Business and Administration, Department of Marketing, Dayton, OH 45435. Awards MBA. Students: 17 full-time (10 women), 19 part-time (10 women); includes 4 minority (2 African Americans, 2 Asian Americans), 10 international. Average age 32. 27 applicants, 78% accepted. In 1997, 17 degrees awarded. *Degree requirements:* Computer language required, foreign language and thesis not required. *Entrance requirements:* GMAT, TOEFL (minimum score 550), minimum AACSB index of 1000. Application fee: $25. *Tuition:* $5109 per year full-time, $161 per credit hour part-time for state residents; $9039 per year full-time, $282 per credit hour part-time for nonresidents. *Financial aid:* In 1997–98, 8 fellowships (all to first-year students), 3 graduate assistantships were awarded; research assistantships, teaching assistantships also available. Aid available to part-time students. Financial aid applicants required to submit FAFSA. • Dr. Thomas D. Dovel, Chair, 937-775-3047. Application contact: James Crawford, Director of Graduate Programs, 937-775-2437. Fax: 937-775-3301.

Yale University, School of Management and Graduate School of Arts and Sciences, Doctoral Program in Management, New Haven, CT 06520. Offerings include marketing (PhD). Terminal master's awarded for partial completion of doctoral program. Program faculty: 36 full-time (4 women). *Degree requirements:* Dissertation required, foreign language not required. *Average time to degree:* doctorate–5 years full-time. *Entrance requirements:* GMAT or GRE General Test (GRE preferred). Application deadline: 1/2. Application fee: $65. *Expenses:* Tuition waived upon acceptance into program. • Application contact: Subrata Sen, Director of Graduate Studies, 203-432-6028. Fax: 203-432-6974. E-mail: subrata.sen@yale.edu.

Youngstown State University, Warren P. Williamson Jr. College of Business Administration, Department of Marketing, Youngstown, OH 44555-0002. Awards MBA. Part-time and evening/weekend programs available. Faculty: 7 full-time (3 women). Students: 8 full-time (3 women), 11 part-time (5 women); includes 2 minority (1 African American, 1 Asian American), 1 international. 10 applicants, 70% accepted. In 1997, 5 degrees awarded. *Degree requirements:* Computer language required, thesis optional, foreign language not required. *Entrance requirements:* GMAT (minimum score 450), TOEFL (minimum score 550), minimum GPA of 2.7. Application deadline: 8/15 (priority date; rolling processing; 2/15 for spring admission). Application fee: $30 ($75 for international students). *Expenses:* Tuition $90 per credit hour for state residents; $144 per credit hour (minimum) for nonresidents. Fees $528 per year full-time, $244 per year (minimum) part-time. *Financial aid:* In 1997–98, 7 students received aid, including 4 research assistantships averaging $666 per month and totaling $34,080, 3 scholarships totaling $2,064; fellowships, teaching assistantships, Federal Work-Study, institutionally sponsored loans also available. Aid available to part-time students. Financial aid application deadline: 3/1. *Faculty research:* Media, international marketing, advanced marketing simulations, ethics in business. • Dr. E. Terry Deiderick, Chair, 330-742-3080. Application contact: Dr. Peter J. Kasvinsky, Dean of Graduate Studies, 330-742-3091. Fax: 330-742-1580. E-mail: amgrad03@ysub.ysu.edu.

Marketing Research

Pace University, Lubin School of Business, Marketing Program, New York, NY 10038. Offerings include marketing research (MBA). *Degree requirements:* Computer language required, foreign language not required. *Entrance requirements:* GMAT. Application deadline: 7/31 (priority date; rolling processing; 11/30 for spring admission). Application fee: $60. *Expenses:* Tuition $545 per credit. Fees $360 per year full-time, $53 per semester (minimum) part-time.

Southern Illinois University at Edwardsville, School of Business, Program in Marketing Research, Edwardsville, IL 62026-0001. Awards MBA, MMR. Students: 10 full-time (8 women), 8 part-time (6 women); includes 3 international. 12 applicants, 58% accepted. In 1997, 8 degrees awarded. *Degree requirements:* Final exam required, foreign language and thesis not required. *Entrance requirements:* GMAT. Application deadline: 7/24. Application fee: $25. *Expenses:* Tuition $1716 per year full-time, $95 per credit hour part-time for state residents; $5149 per year full-time, $286 per credit hour part-time for nonresidents. Fees $463 per year full-time, $433 per year part-time. *Financial aid:* In 1997–98, 8 research assistantships, 4 assistantships were awarded; fellowships, teaching assistantships, Federal Work-Study, institutionally sponsored loans also available. Aid available to part-time students. • Dr. Jack Kaikati, Chairperson, 618-692-3221. Application contact: Dr. Madhav Segal, Graduate Adviser, 618-692-3221.

University of Georgia, Terry College of Business, Program in Marketing Research, Athens, GA 30602. Awards MMR. Faculty: 14 full-time (5 women). Students: 15 full-time, 17 part-time; includes 2 minority (both African Americans), 6 international. 5 applicants, 0% accepted. In 1997, 13 degrees awarded. *Entrance requirements:* GMAT or GRE General Test. Application deadline: 7/1 (priority date; 11/15 for spring admission). Application fee: $30. Electronic applications accepted. *Tuition:* $3290 per year full-time, $643 per semester (minimum) part-time for state residents; $11,300 per year full-time, $1645 per semester (minimum) part-time for nonresidents. *Financial aid:* Research assistantships available. • Dr. Srinivas K. Reddy, Graduate Coordinator, 706-542-0426. Fax: 706-542-3738. E-mail: mmr@blaze.cba.uga.edu.

The University of Texas at Arlington, College of Business Administration, Department of Marketing, Arlington, TX 76019-0407. Offers program in marketing research (MS). *Degree requirements:* Computer language required, foreign language and thesis not required. *Entrance requirements:* GMAT (minimum score 480), minimum GPA of 2.9. Application deadline: rolling. Application fee: $25 ($50 for international students). *Tuition:* $3206 per year full-time, $468 per semester (minimum) part-time for state residents; $8612 per year full-time, $1137 per semester (minimum) part-time for nonresidents. • Carl McDaniel, Chair, 817-272-2876.

University of Wisconsin–Madison, School of Business, Program in Marketing Research, Madison, WI 53706-1380. Awards MS. *Entrance requirements:* GMAT. Application deadline: 6/1 (rolling processing; 10/1 for spring admission). Application fee: $38. *Tuition:* $5950 per year full-time, $1118 per semester (minimum) part-time for state residents; $16,230 per year full-time, $3044 per semester (minimum) part-time for nonresidents.

Cross-Discipline Announcements

Clarkson University, School of Business, Potsdam, NY 13699.

Either the MBA or MS may be completed in 1 year by students with course work equivalent to 1st-year requirements. The more specialized MS program allows for focused course work and research in marketing. Class size averages 20–30 students and allows for strong interaction between faculty members and students.

University of Colorado at Boulder, School of Journalism and Mass Communication, Boulder, CO 80309.

The School of Journalism and Mass Communication at the University of Colorado at Boulder offers an MA in integrated marketing communications, an interdisciplinary program that emphasizes practical application of business theory, including marketing communications, strategic planning, and management. Students study in small classes, develop presentations to corporations using the newest technologies, and create strategies and plans that increase writing and presentation skills in an atmosphere of actual business situations. An MA in integrated marketing communications can be completed in 16 months.

University of Southern California, Graduate School, Annenberg School for Communication, School of Communication, Program in Communication Management, Los Angeles, CA 90089.

The master's in communication management has concentrations in marketing communication, entertainment management, strategic and corporate communication management, communication and information technologies, and communication law and policy. Students may take cognate courses in other units, such as business or cinema/television. Communication management program graduates pursue careers in such areas as market research and analysis, media research, marketing, social marketing, public and political communication campaigns, advertising, public relations, publicity, and media management.

University of Wisconsin–Madison, School of Pharmacy, Madison, WI 53706-1380.

The objective of the graduate program in social and administrative sciences in pharmacy is to prepare students for independent, theory-based research that leads to new knowledge and understanding of drug use, patient and provider communication and behaviors, health outcomes, pharmacy practice, patient care systems, and the pharmacy profession. This is accomplished by integrating theories and concepts from basic disciplines such as economics, sociology, psychology, management sciences, education, epidemiology, history, and law to pharmacy and pharmaceuticals.

ILLINOIS INSTITUTE OF TECHNOLOGY

Stuart School of Business
Marketing Communication Program

Programs of Study

The Stuart School of Business offers an M.S. in marketing communication (MC), which is discussed in detail below. In addition, Stuart offers an M.B.A./M.S. in marketing communication dual-degree program and M.S. degrees in financial markets and trading, environmental management, and operations and technology management. The M.B.A. and Ph.D. in management science are also available.

The Marketing Communication Program teaches a strategy-driven approach that integrates advertising, public relations, database marketing, promotion, media planning, and other marketing tools—all taught from a practical perspective. Students in the program learn to plan, manage, implement, and assess integrated marketing communication programs in a hands-on environment where many of the faculty members are working professionals. In this setting the curriculum duplicates, as nearly as possible, the professional problems encountered in the workplace.

The curriculum includes courses in media strategy and implementation, creative strategies, understanding the target audience, the database as marketing tool, marketing and advertising research, sales promotion techniques, public relations, direct marketing, budgeting, organization dynamics, writing and presentation skills, and marketing communication planning.

Guided by an advisory board of top-level industry executives, the program prepares graduates for senior staff and managerial positions at advertising agencies, public relations firms, convention industry firms, design companies, small total-marketing businesses, and communications departments in corporations, government, and not-for-profit organizations.

The M.S. curriculum consists of fourteen quarter courses and, for full-time students, the completion of a qualified internship. When students demonstrate a mastery of such areas as media planning, promotion, or direct marketing, advanced placement is available. The degree can be completed in as few as four quarters of study. Students may take up to six years to complete the program. Courses are offered once a week in the evenings at Illinois Institute of Technology's (IIT) Downtown Chicago Campus.

Research Facilities

The Downtown Campus Information Center is an open-stack collection of more than 500,000 volumes, including the business holdings of the Stuart Business Library; the Chicago-Kent Law Library, with its large holdings in environmental law; and the Library of International Relations, a depository for numerous government agencies, international organizations, and the United Nations. U.N. Environmental Program documents and environmental treaties and protocols are available to students. Stuart students have access to IIT's full library system, including its extensive holdings in environmental science, and, using the Illinet Online Library catalog, can obtain access to materials and books in hundreds of Illinois libraries.

Stuart's Downtown Campus is equipped with two computer labs offering a total of seventy student workstations linked to the Internet and networked with IIT libraries, including the Downtown Campus Information Center's CD-ROM databases. The labs provide access to a wide range of software and resources through a Windows interface. Computer skills workshops are offered throughout the year.

Financial Aid

Partial tuition scholarships of 25 percent to 50 percent are offered on a merit basis to full-time students. A variety of government-supported loans are available to qualified U.S. residents enrolled in at least two courses per quarter. IIT alumni receive a one-third reduction in tuition in one course per quarter. A tuition installment plan is available, and, for students whose employers offer tuition reimbursement, a tuition deferment plan is available.

Cost of Study

Tuition for 1998–1999 is $1620 per course.

Living and Housing Costs

Stuart's downtown Chicago location makes it easily accessible by public transportation from most locations in the metropolitan area. Housing is available in apartments, at discounted student rates, just one block from the campus. Full-time students may also live in apartment housing on IIT's Main Campus. Room and board costs range from $5005 to $6680, depending on occupancy arrangements and meal plans.

Student Group

About 700 students are enrolled in Stuart graduate programs. Approximately 80 percent are employed in local firms and study part-time in the evenings. Twelve percent are full-time international students.

Location

The Stuart School of Business is located in IIT's state-of-the-art Downtown Chicago Campus, in Chicago's financial and business center. Chicago offers a rich variety of recreation and culture, ranging from professional basketball to the Lyric Opera. The shoreline of Lake Michigan features beaches, parks, and splendid scenery.

The Institute and The School

Illinois Institute of Technology is a private university established in 1890. IIT's Stuart School of Business has focused on unique industry-responsive master's programs. The MC Program was established in 1998 with the assistance of Chicago's top-level industry executives, who now serve on its advisory board.

Applying

Admission to the MC Program is based on a profile combination of GPA, GMAT, or GRE test scores; professional goals; work experience; and letters of recommendation. Applicants from non-English-speaking countries must also submit TOEFL scores. Applications are accepted throughout the year, and students may enter the program any quarter. Stuart follows an academic calendar of four quarters, beginning in August, November, February, and May. To ensure full consideration, early submission of applications is encouraged.

Correspondence and Information

Stuart School of Business
Illinois Institute of Technology
565 West Adams Street
Chicago, Illinois 60661
Telephone: 312-906-6535
Fax: 312-906-6549
E-mail: degrees@stuart.iit.edu
World Wide Web: http://www.stuart.iit.edu

Illinois Institute of Technology

THE FACULTY AND THEIR RESEARCH

Christopher M. Barlow, Assistant Professor; Ph.D., Case Western Reserve. Cross-functional teamwork with a particular emphasis on integrating technical and business perspectives.
Frank Bloom, Adjunct Professor; M.A., IIT. Management consulting in health-care multilevel marketing and other businesses.
Nick Bothfeld, Adjunct Professor; M.B.A., Chicago. Senior Vice President and Account Director, Hal Riney & Partners.
Eve M. Caudill, Visiting Assistant Professor; Ph.D., Illinois at Urbana-Champaign. Marketing research, consumer behavior.
Lynn Miller, Adjunct Professor; Ph.D., Northwestern. Communication.
Marlene Montgomery, Adjunct Professor; M.S., Roosevelt. Marketing communication.
Paul R. Prabhaker, Associate Professor; Ph.D., Rochester. Marketing research and strategy, marketing implications of newer manufacturing technologies.
Bernard Rausch, Lecturer; M.S., Stevens. Innovation, marketing/R&D interactions, entrepreneuriality, business-to-business marketing.
Leonard Rosenstein, Adjunct Professor; M.B.A., Chicago. Marketing research.
John Tarini, Program Director; Ph.D., Chicago. Consumer psychology, advertising effectiveness, new product development.
Mary Whaley, Adjunct Professor; M.B.A., Northwestern. President, MVW Enterprises Ltd.
Serene Wise, Adjunct Professor; M.A., Chicago. Communication skills.

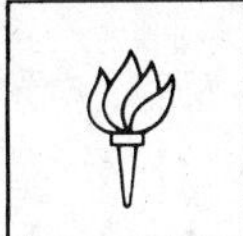

NEW YORK UNIVERSITY

School of Continuing and Professional Studies
Center for Direct Marketing

Program of Study

The Master of Science in Direct Marketing Communications program is designed to meet the growing demand for mid- and senior-level managers who are knowledgeable and skilled in all areas of direct marketing. While these managers are broadly trained, they know how to use databases to pinpoint and understand their markets and how to utilize new media and new computer and modeling tactics to reach customers.

A unique strength of the Master of Science in Direct Marketing Communications is the students' exposure in class and in informal sessions to some of the nation's leading authorities in the field. The instructors and guest lecturers combine academic credentials with impressive accomplishments in the daily practice of direct marketing. The faculty is highly recognized, diversified, and committed, creating an energetic and professional program.

To obtain a degree, students must complete 38 credits of graduate education. The curriculum consists of six required foundation courses, eight core competency courses (six required and two electives), and a master's project. The program can typically be completed in 1½ to 2 years of full-time study or two to three years of part-time study. Courses are offered primarily in the evening.

Research Facilities

NYU's Elmer Holmes Bobst Library and Study Center, one of the largest open-stack research libraries in the world, houses more than 2.5 million volumes. Bobst is one of seven NYU libraries.

The Academic Computing Facility has four instruction computer labs with more than 340 Apple and IBM-compatible computers. All are linked to NYU-NET, the campus data network, and are connected to Novell-based file servers and printers. A collection of more than 100 software packages is available.

Financial Aid

NYU's centralized Office of Financial Aid assists students with loan packages, scholarships, and the NYU monthly payment plan, which enables students to spread out their tuition payments.

Cost of Study

Tuition for the 1998–99 academic year is $570 per credit. Additional nonrefundable fees are charged on a per-credit basis: registration and service fees are charged on the first credit and registration fees are charged on each additional credit. The fee structure by semester is as follows: for fall 1998, $148 on the first credit, $40 on each additional credit; for spring 1999, $162 on the first credit, $40 on each additional credit; and for summer 1999, $89 on the first credit, $40 on each additional credit. Full-time status is 12 or more credits; part-time status is fewer than 12 credits.

Living and Housing Costs

Most graduate student housing, located within walking distance of the Washington Square campus, provides separate kitchen and bathroom facilities and laundry rooms. A free NYU shuttle bus links housing and academic facilities. An off-campus housing office is also available to assist students. Room rates for the academic year (fall and spring) range from approximately $5775 to $10,350, with available meal plans ranging from approximately $1485 to $3625.

Student Group

Beginning with the fall 1998 semester, the student body will number approximately 120 graduate students, with both full- and part-time students in the group.

Location

The School of Continuing and Professional Studies' Center for Direct Marketing is located in historic Greenwich Village, within walking distance of Chinatown, Little Italy, and SoHo, one of New York City's major art centers. NYU's Washington Square campus is within minutes of Broadway and off-Broadway theaters as well as museums, restaurants, and major sightseeing locations. New York City is also the center of the direct marketing industry in America.

The University

NYU is a private university, composed of thirteen schools, colleges, and divisions. The University was founded in 1831, and the School of Continuing and Professional Studies in 1934. The Center for Direct Marketing, which offers the master's degree as well as noncredit courses in direct marketing, was established in 1984.

Applying

Students may apply for fall or spring admission. Factors that are considered in evaluating an applicant include the applicant's academic achievement in previous undergraduate and graduate course work, scores from a standardized graduate admissions test, the nature and extent of previous work experience, letters of recommendation, and a statement of purpose.

Correspondence and Information

For more information and an application package, students should contact:

Master of Science in Direct Marketing Communications
School of Continuing and Professional Studies
New York University
7 East 12th Street, 11th Floor
New York, New York 10003-4475
Telephone: 212-998-7219
Fax: 212-995-3656
E-mail: sce.dirmktng@nyu.edu

New York University

ADVISORY BOARD FOR THE CENTER FOR DIRECT MARKETING

Regina Brady, Vice President of Interactive, Direct Media/Acxiom.
C. Samuel Craig, Professor, Marketing, Stern School of Business, NYU.
G. Steven Dapper, President and CEO, Rapp Collins Worldwide.
Lee Epstein, President, Mailman, Inc.
Aaron Feinsot, Divisional Dean, Division of Professional and Industry Programs, School of Continuing and Professional Studies, NYU.
Thomas Flood, President, Flood Marketing Resources.
Alan M. Glazer, President, Bedford Fair Industries.
Richard Hochhauser, President, Harte-Hanks Direct Marketing.
Myles Megdal, Chief Executive Officer and Senior Adviser, Marketing Information Technologies, Inc.
Murray Miller, Senior Adviser, Direct Marketing, American Express Travel Related Services Company, Inc.
Mitchell Orfuss, President, Lowe Fox.
Pierre Passavant, Director, Marketing and Management Institute, School of Continuing and Professional Studies.
Lance Podell, Vice President, Client Development/Marketing, Savator.
Marilyn Rutland, Vice President, Henry Schein, Inc.
David Shepard, President, David Shepard Associates.
Robin Smith, President, Publishers Clearing House.
George S. Wiedemann, Chairman and Chief Executive Officer, Grey Direct.
Richard C. Wolter, Chairman and Chief Executive Officer, Columbia House.
Wesley Wood, President, Marketing Capital Corporation.
Lester Wunderman, Visiting Clinical Professor of Direct Marketing, NYU; Principal, Wunderman LLC, Marketing Consultancy.

NORTHWESTERN UNIVERSITY

Medill School of Journalism
Integrated Marketing Communications

Programs of Study

Medill offers a Master of Science in integrated marketing communications (IMC) degree, the first such degree in the country, with specializations in advertising/sales promotions, public relations, direct marketing, and general studies. This innovative curriculum gives students the expertise to assess markets through advanced marketing research methods or database segmentation. Students also develop communication skills that measurably improve profitability and success, addressing every segment of an audience with a distinctive, persuasive message. The IMC program is fifteen months in length and begins in September. Students spend one quarter in a professional residency working on marketing communications projects at Fortune 500 companies and smaller emerging firms.

The advertising/sales promotion specialty emphasizes both creative flair and the strategic thinking that produces good advertising and promotions. Students learn media planning, marketing strategies, research techniques, and managerial decision-making.

Those who specialize in direct marketing get hands-on training in today's technology-oriented database gathering techniques while learning how to implement strategies to reach target audiences.

The public relations specialty concentrates on aligning public relations more closely with marketing and management functions to persuasively communicate with customers and all public stakeholders.

The IMC program goes beyond a traditional MBA by preparing students for the future of marketing communications, which requires research and interdisciplinary work in addition to practical training. Courses include studies in research methodology, account planning, database marketing and analysis, creative strategies, and management techniques.

Research Facilities

Medill students have free access to the Internet and obtain e-mail accounts upon enrollment. The full resources of Northwestern University are available, including libraries, which hold more than 3 million volumes and 1,000 international and domestic newspapers. Northwestern's libraries offer a wide range of research information, including current information in print, on electronic resources that are also accessible from home, and a multimedia development center for creating projects with sound, video, and graphics. Librarians provide assistance at the reference desk and offer classes in the use of the library. Northwestern is one of 137 members of the Center for Research Libraries through which students can receive infrequently used materials. Medill also maintains a resource library that features an excellent selection of books, newspapers, reference materials, magazines, online services, and periodicals that are pertinent to the communications industry.

Medill is one of eight schools located on Northwestern's Evanston campus. The others are the Weinberg College of Arts and Sciences, the School of Education and Social Policy, the Graduate School, the J. L. Kellogg Graduate School of Management, the School of Music, the School of Speech, and the Robert R. McCormick School of Engineering and Applied Science of the Technological Institute. The Chicago campus accommodates Medill's newsrooms, the Center for Nursing, the School of Law, the Medical School, the Dental School, the University College, and the McGaw Medical Center.

Financial Aid

Eighty percent of Medill students receive some form of financial assistance. Financial aid packages comprise a combination of loans (self-help), Federal Work-Study awards, and grants or scholarships. The amount of the financial aid package is based on the student's financial need as well as the availability of grant, scholarship, Federal Work-Study, and loan funds.

Cost of Study

For the 1998–99 academic year, tuition is $6810 per quarter for IMC students. Other quarterly costs include $472 for books, $527 for transportation, and $1116 for personal expenses. Generally, tuition during the residency quarter is covered by the sponsoring organization.

Living and Housing Costs

The university acts as a resource in finding suitable accommodations for incoming students. Graduate housing is readily available on both the Evanston and Chicago campuses. Off-campus apartments are plentiful and vary in price. Estimated costs for room and board are $13,500 for twelve months.

Student Group

Enrollment in the IMC program is about 90 students per year. These individuals come from liberal arts institutions that span the globe. The average age of the students is 27. Most have full-time work experience. Currently, about 90 percent of IMC program graduates find immediate employment in a variety of settings in advertising, public relations, or direct marketing.

Location

Medill's IMC program is located in Fisk Hall, which has smart classrooms and computer labs. It is a few steps from Lake Michigan in historic Evanston. Evanston, Chicago's first suburb to the north, blends urban convenience with small-town charm, while Chicago boasts its prominence in the business and cultural world. Chicago is home to some of the nation's most progressive blue chip marketing and service companies.

The University

Established May 31, 1850, Northwestern University is one of the nation's major private research universities. Some 7,500 undergraduates and 5,200 graduate and professional school students study full-time on the Evanston and Chicago campuses with 1,600 full- and part-time faculty members.

Applying

Medill seeks graduate students with relevant full-time work experience who also have academic promise, outstanding career potential, and high motivation. Applicants are required to submit a graduate admission application form, including essay questions, three letters of recommendation, transcripts from all postsecondary institutions attended, the results of the Graduate Record Examinations (GRE) or the Graduate Management Admission Test (GMAT), and a $50 nonrefundable application fee. An on-campus or alumni interview is required. International applicants must submit results from the Test of English as a Foreign Language (TOEFL). The application deadline is March 1, but early application is welcome. Notification will be mailed on or around April 15.

Correspondence and Information

Graduate Admissions and Financial Aid
Medill School of Journalism
1845 Sheridan Road
Northwestern University
Evanston, Illinois 60208-2101

Telephone: 847-491-2052 or 5228
Fax: 847-467-7342
E-mail: medill-admis@nwu.edu
World Wide Web: http://www.medill.nwu.edu/imc/

Northwestern University

THE FACULTY AND THEIR RESEARCH

Integrated Marketing Communications Faculty

Martin Block, Professor; Ph.D., Michigan State. Former Chair, Departments of Advertising, Northwestern University and Michigan State University; senior market analyst, Goodyear Tire & Rubber Company; author, *Analyzing Sales Promotion, Business-to-Business Marketing Research,* and *Cable Advertising: New Ways to New Business.*

Clarke Caywood, Associate Professor and Department Chair; Ph.D., Wisconsin–Madison. Former legislative officer, attorney general; former assistant to governor; editor, *International Handbook of Public Relations and Integrated Communications;* coeditor, *Corporate Communications in Mergers and Restructuring.*

Tom Collinger, Associate Professor and Director of Direct Marketing; B.S., Colorado. Former senior vice president, Leo Burnett Company; former vice president, Ogilvy & Mather Direct.

Lisa Fortini-Campbell, Associate Professor; Ph.D., Washington (Seattle). Former general manager, Hal Riney & Partners/Chicago; former vice president and research director, Young & Rubicam/Chicago; author, *Hitting the Sweet Spot.*

Lee Huebner, Professor; Ph.D., Harvard. Former publisher, *International Herald Tribune;* former special assistant to the President and associate director of the White House writing/research staff.

Edward Malthouse, Assistant Professor of Marketing; Ph.D., Northwestern. Former lecturer, J.L. Kellogg Graduate School of Management.

Francis J. Mulhern, Assistant Professor; Ph.D., Texas at Austin. Former member of the faculty, College of Business, Pennsylvania State University; research on database marketing, retailing, marketing models.

Don Schultz, Professor; Ph.D., Michigan State. Former senior vice president, Tracy-Locke Advertising and Public Relations; founding editor, *Journal of Direct Marketing;* author, *Strategic Advertising Campaigns, Essentials of Sales Promotion, Sales Promotion Management and Strategic Newspaper Marketing;* coauthor, *New Marketing Paradigm, Essentials of Advertising Strategy.*

Edward Spiegel, Associate Professor; M.B.A., Dartmouth. Former senior vice president for marketing and advertising and member of the board of directors, Spiegel, Inc.

Kurt Stocker, Associate Professor and Director of Public Relations; B.S., Marietta. Former chief corporate relations officer for Continental Bank Corporation; senior vice president, United Airlines; senior vice president, Hill & Knowlton.

Stanley Tannenbaum, Associate Professor and Director of Advertising/Sales Promotion; B.S., Temple. Former Chairman, Kenyon & Eckhart Advertising Inc; former executive vice president, Turtle Wax, Inc.; coauthor, *The TV and Radio Commercial, Essentials of Advertising Strategy, New Marketing Paradigm.*

Paul Wang, Associate Professor; Ph.D., Northwestern. Fellow, Newspaper Management Center; coauthor, *Strategic Database Marketing.*

Adjunct Faculty

Kate Bergin, Adjunct Professor, M.M. candidate, Northwestern. President, Kate Bergin & Associates; former integrated marketing communications consultant, Leo Burnett Company.

Roy Bergold, Adjunct Professor, M.S., Illinois. Vice President–Creative, McDonald's Corp.

Alan Fortini-Campbell, Adjunct Professor, J.D., Loyola Chicago; M.B.A., Ohio State. Principal of The Fortini-Campbell Company; former associate director (flow-through entities), Arthur Andersen LLP.

Matthew Gonring, Adjunct Professor; M.S., American. Vice president of communications, USG Corporation.

Behram Hansotia, Adjunct Professor; Ph.D., Illinois. Senior vice president, InfoWorks.

Thomas L. Harris, Adjunct Professor; M.A., Chicago. Former president, Golin/Harris; former president, Foote Cone & Belding Public Relations; managing partner, Thomas L. Harris Associates; author, *The Marketer's Guide to Public Relations, Choosing and Working with Your Public Relations Firm.*

Randy Hlavac, Adjunct Professor; M.B.A., Nebraska. President and CEO, Marketing Synergy.

Nancy Hobor, Adjunct Professor; Ph.D., Chicago. Vice president, communications and investor relations, Morton International.

Ron Jacobs, Adjunct Professor; M.S., Roosevelt. Founder and president, Jacobs & Clevenger, Inc.

Jim Kobs, Adjunct Professor; B.S., Illinois. Chairman and CEO, Kobs Gregory Passavant; author, *Profitable Direct Marketing.*

Kevin Leo, Adjunct Professor, M.B.A., DePaul. Senior vice president, client services, Kobs Gregory Passavant.

Maryclaire Collins, Lecturer; M.S.J., Northwestern. President, Collins Communications; author, *How to Make Money Writing Corporate Communications.*

Sharon McGowan, Lecturer; M.S.J., Northwestern. President, Desktop Edit Shop; consulting editor, *Multi-Channel Marketing and Exposure! How to Make your Message Unavoidable.*

Editorial Faculty

David Abrahamson, Associate Professor of Magazine Publishing; Ph.D., NYU. Journalism educator and management consultant; former editor of trade and consumer magazines.

Ken Bode, Professor and Dean; Ph.D., North Carolina at Chapel Hill. Moderator, PBS's *Washington Week in Review*; former professor of media and political science, DePauw University.

Neil Chase, Assistant Professor; B.A., Michigan. Design, editing, electronic publishing. Member of Board of Directors, Society of Newspaper Design.

Mary Coffman, Associate Professor and Co-Director, Medill Washington, D.C. Program; M.A., Bowling Green State. Former assistant bureau chief of Post Newsweek Stations.

Susan Mango Curtis, Assistant Professor of Editing and Design; B.A., Virginia Commonwealth. Former designer, *Washington Post Sunday Magazine.*

Patricia Dean, Associate Professor and Chair of Broadcast; B.S., Iowa State. Former senior executive producer and program director, WBBM-TV (CBS), Chicago; former producer and writer, WMAQ-TV (NBC), Chicago.

Mary Dedinsky, Associate Dean, Associate Professor, and Director of Teaching Media program; M.S.J., Northwestern. Former managing editor, *Chicago Sun-Times;* former reporter, *Chicago Today.*

Jack Doppelt, Associate Dean and Associate Professor of Reporting and Writing; J.D., Chicago. Investigative reporter, Better Government Association.

Sharon Edwards Downey, Lecturer, Medill Washington, D.C. broadcast program; B.A., Cleveland State. Current member, Board of Trustees WETA; former TV news writer/producer for WUSA and WRC Washington, WABC New York, WDTN Dayton, and WHO Des Moines.

Ava Greenwell, Assistant Professor, broadcast program; M.S.J., Northwestern. Former reporter for WFLA-TV, Tampa; WCCO-TV, Minneapolis; WEHT-TV, Evansville.

George Harmon, Associate Professor of Reporting and Writing and Chair of Newspaper program; M.B.A., Loyola Chicago. Former financial editor, *Chicago Sun-Times;* publisher, *Chicago Daily Law Bulletin.*

John Kupetz, Assistant Professor and Director of Placement; M.S.J., Northwestern. Former assistant professor, Mercyhurst College.

John Lavine, Professor and Executive Director, Newspaper Management Center; B.A., Carleton College. Publisher, Independent Media Group, Inc.; president, Accrediting Council on Education in Journalism and Mass Communications.

Donna Marx Leff, Associate Professor of Reporting and Writing; Ph.D., Berkeley. Former assistant city editor, *Chicago Tribune;* research faculty, Center for Urban Affairs and Policy Research.

Robert McClory, Assistant Professor of Reporting and Writing; M.S.J., Northwestern. Staff writer, *Chicago Reader,* freelance writer, *Chicago* magazine and other publications.

David Nelson, Associate Professor of Reporting and Writing; M.S.J., Northwestern. Former editor and reporter, *Miami Herald;* charter writer, *Money* magazine.

Abe Peck, Professor and Chair of Magazine Publishing; B.A., NYU. Former reporter, *Chicago Daily News;* contributing editor, *Rolling Stone.*

David Protess, Professor and Director of Gannett Urban Journalism Center; Ph.D., Chicago. Former research director, Better Government Association.

Richard Roth, Associate Professor and Associate Dean; M.A., Indiana State. Former editor in chief, the *Tribune Star* (Indiana); guest editor, *Wall Street Journal Online.*

Dick Schwarzlose, Professor; Ph.D., Illinois at Urbana-Champaign. Former reporter and editor, Champaign-Urbana *News Gazette.*

Ellen Shearer, Associate Professor and Co-Director, Medill Washington, D.C., program; B.A., Wisconsin–Madison. Former administrative editor.

Frank Starr, Assistant Professor, Medill Washington, D.C.; B.A., Indiana. Former international reporter and bureau chief, *Chicago Tribune* and *Baltimore Sun.*

Mindy S. Trossman, Senior Lecturer; M.S.J., Northwestern; J.D., Loyola Chicago. Attorney; former investigative reporter.

Mary Ann Damme Weston, Assistant Professor of Reporting and Writing; M.S.J., Columbia. Freelance writer, *Chicago Tribune, Chicago Sun-Times,* and other publications.

Charles Whitaker, Assistant Professor; M.S.J., Northwestern. Former senior staff editor, *Ebony* magazine; former reporter, *Louisville Times* (Kentucky) and *Miami Herald.*

James Ylisela, Lecturer; B.A., DePaul. Consulting editor, the *Chicago Reporter.*

Jon Ziomek, Director of Graduate Editorial Program; M.S.J., Illinois at Urbana-Champaign. Former reporter and editor *Chicago Sun-Times.*

Section 15
Nonprofit Management

This section contains a directory of institutions offering graduate work in nonprofit management, followed by in-depth entries submitted by institutions that chose to prepare detailed program descriptions. Additional information about programs listed in the directory but not augmented by an in-depth entry may be obtained by writing directly to the dean of a graduate school or chair of a department at the address given in the directory.

For programs offering related work, see also in this book Accounting and Finance and Business Administration and Management. In Book 2, see Public, Regional, and Industrial Affairs.

CONTENTS

Nonprofit Management

Boston University, School of Management, Program in Public and Nonprofit Management, Boston, MA 02215. Awards MBA, JD/MBA, MBA/MA, MBA/MS, MBA/MSMIS. Offerings include nonprofit management (MBA), public management (MBA). Part-time and evening/weekend programs available. Faculty: 5 full-time (1 woman), 2 part-time (both women). Students: 29 full-time (23 women), 45 part-time (23 women); includes 5 minority (1 African American, 3 Asian Americans, 1 Hispanic), 3 international. Average age 31. 63 applicants, 71% accepted. In 1997, 24 degrees awarded. *Degree requirements:* Internship required, foreign language and thesis not required. *Entrance requirements:* GMAT. Application deadline: 4/15 (rolling processing; 11/15 for spring admission). Application fee: $50. Electronic applications accepted. *Expenses:* Tuition $22,830 per year full-time, $713 per credit part-time. Fees $218 per year full-time, $40 per semester part-time. *Financial aid:* 35 students received aid; Federal Work-Study, institutionally sponsored loans, and career-related internships or fieldwork available. Aid available to part-time students. Financial aid application deadline: 3/15; applicants required to submit FAFSA. *Faculty research:* Nonprofit marketing, international economic development, managing environmental issues, labor relations, corporate philanthropy. • James Post, Assistant Director, 617-353-2312. E-mail: pubmgmt@bu.edu. Application contact: Sally Locke, Assistant Director, 617-353-2312. Fax: 617-353-9498. E-mail: pubmgmt@bu.edu.

Announcement: Boston University's MBA with concentration in public and nonprofit management combines traditional management education with an emphasis on the unique skills necessary for leadership in government, nonprofit, and socially responsible organizations. An internship is required, and full- or part-time study is available. This degree offers graduates the flexibility to choose careers in the public, nonprofit, and private sectors.

Carlow College, Division of Professional Leadership, Pittsburgh, PA 15213-3165. Offerings include nonprofit management (MS). Division faculty: 2 full-time (both women), 16 part-time (14 women). *Degree requirements:* Thesis or alternative required, foreign language not required. *Average time to degree:* master's–2 years part-time. *Entrance requirements:* Interview, minimum GPA of 3.0. Application deadline: 6/1 (priority date; 11/1 for spring admission). Application fee: $35. • Dr. M. Sandie Turner, Director, 412-578-6669. Application contact: Bonnie Potthoff, Office Manager, Graduate Studies, 412-578-8764. Fax: 412-578-8822.

Case Western Reserve University, Weatherhead School of Management, Mandel Center for Nonprofit Organizations, Cleveland, OH 44106. Awards MNO, CNM. MNO offered jointly with the Mandel School of Applied Social Sciences; CNM offered jointly with the School of Law. Part-time and evening/weekend programs available. Faculty: 3 full-time (1 woman), 19 part-time (1 woman). Students: 24 full-time (20 women), 43 part-time (27 women); includes 12 minority (11 African Americans, 1 Hispanic), 2 international. Average age 32. 65 applicants, 83% accepted. In 1997, 23 master's awarded. *Average time to degree:* master's–1.5 years full-time, 2.5 years part-time. *Entrance requirements:* For master's, GMAT (average 603); for CNM, GMAT. Application deadline: 5/1 (priority date; rolling processing). Application fee: $25. *Tuition:* $18,400 per year full-time, $767 per credit hour part-time. *Financial aid:* In 1997–98, 42 scholarships (14 to first-year students) totaling $126,000 were awarded; fellowships, Federal Work-Study, and career-related internships or fieldwork also available. Financial aid application deadline: 5/1; applicants required to submit FAFSA. *Faculty research:* Structure and government interaction with markets, public policy issues, arts management. Total annual research expenditures: $300,000. • John Palmer Smith, Director, 216-368-2275. Fax: 216-368-8592. Application contact: Michael Fitzgibbon, Director of Graduate Programs, 216-368-8566. Fax: 216-368-4793. E-mail: mjf10@po.cwru.edu.

See in-depth description on page 617.

DePaul University, College of Liberal Arts and Sciences, Programs in Public Services, Chicago, IL 60604-2287. Awards MS, Certificate, MA/MS. Offerings include financial administration management (Certificate), health administration (Certificate), health law and policy (MS), metropolitan planning (Certificate), nonprofit organization management (MS), public administration (MS), public services (Certificate). Part-time and evening/weekend programs available. Faculty: 7 full-time (4 women), 18 part-time (7 women). Students: 41 full-time (27 women), 160 part-time (112 women); includes 50 minority (35 African Americans, 6 Asian Americans, 9 Hispanics), 3 international. Average age 33. 89 applicants, 83% accepted. In 1997, 42 master's awarded. *Degree requirements:* For master's, practicum or thesis required, foreign language not required. *Application deadline:* 7/1 (priority date; rolling processing; 1/20 for spring admission). *Application fee:* $25. *Expenses:* Tuition $320 per credit hour. Fees $30 per year. *Financial aid:* In 1997–98, 15 students received aid, including 2 research assistantships (1 to a first-year student) averaging $500 per month and totaling $10,000; scholarships, partial tuition waivers, Federal Work-Study, institutionally sponsored loans, and career-related internships or fieldwork also available. Aid available to part-time students. Financial aid application deadline: 7/1; applicants required to submit FAFSA. *Faculty research:* Government financing, transportation, leadership, health care, empowerment zones. Total annual research expenditures: $128,000. • Dr. J. Patrick Murphy, Director, 312-362-8441. Fax: 312-362-5506. E-mail: jpmurphy@wppost.depaul.edu. Application contact: Graduate Information, 312-362-5367. Fax: 312-362-5749.

See in-depth description on page 619.

Eastern College, Graduate Business Programs, St. Davids, PA 19087-3696. Offerings include nonprofit management (MBA, MS). M Div/MS and M Div/MBA offered jointly with Eastern Baptist Theological Seminary. Faculty: 32 full-time (18 women), 14 part-time (12 women). *Degree requirements:* Thesis required (for some programs), foreign language not required. *Entrance requirements:* GMAT (MBA), minimum GPA of 2.5. Application deadline: rolling. Application fee: $35. • Dr. John Stapleford, Chair, 610-341-5848. Application contact: Megan Miscioscia, Graduate Admissions Representative, 610-341-5972. Fax: 610-341-1466.

Georgia State University, School of Policy Studies, Department of Public Administration and Urban Studies, Atlanta, GA 30303-3083. Offerings include urban studies (MS), with options in gerontology, human resources, nonprofit administration, planning and economic development, transportation. Department faculty: 18 full-time (7 women), 2 part-time (1 woman). *Average time to degree:* master's–2 years full-time, 3 years part-time. *Application deadline:* 7/1 (rolling processing; 11/1 for spring admission). *Application fee:* $25. *Expenses:* Tuition $2673 per year full-time, $99 per semester hour part-time for state residents; $10,692 per year full-time, $396 per semester hour part-time for nonresidents. Fees $228 per year. • Dr. John Thomas, Chair, 404-651-4591. Application contact: Sue Fagan, Director, 404-651-3504.

Hamline University, Graduate School of Public Administration and Management, St. Paul, MN 55104-1284. Offerings include nonprofit management (MANM). JD/MANM and JD/MAM new for fall 1998. School faculty: 4 full-time, 25 part-time. *Application deadline:* 7/15 (priority date; rolling processing; 12/15 for spring admission). *Application fee:* $30. *Tuition:* $983 per course. • Dr. Jane McPeak, Dean, 651-523-2799. Fax: 651-523-2987. Application contact: Christine Wolf, Program Assistant, 651-523-2284.

Hope International University, Graduate Studies, MBA Program, Fullerton, CA 92831-3138. Offerings include management (MBA), with options in international development, non-profit organizations management; non-profit organizations management (MS). Program faculty: 2 full-time (0 women), 23 part-time (4 women). *Degree requirements:* Computer language, thesis required, foreign language not required. *Average time to degree:* master's–1.5 years full-time, 2 years part-time. *Entrance requirements:* Minimum GPA of 3.0. Application deadline: rolling. Application fee: $100. Electronic applications accepted. • Dr. Raj Singh, Director, 800-762-1294 Ext. 633. Application contact: Connie Born, Director of Admissions, 800-762-1294 Ext. 626. Fax: 714-738-4564. E-mail: cborn@pacificcc.edu.

Indiana University Northwest, Division of Public and Environmental Affairs, Gary, IN 46408-1197. Offerings include non-profit management (NPMC). Division faculty: 7 full-time (2 women), 5 part-time (2 women), 8.25 FTE. *Application deadline:* 8/15 (priority date; rolling processing). *Application fee:* $25. • Joseph M. Pellicciotti, Director, 219-980-6695. E-mail: jpelli@iunhaw1.iun.indiana.edu. Application contact: Suzanne Green, Recorder, 219-980-6695. Fax: 219-980-6737. E-mail: sgreen@iunhaw1.iun.indiana.edu.

Lesley College, School of Management, Cambridge, MA 02138-2790. Offerings include fundraising management (MSM). Postbaccalaureate distance learning degree programs offered (no on-campus study). School faculty: 10 full-time (4 women), 204 part-time (78 women). *Application deadline:* rolling. *Application fee:* $45. *Tuition:* $425 per credit. • Dr. Earl Potter, Dean, 617-349-8682. Fax: 617-349-8678. Application contact: Marilyn Gove, Associate Director, 617-349-8690. Fax: 617-349-8313. E-mail: mgove@mail.lesley.edu.

New School University, Robert J. Milano Graduate School of Management and Urban Policy, Program in Nonprofit Management, New York, NY 10011-8603. Awards MS. Part-time and evening/weekend programs available. Faculty: 1 (woman) full-time, 18 part-time (11 women). Students: 40 full-time (28 women), 55 part-time (39 women); includes 24 minority (16 African Americans, 8 Hispanics), 3 international. Average age 31. In 1997, 45 degrees awarded. *Degree requirements:* Computer language, thesis required, foreign language not required. *Average time to degree:* master's–2 years full-time, 3.5 years part-time. *Entrance requirements:* Interview. Application deadline: 9/1 (priority date; rolling processing). Application fee: $30. *Tuition:* $622 per credit. *Financial aid:* In 1997–98, 66 students received aid, including 5 teaching assistantships totaling $7,500, 63 scholarships (35 to first-year students) totaling $294,560; full and partial tuition waivers, Federal Work-Study, and career-related internships or fieldwork also available. Financial aid application deadline: 3/1; applicants required to submit FAFSA. *Faculty research:* Management of nonprofit organizations, fund raising in minority nonprofit organizations. • Bonnie McEwan, Acting Chair, 212-229-5950. Application contact: Susan Morris, Assistant Dean, 212-229-5388. Fax: 212-229-8935. E-mail: smorris@newschool.edu.

New York University, Robert F. Wagner Graduate School of Public Service, Program in Public Administration, New York, NY 10012-1019. Offerings include management for public and nonprofit organizations (MPA, APC). Program faculty: 14 full-time (6 women), 49 part-time (21 women), 23 FTE. *Degree requirements:* For master's, thesis or alternative. *Average time to degree:* master's–2 years full-time, 4 years part-time; doctorate–5 years full-time, 7 years part-time; other advanced degree–1 year full-time. *Entrance requirements:* For master's, minimum undergraduate GPA of 3.0. Application deadline: 8/1 (rolling processing; 1/1 for spring admission). Application fee: $50 ($70 for international students). • Leanna Stiefel, Director, 212-998-7400. Application contact: Hedy Flanders, Director, Admissions and Financial Aid, 212-998-7414. Fax: 212-995-4164. E-mail: wagner.admissions@nyu.edu.

Northwestern University, J. L. Kellogg Graduate School of Management, Programs in Management, Evanston, IL 60208. Offerings include public and nonprofit management (MM). MMM offered jointly with the Robert R. McCormick School of Engineering and Applied Science; MM/MSN offered jointly with Rush Presbyterian Hospital. Faculty: 129 full-time (24 women), 89 part-time (15 women). *Application deadline:* 3/16. *Application fee:* $125. *Tuition:* $25,872 per year. • Michele Rogers, Assistant Dean of Admissions and Financial Aid, 847-491-3308. Fax: 847-491-4960.

Pace University, Dyson College of Arts and Sciences, Department of Public Administration, New York, NY 10038. Offerings include nonprofit management (MPA). *Entrance requirements:* GRE General Test. Application deadline: 7/31 (priority date; rolling processing; 11/30 for spring admission). Application fee: $60. *Expenses:* Tuition $520 per credit. Fees $360 per year full-time, $53 per semester (minimum) part-time.

Regis University, Program in Nonprofit Management, Denver, CO 80221-1099. Awards MNM, Certificate. Offered at Northwest Denver Campus and Southeast Denver Campus. Part-time and evening/weekend programs available. Postbaccalaureate distance learning degree programs offered. Students: 59 full-time, 37 part-time; includes 13 minority (4 African Americans, 7 Hispanics, 2 Native Americans). Average age 37. 53 applicants, 11% accepted. In 1997, 16 master's awarded. *Degree requirements:* For master's, final research project required, thesis optional, foreign language not required. *Average time to degree:* master's–2 years full-time, 4 years part-time. *Entrance requirements:* For master's, 2 years of work experience or 400-hour internship in nonprofit sector, interview. Application deadline: rolling. Application fee: $75. *Tuition:* $256 per semester hour. *Financial aid:* In 1997–98, 12 fellowships (all to first-year students) were awarded; Federal Work-Study and career-related internships or fieldwork also available. Aid available to part-time students. Financial aid applicants required to submit FAFSA. *Faculty research:* International nonprofits, enterprise, grass roots nonprofits, leadership. • Paul Alexander, Chair. E-mail: paulalex@regis.edu. Application contact: Richard Boorom, Director of Marketing and Admissions, 800-677-9270. Fax: 303-964-5538. E-mail: admarg@regis.edu.

San Francisco State University, College of Behavioral and Social Sciences, Public Administration Program, San Francisco, CA 94132-1722. Offerings include nonprofit administration (MPA). *Degree requirements:* Internship, project or thesis required, foreign language not required. *Entrance requirements:* GRE General Test, essay exam, minimum GPA of 3.0. Application deadline: 3/1 (priority date; rolling processing). Application fee: $55. *Expenses:* Tuition $0 for state residents; $246 per unit for nonresidents. Fees $1982 per year full-time, $1316 per year part-time.

Seattle University, College of Arts and Sciences, Institute of Public Service, Program in Not-for-Profit Leadership, Seattle, WA 98122. Awards MNPL. Faculty: 1 (woman) full-time, 6 part-time (3 women), 2 FTE. Students: 38 part-time (23 women); includes 4 minority (2 African Americans, 2 Asian Americans). Average age 39. 33 applicants, 79% accepted. In 1997, 24 degrees awarded. *Degree requirements:* Thesis or alternative required, foreign language not required. *Entrance requirements:* Interview, professional experience. Application deadline: 2/1. Application fee: $55. *Expenses:* Tuition $367 per credit hour. Fees $70 per year. *Financial aid:* Federal Work-Study and career-related internships or fieldwork available. Aid available to part-time students. Financial aid applicants required to submit FAFSA. • Dr. Mary Hall, Director, 206-296-5435. Fax: 206-596-5997. E-mail: mhall@seattleu.edu. Application contact: Michael McKeon, Dean of Admissions, 206-296-5900. Fax: 206-296-5656. E-mail: admissions@seattleu.edu.

Seton Hall University, College of Arts and Sciences, Center for Public Service, Program in Management of Nonprofit Organizations, South Orange, NJ 07079-2697. Awards MPA. Part-time and evening/weekend programs available. *Degree requirements:* Research project. *Entrance requirements:* GMAT, GRE General Test, or LSAT. Application deadline: rolling. Application fee: $50. *Expenses:* Tuition $500 per credit. Fees $610 per year full-time, $185 per semester part-time. *Financial aid:* Research assistantships, nonprofit management scholarships, and career-related internships or fieldwork available. • Application contact: Barbara Metelsky, Assistant Director, 973-761-9510. Fax: 973-275-2463. E-mail: metelsba@lanmail.shu.edu.

See in-depth description on page 621.

Suffolk University, Sawyer School of Management, Department of Public Management, Boston, MA 02108-2770. Offerings include nonprofit management (MPA). MPA/MS offered jointly with Department of Education and Human Services. Department faculty: 7 full-time (2 women), 20 part-time (12 women). *Application deadline:* 6/15 (priority date; rolling processing; 11/15 for spring admission). *Application fee:* $50. *Expenses:* Tuition $16,122 per year full-time, $1611 per course part-time. Fees $50 per year full-time, $20 per year part-time. • Michael Lavin, Chair, 617-573-8317. Fax: 617-573-8345. E-mail: mlavin@acad.suffolk.edu. Application contact: Judy Reynolds, Acting Director of Graduate Admissions, 617-573-8302. Fax: 617-523-0116. E-mail: grad.admission@admin.suffolk.edu.

Trinity College, School of Professional Studies, Programs in Administration, Washington, DC 20017-1094. Offerings include administration in non-profit management (MA). Faculty: 4 full-time (1 woman), 4 part-time (all women). *Application deadline:* rolling. *Application fee:* $35. *Tuition:* $460 per credit hour. • Dr. Sheri Levin, Division Chair, Human Services, 202-884-9553. Application contact: Karen Goodwin, Director of Graduate Admissions, 202-884-9400. Fax: 202-884-9229.

Tufts University, Division of Graduate and Continuing Studies and Research, Professional and Continuing Studies, Management of Community Organizations Program, Medford, MA 02155. Awards Certificate. Part-time and evening/weekend programs available. Students: 5 part-time (4 women). Average age 35. 2 applicants, 100% accepted. In 1997, 3 degrees awarded. *Average time to degree:* other advanced degree–1 year part-time. *Application deadline:* 8/15 (priority date; 12/12 for spring admission). *Application fee:* $40. *Tuition:* $1100 per course (minimum). *Financial aid:* Career-related internships or fieldwork available. Aid available to part-time students. Financial aid application deadline: 5/1; applicants required to submit FAFSA. • Application contact: Liz Regan, Program Administrator, 617-627-3562. Fax: 617-627-3017. E-mail: pcs@infonet.tufts.edu.

University of Judaism, Graduate School, David Lieber School of Graduate Studies, Program in Business Administration, 15600 Mulholland Drive, Bel Air, CA 90077-1599. Offerings include general nonprofit administration (MBA), Jewish nonprofit administration (MBA). Program faculty: 5 full-time (0 women), 10 part-time (4 women). *Degree requirements:* Thesis, internship required, foreign language not required. *Entrance requirements:* GMAT or GRE General Test, interview, minimum undergraduate GPA of 3.0. Application deadline: 3/31 (priority date; rolling processing; 11/1 for spring admission). Application fee: $35. *Expenses:* Tuition $13,910 per year full-time, $580 per unit part-time. Fees $465 per year. • Dr. Beryl Geber, Director, 310-476-9777. Application contact: Tamara Greenebaum, Dean of Admissions, 310-476-9777. Fax: 310-471-3657.

The University of Memphis, College of Arts and Sciences, Department of Political Science, Program in Public Administration, Memphis, TN 38152. Offerings include non-profit administration (MPA). *Degree requirements:* Thesis or alternative, comprehensive exam, internship. *Entrance requirements:* GRE General Test (minimum combined score of 1000) or GMAT (minimum score 500), minimum GPA of 3.0. Application deadline: 8/1 (rolling processing; 12/1 for spring admission). Application fee: $25 ($50 for international students). *Tuition:* $2862 per year full-time, $166 per credit hour part-time for state residents; $6696 per year full-time, $379 per credit hour part-time for nonresidents. • Dr. Dorothy Norris-Tirrell, Coordinator, 901-678-3360. E-mail: dnrrstrr@memphis.edu. Application contact: James R. Carruth, Coordinator of Graduate Studies, 901-678-3360. Fax: 901-678-2983. E-mail: jrcarrth@memphis.edu.

University of Notre Dame, College of Business Administration, Program in Not-for-Profit Administration, Notre Dame, IN 46556. Awards MSA. Faculty: 1 full-time (0 women), 4 part-time (1 woman). Students: 114 full-time (65 women), 61 part-time (32 women); includes 22 minority (14 African Americans, 2 Asian Americans, 6 Hispanics). Average age 39. 0 applicants. In 1997, 37 degrees awarded. *Application deadline:* 5/1. *Application fee:* $30. *Financial aid:* Career-related internships or fieldwork available. *Faculty research:* Law and public policy, demographics and not-for-profit institutions, motivation and morale in not-for-profit institutions, tax-exempt municipal bond issues, controllership. • Glenn R. Rousey, Director, 219-631-7302. Fax: 219-631-6532. E-mail: glenn.r.rousey.1@nd.edu.

University of St. Thomas, Graduate School of Business, Day MBA Program, St. Paul, MN 55105-1096. Offerings include nonprofit management (MBA). Program faculty: 13 part-time. *Degree requirements:* Computer language required, foreign language and thesis not required. *Entrance requirements:* GMAT (score in 50th percentile or higher). Application deadline: 5/1 (priority date; rolling processing). Application fee: $30. *Tuition:* $473 per credit hour. • Application contact: Jim O'Connor, Student Adviser, 612-962-4233. Fax: 612-962-4260.

University of St. Thomas, Graduate School of Business, Evening MBA Program, St. Paul, MN 55105-1096. Offerings include nonprofit management (MBA, Certificate). Program faculty: 16 full-time (2 women), 89 part-time (17 women). *Degree requirements:* For master's, computer language required, foreign language and thesis not required. *Entrance requirements:* For master's, GMAT (score in 50th percentile or higher). Application deadline: 8/1 (priority date; rolling processing; 12/1 for spring admission). Application fee: $30. *Tuition:* $416 per credit hour. • Dr. Stanford Nyquist, MBA Director, 612-962-4242. Application contact: Martha Ballard, Director of Student Services, 612-962-4226. Fax: 612-962-4260.

University of San Francisco, College of Professional Studies, Department of Public Management, Institute for Nonprofit Administration, San Francisco, CA 94117-1080. Awards MNA. Faculty: 1 full-time (0 women), 11 part-time (4 women). Students: 54 full-time (35 women); includes 4 minority (1 African American, 3 Hispanics). Average age 34. 21 applicants, 90% accepted. In 1997, 20 degrees awarded. *Degree requirements:* Thesis optional, foreign language not required. *Entrance requirements:* Minimum GPA of 3.0. Application fee: $35. *Financial aid:* 26 students received aid. Financial aid application deadline: 3/2. *Faculty research:* Philanthropy in ethnic communities. • Michael O'Neill, Director. Application contact: Advising Office, 415-422-6000.

Worcester State College, Graduate Studies, Program in Non-Profit Management, Worcester, MA 01602-2597. Awards MS. Part-time and evening/weekend programs available. Students: 1 (woman) full-time, 25 part-time (17 women); includes 3 minority (1 African American, 1 Asian American, 1 Hispanic). Average age 40. 4 applicants, 100% accepted. In 1997, 16 degrees awarded. *Degree requirements:* Thesis, comprehensive exam required, foreign language not required. *Entrance requirements:* GRE General Test or MAT. Application deadline: rolling. Application fee: $10 ($40 for international students). *Tuition:* $127 per credit hour. *Financial aid:* Career-related internships or fieldwork available. *Faculty research:* Politics of human services, models of supervision. • Francis Amory, Coordinator, 508-929-8670. Application contact: Andrea Wetmore, Graduate Admissions Counselor, 508-929-8120. E-mail: awetmore@worc.mass.edu.

Cross-Discipline Announcements

The George Washington University, School of Business and Public Management, Department of Public Administration, Washington, DC 20052.

The George Washington University's Master of Public Administration (MPA) program is known for its exceptional faculty, distinctive curricular approaches, and well-established links with business, government, and nonprofit organizations. Located 4 blocks from the White House and 6 subway stops from the US Congress, The George Washington University MPA program places graduates in think tanks, policy advocacy and lobbying organizations, national associations, nonprofit organizations, businesses, and international organizations as well as local, state, and federal government agencies. Students can begin or enhance their career with an MPA or PhD in public administration from The George Washington University School of Business and Public Management.

Indiana University Bloomington, School of Public and Environmental Affairs, Public Affairs Programs, Bloomington, IN 47405.

Students interested in pursuing professional careers in the public or not-for-profit sectors may be interested in the Master of Public Affairs (MPA) degree, ranked 3rd in the nation. In addition to course work in public management, budgeting, and quantitative analysis, the student also selects a concentration area: international affairs, environmental policy, policy analysis, public finance, public management, nonprofit management, or urban management. For more information, see in-depth description in Book 2 of this series or contact the school.

Pepperdine University, School of Public Policy, Malibu, CA 90263-0001.

Pepperdine University's School of Public Policy offers a Master of Public Policy degree, which may be considered an alternative or complement to an MBA, a nonprofit management program, or a law degree. The School plans to offer joint-degree programs with the JD, MBA, and Master of Dispute Resolution. It is the School's firm belief that public policy itself is not limited to the study of government solutions but is broadened to embrace a full range of community-based and free-market approaches to public policy problems. For detailed information, see Book 2 of this series, contact 310-317-7493 or 888-456-1177 (toll-free), fax: 310-317-7494, e-mail: npapen@pepperdine.edu, or visit the Web site: http://www.pepperdine.edu/PublicPolicy

CASE WESTERN RESERVE UNIVERSITY

Mandel Center for Nonprofit Organizations

Programs of Study

Since 1987, the Mandel Center for Nonprofit Organizations has been the standard-setter in graduate education for executive leadership of not-for-profit organizations in the United States. In that year, the center instituted its credit-bearing Certificate in Nonprofit Management (C.N.M.) program. Two years later, it established the groundbreaking Master of Nonprofit Organizations (M.N.O.) degree program. In 1995, the center began to offer the C.N.M. through a unique distance learning format. Students in the M.N.O. and C.N.M. programs benefit from an interdisciplinary curriculum and faculty members drawn from the three sponsoring schools of the Mandel Center: the Mandel School of Applied Social Sciences (MSASS), the Weatherhead School of Management (WSOM), and the School of Law.

The M.N.O. is a rigorous professional degree. It is designed for managers and leaders in human services, fine and performing arts, and cultural, educational, community development, religious, environmental, and other nonprofit organizations. The curriculum recognizes the special concerns of nonprofit organizations in such areas as management of volunteers and professionals; resource development and fund-raising; governance by volunteer boards of trustees and directors; management of multiple sources and types of funding; unique legal and regulatory issues; special values of service, community, and charity; and the entrepreneurial character of nonprofit leadership. The program may be pursued on a seventeen-month full-time basis or on a part-time basis. Students have the opportunity through practicums and carefully selected externships to gain additional experience and skills in nonprofit management.

The C.N.M. is a nondegree program for experienced practitioners. Although it does carry graduate credit, the C.N.M. is not a master's degree, nor is it intended for those seeking extensive graduate or professional course work. Courses for the C.N.M. are drawn from the regular M.N.O. curriculum. The C.N.M. can be completed through a traditional residency format or through a distance learning format. The latter program involves two 12-day residencies and eleven months of supervised, self-directed study through the Internet.

Research Facilities

Students have access to the libraries of the three sponsoring schools and a new campus library. These state-of-the-art facilities offer online access to a wide range of research materials and publications. The Mandel Center maintains a nonprofit reading room in the Lillian F. and Milford J. Harris Library of MSASS. The reading room contains a broad array of books and periodicals related to the nonprofit sector.

Financial Aid

The majority of Mandel Center students support their studies through a combination of loans, personal savings, employer tuition reimbursement plans, and scholarships. The Mandel Center offers a variety of scholarships to assist qualified students in the M.N.O. and C.N.M. programs.

Cost of Study

Tuition for the 1998–99 academic year is $767 per semester credit hour. A one-time application fee of $25 is also charged. Students accepted into one of the programs must make a nonrefundable tuition deposit of $150 to reserve a place in the entering class.

Living and Housing Costs

The cost of on-campus housing ranges from $1500 to $1700 per semester. Off-campus housing costs between $350 and $650 per month.

Student Group

The median age of M.N.O. students is 30. Forty percent of the students are full-time. Eighty percent of the students are female, and 31 percent are people of color. An active student association plans activities among the students and faculty and between students and nonprofit leaders in the Cleveland community.

Student Outcomes

The Mandel Center employs a full-time career consultant who helps place students and alumni in nonprofit agencies. The placement rate is very high, as demand for skilled nonprofit managers has increased in recent years.

Location

Cleveland provides a perfect laboratory for students who study nonprofit management. There are currently more than 3,000 nonprofit organizations in the city, building on a long tradition of innovative nonprofit activity. The attractive campus of Case Western Reserve University (CWRU) is located in University Circle, a 550-acre park-like concentration of nearly forty cultural, medical, educational, religious, and social service institutions at the eastern end of the city of Cleveland. In addition to CWRU, University Circle includes Severance Hall (the home of the Cleveland Orchestra), the Cleveland Museum of Art, the Cleveland Institute of Art, the Cleveland Institute of Music, the Cleveland Museum of Natural History, and much more.

The University

Case Western Reserve University is one of the nation's leading independent research universities. Although its origins date back to 1826, the University in its present form is the result of the 1967 federation of Case Institute of Technology and Western Reserve University. The two institutions had shared adjacent campuses since the late nineteenth century and were involved in cooperative efforts for many years.

Applying

Applications are accepted for both fall and spring semesters. However, fall applications for the M.N.O. are encouraged. Admission deadlines usually precede the semester of admission by two months. Admission to the M.N.O. program requires successful completion of the GMAT (this is not a requirement for the C.N.M.). In addition, students must submit a completed application form, two letters of recommendation, an essay, a recent resume, and official transcripts. International students must submit TOEFL scores.

Correspondence and Information

Denise S. Coleman
Director of Recruitment and Admissions
Case Western Reserve University
10900 Euclid Avenue
Cleveland, Ohio 44106-7167

Telephone: 216-368-6025
800-435-6669 (toll-free)
Fax: 216-368-6624
E-mail: dsc3@po.cwru.edu
World Wide Web: http://www.cwru.edu/msass/mandelcenter/index.html

Case Western Reserve University

MANDEL CENTER PROGRAM FACULTY

Albert Abramovitz, Professor, Mandel School of Applied Social Sciences; Ph.D., Case Western Reserve.
Diana Bilimoria, Associate Professor, Weatherhead School of Management; Ph.D., Michigan.
Arthur Blum, Professor Emeritus, Mandel School of Applied Social Sciences; D.S.W., Case Western Reserve.
William T. Bogart, Associate Professor, Weatherhead School of Management; Ph.D., Case Western Reserve.
Susan Case, Associate Professor, Weatherhead School of Management; Ph.D., SUNY at Buffalo.
Pranab Chatterjee, Professor, Mandel School of Applied Social Sciences; Ph.D., Chicago.
Laura Chisolm, Associate Professor, School of Law; J.D., Case Western Reserve.
Fred Collopy, Assistant Professor, Weatherhead School of Management; Ph.D., Pennsylvania.
David Cooperrider, Associate Professor, Weatherhead School of Management; Ph.D., Case Western Reserve.
Paul Feinberg, Adjunct Professor, School of Law; L.L.M., NYU.
Steve Feldman, Associate Professor, Weatherhead School of Management; Ph.D., Pennsylvania.
Paula FitzGibbon, Instructor, Department of Statistics; M.S., Miami (Florida).
Ronald Fry, Associate Professor, Weatherhead School of Management; Ph.D., MIT.
Karen Grochau, Acting Director of Arts Management Program; Ph.D., Case Western Reserve.
David Hammack, Benton Professor of History, Department of History; Ph.D., Columbia.
Amresh Hanchate, Assistant Professor, Weatherhead School of Management; Ph.D., Wisconsin.
Robert Hisrich, A. Malachi Mixon III Professor, Weatherhead School of Management; Ph.D., Cincinnati.
Alice Johnson, Associate Professor, Mandel School of Applied Social Sciences; Ph.D., Washington (St. Louis).
Peter Joy, Assistant Professor, School of Law; J.D., Case Western Reserve.
Robert Lawry, Professor, School of Law; J.D., Pennsylvania.
Laura Leete, Assistant Professor, Weatherhead School of Management; Ph.D., Harvard.
Miriam Levin, Associate Professor, Department of History; Ph.D., Massachusetts.
Robert Lewis, Adjunct Professor, Mandel Center for Nonprofit Organizations; L.L.B./J.D., Case Western Reserve.
Art Naparstek, Professor, Mandel School of Applied Social Sciences; Ph.D., Brandeis.
August Napoli Jr., Adjunct Clinical Instructor, Mandel School of Applied Social Sciences; B.A., Steubenville.
Duncan Neuhauser, Professor, School of Medicine and Weatherhead School of Management; Ph.D., Chicago.
Karen Owens, Adjunct Clinical Instructor, Mandel School of Applied Social Sciences; B.S., Ohio State.
Roberta Pearlmutter, Assistant Professor, Mandel School of Applied Social Sciences; Ph.D., Kansas.
Vaughan Radcliffe, Assistant Professor, Weatherhead School of Management; Ph.D., MIT.
Mohan Reddy, Associate Professor, Weatherhead School of Management; Ph.D., Case Western Reserve.
Marvin Rosenberg, Associate Professor, Mandel School of Applied Social Sciences; D.S.W., Case Western Reserve.
Paul Salipante, Professor, Weatherhead School of Management; Ph.D., Chicago.
Richard Shatten, Senior Lecturer, Weatherhead School of Management; M.B.A., Harvard.
John Palmer Smith, Executive Director and Professor of Nonprofit Management, Mandel Center for Nonprofit Organizations; Ph.D., Columbia.
James Strachan, Senior Lecturer and Assistant Dean, Weatherhead School of Management; Ph.D., Texas at Austin.
Betty Vandenbosch, Lewis-Progressive Assistant Professor, Weatherhead School of Management; Ph.D., Western Ontario.
Margaret Wyszomirski, Professor, Political Science; Ph.D., Cornell.
John Yankey, Leonard W. Mayo Professor, Mandel School of Applied Social Sciences; Ph.D., Pittsburgh.
Dennis Young, Professor, Mandel School of Applied Social Sciences; Ph.D., Stanford.

DEPAUL UNIVERSITY

Program in Public Services

Programs of Study

The Public Services Graduate Program offers the Master of Science in public services, the Master of Science in health law, the Master of Science in nursing and public service administration, and the Master of Science/Master of Arts in international public service management, as well as certificate programs. These programs prepare students for careers in public, nonprofit, and private organizations as managers, planners, policy analysts, organizers, association executives, and social service and health-care administrators; in philanthropy; and in all levels and agencies of government. Candidates are admitted year-round. Graduates describe the program as "better than an M.B.A. for the nonprofit sector." Founded in 1970, the Public Services Program is one of the oldest programs for nonprofit management in the country and one of the few that combines the benefit of nonprofit management and public administration in a single, flexible, unified program. Students complete a core of courses to build a base of skills and knowledge, then specialize in a wide range of electives. Internships are available but are not required. Master's degrees culminate in either practicum or thesis research projects. The program takes advantage of its Chicago location by offering special courses and guest lecturers. Recent special courses included seminars on urban issues offered by a former mayor of a large, Midwestern city and another on national political convention management. Guest lecturers included department heads, commissioners, budget directors from the city of Chicago, Cook County, the Regional Transportation Authority, and the Chicago Park District as well as leaders from other civic, social, and cultural agencies. The Master of Science in public services is offered at the Downtown Campus on weekday evenings and at the Naperville Campus on weekends. The Master of Science in health law and policy is offered at the Downtown Campus on weekday evenings in conjunction with the College of Law. It is designed for students whose careers require a detailed understanding of case law and policy analysis applicable to the health fields. The Master of Science/Master of Arts in international public service management is offered at the Downtown and Lincoln Park Campuses on weekday evenings in conjunction with the International Studies Program. It is designed to provide professional credentials to managers of nonprofit public services that operate across national borders or transnational organizations with local missions. The Master of Science in nursing and public service administration is offered on the Downtown and Lincoln Park Campuses in conjunction with the Department of Nursing. Application should be made to the Department of Nursing. Master's degrees can normally be completed in two years, but most students take courses at their own pace and complete programs in two to four years. All programs are available full- or part-time. Certificate programs in administrative foundations in public service and financial administration for government and nonprofit professionals are offered at the Downtown and Naperville Campuses. In the tradition of St. Vincent de Paul, the Public Services Graduate Program devotes special attention to policies and practices that promote social equity through delivery of affordable, quality services to those in greatest need.

Research Facilities

The Public Services Program sponsors the Chaddick Institute for Metropolitan Development and is closely allied with the Msgr. John J. Egan Urban Center. Students participate in research projects emanating from these entities. In addition, the DePaul Center at the Downtown Campus with its library, the Richardson Library on the Lincoln Park campus, and extensive computer labs are examples of the latest technological resources available to students and faculty for research. Students may also participate in the research agenda of the Center for Culture and History of Black Diaspora, the Health Law Institute, the Center for Latino Research, the Women's Center, and the Center for University Values.

Financial Aid

Each year competitive research assistantships and Parisi Scholarships are awarded by the Public Services Program. Chicago residents may also apply for the Mayor's Leadership 2000 Scholarships. In addition, several loan programs are available. Students apply for assistantships, scholarships, and loans after admission to the program.

Cost of Study

Tuition during 1998–99 is $1280 per course.

Living and Housing Costs

Off-campus housing is available in the Downtown and Lincoln Park campus areas. Housing in Chicago is considered to be among the most affordable of the country's major cities.

Student Group

The Public Services Program enrolls more than 350 students, one of the largest enrollments of programs of its type. Students come from all over the U.S. and a variety of international sites, many as returning Peace Corps volunteers. Students hold undergraduate degrees in a wide range of fields from more than 100 institutions. Some have earned graduate degrees; most arrive with two or more years of work experience.

Student Outcomes

Public services graduates enter and continue widely varied careers. Recent graduates include a city planner, FBI special agent, health-policy administrator, pharmacist, budget analyst, state human rights program administrator, consultant, deputy commissioner of city services, association executive, controller, quality assurance officer for federal agency, zoo director, museum director of education, human resource administrator, director of state police, and foreign service officer.

Location

The resources of Chicago are a major benefit for DePaul students. The city is the nation's third largest and is a governmental, financial, cultural, and philanthropic center. The Public Services Program is located on DePaul's Downtown campus in the heart of the city; cultural attractions and Lake Michigan are within walking distance.

The University

DePaul University is celebrating its 100th anniversary. More than 17,000 students enroll in 200 undergraduate and graduate programs. Nearly 1,000 public services and 70,000 DePaul alumni provide a powerful network of support for DePaul students. The University's leadership and extraordinary connections with nonprofit organizations, governments, and businesses in Chicago are additional resources of immeasurable value.

Applying

Admission to the Public Services Program is selective. Admission occurs year-round for most terms. Admission decisions are based on an evaluation of all prior academic work, professional experience, two letters of recommendation, and a personal statement. Interviews may be required. International candidates must also demonstrate English proficiency with a TOEFL score of 590 or greater.

Correspondence and Information

Office of Graduate Information
DePaul University
1 East Jackson Boulevard
Chicago, Illinois 60604

Telephone: 312-362-5367
312-362-8441 (Public Services Graduate Program)
Fax: 312-362-5749
E-mail: pubserv@wppost.depaul.edu
World Wide Web: http://www.depaul.edu/~pubserv

DePaul University

THE FACULTY AND THEIR RESEARCH

Faculty members from a wide range of disciplines teach in the Public Services program. Their specialties, which include public policy, organizational behavior, public administration, economics, transportation, law enforcement, political science, and health care, represent an enormous advising resource for students and their research or career interests.

CORE FACULTY IN PUBLIC SERVICES

J. Patrick Murphy, C.M., Associate Professor and Director; Ph.D., Stanford. Organizational behavior, higher education administration, organizational culture.
Ellen J. Benjamin, Assistant Professor; Ph.D., Chicago. Foundation management.
Susan F. Bennett, Associate Professor; Ph.D., Northwestern. Political science, law enforcement, public policy, poverty, research methods.
Barbara C. Berlin, Lecturer; M.U.P., Michigan. Urban planning.
H. Woods Bowman, Assistant Professor; Ph.D., Syracuse; CGFM. Economics, public finance, public administration, internships.
Grace Budrys, Professor; Ph.D., Chicago. Sociology, organizations, health care.
Dean Eitel, Assistant Professor; Ph.D., Illinois at Chicago. Public policy, public administration, fire and police management, planning.
Barbara A. Kraemer, OSF, Lecturer; Ph.D., Illinois at Chicago. Economics, public policy, education, international studies.
Matthew Liao-Troth, Assistant Professor; Ph.D., Arizona. Management, organizational behavior.
Terrence J. Rynne, Lecturer; M.M., Northwestern. Marketing.
William A. Sampson, Visiting Associate Professor; Ph.D., Johns Hopkins. Social relations, urban poverty, community organizations.
Susan M. Sanders, RSM, Associate Professor; Ph.D., Chicago. Public policy, public administration, health care.
Barbara Schaffer, Lecturer; M.A., Washington (St. Louis).
Henry Schaffer, Lecturer; J.D., Berkeley.
Joseph P. Schwieterman, Associate Professor and Director of the Chaddick Institute for Metropolitan Development; Ph.D., Chicago. Public policy, transportation, urban planning, geographic information systems, economics, research methods.
Maureen A. Scott, RSM, Visiting Associate Professor; Ph.D., Illinois at Chicago. Social psychology, policy analysis.
John F. Settich, Lecturer; M.S., DePaul. Association management, external boards, convention management.
Anna L. Waring, Assistant Professor; Ph.D., Stanford. Organizational behavior, higher education administration and policy analysis.

The resources of Chicago are a major benefit for DePaul students.

The latest technological resources are available to students and faculty members for research.

SETON HALL UNIVERSITY

Center for Public Service
Management of Nonprofit Organizations

Programs of Study

The Center for Public Service offers a Master of Public Administration (M.P.A.) degree program for people who currently work for or who seek professional careers in the nonprofit and public sectors. The M.P.A. program is accredited by the National Association of Schools of Public Affairs and Administration (NASPAA).

The nonprofit organization management concentration of the M.P.A. program focuses on the management of all types of nonprofit organizations, such as social service, community development, health-care, and arts organizations. The program also focuses on association and membership organization management. *U.S. News & World Report* ranked the nonprofit management program eighth in the country in February 1998.

Other M.P.A. concentrations include health policy and management, criminal justice, court administration, and public service administration and policy. Students who wish to gain expertise in more than one concentration may select elective courses from any concentration area.

A 12-credit graduate certificate program in nonprofit organization management is also offered, as are certificates in health-care administration and management and law and justice management.

The curriculum stresses the development of managerial and analytical skills, as well as ethical and professional values.

All courses are scheduled for the convenience of working students. Classes meet in the late afternoon, in the evenings, and on alternate Saturdays. To allow for study throughout the year, Wintersession and summer session courses are offered in addition to the fall and spring semester course offerings.

The Center for Public Service houses the Nonprofit Sector Resource Institute of New Jersey (NSRI), which provides continuing education to nonprofit professionals, publishes *The Nonprofit Connection,* conducts applied research, and provides technical assistance to New Jersey nonprofits. The NSRI provides opportunities for students to attend workshops and seminars and to be involved in its other activities that provide valuable experience.

Research Facilities

The library houses 410,000 titles and 2,200 current periodicals. It is equipped with listening tables and more than 2,500 phonodiscs, a microform room with six reader/printers and microfilm reelers, and five copying machines. Personal computers are available for student use. Corrigan Hall houses the University Computer Center, which is supported by time-sharing and microcomputer terminals located throughout the campus.

Financial Aid

Available financial aid includes Nonprofit Management Scholarships, Reiner Scholarships, Goya Scholarships, Nonprofit Management and Leadership Opportunity Scholarships, Graduate Assistantships, and federal financial aid programs.

Nonprofit Management Scholarships are partial scholarships available on a competitive basis to managers of nonprofit organizations, with preference given to candidates who are members of minority groups and individuals who work for small nonprofits. Scholarship funds cover up to half tuition for the Center's nonprofit management courses.

Reiner Scholarships are partial scholarships available on a competitive basis to individuals who presently work for or who are planning careers in the nonprofit sector. These scholarships are awarded based on high academic achievement, with preference given to candidates who are members of minority groups. Scholarship funds provide partial tuition remission for all M.P.A. courses.

Goya Scholarships are partial scholarships awarded based on financial need and on a competitive basis for Hispanic individuals studying in any M.P.A. concentration area.

Seton Hall is one of twenty-nine universities across the nation selected by the Kellogg Foundation to participate in the prestigious Nonprofit Management and Leadership Opportunity Scholarship program. These partial scholarships are open to individuals who are members of a minority historically underrepresented in nonprofit management.

A limited number of graduate assistantships are available for full-time students. Those who receive this assistance are normally assigned administrative and/or research duties in one of the University's offices for 20 hours per week in exchange for full tuition and a monthly stipend.

For applications and information regarding the above scholarship programs, students should contact the Center for Public Service (telephone: 973-761-9510). For information about federal financial aid programs, students should contact Seton Hall's Office of Enrollment Services (telephone: 973-761-9350).

Cost of Study

Graduate tuition for 1998–99 is $500 per semester hour. There is an additional registration fee of $85 per semester for part-time students and $105 per semester for full-time students.

Living and Housing Costs

Seton Hall offers graduate housing both on campus and off campus (in the village of South Orange). The South Orange area provides a broad selection of private housing options. For information about University and private housing options, students should contact the Office of Housing and Residence Life (telephone: 973-761-9172).

Student Group

The Graduate Student Association in the M.P.A. program sponsors many educational and social events. One of its main activities is the Distinguished Lecturer Series.

Location

South Orange is situated about half an hour from Manhattan, where many distinguished libraries, museums, theaters, concert halls, and sports arenas are located. Areas for summer and winter sports are easily accessible.

The University

Founded in 1856, Seton Hall is a private coeducational Catholic institution—the first diocesan college in the United States. It is made up of the College of Arts and Sciences, the College of Education and Human Services, Stillman School of Business, the College of Nursing, Immaculate Conception Seminary School of Theology, the School of Graduate Medical Education, and the School of Law. The total enrollment is about 9,000. The main campus comprises 58 acres in the village of South Orange. Seton Hall is accredited by the Middle States Association of Colleges and Schools and holds additional accreditations by the National Council for Accreditation of Teacher Education, AACSB–The International Association for Management Education, National League for Nursing, and American Bar Association.

Applying

Applicants must forward the following to the Office of Graduate Admissions: a completed application (with a $50 application fee); official transcripts from all colleges and universities attended (undergraduate, graduate, and professional); scores on the Graduate Record Examinations (GRE), the Graduate Management Admission Test (GMAT), or the Law School Admission Test (LSAT) (only required of students who completed their undergraduate work within the past five years); three letters of reference concerning the applicant's work experience and academic performance; a letter of intent from the applicant describing career goals and reasons for applying to the M.P.A. program; and a current resume.

Correspondence and Information

Christopher Gonzalez, Assistant Director of Recruitment
and Student Support Services
Center for Public Service
Seton Hall University
South Orange, New Jersey 07079
Telephone: 973-761-9510
Fax: 973-275-2463
E-mail: gonzalch@shu.edu
World Wide Web: http://www.shu.edu/~centerps/

Seton Hall University

THE FACULTY

Philip S. DiSalvio, Associate Professor of Public Administration; Ed.D., Harvard. Public/nonprofit financial management, budgeting, management information systems, and health-care administration. Former Robert Wood Johnson Faculty Fellow in Healthcare Finance. Author of *Managing Computers and Information in Public and Health Care Organizations.*

Jonathan Engel, Assistant Professor of Public Administration; Ph.D., Yale. Research methods and health-care systems and policy. Former Research Analyst, Advisory Committee on Human Radiation Experiments, Washington, D.C.

William Kleintop, Assistant Professor of Public Administration; Ph.D., Temple. Computers, organizational theory, human resources, and uses of information technology by local governments and nonprofit organizations.

Pamela J. Leland, Assistant Professor of Public Administration; Ph.D., Delaware. Nonprofit management and urban public policy. Research interests include issues in homelessness and affordable housing, charitable tax exemption at the state and local levels, and the dynamics between and among the public, private, and nonprofit sectors in the development of public policy.

Roseanne Mirabella, Assistant Professor of Public Administration; Ph.D., NYU. Public policy, organization theory and behavior, and nonprofit management. Director of Nonprofit Sector Resource Institute of New Jersey.

Naomi Bailin Wish, Professor of Public Administration, Chair of the Graduate Department of Public Administration, and Director of the Center for Public Service; Ph.D., Rutgers. Policy analysis, program evaluation, and quantitative methods. Author of articles in *Public Administration Review, International Journal of Public Administration, American Journal of Economics and Sociology,* and the *Municipal Yearbook.*

John Abbott Worthley, University Professor of Public Administration; D.P.A., SUNY at Albany. Management information systems, budgets and finance, administrative ethics, and health care. Author of more than twenty articles and four books, including *Managing Computers and Information in Public and Health Care Organizations* and *Zero-base Budgeting in State and Local Government.*

Section 16
Organizational Behavior

This section contains a directory of institutions offering graduate work in organizational behavior, followed by in-depth entries submitted by institutions that chose to prepare detailed program descriptions. Additional information about programs listed in the directory but not augmented by an in-depth entry may be obtained by writing directly to the dean of a graduate school or chair of a department at the address given in the directory.

For programs offering related work, see also in this book Business Administration and Management, Human Resources, and Industrial and Manufacturing Management. In Book 2, see Communication and Media and Public, Regional, and Industrial Affairs.

CONTENTS

Organizational Behavior

American International College, School of Continuing Education and Graduate Studies, Program in Organization Development, Springfield, MA 01109-3189. Awards MSOD. Faculty: 8 part-time. Students: 14 part-time (10 women); includes 2 minority (1 African American, 1 Hispanic). 10 applicants, 90% accepted. In 1997, 4 degrees awarded. *Degree requirements:* Project or research report required, foreign language and thesis not required. *Application fee:* $15 ($25 for international students). *Expenses:* Tuition $363 per credit hour. Fees $25 per semester. *Financial aid:* Career-related internships or fieldwork available. Aid available to part-time students. • Dr. Elizabeth A. Ayres, Dean, School of Continuing Education and Graduate Studies, 413-747-6525. Fax: 413-737-2803.

American University, School of Public Affairs, Department of Public Administration, Program in Organization Development, Washington, DC 20016-8001. Awards MSOD. Faculty: 17 full-time (3 women), 18 part-time (8 women). Students: 26 full-time (15 women), 81 part-time (59 women); includes 23 minority (17 African Americans, 3 Asian Americans, 3 Hispanics), 3 international. 35 applicants, 89% accepted. In 1997, 51 degrees awarded. *Degree requirements:* Comprehensive exam required, foreign language and thesis not required. *Entrance requirements:* 2 years of related professional experience. Application deadline: 2/1 (10/1 for spring admission). Application fee: $50. *Expenses:* Tuition $687 per credit hour. Fees $180 per year full-time, $110 per year part-time. *Financial aid:* Application deadline 2/1. • Application contact: Academic Adviser, 202-885-6206.

Antioch Southern California/Los Angeles, Program in Organizational Management, 13274 Fiji Way, Marina del Rey, CA 90292-7090. Offerings include organizational behavior (MA). Program faculty: 2 full-time (1 woman), 5 part-time (3 women). *Degree requirements:* Computer language, thesis required, foreign language not required. *Entrance requirements:* TOEFL (minimum score 600), interview. Application deadline: 8/8 (priority date; 2/6 for spring admission). Application fee: $50. • Scott Schroeder, Chair, 310-578-1080. Fax: 310-822-4824. E-mail: scott_schroeder@antiochla.edu. Application contact: MeHee Hyun, Director of Admissions, 310-578-1090. Fax: 310-822-4842. E-mail: mehee_hyun@antiochla.edu.

Antioch Southern California/Santa Barbara, Graduate Program in Organizational Management, 801 Garden Street, Santa Barbara, CA 93101-1580. Awards MA. Part-time and evening/weekend programs available. Faculty: 1 full-time (0 women), 15 part-time (5 women). Students: 25 full-time (18 women), 13 part-time (9 women); includes 5 minority (3 African Americans, 2 Hispanics). Average age 37. 7 applicants, 100% accepted. In 1997, 15 degrees awarded. *Degree requirements:* Computer language. *Entrance requirements:* TOEFL (minimum score 600). Application deadline: 9/1 (rolling processing). Application fee: $50. *Tuition:* $3200 per quarter full-time, $1920 per quarter part-time. *Financial aid:* 26 students received aid; Federal Work-Study and career-related internships or fieldwork available. Aid available to part-time students. Financial aid application deadline: 9/1; applicants required to submit FAFSA. *Faculty research:* Multicultural communication, organizational change. • Robert Kroes, Chair, 805-962-8179. Application contact: Carol Flores, Admissions Officer, 805-962-8179. Fax: 805-962-4786. E-mail: cflores@antiochsb.edu.

Antioch University Seattle, Program in Whole Systems Design, 2326 Sixth Avenue, Seattle, WA 98121-1814. Offers individualized design (MA), organizational systems renewal (MA). Part-time and evening/weekend programs available. Faculty: 5 full-time (2 women), 6 part-time (4 women). Students: 72 full-time, 44 part-time; includes 4 international. Average age 39. 20 applicants, 85% accepted. In 1997, 19 degrees awarded. *Application deadline:* 8/4 (rolling processing). *Application fee:* $50. *Expenses:* Tuition $2970 per quarter. Fees $30 per quarter full-time, $15 per quarter part-time. *Financial aid:* Federal Work-Study available. Financial aid application deadline: 6/15. • Harold Nelson, Director, 206-441-5352. Application contact: Vicki Tolbert, Admissions Officer, 206-441-5352.

Baruch College of the City University of New York, School of Business, Department of Management, 17 Lexington Avenue, New York, NY 10010-5585. Offerings include organization and policy studies (PhD), organizational behavior (MBA). PhD offered jointly with the Graduate School and University Center of the City University of New York. Department faculty: 33 full-time (6 women), 15 part-time (0 women). *Degree requirements:* For master's, computer language required, foreign language not required; for doctorate, computer language, dissertation required, foreign language not required. *Average time to degree:* master's–2 years full-time, 4 years part-time. *Entrance requirements:* For master's, GMAT, TOEFL (minimum score 570), TWE (minimum score 4.5); for doctorate, GMAT or GRE General Test. Application deadline: 6/15 (11/1 for spring admission). Application fee: $40. *Expenses:* Tuition $4350 per year full-time, $185 per credit part-time for state residents; $7600 per year full-time, $320 per credit part-time for nonresidents. Fees $53 per year. • Harry M. Rosen, Chairman, 212-802-6870. Application contact: Michael S. Wynne, Office of Graduate Admissions, 212-802-2330. Fax: 212-802-2335. E-mail: graduate_admissions@baruch.cuny.edu.

Benedictine University, Program in Management and Organizational Behavior, Lisle, IL 60532-0900. Awards MS, MBA/MS, MPH/MS. Part-time and evening/weekend programs available. Faculty: 2 full-time (1 woman), 45 part-time (13 women). Students: 164 (112 women). *Entrance requirements:* GMAT. Application fee: $30. *Faculty research:* Organizational change, transformation, development, learning organizations, career transitions for academics. • Dr. Peter F. Sorensen, Director, 630-829-6220. Application contact: Dr. Ralph Meeker, Director of Graduate Admissions, 630-829-6200. Fax: 630-960-1126.

Benedictine University, Program in Organizational Development, Lisle, IL 60532-0900. Awards PhD. Students: 18 (8 women). *Application fee:* $30. • Dr. Peter F. Sorensen, Director, 630-829-6220. Application contact: Dr. Ralph Meeker, Director of Graduate Admissions, 630-829-6200. Fax: 630-960-1126.

Bethel College, Center for Graduate and Continuing Studies, Department of Organizational Studies, 3900 Bethel Drive, St. Paul, MN 55112-6999. Awards MA. Faculty: 7 full-time (2 women), 2 part-time (0 women), 7.22 FTE. Students: 41. Average age 37. *Degree requirements:* Thesis required, foreign language not required. *Entrance requirements:* Interview, minimum GPA of 3.0, previous course work in humanities, portfolio. Application fee: $25. *Expenses:* Tuition $270 per credit. Fees $75 per year. • Dr. William Johnson, Chair, 612-638-6325. Fax: 612-638-6001. E-mail: johwil@homer.bethel.edu. Application contact: Andrea Sorensen, Admissions Adviser, 612-635-8014. Fax: 612-635-1464.

Boston College, Wallace E. Carroll Graduate School of Management, Department of Organization Studies/Human Resources Management, Chestnut Hill, MA 02167-9991. Awards MBA, PhD. Part-time and evening/weekend programs available. *Degree requirements:* For doctorate, dissertation required, foreign language not required. *Entrance requirements:* For master's, GMAT (average 610), TOEFL (minimum score 600; average 630). Application deadline: 4/1 (priority date; rolling processing; 11/15 for spring admission). Application fee: $45. *Expenses:* Tuition $22,134 per year full-time, $714 per semester hour part-time. Fees $80 per year (minimum) full-time, $30 per semester part-time. *Financial aid:* Fellowships, research assistantships, teaching assistantships, administrative assistantships, full and partial tuition waivers, Federal Work-Study, and career-related internships or fieldwork available. Financial aid application deadline: 3/1; applicants required to submit FAFSA. *Faculty research:* Organizational transformation, mergers and acquisitions, managerial effectiveness, organizational change, organizational structure. • Dr. Judy Gordon, Chairperson, 617-552-0454. Application contact: Simone Marthers, Director of Admissions, 617-552-3920. Fax: 617-552-8078.

See in-depth description on page 629.

Boston University, School of Management, Boston, MA 02215. Offerings include organizational behavior (DBA). School faculty: 110 full-time, 54 part-time. *Degree requirements:* Dissertation required, foreign language not required. *Entrance requirements:* GMAT or GRE General Test. Application deadline: 5/1 (rolling processing). Application fee: $50. Electronic applications accepted. *Expenses:* Tuition $22,830 per year full-time, $713 per credit part-time. Fees $218 per year full-time, $40 per semester part-time. • Therese M. Hofmann, Assistant Dean, 617-353-2673. Application contact: Peter G. Kelly, Director of Admissions and Financial Aid, 617-353-2670. Fax: 617-353-7368. E-mail: mba@bu.edu.

Bowling Green State University, College of Business Administration, Program in Organization Development, Bowling Green, OH 43403. Awards MOD. Part-time and evening/weekend programs available. Faculty: 11 full-time (2 women). Students: 18 full-time (10 women), 96 part-time (57 women); includes 14 minority (11 African Americans, 1 Asian American, 1 Hispanic, 1 Native American), 16 international. 27 applicants, 67% accepted. In 1997, 9 degrees awarded. *Degree requirements:* Internship required, foreign language and thesis not required. *Entrance requirements:* GMAT, TOEFL (minimum score 550). Application fee: $30. Electronic applications accepted. *Tuition:* $6070 per year full-time, $284 per credit hour part-time for state residents; $11,358 per year full-time, $536 per credit hour part-time for nonresidents. *Financial aid:* In 1997–98, 8 assistantships were awarded; Federal Work-Study and career-related internships or fieldwork also available. Financial aid application deadline: 2/15; applicants required to submit FAFSA. *Faculty research:* Charismatic leadership, self-managing work teams, knowledge workers, stress, effects of change processes. • Dr. Peter Pinto, Director, 419-372-8210. Application contact: Dr. Thomas Choi, Graduate Coordinator, 419-372-2388.

Briercrest Biblical Seminary, Program in Leadership and Management, Caronport, SK S0H 0S0, Canada. Offerings include organizational leadership (MA). *Degree requirements:* Thesis optional, foreign language not required. *Application fee:* $25. *Tuition:* $471 per course. • Application contact: Michael Penner, Enrollment Management Officer, 306-756-3200. Fax: 306-756-7366.

Brigham Young University, Marriott School of Management, Organizational Behavior Program, Provo, UT 84602-1001. Awards MOB, JD/MOB, MOB/MA. MOB/MA offered jointly with the Center for International and Area Studies. Faculty: 17 full-time (4 women), 1 (woman) part-time. Students: 52 full-time (14 women), 11 part-time (6 women); includes 13 minority (3 African Americans, 6 Asian Americans, 2 Hispanics, 2 Native Americans), 13 international. Average age 30. 65 applicants, 48% accepted. In 1997, 17 degrees awarded. *Average time to degree:* master's–2 years full-time, 4 years part-time. *Entrance requirements:* GMAT (minimum score 500; average 600), GRE General Test (minimum combined score of 1600 on three sections; average 1800), TOEFL (minimum score 550), minimum GPA of 3.0 in last 60 hours. Application deadline: 1/15 (priority date). Application fee: $30. *Financial aid:* In 1997–98, 5 research assistantships (1 to a first-year student) totaling $10,000, 20 teaching assistantships (10 to first-year students) totaling $32,000, 17 scholarships (12 to first-year students) totaling $46,630 were awarded; institutionally sponsored loans and career-related internships or fieldwork also available. Financial aid application deadline: 1/15. *Faculty research:* Leadership, change, diversity, strategy, entrepreneurship. • Dr. W. Gibb Dyer, Director, 801-378-2664. E-mail: mob@byu.edu. Application contact: Jean Hawkins, Administrator, 801-378-2665. Fax: 801-378-8098. E-mail: mob@byu.edu.

California Institute of Integral Studies, School of Consciousness and Transformation, Program in Organizational Culture and Social Transformation, San Francisco, CA 94109. Awards MA. Part-time and evening/weekend programs available. Faculty: 3 full-time (1 woman), 12 part-time (6 women). 36 applicants, 78% accepted. *Degree requirements:* Comprehensive exams. *Entrance requirements:* TOEFL (minimum score 550). Application deadline: 7/1 (2/1 for spring admission). Application fee: $60. *Financial aid:* Institutionally sponsored loans and career-related internships or fieldwork available. Aid available to part-time students. Financial aid application deadline: 8/1; applicants required to submit FAFSA. *Faculty research:* Global and social innovation, creativity. • Alfonso Montuori, Associate Dean, 415-674-5500 Ext. 275. Application contact: John Hofmann, Admissions Counselor, 415-674-5500 Ext. 289. Fax: 415-674-5555.

California Lutheran University, School of Business Administration, Thousand Oaks, CA 91360-2787. Offerings include organizational behavior (MBA). School faculty: 8 full-time (3 women), 29 part-time (4 women). *Entrance requirements:* GMAT, minimum GPA of 3.0, interview. Application deadline: 8/1 (priority date; rolling processing). Application fee: $50. *Tuition:* $395 per unit. • Dr. Ronald Hagler, Director, 805-493-3371.

Carnegie Mellon University, College of Humanities and Social Sciences, Department of Social and Decision Sciences, Pittsburgh, PA 15213-3891. Offerings include organization science (MS, PhD). Terminal master's awarded for partial completion of doctoral program. Department faculty: 19 full-time (4 women), 1 (woman) part-time. *Degree requirements:* For doctorate, dissertation, research paper, written comprehensive exams required, foreign language not required. *Average time to degree:* doctorate–6 years full-time. *Entrance requirements:* For master's, GRE General Test, TOEFL; for doctorate, GRE General Test (minimum score 550 on verbal section, 680 on quantitative section, 650 on analytical; average 650 verbal, 720 quantitive, 700 analytical), TOEFL (minimum score 550; average 600). Application deadline: 2/1 (priority date; rolling processing). Application fee: $30. Electronic applications accepted. *Expenses:* Tuition $21,275 per year full-time, $295 per unit part-time. Fees $130 per year. • William Keech, Head, 412-268-8364. E-mail: keech+@andrew.cmu.edu. Application contact: Graduate Admissions, 412-268-2833. Fax: 412-268-6938. E-mail: cd01@andrew.cmu.edu.

Carnegie Mellon University, Graduate School of Industrial Administration, Organizational Behavior and Theory Program, Pittsburgh, PA 15213-3890. Awards PhD. Faculty: 8 full-time (4 women). *Degree requirements:* Dissertation required, foreign language not required. *Entrance requirements:* GMAT or GRE General Test, TOEFL. Application deadline: 2/1. Application fee: $50. *Financial aid:* Fellowships available. Financial aid application deadline: 2/1; applicants required to submit FAFSA. *Faculty research:* Negotiation, organizational learning, interorganizational relations, interorganizational strategy, group processes and performance, communication processes and electronic media, group goal setting, uncertainty in organizations, creation and effect of institutions and psychological contracts. • Application contact: Jackie Cavendish, Administrative Assistant, 412-268-2301.

Case Western Reserve University, Weatherhead School of Management, Department of Organizational Behavior and Analysis, Cleveland, OH 44106. Awards MBA, MS, PhD. MS and PhD offered through the School of Graduate Studies. Part-time and evening/weekend programs available. Faculty: 12 full-time (4 women). Students: 9 full-time (6 women), 5 part-time (4 women); includes 2 minority (both African Americans), 2 international. Average age 28. In 1997, 4 master's, 6 doctorates awarded. *Degree requirements:* For doctorate, dissertation required, foreign language not required. *Average time to degree:* doctorate–5 years full-time. *Entrance requirements:* For master's, GMAT (average 603); for doctorate, GMAT. Application deadline: 4/15 (priority date; rolling processing). Application fee: $50. *Tuition:* $20,900 per year full-time, $871 per credit hour part-time. *Financial aid:* Full and partial tuition waivers, Federal Work-Study, institutionally sponsored loans, and career-related internships or fieldwork available. Financial aid application deadline: 5/1. *Faculty research:* Social innovation in global management, competency-based learning, life-long learning, organizational theory, organizational change. • Richard E. Boyatzis, Chairman, 216-368-2055. Fax: 216-368-4785. Application contact: Linda S. Gaston, Director of Marketing and Admissions, 216-368-2030. Fax: 216-368-5548. E-mail: lxg10@po.cwru.edu.

Chapman University, Professional Studies, Orange, CA 92866. Offerings include organizational leadership (MA). Faculty: 3 full-time (2 women). *Application deadline:* rolling. *Application fee:* $40. • Harry J. Schuler, Vice Provost, 714-997-6730.

Charleston Southern University, Program in Business, Charleston, SC 29423-8087. Offerings include organizational development (MBA). Program faculty: 8 full-time (0 women), 1 (woman) part-time, 8.33 FTE. *Entrance requirements:* GMAT. Application deadline: rolling. Application fee: $25. *Tuition:* $9821 per year full-time, $173 per hour (minimum) part-time. • Dr. Al Parish, MBA Director, 803-863-7904. Fax: 803-863-7919. E-mail: aparish@awdd.com. Application contact: Terri Jordan, MBA Coordinator, 803-863-7955. Fax: 803-863-7922.

Claremont Graduate University, Peter F. Drucker Graduate Management Center, Program in Management, Claremont, CA 91711-6163. Offerings include organizational behavior (MBA). *Entrance requirements:* GMAT, TOEFL. Application deadline: 2/15 (priority date; rolling processing). Application fee: $40. Electronic applications accepted. *Expenses:* Tuition $20,250 per year full-time, $913 per unit part-time. Fees $130 per year. • Dr. Jeffrey Decker, Director, 909-621-8073. Fax: 909-621-8390. E-mail: jeff.decker@cgu.edu. Application contact: Kathy Hubener, Admissions Coordinator, 909-621-8073. Fax: 909-621-8543. E-mail: mba@cgu.edu.

College of St. Catherine, Graduate Program, Program in Organizational Leadership, St. Paul, MN 55105-1789. Awards MA. Part-time and evening/weekend programs available. Faculty: 6 full-time (5 women), 5 part-time (3 women). Students: 10 full-time (8 women), 48 part-time (40 women); includes 5 minority (4 African Americans, 1 Asian American). Average age 40. 29 applicants, 86% accepted. In 1997, 21 degrees awarded. *Degree requirements:* Thesis required, foreign language not required. *Entrance requirements:* GMAT (score in 50th percentile or higher), GRE General Test (score in 50th percentile or higher), or MAT (minimum score 50); Michigan English Language Assessment Battery (minimum score 90) or TOEFL (minimum score o, 2 years of work experience, minimum GPA of 3.0. Application deadline: rolling. Application fee: $25. *Expenses:* Tuition $460 per credit hour. Fees $60 per year. *Financial aid:* 13 students received aid; research assistantships, institutionally sponsored loans, and career-related internships or fieldwork available. Aid available to part-time students. Financial aid application deadline: 4/1; applicants required to submit FAFSA. *Faculty research:* Ethics. • Dr. Julie Belle White, Director, 612-690-6783. Application contact: Office of Admission, 612-690-6505.

Concordia University at St. Paul, Program in Organizational Management, St. Paul, MN 55104-5494. Awards MA. Part-time and evening/weekend programs available. Faculty: 6 full-time (1 woman), 13 part-time (4 women), 9 FTE. Students: 62 full-time. Average age 41. 55 applicants, 95% accepted. *Entrance requirements:* MAT, interview, minimum GPA of 2.5. Application deadline: rolling. Application fee: $20. *Tuition:* $225 per semester hour. *Financial aid:* Research assistantships, teaching assistantships available. Financial aid applicants required to submit FAFSA. *Faculty research:* Creativity, self-directed learning, organizational collaboration, productivity and quality. • Dr. Robert DeWerff, Dean of Graduate and Continuing Studies, 612-641-8277. Fax: 612-659-0207. E-mail: dewerff@luther.csp.edu. Application contact: Dr. Tom Hanson, Director of the School of Accelerated Learning, 612-641-8844. Fax: 612-641-8807. E-mail: hanson@luther.csp.edu.

Cornell University, Graduate Field of Management, Ithaca, NY 14853-0001. Offerings include behavioral decision theory (PhD), organizational behavior (PhD). Terminal master's awarded for partial completion of doctoral program. Faculty: 43 full-time. *Degree requirements:* Dissertation required, foreign language not required. *Entrance requirements:* GMAT or GRE General Test, TOEFL. Application deadline: 1/10 (priority date). Application fee: $65. *Expenses:* Tuition $24,300 per year. Fees $48 per year. • Director of Graduate Studies, 607-255-3669. Application contact: Graduate Field Assistant, 607-255-3669. Fax: 607-254-4590. E-mail: maria@johnson.cornell.edu.

Cornell University, Graduate Fields of Industrial and Labor Relations, Ithaca, NY 14853-0001. Offerings include organizational behavior (MILR, MPS, MS, PhD). Faculty: 48 full-time. *Degree requirements:* For master's, thesis (for some programs); for doctorate, dissertation. *Entrance requirements:* GRE General Test, TOEFL. Application deadline: 2/15. Application fee: $65. • Director of Graduate Studies, 607-255-1522. Application contact: Graduate Field Assistant, 607-255-1522. Fax: 607-255-7774. E-mail: ilrgrad@cornell.edu.

Dallas Baptist University, College of Business, Organizational Management Program, Dallas, TX 75211-9299. Offers conflict resolution management (MA), general management (MA), human resource management (MA). Part-time and evening/weekend programs available. Faculty: 15 full-time (4 women), 26 part-time (5 women). Students: 21 full-time (16 women), 92 part-time (53 women). Average age 39. 66 applicants, 76% accepted. In 1997, 26 degrees awarded. *Entrance requirements:* TOEFL (minimum score 550). Application deadline: rolling. Application fee: $25. *Tuition:* $285 per hour. *Financial aid:* In 1997–98, 6 grants, scholarships (2 to first-year students) totaling $10,868 were awarded. *Faculty research:* Organizational behavior, conflict personalities. • Annette Hoffman, Director of Graduate Business Programs, 214-333-5280. Application contact: Travis Bundrick, Director of Graduate Programs, 214-333-5243. Fax: 214-333-5579. E-mail: graduate@dbu.edu.

Defiance College, Program in Business and Organizational Leadership, Defiance, OH 43512-1610. Awards MBOL. Part-time and evening/weekend programs available. Students: 20 part-time (11 women). Average age 28. *Degree requirements:* Thesis required (for some programs), foreign language not required. *Application deadline:* 8/1 (rolling processing). *Application fee:* $25. *Expenses:* Tuition $255 per credit hour. Fees $25 per semester. • Dale Sullivan, Coordinator, 419-784-4010. Application contact: Sally Bissell, Director of Continuing Education, 419-784-4010.

Dominican University, Graduate School of Business, River Forest, IL 60305-1099. Offerings include organization management (MSOM). School faculty: 52 (15 women). *Application deadline:* 8/1 (priority date; rolling processing). *Application fee:* $25. • Dr. Molly Burke, Dean, 708-524-6810. E-mail: burkemg@email.dom.edu. Application contact: Dr. Dan Condon, Director Admissions and Advising, 708-524-6223. Fax: 708-366-5360. E-mail: condond@email.dom.edu.

Drexel University, College of Business and Administration, Program in Business Administration, 3141 Chestnut Street, Philadelphia, PA 19104-2875. Offerings include business administration (MBA, PhD, APC), with options in accounting (MBA, PhD), decision sciences (PhD), economics (MBA, PhD), finance (MBA, PhD), legal studies (MBA), management (MBA), marketing (MBA, PhD), organizational sciences (PhD), quantitative methods (MBA), strategic management (PhD). Terminal master's awarded for partial completion of doctoral program. *Degree requirements:* Computer language required, foreign language and dissertation not required. *Entrance requirements:* GMAT, TOEFL (minimum score 570). Application deadline: 8/21 (rolling processing; 3/5 for spring admission). Application fee: $35. *Expenses:* Tuition $494 per credit hour. Fees $121 per quarter full-time, $65 per quarter part-time. • Dr. Jerold B. Muskin, Director of Master's Programs in Business, 215-895-2115. Application contact: Denise Bigham, Director of Admissions, 215-895-6700. Fax: 215-895-5969.

Eastern Connecticut State University, School of Education and Professional Studies/ Graduate Division, Program in Organizational Management, Willimantic, CT 06226-2295. Awards MS. Faculty: 2 full-time (1 woman), 3 part-time (1 woman). Students: 39 part-time (23 women); includes 2 minority (1 African American, 1 Hispanic), 2 international. Average age 42. 10 applicants, 100% accepted. In 1997, 12 degrees awarded. *Degree requirements:* Comprehensive exam or thesis required, foreign language not required. *Entrance requirements:* Minimum GPA of 2.7. Application deadline: 3/1 (11/1 for spring admission). Application fee: $40. *Expenses:* Tuition $2632 per year full-time, $175 per credit hour part-time for state residents; $7220 per year full-time, $175 per credit hour part-time for nonresidents. Fees $1851 per year full-time, $20 per semester part-time for state residents; $2748 per year full-time, $20 per semester part-time for nonresidents. *Financial aid:* Application deadline 3/15. • Lyle Yorks, Coordinator, 860-465-5210. E-mail: yorksl@ecsu.ctstateu.edu. Application contact: Edith Mavor, Graduate Division Director, 860-465-4543. E-mail: mavor@ecsuc.ctstateu.edu.

Eastern Michigan University, College of Business, Department of Management, Program in Human Resources Management and Organizational Development, Ypsilanti, MI 48197. Awards MSHROD. *Degree requirements:* Thesis optional, foreign language not required. *Entrance requirements:* GMAT (minimum score 450), TOEFL (minimum score 550). Application deadline: 5/15 (rolling processing; 3/15 for spring admission). Application fee: $30. *Expenses:* Tuition $2691 per year full-time, $150 per credit hour part-time for state residents; $6300 per year full-time, $350 per credit hour part-time for nonresidents. Fees $368 per year full-time, $88 per semester (minimum) part-time. *Financial aid:* Application deadline 3/15. • Dr. Mary Herman, Coordinator, 734-487-3240.

Fairleigh Dickinson University, Florham–Madison Campus, Maxwell Becton College of Arts and Sciences, Department of Psychology, Program in Organizational Behavior, 285 Madison Avenue, Madison, NJ 07940-1099. Awards MA. Faculty: 10. Students: 15 part-time (8 women). *Entrance requirements:* GRE General Test. Application deadline: rolling. Application fee: $35. *Expenses:* Tuition $522 per credit. Fees $302 per year full-time, $138 per year part-time. • Dr. Diane Wentworth, Director, 973-443-8560.

Fielding Institute, Program in Organizational Design and Effectiveness, Santa Barbara, CA 93105-3538. Awards MA. Faculty: 5 full-time (2 women), 8 part-time (3 women). Students: 51 full-time (34 women); includes 6 minority (5 African Americans, 1 Hispanic). 62 applicants, 94% accepted. *Entrance requirements:* Professional experience in field. Application deadline: 6/1 (3/1 for spring admission). Application fee: $75. *Tuition:* $12,750 per year. *Financial aid:* Application deadline 4/1. • Dr. Matthews Hamabata, Co-Director, 805-687-1099 Ext. 2922. Application contact: Judy Brown, Admissions Counselor, 805-687-1099 Ext. 4020. Fax: 805-687-9793. E-mail: jsbrown@fielding.edu.

Fielding Institute, Programs in Human and Organization Development, Santa Barbara, CA 93105-3538. Offerings in human and organizational systems (PhD), human development (MA, PhD), human organization development (Ed D), human services (MA, DHS), organization development (MA). Evening/weekend programs available. Faculty: 28 full-time (13 women), 4 part-time (1 woman). Students: 448 full-time (309 women); includes 73 minority (42 African Americans, 10 Asian Americans, 17 Hispanics, 4 Native Americans), 25 international. Average age 46. 149 applicants, 75% accepted. In 1997, 77 master's, 63 doctorates awarded. Terminal master's awarded for partial completion of doctoral program. *Degree requirements:* For doctorate, dissertation required, foreign language not required. *Average time to degree:* master's–3.2 years full-time; doctorate–5.8 years full-time. *Application deadline:* 6/1 (3/1 for spring admission). *Application fee:* $60. *Tuition:* $12,250 per year. *Financial aid:* Minority scholarships and career-related internships or fieldwork available. Financial aid application deadline: 4/1. • Dr. Barbara Mink, Dean, 805-687-1099 Ext. 2930. Fax: 805-687-4590. Application contact: Judy Brown, Admissions Counselor, 805-687-1099 Ext. 4020. Fax: 805-687-9793. E-mail: jsbrown@fielding.edu.

Geneva College, Program in Organizational Leadership, Beaver Falls, PA 15010-3599. Awards MS. Part-time and evening/weekend programs available. Postbaccalaureate distance learning degree programs offered (no on-campus study). *Degree requirements:* Thesis required, foreign language not required. *Entrance requirements:* GRE, 3-5 years of professional experience; 2.5 GPA (undergraduate). Application fee: $15. *Faculty research:* Virtue ethics, strategic planning, leadership models.

George Mason University, College of Arts and Sciences, Department of Social and Organizational Learning, Fairfax, VA 22030-4444. Awards MA. Faculty: 7 full-time (2 women), 1 part-time (0 women), 7.25 FTE. Students: 6 full-time (2 women), 38 part-time (24 women); includes 7 minority (5 African Americans, 2 Asian Americans), 4 international. *Application fee:* $30. *Tuition:* $4344 per year full-time, $181 per credit hour part-time for state residents; $12,504 per year full-time, $521 per credit hour part-time for nonresidents. *Financial aid:* Application deadline 3/1. • Ann C. Baker, Director, 703-993-3813. E-mail: psol@gmu.edu.

The George Washington University, Columbian School of Arts and Sciences, Program in Administrative Sciences, Washington, DC 20052. Offerings include organizational management (MA). Program faculty: 3 part-time (0 women), 1 FTE. *Degree requirements:* Comprehensive exam required, thesis not required. *Entrance requirements:* GRE General Test, minimum GPA of 3.0. Application deadline: 5/1. Application fee: $50. *Expenses:* Tuition $680 per semester hour. Fees $35 per semester hour. • Dr. Joseph Zeidner, Director, 202-496-8380.

The George Washington University, School of Business and Public Management, Department of Management Science, Washington, DC 20052. Offerings include organizational behavior and development (MBA). Department faculty: 29 full-time (3 women), 23 part-time (5 women), 35 FTE. *Application deadline:* 4/1 (priority date; rolling processing; 10/1 for spring admission). *Application fee:* $50. *Expenses:* Tuition $680 per semester hour. Fees $35 per semester hour. • Dr. Erik K. Winslow, Chair, 202-994-7375. Application contact: Lilly Hastings, Graduate Admissions, 202-994-6584. Fax: 202-994-6382.

Golden Gate University, School of Business, San Francisco, CA 94105-2968. Offerings include organizational behavior and development (MBA, MS). MBA (telecommunications, management information systems) offered jointly with the School of Technology and Industry. *Average time to degree:* master's–2.5 years full-time. *Application deadline:* 7/1 (priority date; rolling processing). *Application fee:* $55 ($70 for international students). *Tuition:* $996 per course (minimum). • Dr. Hamid Shomali, Dean, 415-442-6500. Fax: 415-442-6579. Application contact: Enrollment Services, 415-442-7800. Fax: 415-442-7807. E-mail: info@ggu.edu.

Gonzaga University, Graduate School, School of Professional Studies, Program in Organizational Leadership, Spokane, WA 99258-0001. Awards MOL. *Entrance requirements:* GRE General Test or MAT, TOEFL (minimum score 550), minimum B average in undergraduate course work. Application deadline: 7/20 (priority date; rolling processing; 11/1 for spring admission). Application fee: $40. *Tuition:* $7380 per year (minimum) full-time, $410 per credit (minimum) part-time. *Financial aid:* Application deadline 3/1. • Application contact: Dr. Joseph Albert, 509-328-4220 Ext. 3564.

Graduate School and University Center of the City University of New York, Program in Business, New York, NY 10036-8099. Offerings include behavioral science (PhD). Terminal master's awarded for partial completion of doctoral program. Program faculty: 66 full-time (5 women). *Degree requirements:* Dissertation required, foreign language not required. *Entrance requirements:* GMAT. Application deadline: 3/1. Application fee: $40. *Expenses:* Tuition $4350 per year full-time, $185 per credit (minimum) part-time for state residents; $7600 per year full-time, $320 per credit (minimum) part-time for nonresidents. Fees $69 per year. • Dr. Gloria Thomas, Executive Officer, 212-802-6580.

The Graduate School of America, Graduate School, Management Field, Minneapolis, MN 55401. Offerings include organization and management (PhD), with option in communications technology. Terminal master's awarded for partial completion of doctoral program. Postbaccalaureate distance learning degree programs offered (minimal on-campus study). Faculty: 2 full-time (0 women), 15 part-time (6 women). *Degree requirements:* Dissertation required, foreign language not required. *Entrance requirements:* TOEFL (minimum score 550), minimum GPA of 3.0. Application deadline: rolling. Application fee: $50. Electronic applications accepted. *Expenses:* Tuition $7160 per year (minimum). Fees $795 per year (minimum). • Dr. Frank DeCaro, Chair, 612-339-8650. E-mail: fdecaro@worldnet.att.net. Application contact: Associate Director of Admissions, 800-987-1133. Fax: 612-337-5396. E-mail: tgsainfo@tgsa.edu.

Harvard University, Graduate School of Arts and Sciences and Doctoral Program in Management, Committee on Organizational Behavior, Cambridge, MA 02138. Awards PhD. Students: 23 full-time (11 women); includes 2 minority (both African Americans), 4 international. 98 applicants, 7% accepted. In 1997, 3 degrees awarded. *Entrance requirements:* GRE General Test or GMAT, TOEFL (minimum score 550), major in psychology or sociology, previous course work in statistics or mathematics. Application deadline: 12/30. Application fee: $60. *Expenses:* Tuition $21,342 per year. Fees $686 per year. *Financial aid:* Fellowships, research assistantships, teaching assistantships, Federal Work-Study, institutionally sponsored loans, and career-related internships or fieldwork available. Financial aid application deadline: 12/30. • Dr. Jay Lorsch, Co-Chair, 617-495-6413. Application contact: Office of Admissions and Financial Aid, 617-495-5315.

Directory: Organizational Behavior

Hawaii Pacific University, School of Business Administration, 1166 Fort Street, Honolulu, HI 96813-2785. Offerings include organizational change (MA). School faculty: 30 full-time (3 women), 12 part-time (1 woman), 38 FTE. *Average time to degree:* master's–2 years full-time, 4 years part-time. *Application deadline:* rolling. *Application fee:* $50. Electronic applications accepted. *Tuition:* $7920 per year full-time, $330 per credit part-time. • Dr. Richard Ward, Dean for Graduate Management Studies, 808-544-0279. Application contact: Leina Danao, Admissions Coordinator, 808-544-1120. Fax: 808-544-0280. E-mail: gradservctr@hpu.edu.

Indiana University Bloomington, School of Business, Doctoral Programs in Business, Bloomington, IN 47405. Offerings include organizational behavior (DBA, PhD). PhD offered through the University Graduate School. *Degree requirements:* Computer language, dissertation required, foreign language not required. *Entrance requirements:* GMAT (minimum score 600), GRE General Test. Application deadline: 3/1. Application fee: $35. *Expenses:* Tuition $261 per credit hour for state residents; $523 per credit hour for nonresidents. Fees $343 per year. • Dr. Janet Near, Chairperson, 812-855-3476. Application contact: Barbara Clark, Program Secretary and Assistant to Chairperson, 812-855-3476. Fax: 812-855-8679. E-mail: bclark@ucs.indiana.edu.

John F. Kennedy University, School of Management, Program in Business Administration, Orinda, CA 94563-2689. Offerings include organizational leadership (Certificate). *Application deadline:* rolling. *Application fee:* $50. *Expenses:* Tuition $316 per unit. Fees $9 per quarter. • Jeffrey Newcomb, Chair, 925-295-0600. Application contact: Ellena Bloedorn, Director of Admissions, 925-258-2213. Fax: 925-254-6964.

John Jay College of Criminal Justice, the City University of New York, Programs in Criminal Justice, New York, NY 10019-1093. Offerings include organizational behavior (PhD). Terminal master's awarded for partial completion of doctoral program. Faculty: 17 full-time, 6 part-time. *Degree requirements:* 1 foreign language (computer language can substitute), dissertation. *Entrance requirements:* GRE General Test, TOEFL. Application deadline: 6/30 (priority date; rolling processing; 12/1 for spring admission). Application fee: $40. *Expenses:* Tuition $4350 per year full-time, $185 per credit part-time for state residents; $7600 per year full-time, $320 per credit part-time for nonresidents. Fees $63 per year. • Dr. William Heffernan, Co-Program Director, 212-237-8376. Application contact: Dr. Barry Spunt, Co-Program Director, 212-237-8677. Fax: 212-237-8309.

Loyola University Chicago, Graduate School, Program for the Center for Organizational Development, 820 North Michigan Avenue, Chicago, IL 60611-2196. Awards MSOD, MSHR/MSOD, MSIR/MSOD, MSOD/MSTD. Part-time programs available. Faculty: 3 full-time (0 women), 3 part-time (1 woman). Students: 7 full-time (6 women), 82 part-time (59 women); includes 10 minority (6 African Americans, 2 Asian Americans, 2 Hispanics), 1 international. Average age 35. 18 applicants, 100% accepted. In 1997, 38 degrees awarded (100% found work related to degree). *Entrance requirements:* GMAT (minimum score 500) or GRE General Test (minimum combined score of 1550 on three sections), 5 years of work experience. Application deadline: 8/1. Application fee: $35. *Tuition:* $1665 per course. *Financial aid:* In 1997–98, 1 research assistantship (to a first-year student) was awarded; Federal Work-Study and career-related internships or fieldwork also available. *Faculty research:* Sociotechnical systems, work redesign, total quality management, teams, trust. • Dr. Linda K. Stroh, Director, 312-915-6595. E-mail: lstroh@luc.edu. Application contact: Dr. Fran Daly, Associate Director, 312-915-6595. Fax: 312-915-6231. E-mail: fdaly@luc.edu.

Manhattanville College, Humanities and Social Sciences Programs, Program in Organization Management and Human Resources Development, Purchase, NY 10577-2132. Awards MS. Part-time and evening/weekend programs available. Students: 170. *Degree requirements:* Thesis required, foreign language not required. *Application deadline:* 9/1 (priority date; rolling processing; 3/1 for spring admission). *Application fee:* $45. *Expenses:* Tuition $410 per credit (minimum). Fees $25 per semester. • Application contact: Donald J. Richards, Associate Dean, 914-694-3425. Fax: 914-694-3488. E-mail: drichard@mville.edu.

Marian College of Fond du Lac, Business Division, 45 South National Avenue, Fond du Lac, WI 54935-4699. Offerings include organizational leadership and quality (MS). Postbaccalaureate distance learning degree programs offered (no on-campus study). Division faculty: 3 full-time (0 women), 15 part-time (3 women). *Degree requirements:* Comprehensive group project required, foreign language and thesis not required. *Average time to degree:* master's–1.6 years part-time. *Entrance requirements:* 3 years of managerial experience. Application deadline: rolling. Application fee: $25. *Tuition:* $275 per credit hour. • Richard M. Dienesch, Assistant Dean of Evening/Weekend Programs, 920-923-8125. Fax: 920-923-7167.

Marymount University, School of Business Administration, Program in Organization Development, Arlington, VA 22207-4299. Awards MA. Part-time and evening/weekend programs available. Students: 28. *Degree requirements:* Thesis optional, foreign language not required. *Entrance requirements:* GMAT or GRE General Test, interview. Application deadline: rolling. Application fee: $35. *Expenses:* Tuition $465 per credit hour. Fees $120 per year full-time, $5 per credit hour part-time. *Financial aid:* Career-related internships or fieldwork available. Aid available to part-time students. Financial aid applicants required to submit FAFSA. • Dr. Karen Medsker, Chair, 703-284-5910. Fax: 703-527-3815. E-mail: karen.medsker@marymount.edu.

Marymount University, School of Business Administration, Program in Organizational Leadership and Innovation, Arlington, VA 22207-4299. Awards MS. Part-time and evening/weekend programs available. Students: 37. In 1997, 13 degrees awarded. *Degree requirements:* Thesis optional, foreign language not required. *Entrance requirements:* GMAT or GRE General Test, interview. Application deadline: rolling. Application fee: $35. *Expenses:* Tuition $465 per credit hour. Fees $120 per year full-time, $5 per credit hour part-time. *Financial aid:* Career-related internships or fieldwork available. Aid available to part-time students. Financial aid applicants required to submit FAFSA. *Faculty research:* Linking industrialization and cultural values. • Dr. John Fry, Associate Dean, 703-284-1622. Fax: 703-527-3815. E-mail: john.fry@marymount.edu.

Mercy College, Department of Business, Concentration in Organizational Leadership, Dobbs Ferry, NY 10522-1189. Awards MS. 60 applicants. *Entrance requirements:* Interview. *Tuition:* $390 per credit. • Application contact: Andrew Joppa, Assistant Director, 914-693-4500.

Mercyhurst College, Program in Organizational Leadership, 501 East 38th Street, Erie, PA 16546. Awards MS, Certificate. MS new for fall 1998. Students: 27 part-time (16 women); includes 2 minority (1 Asian American, 1 Hispanic). *Degree requirements:* For master's, thesis required, foreign language not required. *Entrance requirements:* For master's, GRE General Test, MAT, or minimum GPA of 3.0. Application deadline: 8/1 (priority date; rolling processing). Application fee: $35. Electronic applications accepted. *Expenses:* Tuition $681 per course. Fees $250 per year. • Dr. Bruce T. Murphy, Director, 814-824-2020. E-mail: bmurphy@mercyhurst.edu. Application contact: Mary Ellen Dahlkemper, Director, Office of Adult and Graduate Programs, 814-824-2294. Fax: 814-824-2055. E-mail: medahlk@mercyhurst.edu.

Metropolitan State University, Management and Administration Program, St. Paul, MN 55106-5000. Offerings include organizational studies (MBA). Program faculty: 17 full-time (5 women), 150 part-time. *Application deadline:* rolling. *Application fee:* $20. *Tuition:* $133 per credit for state residents; $208 per credit for nonresidents. • Gary Seiler, Graduate Coordinator, 612-373-2754. E-mail: seiler@msus1.msus.edu. Application contact: Gloria Marcus, Recruiter/Admissions Adviser, 612-373-2724. Fax: 612-373-2888. E-mail: marcusg@msus1.msus.edu.

Michigan State University, Eli Broad Graduate School of Management, Department of Management, East Lansing, MI 48824-1020. Offerings include organizational behavior-personnel (PhD). Department faculty: 12 (5 women). *Degree requirements:* Dissertation required, foreign language not required. *Entrance requirements:* GMAT (score in 90th percentile or higher). Application deadline: rolling. Application fee: $30 ($40 for international students). *Expenses:* Tuition $4609 per year full-time, $223 per credit hour (minimum) part-time for state residents; $8704 per year full-time, $450 per credit hour (minimum) part-time for nonresidents. Fees $576 per year full-time, $476 per year part-time. • Dr. John Wagner III, Acting Chairperson, 517-355-1878. Fax: 517-432-1111. E-mail: wagner@pilot.msu.edu.

Newman University, Program in Organizational Leadership, Wichita, KS 67213-2084. Awards MS. Faculty: 3 full-time. Students: 9. *Application deadline:* 8/15. *Application fee:* $25. *Tuition:* $257 per credit hour. • George Smith, Director of Graduate Business Program, 316-942-4291 Ext. 205. Fax: 316-942-4483.

Northwestern University, Division of Interdepartmental Programs, Program in Sociology and Organization Behavior, Evanston, IL 60208. Awards PhD. Program requires admission to both The Graduate School and the J. L. Kellogg Graduate School of Management. Students: 4 full-time (1 woman); includes 1 minority (African American), 1 international. 7 applicants, 0% accepted. *Degree requirements:* Computer language, dissertation required, foreign language not required. *Entrance requirements:* GMAT or GRE General Test, TOEFL (minimum score 550). Application fee: $50 ($55 for international students). *Tuition:* $20,430 per year full-time, $2424 per course part-time. *Financial aid:* Fellowships, research assistantships, teaching assistantships, Federal Work-Study, institutionally sponsored loans, and career-related internships or fieldwork available. Financial aid application deadline: 1/15; applicants required to submit FAFSA. *Faculty research:* Strategic alliances and organizational competitiveness, institutional change and the information of industries, social capital and the creation of financial capital, social networks and the stock market trade in England in the 1600's, attention and adapation. • Brian Uzzi, Director, 847-491-3470. E-mail: uzzi@nwu.edu. Application contact: Mary Lou Manning, Assistant, 847-491-8501. Fax: 847-491-9907. E-mail: mmanning@nwu.edu.

Northwestern University, J. L. Kellogg Graduate School of Management, Department of Organization Behavior, Evanston, IL 60208. Awards PhD. Admissions and degree offered through The Graduate School. Faculty: 17 full-time (4 women). Students: 19 full-time (7 women); includes 4 minority (2 African Americans, 1 Asian American, 1 Native American), 4 international. 80 applicants, 15% accepted. In 1997, 1 degree awarded. *Degree requirements:* Dissertation required, foreign language not required. *Entrance requirements:* GMAT or GRE General Test. Application deadline: 1/15. Application fee: $50 ($55 for international students). *Tuition:* $25,872 per year. *Financial aid:* In 1997–98, 16 students received aid, including fellowships averaging $1,256 per month; tuition scholarships, institutionally sponsored loans, and career-related internships or fieldwork also available. Financial aid application deadline: 1/15; applicants required to submit FAFSA. *Faculty research:* Bargaining and negotiation, organizational design, decision making, organizational change, strategic alliances. Total annual research expenditures: $169,200. • Robert Duncan, Chair, 847-491-4954. Application contact: Lucy Vandenburgh, Contact, 847-491-3400. Fax: 847-491-5071. E-mail: l-vandenburgh@nwu.edu.

Pepperdine University, School of Business and Management, Culver City, CA 90230-7615. Offerings include organizational development (MSOD). School faculty: 72 full-time (10 women), 38 part-time (5 women). *Application deadline:* 5/1. *Application fee:* $45. • Dr. Otis Baskin, Dean, 310-568-5500. Application contact: Dianna Sadlouskos, Director of Career Development and Student Recruitment.

Pfeiffer University, Program in Business Administration, Charlotte, NC 28209. Offerings include organizational management (MS). Postbaccalaureate distance learning degree programs offered. Program faculty: 11 full-time (2 women), 8 part-time (4 women), 15 FTE. *Application deadline:* 8/21. *Application fee:* $50. *Tuition:* $245 per hour (minimum). • Dr. Muhammed Abdullah, Director, 704-521-9116. Fax: 704-521-8617.

Philadelphia College of Bible, Graduate School, Organizational Leadership Program, 200 Manor Avenue, Langhorne, PA 19047-2990. Awards MS. Part-time and evening/weekend programs available. Faculty: 1 full-time (0 women), 10 part-time (3 women), 5 FTE. Students: 1 full-time (0 women), 29 part-time (9 women); includes 10 minority (all African Americans). Average age 34. 17 applicants, 100% accepted. *Average time to degree:* master's–2 years full-time, 4 years part-time. *Entrance requirements:* Minimum undergraduate GPA of 2.5. Application deadline: 9/1 (priority date; rolling processing). Application fee: $25. *Expenses:* Tuition $275 per credit. Fees $10 per year. *Financial aid:* In 1997–98, 10 students received aid, including 10 scholarships (6 to first-year students) totaling $5,514. Financial aid application deadline: 8/1. • Dr. Jay Desko, Chair, 800-572-2472. E-mail: jdesko@pcb.edu. Application contact: Ted McKown, Director of Marketing/Recruiting, 800-572-2472. Fax: 215-702-4359. E-mail: tmckown@pcb.edu.

Phillips Graduate Institute, Program in Marital and Family Therapy and Organizational Behavior, 5445 Balboa Boulevard, Encino, CA 91316-1509. Offers marital and family therapy (MA), organizational behavior (MA). Evening/weekend programs available. Faculty: 13 full-time, 30 part-time. Students: 283. *Degree requirements:* Thesis, comprehensive oral exam required, foreign language not required. *Average time to degree:* master's–2 years full-time. *Entrance requirements:* Minimum GPA of 3.0. Application deadline: 8/15 (priority date; rolling processing; 12/15 for spring admission). Application fee: $0. *Tuition:* $475 per unit. *Financial aid:* Full and partial tuition waivers available. Financial aid application deadline: 8/15; applicants required to submit FAFSA. *Faculty research:* Integration of interpersonal psychological theory, systems approach, firsthand experiential learning. • Dr. Edwin S. Cox, President, 818-386-5650. Application contact: Michelle Browning, Registrar and Admissions Officer, 818-386-5638. Fax: 818-386-5699.

Polytechnic University, Brooklyn Campus, Department of Management, Major in Organizational Behavior, Six Metrotech Center, Brooklyn, NY 11201-2990. Awards MS. Students: 17. 9 applicants, 89% accepted. In 1997, 18 degrees awarded. *Degree requirements:* Thesis or alternative. *Entrance requirements:* GMAT, minimum B average in undergraduate course work. Application deadline: rolling. Application fee: $45. Electronic applications accepted. *Expenses:* Tuition $19,530 per year full-time, $675 per credit part-time. Fees $600 per year full-time, $135 per semester part-time. • Harold Kaufman, Director, 718-260-3485. Fax: 718-260-3874. E-mail: hkaufman@poly.edu. Application contact: John S. Kerge, Dean of Admissions, 718-260-3200. Fax: 718-260-3446. E-mail: admitme@poly.edu.

Polytechnic University, Westchester Graduate Center, Division of Management, Major in Organizational Behavior, Hawthorne, NY 10532-1507. Awards MS. Students: 0. 0 applicants. *Degree requirements:* Computer language. *Application deadline:* rolling. *Application fee:* $45. Electronic applications accepted. *Expenses:* Tuition $19,530 per year full-time, $675 per credit part-time. Fees $600 per year full-time, $135 per semester part-time. • Harold Kaufman, Director, 718-260-3485. Fax: 718-260-3874. E-mail: hkaufman@poly.edu. Application contact: John S. Kerge, Dean of Admissions, 718-260-3200. Fax: 718-260-3446. E-mail: admitme@poly.edu.

Purdue University, Krannert Graduate School of Management, Department of Organizational Behavior and Human Resource Management, West Lafayette, IN 47907. Offers programs in human resource management (MS), organizational behavior and human resource management (PhD). Faculty: 10 full-time (2 women). Students: 52 full-time (34 women), 2 part-time (1 woman); includes 14 minority (7 African Americans, 3 Asian Americans, 4 Hispanics), 11 international. Average age 28. 109 applicants, 36% accepted. In 1997, 19 master's, 2 doctorates awarded. *Degree requirements:* For doctorate, dissertation required, foreign language not required. *Average time to degree:* doctorate–4 years full-time. *Entrance requirements:* For master's, GMAT, TOEFL (minimum score 575); for doctorate, GMAT or GRE General Test, TOEFL (minimum score 575). Application fee: $30. Electronic applications accepted. *Tuition:* $3500 per year full-time, $126 per credit hour part-time for state residents; $11,720 per year full-time, $387 per credit hour part-time for nonresidents. *Financial aid:* In 1997–98, 3 fellowships averaging $960 per month, 10 research assistantships (1 to a first-year student) averaging $960 per month, 5 teaching assistantships averaging $960 per month were awarded; career-related internships or fieldwork also available. Aid available to part-time students.

Financial aid applicants required to submit FAFSA. *Faculty research:* Leadership, staff management and selection, teams, human resource information systems. • Dr. J. J. McConnell, Director of Doctoral Programs, 765-494-4375. Application contact: Kelly Felty, Assistant Director of Administration for Doctoral Programs, 765-494-4375. Fax: 765-494-1526. E-mail: feltyk@mgmt.purdue.edu.

Regent University, Graduate School, Center for Leadership Studies, Virginia Beach, VA 23464-9800. Offers program in organizational leadership (MA, PhD). Faculty: 2 full-time (0 women), 10 part-time (2 women). Students: 3 full-time (2 women), 89 part-time (37 women); includes 20 minority (13 African Americans, 2 Asian Americans, 3 Hispanics, 2 Native Americans). Average age 43. 72 applicants, 61% accepted. *Entrance requirements:* For master's, minimum undergraduate GPA of 2.75. Application deadline: rolling. Application fee: $100. Electronic applications accepted. *Expenses:* Tuition $350 per credit hour (minimum). Fees $18 per semester. *Financial aid:* Application deadline 5/1. • Dr. Kathaleen Reid-Martinez, Director, 757-226-4242. E-mail: kathrei@regent.edu. Application contact: Julia Mattera, Director of Admissions, 757-226-4122. Fax: 757-226-4042. E-mail: leadercenter@regent.edu.

Rensselaer Polytechnic Institute, Lally School of Management and Technology, Troy, NY 12180-3590. Offerings include business administration (MBA, PhD), with options in finance and accounting (MBA), information systems management (MBA), management (PhD), management of technology and entrepreneurships (MBA), manufacturing management (MBA), marketing management (MBA), operations research (MBA), organizational behavior and human resource management (MBA), statistical methods for management (MBA). Postbaccalaureate distance learning degree programs offered (no on-campus study). School faculty: 36 full-time (5 women), 6 part-time (0 women). *Application deadline:* 2/1 (priority date; rolling processing). *Application fee:* $35. *Expenses:* Tuition $630 per credit hour. Fees $1000 per year. • Dr. Joseph G. Ecker, Dean, 518-276-6802. Application contact: Michele Martens, Manager of Enrollment Services, 518-276-4800. Fax: 518-276-8661.

Rutgers, The State University of New Jersey, Newark, Graduate School of Management, Department of Organization Management, Newark, NJ 07102-3192. Awards MBA. *Degree requirements:* Computer language required, thesis not required. *Entrance requirements:* GMAT, TOEFL. Application deadline: 6/1 (rolling processing). Application fee: $40. *Financial aid:* Federal Work-Study, institutionally sponsored loans, and career-related internships or fieldwork available. Financial aid application deadline: 3/15; applicants required to submit FAFSA. • Dr. Fariborz Damanpour, Chair, 973-353-5050. Fax: 973-353-1664. E-mail: fdamanpo@gsmack.rutgers.edu. Application contact: Director of Admissions, 973-353-1234. Fax: 973-353-1592. E-mail: admit@gsmack.rutgers.edu.

Saginaw Valley State University, College of Arts and Behavioral Sciences, Program in Organizational Leadership and Administration, University Center, MI 48710. Awards MA. Faculty: 9 full-time (6 women). Students: 6 full-time (3 women), 14 part-time (7 women); includes 6 minority (5 African Americans, 1 Hispanic). *Entrance requirements:* Minimum GPA of 3.0 in social sciences, 2.75 overall. Application deadline: rolling. Application fee: $25. *Expenses:* Tuition $159 per credit hour for state residents; $311 per credit hour for nonresidents. Fees $8.70 per credit hour. *Faculty research:* Mediation and conciliation, public administration, criminal justice, fiscal administration, professional ethics. • David Weaver, Chair, 517-790-4378. E-mail: drw@tardis.svsu.edu.

Simon Fraser University, Faculty of Business Administration, Burnaby, BC V5A 1S6, Canada. Offerings include organization behavior (MBA). Faculty: 48 full-time (12 women). *Application fee:* $55. *Expenses:* Tuition $2400 per year (minimum). Fees $207 per year. • S. McShane, Director, 604-291-3639. Application contact: Program Assistant, 604-291-3047. Fax: 604-291-3404. E-mail: mba@sfu.ca.

State University of New York at Albany, School of Business, Program in Organizational Studies, Albany, NY 12222-0001. Awards PhD. Students: 20 full-time (11 women), 16 part-time (7 women); includes 3 minority (2 African Americans, 1 Hispanic), 4 international. 28 applicants, 43% accepted. In 1997, 3 degrees awarded. *Degree requirements:* Dissertation. *Entrance requirements:* GMAT or GRE. Application deadline: 7/1 (priority date; rolling processing). Application fee: $50. *Expenses:* Tuition $5100 per year full-time, $213 per credit hour part-time for state residents; $8416 per year full-time, $351 per credit hour part-time for nonresidents. Fees $705 per year full-time, $26.85 per credit hour part-time. *Financial aid:* Application deadline 4/1. *Faculty research:* Organizational stress and burnout, database change, task design. • Dr. Michael Kavanaugh, Director, 518-442-4956. Application contact: Jeffrey Collins, Assistant Director, Graduate Admissions, 518-442-3980.

Syracuse University, School of Management, PhD Program in Business Administration, Syracuse, NY 13244-0003. Offerings include organizational behavior (PhD). Program faculty: 75. *Entrance requirements:* GMAT (minimum score 600). Application deadline: 2/1. Application fee: $40. *Tuition:* $13,320 per year full-time, $555 per credit hour part-time. • S. P. Raj, Associate Dean. Application contact: Barbara Buske, Secretary, 315-443-1001.

Syracuse University, School of Management, Program in Organization and Management, Syracuse, NY 13244-0003. Awards MBA. Students: 51 full-time (16 women), 105 part-time (29 women); includes 14 minority (8 African Americans, 3 Asian Americans, 3 Hispanics), 13 international. 98 applicants, 74% accepted. In 1997, 70 degrees awarded. *Entrance requirements:* GMAT. Application deadline: 2/1. Application fee: $40. *Tuition:* $13,320 per year full-time, $555 per credit hour part-time. *Financial aid:* Application deadline 3/1. • Rod Chesser, Chair, 315-443-2601. Application contact: Associate Dean, 315-443-3850.

Trevecca Nazarene University, Major in Organizational Management, Nashville, TN 37210-2834. Awards MA. Evening/weekend programs available. Faculty: 2 full-time (both women), 1 part-time (0 women). Students: 88 full-time (41 women); includes 18 minority (all African Americans). Average age 35. 38 applicants, 71% accepted. In 1997, 61 degrees awarded. *Entrance requirements:* GMAT, minimum GPA of 2.5. Application deadline: 8/31 (rolling processing; 1/18 for spring admission). Application fee: $25. *Expenses:* Tuition $287 per hour. Fees $125 per year. • Dr. Rondy Smith, Graduate Director, 615-248-1529.

University of Alberta, Faculty of Graduate Studies and Research, Doctoral Program in Business, Edmonton, AB T6G 2E1, Canada. Offerings include organizational analysis (PhD). Terminal master's awarded for partial completion of doctoral program. Program faculty: 34 full-time (5 women). *Degree requirements:* Dissertation required, foreign language not required. *Average time to degree:* doctorate–6 years full-time, 8.5 years part-time. *Entrance requirements:* GMAT (average 675), TOEFL (minimum score 600; average 627). Application deadline: 3/1 (priority date). Application fee: $60. *Expenses:* Tuition $390 per course for Canadian residents; $781 per course for nonresidents. Fees $500 per year full-time, $184 per year part-time. • Dr. Michael Gibbins, Director, 403-492-2361. Application contact: Jeanette Gosine, Department Office, 403-492-2361. Fax: 403-492-3325. E-mail: jgosine@gpu.srv.ualberta.ca.

University of British Columbia, Faculty of Commerce and Business Administration, Doctoral Program in Commerce and Business Administration, Vancouver, BC V6T 1Z2, Canada. Offerings include organizational behavior (PhD). *Degree requirements:* Dissertation required, foreign language not required. *Entrance requirements:* GMAT or GRE, TOEFL. Application deadline: 12/31 (priority date; rolling processing). Application fee: $60.

University of California, Berkeley, Haas School of Business, Doctoral Program in Business, Berkeley, CA 94720-1500. Offerings include organizational behavior and industrial relations (PhD). Program faculty: 64 full-time (11 women). *Degree requirements:* Dissertation, oral exam, written preliminary exams required, foreign language not required. *Entrance requirements:* GMAT or GRE, TOEFL, minimum GPA of 3.0. Application deadline: 2/10. Application fee: $40. *Expenses:* Tuition $0 for state residents; $9384 per year for nonresidents. Fees $4409 per year. • Dr. David C. Mowery, Director, 510-643-9992. E-mail: jan@haas.berkeley.edu. Application contact: Jan Price Greenough, Coordinator, 510-642-1409. Fax: 510-643-6659. E-mail: jan@haas.berkeley.edu.

University of Colorado at Boulder, Graduate School of Business Administration, Division of Organization Management, Boulder, CO 80309. Awards MBA, PhD. Students: 28 full-time (17 women), 1 (woman) part-time; includes 4 minority (3 Asian Americans, 1 Hispanic), 2 international. Average age 29. 49 applicants, 45% accepted. *Degree requirements:* For master's, computer language required, foreign language not required; for doctorate, dissertation, research internship. *Entrance requirements:* GMAT. Application deadline: 3/1 (priority date; rolling processing). Application fee: $40 ($60 for international students). *Expenses:* Tuition $3594 per year (minimum) full-time, $597 per semester (minimum) part-time for state residents; $14,868 per year (minimum) full-time, $2478 per semester (minimum) part-time for nonresidents. Fees $667 per year full-time, $130 per semester (minimum) part-time. *Financial aid:* Application deadline 3/1. • Dale Meyer, Chair, 303-492-4479. Fax: 303-492-5962. E-mail: d.meyer@colorado.edu. Application contact: Diana Marinaro, Graduate Student Admissions, 303-492-1831. Fax: 303-492-1727. E-mail: busgrad@spot.colorado.edu.

University of Colorado at Colorado Springs, Graduate School of Business Administration, Colorado Springs, CO 80933-7150. Offerings include organizational management (MBA). School faculty: 24 full-time (4 women). *Entrance requirements:* GMAT. Application deadline: 6/1 (priority date; 11/1 for spring admission). Application fee: $50. *Expenses:* Tuition $2860 per year full-time, $121 per credit hour part-time for state residents; $10,254 per year full-time, $420 per credit hour part-time for nonresidents. Fees $399 per year (minimum) full-time, $106 per year (minimum) part-time. • Dr. Richard Dicenza, Dean, 719-262-3113. E-mail: rdicenz@mail.uccs.edu. Application contact: Diane Belger, Adviser, 719-262-3408. Fax: 719-262-3494. E-mail: dbelger@mail.uccs.edu.

University of Hartford, Barney School of Business and Public Administration, Program in Business Administration, West Hartford, CT 06117-1599. Offerings include organizational behavior (MBA). Program faculty: 24 full-time (4 women), 15 part-time (1 woman). *Average time to degree:* master's–1.5 years full-time, 3 years part-time. *Entrance requirements:* GMAT, TOEFL. Application deadline: 7/1 (priority date; rolling processing; 12/1 for spring admission). Application fee: $35 ($50 for international students). Electronic applications accepted. • Christopher Galligan, Director, 860-768-4390. Application contact: Claire Silverstein, Assistant Director, 860-768-4900. Fax: 860-768-4821. E-mail: silverste@unavax.hartford.edu.

University of Hartford, Barney School of Business and Public Administration, Department of Management/Marketing, Program in Organizational Behavior, West Hartford, CT 06117-1599. Awards MSOB, MSN/MSOB. Offerings include human resource management (MSOB), organizational development (MSOB). Part-time and evening/weekend programs available. Faculty: 5 full-time (2 women), 2 part-time (1 woman). Students: 8 full-time, 23 part-time; includes 2 international. Average age 31. 18 applicants, 72% accepted. In 1997, 13 degrees awarded. *Average time to degree:* master's–1.5 years full-time, 3 years part-time. *Entrance requirements:* GMAT, GRE, TOEFL. Application deadline: 7/1 (priority date; rolling processing; 12/1 for spring admission). Application fee: $35 ($50 for international students). Electronic applications accepted. *Financial aid:* Research assistantships, institutionally sponsored loans available. Financial aid application deadline: 5/1. • Dr. Sandra Morgan, Director, 860-768-4974. Fax: 860-768-4198. E-mail: morgan@uhavax.hartford.edu. Application contact: Claire Silverstein, Assistant Director, 860-768-4900. Fax: 860-768-4821. E-mail: silverste@unavax.hartford.edu.

The University of Iowa, College of Business Administration, Department of Management and Organizations, Iowa City, IA 52242-1316. Offers program in business administration (PhD). Faculty: 11 full-time (3 women), 4 part-time (2 women). Students: 12 full-time (4 women), 2 part-time (1 woman); includes 1 minority (African American), 2 international. Average age 37. 32 applicants, 16% accepted. In 1997, 2 doctorates awarded (50% entered university research/teaching, 50% found other work related to degree). Terminal master's awarded for partial completion of doctoral program. *Degree requirements:* For doctorate, computer language, dissertation required, foreign language not required. *Average time to degree:* doctorate–4 years full-time, 5 years part-time. *Entrance requirements:* For doctorate, GMAT (minimum score 600; average 650). Application deadline: 3/1. Application fee: $30 ($50 for international students). *Expenses:* Tuition $3166 per year full-time, $176 per semester hour part-time for state residents; $10,202 per year full-time, $176 per semester hour part-time for nonresidents. Fees $202 per year full-time, $52 per year (minimum) part-time. *Financial aid:* In 1997–98, 13 students received aid, including 1 fellowship totaling $3,200, 7 research assistantships averaging $1,278 per month and totaling $32,884, 10 teaching assistantships averaging $1,278 per month and totaling $76,019, 9 summer research grants, tuition grants (1 to a first-year student) totaling $27,456; Federal Work-Study and career-related internships or fieldwork also available. Financial aid application deadline: 3/1; applicants required to submit FAFSA. *Faculty research:* Personality and job performance, behavioral decision making, employment selection, negotiation and conflict management, ethics. • Michael Mount, Chair, 319-335-0927. E-mail: michael-mount@uiowa.edu. Application contact: Murray Barrick, Associate Professor, 319-335-0924. Fax: 319-335-1956. E-mail: mbarrick@uiowa.edu.

University of La Verne, School of Business and Economics, La Verne, CA 91750-4443. Offerings include business organizational management (MS). *Application fee:* $25. *Expenses:* Tuition $335 per unit. Fees $60 per year.

University of La Verne, School of Organizational Management, Department of Public Administration, Program in Leadership and Management, La Verne, CA 91750-4443. Awards MS. Part-time programs available. *Degree requirements:* Major research project required, thesis not required. *Entrance requirements:* TOEFL (minimum score 550), minimum GPA of 2.5. Application fee: $25. *Expenses:* Tuition $315 per unit (minimum). Fees $60 per year.

University of Missouri–St. Louis, School of Business Administration, Program in Business Administration, St. Louis, MO 63121-4499. Offerings include organizational behavior (MBA). Program faculty: 19 (3 women). *Entrance requirements:* GMAT (minimum score 500; average 554). Application deadline: 7/1 (rolling processing; 11/1 for spring admission). Application fee: $0. Electronic applications accepted. *Expenses:* Tuition $3903 per year full-time, $167 per credit hour part-time for state residents; $11,745 per year full-time, $489 per credit hour part-time for nonresidents. Fees $816 per year full-time, $34 per credit hour part-time. • Application contact: Graduate Admissions, 314-516-5458. Fax: 314-516-6759. E-mail: gradadm@umslvma.umsl.edu.

University of New Haven, School of Business, Program in Business Administration, West Haven, CT 06516-1916. Offerings include management and organization (MBA). *Degree requirements:* Thesis or alternative required, foreign language not required. *Application deadline:* rolling. *Application fee:* $50. *Expenses:* Tuition $1125 per course. Fees $13 per trimester. • Dr. Omid Nodoushani, Coordinator, 203-932-7123.

The University of North Carolina at Chapel Hill, Kenan-Flagler Business School, Doctoral Program in Business Administration, Chapel Hill, NC 27599. Offerings include organizational behavior (PhD). Program faculty: 79 full-time (15 women), 29 part-time (6 women). *Degree requirements:* Dissertation required, foreign language not required. *Average time to degree:* doctorate–4 years full-time. *Entrance requirements:* GMAT (average 657) or GRE General Test (minimum combined score of 1350). Application deadline: 1/1 (priority date; rolling processing). Application fee: $55. Electronic applications accepted. *Expenses:* Tuition $1428 per year for state residents; $10,414 per year for nonresidents. Fees $787 per year. • Ann Marucheck, Associate Dean for PhD Programs, 919-962-3193. Application contact: Liz Griffin, Director, 919-962-1657. E-mail: kfphd_app@unc.edu.

University of North Carolina at Pembroke, Graduate Studies, Department of Organizational Leadership and Management, Pembroke, NC 28372-1510. Awards MS. Part-time and evening/weekend programs available. Faculty: 9 full-time (0 women). Students: 4 full-time (1 woman), 28 part-time (18 women); includes 8 minority (2 African Americans, 6 Native Americans). In 1997, 6 degrees awarded. *Degree requirements:* Comprehensive exam required, thesis optional, foreign language not required. *Average time to degree:* master's–2 years full-time, 3 years

Directory: Organizational Behavior; Cross-Discipline Announcement

University of North Carolina at Pembroke (continued)
part-time. *Entrance requirements:* GMAT, GRE General Test, or MAT, minimum GPA of 3.0 in major, 2.5 overall. Application deadline: rolling. Application fee: $25. *Tuition:* $1554 per year full-time, $610 per semester (minimum) part-time for state residents; $8824 per year full-time, $2122 per semester (minimum) part-time for nonresidents. *Financial aid:* In 1997–98, 3 graduate assistantships averaging $700 per month and totaling $16,800 were awarded. Aid available to part-time students. Financial aid application deadline: 4/15. • Dr. Daniel Barbee, Director, 910-521-6637. Application contact: Director of Graduate Studies, 910-521-6271. Fax: 910-521-6497.

University of North Texas, College of Business Administration, Department of Management, Denton, TX 76203-6737. Offerings include organization theory and policy (PhD). Department faculty: 16 full-time (3 women), 5 part-time (3 women). *Degree requirements:* Computer language, dissertation required, foreign language not required. *Entrance requirements:* GMAT or GRE General Test, TOEFL, work experience. Application deadline: 7/17. Application fee: $25 ($50 for international students). *Tuition:* $2063 per year full-time, $815 per year part-time for state residents; $5897 per year full-time, $2100 per year part-time for nonresidents. • Dr. Lewis A. Taylor, Chair, 940-565-3140. Application contact: Dr. J. Lyn Johnson, Graduate Adviser, 940-565-3147. Fax: 940-565-4394.

University of Pennsylvania, School of Arts and Sciences, Graduate Group in Organizational Dynamics, Philadelphia, PA 19104. Awards MS. Part-time and evening/weekend programs available. Faculty: 18 part-time (7 women). Students: 732 part-time (361 women). Average age 38. 85 applicants, 94% accepted. In 1997, 121 degrees awarded (100% found work related to degree). *Degree requirements:* Thesis required, foreign language not required. *Average time to degree:* master's–4 years part-time. *Application deadline:* rolling. *Application fee:* $65. *Expenses:* Tuition $22,716 per year full-time, $2876 per course part-time. Fees $1484 per year full-time, $181 per course part-time. *Financial aid:* Grants available. Aid available to part-time students. • Dr. Stephen Gale, Chairman/Director, 215-898-6967. Application contact: Lois Ginsberg, Associate Director, 215-898-6967. Fax: 215-898-8934.

University of Phoenix, Graduate Programs, Business Administration and Management Programs, Program in Organizational Management, 4615 East Elwood St, PO Box 52069, Phoenix, AZ 85072-2069. Awards MAOM. Programs offered at campuses in Colorado, Colorado Springs, Florida, Hawaii, Louisiana, Michigan, Nevada, New Mexico, Northern California, Phoenix, Sacramento, San Diego, Southern California, Tucson, Utah, on-line, and at the Center for Distance Education. Postbaccalaureate distance learning degree programs offered (no on-campus study). Students: 2,107 full-time (1,237 women); includes 674 minority (329 African Americans, 124 Asian Americans, 181 Hispanics, 40 Native Americans). Average age 36. In 1997, 658 degrees awarded. *Degree requirements:* Thesis or alternative required, foreign language not required. *Entrance requirements:* TOEFL (minimum score 520), minimum undergraduate GPA of 2.5, 3 years of work experience, comprehensive cognitive assessment (COCA). Application deadline: rolling. Application fee: $50. *Tuition:* $248 per credit hour. • Application contact: Campus Information Center, 602-966-9577.

University of San Francisco, College of Professional Studies, Department of Organizational Studies, Program in Human Resources and Organization Development, San Francisco, CA 94117-1080. Awards MHROD. Part-time and evening/weekend programs available. Faculty: 5 full-time (4 women), 44 part-time (12 women). Students: 296 full-time (225 women); includes 72 minority (28 African Americans, 18 Asian Americans, 24 Hispanics, 2 Native Americans). Average age 39. 136 applicants, 82% accepted. In 1997, 104 degrees awarded. *Degree requirements:* Thesis required, foreign language not required. *Average time to degree:* master's–3 years full-time. *Entrance requirements:* Minimum GPA of 3.0. Application fee: $35. *Financial aid:* 87 students received aid. Financial aid application deadline: 3/2. • Application contact: Advising Office, 415-422-6000.

University of Saskatchewan, College of Commerce, Department of Industrial Relations and Organizational Behavior, Saskatoon, SK S7N 5A2, Canada. Awards M Sc. Part-time programs available. *Degree requirements:* Thesis. *Entrance requirements:* GMAT, TOEFL. Application deadline: 7/1 (priority date; rolling processing). Application fee: $0.

University of Scranton, Department of Health Administration and Human Resources, Program in Human Resources Administration, Scranton, PA 18510-4622. Offerings include organizational leadership (MS). *Degree requirements:* Comprehensive exam required, foreign language and thesis not required. *Entrance requirements:* TOEFL (minimum score 575), minimum GPA of 2.75. Application deadline: rolling. Application fee: $35. *Expenses:* Tuition $465 per credit. Fees $25 per semester. • Dr. Daniel J. West, Chair, Department of Health Administration and Human Resources, 717-941-4126. Fax: 717-941-4201. E-mail: westd1@uofs.edu.

University of Tennessee at Chattanooga, School of Business Administration, Program in Business Administration, Chattanooga, TN 37403-2598. Offerings include organizational management (MBA). *Entrance requirements:* GMAT (average 527). Application deadline: rolling. Application fee: $25. *Tuition:* $2864 per year full-time, $160 per credit hour part-time for state residents; $6806 per year full-time, $379 per credit hour part-time for nonresidents. • Ashley Williams, Director, 423-755-4169. Fax: 423-755-5255. Application contact: Dr. Deborah Arfken, Assistant Provost for Graduate Studies, 423-755-4667. Fax: 423-755-4478.

Vanderbilt University, Owen Graduate School of Management and Graduate School, Program in Management, Nashville, TN 37240-1001. Offerings include organizational studies (PhD). PhD offered through the Graduate School. *Degree requirements:* Dissertation required, foreign language not required. *Entrance requirements:* GMAT (minimum score 650), GRE, TOEFL (minimum score 600). Application deadline: 1/15. Application fee: $50. *Tuition:* $871 per semester hour. • Bruce Barry, Director, 615-322-3489. Application contact: Maureen Writesman, 615-343-1989. Fax: 615-343-7177. E-mail: owenphd@ctrvax.vanderbilt.edu.

Cross-Discipline Announcement

University of Southern California, Graduate School, Annenberg School for Communication, School of Communication, Program in Communication Theory and Research, Los Angeles, CA 90089.

The master's in communication management has concentrations in marketing communication, entertainment management, strategic and corporate communication management, communication and information technologies, and communication law and policy. Students may take cognate courses in other units, such as business or cinema/television. Communication management program graduates pursue careers in such areas as marketing, market research and analysis, social marketing, public and political communication campaigns, advertising, public relations, publicity, media management, and entertainment.

BOSTON COLLEGE

Wallace E. Carroll School of Management
Organization Studies Department
Doctoral Program in Organizational Transformation

Program of Study

The doctoral program is designed for individuals who wish to pursue academic careers in teaching, research, consulting, and organizational development. The intellectual theme of the program emphasizes organizational transformation, which refers to fundamental changes in organizations that influence their character and effectiveness.

The program combines courses in theory and applied research, as well as teaching and consulting experience. The program begins with systematic and rigorous training in organizational theory, statistics, research methods, and organizational change. Students take four required theory courses, six required research methods courses, and four required application courses. In addition, students take four elective courses. The four required theory courses are micro-organization theory, macro-organization theory, perspectives on individual and organizational change, and organizational change and transformation. The six required research methods courses are statistical analysis I and II, qualitative research methods, quantitative research methods, and research seminar I and II. The four required application courses are teaching practicum, independent research I and II, and consulting practice, theory, and research.

During the second year, students also receive training in teaching skills, as well as the opportunity to teach. Students serve as teaching assistants and teaching fellows and are required to complete the teaching practicum. This course is designed to accompany a doctoral student's first teaching experience. The course addresses issues associated with teaching in a university. It traces typical course progression and identifies the issues faculty members encounter during various phases of a course. Peer observations and critique through videotaping are integral parts of the course.

The program's practice of offering qualifying exams after the first year of the program frees students to bring their own research and dissertation topics into focus earlier. A research paper prepared during the second year helps develop the student's ability to do original research. This development of research skills culminates in the preparation and defense of a dissertation during the third and fourth years. Within the prescribed requirements of the program, students have sufficient flexibility to develop individual directions to their studies.

Research Facilities

All Ph.D. students are provided with office space, free computing access, and various research tools. In addition, students have access to a library system with over 1 million volumes and approximately 10,000 serial titles. The library also provides a multitude of on-line and high-tech resources.

Financial Aid

The doctoral program offers four-year financial support for all accepted applicants, including full tuition remission and an annual stipend of $16,000 for three years and $12,000 for a fourth year. Travel funds for research presentations are also available.

Cost of Study

All doctoral students are fully supported for tuition. However, books and fees must be paid for by the student.

Living and Housing Costs

Room, board, personal expenses, books, supplies, and transportation for graduate students are estimated to be at least $13,000 per year. There is no university housing available to graduate students. Assistance in locating housing or roommates is available through off-campus housing at 617-552-3075.

Student Group

Currently, there are 20 students enrolled in the doctoral program. Fewer than 1 of 10 applicants is accepted to the program each year. The average GMAT score for the candidates accepted over the past two years was 645. Of the program's 20 students, 4 are international, 10 are women, and all receive full tuition remission plus stipends. All students are aiming toward university faculty positions combining research and teaching; several are also considering joining research institutes or engaging in consulting. Students of the program won three "Best Paper" awards at the Academy of Management in 1995 and 1996. They have offered as many as three papers at the same conference, and more than half of the students have been published. They have also founded or served as officers of four national and local graduate student conferences and consortia.

Student Outcomes

Since 1997–98 represented the sixth year of the program, the first graduates have entered the academic employment market. With a strong faculty and student presence in Academy of Management officerships, consortia, symposia, and journals, dissertating program students have unusually good market visibility.

Location

Boston College, comprising thirteen colleges, schools, and institutes, is situated on 150 acres of tree-covered Chestnut Hill, Massachusetts, within sight of downtown Boston—the financial, educational, and cultural heart of New England—and is near America's technology highway, Route 128. Founded by the Society of Jesus in 1863, Boston College retains its commitment to learning that is joined to ethical practice.

The College and The Department

The Organization Studies Department is one of seven departments in The Wallace E. Carroll School of Management of Boston College. Founded in 1957, the Carroll School was accredited by the American Assembly of Collegiate Schools of Business in 1975. The Carroll School is located on Boston College's main campus in the completely renovated and expanded state-of-the-art School of Management building.

Applying

Admission to the Ph.D. program is open to applicants who show evidence of strong intellectual ability, a commitment to research, and previous work experience. Students are required to have demonstrated competence and basic knowledge in management. This requirement is usually satisfied by the completion of a B.S. in management or a Master of Business Administration (M.B.A.) degree prior to entering the program. Students who have not completed a B.S. in management or an M.B.A. are required to take additional courses. In addition, GMAT scores or GRE scores taken within the previous five years must be submitted prior to acceptance into the program.

Applications for September admission to the Ph.D. program must be submitted by the previous February 1.

Correspondence and Information

Dr. Richard P. Nielsen
Director of Ph.D. Program in Organization Studies
Fulton Hall, Room 430
Boston College
Chestnut Hill, Massachusetts 02167

Boston College

THE FACULTY AND THEIR RESEARCH

Jean M. Bartunek, Professor; Ph.D., Illinois at Chicago, 1977. Organizational change and transformation, conflict, social cognition.

Stephen B. Borgatti, Visiting Associate Professor; Ph.D., California, Irvine, 1989. Social networks, scaling and measurement, cultural domain analysis.

Judith A. Clair, Assistant Professor; Ph.D., USC, 1993. Crisis, natural environmental management, transformational leadership, organizational change, multicultural diversity.

W. E. Douglas Creed, Assistant Professor; Ph.D., Berkeley, 1995. Organizational theory, organizational effectiveness, effects of social trends on the workplace and on individuals' careers.

Dalmar Fisher, Associate Professor; D.B.A., Harvard, 1968. Communication and managerial effectiveness, ways managers inquire and frame problems, relationship between stage of adult development and managers' performance.

Judith Gordon, Associate Professor; Ph.D., MIT, 1977. Organizational design, career development of professional women, information systems, managerial effectiveness.

Candace Jones, Assistant Professor; Ph.D., Utah, 1993. New organizational forms, cooperative interorganizational relations and implications of these for human resource practices.

John W. Lewis III, Associate Professor; Ph.D., Case Western Reserve, 1970. Managerial effectiveness, executive and organization development, human aspects of corporate mergers.

Richard P. Nielsen, Professor; Ph.D., Syracuse, 1974. Organization ethics action and learning methods, cooperative change methods.

William B. Stevenson, Associate Professor; Ph.D., California, Riverside, 1983. Organizational design, communication networks.

William R. Torbert, Professor; Ph.D., Yale, 1970. Psychological and organizational conditions and methods of inquiry conducive to human development and to effective organizational restructuring.

Donald J. White, Dean Emeritus and Distinguished Emeritus Professor; Ph.D., Harvard, 1949. Negotiating, dispute settlement, and collective bargaining.

Section 17
Project Management

This section contains a directory of institutions offering graduate work in project management, followed by in-depth entries submitted by institutions that chose to prepare detailed program descriptions. Additional information about programs listed in the directory but not augmented by an in-depth entry may be obtained by writing directly to the dean of a graduate school or chair of a department at the address given in the directory.

For programs offering related work, see also in this book Business Administration and Management.

CONTENTS

Program Directory

Project Management

City University, School of Business and Management Professions, Bellevue, WA 98004-6442. Offerings include project management (MS, Certificate). Postbaccalaureate distance learning degree programs offered (no on-campus study). School faculty: 14 full-time (6 women), 689 part-time (247 women). *Application deadline:* rolling. *Application fee:* $75 ($175 for international students). Electronic applications accepted. *Tuition:* $280 per credit hour. • Dr. Roman Borboa, Dean, 425-637-1010 Ext. 3759. Fax: 425-277-2439. E-mail: rborboa@cityu.edu. Application contact: Nabil El-Khatib, Vice President, Admissions, 800-426-5596. Fax: 425-277-2437. E-mail: nel-khatib@cityu.edu.

Denver Technical College, Program in Project Management, 925 South Niagara Street, Denver, CO 80224-1658. Awards MS. Part-time and evening/weekend programs available. Faculty: 15. Students: 25. *Application deadline:* rolling. *Application fee:* $30. *Tuition:* $13,220 per year. • Michael Basham, Director of Academic Affairs, 303-329-3340 Ext. 219. Application contact: David Phillips, Director of Admissions, 303-329-3000 Ext. 216.

The George Washington University, School of Business and Public Management, Department of Management Science, Washington, DC 20052. Offerings include project management (MS). Department faculty: 29 full-time (3 women), 23 part-time (5 women), 35 FTE. *Application deadline:* 4/1 (priority date; rolling processing; 10/1 for spring admission). *Application fee:* $50. *Expenses:* Tuition $680 per semester hour. Fees $35 per semester hour. • Dr. Erik K. Winslow, Chair, 202-994-7375. Application contact: Lilly Hastings, Graduate Admissions, 202-994-6584. Fax: 202-994-6382.

Golden Gate University, School of Business, San Francisco, CA 94105-2968. Offerings include project and systems management (MS, Certificate). *Average time to degree:* master's–2.5 years full-time. *Application deadline:* 7/1 (priority date; rolling processing). *Application fee:* $55 ($70 for international students). *Tuition:* $996 per course (minimum). • Dr. Hamid Shomali, Dean, 415-442-6500. Fax: 415-442-6579. Application contact: Enrollment Services, 415-442-7800. Fax: 415-442-7807. E-mail: info@ggu.edu.

Keller Graduate School of Management, 1 Tower Lane, Oak Brook Terrace, IL 60181. Offerings include project management (MPM). School faculty: 604. *Average time to degree:* master's–3 years part-time. *Application deadline:* rolling. *Application fee:* $0. *Tuition:* $1235 per course. • Dr. Sherrill Hole, Director, Academic Affairs, 630-574-1894. Application contact: Michael J. Alexander, Director, Central Services, 630-574-1957. Fax: 630-574-1969.

Lesley College, Graduate School of Arts and Social Sciences, Cambridge, MA 02138-2790. Offerings include intercultural relations (MA, CAGS), with options in development project administration (MA), individually designed (MA), intercultural conflict resolution (MA), intercultural health and human services (MA), intercultural training and consulting (MA), international education exchange (MA), international student advising (MA), managing culturally diverse human resources (MA), multicultural education (MA). Postbaccalaureate distance learning degree programs offered (minimal on-campus study). School faculty: 24 full-time (14 women), 344 part-time (225 women). *Application deadline:* rolling. *Application fee:* $45. *Tuition:* $425 per credit. • Dr. Martha B. McKenna, Dean, 617-349-8467. Application contact: Graduate Admissions, 617-349-8300. Fax: 617-349-8366.

Montana State University–Bozeman, College of Engineering, Department of Chemical Engineering, 211 Montana Hall, Bozeman, MT 59717. Offerings include project engineering and management (MPEM). MPEM offered jointly with Montana Tech of The University of Montana. Department faculty: 5 full-time (1 woman), 2 part-time (0 women). *Application deadline:* 6/1 (priority date; rolling processing; 11/1 for spring admission). *Application fee:* $50. *Tuition:* $3994 per year full-time, $367 per semester (minimum) part-time for state residents; $9507 per year full-time, $957 per semester (minimum) part-time for nonresidents. • Dr. John T. Sears, Head, 406-994-2221. Fax: 406-994-5308. E-mail: cheme@coe.montana.edu.

Montana Tech of The University of Montana, Graduate School, Environmental Engineering Program, Butte, MT 59701-8997. Offerings include project engineering and management (MPEM). MPEM offered jointly with Montana State University–Bozeman. Postbaccalaureate distance learning degree programs offered (minimal on-campus study). Program faculty: 6 full-time (1 woman). *Application deadline:* 4/1 (priority date; rolling processing; 10/1 for spring admission). *Application fee:* $30. *Tuition:* $2976 per year full-time, $373 per semester (minimum) part-time for state residents; $8857 per year full-time, $1118 per semester (minimum) part-time for nonresidents. • Dr. Kumar Ganesan, Department Head, 406-496-4239. Fax: 406-496-4133. E-mail: kganesan@po1.mtech.edu. Application contact: Cindy Dunstan, Administrative Assistant, 406-496-4128. Fax: 406-496-4334. E-mail: cdunstan@po1.mtech.edu.

Northwestern University, Robert R. McCormick School of Engineering and Applied Science, Department of Civil Engineering, Program in Project Management, Evanston, IL 60208. Awards MPM. Part-time programs available. Students: 24 full-time (2 women), 19 part-time (4 women); includes 3 minority (all Asian Americans), 20 international. *Degree requirements:* Computer language required, foreign language not required. *Entrance requirements:* GRE General Test. Application deadline: 8/15 (priority date; rolling processing). Application fee: $50 ($55 for international students). *Tuition:* $20,430 per year full-time, $2424 per course part-time. *Financial aid:* Institutionally sponsored loans available. Financial aid application deadline: 1/15; applicants required to submit FAFSA. • Raymond Krizek, Director, 847-491-4040. Fax: 847-491-4011. E-mail: mpm@nwu.edu.

Stevens Institute of Technology, Wesley J. Howe School of Technology Management, Program in Project Management, Hoboken, NJ 07030. Awards MS, Certificate. 35 applicants, 94% accepted. *Degree requirements:* For Certificate, computer language required, foreign language not required. *Entrance requirements:* For master's, GMAT, GRE, TOEFL. Application deadline: rolling. Application fee: $45. Electronic applications accepted. *Expenses:* Tuition $13,500 per year full-time, $675 per credit part-time. Fees $160 per year. • Dr. James Teitjen, Head, Wesley J. Howe School of Technology Management, 201-216-5384. Fax: 201-216-5385.

Texas A&M University, College of Engineering, Department of Civil Engineering, Program in Construction Engineering and Project Management, College Station, TX 77843. Awards M Eng, MS, D Eng, PhD. D Eng offered through the College of Engineering. Students: 25. *Degree requirements:* For master's, thesis (MS) required, foreign language not required; for doctorate, dissertation (PhD), internship (D Eng) required, foreign language not required. *Entrance requirements:* GRE General Test, TOEFL. Application fee: $35 ($75 for international students). *Financial aid:* Fellowships, research assistantships, teaching assistantships available. *Faculty research:* Engineering management aspects of major engineered construction projects from concept formulation through start-up. • Dr. Joseph Bracci, Head, Constructed Facilities Division, 409-845-3750. Fax: 409-845-6554. E-mail: ce-grad@tamu.edu. Application contact: Dr. Paul Roschke, 409-845-1985. E-mail: ce-grad@tamu.edu.

Towson University, Program in Information Technology Management, Towson, MD 21252-0001. Offerings include information systems project management (MS). Offered jointly with the University of Baltimore. *Application deadline:* rolling. *Application fee:* $40. *Expenses:* Tuition $187 per credit hour for state residents; $364 per credit hour for nonresidents. Fees $40 per credit hour. • Dr. Tom Basuray, Director, 410-830-2124. Fax: 410-830-6091. E-mail: tbasuray@towson.edu. Application contact: Fran Musotto, Office Manager, 410-830-2501. Fax: 410-830-4675. E-mail: fmusotto@towson.edu.

Université du Québec à Chicoutimi, Program in Project Management, Chicoutimi, PQ G7H 2B1, Canada. Awards M Sc. Offered jointly with the Université du Québec à Hull, the Université du Québec à Montréal, the Université du Québec à Rimouski, the Université du Québec à Trois-Rivières, and the Université du Québec en Abitibi-Témiscamingue. Part-time programs available. *Entrance requirements:* Appropriate bachelor's degree, proficiency in French. Application deadline: 5/1. Application fee: $30.

Université du Québec à Hull, Program in Project Management, Hull, PQ J8X 3X7, Canada. Awards M Sc. Offered jointly with the Université du Québec à Chicoutimi, the Université du Québec à Montréal, the Université du Québec à Trois-Riviéres, the Université du Québec à Rimouski, and the Université du Québec en Abitibi-Témiscamingue. Part-time programs available. *Entrance requirements:* Appropriate bachelor's degree, proficiency in French. Application deadline: 8/21. Application fee: $30.

Université du Québec à Montréal, Program in Project Management, Montréal, PQ H3C 3P8, Canada. Awards MGP, Diploma. Offered jointly with the Université du Québec à Chinoutimi, the Université du Québec à Hull, the Université du Québec en Abitibi-Témiscamingue, the Université du Québec à Trois-Riviéres, and the Université du Québec à Chicoutimi. Part-time programs available. *Entrance requirements:* Appropriate bachelor's degree or equivalent and proficiency in French. Application deadline: 5/1 (priority date). Application fee: $50.

Université du Québec à Rimouski, Program in Project Management, Rimouski, PQ G5L 3A1, Canada. Awards M Sc. Offered jointly with the Université du Québec à Chicoutmi, the Univesité du Québec à Hull, the Université du Québec à Montréal, the Université du Québec à Trois-Rivières, and the Université du Québec en Abitibi-Témiscamingue. Part-time programs available. *Entrance requirements:* Proficiency in French, appropriate bachelor's degree. Application deadline: 5/1 (priority date). Application fee: $30.

Université du Québec à Trois-Rivières, Program in Project Management, Trois-Rivières, PQ G9A 5H7, Canada. Awards MGP. Offered jointly with the Université du Québec à Chicoutimi, the Université du Québec à Hull, the Université du Québec à Montréal, the Université du Québec à Rimouski, and the Université du Québec en Abitibi-Témiscamingue. Part-time programs available. Students: 9 full-time (4 women), 43 part-time (9 women). 92 applicants, 76% accepted. *Entrance requirements:* Appropriate bachelor's degree, proficiency in French. Application deadline: 2/1. Application fee: $30. *Financial aid:* Fellowships, research assistantships, teaching assistantships available. • Normand Pettersen, Director, 819-376-5081. Fax: 819-376-5012. E-mail: normand_pettersen@uqtr.uquebec.ca. Application contact: Suzanne Camirand, Admissions Officer, 819-376-5045 Ext. 2591. Fax: 819-376-5210. E-mail: suzanne_camirand@uqtr.uquebec.ca.

Université du Québec en Abitibi-Témiscamingue, Program in Project Management, Rouyn-Noranda, PQ J9X 5E4, Canada. Awards M Sc. Offered jointly with the Université du Québec à Chicoutimi, the Université du Québec à Hull, the Université du Québec à Montréal, the Université du Québec à Rimouski, and the Université du Québec à Trois-Rivières. Part-time programs available. *Entrance requirements:* Appropriate bachelor's degree, proficiency in French. Application deadline: 4/1. Application fee: $30.

Western Carolina University, College of Business, Program in Project Management, Cullowhee, NC 28723. Awards MPM. Part-time and evening/weekend programs available. Students: 16 full-time (3 women), 3 part-time (1 woman); includes 2 minority (1 African American, 1 Hispanic), 7 international. 8 applicants, 75% accepted. In 1997, 14 degrees awarded. *Degree requirements:* Comprehensive exam required, foreign language and thesis not required. *Entrance requirements:* GMAT. Application deadline: rolling. Application fee: $35. *Tuition:* $1799 per year full-time, $144 per credit hour (minimum) part-time for state residents; $9069 per year full-time, $1053 per credit hour (minimum) part-time for nonresidents. *Financial aid:* In 1997–98, 8 students received aid, including 5 research assistantships (1 to a first-year student) totaling $19,300, 3 teaching assistantships (1 to a first-year student) totaling $15,000; fellowships, Federal Work-Study, institutionally sponsored loans also available. Financial aid application deadline: 3/15. • Gary A. Williams, Director, 828-227-7401. Application contact: Kathleen Owen, Assistant to the Dean, 828-227-7398. Fax: 828-227-7480.

Wright State University, College of Business and Administration, Department of Management, Dayton, OH 45435. Offerings include project management (MBA). *Entrance requirements:* GMAT, TOEFL (minimum score 550), minimum AACSB index of 1000. Application fee: $25. *Tuition:* $5109 per year full-time, $161 per credit hour part-time for state residents; $9039 per year full-time, $282 per credit hour part-time for nonresidents. • Dr. Crystal Owen, Chair, 937-775-2290. Application contact: James Crawford, Director of Graduate Programs, 937-775-2437. Fax: 937-775-3301.

Section 18
Quality Management

This section contains a directory of institutions offering graduate work in quality management, followed by in-depth entries submitted by institutions that chose to prepare detailed program descriptions. Additional information about programs listed in the directory but not augmented by an in-depth entry may be obtained by writing directly to the dean of a graduate school or chair of a department at the address given in the directory.

For programs offering related work, see also in this book Business Administration and Management.

CONTENTS

Program Directory

Quality Management

California State University, Dominguez Hills, Program in Quality Assurance, Carson, CA 90747-0001. Awards MS. Students: 2 full-time (0 women), 29 part-time (7 women); includes 13 minority (3 African Americans, 5 Asian Americans, 4 Hispanics, 1 Native American), 8 international. Average age 36. 34 applicants, 94% accepted. In 1997, 28 degrees awarded. *Application deadline:* 6/1. *Application fee:* $55. *Expenses:* Tuition $0 for state residents; $246 per unit for nonresidents. Fees $1896 per year full-time, $1230 per year part-time. • Dr. Eugene Watson, Coordinator, 310-243-3880.

Case Western Reserve University, Weatherhead School of Management, Department of Operations Research and Operations Management, Cleveland, OH 44106. Offerings include management science (MS), with options in finance, information systems, marketing, operations management, operations research, quality management. MS and PhD offered through the School of Graduate Studies. Department faculty: 12 full-time (0 women). *Average time to degree:* doctorate–4 years full-time. *Application deadline:* 4/15 (priority date; rolling processing). *Application fee:* $50. *Tuition:* $20,900 per year full-time, $871 per credit hour part-time. • Hamilton Emmons, Chairman, 216-368-3841. Application contact: Linda S. Gaston, Director of Marketing and Admissions, 216-368-2030. Fax: 216-368-5548. E-mail: lxg10@po.cwru.edu.

Dowling College, School of Business, Oakdale, NY 11769-1999. Offerings include total quality management (MBA, Certificate). School faculty: 17 full-time, 75 part-time. *Degree requirements:* For master's, thesis optional, foreign language not required. *Entrance requirements:* For master's, GMAT, TOEFL. Application deadline: rolling. Application fee: $0. Electronic applications accepted. • Dr. Anthony F. Libertella, Interim Dean, 516-244-3355. Fax: 516-589-6644. Application contact: Kate Rowe, Director of Admissions, 516-244-3030. Fax: 516-563-3827. E-mail: rowek@dowling.edu.

Eastern Michigan University, College of Business, Department of Management, Ypsilanti, MI 48197. Offerings include strategic quality management (MBA). Department faculty: 20 full-time (8 women). *Application deadline:* 5/15 (rolling processing; 3/15 for spring admission). *Application fee:* $30. *Expenses:* Tuition $2691 per year full-time, $150 per credit hour part-time for state residents; $6300 per year full-time, $350 per credit hour part-time for nonresidents. Fees $368 per year full-time, $88 per semester (minimum) part-time. • Dr. Sahab Dayal, Head, 734-487-3240. Application contact: Dr. William Whitmire, Coordinator, 734-487-3240.

Fordham University, Graduate School of Business Administration, New York, NY 10023. Offerings include total quality management (Certificate). School faculty: 85 full-time (22 women), 95 part-time (12 women). *Average time to degree:* master's–2 years full-time, 3 years part-time. *Application deadline:* 6/1 (priority date; rolling processing; 11/1 for spring admission). *Application fee:* $50. • Dr. Ernest J. Scalberg, Dean, 212-636-6111. Fax: 212-307-1779. Application contact: Kathy Pattison, Assistant Dean of Admission, 212-636-6200. Fax: 212-636-7076. E-mail: admission@bschool.bnet.fordham.edu.

Friends University, Graduate Programs, College of Continuing Education, Program in Quality Systems Management, Wichita, KS 67213. Awards MSQSM. Evening/weekend programs available. Faculty: 1 full-time (0 women), 4 part-time (0 women). Students: 44. *Application deadline:* rolling. *Application fee:* $45. *Expenses:* Tuition $326 per credit hour (minimum). Fees $215 per year. • Dr. Graydon Dawson, Director, 800-794-6945 Ext. 5526. Application contact: Director of Graduate Admissions, 800-794-6945 Ext. 5300.

Hawaii Pacific University, School of Business Administration, 1166 Fort Street, Honolulu, HI 96813-2785. Offerings include quality management (MBA). School faculty: 30 full-time (3 women), 12 part-time (1 woman), 38 FTE. *Average time to degree:* master's–2 years full-time, 4 years part-time. *Application deadline:* rolling. *Application fee:* $50. Electronic applications accepted. *Tuition:* $7920 per year full-time, $330 per credit part-time. • Dr. Richard Ward, Dean for Graduate Management Studies, 808-544-0279. Application contact: Leina Danao, Admissions Coordinator, 808-544-1120. Fax: 808-544-0280. E-mail: gradservctr@hpu.edu.

Instituto Tecnológico y de Estudios Superiores de Monterrey, Estado de México Campus, Graduate Division, Atizapán de Zaragoza 52926, Mexico. Offerings include quality systems (MQS). Postbaccalaureate distance learning degree programs offered (minimal on-campus study). Institute faculty: 19 full-time (3 women), 32 part-time (3 women). *Average time to degree:* master's–2 years full-time, 3.3 years part-time. *Application deadline:* 1/12 (priority date; rolling processing; 4/4 for spring admission). *Application fee:* $72. • Emilio Alvarado Badillo, Headmaster, 5-326-5500. Fax: 5-326-5507. E-mail: ealvarad@campus.cem.itesm.mx. Application contact: Lourdes Turrubiates, Admissions Officer, 5-326-5776. E-mail: lturrubi@campus.cem.itesm.mx.

Loyola University New Orleans, Joseph A. Butt, S.J., College of Business Administration, Program in Quality Management, New Orleans, LA 70118-6195. Awards MQM. Part-time programs available. Postbaccalaureate distance learning degree programs offered (minimal on-campus study). Faculty: 6 full-time (4 women), 6 part-time (2 women). Students: 79 part-time (25 women). Average age 43. 41 applicants, 80% accepted. In 1997, 26 degrees awarded. *Entrance requirements:* TOEFL (minimum score 600), minimum GPA of 3.0, 5 years of work experience, resumé. Application deadline: 2/15. Application fee: $20. *Expenses:* Tuition $525 per credit hour. Fees $556 per year full-time, $164 per year part-time. *Financial aid:* 5 students received aid; Federal Work-Study and career-related internships or fieldwork available. Aid available to part-time students. Financial aid application deadline: 5/1; applicants required to submit FAFSA. *Faculty research:* Ethics in total quality management (TQM), TQM and business results, TQM in higher education, quality function deployment. • Application contact: Dr. Caroline Fisher, Director, 504-865-2159. Fax: 504-865-3496. E-mail: fisher@loyno.edu.

Madonna University, Program in Business Administration, Livonia, MI 48150-1173. Offerings include quality and operations management (MSBA). Postbaccalaureate distance learning degree programs offered (minimal on-campus study). Program faculty: 8 full-time (2 women), 13 part-time (2 women). *Degree requirements:* Thesis required (for some programs), foreign language not required. *Entrance requirements:* GMAT, GRE General Test, minimum GPA of 3.0. Application deadline: 8/1 (priority date; rolling processing; 4/1 for spring admission). *Expenses:* Tuition $260 per credit hour (minimum). Fees $50 per semester. • Dr. Stuart Arends, Dean of Business School, 734-432-5366. Fax: 734-432-5364. E-mail: arends@smtp.munet.edu. Application contact: Sandra Kellums, Coordinator of Graduate Admissions, 734-432-5666. Fax: 734-432-5393. E-mail: kellums@smtp.munet.edu.

Marian College of Fond du Lac, Business Division, 45 South National Avenue, Fond du Lac, WI 54935-4699. Offerings include organizational leadership and quality (MS). Postbaccalaureate distance learning degree programs offered (no on-campus study). Division faculty: 3 full-time (0 women), 15 part-time (3 women). *Degree requirements:* Comprehensive group project required, foreign language and thesis not required. *Average time to degree:* master's–1.6 years part-time. *Entrance requirements:* 3 years of managerial experience. Application deadline: rolling. Application fee: $25. *Tuition:* $275 per credit hour. • Richard M. Dienesch, Assistant Dean of Evening/Weekend Programs, 920-923-8125. Fax: 920-923-7167.

North Carolina State University, College of Management, Program in Management, Raleigh, NC 27695. Offerings include total quality management (MS). Program faculty: 53 full-time (7 women), 3 part-time (0 women). *Degree requirements:* Computer language required, foreign language and thesis not required. *Entrance requirements:* GRE or GMAT, TOEFL (minimum score 550), minimum undergraduate GPA of 3.0. Application deadline: 6/25 (rolling processing; 11/25 for spring admission). Application fee: $45. *Tuition:* $2370 per year full-time, $517 per semester (minimum) part-time for state residents; $11,536 per year full-time, $2809 per semester (minimum) part-time for nonresidents. • Dr. Jack W. Wilson, Director of Graduate Programs, 919-515-4327. Fax: 919-515-6943. E-mail: jack_wilson@ncsu.edu. Application contact: Dr. Steven G. Allen, Director of Graduate Programs, 919-515-6941. Fax: 919-515-5073. E-mail: steve_allen@ncsu.edu.

Pennsylvania State University University Park Campus, Intercollege Graduate Programs, Intercollege Program in Quality and Manufacturing Management, University Park, PA 16802-1503. Awards MMM. Students: 27 full-time (10 women), 6 part-time (2 women). *Entrance requirements:* GRE or GMAT. Application fee: $40. *Expenses:* Tuition $6534 per year full-time, $276 per credit part-time for state residents; $13,460 per year full-time, $561 per credit part-time for nonresidents. Fees $252 per year (minimum) full-time, $43 per semester (minimum) part-time. • Dr. M. P. Hottenstein, Co-Director, 814-863-5802.

Rutgers, The State University of New Jersey, New Brunswick, Program in Statistics, New Brunswick, NJ 08903. Offerings include quality and productivity management (MS). Program faculty: 16 full-time (1 woman). *Degree requirements:* Essay, exam required, foreign language and thesis not required. *Average time to degree:* master's–2 years full-time, 5 years part-time; doctorate–5 years full-time, 7 years part-time. *Entrance requirements:* GRE General Test. Application deadline: 5/1 (rolling processing; 12/1 for spring admission). Application fee: $40. Electronic applications accepted. *Expenses:* Tuition $6492 per year full-time, $268 per credit part-time for state residents; $9520 per year full-time, $395 per credit part-time for nonresidents. Fees $208 per year (minimum). • Dr. Kesar Singh, Director, 732-445-3634. Fax: 732-445-3428. E-mail: kesar@stat.rutgers.edu.

San Jose State University, College of Applied Arts and Sciences, Division of Technology, San Jose, CA 95192-0001. Offers program in quality assurance (MS). Faculty: 13 full-time (3 women), 3 part-time (1 woman). Students: 3 full-time (0 women), 24 part-time (4 women); includes 13 minority (1 African American, 11 Asian Americans, 1 Hispanic). Average age 35. 11 applicants, 91% accepted. In 1997, 4 degrees awarded. *Application deadline:* 6/1 (rolling processing). *Application fee:* $59. *Expenses:* Tuition $0 for state residents; $246 per unit for nonresidents. Fees $2017 per year full-time, $1351 per year part-time. • Dr. Seth Bates, Director, 408-924-3190. Application contact: Dr. James Yu, Graduate Adviser, 408-924-3227.

Southern Polytechnic State University, Program in Quality Assurance, South Marietta Parkway, Marietta, GA 30060-2896. Awards MS. Part-time and evening/weekend programs available. Postbaccalaureate distance learning degree programs offered (minimal on-campus study). Faculty: 2 full-time (1 woman), 2 part-time (1 woman), 3 FTE. Students: 16 full-time (7 women), 51 part-time (19 women); includes 14 minority (10 African Americans, 1 Asian American, 2 Hispanics, 1 Native American). Average age 35. 38 applicants, 100% accepted. *Degree requirements:* Thesis optional, foreign language not required. *Average time to degree:* master's–2 years full-time, 4 years part-time. *Entrance requirements:* GRE General Test. Application deadline: 7/15 (priority date; rolling processing; 12/1 for spring admission). Application fee: $0. *Tuition:* $1980 per year full-time, $409 per semester (minimum) part-time for state residents; $6980 per year full-time, $1159 per semester (minimum) part-time for nonresidents. *Financial aid:* In 1997–98, 30 students received aid, including 3 teaching assistantships (1 to a first-year student) averaging $300 per month and totaling $9,000; Federal Work-Study and career-related internships or fieldwork also available. Aid available to part-time students. Financial aid application deadline: 3/15; applicants required to submit FAFSA. • Thomas Carmichael, Head, Industrial Engineering Technology Department, 770-528-7339.

The University of Iowa, Program in Quality Management and Productivity, Iowa City, IA 52242-1316. Awards MS. Students: 7 full-time (3 women), 2 part-time (1 woman); includes 1 minority (Asian American), 6 international. 7 applicants, 71% accepted. In 1997, 3 degrees awarded. *Degree requirements:* Thesis optional. *Entrance requirements:* GRE General Test. Application deadline: rolling. Application fee: $30 ($50 for international students). *Expenses:* Tuition $3166 per year full-time, $176 per semester hour part-time for state residents; $10,202 per year full-time, $176 per semester hour part-time for nonresidents. Fees $202 per year full-time, $52 per year (minimum) part-time. *Financial aid:* In 1997–98, 4 teaching assistantships (1 to a first-year student) were awarded; fellowships, research assistantships also available. Financial aid applicants required to submit FAFSA. • Russell Lenth, Chair, 319-335-0814.

Upper Iowa University, Program in Business Leadership, Fayette, IA 52142-1857. Offerings include quality management (MA). Also available at Des Moines, Iowa campus; Madison, Wisconsin campus; and Waterloo, Iowa campus. Postbaccalaureate distance learning degree programs offered (no on-campus study). Program faculty: 40. *Degree requirements:* Thesis optional, foreign language not required. *Entrance requirements:* GMAT, GRE, or minimum GPA of 2.5 during last 60 hours. Application deadline: 8/26 (rolling processing). Application fee: $50. *Tuition:* $200 per credit. • Dr. Patrick Langan, Director, 800-773-9298. Fax: 319-425-5383.

Section 19
Quantitative Analysis

This section contains a directory of institutions offering graduate work in quantitative analysis, followed by in-depth entries submitted by institutions that chose to prepare detailed program descriptions. Additional information about programs listed in the directory but not augmented by an in-depth entry may be obtained by writing directly to the dean of a graduate school or chair of a department at the address given in the directory.

For programs offering related work, see also in this book Business Administration and Management.

CONTENTS

Program Directory

Quantitative Analysis

Bucknell University, College of Arts and Sciences, Department of Management, Lewisburg, PA 17837. Offerings include quantitative methods and operations management (MSBA). Department faculty: 12 full-time. *Degree requirements:* Thesis required, foreign language not required. *Entrance requirements:* GMAT, TOEFL (minimum score 550), minimum GPA of 2.8. Application deadline: 6/1 (priority date; rolling processing; 12/1 for spring admission). Application fee: $25. *Tuition:* $2410 per course. • Dr. Mark Bettner, Head, 717-524-1306.

California State University, Hayward, School of Business and Economics, Department of Management and Finance, Option in Quantitative Business Methods, Hayward, CA 94542-3000. Awards MS. Part-time and evening/weekend programs available. *Degree requirements:* Comprehensive exam or thesis required, foreign language not required. *Entrance requirements:* GMAT, minimum GPA of 2.75. Application deadline: 4/19 (priority date; rolling processing; 1/5 for spring admission). Application fee: $55. *Expenses:* Tuition $0 for state residents; $164 per unit for nonresidents. Fees $1827 per year full-time, $1161 per year part-time. *Financial aid:* Federal Work-Study, institutionally sponsored loans available. Aid available to part-time students. Financial aid application deadline: 3/1. • Dr. Alan Goldberg, Coordinator, 510-885-3304. Application contact: Dr. Donna L. Wiley, Director of Graduate Programs, 510-885-3964.

Clark Atlanta University, School of Business Administration, Department of Decision Science, Atlanta, GA 30314. Awards MBA. Part-time programs available. Students: 8 full-time (3 women), 1 (woman) part-time; includes 8 minority (all African Americans), 1 international. In 1997, 2 degrees awarded. *Entrance requirements:* GMAT. Application deadline: 4/1 (rolling processing; 11/1 for spring admission). Application fee: $40. *Expenses:* Tuition $9672 per year full-time, $403 per credit hour part-time. Fees $200 per year. *Financial aid:* Application deadline 4/30. • Dr. Young Kim, Chairperson, 404-880-8387. Application contact: Michelle Clark-Davis, Graduate Program Assistant, 404-880-8709.

Cornell University, Graduate Field of Management, Ithaca, NY 14853-0001. Offerings include quantitative analysis (PhD). Terminal master's awarded for partial completion of doctoral program. Faculty: 43 full-time. *Degree requirements:* Dissertation required, foreign language not required. *Entrance requirements:* GMAT or GRE General Test, TOEFL. Application deadline: 1/10 (priority date). Application fee: $65. *Expenses:* Tuition $24,300 per year. Fees $48 per year. • Director of Graduate Studies, 607-255-3669. Application contact: Graduate Field Assistant, 607-255-3669. Fax: 607-254-4590. E-mail: maria@johnson.cornell.edu.

Drexel University, College of Business and Administration, Department of Quantitative Methods, 3141 Chestnut Street, Philadelphia, PA 19104-2875. Awards MS. Faculty: 4 full-time (0 women), 4 part-time (0 women), 5.33 FTE. Students: 0. 1 applicant, 100% accepted. *Degree requirements:* Computer language required, foreign language and thesis not required. *Entrance requirements:* GMAT, TOEFL (minimum score 570), minimum GPA of 2.75. Application deadline: 8/21. Application fee: $35. *Expenses:* Tuition $494 per credit hour. Fees $121 per quarter full-time, $65 per quarter part-time. *Financial aid:* Application deadline 2/1. • Dr. Steve M. Bajgier, Head. Application contact: Denise Bigham, Director of Admissions, 215-895-6700. Fax: 215-895-5969.

Drexel University, College of Business and Administration, Program in Business Administration, 3141 Chestnut Street, Philadelphia, PA 19104-2875. Offerings include business administration (MBA, PhD, APC), with options in accounting (MBA, PhD), decision sciences (PhD), economics (MBA, PhD), finance (MBA, PhD), legal studies (MBA), management (MBA), marketing (MBA, PhD), organizational sciences (PhD), quantitative methods (MBA), strategic management (PhD); decision sciences (MS). Terminal master's awarded for partial completion of doctoral program. *Degree requirements:* Computer language required, foreign language and thesis/dissertation not required. *Entrance requirements:* For master's, GMAT, TOEFL (minimum score 570), minimum GPA of 2.75; for doctorate, GMAT, TOEFL (minimum score 570). Application deadline: 8/21 (rolling processing; 3/5 for spring admission). Application fee: $35. *Expenses:* Tuition $494 per credit hour. Fees $121 per quarter full-time, $65 per quarter part-time. • Dr. Jerold B. Muskin, Director of Master's Programs in Business, 215-895-2115. Application contact: Denise Bigham, Director of Admissions, 215-895-6700. Fax: 215-895-5969.

Fairleigh Dickinson University, Florham–Madison Campus, Samuel J. Silberman College of Business Administration, Program in Quantitative Analysis, 285 Madison Avenue, Madison, NJ 07940-1099. Awards MBA. Part-time and evening/weekend programs available. Faculty: 7 full-time (1 woman), 9 part-time (2 women). Students: 4 full-time (1 woman), 25 part-time (11 women); includes 3 minority (1 African American, 2 Asian Americans). Average age 31. 4 applicants, 75% accepted. In 1997, 2 degrees awarded. *Degree requirements:* Thesis optional, foreign language not required. *Entrance requirements:* GMAT. Application deadline: rolling. Application fee: $35. *Expenses:* Tuition $522 per credit. Fees $302 per year full-time, $138 per year part-time. *Financial aid:* Fellowships available. • Dr. Joel Harmon, Chairperson, 973-443-8850.

Fairleigh Dickinson University, Teaneck–Hackensack Campus, Samuel J. Silberman College of Business Administration, Department of Management, Marketing, and Information Systems and Sciences, Program in Quantitative Analysis, 1000 River Road, Teaneck, NJ 07666-1914. Awards MBA. Students: 1 full-time (0 women), 4 part-time (1 woman); includes 2 minority (1 Asian American, 1 Hispanic), 2 international. Average age 28. In 1997, 5 degrees awarded. *Degree requirements:* Computer language required, thesis optional, foreign language not required. *Entrance requirements:* GMAT. Application deadline: rolling. Application fee: $35. *Expenses:* Tuition $522 per credit. Fees $302 per year full-time, $138 per year part-time. *Financial aid:* Fellowships, research assistantships available. *Faculty research:* Forecasting, production management. • Paul Yoon, Chair, Department of Management, Marketing, and Information Systems and Sciences, 201-692-7223.

Hofstra University, Frank G. Zarb School of Business, Department of Business Computer Information Systems/Quantitative Methods, Hempstead, NY 11549. Awards MBA. Part-time and evening/weekend programs available. Faculty: 15 full-time (2 women), 1 part-time (0 women). Students: 11 full-time (4 women), 59 part-time (18 women); includes 6 minority (2 African Americans, 3 Asian Americans, 1 Hispanic), 5 international. Average age 30. 24 applicants, 71% accepted. In 1997, 23 degrees awarded. *Degree requirements:* Computer language, thesis (for some programs) required, foreign language not required. *Entrance requirements:* GMAT (average 580). Application deadline: rolling. Application fee: $40 ($75 for international students). *Expenses:* Tuition $10,968 per year full-time, $457 per credit hour part-time. Fees $670 per year full-time, $112 per semester (minimum) part-time. *Financial aid:* 10 students received aid; fellowships, research assistantships, Federal Work-Study, and career-related internships or fieldwork available. Financial aid application deadline: 4/1. *Faculty research:* Analysis of industrial performance, adaptation of new computer systems, history of computers, manufacturing and operating strategy, expert systems. • Dr. Farrokh Nasri, Chairperson, 516-463-5716. Fax: 516-463-4834. E-mail: acsfzn@hofstra.edu. Application contact: Susan McTiernan, Senior Assistant Dean, 516-463-5683. Fax: 516-463-5268. E-mail: bizsmm@hofstra.edu.

Louisiana Tech University, College of Administration and Business, Department of Business Analysis and Communication, Ruston, LA 71272. Offers programs in business administration (MBA), quantitative analysis (MBA, DBA). Part-time programs available. Faculty: 8 full-time (2 women). Students: 36 full-time (18 women), 23 part-time (6 women); includes 17 international. Average age 27. In 1997, 21 master's, 1 doctorate awarded. *Degree requirements:* For master's, computer language required, foreign language and thesis not required; for doctorate, computer language, dissertation required, foreign language not required. *Entrance requirements:* GMAT. Application deadline: 7/29 (2/3 for spring admission). Application fee: $20 ($30 for international students). *Tuition:* $2382 per year full-time, $223 per quarter (minimum) part-time for state residents; $5307 per year full-time, $223 per quarter (minimum) part-time for nonresidents. *Financial aid:* Fellowships, research assistantships, teaching assistantships available. Financial aid application deadline: 2/1. • Dr. Tom Means, Head, 318-257-3293.

Loyola College, Sellinger School of Business and Management, Programs in Business Administration, Baltimore, MD 21210-2699. Offerings include decision sciences (MBA). *Application deadline:* 7/20 (11/20 for spring admission). *Application fee:* $35. *Tuition:* $365 per credit. • Dr. Peter Lorenzi, Dean, Sellinger School of Business and Management, 410-617-2301.

Montclair State University, School of Business, Program in Business Administration, Upper Montclair, NJ 07043-1624. Offerings include quantitative analysis (MBA). Program faculty: 57 full-time. *Entrance requirements:* GMAT. Application deadline: 4/1 (rolling processing; 11/1 for spring admission). Application fee: $40. *Expenses:* Tuition $201 per credit for state residents; $257 per credit for nonresidents. Fees $22.05 per credit. • Dr. Eileen Kaplan, Director, 973-655-4306.

New York University, Robert F. Wagner Graduate School of Public Service, Program in Public Administration, New York, NY 10012-1019. Offerings include quantitative analysis and computer applications (APC). Program faculty: 14 full-time (6 women), 49 part-time (21 women), 23 FTE. *Average time to degree:* master's–2 years full-time, 4 years part-time; doctorate–5 years full-time, 7 years part-time; other advanced degree–1 year full-time. *Application deadline:* 8/1 (rolling processing; 1/1 for spring admission). *Application fee:* $50 ($70 for international students). • Leanna Stiefel, Director, 212-998-7400. Application contact: Hedy Flanders, Director, Admissions and Financial Aid, 212-998-7414. Fax: 212-995-4164. E-mail: wagner.admissions@nyu.edu.

Purdue University, Krannert Graduate School of Management, Department of Management, West Lafayette, IN 47907. Offerings include applied optimization (PhD), applied statistics (PhD), quantitative methods (MSM, PhD). Department faculty: 51 full-time (5 women). *Degree requirements:* For doctorate, dissertation required, foreign language not required. *Average time to degree:* doctorate–4 years full-time. *Entrance requirements:* For doctorate, GMAT, TOEFL (minimum score 575). Application fee: $30. Electronic applications accepted. *Tuition:* $3500 per year full-time, $126 per credit hour part-time for state residents; $11,720 per year full-time, $387 per credit hour part-time for nonresidents. • Dr. J. J. McConnell, Director of Doctoral Programs, 765-494-4375. Application contact: Kelly Felty, Assistant Director of Administration for Doctoral Programs, 765-494-4375. Fax: 765-494-1526. E-mail: feltyk@mgmt.purdue.edu.

Rensselaer Polytechnic Institute, Lally School of Management and Technology, Troy, NY 12180-3590. Offerings include business administration (MBA, PhD), with options in finance and accounting (MBA), information systems management (MBA), management (PhD), management of technology and entrepreneurships (MBA), manufacturing management (MBA), marketing management (MBA), operations research (MBA), organizational behavior and human resource management (MBA), statistical methods for management (MBA). Postbaccalaureate distance learning degree programs offered (no on-campus study). School faculty: 36 full-time (5 women), 6 part-time (0 women). *Application deadline:* 2/1 (priority date; rolling processing). *Application fee:* $35. *Expenses:* Tuition $630 per credit hour. Fees $1000 per year. • Dr. Joseph G. Ecker, Dean, 518-276-6802. Application contact: Michele Martens, Manager of Enrollment Services, 518-276-4800. Fax: 518-276-8661.

St. John's University, College of Business Administration, Department of Computer Information Systems and Decision Sciences, Jamaica, NY 11439. Awards MBA, Adv C. Part-time and evening/weekend programs available. Faculty: 16 full-time (0 women), 1 part-time (0 women). Students: 10 full-time (5 women), 76 part-time (22 women); includes 16 minority (5 African Americans, 8 Asian Americans, 3 Hispanics), 17 international. Average age 29. 49 applicants, 61% accepted. In 1997, 38 master's awarded. *Degree requirements:* For master's, thesis optional, foreign language not required. *Entrance requirements:* For master's, GMAT. Application deadline: 6/1 (rolling processing; 10/1 for spring admission). Application fee: $40. *Expenses:* Tuition $600 per credit. Fees $150 per year. *Financial aid:* In 1997–98, 5 research assistantships (1 to a first-year student) averaging $667 per month were awarded; Federal Work-Study also available. Aid available to part-time students. Financial aid application deadline: 3/1; applicants required to submit FAFSA. • Dr. Andrew Rasselkoff, Chair, 718-990-6338. Application contact: Shamus J. McGrenra, TOR, Associate Director, Graduate Admissions, 718-990-6107. Fax: 718-990-5736. E-mail: mcgrenrs@stjohns.edu.

Saint Louis University, School of Business and Administration, Department of Decision Sciences and Management Information Systems, 3674 Lindell Boulevard, St. Louis, MO 63108. Offers programs in decision sciences (MBA, M Dec S, PhD), information systems management (MBA), management information systems (MMIS). Part-time programs available. Faculty: 10 full-time (0 women). Students: 3 full-time (1 woman), 11 part-time (2 women); includes 1 minority (Asian American), 2 international. Average age 26. 16 applicants, 44% accepted. In 1997, 2 doctorates awarded. *Degree requirements:* For master's, oral exam required, thesis not required; for doctorate, dissertation. *Average time to degree:* master's–1.5 years full-time, 3 years part-time. *Entrance requirements:* For master's, GMAT, TOEFL; for doctorate, GMAT. Application deadline: 7/15 (rolling processing; 11/15 for spring admission). Application fee: $40. Electronic applications accepted. *Financial aid:* Fellowships, research assistantships, teaching assistantships, Federal Work-Study available. Aid available to part-time students. • Dr. Mark E. Ferris, Chairman, 314-977-3878.

Seton Hall University, W. Paul Stillman School of Business, Department of Computer and Decision Sciences, South Orange, NJ 07079-2692. Offers programs in information systems (MBA, MS), quantitative analysis (MBA). Part-time and evening/weekend programs available. Faculty: 9 full-time (1 woman), 3 part-time (0 women). *Degree requirements:* Thesis optional, foreign language not required. *Entrance requirements:* GMAT (minimum score 500), TOEFL (minimum score 550). Application deadline: 6/1 (priority date; rolling processing). Application fee: $50. *Expenses:* Tuition $538 per credit. Fees $185 per semester. *Financial aid:* Research assistantships and career-related internships or fieldwork available. Aid available to part-time students. Financial aid applicants required to submit FAFSA. • Dr. David Rosenthal, Acting Chairperson, 973-761-9250. E-mail: rosentdv@shu.edu. Application contact: Student Information Office, 973-761-9222. Fax: 973-761-9217. E-mail: busgrad@shu.edu.

Texas Tech University, Graduate School, College of Business Administration, Program in Information Systems and Quantitative Sciences, Lubbock, TX 79409. Offers business statistics (MSBA, PhD), management information systems (MSBA, PhD), operations management (PhD). Part-time programs available. Faculty: 11 full-time (1 woman). Students: 61 full-time (13 women), 7 part-time (2 women); includes 7 minority (1 African American, 6 Hispanics), 33 international. Average age 33. 33 applicants, 55% accepted. In 1997, 21 master's awarded; 3 doctorates awarded (100% entered university research/teaching). *Degree requirements:* For master's, computer language, comprehensive exam required, foreign language and thesis not required; for doctorate, computer language, dissertation, qualifying exams required, foreign language not required. *Entrance requirements:* For master's, GMAT (minimum score 500; average 560); for doctorate, GMAT (minimum score 580; average 620). Application deadline: 4/15 (priority date; rolling processing; 9/30 for spring admission). Application fee: $25 ($50 for international students). *Expenses:* Tuition $864 per year full-time, $120 per semester (minimum) part-time for state residents; $5976 per year full-time, $747 per semester (minimum) part-time for nonresidents. Fees $2321 per year full-time, $302 per semester (minimum) part-time. *Financial aid:* Teaching assistantships, Federal Work-Study available. *Faculty research:* Database management systems, systems management and engineering, expert systems and adaptive knowledge-based sciences, statistical analysis and design. • Dr. Surya Yadav, Coordinator, 806-742-3192. E-mail: odsby@ttacs.ttu.edu. Application contact: Nancy Dodge, Director, 806-742-3184. Fax: 806-742-3958.

Directory: Quantitative Analysis

Troy State University Dothan, School of Business, Department of Finance and Quantitative Methods, Dothan, AL 36304-0368. Offers programs in finance (MS), quantitative methods (MS). *Entrance requirements:* GMAT, GRE General Test, or MAT, minimum GPA of 2.5. Application deadline: rolling. Application fee: $20. *Expenses:* Tuition $68 per credit hour for state residents; $140 per credit hour for nonresidents. Fees $2 per credit hour. • Dr. Adair Gilbert, Chair. Application contact: Reta Cordell, Director of Admissions and Records, 334-983-6556. Fax: 334-983-6322. E-mail: rcordell@tsud.edu.

University of Cincinnati, College of Business Administration, Department of Quantitative Analysis and Operations Management, Cincinnati, OH 45221. Offers programs in operations management (MBA, PhD), quantitative analysis (MBA, MS, PhD). Part-time and evening/weekend programs available. Faculty: 11 full-time. Students: 30 full-time (13 women), 51 part-time (13 women). 47 applicants, 36% accepted. In 1997, 17 master's, 2 doctorates awarded. *Degree requirements:* For doctorate, computer language, dissertation. *Average time to degree:* master's–2.9 years full-time; doctorate–6.3 years full-time. *Entrance requirements:* GMAT. Application fee: $30. *Tuition:* $7228 per year full-time, $185 per credit hour part-time for state residents; $13,812 per year full-time, $352 per credit hour part-time for nonresidents. *Financial aid:* Fellowships, graduate assistantships available. Financial aid application deadline: 2/15. • Jeffrey D. Camm, Head, 513-556-7140. Fax: 513-556-5499.

University of Hartford, Barney School of Business and Public Administration, Program in Business Administration, West Hartford, CT 06117-1599. Offerings include quantitative decision making (MBA). Program faculty: 24 full-time (4 women), 15 part-time (1 woman). *Average time to degree:* master's–1.5 years full-time, 3 years part-time. *Entrance requirements:* GMAT, TOEFL. Application deadline: 7/1 (priority date; rolling processing; 12/1 for spring admission). Application fee: $35 ($50 for international students). Electronic applications accepted. • Christopher Galligan, Director, 860-768-4390. Application contact: Claire Silverstein, Assistant Director, 860-768-4900. Fax: 860-768-4821. E-mail: silverste@unavax.hartford.edu.

University of Minnesota, Twin Cities Campus, Carlson School of Management, Department of Information and Decision Sciences, Minneapolis, MN 55455-0213. Awards MBA, PhD. MBA offered jointly with the Master's Program in Business Administration; PhD offered jointly with the Doctoral Program in Business Administration. *Degree requirements:* For doctorate, dissertation required, foreign language not required. *Entrance requirements:* GMAT. *Faculty research:* Group decision making, expert systems, information systems management, problem formulation, database design.

University of Missouri–St. Louis, School of Business Administration, Program in Business Administration, St. Louis, MO 63121-4499. Offerings include quantitative management science (MBA). Program faculty: 19 (3 women). *Entrance requirements:* GMAT (minimum score 500; average 554). Application deadline: 7/1 (rolling processing; 11/1 for spring admission). Application fee: $0. Electronic applications accepted. *Expenses:* Tuition $3903 per year full-time, $167 per credit hour part-time for state residents; $11,745 per year full-time, $489 per credit hour part-time for nonresidents. Fees $816 per year full-time, $34 per credit hour part-time. • Application contact: Graduate Admissions, 314-516-5458. Fax: 314-516-6759. E-mail: gradadm@umslvma.umsl.edu.

The University of North Carolina at Chapel Hill, Kenan-Flagler Business School, Doctoral Program in Business Administration, Chapel Hill, NC 27599. Offerings include operations management/quantitative methods (PhD). Program faculty: 79 full-time (15 women), 29 part-time (6 women). *Degree requirements:* Dissertation required, foreign language not required. *Average time to degree:* doctorate–4 years full-time. *Entrance requirements:* GMAT (average 657) or GRE General Test (minimum combined score of 1350). Application deadline: 1/1 (priority date; rolling processing). Application fee: $55. Electronic applications accepted. *Expenses:* Tuition $1428 per year for state residents; $10,414 per year for nonresidents. Fees $787 per year. • Ann Marucheck, Associate Dean for PhD Programs, 919-962-3193. Application contact: Liz Griffin, Director, 919-962-1657. E-mail: kfphd_app@unc.edu.

University of Oregon, Graduate School, Charles H. Lundquist College of Business, Department of Decision Sciences, Eugene, OR 97403. Awards MA, MS, PhD. Faculty: 4 full-time (0 women). Students: 3 full-time (1 woman). 2 applicants, 0% accepted. In 1997, 2 doctorates awarded. *Degree requirements:* For master's, computer language required, foreign language and thesis not required; for doctorate, computer language, dissertation, 2 comprehensive exams required, foreign language not required. *Average time to degree:* doctorate–3 years full-time. *Entrance requirements:* GMAT. Application deadline: 3/1. Application fee: $50. *Tuition:* $6429 per year full-time, $873 per quarter (minimum) part-time for state residents; $10,857 per year full-time, $1360 per quarter (minimum) part-time for nonresidents. *Financial aid:* In 1997–98, 2 teaching assistantships were awarded; Federal Work-Study and career-related internships or fieldwork also available. *Faculty research:* Time-series analysis, production scheduling, nonparametric methods, decision theory. • Larry E. Richards, Head, 541-346-3377. Application contact: Linda Johnson, Graduate Secretary, 541-346-3306.

University of Rhode Island, College of Business Administration, Kingston, RI 02881. Offerings include applied mathematics (PhD). *Entrance requirements:* GMAT, TOEFL (minimum score 575). Application deadline: 4/15 (priority date; rolling processing). Application fee: $35. *Expenses:* Tuition $3446 per year full-time, $191 per credit part-time for state residents; $9850 per year full-time, $547 per credit part-time for nonresidents. Fees $1276 per year full-time, $135 per semester (minimum) part-time.

Virginia Commonwealth University, School of Business, Program in Decision Sciences, Richmond, VA 23284-9005. Awards MS, PhD. *Degree requirements:* For doctorate, dissertation. *Entrance requirements:* For doctorate, GMAT. Application deadline: rolling. Application fee: $30 ($0 for international students). *Tuition:* $4960 per year full-time, $257 per credit part-time for state residents; $12,652 per year full-time, $684 per credit part-time for nonresidents. *Financial aid:* Fellowships, research assistantships, teaching assistantships, full and partial tuition waivers, Federal Work-Study, institutionally sponsored loans available. Financial aid application deadline: 3/15. • Dr. George M. Kasper, Chair, 804-828-1737. Fax: 804-828-3972. E-mail: gmkasper@vcu.edu. Application contact: Dr. Edward L. Millner, Associate Dean of Graduate Studies, 804-828-1741. Fax: 804-828-7174.

Section 20
Real Estate

This section contains a directory of institutions offering graduate work in real estate, followed by in-depth entries submitted by institutions that chose to prepare detailed program descriptions. Additional information about programs listed in the directory but not augmented by an in-depth entry may be obtained by writing directly to the dean of a graduate school or chair of a department at the address given in the directory.

For programs offering related work, see also in this book Business Administration and Management.

CONTENTS

Program Directory

In-Depth Descriptions

Real Estate

American University, Kogod College of Business Administration, Department of Finance, Program in Real Estate and Urban Development, Washington, DC 20016-8001. Awards MBA. Part-time and evening/weekend programs available. Faculty: 9 full-time (1 woman), 4 part-time (3 women). Students: 1 full-time (0 women), 11 part-time (2 women); includes 3 minority (1 African American, 2 Hispanics), 1 international. 11 applicants, 82% accepted. In 1997, 7 degrees awarded. *Entrance requirements:* GMAT. Application deadline: 2/1 (priority date; 10/1 for spring admission). Application fee: $50. *Expenses:* Tuition $19,080 per year full-time, $687 per credit hour (minimum) part-time. Fees $180 per year full-time, $110 per year part-time. *Financial aid:* Fellowships, Federal Work-Study, institutionally sponsored loans, and career-related internships or fieldwork available. Aid available to part-time students. Financial aid application deadline: 2/1. • Dr. Robert L. Losey, Chair, Department of Finance, 202-885-1941. Fax: 202-885-1946.

California State University, Northridge, College of Business Administration and Economics, Department of Finance, Real Estate and Insurance, Northridge, CA 91330. Awards MBA. Faculty: 13 full-time, 5 part-time. 4 applicants, 50% accepted. *Degree requirements:* Thesis or alternative required, foreign language not required. *Entrance requirements:* GMAT (score in 50th percentile or higher), TOEFL, minimum GPA of 3.0 in last 60 units. Application deadline: 11/30. Application fee: $55. *Expenses:* Tuition $0 for state residents; $246 per unit for nonresidents. Fees $1970 per year full-time, $1304 per year part-time. *Financial aid:* Application deadline 3/1. *Faculty research:* Real estate education improvement. • Dr. William Jennings, Chair, 818-677-2459. Application contact: Dr. Richard Moore, Director of Graduate Programs, 818-677-2467.

California State University, Sacramento, School of Business Administration, Program in Business Administration, Sacramento, CA 95819-6048. Offerings include urban land development (MBA). *Degree requirements:* Thesis or alternative, writing proficiency exam required, foreign language not required. *Entrance requirements:* GMAT, TOEFL (minimum score 550). Application deadline: 4/15 (11/1 for spring admission). Application fee: $55. *Expenses:* Tuition $0 for state residents; $246 per unit for nonresidents. Fees $2012 per year full-time, $1346 per year part-time. • Application contact: Dr. Herbert Blake, Graduate Adviser, 916-278-6771.

Columbia University, Graduate School of Architecture, Planning, and Preservation, Program in Real Estate Development, New York, NY 10027. Awards MS. Students: 52 full-time (13 women). In 1997, 16 degrees awarded. *Entrance requirements:* GRE General Test. Application deadline: 2/15. Application fee: $60. *Tuition:* $22,980 per year full-time, $766 per credit part-time. *Financial aid:* Fellowships available. Financial aid application deadline: 2/15. • Irving Fischer, Director, 212-854-3846. Application contact: Office of Admissions, 212-854-3510.

Columbia University, Graduate School of Business, MBA Program, New York, NY 10027. Offerings include real estate (MBA). Program faculty: 105 full-time (15 women), 86 part-time (15 women). *Entrance requirements:* GMAT, TOEFL (minimum score 610). Application deadline: 4/20 (rolling processing; 11/1 for spring admission). Application fee: $125 ($150 for international students). *Expenses:* Tuition $26,520 per year. Fees $1250 per year. • Prof. Safwan Masri, Vice Dean of Students and the MBA Program, 212-854-8716. Fax: 212-854-0545. E-mail: smm1@columbia.edu. Application contact: Linda Meehan, Assistant Dean and Executive Director of Admissions and Financial Aid, 212-854-1961. Fax: 212-662-6754. E-mail: gohermes@claven.gsb.columbia.edu.

Cornell University, Graduate Fields of Architecture, Art and Planning, Field of Real Estate, Ithaca, NY 14853-0001. Awards MPSRE. Faculty: 18 full-time. Students: 16 full-time (7 women); includes 1 minority (Hispanic), 8 international. 23 applicants, 57% accepted. *Entrance requirements:* GMAT or GRE General Test, TOEFL, resume. Application deadline: 3/1. Application fee: $65. Electronic applications accepted. *Expenses:* Tuition $22,780 per year. Fees $48 per year. *Financial aid:* Fellowships, research assistantships, teaching assistantships, institutionally sponsored loans available. Financial aid applicants required to submit FAFSA. *Faculty research:* Development financing, urban economic growth. • Director of Graduate Studies, 607-255-7110. Application contact: Graduate Field Assistant, 607-255-7110. Fax: 607-255-6681. E-mail: real_estate@cornell.edu.

See in-depth description on page 643.

The George Washington University, School of Business and Public Management, Department of Finance, Program in Real Estate Development, Washington, DC 20052. Awards MBA. Part-time and evening/weekend programs available. Faculty: 1 full-time (0 women). Students: 5 part-time (3 women); includes 2 minority (1 African American, 1 Hispanic). Average age 30. 17 applicants, 59% accepted. In 1997, 2 degrees awarded. *Degree requirements:* Computer language required, foreign language and thesis not required. *Entrance requirements:* GMAT, TOEFL (minimum score 550). Application deadline: 4/1 (priority date; rolling processing; 10/1 for spring admission). Application fee: $50. *Expenses:* Tuition $680 per semester hour. Fees $35 per semester hour. *Financial aid:* Fellowships, teaching assistantships, Federal Work-Study, institutionally sponsored loans, and career-related internships or fieldwork available. Financial aid application deadline: 4/1. • Dr. Mark J. Eppli, Head, 202-994-7478. Application contact: Lilly Hastings, Graduate Admissions, 202-994-6584. Fax: 202-994-6382.

Georgia State University, College of Business Administration, Department of Real Estate, Atlanta, GA 30303-3083. Awards MBA, MSRE, PhD. Part-time and evening/weekend programs available. Faculty: 6 full-time. Students: 28 full-time (7 women), 33 part-time (6 women); includes 1 Hispanic. Average age 30. In 1997, 11 master's, 1 doctorate awarded. Terminal master's awarded for partial completion of doctoral program. *Degree requirements:* For doctorate, dissertation required, foreign language not required. *Entrance requirements:* For master's, GMAT (average 566), TOEFL; for doctorate, GMAT (average 670), TOEFL. Application deadline: 5/1 (rolling processing; 10/1 for spring admission). Application fee: $25. *Expenses:* Tuition $2673 per year full-time, $99 per semester hour part-time for state residents; $10,692 per year full-time, $396 per semester hour part-time for nonresidents. Fees $228 per year. *Financial aid:* Fellowships, research assistantships, teaching assistantships, partial tuition waivers, and career-related internships or fieldwork available. Aid available to part-time students. Financial aid applicants required to submit FAFSA. • Dr. Joseph S. Rabianski, Chair, 404-651-2760. Fax: 404-651-3396. Application contact: Office of Academic Assistance and Master's Admissions, 404-651-1913. Fax: 404-651-0219.

John Marshall Law School, Chicago, IL 60604-3968. Offerings include real estate (LL M). School faculty: 52 full-time (14 women), 230 part-time (43 women). *Average time to degree:* master's–1.5 years full-time, 2 years part-time; first professional–3 years full-time, 4 years part-time. *Application deadline:* 3/1 (priority date; rolling processing; 10/1 for spring admission). *Application fee:* $50 ($60 for international students). *Expenses:* Tuition $675 per credit (minimum). Fees $40 per semester. • Robert Gilbert Johnson, Dean, 312-427-2737. Application contact: William B. Powers, Dean of Admission and Student Affairs, 312-987-1403. Fax: 312-427-5136. E-mail: 6alonzo@jmls.edu.

Johns Hopkins University, School of Continuing Studies, Division of Business and Management, Baltimore, MD 21218-2699. Offerings include real estate (MS). Division faculty: 12 full-time, 190 part-time. *Degree requirements:* Project required, foreign language and thesis not required. *Entrance requirements:* Minimum GPA of 3.0. Application deadline: rolling. Application fee: $50. • Dr. Jon Heggan, Director, 410-516-0755. Application contact: Lenora Henry, Admissions Coordinator, 410-872-1234. Fax: 410-872-1251. E-mail: adv_mail@jhuvms.hcf.jhu.edu.

Massachusetts Institute of Technology, School of Architecture and Planning, Center for Real Estate, Cambridge, MA 02139-4307. Awards MSRED. Faculty: 8 full-time (3 women), 1 part-time (0 women). Students: 30 full-time (10 women); includes 4 international. Average age 30. In 1997, 32 degrees awarded (100% found work related to degree). *Degree requirements:* Thesis. *Entrance requirements:* GMAT. Application deadline: 2/15. Application fee: $55. *Tuition:* $24,050 per year. *Financial aid:* In 1997–98, 8 fellowships (all to first-year students) were awarded. *Faculty research:* Real estate finance, foreign investment, land use regulation, affordable housing, design. • William C. Wheaton, Director, 617-253-4373. Fax: 617-258-6991. Application contact: Maria Vieira, Associate Director of Education, 617-253-4373.

New York University, School of Continuing Education, Real Estate Institute, Program in Real Estate, New York, NY 10012-1019. Awards MS. Part-time and evening/weekend programs available. Faculty: 2 full-time (0 women), 48 part-time (4 women). Students: 19 full-time (5 women), 234 part-time (44 women); includes 10 minority (3 African Americans, 6 Asian Americans, 1 Hispanic), 9 international. Average age 33. 190 applicants, 47% accepted. In 1997, 96 degrees awarded (100% found work related to degree). *Entrance requirements:* GMAT, GRE, or LSAT (score in 75th percentile or higher), 2 years of work experience. Application deadline: 5/15 (priority date; rolling processing; 10/15 for spring admission). Application fee: $50. *Financial aid:* 32 students received aid; partial tuition waivers, Federal Work-Study, institutionally sponsored loans available. Aid available to part-time students. Financial aid application deadline: 3/1; applicants required to submit FAFSA. *Faculty research:* Valuation, real estate capital markets, senior housing. • Dr. Arthur Margon, Director, Real Estate Institute, 212-790-1335. Fax: 212-790-1686.

See in-depth description on page 645.

Northwestern University, J. L. Kellogg Graduate School of Management, Programs in Management, Evanston, IL 60208. Offerings include real estate management (MM). MMM offered jointly with the Robert R. McCormick School of Engineering and Applied Science; MM/MSN offered jointly with Rush Presbyterian Hospital. Faculty: 129 full-time (24 women), 89 part-time (15 women). *Application deadline:* 3/16. *Application fee:* $125. *Tuition:* $25,872 per year. • Michele Rogers, Assistant Dean of Admissions and Financial Aid, 847-491-3308. Fax: 847-491-4960.

Pennsylvania State University University Park Campus, The Mary Jean and Frank P. Smeal College of Business Administration, MS Programs in Business Administration, Department of Real Estate, University Park, PA 16802-1503. Awards MS. *Degree requirements:* Thesis or alternative required, foreign language not required. *Entrance requirements:* GMAT. Application fee: $40. *Expenses:* Tuition $6534 per year full-time, $276 per credit part-time for state residents; $13,460 per year full-time, $561 per credit part-time for nonresidents. Fees $252 per year (minimum) full-time, $43 per semester (minimum) part-time. • Dr. Kenneth M. Lusht, Chair, 814-865-1190.

Pennsylvania State University University Park Campus, The Mary Jean and Frank P. Smeal College of Business Administration, PhD Programs in Business Administration, Program in Finance/Insurance and Real Estate, University Park, PA 16802-1503. Awards PhD. *Degree requirements:* Dissertation. *Entrance requirements:* GMAT. Application fee: $40. *Expenses:* Tuition $6534 per year full-time, $276 per credit part-time for state residents; $13,460 per year full-time, $561 per credit part-time for nonresidents. Fees $252 per year (minimum) full-time, $43 per semester (minimum) part-time. • Dr. Dennis P. Sheehan, Field Adviser, 814-863-8512.

Temple University, School of Business and Management, Master's Program in Business Administration, Philadelphia, PA 19122-6096. Offerings include real estate and urban land studies (MBA, MS). Program faculty: 72 full-time (13 women). *Entrance requirements:* GMAT (average 540), TOEFL (minimum score 575). Application fee: $40. *Expenses:* Tuition $323 per semester hour for state residents; $444 per semester hour for nonresidents. Fees $170 per year full-time, $28 per semester (minimum) part-time. • Application contact: Linda Whelan, Director, 215-204-7678. Fax: 215-204-8300. E-mail: linda@astro.ocis.temple.edu.

University of Cincinnati, College of Business Administration, Department of Finance, Program in Real Estate, Cincinnati, OH 45221. Awards MBA. Part-time and evening/weekend programs available. Faculty: 1 full-time. Students: 2 full-time (0 women), 5 part-time (1 woman). 2 applicants, 0% accepted. In 1997, 5 degrees awarded. *Degree requirements:* Thesis or alternative. *Average time to degree:* master's–2.8 years full-time. *Entrance requirements:* GMAT. Application deadline: 5/30. Application fee: $30. *Tuition:* $7228 per year full-time, $185 per credit hour part-time for state residents; $13,812 per year full-time, $352 per credit hour part-time for nonresidents. *Financial aid:* Fellowships, graduate assistantships, full tuition waivers available. Aid available to part-time students. Financial aid application deadline: 2/15. • Application contact: Glenn V. Henderson Jr., Graduate Program Director, 513-556-7079. Fax: 513-556-4891.

University of Denver, Daniels College of Business, Department of Finance, Denver, CO 80208. Offerings include finance/real estate (MBA). Department faculty: 10 full-time (3 women). *Application deadline:* 5/1 (priority date; rolling processing; 1/1 for spring admission). *Application fee:* $50. *Expenses:* Tuition $18,216 per year full-time, $506 per credit hour part-time. Fees $159 per year. • Dr. Maclyn Clouse, Chairman, 303-871-3320. Application contact: Jan Johnson, Executive Director, Student Services, 303-871-3416. Fax: 303-871-4466. E-mail: dcb@du.edu.

University of Denver, Daniels College of Business, School of Real Estate and Construction Management, Denver, CO 80208. Offers programs in real estate (MBA), real estate and construction management (MRECM). Part-time programs available. Faculty: 4 full-time (0 women). Students: 43 full-time (9 women), 10 part-time (2 women); includes 1 minority (Asian American), 10 international. Average age 27. 54 applicants, 80% accepted. In 1997, 9 degrees awarded. *Entrance requirements:* GMAT (average 545). Application deadline: 5/1 (priority date; rolling processing; 1/1 for spring admission). Application fee: $50. *Expenses:* Tuition $18,216 per year full-time, $506 per credit hour part-time. Fees $159 per year. *Financial aid:* In 1997–98, 27 students received aid, including 1 teaching assistantship averaging $634 per month and totaling $7,027, 17 grants, scholarships totaling $13,800; research assistantships, Federal Work-Study, institutionally sponsored loans, and career-related internships or fieldwork also available. Aid available to part-time students. Financial aid application deadline: 2/15; applicants required to submit FAFSA. • Dr. Mark Levine, Director, 303-871-2142. Application contact: Jan Johnson, Executive Director, Student Services, 303-871-3416. Fax: 303-871-4466. E-mail: dcb@du.edu.

University of Florida, College of Business Administration, Department of Finance, Insurance and Real Estate, Gainesville, FL 32611. Offers programs in finance (PhD), real estate and urban analysis (MA, PhD). Faculty: 20. Students: 22 full-time (3 women), 5 part-time (0 women); includes 2 minority (both Asian Americans), 5 international. 113 applicants, 23% accepted. In 1997, 11 master's, 2 doctorates awarded. *Degree requirements:* Thesis/dissertation required, foreign language not required. *Entrance requirements:* GMAT or GRE General Test, minimum GPA of 3.0. Application deadline: 2/16 (rolling processing). Application fee: $20. *Tuition:* $138 per credit hour for state residents; $481 per credit hour for nonresidents. *Financial aid:* In 1997–98, 21 students received aid, including 5 fellowships averaging $1,962 per month, 12 research assistantships averaging $560 per month, 2 teaching assistantships averaging $1,746 per month, 2 graduate assistantships averaging $320 per month; career-related internships or fieldwork also available. *Faculty research:* Financial management, financial markets and institutions, investments, risk and insurance, real estate development. • Dr. David Brown, Chair, 352-392-0153. E-mail: dbrown@dale.cba.ufl.edu. Application contact: Dr. Michael Ryngaert, Graduate Coordinator, 352-392-3184. Fax: 352-392-0301. E-mail: ryngaert@dale.cba.ufl.edu.

The University of Memphis, Fogelman College of Business and Economics, Program in Business Administration, Memphis, TN 38152. Offerings include finance, insurance, and real estate (MBA, MS); real estate development (MS). Program faculty: 92 full-time (15 women), 2 part-time (0 women). *Degree requirements:* Comprehensive exams required, thesis not required.

Entrance requirements: GMAT (minimum score 430; average 535), GRE General Test. Application deadline: 8/1 (12/1 for spring admission). Application fee: $25 ($50 for international students). *Tuition:* $2862 per year full-time, $166 per credit hour part-time for state residents; $6696 per year full-time, $379 per credit hour part-time for nonresidents. • Application contact: Dr. Ravinder Nath, Associate Dean of Academic Programs, 901-678-3721. Fax: 901-678-4705. E-mail: fcbegp@memphis.edu.

University of North Texas, College of Business Administration, Department of Finance, Insurance, Real Estate, and Law, Denton, TX 76203-6737. Offers programs in banking (MBA, PhD), finance (MBA, PhD), insurance (MBA), real estate (MBA). Part-time programs available. Faculty: 22 full-time (3 women), 4 part-time (0 women). Students: 40 full-time (18 women), 138 part-time (47 women); includes 12 minority (4 African Americans, 5 Asian Americans, 3 Hispanics), 29 international. In 1997, 38 master's, 1 doctorate awarded. *Degree requirements:* For master's, computer language required, foreign language and thesis not required; for doctorate, computer language, dissertation required, foreign language not required. *Entrance requirements:* For master's, GMAT, TOEFL; for doctorate, GMAT or GRE General Test, TOEFL. Application deadline: 7/17. Application fee: $25 ($50 for international students). *Tuition:* $2063 per year full-time, $815 per year part-time for state residents; $5897 per year full-time, $2100 per year part-time for nonresidents. *Financial aid:* Fellowships, research assistantships, teaching assistantships, and career-related internships or fieldwork available. Financial aid application deadline: 4/1. *Faculty research:* Financial impact of regulation, risk management, financial instrument rating changes, taxes and valuation, bankruptcy. • Dr. Imre Karafiath, Chair, 940-565-3050.

University of Pennsylvania, Wharton School, Real Estate Department, Philadelphia, PA 19104. Awards MBA. *Entrance requirements:* GMAT. Application fee: $125. *Faculty research:* Public economics and taxation economics and finance of real estate markets, economics of housing markets, real estate development. • Dr. Susan Wachter, Chair, 215-898-9687. E-mail: wachter@finance.upenn.edu. Application contact: Lisa Lord, Fiscal Coordinator, 215-898-9687. Fax: 215-573-2220. E-mail: lordli@wharton.upenn.edu.

University of St. Thomas, Graduate School of Business, Program in Real Estate Appraisal, St. Paul, MN 55105-1096. Awards MS. Part-time programs available. Faculty: 1 full-time, 6 part-time. *Entrance requirements:* GMAT. Application deadline: 6/1 (priority date; rolling processing). Application fee: $30. *Tuition:* $416 per credit hour. *Financial aid:* Career-related internships or fieldwork available. Aid available to part-time students. Financial aid application deadline: 4/1; applicants required to submit FAFSA. • Thomas Musil, Director, 612-962-4289. Fax: 612-962-4125.

University of Southern California, Graduate School, School of Policy, Planning and Development, Program in Real Estate Development, Los Angeles, CA 90089. Awards MRED, JD/MRED, MBA/MRED. Students: 45 full-time (12 women), 6 part-time (0 women); includes 13 minority (5 African Americans, 5 Asian Americans, 3 Hispanics), 14 international. Average age 31. In 1997, 25 degrees awarded. *Entrance requirements:* GRE General Test. Application deadline: 3/1 (priority date). Application fee: $55. *Expenses:* Tuition $25,088 per year full-time, $784 per unit part-time. Fees $414 per year full-time, $32 per year part-time. *Financial aid:* In 1997–98, 11 research assistantships, 1 teaching assistantship were awarded; fellowships, Federal Work-Study, institutionally sponsored loans also available. Aid available to part-time students. Financial aid application deadline: 2/15; applicants required to submit FAFSA. • Dr. Richard B. Peiser, Director, 213-740-8894.

See in-depth description on page 647.

The University of Texas at Arlington, College of Business Administration, Department of Finance and Real Estate, Arlington, TX 76019-0407. Offers program in real estate (MS). Students: 4 full-time (2 women), 5 part-time (1 woman); includes 2 international. 11 applicants, 64% accepted. In 1997, 2 degrees awarded. *Degree requirements:* Thesis optional, foreign language not required. *Entrance requirements:* GMAT (minimum score 480; average 539), minimum GPA of 2.7. Application deadline: rolling. Application fee: $25 ($50 for international students). *Tuition:* $3206 per year full-time, $468 per semester (minimum) part-time for state residents; $8612 per year full-time, $1137 per semester (minimum) part-time for nonresidents. *Financial aid:* Research assistantships, teaching assistantships, Federal Work-Study, institutionally sponsored loans, and career-related internships or fieldwork available. • Dr. Peggy Swanson, Chair, 817-272-3705. Application contact: Dr. Richard Buttimer, Graduate Adviser, 817-272-3004.

The University of Texas at Arlington, College of Business Administration, Program in Business Administration, Arlington, TX 76019-0407. Offerings include real estate (MBA). *Degree requirements:* Computer language required, foreign language not required. *Entrance requirements:* GMAT (minimum score 480; average 550), minimum GPA of 2.9. Application deadline: rolling. Application fee: $25 ($50 for international students). *Tuition:* $3206 per year full-time, $468 per semester (minimum) part-time for state residents; $8612 per year full-time, $1137 per semester (minimum) part-time for nonresidents. • Application contact: Dr. James E. Walther, Graduate Adviser, 817-272-3004. Fax: 817-794-5799.

University of Wisconsin–Madison, School of Business, Program in Real Estate and Urban Land Economics, Madison, WI 53706-1380. Awards MBA, MS, PhD. Faculty: 4 full-time (0 women). Students: 39 full-time (9 women). In 1997, 30 master's awarded (100% found work related to degree); 2 doctorates awarded (100% entered university research/teaching). *Degree requirements:* For doctorate, dissertation. *Entrance requirements:* GMAT. Application deadline: 6/1 (rolling processing; 10/1 for spring admission). Application fee: $45. *Tuition:* $5950 per year full-time, $1118 per semester (minimum) part-time for state residents; $16,230 per year full-time, $3044 per semester (minimum) part-time for nonresidents. *Financial aid:* Fellowships, research assistantships, teaching assistantships, project assistantships available. *Faculty research:* Real estate finance, real estate equity investments, zoning restructurings, home ownership, international real estate and public policy. • James Shilling, Chair, 608-262-8602. Fax: 608-265-2738. E-mail: jshilling@bus.wisc.edu. Application contact: Lisa Urban, Director of Master's Marketing and Recruiting, 608-262-4610. Fax: 608-265-4192.

University of Wisconsin–Madison, School of Business, Program in Real Estate Appraisal and Investment Analysis, Madison, WI 53706-1380. Awards MS. *Entrance requirements:* GMAT. Application deadline: 6/1 (rolling processing; 10/1 for spring admission). Application fee: $45. *Tuition:* $5950 per year full-time, $1118 per semester (minimum) part-time for state residents; $16,230 per year full-time, $3044 per semester (minimum) part-time for nonresidents. • James Shilling, Chair, 608-262-8602. Fax: 608-265-2738. E-mail: jshilling@bus.wisc.edu. Application contact: Lisa Urban, Director of Master's Marketing and Recruiting, 608-262-4610. Fax: 608-265-4192.

Virginia Commonwealth University, School of Business, Program in Real Estate and Urban Land Development, Richmond, VA 23284-9005. Awards MS, Certificate. Students: *Entrance requirements:* For master's, GMAT. Application deadline: rolling. Application fee: $30 ($0 for international students). *Tuition:* $4960 per year full-time, $257 per credit part-time for state residents; $12,652 per year full-time, $684 per credit part-time for nonresidents. *Financial aid:* Fellowships, research assistantships, teaching assistantships, full and partial tuition waivers, Federal Work-Study, institutionally sponsored loans available. Financial aid application deadline: 3/15. • Dr. James H. Boykin, Chair, 804-828-1721. Fax: 804-828-3972. Application contact: Dr. Edward L. Millner, Associate Dean of Graduate Studies, 804-828-1741. Fax: 804-828-7174.

Webster University, School of Business and Technology, Department of Business, St. Louis, MO 63119-3194. Offerings include real estate management (MA, MBA). Department faculty: 5 full-time (1 woman). *Application deadline:* rolling. *Application fee:* $25 ($50 for international students). *Tuition:* $350 per credit hour. • Lucille Berry, Chair, 314-968-7022. Fax: 314-968-7077. E-mail: berrylm@webster.edu. Application contact: Beth Russell, Director of Graduate Admissions, 314-968-7089. Fax: 314-968-7166. E-mail: russellmb@webster.edu.

CORNELL UNIVERSITY

Master of Professional Studies in Real Estate

Program of Study

Cornell University offers a two-year course of study that leads to a Master of Professional Studies (M.P.S.) degree. The program, established to meet a growing need for formal training in real estate, is primarily geared for those beginning or continuing professional real estate careers.

The curriculum is multidisciplinary and addresses all aspects of real estate. Administratively, the program is located in the College of Architecture, Art, and Planning, but faculty and courses are found in seven of the University's distinguished colleges and professional schools, principally the School of Hotel Administration; the Johnson Graduate School of Management; the College of Architecture, Art, and Planning; the College of Human Ecology; and the College of Engineering.

The curriculum emphasizes management skills and real estate principles and capitalizes on Cornell's vast educational resources. Students take twenty courses. A core curriculum of thirteen courses includes real estate finance and investment, management, economics, market analysis, development process, construction planning, real estate law, housing economics and regulation, and facilities management. The balance of a student's curriculum—seven electives—is selected from sixty real estate-related courses offered throughout the University. Students may design a curriculum that concentrates on an aspect of real estate, such as development, asset management, international development, or low-income housing. They may also specialize in a geographic area of the nation or the world, concentrate on entrepreneurship, or study government regulation and public policy.

The flexibility of the real estate program allows students to draw on Cornell's traditional strengths in architecture, engineering, hospitality administration, and business management. The program also offers students extensive contact with professionals in the industry through a number of organizations that have ties to the University, especially the 900-member Cornell Real Estate Council.

Research Facilities

Students enjoy unlimited access to Cornell University's system of nineteen libraries, among them specialized collections and resources in law, management, hotel administration, and the arts. The system contains more than 5 million volumes, 600,000 periodical titles, and extensive microform and other materials. The Johnson Graduate School of Management Library has a collection of approximately 157,000 volumes. The Stouffer Library in the School of Hotel Administration contains more than 25,000 volumes on all aspects of hospitality administration, including real estate and related subjects. Sibley Library in the College of Architecture, Art, and Planning has works on housing, landscape architecture, site planning, land use, and urban planning.

Computing at Cornell is integral to academic life. Network access to e-mail, online library catalogs, public-information servers, microcomputer facilities, and educational programs is available to all. Computer workstations are located throughout the University, including most libraries, and there is round-the-clock access to IBM and Apple Macintosh computers.

Financial Aid

Fellowships are not generally available, but students may be eligible for other sources of aid, such as loans and teaching assistantships. Whenever possible, students should seek fellowships from national, international, industrial, foundation, and governmental sources. Cornell administers several need-based financial aid programs for United States citizens and permanent residents, including the Federal Work-Study Program, Federal Perkins Loan, and the William D. Ford Federal Direct Loan program. GradShare loans are available to United States citizens and permanent residents. Legal residents of New York State may be eligible for New York State Tuition Assistance Program awards. Opportunities for part-time work may be available in connection with faculty research projects.

Cost of Study

The estimated total of tuition and fees for full-time students for the 1998–99 academic year is $22,780. The cost of books and materials is approximately $750.

Living and Housing Costs

The cost of living is lower in Ithaca than in major urban centers. For the 1998–99 academic year, expenses for a single student are between $10,000 and $12,000—including the cost of room and board, books, personal expenses, and medical insurance, but not including tuition, travel, summer living expenses, and applicable income taxes.

Student Group

Cornell University enrolls approximately 4,500 graduate students in eighty-five fields of study. More than one third are women, more than one third are international students, and 15 percent of those who are United States citizens are members of minority groups. Graduate students who study real estate come from a variety of undergraduate backgrounds. Some will have work experience in the real estate field, but experience is not a requirement. An enrollment of 12 new students in 1998–99 and 15 new students in 1999–2000 is expected.

Location

Cornell is located in the Finger Lakes region of central New York State. Surrounded by spectacular gorges and waterfalls, the campus is renowned for its natural beauty. The city of Ithaca and its surrounding residential areas have a population close to 100,000—with a surprising number of bookshops, movie houses, and stores and the greatest number of restaurants per capita of any county in the country. Three state parks are within 10 miles of the city. Within an hour are the cities of Syracuse and Binghamton, the Finger Lakes wine district, Watkins Glen, and several centers for the performing arts. For the serious student, this provides an ideal environment for study.

The University

Founded in 1865 by Ezra Cornell, Cornell University is both the land-grant institution of the state of New York and a privately endowed university. The faculty numbers more than 2,000 and includes Nobel laureates, Pulitzer Prize and MacArthur Fellowship winners, and members of learned societies. More than 19,000 students are enrolled in the thirteen schools and colleges of this Ivy League institution, including graduate, professional, and undergraduate students. Cornell University is an Equal Opportunity/Affirmative Action educator and employer.

Applying

Applicants must have completed a bachelor's degree with a good academic record prior to enrollment, take either the Graduate Record Examinations (GRE) or Graduate Management Admission Test (GMAT), and submit two letters of recommendation from undergraduate college faculty members (or from employers, if appropriate). International students for whom English is a second language must score a minimum of 575 on the Test of English as a Foreign Language (TOEFL). Complete applications must be filed by March 1, but can be submitted earlier for earlier decisions.

Correspondence and Information

Robert H. Abrams
Director of the Program in Real Estate
114 West Sibley Hall
Cornell University
Ithaca, New York 14853-6701
Telephone: 607-255-7110
Fax: 607-255-0242
E-mail: real_estate@cornell.edu

Matthew P. Drennan
Director of Graduate Studies
202 West Sibley Hall
Cornell University
Ithaca, New York 14853-6701
Telephone: 607-255-7436
Fax: 607-255-0242
E-mail: real_estate@cornell.edu

Cornell University

THE FACULTY AND THEIR RESEARCH

Robert H. Abrams, Senior Lecturer, City and Regional Planning; M.B.A., Harvard. A former principal of Abrams Benisch Riker Inc., Robert Abrams has more than thirty years of experience in management and leasing of major New York City office buildings, including the Seagram Building and the Chrysler Building. He teaches real estate development and real estate management and serves as director of the Program in Real Estate.

Franklin Becker, Professor, Design and Environmental Analysis, and Director of the International Facility Management Program; Ph.D., California, Davis. Dr. Becker is the author of several books and articles on environmental design, including *Workplace: Creating Environments in Organization,* and is the leader of an international research consortium studying the organizational and real estate consequences of innovative workplace strategies. He teaches courses in planning and managing the workplace.

Richard Booth, Associate Professor, City and Regional Planning; J.D., George Washington. An expert in land use controls, environmental controls, management of local governments, and political issues pertaining to use and management of land, Richard Booth teaches environmental law, real estate law, and historic preservation law.

Jack Corgel, Associate Professor, Hotel Administration; Ph.D., Georgia. Dr. Corgel has published more than forty articles on real estate investment and real estate finance. His textbook, *Real Estate Perspectives,* is used throughout the country. He teaches courses on the principles of real estate and advanced real estate investment.

Jan deRoos, Assistant Professor, Hotel Administration; Ph.D., Cornell. Research interests include hospitality industry energy conservation and comparative lodging prices. Dr. deRoos consults extensively in the hospitality industry and co-teaches the Real Estate Project Workshop.

Matt Drennan, Professor, City and Regional Planning; Ph.D., NYU. An expert on urban economics and urban public finance, Dr. Drennan consults on economic development issues for the City of New York and other clients. He teaches urban economics, microeconomics, and urban public finance.

James Eyster, Professor, Hotel Administration; Ph.D., Cornell. Dr. Eyster has published numerous articles on valuation, financial analysis, financial management, and contract negotiation and works as a real estate consultant to more than eighty corporations in the hospitality industry. He teaches hospitality property finance.

Kenneth Hover, Associate Professor, Civil and Environmental Engineering; Ph.D., Cornell. A registered professional engineer in New York and Ohio, Dr. Hover has spent twelve years in the design and construction industry, and his research focuses on the impact of construction operations on the quality and durability of concrete buildings, bridges, and pavements. He teaches construction planning and operations.

Nandinee K. Kutty, Assistant Professor, Consumer Economics and Housing; Ph.D., Syracuse. Dr. Kutty's research interests include housing economics and policy and home ownership and housing maintenance, and her study citing the untapped potential of reverse mortgages for the elderly has received national attention. She teaches housing economics.

Vincent Mulcahy, Associate Professor, Architecture; M.Arch., Harvard. Professor Mulcahy's research interests include campus planning and design, and he actively practices architecture and small-town planning. He is part of a team that teaches introductory architecture.

Kermit Parsons, Professor, City and Regional Planning; M.R.P., Cornell. Professor Parsons is the author of several books and more than thirty articles on urban land-use planning, large-scale urban development planning, and urban-growth policy.

Patricia Pollak, Associate Professor, Consumer Economics and Housing; Ph.D., Syracuse. Dr. Pollak's research interests include housing policy, community-based housing, and the impacts of zoning and land-use regulations.

Michael Redlin, Professor, Hotel Administration; Ph.D., Cornell. Dr. Redlin specializes in facilities development and design, maintenance, mechanical systems, and energy conservation for the hospitality industry. A member of the American Hotel and Motel Association's Executive Engineering Committee, he is also a member of the Food-Service Consultants Society International.

Henry Richardson, Associate Professor, Architecture; M.R.P., Cornell. Henry Richardson is a professional architect and planner whose work includes large-scale urban design projects and the design of commercial and laboratory buildings.

Mario Schack, Professor, Architecture; M.Arch., Harvard. Professor Schack's professional practice involves urban design and planning, including feasibility studies for various multiuse projects, and he has served as vice president of two international architectural firms.

William Sims, Professor, Department of Design and Environmental Analysis and Head of Cornell's Program in Facility Planning and Management; Ph.D., MIT. Dr. Sims serves as co-director of the International Facility Management Research Project and is the author of numerous articles on facility planning and management, performance appraisal of buildings, and building programming and evaluation. He teaches courses and conducts research in facility planning and management.

Roger Trancik, Professor, Landscape Architecture; M.L.A., Harvard. Roger Trancik is the author of *Finding Lost Space: Theories of Urban Design* and more than thirty journal articles on urban design and community impact assessment. His professional interests include urban design, landscape architecture, environmental planning, and urban development.

Peter Trowbridge, Professor, Landscape Architecture; M.L.A., Harvard. Professor Trowbridge's research interests include environmental remediation of former industrial sites. He teaches site construction and studios on site redevelopment and urban greenways.

The Cornell University campus.

NEW YORK UNIVERSITY

School of Continuing and Professional Studies
The Real Estate Institute

Program of Study

The analysis, financing, and operation of investment property around the world has evolved into a discipline requiring knowledge of markets, complex capital sources and structures, and sophisticated analytic techniques. The Master of Science in real estate teaches the multiple disciplines required by professionals who shape real estate decisions for investors, institutions, and corporations.

Courses are taught by a combination of full-time faculty members and adjunct faculty members who are active participants in the real estate industry. The program draws upon a faculty pool of approximately 250 lecturers and professors.

The degree consists of 38 credits, with all students required to take a common core of courses before choosing a concentration in development, finance, investment, valuation, or international real estate. The valuation concentration allows students to fulfill the educational requirements for designation as a Member of the Appraisal Institute (MAI). The final course experience is a capstone project that allows the student to demonstrate a broad range of capabilities in real estate.

The program can be completed in twelve months of full-time study or in two to three years on a part-time basis.

Research Facilities

The Real Estate Institute draws upon the specialized resources of the Jack Brause Library and Information Center, which is operated jointly by the Institute and the University Library System. The Brause Library is a unique resource used by students and real estate professionals with a strong collection focused entirely on real estate.

Financial Aid

NYU's centralized Office of Financial Aid assists students with loan packages, and the NYU monthly payment plan enables students to spread out their tuition payments.

Cost of Study

Tuition for the 1998–99 academic year is $570 per credit. Additional nonrefundable fees are charged on a per-credit basis and registration and service fees are charged on the first credit and on each additional credit. The fee structure by semester is as follows: for fall 1998, $148 on the first credit, $40 on each additional credit; for spring 1999, $162 on the first credit, $40 on each additional credit; and for summer 1999, $89 and on the first credit, $40 on each additional credit. Full-time status is 12 or more credits; part-time status is fewer than 12 credits.

Living and Housing Costs

Most graduate student housing, located within walking distance of the Washington Square campus, provides separate kitchen and bathroom facilities and laundry rooms. A free NYU shuttle bus links housing and academic facilities. An off-campus housing office is also available to assist students. Room rates for the academic year (fall and spring) range form approximately $5775 to $10,350, with available meal plans ranging from approximately $1485 to $3625.

Student Group

The student body numbers approximately 275 students in both full-time and part-time study.

Location

The Real Estate Institute is located at 11 West 42nd Street, off Fifth Avenue in midtown Manhattan, close to shops, offices, theaters, and museums. It is directly across the street from the New York Public Library in the heart of New York's most vibrant office location.

The University and The Institute

NYU is a private university, composed of thirteen schools, colleges, and divisions. The University was founded in 1831, and the School of Continuing and Professional Studies in 1934. The Real Estate Institute, which offers the master's degree, a graduate-level advanced professional certificate, a diploma program, summer intensive programs, and noncredit professional development courses, was established in 1966.

Applying

Students may apply for fall, spring, or summer admission. Factors that are considered in evaluating applicants include the applicant's academic achievement in previous undergraduate and graduate course work, scores from a standardized graduate admissions test, the nature and extent of previous work experience, letters of recommendation, and a statement of purpose.

Correspondence and Information

For more information and an application package, students should contact:

Master of Science in Real Estate
School of Continuing and Professional Studies
New York University
7 East 12th Street, 11th Floor
New York, New York 10003-4475

Telephone: 212-790-1335
Fax: 212-995-3656
E-mail: sce.realestate@nyu.edu

New York University

THE FACULTY AND THEIR RESEARCH

Lawrence W. Agne, Adjunct Assistant Professor of Real Estate; CPA, CMA.
Jerome B. Alenick, Adjunct Professor of Real Estate; LL.B. Principal, Jerome B. Alenick Investment and Financial Services; editor, *Real Estate Development Manual.*
Barry S. Auerbach, Adjunct Assistant Professor of Real Estate; J.D., CPA. Partner, KPMG Peat Marwick.
Jerome Block, Adjunct Associate Professor of Real Estate; M.B.A., MAI. President, Wilrock Appraisal.
Robert S. Blumenthal, Adjunct Professor of Real Estate; M.P.A. Managing director, BT Securities Corporation.
Enda Bracken, Instructor of Real Estate; M.S. Senior Vice President, R.E.O., The RCC Group, Inc.
Barry D. Citrin, Adjunct Assistant Professor of Real Estate; M.P.A. Senior vice president, Tri-Quest Financial Service Corporation.
Steven K. Copulsky, Lecturer; M.B.A. Senior Vice President, Schroder Mortgage Associates.
Sylvia Deutsch, Adjunct Associate Professor of Real Estate; B.A. Land use consultant; former chairperson, NYC Board of Standards and Appeals and NYC Planning Commission.
Rudolph de Winter, Adjunct Associate Professor of Real Estate; LL.B. Partner, Kramer, Levin, Naftalis, Nessen, Kamin & Frankel.
Alan M. Di Sciullo, Adjunct Assistant Professor of Real Estate; J.D., M.B.A. First vice president and senior attorney, Dean Witter Reynolds, Inc.
Frederic J. Fatigati, Lecturer; M.S. Vice president, The Garibaldi Group.
Lawrence E. Fiedler, Adjunct Professor of Real Estate; LL.M., CPA. President, JRM Development Enterprises, Inc.
David Fields, Lecturer; B.B.A. Principal, The Fields Company.
John S. Halpern, Adjunct Assistant Professor of Real Estate; B.S. Partner, Hampton Partners.
Richard K. Helman, Adjunct Assistant Professor of Real Estate; LL.B. Real estate attorney.
Hugh F. Kelly, Adjunct Associate Professor of Real Estate; B.A., CRE. Senior vice president, Landauer Associates, Inc.
Richard Kessler, Adjunct Assistant Professor of Real Estate; B.A., B.S. Senior vice president, Benenson Development Corp.
Herve A. Kevenides, Adjunct Associate Professor of Real Estate; M.B.A. President, Metropolitan Analysis & Forecasting Corp.
William Kinn, Adjunct Assistant Professor of Real Estate; B.S. Managing Director, Landauer Associates, Inc.
James D. Kuhn, Adjunct Associate Professor of Real Estate; M.B.A. President, Newmark & Company Real Estate, Inc.
Alan Lapidus, Lecturer; B.Arch. President, Alan Lapidus Architecture, P.C.
Matthew W. Lechner, Adjunct Assistant Professor of Real Estate; B.A. Certified Investment Management Analyst, A.G. Edwards & Sons, Inc.
Marc D. Legman, Lecturer; M.S. Vice President, Grubb & Ellis Company.
Joel Leitner, Adjunct Assistant Professor of Real Estate; M.S. President, Leitner & Borax Inc.
Sheldon Lobel, Adjunct Assistant Professor of Real Estate; J.D. Founder, Sheldon Lobel & Associates.
Demetrios Louziotis Jr., Lecturer; M.S. Consultant, Price Waterhouse LLP.
Richard Marchitelli, Adjunct Assistant Professor of Real Estate; MAI, CRE. Principal, Marchitelli Barnes & Company, Inc.
Arthur Margon, Clinical Professor of Real Estate; Ph.D.
Damiano G. Maruca, Adjunct Assistant Professor of Real Estate; M.S., ASCE. Principal, Damiano G. Maruca, AIA.
Edward R. McGinnis, Adjunct Associate Professor of Real Estate; B.S. Principal, Edward Rory McGinnis, Architect.
Benjamin McGrath, Lecturer; M.B.A. Managing director, Chemical Bank.
Louis P. Mirando, Adjunct Assistant Professor of Real Estate; B.S., B.A. Managing Director, TransAtlantic Capital Company.
Eugene J. Morris, Adjunct Professor of Real Estate; LL.B. Of counsel, Spector Scher & Feldman.
Stephen Pearlman, Adjunct Associate Professor of Real Estate; M.B.A. Director, real estate finance, Jones Lang Wootton USA.
David A. Pearson, Adjunct Assistant Professor of Real Estate; B.B.A., MAI. Principal, Pearson Partners, Inc.
Helen Peng, Lecturer; M.S. Vice president, Bankers Trust.
Glenn J. Rufrano, Adjunct Associate Professor of Real Estate; M.S.M., MAI. Executive vice president, The O'Connor Group.
David Scribner Jr., Adjunct Associate Professor of Real Estate; M.B.A., Ph.D., MAI, SRA.
Ronald Shapiro, Lecturer; M.B.A. Vice president, First Fidelity Bank, N.A.
Carole S. Slater, Adjunct Assistant Professor of Real Estate; J.D. Law Office of Carole S. Slater.
Norman B. Steinberg, Adjunct Assistant Professor of Real Estate; M.B.A. Vice president, valuation, Prudential Realty Group.
Frank D. Tardiff, Adjunct Assistant Professor of Real Estate; M.B.A. Senior real estate finance consultant, Lehman Bros.
Garrett Thelander, Adjunct Assistant Professor of Real Estate; M.P.A. Vice-president, Bankers Trust Co.
Robert G. Von Ancken, Adjunct Assistant Professor of Real Estate; B.B.A., MAI, CRE. President, James Felt Realty Services.
Joan Waters, Lecturer; J.D. Assistant County Attorney, Westchester County Attorney's Office.
Michael F. X. Waters, Clinical Associate Professor of Real Estate; J.D., CPA. Tax consultant, Glickman, Rubin & Gaft.
Robert J. West Jr., Lecturer; J.D. Partner, Parker Duryee Rosoff & Haft.
Gregory A. White, Lecturer; M.B.A. Managing director, Schroeder Mortgage Associates.

UNIVERSITY OF SOUTHERN CALIFORNIA

School of Policy Planning and Development
Master of Real Estate Development Program

Program of Study

The Master of Real Estate Development (M.R.E.D.) degree program consists of 32 credit units of core courses and 8 credit units of electives. Students must pass a written and oral comprehensive examination, normally taken in the third semester. The M.R.E.D. may be pursued on either a full-time or a part-time basis. The full-time program is completed over a ten month period from July to May. Part-time students attend class during the evening hours and complete the program in two years.

The M.R.E.D. program is one of five such programs in the United States and the only one on the West Coast. The integrative, professionally oriented curriculum is designed to provide students with the knowledge and skills they require to successfully compete as professionals in the development industry. The curriculum encompasses those areas of study with which developers must be conversant: real estate finance, law, economics, planning, marketing, architecture, market feasibility, and construction. Elective emphases may be pursued in international development, construction management, asset management, and appraisal. Individual courses combine lectures, projects, case analyses, and exercises that enable students to experience all facets of a developer's tasks and problems. Faculty from the school of planning, including adjunct faculty who are leaders in the industry, create an instructive, exciting, and intensive learning experience. In addition, developers, lawyers, planners, and other professionals make regular contributions to the course of study, helping to link learning to practice. The objective of the program is to prepare students who are particularly qualified to capitalize on development opportunities while contributing to the advancement of the industry and the well-being of the community.

A number of extracurricular programs are sponsored by the M.R.E.D. program to augment the student's educational experience. Each semester, leaders in the real estate industry from southern California are invited to speak at the weekly Speakers Series. The Developer in Residence Program allows students to meet with a prominent developer on a monthly basis, in individual meetings, a monthly lecture, and site visits to actual projects.

The Master of Business Administration/Master of Real Estate Development and the Master of Real Estate Development/Juris Doctor dual-degree programs enable real estate development students to study both fields simultaneously. Students must apply and be admitted to both the Graduate School of Business Administration or the Law School and the School of Policy Planning and Development.

Research Facilities

The Von KleinSmid Library, with a collection of approximately 200,000 volumes, is a research library in public affairs with a specialization in urban planning and development. The Crocker Library contains a substantial collection of materials related to business and real estate development. The University is committed to providing students with up-to-date computer facilities; there are currently four University computer centers with both Macintosh and IBM computers, in addition to the School's own computer lab.

Financial Aid

Financial aid for students enrolled in the Master of Real Estate Development Program is provided in the form of graduate student loans and Federal Work-Study awards administered by the USC Financial Office and awarded on the basis of financial need. A limited number of research assistantships funded by the Lusk Center for Real Estate Development are also available.

Cost of Study

Tuition and fees for the 1998–99 academic year are approximately $31,500 for the entire degree program.

Living and Housing Costs

USC maintains a number of off-campus apartment buildings for graduate students only. Rates for a two-bedroom, 4-person apartment are approximately $2700–$3800 for the 1998–99 academic year. Housing applications are included with the letter of admission. Rates for privately owned apartments near USC and in greater Los Angeles are comparable to those in other large metropolitan areas.

Student Group

There are approximately 30 full-time and 30 part-time students in the Master of Real Estate Development Program. The students enter with a variety of academic backgrounds and professional experiences and include architects, brokers, loan officers, accountants, lawyers, engineers, and planners. There are a number of international students in the program, most from countries on the Pacific Rim.

Student Outcomes

Most graduates enter the real estate development industry with positions in feasibility analysis, site acquisition, entitlement processing, and project management.

Location

Southern California, a national leader in real estate development, is an ideal location for the student who is interested in the field. Los Angeles enjoys the additional advantage of serving as the prototypical international city and is situated strategically to play a leading role in Pacific Rim growth and development.

The University and The School

The School of Policy Planning and Development is heir to a long and distinguished history of policy and planning education at the University of Southern California. Nearly seventy years ago, one of the first planning courses in the country was offered at USC, and in 1975 USC's was the first planning program in the nation to become an independent school. The Master of Real Estate Development Program was founded in 1986 with support from a grant provided by the Urban Land Institute. The Lusk Center for Real Estate Development, established in 1988, is the professional and research arm of the program. It is an unusual organization, furnishing academic support to professionals involved in the development industry. The Lusk Center is designed to promote the progressive aims of the development industry through various outreach activities sponsored each year.

Applying

Admission is highly selective and is limited to approximately 45 students. Scores from either the GRE, GMAT, or LSAT exams are required. Applicants must have a minimum of two years of professional experience in an area related to real estate, such as brokerage, construction, banking, planning, business, architecture, law, or engineering. Applications received before January 15 are given initial consideration; applications should be submitted no later than March 1, except by special permission.

Correspondence and Information

Office of Student Affairs
School of Policy Planning and Development
University of Southern California
University Park, VKC 232
Los Angeles, California 90089-0041

Telephone: 213-740-2052
Fax: 213-740-7573
E-mail: supd@usc.edu
World Wide Web: http://www.usc.edu/dept/supd

University of Southern California

THE FACULTY AND THEIR RESEARCH

Peter Gordon, Professor; Ph.D., Pennsylvania. Urban theory and policy.
Bryan Jackson, Lecturer; J.D., Brigham Young. Project construction management.
Susan Kamei, Lecturer; J.D., Georgetown. Project construction management.
Allan Kotin, Adjunct Professor; M.A., UCLA. Real estate market analysis, financial feasibility, joint ventures, governmental approvals.
Richard Peiser, Associate Professor; Ph.D., Cambridge. Real estate development, urban and regional economics.
Rena Sivitanidou, Assistant Professor; Ph.D., MIT. Real estate market analysis, urban economics.
Richard Smith, Adjunct Professor; J.D., California, Hastings Law. Real estate law.
Kevin Starr, Professor; Ph.D., Harvard. History of cities and development.
Johannes Van Tilburg, Lecturer; B.Arch., The Hague. Architecture.

The M.R.E.D. program attracts professionals from architecture, law, brokerage, planning, banking, construction, and other areas within real estate.

Students visit California Plaza, a multiphase mixed-use development project.

The curriculum is complemented by a weekly Speakers Series that brings leaders from the real estate development industry to campus to discuss case studies and current development projects.

Academic and Professional Programs in Education

This part of Book 6 consists of five sections covering education. Each section has a table of contents (listing the program directories, announcements, and in-depth descriptions); program directories, which consist of brief profiles of programs in the relevant fields (and that include 50-word or 100-word announcements following the profiles, if programs have chosen to include them); Cross-Discipline Announcements, if any programs have chosen to submit such entries; and in-depth descriptions, which are more individualized statements included, if programs have chosen to submit them.

Section 21
Education

This section contains a general directory of institutions that have graduate units in education, followed by in-depth entries submitted by institutions that chose to prepare detailed program descriptions. Additional information about programs listed in the directory but not augmented by an in-depth entry may be obtained by writing directly to the dean of a graduate school or chair of a department at the address given in the directory.

For programs offering related work, see also in this book Administration, Instruction, and Theory; Health-Related Professions; Instructional Levels; Leisure Studies and Recreation; Physical Education and Kinesiology; Special Focus; and Subject Areas; and in Book 2, Psychology and Counseling (School Psychology).

CONTENTS

Program Directory

Announcements

Cross-Discipline Announcements

In-Depth Descriptions

Education—General

Abilene Christian University, College of Arts and Sciences, Department of Education, Abilene, TX 79699-9100. Offers programs in educational diagnosis (M Ed); elementary teaching (M Ed); guidance services (M Ed); reading specialist (M Ed); school administration and supervision (M Ed), including school administration, school supervision; secondary teaching (M Ed). Part-time programs available. Faculty: 11 part-time (4 women). Students: 10 full-time (5 women), 47 part-time (26 women); includes 11 minority (6 African Americans, 4 Hispanics, 1 Native American), 1 international. 42 applicants, 88% accepted. In 1997, 28 degrees awarded (100% found work related to degree). *Degree requirements:* Comprehensive exam required, foreign language and thesis not required. *Average time to degree:* master's–2 years full-time, 3 years part-time. *Entrance requirements:* GRE General Test or MAT. Application deadline: 4/1 (priority date; rolling processing; 11/1 for spring admission). Application fee: $25 ($45 for international students). *Expenses:* Tuition $308 per credit hour. Fees $430 per year full-time, $85 per semester (minimum) part-time. *Financial aid:* In 1997–98, 2 teaching assistantships were awarded; Federal Work-Study and career-related internships or fieldwork also available. Aid available to part-time students. Financial aid application deadline: 4/1. *Faculty research:* Disability learning models, learning style. • Dr. Jerry Whitworth, Chair, 915-674-2112. Application contact: Dr. Carley Dodd, Graduate Dean, 915-674-2354. Fax: 915-674-6717. E-mail: gradinfo@nicanor.acu.edu.

Acadia University, Faculty of Professional Studies, School of Education, Wolfville, NS B0P 1X0, Canada. Offers programs in counseling (M Ed), curriculum studies (M Ed), inclusive education (Certificate), leadership and school development (M Ed), special education (M Ed). Part-time and evening/weekend programs available. Faculty: 9 full-time, 7 part-time. Students: 21 full-time (18 women), 113 part-time (72 women). In 1997, 31 master's awarded. *Degree requirements:* For master's, thesis required, foreign language not required. *Entrance requirements:* Minimum B average in undergraduate course work. Application deadline: 2/1. Application fee: $25. *Expenses:* Tuition $4095 per year for Canadian residents; $8190 per year for nonresidents. Fees $145 per year. *Financial aid:* 6 students received aid; research assistantships, teaching assistantships available. Financial aid application deadline: 2/1. *Faculty research:* Technology in special education, exemplary schools. • Dr. Bryant Griffith, Director, 902-585-1229. E-mail: bryant.griffith@acadiau.ca. Application contact: Sheila Langille, Secretary, 902-585-1229. Fax: 902-585-1071.

Adams State College, School of Education and Graduate Studies, Alamosa, CO 81102. Awards MA. Accredited by NCATE. Part-time programs available. Postbaccalaureate distance learning degree programs offered. In 1997, 173 degrees awarded. *Entrance requirements:* GRE General Test or MAT, minimum undergraduate GPA of 2.75. Application deadline: 5/15 (priority date; rolling processing; 10/15 for spring admission). Application fee: $25. *Tuition:* $2164 per year full-time, $111 per credit part-time for state residents; $7284 per year full-time, $377 per credit part-time for nonresidents. *Financial aid:* In 1997–98, graduate assistantships averaging $500 per month were awarded; Federal Work-Study, institutionally sponsored loans, and career-related internships or fieldwork also available. Aid available to part-time students. Financial aid application deadline: 4/15; applicants required to submit FAFSA. • Dr. Scott Baldwin, Dean, Graduate Studies, 719-587-7936. Fax: 719-587-7873. E-mail: cbrtech@amigo.net.

Announcement: Adams State College offers MA programs in art, guidance and counseling (CACREP accredited), health, physical education and recreation, elementary and secondary education with an emphasis in bilingual education, ESL, educational leadership (principal's licensure), and special education. Initial licensure programs in secondary education. Education programs are NCATE accredited. Part-time, off-campus, and distance learning programs are offered. Graduate assistantships with partial tuition waivers and monthly stipends and federal work-study positions are available. Aid available to part-time students. Financial aid applicants required to submit FAFSA. For more information, call the Office of Graduate Studies at 800-662-3382 (toll-free).

Adelphi University, School of Education, Garden City, NY 11530. Awards MA, MS, DA, Certificate, PD. Part-time and evening/weekend programs available. Students: 302 full-time (253 women), 1,120 part-time (865 women); includes 214 minority (115 African Americans, 15 Asian Americans, 83 Hispanics, 1 Native American), 15 international. Average age 33. In 1997, 616 master's awarded. *Degree requirements:* For doctorate, 1 foreign language, dissertation. *Application deadline:* rolling. *Application fee:* $50. *Expenses:* Tuition $16,000 per year full-time, $485 per credit part-time. Fees $500 per year full-time, $150 per semester part-time. *Financial aid:* Fellowships, research assistantships, teaching assistantships, full tuition waivers, Federal Work-Study, institutionally sponsored loans, and career-related internships or fieldwork available. Aid available to part-time students. Financial aid application deadline: 3/1. *Faculty research:* Bilingual special education, bilingual early childhood special education. • Dr. Elaine Sands, Interim Dean, 516-877-4065.

See in-depth description on page 711.

Alabama Agricultural and Mechanical University, School of Education, PO Box 1357, Normal, AL 35762-1357. Awards M Ed, MS, Ed S. Accredited by NCATE. Ed S (agribusiness education) offered jointly with the School of Agricultural and Environmental Sciences; M Ed (industrial technology) offered jointly with the School of Engineering and Technology. Part-time and evening/weekend programs available. Faculty: 36 full-time (18 women), 4 part-time (1 woman). Students: 259. In 1997, 231 master's awarded. *Degree requirements:* For master's, comprehensive exam required, foreign language not required. *Entrance requirements:* For master's, GRE General Test. Application deadline: 5/1. Application fee: $15 ($20 for international students). *Expenses:* Tuition $2782 per year full-time, $565 per semester (minimum) part-time for state residents; $5164 per year full-time, $1015 per semester (minimum) part-time for nonresidents. Fees $560 per year full-time, $390 per year part-time. *Financial aid:* Fellowships, research assistantships, and career-related internships or fieldwork available. Aid available to part-time students. Financial aid application deadline: 4/1. *Faculty research:* Speech defects, aging, blindness, multicultural education, learning styles. • Dr. Phillip Redrick, Interim Dean, 205-851-5500.

Alabama State University, School of Graduate Studies, College of Education, Montgomery, AL 36101-0271. Awards M Ed, MS, Ed S. Faculty: 19 full-time (12 women), 7 part-time (3 women), 22 FTE. Students: 97 full-time (71 women), 402 part-time (295 women); includes 342 minority (337 African Americans, 2 Asian Americans, 3 Hispanics). In 1997, 153 master's, 22 Ed Ss awarded. *Degree requirements:* For master's, comprehensive exam required, thesis optional; for Ed S, thesis. *Entrance requirements:* For master's, GRE General Test, MAT or NTE. Application deadline: 7/15 (rolling processing; 12/15 for spring admission). Application fee: $10. *Expenses:* Tuition $85 per credit hour for state residents; $170 per credit hour for nonresidents. Fees $486 per year. *Financial aid:* Research assistantships, teaching assistantships available. *Faculty research:* Whole language instruction, African-American children's literature. • Dr. Daniel Vertrees, Dean, 334-229-4252. Fax: 334-229-4904. E-mail: dvertrees@asunet.alasu.edu. Application contact: Dr. Fred Dauser, Dean of Graduate Studies, 334-229-4276. Fax: 334-229-4928.

Alaska Pacific University, Graduate Programs, Education Department, 4101 University Drive, Anchorage, AK 99508-4672. Offers program in teaching (MAT), including K–8. Part-time programs available. Faculty: 5 full-time (4 women), 2 part-time (both women), 5.6 FTE. Students: 31 full-time (22 women), 10 part-time (9 women); includes 8 minority (1 African American, 3 Asian Americans, 2 Hispanics, 2 Native Americans). Average age 36. 14 applicants, 93% accepted. In 1997, 11 degrees awarded. *Degree requirements:* Comprehensive exam or thesis required, foreign language not required. *Entrance requirements:* GRE or MAT, minimum GPA of 3.0. Application deadline: 4/15 (rolling processing; 12/15 for spring admission). Application fee: $25. *Expenses:* Tuition $6600 per year full-time, $370 per credit hour part-time. Fees $80 per year. *Financial aid:* In 1997–98, 9 teaching assistantships (2 to first-year students) totaling $18,900, 26 grants, scholarships (13 to first-year students) totaling $325,000 were awarded; Federal Work-Study and career-related internships or fieldwork also available. Aid available to part-time students. Financial aid application deadline: 3/15; applicants required to submit FAFSA. • Diane Hoffbauer, Director, 907-564-8271. Fax: 907-562-4276. Application contact: Kirsty Gladkoff, Associate Director of Admissions, 907-564-8248. Fax: 907-564-8317. E-mail: apu@corecom.net.

Albany State University, School of Education, Albany, GA 31705-2717. Offers programs in business education (M Ed), early childhood education (M Ed), educational administration and supervision (M Ed, Certificate), English education (M Ed), health and physical education (M Ed), mathematics education (M Ed), middle childhood education (M Ed), music education (M Ed), physical education (M Ed), reading education (M Ed), science education (M Ed), secondary education (M Ed), special education (M Ed). Accredited by NCATE. Part-time programs available. Faculty: 3 full-time (1 woman), 10 part-time (4 women). 14 applicants, 100% accepted. In 1997, 46 master's awarded (100% found work related to degree); 3 Certificates awarded. *Degree requirements:* For master's, comprehensive exam. *Entrance requirements:* For master's, GRE General Test (minimum combined score of 800), MAT (minimum score 44) or NTE (minimum score 550). Application deadline: 9/1. Application fee: $10. *Financial aid:* Fellowships, Federal Work-Study, and career-related internships or fieldwork available. Aid available to part-time students. Financial aid application deadline: 4/1. • Dr. Claude Perkins, Dean, 912-430-4715. Fax: 912-430-4993. E-mail: cperkins@fld94.alsnet.peachnet.edu.

Alcorn State University, School of Psychology and Education, Lorman, MS 39096-9402. Offers programs in administration and supervision (MS Ed); agricultural education (MS Ed); elementary education (MS Ed, Ed S); guidance and counseling (MS Ed); industrial education (MS Ed); secondary education (MS Ed), including health and physical education; special education (MS Ed). Accredited by NCATE. *Degree requirements:* For master's, thesis optional, foreign language not required. *Application deadline:* 7/1 (priority date; rolling processing; 12/1 for spring admission). *Application fee:* $10. *Tuition:* $2470 per year full-time, $378 per semester (minimum) part-time for state residents; $5331 per year full-time, $855 per semester (minimum) part-time for nonresidents.

Alfred University, Graduate School, Division of Education, Alfred, NY 14802-1205. Offers programs in business education (MS Ed); college student development (MS Ed); counseling (MS Ed); elementary education (MS Ed); reading (MS Ed); secondary education (MS Ed), including biology education, chemistry education, earth science education, English education, mathematics education, physics education, social studies education. Part-time programs available. Faculty: 45 full-time (12 women). Students: 43 full-time (30 women), 41 part-time (18 women). Average age 24. 82 applicants, 72% accepted. In 1997, 34 degrees awarded. *Degree requirements:* Thesis required (for some programs), foreign language not required. *Entrance requirements:* TOEFL. Application deadline: rolling. Application fee: $50. *Expenses:* Tuition $20,376 per year full-time, $390 per credit hour (minimum) part-time. Fees $546 per year. *Financial aid:* Assistantships, partial tuition waivers, Federal Work-Study, and career-related internships or fieldwork available. Aid available to part-time students. Financial aid applicants required to submit FAFSA. *Faculty research:* Whole language, ethics in counseling and psychotherapy. • Dr. Katherine D. Wiesendanger, Chair, 607-871-2219. E-mail: fwiesendange@bigvax.alfred.edu. Application contact: Cathleen R. Johnson, Assistant Director of Admissions, 607-871-2141. Fax: 607-871-2198. E-mail: johnsonc@bigvax.alfred.edu.

Allentown College of St. Francis de Sales, Graduate Division, Program in Education, Center Valley, PA 18034-9568. Offers biology (M Ed), chemistry (M Ed), computer education (M Ed), computer science (M Ed), English (M Ed), mathematics (M Ed). Part-time programs available. Faculty: 18 full-time (4 women), 25 part-time (6 women). Students: 203 part-time (131 women). In 1997, 20 degrees awarded (100% found work related to degree). *Degree requirements:* Capstone Course or Project required, foreign language not required. *Average time to degree:* master's–3 years part-time. *Entrance requirements:* Teaching certificate. Application deadline: 8/24 (priority date; rolling processing). Application fee: $35. *Tuition:* $285 per credit. *Financial aid:* Available to part-time students. Financial aid application deadline: 5/1. *Faculty research:* Turn-of-the-century literature, effective teaching, seed pods, computer interfacing in chemistry labs, computer applications to teaching. • Dr. Irene Pompetti-Szul, Director, 610-282-1100 Ext. 1401. Fax: 610-282-2254.

Alverno College, Department of Education, 3401 South 39th St, PO Box 343922, Milwaukee, WI 53234-3922. Offers programs in adaptive education (MA), director of instruction (MA), instructional design (MA), teaching in alternative schools (MA). Part-time and evening/weekend programs available. Faculty: 107 full-time (80 women), 84 part-time (66 women). Students: 50 part-time (44 women); includes 14 minority (10 African Americans, 1 Asian American, 3 Hispanics), 1 international. Average age 37. 28 applicants, 89% accepted. *Application deadline:* 8/1 (priority date; rolling processing; 12/1 for spring admission). *Application fee:* $25. Electronic applications accepted. *Expenses:* Tuition $295 per credit. Fees $115 per year. *Financial aid:* 20 students received aid; Federal Work-Study and career-related internships or fieldwork available. Aid available to part-time students. Financial aid application deadline: 6/1; applicants required to submit FAFSA. *Faculty research:* Student self-assessment, self-reflection, integration of curriculum, identifying needs of students in strategic situations and designing appropriate classroom strategies. • Mary Diez, Graduate Dean, 414-382-6214. Fax: 414-382-6354. E-mail: mary.diez@alverno.edu.

American International College, School of Continuing Education and Graduate Studies, School of Psychology and Education, Department of Education, Springfield, MA 01109-3189. Offers programs in administration (M Ed, CAGS); child development (MA, Ed D), including educational psychology; elementary education (M Ed, CAGS); English (MAT); history (MAT); mathematics (MAT); reading (M Ed, CAGS); secondary education (M Ed, CAGS); special education (M Ed, CAGS); teaching (MA). Part-time programs available. Faculty: 5 full-time (3 women), 15 part-time (9 women). Students: 48 full-time (36 women), 175 part-time (143 women); includes 12 minority (8 African Americans, 2 Asian Americans, 2 Hispanics), 2 international. 60 applicants, 92% accepted. In 1997, 77 master's, 23 CAGSs awarded. Terminal master's awarded for partial completion of doctoral program. *Degree requirements:* For master's, practicum required, foreign language and thesis not required; for doctorate, dissertation required, foreign language not required; for CAGS, practicum required, foreign language not required. *Entrance requirements:* For master's, minimum C average in undergraduate course work; for doctorate, GRE General Test, interview. Application fee: $15 ($25 for international students). *Expenses:* Tuition $363 per credit hour. Fees $25 per semester. *Financial aid:* Career-related internships or fieldwork available. • C. Gerald Weaver, Dean, School of Psychology and Education, 413-747-6338.

American University, College of Arts and Sciences, School of Education, Washington, DC 20016-8001. Awards MA, MAT, PhD. Part-time and evening/weekend programs available. Faculty: 8 full-time (5 women), 10 part-time (8 women), 11.3 FTE. Students: 64 full-time (52 women), 109 part-time (81 women); includes 35 minority (24 African Americans, 6 Asian Americans, 4 Hispanics, 1 Native American), 12 international. 163 applicants, 83% accepted. In 1997, 62 master's, 3 doctorates awarded. *Degree requirements:* For master's, thesis or alternative required, foreign language not required; for doctorate, dissertation required, foreign language not required. *Entrance requirements:* GRE General Test or MAT, minimum GPA of 3.0. Application deadline: 2/1 (10/1 for spring admission). Application fee: $50. *Expenses:* Tuition $687 per credit hour. Fees $180 per year full-time, $110 per year part-time. *Financial aid:* Fellowships, research assistantships, teaching assistantships, Federal Work-Study, institutionally sponsored loans, and career-related internships or fieldwork available. Aid available to part-time students. Financial aid application deadline: 2/1; applicants required to submit

Directory: Education—General

American University (continued)
FAFSA. *Faculty research:* Gender equity. • Dr. Charles Tesconi, Dean, 202-885-3740. Fax: 202-885-1187. E-mail: educate@american.edu.

See in-depth description on page 713.

Andrews University, School of Graduate Studies, School of Education, Berrien Springs, MI 49104. Awards MA, MAT, Ed D, PhD, Ed S. Part-time programs available. Faculty: 22 full-time (8 women). Students: 139 full-time (88 women), 145 part-time (84 women); includes 84 minority (59 African Americans, 4 Asian Americans, 19 Hispanics, 2 Native Americans), 66 international. In 1997, 64 master's, 28 doctorates, 4 Ed Ss awarded. Terminal master's awarded for partial completion of doctoral program. *Degree requirements:* For doctorate, dissertation. *Entrance requirements:* For master's, GRE Subject Test. Application deadline: rolling. Application fee: $30. *Expenses:* Tuition $290 per quarter hour (minimum). Fees $75 per quarter. *Financial aid:* Fellowships, research assistantships, teaching assistantships, partial tuition waivers, Federal Work-Study, institutionally sponsored loans, and career-related internships or fieldwork available. Aid available to part-time students. • Dr. Karen R. Graham, Dean, 616-471-3109.

Angelo State University, College of Professional Studies, Department of Education, San Angelo, TX 76909. Offers programs in curriculum and instruction (MA), educational diagnostics (M Ed), guidance and counseling (M Ed), reading specialist (M Ed), school administration (M Ed), supervision (M Ed). Part-time and evening/weekend programs available. Faculty: 8 full-time (2 women). Students: 12 full-time (10 women), 96 part-time (71 women); includes 8 minority (3 Asian Americans, 5 Hispanics). Average age 39. 44 applicants, 84% accepted. In 1997, 41 degrees awarded. *Degree requirements:* Comprehensive exam required, thesis optional, foreign language not required. *Entrance requirements:* GRE General Test, minimum GPA of 2.5. Application deadline: 8/7 (priority date; rolling processing; 1/2 for spring admission). Application fee: $25 ($50 for international students). *Expenses:* Tuition $1022 per year full-time, $36 per semester hour part-time for state residents; $7382 per year full-time, $246 per semester hour part-time for nonresidents. Fees $1140 per year full-time, $165 per semester (minimum) part-time. *Financial aid:* In 1997–98, 23 fellowships, 3 graduate assistantships were awarded; teaching assistantships, partial tuition waivers, Federal Work-Study, and career-related internships or fieldwork also available. Aid available to part-time students. Financial aid application deadline: 8/1. • Dr. James Hademenos, Head, 915-942-2052.

Anna Maria College, Program in Education, Paxton, MA 01612. Awards M Ed. Part-time and evening/weekend programs available. Faculty: 11. In 1997, 6 degrees awarded. *Entrance requirements:* MAT. Application fee: $30. *Tuition:* $730 per course. • Dr. Doris Brodeur, Director, 508-849-3435. Fax: 508-849-3339.

Antioch New England Graduate School, Graduate School, Department of Education, 40 Avon Street, Keene, NH 03431-3516. Offers programs in elementary education/early childhood education (M Ed), including integrated day education, science and environmental education; experienced educators (M Ed), including education by design, professional development; Waldorf teacher education (M Ed). Faculty: 7 full-time (2 women), 12 part-time (11 women). Students: 116 full-time (90 women), 58 part-time (48 women); includes 3 minority (2 Asian Americans, 1 Native American), 2 international. Average age 37. 118 applicants, 96% accepted. In 1997, 70 degrees awarded. *Application fee:* $40. *Expenses:* Tuition $12,700 per year full-time, $330 per credit part-time. Fees $165 per year. *Financial aid:* 104 students received aid; fellowships, Federal Work-Study, and career-related internships or fieldwork available. Financial aid applicants required to submit FAFSA. *Faculty research:* Classroom and school restructuring, problem-based learning, Waldorf collaborative leadership, ecological literacy. • Peter Eppig, Chairperson, 603-357-3122 Ext. 356. E-mail: peppig@antiochne.edu. Application contact: Diane K. Hewitt, Co-Director of Admissions, 603-357-6265 Ext. 286. Fax: 603-357-0718. E-mail: dhewitt@antiochne.edu.

Announcement: Holistic, progressive, practice-oriented teacher education programs committed to student-centered, activity-based learning. Teacher certification programs (M Ed in elementary/early childhood education) in integrated day education, science and environmental education, and Waldorf education. Experienced Educators Program (M Ed in Foundations of Education) with concentrations in professional development and critical skills/education by design. This program is offered at regionally clustered sites in New Hampshire, Vermont, and Maine.

Antioch University Seattle, Program in Education, 2326 Sixth Avenue, Seattle, WA 98121-1814. Awards MA. Part-time and evening/weekend programs available. Faculty: 10 full-time (6 women), 3 part-time (all women). Students: 160; includes 4 international. Average age 37. In 1997, 40 degrees awarded. *Average time to degree:* master's–2.5 years full-time, 4 years part-time. *Application deadline:* 8/4 (priority date; rolling processing; 2/3 for spring admission). *Application fee:* $50. *Expenses:* Tuition $2460 per quarter. Fees $30 per quarter full-time, $15 per quarter part-time. *Financial aid:* Application deadline 6/15. *Faculty research:* Transformative learning, intercultural studies, gay and lesbian studies. • Beverly Purrington, Director, 206-441-5352. Application contact: Vicki Tolbert, Admissions Officer, 206-441-5352.

Appalachian State University, College of Education, Boone, NC 28608. Awards MA, MLS, MSA, Ed D, Ed S. Accredited by NCATE. Part-time and evening/weekend programs available. Postbaccalaureate distance learning degree programs offered (minimal on-campus study). Faculty: 85. Students: 299 full-time (232 women), 202 part-time (154 women). 577 applicants, 42% accepted. In 1997, 147 master's, 6 doctorates awarded. *Degree requirements:* For master's, thesis or alternative, comprehensive exams required, foreign language not required; for doctorate, dissertation, comprehensive exam; for Ed S, comprehensive exam required, foreign language not required. *Entrance requirements:* For doctorate and Ed S, GRE General Test. Application fee: $35. *Tuition:* $1811 per year full-time, $354 per semester (minimum) part-time for state residents; $9081 per year full-time, $2171 per semester (minimum) part-time for nonresidents. *Financial aid:* In 1997–98, 76 students received aid, including 29 research assistantships, 4 teaching assistantships, 43 assistantships; fellowships, Federal Work-Study, and career-related internships or fieldwork also available. Aid available to part-time students. • Dr. Charles Duke, Dean, 704-262-2232.

Aquinas College, Graduate Education Program, Grand Rapids, MI 49506-1799. Awards MAT. Part-time and evening/weekend programs available. Faculty: 16 full-time (12 women), 24 part-time (14 women). Students: 115 full-time (77 women), 165 part-time (123 women); includes 12 minority (6 African Americans, 2 Asian Americans, 3 Hispanics, 1 Native American). Average age 31. 153 applicants, 99% accepted. In 1997, 31 degrees awarded. *Degree requirements:* Teaching project required, thesis not required. *Entrance requirements:* GRE General Test or teacher competency exam, minimum undergraduate GPA of 3.0, teaching certificate. Application deadline: rolling. Application fee: $35. *Tuition:* $304 per credit hour. *Financial aid:* Application deadline 3/15. • Dr. Joyce McNally, Dean of Graduate Studies, 616-459-8281 Ext. 5427.

Arizona State University, College of Education, Tempe, AZ 85287. Awards MA, MC, M Ed, Ed D, PhD. Part-time programs available. Faculty: 107 full-time (44 women), 7 part-time (3 women). Students: 678 full-time (480 women), 726 part-time (541 women); includes 228 minority (48 African Americans, 34 Asian Americans, 127 Hispanics, 19 Native Americans), 88 international. Average age 35. 891 applicants, 57% accepted. In 1997, 437 master's, 58 doctorates awarded. *Degree requirements:* For doctorate, dissertation. *Entrance requirements:* GRE General Test or MAT. Application fee: $45. *Expenses:* Tuition $2088 per year full-time, $110 per hour part-time for state residents; $9040 per year full-time, $377 per hour part-time for nonresidents. Fees $72 per year full-time, $18 per semester (minimum) part-time. *Financial aid:* In 1997–98, 5 fellowships were awarded; research assistantships, teaching assistantships, institutionally sponsored loans also available. *Faculty research:* Development and education of children and youth from diverse cultural populations. • Dr. David Berliner, Dean, 602-965-1329.

Announcement: The Arizona State University College of Education is rated among the top 20 public graduate colleges in the US. Programs include curriculum and instruction, educational leadership and policy studies, and psychology in education. Visit the Web site for complete, up-to-date information (http://www.ed.asu.edu/).

Arizona State University West, College of Education, Phoenix, AZ 85069-7100. Offers programs in educational administration and supervision (M Ed), elementary education (M Ed), secondary education (M Ed), special education (M Ed). Part-time and evening/weekend programs available. Faculty: 19 full-time (13 women), 12 part-time (7 women), 24.23 FTE. Students: 14 full-time (9 women), 156 part-time (125 women); includes 29 minority (1 African American, 4 Asian Americans, 23 Hispanics, 1 Native American). Average age 35. 44 applicants, 89% accepted. In 1997, 57 degrees awarded (100% found work related to degree). *Degree requirements:* Comprehensive exams required, thesis not required. *Entrance requirements:* GRE or MAT, TOEFL. Application deadline: rolling. Application fee: $40. *Expenses:* Tuition $2088 per year full-time, $330 per course part-time for state residents; $9040 per year full-time, $1131 per course part-time for nonresidents. Fees $10 per year (minimum). *Financial aid:* 13 students received aid; full and partial tuition waivers, institutionally sponsored loans, and career-related internships or fieldwork available. Aid available to part-time students. Financial aid application deadline: 4/1; applicants required to submit FAFSA. *Faculty research:* Performance-based assessment, self-regulated learning in students, collaboration and consultation skills for educators, school reform and restructuring, hands-on science and mathematics programs. • Dr. William S. Svoboda, Dean, 602-543-6300. Application contact: Ray Buss, Assistant Dean, 602-543-6300. Fax: 602-543-6350.

Arkansas State University, College of Education, State University, AR 72467. Awards MRC, MS, MSE, Ed D, Ed S, SCCT. Accredited by NCATE. Part-time programs available. Faculty: 51 full-time (19 women), 3 part-time (2 women). Students: 71 full-time (54 women), 334 part-time (242 women); includes 45 minority (41 African Americans, 1 Asian American, 1 Hispanic, 2 Native Americans), 1 international. Average age 36. In 1997, 111 master's, 5 doctorates, 4 other advanced degrees awarded. *Degree requirements:* For master's, thesis or alternative, comprehensive exam; for doctorate, dissertation, comprehensive exam; for other advanced degree, comprehensive exam required, thesis not required. *Entrance requirements:* For master's, appropriate bachelor's degree; for doctorate and other advanced degree, GRE General Test or MAT, master's degree. Application deadline: 7/1 (priority date; rolling processing; 11/15 for spring admission). Application fee: $15 ($25 for international students). *Expenses:* Tuition $2760 per year full-time, $115 per credit hour part-time for state residents; $6936 per year full-time, $289 per credit hour part-time for nonresidents. Fees $506 per year full-time, $44 per semester (minimum) part-time. *Financial aid:* Teaching assistantships and career-related internships or fieldwork available. Aid available to part-time students. Financial aid application deadline: 7/1; applicants required to submit FAFSA. • Dr. Evelyn Lynch, Dean, 870-972-3057. Fax: 870-972-3828. E-mail: elynch@kiowa.astate.edu.

Arkansas Tech University, School of Education, Russellville, AR 72801-2222. Awards M Ed, MSE, PhD. Accredited by NCATE. Part-time and evening/weekend programs available. Students: 29 full-time (18 women), 89 part-time (76 women); includes 5 minority (2 African Americans, 1 Asian American, 2 Native Americans), 18 international. Average age 38. 70 applicants, 100% accepted. In 1997, 65 master's awarded. *Degree requirements:* For master's, action research project, comprehensive exam required, thesis optional. *Entrance requirements:* For master's, GRE General Test. Application deadline: rolling. Application fee: $0 ($30 for international students). *Expenses:* Tuition $98 per credit hour for state residents; $196 per credit hour for nonresidents. Fees $30 per semester. *Financial aid:* In 1997–98, 4 teaching assistantships averaging $500 per month and totaling $20,914 were awarded; Federal Work-Study also available. Aid available to part-time students. Financial aid application deadline: 4/15. • Dr. Dennis W. Fleniken, Dean, 501-968-0350.

Armstrong Atlantic State University, School of Graduate Studies, Program in Education, Savannah, GA 31419-1997. Offers elementary education (M Ed), middle grades education (M Ed), secondary education (M Ed), special education (M Ed). Accredited by NCATE. Faculty: 25. *Expenses:* Tuition $83 per quarter hour for state residents; $250 per quarter hour for nonresidents. Fees $145 per quarter hour for state residents; $228 per quarter hour for nonresidents. • Dr. Bettye Anne Battiste, Department Head, 912-927-5281.

Ashland University, College of Education, Ashland, OH 44805-3702. Awards M Ed. Accredited by NCATE. Part-time and evening/weekend programs available. Faculty: 45 full-time, 22 part-time. Students: 79 full-time (53 women), 1,363 part-time (1,060 women). In 1997, 632 degrees awarded. *Entrance requirements:* GRE General Test or MAT, teaching certificate. Application deadline: rolling. Application fee: $15. *Tuition:* $275 per credit hour. *Financial aid:* Teaching assistantships, coaching scholarships available. • Dr. Gene A. Telego, Associate Provost and Dean, 419-289-5365. Fax: 419-289-5331. E-mail: gtelego@ashland.edu. Application contact: Dr. Joe Bailey, Director and Chair Graduate Studies in Teacher Education, 419-289-5377. Fax: 419-289-5097. E-mail: jbailey@ashland.edu.

Assumption College, Department of Education, 500 Salisbury Street, PO Box 15005, Worcester, MA 01615-0005. Awards MA. *Degree requirements:* Oral comprehensive exam. *Entrance requirements:* TOEFL. Application fee: $20. *Expenses:* Tuition $297 per credit hour. Fees $10 per semester.

Athabasca University, Centre for Distance Education, Athabasca, AB T9S 3A3, Canada. Awards MDE. Part-time programs available. Postbaccalaureate distance learning degree programs offered (no on-campus study). Faculty: 6 full-time (1 woman), 14 part-time (4 women). Students: 157 part-time (83 women); includes 1 international. Average age 40. 86 applicants, 60% accepted. *Degree requirements:* Thesis optional, foreign language not required. *Application deadline:* 3/1. *Application fee:* $50. *Tuition:* $700 per course for Canadian residents; $800 per course (minimum) for nonresidents. • Dr. Bob Spencer, Director, 403-675-6238. Fax: 403-675-6170. E-mail: bobs@cs.athabascau.ca.

Atlantic Union College, Graduate Education Program, South Lancaster, MA 01561-1000. Awards M Ed. Offered during summer only. Part-time programs available. Postbaccalaureate distance learning degree programs offered (minimal on-campus study). Faculty: 8 part-time (4 women). Students: 46 part-time (39 women); includes 33 minority (29 African Americans, 4 Hispanics). Average age 32. 14 applicants, 100% accepted. In 1997, 8 degrees awarded (88% found work related to degree, 12% continued full-time study). *Degree requirements:* Thesis. *Average time to degree:* master's–4 years part-time. *Entrance requirements:* GRE, minimum GPA of 3.0. Application deadline: rolling. Application fee: $25. *Tuition:* $180 per credit. *Financial aid:* 7 students received aid. Aid available to part-time students. Financial aid applicants required to submit FAFSA. • Dr. Roger Bothwell, Graduate Coordinator, 978-368-2434. Fax: 978-368-2512.

Auburn University, College of Education, Auburn University, AL 36849-0001. Awards M Ed, MS, Ed D, PhD, Ed S. Accredited by NCATE. Part-time programs available. Faculty: 79 full-time (35 women). Students: 318 full-time (204 women), 384 part-time (260 women); includes 101 minority (86 African Americans, 3 Asian Americans, 9 Hispanics, 3 Native Americans), 19 international. 514 applicants, 49% accepted. In 1997, 194 master's, 29 doctorates, 5 Ed Ss awarded. *Degree requirements:* For master's, thesis (MS) required, foreign language not required; for doctorate, dissertation required, foreign language not required. *Entrance requirements:* GRE General Test. Application fee: $25 ($50 for international students). *Expenses:* Tuition $2760 per year full-time, $76 per credit hour part-time for state residents; $8280 per year full-time, $228 per credit hour part-time for nonresidents. Fees $30 per year full-time, $160 per quarter part-time for state residents; $30 per year full-time, $480 per quarter part-time for nonresidents. *Financial aid:* Fellowships, research assistantships, teaching assistantships, Federal Work-Study, and career-related internships or fieldwork available. Aid available to part-time students. Financial aid application deadline: 3/15. *Faculty research:* Dropout phenomena, high school students and substance use and abuse. • Dr. Richard C. Kunkel, Dean, 334-844-4446. Application contact: Dr. John F. Pritchett, Dean of the Graduate School, 334-844-4700.

See in-depth description on page 715.

Auburn University Montgomery, School of Education, Montgomery, AL 36124-4023. Awards M Ed, Ed S. Accredited by NCATE. Part-time and evening/weekend programs available. Faculty: 29 full-time (16 women), 13 part-time (10 women). Students: 207 full-time (157 women), 152 part-time (125 women); includes 128 minority (123 African Americans, 4 Hispanics, 1 Native American), 1 international. Average age 33. 123 applicants, 81% accepted. In 1997, 166 master's, 26 Ed Ss awarded. *Degree requirements:* Comprehensive exam required, foreign language not required. *Entrance requirements:* For master's, GRE General Test or MAT, certification, BS in teaching; for Ed S, GRE General Test or MAT, certification. Application deadline: 9/1 (priority date; rolling processing; 3/28 for spring admission). Application fee: $25. Electronic applications accepted. *Tuition:* $2664 per year full-time, $85 per quarter hour part-time for state residents; $7080 per year full-time, $255 per quarter hour part-time for nonresidents. *Financial aid:* In 1997–98, 7 teaching assistantships were awarded; Federal Work-Study and career-related internships or fieldwork also available. Aid available to part-time students. • Dr. Morgan Simpson, Interim Dean, 334-244-3413.

Augustana College, Department of Education, Sioux Falls, SD 57197. Awards MA. Accredited by NCATE. Part-time programs available. Faculty: 10 full-time (6 women), 2 part-time (0 women). Students: 43 part-time (39 women). *Degree requirements:* Comprehensive and oral exams required, foreign language and thesis not required. *Entrance requirements:* Appropriate bachelor's degree, minimum GPA of 3.0. Application deadline: 6/1 (priority date; rolling processing). Application fee: $50. *Tuition:* $14,726 per year full-time, $250 per credit hour part-time. *Financial aid:* Fellowships, teaching assistantships, coaching assistantships, Federal Work-Study, institutionally sponsored loans, and career-related internships or fieldwork available. Aid available to part-time students. Financial aid application deadline: 2/1. *Faculty research:* Classroom management, stress management, youth at risk. • Dr. Mary Friehe, Chair, 605-336-4615. Application contact: Kay West, Secretary, 605-336-4126. Fax: 605-336-4450.

Augusta State University, College of Education, Augusta, GA 30904-2200. Awards M Ed, Ed S. Accredited by NCATE. Part-time and evening/weekend programs available. Faculty: 22 full-time (12 women). Students: 109 full-time (89 women), 125 part-time (103 women); includes 47 minority (46 African Americans, 1 Hispanic). Average age 35. 65 applicants, 100% accepted. In 1997, 80 master's, 20 Ed Ss awarded. *Degree requirements:* For master's, comprehensive exam; for Ed S, thesis, comprehensive exam. *Entrance requirements:* GRE, MAT. Application deadline: 7/26 (priority date; rolling processing). Application fee: $10. *Tuition:* $2260 per year full-time, $83 per credit hour part-time for state residents; $8260 per year full-time, $333 per credit hour part-time for nonresidents. *Financial aid:* In 1997–98, 3 graduate assistantships (all to first-year students) were awarded; Federal Work-Study, institutionally sponsored loans, and career-related internships or fieldwork also available. Aid available to part-time students. Financial aid application deadline: 4/15; applicants required to submit FAFSA. • Dr. Robert Freeman, Dean, 706-737-1499. E-mail: rfreeman@aug.edu. Application contact: Heather Eakin, Secretary to the Dean, 706-737-1499. Fax: 706-667-4706. E-mail: heakin@aug.edu.

Aurora University, George Williams College, School of Education, Aurora, IL 60506-4892. Offers programs in education (MAT), educational leadership (MEL). Part-time and evening/weekend programs available. Faculty: 7 full-time (4 women), 22 part-time (12 women). Students: 57 full-time (37 women), 424 part-time (357 women). 127 applicants, 72% accepted. In 1997, 242 degrees awarded. *Entrance requirements:* 2 years of teaching experience, valid teaching certificate. Application deadline: rolling. Application fee: $25. *Tuition:* $408 per semester hour. *Financial aid:* Scholarships, institutionally sponsored loans available. Aid available to part-time students. • Dr. Gary Jewel, Dean, 630-844-5498. Application contact: Office of Admissions, 630-844-5533. Fax: 630-844-5463.

Austin College, Sherman, TX 75090-4440. Offers program in teacher education (MA), including elementary education, secondary education. Applicants must meet Austin College's undergraduate curriculum requirements. Part-time programs available. Faculty: 5 full-time (3 women). Students: 25 full-time (15 women), 16 part-time (13 women); includes 4 minority (all Hispanics). Average age 22. In 1997, 21 degrees awarded. *Degree requirements:* 1 foreign language, computer language, thesis or alternative. *Average time to degree:* master's–5 years full-time. *Entrance requirements:* Texas Academic Skills Program (minimum score 220 required on reading, writing, and math sections). Application deadline: 5/1 (priority date; rolling processing). Application fee: $35. Electronic applications accepted. *Expenses:* Tuition $14,080 per year full-time, $2010 per course part-time. Fees $125 per year full-time. *Financial aid:* 13 students received aid; fellowships, Federal Work-Study, institutionally sponsored loans, and career-related internships or fieldwork available. Aid available to part-time students. Financial aid application deadline: 5/1; applicants required to submit FAFSA. • Dr. John White, Director, 903-813-2459. Fax: 903-813-2326.

Austin Peay State University, College of Education, Department of Education, Clarksville, TN 37044-0001. Offers programs in administration and supervision (MA Ed, Ed S), counseling and guidance (Ed S), curriculum and instruction (MA Ed), elementary education (MA Ed, Ed S), reading (MA Ed), school psychology (Ed S), secondary education (Ed S), special education (MA). Accredited by NCATE. Ed S offered jointly with Tennessee State University. Part-time and evening/weekend programs available. Students: 56 full-time (43 women), 151 part-time (132 women); includes 32 minority (25 African Americans, 2 Asian Americans, 5 Hispanics). In 1997, 65 master's, 13 Ed Ss awarded. *Degree requirements:* For master's, teaching license required, thesis optional, foreign language not required. *Entrance requirements:* For master's, GRE General Test; for Ed S, GRE General Test (minimum score 350 on verbal and quantitative sections), master's degree, minimum graduate GPA of 3.0. Application deadline: 7/31 (priority date; rolling processing; 12/4 for spring admission). Application fee: $15. *Expenses:* Tuition $2438 per year full-time, $123 per semester hour part-time for state residents; $7034 per year full-time, $324 per semester hour part-time for nonresidents. Fees $484 per year (minimum) full-time, $154 per semester (minimum) part-time. *Financial aid:* Graduate assistantships, Federal Work-Study, institutionally sponsored loans, and career-related internships or fieldwork available. Aid available to part-time students. Financial aid application deadline: 4/1; applicants required to submit FAFSA. *Faculty research:* Teaching skills, whole language, children's literature, classroom technology, PDS model. Total annual research expenditures: $17,500. • J. Ronald Groseclose, Interim Chair, 931-648-7585. Fax: 931-648-5991. E-mail: groseclosег@apsu.edu.

Averett College, Division of Education, Danville, VA 24541-3692. Offers programs in curriculum and instruction (M Ed), reading (M Ed), teaching (MAT). Part-time and evening/weekend programs available. Faculty: 8 full-time (4 women). Students: 5 full-time (4 women), 36 part-time (30 women); includes 12 minority (9 African Americans, 1 Asian American, 2 Hispanics). Average age 30. 4 applicants, 100% accepted. In 1997, 20 degrees awarded (100% found work related to degree). *Degree requirements:* Comprehensive exam required, foreign language not required. *Average time to degree:* master's–3 years part-time. *Entrance requirements:* Minimum GPA of 3.0 in previous 2 years. Application deadline: 8/1 (priority date; rolling processing; 1/3 for spring admission). Application fee: $25. *Tuition:* $225 per credit hour. *Financial aid:* Federal Work-Study and career-related internships or fieldwork available. Aid available to part-time students. • Dr. Elizabeth Compton, Academic Vice President, 804-791-5656. Fax: 804-791-0658.

Avila College, Department of Education and Psychology, Program in Education, Kansas City, MO 64145-1698. Awards MS. Part-time and evening/weekend programs available. Faculty: 1 (woman) full-time, 4 part-time (3 women). Students: 27 part-time (24 women); includes 3 minority (2 African Americans, 1 Hispanic). Average age 35. 15 applicants, 100% accepted. In 1997, 17 degrees awarded (100% found work related to degree). *Degree requirements:* Final exam, portfolio required, foreign language and thesis not required. *Average time to degree:* master's–2 years full-time, 2 years part-time. *Entrance requirements:* Minimum GPA of 3.0 in last 60 hours. Application deadline: 4/30 (priority date; rolling processing). Application fee: $0. *Expenses:* Tuition $295 per credit hour. Fees $160 per year full-time, $6 per year part-time. *Financial aid:* Career-related internships or fieldwork available. Aid available to part-time students. Financial aid applicants required to submit FAFSA. • Sr. Marie Georgette Eschbacher, Director, 816-942-8400 Ext. 2207. E-mail: eschbachermg@mail.avila.edu. Application contact: Susan Jackson, Admissions Office, 816-942-8400 Ext. 2375. Fax: 816-942-3362.

Azusa Pacific University, School of Education and Behavioral Studies, Department of Education, Azusa, CA 91702-7000. Offers programs in curriculum and instruction (MA), educational leadership and administration (Ed D), educational technology (M Ed), language development (MA), physical education (M Ed), pupil personnel services (MA), school administration (MA), special education (MA). Part-time and evening/weekend programs available. Faculty: 78. Students: 1,586. In 1997, 357 master's awarded. *Degree requirements:* For master's, core exams, oral presentation required, foreign language not required; for doctorate, oral defense of dissertation, qualifying exam. *Entrance requirements:* For master's, minimum GPA of 3.0; for doctorate, GRE General Test (minimum combined score of 1000 or 1500 on three sections) or MAT (minimum score 48), TOEFL (minimum score 600), 5 years of experience, writing sample. Application fee: $45 ($65 for international students). *Expenses:* Tuition $350 per unit. Fees $57 per year. *Financial aid:* Career-related internships or fieldwork available. Aid available to part-time students. Financial aid applicants required to submit FAFSA. • Dr. Alice Watkins, Dean, School of Education and Behavioral Studies, 626-815-5348.

Baker University, Program in Education, Baldwin City, KS 66006-0065. Awards MA Ed. Students: 4 full-time (1 woman), 43 part-time (31 women); includes 1 minority (Hispanic), 1 international. 14 applicants, 100% accepted. In 1997, 23 degrees awarded. *Degree requirements:* Thesis required, foreign language not required. *Entrance requirements:* TOEFL (minimum score 600), 1 year of teaching experience, teaching certificate. Application deadline: rolling. Application fee: $20. *Expenses:* Tuition $310 per credit hour (minimum). Fees $40 per year. • Application contact: Laura Lane, MLA Academic Coordinator, 913-491-4432. Fax: 913-491-0470.

Baldwin-Wallace College, Division of Education, Berea, OH 44017-2088. Offers programs in reading (MA Ed), specific learning disabilities (MA Ed), supervision or administration (MA Ed). Accredited by NCATE. Part-time and evening/weekend programs available. Faculty: 11 full-time (4 women), 6 part-time (2 women). Students: 21 full-time (14 women), 137 part-time (108 women); includes 15 minority (12 African Americans, 1 Asian American, 1 Hispanic, 1 Native American). Average age 32. 62 applicants, 92% accepted. In 1997, 57 degrees awarded. *Average time to degree:* master's–3.7 years part-time. *Entrance requirements:* Bachelor's degree in field, MAT or minimum GPA of 2.75. Application fee: $15. *Financial aid:* Career-related internships or fieldwork available. • Dr. Patrick F. Cosiano, Chairman, 440-826-2168. Fax: 440-826-3779. E-mail: pcosiano@bw.edu. Application contact: Dr. Jane F. Cavanaugh, Director of Continuing Education, 440-826-2222. Fax: 440-826-3640. E-mail: admission@bw.edu.

Ball State University, Teachers College, 2000 University Avenue, Muncie, IN 47306-1099. Awards MA, MAE, Ed D, PhD, Ed S. Accredited by NCATE. Part-time and evening/weekend programs available. Faculty: 104. Students: 202 full-time (141 women), 458 part-time (316 women); includes 53 minority (34 African Americans, 6 Asian Americans, 12 Hispanics, 1 Native American), 16 international. 532 applicants, 54% accepted. In 1997, 246 master's, 35 doctorates, 12 Ed Ss awarded. *Degree requirements:* For doctorate, dissertation; for Ed S, thesis required, foreign language not required. *Entrance requirements:* For doctorate, GRE General Test (minimum combined score of 1000), minimum graduate GPA of 3.2; for Ed S, GRE General Test. Application fee: $15 ($25 for international students). *Expenses:* Tuition $3454 per year full-time, $518 per semester (minimum) part-time for state residents; $9316 per year full-time, $1221 per semester (minimum) part-time for nonresidents. Fees $242 per year full-time, $18 per semester (minimum) part-time. *Financial aid:* Research assistantships, teaching assistantships, Federal Work-Study, and career-related internships or fieldwork available. Aid available to part-time students. • Dr. Roy Weaver, Dean, 765-285-5251.

Bank Street College of Education, Graduate School, 610 West 112th Street, New York, NY 10025-1120. Awards Ed M, MS Ed, Certificate, MSW/MS Ed. Faculty: 58 full-time (45 women), 61 part-time (52 women). Students: 291 full-time (260 women), 588 part-time (535 women); includes 190 minority (96 African Americans, 22 Asian Americans, 71 Hispanics, 1 Native American), 12 international. Average age 31. In 1997, 305 master's awarded. *Degree requirements:* For master's, thesis. *Average time to degree:* master's–2 years full-time, 4 years part-time. *Entrance requirements:* For master's, TOEFL (minimum score 550). Application deadline: 3/1 (priority date; rolling processing; 11/1 for spring admission). Application fee: $50. *Tuition:* $560 per credit. *Financial aid:* 385 students received aid; Federal Work-Study and career-related internships or fieldwork available. Aid available to part-time students. Financial aid application deadline: 3/1; applicants required to submit FAFSA. *Faculty research:* Understanding developmental variations in inclusive classrooms, holistic literacy in urban classrooms, development of administration for small alternative charter schools. Total annual research expenditures: $5.622 million. • Dr. Patricia Wasley, Dean, 212-875-4460. Application contact: Ann Morgan, Director of Admissions, 212-875-4404. Fax: 212-875-4678. E-mail: amorgan@bnkst.edu.

See in-depth description on page 717.

Barat College, Graduate School of Education, Lake Forest, IL 60045-3297. Awards MA. Faculty: 2 full-time (1 woman), 9 part-time (6 women), 3.5 FTE. Students: 10 full-time (7 women), 9 part-time (7 women); includes 4 minority (2 African Americans, 1 Asian American, 1 Hispanic). *Tuition:* $432 per semester hour. *Financial aid:* In 1997–98, 2 graduate assistantships were awarded; Federal Work-Study, institutionally sponsored loans, and career-related internships or fieldwork also available. Aid available to part-time students. Financial aid applicants required to submit FAFSA. *Faculty research:* Follow-up study of students with learning disabilities. • Dr. Pamela Adelman, Dean, 847-604-6320. Application contact: Mary Kay Farrell, Associate Director of Admissions, 847-615-5678. Fax: 847-604-6300.

Barry University, School of Education, Miami Shores, FL 33161-6695. Awards MAT, MS, PhD, Ed S. Part-time and evening/weekend programs available. Postbaccalaureate distance learning degree programs offered. Faculty: 19 full-time (11 women), 23 part-time (14 women). Students: 243 full-time (205 women), 483 part-time (358 women); includes 337 minority (141 African Americans, 8 Asian Americans, 187 Hispanics, 1 Native American), 19 international. Average age 38. 398 applicants, 68% accepted. In 1997, 225 master's, 6 doctorates, 30 Ed Ss awarded. *Degree requirements:* For master's, written comprehensive exam required, foreign language and thesis not required; for doctorate, dissertation. *Entrance requirements:* For master's, GRE General Test or MAT, minimum GPA of 3.0; for doctorate, GRE General Test, minimum GPA of 3.25; for Ed S, GRE General Test, minimum GPA of 3.0. Application deadline: 5/1 (priority date; rolling processing). Application fee: $30. Electronic applications accepted. *Tuition:* $450 per credit (minimum). *Financial aid:* 342 students received aid; research assistantships, partial tuition waivers, and career-related internships or fieldwork available. Aid available to part-time students. Financial aid application deadline: 5/1; applicants required to submit FAFSA. • Sr. Evelyn Piche, OP, Dean, 305-899-3700. Fax: 305-899-3630. Application contact: Angela Scott, Enrollment Services, Assistant Dean, 305-899-3112. Fax: 305-899-3149. E-mail: ascott@jeanne.barry.edu.

Baruch College of the City University of New York, Department of Education, 17 Lexington Avenue, New York, NY 10010-5585. Offers programs in early childhood education (MS Ed), elementary education (MS Ed). Program being phased out; applicants no longer accepted. Part-time and evening/weekend programs available. Faculty: 5 full-time (2 women), 4 part-time (2 women), 6.25 FTE. Students: 120. Average age 35. *Expenses:* Tuition $4350 per year

Directory: Education—General

Baruch College of the City University of New York (continued)
full-time, $185 per credit part-time for state residents; $7600 per year full-time, $320 per credit part-time for nonresidents. Fees $53 per year. *Financial aid:* Research assistantships, full tuition waivers, and career-related internships or fieldwork available. • Dr. Jeffrey H. Golland, Chairperson, 212-389-1731. Fax: 212-387-1748. E-mail: jegbb@cunyvm.cuny.edu.

Baylor University, School of Education, Waco, TX 76798. Awards MA, MS Ed, Ed D, PhD, Ed S. Accredited by NCATE. Part-time programs available. Postbaccalaureate distance learning degree programs offered (minimal on-campus study). Students: 130 full-time (80 women), 151 part-time (90 women); includes 40 minority (20 African Americans, 3 Asian Americans, 16 Hispanics, 1 Native American), 14 international. In 1997, 76 master's, 14 doctorates awarded. *Degree requirements:* For doctorate, dissertation required, foreign language not required. *Entrance requirements:* For master's and doctorate, GRE General Test. Application deadline: rolling. Application fee: $25. Electronic applications accepted. *Expenses:* Tuition $7392 per year full-time, $308 per semester hour part-time. Fees $1024 per year. *Financial aid:* Research assistantships, teaching assistantships, partial tuition waivers, Federal Work-Study, institutionally sponsored loans, and career-related internships or fieldwork available. • Dr. Fred Curtis, Director of Graduate Studies, 254-710-3111.

Beaver College, Department of Education, Glenside, PA 19038-3295. Offers programs in allied health (MA Ed, MHA, MSH Ed); art education (MA Ed, M Ed); biology education (MA Ed); chemistry education (MA Ed); child development (CAS); computer education (M Ed, CAS); computer education 7–12 (MA Ed); curriculum (CAS); early childhood education (M Ed, CAS), including individualized (M Ed), master teacher (M Ed), research in child development (M Ed); educational leadership (M Ed, CAS); educational psychology (CAS); elementary education (M Ed, CAS); English education (MA Ed); environmental education (MA Ed, CAS); history education (MA Ed); language arts (M Ed, CAS); mathematics education (MA Ed, M Ed, CAS); music education (MA Ed); reading (M Ed, CAS); school library science (M Ed); science education (M Ed, CAS); secondary education (M Ed, CAS); special education (M Ed, CAS); written communication (MA Ed). Part-time and evening/weekend programs available. *Application fee:* $35. *Expenses:* Tuition $6570 per year full-time, $365 per credit part-time. Fees $35 per year.

Announcement: Beaver College, Graduate Studies, offers master's degrees and/or certification in art, biology, chemistry, computer education, early childhood education, elementary education, English, environmental education, health education, language arts, mathematics, reading, school librarian certification, science, secondary education, social studies, special education, and written communication. Administrative-level certifications are available through the educational leadership program. These certifications include principal, supervisory, and superintendent's letter of eligibility. School specialist certificates are offered in elementary and secondary school counseling. Study-abroad opportunities are available in Africa, Canada, and England. Faculty members are recognized leaders in their disciplines, and more than 88% have earned doctoral or terminal degrees.

Bellarmine College, College of Arts and Sciences, Graduate Programs in Education, Louisville, KY 40205-0671. Offerings in early elementary education (MA, MAT), elementary education (MA), learning and behavior disorders (MA), middle school education (MA, MAT). Accredited by NCATE. Faculty: 2 full-time (both women). Students: 9 full-time (7 women), 66 part-time (58 women); includes 9 minority (4 African Americans, 2 Asian Americans, 3 Hispanics). Average age 29. 42 applicants, 90% accepted. In 1997, 13 degrees awarded. *Application deadline:* 8/1 (priority date; rolling processing; 12/15 for spring admission). *Application fee:* $25. Electronic applications accepted. *Tuition:* $360 per credit hour. • Dr. Doris Tegart, Director, 502-452-8191.

Belmont Abbey College, School of Graduate Studies, Division of Education, Belmont, NC 28012-1802. Offers programs in elementary education (MA), middle grades education (MA), special education (MA). One or more programs accredited by NCATE. MA (special education) being phased out; applicants no longer accepted. Part-time and evening/weekend programs available. Students: 6. *Application deadline:* 6/1 (rolling processing; 11/1 for spring admission). *Application fee:* $20. *Expenses:* Tuition $530 per course (minimum). Fees $43 per semester (minimum). *Financial aid:* Available to part-time students. Financial aid application deadline: 8/1; applicants required to submit FAFSA. • Dr. Sandra Loehr, Director, 704-825-6728. Application contact: Julia Gunter, Director of Adult Admissions, 704-825-6671. Fax: 704-825-6658.

Belmont University, Graduate Studies in Education, Nashville, TN 37212-3757. Offers programs in childcare administration (M Ed), elementary education (M Ed), English (M Ed), music education (MME). Part-time and evening/weekend programs available. Faculty: 31 full-time (16 women), 1 (woman) part-time. Students: 49 full-time (40 women), 50 part-time (42 women); includes 7 minority (6 African Americans, 1 Asian American), 1 international. Average age 30. 34 applicants, 38% accepted. In 1997, 19 degrees awarded. *Degree requirements:* Thesis, project, recital (optional) required, foreign language not required. *Average time to degree:* master's–2 years full-time, 5 years part-time. *Entrance requirements:* GRE General Test (minimum combined score of 1200), MAT (minimum score 40), NTE, minimum GPA of 2.75. Application deadline: 7/15 (priority date; rolling processing; 11/15 for spring admission). Application fee: $50. *Financial aid:* In 1997–98, 50 students received aid, including 50 partial scholarships (25 to first-year students) totaling $35,000; partial tuition waivers also available. Aid available to part-time students. Financial aid application deadline: 4/15; applicants required to submit FAFSA. *Faculty research:* Internship, pedagogy, assessment, learning styles, Head Start articulation. Total annual research expenditures: $7500. • Dr. Norma Stevens, Associate Dean, 615-460-6233. E-mail: stevensn@belmont.edu. Application contact: Lois Smith, Admissions Counselor, 615-460-5483. Fax: 615-385-5084. E-mail: smithl@belmont.edu.

Bemidji State University, Division of Professional Studies, Bemidji, MN 56601-2699. Awards MS Ed. Accredited by NCATE. Part-time programs available. Students: 11 full-time (3 women), 55 part-time (34 women). Average age 35. In 1997, 10 degrees awarded. *Degree requirements:* Thesis required, foreign language not required. *Application deadline:* 5/1. *Application fee:* $20. *Expenses:* Tuition $128 per credit for state residents; $134 per credit (minimum) for nonresidents. Fees $517 per year full-time, $35 per credit (minimum) part-time. *Financial aid:* Research assistantships, teaching assistantships, Federal Work-Study, and career-related internships or fieldwork available. Aid available to part-time students. Financial aid application deadline: 5/1. • Dr. David Larkin, Dean, Graduate Studies, 218-755-3732. Fax: 218-755-3788. E-mail: dlarkin@vax1.bemidji.msus.edu.

Benedictine University, Program in Education, Lisle, IL 60532-0900. Offers curriculum and instruction and collaborative teaching (M Ed), elementary education (MA Ed), special education (MA Ed). Part-time and evening/weekend programs available. Faculty: 4 full-time (3 women), 3 part-time (1 woman). Students: 184 (163 women). *Degree requirements:* Thesis or alternative required, foreign language not required. *Entrance requirements:* GRE or MAT. Application fee: $30. • Dr. Eileen M. Kolich, Director, 630-829-6280. Fax: 630-960-1126. E-mail: ekolich@ben.edu.

Bennington College, Program in Teaching, Bennington, VT 05201-9993. Awards MAT. Students: 8. *Degree requirements:* Thesis, 1 year teaching practicum. *Application deadline:* 3/1. *Application fee:* $45. *Financial aid:* Teaching assistantships available. • Wendy Hirsch, Associate Dean, 802-440-4400. Application contact: Barbara Caron, Associate Director of Admissions, 802-440-4312. Fax: 802-440-4320. E-mail: admissions@bennington.edu.

Berry College, Graduate Programs in Education, Mount Berry, GA 30149-0159. Offerings in curriculum and instruction (Ed S), early childhood education (M Ed), middle-grades education (M Ed), reading (M Ed). Accredited by NCATE. Part-time programs available. Faculty: 14 part-time (9 women), 4.1 FTE. Students: 15 full-time (14 women), 105 part-time (86 women); includes 1 minority (African American). Average age 34. 45 applicants, 78% accepted. In 1997, 75 master's awarded; 20 Ed Ss awarded (100% found work related to degree). *Degree requirements:* For master's, oral exams required, thesis optional, foreign language not required; for Ed S, computer language, thesis, portfolio and oral exams required, foreign language not required. *Average time to degree:* master's–2 years full-time, 3 years part-time; other advanced degree–2 years full-time, 3 years part-time. *Entrance requirements:* For master's, GRE General Test, MAT, or NTE, minimum GPA of 2.5; for Ed S, M Ed from NCATE accredited school, minimum GPA of 3.25. Application deadline: 7/29 (rolling processing; 12/16 for spring admission). Application fee: $25 ($30 for international students). *Tuition:* $146 per semester hour. *Financial aid:* In 1997–98, 39 students received aid, including 5 assistantships (2 to first-year students) averaging $600 per month and totaling $18,150. Aid available to part-time students. Financial aid application deadline: 4/1; applicants required to submit FAFSA. *Faculty research:* Teacher education, mathematics education, applications of technology, family services, exercise science. Total annual research expenditures: $51,700. • Dr. Jacqueline Anglin, Dean, School of Education and Human Sciences, 706-232-5374 Ext. 1717. Application contact: George Gaddie, Dean of Admissions, 706-236-2215. Fax: 706-290-2178.

Bethany College of the Assemblies of God, Program in Teacher Education, Scotts Valley, CA 95066-2820. Awards MA. Part-time and evening/weekend programs available. Faculty: 2 full-time (1 woman), 11 part-time (10 women). Students: 20 full-time (12 women), 14 part-time (12 women). Average age 35. *Degree requirements:* Thesis, Christian ethics/research classes required, foreign language not required. *Entrance requirements:* GRE General Test (minimum combined score of 1000 r. Application deadline: 7/1 (priority date; rolling processing). Application fee: $35. *Expenses:* Tuition $6500 per year full-time, $325 per credit hour part-time. Fees $70 per year. *Financial aid:* Research assistantships and career-related internships or fieldwork available. Aid available to part-time students. Financial aid application deadline: 3/15; applicants required to submit FAFSA. • Dr. Marilyn Vaughn, Director, 408-438-3800 Ext. 1503. Application contact: Faith Alpher, Admissions Coordinator, 408-438-3800 Ext. 1503. Fax: 408-438-4517.

Bethel College, Center for Graduate and Continuing Studies, Department of Education, 3900 Bethel Drive, St. Paul, MN 55112-6999. Awards M Ed. Accredited by NCATE. Evening/weekend programs available. Faculty: 14 full-time (5 women), 8 part-time (5 women), 15.4 FTE. Students: 92 full-time (68 women), 47 part-time (41 women); includes 1 minority (African American). Average age 34. *Degree requirements:* Thesis required, foreign language not required. *Average time to degree:* master's–2 years full-time. *Entrance requirements:* Interview, current teaching license, minimum GPA of 3.0, teaching experience. Application deadline: rolling. Application fee: $25. *Expenses:* Tuition $255 per credit. Fees $75 per year. *Financial aid:* Institutionally sponsored loans available. Aid available to part-time students. Financial aid applicants required to submit FAFSA. • Dr. Jay B. Rasmussen, Coordinator of Graduate Education, 612-638-6237. Fax: 612-638-6001. E-mail: rasjay@homer.bethel.edu. Application contact: Glen Cleveland, Admissions Adviser, 612-635-8015. Fax: 612-635-1464.

Bethel College, Program in Education, McKenzie, TN 38201. Awards MA Ed, MAT. Part-time and evening/weekend programs available. Faculty: 3 full-time (2 women), 2 part-time (0 women). Students: 17 full-time (11 women), 59 part-time (53 women); includes 10 minority (all African Americans). Average age 36. 32 applicants, 100% accepted. In 1997, 14 degrees awarded. *Degree requirements:* Thesis required (for some programs), foreign language not required. *Average time to degree:* master's–2 years full-time, 3 years part-time. *Entrance requirements:* GRE General Test (combined average 1100) or MAT (minimum score 30), minimum undergraduate GPA of 2.5. Application deadline: 8/24 (priority date; rolling processing; 1/4 for spring admission). Application fee: $10. *Tuition:* $205 per semester hour. *Financial aid:* 17 students received aid; career-related internships or fieldwork available. Aid available to part-time students. Financial aid applicants required to submit FAFSA. • Dr. Ben G. McClure, Director of Graduate Studies, 901-352-4023. Fax: 901-352-4069.

Biola University, School of Arts and Sciences, La Mirada, CA 90639-0001. Awards MA Ed. Part-time and evening/weekend programs available. Faculty: 5 full-time (3 women). Students: 34 full-time (24 women), 95 part-time (65 women); includes 24 minority (3 African Americans, 11 Asian Americans, 10 Hispanics), 1 international. *Degree requirements:* Thesis or alternative required, foreign language not required. *Entrance requirements:* California Basic Educational Skills Test. Application deadline: 6/1 (rolling processing; 1/1 for spring admission). Application fee: $35. *Expenses:* Tuition $9810 per year full-time, $327 per unit part-time. Fees $40 per year full-time. *Financial aid:* Career-related internships or fieldwork available. Financial aid application deadline: 3/2; applicants required to submit FAFSA. • Dr. Lucille Richardson, Chair of Education Department, 562-903-5682. Fax: 562-903-4748. Application contact: Roy Allinson, Director of Graduate Admissions, 562-903-4752. Fax: 562-903-4709. E-mail: admissions@biola.edu.

Bishop's University, School of Education, Lennoxville, PQ J1M 1Z7, Canada. Offers programs in advanced studies in education (Diploma), education (MA, M Ed), teaching English as a second language (Certificate). Part-time programs available. Postbaccalaureate distance learning degree programs offered (minimal on-campus study). Faculty: 4 full-time (3 women), 3 part-time (1 woman). Students: 48 part-time. *Degree requirements:* For master's, thesis required (for some programs), foreign language not required. *Average time to degree:* master's–4 years part-time. *Entrance requirements:* For master's, teaching license, 2 years of teaching experience. Application deadline: 3/1 (priority date). Application fee: $40. *Faculty research:* Integration of special needs students, attitudes towards science education, multigrade classes/small schools, leadership in organizational development. • Dr. W. Duffie Van Balkom, Director, 819-822-9658. Application contact: Jane Wilson, Director of Admissions, 819-822-9600 Ext. 2220. Fax: 819-822-9661. E-mail: jwilson@ubishops.ca.

Black Hills State University, College of Education, Spearfish, SD 57799-9502. Offers program in curriculum and instruction (MS). Accredited by NCATE. Part-time programs available. Faculty: 16 full-time (5 women), 7 part-time (4 women). Students: 3 full-time, 28 part-time. In 1997, 16 degrees awarded. *Degree requirements:* Thesis or portfolio required, foreign language not required. *Entrance requirements:* GRE General Test, bachelor's degree in education. Application deadline: 4/1 (priority date; rolling processing; 10/1 for spring admission). Application fee: $15. *Expenses:* Tuition $85 per credit hour for state residents; $251 per credit hour for nonresidents. Fees $41 per credit hour. *Financial aid:* In 1997–98, 2 students received aid, including 2 research assistantships (both to first-year students) averaging $666 per month and totaling $6,000; partial tuition waivers, Federal Work-Study, and career-related internships or fieldwork also available. Aid available to part-time students. Financial aid application deadline: 2/1. *Faculty research:* Rural education, teacher/student self-concepts, teaching/learning styles, active learning technology in curriculum. • Dr. Dean Myers, Dean, 605-642-6550. Application contact: George Earley, Director of Graduate Studies, 605-642-6270. Fax: 605-642-6273.

Announcement: The institution offers a Master of Science in Curriculum and Instruction (K–12) and a Master of Science in tourism and hospitality management. The MSCI program is designed for teachers who want to improve their skills as classroom instructors. The MS in tourism and hospitality management program is designed for students who plan to enter management positions in the tourism and hospitality industries.

Bloomsburg University of Pennsylvania, School of Graduate Studies, College of Professional Studies, School of Education, Bloomsburg, PA 17815-1905. Awards M Ed, MS. Accredited by NCATE. Students: 60 full-time (46 women), 144 part-time (119 women); includes 10 minority (8 African Americans, 2 Asian Americans), 4 international. 85 applicants, 100% accepted. In 1997, 114 degrees awarded. *Entrance requirements:* Minimum QPA of 2.5. Application fee: $25. *Expenses:* Tuition $3468 per year full-time, $193 per credit part-time for state residents; $6236 per year full-time, $346 per credit part-time for nonresidents. Fees $748 per year full-time, $166 per semester (minimum) part-time. • Robert Gates, Assistant Dean, 717-389-4961. Fax: 717-389-3894. E-mail: rgates@bloomu.edu.

Bluffton College, Program in Education, Bluffton, OH 45817-1196. Awards MAE. Part-time programs available. Faculty: 14. Students: 40. In 1997, 16 degrees awarded. *Application deadline:* rolling. *Application fee:* $20. *Tuition:* $265 per semester hour. • Dr. Elizabeth Hostetler,

Director of Graduate Studies. Application contact: Diane Neal, Graduate Recruitment and Admissions, 419-358-3328. Fax: 419-358-3323. E-mail: neald@bluffton.edu.

Boise State University, College of Education, Boise, ID 83725-0399. Awards MA, MPE, MS, Ed D. Accredited by NCATE. Part-time programs available. Faculty: 51 full-time (22 women), 24 part-time (14 women). Students: 147 full-time (88 women), 439 part-time (327 women); includes 21 minority (3 African Americans, 5 Asian Americans, 10 Hispanics, 3 Native Americans), 9 international. Average age 38. 184 applicants, 95% accepted. In 1997, 105 master's, 4 doctorates awarded. *Degree requirements:* For doctorate, dissertation. *Entrance requirements:* For doctorate, GRE, minimum GPA of 3.0. Application deadline: 7/26 (priority date; rolling processing; 11/29 for spring admission). Application fee: $20 ($30 for international students). Electronic applications accepted. *Tuition:* $3020 per year full-time, $135 per credit part-time for state residents; $8900 per year full-time, $135 per credit part-time for nonresidents. *Financial aid:* In 1997–98, 33 students received aid, including 33 graduate assistantships; Federal Work-Study, institutionally sponsored loans, and career-related internships or fieldwork also available. Aid available to part-time students. Financial aid application deadline: 3/1; applicants required to submit FAFSA. • Dr. Glenn Potter, Interim Dean, 208-385-1134. Fax: 208-385-4365.

Boston College, Graduate School of Education, Chestnut Hill, MA 02167-9991. Awards MA, MAT, M Ed, MST, PhD, CAES, JD/MA, MA/MA. Accredited by NCATE. Part-time programs available. Faculty: 55 full-time (23 women), 43 part-time (29 women). Students: 436 full-time (314 women), 597 part-time (436 women); includes 133 minority (56 African Americans, 36 Asian Americans, 36 Hispanics, 5 Native Americans), 49 international. 1,532 applicants, 60% accepted. In 1997, 352 master's, 38 doctorates, 5 CAESs awarded. *Degree requirements:* For master's and CAES, comprehensive exam required, thesis not required; for doctorate, computer language, dissertation, comprehensive exam. *Entrance requirements:* For master's and doctorate, GRE General Test; for CAES, GRE General Test or MAT. Application fee: $40. *Expenses:* Tuition $626 per semester hour. Fees $80 per year (minimum) full-time, $30 per semester part-time. *Financial aid:* In 1997–98, 216 fellowships, 129 research assistantships, 81 teaching assistantships, 166 administrative assistantships, merit scholarships were awarded; partial tuition waivers, Federal Work-Study, and career-related internships or fieldwork also available. Aid available to part-time students. Financial aid applicants required to submit FAFSA. *Faculty research:* Assessment and public policy, moral education and development, minority perspectives in education, creativity, urban school leadership and organization, school inclusion. • Dr. Mary Brabeck, Dean, 617-552-4200. E-mail: brabeck@bc.edu. Application contact: Arline Riordan, Graduate Admissions Director, 617-552-4214. Fax: 617-552-0812. E-mail: riordana@bc.edu.

See in-depth description on page 719.

Boston University, School of Education, Boston, MA 02215. Awards Ed M, MAT, Ed D, CAGS, MSW/Ed D, MSW/Ed M. Part-time and evening/weekend programs available. Faculty: 49 full-time (24 women), 57 part-time (24 women), 63.04 FTE. Students: 322 full-time (236 women), 385 part-time (279 women); includes 53 minority (23 African Americans, 16 Asian Americans, 11 Hispanics, 3 Native Americans), 64 international. Average age 33. 946 applicants, 76% accepted. In 1997, 256 master's, 28 doctorates, 13 CAGSs awarded. Terminal master's awarded for partial completion of doctoral program. *Degree requirements:* For doctorate, dissertation, comprehensive exam required, foreign language not required; for CAGS, comprehensive exam required, foreign language and thesis not required. *Entrance requirements:* GRE or MAT, TOEFL. Application deadline: 2/15 (priority date; rolling processing). Application fee: $50. *Expenses:* Tuition $22,830 per year full-time, $713 per credit part-time. Fees $218 per year full-time, $40 per semester part-time. *Financial aid:* In 1997–98, 350 students received aid, including 6 fellowships averaging $1,222 per month and totaling $66,000, 40 research assistantships averaging $525 per month and totaling $168,000, 50 teaching assistantships averaging $725 per month and totaling $290,000, 194 scholarships (182 to first-year students) totaling $2.1 million; partial tuition waivers, Federal Work-Study, and career-related internships or fieldwork also available. Aid available to part-time students. Financial aid application deadline: 3/30; applicants required to submit FAFSA. *Faculty research:* Moral development, language development in young children, mathematics curriculum development, educational reform and standards, science curriculum development. • Dr. Edwin J. Delattre, Dean, 617-353-4233. E-mail: ejd@bu.edu. Application contact: Geri Lakey, Graduate Admissions Office, 617-353-4237. Fax: 617-353-8937. E-mail: glakey@bu.edu.

Announcement: The Master of Art in Teaching (MAT) programs offer courses at the master's level leading to classroom certification for students holding undergraduate degrees in appropriate academic fields. Graduates completing the course of study are eligible for Massachusetts certification.

See in-depth description on page 721.

Bowie State University, Programs in Education, 14000 Jericho Park Road, Bowie, MD 20715. Offerings in elementary education (M Ed), guidance and counseling (M Ed), reading education (M Ed), school administration and supervision (M Ed), secondary education (M Ed), special education (M Ed), teaching (MAT). Part-time and evening/weekend programs available. *Degree requirements:* Research paper, written comprehensive exam required, thesis optional. *Entrance requirements:* Teaching experience. Application deadline: 8/16 (priority date; rolling processing). Application fee: $30. *Expenses:* Tuition $169 per credit hour for state residents; $304 per credit hour for nonresidents. Fees $171 per year.

Bowling Green State University, College of Education and Allied Professions, Bowling Green, OH 43403. Awards MA, M Ed, MFCS, MRC, Ed D, PhD, Ed S. Accredited by NCATE. Part-time and evening/weekend programs available. Faculty: 85 full-time (50 women), 16 part-time (8 women). Students: 298 full-time (205 women), 363 part-time (274 women); includes 89 minority (66 African Americans, 5 Asian Americans, 15 Hispanics, 3 Native Americans), 22 international. 529 applicants, 51% accepted. In 1997, 216 master's, 9 doctorates, 2 Ed Ss awarded. *Degree requirements:* For master's, thesis or alternative required, foreign language not required; for doctorate, dissertation required, foreign language not required. *Entrance requirements:* For master's and doctorate, GRE General Test, TOEFL; for Ed S, GRE General Test. Application deadline: rolling. Application fee: $30. Electronic applications accepted. *Tuition:* $6070 per year full-time, $284 per credit hour part-time for state residents; $11,358 per year full-time, $536 per credit hour part-time for nonresidents. *Financial aid:* In 1997–98, 216 assistantships were awarded; full and partial tuition waivers, Federal Work-Study, institutionally sponsored loans, and career-related internships or fieldwork also available. Aid available to part-time students. Financial aid application deadline: 2/15; applicants required to submit FAFSA. • Dr. Les Sternberg, Dean, 419-372-7403.

Bradley University, College of Education and Health Sciences, Peoria, IL 61625-0002. Awards MA, MSN. Accredited by NCATE. Part-time and evening/weekend programs available. *Degree requirements:* Comprehensive exam. *Entrance requirements:* TOEFL (minimum score 500). Application deadline: 7/1 (priority date; rolling processing; 11/1 for spring admission). Application fee: $35. *Tuition:* $13,240 per year full-time, $359 per semester hour (minimum) part-time. *Faculty research:* Health care, professional nurse traineeship, home economics, gifted education.

Brandon University, Faculty of Education, Brandon, MB R7A 6A9, Canada. Offers programs in curriculum studies (M Ed), education (Diploma), education administration (M Ed), guidance and counseling (M Ed), special education (M Ed). Faculty: 27 full-time (3 women), 1 part-time (0 women). Students: 2 full-time (1 woman), 139 part-time (80 women). In 1997, 15 master's, 25 Diplomas awarded. *Degree requirements:* For master's, thesis. *Average time to degree:* master's–2 years full-time; other advanced degree–1 year full-time. *Entrance requirements:* For master's, TOEFL (minimum score 550), minimum GPA of 3.0, teaching certificate or equivalent. Application deadline: 3/1. Application fee: $30. *Expenses:* Tuition $421 per course (minimum). Fees $24.95 per year. *Financial aid:* In 1997–98, 4 research assistantships totaling $6,000 were awarded; fellowships, institutionally sponsored loans also available. Financial aid application deadline: 3/31. *Faculty research:* Comparative education, environmental studies, parent/school council. • Dean, 204-728-9520. Application contact: Faye Douglas, Admissions Director, 204-727-7352. Fax: 204-725-2143. E-mail: douglas@brandonu.ca.

Brenau University, School of Education and Human Development, Gainesville, GA 30501-3697. Offers programs in early childhood education (M Ed, Ed S), including behavior disorders (M Ed); learning disabilities (M Ed), including special education interrelated; middle grades education (M Ed, Ed S). Part-time and evening/weekend programs available. Students: 71 full-time (65 women), 190 part-time (178 women); includes 39 minority (36 African Americans, 1 Asian American, 2 Hispanics), 1 international. Average age 35. *Degree requirements:* For master's, comprehensive exam (M Ed) required, foreign language and thesis not required. *Average time to degree:* master's–2 years part-time; other advanced degree–1.5 years part-time. *Entrance requirements:* For master's, GRE, MAT. Application deadline: rolling. Application fee: $30. *Tuition:* $198 per semester hour. *Financial aid:* Career-related internships or fieldwork available. Financial aid application deadline: 6/1. • Dr. William B. Ware, Dean, 770-534-6220. Application contact: Kathy Cobb, Director of Graduate Admissions, 770-534-6162. Fax: 770-538-4306. E-mail: kcobb@lib.brenau.edu.

Bridgewater State College, School of Education, Bridgewater, MA 02325-0001. Awards MAT, M Ed, MS, CAGS. Accredited by NCATE. Evening/weekend programs available. Students: 1,070. *Degree requirements:* For CAGS, comprehensive exam. *Entrance requirements:* For master's, GRE General Test; for CAGS, master's degree. Application deadline: 4/1 (10/1 for spring admission). Application fee: $25. *Expenses:* Tuition $1675 per year full-time, $70 per credit part-time for state residents; $6450 per year full-time, $269 per credit part-time for nonresidents. Fees $1588 per year full-time, $66 per credit hour part-time for state residents; $1588 per year full-time, $66 per credit part-time for nonresidents. *Financial aid:* Career-related internships or fieldwork available. • Dr. Mary Lou Thornburg, Acting Dean, 508-697-1347. Application contact: Graduate School, 508-697-1300.

Brigham Young University, David O. McKay School of Education, Provo, UT 84602-1001. Awards MA, M Ed, MS, Ed D, PhD, Certificate, JD/Ed D, JD/M Ed. Accredited by NCATE. Part-time programs available. Faculty: 52 full-time (6 women), 22 part-time (8 women). Students: 250 full-time (112 women), 107 part-time (65 women); includes 30 minority (3 African Americans, 17 Asian Americans, 9 Hispanics, 1 Native American), 35 international. Average age 32. 277 applicants, 47% accepted. In 1997, 94 master's, 20 doctorates awarded. *Degree requirements:* For doctorate, dissertation. *Average time to degree:* master's–3 years part-time. *Entrance requirements:* For master's, GRE General Test, minimum GPA of 3.0 in last 60 hours; for doctorate, GRE General Test. Application fee: $30. *Tuition:* $3200 per year full-time, $178 per credit hour part-time for state residents; $4800 per year full-time, $266 per credit hour part-time for nonresidents. *Financial aid:* In 1997–98, 14 fellowships (6 to first-year students), 38 research assistantships (17 to first-year students), 39 teaching assistantships (16 to first-year students), scholarships totaling $1,200 were awarded; partial tuition waivers, institutionally sponsored loans, and career-related internships or fieldwork also available. Aid available to part-time students. Financial aid applicants required to submit FAFSA. *Faculty research:* Reading, learning, teacher education, assessment and evaluation. • Dr. Robert S. Patterson, Dean, 801-378-3695. Fax: 801-378-4017. E-mail: bob_patterson@byu.edu.

Brock University, Faculty of Education, St. Catharines, ON L2S 3A1, Canada. Offers programs in education (M Ed), teaching English as a second language (M Ed). M Ed (teaching English as a second language) new for fall 1998. Part-time and evening/weekend programs available. Faculty: 37 full-time (14 women), 24 part-time (15 women). Students: 67 full-time (50 women), 570 part-time (392 women); includes 4 international. Average age 35. 232 applicants, 68% accepted. In 1997, 106 degrees awarded (80% found work related to degree, 20% continued full-time study). *Degree requirements:* Thesis optional, foreign language not required. *Average time to degree:* master's–2 years full-time, 5 years part-time. *Entrance requirements:* B Ed, 1 year of teaching experience. Application deadline: 4/12 (rolling processing). Application fee: $35. *Expenses:* Tuition $5185 per year full-time, $2074 per year part-time for Canadian residents; $10,800 per year for nonresidents. Fees $90 per year. *Financial aid:* Fellowships, research assistantships, teaching assistantships, and career-related internships or fieldwork available. Aid available to part-time students. *Faculty research:* Curriculum studies, foundations of learning, teaching behavior, educational administration. • Victor D. Cicci, Acting Dean, 905-688-5550 Ext. 3712. Fax: 905-685-4131. E-mail: vcicci@dewey.ed.brocku.ca. Application contact: Ellie Koop, Assistant Registrar, Graduate Studies, 905-688-5550 Ext. 4467. Fax: 905-988-5488. E-mail: ekoop@spartan.ac.brocku.ca.

Brooklyn College of the City University of New York, School of Education, 2900 Bedford Avenue, Brooklyn, NY 11210-2889. Awards MA, MS Ed, CAS. Part-time and evening/weekend programs available. Faculty: 38 full-time, 6 part-time, 41 FTE. Students: 124 full-time (95 women), 1,401 part-time (1,131 women); includes 555 minority (383 African Americans, 37 Asian Americans, 134 Hispanics, 1 Native American), 12 international. In 1997, 458 master's, 115 CASs awarded. *Entrance requirements:* For CAS, master's degree. Application deadline: 3/1 (rolling processing; 11/1 for spring admission). Application fee: $40. *Expenses:* Tuition $4350 per year full-time, $185 per credit part-time for state residents; $7600 per year full-time, $320 per credit part-time for nonresidents. Fees $500 per year for state residents; $806 per year for nonresidents. *Financial aid:* Fellowships, full and partial tuition waivers, Federal Work-Study, institutionally sponsored loans, and career-related internships or fieldwork available. Aid available to part-time students. Financial aid application deadline: 5/1; applicants required to submit FAFSA. • Dr. Rosamond Welchman, Acting Dean, 718-951-5214. Fax: 718-951-4816.

Brown University, Department of Education, Providence, RI 02912. Offers programs in elementary education K–6 (MAT), secondary biology (MAT), secondary English (MAT), secondary social studies (MAT). MAT (elementary education K–6) new for fall 1998. Faculty: 4 full-time (2 women), 20 part-time (15 women). Students: 28 full-time (23 women); includes 6 minority (4 African Americans, 1 Asian American, 1 Hispanic). Average age 25. 95 applicants, 34% accepted. In 1997, 26 degrees awarded. *Average time to degree:* master's–1 year full-time. *Entrance requirements:* GRE (score in 95th percentile or higher). Application deadline: 1/2 (priority date). Application fee: $60. *Expenses:* Tuition $23,616 per year. Fees $436 per year. *Financial aid:* In 1997–98, 3 fellowships, 3 teaching assistantships were awarded; proctorships, full and partial tuition waivers, Federal Work-Study, institutionally sponsored loans, and career-related internships or fieldwork also available. Financial aid application deadline: 2/1; applicants required to submit FAFSA. *Faculty research:* Literacy, human development, minority women. • Lawrence Wakeford, Chairman, 401-863-2407. Application contact: Yvette Nachmias, Teacher Education Coordinator, 401-863-3364. Fax: 401-863-1276. E-mail: yvette_nachmias@brown.edu.

Bucknell University, College of Arts and Sciences, Department of Education, Lewisburg, PA 17837. Offers programs in classroom teaching (MS Ed), educational research (MS Ed), elementary and secondary counseling (MA, MS Ed), elementary and secondary principalship (MA, MS Ed), reading (MA, MS Ed), school psychology (MS Ed), supervision of curriculum and instruction (MA, MS Ed). Faculty: 9 full-time. Students: 34 full-time (28 women), 17 part-time (10 women). *Degree requirements:* Thesis or alternative required, foreign language not required. *Entrance requirements:* GRE General Test (minimum combined score of 1000), TOEFL (minimum score 550), minimum GPA of 2.8. Application deadline: 6/1 (priority date; rolling processing; 12/1 for spring admission). Application fee: $25. *Tuition:* $2410 per course. *Financial aid:* Fellowships, assistantships available. Financial aid application deadline: 3/1. • Dr. Robert Midkiff, Head, 717-524-1133.

Buena Vista University, School of Education, Storm Lake, IA 50588. Offers programs in education administration (MS Ed), school guidance and counseling (MS Ed). Offered in summer only. Part-time programs available. Postbaccalaureate distance learning degree programs offered (minimal on-campus study). Faculty: 7 full-time (2 women). Students: 66 full-time (48 women). 58 applicants, 86% accepted. *Degree requirements:* Thesis, fieldwork/practicum

Directory: Education—General

Buena Vista University (continued)

required, foreign language not required. *Entrance requirements:* GRE, minimum undergraduate GPA of 2.75. Application fee: $0. *Financial aid:* Career-related internships or fieldwork available. Financial aid applicants required to submit FAFSA. *Faculty research:* Reading, curriculum, educational psychology, special education. • F. Kline Capps, Dean, 712-749-2275. E-mail: cappsk@bvu.edu. Application contact: Jon E. Hixon, Director of Graduate Studies, 712-749-2190. Fax: 712-749-2035. E-mail: hixon@bvu.edu.

Butler University, College of Education, Indianapolis, IN 46208-3485. Offers programs in administration (MS, Ed S), counseling psychology (Ed S), elementary education (MS), reading (MS), school counseling (MS, Ed S), school psychology (MS, Ed S), secondary education (MS), special education (MS). Accredited by NCATE. Part-time and evening/weekend programs available. Faculty: 10 full-time (3 women), 22 part-time (8 women), 22.5 FTE. Students: 6 full-time (5 women), 104 part-time (80 women); includes 2 minority (both African Americans). Average age 31. 36 applicants, 86% accepted. In 1997, 44 master's awarded. *Degree requirements:* For Ed S, thesis required, foreign language not required. *Average time to degree:* master's–7 years part-time; other advanced degree–5 years part-time. *Entrance requirements:* For master's, GRE General Test, MAT (minimum score 40), interview. Application deadline: 8/15 (priority date; rolling processing). Application fee: $25. *Tuition:* $220 per credit hour. *Financial aid:* 10 students received aid; institutionally sponsored loans available. Aid available to part-time students. Financial aid application deadline: 7/15. • Dr. Saundra Tracy, Dean, 317-940-9514. Fax: 317-940-6481. E-mail: stracy@butler.edu.

Cabrini College, Graduate Education Programs, Radnor, PA 19087-3698. Awards M Ed. Part-time programs available. Faculty: 9 full-time (4 women), 16 part-time (14 women), 14 FTE. Students: 50 full-time (36 women), 321 part-time (279 women); includes 11 minority (6 African Americans, 2 Asian Americans, 3 Hispanics), 2 international. Average age 33. 80 applicants, 85% accepted. In 1997, 112 degrees awarded. *Degree requirements:* Thesis required (for some programs), foreign language not required. *Average time to degree:* master's–1.5 years full-time, 3 years part-time. *Application deadline:* 5/15 (priority date; rolling processing; 10/15 for spring admission). *Application fee:* $35. Electronic applications accepted. *Financial aid:* In 1997–98, 85 students received aid, including 7 research assistantships totaling $16,600; Federal Work-Study and career-related internships or fieldwork also available. Aid available to part-time students. Financial aid applicants required to submit FAFSA. *Faculty research:* Qualitative research in reading, ethnographic studies. • Dr. Dawn Middleton, Chairperson, 610-902-8350. Fax: 610-902-8520. E-mail: dawn.middleton@cabrini.edu. Application contact: William Firman, Associate Director of Admissions, 610-902-8552. Fax: 610-902-8508. E-mail: admit@cabrini.edu.

Caldwell College, Graduate Studies, Program in Education, Caldwell, NJ 07006-6195. Awards Certificate. Students: 37 part-time (all women). *Application deadline:* rolling. *Application fee:* $25. *Tuition:* $365 per credit. • Dr. Cordelia Twomey, Coordinator, 973-228-4424 Ext. 629. E-mail: ctwomey@caldwell.edu. Application contact: Dr. Rina Spano, Director of Graduate Studies, 973-228-4424 Ext. 408. Fax: 973-364-7618. E-mail: rspano@caldwell.edu.

California Baptist College, Graduate Program in Education, Riverside, CA 92504-3206. Offers cross-cultural language academic development (MA Ed), educational leadership (MS Ed), educational technology (MS Ed), English education (MS Ed), reading (MS Ed), special education (MS Ed), sport leadership (MS Ed), teaching and curriculum (MS Ed). Part-time and evening/weekend programs available. Faculty: 8 full-time (7 women), 4 part-time (2 women). Students: 225. *Degree requirements:* Thesis or alternative. *Application deadline:* rolling. *Application fee:* $40. *Expenses:* Tuition $275 per unit. Fees $100 per year. *Financial aid:* Federal Work-Study and career-related internships or fieldwork available. Financial aid applicants required to submit FAFSA. • Dr. Marsha Savage, Chair, 909-689-5771. Application contact: Gail Ronveaux, Director of Graduate Services, 909-343-4249. Fax: 909-351-1808. E-mail: gradser@cal.baptist.edu.

California Lutheran University, School of Education, Thousand Oaks, CA 91360-2787. Offers programs in counseling and guidance (MS); curriculum and instruction (MA), including reading education; education (M Ed); educational administration (MA); special education (MS). Part-time programs available. Faculty: 10 full-time (8 women), 30 part-time (18 women). Students: 94 full-time (72 women), 378 part-time (291 women). Average age 35. 102 applicants, 93% accepted. In 1997, 55 degrees awarded. *Degree requirements:* Thesis or comprehensive exam. *Entrance requirements:* GRE General Test, minimum GPA of 3.0. Application deadline: 8/1 (priority date; rolling processing; 12/1 for spring admission). Application fee: $50. *Tuition:* $335 per unit. • Dr. Carol Bartell, Dean, 805-493-3420.

California Polytechnic State University, San Luis Obispo, Center for Teacher Education, San Luis Obispo, CA 93407. Offers programs in counseling (MA), including education; curriculum and instruction (MA); educational administration (MA); reading (MA); special education (MA). Part-time and evening/weekend programs available. Faculty: 12 full-time, 19 part-time. Students: 200 full-time (139 women), 141 part-time (107 women); includes 10 Asian Americans, 34 Hispanics, 8 Native Americans. 250 applicants, 61% accepted. In 1997, 76 degrees awarded. *Degree requirements:* Comprehensive exam required, thesis optional, foreign language not required. *Entrance requirements:* Minimum GPA of 3.0 during last 90 quarter units. Application deadline: 4/1 (12/15 for spring admission). Application fee: $55. *Expenses:* Tuition $0 for state residents; $164 per unit for nonresidents. Fees $2102 per year full-time, $1632 per year part-time. *Financial aid:* Federal Work-Study, institutionally sponsored loans, and career-related internships or fieldwork available. *Faculty research:* Rural school counseling, partner school effectiveness. • Dr. Susan Roper, Director, 805-756-2584. Fax: 805-756-5682.

California State Polytechnic University, Pomona, School of Education and Integrative Studies, Pomona, CA 91768-2557. Awards MA. Part-time programs available. Students: 8 full-time (4 women), 109 part-time (78 women); includes 25 minority (4 African Americans, 10 Asian Americans, 10 Hispanics, 1 Native American), 4 international. 42 applicants, 88% accepted. In 1997, 26 degrees awarded. *Degree requirements:* Thesis or alternative. *Application deadline:* rolling. *Application fee:* $55. *Expenses:* Tuition $0 for state residents; $164 per unit for nonresidents. Fees $1953 per year full-time, $1287 per year part-time. *Financial aid:* 55 students received aid; Federal Work-Study, institutionally sponsored loans, and career-related internships or fieldwork available. Aid available to part-time students. Financial aid application deadline: 3/2; applicants required to submit FAFSA. *Faculty research:* Cognitive style, human factors, learning-handicapped children, teaching and learning, severely handicapped children. • Dr. Richard A. Navarro, Dean, 909-869-2307. E-mail: ranavarro@csupomona.edu. Application contact: Dr. Jane McGraw, Chair, Graduate and Professional Studies Department, 909-869-2302. Fax: 909-869-4822. E-mail: jsmcgraw@csupomona.edu.

California State University, Bakersfield, School of Education, 9001 Stockdale Highway, Bakersfield, CA 93311-1099. Offers programs in bilingual/bicultural education (MA); counseling (MS); counseling and personnel services (MA); curriculum and instruction (MA), including elementary curriculum and instruction, secondary curriculum and instruction; early childhood education (MA); educational administration (MA); reading education (MA); special education (MA). Accredited by NCATE. Students: 77 full-time (59 women), 149 part-time (115 women); includes 62 minority (13 African Americans, 7 Asian Americans, 38 Hispanics, 4 Native Americans), 1 international. 52 applicants, 98% accepted. *Degree requirements:* Thesis or alternative, culminating projects. *Application deadline:* rolling. *Application fee:* $55. *Expenses:* Tuition $0 for state residents; $246 per unit full-time, $164 per unit part-time for nonresidents. Fees $1584 per year full-time, $918 per year part-time. • Dr. Lon Kellenberger, Interim Dean, 805-664-2219. Application contact: Dr. Dianne Turner, Graduate Coordinator, 805-664-2422. Fax: 805-664-2063.

California State University, Chico, College of Communication and Education, School of Education, Chico, CA 95929-0722. Awards MA. Students: 37 full-time (35 women), 51 part-time (39 women); includes 14 minority (1 Asian American, 12 Hispanics, 1 Native American), 8 international. In 1997, 39 degrees awarded. *Application deadline:* 4/1 (rolling processing). *Application fee:* $55. *Expenses:* Tuition $0 for state residents; $246 per unit for nonresidents. Fees $2108 per year full-time, $1442 per year part-time. *Financial aid:* Fellowships, teaching assistantships, stipends, and career-related internships or fieldwork available. • Dr. Carolynn Reynolds, Associate Dean, 530-898-6293.

California State University, Dominguez Hills, School of Education, Carson, CA 90747-0001. Awards MA, Certificate. Part-time and evening/weekend programs available. Faculty: 15 full-time (5 women), 6 part-time (3 women). Students: 182 full-time (124 women), 455 part-time (329 women); includes 343 minority (134 African Americans, 38 Asian Americans, 165 Hispanics, 6 Native Americans), 11 international. Average age 35. 273 applicants, 99% accepted. In 1997, 224 master's awarded. *Entrance requirements:* For master's, minimum GPA of 2.75. Application deadline: 6/1. Application fee: $55. *Expenses:* Tuition $0 for state residents; $246 per unit for nonresidents. Fees $1896 per year full-time, $1230 per year part-time. • Dr. Joseph Braun, Dean, 310-243-3519. Application contact: Admissions Office, 310-243-3600.

California State University, Fresno, Division of Graduate Studies, School of Education and Human Development, 5241 North Maple Avenue, Fresno, CA 93740. Awards MA, MS. Accredited by NCATE. Part-time and evening/weekend programs available. Faculty: 49 full-time (26 women). Students: 219 full-time (162 women), 263 part-time (194 women); includes 155 minority (12 African Americans, 29 Asian Americans, 110 Hispanics, 4 Native Americans), 6 international. Average age 31. 171 applicants, 92% accepted. In 1997, 154 degrees awarded. *Average time to degree:* master's–3.5 years full-time. *Entrance requirements:* GRE General Test, TOEFL (minimum score 550), MAT. Application deadline: 4/1 (priority date; rolling processing; 11/1 for spring admission). Application fee: $55. Electronic applications accepted. *Expenses:* Tuition $0 for state residents; $246 per unit for nonresidents. Fees $1872 per year full-time, $1206 per year part-time. *Financial aid:* In 1997–98, 3 fellowships totaling $9,000, 143 research awards, travel grants, scholarships totaling $191,003 were awarded; research assistantships, Federal Work-Study, and career-related internships or fieldwork also available. Financial aid application deadline: 3/1; applicants required to submit FAFSA. *Faculty research:* Adult community education, parenting, gifted and talented curriculum and instruction, peer mediation and conflict resolution. • Dr. Paul Shaker, Dean, 209-278-0210. E-mail: paul_shaker@csufresno.edu. Application contact: Robert Monke, Associate Dean, 209-278-0205. Fax: 209-278-6203. E-mail: robert_monke@csufresno.edu.

California State University, Fullerton, School of Human Development and Community Service, PO Box 34080, Fullerton, CA 92834-9480. Awards MS. Accredited by NCATE. Part-time programs available. Faculty: 47 full-time (30 women), 153 part-time, 78.2 FTE. Students: 91 full-time (74 women), 563 part-time (466 women); includes 143 minority (18 African Americans, 43 Asian Americans, 80 Hispanics, 2 Native Americans), 11 international. Average age 34. 289 applicants, 83% accepted. In 1997, 183 degrees awarded. *Degree requirements:* Thesis or alternative. *Application fee:* $55. *Expenses:* Tuition $0 for state residents; $246 per unit for nonresidents. Fees $1947 per year full-time, $1281 per year part-time. *Financial aid:* Teaching assistantships, state grants, Federal Work-Study, institutionally sponsored loans, and career-related internships or fieldwork available. Aid available to part-time students. Financial aid application deadline: 3/1. *Faculty research:* Nursing and health, exercise and heart disease, time studies and counseling, sex bias and coaching, nutrition and self-image. • Dr. Soraya Coley, Dean, 714-278-3311.

California State University, Hayward, School of Education, Hayward, CA 94542-3000. Awards MS. Accredited by NCATE. Part-time and evening/weekend programs available. Faculty: 68 full-time (30 women). Students: 544. 49 applicants, 78% accepted. In 1997, 53 degrees awarded. *Application deadline:* 4/19 (priority date; rolling processing; 1/5 for spring admission). *Application fee:* $55. *Expenses:* Tuition $0 for state residents; $164 per unit for nonresidents. Fees $1827 per year full-time, $1161 per year part-time. *Financial aid:* Federal Work-Study, institutionally sponsored loans, and career-related internships or fieldwork available. Aid available to part-time students. Financial aid application deadline: 3/1. • Dr. Arthurlene Towner, Dean, 510-885-3942. Application contact: Dr. Maria De Anda-Ramos, Executive Director, Admissions and Outreach, 510-885-2624.

California State University, Long Beach, College of Education, Long Beach, CA 90840-2201. Awards MA, MS, Certificate. Part-time and evening/weekend programs available. Faculty: 53 full-time, 63 part-time. Students: 111 full-time (86 women), 349 part-time (279 women); includes 136 minority (30 African Americans, 37 Asian Americans, 68 Hispanics, 1 Native American), 8 international. Average age 33. 265 applicants, 68% accepted. In 1997, 95 master's awarded. *Entrance requirements:* For master's, GRE General Test, minimum GPA of 2.75. Application deadline: 8/1 (rolling processing; 12/1 for spring admission). Application fee: $55. *Expenses:* Tuition $0 for state residents; $246 per unit for nonresidents. Fees $1846 per year full-time, $1180 per year part-time. *Financial aid:* Application deadline 3/2. • Dr. Jean Houck, Acting Dean, 562-985-4513. Fax: 562-985-1774. E-mail: jhouck@csulb.edu.

California State University, Los Angeles, School of Education, Los Angeles, CA 90032-8530. Awards MA, MS, PhD. Accredited by NCATE. Part-time and evening/weekend programs available. Faculty: 77 full-time, 97 part-time. Students: 416 full-time (305 women), 848 part-time (602 women); includes 769 minority (103 African Americans, 168 Asian Americans, 495 Hispanics, 3 Native Americans), 51 international. In 1997, 338 master's awarded. *Degree requirements:* For doctorate, dissertation. *Entrance requirements:* For master's, TOEFL (minimum score 550), minimum GPA of 2.75 in last 90 units, teaching certificate; for doctorate, GRE General Test (minimum combined score of 1000), TOEFL (minimum score 550), master's degree; minimum GPA of 3.0 (undergraduate), 3.5 (graduate). Application deadline: 6/30 (rolling processing; 2/1 for spring admission). Application fee: $55. *Expenses:* Tuition $0 for state residents; $164 per unit for nonresidents. Fees $1763 per year full-time, $1097 per year part-time. *Financial aid:* 178 students received aid; Federal Work-Study and career-related internships or fieldwork available. Aid available to part-time students. Financial aid application deadline: 3/1. • Dr. Allen Mori, Dean, 213-343-4300.

California State University, Northridge, College of Education, Northridge, CA 91330. Awards MA, MS, MFCC. Accredited by NCATE. Part-time and evening/weekend programs available. Faculty: 79 full-time, 90 part-time. Students: 385 full-time (309 women), 551 part-time (443 women); includes 275 minority (63 African Americans, 65 Asian Americans, 141 Hispanics, 6 Native Americans), 11 international. Average age 35. 365 applicants, 89% accepted. *Entrance requirements:* For master's, TOEFL. Application deadline: 11/30. Application fee: $55. *Expenses:* Tuition $0 for state residents; $246 per unit for nonresidents. Fees $1970 per year full-time, $1304 per year part-time. *Financial aid:* Fellowships, partial tuition waivers, Federal Work-Study, institutionally sponsored loans, and career-related internships or fieldwork available. Aid available to part-time students. Financial aid application deadline: 3/1. *Faculty research:* Federal teacher center support, bilingual teacher training. • Dr. Carolyn L. Ellner, Dean, 818-677-2590.

California State University, Sacramento, School of Education, Sacramento, CA 95819-6048. Awards MA, MS. Part-time programs available. *Degree requirements:* Thesis or alternative, writing proficiency exam. *Entrance requirements:* TOEFL (minimum score 550). Application deadline: 4/15 (11/1 for spring admission). Application fee: $55. *Expenses:* Tuition $0 for state residents; $246 per unit for nonresidents. Fees $2012 per year full-time, $1346 per year part-time. *Financial aid:* Research assistantships, teaching assistantships, Federal Work-Study, and career-related internships or fieldwork available. Aid available to part-time students. Financial aid application deadline: 3/1. • Dr. Diane Cordero De Noriega, Dean, 916-278-6639.

California State University, San Bernardino, Graduate Studies, School of Education, San Bernardino, CA 92407-2397. Offers programs in bilingual/cross-cultural education (MA); counselor education (MA, MS), including counseling/guidance (MS), counselor education (MA); elementary education (MA); English as a second language (MA); environmental education (MA); history and English for secondary teachers (MA); instructional technology (MA); reading (MA); school administration (MA); secondary education (MA); special education and rehabilitation counseling (MA), including rehabilitation counseling, special education; vocational education (MA). Part-time and evening/weekend programs available. Faculty: 77 full-time (38 women). Students: 489 full-time (336 women), 399 part-time (283 women); includes 221 minority (66 African Americans, 20 Asian Americans, 130 Hispanics, 5 Native Americans), 20 international. 422 applicants, 98% accepted. In 1997, 259 degrees awarded. *Entrance requirements:* Minimum GPA of 3.0 in education. Application deadline: 8/31 (priority date). Application fee: $55. *Expenses:* Tuition $0 for state residents; $164 per unit for nonresidents. Fees $1922 per year full-time, $1256 per year part-time. *Financial aid:* Federal Work-Study and career-related internships or fieldwork available. Aid available to part-time students. *Faculty research:* Multicultural education, brain-based learning, science education, social studies/global education. • Patricia Arlin, Dean, 909-880-3600. Fax: 909-880-7011.

California State University, San Marcos, College of Education, San Marcos, CA 92096. Awards MA. One or more programs accredited by NCATE. Part-time and evening/weekend programs available. Students: 5 full-time (4 women), 83 part-time (76 women); includes 16 minority (1 Asian American, 15 Hispanics). Average age 37. 63 applicants, 89% accepted. In 1997, 12 degrees awarded. *Degree requirements:* Thesis. *Entrance requirements:* Minimum GPA of 3.0, teaching credentials, 1 year of teaching experience. Application deadline: 11/2 (priority date; rolling processing). Application fee: $55. *Expenses:* Tuition $0 for state residents; $246 per unit for nonresidents. Fees $1790 per year full-time, $1104 per year part-time. *Financial aid:* Fellowships, teaching assistantships, Federal Work-Study, and career-related internships or fieldwork available. Aid available to part-time students. Financial aid applicants required to submit FAFSA. *Faculty research:* Multicultural literature, art as knowledge, poetry and second language acquisition, restructuring K–12 education and improving the training of K–8 science teachers. • Dr. Steve Lilly, Dean, 760-750-4311. Fax: 760-750-4323. E-mail: steve_lilly@csusm.edu. Application contact: Beverly Mahdavi, Program Support, 760-750-4281.

California State University, Stanislaus, School of Education, Turlock, CA 95382. Awards MA Ed. Accredited by NCATE. Part-time and evening/weekend programs available. Faculty: 34 full-time (18 women), 3 part-time (2 women). Students: 38 (32 women); includes 8 minority (2 Asian Americans, 5 Hispanics, 1 Native American). 64 applicants, 97% accepted. In 1997, 28 degrees awarded. *Entrance requirements:* MAT. Application fee: $55. *Expenses:* Tuition $0 for state residents; $246 per unit for nonresidents. Fees $1779 per year full-time, $1113 per year part-time. *Financial aid:* Federal Work-Study and career-related internships or fieldwork available. Financial aid application deadline: 3/2; applicants required to submit FAFSA. • Dr. Irma Guzman Wagner, Dean, 209-667-3145.

California University of Pennsylvania, School of Education, 250 University Avenue, California, PA 15419-1394. Awards M Ed, MS, MSW. Accredited by NCATE. Part-time and evening/weekend programs available. Faculty: 10 full-time (3 women), 53 part-time (17 women). Students: 284 full-time (219 women), 341 part-time (274 women); includes 15 minority (12 African Americans, 3 Native Americans), 2 international. 333 applicants, 73% accepted. In 1997, 252 degrees awarded. *Degree requirements:* Comprehensive exam required, foreign language not required. *Entrance requirements:* TOEFL. Application fee: $25. *Expenses:* Tuition $3468 per year full-time, $193 per credit part-time for state residents; $6236 per year full-time, $346 per credit part-time for nonresidents. Fees $886 per year full-time, $153 per semester (minimum) part-time. *Financial aid:* Graduate assistantships and career-related internships or fieldwork available. • Dr. Stephen A. Pavlak, Dean, 724-938-4125.

Calvin College, Graduate Programs in Education, Grand Rapids, MI 49546-4388. Offerings in curriculum and instruction (M Ed), learning disabilities (M Ed), reading (M Ed), school administration (M Ed). Accredited by NCATE. M Ed (reading, school administration) admissions temporarily suspended. Part-time programs available. Faculty: 1 (woman) full-time, 15 part-time (6 women). Students: 7 full-time (5 women), 99 part-time (71 women); includes 1 minority (African American), 20 international. 9 applicants, 100% accepted. In 1997, 14 degrees awarded. *Degree requirements:* Thesis required, foreign language not required. *Entrance requirements:* GRE General Test, TOEFL, teaching certificate. Application deadline: 8/15 (priority date; rolling processing; 1/15 for spring admission). Application fee: $0. Electronic applications accepted. *Tuition:* $250 per semester hour. *Financial aid:* In 1997–98, 4 scholarships were awarded; full and partial tuition waivers, Federal Work-Study also available. Aid available to part-time students. Financial aid application deadline: 2/15. • Dr. Robert S. Fortner, Director of Graduate Studies, 616-957-8533. Fax: 616-957-8551. E-mail: forr@calvin.edu.

Cambridge College, Graduate Studies, Program in Education, Cambridge, MA 02138-5304. Offers education/integrated studies (M Ed). Part-time and evening/weekend programs available. Faculty: 5 full-time (3 women), 62 part-time (37 women). Students: 885 full-time (708 women), 53 part-time (42 women); includes 466 minority (393 African Americans, 9 Asian Americans, 64 Hispanics), 6 international. Average age 40. 191 applicants, 79% accepted. In 1997, 686 degrees awarded. *Degree requirements:* Computer language, thesis, internship/practicum. *Average time to degree:* master's–1 year full-time. *Application deadline:* 9/10 (priority date; rolling processing; 1/10 for spring admission). *Application fee:* $30. *Expenses:* Tuition $315 per credit. Fees $60 per semester. *Financial aid:* Teaching assistantships, Federal Work-Study, and career-related internships or fieldwork available. Financial aid applicants required to submit FAFSA. *Faculty research:* Adult education, accelerated learning, mathematics education, brain compatible learning, special education and law. • Application contact: Jacqueline Tynes, Senior Admissions Representative, 617-868-1000 Ext. 140. Fax: 617-349-3561. E-mail: admit@idea.cambridge.edu.

Cameron University, School of Graduate and Professional Studies, Program in Education, Lawton, OK 73505-6377. Awards M Ed. Accredited by NCATE. Part-time and evening/weekend programs available. Faculty: 15 full-time (8 women). Students: 5 full-time (3 women), 39 part-time (35 women); includes 10 minority (4 African Americans, 2 Asian Americans, 2 Hispanics, 2 Native Americans). Average age 38. In 1997, 21 degrees awarded. *Degree requirements:* Comprehensive exams required, thesis optional, foreign language not required. *Average time to degree:* master's–2 years full-time, 3 years part-time. *Entrance requirements:* GRE General Test or MAT, minimum GPA of 2.75 (undergraduate), 3.0 (graduate). Application deadline: 8/18 (priority date; rolling processing; 1/9 for spring admission). Application fee: $15. *Tuition:* $78 per semester hour for state residents; $180 per semester hour for nonresidents. *Financial aid:* Federal Work-Study and career-related internships or fieldwork available. Aid available to part-time students. Financial aid application deadline: 4/15; applicants required to submit FAFSA. • Dr. John Moseley, Associate Dean, 580-581-2319. Fax: 580-581-2553. E-mail: johnmos@cameron.edu. Application contact: Suzanne Cartwright, Admissions Coordinator, 580-581-2986. Fax: 580-581-5532. E-mail: suzannea@cameron.edu.

Cameron University, School of Graduate and Professional Studies, Program in Teaching, Lawton, OK 73505-6377. Awards MAT. Accredited by NCATE. Faculty: 2 full-time (both women). Students: 31 full-time (15 women), 2 part-time (1 woman); includes 7 minority (3 African Americans, 1 Asian American, 2 Hispanics, 1 Native American). Average age 38. In 1997, 15 degrees awarded. *Degree requirements:* Thesis optional, foreign language not required. *Average time to degree:* master's–2 years full-time. *Entrance requirements:* GRE General Test or MAT, minimum GPA of 2.75 (undergraduate), 3.0 (graduate). Application deadline: 8/18 (priority date; rolling processing; 1/9 for spring admission). Application fee: $15. *Tuition:* $78 per semester hour for state residents; $180 per semester hour for nonresidents. *Financial aid:* Federal Work-Study available. Aid available to part-time students. Financial aid application deadline: 4/15; applicants required to submit FAFSA. • Dr. Judy Neale, Associate Dean, 580-581-2339. Fax: 580-581-2553. E-mail: judyn@cameron.edu. Application contact: Suzanne Cartwright, Admissions Coordinator, 580-581-2986. Fax: 580-581-5532. E-mail: suzannea@cameron.edu.

Campbellsville University, Division of Education, Campbellsville, KY 42718-2799. Offers programs in education (MA Ed), music education (MA Ed). Faculty: 11. Students: 69. *Application deadline:* rolling. *Application fee:* $0. *Tuition:* $7800 per year. • Dr. Linda B. Cundiff, Chair, 502-789-5344.

Campbell University, School of Education, Buies Creek, NC 27506. Offers programs in administration (MSA), community counseling (MA), elementary education (M Ed), English education (M Ed), mathematics education (M Ed), middle grades education (M Ed), physical education (M Ed), school counseling (M Ed), secondary education (M Ed), social science education (M Ed). Accredited by NCATE. Part-time and evening/weekend programs available. Faculty: 8 full-time (6 women), 6 part-time (0 women). Students: 15 full-time (10 women), 168 part-time (122 women); includes 27 minority (21 African Americans, 1 Asian American, 4 Hispanics, 1 Native American), 2 international. Average age 29. 79 applicants, 51% accepted. In 1997, 53 degrees awarded (100% found work related to degree). *Degree requirements:* Comprehensive exams required, foreign language and thesis not required. *Entrance requirements:* GRE or MAT, minimum GPA of 2.7. Application deadline: 8/1 (priority date; rolling processing; 1/2 for spring admission). Application fee: $25. *Tuition:* $168 per credit hour (minimum). *Financial aid:* 39 students received aid; institutionally sponsored loans and career-related internships or fieldwork available. Financial aid application deadline: 4/1; applicants required to submit FAFSA. *Faculty research:* Spiritual values and wellness issues in counseling, stress and professional burnout among counselors, thinking strategies, leadership. • Dr. Margaret Giesbrecht, Dean, 910-893-1630. Fax: 910-893-1999. E-mail: giesbrec@mailcenter.campbell.edu. Application contact: James S. Farthing, Director of Graduate Admissions, 910-893-1200 Ext. 1318. Fax: 910-893-1288.

Canisius College, School of Education and Human Services, Buffalo, NY 14208-1098. Awards MS, MS Ed, CAS, SAS. Part-time and evening/weekend programs available. Faculty: 25 full-time (8 women), 94 part-time (26 women). Students: 514 full-time (346 women), 436 part-time (295 women); includes 23 minority (16 African Americans, 4 Hispanics, 3 Native Americans), 350 international. Average age 27. 608 applicants, 85% accepted. *Entrance requirements:* For master's, GRE General Test. Application deadline: rolling. Application fee: $20. *Expenses:* Tuition $415 per credit hour. Fees $15 per credit hour. *Financial aid:* Graduate assistantships, partial tuition waivers, Federal Work-Study, institutionally sponsored loans, and career-related internships or fieldwork available. Aid available to part-time students. *Total annual research expenditures:* $300,000. • Dr. James M. McDonnell, Acting Dean, 716-888-2548. Application contact: Kevin Smith, Graduate Recruitment and Admissions, 716-888-2544. Fax: 716-888-3290.

Cardinal Stritch University, College of Education, Milwaukee, WI 53217-3985. Awards MA, ME, M Ed, MS, Ed D. Accredited by NCATE. Faculty: 16 full-time, 22 part-time. Students: 1,125. Average age 37. *Application deadline:* 4/1 (priority date; rolling processing). *Application fee:* $20. *Expenses:* Tuition $338 per credit. Fees $25 per semester. *Financial aid:* Federal Work-Study available. Financial aid applicants required to submit FAFSA. • Dr. Tia Bojar, Associate Dean, 414-410-4434. Application contact: Amy Knox, Graduate Admissions Officer, 414-410-4042.

Announcement: Cardinal Stritch University has long been known for its innovative programs in teacher education. The University offers exceptional graduate degree programs in the teaching of reading, special education, computer science education, educational computing, professional development, educational leadership, religious studies, and nursing. The University also offers a doctoral degree in leadership. Most programs are offered on campus, with a few offered off campus in an accelerated format.

Carlow College, Division of Education, Pittsburgh, PA 15213-3165. Offers programs in art education (M Ed), early childhood education (M Ed), early childhood supervision (M Ed), educational leadership (M Ed). Part-time and evening/weekend programs available. Faculty: 5 full-time (all women), 15 part-time (13 women). Students: 87 part-time (81 women); includes 2 minority (both African Americans), 2 international. Average age 36. In 1997, 12 degrees awarded. *Entrance requirements:* Interview, minimum GPA of 3.0. Application deadline: rolling. Application fee: $35. *Financial aid:* Partial tuition waivers, Federal Work-Study, and career-related internships or fieldwork available. Aid available to part-time students. Financial aid application deadline: 3/15. • Dr. Roberta Schomburg, Chair, 412-578-6312. Fax: 412-578-8816. Application contact: Bonnie Potthoff, Office Manager, Graduate Studies, 412-578-8764. Fax: 412-578-8822.

Carnegie Mellon University, Center for Innovation in Learning, Pittsburgh, PA 15213-3891. Offers program in instructional science (PhD). *Expenses:* Tuition $21,275 per year full-time, $295 per unit part-time. Fees $130 per year. *Faculty research:* Improvement of undergraduate education, teaching and learning at the college level. • Dr. John R. Hayes, Director. Application contact: Pamela Yocca, Administrator, 412-268-7675.

Carroll College, Graduate Program in Education, Waukesha, WI 53186-5593. Awards M Ed. Part-time and evening/weekend programs available. Faculty: 6 full-time (4 women), 7 part-time (5 women). Students: 83 part-time (65 women); includes 12 minority (5 African Americans, 6 Hispanics, 1 Native American). Average age 35. *Degree requirements:* Thesis required, foreign language not required. *Application deadline:* 8/15 (priority date; rolling processing). *Application fee:* $25. *Financial aid:* Teaching assistantships and career-related internships or fieldwork available. Aid available to part-time students. Financial aid applicants required to submit FAFSA. *Faculty research:* Qualitative research methods, whole language approaches to teaching, the writing process, multicultural education, gifted/talented learners. • Dr. Bruce Strom, Head, 414-524-7288. Fax: 414-524-7139. E-mail: bstrom@carroll1.cc.edu.

Carson-Newman College, Graduate Program in Education, Jefferson City, TN 37760. Offers programs in curriculum and instruction (M Ed), elementary education (MAT), school counseling (M Ed), secondary education (MAT), teaching English as a second language (MATESL). Accredited by NCATE. Part-time and evening/weekend programs available. Faculty: 18 full-time (8 women), 7 part-time (5 women). Students: 143 full-time (104 women), 88 part-time (65 women); includes 5 minority (4 African Americans, 1 Asian American), 20 international. Average age 31. 54 applicants, 89% accepted. In 1997, 67 degrees awarded. *Degree requirements:* Thesis or alternative required, foreign language not required. *Entrance requirements:* NTE (score in 50th percentile or higher), minimum GPA of 3.0 in major, 2.5 overall. Application deadline: 7/15 (priority date; rolling processing). Application fee: $25 ($50 for international students). *Expenses:* Tuition $190 per credit hour. Fees $10 per year. *Financial aid:* In 1997–98, 139 students received aid, including 6 assistantships; Federal Work-Study also available. Financial aid application deadline: 4/1; applicants required to submit FAFSA. • Dr. Margaret A. Hypes, Chair, 423-471-3461. Application contact: Jane W. McGill, Graduate Admissions and Services Adviser, 423-471-3460. Fax: 423-471-3475.

Carthage College, Division of Teacher Education, Kenosha, WI 53140-1994. Offers programs in classroom guidance and counseling (M Ed), creative arts (M Ed), gifted and talented children (M Ed), language arts (M Ed), modern language (M Ed), natural sciences (M Ed), reading (M Ed, Certificate), social sciences (M Ed). Part-time and evening/weekend programs available. Faculty: 6 full-time (4 women), 13 part-time (8 women). Students: 115 part-time (104 women); includes 5 minority (all Hispanics), 11 international. Average age 35. 24 applicants, 100% accepted. In 1997, 22 master's awarded (100% found work related to degree). *Degree requirements:* For master's, thesis optional, foreign language not required. *Average time to degree:* master's–5 years part-time. *Entrance requirements:* For master's, MAT, minimum B average. Application deadline: rolling. Application fee: $25. *Financial aid:* In 1997–98, 6 students received aid, including 6 teaching assistantships (all to first-year students). • Dr. Judith B. Schaumberg, Director of Graduate Programs, 414-551-5876. Fax: 414-551-5704.

Castleton State College, Department of Education, Castleton, VT 05735. Offers programs in curriculum and instruction (MA Ed), educational leadership (MA Ed, CAGS), language arts and reading (MA Ed, CAGS), special education (MA Ed). Part-time and evening/weekend programs available. Faculty: 9 full-time (5 women), 7 part-time (4 women). Students: 19 full-time (13 women), 52 part-time (35 women). *Degree requirements:* For master's, thesis or written exams required, foreign language not required; for CAGS, publishable paper required, foreign language and thesis not required. *Entrance requirements:* For master's, GRE General Test (minimum

Directory: Education—General

Castleton State College (continued)

combined score of 1000), MAT (minimum score 50), interview, minimum undergraduate GPA of 3.0; for CAGS, educational research, master's degree, minimum undergraduate GPA of 3.0. Application deadline: 7/1 (10/1 for spring admission). Application fee: $30. *Expenses:* Tuition $3924 per year full-time, $164 per credit part-time for state residents; $9192 per year full-time, $383 per credit part-time for nonresidents. Fees $902 per year full-time, $26 per credit part-time. *Financial aid:* Federal Work-Study and career-related internships or fieldwork available. Aid available to part-time students. *Faculty research:* Leadership, assessment, narrative, special education, reading. • Dr. Joyce Cunningham, Chairperson, 802-468-1466. Application contact: Mary Frucelli, Graduate Assistant, 802-468-1441. Fax: 802-468-5237.

Catawba College, Program in Education, Salisbury, NC 28144-2488. Offers language arts (M Ed), mathematics (M Ed). Accredited by NCATE. Part-time and evening/weekend programs available. Faculty: 5 full-time (4 women), 2 part-time (both women). Students: 25 part-time (23 women). Average age 30. 6 applicants, 100% accepted. In 1997, 4 degrees awarded. *Degree requirements:* Comprehensive written exams required, thesis not required. *Average time to degree:* master's–4 years part-time. *Entrance requirements:* NTE, PRAXIS. Application deadline: 8/1 (priority date; rolling processing). Application fee: $15. *Tuition:* $90 per semester hour. *Financial aid:* 1 student received aid; Federal Work-Study and career-related internships or fieldwork available. • Dr. Shirley Haworth, Chair, 704-637-4461. Fax: 704-637-4732.

The Catholic University of America, School of Arts and Sciences, Department of Education, Washington, DC 20064. Offers programs in administration, curriculum, and policy studies (MA); Catholic school leadership (MA); counselor education (MA); educational administration (PhD); educational psychology (PhD); English as a second language (MA); learning and instruction (MA); policy studies (PhD); teacher education (MA). Accredited by NCATE. MA (English as a second language) new for fall 1998. Part-time programs available. Faculty: 13 full-time (8 women), 2 part-time (both women), 14 FTE. Students: 17 full-time (13 women), 38 part-time (30 women); includes 10 minority (6 African Americans, 4 Asian Americans), 2 international. Average age 34. 44 applicants, 68% accepted. In 1997, 15 master's, 3 doctorates awarded. *Degree requirements:* For master's, comprehensive exam required, foreign language not required; for doctorate, 1 foreign language, dissertation, comprehensive exam. *Entrance requirements:* GRE General Test, TOEFL. Application deadline: 8/1 (priority date; rolling processing; 12/1 for spring admission). Application fee: $50. *Expenses:* Tuition $17,325 per year full-time, $668 per credit hour part-time. Fees $680 per year full-time, $360 per year part-time. *Financial aid:* Research assistantships, teaching assistantships, scholarships, full and partial tuition waivers, Federal Work-Study, institutionally sponsored loans, and career-related internships or fieldwork available. Aid available to part-time students. Financial aid application deadline: 2/1. *Faculty research:* Catholic school issues, reflective teaching, cognitive psychology, urban education. Total annual research expenditures: $118,856. • Chair, 202-319-5800. Fax: 202-319-5815.

Centenary College, Program in Education, 400 Jefferson Street, Hackettstown, NJ 07840-2100. Offers instructional leadership (MA). Part-time and evening/weekend programs available. Faculty: 6 full-time (2 women), 3 part-time (0 women). Students: 61 part-time (46 women); includes 4 minority (1 African American, 3 Hispanics), 2 international. *Degree requirements:* Comprehensive assessment. *Entrance requirements:* Interview, minimum undergraduate GPA of 2.8. Application deadline: 8/15 (rolling processing; 1/15 for spring admission). Application fee: $30. *Tuition:* $355 per credit. • Dr. Thomas A. Brunner, Director of Graduate Studies, 908-852-1400 Ext. 2299.

Centenary College of Louisiana, Department of Education, Shreveport, LA 71134-1188. Offers programs in administration (M Ed), elementary education (M Ed), supervision of instruction (M Ed). Part-time and evening/weekend programs available. Faculty: 5 full-time (2 women), 6 part-time (1 woman). Students: 8 full-time (4 women), 154 part-time (118 women); includes 56 minority (52 African Americans, 1 Hispanic, 3 Native Americans). Average age 35. In 1997, 25 degrees awarded. *Average time to degree:* master's–2 years full-time, 4 years part-time. *Entrance requirements:* GRE. Application fee: $30. *Tuition:* $360 per course. *Financial aid:* Career-related internships or fieldwork available. • Dr. E. John Turner, Chairman, 318-869-5223.

Central Connecticut State University, School of Education and Professional Studies, New Britain, CT 06050-4010. Awards MS, Sixth Year Certificate. Part-time and evening/weekend programs available. Faculty: 49 full-time (29 women), 70 part-time (45 women), 71.4 FTE. Students: 184 full-time (146 women), 842 part-time (683 women); includes 63 minority (31 African Americans, 13 Asian Americans, 19 Hispanics), 9 international. Average age 34. 650 applicants, 75% accepted. In 1997, 152 master's, 23 Sixth Year Certificates awarded. *Degree requirements:* For master's, thesis or alternative required, foreign language not required; for Sixth Year Certificate, qualifying exam required, foreign language not required. *Entrance requirements:* For master's, TOEFL (minimum score 550), minimum GPA of 2.7. Application deadline: 6/1 (priority date; rolling processing; 12/1 for spring admission). Application fee: $40. *Expenses:* Tuition $4458 per year full-time, $175 per credit hour part-time for state residents; $9943 per year full-time, $175 per credit hour part-time for nonresidents. Fees $45 per semester. *Financial aid:* Fellowships, research assistantships, Federal Work-Study, and career-related internships or fieldwork available. Financial aid application deadline: 3/15; applicants required to submit FAFSA. • Dr. Richard Arends, Dean, 860-832-2100.

Central Methodist College, Program in Education, Fayette, MO 65248-1198. Awards M Ed. Part-time and evening/weekend programs available. Postbaccalaureate distance learning degree programs offered (no on-campus study). Faculty: 13 full-time (7 women), 4 part-time (1 woman), 13.44 FTE. Students: 51 part-time (39 women). Average age 36. 24 applicants, 88% accepted. *Degree requirements:* Thesis. *Average time to degree:* master's–2 years full-time, 3 years part-time. *Application deadline:* rolling. *Application fee:* $25. Electronic applications accepted. *Tuition:* $2970 per year full-time, $165 per hour part-time. *Financial aid:* Available to part-time students. Financial aid applicants required to submit FAFSA. • Ann Oberhaus, Coordinator of Off-Campus Programs, 660-248-6286. Fax: 660-248-2622. E-mail: aoberhau@cmc2.cmc.edu.

Central Michigan University, College of Education and Human Services, Mount Pleasant, MI 48859. Awards MA, MAV Ed, MS, MSA, Certificate, Ed S. Accredited by NCATE. Faculty: 124 full-time (63 women). Students: 104 full-time (63 women), 389 part-time (268 women); includes 26 minority (15 African Americans, 1 Asian American, 8 Hispanics, 2 Native Americans), 8 international. In 1997, 236 master's, 6 other advanced degrees awarded. *Degree requirements:* For master's, thesis or alternative required, foreign language not required. *Application fee:* $30. *Expenses:* Tuition $139 per credit hour (minimum) for state residents; $276 per credit hour (minimum) for nonresidents. Fees $260 per year full-time, $150 per semester part-time. *Financial aid:* In 1997–98, 2 fellowships, 3 research assistantships (2 to first-year students), 12 teaching assistantships (10 to first-year students) were awarded; Federal Work-Study and career-related internships or fieldwork also available. Financial aid application deadline: 3/7. • Dr. Kelvie Comer, Dean, 517-774-6995. Fax: 517-774-4374. E-mail: 3anhgi@cmich.edu.

Central Michigan University, College of Extended Learning, Program in Humanities, Mount Pleasant, MI 48859. Offerings include education (MA). Postbaccalaureate distance learning degree programs offered. *Entrance requirements:* Minimum GPA of 2.5 in major. Application fee: $50. *Tuition:* $211 per credit hour. • Dr. Ronald Primeau, Director, 517-774-3117. Application contact: Marketing Office, 800-950-1144. Fax: 517-774-2461.

Central Missouri State University, College of Education and Human Services, Warrensburg, MO 64093. Awards MA, MS, MSE, Ed D, Ed S. Accredited by NCATE. Part-time programs available. Faculty: 128 full-time. Students: 156 full-time (109 women), 531 part-time (389 women). In 1997, 256 master's, 17 Ed Ss awarded. *Application deadline:* 6/30 (priority date; rolling processing). *Application fee:* $25 ($50 for international students). *Tuition:* $3288 per year full-time, $137 per credit hour part-time for state residents; $5928 per year full-time, $274 per credit hour part-time for nonresidents. *Financial aid:* In 1997–98, 11 research assistantships, 12 teaching assistantships, 51 administrative and laboratory assistantships were awarded; Federal Work-Study and career-related internships or fieldwork also available. Aid available to part-time students. Financial aid application deadline: 3/1; applicants required to submit FAFSA. • Dr. Jim Bowman, Dean, 660-543-4272. Fax: 660-543-4167.

Central State University, Program in Education, Wilberforce, OH 45384. Offers educational technology (M Ed), leadership (M Ed), literacy (M Ed). Faculty: 3 full-time. Students: 120. *Tuition:* $120 per credit hour for state residents; $206 per credit hour for nonresidents. • Constance Robinson, Coordinator, 937-376-6536.

Central Washington University, College of Education and Professional Studies, Department of Teacher Education, Ellensburg, WA 98926. Offers programs in curriculum and instruction (M Ed), educational administration (M Ed), reading education (M Ed), special education (M Ed). Accredited by NCATE. Part-time programs available. Faculty: 21 full-time (10 women). Students: 10 full-time (6 women), 39 part-time (20 women); includes 2 minority (1 Hispanic, 1 Native American), 1 international. 18 applicants, 78% accepted. In 1997, 29 degrees awarded. *Degree requirements:* Thesis or alternative required, foreign language not required. *Entrance requirements:* Minimum GPA of 3.0. Application deadline: 4/1 (priority date; rolling processing; 1/1 for spring admission). Application fee: $35. *Expenses:* Tuition $4200 per year full-time, $140 per credit hour part-time for state residents; $12,780 per year full-time, $426 per credit hour part-time for nonresidents. Fees $240 per year. *Financial aid:* In 1997–98, 1 research assistantship (to a first-year student) averaging $1,108 per month and totaling $9,972, 1 teaching assistantship (to a first-year student) averaging $1,108 per month and totaling $9,972 were awarded; Federal Work-Study also available. Financial aid application deadline: 2/15. • Dr. Joe Schomer, Chairman, 509-963-1461. Application contact: Christie A. Fevergeon, Program Coordinator, Graduate Studies and Research, 509-963-3103. Fax: 509-963-1799. E-mail: masters@cwu.edu.

Chadron State College, Department of Education, Chadron, NE 69337. Offers programs in business (MA Ed), counseling (MA Ed, Sp Ed), educational administration (MS Ed, Sp Ed), elementary education (MS Ed), history (MA Ed), language and literature (MA Ed), secondary administration (MS Ed), secondary education (MS Ed). Accredited by NCATE. Sp Ed (counseling) admissions temporarily suspended. Part-time programs available. Students: 359. *Degree requirements:* For master's, thesis or alternative. *Entrance requirements:* For master's, GRE General Test (minimum score 350 on verbal section, 410 on quantitative, 390 on analytical). Application deadline: rolling. Application fee: $15. *Expenses:* Tuition $1788 per year full-time, $75 per credit hour part-time for state residents; $3588 per year full-time, $149 per credit hour part-time for nonresidents. Fees $388 per year full-time, $1232 per year part-time. *Financial aid:* Federal Work-Study and career-related internships or fieldwork available. Aid available to part-time students. • Dr. Pat Colgate, Dean, School of Graduate Studies, 308-432-6330. Fax: 308-432-6454. E-mail: pcolgate@csc1.csc.edu.

Chaminade University of Honolulu, Program in Education, Honolulu, HI 96816-1578. Offers social science via peace education (M Ed). Part-time and evening/weekend programs available. Faculty: 8 full-time (6 women), 28 part-time (23 women). Students: 64 full-time (55 women), 119 part-time (76 women). In 1997, 6 degrees awarded. *Degree requirements:* Thesis required, foreign language not required. *Average time to degree:* master's–2 years full-time, 2.5 years part-time. *Entrance requirements:* TOEFL (minimum score 550), minimum GPA of 2.75. Application deadline: 9/15 (priority date; rolling processing; 3/1 for spring admission). Application fee: $50. *Financial aid:* 45 students received aid; partial tuition waivers, Federal Work-Study, institutionally sponsored loans, and career-related internships or fieldwork available. Aid available to part-time students. Financial aid application deadline: 3/1; applicants required to submit FAFSA. *Faculty research:* Peace and curriculum education. • Bryan Man, Director, 808-735-4850. Fax: 808-739-4607. E-mail: bman@chaminade.edu.

Chapman University, School of Education, Orange, CA 92866. Awards MA. Part-time and evening/weekend programs available. Faculty: 10 full-time (8 women). Students: 422. *Degree requirements:* Comprehensive exam required, thesis not required. *Entrance requirements:* GRE General Test (minimum combined score of 900), MAT (minimum score 45), or PRAXIS. Application deadline: rolling. Application fee: $40. *Tuition:* $7020 per year full-time, $390 per credit part-time. *Financial aid:* Application deadline 3/1. • Dr. Jim Brown, Dean, 714-997-6781. Application contact: Saundra Hoover, Director of Graduate Admissions, 714-997-6786. Fax: 714-997-6713.

Charleston Southern University, Programs in Education, Charleston, SC 29423-8087. Offerings in administration and supervision (M Ed), including elementary, secondary; elementary education (M Ed); English (MAT); science (MAT); secondary education (M Ed); social studies (MAT). Part-time and evening/weekend programs available. Faculty: 16 full-time (5 women), 5 part-time (3 women), 17.6 FTE. Students: 175 (151 women). Average age 35. 39 applicants, 90% accepted. In 1997, 60 degrees awarded. *Degree requirements:* Thesis optional, foreign language not required. *Entrance requirements:* GRE or MAT. Application deadline: rolling. Application fee: $25. *Tuition:* $9821 per year full-time, $173 per hour (minimum) part-time. *Financial aid:* Research assistantships, Federal Work-Study, and career-related internships or fieldwork available. *Faculty research:* Economic education, multicultural education, restructuring teacher education, participation in mathematics and science by minorities and women, at-risk children. • Dr. Martha Watson, Director of Graduate Programs, 803-863-7555.

Chatham College, School of Graduate Studies, Program in Education, Pittsburgh, PA 15232-2826. Awards MAT, M Ed. M Ed being phased out; applicants no longer accepted. Faculty: 3 full-time (2 women), 3 part-time (2 women). Students: 20 full-time (18 women), 30 part-time (29 women); includes 5 minority (1 African American, 4 Asian Americans). 57 applicants, 82% accepted. In 1997, 16 degrees awarded. *Degree requirements:* Teaching experience. *Average time to degree:* master's–2 years full-time. *Entrance requirements:* Resume. Application deadline: 8/15 (priority date; rolling processing). Application fee: $35. Electronic applications accepted. *Tuition:* $15,792 per year full-time, $395 per credit part-time. *Financial aid:* In 1997–98, 33 students received aid, including 8 research assistantships (all to first-year students) totaling $40,000, 5 graduate assistantships (all to first-year students) totaling $14,668. Aid available to part-time students. Financial aid applicants required to submit FAFSA. • Dr. Helen Faison, Acting Chair, 412-365-1184. Application contact: Melinda Robbins, Evening and Weekend Studies, 412-365-1155. Fax: 412-365-1720. E-mail: admissions@chatham.edu.

Cheyney University of Pennsylvania, School of Education, Cheyney, PA 19319. Awards M Ed, MS. Accredited by NCATE. Part-time and evening/weekend programs available. Faculty: 5 full-time (3 women), 7 part-time (4 women). Students: 43 full-time (34 women), 257 part-time (179 women); includes 271 minority (265 African Americans, 6 Hispanics). Average age 39. 139 applicants, 100% accepted. In 1997, 121 degrees awarded. *Degree requirements:* Thesis or alternative required, foreign language not required. *Entrance requirements:* GRE General Test, MAT, minimum GPA of 2.75. Application deadline: 8/1 (priority date; rolling processing; 12/15 for spring admission). Application fee: $25. *Tuition:* $3848 per year full-time, $193 per credit hour part-time for state residents; $6616 per year full-time, $346 per credit hour part-time for nonresidents. *Financial aid:* Assistantships, institutionally sponsored loans, and career-related internships or fieldwork available. Financial aid application deadline: 5/1. *Faculty research:* Teacher motivation, critical thinking. • Dean, 610-399-2400. Fax: 610-399-2118.

Chicago State University, College of Education, Chicago, IL 60628. Awards MA, MS Ed. Accredited by NCATE. Part-time programs available. *Entrance requirements:* Minimum GPA of 2.75. Application deadline: 7/1 (11/10 for spring admission). *Tuition:* $2268 per year full-time, $95 per credit hour part-time for state residents; $6804 per year full-time, $284 per credit hour part-time for nonresidents.

Christopher Newport University, Graduate Studies, Department of Education, 1 University Place, Newport News, VA 23606-2998. Offers programs in teaching language arts (MAT), including elementary language arts education, high school language arts education, middle school teaching; teaching mathematics (MAT), including elementary mathematics education, high school teaching, middle school teaching; teaching science (MAT), including elementary science education, middle school teaching. Part-time and evening/weekend programs available. Faculty: 25 full-time (12 women), 1 part-time (0 women). Students: 1 (woman) full-time, 18 part-time (17 women); includes 4 minority (3 African Americans, 1 Native American). Average age 41. In 1997, 10 degrees awarded (100% found work related to degree). *Degree requirements:* Thesis or alternative, comprehensive exam required, foreign language not required. *Average time to degree:* master's–3.5 years part-time. *Entrance requirements:* GRE, minimum GPA of 3.0. Application deadline: 8/1 (priority date; rolling processing; 12/15 for spring admission). Application fee: $40. *Expenses:* Tuition $3474 per year full-time, $145 per credit hour part-time for state residents; $8424 per year full-time, $351 per credit hour part-time for nonresidents. Fees $40 per year. *Financial aid:* In 1997–98, 3 research assistantships (1 to a first-year student) totaling $7,000 were awarded; Federal Work-Study and career-related internships or fieldwork also available. Aid available to part-time students. Financial aid application deadline: 4/1; applicants required to submit FAFSA. *Faculty research:* Early literacy development, instructional innovations, professional teaching standards, multicultural issues, aesthetic education. • Dr. Marsha Sprague, Coordinator, 757-594-7973. Fax: 757-594-7862. E-mail: msprague@cnu.edu. Application contact: Graduate Admissions, 800-333-4268. Fax: 757-594-7333. E-mail: admit@cnu.edu.

The Citadel, The Military College of South Carolina, Department of Education, Charleston, SC 29409. Offers programs in curriculum and instruction (M Ed), educational administration (M Ed, Ed S), guidance and counseling (M Ed), reading (M Ed), secondary education (MAT), special education (M Ed). Accredited by NCATE. Faculty: 12 full-time (3 women), 13 part-time (9 women). Students: 96 full-time (61 women), 337 part-time (231 women); includes 80 minority (76 African Americans, 2 Asian Americans, 1 Hispanic, 1 Native American), 2 international. In 1997, 145 master's, 6 Ed Ss awarded. *Entrance requirements:* For master's, GRE, MAT, or 12 hours of graduate course work with a minimum GPA of 3.0. Application deadline: rolling. Application fee: $25. *Expenses:* Tuition $130 per credit hour for state residents; $260 per credit hour for nonresidents. Fees $30 per semester. *Financial aid:* Fellowships available. • Dr. Robert Carter, Head, 803-953-5097.

City College of the City University of New York, Graduate School, School of Education, Convent Avenue at 138th Street, New York, NY 10031-6977. Awards MA, MS, MS Ed, AC. Part-time and evening/weekend programs available. In 1997, 487 master's awarded. *Entrance requirements:* For master's, TOEFL (minimum score 500). Application fee: $40. *Expenses:* Tuition $4350 per year full-time, $185 per credit part-time for state residents; $7600 per year full-time, $320 per credit part-time for nonresidents. Fees $41 per year. *Financial aid:* Fellowships, research assistantships, teaching assistantships, full and partial tuition waivers, Federal Work-Study, and career-related internships or fieldwork available. Aid available to part-time students. • Oliver Patterson, Acting Dean, 212-650-5354. Application contact: Fareed Suarez, Graduate Admissions Adviser, 212-650-6236.

City University, School of Education, Bellevue, WA 98004-6442. Offers programs in curriculum and instruction (M Ed), education technology (M Ed), ESL counseling (Certificate), ESL instructional methods (M Ed), guidance and counseling (M Ed), school administration (M Ed), school principal (Certificate), special education (M Ed), teaching (MIT). Part-time and evening/weekend programs available. Postbaccalaureate distance learning degree programs offered (no on-campus study). Faculty: 21 full-time (13 women), 301 part-time (162 women). Students: 674 full-time, 1,669 part-time. Average age 37. 820 applicants. In 1997, 651 master's awarded. *Application deadline:* rolling. *Application fee:* $75 ($175 for international students). Electronic applications accepted. *Tuition:* $280 per credit hour. *Financial aid:* Federal Work-Study available. Aid available to part-time students. Financial aid applicants required to submit FAFSA. • Roxanne Kelly, Dean, 425-637-1010 Ext. 3712. Fax: 425-277-2439. Application contact: Nabil El-Khatib, Vice President, Admissions, 800-426-5596. Fax: 425-277-2437. E-mail: nel-khatib@cityu.edu.

Claremont Graduate University, Department of Education, Claremont, CA 91711-6163. Awards MA, PhD, MBA/PhD. Programs in comparative and intercultural studies (MA, PhD), cross-cultural studies (MA, PhD), curriculum and teaching (MA, PhD), evaluation and quantitative analysis (MA, PhD), growth and development (MA, PhD), higher education (MA, PhD), mathematics education (MA), organization and administration (MA, PhD), reading and language development (MA, PhD), teaching/learning process (MA, PhD). PhD offered jointly with San Diego State University; MA (mathematics education) offered jointly with the Department of Mathematics. Part-time programs available. Faculty: 13 full-time (6 women), 13 part-time (10 women). Students: 12 full-time (9 women), 363 part-time (269 women); includes 148 minority (32 African Americans, 31 Asian Americans, 79 Hispanics, 6 Native Americans), 5 international. Average age 35. 81 applicants, 75% accepted. In 1997, 97 master's, 37 doctorates awarded. Terminal master's awarded for partial completion of doctoral program. *Degree requirements:* For master's, thesis or alternative; for doctorate, dissertation. *Entrance requirements:* GRE General Test. Application deadline: 2/15 (priority date; rolling processing). Application fee: $40. Electronic applications accepted. *Expenses:* Tuition $20,250 per year full-time, $913 per unit part-time. Fees $130 per year. *Financial aid:* Fellowships, research assistantships, Federal Work-Study, institutionally sponsored loans available. Aid available to part-time students. Financial aid application deadline: 2/15; applicants required to submit FAFSA. *Faculty research:* Education administration, K–12 and higher education, multicultural education, education policy, diversity in higher education, faculty issues. • David Drew, Chair, 909-621-8075. Application contact: Ethel Rogers, Associate Director, 909-621-8317. Fax: 909-621-8734. E-mail: educ@cgu.edu.

Announcement: Individualized program design is emphasized. PhD and MA concentrations include higher education administration, bicultural educational issues, the teaching/learning process, teacher education, human development, elementary/secondary organization and administration, reading and language development, and policy research. A program combining a California teaching credential and the MA is also available.

Clarion University of Pennsylvania, College of Education and Human Services, Clarion, PA 16214. Awards M Ed, MS, MSLS. Accredited by NCATE. Part-time programs available. Faculty: 39 full-time (20 women). Students: 106 full-time (88 women), 139 part-time (114 women). 272 applicants, 46% accepted. *Degree requirements:* Thesis or alternative required, foreign language not required. *Application deadline:* rolling. *Application fee:* $25. *Expenses:* Tuition $3468 per year full-time, $193 per credit hour part-time for state residents; $6236 per year full-time, $346 per credit hour part-time for nonresidents. Fees $921 per year full-time, $90 per credit hour part-time for state residents; $921 per year full-time, $89 per credit hour part-time for nonresidents. *Financial aid:* Research assistantships and career-related internships or fieldwork available. Aid available to part-time students. Financial aid application deadline: 5/1. • Dr. Gail Grejda, Interim Dean, 814-226-2146.

Clark Atlanta University, School of Education, Atlanta, GA 30314. Awards MA, Ed D, PhD, Ed S. Part-time and evening/weekend programs available. Students: 188 full-time (153 women), 238 part-time (180 women); includes 414 minority (412 African Americans, 1 Asian American, 1 Hispanic), 6 international. In 1997, 124 master's, 11 doctorates, 8 Ed Ss awarded. *Degree requirements:* For master's, 1 foreign language (computer language can substitute), thesis; for doctorate, dissertation. *Entrance requirements:* For master's, GRE General Test, minimum undergraduate GPA of 2.5; for doctorate, GRE General Test, minimum graduate GPA of 3.0. Application deadline: 4/1 (rolling processing; 11/1 for spring admission). Application fee: $30. *Expenses:* Tuition $9672 per year full-time, $403 per credit hour part-time. Fees $200 per year. *Financial aid:* Fellowships, Federal Work-Study, and career-related internships or fieldwork available. Aid available to part-time students. Financial aid application deadline: 4/30. • Dr. Trevor Turner, Dean, 404-880-8504. Application contact: Michelle Clark-Davis, Graduate Program Assistant, 404-880-8709.

Clarke College, Program in Education, Dubuque, IA 52001-3198. Offers educational administration: elementary and secondary (MA), educational media: elementary and secondary (MA), reading: elementary (MA), technology in education (MA). One or more programs accredited by NCATE. Part-time and evening/weekend programs available. Faculty: 8 part-time (4 women). Students: 16 part-time (all women). Average age 31. In 1997, 3 degrees awarded. *Degree requirements:* Comprehensive exam, minimum GPA of 3.25 required, thesis optional, foreign language not required. *Average time to degree:* master's–4 years part-time. *Entrance requirements:* GRE General Test or MAT, minimum GPA of 2.75. Application deadline: rolling. Application fee: $25. Electronic applications accepted. *Expenses:* Tuition $12,688 per year full-time, $315 per credit hour part-time. Fees $240 per year. *Financial aid:* Career-related internships or fieldwork available. Financial aid applicants required to submit FAFSA. • Dr. Margaret Feldner, Chair, 319-588-6397. E-mail: mfeldner@clarke.edu. Application contact: Admissions Office, 800-383-2345. Fax: 319-588-6789. E-mail: graduate@clarke.edu.

Clark University, Department of Education, Worcester, MA 01610-1477. Awards MA Ed. Students: 8 (6 women). 9 applicants, 67% accepted. In 1997, 16 degrees awarded. *Degree requirements:* Thesis or alternative, oral exam required, foreign language not required. *Entrance requirements:* GRE General Test or MAT, minimum GPA of 3.0, professional experience. Application deadline: 2/15 (priority date; rolling processing). Application fee: $40. *Tuition:* $21,300 per year full-time, $2663 per course part-time. *Financial aid:* Fellowships, teaching assistantships, partial tuition waivers, institutionally sponsored loans available. Financial aid application deadline: 5/1. *Faculty research:* Developmental learning, instructional theory, educational program management, special education, urban education. • Dr. Thomas DelPrete, Chair, 508-793-7222. Application contact: Lisa Lemerise, Managerial Secretary, 508-793-7222.

Clemson University, College of Health, Education, and Human Development, Clemson, SC 29634. Awards M Ed, MHA, MHRD, M In Ed, MPRTM, MS, Ed D, PhD, Ed S. One or more programs accredited by NCATE. Part-time and evening/weekend programs available. Postbaccalaureate distance learning degree programs offered. Students: 205 full-time (138 women), 770 part-time (552 women); includes 128 minority (117 African Americans, 1 Asian American, 9 Hispanics, 1 Native American), 20 international. 489 applicants, 69% accepted. In 1997, 293 master's, 23 doctorates, 13 Ed Ss awarded. *Degree requirements:* For doctorate, dissertation. *Entrance requirements:* For master's, TOEFL; for doctorate, GRE General Test, TOEFL; for Ed S, GRE General Test or MAT, TOEFL, 1 year of teaching experience. Application fee: $35. Electronic applications accepted. *Expenses:* Tuition $3154 per year full-time, $130 per credit hour part-time for state residents; $6452 per year full-time, $264 per credit hour part-time for nonresidents. Fees $190 per year. *Financial aid:* Fellowships, research assistantships, teaching assistantships, full and partial tuition waivers, Federal Work-Study, and career-related internships or fieldwork available. Aid available to part-time students. Financial aid applicants required to submit FAFSA. • Dr. Harold E. Cheatham, Dean, 864-656-7641. Fax: 864-656-5488.

Cleveland State University, College of Education, Cleveland, OH 44115-2440. Awards M Ed, PhD, Ed S. Part-time programs available. Faculty: 59 full-time (33 women). Students: 85 full-time (67 women), 756 part-time (574 women); includes 146 minority (126 African Americans, 7 Asian Americans, 13 Hispanics), 4 international. Average age 35. 206 applicants, 40% accepted. In 1997, 313 master's, 4 doctorates awarded. *Degree requirements:* For doctorate, 1 foreign language (computer language can substitute), dissertation; for Ed S, comprehensive exam, internship required, thesis optional, foreign language not required. *Entrance requirements:* For master's, GRE General Test or MAT (score in 50th percentile or higher); for doctorate, GRE General Test, minimum graduate GPA of 3.25. Application fee: $25. *Expenses:* Tuition $5252 per year full-time, $202 per credit hour part-time for state residents; $10,504 per year full-time, $404 per credit hour part-time for nonresidents. Fees $2.25 per credit hour (minimum). *Financial aid:* In 1997–98, 4 research assistantships, 9 teaching assistantships, 2 assistantships were awarded; Federal Work-Study and career-related internships or fieldwork also available. Aid available to part-time students. *Faculty research:* Equity issues (race, ethnicity, gender, and socioeconomics), educational developmental consequences for special needs of urban populations, urban educational programming, adult learning and development, urban educational leadership. • Dr. James McLoughlin, Dean, 216-523-7143. E-mail: j.mcloughlin@csuohio.edu. Application contact: Margaret Gallagher, Director, Student Personnel Services, 216-687-4625.

Announcement: The PhD in urban education was designed to prepare students to effect change in urban educational settings. It is one of the few education doctoral programs in the nation in which special focus on urban education is infused across different specializations. Concepts from education, urban policy planning, law, economics, psychology, public administration, sociology, political science, and organizational development constitute the core content that underpins study in the specialty areas. Graduates of the program play leadership roles as instructors, counselors, administrators, and policymakers in schools, colleges, and universities; business or industry; allied health organizations; social and community agencies; and government. Special features of the program include a cohort group, an urban laboratory, a research emphasis, an interdisciplinary core, an emphasis on organizational change, and advanced study in an area of specialized educational practice. The cohort remains continuously enrolled as an intact unit for two years of intensive study and discussion. The continuing intellectual association and support of a group meets the residency requirement of a doctoral program. The dissertation component follows a traditional model, adhering to the scholarship requirements of research in Doctor of Philosophy degrees.

Coastal Carolina University, School of Education, Program in Education, Conway, SC 29528-6054. Offers early childhood education (M Ed), elementary education (M Ed), secondary education (M Ed). Part-time and evening/weekend programs available. Faculty: 6 full-time (3 women). Students: 3 full-time (2 women), 122 part-time (104 women); includes 19 minority (all African Americans). 54 applicants, 100% accepted. In 1997, 22 degrees awarded. *Entrance requirements:* GRE General Test (minimum combined score of 800), MAT (minimum score 35), teacher certification. Application deadline: 8/15 (priority date; rolling processing). Application fee: $25. Electronic applications accepted. *Financial aid:* Fellowships, staff assistantships available. Aid available to part-time students. Financial aid application deadline: 4/15; applicants required to submit FAFSA. • Dr. Sandra Bowden, Head, 843-349-2606.

Coe College, Department of Education, Cedar Rapids, IA 52402-5070. Awards MAT. Part-time and evening/weekend programs available. Faculty: 8 full-time (5 women), 5 part-time (3 women), 9 FTE. Students: 65. Average age 30. *Degree requirements:* Thesis or alternative, endorsement of teaching expertise in 3 subject areas required, foreign language not required. *Average time to degree:* master's–2 years part-time. *Application deadline:* rolling. *Application fee:* $25. *Tuition:* $300 per semester hour. *Financial aid:* Partial tuition waivers, institutionally sponsored loans available. Aid available to part-time students. • Roger Johanson, Chairperson, 319-399-8510. Fax: 319-399-8667. E-mail: rjohanse@coe.edu. Application contact: Dr. Terry McNabb, Director of Graduate Programs, 319-399-8000. E-mail: pmorgan@coe.edu.

Colgate University, Department of Education, Hamilton, NY 13346-1386. Offers programs in education (MAT), secondary education (MAT). Part-time programs available. Faculty: 10 full-time (5 women). Students: 2 full-time (0 women), 5 part-time (3 women); includes 2 minority (1 African American, 1 Native American). Average age 24. 25 applicants, 24% accepted. In 1997, 6 degrees awarded. *Degree requirements:* 1 foreign language, special project or thesis. *Entrance requirements:* GRE General Test. Application deadline: 3/15 (priority date; rolling processing; 9/1 for spring admission). Application fee: $155. *Expenses:* Tuition $2635 per course. Fees $165 per year. *Financial aid:* Research assistantships, institutionally sponsored loans available. Aid available to part-time students. Financial aid application deadline: 2/1; applicants required to submit FAFSA. *Faculty research:* Multicultural education, moral problem solving, China, Native Americans, gender achievement in mathematics and science. • Dr. D. K. Johnston, Chair, 315-228-7256. Application contact: Joan Thompson, Secretary, 315-228-7256. Fax: 315-228-7857. E-mail: jthompson@mail.colgate.edu.

Directory: Education—General

College Misericordia, Division of Professional Studies, Program in Education/Curriculum, Dallas, PA 18612-1098. Awards MS. Part-time and evening/weekend programs available. Faculty: 4 full-time (2 women), 6 part-time (2 women). Students: 25 part-time (23 women). 12 applicants, 75% accepted. In 1997, 7 degrees awarded. *Degree requirements:* Thesis or alternative required, foreign language not required. *Entrance requirements:* GRE or MAT, minimum GPA of 2.5. Application deadline: 8/1 (priority date; rolling processing). Application fee: $20. *Expenses:* Tuition $13,780 per year full-time, $345 per credit part-time. Fees $740 per year. *Financial aid:* In 1997–98, 2 fellowships were awarded. Financial aid application deadline: 5/1. • Dr. Joseph Rogan, Director, 717-674-6347. Fax: 717-675-2441.

College of Mount St. Joseph, Education Department, Cincinnati, OH 45233-1670. Awards MA Ed. Part-time and evening/weekend programs available. Faculty: 20. Students: 126. *Degree requirements:* Comprehensive exam required, foreign language and thesis not required. *Entrance requirements:* GRE General Test (minimum combined score of 825), minimum GPA of 2.7. Application deadline: rolling. Application fee: $0. *Tuition:* $320 per credit hour. *Financial aid:* Institutionally sponsored loans available. Financial aid application deadline: 6/1. *Faculty research:* Language disorders. • Dr. Barbara Reid, Chairperson, 513-244-4812. Fax: 513-244-4222. Application contact: Jean Abrams, Graduate Secretary, 513-244-4812.

College of Mount Saint Vincent, Program in Education, Riverdale, NY 10471-1093. Offers urban and multicultural education (MS). Part-time programs available. *Application deadline:* rolling. *Application fee:* $50.

The College of New Jersey, Graduate Division, School of Education, Ewing, NJ 08628. Awards MA, MAT, M Ed, Certificate. Accredited by NCATE. Part-time and evening/weekend programs available. Faculty: 32 full-time, 12 part-time. Students: 107 full-time (81 women), 583 part-time (470 women); includes 102 minority (27 African Americans, 10 Asian Americans, 61 Hispanics, 4 Native Americans), 25 international. In 1997, 221 master's awarded. *Degree requirements:* For master's, comprehensive exam required, foreign language and thesis not required. *Entrance requirements:* For master's, minimum GPA of 3.0 in field or 2.75 overall; for Certificate, M Ed. Application deadline: 4/15. Application fee: $50. *Expenses:* Tuition $6892 per year full-time, $287 per credit hour part-time for state residents; $9602 per year full-time, $402 per credit hour part-time for nonresidents. Fees $799 per year full-time, $33 per credit hour part-time. *Financial aid:* Graduate assistantships available. Financial aid application deadline: 5/1; applicants required to submit FAFSA. • Dr. Suzanne Pasch, Dean, Graduate Division, 609-771-2100. Fax: 609-637-5117. E-mail: pasch@tcnj.edu. Application contact: Office of Graduate Studies, 609-771-2300. Fax: 609-637-5105. E-mail: gradstud@tcnj.edu.

College of New Rochelle, Division of Education, New Rochelle, NY 10805-2308. Offers programs in elementary education/early childhood education (MS Ed); gifted education (MS Ed, Certificate); reading/adult communication skills (MS Ed); reading/special education (MS Ed); school administration and supervision (MS Ed, Certificate, PD); special education/therapeutic education (MS Ed), including special education, therapeutic education; teaching English as a second language (MS Ed). Part-time and evening/weekend programs available. Faculty: 11 full-time (6 women), 29 part-time (17 women), 21 FTE. Students: 47 full-time (41 women), 574 part-time (499 women); includes 63 minority (44 African Americans, 1 Asian American, 17 Hispanics, 1 Native American), 6 international. 77 applicants, 82% accepted. In 1997, 324 master's awarded. *Average time to degree:* master's–1.2 years full-time, 2.7 years part-time. *Entrance requirements:* For master's, interview; minimum GPA of 3.0 in field, 2.7 overall. Application deadline: 8/1 (priority date; rolling processing; 4/6 for spring admission). Application fee: $35. *Tuition:* $329 per credit. *Financial aid:* In 1997–98, 40 students received aid, including 8 research assistantships totaling $19,142, 4 assistantships, scholarships totaling $7,842; fellowships and career-related internships or fieldwork also available. Aid available to part-time students. • Dr. Melanie Hannigan, Division Head, 914-654-5330.

College of Notre Dame, Department of Education, Belmont, CA 94002-1997. Offers programs in elementary education (M Ed, Certificate), including educational technology (M Ed), elementary education (Certificate), multicultural education (M Ed); Montessori teaching (M Ed); secondary education (MAT, M Ed, Certificate), including educational technology (M Ed), multicultural education (M Ed), secondary education (MAT, Certificate), teaching art (MAT), teaching biology (MAT), teaching English (MAT), teaching French (MAT), teaching music (MAT), teaching religious studies (MAT), teaching social sciences (MAT). Part-time and evening/weekend programs available. Faculty: 7 full-time, 24 part-time. Average age 29. In 1997, 9 master's awarded. *Entrance requirements:* For master's, TOEFL (minimum score 550), interview, minimum GPA of 2.5. Application deadline: rolling. Application fee: $50 ($500 for international students). *Tuition:* $460 per unit. *Financial aid:* Career-related internships or fieldwork available. Aid available to part-time students. • Dr. Diane Guay, Chair, 650-508-3701.

College of Notre Dame of Maryland, Program in Teaching, Baltimore, MD 21210-2476. Awards MA. *Entrance requirements:* Watson-Glaser Critical Thinking Appraisal, writing test, interview. Application deadline: 3/31 (rolling processing; 1/15 for spring admission). Application fee: $25. *Tuition:* $248 per credit. *Financial aid:* Application deadline 6/30; applicants required to submit FAFSA. • Clifton Osborn, Coordinator, 410-532-5895. Fax: 410-532-5793. Application contact: Irma Kalkowski, Graduate Admissions Secretary, 410-532-5317. Fax: 410-532-5333. E-mail: gradadm@ndm.edu.

College of Our Lady of the Elms, Department of Education, Chicopee, MA 01013-2839. Offers programs in early childhood education (MAT); elementary education (MAT); English as a second language (MAT); general education administration (M Ed); reading (MAT); secondary education (MAT), including biology education, English education, Spanish education; special education (MAT). Part-time programs available. Faculty: 7 full-time (all women), 6 part-time (5 women). Students: 27 full-time (25 women), 178 part-time (147 women); includes 20 minority (6 African Americans, 4 Asian Americans, 10 Hispanics), 2 international. Average age 35. 40 applicants, 83% accepted. In 1997, 35 degrees awarded. *Entrance requirements:* Minimum GPA of 3.0. Application deadline: rolling. Application fee: $30. *Expenses:* Tuition $320 per credit. Fees $40 per year. *Financial aid:* In 1997–98, 4 teaching assistantships (2 to first-year students) were awarded; partial tuition waivers also available. Financial aid applicants required to submit FAFSA. • Sr. Kathleen M. Kirley, Dean of Continuing Education and Graduate Studies, 413-594-2761. Fax: 413-592-4871. Application contact: Dr. Mary Janeczek, Director, 413-594-2761.

College of St. Catherine, Graduate Program, Program in Education, St. Paul, MN 55105-1789. Awards MA. Students: 11 full-time (9 women), 33 part-time (32 women); includes 1 minority (Asian American). Average age 36. 50 applicants, 88% accepted. In 1997, 8 degrees awarded. *Degree requirements:* Thesis required, foreign language not required. *Entrance requirements:* Michigan English Language Assessment Battery (minimum score 90) or TOEFL (minimum score 600), current teaching license, classroom experience, minimum GPA of 3.0. Application deadline: 5/1 (priority date; rolling processing). Application fee: $25. *Expenses:* Tuition $350 per credit hour. Fees $20 per trimester. *Financial aid:* 16 students received aid. Financial aid application deadline: 4/1. • Sr. Jean Dummer, Director, 612-690-6613. Application contact: Office of Admission, 612-690-6505.

College of Saint Elizabeth, Department of Education, Morristown, NJ 07960-6989. Offers programs in education: human services leadership (MA), educational technology (MA). Part-time and evening/weekend programs available. Faculty: 4 full-time (3 women), 7 part-time (3 women). Students: 2 full-time (both women), 83 part-time (81 women); includes 3 minority (1 African American, 2 Hispanics). 23 applicants, 100% accepted. In 1997, 13 degrees awarded. *Degree requirements:* Thesis or alternative, portfolio required, foreign language not required. *Average time to degree:* master's–2.5 years part-time. *Entrance requirements:* Interview, minimum undergraduate GPA of 3.0. Application deadline: 6/30 (priority date; rolling processing; 11/30 for spring admission). Application fee: $35. *Expenses:* Tuition $364 per credit. Fees $455 per year full-time, $70 per semester part-time. *Financial aid:* 13 students received aid; research assistantships, teaching assistantships, Federal Work-Study, and career-related internships or fieldwork available. Aid available to part-time students. Financial aid application deadline: 3/15; applicants required to submit FAFSA. *Faculty research:* Developmental stages for teaching and human services professionals, effectiveness of humanities core curriculum. • Dr. Joan T. Walters, SC, Director of Graduate Program, 973-290-4374. Fax: 973-290-4389. E-mail: education@liza.st-elizabeth.edu.

College of St. Joseph, Division of Education, Rutland, VT 05701-3899. Offers programs in elementary education (M Ed), general education (M Ed), reading (M Ed), special education (M Ed). Part-time and evening/weekend programs available. Faculty: 3 full-time (2 women), 9 part-time (7 women). Students: 15 full-time (10 women), 71 part-time (61 women). *Degree requirements:* Comprehensive exams required, foreign language and thesis not required. *Average time to degree:* master's–4 years part-time. *Entrance requirements:* GRE General Test (combined average 1100), interview. Application deadline: rolling. Application fee: $25. *Tuition:* $7950 per year full-time, $220 per credit part-time. *Financial aid:* Federal Work-Study and career-related internships or fieldwork available. Aid available to part-time students. Financial aid application deadline: 3/1. • Dr. Stan Cianfarano, Chair, 802-773-5900 Ext. 246. Application contact: Steve Soba, Director of Admissions, 802-773-5900 Ext. 206. Fax: 802-773-5900 Ext. 258. E-mail: suite9@aol.com.

The College of Saint Rose, School of Education, Albany, NY 12203-1419. Awards MS Ed, Certificate. Part-time and evening/weekend programs available. Faculty: 40 full-time (24 women), 24 part-time (16 women). Students: 173 full-time (147 women), 696 part-time (579 women); includes 23 minority (11 African Americans, 6 Asian Americans, 5 Hispanics, 1 Native American). Average age 31. In 1997, 374 master's awarded. *Degree requirements:* For master's, thesis or alternative. *Entrance requirements:* For master's, minimum undergraduate GPA of 3.0. Application deadline: rolling. Application fee: $30. *Expenses:* Tuition $338 per credit. Fees $60 per year. *Financial aid:* Research assistantships, partial tuition waivers, and career-related internships or fieldwork available. Aid available to part-time students. Financial aid application deadline: 3/1; applicants required to submit FAFSA. • Dr. Penny Axelrod, Associate Dean, 518-454-5258. Application contact: Graduate Office, 518-454-5136. Fax: 518-458-5479. E-mail: ace@rosnet.strose.edu.

College of St. Scholastica, Program in Education, Duluth, MN 55811-4199. Awards M Ed. Also offered via distance learning. Part-time and evening/weekend programs available. Postbaccalaureate distance learning degree programs offered (minimal on-campus study). Faculty: 9 full-time (5 women), 1 (woman) part-time. Students: 38 full-time (31 women), 293 part-time (230 women); includes 5 minority (1 African American, 3 Asian Americans, 1 Hispanic). Average age 37. In 1997, 105 degrees awarded. *Degree requirements:* Thesis. *Entrance requirements:* Interview, minimum GPA of 3.0. Application deadline: rolling. Application fee: $50. *Tuition:* $7968 per year full-time, $332 per credit part-time. *Financial aid:* 78 students received aid. Aid available to part-time students. Financial aid applicants required to submit FAFSA. • Dr. David Rigoni, Director, 218-723-6109. Application contact: Mary Balow, 218-723-6108. Fax: 218-723-6290. E-mail: mbalow@css.edu.

College of Santa Fe, Department of Education, Santa Fe, NM 87505-7634. Offers programs in at-risk youth (MA), including bilingual/multicultural education, classroom teaching, community counseling, educational administration, leadership, school counseling; multicultural special education (MA). Part-time and evening/weekend programs available. Faculty: 8 full-time (6 women), 18 part-time (13 women). Students: 166 part-time (126 women); includes 83 minority (2 African Americans, 60 Hispanics, 21 Native Americans). Average age 36. 69 applicants, 97% accepted. In 1997, 29 degrees awarded. *Entrance requirements:* Minimum GPA of 3.0. Application deadline: rolling. Application fee: $25. *Expenses:* Tuition $237 per credit hour. Fees $25 per year. *Financial aid:* Scholarships, institutionally sponsored loans, and career-related internships or fieldwork available. Aid available to part-time students. Financial aid application deadline: 3/1; applicants required to submit FAFSA. *Faculty research:* Integrated curriculum, child development, brain research, learning styles, systemic issues in education. • Dr. Barbara Reider, Chair, 800-246-2673. Fax: 505-473-6510.

College of Staten Island of the City University of New York, Department of Education, Staten Island, NY 10314-6600. Offers programs in educational supervision and administration (6th Year Certificate), elementary education (MS Ed), secondary education (MS Ed), special education (MS Ed). Part-time and evening/weekend programs available. Faculty: 9 full-time (3 women), 27 part-time (13 women). Students: 21 full-time (19 women), 674 part-time (574 women); includes 32 minority (13 African Americans, 2 Asian Americans, 16 Hispanics, 1 Native American). Average age 33. In 1997, 327 master's, 36 6th Year Certificates awarded. *Entrance requirements:* For 6th Year Certificate, master's degree, 4 years of teaching experience. Application deadline: rolling. Application fee: $40. *Expenses:* Tuition $4350 per year full-time, $185 per credit part-time for state residents; $7600 per year full-time, $320 per credit part-time for nonresidents. Fees $106 per year full-time, $54 per year part-time. *Financial aid:* Career-related internships or fieldwork available. • Dr. David Podell, Chairperson, 718-982-3725. Application contact: Earl Teasley, Director of Admissions, 718-982-2010. Fax: 718-982-2500.

College of the Southwest, School of Education and Professional Studies, Hobbs, NM 88240-9129. Offers programs in curriculum and instruction (MS), educational administration (MS), educational counseling (MS). Part-time and evening/weekend programs available. Postbaccalaureate distance learning degree programs offered. Faculty: 4 full-time (all women), 6 part-time (2 women). Students: 33 full-time (26 women), 55 part-time (44 women); includes 15 minority (2 African Americans, 11 Hispanics, 2 Native Americans). Average age 39. In 1997, 20 degrees awarded. *Entrance requirements:* GRE General Test (minimum combined score of 1200). Application deadline: 3/1 (priority date; rolling processing; 10/1 for spring admission). Application fee: $50. *Expenses:* Tuition $150 per credit hour. Fees $140 per year. *Financial aid:* In 1997–98, 74 students received aid, including 1 research assistantship averaging $150 per month and totaling $1,500, 51 academic scholarships (15 to first-year students) totaling $40,500; full tuition waivers, Federal Work-Study also available. Aid available to part-time students. Financial aid application deadline: 4/1; applicants required to submit FAFSA. • Dr. Marilyn Smith, Dean, 505-392-6561.

College of William and Mary, School of Education, Williamsburg, VA 23187-8795. Awards MA Ed, M Ed, Ed D, PhD. Accredited by NCATE. Part-time and evening/weekend programs available. Faculty: 33 full-time (13 women), 13 part-time (6 women). Students: 160 full-time (123 women), 209 part-time (163 women); includes 53 minority (32 African Americans, 11 Asian Americans, 9 Hispanics, 1 Native American), 1 international. Average age 35. 395 applicants, 65% accepted. In 1997, 149 master's, 18 doctorates awarded. *Degree requirements:* For doctorate, dissertation required, foreign language not required. *Entrance requirements:* For master's, GRE or MAT, minimum GPA of 2.5. Application deadline: 2/15 (priority date). Application fee: $30. *Tuition:* $5262 per year full-time, $165 per semester hour part-time for state residents; $16,138 per year full-time, $500 per semester hour part-time for nonresidents. *Financial aid:* In 1997–98, 1 fellowship, 47 research assistantships, 92 graduate assistantships (26 to first-year students) averaging $643 per month and totaling $765,848 were awarded; teaching assistantships, Federal Work-Study, institutionally sponsored loans, and career-related internships or fieldwork also available. Financial aid application deadline: 2/15. *Faculty research:* Writing, gifted education, curriculum and instruction, special education, leadership, faculty development, cultural diversity. Total annual research expenditures: $1633. • Dr. Virginia McLaughlin, Dean, 757-221-4300. E-mail: vamcla@facstaff.wm.edu. Application contact: James Patton, Associate Dean, 757-221-4300. E-mail: jmpatt@facstaff.wm.edu.

The Colorado College, Department of Education, Colorado Springs, CO 80903-3294. Awards MAT. Faculty: 2 full-time (1 woman), 26 part-time (20 women). Students: 25 full-time (20 women); includes 2 minority (both Hispanics). Average age 28. 51 applicants, 49% accepted. In 1997, 26 degrees awarded (100% found work related to degree). *Degree requirements:* Thesis, internship required, foreign language not required. *Entrance requirements:* GRE Subject Test, Program for Licensing Assessments for Colorado Educators Basic Skills Test. Application deadline: 3/1. Application fee: $40. *Financial aid:* In 1997–98, 23 fellowships (all to first-year students) were awarded; institutionally sponsored loans and career-related internships or fieldwork also available. Financial aid application deadline: 3/1; applicants required to submit

CSS PROFILE or FAFSA. • Charlotte Mendoza, Chair, 719-389-6474. Application contact: Marsha Unruh, Educational Services Coordinator, 719-389-6472. Fax: 719-389-6473.

The Colorado College, Programs for Experienced Teachers, Colorado Springs, CO 80903-3294. Offerings in humanities for secondary school teachers and administrators (MAT), liberal arts for elementary school teachers and administrators (MAT), Southwest studies (MAT). Offered during summer only. Part-time programs available. *Degree requirements:* Thesis, oral exam, 30-50 page paper required, foreign language not required. *Entrance requirements:* Minimum undergraduate GPA of 2.75. Application deadline: rolling. Application fee: $30.

Columbia College, Department of Educational Studies, 600 South Michigan Avenue, Chicago, IL 60605-1997. Offers programs in elementary (MAT), English (MAT), interdisciplinary arts (MAT), multicultural education (MA), urban teaching (MA). Part-time and evening/weekend programs available. *Degree requirements:* Thesis, student teaching, 100 pre-clinical hours required, foreign language not required. *Entrance requirements:* NTE, minimum GPA of 3.0, portfolio. Application deadline: 7/15 (rolling processing; 12/4 for spring admission). Application fee: $35. *Expenses:* Tuition $392 per credit hour. Fees $170 per year full-time, $150 per year part-time.

Columbia College, Program in Teaching, Columbia, MO 65216-0002. Awards MAT. Part-time and evening/weekend programs available. Faculty: 5 full-time (4 women). Students: 4 full-time (all women), 26 part-time (22 women); includes 5 minority (2 African Americans, 3 Hispanics). Average age 33. 15 applicants, 80% accepted. In 1997, 1 degree awarded. *Degree requirements:* Final project required, foreign language and thesis not required. *Average time to degree:* master's–1.5 years part-time. *Entrance requirements:* Bachelor's degree in related area, minimum GPA of 3.0. Application deadline: rolling. Application fee: $25 ($50 for international students). *Tuition:* $180 per credit hour. *Financial aid:* Federal Work-Study and career-related internships or fieldwork available. Aid available to part-time students. Financial aid applicants required to submit FAFSA. • Chair, Evening and Graduate Division, 573-875-7615. Fax: 573-875-7209. Application contact: Virginia Wilson, Assistant Director, Admissions, 573-875-7339. Fax: 573-875-7506. E-mail: vlwilson@ccishp.ccis.edu.

Columbia International University, Columbia Biblical Seminary and Graduate School of Missions, Columbia, SC 29230-3122. Offerings include education (PhD). MACE offered jointly with Erskine Theological Seminary; PhD offered jointly with the University of South Carolina. Seminary faculty: 36 full-time (3 women), 38 part-time (1 woman). *Application deadline:* rolling. *Application fee:* $25. *Expenses:* Tuition $7410 per year full-time, $285 per semester hour part-time. Fees $150 per year. • Dr. Ken B. Mulholland, Dean, 803-754-4100. E-mail: kenm@ciu.edu. Application contact: Brian O'Donnell, Director of Admissions, 803-754-4100. Fax: 803-786-4209. E-mail: bodonell@ciu.edu.

Columbia International University, Graduate Program in Education, Columbia, SC 29230-3122. Offers curriculum and instruction (MA Ed), educational administration (MA Ed), teaching (MAT). Part-time and evening/weekend programs available. Faculty: 4 full-time, 17 part-time. Students: 115 full-time (69 women). In 1997, 23 degrees awarded. *Degree requirements:* Internships, professional project required, foreign language and thesis not required. *Application deadline:* rolling. *Application fee:* $20. *Expenses:* Tuition $7410 per year full-time, $285 per semester hour part-time. Fees $150 per year. *Financial aid:* Federal Work-Study, institutionally sponsored loans, and career-related internships or fieldwork available. Financial aid application deadline: 2/15; applicants required to submit FAFSA. • Dr. Milt Uecker, Associate Dean for Education Programs, 803-754-4100. E-mail: muecker@ciu.edu. Application contact: Yvonne Miranda, Associate Director of Admissions, 803-754-4100 Ext. 3026. Fax: 803-786-4209. E-mail: yvonnem@ciu.edu.

Columbus State University, College of Education, Columbus, GA 31907-5645. Awards M Ed, MS, Ed S. Accredited by NCATE. Part-time and evening/weekend programs available. Postbaccalaureate distance learning degree programs offered (minimal on-campus study). Faculty: 34 full-time (16 women), 12 part-time (9 women), 38 FTE. Students: 234 full-time (167 women), 271 part-time (210 women); includes 152 minority (140 African Americans, 1 Asian American, 9 Hispanics, 2 Native Americans), 3 international. Average age 36. 189 applicants, 99% accepted. In 1997, 90 master's, 32 Ed Ss awarded. *Degree requirements:* For master's, exit exam required, foreign language and thesis not required; for Ed S, thesis or alternative required, foreign language not required. *Average time to degree:* master's–1.5 years full-time, 3 years part-time; other advanced degree–1 year full-time, 2 years part-time. *Entrance requirements:* For master's, GRE General Test (minimum combined score of 800), MAT (minimum score 44); for Ed S, GRE General Test (minimum combined score of 900), MAT (minimum score 44). Application deadline: 7/10 (priority date; rolling processing; 10/23 for spring admission). Application fee: $20. *Tuition:* $1718 per year full-time, $151 per semester hour part-time for state residents; $6218 per year full-time, $401 per semester hour part-time for nonresidents. *Financial aid:* In 1997–98, 7 research assistantships (3 to first-year students) were awarded; teaching assistantships, full tuition waivers, Federal Work-Study, institutionally sponsored loans, and career-related internships or fieldwork also available. Aid available to part-time students. Financial aid application deadline: 7/15; applicants required to submit FAFSA. • Dr. Thomas E. Harrison, Dean, 706-568-2212. Fax: 706-569-3134. E-mail: harrison_thomas@colstate.edu. Application contact: Katie Thornton, Graduate Admissions, 706-568-2279. Fax: 706-568-2462. E-mail: thornton_katie@colstate.edu.

Concordia University, Graduate Programs in Education, Seward, NE 68434-1599. Awards M Ed, MPE, MS. Accredited by NCATE. Part-time and evening/weekend programs available. Faculty: 30 full-time (5 women), 5 part-time (2 women), 31 FTE. Students: 21 full-time (15 women), 271 part-time (143 women); includes 9 minority (7 Asian Americans, 2 Native Americans), 8 international. Average age 40. 56 applicants, 100% accepted. In 1997, 18 degrees awarded (100% found work related to degree). *Degree requirements:* Thesis or alternative required, foreign language not required. *Average time to degree:* master's–2 years full-time, 5 years part-time. *Entrance requirements:* GRE, MAT, or NTE, minimum GPA of 3.0, BS in education or equivalent. Application deadline: 8/1 (priority date; rolling processing; 12/1 for spring admission). Application fee: $15. *Tuition:* $127 per hour. *Financial aid:* Federal Work-Study, institutionally sponsored loans available. Aid available to part-time students. Financial aid applicants required to submit FAFSA. • Dr. Judy Preuss, Dean of Graduate Studies, 402-643-7475. Fax: 402-643-4073.

Concordia University, College of Education, Portland, OR 97211-6099. Offers programs in curriculum and instruction (elementary) (M Ed), educational administration (M Ed), elementary education (MAT), secondary education (MAT). Faculty: 8 part-time (3 women). Students: 56 full-time (27 women), 12 part-time (8 women). *Application deadline:* rolling. *Application fee:* $35. *Tuition:* $350 per credit. • Dr. Joseph Mannion, Dean, 503-493-6233. Application contact: Dr. Peter Johnson, Director of Admissions, 503-280-8501.

Concordia University, Faculty of Arts and Science, Department of Education, Montréal, PQ H3G 1M8, Canada. Offers programs in adult education (Diploma), child studies (MA), early childhood education (Diploma), educational studies (MA), educational technology (MA, PhD), instructional technology (Diploma). Students: 177 full-time (127 women), 125 part-time (93 women); includes 10 international. In 1997, 45 master's, 3 doctorates, 21 Diplomas awarded. *Degree requirements:* For master's, 1 foreign language required, thesis optional; for doctorate, dissertation, comprehensive exam. *Entrance requirements:* For doctorate, MA in educational technology or equivalent. Application fee: $30. *Expenses:* Tuition $56 per credit (minimum) for Canadian residents; $249 per credit (minimum) for nonresidents. Fees $158 per year full-time, $117 per year (minimum) part-time. *Financial aid:* Career-related internships or fieldwork available. • Dr. R. Schmid, Chair, 514-848-2033. Application contact: Dr. Steven Shaw, Director, 514-848-2044. Fax: 514-848-4520.

Concordia University at St. Paul, Program in Education, St. Paul, MN 55104-5494. Offers early childhood education (MA Ed), elementary education (MA Ed), school-age care (MA Ed). Part-time and evening/weekend programs available. Postbaccalaureate distance learning degree programs offered (minimal on-campus study). Faculty: 13 full-time (6 women), 8 part-time (4 women), 15 FTE. Students: 59 full-time, 8 part-time. Average age 32. In 1997, 3 degrees awarded. *Degree requirements:* Thesis or alternative required, foreign language not required. *Application deadline:* rolling. *Application fee:* $20. *Tuition:* $220 per semester hour. *Financial aid:* Available to part-time students. • Dr. Robert DeWerff, Dean of Graduate and Continuing Studies, 612-641-8277. Fax: 612-659-0207. E-mail: dewerff@luther.csp.edu.

Concordia University Wisconsin, Division of Graduate Studies, Education Department, Mequon, WI 53097-2402. Offers programs in counseling (MS Ed), curriculum and instruction (MS Ed), early childhood (MS Ed), educational administration (MS), family studies (MS Ed), reading (MS Ed). Part-time and evening/weekend programs available. Postbaccalaureate distance learning degree programs offered (minimal on-campus study). Faculty: 13 full-time (5 women), 10 part-time (5 women). *Degree requirements:* Thesis or alternative, comprehensive exam. *Entrance requirements:* TOEFL (minimum score 550), minimum GPA of 3.0, teaching license. *Tuition:* $250 per credit. *Financial aid:* Partial tuition waivers and career-related internships or fieldwork available. Financial aid application deadline: 8/1. *Faculty research:* Motivation, developmental learning, learning styles. • Application contact: Brooke Tireman, Graduate Admissions, 414-243-4248. Fax: 414-243-4428. E-mail: btireman@back.cuw.edu.

Connecticut College, Programs in Education, New London, CT 06320-4196. Offerings in elementary education (MAT), secondary education (MAT). Part-time programs available. *Entrance requirements:* MAT. Application deadline: 2/2. Application fee: $35.

Converse College, Department of Education, Spartanburg, SC 29302-0006. Offers programs in educational administration (Ed S), educational curriculum and instruction (Ed S), elementary education (M Ed), gifted education (M Ed), marriage and family therapy (Ed S), secondary education (M Ed), special education (M Ed). Part-time programs available. Faculty: 35 full-time (20 women), 15 part-time (10 women). Students: 500 (400 women); includes 66 minority (55 African Americans, 5 Asian Americans, 6 Hispanics). Average age 35. 84 applicants, 96% accepted. In 1997, 173 master's, 10 Ed Ss awarded. *Entrance requirements:* For master's, NTE, minimum GPA of 2.5; for Ed S, minimum GPA of 3.0. Application deadline: 5/1 (priority date; rolling processing; 1/30 for spring admission). Application fee: $35. *Tuition:* $185 per credit. *Financial aid:* Research assistantships and career-related internships or fieldwork available. Aid available to part-time students. Financial aid applicants required to submit FAFSA. *Faculty research:* Motivation, classroom management, predictors of success in classroom teaching, sex equity in public education, gifted research. Total annual research expenditures: $50,000. • Dr. Martha T. Lovett, Dean of Graduate Education and Special Programs, 864-596-9082. Fax: 864-596-9221. E-mail: martylovett@converse.edu.

Coppin State College, Division of Education, Baltimore, MD 21216-3698. Offers programs in adult and general education (M Ed, MS), curriculum and instruction (M Ed), special education (M Ed). Part-time and evening/weekend programs available. Faculty: 13 full-time (7 women), 9 part-time (7 women). Students: 19 full-time (16 women), 232 part-time (179 women); includes 225 minority (221 African Americans, 4 Hispanics), 6 international. Average age 35. In 1997, 78 degrees awarded. *Degree requirements:* Thesis or alternative required, foreign language not required. *Entrance requirements:* Minimum GPA of 2.5. Application deadline: 7/15 (12/15 for spring admission). Application fee: $20. *Expenses:* Tuition $140 per credit for state residents; $240 per credit for nonresidents. Fees $504 per year. *Financial aid:* Federal Work-Study, institutionally sponsored loans, and career-related internships or fieldwork available. Aid available to part-time students. Financial aid application deadline: 4/1; applicants required to submit FAFSA. • Dr. Julius Chapman, Chair, 410-383-5530. Fax: 410-669-2861. Application contact: Allen Mosley, Director of Admissions, 410-383-5990.

Cornell University, Graduate Fields of Agriculture and Life Sciences, Field of Education, Ithaca, NY 14853-0001. Offers programs in agricultural education (MAT); agricultural, extension, and adult education (MPS, MS, PhD); biology (MAT); chemistry (MAT); curriculum and instruction (MPS, MS, PhD); earth science (MAT); educational psychology and measurement (MPS, MS, PhD); educational research methodology (MPS, MS, PhD); mathematics (MAT, MS); philosophical and social foundations: educational administration (MPS, MS, PhD); physics (MAT). Faculty: 26 full-time. Students: 89 full-time (57 women); includes 13 minority (3 African Americans, 3 Asian Americans, 3 Hispanics, 4 Native Americans), 12 international. 143 applicants, 40% accepted. In 1997, 38 master's, 16 doctorates awarded. Terminal master's awarded for partial completion of doctoral program. *Degree requirements:* For master's, thesis (MS) required, foreign language not required; for doctorate, dissertation required, foreign language not required. *Entrance requirements:* GRE General Test or MAT, TOEFL. Application deadline: 5/1. Application fee: $65. Electronic applications accepted. *Financial aid:* In 1997–98, 43 students received aid, including 9 fellowships (3 to first-year students), 9 research assistantships (2 to first-year students), 25 teaching assistantships (10 to first-year students); full and partial tuition waivers, institutionally sponsored loans also available. Financial aid applicants required to submit FAFSA. • Director of Graduate Studies, 607-255-4278. Application contact: Graduate Field Assistant, 607-255-4278. E-mail: edgrfld@cornell.edu.

Covenant College, Program in Education, Lookout Mountain, GA 30750. Awards M Ed. Part-time programs available. Faculty: 8 full-time (1 woman), 3 part-time (1 woman), 10 FTE. Students: 59 full-time (33 women); includes 3 minority (2 African Americans, 1 Asian American). Average age 35. 30 applicants, 100% accepted. In 1997, 12 degrees awarded. *Degree requirements:* Comprehensive exams, special project. *Average time to degree:* master's–3 years full-time. *Entrance requirements:* GRE General Test, minimum GPA of 3.0, writing sample, 2 years of teaching experience. Application deadline: 4/1 (priority date; rolling processing). Application fee: $35. *Expenses:* Tuition $240 per semester hour. Fees $123 per semester. *Financial aid:* 13 students received aid. Aid available to part-time students. Financial aid application deadline: 3/10; applicants required to submit FAFSA. • Dr. Jeff Hall, Director, 706-820-1560 Ext. 1412. E-mail: hall@covenant.edu. Application contact: Rebecca Dodson, Assistant Director, 706-820-1560 Ext. 1406. Fax: 706-820-2165. E-mail: dodsonr@covenant.edu.

Announcement: The Master of Education program is a 30-semester-hour program offered with 2 specializations: integrated curriculum and instruction, and educational leadership. Minimum of 2 years' teaching experience in K–12 school settings and the General Test of the Graduate Record Examinations required for admission. Accredited by the Southern Association of Colleges and Schools. Format is nontraditional. Each course consists of a pre-campus phase, an on-campus phase, and a post-campus phase. Pre-campus phase includes significant reading, responses to that reading, and data gathering. On-campus phase takes place during the month of July and consists of intensive in-class course work. Post-campus phase involves exams and projects in which students apply learning to their school settings. Comprehensive exams taken at conclusion of course work. Degree can be completed in 3 years.

Creighton University, College of Arts and Sciences, Department of Education, Omaha, NE 68178-0001. Offers programs in educational administration (MS), guidance and counseling (MS). Part-time and evening/weekend programs available. Faculty: 11 full-time, 5 part-time. Students: 5 full-time (2 women), 33 part-time (24 women); includes 4 minority (2 African Americans, 1 Asian American, 1 Hispanic). In 1997, 24 degrees awarded. *Entrance requirements:* GRE General Test, TOEFL (minimum score 550). Application deadline: 3/1 (priority date; rolling processing). Application fee: $30. *Expenses:* Tuition $402 per credit hour. Fees $536 per year full-time, $28 per semester part-time. *Financial aid:* Teaching assistantships available. • Dr. Timothy Dickel, Chair, 402-280-2820. Application contact: Dr. Barbara J. Braden, Dean, Graduate School, 402-280-2870. Fax: 402-280-5762.

Cumberland College, Graduate Programs in Education, 6178 College Station Drive, Williamsburg, KY 40769-1372. Awards MA Ed, Certificate. Part-time and evening/weekend programs available. Faculty: 4 full-time (2 women), 5 part-time (2 women). Students: 10 full-time (6 women), 101 part-time (74 women); includes 1 minority (Hispanic). Average age 30. 62 applicants, 100% accepted. In 1997, 22 master's awarded. *Degree requirements:* For

Directory: Education—General

Cumberland College (continued)
master's, comprehensive exam required, foreign language and thesis not required. *Average time to degree:* master's–2 years full-time, 3 years part-time. *Entrance requirements:* For master's, GRE or NTE, Kentucky teaching certificate; for Certificate, master's degree, 3 years of teaching experience. Application deadline: 8/26 (rolling processing). Application fee: $25. *Tuition:* $175 per credit. *Financial aid:* In 1997–98, 3 assistantships (all to first-year students) were awarded. • Dr. Martha Johnson, Director, 606-549-2200 Ext. 4432. Fax: 606-539-4490. E-mail: mjohnson@cumber.edu. Application contact: Erica Harris, Admissions Office, 606-539-4241.

Cumberland University, Division of Graduate Studies, Program in Education, Lebanon, TN 37087-3554. Awards MAE. Part-time and evening/weekend programs available. Faculty: 8 part-time (4 women). Students: 14 full-time (5 women), 18 part-time (10 women); includes 1 minority (African American). Average age 35. In 1997, 18 degrees awarded (100% found work related to degree). *Average time to degree:* master's–2 years full-time, 3 years part-time. *Entrance requirements:* GRE, MAT, or NTE. Application fee: $50. *Tuition:* $375 per semester hour. *Financial aid:* Institutionally sponsored loans and career-related internships or fieldwork available. Aid available to part-time students. Financial aid application deadline: 8/1; applicants required to submit FAFSA. • Dr. Adria Karle-Wiess, Head, 615-444-2562 Ext. 1128. Application contact: Stephanie Walker, Director of Admissions, 615-444-2562 Ext. 1120. Fax: 615-444-2569. E-mail: swalker@cumberland.edu.

Curry College, Graduate Program in Education, Milton, MA 02186-9984. Offers programs in adult education (M Ed, Certificate), educational studies in and out of the classroom environment (M Ed), learning disabilities across the lifespan (Certificate), post-secondary learning disabilities (M Ed), reading (M Ed, Certificate). Certificate (learning disabilities across the lifespan, adult education) new for fall 1998. Part-time and evening/weekend programs available. Faculty: 10. Students: 60. *Degree requirements:* For master's, research project required, foreign language and thesis not required. *Application deadline:* 8/1 (priority date; 1/1 for spring admission). *Application fee:* $50. Electronic applications accepted. *Tuition:* $325 per credit. *Financial aid:* Partial tuition waivers and career-related internships or fieldwork available. Aid available to part-time students. *Faculty research:* Learning disabilities, classroom trauma, therapeutic writing, inclusionary practices. • Dr. Jane Utley Adelizzi, Director, 617-333-2130. Fax: 617-333-9722. E-mail: jutleyad@curry.edu.

Daemen College, Program in Special Education, Amherst, NY 14226-3592. Offers education (MS). Part-time and evening/weekend programs available. Faculty: 3 full-time (1 woman), 1 (woman) part-time. Students: 6 part-time (all women). Average age 34. *Degree requirements:* Thesis. *Entrance requirements:* Minimum GPA of 2.85, teaching certificate. Application deadline: 3/1 (priority date; rolling processing; 10/1 for spring admission). Application fee: $25. *Expenses:* Tuition $430 per credit. Fees $13 per credit. *Financial aid:* Available to part-time students. Financial aid application deadline: 2/15; applicants required to submit FAFSA. *Faculty research:* Reading remediation, portfolio and other assessments. • Dr. Patrick J. Hartwick, Chair, 716-839-8349. E-mail: phartwic@daemen.edu. Application contact: Deborah Fargo, Associate Director of Admissions, 716-839-8225. Fax: 716-839-8516. E-mail: dfargo@daemen.edu.

Dalhousie University, School of Education, Halifax, NS B3H 3J5, Canada. Offers programs in continuing education (MA, M Ed), curriculum and special subjects (MA, M Ed), educational administration (MA, M Ed), educational psychology (MA, M Ed), foundations of education (MA, M Ed, PhD). Program being phased out; applicants no longer accepted. Part-time programs available. Faculty: 19 full-time, 12 part-time. Students: 30 full-time (21 women), 67 part-time (53 women). In 1997, 45 master's, 2 doctorates awarded. *Degree requirements:* For master's, thesis required (for some programs), foreign language not required; for doctorate, dissertation required, foreign language not required. *Financial aid:* Fellowships available. • Dr. K. C. Sullivan, Director, 902-494-3724.

Dallas Baptist University, Dorothy M. Bush College of Education, Dallas, TX 75211-9299. Awards M Ed. Part-time and evening/weekend programs available. Faculty: 15 full-time (4 women), 5 part-time (3 women). Students: 34 full-time (31 women), 123 part-time (106 women). Average age 36. 61 applicants, 74% accepted. In 1997, 48 degrees awarded. *Entrance requirements:* GRE General Test, TOEFL (minimum score 550). Application deadline: rolling. Application fee: $25. *Tuition:* $285 per hour. *Financial aid:* In 1997–98, 49 scholarships (19 to first-year students) totaling $78,110 were awarded; Federal Work-Study also available. Aid available to part-time students. • Dr. Mike Rosato, Dean, 214-333-5200. Fax: 214-333-5551. Application contact: Travis Bundrick, Director of Graduate Programs, 214-333-5243. Fax: 214-333-5579. E-mail: graduate@dbu.edu.

David Lipscomb University, Graduate Studies in Education, Nashville, TN 37204-3951. Awards M Ed. Part-time and evening/weekend programs available. Faculty: 8 full-time (2 women), 1 part-time (0 women). Students: 20 full-time (13 women), 34 part-time (27 women); includes 6 minority (5 African Americans, 1 Asian American), 2 international. Average age 33. 22 applicants, 100% accepted. In 1997, 13 degrees awarded (100% found work related to degree). *Average time to degree:* master's–1.5 years full-time, 3.5 years part-time. *Entrance requirements:* MAT (minimum score 25; average 51) or GRE General Test (minimum combined score of 750; average 1010). Application deadline: 8/29 (priority date; rolling processing; 1/16 for spring admission). Application fee: $0. *Financial aid:* In 1997–98, 4 assistantships (all to first-year students) totaling $10,000 were awarded; full tuition waivers, Federal Work-Study also available. Aid available to part-time students. Financial aid applicants required to submit FAFSA. *Faculty research:* Facilitative learning styles, leadership, student assessment, interactive multimedia inclusion. • Dr. Wayne Pyle, Director, 615-269-1000 Ext. 2579. E-mail: pylebw@dlu.edu. Application contact: Jackie Sanders, Administrative Assistant, 615-269-1000 Ext. 2579. Fax: 615-386-7628. E-mail: sandersjd@dlu.edu.

Defiance College, Program in Education, Defiance, OH 43512-1610. Awards MA. Part-time programs available. Faculty: 5 full-time (2 women). Students: 53 part-time (32 women). Average age 28. In 1997, 26 degrees awarded (100% found work related to degree). *Degree requirements:* Thesis required (for some programs), foreign language not required. *Average time to degree:* master's–2 years part-time. *Application deadline:* 8/1 (rolling processing). *Application fee:* $25. *Expenses:* Tuition $255 per credit hour. Fees $25 per semester. • James Brey, Coordinator, 419-784-4010. Application contact: Sally Bissell, Director of Continuing Education, 419-784-4010.

Delaware State University, Department of Education, Dover, DE 19901-2277. Offers programs in curriculum and instruction (MA), education (MA), science education (MA), special education (MA). Part-time and evening/weekend programs available. *Degree requirements:* Comprehensive exam required, thesis optional, foreign language not required. *Entrance requirements:* GRE General Test, minimum GPA of 3.0 in major, 2.75 overall. Application deadline: 6/30 (priority date; rolling processing). Application fee: $10.

Delta State University, School of Education, Cleveland, MS 38733-0001. Awards M Ed, Ed D, Ed S. Accredited by NCATE. Part-time and evening/weekend programs available. Faculty: 22 full-time (8 women), 3 part-time (1 woman), 24 FTE. Students: 95 full-time (62 women), 109 part-time (86 women); includes 87 minority (all African Americans). Average age 33. 95 applicants, 97% accepted. In 1997, 57 master's, 4 doctorates, 3 Ed Ss awarded. *Degree requirements:* For master's, thesis optional, foreign language not required; for doctorate, dissertation required, foreign language not required. *Entrance requirements:* For master's, GRE General Test (minimum combined score of 800) or MAT (minimum score 34); for doctorate, GRE General Test (minimum combined score of 1000); for Ed S, master's degree, teaching certificate. Application deadline: 8/1 (priority date; rolling processing; 8/1 for spring admission). Application fee: $0. *Tuition:* $2596 per year full-time, $121 per semester hour part-time for state residents; $5546 per year full-time, $285 per semester hour part-time for nonresidents. *Financial aid:* Research assistantships, Federal Work-Study, institutionally sponsored loans, and career-related internships or fieldwork available. Aid available to part-time students. Financial aid application deadline: 6/1. • Dr. Everett Caston, Dean, 601-846-4402. E-mail: ecaston@dsu.deltast.edu. Application contact: Dr. John Thornell, Dean of Graduate Studies and Continuing Education, 601-846-4310. Fax: 601-846-4016. E-mail: thornell@dsu.deltast.edu.

DePaul University, School for New Learning, Chicago, IL 60604-2287. Offers program in integrated professional studies (MA). Part-time and evening/weekend programs available. Faculty: 10 full-time (4 women), 15 part-time (8 women). Students: 6 full-time (3 women), 107 part-time (77 women); includes 17 minority (15 African Americans, 1 Hispanic, 1 Native American), 24 international. Average age 42. 53 applicants, 100% accepted. In 1997, 15 degrees awarded. *Degree requirements:* Thesis or alternative required, foreign language not required. *Entrance requirements:* 3 years of work experience, current related employment. Application deadline: rolling. Application fee: $25. *Expenses:* Tuition $320 per credit hour. Fees $30 per year. *Faculty research:* Interactive problem-based learning, liberal learning and professional competence, effective instructional practice. • Dr. Suzanne Dumbleton, Dean, 312-362-8512. Fax: 312-362-8809. Application contact: Dr. Dean Bell, Coordinator, 312-362-8448. E-mail: dbell@wppost.depaul.edu.

DePaul University, School of Education, Chicago, IL 60604-2287. Awards MA, M Ed. Accredited by NCATE. Part-time and evening/weekend programs available. Faculty: 33 full-time (22 women), 60 part-time (42 women). Students: 575 full-time (442 women), 430 part-time (328 women); includes 220 minority (126 African Americans, 36 Asian Americans, 55 Hispanics, 3 Native Americans), 7 international. Average age 30. 457 applicants, 91% accepted. In 1997, 112 degrees awarded. *Entrance requirements:* Interview, minimum GPA of 2.75, work experience. Application deadline: rolling. Application fee: $25. *Expenses:* Tuition $320 per credit hour. Fees $30 per year. *Financial aid:* In 1997–98, research assistantships averaging $500 per month were awarded; teaching assistantships, Federal Work-Study, and career-related internships or fieldwork also available. Aid available to part-time students. *Faculty research:* Reflective teaching, children at risk, loss, ethnicity, urban education. • Dr. Barbara Sizemore, Dean, 312-325-7000 Ext. 1666. Fax: 312-325-7748. Application contact: Director of Graduate Admissions, 312-325-7000 Ext. 1666. E-mail: mmurphy@wppost.depaul.edu.

See in-depth description on page 723.

Doane College, Program in Education, Crete, NE 68333-2430. Offers curriculum and instruction (M Ed), educational leadership (M Ed). Accredited by NCATE. Part-time and evening/weekend programs available. In 1997, 145 degrees awarded. *Degree requirements:* Thesis required, foreign language not required. *Average time to degree:* master's–2.7 years part-time. *Entrance requirements:* Minimum GPA of 2.5. Application deadline: rolling. Application fee: $25. *Tuition:* $135 per credit hour. • Dr. Marilyn Kent Byrne, Dean, 402-826-8604. Fax: 402-826-8278. E-mail: mbyrne@doane.edu. Application contact: Wilma Daddario, Director, Office of Graduate Studies, 402-464-1223. Fax: 402-466-4228. E-mail: wdaddario@doane.edu.

Dominican College of Blauvelt, Division of Teacher Education, Orangeburg, NY 10962-1210. Offers program in special education (MS Ed). Part-time and evening/weekend programs available. *Degree requirements:* Practicum, research project required, foreign language and thesis not required. *Entrance requirements:* Interview. Application deadline: rolling. Application fee: $50. *Expenses:* Tuition $400 per credit hour. Fees $155 per year.

Dominican College of San Rafael, School of Education, San Rafael, CA 94901-2298. Awards MS, Certificate. Programs also offered in Ukiah, CA. Part-time programs available. Faculty: 8 full-time (7 women), 17 part-time (13 women), 14.1 FTE. Students: 180 full-time (141 women), 32 part-time (25 women); includes 22 minority (4 Asian Americans, 16 Hispanics, 2 Native Americans). In 1997, 9 master's awarded (100% found work related to degree); 161 Certificates awarded (100% found work related to degree). *Degree requirements:* For master's, research project required, foreign language and thesis not required. *Average time to degree:* master's–2 years part-time. *Entrance requirements:* For master's, Dominican credential program; for Certificate, California Basic Educational Skills Test, PRAXIS, minimum GPA of 2.7, bachelor's degree in area other than education, 48 units of course work in education. Application deadline: rolling. Application fee: $25. *Expenses:* Tuition $12,816 per year full-time, $534 per unit part-time. Fees $320 per year full-time. *Financial aid:* In 1997–98, 20 students received aid, including 20 tuition discounts totaling $35,500; partial tuition waivers, Federal Work-Study, institutionally sponsored loans also available. Financial aid applicants required to submit FAFSA. • Dr. Barry A. Kaufman, Dean, 415-485-3287. Fax: 415-458-3790.

Dominican University, Graduate School of Education, River Forest, IL 60305-1099. Offers programs in early childhood education (MS), education (MAT), educational administration (MA), special education (MS). Part-time and evening/weekend programs available. Faculty: 9 full-time (7 women), 14 part-time (11 women), 14 FTE. Students: 13 full-time (8 women), 185 part-time (146 women); includes 46 minority (26 African Americans, 19 Hispanics, 1 Native American), 2 international. Average age 35. 143 applicants, 45% accepted. In 1997, 63 degrees awarded. *Entrance requirements:* Minimum B average. Application deadline: 8/15 (priority date; rolling processing; 1/16 for spring admission). Application fee: $25. *Expenses:* Tuition $6120 per year full-time, $1020 per course part-time. Fees $10 per course. *Financial aid:* In 1997–98, 74 students received aid, including 6 fellowships (2 to first-year students) totaling $15,070, 43 teaching assistantships (18 to first-year students) totaling $210,150, 25 scholarships (16 to first-year students) totaling $34,029; institutionally sponsored loans and career-related internships or fieldwork also available. Aid available to part-time students. Financial aid application deadline: 8/15; applicants required to submit FAFSA. *Faculty research:* Governance of private education institutions, reading and language arts, inclusion, organizational planning, leadership and vision. • Sr. Colleen McNicholas, Dean, 708-524-6830. E-mail: educate@email.dom.edu. Application contact: Deborah Davison, Coordinator of Admissions, 708-524-6922. Fax: 708-524-6665. E-mail: educate@email.dom.edu.

Dordt College, Program in Education, Sioux Center, IA 51250-1697. Awards M Ed. Part-time programs available. Faculty: 4 full-time (1 woman), 3 part-time (2 women). Students: 15 part-time (10 women). 6 applicants, 100% accepted. In 1997, 2 degrees awarded. *Degree requirements:* Thesis or alternative required, foreign language not required. *Average time to degree:* master's–3 years part-time. *Entrance requirements:* GRE (score in 68th percentile or higher). Application deadline: 5/15 (priority date; rolling processing). Application fee: $25. *Tuition:* $570 per course. • Dr. Jack Fennema, Director of Graduate Education, 712-722-6226. Fax: 712-722-1185. E-mail: jfennema@dordt.edu.

Dowling College, Graduate Programs in Education, Oakdale, NY 11769-1999. Offerings in educational administration (PD), including computers in education, school administration and supervision, school district administration; elementary education (MS Ed); reading (MS Ed); reading/special education (MS Ed); secondary education (MS Ed); special education (MS Ed). Part-time and evening/weekend programs available. Faculty: 85. Students: 21 full-time (15 women), 1,592 part-time (1,210 women); includes 73 minority (20 African Americans, 12 Asian Americans, 38 Hispanics, 3 Native Americans). Average age 32. In 1997, 440 master's, 33 PDs awarded. *Degree requirements:* Comprehensive exam required, foreign language and thesis not required. *Entrance requirements:* For master's, provisional teaching certificate; for PD, teaching certificate. Application deadline: 9/1 (priority date; rolling processing). Application fee: $0. *Financial aid:* General graduate assistantships, Federal Work-Study, and career-related internships or fieldwork available. Aid available to part-time students. Financial aid application deadline: 4/30. *Faculty research:* Natural readers, Korean styles and learning strategies, mothers of children with disabilities, computers in instruction, cultural background and organizational roadblocks to problem solving. • Dr. Kathryn Padovano, Dean, 516-244-3286. Fax: 516-589-6644. Application contact: Kate Rowe, Director of Admissions, 516-244-3030. Fax: 516-563-3827. E-mail: rowek@dowling.edu.

See in-depth description on page 725.

Directory: Education—General

Drake University, School of Education, Des Moines, IA 50311-4516. Awards MAT, MS, MSE, MST, Ed D, Ed S. Part-time and evening/weekend programs available. Faculty: 21 full-time (9 women), 33 part-time (17 women). Students: 18 full-time (16 women), 397 part-time (282 women); includes 4 minority (1 African American, 2 Asian Americans, 1 Hispanic), 1 international. 304 applicants, 79% accepted. In 1997, 203 master's, 18 doctorates awarded. *Degree requirements:* For doctorate, dissertation. *Entrance requirements:* For master's, GRE General Test (minimum combined score of 1000) or MAT (minimum score 36); for doctorate and Ed S, GRE General Test (minimum combined score of 1000) or MAT (minimum score 43). Application deadline: rolling. Application fee: $25. *Tuition:* $16,000 per year full-time, $260 per hour (minimum) part-time. *Financial aid:* In 1997–98, 14 research assistantships were awarded; career-related internships or fieldwork also available. Aid available to part-time students. *Faculty research:* School transformation, educational technology. Total annual research expenditures: $1 million. • Dr. James P. Ferrare, Dean, 515-271-2736. Application contact: Ann J. Martin, Graduate Coordinator, 515-271-3871. Fax: 515-271-2831. E-mail: ajm@admin.drake.edu.

Drexel University, College of Arts and Sciences, School of Education, 3141 Chestnut Street, Philadelphia, PA 19104-2875. Offers program in science of instruction (MS). Part-time and evening/weekend programs available. Faculty: 2 full-time (both women), 5 part-time (4 women), 3.7 FTE. Students: 11 full-time (7 women), 82 part-time (51 women); includes 20 minority (17 African Americans, 3 Asian Americans), 3 international. Average age 33. 23 applicants, 35% accepted. In 1997, 40 degrees awarded. *Entrance requirements:* GRE, TOEFL (minimum score 570), bachelor's degree in related field. Application deadline: 8/21 (3/5 for spring admission). Application fee: $35. *Expenses:* Tuition $494 per credit hour (minimum). Fees $121 per quarter full-time, $65 per quarter part-time. *Financial aid:* In 1997–98, 1 teaching assistantship, 1 graduate assistantship were awarded; research assistantships also available. Financial aid application deadline: 2/1. • Dr. Fredricka Reisman, Head, 215-895-6770. Fax: 215-895-4999.

Drury College, Graduate Programs in Education, Springfield, MO 65802-3791. Offerings in elementary education (M Ed), gifted education (M Ed), human services (M Ed), middle school teaching (M Ed), physical education (M Ed), secondary education (M Ed). Accredited by NCATE. Part-time and evening/weekend programs available. Faculty: 38 full-time, 20 part-time. Students: 285; includes 26 minority (11 African Americans, 4 Asian Americans, 4 Hispanics, 7 Native Americans), 7 international. Average age 27. In 1997, 74 degrees awarded. *Degree requirements:* Thesis required, foreign language not required. *Average time to degree:* master's–1.5 years full-time, 3 years part-time. *Entrance requirements:* MAT (minimum score 35; average 48), minimum GPA of 2.75. Application fee: $15. *Tuition:* $170 per credit hour. *Financial aid:* Minority fellowshowships and career-related internships or fieldwork available. *Faculty research:* Cultural enrichment, research skills, parental involvement relating to reading skills, reading strategies for mainstreaming children. • Dr. Daniel R. Beach, Director, 417-873-7271. Fax: 417-873-7432. E-mail: dbeach@lib.drury.edu.

Duke University, Graduate School, Program in Teaching, Durham, NC 27708-0586. Awards MAT, MAT/MEM. Accredited by NCATE. Students: 25 full-time (7 women); includes 2 minority (both African Americans), 1 international. 38 applicants, 61% accepted. In 1997, 13 degrees awarded. *Entrance requirements:* GRE General Test. Application deadline: 2/28 (11/1 for spring admission). Application fee: $75. *Expenses:* Tuition $16,632 per year full-time, $693 per unit part-time. Fees $2884 per year. *Financial aid:* Application deadline 12/31. • Rosemary Thorne, Director, 919-684-4353.

Duquesne University, School of Education, Pittsburgh, PA 15282-0001. Awards MS Ed, Ed D, CAGS. Part-time and evening/weekend programs available. Students: 270 full-time, 575 part-time; includes 10 international. 340 applicants, 72% accepted. In 1997, 297 master's, 15 doctorates awarded. *Degree requirements:* For doctorate, dissertation required, foreign language not required. *Average time to degree:* master's–1.5 years full-time, 3 years part-time. *Entrance requirements:* For master's, MAT; for doctorate, MAT, interviews, sample of written work. Application deadline: 8/1 (rolling processing; 12/1 for spring admission). Application fee: $40. *Expenses:* Tuition $481 per credit. Fees $39 per credit. *Financial aid:* Research assistantships, teaching assistantships, partial tuition waivers, Federal Work-Study, institutionally sponsored loans, and career-related internships or fieldwork available. Aid available to part-time students. • Dr. James Henderson, Dean, 412-396-5577. Application contact: Director of Education Services, 412-396-6114. Fax: 412-396-5585.

D'Youville College, Division of Education, Buffalo, NY 14201-1084. Offers programs in elementary education (MS Ed), secondary education (MS Ed), special education (MS Ed). Part-time and evening/weekend programs available. Faculty: 5 full-time (4 women), 8 part-time (2 women). Students: 174 full-time, 81 part-time. Average age 29. In 1997, 44 degrees awarded. *Degree requirements:* Computer language, thesis required, foreign language not required. *Entrance requirements:* Minimum GPA of 3.0. Application deadline: rolling. Application fee: $25. *Expenses:* Tuition $357 per credit hour. Fees $350 per year. *Financial aid:* Scholarships and career-related internships or fieldwork available. Aid available to part-time students. Financial aid application deadline: 3/1; applicants required to submit FAFSA. *Faculty research:* Developmentally disabled, multiculturalism, early childhood education. • Dr. Robert DiSibio, Graduate Director, 716-881-3200. Application contact: Joseph Syracuse, Graduate Admissions Director, 716-881-7676. Fax: 716-881-7790.

East Carolina University, School of Education, Greenville, NC 27858-4353. Awards MA, MA Ed, MLS, MS, MSA, Ed D, CAS, Ed S. Accredited by NCATE. Part-time and evening/weekend programs available. Faculty: 42 full-time (17 women), 1 part-time (0 women). Students: 140 full-time (97 women), 387 part-time (304 women); includes 92 minority (88 African Americans, 2 Asian Americans, 1 Hispanic, 1 Native American). Average age 35. 369 applicants, 76% accepted. In 1997, 193 master's, 4 doctorates, 17 other advanced degrees awarded. *Degree requirements:* For master's, comprehensive exams; for doctorate, dissertation. *Entrance requirements:* For doctorate, master's degree. Application deadline: rolling. Application fee: $40. *Tuition:* $1886 per year full-time, $472 per semester (minimum) part-time for state residents; $9156 per year full-time, $2289 per semester (minimum) part-time for nonresidents. *Financial aid:* Research assistantships, teaching assistantships, Federal Work-Study available. Aid available to part-time students. Financial aid application deadline: 6/1. • Dr. Marilyn Sheerer, Dean, 252-328-6172. Application contact: Dr. Paul D. Tschetter, Associate Dean, 252-328-6012. Fax: 252-328-6071. E-mail: grad@mail.ecu.edu.

East Central University, Department of Education, Ada, OK 74820-6899. Awards M Ed. Accredited by NCATE. Evening/weekend programs available. Faculty: 34 part-time (14 women). Students: 68 full-time (47 women), 215 part-time (150 women); includes 34 minority (3 African Americans, 1 Hispanic, 30 Native Americans), 1 international. Average age 35. 145 applicants, 99% accepted. In 1997, 101 degrees awarded. *Entrance requirements:* Minimum GPA of 2.5. Application fee: $0 ($50 for international students). *Expenses:* Tuition $75 per semester hour for state residents; $177 per semester hour for nonresidents. Fees $39 per year full-time, $31 per year part-time. *Financial aid:* Fellowships, partial tuition waivers, and career-related internships or fieldwork available. Aid available to part-time students. • Dr. Kenneth Moore, Dean, 405-332-8000.

Eastern College, Graduate Education Programs, St. Davids, PA 19087-3696. Offerings in English as a second or foreign language (Certificate), multicultural education (M Ed), school health services (M Ed). Part-time programs available. Faculty: 8 full-time (6 women), 23 part-time (11 women). In 1997, 51 master's awarded. *Entrance requirements:* For master's, TOEFL, minimum GPA of 2.5. Application deadline: rolling. Application fee: $35. *Financial aid:* Research assistantships, teaching assistantships, and career-related internships or fieldwork available. Aid available to part-time students. • Dr. Helen Loeb, Director, 610-341-5943. Application contact: Megan Miscioscia, Graduate Admissions Representative, 610-341-5972. Fax: 610-341-1466.

See in-depth description on page 727.

Eastern Connecticut State University, School of Education and Professional Studies/Graduate Division, Willimantic, CT 06226-2295. Awards MS. Part-time and evening/weekend programs available. Faculty: 17 full-time (11 women), 9 part-time (6 women). Students: 14 full-time (8 women), 183 part-time (152 women); includes 7 minority (4 African Americans, 2 Hispanics, 1 Native American), 2 international. Average age 36. 60 applicants, 100% accepted. In 1997, 62 degrees awarded. *Degree requirements:* Comprehensive exam or thesis required, foreign language not required. *Entrance requirements:* Minimum GPA of 2.7. Application fee: $40. *Expenses:* Tuition $2632 per year full-time, $175 per credit hour part-time for state residents; $7220 per year full-time, $175 per credit hour part-time for nonresidents. Fees $1851 per year full-time, $20 per semester part-time for state residents; $2748 per year full-time, $20 per semester part-time for nonresidents. *Financial aid:* Fellowships, research assistantships, teaching assistantships, administrative assistantships, and career-related internships or fieldwork available. Aid available to part-time students. Financial aid application deadline: 3/15. • Dr. David Stoloff, Interim Dean, 860-465-5293. Fax: 860-465-4538. E-mail: stoloffd@ecsuc.ctstateu.edu. Application contact: Edith Mavor, Graduate Division Director, 860-465-4543. E-mail: mavor@ecsuc.ctstateu.edu.

Eastern Illinois University, College of Education and Professional Studies, 600 Lincoln Avenue, Charleston, IL 61920-3099. Awards MS, MS Ed, Ed S. Accredited by NCATE. Part-time and evening/weekend programs available. Faculty: 38 full-time (20 women). Students: 158 full-time (99 women), 515 part-time (380 women); includes 35 minority (32 African Americans, 1 Asian American, 2 Hispanics). In 1997, 236 master's, 22 Ed Ss awarded. *Degree requirements:* For Ed S, thesis required, foreign language not required. *Application deadline:* 7/31 (priority date; rolling processing). *Application fee:* $25. *Expenses:* Tuition $3459 per year full-time, $96 per semester hour part-time for state residents; $10,377 per year full-time, $288 per semester hour part-time for nonresidents. Fees $1566 per year full-time, $37 per semester hour part-time. *Financial aid:* In 1997–98, 12 research assistantships, 13 teaching assistantships were awarded; Federal Work-Study and career-related internships or fieldwork also available. Aid available to part-time students. • Dr. Elizabeth Hitch, Dean, 217-581-2524. Fax: 217-581-2518. E-mail: cfejh@eiu.edu.

Eastern Kentucky University, College of Education, Richmond, KY 40475-3101. Awards MA, MA Ed, Ed S. Accredited by NCATE. Part-time programs available. Postbaccalaureate distance learning degree programs offered (minimal on-campus study). Faculty: 45. In 1997, 197 master's awarded. *Degree requirements:* For Ed S, thesis, research project. *Entrance requirements:* GRE General Test, minimum GPA of 2.5. Application fee: $0. *Tuition:* $2390 per year full-time, $133 per credit hour part-time for state residents; $6630 per year full-time, $365 per credit hour part-time for nonresidents. *Financial aid:* Fellowships, research assistantships, teaching assistantships, scholarships, Federal Work-Study, and career-related internships or fieldwork available. Aid available to part-time students. • Dr. Kenneth Henson, Dean, 606-622-3515.

Eastern Mennonite University, Program in Education, Harrisonburg, VA 22802-2462. Awards MA. Part-time programs available. Faculty: 12 part-time (6 women), 1.5 FTE. Students: 44 part-time (39 women); includes 2 minority (1 Asian American, 1 Hispanic), 1 international. Average age 35. 18 applicants, 100% accepted. *Degree requirements:* Practicum, research projects required, foreign language and thesis not required. *Average time to degree:* master's–2 years full-time, 6 years part-time. *Entrance requirements:* NTE, 2 years of teaching experience, interview. Application deadline: rolling. Application fee: $25. *Tuition:* $250 per credit hour. *Financial aid:* 8 students received aid; Federal Work-Study available. Aid available to part-time students. Financial aid application deadline: 4/15; applicants required to submit FAFSA. *Faculty research:* Literacy, multicultural communication, at-risk populations, peace education, teaching English as a second language. • Judy H. Mullet, Director, 540-432-4146. E-mail: mulletjh@emu.edu. Application contact: Beth Bergman, Administrative Assistant, 540-432-4350. Fax: 540-432-4444. E-mail: bergmane@emu.edu.

Eastern Michigan University, College of Education, Ypsilanti, MI 48197. Awards MA, MS, Ed D, SPA. Accredited by NCATE. Part-time and evening/weekend programs available. Faculty: 116 full-time (65 women). Students: 364 full-time (272 women), 1,123 part-time (906 women). 666 applicants, 56% accepted. In 1997, 432 master's, 5 doctorates, 11 SPAs awarded. *Degree requirements:* For doctorate, dissertation required, foreign language not required. *Entrance requirements:* For master's, GRE, TOEFL; for doctorate, GRE General Test (score in 55th percentile or higher). Application deadline: 5/15 (priority date; rolling processing; 3/15 for spring admission). Application fee: $30. *Expenses:* Tuition $2691 per year full-time, $150 per credit hour part-time for state residents; $6300 per year full-time, $350 per credit hour part-time for nonresidents. Fees $368 per year full-time, $88 per semester (minimum) part-time. *Financial aid:* Fellowships, teaching assistantships, Federal Work-Study, and career-related internships or fieldwork available. Aid available to part-time students. Financial aid application deadline: 3/15; applicants required to submit FAFSA. • Dr. Jerry Robbins, Dean, 734-487-1414.

Eastern Nazarene College, Graduate Studies, Division of Education, Quincy, MA 02170-2999. Offers programs in bilingual education (M Ed, Certificate), early childhood education (M Ed, Certificate), elementary education (M Ed, Certificate), English as a second language (M Ed, Certificate), instructional enrichment and development (M Ed, Certificate), middle school education (M Ed, Certificate), moderate special needs education (M Ed, Certificate), music education (M Ed, Certificate), physical education (M Ed, Certificate), principal (Certificate), program development and supervision (M Ed, Certificate), secondary education (M Ed, Certificate), special education administrator (Certificate), supervisor (Certificate), teacher of reading (M Ed, Certificate). M Ed and Certificate also available through weekend program for administration, special needs, and reading only. Part-time and evening/weekend programs available. Faculty: 9 full-time (5 women), 11 part-time (5 women). Students: 28 full-time (20 women), 72 part-time (55 women); includes 15 minority (9 African Americans, 3 Asian Americans, 3 Hispanics), 4 international. Average age 35. 20 applicants, 100% accepted. In 1997, 2 master's awarded. *Entrance requirements:* For master's, TOEFL (minimum score 500). Application deadline: rolling. Application fee: $35. *Expenses:* Tuition $350 per credit. Fees $125 per semester full-time, $15 per semester part-time. *Financial aid:* Scholarships and career-related internships or fieldwork available. Aid available to part-time students. Financial aid applicants required to submit FAFSA. • Dr. Lorne Ranstrom, Chair, 617-745-3528. Application contact: Cleo P. Cakridas, Graduate Enrollment Counselor, 617-745-3870. Fax: 617-745-3907. E-mail: cakridac@enc.edu.

Eastern New Mexico University, College of Education and Technology, School of Education, Portales, NM 88130. Offers programs in counseling and guidance (M Ed), education (M Ed), special education (M Sp Ed). Part-time programs available. Faculty: 10 full-time (8 women), 8 part-time (3 women). Students: 32 full-time (24 women), 105 part-time (76 women); includes 33 minority (3 African Americans, 2 Asian Americans, 26 Hispanics, 2 Native Americans), 1 international. 17 applicants, 94% accepted. In 1997, 50 degrees awarded. *Degree requirements:* Thesis optional, foreign language not required. *Entrance requirements:* Minimum GPA of 2.5. Application deadline: rolling. Application fee: $10. *Tuition:* $1956 per year full-time, $82 per credit hour part-time for state residents; $6702 per year full-time, $280 per credit hour part-time for nonresidents. *Financial aid:* In 1997–98, 11 research assistantships (5 to first-year students), 4 teaching assistantships (3 to first-year students) were awarded; fellowships, Federal Work-Study, and career-related internships or fieldwork also available. Aid available to part-time students. Financial aid application deadline: 4/1. • Dr. Sherrie Bettenhausen, Graduate Coordinator, 505-562-2603.

Eastern Oregon University, School of Education, La Grande, OR 97850-2899. Awards MTE. Part-time programs available. Postbaccalaureate distance learning degree programs offered (minimal on-campus study). Faculty: 10 full-time (3 women), 12 part-time (6 women). Students: 66 full-time (46 women), 118 part-time (73 women); includes 9 minority (8 Hispanics, 1 Native American). Average age 28. 148 applicants, 60% accepted. In 1997, 35 degrees awarded. *Degree requirements:* Thesis required, foreign language not required. *Average time to degree:*

Directory: Education—General

Eastern Oregon University (continued)

master's–1 year full-time. *Entrance requirements:* NTE. Application deadline: 1/15 (priority date; rolling processing). Application fee: $50. *Expenses:* Tuition $4371 per year for state residents; $8379 per year for nonresidents. Fees $957 per year. *Financial aid:* Full and partial tuition waivers, Federal Work-Study available. Aid available to part-time students. • Dr. R. Doyle Slater, Director of Teacher Education, 541-962-3772. E-mail: dslater@eou.edu. Application contact: Dr. Margo Mack, Professor of Education, 541-962-3586. Fax: 541-962-3701. E-mail: mmack@eou.edu.

Eastern Washington University, College of Education and Human Development, Cheney, WA 99004-2431. Awards MA, M Ed, MS. Accredited by NCATE. Part-time programs available. Faculty: 54 full-time (12 women). Students: 160 full-time (108 women), 84 part-time (58 women); includes 15 minority (2 African Americans, 4 Asian Americans, 6 Hispanics, 3 Native Americans), 4 international. 217 applicants, 73% accepted. In 1997, 109 degrees awarded. *Degree requirements:* Comprehensive exam. *Entrance requirements:* Minimum GPA of 3.0. Application deadline: rolling. Application fee: $35. *Tuition:* $4200 per year full-time, $140 per credit part-time for state residents; $12,780 per year full-time, $415 per credit part-time for nonresidents. *Financial aid:* Research assistantships, teaching assistantships, Federal Work-Study, institutionally sponsored loans, and career-related internships or fieldwork available. Financial aid application deadline: 2/1. • Dr. Phyllis Edmundson, Dean, 509-359-2328.

East Stroudsburg University of Pennsylvania, School of Professional Studies, East Stroudsburg, PA 18301-2999. Awards M Ed. Part-time and evening/weekend programs available. *Degree requirements:* Comprehensive exam required, foreign language and thesis not required. *Application deadline:* 7/31 (priority date; rolling processing; 11/30 for spring admission). *Application fee:* $15 ($25 for international students). *Expenses:* Tuition $3468 per year full-time, $193 per credit part-time for state residents; $6236 per year full-time, $346 per credit part-time for nonresidents. Fees $700 per year full-time, $39 per credit part-time.

East Tennessee State University, College of Education, Johnson City, TN 37614-0734. Awards MA, MAT, M Ed, Ed D, Ed S. Accredited by NCATE. Part-time and evening/weekend programs available. Faculty: 53 full-time (16 women). Students: 240 full-time (173 women), 298 part-time (218 women); includes 30 minority (23 African Americans, 3 Asian Americans, 3 Hispanics, 1 Native American), 11 international. Average age 35. 225 applicants, 61% accepted. In 1997, 161 master's, 23 doctorates, 7 Ed Ss awarded. Terminal master's awarded for partial completion of doctoral program. *Degree requirements:* For doctorate, dissertation, oral and written exams required, foreign language not required; for Ed S, internship, practicum required, foreign language and thesis not required. *Entrance requirements:* For master's, TOEFL (minimum score 550); for doctorate, GRE General Test, GRE Subject Test, TOEFL (minimum score 550); for Ed S, GRE General Test, TOEFL (minimum score 550), teacher certification. Application deadline: 7/15 (priority date; rolling processing). Application fee: $25 ($35 for international students). *Tuition:* $2944 per year full-time, $158 per credit hour part-time for state residents; $7770 per year full-time, $369 per credit hour part-time for nonresidents. *Financial aid:* In 1997–98, 10 fellowships (5 to first-year students), 33 research assistantships (18 to first-year students), 5 teaching assistantships (1 to a first-year student), 10 assistantships, grants (6 to first-year students) were awarded; Federal Work-Study, institutionally sponsored loans, and career-related internships or fieldwork also available. • Dr. Martha Collins, Dean, 423-439-4444. E-mail: collinsm@etsu-tn.edu. Application contact: Dr. Hal Knight, Associate Dean, 423-439-4444. Fax: 423-439-5764. E-mail: knighth@etsu-tn.edu.

Edgewood College, Program in Education, Madison, WI 53711-1998. Offers director of instruction (Certificate), director of special education and pupil services (Certificate), education (MA Ed), educational administration (MA), emotional disturbances (MA, Certificate), learning disabilities (MA, Certificate), learning disabilities and emotional disturbances (MA, Certificate), school business administration (Certificate), school principalship K-12 (Certificate). One or more programs accredited by NCATE. Faculty: 6 full-time (3 women), 3 part-time (0 women), 7 FTE. Students: 145. In 1997, 23 master's awarded. *Degree requirements:* For master's, practicum, research project required, foreign language and thesis not required. *Application deadline:* 8/1 (priority date; rolling processing). *Application fee:* $25. *Tuition:* $330 per credit. • Dr. Joseph Schmiedicke, Chair, 608-257-4861 Ext. 2293. Application contact: Sr. Lucille Marie Frost, Assistant Dean of Graduate Programs, 608-254-4861 Ext. 2382. Fax: 608-257-1455.

Edinboro University of Pennsylvania, School of Education, Edinboro, PA 16444. Awards MA, M Ed, Certificate. Evening/weekend programs available. Faculty: 36 full-time (22 women). Students: 139 full-time (108 women), 229 part-time (170 women); includes 13 minority (11 African Americans, 1 Asian American, 1 Hispanic), 2 international. Average age 32. In 1997, 137 master's, 27 Certificates awarded. *Entrance requirements:* For master's, GRE or MAT (score in 30th percentile or higher). Application deadline: rolling. Application fee: $25. *Expenses:* Tuition $3468 per year full-time, $193 per credit part-time for state residents; $6236 per year full-time, $346 per credit part-time for nonresidents. Fees $898 per year full-time, $50 per semester (minimum) part-time. *Financial aid:* In 1997–98, 64 assistantships were awarded; career-related internships or fieldwork also available. Aid available to part-time students. • Application contact: Dr. Philip Kerstetter, Dean of Graduate Studies, 814-732-2856. Fax: 814-732-2611. E-mail: kerstetter@edinboro.edu.

Elmira College, Graduate Programs in Education, Program in General Education, Elmira, NY 14901. Awards MS Ed. Part-time and evening/weekend programs available. Faculty: 20 full-time (7 women), 31 part-time (12 women). Students: 74. *Degree requirements:* Thesis or alternative required, foreign language not required. *Application fee:* $35. *Tuition:* $344 per credit hour. *Financial aid:* Career-related internships or fieldwork available. Aid available to part-time students. • Dr. John Madison, Director of Education, 607-735-1912. Application contact: Judith B. Clack, Associate Dean for Graduate Studies, 607-735-1825.

Elon College, Program in Education, Elon College, NC 27244. Offers elementary education (M Ed), special education (M Ed). Accredited by NCATE. Part-time and evening/weekend programs available. Faculty: 15 full-time (10 women). Students: 8 full-time (6 women), 84 part-time (71 women); includes 6 minority (5 African Americans, 1 Hispanic). Average age 32. 61 applicants, 97% accepted. In 1997, 10 degrees awarded. *Entrance requirements:* GRE, MAT, NTE (special education). Application deadline: 8/15 (priority date; rolling processing). Application fee: $25. *Tuition:* $210 per credit hour. *Financial aid:* 7 students received aid. Aid available to part-time students. Financial aid application deadline: 8/1; applicants required to submit FAFSA. *Faculty research:* Teaching reading to low-achieving second and third graders, pre- and post-student teaching attitudes toward teaching, children's writing, whole language methodology, critical creative thinking. • Dr. Glenda W. Beamon, Director, 336-584-2126. Fax: 336-538-2609. E-mail: beamon@vax1.elon.edu. Application contact: Alice N. Essen, Director of Graduate Admissions, 800-334-8448. Fax: 336-538-3986. E-mail: essen@numen.elon.edu.

Emmanuel College, Programs in Education, Boston, MA 02115. Awards MAT. *Entrance requirements:* GRE General Test or MAT, interview. Application deadline: 9/7 (priority date; rolling processing). Application fee: $50. *Financial aid:* Federal Work-Study and career-related internships or fieldwork available. Aid available to part-time students. *Faculty research:* Literature/reading, history of education, multicultural education, special education. • Dr. Rosemary Barton Tobin, Chair, 617-735-9955. Fax: 617-735-9877. Application contact: Lorene Ashton-Reed, Graduate Program Assistant, 617-735-9844.

Emory University, Graduate School of Arts and Sciences, Division of Educational Studies, Atlanta, GA 30322-1100. Offers programs in early childhood teaching (MAT, M Ed), educational studies (MA, PhD, DAST), middle grades teaching (MAT, M Ed), secondary teaching (MAT, M Ed). Faculty: 13. Students: 31 full-time (22 women), 24 part-time (19 women); includes 21 minority (19 African Americans, 2 Asian Americans), 3 international. 91 applicants, 53% accepted. In 1997, 22 master's, 2 doctorates, 4 DASTs awarded. Terminal master's awarded for partial completion of doctoral program. *Degree requirements:* For master's, thesis required, foreign language not required; for doctorate, dissertation, comprehensive exams required, foreign language not required. *Entrance requirements:* For master's and doctorate, GRE General Test, TOEFL, minimum GPA of 3.0. Application deadline: 1/20 (3/15 for spring admission). Application fee: $45. *Expenses:* Tuition $21,770 per year. Fees $300 per year. *Financial aid:* In 1997–98, 10 fellowships (4 to first-year students) averaging $1,060 per month and totaling $106,000, tuition scholarships totaling $872,540 were awarded; research assistantships, teaching assistantships, full and partial tuition waivers, and career-related internships or fieldwork also available. Financial aid application deadline: 1/20. *Faculty research:* Educational policy, educational measurement and evaluation, urban and multicultural education, environmental science, social science education. • Dr. Robert Jensen, Acting Director, 404-727-0606. Fax: 404-727-2799. E-mail: rjensen@emory.edu. Application contact: Dr. Glen Avant, Program Development Coordinator, 404-727-0612.

See in-depth description on page 729.

Emporia State University, School of Graduate Studies, The Teachers College, Emporia, KS 66801-5087. Awards MS, Ed S. Accredited by NCATE. Part-time programs available. Postbaccalaureate distance learning degree programs offered. Faculty: 60 full-time (30 women), 32 part-time (21 women). Students: 178 full-time (133 women), 217 part-time (170 women); includes 19 minority (8 African Americans, 3 Asian Americans, 7 Hispanics, 1 Native American), 7 international. 152 applicants, 67% accepted. In 1997, 189 master's, 2 Ed Ss awarded. *Degree requirements:* For master's, comprehensive exam or thesis required, foreign language not required; for Ed S, thesis or alternative required, foreign language not required. *Entrance requirements:* For master's, GRE General Test or MAT, TOEFL (minimum score 550); for Ed S, GRE Subject Test. Application deadline: rolling. Application fee: $30 ($75 for international students). Electronic applications accepted. *Tuition:* $2300 per year full-time, $103 per credit hour part-time for state residents; $6012 per year full-time, $258 per credit hour part-time for nonresidents. *Financial aid:* In 1997–98, 4 fellowships averaging $667 per month, 6 research assistantships averaging $558 per month, 34 teaching assistantships averaging $522 per month were awarded; Federal Work-Study, institutionally sponsored loans, and career-related internships or fieldwork also available. Financial aid application deadline: 3/15; applicants required to submit FAFSA. • Dr. Teresa Mehring, Dean, 316-341-5367. E-mail: mehringt@emporia.edu.

The Evergreen State College, Master's in Teaching Program, Olympia, WA 98505. Awards MIT. Faculty: 8 full-time (6 women). Students: 100 full-time (70 women); includes 10 minority (1 African American, 3 Asian Americans, 3 Hispanics, 3 Native Americans). Average age 30. 78 applicants, 74% accepted. In 1997, 4 degrees awarded. *Degree requirements:* Thesis or alternative, student teaching required, foreign language not required. *Average time to degree:* master's–2 years full-time. *Entrance requirements:* GRE, minimum undergraduate GPA of 3.0, related experience. Application deadline: rolling. Application fee: $35. *Expenses:* Tuition $4215 per year full-time, $141 per credit part-time for state residents; $12,795 per year full-time, $427 per credit part-time for nonresidents. Fees $120 per year full-time. *Financial aid:* In 1997–98, 3 fellowships (all to first-year students) averaging $570 per month and totaling $15,326, 2 research assistantships (both to first-year students) were awarded; full and partial tuition waivers, Federal Work-Study, institutionally sponsored loans, and career-related internships or fieldwork also available. Financial aid application deadline: 3/15; applicants required to submit FAFSA. *Faculty research:* Assessment, multicultural education, ideology and schooling, construcivist psychology. • Dr. Michael Vavrus, Director, 360-866-6000 Ext. 6638. E-mail: vavrusm@elwha.evergreen.edu. Application contact: Susan Hirst, Admissions Officer, 360-866-6000 Ext. 6181. Fax: 360-866-6838. E-mail: hirsts@elwha.evergreen.edu.

Fairfield University, Graduate School of Education and Allied Professions, Fairfield, CT 06430-5195. Awards MA, CAS. Part-time and evening/weekend programs available. Faculty: 18 full-time (10 women), 29 part-time (15 women), 28 FTE. Students: 129 full-time (103 women), 481 part-time (391 women); includes 47 minority (12 African Americans, 6 Asian Americans, 29 Hispanics), 8 international. Average age 30. 212 applicants, 86% accepted. In 1997, 104 master's awarded; 19 CASs awarded (100% found work related to degree). *Degree requirements:* For master's, comprehensive exam. *Average time to degree:* master's–2 years full-time, 4 years part-time; other advanced degree–1 year full-time, 2 years part-time. *Entrance requirements:* For master's, TOEFL. Application deadline: rolling. Application fee: $40. *Expenses:* Tuition $350 per credit hour (minimum). Fees $20 per semester (minimum). *Financial aid:* Partial tuition waivers and career-related internships or fieldwork available. Aid available to part-time students. *Total annual research expenditures:* $167,290. • Dr. Margaret Deignan, Dean, 203-254-4250. Application contact: Karen Creecy, Assistant Dean, 203-254-4250. Fax: 203-254-4241. E-mail: klcreecy@fair1.fairfield.edu.

See in-depth description on page 731.

Fairleigh Dickinson University, Florham–Madison Campus, Maxwell Becton College of Arts and Sciences, Program in Teaching, 285 Madison Avenue, Madison, NJ 07940-1099. Awards MAT. Students: 19 full-time (12 women), 45 part-time (32 women); includes 2 minority (1 African American, 1 Native American). Average age 29. 62 applicants, 90% accepted. *Degree requirements:* Research project required, thesis not required. *Entrance requirements:* GRE General Test, MAT, NTE. Application deadline: rolling. Application fee: $35. *Expenses:* Tuition $522 per credit. Fees $302 per year full-time, $138 per year part-time. • Dr. Eloise Forster, Director, 973-443-8375.

Fairleigh Dickinson University, Teaneck–Hackensack Campus, University College: Arts, Sciences, and Professional Studies, Peter Sammartino School of Education, 1000 River Road, Teaneck, NJ 07666-1914. Awards MA, MAT. Part-time programs available. Faculty: 11 full-time (8 women), 27 part-time (10 women). Students: 42 full-time (33 women), 162 part-time (129 women). Average age 34. In 1997, 69 degrees awarded. *Degree requirements:* Research project (MAT) required, thesis not required. *Application deadline:* rolling. *Application fee:* $35. *Expenses:* Tuition $522 per credit. Fees $302 per year full-time, $138 per year part-time. *Faculty research:* Mathematics for students with learning disabilities, gender issues in education, social problem-solving and conflict resolution in the classroom, multicultural education in the elementary classroom, problems encountered by international students in college programs. • Dr. Eloise Forster, Interim Director, 201-692-2834. Fax: 201-692-2603.

Fayetteville State University, Doctoral Program in Education, 1200 Murchison Road, Fayetteville, NC 28301-4298. Awards Ed D. Accredited by NCATE. *Degree requirements:* Comprehensive exams, internship required, foreign language and dissertation not required. *Application deadline:* 8/1 (rolling processing; 12/15 for spring admission). *Application fee:* $20. *Tuition:* $1498 per year full-time, $327 per semester (minimum) part-time for state residents; $8768 per year full-time, $2144 per semester (minimum) part-time for nonresidents.

Ferris State University, College of Education, Big Rapids, MI 49307-2742. Awards MS. Part-time and evening/weekend programs available. Faculty: 2 full-time (1 woman), 4 part-time (0 women), 3.25 FTE. Students: 12 full-time (5 women), 99 part-time (61 women); includes 10 minority (9 African Americans, 1 Hispanic). Average age 35. 17 applicants, 100% accepted. In 1997, 21 degrees awarded. *Average time to degree:* master's–1 year full-time, 3 years part-time. *Application deadline:* 8/31 (priority date; rolling processing). *Application fee:* $20. *Expenses:* Tuition $220 per credit hour for state residents; $450 per credit hour for nonresidents. Fees $100 per year. *Financial aid:* Full and partial tuition waivers and career-related internships or fieldwork available. Aid available to part-time students. *Faculty research:* Competency testing, teaching methodologies, assessment of teaching effectiveness. • Dr. E. D. Cory, Acting Dean, 616-592-3648. Application contact: Helen Bacon, Administrative Assistant, 616-592-3652. Fax: 616-592-3792. E-mail: hbacon@music.ferris.edu.

Fitchburg State College, Division of Graduate and Continuing Education, Fitchburg, MA 01420-2697. Awards MA, MAT, MBA, M Ed, MS, CAGS, Certificate. Accredited by NCATE. Part-time and evening/weekend programs available. Faculty: 162 part-time (54 women). Students: 114 full-time (95 women), 460 part-time (324 women). Average age 26. In 1997, 267 master's, 43 other advanced degrees awarded. *Average time to degree:* master's–2.5 years part-time. *Entrance requirements:* For other advanced degree, master's degree. Application deadline: rolling. Application fee: $10. *Expenses:* Tuition $147 per credit. Fees $55 per semester. *Financial aid:* Graduate assistantships, Federal Work-Study available. Aid available to part-time students. Financial aid application deadline: 3/30; applicants required to submit FAFSA. • Dr. Michele M. Zide, Associate Vice President, Academic Affairs and Dean, 978-665-3185. Fax: 978-665-3658. E-mail: dgce@fsu.edu. Application contact: James DuPont, Director of Admissions, 978-665-3144. Fax: 978-665-4540. E-mail: admissions@fsc.edu.

See in-depth description on page 733.

Florida Agricultural and Mechanical University, Division of Graduate Studies, Research, and Continuing Education, College of Education, Tallahassee, FL 32307-3200. Awards MBE, M Ed, MS Ed. Accredited by NCATE. Part-time and evening/weekend programs available. Students: 196 (131 women); includes 124 minority (123 African Americans, 1 Hispanic). In 1997, 55 degrees awarded. *Entrance requirements:* GRE General Test (minimum combined score of 1000), minimum GPA of 3.0. Application deadline: 5/13. Application fee: $20. *Expenses:* Tuition $140 per credit hour for state residents; $484 per credit hour for nonresidents. Fees $130 per year. *Financial aid:* Fellowships, teaching assistantships, Federal Work-Study, institutionally sponsored loans available. • Dr. Melvin Gadson, Dean, 850-599-3482. Fax: 850-561-2211.

Florida Atlantic University, College of Education, Boca Raton, FL 33431-0991. Awards M Ed, MS, Ed D, Ed S. Accredited by NCATE. Part-time and evening/weekend programs available. Faculty: 78 full-time (41 women), 36 part-time (18 women). Students: 209 full-time (169 women), 597 part-time (485 women); includes 108 minority (52 African Americans, 9 Asian Americans, 46 Hispanics, 1 Native American), 16 international. Average age 28. 551 applicants, 62% accepted. In 1997, 142 master's, 12 doctorates, 8 Ed Ss awarded. *Degree requirements:* For doctorate, dissertation required, foreign language not required; for Ed S, departmental qualifying exam required, foreign language and thesis not required. *Entrance requirements:* For master's, GRE General Test; for doctorate and Ed S, GRE General Test, GRE Subject Test. Application deadline: rolling. Application fee: $20. *Expenses:* Tuition $2520 per year full-time, $140 per credit hour part-time for state residents; $8712 per year full-time, $484 per credit hour part-time for nonresidents. Fees $5 per year (minimum). *Financial aid:* In 1997–98, 6 fellowships, 6 research assistantships were awarded; teaching assistantships, Federal Work-Study, and career-related internships or fieldwork also available. *Faculty research:* Aging, marriage and family counseling, multicultural education, self-directed learning, assessment. Total annual research expenditures: $2.1 million. • Dr. Jerry Lafferty, Dean, 561-297-3564.

Florida Gulf Coast University, College of Professional Studies, School of Education, Fort Myers, FL 33965-6565. Awards MA, M Ed. Part-time and evening/weekend programs available. Postbaccalaureate distance learning degree programs offered (minimal on-campus study). Students: 6 full-time (all women), 190 part-time (163 women). *Application fee:* $20. Electronic applications accepted. • Dennis Pataniczek, Director, 941-590-7780. Fax: 941-590-7801.

Florida International University, College of Education, Miami, FL 33199. Awards MA, MS, Ed D, Ed S. Accredited by NCATE. Part-time and evening/weekend programs available. Faculty: 66 full-time (34 women), 13 part-time (7 women), 71.43 FTE. Students: 233 full-time (167 women), 804 part-time (633 women); includes 607 minority (129 African Americans, 23 Asian Americans, 454 Hispanics, 1 Native American), 29 international. Average age 35. 486 applicants, 49% accepted. In 1997, 315 master's, 29 doctorates, 19 Ed Ss awarded. *Degree requirements:* For doctorate, dissertation required, foreign language not required. *Entrance requirements:* For master's, GRE General Test (minimum combined score of 1000) or minimum GPA of 3.0. Application deadline: 4/1 (priority date; rolling processing; 10/1 for spring admission). Application fee: $20. *Expenses:* Tuition $138 per credit hour for state residents; $482 per credit hour for nonresidents. Fees $46 per semester. *Financial aid:* In 1997–98, 4 research assistantships (2 to first-year students), 25 teaching assistantships (12 to first-year students) were awarded; fellowships, full and partial tuition waivers, Federal Work-Study, institutionally sponsored loans, and career-related internships or fieldwork also available. Aid available to part-time students. *Faculty research:* School improvement, cognitive processes, international development, urban education, multicultural/multilingual education. • Dr. Ira Goldenberg, Dean, 305-348-3202. Fax: 305-348-3205.

Florida State University, College of Education, Tallahassee, FL 32306. Awards MS, Ed D, PhD, Ed S. Part-time and evening/weekend programs available. Postbaccalaureate distance learning degree programs offered. Faculty: 91 full-time (40 women), 32 part-time (6 women). Students: 617 full-time (406 women), 576 part-time (366 women); includes 286 minority (144 African Americans, 76 Asian Americans, 59 Hispanics, 7 Native Americans), 1 international. 983 applicants, 71% accepted. In 1997, 375 master's, 65 doctorates awarded. Terminal master's awarded for partial completion of doctoral program. *Degree requirements:* For master's and Ed S, comprehensive exam required, thesis optional; for doctorate, dissertation, comprehensive exam. *Entrance requirements:* GRE General Test (minimum combined score of 1000), minimum GPA of 3.0. Application deadline: 7/1 (priority date; rolling processing; 11/1 for spring admission). Application fee: $20. *Tuition:* $139 per credit hour for state residents; $482 per credit hour for nonresidents. *Financial aid:* In 1997–98, 7 fellowships (all to first-year students) were awarded; research assistantships, teaching assistantships, and career-related internships or fieldwork also available. • Dr. John W. Miller, Dean, 850-644-6885. Fax: 850-644-2725. E-mail: miller@mail.coe.fsu.edu. Application contact: Admissions Coordinator, Office of Student Services, 850-644-3760. Fax: 850-644-6868.

Fontbonne College, Department of Education, St. Louis, MO 63105-3098. Awards MA. Faculty: 3 full-time (2 women), 6 part-time (5 women). Students: 4 full-time (all women), 20 part-time (19 women); includes 2 minority (both African Americans). Average age 36. *Entrance requirements:* Minimum GPA of 3.0. Application deadline: 8/1 (priority date; rolling processing). Application fee: $20. *Expenses:* Tuition $10,650 per year full-time, $346 per credit hour part-time. Fees $160 per year full-time, $7 per credit hour part-time. • Dr. William Freeman, Chairperson, 314-889-4536. Fax: 314-889-1451. E-mail: wfreeman@fontbonne.edu.

Fordham University, Graduate School of Education, New York, NY 10023. Awards MAT, MS, MSE, MST, Ed D, PhD, Adv C. Accredited by NCATE. Part-time and evening/weekend programs available. Faculty: 39 full-time (19 women), 90 part-time (50 women). Students: 107 full-time (83 women), 1,076 part-time (839 women); includes 180 minority (106 African Americans, 20 Asian Americans, 54 Hispanics), 24 international. 1,049 applicants, 86% accepted. In 1997, 420 master's, 60 doctorates awarded. *Application fee:* $50. *Financial aid:* Fellowships, research assistantships, Federal Work-Study, and career-related internships or fieldwork available. Aid available to part-time students. • Dr. Regis Bernhardt, Dean, 212-636-6406. Application contact: Joseph Korevec, Director of Admissions, 212-636-6400.

See in-depth description on page 735.

Fort Hays State University, College of Education, Hays, KS 67601-4099. Awards MS, Ed S. Accredited by NCATE. Part-time programs available. Faculty: 22 full-time (8 women). Students: 31 full-time (24 women), 312 part-time (258 women). Average age 36. 76 applicants, 83% accepted. In 1997, 108 master's, 2 Ed Ss awarded. *Application deadline:* 7/1 (priority date; rolling processing). *Application fee:* $25 ($35 for international students). *Tuition:* $94 per credit hour for state residents; $249 per credit hour for nonresidents. *Financial aid:* Research assistantships, teaching assistantships, full tuition waivers, institutionally sponsored loans, and career-related internships or fieldwork available. Aid available to part-time students. • Dr. Charles Leftwich, Dean, 785-625-5866.

Framingham State College, Graduate Programs, Department of Education, Framingham, MA 01701-9101. Offers programs in educational leadership (MA), literacy and language (M Ed), special education (M Ed). Part-time and evening/weekend programs available. Faculty: 1 full-time, 8 part-time. Students: 187 part-time. In 1997, 31 degrees awarded. *Entrance requirements:* MAT. *Tuition:* $4184 per year full-time, $523 per course part-time for state residents; $4848 per year full-time, $606 per course part-time for nonresidents. • Ellen Keretz, Chair, 508-626-4694. Application contact: Graduate Office, 508-626-4550.

Franciscan University of Steubenville, Department of Education, Steubenville, OH 43952-6701. Offers program in administration (MS Ed). Part-time and evening/weekend programs available. Students: 18 full-time (12 women), 124 part-time (71 women). 46 applicants, 100% accepted. In 1997, 41 degrees awarded. *Degree requirements:* Project required, foreign language and thesis not required. *Average time to degree:* master's–3 years full-time, 6 years part-time. *Entrance requirements:* Minimum undergraduate GPA of 2.5 or written exam. Application deadline: 7/1 (rolling processing; 12/15 for spring admission). Application fee: $20. *Expenses:* Tuition $210 per credit hour. Fees $10 per credit hour. *Financial aid:* Federal Work-Study available. Aid available to part-time students. Financial aid application deadline: 7/1; applicants required to submit FAFSA. • Dr. Diane Keenan, Chair, 740-283-6404. Application contact: Mark McGuire, Associate Director of Graduate Admissions, 800-783-6220. Fax: 740-283-6472.

Francis Marion University, School of Education, Florence, SC 29501-0547. Offers programs in early childhood education (M Ed), elementary education (M Ed), learning disabilities (MAT, M Ed), remediation education (M Ed), secondary education (M Ed). Part-time and evening/weekend programs available. Faculty: 65 full-time (14 women). Students: 15 full-time (14 women), 347 part-time (300 women); includes 119 minority (118 African Americans, 1 Native American). In 1997, 39 degrees awarded. *Entrance requirements:* GRE General Test, MAT, or NTE. Application deadline: 8/21 (priority date; rolling processing). Application fee: $25. *Financial aid:* Graduate assistantships available. Aid available to part-time students. Financial aid application deadline: 3/1. *Faculty research:* Identification and alternate assessment of at-risk students. • Dr. Wayne Pruitt, Coordinator, 803-661-1462.

Freed–Hardeman University, Program in Education, 158 East Main Street, Henderson, TN 38340-2399. Offers curriculum and instruction (M Ed). Part-time and evening/weekend programs available. Faculty: 8 full-time (1 woman), 4 part-time (2 women). Students: 63 full-time (44 women), 147 part-time (114 women); includes 67 minority (all African Americans). Average age 32. 75 applicants, 80% accepted. In 1997, 69 degrees awarded. *Degree requirements:* Thesis optional. *Entrance requirements:* GRE General Test (minimum combined score of 800), MAT (minimum score 28), or NTE. Application deadline: 8/1 (rolling processing; 12/1 for spring admission). Application fee: $25. *Tuition:* $159 per semester hour. *Financial aid:* Graduate assistantships, partial tuition waivers, Federal Work-Study, and career-related internships or fieldwork available. Aid available to part-time students. Financial aid application deadline: 8/1; applicants required to submit FAFSA. • Dr. James Murphy, Director, Graduate Studies in Education, 901-989-6082. Fax: 901-989-6065. E-mail: jmurphy@fhu.edu.

Fresno Pacific University, Graduate School, Programs in Education, Fresno, CA 93702-4709. Offerings in administration (MA Ed), including administrative services; foundations, curriculum and teaching (MA Ed), including curriculum and teaching, school library media; language, literacy, and culture (MA Ed), including bilingual/cross-cultural education, language development, reading; mathematics/science/computer education (MA Ed), including integrated mathematics/science education, mathematics education, science education, technology; pupil personnel (MA Ed), including school counseling, school psychology; special education (MA Ed), including learning handicapped, physical and health impairments, severely handicapped. Part-time and evening/weekend programs available. Faculty: 19 full-time (8 women), 67 part-time (28 women). Students: 89 full-time (64 women), 739 part-time (524 women). *Application deadline:* 7/31 (rolling processing). *Application fee:* $75. *Tuition:* $250 per unit. • Dr. John H. Yoder, Dean, Graduate School, 209-453-2248. Fax: 209-453-2001.

Frostburg State University, School of Education, Frostburg, MD 21532-1099. Awards M Ed, MS. Part-time and evening/weekend programs available. *Application deadline:* 7/15 (rolling processing). *Application fee:* $30.

Furman University, Department of Education, Greenville, SC 29613. Offers programs in elementary education (MA Ed), reading (MA Ed), school administration (MA Ed), social studies (MA Ed), special education (MA Ed). Students: 33 full-time (21 women), 174 part-time (155 women). *Degree requirements:* Comprehensive written exam. *Application deadline:* rolling. *Application fee:* $25. *Tuition:* $185 per credit hour. • Dr. Hazel W. Harris, Director, 864-294-2213.

Gallaudet University, School of Education and Human Services, Washington, DC 20002-3625. Awards MA, MS, PhD, Ed S. Accredited by NCATE. Students: 111 full-time (81 women), 61 part-time (51 women); includes 29 minority (18 African Americans, 2 Asian Americans, 8 Hispanics, 1 Native American). *Degree requirements:* For master's, thesis optional; for doctorate, computer language, dissertation. *Entrance requirements:* For master's, GRE General Test or MAT; for doctorate, GRE General Test or MAT, interview. Application deadline: 2/15 (priority date; rolling processing). Application fee: $50. *Expenses:* Tuition $7064 per year full-time, $392 per credit part-time. Fees $50 (one-time charge). *Financial aid:* Federal Work-Study, institutionally sponsored loans, and career-related internships or fieldwork available. Financial aid application deadline: 8/1. *Faculty research:* Full inclusion and deaf education, use of American Sign Language in teaching, bilingual/bicultural education, training and licensure of deaf teachers. • Dr. William P. McCrone, Dean, 202-651-5520. Application contact: Deborah DeStefano, Director of Admissions, 202-651-5253. Fax: 202-651-5744. E-mail: adm_destefan@gallua.bitnet.

Gannon University, School of Graduate Studies, College of Humanities, Business, and Education, School of Education, Erie, PA 16541. Awards M Ed, MS, Certificate. Part-time and evening/weekend programs available. Faculty: 5 full-time (2 women), 3 part-time (1 woman), 6 FTE. Students: 2 full-time (both women), 29 part-time (21 women). Average age 35. 21 applicants, 100% accepted. In 1997, 6 master's awarded. *Degree requirements:* For master's, thesis, comprehensive exam. *Entrance requirements:* For master's, GRE or MAT, interview, teaching certificate. Application deadline: rolling. Application fee: $25. *Expenses:* Tuition $405 per credit. Fees $200 per year full-time, $8 per credit part-time. *Financial aid:* Career-related internships or fieldwork available. Aid available to part-time students. Financial aid application deadline: 3/1; applicants required to submit FAFSA. • Dr. Suzanne Loss, Director, 814-871-5465. Application contact: Beth Nemenz, Director of Admissions, 814-871-7240. Fax: 814-871-5803. E-mail: admissions@gannon.edu.

Gardner–Webb University, Department of Education, Boiling Springs, NC 28017. Offers programs in elementary education (MA), middle grades education (MA), school administration (MA). Accredited by NCATE. Part-time and evening/weekend programs available. Faculty: 6 full-time (3 women), 4 part-time (2 women). Students: 5 full-time (4 women), 130 part-time (99 women); includes 10 minority (all African Americans). Average age 35. 57 applicants, 93% accepted. In 1997, 39 degrees awarded. *Degree requirements:* Comprehensive exam required, foreign language and thesis not required. *Entrance requirements:* GRE General Test (minimum combined score of 900), MAT (minimum score 35), or NTE, minimum GPA of 2.5. Application deadline: 8/1. Application fee: $25. *Tuition:* $178 per semester hour full-time, $220 per semester hour part-time. *Financial aid:* In 1997–98, 3 assistantships (all to first-year students) averaging $450 per month were awarded. • Dr. Ben Carson, Chair, 704-434-4406. Fax: 704-434-3921. E-mail: bcarson@gardner-webb.edu.

Geneva College, Department of Education, Beaver Falls, PA 15010-3599. Offers program in higher education (MA). Part-time and evening/weekend programs available. Postbaccalaureate distance learning degree programs offered (minimal on-campus study). Faculty: 11 part-time (2 women). Students: 55 part-time (25 women); includes 1 minority (African American), 1 international. Average age 24. 17 applicants, 100% accepted. In 1997, 17 degrees awarded. *Degree requirements:* Integrative seminar, practicum required, foreign language and thesis not required. *Average time to degree:* master's–3 years part-time. *Entrance requirements:* Minimum GPA of 2.8. Application deadline: 9/15 (priority date; rolling processing). Application fee: $15. *Financial aid:* Career-related internships or fieldwork available. Financial aid applicants required

Directory: Education—General

Geneva College (continued)

to submit FAFSA. *Faculty research:* Student development and learning theories, college student popular culture use. • Dr. David S. Guthrie, Director, 724-847-5564. E-mail: hed@geneva.edu. Application contact: Debbie Michalik, Administrative Assistant, 724-847-5564. Fax: 724-847-6696. E-mail: hed@geneva.edu.

George Fox University, Department of Teacher Education, Newberg, OR 97132-2697. Awards MAT, M Ed. Postbaccalaureate distance learning degree programs offered (minimal on-campus study). Faculty: 8 full-time (4 women), 1 (woman) part-time. Students: 64 full-time (47 women); includes 1 minority (Native American). Average age 30. 133 applicants, 67% accepted. In 1997, 62 degrees awarded. *Degree requirements:* Thesis required (for some programs), foreign language not required. *Average time to degree:* master's–1 year full-time. *Entrance requirements:* California Basic Educational Skills Test, NTE, minimum undergraduate GPA of 3.0 during previous 2 years. Application deadline: 2/1 (rolling processing). Application fee: $25. Electronic applications accepted. • Dr. Gary Kilburg, MAT Director, 800-765-4369 Ext. 2832. E-mail: gkilburg@georgefox.edu. Application contact: Jackie Baysinger, Director of Graduate Admissions, 800-631-0921. Fax: 503-538-7234. E-mail: jbaysinger@georgefox.edu.

George Mason University, Graduate School of Education, Fairfax, VA 22030-4444. Awards M Ed, MS, DA Ed, PhD. Accredited by NCATE. Part-time and evening/weekend programs available. Faculty: 42 full-time (24 women), 65 part-time (51 women), 58.73 FTE. Students: 390 full-time (309 women), 1,283 part-time (964 women). Average age 36. 936 applicants, 75% accepted. In 1997, 441 master's, 34 doctorates awarded. *Degree requirements:* For master's, computer language required, foreign language not required; for doctorate, computer language, comprehensive exam, final project, internship required, foreign language not required. *Entrance requirements:* For master's, minimum GPA of 3.0 in last 60 hours; for doctorate, GRE or MAT, appropriate master's degree, interview. Application deadline: 5/1 (11/1 for spring admission). Application fee: $30. Electronic applications accepted. *Tuition:* $4344 per year full-time, $181 per credit hour part-time for state residents; $12,504 per year full-time, $521 per credit hour part-time for nonresidents. *Financial aid:* Fellowships, research assistantships, teaching assistantships, Federal Work-Study, and career-related internships or fieldwork available. Aid available to part-time students. Financial aid application deadline: 3/1; applicants required to submit FAFSA. *Faculty research:* Special education/human disabilities, mathematics/science/technology education, education leadership, school/community/agency/higher education, counseling and administration. • Gary Galluzzo, Dean, 703-993-2004. Fax: 703-993-2001. E-mail: ggalluzzo@gmu.edu.

Georgetown College, Graduate Studies, Georgetown, KY 40324-1696. Awards MA Ed. Part-time programs available. Faculty: 3 full-time (1 woman), 10 part-time (3 women), 6.3 FTE. Students: 317 part-time (283 women); includes 4 minority (3 African Americans, 1 Hispanic). Average age 45. 103 applicants, 100% accepted. In 1997, 99 degrees awarded. *Degree requirements:* Portfolio required, foreign language and thesis not required. *Average time to degree:* master's–2 years part-time. *Entrance requirements:* Teaching certificate, minimum GPA of 2.7 or GRE General Test (minimum combined score of 1150). Application deadline: 9/1 (priority date; rolling processing; 1/1 for spring admission). Application fee: $0. *Tuition:* $170 per semester hour. *Financial aid:* Federal Work-Study available. Aid available to part-time students. • Dr. Ben R. Oldham, Dean of Education, 502-863-8176. Fax: 502-863-7041. E-mail: boldham@gtc.georgetown.ky.us.

The George Washington University, Graduate School of Education and Human Development, Washington, DC 20052. Awards MA Ed, MAT, M Ed, Ed D, Certificate, Ed S. Accredited by NCATE. Part-time and evening/weekend programs available. Faculty: 62 full-time (33 women), 44 part-time (28 women), 73 FTE. Students: 313 full-time (213 women), 963 part-time (644 women); includes 294 minority (206 African Americans, 46 Asian Americans, 37 Hispanics, 5 Native Americans), 54 international. Average age 37. 808 applicants, 88% accepted. In 1997, 402 master's, 38 doctorates, 29 other advanced degrees awarded. *Degree requirements:* For master's, comprehensive exam required, foreign language not required; for doctorate, dissertation, comprehensive exam; for other advanced degree, comprehensive exam required, thesis not required. *Entrance requirements:* For master's, GRE General Test or MAT, minimum GPA of 2.75; for doctorate, GRE General Test or MAT, interview, minimum GPA of 3.3; for other advanced degree, GRE General Test or MAT, minimum GPA of 3.3. Application deadline: 3/1 (priority date; rolling processing; 10/1 for spring admission). Application fee: $50. Electronic applications accepted. *Expenses:* Tuition $680 per semester hour. Fees $35 per semester hour. *Financial aid:* Fellowships, research assistantships, full and partial tuition waivers, Federal Work-Study, and career-related internships or fieldwork available. Aid available to part-time students. *Faculty research:* Policy, special education, bilingual education, counseling, human resource development. Total annual research expenditures: $4.625 million. • Dr. Mary Futrell, Dean, 202-994-6160. Application contact: Debra A. Bright, Director of Graduate Admissions, 202-994-6160. Fax: 202-994-7207.

See in-depth description on page 737.

Georgia College and State University, School of Education, Milledgeville, GA 31061. Awards MAT, M Ed, Ed S. Accredited by NCATE. Part-time programs available. Faculty: 26 full-time (10 women). Students: 166 full-time (136 women), 283 part-time (235 women); includes 64 minority (62 African Americans, 2 Hispanics), 2 international. Average age 34. In 1997, 130 master's, 52 Ed Ss awarded. *Degree requirements:* For master's, computer language, comprehensive exit exam required, foreign language and thesis not required; for Ed S, computer language, comprehensive exit exam, oral exam, research project required, foreign language not required. *Entrance requirements:* For master's, GRE General Test (minimum combined score of 800) or NTE (minimum score 550 on each core battery test), MAT (minimum score 44), minimum GPA of 2.5, NT-4 certificate; for Ed S, GRE General Test (minimum combined score of 900) or NTE (minimum score 575 on each core battery test), MAT (minimum score 48), master's degree, minimum graduate GPA of 3.25, NT-5 certificate, 2 years of teaching experience. Application deadline: 7/31 (priority date; rolling processing). Application fee: $10. *Financial aid:* In 1997–98, 7 assistantships were awarded; Federal Work-Study and career-related internships or fieldwork also available. Aid available to part-time students. Financial aid application deadline: 4/15. *Faculty research:* Performance skills of middle school principals in Georgia. • Dr. W. Bee Crews, Graduate Coordinator.

Georgian Court College, Program in Education, Lakewood, NJ 08701-2697. Offers administration, supervision and curriculum planning (management specialization) (MA); administration, supervision, and curriculum planning (MA); reading specialization (MA); special education (MA); teaching certificate (MA). *Application deadline:* 8/25 (rolling processing; 1/15 for spring admission). *Application fee:* $30. *Tuition:* $350 per credit. • Application contact: Renee Loew, Director of Graduate Admissions and Records, 732-367-1717. Fax: 732-364-4516.

Georgia Southern University, College of Education, Statesboro, GA 30460-8126. Awards M Ed, Ed D, Ed S. Accredited by NCATE. Part-time and evening/weekend programs available. Faculty: 66 full-time (30 women). Students: 290 full-time (222 women), 445 part-time (352 women); includes 80 minority (73 African Americans, 2 Asian Americans, 3 Hispanics, 2 Native Americans), 2 international. Average age 33. 301 applicants, 63% accepted. In 1997, 255 master's, 5 doctorates, 81 Ed Ss awarded. *Degree requirements:* For master's and Ed S, exams required, thesis not required; for doctorate, dissertation, exams required, foreign language not required. *Entrance requirements:* For master's, GRE General Test (minimum score 450 on each section) or MAT (minimum score 44); for doctorate, GRE General Test (minimum combined score of 1000) or MAT (minimum score 55), minimum GPA of 3.5; for Ed S, GRE General Test (minimum score 450 on each section) or MAT (minimum score 49), minimum graduate GPA of 3.25. Application deadline: rolling. Application fee: $0. Electronic applications accepted. *Tuition:* $2619 per year full-time, $287 per semester (minimum) part-time for state residents; $8619 per year full-time, $1037 per semester (minimum) part-time for nonresidents. *Financial aid:* In 1997–98, 23 assistantships, doctoral stipends were awarded; fellowships, research assistantships, teaching assistantships, Federal Work-Study, and career-related internships or fieldwork also available. Aid available to part-time students. Financial aid application deadline: 4/15. • Dr. Arnold Cooper, Dean, 912-681-5648. Fax: 912-681-5093. E-mail: acooper@gsvms2.cc.gasou.edu. Application contact: Dr. John R. Diebolt, Associate Graduate Dean, 912-681-5384. Fax: 912-681-0740. E-mail: gradschool@gsvms2.cc.gasou.edu.

Georgia Southwestern State University, School of Education, Americus, GA 31709-4693. Offers programs in business education (M Ed), early childhood education (M Ed, Ed S), health and physical education (M Ed), middle grades education (M Ed, Ed S), reading (M Ed), secondary education (M Ed). Accredited by NCATE. Students: 117 full-time (101 women), 315 part-time (261 women); includes 73 minority (57 African Americans, 10 Asian Americans, 5 Hispanics, 1 Native American). *Entrance requirements:* For master's, GRE General Test (minimum score 400 on each section) or MAT (minimum score 44), minimum GPA of 2.5; for Ed S, GRE General Test (minimum score 450 on each section) or MAT (minimum score 48), minimum GPA of 3.25. Application deadline: 9/1 (rolling processing; 3/15 for spring admission). Application fee: $10. *Financial aid:* Application deadline 9/1. • Dr. Kurt Myers, Chair, 912-931-2145. Application contact: Chris Laney, Graduate Admissions Specialist, 912-931-2027. Fax: 912-931-2059. E-mail: claney@gsw1500.gsw.peachnet.edu.

Georgia State University, College of Education, Atlanta, GA 30303-3083. Awards MBE, M Ed, MLM, MS, PhD, Ed S. Accredited by NCATE. Part-time and evening/weekend programs available. Faculty: 136 full-time (71 women), 63 part-time (46 women). Students: 945 full-time (716 women), 801 part-time (615 women); includes 299 minority (231 African Americans, 34 Asian Americans, 25 Hispanics, 9 Native Americans), 34 international. Average age 34. 968 applicants, 45% accepted. In 1997, 616 master's, 64 doctorates, 105 Ed Ss awarded. *Degree requirements:* For master's, comprehensive exam; for doctorate, dissertation, comprehensive exam. *Entrance requirements:* For doctorate, GRE General Test (minimum score 500 on verbal section, 500 on either quantitative or analytical sections) or MAT (minimum score 53), minimum GPA of 3.3; for Ed S, GRE General Test (minimum combined score of 900) or MAT (minimum score 48), minimum graduate GPA of 3.25. Application fee: $25. *Expenses:* Tuition $2673 per year full-time, $99 per semester hour part-time for state residents; $10,692 per year full-time, $396 per semester hour part-time for nonresidents. Fees $228 per year. *Financial aid:* In 1997–98, 211 research assistantships, 26 teaching assistantships were awarded; fellowships, Federal Work-Study, institutionally sponsored loans, and career-related internships or fieldwork also available. Aid available to part-time students. *Faculty research:* Evaluation and test development, teacher/school administration effectiveness, curriculum strategies and interventions. Total annual research expenditures: $6 million. • Dr. Samuel M. Deitz, Dean, 404-651-2525.

See in-depth description on page 739.

Goddard College, Program in Education and Teaching, Plainfield, VT 05667. Awards MA. Postbaccalaureate distance learning degree programs offered (minimal on-campus study). Faculty: 2 full-time (1 woman), 5 part-time (2 women). Students: 38 full-time; includes 9 minority (2 African Americans, 4 Asian Americans, 2 Hispanics, 1 Native American). Average age 37. 16 applicants, 100% accepted. In 1997, 29 degrees awarded. *Degree requirements:* Thesis. *Application deadline:* rolling. *Application fee:* $40. Electronic applications accepted. • Dr. Kathleen Kesson, Head, 802-454-8311. E-mail: kathk@earth.goddard.edu. Application contact: Ellen Codling, Admissions Office, 802-454-8311. Fax: 802-454-8017. E-mail: admissions@earth.goddard.edu.

Gonzaga University, Graduate School, School of Education, Spokane, WA 99258-0001. Offers programs in administration and curriculum (MAA), anesthesiology education (M Anesth Ed), computer education (MACE), counseling psychology (MAP), educational leadership (PhD), initial teaching (MIT), special education (MES), sports and athletic administration (MASPAA), teaching (MTA). Accredited by NCATE. Part-time and evening/weekend programs available. Faculty: 50 full-time (20 women), 44 part-time (15 women). Students: 613 full-time (431 women); includes 14 minority (6 Asian Americans, 2 Hispanics, 6 Native Americans). Average age 39. 302 applicants, 48% accepted. In 1997, 229 master's, 20 doctorates awarded. *Degree requirements:* For master's, comprehensive exam required, foreign language and thesis not required; for doctorate, dissertation, comprehensive exam required, foreign language not required. *Entrance requirements:* For master's, TOEFL (minimum score 550); for doctorate, TOEFL (minimum score 550), minimum GPA of 3.5. Application fee: $40. *Tuition:* $7380 per year (minimum) full-time, $410 per credit (minimum) part-time. *Financial aid:* Teaching assistantships, full and partial tuition waivers, Federal Work-Study available. Aid available to part-time students. Financial aid application deadline: 3/1. • Dr. Corrine McGuigan, Dean, 509-328-4220 Ext. 3503. Fax: 509-324-5812.

Gordon College, Program in Education, Wenham, MA 01984-1899. Awards M Ed. Faculty: 7 full-time (6 women). Students: 27. *Application deadline:* rolling. *Application fee:* $40. *Expenses:* Tuition $700 per course. Fees $565 per year full-time, $35 per year part-time. • Dr. Muriel Radtke, Director, 978-927-2300 Ext. 4315. Fax: 978-524-3704.

See in-depth description on page 741.

Goucher College, Programs in Education, 1021 Dulaney Valley Road, Baltimore, MD 21204-2794. Awards MAT, M Ed. Part-time and evening/weekend programs available. Faculty: 55 part-time (34 women). Students: 46 full-time (35 women), 163 part-time (127 women); includes 43 minority (37 African Americans, 3 Asian Americans, 3 Hispanics). Average age 26. 94 applicants, 68% accepted. In 1997, 65 degrees awarded (100% found work related to degree). *Degree requirements:* Action research project required, foreign language and thesis not required. *Average time to degree:* master's–1.5 years full-time, 3 years part-time. *Entrance requirements:* Minimum GPA of 3.0. Application deadline: 8/15 (priority date; rolling processing; 1/15 for spring admission). Application fee: $25. *Financial aid:* 47 students received aid; need-based awards and career-related internships or fieldwork available. Aid available to part-time students. Financial aid application deadline: 8/15; applicants required to submit FAFSA. *Faculty research:* Adolescent development, urban education, middle school, school improvement, teacher education. • Phyllis Sunshine, Director, 410-337-6047. Fax: 410-337-6394. E-mail: psunshin@goucher.edu.

Governors State University, College of Education, Division of Education, University Park, IL 60466. Offers programs in education (MA), educational administration and supervision (MA), multi-categorical special education (MA). Part-time and evening/weekend programs available. Faculty: 20 full-time (8 women), 29 part-time (13 women). Average age 36. In 1997, 121 degrees awarded. *Degree requirements:* Comprehensive exam, practicum required, foreign language not required. *Entrance requirements:* Minimum GPA of 2.75 in last 60 hours of undergraduate course work, 3.0 in any graduate work attempted. Application deadline: 7/15 (priority date; rolling processing; 11/10 for spring admission). Application fee: $0. *Expenses:* Tuition $1140 per trimester full-time, $95 per credit hour part-time for state residents; $3420 per trimester full-time, $285 per credit hour part-time for nonresidents. Fees $95 per trimester. *Financial aid:* Graduate assistantships, full and partial tuition waivers, Federal Work-Study, institutionally sponsored loans, and career-related internships or fieldwork available. Aid available to part-time students. Financial aid application deadline: 5/1. *Faculty research:* Staff development in interactive reading. • Dr. Maribeth Kasik, Chairperson, 708-534-4360. Application contact: Nick Battaglia, Adviser, 708-534-4393.

The Graduate School of America, Graduate School, Education Field, Minneapolis, MN 55401. Offers programs in education (MS), school-age care (PhD). Part-time and evening/weekend programs available. Postbaccalaureate distance learning degree programs offered (minimal on-campus study). Faculty: 4 full-time (2 women), 11 part-time (3 women). Students: 65 full-time (39 women); includes 9 minority (6 African Americans, 3 Asian Americans). Average age 49. In 1997, 3 master's awarded. Terminal master's awarded for partial completion of doctoral program. *Degree requirements:* For master's, project required, thesis optional, foreign language not required; for doctorate, dissertation required, foreign language not required. *Entrance requirements:* For master's, TOEFL (minimum score 550), minimum GPA of 2.7; for doctorate, TOEFL (minimum score 550), minimum GPA of 3.0. Application deadline: rolling.

Application fee: $50. Electronic applications accepted. *Expenses:* Tuition $7160 per year (minimum). Fees $795 per year (minimum). *Financial aid:* 18 students received aid; institutionally sponsored loans available. *Faculty research:* School administration, higher education administration, distance learning, adult education. • Dr. Elizabeth Bruch, Chair, 612-339-8650. E-mail: ebruch@tgsa.edu. Application contact: Associate Director of Admissions, 800-987-1133. Fax: 612-337-5396. E-mail: tgsainfo@tgsa.edu.

Grambling State University, College of Education, Grambling, LA 71245. Offers programs in curriculum and instruction (Ed D), developmental education (MS, Ed D), early childhood education (MS), educational leadership (Ed D), elementary education (MS), sports administration (MS). Accredited by NCATE. Ed D (curriculum and instruction, educational leadership) offered jointly with Louisiana Tech University and Northeast Louisiana University. Part-time and evening/weekend programs available. Postbaccalaureate distance learning degree programs offered. Faculty: 23 full-time (8 women), 13 part-time (9 women), 26 FTE. Students: 55 full-time (36 women), 154 part-time (112 women); includes 209 minority (all African Americans). Average age 26. 26 applicants, 62% accepted. In 1997, 20 master's, 8 doctorates awarded. *Degree requirements:* For doctorate, dissertation required, foreign language not required. *Average time to degree:* master's–1.5 years full-time, 3 years part-time; doctorate–3.5 years full-time, 7 years part-time. *Entrance requirements:* GRE. Application deadline: rolling. Application fee: $15. *Tuition:* $1960 per year full-time, $297 per semester (minimum) part-time for state residents; $7110 per year full-time, $297 per semester (minimum) part-time for nonresidents. *Financial aid:* In 1997–98, 11 research assistantships (1 to a first-year student), 5 teaching assistantships averaging $500 per month were awarded; full and partial tuition waivers, institutionally sponsored loans, and career-related internships or fieldwork also available. Financial aid application deadline: 5/31; applicants required to submit FAFSA. *Faculty research:* Curriculum revision, K–12 school improvement projects, teaching strategies, nontraditional learners, developmental studies. • Dr. Andolyn Harrison, Acting Dean, 318-274-2251.

Grand Canyon University, College of Education, Phoenix, AZ 85017-3030. Offers programs in elementary education (MA, M Ed), reading education (MA), secondary education (M Ed), teaching (MAT), teaching English as a second language (MA). Part-time programs available. Faculty: 8 full-time (5 women), 2 part-time (1 woman). Students: 47 full-time (38 women), 345 part-time (267 women); includes 15 minority (1 African American, 4 Asian Americans, 8 Hispanics, 2 Native Americans), 1 international. In 1997, 11 degrees awarded. *Degree requirements:* Publishable research paper (M Ed) required, foreign language and thesis not required. *Entrance requirements:* MAT, GRE or minimum GPA of 3.0. Application deadline: rolling. Application fee: $25. *Financial aid:* In 1997–98, 9 fellowships were awarded; Federal Work-Study, institutionally sponsored loans, and career-related internships or fieldwork also available. Aid available to part-time students. Financial aid application deadline: 3/15. • Dr. Betz Fredrick, Director, 602-589-2472.

Grand Valley State University, School of Education, Allendale, MI 49401-9403. Awards M Ed. Accredited by NCATE. Part-time and evening/weekend programs available. Postbaccalaureate distance learning degree programs offered (minimal on-campus study). Faculty: 15 full-time (6 women), 39 part-time (11 women). Students: 64 full-time (46 women), 542 part-time (415 women); includes 21 minority (11 African Americans, 4 Asian Americans, 2 Hispanics, 4 Native Americans), 3 international. Average age 34. 415 applicants, 94% accepted. In 1997, 209 degrees awarded (100% found work related to degree). *Degree requirements:* Thesis or alternative, applied research project. *Entrance requirements:* GRE General Test (minimum combined score of 1300) or minimum GPA of 3.0. Application deadline: rolling. Application fee: $20. *Financial aid:* In 1997–98, 7 research assistantships were awarded; Federal Work-Study and career-related internships or fieldwork also available. *Faculty research:* Mainstreaming, gifted students, attitudes evaluation of special education program effects, gender, pre-primary student adaptive behaviors. • Dr. Robert Hagerty, Dean, 616-895-2091. Fax: 616-895-2330. Application contact: Admissions Office, 616-895-2025. Fax: 616-895-3081.

Gratz College, Program in Education, Old York Road and Melrose Avenue, Melrose Park, PA 19027. Awards MA. *Degree requirements:* 1 foreign language, project. *Entrance requirements:* Teaching certificate. Application deadline: rolling. Application fee: $50. *Tuition:* $8500 per year full-time, $395 per credit part-time. *Financial aid:* Application deadline 4/1. • Dr. Ilene Schneider, Coordinator, 215-635-7300. Application contact: Evelyn Klein, Director of Admissions, 215-635-7300. Fax: 215-635-7320. E-mail: gratzinfo@aol.com.

Gwynedd–Mercy College, Graduate Education Programs, Gwynedd Valley, PA 19437-0901. Offerings in educational administration (MS), mental health counseling (MS), reading (MS), school counseling (MS), teaching (MS). Part-time and evening/weekend programs available. Faculty: 4 full-time (all women), 11 part-time (7 women). Students: 92 full-time (67 women), 110 part-time (91 women); includes 29 minority (all African Americans). Average age 34. 48 applicants, 96% accepted. In 1997, 12 degrees awarded (100% found work related to degree). *Degree requirements:* Thesis, internship, practicum required, foreign language not required. *Average time to degree:* master's–3 years part-time. *Entrance requirements:* GRE or MAT. Application deadline: rolling. Application fee: $25. *Expenses:* Tuition $299 per credit. Fees $50 per year. *Financial aid:* In 1997–98, 2 research assistantships were awarded; graduate assistantships, Federal Work-Study, and career-related internships or fieldwork also available. *Faculty research:* Language, cognition and reading, multicultural counseling, assessment, learning processes. • Dr. Lorraine Cavaliere, Dean, 215-641-5549. Application contact: Maureen Coyle, Program Administrator, 215-641-5561. Fax: 215-542-4695.

Hamline University, Graduate School of Education, St. Paul, MN 55104-1284. Awards MA Ed, Ed D. One or more programs accredited by NCATE. Part-time and evening/weekend programs available. Faculty: 7 full-time, 10 part-time. Students: 641. *Degree requirements:* For master's, thesis required, foreign language not required. *Application deadline:* 7/15 (priority date; rolling processing; 12/15 for spring admission). *Application fee:* $30. *Tuition:* $983 per course. *Financial aid:* Application deadline 6/1. *Faculty research:* Teacher leadership, quantitative leadership. • Joe Graba, Dean, 651-523-2404. Application contact: Jeanne Schuller, Program Assistant, 651-523-2195. Fax: 651-523-2987.

Hampton University, Department of Education, Hampton, VA 23668. Offers programs in elementary education (MA), special education (MA), teaching (MT). Accredited by NCATE. Part-time and evening/weekend programs available. Faculty: 10 full-time (8 women), 2 part-time (both women). Students: 23 full-time (19 women), 18 part-time (13 women); includes 36 minority (all African Americans), 1 international. In 1997, 20 degrees awarded. *Entrance requirements:* GRE General Test (minimum score 450 on verbal section). Application deadline: 6/1 (priority date; rolling processing; 11/1 for spring admission). Application fee: $25. *Expenses:* Tuition $9038 per year full-time, $220 per credit part-time. Fees $70 per year. *Financial aid:* Fellowships, research assistantships, teaching assistantships, scholarships, Federal Work-Study, institutionally sponsored loans, and career-related internships or fieldwork available. Aid available to part-time students. Financial aid application deadline: 5/1; applicants required to submit FAFSA. • Dr. Mamie Locke, Chair, 757-727-5793. Application contact: Erika Henderson, Director, Graduate Programs, 757-727-5454. Fax: 757-727-5084.

Harding University, School of Education, Searcy, AR 72149-0001. Awards M Ed, MSE. Accredited by NCATE. Part-time programs available. Faculty: 23 part-time (7 women), 3 FTE. Students: 80 full-time (47 women), 80 part-time (52 women); includes 7 minority (4 African Americans, 1 Asian American, 1 Hispanic, 1 Native American), 1 international. Average age 30. 46 applicants, 96% accepted. In 1997, 67 degrees awarded. *Degree requirements:* Comprehensive exam required, foreign language and thesis not required. *Average time to degree:* master's–1 year full-time, 3 years part-time. *Entrance requirements:* GRE, MAT, or NTE. Application deadline: 8/27 (rolling processing). Application fee: $25. *Expenses:* Tuition $212 per credit hour. Fees $39 per credit hour. *Financial aid:* Graduate assistantships, scholarships available. • Dr. Dee Carson, Director, 501-279-4315. Fax: 501-279-4685. E-mail: dcarson@harding.edu.

Hardin–Simmons University, Irvin School of Education, Abilene, TX 79698-0001. Awards M Ed. Part-time and evening/weekend programs available. Faculty: 10 full-time (5 women), 5 part-time (4 women). Students: 27 full-time (17 women), 87 part-time (67 women); includes 13 minority (4 African Americans, 9 Hispanics), 1 international. Average age 33. In 1997, 46 degrees awarded. *Degree requirements:* Project required, foreign language not required. *Application deadline:* 8/15 (priority date; rolling processing; 1/5 for spring admission). *Application fee:* $25. *Expenses:* Tuition $280 per semester hour. Fees $630 per year full-time. *Financial aid:* In 1997–98, 101 students received aid, including 21 fellowships (6 to first-year students) averaging $250 per month and totaling $19,000, 21 recreation assistantships, coaching assistantships (10 to first-year students) totaling $41,000; research assistantships, teaching assistantships, full and partial tuition waivers, Federal Work-Study, and career-related internships or fieldwork also available. Aid available to part-time students. Financial aid application deadline: 3/15; applicants required to submit FAFSA. *Total annual research expenditures:* $13,000. • Dr. Peter Gilman, Dean, 915-670-1347. Fax: 915-670-5859. Application contact: Dr. J. Paul Sorrels, Dean of Graduate Studies, 915-670-1298. Fax: 915-670-1564.

Harvard University, Graduate School of Education, Cambridge, MA 02138. Awards Ed M, Ed D, CAS. Part-time programs available. Faculty: 38 full-time (20 women), 58 part-time (21 women), 48.9 FTE. Students: 884 full-time (617 women), 259 part-time (186 women); includes 288 minority (111 African Americans, 72 Asian Americans, 83 Hispanics, 22 Native Americans), 104 international. Average age 31. 1,762 applicants, 48% accepted. In 1997, 590 master's, 68 doctorates, 18 CASs awarded. Terminal master's awarded for partial completion of doctoral program. *Degree requirements:* For doctorate, dissertation required, foreign language not required. *Average time to degree:* master's–1 year full-time, 2 years part-time; doctorate–6.1 years full-time, 7.8 years part-time; other advanced degree–1 year full-time, 3.5 years part-time. *Entrance requirements:* GRE General Test, TOEFL (minimum score 600), TWE (minimum score 5.0). Application deadline: 1/2. Application fee: $60. *Financial aid:* In 1997–98, 814 students received aid, including 86 fellowships (50 to first-year students) totaling $1.258 million, 40 research assistantships averaging $588 per month, 184 teaching assistantships averaging $670 per month, 518 need-based scholarships, need-based fellowships (320 to first-year students) totaling $2.886 million; Federal Work-Study and career-related internships or fieldwork also available. Aid available to part-time students. Financial aid application deadline: 1/8; applicants required to submit FAFSA. • Jerome T. Murphy, Dean, 617-495-3401. Application contact: Roland Hence, Director of Admissions, 617-495-3414. Fax: 617-496-3577. E-mail: gseadmissions@harvard.edu.

See in-depth description on page 743.

Hastings College, Program in Teacher Education, Hastings, NE 68902-0269. Awards MAT. Accredited by NCATE. Part-time programs available. Faculty: 52. Students: 6 full-time, 11 part-time. In 1997, 7 degrees awarded (100% found work related to degree). *Degree requirements:* Thesis optional, foreign language not required. *Entrance requirements:* GRE General Test. Application deadline: rolling. Application fee: $20. *Expenses:* Tuition $166 per credit. Fees $482 per year full-time, $127 per semester (minimum) part-time. *Financial aid:* Teaching assistantships, partial tuition waivers, institutionally sponsored loans, and career-related internships or fieldwork available. Aid available to part-time students. Financial aid applicants required to submit FAFSA. • Fred Condos, Director, 402-461-7388. Fax: 402-461-7490. E-mail: fcondos@hastings.edu.

Hebrew College, Shoolman Graduate School of Education, 43 Hawes Street, Brookline, MA 02146-5495. Awards MJ Ed. Part-time and evening/weekend programs available. Faculty: 20. Students: 9 full-time, 10 part-time; includes 2 international. Average age 37. In 1997, 4 degrees awarded. *Degree requirements:* 1 foreign language. *Average time to degree:* master's–2.5 years full-time. *Entrance requirements:* GRE General Test, interview. Application deadline: 4/15 (priority date; rolling processing; 11/30 for spring admission). Application fee: $45. *Expenses:* Tuition $395 per credit. Fees $90 per year. *Financial aid:* Partial tuition waivers and career-related internships or fieldwork available. Aid available to part-time students. Financial aid application deadline: 4/15. • Harvey Shapiro, Director, 617-278-4942. E-mail: hshapiro@lynx.neu.edu. Application contact: Norma Frankel, Registrar, 617-278-4947. Fax: 617-264-9264. E-mail: nfrankel@lynx.neu.edu.

Hebrew Union College–Jewish Institute of Religion, Rhea Hirsch School of Education, Los Angeles, CA 90007-3796. Awards MAJE, PhD, MAJCS/MAJE. Faculty: 3 full-time (2 women), 6 part-time (1 woman). Students: 9 full-time (8 women). Average age 27. In 1997, 12 master's awarded (90% found work related to degree, 10% continued full-time study). Terminal master's awarded for partial completion of doctoral program. *Degree requirements:* For master's, 1 foreign language, Hebrew; for doctorate, 1 foreign language, dissertation. *Average time to degree:* master's–3 years full-time; doctorate–5 years part-time. *Entrance requirements:* GRE General Test. Application deadline: 3/15. Application fee: $55. *Expenses:* Tuition $7500 per year full-time, $315 per unit part-time. Fees $296 per year full-time. *Financial aid:* Institutionally sponsored loans and career-related internships or fieldwork available. Financial aid applicants required to submit FAFSA. • Sara Lee, Director, 213-749-3424. Application contact: Rabbi Sheldon Marder, Associate Dean, 213-749-3424. Fax: 213-747-6128. E-mail: marder@mizar.usc.edu.

Hebrew Union College–Jewish Institute of Religion, School of Education, New York, NY 10012-1186. Awards MAJS, MARE. Part-time programs available. *Degree requirements:* 1 foreign language, thesis. *Entrance requirements:* GRE, minimum 1 year of college-level Hebrew. Application fee: $35.

Heidelberg College, Graduate Programs, Program in Education, Tiffin, OH 44883-2462. Awards MA. Part-time and evening/weekend programs available. Faculty: 7 full-time (3 women), 3 part-time (0 women). Students: 1 (woman) full-time, 65 part-time (51 women); includes 1 minority (African American). Average age 37. 49 applicants, 20% accepted. In 1997, 32 degrees awarded (100% found work related to degree). *Degree requirements:* Thesis or alternative, internship, practicum required, foreign language not required. *Average time to degree:* master's–3 years part-time. *Entrance requirements:* TOEFL (minimum score 550), minimum GPA of 2.5, teaching certificate. Application deadline: rolling. Application fee: $20. *Tuition:* $250 per semester hour. *Financial aid:* Available to part-time students. Financial aid application deadline: 4/15; applicants required to submit FAFSA. • Dr. Charles E. Moon, Dean of Graduate Studies, Graduate Programs, 419-448-2288. Fax: 419-448-2124. E-mail: moon@nike.heidelberg.edu.

Henderson State University, School of Education, Arkadelphia, AR 71999-0001. Awards MS, MSE. Accredited by NCATE. Part-time programs available. Postbaccalaureate distance learning degree programs offered (minimal on-campus study). Faculty: 24 full-time (6 women), 7 part-time (6 women). Students: 28 full-time (14 women), 163 part-time (122 women); includes 20 minority (19 African Americans, 1 Native American). In 1997, 71 degrees awarded. *Entrance requirements:* GRE General Test or MAT, minimum GPA of 2.7. Application deadline: 7/31 (priority date; rolling processing). *Expenses:* Tuition $120 per credit hour for state residents; $240 per credit hour for nonresidents. Fees $105 per semester (minimum) full-time, $52 per semester (minimum) part-time. *Financial aid:* Research assistantships, teaching assistantships, Federal Work-Study, institutionally sponsored loans available. Aid available to part-time students. Financial aid application deadline: 7/31. • Dr. Joye Norris, Dean, 870-230-5367. Fax: 870-230-5455.

Heritage College, Graduate Program in Education, Toppenish, WA 98948-9599. Offers programs in community and human resource development (M Ed); counseling (M Ed); educational administration (M Ed); professional development (M Ed), including bilingual education/ESL, early childhood education, special education. Part-time and evening/weekend programs available. Faculty: 9 full-time (3 women), 21 part-time (5 women). Students: 487 (341 women). In 1997, 343 degrees awarded. *Degree requirements:* Comprehensive exam required, thesis optional, foreign language not required. *Application deadline:* rolling. *Application fee:* $35 ($75

Directory: Education—General

Heritage College (continued)
for international students). *Tuition:* $270 per credit. *Financial aid:* Partial tuition waivers, Federal Work-Study, institutionally sponsored loans, and career-related internships or fieldwork available. Aid available to part-time students. • Dean, 509-865-2244 Ext. 1306.

Hofstra University, School of Education and Allied Human Services, Hempstead, NY 11549. Awards MA, MPS, MS, MS Ed, Ed D, PhD, CAS, PD. Accredited by NCATE. Part-time and evening/weekend programs available. Faculty: 72 full-time (47 women), 170 part-time (93 women). Students: 269 full-time (201 women), 1,183 part-time (937 women); includes 66 minority (30 African Americans, 9 Asian Americans, 23 Hispanics, 4 Native Americans), 12 international. Average age 32. 967 applicants, 60% accepted. In 1997, 518 master's, 5 doctorates awarded. Terminal master's awarded for partial completion of doctoral program. *Entrance requirements:* For doctorate, interview. Application deadline: rolling. Application fee: $40 ($75 for international students). *Expenses:* Tuition $10,968 per year full-time, $457 per credit hour part-time. Fees $670 per year full-time, $112 per semester (minimum) part-time. *Financial aid:* Fellowships, research assistantships, teaching assistantships, scholarships, grants, graduate assistantships, full and partial tuition waivers, Federal Work-Study, institutionally sponsored loans, and career-related internships or fieldwork available. Aid available to part-time students. Financial aid applicants required to submit FAFSA. *Faculty research:* Long-term training in rehabilitation counseling, technology, reflective practice, alternative schools. • James Johnson, Dean, 516-463-5740. Fax: 516-463-6503. E-mail: soejrj@hofstra.edu. Application contact: Mary Beth Carey, Dean of Admissions, 516-463-6700. Fax: 516-560-7660. E-mail: hofstra@hofstra.edu.

See in-depth description on page 745.

Hollins University, Program in Teaching, Roanoke, VA 24020-1688. Awards MAT. Part-time and evening/weekend programs available. Faculty: 1 (woman) full-time, 2 part-time (both women). Students: 12 part-time (11 women). Average age 35. 0 applicants. In 1997, 12 degrees awarded. *Degree requirements:* Thesis. *Entrance requirements:* 3 years of teaching experience. Application deadline: 8/14 (priority date; rolling processing; 1/10 for spring admission). Application fee: $25. *Financial aid:* 12 students received aid; Federal Work-Study available. Financial aid applicants required to submit FAFSA. • Dr. Leslie Willett, Chair, 540-362-7431. Fax: 540-362-6642. Application contact: Cathy S. Koon, Administrative Assistant, 540-362-6575. Fax: 540-362-6288. E-mail: ckoon@hollins.edu.

Holy Family College, Graduate Studies, Program in Education, Philadelphia, PA 19114-2094. Offers education (M Ed), elementary education (M Ed), reading specialist (M Ed), secondary education (M Ed). Part-time and evening/weekend programs available. Faculty: 11 full-time (6 women), 22 part-time (10 women), 16.5 FTE. Students: 26 full-time (19 women), 477 part-time (393 women); includes 25 minority (15 African Americans, 1 Asian American, 9 Hispanics). Average age 27. 98 applicants, 97% accepted. In 1997, 61 degrees awarded. *Average time to degree:* master's–3.5 years part-time. *Entrance requirements:* GRE or MAT, interview. Application deadline: 4/30 (priority date; rolling processing; 11/15 for spring admission). Application fee: $25. *Expenses:* Tuition $320 per credit hour. Fees $65 per semester. *Financial aid:* Research assistantships available. Aid available to part-time students. Financial aid application deadline: 2/15; applicants required to submit FAFSA. *Faculty research:* Cognition, developmental issues, sociological issues in education. • Leonard Soroka, Chair, 215-637-7700 Ext. 3565. Fax: 215-824-2438. Application contact: Joseph Canaday, Graduate Coordinator, 215-637-7203. Fax: 215-637-1478. E-mail: jcanaday@hfc.edu.

Holy Names College, Department of Education, 3500 Mountain Boulevard, Oakland, CA 94619-1699. Offers programs in education (M Ed), teaching English as a second language (Certificate). Part-time programs available. Faculty: 5 full-time (all women), 6 part-time (1 woman). Students: 7 full-time (6 women), 25 part-time (20 women); includes 5 minority (2 African Americans, 1 Asian American, 2 Hispanics), 2 international. 9 applicants, 67% accepted. In 1997, 4 master's awarded. *Average time to degree:* master's–1 year full-time, 2 years part-time; other advanced degree–1 year full-time, 2 years part-time. *Entrance requirements:* For master's, TOEFL (minimum score 550), minimum undergraduate GPA of 2.6 overall, 3.0 in major. Application deadline: 8/1 (rolling processing; 12/1 for spring admission). Application fee: $35. *Tuition:* $7650 per year full-time, $425 per unit part-time. *Financial aid:* 11 students received aid; Federal Work-Study and career-related internships or fieldwork available. Aid available to part-time students. Financial aid application deadline: 3/2; applicants required to submit FAFSA. *Faculty research:* Cognitive development, language development, learning handicaps. • Peggy Webster, Chairperson, 510-436-1515. Application contact: Graduate Admissions Office, 800-430-1321. Fax: 510-436-1317. E-mail: garner@admin.hnc.edu.

Hood College, Department of Education, Frederick, MD 21701-8575. Offers programs in curriculum and instruction (MS), including early childhood education, elementary education, elementary school science and mathematics, reading, secondary education, special education; educational leadership (MS). Part-time and evening/weekend programs available. Students: 5 full-time (3 women), 229 part-time (202 women); includes 10 minority (6 African Americans, 3 Asian Americans, 1 Hispanic), 1 international. Average age 33. In 1997, 30 degrees awarded. *Entrance requirements:* Minimum GPA of 2.5. Application deadline: rolling. Application fee: $30. *Tuition:* $285 per credit. *Financial aid:* Partial tuition waivers, institutionally sponsored loans, and career-related internships or fieldwork available. Aid available to part-time students. Financial aid applicants required to submit FAFSA. *Faculty research:* Constructivist curricula for pre–K, methods of teaching spelling, HIV instruction, exemplary science programs. Total annual research expenditures: $500,000. • Dr. Patricia Bartlett, Chairperson, 301-696-3471. E-mail: bartlett@nimue.hood.edu. Application contact: Hood College Graduate School, 301-696-3600. Fax: 301-696-3597. E-mail: postmaster@nimue.hood.edu.

Hope International University, Graduate Studies, Program in Education, Fullerton, CA 92831-3138. Awards ME. Part-time and evening/weekend programs available. Students: 15. *Degree requirements:* Thesis required, foreign language not required. *Entrance requirements:* Minimum GPA of 3.0. Application deadline: 8/1 (priority date; rolling processing). Application fee: $50. Electronic applications accepted. *Financial aid:* Available to part-time students. Financial aid application deadline: 3/31. • Dr. James Whitmore, Director, 800-762-1294 Ext. 260. Application contact: Connie Born, Director of Admissions, 800-762-1294 Ext. 626. Fax: 714-738-4564. E-mail: cborn@pacificcc.edu.

Houston Baptist University, College of Education and Behavioral Sciences, Programs in Education, Houston, TX 77074-3298. Offerings in bilingual education (M Ed), counselor education (M Ed), education (M Ed), educational administration (M Ed), educational diagnostician (M Ed), elementary education (M Ed), generic special education (M Ed), reading education (M Ed), secondary education (M Ed). Part-time programs available. Faculty: 9 full-time (5 women), 4 part-time (3 women). Students: 37 full-time (33 women), 65 part-time (56 women); includes 34 minority (17 African Americans, 5 Asian Americans, 12 Hispanics). 28 applicants, 82% accepted. In 1997, 24 degrees awarded. *Degree requirements:* Comprehensive exam required, foreign language and thesis not required. *Entrance requirements:* GRE General Test (minimum combined score of 850), minimum GPA of 2.5, teaching certificate. Application deadline: 7/1 (priority date; rolling processing; 1/1 for spring admission). Application fee: $25 ($85 for international students). *Expenses:* Tuition $280 per semester hour. Fees $235 per quarter. *Financial aid:* Federal Work-Study available. Financial aid applicants required to submit FAFSA. • Dr. John Lutjemeier, Head, 281-649-3000 Ext. 2336. Application contact: Judy Ferguson, Program Assistant, 281-649-3241.

Howard University, School of Education, 2400 Sixth Street, NW, Washington, DC 20059-0002. Awards MA, MAT, M Ed, MS, Ed D, PhD, CAGS. Accredited by NCATE. Part-time programs available. Faculty: 30. Students: 249; includes 4 Hispanics, 1 Native American, 35 international. In 1997, 79 master's, 8 doctorates, 2 CAGSs awarded. *Degree requirements:* For master's, comprehensive exam required, foreign language not required; for doctorate, 1 foreign language, dissertation, comprehensive exam, expository writing exam, internship. *Average time to degree:* master's–2 years full-time, 4 years part-time. *Entrance requirements:* For master's, GRE General Test, minimum GPA of 2.7; for doctorate, GRE General Test, minimum GPA of 3.4; for CAGS, GRE General Test. Application deadline: 4/1 (priority date; rolling processing). Application fee: $45. *Expenses:* Tuition $10,200 per year full-time, $567 per credit hour part-time. Fees $405 per year. *Financial aid:* Fellowships, research assistantships, teaching assistantships, grants, scholarships, full and partial tuition waivers, Federal Work-Study, institutionally sponsored loans, and career-related internships or fieldwork available. Financial aid applicants required to submit FAFSA. *Faculty research:* Policy affecting education for African-Americans; utilizing information technology with underserved school populations; increasing literacy skills for public school students; violence intervention and prevention; successes, problems, and needs of disabled African-Americans. • Dr. Veronica G. Thomas, Interim Dean, 202-806-7340. Application contact: Dr. Dolores P. Dickerson, Associate Dean, 202-806-7348.

Announcement: The School of Education has 3 departments: Curriculum and Instruction, Educational Administration and Policy, and Human Development and Psychoeducational Studies. The MA, M Ed, and CAGS degrees are offered in early childhood, secondary, and special education; reading; educational administration; educational supervision; counseling and guidance; counseling psychology; educational psychology; and school psychology. The MAT is offered in early childhood education, secondary curriculum and teaching, and reading. The M Ed only is offered in elementary education. The MS is offered in human development. The PhD and Ed D are offered in educational psychology, counseling psychology, and school psychology. The School has distinguished auxiliary services: the Center for Academic Reinforcement, Center for Disability and Socioeconomic Policy Studies, *Journal of Negro Education,* Upward Bound, a Center for Drug Abuse Research, a national Center for Research on the Education of Students Placed at Risk, a Professional Development School, and a preschool center. Howard's numerous resources include a leading repository for information on African Americans and the Center for International Affairs. Resources can be shared with 10 other colleges and universities in the Washington Metropolitan Area Consortium. The nation's capital offers resources at federal, state, and local levels, including teaching, research, policy, and service.

Hunter College of the City University of New York, Division of Education, 695 Park Avenue, New York, NY 10021-5085. Awards MA, MS, MS Ed, AC. Part-time and evening/weekend programs available. *Entrance requirements:* For master's, TOEFL; for AC, TOEFL (minimum score 575). Application fee: $40. *Expenses:* Tuition $4350 per year full-time, $185 per credit part-time for state residents; $7600 per year full-time, $320 per credit part-time for nonresidents. Fees $26 per year. *Faculty research:* Multicultural and multiracial urban education; mentoring new teachers; mathematics and science education; bilingual, bicultural, and special education.

Idaho State University, College of Education, Pocatello, ID 83209. Awards M Ed, MPE, Ed D, Ed S. Accredited by NCATE. Part-time and evening/weekend programs available. Postbaccalaureate distance learning degree programs offered (no on-campus study). Faculty: 30 full-time (10 women), 4 part-time (0 women). Students: 91 full-time (48 women), 177 part-time (98 women); includes 8 minority (2 African Americans, 1 Asian American, 5 Hispanics), 2 international. Average age 38. In 1997, 185 master's, 1 doctorate, 14 Ed Ss awarded. *Degree requirements:* For master's, oral exam, written exam required, thesis optional, foreign language not required; for doctorate, computer language, dissertation, written exam required, foreign language not required; for Ed S, oral exam, written exam required, foreign language and thesis not required. *Average time to degree:* master's–2 years full-time, 4 years part-time; other advanced degree–1 year full-time, 2 years part-time. *Entrance requirements:* For master's, GRE General Test (score in 35th percentile or higher on one section) or MAT (minimum score 48), minimum undergraduate GPA of 3.0; for doctorate, GRE General Test (minimum combined score of 1000) or MAT (minimum score 50), minimum undergraduate GPA of 3.0, minimum graduate GPA of 3.5; for Ed S, GRE, minimum graduate GPA of 3.0. Application deadline: 7/1 (priority date; rolling processing; 12/1 for spring admission). Application fee: $30. *Tuition:* $3130 per year full-time, $136 per credit hour part-time for state residents; $9370 per year full-time, $226 per credit hour part-time for nonresidents. *Financial aid:* In 1997–98, 17 teaching assistantships were awarded; fellowships, research assistantships, full tuition waivers, Federal Work-Study, institutionally sponsored loans, and career-related internships or fieldwork also available. Aid available to part-time students. *Faculty research:* School reform, inclusion, students at risk, teacher education standards, teaching cases. • Dr. Larry Harris, Dean, 208-236-3259. E-mail: harrlarr@isu.edu. Application contact: Dr. Stephanie Salzman, Director, Office of Standards and Assessment, 208-236-3114. Fax: 208-236-4697. E-mail: salzstep@isu.edu.

Illinois State University, College of Education, Normal, IL 61790-2200. Awards MA, MS, MS Ed, Ed D, PhD. Accredited by NCATE. Part-time programs available. Faculty: 59 full-time (22 women), 4 part-time (1 woman). Students: 115 full-time (81 women), 641 part-time (470 women); includes 73 minority (52 African Americans, 7 Asian Americans, 13 Hispanics, 1 Native American), 10 international. 151 applicants, 93% accepted. In 1997, 192 master's, 27 doctorates awarded. *Degree requirements:* For doctorate, dissertation, 2 terms of residency. *Entrance requirements:* GRE General Test. Application deadline: rolling. Application fee: $0. *Expenses:* Tuition $2454 per year full-time, $102 per hour part-time for state residents; $7362 per year full-time, $307 per hour part-time for nonresidents. Fees $1048 per year full-time, $44 per hour part-time. *Financial aid:* In 1997–98, 19 research assistantships, 4 teaching assistantships, 5 assistantships were awarded; full and partial tuition waivers, Federal Work-Study, institutionally sponsored loans, and career-related internships or fieldwork also available. Aid available to part-time students. Financial aid application deadline: 4/1. *Total annual research expenditures:* $1.629 million. • Dr. Sally Pancrazio, Dean, 309-438-5415.

Indiana State University, School of Education, Terre Haute, IN 47809-1401. Awards MA, M Ed, MS, PhD, Ed S. Accredited by NCATE. Part-time and evening/weekend programs available. Faculty: 89 full-time (38 women), 1 (woman) part-time. Students: 207 full-time (141 women), 188 part-time (130 women); includes 32 minority (25 African Americans, 2 Asian Americans, 3 Hispanics, 2 Native Americans), 20 international. Average age 34. 333 applicants, 41% accepted. In 1997, 90 master's, 26 doctorates, 15 Ed Ss awarded. Terminal master's awarded for partial completion of doctoral program. *Degree requirements:* For doctorate, computer language, dissertation. *Entrance requirements:* For master's, minimum undergraduate GPA of 2.5; for doctorate, GRE General Test (minimum score 500 on each section); for Ed S, GRE General Test (minimum combined score of 900), minimum graduate GPA of 3.25. Application deadline: rolling. Application fee: $20. *Tuition:* $143 per credit hour for state residents; $325 per credit hour for nonresidents. *Financial aid:* In 1997–98, 44 fellowships (8 to first-year students), 55 research assistantships, 5 teaching assistantships were awarded; partial tuition waivers, Federal Work-Study, institutionally sponsored loans, and career-related internships or fieldwork also available. Aid available to part-time students. Financial aid application deadline: 3/1. • Dr. Richard Antonak, Dean, 812-237-2919.

Indiana University Bloomington, School of Education, Bloomington, IN 47405. Awards MS, Ed D, PhD, Ed S. Accredited by NCATE. PhD offered through the University Graduate School. Part-time and evening/weekend programs available. Faculty: 87 full-time (33 women). Students: 634 full-time (395 women), 661 part-time (427 women); includes 122 minority (62 African Americans, 29 Asian Americans, 28 Hispanics, 3 Native Americans), 216 international. In 1997, 302 master's, 81 doctorates awarded. Terminal master's awarded for partial completion of doctoral program. *Degree requirements:* For doctorate, dissertation required, foreign language not required; for Ed S, comprehensive exam or project required, foreign language not required. *Entrance requirements:* GRE General Test. Application fee: $35. *Expenses:* Tuition $153 per credit hour for state residents; $446 per credit hour for nonresidents. Fees $343 per year. *Financial aid:* Fellowships, research assistantships, teaching assistantships, graduate assistantships, full and partial tuition waivers, Federal Work-Study, institutionally sponsored loans, and career-related internships or fieldwork available. Aid available to part-time students. • Donald Warren, Dean, 812-856-8001. Fax: 812-856-8440. Application contact: Barbara Hayes, Graduate Admissions, 812-856-8504.

See in-depth description on page 747.

Indiana University Kokomo, Division of Education, Kokomo, IN 46904-9003. Offers programs in education (MS), elementary education (MS). Accredited by NCATE. Part-time and evening/weekend programs available. Faculty: 5 full-time (1 woman). Average age 30. In 1997, 3 degrees awarded. *Degree requirements:* Research project required, thesis optional, foreign language not required. *Entrance requirements:* GRE General Test, minimum GPA of 2.5. Application deadline: 8/1 (rolling processing; 12/1 for spring admission). Application fee: $30 ($50 for international students). *Financial aid:* Minority teacher scholarships available. *Faculty research:* Reading, teaching effectiveness, portfolio, curriculum development. • Dr. Steven Gilbert, Chair, 765-455-9287. E-mail: sgilbert@iuk.edu. Application contact: Cindy Metsker, Counselor, 765-455-9419. Fax: 765-455-9503. E-mail: lmetsker@iuk.edu.

Indiana University Northwest, Division of Education, Gary, IN 46408-1197. Offers programs in elementary education (MS Ed), secondary education (MS Ed). Part-time and evening/weekend programs available. Faculty: 14. Students: 144 part-time; includes 70 minority (46 African Americans, 1 Asian American, 23 Hispanics). Average age 32. *Degree requirements:* Thesis. *Entrance requirements:* GRE General Test or MAT, minimum GPA of 3.0. Application deadline: 7/15 (priority date; 11/15 for spring admission). Application fee: $25. • Dr. William May, Interim Dean, 219-981-4278. Application contact: John Burson, Director of Education Student Services, 219-980-6514. Fax: 219-981-4208. E-mail: jburson@iunhaw1.iun.indiana.edu.

Indiana University of Pennsylvania, College of Education, Indiana, PA 15705-1087. Awards MA, M Ed, MS, D Ed, Certificate. Accredited by NCATE. Part-time and evening/weekend programs available. Faculty: 52 full-time (23 women). Students: 193 full-time (146 women), 355 part-time (260 women); includes 41 minority (32 African Americans, 3 Asian Americans, 2 Hispanics, 4 Native Americans), 16 international. Average age 33. 354 applicants, 61% accepted. In 1997, 154 master's, 10 doctorates, 3 Certificates awarded. Terminal master's awarded for partial completion of doctoral program. *Degree requirements:* For master's, thesis optional, foreign language not required; for doctorate, dissertation. *Entrance requirements:* For master's and doctorate, TOEFL (minimum score 500); for Certificate, GRE General Test, GRE Subject Test, TOEFL (minimum score 500). Application deadline: rolling. Application fee: $30. *Expenses:* Tuition $3468 per year full-time, $193 per credit part-time for state residents; $6236 per year full-time, $346 per credit part-time for nonresidents. Fees $313 per year (minimum) full-time, $84 per year part-time. *Financial aid:* Fellowships, research assistantships, teaching assistantships, Federal Work-Study, and career-related internships or fieldwork available. Aid available to part-time students. Financial aid application deadline: 3/15. • Dr. John Butzow, Dean, 724-357-2480. E-mail: jwbutzow@grove.iup.edu. Application contact: Joyce Garrett, Associate Dean, 724-357-2480.

Indiana University–Purdue University Fort Wayne, School of Education, Fort Wayne, IN 46805-1499. Awards MS Ed. Accredited by NCATE. Part-time and evening/weekend programs available. Faculty: 16 full-time (7 women), 10 part-time (4 women), 18.5 FTE. Students: 8 full-time (6 women), 332 part-time (225 women); includes 13 minority (11 African Americans, 1 Asian American, 1 Hispanic), 1 international. Average age 37. 180 applicants, 98% accepted. In 1997, 122 degrees awarded (100% found work related to degree). *Entrance requirements:* Minimum GPA of 2.5. Application deadline: 8/1 (priority date; rolling processing; 12/1 for spring admission). Application fee: $30. *Expenses:* Tuition $2356 per year full-time, $131 per credit hour part-time for state residents; $5253 per year full-time, $292 per credit hour part-time for nonresidents. Fees $183 per year full-time, $10.15 per credit hour part-time. *Financial aid:* Application deadline 3/1. • Betty Steffy, Dean, 219-481-6456. Fax: 219-481-6083.

Indiana University–Purdue University Indianapolis, School of Education, Indianapolis, IN 46202-2896. Awards MS. Part-time and evening/weekend programs available. Faculty: 25 full-time (5 women), 18 part-time (6 women). Students: 26 full-time (16 women), 198 part-time (145 women); includes 16 minority (10 African Americans, 6 Hispanics), 6 international. Average age 32. In 1997, 83 degrees awarded. *Entrance requirements:* GRE General Test (minimum combined score of 1300; average 1640), minimum GPA of 3.0. Application deadline: 3/1 (priority date; 11/1 for spring admission). Application fee: $35. *Expenses:* Tuition $3602 per year full-time, $150 per credit hour part-time for state residents; $10,392 per year full-time, $433 per credit hour part-time for nonresidents. Fees $100 per year (minimum) full-time, $40 per year (minimum) part-time. *Financial aid:* In 1997–98, 15 research assistantships (8 to first-year students) averaging $500 per month and totaling $45,000 were awarded; fellowships, teaching assistantships, Federal Work-Study, and career-related internships or fieldwork also available. *Faculty research:* Teachers in the process of change, learning cycles, children's concepts of science. • Barbara Wilcox, Executive Associate Dean, 317-274-6862. Application contact: Dr. O. Gilbert Brown, Assistant Dean for Education Student Services, 317-274-0649. Fax: 317-274-6864. E-mail: ogbrown@iupui.edu.

Indiana University South Bend, Division of Education, South Bend, IN 46634-7111. Awards MS Ed. Accredited by NCATE. Part-time and evening/weekend programs available. Faculty: 24 full-time (10 women), 21 part-time (10 women), 31 FTE. Students: 160 full-time (116 women), 342 part-time (265 women); includes 26 minority (19 African Americans, 3 Asian Americans, 3 Hispanics, 1 Native American), 3 international. Average age 35. 191 applicants, 90% accepted. In 1997, 108 degrees awarded. *Degree requirements:* Thesis or alternative, exit project required, foreign language not required. *Entrance requirements:* TOEFL (minimum score 550). Application deadline: rolling. Application fee: $35 ($40 for international students). *Expenses:* Tuition $3024 per year full-time, $126 per credit hour part-time for state residents; $7320 per year full-time, $305 per credit hour part-time for nonresidents. Fees $222 per year full-time, $34 per semester (minimum) part-time. *Financial aid:* Federal Work-Study available. Aid available to part-time students. Financial aid application deadline: 3/1. • Dr. James Smith, Dean, 219-237-4546. Fax: 219-237-4550. E-mail: jsmith@iusb.edu. Application contact: Graduate Director, 219-237-4183. Fax: 219-237-6549.

Indiana University Southeast, Division of Education, New Albany, IN 47150-6405. Offers programs in counselor education (MS Ed), elementary education (MS Ed), secondary education (MS Ed). Accredited by NCATE. Part-time and evening/weekend programs available. Faculty: 18 full-time (12 women), 10 part-time (6 women). Students: 1 (woman) full-time, 358 part-time (254 women); includes 14 minority (13 African Americans, 1 Native American), 2 international. 88 applicants, 100% accepted. In 1997, 83 degrees awarded (100% found work related to degree). *Degree requirements:* Thesis or alternative required, foreign language not required. *Entrance requirements:* Appropriate bachelor's degree. Application deadline: rolling. Application fee: $28. *Expenses:* Tuition $125 per credit hour (minimum) for state residents; $284 per credit hour (minimum) for nonresidents. Fees $33 per year full-time, $2.75 per credit hour part-time. *Financial aid:* Federal Work-Study, institutionally sponsored loans, and career-related internships or fieldwork available. Aid available to part-time students. Financial aid applicants required to submit FAFSA. *Faculty research:* Distance learning-vocational education, service learning, calculator applications. • Dr. Carl DeGraaf, Dean, 812-941-2385. E-mail: cdegraaf@iusmail.indiana.edu. Application contact: Dr. Teesue H. Fields, Director of Graduate Studies, 812-941-2658. Fax: 812-941-2667. E-mail: thfields@iusmail.indiana.edu.

Indiana Wesleyan University, Adult and Professional Studies Program, Program in Graduate Teacher Education, Marion, IN 46953-4999. Offers curriculum and instruction (M Ed). Evening/weekend programs available. Faculty: 50 part-time (15 women). Students: 553 full-time (441 women); includes 22 minority (19 African Americans, 1 Asian American, 2 Hispanics). Average age 33. 512 applicants, 88% accepted. In 1997, 329 degrees awarded. *Entrance requirements:* GRE General Test (minimum combined score of 1000), MAT (minimum score 40), NTE, minimum GPA of 2.75, related experience, teaching license. Application deadline: rolling. Application fee: $20. *Tuition:* $239 per hour. • Dr. Larry Lindsay, Director, 765-677-2894. Fax: 765-677-2380. Application contact: Beth Dickerson, Director of Marketing, 765-677-2863.

Institute for Christian Studies, Institute for Christian Studies, Toronto, ON M5T 1R4, Canada. Offerings include education (MA). Institute faculty: 11 full-time (4 women), 11 part-time (3 women). *Application deadline:* 3/31 (priority date; rolling processing). *Application fee:* $25. *Tuition:* $3750 per year full-time, $550 per course part-time. • Dr. Harry Fernhout, President, 416-979-2331. Application contact: Wanda Coffey-Bailey, Director of Student Services, 416-979-2331. Fax: 416-979-2332.

Instituto Tecnológico y de Estudios Superiores de Monterrey, Estado de México Campus, Graduate Division, Atizapán de Zaragoza 52926, Mexico. Offerings include education (M Ed). Postbaccalaureate distance learning degree programs offered (minimal on-campus study). Institute faculty: 19 full-time (3 women), 32 part-time (3 women). *Average time to degree:* master's–2 years full-time, 3.3 years part-time. *Application deadline:* 1/12 (priority date; rolling processing; 4/4 for spring admission). *Application fee:* $72. • Emilio Alvarado Badillo, Headmaster, 5-326-5500. Fax: 5-326-5507. E-mail: ealvarad@campus.cem.itesm.mx. Application contact: Lourdes Turrubiates, Admissions Officer, 5-326-5776. E-mail: lturrubi@campus.cem.itesm.mx.

Instituto Tecnológico y de Estudios Superiores de Monterrey, Sonora Norte Campus, Program in Education, Hermosillo, Sonora 83000, Mexico. Awards MA. *Entrance requirements:* MAT (minimum score 40).

Inter American University of Puerto Rico, Metropolitan Campus, Division of Education, San Juan, PR 00919-1293. Offers programs in administration and supervision (MA), education (Ed D), elementary education (MA), guidance and counseling (MA), health and physical education (MA), higher education (MA Ed), occupational education (MA), special education (MA Ed), teaching of science (MA Ed), vocational evaluation (MA). Part-time and evening/weekend programs available. Faculty: 23 full-time (16 women), 14 part-time (8 women). Students: 147 full-time (109 women), 271 part-time (193 women); includes 418 minority (all Hispanics). 157 applicants, 74% accepted. In 1997, 81 master's, 11 doctorates awarded. *Degree requirements:* For master's, comprehensive exam; for doctorate, dissertation, comprehensive exam. *Entrance requirements:* For master's, GRE or PAEG, interview; for doctorate, GRE or PAEG. Application deadline: 5/15 (priority date; rolling processing; 11/15 for spring admission). Application fee: $31. Electronic applications accepted. *Expenses:* Tuition $3272 per year full-time, $1740 per year part-time. Fees $328 per year full-time, $176 per year part-time. *Financial aid:* Federal Work-Study and career-related internships or fieldwork available. Aid available to part-time students. *Faculty research:* Curriculum development, student achievement assessment, evaluation of elementary and secondary physical education programs. Total annual research expenditures: $200,000. • Dr. Amalia Charneco, Director, 787-758-5652. Application contact: Jenny Maldonado, Administrative Assistant, 787-250-1912 Ext. 2393. Fax: 787-250-1197.

Inter American University of Puerto Rico, San Germán Campus, Department of Education, San Germán, PR 00683-5008. Offers programs in administration of higher education institutions (MA), curriculum and instruction (MA Ed), educational administration (MA Ed), guidance and counseling (MA Ed), library science (MA), physical education and scientific analysis of human body movement (MA Ed), science education (MA), special education (MS Ed). Part-time and evening/weekend programs available. Faculty: 9 full-time (2 women), 16 part-time (9 women). In 1997, 87 degrees awarded. *Degree requirements:* Comprehensive exam required, foreign language and thesis not required. *Entrance requirements:* Minimum GPA of 3.0, GRE General Test, or PAEG. Application deadline: 4/30 (priority date; rolling processing; 11/15 for spring admission). Application fee: $31. *Expenses:* Tuition $150 per credit. Fees $177 per semester. *Financial aid:* Teaching assistantships available. • Dr. Ivan Calimano, Coordinator of Graduate Programs, 787-264-1912 Ext. 7355. Application contact: Mildred Camacho, Admissions Director, 787-892-3090. Fax: 787-892-6350.

Iowa State University of Science and Technology, College of Education, Ames, IA 50011. Awards M Ed, MS, PhD. Part-time programs available. Faculty: 78 full-time, 6 part-time. Students: 108 full-time (64 women), 320 part-time (203 women); includes 59 minority (41 African Americans, 3 Asian Americans, 14 Hispanics, 1 Native American), 27 international. 226 applicants, 60% accepted. In 1997, 90 master's, 25 doctorates awarded. *Degree requirements:* For master's, thesis or alternative; for doctorate, dissertation. *Entrance requirements:* For master's, TOEFL; for doctorate, TOEFL, GRE General Test. Application fee: $20 ($30 for international students). *Expenses:* Tuition $3166 per year full-time, $176 per credit part-time for state residents; $9324 per year full-time, $518 per credit part-time for nonresidents. Fees $200 per year. *Financial aid:* In 1997–98, 62 research assistantships (15 to first-year students), 34 teaching assistantships (13 to first-year students), 24 scholarships (8 to first-year students) were awarded; fellowships, Federal Work-Study, and career-related internships or fieldwork also available. Aid available to part-time students. • Dr. Camilla P. Benbow, Interim Dean, 515-294-7000. E-mail: cbenbow@iastate.edu.

Jackson State University, School of Education, Jackson, MS 39217. Awards MS, MS Ed, Ed D, PhD, Ed S. Accredited by NCATE. Part-time and evening/weekend programs available. Faculty: 50 full-time (26 women), 11 part-time (4 women). Students: 125 full-time (81 women), 218 part-time (158 women); includes 313 minority (312 African Americans, 1 Native American), 2 international. 203 applicants, 70% accepted. In 1997, 84 master's, 5 doctorates, 6 Ed Ss awarded. Terminal master's awarded for partial completion of doctoral program. *Degree requirements:* For master's, thesis or alternative, comprehensive exam; for doctorate, dissertation, comprehensive exam. *Entrance requirements:* For master's, GRE General Test (minimum combined score of 1000), TOEFL (minimum score 550); for doctorate, MAT (minimum score 45), teaching experience. Application deadline: 3/1 (priority date; rolling processing; 10/1 for spring admission). Application fee: $20. *Tuition:* $2688 per year (minimum) full-time, $150 per semester hour part-time for state residents; $5546 per year (minimum) full-time, $309 per semester hour part-time for nonresidents. *Financial aid:* Federal Work-Study available. Financial aid application deadline: 3/1. • Dr. Johnnie Mills-Jones, Dean, 601-968-2433. Fax: 601-968-7048. Application contact: Mae Robinson, Admissions Coordinator, 601-968-2455. Fax: 601-968-8246. E-mail: mrobinson@ccaix.jsums.edu.

Jacksonville State University, College of Education, Jacksonville, AL 36265-9982. Awards MM Ed, MS, MS Ed, Ed S. Accredited by NCATE. Part-time and evening/weekend programs available. Faculty: 30 full-time (17 women). Students: 156 full-time (119 women), 474 part-time (316 women); includes 176 minority (170 African Americans, 2 Asian Americans, 3 Hispanics, 1 Native American). In 1997, 214 master's, 46 Ed Ss awarded. *Degree requirements:* For master's, thesis optional. *Entrance requirements:* For master's, GRE General Test or MAT. Application deadline: rolling. Application fee: $20. *Expenses:* Tuition $2140 per year full-time, $107 per semester hour part-time for state residents; $4280 per year full-time, $214 per semester hour part-time for nonresidents. Fees $30 per semester. *Financial aid:* Available to part-time students. Financial aid application deadline: 4/1. • Application contact: College of Graduate Studies and Continuing Education, 205-782-5329.

Jacksonville University, College of Arts and Sciences, Division of Education, 2800 University Boulevard North, Jacksonville, FL 32211-3394. Offers programs in art (MAT); computer education (MAT); early childhood education (Certificate); educational leadership (MAT); elementary education (MAT); English (MAT); exceptional child education (Certificate); foreign language (MAT), including French, Spanish; gifted education (Certificate); integrated learning with educational technology (MAT); mathematics (MAT); music (MAT); reading (MAT); secondary education (Certificate). Part-time and evening/weekend programs available. *Degree requirements:* For master's, comprehensive exam required, foreign language and thesis not required. *Average time to degree:* master's–1.5 years full-time, 2.5 years part-time. *Entrance requirements:* For master's, GRE General Test (minimum combined score of 900), TOEFL (minimum score 500), minimum GPA of 3.0; for Certificate, TOEFL (minimum score 500). Application deadline: 8/1 (priority date; rolling processing; 11/1 for spring admission). Application fee: $25.

Announcement: Master of Arts in Teaching (MAT) provides academic and professional education for in-service and prospective teachers. Program offers majors in art, computer education, educational leadership (administration supervision), elementary education, English, French, integrated learning with educational technology, mathematics, music, reading, and Spanish. Teacher certification available in early childhood education and exceptional child education. Limited number of scholarships offered.

Directory: Education—General

James Madison University, College of Education and Psychology, School of Education, Harrisonburg, VA 22807. Awards MAT, M Ed, MS Ed. One or more programs accredited by NCATE. Part-time and evening/weekend programs available. Faculty: 26 full-time (14 women). Students: 57 full-time (46 women), 97 part-time (76 women); includes 5 minority (1 African American, 4 Asian Americans), 2 international. Average age 30. In 1997, 112 degrees awarded. *Entrance requirements:* GRE General Test. Application deadline: 7/1 (priority date; rolling processing). Application fee: $50. *Tuition:* $134 per credit hour for state residents; $404 per credit hour for nonresidents. *Financial aid:* In 1997–98, 16 assistantships totaling $133,982 were awarded; fellowships, teaching assistantships, Federal Work-Study, and career-related internships or fieldwork also available. Financial aid application deadline: 2/15; applicants required to submit FAFSA. • Dr. Linda Blanton, Director, 540-568-2813.

John Carroll University, Department of Education and Allied Studies, University Heights, OH 44118-4581. Offers programs in administration supervision (MA, M Ed), educational psychology (MA, M Ed), guidance and counseling (MA, M Ed), professional teacher education (MA, M Ed), school based elementary education (M Ed), school based secondary education (M Ed). Accredited by NCATE. Faculty: 13 full-time (8 women), 38 part-time (19 women). Students: 106 full-time (79 women), 180 part-time (139 women); includes 46 minority (41 African Americans, 3 Asian Americans, 2 Hispanics), 1 international. In 1997, 122 degrees awarded. *Degree requirements:* Comprehensive exam, research essay or thesis required, foreign language not required. *Entrance requirements:* GRE General Test or MAT, minimum GPA of 2.75. Application deadline: rolling. Application fee: $25 ($35 for international students). *Tuition:* $450 per credit. *Financial aid:* In 1997–98, 5 students received aid, including 5 assistantships; teaching assistantships, partial tuition waivers also available. Financial aid application deadline: 3/1; applicants required to submit FAFSA. • Dr. Kathleen A. Roskos, Chairperson, 216-397-4331.

John F. Kennedy University, School of Liberal Arts, Program in Teaching, Orinda, CA 94563-2689. Awards MAT. Part-time and evening/weekend programs available. Faculty: 1 (woman) full-time, 22 part-time (17 women). Students: 23 full-time (19 women), 19 part-time (13 women); includes 11 minority (6 African Americans, 1 Asian American, 2 Hispanics, 2 Native Americans). Average age 35. 0 applicants. In 1997, 1 degree awarded. *Degree requirements:* Thesis required, foreign language not required. *Entrance requirements:* California Basic Educational Skills Test, NTE, TOEFL (minimum score 550), interview. Application deadline: rolling. Application fee: $50. *Expenses:* Tuition $316 per unit. Fees $9 per quarter. *Financial aid:* Application deadline 3/2. • Dr. Susan Kwock, Chair, 925-258-2232. Application contact: Ellena Bloedorn, Director of Admissions, 925-258-2213. Fax: 925-254-6964.

Johns Hopkins University, School of Continuing Studies, Division of Education, Baltimore, MD 21218-2699. Awards MAT, MS, Ed D, CAGS, Certificate. Part-time and evening/weekend programs available. Faculty: 21 full-time, 105 part-time. Students: 64 full-time (40 women), 1,168 part-time (943 women); includes 203 minority (142 African Americans, 32 Asian Americans, 26 Hispanics, 3 Native Americans), 2 international. Average age 34. 570 applicants, 96% accepted. In 1997, 401 master's, 3 doctorates, 4 other advanced degrees awarded. *Degree requirements:* For doctorate, dissertation, comprehensive exam required, foreign language not required. *Entrance requirements:* For master's, minimum GPA of 3.0, interview; for doctorate, MAT, interview, master's degree, minimum GPA of 3.25; for other advanced degree, master's or doctoral degree. Application deadline: rolling. Application fee: $50. *Financial aid:* 549 students received aid; Federal Work-Study available. Aid available to part-time students. Financial aid application deadline: 7/1; applicants required to submit FAFSA. • Dr. Ralph Fessler, Director, 410-516-8273. Application contact: Lenora Henry, Admissions Coordinator, 410-872-1234. Fax: 410-872-1251. E-mail: adv_mail@jhuvms.hcf.jhu.edu.

See in-depth description on page 749.

Johnson & Wales University, Graduate School, Program in Teacher Education, 8 Abbott Park Place, Providence, RI 02903-3703. Offers business administration (MAT), food service (MAT). Faculty: 2 full-time (1 woman), 5 part-time (0 women). Students: 67 part-time (35 women); includes 6 minority (5 African Americans, 1 Hispanic). Average age 28. 43 applicants, 72% accepted. In 1997, 15 degrees awarded. *Average time to degree:* master's–2.5 years part-time. *Entrance requirements:* MAT, minimum GPA of 2.75. Application deadline: 8/21 (priority date; rolling processing). Application fee: $0. *Expenses:* Tuition $194 per quarter hour (minimum). Fees $477 per year. *Financial aid:* In 1997–98, 2 graduate assistantships averaging $735 per month were awarded. Financial aid application deadline: 5/1. *Faculty research:* Secondary education, student teaching, educational reform, evaluation procedures. • Application contact: Dr. Allan G. Freedman, Director of Graduate Admissions, 401-598-1015. Fax: 401-598-4773. E-mail: clifb@jwu.edu.

Johnson State College, Graduate Program in Education, Johnson, VT 05656-9405. Offers counseling (MA); curriculum and instruction (MA Ed); early childhood education (MA Ed); education of the gifted (MA Ed); educational leadership (MA Ed), including public school principal, school business management; reading education (MA Ed); special education (MA Ed). Part-time programs available. Faculty: 8 full-time (4 women), 5 part-time (3 women). Students: 41 full-time (30 women), 113 part-time (80 women). *Degree requirements:* Comprehensive exam required, foreign language not required. *Entrance requirements:* Interview. Application deadline: (11/1 for spring admission). Application fee: $30. *Expenses:* Tuition $164 per credit for state residents; $383 per credit for nonresidents. Fees $15.90 per credit. *Financial aid:* Federal Work-Study, institutionally sponsored loans, and career-related internships or fieldwork available. Aid available to part-time students. Financial aid application deadline: 3/1; applicants required to submit FAFSA. • Application contact: Catherine H. Higley, Administrative Assistant, 802-635-2356 Ext. 1244. Fax: 802-635-1248. E-mail: higleyc@badger.jsc.vsc.edu.

Kansas State University, College of Education, Manhattan, KS 66506. Awards MS, Ed D, PhD. Accredited by NCATE. Part-time and evening/weekend programs available. Faculty: 66 full-time (19 women), 7 part-time (4 women). Students: 108 full-time (79 women), 468 part-time (341 women). Terminal master's awarded for partial completion of doctoral program. *Degree requirements:* For master's, thesis or alternative required, foreign language not required; for doctorate, dissertation required, foreign language not required. *Entrance requirements:* For master's, minimum B average; for doctorate, GRE, minimum B average. Application deadline: rolling. Application fee: $0 ($25 for international students). Electronic applications accepted. *Tuition:* $2218 per year full-time, $401 per semester (minimum) part-time for state residents; $6336 per year full-time, $1087 per semester (minimum) part-time for nonresidents. *Financial aid:* Fellowships, research assistantships, teaching assistantships, Federal Work-Study, institutionally sponsored loans, and career-related internships or fieldwork available. Aid available to part-time students. • Michael Holen, Dean, 785-532-5525. Application contact: Paul Burden, Assistant Dean, 785-532-5595. Fax: 785-532-7304. E-mail: gradstudy@mail.educ.ksu.edu.

Kean University, School of Education, Union, NJ 07083. Awards MA, Certificate, PMC. Accredited by NCATE. Part-time programs available. Students: 106 full-time (90 women), 701 part-time (579 women); includes 112 minority (59 African Americans, 6 Asian Americans, 46 Hispanics, 1 Native American). Average age 34. In 1997, 279 master's awarded. *Degree requirements:* For master's, thesis, comprehensive exams required, foreign language not required. *Application deadline:* 6/15 (11/15 for spring admission). *Application fee:* $35. *Tuition:* $5926 per year full-time, $248 per credit part-time for state residents; $7312 per year full-time, $304 per credit part-time for nonresidents. *Financial aid:* Fellowships, graduate assistantships, and career-related internships or fieldwork available. • Dr. Ana Maria Schuhmann, Dean, 908-527-2136. Application contact: Joanne Morris, Director of Graduate Admissions, 908-527-2665. Fax: 908-527-2286. E-mail: grad_adm@turbo.kean.edu.

Keene State College, Division of Graduate and Professional Studies, Keene, NH 03435. Awards M Ed. Part-time and evening/weekend programs available. Faculty: 184 full-time, 169 part-time. Students: 8 full-time (all women), 65 part-time (52 women); includes 1 international. Average age 42. 30 applicants, 100% accepted. In 1997, 21 degrees awarded. *Entrance requirements:* Resume. Application deadline: 6/15 (rolling processing; 10/15 for spring admission). Application fee: $25 ($35 for international students). *Financial aid:* Research assistantships, assistantships, Federal Work-Study, institutionally sponsored loans, and career-related internships or fieldwork available. Aid available to part-time students. Financial aid application deadline: 3/1; applicants required to submit FAFSA. • Dr. Ann Britt Waling, Dean, 603-358-2332. E-mail: ptandy@keene.edu. Application contact: Peter Tandy, Academic Counselor, 603-358-2332. Fax: 603-358-2257. E-mail: ptandy@keene.edu.

Kennesaw State University, Leland and Clarice C. Bagwell College of Education, Kennesaw, GA 30144-5591. Awards M Ed. Accredited by NCATE. Part-time programs available. Faculty: 38 full-time (24 women), 2 part-time (both women). Students: 81 full-time (71 women), 194 part-time (170 women); includes 17 minority (15 African Americans, 1 Asian American, 1 Hispanic). Average age 34. 193 applicants, 80% accepted. In 1997, 50 degrees awarded. *Degree requirements:* Thesis or alternative required, foreign language not required. *Entrance requirements:* GRE General Test (minimum combined score of 800), T-4 state certification, minimum GPA of 2.5. Application deadline: 7/1 (2/20 for spring admission). Application fee: $20. *Expenses:* Tuition $2398 per year full-time, $83 per credit hour part-time for state residents; $8398 per year full-time, $333 per credit hour part-time for nonresidents. Fees $338 per year. *Financial aid:* Federal Work-Study available. Aid available to part-time students. Financial aid application deadline: 6/15; applicants required to submit FAFSA. • Dr. Deborah Wallace, Dean, 770-423-6043. Fax: 770-423-6527. E-mail: dwallace@ksumail.kennesaw.edu. Application contact: Susan N. Barrett, Administrative Specialist, Admissions, 770-423-6500. Fax: 770-423-6541. E-mail: sbarrett@ksumail.kennesaw.edu.

Kent State University, Graduate School of Education, Kent, OH 44242-0001. Awards MA, MAT, M Ed, PhD, Ed S. Accredited by NCATE. Part-time and evening/weekend programs available. Faculty: 98 full-time (54 women), 122 part-time (72 women). Students: 606 full-time (454 women), 743 part-time (568 women); includes 89 minority (68 African Americans, 8 Asian Americans, 9 Hispanics, 4 Native Americans), 22 international. 242 applicants. In 1997, 350 master's, 63 doctorates, 15 Ed Ss awarded. *Degree requirements:* For master's, thesis (MA) required, foreign language not required; for doctorate, dissertation required, foreign language not required. *Average time to degree:* master's–2 years full-time, 5 years part-time; doctorate–4.5 years full-time, 6.5 years part-time; other advanced degree–2 years full-time, 5 years part-time. *Entrance requirements:* For doctorate, GRE General Test (minimum score 550 on verbal section). Application deadline: rolling. Application fee: $30. *Tuition:* $4752 per year full-time, $216 per credit hour part-time for state residents; $9213 per year full-time, $419 per credit hour part-time for nonresidents. *Financial aid:* In 1997–98, 45 fellowships, 5 research assistantships, 41 teaching assistantships were awarded; Federal Work-Study and career-related internships or fieldwork also available. Financial aid application deadline: 4/1. • Dr. Joanne R. Whitmore, Dean, 330-672-2808. Fax: 330-672-3407. E-mail: jwhitmore@emerald.educ.kent.edu. Application contact: Deborah Barber, Director, Office of Academic Services, 330-672-2862. Fax: 330-672-3549.

Kutztown University of Pennsylvania, Graduate School, College of Education, Kutztown, PA 19530. Awards MA, M Ed, MLS. Accredited by NCATE. Part-time and evening/weekend programs available. Faculty: 25 full-time (8 women). Students: 97 full-time (67 women), 524 part-time (436 women); includes 21 minority (6 African Americans, 3 Asian Americans, 11 Hispanics, 1 Native American). Average age 32. In 1997, 169 degrees awarded. *Entrance requirements:* GRE, TOEFL, TSE. Application deadline: 3/1 (8/1 for spring admission). Application fee: $25. *Tuition:* $4111 per year full-time, $225 per credit hour part-time for state residents; $6879 per year full-time, $393 per credit hour part-time for nonresidents. *Financial aid:* Graduate assistantships, partial tuition waivers, Federal Work-Study, and career-related internships or fieldwork available. Financial aid application deadline: 3/15; applicants required to submit FAFSA. • Dr. U. Mae Reck, Dean, 610-683-4253.

LaGrange College, Department of Education, LaGrange, GA 30240-2999. Offers programs in early childhood education (M Ed), education (M Ed), middle childhood education (M Ed). Part-time and evening/weekend programs available. Faculty: 1 (woman) full-time, 6 part-time (4 women). Students: 6 full-time (4 women), 12 part-time (10 women); includes 3 minority (2 African Americans, 1 Hispanic), 1 international. Average age 33. 9 applicants, 78% accepted. In 1997, 12 degrees awarded (100% found work related to degree). *Degree requirements:* Comprehensive exam required, thesis not required. *Entrance requirements:* GRE, MAT, or NTE, minimum GPA of 2.5. Application deadline: 8/1 (priority date; rolling processing). Application fee: $20 ($25 for international students). *Expenses:* Tuition $219 per quarter hour. Fees $80 per quarter hour. *Financial aid:* Full and partial tuition waivers available. Aid available to part-time students. • Dr. Evelyn Jordan, Chair, 706-812-7276. Application contact: Andy Geeter, Director of Admissions, 706-812-7260. Fax: 706-812-7348. E-mail: ageeter@mentor.lgc.peachnet.edu.

Lake Erie College, Division of Education, Painesville, OH 44077-3389. Offers programs in education (MS Ed), effective teaching (MS Ed), reading (MS Ed). Part-time and evening/weekend programs available. Faculty: 4 full-time (2 women), 2 part-time (0 women). Students: 39 part-time. Average age 34. 10 applicants, 90% accepted. In 1997, 9 degrees awarded. *Degree requirements:* Thesis, applied research project, comprehensive exam required, foreign language not required. *Entrance requirements:* GRE General Test (minimum score 440 on verbal section, 500 on quantitative) or minimum GPA of 2.75. Application deadline: 8/1 (priority date; rolling processing; 12/15 for spring admission). Application fee: $20 ($50 for international students). *Expenses:* Tuition $294 per credit hour. Fees $20 per credit hour. *Financial aid:* Scholarships available. Financial aid applicants required to submit FAFSA. *Faculty research:* Cooperative learning, portfolio assessment, education systems in England, curriculum, video case-based instruction. • Dr. Carol Ramsay, Associate Dean of Teacher Education and Certification, 440-639-4749. Application contact: Director of Admissions, 440-639-7879. Fax: 440-352-3533.

Lakehead University, Faculty of Education, Thunder Bay, ON P7B 5E1, Canada. Offers programs in curriculum development (M Ed), education administration (M Ed). Part-time and evening/weekend programs available. *Degree requirements:* Thesis optional, foreign language not required. *Entrance requirements:* TOEFL (minimum score 550), honors degree, minimum B average. Application deadline: 2/1 (priority date; rolling processing). Application fee: $0. *Faculty research:* Art education, AIDS education, language arts education, gerontology, women's studies.

Lakeland College, Graduate Studies Division, Program in Education, Sheboygan, WI 53082-0359. Awards M Ed. *Degree requirements:* Thesis. *Application deadline:* rolling. *Application fee:* $25. *Tuition:* $175 per credit hour. • Application contact: Rebecca Hagan, Graduate Program Coordinator, 414-565-1256. Fax: 414-565-1206.

Lamar University, College of Education and Human Development, Beaumont, TX 77710. Awards M Ed, MS, Certificate. Part-time and evening/weekend programs available. Faculty: 26 full-time (11 women), 12 part-time (3 women). Students: 87 full-time (66 women), 175 part-time (111 women). Average age 37. 50 applicants, 72% accepted. In 1997, 58 master's awarded. *Degree requirements:* For master's, thesis optional, foreign language not required. *Entrance requirements:* For master's, GRE General Test, TOEFL (minimum score 500), minimum GPA of 2.5. Application deadline: 8/1 (rolling processing; 12/1 for spring admission). Application fee: $0. *Expenses:* Tuition $1296 per year full-time, $360 per year part-time for state residents; $6432 per year full-time, $1608 per year part-time for nonresidents. Fees $238 per year full-time, $103 per year part-time. *Financial aid:* Fellowships, research assistantships, teaching assistantships, Federal Work-Study, institutionally sponsored loans, and career-related internships or fieldwork available. Aid available to part-time students. Financial aid application deadline: 4/1. *Faculty research:* School dropouts, suicide prevention in public school students, school climate and gifted performance, teacher evaluation. Total annual research expenditures: $600,000. • Dr. LeBland McAdams, Dean, 409-880-8661. Fax: 409-880-8662.

Lander University, School of Education, Greenwood, SC 29649-2099. Offers programs in art (MAT), elementary education (M Ed), English (MAT), science (MAT). Part-time and evening/weekend programs available. Faculty: 9 full-time (5 women). Students: 215. *Degree requirements:* Thesis or alternative, comprehensive exam required, foreign language not required. *Entrance requirements:* GRE. Application deadline: rolling. Application fee: $25. *Tuition:* $3700 per year full-time, $148 per semester hour part-time for state residents; $6326 per year full-time, $253 per semester hour part-time for nonresidents. *Financial aid:* Federal Work-Study available. Aid available to part-time students. Financial aid application deadline: 4/15; applicants required to submit FAFSA. • Dr. Phil Bennett, Dean, 864-388-8225.

Langston University, School of Education and Behavioral Sciences, PO Box 838, Langston, OK 73050-0838. Awards M Ed. One or more programs accredited by NCATE. Part-time programs available. Faculty: 16 full-time (7 women), 8 part-time (6 women). Students: 62 full-time (41 women); includes 55 minority (52 African Americans, 2 Asian Americans, 1 Native American), 3 international. 37 applicants, 100% accepted. *Degree requirements:* Thesis optional, foreign language not required. *Entrance requirements:* GRE, minimum GPA of 2.5. Application deadline: 7/15 (priority date; 12/15 for spring admission). Application fee: $0. *Expenses:* Tuition $62 per credit hour for state residents; $164 per credit hour for nonresidents. Fees $581 per year full-time, $97 per semester (minimum) part-time. *Financial aid:* Research assistantships, teaching assistantships, partial tuition waivers, institutionally sponsored loans available. Financial aid application deadline: 5/15. *Faculty research:* Bilingual/multicultural education, financing post-secondary education. • Dr. Alex O. Lewis, Director, 405-466-3379. Fax: 405-466-3270. E-mail: aolewis@lunet.edu.

La Salle University, School of Arts and Sciences, Program in Education, 1900 West Olney Avenue, Philadelphia, PA 19141-1199. Awards MA. Part-time and evening/weekend programs available. Faculty: 12 full-time (6 women), 10 part-time (5 women), 14.5 FTE. Students: 165 (117 women); includes 11 minority (9 African Americans, 1 Asian American, 1 Hispanic). Average age 29. In 1997, 46 degrees awarded. *Degree requirements:* Written comprehensive exam required, foreign language and thesis not required. *Entrance requirements:* GRE or MAT. Application fee: $30. *Financial aid:* Partial tuition waivers, Federal Work-Study, and career-related internships or fieldwork available. Aid available to part-time students. *Faculty research:* Educational reform and social realities, adult development, curriculum design for special needs children, developmentally based schooling. • Gary K. Clabaugh, Director, 215-951-1593. E-mail: clabaugh@lasalle.edu.

La Sierra University, School of Education, Riverside, CA 92515-8247. Awards MA, Ed D, Ed S. Part-time and evening/weekend programs available. Faculty: 10 full-time (5 women), 17 part-time (8 women), 16 FTE. Students: 26 full-time (13 women), 60 part-time (41 women). Average age 35. In 1997, 30 master's, 2 doctorates, 10 Ed Ss awarded. Terminal master's awarded for partial completion of doctoral program. *Degree requirements:* For doctorate, dissertation required, foreign language not required; for Ed S, thesis optional, foreign language not required. *Entrance requirements:* For master's, minimum GPA of 3.0; for doctorate, GRE General Test, GRE Subject Test, minimum GPA of 3.3; for Ed S, minimum GPA of 3.3. Application deadline: rolling. Application fee: $30. *Financial aid:* 8 students received aid; graduate assistantships, Federal Work-Study, institutionally sponsored loans, and career-related internships or fieldwork available. Aid available to part-time students. Financial aid application deadline: 2/10. • Dr. David S. Penner, Dean, 909-785-2266. Application contact: Myrna Costa-Casado, Director of Admissions, 909-785-2176. Fax: 909-785-2447. E-mail: mcosta@lasierra.edu.

Lawrence Technological University, College of Arts and Sciences, 21000 West Ten Mile Road, Southfield, MI 48075-1058. Offers program in science education (MSE). Part-time and evening/weekend programs available. Faculty: 2 full-time (1 woman), 2 part-time (0 women), 3 FTE. Students: 15 part-time (12 women); includes 2 minority (1 African American, 1 Hispanic). Average age 36. 15 applicants, 67% accepted. *Application deadline:* 8/1 (priority date; rolling processing; 1/1 for spring admission). *Application fee:* $50. Electronic applications accepted. *Expenses:* Tuition $11,400 per year full-time, $380 per credit hour part-time. Fees $100 per year. • Dr. James Rodgers, Dean, 248-204-3500. E-mail: scidean@ltu.edu. Application contact: Paul Kinder, Director of Admissions, 248-204-3160. Fax: 248-204-3188. E-mail: admissions@ltu.edu.

Lee University, Program in Education, Cleveland, TN 37320-3450. Awards M Ed. Faculty: 7. Students: 20. *Application deadline:* rolling. *Application fee:* $25. *Tuition:* $5826 per year full-time, $292 per credit hour part-time. • Dr. Debbie Murray, Director, 423-614-8175.

Lehigh University, College of Education, Bethlehem, PA 18015-3094. Awards MA, M Ed, MS, Ed D, PhD, Certificate, Ed S. Part-time and evening/weekend programs available. Postbaccalaureate distance learning degree programs offered (minimal on-campus study). Faculty: 22 full-time (8 women), 12 part-time (4 women). Students: 133 full-time (102 women), 313 part-time (201 women); includes 26 minority (5 African Americans, 7 Asian Americans, 14 Hispanics), 19 international. 318 applicants, 42% accepted. In 1997, 101 master's, 24 doctorates awarded. Terminal master's awarded for partial completion of doctoral program. *Degree requirements:* For doctorate, dissertation required, foreign language not required. *Entrance requirements:* For master's, TOEFL, minimum GPA of 2.75; for doctorate, TOEFL; for other advanced degree, TOEFL (minimum score 550). Application fee: $40. Electronic applications accepted. *Expenses:* Tuition $470 per credit. Fees $12 per semester full-time, $6 per semester part-time. *Financial aid:* Fellowships, research assistantships, teaching assistantships, assistantships, scholarships, full and partial tuition waivers, Federal Work-Study, institutionally sponsored loans, and career-related internships or fieldwork available. Financial aid application deadline: 1/15. • Roland K. Yoshida, Dean, 610-758-3221. E-mail: rky2@lehigh.edu. Application contact: Betty Shook, Coordinator, 610-758-3235. Fax: 610-758-6223. E-mail: es0d@lehigh.edu.

Lehman College of the City University of New York, Division of Education, 250 Bedford Park Boulevard West, Bronx, NY 10468-1589. Awards MA, MS Ed. Part-time and evening/weekend programs available. Faculty: 40 full-time, 27 part-time. Students: 18 full-time (15 women), 822 part-time (645 women). *Application deadline:* 4/1 (rolling processing; 11/1 for spring admission). *Application fee:* $40. *Expenses:* Tuition $4350 per year full-time, $185 per credit part-time for state residents; $7600 per year full-time, $320 per credit part-time for nonresidents. Fees $120 per year full-time, $80 per year part-time. *Financial aid:* Fellowships, full and partial tuition waivers, Federal Work-Study, institutionally sponsored loans, and career-related internships or fieldwork available. Aid available to part-time students. Financial aid application deadline: 5/15; applicants required to submit FAFSA. • James V. Bruni, Dean, 718-960-8401.

Le Moyne College, Department of Education, Syracuse, NY 13214-1399. Awards MS Ed, MST. Part-time and evening/weekend programs available. Faculty: 8 full-time (5 women), 20 part-time (14 women). Students: 58 full-time (44 women), 195 part-time (138 women); includes 9 minority (6 African Americans, 2 Asian Americans, 1 Hispanic). Average age 32. 76 applicants, 99% accepted. In 1997, 22 degrees awarded. *Degree requirements:* Thesis required, foreign language not required. *Entrance requirements:* GRE General Test (combined average 1500 on three sections), minimum GPA of 3.0. Application deadline: rolling. Application fee: $25. *Tuition:* $333 per credit hour. *Financial aid:* 175 students received aid; partial tuition waivers and career-related internships or fieldwork available. Financial aid applicants required to submit FAFSA. • Rev. Edmund G. Ryan SJ, Interim Director of Graduate Education, 315-445-4376. Fax: 315-445-4540.

LeMoyne–Owen College, Graduate Program in Education, Memphis, TN 38126-6595. Awards MS. Faculty: 3 full-time (all women). Students: 4 full-time (all women), 3 part-time (all women); includes 7 minority (6 African Americans, 1 Asian American). *Entrance requirements:* MAT. Application deadline: 4/1 (priority date; rolling processing; 11/31 for spring admission). Application fee: $25. *Tuition:* $3300 per year full-time, $280 per credit part-time. *Financial aid:* Research assistantships, graduate assistantships available. • Dr. Jesse McClure, Vice President of Academic Affairs, 901-942-7305.

Lenoir–Rhyne College, Division of Graduate Programs, Department of Education, Hickory, NC 28601. Offers programs in academically gifted (MA); early childhood education (MA); elementary education (MA); guidance and counseling (MA, Ed S), including counselor education; middle school education (MA); reading (MA). Part-time and evening/weekend programs available. Faculty: 16 (10 women). Students: 13 full-time (12 women), 100 part-time (91 women); includes 1 international. Average age 35. In 1997, 39 master's awarded (95% found work related to degree, 5% continued full-time study). *Degree requirements:* For master's, thesis optional, foreign language not required; for Ed S, thesis, internship required, foreign language not required. *Entrance requirements:* For master's, GRE General Test (minimum score 450 on verbal section, 1350 combined), minimum GPA of 2.7; for Ed S, GRE General Test (minimum score 450 on verbal section, 1350 combined), minimum GPA of 3.0. Application deadline: 8/1 (12/1 for spring admission). Application fee: $25. *Tuition:* $190 per credit hour. *Financial aid:* Federal Work-Study, institutionally sponsored loans, and career-related internships or fieldwork available. Aid available to part-time students. • Prof. Barbara Andrew, Chair, 828-328-7194. Application contact: Dr. Thomas W. Fauquet, Dean of Graduate Studies, 828-328-7275. Fax: 828-328-7368. E-mail: fauquet@lrc.edu.

Lesley College, School of Education, Cambridge, MA 02138-2790. Offers programs in computers in education (M Ed, CAGS), curriculum and instruction (M Ed, CAGS), early childhood education (M Ed), educational administration (M Ed, CAGS), educational studies (PhD), elementary education (M Ed), individually designed (M Ed), intensive special needs (M Ed), middle school education (M Ed), reading (M Ed, CAGS), special needs (M Ed, CAGS). Part-time and evening/weekend programs available. Postbaccalaureate distance learning degree programs offered (no on-campus study). Faculty: 36 full-time (31 women), 340 part-time (220 women). Students: 168 full-time, 2,392 part-time; includes 149 minority (63 African Americans, 26 Asian Americans, 49 Hispanics, 11 Native Americans), 15 international. Average age 35. In 1997, 1,054 master's, 3 doctorates, 3 CAGSs awarded. *Degree requirements:* For master's and CAGS, computer language required, foreign language and thesis not required; for doctorate, dissertation. *Entrance requirements:* For master's, TOEFL (minimum score 550); for doctorate, GRE General Test or MAT, interview, master's degree; for CAGS, interview, master's degree. Application deadline: rolling. Application fee: $45. *Tuition:* $425 per credit. *Financial aid:* Research assistantships, teaching assistantships, assistantships, Federal Work-Study, and career-related internships or fieldwork available. Aid available to part-time students. Financial aid application deadline: 5/1. *Faculty research:* Literacy and learning, logo algebra, autism, clinical mentorship models. • Dr. William L. Dandridge, Dean, 617-349-8375. Application contact: Graduate Admissions, 617-349-8300. Fax: 617-349-8366.

See in-depth description on page 751.

Lewis & Clark College, Department of Education, Portland, OR 97219-7899. Awards MAT, Certificate, MAT/Certificate, MPA/Certificate, MPA/MAT. Programs in educational administration (Certificate), elementary education (MAT), music education (MAT), secondary education (MAT). Part-time and evening/weekend programs available. *Application deadline:* rolling. *Application fee:* $45.

See in-depth description on page 753.

Lewis University, College of Arts and Sciences, Department of Education, Romeoville, IL 60446. Offers programs in education (MAE, M Ed), education administration (CAS). Part-time and evening/weekend programs available. Faculty: 12 (10 women). Students: 1 full-time, 140 part-time; includes 15 minority (13 African Americans, 1 Asian American, 1 Hispanic). Average age 33. In 1997, 33 master's awarded. *Degree requirements:* For master's, thesis optional, foreign language not required. *Entrance requirements:* For master's, departmental qualifying exam, minimum GPA of 2.75. Application deadline: 9/1. Application fee: $35. *Financial aid:* Research assistantships, scholarships, partial tuition waivers, institutionally sponsored loans, and career-related internships or fieldwork available. Aid available to part-time students. Financial aid application deadline: 4/1. • Dr. Jeanette Mines, Chair, 815-838-0500 Ext. 5316. Fax: 815-836-5879.

Liberty University, School of Education, 1971 University Road, Lynchburg, VA 24502. Offers programs in educational administration (M Ed), elementary education (M Ed), reading (M Ed), secondary education (M Ed). Part-time programs available. Faculty: 3 full-time (1 woman), 4 part-time (2 women). Students: 1 (woman) full-time, 67 part-time (34 women). In 1997, 4 degrees awarded. *Degree requirements:* Thesis optional, foreign language not required. *Entrance requirements:* GRE General Test (minimum combined score of 900). Application deadline: 8/15 (priority date; rolling processing). Application fee: $35. *Tuition:* $280 per credit hour. *Financial aid:* Federal Work-Study available. Financial aid application deadline: 4/15. *Faculty research:* Outcomes assessment, classroom methodology. • Dr. Pauline Donaldson, Dean, 804-582-2314. Application contact: Bill Wegert, Coordinator of Graduate Admissions, 804-582-2175.

Lincoln Memorial University, Program in Education, Cumberland Gap Parkway, Harrogate, TN 37752-1901. Awards M Ed, Ed S. Part-time and evening/weekend programs available. Faculty: 7 full-time (3 women), 11 part-time (5 women), 15 FTE. Students: 349 full-time (278 women), 164 part-time (122 women); includes 12 minority (11 African Americans, 1 Hispanic), 2 international. Average age 38. 347 applicants, 78% accepted. In 1997, 93 master's awarded (100% found work related to degree); 220 Ed Ss awarded (100% found work related to degree). *Degree requirements:* For master's, comprehensive exam required, thesis optional, foreign language not required. *Average time to degree:* master's–1 year full-time, 2 years part-time; other advanced degree–1 year full-time, 2 years part-time. *Entrance requirements:* For master's, GRE, MAT, or NTE. Application deadline: 8/10 (priority date). Application fee: $25. *Expenses:* Tuition $7800 per year full-time, $210 per semester hour part-time. Fees $300 per year full-time, $100 per year part-time. *Financial aid:* In 1997–98, 68 students received aid, including 25 assistantships; career-related internships or fieldwork also available. Aid available to part-time students. Financial aid application deadline: 4/1; applicants required to submit FAFSA. *Faculty research:* Administration and supervision, curriculum and instruction, counseling and guidance. • Dr. Fred Bedelle, Dean, School of Graduate Studies, 423-869-6223. Application contact: Barbara McCune, Senior Assistant, Graduate Office, 423-869-6374. Fax: 423-869-6261.

Lincoln University, Graduate School, College of Arts and Sciences, Department of Education, Jefferson City, MO 65102. Offers programs in elementary and secondary teaching (M Ed), including elementary, secondary; guidance and counseling (M Ed), including agency, elementary, secondary; school administration and supervision (M Ed), including elementary, secondary. Accredited by NCATE. Part-time and evening/weekend programs available. Faculty: 2 full-time (0 women), 10 part-time (6 women). Students: 5 full-time (2 women), 157 part-time (114 women); includes 6 minority (5 African Americans, 1 Hispanic), 1 international. Average age 35. 19 applicants. In 1997, 61 degrees awarded. *Entrance requirements:* GRE General Test or MAT, minimum GPA of 2.75 in major, 2.5 overall. Application deadline: 7/25 (rolling processing; 12/15 for spring admission). Application fee: $17. *Expenses:* Tuition $117 per credit hour for state residents; $234 per credit hour for nonresidents. Fees $552 per year (minimum) for state residents; $1104 per year (minimum) for nonresidents. • Dr. Marilyn Hofmann, Acting Head, 573-681-5250.

Lindenwood University, Department of Education, St. Charles, MO 63301-1695. Awards MA. Accredited by NCATE. Part-time programs available. Faculty: 12 full-time (7 women), 11 part-time (9 women). Students: 548 part-time (454 women); includes 21 minority (13 African Americans, 1 Asian American, 2 Hispanics, 5 Native Americans), 2 international. Average age 28. *Degree requirements:* Thesis required (for some programs), foreign language not required. *Entrance requirements:* Interview, minimum GPA of 3.0, sample of written work. Application deadline: 6/30 (rolling processing). Application fee: $25. Electronic applications accepted. *Tuition:* $5880 per year full-time, $245 per credit hour part-time. *Financial aid:* Partial tuition waivers, institutionally sponsored loans, and career-related internships or fieldwork available.

Directory: Education—General

Lindenwood University (continued)

Financial aid application deadline: 6/30. • Dr. Richard Boyle, Dean, 314-949-4844. Application contact: John Guffey, Director of Graduate Admissions, 314-949-4933. Fax: 314-949-4910.

Lock Haven University of Pennsylvania, Office of Graduate Studies, Department of Education, Lock Haven, PA 17745-2390. Offers program in curriculum and instruction (M Ed). One or more programs accredited by NCATE. Part-time and evening/weekend programs available. Students: 31 part-time (8 women). Average age 35. 5 applicants, 100% accepted. *Entrance requirements:* Minimum undergraduate GPA of 3.0. Application deadline: rolling. Application fee: $25. Electronic applications accepted. *Expenses:* Tuition $3468 per year full-time, $193 per credit hour part-time for state residents; $6236 per year full-time, $346 per credit hour part-time for nonresidents. Fees $604 per year full-time, $46 per credit hour part-time for state residents; $604 per year full-time, $59 per credit hour part-time for nonresidents. *Financial aid:* Application deadline 8/1. • Dr. Susan Ashley, Director, 717-893-2205. E-mail: sashley@eagle.lhup.edu. Application contact: Office of Admissions, 717-893-2027. Fax: 717-893-2201. E-mail: admissions@eagle.lhup.edu.

Long Island University, Brooklyn Campus, School of Education, Brooklyn, NY 11201-8423. Awards MS, MS Ed, Certificate, PD. Part-time and evening/weekend programs available. Faculty: 21 full-time (14 women), 56 part-time (27 women). Students: 282 full-time (232 women), 439 part-time (349 women); includes 466 minority (329 African Americans, 16 Asian Americans, 118 Hispanics, 3 Native Americans). 518 applicants, 86% accepted. In 1997, 260 master's, 18 other advanced degrees awarded. *Degree requirements:* For master's, thesis optional. *Application deadline:* rolling. *Application fee:* $30. Electronic applications accepted. *Expenses:* Tuition $480 per credit. Fees $415 per year full-time, $73 per semester (minimum) part-time. *Financial aid:* In 1997–98, 15 students received aid, including 15 assistantships; partial tuition waivers and career-related internships or fieldwork also available. Aid available to part-time students. Financial aid applicants required to submit FAFSA. • Dr. Ofelia Garcia, Dean, 718-488-1055. Application contact: Bernard W. Sullivan, Associate Director of Admissions, 718-488-1011.

Long Island University, C.W. Post Campus, School of Education, Brookville, NY 11548-1300. Awards MA, MS, MS Ed, CAS, PD. Part-time and evening/weekend programs available. Faculty: 47 full-time (19 women), 98 part-time (42 women). Students: 170 full-time, 1,395 part-time. Average age 28. 1,026 applicants, 69% accepted. In 1997, 719 master's, 53 other advanced degrees awarded. *Application deadline:* rolling. *Application fee:* $30. Electronic applications accepted. *Expenses:* Tuition $480 per credit. Fees $316 per year full-time, $71 per semester (minimum) part-time. *Financial aid:* In 1997–98, 30 research assistantships were awarded; teaching assistantships and career-related internships or fieldwork also available. Aid available to part-time students. Financial aid application deadline: 5/15; applicants required to submit FAFSA. • Dr. Jeffrey Kane, Dean, 516-299-2210. Fax: 516-299-4167. E-mail: jkane@titan.liunet.edu. Application contact: Sally Luzader, Associate Director of Graduate Admissions, 516-299-2417. Fax: 516-299-2137. E-mail: admissions@collegehall.liunet.edu.

Long Island University, Southampton College, Education Division, Southampton, NY 11968-9822. Awards MS Ed. Part-time and evening/weekend programs available. Faculty: 5 full-time (2 women), 7 part-time (4 women). Students: 79. Average age 35. In 1997, 18 degrees awarded. *Degree requirements:* Computer language, thesis. *Entrance requirements:* MAT. Application deadline: 4/15 (priority date; 11/30 for spring admission). Application fee: $30. • Dr. R. Lawrence McCann, Director, 516-287-8211 Ext. 211.

Longwood College, Department of Education, Farmville, VA 23909-1800. Offers programs in administration/supervision (MS); community and college counseling (MS); curriculum and instruction specialist-elementary (MS), including English (MS), mild disabilities (MS), modern language (MS), physical education (MS), speech and drama (MS); guidance and counseling (MS); library science media specialist (MS); reading specialist (MS). Accredited by NCATE. Part-time and evening/weekend programs available. Faculty: 34 part-time. Students: 356 (299 women); includes 86 minority (54 African Americans, 4 Asian Americans, 28 Hispanics). Average age 32. 38 applicants, 92% accepted. In 1997, 84 degrees awarded. *Degree requirements:* Thesis (for some programs), comprehensive exam. *Entrance requirements:* Minimum GPA of 2.5. Application deadline: 5/1 (priority date; rolling processing; 10/15 for spring admission). Application fee: $25. *Expenses:* Tuition $3048 per year full-time, $127 per credit hour part-time for state residents; $8160 per year full-time, $340 per credit hour part-time for nonresidents. Fees $920 per year full-time, $31 per credit hour part-time. *Financial aid:* In 1997–98, 8 students received aid, including 8 research assistantships; teaching assistantships and career-related internships or fieldwork also available. • Dr. Frank Howe, Chair, 804-395-2324. Application contact: Admissions Office, 804-395-2060.

Louisiana State University and Agricultural and Mechanical College, College of Education, Baton Rouge, LA 70803. Awards MA, M Ed, MS, PhD, Ed S. Accredited by NCATE. PhD offered jointly with Louisiana State University in Shreveport. Part-time and evening/weekend programs available. Faculty: 63 full-time, 3 part-time. Students: 261 full-time (194 women), 269 part-time (212 women); includes 89 minority (74 African Americans, 6 Asian Americans, 9 Hispanics), 29 international. Average age 34. 188 applicants, 75% accepted. In 1997, 163 master's, 28 doctorates, 37 Ed Ss awarded. Terminal master's awarded for partial completion of doctoral program. *Degree requirements:* For Ed S, thesis optional, foreign language not required. *Entrance requirements:* For master's, GRE General Test (minimum combined score of 1000; average 1080), minimum GPA of 3.0; for doctorate, GRE General Test (minimum combined score of 1000; average 1100), minimum GPA of 3.0. Application deadline: 1/25 (priority date; rolling processing). Application fee: $25. *Tuition:* $2736 per year full-time, $285 per semester (minimum) part-time for state residents; $6636 per year full-time, $460 per semester (minimum) part-time for nonresidents. *Financial aid:* In 1997–98, 24 fellowships (2 to first-year students), 44 research assistantships (2 to first-year students), 16 teaching assistantships (6 to first-year students), 18 service assistantships (4 to first-year students) were awarded; partial tuition waivers, Federal Work-Study, institutionally sponsored loans, and career-related internships or fieldwork also available. Aid available to part-time students. *Faculty research:* Instructional learning, educational administration, exercise physiology, sports psychology, literacy education curriculum and instruction. Total annual research expenditures: $2.5 million. • Dr. F. Neil Matthews, Dean, 504-388-1258. Application contact: Dr. Earl Cheek, Graduate Adviser, 504-388-6017.

Louisiana State University in Shreveport, College of Education, Shreveport, LA 71115-2399. Awards M Ed, SSP. Part-time and evening/weekend programs available. Faculty: 19 full-time (10 women). Students: 32 full-time (25 women), 256 part-time (210 women); includes 88 minority (84 African Americans, 2 Asian Americans, 1 Hispanic, 1 Native American). Average age 34. In 1997, 13 master's awarded (100% found work related to degree); 6 SSPs awarded (100% found work related to degree). *Degree requirements:* For master's, thesis required, foreign language not required; for SSP, written comprehensive exam required, foreign language and thesis not required. *Entrance requirements:* For master's, GRE General Test, minimum GPA of 2.5; for SSP, GRE General Test (minimum score 400 on each section), minimum GPA of 2.75. Application fee: $10. *Financial aid:* In 1997–98, 2 research assistantships were awarded; teaching assistantships, Federal Work-Study, and career-related internships or fieldwork also available. Aid available to part-time students. Financial aid applicants required to submit FAFSA. • Dr. Gary S. Rush, Dean, 318-797-5381. Fax: 318-798-4105. E-mail: grush@pilot.lsus.edu. Application contact: Dr. Patricia Doerr, Chair, 318-797-5040. Fax: 318-798-4144. E-mail: pdoerr@pilot.lsus.edu.

Louisiana Tech University, College of Education, Ruston, LA 71272. Awards MA, M Ed, MS, Ed D, PhD, Ed S. Accredited by NCATE. Part-time programs available. Faculty: 39 full-time (18 women). Students: 202 full-time (129 women), 135 part-time (109 women); includes 47 minority (40 African Americans, 3 Asian Americans, 4 Hispanics), 13 international. Average age 27. In 1997, 184 master's, 4 Ed Ss awarded. *Degree requirements:* For master's, computer language required, foreign language not required; for doctorate, computer language, dissertation required, foreign language not required. *Entrance requirements:* For master's, GRE General Test; for doctorate, GRE General Test (minimum combined score of 1000). Application deadline: 7/29 (2/3 for spring admission). Application fee: $20 ($30 for international students). *Tuition:* $2382 per year full-time, $223 per quarter (minimum) part-time for state residents; $5307 per year full-time, $223 per quarter (minimum) part-time for nonresidents. *Financial aid:* Fellowships, research assistantships, teaching assistantships, and career-related internships or fieldwork available. Financial aid application deadline: 2/1. • Dr. Jerry W. Andrews, Dean, 318-257-3712.

Loyola College, College of Arts and Sciences, Department of Education, Baltimore, MD 21210-2699. Offers programs in curriculum and instruction (MA, M Ed, CAS), educational management and supervision (MA, M Ed, CAS), foundations of education (MA, M Ed, CAS), guidance and counseling (MA, M Ed, CAS), reading (MA, M Ed, CAS), special education (MA, M Ed, CAS). Part-time and evening/weekend programs available. Faculty: 11 full-time (4 women), 43 part-time (26 women), 25 FTE. Students: 81 full-time (66 women), 916 part-time (747 women); includes 92 minority (78 African Americans, 7 Asian Americans, 7 Hispanics), 4 international. 377 applicants, 86% accepted. In 1997, 250 master's, 4 CASs awarded. *Entrance requirements:* For CAS, master's degree. Application deadline: 8/1 (rolling processing; 12/1 for spring admission). Application fee: $35. *Tuition:* $222 per credit (minimum). *Financial aid:* Research assistantships and career-related internships or fieldwork available. • Dr. John Hollwitz, Acting Chairman, 410-617-2563.

Loyola Marymount University, School of Education, Los Angeles, CA 90045-8350. Awards MA, MAT, M Ed. Part-time and evening/weekend programs available. Faculty: 14 full-time (8 women), 25 part-time (20 women). Students: 194 full-time (168 women), 131 part-time (95 women); includes 125 minority (22 African Americans, 24 Asian Americans, 78 Hispanics, 1 Native American), 6 international. 280 applicants, 72% accepted. In 1997, 104 degrees awarded. *Degree requirements:* Comprehensive exam required, foreign language not required. *Entrance requirements:* GRE General Test, TOEFL (minimum score 550), interview. Application fee: $35. Electronic applications accepted. *Expenses:* Tuition $500 per unit. Fees $111 per year full-time, $28 per year part-time. *Financial aid:* In 1997–98, 211 students received aid, including 19 research assistantships (4 to first-year students) totaling $21,985, teaching assistantships totaling $3,940, 138 grants, scholarships (24 to first-year students) totaling $177,845; Federal Work-Study also available. Aid available to part-time students. Financial aid application deadline: 3/2; applicants required to submit FAFSA. • Dr. Albert P. Koppes, Director, 310-338-7301.

Loyola University Chicago, School of Education, 820 North Michigan Avenue, Chicago, IL 60611-2196. Awards MA, M Ed, Ed D, PhD. Part-time and evening/weekend programs available. Postbaccalaureate distance learning degree programs offered (no on-campus study). Students: 1,162; includes 152 minority (92 African Americans, 29 Asian Americans, 26 Hispanics, 5 Native Americans). Average age 26. 659 applicants, 79% accepted. Terminal master's awarded for partial completion of doctoral program. *Degree requirements:* For doctorate, dissertation, comprehensive exam. *Entrance requirements:* For doctorate, interview. Application fee: $35. *Tuition:* $467 per semester hour. *Financial aid:* Fellowships, research assistantships, teaching assistantships, project assistantships, partial tuition waivers, Federal Work-Study, institutionally sponsored loans, and career-related internships or fieldwork available. Aid available to part-time students. Financial aid applicants required to submit FAFSA. *Faculty research:* Policy studies, child development, historical foundations, politics of education, teacher education. • Dr. Margaret Fong, Dean, 847-853-3000. Application contact: Marie Rosin-Dittmar, Admissions Coordinator, 847-853-3323. Fax: 847-853-3375. E-mail: mrosind@wpo.it.luc.edu.

Loyola University New Orleans, College of Arts and Sciences, Department of Education, New Orleans, LA 70118-6195. Offers programs in counseling (MS), elementary education (MS), reading education (MS), secondary education (MS). Part-time and evening/weekend programs available. Faculty: 8 full-time (6 women), 8 part-time (7 women). Students: 16 full-time (15 women), 40 part-time (32 women); includes 7 minority (5 African Americans, 1 Asian American, 1 Hispanic), 2 international. Average age 32. 46 applicants, 61% accepted. In 1997, 19 degrees awarded. *Degree requirements:* Comprehensive exams required, foreign language and thesis not required. *Entrance requirements:* GRE, MAT (preferred), interview, sample of written work. Application deadline: 8/1 (priority date; rolling processing; 12/1 for spring admission). Application fee: $20. Electronic applications accepted. *Expenses:* Tuition $247 per credit hour. Fees $556 per year full-time, $164 per year part-time. *Financial aid:* In 1997–98, 13 students received aid, including 2 research assistantships; partial tuition waivers, Federal Work-Study, and career-related internships or fieldwork also available. Aid available to part-time students. Financial aid application deadline: 5/1; applicants required to submit FAFSA. *Faculty research:* Special education, counseling theory, education politics, moral development, mathematics education, spirituality and counseling. • Dr. Jane Chauvin, Chair, 504-865-3540. Fax: 504-865-3571. Application contact: Office of Admissions, Graduate Programs, 504-865-3240. Fax: 504-865-3383. E-mail: admit@loyno.edu.

Lynchburg College, School of Education and Human Development, Lynchburg, VA 24501-3199. Offers programs in adapted physical education (M Ed); counseling (M Ed), including agency counseling, school counseling; curriculum and instruction (M Ed); early childhood education (M Ed), including curriculum and instruction: early childhood education, curriculum and instruction: middle education; English education (M Ed); middle school education (M Ed); physical education (M Ed); reading (M Ed); school administration (M Ed); secondary education (M Ed); special education (M Ed), including early childhood special education, mental retardation, severely/profoundly handicapped education, teaching children with learning disabilities, teaching the emotionally disturbed; supervision (M Ed). M Ed (adapted physical education, physical education) admissions temporarily suspended. *Entrance requirements:* Minimum GPA of 3.0 (undergraduate). Application fee: $20.

Lyndon State College, Graduate Programs in Education, Lyndonville, VT 05851. Offerings in education (M Ed), including curriculum and instruction, reading specialist, special education; natural sciences (MST), including science education; psychology (M Ed), including teaching and counseling. Part-time and evening/weekend programs available. Faculty: 17 full-time (7 women), 10 part-time (7 women), 18.2 FTE. Students: 17 part-time (11 women). Average age 40. 0 applicants. *Degree requirements:* Exam or major field project required, foreign language and thesis not required. *Entrance requirements:* GRE General Test or MAT. Application deadline: 2/28 (priority date; 10/31 for spring admission). Application fee: $30. *Expenses:* Tuition $3924 per year full-time, $164 per credit part-time for state residents; $9192 per year full-time, $383 per credit part-time for nonresidents. Fees $632 per year. *Financial aid:* Career-related internships or fieldwork available. Financial aid applicants required to submit FAFSA. *Faculty research:* Impaired reading, cognitive style, counseling relationship. • Dr. Sheryl Hruska, Associate Academic Dean, 802-626-9371 Ext. 6497. E-mail: hruskas@king.lsc.vsc.edu. Application contact: Elaine L. Turner, Administrative Secretary, 802-626-6497. Fax: 802-626-9770. E-mail: turnere@king.lsc.vsc.edu.

Lynn University, School of Graduate Studies, College of Education, Boca Raton, FL 33431-5598. Offers programs in educational leadership with a global perspective (PhD), ESOL and varying exceptionalities (M Ed), varying exceptionalities (M Ed). Part-time and evening/weekend programs available. Faculty: 5 full-time (4 women), 3 part-time (all women). Students: 10 full-time (7 women), 7 part-time (all women). 19 applicants, 63% accepted. In 1997, 6 master's awarded. *Degree requirements:* For master's, thesis (for some programs), comprehensive exam (ESOL and varying exceptionalities), (varying exceptionalities) required, foreign language not required; for doctorate, dissertation. *Average time to degree:* master's–1.8 years full-time. *Entrance requirements:* For master's, MAT, minimum undergraduate GPA of 3.0; for doctorate, GRE General Test (minimum combined score of 1000) or MAT (score in 50th percentile or higher). Application deadline: rolling. Application fee: $50. Electronic applications accepted. *Expenses:* Tuition $375 per credit hour. Fees $60 per year. *Financial aid:* In 1997–98, 1 graduate assistantship (to a first-year student) was awarded; partial tuition waivers and career-related internships or fieldwork also available. Financial aid application deadline: 6/15;

applicants required to submit FAFSA. *Faculty research:* Non-traditional education, innovative curricula, multicultural education, simulation games. • Dr. Carole Warshaw, Dean, 561-994-0770 Ext. 247. Fax: 561-241-3939. E-mail: admission@lynn.edu. Application contact: Peter Gallo, Graduate Admissions Counselor, 800-544-8035. Fax: 561-241-3552. E-mail: admission@lynn.edu.

Madonna University, Programs in Education, Livonia, MI 48150-1173. Offerings in Catholic school leadership (MSA), educational leadership (MSA), learning disabilities (MAT), literacy education (MAT). Accredited by NCATE. Part-time and evening/weekend programs available. Faculty: 7 full-time (4 women), 3 part-time (2 women). Students: 21 full-time (10 women), 134 part-time (120 women); includes 155 international. In 1997, 38 degrees awarded (100% found work related to degree). *Degree requirements:* Thesis or alternative required, foreign language not required. *Entrance requirements:* GRE General Test. Application deadline: 8/1 (priority date; rolling processing). Application fee: $0. *Expenses:* Tuition $260 per credit hour (minimum). Fees $50 per semester. *Financial aid:* Federal Work-Study and career-related internships or fieldwork available. • Dr. Robert Kimball, Chair, Education Department, 734-432-5652. E-mail: kimball@smtp.munet.edu. Application contact: Sandra Kellums, Coordinator of Graduate Admissions, 734-432-5666. Fax: 734-432-5393. E-mail: kellums@smtp.munet.edu.

Maharishi University of Management, Department of Education, Fairfield, IA 52557. Offers programs in elementary education (MA), foundations of education (MA), secondary education (MA). Faculty: 11 (2 women). Students: 9 full-time (4 women). Average age 24. In 1997, 5 degrees awarded. *Degree requirements:* Thesis or alternative required, foreign language not required. *Entrance requirements:* GRE, TOEFL (minimum score 550), minimum GPA of 3.0. Application deadline: 4/15 (priority date; rolling processing). Application fee: $40. *Financial aid:* Fellowships, Federal Work-Study available. Aid available to part-time students. Financial aid application deadline: 4/30. *Faculty research:* Unified field-based approach to education, moral climate, scientific study of teaching. • Dr. Christopher Jones, Associate Chairperson, 515-472-1105. Application contact: Harry Bright, Director of Admissions, 515-472-1166.

Malone College, Graduate School, Program in Education, Canton, OH 44709-3897. Offers community counseling (MA), curriculum and instruction (MA), early childhood education (MA), early childhood special education (MA), instructional technology (MA), middle school (MA), physical education and sport (MA), reading (MA), school counseling (MA), specific learning disabilities (MA), supervision (MA). Part-time and evening/weekend programs available. Faculty: 10 full-time (6 women), 11 part-time (5 women), 12.68 FTE. Students: 5 full-time (all women), 112 part-time (94 women); includes 7 minority (6 African Americans, 1 Asian American). Average age 36. 178 applicants, 100% accepted. In 1997, 23 degrees awarded. *Degree requirements:* Research practicum required, foreign language and thesis not required. *Entrance requirements:* Minimum GPA of 3.0, teaching license. Application deadline: 9/6 (rolling processing; 1/2 for spring admission). Application fee: $20. *Tuition:* $300 per credit hour. *Financial aid:* 63 students received aid. Aid available to part-time students. Financial aid application deadline: 6/30; applicants required to submit FAFSA. *Faculty research:* Family literacy, language proficiency in special education, inclusion, drug education/sex education, teacher mentoring. • Dr. Marietta Daulton, Director, 330-471-8447. Fax: 330-471-8478. E-mail: mdaulton@malone.edu. Application contact: Dan Depasquale, Director of Graduate Student Services, 800-257-4723. Fax: 330-471-8343. E-mail: depasquale@malone.edu.

Manhattan College, School of Education, Riverdale, NY 10471. Offers programs in administration and supervision (MS Ed, Diploma), counseling (MA, Diploma), special education (MS Ed, Diploma). Part-time and evening/weekend programs available. Faculty: 5 full-time (4 women), 15 part-time (8 women). Students: 22 full-time (19 women), 117 part-time (86 women); includes 25 minority (13 African Americans, 1 Asian American, 11 Hispanics), 6 international. Average age 30. 122 applicants, 93% accepted. In 1997, 55 master's awarded (100% entered university research/teaching); 3 Diplomas awarded. *Degree requirements:* For master's, thesis, internship. *Entrance requirements:* For master's, minimum GPA of 3.0. Application deadline: 8/10 (priority date; rolling processing; 1/7 for spring admission). Application fee: $50. *Expenses:* Tuition $385 per credit. Fees $100 per year. *Financial aid:* In 1997–98, 35 scholarships were awarded; Federal Work-Study also available. Financial aid application deadline: 2/1. *Faculty research:* Adapted physical education, cross-training of preschool regular and special education teachers. • Dr. Elizabeth Kosky, Director, Graduate Education Programs, 718-862-7416. Application contact: William J. Bisset Jr., Dean of Admissions/Financial Aid, 718-862-7200. Fax: 718-863-8019. E-mail: admit@manhattan.edu.

Announcement: The School of Education at Manhattan College offers graduate programs in 3 areas. The Counseling Program (MA) is directed toward work in guidance and counseling with a view toward preparing the candidate for certification as a substance abuse counselor or as a school counselor. The program for alcohol/substance abuse counselor consists of 36 credits and provides integrated sequenced training that follows OASAS guidelines. The Special Education Program (MS Ed) is directed toward the professional preparation of teachers of exceptional individuals. This program includes adaptive physical education for the disabled. The Administration and Supervision Program (MS Ed) is directed toward the preparation of school administrators and supervisors. See in-depth description in Book 1 of this series. For further information, contact the Dean of Admissions, 718-862-7200.

Manhattanville College, School of Education, Purchase, NY 10577-2132. Offers programs in art education (MAT); elementary education (MAT); English as a second language (MPS), including teaching English as a second language; music education (MAT); reading and writing (MPS); secondary and special education (MPS); secondary education (MAT), including English, languages, mathematics, science, social studies; special education (MPS, MS), including elementary education and special education (MPS), leadership and strategic management (MS), special education (MPS), special education and reading (MPS). Part-time programs available. Students: 570 (497 women). Average age 34. In 1997, 205 degrees awarded. *Degree requirements:* Thesis, comprehensive exam or research project required, foreign language not required. *Average time to degree:* master's–1.5 years full-time, 3 years part-time. *Entrance requirements:* Minimum undergraduate GPA of 3.0. Application deadline: rolling. Application fee: $40. *Expenses:* Tuition $410 per credit (minimum). Fees $25 per semester. *Financial aid:* Partial tuition waivers, institutionally sponsored loans, and career-related internships or fieldwork available. Aid available to part-time students. • Dr. Sylvia Blake, Dean, 914-323-5137. Application contact: Carol Messar, Director of Admissions, 914-323-5142. Fax: 914-323-5493.

Mankato State University, College of Education, South Rd and Ellis Ave, PO Box 8400, Mankato, MN 56002-8400. Awards MA, MAT, MS, MT, Certificate, SP. Accredited by NCATE. Part-time and evening/weekend programs available. Faculty: 50 full-time (19 women). Students: 345 full-time (250 women), 364 part-time (277 women). Average age 35. 231 applicants, 67% accepted. In 1997, 269 master's, 19 other advanced degrees awarded. *Degree requirements:* For master's, thesis or alternative, comprehensive exam; for other advanced degree, thesis required, foreign language not required. *Entrance requirements:* For master's, minimum GPA of 3.0 during previous 2 years; for other advanced degree, minimum GPA of 3.0. Application deadline: 7/10 (priority date; rolling processing; 10/30 for spring admission). Application fee: $20. *Tuition:* $126 per credit (minimum) for state residents; $200 per credit for nonresidents. *Financial aid:* Fellowships, research assistantships, teaching assistantships, Federal Work-Study, institutionally sponsored loans, and career-related internships or fieldwork available. Aid available to part-time students. Financial aid application deadline: 3/15; applicants required to submit FAFSA. *Faculty research:* Longitudinal studies of alternative education graduates, student achievement scores. • M. Paula Stone, Interim Dean, 507-389-1215. Application contact: Joni Roberts, Admissions Coordinator, 507-389-2321. Fax: 507-389-5974. E-mail: grad@mankato.msus.edu.

Mansfield University of Pennsylvania, Department of Education, Mansfield, PA 16933. Offers programs in elementary education (M Ed), secondary education (MS). One or more programs accredited by NCATE. Part-time and evening/weekend programs available. Faculty: 12 part-time (6 women). Students: 25 full-time (16 women), 45 part-time (35 women); includes 3 minority (1 African American, 1 Asian American, 1 Hispanic), 1 international. Average age 31. 29 applicants, 100% accepted. In 1997, 32 degrees awarded. *Degree requirements:* Thesis optional, foreign language not required. *Entrance requirements:* GRE General Test, MAT, NTE, or minimum GPA of 3.0. Application deadline: rolling. Application fee: $25. *Expenses:* Tuition $3468 per year full-time, $193 per credit part-time for state residents; $6236 per year full-time, $346 per credit part-time for nonresidents. Fees $236 per year full-time, $18.25 per semester (minimum) part-time for state residents; $266 per year full-time, $18.25 per semester (minimum) part-time for nonresidents. *Financial aid:* In 1997–98, 3 graduate assistantships (2 to first-year students) were awarded; career-related internships or fieldwork also available. Aid available to part-time students. Financial aid application deadline: 5/1; applicants required to submit FAFSA. • Dr. Robert Putt, Chairperson, 717-662-4562.

Marian College of Fond du Lac, Education Division, 45 South National Avenue, Fond du Lac, WI 54935-4699. Offers programs in educational leadership (MA), teacher development (MA). Accredited by NCATE. Part-time programs available. Faculty: 8 full-time (3 women), 21 part-time (10 women). Students: 11 full-time (8 women), 588 part-time (414 women); includes 7 African Americans, 5 Hispanics. Average age 38. 110 applicants, 94% accepted. In 1997, 87 degrees awarded. *Degree requirements:* Exam, field-based experience project, portfolio. *Entrance requirements:* Minimum GPA of 3.0, BA in education or related field, teaching license. Application deadline: rolling. Application fee: $25. *Tuition:* $220 per credit hour. *Financial aid:* 26 students received aid; Federal Work-Study available. Aid available to part-time students. Financial aid application deadline: 3/1; applicants required to submit FAFSA. *Faculty research:* At-risk youth, multicultural issues, values in education, teaching/learning strategies. • Dr. Nancy C. Riley, Chair, Educational Studies, 920-923-8143. E-mail: nriley@mariancoll.edu. Application contact: Robert Bohnsack, Admissions, 920-923-8100. Fax: 920-923-7154.

Marietta College, Program in Education, Marietta, OH 45750-4000. Awards MA. Part-time and evening/weekend programs available. Faculty: 18 full-time (8 women). Students: 50 part-time (42 women); includes 1 minority (African American). Average age 37. *Degree requirements:* Writing portfolio required, foreign language and thesis not required. *Entrance requirements:* MAT. Application deadline: 8/23 (priority date). Application fee: $25. *Tuition:* $270 per credit hour. *Financial aid:* Available to part-time students. *Faculty research:* Teaching of reading. • Dr. Constance Golden, Chair, 740-376-4765.

Marquette University, School of Education, Milwaukee, WI 53201-1881. Awards MA, M Ed, Ed D, PhD, Spec. Accredited by NCATE. Part-time programs available. Faculty: 17 full-time (7 women), 7 part-time (0 women). Students: 62 full-time (35 women), 189 part-time (139 women); includes 7 international. Average age 39. 81 applicants, 98% accepted. In 1997, 23 master's, 20 doctorates awarded. Terminal master's awarded for partial completion of doctoral program. *Degree requirements:* For master's, thesis, comprehensive exam required, foreign language not required; for doctorate, dissertation, qualifying exam required, foreign language not required. *Entrance requirements:* For master's, GRE General Test or MAT, TOEFL (minimum score 550); for doctorate, GRE General Test, MAT, TOEFL (minimum score 550), sample of written work; for Spec, GRE General Test or MAT, master's degree. Application fee: $40. *Tuition:* $335 per credit. *Financial aid:* In 1997–98, 5 research assistantships, 5 teaching assistantships were awarded; scholarships, full and partial tuition waivers, Federal Work-Study, institutionally sponsored loans also available. Aid available to part-time students. Financial aid application deadline: 2/15. *Faculty research:* Parenting, psychology of motivation, reading assessment, socialization of educational administrators, education philosophy of Cardinal Newman. Total annual research expenditures: $1.351 million. • Dr. Mary P. Hoy, Dean, 414-288-7376. Fax: 414-288-1578. Application contact: Dr. Terrence Wong, Assistant Dean, 414-288-7375. Fax: 414-288-5333.

Marshall University, College of Education, Huntington, WV 25755-2020. Awards MA, MAT, MS, Ed D, Ed S. Accredited by NCATE. Evening/weekend programs available. Faculty: 56 (20 women). Students: 347 full-time (209 women), 529 part-time (390 women); includes 40 minority (34 African Americans, 2 Asian Americans, 1 Hispanic, 3 Native Americans), 11 international. In 1997, 209 master's awarded. *Degree requirements:* For master's, thesis optional. *Entrance requirements:* For master's, GRE General Test (minimum combined score of 1200); for doctorate, GRE General Test (minimum combined score of 1500 on three sections). *Tuition:* $2364 per year full-time, $132 per hour part-time for state residents; $6894 per year full-time, $383 per hour part-time for nonresidents. *Financial aid:* Career-related internships or fieldwork available. • Dr. Larry Froelich, Dean, 304-696-6703. Application contact: Dr. James Harless, Director of Admissions, 304-696-3160.

Marshall University, Graduate School of Education and Professional Studies, South Charleston, WV 25303-1600. Awards MA, Ed S. Accredited by NCATE. Part-time and evening/weekend programs available. Faculty: 32 full-time (9 women), 62 part-time (28 women), 45.4 FTE. Students: 147 full-time (109 women), 1,098 part-time (822 women); includes 57 minority (50 African Americans, 2 Asian Americans, 3 Hispanics, 2 Native Americans). Average age 40. In 1997, 283 master's, 16 Ed Ss awarded. *Entrance requirements:* For master's, GRE General Test. Application deadline: 8/1 (priority date; rolling processing). Application fee: $0. *Tuition:* $2364 per year full-time, $132 per hour part-time for state residents; $6894 per year full-time, $383 per hour part-time for nonresidents. *Financial aid:* Full tuition waivers and career-related internships or fieldwork available. Aid available to part-time students. Financial aid applicants required to submit FAFSA. • Dr. James Ranson, Dean, 304-746-1998. Fax: 304-746-1942.

Mary Baldwin College, Graduate Studies, Staunton, VA 24401. Offers program in elementary education (MAT). Part-time and evening/weekend programs available. Faculty: 1 (woman) full-time, 38 part-time (24 women). Students: 90 (80 women); includes 9 minority (all African Americans). Average age 30. In 1997, 27 degrees awarded (100% found work related to degree). *Degree requirements:* Final paper, student teaching required, foreign language and thesis not required. *Average time to degree:* master's–2 years full-time, 4 years part-time. *Entrance requirements:* Previous course work in college algebra, English composition. Application deadline: 7/1 (priority date; rolling processing; 12/15 for spring admission). Application fee: $35. *Expenses:* Tuition $305 per credit hour. Fees $250 per year. *Financial aid:* Fellowships, tuition assistance grants, Federal Work-Study, and career-related internships or fieldwork available. Aid available to part-time students. *Faculty research:* Learning styles, single-sex education, teacher research, literacy development. • Dr. Beth Roberts, Director, 540-887-7333.

Marycrest International University, Division of Education, Davenport, IA 52804-4096. Offers programs in early childhood education (MA, MS), education (MA, MAT), reading specialist (MA). Part-time and evening/weekend programs available. Faculty: 4 full-time (all women), 3 part-time (0 women), 4.8 FTE. Students: 277 part-time (232 women); includes 4 international. Average age 32. 50 applicants, 98% accepted. In 1997, 18 degrees awarded (100% found work related to degree). *Degree requirements:* Comprehensive exams required, foreign language and thesis not required. *Average time to degree:* master's–2.5 years part-time. *Entrance requirements:* Interview, minimum undergraduate GPA of 2.8. Application deadline: 4/15 (priority date; rolling processing; 12/1 for spring admission). Application fee: $25. *Expenses:* Tuition of $198 per credit hour for students holding a valid teaching certificate (for MA in education and reading specialist only); $413 per credit hour for other degree programs. *Financial aid:* Partial tuition waivers available. Financial aid application deadline: 3/1. *Faculty research:* Multiple intelligences, professional development schools, multi-age grouping. • Dr. Michelle Schiffgens, Chair, 319-326-9241. Fax: 319-326-9250.

Marygrove College, Division of Education, Detroit, MI 48221-2599. Offers programs in art of teaching (MAT); early childhood education (M Ed); modern language translation (M Ed); reading education (M Ed); special education (M Ed), including education of the emotionally impaired. Accredited by NCATE. Part-time and evening/weekend programs available. Postbaccalaureate distance learning degree programs offered (no on-campus study). *Average time to degree:* master's–2 years full-time, 3 years part-time. *Entrance requirements:* MAT, interview, minimum

Directory: Education—General

Marygrove College (continued)

undergraduate GPA of 3.0, teaching certificate. Application fee: $25. *Faculty research:* Teaching learning styles.

Marymount University, School of Education and Human Services, Arlington, VA 22207-4299. Offers programs in elementary education (M Ed); English as a second language (M Ed); learning disabilities (M Ed); psychology (MA), including counseling psychology, school counseling; secondary education (M Ed). Accredited by NCATE. Part-time and evening/weekend programs available. Students: 568. In 1997, 284 degrees awarded. *Degree requirements:* Thesis or alternative required, foreign language not required. *Entrance requirements:* GRE General Test or MAT, interview. Application deadline: rolling. Application fee: $35. *Expenses:* Tuition $465 per credit hour. Fees $120 per year full-time, $5 per credit hour part-time. *Financial aid:* Research assistantships and career-related internships or fieldwork available. Aid available to part-time students. Financial aid applicants required to submit FAFSA. *Faculty research:* Aging and overconfidence in likelihood judgements, clinical supervision models for student teachers. • Dr. Wayne Lesko, Dean, 703-284-1624. Fax: 703-284-1631. E-mail: wayne.lesko@marymount.edu.

Maryville University of Saint Louis, School of Education, St. Louis, MO 63141-7299. Offers programs in art education (MA), early childhood education (MA), elementary education (MA), environmental education (MA), gifted education (MA), middle grades education (MA), multicultural education (MA), secondary education (MA). Accredited by NCATE. Part-time programs available. Faculty: 9 full-time (7 women), 15 part-time (9 women). Students: 26 full-time (17 women), 264 part-time (230 women); includes 21 minority (19 African Americans, 1 Asian American, 1 Hispanic), 5 international. Average age 38. 78 applicants, 99% accepted. In 1997, 106 degrees awarded (100% found work related to degree). *Degree requirements:* Thesis, project required, foreign language not required. *Average time to degree:* master's–2 years full-time, 4 years part-time. *Entrance requirements:* Minimum GPA of 3.0. Application deadline: rolling. Application fee: $20. Electronic applications accepted. *Expenses:* Tuition $11,480 per year full-time, $345 per credit hour part-time. Fees $120 per year full-time, $60 per year part-time. *Financial aid:* 253 students received aid; partial tuition waivers and career-related internships or fieldwork available. Financial aid application deadline: 7/23; applicants required to submit FAFSA. *Faculty research:* Whole language, collaboration with public schools, professional practice schools, pre-service program development, mathematics. Total annual research expenditures: $40,000. • Dr. Kathe Rasch, Dean, 314-529-9466. Fax: 314-529-9921. E-mail: krasch@maryville.edu.

Marywood University, Graduate School of Arts and Sciences, Department of Education, Scranton, PA 18509-1598. Offers programs in early childhood education (MS), elementary education (MAT, MS), instructional technology (MS), reading education (MS), school leadership (MS). Accredited by NCATE. Part-time and evening/weekend programs available. Faculty: 4 full-time (3 women), 11 part-time (7 women). Students: 18 full-time (8 women), 84 part-time (71 women). Average age 33. 39 applicants, 90% accepted. In 1997, 36 degrees awarded. *Degree requirements:* Thesis or alternative required, foreign language not required. *Entrance requirements:* GRE or MAT, TOEFL (minimum score 550; average 590). Application deadline: 7/15 (priority date; rolling processing; 12/1 for spring admission). Application fee: $20. *Expenses:* Tuition $449 per credit hour. Fees $530 per year full-time, $180 per year part-time. *Financial aid:* Research assistantships, scholarships/tuition reductions, partial tuition waivers, and career-related internships or fieldwork available. Aid available to part-time students. Financial aid application deadline: 2/15; applicants required to submit FAFSA. *Faculty research:* Catholic identity in higher education, school reading programs, teacher practice enhancement, cooperative learning, institutional and instructional leadership. • Dr. Lois K. Draina, Chairperson, 717-348-6289. Application contact: Deborah M. Flynn, Coordinator of Admissions, 717-340-6002. Fax: 717-961-4745.

Massachusetts College of Liberal Arts, Graduate Program in Education, North Adams, MA 01247-4100. Offers curriculum and instruction (M Ed), educational administration (M Ed), reading (M Ed), special education (M Ed). Part-time and evening/weekend programs available. Faculty: 8 full-time (5 women), 4 part-time (2 women). Students: 149 part-time (98 women). In 1997, 25 degrees awarded. *Degree requirements:* Thesis required, foreign language not required. *Average time to degree:* master's–3 years part-time. *Entrance requirements:* Writing sample. Application deadline: rolling. Application fee: $0. *Expenses:* Tuition $130 per credit. Fees $15 per credit. *Financial aid:* Fellowships and career-related internships or fieldwork available. *Faculty research:* Anxiety, methodology, mainstreaming. • Dr. Susanne Chandler, Chair, 413-662-5381.

McGill University, Faculty of Graduate Studies and Research, Faculty of Education, Montréal, PQ H3A 2T5, Canada. Awards MA, M Ed, MLIS, PhD, Diploma. Part-time and evening/weekend programs available. Students: 792. In 1997, 205 master's, 11 doctorates awarded. Terminal master's awarded for partial completion of doctoral program. *Degree requirements:* For doctorate, dissertation. *Entrance requirements:* For master's, TOEFL (minimum score 550), minimum GPA of 3.0; for doctorate, TOEFL (minimum score 550). Application deadline: rolling. Application fee: $60. *Expenses:* Tuition $1668 per year for Canadian residents; $8268 per year for nonresidents. Fees $828 per year for Canadian residents; $1216 per year for nonresidents. *Financial aid:* Fellowships, research assistantships, teaching assistantships, full and partial tuition waivers, institutionally sponsored loans, and career-related internships or fieldwork available. *Faculty research:* Second language education, integrated education, cognitive science and learning, counseling/school/educational psychology. • A. E. Wall, Dean, 514-398-7037. Fax: 514-398-1527. E-mail: walla@education.mcgill.ca.

McMaster University, Program in Teaching, Hamilton, ON L8S 4M2, Canada. Awards MAT, M Sc T. Program being phased out; applicants no longer accepted. Evening/weekend programs available. Faculty: 2 full-time, 4 part-time. Students: 1 (woman) full-time, 48 part-time (36 women). In 1997, 6 degrees awarded (100% found work related to degree). *Degree requirements:* Thesis. *Expenses:* Tuition $4422 per year full-time, $1590 per year part-time for Canadian residents; $12,000 per year full-time, $6165 per year part-time for nonresidents. Fees $257 per year full-time, $188 per year part-time. • Dr. John Ferns, Chair, 905-525-9140 Ext. 24532.

McNeese State University, College of Education, Lake Charles, LA 70609-2495. Awards MA, M Ed, Ed S. Part-time and evening/weekend programs available. Faculty: 33 full-time (9 women). Students: 47 full-time (36 women), 193 part-time (153 women). In 1997, 111 master's awarded. *Degree requirements:* For Ed S, comprehensive exam. *Entrance requirements:* For master's, GRE General Test; for Ed S, teaching certificate, 3 years of teaching experience, 1 year of administration or supervision experience. Application deadline: 7/15 (priority date; rolling processing). Application fee: $10 ($25 for international students). *Tuition:* $2118 per year full-time, $344 per semester (minimum) part-time for state residents; $7308 per year full-time, $344 per semester (minimum) part-time for nonresidents. *Financial aid:* Fellowships, research assistantships, teaching assistantships, Federal Work-Study available. Aid available to part-time students. Financial aid application deadline: 5/1. • Dr. Hugh Frugé, Dean, 318-475-5432.

Medaille College, Program in Education, Buffalo, NY 14214-2695. Awards MS Ed. Evening/weekend programs available. Faculty: 4. *Financial aid:* Federal Work-Study, institutionally sponsored loans available. • Dr. Jerry Mosey, Chairperson, 716-884-3281. Application contact: Kevin Reed, Graduate Admissions Counselor, 716-884-3281 Ext. 323. Fax: 716-884-0291.

Announcement: Medaille College's Master of Science in Education (curriculum and instruction) program is designed to prepare teachers to meet the needs of the 21st century. Unique characteristics include a team-based action research project, a focus on integrating multimedia technology into instructional strategies, and a 2-course concentration in the arts, middle school studies, or technology.

Memorial University of Newfoundland, School of Graduate Studies, Faculty of Education, St. John's, NF A1C 5S7, Canada. Offers programs in leadership (M Ed), post-secondary education (M Ed), psychology (M Ed), teaching-learning (M Ed). Students: 117 full-time (78 women), 236 part-time (153 women); includes 2 international. 85 applicants, 29% accepted. In 1997, 108 degrees awarded. *Degree requirements:* Comprehensive exam required, foreign language not required. *Application deadline:* 2/1. *Application fee:* $40. *Expenses:* Tuition $1896 per year (minimum). Fees $60 per year for Canadian residents; $621 per year for nonresidents. *Financial aid:* Fellowships, research assistantships, teaching assistantships, and career-related internships or fieldwork available. Financial aid application deadline: 6/30. • Dr. Terry Piper, Dean, 709-737-8588. E-mail: tpiper@kean.ucs.mun.ca. Application contact: Dr. Linda M. Phillips, Associate Dean, 709-737-3402. E-mail: lindap@morgan.ucs.mun.ca.

Mercer University, School of Education, 1400 Coleman Avenue, Macon, GA 31207-0003. Offers programs in early childhood education (M Ed, Ed S), English education (M Ed), mathematics education (M Ed), middle grades education (M Ed, Ed S), reading specialist (M Ed), science education (M Ed), social sciences education (M Ed). Part-time and evening/weekend programs available. Faculty: 11 full-time (5 women), 17 part-time (11 women). Students: 14 full-time (8 women), 76 part-time (62 women); includes 26 minority (25 African Americans, 1 Hispanic), 2 international. Average age 35. In 1997, 32 master's, 5 Ed Ss awarded. *Degree requirements:* Research project report required, foreign language and thesis not required. *Entrance requirements:* For master's, GRE, MAT, NTE, minimum GPA of 2.75; for Ed S, GRE, MAT, NTE, minimum GPA of 3.25, 3 years of teaching experience. Application deadline: 8/1 (priority date; rolling processing; 12/1 for spring admission). Application fee: $25. *Tuition:* $180 per credit hour. *Financial aid:* Federal Work-Study, institutionally sponsored loans, and career-related internships or fieldwork available. Aid available to part-time students. Financial aid application deadline: 5/1. *Faculty research:* Teacher effectiveness, specific learning disabilities, inclusion. • Dr. Anne Hathaway, Dean, 912-752-5397. Fax: 912-752-2280. E-mail: hathaway_ha@mercer.edu. Application contact: Dr. Louis Gallien, Chair, Department of Teacher Education, 912-752-2585. Fax: 912-752-2576. E-mail: gallien_lb@mercer.edu.

Mercer University, Cecil B. Day Campus, Graduate Education Programs, 3001 Mercer University Drive, Atlanta, GA 30341-4155. Offerings in early childhood education (M Ed, Ed S), middle grades education (M Ed, Ed S). Part-time and evening/weekend programs available. Faculty: 8 full-time (4 women), 33 part-time (17 women). Students: 141 full-time (127 women), 366 part-time (301 women); includes 184 minority (175 African Americans, 2 Asian Americans, 5 Hispanics, 2 Native Americans), 1 international. Average age 32. 180 applicants, 89% accepted. In 1997, 73 master's, 6 Ed Ss awarded. *Degree requirements:* Research project required, foreign language and thesis not required. *Entrance requirements:* For master's, GRE, MAT, or NTE, minimum undergraduate GPA of 2.75; for Ed S, GRE, MAT, or NTE, minimum GPA of 3.25, 3 years of teaching experience. Application deadline: 8/1 (priority date; rolling processing; 12/1 for spring admission). Application fee: $25. *Tuition:* $220 per semester hour. *Financial aid:* Federal Work-Study and career-related internships or fieldwork available. Aid available to part-time students. Financial aid application deadline: 5/1. *Faculty research:* Educational computing, content area reading, concept learning, importance of play for young children, multicultural literature. • Dr. Anne Hathaway, Dean, 912-752-5397. Fax: 912-752-2280. E-mail: hathaway_ha@mercer.edu. Application contact: Dr. Allison Gilmore, Associate Dean and Director of Graduate Education, 770-986-3330. Fax: 770-986-3292. E-mail: gilmore_a@mercer.edu.

Mercy College, Department of Education, Dobbs Ferry, NY 10522-1189. Offers program in learning technology (MSE). Students: 158 (110 women). *Entrance requirements:* Teaching certificate. *Tuition:* $390 per credit. • Dr. William Pratella, Chairperson, 914-674-7555.

Meredith College, Department of Education, Raleigh, NC 27607-5298. Awards M Ed. Accredited by NCATE. Part-time and evening/weekend programs available. Faculty: 4 full-time (all women). Students: 7 full-time (all women), 19 part-time (all women); includes 3 minority (1 African American, 2 Hispanics). Average age 28. 12 applicants, 83% accepted. In 1997, 4 degrees awarded. *Degree requirements:* Thesis optional, foreign language not required. *Entrance requirements:* MAT (minimum score 35), minimum GPA of 2.5. Application deadline: 8/1 (priority date; rolling processing; 12/1 for spring admission). Application fee: $50. *Tuition:* $4680 per year full-time, $260 per credit hour part-time. *Financial aid:* Partial tuition waivers, institutionally sponsored loans, and career-related internships or fieldwork available. Aid available to part-time students. Financial aid application deadline: 2/15. • Dr. Jerod Kratzer, Head, 919-829-8315. Fax: 919-829-2898. Application contact: Cheryl Martine, Coordinator, 919-829-8315. Fax: 919-829-8303. E-mail: martinec@meredith.edu.

Merrimack College, Department of Education, 315 Turnpike Street, North Andover, MA 01845-5800. Awards M Ed. Program new for fall 1998. Part-time and evening/weekend programs available. Faculty: 5 full-time (2 women). *Degree requirements:* Field experience required, foreign language and thesis not required. *Entrance requirements:* GRE or MAT, teaching certificate. Application deadline: 8/15 (priority date; rolling processing; 1/15 for spring admission). Application fee: $50. *Tuition:* $329 per credit hour. *Financial aid:* Career-related internships or fieldwork available. *Faculty research:* Educational technology, teaching mathematics, leadership. • Dr. Brenda Brown, Chair, 978-837-5000 Ext. 4367. Fax: 978-837-5069.

Miami University, School of Education and Allied Professions, Oxford, OH 45056. Awards MAT, M Ed, MS, Ed D, PhD, Ed S. Accredited by NCATE. Part-time programs available. Faculty: 114. Students: 230 full-time (168 women), 116 part-time (94 women); includes 48 minority (41 African Americans, 4 Asian Americans, 1 Hispanic, 2 Native Americans), 18 international. 446 applicants, 80% accepted. In 1997, 164 master's, 12 doctorates, 6 Ed Ss awarded. *Degree requirements:* For doctorate, dissertation, comprehensive and final exams required, foreign language not required; for Ed S, oral or written exam required, foreign language and thesis not required. *Entrance requirements:* For master's, minimum undergraduate GPA of 3.0 during previous 2 years or 2.75 overall; for doctorate, MAT, minimum undergraduate GPA of 2.75, 3.0 graduate; for Ed S, GRE General Test or MAT. Application deadline: 3/1 (priority date; rolling processing). Application fee: $35. *Tuition:* $5932 per year full-time, $255 per credit hour part-time for state residents; $12,392 per year full-time, $524 per credit hour part-time for nonresidents. *Financial aid:* Fellowships, research assistantships, teaching assistantships, full tuition waivers, Federal Work-Study, and career-related internships or fieldwork available. Financial aid application deadline: 3/1. • Dr. Curtis Ellison, Acting Dean, 513-529-6317.

Michigan State University, College of Education, East Lansing, MI 48824-1020. Awards MA, MS, PhD, Ed S. Part-time and evening/weekend programs available. Postbaccalaureate distance learning degree programs offered (no on-campus study). Faculty: 137 (61 women). Students: 1,027 (696 women); includes 162 minority (95 African Americans, 28 Asian Americans, 34 Hispanics, 5 Native Americans), 118 international. In 1997, 264 master's, 78 doctorates, 18 Ed Ss awarded. *Degree requirements:* For doctorate, dissertation required, foreign language not required. *Application deadline:* rolling. *Application fee:* $30 ($40 for international students). *Expenses:* Tuition $4609 per year full-time, $223 per credit hour (minimum) part-time for state residents; $8704 per year full-time, $450 per credit hour (minimum) part-time for nonresidents. Fees $576 per year full-time, $476 per year part-time. *Financial aid:* Fellowships, research assistantships, teaching assistantships, Federal Work-Study, institutionally sponsored loans, and career-related internships or fieldwork available. Aid available to part-time students. Financial aid applicants required to submit FAFSA. • Dr. Carole Ames, Dean, 517-355-1734.

See in-depth description on page 755.

MidAmerica Nazarene University, Graduate Studies in Education, Olathe, KS 66062-1899. Offers program in curriculum and instruction (M Ed). Evening/weekend programs available. Faculty: 9 full-time (4 women), 1 part-time (0 women). Students: 79 full-time (69 women); includes 5 minority (3 African Americans, 1 Hispanic, 1 Native American). Average age 32. 110 applicants, 72% accepted. In 1997, 81 degrees awarded (100% found work related to degree). *Degree requirements:* Computer language, thesis or alternative, creative project. *Average time* *to degree:* master's–1.2 years full-time. *Entrance requirements:* Minimum undergraduate GPA of 3.0, 2 years of teaching experience. Application deadline: rolling. Application fee: $75. *Tuition:* $7005 per year. *Financial aid:* 39 students received aid. Financial aid applicants required to submit FAFSA. • Dr. Jim Burns, Director, 913-791-3292. Application contact: Aileen Douglas, Graduate Studies Secretary, 913-791-3292. Fax: 913-791-3407. E-mail: adouglas@mnu.edu.

Middle Tennessee State University, College of Education, Murfreesboro, TN 37132. Awards MA, MBE, MCJ, M Ed, MS, DA, Ed S. Accredited by NCATE. Part-time and evening/weekend programs available. Faculty: 110 full-time (53 women), 15 part-time (7 women). Students: 225 full-time (168 women), 539 part-time (397 women); includes 84 minority (73 African Americans, 4 Asian Americans, 5 Hispanics, 2 Native Americans), 5 international. Average age 31. 453 applicants, 47% accepted. In 1997, 226 master's, 1 doctorate, 31 Ed Ss awarded. *Degree requirements:* For master's, comprehensive exams; for doctorate, dissertation, comprehensive exams required, foreign language not required; for Ed S, comprehensive exams required, foreign language and thesis not required. *Entrance requirements:* For doctorate, GRE or MAT. Application deadline: 8/1 (priority date). Application fee: $5. *Expenses:* Tuition $2560 per year full-time, $129 per semester hour part-time for state residents; $7386 per year full-time, $340 per semester hour part-time for nonresidents. Fees $486 per year full-time, $17 per semester (minimum) part-time. *Financial aid:* Research assistantships, teaching assistantships, institutionally sponsored loans, and career-related internships or fieldwork available. Aid available to part-time students. Financial aid application deadline: 5/1; applicants required to submit FAFSA. • Dr. Robert Eaker, Dean, 615-898-2874. Fax: 615-898-2530. E-mail: eaker@mtsu.edu.

Midwestern State University, Division of Education, Wichita Falls, TX 76308-2096. Awards MA, M Ed, MSK. Part-time and evening/weekend programs available. Faculty: 12 full-time (2 women). Students: 17 full-time (11 women), 111 part-time (74 women). In 1997, 40 degrees awarded. *Entrance requirements:* GRE General Test, TOEFL (minimum score 550). Application deadline: 8/7 (12/15 for spring admission). Application fee: $0 ($50 for international students). *Expenses:* Tuition $44 per hour for state residents; $259 per hour for nonresidents. Fees $90 per year (minimum) full-time, $9 per semester (minimum) part-time. *Financial aid:* In 1997–98, 13 teaching assistantships were awarded; assistantships, partial tuition waivers, Federal Work-Study, institutionally sponsored loans, and career-related internships or fieldwork also available. Aid available to part-time students. • Dr. Emerson Capps, Director, 940-397-4313.

Millersville University of Pennsylvania, School of Education, Millersville, PA 17551-0302. Awards M Ed, MS, Certificate. Accredited by NCATE. Part-time and evening/weekend programs available. Faculty: 78 full-time (39 women), 33 part-time (16 women). Students: 100 full-time (67 women), 351 part-time (280 women); includes 18 minority (9 African Americans, 2 Asian Americans, 7 Hispanics), 5 international. Average age 31. 202 applicants, 72% accepted. In 1997, 137 master's awarded. *Entrance requirements:* For master's, minimum undergraduate GPA of 2.75. Application deadline: 5/1 (priority date; rolling processing). Application fee: $25. *Tuition:* $3468 per year full-time, $234 per credit part-time for state residents; $6236 per year full-time, $387 per credit part-time for nonresidents. *Financial aid:* In 1997–98, 74 graduate assistantships (44 to first-year students) averaging $445 per month and totaling $296,000 were awarded; Federal Work-Study, institutionally sponsored loans, and career-related internships or fieldwork also available. Aid available to part-time students. Financial aid application deadline: 5/1. • Dr. Bennett Berhow, Dean, 717-872-3379. Fax: 717-872-3856. Application contact: Dr. Robert J. Labriola, Dean of Graduate Studies, 717-872-3030. Fax: 717-871-2022.

Milligan College, Area of Teacher Education, Milligan College, TN 37682. Awards M Ed. Accredited by NCATE. Part-time programs available. Faculty: 5 full-time (3 women), 5 part-time (2 women). Students: 69 (48 women); includes 4 minority (3 African Americans, 1 Asian American). Average age 30. In 1997, 22 degrees awarded. *Average time to degree:* master's–1.2 years full-time. *Entrance requirements:* MAT (score in 35th percentile or higher), minimum GPA of 2.75. Application deadline: rolling. Application fee: $20. *Tuition:* $170 per hour. *Financial aid:* Institutionally sponsored loans and career-related internships or fieldwork available. Financial aid application deadline: 4/15. *Faculty research:* Teacher education evaluation, professional development centers, internship, early childhood, special education inclusion, reading model. • Rich Aubrey, Director, 423-461-8745. Fax: 423-461-8777. E-mail: raubrey@milligan.edu. Application contact: Mike Johnson, Director of Admissions, 423-461-8730. Fax: 423-461-8982. E-mail: majohnson@milligan.edu.

Mills College, Education Department, Oakland, CA 94613-1000. Offers programs in administration (Ed D); childlife in health care settings (MA); early childhood education (MA); education (MA), including curriculum and instruction, elementary education, English education, mathematics education, science education, secondary education, social sciences education, teaching. Part-time and evening/weekend programs available. Faculty: 8 full-time (6 women), 13 part-time (11 women), 11 FTE. Students: 127 full-time (116 women). 145 applicants, 77% accepted. In 1997, 77 master's awarded. Terminal master's awarded for partial completion of doctoral program. *Degree requirements:* For master's, comprehensive exam required, thesis not required. *Average time to degree:* master's–2 years full-time. *Entrance requirements:* For master's, TOEFL (minimum score 550). Application deadline: 2/1 (priority date; rolling processing; 11/1 for spring admission). Application fee: $50. Electronic applications accepted. *Expenses:* Tuition $10,600 per year full-time, $2560 per year part-time. Fees $468 per year. *Financial aid:* In 1997–98, 47 fellowships (10 to first-year students) totaling $43,633, 28 teaching assistantships (12 to first-year students) totaling $133,785, 1 residence award (to a first-year student) totaling $3,400 were awarded; institutionally sponsored loans and career-related internships or fieldwork also available. Aid available to part-time students. Financial aid application deadline: 2/1; applicants required to submit CSS PROFILE or FAFSA. *Faculty research:* Child development, gender and education, public policy, cross-cultural development, development of literacy. • Jane Bowyer, Chairperson, 510-430-2118. Fax: 510-430-3314. E-mail: grad-studies@mills.edu. Application contact: La Vonna S. Brown, Coordinator of Graduate Studies, 510-430-3309. Fax: 510-430-2159. E-mail: grad-studies@mills.edu.

Mississippi College, School of Education, Clinton, MS 39058. Awards MCP, M Ed, Ed S. Accredited by NCATE. Part-time and evening/weekend programs available. Students: 11 full-time (10 women), 140 part-time (115 women); includes 40 minority (38 African Americans, 2 Hispanics). In 1997, 92 master's awarded. *Degree requirements:* For master's, comprehensive exam required, foreign language and thesis not required. *Entrance requirements:* For master's, GRE or NTE, minimum GPA of 2.5, Class A Certificate; for Ed S, NTE, minimum GPA of 3.0. Application deadline: 8/15 (priority date; rolling processing). Application fee: $25 ($75 for international students). *Expenses:* Tuition $6624 per year full-time, $276 per hour part-time. Fees $230 per year full-time, $35 per semester (minimum) part-time. *Financial aid:* Teaching assistantships, professional development scholarships, and career-related internships or fieldwork available. Aid available to part-time students. Financial aid application deadline: 4/1. • Dr. Thomas Taylor, Dean, 601-925-3402.

Mississippi State University, College of Education, Mississippi State, MS 39762. Awards M Ed, MM Ed, MS, MSIT, Ed D, PhD, Ed S. Accredited by NCATE. Part-time and evening/weekend programs available. Postbaccalaureate distance learning degree programs offered (no on-campus study). Faculty: 98 full-time (44 women), 59 part-time (27 women). Students: 281 full-time (205 women), 396 part-time (286 women); includes 181 minority (179 African Americans, 2 Asian Americans), 22 international. Average age 33. 165 applicants, 90% accepted. In 1997, 258 master's, 32 doctorates, 20 Ed Ss awarded. Terminal master's awarded for partial completion of doctoral program. *Degree requirements:* For doctorate, dissertation required, foreign language not required; for Ed S, thesis or alternative required, foreign language not required. *Entrance requirements:* For master's, minimum QPA of 2.75 in last 2 years; for Ed S, minimum QPA of 3.2 in graduate course work. Application fee: $0 ($25 for international students). Electronic applications accepted. *Tuition:* $3017 per year full-time, $168 per credit hour part-time for state residents; $6119 per year full-time, $340 per credit hour part-time for nonresidents. *Financial aid:* 49 students received aid; research assistantships, teaching assistantships, service assistantships, Federal Work-Study, institutionally sponsored loans, and career-related internships or fieldwork available. Aid available to part-time students. Financial aid application deadline: 4/1. *Faculty research:* Leadership behavior, creativity measures, early childhood education, employability of the blind, quality indicators of professional educators. • Dr. William H. Graves, Dean, 601-325-3717. Fax: 601-325-8784. E-mail: whg1@ra.msstate.edu.

Mississippi University for Women, Division of Education and Human Sciences, Columbus, MS 39701-9998. Offers programs in gifted studies (M Ed), speech/language pathology (MS). Part-time programs available. Faculty: 13 full-time (11 women). Students: 21 full-time (all women), 38 part-time (37 women); includes 9 minority (8 African Americans, 1 Hispanic), 1 international. Average age 31. 111 applicants, 76% accepted. In 1997, 21 degrees awarded. *Degree requirements:* Comprehensive exam required, thesis optional, foreign language not required. *Entrance requirements:* GRE General Test or NTE (M Ed), GRE General Test (MS). Application deadline: 4/1 (priority date; rolling processing). Application fee: $0 ($25 for international students). *Tuition:* $2556 per year full-time, $142 per hour part-time for state residents; $5546 per year full-time, $308 per hour part-time for nonresidents. *Financial aid:* In 1997–98, 10 students received aid, including 10 fellowships averaging $1,100 per month and totaling $110,000; Federal Work-Study, institutionally sponsored loans also available. Financial aid application deadline: 4/1; applicants required to submit FAFSA. • Dr. Suzanne Bean, Head, 601-329-7175. Fax: 601-329-8515. E-mail: sbean@muw.edu.

Mississippi Valley State University, Department of Education, Itta Bena, MS 38941-1400. Offers programs in education (MAT), elementary education (MA). MAT new for fall 1998. Faculty: 5. Students: 15. *Application deadline:* rolling. *Application fee:* $0. *Expenses:* Tuition $97 per hour for state residents; $139 per hour for nonresidents. Fees $30 per hour. • Dr. O. Edward Jack, Chair, 601-254-3619. Application contact: Office of Admissions, 601-254-3344.

Monmouth University, School of Education, West Long Branch, NJ 07764-1898. Offers programs in elementary education (MAT), including certified teachers, non-certified teachers; learning disabilities-teacher consultant (Certificate); principalship (MS Ed); reading specialist (MS Ed, Certificate); special education (MS Ed, Certificate); student personnel services (MS Ed); supervision (Certificate). Certificate (learning disabilities-teacher consultant, reading specialist, supervision) new for fall 1998. Part-time and evening/weekend programs available. Faculty: 9 full-time (7 women), 14 part-time (9 women). Students: 123 full-time (99 women), 240 part-time (199 women); includes 17 minority (11 African Americans, 5 Asian Americans, 1 Hispanic), 1 international. Average age 32. 160 applicants, 96% accepted. In 1997, 147 master's awarded. *Entrance requirements:* For master's, minimum GPA of 3.0 in major, 2.5 overall. Application deadline: 8/1 (priority date; rolling processing; 12/1 for spring admission). Application fee: $35. *Expenses:* Tuition $459 per credit. Fees $274 per semester full-time, $137 per semester part-time. *Financial aid:* In 1997–98, 146 students received aid, including 9 assistantships averaging $326 per month and totaling $21,968; partial tuition waivers, Federal Work-Study, and career-related internships or fieldwork also available. Aid available to part-time students. Financial aid application deadline: 3/1; applicants required to submit FAFSA. *Faculty research:* Literacy centers, electronic communications, spatial relationships and learning. • Dr. Bernice Willis, Dean, 732-571-7518. Fax: 732-263-5277. Application contact: Office of Graduate Admissions, 732-571-3452. Fax: 732-571-5123.

Announcement: The School of Education offers a Master of Arts in Teaching (MAT) for initial certification, an MAT (advanced) for certified teachers, and an MS in Education (MS Ed) with certifications in special education, principal, reading specialist, and student personnel services. There are post-master's certificate programs for learning disabilities teacher-consultant, teacher of the handicapped, reading specialist, and supervisor.

Montana State University–Billings, College of Education and Human Services, Billings, MT 59101-9984. Awards M Ed, MS, MSRC, MS Sp Ed. Accredited by NCATE. Part-time programs available. Postbaccalaureate distance learning degree programs offered (minimal on-campus study). *Degree requirements:* Thesis or alternative required, foreign language not required. *Entrance requirements:* GRE General Test (minimum combined score of 1350 on three sections; average 1450) or MAT (minimum score 38; average 50), minimum GPA of 3.0 (undergraduate), 3.25 (graduate). Application deadline: rolling. Application fee: $30. *Expenses:* Tuition $2253 per year full-time, $397 per semester (minimum) part-time for state residents; $5313 per year full-time, $907 per semester (minimum) part-time for nonresidents. Fees $378 per year full-time, $105 per semester (minimum) part-time. *Faculty research:* Social studies education, science education.

Montana State University–Bozeman, College of Education, Health, and Human Development, Department of Education, 211 Montana Hall, Bozeman, MT 59717. Awards M Ed, Ed D, Ed S. Accredited by NCATE. Part-time programs available. Faculty: 17 full-time (6 women). Students: 32 full-time (18 women), 113 part-time (66 women); includes 10 minority (1 African American, 1 Asian American, 8 Native Americans). Average age 41. 25 applicants, 92% accepted. In 1997, 64 master's, 29 doctorates awarded. *Degree requirements:* For master's, thesis or alternative, comprehensive exam required, foreign language not required; for doctorate, dissertation, oral comprehensive exam required, foreign language not required. *Entrance requirements:* For master's, GRE General Test (minimum combined score of 850), TOEFL; for doctorate, GRE General Test (minimum combined score of 1000), TOEFL (minimum score 550), writing sample. Application deadline: 6/1 (priority date; rolling processing; 11/1 for spring admission). Application fee: $50. *Tuition:* $3994 per year full-time, $367 per semester (minimum) part-time for state residents; $9507 per year full-time, $957 per semester (minimum) part-time for nonresidents. *Financial aid:* In 1997–98, 17 students received aid, including 5 research assistantships averaging $666 per month and totaling $16,650, 12 teaching assistantships (1 to a first-year student) averaging $912 per month and totaling $131,256; career-related internships or fieldwork also available. Financial aid application deadline: 3/1. *Faculty research:* Learning, copyright, multicultural and science education, agricultural literacy, resource policy. Total annual research expenditures: $1.591 million. • Dr. Gloria Gregg, Head, 406-994-6670. Fax: 406-994-3261. E-mail: education@montana.edu.

Montana State University–Northern, Department of Education, Havre, MT 59501-7751. Offers programs in counseling and development (M Ed), elementary education (M Ed), general science (M Ed), learning development (M Ed), vocational education (M Ed). Part-time and evening/weekend programs available. Faculty: 26 full-time (5 women). Students: 68 full-time (41 women), 100 part-time (65 women); includes 11 minority (2 African Americans, 9 Native Americans). Average age 40. *Degree requirements:* Comprehensive and oral exams required, foreign language not required. *Entrance requirements:* GRE General Test, minimum GPA of 3.0. Application deadline: 9/20 (priority date; rolling processing). Application fee: $30. *Tuition:* $3090 per year full-time, $696 per semester (minimum) part-time for state residents; $8044 per year full-time, $1758 per semester (minimum) part-time for nonresidents. *Financial aid:* Teaching assistantships, Federal Work-Study, institutionally sponsored loans, and career-related internships or fieldwork available. Aid available to part-time students. Financial aid application deadline: 4/1; applicants required to submit FAFSA. • Dr. Ben Johnson, Director of Education and Graduate Programs, 406-265-3738. Fax: 406-265-3570. E-mail: johnson@nmcl.nmclites.edu.

Montclair State University, College of Education and Human Services, Upper Montclair, NJ 07043-1624. Awards MA, MAT, M Ed. Accredited by NCATE. Part-time and evening/weekend programs available. Faculty: 75 full-time, 8 part-time. Students: 245 full-time (192 women), 765 part-time (591 women); includes 123 minority (70 African Americans, 7 Asian Americans, 44 Hispanics, 2 Native Americans), 18 international. In 1997, 304 degrees awarded. *Degree requirements:* Comprehensive exam. *Application deadline:* rolling. *Application fee:* $40. *Expenses:* Tuition $201 per credit for state residents; $257 per credit for nonresidents. Fees $22.05 per credit. *Financial aid:* Research assistantships available. Aid available to part-time students. Financial aid application deadline: 3/1; applicants required to submit FAFSA. • Dr. Nicholas M. Michelli, Dean, 973-655-5167.

Directory: Education—General

Moorhead State University, Department of Education, Moorhead, MN 56563-0002. Offers programs in counseling and student affairs (MS), curriculum and instruction (MS), educational administration (MS, Ed S), elementary education (MS), reading (MS), special education (MS). Accredited by NCATE. Part-time and evening/weekend programs available. Students: 21 full-time (18 women), 72 part-time (56 women); includes 2 minority (1 Hispanic, 1 Native American), 1 international. 52 applicants, 98% accepted. In 1997, 24 master's, 1 Ed S awarded. *Degree requirements:* For master's, final oral exam, project or thesis, written comprehensive exam required, foreign language not required. *Entrance requirements:* For master's, TOEFL (minimum score 550). Application deadline: 5/1 (priority date; rolling processing; 9/1 for spring admission). Application fee: $20 ($35 for international students). Electronic applications accepted. *Tuition:* $145 per credit hour for state residents; $220 per credit hour for nonresidents. *Financial aid:* Administrative assistantships, Federal Work-Study, and career-related internships or fieldwork available. Financial aid application deadline: 7/15; applicants required to submit FAFSA. • Dr. Steven Grineski, Interim Dean, 218-236-2095.

Morehead State University, College of Education and Behavioral Sciences, Morehead, KY 40351. Awards MA, MA Ed, MS, Ed D, Ed S. Accredited by NCATE. Part-time and evening/weekend programs available. Faculty: 74 full-time (34 women), 17 part-time (7 women). Students: 97 full-time (58 women), 481 part-time (358 women); includes 9 minority (7 African Americans, 2 Asian Americans), 8 international. Average age 25. 189 applicants, 98% accepted. In 1997, 235 master's, 3 Ed Ss awarded. *Degree requirements:* For Ed S, thesis, oral exam required, foreign language not required. *Entrance requirements:* For master's, GRE General Test; for Ed S, GRE General Test (minimum combined score of 1200), interview, master's degree, minimum GPA of 3.5, work experience. Application deadline: 8/1 (priority date; rolling processing; 12/1 for spring admission). Application fee: $0. *Tuition:* $2470 per year full-time, $138 per semester hour part-time for state residents; $6710 per year full-time, $373 per semester hour part-time for nonresidents. *Financial aid:* In 1997–98, 7 research assistantships, 22 teaching assistantships (12 to first-year students) averaging $471 per month and totaling $116,000 were awarded; Federal Work-Study, institutionally sponsored loans, and career-related internships or fieldwork also available. Financial aid application deadline: 4/1; applicants required to submit FAFSA. *Faculty research:* Regional economic development, computer applications for school administrators, effectiveness of teacher interns, perceptual processes, alcoholism. • Dr. Harold Harty, Dean, 606-783-2040. Fax: 606-783-5029. E-mail: h.harty@morehead-st.edu. Application contact: Betty Cowsert, Graduate Admissions Officer, 606-783-2039. Fax: 606-783-5061.

Morgan State University, School of Education and Urban Studies, Department of Teacher Education and Administration, Baltimore, MD 21251. Offers programs in educational administration and supervision (MS), elementary and middle school education (MS), teaching (MAT), urban educational leadership (Ed D). Accredited by NCATE. Part-time and evening/weekend programs available. Faculty: 5 full-time (1 woman), 4 part-time (1 woman). Students: 10 full-time (6 women), 53 part-time (32 women); includes 63 minority (61 African Americans, 2 Asian Americans). Average age 34. 41 applicants, 20% accepted. In 1997, 11 master's awarded; 5 doctorates awarded (100% found work related to degree). *Degree requirements:* For master's, comprehensive exam required, thesis optional, foreign language not required; for doctorate, dissertation, comprehensive exam required, foreign language not required. *Average time to degree:* master's–2 years full-time, 3 years part-time; doctorate–7 years part-time. *Entrance requirements:* For doctorate, GRE General Test or MAT. Application deadline: 7/1 (rolling processing). Application fee: $0. *Expenses:* Tuition $160 per credit hour for state residents; $286 per credit hour for nonresidents. Fees $326 per year. *Financial aid:* Fellowships, research assistantships available. Financial aid application deadline: 4/1. *Faculty research:* Multicultural education, cooperative learning, psychology of cognition. • Dr. Iola Ragins Smith, Chairperson, 410-319-3292. Fax: 410-319-3871. Application contact: James E. Waller, Admissions and Programs Officer, 410-319-3186. Fax: 410-319-3837.

Morningside College, Department of Education, Sioux City, IA 51106-1751. Offers programs in elementary education (MAT), reading specialist (MAT), special education (MAT), technology based learning (MAT). Accredited by NCATE. Part-time and evening/weekend programs available. Faculty: 33 (17 women). Students: 1 full-time, 179 part-time; includes 1 minority (Native American). *Entrance requirements:* MAT, writing sample. Application deadline: rolling. Application fee: $15. *Tuition:* $245 per credit hour. *Financial aid:* Partial tuition waivers, institutionally sponsored loans available. Aid available to part-time students. • Dr. Glenna Tevis, Director, Graduate Division, 712-274-5375.

Mount Mary College, Graduate Programs, Programs in Education, Milwaukee, WI 53222-4597. Offerings in education (MA), professional development (MA). Part-time and evening/weekend programs available. Faculty: 1 full-time (0 women), 13 part-time (11 women), 5.5 FTE. Students: 123 part-time (118 women); includes 6 minority (4 African Americans, 1 Hispanic, 1 Native American). Average age 36. 11 applicants, 100% accepted. In 1997, 19 degrees awarded (100% found work related to degree). *Degree requirements:* Instructional project required, foreign language and thesis not required. *Average time to degree:* master's–2.5 years part-time. *Entrance requirements:* TOEFL (minimum score 550), minimum GPA of 2.75, teaching license. Application deadline: 8/29 (priority date; rolling processing; 1/20 for spring admission). Application fee: $35. *Tuition:* $370 per credit hour. *Financial aid:* Federal Work-Study available. Aid available to part-time students. Financial aid application deadline: 5/1. *Faculty research:* Staff development, writing across the curriculum, effective schools, critical thinking skills, mathematics education. • Dr. Eileen Schwalbach, Director, 414-256-1214.

Mount Saint Mary College, Division of Education, Newburgh, NY 12550-3494. Offers programs in elementary education (MS Ed), elementary/special education (MS Ed), secondary education (MS Ed), special education (MS Ed). Part-time and evening/weekend programs available. Faculty: 6 full-time (5 women), 15 part-time (8 women). Students: 18 full-time (16 women), 293 part-time (246 women); includes 18 minority (8 African Americans, 3 Asian Americans, 7 Hispanics). Average age 32. In 1997, 86 degrees awarded. *Average time to degree:* master's–1.5 years full-time, 2.5 years part-time. *Application deadline:* rolling. *Application fee:* $20. *Expenses:* Tuition $367 per credit. Fees $30 per year. *Financial aid:* Federal Work-Study and career-related internships or fieldwork available. Aid available to part-time students. Financial aid application deadline: 9/30. *Faculty research:* Learning and teaching styles, computers in special education, language development. • Dr. Lucy DiPaola, Chairperson, 914-569-3263. Application contact: Sr. Frances Berski, Coordinator, 914-569-3267. Fax: 914-562-6762. E-mail: berski@msmc.edu.

Mount St. Mary's College, Department of Education, Los Angeles, CA 90049-1597. Offers programs in administrative studies (MS), elementary education (MS), secondary education (MS), special education (MS). Part-time and evening/weekend programs available. *Degree requirements:* Thesis, research project required, foreign language not required. *Entrance requirements:* MAT, minimum GPA of 3.0. Application fee: $50.

Mount Saint Mary's College and Seminary, Graduate Program in Education, Emmitsburg, MD 21727-7799. Awards M Ed. Part-time and evening/weekend programs available. Faculty: 5 part-time (4 women). Students: 16 full-time (13 women), 55 part-time (46 women); includes 3 minority (1 African American, 1 Asian American, 1 Native American). Average age 31. In 1997, 8 degrees awarded (100% entered university research/teaching). *Degree requirements:* Exit portfolio/presentation required, foreign language and thesis not required. *Entrance requirements:* NTE, minimum GPA of 2.7. Application deadline: rolling. Application fee: $20. *Expenses:* Tuition $3600 per year full-time, $200 per credit hour part-time. Fees $100 per year (minimum) full-time, $5 per credit hour part-time. *Financial aid:* 3 students received aid; research assistantships and career-related internships or fieldwork available. *Faculty research:* Integrated curriculum, literacy, professional development schools, inclusion, portfolio assessment. • Dr. Marie Holahan, Director, 301-447-5371. Fax: 301-447-5250. E-mail: holahan@msmary.edu.

Mount Saint Vincent University, Department of Education, Halifax, NS B3M 2J6, Canada. Offers programs in adult education (MA, MA Ed, MA(R), M Ed), curriculum studies (MA, MA Ed, MA(R), M Ed), educational foundations (MA, MA Ed, MA(R), M Ed), educational psychology (MA, MA Ed, MA(R), M Ed), elementary education (MA, MA Ed, MA(R), M Ed), literacy education (MA, MA Ed, MA(R), M Ed), school psychology (MASP). Part-time and evening/weekend programs available. Postbaccalaureate distance learning degree programs offered (minimal on-campus study). Students: 30 full-time (25 women), 306 part-time (259 women). Average age 35. 313 applicants, 81% accepted. In 1997, 138 degrees awarded. *Degree requirements:* Thesis. *Entrance requirements:* Bachelor's degree in related field. Application deadline: 3/1 (priority date; rolling processing; 9/1 for spring admission). Application fee: $40. *Expenses:* Tuition $1024 per course. Fees $25 per course. *Financial aid:* Fellowships available. Financial aid application deadline: 5/1. *Faculty research:* Critical/feminist pedagogy, relationship between cognitive and behavioral development, gender and education, history of education, diagnosis and remediation in mathematics. • Dr. Mary L. Crowley, Chair, 902-457-6304. Fax: 902-457-4911. E-mail: mary.crowley@msvu.ca. Application contact: Susan Tanner, Assistant Registrar, 902-457-6363. Fax: 902-457-6498. E-mail: susan.tanner@msvu.ca.

Mount Vernon Nazarene College, Department of Education, Mount Vernon, OH 43050-9500. Awards MA Ed. Part-time programs available. Faculty: 5 full-time (3 women), 2 part-time (1 woman). Students: 16 part-time (13 women). In 1997, 8 degrees awarded. *Degree requirements:* Project required, foreign language and thesis not required. *Average time to degree:* master's–2 years part-time. *Application deadline:* 8/1 (rolling processing; 12/1 for spring admission). *Application fee:* $20. *Tuition:* $270 per credit hour. *Financial aid:* 1 student received aid; partial tuition waivers available. Aid available to part-time students. Financial aid application deadline: 8/1. • Dr. Fred Kreamelmeyer, Director, 740-397-1244 Ext. 3403. Fax: 740-397-2769. E-mail: fkreamel@mvnc.edu.

Murray State University, College of Education, Murray, KY 42071-0009. Awards MA, MA Ed, MS, Ed D, PhD, Ed S. Accredited by NCATE. Ed D and PhD offered jointly with the University of Kentucky. Part-time programs available. Faculty: 53 full-time (23 women). Students: 94 full-time (72 women), 682 part-time (568 women); includes 39 African Americans, 1 Hispanic, 1 Native American, 15 international. 256 applicants, 60% accepted. In 1997, 150 master's, 2 Ed Ss awarded. *Entrance requirements:* For master's, TOEFL (minimum score 500). Application deadline: rolling. Application fee: $20. *Expenses:* Tuition $2500 per year full-time, $124 per hour part-time for state residents; $6740 per year full-time, $357 per hour part-time for nonresidents. Fees $360 per year full-time, $180 per year part-time. *Financial aid:* Research assistantships, teaching assistantships, Federal Work-Study available. Financial aid application deadline: 4/1. • Dr. Bill Price, Interim Dean, 502-762-3817.

Muskingum College, Graduate Program in Education, New Concord, OH 43762. Awards MAE. Part-time programs available. Faculty: 19. Students: 162. *Entrance requirements:* Teaching license, minimum GPA of 2.7. Application deadline: rolling. Application fee: $20. *Tuition:* $198 per semester hour. *Faculty research:* Brain behavior relationships, school partnerships, staff development, school law, proficiency testing, multi-age groupings. • Dr. Rolf G. Schmitz, Director of Graduate Studies, 614-826-8037.

National–Louis University, National College of Education, McGaw Graduate School, 2840 Sheridan Road, Evanston, IL 60201-1730. Awards MAT, M Ed, MS Ed, Ed D, CAS, Ed S. Part-time and evening/weekend programs available. Faculty: 163 full-time (118 women), 588 part-time (416 women). Students: 822 full-time (668 women), 1,524 part-time (1,303 women); includes 318 minority (187 African Americans, 36 Asian Americans, 89 Hispanics, 6 Native Americans), 3 international. Average age 37. 726 applicants, 98% accepted. In 1997, 12 doctorates, 70 other advanced degrees awarded. *Degree requirements:* For doctorate, dissertation, comprehensive exams, internship required, foreign language not required. *Entrance requirements:* For master's, minimum GPA of 3.0; for doctorate, GRE General Test, minimum GPA of 3.25. Application fee: $25. *Tuition:* $411 per semester hour. *Financial aid:* Fellowships, research assistantships, teaching assistantships, Federal Work-Study, institutionally sponsored loans, and career-related internships or fieldwork available. Aid available to part-time students. Financial aid applicants required to submit FAFSA. *Faculty research:* Methods of teaching behaviorally challenged, early childhood curriculum planning, individualized learning. • Dr. Linda Tafel, Dean, 847-475-1100 Ext. 5201. Application contact: Dr. David McCulloch, Vice President for University Services, 800-443-5522 Ext. 5127. Fax: 847-465-0593. E-mail: dmcc@wheeling1.nl.edu.

National University, School of Education and Human Services, Department of Teacher Education and Leadership, La Jolla, CA 92037-1011. Offers programs in bilingual crosscultural teaching (ME), cross-cultural teaching (ME), educational technology (MS), instructional leadership (ME), instructional leadership for adult learners (MS), instructional leadership in curriculum and instruction (MS). Students: 845 full-time (598 women), 378 part-time (280 women); includes 381 minority (125 African Americans, 61 Asian Americans, 185 Hispanics, 10 Native Americans), 5 international. Average age 37. *Entrance requirements:* Interview, minimum GPA of 2.5. Application deadline: rolling. Application fee: $60 ($100 for international students). *Tuition:* $7830 per year full-time, $870 per course part-time. *Financial aid:* Application deadline 5/1. • Dr. Helene Mandell, Chair, 619-642-8345. Application contact: Nancy Rohland, Director of Enrollment Management, 619-563-7100. Fax: 619-563-7393.

Nazareth College of Rochester, Graduate Studies, Department of Education, Rochester, NY 14618-3790. Offers programs in computer education (MS Ed), early childhood education (MS Ed), elementary education (MS Ed), general secondary education (MS Ed), reading (MS Ed), special education (MS Ed), teaching English to speakers of other languages (MS Ed). Part-time and evening/weekend programs available. Faculty: 15 full-time (8 women), 52 part-time (29 women). Students: 130 full-time (122 women), 616 part-time (513 women); includes 29 minority (21 African Americans, 2 Asian Americans, 6 Hispanics). Average age 27. 235 applicants, 91% accepted. In 1997, 315 degrees awarded. *Degree requirements:* Comprehensive exam required, foreign language and thesis not required. *Entrance requirements:* Minimum GPA of 2.7. Application fee: $40. *Expenses:* Tuition $436 per credit hour. Fees $20 per semester. • Dr. Mary Palamer, Chairperson, 716-389-2606. Application contact: Dr. Kay F. Marshman, Dean, 716-389-2815. Fax: 716-389-2452.

Neumann College, Program in Education, Aston, PA 19014-1298. Awards MS. Faculty: 2 full-time (1 woman), 3 part-time (1 woman). Students: 5 part-time (3 women). In 1997, 5 degrees awarded. *Entrance requirements:* GRE or MAT, TOEFL. Application deadline: rolling. Application fee: $50. *Tuition:* $410 per credit. *Financial aid:* Available to part-time students. Financial aid application deadline: 3/15; applicants required to submit FAFSA. • Dr. John Kaczenski, Chair, Division of Education and Human Services, 610-558-5640. Fax: 610-459-1370. Application contact: John Pyle, Admissions Counselor, 610-558-5531. Fax: 610-558-5652. E-mail: neumann@smtpgate.neumann.edu.

New Jersey City University, School of Professional Studies and Education, Jersey City, NJ 07305-1957. Awards MA, MS, Certificate. One or more programs accredited by NCATE. Evening/weekend programs available. *Application deadline:* 8/1 (priority date; rolling processing; 12/1 for spring admission). *Application fee:* $0.

Newman University, Program in Education, Wichita, KS 67213-2084. Offers adult education (MS Ed), building leadership (MS Ed), elementary/middle-level education (MS Ed), English as a second language (MS Ed). Faculty: 5 full-time, 9 part-time. Students: 60; includes 5 minority (all African Americans). *Degree requirements:* Thesis or alternative. *Average time to degree:* master's–3 years part-time. *Application deadline:* 8/15 (priority date; rolling processing; 1/10 for spring admission). *Application fee:* $25. *Tuition:* $257 per credit hour. • Dr. Laura McLemore, Division Chair of Institute for Teacher Education, 316-942-4291 Ext. 253. Fax: 316-942-4483.

New Mexico Highlands University, School of Education, Las Vegas, NM 87701. Offers programs in curriculum and instruction (MA), education administration (MA), guidance and counseling (MA), human performance and sport (MA), special education (MA). Part-time programs available. Faculty: 32 full-time (14 women). Students: 63 full-time (21 women), 98 part-time (70 women); includes 106 minority (3 African Americans, 1 Asian American, 97 Hispanics, 5 Native Americans), 3 international. Average age 35. In 1997, 56 degrees awarded. *Degree requirements:* Thesis or alternative required, foreign language not required. *Entrance requirements:* Minimum undergraduate GPA of 3.0. Application deadline: 8/1 (priority date; rolling processing). Application fee: $15. *Expenses:* Tuition $1816 per year full-time, $227 per hour part-time for state residents; $7468 per year full-time, $227 per hour part-time for nonresidents. Fees $10 per year. *Financial aid:* Federal Work-Study available. Financial aid application deadline: 3/1. • Dr. James Abreu, Dean, 505-454-3357. Application contact: Dr. Glen W. Davidson, Academic Vice President, 505-454-3311. Fax: 505-454-3558. E-mail: glendavidson@venus.nmhu.edu.

New Mexico State University, College of Education, Las Cruces, NM 88003-8001. Awards MA, MAT, Ed D, PhD, Ed S. Accredited by NCATE. Part-time programs available. Faculty: 56 full-time (28 women), 1 (woman) part-time. Students: 345 full-time (240 women), 420 part-time (321 women); includes 269 minority (10 African Americans, 5 Asian Americans, 243 Hispanics, 11 Native Americans), 35 international. Average age 36. 443 applicants, 43% accepted. In 1997, 211 master's, 24 doctorates, 2 Ed Ss awarded. *Degree requirements:* For doctorate, dissertation. *Application deadline:* rolling. *Application fee:* $15 ($35 for international students). Electronic applications accepted. *Tuition:* $2514 per year full-time, $105 per credit hour part-time for state residents; $7848 per year full-time, $327 per credit hour part-time for nonresidents. *Financial aid:* Fellowships, research assistantships, teaching assistantships, Federal Work-Study, and career-related internships or fieldwork available. Aid available to part-time students. Financial aid application deadline: 3/1. *Faculty research:* Bilingual special education, early childhood education/Head Start, leadership in border settings, exercise physiology, school-based mental health. • Dr. H. Prentice Baptiste, Dean, 505-646-3404. Fax: 505-646-6032.

New School University, Adult Division, Teacher Education Program, New York, NY 10011-8603. Awards MST. Faculty: 8 part-time (7 women). Students: 43 full-time (32 women); includes 11 minority (9 African Americans, 2 Hispanics). Average age 32. 79 applicants, 68% accepted. In 1997, 44 degrees awarded. *Entrance requirements:* Interview, portfolio. Application deadline: 5/1 (rolling processing). Application fee: $30. *Tuition:* $616 per credit. *Financial aid:* Departmental scholarships, full and partial tuition waivers, Federal Work-Study, institutionally sponsored loans, and career-related internships or fieldwork available. Financial aid application deadline: 5/1; applicants required to submit FAFSA. • Carolina Mancuso, Acting Director, 212-229-5881. Application contact: Gerianne Brusati, Director, Educational Advising and Admissions, 212-229-5630. Fax: 212-989-3887. E-mail: admissions@dialnsa.edu.

See in-depth description on page 995.

New York Institute of Technology, School of Education, Old Westbury, NY 11568-8000. Awards MS, Certificate. Part-time and evening/weekend programs available. Faculty: 11 full-time (4 women), 61 part-time (34 women). Students: 64 full-time (42 women), 796 part-time (561 women); includes 184 minority (125 African Americans, 18 Asian Americans, 40 Hispanics, 1 Native American), 3 international. Average age 35. 187 applicants, 73% accepted. In 1997, 114 master's awarded. *Degree requirements:* For master's, thesis required, foreign language not required. *Average time to degree:* master's–2 years full-time, 3 years part-time. *Entrance requirements:* For master's, GRE General Test, TOEFL, minimum QPA of 2.85. Application deadline: 8/1 (priority date; rolling processing). Application fee: $50. *Tuition:* $413 per credit. *Financial aid:* In 1997–98, 7 research assistantships (3 to first-year students) averaging $300 per month and totaling $11,200 were awarded; full and partial tuition waivers, institutionally sponsored loans, and career-related internships or fieldwork also available. Aid available to part-time students. *Faculty research:* Distance learning, instructional uses of the World Wide Web. • Dr. Helen Greene, Dean, 516-686-7706. Fax: 516-686-7655. Application contact: Glenn Berman, Executive Director of Admissions, 516-686-7519. Fax: 516-626-0419. E-mail: gberman@iris.nyit.edu.

New York University, School of Education, New York, NY 10012-1019. Awards MA, MFA, MM, MPH, MS, DA, DPS, Ed D, PhD, Psy D, AC, CAS, MA/MS. Part-time and evening/weekend programs available. Faculty: 195 full-time, 700 part-time. Students: 1,637 full-time, 2,859 part-time. Average age 25. 4,118 applicants, 46% accepted. In 1997, 1,255 master's, 109 doctorates, 53 other advanced degrees awarded. Terminal master's awarded for partial completion of doctoral program. *Degree requirements:* For doctorate, dissertation. *Entrance requirements:* For master's and other advanced degree, TOEFL; for doctorate, GRE General Test, TOEFL, interview. Application deadline: 2/1 (priority date; rolling processing; 12/1 for spring admission). Application fee: $40 ($60 for international students). *Financial aid:* In 1997–98, fellowships averaging $850 per month, research assistantships averaging $850 per month, teaching assistantships averaging $850 per month were awarded; partial tuition waivers, Federal Work-Study, institutionally sponsored loans, and career-related internships or fieldwork also available. Aid available to part-time students. Financial aid application deadline: 3/1; applicants required to submit FAFSA. *Faculty research:* Gerontology, special education, urban adolescents, Alzheimer's disease, breast cancer. Total annual research expenditures: $14 million. • Dr. Ann Marcus, Dean, 212-998-5000. Application contact: Office of Graduate Admissions, 212-998-5030. Fax: 212-995-4328.

See in-depth description on page 757.

Niagara University, Graduate Division of Education, Niagara University, NY 14109. Offers programs in administration and supervision (MS Ed, PD); biology (MAT); foundations and teaching (MA, MS Ed); mental health counseling (MS Ed); school counseling (MS Ed, PD); teacher education (MS Ed), including elementary education, secondary education. One or more programs accredited by NCATE. Part-time and evening/weekend programs available. Faculty: 10 full-time (2 women), 18 part-time (8 women). Students: 262 full-time (180 women), 202 part-time (145 women); includes 13 minority (9 African Americans, 2 Asian Americans, 2 Hispanics), 64 international. Average age 37. 382 applicants, 75% accepted. In 1997, 221 master's, 6 PDs awarded. *Entrance requirements:* For master's, GRE General Test or MAT. Application deadline: 8/1 (rolling processing). Application fee: $30. *Expenses:* Tuition $4950 per year full-time, $275 per credit hour part-time. Fees $25 per semester. *Financial aid:* In 1997–98, 2 fellowships (both to first-year students), 3 research assistantships were awarded; graduate assistantships, scholarships, Federal Work-Study, and career-related internships or fieldwork also available. Aid available to part-time students. Financial aid application deadline: 3/15. *Faculty research:* Instructional supervision, appraisal and evaluation, career opportunities. • Rev. Daniel F. O'Leary, OMI, Dean, 716-286-8560.

Nicholls State University, College of Education, Department of Teacher Education, Thibodaux, LA 70310. Offers programs in administration and supervision (M Ed), curriculum and instruction (M Ed). Accredited by NCATE. Part-time and evening/weekend programs available. Faculty: 15 full-time (8 women). Students: 5 full-time (4 women), 160 part-time (131 women); includes 28 minority (23 African Americans, 2 Asian Americans, 1 Hispanic, 2 Native Americans), 1 international. In 1997, 76 degrees awarded (100% found work related to degree). *Entrance requirements:* GRE General Test, GRE Subject Test. Application deadline: 6/17 (priority date; rolling processing; 11/15 for spring admission). Application fee: $10 ($60 for international students). *Tuition:* $2136 per year full-time, $283 per semester (minimum) part-time for state residents; $5376 per year full-time, $283 per semester (minimum) part-time for nonresidents. *Financial aid:* Research assistantships available. Financial aid application deadline: 6/17. • Dr. Harrell H. Carpenter, Head, 504-448-4330.

Norfolk State University, School of Education, 2401 Corprew Avenue, Norfolk, VA 23504-3907. Awards MA, MAT. Accredited by NCATE. Part-time programs available. Students: 118 full-time (91 women), 72 part-time (57 women); includes 145 minority (142 African Americans, 3 Asian Americans), 42 international. In 1997, 89 degrees awarded. *Entrance requirements:* GRE. Application deadline: 8/1. Application fee: $30. *Tuition:* $3718 per year full-time, $198 per credit hour part-time for state residents; $7668 per year full-time, $404 per credit hour part-time for nonresidents. *Financial aid:* Fellowships and career-related internships or fieldwork available. *Faculty research:* Urban, pre-elementary, and special education. • Dr. Denise Littleton, Acting Dean, 757-683-8701.

North Carolina Agricultural and Technical State University, Graduate School, School of Education, Greensboro, NC 27411. Awards MS. Accredited by NCATE. Part-time and evening/weekend programs available. Faculty: 70 full-time (28 women). Students: 123 full-time (98 women), 280 part-time (236 women); includes 284 minority (281 African Americans, 1 Asian American, 1 Hispanic, 1 Native American). Average age 35. 216 applicants, 74% accepted. In 1997, 95 degrees awarded. *Degree requirements:* Comprehensive exam, qualifying exam required, foreign language not required. *Entrance requirements:* GRE General Test. Application deadline: 6/1 (priority date; rolling processing; 12/1 for spring admission). Application fee: $35. *Tuition:* $1662 per year full-time, $272 per semester (minimum) part-time for state residents; $8790 per year full-time, $2054 per semester (minimum) part-time for nonresidents. *Financial aid:* Fellowships, research assistantships, teaching assistantships, graduate assistantships, and career-related internships or fieldwork available. Aid available to part-time students. Financial aid application deadline: 6/1. • Dr. David Boger, Dean, 336-334-7757. Fax: 336-334-7132. E-mail: bogerd@ncat.edu.

North Carolina Central University, Division of Academic Affairs, School of Education, Durham, NC 27707-3129. Awards MA, M Ed. Accredited by NCATE. Part-time and evening/weekend programs available. Faculty: 35 full-time (22 women), 7 part-time (5 women). Students: 79 full-time (72 women), 183 part-time (143 women); includes 167 minority (164 African Americans, 2 Hispanics, 1 Native American). Average age 36. 178 applicants, 43% accepted. In 1997, 93 degrees awarded. *Degree requirements:* Thesis or alternative, comprehensive exam required, foreign language not required. *Entrance requirements:* Minimum GPA of 3.0 in major, 2.5 overall. Application deadline: 8/1. Application fee: $30. *Tuition:* $2027 per year full-time, $508 per semester (minimum) part-time for state residents; $9155 per year full-time, $2290 per semester (minimum) part-time for nonresidents. *Financial aid:* Fellowships, research assistantships, teaching assistantships, state grants, Federal Work-Study, institutionally sponsored loans, and career-related internships or fieldwork available. Aid available to part-time students. Financial aid application deadline: 5/1. • Dr. Sammie C. Parrish, Dean, 919-560-6466. Application contact: Dr. Cecelia Steppe-Jones, Associate Dean of Graduate Studies and Administration, 919-560-6478.

North Carolina State University, College of Education and Psychology, Raleigh, NC 27695. Awards M Ed, MS, Ed D, PhD, CAGS, Certificate. Accredited by NCATE. Part-time programs available. Faculty: 104 full-time (34 women), 82 part-time (29 women). Students: 262 full-time (186 women), 647 part-time (444 women); includes 182 minority (149 African Americans, 16 Asian Americans, 9 Hispanics, 8 Native Americans), 11 international. Average age 38. 595 applicants, 39% accepted. In 1997, 135 master's, 82 doctorates awarded. *Degree requirements:* For doctorate, dissertation required, foreign language not required. *Entrance requirements:* GRE General Test or MAT, minimum GPA of 3.0 in major. Application fee: $45. *Tuition:* $2370 per year full-time, $517 per semester (minimum) part-time for state residents; $11,536 per year full-time, $2809 per semester (minimum) part-time for nonresidents. *Financial aid:* In 1997–98, 11 fellowships averaging $838 per month and totaling $48,998, 69 research assistantships (15 to first-year students) averaging $933 per month and totaling $222,439, 137 teaching assistantships (24 to first-year students) totaling $281,292, 6 minority grants were awarded; full tuition waivers, Federal Work-Study, institutionally sponsored loans, and career-related internships or fieldwork also available. Aid available to part-time students. *Faculty research:* Moral/ethical development, financial policy analysis, middle years education, adult education. Total annual research expenditures: $3.01 million. • Dr. Joan J. Michael, Dean, 919-515-2231. E-mail: joan@poe.coe.ncsu.edu. Application contact: Sue Bullard, Administrative Assistant, 919-515-2231. Fax: 919-515-5836. E-mail: bullard@poe.coe.ncsu.edu.

North Central College, Graduate Programs, Department of Education, Naperville, IL 60566-7063. Awards MA Ed. Faculty: 7 full-time (3 women), 4 part-time (2 women). Students: 180. In 1997, 15 degrees awarded. *Degree requirements:* Clinical practicum, project required, thesis not required. *Entrance requirements:* MAT, minimum GPA of 2.75. Application deadline: 8/15 (rolling processing). Application fee: $25. *Financial aid:* Available to part-time students. • Coordinator, 630-637-5742. Fax: 630-637-5844.

North Dakota State University, College of Human Development and Education, School of Education, Fargo, ND 58105. Awards MA, M Ed, MS, Ed S. Accredited by NCATE. Part-time and evening/weekend programs available. Postbaccalaureate distance learning degree programs offered (minimal on-campus study). Faculty: 14 full-time (6 women), 11 part-time (6 women). Students: 22 full-time (15 women), 282 part-time (109 women). In 1997, 59 master's, 4 Ed Ss awarded. *Degree requirements:* For Ed S, thesis required, foreign language not required. *Entrance requirements:* For master's, MAT, TOEFL (minimum score 525); for Ed S, GRE General Test (minimum score 450 on each section), MAT (minimum score 40), TOEFL (minimum score 525), master's degree, minimum GPA of 3.25. Application deadline: rolling. Application fee: $25. *Tuition:* $2572 per year full-time, $107 per credit part-time for state residents; $6868 per year full-time, $286 per credit part-time for nonresidents. *Financial aid:* Research assistantships, teaching assistantships, full tuition waivers, Federal Work-Study, institutionally sponsored loans, and career-related internships or fieldwork available. Financial aid application deadline: 4/15. • Dr. Virginia L. Clark, Dean, College of Human Development and Education, 701-231-8211. Fax: 701-231-7174. E-mail: vclark@badlands.nodak.edu.

Northeastern Illinois University, College of Education, Chicago, IL 60625-4699. Awards MA, MAT, M Ed, MSI. Part-time and evening/weekend programs available. Faculty: 73 full-time (40 women), 39 part-time (21 women). Students: 102 full-time (73 women), 867 part-time (682 women). Average age 35. 454 applicants, 76% accepted. In 1997, 286 degrees awarded. *Entrance requirements:* Minimum GPA of 2.75. Application deadline: 3/18 (priority date; rolling processing; 9/30 for spring admission). Application fee: $0. *Expenses:* Tuition $2226 per year full-time, $93 per credit hour part-time for state residents; $6678 per year full-time, $278 per credit hour part-time for nonresidents. Fees $358 per year full-time, $14.90 per credit hour part-time. *Financial aid:* In 1997–98, 219 students received aid, including 21 research assistantships averaging $450 per month; full and partial tuition waivers, Federal Work-Study, institutionally sponsored loans, and career-related internships or fieldwork also available. Aid available to part-time students. Financial aid applicants required to submit FAFSA. • Dr. Michael Carl, Dean, 773-583-4050 Ext. 5298. Application contact: Dr. Mohan K. Sood, Dean of Graduate College, 773-583-4050 Ext. 6143. Fax: 773-794-6670.

Northeastern State University, College of Education, Tahlequah, OK 74464-2399. Awards M Ed, MS. Part-time and evening/weekend programs available. Students: 507 (373 women); includes 4 international. In 1997, 229 degrees awarded. *Degree requirements:* Thesis or alternative required, foreign language not required. *Entrance requirements:* GRE General Test (minimum combined score of 900) or MAT. Application deadline: 6/1 (priority date; rolling processing). Application fee: $0. *Expenses:* Tuition $74 per credit hour for state residents; $176 per credit hour for nonresidents. Fees $30 per year. *Financial aid:* Teaching assistantships, Federal Work-Study, and career-related internships or fieldwork available. Financial aid application deadline: 3/1. • Dr. Mark Clark, Dean, 918-456-5511 Ext. 3700.

Northeastern University, Graduate School of Arts and Sciences, Department of Education, Boston, MA 02115-5096. Offers programs in curriculum and instruction (M Ed), educational research (M Ed), human development (M Ed), reading (M Ed). Part-time and evening/weekend programs available. Faculty: 11 full-time (3 women), 3 part-time (2 women). Students: 25 full-time (16 women), 22 part-time (15 women). Average age 30. 73 applicants, 63% accepted. In 1997, 13 degrees awarded. *Average time to degree:* master's–3 years full-time, 5 years part-time. *Entrance requirements:* GRE General Test or MAT. Application deadline: 7/15 (rolling processing; 2/1 for spring admission). Application fee: $50. *Expenses:* Tuition $440 per credit hour. Fees $55 per quarter full-time, $13.25 per quarter part-time. *Financial aid:* In 1997–98, 5 tuition assistantships (3 to first-year students) were awarded; full and partial tuition waivers, Federal Work-Study, and career-related internships or fieldwork also available. Aid available to part-time students. Financial aid application deadline: 3/1. *Faculty research:*

Directory: Education—General

Northeastern University (continued)

Self-concept, faculty development and evaluation systems, early childhood and computers. • Dr. James W. Fraser, Acting Chair, 617-373-3302. Application contact: Dr. Mervin Lynch, Director of Graduate Admissions, 617-373-3302. Fax: 617-373-5261.

See in-depth description on page 759.

Northeast Louisiana University, College of Education, Monroe, LA 71209-0001. Awards MA, M Ed, MS, Ed D, PhD, Ed S, SSP. Accredited by NCATE. Part-time and evening/weekend programs available. *Degree requirements:* For doctorate, dissertation. *Entrance requirements:* For master's, GRE General Test. Application fee: $15 ($25 for international students). *Tuition:* $2028 per year full-time, $240 per semester (minimum) part-time for state residents; $6852 per year full-time, $240 per semester (minimum) part-time for nonresidents.

Northern Arizona University, Center for Excellence in Education, Flagstaff, AZ 86011. Awards MA, M Ed, MVE, Ed D. Part-time and evening/weekend programs available. Faculty: 82 full-time (39 women), 230 part-time (125 women). Students: 528 full-time (365 women), 2,580 part-time (1,931 women); includes 580 minority (76 African Americans, 20 Asian Americans, 400 Hispanics, 84 Native Americans), 18 international. 1,333 applicants, 71% accepted. In 1997, 1,183 master's, 51 doctorates awarded. Terminal master's awarded for partial completion of doctoral program. *Degree requirements:* For doctorate, computer language, dissertation required, foreign language not required. *Entrance requirements:* For doctorate, GRE General Test, GRE Subject Test. Application fee: $45. *Expenses:* Tuition $2088 per year full-time, $330 per semester (minimum) part-time for state residents; $8004 per year full-time, $1002 per semester (minimum) part-time for nonresidents. Fees $72 per year full-time, $18 per semester (minimum) part-time. *Financial aid:* In 1997–98, 48 assistantships were awarded; fellowships, research assistantships, teaching assistantships, full and partial tuition waivers, Federal Work-Study, and career-related internships or fieldwork also available. • Dr. Melvin E. Hall, Executive Director, 520-523-7113.

Northern Illinois University, College of Education, De Kalb, IL 60115-2854. Awards MS Ed, Ed D, Ed S. Accredited by NCATE. Part-time and evening/weekend programs available. Postbaccalaureate distance learning degree programs offered. Faculty: 120 full-time (57 women), 7 part-time (3 women). Students: 269 full-time (190 women), 1,388 part-time (970 women); includes 194 minority (134 African Americans, 15 Asian Americans, 41 Hispanics, 4 Native Americans), 43 international. Average age 37. 622 applicants, 63% accepted. In 1997, 429 master's, 58 doctorates, 8 Ed Ss awarded. Terminal master's awarded for partial completion of doctoral program. *Degree requirements:* For master's and Ed S, comprehensive exam required, thesis optional, foreign language not required; for doctorate, candidacy exam, dissertation defense required, foreign language not required. *Entrance requirements:* For master's, TOEFL (minimum score 550), minimum GPA of 2.75; for doctorate, TOEFL (minimum score 550), minimum GPA of 2.75 (undergraduate), 3.2 (graduate); for Ed S, GRE General Test, TOEFL (minimum score 550), minimum graduate GPA of 3.2, master's degree. Application deadline: (11/1 for spring admission). Application fee: $30. *Tuition:* $3984 per year full-time, $154 per credit hour part-time for state residents; $8160 per year full-time, $328 per credit hour part-time for nonresidents. *Financial aid:* In 1997–98, 46 research assistantships, 70 teaching assistantships, 22 staff assistantships were awarded; fellowships, full tuition waivers, Federal Work-Study, and career-related internships or fieldwork also available. Aid available to part-time students. • Dr. Alfonzo Thurman, Dean, 815-753-9056.

Northern Kentucky University, Department of Education, Highland Heights, KY 41099. Offers programs in elementary education (MA Ed), secondary education (MA Ed). Accredited by NCATE. Part-time and evening/weekend programs available. Faculty: 16 full-time (11 women). Students: 6 full-time (3 women), 333 part-time (288 women); includes 4 minority (3 African Americans, 1 Asian American). Average age 33. 264 applicants, 66% accepted. In 1997, 150 degrees awarded. *Entrance requirements:* GRE, teaching certificate. Application deadline: 8/15 (priority date; rolling processing). Application fee: $25. *Tuition:* $2420 per year full-time, $132 per semester hour part-time for state residents; $6660 per year full-time, $368 per semester hour part-time for nonresidents. *Financial aid:* Research assistantships, Federal Work-Study available. • Dr. Darrell Garber, Chairperson, 606-572-5365. Application contact: Peg Griffin, Coordinator, Graduate Program, 606-572-6364.

Northern Michigan University, College of Behavioral Sciences and Human Services, Department of Education, Marquette, MI 49855-5301. Offers programs in administration and supervision (MA Ed), elementary education (MA Ed), secondary education (MA Ed), special education (MA Ed). Accredited by NCATE. Part-time programs available. Faculty: 11 full-time (5 women), 3 part-time (2 women). Students: 38 full-time (35 women), 144 part-time (98 women); includes 1 minority (Native American). 12 applicants, 100% accepted. In 1997, 43 degrees awarded. *Degree requirements:* Thesis or alternative required, foreign language not required. *Entrance requirements:* GRE General Test (minimum combined score of 900), minimum GPA of 2.75. Application deadline: 7/1 (priority date; rolling processing; 11/1 for spring admission). Application fee: $25. *Expenses:* Tuition $135 per credit hour for state residents; $215 per credit hour for nonresidents. Fees $183 per year full-time, $94 per year (minimum) part-time. *Financial aid:* In 1997–98, 2 graduate assistantships averaging $770 per month were awarded; full tuition waivers, Federal Work-Study, institutionally sponsored loans, and career-related internships or fieldwork also available. Aid available to part-time students. Financial aid application deadline: 3/1. • Dr. James D. Hendricks, Head, 906-227-2728.

Northern State University, Division of Graduate Studies in Education, Aberdeen, SD 57401-7198. Awards MS Ed. Accredited by NCATE. Part-time and evening/weekend programs available. Faculty: 98 full-time (28 women). Students: 59 full-time (37 women), 33 part-time (21 women); includes 5 minority (3 Asian Americans, 2 Native Americans). Average age 32. In 1997, 43 degrees awarded. *Average time to degree:* master's–1.5 years full-time. *Entrance requirements:* Minimum GPA of 2.75. Application deadline: 8/15 (priority date; rolling processing; 12/15 for spring admission). Application fee: $15. *Expenses:* Tuition $1999 per year full-time, $83 per credit hour part-time for state residents; $6034 per year full-time, $251 per credit hour part-time for nonresidents. Fees $954 per year full-time, $40 per credit hour part-time. *Financial aid:* Teaching assistantships, Federal Work-Study, institutionally sponsored loans, and career-related internships or fieldwork available. Aid available to part-time students. Financial aid application deadline: 3/1. • Dr. Sharon Tebben, Director of Graduate Studies, 605-626-2558. Fax: 605-626-2542.

North Georgia College & State University, Graduate School, Program in Education, Dahlonega, GA 30597-1001. Offers early childhood education (M Ed); middle grades education (M Ed); secondary education (M Ed), including art education, biology education, chemistry education, English education, mathematics education, modern languages education, physical education, science education, social science education; special education (M Ed), including behavior disorders, interrelated special education, learning disabilities, mental retardation. Accredited by NCATE. Part-time and evening/weekend programs available. Faculty: 57 full-time (15 women), 7 part-time (4 women). Students: 94 full-time (73 women), 198 part-time (162 women); includes 8 minority (2 African Americans, 2 Asian Americans, 4 Hispanics). Average age 33. 136 applicants, 76% accepted. In 1997, 138 degrees awarded. *Degree requirements:* Comprehensive exam required, thesis optional, foreign language not required. *Entrance requirements:* GRE General Test (minimum combined score of 800) or MAT (minimum score 44), minimum GPA of 2.75. Application deadline: 9/1 (priority date; rolling processing). Application fee: $25. *Financial aid:* In 1997–98, 1 scholarship was awarded; teaching assistantships and career-related internships or fieldwork also available. Aid available to part-time students. Financial aid application deadline: 5/1. *Faculty research:* Computers and teachers' attitudes, rural versus urban teacher attitudes, teacher leadership roles, minority recruitment in teaching force. • Dr. Bob Michael, Dean, School of Education, 706-864-1533. Application contact: Mai-Lan Ledbetter, Coordinator of Graduate Admissions, 706-864-1543. Fax: 706-864-1668. E-mail: mledbetter@nugget.ngc.peachnet.edu.

North Park University, Department of Education, Chicago, IL 60625-4895. Awards MA. Faculty: 4 full-time (all women), 8 part-time (4 women). Students: 20 part-time (18 women); includes 1 international. Average age 37. 36 applicants, 61% accepted. *Degree requirements:* Thesis required, foreign language not required. *Entrance requirements:* GRE General Test. Application deadline: 8/1 (priority date; rolling processing). Application fee: $25. *Financial aid:* Grants available. Aid available to part-time students. Financial aid application deadline: 8/15. *Faculty research:* Teacher leadership, research design, teacher education. • Dr. Jill Wettersten, Director of Graduate Studies, 773-244-6200. Application contact: Gloria Gonzalez, Counselor, 773-244-5523. Fax: 773-244-4953.

Northwestern Oklahoma State University, School of Education, Psychology, and Health and Physical Education, Alva, OK 73717. Offers programs in behavioral sciences (MBS), education: non-certificate option (M Ed), elementary education (M Ed), guidance and counseling K–12 (M Ed), library media specialist (M Ed), psychometry (M Ed), reading specialist (M Ed), secondary education (M Ed). One or more programs accredited by NCATE. Part-time programs available. Faculty: 51 full-time (19 women), 1 part-time (0 women). Students: 35 full-time (20 women), 149 part-time (113 women); includes 15 minority (9 African Americans, 4 Hispanics, 2 Native Americans). Average age 31. 83 applicants, 84% accepted. In 1997, 40 degrees awarded. *Entrance requirements:* GRE General Test (minimum combined score of 900) or MAT (minimum score 38), minimum GPA of 2.75. Application deadline: rolling. Application fee: $15. *Tuition:* $73 per semester hour for state residents; $175 per semester hour for nonresidents. *Financial aid:* Fellowships, Federal Work-Study available. Aid available to part-time students. Financial aid application deadline: 5/1. • Dr. James Bowen, Dean, 405-327-8455. Application contact: Dr. Ed Huckeby, Dean of Graduate School, 405-327-8410.

Northwestern State University of Louisiana, Division of Education, Natchitoches, LA 71497. Offers programs in business and distributive education (M Ed); early childhood education (M Ed); educational administration/supervision (M Ed, Ed S); elementary teaching (M Ed, Ed S); home economics education (M Ed); human services (MA, M Ed, Ed S), including counseling and guidance (M Ed, Ed S), special education (M Ed, Ed S), student personnel services (MA); mathematics education (M Ed); reading (M Ed, Ed S); science education (M Ed); secondary teaching (M Ed, Ed S). Accredited by NCATE. Faculty: 10 full-time (7 women), 4 part-time (2 women). Students: 45 full-time (35 women), 171 part-time (149 women). Average age 36. In 1997, 41 master's awarded. *Entrance requirements:* For master's, GRE General Test (minimum combined score of 800), GRE Subject Test, minimum undergraduate GPA of 2.5. Application deadline: 8/1 (priority date; rolling processing; 1/10 for spring admission). Application fee: $15 ($25 for international students). *Tuition:* $2147 per year full-time, $336 per semester (minimum) part-time for state residents; $6437 per year full-time, $336 per semester (minimum) part-time for nonresidents. *Financial aid:* Federal Work-Study and career-related internships or fieldwork available. Financial aid application deadline: 7/15. • Dr. Sue Weaver, Chair, 318-357-5195. Application contact: Dr. Tom Hanson, Dean, Graduate Studies and Research, 318-357-5851. Fax: 318-357-5019.

Northwestern University, School of Education and Social Policy, Evanston, IL 60208. Offers programs in advanced teaching (MS); corporate training and development (MS); education (MS), including education and social policy; education and social policy-counseling psychology (MA); education and social policy-learning sciences (MA, PhD); elementary teaching (MS); higher education administration (MS); human development and social policy (PhD); marital and family therapy (MS); school administration (MS); secondary teaching (MS). MA and PhD admissions and degrees offered through The Graduate School. Part-time and evening/weekend programs available. Faculty: 19 full-time (5 women), 6 part-time (1 woman). Students: 191 full-time (143 women), 43 part-time (30 women); includes 40 minority (20 African Americans, 16 Asian Americans, 3 Hispanics, 1 Native American), 5 international. In 1997, 118 master's, 13 doctorates awarded. Terminal master's awarded for partial completion of doctoral program. *Degree requirements:* For doctorate, dissertation required, foreign language not required. *Entrance requirements:* GRE General Test. *Tuition:* $2424 per course. *Financial aid:* In 1997–98, fellowships averaging $1,297 per month, research assistantships averaging $1,528 per month, teaching assistantships averaging $1,338 per month were awarded; tuition scholarships, partial tuition waivers, Federal Work-Study, institutionally sponsored loans, and career-related internships or fieldwork also available. Financial aid application deadline: 1/15; applicants required to submit FAFSA. • Jean Egmon, Assistant Dean, 847-491-3790. Fax: 847-461-2495. E-mail: egmon@nwu.edu. Application contact: Andrew Ager, Office of Student Affairs, 847-491-3790. Fax: 847-467-2495. E-mail: andrew-ager@nwu.edu.

See in-depth description on page 761.

Northwestern University, School of Education and Social Policy, Program in Education and Social Policy-Learning Sciences, Evanston, IL 60201. Awards MA, PhD. Admissions and degrees offered through The Graduate School. Faculty: 10 full-time (3 women), 3 part-time (0 women). Students: 40 full-time (22 women); includes 12 minority (4 African Americans, 6 Asian Americans, 1 Hispanic, 1 Native American), 2 international. 86 applicants, 28% accepted. In 1997, 23 master's awarded (100% found work related to degree); 3 doctorates awarded. Terminal master's awarded for partial completion of doctoral program. *Degree requirements:* For master's, thesis or alternative, portfolio required, foreign language not required; for doctorate, dissertation, qualifying exam required, foreign language not required. *Average time to degree:* master's–1 year full-time; doctorate–5 years full-time. *Entrance requirements:* For master's, GRE General Test (combined average 1179); for doctorate, GRE General Test (combined average 1223). Application deadline: 2/1 (priority date; rolling processing). Application fee: $50 ($55 for international students). *Tuition:* $2424 per course. *Financial aid:* In 1997–98, 24 students received aid, including 6 fellowships (all to first-year students) averaging $1,169 per month, 17 research assistantships (1 to a first-year student) averaging $1,528 per month, 1 teaching assistantship averaging $1,248 per month; tuition scholarships, Federal Work-Study, institutionally sponsored loans, and career-related internships or fieldwork also available. Financial aid application deadline: 1/15; applicants required to submit FAFSA. *Faculty research:* Technologically supported learning environments; inquiry based learning in math, science, and literacy; learning social contexts; cognitive models of learning and problem solving; changing roles for teachers involved in innovative design and practice. • Dr. Brian J. Reiser, Program Coordinator, 847-491-7494. E-mail: 1s-programs@ils.nwu.edu. Application contact: Carolyn Frazier, Department Assistant, 847-491-7494. Fax: 847-491-8999. E-mail: ls-programs@mail.sesp.nwu.edu.

See in-depth description on page 763.

Northwest Missouri State University, College of Education and Human Services, 800 University Drive, Maryville, MO 64468-6001. Awards MS, MS Ed, Ed S. Accredited by NCATE. Part-time programs available. Faculty: 53 full-time (25 women). Students: 68 full-time (35 women), 271 part-time (225 women); includes 8 minority (5 African Americans, 3 Hispanics), 6 international. 96 applicants, 84% accepted. In 1997, 111 master's, 15 Ed Ss awarded. *Degree requirements:* For master's, comprehensive exam required, foreign language not required; for Ed S, thesis, comprehensive exam required, foreign language not required. *Entrance requirements:* For master's, GRE General Test, TOEFL (minimum score 550), writing sample; for Ed S, minimum graduate GPA of 3.25. Application fee: $0 ($50 for international students). *Expenses:* Tuition $113 per credit hour for state residents; $197 per credit hour for nonresidents. Fees $3 per credit hour. *Financial aid:* In 1997–98, 9 research assistantships (3 to first-year students) averaging $585 per month, 31 teaching assistantships (7 to first-year students) averaging $585 per month, 12 administrative assistantships (3 to first-year students) averaging $585 per month were awarded. Financial aid application deadline: 3/1. *Faculty research:* Great books of educational administration. Total annual research expenditures: $2032. • Dr. Max Ruhl, Dean, 816-562-1231. Application contact: Dr. Frances Shipley, Dean of Graduate School, 816-562-1145. E-mail: gradsch@acad.nwmissouri.edu.

Northwest Nazarene College, Department of Graduate Studies, Graduate Program in Teacher Education, Nampa, ID 83686-5897. Offers curriculum and instruction (M Ed), educational leadership (M Ed), school counseling (M Ed). Accredited by NCATE. Part-time programs available. Postbaccalaureate distance learning degree programs offered. Faculty: 3 full-time (2 women), 13 part-time (3 women). Students: 8 full-time (4 women), 76 part-time (63 women). Average age 34. In 1997, 23 degrees awarded (100% found work related to degree). *Degree requirements:* Action research project required, foreign language and thesis not required. *Application deadline:* 9/1 (rolling processing). *Application fee:* $25. *Faculty research:* Action research, cooperative learning, accountability, institutional accreditation. • Dr. Dennis Cartwright, Chair, 208-467-8258. E-mail: ddcartwright@wiley.nnc.edu.

Notre Dame College, Education Division, Manchester, NH 03104-2299. Offers programs in advanced reading (M Ed), curriculum and instruction (M Ed), elementary teaching (M Ed), emotional and behavioral disorders (M Ed), interdisciplinary studies (M Ed), learning and language disabilities (M Ed), school administration and supervision (M Ed), school counseling (M Ed), secondary teaching (M Ed), teaching English as a second language (M Ed). Part-time programs available. Faculty: 10 full-time (8 women), 52 part-time (36 women). Average age 36. 143 applicants, 76% accepted. In 1997, 89 degrees awarded. *Entrance requirements:* GRE General Test or MAT. Application deadline: rolling. Application fee: $35. *Tuition:* $299 per credit. *Financial aid:* Fellowships, assistantships available. • Sandra S. Metes, Dean, 603-669-4298 Ext. 257.

Notre Dame College of Ohio, Graduate Studies, South Euclid, OH 44121-4293. Awards M Ed. Part-time programs available. Faculty: 5 full-time (4 women), 1 (woman) part-time. Students: 30 part-time (all women); includes 4 minority (3 African Americans, 1 Native American). Average age 35. In 1997, 6 degrees awarded. *Degree requirements:* Thesis. *Entrance requirements:* GRE General Test, MAT, minimum GPA of 2.75, valid teaching certificate. Application deadline: 8/1 (priority date; rolling processing; 1/1 for spring admission). Application fee: $40. *Tuition:* $400 per credit hour. *Financial aid:* 1 student received aid. Aid available to part-time students. Financial aid application deadline: 4/15; applicants required to submit FAFSA. *Faculty research:* Cognitive psychology, teaching critical thinking in the classroom. • Sr. Helene Marie Gregos, SND, Dean, 216-381-1680 Ext. 337. Fax: 216-381-3802.

Nova Southeastern University, Fischler Center for the Advancement of Education, Fort Lauderdale, FL 33314-7721. Awards MS, Au D, Ed D, SLPD, Ed S. Part-time and evening/weekend programs available. Postbaccalaureate distance learning degree programs offered. Faculty: 64 full-time (40 women). Students: 1,144 full-time (878 women), 4,052 part-time (2,871 women); includes 1,592 minority (969 African Americans, 40 Asian Americans, 568 Hispanics, 15 Native Americans), 98 international. Average age 41. In 1997, 883 master's, 375 doctorates, 46 Ed Ss awarded. *Degree requirements:* For master's, practicum required, foreign language not required; for doctorate and Ed S, thesis/dissertation, practicum required, foreign language not required. *Entrance requirements:* For Ed S, master's degree, teaching certificate. Application deadline: rolling. Application fee: $50. *Tuition:* $245 per credit hour (minimum). *Financial aid:* Fellowships, Federal Work-Study, and career-related internships or fieldwork available. Aid available to part-time students. • Dr. H. Wells Singleton, Provost/Dean, 954-262-8730. E-mail: singlew@fcae.nova.edu. Application contact: Carole Benedict, Coordinator of Marketing, 800-986-3223 Ext. 8650. Fax: 954-262-3912. E-mail: benedict@fcae.nova.edu.

Oakland University, School of Education and Human Services, Rochester, MI 48309-4401. Awards MA, MAT, M Ed, MTD, PhD, Certificate, Ed S. Accredited by NCATE. Part-time and evening/weekend programs available. Faculty: 69 full-time. Students: 232 full-time (202 women), 1,021 part-time (912 women); includes 71 minority (44 African Americans, 11 Asian Americans, 11 Hispanics, 5 Native Americans), 22 international. 608 applicants, 89% accepted. In 1997, 314 master's, 9 doctorates, 30 other advanced degrees awarded. *Degree requirements:* For doctorate, dissertation. *Entrance requirements:* For master's, minimum GPA of 3.0 for unconditional admission. Application fee: $30. *Expenses:* Tuition $3852 per year full-time, $214 per credit hour part-time for state residents; $8532 per year full-time, $474 per credit hour part-time for nonresidents. Fees $420 per year. *Financial aid:* Full tuition waivers, Federal Work-Study, institutionally sponsored loans, and career-related internships or fieldwork available. Financial aid application deadline: 3/1; applicants required to submit FAFSA. • Dr. Mary L. Otto, Dean, 248-370-3050.

Occidental College, Department of Education, Los Angeles, CA 90041-3392. Offers programs in elementary education (MAT), including liberal studies; secondary education (MAT), including English and comparative literary studies, French, history, life science, mathematics, music, physical science, Spanish. Part-time programs available. Faculty: 4 full-time (1 woman). Students: 31 full-time (25 women); includes 18 minority (1 African American, 5 Asian Americans, 12 Hispanics). Average age 24. 39 applicants, 92% accepted. *Degree requirements:* Internship required, foreign language and thesis not required. *Entrance requirements:* GRE General Test (minimum score 550 on each section or combined score of 1650 on three sections), TOEFL (minimum score 600), minimum GPA of 3.0. Application deadline: 3/1 (priority date; rolling processing; 10/1 for spring admission). Application fee: $40. *Expenses:* Tuition $21,256 per year full-time, $865 per unit part-time. Fees $314 per year. *Financial aid:* Fellowships, Federal Work-Study, institutionally sponsored loans, and career-related internships or fieldwork available. Aid available to part-time students. Financial aid application deadline: 3/1. *Faculty research:* Preparing teacher-leaders, curriculum development. • Chair, 213-259-2781. Application contact: Susan Molik, Administrative Assistant, Graduate Office, 213-259-2921.

Announcement: The Occidental College Educational Leaders Program is a small, personalized, and rigorous graduate course of study with 2 options: (1) 5th-year, clear credential program to complete requirements for either a single-subject (K–12) or multiple-subjects (K–12) teaching credential in 1 year; and (2) Master of Arts in Teaching degree program to complete requirements for the professional clear credential, plus 3 graduate courses in the field of study. The MAT is available in liberal studies, math, life sciences, physical sciences, music, English and comparative literature, French, German, history, and Spanish. Collegial support, early field experiences, and frequent supervision by college faculty members are key features. Students may begin or conclude their program in summer sessions.

Oglethorpe University, Division of Education, Atlanta, GA 30319-2797. Offers programs in early childhood education (MA), middle grades education (MA). Part-time programs available. Faculty: 4 full-time (3 women), 3 part-time (all women), 5 FTE. Students: 5 full-time (4 women), 70 part-time (61 women). Average age 30. 28 applicants, 86% accepted. In 1997, 23 degrees awarded (100% found work related to degree). *Degree requirements:* Comprehensive exam required, foreign language and thesis not required. *Entrance requirements:* GRE General Test (minimum combined score of 800), MAT (minimum score 44), PRAXIS, minimum GPA of 2.5. Application deadline: rolling. Application fee: $30. *Tuition:* $500 per course. • Dr. Vienna K. Volante, Chair, 404-261-1441 Ext. 385. Application contact: Bill Price, Graduate Admissions Counselor, 404-364-8307. Fax: 404-364-8500.

The Ohio State University, College of Education, Columbus, OH 43210. Awards MA, M Ed, PhD, Certificate. Accredited by NCATE. Part-time programs available. Faculty: 166. Students: 920 full-time (621 women), 1,657 part-time (1,319 women); includes 325 minority (260 African Americans, 29 Asian Americans, 24 Hispanics, 12 Native Americans), 191 international. 1,513 applicants, 55% accepted. In 1997, 696 master's, 87 doctorates awarded. *Degree requirements:* For master's, thesis optional, foreign language not required; for doctorate, dissertation required, foreign language not required. *Application deadline:* 8/15 (rolling processing). *Application fee:* $30 ($40 for international students). *Tuition:* $5472 per year full-time, $554 per quarter (minimum) part-time for state residents; $14,172 per year full-time, $1424 per quarter (minimum) part-time for nonresidents. *Financial aid:* Fellowships, research assistantships, teaching assistantships, administrative assistantships, Federal Work-Study, institutionally sponsored loans available. Aid available to part-time students. • Dr. Nancy Zimpher, Dean, 614-292-2581. Fax: 614-292-4547.

See in-depth description on page 765.

Ohio University, Graduate Studies, College of Education, Athens, OH 45701-2979. Awards MA, M Ed, PhD, Ed S. Accredited by NCATE. Part-time and evening/weekend programs available. Faculty: 33 full-time (10 women), 18 part-time (11 women). Students: 286 full-time (156 women), 241 part-time (159 women); includes 24 minority (16 African Americans, 2 Asian Americans, 4 Hispanics, 2 Native Americans), 113 international. 430 applicants, 63% accepted. In 1997, 165 master's, 34 doctorates awarded. Terminal master's awarded for partial completion of doctoral program. *Degree requirements:* For master's, thesis or alternative required, foreign language not required; for doctorate, dissertation. *Entrance requirements:* For master's, GRE General Test or MAT; for doctorate, GRE General Test, MAT, minimum GPA of 3.0, work experience. Application deadline: rolling. Application fee: $30. *Tuition:* $5430 per year full-time, $216 per quarter hour part-time for state residents; $10,431 per year full-time, $423 per quarter hour part-time for nonresidents. *Financial aid:* In 1997–98, 5 fellowships, 31 research assistantships, 6 teaching assistantships were awarded; assistantships, full tuition waivers, Federal Work-Study, institutionally sponsored loans also available. Financial aid application deadline: 3/15. • Dr. Karen Viechnicki, Interim Dean, 740-593-4449.

Oklahoma City University, Petree College of Arts and Sciences, Division of Education, Oklahoma City, OK 73106-1402. Offers programs in counseling (MACP), early childhood education (M Ed), elementary education (M Ed), gifted and talented education (M Ed), secondary education (M Ed), teaching English as a second language (M Ed). Part-time and evening/weekend programs available. Faculty: 6 full-time (all women), 9 part-time (8 women). Students: 93 full-time (73 women), 46 part-time (35 women); includes 13 minority (4 African Americans, 7 Asian Americans, 2 Native Americans), 57 international. In 1997, 53 degrees awarded. *Degree requirements:* Thesis or alternative required, foreign language not required. *Average time to degree:* master's–1.5 years full-time, 3.3 years part-time. *Entrance requirements:* Minimum GPA of 3.0. Application deadline: 8/25 (priority date; rolling processing; 1/15 for spring admission). Application fee: $35 ($55 for international students). *Expenses:* Tuition $318 per hour. Fees $124 per year. *Financial aid:* Fellowships, full and partial tuition waivers, Federal Work-Study, institutionally sponsored loans, and career-related internships or fieldwork available. Aid available to part-time students. Financial aid application deadline: 8/1; applicants required to submit FAFSA. • Dr. Sherry Sexton, Coordinator, 405-521-5371. E-mail: ssexton@lec.okcu.edu. Application contact: Laura L. Rahhal, Director of Graduate Admissions, 800-633-7242 Ext. 2. Fax: 405-521-5356. E-mail: lrahhal1@froda.okcu.edu.

Oklahoma State University, College of Education, Stillwater, OK 74078. Awards MS, Ed D, PhD, Ed S. Faculty: 76 full-time (32 women). Students: 229 full-time (140 women), 959 part-time (623 women); includes 140 minority (71 African Americans, 12 Asian Americans, 11 Hispanics, 46 Native Americans), 21 international. Average age 38. In 1997, 138 master's, 65 doctorates awarded. *Degree requirements:* For doctorate, dissertation. *Entrance requirements:* For master's and doctorate, TOEFL (minimum score 550). Application deadline: 7/1 (priority date). Application fee: $25. *Financial aid:* In 1997–98, 74 students received aid, including 12 research assistantships (5 to first-year students) totaling $97,350, 53 teaching assistantships (13 to first-year students) totaling $462,057; partial tuition waivers, Federal Work-Study, and career-related internships or fieldwork also available. Aid available to part-time students. Financial aid application deadline: 3/1. • Dr. Ann C. Candler-Lotven, Dean, 405-744-6350.

Old Dominion University, Darden College of Education, Norfolk, VA 23529. Awards MS, MS Ed, PhD, CAS. Accredited by NCATE. Part-time and evening/weekend programs available. Postbaccalaureate distance learning degree programs offered. Faculty: 70 full-time (32 women), 100 part-time (55 women), 103.3 FTE. Students: 607 full-time (427 women), 1,194 part-time (859 women); includes 323 minority (260 African Americans, 24 Asian Americans, 24 Hispanics, 15 Native Americans), 16 international. Average age 35. In 1997, 639 master's, 6 doctorates, 16 CASs awarded. *Degree requirements:* For master's, exam required, foreign language not required; for doctorate, dissertation, comprehensive exams required, foreign language not required; for CAS, comprehensive exam required, foreign language not required. *Entrance requirements:* For doctorate, GRE General Test (minimum combined score of 1350 on three sections), master's degree, minimum GPA of 3.5; for CAS, GRE General Test or MAT. Application fee: $30. Electronic applications accepted. *Expenses:* Tuition $180 per credit hour for state residents; $477 per credit hour for nonresidents. Fees $140 per year full-time, $32 per semester part-time. *Financial aid:* In 1997–98, 611 students received aid, including 18 fellowships (2 to first-year students) totaling $42,214, 78 research assistantships (25 to first-year students) totaling $504,996, 78 teaching assistantships (1 to a first-year student) totaling $34,112, 233 tuition grants (14 to first-year students) totaling $227,436; partial tuition waivers, Federal Work-Study, institutionally sponsored loans, and career-related internships or fieldwork also available. Aid available to part-time students. Financial aid application deadline: 2/15; applicants required to submit CSS PROFILE or FAFSA. *Faculty research:* Effective urban teaching practices, urban school finance, school violence and vandalism, curriculum theory, clinical practices. Total annual research expenditures: $814,256. • Dr. Donna Evans, Dean, 757-683-3938. Fax: 757-683-5406. E-mail: devans@odu.edu.

Olivet Nazarene University, Division of Education, Kankakee, IL 60901-0592. Offers programs in curriculum and instruction (MAE), elementary education (MAT), secondary education (MAT). Evening/weekend programs available. *Degree requirements:* Thesis or alternative required, foreign language not required. *Application deadline:* rolling. *Application fee:* $20.

Oral Roberts University, School of Education, Tulsa, OK 74171-0001. Offers programs in Christian school administration (MA Ed), Christian school teaching (MA Ed), curriculum and instruction (MA Ed), early childhood education (MA Ed), public school administration (MA Ed), public school teaching (MA Ed), teaching English as a second language (MA Ed). Part-time and evening/weekend programs available. Postbaccalaureate distance learning degree programs offered (minimal on-campus study). Faculty: 7 full-time (2 women), 13 part-time (3 women). Students: 76 full-time (61 women), 115 part-time (83 women); includes 38 minority (34 African Americans, 4 Hispanics), 15 international. Average age 32. In 1997, 53 degrees awarded. *Degree requirements:* Thesis (for some programs), comprehensive exam. *Average time to degree:* master's–1.5 years full-time, 3 years part-time. *Entrance requirements:* GRE General Test (minimum combined score of 1000) or MAT, minimum GPA of 3.0. Application deadline: rolling. Application fee: $35. *Financial aid:* Research assistantships, assistantships, and career-related internships or fieldwork available. Aid available to part-time students. Financial aid application deadline: 4/1; applicants required to submit FAFSA. • Dr. David Hand, Dean, 918-495-7084. Fax: 918-495-6050. Application contact: David H. Fulmer III, Coordinator of Graduate Admissions, 918-495-6058. Fax: 918-495-7214. E-mail: dhfulmer@oru.edu.

Oregon State University, Graduate School, College of Home Economics and Education, School of Education, Corvallis, OR 97331. Awards Ed M, MAIS, MAT, MS, Ed D, PhD. Accredited by NCATE. Part-time programs available. Faculty: 22 full-time (9 women), 12 part-time (4 women). Students: 328; includes 14 minority (2 African Americans, 5 Asian Americans, 4 Hispanics, 3 Native Americans), 25 international. Average age 36. 220 applicants, 71% accepted. In 1997, 151 master's, 28 doctorates awarded. Terminal master's awarded for partial completion of doctoral program. *Degree requirements:* For master's, thesis (for some programs), minimum GPA of 3.0; for doctorate, dissertation, minimum GPA of 3.0. *Entrance requirements:* For master's, TOEFL (minimum score 550), minimum GPA of 3.0 in last 90 hours; for doctorate, TOEFL, master's degree, minimum GPA of 3.0 in last 90 hours. Application fee: $50. *Tuition:* $6207 per year full-time, $810 per quarter (minimum) part-time for state residents; $10,551 per year full-time, $1293 per quarter (minimum) part-time for nonresidents. *Financial aid:* In 1997–98, 5 research assistantships (all to first-year students), 5 teaching assistantships (all to first-year students) were awarded; fellowships, Federal Work-Study, institutionally sponsored loans, and career-related internships or fieldwork also available. Aid available to part-time students. Financial aid application deadline: 2/1. *Faculty research:* Adult literacy, classroom behavior, school reform, authentic assessment, AIDS/HIV education. • Dr. Wayne W. Haverson, Director, 541-737-5959.

Ottawa University, Graduate Studies, Major in Education, Phoenix, AZ 85021. Awards MA. Average age 43. *Degree requirements:* Thesis, field experience, practicum required, foreign language not required. *Application deadline:* 7/1 (priority date; rolling processing; 11/1 for spring admission). *Application fee:* $40. *Tuition:* $275 per hour. • Dr. John Mansour, Director,

Directory: Education—General

Ottawa University (continued)

602-371-0993. Application contact: Glenda O'Yates, Graduate Admissions Officer, 602-371-0993. Fax: 602-371-0035.

Otterbein College, Department of Education, Westerville, OH 43081. Awards MAE, MAT. Accredited by NCATE. Part-time and evening/weekend programs available. Faculty: 12 full-time, 8 part-time. Students: 84. In 1997, 15 degrees awarded. *Degree requirements:* Thesis required, foreign language not required. *Average time to degree:* master's–3.5 years part-time. *Entrance requirements:* GRE General Test. Application deadline: rolling. Application fee: $50. *Tuition:* $5216 per quarter. *Financial aid:* Available to part-time students. Financial aid applicants required to submit FAFSA. *Faculty research:* Whole language, alternative teacher certification routes, clinical experiences, portfolio assessment. • Dr. Harriet R. Fayne, Chair, 614-823-1214. Fax: 614-823-3036. Application contact: Dr. Ann Rottersman, Coordinator of Graduate Studies, 614-823-3209. Fax: 614-823-1335.

Our Lady of Holy Cross College, Program in Education, New Orleans, LA 70131-7399. Offers administration and supervision (M Ed); counseling (M Ed), including marriage and family counseling, school counseling; curriculum and instruction (M Ed), including reading. Part-time and evening/weekend programs available. Faculty: 5 full-time (2 women), 7 part-time (3 women). Students: 16 full-time (3 women), 75 part-time (34 women); includes 18 minority (15 African Americans, 3 Asian Americans). Average age 30. In 1997, 35 degrees awarded. *Degree requirements:* Thesis required, foreign language not required. *Entrance requirements:* GRE General Test (minimum combined score of 800), minimum GPA of 2.7. Application deadline: 9/1. Application fee: $20. *Expenses:* Tuition $5760 per year full-time, $240 per semester hour part-time. Fees $167 per year. *Financial aid:* Partial tuition waivers, Federal Work-Study available. Aid available to part-time students. Financial aid application deadline: 6/1. • Dr. Judith G. Miranti, Dean, 504-394-7744.

Our Lady of the Lake University of San Antonio, School of Education and Clinical Studies, 411 Southwest 24th Street, San Antonio, TX 78207-4689. Offers programs in administration/supervision (M Ed); communication and learning disorders (MA); counseling psychology (MS, Psy D), including counseling psychology, psychology; curriculum and instruction (M Ed); human sciences and sociology (MA), including human sciences, sociology; learning resources (M Ed); school counseling (MS); school supervision (M Ed); special education (MA). Part-time and evening/weekend programs available. Postbaccalaureate distance learning degree programs offered (minimal on-campus study). Faculty: 28 full-time (21 women), 27 part-time (12 women). Students: 89 full-time (72 women), 271 part-time (218 women); includes 164 minority (32 African Americans, 3 Asian Americans, 128 Hispanics, 1 Native American), 1 international. Average age 36. In 1997, 83 master's, 2 doctorates awarded. *Degree requirements:* For master's, comprehensive exam required, foreign language not required; for doctorate, computer language, dissertation, internship, qualifying exam required, foreign language not required. *Entrance requirements:* For master's, GRE General Test or MAT; for doctorate, GRE General Test or MAT, interview. Application fee: $15. *Expenses:* Tuition $371 per credit hour. Fees $57 per semester full-time, $32 per semester part-time. *Financial aid:* Research assistantships, teaching assistantships, grants, partial tuition waivers, Federal Work-Study, institutionally sponsored loans, and career-related internships or fieldwork available. Aid available to part-time students. • Dr. Jacquelyn Alexander, Dean, 210-434-6711 Ext. 291. Fax: 210-431-3927. E-mail: alexj@lake.ollusa.edu. Application contact: Debbie Hamilton, Director of Admissions, 210-434-6711 Ext. 314. Fax: 210-436-2314.

Pace University, School of Education, New York, NY 10038. Offers programs in administration and supervision (MS Ed), curriculum and instruction (MS), education (MST), school business management (Certificate). Part-time and evening/weekend programs available. *Degree requirements:* For master's, internship required, foreign language and thesis not required. *Entrance requirements:* For master's, interview, teaching certificate. Application deadline: 7/31 (priority date; rolling processing; 11/30 for spring admission). Application fee: $60. *Expenses:* Tuition $485 per credit. Fees $360 per year full-time, $53 per semester (minimum) part-time.

See in-depth description on page 767.

Pacific Lutheran University, School of Education, Tacoma, WA 98447. Awards MA. Accredited by NCATE. Part-time and evening/weekend programs available. Faculty: 14 full-time (9 women), 1 (woman) part-time. Students: 29 full-time (17 women), 19 part-time (15 women); includes 6 minority (1 African American, 3 Asian Americans, 2 Hispanics), 1 international. Average age 31. 70 applicants, 90% accepted. In 1997, 45 degrees awarded. *Degree requirements:* Comprehensive exam, research project or thesis required, foreign language not required. *Entrance requirements:* GRE General Test or MAT, TOEFL (minimum score 550), interview. Application deadline: rolling. Application fee: $35. *Tuition:* $490 per semester hour. *Financial aid:* Fellowships, research assistantships, scholarships, Federal Work-Study available. Financial aid application deadline: 3/1. • Dr. John L. Brickell, Acting Dean, 253-535-7272. Application contact: Marjo Burdick, Office of Admissions, 253-535-7151. Fax: 253-535-8320. E-mail: admissions@plu.edu.

Pacific Union College, Department of Education, Angwin, CA 94508. Offers programs in education (MA), elementary education (MA). Part-time programs available. Faculty: 4 full-time (3 women), 1 (woman) part-time. Students: 2 full-time (1 woman), 7 part-time (6 women). Average age 29. 4 applicants, 100% accepted. In 1997, 5 degrees awarded (100% found work related to degree). *Degree requirements:* Thesis required, foreign language not required. *Average time to degree:* master's–1 year full-time, 4 years part-time. *Entrance requirements:* GRE, California Basic Educational Skills Test, MSAT, interview, teaching credential. Application deadline: 6/1 (priority date; rolling processing). Application fee: $30. Electronic applications accepted. *Financial aid:* In 1997–98, 2 students received aid, including 2 teaching assistantships (both to first-year students) averaging $150 per month and totaling $1,800; Federal Work-Study also available. Aid available to part-time students. Financial aid application deadline: 3/2. *Faculty research:* New teacher support, school safety, science education, effects of cross-cultural move on identity status of adolescents, reading comprehension. • Dr. Jean Buller, Chair, 707-965-7265. E-mail: jbuller@puc.edu. Application contact: Marsha Crow, Credential Analyst, 707-965-6643. Fax: 707-965-6645. E-mail: mcrow@puc.edu.

Pacific University, School of Education, Forest Grove, OR 97116-1797. Offers programs in early childhood education/elementary education (MAT), education (MAE), elementary/middle school education (MAT), secondary education (MAT). Part-time and evening/weekend programs available. Faculty: 11 full-time, 8 part-time. Students: 113 full-time (76 women), 6 part-time (3 women); includes 7 minority (1 African American, 3 Asian Americans, 2 Hispanics, 1 Native American), 5 international. Average age 30. In 1997, 125 degrees awarded. *Degree requirements:* Research project. *Entrance requirements:* California Basic Educational Skills Test, NTE, minimum GPA of 2.75 (undergraduate), 3.0 (graduate). Application deadline: 3/15 (priority date; rolling processing; 10/15 for spring admission). Application fee: $35. *Financial aid:* Institutionally sponsored loans and career-related internships or fieldwork available. Aid available to part-time students. Financial aid application deadline: 5/1; applicants required to submit FAFSA. • Dr. Willard Kniep, Program Director, 503-359-2205. Application contact: Joel Albin, Admissions Counselor, 503-359-2958. Fax: 503-359-2975. E-mail: admissions@pacificu.edu.

Palm Beach Atlantic College, School of Education and Behavioral Studies, West Palm Beach, FL 33416-4708. Offers programs in counseling psychology (MSCP), including marriage and family therapy, mental health counseling, school guidance counseling; elementary education (M Ed). Faculty: 3 full-time (1 woman), 8 part-time (5 women). Students: 47 full-time (38 women), 65 part-time (54 women); includes 19 minority (15 African Americans, 2 Asian Americans, 2 Hispanics), 2 international. Average age 33. 69 applicants, 70% accepted. In 1997, 34 degrees awarded. *Entrance requirements:* GRE General Test (combined average 1000), minimum GPA of 3.0 in last 60 hours. Application deadline: 7/15 (priority date; rolling processing; 11/15 for spring admission). Application fee: $35. *Tuition:* $280 per credit hour. *Financial aid:* Available to part-time students. Financial aid applicants required to submit FAFSA. • Dr. Dona Thornton, Dean, 561-803-2350. Fax: 561-803-2186. Application contact: Carolanne M. Brown, Director of Graduate Admissions, 800-281-3466. Fax: 561-803-2115. E-mail: grad@pbac.edu.

Park College, Graduate Program in Education, Parkville, MO 64152-4358. Awards M Ed. Students: 22. *Entrance requirements:* GRE General Test (minimum combined score of 1200), minimum GPA of 2.5. Application deadline: 8/1 (priority date; rolling processing). Application fee: $25. *Tuition:* $210 per credit hour. • Dr. Pat McClelland, Director, 816-741-2000 Ext. 6335.

Pennsylvania State University Great Valley School of Graduate Professional Studies, Graduate Studies and Continuing Education, College of Education, Malvern, PA 19355-1488. Offers programs in curriculum and instruction (M Ed, MS), instructional systems (M Ed, MS), special education (M Ed, MS). Students: 22 full-time (20 women), 225 part-time (172 women). *Entrance requirements:* GRE General Test or MAT. Application fee: $40. • Dr. William Milheim, Director, 610-648-3379.

See in-depth description on page 769.

Pennsylvania State University Harrisburg Campus of the Capital College, Division of Behavioral Sciences and Education, Middletown, PA 17057-4898. Awards MA, MCP, M Ed, D Ed. Part-time and evening/weekend programs available. Students: 51 full-time (40 women), 458 part-time (358 women). Average age 33. *Entrance requirements:* For doctorate, GRE General Test or MAT. Application deadline: 7/26. Application fee: $40. *Expenses:* Tuition $6534 per year full-time, $276 per credit part-time for state residents; $12,516 per year full-time, $523 per credit part-time for nonresidents. Fees $232 per year (minimum) full-time, $40 per semester (minimum) part-time. *Financial aid:* Career-related internships or fieldwork available. • Dr. William A. Henk, Head, 717-948-6213.

Pennsylvania State University University Park Campus, College of Education, University Park, PA 16802-1503. Awards MA, M Ed, MS, D Ed, PhD. Accredited by NCATE. Students: 521 full-time (347 women), 528 part-time (350 women). *Entrance requirements:* GRE General Test or MAT. Application fee: $40. *Expenses:* Tuition $6534 per year full-time, $276 per credit part-time for state residents; $13,460 per year full-time, $561 per credit part-time for nonresidents. Fees $252 per year (minimum) full-time, $43 per semester (minimum) part-time. • Dr. Rodney J. Reed, Dean, 814-865-2526.

Pepperdine University, Graduate School of Education and Psychology, Division of Education, Culver City, CA 90230-7615. Awards MA, MS, Ed D. Part-time and evening/weekend programs available. Faculty: 23 full-time (13 women), 38 part-time (20 women). Students: 359 full-time (261 women), 405 part-time (280 women); includes 182 minority (81 African Americans, 40 Asian Americans, 57 Hispanics, 4 Native Americans), 10 international. Average age 38. 454 applicants, 79% accepted. In 1997, 206 master's, 26 doctorates awarded. *Entrance requirements:* For master's, GRE General Test, TOEFL; for doctorate, GRE General Test, MAT, TOEFL. Application fee: $45. *Tuition:* $540 per unit. *Financial aid:* Research assistantships, teaching assistantships, scholarships, institutionally sponsored loans, and career-related internships or fieldwork available. Aid available to part-time students. Financial aid application deadline: 7/1; applicants required to submit CSS PROFILE. • Dr. Terence Cannings, Associate Dean, 310-568-5600. Application contact: Coordinator, 310-568-5600.

See in-depth description on page 771.

Peru State College, Graduate Studies, Program in Education, Peru, NE 68421. Awards MS Ed. Accredited by NCATE. Part-time programs available. Faculty: 68 part-time (42 women). Students: 71 part-time (50 women); includes 2 minority (1 African American, 1 Hispanic). In 1997, 27 degrees awarded. *Degree requirements:* Thesis optional. *Application deadline:* rolling. *Application fee:* $10. • Dr. Daniel J. Cox, Division Chair, Graduate Studies, 402-872-2244. Fax: 402-872-2414. E-mail: cox@bobcat.peru.edu.

Philadelphia College of Bible, Graduate School, Education Program, 200 Manor Avenue, Langhorne, PA 19047-2990. Awards MS. Part-time and evening/weekend programs available. Faculty: 1 (woman) full-time, 9 part-time (4 women), 4.6 FTE. Students: 6 full-time (2 women), 61 part-time (44 women); includes 11 minority (7 African Americans, 1 Asian American, 3 Hispanics), 6 international. Average age 35. 34 applicants, 88% accepted. In 1997, 13 degrees awarded. *Degree requirements:* Thesis required, foreign language not required. *Average time to degree:* master's–2 years full-time, 4 years part-time. *Entrance requirements:* Minimum undergraduate GPA of 2.5. Application deadline: 9/1 (priority date; rolling processing). Application fee: $25. *Expenses:* Tuition $275 per credit. Fees $10 per year. *Financial aid:* In 1997–98, 35 students received aid, including 26 scholarships (25 to first-year students) totaling $13,792. Aid available to part-time students. Financial aid application deadline: 8/1. • Dr. Janet L. Nason, Chair, 800-572-2472. E-mail: jnason@pcb.edu. Application contact: Ted McKown, Director of Marketing/Recruiting, 800-572-2472. Fax: 215-702-4359. E-mail: tmckown@pcb.edu.

Phillips University, School of Education, 100 South University Avenue, Enid, OK 73701-6439. Offers programs in elementary education (M Ed), secondary education (M Ed). Part-time programs available. Faculty: 5 full-time (2 women), 4 part-time (2 women). Students: 12 full-time, 26 part-time. In 1997, 11 degrees awarded (100% found work related to degree). *Degree requirements:* Thesis required (for some programs), foreign language not required. *Entrance requirements:* Minimum GPA of 2.5. Application deadline: 8/1 (1/1 for spring admission). Application fee: $20. *Expenses:* Tuition $97 per credit hour. Fees $10 per credit hour. *Financial aid:* Scholarships, partial tuition waivers, Federal Work-Study, institutionally sponsored loans, and career-related internships or fieldwork available. Aid available to part-time students. Financial aid application deadline: 6/1; applicants required to submit FAFSA. • Dr. Donna Payne, Dean, 405-237-4433 Ext. 207.

Piedmont College, Division of Education, Demorest, GA 30535-0010. Offers programs in early childhood education (MAT), secondary education (MAT). Part-time and evening/weekend programs available. Postbaccalaureate distance learning degree programs offered (no on-campus study). Faculty: 24 full-time (12 women), 25 part-time (13 women), 30 FTE. Students: 193 full-time (146 women), 384 part-time (349 women); includes 35 minority (32 African Americans, 1 Asian American, 2 Hispanics). Average age 34. 142 applicants, 74% accepted. In 1997, 71 degrees awarded. *Degree requirements:* Computer language, thesis, field experience in the teaching classroom required, foreign language not required. *Average time to degree:* master's–1.3 years full-time, 1.5 years part-time. *Entrance requirements:* GRE General Test (minimum combined score of 800; average 835), MAT (minimum score 30; average 45), minimum undergraduate GPA of 2.5. Application deadline: 8/1 (12/1 for spring admission). Application fee: $30. *Tuition:* $2880 per year full-time, $160 per hour part-time. *Financial aid:* In 1997–98, 30 students received aid, including 6 teaching assistantships (3 to first-year students) averaging $830 per month and totaling $41,520; Federal Work-Study, institutionally sponsored loans, and career-related internships or fieldwork also available. Aid available to part-time students. Financial aid applicants required to submit FAFSA. *Faculty research:* Constructivist orientation, critical theory and postmoderinsm as they relate to educational issues, technology, critical thinking, connecting scientific research to classroom. • Dr. Jane McFerrin, Chair, 706-778-3000 Ext. 201. Fax: 706-776-9608. E-mail: jmcferrin@piedmont.edu. Application contact: James L. Clement, Associate Dean for Admissions and Financial Aid, 800-277-7020. Fax: 706-776-6635. E-mail: jclement@piedmont.edu.

Pine Manor College, Program in Education, Chestnut Hill, MA 02167-2332. Offers programs in early childhood education (M Ed), elementary education (M Ed). Part-time programs available. Faculty: 5 full-time (all women). Students: 2 full-time (1 woman), 15 part-time (14 women). *Degree requirements:* Clinical experience, fieldwork. *Application deadline:* rolling. *Application fee:* $25. *Financial aid:* Federal Work-Study and career-related internships or fieldwork available. *Faculty research:* Mentor-teacher activities, gender dynamics, mathematics education. • Dr. Joanna S. Hall, Director of Graduate Studies, 617-731-7075. Application contact: Pat Dunbar, Graduate Admissions, 617-731-7111. Fax: 617-731-7199.

Pittsburg State University, School of Education, Pittsburg, KS 66762-5880. Awards MS, Ed S. Accredited by NCATE. Students: 73 full-time (47 women), 280 part-time (212 women); includes 12 minority (2 African Americans, 1 Asian American, 1 Hispanic, 8 Native Americans), 3 international. In 1997, 120 master's awarded. *Degree requirements:* For master's, thesis or alternative required, foreign language not required. *Application fee:* $40. *Tuition:* $2418 per year full-time, $103 per credit hour part-time for state residents; $6130 per year full-time, $258 per credit hour part-time for nonresidents. *Financial aid:* Teaching assistantships, Federal Work-Study, and career-related internships or fieldwork available. • Dr. Tom Bryant, Dean, 316-235-4517.

Plattsburgh State University of New York, Faculty of Professional Studies, Center for Educational Studies and Services, Plattsburgh, NY 12901-2681. Awards MS, MS Ed, MST, CAS. Students: 100 full-time (70 women), 157 part-time (108 women); includes 5 minority (1 African American, 1 Asian American, 3 Hispanics). 90 applicants, 76% accepted. In 1997, 150 master's, 8 CASs awarded. *Degree requirements:* For master's, comprehensive exam or research project; for CAS, comprehensive exam required, foreign language and thesis not required. *Entrance requirements:* For master's, GRE General Test or MAT, minimum GPA of 2.5. Application deadline: rolling. Application fee: $50. *Expenses:* Tuition $5100 per year full-time, $213 per credit hour part-time for state residents; $8416 per year full-time, $351 per credit hour part-time for nonresidents. Fees $395 per year full-time, $15.10 per credit hour part-time. *Financial aid:* 98 students received aid; Federal Work-Study available. Aid available to part-time students. Financial aid application deadline: 4/15; applicants required to submit FAFSA. • Dr. Raymond Domenico, Director and Associate Dean, 518-564-2122.

Plymouth State College of the University System of New Hampshire, Department of Education, Plymouth, NH 03264-1595. Offers programs in educational administration (M Ed), educational computing (M Ed), elementary education (M Ed), environmental science education (M Ed), guidance and counseling (M Ed), health education (M Ed), heritage studies (M Ed), integrated arts (M Ed), mathematics education (M Ed), reading specialist (M Ed), secondary education (M Ed). One or more programs accredited by NCATE. Part-time and evening/weekend programs available. Faculty: 25 full-time (14 women), 28 part-time (17 women). Students: 48 full-time (34 women), 93 part-time (73 women); includes 2 minority (1 Asian American, 1 Hispanic), 1 international. Average age 37. 56 applicants, 73% accepted. In 1997, 121 degrees awarded. *Entrance requirements:* GRE General Test (average 500 on each section) or MAT (minimum score 50), minimum GPA of 3.0. Application deadline: 9/1 (priority date; rolling processing). Application fee: $25 ($35 for international students). *Tuition:* $232 per credit for state residents; $254 per credit for nonresidents. *Financial aid:* In 1997–98, 8 graduate assistantships were awarded; institutionally sponsored loans and career-related internships or fieldwork also available. Aid available to part-time students. Financial aid application deadline: 3/15; applicants required to submit FAFSA. • Dr. Dennise Bartelo, Director, 603-535-2286. Application contact: Maryann Szabadics, Administrative Assistant, 603-535-2636. Fax: 603-535-2572. E-mail: for.grad@psc.plymouth.edu.

See in-depth description on page 773.

Point Loma Nazarene University, Department of Education, San Diego, CA 92106-2899. Awards MA, Ed D, Ed S. Ed D offered jointly with Northern Arizona University. Part-time and evening/weekend programs available. Faculty: 5 full-time (3 women), 11 part-time (8 women), 7.2 FTE. Students: 219 full-time (163 women), 151 part-time (104 women); includes 73 minority (22 African Americans, 17 Asian Americans, 31 Hispanics, 3 Native Americans), 3 international. Average age 36. In 1997, 51 master's, 6 Ed Ss awarded. *Degree requirements:* For master's, thesis optional, foreign language not required. *Entrance requirements:* For master's and Ed S, GRE General Test or MAT, portfolio. Application deadline: 5/15 (priority date; rolling processing; 11/1 for spring admission). Application fee: $25. *Expenses:* Tuition $450 per unit. Fees $12.50 per unit. *Financial aid:* Career-related internships or fieldwork available. Financial aid application deadline: 4/10. • Dr. Jo Birdsell, Director, 619-849-2358. Application contact: Scott Schoemaker, Director of Admissions, 619-849-2273. Fax: 619-849-2579.

Pontifical Catholic University of Puerto Rico, College of Education, Ponce, PR 00731-6382. Awards MA Ed, M Ed, MRE. Part-time and evening/weekend programs available. Faculty: 4 full-time (2 women), 9 part-time (4 women). Students: 56 full-time (43 women), 250 part-time (175 women); includes 306 minority (all Hispanics). Average age 37. 72 applicants, 100% accepted. In 1997, 61 degrees awarded. *Degree requirements:* Thesis (for some programs), comprehensive exam required, foreign language not required. *Entrance requirements:* Interview, minimum GPA of 2.5. Application deadline: 4/30 (priority date; rolling processing). Application fee: $15. Electronic applications accepted. *Financial aid:* Fellowships, partial tuition waivers, Federal Work-Study, and career-related internships or fieldwork available. Aid available to part-time students. Financial aid application deadline: 7/15. *Faculty research:* Teaching English as a second language, learning styles, leadership styles. • Dr. Gilbert Toro, Chairperson, 787-841-2000 Ext. 319. Application contact: Manuel Luciano, Director of Admissions, 787-841-2000 Ext. 426. Fax: 787-840-4295.

Portland State University, School of Education, Portland, OR 97207-0751. Awards MA, MAT, M Ed, MS, MST, Ed D. Accredited by NCATE. Part-time and evening/weekend programs available. Faculty: 51 full-time (28 women), 9 part-time (5 women), 52 FTE. Students: 299 full-time (214 women), 316 part-time (214 women); includes 68 minority (23 African Americans, 11 Asian Americans, 24 Hispanics, 10 Native Americans), 15 international. Average age 35. 492 applicants, 68% accepted. In 1997, 314 master's, 9 doctorates awarded. *Degree requirements:* For doctorate, dissertation required, foreign language not required. *Entrance requirements:* For master's, TOEFL (minimum score 550), minimum GPA of 3.0 in upper-division course work or 2.75 overall; for doctorate, TOEFL (minimum score 550). Application fee: $50. *Tuition:* $6101 per year full-time, $689 per semester (minimum) part-time for state residents; $10,445 per year full-time, $689 per semester (minimum) part-time for nonresidents. *Financial aid:* In 1997–98, 22 research assistantships (13 to first-year students) were awarded; teaching assistantships, Federal Work-Study, institutionally sponsored loans, and career-related internships or fieldwork also available. Aid available to part-time students. Financial aid application deadline: 3/1; applicants required to submit FAFSA. • Dr. Robert Everhart, Dean, 503-725-4621. Fax: 503-725-8475. E-mail: bob@ed.pdx.edu.

Prairie View A&M University, College of Education, Prairie View, TX 77446-0188. Awards MA, MA Ed, M Ed, MS Ed. Accredited by NCATE. Part-time and evening/weekend programs available. Faculty: 18 full-time (7 women). Students: 258 full-time (181 women), 573 part-time (387 women); includes 621 minority (584 African Americans, 5 Asian Americans, 30 Hispanics, 2 Native Americans), 7 international. Average age 33. In 1997, 268 degrees awarded (100% found work related to degree). *Degree requirements:* Thesis optional, foreign language not required. *Average time to degree:* master's–2.5 years full-time, 4 years part-time. *Entrance requirements:* GRE General Test. Application deadline: 7/1 (priority date; rolling processing; 11/1 for spring admission). Application fee: $10. *Tuition:* $2202 per year full-time, $336 per semester (minimum) part-time for state residents; $6000 per year full-time, $963 per semester (minimum) part-time for nonresidents. *Financial aid:* Federal Work-Study and career-related internships or fieldwork available. Financial aid application deadline: 6/31. *Faculty research:* Administration theory, effective schools, metacognitive strategies, emotionally disturbed, language arts. • Dr. M. Paul Mehta, Dean, 409-857-3880. Fax: 409-857-2911. Application contact: Dr. Willie F. Trotty, Dean, Graduate School and Research, 409-857-2315. Fax: 409-857-4521. E-mail: willie_trotty@pvamu.edu.

Prescott College, Graduate Programs, Program in Education, Prescott, AZ 86301-2990. Offers bilingual education (MA), including English as a second language, Native American bilingual teacher education; education (MA); multicultural education (MA). Postbaccalaureate distance learning degree programs offered (minimal on-campus study). *Degree requirements:* Thesis, fieldwork or internship, practicum required, foreign language not required. *Application deadline:* 6/1 (11/1 for spring admission). *Application fee:* $40. *Tuition:* $9000 per year. • Dr. Gene Hanson, Head, 520-319-9868. Application contact: Joan Clingan, Graduate Director, 520-776-5130. Fax: 520-776-5137. E-mail: mapmail@northlink.com.

Providence College, Department of Education, Providence, RI 02918. Offers programs in administration (M Ed), including elementary administration, secondary administration; guidance and counseling (M Ed); special education (M Ed). Part-time and evening/weekend programs available. Faculty: 9 full-time (7 women), 32 part-time (13 women). Students: 13 full-time (10 women), 242 part-time (196 women); includes 7 minority (5 African Americans, 2 Hispanics). Average age 33. 76 applicants, 95% accepted. In 1997, 125 degrees awarded. *Degree requirements:* Comprehensive exam required, foreign language and thesis not required. *Entrance requirements:* GRE General Test (minimum combined score of 1000) or MAT (minimum score 45), TOEFL. Application deadline: 8/12 (priority date; rolling processing; 12/1 for spring admission). Application fee: $40. *Tuition:* $621 per course. *Financial aid:* In 1997–98, 15 students received aid, including 4 graduate assistantships (all to first-year students) averaging $650 per month and totaling $31,200; institutionally sponsored loans and career-related internships or fieldwork also available. Aid available to part-time students. Financial aid applicants required to submit FAFSA. • Dr. Thomas F. Flaherty, Dean, Graduate School, 401-865-2247. Fax: 401-865-2057.

Purdue University, School of Education, West Lafayette, IN 47907. Awards MS, MS Ed, PhD, Ed S. Accredited by NCATE. Part-time and evening/weekend programs available. Faculty: 60 full-time (28 women), 26 part-time (15 women). Students: 124 full-time (76 women), 275 part-time (185 women); includes 47 minority (27 African Americans, 11 Asian Americans, 7 Hispanics, 2 Native Americans), 45 international. 282 applicants, 73% accepted. In 1997, 125 master's, 32 doctorates, 5 Ed Ss awarded. *Degree requirements:* For master's, thesis optional; for doctorate, dissertation, oral and written exams; for Ed S, oral presentation, project required, thesis not required. *Entrance requirements:* For master's, TOEFL (minimum score 550), minimum B average; for doctorate, GRE General Test (minimum score 500 on each section), TOEFL (minimum score 550); for Ed S, minimum B average. Application fee: $30. Electronic applications accepted. *Tuition:* $3500 per year full-time, $126 per credit hour part-time for state residents; $11,720 per year full-time, $387 per credit hour part-time for nonresidents. *Financial aid:* Fellowships, research assistantships, teaching assistantships, full tuition waivers, and career-related internships or fieldwork available. Aid available to part-time students. Financial aid applicants required to submit FAFSA. • Dr. Marilyn J. Haring, Dean, 765-494-2336.

Purdue University Calumet, School of Professional Studies, Department of Education, Hammond, IN 46323-2094. Offers programs in counseling and personnel services (MS Ed), educational administration (MS Ed), elementary education (MS Ed), instructional development (MS Ed), media sciences (MS Ed), secondary education (MS Ed). One or more programs accredited by NCATE. *Entrance requirements:* TOEFL. Application fee: $30.

Purdue University North Central, Graduate Program in Education, Westville, IN 46391-9528. Offers elementary education (MS Ed). Part-time and evening/weekend programs available. Students: 40 part-time. • Dr. Edward Hackett, Chair, 219-785-5485. Fax: 219-785-5516. E-mail: ehackett@purduenc.edu.

Queens College, Hayworth College, Department of Education, 1900 Selwyn Avenue, Charlotte, NC 28274-0002. Offers program in elementary education (MAT). Accredited by NCATE. Part-time and evening/weekend programs available. Faculty: 4 full-time (all women), 2 part-time (both women). Students: 34 full-time (33 women), 41 part-time (35 women); includes 3 minority (2 African Americans, 1 Hispanic). Average age 27. 50 applicants, 90% accepted. In 1997, 21 degrees awarded. *Degree requirements:* Comprehensive written exam required, foreign language and thesis not required. *Entrance requirements:* GRE General Test (minimum combined score of 850). Application deadline: rolling. Application fee: $25. *Expenses:* Tuition $225 per credit hour. Fees $40 per year. *Financial aid:* Institutionally sponsored loans available. • Dr. Joyce Eckart, Chairperson, 704-337-2565. Application contact: Anne Duplessis, Director of Admissions, 704-337-2314. Fax: 704-337-2415.

Queens College of the City University of New York, Social Science Division, School of Education, 65-30 Kissena Boulevard, Flushing, NY 11367-1597. Awards MS Ed, AC. Part-time and evening/weekend programs available. Students: 209 full-time (163 women), 1,836 part-time (1,436 women); includes 439 minority (192 African Americans, 85 Asian Americans, 154 Hispanics, 8 Native Americans), 6 international. 1,329 applicants, 69% accepted. In 1997, 440 master's, 130 ACs awarded. *Degree requirements:* For master's, research project required, foreign language and thesis not required; for AC, thesis optional, foreign language not required. *Entrance requirements:* For master's, TOEFL (minimum score 600), minimum GPA of 3.0; for AC, TOEFL (minimum score 600). Application deadline: 4/1 (rolling processing; 11/1 for spring admission). Application fee: $40. *Expenses:* Tuition $4350 per year full-time, $185 per credit part-time for state residents; $7600 per year full-time, $320 per credit part-time for nonresidents. Fees $104 per year. *Financial aid:* Partial tuition waivers, Federal Work-Study, institutionally sponsored loans, and career-related internships or fieldwork available. Aid available to part-time students. Financial aid application deadline: 4/1; applicants required to submit FAFSA. • Dr. Sydney L. Schwartz, Acting Dean, 718-997-5220. Application contact: Mario Caruso, Director of Graduate Admissions, 718-997-5200. Fax: 718-997-5193. E-mail: graduate%queens.bitnet@cunyvm.cuny.edu.

Queen's University at Kingston, Faculty of Education, Kingston, ON K7L 3N6, Canada. Awards M Ed. Part-time programs available. Students: 55 full-time (38 women), 90 part-time (60 women). 49 applicants. In 1997, 49 degrees awarded. *Degree requirements:* Thesis optional, foreign language not required. *Entrance requirements:* GRE General Test, MAT, TOEFL (minimum score 580). Application deadline: 2/28 (priority date). Application fee: $60. Electronic applications accepted. *Tuition:* $3803 per year (minimum) full-time, $1901 per year (minimum) part-time for Canadian residents; $7330 per year (minimum) for nonresidents. *Financial aid:* Fellowships, research assistantships, teaching assistantships, institutionally sponsored loans available. Financial aid application deadline: 3/1. *Faculty research:* Reading, instructional computers, French as a second language, impulsivity, science. • Dr. R. Upitis, Dean, 613-545-6210. Application contact: Dr. J. R. Kirby, Graduate Coordinator, 613-545-7231.

Quincy University, Division of Education, Quincy, IL 62301-2699. Awards MS Ed. Faculty: 4 full-time (1 woman), 2 part-time (both women). Students: 48 (41 women); includes 1 Asian American. In 1997, 18 degrees awarded. *Degree requirements:* Thesis or alternative required, foreign language not required. *Entrance requirements:* MAT. Application deadline: rolling. Application fee: $25. *Tuition:* $380 per credit hour. *Financial aid:* 27 students received aid. Aid available to part-time students. Financial aid applicants required to submit FAFSA. • Dr. Alice Mills, Chair, 217-228-5420.

Quinnipiac College, School of Liberal Arts, Program in Secondary and Middle School Teaching, Hamden, CT 06518-1904. Offers biology (MAT), chemistry (MAT), English (MAT), French (MAT), history/social studies (MAT), mathematics (MAT), physics (MAT), Spanish (MAT). Part-time programs available. Faculty: 21 full-time (5 women), 16 part-time (9 women). Students: 55 full-time (35 women), 42 part-time (20 women); includes 4 minority (3 African Americans, 1 Native American). Average age 28. 79 applicants, 91% accepted. In 1997, 48 degrees awarded. *Degree requirements:* Thesis. *Average time to degree:* master's–1.5 years full-time, 3 years part-time. *Entrance requirements:* PRAXIS I, minimum GPA of 2.67. Application deadline: rolling. Application fee: $45. Electronic applications accepted. *Expenses:* Tuition $395 per credit hour. Fees $380 per year full-time. *Financial aid:* Fellowships, partial tuition waivers, and career-related internships or fieldwork available. Aid available to part-time students. Financial aid applicants required to submit FAFSA. • Carol Orticari, Director, 203-281-8978. Fax: 203-281-8709. E-mail: orticari@quinnipiac.edu. Application contact: Scott Farber, Director of Graduate Admissions, 203-281-8795. Fax: 203-287-5238. E-mail: qcgradadmi@quinnipiac.edu.

See in-depth description on page 775.

Directory: Education—General

Radford University, Graduate College, College of Education and Human Development, Radford, VA 24142. Awards MS, MSW. Accredited by NCATE. Part-time programs available. Postbaccalaureate distance learning degree programs offered (minimal on-campus study). Faculty: 37 full-time (21 women), 8 part-time (5 women), 38.6 FTE. Students: 138 full-time (96 women), 247 part-time (187 women); includes 23 minority (20 African Americans, 2 Asian Americans, 1 Hispanic), 3 international. Average age 35. 224 applicants, 73% accepted. In 1997, 104 degrees awarded. *Degree requirements:* Comprehensive exam required, foreign language and thesis not required. *Entrance requirements:* GMAT, GRE General Test, MAT, or NTE; TOEFL (minimum score 550), minimum GPA of 2.7. Application deadline: 2/1 (priority date; rolling processing; 10/1 for spring admission). Application fee: $25. Electronic applications accepted. *Expenses:* Tuition $2302 per year full-time, $147 per credit hour part-time for state residents; $5672 per year full-time, $287 per credit hour part-time for nonresidents. Fees $1222 per year full-time. *Financial aid:* In 1997–98, 27 fellowships totaling $116,814, 29 research assistantships totaling $101,948, 12 teaching assistantships totaling $68,580, 302 scholarships/grants totaling $1.058 million were awarded; Federal Work-Study, institutionally sponsored loans, and career-related internships or fieldwork also available. Financial aid application deadline: 2/1; applicants required to submit FAFSA. • Dr. Robert C. Small Jr., Dean, 540-831-5439. Fax: 540-831-6053. E-mail: rsmall@runet.edu.

Regent University, Graduate School, School of Education, Virginia Beach, VA 23464-9800. Awards M Ed, CAGS, MBA/M Ed, M Div/M Ed, M Ed/MA. Part-time and evening/weekend programs available. Faculty: 6 full-time (3 women), 20 part-time (14 women), 16 FTE. Students: 120 full-time (99 women), 65 part-time (49 women); includes 77 minority (68 African Americans, 3 Asian Americans, 5 Hispanics, 1 Native American). Average age 33. 152 applicants, 73% accepted. In 1997, 91 master's awarded. *Degree requirements:* For master's, thesis or alternative required, foreign language not required. *Average time to degree:* master's–1.5 years full-time, 3.5 years part-time. *Entrance requirements:* For master's, GRE General Test or MAT, minimum undergraduate GPA of 2.75. Application deadline: 6/1 (priority date; rolling processing). Application fee: $40. *Expenses:* Tuition $298 per credit hour full-time, $289 per credit hour part-time for state residents; $289 per credit hour for nonresidents. Fees $18 per semester. *Financial aid:* 63 students received aid; full and partial tuition waivers and career-related internships or fieldwork available. Financial aid application deadline: 5/1. *Faculty research:* Family issues, school and classroom discipline, learner differences, urban issues, integration of faith and learning. Total annual research expenditures: $6000. • Dr. Alan Arroyo, Dean, 757-226-4261. E-mail: alanarr@regent.edu. Application contact: Deanna Malinski, Director of Admissions, 757-226-4395. Fax: 757-226-4318. E-mail: eduschool@regent.edu.

Regis College, Department of Education, Weston, MA 02493. Awards MAT. Faculty: 4 full-time (3 women), 11 part-time (10 women). Students: 5 full-time (all women), 22 part-time (all women). 10 applicants, 80% accepted. In 1997, 4 degrees awarded. *Degree requirements:* Thesis required, foreign language not required. *Average time to degree:* master's–2.5 years part-time. *Entrance requirements:* GRE or MAT. Application deadline: rolling. Application fee: $30. *Expenses:* Tuition $390 per credit hour. Fees $95 per semester. *Financial aid:* 5 students received aid. Aid available to part-time students. Financial aid applicants required to submit FAFSA. *Faculty research:* Reflective teaching, gender-based education, integrated teaching. • Dr. Leona McCaughey-Oreszak, Chair, 781-768-7421. Fax: 781-768-8339.

Regis University, Regis College, Denver, CO 80221-1099. Offers program in whole learning education (MA). Offered at Northwest Denver Campus. Part-time programs available. Students: 2 full-time, 101 part-time; includes 10 minority (1 African American, 2 Asian Americans, 7 Hispanics). Average age 34. 24 applicants, 100% accepted. In 1997, 44 degrees awarded (100% found work related to degree). *Degree requirements:* Capstone Presentation required, foreign language and thesis not required. *Entrance requirements:* 1 year of teaching experience, videotape sample of teaching. Application deadline: rolling. Application fee: $75. *Tuition:* $272 per semester hour. *Financial aid:* Available to part-time students. Financial aid application deadline: 3/15; applicants required to submit FAFSA. • Dr. Steve Doty, Dean. Application contact: Bea Lasky, Director, 303-458-4349. Fax: 303-964-5421. E-mail: blasky@regis.edu.

Rhode Island College, School of Graduate Studies, School of Education and Human Development, Program in Education, Providence, RI 02908-1924. Awards PhD. Accredited by NCATE. Offered jointly with the University of Rhode Island. *Application deadline:* 4/1 (rolling processing). *Application fee:* $25. *Tuition:* $4064 per year full-time, $214 per credit part-time for state residents; $7658 per year full-time, $376 per credit part-time for nonresidents. • Richard Dickson, Director.

Rice University, School of Humanities, Department of Education, Houston, TX 77005. Awards MAT. *Degree requirements:* Variable foreign language requirement, thesis not required. *Entrance requirements:* GRE General Test, TOEFL (minimum score 550), minimum GPA of 3.0. Application deadline: 2/1 (priority date; rolling processing; 11/15 for spring admission). Application fee: $25. *Expenses:* Tuition $15,300 per year full-time, $850 per credit hour part-time. Fees $238 per year.

Rider University, School of Graduate Education and Human Services, Lawrenceville, NJ 08648-3001. Awards MA, Ed S. Accredited by NCATE. Part-time and evening/weekend programs available. Faculty: 13 full-time (5 women), 24 part-time (9 women). Students: 69 full-time, 587 part-time. Average age 36. 250 applicants, 66% accepted. In 1997, 144 master's awarded. *Degree requirements:* For master's, comprehensive exams, research project required, foreign language and thesis not required. *Entrance requirements:* For master's, interview, minimum GPA of 2.5. Application deadline: rolling. Application fee: $35. *Tuition:* $329 per credit hour. *Financial aid:* Research assistantships, Federal Work-Study, and career-related internships or fieldwork available. Aid available to part-time students. *Faculty research:* Gifted students, self-esteem, hope collaboration. • Dr. Jesse DeEsch, Assistant Dean, 609-896-5353. Application contact: Dr. John Carpenter, Dean, Continuing Studies, 609-896-5036. Fax: 609-896-5261.

Rivier College, Graduate Education Department, Nashua, NH 03060-5086. Offers programs in computers in education (MA), counseling and psychotherapy (MA), counselor education (M Ed), early childhood education (M Ed), educational administration (M Ed), elementary education (M Ed), general education (M Ed), learning disabilities (M Ed), reading (M Ed), secondary education (M Ed). Part-time and evening/weekend programs available. *Entrance requirements:* GRE General Test or MAT. Application deadline: rolling. Application fee: $25.

Roberts Wesleyan College, Division of Teacher Education, Program in Teacher Education, Rochester, NY 14624-1997. Awards M Ed. Part-time and evening/weekend programs available. Faculty: 5 full-time (3 women), 11 part-time (5 women). Students: 1 (woman) full-time, 39 part-time (27 women); includes 1 minority (African American). Average age 33. 9 applicants, 89% accepted. In 1997, 15 degrees awarded. *Degree requirements:* Thesis. *Application deadline:* 8/1 (priority date; rolling processing; 12/1 for spring admission). *Application fee:* $35. *Tuition:* $340 per credit hour. *Financial aid:* 7 students received aid; career-related internships or fieldwork available. Financial aid application deadline: 9/1; applicants required to submit FAFSA. • Dr. Jeffrey Altman, Director, 716-594-6448. Fax: 716-594-6316. Application contact: Kathy Merz, Admissions Secretary, 716-594-6600. Fax: 716-594-6585.

Rockford College, Department of Education, Rockford, IL 61108-2393. Offers programs in elementary education (MAT); learning disabilities (MAT); remedial reading (MAT); secondary education (MAT), including art education, English, history, political science, secondary education, social sciences. Part-time and evening/weekend programs available. Faculty: 24 full-time (9 women), 18 part-time (16 women), 28 FTE. Students: 40 full-time (24 women), 164 part-time (128 women); includes 15 minority (9 African Americans, 6 Hispanics). Average age 34. 38 applicants, 100% accepted. In 1997, 43 degrees awarded. *Degree requirements:* Thesis optional, foreign language not required. *Entrance requirements:* GRE General Test (minimum combined score of 1000). Application deadline: rolling. Application fee: $35. *Tuition:* $15,500 per year full-time, $400 per credit part-time. • Barbara Heal, Chair, 815-394-5201.

Rollins College, Program in Education, Winter Park, FL 32789-4499. Offers elementary education (MAT, M Ed); secondary education (MAT), including English, mathematics, music. Part-time and evening/weekend programs available. Faculty: 13 full-time (8 women), 11 part-time (4 women), 17 FTE. Students: 15 full-time (13 women), 34 part-time (29 women); includes 2 minority (both Asian Americans), 1 international. Average age 30. 160 applicants, 56% accepted. In 1997, 14 degrees awarded. *Degree requirements:* Comprehensive exam required, foreign language and thesis not required. *Entrance requirements:* Interview. Application deadline: rolling. Application fee: $50. *Tuition:* $190 per hour. *Financial aid:* In 1997–98, 11 students received aid, including 1 grant totaling $2,160; teaching assistantships also available. Aid available to part-time students. Financial aid application deadline: 3/23. • Dr. Nancy McAleer, Director, 407-646-2305. Application contact: Laura Pfister, Coordinator of Records and Registration, 407-646-2416. Fax: 407-646-1551.

Roosevelt University, College of Education, Chicago, IL 60605-1394. Offers programs in early childhood education (MA), educational administration and supervision (MA, Ed D), elementary education (MA), guidance and counseling (MA), reading education (MA), secondary education (MA). Accredited by NCATE. Part-time and evening/weekend programs available. Students: 153 full-time (109 women), 437 part-time (320 women); includes 206 minority (166 African Americans, 13 Asian Americans, 26 Hispanics, 1 Native American), 4 international. In 1997, 145 master's, 22 doctorates awarded. *Degree requirements:* For doctorate, computer language, dissertation required, foreign language not required. *Entrance requirements:* For doctorate, GRE or MAT. Application deadline: 6/1 (priority date; rolling processing). Application fee: $25 ($35 for international students). *Expenses:* Tuition $445 per credit hour. Fees $100 per year. *Financial aid:* Federal Work-Study available. Aid available to part-time students. Financial aid application deadline: 2/15. • Dr. George Lowery, Dean, 312-341-3700. Application contact: Joanne Canyon-Heller, Coordinator of Graduate Admissions, 312-341-3612.

Rowan University, College of Education, Glassboro, NJ 08028-1701. Awards MA, MST, Ed D, Certificate. Accredited by NCATE. Part-time and evening/weekend programs available. Students: 678 (558 women); includes 65 minority (45 African Americans, 8 Asian Americans, 12 Hispanics). 359 applicants, 59% accepted. In 1997, 234 master's awarded. *Degree requirements:* For master's, thesis, comprehensive exams required, foreign language not required. *Entrance requirements:* For master's, GRE General Test; for doctorate, GRE General Test, master's degree. Application deadline: 11/1 (priority date; rolling processing; 4/1 for spring admission). Application fee: $50. *Tuition:* $5728 per year full-time, $258 per credit hour part-time for state residents; $8968 per year full-time, $393 per credit hour part-time for nonresidents. *Financial aid:* Assistantships, Federal Work-Study, and career-related internships or fieldwork available. Aid available to part-time students. • Dr. David Kapel, Dean, 609-256-4753.

Rutgers, The State University of New Jersey, New Brunswick, Graduate School of Education, New Brunswick, NJ 08903. Awards Ed M, Ed D, Ed S. Part-time and evening/weekend programs available. Faculty: 55 full-time (22 women). Students: 208 full-time (159 women), 763 part-time (582 women). Average age 28. 614 applicants, 67% accepted. In 1997, 185 master's, 36 doctorates awarded. Terminal master's awarded for partial completion of doctoral program. *Degree requirements:* For doctorate, dissertation. *Entrance requirements:* GRE General Test. Application deadline: 3/1 (11/1 for spring admission). Application fee: $40. *Expenses:* Tuition $6492 per year full-time, $268 per credit part-time for state residents; $9520 per year full-time, $395 per credit part-time for nonresidents. Fees $208 per year (minimum). *Financial aid:* In 1997–98, 244 students received aid, including 3 research assistantships, 10 teaching assistantships; fellowships, Federal Work-Study, institutionally sponsored loans, and career-related internships or fieldwork also available. Aid available to part-time students. Financial aid application deadline: 3/1. *Faculty research:* Science, math, early childhood education, counseling, career education. Total annual research expenditures: $8.831 million. • Dr. Louise Cherry Wilkinson, Dean, 732-932-7496 Ext. 117. Application contact: Dr. Jeffrey Smith, Associate Dean, 732-932-7496 Ext. 105. Fax: 732-932-8206. E-mail: jefsmith@rci.rutgers.edu.

Sacred Heart University, College of Education and Health Professions, Faculty of Education and Psychology, 5151 Park Avenue, Fairfield, CT 06432-1000. Offers programs in administration (CAS), education (CAS), elementary education (MAT), secondary education (MAT). Part-time and evening/weekend programs available. Students: 225 full-time (152 women), 432 part-time (320 women); includes 35 minority (14 African Americans, 5 Asian Americans, 15 Hispanics, 1 Native American), 2 international. Average age 35. 171 applicants, 82% accepted. In 1997, 204 master's awarded. *Degree requirements:* For master's, thesis or alternative required, foreign language not required. *Application deadline:* rolling. *Application fee:* $40 ($100 for international students). *Expenses:* Tuition $335 per credit. Fees $78 per semester. *Financial aid:* Research assistantships, traineeships, partial tuition waivers, Federal Work-Study, and career-related internships or fieldwork available. Aid available to part-time students. *Faculty research:* Reading education, learning theory, teacher preparation, education of underachievers. • Dr. A. Harris Stone, Director, 203-371-7800. Application contact: Linda B. Kirby, Dean of Graduate Admissions, 203-371-7880. Fax: 203-365-4732. E-mail: gradstudies@sacredheart.edu.

Sage Graduate School, Graduate School, Division of Education, Troy, NY 12180-4115. Offers programs in elementary education (MS Ed); guidance and counseling (MS Ed, PMC); health education (MS), including community health, nutrition and dietetics, school health; reading (MS Ed); reading/special education (MS Ed); secondary education (MS Ed, PMC); special education (MS Ed). Part-time and evening/weekend programs available. Faculty: 8 full-time (3 women), 20 part-time (15 women). Students: 140 full-time (111 women), 332 part-time (223 women). *Entrance requirements:* For master's, minimum GPA of 2.75. Application deadline: 8/1 (rolling processing; 12/15 for spring admission). Application fee: $25. *Expenses:* Tuition $360 per credit hour. Fees $50 per semester. *Financial aid:* Research assistantships, scholarships, assistantships, and career-related internships or fieldwork available. Aid available to part-time students. Financial aid application deadline: 7/1; applicants required to submit FAFSA. *Faculty research:* Literacy development in at-risk children, effective behavior strategies for class instruction. • Dr. Connell Frazer, Chair, 518-244-2403. Fax: 518-244-2334. E-mail: rothej@sage.edu. Application contact: Melissa Robertson, Associate Director of Admissions, 518-244-6878. Fax: 518-244-6880. E-mail: sgsadm@sage.edu.

Saginaw Valley State University, College of Education, University Center, MI 48710. Awards MAT, M Ed, Ed S. Accredited by NCATE. Part-time and evening/weekend programs available. Postbaccalaureate distance learning degree programs offered (minimal on-campus study). Faculty: 17 full-time (9 women). Students: 23 full-time (17 women), 784 part-time (626 women); includes 35 minority (19 African Americans, 2 Asian Americans, 12 Hispanics, 2 Native Americans), 2 international. 153 applicants, 100% accepted. In 1997, 207 master's awarded. *Entrance requirements:* For master's, minimum GPA of 3.0, teaching certificate. Application deadline: rolling. Application fee: $25. *Expenses:* Tuition $159 per credit hour for state residents; $311 per credit hour for nonresidents. Fees $8.70 per credit hour. *Financial aid:* Federal Work-Study available. Aid available to part-time students. Financial aid applicants required to submit FAFSA. *Faculty research:* Effective schools, foundations of education, children's literature, English education, restructuring of schools. • Dr. Ken Wahl, Interim Dean, 517-790-5648. Application contact: Jean Chipman, Certification Officer, 517-790-4057.

St. Bonaventure University, School of Education, St. Bonaventure, NY 14778-2284. Awards MS, MS Ed, Adv C. Part-time and evening/weekend programs available. Faculty: 18 full-time (8 women), 11 part-time (4 women). Students: 184 full-time (147 women), 247 part-time (162 women); includes 12 minority (7 African Americans, 1 Asian American, 2 Hispanics, 2 Native Americans), 1 international. Average age 25. 255 applicants, 97% accepted. In 1997, 115 master's awarded. *Application deadline:* 8/1 (rolling processing). *Application fee:* $35. *Tuition:* $8100 per year full-time, $450 per credit hour part-time. *Financial aid:* In 1997–98, 8 students received aid, including 5 research assistantships; Federal Work-Study and career-related internships or fieldwork also available. Aid available to part-time students. *Faculty research:*

Learning disabilities, self-concept, reading diagnosis, professional development schools. • Dr. Carol Anne Pierson, Dean, 716-375-2313. E-mail: cpierson@sbu.edu. Application contact: Dean of Graduate Studies, 716-375-2200. Fax: 716-375-7682.

St. Cloud State University, College of Education, St. Cloud, MN 56301-4498. Awards MS, Spt. Accredited by NCATE. Faculty: 113 full-time (46 women), 24 part-time (10 women). Students: 230 full-time (164 women), 257 part-time (164 women). In 1997, 219 master's, 3 Spts awarded. *Degree requirements:* For master's, thesis or alternative required, foreign language not required; for Spt, thesis, field study required, foreign language not required. *Entrance requirements:* For master's, GRE General Test, minimum GPA of 2.75; for Spt, GRE General Test, minimum GPA of 3.25. Application fee: $20 ($100 for international students). *Expenses:* Tuition $128 per credit for state residents; $203 per credit for nonresidents. Fees $16.32 per credit. *Financial aid:* In 1997–98, 83 graduate assistantships were awarded; Federal Work-Study and career-related internships or fieldwork also available. Financial aid application deadline: 3/1. • Dr. Joane McKay, Dean, 320-255-3023. Application contact: Ann Anderson, Graduate Studies Office, 320-255-2113. Fax: 320-654-5371. E-mail: anna@grad.stcloud.msus.edu.

St. Edward's University, School of Education, Austin, TX 78704-6489. Offers program in human services (MA). Part-time and evening/weekend programs available. Faculty: 7 full-time (0 women), 12 part-time (6 women). Students: 37 full-time (32 women), 137 part-time (106 women); includes 30 minority (10 African Americans, 20 Hispanics), 3 international. Average age 36. 88 applicants, 84% accepted. In 1997, 39 degrees awarded. *Average time to degree:* master's–1.5 years full-time, 2.7 years part-time. *Entrance requirements:* GRE General Test (minimum combined score of 1400 on three sections), TOEFL (minimum score 500), minimum GPA of 2.75. Application deadline: 8/1 (priority date; rolling processing; 12/1 for spring admission). Application fee: $25. *Financial aid:* Scholarships, institutionally sponsored loans, and career-related internships or fieldwork available. Aid available to part-time students. Financial aid application deadline: 3/1; applicants required to submit FAFSA. *Faculty research:* Utilization of statistics for managerial decision making, budget and analysis. • Dr. J. Frank Smith, Dean, 512-448-8555. Application contact: Tom Evans, Director of Graduate Admissions, 512-448-8600. Fax: 512-448-8492. E-mail: seu.grad@admin.stedwards.edu.

Saint Francis College, Program in Education, Loretto, PA 15940-0600. Offers leadership (M Ed). Part-time and evening/weekend programs available. Faculty: 2 full-time (both women), 14 part-time (5 women). Students: 131 (94 women); includes 125 minority (all Hispanics). Average age 32. In 1997, 25 degrees awarded. *Degree requirements:* Comprehensive exam required, thesis optional, foreign language not required. *Entrance requirements:* Minimum undergraduate QPA of 2.5. Application deadline: rolling. Application fee: $25. *Financial aid:* Graduate assistantships available. Aid available to part-time students. • Dr. Elizabeth Gensante, Department Chair, 814-472-3058. Fax: 814-472-3864. E-mail: egensante@sfcpa.edu.

St. Francis Xavier University, Programs in Education, Antigonish, NS B2G 2W5, Canada. Awards M Ed, Diploma. Diploma new for fall 1998. Part-time programs available. Postbaccalaureate distance learning degree programs offered (minimal on-campus study). Faculty: 14 part-time (6 women), 4 FTE. Students: 126 part-time (82 women). 130 applicants, 97% accepted. In 1997, 36 master's awarded. *Degree requirements:* For master's, thesis required, foreign language not required. *Average time to degree:* master's–3 years part-time. *Application deadline:* 4/15 (priority date; rolling processing; 2/15 for spring admission). *Application fee:* $30. *Expenses:* Tuition $3965 per year full-time, $850 per course part-time for Canadian residents; $6965 per year full-time, $1450 per course part-time for nonresidents. Fees $123 per year. *Faculty research:* Educational administration, diverse cultures, technology in education. • Dr. Jeff Orr, Chair, 902-867-2214. Fax: 902-867-3887. E-mail: jorr@stfx.ca.

St. John's University, School of Education and Human Services, Jamaica, NY 11439. Awards MS Ed, Ed D, PD. Part-time and evening/weekend programs available. Faculty: 29 full-time (12 women), 50 part-time (27 women). Students: 116 full-time (92 women), 853 part-time (705 women); includes 147 minority (57 African Americans, 11 Asian Americans, 73 Hispanics, 6 Native Americans), 20 international. Average age 32. 561 applicants, 83% accepted. In 1997, 263 master's, 13 doctorates, 29 PDs awarded. *Degree requirements:* For doctorate, 1 foreign language, dissertation. *Entrance requirements:* For doctorate, GRE General Test (minimum combined score of 1100). Application deadline: 6/1 (rolling processing; 10/1 for spring admission). Application fee: $40. *Expenses:* Tuition $525 per credit. Fees $150 per year. *Financial aid:* In 1997–98, 3 fellowships (all to first-year students) averaging $1,111 per month, 2 teaching assistantships (both to first-year students) averaging $833 per month, 11 administrative assistantships (5 to first-year students) averaging $444 per month were awarded; full tuition waivers, Federal Work-Study, and career-related internships or fieldwork also available. Aid available to part-time students. Financial aid application deadline: 3/1; applicants required to submit FAFSA. *Faculty research:* Bilingual education, learning disabilities, counseling special populations, organizational theory, school law. • Dr. Jerrold Ross, Dean, 718-990-1305. Fax: 718-990-6096. Application contact: Shamus J. McGrenra, TOR, Associate Director, Graduate Admissions, 718-990-6107. Fax: 718-990-5736. E-mail: mcgrenrs@stjohns.edu.

Saint Joseph College, Field of Education and Counseling, West Hartford, CT 06117-2700. Offers programs in counseling (MA, Certificate), including counseling (MA, Certificate), marriage and family therapy (MA); education (MA), including early childhood education/special education, elementary education, secondary education; special education (MA), including early childhood education/special education, special education, special education/counseling. Faculty: 11 full-time (9 women), 24 part-time (18 women). Students: 536 (470 women); includes 13 minority (7 African Americans, 2 Asian Americans, 4 Hispanics). Average age 27. In 1997, 150 master's, 2 Certificates awarded. *Degree requirements:* For master's, thesis or alternative required, foreign language not required. *Application deadline:* 8/29 (rolling processing). *Application fee:* $25. *Tuition:* $395 per credit. *Financial aid:* Application deadline 8/31. • Dr. Gerard Thibodeau, Co-Chair, Education Department, 860-232-4571 Ext. 331.

St. Joseph's College, Suffolk Campus, Infant/Toddler Therapeutic Education Major, Patchogue, NY 11772-2399. Awards MA. Faculty: 6 full-time (all women), 6 part-time (5 women). Students: 43 part-time (all women). Average age 31. 42 applicants, 60% accepted. *Degree requirements:* Thesis. *Entrance requirements:* Minimum undergraduate GPA of 3.0, previous course work in child study and special education. Application deadline: 8/15 (priority date; rolling processing). Application fee: $25. *Expenses:* Tuition $360 per credit. Fees $304 per year. • Sr. Frances Solano Carmody, Co-Director, 516-447-3307. Application contact: Marion E. Salgado, Director of Admissions, 516-447-3219. Fax: 516-447-1734.

Saint Joseph's University, Department of Education, Philadelphia, PA 19131-1395. Offers programs in chemistry education (MS), education (MS, Certificate), mathematics education (MS), professional education (MS), reading (MS), secondary education (MS), special education (MS), training and development (MS). Part-time and evening/weekend programs available. *Entrance requirements:* For Certificate, TOEFL. Application deadline: 7/15. Application fee: $30. *Tuition:* $510 per credit hour. *Financial aid:* Fellowships, research assistantships, Federal Work-Study, and career-related internships or fieldwork available. Aid available to part-time students. • Dr. Mary DeKonty Applegate, Director, 610-660-1583.

St. Lawrence University, Department of Education, Canton, NY 13617-1455. Offers programs in counseling and human development (M Ed, CAS), education (Certificate), educational administration (M Ed, CAS), general studies (M Ed). Part-time and evening/weekend programs available. Faculty: 5 full-time (1 woman), 21 part-time (10 women), 8.5 FTE. Students: 28 full-time, 39 part-time. *Degree requirements:* For master's, thesis optional, foreign language not required. *Entrance requirements:* For master's, GRE General Test. Application deadline: rolling. Application fee: $0. *Expenses:* Tuition $460 per credit hour. Fees $35 per year. *Financial aid:* In 1997–98, 3 research assistantships (2 to first-year students) totaling $30,000, 1 teaching assistantship (to a first-year student) totaling $10,000 were awarded; Federal Work-Study and career-related internships or fieldwork also available. Aid available to part-time students. *Faculty research:* Defense mechanisms, conflict negotiations and mediation, teacher educaton policy. • Dr. James Shuman, Chair, 315-229-5847. Fax: 315-229-7423.

Saint Leo College, Leadership Studies and Education Program, Saint Leo, FL 33574-2008. Awards M Ed. Part-time and evening/weekend programs available. Faculty: 5 full-time (3 women), 6 part-time (4 women). Students: 33 full-time (20 women), 35 part-time (25 women); includes 7 minority (5 African Americans, 2 Hispanics), 1 international. Average age 36. 38 applicants, 95% accepted. *Degree requirements:* Portfolio required, foreign language and thesis not required. *Entrance requirements:* GRE General Test or MAT. Application deadline: rolling. Application fee: $45. *Tuition:* $165 per credit hour. *Financial aid:* Available to part-time students. Financial aid applicants required to submit FAFSA. • Dr. Charles Hale, Director of Graduate Studies in Education, 352-588-8309. Fax: 352-588-8861. E-mail: medprog@saintleo.edu. Application contact: Gary Bracken, Dean of Admissions and Financial Aid, 352-588-8283. Fax: 352-588-8257. E-mail: admissns@saintleo.edu.

Saint Louis University, Institute for Leadership and Public Service, Programs in Education, St. Louis, MO 63103-2097. Offerings in counseling and family therapy (MA, PhD), including counseling and family therapy (PhD), human development counseling (MA), school counseling (MA); educational studies (MA, Ed D, PhD), including curriculum and instruction (MA, Ed D, PhD), foundations (MA, Ed D, PhD), special education (MA); leadership and higher education (MA, Ed D, PhD, Ed S), including educational administration, higher education. Accredited by NCATE. Faculty: 22 full-time (11 women), 65 part-time (40 women). Students: 35 full-time (28 women), 402 part-time (264 women); includes 94 minority (83 African Americans, 5 Asian Americans, 3 Hispanics, 3 Native Americans), 7 international. 124 applicants, 56% accepted. In 1997, 26 master's, 61 doctorates, 5 Ed Ss awarded. *Degree requirements:* For master's, comprehensive oral exam required, foreign language and thesis not required; for doctorate, dissertation, preliminary oral and written exams. *Entrance requirements:* For master's, GRE General Test or MAT; for doctorate and Ed S, GRE General Test. Application deadline: (11/1 for spring admission). Application fee: $40. *Tuition:* $542 per credit hour. *Financial aid:* In 1997–98, 1 fellowship, 3 research assistantships, 4 teaching assistantships, 7 assistantships were awarded. Financial aid application deadline: 4/1. *Faculty research:* Legal issues in higher education, effective domain of college students/diversity. • Dr. William Rebore, Associate Director of the Institute, 314-977-2510. Application contact: Dr. Marcia Buresch, Assistant Dean of the Graduate School, 314-977-2240. Fax: 314-977-3943.

Saint Martin's College, Graduate Programs, Department of Education, Lacey, WA 98503-7500. Offers programs in computers in education (M Ed), counseling and guidance (M Ed), instruction (M Ed), reading (M Ed), special education (M Ed), teaching (MIT). Faculty: 8 full-time (3 women), 5 part-time (2 women). Students: 32 full-time (22 women), 39 part-time (27 women); includes 7 minority (4 African Americans, 2 Hispanics, 1 Native American). Average age 36. 20 applicants, 95% accepted. In 1997, 12 degrees awarded (100% found work related to degree). *Degree requirements:* Project required, foreign language and thesis not required. *Entrance requirements:* GRE General Test or MAT. Application deadline: 7/1 (priority date; rolling processing; 12/1 for spring admission). Application fee: $25. *Financial aid:* Federal Work-Study, institutionally sponsored loans, and career-related internships or fieldwork available. Aid available to part-time students. Financial aid application deadline: 3/1. *Faculty research:* Reader's theatre and reader/writer workshops, curriculum and assessment integration, Native American councils. • Dr. Paul Nelson, Director, 360-438-4529. Application contact: Michelle Roman, Administrative Assistant, 360-438-4333.

Saint Mary College, Graduate Programs, Program in Education, Leavenworth, KS 66048-5082. Awards MA. Accredited by NCATE. *Degree requirements:* Thesis required, foreign language not required. *Average time to degree:* master's–1 year full-time, 2 years part-time. *Application deadline:* rolling. *Application fee:* $20. • Dr. Sandra Van Hoose, Vice President for Academic Affairs and Graduate Dean, Graduate Programs, 913-798-6115. Fax: 913-798-6297.

Saint Mary's College of California, School of Education, Moraga, CA 94575. Awards MA, M Ed. Part-time and evening/weekend programs available. Faculty: 22 full-time (18 women), 84 part-time (61 women), 34 FTE. Students: 302 full-time (238 women), 323 part-time (296 women); includes 84 minority (16 African Americans, 16 Asian Americans, 48 Hispanics, 4 Native Americans), 11 international. Average age 31. 160 applicants, 94% accepted. In 1997, 73 degrees awarded (100% found work related to degree). *Degree requirements:* Thesis or alternative required, foreign language not required. *Average time to degree:* master's–2 years part-time. *Entrance requirements:* Interview, minimum GPA of 3.0. Application deadline: rolling. Application fee: $50. *Tuition:* $1319 per course. *Financial aid:* Partial tuition waivers and career-related internships or fieldwork available. Aid available to part-time students. Financial aid application deadline: 2/15. *Faculty research:* Teacher effectiveness, school-based management, multicultural teaching, language and literacy development. Total annual research expenditures: $100,000. • Dr. Fannie Preston, Dean, 925-631-4700. E-mail: fpreston@stmarys-ca.edu. Application contact: Dr. Victoria Courtney, Pre-admissions Adviser, 925-631-4700. Fax: 925-376-8379. E-mail: tory@silcon.com.

Saint Mary's University of Minnesota, Program in Education, Minneapolis, MN 55404. Awards MA. Part-time and evening/weekend programs available. *Degree requirements:* Colloquium, summary paper required, foreign language and thesis not required. *Entrance requirements:* Interview, minimum GPA of 2.75. Application deadline: rolling. Application fee: $20.

St. Mary's University of San Antonio, Department of Education, San Antonio, TX 78228-8507. Offers programs in Catholic school leadership (MA), educational leadership (MA), reading (MA). *Entrance requirements:* GRE General Test. Application deadline: 8/1. Application fee: $15. *Expenses:* Tuition $383 per credit hour (minimum). Fees $217 per year full-time, $58 per semester part-time.

Saint Michael's College, Program in Education, Colchester, VT 05439. Offers administration (M Ed, CAGS), curriculum and instruction (M Ed, CAGS), integrating the arts into education (M Ed), reading (M Ed), self designed (M Ed), special education (M Ed, CAGS), technology (M Ed). Part-time and evening/weekend programs available. Faculty: 5 full-time (4 women), 70 part-time (54 women). Students: 39 full-time (32 women), 313 part-time (242 women); includes 5 minority (3 African Americans, 1 Hispanic, 1 Native American), 3 international. Average age 30. 87 applicants, 86% accepted. In 1997, 31 master's awarded. *Degree requirements:* For master's, computer language, thesis required, foreign language not required. *Entrance requirements:* For master's, minimum GPA of 2.8. Application deadline: rolling. Application fee: $25. *Financial aid:* In 1997–98, 1 fellowship (to a first-year student) was awarded. *Faculty research:* Integrative curriculum, moral and spiritual dimensions of education, learning styles, multiple intelligences. • Dr. Aostre Johnson, Director, 802-654-2436. Fax: 802-654-2664.

St. Norbert College, Program in Adaptive Education and Assistive Technology, De Pere, WI 54115-2099. Awards MS. Part-time programs available. Faculty: 2 full-time (1 woman), 27 part-time (22 women), 16 FTE. Students: 25 part-time (21 women); includes 1 minority (Hispanic). Average age 35. 12 applicants, 42% accepted. In 1997, 3 degrees awarded. *Degree requirements:* Thesis, research project required, foreign language not required. *Entrance requirements:* Minimum GPA of 3.25, 1 year of teaching/professional experience. Application deadline: 7/1 (priority date; rolling processing). *Tuition:* $14,989 per year. *Financial aid:* In 1997–98, 6 students received aid, including teaching assistantships totaling $5,000; partial tuition waivers and career-related internships or fieldwork also available. Aid available to part-time students. *Faculty research:* Assistive technology applications, adaptive art education. • Charles Peterson, Director, 920-403-3076. Fax: 920-403-4057.

Saint Peter's College, Graduate Programs in Education, 2641 Kennedy Boulevard, Jersey City, NJ 07306-5997. Offerings in administration and supervision (MA); reading specialist (MA); teaching (MA, Certificate), including elementary teacher (Certificate), supervisor of instruction (Certificate), teaching (MA); urban education (MA). Part-time and evening/weekend

Directory: Education—General

Saint Peter's College (continued)
programs available. Faculty: 5 full-time (1 woman), 18 part-time (7 women). Students: 25 full-time (11 women), 149 part-time (97 women); includes 28 minority (15 African Americans, 3 Asian Americans, 10 Hispanics), 1 international. Average age 32. 136 applicants, 96% accepted. In 1997, 62 master's awarded. *Degree requirements:* For master's, departmental qualifying exam required, thesis not required. *Entrance requirements:* For master's, GRE or MAT (minimum score 40). Application deadline: 8/1 (priority date; rolling processing). Application fee: $20. *Tuition:* $516 per credit. *Financial aid:* Career-related internships or fieldwork available. Aid available to part-time students. Financial aid application deadline: 7/1. • Dr. Joseph McLaughlin, Director, 201-915-9254. Fax: 201-915-9074. Application contact: Nancy P. Campbell, Associate Vice President for Enrollment, 201-915-9213. Fax: 201-432-5860. E-mail: admissions@spcvxa.spc.edu.

St. Thomas Aquinas College, Division of Teacher Education, Sparkill, NY 10976. Awards MS Ed. Part-time and evening/weekend programs available. Faculty: 6 full-time (4 women), 6 part-time (3 women). Students: 29 full-time (21 women), 89 part-time (77 women); includes 1 minority (Asian American). Average age 28. 75 applicants, 61% accepted. In 1997, 27 degrees awarded. *Degree requirements:* Comprehensive professional portfolio required, thesis not required. *Entrance requirements:* New York State Qualifying Exam, GRE General Test or minimum GPA of 3.0, teaching certificate. Application deadline: 7/31 (priority date; rolling processing; 12/1 for spring admission). Application fee: $35. Electronic applications accepted. *Expenses:* Tuition $390 per credit. Fees $10 per year. *Financial aid:* In 1997–98, 11 students received aid, including 7 assistantships (all to first-year students); partial tuition waivers also available. Aid available to part-time students. Financial aid application deadline: 2/15; applicants required to submit FAFSA. *Faculty research:* Computer applications in education, adolescent special education students. • Dr. Eileen Cunningham, Chairperson, 914-398-4154. Application contact: Joseph L. Chillo, Executive Director of Enrollment Services, 914-398-4100. Fax: 914-398-4224. E-mail: joestacenroll@rockland.net.

St. Thomas University, School of Graduate Studies, Department of Education, Miami, FL 33054-6459. Offers programs in elementary education (MS), guidance and counseling (MS, Certificate). Part-time and evening/weekend programs available. *Degree requirements:* For master's, comprehensive exam required, foreign language and thesis not required. *Average time to degree:* master's–2.5 years full-time. *Entrance requirements:* For master's, TOEFL (minimum score 550), interview, minimum GPA of 3.0 or GRE. Application deadline: 6/15 (priority date; rolling processing; 11/15 for spring admission). Application fee: $30. *Tuition:* $410 per credit.

Saint Xavier University, School of Education, Chicago, IL 60655-3105. Offers programs in curriculum and instruction (MA), education (CAS), educational administration (MA), field-based education (MA), general educational studies (MA), learning disabilities (MA), reading (MA). Part-time and evening/weekend programs available. Faculty: 16 full-time (12 women), 3 part-time (1 woman). Students: 1,287. Average age 33. In 1997, 324 master's awarded. *Degree requirements:* For master's, thesis or project required, thesis optional. *Entrance requirements:* For master's, MAT, minimum GPA of 3.0. Application deadline: 8/15 (priority date; rolling processing). Application fee: $35. *Expenses:* Tuition $435 per hour. Fees $50 per year. *Financial aid:* Career-related internships or fieldwork available. Aid available to part-time students. Financial aid applicants required to submit FAFSA. • Dr. Beverly Gulley, Dean, 773-298-3221. Fax: 773-779-9061. E-mail: gulley@sxu.edu. Application contact: Sr. Evelyn McKenna, Vice President of Enrollment Management, 773-298-3050. Fax: 773-298-3076. E-mail: mckenna@sxu.edu.

Salem College, Department of Education, PO Box 10548, Winston-Salem, NC 27108-0548. Offers programs in early education and leadership (MAT), elementary education (MAT), language and literacy (M Ed), learning disabilities (MAT). Accredited by NCATE. Part-time and evening/weekend programs available. Faculty: 10 full-time (7 women), 2 part-time (both women). Students: 18 full-time (13 women), 97 part-time (90 women); includes 12 minority (10 African Americans, 2 Asian Americans). Average age 33. In 1997, 41 degrees awarded. *Degree requirements:* Practicum (MAT), project (M Ed), oral and written comprehensive exams required, foreign language and thesis not required. *Average time to degree:* master's–1.5 years full-time, 3 years part-time. *Entrance requirements:* GRE, PRAXIS I. Application deadline: rolling. Application fee: $35. *Tuition:* $195 per hour. *Financial aid:* Scholarships, Federal Work-Study available. Aid available to part-time students. Financial aid applicants required to submit FAFSA. *Faculty research:* Educational leadership, elementary school mathematics, whole languages, inclusion, brain-based learning. • Dr. Robin L. Smith, Director of Graduate Studies, 336-721-2656. Fax: 336-721-2683. E-mail: smith@salem.edu.

Salem State College, Department of Education, Salem, MA 01970-5353. Offers programs in chemistry (MAT), early childhood education (M Ed), elementary education (M Ed), English (MAT), English as a second language (MAT), geography (MAT), guidance and counseling (M Ed), history (MAT), library media studies (M Ed), mathematics (MAT), reading (M Ed), school administration (M Ed), special education (M Ed), teaching English as a second language K–9 (M Ed). Accredited by NCATE. MAT (English as a second language) offered jointly with the Department of English. *Application deadline:* rolling. *Application fee:* $25. *Expenses:* Tuition $140 per credit hour for state residents; $230 per credit hour for nonresidents. Fees $20 per credit hour.

Salem–Teikyo University, Department of Education, Salem, WV 26426-0500. Offers programs in elementary education (MA), equestrian education (MA), secondary education (MA). Part-time and evening/weekend programs available. Faculty: 1 (woman) full-time, 6 part-time (1 woman). Students: 2 full-time (1 woman), 73 part-time (59 women). Average age 41. 75 applicants, 100% accepted. In 1997, 60 degrees awarded (100% found work related to degree). *Degree requirements:* Thesis required, foreign language not required. *Average time to degree:* master's–2 years full-time, 5 years part-time. *Entrance requirements:* GRE, MAT, NTE. Application deadline: rolling. Application fee: $25. Electronic applications accepted. *Tuition:* $160 per credit hour. *Financial aid:* Institutionally sponsored loans available. Aid available to part-time students. Financial aid application deadline: 4/15; applicants required to submit FAFSA. *Faculty research:* Improved classroom effectiveness. • Dr. E. G. vander Giessen, Director of Graduate Education, 304-782-5258. Fax: 304-782-5588. E-mail: gabby@salem.wvnet.edu. Application contact: Carolyn Sue Ritter, Director of Admissions, 304-782-5336. Fax: 304-782-5592. E-mail: admiss_new@salem.wvnet.edu.

Salisbury State University, Department of Education, Salisbury, MD 21801-6837. Offers programs in early childhood education (M Ed), educational administration (M Ed), elementary education (M Ed), English (M Ed), geography (M Ed), history (M Ed), mathematics (M Ed), media and technology (M Ed), music (M Ed), psychology (M Ed), reading education (M Ed), science (M Ed), secondary education (M Ed). Part-time and evening/weekend programs available. Faculty: 19 full-time (10 women), 2 part-time (1 woman). Students: 25 full-time (15 women), 150 part-time (120 women); includes 12 minority (6 African Americans, 2 Asian Americans, 3 Hispanics, 1 Native American), 1 international. 23 applicants, 52% accepted. In 1997, 88 degrees awarded. *Application deadline:* 8/1 (priority date; rolling processing; 1/1 for spring admission). *Application fee:* $30. *Expenses:* Tuition $158 per credit hour for state residents; $310 per credit hour for nonresidents. Fees $4 per credit hour. *Financial aid:* Teaching assistantships and career-related internships or fieldwork available. *Faculty research:* Middle-level education, student outcomes. Total annual research expenditures: $75,000. • Dr. Ellen Whitford, Chair, 410-543-6294. E-mail: evwhitford@ssu.edu. Application contact: Phyllis Meyer, Administrative Aide II, 410-543-6281. Fax: 410-548-2593. E-mail: phmeyer@ssu.edu.

Salve Regina University, Program in Education, Newport, RI 02840-4192. Awards M Ed. Program being phased out; applicants no longer accepted. Part-time and evening/weekend programs available. *Expenses:* Tuition $275 per credit hour. Fees $70 per year. *Financial aid:* Federal Work-Study and career-related internships or fieldwork available. Aid available to part-time students. • Dr. Camille Allen, Director, 401-847-6650 Ext. 3153. Fax: 401-847-0372.

Samford University, School of Education, Birmingham, AL 35229-0002. Awards MS Ed, Ed S, M Div/MS Ed. Accredited by NCATE. Part-time programs available. Faculty: 23 full-time (11 women), 42 part-time (28 women). Students: 16 full-time (all women), 61 part-time (53 women); includes 14 minority (all African Americans). Average age 35. 55 applicants, 98% accepted. In 1997, 34 master's awarded. *Entrance requirements:* For master's, GRE or MAT, minimum GPA of 2.75; for Ed S, master's degree, teaching certificate. Application deadline: rolling. Application fee: $25. *Tuition:* $344 per credit hour. *Financial aid:* 77 students received aid; research assistantships, partial tuition waivers, Federal Work-Study, and career-related internships or fieldwork available. Aid available to part-time students. Financial aid applicants required to submit FAFSA. *Faculty research:* School law, the characteristics of beginning teachers, the nature of school reform, school culture, quality improvement in education. • Dr. Ruth Ash, Dean, 205-870-2745. Application contact: Dr. Maurice Persall, Director, Graduate Office, 205-870-2019.

Sam Houston State University, College of Education and Applied Science, Department of Education and Applied Science, Huntsville, TX 77341. Offers programs in curriculum and instruction (MA, M Ed, Ed D, Certificate), including curriculum and instruction (Ed D), elementary education (M Ed, Certificate), secondary education (MA, M Ed, Certificate); educational leadership and counseling (MA, M Ed), including counseling (MA, M Ed), educational administration (M Ed), supervision (M Ed). Accredited by NCATE. Part-time and evening/weekend programs available. Students: 27 full-time (23 women), 294 part-time (224 women); includes 27 minority (10 African Americans, 17 Hispanics), 2 international. In 1997, 108 master's awarded. *Entrance requirements:* For master's, GRE General Test (minimum combined score of 800). Application fee: $15. *Tuition:* $1810 per year full-time, $297 per semester (minimum) part-time for state residents; $6922 per year full-time, $924 per semester (minimum) part-time for nonresidents. *Financial aid:* Teaching assistantships, Federal Work-Study, institutionally sponsored loans, and career-related internships or fieldwork available. Aid available to part-time students. • Dr. Kenneth Craycraft, Chair, 409-294-1101. E-mail: edu_kxc@shsu.edu. Application contact: Dr. Hollis Lowery-Moore, Assistant Dean, 409-294-1103. Fax: 409-294-1102.

San Diego State University, College of Education, San Diego, CA 92182. Awards MA, MS, PhD. Accredited by NCATE. PhD offered jointly with Claremont Graduate University. Part-time and evening/weekend programs available. Students: 262 full-time (166 women), 440 part-time (326 women); includes 220 minority (58 African Americans, 39 Asian Americans, 112 Hispanics, 11 Native Americans), 15 international. Average age 31. In 1997, 333 master's, 10 doctorates awarded. *Degree requirements:* For doctorate, dissertation. *Entrance requirements:* For master's, GRE General Test (minimum combined score of 950), TOEFL (minimum score 550); for doctorate, GRE General Test. Application fee: $55. *Expenses:* Tuition $0 for state residents; $246 per unit for nonresidents. Fees $1932 per year full-time, $1266 per year part-time. *Financial aid:* Fellowships, research assistantships, teaching assistantships, and career-related internships or fieldwork available. Aid available to part-time students. *Faculty research:* Special education, rehabilitation counseling, educational psychology. Total annual research expenditures: $6.68 million. • Ann Morey, Dean, 619-594-1424. Fax: 619-594-7082. E-mail: amorey@sciences.sdsu.edu.

San Francisco State University, College of Education, San Francisco, CA 94132-1722. Awards MA, MS, Ed D, PhD, AC. Accredited by NCATE. Part-time and evening/weekend programs available. *Degree requirements:* For doctorate, dissertation. *Entrance requirements:* For master's, minimum GPA of 2.5 in last 60 units; for doctorate, GRE General Test. Application deadline: 11/30 (priority date; rolling processing). Application fee: $55. *Expenses:* Tuition $0 for state residents; $246 per unit for nonresidents. Fees $1982 per year full-time, $1316 per year part-time.

San Jose State University, College of Education, San Jose, CA 95192-0001. Awards MA, Certificate. Accredited by NCATE. Evening/weekend programs available. Faculty: 152 full-time (63 women), 73 part-time (29 women). Students: 228 full-time (185 women), 327 part-time (251 women); includes 178 minority (29 African Americans, 72 Asian Americans, 76 Hispanics, 1 Native American), 4 international. Average age 36. 388 applicants, 74% accepted. In 1997, 189 master's awarded. *Application deadline:* 6/1 (rolling processing). *Application fee:* $59. *Expenses:* Tuition $0 for state residents; $246 per unit for nonresidents. Fees $2017 per year full-time, $1351 per year part-time. *Financial aid:* Career-related internships or fieldwork available. • Dr. Dolores Escobar, Dean, 408-924-3600.

Santa Clara University, Division of Counseling Psychology and Education, Santa Clara, CA 95053-0001. Awards MA, Certificate. Part-time and evening/weekend programs available. Faculty: 11 full-time (5 women), 21 part-time (13 women). Students: 130 full-time (112 women), 304 part-time (261 women); includes 74 minority (9 African Americans, 41 Asian Americans, 21 Hispanics, 3 Native Americans), 17 international. Average age 35. 200 applicants, 93% accepted. In 1997, 105 master's awarded. *Degree requirements:* For master's, comprehensive exam required, foreign language not required; for Certificate, comprehensive exam required, foreign language and thesis not required. *Entrance requirements:* GRE or MAT, TOEFL, minimum GPA of 3.0. Application deadline: 5/1 (2/1 for spring admission). Application fee: $30. *Financial aid:* Fellowships, teaching assistantships, grants, Federal Work-Study, institutionally sponsored loans, and career-related internships or fieldwork available. Aid available to part-time students. Financial aid application deadline: 2/1. • Dr. Peter A. Facione, Administrator, 408-554-4455. Application contact: Barbara F. Simmons, Assistant to the Dean, 408-554-4355. Fax: 408-554-2392.

Sarah Lawrence College, Program in Art of Teaching, Bronxville, NY 10708. Awards MS Ed. Part-time programs available. *Degree requirements:* Thesis, fieldwork, oral presentation. *Average time to degree:* master's–2 years full-time, 3 years part-time. *Application deadline:* 9/1 (priority date; rolling processing; 12/1 for spring admission). *Application fee:* $45. *Expenses:* Tuition $622 per credit. Fees $290 per year.

Schreiner College, Program in Education, Kerrville, TX 78028-5697. Awards M Ed. Part-time and evening/weekend programs available. Faculty: 2 full-time (1 woman), 1 (woman) part-time. Students: 28 full-time (17 women); includes 4 minority (3 African Americans, 1 Hispanic). *Entrance requirements:* GRE General Test (minimum combined score of 900), departmental exam, minimum GPA of 3.0, interview. Application deadline: 8/12 (12/1 for spring admission). Application fee: $20. Electronic applications accepted. • Dr. Thomas J. Purifoy, Director of Graduate Education Program, 830-896-5411 Ext. 225. Fax: 830-792-7382. E-mail: tpurifoy@schreiner.edu.

Seattle Pacific University, School of Education, Seattle, WA 98119-1997. Awards MAT, M Ed, Ed D. Accredited by NCATE. Part-time and evening/weekend programs available. Faculty: 20 full-time (8 women), 16 part-time (8 women). Students: 33 full-time (24 women), 209 part-time (145 women); includes 19 minority (5 African Americans, 10 Asian Americans, 4 Hispanics), 15 international. Average age 35. In 1997, 66 master's awarded. *Average time to degree:* master's–2 years full-time, 4 years part-time. *Entrance requirements:* For master's, MAT (minimum score 35) or GRE General Test (minimum score 300 on verbal section, 350 on quantitative, 950 combined), minimum GPA of 3.0; for doctorate, MAT, GRE. *Tuition:* $274 per credit. *Financial aid:* In 1997–98, 4 research assistantships were awarded; institutionally sponsored loans and career-related internships or fieldwork also available. • Dr. Ginger MacDonald, Director of Graduate Studies, 206-281-2707. E-mail: gmac@spu.edu. Application contact: Roger M. Long, Graduate Enrollment Manager, 206-281-2378. Fax: 206-281-2756. E-mail: rmlong@spu.edu.

Seattle University, School of Education, Seattle, WA 98122. Awards MA, M Ed, MIT, Ed D, Ed S. Accredited by NCATE. Part-time and evening/weekend programs available. Faculty: 29 full-time (15 women). Students: 166 full-time (127 women), 386 part-time (306 women); includes 71 minority (18 African Americans, 33 Asian Americans, 12 Hispanics, 8 Native Americans), 11 international. Average age 35. 402 applicants, 47% accepted. In 1997, 136 master's, 17 doctorates, 4 Ed Ss awarded. *Degree requirements:* For master's, comprehensive exam required, foreign language not required; for doctorate, dissertation, comprehensive exam required, foreign language not required; for Ed S, comprehensive exam required, foreign language and thesis not required. *Entrance requirements:* For doctorate, GRE General Test, MAT, interview, MA, minimum GPA of 3.5, 3 years of related experience. Application fee: $55. *Expenses:* Tuition $339 per credit hour (minimum). Fees $70 per year. *Financial aid:* Assistantships, Federal Work-Study, and career-related internships or fieldwork available. Aid available to part-time students. Financial aid applicants required to submit FAFSA. *Faculty research:* Service learning, learning and technology, assesment models of professional education, alternative delivery systems. • Dr. Sue Schmitt, Dean, 206-296-5760. E-mail: sschmitt@seattleu.edu. Application contact: Michael McKeon, Dean of Admissions, 206-296-5900. Fax: 206-296-5656. E-mail: admissions@seattleu.edu.

Seton Hall University, College of Education and Human Services, South Orange, NJ 07079-2697. Awards MA, MS, Ed D, Exec Ed D, PhD, Psy D, Ed S. Part-time and evening/weekend programs available. Faculty: 35 full-time. Students: 525. In 1997, 130 master's, 36 doctorates, 30 Ed Ss awarded. *Degree requirements:* For master's, comprehensive exam; for doctorate, dissertation, comprehensive exam, internship required, foreign language not required. *Average time to degree:* master's–2 years full-time, 5 years part-time; doctorate–5 years full-time, 8 years part-time; other advanced degree–3 years full-time, 5 years part-time. *Entrance requirements:* For doctorate, interview. Application fee: $50. Electronic applications accepted. *Expenses:* Tuition $500 per credit. Fees $610 per year full-time, $185 per semester part-time. *Financial aid:* 13 students received aid; fellowships, research assistantships, institutionally sponsored loans, and career-related internships or fieldwork available. Financial aid application deadline: 2/1. *Faculty research:* Information technology and classrooms, adult development including career family systems, therapy effectiveness, management systems, principal effectiveness. Total annual research expenditures: $30,000. • Dr. Sylvester Kohut Jr., Dean, 973-761-9025. E-mail: kohutsyl@shu.edu. Application contact: Rev. Kevin M. Handbury, Associate Dean, 973-761-9668. Fax: 973-275-2187. E-mail: hanburke@shu.edu.

Shenandoah University, School of Arts and Sciences, 1460 University Drive, Winchester, VA 22601-5195. Offers programs in computer education (MSC), education (MSE). Part-time and evening/weekend programs available. Postbaccalaureate distance learning degree programs offered (minimal on-campus study). Faculty: 7 full-time (2 women), 4 part-time (2 women). Students: 15 full-time (11 women), 88 part-time (63 women); includes 3 minority (2 African Americans, 1 Asian American), 17 international. Average age 35. 86 applicants, 92% accepted. In 1997, 91 degrees awarded. *Degree requirements:* Computer language (for some programs), thesis (for some programs), internship, practicum required, foreign language not required. *Application deadline:* 7/1 (priority date; rolling processing). *Application fee:* $30. Electronic applications accepted. *Tuition:* $470 per credit. *Financial aid:* In 1997–98, 56 students received aid, including 1 graduate assistantship (to a first-year student) averaging $720 per month and totaling $8,640; career-related internships or fieldwork also available. Aid available to part-time students. Financial aid application deadline: 3/15; applicants required to submit FAFSA. *Faculty research:* Classroom teaching technique, children's literature, Civil War history, eighteenth- and nineteenth-century American local history, religion and society. • Dr. Catherine Tisinger, Dean, 540-665-4587. Fax: 540-665-4644. E-mail: ctisinge@su.edu. Application contact: Michael Carpenter, Director of Admissions, 540-665-4581. Fax: 540-665-4627. E-mail: admit@su.edu.

Shippensburg University of Pennsylvania, College of Education and Human Services, Shippensburg, PA 17257-2299. Awards M Ed, MS. Accredited by NCATE. Part-time programs available. Faculty: 37 full-time (16 women), 16 part-time (10 women). Students: 117 full-time (87 women), 391 part-time (259 women); includes 29 minority (14 African Americans, 1 Asian American, 6 Hispanics, 8 Native Americans), 5 international. Average age 32. In 1997, 160 degrees awarded. *Application deadline:* rolling. *Application fee:* $25. Electronic applications accepted. *Expenses:* Tuition $3468 per year full-time, $193 per credit hour part-time for state residents; $6236 per year full-time, $346 per credit hour part-time for nonresidents. Fees $678 per year full-time, $108 per semester (minimum) part-time. *Financial aid:* In 1997–98, 93 graduate assistantships were awarded. Aid available to part-time students. Financial aid application deadline: 3/1. • Dr. Robert B. Bartos, Dean, School of Graduate Studies and Research, 717-532-1373. Application contact: A. Renee Mims, Assistant Dean, 717-532-1213.

Siena Heights University, Program in Teacher Education, Adrian, MI 49221-1796. Offers curriculum and instruction (MA); early childhood education (MA), including Montessori education; elementary education (MA), including elementary education/reading; middle school education (MA); secondary education (MA), including secondary education/reading. Part-time programs available. *Degree requirements:* Computer language, thesis, presentation required, foreign language not required. *Entrance requirements:* Minimum GPA of 3.0, interview. Application deadline: 7/1 (priority date; rolling processing; 12/1 for spring admission). Application fee: $25. *Faculty research:* Teaching/learning styles, outcomes-based teaching, multiple intelligences, assessment.

Sierra Nevada College, Program in Teacher Education, Incline Village, NV 89450-4269. Offers programs in elementary education (Certificate), secondary education (Certificate). Faculty: 4 full-time, 17 part-time. Students: 221. *Entrance requirements:* Minimum GPA of 2.75. Application deadline: rolling. Application fee: $35. *Expenses:* Tuition $360 per unit full-time, $250 per unit (minimum) part-time. Fees $50 per year. • Dr. Skip Wenda, Director, 800-332-8666.

Silver Lake College, Graduate Studies, Program in Education, Manitowoc, WI 54220-9319. Awards MA. Part-time and evening/weekend programs available. Postbaccalaureate distance learning degree programs offered (no on-campus study). Faculty: 1 (woman) full-time, 27 part-time (13 women), 9 FTE. Students: 2 full-time (1 woman), 184 part-time (144 women). Average age 35. In 1997, 70 degrees awarded. *Degree requirements:* Thesis or alternative, comprehensive exam required, foreign language not required. *Average time to degree:* master's–2.5 years part-time. *Entrance requirements:* Interview, minimum undergraduate GPA of 3.0, video of performance. Application deadline: rolling. Application fee: $30. *Expenses:* Tuition $4140 per year full-time, $230 per credit (minimum) part-time. Fees $100 per year. *Financial aid:* Federal Work-Study, institutionally sponsored loans, and career-related internships or fieldwork available. Aid available to part-time students. Financial aid application deadline: 4/15; applicants required to submit FAFSA. *Faculty research:* Correspondence between expectations of cooperating teachers and student teachers. • Application contact: Sandra Schwartz, Director of Admissions, 920-684-5955. Fax: 920-684-7082.

Simmons College, Department of Education, Boston, MA 02115. Awards MAT, MS Ed, MAT/MA, MAT/MS, MS Ed/MS. Programs in English as a second language (MAT); middle school and high school teaching (MAT); special education (MS Ed), including inclusion specialist, intensive special needs, special needs; teacher preparation (MAT), including elementary school education. MS Ed/MS offered jointly with the Graduate School of Library and Information Science. Postbaccalaureate distance learning degree programs offered. Faculty: 18 full-time (13 women), 49 part-time (34 women). Students: 205 full-time (173 women), 416 part-time (326 women); includes 33 minority (18 African Americans, 6 Asian Americans, 8 Hispanics, 1 Native American), 5 international. Average age 26. 344 applicants, 85% accepted. In 1997, 225 degrees awarded. *Degree requirements:* Student teaching experience. *Entrance requirements:* Interview. Application deadline: 8/1 (priority date; rolling processing; 12/15 for spring admission). Application fee: $35. *Expenses:* Tuition $587 per credit hour. Fees $20 per year. *Financial aid:* In 1997–98, 84 students received aid, including 6 teaching assistantships (all to first-year students) totaling $6,648; partial tuition waivers, Federal Work-Study, institutionally sponsored loans, and career-related internships or fieldwork also available. Aid available to part-time students. Financial aid application deadline: 3/1; applicants required to submit FAFSA. • Helen Guttentag, Chairperson, 617-521-2553. Fax: 617-521-3199. Application contact: Director, Graduate Studies Admission, 617-521-2910. Fax: 617-521-3058. E-mail: gsa@simmons.edu.

Announcement: Dual Master's Degree Program with Master of Arts in Teaching. Students enroll in the Simmons MAT Internship Program leading to certification and select a 2nd degree program to complement their MAT study. Second master's degrees include MA in children's literature, English, gender/cultural studies, French, or Spanish and MS in communications management.

Simon Fraser University, Faculty of Education, Burnaby, BC V5A 1S6, Canada. Awards MA, M Ed, M Sc, PhD. Faculty: 41 full-time (19 women). Students: 379 full-time (263 women), 153 part-time (118 women). Average age 40. In 1997, 129 master's, 3 doctorates awarded. *Degree requirements:* For master's, project or thesis required, foreign language not required; for doctorate, dissertation. *Entrance requirements:* For master's, TOEFL (minimum score 570), TWE (minimum score 5), or International English Language Test (minimum score 7.5), minimum GPA of 3.0; for doctorate, GRE, TOEFL (minimum score 570), TWE (minimum score 5) or International English Language Test (minimum score 7.5), master's degree or exceptional record in a bachelor's degree, minimum GPA of 3.5. Application fee: $55. *Expenses:* Tuition $768 per trimester. Fees $207 per year full-time, $61 per trimester part-time. *Financial aid:* In 1997–98, 16 fellowships were awarded; research assistantships, teaching assistantships also available. *Faculty research:* Drama education, gender equity, children's literature, theory and curriculum development, counseling psychology. • S. Richmond, Director, Graduate Programs, 604-291-4787. Application contact: Graduate Secretary, 604-291-4787. Fax: 604-291-3203.

Sinte Gleska University, Graduate Education Program, Rosebud, SD 57570-0490. Offers elementary education (M Ed). Part-time and evening/weekend programs available. Faculty: 1 full-time (0 women), 4 part-time (3 women). Students: 30 part-time (28 women); includes 20 minority (all Native Americans). Average age 35. In 1997, 4 degrees awarded (100% found work related to degree). *Degree requirements:* Thesis required, foreign language not required. *Average time to degree:* master's–2 years full-time. *Entrance requirements:* Minimum GPA of 2.5, 2 years experience in elementary education. Application deadline: rolling. Application fee: $0. *Faculty research:* American Indian graduate education teaching of Native American students. • Dr. Archie Beauvais, Chair, 605-747-2263. Fax: 605-747-2098. E-mail: abbeau@rosebud.sinte.edu.

Slippery Rock University of Pennsylvania, College of Education, Slippery Rock, PA 16057. Awards MA, M Ed. Accredited by NCATE. Part-time and evening/weekend programs available. *Degree requirements:* Comprehensive exams. *Entrance requirements:* GRE, minimum GPA of 2.75. Application deadline: 7/1 (priority date; rolling processing; 11/1 for spring admission). Application fee: $25. *Tuition:* $4484 per year full-time, $247 per credit part-time for state residents; $7667 per year full-time, $423 per credit part-time for nonresidents.

Smith College, Department of Education and Child Study, Northampton, MA 01063. Offers programs in education (MA); education and child study (MA); education of the deaf (MA, MED); elementary education (Ed M), including elementary education, preschool education; secondary education (MAT), including art education, biological sciences education, chemistry education, classics education, English education, French education, history education, mathematics education, music education, physics education, Spanish education. Part-time programs available. Faculty: 26 full-time (17 women), 6 part-time (5 women). Students: 40 full-time (36 women), 7 part-time (6 women); includes 1 minority (Asian American), 5 international. Average age 22. 79 applicants, 84% accepted. In 1997, 37 degrees awarded. *Average time to degree:* master's–1 year full-time, 4 years part-time. *Entrance requirements:* GRE General Test or MAT. Application fee: $50. *Tuition:* $21,680 per year full-time, $2720 per course part-time. *Financial aid:* In 1997–98, 6 teaching assistantships (all to first-year students) totaling $53,820, 31 scholarships (28 to first-year students) totaling $442,044 were awarded; fellowships, research assistantships, institutionally sponsored loans also available. Aid available to part-time students. Financial aid application deadline: 1/15; applicants required to submit CSS PROFILE or FAFSA. • Alan Rudnitsky, Chair, 413-585-3261. E-mail: arudnits@sophia.smith.edu.

Sonoma State University, School of Education, Rohnert Park, CA 94928-3609. Awards MA. Part-time and evening/weekend programs available. Faculty: 20 full-time (10 women), 35 part-time (22 women). Students: 39 full-time (27 women), 80 part-time (73 women); includes 14 minority (4 African Americans, 3 Asian Americans, 7 Hispanics), 2 international. Average age 42. 47 applicants, 79% accepted. In 1997, 24 degrees awarded. *Degree requirements:* Thesis or alternative required, foreign language not required. *Entrance requirements:* Minimum GPA of 2.5. Application fee: $55. *Expenses:* Tuition $0 for state residents; $246 per unit for nonresidents. Fees $2130 per year full-time, $1464 per year part-time. *Financial aid:* Fellowships, Federal Work-Study, and career-related internships or fieldwork available. Aid available to part-time students. Financial aid application deadline: 3/2. • Dr. Phyllis Fernlund, Dean, 707-664-2131. E-mail: phyllis.fernlund@sonoma.edu.

South Carolina State University, School of Education, 300 College Street Northeast, Orangeburg, SC 29117-0001. Awards MAT, M Ed, Ed D, Ed S. Accredited by NCATE. Part-time and evening/weekend programs available. Faculty: 14 full-time (4 women), 13 part-time (7 women). Students: 94 full-time (76 women), 121 part-time (90 women); includes 183 minority (181 African Americans, 1 Asian American, 1 Native American). Average age 34. 215 applicants, 67% accepted. In 1997, 53 master's awarded (100% entered university research/teaching); 15 doctorates awarded (100% found work related to degree); 13 Ed Ss awarded. *Degree requirements:* For doctorate, computer language, dissertation, comprehensive and preliminary exams, internship, practicum required, foreign language not required; for Ed S, computer language, thesis required, foreign language not required. *Entrance requirements:* For master's, GRE General Test or MAT (minimum score 35), NTE, interview; for doctorate, GRE General Test (minimum combined score of 1000) or MAT (minimum score 50), teaching certificate, teaching experience; for Ed S, GRE General Test (minimum combined score of 950) or MAT (minimum score 37), interview, teaching certificate, teaching experience. Application deadline: 7/15 (priority date; rolling processing; 11/10 for spring admission). Application fee: $25. *Tuition:* $2974 per year full-time, $165 per credit hour part-time. *Financial aid:* Fellowships, research assistantships, Federal Work-Study, institutionally sponsored loans, and career-related internships or fieldwork available. Financial aid application deadline: 6/1. *Faculty research:* Needs of beginning teachers, appropriate knowledge bases for teacher preparation, principals and superintendents, social skills, coping with violence and crime. • Dr. Casimir Kawalski, Dean, 803-536-7133. Application contact: Dr. Gail Joyner-Fleming, Interim Associate Dean and Director, Graduate Teacher Education, 803-536-8824. Fax: 803-536-8492.

South Dakota State University, College of Education and Counseling, Brookings, SD 57007. Awards M Ed, MS. Accredited by NCATE. Part-time programs available. Faculty: 22 full-time (10 women). Students: 40 full-time (30 women), 164 part-time (110 women); includes 19 minority (6 African Americans, 4 Asian Americans, 1 Hispanic, 8 Native Americans). 53 applicants, 100% accepted. In 1997, 124 degrees awarded. *Degree requirements:* Thesis, comprehensive and oral exams required, foreign language not required. *Entrance requirements:* TOEFL (minimum score 500), minimum GPA of 2.75. Application deadline: rolling. Application fee: $15. *Expenses:* Tuition $82 per credit hour for state residents; $242 per credit hour for nonresidents. Fees $37 per credit hour. *Financial aid:* In 1997–98, 1 research assistantship, 3 teaching assistantships, 20 administrative assistantships (2 to first-year students) were awarded; Federal Work-Study also available. • Dr. Dee Hopkins, Dean, 605-688-4321.

Southeastern Louisiana University, College of Education, Hammond, LA 70402. Awards MA, M Ed, MS, Ed S. Accredited by NCATE. Part-time programs available. Faculty: 43 full-time, 36 part-time. Students: 71 full-time (57 women), 251 part-time (223 women); includes 22 minority (16 African Americans, 1 Asian American, 4 Hispanics, 1 Native American). Average age 32. In 1997, 130 master's awarded. *Entrance requirements:* For master's, GRE. Application deadline: 7/15 (priority date; rolling processing; 12/15 for spring admission). Application fee: $10 ($25 for international students). Electronic applications accepted. *Expenses:* Tuition $2010 per year full-time, $287 per semester (minimum) part-time for state residents; $5232 per year full-time, $287 per semester (minimum) part-time for nonresidents. Fees $5 per year. *Financial aid:* Fellowships, research assistantships, teaching assistantships, administrative assistantships, Federal Work-Study, and career-related internships or fieldwork available. Aid available to part-time students. Financial aid application deadline: 5/1; applicants required to submit FAFSA. • Dr. Stephen Ragan, Dean, 504-549-2217. Fax: 504-549-2070. E-mail: sragan@

Directory: Education—General

Southeastern Louisiana University (continued)
selu.edu. Application contact: Stephen C. Soutullo, Registrar and Director of Enrollment Services, 504-549-2066. Fax: 504-549-5632. E-mail: ssoutullo@selu.edu.

Southeastern Oklahoma State University, School of Education, Durant, OK 74701-0609. Offers programs in educational administration (M Ed), elementary education (M Ed), guidance and counseling (MBS), school counseling (M Ed), secondary education (M Ed). Accredited by NCATE. Part-time and evening/weekend programs available. Faculty: 69 full-time (23 women), 3 part-time (0 women), 69.7 FTE. Students: 37 full-time (27 women), 169 part-time (125 women); includes 23 minority (3 African Americans, 1 Hispanic, 19 Native Americans). Average age 36. 60 applicants, 93% accepted. In 1997, 76 degrees awarded. *Degree requirements:* Thesis optional, foreign language not required. *Entrance requirements:* GRE General Test (MBS), minimum GPA of 3.0 in last 60 hours or 2.75 overall. Application deadline: 8/1. *Tuition:* $76 per credit hour for state residents; $178 per credit hour for nonresidents. *Financial aid:* 148 students received aid; Federal Work-Study, institutionally sponsored loans available. Aid available to part-time students. Financial aid application deadline: 6/15. • Dr. Barbara Decker, Dean, 580-924-0121 Ext. 2251. Fax: 580-920-7473.

Southern Adventist University, School of Education, Collegedale, TN 37315-0370. Offers programs in community counseling (MS), education (MS). Faculty: 8 full-time (5 women), 7 part-time (1 woman). Students: 16 full-time (9 women), 12 part-time (5 women); includes 4 minority (all Hispanics). Average age 36. *Degree requirements:* Thesis (for some programs), written comprehensive exam required, foreign language not required. *Entrance requirements:* GRE. Application deadline: rolling. Application fee: $25. *Tuition:* $275 per credit hour. *Financial aid:* Partial tuition waivers available. Aid available to part-time students. Financial aid application deadline: 4/1; applicants required to submit FAFSA. • Dr. Alberto dos Santos, Dean, 423-238-2779. Fax: 423-238-2468. E-mail: adossant@southern.edu.

Southern Arkansas University–Magnolia, Graduate Program in Education, Magnolia, AR 71753. Awards M Ed. Part-time programs available. Faculty: 32 full-time (18 women), 10 part-time (7 women). Students: 14 full-time (9 women), 94 part-time (79 women); includes 22 minority (20 African Americans, 2 Hispanics). Average age 32. 26 applicants, 96% accepted. In 1997, 57 degrees awarded. *Degree requirements:* Comprehensive exam required, foreign language not required. *Entrance requirements:* GRE, minimum GPA of 2.5. Application deadline: 8/15 (rolling processing). Application fee: $0. *Expenses:* Tuition $95 per hour for state residents; $138 per hour for nonresidents. Fees $2 per hour. *Financial aid:* In 1997–98, 25 research assistantships (all to first-year students), 4 teaching assistantships (all to first-year students) were awarded; full tuition waivers and career-related internships or fieldwork also available. Financial aid application deadline: 8/15. • Dr. Danield L. Bernard, Dean, Graduate Studies, 870-235-4055. Fax: 870-235-5035. E-mail: dlbernard@mail.saumag.edu.

Southern California College, Graduate Department of Education, Costa Mesa, CA 92626-6597. Awards MA. Part-time and evening/weekend programs available. Faculty: 2 full-time (1 woman), 6 part-time (3 women). Students: 46 full-time (27 women); includes 5 minority (1 African American, 2 Asian Americans, 2 Hispanics), 1 international. Average age 25. 40 applicants, 85% accepted. *Entrance requirements:* California Basic Educational Skills Test, PRAXIS, minimum GPA of 3.0. Application deadline: 8/30 (priority date; rolling processing; 11/30 for spring admission). Application fee: $30. *Expenses:* Tuition $8320 per year full-time, $365 per unit part-time. Fees $145 per year. *Financial aid:* In 1997–98, 32 students received aid, including 1 scholarship totaling $1,500. Aid available to part-time students. Financial aid application deadline: 3/1; applicants required to submit FAFSA. • Dr. Magali Gil, Director of Graduate Program in Education, 714-556-3610 Ext. 442. Application contact: Deeanna Routon, Coordinator, 714-556-3610 Ext. 310. Fax: 714-966-5495.

See in-depth description on page 777.

Southern Connecticut State University, School of Education, New Haven, CT 06515-1355. Awards MS, MS Ed, Diploma. Part-time programs available. Faculty: 56 full-time, 31 part-time. *Entrance requirements:* For master's, interview; for Diploma, master's degree. Application fee: $40. *Expenses:* Tuition $2632 per year full-time, $188 per credit part-time for state residents; $7200 per year full-time, $188 per credit part-time for nonresidents. Fees $1806 per year full-time, $45 per semester part-time for state residents; $2703 per year full-time, $45 per semester part-time for nonresidents. *Financial aid:* Research assistantships, teaching assistantships, and career-related internships or fieldwork available. • Dr. Rodney Lane, Dean, 203-392-5900.

Southern Illinois University at Carbondale, College of Education, Carbondale, IL 62901-6806. Awards MS, MS Ed, MSW, PhD, Rh D, JD/MSW. Accredited by NCATE. Part-time programs available. Faculty: 155 full-time (55 women), 30 part-time (17 women). Students: 734 full-time (498 women), 278 part-time (186 women); includes 149 minority (108 African Americans, 17 Asian Americans, 20 Hispanics, 4 Native Americans), 71 international. Average age 34. 542 applicants, 51% accepted. In 1997, 343 master's, 46 doctorates awarded. Terminal master's awarded for partial completion of doctoral program. *Degree requirements:* For doctorate, dissertation. *Entrance requirements:* For master's, TOEFL (minimum score 550), minimum GPA of 2.7; for doctorate, TOEFL (minimum score 550). Application fee: $20. *Expenses:* Tuition $2964 per year full-time, $99 per semester hour part-time for state residents; $8892 per year full-time, $270 per semester hour part-time for nonresidents. Fees $1034 per year full-time, $298 per semester (minimum) part-time. *Financial aid:* In 1997–98, 8 fellowships, 115 research assistantships, 166 teaching assistantships, 113 traineeships, administrative assistantships were awarded; full tuition waivers, Federal Work-Study, institutionally sponsored loans, and career-related internships or fieldwork also available. Aid available to part-time students. *Faculty research:* Safety education, community health, curriculum development, gifted, effective schools. • Nancy Quisenberry, Interim Dean, 618-453-2415.

Southern Illinois University at Edwardsville, School of Education, Edwardsville, IL 62026-0001. Awards MA, MS, MS Ed, Ed D, Ed S. Accredited by NCATE. Part-time programs available. Faculty: 75 full-time (22 women), 17 part-time (13 women). Students: 288 full-time (219 women), 466 part-time (373 women); includes 54 minority (42 African Americans, 5 Asian Americans, 7 Hispanics), 7 international. 432 applicants, 42% accepted. In 1997, 239 master's, 3 doctorates, 10 Ed Ss awarded. *Degree requirements:* For master's, final exam required, foreign language not required; for doctorate, dissertation, final exam required, foreign language not required. *Application deadline:* 7/24. *Application fee:* $25. *Expenses:* Tuition $1716 per year full-time, $95 per credit hour part-time for state residents; $5149 per year full-time, $286 per credit hour part-time for nonresidents. Fees $463 per year full-time, $433 per year part-time. *Financial aid:* In 1997–98, 6 fellowships, 1 research assistantship, 10 teaching assistantships, 82 assistantships were awarded; Federal Work-Study, institutionally sponsored loans, and career-related internships or fieldwork also available. Aid available to part-time students. • Dr. Gary Hull, Dean, 618-692-3350. Application contact: Dr. Mary Polite, Associate Dean, 618-692-2328.

Southern Nazarene University, School of Education, Bethany, OK 73008-2694. Awards MA. Accredited by NCATE. Part-time and evening/weekend programs available. Faculty: 10 full-time (6 women). Students: 51 full-time (28 women), 18 part-time (15 women). Average age 27. In 1997, 11 degrees awarded. *Degree requirements:* Thesis optional, foreign language not required. *Entrance requirements:* MAT, English proficiency exam, minimum GPA of 3.0 in last 60 hours/major, 2.5 overall. Application deadline: 8/1 (priority date; rolling processing). Application fee: $25 ($35 for international students). *Financial aid:* Teaching assistantships and career-related internships or fieldwork available. • Dr. Rex Tullis, Director, 405-491-6317.

Southern Oregon University, School of Social Science, Health and Physical Education, Department of Education, Ashland, OR 97520. Offers programs in elementary education (MA Ed, MS Ed), including classroom teacher, early childhood, handicapped learner, reading, supervision; secondary education (MA Ed, MS Ed), including classroom teacher, handicapped learner, reading, supervision; teaching (MAT). Students: 117 full-time (71 women), 40 part-time (27 women); includes 5 minority (4 Hispanics, 1 Native American). Average age 33. 94 applicants, 77% accepted. In 1997, 42 degrees awarded. *Degree requirements:* Thesis optional. *Entrance requirements:* GRE General Test, minimum GPA of 3.0. Application deadline: 2/1. Application fee: $50. *Tuition:* $5187 per year full-time, $586 per quarter (minimum) part-time for state residents; $9228 per year full-time, $586 per quarter (minimum) part-time for nonresidents. • Dr. Mary-Curtis Gramley, Associate Dean of Education, 541-552-6918.

Southern University and Agricultural and Mechanical College, College of Education, Baton Rouge, LA 70813. Awards MA, M Ed, MS. Accredited by NCATE. Faculty: 25 full-time (8 women), 12 part-time (3 women). Students: 55 full-time (36 women), 208 part-time (154 women); includes 224 minority (all African Americans). Average age 25. 118 applicants, 76% accepted. In 1997, 89 degrees awarded. *Degree requirements:* Thesis optional. *Entrance requirements:* GMAT or GRE General Test, TOEFL. Application deadline: 6/1 (priority date; rolling processing; 11/1 for spring admission). Application fee: $5. *Tuition:* $2226 per year full-time, $267 per semester (minimum) part-time for state residents; $6262 per year full-time, $267 per semester (minimum) part-time for nonresidents. *Financial aid:* Application deadline 4/15. • Dr. Karen Webb, Dean, 504-771-2290.

Southern Utah University, School of Education, Cedar City, UT 84720-2498. Offers programs in elementary education (M Ed), secondary education (M Ed). Part-time programs available. Faculty: 1 full-time (0 women), 18 part-time (3 women). Students: 23 full-time (13 women), 163 part-time (110 women); includes 9 minority (1 Asian American, 5 Hispanics, 3 Native Americans). Average age 33. 57 applicants, 93% accepted. In 1997, 150 degrees awarded. *Degree requirements:* Thesis or alternative required, foreign language not required. *Entrance requirements:* MAT (minimum score 43). Application deadline: 8/1 (rolling processing; 12/1 for spring admission). Application fee: $30. • Dr. Paul Wilford, Director, 435-865-8149.

Southwest Baptist University, School of Graduate Studies, Education Department, 1600 University Avenue, Bolivar, MO 65613-2597. Offers programs in education (MS), educational administration (MS). Part-time and evening/weekend programs available. Faculty: 6 full-time (2 women), 37 part-time (15 women). Students: 201 full-time (163 women), 899 part-time (788 women). Average age 32. 99 applicants, 100% accepted. In 1997, 168 degrees awarded. *Degree requirements:* Thesis required, foreign language not required. *Entrance requirements:* GRE or NTE, interviews, minimum GPA of 2.75. Application deadline: rolling. Application fee: $25. *Tuition:* $123 per credit hour. *Financial aid:* In 1997–98, 5 teaching assistantships (all to first-year students) were awarded; institutionally sponsored loans and career-related internships or fieldwork also available. Aid available to part-time students. Financial aid application deadline: 6/1. *Faculty research:* Critical thinking in the classroom, right brain/left brain. • Dr. Tom Hollis, Director, 417-326-1700. E-mail: gradedu@sbuniv.edu. Application contact: Donna Sybouts, Administrative Assistant, 417-326-1711. Fax: 417-326-1719. E-mail: dsybouts@sbuniv.edu.

Southwestern Adventist University, Graduate School of Education, Keene, TX 76059. Offers program in elementary education (M Ed). Part-time and evening/weekend programs available. Faculty: 10 full-time (3 women). Students: 1 (woman) full-time, 10 part-time (7 women); includes 6 minority (4 African Americans, 1 Asian American, 1 Native American). Average age 38. 4 applicants, 75% accepted. In 1997, 4 degrees awarded. *Degree requirements:* Thesis or alternative, professional paper required, foreign language not required. *Average time to degree:* master's–4 years part-time. *Entrance requirements:* GRE General Test (minimum combined score of 750). Application deadline: 8/24 (priority date; rolling processing; 12/28 for spring admission). Application fee: $0. *Tuition:* $3300 per year full-time, $275 per hour part-time. *Financial aid:* Federal Work-Study, institutionally sponsored loans available. Aid available to part-time students. Financial aid application deadline: 5/1. • Dee Anderson, Director, 817-645-3921. E-mail: andersonde@swau.edu. Application contact: Marie Redwine, Graduate Dean, 817-645-3921 Ext. 211. Fax: 817-556-4744. E-mail: redwinem@swau.edu.

Southwestern Assemblies of God University, School of Graduate Studies, Program in Education, Waxahachie, TX 75165-2397. Awards MS. Students: 7. *Application deadline:* rolling. *Application fee:* $50. • Dr. Mary Campbell, Coordinator, 972-937-4010.

Southwestern College, Center for Teaching Excellence, Winfield, KS 67156-2499. Awards M Ed. Faculty: 5. Students: 19. *Tuition:* $160 per credit hour. • William Medley, Director of Graduate Studies, 800-846-1543.

Southwestern Oklahoma State University, School of Education, Weatherford, OK 73096-3098. Awards M Ed. Accredited by NCATE. Part-time and evening/weekend programs available. Postbaccalaureate distance learning degree programs offered (minimal on-campus study). Students: 62 full-time (40 women), 207 part-time (130 women). 24 applicants, 100% accepted. In 1997, 70 degrees awarded. *Degree requirements:* Exam required, foreign language and thesis not required. *Entrance requirements:* GRE General Test, TOEFL (minimum score 550), minimum GPA of 2.5. Application deadline: rolling. Application fee: $15. *Expenses:* Tuition $60 per credit hour (minimum) for state residents; $147 per credit hour (minimum) for nonresidents. Fees $109 per year full-time, $24 per semester (minimum) part-time. *Financial aid:* Research assistantships, teaching assistantships, partial tuition waivers, Federal Work-Study, institutionally sponsored loans, and career-related internships or fieldwork available. Aid available to part-time students. Financial aid application deadline: 3/1; applicants required to submit FAFSA. • Dr. Greg Moss, Dean, 580-774-3285.

Southwest Missouri State University, College of Education, Springfield, MO 65804-0094. Awards MS, MS Ed, Ed S. Part-time and evening/weekend programs available. Faculty: 42 full-time (10 women), 4 part-time (0 women). Students: 67 full-time (48 women), 919 part-time (696 women); includes 21 minority (6 African Americans, 5 Asian Americans, 1 Hispanic, 9 Native Americans), 7 international. In 1997, 219 master's, 31 Ed Ss awarded. *Degree requirements:* Thesis or alternative, comprehensive exam required, foreign language not required. *Entrance requirements:* For master's, minimum GPA of 2.75; for Ed S, GRE General Test (minimum combined score of 875), MAT, minimum GPA of 2.75. Application deadline: 8/7 (priority date; rolling processing; 12/17 for spring admission). Application fee: $25. *Expenses:* Tuition $1980 per year full-time, $110 per credit hour part-time for state residents; $3960 per year full-time, $220 per credit hour part-time for nonresidents. Fees $274 per year full-time, $73 per semester part-time. *Financial aid:* In 1997–98, 21 graduate assistantships averaging $583 per month and totaling $79,581 were awarded; research assistantships, teaching assistantships, Federal Work-Study, and career-related internships or fieldwork also available. Aid available to part-time students. • Dr. Roger Bennett, Dean, 417-836-5255. Fax: 417-836-4884. E-mail: rvb012f@wpgate.smsu.edu.

Southwest State University, Department of Education, Marshall, MN 56258-1598. Awards MS. Faculty: 7 full-time, 1 part-time, 7.75 FTE. *Application deadline:* rolling. *Application fee:* $20. *Expenses:* Tuition $128 per credit full-time, $120 per credit part-time for state residents; $190 per credit for nonresidents. Fees $389 per semester. • Dr. William Borges, Dean, 507-537-7115. Application contact: Rich Shearer, Director of Admissions, 507-537-6286.

Southwest Texas State University, School of Education, San Marcos, TX 78666. Awards MA, M Ed. Part-time and evening/weekend programs available. Faculty: 60 full-time (29 women), 12 part-time (7 women). Students: 221 full-time (170 women), 600 part-time (471 women); includes 145 minority (45 African Americans, 8 Asian Americans, 90 Hispanics, 2 Native Americans), 8 international. Average age 33. In 1997, 251 degrees awarded. *Degree requirements:* Comprehensive exam required, foreign language not required. *Entrance requirements:* GRE General Test (minimum combined score of 900), TOEFL (minimum score 550). Application deadline: 7/15 (priority date; rolling processing; 11/15 for spring admission). Application fee: $25 ($50 for international students). *Expenses:* Tuition $648 per year full-time, $120 per semester (minimum) part-time for state residents; $4500 per year full-time, $750 per semester (minimum) part-time for nonresidents. Fees $1264 per year full-time, $314 per semester (minimum) part-time. *Financial aid:* Fellowships, research assistantships, teaching assistantships, Federal Work-Study, institutionally sponsored loans, and career-related internships or fieldwork available. Aid available to part-time students. Financial aid application deadline: 4/1; applicants required to submit FAFSA. • Dr. John Beck, Dean, 512-245-2150. Fax: 512-245-8345. E-mail: jb01@swt.edu. Application contact: Dr. J. Michael Willoughby, Dean of the Graduate School, 512-245-2581. Fax: 512-245-8365. E-mail: jw02@swt.edu.

Spalding University, School of Education, Louisville, KY 40203-2188. Awards MA, MAML, MAT, Ed D. Accredited by NCATE. Part-time and evening/weekend programs available. Faculty: 7 full-time (5 women), 12 part-time (8 women). Students: 24 full-time (22 women), 127 part-time (94 women); includes 20 minority (17 African Americans, 2 Hispanics, 1 Native American), 1 international. Average age 39. 67 applicants, 96% accepted. In 1997, 33 master's, 15 doctorates awarded. *Degree requirements:* For doctorate, dissertation required, foreign language not required. *Entrance requirements:* For master's, GRE General Test, portfolio; for doctorate, GRE General Test or MAT, interview, portfolio. Application deadline: 8/15 (priority date; rolling processing). Application fee: $30. *Expenses:* Tuition $350 per credit hour (minimum). Fees $48 per year full-time, $4 per credit hour part-time. *Financial aid:* In 1997–98, 105 students received aid, including 9 research assistantships totaling $19,040, 69 grants, scholarships totaling $102,527; Federal Work-Study and career-related internships or fieldwork also available. Aid available to part-time students. Financial aid application deadline: 3/15; applicants required to submit FAFSA. *Faculty research:* School law, effective school boards, principals' support groups, field experiences, socialization skills for learning-disabled students. • Dr. Mary Burns, Dean, 502-585-7121. E-mail: education@spalding4.win.net. Application contact: Jeanne Anderson, Assistant to the Provost and Director of Graduate Office, 502-585-7105. Fax: 502-585-7158. E-mail: gradoffc@spalding6.win.net.

Spring Arbor College, School of Education, Spring Arbor, MI 49283-9799. Awards MAE. Faculty: 15. Students: 200. *Application deadline:* rolling. *Application fee:* $25. *Expenses:* Tuition $265 per credit hour (minimum). Fees $75 per year (minimum). • Dr. David Hamilton, Dean, 517-750-6411. Application contact: Deborah Scott, Graduate Program Coordinator, 517-750-6410.

Springfield College, Program in Education, Springfield, MA 01109-3797. Offers counseling and secondary education (M Ed, MS), education (M Ed, MS). Part-time and evening/weekend programs available. Faculty: 7 full-time (4 women), 2 part-time (both women), 8 FTE. Students: 37 full-time (21 women), 24 part-time (16 women); includes 3 international. Average age 26. 57 applicants, 82% accepted. In 1997, 19 degrees awarded. *Degree requirements:* Comprehensive exam required, foreign language and thesis not required. *Application deadline:* (12/1 for spring admission). *Application fee:* $40. *Expenses:* Tuition $474 per credit. Fees $25 per year. *Financial aid:* In 1997–98, 2 teaching assistantships (both to first-year students) were awarded; fellowships, full and partial tuition waivers, Federal Work-Study, and career-related internships or fieldwork also available. Financial aid application deadline: 3/1. • Dr. Thomas L. Bernard, Director, 413-748-3251. Application contact: Donald J. Shaw Jr., Director of Graduate Admissions, 413-748-3225. Fax: 413-748-3694. E-mail: dshaw@spfldcol.edu.

Spring Hill College, Graduate Programs, Program in Education, Mobile, AL 36608-1791. Offers early childhood education (MAT, MS Ed), elementary education (MAT, MS Ed), teaching of reading (MS Ed). Part-time and evening/weekend programs available. Faculty: 5 full-time (3 women), 5 part-time (1 woman). Students: 8 full-time (4 women), 136 part-time (122 women). *Degree requirements:* Comprehensive exam required, thesis optional, foreign language not required. *Average time to degree:* master's–2 years part-time. *Entrance requirements:* GRE, MAT, or NTE, minimum undergraduate GPA of 3.0. Application deadline: rolling. Application fee: $25. *Financial aid:* Available to part-time students. Financial aid applicants required to submit FAFSA. • Dr. B. C. Algero, Chair, 334-380-3477.

Stanford University, School of Education, Stanford, CA 94305-9991. Awards AM, MAT, Ed D, PhD. Faculty: 40 full-time (10 women). Students: 299 full-time (207 women), 48 part-time (33 women); includes 93 minority (17 African Americans, 34 Asian Americans, 34 Hispanics, 8 Native Americans), 32 international. Average age 30. 656 applicants, 31% accepted. In 1997, 139 master's, 45 doctorates awarded. *Degree requirements:* For doctorate, dissertation required, foreign language not required. *Entrance requirements:* GRE General Test. Application deadline: 1/2. Application fee: $65 ($75 for international students). *Expenses:* Tuition $22,110 per year. Fees $156 per year. *Financial aid:* In 1997–98, 130 students received aid, including 36 fellowships (32 to first-year students) averaging $1,167 per month, 123 research assistantships (31 to first-year students) averaging $1,167 per month, 62 teaching assistantships (1 to a first-year student) averaging $662 per month, 8 training grants (2 to first-year students) averaging $1,167 per month and totaling $38,594; Federal Work-Study and career-related internships or fieldwork also available. Financial aid application deadline: 2/1; applicants required to submit FAFSA. • Richard Shavelson, Dean, 650-723-2111. Fax: 650-725-7417. E-mail: rich.s@stanford.edu. Application contact: Graduate Admissions Office, 650-723-4794.

See in-depth description on page 779.

State University of New York at Albany, School of Education, Albany, NY 12222-0001. Awards MA, MS, Ed D, PhD, Psy D, CAS. Part-time and evening/weekend programs available. Faculty: 61 full-time (23 women), 12 part-time (6 women). Students: 518 full-time (362 women), 604 part-time (424 women); includes 120 minority (60 African Americans, 9 Asian Americans, 50 Hispanics, 1 Native American), 36 international. 582 applicants, 60% accepted. In 1997, 426 master's, 30 doctorates, 30 CASs awarded. *Degree requirements:* For doctorate, dissertation. *Entrance requirements:* For doctorate, GRE General Test. Application fee: $50. *Expenses:* Tuition $5100 per year full-time, $213 per credit hour part-time for state residents; $8416 per year full-time, $351 per credit hour part-time for nonresidents. Fees $705 per year full-time, $26.85 per credit hour part-time. *Financial aid:* Fellowships, Federal Work-Study, and career-related internships or fieldwork available. • James Fleming, Interim Dean, 518-442-4988. Application contact: Susan Palmer, Graduate Admissions Officer, 518-442-3980.

State University of New York at Binghamton, School of Education and Human Development, Binghamton, NY 13902-6000. Awards MASS, MAT, MS Ed, MST, Ed D, MASS/MSW. Part-time and evening/weekend programs available. Students: 180 full-time (126 women), 229 part-time (168 women); includes 41 minority (16 African Americans, 1 Asian American, 21 Hispanics, 3 Native Americans), 6 international. Average age 34. 234 applicants, 65% accepted. In 1997, 136 master's, 1 doctorate awarded. *Degree requirements:* For doctorate, dissertation. *Entrance requirements:* For master's, GRE General Test, TOEFL; for doctorate, GRE General Test, TOEFL, writing sample. Application deadline: (11/1 for spring admission). Application fee: $50. Electronic applications accepted. *Expenses:* Tuition $5100 per year full-time, $213 per credit hour part-time for state residents; $8416 per year full-time, $351 per credit hour part-time for nonresidents. Fees $654 per year full-time, $75 per semester (minimum) part-time. *Financial aid:* In 1997–98, 8 fellowships (2 to first-year students) averaging $743 per month and totaling $50,800, 2 research assistantships (1 to a first-year student) averaging $480 per month and totaling $9,600, 7 teaching assistantships (2 to first-year students) averaging $810 per month and totaling $43,903, 32 graduate assistantships (17 to first-year students) averaging $517 per month and totaling $148,054 were awarded; Federal Work-Study, institutionally sponsored loans, and career-related internships or fieldwork also available. Aid available to part-time students. Financial aid application deadline: 2/15. • Dr. Linda B. Biemer, Dean, 607-777-2833.

State University of New York at Buffalo, Graduate School, Graduate School of Education, Buffalo, NY 14260. Awards Ed M, MA, MS, Ed D, PhD, Certificate. Part-time programs available. Faculty: 48 full-time (15 women), 11 part-time (6 women). Students: 400 full-time (282 women), 631 part-time (454 women); includes 132 minority (76 African Americans, 15 Asian Americans, 38 Hispanics, 3 Native Americans), 103 international. In 1997, 246 master's, 58 doctorates awarded. Terminal master's awarded for partial completion of doctoral program. *Degree requirements:* For doctorate, dissertation required, foreign language not required. *Entrance requirements:* For master's, GRE General Test, TOEFL; for doctorate, TOEFL. Application fee: $50. *Tuition:* $5970 per year full-time, $288 per credit hour part-time for state residents; $9286 per year full-time, $426 per credit hour part-time for nonresidents. *Financial aid:* Fellowships, research assistantships, teaching assistantships, graduate assistantships, full and partial tuition waivers, Federal Work-Study, institutionally sponsored loans, and career-related internships or fieldwork available. *Faculty research:* Eating disorders, outcome assessment, policy analysis, evaluation of science instruction, early mathematics learning, language and literacy research. Total annual research expenditures: $1.86 million. • Dr. Jacquelyn Mitchell, Dean, 716-645-2491. Fax: 716-645-2479.

See in-depth description on page 781.

State University of New York at New Paltz, Faculty of Education, New Paltz, NY 12561-2499. Awards MAT, MPS, MS Ed, MST, CAS. Part-time and evening/weekend programs available. Faculty: 38 full-time, 112 part-time. Students: 178 full-time (121 women), 605 part-time (463 women); includes 50 minority (23 African Americans, 2 Asian Americans, 21 Hispanics, 4 Native Americans), 14 international. In 1997, 318 master's, 61 CASs awarded. *Entrance requirements:* For master's, minimum GPA of 3.0. Application deadline: 3/15 (priority date; rolling processing). Application fee: $50. *Expenses:* Tuition $5100 per year full-time, $213 per credit hour part-time for state residents; $8416 per year full-time, $351 per credit hour part-time for nonresidents. Fees $493 per year full-time, $48 per semester (minimum) part-time. *Financial aid:* Teaching assistantships, Federal Work-Study, institutionally sponsored loans, and career-related internships or fieldwork available. *Faculty research:* Migrant education, teacher enhancement–science and mathematics, special education teacher preparation, talent search, student special services. • Dr. Robert Michael, Interim Dean, 914-257-2800.

State University of New York at Oswego, School of Education, Oswego, NY 13126. Awards MAT, MS, MS Ed, PhD, CAS, MS/CAS, MS Ed/CAS. Part-time programs available. Faculty: 38 full-time, 20 part-time. Students: 134 full-time (96 women), 385 part-time (273 women); includes 19 minority (12 African Americans, 1 Asian American, 5 Hispanics, 1 Native American). 426 applicants, 79% accepted. In 1997, 274 master's, 42 CASs awarded. *Entrance requirements:* For CAS, GRE General Test, GRE Subject Test, interview, MA or MS, minimum GPA of 3.0. Application deadline: 7/1. Application fee: $50. *Expenses:* Tuition $5100 per year full-time, $213 per credit hour part-time for state residents; $8416 per year full-time, $351 per credit hour part-time for nonresidents. Fees $135 per year (minimum). *Financial aid:* Research assistantships, teaching assistantships, assistantships, partial tuition waivers, Federal Work-Study, institutionally sponsored loans, and career-related internships or fieldwork available. Aid available to part-time students. • Dr. Linda Markert, Interim Dean, 315-341-2102.

State University of New York College at Brockport, School of Professions, Department of Education and Human Development, Brockport, NY 14420-2997. Offers programs in bilingual education (MS Ed); elementary education (MS Ed); reading (MS Ed); secondary education (MS Ed), including biology education, chemistry education, earth science education, English education, mathematics education, physics education, social studies education. Part-time and evening/weekend programs available. Faculty: 15 full-time (6 women), 21 part-time (10 women), 19.5 FTE. Students: 93 full-time (60 women), 247 part-time (185 women); includes 30 minority (24 African Americans, 5 Hispanics, 1 Native American), 1 international. Average age 31. 119 applicants, 85% accepted. In 1997, 119 degrees awarded. *Average time to degree:* master's–3 years full-time, 5 years part-time. *Entrance requirements:* Minimum GPA of 3.0. Application deadline: 1/15 (priority date; 9/15 for spring admission). Application fee: $50. *Expenses:* Tuition $5100 per year full-time, $213 per credit hour part-time for state residents; $8416 per year full-time, $351 per credit hour part-time for nonresidents. Fees $440 per year full-time, $22.60 per credit hour part-time. *Financial aid:* In 1997–98, 2 fellowships (1 to a first-year student), 1 teaching assistantship (to a first-year student) were awarded; Federal Work-Study and career-related internships or fieldwork also available. Aid available to part-time students. Financial aid application deadline: 4/1; applicants required to submit FAFSA. *Faculty research:* Stress management, thinking skills, learning styles. • William Veenis, Chairperson, 716-395-2205.

State University of New York College at Cortland, Division of Professional Studies, Department of Education, Cortland, NY 13045. Offers programs in elementary education (MS Ed), including English education, general science education, mathematics education, social studies education; reading (MS Ed); school administration and supervision (CAS); school business administrator (CAS); secondary education (MS Ed), including biology, chemistry, earth science, French, mathematics, physics. Part-time and evening/weekend programs available. In 1997, 74 master's, 39 CASs awarded. *Application deadline:* rolling. *Application fee:* $50. *Expenses:* Tuition $5100 per year full-time, $213 per credit hour part-time for state residents; $8416 per year full-time, $351 per credit hour part-time for nonresidents. Fees $644 per year full-time, $79 per semester (minimum) part-time. *Financial aid:* Partial tuition waivers, Federal Work-Study, and career-related internships or fieldwork available. Aid available to part-time students. • Mary Ware, Chair, 607-753-2705. Application contact: Jeanne M. Bechtel, Director of Admissions, 607-753-4711. Fax: 607-753-5998.

State University of New York College at Fredonia, Department of Education, Fredonia, NY 14063. Offers programs in educational administration (CAS), elementary education (MS Ed), reading (MS Ed), secondary education (MS Ed). Part-time and evening/weekend programs available. Faculty: 2 full-time (1 woman), 3 part-time (1 woman). Students: 5 full-time (4 women), 113 part-time (89 women); includes 1 minority (Native American). 52 applicants, 87% accepted. In 1997, 85 master's, 20 CASs awarded. *Degree requirements:* Thesis or alternative required, foreign language not required. *Application deadline:* 7/5. *Application fee:* $50. *Expenses:* Tuition $5100 per year full-time, $213 per credit hour part-time for state residents; $8416 per year full-time, $351 per credit hour part-time for nonresidents. Fees $725 per year full-time, $30 per credit hour part-time. *Financial aid:* In 1997–98, 1 teaching assistantship was awarded; research assistantships, full and partial tuition waivers, and career-related internships or fieldwork also available. Aid available to part-time students. Financial aid application deadline: 3/15. • Dr. Julius Adams, Chair, 716-673-3311.

State University of New York College at Geneseo, School of Education, Geneseo, NY 14454-1401. Offers programs in elementary education (MS Ed), reading (MPS, MS Ed), secondary education (MS Ed), special education (MS Ed). Part-time and evening/weekend programs available. Faculty: 31 full-time (15 women), 8 part-time (4 women), 33 FTE. Students: 17 full-time (15 women), 213 part-time (179 women); includes 3 minority (1 African American, 1 Asian American, 1 Hispanic). Average age 24. 180 applicants, 84% accepted. In 1997, 96 degrees awarded. *Entrance requirements:* GRE General Test. Application deadline: 6/1 (priority date; 10/1 for spring admission). Application fee: $35. *Expenses:* Tuition $5100 per year full-time, $213 per credit hour part-time for state residents; $8416 per year full-time, $351 per credit hour part-time for nonresidents. Fees $375 per year full-time, $15.35 per credit hour part-time. *Financial aid:* In 1997–98, 7 students received aid, including 1 fellowship (to a first-year student), 3 teaching assistantships (all to first-year students); Federal Work-Study, institutionally sponsored loans, and career-related internships or fieldwork also available. Financial aid application deadline: 4/1; applicants required to submit FAFSA. *Faculty research:* Whole language. Total annual research expenditures: $88,312. • Dr. Gary DeBolt, Head, 716-245-5558. Fax: 716-245-5220. E-mail: debolt@uno.cc.geneseo.edu.

State University of New York College at Oneonta, Department of Education, Oneonta, NY 13820-4015. Offers programs in counseling (MS, MS Ed, CAS); elementary education (MS Ed), including early secondary English (N–9), early secondary math (N–9), early secondary social science (N–9), general science (N–9); reading (MS Ed); school nurse teacher (MS Ed); secondary education (MS Ed), including biology education, chemistry education, earth science education, English education, home economics education, mathematics education, physics education, social science education. Part-time and evening/weekend programs available. Students: 42 full-time (34 women), 146 part-time (113 women); includes 1 minority (Hispanic). In 1997, 127 master's, 11 CASs awarded. *Entrance requirements:* For master's, GRE General Test. Application deadline: 4/15. Application fee: $50. *Expenses:* Tuition $5100 per year full-time, $213 per credit hour part-time for state residents; $8416 per year full-time, $351 per credit hour part-time for nonresidents. Fees $482 per year full-time, $6.85 per credit hour part-time. • Dr. Ronald Cromwell, Chair, 607-436-2538.

Directory: Education—General

State University of New York College at Potsdam, School of Education, Potsdam, NY 13676. Awards MS Ed, MST. Part-time and evening/weekend programs available. Faculty: 27 full-time (4 women), 16 part-time (6 women). Students: 398; includes 6 minority (1 African American, 2 Asian Americans, 2 Hispanics, 1 Native American), 17 international. *Degree requirements:* Culminating experience. *Entrance requirements:* New York State Teachers Certification Exam Liberal Arts and Science Test (minimum score 220), New York State Teachers Certification Exam Assesment of Teaching Skills-Writing (minimum score 220), minimum GPA of 2.75 in last 60 hours. Application deadline: 4/1 (priority date; 10/15 for spring admission). Application fee: $50. *Expenses:* Tuition $5100 per year full-time, $213 per credit hour part-time for state residents; $8416 per year full-time, $351 per credit hour part-time for nonresidents. Fees $315 per year full-time, $12.50 per credit hour part-time. *Financial aid:* Fellowships, teaching assistantships, Federal Work-Study, and career-related internships or fieldwork available. Aid available to part-time students. Financial aid application deadline: 3/1. • Dr. William Amoriell, Dean of Education and Graduate Studies, 315-267-2515. Fax: 315-267-4802.

State University of West Georgia, College of Education, Carrollton, GA 30118. Awards M Ed, Ed D, Ed S. Accredited by NCATE. Part-time and evening/weekend programs available. Faculty: 60 full-time (34 women), 6 part-time (3 women). Students: 714 full-time (570 women), 1,136 part-time (949 women); includes 288 minority (274 African Americans, 4 Asian Americans, 9 Hispanics, 1 Native American), 4 international. Average age 36. In 1997, 493 master's, 211 Ed Ss awarded. *Degree requirements:* For doctorate, research project; for Ed S, research project required, foreign language and thesis not required. *Entrance requirements:* For master's, GRE General Test (minimum combined score of 800), minimum GPA of 2.5; for Ed S, GRE General Test (minimum combined score of 800), master's degree, minimum graduate GPA of 3.25. Application deadline: 8/30 (rolling processing). Application fee: $15. *Expenses:* Tuition $2428 per year full-time, $83 per semester hour part-time for state residents; $8428 per year full-time, $250 per semester hour part-time for nonresidents. Fees $428 per year. *Financial aid:* Research assistantships, assistantships, and career-related internships or fieldwork available. Aid available to part-time students. Financial aid applicants required to submit FAFSA. *Faculty research:* Language and culture via distance education, speech pathology, staff development, mathematics/science instruction, alternative track: certification of noneducational degree. Total annual research expenditures: $143,609. • Dr. Angela Lumpkin, Dean, 770-836-6570. Fax: 770-836-6729. Application contact: Dr. Jack O. Jenkins, Dean, Graduate School, 770-836-6419. Fax: 770-836-2301. E-mail: jjenkins@cob.as.westga.edu.

Stephen F. Austin State University, College of Education, Nacogdoches, TX 75962. Awards MA, M Ed, MS, Ed D. Accredited by NCATE. Part-time and evening/weekend programs available. Faculty: 74 full-time (27 women), 8 part-time (1 woman). Students: 271 full-time (182 women), 636 part-time (446 women); includes 122 minority (87 African Americans, 2 Asian Americans, 30 Hispanics, 3 Native Americans). 559 applicants, 91% accepted. In 1997, 279 master's awarded. *Degree requirements:* For master's, comprehensive exam required, foreign language not required; for doctorate, dissertation required, foreign language not required. *Entrance requirements:* For master's, GRE General Test (minimum combined score of 1000); for doctorate, GRE General Test (minimum combined score of 1000), TOEFL. Application deadline: rolling. Application fee: $0 ($25 for international students). *Tuition:* $1465 per year full-time, $263 per semester (minimum) part-time for state residents; $5299 per year full-time, $890 per semester (minimum) part-time for nonresidents. *Financial aid:* Research assistantships, teaching assistantships, Federal Work-Study, institutionally sponsored loans, and career-related internships or fieldwork available. Financial aid application deadline: 3/1. • Dr. Thomas Franks, Dean, 409-468-2901.

Stephens College, School of Graduate and Continuing Education, Department of Elementary and Secondary Education, 1200 East Broadway, Columbia, MO 65215-0002. Offers programs in counseling (M Ed), inclusion (M Ed). Part-time programs available. Faculty: 5 full-time (4 women). Students: 11 part-time (all women). *Entrance requirements:* GRE, TOEFL (minimum score 550), minimum GPA of 3.0 in last 60 hours. Application deadline: rolling. Application fee: $25. *Tuition:* $690 per course. *Financial aid:* Available to part-time students. • Dr. Terry Teague, Chair, 573-442-2211 Ext. 261.

Stetson University, College of Arts and Sciences, Division of Education, 421 North Woodland Boulevard, DeLand, FL 32720-3781. Awards MA, M Ed, Ed S. One or more programs accredited by NCATE. Part-time and evening/weekend programs available. Faculty: 11 full-time (8 women), 3 part-time (all women). Students: 2 full-time (1 woman), 23 part-time (19 women); includes 3 minority (1 African American, 1 Asian American, 1 Hispanic). Average age 34. 24 applicants, 96% accepted. In 1997, 22 master's awarded. *Entrance requirements:* For master's, GRE General Test (minimum combined score of 1000) or MAT; for Ed S, GRE General Test or MAT. Application deadline: 3/1 (priority date; rolling processing; 11/1 for spring admission). Application fee: $25. *Tuition:* $370 per credit hour. *Financial aid:* Scholarships, partial tuition waivers, institutionally sponsored loans, and career-related internships or fieldwork available. Aid available to part-time students. *Faculty research:* Values, cultural diversity, cooperative learning, reading. • Dr. Elizabeth Heins, Chair, 904-822-7070. Application contact: Pat LeClaire, Office of Graduate Studies, 904-822-7075.

Suffolk University, College of Liberal Arts and Sciences, Department of Education and Human Services, Boston, MA 02108-2770. Awards M Ed, MS, CAGS, MPA/MS. Programs in adult and organizational learning (MS, CAGS); counseling and human relations (M Ed, MS, CAGS), including counseling and human relations (CAGS), human resource development (MS, CAGS), mental health counseling (MS), school counseling (M Ed); higher education administration (M Ed, CAGS), including educational administration (M Ed), leadership (CAGS); professional teacher/trainer development (M Ed, CAGS); secondary school teaching (MS). Part-time and evening/weekend programs available. Faculty: 9 full-time (3 women), 29 part-time (19 women). Students: 24 full-time (21 women), 115 part-time (88 women). Average age 30. 100 applicants, 94% accepted. In 1997, 59 master's awarded (100% found work related to degree). *Entrance requirements:* For master's, GRE General Test (average 500 on each section) or MAT (average 50). Application deadline: 6/15 (priority date; rolling processing; 11/15 for spring admission). Application fee: $50. *Expenses:* Tuition $14,544 per year full-time, $1452 per course part-time. Fees $20 per year full-time, $10 per year part-time. *Financial aid:* In 1997–98, 5 fellowships were awarded; Federal Work-Study, institutionally sponsored loans, and career-related internships or fieldwork also available. Aid available to part-time students. Financial aid application deadline: 4/1; applicants required to submit FAFSA. *Faculty research:* Administration, personality disorders. • Dr. Glen Eskedal, Chairperson, 617-573-8264. Fax: 617-722-9440. Application contact: Judy Reynolds, Acting Director of Graduate Admissions, 617-573-8302. Fax: 617-523-0116. E-mail: grad.admission@admin.suffolk.edu.

Announcement: The Department of Education and Human Services offers courses of study leading to a Master of Science or Master of Education degree, a 6-course certificate program in human resources, and a 10-course postgraduate certificate of graduate study for candidates who possess a master's degree. The MS degree may be completed in adult/organizational learning, human resources, mental health counseling, or secondary school teaching. The M Ed is offered in administration of higher education and in foundations of education and school counseling. A 20-course dual-degree Master of Public Administration/Mental Health Counseling program and an 18-course dual degree Master of Science in Criminal Justice/Mental Health Counseling program are also offered. For an application and information, contact the Office of Graduate Admission, 617-573-8302, fax: 617-523-0116, e-mail: grad.admission@admin.suffolk.edu

Sul Ross State University, Rio Grande College of Sul Ross State University, Alpine, TX 79832. Offerings include teacher education (M Ed), with options in bilingual education, counseling, educational diagnostics, elementary education, general education, reading, school administration, secondary education. College faculty: 16 full-time (2 women), 2 part-time (1 woman). *Application deadline:* rolling. *Application fee:* $0 ($50 for international students). *Expenses:* Tuition $864 per year full-time, $120 per semester (minimum) part-time for state residents; $5976 per year full-time, $747 per semester (minimum) part-time for nonresidents. Fees $754 per year full-time, $105 per semester (minimum) part-time. • Dr. Frank Abbott, Dean, 512-278-3339. Fax: 512-278-3330.

Sul Ross State University, Department of Teacher Education, Alpine, TX 79832. Offers programs in bilingual education (M Ed), counseling (M Ed), educational diagnostics (M Ed), elementary education (M Ed), reading specialist (M Ed), school administration (M Ed), secondary education (M Ed), supervision (M Ed). Part-time and evening/weekend programs available. Faculty: 9 full-time (5 women), 8 part-time (4 women). Students: 106 full-time (72 women), 312 part-time (197 women); includes 187 minority (11 African Americans, 2 Asian Americans, 172 Hispanics, 2 Native Americans). Average age 39. In 1997, 149 degrees awarded. *Degree requirements:* Thesis optional, foreign language not required. *Entrance requirements:* GMAT (minimum score 400) or GRE General Test (minimum combined score of 850), minimum GPA of 2.5 in last 60 hours of undergraduate work. Application deadline: rolling. Application fee: $0 ($50 for international students). *Expenses:* Tuition $864 per year full-time, $120 per semester (minimum) part-time for state residents; $5976 per year full-time, $747 per semester (minimum) part-time for nonresidents. Fees $754 per year full-time, $105 per semester (minimum) part-time. *Financial aid:* Teaching assistantships, Federal Work-Study, institutionally sponsored loans, and career-related internships or fieldwork available. Aid available to part-time students. Financial aid application deadline: 5/1; applicants required to submit FAFSA. *Faculty research:* Critical thinking skills, adolescent eating disorders, reading-based study skills, cross-cultural adaptations, educational leadership. • Dr. Mary Ann Weinacht, Director, 915-837-8170. Fax: 915-837-8390.

Syracuse University, School of Education, Syracuse, NY 13244-0003. Awards M Mu, MS, Ed D, PhD, CAS, Ed D/PhD. Part-time and evening/weekend programs available. Faculty: 62 full-time (18 women), 2 part-time (1 woman). Students: 448 full-time (306 women), 344 part-time (263 women); includes 61 minority (43 African Americans, 10 Asian Americans, 5 Hispanics, 3 Native Americans), 55 international. 487 applicants, 75% accepted. In 1997, 271 master's, 29 doctorates awarded. *Degree requirements:* For master's, thesis or alternative; for doctorate and CAS, thesis/dissertation. *Entrance requirements:* GRE. Application deadline: rolling. Application fee: $40. *Tuition:* $13,320 per year full-time, $555 per credit hour part-time. *Financial aid:* Fellowships, research assistantships, teaching assistantships, administrative assistantships, Federal Work-Study, institutionally sponsored loans, and career-related internships or fieldwork available. Aid available to part-time students. Financial aid application deadline: 3/1. *Faculty research:* Teaching and curriculum, reading and language arts, literacy, inclusive education, communication sciences and disorders. Total annual research expenditures: $4603. • Dr. Steven T. Bossert, Dean, 315-443-4751. Application contact: Sylvia Groskin, Graduate Admissions Representative, 315-443-2505. Fax: 315-443-5732.

See in-depth description on page 783.

Tarleton State University, College of Education, Stephenville, TX 76402. Awards M Ed, Certificate. Part-time and evening/weekend programs available. Faculty: 28 full-time (9 women). Students: 104 full-time (47 women), 463 part-time (319 women); includes 63 minority (26 African Americans, 7 Asian Americans, 24 Hispanics, 6 Native Americans). In 1997, 113 master's awarded. *Degree requirements:* For master's, comprehensive exam required, foreign language and thesis not required. *Entrance requirements:* For master's, GRE General Test, minimum GPA of 2.9 during last 60 hours. Application deadline: 8/5 (priority date; rolling processing; 12/1 for spring admission). Application fee: $25 ($100 for international students). *Expenses:* Tuition $46 per hour for state residents; $249 per hour for nonresidents. Fees $49 per hour. *Financial aid:* Teaching assistantships, Federal Work-Study, institutionally sponsored loans, and career-related internships or fieldwork available. Aid available to part-time students. Financial aid application deadline: 5/1; applicants required to submit FAFSA. • Dr. Joe Gillespie, Dean, 254-968-9089.

Teachers College, Columbia University, Graduate Faculty of Education, 525 West 120th Street, New York, NY 10027-6696. Awards Ed M, MA, MS, Ed D, Ed DCT, PhD. Part-time and evening/weekend programs available. Faculty: 128 full-time (68 women), 218 part-time (129 women), 222 FTE. Students: 1,557 full-time (1,184 women), 3,488 part-time (2,623 women); includes 1,174 minority (528 African Americans, 339 Asian Americans, 297 Hispanics, 10 Native Americans), 499 international. Average age 34. 3,758 applicants, 59% accepted. In 1997, 1,212 master's, 180 doctorates awarded. Terminal master's awarded for partial completion of doctoral program. *Application fee:* $50. *Expenses:* Tuition $640 per credit. Fees $120 per semester. *Financial aid:* Fellowships, research assistantships, teaching assistantships, full and partial tuition waivers, Federal Work-Study, institutionally sponsored loans, and career-related internships or fieldwork available. Aid available to part-time students. Financial aid application deadline: 2/1. *Faculty research:* Education and the economy, postsecondary governance and finance, career success, dropout prevention evaluation. • Arthur Levine, President, 212-678-3050. Application contact: John Fisher, Executive Director of Admissions and Financial Aid, 212-678-3710. Fax: 212-678-4171.

See in-depth description on page 785.

Temple University, College of Education, Philadelphia, PA 19122-6096. Awards Ed M, MS, Ed D, PhD, Certificate. Accredited by NCATE. Part-time and evening/weekend programs available. Faculty: 75 full-time (31 women). Students: 1,212 (782 women). 995 applicants, 57% accepted. In 1997, 584 master's, 366 doctorates awarded. Terminal master's awarded for partial completion of doctoral program. *Degree requirements:* For doctorate, dissertation required, foreign language not required. *Entrance requirements:* For master's, GRE General Test (minimum combined score of 1000) or MAT (minimum score 39), minimum GPA of 2.8. Application fee: $40. *Expenses:* Tuition $323 per semester hour for state residents; $444 per semester hour for nonresidents. Fees $170 per year full-time, $28 per semester (minimum) part-time. *Financial aid:* Fellowships, research assistantships, teaching assistantships, Federal Work-Study, and career-related internships or fieldwork available. *Faculty research:* School improvement in city schools, teaching strategies, student motivation, individual differences in learning, educational leadership and policy studies. • Dr. Trevor Sewell, Dean, 215-204-8017. Application contact: Dr. Stiles Seay, Director of Advising, 215-204-8011. Fax: 215-204-5622.

See in-depth description on page 787.

Tennessee State University, College of Education, Nashville, TN 37209-1561. Awards MA Ed, M Ed, MS, Ed D, PhD. Accredited by NCATE. Part-time and evening/weekend programs available. Faculty: 44 full-time (18 women), 19 part-time (10 women). Students: 197 full-time (144 women), 255 part-time (174 women); includes 227 minority (212 African Americans, 15 Asian Americans), 9 international. In 1997, 193 master's, 23 doctorates awarded. *Degree requirements:* For doctorate, dissertation. *Entrance requirements:* For doctorate, minimum GPA of 3.25. Application deadline: rolling. Application fee: $15. *Tuition:* $2962 per year full-time, $182 per credit hour part-time for state residents; $7788 per year full-time, $393 per credit hour part-time for nonresidents. *Financial aid:* In 1997–98, 6 fellowships totaling $10,000, 18 research assistantships (6 to first-year students) totaling $7,500 were awarded; teaching assistantships, institutionally sponsored loans, and career-related internships or fieldwork also available. Aid available to part-time students. Financial aid application deadline: 5/1; applicants required to submit FAFSA. *Faculty research:* Class size, biobehavioral research, equity, dropout rate, K–12 teachers: first 5 years of employment. • Dr. Franklin Jones, Dean, 615-963-5451. Application contact: Dr. Clinton M. Lipsey, Dean of the Graduate School, 615-963-5901. Fax: 615-963-5963. E-mail: clipsey@picard.tnstate.edu.

Tennessee Technological University, College of Education, Cookeville, TN 38505. Awards MA, Ed S. Accredited by NCATE. Part-time and evening/weekend programs available. Faculty: 58 full-time (16 women). Students: 117 full-time (76 women), 562 part-time (420 women); includes 11 minority (7 African Americans, 3 Hispanics, 1 Native American). Average age 27. 241 applicants, 95% accepted. In 1997, 179 master's, 43 Ed Ss awarded. *Degree requirements:* For Ed S, thesis or alternative required, foreign language not required. *Entrance requirements:* For master's, MAT, TOEFL (minimum score 525); for Ed S, MAT, NTE. Application deadline:

3/1 (priority date; 8/1 for spring admission). Application fee: $25 ($30 for international students). *Tuition:* $2960 per year full-time, $147 per semester hour part-time for state residents; $7786 per year full-time, $358 per semester hour part-time for nonresidents. *Financial aid:* In 1997–98, 50 students received aid, including 1 fellowship, 26 research assistantships (13 to first-year students), 23 teaching assistantships (16 to first-year students); career-related internships or fieldwork also available. Aid available to part-time students. Financial aid application deadline: 4/1. *Faculty research:* Teacher evaluation. • Dr. Karen I. Adams, Dean, 615-372-3124. Fax: 615-372-6319. E-mail: kadams@tntech.edu. Application contact: Dr. Rebecca F. Quattlebaum, Dean of the Graduate School, 615-372-3233. Fax: 615-372-3497. E-mail: rquattlebaum@tntech.edu.

Tennessee Temple University, Graduate Studies Division, Chattanooga, TN 37404-3587. Awards MS. Faculty: 4 full-time (1 woman), 2 part-time (0 women). Students: 22 (10 women). • Dr. Joe Ray, Director, Graduate Studies in Education, 423-493-4385.

Texas A&M International University, Division of Teacher Education and Psychology, 5201 University Boulevard, Laredo, TX 78041-1900. Offers programs in administration (MS Ed); bilingual education (MS Ed); early childhood education (MS Ed); education (MS Ed); elementary education (MS Ed); gifted and talented (MS Ed); guidance and counseling (MS Ed); reading (MS Ed); secondary education (MS Ed), including business education, secondary education; supervision (MS Ed). Part-time and evening/weekend programs available. *Degree requirements:* Thesis required (for some programs), foreign language not required. *Entrance requirements:* GRE General Test. Application deadline: 7/15 (priority date; rolling processing; 11/12 for spring admission). Application fee: $0.

Texas A&M University, College of Education, College Station, TX 77843. Awards M Ed, MS, Ed D, PhD. Accredited by NCATE. Faculty: 159 full-time (60 women), 43 part-time (32 women), 174.5 FTE. Students: 980 (608 women); includes 154 minority (57 African Americans, 15 Asian Americans, 82 Hispanics), 39 international. 717 applicants, 61% accepted. In 1997, 83 master's, 63 doctorates awarded. *Degree requirements:* For doctorate, dissertation. *Entrance requirements:* GRE General Test, TOEFL. Application fee: $35 ($75 for international students). *Financial aid:* Fellowships, research assistantships, teaching assistantships, partial tuition waivers, Federal Work-Study, institutionally sponsored loans, and career-related internships or fieldwork available. • Jane Conerly, Dean, 409-845-5311.

See in-depth description on page 789.

Texas A&M University–Commerce, College of Education, Commerce, TX 75429-3011. Awards MA, M Ed, MS, Ed D, PhD. Faculty: 64 full-time (20 women), 28 part-time (6 women). Students: 227 full-time (154 women), 799 part-time (554 women); includes 163 minority (108 African Americans, 10 Asian Americans, 34 Hispanics, 11 Native Americans), 12 international. In 1997, 343 master's, 44 doctorates awarded. Terminal master's awarded for partial completion of doctoral program. *Degree requirements:* For master's, comprehensive exam; for doctorate, dissertation, departmental qualifying exam. *Entrance requirements:* GRE General Test. Application deadline: rolling. Application fee: $0 ($25 for international students). *Tuition:* $2382 per year full-time, $343 per semester (minimum) part-time for state residents; $7518 per year full-time, $343 per semester (minimum) part-time for nonresidents. *Financial aid:* Research assistantships, teaching assistantships, Federal Work-Study, institutionally sponsored loans, and career-related internships or fieldwork available. • Dr. Donald Coker, Dean, 903-886-5180. Application contact: Pam Hammonds, Graduate Admissions Adviser, 903-886-5167. Fax: 903-886-5165.

Texas A&M University–Corpus Christi, College of Education, Corpus Christi, TX 78412-5503. Offers programs in curriculum and instruction (MS); educational administration and supervision (MS), including educational administration; educational leadership (Ed D); elementary education (MS); guidance and counseling (MS); occupational education (MS); secondary education (MS); special education (MS). Part-time and evening/weekend programs available. Students: 79 full-time (62 women), 304 part-time (215 women); includes 171 minority (14 African Americans, 2 Asian Americans, 154 Hispanics, 1 Native American), 1 international. Average age 37. In 1997, 271 master's, 4 doctorates awarded. *Degree requirements:* For doctorate, dissertation required, foreign language not required. *Entrance requirements:* For master's, GRE General Test; for doctorate, MS. Application deadline: 7/15 (priority date; rolling processing; 11/15 for spring admission). Application fee: $10 ($30 for international students). *Expenses:* Tuition $648 per year full-time, $120 per semester (minimum) part-time for state residents; $4482 per year full-time, $747 per semester (minimum) part-time for nonresidents. Fees $1010 per year full-time, $205 per semester part-time. *Financial aid:* Federal Work-Study, institutionally sponsored loans, and career-related internships or fieldwork available. Aid available to part-time students. Financial aid application deadline: 3/15; applicants required to submit FAFSA. • Dr. Robert Cox, Dean, 512-994-2661. E-mail: adedu001@tamucc.edu. Application contact: Mary Margaret Dechant, Director of Admissions, 512-994-2624. Fax: 512-994-5887.

Texas A&M University–Kingsville, College of Education, Kingsville, TX 78363. Awards MA, M Ed, MS, Ed D, PhD. Part-time and evening/weekend programs available. Faculty: 23 full-time (5 women), 14 part-time (5 women). Students: 93 full-time (55 women), 557 part-time (389 women); includes 395 minority (29 African Americans, 5 Asian Americans, 360 Hispanics, 1 Native American). *Degree requirements:* For master's, comprehensive exam; for doctorate, 1 foreign language, dissertation, comprehensive exam. *Entrance requirements:* For master's, GRE General Test (minimum combined score of 1000), minimum GPA of 3.0; for doctorate, GRE General Test (minimum combined score of 1000), MAT (minimum score 50), minimum GPA of 3.25. Application deadline: 6/1 (rolling processing; 11/15 for spring admission). Application fee: $15 ($25 for international students). *Tuition:* $1822 per year full-time, $281 per semester (minimum) part-time for state residents; $6934 per year full-time, $908 per semester (minimum) part-time for nonresidents. *Financial aid:* Fellowships, teaching assistantships, partial tuition waivers, Federal Work-Study, institutionally sponsored loans available. Aid available to part-time students. Financial aid application deadline: 5/15. *Faculty research:* Rural schools, facilities planning, linguistics. • Dr. Francisco Hidalgo, Dean, 512-593-2801.

Texas A&M University–Texarkana, Division of Arts and Sciences and Education, Texarkana, TX 75505-5518. Offers programs in counseling psychology (MS), elementary education (MA, M Ed, MS), interdisciplinary studies (MA, MS), secondary education (MA, M Ed, MS), special education (MA, M Ed, MS). Part-time and evening/weekend programs available. Faculty: 9 full-time (3 women), 5 part-time (3 women). Students: 256. In 1997, 48 degrees awarded. *Degree requirements:* Thesis or alternative required, foreign language not required. *Average time to degree:* master's–1.5 years full-time. *Entrance requirements:* GRE General Test, bachelor's degree from a regionally accredited institution, minimum GPA of 3.0, teaching certificate (M Ed). Application deadline: rolling. Application fee: $0 ($25 for international students). *Tuition:* $2136 per year for state residents; $7248 per year for nonresidents. *Financial aid:* Career-related internships or fieldwork available. • Dr. John Anderson, Interim Head, 903-223-3003. Application contact: Pat Black, Registrar, 903-223-3068. Fax: 903-832-8890. E-mail: pat.black@tamut.edu.

Texas Christian University, School of Education, Fort Worth, TX 76129-0002. Awards M Ed, MS. Part-time and evening/weekend programs available. Faculty: 20 full-time. Students: 158 (125 women); includes 25 minority (8 African Americans, 4 Asian Americans, 11 Hispanics, 2 Native Americans), 4 international. 102 applicants, 73% accepted. In 1997, 74 degrees awarded. *Entrance requirements:* TOEFL (minimum score 550). Application deadline: 3/1 (rolling processing; 12/1 for spring admission). Application fee: $0. *Expenses:* Tuition $10,350 per year full-time, $345 per credit hour part-time. Fees $1240 per year full-time, $50 per credit hour part-time. *Financial aid:* Graduate assistantships and career-related internships or fieldwork available. Financial aid application deadline: 3/1. • Dr. Douglas J. Simpson, Dean, 817-257-7663.

Texas Southern University, College of Education, Houston, TX 77004-4584. Awards MA, M Ed, MS, Ed D. Part-time and evening/weekend programs available. Faculty: 35 full-time (14 women), 8 part-time (3 women). 434 applicants, 50% accepted. In 1997, 74 master's, 18 doctorates awarded. *Degree requirements:* For master's, comprehensive exam; for doctorate, dissertation, comprehensive exam required, foreign language not required. *Entrance requirements:* For master's, GRE General Test, TOEFL, minimum GPA of 2.5; for doctorate, GRE General Test or MAT, master's degree, minimum B+ average. Application deadline: 7/15 (priority date; rolling processing). Application fee: $35 ($75 for international students). *Financial aid:* Fellowships, research assistantships, teaching assistantships, Federal Work-Study, institutionally sponsored loans, and career-related internships or fieldwork available. • William Nealy, Acting Dean, 713-313-7342.

Texas Tech University, Graduate School, College of Education, Lubbock, TX 79409. Awards M Ed, Ed D, Certificate. Accredited by NCATE. Part-time programs available. Faculty: 51 full-time (25 women), 3 part-time (1 woman), 52.29 FTE. Students: 268 full-time (181 women), 466 part-time (324 women); includes 78 minority (18 African Americans, 6 Asian Americans, 47 Hispanics, 7 Native Americans), 24 international. Average age 35. 287 applicants, 68% accepted. In 1997, 137 master's, 27 doctorates awarded. *Degree requirements:* For master's, computer language required, thesis optional, foreign language not required; for doctorate, dissertation required, foreign language not required. *Entrance requirements:* For master's, GRE General Test (combined average 1006); for doctorate, GRE General Test. Application deadline: 4/15 (priority date; rolling processing; 11/1 for spring admission). Application fee: $25 ($50 for international students). Electronic applications accepted. *Expenses:* Tuition $864 per year full-time, $120 per semester (minimum) part-time for state residents; $5976 per year full-time, $747 per semester (minimum) part-time for nonresidents. Fees $2321 per year full-time, $302 per semester (minimum) part-time. *Financial aid:* In 1997–98, 363 students received aid, including 35 research assistantships averaging $931 per month and totaling $293,288, 7 teaching assistantships averaging $961 per month and totaling $60,542; fellowships, Federal Work-Study, institutionally sponsored loans, and career-related internships or fieldwork also available. Aid available to part-time students. Financial aid application deadline: 5/15; applicants required to submit FAFSA. *Total annual research expenditures:* $712,120. • Dr. Elaine Jarchow, Dean, 806-742-2377. Fax: 806-742-2179.

Texas Wesleyan University, Programs in Education, Fort Worth, TX 76105-1536. Awards MA Ed, MAT, MS Ed. Part-time and evening/weekend programs available. Postbaccalaureate distance learning degree programs offered (no on-campus study). Faculty: 3 full-time (all women), 22 part-time (11 women). Students: 6 full-time (5 women), 168 part-time (149 women); includes 30 minority (14 African Americans, 1 Asian American, 13 Hispanics, 2 Native Americans), 1 international. Average age 34. In 1997, 31 degrees awarded (100% found work related to degree). *Degree requirements:* Computer language required, thesis optional, foreign language not required. *Average time to degree:* master's–2 years full-time, 5 years part-time. *Entrance requirements:* Minimum GPA of 3.0 in final 60 hours of undergraduate course work, 12 hours in education. Application deadline: rolling. Application fee: $20. *Expenses:* Tuition $275 per hour. Fees $200 per semester. *Financial aid:* In 1997–98, 174 students received aid, including 1 fellowship (to a first-year student); teaching assistantships, Federal Work-Study, institutionally sponsored loans, and career-related internships or fieldwork also available. Aid available to part-time students. Financial aid application deadline: 3/15; applicants required to submit FAFSA. *Faculty research:* Teacher effectiveness, bilingual education, analytic teaching. • Dr. Allen Henderson, Dean, School of Education, 817-531-4940. Application contact: Joyce Breeden, Dean of Admissions, 817-531-4458. Fax: 817-531-4231.

Texas Woman's University, College of Education and Human Ecology, Denton, TX 76204. Awards MA, M Ed, MS, Ed D, PhD. Part-time and evening/weekend programs available. Faculty: 40 full-time (27 women), 42 part-time (36 women). Students: 139 full-time (119 women), 1,269 part-time (1,104 women); includes 347 minority (200 African Americans, 19 Asian Americans, 121 Hispanics, 7 Native Americans), 17 international. Average age 38. 545 applicants, 78% accepted. In 1997, 100 master's awarded (100% found work related to degree); 18 doctorates awarded. Terminal master's awarded for partial completion of doctoral program. *Degree requirements:* For doctorate, dissertation. *Entrance requirements:* GRE General Test. Application fee: $25. *Financial aid:* In 1997–98, 185 students received aid, including 30 fellowships (20 to first-year students), 7 research assistantships (3 to first-year students), 4 teaching assistantships (1 to a first-year student); partial tuition waivers, Federal Work-Study, institutionally sponsored loans, and career-related internships or fieldwork also available. Aid available to part-time students. *Faculty research:* Reading/literacy, inclusion issues, administration styles, aging needs, marital satisfaction studies. Total annual research expenditures: $15,000. • Dr. Michael Wiebe, Dean, 940-898-2202. Fax: 940-898-2209. E-mail: a_wiebe@twu.edu.

Towson University, Program in Teaching, Towson, MD 21252-0001. Awards MAT. Faculty: 6 full-time (3 women). Students: 49 full-time (40 women), 32 part-time (17 women); includes 5 minority (2 African Americans, 2 Asian Americans, 1 Hispanic). In 1997, 31 degrees awarded. *Application deadline:* 10/1. *Application fee:* $40. *Expenses:* Tuition $187 per credit hour for state residents; $364 per credit hour for nonresidents. Fees $40 per credit hour. *Financial aid:* Assistantships available. Financial aid application deadline: 4/1; applicants required to submit FAFSA. *Faculty research:* Professional development. • Dr. Gary Kilarr, Director, 410-830-2611. Fax: 410-830-2733. E-mail: gkilarr@towson.edu. Application contact: Fran Musotto, Office Manager, 410-830-2501. Fax: 410-830-4675. E-mail: fmusotto@towson.edu.

Trevecca Nazarene University, Division of Education, Nashville, TN 37210-2834. Awards M Ed. Part-time and evening/weekend programs available. Faculty: 6 full-time (0 women), 15 part-time (3 women). Students: 212 full-time (153 women), 11 part-time (10 women); includes 22 minority (21 African Americans, 1 Hispanic). Average age 35. 101 applicants, 95% accepted. In 1997, 142 degrees awarded. *Entrance requirements:* GRE General Test, MAT, minimum GPA of 2.7. Application deadline: 8/31 (rolling processing; 1/18 for spring admission). Application fee: $25. *Expenses:* Tuition $230 per hour. Fees $60 per year. *Financial aid:* Career-related internships or fieldwork available. Aid available to part-time students. Financial aid applicants required to submit FAFSA. • Dr. Melvin Welch, Dean of Education, 615-248-1201. Fax: 615-248-7728. E-mail: mwelch@trevecca.edu.

Trinity College, School of Professional Studies, Programs in Education, Washington, DC 20017-1094. Offerings in curriculum and instruction (M Ed), including literacy, urban learner; early childhood education (MAT); elementary education (MAT); guidance and counseling (MA); secondary education (MAT); special education (MAT); student development in higher education (MA). Part-time and evening/weekend programs available. Faculty: 6 full-time (5 women), 18 part-time (13 women). *Degree requirements:* Thesis or alternative. *Entrance requirements:* Minimum GPA of 2.8. Application deadline: rolling. Application fee: $35. *Tuition:* $460 per credit hour. *Financial aid:* Career-related internships or fieldwork available. Financial aid applicants required to submit FAFSA. *Faculty research:* Ongoing professional development, preparing substitute teaching, reading acquisition. • Sr. Rosemarie Bosler, Division Chair, 202-884-9557. Application contact: Karen Goodwin, Director of Graduate Admissions, 202-884-9400. Fax: 202-884-9229.

Trinity College of Vermont, Department of Education, Burlington, VT 05401-1470. Awards M Ed, CAS, CPS. Part-time and evening/weekend programs available. Postbaccalaureate distance learning degree programs offered (minimal on-campus study). Faculty: 9 full-time (6 women), 7 part-time (2 women), 10.8 FTE. Students: 96 part-time (91 women). Average age 33. 17 applicants, 100% accepted. In 1997, 4 master's awarded (100% found work related to degree). *Degree requirements:* For master's, thesis or alternative, action research project required, foreign language not required. *Average time to degree:* master's–3 years part-time. *Entrance requirements:* For master's, current employment as a teacher, external evaluation, teaching certificate. Application deadline: rolling. Application fee: $40. *Tuition:* $278 per credit hour. *Financial aid:* Partial tuition waivers, institutionally sponsored loans available. Aid available to part-time students. Financial aid applicants required to submit FAFSA. *Faculty research:*

Directory: Education—General

Trinity College of Vermont (continued)

Learning styles, authentic evaluation, portfolio assessment, common core curricula, teacher as leader. • Dr. Vanessa C. Zerillo, Director, 802-658-0337. E-mail: vzerillo@charity.trinityvt.edu. Application contact: Maryellen Schaefer, Administrative Assistant, 802-658-0337. Fax: 802-658-5446. E-mail: schaefer@charity.trinityvt.edu.

Trinity University, Division of Behavioral and Administrative Studies, Department of Education, San Antonio, TX 78212-7200. Offers programs in educational administration (M Ed), school psychology (MA), teacher education (MAT). Accredited by NCATE. Part-time and evening/weekend programs available. Faculty: 7 full-time (3 women), 12 part-time (2 women), 12 FTE. Students: 72 full-time (57 women), 52 part-time (42 women); includes 23 minority (1 African American, 3 Asian Americans, 18 Hispanics, 1 Native American), 1 international. Average age 27. 105 applicants, 80% accepted. In 1997, 71 degrees awarded. *Entrance requirements:* GRE General Test (minimum combined score of 1000), minimum GPA of 3.0, interview. Application deadline: 5/1 (priority date). Application fee: $25. *Expenses:* Tuition $14,580 per year full-time, $608 per hour part-time. Fees $18 per year full-time, $6 per hour part-time. *Financial aid:* Fellowships, research assistantships, teaching assistantships, scholarships, grants, Federal Work-Study, institutionally sponsored loans, and career-related internships or fieldwork available. Aid available to part-time students. • Dr. John H. Moore III, Chairman, 210-736-7501.

Troy State University, Graduate School, School of Education, Troy, AL 36082. Awards MS, Ed S. Accredited by NCATE. Part-time and evening/weekend programs available. Students: 523 full-time (387 women), 601 part-time (458 women). Average age 30. In 1997, 296 master's awarded. *Degree requirements:* For master's, thesis, comprehensive exam. *Entrance requirements:* For master's, minimum GPA of 2.5; for Ed S, GRE General Test (minimum combined score of 850) or MAT (minimum score 33), Alabama Class A certificate or equivalent, minimum graduate GPA of 3.0. Application deadline: rolling. Application fee: $20. Electronic applications accepted. *Expenses:* Tuition $2040 per year full-time, $68 per hour part-time for state residents; $4200 per year full-time, $140 per hour part-time for nonresidents. Fees $240 per year full-time, $27 per quarter (minimum) part-time. *Financial aid:* Career-related internships or fieldwork available. Aid available to part-time students. Financial aid applicants required to submit FAFSA. • Dr. Anita Hardin, Dean, 334-670-3365. Fax: 334-670-3474. E-mail: ahardin@trojan.troyst.edu. Application contact: Teresa Rodgers, Director of Graduate Admissions, 334-670-3188. Fax: 334-670-3733. E-mail: trodgers@trojan.troyst.edu.

Troy State University Dothan, School of Education, Dothan, AL 36304-0368. Offers programs in counseling and psychology (MS), educational administration (MS Ed), elementary education (MS Ed, Ed S), foundations of education (MS), pre-elementary education (MS Ed, Ed S), school administration (Ed S), school counseling (MS Ed, Ed S), school psychology (MS Ed), secondary education (MS Ed), special education (MS Ed). Accredited by NCATE. Part-time and evening/weekend programs available. Students: 91. In 1997, 114 master's, 12 Ed Ss awarded. *Degree requirements:* For master's, written comprehensive exam required, thesis optional, foreign language not required. *Entrance requirements:* For master's, GRE General Test or MAT, minimum GPA of 2.5. Application fee: $20. *Expenses:* Tuition $68 per credit hour for state residents; $140 per credit hour for nonresidents. Fees $2 per credit hour. • Dr. Betty Anderson, Dean, 334-983-6556. Application contact: Reta Cordell, Director of Admissions and Records, 334-983-6556. Fax: 334-983-6322. E-mail: rcordell@tsud.edu.

Troy State University Montgomery, Division of Counseling, Education, and Psychology, PO Drawer 4419, Montgomery, AL 36103-4419. Offers programs in adult education (MS); counseling (MS, Ed S), including counseling and human development; elementary education (MS); general education administration (Ed S); teaching (MA). Part-time and evening/weekend programs available. Faculty: 3 full-time (2 women), 7 part-time (4 women). In 1997, 72 master's, 4 Ed Ss awarded. *Degree requirements:* Thesis or alternative. *Entrance requirements:* For master's, TOEFL; for Ed S, GRE General Test, MAT, or NTE; TOEFL. Application deadline: rolling. Application fee: $20. Electronic applications accepted. *Expenses:* Tuition $52 per quarter hour for state residents; $104 per quarter hour for nonresidents. Fees $30 per year. • Dr. Donald Thompson, Dean, 334-241-9594. Fax: 334-241-9586. E-mail: dthompson@tsum.edu.

Truman State University, Division of Education, Kirksville, MO 63501-4221. Awards MAE. *Entrance requirements:* GRE General Test, minimum GPA of 3.0. Application deadline: 2/15 (9/15 for spring admission). Application fee: $0 ($25 for international students). *Tuition:* $2718 per year full-time, $151 per credit part-time for state residents; $4824 per year full-time, $268 per credit part-time for nonresidents.

Tufts University, Division of Graduate and Continuing Studies and Research, Graduate School of Arts and Sciences, Department of Education, Medford, MA 02155. Offers programs in elementary education (MAT), middle and secondary education (MA, MAT), school psychology (MA, CAGS), secondary education (MA). Faculty: 9 full-time, 7 part-time. Students: 141 (109 women); includes 15 minority (6 African Americans, 4 Asian Americans, 5 Hispanics), 2 international. 209 applicants, 78% accepted. In 1997, 75 master's, 9 CAGSs awarded. *Entrance requirements:* For master's, GRE General Test, TOEFL (minimum score 550). Application deadline: 2/15 (rolling processing). Application fee: $50. *Financial aid:* Scholarships, partial tuition waivers, Federal Work-Study, and career-related internships or fieldwork available. Aid available to part-time students. Financial aid application deadline: 2/15; applicants required to submit FAFSA. • Kathleen Camara, Chair, 617-627-3244.

See in-depth description on page 791.

Tulane University, Department of Education, New Orleans, LA 70118-5669. Awards Certificate. Admissions temporarily suspended. Students: 2 full-time (both women). 0 applicants. In 1997, 4 degrees awarded. *Expenses:* Tuition $22,190 per year full-time, $1262 per hour part-time. Fees $852 per year full-time. • Dr. Martha W. Gilliland, Dean, Graduate School, 504-865-5100. E-mail: graduate.school@tulane.edu. Application contact: Kay D. Orrill, Assistant Dean, 504-865-5100. Fax: 504-865-5274.

Tusculum College, Graduate School, Program in Education, Greeneville, TN 37743-9997. Offers adult education (MA Ed), K–12 (MA Ed). Evening/weekend programs available. Students: 263 full-time, 5 part-time. *Degree requirements:* Thesis or alternative required, foreign language not required. *Average time to degree:* master's–1.3 years full-time. *Entrance requirements:* GRE or MAT, NTE, minimum GPA of 2.75, 3 years of work experience. Application fee: $0. *Tuition:* $190 per credit hour (minimum). • Application contact: Don Stout, Executive Director of Professional Studies, 423-636-7330 Ext. 612. Fax: 423-638-5181.

Tuskegee University, College of Liberal Arts and Education, Tuskegee, AL 36088. Awards M Ed, MS. One or more programs accredited by NCATE. Faculty: 3 full-time (all women), 6 part-time (3 women). Students: 13 full-time (7 women), 2 part-time (both women); includes 15 minority (all African Americans). Average age 24. In 1997, 8 degrees awarded. *Entrance requirements:* GRE General Test. Application deadline: 7/15 (rolling processing). Application fee: $25 ($35 for international students). *Financial aid:* Application deadline 4/15. • Dr. Mary A. Jones, Acting Dean, 334-727-8561.

Union College, Department of Education, Barbourville, KY 40906-1499. Offers programs in elementary education (MA Ed), middle grades (MA Ed), music education (MA Ed), reading specialist (MA Ed), secondary education (MA Ed), special education (MA Ed). *Degree requirements:* Thesis optional, foreign language not required. *Entrance requirements:* GRE General Test, NTE. Application deadline: rolling. Application fee: $15. *Tuition:* $220 per hour. • Dr. William E. Bernhardt, Dean of Graduate Academic Affairs, Graduate Programs, 606-546-1210. Fax: 606-546-2217.

Union College, Graduate and Continuing Studies, Programs in Education, Schenectady, NY 12308-2311. Offerings in biology (MAT), chemistry (MAT), earth science (MAT), English (MAT), French (MAT), general science (MAT), German (MAT), Latin (MAT), mathematics (MAT), mathematics/computer science (MS), natural sciences (MS), physical sciences (MS), physics (MAT), social studies (MAT), Spanish (MAT). Students: 51 full-time (32 women), 10 part-time (3 women); includes 1 minority (Hispanic), 2 international. 39 applicants, 97% accepted. In 1997, 49 degrees awarded. *Application deadline:* 5/15. *Application fee:* $35. *Tuition:* $1155 per course. • Dr. Patrick Allen, Educational Studies Director, 518-388-6361.

Union University, School of Education and Human Studies, Jackson, TN 38305-3697. Offers program in education (MA Ed, M Ed). M Ed also available at Germantown campus. Part-time and evening/weekend programs available. Faculty: 8 full-time (2 women), 5 part-time (3 women). Students: 23 full-time (16 women), 61 part-time (50 women); includes 18 minority (16 African Americans, 2 Asian Americans), 2 international. Average age 32. 57 applicants, 100% accepted. In 1997, 31 degrees awarded. *Degree requirements:* Computer language, comprehensive exam or thesis. *Average time to degree:* master's–1.5 years full-time, 2.5 years part-time. *Entrance requirements:* MAT (minimum score 30 required for MA Ed), minimum undergraduate GPA of 2.75 (MA Ed); minimum GPA of 3.0, teaching license (M Ed). Application deadline: 8/24 (priority date; rolling processing; 2/1 for spring admission). Application fee: $25. Electronic applications accepted. *Tuition:* $185 per hour (minimum). *Financial aid:* Career-related internships or fieldwork available. Financial aid applicants required to submit FAFSA. *Faculty research:* Elementary mathematics instruction, staff development, locus of control and retention in grade, biofeedback. • Dr. Tom Rosebrough, Dean, 901-661-5372. E-mail: trosebro@buster.uu.edu. Application contact: Helen F. Butler, Coordinator of Programs, 901-661-5374. Fax: 901-661-5063. E-mail: hbutler@buster.uu.edu.

United States International University, College of Arts and Sciences, Department of Education, San Diego, CA 92131-1799. Offers programs in educational administration (MA, Ed D), teaching (MA), teaching English to speakers of other languages (MA, Ed D), technology and learning (MA, Ed D). Part-time and evening/weekend programs available. Faculty: 10 full-time (7 women), 12 part-time (6 women). Students: 28 full-time (21 women), 249 part-time (185 women); includes 54 minority (18 African Americans, 12 Asian Americans, 23 Hispanics, 1 Native American), 11 international. Average age 40. 106 applicants, 82% accepted. In 1997, 86 master's, 8 doctorates awarded. Terminal master's awarded for partial completion of doctoral program. *Degree requirements:* Thesis/dissertation. *Average time to degree:* master's–1.5 years full-time, 2.5 years part-time; doctorate–3 years full-time, 5 years part-time. *Entrance requirements:* For master's, TOEFL, minimum GPA of 2.5; for doctorate, GRE General Test or MAT, TOEFL, minimum GPA of 3.0. Application deadline: 8/1 (priority date; rolling processing; 3/1 for spring admission). Application fee: $40. *Expenses:* Tuition $255 per unit. Fees $120 per year full-time, $33 per quarter part-time. *Financial aid:* In 1997–98, 194 students received aid, including 8 research assistantships (4 to first-year students) averaging $470 per month; partial tuition waivers, Federal Work-Study, and career-related internships or fieldwork also available. Aid available to part-time students. Financial aid application deadline: 3/2; applicants required to submit FAFSA. *Faculty research:* Critical thinking, second language acquisition, distance learning. • Dr. Mary Ellen Butler-Pascoe, Chair, 619-635-4595. Fax: 619-635-4714. Application contact: Susan Topham, Assistant Director of Admissions, 619-635-4885. Fax: 619-635-4739. E-mail: admissions@usiu.edu.

Universidad de las Américas–Puebla, Division of Graduate Studies, School of Social Sciences, Program in Education, Cholula 72820, Mexico. Awards MA. Part-time and evening/weekend programs available. Faculty: 7 full-time (2 women). Students: 38 full-time (25 women), 11 part-time (9 women); includes 49 minority (all Hispanics). Average age 29. In 1997, 7 degrees awarded. *Degree requirements:* 1 foreign language, thesis. *Average time to degree:* master's–2.5 years full-time, 3.5 years part-time. *Application deadline:* 7/18 (rolling processing). *Application fee:* $0. *Expenses:* Tuition $5400 per year full-time, $113 per year part-time. Fees $361 per year. *Financial aid:* 30 students received aid; research assistantships available. Aid available to part-time students. Financial aid application deadline: 5/15. *Faculty research:* Curriculum development, curriculum evaluation, instructional technology, critical thinking. Total annual research expenditures: $33,000. • Bertha Salinas, Chair, 22-29-20-52. Fax: 22-29-26-35. E-mail: bsalinas@mail.udlap.mx. Application contact: Mauricio Villegas, Chair of Admissions Office, 22-29-20-17. Fax: 22-29-20-18. E-mail: admision@mail.udlap.mx.

Universidad del Turabo, Programs in Education, Gurabo, PR 00778-3030. Offerings in bilingual education (MA), education administration and supervision (MA), school libraries administration (MA), special education (MA), teaching English as a second language (MA). Part-time and evening/weekend programs available. *Entrance requirements:* GRE, PAEG, interview. Application deadline: 8/5. Application fee: $25.

Universidad Metropolitana, Graduate Programs in Education, Río Piedras, PR 00928-1150. Offerings in administration of pre-school (MA), environmental education (MA), teaching (MA). Faculty: 2 full-time (both women), 30 part-time (9 women), 16 FTE. *Application deadline:* rolling. *Application fee:* $0. • Dr. Ana Delgado, Dean, 787-766-1717 Ext. 6409.

Université de Moncton, Faculty of Education, Graduate Studies in Education, Moncton, NB E1A 3E9, Canada. Offers programs in educational psychology (MA Ed, M Ed), guidance (MA Ed, M Ed), school administration (MA Ed, M Ed), teaching (MA Ed, M Ed). Part-time programs available. Faculty: 25 full-time (12 women). Students: 41 full-time (28 women), 34 part-time (17 women); includes 4 international. Average age 33. 60 applicants, 70% accepted. In 1997, 56 degrees awarded. *Degree requirements:* Proficiency in English and French. *Entrance requirements:* Minimum GPA of 3.0. Application deadline: 6/1 (rolling processing). Application fee: $30. *Financial aid:* 10 students received aid; research assistantships, teaching assistantships available. Financial aid application deadline: 2/28. *Faculty research:* Guidance, ethnolinguistic vitality, children's rights, ecological education, entrepreneurship. Total annual research expenditures: $200,000. • Léonard Goguen, Director, 506-858-4409. Fax: 506-858-4317. E-mail: goguenl@umoncton.ca. Application contact: Nicole Savoie, Conseillière à l'admission, 506-858-4115. Fax: 506-858-4544. E-mail: savoien@umoncton.ca.

Université de Montréal, Faculty of Education, Montréal, PQ H3C 3J7, Canada. Awards MA, M Ed, PhD, DESS. Part-time and evening/weekend programs available. Faculty: 94 full-time (39 women), 5 part-time (4 women). 549 applicants, 57% accepted. In 1997, 171 master's, 33 doctorates awarded. Terminal master's awarded for partial completion of doctoral program. *Degree requirements:* For doctorate, dissertation, general exam. *Application fee:* $30. *Financial aid:* Fellowships, research assistantships, teaching assistantships available. • Giséle Painchaud, Dean, 514-343-6658. Application contact: Marcienne Lévesque, Graduate Chairman, 514-343-7844.

Université de Sherbrooke, Faculty of Education, Sherbrooke, PQ J1K 2R1, Canada. Awards MA, M Ed, Diploma. Part-time and evening/weekend programs available. *Degree requirements:* For master's, thesis. *Application deadline:* 6/1. *Application fee:* $15. *Faculty research:* Career education, teaching, professional instruction.

Université du Québec à Chicoutimi, Program in Education, Chicoutimi, PQ G7H 2B1, Canada. Awards MA, M Ed, PhD. PhD offered jointly with the Université du Québec à Hull, the Université du Québec à Montréal, the Université du Québec à Rimouski, the Université du Québec à Trois-Rivières, and the Université du Québec en Abitibi-Témiscamingue. Part-time programs available. *Degree requirements:* For doctorate, dissertation. *Entrance requirements:* For master's, appropriate bachelor's degree, proficiency in French; for doctorate, appropriate master's degree, proficiency in French. Application deadline: 5/1. Application fee: $30.

Université du Québec à Hull, Program in Education, Hull, PQ J8X 3X7, Canada. Awards MA, M Ed, PhD. MA and M Ed offered jointly with the Université du Québec à Rimouski and the Université du Québec en Abitibi-Témiscamingue. PhD offered jointly with the Universités du Québec à Montréal, à Rimouski, à Trois-Riviéres, à Chicoutimi, and en Abitibi-Témiscamingue. Part-time programs available. *Degree requirements:* For master's, thesis optional; for doctorate, dissertation. *Entrance requirements:* For master's, appropriate bachelor's degree, proficiency in French; for doctorate, appropriate master's degree, proficiency in French. Application deadline: 8/21. Application fee: $30.

Université du Québec à Montréal, Program in Education, Montréal, PQ H3C 3P8, Canada. Offers education (MA, M Ed, PhD), education of the environmental sciences (Diploma). PhD offered jointly with the Université du Québec à Chicoutimi, the Université du Québec à Hull, the Université du Québec à Rimouski, the Université du Québec à Trois-Rivières, and the Université du Québec en Abitibi-Témiscamingue; Diploma new for fall 1997. Part-time programs available. *Degree requirements:* For master's, thesis (for some programs); for doctorate, dissertation. *Entrance requirements:* For master's and Diploma, appropriate bachelor's degree or equivalent and proficiency in French; for doctorate, appropriate master's degree or equivalent and proficiency in French. Application deadline: 2/15. Application fee: $50.

Université du Québec à Rimouski, Program in Education, Rimouski, PQ G5L 3A1, Canada. Awards MA, M Ed, PhD. MA and M Ed offered jointly with the Université du Québec à Hull and the Université du Québec en Abitibi-Témiscamingue. PhD offered jointly with the Universités du Québec à Chicoutimi, à Hull, à Trois-Riviéres, and en Abitibi-Témiscamingue. Part-time programs available. *Degree requirements:* For master's, thesis optional; for doctorate, dissertation. *Entrance requirements:* For master's, appropriate bachelor's degree, proficiency in French; for doctorate, appropriate master's degree, proficiency in French. Application deadline: 5/1 (priority date). Application fee: $30.

Université du Québec à Trois-Rivières, Program in Education, Trois-Rivières, PQ G9A 5H7, Canada. Awards MA, M Ed, PhD. PhD offered jointly with the Université du Québec à Chicoutimi, the Université du Québec à Hull, the Université du Québec à Montréal, the Université du Québec à Rimouski, and the Université du Québec en Abitibi-Témiscamingue. Part-time programs available. Students: 11 full-time (9 women), 8 part-time (6 women). 28 applicants, 86% accepted. *Degree requirements:* For master's, research report required, thesis not required; for doctorate, dissertation. *Entrance requirements:* For master's, appropriate bachelor's degree, proficiency in French; for doctorate, appropriate master's degree, proficiency in French. Application deadline: 2/1. Application fee: $30. *Financial aid:* Fellowships, research assistantships, teaching assistantships available. • Colette Baribeau, Director, 819-376-5094. Fax: 819-376-5127. E-mail: colette_baribeau@uqtr.uquebec.ca. Application contact: Suzanne Camirand, Admissions Officer, 819-376-5045 Ext. 2591. Fax: 819-376-5210. E-mail: suzanne_camirand@uqtr.uquebec.ca.

Université du Québec en Abitibi-Témiscamingue, Program in Education, Rouyn-Noranda, PQ J9X 5E4, Canada. Awards MA, M Ed, PhD. MA and M Ed offered jointly with the Université du Québec à Hull and the Université du Québec à Rimouski. PhD offered jointly with the Universités du Québec à Chicoutimi, à Hull, à Montreal, à Rimouski, and à Trois-Rivières. Part-time programs available. *Degree requirements:* For master's, thesis optional; for doctorate, dissertation. *Entrance requirements:* For master's, appropriate bachelor's degree, proficiency in French; for doctorate, appropriate master's degree, proficiency in French. Application deadline: 4/1. Application fee: $30.

Université Laval, Faculty of Education, Sainte-Foy, PQ G1K 7P4, Canada. Awards MA, M Sc, PhD, Diploma. Students: 443 full-time (308 women), 494 part-time (365 women); includes 47 international. Average age 33. 474 applicants, 77% accepted. In 1997, 187 master's, 23 doctorates, 71 Diplomas awarded. *Application deadline:* 3/1. *Application fee:* $30. *Expenses:* Tuition $1334 per year (minimum) full-time, $56 per credit (minimum) part-time for Canadian residents; $5966 per year (minimum) full-time, $249 per credit (minimum) part-time for nonresidents. Fees $150 per year full-time, $6.25 per credit part-time. *Financial aid:* Fellowships available. • Jean-Claude Gagnon, Dean, 418-656-2131 Ext. 2059. Fax: 418-656-2731. E-mail: jean-claude.gagnon@fse.ulaval.ca.

The University of Akron, College of Education, Akron, OH 44325-0001. Awards MA, MA Ed, MS, MS Ed, MSTE, Ed D, PhD. Accredited by NCATE. Part-time programs available. Faculty: 59 full-time, 99 part-time. Students: 269 full-time (179 women), 835 part-time (592 women); includes 153 minority (121 African Americans, 16 Asian Americans, 9 Hispanics, 7 Native Americans), 10 international. Average age 36. 120 applicants, 69% accepted. In 1997, 203 master's, 26 doctorates awarded. Terminal master's awarded for partial completion of doctoral program. *Degree requirements:* For master's, written comprehensive exam required, foreign language not required; for doctorate, variable foreign language requirement, dissertation, written and oral exams. *Application deadline:* 8/15 (rolling processing). *Application fee:* $25 ($50 for international students). *Expenses:* Tuition $178 per credit hour for state residents; $333 per credit hour for nonresidents. Fees $145 per year full-time, $32 per semester (minimum) part-time. *Financial aid:* In 1997–98, 138 students received aid, including 36 research assistantships, 36 teaching assistantships, 22 administrative assistantships; fellowships, full tuition waivers, Federal Work-Study, and career-related internships or fieldwork also available. *Faculty research:* History, philosophy of education, ethnographic research in education, case study methodology in education, multiple linear regression. • Dr. Rita Saslaw, Dean, 330-972-7680. E-mail: rsaslaw@uakron.edu. Application contact: Dr. Robert Eley, Director of Student Services, 330-972-7750. E-mail: reley@uakron.edu.

The University of Alabama, College of Education, Tuscaloosa, AL 35487. Awards MA, Ed D, PhD, Ed S. Accredited by NCATE. Part-time programs available. Faculty: 60 full-time (28 women), 9 part-time (5 women). Students: 324 full-time (237 women), 542 part-time (398 women); includes 115 minority (89 African Americans, 3 Asian Americans, 19 Hispanics, 4 Native Americans). Average age 35. In 1997, 299 master's, 75 doctorates, 57 Ed Ss awarded. *Degree requirements:* For doctorate, 1 foreign language, dissertation. *Entrance requirements:* For master's and doctorate, GRE General Test, MAT (score in 50th percentile or higher), or NTE (minimum score 658 on each core battery test), minimum GPA of 3.0; for Ed S, minimum GPA of 3.0 during previous 2 years. Application deadline: 7/6 (rolling processing). Application fee: $25. *Tuition:* $2684 per year full-time, $594 per semester (minimum) part-time for state residents; $7216 per year full-time, $1248 per semester (minimum) part-time for nonresidents. *Financial aid:* Fellowships, research assistantships, teaching assistantships, Federal Work-Study, institutionally sponsored loans, and career-related internships or fieldwork available. • Dr. John Dolly, Dean, 205-348-6052. Fax: 205-348-6873. E-mail: dolly@bamaed.ua.edu.

The University of Alabama at Birmingham, Graduate School, School of Education, Birmingham, AL 35294. Awards MA, MA Ed, Ed D, PhD, Ed S. Accredited by NCATE. Part-time and evening/weekend programs available. Faculty: 57 full-time, 45 part-time. Students: 317 full-time (247 women), 355 part-time (285 women); includes 134 minority (113 African Americans, 13 Asian Americans, 1 Hispanic, 7 Native Americans). 632 applicants, 96% accepted. In 1997, 365 master's, 14 doctorates, 49 Ed Ss awarded. *Degree requirements:* For master's, thesis optional; for doctorate, dissertation; for Ed S, comprehensive exam. *Entrance requirements:* For master's, GRE General Test, MAT, or NTE, minimum GPA of 3.0. Application deadline: rolling. Application fee: $30 ($60 for international students). Electronic applications accepted. *Expenses:* Tuition $99 per credit hour for state residents; $198 per credit hour for nonresidents. Fees $516 per year (minimum) full-time, $73 per quarter (minimum) part-time for state residents; $516 per year (minimum) full-time, $73 per unit (minimum) part-time for nonresidents. *Financial aid:* Fellowships, Federal Work-Study, and career-related internships or fieldwork available. Aid available to part-time students. • Dr. Clint E. Bruess, Dean, 205-934-5363.

University of Alaska Anchorage, College of Health, Education and Social Welfare, School of Education, Anchorage, AK 99508-8060. Awards MAT, M Ed. Part-time programs available. Students: 76 full-time (58 women), 88 part-time (67 women); includes 23 minority (9 African Americans, 2 Asian Americans, 3 Hispanics, 9 Native Americans). 108 applicants, 69% accepted. In 1997, 87 degrees awarded. *Entrance requirements:* GRE or MAT, interview. Application deadline: 5/1 (rolling processing). Application fee: $45. *Expenses:* Tuition $2988 per year full-time, $1990 per year part-time for state residents; $5814 per year full-time, $3876 per year part-time for nonresidents. Fees $298 per year. *Financial aid:* Federal Work-Study and career-related internships or fieldwork available. Aid available to part-time students. Financial aid application deadline: 4/1. • Application contact: Linda Berg Smith, Associate Vice Chancellor for Enrollment Services, 907-786-1529.

University of Alaska Fairbanks, Graduate School, School of Education, Fairbanks, AK 99775-7480. Offers programs in cross-cultural education (M Ed, Ed S), curriculum and instruction (M Ed), educational administration (M Ed), guidance and counseling (M Ed), language and literature (M Ed). Faculty: 23 full-time (13 women), 2 part-time (both women). Students: 18 full-time (12 women), 10 part-time (8 women); includes 6 minority (1 Hispanic, 5 Native Americans). Average age 36. In 1997, 25 master's awarded. *Degree requirements:* For master's, thesis or alternative, comprehensive exam required, foreign language not required. *Entrance requirements:* For master's, GRE General Test, TOEFL (minimum score 550). Application deadline: 4/1 (10/1 for spring admission). Application fee: $35. *Expenses:* Tuition $162 per credit for state residents; $316 per credit for nonresidents. Fees $520 per year full-time, $45 per semester (minimum) part-time. *Financial aid:* Research assistantships, teaching assistantships, and career-related internships or fieldwork available. • Dr. Joe Kan, Director, 907-474-7341.

University of Alaska Southeast, Program in Education, Juneau, AK 99801-8625. Offers early childhood education (M Ed), elementary education (MAT, M Ed), secondary education (MAT, M Ed). *Degree requirements:* Comprehensive exam or project required, foreign language and thesis not required. *Entrance requirements:* Minimum GPA of 3.0. Application deadline: 8/15 (priority date; rolling processing; 2/15 for spring admission). Application fee: $35. Electronic applications accepted. *Tuition:* $162 per credit for state residents; $316 per credit for nonresidents. *Financial aid:* Federal Work-Study, institutionally sponsored loans, and career-related internships or fieldwork available. Aid available to part-time students. • Application contact: Greg Wagner, Recruiter, 907-465-6239. Fax: 907-465-6365. E-mail: jngaw@acad1.alaska.edu.

The University of Arizona, College of Education, Tucson, AZ 85721. Awards MA, M Ed, MS, MT, Ed D, PhD, Ed S. Part-time programs available. Terminal master's awarded for partial completion of doctoral program. *Degree requirements:* For doctorate, dissertation. *Entrance requirements:* For master's and Ed S, TOEFL (minimum score 550); for doctorate, GRE, TOEFL (minimum score 550). Application deadline: rolling. Application fee: $35. *Tuition:* $2162 per year full-time, $337 per semester (minimum) part-time for state residents; $6860 per year full-time, $1138 per semester (minimum) part-time for nonresidents. *Faculty research:* Teacher effectiveness, pupil achievement, learning skills, program evaluation, instructional method effects.

See in-depth description on page 793.

University of Arkansas, College of Education, Fayetteville, AR 72701-1201. Awards MAT, M Ed, MS, Ed D, PhD, Ed S. Accredited by NCATE. Faculty: 91 full-time (36 women), 3 part-time (2 women). Students: 431 full-time (286 women), 163 part-time (113 women); includes 44 minority (22 African Americans, 4 Asian Americans, 5 Hispanics, 13 Native Americans), 16 international. 392 applicants, 77% accepted. In 1997, 235 master's, 38 doctorates, 15 Ed Ss awarded. *Degree requirements:* For doctorate, dissertation. *Application fee:* $25 ($35 for international students). *Tuition:* $3144 per year full-time, $173 per credit hour part-time for state residents; $7140 per year full-time, $395 per credit hour part-time for nonresidents. *Financial aid:* Research assistantships, teaching assistantships, Federal Work-Study, and career-related internships or fieldwork available. Aid available to part-time students. Financial aid application deadline: 4/1; applicants required to submit FAFSA. • Charles Stegman, Dean, 501-575-3208.

University of Arkansas at Little Rock, College of Education, Little Rock, AR 72204-1099. Awards MA, M Ed, Ed D, Ed S. One or more programs accredited by NCATE. Part-time and evening/weekend programs available. Students: 124 full-time (98 women), 399 part-time (313 women); includes 107 minority (98 African Americans, 3 Asian Americans, 6 Hispanics), 12 international. Average age 37. 381 applicants, 75% accepted. In 1997, 156 master's, 19 doctorates, 3 Ed Ss awarded. *Degree requirements:* For doctorate, comprehensive exam, oral defense of dissertation, residency required, foreign language not required; for Ed S, comprehensive exam required, foreign language not required. *Entrance requirements:* For master's, minimum GPA of 2.75; for doctorate, GRE General Test (minimum combined score of 1500 on three sections) or MAT, minimum graduate GPA of 3.0, teaching certificate, work experience; for Ed S, GRE General Test (minimum combined score of 1350 on three sections) or MAT (minimum score 40), teaching certificate. Application fee: $25 ($30 for international students). *Expenses:* Tuition $2466 per year full-time, $137 per credit hour part-time for state residents; $5256 per year full-time, $292 per credit hour part-time for nonresidents. Fees $216 per year full-time, $36 per semester (minimum) part-time. *Financial aid:* Research assistantships, teaching assistantships, full tuition waivers, Federal Work-Study, institutionally sponsored loans, and career-related internships or fieldwork available. Aid available to part-time students. • Dr. Angela Sewall, Dean, 501-569-3113. Application contact: Dr. Thomas Teeter, Associate Dean, 501-569-3434.

University of Arkansas at Monticello, School of Education, Monticello, AR 71656. Offers programs in elementary education (M Ed), secondary education (M Ed). Part-time and evening/weekend programs available. Faculty: 13 full-time (4 women). Students: 18 full-time (16 women), 118 part-time (110 women); includes 11 minority (7 African Americans, 2 Asian Americans, 2 Hispanics). 92 applicants, 98% accepted. In 1997, 13 degrees awarded. *Degree requirements:* Comprehensive exam required, foreign language and thesis not required. *Entrance requirements:* Minimum GPA of 2.75, teaching certificate. Application deadline: 8/22 (priority date). Application fee: $0. *Financial aid:* Partial tuition waivers, Federal Work-Study available. Aid available to part-time students. *Faculty research:* School improvement, performance assessment, minority retention. • Dr. Gerald Norris, Dean, 870-460-1062. Fax: 870-460-1563.

University of Arkansas at Pine Bluff, Program in Education, Pine Bluff, AR 71601-2799. Offers elementary education (M Ed); secondary education (M Ed), including aquaculture, English, general science, mathematics, physical education, social studies. Accredited by NCATE. Faculty: 51. Students: 75. *Entrance requirements:* GRE, minimum GPA of 2.75; NTE or Standard Arkansas Teaching Certificate. Application deadline: rolling. Application fee: $0. *Expenses:* Tuition $82 per credit hour for state residents; $192 per credit hour for nonresidents. Fees $25 per year. *Faculty research:* Minority representation in early grades. • Dr. Calvin Johnson, Dean, 870-543-8256.

University of Bridgeport, College of Graduate and Undergraduate Studies, School of Education and Human Resources, Division of Education, 380 University Avenue, Bridgeport, CT 06601. Offers programs in education (MS); educational management (Ed D, Diploma); elementary education (MS, Diploma), including early childhood education, elementary education; secondary education (MS, Diploma), including computer specialist, international education, reading specialist, secondary education. Part-time and evening/weekend programs available. Faculty: 10 full-time (2 women), 59 part-time (26 women), 30 FTE. Students: 271 full-time (184 women), 229 part-time (158 women); includes 74 minority (46 African Americans, 6 Asian Americans, 22 Hispanics), 39 international. Average age 30. 270 applicants, 78% accepted. In 1997, 154 master's, 5 doctorates, 23 Diplomas awarded. *Degree requirements:* For master's, computer language, final exam, final project, or thesis required, foreign language not required; for doctorate, dissertation; for Diploma, thesis or alternative, final project required, foreign language not required. *Entrance requirements:* For master's, GRE General Test, MAT (score in 35th percentile or higher), minimum undergraduate QPA of 2.5; for doctorate, GRE, MAT; for Diploma, GRE General Test or MAT (score in 40th percentile or higher), minimum graduate QPA of 3.0. Application fee: $35 ($50 for international students). *Tuition:* $340 per credit. *Financial aid:* In 1997–98, 208 students received aid, including 3 teaching assistantships; fellowships, research assistantships, Federal Work-Study, institutionally sponsored loans, and career-related internships or fieldwork also available. Aid available to part-time students. Financial aid application deadline: 6/1; applicants required to submit FAFSA. *Faculty research:* Self-concept, internship assessment, stress and situational development, follow-up of graduation, trend analysis. • Dr. Allen P. Cook, Associate Dean, 203-576-4206.

See in-depth description on page 795.

Directory: Education—General

University of British Columbia, Faculty of Education, Vancouver, BC V6T 1Z2, Canada. Awards MA, M Ed, MHK, M Sc, Ed D, PhD, Diploma. Part-time and evening/weekend programs available. Terminal master's awarded for partial completion of doctoral program. *Degree requirements:* For doctorate, dissertation required, foreign language not required. *Entrance requirements:* TOEFL. Application fee: $60. *Faculty research:* Schooling, collaborative research, counselling, continuing education, curriculum.

The University of Calgary, Faculty of Education, Calgary, AB T2N 1N4, Canada. Awards MA, M Ed, M Sc, Ed D, PhD. Part-time and evening/weekend programs available. Postbaccalaureate distance learning degree programs offered (minimal on-campus study). Faculty: 60 full-time, 5 part-time. Students: 321 full-time, 276 part-time. Average age 36. In 1997, 150 master's, 23 doctorates awarded. *Degree requirements:* For doctorate, dissertation, candidacy exam. *Entrance requirements:* For master's, minimum GPA of 3.0; for doctorate, minimum GPA of 3.5. *Expenses:* Tuition $5448 per year full-time, $908 per course part-time for Canadian residents; $10,896 per year full-time, $1816 per course part-time for nonresidents. Fees $285 per year full-time, $119 per semester (minimum) part-time. *Financial aid:* 10 students received aid; fellowships, research assistantships, teaching assistantships, institutionally sponsored loans available. • Dr. Ian Winchester, Dean, 403-220-5627. Fax: 403-282-5849. E-mail: 18011@ucdasvm1.admin.ucalgary.ca. Application contact: Dr. Bryant Griffith, Assistant Dean, Division of Educational Research, 403-220-5675. Fax: 403-282-3005. E-mail: griffith@ucalgary.ca.

University of California, Berkeley, School of Education, Berkeley, CA 94720-1500. Awards MA, Ed D, PhD, Certificate, PhD/MA. Faculty: 32 full-time, 29 part-time. Students: 378 full-time (258 women); includes 122 minority (28 African Americans, 50 Asian Americans, 38 Hispanics, 6 Native Americans), 19 international. Average age 31. 694 applicants, 27% accepted. In 1997, 67 master's, 29 doctorates awarded. Terminal master's awarded for partial completion of doctoral program. *Degree requirements:* For master's, exam or thesis required, foreign language not required; for doctorate, dissertation, oral qualifying exam (PhD) required, foreign language not required. *Entrance requirements:* For master's and doctorate, GRE General Test, minimum GPA of 3.0 during last 2 years of undergraduate course work; for Certificate, GRE General Test, minimum GPA of 3.0. Application deadline: 12/15. Application fee: $40. *Expenses:* Tuition $0 for state residents; $9384 per year for nonresidents. Fees $4409 per year. *Financial aid:* Fellowships, research assistantships, teaching assistantships, and career-related internships or fieldwork available. Financial aid application deadline: 12/15. *Faculty research:* Cognition and development; language, literacy and culture. • Dr. Eugene Garcia, Dean, 510-642-3726. Application contact: Francisca Cazares, Admissions Assistant, 510-642-0841. Fax: 510-642-4808. E-mail: fcazares@uclink4.berkeley.edu.

University of California, Davis, Program in Education, Davis, CA 95616. Offers education (Ed D), family and social organization (M Ed), instructional studies (PhD), psychological studies (PhD), sociocultural studies (PhD). Ed D offered jointly with California State University, Fresno; M Ed admissions temporarily suspended. Part-time programs available. Faculty: 19 full-time (9 women). Students: 50. In 1997, 25 master's awarded. *Degree requirements:* For master's, thesis optional, foreign language not required; for doctorate, dissertation. *Entrance requirements:* For master's, GRE General Test, minimum GPA of 3.0. Application deadline: 2/15. Application fee: $40. *Expenses:* Tuition $0 for state residents; $9384 per year for nonresidents. Fees $4466 per year full-time, $2923 per year part-time. *Financial aid:* Fellowships, research assistantships, teaching assistantships, and career-related internships or fieldwork available. *Faculty research:* Language and literacy, mathematics education, science education, teacher development, school psychology. • Johnathan Sandoval, Chair, 530-752-0761. Application contact: Karen Bray, Graduate Adviser, 530-752-0761.

University of California, Irvine, Department of Education, Irvine, CA 92697. Offers program in educational administration (Ed D). Part-time and evening/weekend programs available. Faculty: 6 full-time (2 women), 4 part-time (3 women). Students: 22 part-time (15 women); includes 5 minority (1 African American, 1 Asian American, 3 Hispanics). Average age 43. 16 applicants, 56% accepted. *Degree requirements:* Dissertation. *Entrance requirements:* GRE General Test. Application deadline: 3/1 (priority date). Application fee: $40. Electronic applications accepted. *Expenses:* Tuition $0 for state residents; $9384 per year full-time, $1564 per quarter part-time for nonresidents. Fees $4998 per year full-time, $1152 per quarter part-time. *Financial aid:* Fellowships, research assistantships, institutionally sponsored loans available. Financial aid application deadline: 3/2; applicants required to submit FAFSA. *Faculty research:* Education technology, learning theory, social theory, cultural diversity, postmodernism, education policy, mathematics education. • Louis F. Miron, Chair, 949-824-7840. Application contact: Sarah K. Singh, Admissions and Placement, 949-824-7832. Fax: 949-824-2965. E-mail: sksingh@uci.edu.

University of California, Los Angeles, Graduate School of Education and Information Studies, Department of Education, Los Angeles, CA 90095. Awards MA, M Ed, Ed D, PhD, JD/MA, JD/PhD. Students: 493 full-time (360 women); includes 197 minority (25 African Americans, 88 Asian Americans, 80 Hispanics, 4 Native Americans), 24 international. 493 applicants, 52% accepted. *Degree requirements:* For master's, comprehensive exam required, thesis not required; for doctorate, dissertation, oral and written qualifying exams required, foreign language not required. *Entrance requirements:* For master's, GRE General Test, minimum GPA of 3.0; for doctorate, GRE General Test, minimum undergraduate GPA of 3.0. Application deadline: 12/15. Application fee: $40. Electronic applications accepted. *Expenses:* Tuition $0 for state residents; $9384 per year for nonresidents. Fees $4551 per year. *Financial aid:* In 1997–98, 358 students received aid, including fellowships totaling $1.243 million, research assistantships totaling $1.897 million, teaching assistantships totaling $200,975, federal fellowships and scholarships totaling $90,955. Financial aid application deadline: 3/1. • Dr. H. Levine, Chair, 310-825-8326. Application contact: Departmental Office, 310-825-8326. E-mail: nobody@bert.gse.ucla.edu.

University of California, Riverside, Graduate Division, School of Education, Riverside, CA 92521-0102. Awards MA, PhD. Faculty: 19 full-time (6 women), 7 part-time (6 women). Students: 92 full-time (64 women), 10 part-time (5 women); includes 24 minority (3 African Americans, 11 Asian Americans, 8 Hispanics, 2 Native Americans), 1 international. Average age 37. 52 applicants, 63% accepted. In 1997, 16 master's, 10 doctorates awarded. Terminal master's awarded for partial completion of doctoral program. *Degree requirements:* For master's, comprehensive exams or thesis required, foreign language not required; for doctorate, dissertation, qualifying exams, teaching experience required, foreign language not required. *Average time to degree:* master's–2 years full-time; doctorate–7 years full-time. *Entrance requirements:* For master's, GRE General Test (minimum combined score of 1100), TOEFL (minimum score 550); for doctorate, GRE General Test (minimum combined score of 1100), TOEFL (minimum score 550), master's degree. Application deadline: 5/1 (rolling processing; 12/1 for spring admission). Application fee: $40. *Expenses:* Tuition $0 for state residents; $9384 per year for nonresidents. Fees $4861 per year. *Financial aid:* Fellowships, research assistantships, teaching assistantships, full and partial tuition waivers, Federal Work-Study, institutionally sponsored loans, and career-related internships or fieldwork available. Financial aid application deadline: 2/1; applicants required to submit FAFSA. *Faculty research:* Educational measurement, cognitive development, school organization and administration, school psychology, educational policy. • Dr. Robert Calfee, Dean, 909-787-5225. Application contact: Dr. Donald MacMillan, Graduate Adviser, 909-787-5228. Fax: 909-787-3942. E-mail: donald.macmillan@ucr.edu.

University of California, San Diego, Program in Teacher Education, 9500 Gilman Drive, La Jolla, CA 92093-5003. Awards MA. Students: 12 (all women). In 1997, 15 degrees awarded. *Entrance requirements:* GRE General Test. Application fee: $40. *Expenses:* Tuition $0 for state residents; $9384 per year full-time, $4692 per year part-time for nonresidents. Fees $4887 per year full-time, $3344 per year part-time. • Dr. Hugh Mehan, Chair. Application contact: Student Services, 619-534-1680.

University of California, Santa Barbara, Graduate School of Education, Santa Barbara, CA 93106. Offers programs in clinical/school/counseling psychology (M Ed, PhD), including clinical/school/counseling psychology (PhD), school psychology (M Ed); education (MA, M Ed, PhD). Students: 287 full-time (216 women); includes 103 minority (18 African Americans, 28 Asian Americans, 50 Hispanics, 7 Native Americans), 14 international. 622 applicants, 31% accepted. In 1997, 101 master's, 31 doctorates awarded. *Degree requirements:* For master's, thesis or alternative required, foreign language not required; for doctorate, dissertation required, foreign language not required. *Entrance requirements:* For master's, TOEFL (minimum score 550), minimum GPA of 3.0; for doctorate, GRE General Test or MAT, TOEFL (minimum score 550), minimum GPA of 3.0. Application fee: $40. Electronic applications accepted. *Expenses:* Tuition $0 for state residents; $9384 per year for nonresidents. Fees $4930 per year. *Financial aid:* Fellowships, research assistantships, full and partial tuition waivers, Federal Work-Study, institutionally sponsored loans, and career-related internships or fieldwork available. Financial aid applicants required to submit FAFSA. • Jules Zimmer, Dean, 805-893-3917. Application contact: Lauren Bonar, Graduate Secretary, 805-893-2137. E-mail: jan@education.ucsb.edu.

University of California, Santa Cruz, Division of Social Sciences, Program in Education, Santa Cruz, CA 95064. Awards MA, Certificate. Faculty: 10 full-time. Students: 105 full-time (83 women); includes 35 minority (3 African Americans, 7 Asian Americans, 24 Hispanics, 1 Native American). 173 applicants, 47% accepted. In 1997, 50 master's awarded. *Degree requirements:* For master's, thesis required, foreign language not required. *Application deadline:* 2/1. *Application fee:* $40. *Expenses:* Tuition $0 for state residents; $9384 per year for nonresidents. Fees $5014 per year. *Financial aid:* Fellowships, teaching assistantships, Federal Work-Study, institutionally sponsored loans, and career-related internships or fieldwork available. Financial aid application deadline: 2/1. *Faculty research:* Bilingual/multicultural education, special education, curriculum and instruction, child development. • Dr. Trish Stoddart, Chairperson, 408-459-3850. Application contact: Graduate Admissions, 408-459-2301.

University of Central Arkansas, College of Education, Conway, AR 72035-0001. Awards MS, MSE, Ed S. Accredited by NCATE. Part-time programs available. Faculty: 47 full-time (22 women), 24 part-time (10 women), 55 FTE. Students: 70 full-time (60 women), 325 part-time (268 women); includes 47 minority (43 African Americans, 2 Asian Americans, 1 Hispanic, 1 Native American), 3 international. 156 applicants, 97% accepted. In 1997, 170 master's, 9 Ed Ss awarded. *Degree requirements:* For master's, comprehensive exam. *Entrance requirements:* For master's, GRE General Test, minimum GPA of 2.7. Application deadline: 3/1 (priority date; rolling processing; 10/1 for spring admission). Application fee: $15 ($40 for international students). *Expenses:* Tuition $161 per credit hour for state residents; $298 per credit hour for nonresidents. Fees $50 per year full-time, $30 per year part-time. *Financial aid:* In 1997–98, 25 assistantships were awarded; Federal Work-Study and career-related internships or fieldwork also available. Financial aid application deadline: 2/15. *Faculty research:* Common factors in psychotherapy exercise. • Dr. Fred Litton, Interim Dean, 501-450-5401. Fax: 501-450-5358. E-mail: freddiel@mail.uca.edu.

University of Central Florida, College of Education, Orlando, FL 32816. Awards MA, M Ed, Ed D, Ed S. Accredited by NCATE. Part-time and evening/weekend programs available. Faculty: 99. Students: 669 full-time (503 women), 459 part-time (355 women); includes 142 minority (76 African Americans, 16 Asian Americans, 46 Hispanics, 4 Native Americans), 9 international. Average age 36. 413 applicants, 56% accepted. In 1997, 294 master's, 22 doctorates, 16 Ed Ss awarded. *Degree requirements:* For master's and Ed S, thesis or alternative required, foreign language not required; for doctorate, dissertation required, foreign language not required. *Entrance requirements:* For master's, GRE General Test (minimum combined score of 840); for doctorate and Ed S, GRE General Test (minimum combined score of 1000), GRE Subject Test. Application fee: $20. *Expenses:* Tuition $3288 per year full-time, $137 per credit hour part-time for state residents; $11,520 per year full-time, $480 per credit hour part-time for nonresidents. Fees $105 per year. *Financial aid:* Fellowships, research assistantships, teaching assistantships, partial tuition waivers, Federal Work-Study, institutionally sponsored loans, and career-related internships or fieldwork available. Aid available to part-time students. • Dr. Sandra Robinson, Dean, 407-823-2401. Application contact: Dr. M. Hynes, Graduate Coordinator, 407-823-6076. E-mail: hynes@pegasus.cc.ucf.edu.

University of Central Oklahoma, College of Education, Edmond, OK 73034-5209. Awards MA, M Ed, MS. Accredited by NCATE. Part-time and evening/weekend programs available. *Entrance requirements:* GRE General Test. Application deadline: 8/18. Application fee: $15. *Tuition:* $76 per credit hour for state residents; $178 per credit hour for nonresidents.

University of Charleston, South Carolina, School of Education, Charleston, SC 29424-0001. Awards MAT, M Ed. Part-time and evening/weekend programs available. Faculty: 26 full-time (17 women), 6 part-time (4 women), 28.25 FTE. Students: 101 full-time (84 women), 107 part-time (99 women); includes 11 minority (10 African Americans, 1 Hispanic), 3 international. Average age 32. 138 applicants, 92% accepted. In 1997, 91 degrees awarded. *Degree requirements:* Thesis or alternative, written qualifying exam, student teaching (MAT) required, foreign language not required. *Entrance requirements:* GRE (score in 50th percentile or higher), MAT (score in 50th percentile or higher), or NTE; South Carolina Education Entrance Exam (MAT); TOEFL, teaching certificate (M Ed). Application deadline: rolling. Application fee: $35. *Expenses:* Tuition $2568 per year full-time, $438 per semester (minimum) part-time for state residents; $4596 per year full-time, $876 per semester (minimum) part-time for nonresidents. Fees $51 per year full-time, $21 per semester (minimum) part-time. *Financial aid:* In 1997–98, research assistantships totaling $7,100, teaching assistantships totaling $7,100 were awarded; Federal Work-Study and career-related internships or fieldwork also available. Aid available to part-time students. Financial aid application deadline: 4/1; applicants required to submit FAFSA. *Faculty research:* Computer-assisted instruction, higher education, faculty development, teaching study skills to college students. • Dr. Nancy Sorenson, Dean, 843-953-5613. Fax: 843-953-5407. Application contact: Laura H. Hines, Graduate School Coordinator, 843-953-5614. Fax: 843-953-1434. E-mail: hinesl@cofc.edu.

University of Chicago, Division of Social Sciences, Department of Education, Chicago, IL 60637-1513. Awards AM, MAT, CAS. Part-time programs available. Students: 150. *Degree requirements:* For master's, qualifying paper required, foreign language not required. *Entrance requirements:* For master's, GRE General Test (scores must be submitted by January 5), TOEFL. Application deadline: 1/5. Application fee: $55. *Expenses:* Tuition $23,616 per year full-time, $3258 per course part-time. Fees $378 per year. *Financial aid:* Fellowships, research assistantships, teaching assistantships, Federal Work-Study, institutionally sponsored loans available. Financial aid application deadline: 1/5. • Prof. Robert Dreeban, Chair, 773-702-9458. Application contact: Office of the Dean of Students, 773-702-8415.

University of Cincinnati, College of Education, Cincinnati, OH 45221. Awards MA, M Ed, MS, Ed D, PhD, CAGS, Ed S. Accredited by NCATE. Part-time programs available. Faculty: 59 full-time. Students: 497 full-time (370 women), 466 part-time (351 women); includes 162 minority (137 African Americans, 12 Asian Americans, 9 Hispanics, 4 Native Americans), 47 international. 510 applicants, 39% accepted. In 1997, 202 master's, 47 doctorates awarded. *Degree requirements:* For doctorate, dissertation required, foreign language not required. *Average time to degree:* master's–3 years full-time; doctorate–6.5 years full-time. *Application deadline:* 2/1. *Application fee:* $30. *Tuition:* $7228 per year full-time, $185 per credit hour part-time for state residents; $13,812 per year full-time, $352 per credit hour part-time for nonresidents. *Financial aid:* Fellowships, graduate assistantships, full tuition waivers, and career-related internships or fieldwork available. Aid available to part-time students. • Dr. Louis Castenell Jr., Dean, 513-556-2337. E-mail: louis.castenell@uc.edu. Application contact: Donald Wagner, Director, Graduate Programs, 513-556-3857. Fax: 513-556-2483. E-mail: donald.wagner@uc.edu.

See in-depth description on page 797.

University of Colorado at Boulder, School of Education, Boulder, CO 80309. Awards MA, PhD. Accredited by NCATE. Part-time programs available. Faculty: 29 full-time (12 women). Students: 245 full-time (180 women), 85 part-time (67 women); includes 35 minority (3 African Americans, 4 Asian Americans, 23 Hispanics, 5 Native Americans), 4 international. Average

age 31. 346 applicants, 59% accepted. In 1997, 106 master's, 7 doctorates awarded. *Degree requirements:* For master's, thesis or alternative, comprehensive exam required, foreign language not required; for doctorate, 1 foreign language, dissertation. *Entrance requirements:* For master's, GRE General Test (minimum combined score of 1500 on three sections) or MAT (minimum score 44), minimum undergraduate GPA of 2.75; for doctorate, GRE General Test (minimum combined score of 1500 on three sections). Application deadline: 2/1 (priority date; 8/1 for spring admission). Application fee: $40 ($60 for international students). *Expenses:* Tuition $3170 per year full-time, $531 per semester (minimum) part-time for state residents; $14,652 per year full-time, $2442 per semester (minimum) part-time for nonresidents. Fees $667 per year full-time, $130 per semester (minimum) part-time. *Financial aid:* Fellowships, research assistantships, teaching assistantships, full and partial tuition waivers, Federal Work-Study available. Financial aid application deadline: 2/1. *Total annual research expenditures:* $2.5 million. • Lorrie Shepard, Interim Dean, 303-492-6937. E-mail: lorrie.shepard@colorado.edu. Application contact: Margaret Eisenhart, Director, Graduate Studies, 303-492-6555. Fax: 303-492-7090. E-mail: edadvise@colorado.edu.

University of Colorado at Colorado Springs, School of Education, Colorado Springs, CO 80933-7150. Offers programs in counseling and human services (MA), curriculum and instruction (MA), special education (MA). Accredited by NCATE. Part-time and evening/weekend programs available. Faculty: 13 full-time (6 women). Students: 222 full-time (163 women), 132 part-time (97 women); includes 50 minority (19 African Americans, 5 Asian Americans, 20 Hispanics, 6 Native Americans). Average age 29. 128 applicants, 61% accepted. In 1997, 116 degrees awarded (100% found work related to degree). *Degree requirements:* Thesis or alternative, comprehensive exams, microcomputer proficiency required, foreign language not required. *Entrance requirements:* GRE General Test, MAT. Application deadline: rolling. Application fee: $40 ($50 for international students). *Expenses:* Tuition $2760 per year full-time, $115 per credit hour part-time for state residents; $9960 per year full-time, $415 per credit hour part-time for nonresidents. Fees $399 per year (minimum) full-time, $106 per year (minimum) part-time. *Financial aid:* Fellowships, Federal Work-Study, and career-related internships or fieldwork available. Financial aid application deadline: 5/1. *Faculty research:* Job training for special populations, materials development for classroom. Total annual research expenditures: $175,000. • Dr. Greg R. Weisenstein, Dean, 719-262-4103. E-mail: gweisens@mail.uccs.edu. Application contact: Connie Wroten, Academic Adviser, 719-262-3268. Fax: 719-262-3554. E-mail: cwroten@mail.uccs.edu.

University of Colorado at Denver, School of Education, Denver, CO 80217-3364. Awards MA, PhD, Ed S. Accredited by NCATE. Part-time and evening/weekend programs available. Faculty: 49 full-time (30 women). Students: 330 full-time (261 women), 735 part-time (592 women); includes 139 minority (32 African Americans, 21 Asian Americans, 80 Hispanics, 6 Native Americans), 10 international. Average age 35. 365 applicants, 61% accepted. In 1997, 387 master's, 15 doctorates, 3 Ed Ss awarded. *Degree requirements:* For doctorate, 1 foreign language, dissertation. *Entrance requirements:* For master's, minimum GPA of 2.75. Application deadline: 4/15 (rolling processing; 9/15 for spring admission). Application fee: $50 ($60 for international students). Electronic applications accepted. *Expenses:* Tuition $3530 per year full-time, $199 per semester hour part-time for state residents; $12,722 per year full-time, $764 per semester hour part-time for nonresidents. Fees $252 per year. *Financial aid:* Fellowships, research assistantships, teaching assistantships, Federal Work-Study available. Financial aid applicants required to submit FAFSA. *Total annual research expenditures:* $3.376 million. • G. Thomas Bellamy, Dean, 303-556-2844. Application contact: Sue Green, Administrative Assistant, 303-556-2717. Fax: 303-556-4479.

University of Connecticut, School of Education, Storrs, CT 06269. Awards MA, PhD. Accredited by NCATE. Faculty: 66. Students: 305 full-time (203 women), 424 part-time (287 women); includes 76 minority (29 African Americans, 12 Asian Americans, 33 Hispanics, 2 Native Americans), 45 international. Average age 36. 488 applicants, 69% accepted. In 1997, 265 master's, 54 doctorates awarded. Terminal master's awarded for partial completion of doctoral program. *Degree requirements:* For master's, thesis or alternative; for doctorate, dissertation. *Entrance requirements:* For doctorate, GRE General Test. Application fee: $40 ($45 for international students). *Expenses:* Tuition $5272 per year full-time, $293 per credit part-time for state residents; $13,696 per year full-time, $761 per credit part-time for nonresidents. Fees $948 per year full-time, $640 per year part-time. *Financial aid:* In 1997–98, 22 fellowships totaling $44,430, 91 research assistantships (36 to first-year students) totaling $772,995, 72 teaching assistantships (19 to first-year students) totaling $556,821 were awarded. Financial aid application deadline: 2/15. • Richard L. Schwab, Dean, 860-486-3813. Application contact: Judith A. Meagher, Chairperson, 860-486-3815.

University of Dayton, School of Education, Dayton, OH 45469-1611. Awards MS Ed, MST, PhD, Ed S. Accredited by NCATE. Part-time and evening/weekend programs available. Faculty: 61 full-time (27 women), 31 part-time (10 women). Students: 217 full-time (165 women), 1,556 part-time (1,210 women); includes 211 minority (183 African Americans, 13 Asian Americans, 13 Hispanics, 2 Native Americans), 11 international. Average age 33. 212 applicants, 60% accepted. In 1997, 507 master's, 12 doctorates, 7 Ed Ss awarded. *Degree requirements:* For doctorate, computer language, dissertation, comprehensive exams, residency; for Ed S, thesis or alternative required, foreign language not required. *Entrance requirements:* For master's, GRE General Test (minimum score 430 on verbal section, 490 on analytical), minimum GPA of 2.75; for doctorate, GRE General Test (minimum score 430 on verbal section, 490 on analytical) or MAT, administrative experience, master's degree, minimum GPA of 3.5. Application deadline: rolling. Application fee: $30. *Financial aid:* In 1997–98, 18 research assistantships (8 to first-year students), 8 teaching assistantships (5 to first-year students) were awarded; Federal Work-Study, institutionally sponsored loans, and career-related internships or fieldwork also available. Aid available to part-time students. • Dr. Thomas J. Lasley, Dean, 937-229-3146.

University of Delaware, College of Human Resources, Education and Public Policy, School of Education, Newark, DE 19716. Offers programs in cognition and instruction (MA); cognition, development, and instruction (PhD); curriculum and instruction (M Ed, PhD); educational leadership (M Ed, Ed D); educational policy (MA, PhD); English as a second language/bilingualism (MA); exceptional children (M Ed); exceptionality (PhD); instruction (MI); measurements, statistics, and evaluation (MA, PhD); school counseling (M Ed); school psychology (MA); secondary education (M Ed). PhD (exceptionality; cognition, development, and instruction) new for fall 1998. Part-time and evening/weekend programs available. Faculty: 54 (24 women). Students: 112 full-time (89 women), 354 part-time (257 women); includes 42 minority (25 African Americans, 11 Asian Americans, 6 Hispanics). Terminal master's awarded for partial completion of doctoral program. *Degree requirements:* For doctorate, dissertation required, foreign language not required. *Entrance requirements:* GRE. Application deadline: 7/1 (rolling processing; 1/15 for spring admission). Application fee: $45. *Expenses:* Tuition $4250 per year full-time, $236 per credit hour part-time for state residents; $12,250 per year full-time, $681 per credit hour part-time for nonresidents. Fees $466 per year full-time, $15 per semester (minimum) part-time. *Financial aid:* Fellowships, research assistantships, teaching assistantships, partial tuition waivers, Federal Work-Study, and career-related internships or fieldwork available. Financial aid application deadline: 3/1. *Faculty research:* Conceptual change and teaching, infant language development, curriculum theory and development, covariance structure modelling theory, achievement testing. • Dr. Robert Hampel, Director, 302-831-2573.

University of Denver, College of Education, Denver, CO 80208. Offers programs in counseling psychology (MA, PhD); curriculum and instruction (MA, PhD), including curriculum leadership; educational psychology (MA, PhD, Ed S), including child and family studies (MA, PhD), quantitative research methods (MA, PhD), school psychology (PhD, Ed S); higher education and adult studies (MA, PhD); school administration (PhD). Part-time and evening/weekend programs available. Postbaccalaureate distance learning degree programs offered (no on-campus study). Faculty: 23 full-time (13 women). Students: 128 full-time (97 women), 96 part-time (78 women); includes 34 minority (9 African Americans, 11 Asian Americans, 14 Hispanics), 5 international. Average age 31. 274 applicants, 66% accepted. In 1997, 69 master's, 30 doctorates awarded. *Degree requirements:* For master's, comprehensive exam required, foreign language and thesis not required; for doctorate, 2 foreign languages (computer language can substitute for one), dissertation, comprehensive exam. *Entrance requirements:* For master's, GRE General Test (minimum combined score of 870), TOEFL (minimum score 550), TSE (minimum score 230); for doctorate, GRE General Test (minimum combined score of 930), TOEFL (minimum score 550), TSE (minimum score 230). Application deadline: 1/1 (rolling processing). Application fee: $40 ($45 for international students). *Expenses:* Tuition $18,216 per year full-time, $506 per credit hour part-time. Fees $159 per year. *Financial aid:* In 1997–98, 164 students received aid, including 9 fellowships totaling $25,200, 10 research assistantships averaging $418 per month and totaling $36,443, 22 teaching assistantships averaging $771 per month and totaling $152,715, 87 scholarships totaling $130,425; Federal Work-Study, institutionally sponsored loans, and career-related internships or fieldwork also available. Aid available to part-time students. Financial aid application deadline: 3/1; applicants required to submit FAFSA. • Dr. Elinor Katz, Dean, 303-871-3665. Application contact: Linda McCarthy, 303-871-2509.

University of Detroit Mercy, College of Education and Human Services, Department of Education, Detroit, MI 48219-0900. Offers programs in counseling (MA); curriculum and instruction (MA); early childhood education (MA); educational administration (MA, Ed S); special education (MA), including emotionally impaired, learning disabilities. Part-time and evening/weekend programs available.

See in-depth description on page 799.

University of Dubuque, Program in Education, 2000 University Avenue, Dubuque, IA 52001-5050. Offers multidisciplinary education (MA); special education: multicategorical, elementary and secondary (MA). Part-time programs available. Faculty: 3 full-time (2 women), 3 part-time (2 women), 5 FTE. Students: 2 full-time (1 woman), 23 part-time (15 women); includes 2 Asian Americans, 1 international. Average age 35. 10 applicants, 100% accepted. In 1997, 3 degrees awarded (100% found work related to degree). *Degree requirements:* Comprehensive exam required, thesis optional, foreign language not required. *Average time to degree:* master's–2 years full-time, 4 years part-time. *Entrance requirements:* GRE or MAT. Application deadline: 8/15 (priority date; rolling processing). Application fee: $25. *Financial aid:* Federal Work-Study, institutionally sponsored loans, and career-related internships or fieldwork available. Aid available to part-time students. Financial aid application deadline: 2/1. *Faculty research:* Curriculum, teacher preparation, medication in special education, severe behavior disorders, parent counseling. • Dr. Sally Naylor, Director of Graduate Education, 319-589-3000. Application contact: Clifford D. Bunting, Dean of Admission and Records, 319-589-3270. Fax: 319-589-3690.

University of Evansville, Graduate Programs, School of Education, Evansville, IN 47722-0002. Awards MA, MS Coun. Accredited by NCATE. Part-time and evening/weekend programs available. Students: 1 (woman) full-time, 11 part-time (6 women); includes 3 minority (all African Americans). Average age 31. *Entrance requirements:* GRE. Application deadline: 7/1. Application fee: $20. *Expenses:* Tuition $395 per credit hour. Fees $30 per year. *Financial aid:* Research assistantships and career-related internships or fieldwork available. Financial aid application deadline: 7/1. • Dr. Nealon Gaskey, Dean, 812-479-2367.

The University of Findlay, College of Professional Studies, Division of Education, 1000 North Main Street, Findlay, OH 45840-3653. Offers programs in administration (MA Ed), early childhood (MA Ed), elementary education (MA Ed), special education (MA Ed), technology (MA Ed). Accredited by NCATE. Part-time and evening/weekend programs available. Faculty: 9 full-time (7 women), 8 part-time (4 women), 21 FTE. Students: 17 full-time, 171 part-time; includes 21 minority (4 African Americans, 15 Asian Americans, 1 Hispanic, 1 Native American). Average age 30. 60 applicants, 97% accepted. In 1997, 51 degrees awarded. *Degree requirements:* 4 foreign languages, thesis, cumulative project. *Average time to degree:* master's–1.5 years full-time, 3 years part-time. *Entrance requirements:* Minimum GPA of 3.0. Application deadline: 8/15 (priority date; rolling processing). Application fee: $25. *Tuition:* $236 per semester hour. *Financial aid:* In 1997–98, 8 graduate assistantships averaging $750 per month were awarded. Aid available to part-time students. Financial aid applicants required to submit FAFSA. *Faculty research:* Children's literature, books and artwork, educational technology, professional development. • Dr. Judith Wahrman, Graduate Program Director, 419-424-4864. Fax: 419-424-4822. E-mail: wahrman@lucy.findlay.edu.

University of Florida, College of Education, Gainesville, FL 32611. Awards MAE, M Ed, Ed D, PhD, Ed S, JD/PhD. Accredited by NCATE. Part-time programs available. Faculty: 121. Students: 437 full-time (327 women), 459 part-time (322 women); includes 116 minority (44 African Americans, 13 Asian Americans, 55 Hispanics, 4 Native Americans), 24 international. 549 applicants, 71% accepted. In 1997, 338 master's, 44 doctorates, 80 Ed Ss awarded. Terminal master's awarded for partial completion of doctoral program. *Degree requirements:* For doctorate, dissertation. *Entrance requirements:* For master's and doctorate, GRE General Test, minimum GPA of 3.0; for Ed S, GRE General Test. Application deadline: rolling. Application fee: $20. *Tuition:* $138 per credit hour for state residents; $481 per credit hour for nonresidents. *Financial aid:* In 1997–98, 151 students received aid, including 55 fellowships averaging $608 per month, 32 research assistantships averaging $700 per month, 60 teaching assistantships averaging $640 per month, 4 graduate assistantships averaging $484 per month; Federal Work-Study and career-related internships or fieldwork also available. Aid available to part-time students. • Dr. Roderick McDavis, Dean, 352-392-0728 Ext. 200. E-mail: mcdavis@coe.ufl.edu. Application contact: Dr. Linda Crocker, Assistant Dean for Graduate Studies, 352-392-2315 Ext. 234. Fax: 352-392-7159. E-mail: lcrocker@coe.ufl.edu.

See in-depth description on page 801.

University of Georgia, College of Education, Athens, GA 30602. Awards MA, MA Ed, M Ed, MM Ed, Ed D, PhD, Ed S. Accredited by NCATE. Faculty: 190 full-time (77 women). Students: 1,025 full-time, 1,000 part-time; includes 187 minority (141 African Americans, 14 Asian Americans, 23 Hispanics, 9 Native Americans), 120 international. 1,851 applicants, 37% accepted. In 1997, 489 master's, 82 doctorates, 118 Ed Ss awarded. *Degree requirements:* For master's, thesis (MA) required, foreign language not required; for doctorate, dissertation. *Entrance requirements:* For doctorate, GRE General Test; for Ed S, GRE General Test or MAT. Application deadline: 7/1 (priority date; 11/15 for spring admission). Application fee: $30. Electronic applications accepted. *Tuition:* $3290 per year full-time, $643 per semester (minimum) part-time for state residents; $11,300 per year full-time, $1645 per semester (minimum) part-time for nonresidents. *Financial aid:* Fellowships, research assistantships, teaching assistantships, assistantships available. • Dr. Russell H. Yeany, Dean, 706-542-3866. Fax: 706-542-0360.

University of Great Falls, Graduate Studies Division, Master of Arts in Teaching Program, Great Falls, MT 59405. Offers curriculum and instruction (MAT), elementary education (MAT), secondary education (MAT). Part-time and evening/weekend programs available. Postbaccalaureate distance learning degree programs offered (minimal on-campus study). Faculty: 5 full-time (all women), 6 part-time (4 women), 6 FTE. Students: 19 full-time (14 women), 11 part-time (6 women); includes 2 minority (1 African American, 1 Native American). Average age 35. In 1997, 2 degrees awarded. *Degree requirements:* Thesis or alternative required, foreign language not required. *Entrance requirements:* GRE General Test (minimum score 500 on each section; combined average 1000), bachelor's degree in teaching, teaching certificate, 3 years of teaching experience. Application deadline: 8/15 (priority date; rolling processing). Application fee: $35. *Expenses:* Tuition $327 per credit. Fees $150 per year full-time, $45 per semester (minimum) part-time. *Financial aid:* In 1997–98, 15 students received aid, including 1 research assistantship averaging $500 per month. Financial aid application deadline: 3/1. • Dr. Eleanore Gowen, Head. E-mail: agowen@ugf.edu.

University of Great Falls, Graduate Studies Division, Programs in Education, Great Falls, MT 59405. Offerings in elementary administration (ME), guidance and counseling (ME). Part-time and evening/weekend programs available. Postbaccalaureate distance learning degree programs

Directory: Education—General

University of Great Falls (continued)

offered (minimal on-campus study). Faculty: 4 part-time (2 women). Students: 6 full-time (3 women). Average age 28. 6 applicants, 100% accepted. In 1997, 2 degrees awarded. *Entrance requirements:* GRE General Test (minimum score 500 on each section; combined average 1000). Application deadline: 8/15 (priority date; rolling processing). Application fee: $35. *Expenses:* Tuition $327 per credit. Fees $150 per year full-time, $45 per semester (minimum) part-time. *Financial aid:* In 1997–98, 1 student received aid, including 1 research assistantship averaging $400 per month; Federal Work-Study, institutionally sponsored loans, and career-related internships or fieldwork also available. Aid available to part-time students. Financial aid application deadline: 3/1; applicants required to submit FAFSA. *Faculty research:* Native American attitudinal research. Total annual research expenditures: $5000. • Dr. Al Johnson, Dean, Graduate Studies Division, 406-791-5337. Fax: 406-791-5991. E-mail: ajohnson@ugf.edu.

University of Guam, College of Education, 303 University Drive, UOG Station, Mangilao, GU 96923. Awards MA, M Ed. Part-time and evening/weekend programs available. *Degree requirements:* Comprehensive oral and written exams, special project or thesis required, foreign language not required. *Entrance requirements:* GRE General Test. Application deadline: 5/31. Application fee: $31 ($56 for international students). *Faculty research:* Multicultural issues, computerized student advising.

University of Hartford, College of Education, Nursing, and Health Professions, West Hartford, CT 06117-1599. Awards M Ed, MS, MSN, Ed D, CAGS, Certificate, MSN/MSOB. Accredited by NCATE. Part-time and evening/weekend programs available. Faculty: 21 full-time (14 women), 7 part-time (3 women). Students: 71 full-time (42 women), 299 part-time (255 women); includes 14 minority (9 African Americans, 2 Asian Americans, 1 Hispanic, 2 Native Americans), 5 international. Average age 37. 152 applicants, 73% accepted. In 1997, 119 master's, 11 doctorates, 7 other advanced degrees awarded. *Degree requirements:* For doctorate, dissertation. *Entrance requirements:* For doctorate, MAT; for other advanced degree, GRE General Test or MAT, interview. Application deadline: rolling. Application fee: $40 ($55 for international students). Electronic applications accepted. *Financial aid:* Fellowships, research assistantships, teaching assistantships, graduate assistantships, Federal Work-Study available. Aid available to part-time students. Financial aid application deadline: 6/1; applicants required to submit FAFSA. • Dr. David A. Caruso, Dean. Application contact: Susan Garcia, Coordinator of Student Services, 860-768-5038. E-mail: gettoknow@mail.hartford.edu.

University of Hawaii at Manoa, College of Education, Honolulu, HI 96822. Awards M Ed, M Ed T, Ed D, PhD. Part-time and evening/weekend programs available. Students: 348 full-time (250 women), 295 part-time (217 women). *Degree requirements:* For doctorate, dissertation. *Entrance requirements:* For doctorate, GRE General Test. *Tuition:* $4029 per year full-time, $214 per credit hour part-time for state residents; $9957 per year full-time, $461 per credit hour part-time for nonresidents. *Financial aid:* Fellowships, research assistantships, teaching assistantships, full and partial tuition waivers, Federal Work-Study, institutionally sponsored loans, and career-related internships or fieldwork available. Aid available to part-time students. • Dr. Charles Araki, Interim Dean, 808-956-7703. Fax: 808-956-3106. E-mail: araki@hawaii.edu.

University of Houston, College of Education, 4800 Calhoun, Houston, TX 77204-2163. Awards M Ed, MS, Ed D, PhD. Accredited by NCATE. Part-time and evening/weekend programs available. Faculty: 79 full-time (38 women), 35 part-time (18 women). Students: 418 full-time (306 women), 1,059 part-time (829 women); includes 316 minority (154 African Americans, 42 Asian Americans, 116 Hispanics, 4 Native Americans), 86 international. Average age 36. In 1997, 331 master's, 63 doctorates awarded. *Degree requirements:* For master's, comprehensive exam or thesis required, foreign language not required; for doctorate, dissertation, comprehensive exam required, foreign language not required. *Entrance requirements:* For master's, GRE General Test or MAT; for doctorate, GRE General Test, interview. Application fee: $35 ($75 for international students). *Expenses:* Tuition $1152 per year full-time, $120 per semester (minimum) part-time for state residents; $4482 per year full-time, $249 per credit hour part-time for nonresidents. Fees $977 per year full-time, $119 per semester (minimum) part-time. *Financial aid:* In 1997–98, 3 research assistantships (all to first-year students) averaging $800 per month, 43 teaching assistantships (7 to first-year students) averaging $800 per month were awarded; Federal Work-Study, institutionally sponsored loans, and career-related internships or fieldwork also available. Aid available to part-time students. Financial aid applicants required to submit FAFSA. *Total annual research expenditures:* $3.3 million. • Allen R. Warner, Dean, 713-743-5001. Fax: 713-743-9870. E-mail: awarner@uh.edu.

University of Houston–Clear Lake, School of Education, Houston, TX 77058-1098. Offers programs in counseling (MS), curriculum and instruction (MS), early childhood education (MS), educational management (MS), instructional technology (MS), learning resources (MS), multicultural education (MS), reading (MS), secondary education (MA). Accredited by NCATE. Part-time and evening/weekend programs available. Faculty: 34 full-time (23 women), 17 part-time (12 women), 39 FTE. Students: 627 (517 women); includes 101 minority (43 African Americans, 9 Asian Americans, 47 Hispanics, 2 Native Americans), 5 international. Average age 36. In 1997, 137 degrees awarded. *Degree requirements:* Thesis required (for some programs), foreign language not required. *Entrance requirements:* GRE or minimum GPA of 3.0 in last 60 hours. Application deadline: rolling. Application fee: $30 ($60 for international students). *Tuition:* $207 per credit hour for state residents; $336 per credit hour for nonresidents. *Financial aid:* Federal Work-Study available. Aid available to part-time students. Financial aid application deadline: 5/1. • Dr. Dennis Spuck, Dean, 281-283-3501. Application contact: Dr. Doris L. Prater, Associate Dean, 281-283-3600.

University of Houston–Victoria, Division of Education, 2506 East Red River, Victoria, TX 77901-4450. Awards M Ed. Part-time and evening/weekend programs available. Postbaccalaureate distance learning degree programs offered (no on-campus study). Faculty: 17 full-time (11 women), 4 part-time (all women), 17.8 FTE. Students: 27 full-time (23 women), 224 part-time (179 women); includes 50 minority (25 African Americans, 3 Asian Americans, 22 Hispanics). Average age 39. In 1997, 72 degrees awarded. *Degree requirements:* Comprehensive exam, project, or thesis required, foreign language not required. *Entrance requirements:* GRE General Test (minimum combined score of 800). Application deadline: rolling. *Expenses:* Tuition $1026 per year full-time, $57 per semester hour part-time for state residents; $4464 per year full-time, $248 per semester hour part-time for nonresidents. Fees $540 per year full-time, $30 per semester hour part-time. *Financial aid:* Research assistantships, teaching assistantships, Federal Work-Study, and career-related internships or fieldwork available. Aid available to part-time students. *Faculty research:* Reading and language arts education, evaluation and diagnosis of special children's abilities. • Dr. Cheryl Hines, Chair, 512-788-6247.

University of Idaho, College of Graduate Studies, College of Education, Moscow, ID 83844-4140. Awards MAT, M Ed, MS, Ed D, PhD, CHSS, EAS, Ed S, Sp Ed S, SPS, V Ed S. Accredited by NCATE. Faculty: 45 full-time (19 women), 4 part-time (2 women), 46.93 FTE. Students: 163 full-time (92 women), 636 part-time (417 women); includes 41 minority (23 African Americans, 5 Asian Americans, 4 Hispanics, 9 Native Americans), 16 international. In 1997, 147 master's, 20 doctorates, 35 other advanced degrees awarded. *Degree requirements:* For doctorate, dissertation. *Entrance requirements:* For master's, minimum GPA of 2.8; for doctorate, minimum undergraduate GPA of 2.8, 3.0 graduate. Application deadline: 8/1 (12/15 for spring admission). Application fee: $35 ($45 for international students). *Expenses:* Tuition $0 for state residents; $6000 per year full-time, $95 per credit part-time for nonresidents. Fees $2676 per year full-time, $134 per credit part-time. *Financial aid:* In 1997–98, 22 teaching assistantships (18 to first-year students) averaging $705 per month and totaling $138,993 were awarded; research assistantships, Federal Work-Study also available. Aid available to part-time students. Financial aid application deadline: 2/15. • Dr. Dale Gentry, Dean, 208-885-6772.

University of Illinois at Chicago, College of Education, Chicago, IL 60607-7128. Awards M Ed, PhD. Part-time and evening/weekend programs available. Faculty: 39 full-time (14 women). Students: 150 full-time (110 women), 458 part-time (360 women); includes 195 minority (85 African Americans, 24 Asian Americans, 84 Hispanics, 2 Native Americans), 12 international. Average age 32. 346 applicants, 58% accepted. In 1997, 165 master's, 19 doctorates awarded. Terminal master's awarded for partial completion of doctoral program. *Degree requirements:* For doctorate, dissertation required, foreign language not required. *Entrance requirements:* For master's, TOEFL (minimum score 550), minimum GPA of 3.75 on a 5.0 scale; for doctorate, GRE General Test (minimum combined score of 1000) or MAT (minimum score 55), TOEFL (minimum score 550), minimum GPA of 3.75 on a 5.0 scale. Application deadline: 2/15. Application fee: $40 ($50 for international students). *Financial aid:* Fellowships, research assistantships, teaching assistantships, traineeships, full tuition waivers, institutionally sponsored loans, and career-related internships or fieldwork available. *Faculty research:* Teaching and learning, program design, school and classroom organization with emphasis on urban settings. • Dr. Larry Braskamp, Dean, 312-996-5641. Application contact: Victoria Hare, Director of Graduate Studies, 312-996-4520.

University of Illinois at Urbana–Champaign, College of Education, Urbana, IL 61801. Awards AM, Ed M, MS, Ed D, PhD, AC. Faculty: 106 full-time (41 women), 29 part-time (8 women). Students: 721 full-time (506 women); includes 137 minority (91 African Americans, 21 Asian Americans, 22 Hispanics, 3 Native Americans), 127 international. 549 applicants, 45% accepted. In 1997, 221 master's, 70 doctorates awarded. *Degree requirements:* For doctorate, dissertation. *Application deadline:* rolling. *Application fee:* $40 ($50 for international students). *Financial aid:* In 1997–98, 43 fellowships, 253 research assistantships, 122 teaching assistantships were awarded; full and partial tuition waivers, Federal Work-Study, and career-related internships or fieldwork also available. • Mildred Griggs, Dean, 217-333-0960.

See in-depth description on page 803.

University of Indianapolis, School of Education, Indianapolis, IN 46227-3697. Offers programs in education (MA); elementary education (MA); secondary education (MA), including art education, education, English education, social studies education. Accredited by NCATE. Part-time and evening/weekend programs available. *Average time to degree:* master's–5 years part-time. *Entrance requirements:* GRE Subject Test. Application deadline: rolling. Application fee: $30. *Faculty research:* Assessment of teacher education, perceptions of prospective teachers by parents.

The University of Iowa, College of Education, Iowa City, IA 52242-1316. Awards MA, MAT, PhD, Ed S, JD/MA, JD/PhD. Faculty: 99 full-time, 3 part-time. Students: 325 full-time (212 women), 495 part-time (341 women); includes 106 minority (60 African Americans, 16 Asian Americans, 26 Hispanics, 4 Native Americans), 95 international. 448 applicants, 50% accepted. In 1997, 174 master's, 72 doctorates, 9 Ed Ss awarded. *Degree requirements:* For master's, exam required, foreign language not required; for doctorate, computer language, dissertation, comprehensive exams required, foreign language not required; for Ed S, computer language, exam required, foreign language not required. *Entrance requirements:* For master's and Ed S, GRE General Test, minimum GPA of 2.5; for doctorate, GRE General Test, minimum GPA of 3.0. Application deadline: rolling. Application fee: $30 ($50 for international students). *Expenses:* Tuition $3166 per year full-time, $176 per semester hour part-time for state residents; $10,202 per year full-time, $176 per semester hour part-time for nonresidents. Fees $202 per year full-time, $52 per year (minimum) part-time. *Financial aid:* In 1997–98, 31 fellowships (15 to first-year students), 125 research assistantships (31 to first-year students), 135 teaching assistantships (29 to first-year students) were awarded; Federal Work-Study, institutionally sponsored loans, and career-related internships or fieldwork also available. Financial aid applicants required to submit FAFSA. *Faculty research:* Computer-assisted instrumentation, testing and measurement, instructional design. • Steven R. Yussen, Dean, 319-335-5380. Fax: 319-335-5386.

University of Judaism, Graduate School, Fingerhut School of Education, 15600 Mulholland Drive, Bel Air, CA 90077-1599. Awards MA, MA Ed, MS. Faculty: 6 full-time, 4 part-time. Students: 22 full-time (17 women), 1 (woman) part-time; includes 2 international. Average age 26. 13 applicants, 62% accepted. In 1997, 10 degrees awarded. *Degree requirements:* 1 foreign language, comprehensive exams required, thesis not required. *Entrance requirements:* GRE General Test, interview, minimum undergraduate GPA of 3.0. Application deadline: 3/31 (priority date; rolling processing). Application fee: $35. *Expenses:* Tuition $13,910 per year full-time, $580 per unit part-time. Fees $465 per year. *Financial aid:* Fellowships, full and partial tuition waivers, Federal Work-Study, institutionally sponsored loans, and career-related internships or fieldwork available. Financial aid application deadline: 3/2; applicants required to submit FAFSA. *Faculty research:* Philosophy of education, curriculum development, teacher training. • Application contact: Tamara Greenebaum, Dean of Admissions, 310-476-9777. Fax: 310-471-3657.

University of Kansas, School of Education, Lawrence, KS 66045. Awards MA, MS Ed, Ed D, PhD, Ed S. Accredited by NCATE. Part-time programs available. Faculty: 81. Students: 463 full-time (309 women), 890 part-time (672 women); includes 90 minority (38 African Americans, 19 Asian Americans, 21 Hispanics, 12 Native Americans), 63 international. 500 applicants, 80% accepted. In 1997, 270 master's, 54 doctorates, 5 Ed Ss awarded. Terminal master's awarded for partial completion of doctoral program. *Degree requirements:* For doctorate, dissertation. *Entrance requirements:* For master's and Ed S, minimum GPA of 3.0; for doctorate, GRE General Test, minimum graduate GPA of 3.5. Application fee: $25. Electronic applications accepted. *Expenses:* Tuition $2400 per year full-time, $100 per credit hour part-time for state residents; $7890 per year full-time, $329 per credit hour part-time for nonresidents. Fees $428 per year full-time, $31 per credit hour part-time. *Financial aid:* Fellowships, research assistantships, teaching assistantships, and career-related internships or fieldwork available. *Faculty research:* Effective schools, assessment, students with learning difficulties, learning in school situations, teacher preparation. Total annual research expenditures: $11 million. • Karen Gallagher, Dean, 785-864-3726. Application contact: Mary Ann Williams, Graduate Admissions Coordinator, 785-864-4510. Fax: 785-864-3566. E-mail: mwilliam@kuhub.cc.ukans.edu.

University of Kentucky, Graduate School Programs from the College of Education, Lexington, KY 40506-0032. Awards MA Ed U, MRC, MS, MS Ed U, MSVE, Ed D, PhD, Ed S. Accredited by NCATE. Part-time and evening/weekend programs available. Faculty: 106 full-time (45 women), 14 part-time (1 woman). Students: 433 full-time (266 women), 384 part-time (287 women); includes 68 minority (55 African Americans, 5 Asian Americans, 5 Hispanics, 3 Native Americans), 24 international. 503 applicants, 62% accepted. In 1997, 194 master's, 27 doctorates, 5 Ed Ss awarded. Terminal master's awarded for partial completion of doctoral program. *Degree requirements:* For master's, comprehensive exam required, foreign language not required; for doctorate, dissertation, comprehensive exam; for Ed S, comprehensive exam required, foreign language and thesis not required. *Entrance requirements:* For master's, GRE General Test, minimum undergraduate GPA of 2.5; for doctorate, GRE General Test, minimum graduate GPA of 3.0; for Ed S, GRE General Test. Application deadline: rolling. Application fee: $30 ($35 for international students). *Financial aid:* In 1997–98, 35 fellowships, 25 research assistantships, 32 teaching assistantships, 12 graduate assistantships were awarded; Federal Work-Study, institutionally sponsored loans, and career-related internships or fieldwork also available. Aid available to part-time students. • Dr. Shirley Raines, Dean, 606-257-2813. Application contact: Dr. Constance L. Wood, Associate Dean, 606-257-4613. Fax: 606-323-1928.

University of La Verne, Department of Education, La Verne, CA 91750-4443. Offers programs in child development (MS), child development/child life (MS), multiple subject/single subject teaching (Credential), reading (M Ed), school counseling (MS), special education (MS), special emphasis (classroom guidance) (M Ed). Part-time and evening/weekend programs available. *Entrance requirements:* For master's, TOEFL (minimum score 550), minimum GPA of 2.5. Application fee: $25. *Expenses:* Tuition $370 per unit (minimum). Fees $60 per year.

University of Lethbridge, Faculty of Education, Lethbridge, AB T1K 3M4, Canada. Awards M Ed. Part-time and evening/weekend programs available. Students: 215. *Degree requirements:* Thesis or alternative required, foreign language not required. *Entrance requirements:* TOEFL (minimum score 600), B Ed or equivalent, minimum GPA of 3.0, 2 years of teaching or relevant educational experience, teaching certificate. Application deadline: 6/1 (priority date; rolling processing; 10/1 for spring admission). Application fee: $50. *Tuition:* $402 per semester hour for Canadian residents; $798 per semester hour for nonresidents. *Financial aid:* Research assistantships and career-related internships or fieldwork available. Financial aid application deadline: 4/15. • Dr. L. Walker, Dean, 403-329-2251. E-mail: inquiries@hg.uleth.ca. Application contact: Dr. Peter Heffernan, Coordinator of Graduate Studies, 403-329-2425. Fax: 403-329-2252. E-mail: inquiries@ht.uleth.ca.

University of Louisville, School of Education, Louisville, KY 40292-0001. Awards MA, MAT, M Ed, MS, Ed D, Ed S. Accredited by NCATE. Part-time programs available. Faculty: 78 full-time (32 women), 60 part-time (29 women), 98 FTE. Students: 427 full-time (292 women), 735 part-time (579 women); includes 156 minority (120 African Americans, 20 Asian Americans, 15 Hispanics, 1 Native American), 11 international. Average age 34. In 1997, 406 master's, 7 doctorates, 2 Ed Ss awarded. *Degree requirements:* For doctorate, dissertation. *Entrance requirements:* GRE General Test. Application deadline: rolling. Application fee: $25. *Faculty research:* Health, physical education, and recreation; counseling and student personnel; curriculum and instruction/occupational training and development for elementary, middle, and high schools; administration and higher education; foundations of education. • Dr. Raphael O. Nystrand, Dean, 502-852-6411.

University of Maine, College of Education and Human Development, Orono, ME 04469. Offers programs in counselor education (MAT, M Ed, MS, CAS); educational leadership (M Ed, Ed D, CAS); elementary education (M Ed, MS, CAS); higher education (MAT, M Ed, MS, CAS); human development and family studies (MS), including human development; kinesiology and physical education (MAT, M Ed, MS, CAS); literacy education (MAT, M Ed, MS, Ed D, CAS); science education (M Ed, MS, CAS); secondary education (M Ed, MS, CAS); social studies education (MAT, M Ed, MS, CAS); special education (M Ed, CAS). Accredited by NCATE. Part-time and evening/weekend programs available. Faculty: 34 full-time, 3 part-time. Students: 184 full-time (118 women), 287 part-time (174 women). In 1997, 186 master's, 7 doctorates, 29 CASs awarded. *Degree requirements:* For doctorate, dissertation. *Entrance requirements:* For master's, TOEFL (minimum score 550); for doctorate, GRE General Test, TOEFL (minimum score 550); for CAS, MA, M Ed, or MS. Application deadline: 2/1 (priority date; rolling processing; 10/15 for spring admission). Application fee: $50. *Expenses:* Tuition $194 per credit hour for state residents; $548 per credit hour for nonresidents. Fees $378 per year full-time, $33 per semester (minimum) part-time. *Financial aid:* In 1997–98, 2 research assistantships, 7 teaching assistantships were awarded; fellowships, Federal Work-Study, institutionally sponsored loans, and career-related internships or fieldwork also available. Aid available to part-time students. Financial aid application deadline: 3/1. *Faculty research:* Development of training models for the severely handicapped, marine education, counselor training models. • Dr. Robert A. Cobb, Dean, 207-581-2441. Fax: 207-581-2423. Application contact: Scott Delcourt, Director of the Graduate School, 207-581-3218. Fax: 207-581-3232. E-mail: graduate@maine.edu.

Announcement: NCATE-accredited graduate study at the master's (MAT and M Ed), CAS, and doctoral levels offers the resources and collaboration essential to the development of influential educational leaders. Hallmarks include innovative technology, faculty mentoring, national and statewide research centers, and strong partnerships with public schools. Program areas include educational leadership, literacy, higher education, elementary, secondary, middle level, kinesiology and physical education, special education, social studies, science, counselor, and adult education. The MS in human development offers advanced study in the growth and development of individuals throughout the life span and of the family in its various forms, preparing students for a variety of careers serving children and families. Flexibility allows comprehensive inquiry and concentration on specific interests.

University of Manitoba, Faculty of Education, Winnipeg, MB R3T 2N2, Canada. Awards M Ed, PhD. *Degree requirements:* For master's, thesis or alternative required, foreign language not required; for doctorate, dissertation required, foreign language not required.

University of Mary, Program in Education, 7500 University Drive, Bismarck, ND 58504-9652. Offers elementary education (MS), elementary education administration (MS Ed), higher education (MS Ed), secondary education administration (MS Ed), secondary teaching (MS Ed), special education (MS). Part-time programs available. Faculty: 5 full-time (3 women), 6 part-time (4 women). Students: 7 full-time (5 women), 50 part-time (42 women); includes 2 minority (both Native Americans). In 1997, 23 degrees awarded (100% found work related to degree). *Degree requirements:* Thesis optional, foreign language not required. *Average time to degree:* master's–3 years part-time. *Entrance requirements:* GRE General Test (minimum combined score of 1200), MAT (minimum score 40). Application deadline: 8/1 (12/1 for spring admission). Application fee: $15. *Tuition:* $265 per credit. *Financial aid:* Career-related internships or fieldwork available. Aid available to part-time students. Financial aid application deadline: 8/1; applicants required to submit FAFSA. *Faculty research:* Organizational ethics, validation study, school partnership. • Ramona Klein, Director, 701-255-7500. Application contact: Dr. Diane Fladeland, Director, Graduate Programs, 701-255-7500. Fax: 701-255-7687.

University of Mary Hardin–Baylor, School of Education, Belton, TX 76513. Offers programs in educational administration (M Ed), educational psychology (M Ed), general studies (M Ed), reading education (M Ed). Part-time and evening/weekend programs available. Faculty: 6 full-time (2 women). Students: 11 full-time (8 women), 37 part-time (33 women); includes 5 minority (3 African Americans, 1 Asian American, 1 Hispanic). Average age 40. 20 applicants, 85% accepted. In 1997, 20 degrees awarded (100% found work related to degree). *Average time to degree:* master's–2 years full-time, 3.5 years part-time. *Entrance requirements:* GRE General Test (minimum combined score of 850), minimum GPA of 2.5. Application deadline: 8/1 (priority date; rolling processing; 1/10 for spring admission). Application fee: $35 ($135 for international students). *Expenses:* Tuition $270 per semester hour. Fees $15 per semester hour. *Financial aid:* Available to part-time students. Financial aid application deadline: 6/1. • Dr. Clarence E. Ham, Dean, 254-295-4573. Fax: 254-933-4480. E-mail: ham@tenet.edu.

University of Maryland, Baltimore County, Graduate School, Department of Education, Baltimore, MD 21250-5398. Offers programs in education (MA), instructional systems development (MA). *Entrance requirements:* GRE General Test, GRE Subject Test, TOEFL, minimum GPA of 3.0. Application deadline: 7/1. Application fee: $40. *Expenses:* Tuition $260 per credit hour for state residents; $468 per credit hour for nonresidents. Fees $39 per credit hour.

University of Maryland, College Park, College of Education, College Park, MD 20742-5045. Awards MA, M Ed, Ed D, PhD, CAGS. Accredited by NCATE. Part-time and evening/weekend programs available. Postbaccalaureate distance learning degree programs offered. Faculty: 130 full-time (67 women), 51 part-time (45 women). Students: 398 full-time (313 women), 611 part-time (482 women); includes 227 minority (153 African Americans, 42 Asian Americans, 27 Hispanics, 5 Native Americans), 46 international. 808 applicants, 41% accepted. In 1997, 253 master's, 83 doctorates awarded. *Degree requirements:* For doctorate, dissertation. *Entrance requirements:* For master's, GRE General Test or MAT, minimum GPA of 3.0; for doctorate, GRE General Test or MAT. Application deadline: rolling. Application fee: $50 ($70 for international students). *Expenses:* Tuition $272 per credit hour for state residents; $400 per credit hour for nonresidents. Fees $564 per year full-time, $342 per year part-time. *Financial aid:* In 1997–98, 36 fellowships, 31 research assistantships, 79 teaching assistantships were awarded; career-related internships or fieldwork also available. • Dr. Willis Hawley, Dean, 301-405-2334. Fax: 301-314-9890. Application contact: John Mollish, Director, Graduate Admissions and Records, 301-405-4198. Fax: 301-314-9305.

University of Maryland Eastern Shore, Department of Education, Program in Teaching, Princess Anne, MD 21853-1299. Awards MAT. Offered jointly with Salisbury State University; offered during summer only. Faculty: 3 full-time (all women), 2 part-time (1 woman). Students: 13 part-time (7 women); includes 5 minority (all African Americans), 1 international. Average age 30. 9 applicants, 89% accepted. *Degree requirements:* Comprehensive exam, internship, seminar paper required, foreign language and thesis not required. *Average time to degree:* master's–1.5 years full-time. *Entrance requirements:* NTE, TOEFL (minimum score 550), interview, minimum GPA of 3.0, writing sample. Application fee: $30. *Expenses:* Tuition $143 per credit hour for state residents; $253 per credit hour for nonresidents. Fees $50 per year. *Financial aid:* In 1997–98, 2 students received aid, including 1 research assistantship, 1 teaching assistantship; Federal Work-Study and career-related internships or fieldwork also available. Aid available to part-time students. Financial aid application deadline: 3/1. • Dr. Jodellano Statom, Coordinator, 410-651-6217. Fax: 410-651-7962. E-mail: jstatom@umes-bird.umd.edu.

University of Massachusetts Amherst, School of Education, Amherst, MA 01003-0001. Awards M Ed, Ed D, PhD, CAGS. Accredited by NCATE. Part-time programs available. Faculty: 66 full-time (25 women). Students: 380 full-time (272 women), 466 part-time (326 women); includes 132 minority (56 African Americans, 25 Asian Americans, 43 Hispanics, 8 Native Americans), 89 international. Average age 38. 641 applicants, 53% accepted. In 1997, 245 master's, 71 doctorates awarded. Terminal master's awarded for partial completion of doctoral program. *Degree requirements:* For doctorate, dissertation required, foreign language not required. *Entrance requirements:* For master's and doctorate, GRE General Test. Application deadline: rolling. Application fee: $40. *Expenses:* Tuition $2640 per year full-time, $110 per credit part-time for state residents; $3690 per year (minimum) full-time, $165 per credit (minimum) part-time for nonresidents. Fees $2856 per year full-time, $422 per semester part-time for state residents; $3204 per year full-time, $480 per semester part-time for nonresidents. *Financial aid:* In 1997–98, 101 fellowships, 99 research assistantships, 154 teaching assistantships were awarded; Federal Work-Study and career-related internships or fieldwork also available. Aid available to part-time students. • Dr. Bailey Jackson, Dean, 413-545-0233. Fax: 413-545-4240. Application contact: Nancy Kuminski, Administrator to Dean, 413-545-0233.

See in-depth description on page 805.

University of Massachusetts Boston, Graduate College of Education, Boston, MA 02125-3393. Awards MA, M Ed, Ed D, CAGS, Certificate. Part-time and evening/weekend programs available. Students: 263 full-time (194 women), 737 part-time (516 women); includes 144 minority (80 African Americans, 22 Asian Americans, 40 Hispanics, 2 Native Americans), 13 international. 675 applicants, 60% accepted. In 1997, 292 master's, 49 other advanced degrees awarded. *Degree requirements:* For master's, comprehensive exams required, foreign language not required; for doctorate, dissertation, comprehensive exams required, foreign language not required; for other advanced degree, comprehensive exams required, foreign language and thesis not required. *Entrance requirements:* For master's and doctorate, GRE General Test or MAT, minimum GPA of 2.75; for other advanced degree, minimum GPA of 2.75. Application deadline: 3/1. Application fee: $25 ($35 for international students). *Expenses:* Tuition $2640 per year full-time, $110 per credit part-time for state residents; $8930 per year full-time, $373 per credit part-time for nonresidents. Fees $2650 per year full-time, $420 per semester (minimum) part-time for state residents; $2736 per year full-time, $420 per semester (minimum) part-time for nonresidents. *Financial aid:* In 1997–98, 35 research assistantships (18 to first-year students) averaging $200 per month and totaling $72,600, 14 teaching assistantships (3 to first-year students) averaging $150 per month were awarded; administrative assistantships also available. Financial aid application deadline: 3/1; applicants required to submit FAFSA. • Dr. Richard Clark, Dean, 617-287-7600. Application contact: Lisa Lavely, Director of Graduate Admissions and Records, 617-287-6400. Fax: 617-287-6236.

University of Massachusetts Dartmouth, Graduate School, College of Arts and Sciences, Program in Teaching, North Dartmouth, MA 02747-2300. Awards MAT. Students: 2 full-time (1 woman), 33 part-time (26 women); includes 1 minority (Native American). 49 applicants, 88% accepted. *Entrance requirements:* TOEFL. Application deadline: rolling. Application fee: $40. *Expenses:* Tuition $2950 per year full-time, $82 per credit part-time for state residents; $10,249 per year full-time, $285 per credit part-time for nonresidents. Fees $5002 per year full-time, $143 per credit part-time for state residents; $6830 per year full-time, $194 per credit part-time for nonresidents. *Financial aid:* In 1997–98, 1 graduate assistantship totaling $5,000 was awarded. Financial aid application deadline: 3/15. • Lew Kamm, Director, 508-999-8336. Fax: 508-999-9125. Application contact: Carol A. Novo, Graduate Admissions Office, 508-999-8604. Fax: 508-999-8375. E-mail: graduate@umassd.edu.

University of Massachusetts Lowell, College of Education, 1 University Avenue, Lowell, MA 01854-2881. Awards M Ed, Ed D, CAGS. Accredited by NCATE. Part-time and evening/weekend programs available. Faculty: 18 full-time (8 women), 31 part-time (20 women). Students: 82 full-time (51 women), 443 part-time (290 women); includes 50 minority (22 African Americans, 13 Asian Americans, 13 Hispanics, 2 Native Americans), 8 international. 302 applicants, 65% accepted. In 1997, 96 master's, 16 doctorates, 3 CAGSs awarded. Terminal master's awarded for partial completion of doctoral program. *Degree requirements:* For doctorate, dissertation. *Entrance requirements:* For master's, MAT; for doctorate, GRE General Test. Application deadline: 4/1 (priority date; rolling processing; 10/1 for spring admission). Application fee: $20 ($35 for international students). *Tuition:* $4867 per year full-time, $618 per semester (minimum) part-time for state residents; $10,276 per year full-time, $1294 per semester (minimum) part-time for nonresidents. *Financial aid:* In 1997–98, 1 research assistantship, 13 teaching assistantships were awarded; Federal Work-Study, institutionally sponsored loans, and career-related internships or fieldwork also available. Aid available to part-time students. Financial aid application deadline: 4/1. • Dr. Donald Pierson, Dean, 978-934-4600.

See in-depth description on page 807.

The University of Memphis, College of Education, Memphis, TN 38152. Awards MAT, MS, Ed D, PhD, Ed S. Accredited by NCATE. Part-time and evening/weekend programs available. Faculty: 96 full-time (47 women), 93 part-time (47 women). Students: 388 full-time (281 women), 793 part-time (589 women); includes 217 minority (201 African Americans, 7 Asian Americans, 8 Hispanics, 1 Native American), 26 international. Average age 35. 607 applicants, 56% accepted. In 1997, 270 master's, 51 doctorates, 12 Ed Ss awarded. Terminal master's awarded for partial completion of doctoral program. *Degree requirements:* For master's, comprehensive exam required, foreign language not required; for doctorate, dissertation, comprehensive exam required, foreign language not required; for Ed S, thesis or alternative, comprehensive exams. *Entrance requirements:* For master's, GRE General Test or MAT; for doctorate, GRE General Test; for Ed S, GRE General Test, GRE Subject Test, 2 years of teaching experience. Application deadline: 8/1 (12/1 for spring admission). Application fee: $25 ($50 for international students). *Tuition:* $2862 per year full-time, $166 per credit hour part-time for state residents; $6696 per year full-time, $379 per credit hour part-time for nonresidents. *Financial aid:* In 1997–98, 45 research assistantships totaling $185,002, 12 teaching assistantships totaling $75,046 were awarded; partial tuition waivers and career-related internships or fieldwork also available. *Faculty research:* Urban school effectiveness, literacy development, teacher effectiveness, exercise physiology, crisis counseling. • Dr. Nathan L. Essex, Dean, 901-678-4265. Application contact: Dr. George W. Etheridge, Assistant Dean of Graduate Studies, 901-678-2352. Fax: 901-678-4778. E-mail: getherdg@cc.memphis.edu.

University of Miami, School of Education, Coral Gables, FL 33124. Awards MS Ed, DA, Ed D, PhD, Ed S. Accredited by NCATE. DA offered in cooperation with College of Engineering. Part-time and evening/weekend programs available. Faculty: 37 full-time (16 women), 1 (woman) part-time. Students: 188 full-time (127 women), 199 part-time (162 women); includes 159 minority (62 African Americans, 9 Asian Americans, 87 Hispanics, 1 Native American), 14 international. Average age 31. 420 applicants, 58% accepted. In 1997, 116 master's, 18

Directory: Education—General

University of Miami (continued)
doctorates, 3 Ed Ss awarded. Terminal master's awarded for partial completion of doctoral program. *Degree requirements:* For doctorate, dissertation required, foreign language not required. *Average time to degree:* master's–1.5 years full-time, 2.5 years part-time; doctorate–3.5 years full-time, 4.5 years part-time. *Entrance requirements:* For master's, GRE General Test (minimum combined score of 1000; average 1054), TOEFL (minimum score 550); for doctorate, GRE General Test, GRE Subject Test, TOEFL (minimum score 550); for Ed S, GRE General Test, TOEFL (minimum score 550). Application deadline: rolling. Application fee: $35. *Expenses:* Tuition $815 per credit hour. Fees $174 per year. *Financial aid:* Fellowships, research assistantships, teaching assistantships, graduate assistantships, full and partial tuition waivers, Federal Work-Study, institutionally sponsored loans, and career-related internships or fieldwork available. Aid available to part-time students. Financial aid application deadline: 3/1. *Faculty research:* Social skills and learning disabilities, planning for mainstreamed pupils, alcohol and drug abuse, restructuring education for all learners. Total annual research expenditures: $2.113 million. • Dr. Samuel Yarger, Dean, 305-284-3505. E-mail: syarger@umiami.ir.miami.edu. Application contact: Karen Boss, Graduate Studies Coordinator, 305-284-2167. Fax: 305-284-3003.

Announcement: Master's degree programs are available in counseling, elementary, preprimary, and special education; educational handicaps/learning disabilities; exercise physiology; reading and learning disabilities; sports administration; sports medicine; and teaching English to speakers of other languages (TESOL). MS Ed programs in elementary and special education offer opportunities for individuals without a background in education to enter the teaching profession. For further information, contact University of Miami, School of Education, PO Box 248065, Coral Gables, FL 33146, 305-284-3711, or visit the Web site at http://www/education.miami.edu.

See in-depth description on page 809.

University of Michigan, Interdepartmental Program in Education and Psychology, Ann Arbor, MI 48109. Awards PhD. Faculty: 16. Students: 34 full-time (28 women); includes 9 minority (6 African Americans, 2 Asian Americans, 1 Hispanic), 1 international. 57 applicants, 11% accepted. In 1997, 8 doctorates awarded (75% entered university research/teaching, 25% found other work related to degree). Terminal master's awarded for partial completion of doctoral program. *Degree requirements:* For doctorate, dissertation, oral defense of dissertation, preliminary exam. *Average time to degree:* doctorate–6 years full-time. *Entrance requirements:* For doctorate, GRE General Test (minimum combined score of 1800 on three sections recommended; average 1950), GRE Subject Test (recommend. Application deadline: 1/15. Application fee: $55. *Financial aid:* In 1997–98, 25 fellowships (2 to first-year students) averaging $1,100 per month, 17 research assistantships (2 to first-year students) averaging $1,000 per month, 18 teaching assistantships averaging $1,000 per month were awarded. Financial aid application deadline: 3/15. *Faculty research:* Classroom research, instructional psychology. • Jacquelynne Eccles, Director, 734-647-0626. Application contact: Janie Knieper, Administrative Assistant, 734-647-0626. Fax: 734-936-7370. E-mail: cpep@umich.edu.

University of Michigan, School of Education, Ann Arbor, MI 48109. Awards AM, MA-Certification, MS, Ed D, PhD. Part-time programs available. Faculty: 60 full-time (30 women), 9 part-time (5 women), 64.42 FTE. Students: 306 full-time (192 women), 76 part-time (48 women); includes 98 minority (50 African Americans, 22 Asian Americans, 23 Hispanics, 3 Native Americans), 31 international. 460 applicants, 58% accepted. In 1997, 107 master's, 30 doctorates awarded. Terminal master's awarded for partial completion of doctoral program. *Degree requirements:* For doctorate, dissertation, preliminary exam required, foreign language not required. *Entrance requirements:* GRE General Test (minimum combined score of 1800 on three sections), TOEFL (minimum score 600). Application deadline: 1/15 (priority date). Application fee: $55. Electronic applications accepted. *Financial aid:* In 1997–98, fellowships averaging $700 per month and totaling $2.0 million, 136 research assistantships (25 to first-year students) averaging $675 per month, 72 teaching assistantships (10 to first-year students) averaging $677 per month, 108 staff assistantships, hourly appointments (19 to first-year students) were awarded; full and partial tuition waivers, Federal Work-Study, institutionally sponsored loans, and career-related internships or fieldwork also available. Aid available to part-time students. Financial aid application deadline: 1/15. *Faculty research:* Teaching, learning, policy, leadership, technology. Total annual research expenditures: $6.326 million. • Dr. Cecil Miskel, Dean, 734-764-9470. E-mail: miskel@umich.edu. Application contact: Karen Wixson, Associate Dean, 734-764-9470. Fax: 734-763-1229. E-mail: kwixson@umich.edu.

Announcement: A comprehensive listing of financial aid opportunities is available from the Office of Student Services, 1033 School of Education Building, University of Michigan, 610 East University, Ann Arbor, MI 48109-1259 (telephone: 734-764-7563; e-mail: ed.grad.admit@umich.edu). Early application is suggested; admission to the School is necessary in order to establish fellowship eligibility. Assistance may include stipends, tuition assistance, and some University benefits (with assistantships).

See in-depth description on page 811.

University of Michigan, School of Education, Programs in Educational Studies, Ann Arbor, MI 48109. Offerings in curriculum development (AM), early childhood education (AM, PhD), educational administration and policy (AM, PhD), educational foundations and policy (AM, PhD), educational technology (AM, MS, PhD), elementary education (MA-Certification), English education (AM), learning disabilities and literacy (AM), literacy education (AM, PhD), mathematics education (AM, MS, PhD), science education (AM, MS, PhD), secondary education (MA-Certification), social studies education (AM), special education (PhD), teacher education (PhD). *Degree requirements:* For master's, thesis required (for some programs), foreign language not required; for doctorate, dissertation, preliminary exam required, foreign language not required. *Entrance requirements:* GRE General Test (minimum combined score of 1800 on three sections), TOEFL (minimum score 600). Application deadline: 1/15 (priority date). Application fee: $55. Electronic applications accepted. • Dr. Ronald Marx, Chairperson, 734-763-9497. E-mail: ronmarx@umich.edu. Application contact: Karen Wixson, Associate Dean, 734-764-9470. Fax: 734-763-1229. E-mail: kwixson@umich.edu.

Announcement: Master of Arts with Certification (MAC) Program is an intensive 1-year program for prospective Michigan elementary or secondary teachers who have completed bachelor's degrees in fields other than education. Contact MAC Program, 1225 School of Education Building, University of Michigan, 610 East University, Ann Arbor, MI 48109-1259 (telephone: 734-763-2036; e-mail: ed.grad.admit@umich.edu).

University of Michigan–Dearborn, School of Education, 4901 Evergreen Road, Dearborn, MI 48128-1491. Awards MA, M Ed, MPA. Part-time and evening/weekend programs available. Faculty: 19 full-time (11 women), 40 part-time (33 women). Students: 435. Average age 30. *Application deadline:* rolling. *Expenses:* Tuition $4536 per year full-time, $252 per credit hour part-time for state residents; $13,086 per year full-time, $727 per credit hour part-time for nonresidents. Fees $480 per year (minimum). *Financial aid:* Federal Work-Study and career-related internships or fieldwork available. Aid available to part-time students. Financial aid application deadline: 3/15. *Faculty research:* Children's literature and literacy, curriculum inquiry, creative writing, testing and evaluating, learning disabilities. • Dr. John Poster, Dean, 313-593-5435. E-mail: jposter@fob-f1.umd.umich.edu. Application contact: Rachel Chapman, Academic Services Secretary II, 313-593-5091. E-mail: rchapman@fob-f1.umd.umich.edu.

University of Minnesota, Twin Cities Campus, College of Education and Human Development, Minneapolis, MN 55455-0213. Awards MA, M Ed, Ed D, PhD, Ed S. Part-time programs available. Terminal master's awarded for partial completion of doctoral program. *Financial aid:* Fellowships, research assistantships, teaching assistantships, full and partial tuition waivers, Federal Work-Study, institutionally sponsored loans, and career-related internships or fieldwork available. Aid available to part-time students. • Steve Yussen, Dean, 612-625-6806.

See in-depth description on page 813.

University of Mississippi, Graduate School, School of Education, University, MS 38677-9702. Awards MA, M Ed, MS, Ed D, PhD, Ed S. Accredited by NCATE. Faculty: 47 full-time (25 women). Students: 193 full-time (138 women), 223 part-time (175 women); includes 137 minority (129 African Americans, 1 Asian American, 3 Hispanics, 4 Native Americans), 29 international. In 1997, 175 master's, 40 doctorates, 1 Ed S awarded. *Degree requirements:* For doctorate, dissertation. *Entrance requirements:* For master's, GRE General Test, TOEFL, minimum GPA of 3.0; for doctorate, GRE General Test, TOEFL. Application deadline: 8/1 (rolling processing). Application fee: $0 ($25 for international students). *Financial aid:* Application deadline 3/1. • Dr. James Chambless, Acting Dean, 601-232-7063.

University of Missouri–Columbia, College of Education, Columbia, MO 65211. Awards MA, M Ed, Ed D, PhD, Ed S. Part-time and evening/weekend programs available. Faculty: 103 full-time (40 women), 3 part-time (all women). Students: 315 full-time (190 women), 503 part-time (327 women); includes 72 minority (53 African Americans, 8 Asian Americans, 8 Hispanics, 3 Native Americans), 51 international. In 1997, 311 master's, 66 doctorates awarded. Terminal master's awarded for partial completion of doctoral program. *Degree requirements:* For doctorate, dissertation. *Entrance requirements:* For master's, GRE General Test or MAT, minimum GPA of 3.0; for doctorate, GRE General Test; for Ed S, GRE General Test or MAT. Application deadline: rolling. Application fee: $25 ($50 for international students). *Expenses:* Tuition $3240 per year full-time, $180 per credit hour part-time for state residents; $9108 per year full-time, $506 per credit hour part-time for nonresidents. Fees $55 per year full-time. *Financial aid:* Fellowships, teaching assistantships, Federal Work-Study, and career-related internships or fieldwork available. Aid available to part-time students. • Dr. Richard Andrews, Dean, 573-882-8311.

University of Missouri–Kansas City, School of Education, Kansas City, MO 64110-2499. Awards MA, PhD, Ed S. Accredited by NCATE. Part-time and evening/weekend programs available. Faculty: 46 full-time (21 women). Students: 183 full-time (134 women), 677 part-time (519 women); includes 152 minority (117 African Americans, 13 Asian Americans, 18 Hispanics, 4 Native Americans), 19 international. Average age 35. In 1997, 197 master's, 14 doctorates, 36 Ed Ss awarded. *Degree requirements:* For doctorate, dissertation, internship, practicum required, foreign language not required. *Average time to degree:* master's–2 years full-time, 4 years part-time; doctorate–4 years full-time, 7 years part-time; other advanced degree–2 years full-time, 4 years part-time. *Entrance requirements:* For master's, minimum GPA of 2.75; for doctorate, GRE, minimum GPA of 3.0; for Ed S, minimum GPA of 3.0. Application fee: $25. *Expenses:* Tuition $182 per credit hour for state residents; $508 per credit hour for nonresidents. Fees $60 per year. *Financial aid:* Fellowships, research assistantships, teaching assistantships, full and partial tuition waivers, Federal Work-Study, institutionally sponsored loans, and career-related internships or fieldwork available. Aid available to part-time students. *Faculty research:* Assessment, reading, leadership, teacher education, counseling psychology. • Bernard Oliver, Dean, 816-235-2236. Application contact: Gail Metcalf Schartel, Manager of Student Services, 816-235-2887. Fax: 816-235-5270. E-mail: scharteg@smtpgate.umkc.edu.

University of Missouri–St. Louis, School of Education, St. Louis, MO 63121-4499. Awards M Ed, Ed D. Accredited by NCATE. Part-time and evening/weekend programs available. Faculty: 52 (20 women). Students: 123 full-time (84 women), 936 part-time (770 women); includes 222 minority (195 African Americans, 12 Asian Americans, 10 Hispanics, 5 Native Americans), 11 international. In 1997, 312 master's, 8 doctorates awarded. *Degree requirements:* For doctorate, dissertation. *Entrance requirements:* For doctorate, GRE General Test, GRE Subject Test. Application deadline: 7/1 (priority date; rolling processing; 12/1 for spring admission). Application fee: $0. Electronic applications accepted. *Expenses:* Tuition $3903 per year full-time, $167 per credit hour part-time for state residents; $11,745 per year full-time, $489 per credit hour part-time for nonresidents. Fees $816 per year full-time, $34 per credit hour part-time. *Financial aid:* In 1997–98, 9 teaching assistantships (1 to a first-year student) were awarded. Aid available to part-time students. *Faculty research:* Counseling, remedial reading, literacy, educational policy and research, science education, autism and behavioral disorders, exercise and aging. • Dr. Kathleen Haywood, Director of Graduate Studies, 314-516-5483. Fax: 314-516-5227. E-mail: c1812@umslvma.umsl.edu. Application contact: Graduate Admissions, 314-516-5458. Fax: 314-516-6759. E-mail: gradadm@umslvma.umsl.edu.

University of Mobile, Graduate Programs, Program in Teacher Education, Mobile, AL 36663-0220. Awards MA. Part-time and evening/weekend programs available. Faculty: 6 full-time (4 women), 2 part-time (0 women). Students: 10 full-time (8 women), 41 part-time (27 women); includes 13 minority (all African Americans). Average age 29. 25 applicants, 92% accepted. In 1997, 17 degrees awarded (100% found work related to degree). *Degree requirements:* Comprehensive exams required, thesis optional. *Entrance requirements:* GRE, MAT, or NTE; TOEFL (minimum score 550), Alabama teaching certificate. Application deadline: 8/3 (priority date; rolling processing; 12/23 for spring admission). Application fee: $30. *Tuition:* $160 per semester hour. *Financial aid:* Partial tuition waivers, Federal Work-Study available. Aid available to part-time students. Financial aid application deadline: 8/1. • Dr. Lynda Walden, Dean, School of Education, 334-675-5990 Ext. 354. Fax: 334-679-9314. Application contact: Kaye F. Brown, Dean, Graduate and Special Programs, 334-675-5990 Ext. 289. Fax: 334-675-9816.

The University of Montana–Missoula, School of Education, Missoula, MT 59812-0002. Awards MA, M Ed, MS, Ed D, Ed S. Accredited by NCATE. Part-time programs available. Faculty: 29 full-time (16 women), 4 part-time (1 woman). Students: 43 full-time (22 women), 99 part-time (59 women); includes 9 minority (1 African American, 2 Asian Americans, 2 Hispanics, 4 Native Americans), 8 international. Average age 30. 62 applicants, 74% accepted. In 1997, 42 master's, 7 doctorates awarded. *Degree requirements:* For doctorate, dissertation; for Ed S, thesis required, foreign language not required. *Entrance requirements:* For master's, GRE General Test (minimum score 450 on each section), minimum GPA of 3.0; for doctorate, GRE General Test (minimum score 500 on verbal section, 1100 combined), GRE Subject Test, minimum graduate GPA of 3.5; for Ed S, GRE General Test. Application fee: $30. *Tuition:* $2499 per year (minimum) full-time, $376 per semester (minimum) part-time for state residents; $6528 per year (minimum) full-time, $1048 per semester (minimum) part-time for nonresidents. *Financial aid:* Teaching assistantships, Federal Work-Study, institutionally sponsored loans, and career-related internships or fieldwork available. Financial aid application deadline: 3/1. *Faculty research:* Cooperative learning, administrative styles. • Dr. Don Robson, Dean, 406-243-4911.

University of Montevallo, College of Education, Montevallo, AL 35115. Awards M Ed, Ed S. Accredited by NCATE. Part-time and evening/weekend programs available. *Entrance requirements:* For master's, GRE General Test (minimum combined score of 850), MAT (minimum score 35), minimum undergraduate GPA of 2.75 in last 60 hours or 2.5 overall. Application deadline: 7/15 (11/15 for spring admission). Application fee: $10.

University of Nebraska at Kearney, College of Education, Kearney, NE 68849-0001. Awards MA Ed, MS Ed, Ed S. Accredited by NCATE. Part-time and evening/weekend programs available. Faculty: 28 full-time (11 women). Students: 103 full-time (86 women), 313 part-time (199 women); includes 9 minority (1 African American, 3 Asian Americans, 4 Hispanics, 1 Native American), 6 international. In 1997, 132 master's, 15 Ed Ss awarded. *Degree requirements:* For master's, thesis optional. *Entrance requirements:* GRE General Test. Application deadline: 8/1 (priority date; rolling processing; 12/15 for spring admission). Application fee: $35. *Expenses:* Tuition $1494 per year full-time, $83 per credit hour part-time for state residents; $2826 per year full-time, $157 per credit hour part-time for nonresidents. Fees $229 per year full-time, $11.25 per semester (minimum) part-time. *Financial aid:* In 1997–98, 15 research assistantships, 8 teaching assistantships, 11 graduate assistantships were awarded; career-related internships or fieldwork also available. Aid available to part-time students. Financial aid application deadline: 3/1; applicants required to submit FAFSA. • Dr. Jean Ramage, Dean, 308-865-8502.

University of Nebraska at Omaha, College of Education, Omaha, NE 68182. Awards MA, MS, Ed D, Ed S. Accredited by NCATE. Part-time and evening/weekend programs available. Faculty: 50 full-time (13 women), 3 part-time (0 women). Students: 107 full-time (75 women),

694 part-time (541 women); includes 53 minority (38 African Americans, 7 Asian Americans, 7 Hispanics, 1 Native American), 34 international. Average age 34. In 1997, 243 master's, 3 doctorates awarded. *Degree requirements:* For master's, comprehensive exam required, foreign language not required; for doctorate, dissertation required, foreign language not required. *Entrance requirements:* For master's, minimum GPA of 3.0; for doctorate, GRE General Test, resume, 3 samples of research/written work. Application deadline: rolling. Application fee: $35. *Expenses:* Tuition $1670 per year full-time, $94 per credit hour part-time for state residents; $4082 per year full-time, $227 per credit hour part-time for nonresidents. Fees $302 per year full-time, $108 per semester (minimum) part-time. *Financial aid:* 257 students received aid; fellowships, research assistantships, teaching assistantships, full tuition waivers, Federal Work-Study, institutionally sponsored loans, and career-related internships or fieldwork available. Aid available to part-time students. Financial aid application deadline: 3/1; applicants required to submit FAFSA. • Dr. Richard B. Flynn, Dean, 402-554-2719.

University of Nebraska–Lincoln, Teachers College, Lincoln, NE 68588. Awards MA, M Ed, MPE, MS, MST, Ed D, PhD, Certificate, Ed S, JD/PhD. Accredited by NCATE. Faculty: 79 full-time (21 women), 3 part-time (all women), 81.5 FTE. Students: 287 full-time (201 women), 495 part-time (324 women); includes 58 minority (18 African Americans, 19 Asian Americans, 17 Hispanics, 4 Native Americans), 41 international. Average age 36. 362 applicants, 46% accepted. In 1997, 199 master's, 79 doctorates, 10 other advanced degrees awarded. *Degree requirements:* For doctorate, dissertation, comprehensive exam. *Average time to degree:* doctorate–5.4 years full-time. *Entrance requirements:* For master's and doctorate, TOEFL. Application fee: $35. Electronic applications accepted. *Expenses:* Tuition $110 per credit hour for state residents; $270 per credit hour for nonresidents. Fees $480 per year full-time, $110 per semester part-time. *Financial aid:* In 1997–98, 53 fellowships totaling $128,527, 35 research assistantships totaling $169,300, 69 teaching assistantships totaling $481,468 were awarded; Federal Work-Study also available. Aid available to part-time students. Financial aid application deadline: 2/15. • Dr. James P. O'Hanlon, Dean, 402-472-5400.

University of Nevada, Las Vegas, College of Education, Las Vegas, NV 89154-9900. Awards MA, M Ed, MS, Ed D, PhD, Ed S. Accredited by NCATE. Part-time and evening/weekend programs available. Faculty: 67 full-time (27 women). Students: 197 full-time (144 women), 644 part-time (493 women); includes 119 minority (56 African Americans, 22 Asian Americans, 35 Hispanics, 6 Native Americans), 9 international. 321 applicants, 81% accepted. In 1997, 260 master's, 11 doctorates awarded. *Degree requirements:* For master's, comprehensive exam required, foreign language not required; for doctorate, dissertation, oral exam required, foreign language not required; for Ed S, exam required, foreign language and thesis not required. *Entrance requirements:* For doctorate, MAT, minimum graduate GPA of 3.5. Application fee: $40 ($95 for international students). *Expenses:* Tuition $93 per credit for state residents; $93 per credit full-time, $190 per credit part-time for nonresidents. Fees $5570 per year full-time for nonresidents. *Financial aid:* In 1997–98, 33 research assistantships, 18 teaching assistantships were awarded. Financial aid application deadline: 3/1. • Dr. John Readence, Dean, 702-895-3374. Application contact: Graduate College Admissions Evaluator, 702-895-3320.

University of Nevada, Reno, College of Education, Reno, NV 89557. Awards MA, M Ed, MS, Ed D, PhD, Ed S. Accredited by NCATE. Faculty: 41 (16 women). Students: 166 full-time (123 women), 352 part-time (271 women); includes 49 minority (19 African Americans, 4 Asian Americans, 20 Hispanics, 6 Native Americans), 2 international. 264 applicants, 71% accepted. In 1997, 86 master's, 8 doctorates awarded. Terminal master's awarded for partial completion of doctoral program. *Degree requirements:* For master's, thesis optional, foreign language not required; for doctorate, dissertation required, foreign language not required. *Entrance requirements:* For master's, GRE, TOEFL (minimum score 500), minimum GPA of 2.75; for doctorate, GRE, TOEFL (minimum score 500), minimum GPA of 3.0. Application fee: $40. *Expenses:* Tuition $0 for state residents; $5770 per year full-time, $200 per credit part-time for nonresidents. Fees $93 per credit. *Financial aid:* Research assistantships, teaching assistantships, graduate assistantships, Federal Work-Study, institutionally sponsored loans available. Financial aid application deadline: 3/1. • Dr. Stephen Rock, Acting Dean, 702-784-6905.

University of New Brunswick, Faculty of Education, Fredericton, NB E3B 5A3, Canada. Awards M Ed. Part-time programs available. *Entrance requirements:* TOEFL, TWE, minimum GPA of 3.0. Application deadline: 3/1 (priority date; rolling processing). Application fee: $25.

University of New England, College of Health Professions, Program in Education, Biddeford, ME 04005-9526. Awards MS Ed. Part-time programs available. Postbaccalaureate distance learning degree programs offered (minimal on-campus study). Faculty: 2 full-time (0 women), 5 part-time (3 women). Students: 155 full-time (121 women), 128 part-time (100 women); includes 12 minority (5 African Americans, 1 Asian American, 3 Hispanics, 3 Native Americans). Average age 40. 118 applicants, 85% accepted. In 1997, 15 degrees awarded. *Degree requirements:* Collaborative action research project, integrative seminar portfolio. *Entrance requirements:* Teaching certificate, 2 years of teaching experience. Application deadline: 9/15 (rolling processing; 3/15 for spring admission). Application fee: $40. *Expenses:* Tuition $335 per credit. Fees $230 per year. *Financial aid:* Available to part-time students. Financial aid application deadline: 5/1; applicants required to submit FAFSA. *Faculty research:* Distance learning, effective teaching, transition planning, adult learning. • John E. Brandt, Director, 207-283-0171 Ext. 4382. Fax: 207-797-7225. E-mail: jbrandt@mailbox.une.edu. Application contact: Patricia T. Cribby, Dean of Admissions and Enrollment Management, 207-283-0171 Ext. 2297. Fax: 207-286-3678. E-mail: jshea@mailbox.une.edu.

University of New Hampshire, College of Liberal Arts, Department of Education, Durham, NH 03824. Offers programs in counseling (MA, M Ed); early childhood education (M Ed); education (PhD); educational administration (M Ed, CAGS); elementary education (MAT, M Ed); reading (M Ed, PhD), including reading (M Ed), reading and writing instruction (PhD); secondary education (MAT, M Ed); special education (M Ed). Accredited by NCATE. Part-time programs available. Faculty: 34 full-time. Students: 170 full-time (128 women), 365 part-time (256 women); includes 12 minority (6 African Americans, 3 Asian Americans, 3 Hispanics), 4 international. Average age 35. 252 applicants, 76% accepted. In 1997, 174 master's, 7 doctorates, 9 CAGSs awarded. *Degree requirements:* For doctorate, dissertation required, foreign language not required. *Entrance requirements:* GRE General Test. Application deadline: rolling. Application fee: $50. *Expenses:* Tuition $5440 per year full-time, $302 per credit hour part-time for state residents; $8160 per year (minimum) full-time, $453 per credit hour (minimum) part-time for nonresidents. Fees $868 per year full-time, $15 per year part-time. *Financial aid:* In 1997–98, 1 fellowship, 2 research assistantships, 19 teaching assistantships (9 to first-year students), 36 scholarships (8 to first-year students) were awarded; full and partial tuition waivers, Federal Work-Study, and career-related internships or fieldwork also available. Aid available to part-time students. Financial aid application deadline: 2/15. • Dr. Susan Franzosa, Chairperson, 603-862-2310. Application contact: Dr. Todd DeMitchell, Graduate Coordinator, 603-862-2317.

University of New Haven, College of Arts and Sciences, Programs in Education, West Haven, CT 06516-1916. Awards MS, 6th Year Diploma. Students: 230 full-time (154 women), 100 part-time (72 women); includes 39 minority (30 African Americans, 2 Asian Americans, 7 Hispanics). 180 applicants, 61% accepted. In 1997, 165 master's awarded. *Entrance requirements:* For 6th Year Diploma, master's degree, teaching certificate. Application deadline: rolling. Application fee: $50. *Expenses:* Tuition $1125 per course. Fees $13 per trimester. *Financial aid:* Federal Work-Study and career-related internships or fieldwork available. Financial aid application deadline: 5/1; applicants required to submit FAFSA. • Louise Soares, Director, 203-932-7336.

University of New Mexico, College of Education, Albuquerque, NM 87131-2039. Awards MA, MS, Ed D, PhD, Certificate, Ed S. Accredited by NCATE. Part-time and evening/weekend programs available. Faculty: 111 full-time (67 women), 79 part-time (53 women), 132.4 FTE. Students: 397 full-time (268 women), 627 part-time (464 women); includes 290 minority (28 African Americans, 17 Asian Americans, 200 Hispanics, 45 Native Americans), 45 international. Average age 37. 660 applicants, 49% accepted. In 1997, 484 master's, 41 doctorates, 25 other advanced degrees awarded. Terminal master's awarded for partial completion of doctoral program. *Application fee:* $25. *Expenses:* Tuition $2442 per year full-time, $103 per credit hour part-time for state residents; $8691 per year full-time, $103 per credit hour (minimum) part-time for nonresidents. Fees $32 per year. *Financial aid:* Fellowships, research assistantships, teaching assistantships, full and partial tuition waivers, Federal Work-Study, institutionally sponsored loans, and career-related internships or fieldwork available. Aid available to part-time students. *Total annual research expenditures:* $225,264. • Dr. Viola E. Florez Tighe, Dean, 505-277-2231. E-mail: vflorez@unm.edu. Application contact: Annie Rodgers, Administrative Assistant, 505-277-3638. Fax: 505-277-8427. E-mail: annier@unm.edu.

University of New Orleans, College of Education, New Orleans, LA 70148. Awards MA, M Ed, PhD, Certificate. Accredited by NCATE. Evening/weekend programs available. Faculty: 50 full-time (25 women), 16 part-time (9 women). Students: 353 full-time (254 women), 1,097 part-time (881 women); includes 352 minority (292 African Americans, 19 Asian Americans, 37 Hispanics, 4 Native Americans), 37 international. Average age 35. 583 applicants, 91% accepted. In 1997, 223 master's, 25 doctorates awarded. Terminal master's awarded for partial completion of doctoral program. *Degree requirements:* For doctorate, dissertation. *Entrance requirements:* For master's, GRE General Test; for doctorate, GRE General Test (minimum combined score of 1000). Application deadline: 7/1 (priority date; rolling processing). Application fee: $20. *Expenses:* Tuition $2362 per year full-time, $373 per semester (minimum) part-time for state residents; $7888 per year full-time, $1423 per semester (minimum) part-time for nonresidents. Fees $170 per year full-time, $25 per semester (minimum) part-time. *Financial aid:* Fellowships, research assistantships, teaching assistantships, grants, partial tuition waivers, institutionally sponsored loans, and career-related internships or fieldwork available. *Faculty research:* Special education and habilitation, educational administration, exercise physiology, wellness, effective school instruction. Total annual research expenditures: $1.511 million. • Dr. Robert Wimpelberg, Dean, 504-280-6719. E-mail: rkwel@uno.edu. Application contact: Dr. Cornell Brooks, Associate Dean, 504-280-6028. Fax: 504-280-6065. E-mail: crbel@uno.edu.

University of North Alabama, College of Education, Florence, AL 35632-0001. Awards MA, MA Ed, Ed S. Accredited by NCATE. Part-time and evening/weekend programs available. Faculty: 21 part-time (8 women). Students: 58 full-time (38 women), 319 part-time (209 women); includes 19 minority (18 African Americans, 1 Asian American). Average age 33. In 1997, 168 master's, 9 Ed Ss awarded. *Degree requirements:* For master's, final written comprehensive exam required, foreign language and thesis not required. *Entrance requirements:* For master's, GRE, MAT, or NTE, minimum GPA of 2.5, Alabama Class B Certificate or equivalent, teaching experience. Application deadline: 7/1 (priority date; rolling processing; 12/1 for spring admission). Application fee: $25. *Expenses:* Tuition $2448 per year full-time, $102 per credit hour part-time for state residents; $4896 per year full-time, $204 per credit hour part-time for nonresidents. Fees $3 per semester. *Financial aid:* Federal Work-Study available. Aid available to part-time students. Financial aid application deadline: 4/1. • Dr. Fred L. Hattabaugh, Dean, 205-765-4252. Application contact: Dr. Sue Wilson, Dean of Enrollment Management, 205-765-4316.

The University of North Carolina at Chapel Hill, School of Education, Chapel Hill, NC 27599. Awards MA, MAT, M Ed, MSA, Ed D, PhD. Accredited by NCATE. Part-time programs available. Faculty: 48 full-time (19 women), 61 part-time (28 women). Students: 154 full-time (116 women), 146 part-time (119 women); includes 51 minority (38 African Americans, 4 Asian Americans, 7 Hispanics, 2 Native Americans). Average age 32. 536 applicants, 37% accepted. In 1997, 84 master's, 26 doctorates awarded. *Degree requirements:* For master's, comprehensive exam required, foreign language not required; for doctorate, dissertation, comprehensive exams required, foreign language not required. *Entrance requirements:* GRE General Test (minimum combined score of 1000), minimum GPA of 3.0 during last 2 years of undergraduate course work. Application deadline: 1/1 (rolling processing). Application fee: $55. Electronic applications accepted. *Expenses:* Tuition $1428 per year full-time, $357 per semester (minimum) part-time for state residents; $10,414 per year full-time, $2604 per semester (minimum) part-time for nonresidents. Fees $782 per year full-time, $332 per semester (minimum) part-time. *Financial aid:* In 1997–98, 113 students received aid, including 4 fellowships (1 to a first-year student), 4 general assistantships, traineeships (2 to first-year students); research assistantships, teaching assistantships, Federal Work-Study also available. Aid available to part-time students. Financial aid application deadline: 1/1; applicants required to submit FAFSA. *Faculty research:* Teaching and learning; leadership; early childhood education; culture, curriculum, and change; early childhood, family, and literacy studies; psychological studies in education. • Dr. Madeline R. Grumet, Dean, 919-966-7000. E-mail: grumet@email.unc.edu. Application contact: Janet Carroll, Registrar, 919-966-1346. Fax: 919-962-1533. E-mail: jscarrol@email.unc.edu.

University of North Carolina at Charlotte, College of Education, Charlotte, NC 28223-0001. Offers programs in counseling and guidance (MA), educational administration (CAS), educational leadership (Ed D), elementary education (M Ed), instructional systems technology (M Ed), middle school education (M Ed), reading education (M Ed), school administration (MSA), secondary education (M Ed), special education (M Ed), teaching English as a second language (M Ed). Accredited by NCATE. Part-time and evening/weekend programs available. Faculty: 61 full-time (31 women), 7 part-time (6 women), 62.75 FTE. Students: 177 full-time (143 women), 370 part-time (303 women); includes 93 minority (83 African Americans, 3 Asian Americans, 6 Hispanics, 1 Native American), 7 international. Average age 33. 318 applicants, 74% accepted. In 1997, 177 master's, 2 CASs awarded. *Entrance requirements:* For master's, GRE General Test or MAT, minimum GPA of 2.5. Application deadline: 7/1. Application fee: $35. *Tuition:* $1786 per year full-time, $339 per semester (minimum) part-time for state residents; $8914 per year full-time, $2121 per semester (minimum) part-time for nonresidents. *Financial aid:* In 1997–98, 15 research assistantships averaging $631 per month and totaling $75,745, 8 teaching assistantships averaging $630 per month and totaling $40,350, administrative assistantships averaging $692 per month were awarded; Federal Work-Study and career-related internships or fieldwork also available. Financial aid application deadline: 4/1. *Faculty research:* Education of the handicapped, learning disabilities, physical therapy, human services. • Dr. John M. Nagle, Dean, 704-547-4707. Application contact: Kathy Barringer, Assistant Director of Graduate Admissions, 704-547-3366. Fax: 704-547-3279. E-mail: gradadm@email.uncc.edu.

University of North Carolina at Greensboro, School of Education, Greensboro, NC 27412-0001. Awards MA, M Ed, MLIS, MS, MSA, Ed D, PhD, Ed S, PMC, MS/Ed S. Accredited by NCATE. Part-time and evening/weekend programs available. Faculty: 48 full-time, 16 part-time. Students: 413 full-time (315 women), 358 part-time (285 women). 495 applicants, 44% accepted. In 1997, 190 master's, 32 doctorates, 18 other advanced degrees awarded. *Degree requirements:* For doctorate, dissertation. *Entrance requirements:* GRE General Test. Application fee: $35. *Expenses:* Tuition $1842 per year full-time, $370 per semester (minimum) part-time for state residents; $10,296 per year full-time, $2484 per semester (minimum) part-time for nonresidents. Fees $806 per year full-time, $111 per semester (minimum) part-time. *Financial aid:* Fellowships, research assistantships, teaching assistantships, graduate assistantships, institutionally sponsored loans, and career-related internships or fieldwork available. *Faculty research:* Effects of homogeneous grouping, women in higher education, assessment of student achievement. • Dr. David Armstrong, Dean, 336-334-3403.

University of North Carolina at Pembroke, Graduate Studies, Department of Education, Pembroke, NC 28372-1510. Offers programs in educational administration and supervision (MA Ed), elementary education (MA Ed), middle grades education (MA Ed), reading education (MA Ed), school administration (MSA). Accredited by NCATE. Part-time and evening/weekend programs available. Faculty: 28 full-time (12 women), 4 part-time (0 women). Students: 1 full-time (0 women), 75 part-time (66 women); includes 27 minority (9 African Americans, 2 Asian Americans, 16 Native Americans). In 1997, 35 degrees awarded. *Degree requirements:* Comprehensive exam required, thesis optional, foreign language not required. *Average time to*

Directory: Education—General

University of North Carolina at Pembroke (continued)
degree: master's–2 years full-time, 3 years part-time. *Entrance requirements:* GRE General Test or MAT, minimum GPA of 3.0 in major, 2.5 overall. Application deadline: rolling. Application fee: $25. *Tuition:* $1554 per year full-time, $610 per semester (minimum) part-time for state residents; $8824 per year full-time, $2122 per semester (minimum) part-time for nonresidents. *Financial aid:* Graduate assistantships and career-related internships or fieldwork available. Aid available to part-time students. Financial aid application deadline: 4/15. • Dr. Donald Little, Chair, 910-521-6221. Application contact: Director of Graduate Studies, 910-521-6271. Fax: 910-521-6497.

University of North Carolina at Wilmington, School of Education, Wilmington, NC 28403-3201. Awards MAT, M Ed. Accredited by NCATE. Part-time and evening/weekend programs available. Faculty: 17 full-time (8 women), 2 part-time (0 women). Students: 33 full-time (28 women), 43 part-time (34 women); includes 8 minority (7 African Americans, 1 Native American). Average age 37. 72 applicants, 47% accepted. In 1997, 49 degrees awarded. *Degree requirements:* Comprehensive exam required, foreign language and thesis not required. *Entrance requirements:* GRE General Test, MAT, minimum B average in upper-division undergraduate course work. Application deadline: 7/1 (rolling processing). Application fee: $35. *Tuition:* $1748 per year full-time, $270 per semester (minimum) part-time for state residents; $8882 per year full-time, $2058 per semester (minimum) part-time for nonresidents. *Financial aid:* In 1997–98, 12 assistantships were awarded; teaching assistantships, Federal Work-Study, and career-related internships or fieldwork also available. Aid available to part-time students. Financial aid application deadline: 3/15. • Dr. Robert Tyndall, Dean, 910-962-3354. Application contact: Neil F. Hadley, Dean, Graduate School, 910-962-4117.

University of North Dakota, College of Education and Human Development, Grand Forks, ND 58202. Awards MA, M Ed, MS, MSW, Ed D, PhD, Ed S. Accredited by NCATE. Part-time and evening/weekend programs available. Postbaccalaureate distance learning degree programs offered (minimal on-campus study). Faculty: 39 full-time (23 women). Students: 93 full-time (63 women), 199 part-time (133 women). 182 applicants, 54% accepted. In 1997, 87 master's, 16 doctorates, 3 Ed Ss awarded. *Degree requirements:* For master's, thesis or alternative; for doctorate, dissertation. *Entrance requirements:* For master's, TOEFL (minimum score 550), minimum GPA of 3.0; for doctorate, TOEFL (minimum score 550), minimum GPA of 3.5. Application deadline: 2/1 (priority date; rolling processing). Application fee: $20. *Financial aid:* In 1997–98, 83 students received aid, including 25 fellowships totaling $60,000, 3 research assistantships totaling $14,770, 31 teaching assistantships totaling $135,032, 24 assistantships totaling $175,550; full and partial tuition waivers, Federal Work-Study, institutionally sponsored loans, and career-related internships or fieldwork also available. Financial aid application deadline: 3/15. • Dr. Mary Harris, Dean, 701-777-2674. Fax: 701-777-4393. E-mail: maharris@badlands.nodak.edu.

University of Northern Colorado, College of Education, Greeley, CO 80639. Awards MA, MS, Ed D, PhD, Psy D, Ed S. Accredited by NCATE. Part-time programs available. Faculty: 62 full-time (33 women), 5 part-time (2 women). Students: 580 full-time (431 women), 261 part-time (203 women); includes 77 minority (14 African Americans, 15 Asian Americans, 41 Hispanics, 7 Native Americans), 33 international. Average age 35. 432 applicants, 68% accepted. In 1997, 285 master's, 50 doctorates, 9 Ed Ss awarded. *Degree requirements:* For master's, comprehensive exams; for doctorate and Ed S, thesis/dissertation, comprehensive exams. *Entrance requirements:* For doctorate, GRE General Test. Application deadline: rolling. Application fee: $35. *Expenses:* Tuition $2327 per year full-time, $129 per credit hour part-time for state residents; $9578 per year full-time, $532 per credit hour part-time for nonresidents. Fees $752 per year full-time, $184 per semester (minimum) part-time. *Financial aid:* In 1997–98, 399 students received aid, including 69 fellowships (20 to first-year students) totaling $87,152, 17 teaching assistantships (2 to first-year students) totaling $120,657, 61 graduate assistantships (15 to first-year students) totaling $498,263. Financial aid application deadline: 3/1. • Dr. Allen Huang, Interim Dean, 970-351-2817.

University of Northern Colorado, Interdisciplinary Education Program, Greeley, CO 80639. Awards MA. Students: 9 full-time (all women), 7 part-time (all women); includes 2 minority (1 Asian American, 1 Hispanic). Average age 36. 30 applicants, 77% accepted. In 1997, 39 degrees awarded. *Degree requirements:* Comprehensive exams. *Application deadline:* rolling. *Application fee:* $35. *Expenses:* Tuition $2327 per year full-time, $129 per credit hour part-time for state residents; $9578 per year full-time, $532 per credit hour part-time for nonresidents. Fees $752 per year full-time, $184 per semester (minimum) part-time. *Financial aid:* 10 students received aid. Financial aid application deadline: 3/1. • Dr. Priscilla Kimboko, Associate Dean, 970-351-2831.

University of Northern Iowa, College of Education, Cedar Falls, IA 50614. Awards MA, MA Ed, Ed D, Ed S. Part-time and evening/weekend programs available. Faculty: 94 full-time (32 women). Students: 149 full-time (107 women), 341 part-time (252 women); includes 30 minority (23 African Americans, 5 Asian Americans, 1 Hispanic, 1 Native American), 21 international. Average age 33. 263 applicants, 87% accepted. In 1997, 187 master's, 4 doctorates, 3 Ed Ss awarded. *Degree requirements:* For Ed S, thesis or alternative required, foreign language not required. *Entrance requirements:* For master's, minimum GPA of 3.5, 3 years of educational experience; for doctorate, minimum GPA of 3.2, 3 years of educational experience, master's degree; for Ed S, GRE General Test, GRE Subject Test. Application deadline: rolling. Application fee: $20 ($30 for international students). *Expenses:* Tuition $3166 per year full-time, $176 per hour part-time for state residents; $7805 per year full-time, $176 per hour part-time for nonresidents. Fees $194 per year full-time, $12.50 per semester (minimum) part-time. *Financial aid:* Scholarships, full and partial tuition waivers, Federal Work-Study, institutionally sponsored loans, and career-related internships or fieldwork available. Aid available to part-time students. Financial aid application deadline: 3/1. • Dr. Thomas J. Switzer, Dean, 319-273-2717.

University of North Florida, College of Education, Jacksonville, FL 32224-2645. Awards M Ed, Ed D. Accredited by NCATE. Part-time and evening/weekend programs available. Faculty: 51 full-time (25 women). Students: 90 full-time (72 women), 400 part-time (341 women); includes 82 minority (68 African Americans, 6 Asian Americans, 7 Hispanics, 1 Native American), 1 international. Average age 37. 42 applicants, 67% accepted. In 1997, 194 master's, 3 doctorates awarded. Terminal master's awarded for partial completion of doctoral program. *Degree requirements:* For doctorate, dissertation required, foreign language not required. *Entrance requirements:* For master's, GRE General Test (minimum combined score of 1000), minimum GPA of 3.0; for doctorate, GRE General Test, master's degree. Application deadline: rolling. Application fee: $20. *Tuition:* $3388 per year full-time, $141 per credit hour part-time for state residents; $11,634 per year full-time, $485 per credit hour part-time for nonresidents. *Financial aid:* Fellowships, research assistantships, Federal Work-Study, institutionally sponsored loans, and career-related internships or fieldwork available. Aid available to part-time students. • Dr. Kathrine Kasten, Interim Dean, 904-646-2520.

University of North Texas, College of Education, Denton, TX 76203-6737. Awards M Ed, MS, Ed D, PhD, Certificate. Accredited by NCATE. Part-time and evening/weekend programs available. Faculty: 86 full-time (32 women), 29 part-time (13 women). Students: 467 full-time (327 women), 1,612 part-time (1,164 women); includes 218 minority (102 African Americans, 16 Asian Americans, 83 Hispanics, 17 Native Americans), 58 international. In 1997, 386 master's, 71 doctorates awarded. Terminal master's awarded for partial completion of doctoral program. *Degree requirements:* For doctorate, dissertation. *Entrance requirements:* For master's, GRE General Test; for doctorate, GRE General Test, admissions exam. Application deadline: 7/17. Application fee: $25 ($50 for international students). *Tuition:* $2063 per year full-time, $815 per year part-time for state residents; $5897 per year full-time, $2100 per year part-time for nonresidents. *Financial aid:* Fellowships, research assistantships, teaching assistantships, partial tuition waivers, Federal Work-Study, institutionally sponsored loans, and career-related internships or fieldwork available. Aid available to part-time students. Financial aid application deadline: 4/1. *Faculty research:* Teacher competency, educational measurement, higher education, biological and chemical bases of learning, technology in the classroom. • Dr. Jean Keller, Dean, 940-565-2231. Fax: 940-565-4415. Application contact: Dr. John Williamson, Director of Student Services, 940-565-2736. Fax: 940-565-2728. E-mail: wllmsn@coe.unt.edu.

University of Oklahoma, College of Education, Norman, OK 73019-0390. Awards M Ed, Ed D, PhD, M Ed/MLIS. Accredited by NCATE. Part-time and evening/weekend programs available. Faculty: 54 full-time (27 women), 25 part-time (20 women). Students: 181 full-time (124 women), 426 part-time (301 women); includes 84 minority (33 African Americans, 10 Asian Americans, 7 Hispanics, 34 Native Americans), 15 international. In 1997, 175 master's, 44 doctorates awarded. Terminal master's awarded for partial completion of doctoral program. *Degree requirements:* For doctorate, dissertation. *Entrance requirements:* For master's, TOEFL (minimum score 550), 12 hours of course work in education; for doctorate, GRE General Test, TOEFL (minimum score 550), master's degree. Application fee: $25. *Expenses:* Tuition $1920 per year full-time, $80 per credit hour part-time for state residents; $6108 per year full-time, $255 per credit hour part-time for nonresidents. Fees $468 per year full-time, $12 per semester (minimum) part-time. *Financial aid:* In 1997–98, 33 research assistantships, 20 teaching assistantships were awarded; fellowships, full and partial tuition waivers, Federal Work-Study, institutionally sponsored loans, and career-related internships or fieldwork also available. Aid available to part-time students. *Faculty research:* Single parent families, educational innovation, language acquisition, Piagetian-based science education, counseling psychology. • Dr. Joan Karen Smith, Dean, 405-325-1081. Application contact: Barbi DeLong, Graduate Program Assistant, 405-325-2357.

University of Oregon, Graduate School, College of Education, Eugene, OR 97403. Awards MA, M Ed, MS, D Ed, PhD. Part-time programs available. Faculty: 66 full-time (39 women), 103 part-time (69 women), 119.6 FTE. Students: 319 full-time (238 women), 114 part-time (79 women); includes 61 minority (7 African Americans, 22 Asian Americans, 26 Hispanics, 6 Native Americans), 36 international. 529 applicants, 35% accepted. In 1997, 160 master's, 32 doctorates awarded. Terminal master's awarded for partial completion of doctoral program. *Degree requirements:* For master's, exam, paper, or project required, foreign language not required; for doctorate, dissertation, comprehensive exam required, foreign language not required. *Entrance requirements:* TOEFL. Application fee: $50. *Tuition:* $6429 per year full-time, $873 per quarter (minimum) part-time for state residents; $10,857 per year full-time, $1360 per quarter (minimum) part-time for nonresidents. *Financial aid:* In 1997–98, 78 teaching assistantships (17 to first-year students) were awarded; fellowships, research assistantships, full tuition waivers, Federal Work-Study, institutionally sponsored loans, and career-related internships or fieldwork also available. *Faculty research:* Basic and applied research in teaching, learning and habilitation in all settings, schooling effectiveness. • Martin J. Kaufman, Dean, 541-346-3405. Application contact: Ron Tuomi, Graduate Secretary, 541-346-3528. Fax: 541-346-5818. E-mail: ron_tuomi@ccmail.edu.

University of Ottawa, Faculty of Education, Ottawa, ON K1N 6N5, Canada. Awards MA Ed, M Ed, PhD. Faculty: 41 full-time, 2 part-time. Students: 134 full-time (98 women), 289 part-time (219 women); includes 9 international. Average age 36. In 1997, 187 master's, 5 doctorates awarded. *Degree requirements:* For master's, thesis or alternative required, foreign language not required; for doctorate, dissertation required, foreign language not required. *Entrance requirements:* For master's, honors degree or equivalent, minimum B average; for doctorate, master's degree, minimum B+ average. Application deadline: 4/1 (4/1 for spring admission). Application fee: $35. *Expenses:* Tuition $4677 per year for Canadian residents; $9900 per year for nonresidents. Fees $230 per year. *Financial aid:* Fellowships, research assistantships, teaching assistantships, Federal Work-Study available. *Faculty research:* Item response theory, adult education, cognitive psychology, minority female education. • Richard Maclure, Acting Dean, 613-562-5800 Ext. 4057. Fax: 613-562-5144. Application contact: Cynthea Waddell, Academic Administrator, 613-562-5800 Ext. 4124. Fax: 613-562-5146.

University of Pennsylvania, Graduate School of Education, Philadelphia, PA 19104. Awards MS Ed, Ed D, PhD, DMD/MS Ed. Part-time programs available. Faculty: 36 full-time (16 women), 77 part-time (62 women). Students: 304 full-time (249 women), 441 part-time (318 women); includes 123 minority (76 African Americans, 29 Asian Americans, 12 Hispanics, 6 Native Americans), 102 international. Average age 34. 853 applicants, 61% accepted. In 1997, 216 master's, 56 doctorates awarded. Terminal master's awarded for partial completion of doctoral program. *Degree requirements:* For master's, exam required, foreign language not required; for doctorate, dissertation, exam. *Application fee:* $65. *Expenses:* Tuition $22,716 per year full-time, $2876 per course part-time. Fees $1484 per year full-time, $181 per course part-time. *Financial aid:* In 1997–98, 22 fellowships (7 to first-year students), 260 teaching assistantships were awarded; research assistantships, graduate assistantships, service scholarships, partial tuition waivers, Federal Work-Study, institutionally sponsored loans, and career-related internships or fieldwork also available. Aid available to part-time students. Financial aid applicants required to submit FAFSA. • Dr. Susan Fuhrman, Dean, 215-898-7014. Application contact: Judith Silverman, Admissions Office, 215-898-6455. Fax: 215-573-2166.

See in-depth description on page 815.

University of Phoenix, Graduate Programs, Programs in Education, 4615 East Elwood St, PO Box 52069, Phoenix, AZ 85072-2069. Offerings in administration and supervision (MA Ed), diverse learner (MA Ed), educational counseling (MA Ed). Students: 1,941 full-time (1,260 women); includes 706 minority (60 African Americans, 87 Asian Americans, 532 Hispanics, 27 Native Americans). Average age 35. In 1997, 765 degrees awarded. *Degree requirements:* Thesis or alternative. *Entrance requirements:* Comprehensive cognitive assessment (COCA). Application deadline: rolling. Application fee: $50. *Tuition:* $197 per credit hour. • Dr. Susan Mitchell, Dean, 602-966-9577. Application contact: Campus Information Center, 602-966-9577.

University of Pittsburgh, School of Education, Pittsburgh, PA 15260. Awards MA, MAT, M Ed, MHPE, MS, Ed D, PhD. Part-time and evening/weekend programs available. Faculty: 109 full-time (52 women), 13 part-time (7 women). Students: 669 full-time (449 women), 884 part-time (625 women); includes 174 minority (128 African Americans, 27 Asian Americans, 17 Hispanics, 2 Native Americans), 131 international. 1,416 applicants, 77% accepted. In 1997, 308 master's, 84 doctorates awarded. *Degree requirements:* Thesis/dissertation. *Average time to degree:* master's–2 years full-time, 4 years part-time; doctorate–4 years full-time, 6 years part-time. *Entrance requirements:* For master's, TOEFL (minimum score 650); for doctorate, GRE, TOEFL (minimum score 650). Application deadline: 2/1. Application fee: $30 ($40 for international students). *Expenses:* Tuition $8018 per year full-time, $329 per credit part-time for state residents; $16,508 per year full-time, $680 per credit part-time for nonresidents. Fees $480 per year full-time, $180 per year part-time. *Financial aid:* In 1997–98, 30 fellowships (11 to first-year students), 40 research assistantships (6 to first-year students) averaging $1,100 per month, 22 teaching assistantships averaging $1,250 per month, 40 assistantships (18 to first-year students) averaging $1,100 per month were awarded; partial tuition waivers, Federal Work-Study, institutionally sponsored loans, and career-related internships or fieldwork also available. Aid available to part-time students. Financial aid applicants required to submit FAFSA. • Dr. Kenneth F. Metz, Dean, 412-648-1773. Fax: 412-648-1825. Application contact: Jackie Harden, Manager, 412-648-7060. Fax: 412-648-1899. E-mail: jackie@sched.fsl.pitt.edu.

University of Portland, School of Education, Portland, OR 97203-5798. Awards MA, MAT, M Ed. M Ed also available through the Graduate Outreach Program for teachers residing in the Oregon and Washington State areas. Part-time and evening/weekend programs available. Faculty: 19 full-time (8 women), 10 part-time (5 women). Students: 49 full-time (30 women), 330 part-time (219 women). 379 applicants, 89% accepted. In 1997, 218 degrees awarded. *Entrance requirements:* TOEFL (minimum score 550), minimum GPA of 3.0, teaching certificate. Application deadline: 8/1 (priority date; rolling processing; 12/1 for spring admission). Application fee: $40. *Tuition:* $515 per semester hour. *Financial aid:* Federal Work-Study, institutionally sponsored loans available. Aid available to part-time students. Financial aid application deadline: 3/15. *Faculty research:* Multicultural education, supervision/leadership. • Dr. Maria Ciriello, OP, Dean, 503-283-7135. Fax: 503-283-8042. E-mail: ciriello@up.edu.

University of Puerto Rico, Río Piedras, College of Education, San Juan, PR 00931. Awards M Ed, Ed D. Part-time programs available. *Degree requirements:* For master's, thesis; for doctorate, dissertation required, foreign language not required. *Entrance requirements:* For master's, PAEG, minimum GPA of 3.0; for doctorate, GRE or PAEG, master's degree, minimum GPA of 3.0. Application deadline: 2/21. Application fee: $17. *Faculty research:* Child behavior, use of microcomputers, profile of the Puerto Rican administrator, social studies.

University of Puget Sound, School of Education, Tacoma, WA 98416-0005. Awards MAT, M Ed. Accredited by NCATE. Part-time programs available. Faculty: 12 full-time (9 women), 3 part-time (all women), 12.83 FTE. Students: 61 full-time (39 women), 44 part-time (38 women); includes 10 minority (3 African Americans, 3 Asian Americans, 1 Hispanic, 3 Native Americans). Average age 32. 169 applicants, 82% accepted. In 1997, 100 degrees awarded. *Entrance requirements:* GRE General Test (score in 50th percentile or higher), minimum GPA of 3.0. Application fee: $40. *Expenses:* Tuition $19,640 per year full-time, $2480 per course part-time. Fees $155 per year. *Financial aid:* Federal Work-Study available. • Dr. Carol Merz, Dean, 253-756-3377.

University of Redlands, Alfred North Whitehead College for Lifelong Learning, PO Box 3080, Redlands, CA 92373-0999. Offers programs in administrative services (MA); adult education (MAHRM, MBA), including adult education (MAHRM, MBA), information systems (MBA); curriculum leadership (MA); pupil personnel services (MA). Evening/weekend programs available. Faculty: 25 full-time (11 women), 283 part-time. Students: 684 full-time (273 women), 2 part-time (1 woman). In 1997, 248 degrees awarded. *Application deadline:* 9/1 (priority date; rolling processing; 3/1 for spring admission). *Application fee:* $40. Electronic applications accepted. *Faculty research:* Human resources management, educational leadership, humanities, teacher education. • Dr. Mary Boyce, Dean, 909-793-2121 Ext. 2200.

University of Regina, Faculty of Graduate Studies and Research, Faculty of Education, Regina, SK S4S 0A2, Canada. Awards M Ed, MVT Ed, PhD, Diploma. Part-time programs available. Faculty: 44 full-time (19 women), 10 part-time. Students: 17 full-time, 297 part-time; includes 13 international. 104 applicants, 78% accepted. In 1997, 34 master's, 24 Diplomas awarded. *Degree requirements:* For master's, thesis optional, foreign language not required; for doctorate, dissertation required, foreign language not required. *Entrance requirements:* For master's, TOEFL (minimum score 580), bachelor's degree in education, 2 years of teaching experience. Application deadline: 3/15 (12/15 for spring admission). Application fee: $0. *Tuition:* $196 per credit for Canadian residents; $383 per credit for nonresidents. *Financial aid:* In 1997–98, fellowships averaging $1,142 per month, research assistantships averaging $1,014 per month, 9 teaching assistantships averaging $888 per month, 12 scholarships averaging $750 per month were awarded; career-related internships or fieldwork also available. Financial aid application deadline: 6/15. • Dr. M. Tymchak, Dean, 306-585-4500. E-mail: tymchak@max.cc.uregina.ca. Application contact: Dr. M. Taylor, Chair, Graduate Programs, 306-585-4606. Fax: 306-585-4880. E-mail: marlene.taylor@uregina.ca.

University of Rhode Island, College of Human Science and Services, Department of Education, Kingston, RI 02881. Offers programs in adult education (MA), elementary education (MA), home economics education (MS), reading (MA), secondary education (MA). Accredited by NCATE. Evening/weekend programs available. *Entrance requirements:* MAT or GRE, TOEFL (minimum score 600). Application deadline: 4/15 (priority date; rolling processing; 11/15 for spring admission). Application fee: $35. *Expenses:* Tuition $3446 per year full-time, $191 per credit part-time for state residents; $9850 per year full-time, $547 per credit part-time for nonresidents. Fees $1276 per year full-time, $135 per semester (minimum) part-time.

See in-depth description on page 817.

University of Richmond, Department of Education, University of Richmond, VA 23173. Offers programs in early childhood education (M Ed); learning disabilities (M Ed); reading specialization (M Ed); secondary education (M Ed); teaching (MT), including elementary education, learning disabled, secondary education. Part-time and evening/weekend programs available. Faculty: 5 full-time (3 women), 4 part-time (2 women). Students: 20 full-time (16 women), 17 part-time (all women); includes 1 minority (Hispanic). Average age 28. 46 applicants, 89% accepted. In 1997, 4 degrees awarded. *Average time to degree:* master's–2 years full-time, 4 years part-time. *Entrance requirements:* GRE General Test, PRAXIS I. Application fee: $30. *Tuition:* $18,695 per year full-time, $320 per credit hour part-time. *Financial aid:* 7 students received aid; fellowships, research assistantships, tuition awards, partial tuition waivers, Federal Work-Study, institutionally sponsored loans, and career-related internships or fieldwork available. Financial aid application deadline: 3/15; applicants required to submit FAFSA. *Faculty research:* Transitional early childhood programs, characteristics of low-achieving first graders and reading recovery, writing readiness and whole language in kindergartners, prevalence rates of medical paradigms of dyslexia, personality attributes of special education teachers. • Dr. Mavis Brown, Coordinator, 804-289-8429.

University of Rio Grande, Graduate School, Rio Grande, OH 45674. Offers program in classroom teaching (M Ed), including fine arts, learning disabilities, mathematics, reading education. Part-time and evening/weekend programs available. Faculty: 9 full-time (3 women), 6 part-time (2 women). Students: 250. *Degree requirements:* Final research project, portfolio required, foreign language and thesis not required. *Entrance requirements:* Minimum GPA of 2.7 in major, 2.5 overall. Application deadline: rolling. Application fee: $20. *Financial aid:* Career-related internships or fieldwork available. Aid available to part-time students. Financial aid application deadline: 7/1. *Faculty research:* Interagency collaboration, reading and mathematics, learning styles, college access, literacy. • Dr. Greg Miller, Coordinator, 740-245-7364. Application contact: Dr. Mark Abell, Director of Administration, 740-245-5353.

University of Rochester, Margaret Warner Graduate School of Education and Human Development, Rochester, NY 14627-0001. Awards MAT, MS, Ed D, PhD, MS/PhD. Part-time and evening/weekend programs available. Faculty: 20 full-time. Students: 110 full-time (84 women), 218 part-time (149 women); includes 37 minority (26 African Americans, 5 Asian Americans, 5 Hispanics, 1 Native American), 20 international. 208 applicants, 88% accepted. In 1997, 84 master's, 3 doctorates awarded. Terminal master's awarded for partial completion of doctoral program. *Degree requirements:* For master's, thesis required (for some programs), foreign language not required; for doctorate, dissertation, qualifying exam required, foreign language not required. *Application deadline:* 2/1. *Application fee:* $25. *Expenses:* Tuition $21,485 per year full-time, $672 per credit hour part-time. Fees $336 per year. *Financial aid:* Fellowships, teaching assistantships, full and partial tuition waivers available. Aid available to part-time students. Financial aid application deadline: 2/1. • Philip Wexler, Dean, 716-275-8300. Application contact: Director, Academic Services, 716-275-3950.

See in-depth description on page 819.

University of St. Francis, Graduate Studies, Program in Education, Joliet, IL 60435-6188. Awards M Ed. Part-time programs available. Faculty: 1 (woman) full-time, 8 part-time (5 women). Students: 19 full-time (13 women), 42 part-time (32 women). *Degree requirements:* Computer language. *Average time to degree:* master's–3 years part-time. *Entrance requirements:* Minimum GPA of 2.75. Application deadline: 9/1 (priority date; rolling processing). Application fee: $25. *Tuition:* $285 per credit hour. • Dr. F. William Kelley Jr., Dean, Graduate Studies, 800-735-4723. Fax: 815-740-3537. E-mail: grdinfo@stfrancis.edu.

University of Saint Francis, Department of Education, Fort Wayne, IN 46808-3994. Offers programs in reading (MS Ed), special education (MS Ed). Accredited by NCATE. Faculty: 4 full-time, 9 part-time. Students: 6 full-time, 48 part-time; includes 1 minority (African American). Average age 35. In 1997, 20 degrees awarded. *Entrance requirements:* MAT (average 40), minimum GPA of 2.5. Application deadline: 7/1 (priority date; rolling processing; 11/1 for spring admission). Application fee: $20. *Expenses:* Tuition $350 per semester hour. Fees $390 per year full-time, $69 per semester (minimum) part-time. *Financial aid:* Available to part-time students. • Dr. Nancy Clements, Chair, 219-434-3271. E-mail: nclements@sfc.edu. Application contact: Scott Flanagan, Director of Admissions, 219-434-3264. Fax: 219-434-3183. E-mail: sflanagan@sfc.edu.

University of St. Thomas, School of Education, St. Paul, MN 55105-1096. Offers programs in curriculum and instruction (MA, Ed S); educational leadership and administration (MA, Ed D, Certificate, Ed S); gifted, creative and talented education (MA); learning and human development technology (MA, Certificate); special education (MA); teaching (MA). Accredited by NCATE. Part-time and evening/weekend programs available. Postbaccalaureate distance learning degree programs offered (no on-campus study). Faculty: 32 full-time (18 women), 47 part-time (27 women). Students: 78 full-time (50 women), 953 part-time (678 women); includes 90 minority (62 African Americans, 19 Asian Americans, 6 Hispanics, 3 Native Americans), 5 international. Average age 34. 334 applicants, 93% accepted. In 1997, 249 master's, 16 doctorates, 66 other advanced degrees awarded. *Entrance requirements:* For master's, MAT; for doctorate, MAT, minimum graduate GPA of 3.5; for other advanced degree, minimum graduate GPA of 3.25. Application deadline: rolling. Application fee: $50. *Tuition:* $375 per credit hour. *Financial aid:* In 1997–98, 74 grants (24 to first-year students) totaling $149,138 were awarded; fellowships, research assistantships, teaching assistantships, Federal Work-Study, and career-related internships or fieldwork also available. Aid available to part-time students. Financial aid application deadline: 4/1. • Dr. Richard Podemski, Dean, 612-962-5435. Application contact: Myrna Engebretson, Admissions Counselor, 612-962-5430. Fax: 612-962-5169.

University of St. Thomas, School of Education, Houston, TX 77006-4696. Awards M Ed. Part-time and evening/weekend programs available. Faculty: 10 full-time (6 women), 5 part-time (4 women). Students: 4 full-time (all women), 223 part-time (190 women). *Degree requirements:* Thesis or alternative, comprehensive exam required, foreign language not required. *Average time to degree:* master's–2 years full-time, 3.5 years part-time. *Entrance requirements:* GRE General Test (minimum combined score of 1200), Texas Teacher Certificate or Texas Academic Skills Program Test, minimum GPA of 3.0 in last 60 hours. Application deadline: rolling. Application fee: $35. *Expenses:* Tuition $410 per credit hour. Fees $33 per year full-time, $22.50 per year part-time. *Financial aid:* Grants, institutionally sponsored loans, and career-related internships or fieldwork available. • Dr. Anna Dewald, Dean, 713-525-3540. E-mail: dewald@stthom.edu. Application contact: Paula Hollis, Secretary, 713-525-3541. Fax: 713-525-3871. E-mail: hollisp@stthom.edu.

University of San Diego, School of Education, San Diego, CA 92110-2492. Awards MA, MAT, M Ed, Ed D. Part-time and evening/weekend programs available. Faculty: 15 full-time (7 women), 26 part-time (16 women), 25.6 FTE. Students: 255 full-time (207 women), 239 part-time (177 women); includes 125 minority (20 African Americans, 36 Asian Americans, 64 Hispanics, 5 Native Americans), 25 international. Average age 32. 498 applicants, 79% accepted. In 1997, 126 master's, 9 doctorates awarded. *Degree requirements:* For doctorate, dissertation, comprehensive exam required, foreign language not required. *Entrance requirements:* For doctorate, GRE or MAT, master's degree. Application deadline: 5/1 (priority date; rolling processing). Application fee: $45. *Expenses:* Tuition $585 per unit (minimum). Fees $50 per year full-time, $30 per year part-time. *Financial aid:* Fellowships, assistantships, stipends, Federal Work-Study, institutionally sponsored loans, and career-related internships or fieldwork available. Aid available to part-time students. Financial aid application deadline: 5/1; applicants required to submit FAFSA. *Faculty research:* Teaching, curriculum development, leadership. Total annual research expenditures: $31,000. • Dr. Edward F. DeRoche, Dean, 619-260-4540. Fax: 619-260-6835. Application contact: Mary Jane Tiernan, Director of Graduate Admissions, 619-260-4524. Fax: 619-260-4158. E-mail: grads@acusd.edu.

University of San Francisco, School of Education, San Francisco, CA 94117-1080. Awards MA, Ed D, Psy D. Part-time and evening/weekend programs available. Faculty: 43 full-time (18 women), 75 part-time (40 women). Students: 500 full-time (366 women), 335 part-time (235 women); includes 250 minority (101 African Americans, 59 Asian Americans, 85 Hispanics, 5 Native Americans), 28 international. Average age 38. 581 applicants, 88% accepted. In 1997, 205 master's, 58 doctorates awarded. *Degree requirements:* For doctorate, dissertation required, foreign language not required. *Application fee:* $40. *Tuition:* $658 per unit (minimum). *Financial aid:* 547 students received aid; fellowships, research assistantships, teaching assistantships available. Financial aid application deadline: 3/2. • Dr. Paul Warren, Dean, 415-422-6525.

See in-depth description on page 821.

University of Sarasota, College of Education, Sarasota, FL 34235-8246. Awards MA Ed, Ed D. Part-time and evening/weekend programs available. Postbaccalaureate distance learning degree programs offered (minimal on-campus study). Faculty: 7 full-time (3 women), 10 part-time (5 women). Students: 180 full-time (100 women), 538 part-time (299 women). *Degree requirements:* For master's, thesis optional; for doctorate, dissertation, comprehensive exam. *Average time to degree:* master's–2 years full-time, 3 years part-time; doctorate–3 years full-time, 4 years part-time. *Entrance requirements:* For master's, TOEFL (minimum score 500); for doctorate, TOEFL (minimum score 550), minimum undergraduate GPA of 3.0. Application deadline: rolling. Application fee: $50. *Financial aid:* Available to part-time students. Financial aid applicants required to submit FAFSA. • Dr. Nancy Hoover, Dean, 800-331-5995. Fax: 941-379-9464. E-mail: nancy_hoover@embanet.com. Application contact: Kathy Ketterer, Admissions Representative, 800-331-5995. Fax: 941-371-8910. E-mail: kathy_ketterer@embanet.com.

University of Saskatchewan, College of Education, Saskatoon, SK S7N 5A2, Canada. Awards MC Ed, M Ed, PhD, Diploma. Part-time programs available. *Degree requirements:* For doctorate, dissertation. *Entrance requirements:* For master's, CANTEST (minimum score 4.5) or International English Language Testing System (minimum score 6) or Michigan English Language Assessment Battery (minimum score 80), or TOEFL (minimum score 550; average 560); for doctorate, TOEFL; for Diploma, International English Language Testing System (minimum score 6) or Michigan English Language Assessment Battery (minimum score 80), or TOEFL (minimum score 550). Application deadline: 7/1 (priority date; rolling processing). Application fee: $0.

University of Scranton, Department of Education, Scranton, PA 18510-4622. Offers programs in educational administration (MS), including elementary school administration, secondary school administration; elementary education (MS); reading (MS); secondary education (MS). Accredited by NCATE. Part-time and evening/weekend programs available. Faculty: 11 full-time (3 women), 4 part-time (0 women). Students: 14 full-time (9 women), 61 part-time (40 women). Average age 30. 49 applicants, 98% accepted. In 1997, 29 degrees awarded. *Degree requirements:* Comprehensive exam required, foreign language and thesis not required. *Entrance requirements:* TOEFL (minimum score 500), minimum GPA of 2.75. Application deadline: rolling. Application fee: $35. *Expenses:* Tuition $465 per credit. Fees $25 per semester. *Financial aid:* In 1997–98, 5 students received aid, including 1 teaching assistantship (to a first-year student) averaging $648 per month and totaling $5,835, 4 teaching fellowships (3 to first-year students) averaging $864 per month and totaling $31,120; Federal Work-Study and career-related internships or fieldwork also available. Aid available to part-time students. Financial aid application deadline: 3/1. *Faculty research:* Meta-analysis as a research tool, family involvement in school activities, effect of curriculum integration on student learning and attitude, the effects of inclusion on students, development of emotional intelligence of young children. • Dr. David A. Wiley, Chair, 717-941-4032. Fax: 717-941-7401. E-mail: daw315@uofs.edu.

University of Sioux Falls, Program in Education, Sioux Falls, SD 57105-1699. Offers leadership (M Ed), reading (M Ed), technology (M Ed). Accredited by NCATE. Summer admission only. Part-time and evening/weekend programs available. Faculty: 5 full-time (4 women), 7 part-time (4 women). Students: 68 part-time (57 women); includes 1 minority (Hispanic). *Entrance requirements:* Minimum GPA of 3.0, 1 year of teaching experience. Application

Directory: Education—General

University of Sioux Falls (continued)
deadline: rolling. Application fee: $25. *Tuition:* $195 per credit hour. *Financial aid:* Available to part-time students. • Dr. Donna Goldammer, Chair, 605-331-6713. Application contact: Dr. Nancy Johnson, Director of Graduate Studies, 605-331-6710. Fax: 605-331-6615. E-mail: nancy.johnson@thecoo.edu.

University of South Alabama, College of Education, Mobile, AL 36688-0002. Awards M Ed, MS, PhD, Ed S. Accredited by NCATE. Part-time programs available. Faculty: 49 full-time (17 women). Students: 360 full-time (269 women), 533 part-time (430 women); includes 134 minority (117 African Americans, 7 Asian Americans, 6 Hispanics, 4 Native Americans), 11 international. 381 applicants, 86% accepted. In 1997, 240 master's, 5 doctorates, 8 Ed Ss awarded. *Degree requirements:* For master's, comprehensive exam required, foreign language and thesis not required; for doctorate, computer language, dissertation, comprehensive exam required, foreign language not required. *Entrance requirements:* For master's, GRE General Test (minimum combined score of 1000) or MAT. Application deadline: 9/1 (priority date; rolling processing). Application fee: $25. *Financial aid:* In 1997–98, 23 research assistantships, 10 teaching assistantships were awarded; career-related internships or fieldwork also available. Aid available to part-time students. Financial aid application deadline: 4/1. • George E. Uhlig, Dean, 334-460-6205.

University of South Carolina, Graduate School, College of Education, Columbia, SC 29208. Awards IMA, MA, MAT, M Ed, MS, MT, Ed D, PhD, Certificate, Ed S. Accredited by NCATE. Part-time and evening/weekend programs available. Faculty: 113 full-time, 13 part-time. Students: 554 full-time (404 women), 2,191 part-time (1,739 women); includes 553 minority (514 African Americans, 15 Asian Americans, 18 Hispanics, 6 Native Americans), 28 international. Average age 37. In 1997, 516 master's, 56 doctorates, 65 other advanced degrees awarded. Terminal master's awarded for partial completion of doctoral program. *Degree requirements:* For doctorate, 1 foreign language, dissertation, comprehensive exam. *Application deadline:* rolling. *Application fee:* $35. Electronic applications accepted. *Expenses:* Tuition $3894 per year full-time, $193 per credit hour part-time for state residents; $8114 per year full-time, $404 per credit hour part-time for nonresidents. Fees $125 per year full-time, $37 per semester (minimum) part-time. *Financial aid:* Fellowships, research assistantships, teaching assistantships, assistantships, partial tuition waivers, Federal Work-Study, institutionally sponsored loans, and career-related internships or fieldwork available. Aid available to part-time students. *Faculty research:* Inquiry learning, assessment of student learning, equity issues in education, multicultural education, cultural diversity. Total annual research expenditures: $4.140 million. • Dr. Frederic Melway, Interim Dean, 803-777-3828. Application contact: Office of Intercollegiate Teacher Education and Student Affairs, 803-777-6732. Fax: 803-777-3068.

University of South Carolina–Aiken, Program in Elementary Education, 471 University Parkway, Aiken, SC 29801-6309. Awards M Ed. Part-time and evening/weekend programs available. Faculty: 3 part-time (2 women). Students: 3 full-time (all women), 46 part-time (44 women); includes 7 minority (all African Americans). Average age 33. 12 applicants, 100% accepted. In 1997, 15 degrees awarded. *Degree requirements:* Comprehensive exam required, foreign language and thesis not required. *Entrance requirements:* GRE General Test (minimum score 400 on verbal section, 400 on quantitative) or MAT (minimum score 35). Application deadline: 8/1 (priority date; rolling processing). Application fee: $35. Electronic applications accepted. *Expenses:* Tuition $3894 per year full-time, $193 per credit hour part-time for state residents; $8114 per year full-time, $404 per credit hour part-time for nonresidents. Fees $120 per year full-time, $32 per semester (minimum) part-time. *Financial aid:* Federal Work-Study, institutionally sponsored loans available. Aid available to part-time students. Financial aid application deadline: 3/15; applicants required to submit FAFSA. • Dr. Margaret Riedell, Head, 803-648-6851. Fax: 803-641-3698. Application contact: Karen Morris, Graduate Studies Coordinator, 803-641-3489.

University of South Carolina Spartanburg, Graduate Programs, Spartanburg, SC 29303-4999. Offerings in early childhood development (M Ed), elementary education (M Ed). Part-time and evening/weekend programs available. Postbaccalaureate distance learning degree programs offered. Faculty: 9 full-time (5 women). Students: 337 part-time (308 women); includes 10 minority (9 African Americans, 1 Asian American). Average age 38. In 1997, 5 degrees awarded. *Entrance requirements:* GRE General Test (minimum combined score of 800), MAT (minimum score 35), minimum GPA of 2.5. Application deadline: rolling. Application fee: $25. *Expenses:* Tuition $193 per hour for state residents; $404 per hour for nonresidents. Fees $120 per year full-time, $5 per hour part-time. *Financial aid:* Available to part-time students. Financial aid application deadline: 8/1; applicants required to submit FAFSA. • Dr. Linda Randolph, Director, 864-503-5573. Fax: 864-503-5574.

University of South Dakota, School of Education, Vermillion, SD 57069-2390. Awards MA, Ed D, Ed S, JD/MA. Accredited by NCATE. Part-time programs available. Faculty: 35 full-time (12 women), 8 part-time (2 women). Students: 222 full-time (132 women), 101 part-time (62 women). 166 applicants, 61% accepted. In 1997, 147 master's, 42 doctorates awarded. *Degree requirements:* For doctorate, dissertation required, foreign language not required. *Entrance requirements:* For master's and doctorate, GRE General Test. Application deadline: rolling. Application fee: $15. *Expenses:* Tuition $1530 per year full-time, $85 per credit hour part-time for state residents; $4518 per year full-time, $251 per credit hour part-time for nonresidents. Fees $792 per year full-time, $44 per credit hour part-time. *Financial aid:* Fellowships, research assistantships, teaching assistantships, Federal Work-Study, and career-related internships or fieldwork available. Aid available to part-time students. • Dr. Larry Bright, Dean, 605-677-5437. Application contact: Dr. Sharon Lee, Director of Graduate Studies, 605-677-5451.

University of Southern California, Graduate School, School of Education, Los Angeles, CA 90089. Awards MS, Ed D, PhD, MFCC. Students: 284 full-time (191 women), 335 part-time (213 women); includes 216 minority (61 African Americans, 87 Asian Americans, 67 Hispanics, 1 Native American), 74 international. Average age 34. 451 applicants, 71% accepted. In 1997, 72 master's, 96 doctorates, 22 MFCCs awarded. *Degree requirements:* For doctorate, dissertation. *Entrance requirements:* For master's and doctorate, GRE General Test. Application fee: $55. *Expenses:* Tuition $16,944 per year full-time, $706 per unit part-time. Fees $414 per year full-time, $32 per year part-time. *Financial aid:* In 1997–98, 63 fellowships, 2 research assistantships, 37 teaching assistantships, 41 scholarships were awarded; Federal Work-Study, institutionally sponsored loans also available. Aid available to part-time students. Financial aid application deadline: 2/15; applicants required to submit FAFSA. • Dr. Guilbert Hentschke, Dean, 213-740-8313.

See in-depth description on page 823.

University of Southern Indiana, Graduate Studies, School of Education and Human Services, Department of Teacher Education, Evansville, IN 47712-3590. Offers programs in elementary education (MS), secondary education (MS). Accredited by NCATE. Part-time and evening/weekend programs available. Faculty: 12 full-time (3 women). Students: 1 (woman) full-time, 84 part-time (61 women); includes 1 minority (African American). Average age 37. 27 applicants, 74% accepted. In 1997, 38 degrees awarded. *Entrance requirements:* GRE General Test, NTE, minimum GPA of 3.0. Application deadline: rolling. Application fee: $25. *Tuition:* $129 per credit hour for state residents; $260 per credit hour for nonresidents. • Dr. Charles Price, Director, 812-464-1939. E-mail: cprice.ucs@smtp.usi.edu.

University of Southern Maine, College of Education and Human Development, Portland, ME 04104-9300. Awards MS, MS Ed, CAS, Certificate. Accredited by NCATE. Part-time and evening/weekend programs available. Faculty: 34 full-time (13 women), 49 part-time (34 women). Students: 265 full-time (185 women), 354 part-time (247 women); includes 5 minority (3 Asian Americans, 2 Native Americans), 1 international. Average age 38. 508 applicants, 64% accepted. In 1997, 145 master's awarded. *Degree requirements:* Thesis or alternative required, foreign language not required. *Entrance requirements:* For master's, GRE General Test (minimum combined score of 900), MAT (minimum score 40), TOEFL. Application fee: $25. *Expenses:* Tuition $178 per credit hour for state residents; $267 per credit hour (minimum) for nonresidents. Fees $282 per year full-time, $83 per semester (minimum) part-time. *Financial aid:* In 1997–98, 254 students received aid, including research assistantships totaling $54,808, scholarships totaling $41,950; Federal Work-Study, institutionally sponsored loans, and career-related internships or fieldwork also available. Aid available to part-time students. Financial aid application deadline: 3/1; applicants required to submit FAFSA. *Faculty research:* Alternative assessment, cooperative learning, global education, school/university collaboration, technology in education. • Richard E. Barnes, Dean, 207-780-5371. Application contact: Teresa Belsan, Admissions and Academic Counselor, 207-780-5306. Fax: 207-780-5315. E-mail: belsan@usm.maine.edu.

University of Southern Mississippi, College of Education and Psychology, Hattiesburg, MS 39406-5167. Awards MA, M Ed, MS, Ed D, PhD, Ed S. Part-time programs available. Faculty: 69 full-time (22 women), 11 part-time (2 women). Students: 244 full-time (167 women), 398 part-time (288 women); includes 84 minority (74 African Americans, 5 Asian Americans, 4 Hispanics, 1 Native American), 12 international. Average age 36. 556 applicants, 39% accepted. In 1997, 406 master's, 52 doctorates, 44 Ed Ss awarded. Terminal master's awarded for partial completion of doctoral program. *Degree requirements:* For doctorate, 2 foreign languages, dissertation. *Entrance requirements:* For master's and doctorate, GRE General Test; for Ed S, GRE General Test, minimum GPA of 3.25. Application deadline: rolling. Application fee: $0 ($25 for international students). *Tuition:* $2870 per year full-time, $137 per credit hour part-time for state residents; $5972 per year full-time, $172 per credit hour part-time for nonresidents. *Financial aid:* Research assistantships, teaching assistantships, partial tuition waivers, Federal Work-Study, institutionally sponsored loans, and career-related internships or fieldwork available. Financial aid application deadline: 3/15. • Dr. Bruce Holliman, Acting Dean, 601-266-4568.

University of South Florida, College of Education, Tampa, FL 33620-9951. Awards MA, M Ed, Ed D, PhD, Ed S. Accredited by NCATE. Part-time and evening/weekend programs available. Faculty: 142 full-time (72 women). Students: 425 full-time (341 women), 1,458 part-time (1,124 women); includes 23 African Americans, 3 Asian Americans, 106 Native Americans, 113 international. Average age 36. 545 applicants, 63% accepted. In 1997, 497 master's, 46 doctorates, 11 Ed Ss awarded. *Degree requirements:* For doctorate, dissertation, 2 tools of research in foreign language, statistics, and/or computers. *Entrance requirements:* For master's, GRE General Test (minimum combined score of 1000), minimum GPA of 3.5 in last 60 hours; for doctorate, GRE General Test (minimum combined score of 1000), minimum GPA of 3.0 (undergraduate) or 3.5 (graduate); for Ed S, GRE General Test (minimum combined score of 1000). Application fee: $20. Electronic applications accepted. *Tuition:* $142 per credit hour for state residents; $486 per credit hour for nonresidents. *Financial aid:* In 1997–98, 16 fellowships (2 to first-year students) averaging $758 per month and totaling $109,200, 60 research assistantships averaging $648 per month and totaling $350,000, 37 teaching assistantships averaging $610 per month and totaling $203,000 were awarded; Federal Work-Study, institutionally sponsored loans, and career-related internships or fieldwork also available. Aid available to part-time students. Financial aid applicants required to submit FAFSA. *Total annual research expenditures:* $9.5 million. • Jane Applegate, Dean, 813-974-3406. Fax: 813-974-3826. E-mail: applegat@tempest.coedu.usf.edu. Application contact: Diane Briscoe, Graduate Adviser, 813-974-0544. Fax: 813-974-3391. E-mail: briscoe@tempest.coedu.usf.edu.

See in-depth description on page 825.

University of Southwestern Louisiana, College of Education, Lafayette, LA 70503. Awards M Ed. Accredited by NCATE. Part-time programs available. Faculty: 34 full-time (15 women). Students: 35 full-time (30 women), 148 part-time (116 women); includes 19 minority (15 African Americans, 1 Asian American, 2 Hispanics, 1 Native American), 2 international. 91 applicants, 77% accepted. In 1997, 48 degrees awarded. *Degree requirements:* Thesis or alternative required, foreign language not required. *Entrance requirements:* GRE General Test, teaching certificate. Application deadline: 8/15. Application fee: $5 ($15 for international students). *Tuition:* $2012 per year full-time, $300 per semester (minimum) part-time for state residents; $7244 per year full-time, $300 per semester (minimum) part-time for nonresidents. *Financial aid:* Fellowships, research assistantships, teaching assistantships, Federal Work-Study available. Financial aid application deadline: 5/1. • Dr. Mary Jane Ford, Acting Dean, 318-482-6678.

University of Tennessee at Chattanooga, School of Education, Education Graduate Studies Division, Chattanooga, TN 37403-2598. Offers programs in curriculum and instruction (M Ed), early childhood education (M Ed), elementary administration (M Ed), guidance and counseling (M Ed), reading (M Ed), secondary administration (M Ed), secondary education (M Ed), special education (M Ed). Accredited by NCATE. Part-time and evening/weekend programs available. Faculty: 15 full-time (5 women), 7 part-time (3 women). Students: 78 full-time (56 women), 217 part-time (168 women); includes 40 minority (35 African Americans, 2 Asian Americans, 2 Hispanics, 1 Native American), 3 international. Average age 32. 112 applicants, 97% accepted. In 1997, 104 degrees awarded. *Degree requirements:* Comprehensive exams required, thesis optional, foreign language not required. *Entrance requirements:* GRE General Test or MAT, teaching certificate. Application deadline: rolling. Application fee: $25. *Tuition:* $2864 per year full-time, $160 per credit hour part-time for state residents; $6806 per year full-time, $379 per credit hour part-time for nonresidents. *Financial aid:* Fellowships, research assistantships, Federal Work-Study, institutionally sponsored loans available. Aid available to part-time students. Financial aid application deadline: 4/1. • Dr. Tom Bibler, Acting Head, 423-755-4211. Fax: 423-755-5380. E-mail: tom-bibler@utc.edu. Application contact: Dr. Deborah Arfken, Assistant Provost for Graduate Studies, 423-755-4667. Fax: 423-755-4478.

The University of Tennessee at Martin, School of Education, Martin, TN 38238-1000. Awards MS Ed. Accredited by NCATE. Part-time and evening/weekend programs available. Faculty: 95 full-time (25 women), 10 part-time (7 women). Students: 54 full-time (43 women), 142 part-time (110 women); includes 30 minority (all African Americans). 74 applicants, 82% accepted. In 1997, 24 degrees awarded. *Degree requirements:* Comprehensive exam required, foreign language and thesis not required. *Entrance requirements:* GRE General Test (minimum combined score of 650), MAT (minimum score 32), or NTE (minimum combined score of 1930), minimum GPA of 2.5. Application deadline: rolling. Application fee: $25 ($50 for international students). *Tuition:* $2962 per year full-time, $165 per semester hour part-time for state residents; $7788 per year full-time, $434 per semester hour part-time for nonresidents. *Financial aid:* In 1997–98, 22 students received aid, including 1 research assistantship averaging $545 per month, 5 teaching assistantships (1 to a first-year student) averaging $545 per month, 10 graduate assistantships (3 to first-year students) averaging $545 per month; fellowships, partial tuition waivers also available. Aid available to part-time students. Financial aid application deadline: 3/1. *Faculty research:* Special needs of science instruction, mainstreaming, hands-on science instruction, math manipulatives. • Dr. Linda Murphy, Dean, 901-587-7127. Application contact: Dr. Robbie Kendall-Melton, Coordinator, 901-587-7129. E-mail: rkendall@utm.edu.

University of Tennessee, Knoxville, College of Education, Knoxville, TN 37996. Awards MS, Ed D, PhD, Ed S. Accredited by NCATE. Part-time and evening/weekend programs available. Postbaccalaureate distance learning degree programs offered (no on-campus study). Faculty: 91 full-time (30 women), 3 part-time (1 woman). Students: 668 full-time (454 women), 463 part-time (315 women); includes 84 minority (59 African Americans, 9 Asian Americans, 10 Hispanics, 6 Native Americans), 44 international. 793 applicants, 59% accepted. In 1997, 438 master's, 52 doctorates, 14 Ed Ss awarded. Terminal master's awarded for partial completion of doctoral program. *Degree requirements:* For master's and Ed S, thesis optional, foreign language not required; for doctorate, dissertation. *Entrance requirements:* For master's, TOEFL (minimum score 550), minimum GPA of 2.7; for doctorate, GRE General Test, TOEFL (minimum score 550), minimum GPA of 2.7; for Ed S, TOEFL (minimum score 550), GRE General Test, minimum GPA of 2.7. Application deadline: 2/1 (priority date; rolling processing). Application fee: $35. Electronic applications accepted. *Tuition:* $3354 per year full-time, $181 per semester hour part-time for state residents; $8410 per year full-time, $462 per semester hour part-time for nonresidents. *Financial aid:* In 1997–98, 12 fellowships, 3 research assistantships, 37 teaching assistantships, 48 graduate assistantships were awarded; Federal Work-Study, institutionally sponsored loans, and career-related internships or fieldwork also available. Financial aid application deadline: 2/1. • Dr. Glennon Rowell, Dean, 423-974-2201. E-mail: growell@utk.edu. Application contact: Tom George, Associate Dean, 423-974-0907. Fax: 423-974-8718. E-mail: tgeorge1@utk.edu.

The University of Texas at Arlington, Center for Professional Teacher Education, Arlington, TX 76019-0407. Awards MET. Faculty: 15 full-time (9 women). Students: 47 full-time (34 women), 163 part-time (122 women); includes 46 minority (28 African Americans, 4 Asian Americans, 14 Hispanics), 2 international. 107 applicants, 85% accepted. In 1997, 47 degrees awarded. *Entrance requirements:* GRE General Test. Application deadline: rolling. Application fee: $25 ($50 for international students). *Tuition:* $3206 per year full-time, $468 per semester (minimum) part-time for state residents; $8612 per year full-time, $1137 per semester (minimum) part-time for nonresidents. • Dr. Jeanne Gerlach, Director, 817-272-3339. Application contact: Dr. Sylvia Vardell, Graduate Adviser, 817-272-5058.

The University of Texas at Austin, Graduate School, College of Education, Austin, TX 78712. Awards MA, M Ed, Ed D, PhD. Part-time programs available. Students: 1,461 (1,002 women); includes 329 minority (105 African Americans, 28 Asian Americans, 184 Hispanics, 12 Native Americans), 176 international. 955 applicants, 52% accepted. In 1997, 242 master's, 141 doctorates awarded. Terminal master's awarded for partial completion of doctoral program. *Entrance requirements:* GRE General Test. Application fee: $50 ($75 for international students). Electronic applications accepted. *Expenses:* Tuition $2592 per year full-time, $324 per semester (minimum) part-time for state residents; $7704 per year full-time, $963 per semester (minimum) part-time for nonresidents. Fees $778 per year full-time, $161 per semester (minimum) part-time. *Financial aid:* Fellowships, research assistantships, teaching assistantships, Federal Work-Study, and career-related internships or fieldwork available. Financial aid application deadline: 2/1; applicants required to submit FAFSA. • Dr. Manuel J. Justiz, Dean, 512-471-7255.

The University of Texas at Brownsville, Graduate Studies, School of Education, Brownsville, TX 78520-4991. Offers programs in counseling and guidance (M Ed), curriculum and instruction (M Ed), early childhood education (M Ed), education (Ed D), educational administration (M Ed), educational technology (M Ed), elementary education (M Ed), English as a second language (M Ed), reading (M Ed), special education (M Ed), supervision (M Ed). Ed D offered jointly with the University of Houston. Part-time and evening/weekend programs available. Faculty: 18 full-time (10 women). *Degree requirements:* For master's, thesis optional, foreign language not required. *Entrance requirements:* For master's, GRE General Test, TOEFL (minimum score 550). Application deadline: 8/1 (priority date; rolling processing; 1/1 for spring admission). Application fee: $15. *Expenses:* Tuition $648 per year full-time, $120 per semester hour part-time for state residents; $4698 per year full-time, $783 per semester hour part-time for nonresidents. Fees $593 per year full-time, $109 per year part-time. *Financial aid:* Federal Work-Study and career-related internships or fieldwork available. Aid available to part-time students. Financial aid application deadline: 4/3; applicants required to submit FAFSA. • Dr. Sylvia C. Peña, Dean, 956-983-7219. Fax: 956-982-0293. E-mail: scpena@utb1.utb.edu.

The University of Texas at El Paso, College of Education, 500 West University Avenue, El Paso, TX 79968-0001. Awards MA, M Ed, Ed D. Part-time and evening/weekend programs available. *Degree requirements:* For master's, thesis optional, foreign language not required. *Entrance requirements:* For master's, GRE General Test (minimum combined score of 1400 on three sections), TOEFL (minimum score 550), minimum graduate GPA of 3.0. Application deadline: 7/1 (priority date; rolling processing; 11/1 for spring admission). Application fee: $15 ($65 for international students). Electronic applications accepted. *Tuition:* $1559 per year full-time, $230 per credit hour part-time for state residents; $5393 per year full-time, $405 per credit hour part-time for nonresidents.

The University of Texas at San Antonio, College of Social and Behavioral Sciences, Division of Education, San Antonio, TX 78249-0617. Awards MA. Part-time programs available. Faculty: 43 full-time (24 women), 104 part-time (75 women). Students: 121 full-time (99 women), 512 part-time (408 women); includes 206 minority (27 African Americans, 8 Asian Americans, 170 Hispanics, 1 Native American), 1 international. Average age 34. 219 applicants, 79% accepted. In 1997, 157 degrees awarded. *Degree requirements:* Thesis optional, foreign language not required. *Entrance requirements:* GRE General Test, minimum GPA of 3.0 in last 60 hours. Application deadline: 7/1 (rolling processing). Application fee: $20. *Expenses:* Tuition $2476 per year full-time, $309 per semester (minimum) part-time for state residents; $7584 per year full-time, $948 per semester (minimum) part-time for nonresidents. Fees $361 per year full-time, $133 per semester (minimum) part-time. *Financial aid:* Federal Work-Study and career-related internships or fieldwork available. *Faculty research:* Early childhood, reading, special education, foundations, curriculum and instruction. • Dr. Christopher Borman, Director, 210-458-4410.

The University of Texas at Tyler, School of Education and Psychology, Tyler, TX 75799-0001. Awards MA, MAT, M Ed, MS, Certificate. Part-time and evening/weekend programs available. Faculty: 40 full-time (16 women), 18 part-time (9 women). Students: 700. In 1997, 78 master's awarded. *Application fee:* $0 ($50 for international students). *Tuition:* $2144 per year full-time, $337 per semester (minimum) part-time for state residents; $7256 per year full-time, $964 per semester (minimum) part-time for nonresidents. *Financial aid:* Teaching assistantships, full and partial tuition waivers, Federal Work-Study, institutionally sponsored loans, and career-related internships or fieldwork available. Aid available to part-time students. Financial aid application deadline: 7/1. *Faculty research:* Neuropsychology, bone density, muscle exercise, reading improvement. • Dr. J. Milford Clark, Dean, 903-566-7050. Fax: 903-566-7036. E-mail: mclark@mail.uttyl.edu. Application contact: Martha D. Wheat, Director of Admissions and Student Records, 903-566-7201. Fax: 903-566-7068.

The University of Texas of the Permian Basin, Graduate School, School of Education, Odessa, TX 79762-0001. Awards MA. *Degree requirements:* Thesis required, foreign language not required. *Entrance requirements:* GRE General Test (minimum combined score of 1200). *Expenses:* Tuition $1314 per year full-time, $73 per hour part-time for state residents; $4896 per year full-time, $272 per hour part-time for nonresidents. Fees $383 per year full-time, $111 per semester (minimum) part-time.

The University of Texas–Pan American, College of Education, Edinburg, TX 78539-2999. Awards MA, M Ed, Ed D. Ed D offered jointly with the University of Texas at Austin. Part-time and evening/weekend programs available. *Degree requirements:* For master's, thesis optional. *Entrance requirements:* For master's, GRE General Test. Application deadline: 7/17 (11/16 for spring admission). Application fee: $0. *Tuition:* $2156 per year full-time, $283 per semester (minimum) part-time for state residents; $6788 per year full-time, $862 per semester (minimum) part-time for nonresidents. *Faculty research:* Literacy development, bilingual education, brain mapping.

University of the District of Columbia, College of Arts and Sciences, School of Arts and Education, Division of Education, 4200 Connecticut Avenue, NW, Washington, DC 20008-1175. Offers programs in early childhood education (MA), English composition and rhetoric (MA), speech and language pathology (MS). Part-time programs available. *Degree requirements:* Comprehensive exam required, foreign language not required. *Entrance requirements:* Writing proficiency exam. Application deadline: 6/14 (priority date; rolling processing; 11/15 for spring admission). Application fee: $20. *Expenses:* Tuition $3564 per year full-time, $198 per credit part-time for district residents; $5922 per year full-time, $329 per credit part-time for nonresidents. Fees $990 per year full-time, $55 per credit part-time.

University of the Incarnate Word, School of Graduate Studies, College of Professional Studies, Programs in Education, San Antonio, TX 78209-6397. Offerings in deaf education (M Ed); early childhood education (MA, M Ed); educational diagnostics (MA, M Ed); elementary education (MA, M Ed); physical education (MA, M Ed); reading (MA, M Ed), including reading, reading specialist; secondary teaching (MA, M Ed); special education (MA, M Ed). Evening/weekend programs available. *Entrance requirements:* GRE, MAT, TOEFL (minimum score 550). Application deadline: 8/15 (priority date; rolling processing; 12/31 for spring admission). Application fee: $20. *Expenses:* Tuition $350 per semester hour. Fees $180 per year full-time, $111 per semester (minimum) part-time. • Dr. Charles Slater, Coordinator, 210-829-3137. Fax: 210-829-3134. Application contact: Brian F. Dalton, Dean of Enrollment Services, 210-829-6005. Fax: 210-829-3921.

University of the Pacific, School of Education, Stockton, CA 95211-0197. Awards MA, M Ed, Ed D. Accredited by NCATE. Faculty: 24 full-time (6 women), 1 (woman) part-time. Students: 58 full-time (46 women), 91 part-time (69 women); includes 3 international. In 1997, 32 master's, 8 doctorates awarded. *Degree requirements:* For doctorate, dissertation. *Entrance requirements:* GRE General Test, GRE Subject Test. Application deadline: 3/1 (priority date; rolling processing; 10/15 for spring admission). Application fee: $50. *Expenses:* Tuition $19,000 per year full-time, $594 per unit part-time. Fees $30 per year (minimum). *Financial aid:* In 1997–98, 13 teaching assistantships (8 to first-year students) were awarded; institutionally sponsored loans also available. Aid available to part-time students. Financial aid application deadline: 3/1. • Dr. Fay B. Haisley, Dean, 209-946-2683. E-mail: fhaisley@uop.edu.

University of the Sacred Heart, Graduate Programs, Department of Education, San Juan, PR 00914-0383. Offers program in instruction systems and education technology (M Ed). Part-time and evening/weekend programs available. Faculty: 1 (woman) full-time, 4 part-time (all women), 2.33 FTE. Students: 2 full-time (1 woman), 51 part-time (42 women). 21 applicants, 57% accepted. In 1997, 13 degrees awarded. *Degree requirements:* Computer language, thesis. *Entrance requirements:* PAEG, minimum undergraduate GPA of 2.5. Application deadline: 5/15. Application fee: $25. *Expenses:* Tuition $150 per credit. Fees $240 per credit. • Dr. Fernando Pieras, Director, 787-728-1515 Ext. 2335. Fax: 787-728-1515 Ext. 2334. E-mail: f_pieras@uscac1.usc.clu.edu. Application contact: Dr. Blanca Villamil, Acting Director, Admissions Office, 787-728-1515 Ext. 3237. Fax: 787-728-2066. E-mail: b_villami@uscsi.usc.clu.edu.

University of the Virgin Islands, Division of Education, Charlotte Amalie, St. Thomas, VI 00802-9990. Awards MAE. Part-time and evening/weekend programs available. Faculty: 8 full-time (5 women), 10 part-time (4 women). Students: 11 full-time (10 women), 100 part-time (85 women); includes 96 minority (89 African Americans, 1 Asian American, 6 Hispanics), 1 international. Average age 34. In 1997, 31 degrees awarded. *Degree requirements:* Thesis or alternative required, foreign language not required. *Entrance requirements:* Minimum GPA of 2.5. Application deadline: 4/30 (11/30 for spring admission). Application fee: $20. *Tuition:* $205 per credit for territory residents; $410 per credit for nonresidents. *Financial aid:* Application deadline 4/15. *Faculty research:* Student self-concept and sense of futility. • Dr. Pearl Varlack, Chairperson, 340-693-1327. Fax: 340-693-1185. E-mail: pvarlac@uvi.edu. Application contact: Judith Edwin, Director of Enrollment Management, 340-693-1151. Fax: 340-693-1155. E-mail: jedwin@uvi.edu.

University of Toledo, College of Education and Allied Professions, Toledo, OH 43606-3398. Awards MA Ed, M Ed, MPH, MS, MS Ed, Ed D, PhD, Ed S. Accredited by NCATE. Part-time and evening/weekend programs available. Faculty: 97 full-time (36 women). Students: 244 full-time (173 women), 971 part-time (705 women); includes 127 minority (105 African Americans, 7 Asian Americans, 12 Hispanics, 3 Native Americans), 53 international. Average age 36. 615 applicants, 63% accepted. In 1997, 304 master's, 30 doctorates, 1 Ed S awarded. Terminal master's awarded for partial completion of doctoral program. *Degree requirements:* For doctorate, dissertation, comprehensive exams required, foreign language not required; for Ed S, thesis optional, foreign language not required. *Entrance requirements:* For doctorate, GRE. Application deadline: rolling. Application fee: $30. Electronic applications accepted. *Tuition:* $5907 per year full-time, $246 per hour part-time for state residents; $11,835 per year full-time, $493 per hour part-time for nonresidents. *Financial aid:* In 1997–98, 34 research assistantships, 52 teaching assistantships, 30 administrative assistantships, tuition scholarships were awarded; fellowships, full tuition waivers, Federal Work-Study, institutionally sponsored loans, and career-related internships or fieldwork also available. Aid available to part-time students. Financial aid application deadline: 4/1; applicants required to submit FAFSA. *Faculty research:* Cognitive studies, learning and memory, learning resources, whole language, administration of professional development schools. • Dr. Philip J. Rusche, Dean, 419-530-2025. Fax: 419-530-7719.

University of Toronto, School of Graduate Studies, Social Sciences Division, Department of Education, Toronto, ON M5S 1A1, Canada. Awards MA, MA(T), M Ed, Ed D, PhD. Part-time and evening/weekend programs available. Faculty: 231. Students: 983 full-time (741 women), 1,241 part-time (919 women); includes 58 international. 1,599 applicants, 58% accepted. In 1997, 458 master's, 109 doctorates awarded. *Degree requirements:* For master's, thesis (for some programs); for doctorate, dissertation. *Application fee:* $75. *Expenses:* Tuition $4070 per year for Canadian residents; $7870 per year for nonresidents. Fees $628 per year. • M. Fullan, Dean, 416-923-6641 Ext. 3233. Application contact: Secretary, 416-923-6641 Ext. 2664. Fax: 416-323-9964. E-mail: gradstudy@oise.untoronto.ca.

University of Tulsa, College of Arts and Sciences, School of Education, Tulsa, OK 74104-3189. Offers programs in education (MA), math/science education (MSMSE), teaching arts (MTA). Accredited by NCATE. Part-time programs available. Faculty: 7 full-time (3 women). Students: 26 full-time (17 women), 17 part-time (15 women); includes 8 minority (4 African Americans, 2 Asian Americans, 1 Hispanic, 1 Native American). Average age 32. 28 applicants, 96% accepted. In 1997, 22 degrees awarded. *Entrance requirements:* GRE General Test (minimum combined score of 1000), TOEFL (minimum score 575). Application deadline: rolling. Application fee: $30. Electronic applications accepted. *Expenses:* Tuition $480 per credit hour. Fees $2 per credit hour. *Financial aid:* In 1997–98, 13 students received aid, including 2 research assistantships (1 to a first-year student) totaling $30,668, 11 teaching assistantships (5 to first-year students) totaling $155,542; fellowships, partial tuition waivers, Federal Work-Study also available. Aid available to part-time students. Financial aid application deadline: 2/1; applicants required to submit FAFSA. *Faculty research:* Restructuring of teacher education, new assessment programs, cooperative learning, authentic learning, responsibility-centered management. • Dr. James E. Green, Chairperson, 918-631-2236. Fax: 918-631-2133.

University of Utah, Graduate School of Education, Salt Lake City, UT 84112-1107. Awards MA, M Ed, MS, M Stat, Ed D, PhD, MPA/Ed D, MPA/PhD. Part-time and evening/weekend programs available. Faculty: 60 full-time (24 women), 1,161 part-time (814 women). Students: 219 full-time (140 women), 201 part-time (132 women); includes 43 minority (9 African Americans, 13 Asian Americans, 16 Hispanics, 5 Native Americans), 10 international. Average age 36. In 1997, 144 master's, 16 doctorates awarded. *Entrance requirements:* For master's, TOEFL; for doctorate, GRE, TOEFL. Application deadline: 7/1. Application fee: $30 ($50 for international students). *Tuition:* $2045 per year full-time, $562 per semester (minimum) part-time for state residents; $6129 per year full-time, $1607 per semester (minimum) part-time for nonresidents. *Financial aid:* In 1997–98, 23 teaching assistantships were awarded; fellowships, research assistantships, Federal Work-Study, institutionally sponsored loans, and career-related internships or fieldwork also available. Aid available to part-time students. *Faculty research:* Leadership, autism, reading instruction, mental retardation, diagnosis. • Colleen S. Kennedy, Dean, 801-581-8221. Fax: 801-581-5223. E-mail: kennedy@gse.utah.edu.

University of Vermont, College of Education and Social Services, Burlington, VT 05405-0160. Awards M Ed, MS, MSW, Ed D. Accredited by NCATE. Part-time programs available. Students: 352; includes 23 minority (9 African Americans, 6 Asian Americans, 7 Hispanics, 1 Native American), 4 international. 391 applicants, 55% accepted. In 1997, 120 master's, 13 doctorates awarded. *Degree requirements:* For doctorate, dissertation required, foreign language not required. *Entrance requirements:* GRE General Test, TOEFL (minimum score 550). Application fee: $25. *Expenses:* Tuition $302 per credit for state residents; $755 per credit for

Directory: Education—General

University of Vermont (continued)
nonresidents. Fees $434 per year full-time, $46 per semester (minimum) part-time. *Financial aid:* Fellowships, research assistantships, teaching assistantships, Federal Work-Study, and career-related internships or fieldwork available. • Dr. Jill Tarule, Dean, 802-656-3468.

University of Victoria, Faculty of Education, Victoria, BC V8W 2Y2, Canada. Awards MA, M Ed, M Sc, PhD. Part-time programs available. Postbaccalaureate distance learning degree programs offered (minimal on-campus study). Faculty: 65 full-time (28 women), 23 part-time (11 women). Students: 421 full-time (285 women), 180 part-time (128 women); includes 22 international. Average age 36. 283 applicants, 60% accepted. In 1997, 137 master's, 16 doctorates awarded. *Degree requirements:* For doctorate, dissertation required, foreign language not required. *Average time to degree:* master's–2.3 years full-time; doctorate–4.3 years full-time. *Application deadline:* rolling. *Application fee:* $50. *Tuition:* $2080 per year full-time, $557 per semester part-time. *Financial aid:* Fellowships, research assistantships, teaching assistantships, awards, institutionally sponsored loans, and career-related internships or fieldwork available. Financial aid application deadline: 2/15. • Dr. B. Howe, Dean, 250-721-7757. Application contact: Sarah Baylow, Graduate Secretary, 250-721-7882. Fax: 250-721-7767. E-mail: sbaylow@uvic.ca.

University of Virginia, Curry School of Education, Charlottesville, VA 22903. Awards M Ed, MT, Ed D, PhD, Ed S. Accredited by NCATE. Faculty: 98 full-time (36 women), 5 part-time (3 women), 100 FTE. Students: 617 full-time (446 women), 139 part-time (100 women); includes 104 minority (68 African Americans, 21 Asian Americans, 14 Hispanics, 1 Native American), 14 international. Average age 31. 1,165 applicants, 42% accepted. In 1997, 403 master's, 70 doctorates, 6 Ed Ss awarded. *Entrance requirements:* GRE General Test. Application deadline: 3/1 (11/15 for spring admission). Application fee: $40. *Tuition:* $4876 per year full-time, $944 per semester (minimum) part-time for state residents; $15,824 per year full-time, $2748 per semester (minimum) part-time for nonresidents. *Financial aid:* Fellowships, Federal Work-Study available. • David W. Breneman, Dean, 804-924-3332. Application contact: Linda Berry, Student Enrollment Coordinator, 804-924-0738. E-mail: lrb8e@virginia.edu.

See in-depth description on page 827.

University of Washington, College of Education, Seattle, WA 98195. Offers programs in curriculum and instruction (M Ed, Ed D, PhD); educational leadership and policy studies (M Ed, Ed D, PhD); school counseling and school psychology (M Ed, PhD), including human development and cognition, measurement and research, school counseling, school psychology; special education (M Ed, Ed D, PhD). Faculty: 58 full-time (21 women). Students: 424 full-time (310 women), 167 part-time (114 women); includes 93 minority (19 African Americans, 48 Asian Americans, 18 Hispanics, 8 Native Americans), 31 international. Average age 33. 431 applicants, 58% accepted. In 1997, 205 master's, 32 doctorates awarded. *Degree requirements:* For master's, thesis optional, foreign language not required; for doctorate, dissertation. *Average time to degree:* master's–2 years full-time; doctorate–6 years full-time. *Entrance requirements:* GRE General Test, TOEFL, minimum GPA of 3.0. Application fee: $45. *Tuition:* $5433 per year full-time, $775 per quarter (minimum) part-time for state residents; $13,479 per year full-time, $1925 per quarter (minimum) part-time for nonresidents. *Financial aid:* Fellowships, research assistantships, teaching assistantships, Federal Work-Study, and career-related internships or fieldwork available. Financial aid applicants required to submit FAFSA. *Faculty research:* School restructuring/effective schools, special education interventions, literacy and writing, technology, school partnerships, teacher preparation. Total annual research expenditures: $5.6 million. • Dr. Allen Glenn, Dean, 206-543-5390. Fax: 206-685-1713. E-mail: aglenn@u.washington.edu. Application contact: Richard Neel, Associate Dean, 206-543-7833. Fax: 206-543-8439. E-mail: edinfo@u.washington.edu.

The University of West Alabama, College of Education, Livingston, AL 35470. Awards MAT, M Ed, MSCE. Accredited by NCATE. Part-time and evening/weekend programs available. *Entrance requirements:* GRE General Test, MAT, minimum GPA of 2.75. Application deadline: 9/10 (priority date; rolling processing; 3/24 for spring admission). Application fee: $15. *Tuition:* $70 per quarter hour.

The University of Western Ontario, Social Sciences Division, Faculty of Education, London, ON N6A 5B8, Canada. Awards M Ed. Part-time programs available. In 1997, 54 degrees awarded. *Average time to degree:* master's–2 years full-time, 3 years part-time. *Entrance requirements:* Minimum B average. Application deadline: 2/1. Application fee: $50. *Financial aid:* In 1997–98, 38 teaching assistantships averaging $650 per month were awarded; research assistantships and career-related internships or fieldwork also available. Financial aid application deadline: 4/1. • Dr. B. B. Kymlicka, Dean, 519-661-8687. Application contact: L. Kulak, Graduate Supervisor, 519-661-2099. Fax: 519-661-3833. E-mail: kulak@edu.uwo.ca.

University of West Florida, College of Education, Pensacola, FL 32514-5750. Awards MA, M Ed, Ed D, Ed S. Part-time and evening/weekend programs available. Faculty: 36 full-time (19 women), 19 part-time (10 women), 46.1 FTE. Students: 136 full-time (96 women), 386 part-time (267 women); includes 88 minority (67 African Americans, 11 Asian Americans, 8 Hispanics, 2 Native Americans), 5 international. Average age 40. 170 applicants, 75% accepted. In 1997, 133 master's, 6 doctorates, 30 Ed Ss awarded. *Degree requirements:* For doctorate, dissertation. *Entrance requirements:* For master's, GRE General Test (minimum combined score of 1000) or minimum GPA of 3.0; for doctorate, GMAT (minimum score 450) or GRE General Test (minimum combined score of 1000). Application deadline: 7/1 (rolling processing; 11/1 for spring admission). Application fee: $20. *Tuition:* $131 per credit hour (minimum) for state residents; $436 per credit hour (minimum) for nonresidents. *Financial aid:* Fellowships, Federal Work-Study, and career-related internships or fieldwork available. Aid available to part-time students. • Dr. Wesley Little, Dean, 850-474-2769. Fax: 850-474-3205.

University of Windsor, Faculty of Education, Windsor, ON N9B 3P4, Canada. Awards M Ed. Part-time and evening/weekend programs available. *Degree requirements:* Thesis or alternative required, foreign language not required. *Entrance requirements:* TOEFL (minimum score 600), minimum B average, teaching certificate. Application deadline: 7/1 (priority date; rolling processing). Application fee: $50. *Expenses:* Tuition $4370 per year (minimum) full-time, $345 per course (minimum) part-time for Canadian residents; $8453 per year (minimum) full-time, $915 per course (minimum) part-time for nonresidents. Fees $462 per year (minimum) full-time, $141 per year (minimum) part-time. *Faculty research:* Curriculum and instruction, educational administration, counselor education, special education.

University of Wisconsin–Eau Claire, College of Professional Studies, School of Education, Eau Claire, WI 54702-4004. Awards MAT, MEPD, MSE, MST. Students: 21 full-time (16 women), 105 part-time (90 women); includes 2 minority (both Native Americans). Average age 33. In 1997, 63 degrees awarded. *Degree requirements:* Oral and written comprehensive exams required, thesis optional, foreign language not required. *Application deadline:* 7/1 (rolling processing; 12/1 for spring admission). *Application fee:* $45. *Tuition:* $3651 per year full-time, $611 per semester (minimum) part-time for state residents; $11,295 per year full-time, $1886 per semester (minimum) part-time for nonresidents. *Financial aid:* Federal Work-Study and career-related internships or fieldwork available. Financial aid application deadline: 3/1. • Stephen Kurth, Associate Dean, 715-836-3671.

University of Wisconsin–La Crosse, School of Education, La Crosse, WI 54601-3742. Awards MEPD, MS Ed. Accredited by NCATE. Part-time programs available. Faculty: 27 full-time (15 women), 21 part-time (7 women), 32.5 FTE. Students: 84 full-time (50 women), 67 part-time (52 women); includes 7 minority (3 African Americans, 1 Asian American, 1 Hispanic, 2 Native Americans), 1 international. Average age 33. 120 applicants, 81% accepted. In 1997, 89 degrees awarded. *Application fee:* $38. *Tuition:* $3737 per year full-time, $208 per credit part-time for state residents; $11,921 per year full-time, $633 per credit part-time for nonresidents. *Financial aid:* In 1997–98, 60 students received aid, including 3 research assistantships (2 to first-year students) averaging $546 per month and totaling $14,742, 50 assistantships (13 to first-year students) averaging $637 per month and totaling $282,677; Federal Work-Study, institutionally sponsored loans, and career-related internships or fieldwork also available. Aid available to part-time students. Financial aid application deadline: 3/15; applicants required to submit FAFSA. • Dr. Paul Theobald, Associate Dean, 608-785-8113. Application contact: Tim Lewis, Director of Admissions, 608-785-8939. Fax: 608-785-6695.

University of Wisconsin–Madison, School of Education, Madison, WI 53706-1380. Awards MA, MFA, MS, PhD. *Degree requirements:* For doctorate, dissertation. *Application fee:* $38. *Tuition:* $4928 per year full-time, $926 per semester (minimum) part-time for state residents; $15,190 per year full-time, $2849 per semester (minimum) part-time for nonresidents.

See in-depth description on page 829.

University of Wisconsin–Milwaukee, School of Education, Milwaukee, WI 53201-0413. Awards MS, PhD. Part-time programs available. Faculty: 78 full-time (39 women). Students: 124 full-time (95 women), 591 part-time (451 women); includes 129 minority (82 African Americans, 15 Asian Americans, 26 Hispanics, 6 Native Americans), 5 international. 404 applicants, 61% accepted. In 1997, 205 master's, 90 doctorates awarded. *Degree requirements:* For doctorate, dissertation required, foreign language not required. *Entrance requirements:* For doctorate, GRE General Test. Application deadline: 1/1 (priority date; rolling processing; 9/1 for spring admission). Application fee: $45 ($75 for international students). *Tuition:* $4996 per year full-time, $1030 per semester (minimum) part-time for state residents; $15,216 per year full-time, $2947 per semester (minimum) part-time for nonresidents. *Financial aid:* In 1997–98, 10 fellowships, 2 research assistantships, 6 teaching assistantships, 13 project assistantships were awarded; Federal Work-Study and career-related internships or fieldwork also available. Aid available to part-time students. Financial aid application deadline: 4/15. • William Harvey, Dean, 414-229-6490.

University of Wisconsin–Oshkosh, College of Education and Human Services, Oshkosh, WI 54901-8602. Awards MS, MSE. Accredited by NCATE. Part-time and evening/weekend programs available. Faculty: 40 full-time (22 women), 21 part-time (14 women). Students: 69 full-time (51 women), 469 part-time (373 women); includes 20 minority (4 African Americans, 7 Asian Americans, 4 Hispanics, 5 Native Americans), 5 international. Average age 32. 127 applicants, 78% accepted. In 1997, 106 degrees awarded. *Degree requirements:* Thesis optional, foreign language not required. *Application fee:* $45. *Tuition:* $3638 per year full-time, $609 per semester (minimum) part-time for state residents; $11,882 per year full-time, $1884 per semester (minimum) part-time for nonresidents. *Financial aid:* Federal Work-Study, institutionally sponsored loans, and career-related internships or fieldwork available. Aid available to part-time students. Financial aid application deadline: 3/15. • Dr. Donald W. Mocker, Dean, 920-424-3322.

University of Wisconsin–Platteville, College of Liberal Arts and Education, School of Education, Platteville, WI 53818-3099. Offers programs in adult education (MSE), elementary education (MSE), middle school education (MSE), secondary education (MSE), vocational and technical education (MSE). Accredited by NCATE. Part-time programs available. Faculty: 8 part-time (3 women). Students: 8 full-time (4 women), 32 part-time (27 women); includes 2 minority (1 African American, 1 Asian American), 1 international. 27 applicants, 67% accepted. In 1997, 36 degrees awarded. *Degree requirements:* Thesis or alternative, comprehensive exam required, foreign language not required. *Entrance requirements:* TOEFL (minimum score 500). Application deadline: 7/1 (priority date; rolling processing; 11/1 for spring admission). Application fee: $45. *Financial aid:* In 1997–98, 5 assistantships (3 to first-year students) were awarded; Federal Work-Study and career-related internships or fieldwork also available. • Dr. Sally Standiford, Director, 608-342-1131. Fax: 608-342-1133. E-mail: standiford@uwplatt.edu.

University of Wisconsin–River Falls, College of Education and Graduate Studies, River Falls, WI 54022-5001. Awards MS, MSE. Accredited by NCATE. Students: 247 (196 women). *Application fee:* $45. *Financial aid:* Research assistantships, Federal Work-Study, and career-related internships or fieldwork available. Financial aid application deadline: 3/1. • Application contact: Graduate Admissions, 715-425-3843.

University of Wisconsin–Stevens Point, College of Professional Studies, School of Education, Stevens Point, WI 54481-3897. Offers programs in education—general/reading (MSE), educational administration (MSE), elementary education (MSE), guidance and counseling (MSE). Faculty: 15 (5 women). Students: 1 (woman) full-time, 64 part-time (54 women). In 1997, 78 degrees awarded. *Application deadline:* rolling. *Application fee:* $38. *Tuition:* $3702 per year full-time, $664 per semester (minimum) part-time for state residents; $11,346 per year full-time, $1938 per semester (minimum) part-time for nonresidents. *Financial aid:* Research assistantships, teaching assistantships, graduate assistantships, Federal Work-Study available. Aid available to part-time students. Financial aid application deadline: 5/1; applicants required to submit FAFSA. *Faculty research:* Technology-related societal problems in the science classroom. • Dr. Leslie McClaine-Ruelle, Head, 715-346-2040.

University of Wisconsin–Stout, College of Human Development, Program in Education, Menomonie, WI 54751. Awards MS. Part-time programs available. Students: 3 full-time (0 women), 15 part-time (12 women); includes 3 minority (2 African Americans, 1 Native American). 5 applicants, 100% accepted. In 1997, 14 degrees awarded. *Degree requirements:* Thesis required, foreign language not required. *Application deadline:* rolling. *Application fee:* $45. *Tuition:* $3284 per year full-time, $183 per credit hour part-time for state residents; $7644 per year full-time, $425 per credit hour part-time for nonresidents. *Financial aid:* In 1997–98, 2 research assistantships were awarded; teaching assistantships, full and partial tuition waivers, Federal Work-Study also available. Aid available to part-time students. Financial aid application deadline: 4/1; applicants required to submit FAFSA. • Jill Stanton, Director, 715-232-1622.

University of Wisconsin–Superior, Department of Teacher Education, Superior, WI 54880-2873. Offers programs in instruction (MSE); special education (MSE), including emotionally disturbed learners, learning disabilities; teaching reading (MSE). Part-time and evening/weekend programs available. Postbaccalaureate distance learning degree programs offered (minimal on-campus study). Students: 78 (57 women). 19 applicants, 95% accepted. In 1997, 35 degrees awarded. *Degree requirements:* Research project required, foreign language not required. *Entrance requirements:* Minimum GPA of 2.75, teaching certificate. Application deadline: 4/1 (priority date; rolling processing). Application fee: $45. *Tuition:* $3628 per year full-time, $222 per credit hour part-time for state residents; $11,272 per year full-time, $647 per credit hour part-time for nonresidents. *Financial aid:* In 1997–98, 2 research assistantships (both to first-year students) averaging $850 per month and totaling $15,428 were awarded; partial tuition waivers, Federal Work-Study, and career-related internships or fieldwork also available. Aid available to part-time students. Financial aid application deadline: 5/1. *Faculty research:* Science teaching. • Dr. Cecilia E. Schrenker, Chairperson, 715-394-8156. E-mail: cschrenk@staff.uwsuper.edu.

University of Wisconsin–Whitewater, College of Education, Whitewater, WI 53190-1790. Awards MAT, MEPD, MS, MS Ed. Accredited by NCATE. MAT and MEPD being phased out; applicants no longer accepted. Part-time and evening/weekend programs available. *Application deadline:* rolling. *Application fee:* $38.

University of Wyoming, College of Education, Laramie, WY 82071. Awards MA, MS, Ed D, PhD, Ed S. Accredited by NCATE. Faculty: 51 (18 women). Students: 63 full-time (43 women), 291 part-time (184 women); includes 18 minority (6 African Americans, 2 Asian Americans, 9 Hispanics, 1 Native American), 2 international. 198 applicants, 44% accepted. In 1997, 59 master's, 12 doctorates awarded. *Degree requirements:* For doctorate, dissertation. *Entrance requirements:* GRE General Test, minimum GPA of 3.0. Application deadline: 6/1 (priority date; rolling processing). Application fee: $40. *Expenses:* Tuition $2430 per year full-time, $135 per credit hour part-time for state residents; $7518 per year full-time, $418 per credit hour part-time for nonresidents. Fees $386 per year full-time, $9.25 per credit hour part-time. *Financial aid:* Fellowships, research assistantships, teaching assistantships, Federal Work-Study, and career-related internships or fieldwork available. Financial aid application deadline: 3/1. • Dr. Charles Ksir, Dean, 307-766-3145. Fax: 307-766-6668. E-mail: ksir@uwyo.edu.

Ursuline College, Graduate Studies, Graduate Program in Education, Pepper Pike, OH 44124-4398. Awards MA. Students: 20. *Entrance requirements:* Minimum undergraduate GPA of 3.0. Application deadline: 8/1 (priority date; rolling processing). Application fee: $25. *Expenses:* Tuition $405 per credit hour. Fees $22 per credit hour. *Financial aid:* Application deadline 3/1. • Dr. Denise Davis, Program Director, 440-321-8260.

Utah State University, College of Education, Logan, UT 84322. Awards MA, M Ed, MS, Ed D, PhD, Ed S. Accredited by NCATE. Part-time and evening/weekend programs available. Postbaccalaureate distance learning degree programs offered. Students: 558 full-time (330 women), 243 part-time (153 women). 401 applicants, 45% accepted. In 1997, 281 master's, 34 doctorates, 5 Ed Ss awarded. Terminal master's awarded for partial completion of doctoral program. *Degree requirements:* For doctorate, dissertation. *Entrance requirements:* For master's and doctorate, GRE General Test (score in 40th percentile or higher), TOEFL (minimum score 550), minimum GPA of 3.0; for Ed S, GRE General Test (score in 40th percentile or higher), GRE Subject Test, TOEFL (minimum score 550). Application deadline: (10/15 for spring admission). Application fee: $40. *Expenses:* Tuition $1448 per year full-time, $624 per year part-time for state residents; $5082 per year full-time, $2192 per year part-time for nonresidents. Fees $421 per year full-time, $165 per year part-time. *Financial aid:* Fellowships, research assistantships, teaching assistantships, assistantships, stipends, full and partial tuition waivers, Federal Work-Study, institutionally sponsored loans, and career-related internships or fieldwork available. Aid available to part-time students. • Ron Thorkildsen, Interim Dean, 435-797-1437. E-mail: ront@coe.usu.edu. Application contact: Louann Parkinson, Administrative Assistant, 435-797-1470. Fax: 435-797-3939. E-mail: luannp@coe.usu.edu.

Valdosta State University, College of Education, Valdosta, GA 31698. Awards MAE, M Ed, MME, MS, Ed D, Ed S. Accredited by NCATE. Part-time and evening/weekend programs available. Faculty: 69 full-time (28 women). Students: 439 full-time (369 women), 627 part-time (533 women); includes 93 minority (81 African Americans, 3 Asian Americans, 7 Hispanics, 2 Native Americans), 5 international. 657 applicants, 54% accepted. In 1997, 339 master's awarded. *Entrance requirements:* For master's, GRE General Test; for doctorate, GRE General Test (minimum combined score of 1000); for Ed S, GRE General Test (minimum combined score of 900). Application deadline: 8/1 (rolling processing). Application fee: $10. *Expenses:* Tuition $2472 per year full-time, $83 per semester hour part-time for state residents; $8472 per year full-time, $333 per semester hour part-time for nonresidents. Fees $236 per year full-time. *Financial aid:* Teaching assistantships, Federal Work-Study available. Aid available to part-time students. • Dr. F. D. Toth, Dean, 912-333-5925.

Valparaiso University, Department of Education, Valparaiso, IN 46383-6493. Offers programs in special education (M Ed, MS Sp Ed), including emotionally handicapped (M Ed, MS Sp Ed), learning disabilities (MS Sp Ed), learning disability (M Ed), mild disabilities (M Ed, MS Sp Ed), mild mentally handicapped (M Ed, MS Sp Ed); teaching and learning (M Ed). Accredited by NCATE. Part-time and evening/weekend programs available. Faculty: 6 full-time (4 women). Students: 28 part-time (25 women); includes 1 minority (African American). Average age 36. In 1997, 8 degrees awarded. *Entrance requirements:* Minimum GPA of 3.0. Application deadline: 8/15 (rolling processing). Application fee: $30. *Tuition:* $3870 per year full-time, $215 per credit hour part-time. *Financial aid:* Federal Work-Study, institutionally sponsored loans, and career-related internships or fieldwork available. • Dr. Barbara Livdahl, Chair, 219-464-5078.

Vanderbilt University, Peabody College, Nashville, TN 37240-1001. Awards M Ed, MPP, MS, Ed D, PhD, Ed S. Accredited by NCATE. MS and PhD offered through the Graduate School. Part-time and evening/weekend programs available. Faculty: 103 full-time (31 women), 63 part-time (28 women). Students: 653. Average age 32. *Entrance requirements:* For master's and doctorate, GRE General Test, MAT. Application deadline: 3/1 (priority date; rolling processing). Application fee: $35. *Financial aid:* Fellowships, research assistantships, teaching assistantships, Federal Work-Study, institutionally sponsored loans available. • Dr. James W. Pellegrino, Dean, 615-322-8950. Application contact: Barbara J. Johnston, Director of Admissions and Financial Assistance, 615-322-8410. E-mail: johnstbj@ctrvax.vanderbilt.edu.

See in-depth description on page 831.

Vanderbilt University, Graduate School, Program in Education and Human Development, Nashville, TN 37240-1001. Offers educational leadership (MS, PhD), policy development and program evaluation (MS, PhD), special education (MS, PhD), teaching and learning (MS, PhD). Jointly offered with Peabody College. Part-time programs available. Faculty: 44 full-time (16 women), 1 (woman) part-time. Students: 95 full-time (63 women), 6 part-time (2 women); includes 17 minority (13 African Americans, 2 Asian Americans, 2 Hispanics), 10 international. Average age 36. 73 applicants, 47% accepted. In 1997, 15 doctorates awarded. *Degree requirements:* For master's, thesis required, foreign language not required; for doctorate, dissertation, final and qualifying exams required, foreign language not required. *Entrance requirements:* GRE General Test. Application deadline: 1/15. Application fee: $40. *Expenses:* Tuition $16,452 per year full-time, $914 per semester hour part-time. Fees $236 per year. *Financial aid:* In 1997–98, fellowships averaging $990 per month, research assistantships averaging $990 per month, teaching assistantships averaging $990 per month were awarded; traineeships, Federal Work-Study, institutionally sponsored loans also available. Financial aid application deadline: 1/15. *Faculty research:* Teaching, curriculum, and technology; persons with disabilities; policies in education; mental health, welfare, and criminal justice. • Ellen Goldring, Director, 615-322-8265. Fax: 615-322-8501. E-mail: goldrieb@ctrvax.vanderbilt.edu. Application contact: Barbara J. Johnston, Director of Admissions, 615-322-8410. Fax: 615-322-8401. E-mail: johnstbj@ctrvax.vanderbilt.edu.

Villanova University, Graduate School of Liberal Arts and Sciences, Department of Education and Human Services, Villanova, PA 19085-1699. Offers programs in addictions counseling (MS), including counseling and human relations; community counseling (MS), including counseling and human relations; elementary education (MA); elementary guidance and counseling (MS), including counseling and human relations; rehabilitation counseling (MS), including counseling and human relations; school administration (MA); secondary administration (MS), including counseling and human relations; secondary education (MA); secondary guidance and counseling (MS), including counseling and human relations; supervisory certification (MA). Part-time and evening/weekend programs available. Students: 46 full-time (40 women), 119 part-time (97 women); includes 9 minority (6 African Americans, 3 Hispanics), 2 international. Average age 32. 82 applicants, 55% accepted. In 1997, 81 degrees awarded. *Degree requirements:* Comprehensive exam required, foreign language and thesis not required. *Entrance requirements:* GRE or MAT, minimum GPA of 3.0. Application deadline: 8/1 (priority date; 12/1 for spring admission). Application fee: $40. *Expenses:* Tuition $400 per credit. Fees $60 per year. *Financial aid:* Federal Work-Study and career-related internships or fieldwork available. Financial aid application deadline: 4/1. • Dr. Henry Nichols, Chairperson, 610-519-4620.

Virginia Commonwealth University, School of Education, Richmond, VA 23284-9005. Awards M Ed, MS, MT, PhD, Certificate. Accredited by NCATE. Part-time programs available. Faculty: 60 (23 women). Students: 761. In 1997, 333 master's, 18 doctorates, 1 Certificate awarded. *Degree requirements:* For doctorate, dissertation required, foreign language not required. *Entrance requirements:* For master's, GRE General Test or MAT; for doctorate, GRE, interview, master's degree. Application fee: $30 ($0 for international students). *Tuition:* $4960 per year full-time, $257 per credit part-time for state residents; $12,652 per year full-time, $684 per credit part-time for nonresidents. *Financial aid:* Fellowships, research assistantships, teaching assistantships, full and partial tuition waivers, Federal Work-Study, institutionally sponsored loans, and career-related internships or fieldwork available. Aid available to part-time students. Financial aid application deadline: 3/1. *Faculty research:* College/school-based research, interdisciplinary training, technical assistance for teachers of the disabled. • Dr. John S. Oehler, Dean, 804-828-1309. E-mail: jsoehler@vcu.edu. Application contact: Dr. Michael D. Davis, Interim Director, Graduate Studies, 804-828-6530. Fax: 804-828-1323. E-mail: mddavis@vcu.edu.

Virginia Polytechnic Institute and State University, College of Human Resources and Education, Blacksburg, VA 24061. Awards MA Ed, MS, MS Ed, Ed D, PhD, CAGS. One or more programs accredited by NCATE. Part-time and evening/weekend programs available. Faculty: 67 full-time (48 women), 1 (woman) part-time. Students: 612 full-time (367 women), 954 part-time (674 women); includes 225 minority (178 African Americans, 17 Asian Americans, 22 Hispanics, 8 Native Americans), 81 international. 811 applicants, 54% accepted. In 1997, 285 master's, 121 doctorates, 71 CAGSs awarded. *Degree requirements:* For doctorate, dissertation. *Entrance requirements:* For master's and doctorate, GRE, TOEFL; for CAGS, TOEFL. Application deadline: 12/1 (priority date; rolling processing). Application fee: $25. *Tuition:* $4927 per year full-time, $792 per semester (minimum) part-time for state residents; $7537 per year full-time, $1227 per semester (minimum) part-time for nonresidents. *Financial aid:* In 1997–98, 5 research assistantships, 18 teaching assistantships, 48 assistantships were awarded; fellowships, full and partial tuition waivers, Federal Work-Study, and career-related internships or fieldwork also available. Financial aid application deadline: 4/1. *Faculty research:* New polymer systems for textiles, industrial trends in hotel/restaurant/tourism, lipid/mineral/vitamin metabolism/interactions, social cognition/family/gerontology, management/socio-economics of family. • Dr. J. M. Johnson, Dean, 540-231-6779. Application contact: Associate Dean, 540-231-5380.

Virginia State University, School of Liberal Arts and Education, 1 Hayden Drive, Petersburg, VA 23806-2096. Awards MA, M Ed, MS. Accredited by NCATE. Part-time and evening/weekend programs available. Faculty: 18 full-time (3 women). In 1997, 81 degrees awarded. *Application deadline:* 8/15 (rolling processing). *Application fee:* $25. *Tuition:* $3739 per year full-time, $133 per credit hour part-time for state residents; $9056 per year full-time, $364 per credit hour part-time for nonresidents. *Financial aid:* 12 students received aid; fellowships, Federal Work-Study available. Financial aid application deadline: 5/1. • Dr. Samuel Creighton, Dean, 804-524-5930. Application contact: Dr. Wayne F. Virag, Dean, Graduate Studies and Continuing Education, 804-524-5985. Fax: 804-524-5104. E-mail: wvirag@vsu.edu.

Viterbo College, Graduate Program in Education, La Crosse, WI 54601-4797. Awards MA. Accredited by NCATE. Courses held on weekends and during summer. Part-time and evening/weekend programs available. Faculty: 1 (woman) full-time, 120 part-time (65 women). Students: 812. *Degree requirements:* Thesis. *Entrance requirements:* MAT, teaching certificate, 2 years of teaching experience. Application fee: $50. • John R. Schroeder, Director of Graduate Studies, 608-796-3090. Fax: 608-796-3091.

Wagner College, Department of Education, Staten Island, NY 10301. Offers programs in elementary education (MS Ed), secondary education (MS Ed), special education (MS Ed). Part-time and evening/weekend programs available. Faculty: 8 full-time (7 women), 12 part-time (3 women). Students: 67 full-time (48 women), 69 part-time (55 women); includes 1 minority (Hispanic). 84 applicants, 82% accepted. In 1997, 55 degrees awarded. *Degree requirements:* Thesis optional, foreign language not required. *Entrance requirements:* Minimum GPA of 2.75. Application deadline: 8/1 (priority date; rolling processing; 12/10 for spring admission). Application fee: $50 ($65 for international students). *Tuition:* $580 per credit. *Financial aid:* In 1997–98, 12 teaching assistantships (4 to first-year students) averaging $300 per month and totaling $28,800, 22 alumni fellowships (10 to first-year students) were awarded; partial tuition waivers also available. • Dr. Geoffry Coward, Head, 718-390-3472. Application contact: Admissions Office, 718-390-3411.

Wake Forest University, Department of Education, Winston-Salem, NC 27109. Offers programs in guidance and counseling (MA Ed), secondary education (MA Ed). Accredited by NCATE. Part-time programs available. Faculty: 10 full-time (5 women), 3 part-time (2 women). Students: 48 full-time (37 women), 3 part-time (1 woman); includes 5 minority (all African Americans). Average age 28. 130 applicants, 22% accepted. In 1997, 19 degrees awarded (100% found work related to degree). *Degree requirements:* Thesis optional, foreign language not required. *Entrance requirements:* GRE General Test. Application deadline: 2/15. Application fee: $25. *Tuition:* $17,150 per year full-time, $550 per hour part-time. *Financial aid:* In 1997–98, 22 fellowships (all to first-year students), 5 teaching assistantships (3 to first-year students), 32 scholarships (18 to first-year students) were awarded; research assistantships also available. Aid available to part-time students. Financial aid application deadline: 2/15. *Faculty research:* Cognitive development, teacher performance appraisal, reading styles, teaching assessment and epistemology, reading achievement with heterogeneous classes. Total annual research expenditures: $420,000. • Dr. Joseph O. Milner, Chairman, 336-759-5341. Application contact: Loraine Stewart, Certification Officer, 336-759-5990. Fax: 336-759-4591.

Announcement: The Master Teacher Fellows Program seeks to attract 24 academically talented and professionally committed students who want to teach but have completed their undergraduate degrees with no course work in education. Twenty-four fellows in English, history, mathematics, second language, and science are awarded full tuition scholarships and $4000 stipends ($8000 for minority candidates). They enter the program in June and complete the MA Ed while earning a teaching certificate by July of the following summer. During the 14-month period, they engage in graduate course work in the discipline, rotate through 4 master teachers' classrooms, take part in an intensive 6-week block of pedagogical courses, and teach in the local schools under the guidance of one of the master teachers.

Walden University, Graduate Programs, Program in Education, 155 Fifth Avenue South, Minneapolis, MN 55401. Awards Ed D, PhD. Part-time and evening/weekend programs available. Postbaccalaureate distance learning degree programs offered. *Degree requirements:* Dissertation, brief dispersed residency sessions required, foreign language not required. *Entrance requirements:* 3 years of professional experience, master's degree. Application deadline: rolling. Application fee: $50. Electronic applications accepted. *Tuition:* $3125 per quarter.

Walla Walla College, Department of Education and Psychology, College Place, WA 99324-1198. Offers programs in counseling psychology (MA), curriculum and instruction (MA, M Ed), educational leadership (MA, M Ed), literacy instruction (MA, M Ed), school counseling (MA, M Ed), special education (MA, M Ed), students at risk (MA, M Ed). Part-time programs available. Faculty: 9 full-time (3 women), 4 part-time (2 women). Students: 7 full-time (4 women), 27 part-time (16 women); includes 3 minority (1 Asian American, 2 Hispanics), 1 international. Average age 34. In 1997, 2 degrees awarded. *Average time to degree:* master's–1.5 years full-time, 4 years part-time. *Entrance requirements:* GRE General Test, minimum GPA of 2.75. Application deadline: 4/1 (priority date; rolling processing). Application fee: $40. *Tuition:* $346 per quarter hour. *Financial aid:* In 1997–98, 3 students received aid, including 3 graduate assistantships (all to first-year students) averaging $250 per month and totaling $9,000; partial tuition waivers, Federal Work-Study also available. Aid available to part-time students. Financial aid application deadline: 4/1; applicants required to submit FAFSA. *Faculty research:* Admissions/retention, instructional psychology, moral development, teaching of reading. • Dr. Ralph M. Couplond, Chairman, 509-527-2212. E-mail: coupra@wwc.edu. Application contact: Dr. Joe Galusha, Dean of Graduate Studies, 509-527-2421. Fax: 509-527-2253. E-mail: galujo@wwc.edu.

Walsh University, Graduate Studies, Program in Teacher Education, North Canton, OH 44720-3396. Awards MA. Part-time and evening/weekend programs available. Faculty: 2 full-time (1 woman), 2 part-time (1 woman). Students: 46 part-time. *Degree requirements:* Computer language, comprehensive exam, teaching skills laboratory required, foreign language and thesis not required. *Average time to degree:* master's–3.5 years part-time. *Entrance requirements:* MAT (minimum score 40), interview, minimum GPA of 2.6, writing sample. Application deadline: 7/15 (priority date; rolling processing). Application fee: $25. *Expenses:* Tuition $363 per credit hour. Fees $10 per credit hour. *Financial aid:* Fellowships available. • Dr. Lynn Hutchinson, Director, 330-490-7212. Application contact: Brett Freshour, Dean of Enrollment Management, 330-490-7171. Fax: 330-490-7165.

Washburn University of Topeka, College of Arts and Sciences, Department of Education, Topeka, KS 66621. Offers programs in curriculum and instruction (M Ed), educational administra-

Directory: Education—General

Washburn University of Topeka (continued)

tion (M Ed), reading (M Ed), special education (M Ed). Accredited by NCATE. Part-time programs available. Faculty: 6 full-time, 17 part-time. Students: 6 full-time (4 women), 135 part-time (87 women); includes 6 minority (5 African Americans, 1 Hispanic), 2 international. Average age 28. In 1997, 23 degrees awarded. *Degree requirements:* Thesis or alternative, comprehensive exam required, foreign language not required. *Entrance requirements:* GRE General Test, minimum GPA of 3.0 during previous 2 years. Application deadline: 5/1. Application fee: $0. *Financial aid:* Application deadline 3/15. • Dr. David Van Cleaf, Chairperson, 785-231-1010 Ext. 1430.

Washington State University, College of Education, Pullman, WA 99164-1610. Awards MA, MAT, M Ed, MIT, MS, Ed D, PhD. Accredited by NCATE. Faculty: 47 (15 women). Students: 152 full-time (90 women), 84 part-time (49 women); includes 47 minority (11 African Americans, 12 Asian Americans, 16 Hispanics, 8 Native Americans), 15 international. In 1997, 138 master's, 24 doctorates awarded. Terminal master's awarded for partial completion of doctoral program. *Degree requirements:* For master's, oral exam required, foreign language not required; for doctorate, dissertation, oral exam required, foreign language not required. *Average time to degree:* master's–2 years full-time; doctorate–4 years full-time. *Entrance requirements:* GRE General Test, minimum GPA of 3.0. Application fee: $35. *Tuition:* $5334 per year full-time, $267 per credit hour part-time for state residents; $13,380 per year full-time, $677 per credit hour part-time for nonresidents. *Financial aid:* In 1997–98, 27 research assistantships, 29 teaching assistantships, 13 teaching associateships/staff assistantships were awarded; partial tuition waivers, Federal Work-Study, institutionally sponsored loans, and career-related internships or fieldwork also available. Financial aid application deadline: 4/1; applicants required to submit FAFSA. *Faculty research:* At-risk; bilingual/multicultural, mathematics, special, and cross-cultural education. Total annual research expenditures: $1.41 million. • Dr. Walter Gmelch, Interim Dean, 509-335-4853.

Washington University in St. Louis, Graduate School of Arts and Sciences, Department of Education, St. Louis, MO 63130-4899. Offers programs in early childhood education (MA Ed, AGC), educational research (PhD), elementary education (MA Ed, AGC), secondary education (MA Ed, MAT). One or more programs accredited by NCATE. Part-time and evening/weekend programs available. Students: 14 full-time (11 women). 33 applicants, 48% accepted. In 1997, 19 master's awarded. *Degree requirements:* For master's and AGC, thesis or alternative required, foreign language not required; for doctorate, dissertation. *Entrance requirements:* For master's and AGC, GRE General Test or MAT; for doctorate, GRE General Test. Application deadline: 1/15 (priority date; rolling processing). Application fee: $35. *Tuition:* $22,200 per year full-time, $925 per credit hour part-time. *Financial aid:* Fellowships, teaching assistantships, partial tuition waivers, Federal Work-Study, institutionally sponsored loans, and career-related internships or fieldwork available. Aid available to part-time students. Financial aid application deadline: 1/15. • Dr. James Wertsch, Chair, 314-935-6776.

Announcement: Research may be pursued at the master's or doctoral degree level in these fields: discourse, education history, educational/developmental psychology, language and cognition, pedagogy, public policy, school reform, science education, and sociocultural context. In addition, NCATE-accredited master's degree programs are offered, leading to elementary, early childhood, or secondary teacher certification.

Wayland Baptist University, Program in Education, Plainview, TX 79072-6998. Awards M Ed. Part-time and evening/weekend programs available. Faculty: 13 full-time (4 women), 15 part-time (5 women). Students: 5 full-time (4 women), 57 part-time (32 women); includes 11 minority (4 African Americans, 7 Hispanics). Average age 35. 17 applicants, 82% accepted. In 1997, 27 degrees awarded. *Entrance requirements:* GRE, minimum GPA of 2.7. Application fee: $35. *Expenses:* Tuition $225 per semester hour. Fees $350 per year full-time, $40 per semester part-time. *Financial aid:* Federal Work-Study available. Aid available to part-time students. Financial aid application deadline: 5/1; applicants required to submit FAFSA. • Dr. Jim Todd, Chairman, 806-296-4730.

Wayne State College, Division of Education, Wayne, NE 68787. Awards MSE, Ed S. Accredited by NCATE. Faculty: 18 part-time (11 women). Students: 18 full-time (14 women), 273 part-time (191 women); includes 5 minority (1 Asian American, 2 Hispanics, 2 Native Americans). Average age 36. In 1997, 47 master's, 1 Ed S awarded. *Degree requirements:* For master's, comprehensive exam, research paper required, foreign language not required. *Entrance requirements:* For master's, GRE General Test; for Ed S, GRE General Test, minimum GPA of 3.2. Application deadline: rolling. Application fee: $10. *Expenses:* Tuition $1788 per year full-time, $75 per credit hour part-time for state residents; $3576 per year full-time, $149 per credit hour part-time for nonresidents. Fees $360 per year full-time, $15 per credit hour part-time. *Financial aid:* In 1997–98, 7 teaching assistantships (all to first-year students) were awarded; career-related internships or fieldwork also available. Financial aid application deadline: 5/1; applicants required to submit FAFSA. *Faculty research:* Effective teaching, cooperative learning, effects of alcohol, children-at-risk and control issues, marriage and family. • Dr. Diane Alexander, Head, 402-375-7389.

Wayne State University, College of Education, Detroit, MI 48202. Awards MA, MAT, M Ed, Ed D, PhD, Ed S. Accredited by NCATE. Evening/weekend programs available. Faculty: 258. Students: 677 full-time (451 women), 1,871 part-time (1,345 women); includes 507 minority (432 African Americans, 28 Asian Americans, 37 Hispanics, 10 Native Americans). 716 applicants, 73% accepted. In 1997, 555 master's, 66 doctorates, 154 Ed Ss awarded. Terminal master's awarded for partial completion of doctoral program. *Degree requirements:* For doctorate, dissertation required, foreign language not required. *Application deadline:* 7/1. *Application fee:* $20 ($30 for international students). *Expenses:* Tuition $163 per credit hour for state residents; $355 per credit hour for nonresidents. Fees $498 per year full-time, $114 per semester (minimum) part-time. *Financial aid:* Fellowships, research assistantships, teaching assistantships, Federal Work-Study, institutionally sponsored loans, and career-related internships or fieldwork available. Aid available to part-time students. *Faculty research:* Vocational education curriculum, school improvement, administering education technology, bilingual education, teaching writing. • Dr. Paula Wood, Dean, 313-577-1620. Application contact: Dr. James Boyer, Assistant Dean, 313-577-1605.

See in-depth description on page 833.

Weber State University, College of Education, Ogden, UT 84408-1001. Awards M Ed. Accredited by NCATE. Part-time and evening/weekend programs available. Faculty: 22 full-time (11 women), 6 part-time (2 women). Students: 4 full-time (all women), 84 part-time (55 women); includes 1 minority (Asian American), 2 international. Average age 38. 53 applicants, 96% accepted. In 1997, 36 degrees awarded. *Degree requirements:* Thesis or alternative, project presentation and exam. *Average time to degree:* master's–1 year full-time, 3 years part-time. *Entrance requirements:* GRE General Test (minimum score 480 on each section), MAT (minimum score 40), or minimum GPA of 3.25; minimum GPA of 3.0 in last 90 credits. Application deadline: 8/1 (rolling processing; 2/1 for spring admission). Application fee: $30 ($35 for international students). *Financial aid:* 24 students received aid; full and partial tuition waivers, institutionally sponsored loans available. Aid available to part-time students. Financial aid application deadline: 2/1. • Dr. David M. Greene, Dean, 801-626-6273. E-mail: dgreene@education.weber.edu. Application contact: Dr. Judith Mitchell, Director, 801-626-6278. Fax: 801-626-7427. E-mail: jmitchell@weber.edu.

Webster University, School of Education, St. Louis, MO 63119-3194. Awards MAT. Part-time programs available. Faculty: 14 full-time (11 women). Students: 613 full-time (540 women), 382 part-time (329 women); includes 90 minority (78 African Americans, 4 Asian Americans, 8 Hispanics), 4 international. 216 applicants, 91% accepted. *Entrance requirements:* 2 years of work experience in education, interview, min GPA of 2.5. Application deadline: rolling. Application fee: $25 ($50 for international students). *Tuition:* $350 per credit hour. *Financial aid:* Federal Work-Study and career-related internships or fieldwork available. Aid available to part-time students. Financial aid application deadline: 4/1; applicants required to submit FAFSA. • Judith Walker DeFelix, Dean, 314-968-7423. Fax: 314-968-7118. E-mail: jwafelix@webster.edu. Application contact: Beth Russell, Director of Graduate Admissions, 314-968-7089. Fax: 314-968-7166. E-mail: russelmb@webster.edu.

Wesleyan College, Department of Education, Macon, GA 31210-4462. Offers programs in early childhood education (MA), middle-level mathematics and middle-level science education (MA). Part-time programs available. Students: 7 full-time (all women). Average age 32. 12 applicants, 75% accepted. *Degree requirements:* Practicum, professional portfolio required, thesis optional, foreign language not required. *Entrance requirements:* TOEFL (minimum score 550), interview, teaching certificate. *Tuition:* $150 per semester hour. *Financial aid:* Federal Work-Study available. Financial aid applicants required to submit FAFSA. • Dr. Mary Ellen Durham, Director, 912-757-5226. E-mail: maryellen_durham@post.wesleyan-college.edu. Application contact: Patricia R. Hardeman, Assistant Dean and Registrar, 912-477-1110. Fax: 912-757-4030.

Wesley College, Division of Education and Psychology, Dover, DE 19901. Offers programs in curriculum and instruction (M Ed), middle childhood education (M Ed), secondary education (M Ed). Part-time and evening/weekend programs available. Faculty: 5 full-time (4 women), 1 part-time (0 women). Students: 2 full-time (1 woman), 24 part-time (12 women). *Degree requirements:* Thesis optional, foreign language not required. *Entrance requirements:* GRE. Application deadline: rolling. Application fee: $20. *Faculty research:* Learning styles, community-higher education partnerships, curriculum models, science learning and teaching, literacy development in early elementary. Total annual research expenditures: $150,000. • Dr. B. Patricia Patterson, Chair, 302-736-2448. E-mail: patterpa@mail.wesley.edu. Application contact: Dr. J. Thomas Sturgis, Director of Graduate Studies, 302-736-2414. Fax: 302-736-2301. E-mail: sturgisto@mail.wesley.edu.

West Chester University of Pennsylvania, School of Education, West Chester, PA 19383. Offers programs in childhood studies and reading (M Ed), including elementary education, reading; counselor, secondary and professional education (M Ed, MS), including educational research (MS), school counseling (M Ed, MS), secondary education (M Ed); instructional media (M Ed, MS); special education (M Ed). Accredited by NCATE. Faculty: 26 part-time. Students: 70 full-time (53 women), 306 part-time (268 women); includes 18 minority (12 African Americans, 5 Asian Americans, 1 Hispanic), 2 international. Average age 33. 221 applicants, 73% accepted. In 1997, 138 degrees awarded. *Degree requirements:* Comprehensive exam required, foreign language not required. *Application deadline:* 4/15 (priority date; rolling processing; 10/15 for spring admission). *Application fee:* $25. *Expenses:* Tuition $3468 per year full-time, $193 per credit part-time for state residents; $6236 per year full-time, $346 per credit part-time for nonresidents. Fees $660 per year full-time, $38 per credit part-time. *Financial aid:* Research assistantships available. Aid available to part-time students. Financial aid application deadline: 2/15. • Dr. Tony Johnson, Dean, 610-436-2428.

Western Carolina University, College of Education and Allied Professions, Cullowhee, NC 28723. Awards MA, MA Ed, MAT, MS, MSA, Ed D, Ed S. Accredited by NCATE. Part-time and evening/weekend programs available. Faculty: 55 (22 women). Students: 147 full-time (112 women), 195 part-time (151 women); includes 14 minority (9 African Americans, 5 Native Americans), 6 international. 427 applicants, 38% accepted. In 1997, 114 master's awarded. *Degree requirements:* For master's, comprehensive exam required, foreign language not required; for doctorate, dissertation, comprehensive exam required, foreign language not required; for Ed S, comprehensive exam required, foreign language and thesis not required. *Entrance requirements:* For doctorate and Ed S, GRE General Test, minimum graduate GPA of 3.5. Application deadline: rolling. Application fee: $35. *Tuition:* $1799 per year full-time, $144 per credit hour (minimum) part-time for state residents; $9069 per year full-time, $1053 per credit hour (minimum) part-time for nonresidents. *Financial aid:* In 1997–98, 110 students received aid, including 1 fellowship totaling $5,000, 69 research assistantships (33 to first-year students) totaling $209,980, 40 teaching assistantships (20 to first-year students) totaling $123,935; Federal Work-Study, institutionally sponsored loans also available. Financial aid application deadline: 3/15. • Gurney Chambers, Dean, 828-227-7311. Application contact: Kathleen Owen, Assistant to the Dean, 828-227-7398. Fax: 828-227-7480.

Western Connecticut State University, School of Professional Studies, Department of Education and Educational Psychology, Danbury, CT 06810-6885. Offers programs in education (MS); elementary education (MS); guidance and counseling (MS), including school counselor; music education (MS); reading education (MS), including reading; secondary education (MS). Part-time and evening/weekend programs available. Students: 5 full-time (3 women), 368 part-time (309 women). In 1997, 68 degrees awarded. *Degree requirements:* Thesis or research project required, foreign language not required. *Entrance requirements:* Minimum GPA of 2.67. Application deadline: 8/1 (priority date; rolling processing). Application fee: $40. *Expenses:* Tuition $4127 per year (minimum) full-time, $178 per credit hour part-time for state residents; $9581 per year (minimum) full-time, $178 per credit hour part-time for nonresidents. Fees $25 per year part-time. *Financial aid:* Fellowships, Federal Work-Study, and career-related internships or fieldwork available. Aid available to part-time students. Financial aid application deadline: 5/1. • Dr. Thomas Cordy, Chair, 203-837-8520.

Western Illinois University, College of Education and Human Services, Macomb, IL 61455-1390. Awards MA, MS, MS Ed, Ed S. Accredited by NCATE. Part-time programs available. Faculty: 147 full-time (51 women). Students: 249 full-time (137 women), 892 part-time (646 women); includes 66 minority (39 African Americans, 4 Asian Americans, 21 Hispanics, 2 Native Americans), 32 international. Average age 34. 264 applicants, 59% accepted. In 1997, 331 master's, 14 Ed Ss awarded. *Degree requirements:* For master's, thesis or alternative required, foreign language not required. *Application deadline:* rolling. *Application fee:* $0 ($25 for international students). *Expenses:* Tuition $2304 per year full-time, $96 per semester hour part-time for state residents; $6912 per year full-time, $288 per semester hour part-time for nonresidents. Fees $944 per year full-time, $33 per semester hour part-time. *Financial aid:* In 1997–98, 157 students received aid, including 157 research assistantships averaging $610 per month; full tuition waivers and career-related internships or fieldwork also available. Financial aid applicants required to submit FAFSA. *Faculty research:* Adult education, communications technology, distance learning. • Dr. David Taylor, Dean, 309-298-1690. Application contact: Barbara Baily, Director of Graduate Studies, 309-298-1806. Fax: 309-298-2245. E-mail: barb_baily@ccmail.wiu.edu.

Western Kentucky University, College of Education, Bowling Green, KY 42101-3576. Awards MA, MA Ed, MS, Ed D, PhD, Ed S. Accredited by NCATE. Part-time and evening/weekend programs available. Postbaccalaureate distance learning degree programs offered. Faculty: 99 (42 women). Students: 203 full-time (159 women), 819 part-time (675 women); includes 34 minority (26 African Americans, 2 Asian Americans, 4 Hispanics, 2 Native Americans), 3 international. Average age 31. 430 applicants, 52% accepted. In 1997, 352 master's, 5 Ed Ss awarded. *Degree requirements:* For Ed S, thesis, oral exam required, foreign language not required. *Entrance requirements:* For master's, GRE General Test; for Ed S, GRE General Test (minimum combined score of 1250 on three sections; average 1575), minimum GPA of 3.5. Application deadline: 8/1 (priority date; rolling processing). Application fee: $20. *Tuition:* $2460 per year full-time, $133 per credit hour part-time for state residents; $6700 per year full-time, $369 per credit hour part-time for nonresidents. *Financial aid:* In 1997–98, 94 service awards (50 to first-year students) averaging $474 per month and totaling $328,715 were awarded; research assistantships, teaching assistantships, partial tuition waivers, Federal Work-Study, institutionally sponsored loans, and career-related internships or fieldwork also available. Aid available to part-time students. Financial aid application deadline: 4/1; applicants required to submit FAFSA. *Faculty research:* Teacher career ladder, vision of the elderly. • Dr. Carl Martray, Dean, 502-745-4662. Fax: 502-745-6474.

Western Maryland College, Department of Education, Westminster, MD 21157-4390. Offers programs in education of the deaf (MS), including education of the deaf, sensory impairment; educational administration (MS); elementary and secondary education (MS); guidance and counseling (MS); media/library science (MS); physical education (MS); reading education (MS); special education (MS). Part-time and evening/weekend programs available. Faculty: 10 full-time (4 women), 30 part-time (15 women). Students: 298 full-time (257 women), 1,286 part-time (1,045 women). In 1997, 279 degrees awarded. *Degree requirements:* Thesis optional, foreign language not required. *Entrance requirements:* GRE General Test, MAT, or NTE. Application deadline: rolling. Application fee: $35. *Expenses:* Tuition $210 per credit hour. Fees $30 per semester. *Financial aid:* Institutionally sponsored loans and career-related internships or fieldwork available. Aid available to part-time students. Financial aid application deadline: 3/1. • Dr. Francis Fennell, Chair, 410-857-2501. Application contact: Jeanette Witt, Coordinator of Graduate Records, 410-857-2513. Fax: 410-857-2515. E-mail: jwitt@wmdc.edu.

Western Michigan University, College of Education, Kalamazoo, MI 49008. Awards MA, Ed D, PhD, Ed S. Accredited by NCATE. Part-time programs available. Faculty: 96 full-time, 89 part-time. Students: 170 full-time (117 women), 1,334 part-time (1,030 women); includes 103 minority (76 African Americans, 11 Asian Americans, 12 Hispanics, 4 Native Americans), 41 international. 689 applicants, 48% accepted. In 1997, 503 master's, 20 doctorates awarded. *Degree requirements:* For doctorate, dissertation; for Ed S, thesis, oral exams. *Entrance requirements:* For doctorate and Ed S, GRE General Test. Application deadline: rolling. Application fee: $25. *Expenses:* Tuition $154 per credit hour for state residents; $372 per credit hour for nonresidents. Fees $602 per year full-time, $132 per semester part-time. *Financial aid:* Fellowships, research assistantships, teaching assistantships, Federal Work-Study, and career-related internships or fieldwork available. Financial aid application deadline: 2/15; applicants required to submit FAFSA. • Dr. Frank Rapley, Dean, 616-387-2960. Application contact: Paula J. Boodt, Coordinator, Graduate Admissions and Recruitment, 616-387-2000. E-mail: paulaboodt@wmich.edu.

Western New Mexico University, School of Education, Silver City, NM 88062-0680. Offers programs in counselor education (MA), elementary education (MAT), reading (MAT), school administration (MA), secondary education (MAT), special education (MAT). Faculty: 16 full-time (9 women). In 1997, 87 degrees awarded. *Entrance requirements:* GRE General Test (minimum combined score of 720). Application deadline: rolling. Application fee: $10. *Tuition:* $1516 per year full-time, $55 per credit part-time for state residents; $5604 per year full-time, $55 per credit part-time for nonresidents. *Financial aid:* Graduate assistantships, partial tuition waivers, Federal Work-Study, and career-related internships or fieldwork available. Aid available to part-time students. Financial aid application deadline: 4/1. • Dr. Bonnie Maldonado, Dean, 505-538-6415.

Western Oregon University, School of Education, Monmouth, OR 97361. Awards MAT, MS Ed. Accredited by NCATE. Faculty: 26 full-time (13 women), 72 part-time (44 women), 38.18 FTE. Students: 96 full-time (61 women), 81 part-time (55 women); includes 20 minority (1 African American, 9 Asian Americans, 9 Hispanics, 1 Native American), 1 international. Average age 36. In 1997, 144 degrees awarded. *Degree requirements:* Written exam required, thesis optional, foreign language not required. *Average time to degree:* master's–1 year full-time, 4 years part-time. *Entrance requirements:* GRE General Test (average 450 on each section) or MAT (minimum score 30), minimum GPA of 3.0. Application deadline: rolling. Application fee: $50. *Financial aid:* In 1997–98, 7 research assistantships (2 to first-year students) averaging $1,320 per month, 11 teaching assistantships (7 to first-year students) averaging $680 per month were awarded; full and partial tuition waivers and career-related internships or fieldwork also available. Aid available to part-time students. Financial aid application deadline: 3/1; applicants required to submit FAFSA. *Faculty research:* Motivational determinants of health habits, biomechanical factors of injury prevention and performance enhancement. • Dr. Meredith Brodsky, Dean, 503-838-8825. Fax: 503-838-8228. E-mail: brodskym@wou.edu. Application contact: Alison Marshall, Director of Admissions, 503-838-8211. Fax: 503-838-8289. E-mail: marshaa@wou.edu.

Western Washington University, Woodring College of Education, Bellingham, WA 98225-5996. Awards M Ed. Accredited by NCATE. Part-time programs available. Faculty: 34 (11 women). Students: 196 full-time (113 women), 142 part-time (94 women). 87 applicants, 84% accepted. In 1997, 193 degrees awarded. *Degree requirements:* Thesis optional, foreign language not required. *Entrance requirements:* GRE General Test, TOEFL, minimum GPA of 3.0 in last 60 semester hours or last 90 quarter hours. Application fee: $35. *Expenses:* Tuition $4200 per year full-time, $140 per credit part-time for state residents; $12,780 per year full-time, $426 per credit part-time for nonresidents. Fees $249 per year full-time, $83 per quarter part-time. *Financial aid:* Teaching assistantships, partial tuition waivers, Federal Work-Study, institutionally sponsored loans, and career-related internships or fieldwork available. Aid available to part-time students. Financial aid application deadline: 3/31. • Dr. Larry Marrs, Dean, 360-650-3319.

Westfield State College, Department of Education, Westfield, MA 01086. Offers programs in early childhood education (M Ed), elementary education (M Ed), intensive special needs education (M Ed), middle school education (M Ed), occupational education (M Ed), reading (M Ed), school administration (M Ed, CAGS), secondary education (M Ed), special education (M Ed), special needs education (M Ed), technology for educators (M Ed). Part-time and evening/weekend programs available. Faculty: 20 full-time (10 women), 27 part-time (7 women). Students: 1 (woman) full-time, 151 part-time (120 women); includes 2 minority (1 African American, 1 Hispanic). Average age 32. In 1997, 53 master's, 8 CAGSs awarded. *Degree requirements:* For master's, comprehensive exam, practicum required, foreign language and thesis not required; for CAGS, research-based field internship required, foreign language and thesis not required. *Average time to degree:* master's–3 years part-time. *Entrance requirements:* For master's, GRE General Test or MAT, minimum undergraduate GPA of 2.7; for CAGS, master's degree. Application deadline: rolling. Application fee: $30. *Expenses:* Tuition $145 per credit for state residents; $155 per credit for nonresidents. Fees $90 per semester. *Financial aid:* In 1997–98, 5 research assistantships (4 to first-year students) totaling $6,400 were awarded; teaching assistantships, full and partial tuition waivers, Federal Work-Study, and career-related internships or fieldwork also available. Aid available to part-time students. Financial aid application deadline: 4/1; applicants required to submit CSS PROFILE. *Faculty research:* Collaborative teacher education, developmental early childhood education. • Dr. Jean Rasool, Chair, 413-572-5723. Application contact: Marcia Davio, Graduate Records Clerk, 413-572-8024.

Westminster College, Programs in Education, South Market Street, New Wilmington, PA 16172-0001. Offerings in administration (M Ed, Certificate), elementary education (M Ed, Certificate), general education (M Ed), guidance and counseling (M Ed, Certificate), reading (M Ed, Certificate), supervision and curriculum (M Ed, Certificate). Part-time and evening/weekend programs available. Faculty: 5 full-time (3 women), 7 part-time (3 women), 6 FTE. Students: 1 (woman) full-time, 147 part-time (85 women). In 1997, 26 master's awarded (100% found work related to degree). *Average time to degree:* master's–1.5 years full-time, 2.5 years part-time. *Entrance requirements:* For master's, minimum GPA of 2.75. Application deadline: 8/30 (priority date; rolling processing; 1/15 for spring admission). Application fee: $20. *Expenses:* Tuition $1104 per course. Fees $30 per course. *Financial aid:* Grants and career-related internships or fieldwork available. • Dr. Samuel A. Farmerie, Graduate Director, 724-946-7181. Fax: 724-946-7171. E-mail: farmersa@westminster.edu.

Westminster College of Salt Lake City, School of Education, Program in Education, Salt Lake City, UT 84105-3697. Awards M Ed. Part-time and evening/weekend programs available. Faculty: 7 full-time (5 women), 4 part-time (all women), 7.25 FTE. Students: 6 full-time (3 women), 30 part-time (21 women); includes 2 minority (1 Asian American, 1 Hispanic), 3 international. Average age 41. 20 applicants, 90% accepted. In 1997, 10 degrees awarded. *Degree requirements:* Thesis or alternative, project or thesis required, foreign language not required. *Average time to degree:* master's–2 years full-time, 3 years part-time. *Entrance requirements:* Teaching certificate, resume. Application deadline: 8/1 (priority date; rolling processing). Application fee: $25. Electronic applications accepted. *Expenses:* Tuition $448 per credit hour. Fees $200 per year full-time, $65 per semester (minimum) part-time. *Financial aid:* In 1997–98, 15 students received aid, including 4 scholarships, tuition remissions (1 to a first-year student) totaling $8,680; Federal Work-Study also available. Aid available to part-time students. Financial aid applicants required to submit FAFSA. • Dr. Janet Dynak, Program Chair, 801-488-4188. Fax: 801-487-9507. E-mail: j-dynak@wcslc.edu. Application contact: Philip J. Alletto, Vice President for Student Development and Enrollment Management, 801-488-4200. Fax: 801-484-3252. E-mail: admispub@wcslc.edu.

West Texas A&M University, College of Education and Social Sciences, Division of Education, Canyon, TX 79016-0001. Offers programs in administration (M Ed), counseling education (M Ed), curriculum and instruction (MA, M Ed), educational diagnostician (M Ed), educational technology (M Ed), elementary education (MA, M Ed), professional counseling (M Ed), reading (M Ed), secondary education (MA, M Ed). Part-time and evening/weekend programs available. Postbaccalaureate distance learning degree programs offered (minimal on-campus study). Faculty: 18 full-time (10 women), 8 part-time (7 women). Students: 39 full-time (34 women), 181 part-time (131 women); includes 28 minority (7 African Americans, 3 Asian Americans, 16 Hispanics, 2 Native Americans), 3 international. Average age 34. 77 applicants, 31% accepted. In 1997, 68 degrees awarded. *Degree requirements:* Comprehensive exam required, foreign language not required. *Average time to degree:* master's–3 years full-time, 6 years part-time. *Entrance requirements:* GRE General Test (combined average 964). Application deadline: rolling. Application fee: $0 ($50 for international students). Electronic applications accepted. *Expenses:* Tuition $46 per semester hour for state residents; $259 per semester hour for nonresidents. Fees $156 per semester (minimum). *Financial aid:* Teaching assistantships, partial tuition waivers, Federal Work-Study, institutionally sponsored loans, and career-related internships or fieldwork available. Aid available to part-time students. Financial aid applicants required to submit CSS PROFILE or FAFSA. *Faculty research:* Modified internship for novice teachers, effective instructional strategies, cognitive-relational group. Total annual research expenditures: $12,000. • Dr. George Mann, Head, 806-651-2602. Fax: 806-651-2601. E-mail: george.mann@wtamu.edu.

West Virginia University, College of Human Resources and Education, Morgantown, WV 26506. Awards MA, MS, Ed D, PhD. Accredited by NCATE. Part-time and evening/weekend programs available. Faculty: 85 full-time (38 women), 17 part-time (14 women). Students: 497 full-time (347 women), 899 part-time (716 women); includes 61 minority (36 African Americans, 11 Asian Americans, 11 Hispanics, 3 Native Americans), 26 international. Average age 31. 614 applicants, 56% accepted. In 1997, 381 master's, 58 doctorates awarded. *Degree requirements:* For master's, content exams required, foreign language not required; for doctorate, dissertation, comprehensive exam required, foreign language not required. *Average time to degree:* master's–2 years full-time, 3 years part-time; doctorate–4 years full-time, 6 years part-time. *Entrance requirements:* TOEFL. Application fee: $45. *Tuition:* $2820 per year full-time, $149 per credit hour part-time for state residents; $8104 per year full-time, $443 per credit hour part-time for nonresidents. *Financial aid:* In 1997–98, 124 students received aid, including 12 fellowships (all to first-year students) averaging $1,000 per month, 47 research assistantships (26 to first-year students) averaging $900 per month, 50 teaching assistantships (13 to first-year students) averaging $700 per month, 15 graduate administrative assistantships (4 to first-year students); full and partial tuition waivers, Federal Work-Study, institutionally sponsored loans, and career-related internships or fieldwork also available. Financial aid applicants required to submit FAFSA. *Faculty research:* Internet training and integration for teachers, rural education, teacher preparation, organization of schools, evaluation of personnel, clinical services, web-based courses. Total annual research expenditures: $3.255 million. • Dr. William L. Deaton, Dean, 304-293-5703. E-mail: wdeaton@wvu.edu. Application contact: Dr. Anne Nardi, Coordinator, Graduate Studies, 304-293-5703. Fax: 304-293-7565. E-mail: anardi@wvu.edu.

Wheaton College, Department of Education, Wheaton, IL 60187-5593. Offers program in secondary level (MAT). Accredited by NCATE. *Degree requirements:* Thesis or alternative. *Entrance requirements:* GRE General Test (minimum combined score of 1100; average 1250), MAT (minimum score 50; average 65). Application deadline: 3/1 (priority date; rolling processing; 10/15 for spring admission). Application fee: $20. *Tuition:* $365 per credit hour (minimum).

Wheelock College, Graduate School, Boston, MA 02215. Awards MS, CAGS, MSW/M Ed. One or more programs accredited by NCATE. Part-time and evening/weekend programs available. Postbaccalaureate distance learning degree programs offered (minimal on-campus study). Faculty: 36 full-time (30 women), 32 part-time (27 women). Students: 345 full-time (327 women), 175 part-time (166 women). Average age 28. 236 applicants, 72% accepted. In 1997, 239 master's, 3 CAGSs awarded. *Degree requirements:* For CAGS, thesis. *Average time to degree:* master's–1.2 years full-time, 2 years part-time. *Entrance requirements:* For CAGS, interview. Application deadline: rolling. Application fee: $35 ($40 for international students). Electronic applications accepted. *Tuition:* $525 per credit. *Financial aid:* Fellowships, research assistantships, teaching assistantships, graduate assistantships, grants, Federal Work-Study, institutionally sponsored loans, and career-related internships or fieldwork available. Aid available to part-time students. Financial aid application deadline: 4/1; applicants required to submit FAFSA. *Faculty research:* Teacher development and leadership, national standards science education, high academic achievement for students of color, cultural influences on development, media literacy. • Dr. Jean Krasnow, Interim Dean, 617-734-5200 Ext. 199. E-mail: jkrasnow@wheelock.edu. Application contact: Martha Sheehan, Director of Graduate Admissions, 617-734-5200 Ext. 212. Fax: 617-232-7127. E-mail: msheehan@wheelock.edu.

See in-depth description on page 835.

Whittier College, Department of Education, Whittier, CA 90608-0634. Offers programs in early childhood education (MA Ed), educational administration (MA Ed), elementary education (MA Ed), secondary education (MA Ed). Part-time and evening/weekend programs available. Faculty: 5 full-time (2 women), 6 part-time (4 women), 6 FTE. Students: 51 part-time (43 women); includes 10 minority (1 Asian American, 9 Hispanics). Average age 24. In 1997, 39 degrees awarded (100% found work related to degree). *Degree requirements:* Thesis required, foreign language not required. *Entrance requirements:* GRE General Test, MAT. Application deadline: rolling. Application fee: $60. *Tuition:* $330 per credit. *Financial aid:* In 1997–98, 10 fellowships were awarded; career-related internships or fieldwork also available. • Don Bremme, Chair, 562-907-4200 Ext. 4324. Application contact: Catherine George, Credential Analyst, 562-907-4200 Ext. 4443.

Whitworth College, Graduate Studies in Education, Spokane, WA 99251-0001. Offers programs in education administration (M Ed); English as a second language (MAT); gifted and talented (MAT); guidance and counseling (M Ed), including school counselors, social agency/church setting; physical education and sport administration (MA); reading (MAT); special education (MAT); teaching (MIT). Accredited by NCATE. Part-time and evening/weekend programs available. *Degree requirements:* Comprehensive exams, internship, practicum, research project, or thesis required, foreign language not required. *Entrance requirements:* GRE General Test. Application deadline: 9/1 (priority date; rolling processing; 2/1 for spring admission). Application fee: $25. *Faculty research:* Rural program development, mainstreaming, special needs learners.

Wichita State University, College of Education, Wichita, KS 67260. Awards MA, M Ed, Ed D, PhD, Ed S. Accredited by NCATE. Part-time and evening/weekend programs available. Faculty: 49 full-time (25 women), 210 part-time (139 women). Students: 163 full-time (136 women), 874 part-time (670 women). Average age 38. 328 applicants, 49% accepted. In 1997, 234 master's, 9 doctorates, 5 Ed Ss awarded. *Degree requirements:* For master's, comprehensive exam; for doctorate, 1 foreign language, dissertation; for Ed S, internship, practicum required, foreign language and thesis not required. *Entrance requirements:* For master's, TOEFL (minimum score 550), minimum GPA of 2.75; for doctorate, GRE General Test, TOEFL (minimum score 550). Application deadline: (1/1 for spring admission). Application fee: $25 ($40 for international students). Electronic applications accepted. *Expenses:* Tuition $2303 per year full-time, $96 per credit hour part-time for state residents; $7691 per year full-time, $321 per credit hour

Directory: Education—General

Wichita State University (continued)

part-time for nonresidents. Fees $490 per year full-time, $75 per semester (minimum) part-time. *Financial aid:* In 1997–98, 1 fellowship averaging $1,200 per month and totaling $6,000, 12 research assistantships averaging $560 per month and totaling $40,289, 40 teaching assistantships averaging $658 per month and totaling $190,250, 31 assistantships averaging $659 per month and totaling $154,170 were awarded; Federal Work-Study, institutionally sponsored loans, and career-related internships or fieldwork also available. Aid available to part-time students. Financial aid application deadline: 4/1; applicants required to submit FAFSA. • Dr. Jon Engelhardt, Dean, 316-978-3301. Fax: 316-978-3302. E-mail: engelhardt@wsuhub.uc.twsu.edu.

Widener University, School of Human Service Professions, Center for Education, Chester, PA 19013-5792. Awards M Ed, Ed D. Part-time programs available. Faculty: 20 full-time (10 women), 22 part-time (7 women). Students: 28 full-time (20 women), 690 part-time (520 women); includes 81 minority (70 African Americans, 7 Asian Americans, 4 Hispanics), 5 international. Average age 36. 136 applicants, 98% accepted. In 1997, 139 master's awarded (100% found work related to degree); 26 doctorates awarded (100% entered university research/teaching). Terminal master's awarded for partial completion of doctoral program. *Degree requirements:* For master's, thesis optional; for doctorate, dissertation. *Entrance requirements:* For doctorate, GMAT, GRE General Test, or MAT, minimum GPA of 2.5 (undergraduate), 3.5 (graduate). Application deadline: 9/20 (priority date; rolling processing; 1/13 for spring admission). Application fee: $25. *Financial aid:* Research assistantships, graduate assistantships, partial tuition waivers, and career-related internships or fieldwork available. Aid available to part-time students. *Faculty research:* Reading, cognition, adult education, educational administration, teacher education. • Dr. Shelly Wepner, Associate Dean, 610-499-4345.

Wilkes University, Department of Education, Wilkes-Barre, PA 18766-0002. Offers programs in educational computing (MS Ed); educational development and strategies (MS Ed); educational leadership (MS Ed); elementary education (MS Ed); secondary education (MS Ed), including biology, chemistry, English, history. Evening/weekend programs available. Faculty: 6 full-time, 14 part-time. Students: 5 full-time (all women), 293 part-time (213 women). In 1997, 25 degrees awarded. *Application deadline:* rolling. *Application fee:* $30. *Expenses:* Tuition $12,552 per year full-time, $523 per credit hour part-time. Fees $240 per year full-time, $10 per credit hour part-time. *Financial aid:* Application deadline 2/28; applicants required to submit FAFSA. • Dr. Douglas Lynch, Chair, 717-408-4680.

Willamette University, Graduate Teaching Program, Salem, OR 97301-3931. Awards MAT. Faculty: 10 full-time (6 women), 14 part-time (8 women). Students: 77 full-time (45 women); includes 9 minority (7 Asian Americans, 2 Hispanics). Average age 28. 164 applicants, 49% accepted. In 1997, 90 degrees awarded. *Degree requirements:* Computer language, thesis or alternative required, foreign language not required. *Entrance requirements:* California Basic Educational Skills Test, Multiple Subject Assessment for Teachers, PRAXIS, minimum GPA of 3.0, classroom experience. Application deadline: 2/1 (priority date; rolling processing). Application fee: $35. *Financial aid:* 74 students received aid; partial tuition waivers, institutionally sponsored loans, and career-related internships or fieldwork available. Financial aid application deadline: 2/1; applicants required to submit FAFSA. *Faculty research:* Educational leadership, multicultural education, teacher education, education technology, collaboration, multiple intelligence. • Dr. Richard L. Biffle III, Director, School of Education, 503-370-6294. Fax: 503-375-5478. E-mail: rbiffle@willamette.edu. Application contact: James M. Sumner, Vice President, Enrollment, 503-370-6303. Fax: 503-375-5363. E-mail: jsumner@willamette.edu.

William Carey College, Department of Education, Hattiesburg, MS 39401-5499. Offers programs in educational leadership (M Ed), elementary education (M Ed), gifted education (M Ed), secondary education (M Ed), special education (M Ed), teaching (MA Ed). Evening/weekend programs available. Faculty: 21 full-time (9 women), 11 part-time (4 women). Students: 439. *Entrance requirements:* NTE, minimum GPA of 2.5. Application deadline: 8/15 (priority date; rolling processing). Application fee: $0. *Tuition:* $130 per semester hour. • Dr. William Hetrick, Dean, College of Education and Psychology, Graduate Division, 601-582-6217.

William Paterson University of New Jersey, College of Education, Wayne, NJ 07470-8420. Awards MAT, M Ed. Accredited by NCATE. Faculty: 24 full-time (8 women), 32 part-time (13 women). Students: 10 full-time (9 women), 284 part-time (263 women); includes 9 minority (2 African Americans, 3 Asian Americans, 4 Hispanics). Average age 33. 159 applicants, 52% accepted. In 1997, 113 degrees awarded. *Degree requirements:* Comprehensive exam required, foreign language not required. *Entrance requirements:* GRE General Test (minimum combined score of 850), MAT (minimum score 42), minimum GPA of 2.75, teaching certificate. Application deadline: 4/1 (rolling processing; 10/15 for spring admission). Application fee: $35. *Expenses:* Tuition $230 per credit for state residents; $327 per credit for nonresidents. Fees $3.25 per credit. *Financial aid:* In 1997–98, 41 students received aid, including 2 graduate assistantships totaling $12,000; fellowships, research assistantships, Federal Work-Study, and career-related internships or fieldwork also available. Aid available to part-time students. Financial aid application deadline: 4/1; applicants required to submit FAFSA. *Faculty research:* Urban community service. • Susan Kuveke, Interim Dean, 973-720-2138. Application contact: Office of Graduate Studies, 973-720-2237. Fax: 973-720-2035.

William Woods University, College of Graduate and Adult Studies, Program in Education, Fulton, MO 65251-1098. Offers administration (M Ed), curriculum and instruction (M Ed), equestrian education (M Ed). Faculty: 7 full-time (5 women), 20 part-time (9 women). Students: 218 full-time (171 women); includes 23 minority (3 African Americans, 20 Asian Americans). 232 applicants, 88% accepted. In 1997, 25 degrees awarded. *Degree requirements:* Thesis or alternative required, foreign language not required. *Entrance requirements:* 2 years of teaching experience, minimum GPA of 2.5, teaching certificate. Application deadline: rolling. Application fee: $25. *Tuition:* $240 per credit. • Dr. Larry Ewing, Head, 573-592-4339. Application contact: Mary Henley, Director of Recruitment, 800-995-3199. Fax: 573-592-1164. E-mail: cgas@iris.wmwoods.edu.

Wilmington College, Division of Education, New Castle, DE 19720-6491. Offers programs in elementary and secondary school counseling (M Ed), elementary special education (M Ed), elementary studies (M Ed), innovation and leadership (Ed D), school leadership (M Ed). Part-time and evening/weekend programs available. *Degree requirements:* For doctorate, dissertation. *Entrance requirements:* For doctorate, work experience. Application deadline: rolling. Application fee: $25. *Expenses:* Tuition $4410 per year full-time, $735 per course part-time. Fees $50 per year. • Dr. Barbara Raetsch, Chair, 302-328-9401. Application contact: Michael Lee, Director of Admissions and Financial Aid, 302-328-9401 Ext. 102.

Wingate University, Program in Education, Wingate, NC 28174. Offers education (MAT), elementary education (MA Ed), secondary education (MA Ed). Accredited by NCATE. Part-time programs available. Faculty: 13 part-time (3 women). Students: 1 full-time (0 women), 35 part-time (32 women); includes 1 minority (African American). Average age 35. 39 applicants, 74% accepted. In 1997, 3 degrees awarded (100% found work related to degree). *Average time to degree:* master's–2 years part-time. *Entrance requirements:* GRE General Test or MAT, teaching certificate (MA Ed). Application deadline: 8/15 (priority date; rolling processing). Application fee: $0. *Financial aid:* 5 students received aid. Aid available to part-time students. Financial aid applicants required to submit FAFSA. *Faculty research:* Teaching/learning styles, principles of teaching, homework, stress management, student's rights. • Dr. Robert A. Shaw, Dean, 704-233-8078. Fax: 704-233-8192. Application contact: Phyllis Starnes, Secretary, School of Education, 704-233-8075. Fax: 704-233-8285.

Winona State University, Graduate Studies, College of Education, Winona, MN 55987-5838. Awards MS, Ed S. Accredited by NCATE. Part-time and evening/weekend programs available. Faculty: 13 full-time (6 women). Students: 38 full-time (22 women), 319 part-time (214 women); includes 3 international. 118 applicants, 96% accepted. In 1997, 115 master's, 2 Ed Ss awarded. *Entrance requirements:* For master's, GRE General Test. Application deadline: 8/8 (priority date; rolling processing; 2/17 for spring admission). Application fee: $20. *Financial aid:* In 1997–98, 3 assistantships were awarded; fellowships, Federal Work-Study, and career-related internships or fieldwork also available. Aid available to part-time students. • Dr. Carol Anderson, Dean, 507-457-5570.

Winthrop University, College of Education, Rock Hill, SC 29733. Awards MAT, M Ed, MS, Ed S. Accredited by NCATE. Part-time programs available. Faculty: 32 full-time (15 women). Students: 73 full-time (50 women), 221 part-time (181 women); includes 56 minority (52 African Americans, 2 Hispanics, 2 Native Americans). Average age 33. In 1997, 107 master's, 9 Ed Ss awarded. *Application deadline:* 7/15 (priority date; rolling processing; 12/1 for spring admission). *Application fee:* $35. *Tuition:* $3928 per year full-time, $164 per credit hour part-time for state residents; $7060 per year full-time, $294 per credit hour part-time for nonresidents. *Financial aid:* Graduate assistantships, graduate scholarships, Federal Work-Study, and career-related internships or fieldwork available. Aid available to part-time students. Financial aid application deadline: 2/1; applicants required to submit FAFSA. • Dr. Thomas Powell, Dean, 803-323-2151. Fax: 803-323-4369. E-mail: powellt@winthrop.edu. Application contact: Sharon Johnson, Director of Graduate Studies, 803-323-2204. Fax: 803-323-2292. E-mail: johnsons@winthrop.edu.

Worcester State College, Graduate Studies, Department of Education, Worcester, MA 01602-2597. Offers programs in early childhood education (M Ed), elementary education (M Ed), health education (M Ed), leadership and administration (M Ed), middle school education (M Ed, Certificate), reading (M Ed, Certificate), secondary education (M Ed, Certificate). Part-time and evening/weekend programs available. Students: 12 full-time (3 women), 172 part-time (138 women); includes 5 minority (1 African American, 1 Asian American, 2 Hispanics, 1 Native American). Average age 37. 30 applicants, 83% accepted. In 1997, 65 master's awarded. *Degree requirements:* For master's, comprehensive exam. *Entrance requirements:* For master's, GRE General Test or MAT. Application fee: $10 ($40 for international students). *Tuition:* $127 per credit hour. *Financial aid:* Career-related internships or fieldwork available. • Dr. David Quist, Chair, 508-929-8046. Application contact: Andrea Wetmore, Graduate Admissions Counselor, 508-929-8120. E-mail: awetmore@worc.mass.edu.

Wright State University, College of Education and Human Services, Dayton, OH 45435. Awards MA, M Ed, MRC, MS, PhD, Ed S. Accredited by NCATE. PhD offered jointly with Bowling Green State University. Part-time and evening/weekend programs available. Students: 196 full-time (146 women), 763 part-time (646 women); includes 56 minority (44 African Americans, 2 Asian Americans, 5 Hispanics, 5 Native Americans), 1 international. Average age 34. 390 applicants, 84% accepted. In 1997, 395 master's, 4 Ed Ss awarded. *Entrance requirements:* For master's and Ed S, GRE General Test, MAT, TOEFL (minimum score 550). Application fee: $25. *Tuition:* $5109 per year full-time, $161 per credit hour part-time for state residents; $9039 per year full-time, $282 per credit hour part-time for nonresidents. *Financial aid:* In 1997–98, 4 fellowships (3 to first-year students), 1 teaching assistantship, 33 graduate assistantships were awarded; research assistantships, full and partial tuition waivers, Federal Work-Study, institutionally sponsored loans, and career-related internships or fieldwork also available. Aid available to part-time students. Financial aid applicants required to submit FAFSA. • Dr. Gregory Bernhardt, Dean, 937-775-2821. Fax: 937-775-3301. Application contact: Gerald C. Malicki, Assistant Dean and Director of Graduate Admissions and Records, 937-775-2976. Fax: 937-775-2357. E-mail: wsugrad@wright.edu.

Xavier University, College of Social Sciences, Department of Education, Cincinnati, OH 45207-2111. Offers programs in agency and community counseling (M Ed); art (M Ed); classics (M Ed); educational administration (M Ed); elementary education (M Ed); English (M Ed); human resource development (M Ed); mathematics (M Ed); Montessori (M Ed); multicultural literature for children (M Ed); music (M Ed); reading specialist (M Ed); school counseling (M Ed), including counseling, school counseling; secondary education (M Ed); special education (M Ed), including developmentally handicapped, early childhood education of handicapped, gifted, multiple handicapped, severe behavior handicapped, specific learning disabilities; sport administration (M Ed); theology (M Ed). Part-time and evening/weekend programs available. Faculty: 32 full-time (14 women), 49 part-time (31 women), 44.25 FTE. Students: 228 full-time (169 women), 518 part-time (410 women). Average age 34. 322 applicants, 64% accepted. In 1997, 307 degrees awarded. *Application deadline:* rolling. *Application fee:* $25. *Financial aid:* In 1997–98, 247 students received aid, including 220 scholarships (67 to first-year students); career-related internships or fieldwork also available. Aid available to part-time students. *Faculty research:* Reading achievement, students at risk, school reform, urban school, violence in schools, race in schools. • Dr. James Boothe, Chair, 513-745-2951. Fax: 513-745-1052. E-mail: boothe@admin.xu.edu. Application contact: Sheila Speth, Director of Graduate Services, 513-745-3360. Fax: 513-745-1048. E-mail: xugrad@admin.xu.edu.

Xavier University of Louisiana, Programs in Education, New Orleans, LA 70125-1098. Offerings in administration and supervision (MA), curriculum and instruction (MA), guidance and counseling (MA), teacher education (MAT). Accredited by NCATE. Part-time and evening/weekend programs available. Faculty: 9 full-time (6 women), 12 part-time (5 women). Students: 91 full-time (70 women), 25 part-time (18 women); includes 113 minority (all African Americans). Average age 39. 31 applicants, 81% accepted. In 1997, 46 degrees awarded. *Degree requirements:* Thesis or alternative, comprehensive exam required, foreign language not required. *Average time to degree:* master's–3 years full-time, 7 years part-time. *Entrance requirements:* GRE General Test (minimum combined score of 800), MAT (minimum score 30), minimum GPA of 2.5. Application deadline: 7/1 (rolling processing; 12/1 for spring admission). Application fee: $30. *Tuition:* $200 per semester hour. *Financial aid:* Partial tuition waivers, Federal Work-Study, and career-related internships or fieldwork available. Aid available to part-time students. • Dr. Rosalind Hale, Chair, Division of Education, 504-483-7536. Fax: 504-485-7909. Application contact: Marlene Robinson, Director of Graduate Admissions, 504-483-7487. Fax: 504-485-7921. E-mail: mrobinso@xula.edu.

York University, Faculty of Education, Toronto, ON M3J 1P3, Canada. Awards M Ed. Part-time programs available. *Degree requirements:* Thesis optional, foreign language not required. *Application deadline:* 5/1. *Application fee:* $60.

Youngstown State University, College of Education, Youngstown, OH 44555-0002. Awards MS Ed, Ed D. Accredited by NCATE. Part-time and evening/weekend programs available. Faculty: 43 full-time (23 women), 50 part-time (29 women). Students: 61 full-time (47 women), 578 part-time (420 women); includes 30 minority (24 African Americans, 1 Asian American, 4 Hispanics, 1 Native American), 5 international. 95 applicants, 93% accepted. In 1997, 148 master's awarded. *Degree requirements:* For master's, comprehensive exam required, foreign language not required; for doctorate, dissertation, comprehensive exam required, foreign language not required. *Entrance requirements:* For master's, TOEFL (minimum score 550); for doctorate, GRE General Test, GRE Subject Test (score in 50th percentile or higher), interview, minimum GPA of 3.5. Application deadline: 8/15 (priority date; rolling processing; 2/15 for spring admission). Application fee: $30 ($75 for international students). *Expenses:* Tuition $90 per credit hour for state residents; $144 per credit hour (minimum) for nonresidents. Fees $528 per year full-time, $244 per year (minimum) part-time. *Financial aid:* In 1997–98, 142 students received aid, including 1 fellowship totaling $11,715, 25 research assistantships averaging $666 per month and totaling $213,000, 2 teaching assistantships totaling $17,040, 114 scholarships totaling $63,210; Federal Work-Study, institutionally sponsored loans, and career-related internships or fieldwork also available. Aid available to part-time students. Financial aid application deadline: 3/1. *Faculty research:* Euthanasia, psychometrics, ethical issues, community relations, educational law. • Dr. Clara M. Jennings, Dean, 330-742-3215. Application contact: Dr. Peter J. Kasvinsky, Dean of Graduate Studies, 330-742-3091. Fax: 330-742-1580. E-mail: amgrad03@ysub.ysu.edu.

Cross-Discipline Announcements

Johnson & Wales University, Graduate School, Program in International Business, 8 Abbott Park Place, Providence, RI 02903-3703.

The Graduate School offers an MBA in international business, hospitality administration, management, and accounting. The School also offers an MS in accounting and in instructional technology, an MA in teacher education, and an Ed D in educational leadership.

Tulane University, School of Social Work, New Orleans, LA 70118-5669.

Tulane School of Social Work offers a 16-month graduate program leading to the Master of Social Work degree. Graduate education in social work builds upon a liberal arts baccalaureate education. The first and second semesters of study are devoted to presenting the knowledge, skills, and values that form the foundation or core of the social work profession. The third and fourth semesters prepare the student for advanced practice with individuals, families, and communities. A 12-month field practicum begins in the second semester. Students usually remain in the same field site for the remainder of the program. Contact Lilia Valdez (telephone: 504-865-5314, e-mail: scholar@mailhost.tcs.tulane.edu).

Walden University, Graduate Programs, 155 Fifth Avenue South, Minneapolis, MN 55401.

Nationally recognized faculty members mentor experienced professionals through residency-based and computer-mediated instruction in Walden University's distance learning programs. Degrees are offered in applied management and decision sciences (PhD), education (MS, PhD), health services (PhD), human services (PhD), and psychology (MS, PhD). Accredited by the North Central Association of Colleges and Schools. For more information, see Book 1 of this series.

ADELPHI UNIVERSITY

School of Education

Programs of Study

The School of Education offers graduate programs leading to the M.A. degree in early childhood/elementary education, secondary education, physical education and human performance science, school health education, community health education, and teaching English to speakers of other languages. M.S. degrees are offered in early childhood special education, special education, reading, communicative disorders, deaf studies, and bilingual education. The D.A. in communicative disorders and the Professional Diploma in Reading are also offered. These programs lead to fulfillment of the requirements for New York State certification. There are two tracks in the M.A. in early childhood/elementary education program: the Precertification Program for students who have no previous degree in education (42 credits) and the In-Service Program for students who have previously completed a degree in education (33 credits). There is an innovative five-year B.A./M.A. program, the Scholars Teacher Education Program (STEP). This program is for undergraduates and leads to a B.A. in a liberal arts and sciences discipline and an M.A. in elementary or secondary education. The M.A. in secondary education requires the completion of a minimum of 33 credits. All secondary education students must take the required number of content area credits for certification. This program is restricted to students interested in teaching English, social studies, the sciences, mathematics, Spanish, or art (K–12). The M.A. in physical education and human performance science (K–12) requires the completion of a minimum of 33 credits. Areas of concentration include adapted physical education, exercise physiology, and sports management. The M.A. (K–12) degree leads to New York State certification. The M.A. in school health education requires the completion of a minimum of 36 credits. Candidates are required to have an undergraduate background in health or health-related areas. For New York State certification, 12 credits in professional education courses plus supervised student teaching or one year of teaching experience are required. The M.A. in community health education requires the completion of a minimum of 37 credits. An undergraduate degree in health education or a related field is required. A certificate in community health education is also offered. The M.A. in teaching English to speakers of other languages has two tracks: the Precertification Program for students who have no previous degree in education (48 credits) and the In-Service Program for students who have previously completed a degree in education and hold certification (36 credits). The state education department does not offer a free-standing certificate in bilingual/bicultural education. This program must be taken in conjunction with, or as an extension to certification in, elementary education, special education, or in a secondary education teaching field. Combined programs are offered in bilingual education and elementary education, secondary education, and special education; bilingual certification extensions in each of the major certification areas above are also offered. Advanced certificates for bilingual clinicians leading to bilingual certification are offered to bilingual social workers, speech-language pathologists, and teachers of the speech and hearing handicapped. Two master's programs in special education are offered: special education (33 credits) and early childhood special education (36 credits). Both programs lead to New York State certification. The early childhood special education program prepares students to deal effectively with the special problems that arise in infants, toddlers, and preschool-aged children. Candidates who enter these programs without the required undergraduate training in elementary education competencies are required to complete a minimum of 12 credits of elementary education course work under advisement. The M.S. in reading requires the completion of a minimum of 36 credits. The Professional Diploma requires a previous master's degree and the completion of 30 credits in reading. Both lead to New York State certification in reading. In addition, an advanced graduate certificate in whole language is offered. The whole language certificate requires the completion of 15 credits in whole language courses, all taken at Adelphi. The M.S. in communicative disorders requires the completion of a minimum of 53 credits. Candidates who enter the program without required undergraduate training in communicative disorders are required to complete a minimum of 21 credits of prerequisite courses. The M.S. with a concentration in deaf studies requires the completion of 36–40 credits. The standard background required for acceptance into the program is an undergraduate degree in speech-language pathology and audiology or in elementary education; however, additional course work may be required. In addition to the combined bilingual education programs, a 33-credit M.S. in bilingual education is also available in the areas of elementary, secondary, or special education. Candidates for the M.S. in bilingual education must be certified teachers or within 12 credits of certification completion. The D.A. in communicative disorders requires a minimum of 60 credits beyond the master's degree. Candidates are expected to pass an oral foreign language exam and prepare a doctoral thesis with an oral defense.

Research Facilities

The School of Education has established the Child Activity Center, a model preschool program, on the Garden City Campus. The Curriculum Materials Center has been instituted in Swirbul Library. The Hy Weinberg Center for Communication Disorders serves as a clinical laboratory for students as well as a community service facility for the speech-, language-, and hearing-impaired population. It has an important role in student/faculty research related to speech and hearing science as well as language and voice disorders. The School also maintains an extensive exercise physiology lab as well as a model cardiac rehabilitation and adult fitness program.

Financial Aid

Assistantships are available in nonteaching assignments and provide up to 12 credits of tuition remission per semester. Students who receive 12 credits' tuition remission per semester are required to give 20 hours per week of service. The School offers students with outstanding undergraduate and/or graduate school records positions as paid graduate interns in local public schools. Students enroll in the master's program in their area of certification and serve as interns for a full academic year. A deferred-payment plan, grants from the New York State Tuition Assistance Program, and loans from the New York State Higher Education Services Corporation are also available.

Cost of Study

Tuition for the 1997–98 academic year was $465 per credit hour. The University fees ranged from $100 to $250 per semester.

Living and Housing Costs

Adelphi University assists both single and married students in finding suitable accommodations whenever possible. The cost of living is dependent upon the specific location as well as the number of rooms rented.

Student Group

There are 1,367 full- and part-time graduate students in the School of Education, including those in off-campus programs.

Location

Adelphi University is part of the New York City metropolitan community. Its location enables students to draw upon the city's cultural and social resources as well as the University's own extensive program in the arts.

The University

Adelphi's beautifully landscaped campus of 67 acres is in the attractive residential community of Garden City, Long Island. With the Career Services Center, the School of Education offers career planning services to all students and alumni. Internships are available, and assistance is given in planning a job campaign.

Applying

Applicants must possess a bachelor's degree from an accredited institution and present evidence of qualification for advanced study. Students admitted with degree status have a GPA of 2.75 or better. Students who do not meet degree status criteria may be accepted provisionally. Provisional candidates are eligible for degree status if they maintain a B or better average for the first 12 credits of graded work. Candidates for the M.S. in communicative disorders program are required to take the Graduate Record Examination. The minimum GPA requirement is 3.0, although exceptions may be considered. Provisional acceptance is granted only for those students who were not undergraduate majors and who need to make up prerequisite courses. Application deadlines are April 15 for fall and November 15 for spring.

Correspondence and Information

Graduate Admissions Office
Adelphi University
1 South Avenue
Garden City, New York 11530

Telephone: 800-ADELPHI (toll-free)
E-mail: admissions@adelphi.edu
World Wide Web: http://www.adelphi.edu

Adelphi University

THE FACULTY

Elaine Sands, Ph.D., Acting Dean, School of Education.

Professors
Gary Barrette, Ed.D.
Ronald S. Feingold, Ph.D.
Gerald Glass, Ph.D.
Monica Homer, Ed.D.
Menahem Less, Ph.D.
Florence L. Myers, Ph.D.
Robert Otto, Ph.D.
C. Roger Rees, Ph.D.
Alan Sadovnik, Ph.D.
Roberta Wiener, Ed.D.
Pierre Woog, Ph.D.

Associate Professors
Joan Callahan, D.A.
Stephen A. Cavallo, Ph.D.
Judith Cohen, Ph.D.
H. Robert Perez, Ph.D.
Elaine S. Sands, Ph.D.
Stanley Snegroff, Ed.D.
Devin Thornburg, Ph.D.
Stephen Virgilio, Ph.D.

Assistant Professors
Diana Feige, Ed.D.
Janet Ficke, M.A.
Leah Fiorentino, Ed.D.
Susan Lederer, Ph.D.
Jacqueline McDonald, Ph.D.
Anne Mungai, Ph.D.
Molly Quinn, Ph.D.
Yula Serpanos, Ph.D.
Dale Snauwaert, Ph.D.
Shirley Steinberg, Ph.D.
Julian Wilder, M.A.

Clinical Faculty
Felix Berman, M.S.
Francine Cuccia, M.S.
Diana Feige, Ed.D.
Joseph Hrubes, M.A.
Ellen Kowalski, Ph.D.
Rose Valvezan, M.S.
John Wygand, M.A.

Emeritus Professors
George Benner, M.A.
Patricia Brown, Ph.D.
Norma Cattanach, Ph.D.
Ruth Gold, Ed.D.
Sheila K. Hollander, Ph.D.
Raylah Krevere, Ph.D.
Gertrude Langsam, M.A.
John Matthews, Ed.D.
Ruth Muller, Ed.D.
Arvilla Nolan, M.S.
Julia Pratt, M.A.
Claude Ruggian, M.A.
Ernest Siegel, Ed.D.
Ruth Skinner, Ed.D.
Donald Smith, Ed.D.
Sheldon Stoff, Ph.D.
Meryl Wall, Ph.D.

AMERICAN UNIVERSITY

School of Education

Programs of Study

The School of Education offers interdisciplinary graduate programs to prepare teachers, educational leaders, and specialists for careers in schools, colleges and universities, community and governmental education agencies, and other educational organizations. Students benefit from small classes with a highly qualified and dedicated faculty and opportunities for internships and practicums in schools, agencies, and organizations in the capital area. Degree programs can be completed on a full- or part-time basis. The Master of Arts in Teaching, with concentrations in elementary education, secondary education, and English for speakers of other languages, and the Master of Arts in education: special education–learning disabilities emphasize early and sustained contact with children and youth. Students work closely with master teachers and clinical supervisors in their field placements in both urban and suburban settings in and around Washington, D.C., and have opportunities for internships in such settings as the Challenger Center for Space Science Education and the Washington Lab School, a private school for students with learning disabilities. The M.A. in education: educational leadership is designed for those who want to be effective managers, administrators, and leaders in diverse educational settings. The M.A. in education: specialized studies enables students to develop individually designed advanced specializations in education. The Ph.D. in education provides a strong research foundation, along with the flexibility to pursue academic concentrations that meet professional goals. All programs have opportunities for internships, practicums, and independent study.

The Master of Arts in Teaching (M.A.T.), M.A. in education: special education–learning disabilities and the administration and supervision track in the Master of Arts in education: educational leadership are accredited by the National Association of State Directors of Teacher Education and Certification (NASDTEC). The following secondary subjects are accredited by NASDTEC: biology, chemistry, comprehensive social studies, dance, drama, English, French, general science, German, mathematics, and Spanish (computer science is pending). Students who complete accredited teacher preparation programs and pass the appropriate national teacher examinations are eligible to apply for teacher certification (licensure) in the District of Columbia. Students are eligible for certification in more than thirty states.

Research Facilities

The Bender Library and Learning Resources Center houses more than 600,000 volumes and 3,000 periodical titles as well as extensive microform collections and a nonprint media center. Graduate students have unlimited borrowing privileges, all accessible through the online catalog, at six other college and university libraries in the Washington Research Library Consortium. The Curriculum Materials Center in the Bender Library contains information and materials for developing instructional materials and curricula. This is an invaluable tool for students developing educational projects and for student teaching. The U.S. Department of Education has an education library that students have found to be quite useful. The Media Center provides equipment and materials for research and instructional purposes. Microcomputer resources are extensive and can be used 24 hours a day at various campus locations.

Financial Aid

Fellowships, scholarships, and graduate assistantships are available to full-time students. Special opportunity grants for minority group members parallel the regular honor awards and take the form of assistantships and scholarships. Research and teaching fellowships provide stipends plus tuition. Graduate assistantships provide up to 18 credit hours of tuition remission per year. Students seeking graduate financial aid are advised to include a resume and test scores with their application for admission by February 1.

Cost of Study

For the 1998–99 academic year, tuition is $687 per credit hour.

Living and Housing Costs

Although many graduate students live off campus, the University provides graduate dormitory rooms and apartments. The Off-Campus Housing Office maintains a referral file of rooms and apartments. Housing costs in Washington, D.C., are comparable to those in other major metropolitan areas.

Student Group

The diversity of the students extends beyond racial and ethnic lines to include students of varying ages, nationalities, and experiences. The small class sizes allow for interaction among students and between students and professors. Many graduate students work and attend class part-time, enabling them to begin to integrate professional experiences and interests into their programs of study.

Student Outcomes

Ninety percent of teacher education graduates find positions in elementary and secondary schools within the first year. Teachers who specialize in areas of particular need, such as English for speakers of other languages, special education, Spanish, mathematics, technology, and science, are highly sought in school districts across the country. Students graduating with a master's degree in educational leadership have received positions in schools, colleges and universities, government agencies, and educational organizations. Recent Ph.D. graduates have obtained positions in federal and state educational agencies, higher education institutions, and in the private sector.

Location

The national capital area offers students access to an unparalleled variety of educational, governmental, and cultural resources that enrich their degree programs. Local bus and metro from the campus provide easy access to the greater metropolitan area.

The University

American University was founded as a Methodist institution, chartered by Congress in 1893, and intended originally for graduate study only. The University is located on an 84-acre site in a residential area of northwest Washington. As a member of the Consortium of Universities of the Washington Area, American University can offer its degree candidates the option of taking courses at other consortium universities for residence credit.

Applying

Admission to the master's degree programs requires a bachelor's degree with at least a 3.0 average (on a 4.0 scale) in the last 60 hours, satisfactory scores on the Miller Analogies Test (MAT) or the Graduate Record Examinations (GRE), two recommendations, and a statement of purpose. Admission to the doctoral program requires a master's degree with at least a 3.0 average, satisfactory scores on the MAT, three recommendations, a resume, and a statement of purpose. Students with a 3.5 or better average in a master's program are exempt from the test requirement.

Correspondence and Information

To contact faculty members and for specific program information:

School of Education
American University
4400 Massachusetts Avenue, NW
Washington, D.C. 20016-8030

Telephone: 202-885-3720
E-mail: educate@american.edu
World Wide Web: http://www.american.edu/academic.depts/cas/soe/soemain.html

For an application and a University Catalog:

Graduate Admissions Office
American University
4400 Massachusetts Avenue, NW
Washington, D.C. 20016-8001

Telephone: 202-885-6000
E-mail: afa@american.edu

American University

THE FACULTY AND THEIR RESEARCH

Lynn Fox, Assistant Professor, teaches and conducts research in gender equity, mathematics education, gifted children, and integrating technology into education. *Action in Teacher Education* recently published her article "Computers and curriculum integration in teacher education."

Sarah Irvine, Assistant Professor, researches and teaches integrating technology into education and special education. A recent article, "The digital portfolio as a learning and assessment tool," was published in the *Educational Technology Review.*

Frederic Jacobs, Professor and Director of the Doctoral, Educational Leadership, and Specialized Studies Programs, focuses his research and teaching on higher education, educational management and leadership, and adult learners. He has recently received research grants from the American Educational Research Association, the American Association of University Women, and the Association for Institutional Research.

Andrea Prejean, Assistant Professor, teaches and conducts research in mathematics and science education, teacher professionalism, and action research methods. Prejean is a contributing writer to the NCTM/NASA publication, *Mission Mathematics.*

David Sadker, Professor, has research interests in gender equity in education. He has authored or coauthored six books, including *Failing at Fairness: How America's Schools Cheat Girls.*

Sally Smith, Professor and Director of the Special Education: Learning Disabilities Program has published many articles and eight books, including *Succeeding Against the Odds: How the Learning Disabled Can Realize Their Promise.*

Charles Tesconi, Professor and Dean of the School of Education, teaches and conducts research in social philosophy and educational opportunity, most recently publishing *Good Schools: The Policy Environments of Successful High Schools.*

Deborah Thompson, Assistant Professor, specializes in language and reading education, literacy development of at-risk students, children's literature, and educational technology. She currently chairs the Notable Children's Books section in the Language Arts Committee of the Children's Literature Assembly of the National Council of Teachers of English. She recently wrote *Family Values and Kinship Bonds: An Examination of African American Families in Selected Picture Books, 1974–1993.*

Recent Doctoral Dissertations

Ahmed Asseri (1997). A training model to enhance the effectiveness of school principals in Aseer Educational District in Saudi Arabia.

Catherine Ballou (1996). A comparative assessment of the effectiveness of international/intercultural education in the general education program at American University.

Sharon Briggs (1996). Linking auditory and visual input through audiotapes of text: A technique to enhance reading, academic achievement, and attitude toward reading of at-risk adolescents.

Robin Eggeman (1996). Touchstone mentoring: A multiple mentor model that mirrors women's career development needs.

Maureen Foley (1996). The Internet as a communications innovation: Effects on communication among K–12 teachers.

Anita Henck (1996). Presidential succession and modes of departure in higher education.

Scott Levine (1997). Assessment of student satisfaction.

AUBURN UNIVERSITY

College of Education

Programs of Study

The College of Education prepares professional educators for schools and other educational agencies through innovative programs built on a strong research foundation. Graduate programs in education provide advanced study for teachers, curriculum directors, media specialists (school library and audiovisual personnel), administrators, supervisors, counseling and student personnel specialists, and rehabilitation services personnel.

Programs of study lead to the following graduate degrees: Master of Education (nonthesis), Master of Science (thesis), Specialist in Education, and Doctor of Education. In addition, the Doctor of Philosophy is offered in the Counseling and Counseling Psychology (Counseling Psychology—APA accredited), Curriculum and Teaching, Health and Human Performance, and Rehabilitation and Special Education departments. Ph.D.'s are also offered in educational psychology and school psychology. Research opportunities in each area connect basic research with professional practice and give students a chance to engage in projects that have potential impact on improvement of education.

A Fifth Year Program for teacher certification of non–education baccalaureate degree holders leads to a Master of Education degree and equivalent certification.

The College of Education is accredited by the National Council for Accreditation of Teacher Education and the Southern Association of Colleges and Schools.

Research Facilities

Research facilities for students in the College of Education include the main library, the Truman Pierce Institute for the Advancement of Teacher Education, the Learning Resource Center, the University computer center, microcomputer laboratories, and facilities associated with each department.

The 207,000-square-foot research library is a member of the Association of Research Libraries and provides 2.5 million volumes and a seating capacity of 2,500 designed to serve the study, teaching, and research needs of Auburn students and faculty. The University Libraries' collection includes approximately 2.1 million volumes, 1.8 million government documents, 2.1 million microforms, 133,000 maps, 20,000 current serials, and 160 current newspapers. The library is a U.S. depository library, receiving government publications and documents; a map reference library; and a depository for U.S. patents.

Financial Aid

A number of graduate assistantships and fellowships are available to qualified applicants in the College of Education. Additional assistantships are provided through grants and contracts from external sources. Those receiving assistantships are eligible for Alabama resident fees.

Cost of Study

Full-time (10–15 hours) tuition and fees for 1998–99 are $920 per quarter for Alabama residents and $2760 per quarter for nonresidents. The nonresident fees do not apply to any out-of-state student receiving a one-fourth-time or greater appointment as a graduate assistant.

Living and Housing Costs

Both on-campus and off-campus housing are available to graduate students. The University maintains dormitories for men and women, as well as apartments for married students. The cost of room and board is approximately $1300 per quarter. Off-campus housing includes a wide selection of apartments, private dormitories, and mobile-home facilities. Students interested in additional information should contact the director of housing.

Student Group

Of the 2,667 students enrolled in the College of Education in 1996–97, 678 were graduate students. Among these, 471 were enrolled in master's and specialist programs and 207 in doctoral programs. The College's graduate student population consisted of 450 women and 228 men. Graduate students represent a wide geographical area, including a number of students from other countries, mostly from Asia.

Student Outcomes

Recent doctoral graduates have found positions at major research universities, colleges of education, research centers, and public and private educational settings. Graduates from the master's programs generally are employed in public schools and other community service settings (e.g. community counseling centers, recreation departments, and rehabilitation centers.

Location

Located in eastern Alabama, Auburn University enjoys the beauty of a 1,871-acre campus set in a town of approximately 33,000 (including student residents), with easy access to major metropolitan areas. The city of Auburn is 60 miles northeast of Montgomery, 120 miles southeast of Birmingham, and 110 miles southwest of Atlanta. The Alabama and Florida Gulf coasts are each about a 4-hour drive from the campus.

The University

Auburn University is a land-grant institution and the largest university in the state. Chartered in 1856, Auburn has a rich history of research, teaching, and service. The University comprises twelve colleges and schools in addition to the Graduate School. The College of Education was established in 1915.

Applying

Minimum requirements include a baccalaureate degree from an accredited four-year college or university and satisfactory GRE General Test scores that are no more than five years old. For admission to all programs, international students are required to submit TOEFL scores unless they have completed a degree at a U.S. institution. Formulae combining undergraduate grade point averages and GRE scores are used to determine eligibility for domestic students. Application forms and a copy of the catalog of graduate programs may be obtained from the Graduate School, Hargis Hall. Admission to most programs occurs year-round.

The College of Education has long recognized that cultural and ethnic diversity greatly enhances the quality of its programs. Members of minority groups are strongly encouraged to apply.

Correspondence and Information

Dr. Jeffrey Gorrell, Associate Dean
College of Education
3084 Haley Center
Auburn University
Auburn University, Alabama 36849-5218
Telephone: 334-844-5979
Fax: 334-844-5785
E-mail: jgorrell@mail.auburn.edu

Auburn University

THE DEPARTMENTS AND THEIR FACULTY

Richard C. Kunkel, Dean of the College of Education; Ph.D., Saint Louis.

Counseling and Counseling Psychology: 334-844-5160.
Holly A. Stadler, Head; Ph.D., Purdue.

Elizabeth W. Brazelton, Ph.D., Georgia State.
Joseph Buckhalt, Ph.D., George Peabody.
Keith Byrd, Ph.D., Wisconsin–Madison.
Jamie Carney, Ph.D., Ohio.
Debra C. Cobia, Ed.D., Alabama.
Mark A. Kunkel, Ph.D., Tennessee.
Becky Liddle, Ph.D., North Carolina at Chapel Hill.
Reneé A. Middleton, Ph.D., Auburn.
Randolph Pipes, Ph.D., Texas at Austin.

Curriculum and Teaching: 334-844-4434.
Andrew Weaver, Head; Ed.D., Tennessee.

Barbara H. Ash, Ph.D., Florida State.
William Baird, Ph.D., Texas at Austin.
Mary Sue Barry, Ph.D., Purdue.
Nancy Barry, Ph.D., Florida State.
Pamela C. Boyd, Ed.D., Mississippi State.
Edna Greene Brabham, Ph.D., Florida State.
William Edgington, Ed.D., Oklahoma State.
Betsy Grobecker, Ed.D., Rutgers.
Judith Hayn, Ph.D., Kansas.
Michael Kamen, Ph.D., Texas at Austin.
Terry Ley, Ph.D., Iowa.
Emily Melvin, Ed.D., Virginia.
Bruce Murray, Ph.D., Georgia.
Robert Rowsey, Ed.D., Auburn.
John W. Saye Jr., Ed.D., Georgia.
Elizabeth Senger, Ph.D., Arizona.
Steven Silvern, Ph.D., Wisconsin–Madison.
Janet Taylor, Ph.D., Florida State.
Susan Villaume, Ph.D., Ohio State.
Kimberly C. Walls, Ph.D., Florida State.

Educational Foundations, Leadership and Technology: 334-844-4460.
James S. Kaminsky, Head; Ph.D., Michigan State.

Teresa Akey, Ph.D., Kansas.
Susan Bannon, Ed.D., LSU.
Thomas Brush, Ph.D., Indiana.
Jeffrey Gorrell, Ph.D., Florida.
E. Raymond Hackett, Ph.D., Florida State.
Gerald Halpin, Ed.D., Georgia.
Glennelle Halpin, Ph.D., Georgia.
Kimberly King, Ph.D., Indiana.
Francis Kochan, Ph.D., Florida State.
Richard C. Kunkel, Ph.D., Saint Louis.
Judith Lechner, Ed.D., UCLA.
Bruce Ledford, Ed.D., East Tennessee State.
Jerry G. Matthews, Ph.D., Mississippi State.
Edith Miller, Ed.D., Georgia.
James R. Pennell, Ph.D., Rutgers.
Cynthia J. Reed, Ed.D., Pittsburgh.
Margaret E. Ross, Ph.D., Kansas.
Jill D. Salisbury-Glennon, Ph.D., Penn State.
David Shannon, Ph.D., Virginia.
William Spencer, Ph.D., Illinois.
Darla Twale, Ph.D., Pittsburgh.
Patricia Whang, Ph.D., Berkeley.

Health and Human Performance: 334-844-4483.
Dennis Wilson, Head; Ed.D., Tennessee.

Daniel Blessing, Ph.D, LSU.
Alice Buchanan, Ph.D., Texas A&M.
Seldon Daniels, Ph.D., New Mexico.
Joanna Davenport, Ph.D., Ohio State.
Mark Fischman, Ph.D., Penn State.
Bruce Gladden, Ph.D., Tennessee.
Peter W. Grandjean, Ph.D., Texas A&M.
Peter Hastie, Ph.D., Queensland (Australia).
Sandra Newkirk, M.S., Indiana.
David Pascoe, Ph.D., Ball State.
T. Gilmour Reeve, Ph.D., Texas A&M.
Mary Rudisill, Ph.D., Florida State.
Stephen Sanders, Ph.D., Virginia Tech.
Tai Wang, Ph.D., Illinois at Urbana-Champaign.

Rehabilitation and Special Education: 334-844-5943.
Philip Browning, Head; Ph.D., Wisconsin–Madison.

Samera Baird, Ph.D., Texas at Austin.
Clarence Brown, Ph.D., Georgia.
Craig Darch, Ph.D., Oregon.
Caroline Dunn, Ph.D., Texas at Austin.
Ronald Eaves, Ph.D., Georgia.
Daniel Lustig, Ph.D., Wisconsin
Randall McDaniel, Ed.D., Auburn.
AmySue Reilly, Ph.D., New Mexico.
Robert Simpson, Ph.D., Florida.

Vocational and Adult Education: 334-844-3800.
Bonnie White, Head; Ed.D., Tennessee.

Linda Bean, Ed.D., Oklahoma.
Virginia Hayes, Ed.D., Alabama.
Marie Kraska-Miller, Ph.D., Missouri.
Trellys Morris, Ed.D., Oklahoma.
Gordon Patterson, Ph.D., Maryland.
Jacquelyn Robinson, Ed.D., Alabama.
Elsie Jo Smith, Ed.D., Auburn.
Kirk Swortzel, Ph.D., Ohio State.
Russell Wilson, Ph.D., Iowa.
Baiyin Yang, Ph.D., Georgia.

DEPARTMENTAL RESEARCH AREAS

Counseling and Counseling Psychology
Research centers upon school and community-based action studies related to problems of children and their families: school achievement, disability, substance abuse, violence, suicide, and identity development.

Curriculum and Teaching
Most research in the department involves issues associated with the improvement of teaching and school reform. Some examples are professional development of teachers, children's learning science, portfolio use and evaluation in the classroom, minorities and mathematics success, language and learning in early childhood, and effectiveness of university and public school collaborations.

Educational Foundations, Leadership and Technology
Research focuses upon numerous topics, such as school climate and health, student life in higher education settings, applying networked interactive computing in the classroom, improving efficiency and effectiveness of digital technologies in the classroom, improvement of reasoning and problem solving, children's self-regulation and motivation, and international studies in cognitive development.

Health and Human Performance
Research areas include physical education (teaching and learning in school-based programs), biomechanics (analysis of human movement using mechanical principles of motion), exercise physiology (physiological bases of exercise in preventing disease and improving performance), motor behavior (psychological bases of development, learning and control of skillful movement), and health promotion (risk factors and interventions for healthy lifestyles).

Rehabilitation and Special Education
Faculty members study the transition from school to community for secondary students with disabilities, as well as cognitive and affective factors related to students with disabilities.

Vocational and Adult Education
Research focuses on adult literacy and learning, work place basic skills, and various areas of vocational education, especially business and marketing.

BANK STREET COLLEGE OF EDUCATION

Graduate School of Education

Programs of Study

The Graduate School of Education is a leading institution of progressive education. Grounded in learner-center humanistic traditions, Bank Street College is committed to providing outstanding educational theory and practice for graduate students through small classes combined with extensive supervised fieldwork and advisement.

The College offers master's degree and nondegree programs that prepare adults for professional work in schools and in other educational settings. Recognized for its innovative leadership, the College grants the degree of Master of Science in Education with specializations in bilingual education, early childhood and elementary education, educational leadership, leadership in mathematics education, museum leadership, early childhood leadership, supervision and administration in the visual arts, infant and parent development and early intervention, museum education, reading, early adolescence education, studies in education, and special education. The College also offers an advanced Master of Education (Ed.M.) degree in some programs for qualified students who already hold a master's degree in education or an allied field and have a record of professional competence.

All programs feature ongoing advising and evaluation. Emphasis is placed on understanding patterns of adult and child behavior and on innovations possible within given educational situations. In teaching programs, consideration is given to many aspects of children's experiences in school, such as how they learn, the roles of adults, materials and methods of teaching or guidance, the school's responsibilities as an agent of society, and environmental and historical influences. Direct experience with children, teachers, and parents is integrated with theoretical material.

Research Facilities

Bank Street's School for Children, which enrolls 450 children between the ages of 6 months and 13 years, provides continuing opportunity for study, research, and interaction with children, experienced teachers, and parents. More than 3,000 educators from around the world visit this model school each year to study the Bank Street approach to children's education. Graduate students may also do fieldwork in New York City public schools, with which the College has many cooperative programs, and in private schools. The College maintains an excellent specialized library, and students have access to other libraries in the area.

Financial Aid

Bank Street's financial aid program makes it possible for full- and half-time students to receive support to finance their graduate study. Aid is allocated on the basis of need. The College participates in such federal assistance programs as the Federal Direct Stafford Loan, Federal Perkins Loan, and Federal Work-Study programs. It also offers tuition scholarships and low-interest loans. Internships for qualified students are available through some programs. Approximately 50 percent of all degree students receive some form of financial aid. Financial aid awards are based on the Free Application for Federal Student Aid.

Cost of Study

Tuition for each course or fieldwork credit is $560 in 1998–99.

Living and Housing Costs

Costs vary widely, but students should count on spending approximately $1300 per month to cover rent, food, and books. The College has no residence facilities, but there are many apartments and rooms in the area that can be rented by students, as well as a private graduate student residence. Bank Street's cafeteria is open during the week.

Student Group

The College enrolls about 900 graduate degree students. These students usually have undergraduate degrees in liberal arts and sciences or in education. They may be new to education or they may be seasoned teachers seeking their master's degree while continuing to work in the classroom. Often students come to Bank Street to pursue education as a career change. Many are interested in education careers within museums, clinics, or hospital settings as well as in schools.

Location

New York City offers innumerable opportunities for recreational and cultural pursuits, as well as for serious study. The College's modern nine-story building is located on Manhattan's Upper West Side, only a few short blocks from Columbia University, Barnard College, City College of CUNY, Union Theological Seminary, Jewish Theological Seminary, Manhattan School of Music, Riverside Church, and the Cathedral of St. John the Divine. Public transportation is convenient and close, and it is only a few minutes by bus or subway to the Lincoln Center for the Performing Arts and mid-Manhattan.

The College

Bank Street College of Education is an independent graduate institution committed to improving the quality of education for children. For more than eighty years, it has pioneered in finding better ways to help children learn; in developing improved teaching methods, curricula, and materials; and in preparing education personnel to work effectively with young people, parents, and community groups. It also emphasizes outstanding preparation of teachers, development of educational leadership, and provision of services to public schools, agencies, and child-care centers. It serves as a consultant to schools in twenty states. Faculty members have helped plan such national programs as Head Start, Follow Through, and Right to Read.

Applying

Students who are applying for financial aid and/or supervised fieldwork in the fall semester must apply for admissions and/or financial aid by a March 1 deadline. Because of the limited number of places, students are urged to apply early. Admission is open to candidates who give evidence of superior intellectual ability, a sound background in the liberal arts, potential or demonstrated leadership in the field of education, a high degree of motivation, and personal suitability for the profession. Applicants must submit undergraduate transcripts and recommendations. Written applications are supplemented by interviews with faculty members, a personal essay, and a brief written response to program-related issues. Applicants to the early childhood and elementary education programs are expected to have completed an undergraduate major in one of the liberal arts and sciences and 1 year (or the equivalent) of a foreign language on the college level. Applicants to the early adolescence program need to have completed an undergraduate major in a subject that is taught at the middle school level. Applicants from non-English-speaking countries must submit TOEFL scores.

Correspondence and Information

Director of Admissions
Graduate Programs
Bank Street College of Education
610 West 112th Street
New York, New York 10025
Telephone: 212-875-4404
Fax: 212-875-4678
E-mail: gradcourses@bnkst.edu

Bank Street College of Education

THE FACULTY

Patricia Wasley, Dean of the Graduate School.
Lia Gelb, Associate Dean.
Barbara Coleman, Associate Dean for Administration.

Bilingual Education: Bilingual Special Education, Bilingual Teacher Education, Bilingual Leadership: Olga Romero, Chair.
Educational Leadership: Frank Pignatelli, Chair.
Early Childhood Leadership: Wendy London, Director.
Leadership in Mathematics Education: Barbara Dubitsky, Director.
Leadership in Museum Education: Amy Lawrence, Director.
Supervision and Administration in the Visual Arts: Elaine Wickens, Director.
Special Education: Claire Wurtzel, Chair.
Early Childhood Special Education: Karen Marschke-Tobier, Director.
Elementary and Secondary Special Education: Buffy Smith, Director.
Studies in Education: Lia Gelb, Chair.
Teacher Education: Linda Levine, Chair.
Early Childhood and Elementary Education: Stan Chu, Director; Judy Leipzig, Director; Donald St. John-Parsons, Director.
Early Adolescence Education: Gil Schmerler, Director.
Infant and Parent Development and Early Intervention: Nancy Balaban, Director; Virginia Casper, Director.
Museum Education and Museum Special Education: Nina Jensen, Director.
Reading/Literacy Specialization: Virginia Miller, Director.

Bank Street's Graduate School offers degree (M.S. and Ed.M.) and nondegree programs that prepare professional educators for a variety of roles working with children and youth in schools or other educational settings.

BOSTON COLLEGE

Graduate School of Education

Programs of Study

Programs leading to master's and doctoral degrees are available in a number of areas. Programs in teacher preparation include early childhood, elementary, and secondary levels in both regular and special education, as well as a K–12 reading specialist program. Special education programs include moderate special needs, severe special needs, multiple disabilities and deaf blindness, and visual impairment. Programs in curriculum and instruction offer specialties in reading/literacy, math, science, and technology. Administration programs are available in higher education/student personnel and educational administration for both public and Catholic school settings. Psychology programs are available in counseling psychology (APA accredited), mental health counseling leading to licensure, guidance counseling leading to certification, and developmental and educational psychology. A program in educational research, measurement, and evaluation provides students with expertise in research methodologies, quantitative techniques, and educational assessment. Many of the programs prepare practitioners who are able to apply scholarship to the practical problems encountered in school or clinic activities and who engage in research and evaluation. Other programs focus on the development of research skills that are appropriate for more scholarly activity, leading to university positions. Applicants can obtain additional information by calling the Graduate Admissions office or by writing to the department chairperson of the program in which they are interested. Interdepartmental study with other departments in the Graduate School of Arts and Sciences, the Law School, and the Institute for Religious Education and Pastoral Ministry is possible, and students are allowed to take some of their courses through a consortium of major universities in the Boston area. Both full-time and part-time study are offered in many programs. Typical master's programs require from 30 to 39 credits. A 60-credit master's program in counseling leads to licensure. Doctoral programs require a minimum of 54 credits beyond the master's degree, as well as comprehensive examinations and a dissertation.

Research Facilities

There are several research groups operating within the School, and students often participate in appropriate projects. Many major research projects are conducted under the auspices of the Center for the Study of Testing, Evaluation, and Educational Policy, and many faculty members employ graduate research assistants. The Boston College Campus School, which serves about 50 multiply disabled children, can be used as a research and practicum site for students. Excellent practicum sites are also located in schools, clinics, and hospitals throughout Greater Boston, including the Boston College/Jewish Community Center Preschool collaborative, and students often have opportunities to participate in research projects at these facilities as well. There are nine international practice teaching sites in American schools abroad. The International Center for Higher Education serves as a center of dialogue and communication among academic institutions in the industrialized nations and in the developing countries of the Third World and is home to the journals *Review of Higher Education, Educational Policy,* and *International Higher Education.* The Center for Child, Family, and Community Partnerships engages in outreach scholarship in areas affecting the life chances of youth and their families and is home to the journal *Applied Developmental Science.* Boston College has an extensive network infrastructure that offers Web-based access to student services and scholarly research. Both on-campus and off-campus access to intranet and Internet is available. All classrooms are equipped with data and cable access. A large microcomputer laboratory with an extensive collection of educationally oriented software is housed in the Educational Resource Center in the School of Education. The O'Neill Library houses the University's major collections, including extensive collections in the areas of education and psychology. The online catalog provides access to 1.2 million volumes and periodical articles in the social sciences, humanities, and sciences. An electronic network provides access to numerous Web and CD-ROM scholarly indexes, such as ERIC and PsychLit. Boston College's membership in the Boston Library Consortium provides access to ten major research libraries in the Boston area.

Financial Aid

Financial support is available for many graduate students, particularly those pursuing full-time study. Teaching fellowships are offered to selected doctoral students. Teaching and research assistantships, including the supervision of undergraduates at practicum sites, are available to a wider group of students. Research and training grants also provide support for a large number of students. The amount awarded depends on the source of funds and the amount of work required. Five University-wide Doctoral Minority Fellowships provide tuition remission and a stipend of approximately $16,000, renewable for a period of five years. A number of doctoral programs extend a limited number of four-year fellowships to students with career interests in university research and teaching. The TEAM Scholarship, a special tuition remission scholarship, is available for a select number of highly qualified minority students accepted into graduate degree programs preparing professionals for the nation's schools. The Charles F. Donovan Teaching Scholars program offers an award covering one half of tuition costs to academically talented applicants to teacher education programs who have a desire to teach in an urban setting. Financial aid applications should be submitted as early as possible.

Cost of Study

Tuition is $626 per credit in 1998–99. Full-time students are also charged a $15 registration fee and a $23 activity fee each semester.

Living and Housing Costs

Most graduate students live off campus in nearby apartments, and costs vary widely. The University Off-Campus Housing Office maintains lists of available housing and lists of students looking for roommates, and local realtors are quite helpful. A limited number of on-campus resident assistant positions are available for qualified applicants.

Student Group

There are more than 1,000 graduate students in the Graduate School of Education, representing a wide variety of national and cultural backgrounds. Since the specific program that the student enters has much to do with employment prospects after graduation, it is difficult to generalize about placement, but most programs have a very high placement rate. Students participate in the Graduate Education Association, which is involved in both academic and social activities.

Location

Metropolitan Boston offers a fine setting for graduate study. The numerous local colleges make the city a mecca for students seeking academic, social, and cultural enrichment. The Boston College campus, located in beautiful Chestnut Hill, a short distance from downtown Boston, offers many fine programs and facilities for cultural and athletic pursuits.

The College

Founded in 1863, Boston College is now the largest Jesuit university in the United States. The total graduate student enrollment of approximately 4,500 is distributed among seven schools: the Graduate School of Education, the Law School, the Graduate School of Arts and Sciences, the Graduate School of Social Work, the Wallace E. Carroll Graduate School of Management, the Graduate School of Nursing, and the College of Advancing Studies. Located on two campuses in Boston and suburban Newton, the university enjoys a rich academic and social milieu. The Graduate School of Education at Boston College is ranked nationally in the top twenty-five by *U.S. News & World Report*'s annual survey.

Applying

Applicants are encouraged to contact the Graduate Admissions office to obtain application information. Doctoral programs require the Graduate Record Examinations (GRE), but many master's programs accept either the GRE or the Miller Analogy Test (MAT).

Correspondence and Information

Department Chairperson
(specify program)
School of Education
Boston College
Chestnut Hill, Massachusetts 02167

Arline K. Riordan, Director of Admissions
Office of Graduate Admissions
Campion Hall, Room 103
School of Education
Boston College
Chestnut Hill, Massachusetts 02167
Telephone: 617-552-4214
E-mail: gsoe@bc.edu

Boston College

THE FACULTY AND THEIR RESEARCH

DEPARTMENT OF EDUCATIONAL RESEARCH, MEASUREMENT, AND EVALUATION

Joseph J. Pedulla, Chair; Ph.D., Boston College. Testing and policy, alternative assessment, program evaluation.
Peter Airasian, Ph.D., Chicago. Testing and educational policy, classroom assessment.
Albert Beaton, Ed.D., Harvard. National Assessment of Educational Progress, Third International Mathematics and Science Study, behavioral anchoring and scaling, statistics and research design.
Eugenio J. Gonzalez, Ph.D., Boston College. Psychometrics, statistical analysis and research design, national and international large-scale educational assessment.
Walter Haney, Ed.D., Harvard. Educational testing and public policy, information technology and education, educational evaluation and research methods.
John A. Jensen, Ed.D., Rochester. Computers in measurement and statistics, measurement of abilities, software development.
Larry H. Ludlow, Ph.D., Chicago. Psychometrics, item response theory, statistics.
George F. Madaus, Boisi Chair in Education and Public Policy; Ed.D., Boston College. Test use in public policy, impact of testing on curriculum and instruction, monitoring test use, test standards, program evaluation.
Michael O. Martin, Ph.D., National University (Ireland). International comparisons of student achievement, educational measurement, research methodology, statistical analysis, statistical computing.
Ina V. S. Mullis, Ph.D., Colorado. Design, development, and implementation of large-scale international and national assessments, policy analysis and reporting.
Ronald L. Nuttall, Ph.D., Harvard. Perceptions of sexual abuse, psychometrics of learning disabilities, attitudes toward AIDS, adolescent self-control, math achievement, perceptions of moral behavior.

DEPARTMENT OF COUNSELING, DEVELOPMENTAL, AND EDUCATIONAL PSYCHOLOGY

Maureen Kenny, Chair; Ph.D., Pennsylvania. Adolescent-parent attachment, gender differences in adolescent depression, coping with adolescent transitions.

Program in Counseling Psychology

Etiony Aldarondo, Ph.D., Massachusetts Amherst. Marital violence, Latino mental health, family therapy, child psychology.
Mary Brabeck, Ph.D., Minnesota. Gender, culture, moral and ethical decision making, conceptions of self, mental health and human rights, professional ethics and integrated services.
Janet Helms, Ph.D., Iowa State. Racial identity, psychological testing and assessment, racial and cultural counseling and psychotherapy.
James R. Mahalik, Ph.D., Maryland. Influence of gender role strain on developmental, psychological, and relational well-being; how gender role socialization affects men's utilization and experiences with counseling and psychotherapy.
Bernard A. O'Brien, Ph.D., Catholic University. Research in psychotherapy and group psychotherapy, issues in the practice of psychotherapy.
Elizabeth Sparks, Ph.D., Boston College. Prevention and intervention with children affected by community violence, multicultural issues in counseling psychology, women and sexual abuse.
Mary E. Walsh, Ph.D., Clark. Developmental conceptions of illness (including AIDS) across the lifespan, psychosocial functioning of homeless mothers and children, integrated services in urban schools.

Program in Developmental and Educational Psychology

Martha Bronson, Ed.D., Harvard. Evaluation of social interactions and task-related behaviors of children in natural settings, studies of planning in children in natural and structured settings, early childhood testing and assessment.
M. Beth Casey, Ph.D., Brown. Selective attentional abilities in children, development of effective learning strategies and problem-solving abilities, sex differences in spatial abilities.
John S. Dacey, Ph.D., Cornell. Development in adolescents and facilitating self-control, development of creativity.
Penny Hauser-Cram, Ed.D., Harvard. Policy and program developments for infants and toddlers with disabilities, evaluation of early intervention services.
Lisa Richardson Jackson, Ph.D., Stanford. Theories of the self, educational experiences of students of color, influence of sociocultural contexts on child and adolescent development.
William Kilpatrick, Ph.D., Purdue. Use of stories in moral development, psychology and literature, character education.
Jay King, Ph.D., Rhode Island. Object relations theory; marriage, family, and racial program evaluation and multicultural training; faculty retention; underachievement; attribution theory.
Jacqueline V. Lerner, Ph.D., Penn State. Child development within the school and home contexts, temperament, maternal employment and day-care influences on child development, lifespan development.
Richard M. Lerner, Anita L. Brennan Chair in Education; Ph.D., CUNY. Conceptual and theoretical issues across the lifespan; longitudinal study of the role of individual differences; school, family, and community partnerships.
M. Brinton Lykes, Ph.D., Boston College. Psychosocial and cultural effects of violence on women and children; community strategies for effecting social change; alternative research methodologies; gender, race, class, and notions of the self; mental health and human rights.

DEPARTMENT OF TEACHER EDUCATION/SPECIAL EDUCATION AND CURRICULUM & INSTRUCTION

Marilyn Cochran-Smith, Chair; Ph.D., Pennsylvania. Teacher education across the professional lifespan; teaching and issues of race, class, culture, and gender; teacher research/practical inquiry; children's early language and literacy learning.
Lillie R. Albert, Ph.D., Illinois at Urbana–Champaign. Pedagogical implications of writing to learn, application of Vygotskian Psychology to teaching and learning in mathematical problem solving.
Philip A. DiMattia, Ph.D., Boston College. Issues in changing practices of school leadership, behavior disorders and needs of services.
Sara E. Freedman, Ed.D., Massachusetts Amherst. Urban education, history of urban school desegregation, political economy of schooling, retention and academic success of urban students of color in non-elite white majority institutions of higher education, program evaluation.
Richard Jackson, Ed.D., Columbia. Assistive technology, functional uses of low vision, effective delivery of services for children with disabilities.
George T. Ladd, Ed.D., Indiana. Science education, instructional theory, authentic assessment, systematic change, collaborative building and in-service education.
Jean Mooney, Ph.D., Boston College. Cognitive and metacognitive learning strategies, service models within remedial education, collaborative consultation, strategies for supporting the learning-disabled college student.
Otherine J. Neisler, Ph.D., Syracuse. Adolescent sociopolitical attitude development in relation to social studies instruction, multicultural curriculum design, education and technology, qualitative methodologies.
Alec F. Peck, Ph.D., Penn State. Attention-deficit disorder, transportation of the handicapped, occupational socialization.
Gerald J. Pine, Ed.D., Boston University. Action research as a process of inquiry, as a process of professional development, and as a process of educational change; relationship between teacher development, adult development, and knowledge development; educational change theories and practices; theories and models of leadership.
John Savage, Ed.D., Boston University. Reading instruction, educational publishing, teaching writing and children's literature.
David J. Scanlon, Ph.D., Arizona. Strategic teaching and learning, inclusive education, literacy, adolescents and adults, social implications of special education and schooling.
Michael Schiro, Ed.D., Harvard. Mathematics education, curriculum theory and children's literature.
Polly Ulichny, Ed.D., Harvard. Language, literacy, bilingualism, culture, urban schools, ethnography, qualitative research methods.
Nancy J. Zollers, Ph.D., Syracuse. Effective schooling, transition for students with severe disabilities; school inclusion; urban, public, and parochial schools; students at risk; qualitative research methods.

DEPARTMENT OF EDUCATIONAL ADMINISTRATION AND HIGHER EDUCATION

Robert J. Starratt, Chair; Ed.D., Illinois. Supervision, leadership of schools, creating ethical school environments, social theory in education.

Program in Educational Administration

Irwin Blumer, Ed.D., Boston College. Preparing effective school administrators, the importance of race and active antiracist behavior for teachers and administrators.
Joseph O'Keefe, Ed.D., Harvard. Educational administration theory and ethics, experience of low-income students of color in affluent schools, inner-city Catholic schools, community service.
Diana C. Pullin, Ph.D., J.D., Iowa. Education law and policy, testing and the law, equity issues in testing.

Program in Higher Education

Ana M. Martinez-Alemán, Ed.D., Massachusetts Amherst. Philosophy and theory of higher education; teaching and learning, particularly the impact of race, culture, and gender on college teaching and learning; feminist theory and pedagogy; cross-cultural studies.
Philip P. Altbach, Monan Chair in Education; Ph.D., Chicago. Comparative education, history, and philosophy of higher education; higher education in developing countries; the academic profession.
Karen Arnold, Ph.D., Illinois at Urbana-Champaign. Higher education, the academically talented, student personal issues.
Kathleen Mahoney, Ph.D., Rochester. History of education, religion and higher education, history of women's education.
Ted I. K. Youn, Ph.D., Yale. Qualitative methods, sociology of education, organizational theory in higher education, evolution of the academic profession, politics of education.

BOSTON UNIVERSITY

School of Education

Programs of Study

The School of Education offers graduate degrees in more than twenty program areas. The Master of Education degree, the Master of Arts in Teaching degree, the Certificate of Advanced Graduate Study, and the Doctor of Education degree are available in most areas of study. Although programs are grouped within academic departments that reflect the chief teaching and research interests of the faculty, course work and projects often extend across departmental lines into other areas of the School and University.

Programs in the Department of Administration, Training, and Policy Studies prepare students for diverse responsibilities in administration, training, and policy-centered development work. Graduates can be found in elementary, secondary, and postsecondary school administration, student and alumni affairs, corporate training and development, international educational development, and directing international schools.

Programs in the Department of Curriculum and Teaching prepare professionals for teaching and other leadership responsibilities in education. Students prepare for educational work in schools, media centers, school libraries, community agencies, and educational research projects, as well as state and national educational organizations. Most programs include courses leading to classroom teaching certification.

The Department of Developmental Studies and Counseling includes programs in counseling, health education, and human development and education that focus on applying theory to policy and practice. Other programs emphasize human communication and educational interventions intended to improve effectiveness in communication. Specialty areas include literacy and language study, bilingual education, teaching English to speakers of other languages (TESOL), and education of the deaf.

Programs in the Department of Special Education prepare students for teaching in public schools and colleges as well as in alternative settings. Areas of study include learning disabilities, mental retardation, and behavioral disorders. Graduates may serve as teachers and program evaluators or special education administrators and supervisors. Some become special educators in such alternative settings as group homes and day and residential programs. All degree and certificate programs may include course work offered by other graduate faculties within the University.

Master's degree and C.A.G.S. programs usually require the equivalent of one year of full-time study. Doctoral programs generally require the equivalent of two or more years of full-time study.

Research Facilities

The Educational Resources Library, a curriculum library housing curriculum guides and reference and bibliographic tools, is located in the School. University media services include video services and photographic facilities. The School's Instructional Materials Center supports a wide range of instructional and communications aids: computing and printing resources, telecommunications, photography, audio-visual materials, video technology, and overhead transparencies and graphics. School-based clinics and learning laboratories offer opportunities for research and firsthand learning experiences. Students in the School have access to all libraries within the University system. The University collection contains about 2.1 million volumes, with the equivalent of an additional 3.7 million volumes stored on microform.

Financial Aid

Boston University provides financial assistance to graduate students through scholarships, research and teaching assistantships, grants, Federal Work-Study awards, Federal Perkins Loans, Direct Stafford/Ford Loans, MassPlan Loan, resident assistant positions, tuition payment plans, and special University fellowships. Career-related internships may be available, depending on the student's field of study. The School's Office of Graduate Financial Assistance provides information on eligibility requirements and application procedures.

Cost of Study

For the 1998–99 academic year, tuition for full-time study is $22,830. Part-time students pay $357 per credit.

Living and Housing Costs

Limited dormitory facilities are available for graduate students, most of whom must acquire privately owned apartments or rooms. Annual living expenses for twelve months are about $11,730 for a single student and $16,544 for a married couple.

Student Group

There were 644 graduate students in the School during Semester I of the 1997–98 year. Of these, 73 percent were women and 9 percent were international students from twenty-five countries. The majority of these students had professional experience before enrolling. About 53 percent registered as part-time students—an indication that they were continuing their employment while attending graduate school.

Location

Boston, the largest city in New England, is a seaport whose character reveals a rich blend of historical heritage, an active cultural life, and much contemporary growth in high technology, medicine, and business. Within the city are the Boston Common and the Public Garden, Faneuil Hall Marketplace, the Museum of Fine Arts, a host of art galleries, Chinatown, and the Freedom Trail.

The University

Boston University is independent, coeducational, and nonsectarian, with an enrollment of 23,615 full-time students, 5,785 part-time students, and a faculty of 3,084. Its academic and cultural diversity meets the needs of one of the world's largest bodies of scholars. Incorporated in 1869, it provides today's students with the advantages of a large, contemporary educational complex while maintaining many traditional priorities. The main campus occupies 100 acres on the south bank of the Charles River.

Applying

Most programs offer the option of rolling admissions, that is, applications are reviewed as they are received. Those seeking financial assistance, regardless of the program to which they are applying, must submit a completed application no later than February 15 to be considered for scholarship. Completed admission applications include official transcripts from all universities or colleges attended, two or more letters of reference, a statement of qualifications and objectives, an analytical essay (doctoral applicants only), a $50 application fee, and an official score report for either the Miller Analogies Test (MAT) or Graduate Record Examinations (GRE). International applicants whose bachelor's degree is from an institution where English was not the language of instruction and who are applying to a master's program must also submit a score report for the Test of English as a Foreign Language instead of the MAT or GRE.

Correspondence and Information

Office of Graduate Admissions
School of Education
Boston University
605 Commonwealth Avenue
Boston, Massachusetts 02215

Telephone: 617-353-4237
E-mail: sedgrad@bu.edu

Boston University

THE FACULTY AND THEIR RESEARCH

The departments of the School of Education are listed below. Each departmental section includes a description of faculty research and teaching interests and lists the academic programs and faculty contacts for each program.

Administration, Training, and Policy Studies
Charles L. Glenn, Chairman; Ed.D., Harvard; Ph.D., Boston University.

Faculty research and teaching interests: policy analysis from a comparative perspective; planning, group problem solving, and organizational change in corporate, higher education, and school settings; urban and community education, including parent empowerment; international educational development; school choice and educational reform; immigrant and language-minority pupils; desegregation; religion in public and nonpublic schools; leadership in charter, independent, and international schools.

Community Agency Education: Vivian Johnson, Ed.D., Harvard.
Higher Education Administration: Alan K. Gaynor, Ph.D., NYU.
Human Resource Education: Alan K. Gaynor, Ph.D., NYU.
International Educational Development: Karen Boatman, B.A., Michigan.
Policy, Planning, and Administration: Charles Glenn, Ph.D., Boston University; Kathleen Vaughan, Ed.D., Boston University.

Curriculum and Teaching
Stephan Ellenwood, Chairman; Ph.D., Northwestern.

Faculty research and teaching interests: curriculum development, design, and evaluation; learning theory; diagnosis and correction of difficulties in reading and mathematical problem solving; preschool literacy development; law-focused and intercultural education; character education; ethnographic methodologies for research; interdisciplinary social science, humanities, and science curricula; elementary education; sport theory; equity and access in physical education; media facilities planning and environmental design.

Early Childhood Education: Jane Lannak, Ph.D., USC.
Educational Media and Technology: David Whittier, Ed.D., Boston University.
Elementary Education: Carol Jenkins, Ph.D., Boston College.
English Education/English and Language Arts Education: Thomas Culliton Jr., Ed.D., Boston University.
Human Movement: John Cheffers, Ed.D., Temple.
Master of Arts in Teaching (biology, chemistry, English, French, German, history, Italian, Latin and classical humanities, mathematics, physics, political science, psychology, Russian, sociology): Stephan Ellenwood, Ph.D., Northwestern.
Mathematics Education: Carol Findell, Ed.D., Boston University.
Reading Education: Thomas Culliton Jr., Ed.D., Boston University.
Science Education: Stephan Ellenwood, Ph.D., Northwestern.
Social Studies Education: Stephan Ellenwood, Ph.D., Northwestern.

Developmental Studies and Counseling
Roselmina Indrisano, Chairman; Ed.D., Boston University.

Faculty research and teaching interests: adolescent and adult development; moral education; cultural and ethnic aspects of human development; cross-cultural, bilingual, and multicultural education; literacy and literacy assessment across the life span; bilingual education and second language teaching; theoretical and applied linguistics; acquisition of signed and spoken languages by deaf and hearing-impaired children; counselor effectiveness; family systems and family therapy; counseling women; human sexuality counseling; social psychology of leisure.

Applied Linguistics (joint program with the Graduate School): Bruce Fraser, Ph.D., MIT.
Bilingual Education: Maria Brisk, Ph.D., New Mexico.
Counseling and Counseling Psychology: Mary Ni, Ed.D., Harvard.
Developmental Studies: Roselmina Indrisano, Ed.D., Boston University.
Education of the Deaf: Robert Hoffmeister, Ph.D., Minnesota.
Health Education: Gerald Fain, Ph.D., Maryland.
Human Development and Education: Deborah Youngman, Ed.D., Boston University.
Leisure Studies Education: Gerald Fain, Ph.D., Maryland.
Modern Foreign Language Education: Yuan Feng, Ph.D., Washington (Seattle).
Second Language Education (TESOL): Steven Molinsky, Ph.D., Harvard.

Special Education
Gerald Fain, Chairman; Ph.D., Maryland.

Faculty research and teaching interests: learning disabilities; communicative disorders; developmental disabilities; mental retardation, behavioral and emotional disturbances in children; collaboration with general education teachers and parents of children with disabilities; health and disabilities; implementation and evaluation of curricula; assessment; teaching exceptional children in special and regular settings; learning and cognition.

Department specializations: learning and behavioral disabilities, severe developmental and social disabilities, young children with disabilities, leisure, alternative community settings. The faculty contact for all department specializations: Gerald Fain, Ph.D., Maryland.

Boston University, Charles River Campus.

DEPAUL UNIVERSITY

School of Education

Program of Study

The School of Education offers a Doctor of Education (Ed.D.) degree with concentrations in curriculum studies or educational leadership. The program is designed primarily for professionals who are already engaged in educational practice and who wish to become leaders capable of transforming schools or other educational institutions. It contains a core set of courses that require students to examine themselves as professional practitioners situated within larger social and cultural contexts. It also includes seminars in which students engage in disciplined inquiry in a continuous and ongoing way throughout their doctoral studies. The students are encouraged to examine issues related to the contexts in which they work. In addition to the components of the program required of all, students select an area of concentration. Currently, two areas of concentration are envisioned: educational leadership, which includes the option for the superintendent's endorsement for the Illinois Administrative Certificate, and curriculum studies.

The primary audience for the Ed.D. program consists of educational professionals who wish to improve the quality of their work in their current roles or to prepare themselves for new roles. This Ed.D. program is uniquely designed to link theory with practice.

Also available are master's programs with the following majors: curriculum studies: educational leadership; human development and learning; human services and counseling, with a specialty in early intervention; human services management; higher education, agencies, and families; school guidance; language, literacy, and specialized instruction, with specialties in bilingual education, learning disabilities, reading, and social-emotional disorders; teaching and learning—elementary and secondary for first certificate students. Students should consult the DePaul University Web site for details or write to the Graduate Director.

Research Facilities

The Educational Resource Center is located within the John Richardson Library adjacent to the School of Education Offices. The DePaul libraries provide resources and services to students through seven libraries. The delivery of information and materials is increasingly linked to computer technologies. Access to materials in all the DePaul libraries is provided through ILLINET Online, the libraries' online catalog and circulation system. From the same terminals, students and faculty members can identify and check out books from forty-four other colleges and universities in Illinois. ILLNET Online also allows users to search the catalogs of more than 800 libraries around the state. Materials from libraries across the United States can be located and obtained through other computer networks. Electronic access to periodical articles and other information resources in the social sciences, business, humanities, and sciences is readily available through online and compact disc (CD-ROM) databases.

Financial Aid

The Office of Student Financial Services provides comprehensive educational financial planning and coordinates a variety of federal, state, private, and institutional aid programs. Each financial aid program has its own particular regulations, requirements, procedures, forms, and disbursement schedules. A limited number of graduate assistantships for full time students are available.

Cost of Study

For the 1998–99 academic year, tuition for full-time and part-time study is $320 per credit hour.

Living and Housing Costs

On-campus living is not available for graduate students. The University's Department of Residence Life assists students in finding apartment housing.

Student Group

Student population is multicultural in nature. Seventy-five percent are women and 19.5 percent are members of minority groups.

Location

DePaul's School of Education is located in the scenic Lincoln Park area of Chicago. The campus is readily accessible to the Loop, museums, and cultural events offered by the city.

The School

The School of Education believes that schools require professionals who will exercise skill, understanding, and judgment. It strives for the positive transformation of people and society. The first mission is that as an urban institution, the School is committed to improving primary and secondary education in the metropolitan area and, in particular, in the city of Chicago. The second mission is, in light of the religious character of DePaul, that the School is committed to respect for individuals, an appreciation of diversity, and the ongoing examination of values. Finally, the third mission is that the School is committed to the Vincentian mission of service to the poor and to changing those conditions and settings that perpetuate poverty.

The School of Education seeks students with intellectual promise, social responsibility, and those personal leadership qualities appropriate to graduate-level education. In light of the urban, Catholic, and Vincentian mission of DePaul University and the public need for quality education, the School of Education intends to prepare professionals to work in schools and in settings that support the work of schools and to provide practicing professional educators with degree programs, in-service programs, and other opportunities to develop advanced skills.

Applying

The admissions process must reflect and enact the principles and values of the program regarding engagement, reflection, the exercise of agency, working for change, and a commitment to professional development and learning. The first requirement is an orientation session prior to submitting an application. This session covers the philosophical framework of the program, its values, and its expectations. It includes other activities that would help potential applicants to make an informed decision about whether or not to apply. The second component is a written piece (approximately three pages) in the form of a personal statement in which the applicant discusses why he or she is interested in further study and articulates an issue or problem of interest or concern. Dialogue with two or three faculty members of the Ed.D. program is also required. This conversation will provide an opportunity for candidates to become familiar with the program and the faculty members as well as an opportunity for faculty members to get to know prospective candidates. (Applicants living outside of the Chicago area will engage in an appropriate, reciprocal substitute for this dialogue and for the orientation described above.) Three letters of recommendation are needed: one personal, from someone outside of the immediate workplace, and two additional letters from colleagues, administrators, or supervisors. Finally, all transcripts of undergraduate and graduate work are needed to ascertain the nature of previous educational experiences, course work, and areas of specialization.

Correspondence and Information

Marianne C. Murphy
Director of Graduate Programs
School of Education
DePaul University
2320 North Kenmore Avenue, 3rd Floor
Chicago, Illinois 60614-3298
Telephone: 773-325-7323
E-mail: mmurphy@wppost.depaul.edu
World Wide Web: http://www.depaul.edu/~educate

DePaul University

THE FACULTY

Administration

Barbara A. Sizemore, Dean; Ph.D., Chicago.
Gayle Mindes, Associate Dean; Ed.D., Loyola.
Charles Doyle, Assistant Dean and Certification Officer; M.Ed., Boston University.
Barbara Radner, Director of Ed.D. Program; Ph.D., Chicago.

Doctoral Core

Enora Brown, Ph.D., Chicago.
Anthony Dosen, C.M., Ph.D., Marquette.
Margaret Harrigan, Ed.D., Loyola.
Stephen Haymes, Ph.D., Miami (Ohio).
Peter Pereira, A.M.T., Harvard.
Amira Proweller, Ph.D., SUNY at Buffalo.
Barbara Radner, Ph.D., Chicago.
John Rury, Ph.D., Wisconsin.

Educational Leadership

Anthony Dosen, C.M., Ph.D., Marquette.
Margaret Harrigan, Ed.D., Loyola.
Joan Lakebrink, Ph.D., Wisconsin–Madison.
Angela Miller, Ph.D., Illinois at Chicago.
Vera Rhimes, Ph.D., Miami (Ohio).

Curriculum Studies

Sandra Jackson, Ph.D., Berkeley.
Jeffrey Kuzmic, Ph.D., Indiana.
Carole Mitchener, Ph.D., Denver.
Peter Pereira, A.M.T., Harvard.
Barbara Radner, Ph.D., Chicago.

Students have significant opportunities for hands-on experience.

DOWLING COLLEGE

School of Education

Programs of Study

Dowling, The Personal College®, is committed to encouraging and providing for each individual's potential with small classes and dedicated faculty members. Dowling offers students Master of Science in Education (M.S.Ed.) degree programs in elementary, secondary, special education, reading teacher, and reading/special education. Dowling College's Doctorate of Education (Ed.D.) degree program in educational administration was designed to train leaders for the educational and nonprofit sectors. Dowling College professional diploma programs in educational technology and educational administration and coaching certificate programs are also offered.

While participating in the M.S.Ed. programs, students gain interpersonal, organizational, and decision-making skills for effective teaching. The programs provide students with a comprehensive foundation in curriculum, instructional, professional, and organizational development. Students are actively engaged in curriculum decision making while studying its nature and structure in relation to learning.

Building students' classroom teaching skills is the focus of instructional development. At the other end of the spectrum is professional development, which stresses updating and upgrading skills and the importance of networking with similarly disciplined professionals. Organizational development highlights interpersonal strategies and group techniques needed to function more effectively in a school environment.

The Potentially Gifted Students With Learning Disabilities Program challenges graduate students to tutor people requiring compensating strategies to empower them toward independent learning.

Research Facilities

The Nicholas and Constance Racanelli Center for Learning Resources houses Dowling's library. Its collections include 182,661 volumes, 1,100 current periodicals, 577,097 microforms, and 10,577 government documents.

Another valuable research tool is the Online Computer Library Center (OCLC), used by Dowling's librarians to access the collections of thousands of libraries, universities, and research centers worldwide.

The Academic Computer Center, which has three multimedia classrooms, three labs for individual use, and a faculty resource center, is available to students during extended day and evening hours. The College's membership in the New York State Education and Research Network (Nysernet) serves as a gateway to the Internet, a global network providing access to thousands of computers for research and communication.

Individualized tutorial programs are available for students who need help with the English language.

Financial Aid

While scholarship programs are available, various financing methods can be explored with a personal financial aid counselor. The College offers students individual guidance on flexible payment options, such as a tuition- and fee-deferred payment plan for each semester. Credit cards may also be used to pay tuition and fees. Additionally, for two academic years new students may have their tuition charges frozen at their entering semester's rate.

Cost of Study

Tuition is $440 per graduate credit, and certain student fees are applicable.

Living and Housing Costs

On-campus housing is available in apartment-style suites from $3600 per semester, and there are ample off-campus apartments within a reasonable distance of the College.

Student Group

Dowling's student body is mostly from Long Island, with an increasingly national recruitment scope. Likewise, the College's international range continues to grow since the addition of the National Aviation and Transportation Center®, a unique facility dedicated to studying and researching global transportation issues.

International students represent thirty-one countries. Of Dowling's diverse student population, 37 percent are graduate students. The same percentage of students are enrolled in the School of Education.

Location

The 52-acre, riverside campus is William K. Vanderbilt's former estate. About 50 miles east of midtown Manhattan, it is within reach of the city's sights and near Long Island's beautiful beaches, parks, and cultural attractions.

Dowling also has sites at the World Trade Institute, New York City, and Dowling's Graduate Center, Riverhead, Long Island.

The College and The School

The Oakdale and Riverhead sites offer M.S.Ed., Ed.D., professional diploma, and coaching certificate programs. A practicum can be completed at Dowling's Literacy Center, which provides diagnostic and remedial services for elementary school children who are weak in reading/study skills.

Graduate students must be clear thinkers with oral and written competence and maintain a minimum 3.0 average to prevent academic warning. Students are monitored by the faculty and Teacher Assessment Competency Team. They will be notified if problems are identified and advised of appropriate action.

Applying

Applications are available from Enrollment Services, Dowling College, Idle Hour Boulevard, Oakdale, Long Island, New York 11769-1999. Graduate candidates must have a baccalaureate from an accredited institution and a minimum 3.0 GPA in their undergraduate major. For professional diplomas in educational administration, applicants need permanent teacher certification and an appropriate master's degree. Each candidate's academic record and work experience are considered when being interviewed by a faculty adviser.

Correspondence and Information

Dr. Kathryn Padovano, Dean
School of Education
Dowling College
Idle Hour Boulevard
Oakdale, Long Island, New York 11769-1999

Telephone: 516-244-3171
516-DOWLING
800-DOWLING (toll-free)
Fax: 516-589-6644
E-mail: rowek@dowling.edu (Enrollment Services)
World Wide Web: http://www.dowling.edu

Dowling College

THE FACULTY

Conducted within the personalized atmosphere of a small college, Dowling's graduate education programs are run by highly qualified, experienced professionals. Faculty members are noted for their presentations, scholarly works, expert testimony, professional standing, and national conference participation.

The Racanelli Center is the College's learning resource facility.

A side view of Fortunoff Hall, which was once the summer home of William K. Vanderbilt and now serves as the administrative center of the College.

EASTERN COLLEGE

Graduate Programs in Education

Programs of Study

Eastern College offers graduate programs that speak to the multicultural nature of professional education today. The College offers graduate and professional development programs and courses in supervision, teaching, and training that are designed to develop education professionals for the twenty-first century.

The Master of Education (M.Ed.) in multicultural education requires 30 semester credits and provides educators with the skills needed to work with multicultural populations as well as to diversify their teaching to include materials and resources from many cultures. The program may be combined with the following certifications at Instructional I or II levels: early childhood, elementary education, K–12 foreign language (French and Spanish), reading, secondary education (biology, chemistry, communications, English, mathematics, and social studies), and K–12 special education. General Supervisor I or II certification is also available in the teaching fields listed. The Master of Education in school health services is a 30-credit program designed for those health majors or nurses who hold or wish to earn either Instructional I or II level certification in K–12 health or Education Specialist I or II as a school nurse. The program is designed to broaden and enhance the professional skills appropriate for those who provide health services to children in schools. The Master of Arts (M.A.) in educational counseling is designed for those who wish Education Specialist I or II certification as an elementary and/or secondary counselor. The Master of Science (M.S.) in school psychology is designed for those who wish Education Specialist I or II certification as a school psychologist.

Research Facilities

The Frank Warner Memorial Library houses a wide collection of bound volumes, periodicals, and microfilms. The computer center operates a minicomputer system with more than fifty terminals and IBM-compatible personal computers.

Financial Aid

Financial assistance is available through federally sponsored loan programs and graduate assistantships. Assistantships are limited and awarded competitively to full-time students (enrolled in a minimum of 9 credit hours per semester) for work performed as researchers, grading assistants, and office administrators. Assistantships can provide a waiver for as much as half the cost of tuition in exchange for work hours. The hours worked are determined by the amount of the stipend. Financial aid in the form of assistantships is usually not provided during Winterim or summer sessions and is not available if courses are being repeated.

Cost of Study

For the 1998–99 academic year, graduate tuition is $366 per semester hour. Deferred payment and monthly payments are available. Estimated fees for 1998–99 are $650 for all students. Books and miscellaneous expenses are approximately $3200 per year.

Living and Housing Costs

Eastern College does not have on-campus housing for graduate students. Estimated living expenses for a single student are approximately $4400 for housing and $2700 for food per year. Married couples typically spend $6900 for housing and $3400 for food.

Student Group

The graduate program enrollment for fall 1997, including both full- and part-time students, totaled 555; 165 were enrolled in education programs. Students exhibit a diverse undergraduate educational background, and some hold earned graduate degrees. Full-time students come from across the United States, and part-time students commute from throughout the Philadelphia metropolitan area.

Location

Eastern College is located in St. Davids, one of the western Main Line suburbs of Philadelphia. Center City is 20 minutes away. St. Davids, primarily residential in nature, is complemented by Philadelphia, which provides a variety of cultural, social, spiritual, and athletic activities.

The College

Eastern College is known for its innovative academic programs, caring community, commitment to social action, and exceptionally beautiful campus. Class sizes are small, and professors are both role models to their students and highly accomplished experts in their fields. In addition to integrating faith and learning, Eastern's creative academic programs encourage students to learn from many disciplines. The campus community is highly diverse, with a multiethnic student body that includes representatives from more than thirty countries.

Applying

To apply, interested students should contact the graduate admissions office for an application. Eastern requests that two letters of recommendation and official transcripts from all schools attended accompany all applications. Applications are accepted as received. The nonrefundable application fee is $35.

Correspondence and Information

Graduate Admissions Office
Eastern College
1300 Eagle Road
St. Davids, Pennsylvania 19087
Telephone: 610-341-5972
Fax: 610-341-1466
E-mail: gradadm@eastern.edu
World Wide Web: http://www.eastern.edu

Eastern College

THE FACULTY

Jennifer Addey, Adjunct Professor; M.Ed., Eastern.
Bernice Baxter, Professor of School Health Services and Director of School Health Services Programs; M.Ed., Temple.
Esther Biermann, Adjunct Professor of Education; M.Ed., Eastern.
Patricia Boehne, Professor of Romance Languages; Ph.D., Indiana.
Lynda Bouldin-Hawkins, Adjunct Professor; M.Ed., Beaver.
Heewon Chang, Adjunct Professor; Ph.D., Oregon.
Althea Cousins, Adjunct Professor of Educational Counseling; Ed.D., Walden.
Marguerite Desanctis, Adjunct Professor; M.Ed., Temple.
Patricia Dixon, Adjunct Professor of Education; D.Ed., Penn State.
Joan Eagles, Adjunct Professor; M.Ed., West Chester, M.A., Immaculata.
David Fraser, Professor of Sociology; M.Div., Fuller Theological Seminary; Ph.D., Vanderbilt.
David Greenhalgh, Associate Professor of Education; Ed.D., Boston University.
Marie Koals, Associate Professor of Education; Ed.D., Lehigh.
Barbara Launi, Adjunct Professor; M.Ed., Penn State.
Helen W. Loeb, Professor of Education, Director of Graduate Education, and Chair, Education Department; Ph.D., Bryn Mawr.
Gregory McCord, Adjunct Professor; M.Ed., Millersville.
Allison McFarland, Assistant Professor of Health and Physical Education; Ph.D., Kansas.
Lillian D. McKethan, Associate Professor of Education and Director of Special Education; M.Ed., Temple.
Harry Mercurio, Adjunct Professor; M.Ed., Widener.
Anne Murray, Adjunct Professor; M.A., Kansas State.
Cabrini Carole Ney, Adjunct Professor; M.Ed., Temple.
Zelicia Porter, Adjunct Professor; Ph.D., Pennsylvania.
Josef Ridgway, Adjunct Professor; M.Ed., Virginia.
Deborah Schmeck, Adjunct Professor; Ed.D., Lehigh.
Martha Shalitta, Professor of Psychology; D.Ed., Penn State.
F. Eric Sills, Professor of Health and Physical Education; Ph.D., Temple.
Robert Stremme, Adjunct Professor; M.Ed., Penn State.
David Tyson, Associate Professor of Psychology; Ph.D., Penn State.
Deborah Warrick, Adjunct Professor; M.A., West Chester.
Elaine Wright, Adjunct Professor; M.Ed., Millersville, M.Ed., Immaculata.
Frank Wright, Adjunct Professor; M.A., Villanova.
George Zampetti, Adjunct Professor of Mathematics; M.S., Pennsylvania.

EMORY UNIVERSITY

Division of Educational Studies

Programs of Study

The Division of Educational Studies offers a full range of graduate programs that includes the Ph.D. in educational studies; the Master of Arts (M.A.), which requires a thesis; the Master of Arts in Teaching (M.A.T.), for individuals seeking both a master's degree and their initial teaching field certification; as well as the Master of Education (M.Ed.) and sixth-year Diploma for Advanced Study in Teaching (DAST) programs for previously certified or currently practicing teachers. The Ph.D. in educational studies is designed for individuals with interest in acquiring strong research skills and advanced knowledge in a specialty area within a program that offers an interdisciplinary approach to the study of education with a distinct emphasis on urban and comparative issues. In particular, the Division seeks to provide students with a foundation for understanding the social and cultural context in which education occurs and for interpreting the complex relationships among education, the individual, and society. The Ph.D. program typically takes four years for full-time students to complete and requires two qualifying papers of publishable quality in addition to the dissertation. The three master's (M.A., M.A.T., M.Ed.) and one post-master's (DAST) programs typically take four consecutive semesters, including summers, to complete.

Research Facilities

The Division is housed in the North Decatur Building. Specialized science, mathematics, and statistics lab classrooms are equipped with state-of-the-art facilities. A technology-enhanced Curriculum Learning Center houses PowerMac and Wintel computers, all with direct connections to campus UNIX computers and the Internet. The lab has advanced multimedia capabilities along with research application tools and collections of current K–12 software in the major content areas. Another classroom is fiber-optic–linked to the Next Generation Schools Project with Fernbank Elementary School, Fernbank Science Center, Druid Hills High School, and Egleston Children's Hospital, providing distance learning research and teaching possibilities for faculty and graduate students in the Division. Other research opportunities are possible in conjunction with the Center for Urban Learning/Teaching and Urban Research in Education and Schools, the CULTURES Project, or the IEA Study of Civic Education, the U.S. case study.

Financial Aid

Financial support for full-time Ph.D. students includes a stipend and a tuition waiver. The 1998–99 stipend is set at $11,000, with small increases typical over the four years of funding. Applicants may also request to be considered for the highly competitive University-wide George W. Woodruff Fellowships and/or Emory Minority Graduate Fellowships ($15,000 annually). Additional support for Ph.D. candidates is often available for research-related activities conducted during the summer. A fifth year of funding is possible through the Dean's Teaching Fellowship competition of the Teaching Assistant and Teacher Training (TATTO) Program. Tuition Assistance Grants (TAG) for 50 percent of tuition are available to all local area teachers enrolled in pre- and in-service graduate degree programs (M.A.T., M.Ed., and DAST). To attract individuals, including outstanding minority candidates whose research interests closely match faculty interests and/or currently funded projects, the division recruits aggressively and is often able to supplement the base awards outlined above.

Cost of Study

Tuition for 1998–99 is $21,770, and yearly increases are to be expected.

Living and Housing Costs

A variety of on-campus and off-campus housing is available. On-campus housing includes a graduate, professional, and undergraduate student residential complex offering a wide variety of accommodations ranging from high-rise tower to attractive efficiencies and one- and two-bedroom garden apartments. The complex includes recreational, conference, and seminar facilities and is convenient to campus. A small number of furnished units are available. Further information is available from the Department of Residential Facilities, Graduate and Family Housing, Emory University, 1560 Clairmont Road, Atlanta, Georgia 30322; telephone, 727-8830, or fax, 727-8834.

Student Group

There are 34 current Ph.D. students (14 part-time and 20 full-time). Typically, 4 new fully supported (tuition plus stipend) full-time Ph.D. students are recruited each year. A new cohort group of 21 interns begin the four-semester M.A.T. program each spring term. Their program continues over that summer and following fall and finishes after the second spring semester. Care is taken to provide classroom field experiences in a wide range of teaching situations with culturally diverse student populations. Most M.Ed. and DAST students are carefully selected, experienced, metro-area classroom teachers who provide classroom field sites and supervision for the M.A.T. preservice graduate students. The externs also typically number 10 per cohort group and start their programs in the summer and finish the following summer.

Location

Atlanta is the capital of Georgia and the major city of the southeastern region. The city, host of the 1996 Summer Olympic games, is young, dynamic, and progressive. With metro-area population of more than 2 million, Atlanta is growing not only in size but in maturity: a new rapid transit system is expanding to serve the south, west, and north; increased attention is being paid to the city's past and its historical development; and the renovated old neighborhoods and bold new construction in the downtown area aptly symbolize the city's vital blend of tradition and vision.

The University and The Division

The University campus stands on 620 hilly and wooded acres 6 miles northeast of downtown Atlanta. Since its founding in 1836, Emory University has grown into a national teaching, research, and service center with an enrollment exceeding 9,300. The Division of Educational Studies is one of the twenty-three departments and divisions that comprise the Graduate School of Arts and Sciences.

Applying

Applicants for the Ph.D. degree should have already obtained a master's degree and have had some classroom teaching experience. A complete application requires a written statement of professional goals, three letters of recommendation, transcripts, and an official score report of the GRE taken within 5 years of the application date. The appropriate forms can be obtained from the Graduate School of Arts and Sciences. The application deadline for Ph.D. applicants is January 20, 1999, for fall 1999 entrance. Applicants for Woodruff and EMGF Fellowships competitions should submit applications one month before this date. Applicants for all other graduate degree programs should call 404-727-6468 for their specific application deadline.

Correspondence and Information

Dr. Glen Avant
Program Development Coordinator
Division of Educational Studies
Emory University
Atlanta, Georgia 30322
Telephone: 404-727-0612
Fax: 404-727-2799
E-mail: gavant@emory.edu
World Wide Web: http://www.emory.edu/EDUCATION

Emory University

THE FACULTY AND THEIR RESEARCH

Glen Reed Avant, Program Development Coordinator; Ph.D., Emory. Work role expectations of school principals, effect of individual reading instruction on locus of control and locus of evaluation, diagnosing and remediating specific reading abnormalities. Current projects include recruitment and retention of minority students in teacher education and teachers' awareness of and appreciation for their students' diverse backgrounds.

Joseph P. Cadray, Assistant Professor and Coordinator of Preservice Teaching; Ph.D., New Orleans. Developing reflective classroom teachers who understand the social and cultural contexts of teaching and learning, reflective choice making in teacher education field experiences.

Sandra Damico, Professor; Ph.D., Florida. At-risk adolescents; school policies, especially as they affect adolescents; school improvement; social-cultural school environments and learning; political socialization. Current projects include completing a book on school policies and their effect on general-track adolescents and a series of studies on the relationship between participation in high school extracurricular activities and adult civic and political behavior.

George Engelhard, Professor; Ph.D., Chicago. Role of assessment in improving education, development of affective human characteristics, history of measurement theory, assessment of written composition. Current projects include models of judgment and educational assessment.

Susan H. Frost, Adjunct Associate Professor; Ed.D., Georgia. Planning and decision making in higher education, decision making and college student outcomes. Current projects include public policy and university-level decision making: theory and practice.

Carole L. Hahn, Professor; Ed.D., Indiana. Cross-national studies of citizenship education, gender issues and social studies, controversial issues discussion and classroom climate. Current projects include Adolescent Political Attitudes and Citizenship Education in Selected Western Democracies (U.K., U.S., Germany, Netherlands, Denmark); IEA Study of Civic Education, U.S. case study.

Jacqueline Jordan Irvine, Charles Howard Candler Professor of Urban Education; Ph.D., Georgia State. Effective instructional strategies for African-American students, issues of race, gender, class, and culture in schools. Current projects include position as Director, Center for Urban Learning/Teaching and Urban Research in Education and Schools.

Robert J. Jensen, Associate Professor and Director of Graduate Studies; Ed.D., Georgia. Mathematics education, problem posing, mathematical thinking processes, integrating technology in the teaching of mathematics, learning of algebra. Current projects include professional development in the area of technology with middle grade and high school mathematics and science teachers.

Mary Anne Lindskog, Adjunct Assistant Professor; Ph.D., Penn State. Teacher preparation, history and philosophy of teacher education, social and cultural foundations of education. Current projects include the role of critical pedagogy in teacher preparation.

Jeffrey E. Mirel, Professor and Director of the Division of Educational Studies; Ph.D., Michigan. History of American education, curriculum in the American high school, urban school systems. Current projects include the forthcoming publication of the book *Conflict and Curriculum in the American High School, 1890–1990*.

Jennifer E. Obidah, Assistant Professor; Ph.D., Berkeley. Social and cultural context of urban schooling, focusing on issues of violence, multicultural education, race, and cultural differences between teachers and students; teachers as critical pedagogists. Current projects include completing an article about the classroom practice of critical pedagogy and an article on violence among African-American middle school students.

Frank Pajares, Assistant Professor; Ph.D., Florida. Preservice teachers'/teachers' beliefs, role of self-efficacy in academic settings, self-concepts theory. Current projects include book on self-beliefs and school achievement, completing series of studies and articles on self-efficacy of middle school students, and continuing research on preservice teachers' beliefs.

Donald E. Riechard, Associate Professor; Ph.D., Ohio State. Science concept development, environmental science, science policy, teacher education. Current projects include studies on the perception of risk from environmental hazards.

Charles Strickland, Professor; Ph.D., Wisconsin. History of childhood, families and education. Current projects include History of American Childhood through Autobiography; American Childhood, 1940–1963 (G.K. Hall/Twayne series on the History of American Children).

Emilie Vanessa Siddle Walker, Associate Professor; Ed.D., Harvard. Historical and cultural influences on the teaching and learning of African-American students. Current projects include synthesis of research on the segregated schooling of African-American children and data collection on the experiences of African-American parents and children in desegregated schools.

FAIRFIELD UNIVERSITY

Graduate School of Education and Allied Professions

Programs of Study

The Graduate School's programs prepare students for professional positions in schools, agencies, and corporate settings as well as for entrance into doctoral studies.

Programs lead to the Master of Arts (M.A.), the Certificate of Advanced Study (C.A.S.), and/or state certification. Courses are offered within the following majors: curriculum and teaching, including early childhood education, elementary teaching, secondary teaching, and professional development for teachers; TESOL; bilingual/multicultural education; counselor education, including school counseling, community counseling, student affairs, and college counseling; school psychology; applied psychology, including human services, foundations of advanced psychology (predoctoral study), and industrial/organizational psychology; special education, including bilingual special education, the consulting special education teacher, and teaching the talented and gifted; media/educational technology; computers in education; and marriage and family therapy. Most courses are held in the late afternoon and evening.

An international exchange program leading to a master's degree in multicultural education with study in Lisbon, Portugal, or Shanghai, China, is available.

Master of Arts candidates must complete a minimum of 33 credits (depending on their program) and pass a comprehensive examination or write a master's thesis.

Certificate of Advanced Study (sixth-year) candidates must complete 30 credits, including 15 credits in the major field and other courses required by the program, and an internship or practicum at the end of most programs.

Research Facilities

The Nyselius Library contains 285,000 carefully selected bound volumes, the equivalent of 65,000 volumes in microform, and 1,800 journals and newspapers. A media department provides convenient use of AV and nonprint materials and supervises a microcomputer lab. Interlibrary loan and online and CD-ROM bibliographic search services are available. The library has an automated circulation system and is open more than 104 hours per week.

Financial Aid

A limited number of graduate assistantships providing tuition remission of 6 to 12 credits are available from the Graduate School. Assistantships are also available from other departments such as Residence Life, and some of these provide free tuition plus a stipend. Periodically, funds are available through federal and other grants. The Financial Aid Office assists those applying for loans and other forms of financial aid.

Cost of Study

For 1998–99, tuition is $350 per credit. Most courses are 3 credits. The registration fee is $20 per semester. Laboratory and/or material fees of $15 per credit are charged for selected courses in psychology, computer instruction, and media.

Living and Housing Costs

Limited housing is available on campus for graduate students. Rents for off-campus housing within reasonable commuting distance begin at $450 per month for a room in a private home and $700 per month for an efficiency apartment. Often students share apartments. Student Support Services (telephone: 203-254-4000 Ext. 4211) maintains a computerized list of off-campus housing. The Dean's Office (telephone: 203-254-4000 Ext. 2413) also has off-campus housing information.

Student Group

The majority of students are employed by boards of education in the area and attend classes part-time in the late afternoon and evening. An increasing number of students are seeking state certification as part of a career change. Many others anticipate working outside of school settings in areas such as community counseling, marriage and family therapy, media production, and applied psychology. There are approximately 800 students; 100 are full-time.

Location

Fairfield is a suburban Connecticut town bordering Long Island Sound. It is 1 hour from New York City, 3 hours from Boston, and about 30 minutes from Yale University. Fairfield University occupies a 225-acre landscaped and wooded campus. The town has numerous beaches; a marina; a launching and storage area for small boats; and public athletic facilities, including tennis courts, golf courses, and softball and baseball fields. A public library, town-sponsored concerts, churches of various denominations, a historical society, a train station, an art-film movie house, and two multiplex cinemas are near the campus.

The University and The School

Fairfield University offers Jesuit education at its best. Its long-standing tradition of preparing professionals in education and human services dates back to 1950 when the first classes in graduate education were offered. *U.S. News & World Report* rates Fairfield University among the top three comprehensive universities in the North.

Applying

The counselor education program admits students three times a year, with application deadlines of February 1, July 1, and November 1. The marriage and family therapy program admits students two times a year, with deadlines of February 15 and October 15. The elementary education program admits students twice a year, with a fall deadline of March 1 and a spring deadline of October 15. The school psychology program also admits students twice a year, with deadlines of January 15 for fall and September 1 for spring admission. The remaining programs admit students on a rolling basis. Applicants for the M.A. must hold a bachelor's degree and have a minimum quality point average of 2.67. Applicants for C.A.S. must hold a master's degree and have a minimum quality point average of 3.0. Individual programs may set specific requirements regarding interviews, test scores, course waivers, and undergraduate courses. The application fee for formal admission is $40. Special status students may enroll for a maximum of 9 credits before being admitted.

Correspondence and Information

Assistant Dean Karen Creecy
Graduate School of Education
and Allied Professions
Fairfield University
Fairfield, Connecticut 06430

Telephone: 203-254-4250 or 254-4000 Ext. 2414
Fax: 203-254-4241
E-mail: klcreecy@fair1.fairfield.edu
World Wide Web: http://www.fairfield.edu

Fairfield University

THE FACULTY AND THEIR RESEARCH

Margaret C. Deignan, Associate Professor and Dean; Ph.D., Yeshiva. Cognitive development, learning disabilities, emotional disturbances, consultation and collaboration.
Janine Bernard, Professor; Ph.D., Purdue. Clinical supervision, divorce adjustment, multicultural issues in counseling.
Patricia E. Calderwood, Assistant Professor; Ph.D., Pennsylvania. Teacher education, school transformation, anthropology of education, ethnographic and participatory action research, notion of community.
Anthony Costa, Assistant Professor; C.A.S., Fairfield. Issues in adolescent homosexuality, cooperating teacher proficiency, evaluation and assessment of beginning and student teachers.
Faith-Anne Dohm, Assistant Professor; Ph.D., Maryland. Risk factors for psychological disorders, impression formation and nonverbal behavior, the process of research, deficits in persistence.
Daniel Geller, Professor; Ph.D., Yeshiva. Disabilities, families with disabled members, parent/child relationships, parent/school collaboration.
Harold Hackney, Professor; Ed.D., Massachusetts. Counseling processes, professional issues in counseling.
Lynn M. Haley-Banez, Assistant Professor; Ph.D., Kent State. Multicultural issues in counseling, group work, domestic violence.
Ingeborg Haug, Associate Professor; D.Min., Andover Newton Theological School. Couple therapy, professional ethics, parenting issues.
Ibrahim Hefzallah, Professor; Ph.D., Ohio State. Television advertising, children and television, applications of instructional technologies, multimedia applications, telecommunications and education.
Francis W. Lewis, S.J., Professor; Ed.D., Harvard. Piaget, philosophy and education.
Paula Gill Lopez, Assistant Professor; Ph.D., Berkeley. Dropout prevention, professional support systems for teachers and beginning school psychologists, intervention strategies in urban school systems, collaborative consultation, school-university partnerships.
Alice E. McIntyre, Assistant Professor; Ph.D., Boston College. Multicultural antiracist education, participatory action research.
Julianna Poole, S.S.N.D., Assistant Professor; Ed.D., Rochester. English as a second language, bilingual and multicultural education, teacher education.
Rona Preli, Associate Professor; Ph.D., Virginia Tech. Alcoholism and family structure, multicultural issues in counseling.
David A. Zera, Assistant Professor; Ph.D., Connecticut. Learning disabilities, attention, executive function, cognition, self-organizing systems

FITCHBURG STATE COLLEGE

Division of Graduate and Continuing Education
Education Department

Programs of Study

The Division of Graduate and Continuing Education offers the Certificate of Advanced Graduate Study (CAGS), the Master of Arts in Teaching (M.A.T.), and the Master of Education (M.Ed.) degrees in a total of sixteen program areas in education. CAGS, designed to develop reflective, person-centered educational practitioners who can effectively construct, articulate, and apply educational theory and research, are offered in educational leadership and management, educational staff development, and consultation and peer leadership. M.A.T. degrees are available in biology, earth science, English, history, and mathematics for students wishing to expand their backgrounds and skills in teaching in their subject area, and to expand their strategies for teaching from a multicultural, gender-balanced perspective.

The M.Ed. is offered encompassing ten different areas: arts in education; educational leadership and management; early childhood, elementary, middle school, secondary education, and educational leadership and management; occupational, science, and special education; and technology education. These programs are designed to assist the school educator in developing as a reflective, child/youth-centered practitioner able to effectively articulate and apply child and/or youth development and educational theory and research.

In addition, the M.S. in counseling program offers a concentration in school guidance counseling to prepare professionals for Massachusetts standard certification at either the elementary or secondary levels. The concentration in school adjustment counseling, available through the M.S. in counseling and CAGS in interdisciplinary studies, leads to certification as a school social worker/school adjustment counselor.

All programs are offered evenings on a part-time basis and usually require the equivalent of two to three years to complete at a rate of 6 to 9 credits per semester.

Research Facilities

The College Library provides 96 hours of weekly service, online access to the library's catalog, and more than sixty databases via the library's home page. A CD-ROM local area network provides ready access to heavily utilized subscription services. There are approximately 263,000 volumes and 1,467 current periodicals, supplemented by the 404,000-item Educational Resources Information Center (ERIC).

The College Computer Center serves the general administrative, educational, and research needs of the campus. The Tricord ES8000 and CDC Cyber 932-32 mainframes serve the administrative computer needs of the College. An Alpha Server 2100 acts as the central locus for faculty and staff members and students, providing an enhanced environment for computer science applications and e-mail and Internet access capabilities. A Proliant DHCP server hosts TCP/IP to the entire campus. Five accessible general-purpose labs, five residence hall labs, and one VAX terminal lab exist for general use. Falcon Net, FSC's major telecommuncations upgrade, offers each classroom and residence hall high-speed T-1 network connectivity, making possible the full potential of distance learning and videoconferencing and a scalable infrastructure prepared for the growth of tomorrow.

The McKay Campus School Teacher Education Center provides students in clinical master's degree programs with opportunities to conduct action research in a preschool through grade 5 urban setting.

Financial Aid

Graduate scholarships are available in amounts ranging from $110 to $1790 per year. Scholarships are awarded annually in the form of tuition and fee waivers. Minority students seeking teacher certification are given preference. The application deadline is February 1 of each academic year. Students admitted to a graduate or CAGS program may apply for graduate assistantships in the areas of teaching, research, or administration. Graduate assistants are paid $5500 for the academic year, are awarded a tuition waiver for 24 semester hours over a two-year period, must carry a load of 6 semester hours per semester, and are required to work 20 hours per week. Applications for graduate assistantships, obtainable through the Graduate Office, are due annually by May 15.

Cost of Study

Graduate tuition for 1998–99 is $140 per credit. A comprehensive registration fee of $55 per student and a capital projects fee of $7 per credit are charged at the time of enrollment.

Living and Housing Costs

Fitchburg State College assists students in arranging housing in residence halls or private accommodations. On-campus costs for 1997–98 were: room, $2590 per year; and board, $1500 to $1800 per year. Listings for potential off-campus housing can be found in the Office of Residence Life.

Student Group

Students represent a wide range of communities. Programs of study in early childhood, elementary, and middle school education and educational leadership and management have traditionally been composed of students predominantly on a part-time basis. The vast majority of students are gainfully employed in public or private school settings. Since the department strongly supports initial teacher preparation programs at the undergraduate level and due to changes in Massachusetts Teacher Certification regulations, the College has welcomed a significant growth in numbers of full-time graduate students pursuing continued studies in teacher education.

Student Outcomes

Ninety-nine percent of the students who have completed graduate studies are employed full-time in positions related to their continued studies. A substantial number of students utilize graduate programs of study to experience a job change or salary promotion. Many graduates in early childhood, elementary, and middle school programs continue to be exemplary teachers who continue to develop programs and curricula and provide state-of-the-art knowledge to the teaching-learning process. Graduates in the educational leadership and management program expand their skills to facilitate and effectively lead people, processes, and institutions. Many of these graduates become school principals and directors.

Location

The College is located in the attractive Montachusett region of north-central Massachusetts, an hour's drive from Boston and just minutes from some of New England's finest camping, hiking, and fishing spots. The 90-acre campus includes academic and administrative buildings, the library/campus center, an auditorium/theater, a dining commons, and a gymnasium. A short distance north of the campus is a 36-acre athletic and recreational area and McKay Campus School, a cooperative laboratory facility involving college education students and elementary children.

The College and the Department

Teacher education programs have a century-old tradition of preparing teachers, administrators, and policymakers. The graduate programs in education operate with a teaching university infrastructure, earning them NCATE (National Council of Accreditation of Teacher Education) accreditation. Housed in the McKay Campus School Building, the programs offer excellent practical and research opportunities to graduate students. Faculties are scholarly-oriented professionals engaged in research who provide expertise and programmatic development to schools, students, and agencies in the region. The graduate programs in education also have pioneered intensive field-based degree programs with area school systems and collaboratives and have fostered international liaisons in teacher education.

Applying

Under the College's rolling admissions policy, applications may be submitted at any time. An applicant for enrollment in education programs is required to submit an application (obtainable from the Graduate Office); an official transcript of a bachelor's degree; an official report of the Graduate Record Examinations (GRE) or Miller Analogies Test (MAT); a professional resume; and three letters of recommendation. The Graduate Office accepts a maximum of 6 semester hours in transfer from regionally accredited graduate schools. Applications must be submitted to the Admissions Office.

Correspondence and Information

Division of Graduate and Continuing Education
Fitchburg State College
160 Pearl Street
Fitchburg, Massachusetts 01420-2697
Telephone: 978-665-3181
Fax: 978-665-3658
E-mail: dgce@fsc.edu
World Wide Web: http://www.fsc.edu

Submit applications to:
Admissions Office
Fitchburg State College
160 Pearl Street
Fitchburg, Massachusetts 01420-2697
Telephone: 978-665-3144
Fax: 978-665-3658

Fitchburg State College

THE FACULTY

Michele Moran Zide, Associate Vice President of Academic Affairs and Dean of Graduate and Continuing Education; Ed.D., Massachusetts.

CAGS-Consultation and Peer Leadership
Anne May, Chair, Ed.D., Boston University.

CAGS-Educational Leadership and Management
Ronald Colbert, Chair; Ed.D., Boston University.

CAGS-Staff Development
George Bohrer, Chair; Ph.D., Massachusetts.

M.A./M.A.T.-Biology
George Babich, Chair; Ph.D., New Hampshire.

M.A.T.-Earth Science
Robert Champlin, Chair; Ph.D., Ohio State.

M.A./M.A.T.-English
Marilyn McCaffrey, Chair; Ed.D., Boston University.

M.A./M.A.T.-History
Susan Williams, Chair; Ph.D., Delaware.

M.A.T.-Mathematics
Gerald Higdon, Chair; Ph.D., Lehigh.

M.Ed.-Arts in Education
Harry Semerjian, Chair; Ed.D., Massachusetts.

M.Ed.-Educational Leadership and Management
Ronald Colbert, Chair; Ed.D., Boston University.

M.Ed.-Early Childhood/Elementary/Middle School Education
Patricia Barbaresi, Chair; Ph.D., Cornell.

M.Ed.-Occupational Education
Lloyd Harte, Chair; Ed., Massachusetts.

M.Ed.-Science Education
George Babich, Chair; Ph.D., New Hampshire.

M.Ed.-Secondary Education
Ronald Colbert, Chair; Ed.D., Boston University

M.Ed.-Special Education
Elaine Francis, Co-Chair; Ed.D., Massachusetts.
Anne Howard, Co-Chair; Ph.D., Brandeis.

M.Ed.-Technology Education
Stanley Bucholc, Chair; Ed.D., West Virginia.

M.S.-Counseling (School Guidance Counseling)
Richard Spencer, Chair; Ph.D., SUNY at Buffalo.

FORDHAM UNIVERSITY

Graduate School of Education

Programs of Study

The Fordham University Graduate School of Education offers a number of programs—at the master's, professional diploma, and doctoral levels—to prepare capable men and women for effective service in the many areas and specialties of public and private urban education. At present, Fordham offers the following programs leading to the degree of Master of Science in Education: bilingual special education; bilingual teacher education; counseling and personnel services; creative studies; early childhood; early childhood special education; educational administration and supervision; educational psychology; elementary curriculum; human resource education; reading and literacy education; secondary curriculum: biology, English, or social studies; special education; TESOL; and therapeutic interventions. In addition, the Master of Arts in Teaching (secondary education), the Master of Science in Teaching (elementary education), and the Master of Science in adult education and human resource development are offered.

Programs leading to the professional diploma are offered in the fields of reading, reading administration, counseling, curriculum studies, bilingual school psychology, school psychology, and educational administration and supervision (school administrator–supervisor, school district administrator, and nonpublic school administrator). Doctor of Education programs are available in educational administration and supervision. Programs leading to the Doctor of Philosophy are offered in language, literacy, and learning; counseling psychology; educational psychology; school psychology; and educational administration and supervision. Programs in Catholic educational leadership and administration are offered at the master's, professional diploma, and doctoral levels.

All graduate programs provide for participation in a core of urban multicultural studies and include ample opportunity for interrelating theory and practice through appropriate field activities. Students in the Graduate School of Education may also enroll in suitable courses in the Graduate School of Arts and Sciences, the Graduate School of Social Service, the Graduate School of Business Administration, and the Graduate School of Religion and Religious Education.

All programs offered by the Graduate School of Education are accredited by the National Council for Accreditation of Teacher Education. The doctoral programs in school psychology and counseling psychology are accredited by the American Psychological Association. In addition, the School holds membership in the University Council of Educational Administration, the American Association of Colleges for Teacher Education, and the Council of Graduate Departments of Psychology.

Research Facilities

The University maintains library facilities at the Lincoln Center, Bronx, and Tarrytown campuses. The Lincoln Center campus also maintains a curriculum room, a counseling laboratory, a Center for Technology in Education, and a computer center integrated with the University computer facilities. The Early Childhood/School Consultation Center provides psychoeducational services to children in the public and nonpublic schools. In addition, the rich resources of the New York metropolitan area are available to Fordham students.

Financial Aid

The University offers scholarships, grants, and assistantships to students in the Graduate School of Education. Scholarships and grants are available for most programs of study; some are need-based. The average need-based award for full-time study (12 credits per semester) is approximately $1800 per semester. Assistantships are available in all divisions of the Graduate School of Education and provide tuition remission and/or stipends in return for service to the Graduate School of Education. The average assistantship covers the cost of four courses per year.

Cost of Study

Tuition for graduate courses is $500 per credit hour in 1998–99. Fees for other services are listed in the catalog.

Living and Housing Costs

Fordham's Lincoln Center Residence opened in 1993 and is adjacent to the Graduate School of Education. Off-campus residence costs in the New York metropolitan area will vary considerably according to location and the type of quarters desired.

Student Group

Enrollment in the Graduate School of Education in 1997–98 was approximately 2,300, of whom about 1,200 were degree-seekers. A majority of students attended part-time and most were preparing for teaching or administrative positions in metropolitan elementary and secondary schools or for leadership positions in service-delivery systems.

Location

The Lincoln Center campus is located in the heart of New York City, convenient to centers of finance, industry, community arts, and theater. The School is adjacent to the Lincoln Center for the Performing Arts, one of the world's most famous cultural crossroads.

The Tarrytown facility is located on the beautiful Marymount College campus in Tarrytown, Westchester County, New York.

The School

As a responsive institution located in a world-class city, the Graduate School of Education is dedicated to broadening opportunities and meeting the challenges of urban education for children, ranging from the most academically talented to those struggling with basic education. To stimulate meaningful research and its application to the pressing real-life problems of education, the Graduate School of Education engages in a number of cooperative programs with public and private schools in New York City and surrounding areas and with other professional schools and academic divisions of the University.

Applying

Admissions decisions for master's and most professional diploma programs (except school psychology) are made throughout the year. The deadline for applying to the doctoral programs in counseling psychology, educational psychology, and school psychology; to the professional diploma in school psychology; or to the Intern Fellowship Program (elementary education) is January 10. The deadline for applying to the doctoral programs in administration and supervision is April 15. Applications for assistantships are due by February 1 (January 10 if admissions application is due January 10); applications for scholarships are due by April 15 for fall and by October 15 for spring start dates. All application fees are $50.

Correspondence and Information

Office of Admissions
Graduate School of Education
Fordham University
113 West 60th Street
New York, New York 10023
Telephone: 212-636-6400

Fordham University

THE FACULTY

Graduate School of Education Administration
Regis G. Bernhardt, Dean and Associate Professor; Ph.D., Syracuse.
Jacqueline Kress, Associate Dean and Director of Graduate Studies; Ed.D., Rutgers.
Jane Larkin, Assistant Dean, Tarrytown; Ph.D., Boston College.

Division of Administration, Policy, and Urban Education
Gerald Cattaro, Ph.D., Columbia. Administration, Catholic school leadership, nonpublic school policy.
Bruce Cooper, Ph.D., Chicago. School finance, restructuring, shared decision making, school choice, change processes.
John Elias, Ed.D., Temple. History, philosophy, and ethics in education; adult education.
Anne Gargan, Ed.D., Fordham. Supervision, authentic assessment, results-based teaching/learning, school restructuring.
Ruth Greenblatt, Ed.D., Fordham. Principalship, learning environments, change processes, women in educational administration.
Rita Guare, Ph.D., Fordham. Administration and supervision, leadership, religious education, aesthetics.
Barbara Jackson, Ed.D., Harvard. School/community/family partners, urban schools, women administrators, race and culture.
Sheldon Marcus, Ed.D., Yeshiva. Administration and supervision, college administration, multiculturalism.
Lew Smith, Ed.D., Columbia. Administration, supervision, middle school change, principals' leadership.
Toby Tetenbaum, Ph.D., NYU. Human resource education, workplace issues and trends.

Division of Curriculum and Teaching
Patricia Antonacci, Ph.D., Fordham. Reading, authentic assessment, early childhood education, literacy.
Richard Baecher, Ph.D., Michigan. Bilingual education, bilingual/second language learning, teacher education, literacy.
Anthony Baratta, Ed.D., Penn State. Curriculum and teaching, adult education, teacher education, multicultural education.
Karen Barnhardt, Ph.D., North Carolina. Cultural, historical, and philosophical foundations; ecofeminism.
Kenneth Bates, Ed.D., Hofstra. Initial teacher education, elementary teacher education.
Rita Brause, Ed.D., NYU. Reading, literature and literacy education, teaching/learning, teacher research.
Angela Carrasquillo, Ph.D., NYU. ESL, language, literacy and learning, bilingual/second language education, multicultural education.
Theresa Cicchelli, Ph.D., Syracuse. Professional development, teaching strategies: K–8, teaching/learning styles and processes.
Nancy Ellsworth, Ed.D., Columbia. Special education, reading, technology in education.
Michael Freedman, Ed.D., Temple. Secondary science teacher preparation, secondary science curriculum.
Marshall George, Ed.D., Tennessee. Secondary English education, adolescent literature, secondary school curriculum.
John Hicks, Ed.D., Columbia. Special education, assessment/evaluation in schools, early childhood special education.
Roland Hughes, Ph.D., Fordham. Math education, curriculum and teaching, cognitive skills teaching, mathematics education K–12.
Kathleen P. King, Ed.D., Widener. Adult education, transformational learning, educational technology.
Stephen Kucer, Ph.D., Indiana. Reading, language, literacy and learning, thematic curriculum.
Clement London, Ed.D., Columbia. Curriculum and instructional practices, oral history, ethnographic and multicultural studies.
Anthony Mello, Ed.D., Bridgeport. Professional development, teaching strategies.
Brenda Sheinmel, Ed.D., Harvard. Initial teacher preparation, authentic assessment, professional development, urban education.
Joanna Uhry, Ed.D., Columbia. Reading, initial teacher preparation, at-risk students, early literacy, reading.

Division of Psychological and Educational Services
Vincent Alfonso, Ph.D., Hofstra. School psychology, academic assessment and intervention, cognitive development, early childhood psychology, preschool learning and development.
Francine Blumberg, Ph.D., Purdue. Educational psychology, attention and learning strategies.
Karen Brobst, Ph.D., Columbia. School psychology, learning strategies, parent education.
Anthony Cancelli, Ed.D., Oklahoma State. School psychology, behavioral intervention, consultation.
Eric Chen, Ph.D., Arizona State. Counseling psychology, career development, counseling supervision, cultural diversity.
Giselle Esquivel, Psy.D., Yeshiva. School psychology, bilingual school psychology, gifted/talented/creative students, personality.
Jairo Fuertes, Ph.D., Maryland. Counseling, noncognitive variables in school success, Hispanic students.
Abigail Harris, Ph.D., Berkeley. School psychology, curriculum assessment, multicultural assessment, gender.
James Hennessy, Ph.D., NYU. Counseling psychology, counseling theory, criminal behavior, human development, moral development, personality assessment, violence prevention, measurement, at-risk youth, delinquency, school psychometrics.
John Houtz, Ph.D., Purdue. Educational psychology, creativity, quantitative research, teacher effectiveness.
Merle Keitel, Ph.D., SUNY at Buffalo. Counseling psychology, grief and loss counseling, stress management, health psychology.
Joseph Ponterotto, Ph.D., California, Santa Barbara. Counseling psychology, multicultural counseling.
Mitchell Rabinowitz, Ph.D., California, San Diego. Educational psychology, cognition, educational technology, metacognition.
Amy Reynolds, Ph.D., Ohio State. Counseling HIV/AIDS clients, counseling supervision, gay/lesbian issues, multicultural counseling.
Sigmund Tobias, Ph.D., Columbia. Educational psychology, cognition, interest and metacognition, anxiety, stress and coping.

THE GEORGE WASHINGTON UNIVERSITY

Graduate School of Education and Human Development

Programs of Study

The Graduate School of Education and Human Development offers programs leading to the M.A., M.Ed., M.A.T., Ed.S., and Ed.D. degrees.

Master's programs include the following fields of study: counseling (community counseling, rehabilitation counseling, and school counseling), curriculum and instruction (language and education), educational technology leadership, education policy studies, elementary education, elementary/secondary administration and supervision, higher education administration, human resource development, international education, museum education, secondary education, special education (early childhood special education, infant special education, special education for children and adolescents with serious emotional disturbance, and transition special education), as well as individualized degree programs.

Education specialist programs are available in the fields of administration, counseling, curriculum, higher education administration, human development, human resource development, and special education.

Doctoral programs are offered in counseling, curriculum and instruction, educational administration and policy studies, higher education administration, human development, human resource development, and special education. Each student's program of study is individually planned with a faculty committee and is based on the individual's academic and career goals. Doctoral programs require a research-tool field and a written comprehensive examination in the major field. The doctoral candidate must prepare a dissertation of publishable quality and defend it orally before a committee of examiners.

Students must maintain a quality point index of at least 3.0 during their graduate program.

Research Facilities

The University's libraries contain more than 1 million volumes, to which are added some 40,000 volumes each year. The libraries receive more than 19,000 serials annually. Library collections are housed in the Melvin Gelman Library (the general library of the University) and in the libraries of the National Law Center and the School of Medicine and Health Sciences. Graduate students may be issued a consortium library card that permits direct borrowing from the libraries of most other universities in the Washington area. Interlibrary loan privileges permit graduate students to obtain books and journal articles from other libraries in the city, throughout the United States, and in several other countries. The Library of Congress and libraries of various organizations and associations are available for student use. Museums offer access to art, science, and history collections. The University Computer Center maintains an IBM 4381 mainframe, IBM and Macintosh microcomputers, and extensive peripheral equipment for student use. The Instructional Media and Materials Center (IMMC) provides both technological support and curricular support to school faculty members and teachers in training. The Department of Counseling/Human and Organizational Studies operates a self-contained Community Counseling Service for student use in developing counseling expertise. The Office of Laboratory Experiences (OLE), housed in the Department of Teacher Preparation and Special Education, oversees all clinical placements of master's teachers in training. Current research projects housed within the School include the Center for Equity and Excellence in Education, the Educational Resources Information Center (ERIC) Clearinghouse on Higher Education, the National Clearinghouse for Bilingual Education, the Regional Rehabilitation Continuing Education Program (RRCEP), the Center for Education and National Development, the Institute for Educational Policy Studies, and Collaborative Vocational Evaluation Training.

Financial Aid

A significant number of graduate fellowships and scholarships are offered in specialized areas. In addition, a limited number of doctoral graduate assistantships are available. Tuition benefits are available to employees of the University. Information concerning student loans can be obtained from the University's Office of Student Financial Assistance. In addition, the University's Career and Cooperative Education Center maintains a registry of full- and part-time positions in the Washington area. After enrolling in the program, students may use the services of the University Graduate Fellowship Information Center for information on privately funded awards for graduate study.

Cost of Study

Tuition for the 1998–99 academic year is $680 per credit hour, plus a Marvin Center fee of $30.50 per credit hour. Special fees are charged for dissertation processing.

Living and Housing Costs

The University does not provide housing for graduate students; information on off-campus housing is available from the director of housing and residence life. Housing costs in the area are comparable to those in other major metropolitan areas.

Student Group

Graduate programs have a diverse and international student body. Recent college graduates and experienced professionals are represented. Approximately 90 percent of doctoral students are professionals who are currently employed by metropolitan area school districts, associations, human service agencies, or corporations. Graduates currently serve as district superintendents, principals, educational consultants, teachers, supervisors, counselors, museum staff, program directors, professors, corporate officers, and university administrators.

Location

The University is located in downtown Washington. In adjacent areas are the White House, World Bank, Corcoran Gallery of Art, Department of State, National Academy of Sciences, John F. Kennedy Center for the Performing Arts, and many other governmental and cultural institutions. Special field experiences are available in related national and international agencies because of the University's location.

The School

The central mission of the School is to prepare educators and human services providers who are well grounded in principles of teaching and research and are able to respond creatively to the changing needs of society. The School provides leadership that is recognized locally, nationally, and internationally.

Applying

Applicants must submit completed applications and forms, standardized test scores (MAT or GRE General Test), letters of recommendation, and transcripts by April 1 for the fall semester, October 1 for the spring semester, and March 1 for the summer sessions. The application fee is $55. Students should consult the current *Bulletin* for further admission information. Application forms are available from the Admissions Office.

Correspondence and Information

Debra Bright Harris, Director of Admissions
Graduate School of Education and Human Development
The George Washington University
2134 G Street, NW
Washington, D.C. 20052

Telephone: 202-994-6160
800-449-7343 (toll-free)
Fax: 202-994-7207
E-mail: gsehdapp@gwis2.circ.gwu.edu

The George Washington University

THE FACULTY

Dean: Mary H. Futrell.

DEPARTMENT OF COUNSELING/HUMAN AND ORGANIZATIONAL STUDIES
Chair: Donald C. Linkowski.

Program in Counseling (M.A., Ed.S., Ed.D.). (Includes emphasis in community counseling, school counseling, and rehabilitation counseling.) Professors: Donald W. Dew, Janet C. Heddesheimer, Carol H. Hoare, Donald C. Linkowski. Associate Professor: Patricia Hudson. Assistant Professors: Jorge Garcia, Sylvia Marotta, Terrence J. Martin. Visiting Assistant Professors: Brenda Y. Cartwright, Mary E. Langan.

Program in Human Development (Ed.S, Ed.D.). Professors: Janet C. Heddesheimer, Carol H. Hoare.

Program in Human Resource Development (M.A., Ed.S., Ed.D.). Professors: Carol H. Hoare, Marshall Sashkin, David R. Schwandt. Associate Professors: Neal E. Chalofsky, Sharon Confessore, Dail Fields, Michael Marquardt, Ronald Morgan. Assistant Professors: Nancy Berger, Lisa Horvath. Assistant Research Professor: Andrea J. Casey.

DEPARTMENT OF EDUCATIONAL LEADERSHIP
Chair: Dennis H. Holmes.

Program in Education Administration and Supervision (M.A., Ed.S., Ed.D.). Director: Lee Etta Powell. Professors: Lee Etta Powell, Everett Howerton. Associate Professor: Jane McDonald. Assistant Professor: Henry Willett.

Program in Education Policy (M.A., Ed.D.). Director: Gregg Jackson. Professor: John G. Boswell. Research Professor: Iris C. Rotberg. Associate Professors: Mary H. Futrell, Gregg B. Jackson.

Program in Educational Technology Leadership (M.A.). Director: William Lynch. Professors: Reynolds Ferrante, Dennis H. Holmes, Salvatore R. Paratore. Associate Professor: William Lynch. Assistant Professors: Michael Corry, Badrul Kahn.

Program in Higher Education Administration (M.A., Ed.S., Ed.D.). Director: Reynolds Ferrante. Professors: Gary Confessore, Reynolds Ferrante, Jonathan Fife, Dorothy Moore, Michael J. Worth. Assistant Professor: Walter Brown.

Program in International Education (M.A.). Director: Dorothy A. Moore. Assistant Director: Eileen Evans. Professor: Dorothy A. Moore.

Program in Museum Education (M.A.T.). Director: Carol B. Stapp. Associate Professor: Carol B. Stapp. Instructor: Ellen Willenbecher.

Research Faculty. Professors: Dennis Holmes, Salvatore Paratore. Associate Professor: Ralph Mueller. Assistant Professor: Patricia Freitag.

DEPARTMENT OF TEACHER PREPARATION AND SPECIAL EDUCATION
Chair: Maxine B. Freund.

PROGRAMS IN SPECIAL EDUCATION (M.Ed., M.A., Ed.S., Ed.D.).

Programs in Early Childhood Special Education (M.A., Ed.S., Ed.D.). Coordinator: Marian Jarrett. Professors: Michael Castleberry, Maxine B. Freund. Assistant Professors: Marian Jarrett, Victoria Youcha.

Programs in Infant Special Education (M.A., Ed.S., Ed.D.). Coordinator: Michael Castleberry. Professors: Michael Castleberry, Maxine B. Freund, Marian Jarrett. Assistant Research Professor: Barbara Browne.

Programs in Secondary and Transition Special Education (M.A., Ed.S., Ed.D.). Coordinator: Juliana Taymans. Professors: Robert Ianacone, Juliana Taymans, Lynda West. Associate Professor: Carol Kochhar.

Programs in Special Education for Children and Adolescents with Serious Emotional Disturbance (M.A., Ed.D.). Coordinator: Nancy Belknap. Professor: Nancy Belknap. Assistant Professor: Frank Mosca.

PROGRAMS IN TEACHER PREPARATION (M.Ed., M.A., Ed.S., Ed.D.).

Program in Curriculum and Instruction (M.A., Ed.D.). Professors: Gloria Horrworth, Amy Mazur, Nicholas Paley. Associate Professors: Sylven Beck, Sharon Lynch, Linda Mauro, Kathleen Steeves. Assistant Professors: Carol Muskin, Pat Tate, Jane Neapolitan.

Program in Elementary Education (M.Ed., Ed.S., Ed.D.). Coordinator: Sylven Beck. Professors: Nicholas Paley. Associate Professor: Sylven Beck. Assistant Professor: Pat Tate. Visiting Instructor: Josephine Baker.

Program in Secondary Education (M.Ed., Ed.S., Ed.D.). Coordinator: Libby Hall. Associate Professors: Anna Chamot, Sharon Lynch, Linda Mauro, Kathleen Steeves. Assistant Professor: Libby Hall. Visiting Instructor: Lynda Tredway.

GEORGIA STATE UNIVERSITY

College of Education

Programs of Study

The College of Education is a professional school committed to excellence in preparing people to work in a wide variety of school, business, and governmental educational settings. Excellence in teaching is built on the faculty's commitment to advancing knowledge through scholarship. Georgia State University's programs have prepared outstanding graduates at the baccalaureate through doctoral levels.

The College offers both teacher education and specialized education majors. Teacher education majors lead to certification by the Professional Standards Commission of Georgia and are designed to prepare professional educators. Special emphasis is placed on preparing educators for urban positions. Many graduates have been named teacher, counselor, and administrator of the year throughout Georgia and in other states and have been recipients of national awards presented by scholarly societies.

Specialized education majors, not leading to teacher certification, are designed to prepare students for leadership positions in business, industry, and government. Students earn advanced degrees in specialized areas such as exercise and sport science, higher education, policy analysis, professional counseling, and other nonteaching areas. Graduates have received national honors and acclaim from both public and private sectors.

The Colleges of Education and Arts and Sciences, working as a team, have formed the Professional Educational Faculty, which enhances articulation between content and pedagogical needs. Thus, curriculum decisions about regular and alternative preparation programs are made with the whole program in mind so that students benefit from the best thinking of academicians from both colleges.

A complete list of graduate programs in the College of Education can be found on the reverse of this page. Teacher education programs are approved by the Georgia Professional Standards Commission and the National Council for Accreditation of Teacher Education (NCATE).

Research Facilities

The William Russell Pullen Library supports fifty-three degree programs and 208 academic majors. The collection exceeds 1.3 million books, serials, and U.S. government documents, which can be found through the library's electronic PALS catalog. Electronic access to more than 150 Web-based databases via GALILEO (Georgia Libraries Learning Online) and campuswide access to more than forty-five networked CD-ROM databases. Pullen's special collections include significant resources in labor history, popular music, and the contemporary South. The Library's multimedia collection contains more than 5,000 resources as well as 2.1 million microforms. The library is housed in two adjoining buildings in the center of the downtown campus.

The Wells Computer Center provides a broad range of computing, data communication, and related services. Two mainframes, as well as PC laboratories, are available to all members of the University community 24 hours a day, seven days a week. GSU is also connected to the Internet and to a collection of smaller regional and local networks. Also available to College of Education graduate students are the facilities and services of the College of Law Library, the Educational Research Bureau, and the Instructional Technology Center.

Financial Aid

Many students receive financial assistance from the University in the form of scholarships, grants, loans, or employment. Recipients for all awards are selected on the basis of demonstrated financial need or academic achievement. Application packets for the following academic year are available after January 1. Students are encouraged to apply early for optimum financial aid benefits. Students should obtain information on financial aid in Room 100, Sparks Hall (telephone: 404-651-2227). Numerous teaching, research, and laboratory assistantships are available for graduate students. In addition to a modest salary, graduate assistants receive a tuition waiver. All students must pay student activity, health, and athletic fees.

Cost of Study

Tuition for in-state graduate students is $949 for 9 semester hours, or $82.50 per semester hour. The cost for out-of-state students is $3176.50 for 9 semester hours, or $330 per semester hour. The average cost of books and supplies is $250 per semester.

Living and Housing Costs

Numerous privately owned housing options are located near the campus. In the fall of 1996, Georgia State opened its first student housing, a 2,000-bed, apartment-style facility. For assistance with housing arrangements, students should contact the housing director (telephone: 494-651-4082).

Student Group

The student body is quite diverse. Students come from forty-six states and ninety-five countries. The average age is 34, 58 percent are female, and 25 percent are self-declared minorities. Most students work to finance their education (53 percent work full-time, 25 percent work part-time).

Location

The Georgia State University campus, located in the heart of downtown Atlanta, is expanding. Buildings and facilities are being added to the University each year. The campus is within a 1-hour commuting distance for almost 3 million citizens in the Metropolitan Atlanta area. Two rapid-rail public transportation stations are within one block of the campus, and approximately 10,000 GSU students and faculty and staff members utilize public transportation to commute to campus.

The University

Georgia State was founded in 1913 as part of the Georgia Institute of Technology. It experienced rapid growth, became part of the University of Georgia, and then achieved independence in 1961. It was granted university status in 1969. Georgia State is noted for its quality and size. Faculty members and students have won numerous awards for excellent scholarship. The University is the second largest of seventy-eight accredited institutions of higher learning in Georgia, with almost 250 majors offered in fifty degree programs.

Applying

Students may select from a wide range of master's, specialist, and doctoral programs in the College of Education. Admission requirements, application procedures, and deadlines vary by program. To receive an application, students should contact the address below.

Correspondence and Information

Clarelle Sauls, Director
Office of Academic Assistance/PG
College of Education
Georgia State University
Atlanta, Georgia 30303
Telephone: 404-651-2540
Fax: 404-651-1188
E-mail: educadmissions@gsu.edu

Georgia State University

GRADUATE PROGRAMS AND FACULTY

The graduate programs offered through each department of the College of Education are listed below, with the degrees conferred in each program noted in parentheses. Full-time faculty members are listed after the programs.

Department of Counseling and Psychological Services
Chair: Dr. Richard M. Smith.
Counseling (Ph.D.), Counseling Psychology (Ph.D.), Professional Counseling (M.S., Ed.S.), Rehabilitation Counseling (M.S., Ed.S.), School Counseling (M.Ed., Ed.S.), School Psychology (M.Ed./Ed.S., Ph.D).
Faculty members: Julie Ancis, Gary Arthur, Jeff Ashby, Gregory Brack, Clifford Carter, Barry Chung, Dana Edwards, Gary Evans, Janet Franzoni, Robin Gordon, Joseph Hill, Wayne Jones, Susan Katrin, Roy Kern, Kenneth Matheny, John McDavid, Joel Meyers, Frances Mullis, Richard Riordan, Steve Sampson, Roger Weed, JoAnna White, Phillip Wierson, Doris Wright.

Department of Early Childhood Education
Chair: Dr. Brenda M. Galina.
Early Childhood Education (M.Ed., Ed.S., Ph.D.).
Faculty members: Cheryll D. Barney, Susan Fairley, Edith Guyton, Stephanie Harrell, Olga Jarrett, Clifford Johnson, Margaret Jones, Lynne Jordan, John E. Kesner, Ramona Matthews, Marsha McMurrain, Connie W. Parrish, Lorene Pilcher, Julie Rainer, Ruth Saxton, Laura Smith, Cheryl Turner, LaVern Watkins.

Department of Educational Policy Studies
Chair: Dr. Parker Blount.
Educational Leadership (M.Ed., Ed.S.), Educational Policy Studies (Ph.D.), Educational Research (M.S.), Social Foundations of Education (M.S.).
Faculty members: Benjamin Baez, Deron Boyles, William Curlette, Lisa Delpit, Gary T. Henry, Asa Hilliard III, Dorothy Huenecke, Philo Hutcheson, Russell Irvine, Richard Lakes, Benjamin Layne, James Maxey, Alfred E. McWilliams, John Neel, N. Kathleen O'Neill, Darleen Opfer, Takako Oshima, Lucretia Payton-Stewart, Ross Rubenstein, Susan Talburt, Wayne Urban.

Department of Educational Psychology and Special Education
Chair: Dr. Ronald P. Colarusso.
Behavior/Learning Disabilities (M.Ed.), Communication Disorders (M.Ed.), Education of Students with Exceptionalities (Ph.D.), Educational Psychology (M.S., Ph.D.), Multiple and Severe Disabilities (M.Ed.), Special Education (Ed.S.).
Faculty members: Martha Abbott-Shim, Paul Alberto, David Center, Harry Dangel, Samuel M. Deitz, Susan Easterbrooks, Laura Fredrick, Peggy Gallagher, Juane Heflin, Kathryn Heller, Daniel Hickey, O. Leon Hurley, Marie Keel, Ann Kruger, Amy Lederberg, Lynn Maher, Colleen O'Rourke, Debra Schober-Peterson, Maureen Smith, Linda Sneed-Sanders, Dennis Thompson, Joseph Walker, Rebecca Wilson, Karen Zabrucky.

Department of Kinesiology and Health
Chair: Dr. Jeffrey C. Rupp.
Exercise Science (M.S.), Health and Physical Education (M.Ed., Ed.S.), Sport Science (Ph.D.), Sports Administration (M.S.), Sports Medicine (M.S.).
Faculty members: L. Jerome Brandon, Rankin Cooter, J. Andrew Doyle, Charles Exley, Benjamin Johnson, Michael Metzler, Carol Mushett, Sandra Owen, Terese M. Stratta, Walter Thompson, Laurie Tis, Bonnie Tjeerdsma, Theresa H. Walker.

Department of Middle-Secondary Education and Instructional Technology
Chair: Dr. Beverly J. Armento
English Education (M.Ed.), Instructional Technology (M.S., Ph.D.), Library Media Technology (M.L.M.), Language and Literacy Education (M.Ed.), Mathematics Education (M.Ed.), Middle Childhood Education (M.Ed.), Science Education (M.Ed.), Social Studies Education (M.Ed.), Teaching and Learning (Ed.S., Ph.D.).
Faculty members: Peggy Albers, Francis Atkinson, Janet L. Burns, Virginia Causey, Anne Crane, John Diehl, John Downes, Ramona Frasher, Stephen Harmon, John Hassard, Mary Ann Hindes, Ruth Hough, Hiram Johnston, Edward Lucy, Joyce E. Many, David O'Neil, Robert Probst, Karen Schultz, M. B. Shoffner, Patsy Smith, Lynn Stallings, Shirley Tastad, Christine Thomas, Molly Weinburgh.

GORDON COLLEGE

Division of Education

Program of Study

The Division of Education at Gordon College offers several courses of study that lead to a Master of Education degree (M.Ed.). A degree program in curriculum and instruction may be completed in any of the following concentrations: early childhood, elementary education, special education pre-K–9 or 5–12, middle school (5–9); biology, chemistry, English, history, mathematics, physics, social studies 5–9 or 9–12; and French and Spanish 5–12. Students may also choose to concentrate on teaching in a Christian school.

Students with a bachelor's degree in the arts and sciences or its equivalent and who are certified at the Provisional with Advanced Standing level or above in Massachusetts or the equivalent in another state elect Track I. Upon completion of the master's program, the candidate receives a master's degree and is eligible for the Massachusetts Standard Certificate in the same field and level as their original Provisional Certificate. The total program for Track I candidates is 33 semester hours.

Students who have completed a baccalaureate degree with a liberal arts and sciences major or an interdisciplinary major field in an appropriate content field for the teaching certificate sought but who may or may not have prior teaching experience and do not currently hold or qualify for a teacher certificate elect Track II. Upon completion of 21 semester hours of selected courses, the student becomes eligible for the Provisional with Advanced Standing Certificate and thus eligible for a teaching position. Upon completion of the entire master's degree program, candidates are recommended for the Standard Certificate. The total program for Track II candidates is 45 semester hours.

Students learn in study groups of usually fewer than 10 students. They may begin the program in September, January, or during any of several summer sessions. Courses are offered throughout the twelve-month year.

Research Facilities

The Jenks Learning Resource Center opened in fall 1987. The collection of educational resource literature numbers approximately 279,000 items. The collection includes books, microforms, current periodical titles, record albums, tapes, videocassettes, films, compact discs, specialized collections, and publications of the U.S. Government Printing Office, for which the library is a partial depository. Additions to these holdings are made annually to keep the library abreast of the most recent contributions in scholarship. Gordon uses a GEAC/Plus automated library system, which includes both the circulation and automated public access catalog modules. In addition to searching for books and other resources on the catalog, students can search a periodical database that indexes more than 4,600 periodicals, 2,000 of which are available full-text online. The library subscribes to numerous CD-ROM-based resources. A music and nonprint area with listening carrels, a curriculum library, a microform reading room, word processing rooms, a language lab, and an archives and rare books area are also available.

Students also have access to the Goddard Library of nearby Gordon-Conwell Theological Seminary. The library's participation in the North of Boston Library Exchange (NOBLE) and Gordon's interlibrary loan service with OCLC provide access to the holdings of other excellent libraries. The library provides additional reference services via various online venders.

Financial Aid

There are on- and off-campus opportunities in part-time teaching, advising, and research for supplementing a student's income. In addition, the College has applied for the Federal Stafford Loan Program, which is administered by the Gordon College Financial Aid Office. Qualified students may apply for a limited number of graduate assistantships.

Cost of Study

Tuition per 3-credit course is $700 for 1998–99; most courses are 3 credits. Book and supply costs average $600 per year for a full-time student.

Living and Housing Costs

Housing is not available on campus for graduate students. Information on local housing opportunities is available on campus in the Center for Student Development.

Student Group

The graduate program enrolls about 125 students. Approximately half of the graduate students are entering professional education for the first time. The others are either seeking an advanced certificate, a master's degree, and/or professional development. The men and women in the graduate program range in age from 22 to 65.

Location

Less than 3 miles from the Atlantic Ocean, Gordon is situated in a suburban community near beautiful coastal towns such as the artist colony of Rockport and the yachting capital of Marblehead. Boston, which is just 25 miles south and less than an hour away by train, offers numerous cultural and recreational opportunities as well as many historic attractions, including the Boston Symphony, the Museum of Fine Arts, the Celtics, Old North Church, Copley Square, and colorful Faneuil Hall Market. Gordon's proximity to Boston and its high-technology metropolitan area provides many employment and internship possibilities.

The College

Gordon College was founded as the Boston Missionary Training Institute in 1889 by a small group of Christians who recognized the need for church and society to have educated leadership. Chief among the founders, and the first president, was the Rev. Dr. Adoniram Judson Gordon, whose name the school later adopted. Gordon developed into a liberal arts college with a graduate seminary and moved to its present 730-acre North Shore campus in 1955. In 1970, the divinity school was merged with the Conwell School of Theology from Philadelphia to form the Gordon-Conwell Theological Seminary. Gordon merged with Barrington College as the United College on the Wenham campus in 1985. Building on a long history of quality undergraduate teacher education, Gordon College was approved by the State Board of Education and the Higher Education Coordinating Council (HECC) in May 1996 to offer the Master of Education in curriculum and instruction with thirteen concentration areas. Today, Gordon College is the only nondenominational Christian liberal arts college in New England. In addition to the Master of Education, the College offers thirty-two undergraduate majors and confers three bachelor's degrees. Gordon is a member of the Christian College Consortium, the Coalition of Christian Colleges and Universities, and the Northeast Consortium of Colleges and Universities in Massachusetts.

Applying

Applications are reviewed and acted upon after the completion of at least one course in the program and before the completion of three courses. Admission to the program is on a rolling basis. The requirements for admission to the graduate studies program are a complete application, two official transcripts of all credits earned from accredited undergraduate and graduate schools, an undergraduate grade point average of 3.0 or higher (if a student has less than a 3.0 undergraduate grade point average, he or she may be admitted on a provisional status), agreement to the Statement of Compliance and Respect; three recommendations (a personal reference that speaks to the applicant's character, an academic reference that evaluates the candidate's ability to complete work at the graduate level, and a professional reference that speaks to the applicant's appropriateness for classroom teaching), scores on either the Miller Analogies Test or the General Test of the Graduate Record Examinations, two essays, a $40 nonrefundable fee, and an admissions interview with the Program Director.

Correspondence and Information

Director of Graduate Studies
Gordon College
255 Grapevine Road
Wenham, Massachusetts 01984
Telephone: 978-927-2300 Ext. 4315, 4322
Fax: 978-524-3734
E-mail: radtke@faith.gordonc.edu
lwells@gordonc.edu

Gordon College

THE FACULTY

Janet Arndt, Adjunct Faculty; M.A., Boston University.
Thomas A. Askew Jr., Professor of History; Ph.D., Northwestern.
Deborah Auday, Part-Time Faculty; M.A., Lesley.
Kay Bannon, Professor of Education; Ed.D., Massachusetts.
Russell Bishop, Professor of History; Ph.D., McGill.
Mark Cannister, Assistant Professor of Youth Ministries; Ed.D., Pittsburgh.
Janet Cannon, Adjunct Faculty; M.A., Simmons.
William Davis, Part-Time Faculty; M.Ed., Boston University.
Christine Draper, Assistant Professor of Education; M.Ed., Lesley.
Janis Flint-Ferguson, Associate Professor of Middle School Education and English; D.A., Illinois State.
Daniel Herrell, Part-Time Faculty; Ph.D., North Carolina.
Barry Koops, Adjunct Faculty; Ph.D., Michigan.
Laurie McDonough, Part-Time Faculty; M.A., Lesley.
Priscilla Nelson, Adjunct Faculty; M.Ed., Boston University.
Margaret Niehaus, Part-Time Faculty; Ph.D., Harvard.
Malcolm Patterson, Adjunct Faculty; Ed.D., South Dakota.
Keith Pentz, Assistant Professor of Education; Ed.D., Central Florida.
Rebecca Pitkin, Part-Time Faculty; M.Ed., Nevada, Las Vegas.
Tony Pitkin, Professor of Education (retired); Ed.D., South Dakota.
Muriel Radtke, Professor of Education and Chair, Division of Education; Ed.D., Boston University.
Donna Robinson, Adjunct Faculty; C.A.G.S., Salem State.
Merelyn Smith, Adjunct Faculty; M.S.T., New Hampshire.
Peter W. Stine, Professor of English; Ph.D., Michigan State.
Richard H. Stout, Professor of Mathematics; Ph.D., Penn State.
Doris-Ann I. Vosseler, Assistant Professor of Foreign Languages; Ph.D. candidate, Middlebury.
M. Jane Wells, Assistant Professor of Education; Ed.D., Boston University.
Susan Wood, Adjunct Faculty; M.A., Connecticut

HARVARD UNIVERSITY

Graduate School of Education

Programs of Study

The Harvard Graduate School of Education (HGSE) offers programs of study leading to the Doctor of Education (Ed.D.), the Certificate of Advanced Study (C.A.S.), and the Master of Education (Ed.M.). The Ed.D. is offered in the three program areas of HGSE: Administration, Planning, and Social Policy (APSP); Learning and Teaching (L&T); and Human Development and Psychology (HDP). The Ed.D. generally requires two years of full-time course work, followed by the completion of a qualifying paper and a dissertation. APSP offers six concentrations: higher education, elementary and secondary education, international education, community education and lifelong learning, urban superintendency, and research. Studies in L&T address the philosophical and historical bases of educational practice, the diverse human settings within which teaching and learning occur, the process and content of teaching, the definition of the teacher's role and profession, and the education of teachers. Current topics of faculty teaching and research interest within L&T include the study of teaching, curriculum development and evaluation, schools and schooling, education and community, philosophy of education and curriculum theory, history of education, and research in educational technology. HDP encompasses two doctoral programs: Human Development and Psychology and Language and Literacy. Foci within HDP include acquisition of language and culture; cognitive development; culture, gender, and relational development; and methodology in developmental research.

The C.A.S. program provides an opportunity for an academic year of full-time study for experienced educators and midcareer professionals who ordinarily already have a master's degree. The C.A.S. is offered in all three program areas of HGSE. General Ed.M. programs are available. Students may design an individualized program in consultation with an adviser or may choose a structured program from one of six areas: Language and Literacy, Risk and Prevention, Technology in Education, Arts in Education, Midcareer Math and Science, and Teaching and Curriculum. All Ed.M. programs require an academic year of full-time study except the latter two, which have an additional three-week summer component.

Research Facilities

Gutman Library, with 240,000 volumes relating directly to education, is part of the Harvard library system of 12 million volumes, constituting the largest university library system in the world. Research centers include the Educational Technology Center, the Harvard Family Research Project, the Harvard Native American Program, the Harvard Literacy Laboratory, the Laboratory of Human Development, the National Center for Educational Leadership, the Office of International Education, the Philosophy of Education Research Center, Project Zero, and the Science Education Department, Harvard-Smithsonian Center for Astrophysics.

Financial Aid

To help students meet the cost of study, Harvard offers need-based grants, merit-based fellowships, federal educational loans, and Federal Work-Study.

Cost of Study

Tuition for the 1998–99 academic year is $20,430. The cost of books and supplies averages $1430 annually, and health insurance costs $1246 annually.

Living and Housing Costs

Harvard offers a wide range of housing options. There are studios to three-bedroom apartments available in small buildings and large complexes. Monthly costs range from $500 to $1680. The Housing Office posts approximately 3,000 listings of apartments and houses for rent or sale in the greater Boston area.

Student Group

Students come to HGSE from all walks of professional life, bringing with them a wealth of experience and a maturity that enhances classroom discussions and even casual conversations. Seventy percent of 1,144 students are women, 26 percent are American minorities, and 9 percent are international students from thirty-seven nations. With an average age of 29 (and an age range from 21 to 63), most entering students have seven years of professional experience in a variety of educational settings. Many have been teachers or school/university administrators. Others have experience in educational media, government, community social service agencies, health organizations, and the corporate sector. The majority of HGSE's master's degree and Certificate of Advanced Study recipients work in public school systems, independent schools, and postsecondary institutions. Some select employment in educational service agencies, educational media and technology firms, international organizations, research and consulting firms, foundations, and training and human resources departments. Others elect to go on for further graduate study. Doctoral recipients seek positions in postsecondary teaching, general administration, and research.

Location

The undergraduate, graduate, and professional schools that comprise Harvard are located on the banks of the Charles River, outside Boston, in Cambridge, Massachusetts. Harvard's setting permits a variety of seasonal outdoor activities, and its proximity to Boston adds symphonies, ballet, opera, museums, live theater, music, and restaurants to the wealth of cultural opportunities already available in Cambridge.

The University and The School

Harvard University is a private institution founded in 1636 and named in honor of John Harvard, a young minister who left his library and half his estate to the new institution. Harvard is comprised of ten graduate and professional schools. It has a teaching faculty of 2,278 and an enrollment of 18,273 undergraduate and graduate degree candidates. The Graduate School of Education, created in 1920, includes on its faculty a former U.S. commissioner of education, the author of a landmark study of gender and moral development, 3 recipients of the prestigious MacArthur Award, the principal architect for Sesame Street and other educational programming, a leading sociologist on the comparative study of race and ethnic relations, and top experts in evaluation, literacy, organizational behavior, the theory and practice of teaching, law and education, and immigration and education.

Applying

Information, a catalog, and applications for admission and financial aid can be obtained from the address below. Applicants are judged on the basis of their statement of purpose, work experience, letters of recommendation, academic record, and GRE scores. Applicants whose native language is not English or whose baccalaureate degree is from an institution where English is not the language of instruction must take either the computer-based TOEFL or the paper-based TOEFL and TWE. These applicants must score at least 250 on the computer-based test, including an essay rating of at least 5 on the writing section, or score at least 600 on the paper-based TOEFL and a 5 on the TWE. Doctoral applications are due by January 4, and decisions are sent around March 15; master's and C.A.S. applications are due by January 8, and decisions are sent around April 1. The deadline for all financial aid applications is January 8.

Correspondence and Information

Admissions Office
Graduate School of Education
Harvard University
111 Longfellow Hall, Appian Way
Cambridge, Massachusetts 02138

Telephone: 617-495-3414
Fax: 617-496-3577
E-mail: gseadmissions@harvard.edu

Harvard University

THE FACULTY AND THEIR RESEARCH

Administration, Planning, and Social Policy (APSP)

Stacy Blake, Assistant Professor; Ph.D., Michigan, 1996. Interpersonal relationships within organizations, focusing on antecedents and consequences of mentorships.

Richard Chait, Professor; Ph.D., Wisconsin, 1972. Management and governance of colleges and universities.

Richard Elmore, Professor; Ed.D., Harvard, 1976. Effects of educational policy on schools and classrooms.

Patricia Albjerg Graham, Professor; Ph.D., Columbia, 1964. History of American education, women in higher education.

Emily Hannum, Assistant Professor; Ed.D., Michigan, 1998. Social stratification, sociology of education, poverty and gender inequality in China.

Susan Moore Johnson, Professor; Ed.D., Harvard, 1981. Effects of educational policies on schools.

Sara Lawrence-Lightfoot, Professor; Ed.D., Harvard, 1972. Sociology of education, relationships between culture and schools.

Suzanne Grant Lewis, Assistant Professor; Ph.D., Stanford, 1988. Education policy in the developing world, gender inequity, education in Africa's democratic transition.

Richard Murnane, Professor; Ph.D., Yale, 1974. Teacher labor markets, education and the economy.

Jerome T. Murphy, Professor and Dean; Ed.D., Harvard, 1973. Administrative practice and organizational leadership, government policy, politics of education.

Gary Orfield, Professor; Ph.D., Chicago, 1968. Government policy and minority opportunity.

Fernando Reimers, Associate Professor; Ed.D., Harvard, 1988. Education policy reform and implementation of educational change in developing countries, focusing on improvement of equity; education and poverty in Latin America.

Julie Reuben, Associate Professor; Ph.D., Stanford, 1990. History of American education.

Leslie Santee Siskin, Associate Professor; Ph.D., Stanford, 1992. Structuring of high schools, disciplinary and interdisciplinary organization of knowledge, sociocultural and political contexts of teachers' work.

Carol H. Weiss, Professor; Ph.D., Columbia, 1977. Educational decision making at state, district, and school-site levels.

Charles Willie, Professor; Ph.D., Syracuse, 1957. Desegregation and education, race relations, urban community problems and the family.

Human Development and Psychology (HDP)

Catherine Ayoub, Assistant Professor; Ed.D., Harvard, 1990. Development of young children at risk.

Janine Bempechat, Assistant Professor; Ed.D., Harvard, 1986. Achievement motivation in school-aged children.

Maria Carlo, Assistant Professor; Ph.D., Massachusetts Amherst, 1994. Cognitive processes that underlie reading in a second language and of understanding the role played by the native language in the development of second-language literacy.

Kurt Fischer, Professor; Ph.D., Harvard, 1971. Development and change, relations between cognitive development and brain change.

Howard Gardner, Professor; Ph.D., Harvard, 1971. Development of human symbol using capacities, nature and assessment of human intelligences, growth and nurturance of creativity.

Carol Gilligan, Professor; Ph.D., Harvard, 1964. Psychology of women and girls, relationships between women and girls across racial and cultural differences.

Lowry Hemphill, Assistant Professor; Ed.D., Harvard, 1986. Language and social class, literacy, and developmental pragmatics.

Lawrence P. Hernandez, Assistant Professor; Ph.D., Stanford, 1993. Prevention and intervention efforts for high-risk teens, psychosocial influences on development of risk and resilience.

Robert LeVine, Professor; Ph.D., Harvard, 1958. Cultural aspects of parenthood, child development, and adult personality in African and other societies; influence of maternal schooling on reproduction and infant care in urban Mexico.

Richard Light, Professor; Ph.D., Harvard, 1969. Using statistical information to improve quality of services (e.g., education).

Michael J. Nakkula, Assistant Professor; Ed.D., Harvard, 1993. Psychosocial problems that place urban middle and high school students at risk for academic failure, underachievement, and general educational alienation.

Gil Noam, Associate Professor; Ed.D., Harvard, 1984. Effects of cognitive and emotional development, especially in intimate relationships, on recovery from psychological problems.

Victoria Purcell-Gates, Associate Professor; Ph.D., Berkeley, 1986. Cognitive and linguistic factors contributing to literacy acquisition and development.

Annie G. Rogers, Associate Professor; Ph.D., Washington (St. Louis), 1987. Development of courage in lives of girls and women.

Robert Selman, Professor; Ph.D., Boston University, 1969. Growth of interpersonal understanding and behavior, particularly of both normal and emotionally troubled preadolescents and early adolescents.

Catherine Snow, Professor; Ph.D., McGill, 1971. Infant development and language acquisition, cross-cultural differences in parent-child interaction, role of children's experiences in contributing to school achievement, acquisition of reading skills.

Marcelo Suarez-Orozco, Professor; Ph.D., Berkeley, 1986. Immigration, cultural anthropology, anthropology of education.

Learning and Teaching (L&T)

Robert Coles, Professor; M.D., Columbia, 1954. Social psychiatry, social ethics and public service.

Eileen de los Reyes, Assistant Professor; Ph.D., MIT, 1991. Culture and education, Latin American politics and international relations.

Eleanor Duckworth, Professor; Docteur en sciences de L'education, Geneva, 1977. Experience of teachers and learners of all ages both in and out of schools.

Robert Kegan, Senior Lecturer; Ph.D., Harvard, 1977. Adult education and the development of mental capacities throughout the life span.

Donald Oliver, Professor; Ed.D., Harvard, 1956. Development of teaching, curriculum, and educational programs.

Vito Perrone, Senior Lecturer; Ph.D., Michigan, 1963. Educational equity, curriculum, progressivism in education, testing and evaluation.

Philip Sadler, Assistant Professor; Ed.D., Harvard, 1992. Students' scientific misconceptions and how they change as a result of instruction, computer technologies that allow youngsters to engage in research, models for enhancing skills of experienced teachers.

Judah Schwartz, Professor; Ph.D., NYU, 1963. Use of computers to augment human intuition, process and substance of undergraduate and continuing education, cognitive development.

Marcelo Suarez-Orozco, Professor; Ph.D., Berkeley, 1986. Immigration, cultural anthropology, anthropology of education.

School-Wide Faculty

Judith Singer, Professor; Ph.D., Harvard, 1983. Developing better quantitative methods for addressing questions of educational relevance.

John Willett, Professor; Ph.D., Stanford, 1985. Improving statistical methodology in use in education, psychological and social research.

HOFSTRA UNIVERSITY

School of Education and Allied Human Services

Programs of Study

The School of Education and Allied Human Services offers master's degrees in various subjects, including art education; bilingual/elementary education; bilingual/secondary education; business education; creative arts therapy; elementary education; foundations for education; health administration; managed care; marriage and family therapy; music education; program evaluation; reading, language, and cognition; rehabilitation counseling; special education; teaching English as a second language; teaching special education; teaching speech and hearing handicapped children; and teaching writing. The Ed.D. degree is offered in educational administration and reading, language, and cognition. The Ph.D. degree is offered in reading, language, and cognition. Certificates of advanced study are offered in consultation in special education, deaf education, educational administration, foundations of education, managed care, marriage and family therapy, middle school extension, postsecondary transition specialist, reading teacher studies, school counselor, school counselor bilingual extension, special education assessment and diagnosis, sex counseling, teaching of special education, and teaching of writing.

Research Facilities

It is the philosophy of the School of Education and Allied Human Services that professional research should be carried on in the schools and communities of all social, economic, and cultural levels that are found near Hofstra University. On campus, there are computer facilities, a statistics laboratory, and a special education and counselor education center. The University libraries now contain approximately 1.4 million volumes and volume equivalents. The Hofstra Library is a depository for federal documents. It offers computerized information retrieval services to produce on demand bibliographies on special topics. Library sharing programs are also in place.

Financial Aid

University fellowships, assistantships, and loans are available. The University Placement Bureau can aid the student in finding either part- or full-time employment. Information about graduate financial aid may be obtained by contacting either the director of financial aid or the individual department to which the student is applying. Fellowships are available in the doctoral programs on a competitive basis.

Cost of Study

Tuition was $442 per semester hour in 1997–98. University fees were $275 per semester for 12 or more credits.

Living and Housing Costs

Limited room and board are available for graduate students in the University residence halls. Rates in 1997–98 were as follows: $1930 per semester for a triple room, $2170 per semester for a double room, and $2640 per semester for a single room. The cost of meals ranged from $495 to $1350. There was a $46 Health Center fee as well as a $100 room deposit for breakage. An additional $10 activity charge was required to cover the activities of the Organization of Resident Students.

The Office of Residence Life also maintains listings of off-campus accommodations available for students.

Student Group

The School of Education and Allied Human Services enrolls approximately 1,400 students in graduate degree and diploma programs. Most of these are practicing professionals who bring an element of real life to the theoretical concepts discussed in the classrooms. Close liaison with Long Island school districts provides a living laboratory for graduate research and action programs. Because of the varied socioeconomic structure of the Long Island school districts, the graduate student body represents a broad spectrum of backgrounds, experiences, and viewpoints. The University's total enrollment in fall 1997 was 12,591 students, of whom 7,408 were full-time undergraduates, 1,308 were part-time undergraduates, and 3,875 were graduate and professional students (including 819 law students).

Location

Hofstra is located in a suburban community approximately 25 miles east of New York City, which can be reached by car or railroad in an hour's time. Hofstra has the advantages of both a large university and a small private college. A cosmopolitan population and the recreational facilities of the University and Long Island, with its beautiful beaches and parks, combine with a thriving cultural activity to make a graduate career at Hofstra both exciting and rewarding.

The School

The School of Education and Allied Human Services is an expanding unit in a vital university, offering an ever-increasing number of graduate programs in areas of service to the complex and diverse American population in all educational settings. Surrounded by strong programs in the liberal and fine arts and in business, the graduate student in the School of Education has the opportunity to develop his or her talents and resources to deal successfully with pupils and peers. The Hofstra School of Education is fully accredited by the National Council for Accreditation of Teacher Education at both the basic and advanced levels.

Applying

A student usually should apply at least sixty days in advance of the semester in which he or she wishes to matriculate. Under certain circumstances, limited study as a nonmatriculant is permitted. The Graduate Admissions Office is located in the Admissions Center on South Campus. Application materials, information, and related assistance for graduate applicants may be obtained by calling the number below. The Admissions Center is open from 9 a.m. to 7:30 p.m. Monday through Thursday and from 9 a.m. to 5 p.m. on Friday.

Correspondence and Information

Office of Admissions
100 Hofstra University
Hempstead, New York 11549
Telephone: 516-463-6700
800-HOFSTRA (toll-free)
Fax: 516-463-5100
E-mail: hofstra@hofstra.edu
World Wide Web: http://www.hofstra.edu

Hofstra University

THE FACULTY

James Johnson, Dean; Ph.D., Penn State.
Penelope J. Haile, Associate Dean; Ph.D., CUNY Graduate Center.
Jane M. Goldman, Assistant Dean; M.S., Hofstra.

Questions relating to a specific graduate program may be directed to the telephone numbers listed after the names of the programs below. The area code for all phone numbers is 516. All departmental offices are located in the School of Education and Allied Human Services, Mason Hall, with the exception of Health Studies, Sports Sciences, and Physical Education, which is located in the Hofstra Swim Center, North Campus.

Administration, Policy Studies, and Literacy (463-5758)
Karen Osterman, Associate Professor and Chair; Ph.D., Washington (St. Louis).

Donna Barnes, Professor; Ed.D., Rutgers.
Patricia Brieschke, Associate Professor; Ph.D., Illinois.
Lesley Browder, Professor; Ed.D., Cornell.
Eduardo Duarte, Assistant Professor; Ph.D., New School.
Jeanne Henry, Assistant Professor; Ed.D., Cincinnati.
Robert Kottkamp, Professor; Ph.D., Washington (St. Louis).
Cynthia McCallister, Assistant Professor; Ed.D., Maine.
Michael O'Laughlin, Associate Professor; Ph.D., Columbia.
Charol Shakeshaft, Professor; Ph.D., Texas A&M.
Timothy Smith, Professor; Ed.D., Rutgers.
Elizabeth Unruh, Associate Professor; Ed.D., Hofstra.

Counseling, Research, Special Education, and Rehabilitation (463-5759)
Daniel Wong, Associate Professor and Chair; Ph.D., Northern Colorado.

Joan Atwood, Professor; Ph.D., SUNY at Stony Brook.
Frank Bowe, Professor; Ph.D., NYU.
Estelle Gellman, Professor; Ph.D., Columbia.
Ruth Gold, Professor; Ed.D., Columbia.
Beth Gonzalez-Dolginko, Assistant Professor; M.P.S., Pratt.
Laurie Johnson, Associate Professor; Ph.D., Hofstra.
Joseph Lechowicz, Associate Professor; Ph.D., Georgia.
Diane Schwartz, Assistant Professor; Ed.D., St. John's.
Ralph Zalma, Associate Professor; Ed.D., Columbia.

Curriculum and Teaching (463-5768)
Sharon Whitton, Associate Professor and Chair; Ph.D., Georgia.

Nancy Cloud, Associate Professor; Ph.D., Columbia.
Linda Davey, Special Assistant Professor; M.Ed., Columbia.
Rosebud Elijah, Assistant Professor; Ph.D., Michigan.
Doris Fromberg, Professor; Ed.D., Columbia.
S. Maxwell Hines, Assistant Professor; Ph.D., SUNY at Buffalo.
Judith Kaufman, Assistant Professor; Ph.D., SUNY at Albany.
Sabrina Hope King, Assistant Professor; Ed.D., Columbia.
Janice Koch, Associate Professor; Ph.D., NYU.
Maureen Miletta, Associate Professor; Ed.D., Columbia.
Maureen Murphy, Professor; Ph.D., Indiana.
Anneliese Payne, Assistant Professor; M.S., Eastern Illinois.
Mary Savage, Associate Professor; Ph.D., Catholic University.
Susan Semel, Assistant Professor; Ed.D., Columbia.
Alan Singer, Assistant Professor; Ph.D., Rutgers.
Sandra Stacki, Assistant Professor; M.S., Southern Maine.
Bruce Torff, Assistant Professor; Ed.D., Harvard.

Health Studies, Sport Sciences, and Physical Education (463-5808)
Estelle Weinstein, Professor and Chair; Ph.D., Hofstra.

Carol Alberts, Associate Professor; Ed.D., St. John's (New York).
Rhonda Clements, Associate Professor; Ed.D., Columbia.
Sarah Doolittle, Assistant Professor; Ed.D., Columbia.
Steven Frierman, Assistant Professor; Ph.D., North Carolina.
Nancy Halliday, Assistant Professor; Ph.D., Temple.
Robert Lazow, Assistant Professor; D.P.H., Columbia.
Michael Ludwig, Assistant Professor; Ph.D., Penn State.
Suanne Maurer, Special Assistant Professor; M.S., Canisius; C.A.S., Hofstra.
Israel Schwartz, Assistant Professor; Ph.D., NYU.
Nathalie Smith, Associate Professor; Ph.D., USC.
Linda Zwiren, Professor; Ph.D., Georgia.

INDIANA UNIVERSITY

School of Education

Programs of Study

The School of Education core campus at Indiana University Bloomington and Indiana University–Purdue University Indianapolis (IUPUI) offers nationally recognized programs leading to the degrees of Master of Science in Education, Specialist in Education, Doctor of Education, and Doctor of Philosophy.

Most graduate programs are offered on the Bloomington residential campus. The Master of Science in Education degree is offered in art education; counseling and counselor education; educational psychology; elementary and early childhood education; higher education; history and philosophy; instructional systems technology; international and comparative education; language education; school administration; secondary education, with tracks in mathematics education and science education; social studies education; special education; and student affairs administration. The Specialist in Education degree is offered in counseling and counselor education; elementary and early childhood education; instructional systems technology; language education; school administration; school psychology; science and environmental education; secondary education; and special education. The Ed.D. degree is offered in curriculum and instruction with various specializations; educational psychology; higher education; instructional systems technology; language education; school administration (educational leadership); and special education. The Ph.D. is offered in counseling psychology; curriculum and instruction with various specializations; educational psychology/school psychology; higher education; history, philosophy, and policy studies; instructional systems technology; language education; and special education.

On the Indianapolis campus, master's degrees are offered in counseling and counselor education; elementary and early childhood education; language education; secondary education; and special education. Doctoral-level course work is available in school administration and higher education.

All programs in teacher preparation and school administration have full accreditation from the National Council for Accreditation of Teacher Education (NCATE). In addition, the Indiana Professional Standards Board has accepted all teacher education programs. The American Psychological Association has approved the school psychology and counseling psychology programs.

Research Facilities

The Bloomington campus is a major research center where leading scholars investigate national and international educational issues. The Indianapolis campus provides the opportunity to study in a major urban and policy center and to work in diverse school settings. Research facilities in Bloomington include the Wright Education Building, featuring a distance education studio/classroom, multimedia laboratories, and many other specialized educational settings; the Education Library, containing an extensive collection of 70,000 monographs and journals, access to electronic databases, and a teaching materials center; and the Smith Center for Research in Education, housing the ERIC Clearinghouse for Social Studies/Social Science Education and the ERIC Clearinghouse on Reading, English, and Communication, as well as educational research centers. A highlight of the Indianapolis campus is the state-of-the-art electronic library that allows researchers access to information worldwide. The campus has been a leader in the application of computer and video technology, including a distance education studio/classroom located in the School of Education.

Financial Aid

Graduate students may qualify for financial assistance, including teaching and research assistantships, fellowships, fee remission scholarships, hourly wages, and loans. Most doctoral students are able to secure graduate research or teaching assistantships. Fellowships and scholarships may be granted to doctoral students with superior academic credentials. Minority students may receive financial assistance through the School of Education and the University Graduate School fellowship office. Additional student support opportunities are available through financial aid offices on each campus.

Cost of Study

In 1998–99 tuition for Indiana residents is $147 per graduate credit hour. For nonresidents tuition is $428.25 per graduate credit hour.

Living and Housing Costs

The cost of living in Bloomington and Indianapolis is comparable to other Midwestern college campuses. In 1998–99 students pay $5814 for a single room in a residence hall, including room and board, or $515 a month to rent a furnished efficiency apartment, including utilities, on the Bloomington campus. A furnished, two-bedroom apartment, suitable for married students, ranges from $590 to $630 a month, including utilities. Students also live nearby in off-campus housing. Campus housing is very limited in Indianapolis.

Student Group

About 2,200 graduate students attend the School of Education. These students come from all the states and from many other countries. More than 1,200 doctoral students, 750 master's degree students, and 200 graduate licensure students are enrolled in course work in Bloomington. Graduate students enrolled at Indianapolis include 400 working toward degrees and 450 preparing for teacher licensure.

Location

Bloomington is an exciting college town featuring top-notch athletic and cultural events. The rolling hills of southern Indiana offer excellent recreational facilities within an hour of campus. City life is nearby with Indianapolis only 50 miles away. The modern Indianapolis campus is located close to cultural centers, including symphony orchestra, repertory theater, and museums, as well as many amateur and professional athletic activities.

The School

Established in 1852, the School of Education has a long and distinguished history of service to the state and nation, preparing educators for a broad spectrum of professional responsibilities in classrooms, laboratories, and administrative offices. In national rankings of research productivity and quality of academic programs, the School is acclaimed as one of the leading educational institutions in the world. Its full-time faculty is composed of 105 professors in Bloomington and 25 professors in Indianapolis.

Applying

Applications for master's degrees must be submitted to the campus where the degree is offered. Applications to all Ph.D., Ed.D., and specialist degree programs must be submitted to the Bloomington office. The application can be completed on line (http://php.indiana.edu/~educate/homepage.html) or through a self-managed paper application. An application must include completed application forms, two letters of recommendation, a personal goal statement explaining academic and career objectives, transcripts from all colleges and universities attended, GRE test scores, an application fee, and other materials as required by the degree program. Admission application fees for U.S. citizens and permanent residents are $40 at Bloomington and $30 at IUPUI; for international students, the fees are $40 at Bloomington and $50 at IUPUI.

Correspondence and Information

Education Graduate Studies Office
Wright Education Building, Room 1000
201 North Rose Avenue
Indiana University
Bloomington, Indiana 47405-1006
Telephone: 812-856-8504
Fax: 812-856-8518
World Wide Web: http://education.indiana.edu

Office of Student Services
Education/Social Work Building, Room 3131
902 West New York Street
Indiana University
Indianapolis, Indiana 46202-5155
Telephone: 317-274-0644
Fax: 317-274-6864

Indiana University

THE DEPARTMENTS AND AREAS OF RESEARCH

Bloomington Campus

Department of Counseling and Educational Psychology. Chair: Jack Cummings, Education 4008, 812-856-8300. Programs offered include counseling and counselor education, educational psychology, counseling psychology, and school psychology. The distinguished faculty investigates many important topics using quantitative and qualitative inquiry strategies. Students gain valuable insights through interactive video applications for behavioral observation and analysis of classroom environments.

Department of Curriculum and Instruction. Chair: Peter Kloosterman, Education 3140, 812-856-8100. Programs include art education, curriculum studies, early childhood education, elementary education, mathematics education, multicultural education, science education, secondary education, social studies education, and special education. The department's diverse and internationally known faculty conducts many large-scale research and service projects funded by state, federal, and corporate sources.

Department of Educational Leadership and Policy Studies. Chair: Barry Bull, Education 4228, 812-856-8360. Programs include college student affairs administration, comparative education, educational leadership, higher education, history of education, philosophy of education, policy studies, and school administration. Several of the department's programs are ranked among the best in the United States. Faculty members are internationally recognized for research and publication record in their respective fields.

Department of Instructional Systems Technology. Chair: Thomas Schwen, Education 2276, 812-856-8450. The department has one of the best programs in the nation, preparing students in educational technology using the newest multimedia tools and facilities. Specializations in instructional systems technology are offered in instructional development, product development, or management. The department also develops national and international corporate training projects. Faculty members demonstrate outstanding expertise and research in multimedia instructional design and production.

Department of Language Education. Chair: Larry Mikulecky, Education 3044, 812-856-8260. Programs include English education, English as a second language/bilingual education, foreign language education, and reading education. Bridge courses integrate language study across program areas. Faculty members are known internationally for their excellent teaching, research, and service records.

Indianapolis Campus

Division of Teacher Education. Chair: Michael Cohen, Education/Social Work 3121, 317-274-6801. The division offers an exciting teacher education program that provides educational leadership for a diverse and thriving metropolitan community. The teacher education program collaborates with area schools through the professional development school concept. These schools serve as sites where field experiences and student teaching are concentrated. Prominent faculty members focus their research on issues relevant to the concerns of urban schools.

Division of Human Development, Leadership, and Technology. Chair: Keith Morran, Education/Social Work 3119, 317-274-6815. The division provides study and practice in adult education, applications of technology to educational practice, applied human development, higher education and college student affairs administration, educational foundations, educational psychology, school administration and policy, and school and community counseling. The outstanding faculty is involved in many ongoing research and development activities.

A magnificent limestone structure on the Bloomington campus, the Wendell W. Wright Education Building is a national demonstration site for the application of technology to teaching and learning.

The School of Education on the Indianapolis campus is located in the modern Education/Social Work Building near the heart of downtown.

JOHNS HOPKINS UNIVERSITY

School of Continuing Studies Graduate Division of Education

Programs of Study

The Graduate Division of Education prepares school and human services professionals, at all career levels, to be leaders and change agents in their communities through graduate programs that include master's degrees, graduate certificates, certificates of advanced graduate study, and doctoral degrees.

Teacher certification is offered in early childhood, elementary, and secondary education through the Master of Arts in Teaching (M.A.T.), designed for students pursuing graduate study on a part-time basis, and the full-time School Immersion Master of Arts in Teaching (S.I.-M.A.T.). Certification programs are also available through special education master's degrees and include the following areas: mild to moderate disabilities (infant/primary: birth through grade 3; elementary/middle: grades 1–8; and secondary/adult: grade 6 through age 21) and severe disabilities.

The Master of Science in education (M.S.) and Certificate of Advanced Graduate Study (C.A.G.S.) programs are designed for experienced educators to acquire additional knowledge and skills in an area of specialization. Course requirements vary by program area. Master's degrees require 33–39 credits; a minimum of 30 graduate credits is required for the Certificate of Advanced Graduate Study. Both the M.S. and the C.A.G.S. must be completed within five years. M.S. in education concentrations are offered in school administration and supervision, teacher leadership, gifted education, reading, technology for educators, science and mathematics education, and general education studies. M.S. in special education concentrations include early childhood special education, mild to moderate disabilities, inclusive education, severe disabilities, transition planning, and technology in special education. M.S. in counseling concentrations include school counseling, which leads to certification as a school counselor, and clinical community counseling. Counseling students also have the option to pursue a combined M.S./C.A.G.S. program.

Post-baccalaureate certificate programs cover specialized topics in the areas of teacher development, technology, and special education. These certificate programs, which range between 15–18 credits, can be applied toward a master's degree. Several post-master's certificates are available in counseling.

The Doctor of Education degree is offered with concentrations in special education, counseling, and general education. This program consists of a minimum of 99 credits beyond the baccalaureate (51 of which must be completed at Johns Hopkins) and must be completed within seven years.

Research Facilities

Students in programs leading to teacher or school counseling certification gain hands-on experience in the living laboratory of regional elementary and secondary schools during the field experience component of their training. Johns Hopkins also has formed partnerships with selected public schools, creating Professional Development Schools, comparable to teaching hospitals, in which S.I.-M.A.T. students train as interns in a fully integrated community of learners. The Center for Technology in Education (CTE) conducts research in technology in education for area school systems. Research projects are integral to school partnerships. Students have many opportunities to work with faculty members in developing research for the partnership projects.

Johns Hopkins libraries offer a wide range of services and collections. The Milton S. Eisenhower Library (MSEL) contains more than 2 million volumes in addition to special collections and materials, 11,000 journal subscriptions, and access to fifty databases. MSEL's Resource Services librarians are subject specialists who provide individualized research consultation. Full-service computer labs on each campus are available for student research. The University is connected to both BITNET and the Internet and offers access to its library and other resources through the Internet via JHUniverse, the University's World Wide Web site.

Financial Aid

Financial assistance in the form of federal low-interest loans, tuition assistance grants, and scholarships is available for full- and part-time study. Tuition benefits are available to employees of the University. A limited number of campus-based and private scholarships are available each year. Approximately half of the enrolled students receive financial assistance to meet their educational expenses.

Cost of Study

Course fees in the Graduate Division of Education are $295 per credit on the master's and certificate levels. A $45 nonrefundable fee per semester is required for initial registration. Doctoral program fees include a $500 matriculation fee and a $50 nonrefundable application fee. Tuition for doctoral study is $758 per credit hour.

Living and Housing Costs

Through Hopkins' Off-Campus Housing Service, full-time students (12 or more credits) may obtain information about housing in the Homewood campus area. Rental information, roommate referrals, and information on landlord-tenant laws and regulations also are available.

Student Group

The Graduate Division of Education's diverse student body is composed of teachers, principals, school administrators, and counselors from area schools and human service agencies (50 percent) and early-career and midcareer professionals from varied backgrounds who wish to become educators (50 percent). Students bring a strong commitment to meeting the educational needs of children in grades K–12.

Student Outcomes

Many students are recruited by school systems prior to the completion of their studies to fill positions in teaching, administrative, and counseling services. Student outcomes are measured in every discipline area by national standards, such as INTASC, CEC, and FSLFC. In addition to delivering effective instructional, curricular, and clinical services, students are positioned to become effective leaders. Professional enhancement degrees and certificate programs permit professional educators to progress in their areas of expertise and establish a basis for career-long learning and advancement.

Location

The Baltimore–Washington metropolitan area offers an unmatched array of business, education, and cultural resources. Just 4 miles from downtown Baltimore, the 40-acre, tree-lined Homewood campus houses the University's main administrative offices as well as the Graduate Division of Education offices. In addition to courses at Homewood, the Graduate Division of Education also offers courses at the Montgomery County Center in Rockville, Maryland, and the Columbia Center in Howard County, Maryland.

The University and The School

Established in 1876, Johns Hopkins was the first American university dedicated to both advanced study and scientific research. Since its founding, Johns Hopkins has extended its reach to adult students; in 1909, the University established a division of college-level instruction in education and liberal arts. In 1952, the college offered its first graduate degree, the Master of Education, and today the Graduate Division of Education is responsible for professional education programs. The School of Continuing Studies is one of the eight academic divisions within the University.

Applying

To be considered for admission to any master's or certificate program, individuals must submit a formal application (including an essay), official transcripts from all postsecondary institutions attended, and an application fee. Because specific admissions requirements vary by program, applicants should contact the admissions office or the Division to determine specific admissions criteria, suitability of prior degrees, or certification requirements. Applicants for graduate degrees and certificate programs must hold a bachelor's degree from a regionally accredited college or university. Persons interested in doctoral study should contact the Graduate Division of Education before applying to determine current offerings and to request the doctoral application packet.

Correspondence and Information

Graduate Division of Education
School of Continuing Studies
101 Whitehead Hall
Johns Hopkins University
Baltimore, Maryland 21218-2692
Telephone: 410-516-8273

Johns Hopkins University

THE FACULTY

Ralph Fessler, Ph.D., Professor of Education and Director of Graduate Division of Education.

Department of Teacher Development and Leadership

Chair: Rochelle Ingram, Ph.D., Assistant Professor of Education; Associate Director, Graduate Division of Education; Coordinator, School Administration and Supervision Program; and Adviser, Teacher Leadership, General Educational Studies.

M. Linda Poole, Ph.D., Director, Master of Arts in Teaching Programs, and Assistant Professor.

Lenore J. Cohen, Ed.D., Assistant Professor of Education; Adviser, Master of Arts in Teaching Program; and Coordinator, Professional Development School Partnership with Howard County Public Schools.

Teresa T. Field, Ed.D., Assistant Professor of Education; Adviser, Master of Arts in Teaching Program; and Coordinator, Professional Development School Partnership with Sparrows Point Schools, Baltimore County.

Clarence E. Miller Jr., Ed.D., Visiting Assistant Professor of Education and Adviser, Science and Mathematics Education.

Department of Educational Technology

Chair: Jacqueline A. Nunn, Ed.D., Assistant Professor of Education; Director, Center for Technology in Education; and Adviser, Technology in Special Education, Technology for Educators.

Linda Tsantis, Ed.D., Assistant Professor of Education and Coordinator, Technology for Educators Programs.

Department of Counseling and Human Services (M.S., C.A.G.S. in counseling)

Chair: Mark R. Ginsberg, Ph.D.

Fred Hanna, Ph.D., Associate Professor of Education; Program Coordinator, Certificate of Advanced Graduate Study Program; and Adviser, Counseling and Human Services.

Susan G. Keys, Ph.D., Assistant Professor of Education; Field Experience Coordinator, Clinical Community Counseling and School Counseling; and Adviser, Counseling and Human Services.

Part-Time Appointments:

Leon Rosenberg, Ph.D., Professor of Education (joint appointment with Department of Pediatrics, School of Medicine).

Evelyn R. Kragie, Ed.D., Instructor, Graduate Division of Education, and Coordinator, Montgomery County Programs in Counseling and Human Services.

Department of Special Education (M.S., C.A.G.S., Ed.D. in special education)

Chair: Michael S. Rosenberg, Ph.D., Professor of Education and Adviser, Mild to Moderate Disabilities.

Stephanie L. Carpenter, Ph.D., Assistant Professor of Education; Adviser, Mild to Moderate Disabilities, Inclusive Education; and Field Experience Coordinator, Special Education.

Deborah Carran, Ph.D., Associate Professor of Education and Adviser in Statistics, Measurement, and Research Methodology.

Margaret E. King-Sears, Ph.D., Associate Professor of Education; Coordinator, Montgomery County Programs in Special Education; and Adviser, Mild to Moderate Disabilities, Inclusive Education.

Gloria Lane, Ed.D., Associate Professor of Education and Adviser, Severe Disabilities, Mild to Moderate Disabilities, Transition Planning.

Lawrence A. Larsen, Ph.D., Professor of Education and Adviser, Severe Disabilities, Early Childhood Special Education.

Janeen M. Taylor, Ph.D., Assistant Professor of Education and Coordinator, Early Childhood Special Education.

Part-Time Appointments

Michael Bender, Ed.D., Professor of Education (joint appointment with Department of Pediatrics, School of Medicine).

Robin Church, Ed.D., Associate Professor of Education.

LESLEY COLLEGE

School of Education

Programs of Study

The School of Education offers the Master of Education (M.Ed.), the Certificate of Advanced Graduate Study (C.A.G.S.), and the doctorate (Ph.D.) in educational studies. The Ph.D. program in educational studies is designed for students who wish to pursue advanced study and scholarship in an interdisciplinary area of inquiry. The Educational Administration Program is offered as both a master's degree and a post-master's professional program leading to a Certificate of Advanced Graduate Study (C.A.G.S.). Its successful completion assures provisional and/or standard certification in one of the following areas: Elementary School Principal, Middle School Principal, Administrator of Special Education, or Supervisor/Director. The Education and Special Education Programs offer entry-level and advanced teacher preparation and unique career alternative options. For students with bachelor's degrees who wish to become certified teachers, provisional with advanced standing and standard certification, and master's degree programs in early childhood, elementary, middle school, special education, and instructional technology are available. These programs meet Massachusetts teacher certification regulations and are approved under the Interstate Certification Compact (I.C.C.). For certified or experienced teachers, advanced master's degree and C.A.G.S. programs are offered in technology in education and curriculum and instruction. Curriculum and instruction degree candidates choose an area of specialization in fields such as early childhood, inclusive schooling, literacy, technology in education, conflict resolution and peaceable schools, or teacher leadership. Advanced master's degree, C.A.G.S., or certification-only programs leading to certification as a Consulting Teacher of Reading (K-12) are also offered. The School of Education collaborates with public and independent schools in Massachusetts to offer master's degree programs. The programs are designed to include an ongoing field-based internship at the school site. Collaborative programs are currently offered at Buckingham, Browne & Nichols School, Shady Hill School, the Brookline Public Schools, Pike School, Brookwood School, and Belmont Day School. The School of Education offers its students a superior education through challenging course work, classroom-based reflection, research and clinical experiences that model a strong commitment and belief in cultural pluralism, technology, and inclusive communities. These experiences, in turn, inspire graduates to take leadership roles in helping to initiate reform in their schools and to contribute to the restructuring of education for future generations. The education faculty members, in their various roles as teacher-mentors, facilitators, researchers, consultants, writers, conference speakers, and members of educational boards, commissions, and focus groups, are the primary force in setting the high academic standards and the visionary goals of the School of Education.

Research Facilities

The Ludcke Library maintains a working collection of books, periodicals, microfilm and microfiches, curriculum materials, nonprint materials, and software resources. The Library provides Internet resources and database access to general and subject-specific resources appropriate to the subject focuses of the college. The Kresge Center for Teaching Resources provides instructional resources for individual and group instruction, and the Microcomputer Center houses the Instructional Computing activities of the college, including a collection of educational software. Through the Fenway Consortium students can access thirteen other libraries in Boston-Cambridge area.

Financial Aid

The Lesley College Financial Aid Office administers all federal financial aid programs. There are opportunities in college teaching, advising, and research activities, as well as field placements in public and private schools. A limited number of assistantships are awarded by semester or academic year. Most positions require about 10 to 15 hours of work per week.

Cost of Study

Tuition for on-campus graduate students is $425 per credit in 1998–99; tuition for off-campus graduate students is $300 per credit. Most courses are 3 credits. The total number of credit hours needed to complete graduate degrees varies from 33 to 48, depending upon the student's program and past experience. The cost of books and supplies averages $375 per year.

Living and Housing Costs

Lesley College does not have on-campus housing for its students. Information on housing in the surrounding area and assistance in obtaining it is available from the Residence Life Office of Student Affairs.

Student Group

The total graduate enrollment includes approximately 5,000 on- and off-campus students.

Location

Lesley College occupies a campus adjacent to Harvard Square in Cambridge and is connected to downtown Boston by accessible public transportation. The Boston area has one of the world's greatest concentrations of institutions of higher education and offers an unusual richness of cultural opportunities. Off-campus programs are available across the United States.

The College

Lesley College, founded in 1909 as a women's teaching college, continues its commitment to educating undergraduate women while also offering graduate and Ph.D. programs for women and men in the fields of education, human services, management, and the arts. With the next century's student in mind, Lesley College has successfully pioneered a wide variety of flexible programs for adult learners that share a commitment to quality, innovation, and the integration of theory with practice. Lesley offers degree programs through four schools: the School of Undergraduate Studies, which includes the primarily residential Women's College, the coeducational Adult Baccalaureate College, and the Threshold Program; the Graduate School of Arts and Social Sciences; the School of Education; and the School of Management. The College also supports several centers and hosts a variety of academic and professional conferences and institutes. Lesley programs operate throughout Massachusetts and in fourteen other states, as well as at affiliated international sites.

Applying

Applications are reviewed and acted upon as they are completed. Applications from international students not residing in the United States should be completed by April 1 for the fall semester and October 1 for the spring semester. Requirements for admission to graduate degree programs are a bachelor's degree (for the M.Ed. program) or a master's degree (for the C.A.G.S. and Ph.D. programs) from a regionally accredited college or university as well as a satisfactory grade average, official transcripts of undergraduate and graduate work, three letters of recommendation, a written personal statement, and a nonrefundable $45 application fee. Application materials should be requested from the Office of Admissions for Graduate and Adult Baccalaureate Programs.

Correspondence and Information

Office of Admissions
Graduate and Adult Baccalaureate Programs
Lesley College
29 Everett Street
Cambridge, Massachusetts 02138-2790

Telephone: 617-349-8300
800-999-1959 Ext. 8300 (toll-free)
Fax: 617-349-8313
World Wide Web: http://www.lesley.edu

Lesley College

THE FACULTY AND THEIR RESEARCH

William L. Dandridge, Associate Professor and Dean; Ed.D., Massachusetts Amherst. School reform, organization and administration, studies of educational policy and legal issues in education.
Harriet Deane, Assistant Professor and Assistant Dean; M.Ed., Boston University; M.B.A., Simmons. School, community, and business collaborations.
Susan C. Lane, Assistant Professor and Associate Dean; Ed.D., Harvard. Educational administration and the study of political dimensions in education.
Karen Kuelthau Allan, Professor; Ph.D., Wisconsin–Madison. Reading, writing, collaborative classroom inquiry, teacher research.
George Blakeslee, Associate Professor; Ed.D., Boston University. Technology in education, science education, teacher education.
Sheryl Boris-Schacter, Associate Professor and Director of Educational Administration Program; Ed.D., Harvard. Teacher education, educational administration, professional collaboration, policy-making and curriculum theory and development.
Linda Brion-Meisels, Associate Professor of Education/Psychology; Ph.D., Boston College. Inclusionary education for deaf and hard of hearing students using a coordinated interdisciplinary approach.
Marcia Bromfield, Associate Professor and Director of Field Placement and Professional Development Schools; Ph.D., Syracuse. Teacher education and the development and implementation of Professional Development Schools.
Elaine Bukowiecki, Assistant Professor; C.A.G.S., Lesley. Emergent and early literacy, supervision of reading programs.
Ella Burnett, Associate Professor; Ed.D., UCLA. Curriculum development, program evaluation, mathematics education.
Vivian Dalila Carlo, Assistant Professor; Ed.D., Boston University. Reflective teacher preparation, multicultural education.
Nancy Carlsson-Paige, Professor; Ed.D., Massachusetts Amherst. Children's political socialization, peace education.
Gail M. Carney, Assistant Professor and Director of Undergraduate Education Programs; Ed.D., Boston University. Professional development of experienced teachers, secondary and college reading and study skills.
Stephan Cohen, Assistant Professor; M.Ed., Lesley. Telecommunications, integrating technology into curriculum and its impact on society, html and the Internet.
Catherine Collier, Assistant Professor; Ed.D., Massachusetts Lowell. Integrating technology into education, telecommunications and teacher education.
Constantina Comnenou, Associate Professor; Ed.D., Massachusetts Amherst. Cross-cultural transition, cross-cultural conflict models, interface of cultural differences and systems.
Rebecca Brown Corwin, Professor; Ed.D., Harvard. Mathematics education, elementary school curriculum, connections between mathematics and whole learning.
Frank E. Davis, Professor and Director of the Ph.D. Program; Ed.D., Harvard. Adult learners, mathematics and science education.
Norman E. Dee, Associate Professor of Education; Ed.D., Boston University. Use of the constructivist approach in teaching elementary science method courses.
Karla Baehr DeLetis, Assistant Professor; Ed.D., Boston University. Educational administration, school reform issues, professional development.
Susan J. Doubler, Associate Professor; Ph.D., Liverpool (England). Teacher-student scientist partnerships, using technology to support science learning.
Edna May Duffy, Associate Professor; Ph.D., Boston College. Evolution of women in the sciences.
Angeline Ferris, Assistant Professor; C.A.G.S., Lesley. Integrating technology into the curriculum, telecommunications, distance learning.
Irene Fountas, Professor and Director of Reading Recovery; Ed.D., Boston University. Children's literature, literature-based literacy programs, process learning, thematic teaching.
Barbara P. Gibson, Assistant Professor; C.A.G.S., Lesley. Curriculum and social skill development for inclusive classes at secondary level.
Susan Gurry, Associate Professor and Director of Intensive Special Needs Program; Ed.D., Boston University. Creating inclusive communities and children with developmental disabilities.
Evangeline Harris-Stefanakis, Assistant Professor of Education; Ed.D., Harvard. Assessment of linguistic minority children.
William Holt, Assistant Professor of Education; M.A., California State at Los Angeles. Use of multicultural curriculum and pedagogy.
Judith Hudson, Assistant Professor; M.Ed., Springfield. Multicultural education, research on white identity development and the intersection of racism and sexism.
Susan Hundley, Assistant Professor; M.A., Ohio State. Early literacy, reading recovery, children's literature, at-risk children.
Roberta Jackson, Assistant Professor; M.Ed., Massachusetts Boston. Expansion of knowledge and curriculum about African influences on the societies of the Americas.
Sondra Langer, Associate Professor and Director of Early Childhood Education Program; M.A., Simmons. Early childhood education, teacher approaches to dealing with sensitive issues in the classroom and administration.
Anne Larkin, Professor and Director of Project Promise; Ph.D., Boston College. School reform and restructuring, special education, autism and middle school education.
Solange de Azambuja Lira, Associate Professor; Ph.D., Pennsylvania. Language diversity issues applied to first and second language learning.
Mary McMackin, Assistant Professor and Prepracticum Advisor; Ed.D., Massachusetts Lowell. Developing effective reading and writing instruction for all learners, authentic assessment, staff development, especially teacher inquiry.
Nancy Mehlem, Associate Professor; Ed.D., Boston University. Models of inclusion, continuous quality improvement in off-campus learning communities, role of persons with disabilities in church communities.
Susan Merrifield, Assistant Professor of English/Education; Ed.D., Harvard. Retention of minority and low-income college students, student teacher thinking about lesson planning.
Margery Staman Miller, Professor and Director of Reading Program; Ed.D., Pennsylvania. Integration of reading and writing, assessment, staff development and teacher research, clinician and consultant for literacy issues.
Mary Mindess, Professor of Education; Ed.M., Boston University. Design and evaluation of developmentally based programs.
Deborah O'Brien Morin, Assistant Professor and Acting Director of Curriculum and Instruction Program; Ph.D., Kent State. Gifted education, early childhood and special education curriculum and instruction.
Lenore D. Parker, Professor of Education; Ed.D., Boston University. Use of children's literature to promote moral reasoning.
Janice Philpot, Assistant Professor and Director of DeWitt Wallace Pathways to Teaching Careers Program; C.A.S., Harvard. Development and implementation of full inclusion models for all persons, curriculum development for individuals, intensive special needs.
Diane Powell, Assistant Professor; M.A., Ohio State. Reading recovery and early literacy learning initiatives.
May Carson Reinhardt, Associate Professor and Director of Middle School Education Program; Ed.D., Harvard. Relationships between reading and writing, integrating technology in language arts programs, interdisciplinary curriculum development.
Jose Ribeiro, Associate Professor; Ph.D., Harvard; Ph.D., Boston College. Issues in assessing bilingual and minority populations, cultural differences and emotional development.
Maureen Riley, Associate Professor of Education; M.Ed., Harvard. Ways varies assessment formats facilitate and obstruct the information process of students with learning disabilities.
Nancy Roberts, Professor and Director of Computers in Education Program; Ed.,D., Boston University. Technology in education, computer simulation, development of curriculum materials applying a systems dynamics approach to the teaching of problem solving.
Arlyn Roffman, Professor; Ph.D., Boston College. Special education, learning disabilities in adolescents and adults and social skills remediation.
Maria B. de Lourdes Serpa, Associate Professor and Director of Special Needs Program; Ph.D., Boston University. Nondiscriminatory assessment, bilingualism special education, biliteracy, multicultural education, Portuguese literacy and language development.
Debora Sherman, Professor; Ed.D., NYU. Adult literacy and learning, educational studies on teaching reading and writing.
Winifred Skolnikoff, Assistant Professor; M.Ed., Lesley. Children's literature, writing, cultures and environment.
Beverly J. Smith, Assistant Professor of Education; M.Ed., Harvard. Professional development of experienced teachers, gender and multicultural concerns in schools, factors that influence the achievement of black students.
William Stokes, Associate Professor and Director of Elementary Education; Ed.D., Boston University. Psycholinguistics with special emphasis on literacy development, second language development, literacy and critical literacy.
Joanne M. Szamreta, Associate Professor of Education; Ph.D., Boston College. Development and evaluation of early intervention programs.
Joan Thormann, Professor; Ph.D., Oregon. Technology in education, design and implementation of programs to train teachers.
Maureen Brown Yoder, Associate Professor; Ed.D., Boston University. Technology in education, telecommunications and multimedia.

LEWIS & CLARK COLLEGE

Graduate School of Professional Studies

Programs of Study

The Lewis & Clark College (LC) Graduate School of Professional Studies offers programs of study leading to the Master of Arts in Teaching (M.A.T.), the Master of Education (M.Ed.), the Master of Arts (M.A.), and the Master of Science (M.S.) degrees as well as licensure for teachers, educational administrators, school counselors, and school psychologists.

The M.A.T. is awarded in the teacher education program, which offers preparation for four levels of teaching licensure—early childhood, elementary, middle school, and high school—and multiple endorsement areas, including art, sciences, ESOL/bilingual, foreign languages, language arts, mathematics, reading, social studies, and special education. The preservice program for beginning teachers is a fourteen-month program that begins in summer and leads to an Oregon teaching license. The in-service program, which may be completed over several years, allows experienced teachers to earn a master's degree.

The M.Ed. is awarded in the Special Education: Deaf and Hard of Hearing Program, which offers two types of endorsements—early intervention/early childhood special education and deaf and hard-of-hearing special education (K–12). This is a twelve-month program that begins in the summer and leads to an Oregon teaching license.

The M.A. and M.S. degrees are awarded in the counseling psychology program, which offers three concentrations—school counseling, school psychology, and counseling psychology (child or adult emphasis)—with the opportunity for specific preparation in addictions. These programs range in length from 1½ to 3 years and lead to an Oregon Personnel Service License.

Aspiring administrators and superintendents have the opportunity to earn Oregon administrative licenses through the Educational Administration (EDAD) Program. Because Oregon requires administrators to hold a master's degree, Lewis & Clark also offers a joint M.A.T./EDAD Program. The EDAD programs range in length from one to several years, depending on the number of hours taken per semester.

Research Facilities

Lewis & Clark's library includes more than 600,000 items. In addition, the School's computer facilities support educational research and are linked to multiple national and international networks. Research is also supported through the training that is provided to teachers, which prepares them to become teacher researchers. All teachers-in-training and counselors-in-training also participate in extensive internships.

Financial Aid

To help students meet the cost of study, Lewis & Clark offers need-based grants, multicultural scholarships, educational loans, and a payment plan that enables students to divide tuition into monthly payments.

Cost of Study

The cost for the fourteen-month Pre-Service Teacher Education Program is $18,300. All other students may take courses based on the hourly rate of $423 per semester credit.

Living and Housing Costs

Lewis & Clark students select among several housing options. Some live with other students, others with their families; some live in rented apartments, others elect to purchase homes. Lewis & Clark is fairly centrally located in Portland, and there is an adequate supply of apartments and houses for rent or sale in the Portland metropolitan area.

Student Group

Students come to LC from many walks of life, bringing with them a variety of experiences that enhance classroom discussions. Seventy-five percent of the approximately 600 graduate students are women. The School has some students who are members of minority groups, but it would like to increase the number of these students that are enrolled. With an average age of 31 and an age range from 24 to 55, the majority of students have a number of years of professional experience. Most of LC's master's degree recipients go on to work in public or independent schools; some go to work in community mental health settings both in the U.S. and abroad.

Student Outcomes

Many of the best teachers in the region come out of the Lewis & Clark program in teacher education, including three out of the last four Oregon Teachers of the Year. Graduates of the Educational Administration Program go on to become school leaders and proponents of innovative educational practices. Several counseling psychology students have become presidents of state and national boards. The nationally known Special Education: Deaf and Hard of Hearing Program sends graduates all over the world to provide an education for the hearing impaired.

Location

The beautiful Lewis & Clark campus is situated on 115 wooded acres in a residential area, 6 miles from downtown Portland, Oregon. Oregon's best-known peak, Mount Hood, which is visible from campus, can be reached by car in about an hour, while the Pacific Ocean is less than 2 hours in the other direction. Portland and the surrounding area are home to a wide array of opportunities ranging from cultural attractions, such as the Oregon Ballet Theatre, to outdoor recreation, such as rock climbing, skiing, wind surfing, community soccer leagues, and more.

The College and The School

Founded in 1867, Lewis & Clark College is the largest private liberal arts institution in Oregon. The School has been training teachers for more than 100 years and is well known for its excellent education programs. The Lewis & Clark Graduate School of Professional Studies is in the wonderful position of being a small school (approximately 600 graduate students) within a larger college. The amenities of a major college, including excellent food service, a book store, athletic facilities, a large newly expanded library, computer labs, and more, are all available. Graduate students are part of an intimate community, where the registrar and career specialists are easily accessible, faculty and staff members call students by name, and the Dean's door is always open.

Applying

Information and application forms can be obtained from the address below. Applicants are judged on the basis of their academic record, letters of recommendation, relevant work experience, and test scores, which vary by program and may include the GRE, Miller Analogies Test, or PRAXIS I. The following deadlines apply to full-time students: Pre-service Teacher Education Program applications are due January 8; Special Education: Deaf and Hard of Hearing Program elementary and secondary early decision applications are due December 1; elementary and secondary regular decision applications and all early intervention applications are due March 1; counseling psychology applications are due for spring start by November 1, for summer start by February 1, and for fall start by May 1; in-service teacher education student applicants are admitted once a month, with applications due by the first of the month; part-time students and educational administration students are admitted on an ongoing basis. The deadline for financial aid applications is one month prior to the beginning of a student's starting semester.

Correspondence and Information

Lewis & Clark College
Graduate School of Professional Studies
Campus Box 93
0615 Southwest Palatine Hill Road
Portland, Oregon 97219

Telephone: 503-768-7700
Fax: 503-768-7715
E-mail: grad@lclark.edu
World Wide Web: http://www.lclark.edu

Lewis & Clark College

THE FACULTY AND THEIR RESEARCH

Charles R. Ault Jr., Professor of Education; Ph.D., Cornell, 1980. Science education, environmental and earth science education.
H. William Brelje, Professor of Special Education: Deaf and Hard of Hearing and Program Chair; Ed.D. Portland, 1971.
Celeste Brody, Associate Professor of Education; Ph.D., Ohio State, 1971. Cooperative learning, instructional theory, interdisciplinary graduate programs.
Vicki Brooks, Assistant Professor of Counseling Psychology; Ph.D., Wyoming, 1992. School counseling.
Carolyn Bullard, Professor of Special Education: Deaf and Hard of Hearing; Ph.D., Washington (Seattle), 1973. Special education: early childhood/early intervention.
Mary Burke-Hengen, Visiting Assistant Professor of Education; M.S., Portland State, 1978; M.S., St. Cloud State, 1965. Multicultural literature, secondary teacher education, curriculum and instruction.
Jay Casbon, Associate Professor of Educational Administration and Dean of the Graduate School; Ed.D., Alabama, 1981. Superintendency.
Carol Doyle, Assistant Professor of Counseling Psychology; Ph.D., Nevada, 1996. Adult counseling, research.
Connie Eldridge-Pederson, Assistant Professor of Counseling Psychology; Ph.D., North Texas, 1989. Family counseling, children and women's issues, addictions.
David Hagstrom, Associate Professor of Educational Administration; Ed.D., Illinois, 1966. Leadership.
Nathalie Heger, Instructor of Educational Administration; M.A., Lewis & Clark, 1988. The principalship.
Mary Henning-Stout, Professor of Counseling Psychology; Ph.D., Nebraska–Lincoln, 1986. School counseling, conflict in schools, adolescence and girls, alternatives in academic assessment and evaluation.
Ruth Shagoury Hubbard, Mary Stuart Rogers Professor of Education; Ph.D., New Hampshire, 1988. Child and adolescent literature, art and literacy, and ethnography; writing across the curriculum; literacy development and instruction; teacher research.
Caryl Hurtig, Assistant Professor of Education and Core Coordinator; M.A., Whitworth, 1977. Teacher renewal, interdisciplinary studies, secondary teacher education.
Vern Jones, Professor of Education; Ph.D., Texas at Austin, 1971. Classroom management, special education.
Gordon Lindbloom, Associate Professor of Counseling Psychology and Program Chair; Ph.D., Oregon, 1974. Adult counseling, stress/anxiety in work, addictions, international students.
Andra Makler, Associate Professor of Education and Program Chair; Ed.D., Harvard, 1989. Classroom assessment; curriculum and instruction; teaching of history, policy, social studies, and teacher education; issues of justice.
Joan McIlroy, Associate Professor of Counseling Psychology; Ph.D., Colorado, 1973. Adult counseling, women at midlife, disasters and mental health of survivors.
Peter Mortola, Assistant Professor of Counseling Psychology; Ph.D., California, Santa Barbara, 1998. School psychology.
Nancy Nagel, Associate Professor of Education; Ed.D., Portland State, 1987. Real-world problem solving, elementary education/integrated curriculum, early childhood education.
Glennellen Pace, Associate Professor of Education; Ph.D., Oregon, 1983. Children's literature; early childhood education; literacy, language acquisition, and writing; talented and gifted.
Boyd Pidcock, Assistant Professor of Counseling Psychology; Ph.D., Texas Tech, 1998. Addictions.
Joan Polansky, Assistant Professor of Counseling Psychology; Ph.D., Arizona State, 1994. Adult counseling, abuse survivors.
Tom Ruhl, Assistant Professor of Education Administration and Program Chair; Ph.D., Oregon, 1990. The principalship and superintendency.
Gregory Smith, Associate Professor of Education; Ph.D., Wisconsin–Madison, 1989. Ecology, students at risk, school-community relations.
Kim Stafford, Associate Professor and Director of the Northwest Writing Institute; Ph.D., Oregon, 1979. Northwest independent presses; Northwest folklore; writing instruction, kindergarten through college.
Zaher Wahab, Professor of Education; Ph.D., Stanford, 1972. Race, class, and culture in education; religious fundamentalism; Afghanistan, Southeast Asia, Egypt, Southcentral Asia, and Turkmenistan.
James Wallace, Professor of Education; Ed.D., Harvard, 1966. Educational history, alternative education, urban studies.
Valerie White, Assistant Dean of the Graduate School; M.A., Antioch (Ohio), 1993. Diversity and cross-cultural studies.
Rosemary Williams, Associate Professor of Education; Ph.D., Hawaii, 1984. Assessment and research.
Carol Witherell, Professor of Education; Ph.D., Minnesota, 1978. Character and moral development, narrative and story in education, human development.

In addition to degree-granting programs, Lewis & Clark also offers continuing professional education through the Northwest Writing Institute and the Center for Professional Development.

Lewis & Clark College is located in Portland, Oregon, home of tall trees, mountain views, and 1.8 million people. Oregon's best-known peak, Mount Hood, can be seen from campus.

MICHIGAN STATE UNIVERSITY

College of Education

Programs of Study

The College of Education provides a dynamic atmosphere for graduate study through its strong commitment to excellence in research, teaching, and service. Long recognized for its preparation of practitioners, the College has become one of the leading centers of educational research. Graduate students have many opportunities to study and work with faculty members whose research achievements are recognized worldwide. The College has an international reputation for innovation and leadership. Engaged in dozens of major projects that offer financial support and valuable research experience, the College provides an outstanding atmosphere for graduate study. It is also known for its use of practical experiences at both the graduate and undergraduate levels. The College offers the following degrees in a wide variety of specialties: Master of Arts, Educational Specialist, Doctor of Education, and Doctor of Philosophy. Within the overall requirements for each program, considerable latitude exists for students to plan their studies in collaboration with designated faculty advisers. Through such formative experiences, students develop the insight and skill needed to deal with the many challenges in the education profession today. The College offers graduate studies in its Departments of Teacher Education; Educational Administration; Counseling, Educational Psychology and Special Education; and Kinesiology. The Department of Teacher Education (TE) offers programs in curriculum, teaching, and educational policy. Course work and a master's program are also offered at overseas sites. Programs in adult and continuing education, higher education administration, and elementary and secondary educational administration are offered through the Department of Educational Administration. The Department of Counseling, Educational Psychology and Special Education (CEPSE) offers programs in technology, instructional design, measurement and quantitative methods, rehabilitation counseling, school psychology, counseling, and counseling psychology. The Department of Kinesiology offers a cross-disciplinary program that relates physical activity to human well-being.

Research Facilities

The College is nationally and internationally known for its research on teaching and learning. Several large research efforts are under way at the following centers: the Institute for Research on Teaching, the Center for Policy Research in Education, and the Third International Mathematics and Science Study. In addition, the Institute for the Study of Youth Sports is noted for its research in physical education. A major contract from the state supports a Michigan Center for Career and Technical Education. International research and development take place through the Office of International Networks in Education and Development. The Michigan State University (MSU) libraries have a rapidly growing collection of more than 4 million volumes and 28,000 current serial titles. Graduate students can obtain additional materials through the libraries' participation in interlibrary loan programs and membership in the Center for Research Libraries. The University Computer Laboratory operates an IBM 3090-200J and a Convex 240 UNIX mainframe. This hardware, coupled with an extensive software library and enhanced by the MSU campuswide computer network and electronic mail system (provided free to students), several Macintosh and IBM/PC computer laboratories (available throughout the campus), plus a College-based multifaceted data network, provides the faculty and students with the opportunity to work with state-of-the-art computer technology. The College also maintains a Technology Exploration Center and two microcomputer laboratories. Excellent relationships with the professional development schools, the state Department of Education, school districts, and schools in the surrounding area provide opportunities for field-based research in education.

Financial Aid

Graduate assistantships and fellowships are available on a competitive basis to students who elect full-time study. Half-time assistantships carried a minimum monthly stipend of $1004 in 1997–98, plus a waiver of out-of-state tuition, a 6-credit tuition waiver per semester, and a medical plan.

Cost of Study

Graduate tuition for Michigan residents was $216 per credit hour in 1997–98; nonresidents paid $437 per credit hour. Full-time students were assessed fees of $276 per semester. All fees are subject to change.

Living and Housing Costs

Dormitory costs for a single student in a single room were $4052 per academic year in 1997–98, including meals. Double-room occupancy costs were $3852 per person, including meals. University housing is also available for married students. The costs in 1997–98 ranged from $381 per month for a one-bedroom apartment to $454 per month for a two-bedroom apartment. These fees are subject to change.

Student Group

The University's enrollment is more than 40,000. The total graduate enrollment of the College of Education is more than 1,000, with more than 500 master's students and approximately 500 doctoral students.

Alumni of the College are leaders in virtually all areas of education across the nation and around the world. Many are respected teachers in elementary, middle, and secondary schools. Others are administrators, curriculum specialists, coaches, educational technology specialists, school psychologists, and counselors. Still others are making important contributions to institutions of higher education, government, and industry.

Student Outcomes

Graduates of the College of Education are hired in a variety of settings, including university, college, K–12 institutions, government, and the private sector, depending upon the specific degree obtained. Jobs obtained include teaching, research, coaching, counseling, sports training or administration, education administration, student residence life administration, and other professional education roles.

Location

Michigan State University is located in East Lansing, which is immediately adjacent to Lansing, the state capital. As a Big Ten university, Michigan State offers access to comprehensive cultural and athletic programs and events.

The University

The first land-grant institution, Michigan State University is also a member of the Association of American Universities. Founded in 1855, the University offers programs leading to baccalaureate, master's, specialist's, and doctoral degrees through fourteen colleges. The campus, comprising 2,100 acres, has long been recognized as one of the most attractive in the nation.

Applying

Application forms for admission to the Graduate School can be obtained from the Office of Admissions and Scholarships, Michigan State University, East Lansing, Michigan 48824-1046. Applications must be received at least two months prior to the anticipated first term of enrollment. Ph.D. applicants in CEPSE and TE should apply by January 15 and applicants in Counseling Psychology should apply by January 5. Applicants requesting financial aid should submit their application by February 15. Applicants pay a $30 application fee; international students pay a $40 application fee.

Correspondence and Information

Student Affairs Office
134 Erickson Hall
College of Education
Michigan State University
East Lansing, Michigan 48824-1034

Telephone: 517-353-9680
E-mail: coesao@pilot.msu.edu
World Wide Web: http://www.educ.msu.edu/

Michigan State University

THE FACULTY

Department of Counseling, Educational Psychology and Special Education
Richard S. Prawat, Chairperson; Ph.D., Michigan State; 449 Erickson Hall.

Carole Ames, Ph.D., Purdue. Linda M. Anderson, Ph.D., Texas. Lois A. Bader, Ed.D., Maryland. King Beach, Ph.D., CUNY Graduate Center. Betsy J. Becker, Ph.D., Chicago. Alfiee Breland, Ph.D., Wisconsin. Harvey F. Clarizio, Ed.D., Illinois. Christopher M. Clark, Ph.D., Stanford. Nancy Crewe, Ph.D., Minnesota. W. Patrick Dickson, Ph.D., Stanford. Carol Sue Englert, Ph.D., Indiana. Robert E. Floden, Ph.D., Stanford. Linda Forrest, Ph.D., Washington (Seattle). Kenneth A. Frank, Ph.D., Chicago. Douglas Gordin, Ph.D., Northwestern. Rochelle Habeck, Ph.D., Wisconsin. Don E. Hamachek, Ph.D., Michigan. Walter C. Hapkiewicz, Ph.D., SUNY at Buffalo. Michael Leahy, Ph.D., Wisconsin. Frederick Lopez, Ph.D., Minnesota. Richard J. McLeod, Ph.D., Cornell. William A. Mehrens, Ph.D., Minnesota. Anna Neumann, Ph.D., Michigan. Evelyn R. Oka, Ph.D., Michigan. Aaron Pallas, Ph.D., Johns Hopkins. Linda A. Patriarca, Ph.D., Michigan State. Eugene Pernell, Ph.D., Michigan. Susan J. Peters, Ph.D., Stanford. Susan E. Phillips, Ph.D., Iowa. Leighton Price, Ph.D., Michigan State. Ralph T. Putnam, Ph.D., Stanford. Kenneth Rice, Ph.D., Notre Dame. William H. Schmidt, Ph.D., Chicago. Gloria Smith, Ph.D., Massachusetts. John Smith, Ph.D., Berkeley. Robbie J. Steward, Ph.D., Oklahoma. David A. Stewart, Ed.D., British Columbia. Norman R. Stewart, Ph.D., Wisconsin. David Wong, Ph.D., Stanford. Stephen L. Yelon, Ph.D., Michigan. Yong Zhao, Ph.D., Illinois at Urbana–Champaign.

Department of Educational Administration
Phillip Cusick, Chairperson; Ph.D., Syracuse; 418 Erickson Hall.

Janet Alleman, Ph.D., Iowa. Marilyn Amey, Ph.D., Penn State. Ann Austin, Ph.D., Michigan. Maenette Benham, Ed.D., Hawaii. Michael Boulus, Ph.D., Michigan State. Robert L. Church, Ph.D., Harvard. Marylee Davis, Ph.D., Michigan State. John Dirkx, Ph.D., Wisconsin–Madison. James Fairweather, Ph.D., Stanford. Marvin E. Grandstaff, Ed.D., Indiana. Keith Groty, Ph.D., Michigan. Frederick R. Ignatovich, Ph.D., Iowa. Mary Jim Josephs, Ph.D., Michigan State. Steven Kaagan, Ed.D., Harvard. Gloria Kielbaso, Ph.D., Michigan State. Kathryn M. Moore, Ph.D., Wisconsin. Anna Ortiz, Ph.D., UCLA. David Plank, Ph.D., Chicago. Robert Rhoads, Ph.D., Penn State. Lou Anna Simon, Ph.D., Michigan State. Gary Sykes, Ph.D., Stanford. Mun Tsang, Ph.D., Stanford. Moses Turner, Ed.D., Washington State. George VanDusen, Ph.D., Michigan State. Steven Weiland, Ph.D., Chicago. Lauren S. Young, Ed.D., Harvard.

Department of Kinesiology
Deborah Feltz, Chairperson; Ph.D., Penn State; 138 IM Circle.

Willis R. Baker, H.S.D., Indiana. Crystal F. Branta, Ph.D., Michigan State. Eugene W. Brown, Ph.D., Oregon. Gail Dummer, Ph.D., Berkeley. Martha E. Ewing, Ph.D., Illinois. Jeanne Foley, Ph.D., Michigan State. John L. Haubenstricker, Ph.D., Michigan State. Robert Malina, Ph.D., Pennsylvania and Wisconsin. John Narcy, M.A., Michigan State. Lynnette Overby, Ph.D., Maryland. James Pivarnik, Ph.D., Indiana. Tom Smith, M.A., Michigan State. Yevonne R. Smith, Ph.D., Michigan. V. Dianne Ulibarri, Ph.D., Connecticut.

Department of Teacher Education
Stephen M. Koziol Jr., Chairperson; Ph.D., Stanford: 318 Erickson Hall.

Janet Alleman, Ph.D., Iowa. Charles W. Anderson, Ph.D., Texas. Keith Anderson, Ph.D., Michigan State. Linda Anderson, Ph.D., Texas. Laura Apol, Ph.D., Iowa. Lois A. Bader, Ed.D., Maryland. Henrietta Barnes, Ph.D., Michigan State. Tom Bird, Ph.D., Stanford. Cassandra Book, Ph.D., Purdue. Jere E. Brophy, Ph.D., Chicago. J. Bruce Burke, Ph.D., Syracuse. Douglas R. Campbell, Ph.D., Stanford. Daniel Chazan, Ed.D., Harvard. William Cole, Ed.D., Wayne State. Mark Conley, Ph.D., Syracuse. Brian D. DeLany, Ph.D., Stanford. Patricia Edwards, Ph.D., Wisconsin. Helen Featherstone, Ed.D., Harvard. Joseph Featherstone, A.B., Harvard. Sharon B. Feiman-Nemser, Ed.D., Columbia. Robert E. Floden, Ph.D., Stanford. Susan Florio-Ruane, Ed.D., Harvard. James J. Gallagher, Ed.D., Harvard. Joyce Grant, Ed.D., Harvard. Diane Holt-Reynolds, Ph.D., Michigan. William W. Joyce, Ed.D., Northwestern. Mary Kennedy, Ph.D., Michigan State. David F. Labaree, Ph.D., Pennsylvania. Judith E. Lanier, Ph.D., Michigan State. Perry E. Lanier, Ed.D., Oklahoma. Timothy Little, Ph.D., Northwestern. Wanda T. May, Ph.D., Ohio State. Susan L. Melnick, Ph.D., Wisconsin. Bruce A. Mitchell, Ph.D., Ohio State. Gail Nutter, M.S., Michigan State. Lynn W. Paine, Ph.D., Stanford. P. David Pearson, Ph.D., Minnesota. Susan Peters, Ph.D., Stanford. David Pimm, Ph.D., Open University (England). Joyce G. Putnam, Ph.D., Michigan State. Gail Richmond, Ph.D., Connecticut. Peggy L. Riethmiller, Ph.D., Michigan State. Laura R. Roehler, Ph.D., Michigan State. Cheryl L. Rosaen, Ph.D., Michigan State. Kathleen J. Roth, Ph.D., Michigan State. John Schwille, Ph.D., Chicago. Sharon Schwille, Ph.D. candidate, Michigan State. Michael W. Sedlak, Ph.D., Northwestern. Joanne M. Simmons, Ph.D., Syracuse. Deborah Smith, Ph.D., Delaware. Edward L. Smith, Ph.D., Cornell. Gary Sykes, Ph.D., Stanford. Teresa Tatto, Ed.D., Harvard. Charles Thompson, Ed.D., Harvard. Mun C. Tsang, Ph.D., Stanford. Steven Weiland, Ph.D., Chicago. B. Bradley West, Ph.D., Michigan State. Christopher Wheeler, Ph.D., Columbia. Sandra Wilcox, Ph.D., Michigan State. Suzanne Wilson, Ph.D., Stanford. Lauren S. Young, Ed.D., Harvard.

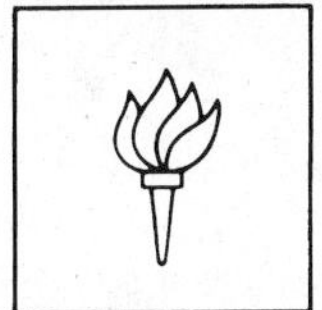

NEW YORK UNIVERSITY

School of Education

Programs of Study

The School of Education, one of the largest graduate schools at New York University, offers a diverse range of graduate programs. Now in its second century of educating professionals, scholars, and researchers, the School is committed to teaching, research, and community service in the urban environment.

The School prepares students for careers in education, health, nursing, communications, and the arts professions. Programs include all areas of elementary and secondary education, special education (including bilingual and early childhood), international education, TESOL, environmental education, studies in arts and humanities education, educational administration and technology, educational psychology, school and counseling psychology, counseling and guidance, community and public health education, rehabilitation counseling, recreation, nursing (including clinical and advanced practice), nutrition, public health nutrition, food and food management, occupational and physical therapy, speech pathology, music performance, music education, music entertainment professions, music technology, music therapy, performing and visual arts administration, studio art and photography, art education, decorative and folk art, art therapy, educational theater, and dance education. Degrees offered include Master of Arts, Master of Fine Arts, Master of Science, Master of Public Health, Master of Music, Certificate of Advanced Study, post-master's advanced certificate in nursing, Doctor of Arts (music therapy), Doctor of Education, Doctor of Philosophy, Doctor of Professional Studies (physical therapy), and Doctor of Psychology.

Research Facilities

Members of the School's faculty direct or participate in several unique research and service centers. These enterprises engage in work that spans the arts, communications, education, music, and policy arenas, serving scholars, students, teachers, and leaders in education, government, and industry. The centers include the New York University Institute for Education and Social Policy, the New York University Nursing Research Center, the New York University Center for Children, the Center for the Study of American Culture and Education, the Center for Urban Community College Leadership, the John A. Hartford Institute for the Advancement of Geriatric Nursing Practice, the Child Health and Family Center, the Metropolitan Center for Urban Education, the Nordoff-Robbins Center for Music Therapy, the Professional Development Laboratory for continuing teacher education, and the Reading Recovery Program Northeast Regional Site. Seven distinct libraries at the University contain more than 3 million volumes.

Financial Aid

The School annually awards more than $3 million in financial assistance to new and continuing graduate students. Assistance is based on merit and need and is offered to both full-time and part-time students. Special merit scholarships include the Deans' Opportunity Scholarship, the Peace Corps Scholarship, the Historically Black Colleges and Universities Scholarship, the Health Professions Opportunity Scholarship, the Centennial Scholarship (for part-time students), and the New York University Opportunity Fellowships. Graduate assistantships, teaching fellowships, resident assistantships, federally insured loans, and student employment are also available.

Cost of Study

Tuition and fees for the 1998–99 school year are $680 per credit, which includes a nonrefundable registration and services fee of $35. Estimated costs for books and supplies are $650 per year. The mandatory health services fee is $450 per year.

Living and Housing Costs

New York University offers a variety of on-campus housing opportunities from shared studios to suites with single bedrooms. Housing costs for the 1998–99 school year range from $5700 to $9000. Optional meal plans, ranging from $1600 to $3200, are also available. The Off-Campus Housing Office can assist students in locating housing in the metropolitan area.

Student Group

The School has a diverse graduate student body of 4,600 (plus 2,100 undergraduate students), which includes students from nearly every state. International students represent 17 percent of the graduate population.

Student Outcomes

Graduates hold leadership roles in schools, hospitals, communities, government and international agencies, and in industry. Graduates are teachers, health-care professionals, administrators, psychologists, counselors, artists, and performers. In addition, they are policy makers; private consultants; producers of children's media; publishers; program directors for museums and science centers; corporate trainers; record and video producers; concert promoters; art dealers; executives in public relations, advertising, television, and corporate communications; registered dietitians; food industry specialists; and researchers.

Location

Located in the historic Greenwich Village neighborhood of New York City, the School provides easy access to the nation's premier educational, cultural, artistic, research, and health institutions.

The University

Founded in 1831, New York University is one of the world's great universities, dedicated to research, scholarship, and the education of leaders for the twenty-first century. From its location in historic Greenwich Village in Manhattan, the University's commitment reaches from the local urban setting to a global involvement with the world community.

Applying

Applicants for degree programs must meet School-wide admissions criteria. Graduate Record Examinations (GRE) scores are required for doctoral applicants only. The fall deadline is March 1 for master's applications and February 1 for doctoral applications. Several programs also accept master's students for the spring term; the application deadline is December 1. The D.P.S. in physical therapy has a December 1 application deadline for summer matriculation. Additional departmental application materials may also be required. The TOEFL is required for all non–native speakers of English.

Correspondence and Information

Office of Graduate Admissions
School of Education
New York University
82 Washington Square East, 2nd Floor
New York, New York 10003-6680

Telephone: 212-998-5030
Fax: 212-995-4328
E-mail: ed.gradadmissions@nyu.edu
World Wide Web: http://www.nyu.edu/education/graduate.admissions

New York University

THE FACULTY

Ann Marcus, Dean
Patricia M. Carey, Associate Dean for Student Services and Public Affairs
W. Gabriel Carras, Associate Dean for Faculty Affairs
James Hurley, Associate Dean for Finance and Administration
Thomas James, Associate Dean for Academic Affairs
Lindsay Wright, Assistant Dean for Planning
Stanislaus Greidus, Director of Enrollment Management

Department of Administration, Leadership, and Technology
Terry A. Astuto, Professor and Chair

Department of Applied Psychology
LaRue Allen, Professor and Chair

Department of Art and Art Professions
Carlo Lamagna, Clinical Associate Professor and Chair

Department of Culture and Communication
Neil M. Postman, Professor and Chair

Department of Health Studies
Vivian P. J. Clarke, Associate Professor and Chair

Department of Music and Performing Arts Professions
Lawrence Ferrara, Professor and Chair

Division of Nursing
Diane O. McGivern, Professor and Head

Department of Nutrition, Food and Hotel Management
Marion Nestle, Professor and Chair

Department of Occupational Therapy
Deborah R. Labovitz, Professor and Chair

Department of Physical Therapy
Wen K. Ling, Clinical Associate Professor and Chair

Department of Speech-Language Pathology and Audiology
Phyllis Tureen, Associate Professor and Chair

Department of Teaching and Learning
Mark Alter, Professor and Chair

The School of Education works closely with New York City's public schools. Progressive graduate programs provide the city's teachers with new skills and methods. Students entering the field gain the finest student teaching experiences.

The Department of Art and Art Professions and the Department of Music and Performing Arts Professions offer the finest professional training and encourage students to explore and develop a wide range of styles and techniques.

New York University's Washington Square campus is located in the heart of historic Greenwich Village. Beyond is New York City—an outstanding resource for career-related internships and field experience.

NORTHEASTERN UNIVERSITY

Graduate Programs in Education

Programs of Study

The Department of Education offers Master of Education (M.Ed.) degrees in curriculum and instruction at elementary, secondary, and middle school levels in English, social studies, mathematics, and the science areas and in educational research. The Master of Arts in Teaching (M.A.T.) degree is offered at the secondary level in English, social sciences, mathematics, and physical sciences.

Research Facilities

The University libraries contain approximately 830,000 volumes; 1.9 million microforms; 170,000 government documents; 8,878 serial subscriptions; and 117,532 audio, video, and software titles. The central library contains technologically sophisticated services, including online catalog and circulation systems, a gateway to external networked information resources, and a network of CD-ROM optical disc databases. Students have access to major research collections through the Boston Library Consortium.

The Department of Education is also associated with the Center for Innovation in Urban Education, which provides a resource for the Department of Education programs.

The University Computing Center provides access to students and faculty members through its NUNET system and its interface with the Internet, Netscape, and Explorer to the campus mainframe and to the World Wide Web. Students have access to microcomputers and to the VAX mainframe, conferencing systems, a multimedia lab, and specialized computing equipment. The Department of Education offers courses in computer applications in education.

Financial Aid

Northeastern University awards need-based financial aid to graduate students through the Federal Perkins Loan, Federal Work-Study, and Federal Stafford Student Loan Programs.

The University also offers a limited number of minority fellowships and Martin Luther King, Jr. Scholarships. The Department of Education also offers a limited number of assistantship awards that include tuition remission for 10 hours per week of work.

Cost of Study

Tuition for the 1997–98 academic year in Department of Education courses was $415 per credit hour. Most department courses are 3 credits; completion of a master's degree in education requires at least fourteen 3-credit courses. Special charges may be made for teaching practicums. Other charges may include a Student Center fee and a health and accident insurance fee, which are required of full-time students.

Living and Housing Costs

Quarterly on-campus room rates for a single bedroom within an apartment ranged from $1460 to $1725 in 1997–98. Off-campus referral service is available (telephone: 617-373-4872). Shared bedrooms in apartments ranged from $1210 to $1425 per quarter.

Student Group

In fall 1998, the graduate M.Ed. and M.A.T. programs included more than 125 graduate students. About half of the students are enrolled full-time. Graduate courses are offered mainly in the late afternoon and evening, which facilitates part-time enrollment.

Location

Northeastern University is located in Boston, which is a center of cultural activities. The Department of Education is located within walking distance of art exhibitions at the Museum of Fine Arts and the Isabella Stuart Gardner Museum and music concerts at Symphony Hall and Jordan Hall.

The University

Northeastern University is a privately endowed nonsectarian institution of higher learning and one of the largest private universities in the country.

Applying

Applications are accepted on a revolving basis. Complete applications from U.S. residents must be received at least one month prior to the beginning of the quarter in which the student is applying. International students must have completed applications submitted at least sixty days prior to the quarter for which they are applying. Either Graduate Record Examinations or Miller Analogies Test scores are required of U.S. students, and TOEFL scores are required of international students. Prospective students should contact the address below for application materials.

Correspondence and Information

Graduate Admissions Office
27 Lake Hall
Northeastern University
Boston, Massachusetts 02115
E-mail: mlynch@lynx.neu.edu
World Wide Web: http://www.casdn.neu.edu/~educate/

Northeastern University

THE FACULTY AND THEIR RESEARCH

Thomas H. Clark, Assistant Professor; M.A., Columbia Teachers College. Mathematics education, science education.
James W. Fraser, Professor and Acting Chair; Ph.D., Columbia Teachers College. History and politics of education, urban education and school reform (telephone: 617-373-4216).
Robert Fried, Visiting Associate Professor; Ed.D., Harvard.
Terry Haywoode, Assistant Professor; Ph.D., City University of New York. Human services, community education, community organizing, middle school reform.
Maurice Kaufman, Professor; Ph.D., NYU. Reading disabilities, remedial education.
Mervin D. Lynch, Professor; Ph.D., Wisconsin–Madison. Educational research, statistics, self-concept and creativity.
Joseph Meier, Associate Professor; Ed.D., Harvard. Educational philosophy, educational technology.
Peter C. Murrell Jr., Associate Professor; Ph.D., Wisconsin–Milwaukee. Cognitive psychology, human learning and acquisition of knowledge, urban education and school reform.
Irene A. Nichols, Associate Professor; Ed.D., Harvard. Psychology in education, early childhood development.

NORTHWESTERN UNIVERSITY

School of Education and Social Policy

Programs of Study

The School of Education and Social Policy offers programs leading to the M.S., M.A., and Ph.D. degrees. Programming is provided in five areas—the M.S. in education, the M.S. in marital and family therapy, the M.S. and Ph.D. in the learning sciences, the M.A. in counseling psychology, and the Ph.D. in human development and social policy. The learning sciences M.A. and Ph.D. programs are dedicated to the preparation of researchers, developers, and practitioners qualified to advance the scientific understanding and practice of teaching and learning. Both interdisciplinary programs in the learning sciences offer a synthesis of computational, educational, and social science research; linguistics; computer science; anthropology; and cognitive science. The Ph.D. program in human development and social policy prepares students to bridge human development, social science, and social policy decisions. Graduates of this program assume positions as teachers, researchers, and policy makers who can bring multidisciplinary knowledge about human development directly to bear upon policy. Concentrations in the M.S. program in education include public and private school teaching, public and private school administration, advanced teaching, higher education administration, and corporate training and development. Students enrolled full-time typically complete the program in twelve months, provided they matriculate with no course deficiencies; opportunities for part-time study are also available. The two-year M.S. program in marital and family therapy prepares students to be family therapists. Master's programs are also offered in counseling psychology and the learning sciences. The M.A. program in counseling psychology emphasizes intensive practitioner training in psychological, career, or corporate/industrial counseling. Closely monitored field training with adolescents, adults, and families, and ongoing integration of theory and applied practice are hallmarks of the program.

Research Facilities

Research libraries contain approximately 3.5 million volumes, 2.3 million microfilm units, and 37,000 serial publications. Research and teaching activities are supported by a state-of-the-art multimedia computing network with full Internet access. The School is actively involved with two University-wide research centers: the Institute for the Learning Sciences, which is devoted to cognitive science research and to educational uses of technology in schools and other educative settings, and the Institute for Policy Research, which promotes interdisciplinary urban policy research and training. Specialized research and service resources within the School include the Center for Talent Development, a nationally prominent center that identifies and provides programming for academically talented youth, their parents, and the professionals who work with them. The School has a formal affiliation with the Family Institute, an institution on the Northwestern campus that provides extensive Chicago-area clinical services, training, and research.

Financial Aid

Several forms of aid are available, including fellowships and scholarships. In addition, there are teaching assistantships awarded to doctoral students who work with the School's undergraduate programs. Special opportunities for research assistantships and other employment also exist within the School's and the University's many research centers. Arrangements for loans are also possible.

Cost of Study

Tuition for full-time study in the M.S. program in 1998–99 amounts to approximately $22,610 for the entire fourteen-course program; part-time enrollment is possible at $1615 per course. Tuition for full-time study in the M.S. in marital and family therapy amounts to approximately $29,070. Part-time enrollment is possible at $1615 per course. Tuition for full-time study (three courses per quarter) in pursuit of the M.A. or Ph.D. in 1998–99 is $20,430 for the academic year, or $6810 per quarter; part-time enrollment is assessed at $2424 per course.

Living and Housing Costs

The University operates a residence in Evanston for the use of graduate students. For those Northwestern students interested in securing off-campus housing near the University, information and assistance are also available.

Student Group

Graduate study occurs within the context of individualized instruction, and enrollments are selective. Currently, 114 students are enrolled in the M.S. programs and 177 in the M.A. and Ph.D. programs. Since an interdisciplinary perspective is valued, students with preparation in a wide range of disciplinary areas are encouraged to apply.

Student Outcomes

Graduates teach and conduct research in academic and nonacademic settings; occupy strategic policy positions in government, corporations, and institutions; and assume positions of responsibility in a wide range of service organizations. Potential professional settings for learning sciences graduates include University research and teaching as well as business, industry, or school system-based careers studying, designing, and/or implementing learning environments. Graduates of the Ph.D. program in human development and social policy assume positions as teachers, researchers, or policy makers who can bring multidisciplinary knowledge about human development directly to bear upon policy. Graduates of the M.A. program in counseling psychology are prepared for a range of service, research, administrative, and policy positions, working with individuals, families, groups, and organizations in a broad spectrum of social service, educational, and corporate/industrial settings. Graduates of the learning sciences M.A. program are practitioners in the vanguard of teaching and learning systems development and instructional resource development. Most students in the M.S. program in Education gain on-site experience through supervised internships for future careers as professional educators. Graduates of the M.S. program in marital and family therapy are qualified to work as systemic family therapists in a wide variety of settings.

Location

The campus is located on Lake Michigan, 12 miles north of Chicago. The beautiful lakefront campus offers a rich cultural environment through a wealth of theatrical, musical, and athletic events.

The University and The School

Established in 1851, Northwestern has grown to become one of the most distinguished private universities in the country. The School of Education and Social Policy has developed from its origins as a department of pedagogy by continually broadening its scope to encompass those educative, learning, and socializing experiences that take place throughout the life span in families, schools, communities, and the workplace.

Applying

Applications for admission are reviewed and acted upon as they are received. Students should consult program brochures for specific application deadlines. Applicants planning to seek financial aid must meet early submission deadlines.

Correspondence and Information

School of Education and Social Policy
(Please specify program)
Northwestern University
2115 North Campus Drive
Evanston, Illinois 60208-2610
Telephone: 847-491-3790 (Office of Student Affairs)
847-467-1458 (M.S. in education)
847-491-3264 (M.A. in counseling psychology)
World Wide Web: http://nuinfo.nwu.edu/education/

Master of Science in Marital and Family Therapy
The Family Institute
618 Library Place
Evanston, Illinois 60201
Telephone: 847-733-4300 Ext. 206

Northwestern University

THE FACULTY AND THEIR RESEARCH

Lee F. Anderson, Ph.D., Illinois at Urbana-Champaign. Global education, political issues in policymaking.
Ray Bareiss, Ph.D., Texas at Austin. Case-based reasoning, intelligent tutoring systems, multimedia computing, automated knowledge acquisition.
Margaret J. Barr, Ph.D., Texas at Austin. Counseling and student services, student affairs administration, student development and intervention.
Lawrence A. Birnbaum, Ph.D., Yale. Natural language understanding, opportunistic planning systems, machine learning.
Rebecca M. Blank, Ph.D., MIT. Labor markets poverty and public policy, income distribution, gender and work.
Lenore S. Blum, Ph.D., Northwestern. Health psychology, clinical education, training and supervision.
Philip J. Bowman, Ph.D., Michigan. Minority youth development, preventative intervention, social psychology of chronic role strain and adaptation processes, family support systems, adult development.
Douglas C. Breunlin, M.S., Case Western Reserve. Marital and family therapy, integrative theory.
Ava Carn-Watkins, Ph.D., Northwestern. Gifted adolescents, psychosocial development, counsel education.
Allan M. Collins, Ph.D., Michigan. Technology and education, portfolio assessment, technologically based school reform.
Donald E. Collins, M.A., Hofstra. Adult education, administration, biography.
Gregg C. Collins, Ph.D., Yale. Machine learning, planning and problem solving, computer models of cognitive processes.
Fay L. Cook, Ph.D., Chicago. Social welfare policy, public attitudes, policy issues in aging, family support systems.
Thomas D. Cook, Ph.D., Stanford. Social-psychological processes, measurement of attitudes, evaluation of social programs.
Solomon Cytrynbaum, Ph.D., Michigan. Developmental and psychodynamic processes, group and organization dynamics, gender and group relations, adult development.
Gregory Duncan, Ph.D., Michigan. Poverty and public policy, longitudinal research methods.
Daniel C. Edelson, Ph.D., Northwestern. Artificial intelligence, case-based teaching systems, collaborative learning environments.
Kenneth D. Forbus, Ph.D., MIT. Qualitative physics, cognitive simulation of analogy, intelligence tutoring systems and learning environments for science and engineering.
Karen C. Fuson, Ph.D., Chicago. Mathematics and learning, cognitive development.
Kathleen M. Galvin, Ph.D., Northwestern. Speech education, communicative studies.
Dedre Gentner, Ph.D., California, San Diego. Learning, reasoning, and conceptual change in adults and children; mental models; acquisition of meaning.
Louis M. Gomez, Ph.D., Berkeley. Applied cognitive science, application of computing and networking technology to learning and instruction, human-computer interaction, computer-supported cooperative work.
Gunhild O. Hagestad, Ph.D., Minnesota. Cross-cultural life span development, the family, older adults.
Sophie Haroutunian-Gordon, Ph.D., Chicago. Philosophy of education, philosophy of psychology, inquiry, interpretive discussion, teacher preparation.
G. Alfred Hess, Ph.D., Northwestern. School reform, urban education, school finance, educational policy.
Barton J. Hirsch, Ph.D., Oregon. Community psychology, social networks, ecology of adolescent development.
Jordan Jacobowitz, Ph.D., Hebrew (Jerusalem). Psychodiagnostics, personality assessment, personality and aging.
Alex Kass, Ph.D., Yale. Case-based reasoning, story understanding, machine learning, models of creativity, computer-based education.
Carol D. Lee, Ph.D., Chicago. Sociocultural foundations of literacy, literacy expertise within specific ethnic speech communities and their implications for learning and teaching processes, cultural models for knowledge representations in literacy-related tasks.
Susan A. Lee, Ph.D., Northwestern. Dance education, counseling.
Dan A. Lewis, Ph.D., California, Santa Cruz. Policy analysis, urban social problems, community organization, urban school reform.
Dan P. McAdams, Ph.D., Harvard. Personality development, identity and life stories, intimacy, adult development.
John L. McKnight, B.S., Northwestern. Communication, urban affairs, community intervention.
Douglas L. Medin, Ph.D., South Dakota. Theories of learning, memory and induction, computational models of cognition, concepts and classification of learning, models of similarity.
Robert J. Menges, Ph.D., Columbia. Teaching and learning in higher education institutions, professional development.
Paula M. Olszewski-Kubilius, Ph.D., Northwestern. Gifted education, child development, minority gifted child development.
Andrew Ortony, Ph.D., London. Knowledge representation and figurative language comprehension; models of cognition, motivation, and emotion.
Janet Osborn, M.A., Syracuse; LAFT. Qualitative research, gay and lesbian issues, survivors of sexual abuse and trauma.
Penelope L. Peterson, Ph.D., Stanford. Learning and teaching in schools and classrooms, particularly in mathematics and literacy; teacher learning in reform contexts; relations among educational research, policy, and practice.
William Pinsof, Ph.D., York. Marital and family therapy.
Michael Radnor, Ph.D., Northwestern. Computer-mediated learning, organization behavior, international technology, intercultural aspects of management.
Cheryl R. Rampage, Ph.D., Loyola. Marital and family therapy, gender and feminist therapy.
Gustave J. Rath, Ph.D., Ohio State. Group process, industrial/organizational psychology, systems analysis, human factors engineering.
Michael M. Ravitch, Ph.D., Stanford. Design and evaluation of instruction in medicine and health sciences, educational measurement and program evaluation, cognition in medicine.
Brian J. Reiser, Ph.D., Yale. Intelligent tutoring systems, interactive learning environments for science and technology, scientific inquiry skills.
Christopher K. Riesbeck, Ph.D., Stanford. Natural language and analyzers, case-based reasoners, intelligent computational media.
Lance J. Rips, Ph.D., Stanford. Theories of reasoning and mathematical problem solving, autobiographical memory, structure of words and sentence meaning.
James E. Rosenbaum, Ph.D., Harvard. Adolescent and adult development, organizational careers.
Linda Rubinowitz, Ph.D., Northwestern. Individual and marital family theory and therapy, life cycle formations.
Roger C. Schank, Ph.D., Texas at Austin. Theories of learning, understanding, teaching, and creativity; applications of artificial intelligence to education, memory processing, natural-language understanding, and case-based reasoning.
Bruce Sherin, Ph.D., Berkeley. Science education, instructional technology, external representations in science and mathematical learning.
Miriam Sherin, Ph.D., Berkeley. Mathematics teaching and learning, teacher cognition, teacher education.
Bruce D. Spencer, Ph.D., Yale. Social and educational measurement, statistics for policy analysis, demography, decision theory.
James P. Spillane, Ph.D., Michigan State. Educational policy, intergovernmental relations, school reform, relations between policy and local practice.
Linda A. Teplin, Ph.D., Northwestern. Mental health services/policies for youth and adult populations in the criminal justice system and community based-samples.
David H. Uttal, Ph.D., Michigan. Mental representation, cognitive development, spatial cognition, early symbolization.
Sandra R. Waxman, Ph.D., Pennsylvania. Language and conceptual development, early cognitive development, language and thought.
Catherine Weigel Foy, M.S.W., Illinois at Chicago. Treatment of adolescent daughters with their mothers, gender issues and therapy.
Samuel P. Whalen, Ph.D., Chicago. Talent and creativity studies, adolescent research.
John W. Wick, Ph.D., Iowa. Student performance improvement programs, psychometrics.
David E. Wiley, Ph.D., Wisconsin–Madison. Statistics and psychometrics; assessment of learning, ability, and performance; public policy and program evaluation.
Jeremy R. Wilson, Ph.D., Northwestern. University administration, institutional studies.
Edward J. Wisniewski, Ph.D., Brown. Cognitive science, conceptual combinations and category learning.

NORTHWESTERN UNIVERSITY

Learning Sciences Programs
School of Education and Social Policy

Programs of Study

The M.A. and Ph.D. programs in the learning sciences are dedicated to the preparation of researchers, developers, and practitioners qualified to advance the scientific understanding and the practice of teaching and learning. The programs are interdisciplinary, drawing on theories and approaches from education, cognitive psychology, developmental psychology, artificial intelligence, computer science, anthropology, and communications. The programs focus on understanding and improving learning environments, not only in schools and classrooms but also in homes, neighborhoods, and work environments. Research projects focus on developing and studying pedagogical, technological, and social policy innovations aimed at improving education. The design of technology plays a special role in the program, exploring ways that technological innovations can facilitate new cognitive and social roles for students and teachers.

Through course work and research apprenticeships, students become engaged in the three major themes that permeate research and theory in the learning sciences: (1) social context: the social, organizational, and cultural dynamics of learning and teaching in classrooms, museums, corporations and homes; (2) cognition: scientific models of the structure and processes of learning and teaching by which knowledge skills are structured; and (3) design: building environments for learning and teaching incorporating multimedia, artificial intelligence, network technologies, and innovative curricular and classroom activity structures.

Research Facilities

The Learning Sciences Ph.D. Program is affiliated with the University-wide research center, the Institute for the Learning Sciences. The institute is a large interdisciplinary center devoted to basic and applied research at the frontiers of artificial intelligence, cognitive science, education, educational software, and affiliated activities. In its research activities, the institute works extensively with schools and industrial training centers. Students have access to the high technology computer and video environments within the institute and the School of Education and Social Policy. Specialized research and service resources within the School include the Center for Talent Development, a nationally prominent center that identifies and provides programming for academically talented youth, their parents, and the professionals who work with them. The School is also involved with the Center for Urban Affairs and Policy Research, which promotes interdisciplinary urban policy research and training. The School has a formal affiliation with the Family Institute of Chicago. Research libraries contain holdings totaling 3.9 million volumes, 3.4 million microfilm units, and 40,100 serial publications.

Financial Aid

Several forms of aid are available, including fellowships and teaching and research assistantships for Ph.D. students. A nine-month stipend of $12,042 and full tuition support are provided to each Ph.D. student accepted to the program. Special opportunities exist within the School's and the University's many research centers. Learning sciences Ph.D. students are eligible for multiyear funding, including summer support, which is competitively awarded.

Cost of Study

Tuition for both the Ph.D. program from September 1998 through August 1999 and for the twelve-month M.A. program is $22,700. Health insurance is available for all graduate students.

Living and Housing Costs

The University operates two residences in Evanston for graduate students. Information and assistance in securing off-campus housing are also available for students who wish to inquire.

Student Group

Graduate study occurs within the context of individualized personalized instruction, and, accordingly, enrollments are selective. The combined enrollment for 1997–98 for the Learning Sciences Program was 40 students. Enrollment in all others programs at the School of Education and Social Policy was 234 students.

Student Outcomes

Recent Ph.D. graduates have joined university faculty in leading departments of education and media arts. M.A. graduates work as educational designers, human factors engineers, and school technologists, employed by schools, universities, large and small software companies, international consulting firms, financial institutions, and training providers.

Location

The campus is located on Lake Michigan, 12 miles north of Chicago. The beautiful lakefront campus offers a rich cultural environment through a wealth of theatrical, musical, and athletic events. Its proximity to a major metropolitan complex further enriches Northwestern's student life.

The University and The School

Established in 1851, Northwestern has grown to become one of the most distinguished private universities in the country. The School of Education and Social Policy has developed from its origins as a department of pedagogy by continually broadening its scope to encompass those educative, learning, and socializing experiences that take place throughout the life span in families, schools, communities, and the workplace. The Learning Sciences Ph.D. Program was established in 1991.

Applying

Applications for admissions are reviewed and acted upon as they are received. Completed applications must be on file at least four weeks before the date of registration for the quarter in which the student expects to begin graduate study. Applicants planning to seek financial aid must meet early submission deadlines. Admission to the Learning Sciences Ph.D. Program is highly selective. Students with preparation in a range of disciplinary areas are encouraged to apply, since an interdisciplinary perspective is valued. No part-time students are accepted at this time.

Correspondence and Information

Learning Sciences Ph.D. Program
or
Learning Sciences M.A. Program
School of Education and Social Policy
Northwestern University
2115 North Campus Drive
Evanston, Illinois 60208-2610
Telephone: 847-491-7494
E-mail: ls-programs@mail.sesp.nwu.edu
World Wide Web: http://www.ls.sesp.nwu.edu

Northwestern University

THE FACULTY AND THEIR RESEARCH

Professors

Allan Collins, Professor of Education; Ph.D., Michigan. Technology and education, situated cognition, school restructuring, cognitive apprenticeship.
Kenneth D. Forbus, Professor of Computer Science; Ph.D., MIT. Qualitative physics, cognitive simulation of analogy, intelligent tutoring systems and learning environments for science and engineering.
Karen C. Fuson, Professor of Education; Ph.D., Chicago. Mathematics teaching and learning, cognitive development, design of teaching/learning activities.
Dedre Gentner, Professor of Psychology; Ph.D., California, San Diego. Learning, reasoning, and conceptual change in adults and children, especially processes of similarity, metaphor, and analogy; mental models; acquisition of meaning.
Douglas L. Medin, Professor of Psychology; Ph.D., South Dakota. Theories of learning, memory and induction, computational models of cognition, concepts and classification of learning, models of similarity.
Andrew Ortony, Professor of Education and Psychology and Area Coordinator, M.A. Program; Ph.D., London. Knowledge representation and figurative language comprehension, models of cognition and emotion, human-computer interaction and interface design.
Penelope Peterson, Professor of Education and Dean, School of Education and Social Policy; Ph.D., Stanford. Teaching and learning in different contexts, particularly in mathematics and literacy; relations among educational research, policy, and practice.
Lance J. Rips, Professor of Psychology; Ph.D., Stanford. Theories of reasoning and mathematical problem solving, autobiographical memory, structure of words and sentence meaning.
Roger C. Shank, John Evans Professor of Computer Science, Psychology, Social Policy, and Education; Ph.D., Texas. Theories of learning, understanding, teaching, and creativity; applications of artificial intelligence to education, memory processing, natural-language understanding, and case-based reasoning.

Associate Professors

Lawrence Birnbaum, Associate Professor of Computer Science; Ph.D., Yale. Semantic analysis, memory organization, learning, information access systems, intelligent performance support.
Louis M. Gomez, Associate Professor of Education and Computer Science; Ph.D., Berkeley. Supporting teaching and learning with computing and networking, applied cognitive science, human-computer interaction, computer-supported collaborative learning.
Carol D. Lee, Associate Professor of Education; Ph.D., Chicago. Sociocultural foundations of literacy, literacy expertise within specific ethnic speech communities and their implications for learning and teaching processes, cultural models for knowledge representations in literacy-related tasks.
Brian J. Reiser, Associate Professor of Education and Area Coordinator, Ph.D. Program; Ph.D., Yale. Interactive learning environments for science education, scientific inquiry and augmentation skills, conceptual change.
Christopher K. Riesbeck, Associate Professor of Computer Science; Ph.D., Stanford. Natural-language analysis, case-based reasoning, tools for authoring intelligent interactive systems.
Sandra R. Waxman, Associate Professor of Psychology; Ph.D., Pennsylvania. Language and conceptual development, early cognitive development, language and thought.

Assistant Professors

Daniel C. Edelson, Assistant Professor of Education and Computer Science; Ph.D., Northwestern. Computer support for open-ended learning, collaborative learning environments, scientific visualization environments for learning, case-based teaching systems.
Marjorie Faulstich Orellana, Assistant Professor of Education; Ph.D., USC. Literacy and language development of linguistic and cultural minority students; the education of immigrant children in urban schools; constructions of ethnicity, gender, social class, and identity through social practices.
Bruce L. Sherin, Assistant Professor of Education; Ph.D., Berkeley. Commonsense beliefs in science, programming environments for learning, external representations in science and mathematics.
Miriam Gamoran Sherin, Assistant Professor of Education; Ph.D., Berkeley. Mathematics teaching and learning, teacher cognition, teacher education.
James P. Spillane, Assistant Professor of Education; Ph.D., Michigan State. Education policy and school reform, intergovernmental relations, policy and practice.
David H. Uttal, Assistant Professor of Psychology; Ph.D., Michigan. Mental representation, cognitive development, spatial cognition, early symbolization.

Faculty Affiliates

Ray Bareiss, Associate Professor (Research) of the Institute for the Learning Sciences; Ph.D., Texas. Case-based reasoning, intelligent tutoring systems, multimedia computing, automated knowledge acquisition.
Sophie Haroutunian-Gordon, Professor of Education and Director, Master of Science in Education Program; Ph.D., Chicago. Philosophy of education, philosophy of psychology, inquiry, interpretive discussion, teacher preparation.
G. Alfred Hess Jr., Professor of Education (Research) and Director, Center for Urban School Policy; Ph.D., Northwestern. Urban school policy, school reform, school and community ethnography, school–community linkages, school finance, school accountability and assessment.
Alex Kass, Associate Professor (Research) of the Institute for the Learning Sciences; Ph.D., Yale. Educational simulation design for elementary, secondary, post-secondary, and professional education and training; architectures and authoring tools for computer-based learning-by-doing environments; distance learning; artificial intelligence, especially case-based reasoning, intelligent tutoring systems, automatic inference, and machine learning.
Eileen Lento, Assistant Professor of Education (Research); Ph.D., Northwestern. Math and science teaching and learning, teacher cognition, teacher education.
Michael M. Ravitch, Associate Professor of Education; Ph.D., Stanford. Problem-based learning, clinical reasoning and decision making, measurement and evaluation, faculty development as educators.
Samuel P. Whalen, Assistant Professor (Research) of the Center for Talent Development; Ph.D., Chicago. Adolescence, talent development, social psychology of creativity, intrinsic motivation and learning, school-linked social services.

High school students discuss the progress of their investigation of an evolution scenario developed by students in Professor Reiser's research group.

THE OHIO STATE UNIVERSITY

College of Education

Programs of Study

The College of Education awards the M.A., M.Ed. and Ph.D. degrees from its three schools. The School of Educational Policy and Leadership includes administration and higher education; cultural studies in education (curriculum, history and policy studies, sport and somatic studies, technologies of instruction and media, and diversity and inclusion); general professional studies (teacher education and humanistic studies); and quantitative research, evaluation and measurement in education. The School of Physical Activity and Educational Services is composed of special education, sport and exercise sciences, wellness and human services (counselor education, school psychology, and rehabilitation services), and workforce education and lifelong learning (adult education, business education, and vocational-technical education). The School of Teaching and Learning offers integrated teaching and learning (early and middle childhood education, and physical and sensory disabilities), language, literacy and culture (English education, foreign language and second language education, social studies and global education, and drama, language arts, children's literature and reading education), and mathematics, science and technology education. Other OSU colleges offer agriculture, art, home economics, and music education programs.

The master's degree thesis plan requires 45 quarter hours of study, a thesis reporting original research, and an oral examination. The nonthesis option involves 50 quarter hours of study and a written comprehensive examination. The Doctor of Philosophy degree requires a minimum of 90 quarter hours beyond the master's level, one year of residence, written and oral examinations on course work, and an oral defense of the dissertation. Practicing administrators who have completed the master's degree can enter the 45-hour Specialists in Educational Administration certificate program. All programs are individualized according to the interests and experiences of the student.

The M.Ed. also is offered at Ohio State's regional campuses at Lima, Mansfield, Marion, and Newark. Information on all degree programs is located on the World Wide Web at http://www-afa.adm.ohio-state.edu/gradbull/fields/educ.html.

Research Facilities

The Ohio State University Libraries is one of the largest in the United States, with 4.8 million volumes. The newly merged Education, Human Ecology, Psychology, and Social Work Library contains 500,000 education volumes and more than 1,400 education and psychology journals. All material is accessible via a computerized catalog. Students can consult via e-mail with librarians familiar with education and expert in associated research techniques.

Financial Aid

Graduate associateships, student personnel assistantships, and Graduate School fellowships are available, along with numerous College awards. All financial aid is competitive and stipends vary. In most cases, resident and nonresident fees are paid also. Information of OSU financial aid and employment opportunities is available on the World Wide Web at http://www-afa.adm.ohio-state.edu/apps/.

Cost of Study

Graduate tuition for three quarters in 1997–98 costs $5,214 for Ohio residents and $13,473 for nonresidents. Part-time students are assessed a fee per quarter hour. A list of estimated expenses is on the World Wide Web at http://www-afa.adm.ohio-state.edu/apps/grad-dom/cost.html.

Living and Housing Costs

An Ohio resident will pay an estimated $8,530 a year for health insurance, books, a single room in a residence hall, and board. Further information is available on the World Wide Web at http://www-afa.adm.ohio-state.edu/apps/grad-dom/cost.html. Graduate student housing costs from $281 to $317 per month for a residence hall room; $365 per month for a one-bedroom apartment; and $465 per month for a two-bedroom apartment. Further information is available at the Web address http://www.rdh.ohio-state.edu/housing/. Off-campus housing can range from $250 to $400 per person.

Student Group

Total OSU enrollment is 54,000 at its Columbus and four regional campuses. The College of Education graduate enrollment totals 3,000, with a minority enrollment of 12 percent.

Location

The main campus is located in Columbus, Ohio, the state capital and one of the fastest growing urban areas in the United States. The city is a global center for high technology.

The University and The College

The Ohio State University is one of the 10 largest campuses in the country. The College of Education has been ranked in the top tier of graduate programs for the past five years and is a national leader in the Holmes Partnership teacher education reform initiative. The College's 130 full-time faculty members and numerous teacher educators also specialize in urban education and lifelong professional development for in-service teachers. Its close partnership with the University District neighborhoods offers opportunities for service learning and action research. A complete list of auxiliary programs can be found at the Web address http://www.osu.edu/units/ucomm/points/index.htm.

Applying

Downloadable applications to The Ohio State University are available from the Office of Admissions at http://www-afa.adm.ohio-state.edu/apps/grad-dom. Applicants can also receive applications by contacting Admissions Office—Graduate Area, The Ohio State University, Lincoln Tower, 1800 Cannon Drive, Columbus, Ohio 43210-1200 (telephone: 614-292-3980; fax: 614-292-4818; e-mail: admissions@osu.edu). There is a $30 application fee for domestic applicants and a $40 fee for international applicants. Applicants with disabilities can learn about services at http://www.acs.ohio-state.edu/units/ods or by calling 614-292-3307 (voice or TDD).

Correspondence and Information

General information about the College of Education can be found at the Web address http://www.coe.ohio-state.edu/ or by contacting the individual school:

School of Physical Activity and Educational Services
215 Pomerene Hall
The Ohio State University
1760 Neil Avenue
Columbus, Ohio 43210
Telephone: 614-292-6787

School of Educational Policy and Leadership
122 Ramseyer Hall
The Ohio State University
29 West Woodruff Avenue
Columbus, Ohio 43210
Telephone: 614-292-5181

School of Teaching and Learning
227 Arps Hall
The Ohio State University
1945 North High Street
Columbus, Ohio 43210
Telephone: 614-292-2332

The Ohio State University

THE FACULTY

School of Educational Policy and Leadership

Melvin Adelman, Associate Professor; Ph.D., Illinois at Chicago.
James Altschuld, Associate Professor; Ph.D., Ohio State.
Leonard Baird; Professor; Ed.D., UCLA.
Marjorie Cambre, Associate Professor; Ph.D., Indiana.
Rafael Cortada, Associate Professor; Ph.D., Fordham.
Suzanne Damarin, Professor; Ph.D., Ohio State.
Philip T. K. Daniel, Associate Professor; Ph.D., Illinois at Urbana-Champaign.
Ayres D'Costa, Associate Professor; Ph.D., Ohio.
Ada Demb, Associate Professor; Ph.D., Harvard.
Robert Donmoyer, Professor and Director; Ph.D., Stanford.
Erwin Epstein, Professor; Ph.D., Chicago.
Antoinette Errante, Assistant Professor; Ph.D., Minnesota.
Beverly Gordon, Associate Professor; Ph.D., Wisconsin–Madison.
Donald Haefele, Associate Professor; Ph.D., Syracuse.
Keith Hall, Professor; Ed.D., Indiana.
Kenneth Howey, Professor; Ph.D., Wisconsin–Madison.
Wayne Hoy, Professor and Fawcett Chair; D.Ed., Penn State.
John Kennedy, Professor; Ed.D., Massachusetts.
Seymour Kleinman, Professor; Ph.D., Ohio State.
Patricia Lather, Associate Professor; Ph.D., Indiana.
Robert Lawson, Professor; Ph.D., Michigan.
Mary Leach, Assistant Professor; Ph.D., Illinois at Urbana-Champaign.
William Loadman, Professor; Ph.D., Michigan State.
Douglas Macbeth, Assistant Professor; Ph.D., Berkeley.
Helen Marks, Assistant Professor; Ph.D., Michigan.
Gail McCutcheon, Associate Professor; Ph.D., Stanford.
Daniel Miller, Associate Professor; Ph.D., Cornell.
Brad Mitchell, Associate Professor; Ph.D., Utah.
Emmalou Norland, Associate Professor; Ph.D., Ohio State.
Gerald Reagan, Professor; Ph.D., Michigan State.
Robert Rodgers, Associate Professor; Ph.D., Ohio State.
Mary Ann Sagaria, Associate Professor; Ed.D., Penn State.
Phillip Smith, Associate Professor; Ph.D., Michigan.
William Taylor, Associate Professor; Ph.D., Indiana.
Cynthia Uline, Assistant Professor; Ph.D., Penn State.
Anita Woolfolk-Hoy, Professor; Ph.D., Texas at Austin.
I. Phillip Young, Professor; Ed.D., Tennessee.
Nancy Zimpher, Professor and Dean; Ph.D., Ohio State.

School of Physical Activity and Educational Services

Ketra Armstrong; Assistant Professor; Ph.D., Ohio state.
Ralph C. Bates, Associate Professor; Ed.D., Oregon.
Fred Bemak, Associate Professor; Ph.D., Massachusetts.
David Boggs, Professor; Ph.D., Michigan State.
Janet Buckworth; Assistant Professor; Ph.D., Georgia.
Gwendolyn Cartledge, Associate Professor; Ph.D., Ohio State.
P. Chelladurai, Professor; Ph.D., Waterloo.
Rita Chung, Assistant Professor; Ph.D., Wellington (New Zealand).
John O. Cooper, Professor; Ph.D., Kansas.
Donna Ford-Harris, Associate Professor; Ph.D., Cleveland State.
Ralph Gardner, Assistant Professor; Ph.D., Ohio State.
Darcy Granello, Assistant Professor; Ph.D., Ohio.
Paul Granello, Assistant Professor; Ph.D., Ohio.
Bruce Growick, Associate Professor; Ph.D., Wisconsin–Madison.
Jackie Herkowitz, Professor; Ph.D., Purdue.
Timothy Heron, Professor; Ed.D., Temple.
William Heward, Professor; Ph.D., Massachusetts.
Samuel Hodge, Assistant Professor, Ph.D., Ohio State.
Richard Howell, Associate Professor; Ph.D., New Mexico.
Ronald Jacobs, Associate Professor; Ph.D., Indiana at Bloomington.
Paul Jansma, Professor; Ph.D., Wisconsin.
Timothy Kirby, Associate Professor; Ph.D., Texas A&M.
Michael Klein, Associate Professor; Ph.D., Penn State.
David Lamb, Professor; P.D., Michigan State.
Jon Linderman, Assistant Professor; Ph.D., Berkeley.
Larry Magliocca, Associate Professor; Ph.D., Ohio State.
Antoinette Miranda, Assistant Professor; Ph.D., Cincinnati.
Jack Naglieri, Professor; Ph.D., Georgia.
Camilla O'Bryant, Assistant Professor; Ph.D., Ohio State.
Anthony Olinzock, Associate Professor; Ph.D., Pennsylvania.
Mary O'Sullivan, Associate Professor; Ph.D., Ohio State.
Donna Pastore, Assistant Professor; Ph.D., Ohio State.
Rick Petosa, Associate Professor; Ph.D., Southern Illinois.
David Porretta, Associate Professor; Ph.D., Temple.
Ray Ryan, Associate Professor; Ed.D., Missouri–Columbia.
Diane Sainato, Associate Professor; Ph.D., Pittsburgh.
Susan Sears, Associate Professor and Associate Dean; Ph.D., Ohio State.
William Sherman, Professor; Ph.D., Texas at Austin.
Daryl Siedentop, Professor and Associate Dean; P.E.D., Indiana.
David Stein, Associate Professor; Ph.D., Michigan.
Sandra Stroot, Associate Professor; Ph.D., Northern Colorado.
Deborah Tannehill, Associate Professor; Ph.D., Idaho.
Nancy Wardwell, Assistant Professor; Ph.D., Toledo.
Joe Wheaton, Assistant Professor; Ph.D., Wisconsin.

School of Teaching and Learning

Deborah Bainer, Associate Professor; Ph.D., Ohio State.
Rhoda Becher, Associate Professor; Ph.D., Ohio State.
Michael Beeth, Assistant Professor; Ph.D., Wisconsin.
Mary Bendixen-Noe, Assistant Professor; Ph.D., Ohio State.
Donna G. Berlin, Associate Professor; Ph.D., Ohio State.
James Bishop, Associate Professor; Ph.D., MIT.
Rudine Sims Bishop, Professor; Ed.D., Wayne State.
Herschell M. Bratt, Associate Professor; Ph.D., Purdue.
Patricia Brosnan, Assistant Professor; Ph.D., SUNY at Buffalo.
Caroline Clark, Assistant Professor; Ph.D., Michigan.
Patricia Connard, Associate Professor; Ph.D., Pittsburgh.
Karin Dahl, Associate Professor; Ph.D., Indiana.
Diane DeFord, Professor; Ed.D., Indiana.
Johanna DeStefano, Professor; Ph.D., Stanford.
Cynthia Dillard, Assistant Professor and Assistant Dean; Ph.D., Washington State.
Brian Edmiston, Assistant Professor; Ph.D., Ohio State.
Patricia Enciso, Assistant Professor.; Ph.D., Ohio State.
David Fernie, Associate Professor; Ed.D., Massachusetts.
Evelyn Freeman, Associate Professor; Ph.D., Ohio State.
Mary Jo Fresch, Assistant Professor; Ph.D., Ohio State.
Maria Galvez-Martin, Assistant Professor; Ph.D., Ohio State.
Charles Hancock, Associate Professor; Ph.D., Ohio State.
David Haury, Associate Professor; Ph.D., Washington (Seattle).
Phillip Heath, Associate Professor; Ed.D., Oklahoma State.
Janet Hickman, Associate Professor; Ph.D., Ohio State.
Lynn Johnson, Associate Professor; Ph.D., Indiana State.
Marilyn Johnston, Associate Professor; Ph.D., Utah.
Rebecca Kantor-Martin, Associate Professor; Ed.D., Boston University.
Susan Kent, Assistant Professor; Ph.D., Ohio State.
Becky Kirschner, Assistant Professor; Ph.D., Michigan.
Barbara Lehman, Associate Professor; Ed.D., Virginia.
Carol Lyons, Associate Professor; Ph.D., Ohio State.
Sandra McCormick, Professor; Ph.D., Ohio State.
Betsy McNeal, Assistant Professor; Ph.D., Purdue.
Merry Merryfield, Associate Professor; Ed.D., Indiana.
Maia Pank Mertz, Professor; Ph.D., Minnesota.
Steve Miller, Associate Professor; Ph.D., Ohio State.
George Newell, Associate Professor; Ph.D., Stanford.
Cecily O'Neill, Associate Professor; Ph.D., Exeter.
Douglas Owens, Professor; Ed.D., Georgia.
Peter Paul, Associate Professor; Ph.D., Illinois at Urbana-Champaign.
Shelley Peterson, Assistant Professor; Ph.D., Alberta.
Gay Su Pinnell, Professor; Ph.D., Ohio State.
Paul Post, Assistant Professor; Ph.D., Purdue.
Richard Remy, Associate Professor; Ph.D., Northwestern.
Theresa Rogers, Associate Professor; Ph.D., Illinois at Urbana-Champaign.
Keiko Samimy, Associate Professor; Ph.D., Illinois at Urbana-Champaign.
Patricia Scharer, Assistant Professor; Ph.D., Ohio State.
Mary Ellen Schmidt, Assistant Professor; Ph.D., Buffalo.
Michael Scott, Associate Professor; Ph.D., Ohio State.
Barbara Seidl, Assistant Professor; Ph.D., Wisconsin–Milwaukee.
David Shutkin, Assistant Professor; Ph.D., Wisconsin–Madison.
Vladimir Sloutsky, Assistant Professor; Ph.D., USSR Academy of Sciences.
Anna Soter, Associate Professor; Ph.D., Illinois at Urbana-Champaign.
Barbara Thomson, Associate Professor; Ph.D., Ohio State.
Robert Tierney, Professor and Director; Ph.D., Georgia.
R. Paul Vellom, Assistant Professor; Ph.D., Michigan State.
Sigrid Wagner, Professor; Ph.S., NYU.
Marjorie Ward, Associate Professor; Ph.D., Pittsburgh.
Arthur L. White, Professor; Ph.D., Colorado.
Deborah Wilburn-Robinson, Assistant Professor; Ph.D., Ohio State.
Karen Zuga, Associate Professor; Ph.D., Ohio State.
Jerome Zutell, Associate Professor; Ph.D., Virginia.

PACE UNIVERSITY

School of Education

Programs of Study

The School of Education of Pace University offers graduate programs leading to the Master of Science in Education degree, with specializations in administration and supervision and in curriculum and instruction, and the Master of Science for Teachers. The Certificate in School Business Management is also offered.

The Master of Science in Education degree in administration and supervision integrates theory with practice. The program is designed to provide future administrators with a sound base of knowledge, enabling them to make thoughtful decisions for schools and in various other settings related to education. To earn the degree, students must successfully complete 33 credits of course work plus a comprehensive examination. Students who enter the program with a master's degree are awarded a Professional Diploma upon completion of the program. Fulfillment of the degree requirements, including an internship, satisfies instructional requirements for School Administrator and Supervisor certification. A 24-credit advanced certificate is offered.

The Master of Science in Education degree in curriculum and instruction offers three concentrations: computers and education (New York City and Westchester campuses), reading (Westchester campus), and special education (Westchester campus). Students elect one concentration. The program requires the completion of ten courses (33–34 credits): five core courses, four courses in the concentration, and one elective course. This degree program fulfills New York state requirements for permanent teaching certification for those who already hold a provisional teaching certificate. Twelve credits from this program may later be applied toward certification as school administrator and supervisor. Advanced certificates are offered in reading and special education.

The Master of Science for Teachers is designed for graduate students with no formal study in the field of education and is intended to satisfy New York State academic requirements in education for provisional teaching certification in elementary and secondary settings. Completion of this degree, a passing score on the NYSTCE, and two years of full-time teaching will result in eligibility for New York State permanent teaching certification. The M.S. for Teachers is a 36-credit graduate program designed to enable students to become academically qualified to teach in school settings. Students may concentrate in early childhood/elementary education or middle school/secondary school education.

The Certificate in School Business Management is offered through a cooperative program administered by the Department of Educational Administration in the School of Education and the Department of Public Administration in the Dyson College of Arts and Sciences. It is an 18-credit program designed for individuals who have earned baccalaureate or master's degrees in education, public administration, or business, and who desire in-depth study in school business management. Completion of this certificate and the master's program in educational administration and supervision will qualify participants for school supervisory certification.

Research Facilities

Pace University's totally integrated online library system holds approximately 825,000 volumes and subscribes to nearly 4,000 serial publications. Electronic access to internal and external information and knowledge sources, including locally mounted CD-ROM databases, online retrieval systems, and Internet, is available. The Pace libraries annually contract with Dialog, BRS, LEXIS-NEXIS, and Dow Jones/News Retrieval to access statistical, bibliographic, directory, and full-text databases covering all major subjects. The University computing network provides access to a range of both mainframe and microcomputing hardware and software. Currently more than 250 computers are located in academic computing facilities. Pace University's wide-area network (Pace Net) can be accessed from labs, dormitory rooms, and offices.

Financial Aid

A number of graduate scholarships and assistantships are available. Grants are made on the basis of outstanding academic performance, as indicated by the applicant's previous college record, and demonstrated financial need. Research and administrative assistantships are available for full- and part-time students. In 1997–98, graduate assistants received stipends of up to $5300 per year and tuition remission for 24 credits. For further information, prospective students should contact the Financial Aid Office at 78 North Broadway, White Plains, New York 10603 (telephone: 914-422-4050) or at 1 Pace Plaza, New York, New York 10038 (telephone: 212-346-1300).

Cost of Study

Tuition is $485 per credit in 1998–99. Registration and library fees vary according to the number of credits taken.

Living and Housing Costs

Dormitory rooms at the Pleasantville and New York City campuses cost $4520 for the 1998–99 academic year. A variety of off-campus housing is available in the vicinity of either campus.

Student Group

Total graduate enrollment in the School of Education exceeds 300. About 5 percent are enrolled on a full-time basis.

Location

The Civic Center campus is located in Manhattan, the cultural and financial focal point of the Eastern Seaboard. The suburban Pleasantville campus in Westchester County, New York, is easily accessible by car, bus, and railroad commuter service and is surrounded by towns and villages that are home to gifted artisans, musical and theatrical groups, rural museums, retail centers, and corporate headquarters.

The University

Founded in 1906, Pace University is a private, nonsectarian, coeducational institution. It has three campuses—one in Manhattan and two in Westchester County. Students interested in any of the graduate programs in education may choose to take courses at the Manhattan location or at the Pleasantville location. In 1948, Pace Institute became Pace College; in 1973, the New York State Board of Regents approved a charter change to designate Pace a university.

Applying

Admission to a degree program in the School of Education on a matriculated basis is open to qualified holders of bachelor's degrees from accredited undergraduate institutions. To qualify, applicants must have completed at least 60 credits in liberal arts and sciences. The Admission Committee carefully reviews each application on the basis of scholastic achievement and a desire to excel, as evidenced by previous academic work; maturity, prior work experience, military service, and/or extracurricular activities; and demonstration of high-level communication skills, both oral and written. Two letters of recommendation are required; an interview may be required as well. Although applications for admission are accepted throughout the year, applicants are urged to submit all materials by August 1 for the fall semester, December 1 for the spring semester, and May 1 for the summer semester.

Correspondence and Information

Office of Graduate Admission
Pace University
1 Pace Plaza
New York, New York 10038
Telephone: 212-346-1531
Fax: 212-346-1585
E-mail: gradnyc@pace.edu

Office of Graduate Admission
Pace University
1 Martine Avenue
White Plains, New York 10606
Telephone: 914-422-4283
Fax: 914-422-4287
E-mail: wp@pace.edu

Pace University

THE FACULTY

Anthony Alfonso, Adjunct Assistant Professor; M.S., Fordham.
David D. Avdul, Professor; Ed.D., Columbia.
Roy Jules Blash, Adjunct Assistant Professor; S.D.A., NYU.
Anthony Ciaglia, Adjunct Associate Professor; Ph.D., Fordham.
Sr. St. John Delany, Associate Professor; Ph.D., Fordham.
Kathryn DeLawter, Assistant Professor; Ed.D., Columbia.
Arthur Doran, Adjunct Associate Professor; LL.B., New York Law.
Carl B. Erdberg, Professor Emeritus; M.S., CCNY.
Bernard Esrig, Adjunct Professor; Ed.D., Columbia.
Ruth Ferguson, Professor Emeritus; Ph.D., Fordham.
Sandra Flank, Professor; Ph.D., Fordham.
Raymond Gerson, Adjunct Lecturer; Ed.D., Columbia.
Glenn Hudak, Professor; Ph.D., Wisconsin–Madison.
Carol Keyes, Professor and Chairperson of Teacher Education (Pleasantville campus); Ph.D., Union (Ohio).
Earl C. Kurtz, Adjunct Assistant Professor; Ed.D., NYU.
Pierre A. Lehmuller, Adjunct Assistant Professor; M.S., Fordham.
Alan Lentin, Adjunct Assistant Professor; Ph.D., Fordham.
Alfred Lodovico, Adjunct Assistant Professor; Ed.D., Bridgeport.
Dorothy Lopez, Adjunct Associate Professor; M.A., Columbia.
Kathy Malu, Assistant Professor; Ph.D., Fordham.
David Martin, Adjunct Assistant Professor; M.A., Adelphi.
Janet Matthews, Adjunct Instructor; M.A., Manhattanville.
Janet McDonald, Professor and Dean; Ph.D., SUNY at Albany.
Bernard Mecklowitz, Adjunct Associate Professor; M.A., Brooklyn.
W. Daniel Morgan, Adjunct Associate Professor; Ed.D., SUNY at Albany.
Anthony Pappalardo, Adjunct Professor; Ph.D., Columbia.
George E. Port, Adjunct Associate Professor; Ed.D., Boston University.
Carol Rhoder, Associate Professor; Ph.D., Columbia.
Carol Rhodes, Associate Professor; Ph.D., NYU.
Lawrence Roder, Professor Emeritus; Ed.D., Columbia.
Rita Silverman, Professor; Ph.D., Pittsburgh.
Natalie Silverstein, Adjunct Assistant Professor; Ph.D., Fordham.
Adrienne Sosin, Assistant Professor; Ed.D., Columbia.
Ann Spindel, Assistant Professor; Ph.D., Fordham.
Regina Toolin, Assistant Professor; Ph.D., Wisconsin–Madison.
Mary Versteck, Associate Professor; Ed.D., Columbia.
Leo Weitz, Professor Emeritus; Ph.D., NYU.
Michael Yazurlo, Adjunct Assistant Professor; Ed.D., Fordham

PENNSYLVANIA STATE UNIVERSITY GREAT VALLEY SCHOOL OF GRADUATE PROFESSIONAL STUDIES

Graduate Programs in Education

Programs of Study

Among the many excellent resources of Pennsylvania State University (Penn State) is the College of Education, acknowledged as one of the finest in the nation. Through the Penn State Great Valley School of Graduate Professional Studies, the College offers graduate and professional development programs and courses in administration, supervision, teaching, and training that are designed to help educators meet the complex challenges of the future. The Master of Education (M.Ed.) in elementary education (K–6) provides practitioners with advanced professional study to extend their knowledge of concepts and skills related to teaching at the elementary school level. The 30-credit program is designed for individuals with the Instructional I or II teaching certificate. The 30-credit M.Ed. in instructional leadership (K–12) provides teachers who exercise leadership among fellow teachers with the knowledge and skills necessary to carry out or improve classroom instruction and school improvement activities. It is designed for educators who work as classroom teachers and wish to undertake an instructional leadership role among their peers. The special education program at Penn State is designed to extend the knowledge and competencies of special and regular education teachers. The program trains individuals in behavior management and instructional design, implementation, and evaluation appropriate for effective work with mildly disabled and at-risk preschool- and school-age students. The program helps prepare educators for inclusive education. Programs range from level I and II certification, which provide basic preparation to become a teacher of the disabled, to graduate work leading to an M.Ed. or Master of Science (M.S.) degree in special education, to supervisory certification that provides leadership training. The instructional systems: training design and development program benefits training professionals, educators, and individuals seeking to enter the training field. Educators choose this program to transfer teaching skills to the private sector or to become better instructors in the classroom. The program combines instructional design, human resource development, and performance technology. Skills in program design, media and production, needs analysis, and program evaluation are enhanced. The M.Ed. option requires 33 semester credits and the M.S. option, 39 semester credits. Students in the training design and development program have the opportunity to participate in an internship within certain guidelines. Supervisory certification is offered in special education. Principal certification (Administrative Level I) and a Post-Master's Certificate in Special Education are also available.

Research Facilities

Research facilities at Penn State Great Valley include extensive computing resources and a research library. The Computer Center provides laboratories and classroom networks of more than 150 Pentium-class and Macintosh microcomputer workstations for student use. These workstations are connected to the campus's local area network (LAN) and to the University's wide area network (WAN). The latter allows student access to the Internet and the World Wide Web. Students are provided with e-mail accounts and dial-up access to facilitate remote use of University-wide computer resources, libraries, and the World Wide Web. The research library at Penn State Great Valley houses more than 22,000 books; 360 current professional, trade, and popular periodicals; and a collection of government publications, microfiche, CD-ROMs, and books on audiotape. Drawing on the resources of the entire University, the library at Great Valley is part of Penn State's University Libraries System, one of the leading academic research library organizations in the nation. Students have access to more than 3 million cataloged volumes, 1.4 million government publications, and 32,000 current journals and serials, plus a number of informational materials at all Big Ten university libraries, other national research centers, and the Tri-State College Library Cooperative, an organization that provides members with access to library resources of more than thirty colleges in the Philadelphia area.

Financial Aid

Financial assistance at Penn State Great Valley exists in the form of scholarships, grants, Federal Stafford Student Loans, graduate research assistantships, a minority fellowship, and Federal Work-Study. For an information packet, specific application forms, and published deadlines, students should contact the Financial Aid Office on campus. External scholarships and information regarding the Taxpayer Act of 1997 may be researched using data in the packet. Many students receive tuition reimbursement.

Cost of Study

Part-time tuition for 1997–98 was $330 per graduate semester credit for Pennsylvania residents. Tuition for nonresidents was $590 per graduate semester credit. Books and supplies cost approximately $80 per course. An administrative computing fee, charged to all students in the fall and spring, is based on the number of credits taken in a semester and averages $50 per semester.

Living and Housing Costs

Most graduate students are enrolled at Penn State Great Valley on a part-time basis, taking evening or Saturday courses. They live and are employed in the greater Philadelphia region.

Student Group

Of the 1,600 part-time graduate students at Great Valley, more than 450 are enrolled in graduate and certification programs in education. The diverse group of students is primarily employed full-time in education but is also employed in areas such as corporate training, human resources, and health and human services.

Location

Penn State Great Valley is one of twenty-five campuses of Pennsylvania State University, an internationally known teaching and research university. The campus is situated in the Great Valley Corporate Center, along the region's high-technology corridor in suburban Philadelphia. It is the nation's first university facility permanently housed in a corporate park, along with world-class companies, and is surrounded by top-ranked school districts.

The University and The College

The College of Education is the professional school established by Pennsylvania State University to conduct and coordinate programs for the preparation of teachers and other educational personnel. The College holds membership in the American Association of Colleges for Teacher Education and the Pennsylvania Association of Colleges and Teacher Educators. Research and development are principal responsibilities of the College; informing and enriching are its other missions. Faculty members engage in sponsored research funded by federal agencies, the commonwealth of Pennsylvania, regional and local school districts, foundations, and the corporate sector. Of the nearly 1,300 colleges and universities that prepare educators nationwide, Penn State's College of Education consistently ranks in the top twenty. Penn State Great Valley is designed specifically for adult learners. To meet the needs of working adults, most courses meet in seven-week sessions, allowing students to take one course at a time and complete two courses each semester. With six sessions offered each year (fall, spring, and summer), students may complete as many as six graduate courses (18 credits) in one year and earn their degrees in about two years on a part-time basis. Evening or Saturday classes enable students to participate in the program while maintaining full-time professional positions. In addition to education programs, the Center offers graduate programs in engineering, information science, and management.

Applying

Qualified students may begin their study in any of six sessions. There are two opportunities to be considered for enrollment in graduate course work. Individuals seeking a degree or certification may apply formally for admission. Individuals interested in beginning their studies prior to formal admission into certain programs or who seek professional development may enroll in courses on a nonmatriculated basis. Detailed program information and applications are available from the Admissions Office at Penn State Great Valley.

Correspondence and Information

JoAnn Korthaus
Graduate Programs Representative
Pennsylvania State University Great Valley School of Graduate Professional Studies
30 East Swedesford Road
Malvern, Pennsylvania 19355
Telephone: 610-648-3312
Fax: 610-889-1334
E-mail: gvinfo@psu.edu
World Wide Web: http://www.psu.edu

Pennsylvania State University Great Valley School of Graduate Professional Studies

THE FACULTY AND THEIR RESEARCH

FULL-TIME FACULTY AND ACADEMIC PROGRAM COORDINATORS

William Milheim, Associate Professor of Instructional Systems and Academic Division Head; Ph.D., Kent State. Instructional design, multimedia, distance education, computer-based learning.

Roy Clariana, Assistant Professor of Instructional Systems; Ed.D., Memphis State. Theory and application of different forms of feedback in computer-based instruction; effectiveness and practical use of computer software in schools; implications of pervasive media on individual cognition and on social systems; effects of individual differences on learning; applications of new technology, such as artificial intelligence, in schools.

Addie Johnson, Assistant Professor of Curriculum and Instruction; Ed.D., Pennsylvania. Curriculum and instruction, teacher professional development, administrative leadership, implementation of school reform.

Ravinder Koul, Assistant Professor of Curriculum and Instruction; Ph.D., Penn State. Design and development of online courses for in-service teachers, assessment of the effectiveness of project-initiated activities to enhance science instruction consistent with prescribed science curriculum framework, development of online evaluation instruments.

Doris Lee, Assistant Professor and Coordinator of Instructional Systems; Ph.D., Texas at Austin. Incorporation of cognitive learning theories of computer-based instruction, use of instructional system models in instructional or training program design, training programs for adult learners in business and industry, human-machine interface design for multimedia learning.

Robert MacMillan, Assistant Professor of Special Education; Ed.D., Alabama. Design of cost-effective service delivery systems for students with special needs. Served as a consultant to school systems committed to the delivery of services to students with disabilities in the least restrictive environment. He is an active presenter at local, national, and international meetings and has completed professional certificates in school counseling and psychology.

Leslie Moller, Assistant Professor of Instructional Systems; Ph.D., Purdue. Contributing editor for *Journal of Performance and Instruction* and author of numerous articles on distance education, motivation, project management, performance technology research foundations, and professional ethics. He has fifteen years of experience as an instructional designer in corporate and consulting firms.

Keith Rose, Associate Adjunct Professor in Educational Administration and Program Coordinator of Principal Certification; Ph.D., Penn State. He has been a teacher and administrator in the Philadelphia public school system for more than twenty-five years and coordinator of the Penn State program for the past thirteen years.

Mary Catherine Scheeler, Instructor and Coordinator of Special Education Programs; M.Ed., Penn State. Supervision of student teachers, curriculum development, developing in-service education programs, classroom and behavior management strategies.

Martin Sharp, Assistant Professor and Coordinator of Curriculum and Instruction; D.Ed., Penn State. His interest in curriculum for diverse populations has aided work completed for the Smithsonian School Program, the Winterthur Museum, and the White House. President of the Eastern Educational Research Association, 1996–97.

Mary Ellen Wrabley, Instructor in Special Education; Ed.D., Temple. Development of alternative assessment and curriculum guidelines for special-needs students in regular education classes, interagency collaboration, legal issues in special education.

PEPPERDINE UNIVERSITY

Graduate School of Education and Psychology

Programs of Study

The Graduate School of Education and Psychology offers degree and credential programs designed to prepare teachers and educational administrators, psychologists and counselors, mental health administrators, consultants, change agents, and technology specialists.

Psychology programs include the Master of Arts in Psychology, the Master of Arts in Clinical Psychology with an emphasis in marriage and family therapy, and the Doctor of Psychology (Psy.D.). Master's programs are designed for students to work at their own pace, with evening classes available for working professionals and a daytime program offered for full-time students. The Psy.D. program is a four-year curriculum culminating with an internship.

Education programs include the Master of Arts in Education, Master of Science in Administration (Educational Leadership Academy), and the Doctor of Education (Ed.D.) with concentrations in educational leadership, administration, and policy; educational technology; organization change; and organizational leadership. Several teaching and administrative credentials are offered as well. Evening and weekend classes are available for the master's programs. Each education doctoral concentration has its own format designed for working professionals. The programs in educational leadership, administration, and policy and organizational leadership offer traditional classes at the Culver City and Orange County campuses during weeknights and weekends; the educational technology program offers classes in a variety of formats including online telecommunications, weekday blocks, weeknights, and weekends; and the organization change program has a sequence-oriented, seminar-style curriculum held at various conference locations in northern and southern California.

Research Facilities

A computer network links all of the School's libraries, which collectively contain more than 800,000 books, bound journals, and microforms. Each facility has computer labs and the West Los Angeles campus houses the Multimedia Center.

Financial Aid

Scholarships, grants, loans, assistantships, and payment plans are available to qualified students. Veterans should follow regular admission procedures and secure the certificate of eligibility from the Veterans Administration or the State of California. More than 70 percent of the students receive federal loans and more than 25 percent receive Pepperdine-funded assistance.

Cost of Study

Charges for one trimester unit of instruction in 1998–99 vary from $515 to $660, depending upon the program.

Living and Housing Costs

While there is a limited amount of graduate housing available for clinical M.A. students at Malibu, the other campuses are in close proximity to apartment buildings and residential areas. Students can expect to budget approximately $15,000 annually for rent, utilities, food, transportation, and personal expenses.

Student Group

Total University enrollment is 7,700 and enrollment at the Graduate School of Education and Psychology is 1,500. Students range in age and experience, with many returning to the workforce or changing their careers, and others entering the programs upon completing their undergraduate degree.

Location

The headquarters for the Graduate School of Education and Psychology is Pepperdine University Plaza, located in Culver City, about 30 minutes west of downtown Los Angeles. The Malibu campus overlooks the Pacific ocean from the Santa Monica Mountains. The San Fernando Valley Center is located in Encino, north of the Santa Monica Mountains. The Orange County center is just east of the John Wayne Airport in Irvine. The Ventura County Center is located in Westlake Village. Program offerings vary by location.

The University

Pepperdine, an independent, medium-sized Christian university, has two major campuses. Seaver College, the undergraduate residential college of letters, arts, and sciences, and the School of Law are on an 830-acre campus overlooking the Pacific Ocean at Malibu. Headquarters for the Graduate School of Education and Psychology and the School of Business and Management are in West Los Angeles.

Applying

Admission requirements vary by program. For more information, prospective students should contact the address given below.

Correspondence and Information

Office of Admissions
Graduate School of Education and Psychology
Pepperdine University
400 Corporate Pointe
Culver City, California 90230
Telephone: 800-347-4849 for education programs (toll-free)
800-888-4849 for psychology programs (toll-free)
World Wide Web: http://moon.pepperdine.edu/gsep/

Pepperdine University

THE FACULTY

Education

J. David Bowick, Senior Lecturer; Ph.D., Claremont.
Terence R. Cannings, Professor; Ed.D., UCLA.
John A. Chandler, Professor; Ed.D., Stanford.
Margot Condon, Visiting Faculty; Ed.D., Pepperdine.
Kay Davis, Lecturer; Ed.D., Pepperdine.
J. L. Fortson, Lecturer; Ed.D., San Francisco.
Cara L. Garcia, Professor; Ph.D., Arizona.
Robert Gelhart, Professor; Ed.D., USC.
Diana Buell Hiatt, Professor; Ed.D., UCLA.
H. Woodrow Hughes, Professor; Ph.D., Oregon.
David W. Jamieson, Visiting Faculty; Ph.D., USC.
Ruth N. Johnson, Associate Professor; Ph.D., California, Davis.
Cheryl Lampe, Visiting Faculty; Ed.D., Pepperdine.
Farzin Madjidi, Visiting Faculty; Ed.D., Pepperdine.
Chester H. McCall Jr. Professor; Ph.D., George Washington.
John F. McManus, Professor; Ph.D., Connecticut.
Kenneth L. Moffett, Distinguished Educator in Residence; Ed.D., USC.
Robert Paull, Associate Professor; Ph.D., USC.
Linda G. Polin, Associate Professor; Ph.D., UCLA.
Reyna G. Garcia Ramos, Assistant Professor; Ph.D., California, Santa Barbara.
June Schmieder, Associate Professor; Ph.D., Stanford.
Jack Scott, Distinguished Professor; Ph.D., Claremont.
Ronald D. Stephens, Associate Professor; Ed.D., USC.
Michele Stimac, Professor; Ed.D., Boston University.
Sue G. Talley, Visiting Faculty; Ed.D. candidate, Pepperdine.

Psychology

Joy Keiko Asamen, Professor; Ph.D., UCLA.
Kathi A. Borden, Associate Professor; Ph.D., Illinois at Urbana–Champaign.
Louis John Cozolino, Professor; Ph.D., UCLA.
Robert A. deMayo, Associate Professor; Ph.D., UCLA.
David N. Elkins, Professor; Ph.D., US International.
Drew Erhardt, Associate Professor; Ph.D., UCLA.
David W. Foy, Professor; Ph.D., Southern Mississippi.
Robert Gelhart, Professor; USC.
Thomas Greening, Visiting Faculty; Ph.D., Michigan.
Joanne Hedgespeth, Associate Professor; Ph.D., Biola.
Clarence Hibbs, Professor; Ph.D., Iowa.
Susan Himelstein, Visiting Professor; Ph.D., UCLA.
Robert Hohenstein, Visiting Faculty; Ph.D., American Commonwealth.
Barbara Ingram, Professor; Ph.D., USC.
William O. Lafitte, Visiting Faculty; Ph.D. candidate, California School of Professional Psychology.
David A. Levy, Associate Professor; Ph.D., UCLA.
Dennis W. Lowe, Professor; Ph.D., Florida State.
Nancy Magnusson-Fagan, Dean; Ph.D., Washington State.
Tomas Martinez, Associate Professor; Ph.D., Michigan.
Cary L. Mitchell, Associate Professor; Ph.D., Kentucky.
Frances W. Neely, Professor; Ph.D., Kansas.
Lynn Rankin-Esquer, Visiting Professor; Ph.D., North Carolina.
Daryl Rowe, Associate Professor; Ph.D., Ohio State.
Edward P. Shafranske, Professor; Ph.D., US International.
Robert S. Weathers, Associate Professor; Ph.D., Fuller School of Psychology.

The Malibu Campus.

Pepperdine University Plaza at Corporate Pointe.

PLYMOUTH STATE COLLEGE

of the University System of New Hampshire

Graduate Programs in Education

Programs of Study

Plymouth State College offers the Master of Education degree in a variety of professional areas that include administration and supervision; counselor education; health education; integrated arts; reading and writing specialist; and elementary or secondary education with options in computer education, environmental science, heritage studies: social science, and mathematics education. Self-designed studies are in such areas as computer education, curriculum and instruction, leadership and adult learning, teacher certification, special education, early childhood education, alternative health and healing courses, and health promotion and wellness management. Other possibilities are available, and a student can pursue them with an adviser. Plymouth State College offers a Certificate of Advanced Graduate Studies (C.A.G.S.) in education. This program addresses the needs of practicing educators who have completed a master's degree and are interested in pursuing advanced academic work in educational restructuring and leadership.

The degree programs are organized around the core courses of research design and philosophy and education, with remaining course work in professional areas, specialization, and electives. The program may be completed through full-time or part-time study. A maximum of 9 credit hours of course work may be transferred into a degree program with the approval of program advisers. An extensive summer graduate program is offered, with many of the graduate students coming from overseas American International (AIS), international, and Department of Defense schools.

Graduates of teacher certification curricula are eligible for recommendation for certification by the New Hampshire State Department of Education. Since New Hampshire is a member of the New England Regional Compact, Plymouth graduates are eligible for certification in any of the compact states upon application to the state education department. The Master of Education programs address the guidelines of various professional organizations, including ASCD, IRA, ACEI, and NAEYC. Plymouth State College is accredited by the New England Association of Schools and Colleges and the New Hampshire Department of Education.

Research Facilities

Research in the field of education is facilitated by the computerized system of expanding holdings (more than 750,000 print and nonprint items) at the Lamson Library. The formal library support services are supplemented by interlibrary agreements with other institutions. In addition, students have access to microcomputers, which include IBMs, available in public clusters on the campus as well as a Macintosh laboratory in Rounds Hall.

Financial Aid

Students should contact the Financial Aid Office for application guidelines. A limited number of graduate assistantships are available to full-time students.

Cost of Study

Tuition in 1998–99 is $232 per credit hour for New Hampshire residents and $254 for nonresidents. Tuition rates are subject to change without notice.

Living and Housing Costs

Graduate students live in single rooms at approximately $1874 per semester, approximately $1000 per summer session, and approximately $265 per winterim in 1998–99. Apartments are available on campus for single students. Off-campus apartments vary widely in cost.

Student Group

Plymouth State College had a student population in 1997–98 of about 4,000 undergraduate and 1,500 part-time graduate students.

Location

Plymouth is located in the Lakes and White Mountain regions of New Hampshire, approximately 2 hours from Boston via Interstate 93 and 40 minutes from the capital city of Concord. The area is a scenic recreation and tourist center for hiking, skiing, and boating activities. Squam Lake (Golden Pond), Waterville Valley, and North Conway are nearby popular tourist and conference areas.

The College

Plymouth State College was founded in 1871 and served as a Normal School. It has grown into a multipurpose institution that offers undergraduate degree programs in a variety of areas, such as early childhood and childhood studies. Graduate programs include the Master of Business Administration (M.B.A.) and Master of Education (M.Ed.) degree programs. Other programs are offered in conjunction with the College for Life-Long Learning at various off-campus sites. Staff development workshops and graduate courses are also offered at area schools through cooperative agreements with the school supervisory units.

Applying

Applications are accepted throughout the year for the M.Ed. program for fall, spring, winter, and summer enrollment. Applicants must hold an undergraduate degree. Three letters of recommendation, official transcripts, and an acceptable score from the Miller Analogies Test (MAT) or the Graduate Record Examinations (GRE) are required. The MAT is offered at the College. An interview with one of the Program Directors is recommended.

Correspondence and Information

Dr. Dennise Bartelo, Program Director
Graduate Studies in Education
Plymouth State College
Plymouth, New Hampshire 03264
Telephone: 603-535-2636
800-FOR-GRAD (800-367-4723, toll-free)
Fax: 603-535-2572
E-mail: for.grad@psc.plymouth.edu

Plymouth State College

THE FACULTY

The Graduate Faculty possess a diversity of experience in teaching, scholarship, research, and service at the local, national, and international levels.

Virginia M. Barry, Associate Professor; Ph.D., Florida State, 1979.
Dennise M. Bartelo, Associate Professor; Ed.D., Virginia Tech, 1987.
Mardie E. Burckes-Miller, Associate Professor; Ed.D., Oklahoma State, 1982.
John C. Carr, Associate Professor; Ed.D., Montana, 1974.
Christopher R. Clarke, Professor; Ed.D., East Tennessee State, 1975.
Katherine Donahue, Assistant Professor; Ph.D., Boston University, 1981.
Richard C. Evans, Professor; Ph.D., Wisconsin–Madison, 1980.
Michael L. Fischler, Professor; Ed.D., Colorado, 1974.
Alison Ford, Assistant Professor; M.F.A., Yale, 1982.
Katharine G. Fralick, Associate Professor; Ed.D., Boston University, 1990.
Richard Fralick, Professor; Ph.D., New Hampshire, 1973.
Joel D. Goldfield, Associate Professor; Ph.D., Universitè Paul Valery, 1985.
Gary E. Goodnough, Assistant Professor; Ph.D., Virginia, 1995.
William C. Haust, Associate Professor; Ed.D., Nova, 1992.
Kenneth H. Heuser, Professor; Ed.D., Illinois at Urbana-Champaign, 1970.
Richard W. Hunnewell, Professor; Ph.D., Boston University, 1982.
Patricia L. Lindberg, Assistant Professor; Ed.D., NYU, 1993.
Robert Morton, Professor; M.F.A., Temple, 1962.
Daniel R. Perkins, Assistant Professor; D.M.A., USC, 1990.
Richard Pfenninger, Assistant Professor; D.M.A., Temple, 1990.
Leonard R. Reitsma, Associate Professor; Ph.D., Dartmouth, 1990.
Gary K. Richey, Assistant Professor; Ph.D., Utah State, 1993.
William J. Roberts, Professor; Ph.D., Massachusetts, 1970.
Leo Sandy, Associate Professor; Ed.D., Boston University, 1983.
Nancy Strapko, Associate Professor; Ph.D., NYU, 1989.
Robert F. Swift, Professor; Ph.D., Rochester (Eastman), 1970.
David Switzer, Professor; Ph.D., Connecticut, 1963.
Warren Tomkiewicz, Associate Professor; Ed.D., Boston University, 1987.
Susan Walsh, Instructor; M.S.W., Boston University, 1989.
Douglas C. Wiseman, Professor; P.E.D., Indiana, 1970.
Eldwin A. Wixson, Professor; Ph.D., Michigan, 1969.

Rounds Hall houses the education department.

QUINNIPIAC COLLEGE

Master of Arts in Teaching Program

Program of Study

Quinnipiac College's Master of Arts in Teaching (M.A.T.) program is a challenging course of study that prepares candidates for certification. It is an intensive sequence of course work and student teaching that is open to individuals who have earned their undergraduate degrees and wish to move directly on to graduate school as well as career changers.

Quinnipiac's M.A.T. program preserves the best of the traditional approaches to teaching while also encouraging students to become professionals who are willing to initiate changes in their schools' curricula and programs. The program offers a careful balance of content and methodology.

The M.A.T. program is a five-semester, intensive course of study (a full-time student who begins in September can finish the program, including student teaching, at the end of the second spring semester). The three basic components of each program are core certification courses that provide eligibility for teacher certification, advanced discipline courses that satisfy master's degree requirements in the subject area(s) for which a candidate is seeking certification, and a yearlong internship/residency experience. This combination of subject area mastery and educational skills prepares teachers to translate academic subjects to the learning needs of students and to make sound educational decisions. The entire program is approximately 42–53 credit hours. Graduates are eligible for both initial certification in the state of Connecticut and the Master of Arts in Teaching degree. Middle grades and secondary certification programs are offered in biology, English, French, history/social studies, mathematics, and Spanish.

Research Facilities

The main research facility for the M.A.T. program is the Curriculum Center of the library. The Curriculum Center provides students with access to the ERIC (Educational Resources Information Center) database and collection. The Center also houses the Kraus Curriculum Library, a young adults' literature collection, hard copies of educational periodicals, and a collection of textbooks. Research opportunities are also available through the program's close links to area school districts.

Financial Aid

Several avenues of financial aid are available to help both full- and part-time students. The Financial Aid Office offers all M.A.T. students assistance in obtaining publicly and privately funded loans and scholarships. M.A.T. candidates may be eligible to apply for Federal Stafford Student Loans. Full-time education students also have the option to participate in an internship/residency program, for which they receive both a stipend and a partial or full tuition waiver for the two internship/residency semesters.

Cost of Study

In 1998–99, the tuition rate for all M.A.T. students is $395 per credit hour. Tuition for the program is approximately $16,000. Part-time students pay a $20 registration fee each semester. Full-time students are charged a student fee of $185 per semester. The College offers a variety of payment plans, including deferred payment and installment programs, and coordinates employer reimbursement programs.

Living and Housing Costs

On-campus housing is available during the summer. Privately owned housing is available, however, near the campus. For more information concerning off-campus housing, interested students should contact the Office of Residential Life at 203-281-8666.

Student Group

Most students in the M.A.T. program attend full-time. Full-time students spend their days in schools as interns or residents and attend classes in the late afternoon or evening. Approximately 50 students from throughout the world begin the program each fall. The average age of M.A.T. students is approximately 27 years, and the class contains a mixture of recent college graduates and professionals seeking a career change. A small number of part-time students also take evening classes.

Location

Quinnipiac is located on a beautiful campus in Hamden, Connecticut, a suburb of New Haven. It is 30 minutes from Hartford, 1½ hours from New York City, and 2 hours from Boston. Quinnipiac is located at the base of Sleeping Giant Park with more than 1,500 acres of wooded trails. New Haven is a vibrant city with much to offer, including theaters, art museums, shops, and restaurants. Hartford, the state capital, also offers historical and cultural attractions, concerts, and athletic events.

The College

Quinnipiac enrolls 3,310 full-time undergraduates and approximately 1,300 graduate students. The College comprises of the Schools of Health Sciences, Business, Law, and Liberal Arts and the College for Adults. A distinguished faculty of more than 170 full-time and nearly 100 part-time faculty members provides instruction for the programs of the College.

Applying

Application for the full-time master's program is on a rolling basis. Applications for part-time study are also considered throughout the year. In addition to a complete application, the applicant must furnish an essay describing the reasons an education career is being pursued, official transcripts, three letters of reference, and the Connecticut PRAXIS I-CBT exam or waiver. An interview is required.

Correspondence and Information

For an application or information:
Graduate Admissions
Quinnipiac College
275 Mount Carmel Avenue
Hamden, Connecticut 06518
Telephone: 203-281-8672
800-462-1944 (toll-free)
Fax: 203-281-5238
E-mail: qcgradadmi@quinnipiac.edu

For a personal interview:
Dr. Sydney Howard
Director, Elementary Education
Quinnipiac College
275 Mount Carmel Avenue
Hamden, Connecticut 06518
Telephone: 203-287-5345
Fax: 203-281-8709
E-mail: howard@quinnipiac.edu

Dr. Cynthia Dubea, Director
Middle Grades and Secondary Education
Quinnipiac College
275 Mount Carmel Avenue
Hamden, Connecticut 06518
Telephone: 203-281-8702
Fax: 203-281-8709
E-mail: dubea@quinnipiac.edu

Quinnipiac College

THE FACULTY AND THEIR RESEARCH

Luis Arata, Assistant Professor of Modern Languages; Ph.D., Cornell. Fine arts.
Daryll Borst, Professor of Biology; Ph.D., Illinois. Biology.
Pearl LeBlanc Brown, Professor of English; Ph.D., Arkansas. English.
Shannon Clarkson, Assistant Professor of Education and Internship Coordinator; Ed.D., Columbia. Curriculum and instruction.
Cynthia Dubea, Assistant Professor of Education and Director of M.A.T. Program; Ed.D., Columbia. Curriculum and instruction.
Len Engel, Professor of English; Ph.D., Fordham. English.
Steve Gottlieb, Professor and Chair, English Department; M.A., NYU. English.
Kim Hartmann, Assistant Professor and Chair; M.H.S., Quinnipiac. Occupational therapy.
Ronald Heiferman, Professor of History; Ph.D., NYU. History.
Sydney Howard, Director of Elementary Education; Ph.D., Kansas. Educational technology and special education.
Mark Johnston Jr., Professor of English; Ph.D., Yale. English.
Kenneth McGeary, Associate Professor of Biology; Ph.D., New Hampshire. Biology.
Neil Nelan, Assistant Professor of Mathematics; Ph.D., Johns Hopkins. Mathematics.
Lakshmi Nigam, Professor of Mathematics; Ph.D., Indian Institute of Technology. Mathematics.
Dennis Opheim, Professor of Biology; Ph.D., Minnesota. Biology.
Rachel Ranis, Professor of Sociology; M.S., Yale. Sociology.
Stanley Rothman, Professor of Mathematics; Ph.D., Wisconsin. Mathematics.
George Schiro, Professor of History; Ph.D., NYU. History.
David Stineback, Dean, School of Liberal Arts; Ph.D., Yale. English.
Alex Welleck, Associate Professor of History and Political Science; Ph.D., Connecticut. History and political science.
David Zucker, Professor of English; Ph.D., Syracuse. English.

SOUTHERN CALIFORNIA COLLEGE

Graduate Program in Education

Programs of Study

The Graduate Program in Education at Southern California College offers a Teacher Education Program that is dedicated to a highly personalized approach to teacher education and graduate training. The mission of the Graduate Program in Education is to provide a supportive and reflective community in which teachers develop the skills, techniques, and professional knowledge base necessary to empower all students to reach their highest spiritual, intellectual, and physical potential. Candidates travel through the program as a cohort, developing strong collaborative relationships throughout their professional training. Southern California College is authorized by the California Commission on Teacher Credentialing to offer California State Teaching Credentials. The College is also accredited by the Western Association of Schools and Colleges (WASC) to offer a Master of Arts in Education degree, with four specific options available.

The Teacher Education Program is designed to support candidates who are seeking the Single Subject Teaching Credential for secondary teaching (grades 7–12) or the Multiple Subject Teaching Credential for elementary teaching (grades K–6). For both types of credentials, the College is authorized to offer the Cross-Cultural, Language and Academic Development (CLAD) emphasis, designed to prepare teachers to work with limited-English-proficient (LEP) students. The CLAD emphasis credential portion of the Teacher Education Program is designed to be completed in two semesters, pending completion of prerequisite course work. The first semester focuses on professional course work during the late afternoons, evenings, and weekends. The second semester focuses on a full-time student teaching component at a public school site. The CLAD Certificate is also available for candidates with a valid California teaching credential.

The Master of Arts options are designed to fulfill specific professional goals and provide graduate training to support professional excellence and instructional leadership. Eligible students who are interested in applying their credential or certificate course work toward a Master of Arts in Education degree are able to do so with additional graduate study.

Research Facilities

Students have access to the O. Cope Budge Library on campus. The library houses an expanding collection of more than 120,000 volumes, 900 periodicals, CDs, CD-ROMs, record albums, tapes, microfilm, and other materials. An Educational Lab, located on the second floor of the library, provides a variety of curriculum materials, lesson plan ideas, and visual aids to support graduate education students during their student teaching and curriculum research. The campus is also in proximity to the libraries at California State University, Fullerton; California State University, Long Beach; and the University of California, Irvine.

Graduate education students have access to the Educational Resource Center (ERC), a curricular technology lab housed in the Graduate Education Offices that is designed specifically to support the Teacher Education Program. The lab currently has PC and Macintosh computers, curricular software and guides, and Internet and e-mail access.

Financial Aid

The Financial Aid Office works with eligible graduate education students to secure Federal Stafford Student Loans for tuition. Limited teaching assistantship grants are available to selected candidates.

Cost of Study

The 1998–99 cost for graduate tuition is $365 per semester unit. A package price of $4160 per semester is available for candidates enrolled in 12 to 17 units.

Living and Housing Costs

Limited on-campus housing is available to graduate education students. Housing for married students ranges from $2500 to $2800 per semester; housing for single students ranges from $1300 to $1500 per semester. Full board is $1090 per semester; partial board is $1005 per semester. The College is in proximity to a large number of housing and apartment complexes at reasonable rates.

Student Group

Total College enrollment is more than 1,300, and the Graduate Program in Education maintains an enrollment of 80 to 100 students per semester. Class sizes are kept small to encourage meaningful personal interaction and mentoring relationships. The student population is varied and composed of candidates completing their graduate work directly out of the undergraduate experience as well as experienced teachers and those who are seeking midcareer changes.

Student Outcomes

The rate of employment upon completion of the Teacher Education Program is 95 percent. The College maintains close ties with local school districts and encourages students to develop personal networks based on its established relationships. A strong Teacher Education Advisory Council, which consists of local school administrators and master teachers, provides an ongoing professional support network to connect graduates with the community.

Location

Southern California College is located in Costa Mesa, in Orange County, 40 miles southeast of Los Angeles. Just minutes from the campus are miles of beautiful ocean, parks, and recreational opportunities. Ski slopes are only 2 hours away. Costa Mesa enjoys an ideal climate. Its winters are tempered by ocean currents, and its summers are cooled by trade winds from the ocean.

The College is centrally located within the heart of the twenty-six public school districts and seventy private Christian schools in Orange County. The Orange County Department of Education is also located in Costa Mesa, minutes from the College.

The College

Founded in 1920, Southern California College is a private, coeducational, liberal arts college that believes its Christian community provides a supportive and challenging environment in which to pursue a high-quality education. In addition to the undergraduate programs, the College offers graduate programs in education, religion, and counseling. The College is scheduled to receive university status in the 1999–2000 academic year.

Applying

Specific admission requirements for each Teacher Education Program option are found in the *Graduate Education Catalog*. Interested students may request an application and information packet by contacting the address listed below.

Correspondence and Information

Deeanna Routon, Coordinator
Graduate Program in Education
Southern California College
55 Fair Drive
Costa Mesa, California 92626
Telephone: 714-556-3610 Ext. 252 or 310
Fax: 714-966-5495
E-mail: grad.ed@sccu.edu
World Wide Web: http://graded.sccu.edu

Southern California College

THE FACULTY AND THEIR RESEARCH

Magali (Mikki) Gil, Professor and Director; Ph.D., California, Irvine. Anthropology and education, educational research, gender studies, multicultural education.

Sandra Ruppert, Assistant Professor; Ph.D., USC. Reading, language acquisition, student teaching supervision.

Teresa Stoops, Assistant Professor; Ed.D. candidate, Seattle Pacific. History and philosophy of education.

Thomas (Tom) Ward, Associate Professor; Ed.D., San Francisco. Curriculum, instructional methodology and reflective teaching.

Raymond (Ray) White, Associate Professor; Ed.D., Northern Arizona. Integration of faith and learning, philosophies of education.

Visiting Faculty

Bonnie Brigman, Elementary School Teacher, Newport-Mesa Unified School District; M.S., Southern California College. School-based action research and curriculum integration.

Anaida Colon-Muniz, Director of K–8 Curriculum, Santa Ana Unified School District; Ed.D., Massachusetts. Multicultural education and instructional methodology.

William (Bill) Knight, Principal, Newport-Mesa Unified School District; Ph.D., California, Riverside. Models of teaching, curriculum assessment, professional development.

Sharon Marshall Johnson, Founder and Director of SCORE for College; M.S., California State, Fullerton. Student study skills, tutorial programs, parent partnerships.

Jan Osborn, Secondary English Teacher, Santa Ana Unified School District; M.A., Michigan. Language acquisition and literacy across the curriculum.

Craig Rusch, Assistant Professor of Anthropology, Southern California College; Ph.D., California, Irvine. Cognitive anthropology, sociolinguistics, culture change.

Bonnie Swann, Director of Special Education, Newport-Mesa Unified School District; M.A., California State, Fullerton. Inclusion, collaborative instruction, action research.

Thomas (Tom) Watt, Elementary School Teacher, Huntington Beach Unified School District; M.A., US International. Technology in education and special education.

STANFORD UNIVERSITY

School of Education

Programs of Study

Doctoral degree programs (Ph.D. and Ed.D.) are designed for students preparing to conduct research and teach in a college or university, to direct research in public school systems or other institutions, or to assume administrative positions in universities, school systems, and government. Ph.D. students must complete a minor in another discipline or hold an acceptable master's degree outside the field of education. A minor is not required for the Ed.D. Doctoral students concentrate in the field of their professional interest, preparing for a professional specialty while mastering an organized body of knowledge. Students are encouraged to design a course of study relevant to their interests and professional objectives.

Doctoral degrees are offered within four program areas with concentrations: curriculum studies and teacher education (art education, English education, general curriculum studies, mathematics education, science education, social studies education, symbolic systems in education, and teacher education); language, literacy, and culture (bilingual education, language policy, second-language education, and writing, reading, and language in English); psychological studies in education (educational psychology, child and adolescent development, counseling psychology, and symbolic systems in education); and social sciences, policy, and educational practice (anthropology, economics, higher education administration, history, interdisciplinary, international comparative education, philosophy, policy analysis, and sociology).

Master's degrees are offered in most areas listed above. In addition, master's (but not doctoral) degrees may be earned in dance education, gender studies, international educational administration and policy analysis, learning design and technology, and policy analysis and evaluation. The Stanford Teacher Education Program (STEP) is a twelve-month program, beginning in summer, leading to a master's degree in education and a California Single Subject Secondary Teaching Credential. The Program for Prospective Principals, taken over three successive summers and including an internship, leads to a master's degree and a California Preliminary Administrative Services Credential.

Research Facilities

Stanford's libraries include more than 5.5 million cataloged volumes and 60 million manuscripts. Cubberley Library contains more than 145,000 volumes relating directly to education. In addition, the School's advanced computer facilities enhance educational research, linking national and international networks. Research programs affiliated with the School include the Accelerated Schools Project, the Center for Policy Research in Education, the Stanford Institute for Higher Education Research, and the Stanford International Development Education Center.

Financial Aid

The School of Education provides a substantial number of doctoral students with financial support.

The primary source of aid for master's students is from loans.

Cost of Study

Tuition at Stanford University is $22,110 for the 1998–99 academic year. The cost of books and supplies is estimated to be $1140 annually.

Living and Housing Costs

Stanford houses 46 percent of its graduate students on campus. Single students choose from among traditional dormitories, cooperative houses, and apartments. Married couples are generally housed in one-bedroom high-rise apartments, while families with children live in larger townhouse apartments. Current campus housing rates for the academic year average $2480 to $7372 for single students, $7372 to $8386 for couples, and $8380 to $13,790 for families.

Student Group

The School enrolls a mature, diverse, and experienced group of approximately 375 graduate students. In recent years, entering Ph.D. students ranged in age from 22 to 50, with an average age of 34. Twenty-seven percent are from American minority groups.

Graduates generally receive positions in college and university teaching, in educational research, and at state and national levels of administration and policymaking.

Location

Stanford University's 8,000-acre campus lies at the base of the Santa Cruz mountains, 25 miles south of San Francisco and less than an hour's drive from the Pacific Ocean. Stanford's mild climate permits outdoor recreation virtually the year round, and San Francisco's symphony, opera, ballet, museums, theaters, and restaurants provide a wealth of cultural and social opportunities.

The University and The School

Stanford University is a private institution founded in 1885 by Senator and Mrs. Leland Stanford. It has seven schools, four of which are professional schools. Of its 13,000 students, approximately half are graduate students. The School of Education has been consistently ranked at the top by surveys over the past two decades. It counts among its affiliated faculty 13 members of the National Academy of Education and members of the American Academy of Arts and Sciences, the National Academy of Sciences, the American Philosophical Society, and the Royal Academy of Arts. The School is committed to addressing issues of equality and issues of quality of educational opportunities and to maintaining an ethnically diverse faculty and student body.

Applying

Information and application forms can be obtained from the address given below. Applicants are judged on the basis of their statement of purpose, letters of recommendation, academic record, GRE scores, and relevant work experience. Doctoral students are admitted in the autumn quarter only; the application deadline is generally December 15 (students should check application packets). The Stanford Teacher Education Program; the Learning, Design and Technology Program; and the Program for Prospective Principals admit master's students for the summer quarter only; applications are generally due January 1 for STEP and March 1 for the Principals' Program. Other master's programs admit in the autumn quarter. Applications are generally due January 15 for most M.A. programs.

Correspondence and Information

Admissions Office
School of Education
485 Lasven Mall
Stanford University
Stanford, California 94305-3096

Telephone: 415-723-4794
E-mail: suse-info@stanford.edu
World Wide Web: http://www.stanford.edu/dept/SUSE

Stanford University

THE FACULTY AND THEIR AREAS OF RESEARCH

J. Myron Atkin, Professor; Ph.D., NYU, 1956. Science education; school-based curriculum development; collaboration among schools, industry, and universities; action research.
Brigid Barron, Assistant Professor; Ph.D., Vanderbilt, 1992. Child development, technology-intensive learning environments and assessment.
John Baugh, Professor; Ph.D., Pennsylvania, 1979. Educational linguistics and anthropology.
Edwin M. Bridges, Professor; Ph.D., Chicago, 1964. Teacher evaluation, training of principals.
Martin Carnoy, Professor; Ph.D., Chicago, 1964. Economics, international studies.
Robbie Case, Professor; Ph.D., Toronto, 1971. Intellectual development, instructional design, developmental theory.
Elizabeth G. Cohen, Professor; Ph.D., Harvard, 1958. Sociology of education, social structure of the classroom, organization of teaching.
Larry Cuban, Professor; Ph.D., Stanford, 1974. History of education, urban education, managing organizations.
William Damon, Professor; Ph.D., Berkeley, 1973. Adolescent development, methods in school and community settings, moral education.
Elliot Eisner, Professor; Ph.D., Chicago, 1962. Qualitative forms of inquiry, education and art, school improvement.
John Gardner, Miriam and Peter Haas Centennial Professor; Ph.D., Berkeley, 1938. Organizational and institutional renewal and leadership.
James G. Greeno, Margaret Jacks Professor; Ph.D., Minnesota, 1961. Mathematical learning theory, cognitive psychology, problem solving in mathematics and science.
Patricia J. Gumport, Associate Professor; Ph.D., Stanford, 1987. Higher education, sociology of education.
Edward Haertel, Professor; Ph.D., Chicago, 1980. Measurement, evaluation, and statistical analysis.
Kenji Hakuta, Professor; Ph.D., Harvard, 1979. Child development, applied linguistics.
Michael L. Kamil, Professor; Ph.D., Wisconsin, 1969. Cognitive psychology, literacy, reading instruction, technology in teaching and learning.
Michael W. Kirst, Professor; Ph.D., Harvard, 1964. Federal and state education policy, school finance.
John D. Krumboltz, Professor; Ph.D., Minnesota, 1955. Counseling psychology, career planning.
Teresa D. LaFromboise, Associate Professor; Ph.D., Oklahoma, 1979. Cross-cultural counseling, American Indian mental health.
Henry M. Levin, David Jacks Professor; Ph.D., Rutgers, 1967. Economics of human resources, education of disadvantaged youth.
James G. March, Professor Emeritus; Ph.D., Yale, 1953. Organizational research.
William F. Massy, Professor Emeritus; Ph.D., MIT, 1960. Finance, management, governance of colleges and universities.
Ray McDermott, Professor; Ph.D., Stanford, 1977. Anthropology, educational issues in classrooms and homes.
Milbrey W. McLaughlin, Professor; Ed.D., Harvard, 1973. Education policy and implementation, context of teaching, disadvantaged youth.
Karen E. Mundy, Assistant Professor; Ph.D., Toronto, 1995. Basic education and literacy, international aid in developing countries.
Ingram Olkin, Professor; Ph.D., North Carolina, 1951. Statistics.
Amado M. Padilla, Professor; Ph.D., New Mexico, 1969. Child psychology, mental health.
Denis C. Phillips, Professor; Ph.D., Melbourne, 1968. Philosophy of social science, educational and social science research methodology.
Francisco O. Ramirez, Professor; Ph.D., Stanford, 1974. Education and nation building, political incorporation of women.
Robert W. Roeser, Assistant Professor; Ph.D., Michigan, 1996. Adolescent development in schools; ecological models of academic motivation, achievement, and psychological adjustment; school reform as a primary prevention and health promotion strategy.
David Rogosa, Associate Professor; Ph.D., Stanford, 1977. Statistical and psychometric methods.
Thomas Rohlen, Professor; Ph.D., Pennsylvania, 1971. Anthropology of education, Japanese education and culture.
Richard J. Shavelson, Professor and I. James Quillen Dean; Ph.D., Stanford, 1971. Measurement theory and application, mathematics and science education, policy analysis.
Lee S. Shulman, Charles E. Ducommun Professor; Ph.D., Chicago, 1963. Educational psychology, cognitive psychology of the practice of teaching.
Marshall Savidge Smith, Professor; Ed.D., Harvard, 1970. Public policy, research methods. (On leave)
Myra H. Strober, Professor; Ph.D., MIT, 1969. Education, work, and family; women's education and employment; child care; occupational segregation; economics education.
Carl E. Thoresen, Professor; Ph.D., Stanford, 1964. Health psychology, counseling, stress.
David B. Tyack, Vida Jacks Professor; Ph.D., Harvard, 1958. Social history of American education.
Guadalupe Valdes, Professor; Ph.D, Florida State, 1972. Bilingual education, foreign language learning.
Decker F. Walker, Professor; Ph.D., Stanford, 1971. Education, general curriculum, educational applications of computers.

View of Stanford's Hoover Tower from Frost Amphitheater.

The Mission Revival architecture of Stanford's Inner Quad.

STATE UNIVERSITY OF NEW YORK AT BUFFALO

Graduate School of Education

Programs of Study

The Graduate School of Education trains scholars, researchers, teachers, counselors, administrators, and other educational personnel for service in such educational organizations as schools, colleges, and universities as well as community and government agencies. Graduate programs lead to the Master of Education (Ed.M.) and Doctor of Education (Ed.D.) and recommendation for New York State certification in teaching, administration, and counseling. Through the Office of the Graduate School, the Graduate School of Education also offers programs leading to the Master of Science (M.S.) in rehabilitation counseling, the Master of Arts (M.A.) in educational psychology and school psychology, and the Doctor of Philosophy (Ph.D.) in various fields of education.

Areas of specialization in the Department of Counseling and Educational Psychology are counselor education, counseling psychology (approved by the American Psychological Association), educational psychology, school counseling, rehabilitation counseling, and school psychology. Department of Learning and Instruction specializations are bilingual education, elementary education, early childhood education, reading education, English education, foreign and second language education, mathematics education, school administration and supervision, science education, social studies education, special education, and teaching English to speakers of other languages. Specializations in the Department of Educational Leadership and Policy are comparative education, educational administration, higher education, school business administration, school district administration, and social foundations.

Research Facilities

The University libraries have more than 3 million volumes and subscribe to more than 21,150 periodicals. Various facilities of the Graduate School of Education give students opportunities for educational research and provide training to complement curricular instruction. These facilities are the Fisher-Price Endowed Early Childhood Research Center, the English Language Institute, the Center for Comparative and Global Studies in Education, and the Center for Educational Resources and Technologies (CERT), which includes the Curriculum Center, the Learning Technologies Laboratory, and the Data Analysis Laboratory. The Data Analysis Laboratory provides facilities and equipment for research, and its staff offers expert advice on research design and measurement, data analysis, and computer use. Through the Buffalo Research Institute on Education for Teaching (BRIET), graduate students have the opportunity to work as supervisors of student teachers and to do research in the public schools.

Financial Aid

Assistantships are available for full-time degree students. Stipends average from $8000 to $8620 for the 1998–99 year. Eligible students may also be considered for Schomburg (for members of minority groups) or Presidential Fellowships. Financial assistance is available for students through the Office of Financial Aid, Hayes C, University at Buffalo, Buffalo, New York 14214 (telephone: 716-829-3724).

Cost of Study

The 1998–99 tuition for full-time graduate students is approximately $5700 per academic year for in-state students and $9000 per year for out-of-state students.

Living and Housing Costs

The University's Off-Campus Housing Office at 100 Allen Hall (telephone: 716-829-2224) assists students in locating accommodations throughout the city and in the suburbs.

Student Group

The Graduate School of Education has about 1,150 graduate students. Out-of-state and international students are well represented. The University enrollment of 23,450 includes more than 6,250 graduate students and 1,650 professional students.

Location

Located at the eastern end of Lake Erie, Buffalo is the second-largest city in New York State. Cultural resources include the Albright-Knox Art Gallery, which houses one of the finest collections of twentieth-century art in the world; the Buffalo Museum of Science; the Buffalo Philharmonic Orchestra; and the Studio Arena Theatre. The area also offers professional sports and many opportunities for outdoor activities.

The University

The Graduate School of Education, housed in Christopher Baldy Hall on the North campus, is one of the academic units of the State University of New York at Buffalo, the largest and most comprehensive graduate center of the State University of New York System.

Applying

All prospective students should contact the appropriate department for admission guidelines well in advance of the academic year in which they wish to enroll. Applications for fall admission in counseling psychology, counselor education, rehabilitation counseling, school counseling, and school psychology must be submitted before February 1; there is no spring admission for these programs. Applications for educational psychology must be submitted by February 1 for fall admission and by November 1 for spring admission. Applications for educational administration and social foundations must be submitted by March 1 for fall admission and by November 15 for spring admission. Applications to the Department of Learning and Instruction must be submitted by February 1 for fall admission and November 15 for spring admission; however, applications for the program in bilingual education are accepted on a continuous basis. Requests for fellowships should be addressed to the department chairperson by February 1. Students who seek campus-based loans should apply by March 1; students who wish to obtain Federal Stafford Student Loans should file the FAFSA as soon as possible after January 1.

Correspondence and Information

Prospective students can contact the Graduate School of Education on the World Wide Web at http://www.gse.buffalo.edu. Students can also contact:

Counseling and Educational Psychology
Graduate School of Education
409 Christopher Baldy Hall
State University of New York at Buffalo
Box 601000
Buffalo, New York 14260-1000
Telephone: 716-645-2484

Learning and Instruction
Graduate School of Education
505 Christopher Baldy Hall
State University of New York at Buffalo
Box 601000
Buffalo, New York 14260-1000
Telephone: 716-645-2455

Educational Leadership and Policy
Graduate School of Education
468 Christopher Baldy Hall
State University of New York at Buffalo
Box 601000
Buffalo, New York 14260-1000
Telephone: 716-645-2471

State University of New York at Buffalo

THE FACULTY

Jacquelyn Mitchell, Dean; Ed.D., Harvard.

Department of Counseling and Educational Psychology
Beth B. Cohen, Assistant Professor; Ph.D., Missouri–Columbia.
Stanley H. Cramer, Professor; Ed.D., Columbia Teachers College.
Janice DeLucia-Waack, Associate Professor; Ph.D., Penn State.
Catherine A. Emihovich, Associate Professor; Ph.D., SUNY at Buffalo.
Jeremy D. Finn, Professor; Ph.D., Chicago.
Thomas T. Frantz, Associate Professor and Chair; Ph.D., Iowa.
J. Ronald Gentile, Professor; Ph.D., Penn State.
Dwight R. Kauppi, Associate Professor; Ph.D., Minnesota.
Scott T. Meier, Associate Professor; Ph.D., Southern Illinois.
LeAdelle Phelps, Professor; Ph.D., Utah.
Thomas J. Shuell, Professor; Ph.D., Berkeley.
Stephen Truscott, Assistant Professor; Ph.D., SUNY at Albany.

Department of Educational Leadership and Policy
Hank Bromley, Assistant Professor; Ph.D., Wisconsin.
Stephen I. Brown, Professor; Ed.D., Harvard.
James A. Conway, Professor; Ed.D., SUNY at Albany.
William K. Cummings, Professor; Ph.D., Harvard.
Lynn S. Ilon, Assistant Professor; Ph.D., Florida State.
Stephen L. Jacobson, Associate Professor; Ph.D., Cornell.
Lauri Johnson, Assistant Professor; Ph.D., Washington (Seattle).
J. Bruce Johnstone, University Professor; Ph.D., Minnesota.
David A. Nyberg, Professor; Ph.D., Stanford.
Albert J. Pautler, Professor; Ed.D., SUNY at Buffalo.
Hugh G. Petrie, Professor; Ph.D., Stanford.
Maxine S. Seller, Professor; Ph.D., Pennsylvania.
Mwalimu Shujaa, Associate Professor; Ed.D., Rutgers.
Robert B. Stevenson, Associate Professor and Chair; Ph.D., Wisconsin.
Austin D. Swanson, Professor; Ed.D., Columbia Teachers College.
Lois Weis, Professor; Ph.D., Wisconsin.

Department of Learning and Instruction
Janice Almasi, Assistant Professor; Ph.D., Maryland.
Stephen I. Brown, Professor; Ed.D., Harvard.
Douglas H. Clements, Professor; Ph.D., SUNY at Buffalo.
James L. Collins, Professor; Ed.D., Massachusetts.
Catherine Cornbleth, Professor; Ph.D., Texas.
Rodney L. Doran, Professor; Ph.D., Wisconsin.
Stephen Dunnett, Professor; Ph.D., SUNY at Buffalo.
James Ernest, Assistant Professor; Ph.D., Alabama.
Patrick J. Finn, Associate Professor; Ph.D., Chicago.
S. G. Grant, Assistant Professor; Ph.D., Michigan State.
James L. Hoot, Professor; Ph.D., Illinois.
Carol Hosenfeld, Associate Professor; Ph.D., Ohio State.
Michael W. Kibby, Professor and Chair; Ph.D., Chicago.
Laura J. Klenk, Assistant Professor; Ph.D., Michigan.
Lilliam Malavé, Associate Professor; Ph.D., SUNY at Buffalo.
Suzanne Miller, Associate Professor; Ph.D., Pittsburgh.
Dorothy Rissel, Associate Professor; Ph.D., SUNY at Buffalo.
Thomas Schroeder, Associate Professor; Ph.D., Indiana.
Barry Shealy, Assistant Professor; Ph.D., Georgia.
Mark Templin, Assistant Professor; Ph.D., Michigan.
Conrad F. Toepfer Jr., Professor; Ed.D., Buffalo.
Lynne Yang, Assistant Professor; Ph.D., Oregon.

SYRACUSE UNIVERSITY

School of Education

Programs of Study

Graduate study in the School of Education offers a comprehensive range of instruction and research opportunities leading to the Master of Science (M.S.) degree, Certificate of Advanced Studies (C.A.S.), Doctor of Education (Ed.D.), and Doctor of Philosophy (Ph.D.). Programs are available for educational practitioners as well as for those aspiring to research careers. Programs include art education; communication sciences and disorders (audiology and speech pathology); counselor education; cultural foundations of education and curriculum; educational leadership; education of infants and young children with special needs; education of the learning disabled; elementary education; English education; exercise science; higher education; instructional design, development, and evaluation; mathematics education; music education; physical education; reading and language arts; rehabilitation counseling; science education; social studies education; special education (severe disorders); and teaching and curriculum.

To receive an M.S., students must earn a minimum of 30 credits and take comprehensive exams or write a thesis. Students in the C.A.S. program are required to earn a minimum of 60 credits, to take qualifying exams, and to participate in a practicum. Requirements for the doctorate include at least 90 credits of course work, examinations, development of research competence, and the dissertation (details of these requirements are specified by the program areas). For more information on individual program requirements, prospective students should contact the appropriate program chairperson.

Graduate programs in education at Syracuse University are varied in scope and purpose. The School has found that the number of students who receive their doctorates and subsequently pursue academic careers (teachers and researchers in institutions of higher education) is about equal to the number of those who enter or continue in administrative, supervisory, or other field positions (school superintendents, deans, and other administrative, supervising, and coordinating positions) in schools and colleges.

Research Facilities

Syracuse University's extensive computer facilities and library collections totaling almost 5 million volumes provide extensive support for learning and research. Other centers that support and enrich the work of the students and faculty of the School of Education include the Educational Resource Center, computer classrooms, the Facilitated Communication Institute, the Center on Human Policy, the Gebbie Speech and Hearing Clinics, the Psychoeducational Teaching Laboratory, the Reading and Language Arts Center, three health and physical education laboratories, and teaching centers located in area school districts.

Financial Aid

Scholarships, fellowships, and graduate assistantships are available from the University and from the School. Assistantships require approximately 20 hours of service per week and provide both a tuition scholarship and a stipend. Federal and state aid is also available in the form of scholarships, fellowships, loans, and work-study programs. Detailed financial aid information can be found in the publication *Graduate Study at Syracuse University*, available from the Office of Financial Aid, 200 Archbold.

Cost of Study

Graduate tuition charges for 1998–99 are $555 per credit hour. Additional expenses include a health services fee for full-time students and graduate student activity fees.

Living and Housing Costs

Minimum living expenses for a single graduate student average $850 a month. The campus and surrounding areas offer excellent housing facilities for single and married graduate students. The University has on-campus residence halls for graduate students and the Skytop Apartment Complex, which overlooks the city. Further information on University housing can be obtained from the South Campus Housing Office, 206 Goldstein Student Center, Syracuse University, Syracuse, New York 13244.

Student Group

Syracuse University has a total enrollment of more than 19,000. Approximately 650 are undergraduate students in education, and more than 900 are registered for graduate study in the School of Education.

Location

Located in a major metropolitan area with a population of more than 500,000 and in a city of almost 200,000, Syracuse University is surrounded by many cultural, recreational, and research opportunities. The Finger Lakes, the Thousand Islands, and the Adirondacks are nearby.

The University and The School

Syracuse University, established in 1870, is a private, chartered institution offering coeducational programs through more than twenty schools, colleges, and departments. The University, with its 200-acre campus, provides a vibrant academic community for its members.

The School of Education has more than 90 full-time, part-time, and adjunct faculty members. Virtually all have attained the highest professional degrees in their specializations, and many hold dual appointments with SU's College of Arts and Sciences, Maxwell School of Citizenship and Public Affairs, and College of Visual and Performing Arts. This broad range of backgrounds provides variety and depth in the academic and research fields available for study. Among the faculty are men and women who are nationally and internationally known in their areas of expertise.

Applying

The regulations governing admission are stated in the application booklet *Graduate Study: School of Education*, available from Central Applications Processing, 212 Archbold. Students, particularly applicants to doctoral programs and those applying for assistantships, should apply well before the semester in which they intend to begin study. There is a nonrefundable application fee of $40.

Correspondence and Information

Graduate Admissions Representative
School of Education
270 Huntington Hall
Syracuse University
Syracuse, New York 13244-2340
Telephone: 315-443-2505
Fax: 315-443-5732

Syracuse University

THE FACULTY AND THEIR RESEARCH

Communication Sciences and Disorders (315-443-9637)

With opportunities to specialize in speech-language pathology or audiology, students experience a blend of quality academic preparation, cutting-edge research, and hands-on clinical experience. Students often pursue careers as speech-language pathologists, audiologists, or administrators in a variety of clinical, hospital, or university settings.

Corinne R. Smith, Interim Chair; Ph.D., Syracuse. School psychological assessment and intervention practices, learning disabilities. Mary Louise Edwards, Ph.D., Stanford. Phonological development and disorders. Karen Doherty, Ph.D., Wisconsin–Madison. Audiology, psychoacoustics, hearing aids. Linda Milosky, Ph.D., Wisconsin–Madison. Child language development and disorders. Beth A. Prieve, Ph.D., Iowa. Audiology, objective measures of hearing.

Counseling and Human Services (315-443-2266)

Through study in counselor education or rehabilitation counseling, students are encouraged to view counseling as a range of interventions that help individuals respond effectively to crucial issues in their lives. The program prepares students for counseling careers in such settings as universities, career placement centers, substance abuse clinics, schools, hospitals, and rehabilitation agencies.

Alan Goldberg, Chair; Ph.D., Michigan State. Counseling theory, substance abuse. James Bellini, Ph.D., Arkansas. Rehabilitation policy research, assessment. Carla Bradley, Ph.D., Kent State. Community agency counseling. Noreen Glover, Ph.D., Southern Illinois. Substance abuse, sexual abuse. Richard Pearson, Ph.D., Illinois. Adult counseling, personal support systems. Paul Salomone, Ph.D., Iowa. Career counseling, vocational psychology.

Cultural Foundations of Education and Curriculum (315-443-3343)

This graduate program focuses on the interdisciplinary study of education as a fundamental human and social activity. Major areas of study include history, philosophy, and sociology of education; curriculum theory; gender and education; and disability studies. Students are prepared for career positions as college and university professors, foundation officers, researchers, and policy analysts, among others.

Sari Knopp Biklen, Chair; Ed.D., Massachusetts. Qualitative research methods, gender in education. Douglas Biklen, Ph.D., Syracuse. Public policy on disability, child advocacy. Robert C. Bogdan, Ph.D., Syracuse. Qualitative research methods, sociology of the handicapped. John Briggs, Ph.D., Minnesota. History of education. Joan N. Burstyn, Ph.D., London. History of higher education, education of women. Gerald Grant, Ed.D., Harvard. Sociology of education. Emily Robertson, Ph.D., Syracuse. Philosophy of education. Steven Taylor, Ph.D., Syracuse. Public policy, sociology of education. Vincent Tinto, Ph.D., Chicago. Sociology of education.

Health and Physical Education (315-443-2114)

With the program's emphasis on pursuing cutting-edge research, students can explore their interests in exercise and sport sciences while using the latest equipment in the department's state-of-the-art laboratory facilities. Students specialize in applied physiology and pursue careers in educational, corporate, clinical, and research settings.

James Graves, Chair; Ph.D., Massachusetts. Exercise and aging, musculoskeletal physiology. Jack Azevedo, Ph.D., Berkeley. Exercise biochemistry. Jill Kanaley, Ph.D., Illinois. Exercise physiology/endocrinology, exercise in aging. Lori Ploutz-Snyder, Ph.D., Ohio. Exercise physiology, skeletal muscle and aging.

Higher Education (315-443-4763)

This program prepares students to participate in the ever-changing collegiate environment by enhancing their understanding of the history, structure, and dynamic role of higher education. Areas of study include student affairs, higher education administration, evaluation and institutional research, counseling in higher education settings, and teaching in higher education.

Vincent Tinto, Chair; Ph.D., Chicago. Attrition, learning communities. Catherine Engstrom, Ph.D., Maryland. Multiculturalism, campus cultures.

Instructional Design, Development, and Evaluation (315-443-3703)

This program prepares students to effectively improve instruction and learning, while fostering their own growth in leadership and professional skills. Areas of study include design, development, and evaluation, where students are prepared for careers in public education, government, human service agencies, or business and industry.

Phil Doughty, Ph.D., Florida State. Instructional development. Nick Smith, Ph.D., Illinois. Evaluation, research. Adjuncts: Ronald Bouverat, M.A., Syracuse. Alexander Romiszowski, Ph.D., Loughborough. Charles Spuches, Ed.D., Syracuse. Barbara Yonai, Ph.D., Syracuse.

Reading and Language Arts (315-443-4755)

With opportunities to earn advance degrees in reading education, literacy education, literacy technology, English education, and learning disabilities, students are prepared to direct reading education programs and serve students with learning disabilities, as well as teach English education in middle, junior high, and senior high schools. Students gain valuable research experiences in public and private schools, where they work to upgrade reading, English, and language arts instruction, as well as impact on broader program assessment and technology issues.

Peter Mosenthal, Chair; Ph.D., Ohio State. Discourse analysis, linguistics, writing. Benita Blachman, Ph.D., Connecticut. Educational psychology, learning disabilities. Marlene Blumin, Ph.D., Cornell. Curriculum and instruction. Kathleen Hinchman, Ph.D., Syracuse. Reading evaluation and curriculum development. Susan Hynds, Ph.D., Vanderbilt. Communicating and the teaching of composition. Donald Leu, Ph.D., Berkeley. Reading education, literacy technology, multimedia.

Teaching and Leadership (315-443-2685)

With an emphasis on addressing student diversity and inclusion, students may pursue programs in art, mathematics, music, science, or social studies, as well as programs in elementary education, special education, educational administration, and teaching and curriculum. Programs provide for initial teacher preparation, continued professional support of in-service teachers, and the education of those who will provide leadership through school administration, policy development, research on teaching, and the practice of teacher education.

Larry Schafer, Chair; Ph.D., Michigan State. Science education. Lon Beery, Ph.D., Ohio State. Choral repertoire, music education. Douglas Biklen, Ph.D., Syracuse. Child advocacy, public policy in special education. Wanda Blanchette, Ph.D., Penn State. Special education. Steven T. Bossert, Dean, School of Education; Ph.D., Chicago. School effectiveness, leadership, organizational analysis. John Coggiola, Ph.D., Florida State. Music education. Helen Doerr, Ph.D., Cornell. Mathematics education, mathematical modeling, functions, and problem solving using computing technology. Marvin Druger, Ph.D., Columbia. Science education. Gail Ensher, Ed.D., Boston University. Educating infants and young children with special needs. Louis Heifetz, Ph.D., Harvard. Community-clinical psychology, developmental disabilities. Hope Irvine, Ph.D., NYU. Art education. Howard Johnson, Ph.D., Northwestern. Mathematics education. Gerald Mager, Ph.D., Ohio State. Teacher education, supervision and curriculum. Joanna Masingila, Ph.D., Indiana. Mathematics education. Adah Randolph, Ph.D., Ohio State. Educational policy and leadership, curriculum theory, urban education. Mara Sapon-Shevin, Ph.D., Rochester. Teacher education, inclusive schools. Joseph Shedd, Ph.D., Cornell. Collective bargaining, labor law and history. Corinne Smith, Ph.D., Syracuse. School psychology, learning disabilities. Marilyn Tallerico, Ph.D., Arizona State. Educational leadership and governance. John Tillotson, Ph.D., Iowa. Science teaching, preparation, constructive teaching. Patricia Tinto, Ph.D., Syracuse. Math education, teaching and curriculum. Brenda Weikel, Ph.D., Washington (Seattle). Methods and curriculum in teaching social studies, multicultural education. Gwen Yarger-Kane, Ph.D., Syracuse. Teacher education.

TEACHERS COLLEGE, COLUMBIA UNIVERSITY

Graduate Faculty of Education

Programs of Study

Teachers College is the largest, most comprehensive graduate school of education in the world. Programs lead to the degrees of Master of Arts, Master of Science, Master of Education, Doctor of Education, and (under the auspices of the Graduate School of Arts and Sciences at Columbia University) Doctor of Philosophy.

The programs range from introductory teacher education for graduates of liberal arts institutions to advanced professional development for scholars and practitioners, and they include an innovative doctoral program to prepare students for entry into the educating professions. A list of programs appears with the faculty directory on the reverse of this page.

The College also offers combined-degree programs with the Columbia University Graduate School of Business in educational resource management, with the Columbia School of Law in the law and educational institutions, and with the Jewish Theological Seminary of America and Union Theological Seminary in religion and education.

Research Facilities

Research institutes and service groups include the Institute for Urban and Minority Education, Institute of Higher Education, Institute of Philosophy and Politics of Education, Institute for Education and the Economy, Institute for Learning Technologies, Research and Demonstration Center for the Education of Handicapped Children, Special Education Child Study Center, Research Institute for the Study of Learning Disabilities, Center for Community Colleges, Center for the Study and Education of the Gifted, Center for the Behavioral Analysis of School and Electronic Learning, Reading Center, Microcomputer Resource Center, Nutrition Education Resource Project, Center for Infants and Parents (which also provides day care), Institute of International Studies, Council on Scholarship on Women and Gender, Center for Nursing Leadership Development, Community English Program, Writing Process Project, Peace Education Project, Literacy Center, National Center for Restructuring Education, Schools, and Teaching, and the Center for the Development and Education of Young Children and Their Parents.

The College's Sequent 2000 and microcomputer services and facilities, which include a network of IBM PC and Macintosh computers, are available for academic use. The Milbank Memorial Library at Teachers College has more than 1 million books and materials and a curriculum resource center, constituting the largest American collection on education, psychology, and the health services. Students also have access to the 6 million volumes in the Columbia University library system.

Financial Aid

In 1996–97, the College granted more than $6 million in scholarships and fellowships, including awards from such sources as an International Student Scholarship program, a Minority Student Scholarship program, Professional Development Incentive Awards for teachers and future teachers in designated fields, and Tuition Assistance Awards. The College provides access to education loans, Federal Work-Study funds, and a variety of payment plans. Information is available from the Office of Student Aid, Box 309, Teachers College.

Students should also ask the Department of Special Education, the Program in Bilingual Education, and other departments and programs about assistantships and traineeships. The Joseph Klingenstein Fellows Program and Summer Institute (Box 125) are open to educators from independent schools.

Cost of Study

Tuition, based on the number of credits taken, is $610 per credit in 1998–99. Fees are specified in the College's catalog.

Living and Housing Costs

In 1996–97, minimum living costs for single students were about $1000 per month. Married students should add about $425 per month for a spouse and $480 per month for each child. Housing information is available from the Office of Residence Halls, Box 312, Teachers College.

Student Group

Teachers College seeks a geographically diverse student body. More than 4,200 men and women from all over the United States and seventy other countries are enrolled. The age range is quite wide, and many students are engaged in professional work while pursuing their studies.

Location

Located in upper Manhattan, the Morningside Heights campus of Columbia University is convenient to theaters, concert halls, museums, parks, sports stadiums, arenas, and other New York City attractions.

The College

Founded in 1887, the privately funded Teachers College has been academically affiliated with Columbia University since 1898 and is designated the Graduate Faculty of Education of the University. The faculty consists of 130 professors representing many university disciplines and professional specialties, as well as an equal number of distinguished lecturers and instructors. Day and evening classes are available to provide the greatest flexibility in program planning. Teachers College places a strong emphasis on consultation and field research and on the close faculty-student relationships essential to the successful pursuit of professional and academic goals.

Applying

Application for admission to degree status should be made by July 1 for fall admission, December 1 for spring admission, and April 15 for summer admission. Some programs have an earlier deadline for fall admission. Applicants seeking financial aid should apply by February 1. Department requirements vary considerably, but, in general, applicants should have a B average or better in their undergraduate work. Some programs require scores on the GRE, MAT, and/or other tests. A personal statement and two letters of reference are also required.

Applications for admission to nondegree status are accepted at any time; proof of a baccalaureate from a regionally accredited institution is the only requirement. Up to 16 credits of course work (with no more than 8 credits taken within the intended major) completed by a nondegree student may be credited toward a degree at a later date. It is important to note, however, that admission to nondegree status does not guarantee admission to a degree program.

Correspondence and Information

Office of Admission
Box 302P
Teachers College, Columbia University
525 West 120th Street
New York, New York 10027
Telephone: 212-678-3710
Fax: 212-678-4171
E-mail: tcinfo@columbia.edu
World Wide Web: http://www.tc.columbia.edu

Teachers College, Columbia University

DEPARTMENT CHAIRS

Department of Arts and Humanities
Chair: Professor Judith M. Burton (Telephone: 212-678-3799)
Arts
- Art and Art Education
- Arts Administration
- Dance and Dance Education
- Music and Music Education

Humanities
- History and Education
- Philosophy and Education
- Religion and Education
- Social Studies

Languages and Literature
- Applied Linguistics
- Teaching of English and English Education
- Teaching of English to Speakers of Other Languages (TESOL)
- Teaching of Spanish

Department of Biobehavioral Studies
Chair: Professor John H. Saxman (Telephone: 212-678-3895)
- Applied Physiology
- Motor Learning
- Speech-Language Pathology and Audiology
- Offered jointly with the Department of Health and Behavioral Studies:
  - Applied Physiology and Nutrition

Department of Counseling and Clinical Psychology
Chair: Professor Barry A. Farber (Telephone: 212-678-3257)
- Psychological Counseling (Master's)
- Counseling Psychology (Doctoral)
- Clinical Psychology (Ph.D. program)

Department of Curriculum and Teaching
Chair: Professor Celia Genishi (Telephone: 212-678-3765)
Curriculum and Teaching
- Early Childhood Education
- Elementary/Childhood Education, Preservice
- Curriculum and Teaching

Special Education
- Early Childhood/Special Education
- Giftedness
- Learning Disabilities

Offered jointly with the Department of Health and Behavior Studies:
- Physical Disabilities (Ed.D. program only)
- Reading and Learning Disabilities
- Cross-Categorical Studies

Department of Health and Behavioral Studies
Chair: Professor Charles E. Basch (Telephone: 212-678-3964)
Applied Educational Psychology
- Neurosciences and Education
- Reading and Learning Disabilities*
- Reading Specialist
- School Psychology

Health Studies
- Health Education
- Nursing Education
- Nutrition Education
- Applied Physiology and Nutrition**
- Physical Education

Special Education
- Administration of Special Education
- Behavior Disorders
- Blindness and Visual Impairment
- Cross-Categorical Studies*
- Guidance and Rehabilitation*
- Hearing Impairment
- Instructional Practice*
- Mental Retardation
- Physical Disabilities (Ph.D. program only)
- Supervision of Education

Department of Human Development
Chair: Professor Jane A. Monroe (Telephone: 212-678-4190)
- Developmental Psychology
- Educational Psychology
- Measurement, Evaluation and Statistics
- Politics and Education
- Psychology in Education
- Sociology in Education

Department of International and Transcultural Studies
Chair: Professor Clifford A. Hill (Telephone: 212-678-3947)
- Comparative and International Education/International Educational Development
- Bilingual/Bicultural Education
- Economics and Education

Concentrations
- Family and Community
- Language and Literacy
- Peace Education

Department of Organization and Leadership
Chair: Professor W. Warner Burke (Telephone: 212-678-3258)
Educational Administration
- Educational Administration
- Inquiry in Educational Administrative Practice
- Resource Management

Higher Education
- Adult and Continuing Education
- Adult Education Guided Independent Study (AEGIS)
- Higher Education
- Student Personnel Administration
- Nurse Executive/Health Administration
- Social-Organizational Psychology

Department of Scientific Foundations
Chair: Professor Charles C. Harrington (Telephone: 212-678-3405)
- Anthropology and Education
- Applied Anthropology
- Communication and Education
- Computing and Education
- Instructional Technology and Media
- Mathematics Education
- Science Education

---

* *Offered jointly with the Department of Curriculum and Teaching*
** *Offered jointly with the Department of Biobehavioral Studies*

TEMPLE UNIVERSITY

of the Commonwealth System of Higher Education

College of Education

Programs of Study

The College of Education at Temple University is a comprehensive, professional college offering academic studies leading to the Master of Education (Ed.M.), Master of Science in Education (M.S.Ed.), Doctor of Philosophy (Ph.D.), and Doctor of Education (Ed.D.).

The College of Education is committed to offering individualized academic experiences for preparing productive scholars and practitioners to provide educational leadership in a wide range of specializations.

The Ed.M. is offered in the following areas: adult and organizational development, counselor education, early childhood and elementary education, educational administration, educational psychology, language/literacy education, mathematics and science education, school psychology, special education, urban education, and vocational/technical education.

The M.S.Ed. is an advanced degree, preparing professionals for higher-level positions within education. The M.S.Ed. is offered in the following academic specializations: early childhood education, elementary education, language education, math/science education, second/foreign language education, special education, and vocational/technical education.

The Ed.D. degree is offered in the following areas: educational administration, language education (including TESOL), mathematics and science education, and urban education.

The Ph.D. degree is offered in counseling psychology, educational psychology, and school psychology.

In addition to these programs, the College offers postbaccalaureate certification in elementary and early childhood education and in all of the content areas in secondary education through the Ed.M. Graduate Certification Program, which provides Pennsylvania certification and a master's degree.

Research Facilities

The University libraries contain more than 2.3 million volumes and provide reading space for 2,500 students. Extensive support facilities are available to students and faculty for research, teaching, and interdisciplinary educational services. Facilities associated with the College of Education include the Psychoeducational Clinics, Educational Computer Center, Teaching Skills Laboratory, and Center for Research in Human Development and Education.

Financial Aid

Aid is available to qualified full-time students in the form of assistantships and fellowships funded by the University and various outside agencies. All forms include a stipend plus tuition. Tuition scholarships are also available to qualified students. The specific type of aid offered to a particular student depends on the student's qualifications and program of study.

Cost of Study

Temple is a state-related university. Tuition for graduate study in 1998–99 is $308 per credit hour for residents of Pennsylvania and $429 per credit hour for nonresidents. Tuition and fees are subject to change.

Living and Housing Costs

University-sponsored furnished and unfurnished apartments are available on campus; rents range from $390 to $525 per month in 1998–99. Rates are subject to change.

Student Group

Temple University is a senior, comprehensive, public research university located in an urban setting. Temple's approximately 30,000 students represent a diverse mix of various racial, ethnic, and age groups. Throughout its history, Temple has provided broad access to students who might not otherwise have the opportunity to attend an outstanding and comprehensive university. The College of Education enrolls about 1,100 graduate students.

Location

Located in the Boston-Washington corridor, Philadelphia is the fifth-largest city in the country, with a metropolitan population of more than 4 million. It offers a varied menu of cultural attractions. The city has a world-renowned symphony orchestra, a ballet company, two professional opera companies, and a chamber music society. Besides attracting touring plays, Philadelphia enjoys a professional repertory theater and many amateur productions. All facilities for sports and recreation are easy to reach. The city is famous for its historic shrines, parks, and eighteenth-century charm, which is carefully maintained in its oldest section.

The University

The development of Temple University has been in line with the ideal of educational opportunity for the able and deserving student of limited means. With a rich heritage of social purpose, Temple provides students an opportunity for education of high quality without regard to their race, creed, or station in life. Affiliation with the Pennsylvania Commonwealth System of Higher Education undergirds Temple's character as a public institution.

Temple's academic programs are conducted on five campuses in central and north Philadelphia and its near suburbs. These locations, as well as numerous extension centers throughout eastern Pennsylvania, give Temple University the distinction of being a fast-growing institution with many superior facilities. Temple also has campuses in Rome and Tokyo.

Applying

Applications for admission must be made on forms furnished by the Graduate School. Departmental deadlines for admissions and financial aid are variable. Applicants should consult the University's Web page at the address below or the Graduate School *Bulletin*.

Correspondence and Information

Director of Student Services
College of Education
238 Ritter Annex
Temple University
Philadelphia, Pennsylvania 19122
Telephone: 215-204-8011
World Wide Web: http://www.temple.edu/department/education

Temple University

THE FACULTY

CURRICULUM, INSTRUCTION, AND TECHNOLOGY IN EDUCATION

Early Childhood and Elementary Education
Colden Garland, Ed.D., Rochester. Smita Guha, Ph.D., Buffalo. Thomas W. Lackman, Ph.D., Delaware. Robert J. Mahar, Ed.D., Wayne State. Susan B. Neuman, Ed.D., University of the Pacific. Aida A. Nevarez-LaTorre, Ed.D., Harvard. Ivan J. Quandt, Ed.D., Indiana. Jayminn S. Sanford, Ph.D., Harvard. Cathleen S. Soundy, Ed.D., Rutgers.

Secondary Education
Susan Albertine, Ph.D., Chicago. Matthew H. Bruce, Ph.D., Penn State. Victor G. Cimino, Ed.M., Temple. Roderick J. Ellis, Ph.D., London. Penny L. Hammrich, Ph.D., Minnesota. Stephen Krulik, Ed.D., Columbia. Jacqueline Leonard, Ph.D., Maryland College Park. Suzanne Levin, Ph.D., Chicago. Kenneth G. Schaefer, Ph.D., Columbia. Joseph S. Schmuckler, Ed.D., Pennsylvania. Stiles N. Seay, Ph.D., Texas. Dolores Silva, Ed.D., Columbia. Ellen Skilton-Sylvester, Ph.D., Pennsylvania. Frank J. Sullivan, Ph.D., Pennsylvania.

Special Education
Saul Axelrod, Ph.D., Florida. Nettie R. Bartel, Ph.D., Indiana. Diane N. Bryen, Ph.D., Temple. Terry D. Meddock, Ph.D., Illinois. Lynda Price, Ph.D., Minnesota. S. Kenneth Thurman, Ph.D., George Peabody. Valaida S. Walker, Ed.D., Temple.

Vocational Education and Educational Media
Edward B. Brower, Ed.D., Temple. Jerome I. Leventhal, Ed.D., SUNY at Buffalo. Raymond S. Lolla, Ph.D., Purdue. Elton V. Robertson, Ph.D., Syracuse. Thomas J. Walker, Ed.D., Temple.

EDUCATIONAL LEADERSHIP AND POLICY STUDIES IN EDUCATION

Educational Administration, Higher Education, and Policy Studies
Vincent Anfara Jr., Ph.D., New Orleans. Corrine A. Caldwell, Ph.D., Pennsylvania. Richard M. Englert, Ed.D., UCLA. Peter J. Goldstone, Ph.D., Wisconsin. Vivian W. Ikpa, Ph.D., Maryland. Barbara N. Pavan, Ed.D., Harvard. James R. Powell, Ed.D., Temple. Joan P. Shapiro, Ed.D., Pennsylvania. Jacqueline A. Stefkovich, Ed.D., Harvard. Leonard J. Waks, Ph.D., Wisconsin. Donald L. Walters, Ed.D., Miami (Florida).

Urban Education
William W. Cutler, Ph.D., Cornell. Erin M. Horvat, Ph.D., UCLA. Novella Z. Keith, Ph.D., Rutgers. Kathleen M. Shaw, Ph.D., Michigan.

PSYCHOLOGICAL STUDIES IN EDUCATION

Adult and Organizational Development
Jerome S. Allender, Ph.D., Chicago. Edmund J. Amidon, Ph.D., Minnesota. Thomas L. Hawkes, Ph.D., Chicago. Larry J. Krafft, Ph.D., Michigan. Melvin L. Silberman, Ph.D., Chicago. Susan Wheelan, Ph.D., Wisconsin.

Counseling Psychology
Lois A. Benishek, Ph.D., Arizona State. James A. Bolden, Ed.D., Temple. Chris Erickson, Ph.D., Michigan Sate. Madonna G. Constantine, Ph.D., Memphis. Gordon M. Hart, Ph.D., Michigan. Portia L. Hunt, Ph.D., Indiana State. Kimberly Kirby, Ph.D., Kansas. Emil Soucar, Ed.D., Rochester. Gregory Tucker, Ph.D., Temple.

Educational Psychology
Helmut W. Bartel, Ph.D., Indiana. Joseph P. DuCette, Associate Dean; Ph.D., Cornell. Frank H. Farley, Ph.D., London. David Fitt, Ph.D., Temple. William G. Fullard Jr., Ph.D., Pennsylvania. Leroy J. Messinger, Ph.D., North Carolina. Cathleen K. Morano, Ph.D., SUNY at Buffalo. James J. Roberge, Ph.D., Connecticut. Glenn E. Snelbecker, Ph.D., Cornell. Margaret C. Wang, Ph.D., Pittsburgh.

School Psychology
Catherine A. Fiorello, Ph.D., Kentucky. Irwin Hyman, Ed.D., Rutgers. Joseph G. Rosenfeld, Ph.D., Temple. Stanley L. Rosner, Ph.D., Temple. Trevor E. Sewell, Dean; Ph.D., Wisconsin. Leslie M. Skinner, Ph.D., Western Michigan.

TEXAS A&M UNIVERSITY

College of Education

Programs of Study

The College of Education offers degrees at both the master's and doctoral levels through the Departments of Educational Administration, Educational Curriculum and Instruction, Educational Human Resource Development, Educational Psychology, and Health and Kinesiology. The College is accredited by the National Council for Accreditation of Teacher Education.

Public school professionals are served through programs for teachers, administrators, and counselors as well as specialty areas, including gifted and talented education, reading, mathematics and science, bilingual/multicultural education, educational technology, early childhood education, career development education, special education, school psychology, health education, and safety education.

In addition to public school preparation, students find programs in teaching; administration; student affairs administration; learning, development, and instruction; and research, measurement, and statistics for higher educational institutions. Specialized programs prepare professionals to work in such fields as adult literacy, adult learning, distance learning, counseling psychology, exercise physiology, cardiac rehabilitation, motor learning, sport management, and sports pedagogy.

Research Facilities

The College of Education is home to numerous centers, laboratories, and institutes that provide the opportunity to focus resources, research capabilities, and personnel on a specific area of interest or need in the field of education. The College supports the following: the Center for Alcohol and Drug Education Studies; the Center for Community Education; the Center for Distance Learning Research; the Center for the Study of Implementation of Collaborative Learning Communities; the Institute for Gifted and Talented Students; the Outdoor Education Institute; the Principal's Center; the Texas Center for Adult Literacy and Learning; the Center for Corporate Training; the Cognition and Instructional Technologies Laboratory; the Human Performance Laboratory; the National Space Biomedical Research Institute; the South Central Region Technology in Education Consortium–Texas; the Texas Alliance for Science, Technology, and Math Education; the Texas Education Collaborative; the Educational Research and Evaluation Laboratory; and the Disabled and At-Risk Children and Youth (DARCY) research group. The College of Education had more than $6 million of external funding through grants and contracts in 1997–98.

Financial Aid

In addition to numerous federal and state loan programs, scholarships, grants, and short-term loans are available through the Texas A&M University Student Financial Aid Office (telephone: 409-845-3236). Graduate students may also support their educational experience through graduate assistantships, lecture positions, and other staff positions. More than 100 teaching and nonteaching graduate assistantships are available to qualified students on a competitive basis in the College of Education. These assistantships aid more than 40 percent of the College's full-time graduate students. Highly competitive fellowships are also available to graduate students with outstanding records. Interested students should contact the individual departments for specific financial aid opportunities.

Cost of Study

During the 1997–98 academic year, full-time resident graduate students paid $3153 in tuition and required fees, and full-time nonresidents paid $8289 in tuition and required fees. These totals are based upon 24 hours of course work during the fall and spring semesters.

Living and Housing Costs

Bryan/College Station has recently been rated as the third most economical place to live in Texas and as number six in the nation. During the 1997–98 academic year, the average living expenses (including room, board, books and supplies, transportation, and various other personal expenses) were approximately $10,000.

Student Group

Texas A&M University ranks sixth in the nation in enrollment figures. More than 43,000 students attend the College Station campus, with students representing all fifty states and 113 other countries. The College of Education is home to 3,000 undergraduate students and 1,000 graduate students. Of the College's graduate student population, 66 percent are women and 24 percent are members of minority groups. The majority of graduate students attend school part-time while they continue to work in full-time professional positions.

Location

Centrally located in College Station, Texas, and among some of the country's largest cities—Austin, Dallas, Houston, and San Antonio—Texas A&M University is home to the George Bush Presidential Library and the newly built Reed Arena. Touring Broadway shows, art exhibitions, the Texas Film Festival, concerts, and numerous lecture series on a variety of subjects are brought to the campus by academic and student organizations.

The University and The College

Established in 1876 as the first public college in Texas, Texas A&M University is the only university to be ranked nationally among the top ten in all four of the following areas: total enrollment, enrollment of national merit scholars, value of research, and endowment. Texas A&M also ranks second nationally in granting doctoral degrees to members of minority groups. *U.S.News & World Report* ranked the College of Education's graduate program in the top 20 percent in 1998.

Applying

An application for admission can be requested from the Office of Admissions and Records. Applicants should also contact the College of Education about additional materials that may be required for admission into the desired academic programs.

Correspondence and Information

Dr. Becky L. Carr, Assistant Dean for Academic Affairs
College of Education
Texas A&M University
College Station, Texas 77843-4222
Telephone: 409-862-1342
Fax: 409-845-6129
E-mail: gradinfo@coe.tamu.edu
World Wide Web: http://www.coe.tamu.edu

Graduate Admissions
Office of Admissions and Records
Texas A&M University
College Station, Texas 77843-0100
Telephone: 409-845-3631

Texas A&M University

THE FACULTY

EDUCATIONAL ADMINISTRATION

Bryan R. Cole, Professor and Head; Ph.D., Texas A&M (telephone: 409-845-2716).

Public School Administration
Maynard Bratlien, Associate Professor; Ph.D., Nebraska.
David A. Erlandson, Professor; Ed.D., Illinois.
John Hoyle, Professor; Ph.D., Texas A&M.
Arnold Oates, Senior Lecturer; Ph.D., East Texas State.
Augustina Reyes, Assistant Professor; Ed.D., Houston.
Linda Skrla, Assistant Professor; Ph.D., Texas.
Robert Slater, Professor; Ph.D., Chicago.
Steve Stark, Associate Professor; Ed.D., Western Michigan.
Julian Treviño, Adjunct Professor; Ed.D., Texas A&M.
Clifford L. Whetten, Associate Professor; Ph.D., Texas A&M.

Higher Education Administration
D. Stan Carpenter, Professor; Ph.D., Georgia.
Dean C. Corrigan, Professor; Ed.D., Columbia Teachers College.
Eddie J. Davis, Professor; Ph.D., Texas A&M.
Yvonna Lincoln, Professor; Ed.D., Indiana.
Carol Patitu, Assistant Professor; Ph.D., Bowling Green State.

EDUCATIONAL CURRICULUM AND INSTRUCTION

Francis E. Clark, Professor and Interim Head; Ed.D., Missouri–Columbia (telephone: 409-845-8384).

Curriculum and Instruction Foundations
Lynn M. Burlbaw, Associate Professor; Ph.D., Texas.
Elizabeth S. Foster-Harrison, Associate Professor; Ed.D., North Carolina State.
James B. Kracht, Professor; Ph.D., Washington (Seattle).
John E. Morris, Professor; Ed.D., Mississippi.
G. Patrick Slattery Jr., Associate Professor; Ph.D., LSU.
Jane A. Stallings, Professor; Ph.D., Stanford.

Early Childhood
Gaile S. Cannella, Associate Professor; Ed.D., Georgia.
Doug C. Godwin, Assistant Professor; Ph.D., Michigan State.

Multicultural/Bilingual/ESL
Hassana Alidou-Ngame, Assistant Professor; Ph.D., Illinois.
Novella P. Carter, Associate Professor; Ph.D., Loyola.
Virginia Gonzalez, Associate Professor; Ph.D. Texas.
Rafael Lara-Alecio, Associate Professor; Ph.D., Utah.
Patricia J. Larke, Professor; Ed.D., Missouri–Columbia.

Reading/Language Arts
Jodi L. Holschuh, Assistant Professor; Ph.D., Georgia.
Diane S. Kaplan, Assistant Professor; Ed.D., Houston.
Donna E. Norton, Professor; Ph.D., Wisconsin.
William H. Peters, Professor; Ed.D., Virginia.
Tom H. Reynolds, Assistant Professor; Ph.D., Wisconsin–Madison.
William H. Rupley, Professor; Ph.D., Illinois.
Mark C. Sadoski, Professor; Ph.D., Connecticut.

Math/Science
Jon J. Denton, Professor; Ed.D., Missouri.
Robert K. James, Professor; Ph.D., Iowa.
Delmar L. Janke, Associate Professor; Ph.D., Wisconsin.
Charles E. Lamb, Professor; Ed.D., Georgia.
Cathleen C. Loving, Assistant Professor; Ph.D., Texas.
Carol L. Stuessy, Associate Professor; Ph.D., Ohio State.

Educational Technology
Lauren D. Cifuentes, Assistant Professor; Ph.D., North Carolina.
Karen L. Murphy, Assistant Professor; Ed.D., Washington (Seattle).
Ronald D. Zellner, Associate Professor; Ph.D., Arizona State.

EDUCATIONAL HUMAN RESOURCE DEVELOPMENT

Paulette Beatty, Professor and Interim Head; Ph.D., Florida State (telephone: 409-845-3016).
Adrianne Bonham, Associate Professor; Ed.D., Georgia.
Carolyn Clark, Associate Professor; Ed.D., Georgia.
Larry Dooley, Associate Professor; Ph.D., Texas A&M.
Dan Householder, Professor; Ed.D., Illinois.
Lloyd Korhonen, Professor; Ph.D., Michigan State.
JoAnn Martin, Assistant Professor; Ed.D., Arkansas.
Kenneth Paprock, Associate Professor; Ph.D., Illinois.
Don Seaman, Professor; Ph.D., Florida State.
Walter Stenning, Professor; Ph.D., Texas.
LaVerne Young-Hawkins, Associate Professor; Ed.D., Virginia Tech.

EDUCATIONAL PSYCHOLOGY

Doug Palmer, Professor and Head; Ph.D., UCLA (telephone: 409-845-1831).

Career Development Education
Gonzalo Garcia, Associate Professor; Ph.D., Ohio State.
Jerome Kapes, Professor; Ph.D., Penn State.
Linda Parrish, Professor; Ph.D., Texas A&M.

Counseling Psychology
Daniel Brossart, Assistant Professor; Ph.D., Missouri–Columbia.
Collie Conoley, Professor; Ph.D., Texas.
Donna Davenport, Associate Professor; Ph.D., Texas.
Michael Duffy, Professor; Ph.D., Texas.
David M. Lawson, Associate Professor; Ph.D., North Texas.
Pamilla Morales, Assistant Professor; Ph.D., Kansas.

Educational Psychology Foundations
Ernest Goetz, Professor; Ph.D., Illinois.
Glenda Griffin, Lecturer; Ph.D., Texas A&M.
Robert Hall, Associate Professor; Ph.D., UCLA.
Joyce Juntune, Lecturer; Ph.D., Texas A&M.
Stephanie Knight, Professor; Ed.D., Houston.
James McNamara, Professor; Ph.D., Penn State.
William Nash, Professor; Ed.D., Georgia.
Andy Stricker, Research Scientist; Ph.D., Texas A&M.
Bruce Thompson, Professor; Ed.D., Houston.
Victor Willson, Professor; Ph.D., Colorado.

School Psychology
Michael J. Ash, Professor; Ph.D., Arizona State.
Jane Close Conoley, Professor; Ph.D., Texas.
Jan Hasbrouck, Assistant Professor; Ph.D., Texas A&M.
Jan Hughes, Professor; Ph.D., Texas.
Salvador Hector Ochoa, Associate Professor; Ph.D., Texas A&M.
Cecil Reynolds, Professor; Ph.D., Georgia.
Cynthia Riccio, Assistant Professor; Ph.D., Georgia.

Special Education
Daniel Boudah, Assistant Professor; Ph.D., Kansas.
Patricia Lynch, Senior Lecturer; Ph.D., Texas A&M.
Richard Parker, Associate Professor; Ph.D., Oregon.
Laura Stough, Senior Lecturer; Ph.D., Texas.

HEALTH AND KINESIOLOGY

Jack Wilmore, Professor and Head; Ph.D., Oregon (telephone: 409-845-3109).

Kinesiology
Robert Armstrong, Professor; Ph.D., Washington State.
Frank Ashley, Associate Professor; Ed.D., Alabama.
William Barnes, Professor; Ph.D., USC.
Susan Bloomfield, Assistant Professor; Ph.D., Ohio State.
Robert Brackett, Research Scientist; Ph.D., Texas A&M.
Camille Bunting, Associate Professor; Ph.D., Texas A&M.
John Chevrette, Professor; Ph.D., Florida State.
Steve Crouse, Professor; Ph.D., New Mexico.
Michael Delp, Assistant Professor; Ph.D., Georgia.
John Dollar, Visiting Assistant Professor; Ph.D., Texas A&M.
Georgia Frey, Assistant Professor; Ph.D., Oregon State.
Carl P. Gabbard, Professor; Ed.D., North Texas.
John Green, Visiting Assistant Professor; Ph.D., Texas A&M.
John Lawler, Assistant Professor; Ph.D., Florida.
Ron McBride, Associate Professor; Ed.D., Stanford.
James Robinson, Visiting Professor; Ed.D., Northern Colorado.
Charles Shea, Professor; Ph.D., Virginia Tech.
Homer Tolson, Professor; Ph.D., Purdue.
David Wright, Associate Professor; Ph.D., Penn State.

Health and Safety
Danny Ballard, Associate Professor; Ed.D., Oklahoma State.
Brian Colwell, Associate Professor; Ph.D., Indiana Bloomington.
Maurice Dennis, Professor; Ph.D., Georgia.
Jerry Elledge, Associate Professor; Ph.D., Texas A&M.
Jeff Guidry, Assistant Professor; Ph.D., Texas.
Linda Jackson Jouridine, Visiting Assistant Professor; Ed.D., Virginia.
Leonard Ponder, Professor; Ed.D., Tennessee.
Buzz Pruitt, Professor; Ed.D., North Texas.
Wayne Wylie, Associate Professor; Ed.D., Tennessee.

TUFTS UNIVERSITY

Department of Education

Programs of Study

Within the framework of a liberal arts college, the Department of Education, established in 1910, offers programs leading to the degrees of Master of Arts (M.A.) in education and in education with a specialization in museum education; Master of Arts in Teaching (M.A.T.); Certificate of Advanced Graduate Study (C.A.G.S.) in education; and a combined M.A./C.A.G.S. in school psychology. The M.A., M.A.T., C.A.G.S., and M.A./C.A.G.S. programs provide a sequence of courses that has been approved by the Commonwealth of Massachusetts Department of Education. Students in these programs are eligible for certification as school psychologists for grades K–12 and as teachers of grades 1–6 (elementary), 5–9, and 9–12 in the following subject areas: biology, chemistry, earth science, English, general science, history, mathematics, physics, and social studies. Students are also eligible for certification as teachers of Latin and classical humanities, French, German, Japanese, Russian, and Spanish for grades preK–9 and 5–12. Through a collaboration with the School of the Museum of Fine Arts in Boston, students may receive certification in art education for grades preK–9 and 5–12. A Ph.D. program in education, with specializations in psychological studies and in science, mathematics, and technology, is being developed.

Courses focus on the study of the processes by which children and youth are engaged in learning; on the institutions that serve children and youth; on the cultural, historical, and philosophical influences on educational thought; and on the practices related to effective professional service. The program maintains a balance between knowledge and research that is discipline-oriented and that which is directed toward the critical analysis of issues in education. Course offerings are complemented with opportunities to observe and work with children and youth in a variety of educational settings as teachers, school psychologists, museum educators, curriculum developers, and other professionals in education. Having a metropolitan location and a long-standing association with neighboring schools, museums, industries, and other educational institutions, the department offers a large variety of field experiences to its students. These applied experiences are an essential part of programs in education where theory and research are integrated into practice.

The department maintains its own Placement Office for its graduates and places more than 95 percent of its graduates, a record that substantially exceeds the experiences of many schools, as indicated in nationwide surveys.

Research Facilities

Faculty members are engaged in a wide range of research, including family influences on achievement, the history of women in education, assessment and evaluation, epistemological beliefs of students learning science, microcomputer-based approaches to teaching physics, technology and education, and the analysis of impediments to writing. Students are encouraged to participate in faculty research projects, as well as to engage in independent research.

Financial Aid

Tuition scholarships, usually ranging from one-quarter to one-half tuition, are available to most students in the programs. Teaching and research assistantships and work-study opportunities are also available through departmental funds and through faculty grants.

Cost of Study

In 1998–99, tuition for the one-year M.A. degree and for the M.A.T. program is $23,839. Tuition for the complete M.A./C.A.G.S. program is paid in a two-year period, with the first year's tuition being $20,859. All graduate tuition charges for the second year of programs reflect increases in the base tuition rate for those years.

Living and Housing Costs

Some on-campus dormitory housing is provided and the local area contains many private apartments that customarily accommodate several persons. Local public transportation is modestly priced and readily accessible.

Student Group

There are about 110 students enrolled in the graduate programs in the Department of Education. The University is committed to establishing a racially and culturally diverse group of students. Currently approximately 20 percent of the students in the education programs are male; approximately 12 percent of students represent international or culturally diverse groups. Ninety-five percent of the students receive some form of financial assistance.

Location

The Boston area offers an unusual combination of historical, cultural, and educational experiences and opportunities. The College of Arts and Sciences at Tufts University, located 5 miles from Boston in the suburb of Medford, is in a convenient location with easy access through public transportation to Cambridge and Boston.

The University

Tufts University was founded in 1852 and has about 4,800 undergraduate students and about 2,500 graduate students. The moderate size of the student body and student-faculty ratio foster an informal environment not found in many larger institutions. The Medford campus covers about 150 acres and contains more than 125 buildings. There are many active student organizations on campus and local activities for student participation. The University has extensive computing facilities. Students have access to the services of the Tisch Library on the Medford campus and to the eleven academic and research libraries belonging to the Boston Library Consortium. Tufts is part of a consortium with Boston College, Boston University, and Brandeis University whereby students may register for courses in these institutions without additional cost. Opportunities for international study are also available.

Applying

Applications for fall admission should be received by February 15. Applications are accepted after this time until July 15 depending on available space in the program. Application materials may be obtained from the Graduate School of Arts and Sciences at Tufts University, Packard Avenue, Medford, Massachusetts 02155. Information about the degree programs in education are available from the Department of Education. Scores from the GRE General Test are required for all programs except art education.

Correspondence and Information

Director of Graduate Studies
Department of Education
Lincoln Filene Center
Tufts University
Medford, Massachusetts 02155
Telephone: 617-627-3244

Tufts University

THE FACULTY

Kathleen A. Camara, Chairperson; Ph.D., Stanford, 1979. Family influences on children's development and education, research methods, teacher education, assessment and evaluation.
Richard Aieta, M.A.T., Salem State, 1974. Geography curriculum.
Linda V. Beardsley, M.Ed., Tufts, 1982. Director of Student Teaching and School Partnerships.
Loring Brinckerhoff, Ph.D., Wisconsin, 1984. Learning disabilities, teaching of exceptional children.
Susan Carlson, M.A., Columbia, 1976. Special education, diversity in the classroom.
Eric Chaisson, Director, H. Dudley Wright Center for Innovations in Science Education; Ph.D., Harvard, 1972. Astrophysics, space curricula for middle and secondary school teachers.
Steven Cohen, Ph.D., Brandeis, 1980. Teacher education, history and social studies, curriculum development.
Steven Cohen, Ph.D., Tufts, 1998. Statistics and learning technologies.
Dennis DiSalvo, M.A., Columbia, 1964. Current issues in education.
David Hammer, Ph.D., Berkeley, 1991. Science and mathematics education, epistemological beliefs of students in learning science.
Fran Lanouette, M.A., Tufts, 1976. Foreign language education.
Marcel Lavergne, Ed.D., Boston University, 1975. Foreign language education.
Steven Luz-Alterman, Coordinator of Internships; Ph.D., Adelphi, 1985. School psychology, clinical psychology and life-span development.
Dorothy Pilla, Director, Art Education; M.A., Tufts, 1995. Curriculum development, expressive arts.
Marion Reynolds, M.A., New Mexico, 1980. Literacy development, assessment and instruction, elementary education, interdisciplinary elementary curriculum.
Christopher Saheed, Ph.D. candidate, Harvard. Secondary language, arts education, professional development.
Analucia Dias Schliemann, Ph.D., London, 1980. Theories of learning, cognitive psychology, developmental psychology, quantitative and qualitative research methods.
Anne Snyder, Education Director, Shady Hill Program; M.A., Lesley, 1977. Middle school education, curriculum development.
Sidney Strauss, Ph.D., Berkeley, 1967. Cognitive psychology, learning and development, teachers' cognition.
Corliss Thompson-Drew, Psy.D., Illinois School of Professional Psychology, 1992. Cognitive assessment, families and family interventions, behavior management, child and adolescent issues.
Ronald Thornton, Director, Center for Science and Mathematics Teaching; Ph.D., Brown, 1976. Microcomputer-based approaches to instruction.
Martha Trudeau Tucker, Ph.D., Massachusetts, Amherst, 1997. English education, middle and secondary education, impediments to writing.
Caroline Wandle, Ph.D., North Carolina, 1980. School psychology, assessment and evaluation.
Kathleen Weiler, Ed.D., Boston, 1986. History of education, social foundations of education, women in education.
Uri Wilensky, Ph.D., MIT, 1993. Mathematics education, computer science, teacher development, learning technologies.

Other Affiliations

Center for Science and Mathematics Teaching. The Center is an associated facility of the department involved in evaluating and developing new methods and materials for the teaching of mathematics and science.

The H. Dudley Wright Center for Innovations in Science Education. The Center focuses on the developing of innovations in science and mathematics education, provides fellowships for talented secondary school mathematics and science teachers, and offers training to high school teachers in the use of creative teaching techniques in science and mathematics education. Graduate students are encouraged to participate in the colloquia and research and professional activities of the Center.

UNIVERSITY OF ARIZONA

College of Education

Programs of Study

The College of Education seeks to advance the study and practice of education at all levels while upholding the highest possible standards of excellence. Its graduates teach, conduct research, hold administrative positions, and in other ways provide leadership in schools, institutions of higher education, and nonacademic settings. Its graduate programs are in the top 20 percent of all institutions, public and private combined, according to the 1998 *U.S. News & World Report* ranking.

The College offers more than twenty programs leading to one of the following degrees: Master of Arts (M.A.), Master of Education (M.Ed.), Educational Specialist (Ed.S.), Doctor of Philosophy (Ph.D.), or Doctor of Education (Ed.D.). Program areas include bilingual/multicultural education; educational leadership; educational psychology; higher education; language, reading, and culture; special education and rehabilitation; and teaching and teacher education. Requirements vary by program and by the student's personal interests and goals. The faculty and program descriptions are listed on the back of this page. For more information, students should write to the individual departments or consult the College homepage on the World Wide Web at http://www.ed.arizona.edu.

Research Facilities

Extensive support facilities are available to students and faculty for research, teaching, and interdisciplinary educational services. Within the College, an Instructional Technology Facility, a Teaching Analysis Lab, and diagnostic/instructional clinics serve faculty and students alike. Other resources include the University Library system, which contains more than 5 million items, the Mexican American Studies and Research Center, the Center for Computing and Information Technology (including a large software library and multimedia/visualization laboratory), and the Bureau for Applied Research in Anthropology.

Financial Aid

Financial aid for graduate students includes scholarships, fellowships, assistantships, University research grants, and loans, including several aid sources designated for minority students. Students should inquire at two levels: University of Arizona Office of Student Financial Aid (Administration Building, 520-621-1858) and the individual College of Education department, as listed on the reverse of this page.

Cost of Study

Tuition and fees for nonresident graduate students taking 12 or more units are $4557 per semester in 1998–99. State resident fees for students taking 7 or more units are $1081 per semester. All costs are subject to change.

Living and Housing Costs

Housing is available to graduate and undergraduate students in the University's apartment complex, Christopher City. Residents may be married or single, with or without children. The complex of 356 ground-level apartments features furnished or unfurnished studio, one-, two-, and three-bedroom apartments; a community center, with study, recreation, and computer rooms; swimming and wading pools; and a playground. Monthly rents range from $313 to $653 and include the cost of water, gas, and electricity. For information, students can write to Residence Life, University of Arizona, P.O. Box 210151, Tucson, Arizona 85721-0151 (telephone: 520-621-4173, fax: 520-621-8533, World Wide Web: http://w3.arizona.edu/~rescomp/family/index/html).

Student Group

Approximately 1,000 full- and part-time students are enrolled in graduate degree programs in the College of Education. The University of Arizona has a total enrollment of about 36,000 students and offers special services and physical accommodations on campus for students with disabilities. The College welcomes students of diverse backgrounds. In fall 1997, students of minority groups comprised 20 percent and international students comprised more than 7 percent of the College's total graduate student population.

Location

The University of Arizona maintains a centrally located, beautifully landscaped campus in metropolitan Tucson, which has a metro population of 750,000. The city is surrounded by four mountain ranges of the high Sonoran Desert plain. Mexican-Americans constitute one fourth of the local community, and many other cultural-ethnic groups have contributed to Tucson's expansive and rapidly growing opportunities for individual fulfillment educationally, vocationally, and culturally.

The University and The College

Founded in 1885 as a land-grant college, the University of Arizona in Tucson ranks eleventh among the top research universities in the nation according to the National Science Foundation and is a member of the prestigious Association of American Universities. The College of Education has acquired a national reputation for the quality of its faculty and programs, attracting more than $2.3 million in grants and contracts during the 1997–98 academic year. It maintains a dynamic, cooperative relationship with the community. For more information on the University, students should consult the homepage at http://www.arizona.edu.

Applying

Applications for admission must be made on forms furnished by the Graduate College. The forms and two official transcripts must be filed at least one month prior to registration. In addition, applicants should contact the appropriate program in the College of Education to obtain other application materials and requirements well in advance of applying to the Graduate College.

Correspondence and Information

Graduate Admissions Office
Administration Building 107
University of Arizona
Tucson, Arizona 85721
Telephone: 520-621-3132
E-mail: gradadm@lorax.adm.arizona.edu

Graduate Secretary (specify department)
College of Education
University of Arizona
Tucson, Arizona 85721
Telephone: 520-621-1462

University of Arizona

THE FACULTY AND RESEARCH AREAS

The College of Education (John L. Taylor, Dean) is divided into five academic units. Individual programs are housed within these departments.

DEPARTMENT OF EDUCATIONAL ADMINISTRATION AND HIGHER EDUCATION.

Educational Administration/Leadership Program (Ed.D.): Donald Clark, Program Head.
Professor: Donald C. Clark. Associate Professors: L. Kris Bosworth, J. Robert Hendricks. Assistant Professor: Stephanie Parker.

The Educational Administration/Leadership Program is designed to prepare principals and superintendents to lead the nation's schools by translating theory and knowledge into practice, applying skills in interpersonal relations and political diplomacy, and following ethical principles. The program offers two options: a certification doctorate (for those who wish to acquire an administrative certificate as part of a Doctor of Education program) and an executive doctorate (for those who have already achieved certification and wish to obtain a Doctor of Education).

Center for the Study of Higher Education (M.A., Ph.D.): Gary Rhoades, Program Head.
Professors: Larry Leslie, Gary Rhoades, Sheila Slaughter, Dudley Woodard. Associate Professor: John Levin.

The Center for the Study of Higher Education provides for teaching, practice, and research in such areas as academic administration, finance, college student personnel, community college administration, international education, administrative leadership, and planning and finance in higher education.

DEPARTMENT OF EDUCATIONAL PSYCHOLOGY. Darrell Sabers, Head.

Educational Psychology Program (M.A., Ph.D.)
Professors: Sarah Dinham, Thomas Good, Anthony J. Nitko, Darrell Sabers, Janice Streitmatter. Associate Professors: L. Kris Bosworth, Mary McCaslin, Rosemary Rosser. Assistant Professors: Jerome V. D'Agostino, Virginia González.

Research emphases include systemic study of teaching effectiveness, motivated learning in classroom settings, measurement and evaluation of learning outcomes, applied psychometrics, preadolescent and adolescent development, mathematical problem solving, early childhood cognition and language learning, and nondiscriminatory assessment. The department offers graduate programs in two concentration areas: measurement and research methodology and teaching, learning, and development.

DEPARTMENT OF LANGUAGE, READING AND CULTURE. Richard Ruiz, Head.

Language, Reading and Culture Program (M.A., Ed.S., Ed.D., Ph.D.); Bilingual/Multicultural Education Program (M.A.); Bilingual/Bicultural Education Program (M.Ed.)
Professors: Patricia Anders, Kenneth Goodman, Yetta Goodman, Judy Mitchell, Luis Moll, Richard Ruiz, William Valmont. Associate Professors: Adela Allen, John Bradley, Dana Fox, Teresa McCarty, Marcello Medina Jr., Kathy Short. Clinical Assistant Professor: Arminda Fuentevilla.

Research emphases include language development, applied linguistics, the writing process, the relationship of reading and writing, developmental reading, reading comprehension, reading instruction, reading assessment, bilingualism, bilingual/multicultural education, technology and literacy, children's literature, American Indian education, community literacy, biliteracy, and language planning.

DEPARTMENT OF SPECIAL EDUCATION AND REHABILITATION. Lawrence Aleamoni, Head.

Special Education and Rehabilitation Program (M.Ed., M.A., Ed.S., Ed.D., Ph.D.)
Professors: Lawrence Aleamoni, Shirin Antia, Candace Bos, James Chalfant, C. June Maker, Shitala Mishra, Richard Morris, John Obrzut, Amos Sales, John Umbreit. Associate Professors: Jane Erin, Charlene Kampfe, S. Mae Smith, Samuel Supalla,. Assistant Professors: Todd Fletcher, Kathleen L. Lane, Les McAllan, Elba Reyes.

Research in this department focuses on promoting the empowerment of individuals with disabilities and special abilities across the age span by increasing knowledge and understanding of abilities, disabilities, adaptations, interventions, and support systems. Research emphases include such areas as nondiscriminatory assessment; policy analysis; inclusion and mainstreaming; service delivery models and system change; transitions and interventions in social, language, cognitive, academic, emotional/affective, and vocational domains.

DEPARTMENT OF TEACHING AND TEACHER EDUCATION. Alice Paul, Head.

Teaching and Teacher Education Program (M.Ed., M.A., Ed.D., Ph.D.)
Professors: Wilbur Ames, Kathy Carter, Walter Doyle, Daniel Kirby, John L. Taylor. Associate Professors: Ruth Beeker, Carol Evans, Toni Griego Jones, Paul Heckman, Willis Horak, Carol Larson, Alice Paul, Stanley Pogrow, D. Paul Robinson. Assistant Professors: Maria Fernandez, Katharina Heyning, Julie Luft, Barbara McKean. Senior Lecturer: Richard López.

The M.A. is a research degree, and the M.Ed. is designed for teacher leaders. The Ph.D. focuses on preparation for careers in higher education and research organizations, the Ed.D. on leadership in school settings. Areas of research include teaching, teacher education, curriculum theory and practice, teacher and student cognition, staff development, bilingual education, and school subject matter/age group specializations, including early childhood education, middle level education, English education, mathematics education, reading/language arts education, science education, and social studies education.

Student projects provide opportunities for peer collaboration and faculty-student interaction.

Small-group discussion is typical of graduate-level study at the University of Arizona College of Education.

UNIVERSITY OF BRIDGEPORT

School of Education and Human Resources
Graduate Programs in Education

Programs of Study

The School of Education offers the master's degree in education with two options: a Connecticut certification track and a noncertification track (for those who will teach in other states). Within both tracks, innovative internship options for students are available. They consist of a 33-credit academic requirement combined with a school-year internship at a collaborating school. The intern earns tuition credits for the degree and a living stipend. The final certification requirement is twelve weeks of student teaching following the master's degree year. This format provides a maximum of practical experience combined with the theoretical course work.

Master's-level courses are available in a flexible format for certified teachers. This Modified Alternative Program (MOD MAP) awards 33 credits that require two anchor courses at the beginning and two at the end of the program. The remaining courses may be selected from a range of electives, which provide flexibility for the students to concentrate on areas of professional development most germane to them.

There is a sixth-year degree in elementary or secondary education, also a Modified Alternative Program (MOD MAP), similar to the master's degree MOD MAP. Two anchor requirements that total a minimum of 6 credits permit a range of electives for the 30-credit program. Many of the electives are offered in convenient 1-credit MODs scheduled on a Friday evenings and the following Saturday.

The sixth-year professional diploma in educational leadership is a 30-credit program that offers the courses required for an Intermediate Administrator Certificate. These include courses in psychology/pedagogy, supervision/personnel, curriculum, school management/administration, and policy. The courses are in a traditional semester format, meeting once a week. Two courses are always scheduled back to back on the same evening.

The Doctor of Education (Ed.D.) in educational leadership is an advanced degree program organized in a cohort format and is offered in a flexible format for working adults. Each entering group in September follows the same program for a three-year cycle, including a residency requirement. This residency entails six Friday/Saturday combinations during the academic year plus two weeks in the summer (July). Courses focus on areas such as program development, analysis for administrative decisions, analysis for organizational decisions, statistics, and research. The thesis work takes at least one year and is supported by a continuing doctoral seminar.

Research Facilities

The University's Wahlstrom Library contains approximately 275,000 bound volumes, including bound journals and indexes, and more than 1 million microforms and subscribes to more than 1,500 periodicals and other serials. Online database searching is available on the Internet, DIALOG, First Search, EBSCO's Academic Search Full Text 1,000, and LEXIS-NEXIS. CD/ROM databases include ERIC, Moody's Company Data, MEDLINE, reQuest, Books in Print Plus (BIP Plus), and the National Trade Data Bank. All students have access to e-mail, Netscape, and word processing. Residence halls are wired for individual computer hook-ups.

Financial Aid

Financial aid is available to U.S. citizens in the form of endowed scholarships, Federal Stafford Student Loans, graduate assistantships, and internships. The University also hires graduate students as residence hall directors and assistant hall directors. Further information can be obtained from the Office of Financial Aid at 203-576-4568. International students must demonstrate sufficient funds to finance their studies in the U.S. They must complete the financial aid statement for international students included in the International Application for Admissions.

Cost of Study

In 1998–99, tuition is $340 per credit hour. Students choosing the intern option only pay tuition for student teaching, for a total of $1970. The other 33 tuition credits are paid by the collaborating school system. Students taking 9 credits per semester are considered full-time.

Living and Housing Costs

Dormitory housing is available. Additional information related to on-campus residency can be obtained from the Office of Residential Life at 203-576-4395.

Student Group

There are approximately 150 full-time students in the master's degree program. There are another 30 part-time students.

The University

Founded in 1927, the University of Bridgeport is a private, nonsectarian, comprehensive, urban university of more than 2,600 students. Approximately half of the total student body are graduate students. The University's campus is composed of ninety-one buildings of diverse architectural styles. The Bernard Arts and Humanities Center is a cultural hub, and the Wheeler Recreation Center is a complete recreation and physical fitness facility.

Location

The University of Bridgeport's 86-acre campus is situated on Long Island Sound. The Stamford Campus is a convenient location for students from Connecticut as well as Westchester County, New York, and New Jersey. A Waterbury location, just off Routes 84 and 8, offers a full program for the master's degree.

Applying

Students applying for teacher certification programs should submit all official undergraduate transcripts, two professional references, and a personal statement about reasons for wanting to teach with their applications. Requirements include a minimum undergraduate GPA of 2.75 and passage of a PRAXIS I exam or proof of SAT scores higher than 1000. No previous education courses are necessary. A minimum TOEFL score of 550 is required of students whose native language is not English. Students applying for the doctoral program must have a master's degree and demonstrate an ability to do advanced graduate work. Official transcripts and two professional references must support the application. The Miller's Analogy Test is a requisite. Electronic applications are welcome through the University's Web site and Polaris.

Correspondence and Information

Office of Admissions
University of Bridgeport
126 Park Avenue
Bridgeport, Connecticut 06601
Telephone: 203-576-4552
800-EXCEL-UB (392-3582) (toll-free)
Fax: 203-576-4941
E-mail: admit@cse.bridgeport.edu
World Wide Web: http://www.bridgeport.edu

School of Education
Carlson Hall
University of Bridgeport
Bridgeport, Connecticut 06601
Telephone: 203-576-4198 or 4192
Fax: 203-576-4200

University of Bridgeport

THE FACULTY

Allen Cook, Ph.D., Stanford. Teaching of mathematics.
James T. Hamilton, Ph.D., Ohio State. Educational leadership.
Richard C. Harper, Ed.D., Columbia Teachers College. Teaching social studies.
Robert Kirschmann, Ph.D., Oregon. Educational curriculum and administration.
E. Wesley Menzel, Ph.D., Temple. Teaching of science.
John Mulcahy, Ph.D., Fordham. Educational leadership.
Patricia Mulcahy-Ernt, Ph.D., Minnesota. Teaching of reading.
Nelson Ngoh, Ph.D., Surrey (England). Science education.
James J. Ritchie, Dean; Ed.D., Columbia Teachers College. Educational administration.
Anthony Soares, Ph.D., Illinois. Educational psychology.
Angela Speck, Ph.D., Connecticut. Teaching of language arts.
T. Mathai Thomas, Ph.D., Boston University. History and philosophy of education.

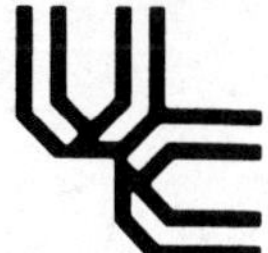

UNIVERSITY OF CINCINNATI

College of Education

Programs of Study

The College of Education at the University of Cincinnati pursues excellence through research and the dissemination of knowledge in the areas of teaching, research, training and development, and administration. The College encourages individuality, thought, and creativity and emphasizes diversity as an integral part of the educational experience. The degree programs offered are the Master of Education (M.Ed.), Master of Arts (M.A.), Master of Science (M.S.), Doctor of Education (Ed.D.), Doctor of Philosophy (Ph.D.), and Educational Specialist (Ed.S.).

The Ed.D. is offered in curriculum and instruction, education foundations, literacy, ESL, and special education. The Ph.D. is offered in criminal justice and school psychology. The M.Ed. is offered in curriculum and instruction, early childhood, educational administration, educational foundations, elementary education, health promotion and education, literacy/ESL, school psychology, secondary education, and special education. The M.A. is offered in counseling, and the M.S. is offered in criminal justice. The Ed.S. is offered in educational administration.

Research Facilities

The University of Cincinnati's Langsam Library is one of the leading state-supported institutions of its kind in Ohio. It is also part of a metropolitan-area consortium that includes the 3-million-volume library of the city of Cincinnati and Hamilton County. The Curriculum Resource Center and the recently constructed College of Education Computer Laboratory provide additional research facilities. In assisting students and faculty in data analysis, the Institute for Policy Research provides extensive consulting services at no cost.

Financial Aid

The two primary forms of financial aid are University Graduate Scholarships, which cover tuition only, and graduate assistantships, which cover tuition and general fees and are accompanied by a stipend. Students from underrepresented groups are especially invited to apply for the College of Education Scholarship fund and the University Yates Fellowship program, which provides a stipend, full tuition, and a waiver of general fees for one year or a full tuition award for the academic year.

Cost of Study

For the 1998–99 academic year, tuition is $1863 per quarter for Ohio residents and $3509 per quarter for out-of-state residents. Costs are subject to change.

Living and Housing Costs

The campus and surrounding area offer excellent housing facilities for single and married graduate students. Further information can be obtained from the Graduate and Guest Housing Main Apartment Office, 2920 Scioto Hall.

Student Group

The College of Education currently has a student body of more than 3,000. As an equal educational opportunity institution, the College enjoys a student population representing most of the United States and nations in Asia, Africa, the Caribbean, and the Middle East. Graduates find positions as college and university professors; researchers; counselors; psychologists; educational administrators; early childhood, elementary, and secondary school teachers; and health promotion specialists.

Location

The city of Cincinnati is located in southwestern Ohio and is part of a metropolitan area of approximately 1.9 million residents. Coupled with the city's outstanding musical heritage are many cultural attractions. Cincinnati is famous for its zoo and for its professional athletic teams—the Reds and the Bengals.

The University and The College

The origin of the University of Cincinnati can be traced to 1819, the year following the founding of the Cincinnati College and the Medical College of Ohio. In 1870 the University was established by a charter of the city of Cincinnati. The University operated as a municipal institution until becoming a member of the higher education system of the state of Ohio in 1977. The current University enrollment is approximately 34,000.

The College of Education traces its founding to the establishment of the Cincinnati Board of Education's City Normal Schools, which operated from 1868 to 1890, when that system was replaced by university courses taught specifically for public school teachers. By 1905, the College of Education was established under the name "A College for Teachers." By 1922, the board changed the name to College of Education, and the College of Education was put on a cooperative basis. By 1926, the College of Education began to offer the strictly professional degrees of Master of Arts and Doctor of Philosophy.

Applying

Applicants are encouraged to submit an application packet, consisting of the application form, three letters of recommendation, a goal statement, official transcripts of previous academic work, and GRE General Test scores not more than seven years old. Some programs also require GRE Subject Test scores. Application deadlines for admission vary, depending on the division, but the deadline for applications for financial aid is February 15 for students intending to matriculate in the fall.

Correspondence and Information

Office of Graduate Studies
College of Education
University of Cincinnati
Cincinnati, Ohio 45221-0002
Telephone: 513-556-4430

University of Cincinnati

THE FACULTY

Louis A. Castenell Jr., Dean; Ph.D., Illinois.
Arlene Harris Mitchell, Associate Dean for Academic Affairs; Ph.D., Penn State.
Lawrence Johnson, Associate Dean for Research and Development; Ph.D., Illinois.
Donald I. Wagner, Director of Graduate Studies; H.S.D., Indiana.

Counseling. Robert K. Conyne, Acting Program Coordinator; Ph.D., Purdue: group work. Ellen P. Cook, Ph.D., Iowa: community counseling. Mei Tang, Ph.D., Wisconsin–Milwaukee: school counseling. Albert Watson, Ph.D., Michigan: community counseling. F. Robert Wilson, Ph.D., Michigan State: community counseling. Geoffrey G. Yager, Ph.D., Michigan State: counseling supervision.

Criminal Justice. Program includes policing and corrections. Edward Latessa, Head; Ph.D., Ohio State: community connections. Joanne Belknap, Ph.D., Michigan State: women and crime. Sandra Browning, M.S., Cincinnati: criminological theory, race and crime. Mitchell Chamlin, Ph.D., SUNY at Albany: criminological theory, history and philosophy of criminal justice. Francis T. Cullen, Ph.D., Columbia: criminological theory. James Frank, Graduate Program Coordinator; Ph.D., Michigan State: police behavior. Lorraine Mazerolle, Ph.D., Rutgers: crime prevention. Paul Mazerolle, Ph.D., Maryland: criminology and juvenile delinquency. Lawrence F. Travis III, Ph.D., SUNY at Albany: sentencing, corrections. Patricia Van Voorhis, Ph.D., SUNY at Albany: correctional treatment. John Wooldredge, Ph.D., Illinois: institutional corrections, statistics.

Curriculum and Instruction. Linda B. Amspaugh, Ph.D., Ohio State: reading. Keith Barton, Ed.D., Kentucky: social studies education. Harriett C. Bebout, Ph.D., Wisconsin–Madison: mathematics education. Janet B. Bobango, Ph.D., Penn State: mathematics education. Janet L. Bohren, Ph.D., Ohio State: computer-based education. Bob M. Drake, Ed.D., Indiana: mathematics education. Thaddeus W. Fowler, Ed.D., Houston: science education. Jeffrey S. Gordon, Ph.D., Illinois: mathematics and computer education. Nancy B. Hamant, Ed.D., Cincinnati: curriculum and instruction. Susan Jenkins, Ph.D., Penn State: TESL. Glenn C. Markle, Ed.D., Georgia: science education. Kenneth E. Martin, Ph.D., Indiana: business education. Estela C. Matriano, Ed.D., Indiana: multicultural education. David T. Naylor, Ed.D., Rutgers: social studies education. Bruce D. Smith, Ed.D., Indiana: social studies education. Linda Taylor, Ph.D., Ohio State: mathematics education.

Early Childhood. Annie Bauer, Ed.D., Southern Illinois at Edwardsville: young children at risk. Anne G. Dorsey, M.Ed., Cincinnati: early childhood curriculum. Peggy Elgas, Ph.D., Ohio State: play styles. Darwin Henderson, Ed.D., Northern Illinois: children's literature and literacy. Lawrence Johnson, Ph.D., Illinois: assessment, collaboration. David Kuschner, Ed.D., Massachusetts Amherst: play, children's development, historical foundations of early childhood education. Michael Malone, Ph.D., Georgia: contexts of children's play, team process, observational methodology, early intervention, personnel preparation and program development.

Educational Administration. Nancy A. Evers, Ph.D., Wisconsin–Madison: leadership, change, and interpersonal relations.

Educational Foundations. Vanessa Allen-Brown, Ph.D., Missouri: social foundation of education. Marvin J. Berlowitz, Ph.D., SUNY at Buffalo: Marxist analysis of education. Lanthan D. Camblin, Ph.D., Missouri: human development. Roger L. Collins, Ph.D., Harvard: education and mental health. Judith Frankel, Ph.D., Ohio State: developmental psychology—life span. Annette Hemmings, Ph.D., Wisconsin–Madison: anthropology, sociology. Leo Krzywkowski, Ph.D., Ball State: educational and immigration history. Joel I. Milgram, Ph.D., Maryland: child development. Patricia O'Reilly, Program Coordinator; Ph.D., Cincinnati: gender roles, women's studies. Mary Anne Pitman, Division Head; Ph.D., Minnesota: educational anthropology and women's studies. Suzanne W. Soled, Ph.D., Chicago: measurement and evaluation. James Stevens, Ph.D., SUNY at Buffalo: multivariate statistics. Daniel Wheeler, Ph.D., Michigan: cognition and thought. Robert Yinger, Ph.D., Michigan State: cognitive psychology.

Elementary Education. Linda B. Amspaugh, Ph.D., Ohio State: reading. Harriet C. Bebout, Ph.D., Wisconsin–Madison: mathematics education. Alfred J. Ciani, Ph.D., Indiana: reading. Estela C. Matriano, Ed.D., Indiana: multicultural education. Florence Newell, Ed.D., Cincinnati: literacy and elementary education. Ronald E. Sterling, Ed.D., Indiana: social studies education. Sardar Tanveer, Ed.D., Indiana: science education. Cheri L. Williams, Ph.D., Ohio State: literacy and elementary education.

Health Promotion and Education. Amy Bernard, Ph.D., Ohio State: health science research and statistics, health behavioral theory. Randall R. Cottrell, Ed.D., Penn State: community health planning and evaluation, research design. Patricia M. Graman, M.A., ATC, Ball State: athletic training. Keith King, Ed.D., Toledo: adolescent health. Donald I. Wagner, H.S.D., Indiana: community health. Bradley R. A. Wilson, Program Coordinator; Ph.D., Michigan State: worksite health promotion.

Literacy. Linda B. Amspaugh, Program Coordinator; Ph.D., Ohio State: reading. Alfred J. Ciani, Ph.D., Indiana: reading. Penny A. Freppon, Ed.D., Cincinnati: literacy and elementary education. Deborah Hicks, Ed.D., Harvard: narrative discourse in literacy. Susan Jenkins, Ph.D., Penn State: TESL. Chester H. Laine, Ph.D., Penn State: literacy. Arlene H. Mitchell, Ph.D., Penn State: literacy and secondary English. Florence M. Newell, Ed.D., Cincinnati: literacy and elementary education. Elizabeth Peavy, Ph.D., Temple: adult literacy. Cheri L. Williams, Ph.D., Ohio State: literacy and elementary education.

School Psychology. Sarah J. Allen, Ph.D., Nebraska: consultation. David W. Barnett, Ph.D., Indiana State: social and cognitive theory and intervention. Edward J. Daly, Ph.D., Syracuse: academic and behavioral intervention. Janet L. Graden, Program Coordinator; Ph.D., Minnesota: family interventions and organizational change. Francis E. Lentz Jr., Ph.D., Tennessee: academic assessment and interventions.

Secondary Education. Janet C. Bobango, Ph.D., Penn State: mathematics education. Janet L. Bohren, Ph.D., Ohio State: computer-based education. Robert Burroughs, Ph.D., SUNY at Albany: English literature. Thaddeus W. Fowler, Ed.D., Houston: science education. Jeffrey S. Gordon, Ph.D., Illinois: mathematics and computer education. Nancy B. Hamant, Ed.D., Cincinnati: curriculum and instruction. Chester H. Laine, Ph.D., Penn State: reading. Glenn C. Markle, Ed.D., Georgia: science and teacher education. Kenneth E. Martin, Ph.D., Indiana: business education. Arlene H. Mitchell, Ph.D., Penn State: literacy and secondary English. David T. Naylor, Ed.D., Rutgers: social studies education. Bruce D. Smith, Ed.D., Indiana: social studies education. Piyush Swami, Ed.D., Ohio State: science education. Linda Taylor, Ph.D., Ohio State: mathematics education. Lee F. Wilberschied, Ph.D., Ohio State: applied linguistics and Spanish literature, teacher education and cognitive processes in language learning and teaching.

Special Education. Anne M. Bauer, Ed.D., Southern Illinois at Edwardsville: behavioral disorders. Peter Cardullias, Ed.D., Cincinnati: orthopedic and other health impairments in children. Carole Donnelly, Ph.D., Cincinnati: communication disorders. Dorothy A. Feldis, Ph.D., Michigan: assessment. Mary E. Franklin, Ph.D., Southern Illinois at Carbondale: mild disabilities. Richard R. Kretschmer, Ed.D., Columbia: language and hearing impairment. Regina Sapona, Ph.D., Virginia: learning disabilities. Roberta Truax, Ph.D., Cincinnati: hearing impairments. Joseph Zins, Ed.D., Cincinnati: consultation, prevention, behavioral intervention.

UNIVERSITY OF DETROIT MERCY

College of Education and Human Services
Department of Education

Programs of Study

The Department of Education offers the Master of Arts degree in six areas, including counseling, curriculum and instruction, early childhood education, educational administration, special education, and teaching and learning.

The Master of Arts in counseling combines practical, experiential, and theoretical perspectives in learning that stimulate academic and personal growth in graduate students. Persons planning to be counselors in school settings, community agencies, business, and industrial or health settings may elect one of the following: school counseling, agency counseling, or agency counseling with a certificate in addiction studies. School counseling is for certified teachers planning to work in a school setting as school counselors or guidance counselors or for teachers interested in a guidance-oriented background. Agency counseling is for those who are interested in working with people outside of education such as career counseling, the ministry, employment and assistance programs, mental health and social service agencies, and private practice. Agency counseling with a certificate in addiction studies is for those interested in working in the prevention, intervention, or treatment of chemical dependence. Additional information about each of these options is available upon request.

The Master of Arts in curriculum and instruction is designed for educators who wish to combine advanced study in curriculum planning and techniques, from K through adult education, with their special educational interests and goals. The program has a flexible and open design to provide specialized study in an area of concentration leading to curriculum leadership roles, including supervision and in-service development; curriculum planning in subject matter areas; studies relating to children with special needs; urban education; or curriculum and methods for ethical and moral development and decision making.

The Master of Arts in early childhood education is designed for active participation in advanced study of theories of curriculum and instruction, research skills, and educational foundations pertaining to pre-school, kindergarten, and primary education. Studies involve the designing of early learning strategies for instruction based on developmental theories. Each student is given the opportunity to make direct application of learning activities in a supervised laboratory setting.

The Master of Arts in educational administration is designed for those individuals who are interested in some phase of educational administration, whether as assistant superintendent, principal, assistant principal, or some other form of administration.

The Master of Arts in special education (emotionally impaired program) is designed to meet the needs of teachers who wish to prepare themselves for working with individuals experiencing mild to severe emotional problems at the elementary- and middle- or middle- and secondary-school levels. The Master of Arts in special education (learning disabilities program) is designed to meet the needs of teachers who wish to prepare themselves for working with individuals experiencing specific and general learning problems at the elementary- and middle- or middle- and secondary-school levels.

The Master of Arts in teaching and learning is a field-based program developed for teachers. It is practical and research-based in its approach to the difficulties within urban education today. It uses mediated learning as the way to define the teaching relationship from which students learn how to learn. The program focuses on teachers interested in becoming better practitioners within the metro-Detroit geographic areas. Classes and mentoring are offered within designated field sites.

Financial Aid

The Scholarship and Financial Aid Office provides applications for grants, loans, and work-study assistance. Aid includes the Michigan Tuition Grant for Michigan residents, various work-study programs, and a variety of low-interest loans providing up to 10 years for repayment. UDM accepts third-party payment from employers and government agencies and offers deferred payment plans for equal installments throughout the academic year.

Cost of Study

Graduate tuition for 1998–99 is $490 per credit hour for both regular semesters and summer sessions. Graduate students also pay a registration and student activities fee.

Living and Housing Costs

Housing is available in University residence halls. Double-occupancy rates begin at $1390 per semester, single-occupancy rates begin at $2400 per semester, and married student rates begin at $2590 per semester. A variety of meal plans are available for $575 to $1200 per semester.

Students

UDM enrolls about 7,500 students, including more than 1,750 graduate students. About 400 graduate students are enrolled in the College of Education and Human Services. Of these students, 78 percent are women and 22 percent are men; 56 percent are African-American and 4 percent are international students; the average age is 37. The majority enroll as part-time students and earn an average GPA of 3.53.

Location

UDM's location in southeastern Michigan places it amidst a corporate and educational community that rivals any other in the world for size and importance. Metropolitan Airport provides easy access from almost anywhere in the United States and daily international flights offer links with major centers around the globe. From the Midwest, interstate highways allow reasonable driving from cities such as Buffalo, Chicago, Cincinnati, Milwaukee, and Pittsburgh. The College of Education and Human Services offers courses at two campuses in residential areas of northwest Detroit. The campus and the Detroit area offer a wide variety of cultural and recreational activities, including concerts and theatrical performances of national reputation plus museums, libraries, and four professional sports teams. Canada is just a few minutes away.

The University

The University of Detroit Mercy is an independent Catholic institution of higher learning that exists primarily for teaching, learning, and research. Its mission includes compassionate service to people in need, the service of faith, the promotion of justice, and a commitment to quality education. UDM is the largest private university in Michigan, operated under the sponsorship of the Society of Jesus and the Religious Sisters of Mercy.

Applying

A bachelor's degree is required for admission to all programs. The Master of Arts in counseling requires at least a B average, a minimum of 15 hours in the behavioral sciences (including statistics), the Miller Analogies Test, and a personal letter explaining interests and plans in this program. The Master of Arts in curriculum and instruction normally requires at least a B average and a state teaching certificate. The Master of Arts in early childhood education normally requires at least a B average and fulfillment of requirements for a state teaching certificate, or a background of education and experience satisfactory to the department. The Master of Arts in educational administration normally requires at least a B average and fulfillment of requirements for a state teaching certificate, or a background of education and experience satisfactory to the department. The Master of Arts in special education normally requires at least a B average and fulfillment of requirements for a state teaching certificate, or a background of education and experience satisfactory to the department. The Master of Arts in teaching and learning normally requires at least a B average and a state teaching certificate. Applicants to all programs are required to give evidence of their fitness to pursue a professional career in the area of interest by submitting three letters of recommendation attesting to academic, personal, and professional qualifications.

Correspondence and Information

Chair, Department of Education
University of Detroit Mercy
P.O. Box 19900
Detroit, Michigan 48219
Telephone: 313-993-6305
E-mail: admissions@udmercy.edu

University of Detroit Mercy

THE FACULTY

Elizabeth U. Carlson, Assistant Professor of Education; Ed.D., Michigan.
W. Robert Docking, Assistant Professor of Education; Ed.D., Michigan State.
Josephine M. Gambini, Professor of Special Education; Ph.D., Wayne State.
Nancy Gibney, Assistant Professor of Education; Ph.D., Walden.
Jerry D. Goldberg, Assistant Professor of Education; Ed.D., Michigan.
Joslen L. Letscher, Assistant Professor of Education; Ph.D., Michigan.
Richard Sinacola, Assistant Professor of Counseling; Ph.D., Wayne State.
Carolyn Stoecklin, R.S.M., Assistant Professor of Education; Ph.D., St. Louis.
Donna Wilson, Associate Professor and Chair of the Department of Education; Ph.D., Oklahoma.

UNIVERSITY OF FLORIDA

College of Education

Programs of Study

The College of Education offers a variety of challenging graduate programs leading to the M.Ed., M.A.E., Ed.S., Ed.D., and Ph.D. degrees. A minimum of 30–36 credits is required in master's programs. The Ed.S. program requires a minimum of 72 credits; the Ed.D. and Ph.D. programs require a minimum of 90 credits beyond the bachelor's degree (including up to 30 credits from master's program course work). A thesis is required for the M.A.E., Ed.D., and Ph.D. degrees.

The instructional programs of the College are organized into five major departments: in Counselor Education, the programs are mental health counseling, marriage and family counseling, school counseling and guidance, and student services in higher education. In Educational Leadership, the programs include curriculum and instructional leadership, educational administration, and higher education. Foundations of Education offers specializations in comparative education; educational psychology; history, philosophy, and sociology of education; school psychology; and statistics, measurement, and evaluation methodology. Instruction and Curriculum offers specializations in bilingual education, computer education, early childhood education, elementary education, English education, foreign language education, mathematics education, media and instructional design, middle school education, reading and language arts, science education, secondary education, and social studies education. Special Education offers specializations in administration of special education programs and instruction of students with a broad range of exceptionalities.

Research Facilities

The University of Florida libraries form one of the most comprehensive collections in the country. Most educational resources are housed in the College of Education Library. Extensive mainframe computing facilities and a wide variety of computing services for students and faculty are available on campus, and a large PC lab is located in the College. The P. K. Yonge Developmental Research School, Multidisciplinary Diagnostic/Training Clinic for children with disabilities, Center for School Improvement, Center for Economic Education, Institute for Educational Finance, and Institute for Higher Education are illustrative of interdisciplinary research centers in the College.

Financial Aid

Financial aid is available for qualified students in the form of fellowships, teaching and research assistantships, and tuition waivers. In 1998–99, a half-time assistantship provides a minimum of $6630 plus tuition payment. Application for fellowships and assistantships should be made directly to the department in which the student plans to study. Information on student loans can be obtained from the Office for Student Financial Affairs.

Cost of Study

In 1997–98, tuition was $129.01 per credit hour for Florida residents and $434.40 per credit hour for nonresidents.

Living and Housing Costs

The University operates five apartment villages for graduate students with families. These typically range in cost from $261 to $344 per month in 1998–99. Two residence halls and one apartment village are open to single graduate students. A variety of privately owned housing is also available in the community.

Student Group

Students attending the University of Florida come from every state within the United States and more than 100 other countries. Of the 6,500 graduate students enrolled at the University, approximately 900 are in education.

Location

The University is located in Gainesville, a city of more than 88,000 situated in north-central Florida. It lies 80 miles west of the Atlantic Ocean and 70 miles east of the Gulf of Mexico. The city is an agricultural, medical, and industrial technology center, accessible in a 2-hour drive to Jacksonville, Orlando, and Tampa. The area, which is noted for its mild climate and natural beauty, has an abundance of springs, rivers, and lakes.

The University

Founded in 1853, the University of Florida is nationally distinguished. It is a member of the prestigious Association of American Universities and is the largest university in the Southeast and the eighth largest in the nation. It ranks third nationally in the number of academic programs offered on a single campus. This land-grant university comprises 20 colleges and schools and 100 interdisciplinary research and education centers located on a residential campus of more than 2,000 acres. The faculty includes some of the nation's leading scholars and researchers. The College of Education is accredited at the doctoral level in every area recognized by the National Council for Accreditation of Teacher Education. Because of its size and diversity, the University provides a rich variety of educational, leadership, cultural, athletic, and recreational opportunities for every student.

Applying

A completed application form, three letters of recommendation, GRE General Test scores, and transcripts from all institutions attended are required. Individual departments may have additional requirements. Application forms are available from the Office of Graduate Studies. International applicants whose native language is not English must also supply TOEFL scores.

Correspondence and Information

Dean of Graduate Studies
146 Norman Hall
College of Education
University of Florida
Gainesville, Florida 32611

University of Florida

THE FACULTY

Counselor Education. Ellen S. Amatea, Professor; Ph.D., Florida State. Family therapy. James Archer Jr., Professor; Ph.D., Michigan State. Counseling psychology. M. Harry Daniels, Professor; Ph.D., Iowa. Family therapy. Silvia Echevarria-Rafuls, Assistant Professor; Ph.D., Purdue. Family therapy. Mary A. Fukuyama, Assistant Professor; Ph.D., Washington State. Gerardo M. Gonzalez, Professor; Ph.D., Florida. Substance abuse. Mary Howard-Hamilton, Associate Professor; Ed.D., North Carolina State. Multicultural development. James Joiner, Associate Professor; Ph.D., Alabama. Larry C. Loesch, Professor; Ph.D., Kent State. Assessment. Roderick J. McDavis, Professor; Ph.D., Toledo. Multicultural counseling. Marvin R. McMillin, Associate Professor; Ed.D., Florida. Phyllis M. Meek, Associate Professor; Ed.D., Florida. James I. Morgan, Associate Professor; Ed.D., Florida. Robert D. Myrick, Professor; Ph.D., Arizona State. Peer counseling. Woodroe M. Parker, Professor; Ph.D., Florida. Multicultural counseling. James H. Pitts, Associate Professor; Ph.D., Northern Colorado. Conflict resolution. Jacquelyn L. Resnick, Professor; Ph.D., Florida. John P. Saxon, Professor; Ph.D., Georgia. Paul G. Schauble, Professor; Ph.D., Michigan State. Peter A. Sherrard, Associate Professor; Ed.D., Massachusetts. Legal and ethical issues. Paul J. Wittmer, Distinguished Service Professor; Ph.D., Indiana State. Peer meditation.

Educational Leadership. Linda Behar-Horenstein, Associate Professor; Ph.D., Loyola–Chicago. Education policy. Dale F. Campbell, Professor; Ph.D., Texas at Austin. Higher education. Phillip A. Clark, Professor; Ed.D., Western Michigan. Leadership. James L. Doud, Professor; Ph.D., Iowa. Elementary curriculum. Paul S. George, Professor; Ed.D., Vanderbilt (Peabody). Instruction. James W. Hensel, Professor Emeritus; Ph.D., Iowa State. Adult vocational administration. David Honeyman, Associate Professor; Ph.D., Virginia. Educational finance. Barbara Keener, Lecturer; Ph.D., Florida. John M. Nickens, Professor; Ph.D., Florida State. Higher education research. Michael Y. Nunnery, Professor Emeritus; Ed.D., Tennessee. Carl A. Sandeen, Professor; Ph.D., Michigan State. David C. Smith, Professor; Ph.D., Northwestern. Educational policy. Walter L. Smith, Visiting Professor; Ph.D., Florida State. Organization and management. James L. Wattenbarger, Distinguished Service Professor Emeritus; Ed.D., Florida. R. Craig Wood, Professor; Ed.D., Virginia Tech. Education administration.

Foundations of Education. James J. Algina, Professor; Ed.D., Massachusetts. Psychometrics. Patricia T. Ashton, Professor; Ph.D., Georgia. Child development. John K. Bengston, Associate Professor; Ph.D., Toledo. Language acquisition/use. Linda M. Crocker, Professor; Ph.D., Michigan State. Test development. Bridget A. Franks, Associate Professor; Ph.D., Nebraska. Cognitive development. Gordon E. Greenwood, Professor; Ed.D., Indiana. Parent involvement in education. Barry J. Guinagh, Associate Professor; Ph.D., Michigan State. Distance education. Jin-Wen Hsu, Assistant Professor; Ph.D., UCLA. Structural equation modeling. Mary L. Koran, Professor; Ph.D., Stanford. Learning in informal settings. John Kranzler, Associate Professor; Ph.D., Berkeley. Psychoeducational assessment. M. David Miller, Professor; Ph.D., UCLA. Large-scale assessment. Arthur J. Newman, Professor; Ed.D., Indiana. Constitutional law. Thomas D. Oakland, Professor; Ph.D., Indiana. School psychology. Richard R. Renner, Professor; Ph.D., Texas at Austin. Comparative education. Robert R. Sherman, Professor; Ed.D., Rutgers. Philosophy of education. Rodman B. Webb, Professor; Ed.D., Rutgers. Educational sociology. Arthur O. White, Professor; Ed.D., SUNY College at Buffalo. History of education. Edward W. Wolfe, Assistant Professor; Ph.D., Berkeley. Measurement.

Instruction and Curriculum. Thomasenia L. Adams, Associate Professor; Ph.D., Florida. Mathematics methods. Donald H. Bernard, Associate Professor Emeritus; Ed.D., Columbia Teachers College. Learning and teaching mathematics. Elroy J. Bolduc Jr., Professor Emeritus; Ed.D., Tennessee. Mathematics. Elizabeth Bondy, Associate Professor; Ph.D., Florida. Elementary education. Glenna D. Carr, Professor; Ed.D., Florida. Economic education. James D. Casteel, Professor Emeritus; Ph.D., Vanderbilt (Peabody). Social studies. Linda L. Cronin-Jones, Associate Professor; Ph.D., Georgia. Science and environmental education. Zhihui Fang, Assistant Professor; Ph.D., Purdue. Literacy. Henry T. Fillmer, Professor Emeritus; Ph.D., Ohio. Literacy. Sebastian L. Foti, Assistant Professor; Ph.D., Florida. Instructional technology. Danling Fu, Assistant Professor; Ph.D., New Hampshire. Whole language. John W. Gregory, Professor; Ph.D., Ohio State. Math methods. Clemens L. Hallman, Professor; Ph.D., Indiana. Foreign language education. Nora L. Hoover, Associate Professor; Ed.D., Virginia. Literacy. Jeff A. Hurt, Associate Professor; Ph.D., Kansas. Library/media education. Simon O. Johnson, Professor Emeritus; Ed.D., Indiana. General science methods. Eleanor L. Kantowski, Professor; Ed.D., Georgia. Mathematics education. Kristen M. Kemple, Associate Professor; Ph.D., Texas at Austin. Early childhood education. John J. Koran Jr., Professor; Ph.D., Stanford. Science education. Linda L. Lamme, Professor; Ph.D., Syracuse. Children's literature. Lee J. Mullally, Associate Professor; Ph.D., Michigan State. Media and instructional design. Ben F. Nelms, Professor; Ph.D., Iowa. English education. Lynn C. Oberlin, Professor; Ed.D., Michigan State. Elementary education. William R. Powell, Professor; Ed.D., Indiana. Dorene D. Ross, Professor; Ed.D., Virginia. Elementary curriculum. Coleen Swain, Assistant Professor; Ph.D., North Texas. Instructional technology. Eugene A. Todd, Professor; D.Ed., Houston. Social studies methods. Jane S. Townsend, Assistant Professor; Ph.D., Texas at Austin. English language arts. Edward C. Turner, Associate Professor; Ph.D., Michigan State. Reading. Regina Weade Lamme, Associate Professor; Ph.D., Ohio State. Language and social processes. Robert G. Wright, Associate Professor; Ph.D., Kansas. English education. Elizabeth Yeager, Assistant Professor; Ph.D., Texas at Austin. Social studies.

Special Education. Mary T. Brownell, Assistant Professor; Ph.D., Kansas. Learning disabilities. Vivian I. Correa, Professor; Ph.D., Vanderbilt. Early childhood special education. Mary K. Dykes, Professor; Ph.D., Texas at Austin. Special populations. Cynthia C. Griffin, Associate Professor; Ph.D., Purdue. Reading. Hazel Jones, Assistant Professor; Ph.D., Vanderbilt (Peabody). Early childhood special education. Cecil D. Mercer, Professor; Ed.D., Virginia. Learning disabilities. Cary L. Reichard, Professor; Ed.D., Northern Colorado. Mental disabilities. Jeanne B. Repetto, Assistant Professor; Ph.D., Missouri. Transition. Diane L. Ryndak, Assistant Professor; Ph.D., Illinois. Moderate and severe disabilities. Stuart E. Schwartz, Professor; Ed.D., Kansas. Transition. Paul T. Sindelar, Professor; Ph.D., Minnesota. School inclusion and reform. Stephen W. Smith, Associate Professor; Ph.D., Kansas. Violence/aggression of children.

UNIVERSITY OF ILLINOIS AT URBANA–CHAMPAIGN

College of Education

Programs of Study

The College of Education is organized into six major instructional departments: curriculum and instruction, educational organization and leadership, educational policy studies, educational psychology, special education, and human resource education. Through these six departments, the College offers more than forty specializations. The College offers master's programs leading to the Ed.M., A.M., and M.S. degrees, each of which requires a minimum of 8 units of study. Programs leading to the Ed.D or Ph.D. requires a minimum of 16 units of study beyond the master's level. A thesis is required for the A.M., M.S., Ed.D., and Ph.D. Joint degree programs are offered in two areas: a Ph.D. degree in educational administration in conjunction with the J.D. degree in law; and through the Medical Scholars Program, a combined M.D. and Ph.D. in education. Other specializations are developed by students and their advisers.

Research Facilities

Research facilities located in the College include the Bureau of Educational Research, the Center for the Study of Reading, the ERIC Clearinghouse for Elementary and Early Childhood Education, the Illinois Alliance for Essential Schools, the National Center for School Leadership, the National Center on Research in Vocational Education, the Office of Career Development for Special Populations and Transition Institute, the Office of Educational Policy and Leadership, the Office of School-University Research Relations, and the Teaching Teleapprenticeship Office. The University also has the third largest academic library in the nation, and the Education and Social Science Library is one of the finest in the world.

Financial Aid

Fellowships, tuition and service fee waivers, and teaching and research assistantships are available for graduate students, with more than 40 percent of graduate students in education receiving assistance for fall 1997. Competitions for most awards take place in March, with applications due on February 15. In 1998–99, a 50-percent assistantship provides a minimum of $9500 plus tuition and service fee waivers. Students apply directly to the departments for financial aid.

Cost of Study

In 1998–98, tuition and fees for an academic year of full-time study are $4834 for Illinois residents and $11,506 for nonresidents (subject to change).

Living and Housing Costs

The University maintains two residence halls for graduate students. For the 1997–98 academic year, rates in Daniels Hall and Sherman Hall, respectively, are $2110 and $2580 for double occupancy and $2360 and $2640 for single occupancy. A meal contract for twenty meals per week is $3004. Other campus and private housing is also readily available for students at a very reasonable cost.

Student Group

The University has approximately 9,800 graduate and professional students, with 951 registered as College of Education students for fall 1997. Approximately 72 percent were women, 18 percent were minority students, and 12 percent were international students.

Student Outcomes

UIUC graduates in education are highly sought by universities, state agencies, and other educational entities in both the private and public sectors. The College has a 90–100 percent placement rate for their graduate students.

Location

Champaign/Urbana, home of UIUC, is located midway between Chicago, St. Louis, and Indianapolis. Its 200 major buildings cover a 1,470-acre area in the heart of the central Illinois prairie land.

The University

Founded in 1867 as one of the original public land-grant institutions, UIUC is respected internationally for its leadership in research and its quality of instruction. Both UIUC and the College of Education consistently rank among the nation's best. UIUC recently ranked first in academic quality in relation to expenditures per student on educational programs. Three of the six departments in the College rank among the top five in the nation.

Ten university alumni have been awarded the Nobel Prize, 16 have won the Pulitzer Prize, numerous others have been honored for their scholarship by world-renowned organizations and foundations; still others fill chief executive positions in a large number of Fortune 500 companies. The environment at UIUC is rich in cultural diversity and supports a wealth of unique learning opportunities.

Applying

Graduate applications are made directly to the department head/chair. Applications are reviewed on a continuing basis, but prospective students should apply no later than February 15 to be considered for admission and financial aid. The Graduate College requires a grade point average of 3.0 (A = 4.0) during the last 60 hours of undergraduate work. Also required are a completed application for admission form (available from individual departments, the College of Education, or the Graduate College, [202 Coble Hall]), three letters of reference, and transcripts from all the institutions attended. Individual departments may also have special requirements, such as MAT or GRE test scores.

Correspondence and Information

Head/Chair, Department of (specify)
College of Education
University of Illinois at Urbana-Champaign
1310 South Sixth Street
Champaign, Illinois 61820
World Wide Web: http://www.ed.uiuc.edu/COE/IPO

Dr. James A. Leach, Associate Dean
College of Education, Instructional Programs Office
University of Illinois at Urbana-Champaign
1310 South Sixth Street
Champaign, Illinois 61820

University of Illinois at Urbana-Champaign

THE FACULTY

Department of Curriculum and Instruction: Mildred B. Griggs, Interim Head.
Richard C. Anderson, Professor; Ed.D., Harvard. Bonnie B. Armbruster, Professor; Ph.D., Illinois. Arthur Baroody, Professor; Ph.D., Cornell. Sheryl Benson, Associate Professor; Ph.D., Illinois. Liora Bresler, Associate Professor; Ph.D., Stanford. David Brown, Associate Professor; Ph.D., Illinois, Ed.D., Massachusetts. Bertram C. Bruce, Professor; Ph.D., Texas at Austin. Renée Clift, Professor; Ph.D., Stanford. Janet Gaffney, Associate Professor; Ph.D., Stanford. Georgia Garcia, Associate Professor; Ph.D., Illinois. Jesus Garcia, Professor; Ph.D., Berkeley. Kim C. Graber, Assistant Professor; Ed.D., Massachusetts at Amherst. Joe Walter Grant Jr., Associate Professor; Ed.D., Illinois. John Grashel, Associate Professor; Ph.D., Ohio State. Rochelle Gutierrez, Assistant Professor, Ph.D., Chicago. Violet Harris, Associate Professor; Ph.D., Georgia. Eve E. Harwood, Associate Professor; Ed.D, Illinois. Robert Jimenez, Assistant Professor; Ph.D., Illinois. Lilian G. Katz, Professor; Ph.D., Stanford. Karl Koenke, Associate Professor; Ph.D., Wisconsin. James A. Levin, Associate Professor; Ph.D., California, San Diego. Brent A. McBride, Associate Professor; Ph.D., Maryland College Park. Thomas McGreal, Professor; Ed.D., Illinois. Susan E. Noffke, Assistant Professor; Ph.D., Wisconsin–Madison. Margery Osborne, Assistant Professor; Ph.D., Michigan State; Ph.D., Western Ontario. Frederick A. Rodgers, Professor; Ed.D., Illinois. Louis J. Rubin, Professor; Ph.D., Berkeley. Deborah A. Sheldon, Assistant Professor; Ph.D., Florida State. Stephen J. Silverman, Professor; Ed.D., Massachusetts Amherst. Robert Stake, Professor; Ph.D., Princeton. René Stofflett, Assistant Professor; Ph.D., Utah. Kenneth J. Travers, Professor; Ph.D., Illinois. Daniel Walsh, Associate Professor; Ph.D., Wisconsin. James Ward, Professor; Ph.D., Virginia Tech. Michael L. Waugh, Associate Professor; Ed.D., Georgia. Ian Westbury, Professor; Ph.D., Alberta. Arlette Willis, Assistant Professor; Ph.D., Ohio State. Klaus G. Witz, Associate Professor; Ph.D., North Carolina.

Department of Educational Organization and Leadership: Paul W. Thurston, Head.
F. King Alexander, Assistant Professor; Ph.D., Wisconsin. Debra Bragg, Associate Professor; Ph.D., Ohio State. Thomas McGreal, Professor; Ed.D., Illinois. Betty Merchant, Assistant Professor; Ph.D., Stanford. Nona Prestine, Associate Professor; Ph.D., Wisconsin. Paul W. Thurston, Professor; Ph.D., Iowa. James G. Ward, Professor; Ph.D., Virginia Tech.

Department of Educational Policy Studies: James D. Anderson, Head.
Kal Alston, Associate Professor; Ph.D., Chicago. James D. Anderson, Professor; Ph.D., Illinois. Berneice Barnett, Assistant Professor; Ph.D., Georgia. Nicholas Burbules, Professor; Ph.D., Stanford. Walter Feinberg, Professor; Ph.D., Boston University. Ralph C. Page, Associate Professor; Ph.D., Illinois. Pradeep Dhillon, Assistant Professor; Ph.D., Stanford. Wanda Pillow, Assistant Professor; Ph.D., Ohio State. Laurence Parker, Associate Professor; Ph.D., Illinois. Mobin Shorish, Associate Professor; Ph.D., Chicago. William T. Trent, Professor; Ph.D., North Carolina.

Department of Educational Psychology: Lenore W. Harmon, Chair.
Terry A. Ackerman, Associate Professor; Ph.D., Wisconsin. Carolyn J. Anderson, Assistant Professor; Ph.D., Illinois. Richard C. Anderson, Professor; Ed.D., Harvard. Thomas H. Anderson, Professor; Ed.D., Illinois. Steven R. Asher, Professor; Ph.D., Wisconsin. A. Toy Caldwell-Colbert, Professor, Ph.D., Georgia. Elaine J. Copeland, Associate Professor; Ph.D., Oregon State. Gary A. Cziko, Associate Professor; Ph.D., McGill. Lizanne DeStefano, Associate Professor; Ph.D., Pittsburgh. Dorothy Espelage, Assistant Professor; Ph.D., Indiana. Diane L. Essex-Sorlie, Associate Professor; Ph.D., Illinois. Helen S. Farmer, Professor; Ph.D., UCLA. Robert D. Felner, Professor; Ph.D., Rochester. Louise F. Fitzgerald, Professor; Ph.D., Ohio State. James W. Hannum, Adjunct Assistant Professor; Ph.D., Stanford. Lenore W. Harmon, Professor; Ph.D., Minnesota. Delwyn L. Harnisch, Associate Professor; Ph.D., Illinois. Jacquetta F. Hill, Professor; Ph.D., Columbia. Lawrence J. Hubert, Professor; Ph.D., Stanford. Gary W. Ladd, Professor; Ed.D., Rochester. Ira W. Langston, Assistant Professor; Ph.D., Illinois. James A. Levin, Associate Professor; Ph.D., California, San Diego. Michael V. Levine, Associate Professor; Ph.D., Stanford. Jane W. Loeb, Professor; Ph.D., USC. Erica F. McClure, Associate Professor; Ph.D., Berkeley. George W. McConkie, Professor; Ph.D., Stanford. Michelle Perry, Associate Professor; Ph.D., Chicago. Alan J. Peshkin, Professor; Ph.D., Illinois. James B. Rounds, Professor; Ph.D., Minnesota. Katherine E. Ryan, Assistant Professor; Ph.D., Illinois. Jenny L. Singleton, Assistant Professor; Ph.D., Illinois. Rand J. Spiro, Professor; Ph.D., Penn State. Robert E. Stake, Professor; Ph.D., Princeton. William F. Stout, Professor; Ph.D., Purdue. Terence J. Tracey, Professor; Ph.D., Maryland. James L. Wardrop, Associate Professor; Ph.D., Washington (St. Louis). Charles K. West, Professor; Ph.D., Alabama. David Zola, Assistant Professor; Ph.D., Cornell.

Department of Special Education: Adelle Renzaglia, Head.
Tess Bennett, Assistant Professor; Ph.D., Florida. Janis Chadsey, Associate Professor; Ph.D., Illinois. Susan A. Fowler, Professor; Ph.D., Kansas. Janet S. Gaffney, Associate Professor; Ph.D., Arizona. James W. Halle, Professor; Ph.D., Kansas. Laird W. Heal, Professor Emeritus; Ph.D., Wisconsin. Robert A. Henderson, Professor Emeritus; Ed.D., Illinois. Nancy Hertzog, Assistant Professor; Ph.D., Illinois. Robert Jimenez, Assistant Professor; Ph.D., Illinois. Jeanette McCollum, Professor; Ph.D., Texas at Austin. Lisa Monda-Amaya, Associate Professor; Ph.D., Florida State. Michaelene Ostrosky, Associate Professor; Ph.D., Vanderbilt. Adelle Renzaglia, Professor; Ph.D., Wisconsin. Frank R. Rusch, Professor; Ph.D., Washington (Seattle). James Shriner, Assistant Professor; Ph.D., Minnesota. Jenny Singleton, Assistant Professor; Ph.D., Illinois. Robert L. Sprague, Professor; Ph.D., Indiana. John Trach, Assistant Professor; Ph.D., Illinois.

Department of Human Resource Education: Tim L. Wentling, Head.
Steven R. Aragon, Assistant Professor; Ph.D., New Mexico. Debra Bragg, Associate Professor; Ph.D., Ohio State. Rose Mary Cordova-Wentling, Associate Professor; Ph.D., Illinois. Mildred B. Griggs, Professor; Ed.D., Illinois. Scott Johnson, Associate Professor; Ph.D., Minnesota. Paul Hardin, Adjunct Assistant Professor; Ph.D., Illinois. K. Peter Kuchinke, Assistant Professor; Ph.D., Minnesota. James Leach, Professor; Ph.D., Illinois. Carolyn Maddy-Bernstein, Assistant Professor; Ed.D., Virginia Tech. Robert E. Nelson, Associate Professor; Ed.D., Northern Illinois. John Ory, Adjunct Associate Professor; Ph.D., Kansas. John Schmitz, Assistant Professor; Ph.D., Illinois. Tim L. Wentling, Professor; Ph.D., Illinois.

The University of Illinois, College of Education Building.

UNIVERSITY OF MASSACHUSETTS AMHERST

School of Education

Programs of Study

The School of Education at the University of Massachusetts Amherst is an NCATE-approved comprehensive professional school providing specialized preparation in diverse areas of education. The School offers graduate programs leading to the Master of Education (M.Ed.) and Doctor of Education (Ed.D.). The Doctor of Philosophy (Ph.D.) is granted to those who successfully complete the American Psychological Association–accredited School Psychology Program. The School also awards a Certificate of Advanced Graduate Study (CAGS). Graduate programs in the School provide opportunities for advanced study and research in education and foster the development of innovative responses to challenges in the field of education. They can be designed to meet certification guidelines, licensing requirements, professional association recommendations, School and University requirements, and individual student goals. As a research-oriented land-grant institution, the School of Education recognizes its responsibility to offer two types of graduate academic programs: programs that prepare educational scholars to further educational theory, policy, and research; and programs that prepare educational practitioners for roles in public education.

The M.Ed. degree program is designed to further the professional development of elementary and secondary school teachers and other school-based practitioners in the various fields of education. Within the framework of the requirements and with the guidance of a faculty adviser, M.Ed. candidates must complete a minimum of 33 graduate credits. Eighteen of these must be graded, 12 must be at or above the 600 level, and a minimum of 21 must be taken in the School of Education. Individual programs may specify a particular course sequence. The School Psychology Program requires 48 credits.

The CAGS is offered to provide an intensive, cohesive program of professional development for educational specialists beyond the master's level. It requires an academic-specific specialty area, without the extended commitment and formal examination of the doctoral program. It is not a University degree program but a School of Education certificate program. The certificate is awarded upon completion of a 30-credit-hour program beyond the master's degree. All 30 credits must be taken at the University within a four-year period, and at least 15 credits must be taken in the School of Education.

The doctoral program is designed to prepare educators for teaching, administration and policy positions, and other leadership roles in the field of education. The goal of the Ed.D. program is to prepare education leaders who can conduct scholarship and research that promote education in a broad range of settings and add to the knowledge base of the field; encourage the diversity of people and practice in education; and influence state, national, and international educational policies and practices. Within the framework of the School requirements and with the advice and approval of a doctoral guidance committee, candidates plan a program commensurate with their academic needs and professional goals. Such programs usually involve at least three years of course work beyond the bachelor's degree. Students are expected to spend at least two consecutive semesters in full-time study, participate in research, become familiar with contemporary problems in education, and take a comprehensive exam prior to writing a dissertation.

Research Facilities

The University library system maintains collections in the twenty-eight-story University Library, two science branch libraries, a music library, and several reading rooms. The University Computing Services supports the instruction and research activities of the University's faculty members and students. The Statistical Consulting Center provides students and faculty members with advice on the statistical aspects of research projects and other studies. This includes design of experiments and surveys, sampling, statistical analysis of data, time series, stochastic modeling, and probability theory.

Financial Aid

A limited number of assistantships and associateships in the instructional programs are available. Graduate assistants and associates are not required to pay tuition if they are enrolled in a degree-granting program and their stipend is $2350 or more for the semester. In addition, applicants may be considered for work-study, Federal Perkins Loans, Federal Stafford Student Loans, or federal fellowship programs. For additional information, students should contact the Financial Aid Office, Whitmore Administration Building.

Cost of Study

For the 1998–99 academic year, full-time tuition for residents of Massachusetts is $1320 per semester or $110 per credit; for nonresidents, it is $4509 per semester or $375.75 per credit. For Massachusetts residents, general fees (which include the University health, fine arts, performing arts, authority, and curriculum fees and the Graduate Student Senate Tax) total $1428 per semester for students taking 9 credits or more, $1045 per semester for students taking 5 to 8 credits, and $422 per semester for students taking fewer than 4 credit hours per semester. The general fee cannot be waived.

Living and Housing Costs

Although most graduate students live off campus, the University provides a limited amount of housing for graduate students at two locations on or near campus. Students can obtain off-campus housing information from the Commuter Services and Housing Resource Center in Room 428, Student Union.

Student Group

The University had an enrollment in the fall of 1997 of 23,932 students, of whom 5,819 were graduate students. There were 906 graduate students in the School of Education. The University has a diverse student body and is committed to the principles of affirmative action, civility, equal opportunity, and the free exchange of ideas. The School actively recruits and supports students from minority groups.

Location

Amherst, Massachusetts, is situated in one of the most picturesque sections of the state. The University of Massachusetts joins its academic neighbors—Amherst, Smith, Mount Holyoke, and Hampshire Colleges—in maintaining the rich tradition of educational and cultural activity associated with the Connecticut Valley region.

The University

The University is one of today's leading centers of public higher education in the Northeast. Located 90 miles west of Boston, it was founded in 1863 under the original Land Grant Act. In recent decades, it has achieved a growing reputation for excellence in an increasing number of disciplines, for the breadth of its academic offerings, and for the expansion of its historic roles in education, research, and public service.

Applying

The deadline for application to the School Psychology Program is January 15. The deadline for other programs is March 1 for summer/fall entrance and October 1 for spring admission. Since graduate admissions are limited and competitive, applicants are encouraged to apply early and to be sure that all required materials (application, fee, two official transcripts from each institution attended, two academic letters of recommendation, and all required test scores) have been received before the appropriate deadline. Nonrefundable application fees of $25 for Massachusetts residents and $40 for nonresidents must be submitted with each application. All applications require submission of a completed Residency Statement. Applicants whose native language is not English must achieve a score of 550 or above on the TOEFL.

Correspondence and Information

Graduate Admissions Office
Graduate School
Goodell Building, Room 530
University of Massachusetts
Amherst, Massachusetts 01003
Telephone: 413-545-0721

Office for Academic Affairs
School of Education
Furcolo Hall, Room 123
University of Massachusetts
Amherst, Massachusetts 01003
Telephone: 413-545-0236
World Wide Web: http://www.umass.edu/education/

University of Massachusetts Amherst

THE FACULTY

Bailey W. Jackson, Dean.
John C. Carey, Associate Dean for Academic Affairs and Graduate Program Director.

The School of Education is dedicated to enhancing the practice of education through scholarship that informs the preparation of educational professionals, the improvement of educational systems, and the development of educational policy. The School's approach is shaped by its fundamental commitment to social justice and diversity and by a belief in the essential importance of national and international perspectives as it advances education in the Commonwealth as a model for the nation. The School is organized into the following three major departments:

Teacher Education and Curriculum Studies

Graduate degree programs of study are offered at the doctoral level in child and family studies; language, literacy, and culture; mathematics and science education; and teacher education and school improvement. At the master's level, graduate degree programs of study are offered in bilingual/English as a second language/multicultural education; child study and early education; elementary education; reading and writing; secondary teacher education; and technology education. State-approved teacher certification programs are offered in agricultural/vocational education, biology, chemistry, early childhood education, earth sciences, elementary teacher, English, English as a second language, general science, history, mathematics, physics, reading, social studies, and modern foreign languages (including Chinese, French, Italian, Japanese, Portuguese, and Spanish).

Deirdre A. Almeida, Assistant Professor; Ed.D., Massachusetts, 1992. Theresa Y. Austin, Associate Professor; Ph.D., UCLA, 1991. Liane Brandon, Professor; M.Ed., Boston University, 1967. Lenore R. Carlisle, Assistant Professor; Ed.D., Massachusetts, 1988. John J. Clement, Professor; Ed.D., Massachusetts, 1976. Grace J. Craig, Professor; Ph.D., Massachusetts, 1967. Kathleen S. Davis, Assistant Professor; Ph.D., Colorado, 1996. Patt S. Dodds, Professor; Ph.D., Ohio State, 1975. Portia C. Elliott, Professor; Ed.D., Massachusetts, 1974. Allan Feldman, Associate Professor; Ph.D., Stanford, 1993. George E. Forman, Professor; Ph.D., Alabama, 1967. Atron A. Gentry, Professor; Ed.D., Massachusetts, 1970. Linda L. Griffin, Assistant Professor; Ph.D., Ohio State, 1991. Alfred L. Karlson, Associate Professor; Ph.D., Chicago, 1972. Catherine E. Luna, Assistant Professor; Ph.D., Pennsylvania, 1977. Robert W. Maloy, Lecturer; Ed.D., Boston University, 1976. William J. Masalski, Professor; Ed.D., Massachusetts, 1970. Dorothy A. Meyer, Lecturer; M.Ed., Massachusetts, 1988. Sonia M. Nieto, Professor; Ed.D., Massachusetts, 1979. J. Kevin Nugent, Professor; Ph.D., Boston College, 1980. Kenneth A. Parker, Associate Professor; Ph.D., Ohio State, 1974. Howard A. Peelle, Professor; Ed.D., Massachusetts, 1971. Judith H. Placek, Professor; Ed.D., Massachusetts, 1982. Cynthia J. Rosenberger, Lecturer; M.Ed., Tufts, 1966. Masha K. Rudman, Professor; Ed.D., Massachusetts, 1970. Irving Seidman, Professor; Ph.D., Stanford, 1967. Clement A. Seldin, Associate Professor; Ed.D., Massachusetts, 1976. Robert L. Sinclair, Professor; Ed.D., UCLA, 1968. Judith W. Solsken, Professor; Ph.D., Cornell, 1974. Patrick J. Sullivan, Professor; Ph.D., Berkeley, 1967. William L. Thuemmel, Associate Professor; Ph.D., Michigan State, 1970. Ernest D. Washington, Professor; Ph.D., Illinois, 1968. Jerri Willett, Associate Professor; Ph.D., Stanford, 1987.

Student Development and Pupil Personnel Services

Graduate degree programs of study are offered at the doctoral level in school psychology and student development. At the master's level, graduate degree programs of study are offered in school counselor education, social justice education, and special education. Graduate students may also pursue state-approved pupil personnel service certification in school guidance counselor, school psychologist, administrator of special education, and teacher of special education. Licensure as a psychologist is available at the doctoral level in the APA-approved program in school psychology.

Maurianne Adams, Lecturer; Ph.D., Indiana, 1967. Mary Lynn Boscardin, Associate Professor; Ph.D., Illinois, 1984. John C. Carey, Associate Professor; Ph.D., Wisconsin, 1979; Ph.D., Wyoming, 1984. Robert D. Colbert, Associate Professor; Ph.D., Wisconsin, 1987. William E. Cross Jr., Professor; Ph.D., Princeton, 1976. Brunilda deLeon, Associate Professor; Ed.D., Massachusetts, 1989. Patricia S. Griffin, Professor; Ed.D., Massachusetts, 1980. John M. Hintze, Assistant Professor; Ph.D., Lehigh, 1994. Barbara J. Love, Associate Professor; Ed.D., Massachusetts, 1972. William J. Matthews, Professor; Ph.D., Connecticut, 1979. Janine Roberts, Professor; Ed.D., Massachusetts, 1982. Stanley E. Scarpati, Associate Professor; Ed.D., Northern Colorado, 1980. Patricia H. Silver, Professor; Ed.D., West Virginia, 1970. Nola V. Stephen, Lecturer; M.Ed., Manchester (England), 1976. Gary Stoner, Associate Professor; Ph.D., Rhode Island, 1986. Ximena U. Zuniga, Lecturer; Ph.D., Michigan, 1992.

Educational Policy, Research, and Administration

Graduate degree programs of study are offered at the doctoral level in education policy and leadership and in research and evaluation methods. At the master's level, graduate degree programs of study are offered in educational administration, higher education, international education, and policy studies in education. Graduate students may also pursue state-approved educational administrator certification in the areas of school principal/assistant school principal, superintendent/assistant superintendent, and supervisor/director.

Johnstone Campbell, Lecturer; Ph.D., Stanford, 1976. Patricia H. Crosson, Professor; Ed.D., Massachusetts, 1974. Jeffrey W. Eiseman, Associate Professor; Ph.D., Michigan, 1971. David R. Evans, Professor; Ph.D., Stanford, 1969. Arthur W. Eve, Professor; Ph.D., Chicago, 1964. Andrew Effrat, Professor; Ph.D., Harvard, 1970. Preston C. Green, Assistant Professor; J.D., Columbia, 1992; Ed.D., Columbia Teachers College, 1995. Kevin F. Grennan, Lecturer; Ed.D., Massachusetts, 1981. Ronald K. Hambleton, Professor; Ph.D., Toronto, 1969. David C. Kinsey, Professor; Ph.D., Harvard, 1965. Robert J. Miltz, Associate Professor; Ed.D., Stanford, 1971. Gretchen B. Rossman, Professor; Ph.D., Pennsylvania, 1983. David M. Schimmel, Professor; J.D., Yale, 1958; B.H.L., Hebrew Union, 1967. David F. Schuman, Professor; Ph.D., Berkeley, 1971. Stephen G. Sireci, Assistant Professor; Ph.D., Fordham, 1993. Hariharan Swaminathan, Professor; Ph.D., Toronto, 1971.

The Murray D. Lincoln Campus Center.

The School of Education.

The Old Chapel.

UNIVERSITY OF MASSACHUSETTS LOWELL

College of Education

COLLEGE OF EDUCATION
UNIVERSITY OF MASSACHUSETTS LOWELL

Programs of Study

The College of Education at the University of Massachusetts Lowell is an entirely graduate education program, reaccredited by NCATE in 1998, with a mission of promoting excellence in teaching, scholarship, and community service. A theme of perspectives and vision unifies its programs, as novice and experienced educators from diverse backgrounds come to share and inform viewpoints and gain enhanced capabilities for teaching and educational leadership roles. All programs operate on a year-round, three-semester schedule to accommodate the work and vacation schedules of a mature graduate student body.

Three Master of Education (M.Ed.) programs support the professional development of beginning and experienced educators who already have a strong background in the liberal arts and sciences. Degrees are offered in curriculum and instruction, educational administration, and reading and language. M.Ed. candidates must complete a minimum of 30 credits of approved course work as well as the corresponding practicum and seminar within five years. A master's degree with certification may be completed with full-time study in one calendar year. Teacher certification options within the M.Ed. curriculum and instruction program include elementary teaching; middle school; early childhood; English as a second language; secondary math, English, biology, chemistry, earth science, physics, history, and social studies; music education; and health education.

Three Certificate of Advanced Graduate Study (C.A.G.S.) programs are designed to provide coherent professional development for experienced practitioners. Degrees are offered in curriculum and instruction; administration, planning, and policy; and reading and language. C.A.G.S. candidates must complete a minimum of 30 credits of approved course work beyond the master's degree, pass a comprehensive exam, and satisfactorily complete a qualifying paper within five years.

Three Doctor of Education (Ed.D.) programs prepare experienced educators with a strong knowledge base, research skills, and scholarly foundation for leadership positions in teaching, administration, and policy planning. Degrees are offered in leadership in schooling, language arts and literacy, and mathematics and science education. In each program area, students are exposed to a variety of perspectives of schooling and are expected not only to show growth in knowledge and scholarship, but also to articulate their own emerging vision of education to face the complex, continually changing challenges of society. Ed.D. candidates are required to complete a minimum of 60 credits, fulfill a two-semester residency requirement, satisfy computer literacy and research proficiency requirements, pass two comprehensive exams, and satisfactorily defend a completed dissertation within seven years.

Research Facilities

The University libraries consist of the Alumni/Lydon Library, the O'Leary Library, and the Center for Lowell History. The reference departments provide interlibrary loan services, computer and manual literature searches, and end-user database searching through the use of CD-based systems. The O'Leary Library incorporates a media center that can accommodate more than 230 students in five instructional and presentation areas. All students are issued computer accounts with public access to clusters of terminals and microcomputers distributed around the campus.

Financial Aid

Sources of financial aid include the Federal Stafford Student Loan Program, Federal Perkins Loans, College Work-Study Program, and other non-need-based loans. A limited number of teaching assistantships are available for qualified full-time students; K–12 teaching experience and technology expertise are required. Research assistantships are available for a limited number of advanced graduate students through arrangements with individual research advisers. Graduate student assistants are paid an hourly rate and are obligated to pay tuition and fees. For additional information, students should contact the Financial Aid Office, McGauvran Student Union Building.

Cost of Study

In 1997–98, full-time (9-credit) tuition and fees for residents of Massachusetts were $2324.39 per semester ($618.13 per course); for nonresidents, it was $4274.42 per semester ($1268.14 per course).

Living and Housing Costs

The majority of graduate students commute from an extensive variety of private housing options in the region. Single graduate students may choose to live in on-campus housing arrangements. Married graduate students and their families may reside at the University's East Meadow Lane apartments; to apply for this housing option, students should call the Office of Residence Life (978-934-2112).

Student Group

The University of Massachusetts Lowell had an enrollment of 8,645 students in the fall of 1997, of whom 2,780 were graduate students. The College of Education enrollment was 613, of whom 12 percent were members of minority groups; approximately 65 percent of participants were women. The University is committed to an affirmative action policy for recruiting increased diversity among its students and faculty members.

Student Outcomes

Graduates of the master's degree programs have successfully obtained teaching positions in the region's elementary and secondary schools. The placement rate was approximately 95 percent for the 1996–97 academic year. Examples of positions that graduates from the doctoral programs have obtained include superintendent of schools, director of teacher training, curriculum supervisor, school principal, director of staff development, and assistant professor.

Location

Located on the banks of the Merrimack River, 26 miles north of Boston and adjacent to the New Hampshire border, Lowell, Massachusetts, has been a leader in urban revitalization and historic preservation. Cultural activities include the Merrimack Repertory Theater and Center for Performing Arts. Recreational facilities of the Massachusetts coast and the New Hampshire lakes and mountains are readily accessible.

The University and The College

The history of the College can be traced to the founding of Lowell Normal School in 1894. In 1989, the then University of Lowell was merged with four other Massachusetts state universities to become the Lowell campus of the University of Massachusetts. UMass Lowell is a technologically advanced campus with a specific mission for regional economic development. The College is distinguished by strong partnership programs with local school systems, including an on-campus, trilingual Demonstration School (serving age 3 to grade 4, Spanish, Khmer, and English languages); a Center for Field Services and Studies (sponsoring K-12 teacher and leadership professional development, two-way television programming, and urban school drop-out prevention programs); and the Tsongas Industrial History Center (hosting 48,000 children for annual field trips in collaboration with Lowell National Historic Park).

Applying

Although the University has a rolling admissions policy, a completed application should be received by April 1 for a candidate who seeks admission for the subsequent summer semester, by June 1 for the fall, and by November 1 for the subsequent spring semester. Applications include a statement of purpose, official transcripts, three letters of recommendation, and either the Graduate Record Examinations or Miller Analogies Test results. Applicants whose native language is not English must achieve a minimum score of 550 on the TOEFL.

Correspondence and Information

Professor Brenda Jochums-Slez
Graduate Coordinator for Doctoral and C.A.G.S. Degree Programs

or

Professor Anita Greenwood
Graduate Coordinator for Master's Programs
College of Education—West Campus
University of Massachusetts Lowell
One University Avenue
Lowell, Massachusetts 01854-2881

Telephone: 978-934-4601
Fax: 978-934-3005
World Wide Web: http://woods.uml.edu/College/Education/

University of Massachusetts Lowell

THE FACULTY AND THEIR RESEARCH

Donald E. Pierson, Professor and Dean; Ph.D., Harvard, 1970. School/college partnerships, early childhood education, urban school improvement.
Richard Ackerman, Associate Professor; Ed.D., Harvard, 1989. Leadership in schooling, case story pedagogy and research.
Ann Benjamin, Assistant Professor and Director, Demonstration School; Ph.D., Tufts, 1989. Child development, early childhood education, diversity.
Norman F. Benson, Professor; Ed.D., Ball State, 1965. History of American education, theory of curriculum and instruction, economic education.
Judith A. Boccia, Assistant Professor and Director, Center for Field Services and Studies; Ed.D., Columbia, 1982. Teacher and leadership development, teaching of English, curriculum frameworks.
James M. Carifio, Associate Professor; Ed.D., Boston University, 1986. Cognition, adult learners, research methods and measurement, math and science education.
John J. Catallozzi, Associate Professor; Ed.D., Boston University, 1970. Educational psychology, teaching and learning strategies, philosophy of education, developmental psychology, social psychology.
Charles Christensen, Lecturer; Ed.D., Harvard, 1990. Middle schools, leadership development, assessment of learning, curriculum frameworks.
Lorraine Dagostino, Associate Professor; Ph.D., Syracuse, 1981. Language arts and literacy, evaluative reading.
Thomas G. Devine, Professor; Ed.D., Boston University, 1961. Teaching of reading, language arts and literacy; study skills.
Joyce T. Gibson, Assistant Professor; Ph.D., Florida, 1983. Multicultural leadership in education, managing change in schools, teaching through case studies, family-school partnerships.
Robert R. Gower, Professor; Ed.D., Columbia, 1974. Skillful teaching, teaching with multimedia, principles of supervision.
Anita Greenwood, Assistant Professor; Ed.D., Massachusetts Lowell, 1992. Science education, constructivist approaches to teaching and learning, curriculum frameworks.
M. William Harp, Professor; Ed.D., Oregon, 1971. Teaching of reading, language arts and literacy; assessment of reading and writing.
Paul C. Jablon, Associate Professor; Ph.D., NYU, 1989. Science education, environmental education, curriculum and teaching in urban schools.
Brenda L. Jochums-Slez, Professor; Ph.D., Indiana, 1982. Program evaluation, cognitive development, research methods and data analysis, museum education.
John F. LeBaron, Professor; Ed.D., Massachusetts Amherst, 1976. Educational technology policies, technology and learning environments, higher education.
Patricia Luongo-Fontaine, Lecturer; Ed.D., Massachusetts Lowell, 1996. Teaching of social studies and history, values in education, bilingual education.
Richard G. Lyons, Professor; Ph.D., Boston University, 1964. Philosophy of education, contemporary issues in education, gender issues in curriculum and instruction.
Dorothy V. Meyer, Associate Professor; Ed.D., Boston University, 1976. Educational and human service administration, planning processes.
Peter S. O'Connell, Assistant Professor and Director, Tsongas Center for Industrial History; Ph.D., Connecticut, 1990. Museum education, cross-disciplinary approaches to curriculum development, use of community resources for curriculum planning.
Vera Ossen, Lecturer; Ed.D., Massachusetts Lowell, 1990. Professional development of teachers; reading, language arts, and children's literature.
Regina M. Panasuk, Assistant Professor; Ph.D., Leningrad Institute of Adult Education of the Academy of Pedagogical Sciences, 1986. Mathematics education, teacher preparation and supervision.
William T. Phelan, Professor and Department Chair; Ph.D., Chicago, 1976. Sociology of education, at-risk students, research methods, academic engagement, survey research.
Juan C. Rodriguez, Associate Professor; Ed.D., Massachusetts Amherst, 1975. Language and cognition, second language acquisition and assessment, bilingual children with special education needs, teaching with multimedia.

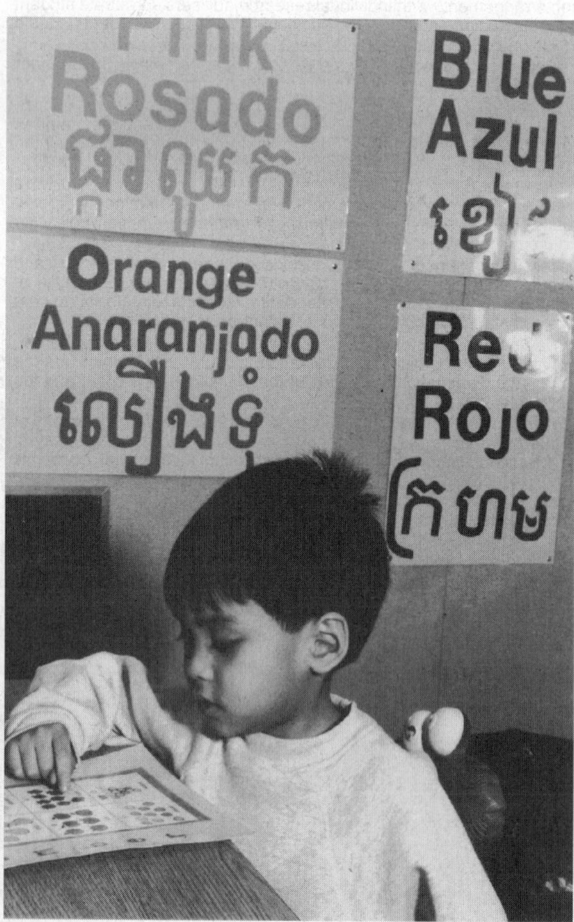

Demonstration School, College of Education.

Read Hall, College of Education.

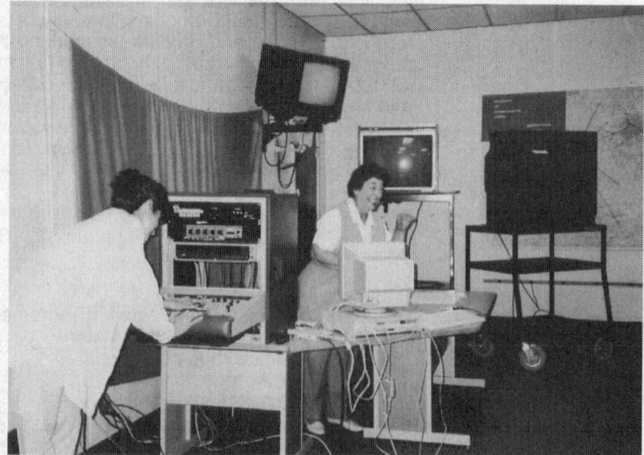
Teaching for two-way television.

UNIVERSITY OF MIAMI

School of Education

Programs of Study

The School of Education of the University of Miami offers curricula leading to the degrees of Master of Science in Education, Specialist in Education, Doctor of Education, and Doctor of Philosophy in education.

At the master's level, separate areas of concentration are available in counseling (marriage and family therapy and mental health counseling), early childhood/special education, elementary education, emotional handicaps/learning disabilities, exercise physiology, pre-K–primary education, reading and learning disabilities, sports administration, sports medicine, and Teaching English to Speakers of Other Languages (TESOL).

Specialist degrees are offered in reading and learning disabilities, TESOL, early childhood/special education, and elementary education.

Doctoral degrees are offered in counseling psychology, educational research, exercise physiology, teaching and learning, and special education and reading.

All programs in teacher preparation are approved by the state of Florida and accredited by NCATE. The counseling psychology doctoral program is APA-accredited.

Research Facilities

All students may use the University library. In addition, a special computer laboratory, administered by the School of Education, is available. The School also operates an exercise physiology laboratory and a training clinic for counseling students.

Financial Aid

Graduate assistantships and partial tuition scholarships are available. Only full-time degree-seeking students are considered for aid.

Cost of Study

Tuition is $815 per credit for graduate course work in 1998–99. Full-time teachers under contract and teachers on official leave or sabbatical may be eligible for the teacher tuition discount scholarship.

Living and Housing Costs

Residential colleges are available for single students, and dining facilities are located on the campus. For students desiring to eat off campus, a wide variety of attractive eating places are nearby.

Student Group

Approximately 1,000 students are enrolled in the School of Education for study in programs leading to graduate degrees. These include students from all the states and from many countries.

Location

The suburb of Coral Gables is one of the municipalities that make up metropolitan Miami. This subtropical area, which stretches from Fort Lauderdale to the Florida Keys, is an exciting, multicultural cosmopolitan community that offers substantial cultural and recreational attractions. For those interested in outdoor recreation, the Florida Keys, Biscayne Bay, and Everglades National Park are nearby.

The University

The University, founded in Coral Gables in 1925, is an independent, nonprofit, nonsectarian institution open to all qualified men and women. Its schools, colleges, and research institutes now occupy four campuses. The main campus is in Coral Gables, the medical campus is in Miami, the marine sciences campus is on Virginia Key, and the south campus—primarily a research campus—is in South Dade County. The University supports a full calendar of significant events during the year. Almost all departments and schools sponsor weekly seminars open to graduate students.

The University is a member of a number of consortia established for teaching or research purposes with other universities in the United States and with universities in Latin America and the Caribbean.

Applying

All applications for admission to graduate study must be sent to the Associate Dean, School of Education, at the address below. All applicants for the master's and specialist's programs must submit transcripts from all institutions attended, recommendations, and scores on the Graduate Record Examinations (General Test). For admission to the doctoral program, an applicant must submit transcripts of undergraduate and graduate work, scores on the Graduate Record Examinations (the General Test and the Subject Test in Education, if required by the department, or the General Test and the Subject Test in Psychology for applicants to the counseling programs), and three letters of recommendation from people who are familiar with the applicant's academic and professional background. Doctoral applications for counseling psychology are reviewed once each year. Completed applications are due no later than January 15 for consideration for the fall semester. Applicants to the counseling psychology master's program are encouraged to apply by May 1. Other doctoral and master's applications are accepted throughout the academic year.

Correspondence and Information

Associate Dean
School of Education
University of Miami
Coral Gables, Florida 33124
Telephone: 305-284-3711

University of Miami

THE FACULTY

Thomas A. Angelo, Associate Professor of Educational and Psychological Studies; Ed.D., Harvard, 1987.
Arlene T. Brett, Professor and Associate Chair of Teaching and Learning; Ed.D., Miami (Florida), 1973.
Joseph F. Brownholtz, Associate Professor of Exercise and Sport Sciences; Ed.D., Florida State, 1968.
Kent Burnett, Associate Professor of Educational and Psychological Studies; Ph.D., Stanford, 1984.
Margaret Crosbie-Burnett, Associate Professor and Chair of Educational and Psychological Studies; Ph.D., Stanford, 1983.
Gilberto J. Cuevas, Professor of Teaching and Learning; Ph.D., Miami (Florida), 1975.
Herbert M. Dandes, Professor of Educational and Psychological Studies; Ph.D., Syracuse, 1964.
Harry W. Forgan Jr., Professor of Teaching and Learning; Ph.D., Kent State, 1969.
Blaine Fowers, Associate Professor of Educational and Psychological Studies; Ph.D., Texas, 1987.
Sandra Fradd, Professor of Teaching and Learning; Ph.D., Florida, 1983.
Robert L. Gropper, Associate Professor of Educational and Psychological Studies; Ph.D., Vanderbilt (Peabody), 1969.
Charles E. Hannemann, Associate Professor of Teaching and Learning; Ph.D., Ohio, 1969.
Beth Harry, Associate Professor of Teaching and Learning; Ph.D., Syracuse, 1989.
Janette K. Klingner, Assistant Professor of Teaching and Learning; Ph.D., Miami (Florida), 1994.
Carol Klopfer, Clinical Assistant Professor of Educational and Psychological Studies; Ph.D., Florida, 1977.
James E. Lance, Associate Professor of Exercise and Sport Sciences; Ph.D., Southern Mississippi, 1974.
Okhee Lee, Associate Professor of Teaching and Learning; Ph.D., Michigan State, 1989.
Kay Lopate, Associate Professor of Teaching and Learning; Ph.D., Miami (Florida), 1986.
Eveleen Lorton, Professor of Teaching and Learning; Ph.D., LSU, 1966.
Harry C. Mallios, Professor and Chairperson of Exercise and Sport Sciences; Ed.D., Miami (Florida), 1970.
Charles T. Mangrum II, Professor of Teaching and Learning; Ed.D., Indiana, 1968.
James McKinney, Professor of Educational and Psychological Studies; Ph.D., North Carolina State, 1969.
Robert C. McMahon, Professor of Educational and Psychological Studies; Ph.D., Wisconsin–Madison, 1973.
Marjorie Montague, Professor of Teaching and Learning; Ph.D., Arizona, 1984.
Robert F. Moore, Associate Professor of Teaching and Learning; Ed.D., Indiana, 1969.
Susan P. Mullane, Assistant Professor of Exercise and Sport Sciences; Ph.D., Miami (Florida), 1995.
Arlette C. Perry, Associate Professor of Exercise and Sport Sciences; Ph.D., NYU, 1981.
Shawn Post, Associate Professor of Teaching and Learning and Assistant Dean; Ph.D., Miami (Florida), 1977.
Eugene F. Provenzo Jr., Professor of Teaching and Learning; Ph.D., Washington (St. Louis), 1976.
Peggy Rios, Assistant Professor of Educational and Psychological Studies; Ph.D., Maryland, 1985.
Bobby Lee Robertson, Professor of Exercise and Sport Sciences; Ed.D., Oregon, 1972.
Liz Rothlein, Professor of Teaching and Learning and Associate Dean; Ed.D., Ball State, 1975.
Jeanne Schumm, Professor and Chair of Teaching and Learning; Ph.D., Miami (Florida), 1984.
Joseph F. Signorile, Associate Professor of Exercise and Sport Sciences; Ph.D., Texas A&M, 1989.
Richard H. Williams, Professor of Educational and Psychological Studies; Ph.D., Indiana, 1964.
Sam J. Yarger, Professor of Teaching and Learning and Dean of School of Education; Ph.D., Wayne State, 1968.

UNIVERSITY OF MICHIGAN

School of Education

Programs of Study

Graduate studies at the School of Education are organized into two programs: Educational Studies and the Center for the Study of Higher and Postsecondary Education.

The Program in Educational Studies offers Master of Arts, Master of Science, and Doctor of Philosophy degrees. Specializations and degree opportunities are available in curriculum development, early childhood education, educational administration and policy, educational foundations and policy, educational technology, English education, learning disabilities and literacy, literacy education, mathematics education, science education, social studies education, special education, and teacher education. In addition, graduate students may enroll in the Master of Arts in education with teaching certification (MAC) program, a one-year intensive course of study available for prospective elementary or secondary school teachers.

The Center for the Study of Higher and Postsecondary Education offers Doctor of Philosophy and Doctor of Education degrees in higher education with concentrations in academic affairs; community college governance and leadership; organizational behavior and management; public policy in postsecondary education; research, evaluation, and assessment; and an opportunity for an individually designed concentration. The Master of Arts degree is offered with specializations in community college administration, higher education, and public policy or student development and academic affairs.

The interdisciplinary Combined Program in Education and Psychology and the Joint Program in English and Education also offer courses of study leading to the Ph.D.

Research Facilities

As part of one of the nation's primary research universities, the School of Education has access to superior research facilities and resources, including more than 24,000 computer workstations throughout the campus and a library system with more than 6.6 million volumes and nearly 70,000 periodical and newspaper subscriptions. The School itself provides research centers, traditional library resources, microcomputer workstations with software for statistical analysis, multimedia materials, a multimedia laboratory, and two interactive multimedia classrooms. In addition, a recent $1.2-million Spencer Foundation Research Training Grant has enabled the School to upgrade research education and fund research awards to graduate students.

Financial Aid

Sources of financial aid for School of Education graduate students include teaching, research, and staff assistantships, which offer a stipend and some University benefits and may offer tuition assistance. A complete listing of current financial aid resources is available from the School of Education Office of Student Services. The deadline for most financial aid consideration is January 15; early application is suggested.

Cost of Study

In 1997–98, graduate student tuition per semester was $4911 for Michigan residents and $9965 for nonresidents. Tuition for doctoral candidates was $3176 for one semester for both residents and nonresidents. A mandatory fee of $92.08 per term applied to all students. Tuition charges are subject to change by the Board of Regents.

Living and Housing Costs

The School of Education estimated that living expenses for a single graduate student were approximately $10,300 for the 1997–98 academic year.

Student Group

In fall 1997, the School of Education enrolled 719 students, 437 of whom were graduate students. Members of minority groups comprised more than 30 percent of the School's graduate students. Overall, approximately 36,000 students, including 13,000 graduate students, attend the University of Michigan at Ann Arbor.

Student Outcomes

Educational Studies graduates become K–12 administrators, professors and researchers, education and government agency leaders, and teachers. Graduates of the Center for the Study of Higher and Postsecondary Education serve as presidents and executive officers at public and private universities, liberal arts colleges, and community colleges; as policy makers and administrators in government; and as leaders in faculty and research roles. Graduates of the Joint Program in English and Education become university English and education teachers and leaders in writing programs. Combined Program in Education and Psychology graduates become researchers and teachers in colleges and universities and researchers at federal and state agencies and foundations.

Location

Ann Arbor and the University of Michigan are located 40 miles west of Detroit and 40 minutes from Detroit Metropolitan Airport. Ann Arbor has a permanent population of nearly 110,000. The community offers a wide range of easily accessible, year-round cultural and recreational opportunities.

The University and The School

As one of the University of Michigan's smaller units, the School of Education provides an environment that fosters close interaction and collaboration between graduate students and faculty, together with all the resources of a large, internationally renowned university. *U.S. News & World Report* ranked the School's graduate programs sixth in the nation in 1998.

Applying

All applicants for admission to graduate studies in the School of Education must apply through the School of Education Office of Student Services. Students also must be accepted in the Horace H. Rackham School of Graduate Studies with a specialization in education. Applications must include the results of the GRE General Test.

Spring, summer, and fall term applications to Educational Studies are due January 15. Master's students not applying for financial aid may apply through May 1. Winter term applications are due November 1. Students applying to the MAC program are admitted to the summer term only. The Center for the Study of Higher and Postsecondary Education accepts applications for fall term only. The application deadline is January 15; students not applying for financial aid may apply through May 1.

Master's students interested in Residence Life positions on campus must submit graduate school applications by November 15. International graduate applicants are considered for fall admission only.

Correspondence and Information

Office of Student Services, Department CP
1033 School of Education Building
University of Michigan
610 East University Avenue
Ann Arbor, Michigan 48109-1259
Telephone: 734-764-7563
E-mail: ed.grad.admit@umich.edu

University of Michigan

THE FACULTY AND THEIR RESEARCH

PROGRAM IN EDUCATIONAL STUDIES

Professors

David Angus, Ph.D. History of education, especially family, school, and community.
Deborah Loewenberg Ball, Ph.D. Mathematics education, mathematics and teaching through hypermedia, teacher preparation, educational policy and practice.
Loren Barritt, Ph.D. Human science approaches to educational research, research on rhetoric.
Percy Bates, Ph.D. Special education of the mentally impaired, educational assessment.
Carl Berger, Ed.D. Microcomputers in learning and teaching, science education, cognitive development of young adolescents.
Phyllis Blumenfeld, Ph.D. Cognitive and social development and school practices, classroom processes, motivation.
David Cohen, Ph.D. Relationship between policy and instruction, the nature of teaching practice.
Arthur Coxford, Ph.D. Mathematics teaching, learning and curriculum, microcomputer education.
Holly Craig, Ph.D. Special education, speech and language pathology.
Jacquelynne Eccles, Ph.D. Educational psychology, adolescent development.
Gary Fenstermacher, Ph.D. Philosophy of education, foundations of education, educational policy.
Anne Gere, Ph.D. English and education, writing, teaching writing.
Frederick Goodman, Ph.D. Design of simulations and games for schools.
Elfrieda Hiebert, Ph.D. Literacy and reading.
Deborah Keller-Cohen, Ph.D. Linguistics, literacy.
Magdalene Lampert, Ed.D. Teacher education, mathematics education.
Valerie Lee, Ed.D. Statistics, data analysis, quantitative methods of educational and social science research.
Martin Maehr, Ph.D. Educational psychology, motivation and achievement.
Ronald Marx, Ph.D., Chair. Educational psychology.
Samuel Meisels, Ed.D. Early childhood special education, developmental consequences of high-risk birth.
Cecil Miskel, Ed.D., Dean. Educational administration, organizational and administration theory.
Annemarie Sullivan Palincsar, Ph.D. Special education, teaching reading as thinking, strategies for teaching learning disabled.
Scott Paris, Ph.D. Cognitive development, reading, memory, and learning.
Stephen W. Raudenbush, Ed.D., Educational statistics, research methods.
Virginia Richardson, Ph.D. Research methods, teaching and schooling, staff development, teacher education.
Brian Rowan, Ph.D., Associate Dean. Educational administration, formal organizations, sociology of education.
Elliot Soloway, Ph.D. Computer and information science, interactive technology.
Elizabeth Sulzby, Ph.D. Elementary education, reading education, psycholinguistics.
Cho-Yee To, Ph.D. Pragmatic naturalism, application of philosophical studies to analysis of educational process.
Karen Wixson, Ph.D., Associate Dean. Reading and learning disabilities, cognitive processes in comprehension and learning.

Associate Professors

David Daly, Ed.D. Communication and learning disabilities, special education of mentally impaired, assessment procedures.
Helen Harrington, Ph.D. Teacher education.
Joseph Krajcik, Ph.D. Science education.
Pamela Moss, Ph.D. Educational research methodology.
Paul Pintrich, Ph.D. Instructional psychology, educational psychology, motivation.
Nancy B. Songer, Ph.D. Science education, educational technology.

Assistant Professors

Ron Astor, Ph.D. School psychology, family and child.
Robert Bain, Ph.D. Social studies education.
Arnetha Ball, Ph.D. Language, literacy, and culture.
Gail Baxter, Ph.D. Measurement and quantitative methods, development and psychometric evaluation of performance assessments.
Elizabeth Davis, Ph.D. Science education, educational technology.
Todd Dinkelman, Ph.D. Social studies.
Terrie Epstein, Ed.D. Social studies education.
Barry Fishman, Ph.D. Educational technology, telecommunication.
Sally Lubeck, Ed.D. Early childhood education, child and family policy.
Elizabeth Moje, Ph.D. Literacy in secondary education.
Arie Nettles, Ph.D. Psychosocial development of children and adolescents, chronic illness.
Carla O'Connor, Ph.D. Urban education, social psychology of education, sociology of education, qualitative methods, school leadership and reform.
Nichole Pinkard, Ph.D. Educational technology, software design.
Leslie Rex, Ph.D. English and education.
Melvin Wilson, Ph.D. Mathematics education, teachers' thinking about mathematics.

Instructors

Henry Meares, Ed.D. Teacher education, educational administration.
Stella Raudenbush, Ed.M. Service learning, youth subcultures.

CENTER FOR THE STUDY OF HIGHER AND POSTSECONDARY EDUCATION

Professors

Michael Nettles, Ph.D. Public policy, assessment, research design and methods.
Marvin Peterson, Ph.D. Organizational and administrative behavior, institutional research and planning, research methodology.
Joan Stark, Ed.D. Administrative behavior and personnel, curriculum and academic administration, research design and methodology.
Teshome Wagaw, Ph.D. Postsecondary education in developing nations, comparative postsecondary education.

Associate Professors

Richard Alfred, D.Ed. Community college governance and administration, financial management, public policy of postsecondary education.
Constance Cook, Ph.D. Public policy and politics of postsecondary education.
Eric Dey, Ph.D. College student research, statistics and research design.
Sylvia Hurtado, Ph.D. College student development, social context of higher education, research design and methods.
Janet Lawrence, Ph.D., Director. Learning and teaching, college and university faculty.

Assistant Professors

Donald Heller, Ed.D. Effects of policy and economic factors on access and choice in higher education.
Jana Nidiffer, Ed.D. Access and opportunity in higher education

UNIVERSITY
OF MINNESOTA

UNIVERSITY OF MINNESOTA

College of Education and Human Development

Programs of Study

The mission of the College of Education and Human Development is to generate knowledge about teaching, learning, and human development and to apply that knowledge to improve education for all individuals. The College, with 125 faculty members and more than 2,300 students, is organized into six academic units and more than twenty research and service centers with an emphasis on collaborative approaches to addressing critical issues in preschool through postsecondary education, lifelong learning, and human development. Consistently ranked as one of the most productive professional schools of education in the country—public or private—the College is a state, national, and international leader in teaching, research, and outreach.

Degree programs are available through six academic departments. The Department of Curriculum and Instruction prepares teachers and educational leaders for preK–12 schools. The Department of Educational Policy and Administration offers graduate programs in educational administration, higher education, comparative and international development education, and evaluation studies. Graduate programs in the Department of Educational Psychology include counseling and student personnel psychology, psychological foundations of education, school psychology, and special education. The Institute of Child Development provides a doctoral program in child psychology. The School on Kinesiology and Leisure Studies offers graduate programs within the broad study of physical activity, leisure, and movement science. Academic programs within the Department of Work, Community, and Family are organized into five areas: agricultural education and extension, business and industry education, education for work and community, family education, and human resource development.

Research Facilities

The College's faculty and staff members are widely recognized for exemplary research in education and human development. In recent years, they have averaged more than $13 million in external grants and contacts annually, placing the college among the top five U.S. colleges of education. The College is home to more than twenty college-wide and nationally designated research and service centers, providing a programmatic and financial framework for graduate student research. As part of the state's flagship land-grant, public research university, access to state-of-the-art research facilities and dozens of computing laboratories is available to students. The University's library collections, which include comprehensive retrospective journal holdings, monographs, and the complete ERIC microfiche file, are considered excellent in quality and scope. Through LUMINA, the online catalog of 1.9 million holdings, and MINITEX, a statewide library resource sharing agency, University libraries are consistently the leading supplier of interlibrary loans in the country.

Financial Aid

The University offers several forms of financial aid, including fellowships, scholarships, research assistantships, and teaching assistantships. In addition, the College offers a number of competitive scholarships for undergraduate, initial licensure, and graduate students.

Cost of Study

The 1997–98 graduate tuition rate of Minnesota residents attending full-time was $1860 per quarter; the rate for nonresidents attending full-time was $3260 per quarter.

Living and Housing Costs

Living and housing costs vary depending on personal preference. Undergraduate and graduate student dormitories, married student housing, and apartment-style living are available on campus. Ample rental property is available near campus and throughout the Twin Cities area.

Student Group

The College of Education and Human Development is committed to recruiting, enrolling, and educating a diverse population of students who represent the overall composition of society. More than 2,300 students are enrolled in the College, including approximately 800 M.Ed. and 900 master's, doctoral, and advanced graduate students. Overall, the University enrolls 18,500 undergraduate, 9,500 graduate, and 3,300 professional students, with an additional 18,000 students enrolled in continuing education and extension, making it one of the largest university systems in the country.

Student Outcomes

Education and human development fields are among the fastest-growing career tracks in the country. Demographic changes will mean increased demand for professionals in such fields as early childhood education, special education, English as a second language, recreation, child psychology, and human resource development. Graduates of the College work in school and clinical settings, higher education institutions, corporate settings, human service agencies, and a broad range of other occupations.

Location

The University has campuses in both Minneapolis and St. Paul as well as three coordinate campuses in greater Minnesota. Often ranked as one of the best places to live in the country, the twin cities of Minneapolis/St. Paul offer a rich cultural environment in a vibrant urban setting.

The University and The College

Founded in 1905 as the Department of Pedagogy, the College today ranks among the top colleges of education in the country; several of its programs (including child psychology, higher education, reading and literacy, school psychology, special education, and vocational and technical educational) rank among the best nationally. In 1995, the University approved a name change to the College of Education and Human Development to reflect the College's deep commitment to broadly improving the well-being of children, youth, families, and communities.

Applying

Applications for M.A., Ed.D., Ph.D., and specialist certificate degree programs are available from the Graduate School, University of Minnesota, 309 Johnston Hall, 101 Pleasant Street S.E., Minneapolis, Minnesota 55455. Application materials for M.Ed. degree programs, including both initial licensure and in-service programs, are available from Student and Professional Services, 110 Wulling Hall, 86 Pleasant Street S.E., Minneapolis, Minnesota 55455.

Correspondence and Information

Student and Professional Services
110 Wulling Hall
86 Pleasant Street SE
University of Minnesota
Minneapolis, Minnesota 55455

Telephone: 612-625-6501
Fax: 612-626-1580
E-mail: spsinfo@coled.umn.edu
World Wide Web: http://www.coled.umn.edu/

University of Minnesota

THE FACULTY

Department of Curriculum and Instruction
Margaret DiBlasio, Director of Graduate Studies, 145 Peik Hall, 159 Pillsbury Drive S.E., Minneapolis, Minnesota 55455 (612-625-3543).
Eugene Anderson, Ed.D., Illinois. Patricia Avery, Ph.D., Emory. Richard W. Beach, Ph.D., Illinois. Deborah Ceglowski, Ph.D., Illinois. John Cogan, Ph.D., Ohio State. Margaret DiBlasio, Ph.D., Ohio State. Fred Finley, Chair; Ph.D., Michigan State. Kerry J. Freedman-Norberg, Ph.D., Wisconsin. Michael F. Graves; Ph.D., Stanford. Patricia Heller, Ph.D., Michigan. Simon R. Hooper, Ph.D., Penn State. Roger T. Johnson, Ed.D., Berkeley. Judith Lambrecht, Ph.D., Wisconsin. Frances Lawrenz, Ph.D., Minnesota. John Manning, Ed.D., Boston University. Darcia Narváez, Ph.D., Minnesota. Robert E. Orton III, Ph.D., Stanford. R. Michael Paige, Ph.D., Stanford. Margaret Phinney, Ph.D., Massachusetts. Thomas R. Post, Ph.D., Indiana. Barbara M. Taylor, Ed.D., Virginia Tech. Dianne J. Tedick, Ph.D., Ohio State. Constance L. Walker, Ph.D., Illinois. Susan Watts-Taffe, Ed.D., SUNY at Buffalo.

Department of Educational Policy and Administration
Ayers L. Bagley, Director of Graduate Studies, 330 Wulling Hall, 86 Pleasant Street S.E., Minneapolis, Minnesota 55455 (612-624-1006).
Gary F. Alkire, Ed.D., Michigan State. William M. Ammentorp, Ph.D., Chicago. Melissa S. Anderson, Ph.D., Minnesota. Ayers L. Bagley, Ph.D., Indiana. David W. Chapman, Ph.D., Syracuse. John J. Cogan, Ph.D., Ohio State. Arthur M. Harkins, Ph.D., Kansas. David R. Johnson, Ph.D., Minnesota. Jean A. King, Ph.D., Cornell. Dale L. Lange, Ph.D., Minnesota. Darrell R. Lewis, Acting Chair; Ph.D., LSU. Karen Seashore Louis, Ph.D., Columbia. Marion L. Lundy-Dobbert, Ph.D., Wisconsin. Josef A. Mestenhauser, Ph.D., Minnesota. R. Michael Paige, Ph.D., Stanford. Byron J. Schneider, Ph.D., Chicago. Caroline Sotello Viernes Turner, Ph.D., Stanford. Jennifer York-Barr, Ph.D., Wisconsin.

Department of Educational Psychology
S. Jay Samuels, Director of Graduate Studies, 204 Burton Hall, 178 Pillsbury Drive S.E., Minneapolis, Minnesota 55455 (612-625-5586).
William M. Bart, Ph.D., Chicago. Sandra L. Christenson, Ph.D., Minnesota. Ernest C. Davenport, Ph.D., North Carolina at Chapel Hill. Carol A. Davis, Ed.D., Houston. Mark L. Davison, Ph.D., Illinois. Stanley L. Deno, Ph.D., Minnesota. Lynne K. Edwards, Ph.D., Washington (Seattle). V. Lois Erickson, Ph.D., Minnesota. Christine A. Espin, Ph.D., Minnesota. Joan Garfield, Ph.D., Minnesota. L. Sunny Hansen, Ph.D., Minnesota. Thomas J. Hummel, Ph.D., Ohio. Susan C. Hupp, Chair; Ph.D., Illinois. David W. Johnson, Ed.D., Columbia. Marie Knowlton, Ph.D., Cornell. Geoffrey M. Maruyama, Ph.D., USC. Scott R. McConnell, Ph.D., Oregon. Mary A. McEvoy, Ph.D., Tennessee. Darcia F. Narváez, Ph.D., Minnesota. James R. Rest, Ph.D., Chicago. John L. Romano, Ph.D., Arizona State. Susan Rose, Ph.D., Ohio State. John E. Rynders, Ph.D., Wisconsin. S. Jay Samuels, Ed.D., California. Thomas M. Skovholt, Ph.D., Missouri. John Taborn, Ph.D., Minnesota. Robert D. Tennyson, Ph.D., Brigham Young. Paulus van den Broek, Doctoraals, Leiden (the Netherlands), Ph.D., Chicago. Patricia McCarthy Veach, Ph.D., Ohio State. Frank B. Wilderson Jr., Ph.D., Michigan. James E. Ysseldyke, Ph.D. Illinois.

Institute of Child Development
Charles A. Nelson, Director of Graduate Studies, 180 Child Development Building, 51 East River Road, Minneapolis, Minnesota 55455 (612-624-0526).
Patricia J. Bauer, Ph.D., Miami (Ohio). W. Andrew Collins, Ph.D., Stanford. Nicki R. Crick, Ph.D., Vanderbilt. Byron Egeland, Ph.D., Iowa State. Megan R. Gunnar, Ph.D., Stanford. Michael P. Maratsos, Ph.D., Harvard. Ann S. Masten, Ph.D., Minnesota. Charles A. Nelson, Ph.D., Kansas. Anne D. Pick, Ph.D., Cornell. Herbert L. Pick Jr., Ph.D., Cornell. Maria D. Sera, Ph.D., Indiana. L. Alan Sroufe, Ph.D., Wisconsin. Richard A. Weinberg, Director; Ph.D., Minnesota. Albert Yonas, Ph.D., Cornell.

School of Kinesiology and Leisure Studies
Allen Burton, Director of Graduate Studies, 110 Cooke Hall, 1900 University Avenue S.E., Minneapolis, Minnesota 55455 (612-625-5300).
Bruce Anderson, Ph.D., Minnesota. Allen Burton, Ph.D., Oregon. Peter Hancock, Ph.D., Illinois. Mary Jo Kane, Ph.D., Illinois. March Krotee, Ph.D., Pittsburgh. Art Leon, M.D., Wisconsin. Leo McAvoy, Ph.D., Minnesota. Robert Pickert, M.A., South Dakota. Stuart J. Schleien, Ph.D., Maryland. Robert Serfass, Ph.D., Minnesota. Carla Tabourne, Ph.D., NYU. Michael Wade, Director; Ph.D., Illinois. Diane Wiese-Bjornstal, Ph.D., Oregon.

Department of Work, Community, and Family Education
Gary W. Leske, Director of Graduate Studies, 210A Vocational and Technical Education Building, 1954 Buford Avenue, St. Paul, Minnesota 55108 (612-625-3757).
James Brown, Ph.D., Bowling Green State. George H. Copa, Ph.D., Minnesota. Richard A. Krueger, Ph.D., Minnesota. Judith Lambrecht, Ph.D., Wisconsin. Gary W. Leske, Ph.D., Minnesota. Theodore Lewis, Ph.D., Ohio State. Jerry McClelland, Ph.D., Iowa State. Gary N. McLean, Ed.D., Columbia. Curtis D. Norenberg, Ph.D., Minnesota. Rosemarie Park, Ed.D., Harvard. Roland Peterson, Ed.D., Nebraska. Shari L. Peterson, Ph.D., Minnesota. Jane Plihal, Interim Chair; Ph.D., Chicago. David J. Pucel, Ph.D., Minnesota. Nancy J. Rohde, M.A., Minnesota, C.A.S., Wisconsin. Marilyn Martin Rossmann, Ph.D., Minnesota. James R. Stone III, Ed.D., Virginia Tech. Richard A. Swanson, Ed.D., Illinois. Ruth G. Thomas, Ph.D., Minnesota.

UNIVERSITY OF PENNSYLVANIA

Graduate School of Education

Programs of Study

The mission of the Graduate School of Education (GSE) at the University of Pennsylvania is to provide leadership in the preparation of education professionals and in research designed to enhance professional practice and student learning. GSE is unique among the nation's schools of education in its emphasis on the interactive relationships of theory, research, and practice. The essence of the school's philosophy is that all people must be students of their settings and practice, that improvement requires continual systematic inquiry and new learning, and that researchers and practitioners must work closely together to understand and serve emerging needs.

GSE has unparalleled strength in three focal areas: environmental context of education, evaluation of educational programs and policies, and issues in urban education. Programs leading to the master's degree (M.S.Ed.) and the doctoral degree (Ed.D. or Ph.D.) are offered in the four divisions of the School: Higher Education, Language in Education, Psychology in Education, and Educational Leadership.

Programs leading to certification are elementary and secondary teaching; principalship; supervision of curriculum and instruction; general supervision; superintendency; reading specialist and reading supervisor; elementary and secondary guidance counseling; and school psychologist. Most of the programs provide the opportunity for fieldwork and internship experiences. The School has developed cooperative links with Philadelphia-area service agencies, public and private schools, and postsecondary institutions that give students many opportunities for practical experience and research.

Research Facilities

Research centers at GSE bring faculty members and students together to study the complex interactions of education and society. Research centers within the School include the National Center on Adult Literacy; Center for Urban Ethnography; Center for Research and Evaluation in Social Policy; Center for School Study Councils; Institute for Research on Higher Education; Center for Health, Achievement, Neighborhood Growth, and Ethnic Studies; National Center on Fathers and Families; Cantor-Fitzgerald Center for Research on Diversity in Education; Collaborative for West Philadelphia Public Schools; Consortium for Policy Research in Education; International Literacy Institute; Literacy Research Center; National Center on the Educational Quality of the Workforce; Penn-Merck Collaborative for the Enhancement of Science Education; Penn Literacy Network; Philadelphia Writing Project; "Say Yes to Education;" and National Center for Postsecondary Improvement.

Financial Aid

Seventy-five percent of the students receive some form of financial aid. The School spends approximately $2 million per year for assistantships, scholarships, fellowships, research assistantships, work-study jobs, and part-time student workers. The average award in the 1997–98 academic year ranged from $2000 to fellowships that provided full tuition and a stipend.

Cost of Study

Full-time students paid a tuition of $21,738, plus a general fee of $1420 for the 1997–98 academic year. Part-time students paid $2752 per course, plus a $163 general fee.

Living and Housing Costs

University graduate housing is available on campus for single students as well as married students and their families. On-campus housing ranges from a single room for $435 per month to a three-bedroom apartment for $1020 per month. Off-campus apartment rents range upward from $400 per month.

Student Group

The approximately 800 students at GSE are a diverse group from a broad geographic range and include 11 percent international students from twenty-seven countries. Seventeen percent are students of color, 58 percent are full-time, and 40 percent are master's students. The programs at GSE attract recent college graduates as well as experienced practitioners seeking to grow professionally and to move into leadership positions in their field.

Student Outcomes

Graduates of the School currently serve as school superintendents, teachers, supervisors, guidance counselors, college and university faculty members and administrators, educational consultants, professional psychologists, educational researchers, and public policy planners and researchers.

Location

The commitment to innovative change is enhanced by the location of GSE in a major metropolitan region. The School's faculty members and students are able to address the problems of urban education—issues of equity and diversity, educational opportunity and educational excellence, and the management of complex organizations.

The campus is located ten blocks from downtown Philadelphia, home of the Liberty Bell, the Philadelphia Orchestra, the Philadelphia Art Museum, and many other rich cultural offerings.

The School

The Graduate School of Education is part of a university that is distinguished both for excellence in its academic disciplines and for the vital interactions of thought that cross disciplinary lines. Because the practice and study of education necessarily entail proficiency in a variety of academic fields, the School extends outward to the University community. GSE students regularly take courses in the Wharton School of Business, the School of Social Work, and the School of Arts and Sciences. In addition, a number of dual-degree programs bring other University students to the School.

Applying

Applicants should contact the office of admissions for a bulletin, the program deadlines, and application materials. Fellowship applications should be completed by February 15. Information on the Graduate School of Education can also be found on the Internet at the World Wide Web address below.

Correspondence and Information

Admissions Office
Graduate School of Education
University of Pennsylvania
3700 Walnut Street
Philadelphia, Pennsylvania 19104-6216
Telephone: 215-898-6415
E-mail: admissions.@nwfs.gse.upenn.edu
World Wide Web: http://www.upenn.edu/gse/

University of Pennsylvania

THE FACULTY

Kristine Billmyer, Ph.D., Adjunct Assistant Professor. Sociolinguistics and its application to second language learning and teaching.
Erling E. Boe, Ph.D., Professor. Teacher work force, educational reform, incentives in education, evaluation research, educational policy.
Robert F. Boruch, Ph.D., Professor. Evaluation, statistics, evaluation policy, research design and methods, vulnerable populations.
Morton Botel, Ed.D., Professor. Reading/writing/talking across the curriculum, assessment, mathematics education, professional development.
Myrna Cohen, Ph.D., Adjunct Assistant Professor. Academic literacies (academic reading, writing, and studying) and adult learners.
Charles Dwyer, Ph.D., Associate Professor. Concepts concerning the nature of organizations, self-design and self-management, conflict avoidance and dissolution, problem resolution, management.
Frederick Erickson, Ph.D., Professor. Multicultural diversity in schools and workplaces; formal and informal educational processes; methods of ethnography; sociolinguistic research on face-to-face interaction; race, class, ethnic, and gender equality.
John Fantuzzo, Ph.D., Professor. Child maltreatment, urban educational reform, social interaction in children's play, social development, peer tutoring and collaborative learning.
Rebecca Freeman, Ph.D., Assistant Professor. Multicultural education, bilingual education, teaching English as a second language, intercultural communication, language and gender, discourse analysis.
Jean Fridy, Ph.D., Adjunct Assistant Professor. Development of young children, developmental disabilities, developmental psychopathology.
Susan Fuhrman, Ph.D., Dean. National, state, and local politics, policy and policymaking, and accountability; intergovernmental relationships; educational reform.
Vivian Gadsden, Ph.D., Associate Professor. African-American family development, educational issues of culture and race, families and literacy in cultural and social contexts, life-span family development and literacy, life-span literacy.
Kenneth D. George, Ed.D., Professor. Sex education, human sexuality, relationships, gay/lesbian studies, love.
Richard A. Gibboney, Ed.D., Associate Professor. Curriculum development, educational history (the progressive movement), John Dewey's comprehensive educational theory, linking practice and ideas.
Ralph B. Ginsberg, Ph.D., Professor. Cognition and learning, reflective practice, comparative advantages of different modes of organization.
Margaret E. Goertz, Ph.D., Professor. Education finance, education policy and intergovernmental relations, fiscal and programmatic equity and the recruitment of minority teachers.
Joan Goodman, Ed.D., Professor. Preschool education and care, early intervention with the developmentally disabled, mental retardation, psychological assessment, adoption.
Kathleen Hall, Ph.D., Assistant Professor. Qualitative urban research, contemporary social theory, social stratification, and education and multiculturalism.
Nancy H. Hornberger, Ph.D., Professor. Bilingualism, bilingual education, intercultural communication, international educational development, language educational development, language and education policy, minorities and education.
Loretta Sweet Jemmott, Ph.D., Secondary Associate Professor. Designing and testing theoretically based HIV prevention studies for urban inner-city populations.
Peter Kuriloff, Ed.D., Professor. Minority retention, sexual socialization and conduct, organizational behavior, small group processes, organizational dynamics, group behavior.
James M. Larkin, Ph.D., Adjunct Associate Professor. Teacher education, urban education, school reform/teacher research, teaching learning and curriculum, history.
Marvin Lazerson, Ph.D., Professor. History, education and social policy, educational administration, higher education.
James Lytle, Ed.D., Adjunct Professor. Effective and responsive schooling for urban students.
Susan Lytle, Ph.D., Associate Professor. Reading/writing/literacy, teacher education, assessment, inquiry and educational reform.
Rebecca Maynard, Ph.D., Professor. Analysis-multivariate; evaluation-general; evaluation-policy; literacy-adult; research methods–design, quantitative; educational reform.
Paul McDermott, Ph.D., Professor. Measurement of observable behavior; study of categorical agreement; application of multivariate statistical analyses for scale development, prediction, classification, and typological research.
Larry Moneta, Ed.D., Adjunct Assistant Professor. Student affairs management practices, privatization and corporate alliances.
Nancy A. Neef, Ph.D., Senior Fellow. Behavior analysis addressing problems of individuals with special needs.
Norman Newberg, Ph.D., Senior Fellow. Urban education, international educational development, school restructuring, staff development, participatory action researching.
Teresa Pica, Ph.D., Associate Professor. Second/foreign language learning, language pedagogy, classroom discourse analysis, context-based language teaching, international teaching assistants of U.S. universities.
John L. Puckett, Ph.D., Associate Professor. Educational history, participatory action research, curriculum, progressive educational reform.
Janine Remillard, Ph.D., Assistant Professor. Mathematics teacher education, curriculum, policy-practice relationships, role of curriculum materials in mathematics education reform.
Ryda D. Rose, Ed.D., Lecturer. Methods, materials in science education, curriculum innovations, implementation: preservice and in-service science education.
Katherine Schultz, Ph.D., Assistant Professor. Literacy learning and issues of identity and discourse in multiracial educational settings.
Vivian C. Seltzer, Ph.D., Secondary Professor. Adolescent psychosocial development and the impact of peer dynamics on adolescent development.
Amy Sichel, Ph.D., Adjunct Associate Professor. Psychological assessment, school psychological services, individual and group counseling.
Lawrence Sipe, Ph.D., Assistant Professor. Literature for children and adolescents, how culture, ethnicity, and gender are related to children's literary responses.
Diana T. Slaughter-Defoe, Ph.D., Constance E. Clayton Professor of Urban Education. Relationship between parental socialization and children's school-related behavior and achievement.
Harris Sokoloff, Ph.D., Executive Director, Center for School Study Councils. Restructuring relationships with schools to enable administrators, teachers, and students to create collaborative learning environments.
Margaret Beale Spencer, Ph.D., Professor. Development of children, particularly minority children; identity formation processes among African-American youth; risk and resilience among vulnerable youth.
Jeanne L. Stanley, Ph.D., Lecturer. Educational and counseling issues regarding HIV/AIDS, addictions, sexual minorities, and group psychotherapy.
William Stayton, Th.D., Adjunct Associate Professor. Issues of gender orientation, sexual response and dysfunction, and sexuality and spirituality.
Howard Stevenson, Ph.D., Assistant Professor. Cultural relevance and empowerment, education-health psychology interface, racial socialization, urban education.
Brian V. Street, Ph.D., Adjunct Professor. Literacy practices in international perspective, cultural dimensions of language, academic literacy.
Michael Tierney, Ph.D., Associate Professor. Strategic planning, administration and governance, budgeting and resource allocation, public policy analysis.
Daniel A. Wagner, Ph.D., Professor. International education, adult literacy, literacy development, psycholinguistics, bilingualism.
Ursula Wagener, Ed.D., Adjunct Associate Professor. Access and successful graduation of minorities within higher education, development of historically black colleges and universities.
Gay Washburn, Ph.D., Adjunct Assistant Professor. Second language acquisition, especially fossilization, and applications of Vygotksian theory.
Robert Zemsky, Ph.D., Professor. Faculty, higher education, quantitative research methods.

UNIVERSITY OF RHODE ISLAND

College of Human Science and Services

Programs of Study

The College of Human Science and Services, the newest of the University's degree-granting colleges, was established in 1978. Its graduate programs are a mix of new and old; all have established traditions of excellence. The College, with a focus on programs that are oriented toward helping people lead more satisfying and self-directed lives, offers graduate programs through the following five departments: Communicative Disorders; Education; Human Development, Counseling and Family Studies; Physical Education and Exercise Science; and Textiles, Fashion Merchandising and Design, as well as the University-wide Program in Gerontology.

This college offers a joint Ph.D. program in education with Rhode Island College. This is an innovative program designed to produce scholar practitioners prepared to address the complex issues in K–12 education and to undertake new professional roles as educational leaders, mentors, and scholars. Graduate programs at the master's level are offered in adult education; audiology; college student personnel; elementary and secondary education; human development and family studies; marriage and family therapy; physical education and exercise science; physical therapy; reading education; speech-language pathology; and textiles, fashion merchandising, and design.

Research Facilities

The University houses the National Center on Public Education and Social Policy and ranks among the top 5 percent of the country's colleges and universities in the amount of research funding received. Research in the College is fostered and administered by the Institute of Human Science and Services, which is an integral part of the College and draws its professional staff from all departments. Each of the College's departments has a special facility to encourage and enable graduate student research. Research in communicative disorders is centered in the URI Speech and Hearing Clinic, a training and service facility serving the URI community and surrounding areas. Research facilities in the Department of Education include the Microcomputer Laboratory and the Micro-Teaching Laboratory, while the Department of Human Development, Counseling and Family Studies provides research and training opportunities in the Child Development Center and the Family Therapy Clinic. The Human Performance Laboratory in the Department of Physical Education and Exercise Science offers programs in adult fitness and cardiac rehabilitation. The Physical Therapy clinic, located in the Independence Square facility, offers training and research opportunities for students. Research in the Department of Textiles, Fashion Merchandising and Design is supported, in part, by the Historic Textile and Costume Collection, one of the largest and best university-based collections of its kind.

Financial Aid

Many different forms of financial aid are available. To be eligible, a student must first be admitted as a degree candidate. Fellowships and scholarships are awarded by the Dean of the Graduate School to students selected from nominees submitted by department chairpersons.

Graduate teaching assistantships and graduate research assistantships are available in every department offering graduate work. In 1997–98, graduate teaching and research assistants received stipends of $8955 for level I and $9395 for level II, and were granted remission of tuition and registration fees for the academic year. Other support available includes Graduate School tuition scholarships, assistance in the form of loans under the National Defense Education Act, and additional summer employment opportunities.

Cost of Study

Tuition and fees vary according to whether or not the student is a legal resident of the state of Rhode Island and according to full- or part-time enrollment. In 1997–98, tuition and fees for full-time students registered for 9 to 15 credits were $3362 per year for Rhode Island residents and $9380 per year for out-of-state students. Full-time students also paid $1210 in additional fees. Part-time students who are Rhode Island residents paid $187 per credit; part-time out-of-state students paid $521 per credit. Fees for part-time students are prorated.

Living and Housing Costs

The University Housing Office maintains a list of off-campus rooms, apartments, and houses that may be rented by graduate students. The use of a car is necessary for most of these locations. The University maintains a very limited number of graduate student apartments ranging from efficiencies to three-bedroom units. Rents range from $446 to $524 per month plus utilities.

Student Group

The College serves approximately 300 graduate students, many of whom are enrolled part-time, and approximately 1,700 undergraduates. The total University graduate enrollment is around 3,200, which includes students on the Kingston campus and at the College of Continuing Education. The total undergraduate student enrollment is approximately 12,000.

Location

The University of Rhode Island is located in Kingston, a small village about 30 miles south of Providence, the state capital. Kingston is in the northeastern metropolitan corridor between Boston (75 miles) and New York (160 miles), a location that provides outstanding cultural and professional opportunities. The area is served by the Amtrak station in West Kingston, 2 miles west of the main campus. T. F. Green Airport, which serves all of Rhode Island, is 20 miles north, and Interstate I-95, which extends from northern Maine to southern Florida, is 10 miles west of Kingston. In addition, there is regular bus service from Providence to Newport.

The University

The University was founded in 1892; it is a medium-sized state land-grant and sea-grant university enrolling about 11,000 students. The University has a faculty of 750 and offers seventy undergraduate majors, sixty-five master's degree programs, and thirty areas of doctoral study. The University's programs are offered at its four campuses. The main campus is located on 1,200 acres of hilly, wooded countryside in Kingston. The Narragansett Bay Campus, home of URI's Graduate School of Oceanography, lies on Narragansett Bay, 6 miles to the east. The College of Continuing Education is located in downtown Providence. The W. Alton Jones Campus, located on 2,300 wooded acres in West Greenwich, is the University's Environmental Educational Center and a conference center.

Applying

A bachelor's degree from an accredited institution, or its equivalent, is required of all applicants. A package of self-managed application materials and the *Bulletin of the University of Rhode Island* can be obtained from the Graduate Admissions Office. The completed application package must be sent directly to the department or program to which admission is sought. Information concerning admissions requirements and application deadlines can be found in the Graduate Programs section of the *Bulletin*. Specific information regarding programs may be obtained by contacting the departments or programs directly.

Correspondence and Information

Graduate School
University of Rhode Island
Kingston, Rhode Island 02881
Telephone: 401-874-2262

Dean's Office
College of Human Science and Services
University of Rhode Island
Kingston, Rhode Island 02881
Telephone: 401-874-2244

University of Rhode Island

THE FACULTY

Faculty members of the College are engaged in a wide variety of research projects. Current areas of research include program evaluation, audiology, speech pathology, cardiac rehabilitation, diving fatalities, long-term care of the elderly, structuring education for adults, student achievement, compensatory education, learning, exercise physiology, health-care ethics, family dynamics, human services policy and management, and volunteerism.

College of Human Sciences and Services (Quinn Hall, 401-874-2244)
Barbara Brittingham, Dean and Professor of Education; Ph.D., Iowa State, 1973.
Leo E. O'Donnell, Associate Dean and Associate Professor of Physical Education and Exercise Science; Ed.D., Temple, 1970.

Department of Communicative Disorders (Adams Hall, 401-874-5969)
Barbara Culatta, Professor; Ph.D., Pittsburgh, 1975.
Stephen D. Grubman-Black, Professor; Ph.D., SUNY at Buffalo, 1972.
Colleen Karow, Assistant Professor; Ph.D., Texas, 1997.
Dana Kovarsky, Assistant Professor; Ph.D., Texas, 1989.
Robert Marshall, Associate Professor; Ph.D., Oklahoma, 1969.
John P. Preece, Associate Professor; Ph.D., Iowa, 1985.
Jay Singer, Department Chair and Associate Professor; Ph.D., Case Western Reserve, 1976.

Department of Education (Chafee Building, 401-874-2564)
James Barton, Associate Professor; Ph.D., Stanford, 1990.
John Boulmetis, Professor; Ph.D., Ohio State, 1982.
David Byrd, Professor; Ph.D., Syracuse, 1980.
William Croasdale, Professor; Ed.D., Columbia, 1966.
Robert Felner, Professor and Chair; Ph.D., Rochester, 1977.
Sandy Jean Hicks, Assistant Professor; Ph.D., Arizona, 1993.
Theodore M. Kellogg, Professor; Ph.D., Florida State, 1971.
John V. Long Jr., Professor; Ph.D., Syracuse, 1971.
William Lynn McKinney, Professor; Ph.D., Chicago, 1973.
Richard F. Purnell, Professor; Ph.D., Texas, 1966.
Richard E. Sullivan, Associate Professor; Ph.D., Texas at Austin, 1971.
Susan L. Trostle, Associate Professor; D.Ed., Penn State, 1984.
George H. Willis, Professor; Ph.D., Johns Hopkins, 1971.
Betty Young, Associate Professor; Ph.D., UCLA, 1988.

Department of Human Development, Counseling, and Family Studies (Transition Center, 401-874-2150)
Jerome Adams, Associate Professor; Ph.D., Purdue, 1989.
Joan Anderson, Professor; Ph.D., California, Davis, 1984.
David Caruso, Professor; Ph.D., Cornell, 1989.
Phillip G. Clark, Acting Director of the Program in Gerontology and Professor; Sc.D., Harvard, 1979.
Stewart Cohen, Professor; Ph.D., Purdue, 1967.
Katherine Douglas, Assistant Professor; Ph.D., Indiana, 1997.
Diane Horm-Wingerd, Director of the Child Development Center and Professor; Ph.D., Virginia Tech, 1985.
Mary Kalymun, Associate Professor; Ph.D., Penn State, 1982.
Peter E. Maynard, Professor; Ph.D., SUNY at Buffalo, 1969.
Gwenneth Rae, Professor; Ed.D., UCLA, 1972.
Jayne E. Richmond, Associate Professor; Ph.D., Florida, 1982.
Jerome Schaffran, Associate Professor; Ph.D., Iowa, 1971.
Karen A. Schroeder, Associate Professor; Ph.D., Connecticut, 1977.
Jingjian Xiao, Associate Professor; Ph.D., Oregon State, 1991.

Department of Physical Education and Exercise Science (Tootell Physical Education Center, 401-874-2976)
James Agostinucci, Associate Professor; Sc.D., Boston University, 1988.
Peter Blanpied, Associate Professor; Ph.D., Iowa, 1989.
Greta L. Cohen, Professor; Ed.D., Boston University, 1981.
Ann Marie Dupre, Clinical Assistant Professor; M.S., Massachusetts General Hospital, 1992.
Linda Lamont, Associate Professor; Ph.D., Kent State, 1985.
Thomas Manfredi, Professor; Ph.D., Massachusetts, 1976.
Raymond A. Nedwidek, Professor; Ed.D., Pittsburgh, 1965.
John O'Leary, Department Cochair and Associate Professor; M.S., Southern Connecticut State, 1963.
J. Richard Polidoro, Associate Professor; D.P.E., Springfield, 1969.
Deborah Riebe, Assistant Professor; Ph.D., Connecticut, 1995.
Susan Roush, Associate Professor; Ph.D., Washington (Seattle), 1990.
Mark Rowinski, Director of the Program in Physical Therapy and Professor; Ph.D., Medical College of Georgia, 1976.
Diane Seleen, Department Cochair and Associate Professor; Ed.D., Boston University, 1981.

Textiles, Fashion Merchandising and Design (Quinn Hall, 401-874-4525)
Martin Bide, Professor; Ph.D., Bradford (United Kingdom), 1979.
Yvette Harps-Logan, Associate Professor; Ph.D., Virginia Tech, 1990.
Patricia A. Helms, Associate Professor; Ph.D., Florida State, 1971.
Josephine Moreno, Assistant Professor; Ph.D., Iowa State, 1995.
Margaret Ordoñez, Associate Professor; Ph.D., Florida State, 1978.
Linda M. Welters, Department Chair and Professor; Ph.D., Minnesota, 1981.

UNIVERSITY OF ROCHESTER

Margaret Warner Graduate School of Education and Human Development

Programs of Study

The Warner School offers programs leading to the degrees of Master of Science (M.S.), Master of Arts in Teaching (M.A.T.), Doctor of Education (Ed.D.), and Doctor of Philosophy (Ph.D.) in three program areas or concentrations: teaching and curriculum, counseling and human development, and educational leadership (school administration and higher education).

Specifically, Warner offers the Master of Arts in Teaching and the Master of Science in the following concentrations: teaching and curriculum, elementary teacher education, secondary education, teaching English to speakers of other languages (TESOL), human development, school counseling, community counseling, human development with a concentration in school counseling, human development with a concentration in community counseling, human development with a concentration in psychological development, administration, administration with a concentration in higher education, and a Catholic school administrator's program. Ed.D. concentrations are offered in administration, higher education, counseling, and human development. The Ph.D. programs include concentrations in teaching, curriculum, and change; human development in educational contexts; leadership, thought, and policy; and higher education and a Ph.D. program for Warner Scholars.

Research Facilities

The University Library system houses more than 2,750,000 volumes and subscribes to about 13,000 current periodicals and other serial publications. Rush Rhees Library is the principal library and holds about 2 million volumes, primarily in the humanities and social sciences. The Computing Library and Resources Center (CLARC) in Rush Rhees is jointly operated by the library and the University Computing Center. Hundreds of software titles are available for use on CLARC's abundant microcomputers. In addition, the University offers a broad range of advanced computing facilities that are readily available to all graduate students. The University participates in NYSERNet, a link among universities and industries throughout New York and supercomputer centers at Cornell and other universities nationwide that provides access to worldwide databases, library facilities, e-mail, and remote computing. Altogether, the variety of computers, the availability of terminals, and the emphasis on usage in regular and special courses make the computer facilities of the University an impressive resource for graduate students.

Financial Aid

Funding for the Warner School in the form of tuition waivers, assistantships, or fellowships is very limited, and the award process is highly competitive. For master's degree programs, financial aid is available only to minority applicants who qualify for the Fifth Year in Teaching Program. For doctoral students, tuition remission and/or assistantships are available only for those who will be full-time students during the academic year.

Cost of Study

The tuition cost for 1998–99 is $672 per credit hour; the cost of books and supplies averages $1200.

Living and Housing Costs

Living expenses are estimated at $10,800 for 1998–99. Living expenses include rent, food, personal expenses, and health insurance.

Student Group

Approximately 350 students are enrolled at the Warner School, of whom slightly fewer than two thirds are master's students. There are both full- and part-time students, many of whom are working and have families. Most students enter the Warner School with educational work experience.

Location

Located on Lake Ontario, the Rochester area, with a population of nearly 1 million, is large enough to offer diverse opportunities for living, working, and enjoying recreation. Rochester and the surrounding metropolitan area gain much of their character and stability from industries that are, for the most part, highly technical. These industries, represented by such companies as Eastman-Kodak and Bausch & Lomb, provide the Rochester-area labor force with a large percentage of skilled and professional employees.

The University

The University of Rochester, located in upstate New York, is coeducational, nonsectarian, independent, and privately endowed. Approximately 9,000 students are enrolled, 33 percent of whom are studying at the graduate level. Programs that range from the undergraduate through the postdoctoral levels are offered in about fifty major disciplines. The University is large enough to attract and retain a distinguished faculty and to offer all other resources that students require for graduate study. The Graduate School of Education, founded in 1958, was renamed the Margaret Warner School of Education and Human Development in 1993.

Applying

Each applicant is considered individually by the Admissions Committee of the School. Admission to the program is based on evidence of success in undergraduate study, letters of recommendation, a writing sample, work experience, and faculty interviews. Scores on the Graduate Record Examinations (GRE) are not required for admission to the Warner School; should an applicant wish to submit test scores, however, these will be considered by the Admissions Committee.

To be considered for admission in the fall quarter and for financial aid, all applicants must send their completed forms and supporting materials by February 1. Program information and application deadlines for those not seeking financial aid can be obtained by contacting the address below.

Correspondence and Information

Admissions
Margaret Warner Graduate School of Education and Human Development
Dewey Hall
University of Rochester
Rochester, New York 14627-0425
Telephone: 716-275-3950
Fax: 716-473-7598
E-mail: tmug@db1.cc.rochester.edu

University of Rochester

THE FACULTY AND THEIR RESEARCH

Craig Barclay, Associate Professor, Counseling and Human Development; Ph.D., Illinois. Cognitive development and the cognitive consequences of developmental disabilities, autobiographical memory.

Raffaella Borasi, Associate Professor, Teaching and Curriculum; Ph.D., SUNY at Buffalo. Mathematical educator, with special interests in the humanistic and contextualized aspects of mathematics and in critical thinking.

Brian O. Brent, Assistant Professor, Educational Leadership Program; Ph.D., Cornell. Fiscal and economic policy issues in educational settings, matters related to educational productivity and alternative revenue sources for schools and universities.

Randall R. Curren, Associate Professor, Educational Leadership Program; Ph.D., Pittsburgh. Philosophy of education, education policy and ethics.

Dale Dannefer, Professor, Counseling and Human Development; Ph.D., Rutgers. Work, life course, and adult development; the problems of diversity, structure, and action in studying human development and the life course.

Lucia French, Associate Professor, Counseling and Human Development; Ph.D., Illinois. Developmental psychology, cognitive development; relations between language and reasoning, the role of receptive and expressive language in early education, comparisons of Asian and American approaches to early childhood education.

Ivor Goodson, Professor, Teaching and Curriculum; D.Phil., Sussex (England). History and sociology of the school curriculum and life histories of teachers and other professional groups.

Lynn D. Gordon, Associate Professor, Educational Leadership Program; Ph.D., Chicago. History of education and higher education, American history and women's studies.

David Hursh, Associate Professor and Chair of the Teaching and Curriculum Program; Ph.D., Wisconsin. Connection between epistemological, ethical, and political aspects of teaching and curriculum to the development of teachers; curriculum theory and practice, teacher education, and social studies methods.

Patricia Irvine, Assistant Professor, Teaching and Curriculum; Ph.D., New Mexico. Literacy practices as they are constructed in a variety of social and cultural contexts, critical approaches to curriculum and pedagogy, qualitative research that documents the effects of social context on the educational experiences of secondary students.

Frederick Jefferson, Professor, Counseling and Human Development; Ed.D., Massachusetts. Group dynamics and organizations, group therapy and practice, systems theory and practice for counselors.

Bruce A. Kimball, Professor, Educational Leadership Program; Ed.D., Harvard. History of curriculum and teaching, particularly in higher education; the history and theory of pedagogy; liberal education and case-method teaching.

Howard Kirschenbaum, Frontier Professor, Counseling and Human Development; Ed.D., Temple. Values education and character education in the schools, family and community, human relations training, holistic curriculum development, museum education.

Joanne Larson, Assistant Professor, Teaching and Curriculum; Ph.D., UCLA. Classroom language and literacy practices; curriculum, diversity, qualitative methods, and literacy learning.

Lisa Lopez Levers, Assistant Professor and Chair of the Counseling and Human Development Program; Ph.D., Kent State; licensed clinical counselor. Effects of violence on children and women, medical anthropology.

Michael Mason, Assistant Professor, Counseling and Human Development; Ph.D., Oregon State. Adolescent substance abuse, ritual theory, social critiques of psychotherapy.

Joy Moss, Adjunct Associate Professor, Teaching and Curriculum; M.A., Rochester. Children's literature, literacy learning, reader response, thematic teaching.

Bonnie Rubenstein, Associate Professor, Counseling and Human Development; Ed.D., Rochester. Impact of divorce on teenagers' home lives and nonschool skill development and school counseling.

Julia B. Smith, Assistant Professor, Educational Leadership Program; Ed.D., Michigan. Organizational process of schools; equity and access to curriculum, particularly concerning issues of gender, racial, and class equity in schools.

Tyll van Geel, Earl B. Taylor Professor and Chair of the Educational Leadership Program; J.D., Northwestern; Ed.D., Harvard. Legal issues in education.

Linda P. Ware, Assistant Professor, Teaching and Curriculum; Ph.D., Kansas. Special education, issues of access and inclusion, technology and the special needs learner.

Edwardine Weaver, Assistant Professor, Teaching and Curriculum and Director of the Catholic School Administrator's Program and the Professional Development Program; Ed.D., Pacific Western.

Harold Wechsler, Professor, Educational Leadership Program; Ph.D., Columbia. Access, governance, business education, and the formation of curriculum and disciplines in twentieth-century American higher education.

Philip Wexler, Michael Scandling Professor and Dean; Ph.D., Princeton. Sociology of education and social theory.

John Wills, Assistant Professor, Teaching and Curriculum; Ph.D., California, San Diego. Social construction of school knowledge, popular political culture, multicultural education, and qualitative methods; social studies methods, sociology of education, and qualitative research methods.

UNIVERSITY OF SAN FRANCISCO

School of Education

Programs of Study

The University of San Francisco (USF) offers programs in counseling psychology, curriculum and instruction, international and multicultural education, organization and leadership, private school education, and teacher education. the program in counseling psychology is designed to prepare professional counselors and psychologists for effective performance in the helping professions. Academic work is complemented by traineeship assignments in a wide variety of social and health helping professions. Academic work is complemented by traineeship assignments in a wide variety of social and health service agencies in the greater Bay Area. Degree programs include the Doctor of Education (Ed.D.), the Doctor of Psychology (Psy.D.), and the Master of Arts (M.A.) in counseling. The Psy.D., which was granted provisional APA approval in 1998, requires 73 units and can be completed in four to five years. The M.A. in counseling has emphases in life transitions counseling (48 units, thirty months to complete); marriage, family, and child counseling (48 units, thirty months to complete); and school counseling (30 units, twelve months to complete). A credential program in pupil personnel services requires 36 units and takes eighteen months to complete. The program in learning and instruction is designed to train administrators and specialists in curriculum design and supervision, instructional leadership and technology, and evaluation, research, and instructional design. Degree programs include the Ed.D. and the M.A. in learning and instruction, with the mild/moderate education specialist credential (30–36 units, twelve months to complete). The Ed.D. has emphases in curriculum design and instructional supervision (60 units, four to five years to complete), instructional leadership and technology (60 units, five years to complete), and evaluation, research, and instructional design (60 units, five years to complete). The M.A. in curriculum and instruction has an emphasis in instructional design and supervision (30 units, twelve months to complete). The M.A. in special education requires 30 units and takes twelve months to complete. The program in international and multicultural education is designed to prepare educators and community leaders to advance their professional understanding and skills in education, cross-cultural communication, bilingual education, English language instruction, and second language acquisition. Degree programs include the Ed.D. in multicultural education, the M.A. in international and multicultural education, and the M.A. in teaching English as a second language (TESL). The Ed.D. in multicultural education requires 60 units and takes forty-eight months to complete. The M.A. in international and multicultural education requires 30 units and takes twelve months to complete. The M.A. in TESL requires 30 units and takes twelve months to complete. An emphasis in educational technology may be added to the M.A. in TESL by completing 3–6 additional units. The program in organization and leadership is designed to prepare administrators and leaders in education, industry, business, health, human services, and government. Studies assist students in exploring relationships among individuals, organizations, and society. Degree programs include the Ed.D. in organization and leadership and the M.A. in organization and leadership. The Ed.D. in organization and leadership requires 60 units and takes forty-eight months to complete. The M.A. in organization and leadership has an optional emphasis in Pacific leadership international studies. Credential programs include preliminary administrative services (27 units, twelve months to complete) and professional administrative services (25 units, twelve months to complete). Lacking the resources of public counterparts, private schools depend on the excellence and commitment of their personnel. The programs in private school education are designed to develop educators to provide leadership for private and Catholic schools. Degree programs include the Ed.D. in private school administration, the M.A. in private school administration, and the M.A. in Catholic school teaching. The Ed.D. in private school administration requires 60 units and takes four to five years to complete. The program in teacher education is designed to prepare exemplary classroom teachers who are ready and able to assume duties in multicultural and multilingual classroom. Course work, research, and service are all designed to assist students in becoming proficient in the use of new technology to enhance learning, developing skill in human relations and communication, and strengthening their capacity for moral leadership and independent thinking. Degree programs include the Master of Arts in education with an emphasis in educational technology (30 units, twelve months to complete). Credential programs are offered in multiple subjects (preliminary or clear), with or without the bilingual–cross-cultural emphasis in Filipino or Spanish; multiple subjects cross-cultural language and development; multiple subjects bilingual, cross-cultural language and academic development; single subject, with an emphasis in cross-cultural language and academic development; and single subject with cross-cultural language and academic development, with or without Filipino or Spanish.

Research Facilities

The School of Education is located in a campus building that houses faculty offices, modern classrooms, conference rooms, counseling and observation rooms, and a computer technology center. Academic and professional programs are complemented by programs of applied research and community-based service that are sponsored by various centers and institutes of the School. Gleeson Library's holdings of more than 1.6 million items include 488,000 books, 243,500 government documents, 100,300 bound periodicals, and 653,000 other items.

Financial Aid

The School of Education receives strong scholarship support from various sources, including the University and the federal government. Approximately 70 percent of students take advantage of some form of financial aid. Information may be obtained from the School of Education and the Office of Financial Aid at 415-422-6303.

Cost of Study

Tuition for the 1998–99 school year is $658 per unit for on-campus master's and credential programs, $546 per unit for off-campus master's and credential programs, and $724 per unit for doctoral programs. The University offers a budget payment plan.

Living and Housing Costs

Graduate on-campus housing is available for single students. The central location of the University makes it easily accessible to students who choose to live in one of the many unique neighborhoods of San Francisco. Information on housing costs is available from the Office of Residence Life at 415-422-6824.

Student Group

The University's richly diverse multicultural student population numbers about 8,000, with close to half of the students attending graduate programs. The School of Education currently has 857 students enrolled. Classes are small, and courses are held on weekday evenings and Saturdays, which allows students the opportunity to continue their careers.

Student Outcomes

Graduates from the School of Education have gone on to a vast variety of positions as prominent administrators, counselors, educators, and psychologists. Graduates join a worldwide alumni network of more than 60,000 advancement professionals working around the globe.

Location

The University is located in the heart of the city of San Francisco. The 55-acre hilltop campus overlooks Golden Gate Park, the Pacific Ocean, and downtown San Francisco. The climate is world renowned, and every conceivable type of recreation can be found in or near the Bay Area.

The University

The University of San Francisco is a private Jesuit university. Founded in 1855 as San Francisco's first institution of higher education, USF has continually prepared graduates to meet the challenges of the ever-changing culture and society.

Applying

For application materials and program information, students should contact the School of Education or the Office of Graduate Admissions. The University of San Francisco does not discriminate on the basis of race, color, age, religion, ancestry, national origin, sex, sexual orientation, or disability.

Correspondence and Information

School of Education
University of San Francisco
2130 Fulton Street
San Francisco, California 94117-1080
Telephone: 415-422-6525

Office of Graduate Admissions
University of San Francisco
2130 Fulton Street
San Francisco, California 94117-1080
Telephone: 415-422-GRAD
800-CALL-USF (toll-free outside CA)
Fax: 415-422-2217
World Wide Web: http://graduate.usfca.edu

University of San Francisco

THE FACULTY AND THEIR RESEARCH

Mary Abascal-Hildebrand, Ed.D. Organization and leadership; applied critical hermeneutics, especially participatory governance; democratic workplace practice; international applications; urban issues; immigration; homelessness; school reform; higher education.

Alma Flor Ada, Ph.D. Sociopolitical issues in education, education for personal liberation and social change, children's literature and critical thinking.

Lanna Andrews, Ed.D. Special education, work in urban education settings with culturally and linguistically diverse learners, collaborative consultation, case method.

Joan Avis, Ph.D. Counseling psychology, adult development and life transitions counseling, life planning and consultation, hypnotherapy, personality and social psychology.

Deborah P. Bloch, Ph.D. Educational leadership, particularly in urban settings and with diverse populations; work and spirituality; career development and counseling; links between school programs and workforce preparation (school-to-work); information systems in educational settings.

Robert Burns, Ph.D. Research on teaching and instruction, particularly the effects of class composition on student learning; research methodology; statistics.

Patricia L. Busk, Ph.D. Education statistics and research methods: meta-analysis, nonparametrics methods applied to analysis of single-case data, randomization tests, test construction, performance assessment, log-linear models and survey methodology, assessment in higher education, research on women, teaching statistics.

Allen D. Calvin, Ph.D. Organizational psychology, operational management in higher education, fund/organizational development, applied educational statistics, administrative research, fundamental management.

Denis E. Collins, S.J., Ph.D. Social and philosophical foundations of education, the educational philosophy of Paulo Freire, educational issues of the third world or oppressed populations, international education.

Robert G. Curley, Ph.D. Language and literacy, reading acquisition and study strategies, research design and methodologies, philosophy and psychology, development of teacher training programs.

Anita P. DeFrantz, Ph.D. Language development; African-American education; communication sociology; developmental psychology; language usage and language power, with emphasis on ethnic diversity for research and publications.

Geoffrey R. Dillon, S.J., Ed.D. Educational leadership, private school administration, school psychology and counseling, teacher and administrator supervision and development, MBTI and leadership styles, moral development, philosophical foundations of education.

Susan Evans, Ed.D. Special education, survey research, teacher training, grant writing, female adult development.

Elena Flores, Ph.D. Latino adolescent sexuality and substance use, family functioning and adolescent health-risk behaviors, counseling Latino families, Latina family relations and depression.

Mary Furlong, Ed.D., Director of the Senior Net Telecommunications Project. Teacher educational software design, telecommunications and aging.

Rosita Galang, Ph.D. Theories, research, and issues in language development and language use; sociolinguistic issues in education, bilingualism and bilingual education, first and second language acquisition and teaching, language maintenance and language shift, Filipino American education.

William T. Garner, Ph.D. Economics and finance of education, higher education planning and management, educational governance and policy, educational technology.

Brian Gerrard, Ph.D. Marital and family therapy, counseling techniques, research methods, psychological type.

Ellen A. Herda, Ph.D. Pacific Rim issues, communication and organizational change, policy analysis, participatory research within the hermeneutic tradition.

Caryl Hodges, Ed.D. Curriculum and instruction; science, mathematics, and humanities; portfolio development; beginning teacher induction; issues in multicultural education, with focus on impact of culture on teaching strategies.

Kathleen Jonson, Ed.D. Reading, language arts, and literacy; issues in beginning teacher development, including mentoring the new teacher and supervision; curriculum and instruction.

Aida A. Joshi, Ph.D. Multicultural curriculum and instruction/social sciences, comparative and international education, Asian studies, cross-cultural similarities and differences.

Susan Katz, Ph.D. Immigration to the U.S. and its impact upon education, particularly for youth from Latin America; examination of youth violence and its link to schooling; issues in multicultural education, especially as related to language and literacy.

Edwin J. McDermott, S.J. Foundations of private education, policy issues on private schooling, history of Catholic education, moral development theories, faith development theories.

Dan McPherson, Ph.D. Family counseling, law and ethics in counseling, lesbian and gay counseling, long-term and brief psychotherapy.

Dorothy S. Messerschmitt, Ph.D. First and second language acquisition, teaching English as a second language, syntax, discourse analysis, linguistics.

Nikki Miller, Ed.D. Literacy development: reading and listening comprehension, urban education, special education issues in urban settings, teacher preparation.

Mathew Mitchell, Ph.D. Mathematics education, student motivation, outcome-based instruction, computers as cognitive tools, creativity.

Patricia Mitchell, Ph.D. Organizational development, leadership styles, management issues, women issues, K–12 administration, K–12 teaching, language development, literacy.

Larry Palmatier, Ph.D. Counseling psychology and marriage, family, and child counseling outcome studies; solution-focused methods; choice theory; counseling and consulting in schools and cross-cultural grief counseling.

Terence Patterson, Ed.D. Ethical and professional issues in psychology, assessment and documentation of couples therapy, choice of theoretical orientation and clinical decision making by practitioners, use of multimedia in professional activities.

Gini Shimabukuro, Ed.D. Private school education, curriculum development, educational technology, moral development, problem solving, development of thinking abilities with the assistance of educational technology, elementary school curriculum and instruction.

Terrence Soo-Hoo, Ph.D. Working with adults, children, and families; clinical psychology, assessment of Asian children; multicultural counseling; brief psychotherapy; consultation in mental health services.

Sr. Mary Peter Traviss, O.P., Ph.D. Cognitive moral development theory, Catholic school research and practice, supervision and administration of Catholic schools, stress management research, MBTI research.

Emile Wilson, Ph.D. International and multicultural issues in education, philosophical foundations of education, research methodologies, working with students of varied cultural backgrounds.

Steven Zlutnick, Ph.D. Behavior therapy and behavioral health/medicine; single-subject experimental research; accountable mental health systems; iatrogenic issues in education, psychology, and medicine.

UNIVERSITY OF SOUTHERN CALIFORNIA

School of Education

Programs of Study

Programs offered by the USC School of Education blend research and theory-based academic experience with field-based practice, research, development, and evaluation activities to prepare present and future educational leaders. These programs are the Ed.D. in leadership, preschool through higher education (with specializations available in business, community college, higher education curriculum, personnel, policy, principalship, superintendency, and teacher education); the Ph.D. (with a specialization in policy and organization; educational psychology; curriculum and teaching; language, literacy, and learning; international and intercultural education; and counseling psychology); the M.S. in education (with a specialization in postsecondary administration and student affairs, curriculum and teaching, communication handicapped–deaf, and instructional technology); the Master in Marriage, Family, and Child Counseling; and the M.S. in teaching English as a second language. Credential programs in teaching (elementary, secondary, and bilingual) and administrative services may be pursued in conjunction with a degree program. The University's programs in higher education are ranked among the top ten in the nation (*U.S. News & World Report*, 1998).

The master's degree programs require from 28 to 50 semester units; 4 to 8 units may be transferred. The Ed.D. and Ph.D. degree programs require a minimum of 66 units; 20 transfer units may be accepted. Master's degree requirements must be completed within five years; Ed.D., within ten years; and Ph.D., within six to eight years.

Classes may be taken in the late afternoons and evenings.

Research Facilities

Waite Phillips Hall, the USC School of Education building, houses offices, classrooms, conference rooms, counseling and observation rooms, and a computer laboratory. To serve the information needs of instruction, research, and the library system, USC supports computer systems ranging from IBM mainframes and UNIX workstations to a variety of personal computers. These are integrated into USCnet, a campuswide network that is linked to the major national networks including Internet, NSFNET, and BITNET.

The Emery Stoops and Joyce King-Stoops Education Library, one of seventeen campus libraries, holds more than 153,900 books and journals, 350,000 ERIC microforms, dissertations, theses, curriculum guides, and a special juvenile literature section. Automated circulation, computerized searching, and reference assistance are provided. An interlibrary loan service is available for accessing research libraries nationwide.

Financial Aid

Scholarships, fellowships, assistantships, tuition awards, loans, and part-time employment are available. Information may be sought from any one of three University offices: (1) the School of Education; (2) the USC Financial Aid Office; and (3) the Graduate School. USC also offers a number of payment plan opportunities.

Cost of Study

Tuition is based on a per-unit rate of $706 for the 1998–99 academic year. Graduate students may take advantage of a flat-fee semester rate of $10,481 when registering for 15–18 units per semester.

Living and Housing Costs

Graduate students may opt for apartment-style furnished accommodations in one of the University-owned units near the campus. Most apartments are designed to house 1 to 4 students per unit; some studio apartments are available. The 1998–99 rate in the residential halls is $3900 per year, plus an additional $3180 for a meal plan. Apartment costs range from $260 to $805 per student per month. A referral service for off-campus apartments and rooms in private homes, as well as roommate listings, is provided by the Information Center (telephone: 213-740-6283).

Student Group

Nearly half of the University's 30,000 students are enrolled in graduate and professional study programs. The School of Education maintains a steady enrollment of approximately 800 graduate students. Most graduate students in the School of Education maintain their full-time teaching or administrative jobs while pursuing their advanced degrees and credentials.

Location

Located at the same site since USC's founding, the University Park Campus now includes 130 major buildings spread over approximately 150 acres in the city of Los Angeles.

Situated 3 miles south of the Los Angeles Civic Center, the University Park Campus is adjacent to museums and recreational facilities and is served by a network of freeways that provide access to cultural, business, and residential areas; shopping and entertainment centers; beaches; and mountains.

The University and The School

Founded in 1880, the University of Southern California is the oldest independent research university in the West. USC has grown into a major center of learning, offering degrees in more than 200 fields of study through eighteen professional schools, as well as the College of Letters, Arts and Sciences and the Graduate School. USC now ranks in the top ten among private research universities and in the top twenty among all universities in the United States (based on federal research and development support).

Counted among the top tier of private professional education schools in the country, the School of Education has a reputation extending beyond national boundaries. Its international visibility is maintained, in part, by nearly 18,000 alumni, many of whom hold prominent positions at local, state, and federal levels.

Applying

All applicants for graduate study at USC must have earned a baccalaureate degree from an accredited college or university prior to initial enrollment. Admission is based upon a careful evaluation of the various competencies and attributes evidenced by the application for admission, grade point average, and results of the General Test of the Graduate Record Examinations (GRE). Each application is further evaluated in light of the individual's potential for success in the program. The admission application deadline for fall is July 1; the deadline for spring is November 1. The Ph.D. program in counseling psychology has an annual deadline of December 15.

Correspondence and Information

School of Education
Waite Phillips Hall, 802
University of Southern California
Los Angeles, California 90089-0031
Telephone: 213-740-7072

University of Southern California

THE FACULTY AND THEIR RESEARCH

Jose M. Abreu, Ph.D., Assistant Professor. Cross-cultural and career counseling.
Robert L. Baker, Ph.D., Professor. Learning and development, technology, research design, organizational behavior.
Estela M. Bensimon, Ed.D., Professor. Academic leadership, organizational change in colleges and universities.
Ruth Gim Chung, Ph.D., Assistant Professor. Acculturation and mental health of Asian Americans, crosscultural conceptualizations of healthy family functioning.
Richard Clark, Ed.D., Professor. Instructional psychology applied to training, instructional uses of computers.
Myron H. Dembo, Ph.D., Professor. Teacher and parent education, social psychology of education, motivation, cooperative learning.
David E. Eskey, Ph.D., Associate Professor. International education, second-language teaching, applied linguistics, administration of multilingual-multicultural programs.
Robert E. Ferris, Ed.D., Associate Professor. Personnel administration, collective bargaining, school-board relationships.
S. Michael Genzuk, Ph.D., Assistant Professor. Theory and application of bilingual education, academic achievement of language minority students.
Rodney K. Goodyear, Ph.D., Associate Professor. Clinical supervision, professional issues, test interpretation.
Gretchen Guiton, Ph.D., Assistant Professor. Research methodology, assessment.
Linda S. Hagedorn, Ph.D., Assistant Professor. The community college, postsecondary student development, quantitative methods.
Dennis Hocevar, Ph.D., Professor. Measurement, individual differences, research methodology.
Edward J. Kazlauskas, Ph.D., Associate Professor. Information technologies, microcomputing, library/media center management.
Frederick G. Knirk, Ed.D., Professor. Educational analysis and design, human factors analysis, media management, logistics.
Stephen D. Krashen, Ph.D., Professor. Language acquisition, literacy, bilingual education.
William B. Lee, Ph.D., Associate Professor. International and intercultural education.
Johanna K. Lemlech, Ed.D., Professor. Instructional leadership, elementary school curriculum, teaching models, teachers' values.
Laurie MacGillivray, Ed.D., Assistant Professor. Emergent literacy, teacher education.
David Marsh, Ph.D., Professor. Curriculum development and change, in-service education, curriculum and program evaluation.
William Maxwell, Ph.D., Associate Professor. Community college administration and planning, international higher education development.
William McComas, Ph.D., Assistant Professor. Science education, teacher education, museum learning.
Birgitte R. Mednick, Ph.D., Associate Professor. Infant through adult development, interaction effects of environmental and congenital variables.
William B. Michael, Ph.D., Professor. Evaluation and measurement, intelligence, creativity, institutional research in higher education.
Michael D. Newcomb, Ph.D., Associate Professor. Substance abuse, human sexuality, marriage and divorce.
Harold F. O'Neil Jr., Ph.D., Professor. Computer-assisted and computer-managed instruction, research and development program planning.
Lawrence O. Picus, Ph.D., Associate Professor. School business administration, budgeting, uses of computers, resource allocation.
Donald Polkinghorne, Ph.D., Professor. Using narrative to organize clinical information, qualitative research methods.
William M. Rideout, Ph.D., Professor. International and intercultural education.
Joan Rosenberg, Ph.D., Assistant Professor. Education and clinical training of counselors and psychologists.
Robert Rueda, Ph.D., Associate Professor. Interaction of social and cognitive activities, language minority students in special education.
Nelly P. Stromquist, Ph.D., Associate Professor. Educational systems in Third World countries, evaluation of educational reforms and policies.
William G. Tierney, Ph.D., Professor. Governance and administration in higher education, leadership issues of equity and multicultural education.
Betty A. Walker, Ph.D., Associate Professor. Existential and phenomenological bases, choices of women.
Edgar H. Williams, Ed.D., Associate Professor. Characteristics of handicapped students, educational strategies.
Priscilla Wohlstetter, Ph.D., Associate Professor. Politics of education, state politics, policy implementation, program evaluation.
Kathleen M. Wulf, Ph.D., Professor. Curriculum design, evaluation, psychology of learning, cognitive and affective growth.
David Yaden, Ph.D., Associate Professor. Intergenerational literacy development, early reading ability, theories of reading disability.

University of South Florida

USF

UNIVERSITY OF SOUTH FLORIDA

College of Education

Programs of Study

The College of Education is committed to excellence in teaching, research, and service. It offers a variety of graduate programs that lead to the Doctor of Philosophy (Ph.D.), Doctor of Education (Ed.D.), Education Specialist (Ed.S.), Master of Education (M.Ed.), and Master of Arts (M.A.) degrees. Doctoral degrees are designed to prepare graduates to conduct research, teach in a college or university setting, and hold administrative or leadership positions in educational institutions, school systems, and other public or private agencies. The master's and education specialist programs are designed to prepare educational practitioners in advanced studies in their field.

The Ph.D. in curriculum and instruction offers specializations in the areas of adult education, English education, foreign language education, higher education, instructional technology, interdisciplinary education, mathematics education, measurement and evaluation, reading/language arts education, school psychology, science education, special education, and vocational education. The Ed.D is offered in educational leadership (K–12), community college leadership, and educational program development. The Ed.S., M.Ed., and M.A. degrees are offered in most of the areas listed above. In addition, master's degrees are offered in the areas of counselor education, physical education, and social science education. The doctoral programs require completion of core courses and courses in the specialization area, satisfactory performance on a qualifying examination, and completion of a dissertation. The Ph.D. program requires two semesters of full-time residency on the Tampa Campus. The Ed.S. programs require a minimum of 36 credit hours, including completion of a thesis and a written comprehensive examination. The master's programs require a minimum of 30 to 33 credit hours and a comprehensive examination.

Research Facilities

The University of South Florida (USF) library system is among the finest in the Florida State University System. It houses close to 1.5 million volumes, 20,000 journals and periodicals, a Special Collections Department with more than 1 million items, and a Government Documents Collection. College of Education students have access to a number of research centers and institutes that are housed within the College and in the broader USF community. The College's state-of-the-art technology system serves to enhance teaching and research and link faculty members and graduate students to national and international networks.

Financial Aid

Financial aid is available to qualified graduate students in the form of graduate assistantships, fellowships, scholarships, and loan programs. For the 1998–99 academic year, graduate assistantship stipends range from $6800 (master's students) to $10,000 (doctoral students) for 20 hours of work per week for two semesters (fall and spring); additional summer employment is available. Students on graduate assistantships and some fellowships are granted tuition waivers. Inquiries about fellowships, grants, and scholarships should be directed to the USF Graduate School or the College of Education's Office of Graduate Studies.

Cost of Study

For the 1998–99 academic year, graduate tuition is $134.34 per credit hour for Florida residents and $439.73 per credit hour for nonresidents.

Living and Housing Costs

On-campus and off-campus housing is available to graduate students, although on-campus housing is limited. The University operates an apartment village that provides housing for graduate students at annual rates of $2536 (double occupancy) and $3650 (single occupancy). Most graduate students live off campus, selecting from a variety of housing options available in the USF and greater Tampa Bay areas. The average cost of apartment rentals in the USF area ranges from $420 per month for a one-bedroom to $520 per month for a two-bedroom unit.

Student Group

The University's total enrollment for the 1997–98 academic year was more than 34,000, with a graduate enrollment of approximately 6,000 students. Graduate enrollment in the College of Education was approximately 1,400. Full-time graduate students account for approximately 42 percent of the College's graduate enrollment, and part-time students comprise the remaining 58 percent. Approximately 70 percent of the graduate students are women; 15 percent are members of minority groups; and 4 percent are international students from thirty-one nations.

Student Outcomes

Graduates of the College of Education are employed in a variety of settings, including universities, four- and two-year colleges, K–12 schools and school systems, central offices of school systems, business, and industry. A number of alumni of the College are recipients of outstanding teaching and leadership awards.

Location

USF is a multicampus university with its main campus in Tampa, Florida, and its three regional campuses in Sarasota, St. Petersburg, and Lakeland. Located in the vibrant Tampa Bay area on the west coast of Florida, it is in one of the fastest-growing metropolitan areas of the nation. It is easily accessible to the waters of the Gulf of Mexico and Tampa Bay and within a 90- minute drive of the Orlando area. The region thrives with its variety of cultural and sports activities.

The University and The College

The University of South Florida, founded in 1956, is a multicampus, comprehensive research university and is strongly committed to the balanced pursuit of teaching, research, and service. The thirteenth-largest university in the nation, it comprises ten colleges on four campuses and is home to a medical school, a major mental health research institute, and four public broadcasting stations. The College of Education, the largest in the Southeast, has a student enrollment of approximately 5,000 and is accredited by the National Council for Accreditation of Teacher Education (NCATE).

Applying

A completed graduate application form, GRE General Test scores, and official transcripts from all institutions of higher education attended are required. Individual departments may have additional requirements. Applicants whose native language is not English are required to submit scores from the Test of English as a Foreign Language (TOEFL). Application forms may be obtained from the Office of Graduate Admissions at the address below. Completed applications are due no later than June 1 (for fall semester), October 15 (for spring semester), and March 2 (for summer semester). Some programs may have earlier application deadlines. Applications for graduate assistantships should be made directly to the department in which the student's program is housed.

Correspondence and Information

Coordinator of Graduate Studies
Office of Student Academic Services, EDU 106
University of South Florida
Tampa, Florida 33620-5650
Telephone: 813-974-3406
Fax: 813-974-3391
E-mail: briscoe@tempest.coedu.usf.edu
World Wide Web: http://www.coedu.usf.edu

Office of Graduate Admissions
University of South Florida
4202 Fowler Avenue—FAO 100 N
Tampa, Florida 33620

University of South Florida

THE FACULTY

Anchin Center. Katherine M. Borman, Professor; Ph.D., Minnesota, 1976.

Childhood/Language Arts/Reading Education. Nancy Anderson, Associate Professor; Ed.D., Southern Mississippi, 1982. Mary Alice Barksdale-Ladd, Associate Professor; Ed.D., Virginia Tech, 1988. Roger Brindley, Assistant Professor; Ed.D., Georgia, 1996. Barbara K. Clarke, Professor; Ph.D., Florida State, 1977. Josue Cruz, Professor; Ph.D., Wisconsin–Madison, 1973. Pamela Fleege, Assistant Professor; Ph.D., LSU, 1990. Barbara J. Frye, Associate Professor; Ph.D., Minnesota, 1990. Stephen Graves, Professor; Ph.D., South Carolina, 1986. Priscilla L. Griffith, Associate Professor; Ph.D., Texas at Austin, 1986. Patricia E. Hanley, Associate Professor; Ph.D., Florida, 1976. Martha M. Harrison, Associate Professor; M.S., Memphis, 1992. Bena R. Hefflin, Assistant Professor; Ed.D., Pittsburgh, 1996. Sonia D. Helton, Professor; Ph.D., Minnesota, 1976. Margaret A. Hewitt, Assistant Professor; Ed.D., South Florida, 1989. Susan P. Homan, Professor; Ph.D., Florida, 1978. James R. King, Associate Professor; Ed.D., West Virginia, 1980. Janell P. Klesius, Professor; Ph.D., Florida State, 1980. Stephen J. Micklo, Associate Professor; Ph.D., Florida State, 1991. Kathleen A. Oropallo, Assistant Professor; Ph.D., Florida State, 1994. Marguerite Radencich, Associate Professor; Ph.D., Miami (Florida), 1983. Nancy Ratcliff, Assistant Professor; Ph.D., Indiana State, 1991. Jenifer J. Schneider, Assistant Professor; Ph.D., Ohio State, 1996. Marjorie J. Wynn, Associate Professor; Ph.D., South Florida, 1986.

Educational Measurement/Research. Madhabi Banerji, Assistant Professor; Ph.D., South Florida, 1990. Lou M. Carey, Professor; Ph.D., Florida State, 1976. Robert F. Dedrick, Associate Professor; Ph.D., Michigan, 1988. John M. Ferron, Assistant Professor; Ph.D., North Carolina at Chapel Hill, 1993. Bruce W. Hall, Professor; Ed.D., Florida State, 1969. Constance V. Hines, Professor; Ph.D., Ohio State, 1981. William G. Katzenmeyer, Professor; Ed.D., Duke, 1962. Jeffrey D. Kromrey, Associate Professor; Ph.D., South Florida, 1989. William S. Lang, Associate Professor; Ph.D., Georgia, 1984. Susan Maller, Assistant Professor; Ph.D., Arizona, 1994. Douglas Stone, Professor; Ph.D., Chicago, 1962.

Leadership Development. William F. Benjamin, Professor; Ph.D., George Peabody, 1961. William E. Blank, Professor; Ph.D., Florida State, 1976. Joseph C. Bondi Jr., Professor; Ed.D., Florida, 1968. Charles W. Gagel, Assistant Professor; Ph.D., Minnesota, 1995. Waynne B. James, Professor; Ed.D., Tennessee, 1976. Steven B. Permuth, Professor; Ed.D., Minnesota, 1973. Daniel M. Purdom, Professor; Ed.D., UCLA, 1967. Janet Scaglione, Associate Professor; Ph.D., South Florida, 1990. Arthur S. Shapiro, Professor; Ph.D., Chicago, 1965. Karolyn J. Snyder, Professor; Ed.D., Texas Tech, 1977. Lester W. Tuttle, Professor; Ed.D., Florida, 1962. Jon W. Wiles, Professor; Ed.D., Florida, 1972.

School of Physical Education, Wellness, and Sport Studies. Candi D. Ashley, Assistant Professor; Ph.D., LSU, 1964. Louis E. Bowers, Distinguished Service Professor; Ph.D., LSU, 1964. Peter J. Ellery, Assistant Professor; Ph.D., Ohio State, 1991. Nell Faucette, Professor; Ed.D., Georgia, 1984. James W. Rauschenbach, Assistant Professor; Ph.D., Ohio State, 1992.

Psychological and Social Foundations. Donna J. Anderson, Associate Professor; Ph.D., South Florida, 1984. James Barnard, Professor; Ph.D., Yale, 1963. George M. Batsche Jr., Professor; Ed.D., Ball State, 1978. Darrel E. Bostow, Professor; Ph.D., Southern Illinois, 1970. Kathy L. Bradley-Klug, Assistant Professor; Ph.D., Lehigh, 1996. Debra J. Chandler, Assistant Professor; Ph.D., UCLA, 1997. Deirdre L. Cobb-Roberts, Assistant Professor; Ph.D., Illinois at Urbana-Champaign, 1998. Michael Curtis, Professor; Ph.D., Texas at Austin, 1974. Sherman J. Dorn, Assistant Professor; Ph.D., Pennsylvania, 1992. Timothy D. Evans, Associate Professor; Ph.D., Georgia, 1984. John C. Follman, Professor; Ph.D., Indiana, 1969. O. Glenn Geiger, Professor; Ph.D., South Carolina, 1968. Erwin V. Johanningmeier, Professor; Ph.D., Illinois, 1967. M. E. Kimmel, Distinguished Service Professor; Ph.D., Florida, 1965. Howard M. Knoff, Professor; Ph.D., Syracuse, 1980. Elisabeth L. McFalls, Assistant Professor; Ph.D., Georgia, 1997. Christine A. Ogren, Assistant Professor; Ph.D., Wisconsin, 1996. Edward E. Panther, Professor; Ed.D., SUNY at Buffalo, 1969. Kelly A. Powell-Smith, Assistant Professor; Ph.D., Oregon, 1993. Linda M. Raffaele, Assistant Professor; Ph.D., Texas at Austin, 1993. Theresa M. Richardson, Assistant Professor; Ph.D., British Columbia, 1990. Marian S. Street, Associate Professor; Ph.D., Florida, 1980.

Secondary Education. Jane Applegate, Professor; Ph.D., Ohio State, 1978. Richard A. Austin, Associate Professor; Ph.D., Florida, 1983. Ann Barron, Associate Professor; Ed.D., Central Florida, 1991. Frank D. Breit, Associate Professor; Texas at Austin, 1968. Michaele F. Chappell, Associate Professor; Ph.D., Florida State, 1991. Barbara C. Cruz, Associate Professor; Ed.D., Florida International, 1990. Patricia L. Daniel, Assistant Professor; Ph.D., Oklahoma, 1991. James A. Duplass, Professor; Ph.D., Saint Louis, 1974. Carine M. Feyten, Associate Professor; Ph.D., South Florida, 1988. Jeffrey N. Golub, Associate Professor; Ph.D., Washington (Seattle), 1983. J. Howard Johnston, Professor; Ph.D., Wyoming, 1974. Joan F. Kaywell, Associate Professor; Ph.D., Florida, 1987. Joyce W. Nutta, Assistant Professor; Ph.D., South Florida, 1996. Fred L. Prince, Associate Professor; Ed.D., Houston, 1971. Dick J. Puglisi, Professor; Ph.D., Georgia State, 1973. Sandra L. Schurr, Associate Professor; Ph.D., Nova, 1985. Barbara Spector, Professor; Ph.D., Syracuse, 1977. H. Edwin Steiner, Professor; Ph.D., Texas at Austin, 1970. Denisse R. Thompson, Associate Professor; Ph.D., Chicago, 1992. James A. White, Associate Professor; Ph.D., South Florida, 1989. Dana L. Zeidler, Associate Professor; Ph.D., Syracuse, 1982.

Special Education. Neal H. Berger, Assistant Professor; Ph.D., Florida State, 1984. Ann M. Cranston-Gingras, Associate Professor; Ph.D., South Florida, 1987. Albert J. Duchnowski, Professor; Ph.D., Vanderbilt, 1969. Betty C. Epanchin, Professor; Ed.D., Duke, 1975. Eleanor C. Guetzloe, Professor; Ed.D., Florida, 1975. Deborah M. Harris, Associate Professor; Ph.D., North Carolina at Chapel Hill, 1985. Carolyn D. Lavely, Professor; Ph.D., Syracuse, 1967. Kofi Marfo, Professor; Ph.D., Alberta, 1985. August J. Mauser, Professor; Ed.D., Indiana, 1968. James L. Paul, Professor; Ed.D., Syracuse, 1967. Terry L. Rose, Professor; Ph.D., Florida, 1977. Hilda C. Rosselli, Associate Professor; Ph.D., South Florida, 1989. Surendra P. Singh, Professor; Ed.D., UCLA, 1967. H. Allan Sproles, Associate Professor; Ed.D., Georgia, 1973. Kim Stoddard, Associate Professor; Ph.D., Florida, 1988. Daphne L. Thomas, Associate Professor; Ph.D., North Carolina at Chapel Hill, 1989. Brenda L Townsend, Associate Professor; Ph.D., Kansas, 1991.

UNIVERSITY OF VIRGINIA

Curry School of Education

Programs of Study

The Curry School of Education offers graduate programs leading to Master of Education, Master of Teaching, Education Specialist, Doctor of Education, and Doctor of Philosophy degrees.

There are three clusters of curricular emphases within the School. The Department of Curriculum, Instruction, and Special Education provides programs in the development and delivery of instruction in schools and specialized educational institutions. It offers specializations in curriculum, elementary education, instruction, reading, special education, and secondary teaching specializations in English, foreign languages, math, science, and social studies. The Department of Education Leadership, Foundations, and Policy houses programs in higher education, policy studies, school administration, school supervision, educational psychology, psychology and education of the gifted, educational research, methodology and statistics, educational evaluation, instructional technology, and foundations of education–historical, philosophical, and social. Students wishing to prepare for leadership roles in the nation's schools, colleges, universities, and governmental or research agencies pursue degrees in this department. The Department of Human Services provides programs related to clinical service in both the physical and psychological domains, including clinical psychology, communication disorders, counselor education, and physical education (including adapted physical education, athletic training, exercise physiology, motor learning, sport and exercise psychology, and sports medicine).

Programs of study differ widely. Master of Education degrees require 30–48 hours and generally include a thesis or comprehensive examination; Master of Teaching degrees require full-time study and an extensive internship in a school setting. Both the Ed.D. and Ph.D. require satisfactory performance on examinations in a major field, in two areas of minor concentration (for the Ed.D. only), and a dissertation. The Ph.D. candidate must also demonstrate competence in specific qualitative and quantitative research skills, while Ed.D. candidates must complete a practicum.

Research Facilities

The Curry School provides outstanding research and clinical facilities for its students and provides service to the Commonwealth of Virginia and the nation. There are a wide variety of laboratories and field experiences available to support educational endeavors, including an acclaimed library of more than 150,000 volumes and 400,000 ERIC microfiche titles as well as optical disc databased systems that provide access to materials from throughout the world. There are thirteen centers, including the Center for Technology and Teacher Education, the Educational Technology Center, the McGuffey Reading Center, the Evaluation Research Center, the Center for the Study of Higher Education, the Speech-Language-Hearing Center, the Center for the Improvement of Early Reading Achievement, the Center for Minority Research on Special Education, the National Research Center on the Gifted and Talented, the Virginia Center for Educational Policy Studies, the Center for Clinical Psychology Services, the Center for Personal and Career Development, and the Thomas Jefferson Center for Educational Design. In addition, there are six laboratories, including Adapted Physical Education, Athletic Training and Sports Medicine, Cardiac Health and Fitness, Communication Disorders, Sport and Exercise Psychology, and the Instructional Technology Laboratory.

Financial Aid

Students may be eligible to apply for a fellowship and/or assistantship. In 1998, stipends range from $1000 to $18,000, depending on academic qualifications, need, and the availability of funds. Loans and part-time employment are also available. Funds are available through the University's Office of Financial Aid and through individual departments in the Curry School. Those interested should contact these areas directly.

Cost of Study

Tuition and required fees, including activity fees for full-time students, are $4786 per year for Virginia residents in 1998–99. The annual cost for out-of-state students is approximately $15,500. Books and supplies cost between $600 and $900 for the nine-month session.

Living and Housing Costs

Dormitory accommodation rates for single students average $2200 for a nine-month session. Married student housing costs range from $425 per month for a one-bedroom unfurnished apartment to $505 per month for a furnished three-bedroom apartment. Estimated food expenses are $1800 for a nine-month session.

Student Group

The University of Virginia is a medium-sized, state-supported, coeducational university. Its enrollment consists of about 12,000 undergraduate students and 6,300 graduate students. Women constitute 51 percent of the enrollment. Sixty-one percent of the students are residents of Virginia. The Curry School of Education has approximately 1,000 graduate students and 300 undergraduates.

Location

Charlottesville has a population of about 41,000, with 72,000 in the surrounding county. Many nearby places of historic interest provide hours of rewarding sightseeing and touring. Recreational facilities include those for swimming, fishing, hunting, and skiing in the surrounding countryside; the camping facilities along the Blue Ridge Parkway, Skyline Drive, and Appalachian Trail are available free or at nominal cost. The climate is warm during the spring, summer, and fall (average 74°), but winters are cool (average 37°). The athletic, cultural, and recreational opportunities of the area are diverse and available to all. Richmond, the state capital, is within a 1-hour drive, and Washington, D.C., is approximately 100 miles away.

The University and The School

The University of Virginia was founded by Thomas Jefferson in 1819. The University's central purpose is to enrich the human mind by stimulating and sustaining a spirit of free inquiry. The focal point of the University today is the central area of the Rotunda, the Lawn, and the Pavilions originally designed by Thomas Jefferson.

The Curry School of Education was ranked nineteenth in the nation as part of the *U.S. Business and World Report* (1998), with the University of Virginia ranked as the number-one public institution. It offers outstanding programs in more than twenty specialization areas and has a nationally renowned teacher education program. Classes in the Curry School of Education are moderate in size and are conducted in a stimulating modern atmosphere. Computer facilities are available in every area.

Applying

Deadline for receipt of all application materials for most programs is March 1 for fall semester admission; November 15 for spring semester admission; and March 1 for summer term admission. Exceptions are January 15 for fall semester and summer term admission to School/Clinical Child Psychology. There is no spring semester admission to the School/Clinical Child Psychology, Communication Disorders, Counselor Education, or Master of Teaching programs.

Applicants must have earned a grade average of B or better during the last two years of undergraduate work and must provide an official report of results on the Graduate Record Examinations, a statement of goals, and two letters of recommendation. International students must submit acceptable TOEFL scores (at least 600). A $40 fee must accompany the application. Soon after the application is complete, the applicant is notified of the action taken on the application. Application for financial aid should be made before March 1 for the following year.

Correspondence and Information

Office of Admissions and Student Affairs
Curry School of Education
104 Ruffner Hall
405 Emmet Street South
University of Virginia
Charlottesville, Virginia 22903-2495

Telephone: 804-924-3334
Fax: 804-924-0747
E-mail: sgs9w@virginia.edu
World Wide Web: http://curry.edschool.virginia.edu/

University of Virginia

THE FACULTY

Dean: David W. Breneman.
Associate Dean for Administration: Robert H. Pate Jr.
Associate Dean for Academic Affairs: Rebecca D. Kneedler
Assistant Dean for Admissions and Student Affairs: Spencer G. Niles

Curriculum, Instruction, and Special Education: Daniel P. Hallahan, Chair.
Mary P. Abouzeid, Associate Professor; Ph.D., Virginia. Clifford T. Bennett, Associate Professor; D.Ed., Penn State. Frederick J. Brigham, Assistant Professor; Ph.D., Purdue. Sandra B. Colnen, Associate Professor; Ph.D., Georgia State. Ronald E. Comfort, Associate Professor; Ed.D., Florida. James M. Cooper, Professor; Ph.D., Stanford. Peter A. Dewitz, Professor; Ph.D., UCLA. Thomas H. Estes, Professor; Ph.D., Syracuse. Margo A. Figgins, Associate Professor; Ed.D., Virginia. Joe Garofalo, Associate Professor; Ph.D., Indiana. Daniel P. Hallahan, Professor; Ph.D., Michigan. Joanne E. Herbert, Associate Professor; Ph.D., Virginia. E. D. Hirsch, Professor; Ph.D., Yale. Marcia Invernizzi, Associate Professor; Ph.D., Virginia. Connie Juel, Professor; Ph.D., Stanford. James M. Kauffman, Professor; Ed.D., Kansas. Rebecca D. Kneedler, Associate Professor; Ed.D., Virginia. John W. Lloyd, Professor; Ph.D., Oregon. Cheryl L. Mason, Assistant Professor; Ph.D., North Carolina State. Juanita J. Matkins, Assistant Professor; Ed.D., Virginia. Jerry R. Moore, Professor; Ph.D., Iowa. Stephen R. Plaskon, Associate Professor; Ph.D., Connecticut. Laura B. Smolkin, Assistant Professor; Ed.D., Houston. Martha E. Snell, Professor; Ph.D., Michigan State. Joseph E. Strzepek, Associate Professor; Ph.D., Stanford. Ertle Thompson, Professor; Ed.D., Virginia. Maria A. Timmerman, Acting Assistant Professor; Ph.D., Penn State. Stanley C. Trent, Assistant Professor; Ph.D., Virginia. Dororthy Vasquez-Levy, Assistant Professor; Ph.D., Arizona.

Human Services: Luke Kelly, Chair.

Clinical and School Psychology: Richard A. Abidin, Professor; Ed.D., Rutgers. Dewey G. Cornell, Associate Professor; Ph.D., Michigan. Ann B. Loper, Associate Professor; Ph.D., Texas. Robert C. Pianta, Professor; Ph.D., Minnesota. Ronald E. Reeve, Professor; Ph.D., Michigan. Peter L. Sheras, Associate Professor; Ph.D., Princeton. Antoinette Thomas, Assistant Professor; Ph.D., North Carolina.

Communication Disorders: Susan D. Dalebout, Assistant Professor; Ph.D., Ohio State. Aliaa A. Khidr, Assistant Professor; Ph.D., Ain Shams (Egypt). Robert E. Novak, Associate Professor; Ph.D., Iowa. Randall R. Robey, Assistant Professor; Ph.D., Ohio. Zahrl G. Schoeny, Associate Professor; Ph.D., Northwestern. Janet W. Stack, Assistant Professor; Ph.D., South Florida. Linda K. Swank, Assistant Professor; Ph.D., Kansas.

Counselor Education: Joan C. Franks, Associate Professor; Ph.D., Wayne State. N. Kenneth LaFleur, Associate Professor; Ph.D., Michigan State. Courtland C. Lee, Professor; Ph.D., Michigan State. Kathleen May, Associate Professor; Ph.D., Florida. Spencer G. Niles, Associate Professor; D.Ed., Penn State. Robert H. Pate Jr., Professor; Ph.D., North Carolina. Kenneth W. Simington, Assistant Professor; Ph.D., North Carolina at Greensboro. Claudia J. Sowa, Associate Professor; Ph.D., Michigan State.

Health and Physical Education: Brent L. Arnold, Assistant Professor; Ph.D., Virginia. Martin E. Block, Associate Professor; Ph.D., Maryland. B. Ann Boyce, Associate Professor; Ph.D., Florida State. Linda K. Bunker, Professor; Ph.D., Illinois. Glenn A. Gaesser, Associate Professor; Ph.D., Berkeley. Luke E. Kelly, Associate Professor; Ph.D., Texas Woman's. David H. Perrin, Professor; Ph.D., Pittsburgh. Maureen A. Weiss, Professor; Ph.D., Michigan State. Arthur L. Weltman, Professor; Ph.D., Michigan. Diane E. Whaley, Assistant Professor; Ph.D., Oregon State.

Leadership, Foundations, and Policy: Harold J. Burbach, Chair.
Donald W. Ball, Associate Professor; Ed.D., Kansas. Eric R. Bredo, Associate Professor; Ph.D., Stanford. David W. Breneman, Professor; Ph.D., Berkeley. Glen L. Bull, Associate Professor; Ph.D., Ohio State. John B. Bunch, Associate Professor; Ph.D., Indiana. Harold J. Burbach, Professor; Ph.D., SUNY at Buffalo. Alfred R. Butler IV, Associate Professor; Ed.D., Virginia. Michael S. Caldwell, Associate Professor; Ph.D., Ohio State. Carolyn M. Callahan, Professor; Ph.D., Connecticut. R. Lynn Canady, Professor; Ed.D., Tennessee. Jay L. Chronister, Professor; Ed.D., Pittsburgh. Robert W. Covert, Associate Professor; Ph.D., Temple. Daniel L. Duke, Professor; Ed.D., SUNY at Albany. James P. Esposito, Associate Professor; Ph.D., Florida State. Bruce M. Gansneder, Professor; Ph.D., Ohio State. Annette Gibbs, Professor; Ph.D., Florida State. Margaret M. Grogan, Assistant Professor; Ph.D., Washington State. Walter F. Heinecke, Assistant Professor; Ph.D., Arizona State. Frederick M. Hess, Assistant Professor; Ph.D., Harvard. Diane M. Hoffman, Assistant Professor; Ph.D., Stanford. Samuel E. Kellams, Associate Professor; Ph.D., Wisconsin–Madison. Mable B. Kinzie, Associate Professor; Ph.D., Arizona State. Timothy R. Konold, Assistant Professor; Ph.D., Delaware. Robert F. McNergney, Professor; Ph.D., Syracuse. Tonya Moon, Assistant Professor; Ph.D., Virginia. Herbert C. Richards, Professor; Ph.D., Emory. John A. Sanderson, Associate Professor; Ed.D., Indiana. Jerry G. Short, Professor; Ph.D., Houston. Harold R. Strang, Professor; Ph.D., Kansas. Valerie O. Sutter, Associate Professor; Ph.D., Virginia. Alton L. Taylor, Professor; Ed.D., Virginia. Carol A. Tomlinson, Associate Professor; Ed.D., Virginia. Pamela D. Tucker, Assistant Professor; Ed.D., William and Mary. Sarah E. Turner, Assistant Professor; Ph.D., Michigan. Deborah A. Verstegen, Associate Professor; Ph.D., Wisconsin–Madison. Jennings L. Wagoner, Professor; Ph.D., Ohio State. Carol Camp Yeakey, Professor; Ph.D., Northwestern.

UNIVERSITY OF WISCONSIN–MADISON

School of Education

Programs of Study

The School of Education comprises diverse departments related to pedagogy, schooling, human development, psychological sciences, and learning across the life span. It also includes departments associated with the visual arts, dance, human movement, and occupational therapy. The School of Education offers the Master of Arts, Master of Fine Arts, Master of Science, and Doctor of Philosophy degrees, as well as Educational Specialist certificates.

Programs are available in the following areas: art (two-dimensional art, three-dimensional art, graphics, art education), continuing and vocational education (adult education), counseling psychology (school counseling, counseling in community/agency settings, counseling in higher education settings, counseling psychology), curriculum and instruction (art education, bilingual/bicultural education, computer education, curriculum theory and research, early childhood education, educational communications and technology, elementary education, English/language arts education, foreign language education, health education, instructional theory, mathematics education, multicultural education, music education, nursing education, reading education, science education, social studies education, teacher education), educational administration (educational administration—elementary, middle, and secondary; higher, postsecondary, and vocational education; professional administrative certifications), educational policy studies (comparative and international education, history of education, philosophy of education, public policy and educational institutions, social sciences of education), educational psychology (cognitive science applied to education; human development; quantitative methods; school psychology), kinesiology (exercise physiology, biomechanics, measurement, motor control and behavior, sport psychology, occupational therapy), and rehabilitation psychology and special education (behavioral/emotional disabilities, intellectual disabilities, learning disabilities, rehabilitational counseling, rehabilitation psychology).

Research Facilities

The University of Wisconsin–Madison has one of the largest research library systems in the country, with total holdings of more than 6 million volumes. The School of Education's Instructional Materials Center (IMC), which has a collection of 57,300 items, is a special library of educational resources and services related primarily to teacher education and preparation. Also available in the IMC is the ERIC CD-ROM database, which provides access to 400,000 documents and to articles in more than 750 journals. The Cooperative Children's Book Center is a nationally unique noncirculating library of children's and young adult literature. Special research facilities of particular value to students in the School of Education include the Center on Education and Work, the Wisconsin Center for Education Research, the Waisman Center on Mental Retardation and Human Development, the Biodynamics Laboratory, and the Educational and Psychological Training Center.

Financial Aid

Graduate fellowships, scholarships, teaching assistantships, research or project assistantships, and loans are available to students. Many financial awards reduce tuition. Prospective students should contact individual departments to learn about opportunities for financial aid.

Cost of Study

The tuition and fee rates for 1997–98 were $2346 per semester for a full-time Wisconsin resident and $7197 per semester for a full-time nonresident.

Living and Housing Costs

The 1997–98 rates for University graduate housing were between $2118 and $3153 per academic year for a single room and $2015 per person per year for a double room. A limited number of University apartments are available for single graduate students; 1997–98 rates were $4233 per academic year for a one-bedroom apartment and $3053 yearly per person for a two-bedroom apartment. The 1998–99 University apartment rates for graduate students and their families range in cost from $380 per month for a one-bedroom apartment to $810 per month for a three-bedroom townhouse. Shared off-campus apartment costs average $250–$450 monthly per person.

Student Group

The graduate enrollment of the School of Education is 1,168. The campus enrollment is 37,500, including 8,200 graduate students. Graduate students come from all areas of the United States and from many other countries.

Student Outcomes

UW–Madison graduates with advanced degrees find positions throughout the world as college and university professors, elementary and secondary school teachers, and educational administrators at all levels. Graduates also find positions as counselors and researchers in local, state, federal, and private agencies; postdoctoral fellows; and self-employed educational professionals.

Location

The University is situated near the center of Madison, the state capital, with an approximate population of 201,000. Consistently ranked among the nation's "most livable" cities, Madison is located 146 miles from Chicago, 77 miles from Milwaukee, and 258 miles from Minneapolis/St. Paul.

The University and The School

In the course of its 148-year history, the University of Wisconsin–Madison has become one of the major centers of graduate study in the United States, with a significant enrollment of international students. It is a comprehensive university with nationally recognized research and graduate programs in the arts, sciences, and humanities, as well as professional schools of law, medicine, education, business, pharmacy, nursing, veterinary medicine, and engineering. There are 143 tenure-track faculty members in the School of Education.

Applying

Applicants should write to the department in which they are interested for an application form and information about deadlines. Application materials must be submitted to both the department and the Graduate School. All credentials must be in the Graduate School Office at least six weeks before the student plans to start graduate work; the department may have an earlier deadline. Students admitted with full graduate standing must satisfy the requirements of the department and have a bachelor's degree from an approved (accredited) institution, an appropriate background for entering the proposed field, and a minimum undergraduate grade point average (GPA) of at least 3.0 (on a 4.0 scale) for the equivalent of the last 60 semester hours (approximately two years of work). There is a $45 Graduate School application fee. The application for most forms of financial aid should be made through departmental offices by January 1.

Correspondence and Information

There is no centralized graduate admissions office in the School of Education. Applicants should write directly to the appropriate department office using the building and street address indicated in parentheses with the general address given below: Art (6241 Humanities Building, 455 North Park Street), Continuing and Vocational Education (126 Lathrop Hall, 1050 University Avenue), Counseling Psychology (321 Education Building, 1000 Bascom Mall), Curriculum and Instruction (210 Teacher Education, 225 North Mills Street), Educational Administration (1152 Educational Sciences, 1025 West Johnson Street), Educational Policy Studies (221 Education Building, 1000 Bascom Mall), Educational Psychology (880 Educational Sciences, 1025 West Johnson Street), Kinesiology (2001 Gymnasium Unit II, 2000 Observatory Drive), and Rehabilitation Psychology and Special Education (432 North Murray Street).

Department of (specify)
University of Wisconsin–Madison
(specify street address)
Madison, Wisconsin 53706

University of Wisconsin–Madison

THE FACULTY

ART

David Becker, Bruce Breckenridge, Derrick Buisch, Laurie Beth Clark, George Cramer, Jack Damer, Jim Escalante, Patricia Fennell, Fred Fenster, Steven Feren, Michelle Grabner, Philip Hamilton, Cavalliere Ketchum, Thomas Loeser, Richard Long, Truman Lowe, Theresa Marché, Douglas Marschalek, Eleanor Moty, Frances Myers, Leslee Nelson, Edward Pope, Carol Pylant, Daniel Ramirez, John Rieben, Elaine Scheer, T. L. Solien, William Weege.

CONTINUING AND VOCATIONAL EDUCATION (STANDING COMMITTEE DEGREE PROGRAM)

Mark Albanese, Lin Compton, Chère Gibson, Terry Gibson, Craig Gjerde, Elisabeth Hayes, Alan Knox, Patrick McBride, Allen Phelps, Robert Ray, Boyd Rossing, Stephanie Smith, Wendy Way, Darlene Weingand.

COUNSELING PSYCHOLOGY

Angela Byars, Hardin Coleman, Alberta Gloria, Elizabeth Holloway, Michael Karcher, Stephen Quintana, Bruce Wampold, Patricia Wolleat.

CURRICULUM AND INSTRUCTION

Michael Apple, Anthony Barresi, Marianne Bloch, Thomas Carpenter, Ann De Vaney, Joel Dworin, Ann Egan-Robertson, Elizabeth Ellsworth, Renée Fountain, James Gee, Mary Gomez, Carl Grant, Elizabeth Graue, John Harvey, Margaret Hawkins, Peter Hewson, Charles James, John Kean, Julia Koza, Gloria Ladson-Billings, Alan Lockwood, Susan McMahon, Fred Newmann, Gerald Olson, Thomas Popkewitz, Gary Price, Charles Read, Alberto Rodriguez, Thomas Romberg, Walter Secada, James Stewart, Michael Streibel, William Tate, Alice Udvari-Solner, Mariamne Whatley, Kenneth Zeichner.

DANCE

Sally Banes, Mary Brennan, Joseph Koykkar, Li Chiao-Ping, Claudia Melrose, Douglas Rosenberg, James Sutton, Jin-Wen Yu.

EDUCATIONAL ADMINISTRATION

Dean Bowles, Paul Bredeson, Cryss Brunner, Colleen Capper, Clifton Conrad, Lloyd Frohreich, Christine Golde, Carolyn Kelley, Allan Odden, Kent Peterson, Allen Phelps, Jacob Stampen.

EDUCATIONAL POLICY STUDIES

Michael Apple, Michael Fultz, Andreas Kazamias, Stacey Lee, Mary Haywood Metz, Jennifer O'Day, Michael Olneck, Daniel Pekarsky, William Reese, Francis Schrag, Amy Stambach.

EDUCATIONAL PSYCHOLOGY

Leonard Abbeduto, Jeffery Braden, Bradford Brown, Sharon Derry, Stephen Elliott, Robert Enright, Maribeth Gettinger, Charles Kalish, Thomas Kratochwill, Richard Lehrer, Joel Levin, David Penner, Andrew Porter, Leona Schauble, Ronald Serlin, Michael Subkoviak, Deborah Vandell.

KINESIOLOGY

Gregory Cartee, Robert Christiaansen, Gary Diffee, Kreg Gruben, Betty Hasselkus, Essie Jacobs, Li Li Ji, Michael Kane, Kelli Koltyn, Gary Kraemer, Jo-Anne Lazarus, William Morgan, Mary Schneider, Peter van Kan.

REHABILITATION PSYCHOLOGY AND SPECIAL EDUCATION

Norman Berven, Brian Bottge, Louis Brown, Fong Chan, Anne Donnellan, Cheryl Hanley-Maxwell, Ruth Torkelson Lynch, Edna Mora Szymanski, Sara Tarver, Kenneth Thomas, Alice Udvari-Solner, Clark Wambold.

Lying along the shores of Lake Mendota, the UW-Madison campus covers 919 acres and has two student unions, three museums, numerous research centers, and twenty-four libraries.

This scenic view of the campus looks eastward toward Madison's downtown isthmus and its surrounding lakes.

VANDERBILT UNIVERSITY

Peabody College

Programs of Study

Peabody College, the school of education and human development of Vanderbilt University, offers programs leading to the Master of Education and Doctor of Education degrees. The Vanderbilt Graduate School, through Peabody departments, offers the Master of Arts in Teaching, Master of Science, and Doctor of Philosophy degrees. Peabody is committed to preparing students who will become research scholars or innovative practitioners in the field of education and human development. Students may attend full- or part-time. Weekend courses are offered in several programs for working professionals who want to earn an advanced degree.

Students may major in counseling, curriculum and instructional leadership, early childhood education, elementary education, general administrative leadership, higher education administration (including specializations in administration, college student personnel services, and institutional advancement), health promotion and education, human resource development, language and literacy education, policy development and program evaluation, psychology (including specializations in clinical psychology, cognitive studies, community psychology, developmental psychology, and quantitative methods), reading education, school administration (elementary or secondary), secondary education, special education (including specializations in early childhood, mild-to-moderate handicaps, multiple and severe handicaps, and visual impairment), and the teaching of English, foreign languages, mathematics, science, and social studies. Teacher education and advanced certification programs of Peabody College are approved by the National Council for Accreditation of Teacher Education (NCATE). The programs in psychology and counseling are accredited by the appropriate accrediting agencies as well.

Research Facilities

In addition to the Vanderbilt University Library, which has more than 2 million volumes, excellent research facilities are available through the John F. Kennedy Center for Research on Education and Human Development and the Vanderbilt Institute for Public Policy Studies. Other research facilities include the Program Evaluation Laboratory, Family and Child Study Center, Microcomputer Laboratory, and Learning Technology Center. The many field sites available for research include hospitals, the Metropolitan Nashville Public School System, rehabilitation centers, schools for the handicapped, government agencies, corporations, and day-care centers.

Financial Aid

More than 60 percent of new students at Peabody College receive financial aid. The College sponsors several substantial scholarship programs with offerings that range from partial to full tuition, including several especially designated for outstanding students from minority groups. In addition, assistantships, traineeships, loans, and part-time employment are available. Awards are made annually, and every attempt is made to meet a student's financial need. Application for financial aid does not affect the admission decision.

Cost of Study

Tuition for study at Peabody College for the 1998–99 academic year is $650 per semester credit hour, and tuition for degrees offered through the Graduate School is $914 per semester credit hour. The cost of books and supplies averages about $750 for the nine-month session. Health insurance, fees, and personal living expenses are additional.

Living and Housing Costs

Vanderbilt's location in Nashville offers students the advantage of a wide variety of living choices. Costs for housing, food, and other expenses are moderate when compared with other metropolitan areas nationwide. A single student living on campus can expect to pay approximately $650 per month for room and board. Costs for married students or students living off campus will vary. Additional information on housing is available from the Office of Residential Affairs, Box 1677, Station B, Vanderbilt University, Nashville, Tennessee 37240.

Student Group

Vanderbilt University has a diverse student body of just under 10,000. Peabody College has an enrollment of approximately 1,500 students, of whom 675 are graduate students. Women make up about 70 percent and students from minority groups about 10 percent of Peabody's postbaccalaureate students. Students have a broad range of academic backgrounds and include recent graduates of baccalaureate programs as well as men and women who have many years of professional experience. The average age of entering students is in the early 30s.

Student Outcomes

Graduates who earn a master's or doctoral degree from Peabody College are prepared to work for educational, corporate, government, and service organizations in a variety of roles. More than 10,000 alumni are practicing teachers, more than 175 are school superintendents, and more than 30 are college or university presidents.

Location

Located halfway between the northern and southern boundaries of the nation, Nashville is a progressive southern city with a population of approximately 500,000. It is the capital of the state and the educational and cultural center of its region. Vanderbilt University is one of thirteen institutions of higher learning located in Nashville and the surrounding area, leading Nashville to be called the "Athens of the South." The city is particularly responsive to the needs of the academic community.

Nashville's involvement with music and publishing companies, business, industry, and education makes it a cosmopolitan city with excellent cultural and recreational opportunities, including two theater groups. There are more than 6,000 acres of public parks in the city, and the surrounding region of lakes and rolling hills is dotted with parks and recreation areas. Nashville is a popular vacation spot, hosting more than 8 million tourists annually.

The University and The College

Vanderbilt University, founded in 1873, is a private nondenominational institution with a strong tradition of graduate and professional education. Peabody College, recognized for more than a century as one of the nation's foremost independent colleges of teacher education, merged with Vanderbilt University in 1979. Peabody, the ninth school of Vanderbilt, focuses on the development of new knowledge in the field of education and human development and the application of that knowledge to societal problems.

Applying

Admission to professional degree programs is based on an evaluation of the applicant's potential for academic success and professional service, with consideration given to transcripts of previous course work, GRE General Test or MAT scores, letters of reference, and a letter outlining personal goals. Additional supporting credentials, such as a sample of the applicant's scholarly writing or a personal interview, may also be required. A nonrefundable $40 fee must accompany each application.

Applicants seeking admission and financial assistance are encouraged to complete the application process as early as possible. Applicants who apply late should realize that admission and financial assistance depend on the availability of space and funds in the department to which they are applying.

Correspondence and Information

Director of Admissions and Financial Assistance
Peabody College of Vanderbilt University
Peabody Station, Box 327
Nashville, Tennessee 37203

Telephone: 615-322-8410
Fax: 615-322-8401
E-mail: gpcadm@ctrvax.vanderbilt.edu

Vanderbilt University

THE FACULTY

Department of Educational Leadership
Jacob Adams, Assistant Professor; Ph.D., Stanford. Patricia Arnold, Lecturer; Ph.D., Vanderbilt. John Braxton, Associate Professor; D.Ed., Penn State. Bruce T. Caine, Assistant Professor of the Practice; Ph.D., Florida. Alma Clayton-Pederson, Assistant Professor of the Practice; Ph.D., Vanderbilt. R. Wilburn Clouse, Associate Professor; Ph.D., George Peabody. Robert L. Crowson, Professor; Ph.D., Chicago. Bonnie Daniel, Lecturer; Ed.D., Vanderbilt. Terrence E. Deal, Professor; Ph.D., Stanford. Linton Deck, Research Professor; Ed.D., Harvard. Janet Eyler, Associate Professor of the Practice; Ph.D., Indiana. Chester E. Finn Jr., Professor; Ed.D., Harvard. Kassie Freeman, Assistant Professor; Ph.D., Emory. Dwight E. Giles, Professor of the Practice; Ph.D., Pennsylvania. Ellen Goldring, Professor; Ph.D., Chicago. James W. Guthrie, Professor; Ph.D., Stanford. Philip Hallinger, Professor; Ed.D., Stanford. Berta Laden, Assistant Professor; Ph.D., Stanford. Johan A. Madson, Associate Professor of the Practice; Ph.D., Ohio. Dorothy Marcic, Senior Lecturer; Ed.D., Massachusetts. Edward A. Martin, Associate Professor of the Practice; M.S., Temple. John M. Maslyn, Assistant Professor; Ph.D., Georgia Tech. Joseph Murphy, Professor; Ph.D., Ohio State. Steven H. Smartt, Assistant Professor of the Practice; Ph.D., Florida State. Claire Smrekar, Associate Professor; Ph.D., Stanford. Mary Watson, Assistant Professor; Ph.D., Vanderbilt. Kent M. Weeks, Professor of the Practice; Ph.D., Case Western Reserve.

Department of Psychology and Human Development
Alfred A. Baumeister, Professor; Ph.D., George Peabody. Leonard Bickman, Professor; Ph.D., CUNY. Penelope Brooks, Professor; Ph.D., Minnesota. Vera Chatman, Professor of the Practice; Ph.D., George Peabody. David Cordray, Professor; Ph.D., Claremont. Gideon Deak, Assistant Professor; Ph.D., Minnesota. Kenneth A. Dodge, Professor; Ph.D., Duke. Paul R. Dokecki, Professor; Ph.D., George Peabody. Gina Frieden, Assistant Professor of the Practice; Ph.D., Memphis State. Judy Garber, Associate Professor; Ph.D., Minnesota. Susan R. Goldman, Professor; Ph.D., Pittsburgh. James H. Hogge, Professor; Ph.D., Texas. Kathleen Hoover-Dempsey, Associate Professor; Ph.D., Michigan State. Robert B. Innes, Associate Professor; Ph.D., Michigan. Mark Lipsey, Professor; Ph.D., Johns Hopkins. John R. Newbrough, Professor; Ph.D., Utah. Laura R. Novick, Assistant Professor; Ph.D., Stanford. James W. Pellegrino, Professor; Ph.D., Colorado. Richard L. Percy, Associate Professor; Ed.D., Virginia. Ellen Pinderhughes, Assistant Professor; Ph.D., Yale. Jeanne M. Plas, Associate Professor; Ph.D., Georgia. Richard H. Porter, Professor; Ph.D., Wayne State. John R. Rieser, Professor; Ph.D., Minnesota. Clifford Russell, Professor; Ph.D., Harvard. Howard M. Sandler, Professor; Ph.D., Northwestern. Daniel L. Schwartz, Assistant Professor; Ph.D., Columbia. Stephen Schilling, Assistant Professor; Ph.D., Chicago. Sharon L. Shields, Professor of the Practice; Ph.D., George Peabody. Craig A. Smith, Associate Professor; Ph.D., Stanford. Travis I. Thompson, Professor; Ph.D., Minnesota. Patti Van Eys, Assistant Professor of the Practice; Ph.D., Bowling Green State. Tedra Ann Walden, Professor; Ph.D., Florida. Bahr Weiss, Associate Professor; Ph.D., North Carolina.

Department of Special Education
Janice Baker, Assistant Professor; Ph.D., Pittsburgh. Anne L. Corn, Professor; Ed.D., Columbia. Joseph Cunningham, Associate Professor; Ed.D., Illinois. Laura B. Davis, Assistant Professor of the Practice; Ed.D., Vanderbilt. Susan De La Paz, Assistant Professor; Ph.D., Maryland. Douglas Fuchs, Professor; Ph.D., Minnesota. Lynn S. Fuchs, Professor; Ph.D., Minnesota. Ted S. Hasselbring, Professor; Ed.D., Indiana. Eva Horn, Assistant Professor; Ph.D., Vanderbilt. Carolyn Hughes, Associate Professor; Ph.D., Illinois at Urbana-Champaign. Ann Kaiser, Professor; Ph.D., Kansas. Craig Kennedy, Associate Professor; Ph.D., California, Santa Barbara. Dan Reschly, Professor; Ph.D., Oregon. Heraldo V. Richards, Senior Lecturer; Ph.D., Northwestern. Steven F. Warren, Professor; Ph.D., Kansas. Joseph H. Wehby, Senior Lecturer; Ph.D., Vanderbilt. Paul J. Yoder, Research Associate Professor; Ph.D, North Carolina.

Department of Teaching and Learning
Linda Barron, Research Associate Professor; Ph.D., Vanderbilt. Jerold P. Bauch, Professor Emeritus; Ed.D., Florida. David M. Bloome, Professor; Ph.D., Kent State. Paul A. Cobb, Professor; Ph.D., Georgia. Angelo Collins, Associate Professor; Ph.D., Wisconsin. Richard A. Duschl, Professor; Ph.D., Maryland College Park. Carolyn M. Evertson, Professor; Ph.D., Texas at Austin. Dale C. Farran, Professor; Ph.D., Bryn Mawr. Elizabeth Spencer Goldman, Associate Professor; Ph.D., Vanderbilt. Alene H. Harris, Research Assistant Professor; Ph.D., Vanderbilt. Clifford A. Hofwolt, Associate Professor; Ed.D., Northern Colorado. Laurie Katz, Lecturer; Ed.D., Massachusetts. Earline D. Kendall, Professor of the Practice Emerita; Ph.D., George Peabody. Charles K. Kinzer, Associate Professor; Ph.D., Berkeley. Xiadong Lin, Assistant Professor; Ph.D., Purdue. Kay J. McClain, Lecturer; Ed.D., Vanderbilt. Charles B. Myers, Professor; Ph.D., George Peabody. Ann M. Neely, Associate Professor of the Practice; Ed.D., Georgia. Jacqueline Palka, Assistant Professor of the Practice; Ed.D., LSU. Amy Palmeri, Lecturer in Education; Ph.D., Indiana Bloomington. Victoria J. Risko, Professor; Ed.D., West Virginia. Deborah W. Rowe, Associate Professor; Ph.D., Indiana. Robert D. Sherwood, Associate Professor; Ph.D., Indiana. Margaret W. Smithey, Senior Lecturer; Ph.D., Vanderbilt. Patrick Thompson, Professor; Ed.D., Georgia.

WAYNE STATE UNIVERSITY

College of Education

Programs of Study

Programs of study lead to the following degrees: M.A., M.A.T., M.Ed., Ed.D., Ph.D., and the Education Specialist Certificate. Programs are offered in elementary, secondary, and K–12 education. Secondary specializations include English education, foreign language education, mathematics education, science education, social studies education, and career and technical education. K–12 areas include special education, reading, art education, and health and physical education.

Graduate degrees are also offered in bilingual-bicultural education, early childhood education, instructional technology, administration and supervision, counseling, educational psychology, school and community psychology, evaluation and research, rehabilitation and community inclusion, recreation and park services, and sports administration.

Graduate programs are designed to prepare leaders in teaching, administration, curriculum, and research at all levels, extending beyond schools and universities to corporations seeking to expand education and training programs. College faculty are making significant contributions toward infusing instructional technology into the full range of instructional programs.

Research Facilities

Students have access not only to the vast library collections at Wayne State, but also to the collections of Michigan's two other research institutions through the interlibrary loan system that utilizes a state-of-the-art online cataloging system.

The College has three classrooms equipped with more than 100 networked Macintosh and IBM computers for instructional purposes. In addition, the College maintains an instructional technology laboratory, a video production studio, a distance education room, an adolescent research laboratory, and a counseling laboratory and houses a research support laboratory, all of which contain some of the most advanced hardware and software available.

The College also operates a full-day early childhood center (toddlers to 4-year-olds) as part of the teacher education program, which offers a wide range of training and research opportunities.

Financial Aid

The University provides a range of graduate scholarships and fellowships to outstanding students. Some of these, such as the Rumble Fellowship, cover tuition, books, and housing, with an additional stipend for living expenses. The College also provides several graduate tuition scholarships annually.

Cost of Study

The 1998–99 tuition ranges from $781 for 4 hours taken by a Michigan resident to $2205 for a full 12-hour course load. Comparable expenses for a nonresident are $1549 and $4509.

Living and Housing Costs

The cost of living in metropolitan Detroit is moderate in comparison to the living expenses in metropolitan areas of the eastern or western parts of the nation. The University Housing Office can provide housing information and assist students in locating housing on campus.

Student Group

The College of Education has the largest number of graduate students of any college in the University. The majority of students work as faculty and administrators in schools and colleges throughout southeast Michigan. Graduates of the College have assumed leadership positions both inside and outside education throughout the country.

Location

The main campus is located in the center of Detroit's expanding cultural center. In addition to its own Hilberry and Bonstelle theaters, the University is in proximity to the Fisher Theater, the Detroit Institute of Arts, The Museum of African-American History, The Detroit Historical Museum, and the Detroit Main Library. The world headquarters of General Motors is also located in this area, along with the Detroit Medical Center.

The University

As one of the fifty-six public universities classified as a major research university by the Carnegie Commission on Higher Education, Wayne State has schools and colleges of Medicine; Law; Engineering; Education; Science; Liberal Arts; Business Administration; Nursing; Social Work; Fine Performing and Communication Arts; Urban, Labor and Metropolitan Affairs; Pharmacy and Allied Health Professions; and Lifelong Learning.

The College of Education is located in the heart of the main campus and within walking distance of the central offices of the Detroit Public Schools. The College has a long history of working cooperatively with Detroit and suburban teachers and administrators in joint research and teaching initiatives.

Applying

Students who have not been formally admitted to the Graduate School should file their initial applications with the University Admissions Office, 3 East, Helen Newberry Joy Building.

Correspondence and Information

Dr. Janice W. Green
Assistant Dean, Academic Services
489 Education Building
Wayne State University
Detroit, Michigan 48202-3489
Telephone: 313-577-1605
E-mail: sitzkow@cms.cc.wayne.edu
World Wide Web: http://www.coe.wayne.edu/

Wayne State University

THE FACULTY

Administrative and Organizational Studies (AOS)
JoAnne Holbert, Interim Assistant Dean; Ed.D., Indiana, 341 Education.

Michael Addonizio, Ph.D., Michigan State. Roger A. DeMont, Ed.D., Tennessee. Richarde Donelan, Ed.D., Michigan. Alvin Edelson, Ph.D., Wayne State. Joella Gipson-Simpson, Ph.D., Illinois. Burnis Hall Jr., Ed.D., Tennessee. Frances LaPlante-Sosnowsky, Ed.D., Wayne State. Thomas McLennan, Ed.D., Wayne State. Lynn Miller-Wietecha, M.Ed., Wayne State. Gary Morrison, Ed.D., Indiana. Gary Powell, Ed.D., Georgia. Lee Randall, Ed.D., Nova. Rita C. Richey, Ph.D., Wayne State.

Health, Physical Education, and Recreation (HPR)
Sarah J. Erbaugh, Assistant Dean, Ph.D., Wisconsin–Madison, 261 Matthaei.

Roy Allen, M.Ed., Wayne State. David L. Blievernicht, Ph.D., Wisconsin–Madison. Judith S. Bowen, M.A., Wayne State. Timothy G. Domke, M.A., Eastern Michigan. Hermann-Josef Engels, Ph.D., Florida State. Mariane Fahlman, Ph.D., Toledo. Mary Jane Heaney, Ph.D., Wayne State. Avanelle Kidwell, M.A., Ohio State. Susan Kolp, M.S., Purdue. Pamela Hodges Kulinna, Ph.D., Illinois at Urbana-Champaign. Jeffrey J. Martin, Ph.D., North Carolina at Greensboro. Peter A. Roberts, M.A., Michigan State. Steven Singleton, M.A., Michigan. William W. Sloan, M.A., Maryland. Delano Tucker, M.A., Michigan State. John C. Wirth, Ph.D., Illinois. Weimo Zhu, Ph.D., Wisconsin–Madison.

Teacher Education (TED)
Sharon L. Elliott, Assistant Dean, Ed.D., Wayne State, 241 Education.

Rudi Alec, Ph.D., Michigan State. Navaz Bhavnagri, Ph.D., Illinois. Anne W. Blake, M.S.L.S., Wayne State. James H. Blake, Ph.D., Wayne State. John S. Camp, Ph.D., Columbia. Hal Dittenber, M.A., Eastern Michigan. Thomas Edwards, Ph.D., Ohio State. Karen Feathers, Ed.D., Indiana. Holly Feen-Calligan, M.A., Wright State. Maria Ferreira, Ph.D., Indiana. Richard Gibson, Ph.D., Penn State. Rivka Greenberg, Ph.D., Michigan. Janice E. Hale, Ph.D., Georgia State. Carole J. Hamilton, M.Ed., Wayne State. Steven Ilmer, Ph.D., Michigan. Lola Jackson, Ph.D., Michigan. Leonard Kaplan, Ed.D., Rochester. Mark Larson, Ed.D., Washington. Randy Lattimore, Ph.D., Ohio State. Rodolfo Martinez, Ph.D., Utah. Manuel R. Mazon, Ph.D., Texas. John T. Norman, Ph.D., Michigan State. Gerald Oglan, Ph.D., Windsor. J. Michael Peterson, Ph.D., North Texas State. Robert Pettapiece, Ed.D., Wayne State. Sally Roberts, Ed.D., Wayne State. R. Craig Roney, Ph.D., Colorado. Lorraine Ross, Ph.D., Iowa State. Joseph Sales Sr., Ed.D., Wayne State. Julie Sarama, Ph.D., SUNY at Buffalo. Gary R. Smith, Ph.D., Northwestern. Jo-Ann Snyder, Ed.D., Wayne State. Mary Stein, Ph.D., SUNY at Buffalo. Geralyn Stephens, Ed.D., Wayne State. Kathi Tarrant, M.A., Michigan State. Jacqueline Tilles, Ph.D., Michigan. Paula C. Wood, Ph.D., Michigan State. Anga Youssef, Ph.D., Penn State. Marshall F. Zumberg, Ph.D., Michigan State.

Theoretical and Behavioral Foundations (TBF)
JoAnne Holbert, Assistant Dean, Ed.D., Indiana, 341 Education.

Arnold B. Coven, Ed.D., Arizona. Daisy Ellington, Ph.D., Wayne State. Stephen B. Hillman, Ph.D., Indiana. Alan M. Hoffman, Ed.D., Penn State. Tyrone Holmes, Ed.D., Penn State. Patricia Leonard, Ph.D., Michigan State. Donald R. Marcotte, Ph.D., Connecticut. Barry S. Markman, Ph.D., Emory. John J. Pietrofesa, Ed.D., Miami (Florida). Lori Rothenberg, Ph.D., North Carolina at Chapel Hill. Shlomo Sawilowsky, Ph.D., South Florida. Cheryl Somers, Ph.D., Ball State.

WHEELOCK COLLEGE

Graduate School

Programs of Study

Wheelock Graduate School offers graduate-level study leading to Master of Science degrees and Certificates of Advanced Graduate Study. These programs reflect the College's mission to improve the quality of life for children and their families. Students choose from Massachusetts teaching certification programs in early childhood education, elementary education, special education, reading, and school leadership (principal, supervisor/director), as well as degrees in child development, human development, family studies, infant and toddler studies, child life, early intervention, and other areas related to careers working with children and families.

Small classes, individualized study plans, and close faculty-student relationships contribute to the rich, multifaceted academic experience. Graduate students select from a wide variety of courses and practicum experiences. Weekday courses meet in the late afternoon and evening at the Boston campus and on weekends at several off-campus sites. In addition, a master's degree program in child development/early childhood education and several professional development certificates are offered in Boston in a weekend format. All programs stress a sound theoretical knowledge base, integrated with practical work with children and adults. To support the Graduate School's commitment to urban schools, a Summer Urban Teaching program is available to adults holding a B.A. who demonstrate promise and competence in the field of urban elementary education. While some programs offer internships with significant stipends, others include independent study and carefully supervised practica. Interdisciplinary programs may be designed based on personal and professional goals.

Most M.S. degree programs offer flexible scheduling to allow students to pursue a master's degree on a full-time or part-time basis. Prospective students should refer to the Graduate School catalog for specific programming information. All the teacher preparation programs comply with the revised M.A. certification requirements. The C.A.G.S. is designed for educational practitioners who wish to pursue concentrated study beyond the master's degree. This specialized study allows adults with master's degrees to pursue additional research and skill development in order to advance their professional opportunities.

Graduates of Wheelock College are prepared for a variety of leadership roles in education and human services, including early-care, preschool, classroom teaching, special education programs, educational administration, early intervention, resource and referral services, early childhood advocacy and policy, family support and parent education, intergenerational studies, child life, and related fields. The latest statistics show that 92 percent of the 1997 graduates who sought jobs found positions in their respective fields within six months of graduation.

Research Facilities

The College library has a rich collection that includes more than 80,000 volumes and 500 periodical titles. Through a cooperative arrangement, students have access to other libraries in the area. The library's curriculum resources include an extensive collection of audiovisual materials, microforms, and computer software. A separate Curriculum Resource Center is one of the best equipped in the Boston area and serves a dual purpose: it offers workshops and materials for creating teaching aids and serves as a lending library for some of the newer educational materials designed for use in classrooms and other centers where graduate students are working. The College subscribes to and trains faculty, administrators, and staff for Internet to expedite communication among faculty, administrators, and staff around the world.

Financial Aid

Applicants seeking Wheelock College graduate assistantships and scholarships should submit the Free Application for Federal Student Aid and the Wheelock College Financial Aid Application by March 15 for the fall or summer semester and December 1 for the spring semester. Both need-based and merit scholarships are available through Wheelock.

Cost of Study

General tuition for the 1998–99 academic year is $525 per credit. In addition, there is a nonrefundable $100 enrollment fee and a late registration fee of $25 due after the initial registration deadline each semester. Tuition for off-campus programs, on-campus Weekend College, certificate programs, and Summer Urban Teaching programs are available upon request.

Living and Housing Costs

Dormitory housing is available on campus during the summer and on a limited basis during the fall and spring semesters. Most graduate students choose to live off campus. Housing costs in the Boston area vary considerably according to the location and type of housing desired.

Student Group

The Graduate School has more than 550 enrolled full-time and part-time students each semester and welcomes many more nonmatriculating students. These women and men represent a diversity of geographic, ethnic, racial, and professional backgrounds, develop new areas of expertise through their individual and collective classroom, social, and practical experiences.

Location

Wheelock is located in the "green belt" of Boston, which extends from the Boston Common and the Public Gardens into suburbia. Within walking distance are the Boston Museum of Fine Arts, the Gardner Museum, five colleges and universities, and a vast complex of hospital and medical school facilities. Graduate students can take advantage of a wide range of child-related resources in hospital care, research programs, public and private schools, child-care programs, and government agencies.

The College

Wheelock College is a small private institution. All of its programs focus on work with young children and their families. The College began in 1888 to train kindergarten teachers. In 1941, it became a four-year, degree-granting institution with interdisciplinary liberal arts majors. Graduate programs began in 1952. From its initial focus on teaching, the College has grown to include preparation for work with children in museums and hospitals, on interdisciplinary early intervention teams, and with parents and community groups.

Applying

Applications are considered on a rolling basis for most programs and should be submitted at least two months prior to the semester in which enrollment is desired. Applicants should refer to the catalog for specific admission guidelines. The application includes a $35 fee ($40 for international students); a completed form; an essay; a resume; official, sealed transcripts representing all undergraduate and relevant graduate study; and three official (sealed) references. Interviews are required for some programs and are optional for others. Students applying for financial aid should submit applications for admission and financial aid by March 15 for the fall or summer semester and December 1 for the spring semester.

Correspondence and Information

Director of Graduate Admissions
Wheelock College
200 The Riverway
Boston, Massachusetts 02215

Telephone: 617-734-5200 Ext. 195
800-734-5215 (toll-free)
Fax: 617-232-7127
E-mail: graduate@wheelock.edu

Wheelock College

THE FACULTY

The faculty of the Wheelock Graduate School has a national reputation in the field of early childhood education and development, and many faculty members are actively engaged in writing, research, and consulting.

Jill Ardley, Ph.D., Florida State.
Jane Attannucci, Ed.D., Harvard.
Joan Bergstrom, Ed.D., Massachusetts.
Joni Block, M.Ed., Rhode Island College.
Linda Braun, M.A., Columbia Teachers College.
Cheryl Render Brown, M.Ed., Tufts.
Emily Cahan, Ph.D., Yale.
Joseph Cambone, Ed.D., Harvard.
Eleanor H. Chasdi, Ph.D., Radcliffe.
Nancy Clark-Chiarelli, Ed.D., Harvard.
Virginia Coleman, M.S., Wheelock.
Stephanie Cox-Suarez, Ph.D., Boston College.
Costanza Eggers-Pierola, Ed.D., Harvard.
Catherine Finn, Ed.D., Masachussetts Amherst.
Susan Harris-Sharples, Ed.D., Harvard.
Marcia Hartley, M.S., Wheelock.
Donna Haynes, Ed.M., Harvard.
Patricia Hogan, D.S.W., Berkeley.
Mieko Kamii, Ed.D., Harvard.
Edgar Klugman, Ed.D., Columbia Teachers College.
Jean Krasnow, M.B.A., Simmons; Ed.D., Boston University.
Elizabeth Larkin, Ed.D., Harvard.
Patricia P. Lawrence, M.Ed., Harvard.
Frances Litman, Ed.M., Harvard.
Shirley Malone-Fenner, Ed.D., Vanderbilt.
Catherine Marchant, Ed.D., Harvard.
Kathleen McDonough, M.Ed., Lesley.
Terry Meier, Ed.D., Harvard.
Gwen Morgan, M.S., Wheelock.
Marcie Osinsky, M.A., Lesley.
Susan Redditt, Ed.D., Boston University.
Kathleen N. Reed, Ph.D., Connecticut.
Florence Rossman, Ed.D., Boston University.
Stefi Rubin, Ph.D., Harvard.
William B. D. Thompson Jr., Ed.D., Harvard.
Eleanora Villegas-Reimers, Ed.D., Harvard.
Jeffrey Winokur, M.Ed., Antioch.
Karen Worth, M.A., Bank Street College of Education.
Alana Zambone, Ph.D., Vanderbilt.

Section 22
Administration, Instruction, and Theory

This section contains directories of institutions offering graduate work in curriculum and instruction, educational administration, educational measurement and evaluation, educational media/instructional technology, educational psychology, foundations and philosophy of education, and international and comparative education, followed by in-depth entries submitted by institutions that chose to prepare detailed program descriptions. Additional information about programs listed in the directories but not augmented by an in-depth entry may be obtained by writing directly to the dean of a graduate school or chair of a department at the address given in the directory.

For programs offering related work, see also in this book Education, Health-Related Professions, Instructional Levels, Leisure Studies and Recreation, Physical Education and Kinesiology, Special Focus, and Subject Areas; and in Book 2, Psychology and Counseling (School Psychology).

CONTENTS

Program Directories

Announcement

In-Depth Descriptions

See also:

Curriculum and Instruction

Acadia University, Faculty of Professional Studies, School of Education, Program in Curriculum Studies, Wolfville, NS B0P 1X0, Canada. Awards M Ed. Evening/weekend programs available. *Degree requirements:* Thesis required, foreign language not required. *Entrance requirements:* Minimum B average in undergraduate course work, 2 years of teaching experience. Application deadline: 2/1 (rolling processing). Application fee: $25. *Expenses:* Tuition $4095 per year for Canadian residents; $8190 per year for nonresidents. Fees $145 per year. *Financial aid:* Teaching assistantships available. Financial aid application deadline: 2/1. *Faculty research:* Counselor education, analysis of teaching, education law, program evaluation, elementary school science. • Dr. Bryant Griffith, Director, School of Education, 902-585-1229. E-mail: bryant.griffith@acadiau.ca. Application contact: Sheila Langille, Secretary, 902-585-1229. Fax: 902-585-1071.

Alverno College, Department of Education, 3401 South 39th St, PO Box 343922, Milwaukee, WI 53234-3922. Offerings include director of instruction (MA), instructional design (MA). Department faculty: 107 full-time (80 women), 84 part-time (66 women). *Application deadline:* 8/1 (priority date; rolling processing; 12/1 for spring admission). *Application fee:* $25. Electronic applications accepted. *Expenses:* Tuition $295 per credit. Fees $115 per year. • Mary Diez, Graduate Dean, 414-382-6214. Fax: 414-382-6354. E-mail: mary.diez@alverno.edu.

Andrews University, School of Graduate Studies, School of Education, Department of Teaching/Learning/Administration, Program in Curriculum and Instruction, Berrien Springs, MI 49104. Awards MA, Ed D, PhD, Ed S. Faculty: 5 full-time (1 woman). *Degree requirements:* For master's, thesis optional, foreign language not required; for doctorate, dissertation. *Entrance requirements:* For master's, GRE Subject Test. Application deadline: 8/15 (rolling processing). Application fee: $30. *Expenses:* Tuition $290 per quarter hour (minimum). Fees $75 per quarter. *Financial aid:* Fellowships, research assistantships, teaching assistantships, partial tuition waivers, Federal Work-Study, institutionally sponsored loans, and career-related internships or fieldwork available. Aid available to part-time students. • Dr. William H. Green, Chair, Department of Teaching/Learning/Administration, 616-471-3465.

Angelo State University, College of Professional Studies, Department of Education, Program in Curriculum and Instruction, San Angelo, TX 76909. Awards MA. Program new for spring 1998. *Degree requirements:* Comprehensive exam required, thesis optional, foreign language not required. *Entrance requirements:* GRE General Test, minimum GPA of 2.5. Application deadline: 8/7 (priority date; rolling processing; 1/2 for spring admission). Application fee: $25 ($50 for international students). *Expenses:* Tuition $1022 per year full-time, $36 per semester hour part-time for state residents; $7382 per year full-time, $246 per semester hour part-time for nonresidents. Fees $1140 per year full-time, $165 per semester (minimum) part-time. *Financial aid:* Application deadline 8/1. • Application contact: Dr. Douglas John, Professor of Education, 915-942-2052.

Arizona State University, Interdisciplinary Program in Curriculum and Instruction, Tempe, AZ 85287. Awards PhD. *Application fee:* $45. *Expenses:* Tuition $2088 per year full-time, $110 per hour part-time for state residents; $9040 per year full-time, $377 per hour part-time for nonresidents. Fees $72 per year full-time, $18 per semester (minimum) part-time. • Dr. Robert Rutherford, Director, 602-965-1450.

Arizona State University, College of Education, Division of Curriculum and Instruction, Academic Program in Curriculum and Instruction, Tempe, AZ 85287. Awards MA, M Ed, Ed D. *Degree requirements:* For doctorate, dissertation. *Entrance requirements:* GRE General Test or MAT. Application fee: $45. *Expenses:* Tuition $2088 per year full-time, $110 per hour part-time for state residents; $9040 per year full-time, $377 per hour part-time for nonresidents. Fees $72 per year full-time, $18 per semester (minimum) part-time. *Faculty research:* Early childhood, media and computers, elementary education, English education, exercise and wellness education. • Dr. Nicholas Appleton, Director, Division of Curriculum and Instruction, 602-965-1644. E-mail: ifkas@asu.edu. Application contact: Admissions Secretary, 602-965-1644.

Arkansas State University, College of Education, Department of Educational Administration and Secondary Education, State University, AR 72467. Offerings include curriculum and instruction (MSE, Ed S). Accredited by NCATE. Department faculty: 12 full-time (3 women), 2 part-time (both women). *Degree requirements:* For master's, thesis or alternative, comprehensive exam; for Ed S, 2 years of professional experience, oral and written comprehensive exams required, thesis not required. *Entrance requirements:* For master's, GRE General Test or MAT, appropriate bachelor's degree; for Ed S, GRE General Test or MAT, master's degree. Application deadline: 7/1 (priority date; rolling processing; 11/15 for spring admission). Application fee: $15 ($25 for international students). *Expenses:* Tuition $2760 per year full-time, $115 per credit hour part-time for state residents; $6936 per year full-time, $289 per credit hour part-time for nonresidents. Fees $506 per year full-time, $44 per semester (minimum) part-time. • Dr. David Cox, Chair, 870-972-3062. Fax: 870-972-3945. E-mail: dwcox@pawnee.astate.edu.

Arkansas Tech University, School of Education, Department of Curriculum and Instruction, Russellville, AR 72801-2222. Offers programs in educational leadership (M Ed), elementary education (M Ed), English (M Ed), gifted education (MSE), instructional improvement (M Ed), instructional technology (M Ed), mathematics (M Ed), social studies (M Ed). Accredited by NCATE. Part-time programs available. Students: 29 full-time (18 women), 89 part-time (76 women); includes 5 minority (2 African Americans, 1 Asian American, 2 Native Americans), 18 international. Average age 38. 65 applicants, 100% accepted. In 1997, 65 degrees awarded. *Degree requirements:* Action research project, comprehensive exam required, thesis optional. *Entrance requirements:* GRE General Test. Application deadline: 3/1 (priority date; rolling processing; 10/1 for spring admission). Application fee: $0 ($30 for international students). *Expenses:* Tuition $98 per credit hour for state residents; $196 per credit hour for nonresidents. Fees $30 per semester. *Financial aid:* In 1997–98, 4 teaching assistantships averaging $500 per month and totaling $20,914 were awarded; Federal Work-Study also available. Aid available to part-time students. Financial aid application deadline: 4/15. • Head, 501-968-0290. Fax: 501-964-0811.

Ashland University, College of Education, Graduate Studies in Teacher Education, Program in Curriculum and Instruction, Ashland, OH 44805-3702. Offers classroom instruction (M Ed), computer education (M Ed), developmentally handicapped education (M Ed), early childhood education (M Ed), early education of the handicapped child (M Ed), economics education (M Ed), gifted education (M Ed), multihandicapped education (M Ed), special education (M Ed), specific learning disabled education (M Ed). One or more programs accredited by NCATE. Part-time and evening/weekend programs available. Faculty: 8 full-time (4 women), 24 part-time (9 women). In 1997, 428 degrees awarded. *Degree requirements:* Practicum or thesis. *Entrance requirements:* GRE General Test or MAT, teaching certificate. Application deadline: rolling. Application fee: $15. *Tuition:* $275 per credit hour. *Financial aid:* In 1997–98, 1 teaching assistantship (to a first-year student) was awarded. • Carl Walley, Program Team Leader, 419-289-5355. E-mail: cwalley@ashland.edu. Application contact: Dr. Joe Bailey, Director, 419-289-5377. Fax: 419-289-5097. E-mail: jbailey@ashland.edu.

Auburn University, College of Education, Department of Educational Foundations, Leadership, and Technology, Auburn University, AL 36849-0001. Offerings include curriculum and instruction (M Ed, MS, Ed D, Ed S), curriculum supervision (M Ed, MS, Ed D, Ed S). One or more programs accredited by NCATE. Department faculty: 18 full-time (9 women). *Degree requirements:* For master's, thesis (MS) required, foreign language not required; for Ed S, field project required, foreign language and thesis not required. *Entrance requirements:* For master's and Ed S, GRE General Test. Application deadline: 9/1 (rolling processing; 3/1 for spring admission). Application fee: $25 ($50 for international students). *Expenses:* Tuition $2760 per year full-time, $76 per credit hour part-time for state residents; $8280 per year full-time, $228 per credit hour part-time for nonresidents. Fees $30 per year full-time, $160 per quarter part-time for state residents; $30 per year full-time, $480 per quarter part-time for nonresidents. • Dr. James S. Kaminsky, Head, 334-844-4460. Application contact: Dr. John F. Pritchett, Dean of the Graduate School, 334-844-4700.

Austin Peay State University, College of Education, Department of Education, Clarksville, TN 37044-0001. Offerings include curriculum and instruction (MA Ed). Accredited by NCATE. *Application deadline:* 7/31 (priority date; rolling processing; 12/4 for spring admission). *Application fee:* $15. *Expenses:* Tuition $2438 per year full-time, $123 per semester hour part-time for state residents; $7034 per year full-time, $324 per semester hour part-time for nonresidents. Fees $484 per year (minimum) full-time, $154 per semester (minimum) part-time. • J. Ronald Groseclose, Interim Chair, 931-648-7585. Fax: 931-648-5991. E-mail: grosecloseg@apsu.edu.

Averett College, Division of Education, Program in Curriculum and Instruction, Danville, VA 24541-3692. Awards M Ed. Part-time and evening/weekend programs available. Faculty: 4 full-time (2 women). Students: 22 part-time (all women); includes 3 minority (all African Americans). 3 applicants, 100% accepted. In 1997, 16 degrees awarded (100% found work related to degree). *Degree requirements:* Comprehensive exam required, foreign language not required. *Entrance requirements:* GRE, MAT, or PRAXIS (test scores should be no older than 5 years), minimum GPA of 3.0 in previous 2 years, teaching certificate. Application deadline: 8/1 (priority date; rolling processing; 1/2 for spring admission). Application fee: $25. *Tuition:* $225 per credit hour. • Dr. Elizabeth Compton, Academic Vice President, Division of Education, 804-791-5656. Fax: 804-791-0658.

Azusa Pacific University, School of Education and Behavioral Studies, Department of Education, Program in Curriculum and Instruction, Azusa, CA 91702-7000. Awards MA. Part-time and evening/weekend programs available. Faculty: 7 full-time (4 women), 9 part-time (4 women). Students: 110. In 1997, 20 degrees awarded. *Degree requirements:* Core exams, oral presentation required, foreign language and thesis not required. *Average time to degree:* master's–1 year full-time, 2 years part-time. *Entrance requirements:* 12 units of previous course work in education, minimum GPA of 3.0. Application fee: $45 ($65 for international students). *Expenses:* Tuition $350 per unit. Fees $57 per year. *Faculty research:* Diversity in teacher education programs, teacher morale, student perception of school, case study instruction. • Application contact: Dr. Beverly Stanford, Director, 626-815-5363. Fax: 626-815-5416.

Ball State University, Teachers College, Department of Educational Leadership, Program in Curriculum and Instruction, 2000 University Avenue, Muncie, IN 47306-1099. Awards MAE, Ed S. Accredited by NCATE. Students: 2 part-time (1 woman). Average age 37. 4 applicants, 75% accepted. *Degree requirements:* For Ed S, thesis required, foreign language not required. *Entrance requirements:* For Ed S, GRE General Test. Application fee: $15 ($25 for international students). *Expenses:* Tuition $3454 per year full-time, $518 per semester (minimum) part-time for state residents; $9316 per year full-time, $1221 per semester (minimum) part-time for nonresidents. Fees $242 per year full-time, $18 per semester (minimum) part-time. • Jay Thompson, Head, 785-285-8488.

Baylor University, School of Education, Department of Curriculum and Instruction, Waco, TX 76798. Awards MA, MS Ed, Ed D, Ed S. Accredited by NCATE. Postbaccalaureate distance learning degree programs offered (minimal on-campus study). Faculty: 11 full-time (5 women), 2 part-time (1 woman). Students: 24 full-time (19 women), 34 part-time (31 women); includes 2 minority (1 African American, 1 Native American), 5 international. Average age 30. 19 applicants, 79% accepted. In 1997, 15 master's, 3 doctorates awarded. *Degree requirements:* For doctorate, dissertation required, foreign language not required. *Entrance requirements:* For master's and doctorate, GRE General Test (minimum combined score of 1000) or GMAT. Application deadline: 7/30 (priority date; rolling processing; 12/1 for spring admission). Application fee: $25. *Expenses:* Tuition $7392 per year full-time, $308 per semester hour part-time. Fees $1024 per year. *Financial aid:* Research assistantships, teaching assistantships, Federal Work-Study, institutionally sponsored loans available. *Faculty research:* Teacher education, language and literacy. • Dr. Betty Conaway, Chairman, 254-710-3113.

Beaver College, Department of Education, Glenside, PA 19038-3295. Offerings include curriculum (CAS). *Application fee:* $35. *Expenses:* Tuition $6570 per year full-time, $365 per credit part-time. Fees $35 per year.

Bemidji State University, Division of Professional Studies, Program in Curriculum and Instruction, Bemidji, MN 56601-2699. Awards MS Ed. Accredited by NCATE. Part-time programs available. Students: 2 full-time (both women), 17 part-time (14 women). Average age 41. In 1997, 4 degrees awarded. *Degree requirements:* Thesis required, foreign language not required. *Application deadline:* 5/1. *Application fee:* $20. *Expenses:* Tuition $128 per credit for state residents; $134 per credit (minimum) for nonresidents. Fees $517 per year full-time, $35 per credit (minimum) part-time. *Financial aid:* Application deadline 5/1. • Dr. Jack Reynolds, Chair, 218-755-2931. Fax: 218-755-3788. E-mail: caravan@vax1.bemidji.msus.edu.

Benedictine University, Program in Education, Lisle, IL 60532-0900. Offerings include curriculum and instruction and collaborative teaching (M Ed). Program faculty: 4 full-time (3 women), 3 part-time (1 woman). *Application fee:* $30. • Dr. Eileen M. Kolich, Director, 630-829-6280. Fax: 630-960-1126. E-mail: ekolich@ben.edu.

Berry College, Graduate Programs in Education, Program in Curriculum and Instruction, Mount Berry, GA 30149-0159. Awards Ed S. Accredited by NCATE. Faculty: 2 part-time (1 woman).5 FTE. Students: 23 part-time (20 women). Average age 35. 0 applicants. In 1997, 20 degrees awarded (95% found work related to degree, 5% continued full-time study). *Degree requirements:* Computer language, thesis, portfolio and oral exams required, foreign language not required. *Average time to degree:* other advanced degree–2 years full-time, 3 years part-time. *Entrance requirements:* M Ed from NCATE accredited school, minimum GPA of 3.25. Application deadline: 7/29 (rolling processing; 12/16 for spring admission). Application fee: $25 ($30 for international students). *Tuition:* $146 per semester hour. *Financial aid:* Assistantships available. Financial aid application deadline: 4/1. • Application contact: George Gaddie, Dean of Admissions, 706-236-2215. Fax: 706-290-2178.

Black Hills State University, College of Education, Spearfish, SD 57799-9502. Offers program in curriculum and instruction (MS). Accredited by NCATE. Part-time programs available. Faculty: 16 full-time (5 women), 7 part-time (4 women). Students: 3 full-time, 28 part-time. In 1997, 16 degrees awarded. *Degree requirements:* Thesis or portfolio required, foreign language not required. *Entrance requirements:* GRE General Test, bachelor's degree in education. Application deadline: 4/1 (priority date; rolling processing; 10/1 for spring admission). Application fee: $15. *Expenses:* Tuition $85 per credit hour for state residents; $251 per credit hour for nonresidents. Fees $41 per credit hour. *Financial aid:* In 1997–98, 2 students received aid, including 2 research assistantships (both to first-year students) averaging $666 per month and totaling $6,000; partial tuition waivers, Federal Work-Study, and career-related internships or fieldwork also available. Aid available to part-time students. Financial aid application deadline: 2/1. *Faculty research:* Rural education, teacher/student self-concepts, teaching/learning styles, active learning technology in curriculum. • Dr. Dean Myers, Dean, 605-642-6550. Application contact: George Earley, Director of Graduate Studies, 605-642-6270. Fax: 605-642-6273.

Bloomsburg University of Pennsylvania, School of Graduate Studies, College of Professional Studies, School of Education, Department of Curriculum and Foundations, Program in Curriculum and Instruction, Bloomsburg, PA 17815-1905. Awards M Ed. Accredited by NCATE. Faculty: 4 full-time (1 woman). Students: 7 full-time (2 women), 21 part-time (14 women); includes 4 minority (all African Americans), 2 international. Average age 31. 22 applicants, 100% accepted. In 1997, 2 degrees awarded. *Degree requirements:* Thesis required, foreign language not required. *Entrance requirements:* MAT, minimum QPA of 2.5. Application deadline:

rolling. Application fee: $25. *Expenses:* Tuition $3468 per year full-time, $193 per credit part-time for state residents; $6236 per year full-time, $346 per credit part-time for nonresidents. Fees $748 per year full-time, $166 per semester (minimum) part-time. *Faculty research:* Administration. • Dr. John Hranitz, Chair, Department of Curriculum and Foundations, 717-389-4025. Fax: 717-389-3894. E-mail: hral@bf486.bloomu.edu.

Boise State University, College of Education, Doctoral Program in Curriculum and Instruction, Boise, ID 83725-0399. Awards Ed D. Accredited by NCATE. Part-time programs available. Students: 12 full-time (8 women), 20 part-time (15 women); includes 2 minority (1 African American, 1 Hispanic), 1 international. Average age 46. 3 applicants, 100% accepted. In 1997, 4 degrees awarded. *Degree requirements:* Dissertation. *Entrance requirements:* GRE, minimum GPA of 3.0. Application deadline: 7/26 (priority date; rolling processing; 11/29 for spring admission). Application fee: $20 ($30 for international students). Electronic applications accepted. *Tuition:* $3020 per year full-time, $135 per credit part-time for state residents; $8900 per year full-time, $135 per credit part-time for nonresidents. *Financial aid:* In 1997–98, 8 students received aid, including 8 graduate assistantships; Federal Work-Study, institutionally sponsored loans, and career-related internships or fieldwork also available. Aid available to part-time students. Financial aid application deadline: 3/1. • Dr. Roger Stewart, Coordinator, 208-385-1731. Fax: 208-385-4365.

Boise State University, College of Education, Programs in Teacher Education, Program in Curriculum and Instruction, Boise, ID 83725-0399. Awards MA. Accredited by NCATE. Part-time programs available. Faculty: 15 full-time (5 women), 9 part-time (5 women). Students: 71 full-time (41 women), 144 part-time (90 women). Average age 37. 66 applicants, 98% accepted. In 1997, 48 degrees awarded. *Degree requirements:* Thesis optional. *Application deadline:* 7/26 (priority date; rolling processing; 11/29 for spring admission). *Application fee:* $20 ($30 for international students). Electronic applications accepted. *Tuition:* $3020 per year full-time, $135 per credit part-time for state residents; $8900 per year full-time, $135 per credit part-time for nonresidents. *Financial aid:* Graduate assistantships, Federal Work-Study, institutionally sponsored loans, and career-related internships or fieldwork available. Aid available to part-time students. Financial aid application deadline: 3/1. • Dr. Roger Stewart, Coordinator, Programs in Teacher Education, 208-385-1731. Fax: 208-385-4365.

Boston College, Graduate School of Education, Department of Teacher Education/Special Education and Curriculum and Instruction, Curriculum and Instruction Specialization, Chestnut Hill, MA 02167-9991. Awards M Ed, PhD, CAES. Accredited by NCATE. Students: 30 full-time (22 women), 42 part-time (30 women); includes 7 minority (4 African Americans, 2 Asian Americans, 1 Hispanic), 4 international. 68 applicants, 57% accepted. In 1997, 22 master's, 1 doctorate, 1 CAES awarded. *Degree requirements:* For master's and CAES, comprehensive exam required, thesis not required; for doctorate, computer language, dissertation, comprehensive exam. *Entrance requirements:* For master's and doctorate, GRE General Test; for CAES, GRE General Test or MAT. Application deadline: 3/15 (11/15 for spring admission). Application fee: $40. *Expenses:* Tuition $626 per semester hour. Fees $80 per year (minimum) full-time, $30 per semester part-time. *Financial aid:* Fellowships, research assistantships, teaching assistantships, administrative assistantships, merit scholarships, partial tuition waivers, Federal Work-Study, and career-related internships or fieldwork available. Aid available to part-time students. *Faculty research:* In-service education, language, bilingualism, urban education. • Application contact: Arline Riordan, Graduate Admissions Director, 617-552-4214. Fax: 617-552-0812. E-mail: riordana@bc.edu.

Boston University, School of Education, Department of Curriculum and Teaching, Program in Curriculum and Teaching, Boston, MA 02215. Awards Ed D. Students: 20 full-time (14 women), 88 part-time (54 women); includes 4 minority (3 African Americans, 1 Asian American), 21 international. Average age 38. In 1997, 10 degrees awarded. *Degree requirements:* Dissertation, comprehensive exam required, foreign language not required. *Entrance requirements:* GRE General Test or MAT, TOEFL. Application deadline: 2/15 (priority date; rolling processing). Application fee: $50. *Expenses:* Tuition $22,830 per year full-time, $713 per credit part-time. Fees $218 per year full-time, $40 per semester part-time. *Financial aid:* Application deadline 3/30. • Dr. Stephan Ellenwood, Coordinator, 617-353-3238. E-mail: ellenwoo@bu.edu. Application contact: Geri Lakey, Graduate Admissions Office, 617-353-4237. E-mail: glakey@bu.edu.

Bradley University, College of Education and Health Sciences, Department of Curriculum and Instruction, Peoria, IL 61625-0002. Awards MA. Accredited by NCATE. *Degree requirements:* Comprehensive exams required, thesis not required. *Entrance requirements:* MAT, TOEFL (minimum score 500). Application deadline: 7/1 (priority date; rolling processing; 11/1 for spring admission). Application fee: $35. *Tuition:* $13,240 per year full-time, $359 per semester hour (minimum) part-time.

Brandon University, Faculty of Education, Brandon, MB R7A 6A9, Canada. Offerings include curriculum studies (M Ed). Faculty: 27 full-time (3 women), 1 part-time (0 women). *Degree requirements:* Thesis. *Average time to degree:* master's–2 years full-time; other advanced degree–1 year full-time. *Entrance requirements:* TOEFL (minimum score 550), minimum GPA of 3.0, teaching certificate or equivalent. Application deadline: 3/1. Application fee: $30. *Expenses:* Tuition $421 per course (minimum). Fees $24.95 per year. • Dean, 204-728-9520. Application contact: Faye Douglas, Admissions Director, 204-727-7352. Fax: 204-725-2143. E-mail: douglas@brandonu.ca.

Bucknell University, College of Arts and Sciences, Department of Education, Specialization in Supervision of Curriculum and Instruction, Lewisburg, PA 17837. Awards MA, MS Ed. Faculty: 8 full-time. *Degree requirements:* Thesis or alternative required, foreign language not required. *Entrance requirements:* GRE General Test (minimum combined score of 1000), TOEFL (minimum score 550), minimum GPA of 2.8. Application deadline: 6/1 (priority date; rolling processing; 12/1 for spring admission). Application fee: $25. *Tuition:* $2410 per course. *Financial aid:* Assistantships available. Financial aid application deadline: 3/1. • Russell E. Dennis, Adviser, 717-524-1133.

Caldwell College, Graduate Studies, Program in Curriculum and Instruction, Caldwell, NJ 07006-6195. Awards MA. Part-time and evening/weekend programs available. Faculty: 5 full-time (3 women), 5 part-time (2 women). Students: 43 part-time (33 women). Average age 40. In 1997, 11 degrees awarded. *Degree requirements:* Thesis, research paper required, foreign language not required. *Average time to degree:* master's–4 years part-time. *Entrance requirements:* GRE General Test, MAT, interview, writing sample. Application deadline: rolling. Application fee: $25. *Tuition:* $365 per credit. *Faculty research:* Early childhood, information technology, educational leadership. • Dr. Joanne Seelaus, Coordinator, 973-228-4424 Ext. 789. E-mail: jseelaus@caldwell.edu. Application contact: Dr. Rina Spano, Director of Graduate Studies, 973-228-4424 Ext. 408. Fax: 973-364-7618. E-mail: rspano@caldwell.edu.

California Baptist College, Graduate Program in Education, Riverside, CA 92504-3206. Offerings include teaching and curriculum (MS Ed). Program faculty: 8 full-time (7 women), 4 part-time (2 women). *Application deadline:* rolling. *Application fee:* $40. *Expenses:* Tuition $275 per unit. Fees $100 per year. • Dr. Marsha Savage, Chair, 909-689-5771. Application contact: Gail Ronveaux, Director of Graduate Services, 909-343-4249. Fax: 909-351-1808. E-mail: gradser@cal.baptist.edu.

California Polytechnic State University, San Luis Obispo, Center for Teacher Education, Program in Curriculum and Instruction, San Luis Obispo, CA 93407. Awards MA. *Degree requirements:* Comprehensive exam required, thesis optional, foreign language not required. *Entrance requirements:* Minimum GPA of 3.0, teaching experience. Application deadline: 4/1 (rolling processing; 12/15 for spring admission). Application fee: $55. *Expenses:* Tuition $0 for state residents; $164 per unit for nonresidents. Fees $2102 per year full-time, $1632 per year part-time. *Faculty research:* Literature-based teaching of reading, language arts, and social studies; cooperative learning; bilingual/multicultural education; simulation games; learning games. • Sue McBride, Coordinator, 805-756-1577.

California State University, Bakersfield, School of Education, Program in Curriculum and Instruction, 9001 Stockdale Highway, Bakersfield, CA 93311-1099. Offers elementary curriculum and instruction (MA), secondary curriculum and instruction (MA). Accredited by NCATE. *Degree requirements:* Thesis or alternative, culminating projects. *Application deadline:* rolling. *Application fee:* $55. *Expenses:* Tuition $0 for state residents; $246 per unit full-time, $164 per unit part-time for nonresidents. Fees $1584 per year full-time, $918 per year part-time. • Dr. Dianne Turner, Coordinator, 805-664-2422.

California State University, Chico, College of Communication and Education, School of Education, Department of Education, Chico, CA 95929-0722. Offers program in education (MA), including curriculum and instruction, linguistically and culturally diverse learners. Faculty: 24 full-time (11 women), 11 part-time (7 women). Students: 37 full-time (35 women), 51 part-time (39 women); includes 14 minority (1 Asian American, 12 Hispanics, 1 Native American), 8 international. Average age 36. In 1997, 39 degrees awarded. *Degree requirements:* Thesis or alternative, oral exam. *Application deadline:* 4/1 (rolling processing). *Application fee:* $55. *Expenses:* Tuition $0 for state residents; $246 per unit for nonresidents. Fees $2108 per year full-time, $1442 per year part-time. *Financial aid:* Fellowships, teaching assistantships, stipends, and career-related internships or fieldwork available. • Dr. Mike Kotar, Graduate Coordinator, 530-898-6421.

California State University, Dominguez Hills, School of Education, Department of Graduate Education, Program in Teaching/Curriculum, Carson, CA 90747-0001. Awards MA. *Entrance requirements:* Minimum GPA of 2.75. Application deadline: 6/1. Application fee: $55. *Expenses:* Tuition $0 for state residents; $246 per unit for nonresidents. Fees $1896 per year full-time, $1230 per year part-time. • Application contact: Admissions Office, 310-243-3600.

California State University, Fresno, Division of Graduate Studies, School of Education and Human Development, Department of Curriculum, Teaching, and Educational Technology, 5241 North Maple Avenue, Fresno, CA 93740. Offers program in education (MA), including curriculum and instruction. Accredited by NCATE. Part-time and evening/weekend programs available. Faculty: 7 full-time (5 women). Students: 6 full-time (3 women), 25 part-time (17 women); includes 9 minority (all Hispanics), 1 international. Average age 31. 12 applicants, 92% accepted. In 1997, 5 degrees awarded. *Degree requirements:* Thesis or alternative required, foreign language not required. *Average time to degree:* master's–3.5 years full-time. *Entrance requirements:* GRE General Test, TOEFL (minimum score 550), MAT, minimum GPA of 2.75. Application deadline: 4/1 (priority date; rolling processing; 11/1 for spring admission). Application fee: $55. Electronic applications accepted. *Expenses:* Tuition $0 for state residents; $246 per unit for nonresidents. Fees $1872 per year full-time, $1206 per year part-time. *Financial aid:* In 1997–98, 2 research awards, travel grants, scholarships totaling $1,582 were awarded; fellowships, research assistantships, Federal Work-Study, and career-related internships or fieldwork also available. Financial aid application deadline: 3/1; applicants required to submit FAFSA. • Dr. Joan Henderson-Sparks, Chair, 209-278-0240. Fax: 209-278-0404.

California State University, Sacramento, School of Education, Department of Teacher Education, Program in Curriculum and Instruction, Sacramento, CA 95819-6048. Awards MA. Part-time programs available. *Degree requirements:* Thesis or alternative, writing proficiency exam. *Entrance requirements:* TOEFL (minimum score 550), minimum GPA of 3.0, teaching credentials. Application deadline: 4/15 (11/1 for spring admission). Application fee: $55. *Expenses:* Tuition $0 for state residents; $246 per unit for nonresidents. Fees $2012 per year full-time, $1346 per year part-time. *Financial aid:* Federal Work-Study and career-related internships or fieldwork available. Aid available to part-time students. Financial aid application deadline: 3/1. • Dr. Ed Arnsdorf, Chair, Department of Teacher Education, 916-278-6155. Application contact: Dr. Robert Edwards, Graduate Coordinator, 916-278-5559.

California State University, Stanislaus, School of Education, Department of Teacher Education, Program in Curriculum and Instruction, Turlock, CA 95382. Offers elementary education (MA Ed), multilingual education (MA Ed), reading education (MA Ed), secondary education (MA Ed). Accredited by NCATE. Part-time and evening/weekend programs available. Faculty: 19 full-time (13 women), 1 (woman) part-time. Students: 12 (10 women); includes 3 minority (1 Asian American, 2 Hispanics). 30 applicants, 100% accepted. In 1997, 17 degrees awarded. *Entrance requirements:* MAT. Application fee: $55. *Expenses:* Tuition $0 for state residents; $246 per unit for nonresidents. Fees $1779 per year full-time, $1113 per year part-time. *Financial aid:* Federal Work-Study available. Financial aid application deadline: 3/2; applicants required to submit FAFSA. • Dr. Mimi Bradley, Coordinator, 209-667-3367.

Calvin College, Graduate Programs in Education, Grand Rapids, MI 49546-4388. Offerings include curriculum and instruction (M Ed). Accredited by NCATE. M Ed (reading, school administration) admissions temporarily suspended. Faculty: 1 (woman) full-time, 15 part-time (6 women). *Degree requirements:* Thesis required, foreign language not required. *Entrance requirements:* GRE General Test, TOEFL, teaching certificate. Application deadline: 8/15 (priority date; rolling processing; 1/15 for spring admission). Application fee: $0. Electronic applications accepted. *Tuition:* $250 per semester hour. • Dr. Robert S. Fortner, Director of Graduate Studies, 616-957-8533. Fax: 616-957-8551. E-mail: forr@calvin.edu.

Carson-Newman College, Graduate Program in Education, Jefferson City, TN 37760. Offerings include curriculum and instruction (M Ed). Accredited by NCATE. College faculty: 18 full-time (8 women), 7 part-time (5 women). *Application deadline:* 7/15 (priority date; rolling processing). *Application fee:* $25 ($50 for international students). *Expenses:* Tuition $190 per credit hour. Fees $10 per year. • Dr. Margaret A. Hypes, Chair, 423-471-3461. Application contact: Jane W. McGill, Graduate Admissions and Services Adviser, 423-471-3460. Fax: 423-471-3475.

Castleton State College, Department of Education, Program in Curriculum and Instruction, Castleton, VT 05735. Awards MA Ed. Part-time and evening/weekend programs available. Faculty: 9 full-time (5 women), 7 part-time (4 women). *Degree requirements:* Thesis or written exams required, foreign language not required. *Entrance requirements:* GRE General Test (minimum combined score of 1000), MAT (minimum score 50), interview, minimum undergraduate GPA of 3.0. Application deadline: 7/1 (10/1 for spring admission). Application fee: $30. *Expenses:* Tuition $3924 per year full-time, $164 per credit part-time for state residents; $9192 per year full-time, $383 per credit part-time for nonresidents. Fees $902 per year full-time, $26 per credit part-time. *Financial aid:* Federal Work-Study and career-related internships or fieldwork available. • Application contact: Mary Frucelli, Graduate Assistant, 802-468-1441. Fax: 802-468-5237.

The Catholic University of America, School of Arts and Sciences, Department of Education, Washington, DC 20064. Offerings include administration, curriculum, and policy studies (MA); learning and instruction (MA). One or more programs accredited by NCATE. MA (English as a second language) new for fall 1998. Department faculty: 13 full-time (8 women), 2 part-time (both women), 14 FTE. *Degree requirements:* Comprehensive exam required, foreign language not required. *Entrance requirements:* GRE General Test, TOEFL. Application deadline: 8/1 (priority date; rolling processing; 12/1 for spring admission). Application fee: $50. *Expenses:* Tuition $17,325 per year full-time, $668 per credit hour part-time. Fees $680 per year full-time, $360 per year part-time. • Chair, 202-319-5800. Fax: 202-319-5815.

Centenary College of Louisiana, Department of Education, Shreveport, LA 71134-1188. Offerings include supervision of instruction (M Ed). Department faculty: 5 full-time (2 women), 6 part-time (1 woman). *Average time to degree:* master's–2 years full-time, 4 years part-time. *Entrance requirements:* GRE. Application fee: $30. *Tuition:* $360 per course. • Dr. E. John Turner, Chairman, 318-869-5223.

Central Connecticut State University, School of Education and Professional Studies, Department of Educational Leadership, Program in Administration, Supervision and Curriculum, New Britain, CT 06050-4010. Awards MS. In 1997, 12 degrees awarded. *Degree requirements:* Thesis or alternative, comprehensive exam required, foreign language not required. *Entrance requirements:* TOEFL (minimum score 550), minimum GPA of 2.7. Application deadline: 6/1

Directory: Curriculum and Instruction

Central Connecticut State University (continued)

(priority date; rolling processing; 12/1 for spring admission). Application fee: $40. *Expenses:* Tuition $4458 per year full-time, $175 per credit hour part-time for state residents; $9943 per year full-time, $175 per credit hour part-time for nonresidents. Fees $45 per semester. *Financial aid:* Application deadline 3/15. • Dr. Penelope Lisi, Interim Chair, Department of Educational Leadership, 860-832-2130.

Central Missouri State University, College of Education and Human Services, Department of Curriculum and Instruction, Warrensburg, MO 64093. Offers programs in adult education (MSE), curriculum and instruction (Ed S), elementary education (MSE), K–12 education (MSE), reading (MSE), secondary education (MSE). Accredited by NCATE. Part-time programs available. Faculty: 20 full-time. Students: 5 full-time (2 women), 115 part-time (98 women). In 1997, 58 master's, 1 Ed S awarded. *Degree requirements:* For master's, comprehensive exam or thesis; for Ed S, thesis, comprehensive exam. *Entrance requirements:* For master's, GRE General Test, minimum GPA of 2.75, teaching certificate; for Ed S, GRE General Test, minimum GPA of 3.25, teaching certificate. Application deadline: 6/30 (priority date; rolling processing). Application fee: $25 ($50 for international students). *Tuition:* $3288 per year full-time, $137 per credit hour part-time for state residents; $5928 per year full-time, $274 per credit hour part-time for nonresidents. *Financial aid:* In 1997–98, 4 administrative and laboratory assistantships were awarded; research assistantships, teaching assistantships, Federal Work-Study also available. Aid available to part-time students. Financial aid application deadline: 3/1; applicants required to submit FAFSA. • Dr. Ted Garten, Chair, 660-543-4235. Fax: 660-543-4167.

Central Washington University, College of Education and Professional Studies, Department of Teacher Education, Program in Curriculum and Instruction, Ellensburg, WA 98926. Awards M Ed. Accredited by NCATE. Part-time programs available. Faculty: 21 full-time (10 women). Students: 2 full-time (both women). 2 applicants, 100% accepted. In 1997, 1 degree awarded. *Degree requirements:* Thesis or alternative required, foreign language not required. *Entrance requirements:* Minimum GPA of 3.0. Application deadline: 4/1 (priority date; rolling processing; 1/1 for spring admission). Application fee: $35. *Expenses:* Tuition $4200 per year full-time, $140 per credit hour part-time for state residents; $12,780 per year full-time, $426 per credit hour part-time for nonresidents. Fees $240 per year. *Financial aid:* Research assistantships, Federal Work-Study available. Financial aid application deadline: 2/15. • Application contact: Christie A. Fevergeon, Program Coordinator, Graduate Studies and Research, 509-963-3103. Fax: 509-963-1799. E-mail: masters@cwu.edu.

Chapman University, School of Education, Concentration in Curriculum and Instruction, Orange, CA 92866. Awards MA. Evening/weekend programs available. Faculty: 10 full-time (8 women). Students: 10. *Degree requirements:* Comprehensive exam required, thesis not required. *Entrance requirements:* GRE General Test (minimum combined score of 900), MAT (minimum score 45), or PRAXIS. Application deadline: rolling. Application fee: $40. *Tuition:* $7020 per year full-time, $390 per credit part-time. *Financial aid:* Application deadline 3/1. • Dr. Barbara Tye, Coordinator, 714-997-6781.

Chicago State University, College of Education, Department of Curriculum and Instruction, Chicago, IL 60628. Offerings include curriculum and instruction (MS Ed). Accredited by NCATE. *Application deadline:* 7/1 (11/10 for spring admission). *Tuition:* $2268 per year full-time, $95 per credit hour part-time for state residents; $6804 per year full-time, $284 per credit hour part-time for nonresidents.

The Citadel, The Military College of South Carolina, Department of Education, Program in Curriculum and Instruction, Charleston, SC 29409. Awards M Ed. Accredited by NCATE. Students: 2 full-time (1 woman), 17 part-time (14 women); includes 2 minority (both African Americans). In 1997, 3 degrees awarded. *Entrance requirements:* GRE, MAT, or 12 hours of graduate course work with a minimum GPA of 3.0. Application deadline: rolling. Application fee: $25. *Expenses:* Tuition $130 per credit hour for state residents; $260 per credit hour for nonresidents. Fees $30 per semester. • Dr. Robert Carter, Head, Department of Education, 803-953-5097.

City University, School of Education, Bellevue, WA 98004-6442. Offerings include curriculum and instruction (M Ed), teaching (MIT). Postbaccalaureate distance learning degree programs offered (no on-campus study). School faculty: 21 full-time (13 women), 301 part-time (162 women). *Application deadline:* rolling. *Application fee:* $75 ($175 for international students). Electronic applications accepted. *Tuition:* $280 per credit hour. • Roxanne Kelly, Dean, 425-637-1010 Ext. 3712. Fax: 425-277-2439. Application contact: Nabil El-Khatib, Vice President, Admissions, 800-426-5596. Fax: 425-277-2437. E-mail: nel-khatib@cityu.edu.

Claremont Graduate University, Department of Education, Claremont, CA 91711-6163. Offerings include curriculum and teaching (MA, PhD). PhD offered jointly with San Diego State University; MA (mathematics education) offered jointly with the Department of Mathematics. Terminal master's awarded for partial completion of doctoral program. Department faculty: 13 full-time (6 women), 13 part-time (10 women). *Degree requirements:* For master's, thesis or alternative; for doctorate, dissertation. *Entrance requirements:* GRE General Test. Application deadline: 2/15 (priority date; rolling processing). Application fee: $40. Electronic applications accepted. *Expenses:* Tuition $20,250 per year full-time, $913 per unit part-time. Fees $130 per year. • David Drew, Chair, 909-621-8075. Application contact: Ethel Rogers, Associate Director, 909-621-8317. Fax: 909-621-8734. E-mail: educ@cgu.edu.

Clark Atlanta University, School of Education, Department of Curriculum, Atlanta, GA 30314. Awards MA, Ed S. Students: 14 full-time (12 women), 26 part-time (19 women); includes 39 minority (all African Americans), 1 international. In 1997, 10 master's awarded. *Degree requirements:* For master's, 1 foreign language (computer language can substitute), thesis. *Entrance requirements:* For master's, GRE General Test, minimum undergraduate GPA of 2.5. Application deadline: 4/1 (rolling processing; 11/1 for spring admission). Application fee: $30. *Expenses:* Tuition $9672 per year full-time, $403 per credit hour part-time. Fees $200 per year. *Financial aid:* Application deadline 4/30. • Dr. James Young, Chairperson, 404-880-8486. Application contact: Michelle Clark-Davis, Graduate Program Assistant, 404-880-8709.

Clemson University, College of Health, Education, and Human Development, Department of Curriculum and Instruction, Program in Curriculum and Instruction, Clemson, SC 29634. Awards PhD. Accredited by NCATE. Students: 11 full-time (all women), 27 part-time (21 women); includes 2 minority (both African Americans), 1 international. 19 applicants, 58% accepted. In 1997, 1 degree awarded. *Degree requirements:* Dissertation. *Entrance requirements:* GRE General Test, TOEFL, teaching certificate. Application deadline: 6/1. Application fee: $35. *Expenses:* Tuition $3154 per year full-time, $130 per credit hour part-time for state residents; $6452 per year full-time, $264 per credit hour part-time for nonresidents. Fees $190 per year. *Financial aid:* Application deadline 6/1. • Dr. Beatrice Naff, Graduate Coordinator, 864-656-5126. Fax: 864-656-1322. E-mail: cbeatri@clemson.edu.

Cleveland State University, College of Education, Department of Specialized Instructional Programs, Cleveland, OH 44115-2440. Offers program in curriculum and instruction (M Ed), including bilingual education, early childhood education, early childhood/special education, education of emerging adolescents, elementary education, English as a second language, learning disabilities, Montessori education, multihandicapped, reading, secondary education. Faculty: 18 full-time (12 women). *Entrance requirements:* GRE General Test or MAT (score in 50th percentile or higher). Application deadline: 9/1 (priority date; rolling processing). Application fee: $25. *Expenses:* Tuition $5252 per year full-time, $202 per credit hour part-time for state residents; $10,504 per year full-time, $404 per credit hour part-time for nonresidents. Fees $2.25 per credit hour (minimum). *Financial aid:* In 1997–98, 2 research assistantships were awarded; assistantships also available. *Faculty research:* Cooperative learning, very low birthweight children, reading recovery, induction programs. • Dr. Jane Zaharias, Chairperson, 216-687-4585. Fax: 216-687-5379. E-mail: j.zaharias@csuohio.edu.

College Misericordia, Division of Professional Studies, Program in Education/Curriculum, Dallas, PA 18612-1098. Awards MS. Part-time and evening/weekend programs available. Faculty: 4 full-time (2 women), 6 part-time (2 women). Students: 25 part-time (23 women). 12 applicants, 75% accepted. In 1997, 7 degrees awarded. *Degree requirements:* Thesis or alternative required, foreign language not required. *Entrance requirements:* GRE or MAT, minimum GPA of 2.5. Application deadline: 8/1 (priority date; rolling processing). Application fee: $20. *Expenses:* Tuition $13,780 per year full-time, $345 per credit part-time. Fees $740 per year. *Financial aid:* In 1997–98, 2 fellowships were awarded. Financial aid application deadline: 5/1. • Dr. Joseph Rogan, Director, 717-674-6347. Fax: 717-675-2441.

College of the Southwest, School of Education and Professional Studies, Hobbs, NM 88240-9129. Offerings include curriculum and instruction (MS). Postbaccalaureate distance learning degree programs offered. School faculty: 4 full-time (all women), 6 part-time (2 women). *Entrance requirements:* GRE General Test (minimum combined score of 1200). Application deadline: 3/1 (priority date; rolling processing; 10/1 for spring admission). Application fee: $50. *Expenses:* Tuition $150 per credit hour. Fees $140 per year. • Dr. Marilyn Smith, Dean, 505-392-6561.

College of William and Mary, School of Education, Program in Curriculum and Instruction, Williamsburg, VA 23187-8795. Awards MA Ed. Accredited by NCATE. Students: 51 full-time (39 women), 28 part-time (25 women); includes 6 minority (1 African American, 2 Asian Americans, 2 Hispanics, 1 Native American). Average age 29. 105 applicants, 77% accepted. In 1997, 60 degrees awarded. *Entrance requirements:* GRE or MAT, minimum GPA of 2.5. Application deadline: 2/15 (priority date). Application fee: $30. *Tuition:* $5262 per year full-time, $165 per semester hour part-time for state residents; $16,138 per year full-time, $500 per semester hour part-time for nonresidents. *Financial aid:* In 1997–98, 24 graduate assistantships (9 to first-year students) averaging $463 per month were awarded; research assistantships and career-related internships or fieldwork also available. Financial aid application deadline: 2/15. • Dr. George Bass, Coordinator, 757-221-4300. E-mail: gmbass@facstaff.wm.edu.

Colorado Christian University, Graduate Division, 180 South Garrison Street, Lakewood, CO 80226-7499. Offerings include curriculum and instruction (MA). Division faculty: 29 (13 women). *Application deadline:* 8/15 (1/10 for spring admission). *Application fee:* $35. • Thomas Varney, Director of Graduate Studies, 303-697-8135. Application contact: Director of Graduate Admissions, 303-202-0100 Ext. 520. Fax: 303-235-0617.

Columbia International University, Graduate Program in Education, Columbia, SC 29230-3122. Offerings include curriculum and instruction (MA Ed). Program faculty: 4 full-time, 17 part-time. *Application deadline:* rolling. *Application fee:* $20. *Expenses:* Tuition $7410 per year full-time, $285 per semester hour part-time. Fees $150 per year. • Dr. Milt Uecker, Associate Dean for Education Programs, 803-754-4100. E-mail: muecker@ciu.edu. Application contact: Yvonne Miranda, Associate Director of Admissions, 803-754-4100 Ext. 3026. Fax: 803-786-4209. E-mail: yvonnem@ciu.edu.

Concordia University, School of Graduate Studies, 1530 Concordia West, Irvine, CA 92612-3299. Offerings include curriculum and instruction (MA), with option in curriculum and instruction–early childhood. School faculty: 12 full-time (4 women), 19 part-time (13 women), 18 FTE. *Degree requirements:* Thesis or alternative. *Entrance requirements:* GRE General Test (minimum combined score of 900), minimum GPA of 3.0. Application deadline: 8/15 (priority date; rolling processing; 11/15 for spring admission). Application fee: $0. *Tuition:* $320 per unit. • Dr. Thomas Doyle, Dean of the School of Graduate Studies, 949-854-8002. Fax: 949-854-6854. E-mail: doyletj@cui.edu.

Concordia University, Program in Curriculum and Instruction, River Forest, IL 60305-1499. Offers curriculum and instruction (MA, CAS), urban teaching (MA). Accredited by NCATE. MA offered jointly with the Chicago Consortium of Colleges and Universities. Part-time and evening/weekend programs available. Faculty: 11 full-time (4 women), 42 part-time (26 women). Students: 307 (254 women); includes 22 minority (16 African Americans, 4 Asian Americans, 1 Hispanic, 1 Native American), 1 international. In 1997, 226 master's awarded. *Degree requirements:* For master's, thesis, comprehensive exams required, foreign language not required; for CAS, thesis, final project required, foreign language not required. *Entrance requirements:* For master's, minimum GPA of 2.9; for CAS, master's degree. Application deadline: rolling. Application fee: $0. *Tuition:* $372 per semester hour. *Financial aid:* Research assistantships, institutionally sponsored loans available. Aid available to part-time students. *Faculty research:* School discipline, school improvement, leadership. • Dr. Daniel Tomal, Coordinator, 708-209-3476. Application contact: Mary Betancourt, Admissions Secretary, 708-209-4093. Fax: 708-209-3454. E-mail: crfdngrad@curf.edu.

Concordia University, College of Education, Portland, OR 97211-6099. Offerings include curriculum and instruction (elementary) (M Ed). College faculty: 8 part-time (3 women). *Application deadline:* rolling. *Application fee:* $35. *Tuition:* $350 per credit. • Dr. Joseph Mannion, Dean, 503-493-6233. Application contact: Dr. Peter Johnson, Director of Admissions, 503-280-8501.

Concordia University Wisconsin, Division of Graduate Studies, Education Department, Program in Curriculum and Instruction, Mequon, WI 53097-2402. Awards MS Ed. Postbaccalaureate distance learning degree programs offered (minimal on-campus study). *Degree requirements:* Thesis or alternative, comprehensive exam. *Entrance requirements:* TOEFL (minimum score 550), minimum GPA of 3.0, teaching license. *Tuition:* $250 per credit. *Financial aid:* Application deadline 8/1. • Application contact: Brooke Tireman, Graduate Admissions, 414-243-4248. Fax: 414-243-4428. E-mail: btireman@back.cuw.edu.

Converse College, Department of Education, Program in Educational Curriculum and Instruction, Spartanburg, SC 29302-0006. Awards Ed S. Faculty: 7 full-time, 15 part-time. Students: 5 part-time (0 women). Average age 35. *Entrance requirements:* NTE, minimum GPA of 3.0. Application deadline: 5/1 (priority date; rolling processing; 1/30 for spring admission). Application fee: $35. *Tuition:* $185 per credit. • Dr. Nancy Breard, Assistant Director of Graduate Education, 864-596-9732.

Coppin State College, Division of Education, Department of Curriculum and Instruction, Baltimore, MD 21216-3698. Awards M Ed. Part-time and evening/weekend programs available. Faculty: 4 full-time (3 women), 2 part-time (both women). Students: 3 full-time (all women), 44 part-time (37 women); includes 46 minority (all African Americans), 1 international. Average age 35. In 1997, 5 degrees awarded. *Degree requirements:* Thesis or alternative required, foreign language not required. *Entrance requirements:* Minimum GPA of 2.5. Application deadline: 7/15 (12/15 for spring admission). Application fee: $20. *Expenses:* Tuition $140 per credit for state residents; $240 per credit for nonresidents. Fees $504 per year. *Financial aid:* Federal Work-Study, institutionally sponsored loans, and career-related internships or fieldwork available. Aid available to part-time students. Financial aid application deadline: 4/1; applicants required to submit FAFSA. • Dr. Frank Kober, Chair, 410-383-5663.

Cornell University, Graduate Fields of Agriculture and Life Sciences, Field of Education, Ithaca, NY 14853-0001. Offerings include curriculum and instruction (MPS, MS, PhD). Terminal master's awarded for partial completion of doctoral program. Faculty: 26 full-time. *Degree requirements:* For doctorate, dissertation required, foreign language not required. *Entrance requirements:* For doctorate, GRE General Test or MAT, TOEFL. Application deadline: 5/1. Application fee: $65. Electronic applications accepted. • Director of Graduate Studies, 607-255-4278. Application contact: Graduate Field Assistant, 607-255-4278. E-mail: edgrfld@cornell.edu.

Dalhousie University, School of Education, Halifax, NS B3H 3J5, Canada. Offerings include curriculum and special subjects (MA, M Ed). Program being phased out; applicants no longer accepted. School faculty: 19 full-time, 12 part-time. *Degree requirements:* Thesis required (for some programs), foreign language not required. • Dr. K. C. Sullivan, Director, 902-494-3724.

Delaware State University, Department of Education, Program in Curriculum and Instruction, Dover, DE 19901-2277. Awards MA. Part-time and evening/weekend programs available. *Degree requirements:* Comprehensive exam required, thesis optional, foreign language not required. *Entrance requirements:* GRE General Test, minimum GPA of 3.0 in major, 2.75 overall. Application deadline: 6/30 (priority date; rolling processing). Application fee: $10.

DePaul University, School of Education, Program in Urban Education, Chicago, IL 60604-2287. Offerings include curriculum development (MA, M Ed). Accredited by NCATE. Program faculty: 1 full-time (0 women). *Degree requirements:* Thesis optional, foreign language not required. *Entrance requirements:* Interview, minimum GPA of 2.75, work experience. Application deadline: rolling. Application fee: $25. *Expenses:* Tuition $320 per credit hour. Fees $30 per year. • Barbara Radner, Chairperson, 312-362-8828.

Doane College, Program in Education, Crete, NE 68333-2430. Offerings include curriculum and instruction (M Ed). Accredited by NCATE. *Degree requirements:* Thesis required, foreign language not required. *Average time to degree:* master's–2.7 years part-time. *Entrance requirements:* Minimum GPA of 2.5. Application deadline: rolling. Application fee: $25. *Tuition:* $135 per credit hour. • Dr. Marilyn Kent Byrne, Dean, 402-826-8604. Fax: 402-826-8278. E-mail: mbyrne@doane.edu. Application contact: Wilma Daddario, Director, Office of Graduate Studies, 402-464-1223. Fax: 402-466-4228. E-mail: wdaddario@doane.edu.

Dominican College of San Rafael, School of Education, Program in Curriculum and Instruction, San Rafael, CA 94901-2298. Awards MS. Program also offered in Ukiah, CA. Part-time programs available. Students: 21 part-time (19 women); includes 2 minority (1 Asian American, 1 Native American). 19 applicants, 100% accepted. In 1997, 9 degrees awarded (100% found work related to degree). *Degree requirements:* Research project required, foreign language and thesis not required. *Average time to degree:* master's–2 years part-time. *Entrance requirements:* Dominican credential program. Application deadline: 7/31 (priority date; rolling processing). Application fee: $25. *Expenses:* Tuition $12,816 per year full-time, $534 per unit part-time. Fees $320 per year full-time. *Financial aid:* Federal Work-Study available. Financial aid application deadline: 3/15; applicants required to submit FAFSA. *Faculty research:* Parent education. • Dr. Barry A. Kaufmann, Chairperson, 415-485-3287. Fax: 415-485-3790.

Drake University, School of Education, Department of Teaching and Learning, Program in Teacher Education and Curriculum Studies, Des Moines, IA 50311-4516. Awards MSE, Ed D, Ed S. Faculty: 5 full-time (3 women), 6 part-time (5 women). Students: 8 full-time (all women), 97 part-time (64 women); includes 1 minority (Asian American). 65 applicants, 82% accepted. In 1997, 71 master's, 1 doctorate awarded. *Degree requirements:* For master's and Ed S, thesis or alternative; for doctorate, dissertation. *Entrance requirements:* For master's, GRE General Test (minimum combined score of 1000) or MAT (minimum score 36); for doctorate, GRE General Test (minimum combined score of 1000) or MAT (minimum score 43); for Ed S, GRE General Test or MAT. Application deadline: rolling. Application fee: $25. *Tuition:* $16,000 per year full-time, $260 per hour (minimum) part-time. *Financial aid:* Career-related internships or fieldwork available. Aid available to part-time students. • Dr. Eunice Merideth, Chair, Department of Teaching and Learning, 515-271-3911. Application contact: Ann J. Martin, Graduate Coordinator, 515-271-3871. Fax: 515-271-2831. E-mail: ajm@admin.drake.edu.

Drexel University, College of Arts and Sciences, School of Education, 3141 Chestnut Street, Philadelphia, PA 19104-2875. Offerings include science of instruction (MS). School faculty: 2 full-time (both women), 5 part-time (4 women), 3.7 FTE. *Entrance requirements:* GRE, TOEFL (minimum score 570), bachelor's degree in related field. Application deadline: 8/21 (3/5 for spring admission). Application fee: $35. *Expenses:* Tuition $494 per credit hour (minimum). Fees $121 per quarter full-time, $65 per quarter part-time. • Dr. Fredricka Reisman, Head, 215-895-6770. Fax: 215-895-4999.

Duquesne University, School of Education, Department of Elementary, Secondary, and Reading Education, Instructional Leadership Excellence Doctoral Program (ILEAD), Pittsburgh, PA 15282-0001. Awards Ed D. Part-time and evening/weekend programs available. Faculty: 14 full-time (7 women). Students: 37 full-time (23 women). 55 applicants, 67% accepted. *Degree requirements:* Computer language, dissertation required, foreign language not required. *Entrance requirements:* MAT, GRE General Test. Application deadline: 3/1 (priority date). Application fee: $100. *Expenses:* Tuition $481 per credit. Fees $39 per credit. *Financial aid:* In 1997–98, 14 students received aid, including 10 research assistantships (all to first-year students) averaging $150 per month and totaling $11,250, 10 scholarships (all to first-year students) averaging $150 per month; Federal Work-Study, institutionally sponsored loans, and career-related internships or fieldwork also available. Financial aid applicants required to submit FAFSA. • Application contact: Dr. Robert Agostino, Director of Admissions, 412-396-6104. Fax: 412-396-5585.

Eastern Michigan University, College of Education, Department of Teacher Education, Program in Advanced Study in Curriculum and Instruction, Ypsilanti, MI 48197. Awards MA. Accredited by NCATE. Evening/weekend programs available. *Application deadline:* 5/15 (rolling processing; 3/15 for spring admission). *Application fee:* $30. *Expenses:* Tuition $2691 per year full-time, $150 per credit hour part-time for state residents; $6300 per year full-time, $350 per credit hour part-time for nonresidents. Fees $368 per year full-time, $88 per semester (minimum) part-time. *Financial aid:* Fellowships, teaching assistantships available. Aid available to part-time students. Financial aid application deadline: 3/15; applicants required to submit FAFSA. • Dr. Georgea Langer, Coordinator, 734-487-3185.

Eastern Michigan University, College of Education, Department of Teacher Education, Program in K–12 Curriculum, Ypsilanti, MI 48197. Awards MA. Accredited by NCATE. In 1997, 4 degrees awarded. *Entrance requirements:* GRE, TOEFL (minimum score 500). Application deadline: 5/15 (rolling processing; 3/15 for spring admission). Application fee: $30. *Expenses:* Tuition $2691 per year full-time, $150 per credit hour part-time for state residents; $6300 per year full-time, $350 per credit hour part-time for nonresidents. Fees $368 per year full-time, $88 per semester (minimum) part-time. *Financial aid:* Fellowships, teaching assistantships available. Aid available to part-time students. Financial aid application deadline: 3/15; applicants required to submit FAFSA. • Dr. Georgea Langer, Coordinator, 734-487-3185.

Eastern Washington University, College of Education and Human Development, Department of Education, Program in Curriculum and Instruction, Cheney, WA 99004-2431. Awards M Ed. Accredited by NCATE. *Degree requirements:* Comprehensive exam required, thesis not required. *Entrance requirements:* Minimum GPA of 3.0. Application deadline: 4/1 (priority date; rolling processing; 1/15 for spring admission). Application fee: $35. *Tuition:* $4200 per year full-time, $140 per credit part-time for state residents; $12,780 per year full-time, $415 per credit part-time for nonresidents. *Financial aid:* Application deadline 2/1. • Dr. Neville Hosking, Adviser, 509-359-6492.

Emporia State University, School of Graduate Studies, The Teachers College, Division of Early Childhood/Elementary Teacher Education, Program in Curriculum and Instruction, Emporia, KS 66801-5087. Offers reading, elementary/secondary (MS). Students: 6 part-time (all women). 0 applicants. In 1997, 2 degrees awarded. *Degree requirements:* Comprehensive exam or thesis required, foreign language not required. *Entrance requirements:* GRE General Test or MAT, TOEFL (minimum score 550), written exam. Application deadline: 8/15 (priority date; rolling processing). Application fee: $30 ($75 for international students). Electronic applications accepted. *Tuition:* $2300 per year full-time, $103 per credit hour part-time for state residents; $6012 per year full-time, $258 per credit hour part-time for nonresidents. *Financial aid:* Federal Work-Study, institutionally sponsored loans available. Financial aid application deadline: 3/15; applicants required to submit FAFSA. • Dr. Eileen Hogan, Chair, Division of Early Childhood/Elementary Teacher Education, 316-341-5751. E-mail: hoganeil@emporia.edu.

Emporia State University, School of Graduate Studies, The Teachers College, Division of School Leadership/Middle and Secondary Teacher Education, Program in Curriculum and Instruction, Emporia, KS 66801-5087. Offers supervision and curriculum (MS). Accredited by NCATE. Students: 3 full-time (2 women), 10 part-time (7 women); includes 1 minority (Hispanic). 3 applicants, 100% accepted. In 1997, 10 degrees awarded. *Degree requirements:* Comprehensive exam or thesis required, foreign language not required. *Entrance requirements:* GRE General Test (minimum score 480 on each section) or MAT (minimum score 42), TOEFL (minimum score 550). Application deadline: 8/15 (priority date; rolling processing). Application fee: $30 ($75 for international students). Electronic applications accepted. *Tuition:* $2300 per year full-time, $103 per credit hour part-time for state residents; $6012 per year full-time, $258 per credit hour part-time for nonresidents. *Financial aid:* Federal Work-Study, institutionally sponsored loans, and career-related internships or fieldwork available. Financial aid application deadline: 3/15; applicants required to submit FAFSA. • Dr. Jerry Will, Chair, Division of School Leadership/Middle and Secondary Teacher Education, 316-341-5777.

Fairleigh Dickinson University, Teaneck–Hackensack Campus, University College: Arts, Sciences, and Professional Studies, Peter Sammartino School of Education, Teaching Program, 1000 River Road, Teaneck, NJ 07666-1914. Awards MAT. Faculty: 11 full-time (8 women), 27 part-time (10 women). *Degree requirements:* Research project required, foreign language and thesis not required. *Entrance requirements:* GRE, MAT, PRAXIS. Application deadline: rolling. Application fee: $35. *Expenses:* Tuition $522 per credit. Fees $302 per year full-time, $138 per year part-time. *Faculty research:* Mathematics for students with learning disabilities, gender issues in education, social problem-solving and conflict resolution in the classroom, multicultural education in the elementary classroom, problems encountered by international students in college programs. • Dr. Eloise Forster, Interim Director, Peter Sammartino School of Education, 201-692-2834. Fax: 201-692-2603.

Florida Atlantic University, College of Education, Department of Teacher Education, Boca Raton, FL 33431-0991. Offerings include curriculum and instruction (Ed D, Ed S). Department faculty: 24 full-time (18 women), 6 part-time (4 women). *Degree requirements:* For doctorate, dissertation, departmental qualifying exam required, foreign language not required; for Ed S, departmental qualifying exam required, foreign language and thesis not required. *Entrance requirements:* For doctorate, GRE General Test (minimum combined score of 1000), GRE Subject Test (score in 50th percentile or higher), minimum graduate GPA of 3.25, 3.0 in last 2 years of undergraduate course work; for Ed S, GRE General Test (minimum combined score of 1000), GRE Subject Test (score in 50th percentile or higher). Application deadline: rolling. Application fee: $20. *Expenses:* Tuition $2520 per year full-time, $140 per credit hour part-time for state residents; $8712 per year full-time, $484 per credit hour part-time for nonresidents. Fees $5 per year (minimum). • Dr. Valerie Bristor, Chairperson, 561-297-3584. Application contact: University Registrar, 561-297-3040.

Florida Gulf Coast University, College of Professional Studies, School of Education, Program in Educational Technology, Fort Myers, FL 33965-6565. Offers curriculum and instruction (MA, M Ed). Part-time and evening/weekend programs available. Postbaccalaureate distance learning degree programs offered (minimal on-campus study). Faculty: 2 full-time (0 women). *Degree requirements:* Computer language, final project or portfolio required, foreign language and thesis not required. *Entrance requirements:* GRE General Test (minimum combined score of 900), MAT (minimum score 42), minimum undergraduate GPA of 3.0 in last 2 years. Application fee: $20. Electronic applications accepted. *Faculty research:* Internet in schools, technology in pre-service and in-service teacher training. • Application contact: Ed George, Coordinator, 941-590-7803. E-mail: ejgeorge@fgcu.edu.

Florida International University, College of Education, Department of Educational Leadership and Policy Studies, Program in Curriculum and Instruction, Miami, FL 33199. Awards Ed D, Ed S. Accredited by NCATE. Part-time and evening/weekend programs available. Students: 13 full-time (6 women), 91 part-time (57 women); includes 32 minority (13 African Americans, 3 Asian Americans, 16 Hispanics), 13 international. Average age 42. 26 applicants, 31% accepted. In 1997, 5 doctorates awarded. *Degree requirements:* For doctorate, dissertation, 3 years of teaching experience required, foreign language not required. *Entrance requirements:* For doctorate, GRE General Test (minimum combined score of 1000) or minimum GPA of 3.0. Application deadline: 4/1 (priority date; rolling processing; 10/1 for spring admission). Application fee: $20. *Expenses:* Tuition $138 per credit hour for state residents; $482 per credit hour for nonresidents. Fees $46 per semester. *Financial aid:* Fellowships, research assistantships, teaching assistantships, full and partial tuition waivers, Federal Work-Study available. Aid available to part-time students. *Faculty research:* Teacher training, elementary and secondary education. • Dr. Kingsley Banya, Chairperson, Department of Educational Leadership and Policy Studies, 305-348-2724. Fax: 305-348-2081. E-mail: banyak@fiu.edu.

Fordham University, Graduate School of Education, Division of Curriculum and Teaching, New York, NY 10023. Offerings include curriculum and teaching (MSE); language, literacy, and learning (PhD). One or more programs accredited by NCATE. *Degree requirements:* For doctorate, dissertation required, foreign language not required. *Entrance requirements:* For doctorate, MAT. Application fee: $50. • Dr. Angela Carrasquillo, Chairperson, 212-636-6427.

Freed–Hardeman University, Program in Education, 158 East Main Street, Henderson, TN 38340-2399. Offers curriculum and instruction (M Ed). Part-time and evening/weekend programs available. Faculty: 8 full-time (1 woman), 4 part-time (2 women). Students: 63 full-time (44 women), 147 part-time (114 women); includes 67 minority (all African Americans). Average age 32. 75 applicants, 80% accepted. In 1997, 69 degrees awarded. *Degree requirements:* Thesis optional. *Entrance requirements:* GRE General Test (minimum combined score of 800), MAT (minimum score 28), or NTE. Application deadline: 8/1 (rolling processing; 12/1 for spring admission). Application fee: $25. *Tuition:* $159 per semester hour. *Financial aid:* Graduate assistantships, partial tuition waivers, Federal Work-Study, and career-related internships or fieldwork available. Aid available to part-time students. Financial aid application deadline: 8/1; applicants required to submit FAFSA. • Dr. James Murphy, Director, Graduate Studies in Education, 901-989-6082. Fax: 901-989-6065. E-mail: jmurphy@fhu.edu.

Fresno Pacific University, Graduate School, Programs in Education, Division of Foundations, Curriculum and Teaching, Program in Curriculum and Teaching, Fresno, CA 93702-4709. Awards MA Ed. Faculty: 1 full-time (0 women), 6 part-time (3 women). Students: 41 part-time (31 women). Average age 38. *Degree requirements:* Thesis or alternative. *Application deadline:* 7/31. *Application fee:* $75. *Tuition:* $250 per unit. • Dr. Rod Janzen, Head, Division of Foundations, Curriculum and Teaching, 209-453-2210. Fax: 209-453-2001.

Frostburg State University, School of Education, Department of Educational Professions, Program in Curriculum and Instruction, Frostburg, MD 21532-1099. Offers elementary education (M Ed), secondary education (M Ed). Part-time and evening/weekend programs available. *Application deadline:* 7/15 (rolling processing). *Application fee:* $30.

Gannon University, School of Graduate Studies, College of Humanities, Business, and Education, School of Education, Program in Curriculum and Instruction, Erie, PA 16541. Awards M Ed. Part-time and evening/weekend programs available. Students: 1 (woman) full-time, 16 part-time (14 women). Average age 34. 11 applicants, 100% accepted. In 1997, 3 degrees awarded. *Degree requirements:* Thesis, comprehensive exam, research project. *Entrance requirements:* GRE General Test or MAT, interview, teaching certificate. Application deadline: rolling. Application fee: $25. *Expenses:* Tuition $405 per credit. Fees $200 per year full-time, $8 per credit part-time. *Financial aid:* Available to part-time students. Financial aid application deadline: 3/1; applicants required to submit FAFSA. • Application contact: Beth Nemenz, Director of Admissions, 814-871-7240. Fax: 814-871-5803. E-mail: admissions@gannon.edu.

The George Washington University, Graduate School of Education and Human Development, Department of Teacher Preparation and Special Education, Program in Curriculum and Instruction, Washington, DC 20052. Awards MA Ed, Ed D, Ed S. Accredited by NCATE. Evening/weekend programs available. Faculty: 2 full-time (both women), 2 part-time (both women), 3 FTE. Students: 3 full-time (all women), 56 part-time (50 women); includes 16 minority (11 African Americans, 1 Asian American, 4 Hispanics). Average age 39. 16 applicants, 81% accepted. In 1997, 7 master's, 1 doctorate, 2 Ed Ss awarded. *Degree requirements:* For

Directory: Curriculum and Instruction

The George Washington University (continued)
master's and Ed S, comprehensive exam required, foreign language and thesis not required; for doctorate, dissertation, comprehensive exam required, foreign language not required. *Entrance requirements:* For master's, GRE General Test or MAT, minimum GPA of 2.75, resume; for doctorate and Ed S, GRE General Test or MAT, interview, minimum GPA of 3.3. Application deadline: 3/1 (priority date; rolling processing; 10/1 for spring admission). Application fee: $50. *Expenses:* Tuition $680 per semester hour. Fees $35 per semester hour. *Financial aid:* Fellowships, research assistantships, partial tuition waivers, Federal Work-Study, and career-related internships or fieldwork available. Financial aid applicants required to submit FAFSA. *Faculty research:* Cognitive skills-teaching, metacognitive strategies, adult basic literacy. • Dr. Gloria Horrworth, Faculty Coordinator, 202-994-6170.

Georgia Southern University, College of Education, Department of Curriculum, Foundations and Research, Statesboro, GA 30460-8126. Offerings include curriculum studies (Ed D). Accredited by NCATE. Department faculty: 15 full-time (7 women). *Degree requirements:* Dissertation, exams. *Entrance requirements:* GRE General Test (minimum combined score of 1000) or MAT (minimum score 55), minimum GPA of 3.5. Application deadline: 8/1 (priority date; rolling processing; 2/15 for spring admission). Application fee: $0. *Tuition:* $2619 per year full-time, $287 per semester (minimum) part-time for state residents; $8619 per year full-time, $1037 per semester (minimum) part-time for nonresidents. • Dr. Jane Page, Chair, 912-681-5091. Fax: 912-681-8144. Application contact: Dr. John R. Diebolt, Associate Graduate Dean, 912-681-5384. Fax: 912-681-0740. E-mail: gradschool@gsvms2.cc.gasou.edu.

Georgia State University, College of Education, Department of Educational Policy Studies, Program in Curriculum Development and Instruction Processes, Atlanta, GA 30303-3083. Awards PhD. Accredited by NCATE. Program being phased out; applicants no longer accepted. Students: 6 full-time (5 women), 2 part-time (both women); includes 4 minority (3 African Americans, 1 Asian American), 1 international. Average age 42. *Degree requirements:* Dissertation, comprehensive exam. *Expenses:* Tuition $2673 per year full-time, $99 per semester hour part-time for state residents; $10,692 per year full-time, $396 per semester hour part-time for nonresidents. Fees $228 per year. *Financial aid:* Federal Work-Study, institutionally sponsored loans available. *Faculty research:* Curriculum criticism, development and evaluation. • Dr. H. Parker Blount, Chair, Department of Educational Policy Studies, 404-651-2582.

Gonzaga University, Graduate School, School of Education, Program in Administration and Curriculum, Spokane, WA 99258-0001. Awards MAA. Accredited by NCATE. Faculty: 18 full-time (5 women), 20 part-time (9 women). Students: 240 full-time (158 women); includes 13 minority (7 African Americans, 4 Asian Americans, 1 Hispanic, 1 Native American), 100 international. Average age 39. 135 applicants, 39% accepted. In 1997, 165 degrees awarded. *Degree requirements:* Comprehensive exam required, foreign language and thesis not required. *Entrance requirements:* GRE General Test or MAT, TOEFL (minimum score 550), minimum B average in undergraduate course work. Application deadline: 7/20 (priority date; rolling processing; 11/1 for spring admission). Application fee: $40. *Tuition:* $7380 per year (minimum) full-time, $410 per credit (minimum) part-time. *Financial aid:* Teaching assistantships available. Aid available to part-time students. Financial aid application deadline: 3/1. • Dr. Robert Bialozer, Director, 509-328-4220 Ext. 3491.

Grambling State University, College of Education, Grambling, LA 71245. Offerings include curriculum and instruction (Ed D). Accredited by NCATE. Ed D (curriculum and instruction, educational leadership) offered jointly with Louisiana Tech University and Northeast Louisiana University. Postbaccalaureate distance learning degree programs offered. College faculty: 23 full-time (8 women), 13 part-time (9 women), 26 FTE. *Degree requirements:* Dissertation required, foreign language not required. *Average time to degree:* master's–1.5 years full-time, 3 years part-time; doctorate–3.5 years full-time, 7 years part-time. *Entrance requirements:* GRE. Application deadline: rolling. Application fee: $15. *Tuition:* $1960 per year full-time, $297 per semester (minimum) part-time for state residents; $7110 per year full-time, $297 per semester (minimum) part-time for nonresidents. • Dr. Andolyn Harrison, Acting Dean, 318-274-2251.

Harvard University, Graduate School of Education, Area of Learning and Teaching, Cambridge, MA 02138. Offers programs in arts in education (Ed M); education in the community (Ed D); experienced teachers program (Ed M, CAS); individualized program (Ed M); learning and teaching (Ed M, Ed D), including curriculum development and evaluation (Ed D), study of teaching (Ed D); mid-career mathematics and science (teaching certification) (Ed M, CAS); philosophy of education and curriculum theory (Ed D); schools and schooling (Ed D); teaching and curriculum (teaching certification) (Ed M); technology in education (Ed M). Part-time programs available. Faculty: 7 full-time (5 women), 16 part-time (8 women), 10.3 FTE. Students: 176 full-time (111 women), 48 part-time (32 women); includes 62 minority (20 African Americans, 25 Asian Americans, 13 Hispanics, 4 Native Americans), 13 international. Average age 35. 136 applicants, 17% accepted. In 1997, 218 master's, 11 doctorates, 5 CASs awarded. Terminal master's awarded for partial completion of doctoral program. *Degree requirements:* For doctorate, dissertation required, foreign language not required. *Average time to degree:* master's–1 year full-time, 2.1 years part-time; doctorate–6.3 years full-time, 9 years part-time; other advanced degree–1 year full-time, 2 years part-time. *Entrance requirements:* GRE General Test, TOEFL (minimum score 600), TWE (minimum score 5.0). Application deadline: 1/2. Application fee: $60. *Financial aid:* In 1997–98, 67 students received aid, including 21 fellowships (10 to first-year students) totaling $344,113, 8 research assistantships averaging $588 per month, 60 teaching assistantships averaging $670 per month, 49 need-based scholarships (3 to first-year students) totaling $416,012; Federal Work-Study and career-related internships or fieldwork also available. Aid available to part-time students. Financial aid application deadline: 1/8; applicants required to submit FAFSA. *Faculty research:* Science education, philosophy of education, community education, perceived and actual participation in secondary school classrooms. • Robert Kegan, Chair, 617-496-2974. Fax: 617-495-7843. Application contact: Roland Hence, Director of Admissions, 617-495-3414. Fax: 617-496-3577. E-mail: gseadmissions@harvard.edu.

Hood College, Department of Education, Frederick, MD 21701-8575. Offerings include curriculum and instruction (MS), with options in early childhood education, elementary education, elementary school science and mathematics, reading, secondary education, special education. *Entrance requirements:* Minimum GPA of 2.5. Application deadline: rolling. Application fee: $30. *Tuition:* $285 per credit. • Dr. Patricia Bartlett, Chairperson, 301-696-3471. E-mail: bartlett@nimue.hood.edu. Application contact: Hood College Graduate School, 301-696-3600. Fax: 301-696-3597. E-mail: postmaster@nimue.hood.edu.

Idaho State University, College of Education, Division I, Pocatello, ID 83209. Offerings include curriculum and instruction (M Ed). Accredited by NCATE. Postbaccalaureate distance learning degree programs offered (no on-campus study). Division faculty: 19 full-time (8 women), 4 part-time (0 women). *Degree requirements:* Oral exam, written exam required, thesis optional, foreign language not required. *Average time to degree:* master's–2 years full-time, 4 years part-time; other advanced degree–1 year full-time, 2 years part-time. *Entrance requirements:* GRE General Test (score in 35th percentile or higher on one section) or MAT (minimum score 48), minimum undergraduate GPA of 3.0. Application deadline: 7/1 (priority date; rolling processing; 12/1 for spring admission). Application fee: $30. *Tuition:* $3130 per year full-time, $136 per credit hour part-time for state residents; $9370 per year full-time, $226 per credit hour part-time for nonresidents. • Dr. Peter Denner, Director, 208-236-4230. E-mail: dennpete@isu.edu. Application contact: Dr. Stephanie Salzman, Director, Office of Standards and Assessment, 208-236-3114. Fax: 208-236-4697. E-mail: salzstep@isu.edu.

Illinois State University, College of Education, Department of Curriculum and Instruction, Normal, IL 61790-2200. Offers programs in curriculum and instruction (MA, MS, MS Ed, Ed D), educational policies (Ed D), postsecondary education (Ed D), supervision (Ed D). Accredited by NCATE. Faculty: 28 full-time (11 women), 3 part-time (1 woman), 28.78 FTE. Students: 17 full-time (14 women), 117 part-time (89 women); includes 14 minority (10 African Americans, 1 Asian American, 3 Hispanics), 4 international. 28 applicants, 89% accepted. In 1997, 27 master's, 7 doctorates awarded. *Degree requirements:* For master's, variable foreign language requirement, thesis or alternative; for doctorate, variable foreign language requirement, dissertation, 2 terms of residency, internship. *Entrance requirements:* For master's, GRE General Test (minimum combined score of 800), minimum GPA of 3.0 in last 60 hours; for doctorate, GRE General Test. Application deadline: rolling. Application fee: $0. *Expenses:* Tuition $2454 per year full-time, $102 per hour part-time for state residents; $7362 per year full-time, $307 per hour part-time for nonresidents. Fees $1048 per year full-time, $44 per hour part-time. *Financial aid:* In 1997–98, 5 research assistantships averaging $880 per month, 3 teaching assistantships, 2 assistantships were awarded; full tuition waivers also available. Financial aid application deadline: 4/1. *Total annual research expenditures:* $142,642. • Dr. John Godbold, Acting Chairperson, 309-438-5425.

Indiana State University, School of Education, Department of Curriculum and Instruction and Media Technology, Terre Haute, IN 47809-1401. Offers programs in business education (MA, MS, PhD, Ed S), curriculum and instruction (M Ed, PhD), educational media (MA, MS, Ed S), industrial arts education (PhD), secondary education (M Ed, MS, PhD, Ed S). Accredited by NCATE. Faculty: 16 full-time (4 women). Students: 13 full-time (6 women), 22 part-time (12 women); includes 2 minority (both African Americans), 5 international. Average age 36. 23 applicants, 65% accepted. In 1997, 12 master's, 2 doctorates awarded. *Degree requirements:* For doctorate, 2 foreign languages, computer language, dissertation. *Entrance requirements:* For master's, minimum undergraduate GPA of 2.5; for doctorate, GRE General Test (minimum score 500 on each section); for Ed S, GRE General Test (minimum combined score of 900), minimum graduate GPA of 3.25. Application deadline: rolling. Application fee: $20. *Tuition:* $143 per credit hour for state residents; $325 per credit hour for nonresidents. *Financial aid:* In 1997–98, 8 fellowships (2 to first-year students), 7 research assistantships (6 to first-year students), 1 teaching assistantship were awarded; partial tuition waivers also available. Financial aid application deadline: 3/1. *Faculty research:* Discipline FERPA reading, teacher strengths and needs. • Dr. Jerry A. Summers, Chairperson, 812-237-2960. Application contact: Dr. Robert Williams, Graduate Adviser, 812-237-2952.

Indiana University Bloomington, School of Education, Department of Curriculum and Instruction, Bloomington, IN 47405. Offers programs in art education (MS), curriculum and instruction (Ed D, PhD), early childhood education (MS, Ed S), elementary education (MS, Ed S), secondary education (MS, Ed S), social studies education (MS), special education (MS, Ed D, PhD, Ed S). PhD offered through the University Graduate School. Part-time and evening/weekend programs available. Faculty: 23 full-time (9 women). Students: 47 full-time (32 women), 68 part-time (53 women); includes 17 minority (7 African Americans, 4 Asian Americans, 6 Hispanics), 28 international. In 1997, 13 doctorates awarded. Terminal master's awarded for partial completion of doctoral program. *Degree requirements:* For doctorate, dissertation required, foreign language not required; for Ed S, comprehensive exam or project required, foreign language not required. *Entrance requirements:* For master's, GRE General Test (minimum combined score of 1300 on three sections); for doctorate and Ed S, GRE General Test (minimum combined score of 1500 on three sections). Application deadline: 3/1 (priority date; rolling processing). Application fee: $35. *Expenses:* Tuition $153 per credit hour for state residents; $446 per credit hour for nonresidents. Fees $343 per year. *Financial aid:* Fellowships, research assistantships, teaching assistantships, partial tuition waivers, Federal Work-Study, institutionally sponsored loans, and career-related internships or fieldwork available. Aid available to part-time students. • Peter Kloosterman, Chairperson, 812-856-8100. Application contact: Sara White, 812-856-8100.

Indiana Wesleyan University, Adult and Professional Studies Program, Program in Graduate Teacher Education, Marion, IN 46953-4999. Offerings include curriculum and instruction (M Ed). Program faculty: 50 part-time (15 women). *Entrance requirements:* GRE General Test (minimum combined score of 1000), MAT (minimum score 40), NTE, minimum GPA of 2.75, related experience, teaching license. Application deadline: rolling. Application fee: $20. *Tuition:* $239 per hour. • Dr. Larry Lindsay, Director, 765-677-2894. Fax: 765-677-2380. Application contact: Beth Dickerson, Director of Marketing, 765-677-2863.

Inter American University of Puerto Rico, San Germán Campus, Department of Education, San Germán, PR 00683-5008. Offerings include curriculum and instruction (MA Ed). Department faculty: 9 full-time (2 women), 16 part-time (9 women). *Application deadline:* 4/30 (priority date; rolling processing; 11/15 for spring admission). *Application fee:* $31. *Expenses:* Tuition $150 per credit. Fees $177 per semester. • Dr. Ivan Calimano, Coordinator of Graduate Programs, 787-264-1912 Ext. 7355. Application contact: Mildred Camacho, Admissions Director, 787-892-3090. Fax: 787-892-6350.

Iowa State University of Science and Technology, College of Education, Department of Curriculum and Instruction, Program in Curriculum and Instruction Technology, Ames, IA 50011. Awards M Ed, MS, PhD. *Degree requirements:* For master's, thesis or alternative; for doctorate, dissertation. *Entrance requirements:* For master's, TOEFL; for doctorate, GRE General Test, TOEFL. Application deadline: 6/1 (priority date; 9/1 for spring admission). Application fee: $20 ($30 for international students). *Expenses:* Tuition $3166 per year full-time, $176 per credit part-time for state residents; $9324 per year full-time, $518 per credit part-time for nonresidents. Fees $200 per year. • Application contact: Daniel Robinson, 515-294-1241.

Johnson State College, Graduate Program in Education, Program in Curriculum and Instruction, Johnson, VT 05656-9405. Awards MA Ed. Part-time programs available. Students: 1 (woman) full-time, 19 part-time (15 women). *Degree requirements:* Thesis or alternative, comprehensive exam required, foreign language not required. *Entrance requirements:* Interview. Application deadline: 7/15 (priority date; rolling processing; 11/1 for spring admission). Application fee: $30. *Expenses:* Tuition $164 per credit for state residents; $383 per credit for nonresidents. Fees $15.90 per credit. *Financial aid:* Federal Work-Study, institutionally sponsored loans, and career-related internships or fieldwork available. Aid available to part-time students. Financial aid application deadline: 3/1; applicants required to submit FAFSA. • Application contact: Catherine H. Higley, Administrative Assistant, 802-635-2356 Ext. 1244. Fax: 802-635-1248. E-mail: higleyc@badger.jsc.vsc.edu.

Kansas State University, College of Education, Department of Curriculum and Instruction, Manhattan, KS 66506. Awards Ed D, PhD. Accredited by NCATE. Part-time programs available. Students: 26 full-time (19 women), 91 part-time (75 women); includes 16 minority (10 African Americans, 6 Hispanics), 16 international. 27 applicants, 70% accepted. *Degree requirements:* Dissertation required, foreign language not required. *Entrance requirements:* GRE, MAT (average 56), minimum B average. Application deadline: 4/1 (priority date; rolling processing; 10/1 for spring admission). Application fee: $0 ($25 for international students). Electronic applications accepted. *Tuition:* $2218 per year full-time, $401 per semester (minimum) part-time for state residents; $6336 per year full-time, $1087 per semester (minimum) part-time for nonresidents. • Application contact: Paul Burden, Assistant Dean, 785-532-5595. Fax: 785-532-7304. E-mail: gradstudy@mail.educ.ksu.edu.

Kean University, School of Education, Department of Instruction, Curriculum and Administration, Instruction and Curriculum Program, Union, NJ 07083. Offers bilingual education (Certificate), bilingual/bicultural education (MA), classroom instruction (MA), earth science (MA), English as a second language (Certificate), mathematics/science/computer education (MA), teaching (MA), teaching English as a second language (MA). Accredited by NCATE. Part-time programs available. Students: 7 full-time (6 women), 157 part-time (132 women); includes 36 minority (16 African Americans, 20 Hispanics). Average age 35. In 1997, 77 master's awarded. *Degree requirements:* For master's, thesis, comprehensive exams required, foreign language not required. *Entrance requirements:* For master's, GRE General Test or MAT. Application deadline: 6/15 (rolling processing; 11/15 for spring admission). Application fee: $35. *Tuition:* $5926 per year full-time, $248 per credit part-time for state residents; $7312 per year full-time, $304 per credit part-time for nonresidents. *Financial aid:* Graduate assistantships available. • Dr. Janet Prince, Coordinator, 908-527-2525. Application contact: Joanne Morris, Director of Graduate Admissions, 908-527-2665. Fax: 908-527-2286. E-mail: grad_adm@turbo.kean.edu.

Keene State College, Program in Curriculum and Instruction, Keene, NH 03435. Awards M Ed. Part-time and evening/weekend programs available. Students: 3 full-time (all women), 14 part-time (12 women); includes 1 international. Average age 40. 8 applicants, 100% accepted. In 1997, 12 degrees awarded. *Degree requirements:* Project or thesis required, foreign language not required. *Entrance requirements:* Resume. Application deadline: 6/15 (rolling processing; 10/15 for spring admission). Application fee: $25 ($35 for international students). *Financial aid:* Research assistantships, Federal Work-Study, institutionally sponsored loans, and career-related internships or fieldwork available. Financial aid application deadline: 3/1; applicants required to submit FAFSA. • Dr. David Hill, Coordinator, 603-358-2331. Application contact: Peter Tandy, Academic Counselor, 603-358-2332. Fax: 603-358-2257. E-mail: ptandy@keene.edu.

Kent State University, Graduate School of Education, Department of Teaching, Leadership, and Curriculum Studies, Program in Curriculum and Instruction, Kent, OH 44242-0001. Awards MA, M Ed, PhD, Ed S. Accredited by NCATE. Part-time and evening/weekend programs available. Faculty: 12 full-time (8 women), 8 part-time (all women). Students: 68 full-time (59 women), 118 part-time (97 women); includes 16 minority (12 African Americans, 1 Asian American, 2 Hispanics, 1 Native American), 5 international. In 1997, 14 master's, 12 doctorates awarded. *Degree requirements:* For master's, thesis (MA) required, foreign language not required; for doctorate, dissertation required, foreign language not required. *Entrance requirements:* For master's, GRE General Test; for doctorate, GRE General Test (minimum score 550 on verbal section). Application deadline: rolling. Application fee: $30. *Tuition:* $4752 per year full-time, $216 per credit hour part-time for state residents; $9213 per year full-time, $419 per credit hour part-time for nonresidents. *Financial aid:* Application deadline 4/1. • Dr. Tim Rasinski, Coordinator, 330-672-2580. Application contact: Deborah Barber, Director, Office of Academic Services, 330-672-2862. Fax: 330-672-3549.

Kutztown University of Pennsylvania, Graduate School, College of Education, Program in Secondary Education, Kutztown, PA 19530. Offerings include curriculum and instruction (M Ed). Accredited by NCATE. Program faculty: 7 full-time (1 woman). *Degree requirements:* Comprehensive exam required, thesis optional, foreign language not required. *Entrance requirements:* GRE General Test, TOEFL, TSE. Application deadline: 3/1 (8/1 for spring admission). Application fee: $25. *Tuition:* $4111 per year full-time, $225 per credit hour part-time for state residents; $6879 per year full-time, $393 per credit hour part-time for nonresidents. • Kathleen Dolgos, Chairperson, 610-683-4259.

Lakehead University, Faculty of Education, Thunder Bay, ON P7B 5E1, Canada. Offerings include curriculum development (M Ed). *Degree requirements:* Thesis optional, foreign language not required. *Entrance requirements:* TOEFL (minimum score 550), honors degree, minimum B average. Application deadline: 2/1 (priority date; rolling processing). Application fee: $0.

La Sierra University, School of Education, Department of Curriculum and Instruction, Riverside, CA 92515-8247. Offers programs in curriculum and instruction (MA, Ed D, Ed S), special education (MA). Part-time and evening/weekend programs available. Faculty: 4 full-time (3 women), 7 part-time (3 women), 5 FTE. Students: 29. Average age 35. In 1997, 15 master's awarded. *Degree requirements:* For master's, computer language required, foreign language and thesis not required; for doctorate, dissertation required, foreign language not required; for Ed S, thesis optional, foreign language not required. *Entrance requirements:* For master's, minimum GPA of 3.0; for doctorate, GRE General Test, GRE Subject Test, minimum GPA of 3.3; for Ed S, minimum GPA of 3.3. Application deadline: rolling. Application fee: $30. *Financial aid:* Graduate assistantships, Federal Work-Study, and career-related internships or fieldwork available. Aid available to part-time students. Financial aid application deadline: 2/10. *Faculty research:* New teacher success, politics of knowledge, computer-assisted instruction, diversity issues. • Dr. Anita Oliver, Chair, 909-785-2203. Fax: 909-785-2205. Application contact: Myrna Costa-Casado, Director of Admissions, 909-785-2176. Fax: 909-785-2447. E-mail: mcosta@lasierra.edu.

Lehigh University, College of Education, Department of Education and Human Services, Program in Teacher Education and Reading, Bethlehem, PA 18015-3094. Offerings include curriculum and instruction (Ed D). Program faculty: 4 full-time (1 woman), 4 part-time (0 women). *Degree requirements:* Dissertation required, foreign language not required. *Entrance requirements:* GRE General Test, TOEFL, minimum graduate GPA of 3.3. Application deadline: rolling. Application fee: $40. *Expenses:* Tuition $470 per credit. Fees $12 per semester full-time, $6 per semester part-time. • Dr. H. Lynn Columba, Coordinator, 610-758-3230. Fax: 610-758-6223. E-mail: hlc0@lehigh.edu.

Lesley College, School of Education, Cambridge, MA 02138-2790. Offerings include curriculum and instruction (M Ed, CAGS). Postbaccalaureate distance learning degree programs offered (no on-campus study). School faculty: 36 full-time (31 women), 340 part-time (220 women). *Degree requirements:* Computer language required, foreign language and thesis not required. *Entrance requirements:* For master's, TOEFL (minimum score 550); for CAGS, interview, master's degree. Application deadline: rolling. Application fee: $45. *Tuition:* $425 per credit. • Dr. William L. Dandridge, Dean, 617-349-8375. Application contact: Graduate Admissions, 617-349-8300. Fax: 617-349-8366.

Lock Haven University of Pennsylvania, Office of Graduate Studies, Department of Education, Lock Haven, PA 17745-2390. Offers program in curriculum and instruction (M Ed). One or more programs accredited by NCATE. Part-time and evening/weekend programs available. Students: 31 part-time (8 women). Average age 35. 5 applicants, 100% accepted. *Entrance requirements:* Minimum undergraduate GPA of 3.0. Application deadline: rolling. Application fee: $25. Electronic applications accepted. *Expenses:* Tuition $3468 per year full-time, $193 per credit hour part-time for state residents; $6236 per year full-time, $346 per credit hour part-time for nonresidents. Fees $604 per year full-time, $46 per credit hour part-time for state residents; $604 per year full-time, $59 per credit hour part-time for nonresidents. *Financial aid:* Application deadline 8/1. • Dr. Susan Ashley, Director, 717-893-2205. E-mail: sashley@eagle.lhup.edu. Application contact: Office of Admissions, 717-893-2027. Fax: 717-893-2201. E-mail: admissions@eagle.lhup.edu.

Loras College, Program in Effective Teaching, Dubuque, IA 52004-0178. Awards MA. Program new for fall 1998. *Application deadline:* rolling. *Application fee:* $25. *Tuition:* $320 per credit. • Dr. James Allan, Chair, Department of Education, 319-588-7157. E-mail: jallan@loras.edu. Application contact: Office of Admissions, 319-588-7236. Fax: 319-588-7964.

Louisiana State University and Agricultural and Mechanical College, College of Education, Department of Curriculum and Instruction, Baton Rouge, LA 70803. Offers programs in curriculum and instruction (MA, PhD, Ed S), elementary education (M Ed), secondary education (M Ed). Accredited by NCATE. Faculty: 27 full-time (15 women), 1 (woman) part-time. Students: 124 full-time (109 women), 144 part-time (123 women); includes 33 minority (24 African Americans, 2 Asian Americans, 7 Hispanics), 13 international. Average age 36. 77 applicants, 90% accepted. In 1997, 110 master's, 11 doctorates, 30 Ed Ss awarded. Terminal master's awarded for partial completion of doctoral program. *Degree requirements:* For doctorate, residency required, foreign language not required; for Ed S, thesis optional, foreign language not required. *Entrance requirements:* For master's, GRE General Test (minimum combined score of 1000; average 1080), minimum GPA of 3.0; for doctorate, GRE General Test (minimum combined score of 1000; average 1100), minimum GPA of 3.0. Application deadline: 1/25 (priority date; rolling processing). Application fee: $25. *Tuition:* $2736 per year full-time, $285 per semester (minimum) part-time for state residents; $6636 per year full-time, $460 per semester (minimum) part-time for nonresidents. *Financial aid:* In 1997–98, 11 fellowships (1 to a first-year student), 27 research assistantships (1 to a first-year student), 4 service assistantships (1 to a first-year student) were awarded; teaching assistantships also available. *Faculty research:* Science and mathematics education, reading, curriculum theory, art education, foreign language and language arts. • Dr. Robert Lafayette, Interim Chair, 504-388-6867. Application contact: Dr. Earl Cheek, Professor, 504-388-6867. Fax: 504-388-1045.

Louisiana Tech University, College of Education, Department of Curriculum, Instruction and Leadership, Ruston, LA 71272. Offerings include curriculum and instruction (MS, Ed D). Accredited by NCATE. Department faculty: 16 full-time (11 women). *Degree requirements:* For doctorate, computer language, dissertation required, foreign language not required. *Entrance requirements:* For doctorate, GRE General Test (minimum combined score of 1000). Application deadline: 7/29 (2/3 for spring admission). Application fee: $20 ($30 for international students). *Tuition:* $2382 per year full-time, $223 per quarter (minimum) part-time for state residents; $5307 per year full-time, $223 per quarter (minimum) part-time for nonresidents. • Dr. Samuel V. Dauzat, Head, 318-257-4609.

Loyola College, College of Arts and Sciences, Department of Education, Program in Curriculum and Instruction, Baltimore, MD 21210-2699. Awards MA, M Ed, CAS. Part-time and evening/weekend programs available. Students: 31 full-time (21 women), 241 part-time (183 women); includes 26 minority (21 African Americans, 4 Asian Americans, 1 Hispanic), 2 international. In 1997, 72 master's, 1 CAS awarded. *Entrance requirements:* For CAS, master's degree. Application deadline: 8/1 (rolling processing; 12/1 for spring admission). Application fee: $35. *Tuition:* $222 per credit (minimum). *Financial aid:* Career-related internships or fieldwork available. • Dr. Beatrice Sarlos, Coordinator, 410-617-2492.

Loyola University Chicago, School of Education, Department of Curriculum, Instruction and Educational Psychology, Program in Curriculum and Instruction, 820 North Michigan Avenue, Chicago, IL 60611-2196. Awards MA, M Ed, Ed D. MA offered through the Graduate School. Students: 102. *Degree requirements:* For master's, comprehensive exam required, foreign language not required; for doctorate, computer language, dissertation, comprehensive exam required, foreign language not required. *Average time to degree:* master's–2 years full-time, 3 years part-time; doctorate–3 years full-time, 5 years part-time. *Entrance requirements:* For doctorate, GRE or MAT, interview. Application fee: $35. *Tuition:* $467 per semester hour. *Financial aid:* Application deadline 5/1. • Dr. Barney Berlin, Co-Director, 847-853-3303. Application contact: Marie Rosin-Dittmar, Admissions Coordinator, 847-853-3323. Fax: 847-853-3375. E-mail: mrosind@wpo.it.luc.edu.

Lynchburg College, School of Education and Human Development, Lynchburg, VA 24501-3199. Offerings include curriculum and instruction (M Ed). M Ed (adapted physical education, physical education) admissions temporarily suspended. *Entrance requirements:* Minimum GPA of 3.0 (undergraduate). Application fee: $20.

Lyndon State College, Graduate Programs in Education, Department of Education, Lyndonville, VT 05851. Offerings include curriculum and instruction (M Ed). *Degree requirements:* Exam or major field project required, foreign language and thesis not required. *Entrance requirements:* GRE General Test or MAT. Application deadline: 2/28 (priority date; 10/31 for spring admission). Application fee: $30. *Expenses:* Tuition $3924 per year full-time, $164 per credit part-time for state residents; $9192 per year full-time, $383 per credit part-time for nonresidents. Fees $632 per year. • Application contact: Elaine L. Turner, Administrative Secretary, 802-626-6497. Fax: 802-626-9770. E-mail: turnere@king.lsc.vsc.edu.

Malone College, Graduate School, Program in Education, Canton, OH 44709-3897. Offerings include curriculum and instruction (MA). Program faculty: 10 full-time (6 women), 11 part-time (5 women), 12.68 FTE. *Degree requirements:* Research practicum required, foreign language and thesis not required. *Entrance requirements:* Minimum GPA of 3.0, teaching license. Application deadline: 9/6 (rolling processing; 1/2 for spring admission). Application fee: $20. *Tuition:* $300 per credit hour. • Dr. Marietta Daulton, Director, 330-471-8447. Fax: 330-471-8478. E-mail: mdaulton@malone.edu. Application contact: Dan Depasquale, Director of Graduate Student Services, 800-257-4723. Fax: 330-471-8343. E-mail: depasquale@malone.edu.

Mankato State University, College of Education, Department of Curriculum and Instruction, South Rd and Ellis Ave, PO Box 8400, Mankato, MN 56002-8400. Offers programs in bilingual/bicultural education (MS), curriculum and instruction (MAT, MT), early childhood education (MS), education of the gifted and talented (MS), reading consultant (MS), secondary teaching (MA, MS, SP). Accredited by NCATE. Part-time programs available. Faculty: 14 full-time (5 women). Students: 21 full-time (14 women), 34 part-time (26 women). Average age 32. 16 applicants, 25% accepted. In 1997, 29 master's, 1 SP awarded. *Degree requirements:* For master's, thesis or alternative, comprehensive exam required, foreign language not required; for SP, thesis, comprehensive exam required, foreign language not required. *Entrance requirements:* For master's, GRE General Test or MAT, minimum GPA of 3.0 during previous 2 years; for SP, GRE, minimum GPA of 3.0. Application deadline: 7/10 (priority date; rolling processing; 10/30 for spring admission). Application fee: $20. *Tuition:* $126 per credit (minimum) for state residents; $200 per credit for nonresidents. *Financial aid:* Teaching assistantships, Federal Work-Study, institutionally sponsored loans, and career-related internships or fieldwork available. Aid available to part-time students. Financial aid application deadline: 3/15; applicants required to submit FAFSA. • Elizabeth Borchardt, Chairperson, 507-389-1516. Fax: 507-389-5853. Application contact: Joni Roberts, Admissions Coordinator, 507-389-2321. Fax: 507-389-5974. E-mail: grad@mankato.msus.edu.

Massachusetts College of Liberal Arts, Graduate Program in Education, North Adams, MA 01247-4100. Offerings include curriculum and instruction (M Ed). Program faculty: 8 full-time (5 women), 4 part-time (2 women). *Degree requirements:* Thesis required, foreign language not required. *Average time to degree:* master's–3 years part-time. *Entrance requirements:* Writing sample. Application deadline: rolling. Application fee: $0. *Expenses:* Tuition $130 per credit. Fees $15 per credit. • Dr. Susanne Chandler, Chair, 413-662-5381.

McGill University, Faculty of Graduate Studies and Research, Faculty of Education, Department of Educational Studies, Montréal, PQ H3A 2T5, Canada. Offerings include curriculum and instruction (M Ed), with options in curriculum studies, literacy studies. Department faculty: 24 full-time (10 women), 1 part-time. *Application deadline:* 3/1 (priority date; rolling processing; 3/1 for spring admission). *Application fee:* $60. *Expenses:* Tuition $1668 per year for Canadian residents; $8268 per year for nonresidents. Fees $828 per year for Canadian residents; $1216 per year for nonresidents. • Dr. Lynn Butler-Kisber, Director of Graduate Studies, 514-398-4531. E-mail: lbk@cel.lan.mcgill.ca. Application contact: Tina Shiavone, Graduate Program Coordinator, 514-398-4531. Fax: 514-398-7436.

Miami University, School of Education and Allied Professions, Department of Educational Leadership, Program in Curriculum and Teacher Leadership, Oxford, OH 45056. Awards M Ed. Accredited by NCATE. Part-time programs available. Students: 5 full-time (4 women), 35 part-time (31 women); includes 1 minority (African American), 5 international. 51 applicants, 88% accepted. In 1997, 12 degrees awarded. *Degree requirements:* Thesis or alternative, oral or written exam required, foreign language not required. *Entrance requirements:* MAT, minimum undergraduate GPA of 3.0 during previous 2 years or 2.75 overall. Application deadline: 3/1 (priority date; rolling processing; 12/15 for spring admission). Application fee: $35. *Tuition:* $5932 per year full-time, $255 per credit hour part-time for state residents; $12,392 per year full-time, $524 per credit hour part-time for nonresidents. *Financial aid:* Fellowships, research assistantships, teaching assistantships, full tuition waivers, Federal Work-Study available. Financial aid application deadline: 3/1. *Faculty research:* Curriculum theory. • Dr. Richard Quantz, Director of Graduate Study, 513-529-6825.

Michigan State University, College of Education, Department of Teacher Education, East Lansing, MI 48824-1020. Offers programs in curriculum and teaching (MA); curriculum, teaching and education policy (PhD, Ed S). Part-time and evening/weekend programs available. Postbaccalaureate distance learning degree programs offered (no on-campus study). Faculty: 55 (29 women). Students: 261 (184 women); includes 33 minority (23 African Americans, 4 Asian Americans, 5 Hispanics, 1 Native American), 36 international. In 1997, 100 master's, 15 doctorates awarded. *Degree requirements:* For doctorate, dissertation required, foreign language

Directory: Curriculum and Instruction

Michigan State University (continued)

not required. *Entrance requirements:* For doctorate and Ed S, GRE General Test or MAT. Application deadline: rolling. Application fee: $30 ($40 for international students). *Expenses:* Tuition $4609 per year full-time, $223 per credit hour (minimum) part-time for state residents; $8704 per year full-time, $450 per credit hour (minimum) part-time for nonresidents. Fees $576 per year full-time, $476 per year part-time. *Financial aid:* Fellowships, research assistantships, teaching assistantships available. *Faculty research:* Teacher learning, educational policy and social analysis, professional development, subject matter pedagogy. Total annual research expenditures: $1.285 million. • Dr. Stephen Koziol, Acting Chairperson, 517-355-9628.

MidAmerica Nazarene University, Graduate Studies in Education, Olathe, KS 66062-1899. Offerings include curriculum and instruction (M Ed). Faculty: 9 full-time (4 women), 1 part-time (0 women). *Degree requirements:* Computer language, thesis or alternative, creative project. *Average time to degree:* master's–1.2 years full-time. *Entrance requirements:* Minimum undergraduate GPA of 3.0, 2 years of teaching experience. Application deadline: rolling. Application fee: $75. *Tuition:* $7005 per year. • Dr. Jim Burns, Director, 913-791-3292. Application contact: Aileen Douglas, Graduate Studies Secretary, 913-791-3292. Fax: 913-791-3407. E-mail: adouglas@mnu.edu.

Middle Tennessee State University, College of Education, Department of Educational Leadership, Major in Curriculum and Instruction, Murfreesboro, TN 37132. Offers programs in curriculum specialist (M Ed, Ed S), secondary education (M Ed, Ed S). Accredited by NCATE. Students: 6 full-time (all women), 51 part-time (39 women); includes 7 minority (all African Americans). Average age 37. 11 applicants, 64% accepted. In 1997, 16 master's, 6 Ed Ss awarded. *Degree requirements:* Comprehensive exams required, foreign language and thesis not required. *Entrance requirements:* Cooperative English Test, MAT. Application deadline: 8/1 (priority date). Application fee: $5. *Expenses:* Tuition $2560 per year full-time, $129 per semester hour part-time for state residents; $7386 per year full-time, $340 per semester hour part-time for nonresidents. Fees $486 per year full-time, $17 per semester (minimum) part-time. *Financial aid:* Application deadline 5/1. • Dr. Nancy Keese, Chair, Department of Educational Leadership, 615-898-2855. Fax: 615-898-2859. E-mail: nkeese@mtsu.edu.

Mills College, Education Department, Oakland, CA 94613-1000. Offerings include education (MA), with options in curriculum and instruction, elementary education, English education, mathematics education, science education, secondary education, social sciences education, teaching. Department faculty: 8 full-time (6 women), 13 part-time (11 women), 11 FTE. *Degree requirements:* Comprehensive exam required, thesis not required. *Average time to degree:* master's–2 years full-time. *Entrance requirements:* TOEFL (minimum score 550). Application deadline: 2/1 (priority date; rolling processing; 11/1 for spring admission). Application fee: $50. Electronic applications accepted. *Expenses:* Tuition $10,600 per year full-time, $2560 per year part-time. Fees $468 per year. • Jane Bowyer, Chairperson, 510-430-2118. Fax: 510-430-3314. E-mail: grad-studies@mills.edu. Application contact: La Vonna S. Brown, Coordinator of Graduate Studies, 510-430-3309. Fax: 510-430-2159. E-mail: grad-studies@mills.edu.

Montana State University–Billings, College of Education and Human Services, Department of Curriculum and Instruction, Option in General Curriculum, Billings, MT 59101-9984. Awards M Ed. Accredited by NCATE. Part-time programs available. *Degree requirements:* Thesis or professional paper and/or field experience required, foreign language not required. *Entrance requirements:* GRE General Test (minimum combined score of 1350 on three sections) or MAT (minimum score 38), minimum GPA of 3.0 (undergraduate), 3.25 (graduate). Application deadline: 8/1 (priority date; rolling processing; 1/1 for spring admission). Application fee: $30. *Expenses:* Tuition $2253 per year full-time, $397 per semester (minimum) part-time for state residents; $5313 per year full-time, $907 per semester (minimum) part-time for nonresidents. Fees $378 per year full-time, $105 per semester (minimum) part-time. *Faculty research:* Social studies education, science education.

Moorhead State University, Department of Education, Program in Curriculum and Instruction, Moorhead, MN 56563-0002. Awards MS. Accredited by NCATE. Part-time programs available. Students: 16 part-time (15 women). 25 applicants, 100% accepted. *Degree requirements:* Final oral exam, project or thesis, written comprehensive exam required, foreign language not required. *Entrance requirements:* TOEFL (minimum score 550). Application deadline: 5/1 (priority date; rolling processing; 9/1 for spring admission). Application fee: $20 ($35 for international students). Electronic applications accepted. *Tuition:* $145 per credit hour for state residents; $220 per credit hour for nonresidents. *Financial aid:* Administrative assistantships, Federal Work-Study available. Financial aid application deadline: 7/15; applicants required to submit FAFSA. • Sandra Gordon, Coordinator, 218-236-3580.

Morehead State University, College of Education and Behavioral Sciences, Department of Leadership and Secondary Education, Morehead, KY 40351. Offerings include instruction and administration (Ed D). Accredited by NCATE. Ed D offered jointly with the University of Kentucky. Department faculty: 12 full-time (6 women), 7 part-time (3 women). *Application deadline:* 8/1 (priority date; rolling processing; 12/1 for spring admission). *Application fee:* $0. *Tuition:* $2470 per year full-time, $138 per semester hour part-time for state residents; $6710 per year full-time, $373 per semester hour part-time for nonresidents. • Dr. Deborah Grubb, Chair, 606-783-5207. Application contact: Betty Cowsert, Graduate Admissions Officer, 606-783-2039. Fax: 606-783-5061.

Morehead State University, College of Education and Behavioral Sciences, Department of Elementary, Reading, and Special Education, Program in Curriculum and Instruction, Morehead, KY 40351. Awards Ed D, Ed S. Accredited by NCATE. Ed D offered jointly with the University of Kentucky. Part-time and evening/weekend programs available. Faculty: 13 full-time (7 women). Students: 0. Average age 25. 0 applicants. *Degree requirements:* For Ed S, thesis, oral exam required, foreign language not required. *Entrance requirements:* For Ed S, GRE General Test (minimum combined score of 1200), interview, master's degree, minimum GPA of 3.5, work experience. Application deadline: 8/1 (priority date; rolling processing; 12/1 for spring admission). Application fee: $0. *Tuition:* $2470 per year full-time, $138 per semester hour part-time for state residents; $6710 per year full-time, $373 per semester hour part-time for nonresidents. *Financial aid:* Research assistantships, teaching assistantships, Federal Work-Study available. Financial aid application deadline: 4/1; applicants required to submit FAFSA. *Faculty research:* Ungraded primary school organization. • Application contact: Betty Cowsert, Graduate Admissions Officer, 606-783-2039. Fax: 606-783-5061.

Mount Saint Vincent University, Department of Education, Program in Curriculum Studies, Halifax, NS B3M 2J6, Canada. Awards MA, MA Ed, MA(R), M Ed. Faculty: 7 full-time (4 women), 5 part-time (3 women). Students: 17. 21 applicants, 81% accepted. In 1997, 1 degree awarded. *Degree requirements:* Thesis. *Entrance requirements:* Bachelor's degree in related field, minimum B average, 1 year of teaching experience. Application deadline: 3/1 (priority date; rolling processing; 9/1 for spring admission). Application fee: $40. *Expenses:* Tuition $1024 per course. Fees $25 per course. *Financial aid:* Fellowships available. Financial aid application deadline: 5/1. *Faculty research:* Science education, cultural studies, international education, curriculum development, critical and popular literacies. • Dr. Robert Sargent, Head, 902-457-6336. Fax: 902-457-4911. E-mail: robert.sargent@msvu.ca. Application contact: Susan Tanner, Assistant Registrar, 902-457-6363. Fax: 902-457-6498. E-mail: susan.tanner@msvu.ca.

National–Louis University, National College of Education, McGaw Graduate School, Program in Curriculum and Instruction, 2840 Sheridan Road, Evanston, IL 60201-1730. Awards M Ed, MS Ed, CAS. Part-time and evening/weekend programs available. Students: 9 full-time (8 women), 165 part-time (147 women); includes 51 minority (8 African Americans, 5 Asian Americans, 37 Hispanics, 1 Native American). Average age 40. In 1997, 85 master's, 1 CAS awarded. *Entrance requirements:* For master's, GRE or MAT, minimum GPA of 3.0. Application deadline: rolling. Application fee: $25. *Tuition:* $411 per semester hour. *Financial aid:* Fellowships available. Aid available to part-time students. Financial aid applicants required to submit FAFSA. • Dr. Darrell Bloom, Coordinator, 847-475-1100 Ext. 5622. Application contact: Dr. David McCulloch, Vice President for University Services, 800-443-5522 Ext. 5127. Fax: 847-465-0593. E-mail: dmcc@wheeling1.nl.edu.

National–Louis University, National College of Education, McGaw Graduate School, Program in Interdisciplinary Studies in Curriculum and Instruction, 2840 Sheridan Road, Evanston, IL 60201-1730. Awards M Ed. Part-time and evening/weekend programs available. Students: 659 full-time (529 women), 58 part-time (55 women); includes 93 minority (70 African Americans, 3 Asian Americans, 18 Hispanics, 2 Native Americans). Average age 37. In 1997, 1,165 degrees awarded. *Degree requirements:* Research project required, foreign language not required. *Entrance requirements:* MAT, minimum GPA of 3.0. Application deadline: rolling. Application fee: $25. *Tuition:* $411 per semester hour. *Financial aid:* Fellowships available. Aid available to part-time students. Financial aid applicants required to submit FAFSA. • Dr. Judith Christensen, Coordinator, 608-265-9092 Ext. 5141. Application contact: Dr. David McCulloch, Vice President for University Services, 800-443-5522 Ext. 5127. Fax: 847-465-0593. E-mail: dmcc@wheeling1.nl.edu.

National–Louis University, National College of Education, McGaw Graduate School, Doctoral Programs in Education, Program in Curriculum and Social Inquiry, 2840 Sheridan Road, Evanston, IL 60201-1730. Awards Ed D. Part-time and evening/weekend programs available. Students: 1 (woman) full-time, 15 part-time (11 women); includes 1 minority (African American). Average age 44. In 1997, 4 degrees awarded. *Degree requirements:* Dissertation, comprehensive exams, internship required, foreign language not required. *Entrance requirements:* GRE General Test, minimum GPA of 3.25. Application deadline: 12/15. Application fee: $25. *Tuition:* $411 per semester hour. *Financial aid:* Fellowships, research assistantships available. Aid available to part-time students. Financial aid application deadline: 4/15. • Dr. Janet Miller, Coordinator, 847-475-1100 Ext. 6841. Application contact: Dr. David McCulloch, Vice President for University Services, 800-443-5522 Ext. 5127. Fax: 847-465-0593. E-mail: dmcc@wheeling1.nl.edu.

National University, School of Education and Human Services, Department of Teacher Education and Leadership, La Jolla, CA 92037-1011. Offerings include instructional leadership in curriculum and instruction (MS). *Application deadline:* rolling. *Application fee:* $60 ($100 for international students). *Tuition:* $7830 per year full-time, $870 per course part-time. • Dr. Helene Mandell, Chair, 619-642-8345. Application contact: Nancy Rohland, Director of Enrollment Management, 619-563-7100. Fax: 619-563-7393.

New Mexico Highlands University, School of Education, Las Vegas, NM 87701. Offerings include curriculum and instruction (MA). School faculty: 32 full-time (14 women). *Degree requirements:* Thesis or alternative required, foreign language not required. *Entrance requirements:* Minimum undergraduate GPA of 3.0. Application deadline: 8/1 (priority date; rolling processing). Application fee: $15. *Expenses:* Tuition $1816 per year full-time, $227 per hour part-time for state residents; $7468 per year full-time, $227 per hour part-time for nonresidents. Fees $10 per year. • Dr. James Abreu, Dean, 505-454-3357. Application contact: Dr. Glen W. Davidson, Academic Vice President, 505-454-3311. Fax: 505-454-3558. E-mail: glendavidson@venus.nmhu.edu.

New Mexico State University, College of Education, Department of Curriculum and Instruction, Las Cruces, NM 88003-8001. Offers programs in curriculum and instruction (MAT, Ed D, PhD, Ed S), general education (MA), reading (Ed S). Accredited by NCATE. Part-time programs available. Faculty: 20 full-time (12 women). Students: 252 full-time (180 women), 307 part-time (247 women); includes 190 minority (6 African Americans, 4 Asian Americans, 171 Hispanics, 9 Native Americans), 28 international. Average age 36. 164 applicants, 79% accepted. In 1997, 16 doctorates, 2 Ed Ss awarded. *Degree requirements:* For master's, computer language required, thesis optional, foreign language not required; for doctorate, computer language, dissertation. *Entrance requirements:* For master's, minimum GPA of 2.5 in last 12 hours; for doctorate, portfolio. Application deadline: 7/1 (priority date; rolling processing; 11/1 for spring admission). Application fee: $15 ($35 for international students). *Tuition:* $2514 per year full-time, $105 per credit hour part-time for state residents; $7848 per year full-time, $327 per credit hour part-time for nonresidents. *Financial aid:* Fellowships, teaching assistantships, Federal Work-Study, and career-related internships or fieldwork available. Aid available to part-time students. Financial aid application deadline: 3/1. *Faculty research:* Multicultural education, students placed at risk, literacy/biliteracy education, bilingual and English as a second language education, early childhood education. • Dr. Jeanette Martin, Head, 505-646-4820. Fax: 505-646-5436. E-mail: jeamarti@nmsu.edu.

Nicholls State University, College of Education, Department of Teacher Education, Thibodaux, LA 70310. Offerings include curriculum and instruction (M Ed). Accredited by NCATE. Department faculty: 15 full-time (8 women). *Entrance requirements:* GRE General Test, GRE Subject Test. Application deadline: 6/17 (priority date; rolling processing; 11/15 for spring admission). Application fee: $10 ($60 for international students). *Tuition:* $2136 per year full-time, $283 per semester (minimum) part-time for state residents; $5376 per year full-time, $283 per semester (minimum) part-time for nonresidents. • Dr. Harrell H. Carpenter, Head, 504-448-4330.

North Carolina State University, College of Education and Psychology, Department of Curriculum and Instruction, Program in Curriculum and Instruction, Raleigh, NC 27695. Awards M Ed, MS, Ed D. Accredited by NCATE. Faculty: 19 full-time (12 women), 9 part-time (5 women). Students: 27 full-time (15 women), 57 part-time (49 women); includes 10 minority (9 African Americans, 1 Asian American). Average age 35. 44 applicants, 61% accepted. In 1997, 16 master's, 4 doctorates awarded. *Degree requirements:* For master's, thesis required (for some programs), foreign language not required; for doctorate, dissertation required, foreign language not required. *Entrance requirements:* GRE General Test or MAT, minimum GPA of 3.0 in major. Application deadline: 5/25 (priority date; 10/25 for spring admission). Application fee: $45. *Tuition:* $2370 per year full-time, $517 per semester (minimum) part-time for state residents; $11,536 per year full-time, $2809 per semester (minimum) part-time for nonresidents. *Financial aid:* Fellowships, research assistantships, teaching assistantships, and career-related internships or fieldwork available. • Dr. Barbara J. Fox, Director of Graduate Programs, 919-515-1781. E-mail: fox@poe.coe.ncsu.edu. Application contact: Peggy Price, Graduate Secretary, 919-515-1772. Fax: 919-515-6978. E-mail: peggy@poe.coe.ncsu.edu.

Northeastern State University, College of Education, Department of Education, Program in Curriculum and Instruction, Tahlequah, OK 74464-2399. Awards M Ed. Faculty: 3 full-time (0 women), 2 part-time (0 women). Students: 17 (14 women). In 1997, 15 degrees awarded. *Degree requirements:* Thesis or alternative required, foreign language not required. *Entrance requirements:* GRE General Test (minimum combined score of 900) or MAT (minimum score 35), minimum GPA of 3.0. Application deadline: 6/1 (priority date; rolling processing). Application fee: $0. *Expenses:* Tuition $74 per credit hour for state residents; $176 per credit hour for nonresidents. Fees $30 per year. *Financial aid:* Teaching assistantships, Federal Work-Study available. Financial aid application deadline: 3/1. • Dr. Sue Ellen Read, Head, 918-456-5511 Ext. 3759.

Northeastern University, Graduate School of Arts and Sciences, Department of Education, Boston, MA 02115-5096. Offerings include curriculum and instruction (M Ed). Department faculty: 11 full-time (3 women), 3 part-time (2 women). *Average time to degree:* master's–3 years full-time, 5 years part-time. *Entrance requirements:* GRE General Test or MAT. Application deadline: 7/15 (rolling processing; 2/1 for spring admission). Application fee: $50. *Expenses:* Tuition $440 per credit hour. Fees $55 per quarter full-time, $13.25 per quarter part-time. • Dr. James W. Fraser, Acting Chair, 617-373-3302. Application contact: Dr. Mervin Lynch, Director of Graduate Admissions, 617-373-3302. Fax: 617-373-5261.

Northeast Louisiana University, College of Education, Department of Curriculum and Instruction, Program in Curriculum and Instruction, Monroe, LA 71209-0001. Awards Ed D. Accredited by NCATE. Offered jointly with Grambling State University and Louisiana Tech University. *Degree requirements:* Dissertation. *Entrance requirements:* GRE General Test (minimum combined score of 1000), minimum GPA of 2.75 (undergraduate), 3.25 (graduate). Application fee: $15 ($25 for international students). *Tuition:* $2028 per year full-time, $240 per semester (minimum) part-time for state residents; $6852 per year full-time, $240 per semester (minimum) part-time for nonresidents.

Northern Arizona University, Center for Excellence in Education, Program in Curriculum and Instruction, Flagstaff, AZ 86011. Awards Ed D. Students: 10 full-time (8 women), 30 part-time (21 women); includes 4 minority (1 Asian American, 3 Hispanics), 5 international. Average age 30. 15 applicants, 7% accepted. In 1997, 6 degrees awarded. *Degree requirements:* Computer language, dissertation required, foreign language not required. *Entrance requirements:* GRE General Test, GRE Subject Test, 3 years of professional experience, interview, master's degree, minimum graduate GPA of 3.3. Application deadline: 2/15 (priority date; rolling processing; 9/15 for spring admission). Application fee: $45. *Expenses:* Tuition $2088 per year full-time, $330 per semester (minimum) part-time for state residents; $8004 per year full-time, $1002 per semester (minimum) part-time for nonresidents. Fees $72 per year full-time, $18 per semester (minimum) part-time. *Financial aid:* Research assistantships, teaching assistantships, full and partial tuition waivers, Federal Work-Study, and career-related internships or fieldwork available. *Faculty research:* Leadership issues, evaluation of education, personnel evaluation, international education, multicultural education. • Dr. Stephen Lapan, Interim Coordinator, 520-523-5342.

Northern Illinois University, College of Education, Department of Curriculum and Instruction, Program in Curriculum and Instruction, De Kalb, IL 60115-2854. Awards MS Ed, Ed D. Accredited by NCATE. Part-time and evening/weekend programs available. Faculty: 28 full-time (18 women). Students: 34 full-time (27 women), 210 part-time (157 women); includes 13 minority (5 African Americans, 2 Asian Americans, 5 Hispanics, 1 Native American), 5 international. Average age 36. 102 applicants, 77% accepted. In 1997, 54 master's, 8 doctorates awarded. *Degree requirements:* For master's, comprehensive exam required, thesis optional, foreign language not required; for doctorate, candidacy exam, dissertation defense required, foreign language not required. *Entrance requirements:* For master's, GRE General Test or MAT, TOEFL (minimum score 550), minimum GPA of 2.75; for doctorate, GRE General Test or MAT, TOEFL (minimum score 550), minimum GPA of 2.75 (undergraduate), 3.2 (graduate). Application deadline: (11/1 for spring admission). *Tuition:* $3984 per year full-time, $154 per credit hour part-time for state residents; $8160 per year full-time, $328 per credit hour part-time for nonresidents. *Financial aid:* Fellowships, research assistantships, teaching assistantships, staff assistantships, full tuition waivers, Federal Work-Study, and career-related internships or fieldwork available. Aid available to part-time students. • Dr. Norman Stahl, Chair, Department of Curriculum and Instruction, 815-753-9032.

Northwest Nazarene College, Department of Graduate Studies, Graduate Program in Teacher Education, Nampa, ID 83686-5897. Offerings include curriculum and instruction (M Ed). Accredited by NCATE. Postbaccalaureate distance learning degree programs offered. Program faculty: 3 full-time (2 women), 13 part-time (3 women). *Degree requirements:* Action research project required, foreign language and thesis not required. *Application deadline:* 9/1 (rolling processing). *Application fee:* $25. • Dr. Dennis Cartwright, Chair, 208-467-8258. E-mail: ddcartwright@wiley.nnc.edu.

Notre Dame College, Education Division, Program in Curriculum and Instruction, Manchester, NH 03104-2299. Awards M Ed. Part-time programs available. Faculty: 1 (woman) full-time, 2 part-time (1 woman). Students: 1 full-time (0 women), 16 part-time (13 women). Average age 37. 8 applicants, 100% accepted. In 1997, 21 degrees awarded. *Degree requirements:* Comprehensive exams, portfolio, or thesis required, foreign language not required. *Entrance requirements:* GRE General Test or MAT, teaching certificate. Application deadline: rolling. Application fee: $35. *Tuition:* $299 per credit. • Dr. Ann McGreevy, Director, 603-669-4298 Ext. 185.

Oakland University, School of Education and Human Services, Program in Curriculum, Instruction and Leadership, Rochester, MI 48309-4401. Awards MAT, M Ed, Certificate. Accredited by NCATE. Faculty: 16 full-time. Students: 15 full-time (12 women), 120 part-time (90 women); includes 8 minority (3 African Americans, 2 Asian Americans, 1 Hispanic, 2 Native Americans), 1 international. Average age 35. In 1997, 48 master's awarded. *Entrance requirements:* For master's; minimum GPA of 3.0 for unconditional admission. Application deadline: 7/15 (3/15 for spring admission). Application fee: $30. *Expenses:* Tuition $3852 per year full-time, $214 per credit hour part-time for state residents; $8532 per year full-time, $474 per credit hour part-time for nonresidents. Fees $420 per year. *Financial aid:* Full tuition waivers, Federal Work-Study, institutionally sponsored loans available. Financial aid application deadline: 3/1; applicants required to submit FAFSA. • Dr. Eric Follo, Chair, 248-370-3070. Application contact: Dr. Jacqueline Lougheed, Coordinator, 248-370-3070.

The Ohio State University, College of Education, School of Teaching and Learning, Program in Educational Studies: Humanities, Science, Technological and Vocational, Columbus, OH 43210. Awards MA, M Ed, PhD. Accredited by NCATE. Faculty: 3. Students: 270 full-time (168 women), 161 part-time (110 women); includes 44 minority (25 African Americans, 11 Asian Americans, 7 Hispanics, 1 Native American), 93 international. 344 applicants, 45% accepted. In 1997, 142 master's, 24 doctorates awarded. *Degree requirements:* For master's, thesis optional, foreign language not required; for doctorate, dissertation required, foreign language not required. *Application deadline:* 8/15 (rolling processing). *Application fee:* $30 ($40 for international students). *Tuition:* $5472 per year full-time, $554 per quarter (minimum) part-time for state residents; $14,172 per year full-time, $1424 per quarter (minimum) part-time for nonresidents. *Financial aid:* Fellowships, research assistantships, teaching assistantships, administrative assistantships, Federal Work-Study, institutionally sponsored loans available. Aid available to part-time students. • Dr. Robert J. Tierney, Director, School of Teaching and Learning, 614-292-1257. Fax: 614-292-7695. E-mail: tierney.4@osu.edu.

Oklahoma State University, College of Education, Department of Curriculum and Instruction, Stillwater, OK 74078. Awards MS, Ed D, Ed S. Faculty: 19 full-time (10 women). Students: 34 full-time (24 women), 156 part-time (128 women); includes 19 minority (12 African Americans, 7 Native Americans), 4 international. Average age 36. In 1997, 40 master's, 16 doctorates awarded. *Degree requirements:* For master's and doctorate, thesis/dissertation. *Entrance requirements:* For master's, TOEFL (minimum score 550); for doctorate, GRE General Test or MAT, TOEFL (minimum score 550). Application deadline: 7/1 (priority date). Application fee: $25. *Financial aid:* In 1997–98, 23 students received aid, including 5 research assistantships (3 to first-year students) averaging $820 per month and totaling $36,915, 18 teaching assistantships (4 to first-year students) averaging $1,155 per month and totaling $187,137; partial tuition waivers, Federal Work-Study, and career-related internships or fieldwork also available. Aid available to part-time students. Financial aid application deadline: 3/1. • Dr. Bruce Petty, Interim Head, 405-744-7125.

Olivet Nazarene University, Division of Education, Program in Curriculum and Instruction, Kankakee, IL 60901-0592. Awards MAE. Evening/weekend programs available. *Degree requirements:* Thesis or alternative required, foreign language not required. *Application deadline:* rolling. *Application fee:* $20.

Oral Roberts University, School of Education, Tulsa, OK 74171-0001. Offerings include curriculum and instruction (MA Ed). Postbaccalaureate distance learning degree programs offered (minimal on-campus study). School faculty: 7 full-time (2 women), 13 part-time (3 women). *Degree requirements:* Thesis (for some programs), comprehensive exam. *Average time to degree:* master's–1.5 years full-time, 3 years part-time. *Entrance requirements:* GRE General Test (minimum combined score of 1000) or MAT, minimum GPA of 3.0. Application deadline: rolling. Application fee: $35. • Dr. David Hand, Dean, 918-495-7084. Fax: 918-495-6050. Application contact: David H. Fulmer III, Coordinator of Graduate Admissions, 918-495-6058. Fax: 918-495-7214. E-mail: dhfulmer@oru.edu.

Our Lady of Holy Cross College, Program in Education, New Orleans, LA 70131-7399. Offerings include curriculum and instruction (M Ed), with option in reading. Program faculty: 5 full-time (2 women), 7 part-time (3 women). *Degree requirements:* Thesis required, foreign language not required. *Entrance requirements:* GRE General Test (minimum combined score of 800), minimum GPA of 2.7. Application deadline: 9/1. Application fee: $20. *Expenses:* Tuition $5760 per year full-time, $240 per semester hour part-time. Fees $167 per year. • Dr. Judith G. Miranti, Dean, 504-394-7744.

Our Lady of the Lake University of San Antonio, School of Education and Clinical Studies, 411 Southwest 24th Street, San Antonio, TX 78207-4689. Offerings include curriculum and instruction (M Ed). Postbaccalaureate distance learning degree programs offered (minimal on-campus study). School faculty: 28 full-time (21 women), 27 part-time (12 women). *Application fee:* $15. *Expenses:* Tuition $371 per credit hour. Fees $57 per semester full-time, $32 per semester part-time. • Dr. Jacquelyn Alexander, Dean, 210-434-6711 Ext. 291. Fax: 210-431-3927. E-mail: alexj@lake.ollusa.edu. Application contact: Debbie Hamilton, Director of Admissions, 210-434-6711 Ext. 314. Fax: 210-436-2314.

Pace University, School of Education, New York, NY 10038. Offerings include curriculum and instruction (MS). *Application deadline:* 7/31 (priority date; rolling processing; 11/30 for spring admission). *Application fee:* $60. *Expenses:* Tuition $485 per credit. Fees $360 per year full-time, $53 per semester (minimum) part-time.

Pacific Lutheran University, School of Education, Program in Classroom Teaching, Tacoma, WA 98447. Offers elementary education (MA), secondary education (MA). Accredited by NCATE. Part-time and evening/weekend programs available. Faculty: 2 full-time (1 woman). Students: 3 part-time (all women). Average age 46. 5 applicants, 100% accepted. In 1997, 7 degrees awarded. *Degree requirements:* Comprehensive exam, research project or thesis required, foreign language not required. *Entrance requirements:* GRE General Test or MAT, TOEFL (minimum score 550), interview. Application deadline: rolling. Application fee: $35. *Tuition:* $490 per semester hour. *Financial aid:* Fellowships, research assistantships, scholarships, Federal Work-Study available. Financial aid application deadline: 3/1. • Dr. Leon Reisberg, Graduate Director, 253-535-7272. Application contact: Marjo Burdick, Office of Admissions, 253-535-7151. Fax: 253-535-8320. E-mail: admissions@plu.edu.

Pacific Lutheran University, School of Education, Program in Teaching, Tacoma, WA 98447. Awards MA. Accredited by NCATE. Faculty: 5 full-time (4 women). Students: 28 full-time (16 women); includes 4 minority (2 Asian Americans, 2 Hispanics), 1 international. Average age 27. 54 applicants, 87% accepted. In 1997, 20 degrees awarded. *Degree requirements:* Comprehensive exam, research project or thesis required, foreign language not required. *Average time to degree:* master's–1.2 years full-time. *Entrance requirements:* GRE General Test or MAT, TOEFL (minimum score 550), interview. Application deadline: 1/31 (priority date). Application fee: $35. *Tuition:* $490 per semester hour. *Financial aid:* Fellowships, research assistantships, scholarships, Federal Work-Study available. Financial aid application deadline: 3/1. • Dr. C. Douglas Lamoreaux, Director, 253-535-8342. Application contact: Marjo Burdick, Office of Admissions, 253-535-7151. Fax: 253-535-8320. E-mail: admissions@plu.edu.

Pennsylvania State University Great Valley School of Graduate Professional Studies, Graduate Studies and Continuing Education, College of Education, Program in Curriculum and Instruction, Malvern, PA 19355-1488. Awards M Ed, MS. Students: 3 full-time (all women), 71 part-time (53 women). Average age 34. In 1997, 33 degrees awarded. *Entrance requirements:* GRE General Test or MAT. Application fee: $40. • Dr. Martin Sharp, Coordinator, 610-648-3284.

Pennsylvania State University Harrisburg Campus of the Capital College, Division of Behavioral Sciences and Education, Program in Teaching and Curriculum, Middletown, PA 17057-4898. Awards M Ed. Evening/weekend programs available. Students: 15 full-time (7 women), 206 part-time (175 women). Average age 33. In 1997, 46 degrees awarded. *Degree requirements:* Thesis or alternative required, foreign language not required. *Entrance requirements:* Minimum GPA of 2.5 during previous 2 years. Application deadline: 7/26. Application fee: $40. *Expenses:* Tuition $6534 per year full-time, $276 per credit part-time for state residents; $12,516 per year full-time, $523 per credit part-time for nonresidents. Fees $232 per year (minimum) full-time, $40 per semester (minimum) part-time. *Faculty research:* Preschool through adult classroom teaching, curriculum and reading. • Dr. Steven Melnick, Head, 717-948-6213.

Pennsylvania State University University Park Campus, College of Education, Department of Curriculum and Instruction, University Park, PA 16802-1503. Offers programs in bilingual education (M Ed, MS, D Ed, PhD), early childhood education (M Ed, MS, D Ed, PhD), elementary education (M Ed, MS, D Ed, PhD), instructional systems (M Ed, MS, D Ed, PhD), language arts and reading (M Ed, MS, D Ed, PhD), science education (M Ed, MS, D Ed, PhD), social studies education (MS, D Ed, PhD), supervisor and curriculum development (M Ed, MS, D Ed, PhD). Accredited by NCATE. Students: 153 full-time (112 women), 85 part-time (66 women). In 1997, 42 master's, 25 doctorates awarded. *Degree requirements:* For doctorate, dissertation. *Entrance requirements:* GRE General Test or MAT. Application fee: $40. *Expenses:* Tuition $6534 per year full-time, $276 per credit part-time for state residents; $13,460 per year full-time, $561 per credit part-time for nonresidents. Fees $252 per year (minimum) full-time, $43 per semester (minimum) part-time. • Dr. Peter A. Rubb, Head, 814-865-5433.

Portland State University, School of Education, Department of Curriculum and Instruction, Portland, OR 97207-0751. Offers programs in early childhood education (MA, MS), education (MA, M Ed, MS), educational leadership: curriculum and instruction (Ed D), educational media/school librarianship (MA, MS), elementary education (MAT, M Ed, MST), reading (MA, MS), secondary education (MAT, M Ed, MST). Accredited by NCATE. Part-time programs available. Students: 175 full-time (123 women), 108 part-time (73 women); includes 40 minority (14 African Americans, 9 Asian Americans, 11 Hispanics, 6 Native Americans), 6 international. Average age 33. 263 applicants, 67% accepted. *Degree requirements:* For master's, special project or thesis, written exam; for doctorate, dissertation required, foreign language not required. *Entrance requirements:* For master's, California Basic Educational Skills Test, TOEFL (minimum score 550), minimum GPA of 3.0 in upper-division course work or 2.75 overall; for doctorate, TOEFL (minimum score 550). Application deadline: 4/1 (rolling processing; 11/1 for spring admission). Application fee: $50. *Tuition:* $6101 per year full-time, $689 per semester (minimum) part-time for state residents; $10,445 per year full-time, $689 per semester (minimum) part-time for nonresidents. *Financial aid:* In 1997–98, 9 research assistantships (4 to first-year students) were awarded; teaching assistantships, Federal Work-Study, institutionally sponsored loans, and career-related internships or fieldwork also available. Aid available to part-time students. Financial aid application deadline: 3/1; applicants required to submit FAFSA. *Faculty research:* Early literacy, characteristics of successful teachers of at-risk students, participation of women/minorities in technology courses, selection of cooperating teachers. Total annual research expenditures: $20,000. • Dr. Ulrich Hardt, Head, 503-725-4756. Fax: 503-725-8475. E-mail: hardtu@ed.pdx.edu.

Prairie View A&M University, College of Education, Department of Curriculum and Instruction, Prairie View, TX 77446-0188. Offers programs in curriculum and instruction (M Ed, MS Ed), special education (M Ed, MS Ed). Accredited by NCATE. Part-time and evening/weekend programs available. Faculty: 8 full-time (5 women). Students: 34 full-time (25 women), 65 part-time (56 women); includes 70 minority (66 African Americans, 3 Asian Americans, 1 Hispanic), 5 international. Average age 32. In 1997, 29 degrees awarded (100% found work related to degree). *Degree requirements:* Seminar paper required, thesis optional, foreign language not required. *Average time to degree:* master's–2.5 years full-time, 4 years part-time. *Entrance requirements:* GRE General Test. Application deadline: 7/1 (priority date; rolling processing; 11/1 for spring admission). Application fee: $10. *Tuition:* $2202 per year full-time, $336 per semester (minimum) part-time for state residents; $6000 per year full-time, $963 per semester (minimum) part-time for nonresidents. *Financial aid:* Career-related internships or fieldwork available. Financial aid application deadline: 6/31. *Faculty research:* Metacognitive strategies, emotionally disturbed, language arts. • Dr. Joan B. Clark, Head, 409-857-3921. Fax: 409-857-2911.

Directory: Curriculum and Instruction

Purdue University, School of Education, Department of Curriculum and Instruction, West Lafayette, IN 47907. Offerings include curriculum theory (MS Ed, PhD, Ed S), instructional development (MS Ed). One or more programs accredited by NCATE. Department faculty: 34 full-time (15 women), 3 part-time (1 woman). *Degree requirements:* For master's, thesis optional; for doctorate, dissertation, oral and written exams; for Ed S, oral presentation, project required, thesis not required. *Entrance requirements:* For master's, TOEFL (minimum score 550), minimum B average; for doctorate, GRE General Test (minimum score 500 on each section), TOEFL (minimum score 550); for Ed S, minimum B average. Application deadline: 1/15 (priority date; 9/15 for spring admission). Application fee: $30. Electronic applications accepted. *Tuition:* $3500 per year full-time, $126 per credit hour part-time for state residents; $11,720 per year full-time, $387 per credit hour part-time for nonresidents. • Dr. J. L. Peters, Head, 765-494-9172. Fax: 765-496-1622. E-mail: peters@purdue.edu. Application contact: Christine Larsen, Coordinator of Graduate Studies, 765-494-2345. Fax: 765-494-5832. E-mail: gradoffice@soe.purdue.edu.

Purdue University Calumet, School of Professional Studies, Department of Education, Program in Instructional Development, Hammond, IN 46323-2094. Awards MS Ed. *Entrance requirements:* TOEFL. Application fee: $30.

Radford University, Graduate College, College of Education and Human Development, Department of Educational Studies, Program in Curriculum and Instruction, Radford, VA 24142. Awards MS. Accredited by NCATE. Part-time programs available. Postbaccalaureate distance learning degree programs offered (minimal on-campus study). Faculty: 16 full-time (11 women), 5 part-time (3 women), 17.3 FTE. Students: 63 full-time (40 women), 86 part-time (67 women); includes 6 minority (5 African Americans, 1 Asian American), 3 international. Average age 31. 65 applicants, 82% accepted. In 1997, 30 degrees awarded. *Degree requirements:* Comprehensive exam required, foreign language and thesis not required. *Entrance requirements:* GMAT, GRE General Test, MAT, or NTE; TOEFL (minimum score 550), minimum GPA of 2.7. Application deadline: 2/1 (priority date; rolling processing; 10/1 for spring admission). Application fee: $25. Electronic applications accepted. *Expenses:* Tuition $2302 per year full-time, $147 per credit hour part-time for state residents; $5672 per year full-time, $287 per credit hour part-time for nonresidents. Fees $1222 per year full-time. *Financial aid:* In 1997–98, 10 fellowships totaling $43,600, 11 research assistantships totaling $40,126, 1 teaching assistantship totaling $6,820, 148 scholarships/grants totaling $472,983 were awarded; Federal Work-Study, institutionally sponsored loans, and career-related internships or fieldwork also available. Financial aid application deadline: 2/1; applicants required to submit FAFSA. • Dr. Sheila S. Reyna, Acting Chairperson, Department of Educational Studies, 540-831-5302. Fax: 540-831-6053. E-mail: aproffit@runet.edu.

Rhode Island College, School of Graduate Studies, School of Education and Human Development, Department of Educational Studies, Program in Curriculum, Providence, RI 02908-1924. Awards CAGS. Accredited by NCATE. Faculty: 7 full-time (2 women), 12 part-time (4 women). Students: 2 part-time (1 woman). *Degree requirements:* Thesis required, foreign language not required. *Application deadline:* 4/1 (rolling processing). *Application fee:* $25. *Tuition:* $4064 per year full-time, $214 per credit part-time for state residents; $7658 per year full-time, $376 per credit part-time for nonresidents. *Financial aid:* Application deadline 4/1. • Dr. Carolyn Panofsky, Chair, Department of Educational Studies, 401-456-8170.

Rider University, School of Graduate Education and Human Services, Program in Curriculum, Instruction and Supervision, Lawrenceville, NJ 08648-3001. Awards MA. Accredited by NCATE. Part-time and evening/weekend programs available. Faculty: 2 full-time (0 women), 3 part-time (2 women), 3 FTE. Students: 38 part-time. Average age 35. 5 applicants, 100% accepted. In 1997, 5 degrees awarded. *Degree requirements:* Comprehensive exams, research project required, foreign language and thesis not required. *Entrance requirements:* Interview, minimum GPA of 2.5. Application deadline: 8/15 (priority date; rolling processing; 12/15 for spring admission). Application fee: $35. *Tuition:* $329 per credit hour. *Financial aid:* Career-related internships or fieldwork available. Aid available to part-time students. *Faculty research:* Analysis of teaching and learning styles to improve instruction and learning. • Dr. Dennis Buss, Adviser, 609-895-5474. Application contact: Dr. John Carpenter, Dean, Continuing Studies, 609-896-5036. Fax: 609-896-5261.

Rowan University, College of Education, Department of Educational Leadership, Program in Supervision and Curriculum Development, Glassboro, NJ 08028-1701. Awards MA, Certificate. Accredited by NCATE. Part-time and evening/weekend programs available. Students: 25 (19 women); includes 1 minority (African American). 24 applicants, 88% accepted. In 1997, 3 master's awarded. *Degree requirements:* For master's, thesis, comprehensive exams, internship required, foreign language not required. *Entrance requirements:* For master's, GRE General Test (minimum combined score of 840), minimum GPA of 2.8, 2 years of teaching experience. Application deadline: 11/1 (priority date; rolling processing; 4/1 for spring admission). Application fee: $50. *Tuition:* $5728 per year full-time, $258 per credit hour part-time for state residents; $8968 per year full-time, $393 per credit hour part-time for nonresidents. *Financial aid:* Federal Work-Study and career-related internships or fieldwork available. • Dr. Ted White, Adviser, 609-256-4702.

St. Bonaventure University, School of Education, Program in Advanced Instructional Processes (Elementary and Secondary), St. Bonaventure, NY 14778-2284. Awards MS Ed. Faculty: 19 full-time (7 women). Students: 26 full-time (20 women), 72 part-time (60 women). *Degree requirements:* Thesis required, foreign language not required. *Entrance requirements:* GRE General Test, TOEFL (minimum score 600). Application deadline: 8/1 (rolling processing). Application fee: $35. *Tuition:* $8100 per year full-time, $450 per credit hour part-time. *Financial aid:* Research assistantships, Federal Work-Study available. Aid available to part-time students. *Faculty research:* Foundations, academic content area. • Phil Ebrel, Director, 716-375-2313.

Saint Louis University, Institute for Leadership and Public Service, Programs in Education, Department of Educational Studies, St. Louis, MO 63103-2097. Offerings include curriculum and instruction (MA, Ed D, PhD). Accredited by NCATE. *Degree requirements:* For master's, comprehensive oral exam required, foreign language and thesis not required; for doctorate, dissertation, preliminary oral and written exams. *Entrance requirements:* For master's, GRE General Test or MAT; for doctorate, GRE General Test. Application deadline: 7/1 (rolling processing; 11/1 for spring admission). Application fee: $40. *Tuition:* $542 per credit hour. • Dr. Ann Rule, Director, 314-977-2486. Application contact: Dr. Marcia Buresch, Assistant Dean of the Graduate School, 314-977-2240. Fax: 314-977-3943.

Saint Martin's College, Graduate Programs, Department of Education, Lacey, WA 98503-7500. Offerings include instruction (M Ed). Department faculty: 8 full-time (3 women), 5 part-time (2 women). *Application deadline:* 7/1 (priority date; rolling processing; 12/1 for spring admission). *Application fee:* $25. • Dr. Paul Nelson, Director, 360-438-4529. Application contact: Michelle Roman, Administrative Assistant, 360-438-4333.

Saint Michael's College, Program in Education, Colchester, VT 05439. Offerings include curriculum and instruction (M Ed, CAGS). Program faculty: 5 full-time (4 women), 70 part-time (54 women). *Degree requirements:* For master's, computer language, thesis required, foreign language not required. *Entrance requirements:* For master's, minimum GPA of 2.8. Application deadline: rolling. Application fee: $25. • Dr. Aostre Johnson, Director, 802-654-2436. Fax: 802-654-2664.

Saint Peter's College, Graduate Programs in Education, Program in Teaching, 2641 Kennedy Boulevard, Jersey City, NJ 07306-5997. Offers elementary teacher (Certificate), supervisor of instruction (Certificate), teaching (MA). Part-time and evening/weekend programs available. Faculty: 2 full-time (0 women), 10 part-time (4 women). Students: 13 full-time (7 women), 73 part-time (47 women); includes 10 minority (3 African Americans, 1 Asian American, 6 Hispanics). Average age 31. In 1997, 34 master's awarded. *Degree requirements:* For master's, departmental qualifying exam required, thesis not required. *Entrance requirements:* For master's, GRE General Test or MAT (minimum score 40). Application deadline: 8/1 (priority date; rolling processing). Application fee: $20. *Tuition:* $516 per credit. *Financial aid:* Career-related internships or fieldwork available. Aid available to part-time students. Financial aid application deadline: 7/1. • Dr. Joseph McLaughlin, Director, Graduate Programs in Education, 201-915-9254. Fax: 201-915-9074. Application contact: Nancy P. Campbell, Associate Vice President for Enrollment, 201-915-9213. Fax: 201-432-5860. E-mail: admissions@spcvxa.spc.edu.

Saint Xavier University, School of Education, Chicago, IL 60655-3105. Offerings include curriculum and instruction (MA). School faculty: 16 full-time (12 women), 3 part-time (1 woman). *Degree requirements:* Thesis or project required, thesis optional. *Entrance requirements:* MAT, minimum GPA of 3.0. Application deadline: 8/15 (priority date; rolling processing). Application fee: $35. *Expenses:* Tuition $435 per hour. Fees $50 per year. • Dr. Beverly Gulley, Dean, 773-298-3221. Fax: 773-779-9061. E-mail: gulley@sxu.edu. Application contact: Sr. Evelyn McKenna, Vice President of Enrollment Management, 773-298-3050. Fax: 773-298-3076. E-mail: mckenna@sxu.edu.

Sam Houston State University, College of Education and Applied Science, Department of Education and Applied Science, Department of Curriculum and Instruction, Huntsville, TX 77341. Offerings include curriculum and instruction (Ed D). Accredited by NCATE. Ed D offered jointly with Texas A&M University. *Application fee:* $15. *Tuition:* $1810 per year full-time, $297 per semester (minimum) part-time for state residents; $6922 per year full-time, $924 per semester (minimum) part-time for nonresidents. • Dr. John C. Huber, Chair, 409-294-1146.

Seattle Pacific University, School of Education, Program in Curriculum and Instruction, Seattle, WA 98119-1997. Offers reading/language arts education (M Ed). Accredited by NCATE. Part-time and evening/weekend programs available. Faculty: 8 full-time (1 woman), 8 part-time (5 women). Students: 5 full-time (all women), 25 part-time (20 women); includes 1 minority (Asian American), 1 international. Average age 32. In 1997, 16 degrees awarded (100% found work related to degree). *Average time to degree:* master's–3 years part-time. *Entrance requirements:* MAT (minimum score 35) or GRE General Test (minimum score 300 on verbal section, 350 on quantitative, 950 combined), minimum GPA of 3.0. Application deadline: 7/1 (priority date; rolling processing; 3/1 for spring admission). Application fee: $35. *Tuition:* $274 per credit. *Financial aid:* In 1997–98, 4 research assistantships were awarded. *Faculty research:* Educational technology, classroom environments, character education. • Patricia Hammill, Chair, 206-281-2380. Fax: 206-281-2756.

Seattle University, School of Education, Division of Teaching and Learning, Program in Curriculum and Instruction, Seattle, WA 98122. Awards MA, M Ed. Accredited by NCATE. Part-time and evening/weekend programs available. Faculty: 7 full-time (5 women). Students: 4 full-time (all women), 48 part-time (43 women); includes 4 minority (1 African American, 2 Asian Americans, 1 Native American), 2 international. Average age 38. 22 applicants, 50% accepted. In 1997, 16 degrees awarded. *Degree requirements:* Comprehensive exam required, foreign language and thesis not required. *Entrance requirements:* GRE, MAT, or minimum GPA of 2.75; 1 year of related experience. Application deadline: 8/20 (rolling processing; 2/20 for spring admission). Application fee: $55. *Expenses:* Tuition $339 per credit hour (minimum). Fees $70 per year. *Financial aid:* Federal Work-Study and career-related internships or fieldwork available. Aid available to part-time students. Financial aid applicants required to submit FAFSA. • Dr. Andrea Sledge, Head, 206-296-5768. E-mail: acsledge@seattleu.edu.

Siena Heights University, Program in Teacher Education, Adrian, MI 49221-1796. Offerings include curriculum and instruction (MA). *Degree requirements:* Computer language, thesis, presentation required, foreign language not required. *Entrance requirements:* Minimum GPA of 3.0, interview. Application deadline: 7/1 (priority date; rolling processing; 12/1 for spring admission). Application fee: $25.

Simon Fraser University, Faculty of Education, Programs in Curriculum and Instruction, Burnaby, BC V5A 1S6, Canada. Awards MA, M Ed, M Sc, PhD. *Degree requirements:* For master's, thesis (for some programs), project or thesis required, foreign language not required; for doctorate, dissertation. *Entrance requirements:* For master's, TOEFL (minimum score 570), TWE (minimum score 5), or International English Language Test (minimum score 7.5), minimum GPA of 3.0; for doctorate, GRE, TOEFL (minimum score 570), TWE (minimum score 5) or International English Language Test (minimum score 7.5), master's degree or exceptional record in a bachelor's degree, minimum GPA of 3.5. Application fee: $55. *Expenses:* Tuition $768 per trimester. Fees $207 per year full-time, $61 per trimester part-time. *Faculty research:* Theory and implementation. • Application contact: Graduate Secretary, 604-291-4787. Fax: 604-291-3203.

Simpson College and Graduate School, Program in Curriculum and Instruction, 2211 College View Drive, Redding, CA 96003-8606. Awards MA. Part-time programs available. Faculty: 3 full-time (1 woman), 7 part-time (2 women). Students: 16 full-time (11 women), 69 part-time (41 women); includes 2 minority (1 Asian American, 1 Native American), 2 international. Average age 40. 22 applicants, 91% accepted. In 1997, 15 degrees awarded. *Degree requirements:* Thesis optional, foreign language not required. *Entrance requirements:* GRE General Test (minimum combined score of 1500 on three sections) or GRE Subject Test (score in 60th percentile or higher), minimum GPA of 2.5 in last 60 credit hours. Application deadline: 8/15 (priority date; rolling processing). Application fee: $20. *Expenses:* Tuition $8850 per year full-time, $375 per credit part-time. Fees $470 per year. *Financial aid:* Partial tuition waivers, Federal Work-Study, and career-related internships or fieldwork available. Aid available to part-time students. Financial aid application deadline: 3/1. *Faculty research:* Educational leadership. • Dr. Carol Whitmer, Dean of Education, 530-224-5600. Fax: 530-224-2057. Application contact: Murry Evans, Vice President for Enrollment Management and Marketing, 530-224-5606. Fax: 530-224-5627.

Sonoma State University, School of Education, Program in Curriculum and Instruction, Rohnert Park, CA 94928-3609. Awards MA. Part-time and evening/weekend programs available. Students: 3 full-time (2 women), 28 part-time (23 women); includes 2 minority (1 African American, 1 Asian American), 1 international. Average age 43. 12 applicants, 50% accepted. In 1997, 5 degrees awarded. *Degree requirements:* Thesis or alternative required, foreign language not required. *Entrance requirements:* Minimum GPA of 2.5. Application fee: $55. *Expenses:* Tuition $0 for state residents; $246 per unit for nonresidents. Fees $2130 per year full-time, $1464 per year part-time. *Financial aid:* Application deadline 3/2. • Dr. Andrea Neves, Advocate, 707-664-2705. E-mail: andrea.neves@sonoma.edu.

South Dakota State University, College of Education and Counseling, Department of Educational Leadership, Program in Curriculum and Instruction, Brookings, SD 57007. Awards M Ed. Accredited by NCATE. Students: 3 full-time (all women), 41 part-time (30 women); includes 2 Asian Americans. 18 applicants, 100% accepted. In 1997, 18 degrees awarded. *Degree requirements:* Thesis, comprehensive and oral exams required, foreign language not required. *Average time to degree:* master's–2 years full-time, 4 years part-time. *Entrance requirements:* TOEFL (minimum score 550), minimum GPA of 2.75. Application deadline: rolling. Application fee: $15. *Expenses:* Tuition $82 per credit hour for state residents; $242 per credit hour for nonresidents. Fees $37 per credit hour. *Faculty research:* Constructivism, educational leadership, learning styles, group processes, special needs children, rural development. • Dr. R. L. Erion, Head, Department of Educational Leadership, 605-688-4448.

Southern Illinois University at Carbondale, College of Education, Department of Curriculum and Instruction, Carbondale, IL 62901-6806. Awards MS Ed, PhD. Accredited by NCATE. Part-time programs available. Faculty: 37 full-time (19 women). Students: 91 full-time (69 women), 61 part-time (52 women). 107 applicants, 30% accepted. In 1997, 63 master's, 7 doctorates awarded. *Degree requirements:* For doctorate, variable foreign language requirement, dissertation. *Entrance requirements:* For master's, TOEFL (minimum score 550), minimum GPA of 2.7; for doctorate, GRE or MAT, TOEFL (minimum score 550), minimum GPA of 3.25. Application deadline: rolling. Application fee: $20. *Expenses:* Tuition $2964 per year full-time, $99 per semester hour part-time for state residents; $8892 per year full-time, $270 per semester hour part-time for nonresidents. Fees $1034 per year full-time, $298 per semester (minimum) part-time. *Financial aid:* In 1997–98, 4 fellowships, 10 research assistantships, 45 teaching assistantships were awarded; full tuition waivers, Federal Work-Study, institutionally sponsored loans, and career-related internships or fieldwork also available. Aid available to part-time students. *Faculty research:* Early childhood, science/environmental education, teacher education, instructional development/technology, reading. Total annual research expenditures: $3 million. • Dr. Billy G. Dixon, Chairperson, 618-536-2441. Application contact: Peggy Johnson, Assistant to the Chair, 618-536-2441. Fax: 618-453-4244. E-mail: ga4051@siuvmb.siu.edu.

Southern Illinois University at Edwardsville, School of Education, Program in Instructional Process, Edwardsville, IL 62026-0001. Awards Ed D. Accredited by NCATE. Program being phased out; applicants no longer accepted. Students: 3 full-time (all women), 4 part-time (2 women); includes 1 minority (African American). In 1997, 3 degrees awarded. *Degree requirements:* Dissertation, final exam required, foreign language not required. *Expenses:* Tuition $1716 per year full-time, $95 per credit hour part-time for state residents; $5149 per year full-time, $286 per credit hour part-time for nonresidents. Fees $463 per year full-time, $433 per year part-time. *Financial aid:* Fellowships, research assistantships, teaching assistantships, assistantships, Federal Work-Study, institutionally sponsored loans, and career-related internships or fieldwork available. Aid available to part-time students. • Dr. William Ahlbrand, Director, 618-692-3643.

Stanford University, School of Education, Program in Curriculum Studies and Teacher Education, Stanford, CA 94305-9991. Offers art (MAT), art education (AM, PhD), biology (MAT), curriculum studies and teacher education (AM, PhD), dance education (AM), English (AM, PhD), French (MAT), German (MAT), history (MAT), Italian (MAT), Latin American studies (MAT), mathematics (MAT), physics (MAT), science (AM, PhD), Slavic (MAT), social science (AM, PhD). *Degree requirements:* For doctorate, dissertation required, foreign language not required. *Entrance requirements:* GRE General Test. Application deadline: 1/2. Application fee: $65 ($75 for international students). *Expenses:* Tuition $22,110 per year. Fees $156 per year. *Financial aid:* Fellowships available. Financial aid application deadline: 2/1; applicants required to submit FAFSA. • Application contact: Graduate Admissions Office, 650-723-4794.

State University of New York at Albany, School of Education, Department of Educational Theory and Practice, Albany, NY 12222-0001. Offers programs in curriculum and instruction (MS, Ed D, CAS), curriculum planning and development (MA), educational communications (MS, CAS). Evening/weekend programs available. Faculty: 13 full-time (7 women), 6 part-time (4 women). Students: 202 full-time (123 women), 171 part-time (109 women); includes 44 minority (22 African Americans, 4 Asian Americans, 18 Hispanics), 10 international. 244 applicants, 68% accepted. In 1997, 165 master's, 7 doctorates awarded. *Degree requirements:* For doctorate, 1 foreign language, dissertation. *Entrance requirements:* For doctorate, GRE General Test. Application fee: $50. *Expenses:* Tuition $5100 per year full-time, $213 per credit hour part-time for state residents; $8416 per year full-time, $351 per credit hour part-time for nonresidents. Fees $705 per year full-time, $26.85 per credit hour part-time. *Financial aid:* Fellowships available. • Judith Langer, Chair, 518-442-5020.

Syracuse University, School of Education, Instructional Design, Development, and Evaluation Program, Syracuse, NY 13244-0003. Awards MS, Ed D, PhD, CAS. Part-time programs available. Faculty: 6 full-time (1 woman), 1 part-time (0 women). Students: 46 full-time (33 women), 29 part-time (19 women); includes 4 minority (3 African Americans, 1 Asian American), 16 international. 32 applicants, 75% accepted. In 1997, 21 master's, 5 doctorates awarded. *Degree requirements:* For master's, thesis or alternative required, foreign language not required; for doctorate and CAS, thesis/dissertation required, foreign language not required. *Entrance requirements:* GRE. Application deadline: rolling. Application fee: $40. *Tuition:* $13,320 per year full-time, $555 per credit hour part-time. *Financial aid:* Fellowships, research assistantships, teaching assistantships, administrative assistantships, Federal Work-Study, and career-related internships or fieldwork available. Aid available to part-time students. Financial aid application deadline: 3/1. *Faculty research:* Cultural pluralism and instructional design, corrections training, aging and learning, the University and social change, investigative evaluation. • James Winschel, Chair. Application contact: Donald Ely, Contact, 315-443-3704.

Syracuse University, School of Education, Teaching and Leadership Programs, Program in Teaching and Curriculum, Syracuse, NY 13244-0003. Awards MS, Ed D, PhD, CAS. Students: 12 full-time (9 women), 9 part-time (8 women); includes 3 minority (all African Americans), 1 international. 6 applicants, 83% accepted. In 1997, 2 master's awarded. *Degree requirements:* For master's, thesis or alternative; for doctorate and CAS, thesis/dissertation. *Entrance requirements:* GRE. Application fee: $40. *Tuition:* $13,320 per year full-time, $555 per credit hour part-time. *Financial aid:* Application deadline 3/1. • Gerald Mager, Director, 315-443-2684. Application contact: Dr. Berj Harootunian, Contact, 315-443-2685.

Teachers College, Columbia University, Graduate Faculty of Education, Department of Curriculum and Teaching, Program in Curriculum and Teaching, 525 West 120th Street, New York, NY 10027-6696. Awards Ed M, MA, Ed D. Faculty: 9 full-time (7 women), 4 part-time (all women), 10.2 FTE. Students: 63 full-time (48 women), 196 part-time (162 women); includes 48 minority (31 African Americans, 12 Asian Americans, 5 Hispanics), 11 international. Average age 35. 117 applicants, 71% accepted. In 1997, 43 master's, 6 doctorates awarded. *Degree requirements:* For doctorate, dissertation. *Entrance requirements:* For doctorate, GRE General Test or MAT. Application deadline: 5/15 (12/1 for spring admission). Application fee: $50. *Expenses:* Tuition $640 per credit. Fees $120 per semester. *Financial aid:* Full and partial tuition waivers, Federal Work-Study, institutionally sponsored loans, and career-related internships or fieldwork available. Aid available to part-time students. Financial aid application deadline: 2/1. *Faculty research:* Teacher education, reading education, curriculum development. • Application contact: Victor Singletary, Office of Admissions, 212-678-3710. Fax: 212-678-4171.

Tennessee State University, College of Education, Department of Teaching and Learning, Program in Curriculum and Instruction, Nashville, TN 37209-1561. Offers curriculum planning (Ed D). Accredited by NCATE. *Degree requirements:* Dissertation. *Entrance requirements:* GRE General Test (minimum combined score of 870), GRE Subject Test, or MAT (minimum score 25), minimum GPA of 3.25. Application deadline: rolling. Application fee: $15. *Tuition:* $2962 per year full-time, $182 per credit hour part-time for state residents; $7788 per year full-time, $393 per credit hour part-time for nonresidents. *Financial aid:* Fellowships available. Financial aid application deadline: 5/1. *Faculty research:* Teacher education, special child education. • Application contact: Dr. Clinton M. Lipsey, Dean of the Graduate School, 615-963-5901. Fax: 615-963-5963. E-mail: clipsey@picard.tnstate.edu.

Tennessee Technological University, College of Education, Department of Curriculum and Instruction, Program in Curriculum, Cookeville, TN 38505. Awards MA, Ed S. Accredited by NCATE. Part-time and evening/weekend programs available. Faculty: 2 full-time (1 woman). Students: 3 full-time (all women), 10 part-time (8 women). Average age 27. 17 applicants, 94% accepted. In 1997, 2 master's awarded. *Degree requirements:* For Ed S, thesis or alternative required, foreign language not required. *Entrance requirements:* For master's, MAT, TOEFL (minimum score 525); for Ed S, MAT, NTE. Application deadline: 3/1 (priority date; 8/1 for spring admission). Application fee: $25 ($30 for international students). *Tuition:* $2960 per year full-time, $147 per semester hour part-time for state residents; $7786 per year full-time, $358 per semester hour part-time for nonresidents. *Financial aid:* In 1997–98, 1 student received aid, including 1 teaching assistantship (to a first-year student); research assistantships also available. Financial aid application deadline: 4/1. • Application contact: Dr. Rebecca F. Quattlebaum, Dean of the Graduate School, 615-372-3233. Fax: 615-372-3497. E-mail: rquattlebaum@tntech.edu.

Texas A&M University, College of Education, Department of Educational Curriculum and Instruction, Unit in Curriculum Development, College Station, TX 77843. Awards M Ed, MS, Ed D, PhD. Accredited by NCATE. *Degree requirements:* For doctorate, dissertation required, foreign language not required. *Entrance requirements:* GRE General Test, TOEFL. Application fee: $35 ($75 for international students). *Financial aid:* Fellowships, research assistantships, teaching assistantships available. • Carol Anderson, Coordinator, 409-845-8252.

Texas A&M University–Corpus Christi, College of Education, Program in Curriculum and Instruction, Corpus Christi, TX 78412-5503. Awards MS. Part-time and evening/weekend programs available. Students: 10 full-time (8 women), 63 part-time (50 women); includes 30 minority (2 African Americans, 1 Asian American, 26 Hispanics, 1 Native American). Average age 37. In 1997, 66 degrees awarded. *Entrance requirements:* GRE General Test. Application deadline: 7/15 (priority date; rolling processing; 11/15 for spring admission). Application fee: $10 ($30 for international students). *Expenses:* Tuition $648 per year full-time, $120 per semester (minimum) part-time for state residents; $4482 per year full-time, $747 per semester (minimum) part-time for nonresidents. Fees $1010 per year full-time, $205 per semester part-time. *Financial aid:* Federal Work-Study, institutionally sponsored loans, and career-related internships or fieldwork available. Aid available to part-time students. Financial aid application deadline: 3/15; applicants required to submit FAFSA. • Dr. Arturo Medina, Graduate Adviser, 512-994-2667. E-mail: adedu005@tamucc.edu. Application contact: Mary Margaret Dechant, Director of Admissions, 512-994-2624. Fax: 512-994-5887.

Texas Southern University, College of Education, Area of Curriculum and Instruction, Houston, TX 77004-4584. Offers programs in bilingual education (M Ed); curriculum, instruction, and urban education (Ed D); early childhood education (M Ed); elementary education (M Ed); reading education (M Ed); secondary education (M Ed); special education (M Ed). Part-time and evening/weekend programs available. Faculty: 15 full-time (7 women), 4 part-time (all women). Students: 39 full-time (33 women), 30 part-time (25 women). 110 applicants, 72% accepted. In 1997, 6 master's awarded. *Degree requirements:* For master's, comprehensive exam required, foreign language not required; for doctorate, dissertation, comprehensive exam required, foreign language not required. *Entrance requirements:* For master's, GRE General Test, TOEFL, minimum GPA of 2.5; for doctorate, GRE General Test or MAT, master's degree, minimum B+ average. Application deadline: 7/15 (priority date; rolling processing). Application fee: $35 ($75 for international students). *Financial aid:* Federal Work-Study, institutionally sponsored loans available. Financial aid application deadline: 5/1. • Dr. Claudette Ligon, Chairperson, 713-313-7775.

Texas Tech University, Graduate School, College of Education, Division of Curriculum and Instruction, Lubbock, TX 79409. Offers programs in art education (Certificate), bilingual education (M Ed, Ed D), curriculum and instruction (M Ed, Ed D), elementary education (M Ed, Ed D, Certificate), music education (Certificate), physical education (Certificate), reading education (M Ed, Ed D), secondary education (M Ed, Ed D, Certificate). Accredited by NCATE. Part-time programs available. Faculty: 23 full-time (12 women). Students: 37 full-time (30 women), 64 part-time (56 women); includes 11 minority (4 African Americans, 7 Hispanics), 10 international. Average age 32. 38 applicants, 61% accepted. In 1997, 35 master's, 2 doctorates awarded. *Degree requirements:* For master's, computer language required, thesis optional, foreign language not required; for doctorate, dissertation required, foreign language not required. *Entrance requirements:* For master's, GRE General Test (combined average 992); for doctorate, GRE General Test. Application deadline: 4/15 (priority date; rolling processing; 11/1 for spring admission). Application fee: $25 ($50 for international students). Electronic applications accepted. *Expenses:* Tuition $864 per year full-time, $120 per semester (minimum) part-time for state residents; $5976 per year full-time, $747 per semester (minimum) part-time for nonresidents. Fees $2321 per year full-time, $302 per semester (minimum) part-time. *Financial aid:* 49 students received aid; fellowships, research assistantships, teaching assistantships, Federal Work-Study, institutionally sponsored loans, and career-related internships or fieldwork available. Aid available to part-time students. Financial aid application deadline: 5/15; applicants required to submit FAFSA. *Faculty research:* Teaching strategies for K–6 science teachers. • Dr. William E. Sparkman, Chair, 805-742-2371.

Trevecca Nazarene University, Division of Education, Major in Instructional Effectiveness, Nashville, TN 37210-2834. Awards M Ed. Part-time and evening/weekend programs available. Students: 64 full-time (53 women), 10 part-time (all women). 25 applicants, 96% accepted. In 1997, 29 degrees awarded. *Degree requirements:* Exit assessment required, foreign language and thesis not required. *Entrance requirements:* GRE General Test, MAT, minimum GPA of 2.7. Application deadline: 8/31 (rolling processing; 1/18 for spring admission). Application fee: $25. *Expenses:* Tuition $230 per hour. Fees $60 per year. • Dr. Melvin Welch, Dean of Education, Division of Education, 615-248-1201. Fax: 615-248-7728. E-mail: mwelch@trevecca.edu.

Trinity College, School of Professional Studies, Programs in Education, Washington, DC 20017-1094. Offerings include curriculum and instruction (M Ed), with options in literacy, urban learner. Faculty: 6 full-time (5 women), 18 part-time (13 women). *Application deadline:* rolling. *Application fee:* $35. *Tuition:* $460 per credit hour. • Sr. Rosemarie Bosler, Division Chair, 202-884-9557. Application contact: Karen Goodwin, Director of Graduate Admissions, 202-884-9400. Fax: 202-884-9229.

Université de Montréal, Faculty of Education, Department of Didactics, Montréal, PQ H3C 3J7, Canada. Awards MA, M Ed, PhD. Faculty: 28 full-time (17 women), 2 part-time (both women). Students: 110 full-time (61 women), 51 part-time (39 women). 63 applicants, 59% accepted. In 1997, 7 master's, 8 doctorates awarded. Terminal master's awarded for partial completion of doctoral program. *Degree requirements:* For master's, thesis (for some programs); for doctorate, dissertation, general exam. *Application deadline:* 3/11. *Application fee:* $30. *Financial aid:* Fellowships, teaching assistantships available. *Faculty research:* Teaching of French as a first or second language, teaching of science and technology, teaching of mathematics, teaching of arts. • Nicole van Grunderbeeck, Director, 514-343-7246.

Université Laval, Faculty of Education, Department of Didactics, Department of Educational Psychology and Instructional Technology, Program in Didactics, Sainte-Foy, PQ G1K 7P4, Canada. Awards MA, PhD. Students: 13 full-time (9 women), 37 part-time (18 women). 24 applicants, 75% accepted. In 1997, 14 master's, 1 doctorate awarded. *Application deadline:* 3/1. *Application fee:* $30. *Expenses:* Tuition $1334 per year (minimum) full-time, $56 per credit (minimum) part-time for Canadian residents; $5966 per year (minimum) full-time, $249 per credit (minimum) part-time for nonresidents. Fees $150 per year full-time, $6.25 per credit part-time. • Jacques Désautels, Director, 418-656-2131 Ext. 7602. Fax: 418-656-2905. E-mail: did@did.ulaval.ca.

The University of Alabama, College of Education, Area of Professional Studies, Program in Instructional Leadership, Tuscaloosa, AL 35487. Awards Ed D, PhD. Accredited by NCATE. *Degree requirements:* 1 foreign language, computer language, dissertation. *Entrance requirements:* GRE General Test, MAT (score in 50th percentile or higher), or NTE (minimum score 658 on each core battery test), minimum GPA of 3.0. Application deadline: 7/6 (rolling processing). Application fee: $25. *Tuition:* $2684 per year full-time, $594 per semester (minimum) part-time for state residents; $7216 per year full-time, $1248 per semester (minimum) part-time for nonresidents. *Financial aid:* Application deadline 7/14. • Dr. R. Carl Westerfield, Head, Area of Professional Studies, 205-348-8362. Fax: 205-348-0867. E-mail: cwesterf@bamaed.ua.edu.

University of Alaska Fairbanks, Graduate School, School of Education, Fairbanks, AK 99775-7480. Offerings include curriculum and instruction (M Ed). School faculty: 23 full-time (13 women), 2 part-time (both women). *Degree requirements:* Thesis or alternative, comprehensive exam required, foreign language not required. *Entrance requirements:* GRE General Test, TOEFL (minimum score 550). Application deadline: 4/1 (10/1 for spring admission). Application fee: $35. *Expenses:* Tuition $162 per credit for state residents; $316 per credit for nonresidents. Fees $520 per year full-time, $45 per semester (minimum) part-time. • Dr. Joe Kan, Director, 907-474-7341.

University of Arkansas, College of Education, Department of Curriculum and Instruction, Fayetteville, AR 72701-1201. Offerings include curriculum and instruction (PhD). Accredited by NCATE. Department faculty: 26 full-time (16 women). *Degree requirements:* Dissertation.

Directory: Curriculum and Instruction

University of Arkansas (continued)

Application fee: $25 ($35 for international students). *Tuition:* $3144 per year full-time, $173 per credit hour part-time for state residents; $7140 per year full-time, $395 per credit hour part-time for nonresidents. • Dr. John Helfeldt, Head, 501-575-4209.

University of British Columbia, Faculty of Education, Centre for the Study of Curriculum and Instruction, Vancouver, BC V6T 1Z4, Canada. Offers programs in curriculum and instruction (MA, M Ed, PhD), early childhood education (MA, M Ed). Part-time and evening/weekend programs available. Terminal master's awarded for partial completion of doctoral program. *Degree requirements:* For master's, thesis (MA) required, foreign language not required; for doctorate, dissertation required, foreign language not required. *Entrance requirements:* TOEFL. Application deadline: 4/30 (2/1 for spring admission). Application fee: $60.

The University of Calgary, Faculty of Education, Graduate Division of Educational Research, Calgary, AB T2N 1N4, Canada. Offerings include curriculum (MA, M Ed, M Sc, Ed D, PhD). Postbaccalaureate distance learning degree programs offered (minimal on-campus study). Division faculty: 60 full-time, 25 part-time. *Degree requirements:* For master's, thesis (for some programs), comprehensive exam required, foreign language not required; for doctorate, dissertation. *Entrance requirements:* For master's, minimum GPA of 3.0; for doctorate, minimum GPA of 3.5. Application deadline: 2/1. Application fee: $60. Electronic applications accepted. *Expenses:* Tuition $5448 per year full-time, $908 per course part-time for Canadian residents; $10,896 per year full-time, $1816 per course part-time for nonresidents. Fees $285 per year full-time, $119 per semester (minimum) part-time. • Dr. Bryant Griffith, Assistant Dean, 403-220-5675. Fax: 403-282-3005. E-mail: griffith@acs.ucalgary.ca.

University of California, Davis, Program in Education, Davis, CA 95616. Offerings include instructional studies (PhD). Program faculty: 19 full-time (9 women). *Application deadline:* 2/15. *Application fee:* $40. *Expenses:* Tuition $0 for state residents; $9384 per year for nonresidents. Fees $4466 per year full-time, $2923 per year part-time. • Johnathan Sandoval, Chair, 530-752-0761. Application contact: Karen Bray, Graduate Adviser, 530-752-0761.

University of Central Florida, College of Education, Department of Educational Foundations, Orlando, FL 32816. Offers program in curriculum and instruction (Ed D, Ed S). Accredited by NCATE. Part-time and evening/weekend programs available. Students: 58 full-time (42 women), 72 part-time (50 women); includes 18 minority (9 African Americans, 4 Asian Americans, 3 Hispanics, 2 Native Americans), 2 international. Average age 43. 34 applicants, 59% accepted. In 1997, 15 doctorates, 1 Ed S awarded. *Degree requirements:* For doctorate, dissertation required, foreign language not required; for Ed S, thesis or alternative required, foreign language not required. *Entrance requirements:* GRE General Test (minimum combined score of 1000), GRE Subject Test. Application deadline: 2/20 (9/20 for spring admission). Application fee: $20. *Expenses:* Tuition $3288 per year full-time, $137 per credit hour part-time for state residents; $11,520 per year full-time, $480 per credit hour part-time for nonresidents. Fees $105 per year. *Financial aid:* Teaching assistantships, Federal Work-Study, institutionally sponsored loans, and career-related internships or fieldwork available. Aid available to part-time students. • Dr. Karen Biraimah, Chair, 407-823-2428. E-mail: biraimah@pegasus.cc.ucf.edu. Application contact: Dr. Marcy Kysilka, Coordinator, 407-823-2011. E-mail: kysilka@pegasus.cc.ucf.edu.

University of Cincinnati, College of Education, Division of Teacher Education, Department of Curriculum and Instruction, Program in Curriculum and Instruction, Cincinnati, OH 45221. Awards M Ed, Ed D. Accredited by NCATE. Part-time programs available. Students: 82; includes 16 minority (13 African Americans, 2 Asian Americans, 1 Hispanic), 13 international. 7 applicants, 14% accepted. In 1997, 14 master's, 6 doctorates awarded. *Degree requirements:* Thesis/dissertation required, foreign language not required. *Average time to degree:* master's–3.7 years full-time; doctorate–5.1 years full-time. *Entrance requirements:* For master's, GRE General Test; for doctorate, GRE General Test, GRE Subject Test. Application deadline: 2/1. Application fee: $30. *Tuition:* $7228 per year full-time, $185 per credit hour part-time for state residents; $13,812 per year full-time, $352 per credit hour part-time for nonresidents. *Financial aid:* Fellowships, full tuition waivers available. Aid available to part-time students. Financial aid application deadline: 5/1. • Application contact: Dr. Glenn Markle, Graduate Program Director, 513-556-3582. Fax: 513-556-2483. E-mail: glenn.markle@uc.edu.

University of Colorado at Boulder, School of Education, Division of Instruction and Curriculum, Boulder, CO 80309. Awards MA, PhD. Accredited by NCATE. Part-time programs available. Students: 167 full-time (122 women), 49 part-time (40 women); includes 9 minority (1 African American, 2 Asian Americans, 4 Hispanics, 2 Native Americans), 1 international. Average age 30. 244 applicants, 61% accepted. In 1997, 74 master's, 2 doctorates awarded. *Degree requirements:* For master's, thesis or alternative, comprehensive exam required, foreign language not required; for doctorate, 1 foreign language, dissertation. *Entrance requirements:* For master's, GRE General Test (minimum combined score of 1500 on three sections) or MAT (minimum score 44), minimum undergraduate GPA of 2.75; for doctorate, GRE General Test (minimum combined score of 1500 on three sections). Application deadline: 2/1 (priority date; 8/1 for spring admission). Application fee: $40 ($60 for international students). *Expenses:* Tuition $3170 per year full-time, $531 per semester (minimum) part-time for state residents; $14,652 per year full-time, $2442 per semester (minimum) part-time for nonresidents. Fees $667 per year full-time, $130 per semester (minimum) part-time. *Financial aid:* Application deadline 2/1. • Michael Meloth, Chair, 303-492-5204. E-mail: michael.meloth@colorado.edu. Application contact: Office of Graduate Studies, 303-492-8430. Fax: 303-492-7090. E-mail: edadvise@colorado.edu.

University of Colorado at Colorado Springs, School of Education, Colorado Springs, CO 80933-7150. Offerings include curriculum and instruction (MA). Accredited by NCATE. School faculty: 13 full-time (6 women). *Degree requirements:* Thesis or alternative, comprehensive exams, microcomputer proficiency required, foreign language not required. *Entrance requirements:* GRE General Test, MAT. Application deadline: rolling. Application fee: $40 ($50 for international students). *Expenses:* Tuition $2760 per year full-time, $115 per credit hour part-time for state residents; $9960 per year full-time, $415 per credit hour part-time for nonresidents. Fees $399 per year (minimum) full-time, $106 per year (minimum) part-time. • Dr. Greg R. Weisenstein, Dean, 719-262-4103. E-mail: gweisens@mail.uccs.edu. Application contact: Connie Wroten, Academic Adviser, 719-262-3268. Fax: 719-262-3554. E-mail: cwroten@mail.uccs.edu.

University of Colorado at Denver, School of Education, Program in Curriculum and Instruction, Denver, CO 80217-3364. Awards MA. Accredited by NCATE. Part-time and evening/weekend programs available. Students: 152 full-time (117 women), 260 part-time (223 women); includes 55 minority (5 African Americans, 6 Asian Americans, 43 Hispanics, 1 Native American), 3 international. Average age 34. 81 applicants, 69% accepted. In 1997, 210 degrees awarded. *Degree requirements:* Thesis required, foreign language not required. *Entrance requirements:* GRE or MAT, minimum GPA of 2.75. Application deadline: 4/15 (rolling processing; 9/15 for spring admission). Application fee: $50 ($60 for international students). Electronic applications accepted. *Expenses:* Tuition $3530 per year full-time, $199 per semester hour part-time for state residents; $12,722 per year full-time, $764 per semester hour part-time for nonresidents. Fees $252 per year. *Financial aid:* Research assistantships, teaching assistantships, Federal Work-Study available. Financial aid application deadline: 3/1; applicants required to submit FAFSA. • Bill Juraschek, Area Coordinator, 303-556-4355. Application contact: Debra Buck, Administrative Assistant, 303-556-2290. Fax: 303-556-4479.

University of Connecticut, School of Education, Field of Curriculum and Instruction, Storrs, CT 06269. Awards MA, PhD. Accredited by NCATE. Faculty: 14. Students: 5 full-time (2 women), 27 part-time (18 women); includes 1 international. Average age 39. 22 applicants, 36% accepted. In 1997, 7 master's, 2 doctorates awarded. Terminal master's awarded for partial completion of doctoral program. *Degree requirements:* For master's, thesis or alternative; for doctorate, dissertation. *Entrance requirements:* For doctorate, GRE General Test. Application deadline: 6/1 (priority date; rolling processing; 11/1 for spring admission). Application fee: $40 ($45 for international students). *Expenses:* Tuition $5272 per year full-time, $293 per credit part-time for state residents; $13,696 per year full-time, $761 per credit part-time for nonresidents. Fees $948 per year full-time, $640 per year part-time. *Financial aid:* In 1997–98, 3 fellowships totaling $3,000, 1 research assistantship totaling $25,875, 2 teaching assistantships totaling $10,500 were awarded. Financial aid application deadline: 2/15. • Thomas P. Weinland, Head, 860-486-2433.

University of Delaware, College of Human Resources, Education and Public Policy, School of Education, Newark, DE 19716. Offerings include cognition and instruction (MA), curriculum and instruction (M Ed, PhD), instruction (MI). PhD (exceptionality; cognition, development, and instruction) new for fall 1998. Terminal master's awarded for partial completion of doctoral program. School faculty: 54 (24 women). *Entrance requirements:* For master's, GRE. Application deadline: 7/1 (rolling processing; 1/15 for spring admission). Application fee: $45. *Expenses:* Tuition $4250 per year full-time, $236 per credit hour part-time for state residents; $12,250 per year full-time, $681 per credit hour part-time for nonresidents. Fees $466 per year full-time, $15 per semester (minimum) part-time. • Dr. Robert Hampel, Director, 302-831-2573.

University of Denver, College of Education, Denver, CO 80208. Offerings include curriculum and instruction (MA, PhD), with option in curriculum leadership. Postbaccalaureate distance learning degree programs offered (no on-campus study). College faculty: 23 full-time (13 women). *Degree requirements:* For master's, comprehensive exam required, foreign language and thesis not required; for doctorate, 2 foreign languages (computer language can substitute for one), dissertation, comprehensive exam. *Entrance requirements:* For master's, GRE General Test (minimum combined score of 870), TOEFL (minimum score 550), TSE (minimum score 230); for doctorate, GRE General Test (minimum combined score of 930), TOEFL (minimum score 550), TSE (minimum score 230). Application deadline: 1/1 (rolling processing). Application fee: $40 ($45 for international students). *Expenses:* Tuition $18,216 per year full-time, $506 per credit hour part-time. Fees $159 per year. • Dr. Elinor Katz, Dean, 303-871-3665. Application contact: Linda McCarthy, 303-871-2509.

University of Detroit Mercy, College of Education and Human Services, Department of Education, Program in Curriculum and Instruction, Detroit, MI 48219-0900. Awards MA. *Degree requirements:* Thesis or alternative. *Entrance requirements:* Minimum GPA of 2.75. Application deadline: 8/1. Application fee: $25. *Faculty research:* Integrative curriculum planning, curriculum planning for ethical and character education.

University of Great Falls, Graduate Studies Division, Master of Arts in Teaching Program, Great Falls, MT 59405. Offerings include curriculum and instruction (MAT). Postbaccalaureate distance learning degree programs offered (minimal on-campus study). Program faculty: 5 full-time (all women), 6 part-time (4 women), 6 FTE. *Degree requirements:* Thesis or alternative required, foreign language not required. *Entrance requirements:* GRE General Test (minimum score 500 on each section; combined average 1000), bachelor's degree in teaching, teaching certificate, 3 years of teaching experience. Application deadline: 8/15 (priority date; rolling processing). Application fee: $35. *Expenses:* Tuition $327 per credit. Fees $150 per year full-time, $45 per semester (minimum) part-time. • Dr. Eleanore Gowen, Head. E-mail: agowen@ugf.edu.

University of Hawaii at Manoa, College of Education, Education Program, Honolulu, HI 96822. Offerings include curriculum and instruction (Ed D). Program faculty: 53 full-time (25 women). *Degree requirements:* Dissertation required, foreign language not required. *Entrance requirements:* GRE General Test, MAT (optional), TOEFL (minimum score 600), sample of written work. Application deadline: 2/1. Application fee: $0. *Tuition:* $4029 per year full-time, $214 per credit hour part-time for state residents; $9957 per year full-time, $461 per credit hour part-time for nonresidents. • Dr. Royal T. Fruehling, Graduate Chair, 808-956-4243. E-mail: fruehlin@hawaii.edu. Application contact: Melanie Bock, Clerk Typist III, 808-956-7817. Fax: 808-956-9100. E-mail: mbock@hawaii.edu.

University of Houston, College of Education, Department of Curriculum and Instruction, 4800 Calhoun, Houston, TX 77204-2163. Offers programs in art education (M Ed), bilingual education (M Ed), curriculum and instruction (Ed D), early childhood education (M Ed), education of the gifted (M Ed), elementary education (M Ed), mathematics education (M Ed), reading and language arts education (M Ed), science education (M Ed), second language education (M Ed), secondary education (M Ed), social studies education (M Ed), teaching (M Ed). Accredited by NCATE. Part-time and evening/weekend programs available. Faculty: 37 full-time (19 women), 10 part-time (7 women). Students: 225 full-time (162 women), 553 part-time (451 women); includes 139 minority (63 African Americans, 21 Asian Americans, 54 Hispanics, 1 Native American), 70 international. Average age 35. In 1997, 201 master's, 22 doctorates awarded. *Degree requirements:* For master's, comprehensive exam or thesis required, foreign language not required; for doctorate, dissertation, comprehensive exam required, foreign language not required. *Entrance requirements:* For master's, GRE General Test or MAT; for doctorate, GRE General Test, interview. Application deadline: 7/3 (priority date; rolling processing). Application fee: $35 ($75 for international students). *Expenses:* Tuition $1152 per year full-time, $120 per semester (minimum) part-time for state residents; $4482 per year full-time, $249 per credit hour part-time for nonresidents. Fees $977 per year full-time, $119 per semester (minimum) part-time. *Financial aid:* Research assistantships, teaching assistantships, Federal Work-Study, institutionally sponsored loans, and career-related internships or fieldwork available. *Faculty research:* Teaching-learning process, instructional technology in schools, teacher education, classroom management, at-risk students. • Wilford Weber, Chair, 713-743-4970. Fax: 713-743-9870. E-mail: wweber@uh.edu.

University of Houston–Clear Lake, School of Education, Houston, TX 77058-1098. Offerings include curriculum and instruction (MS). Accredited by NCATE. School faculty: 34 full-time (23 women), 17 part-time (12 women), 39 FTE. *Application deadline:* rolling. *Application fee:* $30 ($60 for international students). *Tuition:* $207 per credit hour for state residents; $336 per credit hour for nonresidents. • Dr. Dennis Spuck, Dean, 281-283-3501. Application contact: Dr. Doris L. Prater, Associate Dean, 281-283-3600.

University of Illinois at Chicago, College of Education, Department of Curriculum and Instruction, Chicago, IL 60607-7128. Offers programs in curriculum and instruction (PhD); educational policy and administration (PhD); instructional leadership (M Ed), including elementary education, reading, secondary education; leadership and administration (M Ed). Part-time and evening/weekend programs available. Faculty: 28 full-time (13 women), 1 part-time (0 women). Students: 121 full-time (83 women), 372 part-time (286 women); includes 158 minority (73 African Americans, 19 Asian Americans, 64 Hispanics, 2 Native Americans), 9 international. 292 applicants, 58% accepted. In 1997, 142 master's, 18 doctorates awarded. *Degree requirements:* For doctorate, dissertation required, foreign language not required. *Entrance requirements:* For master's, TOEFL (minimum score 550), minimum GPA of 3.75 on a 5.0 scale; for doctorate, GRE General Test (minimum combined score of 1000) or MAT (minimum score 55), TOEFL (minimum score 550), minimum GPA of 3.75 on a 5.0 scale. Application deadline: 2/15. Application fee: $40 ($50 for international students). *Financial aid:* In 1997–98, 10 fellowships, 30 research assistantships, 4 teaching assistantships were awarded; traineeships, full tuition waivers, institutionally sponsored loans, and career-related internships or fieldwork also available. *Faculty research:* Curriculum theory, curriculum development, research on teaching, curriculum and context, reading/literacy. • Dr. John Smart, Area Chair, 312-996-4526. Application contact: Victoria Hare, Director of Graduate Studies, 312-996-4520.

University of Illinois at Urbana–Champaign, College of Education, Department of Curriculum and Instruction, Urbana, IL 61801. Awards AM, Ed M, MS, Ed D, PhD, AC. Faculty: 38 full-time (11 women). Students: 214 full-time (155 women); includes 37 minority (23 African Americans, 6 Asian Americans, 5 Hispanics, 3 Native Americans), 38 international. 176 applicants, 60% accepted. In 1997, 90 master's, 26 doctorates awarded. *Degree requirements:* For doctorate, dissertation. *Entrance requirements:* For master's and doctorate, GRE General Test. Application deadline: rolling. Application fee: $40 ($50 for international students). *Financial aid:* In 1997–98, 44 research assistantships, 59 teaching assistantships were awarded; full and partial tuition waivers, Federal Work-Study also available. Financial aid application deadline: 2/15. • Mildred Griggs, Interim Head, 217-244-8061.

The University of Iowa, College of Education, Division of Early Childhood and Elementary Education, Iowa City, IA 52242-1316. Offerings include curriculum and instruction (Ed S). Division faculty: 12 full-time. *Application deadline:* rolling. *Application fee:* $30 ($50 for international students). *Expenses:* Tuition $3166 per year full-time, $176 per semester hour part-time for state residents; $10,202 per year full-time, $176 per semester hour part-time for nonresidents. Fees $202 per year full-time, $52 per year (minimum) part-time. • William Nibbelink, Chair, 319-335-5324. Fax: 319-335-5608.

University of Kentucky, Graduate School Programs from the College of Education, Program in Curriculum and Instruction, Lexington, KY 40506-0032. Offers clinical and college teaching (MS Ed U), curriculum and instruction (Ed D), instruction and administration (Ed D). Accredited by NCATE. Faculty: 22 full-time (13 women), 3 part-time (1 woman). Students: 84 full-time (46 women), 102 part-time (89 women); includes 13 minority (9 African Americans, 1 Asian American, 2 Hispanics, 1 Native American), 3 international. 89 applicants, 66% accepted. In 1997, 89 master's, 5 doctorates awarded. *Degree requirements:* For master's, comprehensive exam required, thesis optional, foreign language not required; for doctorate, dissertation, comprehensive exam required, foreign language not required. *Entrance requirements:* For master's, GRE General Test, minimum undergraduate GPA of 2.5; for doctorate, GRE General Test, minimum graduate GPA of 3.0. Application deadline: 7/19 (rolling processing; 12/15 for spring admission). Application fee: $30 ($35 for international students). *Financial aid:* In 1997–98, 9 fellowships, 4 research assistantships, 12 teaching assistantships were awarded; Federal Work-Study, institutionally sponsored loans, and career-related internships or fieldwork also available. Aid available to part-time students. *Faculty research:* Educational reform, multicultural education, classroom instructional practices, performance based assessment, primary school programs. • Dr. Douglas C. Smith, Director of Graduate Studies, 606-257-1643. Application contact: Dr. Constance L. Wood, Associate Dean, 606-257-4613. Fax: 606-323-1928.

University of Manitoba, Faculty of Education, Department of Curriculum: Humanities and Social Sciences, Winnipeg, MB R3T 2N2, Canada. Offerings include curriculum studies (M Ed). *Degree requirements:* Thesis or alternative required, foreign language not required.

University of Massachusetts Amherst, School of Education, Program in Education, Amherst, MA 01003-0001. Offerings include cultural diversity and curriculum reform (M Ed, Ed D, CAGS). Accredited by NCATE. *Degree requirements:* For doctorate, dissertation required, foreign language not required. *Entrance requirements:* For master's and doctorate, GRE General Test. Application deadline: 3/1 (rolling processing; 10/1 for spring admission). Application fee: $40. *Expenses:* Tuition $2640 per year full-time, $110 per credit part-time for state residents; $3690 per year (minimum) full-time, $165 per credit (minimum) part-time for nonresidents. Fees $2856 per year full-time, $422 per semester part-time for state residents; $3204 per year full-time, $480 per semester part-time for nonresidents. • John C. Carey, Director, 413-545-0236.

University of Massachusetts Boston, Graduate College of Education, Program in Instructional Design, Boston, MA 02125-3393. Awards M Ed. Students: 6 full-time (4 women), 80 part-time (55 women); includes 3 minority (1 African American, 2 Hispanics), 3 international. 36 applicants, 78% accepted. In 1997, 25 degrees awarded. *Degree requirements:* Comprehensive exams required, foreign language and thesis not required. *Entrance requirements:* GRE General Test, minimum GPA of 2.75. Application deadline: 3/1 (priority date; 11/1 for spring admission). Application fee: $25 ($35 for international students). *Expenses:* Tuition $2640 per year full-time, $110 per credit part-time for state residents; $8930 per year full-time, $373 per credit part-time for nonresidents. Fees $2650 per year full-time, $420 per semester (minimum) part-time for state residents; $2736 per year full-time, $420 per semester (minimum) part-time for nonresidents. *Financial aid:* In 1997–98, 3 research assistantships (1 to a first-year student) averaging $225 per month and totaling $6,000, 4 teaching assistantships (1 to a first-year student) averaging $225 per month and totaling $8,000 were awarded; administrative assistantships also available. Financial aid application deadline: 3/1; applicants required to submit FAFSA. • Dr. Donald Babcock, Director, 617-287-5400. Application contact: Lisa Lavely, Director of Graduate Admissions and Records, 617-287-6400. Fax: 617-287-6236.

University of Massachusetts Lowell, College of Education, Program in Curriculum and Instruction, 1 University Avenue, Lowell, MA 01854-2881. Awards M Ed, Ed D, CAGS. Accredited by NCATE. Part-time and evening/weekend programs available. Students: 61 full-time (38 women), 203 part-time (141 women); includes 27 minority (15 African Americans, 6 Asian Americans, 4 Hispanics, 2 Native Americans), 3 international. 229 applicants, 67% accepted. In 1997, 114 master's awarded. Terminal master's awarded for partial completion of doctoral program. *Degree requirements:* For master's, thesis required (for some programs), foreign language not required; for doctorate, dissertation. *Entrance requirements:* For master's, MAT; for doctorate, GRE General Test. Application deadline: 4/1 (priority date; rolling processing; 10/1 for spring admission). Application fee: $20 ($35 for international students). *Tuition:* $4867 per year full-time, $618 per semester (minimum) part-time for state residents; $10,276 per year full-time, $1294 per semester (minimum) part-time for nonresidents. *Financial aid:* Teaching assistantships and career-related internships or fieldwork available. Financial aid application deadline: 4/1. • Dr. Anita Greenwood, Coordinator, 978-934-4658.

The University of Memphis, College of Education, Department of Instruction and Curriculum Leadership, Memphis, TN 38152. Offers programs in early childhood education (MAT, MS, Ed D), elementary education (MAT), instruction and curriculum (MS, Ed D), instruction design and technology (MS, Ed D), reading (MS, Ed D), secondary education (MAT), special education (MAT, MS, Ed D). One or more programs accredited by NCATE. Part-time programs available. Faculty: 34 full-time (17 women), 22 part-time (13 women). Students: 217 full-time (161 women), 430 part-time (340 women); includes 110 minority (104 African Americans, 5 Hispanics, 1 Native American), 14 international. Average age 34. 297 applicants, 64% accepted. In 1997, 147 master's, 18 doctorates awarded. Terminal master's awarded for partial completion of doctoral program. *Degree requirements:* For master's, thesis or alternative, comprehensive exam required, foreign language not required; for doctorate, dissertation, comprehensive exam required, foreign language not required. *Entrance requirements:* For master's, GRE General Test or MAT, minimum GPA of 2.5; for doctorate, GRE General Test, GRE Subject Test, 2 years of teaching experience. Application deadline: 8/1 (12/1 for spring admission). Application fee: $25 ($50 for international students). *Tuition:* $2862 per year full-time, $166 per credit hour part-time for state residents; $6696 per year full-time, $379 per credit hour part-time for nonresidents. *Financial aid:* In 1997–98, 10 research assistantships totaling $51,420 were awarded. *Faculty research:* Attitudes in Tennessee schools; kindergarten retention; statistical report on Tennessee math teachers; evaluation of Sing, Spell, Read, and Write; teaching the Bill of Rights in elementary school. • Dr. Dennie Smith, Interim Chair, 901-678-2771. Application contact: Dr. Carole L. Bond, Coordinator of Graduate Studies, 901-678-3490.

University of Michigan, School of Education, Programs in Educational Studies, Ann Arbor, MI 48109. Offerings include curriculum development (AM). *Application deadline:* 1/15 (priority date). *Application fee:* $55. Electronic applications accepted. • Dr. Ronald Marx, Chairperson, 734-763-9497. E-mail: ronmarx@umich.edu. Application contact: Karen Wixson, Associate Dean, 734-764-9470. Fax: 734-763-1229. E-mail: kwixson@umich.edu.

University of Minnesota, Twin Cities Campus, College of Education and Human Development, Department of Curriculum and Instruction, Minneapolis, MN 55455-0213. Offers programs in art education (MA, M Ed, PhD), communications (PhD), curriculum studies (MA, PhD), early childhood education (MA, M Ed, PhD), elementary education (MA, M Ed, PhD), English education (MA, M Ed), instructional systems (MA, PhD), literacy (MA), mathematics education (MA, M Ed, PhD), remedial and reading supervisor endorsement (MA), science education (MA, M Ed, PhD), second languages and cultures (MA, M Ed, PhD), social studies education (MA, M Ed, PhD). • Fred Finley, Chairman, 612-625-2545.

University of Mississippi, Graduate School, School of Education, Department of Curriculum and Instruction, University, MS 38677-9702. Offers programs in curriculum and instruction (M Ed, Ed D, Ed S), education (PhD), secondary education (MA). Accredited by NCATE. Faculty: 19 full-time (15 women). Students: 111 full-time (84 women), 135 part-time (112 women); includes 83 minority (78 African Americans, 1 Asian American, 1 Hispanic, 3 Native Americans), 25 international. In 1997, 80 master's, 34 doctorates, 1 Ed S awarded. *Degree requirements:* For master's, thesis required (for some programs), foreign language not required; for doctorate, 1 foreign language, dissertation. *Entrance requirements:* For master's, GRE General Test, TOEFL, minimum GPA of 3.0; for doctorate, GRE General Test, TOEFL. Application deadline: 8/1 (rolling processing). Application fee: $0 ($25 for international students). *Financial aid:* Application deadline 3/1. • Dr. Peggy Emerson, Acting Chair, 601-232-7123.

University of Missouri–Columbia, College of Education, Department of Curriculum and Instruction, Columbia, MO 65211. Awards MA, M Ed, Ed D, PhD, Ed S. Part-time programs available. Faculty: 24 full-time (13 women), 1 (woman) part-time. Students: 97 full-time (57 women), 155 part-time (110 women); includes 9 minority (6 African Americans, 2 Asian Americans, 1 Hispanic), 22 international. In 1997, 103 master's, 16 doctorates awarded. Terminal master's awarded for partial completion of doctoral program. *Degree requirements:* For doctorate, dissertation. *Entrance requirements:* For master's and Ed S, GRE General Test or MAT, minimum GPA of 3.0; for doctorate, GRE General Test, minimum GPA of 3.0. Application deadline: rolling. Application fee: $25 ($50 for international students). *Expenses:* Tuition $3240 per year full-time, $180 per credit hour part-time for state residents; $9108 per year full-time, $506 per credit hour part-time for nonresidents. Fees $55 per year full-time. *Financial aid:* Fellowships available. • Dr. Larry Kantner, Director of Graduate Studies, 573-882-6462.

University of Missouri–Kansas City, School of Education, Division of Curriculum and Instruction, Kansas City, MO 64110-2499. Offers programs in curriculum and instruction (Ed S), education (PhD), elementary education (MA), secondary education (MA), special education (MA). Accredited by NCATE. PhD offered through the School of Graduate Studies. Part-time and evening/weekend programs available. Students: 68 full-time (54 women), 217 part-time (183 women); includes 45 minority (32 African Americans, 4 Asian Americans, 8 Hispanics, 1 Native American), 11 international. Average age 35. In 1997, 90 master's, 3 doctorates, 4 Ed Ss awarded. *Degree requirements:* For master's, thesis optional, foreign language not required; for doctorate, dissertation, internship, practicum required, foreign language not required; for Ed S, practicum required, thesis optional, foreign language not required. *Entrance requirements:* For master's, minimum GPA of 2.75; for doctorate, GRE, minimum GPA of 3.0; for Ed S, minimum GPA of 3.0. Application deadline: 7/1 (priority date; rolling processing; 12/1 for spring admission). Application fee: $25. *Expenses:* Tuition $182 per credit hour for state residents; $508 per credit hour for nonresidents. Fees $60 per year. *Financial aid:* In 1997–98, 1 research assistantship averaging $858 per month was awarded; teaching assistantships, full and partial tuition waivers, Federal Work-Study, institutionally sponsored loans also available. Aid available to part-time students. *Faculty research:* Assessment, teacher education, early childhood, learning disabilities, motivational aspects of education. • Dr. Cheryl Grossman, Chairperson, 816-235-2245.

The University of Montana–Missoula, School of Education, Department of Professional Education, Program in Curriculum and Instruction, Missoula, MT 59812-0002. Awards MA, M Ed, Ed S. Accredited by NCATE. *Degree requirements:* For Ed S, thesis required, foreign language not required. *Entrance requirements:* For master's, GRE General Test (minimum score 450 on each section), minimum GPA of 3.0; for Ed S, GRE General Test. Application deadline: 3/1 (priority date; 10/1 for spring admission). Application fee: $30. *Tuition:* $2499 per year (minimum) full-time, $376 per semester (minimum) part-time for state residents; $6528 per year (minimum) full-time, $1048 per semester (minimum) part-time for nonresidents. *Financial aid:* Application deadline 3/1. • Chair, Department of Professional Education, 406-243-2032.

University of Nebraska at Kearney, College of Education, Department of Professional Teacher Education, Kearney, NE 68849-0001. Offerings include curriculum and instruction (MS Ed). Accredited by NCATE. Department faculty: 6 full-time (4 women). *Degree requirements:* Thesis optional. *Entrance requirements:* GRE General Test. Application deadline: 8/1 (priority date; rolling processing; 12/15 for spring admission). Application fee: $35. *Expenses:* Tuition $1494 per year full-time, $83 per credit hour part-time for state residents; $2826 per year full-time, $157 per credit hour part-time for nonresidents. Fees $229 per year full-time, $11.25 per semester (minimum) part-time. • Dr. Lynn Johnson, Chair, 308-865-8513.

University of Nebraska–Lincoln, Teachers College, Center for Curriculum and Instruction, Lincoln, NE 68588. Awards MA, M Ed, MST, Ed S. Accredited by NCATE. Faculty: 23 full-time (6 women). Students: 16 full-time (13 women), 60 part-time (45 women); includes 6 minority (3 African Americans, 3 Hispanics), 2 international. Average age 33. 18 applicants, 78% accepted. In 1997, 46 master's awarded. *Degree requirements:* For master's, thesis optional. *Entrance requirements:* For master's, GRE General Test or MAT, TOEFL (minimum score 550). Application deadline: rolling. Application fee: $35. Electronic applications accepted. *Expenses:* Tuition $110 per credit hour for state residents; $270 per credit hour for nonresidents. Fees $480 per year full-time, $110 per semester part-time. *Financial aid:* In 1997–98, 7 fellowships totaling $17,394, 1 research assistantship totaling $10,000, 18 teaching assistantships totaling $191,250 were awarded; Federal Work-Study also available. Aid available to part-time students. Financial aid application deadline: 2/15. *Faculty research:* Teacher education, instructional leadership, literacy education, technology, improvement of school curriculum. • Dr. Elizabeth Franklin, Chair, 402-472-2231.

University of Nebraska–Lincoln, Teachers College, Interdepartmental Area of Administration, Curriculum and Instruction, Lincoln, NE 68588. Awards Ed D, PhD, JD/PhD. Accredited by NCATE. Students: 35 full-time (18 women), 145 part-time (87 women); includes 15 minority (4 African Americans, 5 Asian Americans, 3 Hispanics, 3 Native Americans), 15 international. Average age 44. 31 applicants, 55% accepted. In 1997, 42 degrees awarded. *Degree requirements:* Dissertation, comprehensive exam. *Average time to degree:* doctorate–5.6 years full-time. *Entrance requirements:* GRE General Test or MAT, TOEFL (minimum score 500), writing samples. Application deadline: 6/1 (10/1 for spring admission). Application fee: $35. Electronic applications accepted. *Expenses:* Tuition $110 per credit hour for state residents; $270 per credit hour for nonresidents. Fees $480 per year full-time, $110 per semester part-time. *Financial aid:* In 1997–98, 10 fellowships totaling $27,233 were awarded; research assistantships, teaching assistantships, Federal Work-Study also available. Aid available to part-time students. Financial aid application deadline: 2/15. • Dr. Miles Bryant, Graduate Committee Chair, 402-472-3729. E-mail: bryant@unlinfo.unl.edu.

University of Nevada, Las Vegas, College of Education, Department of Instructional and Curricular Studies, Las Vegas, NV 89154-9900. Offers programs in educational computing and technology (M Ed, MS), English/language arts (M Ed, MS), general elementary curriculum (M Ed, MS), general secondary education (M Ed, MS), instructional and curricular studies (Ed D, PhD, Ed S), language and literacy education (M Ed, MS), library science and audiovisual education (M Ed, MS), mathematics education (M Ed, MS), middle school education (M Ed, MS), postsecondary education (M Ed, MS), teaching English as a second language (M Ed, MS), vocational education (M Ed, MS). Accredited by NCATE. Part-time and evening/weekend programs available. Faculty: 34 full-time (16 women). Students: 121 full-time (87 women), 352 part-time (278 women); includes 65 minority (30 African Americans, 10 Asian Americans, 23 Hispanics, 2 Native Americans), 3 international. 181 applicants, 84% accepted. In 1997, 138 master's, 4 doctorates awarded. *Degree requirements:* For master's, thesis (for some programs), oral or written comprehensive exam required, foreign language not required; for doctorate, dissertation, oral exam required, foreign language not required; for Ed S, oral exam required, foreign language and thesis not required. *Entrance requirements:* For master's, minimum GPA

Directory: Curriculum and Instruction

University of Nevada, Las Vegas (continued)

of 3.0; for doctorate, GRE General Test, MAT, minimum graduate GPA of 3.5. Application deadline: 2/15 (9/30 for spring admission). Application fee: $40 ($95 for international students). *Expenses:* Tuition $93 per credit for state residents; $93 per credit full-time, $190 per credit part-time for nonresidents. Fees $5570 per year full-time for nonresidents. *Financial aid:* In 1997–98, 25 research assistantships, 8 teaching assistantships were awarded. Financial aid application deadline: 3/1. • Dr. Jan McCarthy, Chair, 702-895-3241. Application contact: Graduate College Admissions Evaluator, 702-895-3320.

University of Nevada, Reno, College of Education, Department of Curriculum and Instruction, Reno, NV 89557. Offers programs in curriculum and instruction (Ed D, PhD, Ed S), elementary education (MA, M Ed, MS), secondary education (MA, M Ed, MS), special education (MA, M Ed, MS). Accredited by NCATE. Faculty: 19 (7 women). Students: 92 full-time (67 women), 206 part-time (177 women); includes 24 minority (9 African Americans, 11 Hispanics, 4 Native Americans), 2 international. Average age 35. 164 applicants, 79% accepted. In 1997, 42 master's, 4 doctorates awarded. Terminal master's awarded for partial completion of doctoral program. *Degree requirements:* For master's, thesis optional, foreign language not required; for doctorate, dissertation required, foreign language not required. *Entrance requirements:* For master's, GRE, TOEFL (minimum score 500), minimum GPA of 2.75; for doctorate, GRE, TOEFL (minimum score 500), minimum GPA of 3.0. Application deadline: 3/1 (priority date; rolling processing; 10/1 for spring admission). Application fee: $40. *Expenses:* Tuition $0 for state residents; $5770 per year full-time, $200 per credit part-time for nonresidents. Fees $93 per credit. *Financial aid:* Research assistantships, teaching assistantships, graduate assistantships, Federal Work-Study, institutionally sponsored loans available. Financial aid application deadline: 3/1. *Faculty research:* Science, mathematics, English as a second language. • Dr. Vernon D. Luft, Chair, 702-784-4961. Application contact: Dr. J. Randall Koetting, Graduate Director, 702-784-4961 Ext. 2008. E-mail: koetting@unr.edu.

University of New Brunswick, Faculty of Education, Division of Curriculum and Instruction, Fredericton, NB E3B 5A3, Canada. Awards M Ed. Part-time programs available. *Entrance requirements:* TOEFL, TWE, minimum GPA of 3.0. Application deadline: 3/1 (priority date; rolling processing). Application fee: $25.

University of New Mexico, College of Education, Program in Multicultural Teacher and Childhood Education, Albuquerque, NM 87131-2039. Offerings include curriculum and instruction (Ed S). Accredited by NCATE. Program faculty: 11 full-time (5 women), 28 part-time (18 women), 18.72 FTE. *Application deadline:* 3/31 (10/10 for spring admission). *Application fee:* $25. *Expenses:* Tuition $2442 per year full-time, $103 per credit hour part-time for state residents; $8691 per year full-time, $103 per credit hour (minimum) part-time for nonresidents. Fees $32 per year. • Dr. Peter Winograd, Graduate Coordinator, 505-277-4533. E-mail: winograd@unm.edu. Application contact: Irene Martinez, Division Administrator, 505-277-4533. Fax: 505-277-4166. E-mail: icmartin@unm.edu.

University of New Orleans, College of Education, Department of Curriculum and Instruction, New Orleans, LA 70148. Awards M Ed, PhD, Certificate. Accredited by NCATE. Evening/weekend programs available. Faculty: 15 full-time (8 women), 6 part-time (5 women). Students: 48 full-time (38 women), 165 part-time (136 women); includes 34 minority (25 African Americans, 5 Asian Americans, 3 Hispanics, 1 Native American), 5 international. Average age 35. 51 applicants, 69% accepted. In 1997, 81 master's, 9 doctorates awarded. *Degree requirements:* For doctorate, variable foreign language requirement, dissertation. *Entrance requirements:* For master's, GRE General Test; for doctorate, GRE General Test (minimum combined score of 1000), GRE Subject Test (minimum score 500). Application deadline: 7/1 (priority date; rolling processing). Application fee: $20. *Expenses:* Tuition $2362 per year full-time, $373 per semester (minimum) part-time for state residents; $7888 per year full-time, $1423 per semester (minimum) part-time for nonresidents. Fees $170 per year full-time, $25 per semester (minimum) part-time. *Financial aid:* Teaching assistantships, partial tuition waivers, institutionally sponsored loans, and career-related internships or fieldwork available. • Dr. John Barnitz, Chairperson, 504-280-6607. E-mail: jgbci@uno.edu. Application contact: Dr. Richard Speaker, Graduate Coordinator, 504-280-6534. Fax: 504-280-6065. E-mail: rbsci@uno.edu.

The University of North Carolina at Chapel Hill, School of Education, Doctoral Program in Education, Chapel Hill, NC 27599. Offerings include culture, curriculum and change (PhD). Accredited by NCATE. Program new for fall 1998. *Degree requirements:* Dissertation, comprehensive exams required, foreign language not required. *Entrance requirements:* GRE General Test (minimum combined score of 1000), minimum GPA of 3.0 during last 2 years of undergraduate course work. Application deadline: 1/1 (priority date). *Expenses:* Tuition $1428 per year full-time, $357 per semester (minimum) part-time for state residents; $10,414 per year full-time, $2604 per semester (minimum) part-time for nonresidents. Fees $782 per year full-time, $332 per semester (minimum) part-time. • Dr. Walter Pryzwansky, Director of Graduate Studies, 919-966-7000. Application contact: Janet Carroll, Registrar, 919-966-1346. Fax: 919-962-1533. E-mail: jscarrol@email.unc.edu.

The University of North Carolina at Chapel Hill, School of Education, Program in Curriculum and Instruction, Chapel Hill, NC 27599. Awards MA, Ed D. Accredited by NCATE. Students: 8 full-time (5 women), 20 part-time (17 women). 37 applicants, 30% accepted. *Degree requirements:* For master's, thesis, comprehensive exam required, foreign language not required; for doctorate, dissertation, comprehensive exams required, foreign language not required. *Entrance requirements:* GRE General Test (minimum combined score of 1000), minimum GPA of 3.0 during last 2 years of undergraduate course work. Application deadline: 1/1 (priority date; rolling processing). Application fee: $55. *Expenses:* Tuition $1428 per year full-time, $357 per semester (minimum) part-time for state residents; $10,414 per year full-time, $2604 per semester (minimum) part-time for nonresidents. Fees $782 per year full-time, $332 per semester (minimum) part-time. *Financial aid:* Federal Work-Study available. Aid available to part-time students. Financial aid application deadline: 1/1. *Faculty research:* Professional development. • Dr. Barbara Day, Coordinator, 919-966-3291. Application contact: Janet Carroll, Registrar, 919-966-1346. Fax: 919-962-1533. E-mail: jscarrol@email.unc.edu.

University of North Carolina at Greensboro, School of Education, Department of Curriculum and Instruction, Program in Curriculum and Teaching, Greensboro, NC 27412-0001. Awards PhD. Accredited by NCATE. PhD offered jointly with the Department of Educational Leadership and Cultural Foundations. Students: 71 full-time (52 women), 52 part-time (38 women); includes 20 minority (16 African Americans, 3 Hispanics, 1 Native American). 29 applicants, 55% accepted. In 1997, 19 degrees awarded. *Degree requirements:* Dissertation, comprehensive exam. *Entrance requirements:* GRE General Test. Application deadline: 7/1 (priority date; rolling processing; 11/1 for spring admission). Application fee: $35. *Expenses:* Tuition $1842 per year full-time, $370 per semester (minimum) part-time for state residents; $10,296 per year full-time, $2484 per semester (minimum) part-time for nonresidents. Fees $806 per year full-time, $111 per semester (minimum) part-time. *Financial aid:* 16 students received aid; fellowships, research assistantships, teaching assistantships available. • Dr. Gerald Ponder, Chair, Department of Curriculum and Instruction, 336-334-3437.

University of Northern Iowa, College of Education, Department of Curriculum and Instruction, Program in Curriculum and Instruction, Cedar Falls, IA 50614. Awards MA Ed, Ed D. Part-time and evening/weekend programs available. Students: 15 full-time (11 women), 43 part-time (26 women); includes 4 minority (3 African Americans, 1 Hispanic), 4 international. Average age 33. 13 applicants, 77% accepted. In 1997, 17 master's, 1 doctorate awarded. *Degree requirements:* For master's, thesis or alternative required, foreign language not required; for doctorate, dissertation required, foreign language not required. *Entrance requirements:* For master's, minimum GPA of 3.5, 3 years of educational experience; for doctorate, minimum GPA of 3.2, 3 years of educational experience, master's degree. Application deadline: 8/1 (priority date; rolling processing). Application fee: $20 ($30 for international students). *Expenses:* Tuition $3166 per year full-time, $176 per hour part-time for state residents; $7805 per year full-time, $176 per hour part-time for nonresidents. Fees $194 per year full-time, $12.50 per semester (minimum) part-time. *Financial aid:* Full and partial tuition waivers, Federal Work-Study, and career-related internships or fieldwork available. Aid available to part-time students. Financial aid application deadline: 3/1. • Dr. Gregory P. Stefanich, Head, 319-273-2073.

University of North Texas, College of Education, Department of Teacher Education and Administration, Program in Curriculum and Instruction, Denton, TX 76203-6737. Awards Ed D, PhD. Accredited by NCATE. Ed D offered jointly with Texas Woman's University. *Degree requirements:* Dissertation. *Entrance requirements:* GRE General Test (minimum score 400 on each section, 1000 combined). Application fee: $25 ($50 for international students). *Tuition:* $2063 per year full-time, $815 per year part-time for state residents; $5897 per year full-time, $2100 per year part-time for nonresidents. *Financial aid:* Fellowships, research assistantships, teaching assistantships, Federal Work-Study, institutionally sponsored loans, and career-related internships or fieldwork available. Financial aid application deadline: 4/1. • Application contact: Pat Moseley, Adviser, 940-565-2920.

University of Oklahoma, College of Education, Department of Instructional Leadership and Academic Curriculum, Program in Instructional Leadership and Academic Curriculum, Norman, OK 73019-0390. Offers early childhood education (M Ed, PhD), elementary education (M Ed, PhD), English education (M Ed, PhD), math education (M Ed, PhD), reading education (M Ed, PhD), science education (M Ed, PhD), secondary education (M Ed, PhD), social studies education (M Ed, PhD). Accredited by NCATE. Part-time and evening/weekend programs available. Faculty: 19 full-time (12 women), 12 part-time (11 women). Students: 31 full-time (23 women), 113 part-time (94 women); includes 12 minority (3 African Americans, 3 Asian Americans, 1 Hispanic, 5 Native Americans), 6 international. In 1997, 19 master's, 2 doctorates awarded. *Degree requirements:* For doctorate, variable foreign language requirement, dissertation. *Entrance requirements:* For master's, TOEFL (minimum score 550), 12 hours of course work in education; for doctorate, GRE General Test (minimum combined score of 1000), TOEFL (minimum score 500), master's degree, minimum graduate GPA of 3.0. Application deadline: 6/1 (priority date; rolling processing). Application fee: $25. *Expenses:* Tuition $1920 per year full-time, $80 per credit hour part-time for state residents; $6108 per year full-time, $255 per credit hour part-time for nonresidents. Fees $468 per year full-time, $12 per semester (minimum) part-time. *Financial aid:* In 1997–98, 5 research assistantships, 7 teaching assistantships were awarded. • Dr. Bonnie Konopak, Chair, Department of Instructional Leadership and Academic Curriculum, 405-325-1498.

University of Puerto Rico, Río Piedras, College of Education, Program in Curriculum and Teaching, San Juan, PR 00931. Offers biology education (M Ed), chemistry education (M Ed), curriculum and teaching (Ed D), English education (M Ed), history education (M Ed), mathematics education (M Ed), physics education (M Ed), secondary education (M Ed), Spanish education (M Ed). Part-time programs available. *Degree requirements:* Thesis/dissertation required, foreign language not required. *Entrance requirements:* For master's, PAEG, minimum GPA of 3.0; for doctorate, GRE or PAEG, master's degree, minimum GPA of 3.0. Application deadline: 2/21. Application fee: $17.

University of Redlands, Alfred North Whitehead College for Lifelong Learning, Program in Curriculum Leadership, PO Box 3080, Redlands, CA 92373-0999. Awards MA. Students: 21 full-time (18 women); includes 4 minority (all Asian Americans). Average age 37. In 1997, 12 degrees awarded. *Application deadline:* 9/1 (priority date; rolling processing; 3/1 for spring admission). *Application fee:* $40. Electronic applications accepted. • Dr. June Lemke, Director, 909-793-2121 Ext. 6016.

University of Regina, Faculty of Graduate Studies and Research, Faculty of Education, Department of Curriculum and Instruction, Regina, SK S4S 0A2, Canada. Awards M Ed, Diploma. Part-time programs available. Students: 6 full-time, 117 part-time. 42 applicants, 93% accepted. In 1997, 16 master's, 9 Diplomas awarded. *Degree requirements:* For master's, practicum, project, or thesis required, thesis optional, foreign language not required. *Entrance requirements:* For master's, TOEFL (minimum score 580), bachelor's degree in education, 2 years of teaching experience. Application deadline: 3/15 (12/15 for spring admission). Application fee: $0. *Tuition:* $196 per credit for Canadian residents; $383 per credit for nonresidents. *Financial aid:* Fellowships, research assistantships, teaching assistantships available. Financial aid application deadline: 6/15. • Dr. David Bale, Associate Dean, 306-585-5353. Fax: 306-585-5330. E-mail: david.bale@uregina.ca. Application contact: Dr. M. Taylor, Chair, Graduate Programs, 306-585-4606. Fax: 306-585-4880. E-mail: marlene.taylor@uregina.ca.

University of St. Thomas, School of Education, Program in Curriculum and Instruction, St. Paul, MN 55105-1096. Awards MA, Ed S. Accredited by NCATE. Students: 3 full-time (2 women), 158 part-time (120 women); includes 18 minority (15 African Americans, 2 Asian Americans, 1 Native American), 1 international. Average age 34. 63 applicants, 100% accepted. In 1997, 108 master's awarded. *Entrance requirements:* For master's, MAT, minimum GPA of 2.75; for Ed S, minimum graduate GPA of 3.25. Application deadline: rolling. Application fee: $50. *Tuition:* $375 per credit hour. *Financial aid:* In 1997–98, 11 grants (1 to a first-year student) totaling $14,868 were awarded. Financial aid application deadline: 4/1. • Dr. Eleni Roulis, Director, 612-962-5410. Fax: 612-962-5169.

University of San Diego, School of Education, Program in Curriculum and Instruction, San Diego, CA 92110-2492. Awards MA, MAT, M Ed. Part-time and evening/weekend programs available. Faculty: 5 full-time (3 women), 15 part-time (7 women), 6 FTE. Students: 126 full-time (94 women), 52 part-time (44 women); includes 48 minority (6 African Americans, 14 Asian Americans, 25 Hispanics, 3 Native Americans), 3 international. 51 applicants, 94% accepted. In 1997, 22 degrees awarded. *Degree requirements:* Thesis (for some programs), comprehensive exam required, foreign language not required. *Entrance requirements:* TOEFL (minimum score 580), TWE, minimum GPA of 2.75. Application deadline: 5/1 (priority date; rolling processing; 11/15 for spring admission). Application fee: $45. *Expenses:* Tuition $585 per unit (minimum). Fees $50 per year full-time, $30 per year part-time. *Financial aid:* Fellowships, stipends, Federal Work-Study, institutionally sponsored loans, and career-related internships or fieldwork available. Aid available to part-time students. Financial aid application deadline: 5/1; applicants required to submit FAFSA. *Faculty research:* Historical research, computers in the professions. • Dr. Robert L. Infantino, Coordinator, 619-260-4600 Ext. 4285. Fax: 619-260-6835. Application contact: Mary Jane Tiernan, Director of Graduate Admissions, 619-260-4524. Fax: 619-260-4158. E-mail: grads@acusd.edu.

University of San Francisco, School of Education, Department of Curriculum and Instruction, San Francisco, CA 94117-1080. Awards MA, Ed D. Faculty: 6 full-time (4 women), 5 part-time (2 women). Students: 62 full-time (39 women), 28 part-time (20 women); includes 24 minority (18 African Americans, 4 Asian Americans, 2 Hispanics). Average age 41. 55 applicants, 89% accepted. In 1997, 13 master's, 8 doctorates awarded. *Degree requirements:* For doctorate, dissertation required, foreign language not required. *Application fee:* $40. *Tuition:* $658 per unit (minimum). *Financial aid:* 53 students received aid; fellowships, research assistantships, teaching assistantships available. Financial aid application deadline: 3/2. • Dr. Robert Burns, Chair, 415-422-6289.

University of Sarasota, College of Education, Program in Curriculum and Instruction, Sarasota, FL 34235-8246. Awards MA Ed, Ed D. Part-time and evening/weekend programs available. Postbaccalaureate distance learning degree programs offered (minimal on-campus study). Faculty: 4 full-time (3 women). Students: 73 full-time (36 women), 174 part-time (88 women). *Degree requirements:* For master's, thesis optional; for doctorate, dissertation, comprehensive exam. *Average time to degree:* master's–2 years full-time, 3 years part-time; doctorate–3 years full-time, 4 years part-time. *Entrance requirements:* For master's, TOEFL (minimum score 500); for doctorate, TOEFL (minimum score 550), minimum undergraduate GPA of 3.0. Application deadline: rolling. Application fee: $50. *Financial aid:* Available to part-time students. Financial aid applicants required to submit FAFSA. • Application contact: Kathy Ketterer, Admissions Representative, 800-331-5995. Fax: 941-371-8910. E-mail: kathy_ketterer@embanet.com.

University of Saskatchewan, College of Education, Department of Curriculum Studies, Saskatoon, SK S7N 5A2, Canada. Awards M Ed, PhD, Diploma. Part-time programs available. *Degree requirements:* For master's, thesis (for some programs); for doctorate, dissertation. *Entrance requirements:* For master's, MAT, TOEFL; for doctorate, TOEFL; for Diploma, International English Language Testing System (minimum score 6) or Michigan English Language Assessment Battery (minimum score 80), or TOEFL (minimum score 550). Application deadline: 7/1 (priority date; rolling processing). Application fee: $0.

University of South Carolina, Graduate School, College of Education, Department of Educational Leadership and Policies, Program in Curriculum and Instruction, Columbia, SC 29208. Awards Ed D. Accredited by NCATE. Part-time and evening/weekend programs available. Faculty: 5 full-time (2 women). Students: 12 full-time (9 women), 113 part-time (88 women); includes 18 minority (17 African Americans, 1 Hispanic), 3 international. Average age 45. In 1997, 16 doctorates awarded. Terminal master's awarded for partial completion of doctoral program. *Degree requirements:* For doctorate, 1 foreign language (computer language can substitute), dissertation, comprehensive exam. *Entrance requirements:* For doctorate, GRE General Test or MAT, interview. Application deadline: 2/1 (priority date; rolling processing). Application fee: $35. Electronic applications accepted. *Expenses:* Tuition $3894 per year full-time, $193 per credit hour part-time for state residents; $8114 per year full-time, $404 per credit hour part-time for nonresidents. Fees $125 per year full-time, $37 per semester (minimum) part-time. *Financial aid:* Assistantships, partial tuition waivers, Federal Work-Study, institutionally sponsored loans, and career-related internships or fieldwork available. *Faculty research:* Teacher education, historian recording project, curriculum development in international areas, human sexuality. • Application contact: Office of Intercollegiate Teacher Education and Student Affairs, 803-777-6732. Fax: 803-777-3068.

University of South Dakota, School of Education, Division of Curriculum and Instruction, Vermillion, SD 57069-2390. Offers programs in curriculum and instruction (Ed D, Ed S), elementary education (MA), secondary education (MA), special education (MA). Accredited by NCATE. Part-time programs available. Faculty: 12 full-time (5 women), 2 part-time (0 women). Students: 47 full-time (33 women), 27 part-time (22 women). 36 applicants, 53% accepted. In 1997, 58 master's, 12 doctorates awarded. *Degree requirements:* For doctorate, dissertation required, foreign language not required. *Entrance requirements:* For master's, GRE General Test, MAT; for doctorate, GRE General Test. Application deadline: rolling. Application fee: $15. *Expenses:* Tuition $1530 per year full-time, $85 per credit hour part-time for state residents; $4518 per year full-time, $251 per credit hour part-time for nonresidents. Fees $792 per year full-time, $44 per credit hour part-time. *Financial aid:* Teaching assistantships, Federal Work-Study available. • Dr. Linda Reetz, Chair, 605-677-5210.

University of Southern California, Graduate School, School of Education, Department of Curriculum and Instruction, Los Angeles, CA 90089. Offers programs in communication handicapped (MS); curriculum and instruction (Ed D, PhD); curriculum and teaching (MS); instructional technology (MS); language, literacy, and learning (PhD); learning handicapped (MS); teaching English as a second language (MS). Students: 86 full-time (64 women), 93 part-time (69 women); includes 67 minority (13 African Americans, 34 Asian Americans, 19 Hispanics, 1 Native American), 17 international. Average age 38. 126 applicants, 70% accepted. In 1997, 50 master's, 9 doctorates awarded. *Degree requirements:* For doctorate, dissertation. *Entrance requirements:* GRE General Test. Application deadline: 7/1 (priority date; 11/1 for spring admission). Application fee: $55. *Expenses:* Tuition $16,944 per year full-time, $706 per unit part-time. Fees $414 per year full-time, $32 per year part-time. *Financial aid:* In 1997–98, 33 fellowships, 18 teaching assistantships, 15 scholarships were awarded; research assistantships, Federal Work-Study, institutionally sponsored loans also available. Aid available to part-time students. Financial aid application deadline: 2/15; applicants required to submit FAFSA. • Dr. Edgar Williams, Chair.

University of Southern Mississippi, College of Education and Psychology, Department of Curriculum and Instruction, Hattiesburg, MS 39406-5167. Offers programs in early childhood education (M Ed, Ed S), elementary education (M Ed, Ed D, PhD, Ed S), reading (M Ed, MS, Ed S), secondary education (M Ed, MS, Ed D, PhD, Ed S). Faculty: 11 full-time (7 women), 1 part-time (0 women). Students: 23 full-time (19 women), 61 part-time (50 women); includes 10 minority (8 African Americans, 1 Asian American, 1 Hispanic), 3 international. Average age 36. 49 applicants, 73% accepted. In 1997, 113 master's, 2 doctorates, 12 Ed Ss awarded. *Degree requirements:* For master's, thesis or alternative required, foreign language not required; for doctorate, 2 foreign languages, dissertation; for Ed S, thesis required, foreign language not required. *Entrance requirements:* For master's, GRE General Test, minimum GPA of 2.75; for doctorate and Ed S, GRE General Test, minimum GPA of 3.25. Application deadline: 8/9 (priority date; rolling processing). Application fee: $0 ($25 for international students). *Tuition:* $2870 per year full-time, $137 per credit hour part-time for state residents; $5972 per year full-time, $172 per credit hour part-time for nonresidents. *Financial aid:* Teaching assistantships, partial tuition waivers, Federal Work-Study, institutionally sponsored loans available. Financial aid application deadline: 3/15. *Faculty research:* Mathematical problem solving, integrative curriculum, writing process, teacher education models. • Dr. Carolyn Reeves-Kazelskis, Acting Chair, 601-266-4547. Fax: 601-266-4175.

University of Southwestern Louisiana, College of Education, Graduate Studies and Research in Education, Program in Curriculum and Instruction, Lafayette, LA 70503. Awards M Ed. Accredited by NCATE. Faculty: 13 full-time (10 women). Students: 29 full-time (24 women), 60 part-time (50 women); includes 7 minority (4 African Americans, 1 Asian American, 2 Hispanics), 2 international. 54 applicants, 81% accepted. In 1997, 24 degrees awarded. *Degree requirements:* Thesis or alternative required, foreign language not required. *Entrance requirements:* GRE General Test, teaching certificate. Application deadline: 8/15. Application fee: $5 ($15 for international students). *Tuition:* $2012 per year full-time, $300 per semester (minimum) part-time for state residents; $7244 per year full-time, $300 per semester (minimum) part-time for nonresidents. *Financial aid:* Fellowships, research assistantships, Federal Work-Study available. Financial aid application deadline: 5/1. • Dr. Daniel Jordan, Director, Graduate Studies and Research in Education, 318-482-6747.

University of Tennessee at Chattanooga, School of Education, Education Graduate Studies Division, Chattanooga, TN 37403-2598. Offerings include curriculum and instruction (M Ed). Accredited by NCATE. Division faculty: 15 full-time (5 women), 7 part-time (3 women). *Degree requirements:* Comprehensive exams required, thesis optional, foreign language not required. *Entrance requirements:* GRE General Test or MAT, teaching certificate. Application deadline: rolling. Application fee: $25. *Tuition:* $2864 per year full-time, $160 per credit hour part-time for state residents; $6806 per year full-time, $379 per credit hour part-time for nonresidents. • Dr. Tom Bibler, Acting Head, 423-755-4211. Fax: 423-755-5380. E-mail: tom-bibler@utc.edu. Application contact: Dr. Deborah Arfken, Assistant Provost for Graduate Studies, 423-755-4667. Fax: 423-755-4478.

University of Tennessee, Knoxville, College of Education, Program in Education II, Knoxville, TN 37996. Offerings include curriculum (MS, Ed D, Ed S), teaching and learning (Ed S). One or more programs accredited by NCATE. *Degree requirements:* For master's and Ed S, thesis optional, foreign language not required; for doctorate, dissertation required, foreign language not required. *Entrance requirements:* For master's, TOEFL (minimum score 550), minimum GPA of 2.7; for doctorate, GRE General Test, TOEFL (minimum score 550), minimum GPA of 2.7; for Ed S, TOEFL (minimum score 550), GRE General Test, minimum GPA of 2.7. Application deadline: 2/1 (priority date; rolling processing). Application fee: $35. Electronic applications accepted. *Tuition:* $3354 per year full-time, $181 per semester hour part-time for state residents; $8410 per year full-time, $462 per semester hour part-time for nonresidents. • Dr. Tom George, Associate Dean, 423-974-0907. Fax: 423-974-8718. E-mail: tgeorge1@utk.edu.

The University of Texas at Austin, Graduate School, College of Education, Department of Curriculum and Instruction, Austin, TX 78712. Awards MA, M Ed, Ed D, PhD. Students: 290 (214 women); includes 53 minority (7 African Americans, 7 Asian Americans, 38 Hispanics, 1 Native American), 38 international. 119 applicants, 60% accepted. In 1997, 60 master's, 22 doctorates awarded. *Degree requirements:* For doctorate, dissertation. *Entrance requirements:* GRE General Test. Application deadline: 3/1 (rolling processing; 10/1 for spring admission). Application fee: $50 ($75 for international students). Electronic applications accepted. *Expenses:* Tuition $2592 per year full-time, $324 per semester (minimum) part-time for state residents; $7704 per year full-time, $963 per semester (minimum) part-time for nonresidents. Fees $778 per year full-time, $161 per semester (minimum) part-time. *Financial aid:* In 1997–98, 2 fellowships averaging $1,222 per month, 60 teaching assistantships averaging $852 per month were awarded. Financial aid application deadline: 2/1. • Dr. Joe L. Frost, Acting Chairman, 512-471-5942. Application contact: Elaine Fowler Costas, Graduate Adviser, 512-471-4116. Fax: 512-471-8460. E-mail: e.f.costas@mail.utexas.edu.

The University of Texas at Brownsville, Graduate Studies, School of Education, Brownsville, TX 78520-4991. Offerings include curriculum and instruction (M Ed). School faculty: 18 full-time (10 women). *Degree requirements:* Thesis optional, foreign language not required. *Entrance requirements:* GRE General Test, TOEFL (minimum score 550). Application deadline: 8/1 (priority date; rolling processing; 1/1 for spring admission). Application fee: $15. *Expenses:* Tuition $648 per year full-time, $120 per semester hour part-time for state residents; $4698 per year full-time, $783 per semester hour part-time for nonresidents. Fees $593 per year full-time, $109 per year part-time. • Dr. Sylvia C. Peña, Dean, 956-983-7219. Fax: 956-982-0293. E-mail: scpena@utb1.utb.edu.

University of the Pacific, School of Education, Department of Curriculum and Instruction, Stockton, CA 95211-0197. Offers programs in curriculum and instruction (MA, Ed D), education (M Ed). Accredited by NCATE. Ed D being phased out; applicants no longer accepted. Faculty: 10 full-time (4 women). Students: 23 full-time (19 women), 22 part-time (20 women); includes 3 international. In 1997, 16 master's, 3 doctorates awarded. *Degree requirements:* For master's, thesis required (for some programs), foreign language not required; for doctorate, dissertation. *Entrance requirements:* For master's, GRE General Test, GRE Subject Test. Application deadline: 3/1 (priority date; rolling processing; 10/15 for spring admission). Application fee: $50. *Expenses:* Tuition $19,000 per year full-time, $594 per unit part-time. Fees $30 per year (minimum). *Financial aid:* In 1997–98, 7 teaching assistantships were awarded. Financial aid application deadline: 3/1. • Dr. Marilyn Draheim, Chairperson, 209-946-2336.

University of Toledo, College of Education and Allied Professions, Department of Curriculum and Instruction, Toledo, OH 43606-3398. Offers programs in business education (M Ed), curriculum and instruction (MA Ed, M Ed, MS Ed, Ed D, PhD, Ed S), early childhood education (M Ed), educational technology (M Ed), elementary education (M Ed), secondary education (M Ed). Accredited by NCATE. Evening/weekend programs available. Faculty: 27 full-time (9 women). Students: 87 full-time (64 women), 307 part-time (239 women); includes 65 minority (58 African Americans, 5 Hispanics, 2 Native Americans), 15 international. 160 applicants, 70% accepted. In 1997, 99 master's, 7 doctorates, 1 Ed S awarded. *Degree requirements:* For master's, thesis or alternative, comprehensive exam required, foreign language not required; for doctorate, dissertation, comprehensive exams required, foreign language not required; for Ed S, thesis optional, foreign language not required. *Entrance requirements:* For master's, minimum GPA of 2.7; for doctorate, GRE, minimum GPA of 2.7 (undergraduate), 3.0 (graduate); for Ed S, minimum GPA of 2.7 (undergraduate), 3.0 (graduate). Application deadline: 8/1 (priority date; rolling processing). Application fee: $30. *Tuition:* $5907 per year full-time, $246 per hour part-time for state residents; $11,835 per year full-time, $493 per hour part-time for nonresidents. *Financial aid:* In 1997–98, 1 research assistantship, 17 teaching assistantships were awarded; administrative assistantships, tuition scholarships, full tuition waivers, Federal Work-Study, institutionally sponsored loans, and career-related internships or fieldwork also available. Aid available to part-time students. Financial aid application deadline: 4/1; applicants required to submit FAFSA. • Dr. James R. Gress, Chair, 419-530-2468. Fax: 419-530-7719. E-mail: jgress@uoft02.utoledo.edu.

University of Vermont, College of Education and Social Services, Department of Education, Programs in Curriculum and Instruction, Burlington, VT 05405-0160. Awards M Ed. Accredited by NCATE. Students: 51; includes 5 minority (2 African Americans, 1 Asian American, 1 Hispanic, 1 Native American). 67 applicants, 79% accepted. In 1997, 19 degrees awarded. *Entrance requirements:* GRE General Test, TOEFL (minimum score 550). Application deadline: 4/1 (priority date; rolling processing). Application fee: $25. *Expenses:* Tuition $302 per credit for state residents; $755 per credit for nonresidents. Fees $434 per year full-time, $46 per semester (minimum) part-time. *Financial aid:* Fellowships, teaching assistantships, and career-related internships or fieldwork available. Financial aid application deadline: 3/1. • Dr. R. Agne, Coordinator, 802-656-3356.

University of Victoria, Faculty of Education, Department of Communication and Social Foundations, Victoria, BC V8W 2Y2, Canada. Offerings include curriculum studies (MA, M Ed). Postbaccalaureate distance learning degree programs offered (minimal on-campus study). Department faculty: 17 full-time (9 women), 14 part-time (9 women). *Degree requirements:* Thesis, project (M Ed) required, foreign language not required. *Average time to degree:* master's–3.3 years full-time; doctorate–4.4 years full-time. *Entrance requirements:* Minimum B average. Application deadline: 4/30 (rolling processing). Application fee: $50. *Tuition:* $2080 per year full-time, $557 per semester part-time. • Dr. G. Potter, Chair, 250-721-7802. Application contact: Sarah Baylow, Graduate Secretary, 250-721-7882. Fax: 250-721-7767. E-mail: sbaylow@uvic.ca.

University of Virginia, Curry School of Education, Department of Curriculum, Instruction, and Special Education, Program in Curriculum and Instruction, Charlottesville, VA 22903. Awards M Ed, Ed D, Ed S. Accredited by NCATE. Faculty: 27 full-time (12 women), 2 part-time (both women), 28 FTE. Students: 39 full-time (33 women), 22 part-time (18 women); includes 5 minority (4 African Americans, 1 Hispanic), 3 international. Average age 32. 126 applicants, 85% accepted. In 1997, 92 master's, 5 doctorates awarded. *Degree requirements:* For doctorate, dissertation required, foreign language not required. *Entrance requirements:* GRE General Test. Application deadline: 3/1 (11/15 for spring admission). Application fee: $40. *Tuition:* $4876 per year full-time, $944 per semester (minimum) part-time for state residents; $15,824 per year full-time, $2748 per semester (minimum) part-time for nonresidents. • Application contact: Linda Berry, Student Enrollment Coordinator, 804-924-0738. E-mail: lrb8e@virginia.edu.

University of Washington, College of Education, Program in Curriculum and Instruction, Seattle, WA 98195. Awards M Ed, Ed D, PhD. *Degree requirements:* For master's, thesis optional, foreign language not required; for doctorate, dissertation required, foreign language not required. *Entrance requirements:* GRE General Test, TOEFL, minimum GPA of 3.0. Application deadline: 2/1. Application fee: $45. *Tuition:* $5433 per year full-time, $775 per quarter (minimum) part-time for state residents; $13,479 per year full-time, $1925 per quarter (minimum) part-time for nonresidents. *Faculty research:* Educational technology, reading, multiethnic education, science, teacher preparation. • Dr. Allen Glenn, Dean, College of Education, 206-543-5390. Fax: 206-685-1713. E-mail: aglenn@u.washington.edu. Application contact: Richard Neel, Associate Dean, 206-543-7833. Fax: 206-543-8439. E-mail: edinfo@u.washington.edu.

The University of Western Ontario, Social Sciences Division, Faculty of Education, Program in Educational Studies, London, ON N6A 5B8, Canada. Offerings include curriculum studies (M Ed). Program faculty: 30 full-time (10 women). *Average time to degree:* master's–2 years full-time, 3 years part-time. *Application deadline:* 2/1. *Application fee:* $50. • Dr. S. Haggerty, Graduate Chair, 519-661-2099. E-mail: haggerty@edu.uwo.ca. Application contact: L. Kulak, Graduate Supervisor, 519-661-2099. Fax: 519-661-3833. E-mail: kulak@edu.uwo.ca.

University of West Florida, College of Education, Department of Professional Studies, Educational Foundations, and Technology, Program in Curriculum and Instruction, Pensacola, FL 32514-5750. Awards Ed D, Ed S. Accredited by NCATE. Students: 15 full-time (9 women), 135 part-time (84 women); includes 17 minority (10 African Americans, 3 Asian Americans, 4 Hispanics). Average age 40. In 1997, 6 doctorates, 22 Ed Ss awarded. *Degree requirements:* For doctorate, dissertation. *Entrance requirements:* For doctorate, GMAT (minimum score

Directory: Curriculum and Instruction

University of West Florida (continued)

450) or GRE General Test (minimum combined score of 1000). Application deadline: 7/1 (rolling processing); 11/1 for spring admission). Application fee: $20. *Tuition:* $131 per credit hour (minimum) for state residents; $436 per credit hour (minimum) for nonresidents. • Dr. Janet Pilcher, Interim Chairperson, Department of Professional Studies, Educational Foundations, and Technology, 850-474-2300.

University of Wisconsin–Madison, School of Education, Department of Curriculum and Instruction, Program in Curriculum and Instruction, Madison, WI 53706-1380. Awards MS, PhD. *Degree requirements:* For doctorate, dissertation. *Application fee:* $38. *Tuition:* $4928 per year full-time, $926 per semester (minimum) part-time for state residents; $15,190 per year full-time, $2849 per semester (minimum) part-time for nonresidents.

University of Wisconsin–Milwaukee, School of Education, Department of Curriculum and Instruction, Milwaukee, WI 53201-0413. Offers programs in curriculum planning and instruction improvement (MS), early childhood education (MS), elementary education (MS), junior high/middle school education (MS), reading education (MS), secondary education (MS), teaching in an urban setting (MS). Offered jointly with University of Wisconsin–Green Bay. Part-time programs available. Faculty: 28 full-time (17 women). Students: 10 full-time (9 women), 90 part-time (78 women); includes 18 minority (9 African Americans, 4 Asian Americans, 5 Hispanics), 2 international. 15 applicants, 67% accepted. In 1997, 63 degrees awarded. *Degree requirements:* Thesis or alternative required, foreign language not required. *Application deadline:* 1/1 (priority date; rolling processing; 9/1 for spring admission). *Application fee:* $45 ($75 for international students). *Tuition:* $4996 per year full-time, $1030 per semester (minimum) part-time for state residents; $15,216 per year full-time, $2947 per semester (minimum) part-time for nonresidents. *Financial aid:* Fellowships, research assistantships, teaching assistantships, project assistantships, and career-related internships or fieldwork available. Aid available to part-time students. Financial aid application deadline: 4/15. • Linda Post, Chair, 414-229-4884.

University of Wisconsin–Oshkosh, College of Education and Human Services, Department of Curriculum and Instruction, Oshkosh, WI 54901-8602. Awards MSE. Accredited by NCATE. Part-time and evening/weekend programs available. Faculty: 8 full-time (5 women), 2 part-time (both women). Students: 46 part-time (43 women). Average age 30. 11 applicants, 100% accepted. In 1997, 8 degrees awarded (100% found work related to degree). *Degree requirements:* Seminar paper required, thesis optional, foreign language not required. *Entrance requirements:* Teaching license. Application deadline: rolling. Application fee: $45. *Tuition:* $3638 per year full-time, $609 per semester (minimum) part-time for state residents; $11,282 per year full-time, $1884 per semester (minimum) part-time for nonresidents. *Financial aid:* Career-related internships or fieldwork available. Financial aid application deadline: 3/15. *Faculty research:* Early childhood, middle school teaching, literacy, elementary teaching. • Dr. Jean Erdman, Chair, 920-424-2477. Fax: 920-424-0858. E-mail: erdman@uwosh.edu.

University of Wisconsin–Superior, Department of Teacher Education, Program in Instruction, Superior, WI 54880-2873. Awards MSE. Part-time and evening/weekend programs available. Students: 25 (17 women). 4 applicants, 100% accepted. In 1997, 10 degrees awarded (100% found work related to degree). *Degree requirements:* Thesis or alternative, comprehensive exam, research project required, foreign language not required. *Entrance requirements:* Minimum GPA of 2.75, teaching certificate. Application deadline: 4/1 (priority date; rolling processing). Application fee: $45. *Tuition:* $3628 per year full-time, $222 per credit hour part-time for state residents; $11,272 per year full-time, $647 per credit hour part-time for nonresidents. *Financial aid:* In 1997–98, 1 research assistantship (to a first-year student) averaging $850 per month and totaling $7,714 was awarded; partial tuition waivers, Federal Work-Study, and career-related internships or fieldwork also available. Aid available to part-time students. Financial aid application deadline: 5/1. • Coordinator, 715-394-8145.

University of Wisconsin–Whitewater, College of Education, Department of Curriculum and Instruction, Whitewater, WI 53190-1790. Offers programs in curriculum and instruction (MS), reading (MS Ed). Accredited by NCATE. Part-time and evening/weekend programs available. *Degree requirements:* Thesis or alternative required, foreign language not required. *Application deadline:* rolling. *Application fee:* $38.

Utah State University, College of Education, Doctoral Program in Education, Logan, UT 84322. Offerings include curriculum and instruction (Ed D, PhD). Accredited by NCATE. Program faculty: 65 full-time (17 women). *Degree requirements:* Dissertation required, foreign language not required. *Entrance requirements:* GRE General Test (score in 40th percentile or higher), TOEFL (minimum score 550), minimum GPA of 3.0. Application deadline: 6/15 (priority date; rolling processing; 10/15 for spring admission). Application fee: $40. *Expenses:* Tuition $1448 per year full-time, $624 per year part-time for state residents; $5082 per year full-time, $2192 per year part-time for nonresidents. Fees $421 per year full-time, $165 per year part-time. • Application contact: Louann Parkinson, Administrative Assistant, 435-797-1470. Fax: 435-797-3939. E-mail: luannp@coe.usu.edu.

Valdosta State University, College of Education, Department of Secondary Education, Valdosta, GA 31698. Offerings include curriculum and instruction (Ed D). Accredited by NCATE. Department faculty: 8 full-time (5 women). *Degree requirements:* Computer language, dissertation required, foreign language not required. *Entrance requirements:* GRE General Test (minimum combined score of 1000). Application deadline: 8/1 (rolling processing; 11/15 for spring admission). Application fee: $10. *Expenses:* Tuition $2472 per year full-time, $83 per semester hour part-time for state residents; $8472 per year full-time, $333 per semester hour part-time for nonresidents. Fees $236 per year full-time. • Dr. Catherine Price, Head, 912-333-5927. Fax: 912-333-7167. E-mail: cprice@grits.valdosta.peachnet.edu.

Valparaiso University, Department of Education, Program in Teaching and Learning, Valparaiso, IN 46383-6493. Awards M Ed. Accredited by NCATE. Faculty: 6 full-time (4 women). Students: 4 part-time (all women). Average age 34. In 1997, 3 degrees awarded. *Entrance requirements:* Minimum GPA of 3.0. Application deadline: 8/15 (rolling processing). Application fee: $30. *Tuition:* $3870 per year full-time, $215 per credit hour part-time. • Dr. Barbara Livdahl, Chair, Department of Education, 219-464-5078.

Vanderbilt University, Peabody College, Department of Teaching and Learning, Nashville, TN 37240-1001. Offerings include curriculum and instruction (M Ed). Accredited by NCATE. *Entrance requirements:* GRE General Test, MAT. Application deadline: 3/1 (priority date; rolling processing). Application fee: $35. • Carolyn Evertson, Chair, 615-322-8100.

Virginia Commonwealth University, School of Education, Program in Curriculum and Instruction, Richmond, VA 23284-9005. Awards M Ed. Accredited by NCATE. Part-time programs available. Faculty: 7 full-time. Students: 6 full-time (all women), 75 part-time (73 women); includes 7 minority (6 African Americans, 1 Asian American). Average age 36. 32 applicants, 91% accepted. In 1997, 18 degrees awarded. *Entrance requirements:* GRE General Test or MAT. Application deadline: 7/1 (rolling processing; 11/15 for spring admission). Application fee: $30 ($0 for international students). *Tuition:* $4960 per year full-time, $257 per credit part-time for state residents; $12,652 per year full-time, $684 per credit part-time for nonresidents. *Financial aid:* Partial tuition waivers available. Financial aid application deadline: 3/1. • Dr. Alan M. McLeod, Division Head, 804-828-1305. Application contact: Dr. Michael D. Davis, Interim Director, Graduate Studies, 804-828-6530. Fax: 804-828-1323. E-mail: mddavis@vcu.edu.

Virginia Polytechnic Institute and State University, College of Human Resources and Education, Department of Teaching and Learning, Blacksburg, VA 24061. Offerings include curriculum and instruction (MA Ed, Ed D, PhD, CAGS). Accredited by NCATE. *Degree requirements:* For doctorate, dissertation. *Entrance requirements:* For doctorate, GRE, TOEFL; for CAGS, TOEFL. Application deadline: 12/1 (priority date; rolling processing). Application fee: $25. *Tuition:* $4927 per year full-time, $792 per semester (minimum) part-time for state residents; $7537 per year full-time, $1227 per semester (minimum) part-time for nonresidents. • Dr. John Burton, Head, 540-231-5347. E-mail: teach@vt.edu.

Walla Walla College, Department of Education and Psychology, Specialization in Curriculum and Instruction, College Place, WA 99324-1198. Awards MA, M Ed. *Degree requirements:* Thesis (for some programs), 9 months of work experience in education required, foreign language not required. *Entrance requirements:* GRE General Test, minimum GPA of 2.75, 30 hours in professional education. Application deadline: 4/1 (priority date; rolling processing). Application fee: $40. *Tuition:* $346 per quarter hour. *Financial aid:* Application deadline 4/1; applicants required to submit FAFSA. *Faculty research:* Instructional psychology. • Application contact: Dr. Joe Galusha, Dean of Graduate Studies, 509-527-2421. Fax: 509-527-2253. E-mail: galujo@wwc.edu.

Washburn University of Topeka, College of Arts and Sciences, Department of Education, Program in Curriculum and Instruction, Topeka, KS 66621. Awards M Ed. Accredited by NCATE. Part-time programs available. Faculty: 2 full-time, 6 part-time. Students: 20 part-time (10 women). Average age 26. In 1997, 2 degrees awarded. *Degree requirements:* Thesis or alternative, comprehensive exam required, foreign language not required. *Entrance requirements:* GRE General Test, minimum GPA of 3.0 during previous 2 years. Application deadline: 5/1. Application fee: $0. *Financial aid:* Application deadline 3/15. • Dr. David Van Cleaf, Chairperson, Department of Education, 785-231-1010 Ext. 1430.

Washington State University, College of Education, Department of Teaching and Learning, Pullman, WA 99164-1610. Offerings include curriculum development (Ed D, PhD). Accredited by NCATE. Department faculty: 24 full-time (10 women). *Degree requirements:* Dissertation, oral exam required, foreign language not required. *Average time to degree:* master's–2 years full-time; doctorate–4 years full-time. *Entrance requirements:* GRE General Test, minimum GPA of 3.0. Application deadline: 3/1 (priority date; rolling processing). Application fee: $35. *Tuition:* $5334 per year full-time, $267 per credit hour part-time for state residents; $13,380 per year full-time, $677 per credit hour part-time for nonresidents. • Dr. Darcy Miller, Chair, 509-335-7296.

Wayne State College, Division of Education, Program in Curriculum and Instruction, Wayne, NE 68787. Offers art education (MSE), business education (MSE), communication arts education (MSE), curriculum and instruction (MSE), elementary education (MSE), English as a second language (MSE), health and physical education/health (MSE), health and physical education/pedagogy (MSE), industrial technology education (MSE), mathematics education (MSE), music education (MSE), science education (MSE). Accredited by NCATE. Students: 1 (woman) full-time, 53 part-time (40 women); includes 1 minority (Asian American). Average age 38. In 1997, 7 degrees awarded. *Degree requirements:* Comprehensive exam, research paper required, foreign language not required. *Entrance requirements:* GRE General Test. Application deadline: rolling. Application fee: $10. *Expenses:* Tuition $1788 per year full-time, $75 per credit hour part-time for state residents; $3576 per year full-time, $149 per credit hour part-time for nonresidents. Fees $360 per year full-time, $15 per credit hour part-time. *Financial aid:* Application deadline 5/1. • Dr. Diane Alexander, Head, Division of Education, 402-375-7389.

Wayne State University, College of Education, Division of Teacher Education, Detroit, MI 48202. Offerings include curriculum and instruction (Ed D, PhD, Ed S). Accredited by NCATE. Division faculty: 53. *Degree requirements:* For doctorate, dissertation required, foreign language not required. *Entrance requirements:* For doctorate, minimum GPA of 3.0 (undergraduate), 3.5 (graduate); interview. Application deadline: 7/1. Application fee: $20 ($30 for international students). *Expenses:* Tuition $163 per credit hour for state residents; $355 per credit hour for nonresidents. Fees $498 per year full-time, $114 per semester (minimum) part-time. • Dr. Sharon Elliott, Assistant Dean, 313-577-0902.

Weber State University, College of Education, Program in Curriculum and Instruction, Ogden, UT 84408-1001. Awards M Ed. Accredited by NCATE. Part-time and evening/weekend programs available. Faculty: 22 full-time (11 women), 6 part-time (2 women). Students: 4 full-time (all women), 84 part-time (55 women); includes 1 minority (Asian American), 2 international. Average age 38. 53 applicants, 96% accepted. In 1997, 36 degrees awarded. *Degree requirements:* Thesis or alternative, project presentation and exam. *Average time to degree:* master's–1 year full-time, 3 years part-time. *Entrance requirements:* GRE General Test (minimum score 480 on each section), MAT (minimum score 40), or minimum GPA of 3.25; minimum GPA of 3.0 in last 90 credits. Application deadline: 8/1 (rolling processing; 2/1 for spring admission). Application fee: $30 ($35 for international students). *Financial aid:* 24 students received aid; partial tuition waivers, institutionally sponsored loans available. Aid available to part-time students. Financial aid application deadline: 2/1. • Dr. Judith Mitchell, Director, 801-626-6278. Fax: 801-626-7427. E-mail: jmitchell@weber.edu.

Wesley College, Division of Education and Psychology, Dover, DE 19901. Offerings include curriculum and instruction (M Ed). Division faculty: 5 full-time (4 women), 1 part-time (0 women). *Degree requirements:* Thesis optional, foreign language not required. *Entrance requirements:* GRE. Application deadline: rolling. Application fee: $20. • Dr. B. Patricia Patterson, Chair, 302-736-2448. E-mail: patterpa@mail.wesley.edu. Application contact: Dr. J. Thomas Sturgis, Director of Graduate Studies, 302-736-2414. Fax: 302-736-2301. E-mail: sturgisto@mail.wesley.edu.

Westminster College, Programs in Education, Program in Supervision and Curriculum, South Market Street, New Wilmington, PA 16172-0001. Awards M Ed, Certificate. Part-time and evening/weekend programs available. Students: 0. *Entrance requirements:* For master's, minimum GPA of 2.75. Application deadline: 8/30 (priority date; rolling processing; 1/15 for spring admission). Application fee: $20. *Expenses:* Tuition $1104 per course. Fees $30 per course. *Financial aid:* Grants and career-related internships or fieldwork available. • Dr. Allen C. Johnston, Coordinator, 724-946-7188.

West Texas A&M University, College of Education and Social Sciences, Division of Education, Program in Curriculum and Instruction, Canyon, TX 79016-0001. Awards MA, M Ed. MA being phased out; applicants no longer accepted. Part-time and evening/weekend programs available. Postbaccalaureate distance learning degree programs offered. Students: 1 (woman) full-time, 6 part-time (all women). Average age 34. 4 applicants, 25% accepted. In 1997, 2 degrees awarded. *Degree requirements:* Comprehensive exam required, foreign language and thesis not required. *Average time to degree:* master's–3 years full-time, 6 years part-time. *Entrance requirements:* GRE General Test (combined average 964). Application deadline: rolling. Application fee: $0 ($50 for international students). Electronic applications accepted. *Expenses:* Tuition $46 per semester hour for state residents; $259 per semester hour for nonresidents. Fees $156 per semester (minimum). *Financial aid:* Partial tuition waivers, Federal Work-Study, institutionally sponsored loans available. Aid available to part-time students. Financial aid applicants required to submit FAFSA. • Dr. George Mann, Head, Division of Education, 806-651-2602. Fax: 806-651-2601. E-mail: george.mann@wtamu.edu.

West Virginia University, College of Human Resources and Education, Department of Educational Theory and Practice, Morgantown, WV 26506. Offers programs in curriculum and instruction (Ed D), including education; elementary education (MA); reading (MA), including reading; secondary education (MA); special education (MA, Ed D), including education (Ed D), special education (MA). Accredited by NCATE. Part-time and evening/weekend programs available. Students: 170 full-time (117 women), 554 part-time (482 women); includes 23 minority (14 African Americans, 5 Asian Americans, 2 Hispanics, 2 Native Americans), 5 international. Average age 34. 61 applicants, 100% accepted. In 1997, 251 master's, 27 doctorates awarded. *Degree requirements:* For doctorate, computer language, dissertation, comprehensive exam required, foreign language not required. *Entrance requirements:* For master's, TOEFL (minimum score 550); for doctorate, GRE General Test (minimum combined score of 1050), MAT (minimum score 50), TOEFL (minimum score 550). Application deadline: rolling. Application fee: $45. *Tuition:* $2820 per year full-time, $149 per credit hour part-time for state residents; $8104 per year full-time, $443 per credit hour part-time for nonresidents. *Financial aid:* In 1997–98, 1 fellowship (to a first-year student), 13 teaching assistantships (8 to first-year students), 3 graduate administrative assistantships were awarded; research assistantships, full and partial tuition waivers, Federal Work-Study, institutionally sponsored loans, and career-related internships or fieldwork also available. Financial aid application deadline: 2/1; applicants required to submit FAFSA. *Faculty research:* Teacher education, curriculum development, educational technology, curriculum assessment. • Dr. Jerrald Shive, Chair, 304-293-3441. Fax: 304-293-3802.

Wichita State University, College of Education, Department of Curriculum and Instruction, Program in Curriculum and Instruction, Wichita, KS 67260. Awards M Ed. Accredited by NCATE. *Degree requirements:* Comprehensive exam, portfolio required, thesis optional, foreign language not required. *Entrance requirements:* MAT, TOEFL (minimum score 550), minimum GPA of 2.75. Application deadline: 3/1 (priority date; rolling processing; 1/1 for spring admission). Application fee: $25 ($40 for international students). Electronic applications accepted. *Expenses:* Tuition $2303 per year full-time, $96 per credit hour part-time for state residents; $7691 per year full-time, $321 per credit hour part-time for nonresidents. Fees $490 per year full-time, $75 per semester (minimum) part-time. *Financial aid:* Application deadline 4/1. • Application contact: Dr. Bryant Fillion, Graduate Coordinator, 316-978-3322. Fax: 316-978-3302. E-mail: fillion@wsuhub.uc.twsu.edu.

William Woods University, College of Graduate and Adult Studies, Program in Education, Fulton, MO 65251-1098. Offerings include curriculum and instruction (M Ed). Program faculty: 7 full-time (5 women), 20 part-time (9 women). *Degree requirements:* Thesis or alternative required, foreign language not required. *Entrance requirements:* 2 years of teaching experience, minimum GPA of 2.5, teaching certificate. Application deadline: rolling. Application fee: $25. *Tuition:* $240 per credit. • Dr. Larry Ewing, Head, 573-592-4339. Application contact: Mary Henley, Director of Recruitment, 800-995-3199. Fax: 573-592-1164. E-mail: cgas@iris.wmwoods.edu.

Winthrop University, College of Education, Program in Curriculum and Instruction, Rock Hill, SC 29733. Offers curriculum development (Ed S), including elementary education, secondary education, special education. Accredited by NCATE. Part-time programs available. Students: 3 part-time (all women); includes 1 minority (African American). Average age 33. *Entrance requirements:* NTE, master's degree, 2 years of teaching experience, minimum GPA of 3.0. Application deadline: 7/15 (priority date; rolling processing; 12/1 for spring admission). Application fee: $35. *Tuition:* $3928 per year full-time, $164 per credit hour part-time for state residents; $7060 per year full-time, $294 per credit hour part-time for nonresidents. *Financial aid:* Graduate assistantships, graduate scholarships, Federal Work-Study available. Aid available to part-time students. Financial aid application deadline: 2/1; applicants required to submit FAFSA. • Dr. Richard Ingram, Chairman, 803-323-2151. Fax: 803-323-2585. E-mail: ingramr@winthrop.edu. Application contact: Sharon Johnson, Director of Graduate Studies, 803-323-2204. Fax: 803-323-2292. E-mail: johnsons@winthrop.edu.

Xavier University of Louisiana, Programs in Education, New Orleans, LA 70125-1098. Offerings include curriculum and instruction (MA). Accredited by NCATE. Faculty: 9 full-time (6 women), 12 part-time (5 women). *Average time to degree:* master's–3 years full-time, 7 years part-time. *Application deadline:* 7/1 (rolling processing; 12/1 for spring admission). *Application fee:* $30. *Tuition:* $200 per semester hour. • Dr. Rosalind Hale, Chair, Division of Education, 504-483-7536. Fax: 504-485-7909. Application contact: Marlene Robinson, Director of Graduate Admissions, 504-483-7487. Fax: 504-485-7921. E-mail: mrobinso@xula.edu.

Educational Administration

Abilene Christian University, College of Arts and Sciences, Department of Education, Programs in School Administration and Supervision, Abilene, TX 79699-9100. Offerings in school administration (M Ed), school supervision (M Ed). Part-time programs available. Faculty: 11 part-time (4 women). Students: 3 full-time (1 woman), 30 part-time (14 women); includes 8 minority (4 African Americans, 4 Hispanics), 1 international. 16 applicants, 100% accepted. In 1997, 10 degrees awarded. *Degree requirements:* Comprehensive exam required, foreign language and thesis not required. *Entrance requirements:* GRE General Test or MAT. Application deadline: 4/1 (priority date; rolling processing; 11/1 for spring admission). Application fee: $25 ($45 for international students). *Expenses:* Tuition $308 per credit hour. Fees $430 per year full-time, $85 per semester (minimum) part-time. *Financial aid:* Federal Work-Study and career-related internships or fieldwork available. Aid available to part-time students. Financial aid application deadline: 4/1. • Dr. Roger Gee, Graduate Adviser, 915-674-2122. Application contact: Dr. Carley Dodd, Graduate Dean, 915-674-2354. Fax: 915-674-6717. E-mail: gradinfo@nicanor.acu.edu.

Acadia University, Faculty of Professional Studies, School of Education, Program in Leadership and School Development, Wolfville, NS B0P 1X0, Canada. Awards M Ed. Program new for fall 1998. *Degree requirements:* Thesis required, foreign language not required. *Entrance requirements:* Minimum B average in undergraduate course work. Application deadline: 2/1. Application fee: $25. *Expenses:* Tuition $4095 per year for Canadian residents; $8190 per year for nonresidents. Fees $145 per year. *Financial aid:* Application deadline 2/1. • Dr. Bryant Griffith, Director, School of Education, 902-585-1229. E-mail: bryant.griffith@acadiau.ca. Application contact: Sheila Langille, Secretary, 902-585-1229. Fax: 902-585-1071.

Alabama Agricultural and Mechanical University, School of Education, Department of Curriculum and Instruction, Area in Secondary Education, PO Box 1357, Normal, AL 35762-1357. Offerings include higher administration (MS). Accredited by NCATE. Faculty: 7 full-time (2 women), 2 part-time (0 women). *Application deadline:* 5/1. *Application fee:* $15 ($20 for international students). *Expenses:* Tuition $2782 per year full-time, $565 per semester (minimum) part-time for state residents; $5164 per year full-time, $1015 per semester (minimum) part-time for nonresidents. Fees $560 per year full-time, $390 per year part-time. • Dr. Earnest Dees, Chair, Department of Curriculum and Instruction, 205-851-5520. Fax: 205-851-5526.

Alabama State University, School of Graduate Studies, College of Education, Department of Instructional Support, Program in Educational Administration, Montgomery, AL 36101-0271. Awards M Ed, Ed S. Students: 4 full-time (3 women), 61 part-time (38 women); includes 39 minority (38 African Americans, 1 Asian American). In 1997, 1 master's, 9 Ed Ss awarded. *Degree requirements:* For master's, comprehensive exam required, thesis optional; for Ed S, thesis. *Entrance requirements:* For master's, GRE General Test, MAT or NTE. Application deadline: 7/15 (rolling processing; 12/15 for spring admission). Application fee: $10. *Expenses:* Tuition $85 per credit hour for state residents; $170 per credit hour for nonresidents. Fees $486 per year. *Faculty research:* Nontraditional roles, computer applications for principals, women in educational administration. • Dr. Paul Goodwin, Associate Professor, 334-229-4881. Fax: 334-229-4904. Application contact: Dr. Fred Dauser, Dean of Graduate Studies, 334-229-4276. Fax: 334-229-4928.

Albany State University, School of Education, Program in Educational Administration and Supervision, Albany, GA 31705-2717. Awards M Ed, Certificate. Accredited by NCATE. Faculty: 2 full-time (1 woman), 1 part-time (0 women). Students: 5 full-time (3 women), 3 part-time (1 woman). In 1997, 3 master's, 3 Certificates awarded. *Degree requirements:* For master's, comprehensive exam. *Entrance requirements:* For master's, GRE General Test (minimum combined score of 800), MAT (minimum score 44) or NTE (minimum score 550 required, minimum GPA of 2.5. Application deadline: 9/1. Application fee: $10. *Financial aid:* Application deadline 4/1. • Dr. Claude Perkins, Dean, School of Education, 912-430-4715. Fax: 912-430-4993. E-mail: cperkins@fld94.alsnet.peachnet.edu.

Alcorn State University, School of Psychology and Education, Lorman, MS 39096-9402. Offerings include administration and supervision (MS Ed). Accredited by NCATE. *Degree requirements:* Thesis optional, foreign language not required. *Application deadline:* 7/1 (priority date; rolling processing; 12/1 for spring admission). *Application fee:* $10. *Tuition:* $2470 per year full-time, $378 per semester (minimum) part-time for state residents; $5331 per year full-time, $855 per semester (minimum) part-time for nonresidents.

American International College, School of Continuing Education and Graduate Studies, School of Psychology and Education, Department of Education, Springfield, MA 01109-3189. Offerings include administration (M Ed, CAGS). Department faculty: 5 full-time (3 women), 15 part-time (9 women). *Degree requirements:* For CAGS, practicum required, foreign language not required. *Application fee:* $15 ($25 for international students). *Expenses:* Tuition $363 per credit hour. Fees $25 per semester. • C. Gerald Weaver, Dean, School of Psychology and Education, 413-747-6338.

American University, College of Arts and Sciences, School of Education, Program in Educational Leadership, Washington, DC 20016-8001. Awards MA. Part-time and evening/weekend programs available. Faculty: 8 full-time (5 women), 10 part-time (8 women), 11.3 FTE. Students: 7 full-time (4 women), 7 part-time (5 women); includes 2 minority (both African Americans), 1 international. 19 applicants, 89% accepted. In 1997, 7 degrees awarded. *Degree requirements:* Thesis or alternative required, foreign language not required. *Entrance requirements:* GRE General Test or MAT, minimum GPA of 3.0. Application deadline: 2/1 (10/1 for spring admission). Application fee: $50. *Expenses:* Tuition $687 per credit hour. Fees $180 per year full-time, $110 per year part-time. *Financial aid:* Federal Work-Study, institutionally sponsored loans, and career-related internships or fieldwork available. Aid available to part-time students. Financial aid application deadline: 2/1; applicants required to submit FAFSA. • Dr. Frederic Jacobs, Director, 202-885-2124. Fax: 202-885-1187. E-mail: fredj@american.edu.

Andrews University, School of Graduate Studies, School of Education, Department of Teaching/Learning/Administration, Program in Educational Administration and Supervision, Berrien Springs, MI 49104. Awards MA, Ed D, PhD, Ed S. Faculty: 4 full-time (0 women). *Degree requirements:* For master's, thesis or alternative required, foreign language not required; for doctorate, dissertation. *Entrance requirements:* For master's and doctorate, GRE Subject Test. Application deadline: 8/15 (rolling processing). Application fee: $30. *Expenses:* Tuition $290 per quarter hour (minimum). Fees $75 per quarter. *Financial aid:* Research assistantships available. • Dr. William H. Green, Chair, Department of Teaching/Learning/Administration, 616-471-3465.

Andrews University, School of Graduate Studies, School of Education, Department of Teaching/Learning/Administration, Program in Leadership, Berrien Springs, MI 49104. Awards Ed D, PhD. *Degree requirements:* Dissertation. *Application deadline:* 8/15 (rolling processing). *Application fee:* $30. *Expenses:* Tuition $290 per quarter hour (minimum). Fees $75 per quarter. • Dr. William H. Green, Chair, Department of Teaching/Learning/Administration, 616-471-3465.

Angelo State University, College of Professional Studies, Department of Education, Program in School Administration, San Angelo, TX 76909. Awards M Ed. Part-time and evening/weekend programs available. Students: 10 full-time (9 women), 49 part-time (30 women); includes 3 minority (all Hispanics). Average age 39. 19 applicants, 84% accepted. In 1997, 23 degrees awarded. *Degree requirements:* Comprehensive exam required, thesis optional, foreign language not required. *Entrance requirements:* GRE General Test, minimum GPA of 2.5. Application deadline: 8/7 (priority date; rolling processing; 1/2 for spring admission). Application fee: $25 ($50 for international students). *Expenses:* Tuition $1022 per year full-time, $36 per semester hour part-time for state residents; $7382 per year full-time, $246 per semester hour part-time for nonresidents. Fees $1140 per year full-time, $165 per semester (minimum) part-time. *Financial aid:* In 1997–98, 12 fellowships were awarded; teaching assistantships, graduate assistantships, partial tuition waivers, Federal Work-Study, and career-related internships or fieldwork also available. Aid available to part-time students. Financial aid application deadline: 8/1. • Dr. James Hademenos, Head, Department of Education, 915-942-2052.

Angelo State University, College of Professional Studies, Department of Education, Program in Supervision, San Angelo, TX 76909. Awards M Ed. Part-time and evening/weekend programs available. Students: 3 part-time (all women); includes 1 minority (Hispanic). Average age 42. 0 applicants. *Degree requirements:* Comprehensive exam required, thesis optional, foreign language not required. *Entrance requirements:* GRE General Test, minimum GPA of 2.5. Application deadline: 8/7 (priority date; rolling processing; 1/2 for spring admission). Application fee: $25 ($50 for international students). *Expenses:* Tuition $1022 per year full-time, $36 per semester hour part-time for state residents; $7382 per year full-time, $246 per semester hour part-time for nonresidents. Fees $1140 per year full-time, $165 per semester (minimum) part-time. *Financial aid:* In 1997–98, 1 fellowship was awarded; teaching assistantships, graduate assistantships, partial tuition waivers, Federal Work-Study, and career-related internships or fieldwork also available. Aid available to part-time students. Financial aid application deadline: 8/1. • Dr. James Hademenos, Head, Department of Education, 915-942-2052.

Antioch New England Graduate School, Graduate School, Department of Organization and Management, Program in Educational Administration and Supervision, 40 Avon Street, Keene, NH 03431-3516. Awards M Ed. Faculty: 1 (woman) full-time, 18 part-time (9 women). Students: 14 full-time (11 women), 10 part-time (6 women); includes 2 minority (1 African American, 1 Native American). Average age 40. In 1997, 11 degrees awarded. *Degree requirements:* Practicum required, foreign language and thesis not required. *Entrance requirements:* Previous course work and work experience in organization and management. Application deadline: 8/1 (rolling processing; 12/1 for spring admission). Application fee: $40. *Expenses:* Tuition $12,700 per year full-time, $330 per credit part-time. Fees $165 per year. *Financial aid:* 14 students received aid; Federal Work-Study and career-related internships or fieldwork available. Financial aid applicants required to submit FAFSA. *Faculty research:* Collaborative research programs in Waldorf schools and communities, shared decision making in schools, rational to creative problem solving, competency to shift paradigms of thinking. • Application contact: Carolyn S. Bassett, Co-Director of Admissions, 603-357-6265 Ext. 287. Fax: 603-357-0718. E-mail: cbassett@antiochne.edu.

Appalachian State University, College of Education, Program in Educational Leadership, Boone, NC 28608. Awards Ed D. Accredited by NCATE. Students: 9 full-time (6 women), 4 part-time (2 women); includes 1 minority (African American). 9 applicants, 56% accepted. In 1997, 6 degrees awarded. *Degree requirements:* Dissertation, comprehensive exam. *Entrance requirements:* GRE General Test. Application fee: $35. *Tuition:* $1811 per year full-time, $354 per semester (minimum) part-time for state residents; $9081 per year full-time, $2171 per semester (minimum) part-time for nonresidents. *Financial aid:* In 1997–98, 9 research assistantships, 2 assistantships were awarded. • Duncan Waite, Director, 704-262-3168.

Directory: Educational Administration

Appalachian State University, College of Education, Department of Leadership and Educational Studies, Program in School Administration, Boone, NC 28608. Awards MSA. Accredited by NCATE. Faculty: 8. Students: 10 full-time (6 women), 16 part-time (7 women). In 1997, 7 degrees awarded. *Degree requirements:* Thesis or alternative, comprehensive exams required, foreign language not required. *Entrance requirements:* GRE General Test. Application deadline: 7/31 (priority date). Application fee: $35. *Tuition:* $1811 per year full-time, $354 per semester (minimum) part-time for state residents; $9081 per year full-time, $2171 per semester (minimum) part-time for nonresidents. • Dr. Kenneth Jenkins, Director, 704-262-6093.

Arizona State University, College of Education, Division of Educational Leadership and Policy Studies, Academic Program in Educational Leadership and Policy Studies, Tempe, AZ 85287. Awards PhD. *Degree requirements:* Dissertation. *Entrance requirements:* GRE General Test or MAT. Application fee: $45. *Expenses:* Tuition $2088 per year full-time, $110 per hour part-time for state residents; $9040 per year full-time, $377 per hour part-time for nonresidents. Fees $72 per year full-time, $18 per semester (minimum) part-time. *Faculty research:* Culture, language and the school, financing higher education, role of education leaders. • Dr. Mary Lee Smith, Coordinator, 602-965-6357. E-mail: delps@asu.edu.

Arizona State University, College of Education, Division of Educational Leadership and Policy Studies, Academic Program of Educational Administration and Supervision, Tempe, AZ 85287. Awards M Ed, Ed D. *Degree requirements:* For master's, thesis or alternative; for doctorate, dissertation. *Entrance requirements:* GRE General Test or MAT. Application fee: $45. *Expenses:* Tuition $2088 per year full-time, $110 per hour part-time for state residents; $9040 per year full-time, $377 per hour part-time for nonresidents. Fees $72 per year full-time, $18 per semester (minimum) part-time. *Faculty research:* Economics of education, competency performance, administrator preparation, roles of school administrators, educational demographics. • Dr. Thomas H. Metos, Program Coordinator, Division of Educational Leadership and Policy Studies, 602-965-6357. E-mail: delps@asu.edu. Application contact: Admissions Secretary, 602-965-6357.

Arizona State University West, College of Education, Phoenix, AZ 85069-7100. Offerings include educational administration and supervision (M Ed). College faculty: 19 full-time (13 women), 12 part-time (7 women), 24.23 FTE. *Degree requirements:* Comprehensive exams required, thesis not required. *Entrance requirements:* GRE or MAT, TOEFL. Application deadline: rolling. Application fee: $40. *Expenses:* Tuition $2088 per year full-time, $330 per course part-time for state residents; $9040 per year full-time, $1131 per course part-time for nonresidents. Fees $10 per year (minimum). • Dr. William S. Svoboda, Dean, 602-543-6300. Application contact: Ray Buss, Assistant Dean, 602-543-6300. Fax: 602-543-6350.

Arkansas State University, College of Education, Department of Educational Administration and Secondary Education, State University, AR 72467. Offers programs in curriculum and instruction (MSE, Ed S), educational administration (MSE, Ed S), educational leadership (Ed D), secondary education teaching (MSE). Accredited by NCATE. Part-time programs available. Faculty: 12 full-time (3 women), 2 part-time (both women). Students: 16 full-time (9 women), 140 part-time (76 women); includes 21 minority (all African Americans). Average age 39. In 1997, 32 master's, 5 doctorates, 3 Ed Ss awarded. *Degree requirements:* For master's, thesis or alternative, comprehensive exam; for doctorate, dissertation, comprehensive exam; for Ed S, 2 years of professional experience, oral and written comprehensive exams required, thesis not required. *Entrance requirements:* For master's, GRE General Test or MAT, appropriate bachelor's degree; for doctorate and Ed S, GRE General Test or MAT, master's degree. Application deadline: 7/1 (priority date; rolling processing; 11/15 for spring admission). Application fee: $15 ($25 for international students). *Expenses:* Tuition $2760 per year full-time, $115 per credit hour part-time for state residents; $6936 per year full-time, $289 per credit hour part-time for nonresidents. Fees $506 per year full-time, $44 per semester (minimum) part-time. *Financial aid:* Teaching assistantships and career-related internships or fieldwork available. Aid available to part-time students. Financial aid application deadline: 7/1; applicants required to submit FAFSA. • Dr. David Cox, Chair, 870-972-3062. Fax: 870-972-3945. E-mail: dwcox@pawnee.astate.edu.

Arkansas Tech University, School of Education, Department of Curriculum and Instruction, Russellville, AR 72801-2222. Offerings include educational leadership (M Ed). Accredited by NCATE. *Application deadline:* 3/1 (priority date; rolling processing; 10/1 for spring admission). *Application fee:* $0 ($30 for international students). *Expenses:* Tuition $98 per credit hour for state residents; $196 per credit hour for nonresidents. Fees $30 per semester. • Head, 501-968-0290. Fax: 501-964-0811.

Ashland University, College of Education, Graduate Studies in Teacher Education, Program in Administration, Ashland, OH 44805-3702. Awards M Ed. Accredited by NCATE. Part-time and evening/weekend programs available. Faculty: 3 full-time (0 women), 9 part-time (0 women). In 1997, 90 degrees awarded (100% found work related to degree). *Degree requirements:* Practicum. *Entrance requirements:* GRE General Test or MAT, teaching certificate. Application deadline: rolling. Application fee: $15. *Tuition:* $275 per credit hour. *Financial aid:* In 1997–98, 1 teaching assistantship (to a first-year student) was awarded. • Bill Hughes, Program Team Leader, 419-289-5387. E-mail: bhughes@ashland.edu. Application contact: Dr. Joe Bailey, Director, 419-289-5377. Fax: 419-289-5097. E-mail: jbailey@ashland.edu.

Ashland University, College of Education, Graduate Studies in Teacher Education, Program in School Treasurer or Business Manager, Ashland, OH 44805-3702. Offers business manager (M Ed), school treasurer (M Ed). Accredited by NCATE. Part-time and evening/weekend programs available. Faculty: 1 (woman) full-time, 2 part-time (0 women). In 1997, 3 degrees awarded. *Degree requirements:* Practicum. *Entrance requirements:* GRE General Test or MAT, teaching certificate. Application deadline: rolling. Application fee: $15. *Tuition:* $275 per credit hour. • Marjorie Fenton, Coordinator, 419-289-5192. Application contact: Dr. Joe Bailey, Director, 419-289-5377. Fax: 419-289-5097. E-mail: jbailey@ashland.edu.

Ashland University, College of Education, Graduate Studies in Teacher Education, Programs in Supervision, Ashland, OH 44805-3702. Awards M Ed. Accredited by NCATE. Part-time and evening/weekend programs available. Faculty: 2 full-time (0 women), 3 part-time (1 woman). In 1997, 32 degrees awarded. *Degree requirements:* Practicum. *Entrance requirements:* GRE General Test or MAT, teaching certificate. Application deadline: rolling. Application fee: $15. *Tuition:* $275 per credit hour. • Bill Hughes, Program Team Leader, 419-289-5387. E-mail: bhughes@ashland.edu. Application contact: Dr. Joe Bailey, Director, 419-289-5377. Fax: 419-289-5097. E-mail: jbailey@ashland.edu.

Auburn University, College of Education, Department of Educational Foundations, Leadership, and Technology, Auburn University, AL 36849-0001. Offers programs in curriculum and instruction (M Ed, MS, Ed D, Ed S), curriculum supervision (M Ed, MS, Ed D, Ed S), educational psychology (PhD), higher education administration (M Ed, MS, Ed D, Ed S), media instructional design (MS), media specialist (M Ed), school administration (M Ed, MS, Ed D, Ed S). Accredited by NCATE. Part-time programs available. Faculty: 18 full-time (9 women). Students: 37 full-time (16 women), 102 part-time (65 women); includes 27 minority (25 African Americans, 2 Asian Americans), 3 international. 36 applicants, 64% accepted. In 1997, 12 master's, 7 doctorates awarded. *Degree requirements:* For master's, thesis (MS) required, foreign language not required; for doctorate, dissertation required, foreign language not required; for Ed S, field project required, foreign language and thesis not required. *Entrance requirements:* For master's and Ed S, GRE General Test; for doctorate, GRE General Test (minimum score 400 on each section). Application deadline: 9/1 (rolling processing; 3/1 for spring admission). Application fee: $25 ($50 for international students). *Expenses:* Tuition $2760 per year full-time, $76 per credit hour part-time for state residents; $8280 per year full-time, $228 per credit hour part-time for nonresidents. Fees $30 per year full-time, $160 per quarter part-time for state residents; $30 per year full-time, $480 per quarter part-time for nonresidents. *Financial aid:* Teaching assistantships, Federal Work-Study available. Aid available to part-time students. Financial aid application deadline: 3/15. • Dr. James S. Kaminsky, Head, 334-844-4460. Application contact: Dr. John F. Pritchett, Dean of the Graduate School, 334-844-4700.

Auburn University Montgomery, School of Education, Department of Counselor Leadership and Special Education, Montgomery, AL 36124-4023. Offerings include education administration (M Ed, Ed S). Accredited by NCATE. *Degree requirements:* For master's, comprehensive exam required, foreign language and thesis not required; for Ed S, comprehensive exam required, foreign language not required. *Entrance requirements:* For master's, GRE General Test or MAT, certification, BS in teaching; for Ed S, GRE General Test or MAT, certification. Application deadline: 9/1 (priority date; rolling processing; 3/28 for spring admission). Application fee: $25. Electronic applications accepted. *Tuition:* $2664 per year full-time, $85 per quarter hour part-time for state residents; $7080 per year full-time, $255 per quarter hour part-time for nonresidents. • Dr. James Wright, Head, 334-244-3457.

Augusta State University, College of Education, Program in Educational Administration, Augusta, GA 30904-2200. Awards M Ed, Ed S. Accredited by NCATE. Part-time and evening/weekend programs available. Faculty: 3 full-time (2 women). Students: 31 full-time (19 women), 38 part-time (26 women). Average age 35. 21 applicants, 100% accepted. In 1997, 20 master's, 11 Ed Ss awarded. *Degree requirements:* Thesis, comprehensive exam. *Entrance requirements:* GRE, MAT. Application deadline: 7/26 (priority date; rolling processing). Application fee: $10. *Tuition:* $2260 per year full-time, $83 per credit hour part-time for state residents; $8260 per year full-time, $333 per credit hour part-time for nonresidents. *Financial aid:* In 1997–98, 2 students received aid, including 2 graduate assistantships (both to first-year students); Federal Work-Study, institutionally sponsored loans, and career-related internships or fieldwork also available. Aid available to part-time students. Financial aid application deadline: 4/15; applicants required to submit FAFSA. *Faculty research:* Restructuring schools, financing education, student transition. • Dr. C. Jay Hertzog, Chair, 706-737-1497. E-mail: jhertzog@aug.edu. Application contact: Heather Eakin, Secretary to the Dean, 706-737-1499. Fax: 706-667-4706. E-mail: heakin@aug.edu.

Aurora University, George Williams College, School of Education, Aurora, IL 60506-4892. Offerings include educational leadership (MEL). School faculty: 7 full-time (4 women), 22 part-time (12 women). *Application deadline:* rolling. *Application fee:* $25. *Tuition:* $408 per semester hour. • Dr. Gary Jewel, Dean, 630-844-5498. Application contact: Office of Admissions, 630-844-5533. Fax: 630-844-5463.

Austin Peay State University, College of Education, Department of Education, Clarksville, TN 37044-0001. Offerings include administration and supervision (MA Ed, Ed S). Accredited by NCATE. Ed S offered jointly with Tennessee State University. *Entrance requirements:* For Ed S, GRE General Test (minimum score 350 on verbal and quantitative sections), master's degree, minimum graduate GPA of 3.0. Application deadline: 7/31 (priority date; rolling processing; 12/4 for spring admission). Application fee: $15. *Expenses:* Tuition $2438 per year full-time, $123 per semester hour part-time for state residents; $7034 per year full-time, $324 per semester hour part-time for nonresidents. Fees $484 per year (minimum) full-time, $154 per semester (minimum) part-time. • J. Ronald Groseclose, Interim Chair, 931-648-7585. Fax: 931-648-5991. E-mail: groseclosег@apsu.edu.

Azusa Pacific University, School of Education and Behavioral Studies, Department of College Student Affairs and Leadership Studies, Program in College Student Affairs and Leadership Studies, Azusa, CA 91702-7000. Offerings include social science leadership studies (MA). Program faculty: 3 full-time (1 woman), 5 part-time (1 woman). *Application fee:* $45 ($65 for international students). *Expenses:* Tuition $350 per unit. Fees $57 per year. • Application contact: Grace Barnes, Coordinator, 626-815-3848. Fax: 626-815-3868.

Azusa Pacific University, School of Education and Behavioral Studies, Department of Education, Program in Educational Leadership and Administration, Azusa, CA 91702-7000. Awards Ed D. Part-time and evening/weekend programs available. Students: 61 part-time. *Degree requirements:* Oral defense of dissertation, qualifying exam. *Entrance requirements:* GRE General Test (minimum combined score of 1000 or 1500 on three sections) or MAT (minimum score 48), TOEFL (minimum score 600), 5 years of experience, writing sample. Application deadline: 6/16 (priority date; rolling processing; 11/18 for spring admission). Application fee: $45 ($65 for international students). *Expenses:* Tuition $500 per unit. Fees $57 per year. *Financial aid:* Career-related internships or fieldwork available. Aid available to part-time students. Financial aid applicants required to submit FAFSA. *Faculty research:* Ethics in educational administration. Total annual research expenditures: $2750. • Dr. Lillian Wehmeyer, Director, 626-815-5364. Fax: 626-815-5416. E-mail: lwehmeyer@apu.edu.

Azusa Pacific University, School of Education and Behavioral Studies, Department of Education, Program in School Administration, Azusa, CA 91702-7000. Awards MA. Part-time and evening/weekend programs available. Faculty: 6 full-time (1 woman), 28 part-time (3 women), 15 FTE. Students: 234. In 1997, 100 degrees awarded. *Degree requirements:* Comprehensive exam or thesis, core exams, oral presentation required, foreign language not required. *Entrance requirements:* 12 units of previous course work in education, minimum GPA of 3.0. Application deadline: 9/15 (priority date; rolling processing; 2/5 for spring admission). Application fee: $45 ($65 for international students). *Expenses:* Tuition $350 per unit. Fees $57 per year. *Faculty research:* Instructional supervision, outcome-based education, technology and on-line searching, teacher preparation. • Dr. Daniel C. Elliott, Director, 626-815-5352. Fax: 626-815-5416. E-mail: drdelliott@aol.com.

Baldwin-Wallace College, Division of Education, Specialization in Supervision or Administration, Berea, OH 44017-2088. Awards MA Ed. Accredited by NCATE. Part-time and evening/weekend programs available. *Entrance requirements:* Bachelor's degree in field, MAT or minimum GPA of 2.75. Application fee: $15. *Financial aid:* Career-related internships or fieldwork available. • Dr. Patrick F. Cosiano, Chairman, Division of Education, 440-826-2168. Fax: 440-826-3779. E-mail: pcosiano@bw.edu. Application contact: Dr. Jane F. Cavanaugh, Director of Continuing Education, 440-826-2222. Fax: 440-826-3640. E-mail: admission@bw.edu.

Ball State University, Teachers College, Department of Educational Leadership, Program in Educational Administration, 2000 University Avenue, Muncie, IN 47306-1099. Awards MAE, Ed D. Accredited by NCATE. In 1997, 3 doctorates awarded. *Degree requirements:* For doctorate, dissertation required, foreign language not required. *Entrance requirements:* For doctorate, GRE General Test (minimum combined score of 1000), minimum graduate GPA of 3.2. Application fee: $15 ($25 for international students). *Expenses:* Tuition $3454 per year full-time, $518 per semester (minimum) part-time for state residents; $9316 per year full-time, $1221 per semester (minimum) part-time for nonresidents. Fees $242 per year full-time, $18 per semester (minimum) part-time. • Bobby G. Malone, Chairman, Department of Educational Leadership, 765-285-8488.

Ball State University, Teachers College, Department of Educational Leadership, Program in Executive Development, 2000 University Avenue, Muncie, IN 47306-1099. Awards MA. Accredited by NCATE. *Application fee:* $15 ($25 for international students). *Expenses:* Tuition $3454 per year full-time, $518 per semester (minimum) part-time for state residents; $9316 per year full-time, $1221 per semester (minimum) part-time for nonresidents. Fees $242 per year full-time, $18 per semester (minimum) part-time. • Bobby G. Malone, Chairman, Department of Educational Leadership, 765-285-8488.

Ball State University, Teachers College, Department of Educational Leadership, Program in School Superintendency, 2000 University Avenue, Muncie, IN 47306-1099. Awards Ed S. Accredited by NCATE. In 1997, 11 degrees awarded. *Degree requirements:* Thesis required, foreign language not required. *Entrance requirements:* GRE General Test. Application fee: $15 ($25 for international students). *Expenses:* Tuition $3454 per year full-time, $518 per semester (minimum) part-time for state residents; $9316 per year full-time, $1221 per semester (minimum) part-time for nonresidents. Fees $242 per year full-time, $18 per semester (minimum) part-time. • Bobby G. Malone, Chairman, Department of Educational Leadership, 765-285-8488.

Ball State University, Teachers College, Department of Secondary, Higher, and Foundations of Education, Program in Student Personnel Administration in Higher Education, 2000 University

Avenue, Muncie, IN 47306-1099. Awards MA. Accredited by NCATE. Students: 21 full-time (13 women), 19 part-time (11 women); includes 9 minority (6 African Americans, 1 Asian American, 2 Hispanics). Average age 27. 36 applicants, 53% accepted. In 1997, 17 degrees awarded. *Application fee:* $15 ($25 for international students). *Expenses:* Tuition $3454 per year full-time, $518 per semester (minimum) part-time for state residents; $9316 per year full-time, $1221 per semester (minimum) part-time for nonresidents. Fees $242 per year full-time, $18 per semester (minimum) part-time. *Financial aid:* Research assistantships available. • Dr. Donald Mikesell, Head, 765-285-5343.

Bank Street College of Education, Program in Educational Leadership, 610 West 112th Street, New York, NY 10025-1120. Offers early child leadership (MS Ed), educational leadership (Ed M, MS Ed), leadership in mathematics education (MS Ed), leadership in museum education (MS Ed), supervision and administration in the visual arts (MS Ed). MS Ed (supervision and administration in the visual arts) offered jointly with Parsons School of Design, New School of Social Research. *Degree requirements:* Thesis required, foreign language not required. *Entrance requirements:* TOEFL (minimum score 550). Application deadline: 3/1 (priority date; rolling processing; 11/1 for spring admission). Application fee: $50. *Tuition:* $560 per credit. *Financial aid:* Career-related internships or fieldwork available. Financial aid application deadline: 3/1. • Dr. Frank Pignatelli, Chairperson, 212-875-4710. Application contact: Ann Morgan, Director of Admissions, 212-875-4404. Fax: 212-875-4678. E-mail: amorgan@bnkst.edu.

Barry University, School of Education, Program in Educational Leadership, Miami Shores, FL 33161-6695. Awards MS, Ed S. Part-time and evening/weekend programs available. Faculty: 1 (woman) full-time, 1 part-time (0 women). Students: 11 full-time (6 women), 38 part-time (26 women); includes 25 minority (9 African Americans, 16 Hispanics), 2 international. Average age 38. In 1997, 33 master's, 9 Ed Ss awarded. *Degree requirements:* Written comprehensive exam required, foreign language and thesis not required. *Entrance requirements:* For master's, GRE General Test or MAT, minimum GPA of 3.0; for Ed S, GRE General Test, minimum GPA of 3.0. Application deadline: 5/1 (priority date; rolling processing). Application fee: $30. Electronic applications accepted. *Tuition:* $450 per credit (minimum). *Financial aid:* Partial tuition waivers available. Aid available to part-time students. Financial aid application deadline: 5/1; applicants required to submit FAFSA. • Dr. Patrick Gray, Director, 305-899-3701. Fax: 305-899-3630. E-mail: pgray@aquinas.barry.edu. Application contact: Angela Scott, Enrollment Services, Assistant Dean, 305-899-3112. Fax: 305-899-3149. E-mail: ascott@jeanne.barry.edu.

Barry University, School of Education, Program in Higher Education Administration, Miami Shores, FL 33161-6695. Awards MS. Part-time and evening/weekend programs available. Students: 6 full-time (5 women), 16 part-time (12 women); includes 8 minority (3 African Americans, 5 Hispanics), 1 international. Average age 39. In 1997, 8 degrees awarded. *Degree requirements:* Written comprehensive exam required, foreign language and thesis not required. *Entrance requirements:* GRE General Test or MAT, minimum GPA of 3.0. Application deadline: 5/1 (priority date; rolling processing). Application fee: $30. Electronic applications accepted. *Tuition:* $450 per credit (minimum). *Financial aid:* Partial tuition waivers and career-related internships or fieldwork available. Aid available to part-time students. Financial aid application deadline: 5/1; applicants required to submit FAFSA. • Dr. George Wanko, Director, 305-899-3085. Fax: 305-899-3959. E-mail: wanko@jeanne.barry.edu. Application contact: Angela Scott, Enrollment Services, Assistant Dean, 305-899-3112. Fax: 305-899-3149. E-mail: ascott@jeanne.barry.edu.

Barry University, School of Education, Program in Leadership and Education, Miami Shores, FL 33161-6695. Offers counseling (PhD), educational computing and technology (PhD), exceptional student education (PhD), higher education administration (PhD), human resource development (PhD), leadership (PhD). Part-time and evening/weekend programs available. Faculty: 1 full-time (0 women), 2 part-time (1 woman), 2 FTE. Students: 9 full-time (6 women), 76 part-time (52 women); includes 26 minority (8 African Americans, 2 Asian Americans, 16 Hispanics), 6 international. Average age 40. In 1997, 6 degrees awarded. *Degree requirements:* Dissertation. *Entrance requirements:* GRE General Test, minimum GPA of 3.25. Application deadline: 5/1 (priority date; rolling processing). Application fee: $30. Electronic applications accepted. *Tuition:* $450 per credit (minimum). *Financial aid:* Partial tuition waivers available. Aid available to part-time students. Financial aid application deadline: 5/1; applicants required to submit FAFSA. • Dr. Jack Dezek, Chair, 305-899-3700. Fax: 305-899-3630. E-mail: dezek@aquinas.barry.edu. Application contact: Angela Scott, Enrollment Services, Assistant Dean, 305-899-3112. Fax: 305-899-3149. E-mail: ascott@jeanne.barry.edu.

Baruch College of the City University of New York, School of Public Affairs, Program in Educational Administration and Supervision, 17 Lexington Avenue, New York, NY 10010-5585. Awards MS Ed. Part-time programs available. Faculty: 3 full-time (all women), 5 part-time (2 women). Students: 2 full-time (1 woman), 74 part-time (46 women); includes 2 international. Average age 35. 70 applicants, 67% accepted. In 1997, 5 degrees awarded (100% found work related to degree). *Degree requirements:* Internship required, foreign language and thesis not required. *Average time to degree:* master's–3 years part-time. *Entrance requirements:* Relevant work experience, minimum GPA of 3.0, teaching certificate. Application deadline: 7/15 (priority date; rolling processing; 12/15 for spring admission). Application fee: $40. *Expenses:* Tuition $4350 per year full-time, $185 per credit part-time for state residents; $7600 per year full-time, $320 per credit part-time for nonresidents. Fees $53 per year. *Financial aid:* Fellowships, research assistantships, Federal Work-Study, and career-related internships or fieldwork available. Aid available to part-time students. Financial aid application deadline: 5/3; applicants required to submit FAFSA. *Faculty research:* School administration, governmental relations, program development, college administration. • Application contact: Pamela S. Ferner, Director of Admissions, 212-802-5912. Fax: 212-802-5928. E-mail: spa_admissions@baruch.cuny.edu.

Baruch College of the City University of New York, School of Public Affairs, Program in Higher Education Administration, 17 Lexington Avenue, New York, NY 10010-5585. Awards MS Ed. Part-time programs available. Faculty: 1 full-time, 2 part-time. Students: 1 (woman) full-time, 47 part-time (30 women); includes 1 international. Average age 35. 26 applicants, 85% accepted. In 1997, 12 degrees awarded. *Degree requirements:* Internship required, foreign language and thesis not required. *Entrance requirements:* GRE General Test, minimum GPA of 3.0. Application deadline: 7/15 (priority date; rolling processing; 12/15 for spring admission). Application fee: $40. *Expenses:* Tuition $4350 per year full-time, $185 per credit part-time for state residents; $7600 per year full-time, $320 per credit part-time for nonresidents. Fees $53 per year. *Financial aid:* Research assistantships, full tuition waivers, and career-related internships or fieldwork available. Financial aid application deadline: 5/3. • Application contact: Pamela S. Ferner, Director of Admissions, 212-802-5912. Fax: 212-802-5928. E-mail: spa_admissions@baruch.cuny.edu.

Baylor University, School of Education, Department of Educational Administration, Waco, TX 76798. Awards MA, MS Ed, Ed D, Ed S. Accredited by NCATE. Students: 45 full-time (25 women), 74 part-time (35 women); includes 29 minority (13 African Americans, 2 Asian Americans, 14 Hispanics), 3 international. 90 applicants, 44% accepted. In 1997, 11 master's, 9 doctorates awarded. *Degree requirements:* For doctorate, dissertation required, foreign language not required. *Entrance requirements:* For master's and doctorate, GRE General Test. Application deadline: rolling. Application fee: $25. *Expenses:* Tuition $7392 per year full-time, $308 per semester hour part-time. Fees $1024 per year. *Financial aid:* In 1997–98, 20 students received aid, including 2 research assistantships totaling $2, teaching assistantships averaging $500 per month and totaling $3, 18 scholarships totaling $18; Federal Work-Study, institutionally sponsored loans also available. • Dr. James Williamson, Chairman, 254-710-3111.

Beaver College, Department of Education, Glenside, PA 19038-3295. Offerings include educational leadership (M Ed, CAS). *Application fee:* $35. *Expenses:* Tuition $6570 per year full-time, $365 per credit part-time. Fees $35 per year.

Belmont University, Graduate Studies in Education, Nashville, TN 37212-3757. Offerings include childcare administration (M Ed). Accredited by NCATE. Faculty: 31 full-time (16 women), 1 (woman) part-time. *Average time to degree:* master's–2 years full-time, 5 years part-time. *Application deadline:* 7/15 (priority date; rolling processing; 11/15 for spring admission). *Application fee:* $50. • Dr. Norma Stevens, Associate Dean, 615-460-6233. E-mail: stevensn@belmont.edu. Application contact: Lois Smith, Admissions Counselor, 615-460-5483. Fax: 615-385-5084. E-mail: smithl@belmont.edu.

Bemidji State University, Division of Professional Studies, Program in School Administration, Bemidji, MN 56601-2699. Awards MS Ed. Accredited by NCATE. Part-time programs available. Students: 1 full-time (0 women), 8 part-time (3 women). Average age 37. In 1997, 3 degrees awarded. *Degree requirements:* Thesis required, foreign language not required. *Application deadline:* 5/1. *Application fee:* $20. *Expenses:* Tuition $128 per credit for state residents; $134 per credit (minimum) for nonresidents. Fees $517 per year full-time, $35 per credit (minimum) part-time. *Financial aid:* Federal Work-Study and career-related internships or fieldwork available. Aid available to part-time students. Financial aid application deadline: 5/1. • Dr. Jack Reynolds, Chair, 218-755-2931. Fax: 218-755-3788. E-mail: caravan@vax1.bemidji.msus.edu.

Benedictine College, Program in Educational Administration, 1020 North 2nd Street, Atchison, KS 66002-1499. Awards MA. Part-time and evening/weekend programs available. Faculty: 2 part-time (0 women), 1 FTE. Students: 14 part-time (5 women). Average age 39. *Degree requirements:* Thesis or alternative, practicum required, foreign language not required. *Average time to degree:* master's–2 years part-time. *Entrance requirements:* GRE or MAT (minimum score 42), minimum GPA of 3.0. Application deadline: rolling. Application fee: $25. *Tuition:* $160 per credit hour. *Financial aid:* Federal Work-Study and career-related internships or fieldwork available. Aid available to part-time students. Financial aid application deadline: 3/1; applicants required to submit FAFSA. *Faculty research:* Collaborative learning, career mobility, multicultural education. • Dr. Charles Osborn, Director, 913-367-5340 Ext. 2601. E-mail: chucko@raven.benedictine.edu.

Boston College, Graduate School of Education, Department of Educational Administration and Higher Education Administration, Catholic School Leadership Program, Chestnut Hill, MA 02167-9991. Awards M Ed, CAES. Accredited by NCATE. Students: 10 full-time (4 women), 12 part-time (5 women); includes 1 minority (African American), 1 international. 10 applicants, 80% accepted. In 1997, 14 master's awarded. *Degree requirements:* Comprehensive exam required, thesis not required. *Entrance requirements:* For master's, GRE General Test; for CAES, GRE General Test or MAT. Application deadline: 3/15 (11/15 for spring admission). Application fee: $40. *Expenses:* Tuition $626 per semester hour. Fees $80 per year (minimum) full-time, $30 per semester part-time. *Financial aid:* Fellowships, research assistantships, teaching assistantships, administrative assistantships, merit scholarships, Federal Work-Study, and career-related internships or fieldwork available. *Faculty research:* Administration and leadership in Catholic schools, global education, American studies, interdisciplinary education. • Rev. Joseph O'Keefe, SJ, Coordinator, 617-552-8426. E-mail: okeefejo@bc.edu. Application contact: Arline Riordan, Graduate Admissions Director, 617-552-4214. Fax: 617-552-0812. E-mail: riordana@bc.edu.

Boston College, Graduate School of Education, Department of Educational Administration and Higher Education Administration, Educational Administration Specialization, Chestnut Hill, MA 02167-9991. Awards M Ed, PhD, CAES. Students: 20 full-time (12 women), 29 part-time (18 women); includes 13 minority (9 African Americans, 2 Asian Americans, 1 Hispanic, 1 Native American), 1 international. 40 applicants, 70% accepted. In 1997, 5 master's, 4 doctorates, 4 CAESs awarded. *Degree requirements:* For master's and CAES, comprehensive exam required, thesis not required; for doctorate, computer language, dissertation, comprehensive exam. *Entrance requirements:* For master's and doctorate, GRE General Test; for CAES, GRE General Test or MAT. Application deadline: 3/15 (11/15 for spring admission). Application fee: $40. *Expenses:* Tuition $626 per semester hour. Fees $80 per year (minimum) full-time, $30 per semester part-time. *Financial aid:* Fellowships, research assistantships, teaching assistantships, administrative assistantships, merit scholarships, Federal Work-Study, and career-related internships or fieldwork available. *Faculty research:* Politics of urban education, principalship, cultural aspects of teaching, urban school leadership, experience of low-income minority students in private schools. • Application contact: Arline Riordan, Graduate Admissions Director, 617-552-4214. Fax: 617-552-0812. E-mail: riordana@bc.edu.

Boston College, Graduate School of Education, Department of Educational Administration and Higher Education Administration, Higher Education Administration Specialization, Chestnut Hill, MA 02167-9991. Awards MA, PhD, JD/MA. Accredited by NCATE. Students: 40 full-time (24 women), 58 part-time (36 women); includes 11 minority (7 African Americans, 2 Asian Americans, 2 Hispanics), 6 international. 128 applicants, 57% accepted. In 1997, 38 master's, 6 doctorates awarded. *Degree requirements:* For master's, comprehensive exam required, thesis not required; for doctorate, computer language, dissertation, comprehensive exam. *Entrance requirements:* GRE General Test. Application deadline: 3/15 (11/15 for spring admission). Application fee: $40. *Expenses:* Tuition $626 per semester hour. Fees $80 per year (minimum) full-time, $30 per semester part-time. *Financial aid:* Fellowships, research assistantships, teaching assistantships, administrative assistantships, merit scholarships, partial tuition waivers, Federal Work-Study, and career-related internships or fieldwork available. *Faculty research:* Administration and leadership theory, change process in policy making, organizational analysis, comparative education, higher education in developing countries. • Application contact: Arline Riordan, Graduate Admissions Director, 617-552-4214. Fax: 617-552-0812. E-mail: riordana@bc.edu.

Boston College, Graduate School of Education, Department of Educational Administration and Higher Education Administration, Professional School Administrator Program, Chestnut Hill, MA 02167-9991. Awards PhD. Accredited by NCATE. Offered every three years; next class entering fall 2000. Part-time programs available. Students: 18 full-time (8 women), 26 part-time (12 women); includes 5 minority (4 African Americans, 1 Native American). 31 applicants, 48% accepted. In 1997, 8 degrees awarded. *Degree requirements:* Computer language, dissertation, comprehensive exam. *Entrance requirements:* GRE General Test. Application deadline: 3/15. Application fee: $40. *Expenses:* Tuition $626 per semester hour. Fees $80 per year (minimum) full-time, $30 per semester part-time. *Financial aid:* Administrative assistantships, merit scholarships, Federal Work-Study, and career-related internships or fieldwork available. *Faculty research:* Administrator performance and expectation, school finance, administrative organizational problems. • Application contact: Arline Riordan, Graduate Admissions Director, 617-552-4214. Fax: 617-552-0812. E-mail: riordana@bc.edu.

Boston University, School of Education, Dual Degree Program in Administration, Training, and Policy Studies and Social Work, Boston, MA 02215. Awards MSW/Ed M. Students: 0. Average age 37. *Expenses:* Tuition $22,830 per year full-time, $713 per credit part-time. Fees $218 per year full-time, $40 per semester part-time. • Dr. Vivian Johnson, Coordinator, 617-353-3832. E-mail: vjohnson@bu.edu. Application contact: Office of Graduate Admissions, 617-353-4237. E-mail: sedgrad@bu.edu.

Boston University, School of Education, Department of Administration, Training, and Policy Studies, Program in Human Resource Education, Boston, MA 02215. Awards Ed M, Ed D, CAGS. Students: 8 full-time (5 women), 22 part-time (15 women); includes 4 minority (1 African American, 2 Asian Americans, 1 Native American). Average age 40. In 1997, 15 master's, 2 doctorates awarded. *Degree requirements:* For doctorate, dissertation, comprehensive exam required, foreign language not required; for CAGS, comprehensive exam required, foreign language and thesis not required. *Entrance requirements:* GRE or MAT, TOEFL. Application deadline: 2/15 (priority date; rolling processing). Application fee: $50. *Expenses:* Tuition $22,830 per year full-time, $713 per credit part-time. Fees $218 per year full-time, $40 per semester part-time. *Financial aid:* Application deadline 3/30. • Dr. Alan Gaynor, Coordinator, 617-353-3307. E-mail: agaynor@bu.edu.

Directory: Educational Administration

Boston University, School of Education, Department of Administration, Training, and Policy Studies, Program in Policy, Planning, and Administration, Boston, MA 02215. Awards Ed M, Ed D, CAGS, MSW/Ed M. Offerings include higher education administration (Ed M); policy, planning, and administration (Ed M, Ed D, CAGS). Students: 10 part-time (8 women). Average age 48. In 1997, 26 master's, 5 doctorates, 2 CAGSs awarded. *Degree requirements:* For doctorate, dissertation, comprehensive exam required, foreign language not required; for CAGS, comprehensive exam required, foreign language and thesis not required. *Entrance requirements:* GRE or MAT, TOEFL. Application deadline: 2/15 (priority date; rolling processing). Application fee: $50. *Expenses:* Tuition $22,830 per year full-time, $713 per credit part-time. Fees $218 per year full-time, $40 per semester part-time. *Financial aid:* Application deadline 3/30. *Faculty research:* School effectiveness, creative problem solving, parent involvement, community education, curriculum theory and evaluation. • Dr. Charles Glenn, Coordinator, 617-353-7108. E-mail: glennsed@bu.edu.

Bowie State University, Programs in Education, Program in School Administration and Supervision, 14000 Jericho Park Road, Bowie, MD 20715. Awards M Ed. Part-time and evening/weekend programs available. *Degree requirements:* Research paper, written comprehensive exam required, thesis optional. *Entrance requirements:* Minimum undergraduate GPA of 3.0, 3 years of teaching experience, teaching certificate. Application deadline: 8/16 (priority date; rolling processing). Application fee: $30. *Expenses:* Tuition $169 per credit hour for state residents; $304 per credit hour for nonresidents. Fees $171 per year.

Bowling Green State University, College of Education and Allied Professions, Department of Educational Administration and Supervision, Bowling Green, OH 43403. Offers programs in educational administration and supervision (M Ed, Ed S), leadership studies (Ed D), math supervision (Ed S). Accredited by NCATE. Part-time programs available. Faculty: 5 full-time (2 women), 5 part-time (2 women). Students: 16 full-time (10 women), 85 part-time (51 women); includes 12 minority (11 African Americans, 1 Asian American), 2 international. 63 applicants, 73% accepted. In 1997, 17 master's, 3 doctorates, 1 Ed S awarded. *Degree requirements:* For master's, thesis or alternative required, foreign language not required; for doctorate, dissertation required, foreign language not required; for Ed S, field experience or internship required, foreign language and thesis not required. *Entrance requirements:* For master's, GRE General Test, TOEFL (minimum score 565); for doctorate, GRE General Test, TOEFL (minimum score 590); for Ed S, GRE General Test. Application deadline: rolling. Application fee: $30. *Tuition:* $6070 per year full-time, $284 per credit hour part-time for state residents; $11,358 per year full-time, $536 per credit hour part-time for nonresidents. *Financial aid:* In 1997–98, 10 assistantships were awarded; partial tuition waivers, Federal Work-Study, institutionally sponsored loans, and career-related internships or fieldwork also available. Aid available to part-time students. Financial aid application deadline: 2/15; applicants required to submit FAFSA. *Faculty research:* Professional development for school leaders, organizational development, school finance, legal challenges to school decision making, administering urban schools. • Dr. Eugene Sanders, Chair, 419-372-7377.

Bowling Green State University, College of Education and Allied Professions, Department of Higher Education and Student Affairs, Program in College Student Personnel, Bowling Green, OH 43403. Awards MA. Accredited by NCATE. Part-time programs available. Students: 68 full-time (44 women), 5 part-time (2 women); includes 16 minority (10 African Americans, 2 Asian Americans, 4 Hispanics), 1 international. 138 applicants, 15% accepted. In 1997, 34 degrees awarded. *Degree requirements:* Thesis or alternative required, foreign language not required. *Entrance requirements:* GRE General Test, TOEFL (minimum score 565). Application deadline: 1/31 (rolling processing). Application fee: $30. Electronic applications accepted. *Tuition:* $6070 per year full-time, $284 per credit hour part-time for state residents; $11,358 per year full-time, $536 per credit hour part-time for nonresidents. *Financial aid:* In 1997–98, 61 assistantships were awarded; institutionally sponsored loans and career-related internships or fieldwork also available. Financial aid application deadline: 2/15; applicants required to submit FAFSA. • Dr. Patricia King, Chair, Department of Higher Education and Student Affairs, 419-372-7382.

Bowling Green State University, College of Education and Allied Professions, Department of Higher Education and Student Affairs, Program in Higher Education Administration, Bowling Green, OH 43403. Awards PhD. Accredited by NCATE. Part-time programs available. Students: 32 full-time (17 women), 20 part-time (12 women); includes 12 minority (10 African Americans, 1 Hispanic, 1 Native American), 7 international. 24 applicants, 54% accepted. In 1997, 6 degrees awarded. *Degree requirements:* Dissertation, global higher education research required, foreign language not required. *Entrance requirements:* GRE General Test, TOEFL (minimum score 600). Application deadline: 3/31 (rolling processing). Application fee: $30. *Tuition:* $6070 per year full-time, $284 per credit hour part-time for state residents; $11,358 per year full-time, $536 per credit hour part-time for nonresidents. *Financial aid:* In 1997–98, 23 assistantships were awarded; Federal Work-Study, institutionally sponsored loans, and career-related internships or fieldwork also available. Aid available to part-time students. Financial aid application deadline: 2/15; applicants required to submit FAFSA. • Dr. Donald Gehring, Director, 419-372-7305.

Bradley University, College of Education and Health Sciences, Department of Counseling and Human Development, Peoria, IL 61625-0002. Offerings include leadership in educational administration (MA), leadership in human services administration (MA). One or more programs accredited by NCATE. *Degree requirements:* Comprehensive exams required, foreign language and thesis not required. *Entrance requirements:* MAT, TOEFL (minimum score 500), interview. Application deadline: 7/1 (priority date; rolling processing; 11/1 for spring admission). Application fee: $35. *Tuition:* $13,240 per year full-time, $359 per semester hour (minimum) part-time.

Brandon University, Faculty of Education, Brandon, MB R7A 6A9, Canada. Offerings include education administration (M Ed). Faculty: 27 full-time (3 women), 1 part-time (0 women). *Degree requirements:* Thesis. *Average time to degree:* master's–2 years full-time; other advanced degree–1 year full-time. *Entrance requirements:* TOEFL (minimum score 550), minimum GPA of 3.0, teaching certificate or equivalent. Application deadline: 3/1. Application fee: $30. *Expenses:* Tuition $421 per course (minimum). Fees $24.95 per year. • Dean, 204-728-9520. Application contact: Faye Douglas, Admissions Director, 204-727-7352. Fax: 204-725-2143. E-mail: douglas@brandonu.ca.

Bridgewater State College, School of Education, Department of Secondary Education and Professional Programs, Program in School Administration, Bridgewater, MA 02325-0001. Awards M Ed, CAGS. Accredited by NCATE. Evening/weekend programs available. *Degree requirements:* For CAGS, comprehensive exam. *Entrance requirements:* For master's, GRE General Test, work experience; for CAGS, master's degree. Application deadline: 4/1 (10/1 for spring admission). Application fee: $25. *Expenses:* Tuition $1675 per year full-time, $70 per credit part-time for state residents; $6450 per year full-time, $269 per credit part-time for nonresidents. Fees $1588 per year full-time, $66 per credit hour part-time for state residents; $1588 per year full-time, $66 per credit part-time for nonresidents. *Financial aid:* Career-related internships or fieldwork available. • Application contact: Graduate School, 508-697-1300.

Brigham Young University, David O. McKay School of Education, Department of Educational Leadership and Foundations, Provo, UT 84602-1001. Awards M Ed, Ed D, PhD. Accredited by NCATE. Faculty: 11 full-time (1 woman). Students: 57 full-time (23 women), 60 part-time (25 women); includes 24 minority (3 African Americans, 15 Asian Americans, 5 Hispanics, 1 Native American), 12 international. Average age 35. 88 applicants, 55% accepted. In 1997, 40 master's, 15 doctorates awarded. *Degree requirements:* For doctorate, 1 foreign language, dissertation. *Entrance requirements:* For master's, minimum GPA of 3.0 in last 60 hours; for doctorate, minimum GPA of 3.25 in last 60 hours. Application deadline: 2/15. Application fee: $30. *Tuition:* $3200 per year full-time, $178 per credit hour part-time for state residents; $4800 per year full-time, $266 per credit hour part-time for nonresidents. *Financial aid:* In 1997–98, 4 research assistantships were awarded; career-related internships or fieldwork also available. *Faculty research:* Cognition, mentoring, pre-service training of administrators, policy development. • Dr. E. Vance Randall, Chair, 801-378-5073. Fax: 801-378-7740. E-mail: vance_randall@byu.edu.

Brooklyn College of the City University of New York, School of Education, Program in School Administration and Supervision, 2900 Bedford Avenue, Brooklyn, NY 11210-2889. Awards CAS. Part-time and evening/weekend programs available. Students: 18 full-time (16 women), 115 part-time (89 women); includes 49 minority (39 African Americans, 1 Asian American, 9 Hispanics). 68 applicants, 88% accepted. In 1997, 60 degrees awarded. *Degree requirements:* Internship required, foreign language and thesis not required. *Entrance requirements:* TOEFL (minimum score 500), master's degree, minimum GPA of 3.0, teaching certificate, 3 years of teaching experience. Application deadline: 3/1 (11/1 for spring admission). Application fee: $40. *Expenses:* Tuition $4350 per year full-time, $185 per credit part-time for state residents; $7600 per year full-time, $320 per credit part-time for nonresidents. Fees $500 per year for state residents; $806 per year for nonresidents. *Financial aid:* Career-related internships or fieldwork available. Financial aid application deadline: 5/1; applicants required to submit FAFSA. • Dr. Stephan Brumberg, Head, 718-951-5213.

Bucknell University, College of Arts and Sciences, Department of Education, Specialization in Elementary and Secondary Principalship, Lewisburg, PA 17837. Awards MA, MS Ed. Faculty: 8 full-time. *Degree requirements:* Thesis or alternative required, foreign language not required. *Entrance requirements:* GRE General Test (minimum combined score of 1000), TOEFL (minimum score 550), minimum GPA of 2.8. Application deadline: 6/1 (priority date; rolling processing; 12/1 for spring admission). Application fee: $25. *Tuition:* $2410 per course. *Financial aid:* Assistantships available. Financial aid application deadline: 3/1. • Adviser, 717-524-1133.

Buena Vista University, School of Education, Storm Lake, IA 50588. Offerings include education administration (MS Ed). Offered in summer only. Postbaccalaureate distance learning degree programs offered (minimal on-campus study). School faculty: 7 full-time (2 women). *Degree requirements:* Thesis, fieldwork/practicum required, foreign language not required. *Entrance requirements:* GRE, minimum undergraduate GPA of 2.75. Application fee: $0. • F. Kline Capps, Dean, 712-749-2275. E-mail: cappsk@bvu.edu. Application contact: Jon E. Hixon, Director of Graduate Studies, 712-749-2190. Fax: 712-749-2035. E-mail: hixon@bvu.edu.

Butler University, College of Education, Indianapolis, IN 46208-3485. Offerings include administration (MS, Ed S). Accredited by NCATE. College faculty: 10 full-time (3 women), 22 part-time (8 women), 22.5 FTE. *Degree requirements:* For Ed S, thesis required, foreign language not required. *Average time to degree:* master's–7 years part-time; other advanced degree–5 years part-time. *Entrance requirements:* For master's, GRE General Test, MAT (minimum score 40), interview. Application deadline: 8/15 (priority date; rolling processing). Application fee: $25. *Tuition:* $220 per credit hour. • Dr. Saundra Tracy, Dean, 317-940-9514. Fax: 317-940-6481. E-mail: stracy@butler.edu.

Caldwell College, Graduate Studies, Program in Educational Administration, Caldwell, NJ 07006-6195. Awards MA. Part-time and evening/weekend programs available. Faculty: 2 full-time (1 woman), 3 part-time (1 woman). Students: 6 part-time (4 women). Average age 40. 6 applicants, 100% accepted. *Degree requirements:* Thesis, research paper required, foreign language not required. *Entrance requirements:* GRE or MAT, interview, minimum GPA of 2.75, teaching certificate, 3 years of teaching experience, writing sample. Application deadline: rolling. Application fee: $25. *Tuition:* $365 per credit. • Dr. John McIntyre, Coordinator, 973-228-4424 Ext. 572. E-mail: jmcintyr@caldwell.edu. Application contact: Dr. Rina Spano, Director of Graduate Studies, 973-228-4424 Ext. 408. Fax: 973-364-7618. E-mail: rspano@caldwell.edu.

California Baptist College, Graduate Program in Education, Riverside, CA 92504-3206. Offerings include educational leadership (MS Ed). Program faculty: 8 full-time (7 women), 4 part-time (2 women). *Application deadline:* rolling. *Application fee:* $40. *Expenses:* Tuition $275 per unit. Fees $100 per year. • Dr. Marsha Savage, Chair, 909-689-5771. Application contact: Gail Ronveaux, Director of Graduate Services, 909-343-4249. Fax: 909-351-1808. E-mail: gradser@cal.baptist.edu.

California Lutheran University, School of Education, Emphasis in Educational Administration, Thousand Oaks, CA 91360-2787. Awards MA. Part-time programs available. Students: 22 full-time (14 women), 90 part-time (57 women). 29 applicants, 59% accepted. In 1997, 17 degrees awarded. *Degree requirements:* Thesis or comprehensive exam required, foreign language not required. *Entrance requirements:* GRE General Test, minimum GPA of 3.0. Application deadline: 8/1 (priority date; rolling processing; 12/1 for spring admission). Application fee: $50. *Tuition:* $335 per unit. • Dr. Robert Amenta, Director.

California Polytechnic State University, San Luis Obispo, Center for Teacher Education, Program in Educational Administration, San Luis Obispo, CA 93407. Awards MA. In 1997, 6 degrees awarded. *Degree requirements:* Comprehensive exam required, thesis optional, foreign language not required. *Entrance requirements:* Minimum GPA of 3.0. Application deadline: 4/1 (12/15 for spring admission). Application fee: $55. *Expenses:* Tuition $0 for state residents; $164 per unit for nonresidents. Fees $2102 per year full-time, $1632 per year part-time. • Rita King, Coordinator, 805-756-1576.

California State University, Bakersfield, School of Education, 9001 Stockdale Highway, Bakersfield, CA 93311-1099. Offerings include educational administration (MA). Accredited by NCATE. *Application deadline:* rolling. *Application fee:* $55. *Expenses:* Tuition $0 for state residents; $246 per unit full-time, $164 per unit part-time for nonresidents. Fees $1584 per year full-time, $918 per year part-time. • Dr. Lon Kellenberger, Interim Dean, 805-664-2219. Application contact: Dr. Dianne Turner, Graduate Coordinator, 805-664-2422. Fax: 805-664-2063.

California State University, Dominguez Hills, School of Education, Department of Graduate Education, Program in Educational Administration, Carson, CA 90747-0001. Awards MA. *Entrance requirements:* Minimum GPA of 2.75. Application deadline: 6/1. Application fee: $55. *Expenses:* Tuition $0 for state residents; $246 per unit for nonresidents. Fees $1896 per year full-time, $1230 per year part-time. • Application contact: Admissions Office, 310-243-3600.

California State University, Fresno, Division of Graduate Studies, Joint Doctoral Program in Educational Leadership, 5241 North Maple Avenue, Fresno, CA 93740. Awards Ed D. Offered jointly with the University of California, Davis. Part-time programs available. Faculty: 36 part-time (17 women). Students: 2 full-time (1 woman), 39 part-time (19 women); includes 17 minority (6 African Americans, 2 Asian Americans, 8 Hispanics, 1 Native American), 1 international. Average age 31. 15 applicants, 87% accepted. In 1997, 8 degrees awarded. *Degree requirements:* Dissertation required, foreign language not required. *Average time to degree:* doctorate–4 years part-time. *Entrance requirements:* GRE or MAT, minimum GPA of 3.2, master's degree. Application deadline: 3/6. Application fee: $55. *Expenses:* Tuition $0 for state residents; $246 per unit for nonresidents. Fees $1872 per year full-time, $1206 per year part-time. *Financial aid:* In 1997–98, 1 scholarship totaling $1,000 was awarded; career-related internships or fieldwork also available. Aid available to part-time students. Financial aid application deadline: 3/1; applicants required to submit FAFSA. *Faculty research:* Minority special education leadership, literacy, ethics of leadership, organizational planning, language development. • Karen Carey, Co-Director, 209-278-0427. Fax: 209-278-0457. E-mail: karen_carey@csufresno.edu.

California State University, Fresno, Division of Graduate Studies, School of Education and Human Development, Department of Educational Research, Administration and Foundations, 5241 North Maple Avenue, Fresno, CA 93740. Offers program in education (MA), including administration and supervision. Accredited by NCATE. Part-time and evening/weekend programs available. Faculty: 15 full-time (7 women). Students: 41 full-time (23 women), 51 part-time (26 women); includes 25 minority (2 African Americans, 4 Asian Americans, 19 Hispanics). Average age 31. 31 applicants, 90% accepted. In 1997, 47 degrees awarded. *Degree requirements:*

Thesis or alternative required, foreign language not required. *Average time to degree:* master's–3.5 years full-time. *Entrance requirements:* GRE General Test, TOEFL (minimum score 550), MAT, minimum GPA of 2.75. Application deadline: 4/1 (priority date; rolling processing; 11/1 for spring admission). Application fee: $55. Electronic applications accepted. *Expenses:* Tuition $0 for state residents; $246 per unit for nonresidents. Fees $1872 per year full-time, $1206 per year part-time. *Financial aid:* In 1997–98, 3 research awards, travel grants, scholarships totaling $2,014 were awarded; fellowships, research assistantships, Federal Work-Study, and career-related internships or fieldwork also available. Financial aid application deadline: 3/1; applicants required to submit FAFSA. • Dr. Atilano Valencia, Chair, 209-278-0350. Fax: 209-278-0404. E-mail: atilano_valencia@csufresno.edu. Application contact: Curtis Guaglianone, Graduate Coordinator, 209-278-0292. E-mail: curtis_guaglianone@csufresno.edu.

California State University, Fullerton, School of Human Development and Community Service, Department of Educational Leadership, PO Box 34080, Fullerton, CA 92834-9480. Awards MS. Accredited by NCATE. Part-time programs available. Faculty: 3 full-time (0 women), 1 part-time, 3.2 FTE. Students: 37 part-time (23 women); includes 8 minority (2 African Americans, 1 Asian American, 5 Hispanics). Average age 34. 5 applicants, 60% accepted. In 1997, 42 degrees awarded. *Degree requirements:* Thesis or alternative, project required, foreign language not required. *Entrance requirements:* Minimum GPA of 2.5. Application fee: $55. *Expenses:* Tuition $0 for state residents; $246 per unit for nonresidents. Fees $1947 per year full-time, $1281 per year part-time. *Financial aid:* State grants, Federal Work-Study, institutionally sponsored loans, and career-related internships or fieldwork available. Aid available to part-time students. Financial aid application deadline: 3/1. *Faculty research:* Creation of a substance abuse training and demonstration program. • Dr. Louise Adler, Head, 714-278-3911.

California State University, Hayward, School of Education, Department of Educational Leadership, Hayward, CA 94542-3000. Awards MS. Accredited by NCATE. Part-time and evening/weekend programs available. Faculty: 5 full-time (3 women). Students: 25 full-time (18 women), 57 part-time (37 women); includes 28 minority (13 African Americans, 3 Asian Americans, 12 Hispanics). 56 applicants, 95% accepted. In 1997, 22 degrees awarded. *Degree requirements:* Comprehensive exam, project, or thesis required, foreign language not required. *Entrance requirements:* Teaching or services credential and experience. Application deadline: 4/19 (priority date; rolling processing; 1/5 for spring admission). Application fee: $55. *Expenses:* Tuition $0 for state residents; $164 per unit for nonresidents. Fees $1827 per year full-time, $1161 per year part-time. *Financial aid:* Federal Work-Study, institutionally sponsored loans, and career-related internships or fieldwork available. Aid available to part-time students. Financial aid application deadline: 3/1. • Dr. Linda Lambert, Chair, 510-885-4145. Application contact: Dr. Maria De Anda-Ramos, Executive Director, Admissions and Outreach, 510-885-2624.

California State University, Long Beach, College of Education, Department of Educational Psychology and Administration, Program in Educational Administration, Long Beach, CA 90840-2201. Awards MA. Students: 8 full-time (4 women), 52 part-time (37 women); includes 14 minority (2 African Americans, 1 Asian American, 11 Hispanics), 1 international. Average age 34. 40 applicants, 78% accepted. In 1997, 11 degrees awarded. *Degree requirements:* Comprehensive exam, project, or thesis required, foreign language not required. *Entrance requirements:* GRE General Test, minimum GPA of 2.75. Application deadline: 8/1 (rolling processing; 12/1 for spring admission). Application fee: $55. *Expenses:* Tuition $0 for state residents; $246 per unit for nonresidents. Fees $1846 per year full-time, $1180 per year part-time. *Financial aid:* Application deadline 3/2. • Dr. Robert Berdan, Chair, Department of Educational Psychology and Administration, 562-985-4517. Fax: 562-985-4534. E-mail: rberdan@csulb.edu.

California State University, Los Angeles, School of Education, Division of Administration and Counseling, Major in Educational Administration, Los Angeles, CA 90032-8530. Awards MA. Accredited by NCATE. Part-time and evening/weekend programs available. Students: 82 full-time (46 women), 139 part-time (78 women); includes 149 minority (15 African Americans, 25 Asian Americans, 107 Hispanics, 2 Native Americans), 4 international. In 1997, 126 degrees awarded. *Degree requirements:* Comprehensive exam required, foreign language and thesis not required. *Entrance requirements:* TOEFL (minimum score 550), minimum GPA of 2.75 in last 90 units, teaching certificate. Application deadline: 6/30 (rolling processing; 2/1 for spring admission). Application fee: $55. *Expenses:* Tuition $0 for state residents; $164 per unit for nonresidents. Fees $1763 per year full-time, $1097 per year part-time. *Financial aid:* 4 students received aid; Federal Work-Study available. Aid available to part-time students. Financial aid application deadline: 3/1. *Faculty research:* Drug-free schools. • Dr. Raymond Hillis, Chair, Division of Administration and Counseling, 213-343-4250.

California State University, Northridge, College of Education, Department of Educational Leadership and Policy Studies, Program in Administration and Supervision, Northridge, CA 91330. Offers administration and supervision (MA), educational foundations (MA). Accredited by NCATE. Part-time and evening/weekend programs available. Students: 25 full-time (20 women), 87 part-time (58 women); includes 47 minority (9 African Americans, 7 Asian Americans, 30 Hispanics, 1 Native American). Average age 35. 39 applicants, 92% accepted. *Entrance requirements:* GRE General Test, MAT, TOEFL. Application deadline: 11/30. Application fee: $55. *Expenses:* Tuition $0 for state residents; $246 per unit for nonresidents. Fees $1970 per year full-time, $1304 per year part-time. *Financial aid:* Application deadline 3/1. • Application contact: John Schulte, Graduate Coordinator, 818-677-2517.

California State University, Sacramento, School of Education, Department of Educational Administration, Sacramento, CA 95819-6048. Awards MA. Part-time programs available. *Degree requirements:* Thesis or alternative, writing proficiency exam. *Entrance requirements:* TOEFL (minimum score 550), minimum GPA of 2.5. Application deadline: 4/15 (11/1 for spring admission). Application fee: $55. *Expenses:* Tuition $0 for state residents; $246 per unit for nonresidents. Fees $2012 per year full-time, $1346 per year part-time. *Financial aid:* Federal Work-Study and career-related internships or fieldwork available. Aid available to part-time students. Financial aid application deadline: 3/1. • Dr. C. Rodriguez, Chair, 916-278-5388. Application contact: Coordinator, 916-278-7023.

California State University, San Bernardino, Graduate Studies, School of Education, Program in School Administration, San Bernardino, CA 92407-2397. Awards MA. Part-time and evening/weekend programs available. Faculty: 8 full-time (2 women), 4 part-time (2 women). Students: 144 full-time (88 women), 47 part-time (29 women); includes 44 minority (15 African Americans, 1 Asian American, 26 Hispanics, 2 Native Americans). 100 applicants, 98% accepted. In 1997, 45 degrees awarded. *Degree requirements:* Thesis or alternative required, foreign language not required. *Entrance requirements:* Minimum GPA of 3.0 in education. Application deadline: 8/31 (priority date). Application fee: $55. *Expenses:* Tuition $0 for state residents; $164 per unit for nonresidents. Fees $1922 per year full-time, $1256 per year part-time. *Financial aid:* Career-related internships or fieldwork available. Aid available to part-time students. • Dr. Cheryl Fisher, Coordinator, 909-880-5659.

California State University, Stanislaus, School of Education, Department of Advanced Studies in Education, Program in Educational Administration, Turlock, CA 95382. Awards MA Ed. Accredited by NCATE. Part-time programs available. Faculty: 5 full-time (0 women). Students: 10 (9 women). 19 applicants, 100% accepted. In 1997, 5 degrees awarded. *Degree requirements:* Thesis or alternative required, foreign language not required. *Entrance requirements:* MAT. Application fee: $55. *Expenses:* Tuition $0 for state residents; $246 per unit for nonresidents. Fees $1779 per year full-time, $1113 per year part-time. *Financial aid:* Application deadline 3/2; applicants required to submit FAFSA. *Faculty research:* Collective bargaining, school principalship. • Dr. John Borba, Coordinator, 209-667-3364.

California University of Pennsylvania, School of Education, Program in Educational Administration, 250 University Avenue, California, PA 15419-1394. Awards M Ed. Accredited by NCATE. Part-time and evening/weekend programs available. Faculty: 3 full-time (1 woman), 2 part-time (0 women). Students: 3 full-time (1 woman), 45 part-time (28 women). 17 applicants, 94% accepted. In 1997, 10 degrees awarded. *Degree requirements:* Comprehensive exam required, thesis optional, foreign language not required. *Entrance requirements:* MAT (minimum score 35), TOEFL (minimum score 550), interview, minimum GPA of 3.0, teaching certificate, 2 years of teaching experience. Application deadline: rolling. Application fee: $25. *Expenses:* Tuition $3468 per year full-time, $193 per credit part-time for state residents; $6236 per year full-time, $346 per credit part-time for nonresidents. Fees $886 per year full-time, $153 per semester (minimum) part-time. • Dr. Lizabeth Gillette, Coordinator, 724-938-4140.

Calvin College, Graduate Programs in Education, Grand Rapids, MI 49546-4388. Offerings include school administration (M Ed). Accredited by NCATE. M Ed (reading, school administration) admissions temporarily suspended. Faculty: 1 (woman) full-time, 15 part-time (6 women). *Degree requirements:* Thesis required, foreign language not required. *Entrance requirements:* GRE General Test, TOEFL, teaching certificate. Application deadline: 8/15 (priority date; rolling processing; 1/15 for spring admission). Application fee: $0. Electronic applications accepted. *Tuition:* $250 per semester hour. • Dr. Robert S. Fortner, Director of Graduate Studies, 616-957-8533. Fax: 616-957-8551. E-mail: forr@calvin.edu.

Campbell University, School of Education, Buies Creek, NC 27506. Offerings include administration (MSA). Accredited by NCATE. School faculty: 8 full-time (6 women), 6 part-time (0 women). *Application deadline:* 8/1 (priority date; rolling processing; 1/2 for spring admission). *Application fee:* $25. *Tuition:* $168 per credit hour (minimum). • Dr. Margaret Giesbrecht, Dean, 910-893-1630. Fax: 910-893-1999. E-mail: giesbrec@mailcenter.campbell.edu. Application contact: James S. Farthing, Director of Graduate Admissions, 910-893-1200 Ext. 1318. Fax: 910-893-1288.

Canisius College, School of Education and Human Services, Program in Educational Administration and Supervision, Buffalo, NY 14208-1098. Awards MS, SAS. Part-time and evening/weekend programs available. Faculty: 2 full-time (0 women), 14 part-time (0 women). Students: 1 full-time (0 women), 40 part-time (24 women). 24 applicants, 100% accepted. *Degree requirements:* For master's, research project required, foreign language and thesis not required. *Entrance requirements:* For master's, GRE General Test, teaching certificate and experience. Application deadline: 8/15 (priority date; rolling processing). Application fee: $20. *Expenses:* Tuition $415 per credit hour. Fees $15 per credit hour. *Financial aid:* Graduate assistantships, Federal Work-Study, institutionally sponsored loans, and career-related internships or fieldwork available. Aid available to part-time students. • Dr. Donald J. Murphy, Director, 716-888-2390. Application contact: Kevin Smith, Graduate Recruitment and Admissions, 716-888-2544. Fax: 716-888-3290.

Cardinal Stritch University, College of Education, Department of Education, Milwaukee, WI 53217-3985. Offerings include educational leadership (MS), with options in administration, staff development; leadership (Ed D). One or more programs accredited by NCATE. *Application deadline:* 4/1 (priority date; rolling processing). *Application fee:* $20. *Expenses:* Tuition $338 per credit. Fees $25 per semester. • Dr. Nancy Blair, Chair, 414-410-4367. Application contact: Amy Knox, Graduate Admissions Officer, 414-410-4042.

Carlow College, Division of Education, Program in Educational Leadership, Pittsburgh, PA 15213-3165. Awards M Ed. Part-time and evening/weekend programs available. Faculty: 1 (woman) full-time, 5 part-time (4 women). Students: 41 part-time (35 women). Average age 36. 15 applicants, 100% accepted. In 1997, 31 degrees awarded. *Degree requirements:* Thesis or alternative required, foreign language not required. *Average time to degree:* master's–2.3 years part-time. *Entrance requirements:* Interview, minimum GPA of 3.0. Application deadline: 4/1 (rolling processing; 10/15 for spring admission). Application fee: $35. *Financial aid:* Available to part-time students. Financial aid application deadline: 3/15. *Faculty research:* Student assessment. • Dr. Mary F. Toll, Director, 412-578-6333. Application contact: Bonnie Potthoff, Office Manager, Graduate Studies, 412-578-8764. Fax: 412-578-8822.

Castleton State College, Department of Education, Program in Educational Leadership, Castleton, VT 05735. Awards MA Ed, CAGS. Part-time and evening/weekend programs available. Faculty: 9 full-time (5 women), 7 part-time (4 women). *Degree requirements:* For master's, thesis or written exams required, foreign language not required; for CAGS, publishable paper required, foreign language and thesis not required. *Entrance requirements:* For master's, GRE General Test (minimum combined score of 1000), MAT (minimum score 50), interview, minimum undergraduate GPA of 3.0; for CAGS, educational research, master's degree, minimum undergraduate GPA of 3.0. Application deadline: 7/1 (10/1 for spring admission). Application fee: $30. *Expenses:* Tuition $3924 per year full-time, $164 per credit part-time for state residents; $9192 per year full-time, $383 per credit part-time for nonresidents. Fees $902 per year full-time, $26 per credit part-time. *Financial aid:* Federal Work-Study and career-related internships or fieldwork available. • Application contact: Mary Frucelli, Graduate Assistant, 802-468-1441. Fax: 802-468-5237.

The Catholic University of America, School of Arts and Sciences, Department of Education, Washington, DC 20064. Offerings include administration, curriculum, and policy studies (MA); Catholic school leadership (MA); educational administration (PhD). One or more programs accredited by NCATE. MA (English as a second language) new for fall 1998. Department faculty: 13 full-time (8 women), 2 part-time (both women), 14 FTE. *Degree requirements:* For master's, comprehensive exam required, foreign language not required; for doctorate, 1 foreign language, dissertation, comprehensive exam. *Entrance requirements:* GRE General Test, TOEFL. Application deadline: 8/1 (priority date; rolling processing; 12/1 for spring admission). Application fee: $50. *Expenses:* Tuition $17,325 per year full-time, $668 per credit hour part-time. Fees $680 per year full-time, $360 per year part-time. • Chair, 202-319-5800. Fax: 202-319-5815.

Centenary College, Program in Education, 400 Jefferson Street, Hackettstown, NJ 07840-2100. Offerings include instructional leadership (MA). Program faculty: 6 full-time (2 women), 3 part-time (0 women). *Degree requirements:* Comprehensive assessment. *Entrance requirements:* Interview, minimum undergraduate GPA of 2.8. Application deadline: 8/15 (rolling processing; 1/15 for spring admission). Application fee: $30. *Tuition:* $355 per credit. • Dr. Thomas A. Brunner, Director of Graduate Studies, 908-852-1400 Ext. 2299.

Centenary College of Louisiana, Department of Education, Shreveport, LA 71134-1188. Offerings include administration (M Ed). Department faculty: 5 full-time (2 women), 6 part-time (1 woman). *Average time to degree:* master's–2 years full-time, 4 years part-time. *Entrance requirements:* GRE. Application fee: $30. *Tuition:* $360 per course. • Dr. E. John Turner, Chairman, 318-869-5223.

Central Connecticut State University, School of Education and Professional Studies, Department of Educational Leadership, Program in Administration, Supervision and Curriculum, New Britain, CT 06050-4010. Awards MS. In 1997, 12 degrees awarded. *Degree requirements:* Thesis or alternative, comprehensive exam required, foreign language not required. *Entrance requirements:* TOEFL (minimum score 550), minimum GPA of 2.7. Application deadline: 6/1 (priority date; rolling processing; 12/1 for spring admission). Application fee: $40. *Expenses:* Tuition $4458 per year full-time, $175 per credit hour part-time for state residents; $9943 per year full-time, $175 per credit hour part-time for nonresidents. Fees $45 per semester. *Financial aid:* Application deadline 3/15. • Dr. Penelope Lisi, Interim Chair, Department of Educational Leadership, 860-832-2130.

Central Connecticut State University, School of Education and Professional Studies, Department of Educational Leadership, Program in Educational Leadership, New Britain, CT 06050-4010. Awards Sixth Year Certificate. In 1997, 20 degrees awarded. *Degree requirements:* Thesis or alternative, qualifying exam required, foreign language not required. *Application deadline:* 6/1 (priority date; rolling processing; 12/1 for spring admission). *Application fee:* $40. *Expenses:* Tuition $4458 per year full-time, $175 per credit hour part-time for state residents; $9943 per year full-time, $175 per credit hour part-time for nonresidents. Fees $45 per semester. *Financial aid:* Application deadline 3/15. • Dr. Penelope Lisi, Interim Chair, Department of Educational Leadership, 860-832-2130.

Directory: Educational Administration

Central Michigan University, College of Education and Human Services, Department of Educational Administration and Community Leadership, Mount Pleasant, MI 48859. Offers program in educational administration (MA, Ed S). Accredited by NCATE. Faculty: 15 full-time (2 women). Students: 3 full-time (1 woman), 64 part-time (30 women); includes 4 minority (2 African Americans, 1 Hispanic, 1 Native American). Average age 35. In 1997, 58 master's, 6 Ed Ss awarded. *Degree requirements:* Thesis or alternative required, foreign language not required. *Entrance requirements:* For master's, GRE General Test (minimum score 520 on verbal section, 580 on quantitative), minimum GPA of 2.9; for Ed S, GRE, minimum GPA of 3.7. Application deadline: 3/1. Application fee: $30. *Expenses:* Tuition $139 per credit hour (minimum) for state residents; $276 per credit hour (minimum) for nonresidents. Fees $260 per year full-time, $150 per semester part-time. *Financial aid:* Fellowships, Federal Work-Study, and career-related internships or fieldwork available. Financial aid application deadline: 3/7. *Faculty research:* Elementary administration, secondary administration, student achievement, in-service training, internships in administration. • Dr. Roger Grabinski, Chairperson, 517-774-3204. Fax: 517-774-4374. E-mail: roger.grabinski@cmich.edu.

Central Missouri State University, College of Education and Human Services, Department of Education, Administration and Higher Education, Warrensburg, MO 64093. Offers programs in administration (Ed S), including school principalship, superintendency; human services (Ed S); school administration (MSE), including elementary, secondary; student personnel administration (MS). Accredited by NCATE. Part-time programs available. Faculty: 6 full-time. Students: 21 full-time (12 women), 151 part-time (83 women). In 1997, 37 master's, 16 Ed Ss awarded. *Degree requirements:* For master's, internship, Missouri Assessment Center exam (MSE); for Ed S, thesis or alternative, Missouri Assessment Center exam. *Entrance requirements:* For master's, GRE (MSE), minimum GPA of 2.75, teaching certificate, 2 years of teaching experience (MSE); for Ed S, GRE General Test, minimum GPA of 3.25. Application deadline: 6/30 (priority date; rolling processing). Application fee: $25 ($50 for international students). *Tuition:* $3288 per year full-time, $137 per credit hour part-time for state residents; $5928 per year full-time, $274 per credit hour part-time for nonresidents. *Financial aid:* In 1997–98, 14 administrative and laboratory assistantships were awarded; Federal Work-Study and career-related internships or fieldwork also available. Aid available to part-time students. Financial aid application deadline: 3/1; applicants required to submit FAFSA. • Dr. Gordon Warren, Chair, 660-543-4341. Fax: 660-543-4167. E-mail: gcw8803@cmsu2.cmsu.edu.

Central Missouri State University, College of Education and Human Services, Department of Educational Leadership, Warrensburg, MO 64093. Awards Ed D. Accredited by NCATE. Offered jointly with University of Missouri–Columbia. Students: 1 part-time (0 women). *Entrance requirements:* GRE, MS, Ed S, or equivalent. Application deadline: 6/30 (priority date; rolling processing). Application fee: $25 ($50 for international students). *Tuition:* $3288 per year full-time, $137 per credit hour part-time for state residents; $5928 per year full-time, $274 per credit hour part-time for nonresidents. *Financial aid:* Application deadline 3/1. • Jim Machell, Coordinator, 660-543-8823.

Central State University, Program in Education, Wilberforce, OH 45384. Offerings include leadership (M Ed). Program faculty: 3 full-time. *Tuition:* $120 per credit hour for state residents; $206 per credit hour for nonresidents. • Constance Robinson, Coordinator, 937-376-6536.

Central Washington University, College of Education and Professional Studies, Department of Teacher Education, Program in Educational Administration, Ellensburg, WA 98926. Awards M Ed. Part-time programs available. Faculty: 21 full-time (10 women). Students: 7 full-time (3 women), 27 part-time (9 women); includes 2 minority (1 Hispanic, 1 Native American), 2 international. 6 applicants, 83% accepted. In 1997, 19 degrees awarded. *Degree requirements:* Thesis or alternative required, foreign language not required. *Entrance requirements:* Minimum GPA of 3.0. Application deadline: 4/1 (priority date; rolling processing; 1/1 for spring admission). Application fee: $35. *Expenses:* Tuition $4200 per year full-time, $140 per credit hour part-time for state residents; $12,780 per year full-time, $426 per credit hour part-time for nonresidents. Fees $240 per year. *Financial aid:* In 1997–98, 1 research assistantship (to a first-year student) averaging $1,108 per month and totaling $9,972 was awarded; teaching assistantships, Federal Work-Study also available. Financial aid application deadline: 2/15. • Application contact: Christie A. Fevergeon, Program Coordinator, Graduate Studies and Research, 509-963-3103. Fax: 509-963-1799. E-mail: masters@cwu.edu.

Chadron State College, Department of Education, Chadron, NE 69337. Offerings include educational administration (MS Ed, Sp Ed), secondary administration (MS Ed). One or more programs accredited by NCATE. Sp Ed (counseling) admissions temporarily suspended. *Application deadline:* rolling. *Application fee:* $15. *Expenses:* Tuition $1788 per year full-time, $75 per credit hour part-time for state residents; $3588 per year full-time, $149 per credit hour part-time for nonresidents. Fees $388 per year full-time, $1232 per year part-time. • Dr. Pat Colgate, Dean, School of Graduate Studies, 308-432-6330. Fax: 308-432-6454. E-mail: pcolgate@csc1.csc.edu.

Chapman University, School of Education, Concentration in Educational Administration, Orange, CA 92866. Awards MA. Faculty: 10 full-time (8 women). Students: 4. *Degree requirements:* Comprehensive exam required, thesis not required. *Entrance requirements:* GRE General Test (minimum combined score of 900), MAT (minimum score 45), or PRAXIS. Application deadline: rolling. Application fee: $40. *Tuition:* $7020 per year full-time, $390 per credit part-time. *Financial aid:* Application deadline 3/1. • Dr. Penny Bryan, Coordinator, 714-997-6781.

Charleston Southern University, Programs in Education, Charleston, SC 29423-8087. Offerings include administration and supervision (M Ed), with options in elementary, secondary. Faculty: 16 full-time (5 women), 5 part-time (3 women), 17.6 FTE. *Application deadline:* rolling. *Application fee:* $25. *Tuition:* $9821 per year full-time, $173 per hour (minimum) part-time. • Dr. Martha Watson, Director of Graduate Programs, 803-863-7555.

Cheyney University of Pennsylvania, Program in Educational Administration and Supervision, Cheyney, PA 19319. Awards M Ed. Accredited by NCATE. Part-time and evening/weekend programs available. Faculty: 5 full-time (3 women), 7 part-time (4 women). Students: 9 full-time (8 women), 132 part-time (99 women); includes 129 minority (126 African Americans, 3 Hispanics). Average age 39. In 1997, 46 degrees awarded. *Degree requirements:* Thesis or alternative required, foreign language not required. *Entrance requirements:* GRE General Test, MAT, minimum GPA of 2.75. Application deadline: 8/1 (priority date; rolling processing; 12/15 for spring admission). Application fee: $25. *Tuition:* $3848 per year full-time, $193 per credit hour part-time for state residents; $6616 per year full-time, $346 per credit hour part-time for nonresidents. *Financial aid:* Assistantships, institutionally sponsored loans, and career-related internships or fieldwork available. Financial aid application deadline: 5/1. *Faculty research:* Teacher motivation, critical thinking. • Dr. William Magill, Coordinator, 610-399-2406. Application contact: Dean of Graduate Studies, 610-399-2400. Fax: 610-399-2118.

Chicago State University, College of Education, Department of Curriculum and Instruction, Program in Educational Administration and Supervision, Chicago, IL 60628. Awards MA. Accredited by NCATE. *Degree requirements:* Comprehensive exams required, thesis optional, foreign language not required. *Entrance requirements:* Minimum GPA of 2.75. Application deadline: 7/1 (11/10 for spring admission). *Tuition:* $2268 per year full-time, $95 per credit hour part-time for state residents; $6804 per year full-time, $284 per credit hour for nonresidents.

The Citadel, The Military College of South Carolina, Department of Education, Program in Educational Administration, Charleston, SC 29409. Awards M Ed, Ed S. Accredited by NCATE. Students: 9 full-time (4 women), 89 part-time (49 women); includes 38 minority (37 African Americans, 1 Hispanic). In 1997, 29 master's, 6 Ed Ss awarded. *Entrance requirements:* For master's, GRE, MAT, or 12 hours of graduate course work with a minimum GPA of 3.0. Application deadline: rolling. Application fee: $25. *Expenses:* Tuition $130 per credit hour for state residents; $260 per credit hour for nonresidents. Fees $30 per semester. • Dr. Robert Carter, Head, Department of Education, 803-953-5097.

City College of the City University of New York, Graduate School, School of Education, Department of School Services, Program in Educational Administration, Convent Avenue at 138th Street, New York, NY 10031-6977. Awards MS, AC. Students: 124 part-time (82 women). In 1997, 40 master's, 37 ACs awarded. *Degree requirements:* For master's, thesis, research paper required, foreign language not required. *Entrance requirements:* For master's, TOEFL (minimum score 500), interview, minimum GPA of 3.0 in major, 2.5 overall. Application fee: $40. *Expenses:* Tuition $4350 per year full-time, $185 per credit part-time for state residents; $7600 per year full-time, $320 per credit part-time for nonresidents. Fees $41 per year. *Financial aid:* Career-related internships or fieldwork available. Financial aid application deadline: 5/1. *Faculty research:* Dynamics of organizational change, impact of laws on educational policy, leadership development in schools. • Edward Lilly, Head, 212-650-7983.

City University, School of Education, Bellevue, WA 98004-6442. Offerings include school administration (M Ed), school principal (Certificate). Postbaccalaureate distance learning degree programs offered (no on-campus study). School faculty: 21 full-time (13 women), 301 part-time (162 women). *Application deadline:* rolling. *Application fee:* $75 ($175 for international students). Electronic applications accepted. *Tuition:* $280 per credit hour. • Roxanne Kelly, Dean, 425-637-1010 Ext. 3712. Fax: 425-277-2439. Application contact: Nabil El-Khatib, Vice President, Admissions, 800-426-5596. Fax: 425-277-2437. E-mail: nel-khatib@cityu.edu.

Claremont Graduate University, Department of Education, Claremont, CA 91711-6163. Offerings include organization and administration (MA, PhD). PhD offered jointly with San Diego State University; MA (mathematics education) offered jointly with the Department of Mathematics. Terminal master's awarded for partial completion of doctoral program. Department faculty: 13 full-time (6 women), 13 part-time (10 women). *Degree requirements:* For master's, thesis or alternative; for doctorate, dissertation. *Entrance requirements:* GRE General Test. Application deadline: 2/15 (priority date; rolling processing). Application fee: $40. Electronic applications accepted. *Expenses:* Tuition $20,250 per year full-time, $913 per unit part-time. Fees $130 per year. • David Drew, Chair, 909-621-8075. Application contact: Ethel Rogers, Associate Director, 909-621-8317. Fax: 909-621-8734. E-mail: educ@cgu.edu.

Clark Atlanta University, School of Education, Department of Educational Leadership, Atlanta, GA 30314. Awards MA, Ed D, Ed S. Students: 18 full-time (17 women), 23 part-time (15 women); includes 41 minority (all African Americans). In 1997, 6 master's, 2 Ed Ss awarded. *Degree requirements:* For master's and doctorate, 1 foreign language (computer language can substitute), thesis/dissertation; for Ed S, thesis. *Entrance requirements:* For master's, GRE General Test, minimum undergraduate GPA of 2.5; for doctorate and Ed S, GRE General Test, minimum graduate GPA of 3.0. Application deadline: 4/1 (rolling processing; 11/1 for spring admission). Application fee: $30. *Expenses:* Tuition $9672 per year full-time, $403 per credit hour part-time. Fees $200 per year. *Financial aid:* Application deadline 4/30. • Dr. Olivia Boggs, Chairperson, 404-880-8498. Application contact: Michelle Clark-Davis, Graduate Program Assistant, 404-880-8709.

Clarke College, Program in Education, Dubuque, IA 52001-3198. Offerings include educational administration: elementary and secondary (MA). Accredited by NCATE. Program faculty: 8 part-time (4 women). *Degree requirements:* Comprehensive exam, minimum GPA of 3.25 required, thesis optional, foreign language not required. *Average time to degree:* master's–4 years part-time. *Entrance requirements:* GRE General Test or MAT, minimum GPA of 2.75. Application deadline: rolling. Application fee: $25. Electronic applications accepted. *Expenses:* Tuition $12,688 per year full-time, $315 per credit hour part-time. Fees $240 per year. • Dr. Margaret Feldner, Chair, 319-588-6397. E-mail: mfeldner@clarke.edu. Application contact: Admissions Office, 800-383-2345. Fax: 319-588-6789. E-mail: graduate@clarke.edu.

Clemson University, College of Health, Education, and Human Development, Department of Counseling and Educational Leadership, Program in Administration and Supervision, Clemson, SC 29634. Awards M Ed, Ed S. Accredited by NCATE. Students: 77 part-time (41 women); includes 7 minority (6 African Americans, 1 Hispanic). 37 applicants, 62% accepted. In 1997, 9 master's, 13 Ed Ss awarded. *Entrance requirements:* GRE General Test or MAT, TOEFL, 1 year of teaching experience. Application deadline: 6/1. Application fee: $35. *Expenses:* Tuition $3154 per year full-time, $130 per credit hour part-time for state residents; $6452 per year full-time, $264 per credit hour part-time for nonresidents. Fees $190 per year. *Financial aid:* Application deadline 6/1. • Dr. Jack Flanigan, Chair, Department of Counseling and Educational Leadership, 864-656-3484. Fax: 864-656-1322. E-mail: fjackso@clemson.edu.

Clemson University, College of Health, Education, and Human Development, Department of Counseling and Educational Leadership, Program in Educational Leadership, Clemson, SC 29634. Awards PhD. Accredited by NCATE. Students: 9 full-time (4 women), 41 part-time (17 women); includes 3 minority (all African Americans). 22 applicants, 36% accepted. In 1997, 8 degrees awarded. *Degree requirements:* Dissertation required, foreign language not required. *Entrance requirements:* GRE General Test, TOEFL, master's degree in related field. Application fee: $35. *Expenses:* Tuition $3154 per year full-time, $130 per credit hour part-time for state residents; $6452 per year full-time, $264 per credit hour part-time for nonresidents. Fees $190 per year. *Financial aid:* Application deadline 6/1. • Dr. Jack Flanigan, Chair, Department of Counseling and Educational Leadership, 864-656-3484. Fax: 864-656-1322. E-mail: fjackso@clemson.edu.

Cleveland State University, College of Education, Department of Counseling, Administration, Supervision and Adult Learning, Program in Educational Administration and Supervision, Cleveland, OH 44115-2440. Awards M Ed, Ed S. Students: 1 (woman) full-time, 45 part-time (26 women); includes 9 minority (8 African Americans, 1 Hispanic). Average age 34. 3 applicants, 100% accepted. In 1997, 33 master's awarded. *Degree requirements:* For master's, comprehensive exam required, thesis optional, foreign language not required; for Ed S, comprehensive exam, internship required, thesis optional, foreign language not required. *Entrance requirements:* For master's, GRE General Test or MAT (score in 50th percentile or higher). Application deadline: 9/1 (priority date; rolling processing). Application fee: $25. *Expenses:* Tuition $5252 per year full-time, $202 per credit hour part-time for state residents; $10,504 per year full-time, $404 per credit hour part-time for nonresidents. Fees $2.25 per credit hour (minimum). *Financial aid:* Career-related internships or fieldwork available. *Faculty research:* Faculty performance, clinical supervision. • Dr. Bernadette Marczely, Coordinator, 216-687-4614.

The College of New Jersey, Graduate Division, School of Education, Department of Educational Administration and Secondary Education, Ewing, NJ 08628. Offers programs in educational leadership (M Ed), secondary education (MAT). Accredited by NCATE. Part-time and evening/weekend programs available. Students: 20 full-time (8 women), 103 part-time (57 women); includes 26 minority (10 African Americans, 1 Asian American, 14 Hispanics, 1 Native American), 5 international. Average age 28. In 1997, 47 degrees awarded. *Degree requirements:* Comprehensive exam required, foreign language and thesis not required. *Average time to degree:* master's–2 years full-time. *Entrance requirements:* GRE General Test, minimum GPA of 3.0 in field or 2.75 overall. Application deadline: 4/15 (10/15 for spring admission). Application fee: $50. *Expenses:* Tuition $6892 per year full-time, $287 per credit hour part-time for state residents; $9602 per year full-time, $402 per credit hour part-time for nonresidents. Fees $799 per year full-time, $33 per credit hour part-time. *Financial aid:* Graduate assistantships available. Financial aid application deadline: 5/1; applicants required to submit FAFSA. • Dr. Richard Farber, Chair, 609-771-3470. Fax: 609-637-5197.

College of New Rochelle, Division of Education, Program in School Administration and Supervision, New Rochelle, NY 10805-2308. Awards MS Ed, Certificate, PD. Offered jointly with Iona College. Faculty: 2 full-time (0 women), 5 part-time (0 women), 4 FTE. Students: 6 full-time (all women), 75 part-time (57 women); includes 14 minority (10 African Americans, 4 Hispanics). 58 applicants, 100% accepted. In 1997, 63 master's awarded. *Degree requirements:*

For master's, internship required, foreign language not required. *Average time to degree:* master's–1.2 years full-time, 2.5 years part-time. *Entrance requirements:* For master's, interview; minimum GPA of 3.0 in field, 2.7 overall. Application deadline: 8/1 (priority date; rolling processing). Application fee: $35. *Tuition:* $329 per credit. *Financial aid:* In 1997–98, 1 research assistantship totaling $948 was awarded; scholarships also available. *Faculty research:* Training administrators in Eastern Europe, leadership. • Dr. Lawrence Finkel, Coordinator, 914-654-5323.

College of Notre Dame of Maryland, Leadership in Teaching Program, Baltimore, MD 21210-2476. Awards MA. *Entrance requirements:* Watson-Glaser Critical Thinking Appraisal, writing test, interview, 1 year of teaching experience. Application deadline: 8/15 (priority date; rolling processing; 1/15 for spring admission). Application fee: $25. *Tuition:* $248 per credit. *Financial aid:* Institutionally sponsored loans available. Financial aid application deadline: 6/30. • Application contact: Irma Kalkowski, Graduate Admissions Secretary, 410-532-5317. Fax: 410-532-5333. E-mail: gradadm@ndm.edu.

College of Our Lady of the Elms, Department of Education, Chicopee, MA 01013-2839. Offerings include general education administration (M Ed). Department faculty: 7 full-time (all women), 6 part-time (5 women). *Application deadline:* rolling. *Application fee:* $30. *Expenses:* Tuition $320 per credit. Fees $40 per year. • Sr. Kathleen M. Kirley, Dean of Continuing Education and Graduate Studies, 413-594-2761. Fax: 413-592-4871. Application contact: Dr. Mary Janeczek, Director, 413-594-2761.

College of Saint Elizabeth, Department of Education, Morristown, NJ 07960-6989. Offerings include education: human services leadership (MA). Department faculty: 4 full-time (3 women), 7 part-time (3 women). *Degree requirements:* Thesis or alternative, portfolio required, foreign language not required. *Average time to degree:* master's–2.5 years part-time. *Entrance requirements:* Interview, minimum undergraduate GPA of 3.0. Application deadline: 6/30 (priority date; rolling processing; 11/30 for spring admission). Application fee: $35. *Expenses:* Tuition $364 per credit. Fees $455 per year full-time, $70 per semester part-time. • Dr. Joan T. Walters, SC, Director of Graduate Program, 973-290-4374. Fax: 973-290-4389. E-mail: education@liza.st-elizabeth.edu.

The College of Saint Rose, School of Education, Educational Support Department, Program in Counseling, Albany, NY 12203-1419. Offerings include college student personnel (MS Ed). Program faculty: 2 full-time (1 woman), 3 part-time (1 woman). *Degree requirements:* Thesis or alternative, comprehensive exam. *Entrance requirements:* Interview, minimum undergraduate GPA of 3.0. Application deadline: 7/15 (priority date; rolling processing; 12/1 for spring admission). Application fee: $30. *Expenses:* Tuition $338 per credit. Fees $60 per year. • Application contact: Graduate Office, 518-454-5136. Fax: 518-458-5479. E-mail: ace@rosnet.strose.edu.

The College of Saint Rose, School of Education, Educational Support Department, Program in Educational Administration and Supervision, Albany, NY 12203-1419. Awards MS Ed, Certificate. Part-time and evening/weekend programs available. Faculty: 1 (woman) full-time, 3 part-time (2 women). Students: 13 part-time (9 women); includes 2 minority (both African Americans). Average age 31. In 1997, 3 master's awarded. *Degree requirements:* For master's, thesis or alternative, comprehensive exam required, foreign language not required. *Entrance requirements:* For master's, minimum undergraduate GPA of 3.0. Application deadline: 7/15 (priority date; rolling processing; 12/1 for spring admission). Application fee: $30. *Expenses:* Tuition $338 per credit. Fees $60 per year. *Financial aid:* Research assistantships, partial tuition waivers, and career-related internships or fieldwork available. Aid available to part-time students. Financial aid application deadline: 3/1; applicants required to submit FAFSA. • Dr. RoseAnne Fogarty, Head, 518-454-5125. Application contact: Graduate Office, 518-454-5136. Fax: 518-458-5479. E-mail: ace@rosnet.strose.edu.

College of Santa Fe, Department of Education, Program in At-Risk Youth, Santa Fe, NM 87505-7634. Offerings include educational administration (MA), leadership (MA). Program faculty: 7 full-time (5 women), 14 part-time (10 women). *Entrance requirements:* Minimum GPA of 3.0. Application deadline: rolling. Application fee: $25. *Expenses:* Tuition $237 per credit hour. Fees $25 per year. • Dr. Barbara Reider, Chair, Department of Education, 800-246-2673. Fax: 505-473-6510.

College of Staten Island of the City University of New York, Department of Education, Program in Educational Supervision and Administration, Staten Island, NY 10314-6600. Awards 6th Year Certificate. New students enter during summer. Evening/weekend programs available. Faculty: 2 full-time (1 woman), 4 part-time (1 woman). Students: 93 part-time (62 women); includes 6 minority (3 African Americans, 1 Asian American, 2 Hispanics). Average age 37. In 1997, 36 degrees awarded. *Entrance requirements:* Master's degree, 4 years of teaching experience. Application deadline: rolling. Application fee: $40. *Expenses:* Tuition $4350 per year full-time, $185 per credit part-time for state residents; $7600 per year full-time, $320 per credit part-time for nonresidents. Fees $106 per year full-time, $54 per year part-time. *Faculty research:* Educational restructuring, educational leadership. • Dr. David Seeley, Coordinator, 718-982-3735. Application contact: Earl Teasley, Director of Admissions, 718-982-2010. Fax: 718-982-2500.

College of the Southwest, School of Education and Professional Studies, Hobbs, NM 88240-9129. Offerings include educational administration (MS). Postbaccalaureate distance learning degree programs offered. School faculty: 4 full-time (all women), 6 part-time (2 women). *Entrance requirements:* GRE General Test (minimum combined score of 1200). Application deadline: 3/1 (priority date; rolling processing; 10/1 for spring admission). Application fee: $50. *Expenses:* Tuition $150 per credit hour. Fees $140 per year. • Dr. Marilyn Smith, Dean, 505-392-6561.

College of William and Mary, School of Education, Program in Education Policy, Planning, and Leadership, Williamsburg, VA 23187-8795. Awards M Ed, Ed D, PhD. Accredited by NCATE. Part-time and evening/weekend programs available. Students: 46 full-time (34 women), 97 part-time (67 women); includes 25 minority (20 African Americans, 2 Asian Americans, 3 Hispanics), 1 international. Average age 38. 93 applicants, 69% accepted. In 1997, 16 master's, 7 doctorates awarded. *Degree requirements:* For doctorate, dissertation required, foreign language not required. *Entrance requirements:* For master's, GRE or MAT, minimum GPA of 2.5. Application deadline: 2/15 (priority date). Application fee: $30. *Tuition:* $5262 per year full-time, $165 per semester hour part-time for state residents; $16,138 per year full-time, $500 per semester hour part-time for nonresidents. *Financial aid:* In 1997–98, 19 graduate assistantships (5 to first-year students) averaging $622 per month were awarded; research assistantships and career-related internships or fieldwork also available. Financial aid application deadline: 2/15. • Dr. James Stronge, Coordinator, 757-221-4300. E-mail: jhstro@facstaff.wm.edu.

Columbia International University, Graduate Program in Education, Columbia, SC 29230-3122. Offerings include educational administration (MA Ed). Program faculty: 4 full-time, 17 part-time. *Application deadline:* rolling. *Application fee:* $20. *Expenses:* Tuition $7410 per year full-time, $285 per semester hour part-time. Fees $150 per year. • Dr. Milt Uecker, Associate Dean for Education Programs, 803-754-4100. E-mail: muecker@ciu.edu. Application contact: Yvonne Miranda, Associate Director of Admissions, 803-754-4100 Ext. 3026. Fax: 803-786-4209. E-mail: yvonnem@ciu.edu.

Columbus State University, College of Education, Department of Educational Technology, Administration, and Foundations, Columbus, GA 31907-5645. Offers program in educational administration (M Ed, Ed S). Accredited by NCATE. *Degree requirements:* For master's, exit exam required, foreign language and thesis not required; for Ed S, thesis or alternative required, foreign language not required. *Entrance requirements:* For master's, GRE General Test (minimum combined score of 800), MAT (minimum score 44); for Ed S, GRE General Test (minimum combined score of 900), MAT (minimum score 44). Application deadline: 7/10 (priority date; rolling processing; 10/23 for spring admission). Application fee: $20. *Tuition:* $1718 per year full-time, $151 per semester hour part-time for state residents; $6218 per year full-time, $401 per semester hour part-time for nonresidents. *Financial aid:* Research assistantships, teaching assistantships, full tuition waivers, Federal Work-Study, institutionally sponsored loans, and career-related internships or fieldwork available. Aid available to part-time students. Financial aid application deadline: 7/15; applicants required to submit FAFSA. • Dr. Pat Barnes, Acting Chair, 706-568-2250. Fax: 706-569-3134. E-mail: barnes_pat@colstate.edu. Application contact: Katie Thornton, Graduate Admissions, 706-568-2279. Fax: 706-568-2462. E-mail: thornton_katie@colstate.edu.

Concordia University, School of Graduate Studies, 1530 Concordia West, Irvine, CA 92612-3299. Offerings include Christian leadership (MA), educational administration (MA). School faculty: 12 full-time (4 women), 19 part-time (13 women), 18 FTE. *Degree requirements:* Thesis or alternative. *Entrance requirements:* GRE General Test (minimum combined score of 900), minimum GPA of 3.0. Application deadline: 8/15 (priority date; rolling processing; 11/15 for spring admission). Application fee: $0. *Tuition:* $320 per unit. • Dr. Thomas Doyle, Dean of the School of Graduate Studies, 949-854-8002. Fax: 949-854-6854. E-mail: doyletj@cui.edu.

Concordia University, Program in School Administration, River Forest, IL 60305-1499. Offers school administration (MA, CAS), supervision of instruction (MA, CAS). Accredited by NCATE. MA offered jointly with the Chicago Consortium of Colleges and Universities. Part-time and evening/weekend programs available. Faculty: 10 full-time (2 women), 12 part-time (3 women). Students: 106 (69 women); includes 43 minority (41 African Americans, 1 Asian American, 1 Hispanic). In 1997, 58 master's awarded. *Degree requirements:* For master's, comprehensive exams required, thesis optional, foreign language not required; for CAS, thesis, final project required, foreign language not required. *Entrance requirements:* For master's, minimum GPA of 2.9; for CAS, master's degree. Application deadline: rolling. Application fee: $0. *Tuition:* $372 per semester hour. *Financial aid:* Research assistantships, institutionally sponsored loans available. Aid available to part-time students. *Faculty research:* Effectiveness of urban Lutheran schools in impacting children's faith development, effectiveness of centers for urban ministries in supporting urban ministry and teaching science. • Dr. Cynthia Kuck, Coordinator, 708-209-3127. Application contact: Mary Betancourt, Admissions Secretary, 708-209-4093. Fax: 708-209-3454. E-mail: crfdngrad@curf.edu.

Concordia University, Graduate Programs in Education, Program in Educational Administration, Seward, NE 68434-1599. Awards M Ed. Accredited by NCATE. Part-time programs available. Faculty: 7 full-time (0 women), 2 part-time (0 women). Students: 1 full-time (0 women), 43 part-time (10 women); includes 1 minority (Native American), 3 international. 8 applicants, 100% accepted. In 1997, 4 degrees awarded (100% found work related to degree). *Degree requirements:* Thesis or alternative required, foreign language not required. *Entrance requirements:* GRE, MAT, or NTE, minimum GPA of 3.0, BS in education or equivalent. Application deadline: 8/1 (priority date; rolling processing; 12/1 for spring admission). Application fee: $15. *Tuition:* $127 per hour. *Financial aid:* Federal Work-Study, institutionally sponsored loans available. Aid available to part-time students. Financial aid applicants required to submit FAFSA. • Dr. Lee Schluckebier, Coordinator, 402-643-7377.

Concordia University, College of Education, Portland, OR 97211-6099. Offerings include educational administration (M Ed). College faculty: 8 part-time (3 women). *Application deadline:* rolling. *Application fee:* $35. *Tuition:* $350 per credit. • Dr. Joseph Mannion, Dean, 503-493-6233. Application contact: Dr. Peter Johnson, Director of Admissions, 503-280-8501.

Concordia University Wisconsin, Division of Graduate Studies, Program in Student Personnel Administration, Mequon, WI 53097-2402. Awards MSSPA. *Degree requirements:* Thesis or alternative, comprehensive exam. *Entrance requirements:* TOEFL (minimum score 550). Application fee: $25 ($125 for international students). *Tuition:* $250 per credit. *Financial aid:* Application deadline 8/1. • Dr. Andrew Luptak, Director, 414-243-4331.

Concordia University Wisconsin, Division of Graduate Studies, Education Department, Program in Educational Administration, Mequon, WI 53097-2402. Awards MS. Part-time and evening/weekend programs available. Postbaccalaureate distance learning degree programs offered (minimal on-campus study). *Degree requirements:* Thesis or alternative, comprehensive exam. *Entrance requirements:* TOEFL (minimum score 550), minimum GPA of 3.0, teaching license. *Tuition:* $250 per credit. *Financial aid:* Application deadline 8/1. • Dr. James Juergensen, Director, 414-243-4214. E-mail: jjuergen@bach.cuw.edu. Application contact: Brooke Tireman, Graduate Admissions, 414-243-4248. Fax: 414-243-4428. E-mail: btireman@back.cuw.edu.

Converse College, Department of Education, Program in Educational Administration, Spartanburg, SC 29302-0006. Awards Ed S. Part-time programs available. Faculty: 7 full-time, 15 part-time. Students: 28 part-time (20 women); includes 1 minority (African American). Average age 35. 9 applicants, 100% accepted. In 1997, 9 degrees awarded. *Entrance requirements:* NTE, minimum GPA of 3.0. Application deadline: 5/1 (priority date; rolling processing; 1/30 for spring admission). Application fee: $35. *Tuition:* $185 per credit. • Dr. Martha T. Lovett, Dean of Graduate Education and Special Programs, Department of Education, 864-596-9082. Fax: 864-596-9221. E-mail: martylovett@converse.edu.

Cornell University, Graduate Fields of Agriculture and Life Sciences, Field of Education, Ithaca, NY 14853-0001. Offerings include philosophical and social foundations: educational administration (MPS, MS, PhD). Terminal master's awarded for partial completion of doctoral program. Faculty: 26 full-time. *Degree requirements:* For doctorate, dissertation required, foreign language not required. *Entrance requirements:* For doctorate, GRE General Test or MAT, TOEFL. Application deadline: 5/1. Application fee: $65. Electronic applications accepted. • Director of Graduate Studies, 607-255-4278. Application contact: Graduate Field Assistant, 607-255-4278. E-mail: edgrfld@cornell.edu.

Creighton University, College of Arts and Sciences, Department of Education, Program in Educational Administration, Omaha, NE 68178-0001. Awards MS. Faculty: 3 full-time. Students: 5 part-time (3 women). In 1997, 6 degrees awarded. *Entrance requirements:* GRE General Test, TOEFL (minimum score 550). Application deadline: 3/1 (rolling processing). Application fee: $30. *Expenses:* Tuition $402 per credit hour. Fees $536 per year full-time, $28 per semester part-time. • Dr. Barbara Brock, Director, 402-280-2551. Application contact: Dr. Barbara J. Braden, Dean, Graduate School, 402-280-2870. Fax: 402-280-5762.

Cumberland College, Program in Elementary/Secondary Principalship, 6178 College Station Drive, Williamsburg, KY 40769-1372. Awards Certificate. Faculty: 4 full-time (2 women), 5 part-time (2 women). Students: 0. *Entrance requirements:* Master's degree, 3 years of teaching experience. Application deadline: 8/26 (rolling processing). Application fee: $25. *Tuition:* $175 per credit. • Application contact: Erica Harris, Admissions Office, 606-539-4241.

Dalhousie University, School of Education, Halifax, NS B3H 3J5, Canada. Offerings include educational administration (MA, M Ed). Program being phased out; applicants no longer accepted. School faculty: 19 full-time, 12 part-time. *Degree requirements:* Thesis required (for some programs), foreign language not required. • Dr. K. C. Sullivan, Director, 902-494-3724.

Dallas Baptist University, Dorothy M. Bush College of Education, Education Program, Dallas, TX 75211-9299. Offerings include educational organization and administration (M Ed). Program faculty: 15 full-time (4 women), 5 part-time (3 women). *Entrance requirements:* GRE General Test, TOEFL (minimum score 550). Application deadline: rolling. Application fee: $25. *Tuition:* $285 per hour. • Dr. Bill Gilbert, Director, 214-333-5404. Fax: 214-333-5551. Application contact: Travis Bundrick, Director of Graduate Programs, 214-333-5243. Fax: 214-333-5579. E-mail: graduate@dbu.edu.

Delta State University, School of Education, Division of Curriculum, Instruction, Leadership and Research, Program in Administration and Supervision, Cleveland, MS 38733-0001. Offers administration (M Ed), administration and supervision (Ed S), elementary principalship (M Ed), elementary supervision (M Ed), secondary principalship (M Ed), secondary supervision (M Ed). Accredited by NCATE. Part-time and evening/weekend programs available. *Degree requirements:* For master's, thesis optional, foreign language not required. *Entrance requirements:* For

Directory: Educational Administration

Delta State University (continued)
master's, GRE General Test (minimum combined score of 800) or MAT (minimum score 34); for Ed S, master's degree, teaching certificate. Application deadline: 8/1 (priority date; rolling processing). Application fee: $0. *Tuition:* $2596 per year full-time, $121 per semester hour part-time for state residents; $5546 per year full-time, $285 per semester hour part-time for nonresidents. *Financial aid:* Research assistantships, Federal Work-Study, institutionally sponsored loans, and career-related internships or fieldwork available. Aid available to part-time students. Financial aid application deadline: 6/1. • Application contact: Dr. John Thornell, Dean of Graduate Studies and Continuing Education, 601-846-4310. Fax: 601-846-4016.

DePaul University, School of Education, Program in Educational Leadership, Chicago, IL 60604-2287. Offers administration and supervision (MA, M Ed), Catholic school leadership (MA, M Ed), physical education (MA, M Ed). Accredited by NCATE. Faculty: 2 full-time (1 woman), 2 part-time (0 women). Students: 28 full-time (19 women), 46 part-time (35 women); includes 32 minority (28 African Americans, 4 Hispanics), 2 international. Average age 36. 37 applicants, 81% accepted. In 1997, 6 degrees awarded. *Degree requirements:* Oral exam or thesis required, foreign language not required. *Entrance requirements:* Interview, minimum GPA of 2.75, work experience. Application deadline: rolling. Application fee: $25. *Expenses:* Tuition $320 per credit hour. Fees $30 per year. *Financial aid:* Career-related internships or fieldwork available. • Dr. Barbara Sizemore, Dean, School of Education, 312-325-7000 Ext. 1666. Fax: 312-325-7748. Application contact: Director of Graduate Admissions, 312-325-7000 Ext. 1666. E-mail: mmurphy@wppost.depaul.edu.

Doane College, Program in Education, Crete, NE 68333-2430. Offerings include educational leadership (M Ed). Accredited by NCATE. *Degree requirements:* Thesis required, foreign language not required. *Average time to degree:* master's–2.7 years part-time. *Entrance requirements:* Minimum GPA of 2.5. Application deadline: rolling. Application fee: $25. *Tuition:* $135 per credit hour. • Dr. Marilyn Kent Byrne, Dean, 402-826-8604. Fax: 402-826-8278. E-mail: mbyrne@doane.edu. Application contact: Wilma Daddario, Director, Office of Graduate Studies, 402-464-1223. Fax: 402-466-4228. E-mail: wdaddario@doane.edu.

Dominican University, Graduate School of Education, River Forest, IL 60305-1099. Offerings include educational administration (MA). School faculty: 9 full-time (7 women), 14 part-time (11 women), 14 FTE. *Application deadline:* 8/15 (priority date; rolling processing; 1/16 for spring admission). *Application fee:* $25. *Expenses:* Tuition $6120 per year full-time, $1020 per course part-time. Fees $10 per course. • Sr. Colleen McNicholas, Dean, 708-524-6830. E-mail: educate@email.dom.edu. Application contact: Deborah Davison, Coordinator of Admissions, 708-524-6922. Fax: 708-524-6665. E-mail: educate@email.dom.edu.

Dowling College, Professional Program in Educational Administration, Oakdale, NY 11769-1999. Offers computers in education (PD), school administration and supervision (PD), school district administration (PD). Part-time and evening/weekend programs available. Faculty: 1 full-time (0 women), 4 part-time (2 women). Students: 33 part-time (19 women). Average age 32. In 1997, 33 degrees awarded. *Degree requirements:* Comprehensive exam required, foreign language and thesis not required. *Entrance requirements:* Teaching certificate. Application deadline: 9/1 (priority date; rolling processing). Application fee: $0. *Financial aid:* Federal Work-Study and career-related internships or fieldwork available. Aid available to part-time students. Financial aid application deadline: 4/30. • Dr. Jerome Traiger, Discipline Coordinator, 516-244-3459. Fax: 516-244-5036. Application contact: Kate Rowe, Director of Admissions, 516-244-3030. Fax: 516-563-3827. E-mail: rowek@dowling.edu.

Drake University, School of Education, Department of Leadership and Adult Development, Program in Educational Administration, Des Moines, IA 50311-4516. Awards MSE, Ed D, Ed S. Faculty: 4 full-time (3 women), 7 part-time (0 women). Students: 3 full-time (all women), 93 part-time (57 women); includes 1 minority (African American), 1 international. 71 applicants, 85% accepted. In 1997, 55 master's, 11 doctorates awarded. *Degree requirements:* For master's and Ed S, thesis or alternative; for doctorate, dissertation. *Entrance requirements:* For master's, GRE General Test (minimum combined score of 1000) or MAT (minimum score 36); for doctorate and Ed S, GRE General Test (minimum combined score of 1000) or MAT (minimum score 43). Application deadline: rolling. Application fee: $25. *Tuition:* $16,000 per year full-time, $260 per hour (minimum) part-time. *Financial aid:* Career-related internships or fieldwork available. Aid available to part-time students. • Application contact: Ann J. Martin, Graduate Coordinator, 515-271-3871. Fax: 515-271-2831. E-mail: ajm@admin.drake.edu.

Duquesne University, School of Education, Interdisciplinary Doctoral Program for Educational Leaders, Pittsburgh, PA 15282-0001. Awards Ed D. Faculty: 57. Students: 44 full-time; includes 6 African Americans. Average age 36. 0 applicants. In 1997, 15 degrees awarded. *Degree requirements:* Dissertation required, foreign language not required. *Entrance requirements:* MAT, interviews, writing sample. Application deadline: 3/29. Application fee: $100. *Expenses:* Tuition $481 per credit. Fees $39 per credit. *Financial aid:* Teaching assistantships, partial tuition waivers, institutionally sponsored loans, and career-related internships or fieldwork available. Aid available to part-time students. Financial aid application deadline: 5/31. *Faculty research:* Leader effectiveness, shared decision making, organizational climate and health, leader authenticity. • Dr. James Henderson, Dean, School of Education, 412-396-5577. Application contact: Director of Education Services, 412-396-6114. Fax: 412-396-5585.

Duquesne University, School of Education, Department of Foundations and Leadership, Program in School Administration and Supervision, Pittsburgh, PA 15282-0001. Offers school administration (MS Ed), including elementary administration, secondary administration; school supervision (MS Ed). Faculty: 3 full-time (1 woman), 2 part-time (0 women). Students: 70. 25 applicants, 52% accepted. In 1997, 23 degrees awarded. *Average time to degree:* master's–2 years full-time, 3.5 years part-time. *Entrance requirements:* MAT. Application deadline: 8/1 (rolling processing; 12/1 for spring admission). Application fee: $40. *Expenses:* Tuition $481 per credit. Fees $39 per credit. • Application contact: Dr. Wil Barber, Coordinator, 412-396-5192. Fax: 412-396-5585.

East Carolina University, School of Education, Department of Educational Leadership, Greenville, NC 27858-4353. Offers programs in educational administration (Ed S), educational leadership (Ed D), school administration (MSA), supervision (MA Ed, Ed S). Accredited by NCATE. Part-time and evening/weekend programs available. Faculty: 5 full-time (1 woman). Students: 54 full-time (39 women), 150 part-time (95 women); includes 50 minority (47 African Americans, 1 Asian American, 1 Hispanic, 1 Native American). Average age 37. 138 applicants, 81% accepted. In 1997, 58 master's, 4 doctorates, 17 Ed Ss awarded. *Degree requirements:* For master's, comprehensive exams required, thesis optional; for doctorate, dissertation. *Entrance requirements:* For master's, GRE General Test or MAT, TOEFL; for doctorate and Ed S, master's degree. Application deadline: 6/1 (priority date; rolling processing). Application fee: $40. *Tuition:* $1886 per year full-time, $472 per semester (minimum) part-time for state residents; $9156 per year full-time, $2289 per semester (minimum) part-time for nonresidents. *Financial aid:* Research assistantships, teaching assistantships, Federal Work-Study available. Aid available to part-time students. Financial aid application deadline: 6/1. • Dr. Edwin Bell, Chairperson, 252-328-6862. Fax: 252-328-4219. E-mail: belle@mail.ecu.edu. Application contact: Dr. Paul D. Tschetter, Associate Dean, 252-328-6012. Fax: 252-328-6071. E-mail: grad@mail.ecu.edu.

Eastern Illinois University, College of Education and Professional Studies, Department of Educational Administration, 600 Lincoln Avenue, Charleston, IL 61920-3099. Offers program in educational administration and supervision (MS Ed, Ed S). Accredited by NCATE. Part-time and evening/weekend programs available. Faculty: 5 full-time (1 woman). Students: 11 full-time (7 women), 218 part-time (136 women); includes 9 minority (8 African Americans, 1 Asian American). In 1997, 78 master's, 21 Ed Ss awarded. *Degree requirements:* For master's, fieldwork required, foreign language and thesis not required; for Ed S, thesis required, foreign language not required. *Application deadline:* 7/31 (priority date; rolling processing). *Application fee:* $25. *Expenses:* Tuition $3459 per year full-time, $96 per semester hour part-time for state residents; $10,377 per year full-time, $288 per semester hour part-time for nonresidents. Fees $1566 per year full-time, $37 per semester hour part-time. *Financial aid:* In 1997–98, 4 research assistantships were awarded; career-related internships or fieldwork also available. • Dr. Beverly Findley, Chairperson, 217-581-2919. Fax: 217-581-7147. E-mail: cfbcf@eiu.edu.

Eastern Kentucky University, College of Education, Department of Administration, Counseling, and Educational Studies, Richmond, KY 40475-3101. Offers programs in administration and supervision (Ed S), community counseling (MA), elementary counseling (MA Ed), secondary counseling (MA Ed), student personnel counseling (MA, Ed S). Accredited by NCATE. Part-time programs available. Postbaccalaureate distance learning degree programs offered. Faculty: 17 full-time (5 women), 8 part-time (4 women), 19 FTE. Students: 242. In 1997, 79 master's awarded. *Degree requirements:* For Ed S, thesis, research project. *Entrance requirements:* GRE General Test, minimum GPA of 2.5. Application fee: $0. *Tuition:* $2390 per year full-time, $133 per credit hour part-time for state residents; $6630 per year full-time, $365 per credit hour part-time for nonresidents. *Financial aid:* In 1997–98, 2 research assistantships totaling $5,500, 10 scholarships were awarded; teaching assistantships, Federal Work-Study, and career-related internships or fieldwork also available. Aid available to part-time students. • Dr. Leonard Burns, Chair, 606-622-1124. E-mail: eadburns@acs.eku.edu.

Eastern Michigan University, College of Education, Department of Leadership and Counseling, Program in Educational Leadership, Ypsilanti, MI 48197. Awards MA, Ed D, SPA. Accredited by NCATE. Evening/weekend programs available. In 1997, 87 master's, 5 doctorates, 10 SPAs awarded. *Degree requirements:* For doctorate, dissertation required, foreign language not required; for SPA, thesis or alternative required, foreign language not required. *Entrance requirements:* For master's, GRE General Test, TOEFL (minimum score 550); for doctorate, GRE General Test (score in 55th percentile or higher). Application deadline: 5/15 (priority date; rolling processing; 3/15 for spring admission). Application fee: $30. *Expenses:* Tuition $2691 per year full-time, $150 per credit hour part-time for state residents; $6300 per year full-time, $350 per credit hour part-time for nonresidents. Fees $368 per year full-time, $88 per semester (minimum) part-time. *Financial aid:* Fellowships, teaching assistantships available. Aid available to part-time students. Financial aid application deadline: 3/15; applicants required to submit FAFSA. • Dr. Jackie Tracey, Coordinator, 734-487-0255.

Eastern Nazarene College, Graduate Studies, Division of Education, Quincy, MA 02170-2999. Offerings include principal (Certificate), program development and supervision (M Ed, Certificate), special education administrator (Certificate), supervisor (Certificate). M Ed and Certificate also available through weekend program for administration, special needs, and reading only. Division faculty: 9 full-time (5 women), 11 part-time (5 women). *Entrance requirements:* For master's, TOEFL (minimum score 500). Application deadline: rolling. Application fee: $35. *Expenses:* Tuition $350 per credit. Fees $125 per semester full-time, $15 per semester part-time. • Dr. Lorne Ranstrom, Chair, 617-745-3528. Application contact: Cleo P. Cakridas, Graduate Enrollment Counselor, 617-745-3870. Fax: 617-745-3907. E-mail: cakridac@enc.edu.

Eastern Washington University, College of Education and Human Development, Department of Education, Program in Administration—School Principal, Cheney, WA 99004-2431. Awards M Ed. Accredited by NCATE. *Degree requirements:* Thesis or alternative, comprehensive exam. *Entrance requirements:* Minimum GPA of 3.0. Application deadline: 4/1 (priority date; rolling processing; 1/15 for spring admission). Application fee: $35. *Tuition:* $4200 per year full-time, $140 per credit part-time for state residents; $12,780 per year full-time, $415 per credit part-time for nonresidents. *Financial aid:* Application deadline 2/1. • Dr. Harvey Alvy, Adviser, 509-359-2207.

Eastern Washington University, College of Education and Human Development, Department of Education, Program in Supervising (Clinic) Teaching, Cheney, WA 99004-2431. Awards M Ed. Accredited by NCATE. *Degree requirements:* Comprehensive exam required, thesis not required. *Entrance requirements:* Minimum GPA of 3.0. Application deadline: 4/1 (priority date; rolling processing; 1/15 for spring admission). Application fee: $35. *Tuition:* $4200 per year full-time, $140 per credit part-time for state residents; $12,780 per year full-time, $415 per credit part-time for nonresidents. *Financial aid:* Application deadline 2/1. • Dr. William Shreeve, Adviser, 509-359-6492.

East Tennessee State University, College of Education, Department of Educational Leadership and Policy Analysis, Johnson City, TN 37614-0734. Offers programs in educational leadership (M Ed, Ed D, Ed S), supervision of instruction (M Ed). Accredited by NCATE. Faculty: 9 full-time (2 women), 14 part-time (7 women). Students: 28 full-time (17 women), 123 part-time (77 women); includes 10 minority (9 African Americans, 1 Asian American), 5 international. Average age 42. 40 applicants, 30% accepted. In 1997, 13 master's, 23 doctorates, 7 Ed Ss awarded. Terminal master's awarded for partial completion of doctoral program. *Degree requirements:* For master's, oral exam or thesis required, foreign language not required; for doctorate, dissertation, oral and written exams required, foreign language not required; for Ed S, internship, practicum required, foreign language and thesis not required. *Entrance requirements:* For master's, TOEFL (minimum score 550), interview, minimum GPA of 2.75, teacher certification, interview; for doctorate, GRE General Test, GRE Subject Test, TOEFL (minimum score 550); for Ed S, GRE General Test, TOEFL (minimum score 550), teacher certification. Application deadline: 7/15 (priority date; rolling processing; 11/1 for spring admission). Application fee: $25 ($35 for international students). *Tuition:* $2944 per year full-time, $158 per credit hour part-time for state residents; $7770 per year full-time, $369 per credit hour part-time for nonresidents. *Financial aid:* In 1997–98, 10 fellowships (5 to first-year students) were awarded; institutionally sponsored loans and career-related internships or fieldwork also available. Financial aid application deadline: 5/15. • Dr. Ronald A. Lindahl, Chair, 423-439-4226.

Edgewood College, Program in Education, Madison, WI 53711-1998. Offerings include director of instruction (Certificate), director of special education and pupil services (Certificate), educational administration (MA), school business administration (Certificate), school principalship K-12 (Certificate). One or more programs accredited by NCATE. Program faculty: 6 full-time (3 women), 3 part-time (0 women), 7 FTE. *Application deadline:* 8/1 (priority date; rolling processing). *Application fee:* $25. *Tuition:* $330 per credit. • Dr. Joseph Schmiedicke, Chair, 608-257-4861 Ext. 2293. Application contact: Sr. Lucille Marie Frost, Assistant Dean of Graduate Programs, 608-254-4861 Ext. 2382. Fax: 608-257-1455.

Edinboro University of Pennsylvania, School of Education, Department of Educational Services, Program in School Administration, Edinboro, PA 16444. Offers elementary school administration (M Ed, Certificate), secondary school administration (M Ed, Certificate). Evening/weekend programs available. Students: 5 full-time (0 women), 34 part-time (17 women); includes 2 minority (both African Americans). Average age 35. In 1997, 21 master's, 16 Certificates awarded. *Entrance requirements:* For master's, GRE or MAT (score in 30th percentile or higher). Application deadline: rolling. Application fee: $25. *Expenses:* Tuition $3468 per year full-time, $193 per credit part-time for state residents; $6236 per year full-time, $346 per credit part-time for nonresidents. Fees $898 per year full-time, $50 per semester (minimum) part-time. *Financial aid:* In 1997–98, 2 assistantships were awarded; career-related internships or fieldwork also available. • Dr. Donald Beckman, Head, 814-732-2355. E-mail: dbeckman@edinboro.edu. Application contact: Dr. Philip Kerstetter, Dean of Graduate Studies, 814-732-2856. Fax: 814-732-2611. E-mail: kerstetter@edinboro.edu.

Emporia State University, School of Graduate Studies, The Teachers College, Division of School Leadership/Middle and Secondary Teacher Education, Program in Educational Administration, Emporia, KS 66801-5087. Offers elementary administration (MS), secondary administration (MS). Accredited by NCATE. Part-time programs available. Students: 4 full-time (all women), 34 part-time (18 women); includes 3 minority (2 African Americans, 1 Hispanic). 4 applicants, 0% accepted. In 1997, 21 degrees awarded. *Degree requirements:* Comprehensive exam or thesis required, foreign language not required. *Entrance requirements:* GRE General Test (minimum score 480 on each section) or MAT (minimum score 42), TOEFL (minimum score 550). Application deadline: 8/15 (priority date; rolling processing). Application fee: $30 ($75 for international students). Electronic applications accepted. *Tuition:* $2300 per year full-time, $103 per credit hour part-time for state residents; $6012 per year full-time, $258 per credit hour part-time for nonresidents. *Financial aid:* Federal Work-Study, institutionally sponsored loans, and career-related internships or fieldwork available. Financial aid application deadline: 3/15; applicants required to submit FAFSA. • Dr. Jerry Will, Chair, Division of School Leadership/ Middle and Secondary Teacher Education, 316-341-5777.

Fayetteville State University, Programs in Educational Leadership and Secondary Education, 1200 Murchison Road, Fayetteville, NC 28301-4298. Offerings in biology (MAT), educational leadership and secondary education (MA Ed), history (MAT), mathematics (MAT), political science (MAT), sociology (MAT). One or more programs accredited by NCATE. Part-time and evening/weekend programs available. *Degree requirements:* Internship, written and oral exams required, foreign language and thesis not required. *Entrance requirements:* GRE or MAT, minimum GPA of 2.5. Application deadline: 8/1 (rolling processing; 12/15 for spring admission). Application fee: $20. *Tuition:* $1498 per year full-time, $327 per semester (minimum) part-time for state residents; $8768 per year full-time, $2144 per semester (minimum) part-time for nonresidents.

Fielding Institute, Program in Educational Leadership and Change, Santa Barbara, CA 93105-3538. Offers educational leadership (Ed D). Faculty: 10 full-time (6 women), 34 part-time (22 women). Students: 112 full-time (80 women); includes 77 minority (69 African Americans, 6 Asian Americans, 2 Native Americans). 112 applicants, 95% accepted. *Degree requirements:* Dissertation required, foreign language not required. *Application deadline:* 6/1 (3/1 for spring admission). *Application fee:* $75. *Tuition:* $11,550 per year. *Financial aid:* Partial tuition waivers available. Financial aid application deadline: 4/1. • Dr. Willy DeMarcell Smith, Director, 805-687-1099 Ext. 2921. Application contact: Judy Brown, Admissions Counselor, 805-687-1099 Ext. 4020. Fax: 805-687-9793. E-mail: jsbrown@fielding.edu.

Fitchburg State College, Program in Consultation and Peer Leadership, Fitchburg, MA 01420-2697. Awards CAGS. Accredited by NCATE. Part-time and evening/weekend programs available. *Entrance requirements:* Master's degree, teaching certification. Application deadline: rolling. Application fee: $10. *Expenses:* Tuition $147 per credit. Fees $55 per semester. *Financial aid:* Graduate assistantships, Federal Work-Study available. Aid available to part-time students. Financial aid application deadline: 3/30; applicants required to submit FAFSA. • Dr. Anne May, Chair, 978-665-3238. Fax: 978-665-3658. E-mail: dgce@fsc.edu. Application contact: James DuPont, Director of Admissions, 978-665-3144. Fax: 978-665-4540. E-mail: admissions@fsc.edu.

Fitchburg State College, Program in Educational Leadership and Management, Fitchburg, MA 01420-2697. Awards M Ed, CAGS. Accredited by NCATE. Part-time and evening/weekend programs available. *Degree requirements:* For master's, comprehensive exam required, foreign language and thesis not required. *Entrance requirements:* For master's, GRE General Test or MAT (minimum score 47), interview, 3 years of teaching experience, teaching certificate; for CAGS, master's degree. Application deadline: rolling. Application fee: $10. *Expenses:* Tuition $147 per credit. Fees $55 per semester. *Financial aid:* Graduate assistantships, Federal Work-Study available. Aid available to part-time students. Financial aid application deadline: 3/30; applicants required to submit FAFSA. • Dr. Ronald Colbert, Chairperson, 978-665-3493. Fax: 978-665-3658. E-mail: dgce@fsc.edu. Application contact: James DuPont, Director of Admissions, 978-665-3144. Fax: 978-665-4540. E-mail: admissions@fsc.edu.

Fitchburg State College, Program in Professional Staff Development in Education, Fitchburg, MA 01420-2697. Awards CAGS. Accredited by NCATE. Part-time and evening/weekend programs available. *Entrance requirements:* Interview, master's degree. Application deadline: rolling. Application fee: $10. *Expenses:* Tuition $147 per credit. Fees $55 per semester. *Financial aid:* Application deadline 3/30; applicants required to submit FAFSA. • Dr. George Bohrer, Chair, 978-665-3418. Fax: 978-665-3658. E-mail: dgce@fsc.edu. Application contact: James DuPont, Director of Admissions, 978-665-3144. Fax: 978-665-4540. E-mail: admissions@fsc.edu.

Florida Agricultural and Mechanical University, Division of Graduate Studies, Research, and Continuing Education, College of Education, Department of Educational Leadership and Human Services, Tallahassee, FL 32307-3200. Offerings include administration and supervision (M Ed, MS Ed). Accredited by NCATE. *Entrance requirements:* GRE General Test (minimum combined score of 1000), minimum GPA of 3.0. Application deadline: 5/13. Application fee: $20. *Expenses:* Tuition $140 per credit hour for state residents; $484 per credit hour for nonresidents. Fees $130 per year. • Dr. Ada Burnette, Chairperson, 850-599-3191. Fax: 850-561-2211.

Florida Atlantic University, College of Education, Department of Educational Leadership, Boca Raton, FL 33431-0991. Offers programs in adult/community education (M Ed, Ed D, Ed S), educational leadership (M Ed, Ed D, Ed S). Accredited by NCATE. Part-time programs available. Faculty: 13 full-time (4 women), 6 part-time (2 women). Students: 40 full-time (30 women), 214 part-time (151 women); includes 35 minority (22 African Americans, 13 Hispanics), 2 international. Average age 31. 146 applicants, 75% accepted. In 1997, 45 master's, 11 doctorates, 8 Ed Ss awarded. *Degree requirements:* For doctorate, dissertation, departmental qualifying exam required, foreign language not required; for Ed S, departmental qualifying exam required, foreign language and thesis not required. *Entrance requirements:* For master's, GRE General Test, minimum GPA of 3.0 during previous 2 years; for doctorate, GRE General Test, GRE Subject Test, minimum GPA of 3.0; for Ed S, GRE General Test, GRE Subject Test. Application deadline: rolling. Application fee: $20. *Expenses:* Tuition $2520 per year full-time, $140 per credit hour part-time for state residents; $8712 per year full-time, $484 per credit hour part-time for nonresidents. Fees $5 per year (minimum). *Financial aid:* In 1997–98, 6 students received aid, including 1 fellowship, 2 research assistantships averaging $800 per month, 2 teaching assistantships averaging $800 per month; career-related internships or fieldwork also available. *Faculty research:* Self-directed learning, school reform issues, legal issues, mentoring. • Dr. John Pisapia, Chairperson, 561-297-3550.

Florida Atlantic University, College of Education, Department of Exceptional Student Education, Boca Raton, FL 33431-0991. Offerings include special education administration (Ed D). Accredited by NCATE. Department faculty: 10 full-time (7 women), 4 part-time (2 women). *Degree requirements:* Computer language, dissertation required, foreign language not required. *Entrance requirements:* GRE General Test (minimum combined score of 1000), GRE Subject Test. Application deadline: rolling. Application fee: $20. *Expenses:* Tuition $2520 per year full-time, $140 per credit hour part-time for state residents; $8712 per year full-time, $484 per credit hour part-time for nonresidents. Fees $5 per year (minimum). • Dr. Mary Lou Caldwell, Chairperson, 561-297-3280.

Florida Gulf Coast University, College of Professional Studies, School of Education, Program in Educational Leadership, Fort Myers, FL 33965-6565. Awards M Ed. Part-time and evening/weekend programs available. Faculty: 2 full-time (0 women), 4 part-time (2 women), 4 FTE. Students: 30 part-time (20 women). Average age 30. 25 applicants, 88% accepted. In 1997, 25 degrees awarded (100% found work related to degree). *Degree requirements:* Thesis or alternative, learning and professional portfolios required, foreign language not required. *Entrance requirements:* GRE General Test (minimum combined score of 800), MAT (minimum score 40), minimum GPA of 3.0. Application fee: $20. Electronic applications accepted. *Faculty research:* Inclusion, technology in teaching, curriculum development in educational leadership. • Application contact: Tom Valesky, Coordinator, 941-590-7793. E-mail: tvalesky@fgcu.edu.

Florida International University, College of Education, Department of Educational Leadership and Policy Studies, Program in Educational Administration and Supervision, Miami, FL 33199. Awards Ed D. Accredited by NCATE. Part-time and evening/weekend programs available. Students: 2 full-time (0 women), 22 part-time (11 women); includes 8 minority (4 African Americans, 2 Asian Americans, 2 Hispanics). Average age 39. 9 applicants, 33% accepted. *Degree requirements:* Dissertation required, foreign language not required. *Entrance requirements:* GRE General Test (minimum combined score of 1000), teaching certificate. Application deadline: 4/1 (priority date; rolling processing; 10/1 for spring admission). Application fee: $20. *Expenses:* Tuition $138 per credit hour for state residents; $482 per credit hour for nonresidents. Fees $46 per semester. *Financial aid:* In 1997–98, 3 teaching assistantships were awarded; research assistantships also available. • Dr. Kingsley Banya, Chairperson, Department of Educational Leadership and Policy Studies, 305-348-2724. Fax: 305-348-2081. E-mail: banyak@fiu.edu.

Florida International University, College of Education, Department of Educational Leadership and Policy Studies, Program in Educational Leadership, Miami, FL 33199. Awards Ed D, Ed S. Accredited by NCATE. Part-time and evening/weekend programs available. Students: 30 part-time (18 women); includes 20 minority (1 African American, 1 Asian American, 18 Hispanics). Average age 33. 14 applicants, 21% accepted. *Degree requirements:* For doctorate, dissertation required, foreign language not required. *Application deadline:* 4/1 (priority date; rolling processing; 10/1 for spring admission). *Application fee:* $20. *Expenses:* Tuition $138 per credit hour for state residents; $482 per credit hour for nonresidents. Fees $46 per semester. *Financial aid:* Research assistantships, teaching assistantships available. • Dr. Kingsley Banya, Chairperson, Department of Educational Leadership and Policy Studies, 305-348-2724. Fax: 305-348-2081. E-mail: banyak@fiu.edu.

Florida State University, College of Education, Department of Educational Leadership, Program in Educational Administration/Leadership, Tallahassee, FL 32306. Offers educational administration/leadership (MS, Ed D, PhD, Ed S), policy planning and analysis (MS, Ed D, PhD, Ed S). Part-time and evening/weekend programs available. Faculty: 5 full-time (1 woman), 4 part-time (2 women). Students: 12 full-time (7 women), 81 part-time (52 women); includes 15 minority (12 African Americans, 2 Asian Americans, 1 Hispanic). 66 applicants, 85% accepted. In 1997, 20 master's, 11 doctorates awarded. Terminal master's awarded for partial completion of doctoral program. *Degree requirements:* For master's and Ed S, comprehensive exam required, thesis optional; for doctorate, dissertation, comprehensive exam. *Entrance requirements:* For master's, GRE General Test (minimum combined score of 1000), minimum GPA of 3.0; for doctorate and Ed S, GRE General Test (minimum combined score of 1000), minimum graduate GPA of 3.0. Application deadline: 7/1 (priority date; rolling processing; 11/1 for spring admission). Application fee: $20. *Tuition:* $139 per credit hour for state residents; $482 per credit hour for nonresidents. *Financial aid:* Fellowships, research assistantships, teaching assistantships, and career-related internships or fieldwork available. • Dr. Hollie Thomas, Head, Department of Educational Leadership, 850-644-6777. E-mail: thomas@mail.coe.fsu.edu. Application contact: Admissions Secretary, 850-644-6777. Fax: 850-644-1258.

Fordham University, Graduate School of Education, Division of Administration, Policy, and Urban Education, New York, NY 10023. Offers programs in administration and supervision (MSE, Adv C), administration and supervision for church leaders (PhD), educational administration and supervision (Ed D, PhD), human resource program administration (MS). Accredited by NCATE. Faculty: 11 full-time, 7 part-time. Students: 26 full-time (20 women), 264 part-time (206 women); includes 47 minority (26 African Americans, 6 Asian Americans, 15 Hispanics), 12 international. In 1997, 48 master's, 29 doctorates awarded. *Degree requirements:* For doctorate, dissertation required, foreign language not required. *Entrance requirements:* For doctorate, MAT. Application fee: $50. *Financial aid:* Career-related internships or fieldwork available. • Dr. Barbara Jackson, Chairperson, 212-636-6430.

Fort Hays State University, College of Education, Department of Education, Administration and Counseling, Program in Education Administration, Hays, KS 67601-4099. Awards MS, Ed S. Accredited by NCATE. Faculty: 10 full-time (1 woman). Students: 2 full-time (both women), 72 part-time (38 women); includes 4 minority (2 African Americans, 2 Hispanics). Average age 37. 22 applicants, 82% accepted. In 1997, 34 master's, 2 Ed Ss awarded. *Degree requirements:* For master's, thesis or alternative required, foreign language not required. *Entrance requirements:* For master's, GRE General Test or MAT. Application deadline: 7/1 (priority date; rolling processing). Application fee: $25 ($35 for international students). *Tuition:* $94 per credit hour for state residents; $249 per credit hour for nonresidents. *Financial aid:* Research assistantships, teaching assistantships, full tuition waivers, institutionally sponsored loans available. *Faculty research:* Guide to negotiations, nutrition program for disadvantaged, accountability, student insurance practices, student liability. • Dr. Edward Stehno, Coordinator, 785-628-4547.

Framingham State College, Graduate Programs, Department of Education, Program in Educational Leadership, Framingham, MA 01701-9101. Awards MA. Part-time and evening/weekend programs available. Faculty: 1 full-time, 2 part-time. Students: 21 part-time. In 1997, 3 degrees awarded. *Entrance requirements:* MAT. *Tuition:* $4184 per year full-time, $523 per course part-time for state residents; $4848 per year full-time, $606 per course part-time for nonresidents. • Dr. Joseph Caruso, Chairperson. Application contact: Graduate Office, 508-626-4550.

Franciscan University of Steubenville, Department of Education, Steubenville, OH 43952-6701. Offerings include administration (MS Ed). *Degree requirements:* Project required, foreign language and thesis not required. *Average time to degree:* master's–3 years full-time, 6 years part-time. *Entrance requirements:* Minimum undergraduate GPA of 2.5 or written exam. Application deadline: 7/1 (rolling processing; 12/15 for spring admission). Application fee: $20. *Expenses:* Tuition $210 per credit hour. Fees $10 per credit hour. • Dr. Diane Keenan, Chair, 740-283-6404. Application contact: Mark McGuire, Associate Director of Graduate Admissions, 800-783-6220. Fax: 740-283-6472.

Fresno Pacific University, Graduate School, Programs in Education, Division of Administration, Program in Administrative Services, Fresno, CA 93702-4709. Awards MA Ed. Faculty: 2 full-time (1 woman), 9 part-time (1 woman). Students: 180 part-time (100 women). *Degree requirements:* Thesis or alternative, 4 practica required, foreign language not required. *Application deadline:* 7/31 (rolling processing). *Application fee:* $75. *Tuition:* $250 per unit. • Dr. Kenneth G. Engstrom, Head, Division of Administration, 209-453-2203. Fax: 209-453-2001.

Friends University, Graduate Programs, College of Arts and Sciences, Program in School Leadership, Wichita, KS 67213. Awards MSL. Evening/weekend programs available. Faculty: 7 full-time (4 women). Students: 26 full-time. *Application deadline:* rolling. *Application fee:* $45. *Expenses:* Tuition $326 per credit hour (minimum). Fees $215 per year. • Brenda L. Cain, Director, 800-794-6945 Ext. 5592. Application contact: Director of Graduate Admissions, 800-794-6945 Ext. 5583.

Frostburg State University, School of Education, Department of Educational Professions, Program in Educational Administration, Frostburg, MD 21532-1099. Awards M Ed. Part-time and evening/weekend programs available. *Application deadline:* 7/15 (rolling processing). *Application fee:* $30. *Faculty research:* Practicum experience in schools.

Furman University, Department of Education, Greenville, SC 29613. Offerings include school administration (MA Ed). *Degree requirements:* Comprehensive written exam. *Application deadline:* rolling. *Application fee:* $25. *Tuition:* $185 per credit hour. • Dr. Hazel W. Harris, Director, 864-294-2213.

Gallaudet University, School of Education and Human Services, Department of Administration and Supervision, Washington, DC 20002-3625. Offers programs in administration (MS), administration and supervision (PhD, Ed S), instructional supervision (Ed S), leadership training (MS), special education administration (PhD). Accredited by NCATE. *Degree requirements:* For master's, thesis optional; for doctorate, 2 foreign languages, computer language, dissertation; for Ed S, 2 foreign languages (computer language can substitute for one), thesis (for some programs). *Entrance requirements:* For master's, GRE General Test or MAT; for doctorate, GRE General Test or MAT, interview. Application deadline: 2/15 (priority date; rolling processing). Application fee: $50. *Expenses:* Tuition $7064 per year full-time, $392 per credit part-time. Fees $50 (one-time charge). *Financial aid:* Federal Work-Study, institutionally

Directory: Educational Administration

Gallaudet University (continued)
sponsored loans, and career-related internships or fieldwork available. Financial aid application deadline: 8/1. • Dr. William Marshall, Chair, 202-651-5525. Application contact: Deborah DeStefano, Director of Admissions, 202-651-5253. Fax: 202-651-5744. E-mail: adm_destefan@gallua.bitnet.

Gardner–Webb University, Department of Education, Program in School Administration, Boiling Springs, NC 28017. Awards MA. Accredited by NCATE. Part-time and evening/weekend programs available. Faculty: 4 full-time (1 woman), 2 part-time (0 women). Students: 3 full-time (2 women), 67 part-time (36 women); includes 8 minority (all African Americans). Average age 41. 7 applicants, 86% accepted. In 1997, 23 degrees awarded. *Degree requirements:* Comprehensive exam required, foreign language and thesis not required. *Entrance requirements:* GRE General Test (minimum combined score of 900), MAT (minimum score 35), or NTE, minimum GPA of 2.5. Application deadline: 8/1. Application fee: $25. *Tuition:* $178 per semester hour full-time, $220 per semester hour part-time. *Financial aid:* Assistantships available. • Dr. Ben Carson, Chair, Department of Education, 704-434-4406. Fax: 704-434-3921. E-mail: bcarson@gardner-webb.edu.

George Mason University, Graduate School of Education, Program in Education Leadership, Fairfax, VA 22030-4444. Awards M Ed. Accredited by NCATE. Part-time and evening/weekend programs available. Faculty: 42 full-time (24 women), 65 part-time (51 women), 58.73 FTE. Students: 10 full-time (6 women), 175 part-time (119 women); includes 43 minority (33 African Americans, 3 Asian Americans, 7 Hispanics), 2 international. Average age 38. 95 applicants, 93% accepted. In 1997, 33 degrees awarded. *Degree requirements:* Computer language required, foreign language not required. *Entrance requirements:* Minimum GPA of 3.0 in last 60 hours, 2 years of teaching experience. Application deadline: 5/1 (11/1 for spring admission). Application fee: $30. Electronic applications accepted. *Tuition:* $4344 per year full-time, $181 per credit hour part-time for state residents; $12,504 per year full-time, $521 per credit hour part-time for nonresidents. *Financial aid:* Career-related internships or fieldwork available. Aid available to part-time students. Financial aid application deadline: 3/1; applicants required to submit FAFSA. • Dr. Clark Dobson, Coordinator, 703-993-4648. Fax: 703-993-2082.

The George Washington University, Graduate School of Education and Human Development, Department of Educational Leadership, Program in Education Administration and Policy Studies, Washington, DC 20052. Awards Ed D. Accredited by NCATE. Faculty: 2 full-time (1 woman). Students: 8 full-time (6 women), 48 part-time (32 women); includes 21 minority (19 African Americans, 1 Hispanic, 1 Native American), 3 international. Average age 44. 221 applicants, 92% accepted. In 1997, 21 degrees awarded. *Degree requirements:* Dissertation, comprehensive exam. *Entrance requirements:* GRE General Test or MAT, interview, minimum GPA of 3.3. Application deadline: 3/1 (priority date; rolling processing; 10/1 for spring admission). Application fee: $50. *Expenses:* Tuition $680 per semester hour. Fees $35 per semester hour. *Financial aid:* Fellowships, research assistantships, partial tuition waivers, Federal Work-Study, and career-related internships or fieldwork available. Financial aid applicants required to submit FAFSA. • John Boswell, Head. Application contact: Dr. Dennis Holmes, Chair, 202-994-6940.

The George Washington University, Graduate School of Education and Human Development, Department of Educational Leadership, Program in Elementary/Secondary Administration and Supervision, Washington, DC 20052. Awards MA Ed. Accredited by NCATE. Evening/weekend programs available. Students: 4 part-time (all women); includes 1 minority (African American). Average age 38. 14 applicants, 100% accepted. In 1997, 3 degrees awarded. *Degree requirements:* Comprehensive exam required, foreign language and thesis not required. *Entrance requirements:* GRE General Test or MAT, interview, minimum GPA of 2.75. Application deadline: 3/1 (priority date; rolling processing; 10/1 for spring admission). Application fee: $50. *Expenses:* Tuition $680 per semester hour. Fees $35 per semester hour. *Financial aid:* Fellowships, Federal Work-Study, and career-related internships or fieldwork available. Financial aid applicants required to submit FAFSA. *Faculty research:* Organizational learning. • Dr. Lee Etta Powell, Faculty Coordinator, 202-994-6940.

The George Washington University, Graduate School of Education and Human Development, Department of Educational Leadership, Program in Higher Education Administration, Washington, DC 20052. Offers higher education (Ed D, Ed S), higher education administration (MA Ed). Accredited by NCATE. Faculty: 3 full-time (1 woman), 3 part-time (1 woman), 4 FTE. Students: 41 full-time (27 women), 84 part-time (46 women); includes 44 minority (38 African Americans, 2 Asian Americans, 2 Hispanics, 2 Native Americans), 14 international. Average age 40. 66 applicants, 94% accepted. In 1997, 27 master's, 15 doctorates awarded. *Degree requirements:* For master's and Ed S, comprehensive exam required, foreign language and thesis not required; for doctorate, dissertation, comprehensive exam required, foreign language not required. *Entrance requirements:* For master's, GRE General Test or MAT, minimum GPA of 2.75; for doctorate, GRE General Test or MAT, interview, minimum GPA of 3.3; for Ed S, GRE General Test or MAT, minimum GPA of 3.3. Application deadline: 3/1 (priority date; rolling processing; 10/1 for spring admission). Application fee: $50. *Expenses:* Tuition $680 per semester hour. Fees $35 per semester hour. *Financial aid:* Fellowships, research assistantships, partial tuition waivers, Federal Work-Study, and career-related internships or fieldwork available. Financial aid applicants required to submit FAFSA. *Faculty research:* Technology in higher education administration. • Dr. Reynolds Ferrante, Faculty Coordinator, 202-994-2767.

Georgia College and State University, School of Education, Department of Special Education and Administration, Program in Administration and Supervision, Milledgeville, GA 31061. Awards M Ed, Ed S. Accredited by NCATE. Students: 26 full-time (15 women), 52 part-time (35 women); includes 14 minority (13 African Americans, 1 Hispanic), 1 international. Average age 38. In 1997, 10 master's, 19 Ed Ss awarded. *Degree requirements:* For master's, computer language, comprehensive exit exam required, foreign language and thesis not required; for Ed S, computer language, comprehensive exit exam, oral exam, research project required, thesis optional, foreign language not required. *Entrance requirements:* For master's, GRE General Test (minimum combined score of 800) or NTE (minimum score 550 on each core battery test), MAT (minimum score 44), minimum GPA of 2.5, NT-4 certificate; for Ed S, GRE General Test (minimum combined score of 900) or NTE (minimum score 575 on each core battery test), MAT (minimum score 48), master's degree, minimum graduate GPA of 3.25, NT-5 certificate, 2 years of teaching experience. Application deadline: 7/31 (priority date; rolling processing). Application fee: $10. *Financial aid:* Federal Work-Study and career-related internships or fieldwork available. Aid available to part-time students. Financial aid application deadline: 4/15. • Dr. Craig Smith, Chairperson, Department of Special Education and Administration, 912-445-4577.

Georgian Court College, Program in Education, Lakewood, NJ 08701-2697. Offerings include administration, supervision and curriculum planning (management specialization) (MA); administration, supervision, and curriculum planning (MA). *Application deadline:* 8/25 (rolling processing; 1/15 for spring admission). *Application fee:* $30. *Tuition:* $350 per credit. • Application contact: Renee Loew, Director of Graduate Admissions and Records, 732-367-1717. Fax: 732-364-4516.

Georgia Southern University, College of Education, Department of Leadership, Technology, and Human Development, Program in Educational Leadership, Statesboro, GA 30460-8126. Awards M Ed, Ed D, Ed S. Accredited by NCATE. Evening/weekend programs available. Students: 27 full-time (17 women), 84 part-time (57 women); includes 9 minority (all African Americans). Average age 40. 41 applicants, 88% accepted. In 1997, 7 master's, 5 doctorates, 15 Ed Ss awarded. *Degree requirements:* For master's and Ed S, exams required, foreign language and thesis not required; for doctorate, dissertation, exams required, foreign language not required. *Entrance requirements:* For master's, GRE General Test (minimum score 450 on each section) or MAT (minimum score 44), minimum GPA of 2.75; for doctorate, GRE General Test (minimum combined score of 1000) or MAT (minimum score 55), minimum GPA of 3.5; for Ed S, GRE General Test (minimum score 450 on each section) or MAT (minimum score 49), minimum graduate GPA of 3.25. Application deadline: 7/15 (priority date; rolling processing; 11/15 for spring admission). Application fee: $0. Electronic applications accepted. *Tuition:* $2619 per year full-time, $287 per semester (minimum) part-time for state residents; $8619 per year full-time, $1037 per semester (minimum) part-time for nonresidents. *Financial aid:* Research assistantships, teaching assistantships, Federal Work-Study, and career-related internships or fieldwork available. Aid available to part-time students. Financial aid application deadline: 4/15. • Application contact: Dr. John R. Diebolt, Associate Graduate Dean, 912-681-5384. Fax: 912-681-0740. E-mail: gradschool@gsvms2.cc.gasou.edu.

Georgia Southern University, College of Education, Department of Leadership, Technology, and Human Development, Program in Higher Education and Student Services, Statesboro, GA 30460-8126. Awards M Ed. Accredited by NCATE. Students: 13 full-time (8 women), 7 part-time (5 women); includes 4 minority (all African Americans). Average age 31. 12 applicants, 58% accepted. In 1997, 8 degrees awarded. *Degree requirements:* Exams required, foreign language and thesis not required. *Entrance requirements:* GRE General Test (minimum score 450 on each section) or MAT (minimum score 44), minimum GPA of 2.5. Application deadline: 7/15 (priority date; rolling processing; 11/15 for spring admission). Application fee: $0. Electronic applications accepted. *Tuition:* $2619 per year full-time, $287 per semester (minimum) part-time for state residents; $8619 per year full-time, $1037 per semester (minimum) part-time for nonresidents. *Financial aid:* Application deadline 4/15. • Application contact: Dr. John R. Diebolt, Associate Graduate Dean, 912-681-5384. Fax: 912-681-0740. E-mail: gradschool@gsvms2.cc.gasou.edu.

Georgia State University, College of Education, Department of Educational Policy Studies, Program in Educational Administration, Atlanta, GA 30303-3083. Awards M Ed, PhD, Ed S. Accredited by NCATE. Part-time and evening/weekend programs available. Students: 32 full-time (23 women), 76 part-time (50 women); includes 39 minority (34 African Americans, 2 Asian Americans, 2 Hispanics, 1 Native American), 2 international. Average age 39. 34 applicants, 85% accepted. In 1997, 18 master's, 8 doctorates, 18 Ed Ss awarded. *Degree requirements:* For master's, comprehensive exams; for doctorate, dissertation, comprehensive exams. *Entrance requirements:* For master's, GRE General Test (minimum combined score of 900) or MAT (minimum score 48), minimum GPA of 2.5; for doctorate, GRE General Test (minimum score 500 on verbal section, 500 on either quantitative or analytical sections) or MAT (minimum score 53), minimum GPA of 3.3; for Ed S, GRE General Test (minimum combined score of 900) or MAT (minimum score 48), minimum graduate GPA of 3.25. Application fee: $25. *Expenses:* Tuition $2673 per year full-time, $99 per semester hour part-time for state residents; $10,692 per year full-time, $396 per semester hour part-time for nonresidents. Fees $228 per year. *Financial aid:* Research assistantships, Federal Work-Study available. Aid available to part-time students. *Faculty research:* Principal effectiveness, teacher empowerment, restructuring of schools. • Dr. H. Parker Blount, Chair, Department of Educational Policy Studies, 404-651-2582.

Gonzaga University, Graduate School, School of Education, Program in Administration and Curriculum, Spokane, WA 99258-0001. Awards MAA. Accredited by NCATE. Faculty: 18 full-time (5 women), 20 part-time (9 women). Students: 240 full-time (158 women); includes 13 minority (7 African Americans, 4 Asian Americans, 1 Hispanic, 1 Native American), 100 international. Average age 39. 135 applicants, 39% accepted. In 1997, 165 degrees awarded. *Degree requirements:* Comprehensive exam required, foreign language and thesis not required. *Entrance requirements:* GRE General Test or MAT, TOEFL (minimum score 550), minimum B average in undergraduate course work. Application deadline: 7/20 (priority date; rolling processing; 11/1 for spring admission). Application fee: $40. *Tuition:* $7380 per year (minimum) full-time, $410 per credit (minimum) part-time. *Financial aid:* Teaching assistantships available. Aid available to part-time students. Financial aid application deadline: 3/1. • Dr. Robert Bialozer, Director, 509-328-4220 Ext. 3491.

Gonzaga University, Graduate School, School of Education, Program in Educational Leadership, Spokane, WA 99258-0001. Awards PhD. Accredited by NCATE. Evening/weekend programs available. Faculty: 4 full-time (1 woman), 7 part-time (0 women). Students: 101 full-time (64 women); includes 7 international. Average age 43. 15 applicants, 67% accepted. In 1997, 20 degrees awarded. *Degree requirements:* Dissertation, comprehensive exam required, foreign language not required. *Entrance requirements:* GRE General Test, MAT, TOEFL (minimum score 550), minimum GPA of 3.5. Application deadline: 7/20 (priority date; rolling processing; 11/1 for spring admission). Application fee: $40. *Tuition:* $7380 per year (minimum) full-time, $410 per credit (minimum) part-time. *Financial aid:* Application deadline 3/1. • Dr. James Beebe, Department Head, 509-328-4220 Ext. 3484.

Governors State University, College of Education, Division of Education, Program in Educational Administration and Supervision, University Park, IL 60466. Awards MA. Offered jointly with Chicago State University and Northeastern Illinois University. Part-time and evening/weekend programs available. Faculty: 4 full-time (0 women), 5 part-time (0 women). Average age 37. In 1997, 60 degrees awarded. *Degree requirements:* Comprehensive exam, practicum required, foreign language and thesis not required. *Entrance requirements:* Minimum GPA of 2.75 in last 60 hours of undergraduate course work, 3.0 in any graduate work attempted. Application deadline: 7/15 (priority date, rolling processing; 11/10 for spring admission). Application fee: $0. *Expenses:* Tuition $1140 per trimester full-time, $95 per credit hour part-time for state residents; $3420 per trimester full-time, $285 per credit hour part-time for nonresidents. Fees $95 per trimester. *Financial aid:* Full and partial tuition waivers, Federal Work-Study, institutionally sponsored loans, and career-related internships or fieldwork available. Aid available to part-time students. Financial aid application deadline: 5/1. • Application contact: Nick Battaglia, Adviser, 708-534-4393.

Grambling State University, College of Education, Grambling, LA 71245. Offerings include educational leadership (Ed D). Accredited by NCATE. Ed D (curriculum and instruction, educational leadership) offered jointly with Louisiana Tech University and Northeast Louisiana University. Postbaccalaureate distance learning degree programs offered. College faculty: 23 full-time (8 women), 13 part-time (9 women), 26 FTE. *Degree requirements:* Dissertation required, foreign language not required. *Average time to degree:* master's–1.5 years full-time, 3 years part-time; doctorate–3.5 years full-time, 7 years part-time. *Entrance requirements:* GRE. Application deadline: rolling. Application fee: $15. *Tuition:* $1960 per year full-time, $297 per semester (minimum) part-time for state residents; $7110 per year full-time, $297 per semester (minimum) part-time for nonresidents. • Dr. Andolyn Harrison, Acting Dean, 318-274-2251.

Grand Valley State University, School of Education, Program in Special Education, Allendale, MI 49401-9403. Offerings include special education administration (M Ed). Accredited by NCATE. Program faculty: 4 full-time (1 woman), 23 part-time (9 women). *Degree requirements:* Thesis or alternative, applied research project. *Entrance requirements:* GRE General Test (minimum combined score of 1300) or minimum GPA of 3.0. Application deadline: rolling. Application fee: $20. • Dr. James Grant, Coordinator, 616-771-6650. Application contact: Admissions Office, 616-895-2025. Fax: 616-895-3081.

Grand Valley State University, School of Education, Programs in General Education, Program in Educational Leadership, Allendale, MI 49401-9403. Awards M Ed. Accredited by NCATE. *Degree requirements:* Thesis or alternative, applied research project. *Entrance requirements:* GRE General Test (minimum combined score of 1300) or minimum GPA of 3.0. Application deadline: rolling. Application fee: $20. • Application contact: Admissions Office, 616-895-2025. Fax: 616-895-3081.

Gwynedd–Mercy College, Graduate Education Programs, Gwynedd Valley, PA 19437-0901. Offerings include educational administration (MS). Faculty: 4 full-time (all women), 11 part-time (7 women). *Degree requirements:* Thesis, internship, practicum required, foreign language not required. *Average time to degree:* master's–3 years part-time. *Entrance requirements:* GRE or MAT. Application deadline: rolling. Application fee: $25. *Expenses:* Tuition $299 per credit.

Fees $50 per year. • Dr. Lorraine Cavaliere, Dean, 215-641-5549. Application contact: Maureen Coyle, Program Administrator, 215-641-5561. Fax: 215-542-4695.

Harding University, School of Education, Program in Elementary School Administration, Searcy, AR 72149-0001. Awards M Ed. Accredited by NCATE. Part-time programs available. Faculty: 4 part-time (2 women), 1 FTE. Students: 2 full-time (1 woman), 3 part-time (all women). Average age 32. 2 applicants, 100% accepted. In 1997, 4 degrees awarded. *Degree requirements:* Comprehensive exam required, foreign language and thesis not required. *Average time to degree:* master's–1 year full-time, 3 years part-time. *Entrance requirements:* GRE, MAT, or NTE. Application deadline: 8/27 (rolling processing). Application fee: $25. *Expenses:* Tuition $212 per credit hour. Fees $39 per credit hour. *Financial aid:* Graduate assistantships, scholarships available. • Dr. Dee Carson, Director, School of Education, 501-279-4315. Fax: 501-279-4685. E-mail: dcarson@harding.edu.

Harvard University, Graduate School of Education, Area of Administration, Planning and Social Policy, Cambridge, MA 02138. Offers programs in administration, planning and social policy (Ed M, CAS); community and lifelong learning (Ed D); elementary and secondary education (Ed D); higher education (Ed D); individualized program (Ed M); international education (Ed M, Ed D); research (Ed D); urban superintendency (Ed D). Part-time programs available. Faculty: 14 full-time (6 women), 21 part-time (8 women), 15.7 FTE. Students: 157 full-time (97 women), 38 part-time (25 women); includes 69 minority (40 African Americans, 7 Asian Americans, 20 Hispanics, 2 Native Americans), 20 international. Average age 38. 232 applicants, 16% accepted. In 1997, 174 master's, 29 doctorates, 7 CASs awarded. Terminal master's awarded for partial completion of doctoral program. *Degree requirements:* For doctorate, dissertation required, foreign language not required. *Average time to degree:* master's–1 year full-time, 2 years part-time; doctorate–6.3 years full-time, 7.2 years part-time; other advanced degree–1 year full-time, 4.7 years part-time. *Entrance requirements:* GRE General Test, TOEFL (minimum score 600), TWE (minimum score 5.0). Application deadline: 1/2. Application fee: $60. *Financial aid:* In 1997–98, 104 students received aid, including 23 fellowships (15 to first-year students) totaling $333,748, 12 research assistantships averaging $588 per month, 52 teaching assistantships averaging $670 per month, 68 need-based scholarships (15 to first-year students) totaling $711,985; Federal Work-Study and career-related internships or fieldwork also available. Aid available to part-time students. Financial aid application deadline: 1/8; applicants required to submit FAFSA. *Faculty research:* Educational policy, economics of education, sociology of schools and communities. • Richard Murnane, Chair, 617-496-4813. Application contact: Roland Hence, Director of Admissions, 617-495-3414. Fax: 617-496-3577. E-mail: gseadmissions@harvard.edu.

Henderson State University, School of Education, Department of Elementary Education, Arkadelphia, AR 71999-0001. Offerings include elementary school administration (MSE). Accredited by NCATE. *Entrance requirements:* GRE General Test or MAT, minimum GPA of 2.7, teacher certification. Application deadline: 7/31 (priority date; rolling processing). Application fee: $0. Electronic applications accepted. *Expenses:* Tuition $120 per credit hour for state residents; $240 per credit hour for nonresidents. Fees $105 per semester (minimum) full-time, $52 per semester (minimum) part-time. • Dr. Kenneth Harris, Chairperson, 870-230-5203. Fax: 870-230-5455. E-mail: harris@holly.hsu.edu.

Henderson State University, School of Education, Department of Secondary Education, Arkadelphia, AR 71999-0001. Offerings include secondary school administration (MSE). Accredited by NCATE. Postbaccalaureate distance learning degree programs offered (minimal on-campus study). *Degree requirements:* Thesis optional, foreign language not required. *Entrance requirements:* GRE General Test or MAT, minimum GPA of 2.7, teacher certification. Application deadline: 7/31 (priority date; rolling processing). Application fee: $15. Electronic applications accepted. *Expenses:* Tuition $120 per credit hour for state residents; $240 per credit hour for nonresidents. Fees $105 per semester (minimum) full-time, $52 per semester (minimum) part-time. • Dr. Charles Weiner, Chairperson, 870-230-5163. Fax: 870-230-5455. E-mail: weinerc@holly.hsu.edu.

Heritage College, Graduate Program in Education, Program in Educational Administration, Toppenish, WA 98948-9599. Awards M Ed. *Degree requirements:* Comprehensive exam required, thesis optional, foreign language not required. *Entrance requirements:* GRE General Test. Application deadline: rolling. Application fee: $35 ($75 for international students). *Tuition:* $270 per credit. *Financial aid:* Partial tuition waivers, Federal Work-Study, institutionally sponsored loans, and career-related internships or fieldwork available. Aid available to part-time students. • Application contact: Dr. David Zufelt, Adviser, 509-865-2244.

Hofstra University, School of Education and Allied Human Services, Department of Administration and Policy Studies, Specialization in Educational Administration, Hempstead, NY 11549. Awards MS Ed, Ed D, CAS, PD. Accredited by NCATE. Part-time and evening/weekend programs available. Faculty: 9 full-time (5 women), 8 part-time (3 women). Students: 2 full-time (both women), 113 part-time (79 women); includes 8 minority (4 African Americans, 3 Hispanics, 1 Native American), 4 international. Average age 43. 36 applicants, 36% accepted. In 1997, 23 master's, 5 doctorates awarded. *Degree requirements:* For master's, departmental qualifying exam required, foreign language and thesis not required; for doctorate, computer language, dissertation, oral and written comprehensive exams required, foreign language not required. *Entrance requirements:* For master's, public school teaching certificate, 2 years of teaching experience; for doctorate, GMAT, GRE General Test or LSAT, interview; for other advanced degree, GMAT or MAT, GRE General Test or LSAT, minimum GPA of 2.9. Application deadline: rolling. Application fee: $40 ($75 for international students). *Expenses:* Tuition $10,968 per year full-time, $457 per credit hour part-time. Fees $670 per year full-time, $112 per semester (minimum) part-time. *Financial aid:* In 1997–98, 52 students received aid, including 48 fellowships (15 to first-year students), 4 research assistantships, 3 teaching assistantships; partial tuition waivers and career-related internships or fieldwork also available. Aid available to part-time students. Financial aid application deadline: 4/1. *Faculty research:* Gender in education, reflective practice, teacher empowerment. • Dr. Charol Shakeshaft, Director, Doctoral Program, 516-463-5762. Fax: 516-463-6503. E-mail: edacss@hofstra.edu. Application contact: Mary Beth Carey, Dean of Admissions, 516-463-6700. Fax: 516-560-7660. E-mail: hofstra@hofstra.edu.

Hood College, Department of Education, Frederick, MD 21701-8575. Offerings include educational leadership (MS). *Entrance requirements:* Minimum GPA of 2.5. Application deadline: rolling. Application fee: $30. *Tuition:* $285 per credit. • Dr. Patricia Bartlett, Chairperson, 301-696-3471. E-mail: bartlett@nimue.hood.edu. Application contact: Hood College Graduate School, 301-696-3600. Fax: 301-696-3597. E-mail: postmaster@nimue.hood.edu.

Houston Baptist University, College of Education and Behavioral Sciences, Programs in Education, Houston, TX 77074-3298. Offerings include educational administration (M Ed). Faculty: 9 full-time (5 women), 4 part-time (3 women). *Degree requirements:* Comprehensive exam required, foreign language and thesis not required. *Entrance requirements:* GRE General Test (minimum combined score of 850), minimum GPA of 2.5, teaching certificate. Application deadline: 7/1 (priority date; rolling processing; 1/1 for spring admission). Application fee: $25 ($85 for international students). *Expenses:* Tuition $280 per semester hour. Fees $235 per quarter. • Dr. John Lutjemeier, Head, 281-649-3000 Ext. 2336. Application contact: Judy Ferguson, Program Assistant, 281-649-3241.

Howard University, School of Education, Department of Educational Administration and Policy, Program in Educational Administration, 2400 Sixth Street, NW, Washington, DC 20059-0002. Awards MA, M Ed, CAGS. Accredited by NCATE. MA offered through the Graduate School of Arts and Sciences. In 1997, 5 master's awarded. *Degree requirements:* For master's, thesis (for some programs), comprehensive exam required, foreign language not required; for CAGS, thesis. *Entrance requirements:* For master's, GRE General Test, minimum GPA of 2.7, 3 years of teaching experience; for CAGS, GRE General Test. Application deadline: 4/1 (priority date; rolling processing; 10/1 for spring admission). Application fee: $45. *Expenses:* Tuition $10,200 per year full-time, $567 per credit hour part-time. Fees $405 per year. *Financial aid:* Fellowships, research assistantships, teaching assistantships, grants, scholarships, full and partial tuition waivers, Federal Work-Study, institutionally sponsored loans, and career-related internships or fieldwork available. Financial aid application deadline: 4/1. • Dr. Beverly Glenn, Coordinator, 202-806-7347. Fax: 202-806-7018.

Howard University, School of Education, Department of Educational Administration and Policy, Program in Educational Supervision, 2400 Sixth Street, NW, Washington, DC 20059-0002. Awards MA, M Ed, CAGS. Accredited by NCATE. MA offered through the Graduate School of Arts and Sciences. *Degree requirements:* For master's, thesis (for some programs), comprehensive exam required, foreign language not required; for CAGS, thesis. *Entrance requirements:* For master's, GRE General Test, minimum GPA of 2.7, 3 years of teaching experience; for CAGS, GRE General Test. Application deadline: 4/1 (priority date; rolling processing; 10/1 for spring admission). Application fee: $45. *Expenses:* Tuition $10,200 per year full-time, $567 per credit hour part-time. Fees $405 per year. *Financial aid:* Fellowships, research assistantships, grants, scholarships, full and partial tuition waivers, Federal Work-Study, institutionally sponsored loans, and career-related internships or fieldwork available. Financial aid application deadline: 4/1. • Dr. Edwin Hamilton Jr., Chairman, Department of Educational Administration and Policy, 202-806-7347. Fax: 202-806-7018.

Hunter College of the City University of New York, Division of Education, Department of Curriculum and Teaching, Program in Educational Supervision and Administration, 695 Park Avenue, New York, NY 10021-5085. Awards AC. Part-time and evening/weekend programs available. *Average time to degree:* other advanced degree–2.5 years full-time, 3 years part-time. *Entrance requirements:* TOEFL (minimum score 575), minimum B average in graduate course work, teaching certificate, minimum 3 years of full-time teaching experience. Application deadline: 4/28 (priority date; rolling processing; 11/21 for spring admission). Application fee: $40. *Expenses:* Tuition $4350 per year full-time, $185 per credit part-time for state residents; $7600 per year full-time, $320 per credit part-time for nonresidents. Fees $26 per year. *Faculty research:* Supervision of instruction, theory in action, human relations and leadership.

Idaho State University, College of Education, Division II, Pocatello, ID 83209. Offerings include educational administration (M Ed, Ed S), educational leadership (Ed D). One or more programs accredited by NCATE. Postbaccalaureate distance learning degree programs offered (no on-campus study). Division faculty: 11 full-time (2 women). *Degree requirements:* For doctorate, computer language, dissertation, written exam required, foreign language not required; for Ed S, oral exam, written exam required, foreign language and thesis not required. *Average time to degree:* master's–2 years full-time, 4 years part-time; other advanced degree–1 year full-time, 2 years part-time. *Entrance requirements:* For doctorate, GRE General Test (minimum combined score of 1000) or MAT (minimum score 50), minimum undergraduate GPA of 3.0, minimum graduate GPA of 3.5; for Ed S, GRE, minimum graduate GPA of 3.0. Application deadline: 7/1 (priority date; rolling processing; 12/1 for spring admission). Application fee: $30. *Tuition:* $3130 per year full-time, $136 per credit hour part-time for state residents; $9370 per year full-time, $226 per credit hour part-time for nonresidents. • Dr. T. C. Mattocks, Director. E-mail: matttheo@isu.edu. Application contact: Dr. Stephanie Salzman, Director, Office of Standards and Assessment, 208-236-3114. Fax: 208-236-4697. E-mail: salzstep@isu.edu.

Illinois State University, College of Education, Department of Educational Administration, Normal, IL 61790-2200. Awards MA, MS, MS Ed, Ed D, PhD. Accredited by NCATE. Faculty: 16 full-time (4 women), 1 part-time (0 women), 16.25 FTE. Students: 41 full-time (18 women), 284 part-time (163 women); includes 38 minority (25 African Americans, 6 Asian Americans, 7 Hispanics), 5 international. 79 applicants, 94% accepted. In 1997, 56 master's, 16 doctorates awarded. *Degree requirements:* For doctorate, variable foreign language requirement, dissertation, 2 terms of residency. *Entrance requirements:* For master's, GRE General Test, minimum GPA of 2.6 in last 60 hours; for doctorate, GRE General Test, master's degree or equivalent, minimum GPA of 3.5. Application deadline: rolling. Application fee: $0. *Expenses:* Tuition $2454 per year full-time, $102 per hour part-time for state residents; $7362 per year full-time, $307 per hour part-time for nonresidents. Fees $1048 per year full-time, $44 per hour part-time. *Financial aid:* In 1997–98, 2 research assistantships, 3 assistantships averaging $879 per month were awarded; teaching assistantships, full tuition waivers also available. Financial aid application deadline: 4/1. *Total annual research expenditures:* $368,429. • Dr. Diane Ashby, Acting Chairperson, 309-438-5422.

Immaculata College, Graduate Division, Program in Educational Leadership and Administration, Immaculata, PA 19345-0500. Offers educational leadership and administration (MA, Ed D), elementary education (Certificate), intermediate unit director (Certificate), school principal (Certificate), school superintendent (Certificate). Part-time and evening/weekend programs available. Students: 4 full-time (3 women), 158 part-time (103 women). Average age 33. 49 applicants, 76% accepted. In 1997, 15 master's awarded (100% found work related to degree); 7 doctorates awarded. *Degree requirements:* For master's, comprehensive exam required, thesis optional, foreign language not required; for doctorate, dissertation, comprehensive exam required, foreign language not required. *Entrance requirements:* For master's, GRE or MAT, TOEFL, minimum GPA of 3.0; for doctorate, GRE General Test (minimum score 600 on each section, 1200 combined) or MAT (minimum score 65), TOEFL (minimum score 550), minimum GPA of 3.5. Application fee: $25. *Expenses:* Tuition $345 per credit (minimum). Fees $60 per year. *Financial aid:* Application deadline 5/1. *Faculty research:* Cooperative learning, school-based management, whole language, performance assessment. • Sr. Anne Marie Burton, Chair, 610-647-4400 Ext. 3280. Application contact: Office of Graduate Admission, 610-647-4400 Ext. 3211.

Indiana State University, School of Education, Department of Educational Leadership, Administration, and Foundations, Terre Haute, IN 47809-1401. Offers programs in educational administration (PhD, Ed S), elementary school administration (M Ed), secondary school administration (M Ed). Accredited by NCATE. Part-time and evening/weekend programs available. Faculty: 18 full-time (6 women). Students: 25 full-time (14 women), 32 part-time (15 women); includes 6 minority (all African Americans), 1 international. Average age 41. 39 applicants, 79% accepted. In 1997, 10 master's, 8 doctorates, 9 Ed Ss awarded. Terminal master's awarded for partial completion of doctoral program. *Degree requirements:* For master's, 1 foreign language, thesis; for doctorate, 3 foreign languages, computer language, dissertation. *Entrance requirements:* For master's, minimum undergraduate GPA of 2.5; for doctorate, GRE General Test (minimum score 500 on each section), minimum undergraduate GPA of 3.5; for Ed S, GRE General Test (minimum combined score of 900), minimum graduate GPA of 3.25. Application deadline: rolling. Application fee: $20. *Tuition:* $143 per credit hour for state residents; $325 per credit hour for nonresidents. *Financial aid:* In 1997–98, 3 fellowships (1 to a first-year student) were awarded; teaching assistantships and career-related internships or fieldwork also available. Financial aid application deadline: 3/1. • Dr. Rebecca Libler, Acting Chairperson, 812-237-2920.

Indiana State University, School of Education, Department of Counseling, Program in College Student Personnel, Terre Haute, IN 47809-1401. Offers college student personnel work (MA, MS), student personnel work in higher education (PhD). Accredited by NCATE. Students: 21 full-time (14 women), 4 part-time (3 women); includes 5 minority (4 African Americans, 1 Hispanic). 55 applicants, 27% accepted. In 1997, 8 master's awarded. *Degree requirements:* For doctorate, 2 foreign languages, computer language, dissertation. *Entrance requirements:* For master's, minimum undergraduate GPA of 2.5; for doctorate, GRE General Test (minimum score 500 on each section), master's degree, minimum undergraduate GPA of 3.5. Application deadline: 2/15 (rolling processing). Application fee: $20. *Tuition:* $143 per credit hour for state residents; $325 per credit hour for nonresidents. *Financial aid:* Career-related internships or fieldwork available. Financial aid application deadline: 3/1. • Dr. Will Barratt, Coordinator, 812-237-2868.

Indiana University Bloomington, School of Education, Department of Educational Leadership and Policy Studies, Program in Higher Education and College Student Personnel Administration, Bloomington, IN 47405. Offers college student personnel administration (MS), higher

Directory: Educational Administration

Indiana University Bloomington (continued)

education (Ed D, PhD). Accredited by NCATE. PhD offered through the University Graduate School. Evening/weekend programs available. Students: 49 full-time (29 women), 12 part-time (10 women); includes 12 minority (6 African Americans, 2 Asian Americans, 4 Hispanics), 2 international. In 1997, 30 doctorates awarded. *Degree requirements:* For doctorate, dissertation required, foreign language not required. *Entrance requirements:* For master's, GRE General Test (minimum combined score of 1300 on three sections); for doctorate, GRE General Test (minimum combined score of 1500 on three sections). Application deadline: 6/1. Application fee: $35. *Expenses:* Tuition $153 per credit hour for state residents; $446 per credit hour for nonresidents. Fees $343 per year. *Financial aid:* Fellowships, research assistantships, full tuition waivers, Federal Work-Study, institutionally sponsored loans, and career-related internships or fieldwork available. Aid available to part-time students. • Dr. Michael D. Parsons, Chair, 812-856-8364. Fax: 812-856-8394. Application contact: Dr. Dale P. Scannell, Director of Graduate Studies, 812-856-8540.

Indiana University Bloomington, School of Education, Department of Educational Leadership and Policy Studies, Program in School Administration, Bloomington, IN 47405. Awards MS, Ed D, Ed S. Accredited by NCATE. Students: 4 full-time (3 women), 83 part-time (46 women); includes 6 minority (5 African Americans, 1 Hispanic), 1 international. In 1997, 9 master's, 14 doctorates awarded. *Degree requirements:* For doctorate, dissertation, administrative experience required, foreign language not required; for Ed S, comprehensive exam or project required, foreign language and thesis not required. *Entrance requirements:* For master's and Ed S, GRE General Test (minimum combined score of 1300 on three sections); for doctorate, GRE General Test (minimum combined score of 1500 on three sections). Application deadline: 6/1. Application fee: $35. *Expenses:* Tuition $153 per credit hour for state residents; $446 per credit hour for nonresidents. Fees $343 per year. *Financial aid:* Fellowships, research assistantships, full tuition waivers, and career-related internships or fieldwork available. *Faculty research:* Law (teacher/student rights), microcomputer technology and decision making, monitoring/simulation. • Dr. William Foster, Coordinator, 812-856-8390. Application contact: Dr. Dale P. Scannell, Director of Graduate Studies, 812-856-8540.

Indiana University of Pennsylvania, College of Education, Department of Student Affairs in Higher Education, Indiana, PA 15705-1087. Offers programs in student affairs in higher education (MA), student personnel services (MA). Accredited by NCATE. Part-time programs available. Students: 56 full-time (37 women), 18 part-time (9 women); includes 11 minority (9 African Americans, 1 Hispanic, 1 Native American). Average age 25. 52 applicants, 79% accepted. In 1997, 24 degrees awarded. *Degree requirements:* Thesis optional, foreign language not required. *Entrance requirements:* TOEFL (minimum score 500). Application deadline: 7/1 (priority date; rolling processing; 11/1 for spring admission). Application fee: $30. *Expenses:* Tuition $3468 per year full-time, $193 per credit part-time for state residents; $6236 per year full-time, $346 per credit part-time for nonresidents. Fees $313 per year (minimum) full-time, $84 per year part-time. *Financial aid:* Research assistantships, Federal Work-Study, and career-related internships or fieldwork available. Aid available to part-time students. Financial aid application deadline: 3/15. • Dr. Ronald W. Thomas, Chairperson and Graduate Coordinator, 724-357-1251. E-mail: rwt@grove.iup.edu.

Indiana University of Pennsylvania, College of Education, Department of Professional Studies in Education, Certificate Program in Administration and Leadership Studies, Indiana, PA 15705-1087. Awards Certificate. Accredited by NCATE. Students: 17 part-time (13 women). 7 applicants, 100% accepted. *Entrance requirements:* GRE General Test, GRE Subject Test, TOEFL (minimum score 500). Application deadline: 7/1 (priority date; rolling processing; 11/1 for spring admission). Application fee: $30. *Expenses:* Tuition $3468 per year full-time, $193 per credit part-time for state residents; $6236 per year full-time, $346 per credit part-time for nonresidents. Fees $313 per year (minimum) full-time, $84 per year part-time. *Financial aid:* Application deadline 3/15. • Dr. Edwina Vold, Chairperson, Department of Professional Studies in Education, 724-357-2400. E-mail: ebvold@grove.iup.edu. Application contact: Dr. Gail Gerlach, Assistant Chair, 724-357-2400. E-mail: ggerlach@grove.iup.edu.

Indiana University of Pennsylvania, College of Education, Department of Professional Studies in Education, Doctoral Program in Administration and Leadership Studies, Indiana, PA 15705-1087. Awards D Ed. Accredited by NCATE. Students: 33 part-time (13 women); includes 4 minority (3 African Americans, 1 Native American). Average age 43. 1 applicant, 0% accepted. *Degree requirements:* 1 foreign language (computer language can substitute), dissertation. *Entrance requirements:* TOEFL (minimum score 500). Application deadline: 7/1 (priority date; rolling processing; 11/1 for spring admission). Application fee: $30. *Expenses:* Tuition $3468 per year full-time, $193 per credit part-time for state residents; $6236 per year full-time, $346 per credit part-time for nonresidents. Fees $313 per year (minimum) full-time, $84 per year part-time. *Financial aid:* Application deadline 3/15. • Dr. Robert Millward, Graduate Coordinator, 724-357-5593. E-mail: millward@grove.iup.edu.

Indiana University of Pennsylvania, College of Humanities and Social Sciences, Department of Sociology, Program in Administration and Leadership Studies, Indiana, PA 15705-1087. Awards PhD. *Entrance requirements:* TOEFL (minimum score 500). Application deadline: 7/1 (priority date; rolling processing; 11/1 for spring admission). Application fee: $30. *Expenses:* Tuition $3468 per year full-time, $193 per credit part-time for state residents; $6236 per year full-time, $346 per credit part-time for nonresidents. Fees $313 per year (minimum) full-time, $84 per year part-time. • Application contact: Dr. Rosalyn Darling, Graduate Coordinator, 724-357-3930. E-mail: rdarling@grove.iup.edu.

Indiana University–Purdue University Fort Wayne, School of Education, Program in Educational Administration, Fort Wayne, IN 46805-1499. Awards MS Ed. Accredited by NCATE. Part-time and evening/weekend programs available. Faculty: 2 full-time (0 women). Students: 3 full-time (all women), 110 part-time (56 women); includes 6 minority (4 African Americans, 1 Asian American, 1 Hispanic). Average age 36. 42 applicants, 100% accepted. In 1997, 30 degrees awarded (100% found work related to degree). *Entrance requirements:* Minimum GPA of 2.5. Application deadline: 8/1 (priority date; rolling processing; 12/1 for spring admission). Application fee: $30. *Expenses:* Tuition $2356 per year full-time, $131 per credit hour part-time for state residents; $5253 per year full-time, $292 per credit hour part-time for nonresidents. Fees $183 per year full-time, $10.15 per credit hour part-time. *Financial aid:* Application deadline 3/1. • Betty Steffy, Dean, School of Education, 219-481-6456. Fax: 219-481-6083.

Indiana University–Purdue University Indianapolis, School of Education, Department of School Administration, Indianapolis, IN 46202-2896. Awards MS. Evening/weekend programs available. Faculty: 6 full-time, 12 part-time. Students: 20 part-time (6 women); includes 1 minority (African American). Average age 29. In 1997, 7 degrees awarded. *Degree requirements:* Thesis optional, foreign language not required. *Entrance requirements:* GRE General Test (minimum combined score of 1300), minimum GPA of 3.0. Application deadline: 3/1 (priority date; 11/1 for spring admission). Application fee: $35. *Expenses:* Tuition $3602 per year full-time, $150 per credit hour part-time for state residents; $10,392 per year full-time, $433 per credit hour part-time for nonresidents. Fees $100 per year (minimum) full-time, $40 per year (minimum) part-time. *Financial aid:* Federal Work-Study available. *Faculty research:* Principalship, leadership, organizational culture, finance. • Neil Theobald, Chair, 812-856-8397. Application contact: Dr. O. Gilbert Brown, Assistant Dean for Education Student Services, 317-274-0649. Fax: 317-274-6864. E-mail: ogbrown@iupui.edu.

Inter American University of Puerto Rico, Metropolitan Campus, Division of Education, Program in Administration and Supervision, San Juan, PR 00919-1293. Awards MA. Students: 15 full-time (10 women), 22 part-time (14 women); includes 37 minority (all Hispanics). In 1997, 41 degrees awarded. *Degree requirements:* Comprehensive exam required, foreign language and thesis not required. *Entrance requirements:* GRE or PAEG, interview. Application deadline: 5/15 (priority date; rolling processing; 11/15 for spring admission). Application fee: $31. Electronic applications accepted. *Expenses:* Tuition $3272 per year full-time, $1740 per year part-time. Fees $328 per year full-time, $176 per year part-time. • Application contact: Jenny Maldonado, Administrative Assistant, 787-250-1912 Ext. 2393. Fax: 787-250-1197.

Inter American University of Puerto Rico, San Germán Campus, Department of Education, Program in Administration of Higher Education Institutions, San Germán, PR 00683-5008. Awards MA. Part-time and evening/weekend programs available. Faculty: 8 full-time (1 woman), 13 part-time (7 women). In 1997, 10 degrees awarded. *Degree requirements:* Comprehensive exam required, foreign language and thesis not required. *Entrance requirements:* Minimum GPA of 3.0, GRE General Test, or PAEG. Application deadline: 4/30 (priority date; rolling processing; 11/15 for spring admission). Application fee: $31. *Expenses:* Tuition $150 per credit. Fees $177 per semester. *Financial aid:* Teaching assistantships available. • Application contact: Mildred Camacho, Admissions Director, 787-892-3090. Fax: 787-892-6350.

Inter American University of Puerto Rico, San Germán Campus, Department of Education, Program in Educational Administration, San Germán, PR 00683-5008. Awards MA Ed. Part-time and evening/weekend programs available. Faculty: 8 full-time (1 woman), 13 part-time (7 women). In 1997, 7 degrees awarded. *Degree requirements:* Comprehensive exam required, foreign language and thesis not required. *Entrance requirements:* Minimum GPA of 3.0, GRE General Test, or PAEG. Application deadline: 4/30 (priority date; rolling processing; 11/15 for spring admission). Application fee: $31. *Expenses:* Tuition $150 per credit. Fees $177 per semester. *Financial aid:* Teaching assistantships available. • Application contact: Mildred Camacho, Admissions Director, 787-892-3090. Fax: 787-892-6350.

Iona College, School of Arts and Science, Program in School Administration and Supervision, 715 North Avenue, New Rochelle, NY 10801-1890. Awards MS Ed. Part-time and evening/weekend programs available. Faculty: 1 full-time (0 women), 2 part-time (0 women). Students: 14 part-time (9 women); includes 2 minority (both Hispanics). Average age 36. In 1997, 9 degrees awarded. *Degree requirements:* Internships. *Entrance requirements:* New York teaching certificate, 3 years of teaching or supervisory experience. Application deadline: rolling. Application fee: $25. *Expenses:* Tuition $410 per credit hour. Fees $25 per semester. *Financial aid:* Graduate assistantships, partial tuition waivers, and career-related internships or fieldwork available. Aid available to part-time students. *Faculty research:* Educational technology, staff development, multicultural education, reading and writing. • Dr. Lucy Murphy, Chair, 914-633-2210. Fax: 914-633-2608. Application contact: Arlene Melillo, Director of Graduate Recruitment, 914-633-2328. Fax: 914-633-2023.

Iona College, School of Arts and Science, Program in School District Administration, 715 North Avenue, New Rochelle, NY 10801-1890. Awards Diploma. Part-time and evening/weekend programs available. Faculty: 1 full-time (0 women), 2 part-time (0 women). Students: 9 part-time (8 women). Average age 40. In 1997, 8 degrees awarded. *Degree requirements:* Internships. *Entrance requirements:* 3 years of teaching or supervisory experience, New York teaching certificate. Application deadline: rolling. Application fee: $25. *Expenses:* Tuition $410 per credit hour. Fees $25 per semester. *Financial aid:* Graduate assistantships, partial tuition waivers, and career-related internships or fieldwork available. Aid available to part-time students. *Faculty research:* Reading/writing, educational technology, multicultural education. • Dr. Lucy Murphy, Chair, 914-633-2210. Fax: 914-633-2608. Application contact: Arlene Melillo, Director of Graduate Recruitment, 914-633-2328. Fax: 914-633-2023.

Iowa State University of Science and Technology, College of Education, Department of Educational Leadership and Policy Studies, Program in Educational Administration, Ames, IA 50011. Awards MS, PhD. *Degree requirements:* For master's, thesis or alternative; for doctorate, dissertation. *Entrance requirements:* For master's, TOEFL; for doctorate, GRE General Test, TOEFL. Application fee: $20 ($30 for international students). *Expenses:* Tuition $3166 per year full-time, $176 per credit part-time for state residents; $9324 per year full-time, $518 per credit part-time for nonresidents. Fees $200 per year. • Dr. Richard P. Manatt, Coordinator, 515-294-9995. E-mail: manatt@iastate.edu.

Jackson State University, School of Education, Department of Educational Foundations and Leadership, Jackson, MS 39217. Offers programs in education administration (Ed S); educational administration (MS Ed, PhD); secondary education (MS Ed, Ed S), including educational technology (MS Ed). Accredited by NCATE. Part-time and evening/weekend programs available. Faculty: 21 full-time (10 women), 5 part-time (1 woman). Students: 36 full-time (12 women), 54 part-time (37 women); includes 80 minority (all African Americans), 2 international. 57 applicants, 67% accepted. In 1997, 18 master's, 5 doctorates, 4 Ed Ss awarded. *Degree requirements:* For master's, thesis or alternative, comprehensive exam; for doctorate and Ed S, thesis/dissertation, comprehensive exam. *Entrance requirements:* For master's, GRE General Test (minimum combined score of 1000), TOEFL (minimum score 550); for doctorate, MAT (minimum score 45), teaching experience. Application deadline: 3/1 (priority date; rolling processing; 10/1 for spring admission). Application fee: $20. *Tuition:* $2688 per year (minimum) full-time, $150 per semester hour part-time for state residents; $5546 per year (minimum) full-time, $309 per semester hour part-time for nonresidents. *Financial aid:* Federal Work-Study available. Financial aid application deadline: 3/1. • Dr. George Vincent, Chair, 601-968-2351. Fax: 601-968-2213. E-mail: gvincent@ccaix.jsums.edu. Application contact: Mae Robinson, Admissions Coordinator, 601-968-2455. Fax: 601-968-8246. E-mail: mrobinson@ccaix.jsums.edu.

Jacksonville State University, College of Education, Program in School Administration, Jacksonville, AL 36265-9982. Awards MS Ed, Ed S. Accredited by NCATE. Faculty: 2 full-time (0 women). Students: 16 full-time (9 women), 111 part-time (59 women); includes 52 minority (51 African Americans, 1 Hispanic). In 1997, 1 master's, 46 Ed Ss awarded. *Degree requirements:* For master's, thesis optional. *Entrance requirements:* For master's, GRE General Test or MAT. Application deadline: rolling. Application fee: $20. *Expenses:* Tuition $2140 per year full-time, $107 per semester hour part-time for state residents; $4280 per year full-time, $214 per semester hour part-time for nonresidents. Fees $30 per semester. *Financial aid:* Available to part-time students. Financial aid application deadline: 4/1. • Application contact: College of Graduate Studies and Continuing Education, 205-782-5329.

Jacksonville University, College of Arts and Sciences, Division of Education, Program in Educational Leadership, 2800 University Boulevard North, Jacksonville, FL 32211-3394. Awards MAT. Part-time and evening/weekend programs available. *Degree requirements:* Comprehensive exam required, foreign language and thesis not required. *Entrance requirements:* GRE General Test (minimum combined score of 900), TOEFL (minimum score 500), minimum GPA of 3.0. Application deadline: 8/1 (priority date; rolling processing; 11/1 for spring admission). Application fee: $25.

James Madison University, College of Education and Psychology, School of Education, Program in Educational Leadership, Harrisonburg, VA 22807. Awards M Ed. Accredited by NCATE. Program being phased out; applicants no longer accepted. Part-time and evening/weekend programs available. Students: 14 part-time (9 women). Average age 30. In 1997, 8 degrees awarded. *Tuition:* $134 per credit hour for state residents; $404 per credit hour for nonresidents. *Financial aid:* Fellowships, teaching assistantships, Federal Work-Study available. Financial aid applicants required to submit FAFSA. • Dr. Elizabeth Morie, Coordinator, 540-568-6193.

John Carroll University, Department of Education and Allied Studies, Program in Administration Supervision, University Heights, OH 44118-4581. Awards MA, M Ed. Accredited by NCATE. Faculty: 2 full-time (0 women), 16 part-time (4 women). Students: 15 full-time (12 women), 63 part-time (43 women); includes 18 minority (16 African Americans, 2 Hispanics), 1 international. In 1997, 15 degrees awarded. *Degree requirements:* Comprehensive exam, research essay or thesis required, foreign language not required. *Entrance requirements:* GRE General Test or MAT, minimum GPA of 2.75. Application deadline: 8/15 (priority date; rolling processing; 1/3 for spring admission). Application fee: $25 ($35 for international students). *Tuition:* $450 per credit. *Financial aid:* Teaching assistantships, partial tuition waivers available. Financial aid application deadline: 3/1; applicants required to submit FAFSA. • Dr. William P. Deighan, Coordinator, 216-397-4331.

Johns Hopkins University, School of Continuing Studies, Division of Education, Department of Teacher Development and Leadership, Baltimore, MD 21218-2699. Offerings include administration and supervision (MS, CAGS), discipline and positive behavior management (Certificate), general education (MS, Ed D, CAGS), school principalship (Certificate), teacher leadership (MS). *Degree requirements:* For doctorate, dissertation, comprehensive exam required, foreign language not required. *Entrance requirements:* For doctorate, MAT, interview, master's degree, minimum GPA of 3.25; for other advanced degree, master's or doctoral degree. Application fee: $50. • Rochelle Ingram, Chair, 410-516-4957.

Johnson & Wales University, Graduate School, Program in Educational Leadership, 8 Abbott Park Place, Providence, RI 02903-3703. Awards Ed D. Faculty: 4 full-time. Students: 47 full-time (16 women); includes 3 minority (all African Americans). Average age 36. *Degree requirements:* Dissertation. *Entrance requirements:* MAT, minimum GPA of 3.25. Application deadline: 8/21 (priority date; rolling processing). Application fee: $0. *Expenses:* Tuition $194 per quarter hour (minimum). Fees $477 per year. *Financial aid:* Application deadline 5/1. *Faculty research:* Site-based management, collaborative learning, technology and education, K–16 education. • Dr. Clifton J. Boyle, Director, 401-598-4739. Fax: 401-598-1825. Application contact: Dr. Allan G. Freedman, Director of Graduate Admissions, 401-598-1015. Fax: 401-598-4773. E-mail: clifb@jwu.edu.

Johnson State College, Graduate Program in Education, Program in Educational Leadership, Johnson, VT 05656-9405. Offers public school principal (MA Ed), school business management (MA Ed). Students: 1 full-time (0 women), 15 part-time (12 women). *Degree requirements:* Thesis or alternative, comprehensive exam required, foreign language not required. *Entrance requirements:* Interview. Application deadline: 7/15 (priority date; rolling processing; 11/1 for spring admission). Application fee: $30. *Expenses:* Tuition $164 per credit for state residents; $383 per credit for nonresidents. Fees $15.90 per credit. *Financial aid:* Federal Work-Study, institutionally sponsored loans, and career-related internships or fieldwork available. Aid available to part-time students. Financial aid application deadline: 3/1; applicants required to submit FAFSA. • Application contact: Catherine H. Higley, Administrative Assistant, 802-635-2356 Ext. 1244. Fax: 802-635-1248. E-mail: higleyc@badger.jsc.vsc.edu.

Kansas State University, College of Education, Department of Educational Administration and Leadership, Manhattan, KS 66506. Awards MS, Ed D. Accredited by NCATE. Faculty: 25 full-time (6 women). Students: 8 full-time (5 women), 74 part-time (38 women); includes 4 minority (2 African Americans, 2 Hispanics). 12 applicants, 58% accepted. *Degree requirements:* For master's, thesis or alternative required, foreign language not required; for doctorate, dissertation required, foreign language not required. *Entrance requirements:* For master's, GRE General Test (minimum combined score of 960), MAT (minimum score 42; average 52), minimum B average; for doctorate, GRE General Test (minimum combined score of 1000; average 1040), MAT (minimum score 46; average 58), minimum B average. Application deadline: 4/1 (priority date; rolling processing; 10/1 for spring admission). Application fee: $0 ($25 for international students). Electronic applications accepted. *Tuition:* $2218 per year full-time, $401 per semester (minimum) part-time for state residents; $6336 per year full-time, $1087 per semester (minimum) part-time for nonresidents. *Financial aid:* Career-related internships or fieldwork available. • David C. Thompson, Chair, 785-532-5543. Application contact: Paul Burden, Assistant Dean, 785-532-5595. Fax: 785-532-7304. E-mail: gradstudy@mail.educ.ksu.edu.

Kean University, School of Education, Department of Instruction, Curriculum and Administration, Educational Administration Program, Union, NJ 07083. Awards MA, Certificate. Accredited by NCATE. Part-time programs available. Students: 17 full-time (9 women), 154 part-time (89 women); includes 33 minority (18 African Americans, 2 Asian Americans, 13 Hispanics). Average age 39. In 1997, 49 master's awarded. *Degree requirements:* For master's, thesis, comprehensive exams required, foreign language not required. *Entrance requirements:* For master's, GRE General Test or MAT. Application deadline: 6/15 (11/15 for spring admission). Application fee: $35. *Tuition:* $5926 per year full-time, $248 per credit part-time for state residents; $7312 per year full-time, $304 per credit part-time for nonresidents. *Financial aid:* Graduate assistantships available. • Dr. Nicholas Celso, Coordinator, 908-527-2528. Application contact: Joanne Morris, Director of Graduate Admissions, 908-527-2665. Fax: 908-527-2286. E-mail: grad_adm@turbo.kean.edu.

Keene State College, Program in Educational Administration, Keene, NH 03435. Awards M Ed. Part-time and evening/weekend programs available. Students: 1 (woman) full-time, 10 part-time (5 women). Average age 39. 5 applicants, 100% accepted. In 1997, 1 degree awarded. *Degree requirements:* Thesis, comprehensive exam, project required, foreign language not required. *Entrance requirements:* Teaching certificate, 5 years of work experience, resume. Application deadline: 6/15 (rolling processing; 10/15 for spring admission). Application fee: $25 ($35 for international students). *Financial aid:* Research assistantships available. Financial aid application deadline: 3/1; applicants required to submit FAFSA. • Dr. John Couture, Coordinator, 603-358-2350. E-mail: jcouture@keene.edu. Application contact: Peter Tandy, Academic Counselor, 603-358-2332. Fax: 603-358-2257. E-mail: ptandy@keene.edu.

Kent State University, Graduate School of Education, Department of Teaching, Leadership, and Curriculum Studies, Program in Educational Administration, Kent, OH 44242-0001. Offers K–12 leadership (MA, M Ed, PhD, Ed S). Accredited by NCATE. Part-time and evening/weekend programs available. Faculty: 7 full-time (4 women), 8 part-time (4 women). Students: 12 full-time (9 women), 51 part-time (31 women); includes 4 minority (all African Americans), 1 international. In 1997, 9 master's, 3 doctorates, 5 Ed Ss awarded. *Degree requirements:* For master's, thesis (MA) required, foreign language not required; for doctorate, dissertation required, foreign language not required. *Entrance requirements:* For doctorate, GRE General Test (minimum score 550 on verbal section). Application deadline: rolling. Application fee: $30. *Tuition:* $4752 per year full-time, $216 per credit hour part-time for state residents; $9213 per year full-time, $419 per credit hour part-time for nonresidents. *Financial aid:* Application deadline 4/1. • Dr. William Konnert, Coordinator, 330-672-2477. Application contact: Deborah Barber, Director, Office of Academic Services, 330-672-2862. Fax: 330-672-3549.

Kent State University, Graduate School of Education, Department of Teaching, Leadership, and Curriculum Studies, Program in Higher Education Administration and Student Personnel, Kent, OH 44242-0001. Awards MA, M Ed, PhD, Ed S. Accredited by NCATE. Faculty: 3 full-time (0 women). Students: 52 full-time (30 women), 29 part-time (19 women); includes 11 minority (10 African Americans, 1 Hispanic), 1 international. In 1997, 14 master's, 2 doctorates, 2 Ed Ss awarded. *Degree requirements:* For master's, thesis (MA) required, foreign language not required; for doctorate, dissertation required, foreign language not required. *Entrance requirements:* For doctorate, GRE General Test (minimum score 550 on verbal section); for Ed S, MAT or minimum graduate GPA of 3.5. Application deadline: rolling. Application fee: $30. *Tuition:* $4752 per year full-time, $216 per credit hour part-time for state residents; $9213 per year full-time, $419 per credit hour part-time for nonresidents. *Financial aid:* Application deadline 4/1. • Dr. William Konnert, Coordinator, 330-672-2477. Application contact: Deborah Barber, Director, Office of Academic Services, 330-672-2862. Fax: 330-672-3549.

Kutztown University of Pennsylvania, Graduate School, College of Education, Program in Counseling, Kutztown, PA 19530. Offers student affairs in higher education (M Ed). Accredited by NCATE. Part-time and evening/weekend programs available. Faculty: 6 full-time (3 women). Students: 6 full-time (5 women), 16 part-time (13 women); includes 2 Hispanics. Average age 32. In 1997, 7 degrees awarded. *Degree requirements:* Comprehensive exams required, foreign language and thesis not required. *Entrance requirements:* GRE General Test, TOEFL, TSE, interview. Application deadline: 3/1 (8/1 for spring admission). Application fee: $25. *Tuition:* $4111 per year full-time, $225 per credit hour part-time for state residents; $6879 per year full-time, $393 per credit hour part-time for nonresidents. *Financial aid:* Graduate assistantships, partial tuition waivers, Federal Work-Study, and career-related internships or fieldwork available. Financial aid application deadline: 3/15; applicants required to submit FAFSA. • Dr. Frank A. Bucci, Graduate Coordinator, 610-683-4223.

Lakehead University, Faculty of Education, Thunder Bay, ON P7B 5E1, Canada. Offerings include education administration (M Ed). *Degree requirements:* Thesis optional, foreign language not required. *Entrance requirements:* TOEFL (minimum score 550), honors degree, minimum B average. Application deadline: 2/1 (priority date; rolling processing). Application fee: $0.

Lamar University, College of Education and Human Development, Department of Educational Leadership, Program in Administration, Beaumont, TX 77710. Awards M Ed. Faculty: 2 full-time (0 women), 5 part-time (0 women). Students: 7 full-time (5 women), 74 part-time (31 women); includes 9 minority (7 African Americans, 2 Hispanics). Average age 40. In 1997, 11 degrees awarded. *Degree requirements:* Computer language required, thesis optional, foreign language not required. *Entrance requirements:* GRE General Test (minimum combined score of 900), TOEFL (minimum score 500), minimum GPA of 2.5. Application deadline: 8/1 (rolling processing; 12/1 for spring admission). Application fee: $0. *Expenses:* Tuition $1296 per year full-time, $360 per year part-time for state residents; $6432 per year full-time, $1608 per year part-time for nonresidents. Fees $238 per year full-time, $103 per year part-time. *Financial aid:* Application deadline 4/1. • Dr. Carolyn Crawford, Chair, Department of Educational Leadership, 409-880-8689.

Lamar University, College of Education and Human Development, Department of Educational Leadership, Program in Supervision, Beaumont, TX 77710. Awards M Ed. Faculty: 2 full-time (0 women), 1 part-time (0 women). Students: 4 full-time (1 woman), 54 part-time (41 women); includes 12 minority (11 African Americans, 1 Asian American). Average age 25. In 1997, 1 degree awarded. *Degree requirements:* Thesis optional, foreign language not required. *Average time to degree:* master's–2 years full-time, 3.5 years part-time. *Entrance requirements:* GRE General Test (minimum combined score of 900), TOEFL (minimum score 500), minimum GPA of 2.5. Application deadline: 8/1 (rolling processing; 12/1 for spring admission). Application fee: $0. *Expenses:* Tuition $1296 per year full-time, $360 per year part-time for state residents; $6432 per year full-time, $1608 per year part-time for nonresidents. Fees $238 per year full-time, $103 per year part-time. *Financial aid:* Application deadline 4/1. • Dr. Carolyn Crawford, Chair, Department of Educational Leadership, 409-880-8689.

La Sierra University, School of Education, Department of Administration and Leadership, Riverside, CA 92515-8247. Awards MA, Ed D, Ed S. Part-time and evening/weekend programs available. Faculty: 3 full-time (0 women), 3 part-time (0 women), 3.5 FTE. Students: 30. Average age 35. In 1997, 11 master's, 2 doctorates, 6 Ed Ss awarded. Terminal master's awarded for partial completion of doctoral program. *Degree requirements:* For master's, thesis optional, foreign language not required; for doctorate, dissertation, fieldwork, qualifying exam required, foreign language not required; for Ed S, fieldwork required, thesis optional, foreign language not required. *Entrance requirements:* For master's, minimum GPA of 3.0; for doctorate, GRE General Test, GRE Subject Test, minimum GPA of 3.3, Ed S; for Ed S, master's degree, minimum GPA of 3.3. Application deadline: rolling. Application fee: $30. *Financial aid:* Graduate assistantships, Federal Work-Study, and career-related internships or fieldwork available. Financial aid application deadline: 2/10. • Dr. Norman Powell, Chair, 909-785-2074. Application contact: Myrna Costa-Casado, Director of Admissions, 909-785-2176. Fax: 909-785-2447. E-mail: mcosta@lasierra.edu.

Lehigh University, College of Education, Department of Education and Human Services, Program in Educational Leadership, Bethlehem, PA 18015-3094. Awards M Ed, Ed D, Certificate. Part-time and evening/weekend programs available. Postbaccalaureate distance learning degree programs offered (minimal on-campus study). Faculty: 5 full-time (1 woman). Students: 5 full-time (all women), 70 part-time (40 women); includes 2 minority (1 African American, 1 Asian American), 3 international. 7 applicants, 71% accepted. In 1997, 9 master's, 4 doctorates awarded. *Degree requirements:* For doctorate, dissertation required, foreign language not required. *Entrance requirements:* For master's, GRE General Test (score in 75th percentile or higher) or MAT, TOEFL, minimum GPA of 2.75; for doctorate, GRE General Test (score in 75th percentile or higher) or MAT, TOEFL, minimum graduate GPA of 3.6; for Certificate, TOEFL (minimum score 550). Application deadline: 7/15 (rolling processing; 12/1 for spring admission). Application fee: $40. Electronic applications accepted. *Expenses:* Tuition $470 per credit. Fees $12 per semester full-time, $6 per semester part-time. *Financial aid:* Scholarships, full and partial tuition waivers, Federal Work-Study, institutionally sponsored loans, and career-related internships or fieldwork available. Financial aid application deadline: 1/15. *Faculty research:* School finance and law, supervision of instruction, curriculum development, middle-level education, organizational change. • Dr. George P. White, Coordinator, 610-758-3250. Fax: 610-758-6223. E-mail: gpw1@lehigh.edu.

Lesley College, School of Education, Cambridge, MA 02138-2790. Offerings include educational administration (M Ed, CAGS). Postbaccalaureate distance learning degree programs offered (no on-campus study). School faculty: 36 full-time (31 women), 340 part-time (220 women). *Degree requirements:* Computer language required, foreign language and thesis not required. *Entrance requirements:* For master's, TOEFL (minimum score 550); for CAGS, interview, master's degree. Application deadline: rolling. Application fee: $45. *Tuition:* $425 per credit. • Dr. William L. Dandridge, Dean, 617-349-8375. Application contact: Graduate Admissions, 617-349-8300. Fax: 617-349-8366.

Lewis & Clark College, Department of Education, Program in Educational Administration, Portland, OR 97219-7899. Awards Certificate, MAT/Certificate, MPA/Certificate. Part-time and evening/weekend programs available. *Application deadline:* rolling. *Application fee:* $45. *Faculty research:* Socialization of administrators, teacher evaluation effectiveness, instructional leadership, gender and leadership.

Lewis University, College of Arts and Sciences, Department of Education, Romeoville, IL 60446. Offerings include education administration (CAS). Department faculty: 12 (10 women). *Application deadline:* 9/1. *Application fee:* $35. • Dr. Jeanette Mines, Chair, 815-838-0500 Ext. 5316. Fax: 815-836-5879.

Liberty University, School of Education, 1971 University Road, Lynchburg, VA 24502. Offerings include educational administration (M Ed). School faculty: 3 full-time (1 woman), 4 part-time (2 women). *Degree requirements:* Thesis optional, foreign language not required. *Entrance requirements:* GRE General Test (minimum combined score of 900). Application deadline: 8/15 (priority date; rolling processing). Application fee: $35. *Tuition:* $280 per credit hour. • Dr. Pauline Donaldson, Dean, 804-582-2314. Application contact: Bill Wegert, Coordinator of Graduate Admissions, 804-582-2175.

Lincoln University, Graduate School, College of Arts and Sciences, Department of Education, Jefferson City, MO 65102. Offerings include school administration and supervision (M Ed), with options in elementary, secondary. Accredited by NCATE. Department faculty: 2 full-time (0 women), 10 part-time (6 women). *Entrance requirements:* GRE General Test or MAT, minimum GPA of 2.75 in major, 2.5 overall. Application deadline: 7/25 (rolling processing; 12/15 for spring admission). Application fee: $17. *Expenses:* Tuition $117 per credit hour for state residents; $234 per credit hour for nonresidents. Fees $552 per year (minimum) for state residents; $1104 per year (minimum) for nonresidents. • Dr. Marilyn Hofmann, Acting Head, 573-681-5250.

Long Island University, Brooklyn Campus, School of Education, Department of Educational Leadership and Technology, Brooklyn, NY 11201-8423. Offers programs in computers in education (MS), educational leadership (PD). Part-time and evening/weekend programs available. Faculty: 1 full-time (0 women). Students: 4 full-time (all women), 44 part-time (31 women); includes 32 minority (27 African Americans, 5 Hispanics). 32 applicants, 94% accepted. In 1997, 8 master's, 18 PDs awarded. *Degree requirements:* For master's, thesis optional. *Entrance requirements:* For PD, master's degree in education. Application deadline: rolling. Application fee: $30. Electronic applications accepted. *Expenses:* Tuition $480 per credit. Fees $415 per year full-time, $73 per semester (minimum) part-time. • Dr. Philip Segan, Chair, 718-488-1103. Application contact: Bernard W. Sullivan, Associate Director of Admissions, 718-488-1011.

Directory: Educational Administration

Long Island University, C.W. Post Campus, School of Education, Department of Educational Leadership and Administration, Brookville, NY 11548-1300. Offers programs in educational administration (PD), school administration and supervision (MS), school business administration (PD). Part-time and evening/weekend programs available. Faculty: 5 full-time (1 woman), 5 part-time (0 women). Students: 9 full-time, 120 part-time. 59 applicants, 98% accepted. In 1997, 11 master's, 53 PDs awarded. *Degree requirements:* For master's, comprehensive exam or research project, internship required, foreign language not required; for PD, internship. *Entrance requirements:* For master's, minimum GPA of 2.75 in major, 2.5 overall. Application deadline: rolling. Application fee: $30. Electronic applications accepted. *Expenses:* Tuition $480 per credit. Fees $316 per year full-time, $71 per semester (minimum) part-time. *Financial aid:* In 1997–98, 3 research assistantships were awarded; career-related internships or fieldwork also available. Aid available to part-time students. Financial aid application deadline: 5/15; applicants required to submit FAFSA. *Faculty research:* Leadership administration, computers in decision making, curricular innovation and school business administration. • Dr. Dennis Murphy, Chairperson, 516-299-2244. E-mail: murphy@eagle.liunet.edu. Application contact: Camille Marziliano, Academic Counselor, 516-299-2123. Fax: 516-299-4167. E-mail: cmarzili@eagle.liunet.edu.

Longwood College, Department of Education, Farmville, VA 23909-1800. Offerings include administration/supervision (MS). Department faculty: 34 part-time. *Degree requirements:* Thesis (for some programs), comprehensive exam. *Entrance requirements:* Minimum GPA of 2.5. Application deadline: 5/1 (priority date; rolling processing; 10/15 for spring admission). Application fee: $25. *Expenses:* Tuition $3048 per year full-time, $127 per credit hour part-time for state residents; $8160 per year full-time, $340 per credit hour part-time for nonresidents. Fees $920 per year full-time, $31 per credit hour part-time. • Dr. Frank Howe, Chair, 804-395-2324. Application contact: Admissions Office, 804-395-2060.

Loras College, Program in Educational Administration: Elementary and Secondary, Dubuque, IA 52004-0178. Awards MA. Faculty: 4. Students: 8. *Application deadline:* rolling. *Application fee:* $25. *Tuition:* $320 per credit. • Dr. James Allan, Chair, 319-588-7157. Application contact: Office of Admissions, 319-588-7157. Fax: 319-588-7964.

Louisiana State University and Agricultural and Mechanical College, College of Education, Department of Administrative and Foundational Services, Baton Rouge, LA 70803. Offers programs in counseling (MA, M Ed, Ed S), educational administration (MA, M Ed, PhD, Ed S), research methodology (PhD). Accredited by NCATE. Part-time and evening/weekend programs available. Faculty: 16 full-time (5 women), 1 part-time (0 women). Students: 67 full-time (49 women), 100 part-time (75 women); includes 44 minority (41 African Americans, 3 Asian Americans), 8 international. Average age 36. 44 applicants, 59% accepted. In 1997, 29 master's, 12 doctorates, 7 Ed Ss awarded. Terminal master's awarded for partial completion of doctoral program. *Degree requirements:* For doctorate, dissertation required, foreign language not required; for Ed S, thesis optional, foreign language not required. *Entrance requirements:* For master's, GRE General Test (minimum combined score of 1000; average 1080), minimum GPA of 3.0; for doctorate, GRE General Test (minimum combined score of 1000; average 1100), minimum GPA of 3.0. Application deadline: 1/25 (priority date; rolling processing). Application fee: $25. *Tuition:* $2736 per year full-time, $285 per semester (minimum) part-time for state residents; $6636 per year full-time, $460 per semester (minimum) part-time for nonresidents. *Financial aid:* In 1997–98, 37 students received aid, including 10 fellowships, 16 research assistantships (1 to a first-year student), 8 service assistantships (1 to a first-year student); teaching assistantships, Federal Work-Study, institutionally sponsored loans, and career-related internships or fieldwork also available. Aid available to part-time students. *Faculty research:* Educational evaluation, principal leadership, school organization, higher education. • Barbara Fuhrmann, Chair, 504-388-6900. Application contact: Jim Fox, Graduate Adviser, 504-388-6933. Fax: 504-388-6918.

Louisiana Tech University, College of Education, Department of Curriculum, Instruction and Leadership, Ruston, LA 71272. Offerings include educational leadership (Ed D). Accredited by NCATE. Department faculty: 16 full-time (11 women). *Degree requirements:* Computer language, dissertation required, foreign language not required. *Entrance requirements:* GRE General Test (minimum combined score of 1000). Application deadline: 7/29 (2/3 for spring admission). Application fee: $20 ($30 for international students). *Tuition:* $2382 per year full-time, $223 per quarter (minimum) part-time for state residents; $5307 per year full-time, $223 per quarter (minimum) part-time for nonresidents. • Dr. Samuel V. Dauzat, Head, 318-257-4609.

Loyola College, College of Arts and Sciences, Department of Education, Program in Educational Management and Supervision, Baltimore, MD 21210-2699. Awards MA, M Ed, CAS. Part-time and evening/weekend programs available. Students: 5 full-time (all women), 197 part-time (137 women); includes 28 minority (27 African Americans, 1 Asian American), 1 international. In 1997, 34 master's, 1 CAS awarded. *Entrance requirements:* For CAS, master's degree. Application deadline: 8/1 (rolling processing; 12/1 for spring admission). Application fee: $35. *Tuition:* $222 per credit (minimum). *Financial aid:* Career-related internships or fieldwork available. • Kathleen Cornell, Coordinator, 410-617-2847.

Loyola Marymount University, School of Education, Program in Administration, Los Angeles, CA 90045-8350. Awards M Ed. Part-time and evening/weekend programs available. Faculty: 14 full-time (8 women), 25 part-time (20 women). Students: 2 full-time (1 woman), 15 part-time (9 women); includes 8 minority (2 African Americans, 3 Asian Americans, 3 Hispanics), 1 international. In 1997, 8 degrees awarded. *Degree requirements:* Comprehensive exam required, foreign language and thesis not required. *Entrance requirements:* GRE General Test, TOEFL (minimum score 550), interview. Application fee: $35. Electronic applications accepted. *Expenses:* Tuition $500 per unit. Fees $111 per year full-time, $28 per year part-time. *Financial aid:* In 1997–98, 1 research assistantship totaling $1,200, 1 teaching assistantship totaling $1,300, 9 grants totaling $22,290 were awarded. Aid available to part-time students. Financial aid application deadline: 3/2; applicants required to submit FAFSA. • Dr. Mary McCullough, Coordinator, 310-338-7312.

Loyola University Chicago, School of Education, Department of Curriculum, Instruction and Educational Psychology, Program in Instructional Leadership, 820 North Michigan Avenue, Chicago, IL 60611-2196. Awards M Ed. Students: 10. *Degree requirements:* Comprehensive exam required, foreign language not required. *Average time to degree:* master's–2 years full-time, 3 years part-time. *Application fee:* $35. *Tuition:* $467 per semester hour. *Financial aid:* Application deadline 5/1. • Dr. Diane Schiller, Director, 847-853-3342. Application contact: Marie Rosin-Dittmar, Admissions Coordinator, 847-853-3323. Fax: 847-853-3375. E-mail: mrosind@wpo.it.luc.edu.

Loyola University Chicago, School of Education, Department of Educational Leadership and Policy Studies, Program in Administration/Supervision, 820 North Michigan Avenue, Chicago, IL 60611-2196. Awards MA, M Ed, Ed D, PhD. MA and PhD offered through the Graduate School. Part-time programs available. Faculty: 5 full-time (1 woman), 6 part-time (3 women), 7.3 FTE. Students: 182 (120 women); includes 37 minority (31 African Americans, 3 Asian Americans, 3 Hispanics), 4 international. Average age 35. 55 applicants, 64% accepted. In 1997, 28 master's awarded (100% found work related to degree); 11 doctorates awarded (100% found work related to degree). *Degree requirements:* For master's, comprehensive exam (M Ed), thesis (MA) required, foreign language not required; for doctorate, dissertation, comprehensive exam required, foreign language not required. *Average time to degree:* master's–2 years full-time, 4 years part-time; doctorate–3 years full-time, 6 years part-time. *Entrance requirements:* For doctorate, GRE General Test, MAT, interview. Application deadline: 8/1 (rolling processing; 12/1 for spring admission). Application fee: $35. *Tuition:* $467 per semester hour. *Financial aid:* Research assistantships, institutionally sponsored loans, and career-related internships or fieldwork available. Financial aid application deadline: 2/1; applicants required to submit FAFSA. *Faculty research:* Policy, leadership, staff development, school law, school administration. • Dr. L. A. Safer, Acting Director, 847-853-3353. Application contact: Marie Rosin-Dittmar, Admissions Coordinator, 847-853-3323. Fax: 847-853-3375. E-mail: mrosind@wpo.it.luc.edu.

Loyola University Chicago, School of Education, Department of Educational Leadership and Policy Studies, Program in College Student Personnel, 820 North Michigan Avenue, Chicago, IL 60611-2196. Awards M Ed. Part-time and evening/weekend programs available. Faculty: 3 full-time (1 woman), 3 part-time (2 women). Students: 25 full-time (18 women), 23 part-time (19 women); includes 11 minority (6 African Americans, 4 Asian Americans, 1 Hispanic). Average age 26. 40 applicants, 88% accepted. In 1997, 18 degrees awarded (100% found work related to degree). *Degree requirements:* Comprehensive exam required, foreign language and thesis not required. *Average time to degree:* master's–2 years full-time, 4 years part-time. *Application deadline:* 8/1 (rolling processing; 12/1 for spring admission). *Application fee:* $35. *Tuition:* $467 per semester hour. *Financial aid:* 25 students received aid; research assistantships, institutionally sponsored loans, and career-related internships or fieldwork available. Financial aid application deadline: 2/1; applicants required to submit FAFSA. *Faculty research:* Enrollment management, community colleges, church-affiliated higher education, community service programs, curriculum, evaluation, academic program quality. • Dr. Terry Williams, Director, 847-853-3354. E-mail: twillia@orion.it.luc.edu. Application contact: Marie Rosin-Dittmar, Admissions Coordinator, 847-853-3323. Fax: 847-853-3375. E-mail: mrosind@wpo.it.luc.edu.

Lynchburg College, School of Education and Human Development, Program in School Administration, Lynchburg, VA 24501-3199. Awards M Ed. *Entrance requirements:* Minimum GPA of 3.0 (undergraduate). Application fee: $20.

Lynchburg College, School of Education and Human Development, Program in Supervision, Lynchburg, VA 24501-3199. Awards M Ed. *Entrance requirements:* Minimum GPA of 3.0 (undergraduate). Application fee: $20.

Lynn University, School of Graduate Studies, College of Education, Boca Raton, FL 33431-5598. Offerings include educational leadership with a global perspective (PhD). College faculty: 5 full-time (4 women), 3 part-time (all women). *Degree requirements:* Dissertation. *Average time to degree:* master's–1.8 years full-time. *Entrance requirements:* GRE General Test (minimum combined score of 1000) or MAT (score in 50th percentile or higher). Application deadline: rolling. Application fee: $50. Electronic applications accepted. *Expenses:* Tuition $375 per credit hour. Fees $60 per year. • Dr. Carole Warshaw, Dean, 561-994-0770 Ext. 247. Fax: 561-241-3939. E-mail: admission@lynn.edu. Application contact: Peter Gallo, Graduate Admissions Counselor, 800-544-8035. Fax: 561-241-3552. E-mail: admission@lynn.edu.

Madonna University, Programs in Education, Livonia, MI 48150-1173. Offerings include Catholic school leadership (MSA), educational leadership (MSA). One or more programs accredited by NCATE. Faculty: 7 full-time (4 women), 3 part-time (2 women). *Application deadline:* 8/1 (priority date; rolling processing). *Application fee:* $0. *Expenses:* Tuition $260 per credit hour (minimum). Fees $50 per semester. • Dr. Robert Kimball, Chair, Education Department, 734-432-5652. E-mail: kimball@smtp.munet.edu. Application contact: Sandra Kellums, Coordinator of Graduate Admissions, 734-432-5666. Fax: 734-432-5393. E-mail: kellums@smtp.munet.edu.

Malone College, Graduate School, Program in Education, Canton, OH 44709-3897. Offerings include supervision (MA). Program faculty: 10 full-time (6 women), 11 part-time (5 women), 12.68 FTE. *Degree requirements:* Research practicum required, foreign language and thesis not required. *Entrance requirements:* Minimum GPA of 3.0, teaching license. Application deadline: 9/6 (rolling processing; 1/2 for spring admission). Application fee: $20. *Tuition:* $300 per credit hour. • Dr. Marietta Daulton, Director, 330-471-8447. Fax: 330-471-8478. E-mail: mdaulton@malone.edu. Application contact: Dan Depasquale, Director of Graduate Student Services, 800-257-4723. Fax: 330-471-8343. E-mail: depasquale@malone.edu.

Manhattan College, School of Education, Program in Administration and Supervision, Riverdale, NY 10471. Awards MS Ed, Diploma. Part-time and evening/weekend programs available. Faculty: 2 full-time (1 woman), 1 (woman) part-time. Students: 1 (woman) full-time, 19 part-time (11 women); includes 2 minority (both Hispanics), 2 international. Average age 39. 28 applicants, 86% accepted. In 1997, 11 master's awarded (100% entered university research/teaching). *Degree requirements:* For master's, thesis, internship. *Entrance requirements:* For master's, minimum GPA of 3.0. Application deadline: 8/10 (priority date; rolling processing; 1/7 for spring admission). Application fee: $50. *Expenses:* Tuition $385 per credit. Fees $100 per year. *Financial aid:* In 1997–98, 5 scholarships were awarded. Financial aid application deadline: 2/1. • Sr. Remigia Kushner, Adviser, 718-862-7473. Application contact: William J. Bisset Jr., Dean of Admissions/Financial Aid, 718-862-7200. Fax: 718-863-8019. E-mail: admit@manhattan.edu.

Manhattanville College, School of Education, Program in Special Education, Purchase, NY 10577-2132. Offerings include leadership and strategic management (MS). *Application deadline:* rolling. *Application fee:* $40. *Expenses:* Tuition $410 per credit (minimum). Fees $25 per semester. • Dr. Rebecca Rich, Coordinator, 914-323-5143. Application contact: Carol Messar, Director of Admissions, 914-323-5142. Fax: 914-323-5493.

Mankato State University, College of Education, Department of Educational Administration, Program in Educational Leadership, South Rd and Ellis Ave, PO Box 8400, Mankato, MN 56002-8400. Offers computer services administration (MS), educational administration (Certificate), educational leadership (MS), elementary school administration (MS, SP), general educational administration (MS), higher education administration (MS), secondary administration (MS, SP), vocational-technical administration (MS). Accredited by NCATE. Part-time and evening/weekend programs available. Faculty: 6 full-time (2 women). Students: 32 full-time (18 women), 51 part-time (36 women); includes 1 minority (Asian American), 1 international. Average age 37. 0 applicants. In 1997, 20 master's, 2 other advanced degrees awarded. *Degree requirements:* For master's, thesis or alternative, comprehensive exam required, foreign language not required; for other advanced degree, thesis required, foreign language not required. *Entrance requirements:* For master's, minimum GPA of 3.0 during previous 2 years; for other advanced degree, minimum GPA of 3.0. Application deadline: 7/10 (priority date; rolling processing; 10/30 for spring admission). Application fee: $20. *Tuition:* $126 per credit (minimum) for state residents; $200 per credit for nonresidents. *Financial aid:* Research assistantships, teaching assistantships, Federal Work-Study, and career-related internships or fieldwork available. Aid available to part-time students. Financial aid application deadline: 3/15; applicants required to submit FAFSA. • Application contact: Joni Roberts, Admissions Coordinator, 507-389-2321. Fax: 507-389-5974. E-mail: grad@mankato.msus.edu.

Marian College of Fond du Lac, Education Division, 45 South National Avenue, Fond du Lac, WI 54935-4699. Offerings include educational leadership (MA). Accredited by NCATE. Division faculty: 8 full-time (3 women), 21 part-time (10 women). *Degree requirements:* Exam, field-based experience project, portfolio. *Entrance requirements:* Minimum GPA of 3.0, BA in education or related field, teaching license. Application deadline: rolling. Application fee: $25. *Tuition:* $220 per credit hour. • Dr. Nancy C. Riley, Chair, Educational Studies, 920-923-8143. E-mail: nriley@mariancoll.edu. Application contact: Robert Bohnsack, Admissions, 920-923-8100. Fax: 920-923-7154.

Marshall University, Graduate School of Education and Professional Studies, Program in Leadership Studies, South Charleston, WV 25303-1600. Awards MA, Ed S. Accredited by NCATE. Part-time and evening/weekend programs available. Faculty: 6 full-time (1 woman), 4 part-time (2 women), 7 FTE. Students: 18 full-time (12 women), 178 part-time (102 women); includes 13 minority (12 African Americans, 1 Asian American). Average age 42. In 1997, 48 master's, 6 Ed Ss awarded. *Degree requirements:* For master's, comprehensive or oral exam required, foreign language and thesis not required; for Ed S, internship required, foreign language and thesis not required. *Entrance requirements:* For master's, GRE General Test, minimum undergraduate GPA of 2.5. Application deadline: 8/1 (priority date; rolling processing). Application fee: $0. *Tuition:* $2364 per year full-time, $132 per hour part-time for state residents; $6894 per year full-time, $383 per hour part-time for nonresidents. *Financial aid:* Full tuition waivers and career-related internships or fieldwork available. Aid available to part-time students.

Financial aid applicants required to submit FAFSA. • Dr. James Ranson, Dean, Graduate School of Education and Professional Studies, 304-746-1998. Fax: 304-746-1942.

Marshall University, College of Education, Division of Educational Leadership, Program in Educational Administration, Huntington, WV 25755-2020. Awards MA, Ed D, Ed S. Accredited by NCATE. Ed D offered jointly with West Virginia University. Evening/weekend programs available. Faculty: 2 (1 woman). Students: 9 full-time (6 women), 63 part-time (36 women); includes 4 minority (2 African Americans, 1 Asian American, 1 Native American), 1 international. In 1997, 6 master's awarded. *Degree requirements:* For master's, thesis optional, foreign language not required. *Entrance requirements:* For master's, GRE General Test (minimum combined score of 1200); for doctorate, GRE General Test (minimum combined score of 1500 on three sections). *Tuition:* $2364 per year full-time, $132 per hour part-time for state residents; $6894 per year full-time, $383 per hour part-time for nonresidents. • Dr. Powell Toth, Coordinator, 304-746-2516. Application contact: Dr. James Harless, Director of Admissions, 304-696-3160.

Marshall University, College of Education, Division of Educational Leadership, Program in Educational Supervision, Huntington, WV 25755-2020. Awards MA. Accredited by NCATE. Faculty: 6 (1 woman). Students: 1 (woman) part-time. *Degree requirements:* Thesis optional. *Entrance requirements:* GRE General Test (minimum combined score of 1200). *Tuition:* $2364 per year full-time, $132 per hour part-time for state residents; $6894 per year full-time, $383 per hour part-time for nonresidents. • Dr. Powell Toth, Coordinator, 304-746-2516. Application contact: Dr. James Harless, Director of Admissions, 304-696-3160.

Marygrove College, Department of Administration, Detroit, MI 48221-2599. Offerings include educational administration (MA). *Degree requirements:* Research project required, foreign language and thesis not required. *Average time to degree:* master's–2 years full-time, 3.5 years part-time. *Entrance requirements:* MAT, interview, minimum undergraduate GPA of 3.0. Application deadline: 8/15 (rolling processing). Application fee: $25.

Marywood University, Graduate School of Arts and Sciences, Department of Education, Program in School Leadership, Scranton, PA 18509-1598. Awards MS. Accredited by NCATE. Part-time programs available. Students: 17 part-time (13 women). Average age 37. 6 applicants, 100% accepted. In 1997, 4 degrees awarded. *Degree requirements:* Thesis or alternative, internship required, foreign language not required. *Entrance requirements:* GRE or MAT, TOEFL (minimum score 550; average 590), interview. Application deadline: 7/15 (priority date; rolling processing; 12/1 for spring admission). Application fee: $20. *Expenses:* Tuition $449 per credit hour. Fees $530 per year full-time, $180 per year part-time. *Financial aid:* Research assistantships, scholarships/tuition reductions, partial tuition waivers, and career-related internships or fieldwork available. Aid available to part-time students. Financial aid application deadline: 2/15; applicants required to submit FAFSA. *Faculty research:* School board leadership and development, site-based decision making, educational administration. • Dr. Douglas Lare, Director, 717-348-6211 Ext. 2628. Application contact: Deborah M. Flynn, Coordinator of Admissions, 717-340-6002. Fax: 717-961-4745.

Massachusetts College of Liberal Arts, Graduate Program in Education, North Adams, MA 01247-4100. Offerings include educational administration (M Ed). Program faculty: 8 full-time (5 women), 4 part-time (2 women). *Degree requirements:* Thesis required, foreign language not required. *Average time to degree:* master's–3 years part-time. *Entrance requirements:* Writing sample. Application deadline: rolling. Application fee: $0. *Expenses:* Tuition $130 per credit. Fees $15 per credit. • Dr. Susanne Chandler, Chair, 413-662-5381.

McGill University, Faculty of Graduate Studies and Research, Faculty of Education, Department of Educational Studies, Montréal, PQ H3A 2T5, Canada. Offerings include administration and policy studies (MA, M Ed), with option in educational administration (M Ed). Department faculty: 24 full-time (10 women), 1 part-time. *Entrance requirements:* TOEFL (minimum score 550), minimum GPA of 3.0. Application deadline: 3/1 (priority date; rolling processing; 3/1 for spring admission). Application fee: $60. *Expenses:* Tuition $1668 per year for Canadian residents; $8268 per year for nonresidents. Fees $828 per year for Canadian residents; $1216 per year for nonresidents. • Dr. Lynn Butler-Kisber, Director of Graduate Studies, 514-398-4531. E-mail: lbk@cel.lan.mcgill.ca. Application contact: Tina Shiavone, Graduate Program Coordinator, 514-398-4531. Fax: 514-398-7436.

McNeese State University, College of Education, Department of Educational Leadership and Instructional Technology, Program in Administration and Supervision, Lake Charles, LA 70609-2495. Awards M Ed, Ed S. Evening/weekend programs available. Faculty: 5 full-time (1 woman). Students: 13 full-time (11 women), 75 part-time (50 women). In 1997, 36 master's awarded. *Degree requirements:* For Ed S, comprehensive exam. *Entrance requirements:* For master's, GRE General Test, teaching certificate, 18 hours in professional education; for Ed S, teaching certificate, 3 years of teaching experience, 1 year of administration or supervision experience. Application deadline: 7/15 (priority date; rolling processing). Application fee: $10 ($25 for international students). *Tuition:* $2118 per year full-time, $344 per semester (minimum) part-time for state residents; $7308 per year full-time, $344 per semester (minimum) part-time for nonresidents. *Financial aid:* Fellowships available. Financial aid application deadline: 5/1. • Joe E. Savoie, Head, Department of Educational Leadership and Instructional Technology, 318-475-5423.

Memorial University of Newfoundland, School of Graduate Studies, Faculty of Education, St. John's, NF A1C 5S7, Canada. Offerings include leadership (M Ed). *Degree requirements:* Comprehensive exam required, foreign language not required. *Application deadline:* 2/1. *Application fee:* $40. *Expenses:* Tuition $1896 per year (minimum). Fees $60 per year for Canadian residents; $621 per year for nonresidents. • Dr. Terry Piper, Dean, 709-737-8588. E-mail: tpiper@kean.ucs.mun.ca. Application contact: Dr. Linda M. Phillips, Associate Dean, 709-737-3402. E-mail: lindap@morgan.ucs.mun.ca.

Miami University, School of Education and Allied Professions, Department of Educational Leadership, Program in College Student Personnel Services, Oxford, OH 45056. Awards MS. Accredited by NCATE. Faculty: 4 full-time (3 women). Students: 36 full-time (28 women), 5 part-time (3 women); includes 9 minority (8 African Americans, 1 Hispanic), 2 international. 87 applicants, 51% accepted. In 1997, 20 degrees awarded. *Degree requirements:* Thesis or alternative, oral or written exam required, foreign language not required. *Entrance requirements:* MAT, minimum undergraduate GPA of 3.0 during previous 2 years or 2.75 overall. Application deadline: 3/1 (priority date; rolling processing). Application fee: $35. *Tuition:* $5932 per year full-time, $255 per credit hour part-time for state residents; $12,392 per year full-time, $524 per credit hour part-time for nonresidents. *Financial aid:* In 1997–98, 39 students received aid, including 4 research assistantships, 35 residence hall assistantships; full tuition waivers, Federal Work-Study, and career-related internships or fieldwork also available. Financial aid application deadline: 3/1. • Dr. Judy Rogers, Director of Graduate Study, 513-529-6825.

Miami University, School of Education and Allied Professions, Department of Educational Leadership, Program in Educational Administration, Oxford, OH 45056. Awards M Ed, Ed D, PhD. Accredited by NCATE. *Degree requirements:* For master's, thesis or alternative, oral or written exam required, foreign language not required; for doctorate, dissertation, comprehensive and final exams required, foreign language not required. *Entrance requirements:* For master's, MAT, minimum undergraduate GPA of 3.0 during previous 2 years or 2.75 overall; for doctorate, MAT, minimum undergraduate GPA of 2.75, 3.0 graduate. Application deadline: 3/1 (priority date; rolling processing; 12/15 for spring admission). Application fee: $35. *Tuition:* $5932 per year full-time, $255 per credit hour part-time for state residents; $12,392 per year full-time, $524 per credit hour part-time for nonresidents. *Financial aid:* Application deadline 3/1. • Dr. Richard Quantz, Director of Graduate Study, 513-529-6825.

Michigan State University, College of Education, Department of Educational Administration, East Lansing, MI 48824-1020. Offers programs in adult and continuing education (MA); higher, adult and lifelong education (PhD); K–12 educational administration (MA, PhD, Ed S); student affairs administration (MA). Faculty: 17 (6 women). Students: 293 (182 women); includes 57 minority (38 African Americans, 7 Asian Americans, 11 Hispanics, 1 Native American), 19 international. In 1997, 53 master's, 10 doctorates, 7 Ed Ss awarded. *Degree requirements:* For doctorate, dissertation required, foreign language not required. *Application deadline:* rolling. *Application fee:* $30 ($40 for international students). *Expenses:* Tuition $4609 per year full-time, $223 per credit hour (minimum) part-time for state residents; $8704 per year full-time, $450 per credit hour (minimum) part-time for nonresidents. Fees $576 per year full-time, $476 per year part-time. *Financial aid:* Research assistantships available. *Faculty research:* School reform and public policy, university reform, school to work transitions. • Dr. Philip Cusick, Chairperson, 517-355-4538.

Middle Tennessee State University, College of Education, Department of Educational Leadership, Major in Administration and Supervision, Murfreesboro, TN 37132. Awards M Ed, Ed S. Accredited by NCATE. Students: 14 full-time (11 women), 124 part-time (86 women); includes 15 minority (13 African Americans, 1 Asian American, 1 Native American). Average age 34. 51 applicants, 51% accepted. In 1997, 49 master's, 19 Ed Ss awarded. *Degree requirements:* Comprehensive exams required, foreign language and thesis not required. *Entrance requirements:* Cooperative English Test, MAT. Application deadline: 8/1 (priority date). Application fee: $5. *Expenses:* Tuition $2560 per year full-time, $129 per semester hour part-time for state residents; $7386 per year full-time, $340 per semester hour part-time for nonresidents. Fees $486 per year full-time, $17 per semester (minimum) part-time. *Financial aid:* Application deadline 5/1. • Dr. Nancy Keese, Chair, Department of Educational Leadership, 615-898-2855. Fax: 615-898-2859. E-mail: nkeese@mtsu.edu.

Midwestern State University, Division of Education, Program in Educational Administration, Wichita Falls, TX 76308-2096. Awards M Ed. Part-time and evening/weekend programs available. Students: 36 part-time. Average age 35. 4 applicants, 100% accepted. In 1997, 4 degrees awarded. *Entrance requirements:* GRE General Test, MAT (average 46), TOEFL (minimum score 550). Application deadline: 8/7 (12/15 for spring admission). Application fee: $0 ($50 for international students). *Expenses:* Tuition $44 per hour for state residents; $259 per hour for nonresidents. Fees $90 per year (minimum) full-time, $9 per semester (minimum) part-time. *Financial aid:* Teaching assistantships, institutionally sponsored loans available. • Dr. Emerson Capps, Director, Division of Education, 940-397-4313.

Mills College, Education Department, Oakland, CA 94613-1000. Offerings include administration (Ed D). Terminal master's awarded for partial completion of doctoral program. Department faculty: 8 full-time (6 women), 13 part-time (11 women), 11 FTE. *Average time to degree:* master's–2 years full-time. *Application deadline:* 2/1 (priority date; rolling processing; 11/1 for spring admission). *Application fee:* $50. Electronic applications accepted. *Expenses:* Tuition $10,600 per year full-time, $2560 per year part-time. Fees $468 per year. • Jane Bowyer, Chairperson, 510-430-2118. Fax: 510-430-3314. E-mail: grad-studies@mills.edu. Application contact: La Vonna S. Brown, Coordinator of Graduate Studies, 510-430-3309. Fax: 510-430-2159. E-mail: grad-studies@mills.edu.

Mississippi College, School of Education, Program in School Administration, Clinton, MS 39058. Awards M Ed. Accredited by NCATE. Evening/weekend programs available. *Degree requirements:* Comprehensive exam required, foreign language and thesis not required. *Entrance requirements:* GRE or NTE, minimum GPA of 2.5, Class A Certificate. Application deadline: 8/15 (priority date; rolling processing). Application fee: $25 ($75 for international students). *Expenses:* Tuition $6624 per year full-time, $276 per hour part-time. Fees $230 per year full-time, $35 per semester (minimum) part-time. *Financial aid:* Professional development scholarships and career-related internships or fieldwork available. Aid available to part-time students. Financial aid application deadline: 4/1. • Dr. Alan O'Dell, Head, 601-925-3403.

Mississippi State University, College of Education, Department of Educational Leadership, Mississippi State, MS 39762. Offers program in school administration (MS). Accredited by NCATE. Faculty: 5 full-time (1 woman), 2 part-time (both women). Students: 5 full-time (2 women), 22 part-time (9 women); includes 10 minority (all African Americans). Average age 27. In 1997, 35 degrees awarded. *Degree requirements:* Comprehensive oral or written exam required, foreign language and thesis not required. *Entrance requirements:* NTE, minimum QPA of 2.75 in last 2 years. Application deadline: 7/26 (priority date; rolling processing; 11/10 for spring admission). Application fee: $0 ($25 for international students). *Tuition:* $3017 per year full-time, $168 per credit hour part-time for state residents; $6119 per year full-time, $340 per credit hour part-time for nonresidents. *Financial aid:* In 1997–98, service assistantships averaging $600 per month and totaling $26,000 were awarded; Federal Work-Study and career-related internships or fieldwork also available. Aid available to part-time students. Financial aid application deadline: 4/1. *Faculty research:* Performance appraisal of school administrators, leadership styles. • Dr. Ned B. Lovell, Head, 601-325-3041.

Mississippi State University, College of Education, Program Under Dean of Education, Mississippi State, MS 39762. Offerings include school administration (Ed D, PhD, Ed S). Accredited by NCATE. *Degree requirements:* For doctorate, computer language (for some programs), dissertation required, foreign language not required; for Ed S, thesis or alternative required, foreign language not required. *Entrance requirements:* For Ed S, minimum QPA of 3.2 in graduate course work. *Tuition:* $3017 per year full-time, $168 per credit hour part-time for state residents; $6119 per year full-time, $340 per credit hour part-time for nonresidents. • Dr. William H. Graves, Dean, College of Education, 601-325-3717. Fax: 601-325-8784. E-mail: whg1@ra.msstate.edu.

Monmouth University, School of Education, West Long Branch, NJ 07764-1898. Offerings include principalship (MS Ed), student personnel services (MS Ed), supervision (Certificate). Certificate (learning disabilities-teacher consultant, reading specialist, supervision) new for fall 1998. School faculty: 9 full-time (7 women), 14 part-time (9 women). *Application deadline:* 8/1 (priority date; rolling processing; 12/1 for spring admission). *Application fee:* $35. *Expenses:* Tuition $459 per credit. Fees $274 per semester full-time, $137 per semester part-time. • Dr. Bernice Willis, Dean, 732-571-7518. Fax: 732-263-5277. Application contact: Office of Graduate Admissions, 732-571-3452. Fax: 732-571-5123.

Montclair State University, College of Education and Human Services, Department of Counseling, Human Development, and Educational Leadership, Program in Administration and Supervision, Upper Montclair, NJ 07043-1624. Awards MA. Accredited by NCATE. Part-time and evening/weekend programs available. Faculty: 12 full-time. Students: 28 full-time (22 women), 131 part-time (83 women); includes 28 minority (22 African Americans, 1 Asian American, 5 Hispanics). In 1997, 50 degrees awarded. *Degree requirements:* Thesis or alternative, comprehensive exam. *Entrance requirements:* GRE General Test, interview. Application deadline: 4/1 (rolling processing; 11/1 for spring admission). Application fee: $40. *Expenses:* Tuition $201 per credit for state residents; $257 per credit for nonresidents. Fees $22.05 per credit. *Financial aid:* Application deadline 3/1; applicants required to submit FAFSA. • Dr. Arlene King, Chairperson, Department of Counseling, Human Development, and Educational Leadership, 973-655-5175.

Moorhead State University, Department of Education, Program in Educational Administration, Moorhead, MN 56563-0002. Awards MS, Ed S. Accredited by NCATE. MS and Ed S offered jointly with North Dakota State University. Part-time programs available. Faculty: 1 full-time (0 women). Students: 2 full-time (1 woman), 16 part-time (7 women). 19 applicants, 100% accepted. In 1997, 2 master's, 1 Ed S awarded. *Degree requirements:* For master's, final oral exam, project or thesis, written comprehensive exam required, foreign language not required. *Entrance requirements:* For master's, TOEFL (minimum score 550). Application deadline: 5/1 (priority date; rolling processing; 9/1 for spring admission). Application fee: $20 ($35 for international students). Electronic applications accepted. *Tuition:* $145 per credit hour for state residents; $220 per credit hour for nonresidents. *Financial aid:* Administrative assistantships, Federal Work-Study available. Financial aid application deadline: 7/15; applicants required to submit FAFSA. • Dennis Van Berkum, Coordinator, 218-236-2014.

Directory: Educational Administration

Morehead State University, College of Education and Behavioral Sciences, Department of Leadership and Secondary Education, Program in Elementary and Secondary Education Administration, Morehead, KY 40351. Offers instructional leadership (Ed S). Accredited by NCATE. Part-time and evening/weekend programs available. Faculty: 1 full-time (0 women), 1 part-time (0 women). Students: 0. Average age 25. In 1997, 2 degrees awarded. *Degree requirements:* Thesis, oral exam required, foreign language not required. *Entrance requirements:* GRE General Test (minimum combined score of 1200), interview, master's degree, minimum GPA of 3.5, work experience. Application deadline: 8/1 (priority date; rolling processing; 12/1 for spring admission). Application fee: $0. *Tuition:* $2470 per year full-time, $138 per semester hour part-time for state residents; $6710 per year full-time, $373 per semester hour part-time for nonresidents. *Financial aid:* Research assistantships, teaching assistantships, Federal Work-Study, and career-related internships or fieldwork available. Financial aid application deadline: 4/1; applicants required to submit FAFSA. *Faculty research:* Computer applications for school administrators. • Application contact: Betty Cowsert, Graduate Admissions Officer, 606-783-2039. Fax: 606-783-5061.

Morgan State University, School of Education and Urban Studies, Department of Teacher Education and Administration, Program in Educational Administration and Supervision, Baltimore, MD 21251. Awards MS. Accredited by NCATE. Part-time and evening/weekend programs available. Faculty: 5 full-time (1 woman), 4 part-time (1 woman). Students: 3 full-time (all women), 4 part-time (3 women); includes 6 minority (all African Americans). Average age 35. In 1997, 4 degrees awarded. *Degree requirements:* Comprehensive exam required, thesis optional, foreign language not required. *Average time to degree:* master's–3 years part-time. *Entrance requirements:* GRE General Test or MAT. Application deadline: 7/1 (rolling processing; 11/1 for spring admission). Application fee: $0. *Expenses:* Tuition $160 per credit hour for state residents; $286 per credit hour for nonresidents. Fees $326 per year. *Financial aid:* In 1997–98, 6 fellowships (all to first-year students) totaling $6,000 were awarded. Financial aid application deadline: 4/1. *Faculty research:* Multicultural education, cooperative learing, psychology of cognition. • Paul McElroy, Coordinator, 410-319-3395. Fax: 410-319-3871. Application contact: James E. Waller, Admissions and Programs Officer, 410-319-3186. Fax: 410-319-3837.

Morgan State University, School of Education and Urban Studies, Department of Teacher Education and Administration, Program in Urban Educational Leadership, Baltimore, MD 21251. Awards Ed D. Accredited by NCATE. Part-time and evening/weekend programs available. Faculty: 5 full-time (1 woman), 4 part-time (1 woman). Students: 2 full-time (0 women), 47 part-time (27 women); includes 43 minority (42 African Americans, 1 Asian American). Average age 40. 29 applicants, 28% accepted. In 1997, 5 degrees awarded (100% found work related to degree). *Degree requirements:* Dissertation, comprehensive exam required, foreign language not required. *Average time to degree:* doctorate–7 years part-time. *Entrance requirements:* GRE General Test or MAT. Application deadline: 7/1 (rolling processing). Application fee: $0. *Expenses:* Tuition $160 per credit hour for state residents; $286 per credit hour for nonresidents. Fees $326 per year. *Financial aid:* Application deadline 4/1. *Faculty research:* Multicultural education, cooperative learning, psychology of cognition. • Dr. Iola Ragins Smith, Chair, 410-319-3292. Application contact: James E. Waller, Admissions and Programs Officer, 410-319-3186. Fax: 410-319-3837.

Mount St. Mary's College, Department of Education, Specialization in Administrative Studies, Los Angeles, CA 90049-1597. Awards MS. Part-time and evening/weekend programs available. *Degree requirements:* Thesis, research project required, foreign language not required. *Entrance requirements:* MAT, minimum GPA of 3.0. Application fee: $50.

Murray State University, College of Education, Department of Educational Leadership and Counseling, Program in Educational Administration, Murray, KY 42071-0009. Awards Ed S. Accredited by NCATE. Part-time programs available. Students: 3 full-time (2 women), 72 part-time (52 women); includes 3 minority (all African Americans). 9 applicants, 100% accepted. In 1997, 2 degrees awarded. *Entrance requirements:* GRE General Test, TOEFL (minimum score 500). Application deadline: rolling. Application fee: $20. *Expenses:* Tuition $2500 per year full-time, $124 per hour part-time for state residents; $6740 per year full-time, $357 per hour part-time for nonresidents. Fees $360 per year full-time, $180 per year part-time. *Financial aid:* Research assistantships, teaching assistantships, Federal Work-Study available. Financial aid application deadline: 4/1. • Dr. Steve Traw, Director, 502-762-2794. Fax: 502-762-3799.

National–Louis University, National College of Education, McGaw Graduate School, Program in Early Childhood Administration, 2840 Sheridan Road, Evanston, IL 60201-1730. Awards M Ed, CAS. Program new for fall 1998. *Entrance requirements:* For master's, GRE or MAT, minimum GPA of 3.0. Application fee: $25. *Tuition:* $411 per semester hour. • Dr. Paula Jorde-Bloom, Coordinator, 847-475-1100 Ext. 5551. Application contact: Dr. David McCulloch, Vice President for University Services, 800-443-5522 Ext. 5127. Fax: 847-465-0593. E-mail: dmcc@wheeling1.nl.edu.

National–Louis University, National College of Education, McGaw Graduate School, Program in Early Childhood Leadership and Advocacy, 2840 Sheridan Road, Evanston, IL 60201-1730. Awards M Ed. Students: 25 full-time (all women), 3 part-time (all women); includes 2 minority (both African Americans). In 1997, 62 degrees awarded. *Entrance requirements:* GRE or MAT, minimum GPA of 3.0. Application fee: $25. *Tuition:* $411 per semester hour. *Financial aid:* Fellowships, Federal Work-Study, institutionally sponsored loans available. Aid available to part-time students. Financial aid applicants required to submit FAFSA. • Dr. Marjorie Lee, Coordinator, 847-475-1100 Ext. 3523. Application contact: Dr. David McCulloch, Vice President for University Services, 800-443-5522 Ext. 5127. Fax: 847-465-0593. E-mail: dmcc@wheeling1.nl.edu.

National–Louis University, National College of Education, McGaw Graduate School, Program in Educational Leadership, 2840 Sheridan Road, Evanston, IL 60201-1730. Offers administration and supervision (M Ed, CAS, Ed S), including superintendent endorsement (Ed S). Part-time and evening/weekend programs available. Students: 5 full-time (2 women), 215 part-time (149 women); includes 55 minority (45 African Americans, 2 Asian Americans, 7 Hispanics, 1 Native American). Average age 40. In 1997, 86 master's, 48 other advanced degrees awarded. *Entrance requirements:* For master's, GRE or MAT, minimum GPA of 3.0; for other advanced degree, GRE. Application deadline: rolling. Application fee: $25. *Tuition:* $411 per semester hour. *Financial aid:* Fellowships and career-related internships or fieldwork available. Aid available to part-time students. Financial aid applicants required to submit FAFSA. • Dr. Paul Jung, Coordinator, 847-475-1100 Ext. 5108. Application contact: Dr. David McCulloch, Vice President for University Services, 800-443-5522 Ext. 5127. Fax: 847-465-0593. E-mail: dmcc@wheeling1.nl.edu.

National–Louis University, National College of Education, McGaw Graduate School, Doctoral Programs in Education, Program in Educational Leadership, 2840 Sheridan Road, Evanston, IL 60201-1730. Offers educational leadership/superintendent endorsement (Ed D). Part-time and evening/weekend programs available. Students: 1 full-time (0 women), 38 part-time (25 women); includes 7 minority (5 African Americans, 2 Hispanics). Average age 44. *Degree requirements:* Dissertation, comprehensive exams, internship required, foreign language not required. *Entrance requirements:* GRE General Test, minimum GPA of 3.25. Application deadline: 12/15. Application fee: $25. *Tuition:* $411 per semester hour. *Financial aid:* Fellowships, research assistantships, teaching assistantships, institutionally sponsored loans available. Aid available to part-time students. Financial aid application deadline: 4/15; applicants required to submit FAFSA. • Dr. Kathryn Tooredman, Coordinator, 847-475-1100 Ext. 5516. Application contact: Dr. David McCulloch, Vice President for University Services, 800-443-5522 Ext. 5127. Fax: 847-465-0593. E-mail: dmcc@wheeling1.nl.edu.

National University, School of Education and Human Services, Department of Special Education and Pupil Personnel Services, La Jolla, CA 92037-1011. Offers programs in educational administration (MS), educational counseling (MS), school psychology (MS), special education (MS). Students: 301 full-time (196 women), 182 part-time (122 women); includes 169 minority (62 African Americans, 18 Asian Americans, 83 Hispanics, 6 Native Americans). Average age 36. In 1997, 237 degrees awarded. *Entrance requirements:* Interview, minimum GPA of 2.5. Application deadline: rolling. Application fee: $60 ($100 for international students). *Tuition:* $7830 per year full-time, $870 per course part-time. *Financial aid:* Application deadline 5/1. • Dr. Judy Mantel, Chair, 619-642-8347. Application contact: Nancy Rohland, Director of Enrollment Management, 619-563-7100. Fax: 619-563-7393.

National University, School of Education and Human Services, Department of Teacher Education and Leadership, La Jolla, CA 92037-1011. Offerings include instructional leadership (ME). *Application deadline:* rolling. *Application fee:* $60 ($100 for international students). *Tuition:* $7830 per year full-time, $870 per course part-time. • Dr. Helene Mandell, Chair, 619-642-8345. Application contact: Nancy Rohland, Director of Enrollment Management, 619-563-7100. Fax: 619-563-7393.

New Jersey City University, School of Professional Studies and Education, Programs in Urban Education, Concentration in Administration and Supervision, Jersey City, NJ 07305-1957. Awards MA. Accredited by NCATE. Evening/weekend programs available. *Degree requirements:* Internship required, foreign language and thesis not required. *Entrance requirements:* GRE General Test, TOEFL or MAT. Application deadline: 8/1 (priority date; rolling processing; 12/1 for spring admission). Application fee: $0.

New Jersey City University, School of Professional Studies and Education, Programs in Urban Education, Program in Administration, Curriculum and Instruction, Jersey City, NJ 07305-1957. Offerings include urban education (MA), with options in administration and supervision, basics and urban studies, bilingual/bicultural education and English as a second language. Accredited by NCATE. *Entrance requirements:* GRE General Test, MAT or TOEFL. Application deadline: 8/1 (priority date; rolling processing; 12/1 for spring admission). Application fee: $0.

Newman University, Program in Education, Wichita, KS 67213-2084. Offerings include building leadership (MS Ed). Program faculty: 5 full-time, 9 part-time. *Degree requirements:* Thesis or alternative. *Average time to degree:* master's–3 years part-time. *Application deadline:* 8/15 (priority date; rolling processing; 1/10 for spring admission). *Application fee:* $25. *Tuition:* $257 per credit hour. • Dr. Laura McLemore, Division Chair of Institute for Teacher Education, 316-942-4291 Ext. 253. Fax: 316-942-4483.

New Mexico Highlands University, School of Education, Las Vegas, NM 87701. Offerings include education administration (MA). School faculty: 32 full-time (14 women). *Degree requirements:* Thesis or alternative required, foreign language not required. *Entrance requirements:* Minimum undergraduate GPA of 3.0. Application deadline: 8/1 (priority date; rolling processing). Application fee: $15. *Expenses:* Tuition $1816 per year full-time, $227 per hour part-time for state residents; $7468 per year full-time, $227 per hour part-time for nonresidents. Fees $10 per year. • Dr. James Abreu, Dean, 505-454-3357. Application contact: Dr. Glen W. Davidson, Academic Vice President, 505-454-3311. Fax: 505-454-3558. E-mail: glendavidson@venus.nmhu.edu.

New Mexico State University, College of Education, Department of Educational Management and Development, Las Cruces, NM 88003-8001. Offers programs in educational administration (MA, PhD, Ed S), educational management and development (Ed D). Accredited by NCATE. Part-time programs available. Faculty: 9 full-time (4 women). Students: 37 full-time (17 women), 88 part-time (57 women); includes 53 minority (1 African American, 1 Asian American, 49 Hispanics, 2 Native Americans), 6 international. Average age 40. 53 applicants, 34% accepted. In 1997, 26 master's, 4 doctorates awarded. *Degree requirements:* For master's, internship required, thesis optional, foreign language not required; for doctorate, dissertation, internship. *Entrance requirements:* For master's, minimum GPA of 3.0; for doctorate, GRE General Test, minimum GPA of 3.0; for Ed S, GRE General Test or MAT. Application deadline: 7/1 (priority date; rolling processing; 11/1 for spring admission). Application fee: $15 ($35 for international students). Electronic applications accepted. *Tuition:* $2514 per year full-time, $105 per credit hour part-time for state residents; $7848 per year full-time, $327 per credit hour part-time for nonresidents. *Financial aid:* Research assistantships, teaching assistantships, Federal Work-Study, and career-related internships or fieldwork available. Aid available to part-time students. Financial aid application deadline: 3/1. *Faculty research:* Leadership in K–12 and postsecondary education, management technology, community college administration, diversity in educational administration. • Dr. Maria Luisa Gonzalez, Head, 505-646-3825. Fax: 505-646-4767. E-mail: edmandev@nmsu.edu.

New York University, School of Education, Department of Administration, Leadership, and Technology, Program in Educational Administration and Supervision, New York, NY 10012-1019. Awards MA, Ed D, PhD, CAS. Part-time and evening/weekend programs available. Faculty: 4 full-time, 1 part-time. Students: 20 full-time, 64 part-time. 67 applicants, 45% accepted. In 1997, 17 master's, 5 doctorates, 3 CASs awarded. Terminal master's awarded for partial completion of doctoral program. *Degree requirements:* For master's, thesis required (for some programs), foreign language not required; for doctorate, dissertation. *Entrance requirements:* For master's, TOEFL; for doctorate, GRE General Test, TOEFL, interview; for CAS, TOEFL, master's degree. Application deadline: 2/1 (priority date; rolling processing; 12/1 for spring admission). Application fee: $40 ($60 for international students). *Financial aid:* In 1997–98, teaching assistantships averaging $850 per month were awarded; partial tuition waivers, Federal Work-Study, institutionally sponsored loans, and career-related internships or fieldwork also available. Aid available to part-time students. Financial aid application deadline: 3/1; applicants required to submit FAFSA. *Faculty research:* School restructuring, educational reform, social organization of schools, factors affecting teachers' work. • Terry A. Astuto, Director, 212-998-5179. Application contact: Office of Graduate Admissions, 212-998-5030. Fax: 212-995-4328.

New York University, School of Education, Department of Administration, Leadership, and Technology, Program in Higher Education, New York, NY 10012-1019. Offerings include student personnel administration in higher education (MA). Program faculty: 4 full-time, 10 part-time. *Degree requirements:* Thesis required (for some programs), foreign language not required. *Entrance requirements:* TOEFL. Application deadline: 2/1 (priority date; rolling processing; 12/1 for spring admission). Application fee: $40 ($60 for international students). • Joshua Smith, Director, 212-998-5656. Application contact: Office of Graduate Admissions, 212-998-5030. Fax: 212-995-4328.

New York University, School of Education, Department of Administration, Leadership, and Technology, Program in School Business Administration, New York, NY 10012-1019. Awards CAS. Part-time and evening/weekend programs available. Faculty: 1 full-time. Students: 2 full-time, 2 part-time. In 1997, 3 degrees awarded. *Entrance requirements:* TOEFL, master's degree. Application deadline: 2/1 (priority date; rolling processing; 12/1 for spring admission). Application fee: $40 ($60 for international students). *Financial aid:* Partial tuition waivers, Federal Work-Study, institutionally sponsored loans, and career-related internships or fieldwork available. Aid available to part-time students. Financial aid application deadline: 3/1; applicants required to submit FAFSA. • Terry A. Astuto, Director, 212-998-5179. Application contact: Office of Graduate Admissions, 212-998-5030. Fax: 212-995-4328.

Niagara University, Graduate Division of Education, Concentration in Administration and Supervision, Niagara University, NY 14109. Awards MS Ed, PD. Accredited by NCATE. Part-time and evening/weekend programs available. Faculty: 2 full-time (0 women), 7 part-time (1 woman). Students: 5 full-time (4 women), 50 part-time (35 women); includes 1 minority (African American), 16 international. In 1997, 28 master's awarded. *Entrance requirements:* For master's, GRE General Test or MAT; for PD, GRE General Test and GRE Subject Test or MAT. Application deadline: 8/1 (rolling processing). Application fee: $30. *Expenses:* Tuition $4950 per year full-time, $275 per credit hour part-time. Fees $25 per semester. *Financial aid:* In 1997–98, 1 research assistantship (to a first-year student) was awarded; graduate assistantships, Federal Work-Study, and career-related internships or fieldwork also available. Aid available to part-time students. Financial aid application deadline: 3/15. • Dr. Paul J. Vermette,

Chairman, 716-286-8550. Application contact: Rev. Daniel F. O'Leary, OMI, Dean of Education, 716-286-8560.

Nicholls State University, College of Education, Department of Teacher Education, Thibodaux, LA 70310. Offerings include administration and supervision (M Ed). Accredited by NCATE. Department faculty: 15 full-time (8 women). *Entrance requirements:* GRE General Test, GRE Subject Test. Application deadline: 6/17 (priority date; rolling processing; 11/15 for spring admission). Application fee: $10 ($60 for international students). *Tuition:* $2136 per year full-time, $283 per semester (minimum) part-time for state residents; $5376 per year full-time, $283 per semester (minimum) part-time for nonresidents. • Dr. Harrell H. Carpenter, Head, 504-448-4330.

Norfolk State University, School of Education, Department of Secondary Education and School Management, Program in Urban Education/Administration, 2401 Corprew Avenue, Norfolk, VA 23504-3907. Awards MA. Accredited by NCATE. Part-time programs available. Faculty: 3 full-time, 1 part-time. Students: 46 full-time (39 women), 47 part-time (33 women); includes 68 minority (67 African Americans, 1 Asian American), 23 international. Average age 35. In 1997, 43 degrees awarded. *Entrance requirements:* GRE General Test, minimum GPA of 3.0 in major, 2.5 overall. Application deadline: 8/1. Application fee: $30. *Tuition:* $3718 per year full-time, $198 per credit hour part-time for state residents; $7668 per year full-time, $404 per credit hour part-time for nonresidents. *Financial aid:* Fellowships and career-related internships or fieldwork available. • Dr. Mary Kimble, Acting Head, Department of Secondary Education and School Management, 757-683-8178.

North Carolina Agricultural and Technical State University, Graduate School, School of Education, Department of Educational Leadership and Policy, Greensboro, NC 27411. Offerings include educational administration (MS), with options in educational administration, educational supervision. Accredited by NCATE. *Degree requirements:* Thesis or alternative, comprehensive exam, qualifying exam required, foreign language not required. *Entrance requirements:* GRE General Test, minimum GPA of 2.6. Application deadline: 6/1 (priority date; rolling processing; 12/1 for spring admission). Application fee: $35. *Tuition:* $1662 per year full-time, $272 per semester (minimum) part-time for state residents; $8790 per year full-time, $2054 per semester (minimum) part-time for nonresidents. • Dr. Fred Wood, Interim Chairperson, 336-334-7522. E-mail: woodf@ncat.edu.

North Carolina Central University, Division of Academic Affairs, School of Education, Program in Educational Leadership, Durham, NC 27707-3129. Awards MA. Accredited by NCATE. Part-time and evening/weekend programs available. Students: 6 part-time (3 women); includes 5 minority (all African Americans). Average age 43. 0 applicants. In 1997, 11 degrees awarded. *Degree requirements:* Thesis or alternative, comprehensive exam required, foreign language not required. *Entrance requirements:* Minimum GPA of 3.0 in major, 2.5 overall. Application deadline: 8/1. Application fee: $30. *Tuition:* $2027 per year full-time, $508 per semester (minimum) part-time for state residents; $9155 per year full-time, $2290 per semester (minimum) part-time for nonresidents. *Financial aid:* Fellowships, teaching assistantships, Federal Work-Study, institutionally sponsored loans, and career-related internships or fieldwork available. Aid available to part-time students. Financial aid application deadline: 5/1. *Faculty research:* Simulation of decision-making behavior of school boards. • Dr. Pamela G. George, Director, 919-560-5175. Application contact: Dr. Cecelia Steppe-Jones, Associate Dean of Graduate Studies and Administration, 919-560-6478.

North Dakota State University, College of Human Development and Education, School of Education, Program in Educational Administration, Fargo, ND 58105. Awards MS, Ed S. Accredited by NCATE. Offered jointly with Moorhead State University. Part-time and evening/weekend programs available. Postbaccalaureate distance learning degree programs offered (minimal on-campus study). Faculty: 3 full-time (0 women), 9 part-time (6 women). Students: 219 part-time (73 women); includes 4 minority (all Native Americans). Average age 31. 36 applicants, 97% accepted. In 1997, 17 master's, 5 Ed Ss awarded. *Degree requirements:* Thesis required, foreign language not required. *Entrance requirements:* For master's, GRE General Test (minimum score 450 on each section), MAT (minimum score 40), TOEFL (minimum score 525), minimum GPA of 3.0; for Ed S, GRE General Test (minimum score 450 on each section), MAT (minimum score 40), TOEFL (minimum score 525), master's degree, minimum GPA of 3.25. Application deadline: rolling. Application fee: $25. *Tuition:* $2572 per year full-time, $107 per credit part-time for state residents; $6868 per year full-time, $286 per credit part-time for nonresidents. *Financial aid:* Full tuition waivers, Federal Work-Study, institutionally sponsored loans, and career-related internships or fieldwork available. Financial aid application deadline: 4/15. *Faculty research:* Organizational change and development, goal setting and systematic planning, beginning teacher assistance. • Dr. Dennis Van Berkum, Chair, TCU Educational Administration, 218-236-2014. Fax: 218-299-5850. E-mail: vanberku@mhdl.moorhead.msus.edu.

Northeastern Illinois University, College of Education, Department of Educational Leadership and Development, Program in Educational Administration, Chicago, IL 60625-4699. Offers educational administration and supervision (MA), including chief school business official, community college administration. Part-time and evening/weekend programs available. Faculty: 14 full-time (7 women), 20 part-time (7 women). Students: 15 full-time (8 women), 200 part-time (135 women); includes 44 minority (22 African Americans, 2 Asian Americans, 20 Hispanics). Average age 41. 86 applicants, 73% accepted. In 1997, 70 degrees awarded. *Degree requirements:* Comprehensive exam, practicum required, foreign language and thesis not required. *Entrance requirements:* Minimum GPA of 2.75, 2 years of teaching experience. Application deadline: 3/18 (priority date; rolling processing; 9/30 for spring admission). Application fee: $0. *Expenses:* Tuition $2226 per year full-time, $93 per credit hour part-time for state residents; $6678 per year full-time, $278 per credit hour part-time for nonresidents. Fees $358 per year full-time, $14.90 per credit hour part-time. *Financial aid:* In 1997–98, 27 students received aid, including 3 research assistantships; full and partial tuition waivers, Federal Work-Study, institutionally sponsored loans, and career-related internships or fieldwork also available. Aid available to part-time students. *Faculty research:* Student motivation, leadership, teacher expectation. • Dr. Clyde Bradley, Coordinator, 773-794-6517. Application contact: Dr. Mohan K. Sood, Dean of Graduate College, 773-583-4050 Ext. 6143. Fax: 773-794-6670.

Northeastern State University, College of Education, Department of Education, Program in School Administration, Tahlequah, OK 74464-2399. Awards M Ed. Faculty: 4 full-time (0 women), 4 part-time (0 women). Students: 138 (58 women). In 1997, 42 degrees awarded. *Degree requirements:* Thesis or alternative required, foreign language not required. *Entrance requirements:* GRE General Test (minimum combined score of 900) or MAT (minimum score 35), minimum GPA of 3.0. Application deadline: 6/1 (priority date; rolling processing). Application fee: $0. *Expenses:* Tuition $74 per credit hour for state residents; $176 per credit hour for nonresidents. Fees $30 per year. *Financial aid:* Teaching assistantships, Federal Work-Study available. Financial aid application deadline: 3/1. • Dr. James King, Coordinator, 918-456-5511 Ext. 3717.

Northeast Louisiana University, College of Education, Department of Educational Leadership and Counseling, Program in Administration and Supervision, Monroe, LA 71209-0001. Awards M Ed, Ed S. Accredited by NCATE. Part-time and evening/weekend programs available. *Degree requirements:* For master's, comprehensive exam required, foreign language and thesis not required; for Ed S, thesis, comprehensive exam. *Entrance requirements:* GRE General Test, minimum undergraduate GPA of 2.5. Application deadline: 6/1 (priority date; rolling processing; 11/1 for spring admission). Application fee: $15 ($25 for international students). *Tuition:* $2028 per year full-time, $240 per semester (minimum) part-time for state residents; $6852 per year full-time, $240 per semester (minimum) part-time for nonresidents. *Faculty research:* School facilities utilization.

Northeast Louisiana University, College of Education, Department of Educational Leadership and Counseling, Program in Educational Leadership, Monroe, LA 71209-0001. Awards Ed D. Accredited by NCATE. Offered jointly with Grambling State University and Louisiana Tech University. *Degree requirements:* Dissertation. *Entrance requirements:* GRE General Test (minimum combined score of 1000). Application deadline: 6/1 (priority date; rolling processing; 11/1 for spring admission). Application fee: $15 ($25 for international students). *Tuition:* $2028 per year full-time, $240 per semester (minimum) part-time for state residents; $6852 per year full-time, $240 per semester (minimum) part-time for nonresidents.

Northern Arizona University, Center for Excellence in Education, Program in Educational Leadership, Flagstaff, AZ 86011. Awards M Ed, Ed D. Part-time programs available. Students: 177 full-time (94 women), 889 part-time (532 women); includes 196 minority (29 African Americans, 5 Asian Americans, 143 Hispanics, 19 Native Americans), 3 international. Average age 35. 479 applicants, 76% accepted. In 1997, 355 master's, 40 doctorates awarded. *Degree requirements:* For master's, thesis or alternative required, foreign language not required; for doctorate, computer language, dissertation required, foreign language not required. *Entrance requirements:* For master's, GRE General Test, GRE Subject Test, or minimum GPA of 3.0; for doctorate, GRE General Test, GRE Subject Test, 3 years of work experience, interview, master's degree. Application fee: $45. *Expenses:* Tuition $2088 per year full-time, $330 per semester (minimum) part-time for state residents; $8004 per year full-time, $1002 per semester (minimum) part-time for nonresidents. Fees $72 per year full-time, $18 per semester (minimum) part-time. *Financial aid:* Fellowships, research assistantships, teaching assistantships, full and partial tuition waivers, Federal Work-Study, and career-related internships or fieldwork available. *Faculty research:* Change processes, African education, law and education, program evaluation. • Dr. Henry Clark III, Interim Chair, 520-523-2080.

Northern Illinois University, College of Education, Department of Leadership and Educational Policy Studies, Program in Educational Administration, De Kalb, IL 60115-2854. Awards MS Ed, Ed D, Ed S. Accredited by NCATE. Part-time and evening/weekend programs available. Faculty: 10 full-time (4 women), 2 part-time (1 woman). Students: 15 full-time (6 women), 337 part-time (202 women); includes 56 minority (35 African Americans, 2 Asian Americans, 17 Hispanics, 2 Native Americans), 1 international. Average age 39. 81 applicants, 75% accepted. In 1997, 57 master's, 17 doctorates, 7 Ed Ss awarded. *Degree requirements:* For master's and Ed S, comprehensive exam required, thesis optional, foreign language not required; for doctorate, candidacy exam, dissertation defense required, foreign language not required. *Entrance requirements:* For master's, GRE General Test, TOEFL (minimum score 550), minimum GPA of 2.75; for doctorate, GRE General Test, TOEFL (minimum score 550), minimum GPA of 2.75 (undergraduate), 3.2 (graduate); for Ed S, GRE General Test, TOEFL (minimum score 550), minimum graduate GPA of 3.2, master's degree. Application deadline: 6/1 (rolling processing; 11/1 for spring admission). Application fee: $30. *Tuition:* $3984 per year full-time, $154 per credit hour part-time for state residents; $8160 per year full-time, $328 per credit hour part-time for nonresidents. *Financial aid:* Fellowships, research assistantships, teaching assistantships, staff assistantships, full tuition waivers, Federal Work-Study, and career-related internships or fieldwork available. Aid available to part-time students. • Dr. Rosita Marcano, Faculty Chair, 815-753-1465.

See in-depth description on page 921.

Northern Illinois University, College of Education, Department of Leadership and Educational Policy Studies, Program in School Business Management, De Kalb, IL 60115-2854. Awards MS Ed. Accredited by NCATE. Part-time and evening/weekend programs available. Faculty: 10 full-time (4 women), 2 part-time (1 woman). Students: 11 part-time (6 women); includes 2 minority (both African Americans). Average age 34. 3 applicants, 67% accepted. In 1997, 8 degrees awarded. *Degree requirements:* Comprehensive exam required, thesis optional, foreign language not required. *Entrance requirements:* GRE General Test, TOEFL (minimum score 550), minimum GPA of 2.75. Application deadline: 6/1 (rolling processing; 11/1 for spring admission). Application fee: $30. *Tuition:* $3984 per year full-time, $154 per credit hour part-time for state residents; $8160 per year full-time, $328 per credit hour part-time for nonresidents. *Financial aid:* Fellowships, research assistantships, teaching assistantships, staff assistantships, full tuition waivers, Federal Work-Study, and career-related internships or fieldwork available. Aid available to part-time students. • Application contact: Dr. Ron Everett, Professor, 815-753-9369.

See in-depth description on page 921.

Northern Michigan University, College of Behavioral Sciences and Human Services, Department of Education, Program in Administration and Supervision, Marquette, MI 49855-5301. Awards MA Ed. Accredited by NCATE. Part-time programs available. Students: 3 full-time (1 woman), 77 part-time (48 women). 13 applicants, 100% accepted. In 1997, 19 degrees awarded. *Degree requirements:* Thesis or alternative required, foreign language not required. *Entrance requirements:* GRE General Test (minimum combined score of 900), minimum GPA of 2.75. Application deadline: 7/1 (priority date; rolling processing; 11/1 for spring admission). Application fee: $25. *Expenses:* Tuition $135 per credit hour for state residents; $215 per credit hour for nonresidents. Fees $183 per year full-time, $94 per year (minimum) part-time. *Financial aid:* Federal Work-Study, institutionally sponsored loans available. Aid available to part-time students. Financial aid application deadline: 3/1. *Faculty research:* Supervision and improvement of instruction, the principal as educational leader, women in K–12 educational administration. • Application contact: Dr. Lois Hirst, Co-Coordinator, 906-227-1858.

Northern State University, Division of Graduate Studies in Education, Program in Elementary and Secondary School Administration, Aberdeen, SD 57401-7198. Offers elementary school administration (MS Ed), secondary school administration (MS Ed). Accredited by NCATE. Offered jointly with Huron University, Jamestown College, and the University of Mary. Part-time and evening/weekend programs available. Faculty: 6 full-time (3 women). Students: 4 full-time (3 women), 12 part-time (6 women). Average age 32. In 1997, 11 degrees awarded. *Degree requirements:* Thesis optional, foreign language not required. *Average time to degree:* master's–1.5 years full-time. *Entrance requirements:* Minimum GPA of 2.75. Application deadline: 8/15 (priority date; rolling processing; 12/15 for spring admission). Application fee: $15. *Expenses:* Tuition $1999 per year full-time, $83 per credit hour part-time for state residents; $6034 per year full-time, $251 per credit hour part-time for nonresidents. Fees $954 per year full-time, $40 per credit hour part-time. *Financial aid:* 4 students received aid; teaching assistantships, Federal Work-Study, institutionally sponsored loans, and career-related internships or fieldwork available. Aid available to part-time students. Financial aid application deadline: 3/1. • Dr. Paul Deputy, Head, 605-626-2415. Application contact: Dr. Sharon Tebben, Director of Graduate Studies, 605-626-2558. Fax: 605-626-2542.

Northwestern State University of Louisiana, Division of Education, Emphasis in Educational Administration/Supervision, Natchitoches, LA 71497. Awards M Ed, Ed S. Accredited by NCATE. Faculty: 2 full-time (1 woman), 3 part-time (1 woman). Students: 4 full-time (3 women), 58 part-time (48 women); includes 8 minority (all African Americans). Average age 36. In 1997, 10 master's awarded. *Degree requirements:* For Ed S, thesis required, foreign language not required. *Entrance requirements:* For master's, GRE General Test (minimum combined score of 800), GRE Subject Test, minimum undergraduate GPA of 2.5; for Ed S, GRE General Test, GRE Subject Test. Application deadline: 8/1 (priority date; rolling processing; 1/10 for spring admission). Application fee: $15 ($25 for international students). *Tuition:* $2147 per year full-time, $336 per semester (minimum) part-time for state residents; $6437 per year full-time, $336 per semester (minimum) part-time for nonresidents. *Financial aid:* Career-related internships or fieldwork available. Financial aid application deadline: 7/15. • Application contact: Dr. Tom Hanson, Dean, Graduate Studies and Research, 318-357-5851. Fax: 318-357-5019.

Northwestern State University of Louisiana, Division of Education, Program in Human Services, Natchitoches, LA 71497. Offerings include student personnel services (MA). Accredited by NCATE. Program faculty: 3 full-time (2 women), 2 part-time (1 woman). *Application deadline:* 8/1 (priority date; rolling processing; 1/10 for spring admission). *Application fee:* $15 ($25 for international students). *Tuition:* $2147 per year full-time, $336 per semester (minimum) part-time for state residents; $6437 per year full-time, $336 per semester (minimum) part-time for

Directory: Educational Administration

Northwestern State University of Louisiana (continued)
nonresidents. • Dr. Hurst Hall, Head, 318-357-4169. Application contact: Dr. Tom Hanson, Dean, Graduate Studies and Research, 318-357-5851. Fax: 318-357-5019.

Northwestern University, School of Education and Social Policy, Evanston, IL 60208. Offerings include higher education administration (MS), school administration (MS). School faculty: 19 full-time (5 women), 6 part-time (1 woman). *Tuition:* $2424 per course. • Jean Egmon, Assistant Dean, 847-491-3790. Fax: 847-461-2495. E-mail: egmon@nwu.edu. Application contact: Andrew Ager, Office of Student Affairs, 847-491-3790. Fax: 847-467-2495. E-mail: andrew-ager@nwu.edu.

Northwest Missouri State University, College of Education and Human Services, Department of Educational Leadership, Program in Educational Administration and Supervision, 800 University Drive, Maryville, MO 64468-6001. Awards MS Ed, Ed S. Accredited by NCATE. Part-time programs available. Faculty: 12 full-time (2 women). Students: 10 full-time (3 women), 65 part-time (29 women). 22 applicants, 95% accepted. In 1997, 43 master's, 15 Ed Ss awarded. *Degree requirements:* For master's, comprehensive exam required, foreign language and thesis not required; for Ed S, thesis, comprehensive exam required, foreign language not required. *Entrance requirements:* For master's, GRE General Test (minimum combined score of 700), TOEFL (minimum score 550), minimum undergraduate GPA of 2.5, teaching certificate, writing sample; for Ed S, minimum graduate GPA of 3.25. Application fee: $0 ($50 for international students). *Expenses:* Tuition $113 per credit hour for state residents; $197 per credit hour for nonresidents. Fees $3 per credit hour. *Financial aid:* In 1997–98, 1 research assistantship averaging $585 per month, 4 teaching assistantships averaging $585 per month, 2 administrative assistantships averaging $585 per month were awarded. Financial aid application deadline: 3/1. • Dr. Gary Bennerotte, Director, 816-562-1768. Application contact: Dr. Frances Shipley, Dean of Graduate School, 816-562-1145. E-mail: gradsch@acad.nwmissouri.edu.

Northwest Nazarene College, Department of Graduate Studies, Graduate Program in Teacher Education, Nampa, ID 83686-5897. Offerings include educational leadership (M Ed). Accredited by NCATE. Postbaccalaureate distance learning degree programs offered. Program faculty: 3 full-time (2 women), 13 part-time (3 women). *Degree requirements:* Action research project required, foreign language and thesis not required. *Application deadline:* 9/1 (rolling processing). *Application fee:* $25. • Dr. Dennis Cartwright, Chair, 208-467-8258. E-mail: ddcartwright@wiley.nnc.edu.

Notre Dame College, Education Division, Program in School Administration and Supervision, Manchester, NH 03104-2299. Awards M Ed. Part-time programs available. Faculty: 1 (woman) full-time, 2 part-time (1 woman). Students: 8 full-time (7 women), 25 part-time (11 women). Average age 39. 6 applicants, 100% accepted. In 1997, 5 degrees awarded. *Degree requirements:* Comprehensive exams, portfolio, or thesis required, foreign language not required. *Entrance requirements:* GRE General Test or MAT, teaching certificate. Application deadline: rolling. Application fee: $35. *Tuition:* $299 per credit. *Financial aid:* Assistantships available. • Dr. Barbara Stone, Director, 603-669-4298.

Nova Southeastern University, Fischler Center for the Advancement of Education, Graduate Teacher Education Program, Fort Lauderdale, FL 33314-7721. Offerings include educational leadership (administration K–12) (MS, Ed S). *Degree requirements:* Thesis, practicum required, foreign language not required. *Entrance requirements:* For master's, teaching certificate; for Ed S, master's degree, teaching certificate. Application deadline: rolling. Application fee: $50. *Tuition:* $245 per credit hour (minimum). • Dr. Deo Nellis, Dean, 954-262-8601. E-mail: deo@fcae.nova.edu. Application contact: Dr. Mark Seldine, Director of Student Affairs, 954-262-8689. Fax: 954-262-3910. E-mail: seldines@fcae.nova.edu.

Nova Southeastern University, Fischler Center for the Advancement of Education, National Program for Educational Leaders, Fort Lauderdale, FL 33314-7721. Awards Ed D. Part-time and evening/weekend programs available. Postbaccalaureate distance learning degree programs offered. Students: 7 full-time (3 women), 829 part-time (486 women); includes 240 minority (207 African Americans, 2 Asian Americans, 28 Hispanics, 3 Native Americans), 23 international. In 1997, 159 degrees awarded. *Degree requirements:* Dissertation, research project required, foreign language not required. *Entrance requirements:* Master's degree, professional certification, practicing school administrator. Application deadline: rolling. Application fee: $50. *Tuition:* $8460 per year. • Dr. Charles Faires, Dean, 954-262-8595. E-mail: fairesc@fcae.nova.edu. Application contact: N. Borders, Coordinator of Marketing, 954-262-8580. Fax: 954-262-3906. E-mail: edlinfo@fcae.nova.edu.

Nova Southeastern University, Fischler Center for the Advancement of Education, Program in Life-Span Care and Administration, Fort Lauderdale, FL 33314-7721. Offerings include early childhood education administration (MS). MS (applied gerontology administration) new for fall 1998. Postbaccalaureate distance learning degree programs offered. *Degree requirements:* Thesis, practicum required, foreign language not required. *Entrance requirements:* Work experience in field. Application deadline: rolling. Application fee: $50. *Tuition:* $300 per credit hour. • Dr. Norman Powell, Dean, 954-262-8701. E-mail: powell@fcae.nova.edu. Application contact: Sara Sauceda, Program Secretary, 800-986-3223 Ext. 8302. Fax: 954-262-3907. E-mail: powell@fcae.nova.edu.

Oakland University, School of Education and Human Services, Program in Curriculum, Instruction and Leadership, Rochester, MI 48309-4401. Awards MAT, M Ed, Certificate. Accredited by NCATE. Faculty: 16 full-time. Students: 15 full-time (12 women), 120 part-time (90 women); includes 8 minority (3 African Americans, 2 Asian Americans, 1 Hispanic, 2 Native Americans), 1 international. Average age 35. In 1997, 48 master's awarded. *Entrance requirements:* For master's, minimum GPA of 3.0 for unconditional admission. Application deadline: 7/15 (3/15 for spring admission). Application fee: $30. *Expenses:* Tuition $3852 per year full-time, $214 per credit hour part-time for state residents; $8532 per year full-time, $474 per credit hour part-time for nonresidents. Fees $420 per year. *Financial aid:* Full tuition waivers, Federal Work-Study, institutionally sponsored loans available. Financial aid application deadline: 3/1; applicants required to submit FAFSA. • Dr. Eric Follo, Chair, 248-370-3070. Application contact: Dr. Jacqueline Lougheed, Coordinator, 248-370-3070.

The Ohio State University, College of Education, School of Educational Policy and Leadership, Columbus, OH 43210. Offers programs in educational administration (Certificate), educational policy and leadership (MA, M Ed, PhD). Accredited by NCATE. Faculty: 41. Students: 150 full-time (100 women), 227 part-time (156 women); includes 63 minority (58 African Americans, 1 Asian American, 3 Hispanics, 1 Native American), 28 international. 316 applicants, 52% accepted. In 1997, 86 master's, 17 doctorates awarded. *Degree requirements:* For master's, thesis optional, foreign language not required; for doctorate, dissertation required, foreign language not required. *Application deadline:* 8/15 (rolling processing). *Application fee:* $30 ($40 for international students). *Tuition:* $5472 per year full-time, $554 per quarter (minimum) part-time for state residents; $14,172 per year full-time, $1424 per quarter (minimum) part-time for nonresidents. *Financial aid:* Fellowships, research assistantships, teaching assistantships, administrative assistantships, Federal Work-Study, institutionally sponsored loans available. Aid available to part-time students. • Dr. Robert B. Donmoyer, Director, 614-292-5181. Fax: 614-292-7900. E-mail: donmoyer.1@osu.edu.

Ohio University, Graduate Studies, College of Education, School of Curriculum and Instruction, Athens, OH 45701-2979. Offerings include supervision (PhD). Accredited by NCATE. Terminal master's awarded for partial completion of doctoral program. School faculty: 21 full-time (7 women), 16 part-time (11 women). *Degree requirements:* Dissertation. *Entrance requirements:* GRE General Test, MAT, minimum GPA of 3.0, work experience. Application deadline: rolling. Application fee: $30. *Tuition:* $5430 per year full-time, $216 per quarter hour part-time for state residents; $10,431 per year full-time, $423 per quarter hour part-time for nonresidents. • Dr. Ralph Martin, Director, 740-593-4422. Application contact: Dr. Bonnie Beach, Graduate Chair, 740-593-0523.

Ohio University, Graduate Studies, College of Education, School of Applied Behavioral Sciences and Educational Leadership, Program in Educational Administration, Athens, OH 45701-2979. Awards M Ed, PhD, Ed S. Accredited by NCATE. Part-time and evening/weekend programs available. Students: 91 full-time (40 women), 84 part-time (50 women); includes 17 minority (10 African Americans, 2 Asian Americans, 3 Hispanics, 2 Native Americans), 28 international. 151 applicants, 62% accepted. Terminal master's awarded for partial completion of doctoral program. *Degree requirements:* For master's, thesis or alternative required, foreign language not required; for doctorate, dissertation. *Entrance requirements:* For master's, GRE General Test (minimum combined score of 1000) or MAT (minimum score 48); for doctorate, GRE General Test (minimum combined score of 1000), MAT (minimum score 45), minimum GPA of 3.0, work experience. Application deadline: rolling. Application fee: $30. *Tuition:* $5430 per year full-time, $216 per quarter hour part-time for state residents; $10,431 per year full-time, $423 per quarter hour part-time for nonresidents. *Financial aid:* In 1997–98, 2 assistantships (both to first-year students) were awarded; teaching assistantships, full tuition waivers, Federal Work-Study, institutionally sponsored loans also available. Financial aid application deadline: 3/15. • Application contact: Dr. Patricia Beamish, Graduate Chair, 740-593-4440.

Oklahoma State University, College of Education, Department of Educational Administration and Higher Education, Stillwater, OK 74078. Offers programs in educational administration (MS, Ed S), higher education (MS, Ed D). Faculty: 11 full-time (3 women). Students: 17 full-time (7 women), 144 part-time (79 women); includes 28 minority (17 African Americans, 2 Asian Americans, 3 Hispanics, 6 Native Americans), 3 international. Average age 42. In 1997, 2 master's, 16 doctorates awarded. *Degree requirements:* For master's, thesis or alternative; for doctorate, dissertation. *Entrance requirements:* For master's and doctorate, TOEFL (minimum score 550). Application deadline: 7/1 (priority date). Application fee: $25. *Financial aid:* 1 student received aid; partial tuition waivers, Federal Work-Study, and career-related internships or fieldwork available. Aid available to part-time students. Financial aid application deadline: 3/1. • Dr. Joseph Licata, Head, 405-744-7244.

Oklahoma State University, College of Education, Department of Applied Behavioral Studies, Program in Counseling and Student Personnel, Stillwater, OK 74078. Awards MS. *Application deadline:* 7/1 (priority date). *Application fee:* $25. *Financial aid:* Partial tuition waivers, Federal Work-Study, and career-related internships or fieldwork available. Aid available to part-time students. Financial aid application deadline: 3/1. • Dr. Dale Fuqua, Head, Department of Applied Behavioral Studies, 405-744-6040.

Old Dominion University, Darden College of Education, Department of Educational Leadership and Counseling, Programs in Educational Administration, Norfolk, VA 23529. Awards MS, CAS. Accredited by NCATE. Part-time and evening/weekend programs available. Postbaccalaureate distance learning degree programs offered (no on-campus study). Students: 24 full-time (16 women), 133 part-time (86 women); includes 54 minority (45 African Americans, 5 Asian Americans, 1 Hispanic, 3 Native Americans), 1 international. Average age 38. In 1997, 44 master's, 13 CASs awarded. *Degree requirements:* For master's, comprehensive exam, practicum required, thesis optional, foreign language not required; for CAS, comprehensive exam, fieldwork required, thesis optional, foreign language not required. *Entrance requirements:* For master's, GRE General Test or MAT, minimum GPA of 3.0 in major; for CAS, GRE General Test or MAT. Application deadline: 7/1 (rolling processing). Application fee: $30. *Expenses:* Tuition $180 per credit hour for state residents; $477 per credit hour for nonresidents. Fees $140 per year full-time, $32 per semester part-time. *Financial aid:* In 1997–98, 50 students received aid, including 1 research assistantship totaling $5,936, 33 tuition grants (2 to first-year students) totaling $34,302; teaching assistantships, partial tuition waivers, and career-related internships or fieldwork also available. Aid available to part-time students. Financial aid application deadline: 2/15; applicants required to submit FAFSA. *Faculty research:* Urban education, principal and leadership preparation, higher education, supervision, policy studies. • Dr. Petra Snowden, Graduate Director, 757-683-3326. Fax: 757-683-5756. E-mail: psnowden@odu.edu.

Oral Roberts University, School of Education, Tulsa, OK 74171-0001. Offerings include Christian school administration (MA Ed), public school administration (MA Ed). Postbaccalaureate distance learning degree programs offered (minimal on-campus study). School faculty: 7 full-time (2 women), 13 part-time (3 women). *Degree requirements:* Thesis (for some programs), comprehensive exam. *Average time to degree:* master's–1.5 years full-time, 3 years part-time. *Entrance requirements:* GRE General Test (minimum combined score of 1000) or MAT, minimum GPA of 3.0. Application deadline: rolling. Application fee: $35. • Dr. David Hand, Dean, 918-495-7084. Fax: 918-495-6050. Application contact: David H. Fulmer III, Coordinator of Graduate Admissions, 918-495-6058. Fax: 918-495-7214. E-mail: dhfulmer@oru.edu.

Oregon State University, Graduate School, College of Home Economics and Education, School of Education, Program in College Student Service Administration, Corvallis, OR 97331. Awards Ed M, MS. Accredited by NCATE. Faculty: 14 part-time (4 women). Students: 33 full-time (20 women); includes 4 minority (1 African American, 2 Asian Americans, 1 Hispanic). Average age 26. 41 applicants, 22% accepted. In 1997, 13 degrees awarded. *Degree requirements:* Thesis or alternative, minimum GPA of 3.0 required, foreign language not required. *Entrance requirements:* TOEFL (minimum score 550), minimum GPA of 3.0 in last 90 hours. Application deadline: 3/1 (rolling processing). Application fee: $50. *Tuition:* $6207 per year full-time, $810 per quarter (minimum) part-time for state residents; $10,551 per year full-time, $1293 per quarter (minimum) part-time for nonresidents. *Financial aid:* Teaching assistantships, Federal Work-Study, institutionally sponsored loans, and career-related internships or fieldwork available. Aid available to part-time students. Financial aid application deadline: 2/1. *Faculty research:* Improvement of student activities, administering recreational sports programs. • Dr. J. Roger Penn, Director, 541-737-3657.

Our Lady of Holy Cross College, Program in Education, New Orleans, LA 70131-7399. Offerings include administration and supervision (M Ed). Program faculty: 5 full-time (2 women), 7 part-time (3 women). *Degree requirements:* Thesis required, foreign language not required. *Entrance requirements:* GRE General Test (minimum combined score of 800), minimum GPA of 2.7. Application deadline: 9/1. Application fee: $20. *Expenses:* Tuition $5760 per year full-time, $240 per semester hour part-time. Fees $167 per year. • Dr. Judith G. Miranti, Dean, 504-394-7744.

Our Lady of the Lake University of San Antonio, School of Education and Clinical Studies, Program in Administration/Supervision, 411 Southwest 24th Street, San Antonio, TX 78207-4689. Awards M Ed. Part-time and evening/weekend programs available. Faculty: 1 (woman) full-time, 2 part-time (0 women). Students: 21 part-time (13 women); includes 12 minority (4 African Americans, 1 Asian American, 7 Hispanics). Average age 35. In 1997, 5 degrees awarded. *Degree requirements:* Computer language, exam, internship required, foreign language and thesis not required. *Entrance requirements:* GRE General Test or MAT. Application deadline: 8/6 (priority date; rolling processing). Application fee: $15. *Expenses:* Tuition $371 per credit hour. Fees $57 per semester full-time, $32 per semester part-time. *Financial aid:* Grants, institutionally sponsored loans, and career-related internships or fieldwork available. Financial aid application deadline: 4/15. *Faculty research:* Leadership, organizational behavior. • Dr. Jean Kueker, Head, 210-434-6711 Ext. 291. Fax: 210-431-3927. E-mail: kuekj@lake.ollusa.edu. Application contact: Debbie Hamilton, Director of Admissions, 210-434-6711 Ext. 314. Fax: 210-436-2314.

Pace University, School of Education, New York, NY 10038. Offerings include administration and supervision (MS Ed), school business management (Certificate). *Application deadline:* 7/31 (priority date; rolling processing; 11/30 for spring admission). *Application fee:* $60. *Expenses:* Tuition $485 per credit. Fees $360 per year full-time, $53 per semester (minimum) part-time.

Pacific Lutheran University, School of Education, Program in Education Administration, Tacoma, WA 98447. Awards MA. Accredited by NCATE. Part-time and evening/weekend programs available. Faculty: 2 full-time (1 woman), 1 (woman) part-time. Students: 7 part-time

(4 women); includes 1 minority (African American). Average age 37. 3 applicants, 100% accepted. In 1997, 6 degrees awarded. *Degree requirements:* Comprehensive exam, research project or thesis required, foreign language not required. *Entrance requirements:* GRE General Test or MAT, TOEFL (minimum score 550), interview. Application deadline: rolling. Application fee: $35. *Tuition:* $490 per semester hour. *Financial aid:* Fellowships, research assistantships, scholarships, Federal Work-Study available. Financial aid application deadline: 3/1. • Dr. Leon Reisberg, Graduate Director, 253-535-7272. Application contact: Marjo Burdick, Office of Admissions, 253-535-7151. Fax: 253-535-8320. E-mail: admissions@plu.edu.

Pennsylvania State University University Park Campus, College of Education, Department of Education Policy Studies, Program in Educational Administration, University Park, PA 16802-1503. Awards M Ed, MS, D Ed, PhD. Accredited by NCATE. Students: 16 full-time (10 women), 75 part-time (35 women). In 1997, 19 master's, 21 doctorates awarded. *Entrance requirements:* GRE General Test or MAT. Application fee: $40. *Expenses:* Tuition $6534 per year full-time, $276 per credit part-time for state residents; $13,460 per year full-time, $561 per credit part-time for nonresidents. Fees $252 per year (minimum) full-time, $43 per semester (minimum) part-time. • Dr. Donald J. Willower, Professor in Charge, 814-865-1487.

Pepperdine University, Graduate School of Education and Psychology, Division of Education, Program in Educational Administration, Culver City, CA 90230-7615. Offers administration and educational technology (MS), school business administration (MS), school management and administration (MS). Students: 45 full-time (31 women), 40 part-time (29 women); includes 25 minority (11 African Americans, 2 Asian Americans, 12 Hispanics). Average age 39. 79 applicants, 94% accepted. In 1997, 52 degrees awarded. *Entrance requirements:* GRE General Test, TOEFL. Application deadline: 7/1. Application fee: $45. *Tuition:* $540 per unit. *Financial aid:* Research assistantships, teaching assistantships available. Financial aid application deadline: 7/1. • Dr. Robert Paull, Director, 310-568-5738. Application contact: Jo Witte, Coordinator, 310-568-5604.

Pepperdine University, Graduate School of Education and Psychology, Division of Education, Program in Educational Leadership, Administration, and Policy, Culver City, CA 90230-7615. Awards Ed D. Students: 7 full-time (4 women), 8 part-time (4 women); includes 5 minority (2 African Americans, 2 Asian Americans, 1 Hispanic). 19 applicants, 100% accepted. *Entrance requirements:* GRE General Test, MAT, TOEFL. Application deadline: 3/30 (priority date). Application fee: $45. *Tuition:* $690 per unit. *Financial aid:* Application deadline 7/1. • Dr. Ken Moffett, Director, 310-568-5600. Application contact: Christie Dailo, Administrator, 310-568-5612.

Pepperdine University, Graduate School of Education and Psychology, Division of Education, Program in Institutional Management, Culver City, CA 90230-7615. Awards Ed D. Program being phased out; applicants no longer accepted. Part-time and evening/weekend programs available. Students: 110 full-time (73 women), 70 part-time (43 women); includes 59 minority (35 African Americans, 13 Asian Americans, 11 Hispanics), 5 international. Average age 45. In 1997, 26 degrees awarded. *Degree requirements:* Dissertation, comprehensive exams required, foreign language not required. *Financial aid:* Research assistantships, teaching assistantships, scholarships available. Aid available to part-time students. • Dr. Chester H. McCall Jr., Director, 310-568-5600.

Pepperdine University, Graduate School of Education and Psychology, Division of Education, Program in Organization Change, Culver City, CA 90230-7615. Awards Ed D. Students: 13 full-time (5 women), 21 part-time (9 women); includes 7 minority (4 African Americans, 3 Asian Americans), 1 international. Average age 45. 46 applicants, 52% accepted. *Entrance requirements:* GMAT, GRE General Test, MAT, TOEFL. Application deadline: 3/30 (priority date). Application fee: $45. *Tuition:* $14,100 per year. *Financial aid:* Research assistantships, teaching assistantships, scholarships, institutionally sponsored loans available. Aid available to part-time students. Financial aid application deadline: 7/1; applicants required to submit FAFSA. • Dr. Kay Davis, Director, 310-568-5660. Application contact: Christie Dailo, Administrator, 310-568-5612.

Pepperdine University, Graduate School of Education and Psychology, Division of Education, Program in Organizational Leadership, Culver City, CA 90230-7615. Awards Ed D. Students: 38 part-time (18 women); includes 9 minority (5 African Americans, 3 Asian Americans, 1 Hispanic), 1 international. 45 applicants, 89% accepted. *Entrance requirements:* GRE General Test, MAT, TOEFL. Application fee: $45. *Tuition:* $690 per unit. *Financial aid:* Application deadline 7/1. • Dr. Chester H. McCall Jr., Director, 310-568-5600. Application contact: Christie Dailo, Administrator, 310-568-5612.

Pittsburg State University, School of Education, Department of Special Services and Leadership Studies, Program in Educational Administration and Supervision, Pittsburg, KS 66762-5880. Offers elementary school administration (MS, Ed S), secondary school administration (MS, Ed S). Accredited by NCATE. Students: 2 full-time (0 women), 37 part-time (18 women); includes 4 minority (all Native Americans). In 1997, 15 master's awarded. *Degree requirements:* For master's, thesis or alternative required, foreign language not required. *Entrance requirements:* For master's, GRE General Test or MAT. Application fee: $40. *Tuition:* $2418 per year full-time, $103 per credit hour part-time for state residents; $6130 per year full-time, $258 per credit hour part-time for nonresidents. *Financial aid:* Teaching assistantships, Federal Work-Study, and career-related internships or fieldwork available. • Dr. Steve Scott, Chairman, Department of Special Services and Leadership Studies, 316-235-4487.

Pittsburg State University, School of Education, Department of Special Services and Leadership Studies, Program in Secondary Education, Pittsburg, KS 66762-5880. Offerings include secondary school administration (Ed S). Accredited by NCATE. *Application fee:* $40. *Tuition:* $2418 per year full-time, $103 per credit hour part-time for state residents; $6130 per year full-time, $258 per credit hour part-time for nonresidents. • Dr. Steve Scott, Chairman, Department of Special Services and Leadership Studies, 316-235-4487.

Plattsburgh State University of New York, Faculty of Professional Studies, Center for Educational Studies and Services, Program in Educational Administration, Plattsburgh, NY 12901-2681. Awards MS, CAS. Students: 7 full-time (3 women), 54 part-time (27 women). 25 applicants, 84% accepted. In 1997, 35 master's, 8 CASs awarded. *Degree requirements:* Comprehensive exam required, foreign language and thesis not required. *Entrance requirements:* For master's, GRE General Test or MAT, minimum GPA of 2.5. Application deadline: rolling. Application fee: $50. *Expenses:* Tuition $5100 per year full-time, $213 per credit hour part-time for state residents; $8416 per year full-time, $351 per credit hour part-time for nonresidents. Fees $395 per year full-time, $15.10 per credit hour part-time. *Financial aid:* 3 students received aid; Federal Work-Study available. Aid available to part-time students. Financial aid application deadline: 4/15; applicants required to submit FAFSA. • Dr. Raymond Domenico, Director and Associate Dean, Center for Educational Studies and Services, 518-564-2122.

Plymouth State College of the University System of New Hampshire, Department of Education, Program in Educational Administration, Plymouth, NH 03264-1595. Awards M Ed. Accredited by NCATE. Part-time and evening/weekend programs available. Students: 3 full-time (2 women), 9 part-time (6 women). Average age 33. 5 applicants, 80% accepted. In 1997, 23 degrees awarded. *Entrance requirements:* GRE General Test (average 500 on each section) or MAT (minimum score 50), minimum GPA of 3.0. Application deadline: 9/1 (priority date; rolling processing). Application fee: $25 ($35 for international students). *Tuition:* $232 per credit for state residents; $254 per credit for nonresidents. *Financial aid:* Graduate assistantships, institutionally sponsored loans, and career-related internships or fieldwork available. Aid available to part-time students. Financial aid application deadline: 3/15; applicants required to submit FAFSA. • Dr. Kenneth Heuser, Adviser, 603-535-2479. Application contact: Maryann Szabadics, Administrative Assistant, 603-535-2636. Fax: 603-535-2572. E-mail: for.grad@psc.plymouth.edu.

Portland State University, School of Education, Department of Educational Policy, Foundations, and Administrative Studies, Program in Educational Administration and Leadership, Portland, OR 97207-0751. Offers educational administration (MA, MS), educational leadership/educational administration (Ed D). Accredited by NCATE. Part-time and evening/weekend programs available. Faculty: 11 full-time (6 women), 2 part-time (1 woman), 12 FTE. Students: 15 full-time (9 women), 88 part-time (59 women); includes 11 minority (4 African Americans, 1 Asian American, 5 Hispanics, 1 Native American), 5 international. Average age 41. 47 applicants, 74% accepted. *Degree requirements:* For master's, variable foreign language requirement, thesis or alternative, written exam; for doctorate, dissertation, comprehensive exam required, foreign language not required. *Entrance requirements:* For master's, California Basic Educational Skills Test, TOEFL (minimum score 550), minimum GPA of 3.0 in upper-division course work or 2.75 overall; for doctorate, GRE General Test or MAT, TOEFL (minimum score 550). Application deadline: 4/1 (rolling processing; 11/1 for spring admission). Application fee: $50. *Tuition:* $6101 per year full-time, $689 per semester (minimum) part-time for state residents; $10,445 per year full-time, $689 per semester (minimum) part-time for nonresidents. *Financial aid:* Research assistantships, teaching assistantships, Federal Work-Study, institutionally sponsored loans available. Aid available to part-time students. Financial aid application deadline: 3/1; applicants required to submit FAFSA. *Faculty research:* Integrated services models, site-based decision making, principalship, accelerated schools, school change process. Total annual research expenditures: $5000. • Dr. Tom Chenoweth, Head, 503-725-4754. Fax: 503-725-5599. E-mail: tom@ed.pdx.edu.

Prairie View A&M University, College of Education, Department of School Services, Prairie View, TX 77446-0188. Offerings include school administration (M Ed, MS Ed), school supervision (M Ed, MS Ed). One or more programs accredited by NCATE. Department faculty: 8 full-time (1 woman). *Average time to degree:* master's–2.5 years full-time, 4 years part-time. *Application deadline:* 7/1 (priority date; rolling processing; 11/1 for spring admission). *Application fee:* $10. *Tuition:* $2202 per year full-time, $336 per semester (minimum) part-time for state residents; $6000 per year full-time, $963 per semester (minimum) part-time for nonresidents. • Dr. William H. Parker, Head, 409-857-2312. Fax: 409-857-2911.

Providence College, Department of Education, Programs in Administration, Providence, RI 02918. Offerings in elementary administration (M Ed), secondary administration (M Ed). Part-time and evening/weekend programs available. Faculty: 10 part-time (2 women). Students: 3 full-time (1 woman), 55 part-time (31 women); includes 3 minority (2 African Americans, 1 Hispanic). Average age 35. 24 applicants, 96% accepted. In 1997, 25 degrees awarded (100% found work related to degree). *Degree requirements:* Comprehensive exam required, foreign language and thesis not required. *Entrance requirements:* GRE General Test (minimum combined score of 1000) or MAT (minimum score 45), TOEFL. Application deadline: 8/12 (priority date; rolling processing; 12/1 for spring admission). Application fee: $40. *Tuition:* $621 per course. *Financial aid:* Institutionally sponsored loans and career-related internships or fieldwork available. Aid available to part-time students. Financial aid applicants required to submit FAFSA. • Dr. Thomas F. Flaherty, Dean, Graduate School, 401-865-2247. Fax: 401-865-2057.

Purdue University, School of Education, Department of Educational Studies, West Lafayette, IN 47907. Offerings include administration (MS Ed, PhD, Ed S). Accredited by NCATE. Department faculty: 26 full-time (13 women), 23 part-time (14 women). *Degree requirements:* For doctorate, dissertation, oral and written exams; for Ed S, oral presentation, project required, thesis not required. *Entrance requirements:* For doctorate, GRE General Test (minimum score 500 on each section), TOEFL (minimum score 550); for Ed S, minimum B average. Application deadline: 2/1 (9/15 for spring admission). Application fee: $30. Electronic applications accepted. *Tuition:* $3500 per year full-time, $126 per credit hour part-time for state residents; $11,720 per year full-time, $387 per credit hour part-time for nonresidents. • Dr. D. H. Schunk, Head, 765-494-9170. Fax: 765-496-1228. E-mail: dschunk@purdue.edu. Application contact: Christine Larsen, Coordinator of Graduate Studies, 765-494-2345. Fax: 765-494-5832. E-mail: gradoffice@soe.purdue.edu.

Purdue University Calumet, School of Professional Studies, Department of Education, Program in Educational Administration, Hammond, IN 46323-2094. Awards MS Ed. *Entrance requirements:* TOEFL. Application fee: $30.

Queens College of the City University of New York, Social Science Division, School of Education, Department of Educational and Community Programs, Program in Administration and Supervision, 65-30 Kissena Boulevard, Flushing, NY 11367-1597. Awards AC. Part-time programs available. Students: 1 (woman) full-time, 161 part-time (118 women); includes 28 minority (15 African Americans, 4 Asian Americans, 9 Hispanics). 95 applicants, 96% accepted. In 1997, 45 degrees awarded. *Degree requirements:* Internship required, thesis optional, foreign language not required. *Entrance requirements:* TOEFL (minimum score 600), master's degree or equivalent. Application deadline: 4/1 (rolling processing; 11/1 for spring admission). Application fee: $40. *Expenses:* Tuition $4350 per year full-time, $185 per credit part-time for state residents; $7600 per year full-time, $320 per credit part-time for nonresidents. Fees $104 per year. *Financial aid:* Partial tuition waivers, Federal Work-Study, institutionally sponsored loans, and career-related internships or fieldwork available. Aid available to part-time students. Financial aid application deadline: 4/1; applicants required to submit FAFSA. • Prof. Jack Seiferth, Coordinator and Graduate Adviser, 718-997-5240. Application contact: Mario Caruso, Director of Graduate Admissions, 718-997-5200. Fax: 718-997-5193. E-mail: graduate%queens.bitnet@cunyvm.cuny.edu.

Radford University, Graduate College, College of Education and Human Development, Department of Educational Studies, Program in Educational Leadership, Radford, VA 24142. Awards MS. Accredited by NCATE. Part-time programs available. Postbaccalaureate distance learning degree programs offered (minimal on-campus study). Students: 2 full-time (both women), 59 part-time (33 women); includes 4 minority (all African Americans). Average age 37. 40 applicants, 83% accepted. In 1997, 26 degrees awarded. *Degree requirements:* Comprehensive exam required, foreign language and thesis not required. *Entrance requirements:* GMAT, GRE General Test, MAT, or NTE; TOEFL (minimum score 550), minimum GPA of 2.7. Application deadline: 2/1 (priority date; rolling processing; 10/1 for spring admission). Application fee: $25. Electronic applications accepted. *Expenses:* Tuition $2302 per year full-time, $147 per credit hour part-time for state residents; $5672 per year full-time, $287 per credit hour part-time for nonresidents. Fees $1222 per year full-time. *Financial aid:* In 1997–98, 11 scholarships/grants totaling $21,131 were awarded; fellowships, research assistantships, teaching assistantships, Federal Work-Study, institutionally sponsored loans, and career-related internships or fieldwork also available. Financial aid application deadline: 2/1; applicants required to submit FAFSA. • Dr. Sheila S. Reyna, Acting Chairperson, Department of Educational Studies, 540-831-5302. Fax: 540-831-6053. E-mail: aproffit@runet.edu.

Rhode Island College, School of Graduate Studies, School of Education and Human Development, Department of Educational Studies, Program in Educational Administration, Providence, RI 02908-1924. Awards M Ed, CAGS. Accredited by NCATE. Evening/weekend programs available. Faculty: 7 full-time (2 women), 12 part-time (4 women). Students: 5 full-time (1 woman), 38 part-time (21 women). In 1997, 9 master's, 3 CAGSs awarded. *Degree requirements:* For CAGS, thesis required, foreign language not required. *Entrance requirements:* For master's, GRE General Test or MAT. Application deadline: 4/1 (rolling processing). Application fee: $25. *Tuition:* $4064 per year full-time, $214 per credit part-time for state residents; $7658 per year full-time, $376 per credit part-time for nonresidents. *Financial aid:* Career-related internships or fieldwork available. Financial aid application deadline: 4/1. • Dr. Carolyn Panofsky, Chair, Department of Educational Studies, 401-456-8170.

Rider University, School of Graduate Education and Human Services, Program in Educational Administration, Lawrenceville, NJ 08648-3001. Awards MA. Accredited by NCATE. Part-time and evening/weekend programs available. Faculty: 1 full-time (0 women), 6 part-time (1 woman). Students: 1 full-time, 84 part-time. Average age 36. 13 applicants, 77% accepted. In 1997, 23 degrees awarded. *Degree requirements:* Comprehensive exams, research project required, foreign language and thesis not required. *Entrance requirements:* Interview, minimum GPA of 2.5. Application deadline: 8/15 (priority date; rolling processing; 12/15 for spring

Directory: Educational Administration

Rider University (continued)

admission). Application fee: $35. *Tuition:* $329 per credit hour. *Financial aid:* Career-related internships or fieldwork available. Aid available to part-time students. *Faculty research:* Use of new technologies (microcomputers and word processors) in school settings. • Dr. Stephen Philips, Adviser, 609-895-5473. Application contact: Dr. John Carpenter, Dean, Continuing Studies, 609-896-5036. Fax: 609-896-5261.

Rivier College, Graduate Education Department, Program in Educational Administration, Nashua, NH 03060-5086. Awards M Ed. Part-time and evening/weekend programs available. *Entrance requirements:* GRE General Test or MAT. Application deadline: rolling. Application fee: $25.

Robert Morris College, Program in Instructional Leadership, 881 Narrows Run Road, Moon Township, PA 15108-1189. Awards MS. Only part-time programs offered. Faculty: 35 full-time (6 women), 35 part-time (5 women). Students: 19 part-time. In 1997, 3 degrees awarded. *Entrance requirements:* Minimum GPA of 2.5. Application deadline: 8/1 (priority date; rolling processing; 11/30 for spring admission). Application fee: $25 ($35 for international students). *Expenses:* Tuition $328 per credit. Fees $15 per credit. *Financial aid:* Available to part-time students. Financial aid application deadline: 5/1; applicants required to submit FAFSA. • Dr. Jon A. Shank, Dean, School of Applied Sciences and Education, 412-262-8279. Fax: 412-262-8494. E-mail: shank@robert-morris.edu. Application contact: Vincent J. Kane, Recruiting Coordinator, 412-262-8535. Fax: 412-299-2425.

Roosevelt University, College of Education, Chicago, IL 60605-1394. Offerings include educational administration and supervision (MA, Ed D). Accredited by NCATE. *Degree requirements:* For doctorate, computer language, dissertation required, foreign language not required. *Entrance requirements:* For doctorate, GRE or MAT. Application deadline: 6/1 (priority date; rolling processing). Application fee: $25 ($35 for international students). *Expenses:* Tuition $445 per credit hour. Fees $100 per year. • Dr. George Lowery, Dean, 312-341-3700. Application contact: Joanne Canyon-Heller, Coordinator of Graduate Admissions, 312-341-3612.

Rowan University, College of Education, Department of Educational Leadership, Program in Educational Leadership, Glassboro, NJ 08028-1701. Awards Ed D. Accredited by NCATE. Students: 17 (14 women); includes 2 minority (both African Americans). *Entrance requirements:* GRE General Test, master's degree. Application deadline: 11/1 (priority date; rolling processing; 4/1 for spring admission). Application fee: $50. *Tuition:* $5728 per year full-time, $258 per credit hour part-time for state residents; $8968 per year full-time, $393 per credit hour part-time for nonresidents. • Dr. Ted White, Chairperson, Department of Educational Leadership, 609-256-4702.

Rowan University, College of Education, Department of Educational Leadership, Program in Higher Education Administration, Glassboro, NJ 08028-1701. Awards MA. Accredited by NCATE. Part-time and evening/weekend programs available. Students: 14 (9 women). 4 applicants, 25% accepted. In 1997, 7 degrees awarded. *Degree requirements:* Thesis, comprehensive exams required, foreign language not required. *Entrance requirements:* GRE General Test (minimum combined score of 840), minimum GPA of 2.8, 2 years of teaching experience. Application deadline: 11/1 (priority date; rolling processing; 4/1 for spring admission). Application fee: $50. *Tuition:* $5728 per year full-time, $258 per credit hour part-time for state residents; $8968 per year full-time, $393 per credit hour part-time for nonresidents. *Financial aid:* Career-related internships or fieldwork available. • Dr. Richard Smith, Adviser, 609-256-4500 Ext. 3820.

Rowan University, College of Education, Department of Educational Leadership, Program in School Administration, Glassboro, NJ 08028-1701. Offers school administration (MA), school administration-business administration (MA), school business administration (Certificate). Accredited by NCATE. Part-time and evening/weekend programs available. Students: 107 (71 women); includes 15 minority (13 African Americans, 1 Asian American, 1 Hispanic). 50 applicants, 40% accepted. In 1997, 53 master's awarded. *Degree requirements:* For master's, thesis, comprehensive exams, internship required, foreign language not required. *Entrance requirements:* For master's, GRE General Test (minimum combined score of 840), NTE, minimum GPA of 2.8, 2 years of teaching experience. Application deadline: 11/1 (priority date; rolling processing; 4/1 for spring admission). Application fee: $50. *Tuition:* $5728 per year full-time, $258 per credit hour part-time for state residents; $8968 per year full-time, $393 per credit hour part-time for nonresidents. *Financial aid:* Career-related internships or fieldwork available. • Jack Collins, Adviser (Secondary), 609-256-4703. Application contact: Dr. Christine Johnston, Adviser (Elementary), 609-256-4701.

Rowan University, College of Education, Department of Health and Exercise Science, Program in Administration and Supervision in Health and Physical Education or Athletics, Glassboro, NJ 08028-1701. Awards MA. Accredited by NCATE. 4 applicants, 50% accepted. *Application deadline:* 11/1 (priority date; rolling processing; 4/1 for spring admission). *Application fee:* $50. *Tuition:* $5728 per year full-time, $258 per credit hour part-time for state residents; $8968 per year full-time, $393 per credit hour part-time for nonresidents. • Dr. James Burd, Adviser, Department of Health and Exercise Science, 609-256-4783.

Rowan University, College of Education, Department of Special Educational Services/Instruction, Program in Student Personnel Services, Glassboro, NJ 08028-1701. Awards MA, Certificate. Accredited by NCATE. Evening/weekend programs available. Students: 123 (98 women); includes 15 minority (10 African Americans, 2 Asian Americans, 3 Hispanics). 51 applicants, 63% accepted. In 1997, 53 master's awarded. *Degree requirements:* For master's, thesis, comprehensive exams required, foreign language not required; for Certificate, thesis or alternative required, foreign language not required. *Entrance requirements:* For master's, GRE General Test (minimum combined score of 800), minimum GPA of 2.8, 1 year of teaching experience; for Certificate, GRE General Test. Application deadline: 11/1 (priority date; rolling processing; 4/1 for spring admission). Application fee: $50. *Tuition:* $5728 per year full-time, $258 per credit hour part-time for state residents; $8968 per year full-time, $393 per credit hour part-time for nonresidents. *Financial aid:* Federal Work-Study and career-related internships or fieldwork available. • Dr. Gerald Ognibene, Adviser, 609-256-4500 Ext. 3828.

Rutgers, The State University of New Jersey, New Brunswick, Graduate School of Education, Department of Educational Theory, Policy and Administration, Program in School Business Administration, New Brunswick, NJ 08903. Awards Ed M. Faculty: 7 full-time (1 woman), 6 part-time (0 women). Students: 10 part-time. In 1997, 2 degrees awarded. *Entrance requirements:* GRE General Test (minimum combined score of 1000), minimum GPA of 3.0. Application deadline: 3/1 (11/1 for spring admission). Application fee: $40. *Expenses:* Tuition $6492 per year full-time, $268 per credit part-time for state residents; $9520 per year full-time, $395 per credit part-time for nonresidents. Fees $208 per year (minimum). *Financial aid:* Application deadline 3/1. *Faculty research:* Accounting and school finance. • James Bliss, Coordinator, 732-932-7496 Ext. 221.

Rutgers, The State University of New Jersey, New Brunswick, Graduate School of Education, Department of Educational Theory, Policy and Administration, Programs in Educational Administration and Supervision, New Brunswick, NJ 08903. Offerings in education administration (Ed M), educational administration and supervision (Ed D, Ed S). Faculty: 7 full-time (1 woman), 6 part-time (0 women). Students: 17 full-time, 142 part-time; includes 21 minority (9 African Americans, 10 Asian Americans, 1 Hispanic, 1 Native American). In 1997, 17 master's, 16 doctorates, 3 Ed Ss awarded. *Degree requirements:* For doctorate, dissertation. *Entrance requirements:* For master's, GRE General Test (minimum combined score of 1000), minimum GPA of 3.0; for doctorate, GRE General Test (minimum combined score of 1100), minimum GPA of 3.0; for Ed S, GRE General Test. Application deadline: 3/1 (11/1 for spring admission). Application fee: $40. *Expenses:* Tuition $6492 per year full-time, $268 per credit part-time for state residents; $9520 per year full-time, $395 per credit part-time for nonresidents. Fees $208 per year (minimum). *Financial aid:* Application deadline 3/1. • James Bliss, Coordinator, 732-932-7496 Ext. 221.

Sacred Heart University, College of Education and Health Professions, Faculty of Education and Psychology, 5151 Park Avenue, Fairfield, CT 06432-1000. Offerings include administration (CAS). *Application deadline:* rolling. *Application fee:* $40 ($100 for international students). *Expenses:* Tuition $335 per credit. Fees $78 per semester. • Dr. A. Harris Stone, Director, 203-371-7800. Application contact: Linda B. Kirby, Dean of Graduate Admissions, 203-371-7880. Fax: 203-365-4732. E-mail: gradstudies@sacredheart.edu.

Saginaw Valley State University, College of Education, Program in Educational Administration, University Center, MI 48710. Offers chief business officers (M Ed), education leadership (Ed S), educational administration and supervision (M Ed), principalship (M Ed), superintendency (M Ed). Accredited by NCATE. Ed S new for fall 1998. Part-time and evening/weekend programs available. Faculty: 5 full-time (0 women). Students: 13 full-time (9 women), 257 part-time (163 women); includes 20 minority (9 African Americans, 10 Hispanics, 1 Native American), 1 international. In 1997, 82 master's awarded. *Entrance requirements:* For master's, minimum GPA of 3.0, teaching certificate. Application deadline: rolling. Application fee: $25. *Expenses:* Tuition $159 per credit hour for state residents; $311 per credit hour for nonresidents. Fees $8.70 per credit hour. • Application contact: Dr. Gamal Elashhab, Chair, 517-790-4322.

St. Bonaventure University, School of Education, Program in Educational Administration, Supervision, and Curriculum, St. Bonaventure, NY 14778-2284. Awards MS Ed, Adv C. Part-time and evening/weekend programs available. Faculty: 1 (woman) full-time, 6 part-time (2 women), 2 FTE. Students: 34 part-time (11 women); includes 1 minority (Native American), 1 international. 12 applicants, 100% accepted. In 1997, 8 master's, 1 Adv C awarded. *Degree requirements:* For master's, thesis optional, foreign language not required. *Entrance requirements:* For master's, TOEFL (minimum score 600). Application deadline: 8/1 (rolling processing). Application fee: $35. *Tuition:* $8100 per year full-time, $450 per credit hour part-time. *Financial aid:* In 1997–98, 1 student received aid, including 1 research assistantship (to a first-year student); Federal Work-Study and career-related internships or fieldwork also available. Aid available to part-time students. *Faculty research:* Collective bargaining, curriculum development, self-esteem, rural schools program, leadership issues. • William O'Connell, Director, 716-375-2313. Fax: 716-375-2360.

St. Cloud State University, College of Education, Center for Educational Administration and Leadership, St. Cloud, MN 56301-4498. Awards MS, Spt. Accredited by NCATE. Faculty: 11 full-time (5 women), 9 part-time (4 women). Students: 15 full-time (7 women), 11 part-time (4 women). In 1997, 8 master's awarded. *Degree requirements:* For master's, thesis or alternative required, foreign language not required; for Spt, thesis, field study required, foreign language not required. *Entrance requirements:* For master's, GRE General Test, minimum GPA of 2.75; for Spt, GRE General Test, minimum GPA of 3.25 in course work above master's degree. Application fee: $20 ($100 for international students). *Expenses:* Tuition $128 per credit for state residents; $203 per credit for nonresidents. Fees $16.32 per credit. *Financial aid:* In 1997–98, 3 graduate assistantships were awarded; Federal Work-Study also available. Financial aid application deadline: 3/1. • Dr. Charles Moore, Chair, 320-255-2160. Application contact: Ann Anderson, Graduate Studies Office, 320-255-2113. Fax: 320-654-5371. E-mail: anna@grad.stcloud.msus.edu.

St. Cloud State University, College of Education, Department of Special Education, St. Cloud, MN 56301-4498. Offerings include administration of special education (Spt). Accredited by NCATE. Department faculty: 9 full-time (4 women), 4 part-time (2 women). *Degree requirements:* Thesis, field study required, foreign language not required. *Entrance requirements:* GRE General Test, minimum GPA of 3.25. Application fee: $20 ($100 for international students). *Expenses:* Tuition $128 per credit for state residents; $203 per credit for nonresidents. Fees $16.32 per credit. • Dr. Joan Kellet, Chairperson, 320-255-2041. Application contact: Ann Anderson, Graduate Studies Office, 320-255-2113. Fax: 320-654-5371. E-mail: anna@grad.stcloud.msus.edu.

Saint Francis College, Program in Education, Loretto, PA 15940-0600. Offerings include leadership (M Ed). Program faculty: 2 full-time (both women), 14 part-time (5 women). *Degree requirements:* Comprehensive exam required, thesis optional, foreign language not required. *Entrance requirements:* Minimum undergraduate QPA of 2.5. Application deadline: rolling. Application fee: $25. • Dr. Elizabeth Gensante, Department Chair, 814-472-3058. Fax: 814-472-3864. E-mail: egensante@sfcpa.edu.

St. John's University, School of Education and Human Services, Division of Administration and Instructional Leadership, Instructional Leadership Program, Jamaica, NY 11439. Awards Ed D, PD. Part-time and evening/weekend programs available. Students: 6 full-time (5 women), 77 part-time (61 women); includes 5 minority (4 African Americans, 1 Hispanic), 1 international. Average age 43. 46 applicants, 39% accepted. In 1997, 8 doctorates, 3 PDs awarded. *Degree requirements:* For doctorate, 1 foreign language, dissertation. *Entrance requirements:* For doctorate, GRE General Test (minimum combined score of 1100). Application deadline: 6/1 (rolling processing; 10/1 for spring admission). Application fee: $40. *Expenses:* Tuition $525 per credit. Fees $150 per year. *Financial aid:* In 1997–98, 3 fellowships (all to first-year students) averaging $1,111 per month were awarded; administrative assistantship, Federal Work-Study, and career-related internships or fieldwork also available. Aid available to part-time students. Financial aid application deadline: 3/1; applicants required to submit FAFSA. *Faculty research:* Learning styles, gifted and talented. • Application contact: Shamus J. McGrenra, TOR, Associate Director, Graduate Admissions, 718-990-6107. Fax: 718-990-5736. E-mail: mcgrenrs@stjohns.edu.

St. John's University, School of Education and Human Services, Division of Administration and Instructional Leadership, Program in Administration and Supervision, Jamaica, NY 11439. Awards MS Ed, Ed D, PD. Part-time and evening/weekend programs available. Students: 4 full-time (3 women), 108 part-time (71 women); includes 9 minority (4 African Americans, 1 Asian American, 4 Hispanics), 4 international. Average age 42. 90 applicants, 68% accepted. In 1997, 2 master's, 4 doctorates, 24 PDs awarded. *Degree requirements:* For doctorate, 1 foreign language, dissertation. *Entrance requirements:* For doctorate, GRE General Test (minimum combined score of 1100). Application deadline: 6/1 (rolling processing; 10/1 for spring admission). Application fee: $40. *Expenses:* Tuition $525 per credit. Fees $150 per year. *Financial aid:* Teaching assistantships, administrative assistantship, Federal Work-Study, and career-related internships or fieldwork available. Aid available to part-time students. Financial aid application deadline: 3/1; applicants required to submit FAFSA. *Faculty research:* Organizational theory, economics, collective bargaining and restructuring. • Application contact: Shamus J. McGrenra, TOR, Associate Director, Graduate Admissions, 718-990-6107. Fax: 718-990-5736. E-mail: mcgrenrs@stjohns.edu.

St. Lawrence University, Department of Education, Program in Educational Administration, Canton, NY 13617-1455. Awards M Ed, CAS. Part-time and evening/weekend programs available. Faculty: 3 full-time (0 women), 4 part-time (2 women). Students: 10 part-time. *Entrance requirements:* For master's, GRE General Test. Application deadline: rolling. Application fee: $0. *Expenses:* Tuition $460 per credit hour. Fees $35 per year. *Financial aid:* Research assistantships and career-related internships or fieldwork available. *Faculty research:* Leadership. • Dr. William Fox, Coordinator, 315-229-5842.

Saint Louis University, Institute for Leadership and Public Service, Programs in Education, Department of Leadership and Higher Education, St. Louis, MO 63103-2097. Offers programs in educational administration (MA, Ed D, PhD, Ed S), higher education (MA, Ed D, PhD, Ed S). Accredited by NCATE. *Degree requirements:* For master's, comprehensive oral exam required, foreign language and thesis not required; for doctorate, dissertation, preliminary oral and written exams. *Entrance requirements:* For master's, GRE General Test or MAT; for doctorate and Ed S, GRE General Test. Application deadline: 7/1 (rolling processing; 11/1 for spring admission). Application fee: $40. *Tuition:* $542 per credit hour. *Financial aid:* Application deadline 4/1. *Faculty research:* Urban leadership, executive leadership development ethics, mediation and arbitration, comparative systems in higher education. • Dr. William T. Rebore, Director, 314-977-2510. Application contact: Dr. Marcia Buresch, Assistant Dean of the Graduate School, 314-977-2240. Fax: 314-977-3943.

Saint Mary's College of California, School of Education, Program in Administration and Supervision, Moraga, CA 94575. Awards MA. Part-time and evening/weekend programs available. Faculty: 2 full-time (0 women), 20 part-time (4 women). Students: 77 full-time (60 women), 41 part-time (34 women); includes 20 minority (6 African Americans, 4 Asian Americans, 9 Hispanics, 1 Native American). Average age 35. 40 applicants, 90% accepted. In 1997, 46 degrees awarded. *Degree requirements:* Thesis or alternative required, foreign language not required. *Entrance requirements:* Interview, minimum GPA of 3.0, teaching credential. Application deadline: rolling. Application fee: $50. *Tuition:* $1319 per course. *Financial aid:* Career-related internships or fieldwork available. Aid available to part-time students. Financial aid application deadline: 2/15. • Rudie Tretten, Director, 925-631-4700.

Saint Mary's University of Minnesota, Program in Educational Administration, Minneapolis, MN 55404. Awards MA. Part-time and evening/weekend programs available. *Degree requirements:* Internship required, foreign language and thesis not required. *Entrance requirements:* Interview, minimum GPA of 2.75. Application deadline: rolling. Application fee: $20.

Saint Mary's University of Minnesota, Program in Educational Leadership, 700 Terrace Heights, Winona, MN 55987-1399. Awards Ed D. *Application deadline:* rolling. *Application fee:* $20.

St. Mary's University of San Antonio, Department of Education, San Antonio, TX 78228-8507. Offerings include Catholic school leadership (MA), educational leadership (MA). *Entrance requirements:* GRE General Test. Application deadline: 8/1. Application fee: $15. *Expenses:* Tuition $383 per credit hour (minimum). Fees $217 per year full-time, $58 per semester part-time.

Saint Michael's College, Program in Education, Colchester, VT 05439. Offerings include administration (M Ed, CAGS). Program faculty: 5 full-time (4 women), 70 part-time (54 women). *Degree requirements:* For master's, computer language, thesis required, foreign language not required. *Entrance requirements:* For master's, minimum GPA of 2.8. Application deadline: rolling. Application fee: $25. • Dr. Aostre Johnson, Director, 802-654-2436. Fax: 802-654-2664.

Saint Peter's College, Graduate Programs in Education, Program in Administration and Supervision, 2641 Kennedy Boulevard, Jersey City, NJ 07306-5997. Awards MA. Part-time and evening/weekend programs available. Faculty: 2 full-time (1 woman), 7 part-time (1 woman). Students: 11 full-time (4 women), 49 part-time (27 women); includes 13 minority (9 African Americans, 1 Asian American, 3 Hispanics), 1 international. Average age 34. In 1997, 22 degrees awarded. *Degree requirements:* Departmental qualifying exam required, foreign language and thesis not required. *Entrance requirements:* GRE or MAT (minimum score 40), matriculation exam. Application deadline: 8/1 (priority date; rolling processing). Application fee: $20. *Tuition:* $516 per credit. *Financial aid:* Career-related internships or fieldwork available. Aid available to part-time students. Financial aid application deadline: 7/1. • Dr. Joseph McLaughlin, Director, Graduate Programs in Education, 201-915-9254. Fax: 201-915-9074. Application contact: Nancy P. Campbell, Associate Vice President for Enrollment, 201-915-9213. Fax: 201-432-5860. E-mail: admissions@spcvxa.spc.edu.

Saint Peter's College, Graduate Programs in Education, Program in Teaching, 2641 Kennedy Boulevard, Jersey City, NJ 07306-5997. Offerings include supervisor of instruction (Certificate). Program faculty: 2 full-time (0 women), 10 part-time (4 women). *Application deadline:* 8/1 (priority date; rolling processing). *Application fee:* $20. *Tuition:* $516 per credit. • Dr. Joseph McLaughlin, Director, Graduate Programs in Education, 201-915-9254. Fax: 201-915-9074. Application contact: Nancy P. Campbell, Associate Vice President for Enrollment, 201-915-9213. Fax: 201-432-5860. E-mail: admissions@spcvxa.spc.edu.

Saint Xavier University, School of Education, Chicago, IL 60655-3105. Offerings include educational administration (MA). School faculty: 16 full-time (12 women), 3 part-time (1 woman). *Degree requirements:* Thesis or project required, thesis optional. *Entrance requirements:* MAT, minimum GPA of 3.0. Application deadline: 8/15 (priority date; rolling processing). Application fee: $35. *Expenses:* Tuition $435 per hour. Fees $50 per year. • Dr. Beverly Gulley, Dean, 773-298-3221. Fax: 773-779-9061. E-mail: gulley@sxu.edu. Application contact: Sr. Evelyn McKenna, Vice President of Enrollment Management, 773-298-3050. Fax: 773-298-3076. E-mail: mckenna@sxu.edu.

Salem State College, Department of Education, Program in School Administration, Salem, MA 01970-5353. Awards M Ed. Accredited by NCATE. *Entrance requirements:* GRE General Test. Application deadline: rolling. Application fee: $25. *Expenses:* Tuition $140 per credit hour for state residents; $230 per credit hour for nonresidents. Fees $20 per credit hour.

Salisbury State University, Department of Education, Concentration in Educational Administration, Salisbury, MD 21801-6837. Awards M Ed. Part-time and evening/weekend programs available. Students: 28 part-time (16 women); includes 1 minority (African American). 31 applicants, 39% accepted. In 1997, 8 degrees awarded. *Application deadline:* 8/1 (priority date; rolling processing; 1/1 for spring admission). *Application fee:* $30. *Expenses:* Tuition $158 per credit hour for state residents; $310 per credit hour for nonresidents. Fees $4 per credit hour. *Financial aid:* Teaching assistantships available. • Dr. Ellen Whitford, Chair, Department of Education, 410-543-6294. E-mail: evwhitford@ssu.edu. Application contact: Phyllis Meyer, Administrative Aide II, 410-543-6281. Fax: 410-548-2593. E-mail: phmeyer@ssu.edu.

Samford University, School of Education, Program in Educational Administration, Birmingham, AL 35229-0002. Awards MS Ed, Ed S, M Div/MS Ed. Accredited by NCATE. 24 applicants, 96% accepted. In 1997, 4 master's awarded. *Entrance requirements:* For master's, GRE or MAT, minimum GPA of 2.75; for Ed S, master's degree, teaching certificate. Application deadline: rolling. Application fee: $25. *Tuition:* $344 per credit hour. • Dr. Maurice Persall, Director, Graduate Office, 205-870-2019.

Sam Houston State University, College of Education and Applied Science, Department of Education and Applied Science, Department of Educational Leadership and Counseling, Program in Educational Administration, Huntsville, TX 77341. Awards M Ed. Accredited by NCATE. Part-time programs available. Students: 7 full-time (5 women), 141 part-time (95 women); includes 16 minority (5 African Americans, 11 Hispanics), 1 international. Average age 34. In 1997, 27 degrees awarded. *Entrance requirements:* GRE General Test (minimum combined score of 800). Application fee: $15. *Tuition:* $1810 per year full-time, $297 per semester (minimum) part-time for state residents; $6922 per year full-time, $924 per semester (minimum) part-time for nonresidents. *Financial aid:* Federal Work-Study and career-related internships or fieldwork available. Aid available to part-time students. *Faculty research:* Principalship, administrative theory, leadership, appraisal. • Dr. Genevieve Brown, Chair, Department of Educational Leadership and Counseling, 409-294-1144. Fax: 409-294-1102. E-mail: edu_gxb@shsu.edu.

Sam Houston State University, College of Education and Applied Science, Department of Education and Applied Science, Department of Educational Leadership and Counseling, Program in Supervision, Huntsville, TX 77341. Awards M Ed. Accredited by NCATE. Part-time programs available. Students: 9 part-time (7 women). Average age 35. In 1997, 3 degrees awarded. *Entrance requirements:* GRE General Test (minimum combined score of 800). Application fee: $15. *Tuition:* $1810 per year full-time, $297 per semester (minimum) part-time for state residents; $6922 per year full-time, $924 per semester (minimum) part-time for nonresidents. *Faculty research:* Principalship, administration theory, leadership appraisal. • Dr. Genevieve Brown, Chair, Department of Educational Leadership and Counseling, 409-294-1144. Fax: 409-294-1102. E-mail: edu_gxb@shsu.edu.

San Diego State University, College of Education, Department of Administration, Rehabilitation and Post-Secondary Education, Program in Educational Administration and Supervision, San Diego, CA 92182. Awards MA. Accredited by NCATE. Evening/weekend programs available. Students: 36 full-time (20 women), 39 part-time (25 women); includes 36 minority (14 African Americans, 5 Asian Americans, 16 Hispanics, 1 Native American), 2 international. Average age 28. In 1997, 122 degrees awarded. *Entrance requirements:* GRE General Test (minimum combined score of 950), TOEFL (minimum score 550). Application deadline: 6/1 (priority date; rolling processing; 12/1 for spring admission). Application fee: $55. *Expenses:* Tuition $0 for state residents; $246 per unit for nonresidents. Fees $1932 per year full-time, $1266 per year part-time. *Financial aid:* Career-related internships or fieldwork available. • Fred McFarlane, Chair, Department of Administration, Rehabilitation and Post-Secondary Education, 619-594-6115. Fax: 619-594-4208. E-mail: fmcfarlane@sciences.sdsu.edu.

San Francisco State University, College of Education, Department of Administration and Interdisciplinary Studies, Program in Educational Administration, San Francisco, CA 94132-1722. Awards MA, AC. Accredited by NCATE. Part-time programs available. *Entrance requirements:* For master's, minimum GPA of 2.5 in last 60 units. Application deadline: 11/30 (priority date; rolling processing). Application fee: $55. *Expenses:* Tuition $0 for state residents; $246 per unit for nonresidents. Fees $1982 per year full-time, $1316 per year part-time.

San Jose State University, College of Education, Program in Administration/Higher Education, San Jose, CA 95192-0001. Awards MA, Certificate. Accredited by NCATE. Faculty: 6 full-time (2 women), 1 part-time (0 women). Students: 28 full-time (17 women), 66 part-time (40 women); includes 34 minority (6 African Americans, 7 Asian Americans, 21 Hispanics). Average age 36. 68 applicants, 84% accepted. In 1997, 24 master's awarded. *Degree requirements:* For master's, thesis or alternative required, foreign language not required. *Application deadline:* 6/1 (rolling processing). *Application fee:* $59. *Expenses:* Tuition $0 for state residents; $246 per unit for nonresidents. Fees $2017 per year full-time, $1351 per year part-time. *Financial aid:* Career-related internships or fieldwork available. • Dr. Marsha Speck, Director, 408-924-3625.

Santa Clara University, Division of Counseling Psychology and Education, Program in Educational Administration, Santa Clara, CA 95053-0001. Awards MA. Part-time and evening/weekend programs available. Students: 9 full-time (7 women), 51 part-time (41 women); includes 10 minority (2 African Americans, 4 Asian Americans, 3 Hispanics, 1 Native American), 1 international. Average age 41. 32 applicants, 97% accepted. In 1997, 22 degrees awarded. *Degree requirements:* Comprehensive exams required, foreign language and thesis not required. *Entrance requirements:* GRE or MAT, TOEFL, minimum GPA of 3.0. Application deadline: 5/1 (2/1 for spring admission). Application fee: $30. *Financial aid:* Fellowships, teaching assistantships, Federal Work-Study, and career-related internships or fieldwork available. Aid available to part-time students. Financial aid application deadline: 2/1. • Dr. Pauline Lee Mahon, Director, 408-554-4696. Application contact: Barbara F. Simmons, Assistant to the Dean, 408-554-4355. Fax: 408-554-2392.

Seattle Pacific University, School of Education, Doctoral Program in Education, Seattle, WA 98119-1997. Awards Ed D. Accredited by NCATE. Faculty: 17 full-time (5 women). Students: 49 part-time (31 women); includes 3 minority (2 African Americans, 1 Hispanic). Average age 40. 25 applicants, 60% accepted. In 1997, 6 degrees awarded (83% entered university research/teaching, 17% found other work related to degree). *Degree requirements:* Dissertation. *Average time to degree:* doctorate–3 years part-time. *Entrance requirements:* MAT, GRE. Application deadline: rolling. Application fee: $40. *Tuition:* $349 per credit. *Financial aid:* Career-related internships or fieldwork available. *Faculty research:* International education, curriculum and instruction, values and morals, school reform. • Dr. Chris Sink, Director, 206-281-2453. Fax: 206-281-2756. E-mail: csink@spu.edu.

Seattle Pacific University, School of Education, Program in Educational Leadership, Seattle, WA 98119-1997. Awards M Ed. Accredited by NCATE. Part-time and evening/weekend programs available. Faculty: 2 full-time (0 women), 3 part-time (0 women). Students: 3 full-time (1 woman), 94 part-time (56 women); includes 6 minority (1 African American, 3 Asian Americans, 2 Hispanics), 3 international. Average age 44. In 1997, 10 degrees awarded (100% found work related to degree). *Average time to degree:* master's–3 years part-time. *Entrance requirements:* MAT (minimum score 35) or GRE General Test (minimum score 300 on verbal section, 350 on quantitative, 950 combined), minimum GPA of 3.0. Application deadline: 7/1 (priority date; rolling processing; 3/1 for spring admission). Application fee: $35. *Tuition:* $316 per credit. *Financial aid:* In 1997–98, 4 research assistantships were awarded; career-related internships or fieldwork also available. • Dr. Richard Smith, Chair, 206-281-2375. Fax: 206-281-2756. E-mail: rsmith@spu.edu.

Seattle University, School of Education, Division of Leadership and Service, Program in Educational Leadership, Seattle, WA 98122. Awards Ed D. Accredited by NCATE. Part-time and evening/weekend programs available. Faculty: 3 full-time (1 woman). Students: 19 full-time (14 women), 63 part-time (42 women); includes 16 minority (5 African Americans, 4 Asian Americans, 4 Hispanics, 3 Native Americans), 1 international. Average age 45. 36 applicants, 58% accepted. In 1997, 17 degrees awarded. *Degree requirements:* Dissertation, comprehensive exam required, foreign language not required. *Entrance requirements:* GRE General Test, MAT, interview, MA, minimum GPA of 3.5, 3 years of related experience. Application deadline: 3/1. Application fee: $55. *Expenses:* Tuition $412 per credit hour. Fees $70 per year. *Financial aid:* Federal Work-Study and career-related internships or fieldwork available. Aid available to part-time students. Financial aid applicants required to submit FAFSA. • Coordinator, 206-296-6170.

Seattle University, School of Education, Division of Leadership and Service, Program in Student Development Administration, Seattle, WA 98122. Awards MA, M Ed. Accredited by NCATE. Part-time and evening/weekend programs available. Faculty: 1 full-time. Students: 10 full-time (8 women), 21 part-time (17 women); includes 6 minority (3 African Americans, 2 Asian Americans, 1 Hispanic). Average age 29. 15 applicants, 87% accepted. In 1997, 7 degrees awarded. *Degree requirements:* Comprehensive exam required, foreign language and thesis not required. *Entrance requirements:* GRE, MAT, or minimum GPA of 3.0. Application deadline: 8/20 (priority date; rolling processing; 2/20 for spring admission). Application fee: $55. *Expenses:* Tuition $339 per credit hour (minimum). Fees $70 per year. *Financial aid:* Assistantships, Federal Work-Study, and career-related internships or fieldwork available. Aid available to part-time students. Financial aid applicants required to submit FAFSA. • Dr. Jeremy Stringer, Coordinator, 206-296-5910. E-mail: stringer@seattleu.edu.

Seattle University, School of Education, Division of Teaching and Learning, Program in Educational Administration, Seattle, WA 98122. Awards MA, M Ed, Ed S. Accredited by NCATE. Part-time and evening/weekend programs available. Faculty: 1 full-time. Students: 2 full-time (both women), 29 part-time (18 women); includes 7 minority (4 African Americans, 1 Asian American, 2 Hispanics), 1 international. Average age 37. 17 applicants, 76% accepted. In 1997, 11 master's awarded. *Degree requirements:* Comprehensive exam required, foreign language and thesis not required. *Entrance requirements:* For master's, GRE, MAT, or minimum GPA of 2.75; interview; 1 year of related experience. Application deadline: 8/20 (priority date; rolling processing; 2/20 for spring admission). Application fee: $55. *Expenses:* Tuition $339 per credit hour (minimum). Fees $70 per year. *Financial aid:* Federal Work-Study and career-related internships or fieldwork available. Aid available to part-time students. Financial aid applicants required to submit FAFSA. • Dr. Sandra Barker, Chair, Division of Teaching and Learning, 206-296-5798. Fax: 206-296-2053. E-mail: sbarker@seattleu.edu.

Seton Hall University, College of Education and Human Services, Department of Educational Administration and Supervision, South Orange, NJ 07079-2697. Offers programs in Catholic school leadership (MA), educational administration and supervision (Ed D, Exec Ed D, PhD), elementary and secondary educational administration (MA, Ed D, Ed S), higher education administration (Ed D, Exec Ed D, PhD, Ed S), human resource training and development (MA). MA (Catholic school leadership) and PhD new for fall 1998. Evening/weekend programs

Directory: Educational Administration

Seton Hall University (continued)
available. Students: 255. In 1997, 17 doctorates awarded. *Degree requirements:* For master's, thesis or alternative, comprehensive exam required, foreign language not required; for doctorate, dissertation, comprehensive exam, internship required, foreign language not required; for Ed S, internship, research project required, foreign language not required. *Entrance requirements:* For master's, GRE or MAT, minimum GPA of 3.0; for doctorate, GRE or MAT, interview, minimum GPA of 3.5; for Ed S, GRE or MAT, minimum GPA of 3.5. Application fee: $50. *Expenses:* Tuition $500 per credit. Fees $610 per year full-time, $185 per semester part-time. *Financial aid:* Fellowships available. Financial aid application deadline: 2/1. *Faculty research:* Leadership, principalship, management of careers, effective schools, cooperative learning. • Dr. Charles Mitchell, Chairman, 973-761-9397. E-mail: mitcheca@shu.edu.

Seton Hall University, College of Education and Human Services, Department of Professional Psychology and Family Therapy, Program in Student Personnel Services (K-12), South Orange, NJ 07079-2697. Awards MA. *Degree requirements:* Comprehensive exam required, foreign language and thesis not required. *Entrance requirements:* GRE or MAT, teaching certificate, 1 year of teaching experience. Application deadline: rolling. Application fee: $50. *Expenses:* Tuition $500 per credit. Fees $610 per year full-time, $185 per semester part-time. *Financial aid:* Career-related internships or fieldwork available. Financial aid application deadline: 2/1. • Dr. John Smith, Coordinator, 973-275-2741. E-mail: smithjoh@shu.edu.

Shippensburg University of Pennsylvania, College of Education and Human Services, Department of Educational Administration and Foundations, Shippensburg, PA 17257-2299. Offers programs in elementary school administration (M Ed), secondary school administration (M Ed). Accredited by NCATE. Faculty: 4 full-time (1 woman), 3 part-time (2 women). Students: 3 full-time (2 women), 69 part-time (24 women); includes 3 minority (2 Hispanics, 1 Native American). Average age 31. In 1997, 17 degrees awarded. *Entrance requirements:* Interview or minimum GPA of 2.5. Application deadline: rolling. Application fee: $25. Electronic applications accepted. *Expenses:* Tuition $3468 per year full-time, $193 per credit hour part-time for state residents; $6236 per year full-time, $346 per credit hour part-time for nonresidents. Fees $678 per year full-time, $108 per semester (minimum) part-time. *Financial aid:* In 1997–98, 3 graduate assistantships were awarded. Financial aid application deadline: 3/1. • Dr. Nancy H. Stankus, Chairperson, 717-532-1591.

Simon Fraser University, Faculty of Education, Program in Administrative Leadership, Burnaby, BC V5A 1S6, Canada. Awards MA, M Ed. *Degree requirements:* Thesis (for some programs), project or thesis required, foreign language not required. *Entrance requirements:* TOEFL (minimum score 570), TWE (minimum score 5), or International English Language Test (minimum score 7.5), minimum GPA of 3.0. Application fee: $55. *Expenses:* Tuition $768 per trimester. Fees $207 per year full-time, $61 per trimester part-time. • Application contact: Graduate Secretary, 604-291-4787. Fax: 604-291-3203.

Sonoma State University, School of Education, Program in Educational Administration, Rohnert Park, CA 94928-3609. Awards MA. Part-time and evening/weekend programs available. Students: 27 full-time (18 women), 12 part-time (11 women); includes 7 minority (2 African Americans, 1 Asian American, 4 Hispanics). Average age 44. 22 applicants, 91% accepted. In 1997, 11 degrees awarded. *Degree requirements:* Thesis or alternative required, foreign language not required. *Entrance requirements:* GRE General Test, minimum GPA of 2.5. Application fee: $55. *Expenses:* Tuition $0 for state residents; $246 per unit for nonresidents. Fees $2130 per year full-time, $1464 per year part-time. *Financial aid:* Application deadline 3/2. • Dr. Linda Webster, Coordinator, 707-664-3117. E-mail: linda.webster@sonoma.edu.

South Carolina State University, School of Education, Department of Educational Administration, 300 College Street Northeast, Orangeburg, SC 29117-0001. Awards Ed D, Ed S. Accredited by NCATE. Part-time and evening/weekend programs available. Faculty: 8 full-time (1 woman), 1 part-time (0 women). Students: 12 full-time (6 women), 62 part-time (42 women); includes 56 minority (54 African Americans, 1 Asian American, 1 Native American). Average age 40. 101 applicants, 62% accepted. In 1997, 15 doctorates awarded (100% found work related to degree); 13 Ed Ss awarded. *Degree requirements:* For doctorate, computer language, dissertation, comprehensive and preliminary exams, internship, practicum required, foreign language not required; for Ed S, computer language, thesis required, foreign language not required. *Average time to degree:* doctorate–6 years full-time. *Entrance requirements:* For doctorate, GRE General Test (minimum combined score of 1000) or MAT (minimum score 50), teaching certificate, teaching experience; for Ed S, GRE General Test (minimum combined score of 950) or MAT (minimum score 37), interview, teaching certificate, teaching experience. Application deadline: 7/15 (priority date; rolling processing; 11/10 for spring admission). Application fee: $25. *Tuition:* $2974 per year full-time, $165 per credit hour part-time. *Financial aid:* Institutionally sponsored loans and career-related internships or fieldwork available. Financial aid application deadline: 6/1. *Faculty research:* Middle schools, organization leadership, school personnel, efficacy of teachers. • Dr. George Bradley, Interim Chairperson, 803-536-8381. Application contact: Dr. Gail Joyner-Fleming, Interim Associate Dean and Director, Graduate Teacher Education, 803-536-8824. Fax: 803-536-8492.

South Dakota State University, College of Education and Counseling, Department of Educational Leadership, Program in Educational Administration, Brookings, SD 57007. Awards M Ed. Accredited by NCATE. Students: 2 full-time (both women), 40 part-time (21 women). 9 applicants, 100% accepted. In 1997, 47 degrees awarded. *Degree requirements:* Thesis, comprehensive and oral exams required, foreign language not required. *Average time to degree:* master's–2 years full-time, 4 years part-time. *Entrance requirements:* TOEFL (minimum score 550), minimum GPA of 2.75. Application deadline: rolling. Application fee: $15. *Expenses:* Tuition $82 per credit hour for state residents; $242 per credit hour for nonresidents. Fees $37 per credit hour. *Faculty research:* School improvement, total quality management and schools, constructiveism, leadership, educational rural development. • Dr. R. L. Erion, Head, Department of Educational Leadership, 605-688-4448.

Southeastern Louisiana University, College of Education, Department of Counseling, Family Studies, and Educational Leadership, Hammond, LA 70402. Offers programs in counselor education (M Ed), educational administration (Ed S), school administration and supervision (M Ed). Accredited by NCATE. Ed S being phased out; applicants no longer accepted. Part-time programs available. Faculty: 7 full-time, 6 part-time. Students: 28 full-time (21 women), 122 part-time (100 women); includes 15 minority (12 African Americans, 3 Asian Americans). Average age 34. In 1997, 51 master's awarded. *Entrance requirements:* For master's, GRE. Application deadline: 7/15 (priority date; rolling processing; 12/15 for spring admission). Application fee: $10 ($25 for international students). Electronic applications accepted. *Expenses:* Tuition $2010 per year full-time, $287 per semester (minimum) part-time for state residents; $5232 per year full-time, $287 per semester (minimum) part-time for nonresidents. Fees $5 per year. *Financial aid:* Research assistantships, teaching assistantships, administrative assistantships, Federal Work-Study, and career-related internships or fieldwork available. Aid available to part-time students. Financial aid application deadline: 5/1; applicants required to submit FAFSA. *Faculty research:* Transformational leadership, contraceptive implants, women's issues, family resource centers, leadership for the twenty-first century. Total annual research expenditures: $60,000. • Dr. Peter Emerson, Head, 504-549-2309. E-mail: pemerson@selu.edu. Application contact: Dr. Sue Austin, Graduate Coordinator, 504-549-2181. Fax: 504-549-3758. E-mail: saustin@selu.edu.

Southeastern Oklahoma State University, School of Education, Durant, OK 74701-0609. Offerings include educational administration (M Ed). Accredited by NCATE. School faculty: 69 full-time (23 women), 3 part-time (0 women), 69.7 FTE. *Application deadline:* 8/1. *Tuition:* $76 per credit hour for state residents; $178 per credit hour for nonresidents. • Dr. Barbara Decker, Dean, 580-924-0121 Ext. 2251. Fax: 580-920-7473.

Southeast Missouri State University, Department of Educational Administration and Counseling, Program in Educational Administration, Cape Girardeau, MO 63701-4799. Awards MA, Ed D, Ed S. Accredited by NCATE. Ed D offered jointly with the University of Missouri–Columbia and new for fall 1998. Part-time and evening/weekend programs available. In 1997, 17 Ed Ss awarded. *Degree requirements:* For master's, thesis or alternative required, foreign language not required. *Entrance requirements:* For master's, GRE General Test (score in 50th percentile or higher), minimum GPA of 2.75; for Ed S, GRE General Test, minimum GPA of 2.5. Application deadline: 4/1 (priority date; rolling processing; 11/21 for spring admission). Application fee: $20 ($100 for international students). *Tuition:* $2034 per year full-time, $113 per credit hour part-time for state residents; $3672 per year full-time, $204 per credit hour part-time for nonresidents. *Financial aid:* Research assistantships and career-related internships or fieldwork available. • Wayne Gould, Head, 573-651-2137. Application contact: Office of Graduate Studies, 573-651-2192.

Southern Connecticut State University, School of Education, Department of Educational Leadership, New Haven, CT 06515-1355. Awards Diploma. Faculty: 3 full-time, 3 part-time. Students: 6 full-time (3 women), 246 part-time (169 women); includes 13 minority (9 African Americans, 1 Asian American, 3 Hispanics). 192 applicants, 68% accepted. In 1997, 95 degrees awarded. *Entrance requirements:* Master's degree, minimum GPA of 3.0. Application deadline: 7/15 (priority date; rolling processing). Application fee: $40. *Expenses:* Tuition $2632 per year full-time, $188 per credit part-time for state residents; $7200 per year full-time, $188 per credit part-time for nonresidents. Fees $1806 per year full-time, $45 per semester part-time for state residents; $2703 per year full-time, $45 per semester part-time for nonresidents. • Dr. John Onofrio, Chairperson, 203-392-5341.

Southern Illinois University at Carbondale, College of Education, Department of Educational Administration and Higher Education, Program in Educational Administration, Carbondale, IL 62901-6806. Awards MS Ed, PhD. Accredited by NCATE. PhD offered jointly with Southeast Missouri State University. Part-time programs available. Faculty: 9 full-time (1 woman). Students: 27 full-time (12 women), 26 part-time (14 women); includes 3 minority (2 African Americans, 1 Native American), 3 international. 26 applicants, 50% accepted. In 1997, 12 master's, 9 doctorates awarded. *Degree requirements:* For master's, thesis or alternative required, foreign language not required; for doctorate, dissertation. *Entrance requirements:* For master's, GRE General Test, MAT, TOEFL (minimum score 550), minimum GPA of 2.7; for doctorate, GRE General Test, MAT, TOEFL (minimum score 550), minimum GPA of 3.5. Application deadline: 5/15 (rolling processing; 9/15 for spring admission). Application fee: $20. *Expenses:* Tuition $2964 per year full-time, $99 per semester hour part-time for state residents; $8892 per year full-time, $270 per semester hour part-time for nonresidents. Fees $1034 per year full-time, $298 per semester (minimum) part-time. *Financial aid:* In 1997–98, 1 research assistantship, 3 teaching assistantships were awarded; fellowships, full tuition waivers, Federal Work-Study, institutionally sponsored loans, and career-related internships or fieldwork also available. Aid available to part-time students. Financial aid application deadline: 4/1. *Faculty research:* School principalship, history and philosophy of education, supervision. • Application contact: Debra Mibb, Admissions Secretary, 618-536-4434. Fax: 618-453-4338. E-mail: dmibb@siu.edu.

Southern Illinois University at Edwardsville, School of Education, Department of Educational Administration and Instructional Technology, Program in Educational Administration and Supervision, Edwardsville, IL 62026-0001. Awards MS Ed, Ed S. Accredited by NCATE. Part-time programs available. Students: 54 full-time (36 women), 98 part-time (55 women); includes 14 minority (13 African Americans, 1 Hispanic). 42 applicants, 64% accepted. In 1997, 29 master's awarded. *Degree requirements:* For master's, thesis or alternative, final exam required, foreign language not required. *Entrance requirements:* For master's, GRE General Test or MAT. Application deadline: 7/24. Application fee: $25. *Expenses:* Tuition $1716 per year full-time, $95 per credit hour part-time for state residents; $5149 per year full-time, $286 per credit hour part-time for nonresidents. Fees $463 per year full-time, $433 per year part-time. *Financial aid:* In 1997–98, 1 research assistantship, 2 assistantships were awarded; fellowships, teaching assistantships, Federal Work-Study, institutionally sponsored loans also available. Aid available to part-time students. • Dr. Wayne Nelson, Chair, Department of Educational Administration and Instructional Technology, 618-692-3286.

Southern Oregon University, School of Social Science, Health and Physical Education, Department of Education, Ashland, OR 97520. Offerings include elementary education (MA Ed, MS Ed), with options in classroom teacher, early childhood, handicapped learner, reading, supervision; secondary education (MA Ed, MS Ed), with options in classroom teacher, handicapped learner, reading, supervision. *Application deadline:* 2/1. *Application fee:* $50. *Tuition:* $5187 per year full-time, $586 per quarter (minimum) part-time for state residents; $9228 per year full-time, $586 per quarter (minimum) part-time for nonresidents. • Dr. Mary-Curtis Gramley, Associate Dean of Education, 541-552-6918.

Southern University and Agricultural and Mechanical College, College of Education, Department of Behavioral Studies and Educational Leadership, Baton Rouge, LA 70813. Offers programs in administration and supervision (M Ed), counselor education (MA), mental health counseling (MA). Accredited by NCATE. Faculty: 10 full-time (3 women). Students: 39 full-time (25 women), 139 part-time (97 women); includes 157 minority (all African Americans). Average age 30. 72 applicants, 79% accepted. In 1997, 59 degrees awarded. *Degree requirements:* Thesis optional. *Entrance requirements:* GMAT or GRE General Test, TOEFL. Application deadline: 6/1 (priority date; rolling processing; 11/1 for spring admission). Application fee: $5. *Tuition:* $2226 per year full-time, $267 per semester (minimum) part-time for state residents; $6262 per year full-time, $267 per semester (minimum) part-time for nonresidents. *Financial aid:* Application deadline 4/15. • Dr. Harry Albert, Chairman, 504-771-2890.

Southwest Baptist University, School of Graduate Studies, Education Department, 1600 University Avenue, Bolivar, MO 65613-2597. Offerings include educational administration (MS). Department faculty: 6 full-time (2 women), 37 part-time (15 women). *Degree requirements:* Thesis required, foreign language not required. *Entrance requirements:* GRE or NTE, interviews, minimum GPA of 2.75. Application deadline: rolling. Application fee: $25. *Tuition:* $123 per credit hour. • Dr. Tom Hollis, Director, 417-326-1700. E-mail: gradedu@sbuniv.edu. Application contact: Donna Sybouts, Administrative Assistant, 417-326-1711. Fax: 417-326-1719. E-mail: dsybouts@sbuniv.edu.

Southwestern Oklahoma State University, School of Education, Program in Educational Administration, Weatherford, OK 73096-3098. Awards M Ed. Accredited by NCATE. M Ed distance learning degree program offered to Oklahoma residents only. Part-time programs available. Postbaccalaureate distance learning degree programs offered (minimal on-campus study). Students: 20 full-time (7 women), 81 part-time (35 women); includes 8 minority (4 African Americans, 1 Asian American, 2 Hispanics, 1 Native American). 6 applicants, 100% accepted. In 1997, 21 degrees awarded. *Degree requirements:* Exam required, foreign language and thesis not required. *Entrance requirements:* GRE General Test, TOEFL (minimum score 550), minimum GPA of 2.5, portfolio. Application deadline: rolling. Application fee: $15. *Expenses:* Tuition $60 per credit hour (minimum) for state residents; $147 per credit hour (minimum) for nonresidents. Fees $109 per year full-time, $24 per semester (minimum) part-time. *Financial aid:* Research assistantships, teaching assistantships, partial tuition waivers, Federal Work-Study, institutionally sponsored loans, and career-related internships or fieldwork available. Aid available to part-time students. Financial aid application deadline: 3/1; applicants required to submit FAFSA. • Dr. Greg Moss, Chair, School Service Programs, 580-774-3140.

Southwest Missouri State University, College of Education, Department of Educational Administration, Springfield, MO 65804-0094. Awards MS Ed, Ed S. Part-time and evening/weekend programs available. Faculty: 5 full-time (0 women), 2 part-time (0 women). Students: 10 full-time (5 women), 317 part-time (170 women); includes 5 minority (2 African Americans, 1 Asian American, 2 Native Americans). Average age 33. In 1997, 47 master's, 31 Ed Ss awarded. *Degree requirements:* Thesis or alternative, comprehensive exam required, foreign language not required. *Entrance requirements:* For master's, minimum GPA of 2.75; for Ed S, GRE General Test (minimum combined score of 875), MAT, minimum GPA of 2.75. Application deadline: 8/7 (priority date; rolling processing; 12/17 for spring admission). Application fee:

$25. *Expenses:* Tuition $1980 per year full-time, $110 per credit hour part-time for state residents; $3960 per year full-time, $220 per credit hour part-time for nonresidents. Fees $274 per year full-time, $73 per semester part-time. *Financial aid:* In 1997–98, 2 graduate assistantships averaging $583 per month and totaling $10,500 were awarded; research assistantships and career-related internships or fieldwork also available. *Faculty research:* Cultural diversity, instructional improvement, leadership correlates. Total annual research expenditures: $2000. • Dr. Jack Israel, Head, 417-836-5392. Fax: 417-836-6905. E-mail: jwi956f@wpgate.smsu.edu.

Southwest Texas State University, School of Education, Department of Educational Administration and Psychological Services, Program in Educational Administration, San Marcos, TX 78666. Awards MA, M Ed. Part-time and evening/weekend programs available. Students: 10 full-time (7 women), 105 part-time (71 women); includes 16 minority (3 African Americans, 13 Hispanics), 1 international. Average age 36. In 1997, 44 degrees awarded. *Degree requirements:* Comprehensive exam required, foreign language and thesis not required. *Entrance requirements:* GRE General Test (minimum combined score of 900), TOEFL (minimum score 550), minimum GPA of 2.75 in last 60 hours. Application deadline: 7/15 (rolling processing; 11/15 for spring admission). Application fee: $25 ($50 for international students). *Expenses:* Tuition $648 per year full-time, $120 per semester (minimum) part-time for state residents; $4500 per year full-time, $750 per semester (minimum) part-time for nonresidents. Fees $1264 per year full-time, $314 per semester (minimum) part-time. *Financial aid:* Federal Work-Study, institutionally sponsored loans, and career-related internships or fieldwork available. Aid available to part-time students. Financial aid application deadline: 4/1; applicants required to submit FAFSA. *Faculty research:* Superintendency, middle management, supervision, junior college. • Dr. Marianne Reese, Graduate Adviser, 512-245-2575. E-mail: mr11@swt.edu.

Spalding University, School of Education, Doctoral Program in Leadership Education, Louisville, KY 40203-2188. Awards Ed D. Accredited by NCATE. Faculty: 7 full-time (5 women), 5 part-time (4 women). Students: 3 full-time (all women), 60 part-time (39 women); includes 13 minority (all African Americans). Average age 44. 26 applicants, 85% accepted. In 1997, 15 degrees awarded. *Degree requirements:* Dissertation required, foreign language not required. *Entrance requirements:* GRE General Test or MAT, interview, portfolio. Application deadline: 8/15 (priority date; rolling processing). Application fee: $30. *Expenses:* Tuition $350 per credit hour (minimum). Fees $48 per year full-time, $4 per credit hour part-time. *Financial aid:* In 1997–98, 4 research assistantships totaling $9,000, 1 scholarship totaling $2,813 were awarded; Federal Work-Study and career-related internships or fieldwork also available. Aid available to part-time students. Financial aid application deadline: 3/15; applicants required to submit FAFSA. • Dr. Mary Angela Shaughnessy, Director, 502-588-7171. Fax: 502-588-7172. E-mail: angie@spalding14.win.net. Application contact: Jeanne Anderson, Assistant to the Provost and Director of Graduate Office, 502-585-7105. Fax: 502-585-7158. E-mail: gradoffc@spalding6.win.net.

Spalding University, School of Education, Programs in Teacher Education and Administration, Louisville, KY 40203-2188. Offerings in 5–8 (MA, MAT), 9–12 (MA, MAT), guidance (MA), K–4 (MA, MAT), reading specialist (MA). Accredited by NCATE. Part-time and evening/weekend programs available. Faculty: 7 full-time (5 women), 5 part-time (4 women). Students: 20 full-time (18 women), 53 part-time (43 women); includes 4 minority (3 African Americans, 1 Hispanic), 1 international. Average age 36. 26 applicants, 65% accepted. In 1997, 33 degrees awarded. *Entrance requirements:* GRE General Test, interview, portfolio. Application deadline: 8/15 (priority date; rolling processing). Application fee: $30. *Expenses:* Tuition $350 per credit hour (minimum). Fees $48 per year full-time, $4 per credit hour part-time. *Financial aid:* In 1997–98, 64 students received aid, including 2 research assistantships totaling $4,200, 49 scholarships totaling $64,155; Federal Work-Study and career-related internships or fieldwork also available. Financial aid application deadline: 3/15; applicants required to submit FAFSA. • Application contact: Jeanne Anderson, Assistant to the Provost and Director of Graduate Office, 502-585-7105. Fax: 502-585-7158. E-mail: gradoffc@spalding6.win.net.

Springfield College, Programs in Counseling and Psychological Services, Springfield, MA 01109-3797. Offerings include student personnel in higher education (M Ed, MS, CAS). Faculty: 9 full-time (5 women), 15 part-time (8 women), 13 FTE. *Degree requirements:* For master's, thesis (for some programs), comprehensive exam required, foreign language not required. *Entrance requirements:* Interview. Application deadline: 2/1 (priority date; rolling processing; 12/1 for spring admission). Application fee: $40. *Expenses:* Tuition $474 per credit. Fees $25 per year. • Dr. Barbara Mandell, Director, 413-748-3328. Application contact: Donald J. Shaw Jr., Director of Graduate Admissions, 413-748-3225. Fax: 413-748-3694. E-mail: dshaw@spfldcol.edu.

Stanford University, School of Education, Program in Social Sciences in Educational Practice, Stanford, CA 94305-9991. Offers anthropology of education (PhD); economics of education (PhD); higher education administration (AM, Ed D, PhD); history of education (PhD); international comparative education (AM, PhD); international education administration and policy analysis (AM); philosophy of education (PhD); policy analysis (AM, Ed D, PhD); prospective principal's program (AM); social science in education (AM), including gender studies; interdisciplinary; social sciences in education (PhD); sociology of education (PhD). *Degree requirements:* For doctorate, dissertation required, foreign language not required. *Entrance requirements:* GRE General Test. Application deadline: 1/2. Application fee: $65 ($75 for international students). *Expenses:* Tuition $22,110 per year. Fees $156 per year. *Financial aid:* Fellowships available. Financial aid application deadline: 2/1; applicants required to submit FAFSA. • Application contact: Graduate Admissions Office, 650-723-4794.

State University of New York at Albany, School of Education, Department of Educational Administration, Albany, NY 12222-0001. Awards MS, Ed D, CAS. Evening/weekend programs available. Faculty: 14 full-time (2 women), 2 part-time (0 women). Students: 66 full-time (33 women), 136 part-time (73 women); includes 22 minority (14 African Americans, 8 Hispanics), 7 international. 75 applicants, 87% accepted. In 1997, 44 master's, 11 doctorates, 4 CASs awarded. *Degree requirements:* For doctorate, 1 foreign language, dissertation. *Entrance requirements:* For doctorate, GRE General Test, GRE Subject Test. Application fee: $50. *Expenses:* Tuition $5100 per year full-time, $213 per credit hour part-time for state residents; $8416 per year full-time, $351 per credit hour part-time for nonresidents. Fees $705 per year full-time, $26.85 per credit hour part-time. *Financial aid:* Fellowships and career-related internships or fieldwork available. • Dr. Fred Dembrowski, Chair, 518-442-5080.

State University of New York at Buffalo, Graduate School, Graduate School of Education, Department of Educational Leadership and Policy, Buffalo, NY 14260. Offers programs in educational administration (Ed M, Ed D, PhD, Certificate); social, philosophical, and historical foundations (Ed D, PhD). Faculty: 17 full-time (3 women), 1 (woman) part-time. Students: 58 full-time (34 women), 204 part-time (122 women); includes 55 minority (46 African Americans, 3 Asian Americans, 5 Hispanics, 1 Native American), 34 international. Average age 37. 107 applicants, 68% accepted. In 1997, 4 master's, 27 doctorates awarded. Terminal master's awarded for partial completion of doctoral program. *Degree requirements:* For master's, thesis required (for some programs), foreign language not required; for doctorate, dissertation required, foreign language not required. *Entrance requirements:* For master's, GRE General Test, TOEFL (minimum score 550); for doctorate, GRE General Test or MAT, TOEFL (minimum score 550), sample of written work. Application deadline: 3/1 (rolling processing; 11/15 for spring admission). Application fee: $50. *Tuition:* $5970 per year full-time, $288 per credit hour part-time for state residents; $9286 per year full-time, $426 per credit hour part-time for nonresidents. *Financial aid:* In 1997–98, 50 students received aid, including 1 fellowship averaging $1,000 per month and totaling $10,000, 8 graduate assistantships (4 to first-year students) averaging $800 per month and totaling $65,280; research assistantships, teaching assistantships, full and partial tuition waivers, Federal Work-Study, institutionally sponsored loans, and career-related internships or fieldwork also available. Financial aid application deadline: 3/15. *Faculty research:* At-risk students, comparative educational leadership, higher education. • Dr. Robert B. Stevenson, Chairman, 716-645-2471. Fax: 716-645-2481. E-mail: eoastevo@acsu.buffalo.edu.

State University of New York at Buffalo, Graduate School, Graduate School of Education, Department of Learning and Instruction, Buffalo, NY 14260. Offerings include school administrator and supervisor (Certificate). Department faculty: 20 full-time (9 women), 7 part-time (2 women). *Application deadline:* 2/1 (11/15 for spring admission). *Application fee:* $50. *Tuition:* $5970 per year full-time, $288 per credit hour part-time for state residents; $9286 per year full-time, $426 per credit hour part-time for nonresidents. • Dr. Michael Kibby, Chair, 716-645-2455. Application contact: Barbara Cracchiolo, Admissions Secretary, 716-645-2457. Fax: 716-645-3161.

State University of New York at New Paltz, Faculty of Education, Department of Educational Administration, New Paltz, NY 12561-2499. Awards MS Ed, CAS. Students: 18 full-time (8 women), 90 part-time (54 women); includes 10 minority (8 African Americans, 2 Hispanics), 6 international. In 1997, 34 master's, 61 CASs awarded. *Entrance requirements:* For master's, GRE General Test or MAT, minimum GPA of 3.0, teaching certificate. Application deadline: 3/15 (priority date; rolling processing). Application fee: $50. *Expenses:* Tuition $5100 per year full-time, $213 per credit hour part-time for state residents; $8416 per year full-time, $351 per credit hour part-time for nonresidents. Fees $493 per year full-time, $48 per semester (minimum) part-time. *Financial aid:* Federal Work-Study, institutionally sponsored loans, and career-related internships or fieldwork available. • Dr. Irene Lober, Chair, 914-257-2810.

State University of New York at Oswego, School of Education, Department of Educational Administration, Oswego, NY 13126. Awards MS Ed, PhD, CAS, MS Ed/CAS. Programs in educational administration (PhD), instructional administration (MS Ed, CAS). PhD (educational administration) offered jointly with University of Albany, State University of New York. Faculty: 3 full-time, 2 part-time. Students: 2 full-time (0 women), 40 part-time (24 women); includes 2 minority (both African Americans). Average age 40. 36 applicants, 83% accepted. In 1997, 49 CASs awarded. *Degree requirements:* For master's and CAS, comprehensive exam, internship required, foreign language and thesis not required. *Entrance requirements:* For master's, GRE General Test, GRE Subject Test, teaching certificate; for CAS, GRE General Test, GRE Subject Test, interview, MA or MS, minimum GPA of 3.0, teaching certificate. Application deadline: 7/1. Application fee: $50. *Expenses:* Tuition $5100 per year full-time, $213 per credit hour part-time for state residents; $8416 per year full-time, $351 per credit hour part-time for nonresidents. Fees $135 per year (minimum). *Financial aid:* Teaching assistantships and career-related internships or fieldwork available. *Faculty research:* Professional growth and development, leadership, governance, strategic planning, shared decision making. • Dr. William Silky, Chair, 315-341-2264.

State University of New York at Stony Brook, School of Professional Development and Continuing Studies, Stony Brook, NY 11794. Offerings include school administration and supervision (Certificate), school district administration (Certificate). School faculty: 1 full-time, 101 part-time. *Application deadline:* 1/15. *Application fee:* $50. *Expenses:* Tuition $5100 per year full-time, $213 per credit hour part-time for state residents; $8416 per year full-time, $351 per credit hour part-time for nonresidents. Fees $529 per year full-time, $77 per semester (minimum) part-time. • Dr. Paul J. Edelson, Dean, 516-632-7052. E-mail: paul.edelson@sunysb.edu. Application contact: Sandra Romansky, Director of Admissions and Advisement, 516-632-7050. Fax: 516-632-9046. E-mail: sandra.romansky@sunysb.edu.

State University of New York College at Brockport, School of Professions, Department of Educational Administration, Brockport, NY 14420-2997. Offers programs in school administration and supervision (MS Ed, CAS), school business administration (CAS), school district administration (CAS). Part-time and evening/weekend programs available. Faculty: 6 full-time (3 women), 15 part-time (7 women), 9 FTE. Students: 21 full-time (10 women), 228 part-time (128 women); includes 27 minority (19 African Americans, 1 Asian American, 6 Hispanics, 1 Native American). Average age 35. 62 applicants, 98% accepted. In 1997, 43 master's, 97 CASs awarded. *Degree requirements:* For CAS, 6 hour internship required, foreign language and thesis not required. *Entrance requirements:* For master's, minimum GPA of 3.0; for CAS, minimum GPA of 3.0 (undergraduate), 3.5 (graduate); MS. Application deadline: rolling. Application fee: $50. *Expenses:* Tuition $5100 per year full-time, $213 per credit hour part-time for state residents; $8416 per year full-time, $351 per credit hour part-time for nonresidents. Fees $440 per year full-time, $22.60 per credit hour part-time. *Financial aid:* Federal Work-Study and career-related internships or fieldwork available. Aid available to part-time students. Financial aid application deadline: 4/1; applicants required to submit FAFSA. *Faculty research:* Special education, new faculty perceptions, gender bias, the superintendency. • Dr. Sandra Graczyk, Chairperson, 716-395-2661. Fax: 716-395-2172. E-mail: slgraczyk@aol.com.

State University of New York College at Buffalo, Faculty of Applied Science and Education, Department of Educational Foundations, Program in Student Personnel Administration, Buffalo, NY 14222-1095. Awards MS. Accredited by NCATE. Students: 59 full-time (39 women), 43 part-time (29 women); includes 32 minority (26 African Americans, 6 Hispanics). Average age 31. 68 applicants, 88% accepted. In 1997, 41 degrees awarded. *Entrance requirements:* Minimum GPA of 2.75 in last 60 hours of undergraduate course work. Application deadline: 5/1 (10/1 for spring admission). Application fee: $50. *Expenses:* Tuition $5100 per year full-time, $213 per credit hour part-time for state residents; $8416 per year full-time, $351 per credit hour part-time for nonresidents. Fees $195 per year full-time, $8.60 per credit hour part-time. *Financial aid:* Assistantships available. • Dr. James Gold, Coordinator, 716-878-4303.

State University of New York College at Buffalo, Faculty of Applied Science and Education, Department of Elementary Education and Reading, Program in School Administration and Supervision, Buffalo, NY 14222-1095. Awards CAS. Accredited by NCATE. Part-time and evening/weekend programs available. Faculty: 4 full-time (1 woman). Students: 2 full-time (both women), 63 part-time (47 women); includes 13 minority (11 African Americans, 1 Hispanic, 1 Native American). Average age 40. 15 applicants, 80% accepted. In 1997, 21 degrees awarded. *Degree requirements:* Internship required, foreign language and thesis not required. *Entrance requirements:* Master's degree, New York teaching certificate, 3 years of teaching experience. Application deadline: 5/1 (10/1 for spring admission). Application fee: $50. *Expenses:* Tuition $5100 per year full-time, $213 per credit hour part-time for state residents; $8416 per year full-time, $351 per credit hour part-time for nonresidents. Fees $195 per year full-time, $8.60 per credit hour part-time. *Financial aid:* Fellowships, Federal Work-Study available. Aid available to part-time students. Financial aid application deadline: 3/1. • Dr. Peter Loehr, Coordinator, 716-878-5916.

State University of New York College at Cortland, Division of Professional Studies, Department of Education, Program in School Administration and Supervision, Cortland, NY 13045. Awards CAS. Part-time and evening/weekend programs available. In 1997, 39 degrees awarded. *Degree requirements:* 1 foreign language required, thesis not required. *Entrance requirements:* MS in education, permanent New York teaching certificate. Application deadline: rolling. Application fee: $50. *Expenses:* Tuition $5100 per year full-time, $213 per credit hour part-time for state residents; $8416 per year full-time, $351 per credit hour part-time for nonresidents. Fees $644 per year full-time, $79 per semester (minimum) part-time. • Application contact: Jeanne M. Bechtel, Director of Admissions, 607-753-4711. Fax: 607-753-5998.

State University of New York College at Fredonia, Department of Education, Program in Educational Administration, Fredonia, NY 14063. Awards CAS. Part-time and evening/weekend programs available. Faculty: 1 part-time (0 women). Students: 0. 0 applicants. In 1997, 20 degrees awarded. *Degree requirements:* Thesis or alternative required, foreign language not required. *Application deadline:* 7/5. *Application fee:* $50. *Expenses:* Tuition $5100 per year full-time, $213 per credit hour part-time for state residents; $8416 per year full-time, $351 per credit hour part-time for nonresidents. Fees $725 per year full-time, $30 per credit hour part-time. *Financial aid:* Research assistantships, teaching assistantships, full and partial tuition waivers, and career-related internships or fieldwork available. Aid available to

Directory: Educational Administration

State University of New York College at Fredonia (continued)
part-time students. Financial aid application deadline: 3/15. • Dr. Julius Adams, Chair, Department of Education, 716-673-3311.

State University of West Georgia, College of Education, Department of Educational Leadership, Carrollton, GA 30118. Offers programs in administration and supervision (M Ed, Ed S), educational leadership (Ed D, Ed S). Accredited by NCATE. Ed D offered jointly with the University of Georgia. Part-time and evening/weekend programs available. Faculty: 9 full-time (2 women). Students: 69 full-time (43 women), 228 part-time (163 women); includes 70 minority (69 African Americans, 1 Hispanic). Average age 35. In 1997, 57 master's, 61 Ed Ss awarded. *Degree requirements:* For doctorate, research project; for Ed S, research project required, foreign language and thesis not required. *Entrance requirements:* For master's, GRE General Test (minimum combined score of 800), minimum GPA of 2.5; for Ed S, GRE General Test (minimum combined score of 800), master's degree, minimum graduate GPA of 3.25. Application deadline: 8/30 (rolling processing). Application fee: $15. *Expenses:* Tuition $2428 per year full-time, $83 per semester hour part-time for state residents; $8428 per year full-time, $250 per semester hour part-time for nonresidents. Fees $428 per year. *Financial aid:* Research assistantships, assistantships, and career-related internships or fieldwork available. Aid available to part-time students. Financial aid applicants required to submit FAFSA. *Total annual research expenditures:* $5000. • Dr. Price M. Michael, Chairman, 770-836-6557. Application contact: Dr. Jack O. Jenkins, Dean, Graduate School, 770-836-6419. Fax: 770-836-2301. E-mail: jjenkins@cob.as.westga.edu.

Stephen F. Austin State University, College of Education, Department of Secondary Education and Educational Leadership, Nacogdoches, TX 75962. Offers programs in educational leadership (Ed D), secondary education (M Ed). Accredited by NCATE. Faculty: 12 full-time (4 women), 4 part-time (0 women). Students: 154 full-time (98 women), 425 part-time (261 women); includes 92 minority (71 African Americans, 1 Asian American, 17 Hispanics, 3 Native Americans). Average age 33. 425 applicants, 98% accepted. In 1997, 175 master's awarded. *Degree requirements:* For master's, comprehensive exam required, foreign language and thesis not required; for doctorate, dissertation required, foreign language not required. *Entrance requirements:* For master's, GRE General Test (minimum combined score of 1000); for doctorate, GRE General Test (minimum combined score of 1000), TOEFL. Application deadline: 8/1 (priority date; rolling processing; 12/15 for spring admission). Application fee: $0 ($25 for international students). *Tuition:* $1465 per year full-time, $263 per semester (minimum) part-time for state residents; $5299 per year full-time, $890 per semester (minimum) part-time for nonresidents. *Financial aid:* Teaching assistantships available. Financial aid application deadline: 3/1. • Dr. Patrick Jenlink, Chair, 409-468-2908.

Stetson University, College of Arts and Sciences, Division of Education, Department of Teacher Education, Program in Educational Leadership, 421 North Woodland Boulevard, DeLand, FL 32720-3781. Awards M Ed, Ed S. Accredited by NCATE. Evening/weekend programs available. Students: 4 part-time (3 women). Average age 32. 13 applicants, 92% accepted. In 1997, 5 master's awarded. *Degree requirements:* For master's, comprehensive exam required, foreign language and thesis not required. *Entrance requirements:* For master's, GRE General Test (minimum combined score of 1000) or MAT; for Ed S, GRE General Test or MAT. Application deadline: 3/1 (priority date; rolling processing; 11/1 for spring admission). Application fee: $25. *Tuition:* $370 per credit hour. *Financial aid:* Career-related internships or fieldwork available. • Application contact: Pat LeClaire, Office of Graduate Studies, 904-822-7075.

Suffolk University, College of Liberal Arts and Sciences, Department of Education and Human Services, Program in Higher Education Administration, Boston, MA 02108-2770. Offers educational administration (M Ed), leadership (CAGS). Part-time and evening/weekend programs available. Faculty: 1 full-time (0 women), 2 part-time (1 woman). *Entrance requirements:* For master's, GRE General Test (average 500 on each section) or MAT (average 50). Application deadline: 6/15 (priority date; rolling processing; 11/15 for spring admission). Application fee: $50. *Expenses:* Tuition $14,544 per year full-time, $1452 per course part-time. Fees $20 per year full-time, $10 per year part-time. *Financial aid:* Fellowships, Federal Work-Study, institutionally sponsored loans, and career-related internships or fieldwork available. Aid available to part-time students. Financial aid application deadline: 4/1; applicants required to submit FAFSA. *Faculty research:* History of universities, student financial aid. • Dr. Joseph McCarthy, Director, 617-573-8262. Fax: 617-722-9440. E-mail: jmccarth@acad.suffolk.edu. Application contact: Judy Reynolds, Acting Director of Graduate Admissions, 617-573-8302. Fax: 617-523-0116. E-mail: grad.admission@admin.suffolk.edu.

Sul Ross State University, Rio Grande College of Sul Ross State University, Alpine, TX 79832. Offerings include teacher education (M Ed), with options in bilingual education, counseling, educational diagnostics, elementary education, general education, reading, school administration, secondary education. College faculty: 16 full-time (2 women), 2 part-time (1 woman). *Application deadline:* rolling. *Application fee:* $0 ($50 for international students). *Expenses:* Tuition $864 per year full-time, $120 per semester (minimum) part-time for state residents; $5976 per year full-time, $747 per semester (minimum) part-time for nonresidents. Fees $754 per year full-time, $105 per semester (minimum) part-time. • Dr. Frank Abbott, Dean, 512-278-3339. Fax: 512-278-3330.

Sul Ross State University, Department of Teacher Education, Program in School Administration, Alpine, TX 79832. Awards M Ed. Part-time and evening/weekend programs available. Students: 34 full-time (20 women), 136 part-time (54 women); includes 73 minority (7 African Americans, 65 Hispanics, 1 Native American). Average age 39. In 1997, 49 degrees awarded. *Degree requirements:* Thesis optional, foreign language not required. *Entrance requirements:* GMAT (minimum score 400) or GRE General Test (minimum combined score of 850), minimum GPA of 2.5 in last 60 hours of undergraduate work. Application deadline: rolling. Application fee: $0 ($50 for international students). *Expenses:* Tuition $864 per year full-time, $120 per semester (minimum) part-time for state residents; $5976 per year full-time, $747 per semester (minimum) part-time for nonresidents. Fees $754 per year full-time, $105 per semester (minimum) part-time. *Financial aid:* Federal Work-Study, institutionally sponsored loans, and career-related internships or fieldwork available. Aid available to part-time students. Financial aid application deadline: 5/1; applicants required to submit FAFSA. • Dr. Mary Ann Weinacht, Director, Department of Teacher Education, 915-837-8170. Fax: 915-837-8390.

Sul Ross State University, Department of Teacher Education, Program in Supervision, Alpine, TX 79832. Awards M Ed. Part-time and evening/weekend programs available. Students: 2 part-time (both women). Average age 39. *Degree requirements:* Thesis optional, foreign language not required. *Entrance requirements:* GMAT (minimum score 400) or GRE General Test (minimum combined score of 850), minimum GPA of 2.5 in last 60 hours of undergraduate work. Application deadline: rolling. Application fee: $0 ($50 for international students). *Expenses:* Tuition $864 per year full-time, $120 per semester (minimum) part-time for state residents; $5976 per year full-time, $747 per semester (minimum) part-time for nonresidents. Fees $754 per year full-time, $105 per semester (minimum) part-time. *Financial aid:* Federal Work-Study, institutionally sponsored loans, and career-related internships or fieldwork available. Aid available to part-time students. Financial aid application deadline: 5/1; applicants required to submit FAFSA. • Dr. Mary Ann Weinacht, Director, Department of Teacher Education, 915-837-8170. Fax: 915-837-8390.

Syracuse University, School of Education, Teaching and Leadership Programs, Program in Educational Administration, Syracuse, NY 13244-0003. Awards M Ed, Ed D, PhD, CAS. Students: 14 full-time (9 women), 16 part-time (9 women). 0 applicants. In 1997, 5 master's, 2 doctorates awarded. *Degree requirements:* For master's, thesis or alternative; for doctorate and CAS, thesis/dissertation. *Entrance requirements:* GRE. Application fee: $40. *Tuition:* $13,320 per year full-time, $555 per credit hour part-time. *Financial aid:* Application deadline 3/1. • Application contact: Dr. Berj Harootunian, Contact, 315-443-2685.

Syracuse University, School of Education, Teaching and Leadership Programs, Program in Educational Leadership, Syracuse, NY 13244-0003. Awards MS, Ed D, CAS. *Degree requirements:* For master's, thesis or alternative; for doctorate and CAS, thesis/dissertation. *Entrance requirements:* GRE. Application deadline: rolling. Application fee: $40. *Tuition:* $13,320 per year full-time, $555 per credit hour part-time. *Financial aid:* Federal Work-Study and career-related internships or fieldwork available. Aid available to part-time students. Financial aid application deadline: 3/1. • Gerald Mager, Coordinator, 315-443-2684.

Tarleton State University, College of Education, Department of Education and Psychology, Program in Educational Administration, Stephenville, TX 76402. Awards M Ed, Certificate. Part-time and evening/weekend programs available. Postbaccalaureate distance learning degree programs offered (minimal on-campus study). Faculty: 24 full-time (9 women). Students: 60 full-time (28 women), 124 part-time (58 women); includes 32 minority (16 African Americans, 4 Asian Americans, 7 Hispanics, 5 Native Americans). 51 applicants, 90% accepted. In 1997, 50 master's awarded. *Degree requirements:* For master's, comprehensive exam required, thesis optional, foreign language not required. *Entrance requirements:* For master's, GRE General Test, minimum GPA of 2.9 during last 60 hours. Application deadline: 8/5 (priority date; rolling processing; 12/1 for spring admission). Application fee: $25 ($100 for international students). *Expenses:* Tuition $46 per hour for state residents; $249 per hour for nonresidents. Fees $49 per hour. *Financial aid:* Teaching assistantships, Federal Work-Study, institutionally sponsored loans, and career-related internships or fieldwork available. Aid available to part-time students. Financial aid application deadline: 5/1; applicants required to submit FAFSA. • Dr. Don Beach, Coordinator, 254-968-9097.

Teachers College, Columbia University, Graduate Faculty of Education, Department of Health and Behavior Studies, Program in Special Education Administration and Supervision, Instructional Practice, 525 West 120th Street, New York, NY 10027-6696. Awards Ed M, MA, Ed D. Part-time and evening/weekend programs available. Faculty: 1 full-time (0 women), 3 part-time (2 women), 2.2 FTE. Students: 1 (woman) full-time, 25 part-time (18 women); includes 2 minority (1 African American, 1 Native American), 4 international. Average age 35. 9 applicants, 78% accepted. In 1997, 8 master's, 1 doctorate awarded. Terminal master's awarded for partial completion of doctoral program. *Application deadline:* 5/15 (12/1 for spring admission). *Application fee:* $50. *Expenses:* Tuition $640 per credit. Fees $120 per semester. *Financial aid:* Full and partial tuition waivers, Federal Work-Study, institutionally sponsored loans, and career-related internships or fieldwork available. Aid available to part-time students. Financial aid application deadline: 2/1. • Application contact: Ursula Felton, Office of Admissions, 212-678-3710. Fax: 212-678-4171.

Teachers College, Columbia University, Graduate Faculty of Education, Department of Organization and Leadership, Program in College Teaching and Academic Leadership, 525 West 120th Street, New York, NY 10027-6696. Awards Ed D. Part-time and evening/weekend programs available. Faculty: 2 full-time (1 woman), 5 part-time (3 women). Terminal master's awarded for partial completion of doctoral program. *Degree requirements:* For doctorate, dissertation. *Entrance requirements:* For doctorate, master's degree, 2 years of professional experience. Application deadline: 5/15. Application fee: $50. *Expenses:* Tuition $640 per credit. Fees $120 per semester. *Financial aid:* Full and partial tuition waivers, Federal Work-Study, institutionally sponsored loans, and career-related internships or fieldwork available. Aid available to part-time students. Financial aid application deadline: 2/1. *Faculty research:* Scholarship of race, class, and gender in higher education; faculty careers and evaluation; theories of intellectual and moral development; curriculum transformation. • Application contact: Christine Souders, Office of Admissions, 212-678-3710. Fax: 212-678-4171.

Teachers College, Columbia University, Graduate Faculty of Education, Department of Organization and Leadership, Program in Educational Administration, 525 West 120th Street, New York, NY 10027-6696. Awards Ed M, MA, Ed D, PhD. Faculty: 8 full-time (2 women), 3 part-time (1 woman), 9 FTE. Students: 80 full-time (49 women), 177 part-time (101 women); includes 89 minority (57 African Americans, 6 Asian Americans, 26 Hispanics), 16 international. Average age 38. 129 applicants, 62% accepted. In 1997, 46 master's, 16 doctorates awarded. *Degree requirements:* For doctorate, dissertation. *Application deadline:* 5/15. *Application fee:* $50. *Expenses:* Tuition $640 per credit. Fees $120 per semester. *Financial aid:* Full and partial tuition waivers, Federal Work-Study, institutionally sponsored loans, and career-related internships or fieldwork available. Aid available to part-time students. Financial aid application deadline: 2/1. *Faculty research:* Database decision support systems for administrators, education policy, public school governance and finance, school-business partnerships, evaluation issues in school restructuring and reform. • Application contact: Christine Souders, Office of Admissions, 212-678-3710. Fax: 212-678-4171.

Teachers College, Columbia University, Graduate Faculty of Education, Department of Organization and Leadership, Program in Inquiry in Educational Administration, 525 West 120th Street, New York, NY 10027-6696. Awards Ed D. Faculty: 1 (woman) full-time, 3 part-time (2 women), 2.6 FTE. Students: 34 full-time (20 women), 41 part-time (27 women); includes 18 minority (15 African Americans, 1 Asian American, 2 Hispanics), 1 international. Average age 48. 1 applicant, 0% accepted. In 1997, 10 degrees awarded. *Degree requirements:* Dissertation. *Application deadline:* 5/15. *Application fee:* $50. *Expenses:* Tuition $640 per credit. Fees $120 per semester. *Financial aid:* Full and partial tuition waivers, Federal Work-Study, institutionally sponsored loans, and career-related internships or fieldwork available. Aid available to part-time students. Financial aid application deadline: 2/1. *Faculty research:* Field research in school systems. • Application contact: Christine Souders, Office of Admissions, 212-678-3710. Fax: 212-678-4171.

Teachers College, Columbia University, Graduate Faculty of Education, Department of Organization and Leadership, Program in Student Personnel Administration, 525 West 120th Street, New York, NY 10027-6696. Awards Ed M, MA, Ed D. Part-time and evening/weekend programs available. Faculty: 1 (woman) full-time, 3 part-time (2 women), 2.6 FTE. Students: 13 full-time (11 women), 15 part-time (10 women); includes 11 minority (5 African Americans, 5 Asian Americans, 1 Hispanic). Average age 27. 57 applicants, 74% accepted. In 1997, 15 master's awarded. Terminal master's awarded for partial completion of doctoral program. *Degree requirements:* For doctorate, dissertation. *Entrance requirements:* For doctorate, master's degree, 2 years of professional experience. Application deadline: 5/15. Application fee: $50. *Expenses:* Tuition $640 per credit. Fees $120 per semester. *Financial aid:* Research assistantships, full and partial tuition waivers, Federal Work-Study, institutionally sponsored loans, and career-related internships or fieldwork available. Aid available to part-time students. Financial aid application deadline: 2/1. *Faculty research:* Multicultural campus environments, college student development, leadership and higher education. • Application contact: Christine Souders, Office of Admissions, 212-678-3710. Fax: 212-678-4171.

Temple University, College of Education, Department of Educational Leadership and Policy Studies, Philadelphia, PA 19122-6096. Offers programs in educational administration (Ed M, Ed D), urban education (Ed M, Ed D). Accredited by NCATE. Part-time and evening/weekend programs available. Faculty: 14 full-time (8 women). Students: 200 (114 women). 149 applicants, 60% accepted. In 1997, 252 master's, 25 doctorates awarded. Terminal master's awarded for partial completion of doctoral program. *Degree requirements:* For master's, thesis or alternative, comprehensive exam required, foreign language not required; for doctorate, dissertation, preliminary exam required, foreign language not required. *Entrance requirements:* For master's, GRE General Test (minimum combined score of 1000) or MAT (minimum score 39), minimum GPA of 2.8; for doctorate, GRE General Test (minimum combined score of 1000) or MAT (minimum score 48), minimum GPA of 2.8 undergraduate, 3.0 graduate. Application deadline: 7/1 (11/1 for spring admission). Application fee: $40. *Expenses:* Tuition $323 per semester hour for state residents; $444 per semester hour for nonresidents. Fees $170 per year full-time, $28 per semester (minimum) part-time. *Financial aid:* Fellowships, research assistantships, teaching assistantships, Federal Work-Study, and career-related internships or fieldwork available. *Faculty research:* Women in education, school effectiveness, financial policy, school improvement in city schools, nongraded schools. • Dr. Donald Walters, Chair, 215-204-6169. Application contact: Dr. Stiles Seay, Director of Advising, 215-204-8011. Fax: 215-204-5622.

Tennessee State University, College of Education, Department of Educational Administration, Nashville, TN 37209-1561. Awards MA Ed, M Ed, Ed D. Accredited by NCATE. Faculty: 9 full-time (2 women), 7 part-time (4 women). Students: 19 full-time (11 women), 59 part-time (43 women); includes 54 minority (50 African Americans, 4 Asian Americans), 3 international. Average age 33. In 1997, 39 master's, 13 doctorates awarded. *Degree requirements:* For master's, comprehensive exam (M Ed), thesis (MA Ed) required, foreign language not required; for doctorate, dissertation, comprehensive exam. *Average time to degree:* master's–2.5 years part-time; doctorate–5 years part-time. *Entrance requirements:* For master's, GRE General Test, GRE Subject Test, minimum GPA of 2.5; for doctorate, GRE General Test (minimum combined score of 900), MAT (minimum score 44), interview, minimum GPA of 3.25, work experience. Application deadline: rolling. Application fee: $15. *Tuition:* $2962 per year full-time, $182 per credit hour part-time for state residents; $7788 per year full-time, $393 per credit hour part-time for nonresidents. *Financial aid:* In 1997–98, 3 research assistantships (all to first-year students) averaging $756 per month and totaling $10,000 were awarded. Financial aid application deadline: 5/1. • Dr. Paul F. Caraher, Head, 615-963-5452. Application contact: Dr. Clinton M. Lipsey, Dean of the Graduate School, 615-963-5901. Fax: 615-963-5963. E-mail: clipsey@picard.tnstate.edu.

Tennessee Technological University, College of Education, Department of Curriculum and Instruction, Program in Instructional Leadership, Cookeville, TN 38505. Awards MA, Ed S. Accredited by NCATE. Part-time and evening/weekend programs available. Faculty: 9 full-time (3 women). Students: 14 full-time (7 women), 337 part-time (241 women); includes 4 minority (2 African Americans, 1 Hispanic, 1 Native American). Average age 27. 103 applicants, 98% accepted. In 1997, 56 master's, 34 Ed Ss awarded. *Degree requirements:* For Ed S, thesis or alternative required, foreign language not required. *Entrance requirements:* For master's, MAT, TOEFL (minimum score 525); for Ed S, MAT, NTE. Application deadline: 3/1 (priority date; 8/1 for spring admission). Application fee: $25 ($30 for international students). *Tuition:* $2960 per year full-time, $147 per semester hour part-time for state residents; $7786 per year full-time, $358 per semester hour part-time for nonresidents. *Financial aid:* In 1997–98, 9 students received aid, including 5 research assistantships (2 to first-year students), 4 teaching assistantships (all to first-year students); fellowships and career-related internships or fieldwork also available. Financial aid application deadline: 4/1. *Faculty research:* School board member training, community school education. • Application contact: Dr. Rebecca F. Quattlebaum, Dean of the Graduate School, 615-372-3233. Fax: 615-372-3497. E-mail: rquattlebaum@tntech.edu.

Tennessee Temple University, Program in Educational Administration and Supervision, Chattanooga, TN 37404-3587. Awards MS. Faculty: 4 full-time (1 woman), 2 part-time (0 women). Students: 22 (10 women). • Application contact: Dr. Connie Pierson, Dean of the School of Education, 423-493-4260.

Texas A&M International University, Division of Teacher Education and Psychology, 5201 University Boulevard, Laredo, TX 78041-1900. Offerings include administration (MS Ed), supervision (MS Ed). *Degree requirements:* Thesis required (for some programs), foreign language not required. *Entrance requirements:* GRE General Test. Application deadline: 7/15 (priority date; rolling processing; 11/12 for spring admission). Application fee: $0.

Texas A&M University, College of Education, Department of Educational Administration, College Station, TX 77843. Awards M Ed, MS, Ed D, PhD. Accredited by NCATE. Faculty: 13 full-time (3 women), 3 part-time (0 women), 14.3 FTE. Students: 93 full-time (55 women), 228 part-time (128 women); includes 54 minority (24 African Americans, 1 Asian American, 29 Hispanics), 2 international. Average age 37. 166 applicants, 64% accepted. In 1997, 42 master's, 16 doctorates awarded. *Degree requirements:* For doctorate, dissertation required, foreign language not required. *Entrance requirements:* GRE General Test, TOEFL. Application fee: $35 ($75 for international students). *Financial aid:* Fellowships, research assistantships, institutionally sponsored loans, and career-related internships or fieldwork available. • Dr. Yvonna Lincoln, Head, 409-845-2716. Application contact: Joyce Nelson, Admissions and Certification Adviser, 409-847-9098. Fax: 409-862-4347.

Texas A&M University, College of Education, Department of Educational Human Resource Development, College Station, TX 77843. Offers programs in adult education (M Ed, MS, Ed D, PhD), educational human resource development (M Ed, MS, Ed D, PhD), industrial education (M Ed, MS, Ed D, PhD). Accredited by NCATE. Faculty: 14 full-time (5 women). Students: 46 full-time (26 women), 77 part-time (42 women); includes 17 minority (5 African Americans, 3 Asian Americans, 9 Hispanics), 6 international. Average age 37. 75 applicants, 63% accepted. In 1997, 13 master's, 19 doctorates awarded. *Degree requirements:* For doctorate, dissertation required, foreign language not required. *Entrance requirements:* GRE General Test, TOEFL. Application fee: $35 ($75 for international students). *Financial aid:* Fellowships, research assistantships, teaching assistantships, and career-related internships or fieldwork available. *Faculty research:* Adult and family literacy, distance education, adult learning and development, training and development. • Lloyd Korhonan, Head, 409-845-3016. E-mail: lloyd@summa.tamu.edu. Application contact: Anne Koppa, Graduate Admissions Supervisor, 409-862-4154. Fax: 409-845-0409. E-mail: cak5866@zeys.tamu.edu.

Texas A&M University–Commerce, College of Education, Department of Educational Administration, Commerce, TX 75429-3011. Awards M Ed, MS, Ed D. Faculty: 7 full-time (2 women), 14 part-time (0 women). Students: 32 full-time (20 women), 247 part-time (145 women); includes 60 minority (37 African Americans, 2 Asian Americans, 18 Hispanics, 3 Native Americans). In 1997, 106 master's, 12 doctorates awarded. Terminal master's awarded for partial completion of doctoral program. *Degree requirements:* For master's, thesis (for some programs), comprehensive exam; for doctorate, dissertation, departmental qualifying exam. *Entrance requirements:* For master's, GRE General Test; for doctorate, GRE General Test, writing skills exam, interview. Application deadline: rolling. Application fee: $0 ($25 for international students). *Tuition:* $2382 per year full-time, $343 per semester (minimum) part-time for state residents; $7518 per year full-time, $343 per semester (minimum) part-time for nonresidents. *Financial aid:* Research assistantships, teaching assistantships, Federal Work-Study, institutionally sponsored loans available. *Faculty research:* Property tax reform, politics of education, administrative stress. • Dr. David Thompson, Head, 903-886-5520. Application contact: Pam Hammonds, Graduate Admissions Adviser, 903-886-5167. Fax: 903-886-5165.

Texas A&M University–Corpus Christi, College of Education, Program in Educational Leadership, Corpus Christi, TX 78412-5503. Awards Ed D. Offered jointly with Texas A&M University–Kingsville. Part-time and evening/weekend programs available. Students: 2 full-time (both women), 52 part-time (32 women); includes 29 minority (2 African Americans, 27 Hispanics). Average age 42. In 1997, 4 degrees awarded. *Degree requirements:* Dissertation required, foreign language not required. *Entrance requirements:* MS. Application deadline: 7/15 (priority date; rolling processing; 11/15 for spring admission). Application fee: $10 ($30 for international students). *Expenses:* Tuition $648 per year full-time, $120 per semester (minimum) part-time for state residents; $4482 per year full-time, $747 per semester (minimum) part-time for nonresidents. Fees $1010 per year full-time, $205 per semester part-time. *Financial aid:* Federal Work-Study, institutionally sponsored loans available. Aid available to part-time students. Financial aid application deadline: 3/15; applicants required to submit FAFSA. • Dr. Jane Wilhour, Adviser, 512-994-2440. Application contact: Mary Margaret Dechant, Director of Admissions, 512-994-2624. Fax: 512-994-5887.

Texas A&M University–Corpus Christi, College of Education, Programs in Educational Administration and Supervision, Corpus Christi, TX 78412-5503. Offering in educational administration (MS). Part-time and evening/weekend programs available. Students: 7 full-time (6 women), 58 part-time (37 women); includes 22 minority (1 African American, 21 Hispanics). Average age 36. In 1997, 47 degrees awarded. *Entrance requirements:* GRE General Test. Application deadline: 7/15 (priority date; rolling processing; 11/15 for spring admission). Application fee: $10 ($30 for international students). *Expenses:* Tuition $648 per year full-time, $120 per semester (minimum) part-time for state residents; $4482 per year full-time, $747 per semester (minimum) part-time for nonresidents. Fees $1010 per year full-time, $205 per semester part-time. *Financial aid:* Federal Work-Study, institutionally sponsored loans available. Aid available to part-time students. Financial aid application deadline: 3/15; applicants required to submit FAFSA. • Dr. Arturo Medina, Graduate Adviser, 512-994-2667. E-mail: adedu005@tamucc.edu. Application contact: Mary Margaret Dechant, Director of Admissions, 512-994-2624. Fax: 512-994-5887.

Texas A&M University–Kingsville, College of Education, Department of Education, Program in Higher Education Administration, Kingsville, TX 78363. Awards PhD. Offered jointly with Texas A&M University. *Degree requirements:* 1 foreign language, dissertation, comprehensive exam. *Entrance requirements:* GRE General Test (minimum combined score of 1000), MAT (minimum score 50), minimum GPA of 3.25. Application deadline: 6/1 (rolling processing; 11/15 for spring admission). Application fee: $15 ($25 for international students). *Tuition:* $1822 per year full-time, $281 per semester (minimum) part-time for state residents; $6934 per year full-time, $908 per semester (minimum) part-time for nonresidents. *Financial aid:* Application deadline 5/15. • Dr. Travis Polk, Chair, Department of Education, 512-593-3204.

Texas A&M University–Kingsville, College of Education, Department of Education, Program in School Administration, Kingsville, TX 78363. Awards MA, MS, Ed D. Ed D offered jointly with Texas A&M University–Corpus Christi. Part-time and evening/weekend programs available. Faculty: 5 full-time, 1 part-time (0 women). *Degree requirements:* For master's, comprehensive exam, mini-thesis required, foreign language not required; for doctorate, 1 foreign language, dissertation, comprehensive exam. *Entrance requirements:* For master's, GRE General Test (minimum combined score of 1000), MAT (minimum score 34), minimum GPA of 3.0; for doctorate, GRE General Test (minimum combined score of 1000), MAT (minimum score 50), minimum GPA of 3.25. Application deadline: 6/1 (rolling processing; 11/15 for spring admission). Application fee: $15 ($25 for international students). *Tuition:* $1822 per year full-time, $281 per semester (minimum) part-time for state residents; $6934 per year full-time, $908 per semester (minimum) part-time for nonresidents. *Financial aid:* Application deadline 5/15. *Faculty research:* Funding sources in public education. • Dr. Ronald McKenzie, Director, 512-593-3203.

Texas A&M University–Kingsville, College of Education, Department of Education, Program in Supervision, Kingsville, TX 78363. Awards MA, MS. Part-time programs available. Faculty: 3 full-time. *Degree requirements:* Comprehensive exam, mini-thesis required, foreign language not required. *Entrance requirements:* GRE General Test (minimum combined score of 1000), MAT (minimum score 34), minimum GPA of 3.0. Application deadline: 6/1 (rolling processing; 11/15 for spring admission). Application fee: $15 ($25 for international students). *Tuition:* $1822 per year full-time, $281 per semester (minimum) part-time for state residents; $6934 per year full-time, $908 per semester (minimum) part-time for nonresidents. *Financial aid:* Application deadline 5/15. • Dr. Robert Blomstedt, Director, 512-593-3203.

Texas Christian University, School of Education, Department of Educational Foundations and Administration, Program in Administration Education, Fort Worth, TX 76129-0002. Awards M Ed. Part-time and evening/weekend programs available. Students: 39 (30 women); includes 5 minority (3 African Americans, 1 Hispanic, 1 Native American), 1 international. 17 applicants, 76% accepted. In 1997, 20 degrees awarded. *Entrance requirements:* TOEFL (minimum score 550), interview. Application deadline: 3/1 (rolling processing; 12/1 for spring admission). Application fee: $0. *Expenses:* Tuition $10,350 per year full-time, $345 per credit hour part-time. Fees $1240 per year full-time, $50 per credit hour part-time. *Financial aid:* Graduate assistantships available. Financial aid application deadline: 3/1. • Dr. Cornell Thomas, Chairperson, Department of Educational Foundations and Administration, 817-257-7943.

Texas Southern University, College of Education, Department of Administration and Higher Education, Houston, TX 77004-4584. Offers programs in educational administration (M Ed, Ed D), higher education administration (Ed D). Faculty: 12 full-time (4 women), 3 part-time (0 women). Students: 5 full-time (all women), 13 part-time (2 women); includes 19 international. Average age 30. 110 applicants, 55% accepted. In 1997, 4 doctorates awarded (100% found work related to degree). *Degree requirements:* For master's, comprehensive exam; for doctorate, dissertation, comprehensive exam required, foreign language not required. *Entrance requirements:* For master's, GRE General Test, TOEFL, minimum GPA of 2.5; for doctorate, GRE General Test or MAT, master's degree, minimum B+ average. Application deadline: 7/15 (priority date; rolling processing). Application fee: $35 ($75 for international students). *Financial aid:* Federal Work-Study, institutionally sponsored loans available. Financial aid application deadline: 5/1. • Dr. Lonnie Sadberry, Chairperson, 713-313-7256.

Texas Tech University, Graduate School, College of Education, Division of Educational Psychology and Leadership, Lubbock, TX 79409. Offers programs in counselor education (M Ed, Ed D, Certificate), early childhood education (M Ed, Certificate), education diagnostician (Certificate), educational leadership (M Ed, Ed D), educational psychology (M Ed, Ed D), higher education (M Ed, Ed D), instructional technology (M Ed, Ed D), principal (Certificate), reading specialist (Certificate), special education (M Ed, Ed D), special education counselor (Certificate), special education supervisor (Certificate), superintendent (Certificate), supervision (M Ed), supervisor (Certificate). Accredited by NCATE. Part-time programs available. Faculty: 28 full-time (13 women), 3 part-time (1 woman), 29.29 FTE. Students: 99 full-time (62 women), 257 part-time (160 women); includes 23 minority (5 African Americans, 4 Asian Americans, 10 Hispanics, 4 Native Americans), 12 international. Average age 37. 136 applicants, 46% accepted. In 1997, 102 master's, 25 doctorates awarded. *Degree requirements:* For master's, computer language required, thesis optional, foreign language not required; for doctorate, dissertation required, foreign language not required. *Entrance requirements:* For master's, GRE General Test (combined average 1034); for doctorate, GRE General Test. Application deadline: 4/15 (priority date; rolling processing; 11/1 for spring admission). Application fee: $25 ($50 for international students). Electronic applications accepted. *Expenses:* Tuition $864 per year full-time, $120 per semester (minimum) part-time for state residents; $5976 per year full-time, $747 per semester (minimum) part-time for nonresidents. Fees $2321 per year full-time, $302 per semester (minimum) part-time. *Financial aid:* In 1997–98, 162 students received aid, including 1 research assistantship averaging $909 per month; teaching assistantships, Federal Work-Study, institutionally sponsored loans, and career-related internships or fieldwork also available. Aid available to part-time students. Financial aid application deadline: 5/15; applicants required to submit FAFSA. *Faculty research:* Field test of speech/language for visually impaired, medication side effects on handicapped students, adult literacy in visually impaired. • Dr. Loretta J. Bradley, Chair, 806-742-2393.

Texas Woman's University, College of Education and Human Ecology, Department of Educational Leadership, Programs in Administration and Supervision, Denton, TX 76204. Awards MA, M Ed. Part-time and evening/weekend programs available. Faculty: 4 full-time (2 women), 6 part-time (2 women), 5.75 FTE. Students: 8 full-time (7 women), 271 part-time (205 women); includes 85 minority (56 African Americans, 1 Asian American, 26 Hispanics, 2 Native Americans), 1 international. Average age 40. 66 applicants, 86% accepted. In 1997, 39 degrees awarded (100% found work related to degree). *Degree requirements:* Thesis or professional paper required, foreign language not required. *Average time to degree:* master's–1.5 years full-time, 2.5 years part-time. *Entrance requirements:* GRE General Test (minimum combined score of 750), minimum GPA of 3.0. Application fee: $25. *Financial aid:* Partial tuition waivers, Federal Work-Study, institutionally sponsored loans, and career-related internships or fieldwork available. Aid available to part-time students. Financial aid application deadline: 4/1. *Faculty research:* Supervising the marginal teacher, in-school suspension programs, women in leadership, teacher appraisal. • Dr. Howard L. Stone, Chair, Department of Educational Leadership, 940-898-2241. Fax: 940-898-2224. E-mail: d_stone@twu.edu.

Trevecca Nazarene University, Division of Education, Major in Educational Leadership, Nashville, TN 37210-2834. Awards M Ed. Part-time and evening/weekend programs available. Students: 148 full-time (100 women), 1 part-time (0 women); includes 13 minority (12 African Americans, 1 Hispanic). 20 applicants, 95% accepted. In 1997, 73 degrees awarded. *Degree*

Directory: Educational Administration

Trevecca Nazarene University (continued)

requirements: Exit assessment required, foreign language and thesis not required. *Entrance requirements:* GRE General Test, MAT, minimum GPA of 2.7. Application deadline: 8/31 (rolling processing; 1/18 for spring admission). Application fee: $25. *Expenses:* Tuition $230 per hour. Fees $60 per year. *Financial aid:* Career-related internships or fieldwork available. Aid available to part-time students. • Dr. Melvin Welch, Dean of Education, 615-248-1201. Fax: 615-248-7728. E-mail: mwelch@trevecca.edu.

Tri-College University, see North Dakota State University.

Trinity College, School of Professional Studies, Programs in Administration, Washington, DC 20017-1094. Offerings include educational administration (MSA), with options in instructional leadership, principalship. Faculty: 4 full-time (1 woman), 4 part-time (all women). *Application deadline:* rolling. *Application fee:* $35. *Tuition:* $460 per credit hour. • Dr. Sheri Levin, Division Chair, Human Services, 202-884-9553. Application contact: Karen Goodwin, Director of Graduate Admissions, 202-884-9400. Fax: 202-884-9229.

Trinity University, Division of Behavioral and Administrative Studies, Department of Education, Program in Educational Administration, San Antonio, TX 78212-7200. Awards M Ed. Accredited by NCATE. Part-time and evening/weekend programs available. Faculty: 2 full-time (0 women), 4 part-time (0 women), 3 FTE. Students: 36 part-time (26 women); includes 7 minority (all Hispanics). Average age 33. 24 applicants, 75% accepted. In 1997, 16 degrees awarded. *Average time to degree:* master's–2 years part-time. *Entrance requirements:* GRE General Test (minimum combined score of 1000), minimum GPA of 3.0, interview. Application deadline: 5/1 (priority date). Application fee: $25. *Expenses:* Tuition $14,580 per year full-time, $608 per hour part-time. Fees $18 per year full-time, $6 per hour part-time. *Financial aid:* Fellowships, research assistantships, grants, Federal Work-Study, institutionally sponsored loans, and career-related internships or fieldwork available. Aid available to part-time students. Financial aid application deadline: 5/1. • Dr. Thomas Sergiovanni, Director, 210-736-7501.

Troy State University, Graduate School, School of Education, Program in Educational Leadership/Administration, Troy, AL 36082. Awards MS. Accredited by NCATE. Part-time and evening/weekend programs available. Students: 34 full-time (22 women), 80 part-time (47 women); includes 75 minority (all African Americans). Average age 30. In 1997, 7 degrees awarded. *Degree requirements:* Thesis, comprehensive exam. *Entrance requirements:* Minimum GPA of 2.5. Application deadline: rolling. Application fee: $20. Electronic applications accepted. *Expenses:* Tuition $2040 per year full-time, $68 per hour part-time for state residents; $4200 per year full-time, $140 per hour part-time for nonresidents. Fees $240 per year full-time, $27 per quarter (minimum) part-time. *Financial aid:* Available to part-time students. Financial aid applicants required to submit FAFSA. • Martha Hall, Chair, 334-448-5140. Fax: 334-448-5205. Application contact: Teresa Rodgers, Director of Graduate Admissions, 334-670-3188. Fax: 334-670-3733. E-mail: trodgers@trojan.troyst.edu.

Troy State University Dothan, School of Education, Dothan, AL 36304-0368. Offerings include educational administration (MS Ed), school administration (Ed S). One or more programs accredited by NCATE. *Application fee:* $20. *Expenses:* Tuition $68 per credit hour for state residents; $140 per credit hour for nonresidents. Fees $2 per credit hour. • Dr. Betty Anderson, Dean, 334-983-6556. Application contact: Reta Cordell, Director of Admissions and Records, 334-983-6556. Fax: 334-983-6322. E-mail: rcordell@tsud.edu.

Troy State University Montgomery, Division of Counseling, Education, and Psychology, Program in General Education Administration, PO Drawer 4419, Montgomery, AL 36103-4419. Awards Ed S. Part-time and evening/weekend programs available. In 1997, 2 degrees awarded. *Degree requirements:* Thesis or alternative. *Entrance requirements:* GRE General Test, MAT, or NTE; TOEFL. Application deadline: rolling. Application fee: $20. Electronic applications accepted. *Expenses:* Tuition $52 per quarter hour for state residents; $104 per quarter hour for nonresidents. Fees $30 per year. • Dr. James Macey, Coordinator, 334-241-9553. Fax: 334-240-7320. E-mail: jmacey@tsum.edu.

Tuskegee University, College of Liberal Arts and Education, Department of Curriculum, Instruction and Administration, Program in Personnel Administration, Tuskegee, AL 36088. Awards M Ed, MS. Accredited by NCATE. Faculty: 2 full-time (both women), 4 part-time (1 woman). Students: 2 full-time (0 women); includes 2 minority (both African Americans). Average age 24. *Entrance requirements:* GRE General Test. Application deadline: 7/15 (rolling processing). Application fee: $25 ($35 for international students). *Financial aid:* Application deadline 4/15. • H. Frank Leftwich, Acting Head, Department of Curriculum, Instruction and Administration, 334-727-8599.

Union College, Educational Leadership Program, Barbourville, KY 40906-1499. Offers elementary principalship (Certificate), middle grades principalship (Certificate), secondary school principalship (Certificate), supervisor of instruction (Certificate). Faculty: 2 full-time (0 women). *Application deadline:* rolling. *Application fee:* $15. *Tuition:* $220 per hour. • Dr. William E. Bernhardt, Head, 606-546-1209.

United States International University, College of Arts and Sciences, Department of Education, San Diego, CA 92131-1799. Offerings include educational administration (MA, Ed D). Terminal master's awarded for partial completion of doctoral program. Department faculty: 10 full-time (7 women), 12 part-time (6 women). *Degree requirements:* Thesis/dissertation. *Average time to degree:* master's–1.5 years full-time, 2.5 years part-time; doctorate–3 years full-time, 5 years part-time. *Entrance requirements:* For master's, TOEFL, minimum GPA of 2.5; for doctorate, GRE General Test or MAT, TOEFL, minimum GPA of 3.0. Application deadline: 8/1 (priority date; rolling processing; 3/1 for spring admission). Application fee: $40. *Expenses:* Tuition $255 per unit. Fees $120 per year full-time, $33 per quarter part-time. • Dr. Mary Ellen Butler-Pascoe, Chair, 619-635-4595. Fax: 619-635-4714. Application contact: Susan Topham, Assistant Director of Admissions, 619-635-4885. Fax: 619-635-4739. E-mail: admissions@usiu.edu.

Universidad del Turabo, Programs in Education, Program in Education Administration and Supervision, Gurabo, PR 00778-3030. Awards MA. *Entrance requirements:* GRE, PAEG, interview. Application deadline: 8/5. Application fee: $25.

Universidad del Turabo, Programs in Education, Program in School Libraries Administration, Gurabo, PR 00778-3030. Awards MA. *Entrance requirements:* GRE, PAEG, interview. Application deadline: 8/5. Application fee: $25.

Universidad Metropolitana, Graduate Programs in Education, Program in Administration of Pre-school, Río Piedras, PR 00928-1150. Awards MA. *Application deadline:* rolling. *Application fee:* $0. • Dr. Ana Delgado, Dean, Graduate Programs in Education, 787-766-1717 Ext. 6409.

Université de Moncton, Faculty of Education, Graduate Studies in Education, Moncton, NB E1A 3E9, Canada. Offerings include school administration (MA Ed, M Ed). Faculty: 25 full-time (12 women). *Degree requirements:* Proficiency in English and French. *Entrance requirements:* Minimum GPA of 3.0. Application deadline: 6/1 (rolling processing). Application fee: $30. • Léonard Goguen, Director, 506-858-4409. Fax: 506-858-4317. E-mail: goguenl@umoncton.ca. Application contact: Nicole Savoie, Conseillière à l'admission, 506-858-4115. Fax: 506-858-4544. E-mail: savoien@umoncton.ca.

Université de Montréal, Faculty of Education, Department of Studies in Education and Educational Administration, Montréal, PQ H3C 3J7, Canada. Awards MA, M Ed, PhD, DESS. Part-time programs available. Faculty: 39 full-time (7 women), 2 part-time (1 woman). Students: 46 full-time (26 women), 98 part-time (56 women). 65 applicants, 58% accepted. In 1997, 31 master's, 3 doctorates awarded. *Degree requirements:* For master's, thesis; for doctorate, dissertation, general exam. *Entrance requirements:* For master's and DESS, bachelor's degree in related field, minimum B average; for doctorate, master's degree in related field, minimum B average. Application deadline: 3/1. Application fee: $30. *Financial aid:* Teaching assistantships available. *Faculty research:* Pluriethnicity, formative education, comparative education, diagnostic evaluation. • André Brassard, Director, 514-343-7251.

Université de Sherbrooke, Faculty of Education, Program in School Administration, Sherbrooke, PQ J1K 2R1, Canada. Awards M Ed. Part-time and evening/weekend programs available. *Degree requirements:* Thesis. *Application deadline:* 6/1. *Application fee:* $15.

Université du Québec à Trois-Rivières, Program in Educational Administration, Trois-Rivières, PQ G9A 5H7, Canada. Awards DESS. Students: 46 part-time (7 women). *Entrance requirements:* Appropriate bachelor's degree, proficiency in French. Application deadline: 2/1. Application fee: $30. *Financial aid:* Fellowships, research assistantships, teaching assistantships available. • Marc Dussault, Director, 819-376-5095 Ext. 3617. E-mail: marc_dussault@uqtr.uquebec.ca. Application contact: Suzanne Camirand, Admissions Officer, 819-376-5045 Ext. 2591. Fax: 819-376-5210. E-mail: suzanne_camirand@uqtr.uquebec.ca.

Université Laval, Faculty of Education, Department of Guidance and Counseling, Administration and Evaluation in Education, Program in Educational Policy and Administrative Studies, Sainte-Foy, PQ G1K 7P4, Canada. Awards MA, PhD. Students: 41 full-time (16 women), 44 part-time (24 women). 37 applicants, 76% accepted. In 1997, 16 master's, 1 doctorate awarded. *Degree requirements:* Thesis/dissertation. *Application deadline:* 3/1. *Application fee:* $30. *Expenses:* Tuition $1334 per year (minimum) full-time, $56 per credit (minimum) part-time for Canadian residents; $5966 per year (minimum) full-time, $249 per credit (minimum) part-time for nonresidents. Fees $150 per year full-time, $6.25 per credit part-time. • Pierre W. Belanger, Director, 418-656-2131 Ext. 3799. Fax: 418-656-3071. E-mail: pierre.belanger@ads.ulaval.ca.

Université Laval, Faculty of Education, Department of Guidance and Counseling, Administration and Evaluation in Education, Program in Group Leadership Study and Training, Sainte-Foy, PQ G1K 7P4, Canada. Awards Diploma. Students: 4 part-time (3 women). 5 applicants, 20% accepted. In 1997, 5 degrees awarded. *Application deadline:* 3/1. *Application fee:* $30. *Expenses:* Tuition $1334 per year (minimum) full-time, $56 per credit (minimum) part-time for Canadian residents; $5966 per year (minimum) full-time, $249 per credit (minimum) part-time for nonresidents. Fees $150 per year full-time, $6.25 per credit part-time. • Jean-Guy Bernard, Director, 418-656-2131 Ext. 3789. Fax: 418-656-2905. E-mail: jean-guy.bernard@did.ulaval.ca.

The University of Akron, College of Education, Department of Educational Foundations and Leadership, Program in Administrative Specialist, Akron, OH 44325-0001. Awards MA, MS. Accredited by NCATE. Students: 11 part-time (6 women); includes 3 minority (all African Americans). Average age 41. *Degree requirements:* Thesis or alternative, written comprehensive exam required, foreign language not required. *Entrance requirements:* Bernreuter Personality Inventory, Guilford-Zimmerman Temperament Survey, Watson-Glaser Critical Thinking Appraisal, minimum GPA of 2.75. Application deadline: 8/15 (rolling processing). Application fee: $25 ($50 for international students). *Expenses:* Tuition $178 per credit hour for state residents; $333 per credit hour for nonresidents. Fees $145 per year full-time, $32 per semester (minimum) part-time. • Application contact: Dr. Robert Eley, Director of Student Services, 330-972-7750. E-mail: reley@uakron.edu.

The University of Akron, College of Education, Department of Educational Foundations and Leadership, Program in Educational Administration, Akron, OH 44325-0001. Awards MA, MS, Ed D. Accredited by NCATE. Students: 22 full-time (11 women), 76 part-time (42 women); includes 24 minority (23 African Americans, 1 Asian American), 1 international. Average age 40. In 1997, 35 master's, 5 doctorates awarded. *Degree requirements:* For master's, thesis or alternative, written comprehensive exam required, foreign language not required. *Entrance requirements:* For master's, Bernreuter Personality Inventory, Guilford-Zimmerman Temperament Survey, Watson-Glaser Critical Thinking Appraisal, minimum GPA of 2.75. Application deadline: 8/15 (rolling processing). Application fee: $25 ($50 for international students). *Expenses:* Tuition $178 per credit hour for state residents; $333 per credit hour for nonresidents. Fees $145 per year full-time, $32 per semester (minimum) part-time. • Application contact: Dr. Robert Eley, Director of Student Services, 330-972-7750. E-mail: reley@uakron.edu.

The University of Akron, College of Education, Department of Educational Foundations and Leadership, Program in Elementary School Administration, Akron, OH 44325-0001. Awards MA, MS. Accredited by NCATE. Students: 3 full-time (all women), 50 part-time (34 women); includes 6 minority (4 African Americans, 2 Asian Americans). Average age 35. In 1997, 4 degrees awarded. *Degree requirements:* Thesis or alternative, written comprehensive exam required, foreign language not required. *Entrance requirements:* Bernreuter Personality Inventory, Guilford-Zimmerman Temperament Survey, Watson-Glaser Critical Thinking Appraisal, minimum GPA of 2.75. Application deadline: 8/15 (rolling processing). Application fee: $25 ($50 for international students). *Expenses:* Tuition $178 per credit hour for state residents; $333 per credit hour for nonresidents. Fees $145 per year full-time, $32 per semester (minimum) part-time. • Application contact: Dr. Robert Eley, Director of Student Services, 330-972-7750. E-mail: reley@uakron.edu.

The University of Akron, College of Education, Department of Educational Foundations and Leadership, Program in Higher Education Administration, Akron, OH 44325-0001. Awards MA, MS. Accredited by NCATE. Admissions temporarily suspended. Students: 22 full-time (12 women), 40 part-time (17 women); includes 17 minority (15 African Americans, 1 Asian American, 1 Hispanic). Average age 37. In 1997, 7 degrees awarded. *Application deadline:* 8/15 (rolling processing). *Application fee:* $25 ($50 for international students). *Expenses:* Tuition $178 per credit hour for state residents; $333 per credit hour for nonresidents. Fees $145 per year full-time, $32 per semester (minimum) part-time. *Financial aid:* Fellowships, research assistantships, teaching assistantships, administrative assistantships, and career-related internships or fieldwork available. • Application contact: Dr. Robert Eley, Director of Student Services, 330-972-7750. E-mail: reley@uakron.edu.

The University of Akron, College of Education, Department of Educational Foundations and Leadership, Program in School Superintendent, Akron, OH 44325-0001. Awards MA, MS. Accredited by NCATE. Students: 3 part-time (2 women). Average age 47. *Degree requirements:* Thesis or alternative, written comprehensive exam required, foreign language not required. *Entrance requirements:* Bernreuter Personality Inventory, Guilford-Zimmerman Temperament Survey, Watson-Glaser Critical Thinking Appraisal, minimum GPA of 2.75. Application fee: $25 ($50 for international students). *Expenses:* Tuition $178 per credit hour for state residents; $333 per credit hour for nonresidents. Fees $145 per year full-time, $32 per semester (minimum) part-time. • Application contact: Dr. Robert Eley, Director of Student Services, 330-972-7750. E-mail: reley@uakron.edu.

The University of Akron, College of Education, Department of Educational Foundations and Leadership, Program in Secondary School Administration, Akron, OH 44325-0001. Awards MA, MS. Accredited by NCATE. Students: 5 full-time (0 women), 56 part-time (28 women); includes 7 minority (all African Americans). Average age 33. In 1997, 1 degree awarded. *Degree requirements:* Thesis or alternative, written comprehensive exam required, foreign language not required. *Entrance requirements:* Bernreuter Personality Inventory, Guilford-Zimmerman Temperament Survey, Watson-Glaser Critical Thinking Appraisal, minimum GPA of 2.75. Application deadline: 8/15 (rolling processing). Application fee: $25 ($50 for international students). *Expenses:* Tuition $178 per credit hour for state residents; $333 per credit hour for nonresidents. Fees $145 per year full-time, $32 per semester (minimum) part-time. • Application contact: Dr. Robert Eley, Director of Student Services, 330-972-7750. E-mail: reley@uakron.edu.

The University of Akron, College of Education, Department of Educational Foundations and Leadership, Program in Supervisor, Akron, OH 44325-0001. Awards MA, MS. Accredited by NCATE. Students: 1 (woman) full-time, 5 part-time (4 women). Average age 39. In 1997, 1 degree awarded. *Degree requirements:* Thesis or alternative, written comprehensive exam required, foreign language not required. *Entrance requirements:* Bernreuter Personality Inventory, Guilford-Zimmerman Temperament Survey, Watson-Glaser Critical Thinking Appraisal, minimum GPA of 2.75. Application deadline: 8/15 (rolling processing). Application fee: $25 ($50 for international students). *Expenses:* Tuition $178 per credit hour for state residents; $333 per credit hour for nonresidents. Fees $145 per year full-time, $32 per semester (minimum) part-time. • Application contact: Dr. Robert Eley, Director of Student Services, 330-972-7750. E-mail: reley@uakron.edu.

The University of Alabama, College of Education, Area of Professional Studies, Program in Educational Administration, Tuscaloosa, AL 35487. Awards MA, Ed D, PhD. Accredited by NCATE. Ed D and PhD offered jointly with the University of Alabama at Birmingham. PhD admissions temporarily suspended. *Degree requirements:* For doctorate, 1 foreign language, computer language, dissertation. *Average time to degree:* doctorate–3 years full-time, 6 years part-time. *Entrance requirements:* GRE General Test, MAT (score in 50th percentile or higher), or NTE (minimum score 658 on each core battery test), minimum GPA of 3.0. Application deadline: 7/6 (rolling processing). Application fee: $25. *Tuition:* $2684 per year full-time, $594 per semester (minimum) part-time for state residents; $7216 per year full-time, $1248 per semester (minimum) part-time for nonresidents. *Financial aid:* Fellowships, research assistantships, teaching assistantships, Federal Work-Study, institutionally sponsored loans, and career-related internships or fieldwork available. Financial aid application deadline: 7/14. • Dr. Lynn Beck, Head, 205-348-1152. Fax: 205-348-2161. E-mail: lbeck@bamaed.ua.edu.

The University of Alabama, College of Education, Area of Professional Studies, Program in Educational Leadership, Tuscaloosa, AL 35487. Awards MA, Ed S. Accredited by NCATE. *Entrance requirements:* For master's, GRE General Test, MAT (score in 50th percentile or higher), or NTE (minimum score 658 on each core battery test), minimum GPA of 3.0; for Ed S, minimum GPA of 3.0 during previous 2 years. Application deadline: 7/6 (rolling processing). Application fee: $25. *Tuition:* $2684 per year full-time, $594 per semester (minimum) part-time for state residents; $7216 per year full-time, $1248 per semester (minimum) part-time for nonresidents. *Financial aid:* Application deadline 7/14. • Dr. R. Carl Westerfield, Head, Area of Professional Studies, 205-348-8362. Fax: 205-348-0867. E-mail: cwesterf@bamaed.ua.edu.

The University of Alabama, College of Education, Area of Professional Studies, Program in Higher Education Administration, Tuscaloosa, AL 35487. Awards MA, Ed D, PhD, Ed S. Accredited by NCATE. *Degree requirements:* For doctorate, 1 foreign language, computer language, dissertation. *Entrance requirements:* For master's and doctorate, GRE General Test, MAT (score in 50th percentile or higher), or NTE (minimum score 658 on each core battery test), minimum GPA of 3.0; for Ed S, minimum GPA of 3.0 during previous 2 years. Application deadline: 7/6 (rolling processing). Application fee: $25. *Tuition:* $2684 per year full-time, $594 per semester (minimum) part-time for state residents; $7216 per year full-time, $1248 per semester (minimum) part-time for nonresidents. *Financial aid:* Application deadline 7/14. • Dr. R. Carl Westerfield, Head, Area of Professional Studies, 205-348-8362. Fax: 205-348-0867. E-mail: cwesterf@bamaed.ua.edu.

The University of Alabama at Birmingham, Graduate School, School of Education, Department of Leadership, Special Education and Foundations, Program in Educational Leadership, Birmingham, AL 35294. Awards MA Ed, Ed D, PhD, Ed S. Accredited by NCATE. Ed D and PhD offered jointly with The University of Alabama–Tuscaloosa. Students: 22 full-time (17 women), 40 part-time (27 women); includes 23 minority (21 African Americans, 2 Asian Americans). 125 applicants, 98% accepted. In 1997, 5 master's, 7 doctorates, 33 Ed Ss awarded. *Degree requirements:* For master's, thesis optional; for doctorate, dissertation; for Ed S, comprehensive exam. *Entrance requirements:* For master's, GRE General Test, MAT, or NTE, minimum GPA of 3.0. Application deadline: rolling. Application fee: $30 ($60 for international students). Electronic applications accepted. *Expenses:* Tuition $99 per credit hour for state residents; $198 per credit hour for nonresidents. Fees $516 per year (minimum) full-time, $73 per quarter (minimum) part-time for state residents; $516 per year (minimum) full-time, $73 per unit (minimum) part-time for nonresidents. • Dr. W. Boyd Rogan, Chair, Department of Leadership, Special Education and Foundations, 205-934-4892.

University of Alaska Anchorage, College of Health, Education and Social Welfare, School of Education, Program in Educational Leadership, Anchorage, AK 99508-8060. Awards M Ed. Part-time programs available. Students: 6 full-time (all women), 13 part-time (8 women); includes 2 African Americans, 2 Native Americans. 12 applicants, 92% accepted. In 1997, 6 degrees awarded. *Entrance requirements:* GRE Subject Test, interview. Application deadline: 5/1 (rolling processing). Application fee: $45. *Expenses:* Tuition $2988 per year full-time, $1990 per year part-time for state residents; $5814 per year full-time, $3876 per year part-time for nonresidents. Fees $298 per year. *Financial aid:* Federal Work-Study and career-related internships or fieldwork available. Aid available to part-time students. Financial aid application deadline: 4/1. • Dr. Chris Jensen, Head, 907-786-4415. Fax: 907-786-4444. Application contact: Linda Berg Smith, Associate Vice Chancellor for Enrollment Services, 907-786-1529.

University of Alaska Fairbanks, Graduate School, School of Education, Fairbanks, AK 99775-7480. Offerings include educational administration (M Ed). School faculty: 23 full-time (13 women), 2 part-time (both women). *Degree requirements:* Thesis or alternative, comprehensive exam required, foreign language not required. *Entrance requirements:* GRE General Test, TOEFL (minimum score 550). Application deadline: 4/1 (10/1 for spring admission). Application fee: $35. *Expenses:* Tuition $162 per credit for state residents; $316 per credit for nonresidents. Fees $520 per year full-time, $45 per semester (minimum) part-time. • Dr. Joe Kan, Director, 907-474-7341.

University of Alberta, Faculty of Graduate Studies and Research, Department of Educational Policy Studies, Edmonton, AB T6G 2E1, Canada. Offers programs in administration of postsecondary education (M Ed, PhD), adult education (M Ed), educational administration (M Ed, Ed D, PhD, Postgraduate Diploma), educational leadership (M Ed), First Nations education (M Ed, PhD), international and global education (M Ed, PhD), social and cultural education (M Ed, PhD). Part-time programs available. Faculty: 25 full-time (7 women), 3 part-time (1 woman). Students: 109 full-time (61 women), 259 part-time (166 women); includes 17 international. In 1997, 53 master's, 18 doctorates awarded. *Degree requirements:* For master's, thesis (for some programs); for doctorate, dissertation. *Average time to degree:* master's–1 year full-time, 3 years part-time; doctorate–2 years full-time, 4 years part-time. *Entrance requirements:* For master's and doctorate, TOEFL (minimum score 580). Application deadline: 8/1 (priority date; rolling processing; 4/1 for spring admission). Application fee: $60. *Expenses:* Tuition $390 per course for Canadian residents; $781 per course for nonresidents. Fees $500 per year full-time, $184 per year part-time. *Financial aid:* In 1997–98, 10 tuition scholarships were awarded. • Dr. D. M. Richards, Chair, 403-492-3679. E-mail: don.richards@ualberta.ca. Application contact: Joan White, Graduate Secretary, 403-492-3679. Fax: 403-492-2024. E-mail: joan.white@ualberta.ca.

The University of Arizona, College of Education, Department of Educational Administration and Higher Education, Program in Educational Administration, Tucson, AZ 85721. Awards MA, M Ed, Ed D, PhD, Ed S. *Degree requirements:* For master's, thesis (MA) required, foreign language not required; for doctorate, dissertation required, foreign language not required. *Entrance requirements:* For master's, TOEFL (minimum score 550); for doctorate, GRE General Test (minimum combined score of 1100) or MAT, TOEFL (minimum score 550), master's degree; for Ed S, TOEFL (minimun score of 550). Application deadline: 4/15 (rolling processing). Application fee: $35. *Tuition:* $2162 per year full-time, $337 per semester (minimum) part-time for state residents; $6860 per year full-time, $1138 per semester (minimum) part-time for nonresidents. *Faculty research:* School governance, higher order thinking, restructuring schools, bilingual education policy, authority in education.

University of Arkansas, College of Education, Department of Educational Leadership, Counseling and Foundations, Program in Educational Administration, Fayetteville, AR 72701-1201. Awards M Ed, Ed D, Ed S. Accredited by NCATE. Students: 42 full-time (18 women), 33 part-time (19 women); includes 6 minority (4 African Americans, 2 Native Americans), 2 international. 38 applicants, 66% accepted. In 1997, 11 master's, 9 doctorates, 10 Ed Ss awarded. *Degree requirements:* For doctorate, dissertation. *Entrance requirements:* For master's, GRE General Test or MAT. Application fee: $25 ($35 for international students). *Tuition:* $3144 per year full-time, $173 per credit hour part-time for state residents; $7140 per year full-time, $395 per credit hour part-time for nonresidents. *Financial aid:* Research assistantships, teaching assistantships, Federal Work-Study, and career-related internships or fieldwork available. Aid available to part-time students. Financial aid application deadline: 4/1; applicants required to submit FAFSA. • Dr. John Murry, Coordinator, 501-575-2207.

University of Arkansas at Little Rock, College of Education, Department of Educational Leadership, Program in Educational Administration, Little Rock, AR 72204-1099. Offers educational administration and supervision (M Ed, Ed D, Ed S). Part-time and evening/weekend programs available. Students: 9 full-time (6 women), 77 part-time (48 women); includes 31 minority (30 African Americans, 1 Hispanic). Average age 40. 63 applicants, 62% accepted. In 1997, 8 master's, 6 doctorates awarded. *Degree requirements:* For master's, comprehensive exam required, foreign language and thesis not required; for doctorate, comprehensive exam, oral defense of dissertation, residency required, foreign language not required; for Ed S, comprehensive exam, professional project required, foreign language and thesis not required. *Entrance requirements:* For master's, GRE General Test (minimum combined score of 1000 on three sections) or MAT (minimum score 40), teaching certificate, minimum GPA of 2.75, 4 years of work experience (minimum 3 in teaching), interview; for doctorate, GRE General Test (minimum combined score of 1500 on three sections) or MAT (minimum score 40), minimum graduate GPA of 3.0, teaching certificate, 4 years of work experience; for Ed S, GRE General Test (minimum combined score of 1350 on three sections) or MAT (minimum score 40), minimum GPA of 2.75, 4 years of work experience, teaching certificate. Application fee: $25 ($30 for international students). *Expenses:* Tuition $2466 per year full-time, $137 per credit hour part-time for state residents; $5256 per year full-time, $292 per credit hour part-time for nonresidents. Fees $216 per year full-time, $36 per semester (minimum) part-time. *Financial aid:* Research assistantships, teaching assistantships, Federal Work-Study available. • Dr. Richard Henderson, Adviser, 501-569-3267.

University of Arkansas at Little Rock, College of Education, Department of Educational Leadership, Program in Higher Education Administration, Little Rock, AR 72204-1099. Awards Ed D. Students: 16 full-time (11 women), 102 part-time (68 women); includes 18 minority (15 African Americans, 1 Asian American, 2 Hispanics), 4 international. Average age 42. 91 applicants, 84% accepted. In 1997, 13 degrees awarded. *Degree requirements:* Comprehensive exam, oral defense of dissertation, residency required, foreign language not required. *Entrance requirements:* GRE General Test (minimum combined score of 1500 on three sections) or MAT (minimum score 55), interview, minimum graduate GPA of 3.0, teaching certificate, work experience. Application deadline: 8/1 (priority date). Application fee: $25 ($30 for international students). *Expenses:* Tuition $2466 per year full-time, $137 per credit hour part-time for state residents; $5256 per year full-time, $292 per credit hour part-time for nonresidents. Fees $216 per year full-time, $36 per semester (minimum) part-time. *Financial aid:* Research assistantships available. • Dr. David Spillers, Chairperson, Department of Educational Leadership, 501-569-3267.

University of Bridgeport, College of Graduate and Undergraduate Studies, School of Education and Human Resources, Division of Education, Program in Educational Management, 380 University Avenue, Bridgeport, CT 06601. Awards Ed D, Diploma. Faculty: 2 full-time (0 women), 2 part-time (0 women), 3 FTE. Students: 2 full-time (0 women), 56 part-time (34 women); includes 9 minority (all African Americans), 7 international. 19 applicants, 95% accepted. In 1997, 5 doctorates, 10 Diplomas awarded. *Degree requirements:* For doctorate, dissertation; for Diploma, thesis or alternative, final project required, foreign language not required. *Entrance requirements:* For doctorate, GRE, MAT; for Diploma, GRE General Test or MAT (score in 40th percentile or higher), minimum graduate QPA of 3.0. Application deadline: rolling. Application fee: $35 ($50 for international students). *Tuition:* $7400 per year. *Financial aid:* 28 students received aid; fellowships, research assistantships, teaching assistantships, Federal Work-Study, institutionally sponsored loans, and career-related internships or fieldwork available. Aid available to part-time students. Financial aid application deadline: 6/1; applicants required to submit FAFSA. • Dr. John W. Mulcahy, Coordinator, 203-576-4028.

University of British Columbia, Faculty of Education, Department of Educational Studies, Program in Educational Administration, Vancouver, BC V6T 1Z2, Canada. Awards MA, M Ed. Part-time and evening/weekend programs available. *Degree requirements:* Thesis (MA) required, foreign language not required. *Entrance requirements:* TOEFL (minimum score 550). Application deadline: 6/1 (priority date; 2/1 for spring admission). Application fee: $60. *Faculty research:* Supervision, decentralization, problem formulation and analysis, teacher research.

University of British Columbia, Faculty of Education, Department of Educational Studies, Program in Educational Leadership and Policy, Vancouver, BC V6T 1Z2, Canada. Awards Ed D. *Degree requirements:* Dissertation required, foreign language not required. *Entrance requirements:* TOEFL (minimum score 550). Application fee: $60.

The University of Calgary, Faculty of Education, Graduate Division of Educational Research, Calgary, AB T2N 1N4, Canada. Offerings include educational leadership (MA, M Ed, M Sc, Ed D, PhD). Postbaccalaureate distance learning degree programs offered (minimal on-campus study). Division faculty: 60 full-time, 25 part-time. *Degree requirements:* For master's, thesis (for some programs), comprehensive exam required, foreign language not required; for doctorate, dissertation. *Entrance requirements:* For master's, minimum GPA of 3.0; for doctorate, minimum GPA of 3.5. Application deadline: 2/1. Application fee: $60. Electronic applications accepted. *Expenses:* Tuition $5448 per year full-time, $908 per course part-time for Canadian residents; $10,896 per year full-time, $1816 per course part-time for nonresidents. Fees $285 per year full-time, $119 per semester (minimum) part-time. • Dr. Bryant Griffith, Assistant Dean, 403-220-5675. Fax: 403-282-3005. E-mail: griffith@acs.ucalgary.ca.

University of California, Berkeley, School of Education, Division of Policy, Organization, Measurement and Evaluation, Berkeley, CA 94720-1500. Offers programs in educational leadership (Ed D), policy (MA), policy research (PhD), program evaluation and assessment (Ed D), quantitative methods in education (PhD). Terminal master's awarded for partial completion of doctoral program. *Degree requirements:* For master's, exam or thesis required, foreign language not required; for doctorate, dissertation, oral qualifying exam (PhD) required, foreign language not required. *Entrance requirements:* GRE General Test, minimum GPA of 3.0 during last 2 years of undergraduate course work. Application deadline: 12/15 (rolling processing). Application fee: $40. *Expenses:* Tuition $0 for state residents; $9384 per year for nonresidents. Fees $4409 per year. *Financial aid:* Fellowships, research assistantships, teaching assistantships available. Financial aid application deadline: 12/15. • Mark Wilson, Chair, 510-642-0709.

University of California, Irvine, Department of Education, Irvine, CA 92697. Offerings include educational administration (Ed D). Department faculty: 6 full-time (2 women), 4 part-time (3 women). *Degree requirements:* Dissertation. *Entrance requirements:* GRE General Test. Application deadline: 3/1 (priority date). Application fee: $40. Electronic applications accepted. *Expenses:* Tuition $0 for state residents; $9384 per year full-time, $1564 per quarter part-time for nonresidents. Fees $4998 per year full-time, $1152 per quarter part-time. • Louis F. Miron, Chair, 949-824-7840. Application contact: Sarah K. Singh, Admissions and Placement, 949-824-7832. Fax: 949-824-2965. E-mail: sksingh@uci.edu.

University of California, Los Angeles, Graduate School of Education and Information Studies, Program in Educational Leadership, Los Angeles, CA 90095. Awards Ed D. Students: 77 full-time (41 women); includes 30 minority (10 African Americans, 5 Asian Americans, 15 Hispanics). 52 applicants, 54% accepted. *Entrance requirements:* GRE General Test, minimum undergraduate GPA of 3.0, resume. Application deadline: 3/1. Application fee: $40. Electronic applications accepted. *Expenses:* Tuition $0 for state residents; $9384 per year for nonresidents. Fees $4551 per year. *Financial aid:* 57 students received aid. • Application contact: Departmental Office, 310-206-1637. E-mail: edwards@gseis.ucla.edu.

Directory: Educational Administration

University of Central Arkansas, College of Education, Department of Administration and Secondary Education, Program in Educational Leadership, Conway, AR 72035-0001. Awards Ed S. Accredited by NCATE. Students: 7 part-time (3 women); includes 1 minority (African American). 3 applicants, 100% accepted. In 1997, 9 degrees awarded. *Degree requirements:* Comprehensive exam required, thesis not required. *Entrance requirements:* GRE General Test, minimum GPA of 2.7. Application deadline: 3/1 (priority date; rolling processing; 10/1 for spring admission). Application fee: $15 ($40 for international students). *Expenses:* Tuition $161 per credit hour for state residents; $298 per credit hour for nonresidents. Fees $50 per year full-time, $30 per year part-time. *Financial aid:* Federal Work-Study and career-related internships or fieldwork available. Financial aid application deadline: 2/15. • Dr. David Skotko, Interim Chairperson, Department of Administration and Secondary Education, 501-450-5407. Fax: 501-450-5671. E-mail: davids@mail.uca.edu.

University of Central Arkansas, College of Education, Department of Administration and Secondary Education, Programs in Elementary and Secondary School Leadership, Conway, AR 72035-0001. Offerings in elementary school leadership (MSE), secondary school leadership (MSE). Accredited by NCATE. Part-time programs available. Students: 5 full-time (3 women), 60 part-time (35 women); includes 10 minority (all African Americans). 14 applicants, 100% accepted. In 1997, 44 degrees awarded. *Degree requirements:* Comprehensive exam required, thesis not required. *Entrance requirements:* GRE General Test, minimum GPA of 2.7. Application deadline: 3/1 (priority date; rolling processing; 10/1 for spring admission). Application fee: $15 ($40 for international students). *Expenses:* Tuition $161 per credit hour for state residents; $298 per credit hour for nonresidents. Fees $50 per year full-time, $30 per year part-time. *Financial aid:* Application deadline 2/15. • Dr. David Skotko, Interim Chairperson, Department of Administration and Secondary Education, 501-450-5407. Fax: 501-450-5671. E-mail: davids@mail.uca.edu.

University of Central Arkansas, College of Education, Department of Counseling and Psychology, Program in Community Service Counseling, Conway, AR 72035-0001. Offerings include student personnel services in higher education (MS). Accredited by NCATE. *Degree requirements:* Comprehensive exam required, thesis optional. *Entrance requirements:* GRE General Test, minimum GPA of 2.7. Application deadline: 3/1 (priority date; rolling processing; 10/1 for spring admission). Application fee: $15 ($40 for international students). *Expenses:* Tuition $161 per credit hour for state residents; $298 per credit hour for nonresidents. Fees $50 per year full-time, $30 per year part-time. • Application contact: Dr. Lauren Bush, Assistant Professor, 501-450-3193. Fax: 501-450-5424. E-mail: laurenb@mail.uca.edu.

University of Central Florida, College of Education, Department of Educational Services, Program in Educational Leadership, Orlando, FL 32816. Awards MA, M Ed, Ed D, Ed S. Accredited by NCATE. Part-time and evening/weekend programs available. Students: 123 full-time (77 women), 91 part-time (65 women); includes 30 minority (21 African Americans, 1 Asian American, 8 Hispanics), 1 international. Average age 38. 71 applicants, 59% accepted. In 1997, 57 master's, 7 doctorates awarded. *Degree requirements:* For master's and Ed S, thesis or alternative required, foreign language not required; for doctorate, dissertation required, foreign language not required. *Entrance requirements:* For master's, GRE General Test (minimum combined score of 840); for doctorate and Ed S, GRE General Test (minimum combined score of 1000), GRE Subject Test. Application deadline: 2/20 (9/20 for spring admission). Application fee: $20. *Expenses:* Tuition $3288 per year full-time, $137 per credit hour part-time for state residents; $11,520 per year full-time, $480 per credit hour part-time for nonresidents. Fees $105 per year. *Financial aid:* Teaching assistantships, Federal Work-Study, institutionally sponsored loans, and career-related internships or fieldwork available. Aid available to part-time students. • Application contact: Dr. Mary Ann Lynn, Coordinator, 407-384-2191.

University of Central Oklahoma, College of Education, Department of Professional Teacher Education, Program in School Administration, Edmond, OK 73034-5209. Awards M Ed. Accredited by NCATE. Part-time and evening/weekend programs available. *Entrance requirements:* GRE General Test. Application deadline: 8/18. Application fee: $15. *Tuition:* $76 per credit hour for state residents; $178 per credit hour for nonresidents.

University of Cincinnati, College of Education, Division of Educational Studies, Department of Education Administration, Cincinnati, OH 45221. Awards M Ed, Ed D, Ed S. Accredited by NCATE. Part-time programs available. Students: 34 full-time (16 women), 43 part-time (24 women); includes 14 minority (13 African Americans, 1 Native American), 1 international. 66 applicants, 83% accepted. In 1997, 34 master's, 6 doctorates awarded. *Degree requirements:* For master's, thesis or alternative required, foreign language not required; for doctorate, dissertation required, foreign language not required. *Average time to degree:* master's–2.8 years full-time; doctorate–8 years full-time. *Entrance requirements:* For master's, GRE General Test; for doctorate, GRE General Test, GRE Subject Test. Application deadline: 2/1. Application fee: $30. *Tuition:* $7228 per year full-time, $185 per credit hour part-time for state residents; $13,812 per year full-time, $352 per credit hour part-time for nonresidents. *Financial aid:* Fellowships, graduate assistantships, full tuition waivers available. Aid available to part-time students. Financial aid application deadline: 5/1. • Application contact: Nancy Evers, Program Coordinator, 513-556-6623. Fax: 513-556-2483. E-mail: nancy.evers@uc.edu.

University of Colorado at Denver, School of Education, Program in Educational Administration, Denver, CO 80217-3364. Offers administration, supervision, and curriculum development (MA); educational administration, curriculum and supervision (Ed S); educational leadership and innovation (PhD). Accredited by NCATE. Part-time and evening/weekend programs available. Students: 28 full-time (17 women), 165 part-time (112 women); includes 31 minority (10 African Americans, 4 Asian Americans, 15 Hispanics, 2 Native Americans), 2 international. Average age 40. 86 applicants, 56% accepted. In 1997, 25 master's, 15 doctorates, 3 Ed Ss awarded. *Degree requirements:* For master's, thesis or alternative required, foreign language not required; for doctorate, 1 foreign language, dissertation. *Entrance requirements:* For master's, GRE, MAT, minimum GPA of 2.75. Application deadline: 4/15 (rolling processing; 9/15 for spring admission). Application fee: $50 ($60 for international students). Electronic applications accepted. *Expenses:* Tuition $3530 per year full-time, $199 per semester hour part-time for state residents; $12,722 per year full-time, $764 per semester hour part-time for nonresidents. Fees $252 per year. *Financial aid:* Research assistantships, teaching assistantships, Federal Work-Study available. Financial aid application deadline: 3/1; applicants required to submit FAFSA. • Rodney Muth, Area Coordinator, 303-556-4657. Fax: 303-556-4479.

University of Connecticut, School of Education, Field of Educational Administration, Storrs, CT 06269. Awards MA, PhD. Accredited by NCATE. Faculty: 14. Students: 78 part-time (48 women); includes 8 minority (6 African Americans, 2 Hispanics), 1 international. Average age 45. 17 applicants, 24% accepted. In 1997, 1 master's, 4 doctorates awarded. Terminal master's awarded for partial completion of doctoral program. *Degree requirements:* For master's, thesis or alternative; for doctorate, dissertation. *Entrance requirements:* For doctorate, GRE General Test. Application deadline: 6/1 (priority date; rolling processing; 11/1 for spring admission). Application fee: $40 ($45 for international students). *Expenses:* Tuition $5272 per year full-time, $293 per credit part-time for state residents; $13,696 per year full-time, $761 per credit part-time for nonresidents. Fees $948 per year full-time, $640 per year part-time. *Financial aid:* In 1997–98, 1 teaching assistantship totaling $12,825 was awarded; fellowships, research assistantships also available. Financial aid application deadline: 2/15. • Patrick B. Mullarney, Head, 860-486-6278.

University of Connecticut, School of Education, Field of Professional Higher Education Administration, Storrs, CT 06269. Awards MA, PhD. Accredited by NCATE. Faculty: 7. Students: 7 full-time (5 women), 24 part-time (16 women); includes 3 minority (2 African Americans, 1 Asian American), 1 international. Average age 40. 4 applicants, 0% accepted. In 1997, 14 master's, 7 doctorates awarded. Terminal master's awarded for partial completion of doctoral program. *Degree requirements:* For master's, thesis or alternative; for doctorate, dissertation. *Entrance requirements:* For doctorate, GRE General Test. Application deadline: 6/1 (priority date; rolling processing; 11/1 for spring admission). Application fee: $40 ($45 for international students). *Expenses:* Tuition $5272 per year full-time, $293 per credit part-time for state residents; $13,696 per year full-time, $761 per credit part-time for nonresidents. Fees $948 per year full-time, $640 per year part-time. *Financial aid:* In 1997–98, 1 fellowship totaling $1,910, 11 research assistantships (3 to first-year students) totaling $110,148, 2 teaching assistantships (1 to a first-year student) totaling $16,875 were awarded. Financial aid application deadline: 2/15. • Patrick B. Mullarney, Head, 860-486-6278.

University of Dayton, School of Education, Department of Counselor Education and Human Services, Dayton, OH 45469-1611. Offerings include college student personnel services (MS Ed). Accredited by NCATE. Department faculty: 8 full-time (1 woman), 5 part-time (4 women). *Degree requirements:* Exit exam required, thesis optional, foreign language not required. *Average time to degree:* master's–2 years full-time, 3.5 years part-time. *Entrance requirements:* GRE General Test (minimum score 430 on verbal section, 490 on analytical), minimum GPA of 2.75. Application deadline: 2/15 (priority date; rolling processing). Application fee: $30. • Dr. William Drury, Chairperson, 937-229-3644.

University of Dayton, School of Education, Department of Educational Administration, Dayton, OH 45469-1611. Offers programs in educational leadership (PhD, Ed S), school administration (MS Ed). Accredited by NCATE. Part-time and evening/weekend programs available. Faculty: 14 full-time (3 women), 13 part-time (1 woman). Students: 63 full-time (48 women), 400 part-time (311 women); includes 53 minority (48 African Americans, 2 Asian Americans, 3 Hispanics), 4 international. Average age 38. 30 applicants, 80% accepted. In 1997, 120 master's, 12 doctorates, 7 Ed Ss awarded. *Degree requirements:* For doctorate, computer language, dissertation, comprehensive exams, residency; for Ed S, thesis or alternative required, foreign language not required. *Entrance requirements:* For master's, GRE General Test (minimum score 430 on verbal section, 490 on analytical), minimum GPA of 2.75; for doctorate, GRE General Test (minimum score 430 on verbal section, 490 on analytical) or MAT, administrative experience, master's degree, minimum GPA of 3.5. Application deadline: 3/1 (priority date; rolling processing). Application fee: $30. *Financial aid:* In 1997–98, 4 research assistantships (3 to first-year students), 3 teaching assistantships (2 to first-year students) were awarded. *Faculty research:* Under-represented population urban school restructuring; leadership styles of principals and central office administrators; student science achievement; e-mail communication between teachers, scientists, engineers, universities, business, and industry. • Dr. Charles Russo, Chairperson, 937-229-3737. Fax: 937-229-4188.

University of Delaware, College of Human Resources, Education and Public Policy, School of Education, Newark, DE 19716. Offerings include educational leadership (M Ed, Ed D), educational policy (MA, PhD). PhD (exceptionality; cognition, development, and instruction) new for fall 1998. Terminal master's awarded for partial completion of doctoral program. School faculty: 54 (24 women). *Degree requirements:* For doctorate, dissertation required, foreign language not required. *Entrance requirements:* For doctorate, GRE. Application deadline: 7/1 (rolling processing; 1/15 for spring admission). Application fee: $45. *Expenses:* Tuition $4250 per year full-time, $236 per credit hour part-time for state residents; $12,250 per year full-time, $681 per credit hour part-time for nonresidents. Fees $466 per year full-time, $15 per semester (minimum) part-time. • Dr. Robert Hampel, Director, 302-831-2573.

University of Denver, College of Education, Denver, CO 80208. Offerings include school administration (PhD). Postbaccalaureate distance learning degree programs offered (no on-campus study). College faculty: 23 full-time (13 women). *Degree requirements:* 2 foreign languages (computer language can substitute for one), dissertation, comprehensive exam. *Entrance requirements:* GRE General Test (minimum combined score of 930), TOEFL (minimum score 550), TSE (minimum score 230). Application deadline: 1/1 (rolling processing). Application fee: $40 ($45 for international students). *Expenses:* Tuition $18,216 per year full-time, $506 per credit hour part-time. Fees $159 per year. • Dr. Elinor Katz, Dean, 303-871-3665. Application contact: Linda McCarthy, 303-871-2509.

University of Denver, Daniels College of Business, General Business Administration Program, Denver, CO 80208. Offerings include education management (MSM). MSMGEN offered jointly with the Department of Engineering; MSMC new for fall 1998. Program faculty: 76 full-time (15 women). *Application deadline:* 5/1 (priority date; rolling processing; 1/1 for spring admission). *Application fee:* $50. *Expenses:* Tuition $18,216 per year full-time, $506 per credit hour part-time. Fees $159 per year. • Dr. Tom Howard, Director, 303-871-4402. Application contact: Jan Johnson, Executive Director, Student Services, 303-871-3416. Fax: 303-871-4466. E-mail: dcb@du.edu.

University of Detroit Mercy, College of Education and Human Services, Department of Education, Program in Educational Administration, Detroit, MI 48219-0900. Awards MA, Ed S. *Degree requirements:* For master's, thesis or alternative. *Entrance requirements:* For master's, minimum GPA of 2.75. Application deadline: 8/1. Application fee: $25.

The University of Findlay, College of Professional Studies, Division of Education, 1000 North Main Street, Findlay, OH 45840-3653. Offerings include administration (MA Ed). Accredited by NCATE. Division faculty: 9 full-time (7 women), 8 part-time (4 women), 21 FTE. *Degree requirements:* 4 foreign languages, thesis, cumulative project. *Average time to degree:* master's–1.5 years full-time, 3 years part-time. *Entrance requirements:* Minimum GPA of 3.0. Application deadline: 8/15 (priority date; rolling processing). Application fee: $25. *Tuition:* $236 per semester hour. • Dr. Judith Wahrman, Graduate Program Director, 419-424-4864. Fax: 419-424-4822. E-mail: wahrman@lucy.findlay.edu.

University of Florida, College of Education, Department of Counselor Education, Gainesville, FL 32611. Offerings include student personnel services in higher education (M Ed, Ed D, PhD, Ed S). Accredited by NCATE. Terminal master's awarded for partial completion of doctoral program. Department faculty: 25. *Degree requirements:* For doctorate, dissertation required, foreign language not required. *Entrance requirements:* For master's and doctorate, GRE General Test, minimum GPA of 3.0 (undergraduate), 3.5 (graduate); for Ed S, GRE General Test. Application deadline: 2/27 (priority date; rolling processing). Application fee: $20. *Tuition:* $138 per credit hour for state residents; $481 per credit hour for nonresidents. • Dr. Harry Daniels, Chairman, 352-392-0731 Ext. 226. Application contact: Dr. Peter Sherrard, Graduate Coordinator, 352-392-0731 Ext. 234. Fax: 352-392-7159 Ext. 225. E-mail: psherrard@coe.ufl.edu.

University of Florida, College of Education, Department of Educational Leadership, Gainesville, FL 32611. Awards MAE, M Ed, Ed D, PhD, Ed S, JD/PhD. Programs in curriculum and instructional leadership (Ed D, PhD, Ed S), educational administration (MAE, M Ed, Ed D, PhD, Ed S), educational leadership (PhD), higher education (Ed D, PhD, Ed S). Accredited by NCATE. Faculty: 18. Students: 19 full-time (10 women), 152 part-time (97 women); includes 20 minority (11 African Americans, 1 Asian American, 7 Hispanics, 1 Native American), 1 international. 65 applicants, 89% accepted. In 1997, 10 master's, 12 doctorates, 20 Ed Ss awarded. *Degree requirements:* For master's, thesis optional, foreign language not required; for doctorate, variable foreign language requirement, dissertation. *Entrance requirements:* For master's, GRE General Test, minimum GPA of 3.0, teaching experience; for doctorate and Ed S, GRE General Test, minimum GPA of 3.0. Application deadline: 6/5 (priority date; rolling processing). Application fee: $20. *Tuition:* $138 per credit hour for state residents; $481 per credit hour for nonresidents. *Financial aid:* In 1997–98, 13 students received aid, including 3 fellowships averaging $950 per month, 8 research assistantships averaging $564 per month, 2 teaching assistantships averaging $514 per month; graduate assistantships and career-related internships or fieldwork also available. *Faculty research:* Educational finance, community education, middle school curriculum, community college administration. • Dr. James L. Doud, Chair, 352-392-2391 Ext. 263. E-mail: jldoud@coe.ufl.edu. Application contact: Dr. Walter Smith, Graduate Coordinator, 352-392-2391 Ext. 274. Fax: 352-392-0038. E-mail: wis@coe.ufl.edu.

University of Georgia, College of Education, Department of Counseling and Human Development Services, Athens, GA 30602. Offerings include counseling and student personnel services (PhD), student personnel in higher education (M Ed). One or more programs accredited by

NCATE. Department faculty: 10 full-time (4 women). *Degree requirements:* For doctorate, variable foreign language requirement, dissertation. *Entrance requirements:* For doctorate, GRE General Test. Application deadline: 7/1 (priority date; 11/15 for spring admission). Application fee: $30. Electronic applications accepted. *Tuition:* $3290 per year full-time, $643 per semester (minimum) part-time for state residents; $11,300 per year full-time, $1645 per semester (minimum) part-time for nonresidents. • Dr. John C. Dagley Jr., Graduate Coordinator, 706-542-1813. Fax: 706-542-4130.

University of Georgia, College of Education, Department of Educational Leadership, Athens, GA 30602. Awards MA, M Ed, Ed D, Ed S. Accredited by NCATE. Faculty: 15 full-time (3 women). Students: 103 full-time, 228 part-time; includes 38 minority (33 African Americans, 4 Hispanics, 1 Native American), 2 international. 112 applicants, 73% accepted. In 1997, 24 master's, 9 doctorates, 60 Ed Ss awarded. *Degree requirements:* For master's, thesis (MA) required, foreign language not required; for doctorate, dissertation required, foreign language not required. *Entrance requirements:* For master's and Ed S, GRE General Test or MAT; for doctorate, GRE General Test. Application deadline: 7/1 (priority date; 11/15 for spring admission). Application fee: $30. Electronic applications accepted. *Tuition:* $3290 per year full-time, $643 per semester (minimum) part-time for state residents; $11,300 per year full-time, $1645 per semester (minimum) part-time for nonresidents. *Financial aid:* Fellowships, research assistantships, teaching assistantships, assistantships available. • Dr. C. Thomas Holmes, Graduate Coordinator, 706-542-4146. Fax: 706-542-5873.

University of Great Falls, Graduate Studies Division, Programs in Education, Great Falls, MT 59405. Offerings include elementary administration (ME). Postbaccalaureate distance learning degree programs offered (minimal on-campus study). Faculty: 4 part-time (2 women). *Entrance requirements:* GRE General Test (minimum score 500 on each section; combined average 1000). Application deadline: 8/15 (priority date; rolling processing). Application fee: $35. *Expenses:* Tuition $327 per credit. Fees $150 per year full-time, $45 per semester (minimum) part-time. • Dr. Al Johnson, Dean, Graduate Studies Division, 406-791-5337. Fax: 406-791-5991. E-mail: ajohnson@ugf.edu.

University of Guam, College of Arts and Sciences, Instructional Leadership Program, 303 University Drive, UOG Station, Mangilao, GU 96923. Awards MA. *Degree requirements:* Thesis. *Entrance requirements:* GRE General Test. Application deadline: 5/31. Application fee: $31 ($56 for international students).

University of Guam, College of Education, Program in Administration and Supervision, 303 University Drive, UOG Station, Mangilao, GU 96923. Awards M Ed. *Degree requirements:* Comprehensive oral and written exams, special project or thesis required, foreign language not required. *Entrance requirements:* GRE General Test. Application deadline: 5/31. Application fee: $31 ($56 for international students).

University of Hartford, College of Education, Nursing, and Health Professions, Program in Administration and Supervision, West Hartford, CT 06117-1599. Awards M Ed, CAGS, Certificate. Accredited by NCATE. Part-time and evening/weekend programs available. Faculty: 6 full-time (2 women), 1 (woman) part-time. Students: 26 part-time (19 women); includes 1 minority (African American). Average age 38. 12 applicants, 67% accepted. In 1997, 4 master's, 6 other advanced degrees awarded. *Degree requirements:* For master's, comprehensive exam required, foreign language and thesis not required; for other advanced degree, comprehensive research project required, foreign language and thesis not required. *Entrance requirements:* GRE General Test or MAT, interview. Application deadline: 5/15 (priority date; rolling processing; 12/15 for spring admission). Application fee: $40 ($55 for international students). Electronic applications accepted. *Financial aid:* Federal Work-Study available. Aid available to part-time students. Financial aid application deadline: 6/1; applicants required to submit FAFSA. • Dr. Barbara Intriligator, Director, 860-768-4772. Application contact: Susan Garcia, Coordinator of Student Services, 860-768-5038. E-mail: gettoknow@mail.hartford.edu.

University of Hartford, College of Education, Nursing, and Health Professions, Program in Educational Leadership, West Hartford, CT 06117-1599. Awards Ed D. Accredited by NCATE. Part-time and evening/weekend programs available. Faculty: 5 full-time (2 women). Students: 30 full-time (18 women), 17 part-time (15 women); includes 4 minority (3 African Americans, 1 Native American), 2 international. Average age 41. 21 applicants, 90% accepted. In 1997, 11 degrees awarded. *Degree requirements:* Dissertation. *Entrance requirements:* MAT. Application deadline: rolling. Application fee: $40 ($55 for international students). *Expenses:* Tuition $7920 per year full-time, $440 per credit hour part-time. Fees $60 per year. *Financial aid:* Federal Work-Study available. Aid available to part-time students. Financial aid application deadline: 6/1; applicants required to submit FAFSA. • Dr. Barbara Intriligator, Director, 860-768-4772. Application contact: Heske Zelermyer, Coordinator, 860-768-5263. E-mail: gettoknow@mail.hartford.edu.

University of Hawaii at Manoa, College of Education, Department of Educational Administration, Honolulu, HI 96822. Awards M Ed. Part-time programs available. Faculty: 6 full-time (4 women). Students: 23 full-time (15 women), 79 part-time (46 women); includes 69 minority (all Asian Americans), 3 international. Average age 40. 58 applicants, 67% accepted. In 1997, 34 degrees awarded (80% found work related to degree, 20% continued full-time study). *Degree requirements:* Thesis or alternative. *Average time to degree:* master's–2 years full-time, 4 years part-time. *Application deadline:* 3/1 (9/1 for spring admission). *Application fee:* $25 ($50 for international students). *Tuition:* $4029 per year full-time, $214 per credit hour part-time for state residents; $9957 per year full-time, $461 per credit hour part-time for nonresidents. *Financial aid:* 8 students received aid; research assistantships, teaching assistantships, full and partial tuition waivers, Federal Work-Study, institutionally sponsored loans, and career-related internships or fieldwork available. *Faculty research:* Leadership, educational policy, organizational processes, finance. • Dr. Ronald H. Heck, Chairperson, 808-956-7843.

University of Hawaii at Manoa, College of Education, Education Program, Honolulu, HI 96822. Offerings include educational administration (Ed D). Program faculty: 53 full-time (25 women). *Degree requirements:* Dissertation required, foreign language not required. *Entrance requirements:* GRE General Test, MAT (optional), TOEFL (minimum score 600), sample of written work. Application deadline: 2/1. Application fee: $0. *Tuition:* $4029 per year full-time, $214 per credit hour part-time for state residents; $9957 per year full-time, $461 per credit hour part-time for nonresidents. • Dr. Royal T. Fruehling, Graduate Chair, 808-956-4243. E-mail: fruehlin@hawaii.edu. Application contact: Melanie Bock, Clerk Typist III, 808-956-7817. Fax: 808-956-9100. E-mail: mbock@hawaii.edu.

University of Houston, College of Education, Department of Educational Leadership and Cultural Studies, 4800 Calhoun, Houston, TX 77204-2163. Offers programs in educational administration (M Ed, Ed D); higher education (M Ed); historical, social, and cultural foundations of education (M Ed, Ed D). Accredited by NCATE. Part-time and evening/weekend programs available. Faculty: 15 full-time (9 women), 10 part-time (3 women), 20 FTE. Students: 53 full-time (41 women), 287 part-time (206 women); includes 96 minority (51 African Americans, 8 Asian Americans, 37 Hispanics), 1 international. Average age 39. 75 applicants, 61% accepted. In 1997, 48 master's, 24 doctorates awarded. *Degree requirements:* For master's, comprehensive exam or thesis required, foreign language not required; for doctorate, dissertation, comprehensive exam required, foreign language not required. *Average time to degree:* master's–1.5 years full-time, 3 years part-time; doctorate–3 years full-time, 6 years part-time. *Entrance requirements:* For master's, GRE General Test (minimum score 460 on verbal section) or MAT (minimum score 43), minimum GPA of 3.0 in last 60 hours; for doctorate, GRE General Test (minimum score 500 on verbal section), interview, minimum GPA of 3.0 in last 60 hours. Application deadline: 7/18 (priority date; rolling processing; 12/18 for spring admission). Application fee: $35 ($75 for international students). *Expenses:* Tuition $1152 per year full-time, $120 per semester (minimum) part-time for state residents; $4482 per year full-time, $249 per credit hour part-time for nonresidents. Fees $977 per year full-time, $119 per semester (minimum) part-time. *Financial aid:* Research assistantships, teaching assistantships, Federal Work-Study, institutionally sponsored loans, and career-related internships or fieldwork available. Aid available to part-time students. Financial aid application deadline: 4/1; applicants required to submit FAFSA. *Faculty research:* Change, supervision, multiculturalism, evaluation, policy. • Richard L. Hooker, Chairperson, 713-743-5035. Application contact: Rose L. Hernandez, Office Assistant, 713-743-5044. Fax: 713-743-4979.

University of Houston–Clear Lake, School of Education, Houston, TX 77058-1098. Offerings include educational management (MS). Accredited by NCATE. School faculty: 34 full-time (23 women), 17 part-time (12 women), 39 FTE. *Application deadline:* rolling. *Application fee:* $30 ($60 for international students). *Tuition:* $207 per credit hour for state residents; $336 per credit hour for nonresidents. • Dr. Dennis Spuck, Dean, 281-283-3501. Application contact: Dr. Doris L. Prater, Associate Dean, 281-283-3600.

University of Idaho, College of Graduate Studies, College of Education, Division of Teacher Education, Department of Educational Administration, Moscow, ID 83844-4140. Awards M Ed, MS, Ed D, PhD, EAS. Accredited by NCATE. Ed D and PhD offered through the College of Education. Students: 13 full-time (7 women), 192 part-time (100 women); includes 11 minority (7 African Americans, 2 Hispanics, 2 Native Americans). In 1997, 35 master's, 14 EASs awarded. *Entrance requirements:* For master's, minimum GPA of 2.8. Application deadline: 8/1 (12/15 for spring admission). Application fee: $35 ($45 for international students). *Expenses:* Tuition $0 for state residents; $6000 per year full-time, $95 per credit part-time for nonresidents. Fees $2676 per year full-time, $134 per credit part-time. *Financial aid:* Application deadline 2/15. • Dr. Grace Goc Karp, Acting Head, Division of Teacher Education, 208-885-6586.

University of Idaho, College of Graduate Studies, College of Education, Division of Teacher Education, Department of Teacher Education, Moscow, ID 83844-4140. Offerings include educational administration (M Ed). Accredited by NCATE. *Application deadline:* 8/1 (12/15 for spring admission). *Application fee:* $35 ($45 for international students). *Expenses:* Tuition $0 for state residents; $6000 per year full-time, $95 per credit part-time for nonresidents. Fees $2676 per year full-time, $134 per credit part-time. • Dr. Grace Goc Karp, Acting Head, Division of Teacher Education, 208-885-6586.

University of Illinois at Chicago, College of Education, Department of Curriculum and Instruction, Chicago, IL 60607-7128. Offerings include educational policy and administration (PhD), leadership and administration (M Ed). Department faculty: 28 full-time (13 women), 1 part-time (0 women). *Degree requirements:* For doctorate, dissertation required, foreign language not required. *Entrance requirements:* For master's, TOEFL (minimum score 550), minimum GPA of 3.75 on a 5.0 scale; for doctorate, GRE General Test (minimum combined score of 1000) or MAT (minimum score 55), TOEFL (minimum score 550), minimum GPA of 3.75 on a 5.0 scale. Application deadline: 2/15. Application fee: $40 ($50 for international students). • Dr. John Smart, Area Chair, 312-996-4526. Application contact: Victoria Hare, Director of Graduate Studies, 312-996-4520.

University of Illinois at Springfield, School of Health and Human Services, Program in Educational Administration, Springfield, IL 62794-9243. Awards MA. Offered jointly with Illinois State University, Southern Illinois University, and Western Illinois University. Part-time and evening/weekend programs available. Faculty: 2 full-time (1 woman), 2 part-time (1 woman), 2.75 FTE. Students: 3 full-time (2 women), 124 part-time (86 women); includes 17 minority (14 African Americans, 3 Hispanics), 1 international. Average age 38. 31 applicants, 97% accepted. In 1997, 33 degrees awarded. *Degree requirements:* Thesis or alternative required, foreign language not required. *Application deadline:* rolling. *Application fee:* $0. *Expenses:* Tuition $99 per credit hour for state residents; $296 per credit hour for nonresidents. Fees $242 per year full-time, $63 per semester (minimum) part-time. *Financial aid:* In 1997–98, 11 students received aid, including 4 assistantships averaging $606 per month; partial tuition waivers, Federal Work-Study, and career-related internships or fieldwork also available. Aid available to part-time students. Financial aid application deadline: 6/1; applicants required to submit FAFSA. • James Cherry, Convener, 217-786-6306.

University of Illinois at Urbana–Champaign, College of Education, Department of Educational Organization and Leadership, Urbana, IL 61801. Awards AM, Ed M, MS, Ed D, PhD, AC. Faculty: 6 full-time (2 women). Students: 288 (184 women); includes 9 international. 132 applicants, 72% accepted. In 1997, 25 master's, 14 doctorates awarded. *Degree requirements:* For doctorate, dissertation. *Entrance requirements:* For doctorate, GRE General Test or MAT. Application deadline: rolling. Application fee: $40 ($50 for international students). *Financial aid:* In 1997–98, 3 fellowships, 2 research assistantships were awarded; full and partial tuition waivers also available. Financial aid application deadline: 1/15. • Paul W. Thurston, Head, 217-333-2155.

The University of Iowa, College of Education, Division of Educational Administration, Iowa City, IA 52242-1316. Awards MA, PhD, Ed S, JD/PhD. Faculty: 5 full-time, 1 part-time. Students: 7 full-time (3 women), 51 part-time (29 women); includes 5 minority (all African Americans), 4 international. 19 applicants, 79% accepted. In 1997, 12 master's, 4 doctorates, 3 Ed Ss awarded. *Degree requirements:* For master's, exam required, foreign language and thesis not required; for doctorate, computer language, dissertation, comprehensive exams required, foreign language not required; for Ed S, computer language, exam required, foreign language not required. *Entrance requirements:* For master's and Ed S, minimum GPA of 2.5; for doctorate, minimum GPA of 3.0. Application fee: $30 ($50 for international students). *Expenses:* Tuition $3166 per year full-time, $176 per semester hour part-time for state residents; $10,202 per year full-time, $176 per semester hour part-time for nonresidents. Fees $202 per year full-time, $52 per year (minimum) part-time. *Financial aid:* In 1997–98, 3 teaching assistantships were awarded; fellowships, research assistantships also available. Financial aid applicants required to submit FAFSA. • David B. Bills, Chair, 319-335-5366. Fax: 319-384-0587.

University of Kansas, School of Education, Department of Teaching and Leadership, Program in Educational Administration, Lawrence, KS 66045. Awards MS Ed, Ed D, PhD, Ed S. Accredited by NCATE. Students: 51 part-time (33 women); includes 3 minority (all African Americans). *Degree requirements:* For doctorate, variable foreign language requirement, dissertation. *Entrance requirements:* For master's and Ed S, minimum GPA of 3.0; for doctorate, GRE General Test (combined average 1000), minimum graduate GPA of 3.5. Application deadline: 7/1. Application fee: $25. *Expenses:* Tuition $2400 per year full-time, $100 per credit hour part-time for state residents; $7890 per year full-time, $329 per credit hour part-time for nonresidents. Fees $428 per year full-time, $31 per credit hour part-time. *Faculty research:* Law, teacher effectiveness. • Marc Mahlios, Chair, Department of Teaching and Leadership, 785-864-4435.

University of Kansas, School of Education, Department of Teaching and Leadership, Program in Educational Policy and Leadership, Lawrence, KS 66045. Awards Ed D, PhD. Accredited by NCATE. Students: 21 full-time (9 women), 91 part-time (51 women); includes 12 minority (9 African Americans, 2 Hispanics, 1 Native American), 7 international. *Degree requirements:* Dissertation. *Entrance requirements:* GRE General Test (combined average 1000), minimum graduate GPA of 3.5. Application deadline: 7/1. Application fee: $25. *Expenses:* Tuition $2400 per year full-time, $100 per credit hour part-time for state residents; $7890 per year full-time, $329 per credit hour part-time for nonresidents. Fees $428 per year full-time, $31 per credit hour part-time. • Marc Mahlios, Chair, Department of Teaching and Leadership, 785-864-4435.

University of Kentucky, Graduate School Programs from the College of Education, Program in Administration and Supervision, Lexington, KY 40506-0032. Awards Ed D, Ed S. Accredited by NCATE. Faculty: 12 full-time (5 women), 2 part-time (0 women). Students: 44 full-time (25 women), 44 part-time (25 women); includes 3 minority (all African Americans). 59 applicants, 83% accepted. In 1997, 6 doctorates, 1 Ed S awarded. *Degree requirements:* For doctorate, dissertation, comprehensive exam required, foreign language not required; for Ed S, comprehensive exam required, foreign language and thesis not required. *Entrance requirements:* For doctorate, GRE General Test, minimum graduate GPA of 3.0; for Ed S, GRE General Test. Application deadline: (12/15 for spring admission). *Financial aid:* In 1997–98, 3 fellowships were awarded. *Faculty research:* School governance, teacher empowerment, planned change,

Directory: Educational Administration

University of Kentucky (continued)
systemic reform, issues of equity and fairness. Total annual research expenditures: $100,000. • Dr. Susan Scollay, Director of Graduate Studies, 606-257-7834. E-mail: scollay@ukcc.uky.edu. Application contact: Dr. Constance L. Wood, Associate Dean, 606-257-4613. Fax: 606-323-1928.

University of La Verne, School of Organizational Management, Department of Educational Management, La Verne, CA 91750-4443. Offers programs in educational management (Ed D); educational management/administrative services (M Ed, Credential), including administrative services (Credential), educational management (M Ed). *Degree requirements:* For doctorate, dissertation. *Entrance requirements:* For master's, TOEFL (minimum score 550), minimum GPA of 2.5; for doctorate, GRE or MAT, minimum graduate GPA of 3.0. Application fee: $25. *Expenses:* Tuition $315 per unit (minimum). Fees $60 per year.

University of Louisville, School of Education, Department of Educational Psychology and Counseling, Louisville, KY 40292-0001. Offerings include college student personnel services (M Ed), counseling and student personnel (Ed D), guidance and personnel (Ed S). One or more programs accredited by NCATE. Department faculty: 11 full-time (2 women), 9 part-time (3 women), 14 FTE. *Degree requirements:* For doctorate, dissertation required, foreign language not required. *Entrance requirements:* GRE General Test. Application deadline: rolling. Application fee: $25. • Dr. Daya S. Sandhu, Chair, 502-852-6884.

University of Louisville, School of Education, Department of Administration and Higher Education, Program in Educational Supervision, Louisville, KY 40292-0001. Awards Ed D, Ed S. Accredited by NCATE. Students: 22 full-time (13 women), 26 part-time (19 women); includes 6 minority (5 African Americans, 1 Asian American), 3 international. Average age 42. *Degree requirements:* For Ed S, thesis required, foreign language not required. *Entrance requirements:* For Ed S, GRE General Test. Application deadline: rolling. Application fee: $25. • Dr. John L. Strope Jr., Chairman, Department of Administration and Higher Education, 502-852-6428.

University of Maine, College of Education and Human Development, Program in Educational Leadership, Orono, ME 04469. Awards M Ed, Ed D, CAS. Accredited by NCATE. Part-time and evening/weekend programs available. *Degree requirements:* For master's, thesis or alternative required, foreign language not required; for doctorate, dissertation required, foreign language not required. *Entrance requirements:* For master's, MAT, TOEFL (minimum score 550); for doctorate, GRE General Test, TOEFL (minimum score 550); for CAS, MA, M Ed, or MS. Application deadline: 2/1 (priority date; rolling processing; 10/15 for spring admission). Application fee: $50. *Expenses:* Tuition $194 per credit hour for state residents; $548 per credit hour for nonresidents. Fees $378 per year full-time, $33 per semester (minimum) part-time. *Financial aid:* Research assistantships, teaching assistantships, and career-related internships or fieldwork available. Aid available to part-time students. Financial aid application deadline: 3/1. • Application contact: Scott Delcourt, Director of the Graduate School, 207-581-3218. Fax: 207-581-3232. E-mail: graduate@maine.edu.

University of Manitoba, Faculty of Education, Department of Educational Administration and Foundations, Winnipeg, MB R3T 2N2, Canada. Offerings include educational administration (M Ed, PhD). PhD admissions temporarily suspended. *Degree requirements:* For master's, thesis or alternative required, foreign language not required; for doctorate, dissertation required, foreign language not required.

University of Mary, Program in Education, 7500 University Drive, Bismarck, ND 58504-9652. Offerings include elementary education administration (MS Ed), secondary education administration (MS Ed). Program faculty: 5 full-time (3 women), 6 part-time (4 women). *Average time to degree:* master's–3 years part-time. *Application deadline:* 8/1 (12/1 for spring admission). *Application fee:* $15. *Tuition:* $265 per credit. • Ramona Klein, Director, 701-255-7500. Application contact: Dr. Diane Fladeland, Director, Graduate Programs, 701-255-7500. Fax: 701-255-7687.

University of Mary Hardin–Baylor, School of Education, Belton, TX 76513. Offerings include educational administration (M Ed). School faculty: 6 full-time (2 women). *Average time to degree:* master's–2 years full-time, 3.5 years part-time. *Entrance requirements:* GRE General Test (minimum combined score of 850), minimum GPA of 2.5. Application deadline: 8/1 (priority date; rolling processing; 1/10 for spring admission). Application fee: $35 ($135 for international students). *Expenses:* Tuition $270 per semester hour. Fees $15 per semester hour. • Dr. Clarence E. Ham, Dean, 254-295-4573. Fax: 254-933-4480. E-mail: ham@tenet.edu.

University of Maryland, College Park, College of Education, Department of Counseling and Personnel Services, College Park, MD 20742-5045. Offerings include college student personnel (MA, M Ed), college student personnel administration (PhD). One or more programs accredited by NCATE. Department faculty: 15 full-time (8 women), 2 part-time (both women). *Degree requirements:* For master's, thesis or alternative required, foreign language not required; for doctorate, dissertation required, foreign language not required. *Entrance requirements:* For master's, GRE General Test or MAT, minimum GPA of 3.0; for doctorate, GRE General Test or MAT, minimum GPA of 3.5. Application deadline: rolling. Application fee: $50 ($70 for international students). *Expenses:* Tuition $272 per credit hour for state residents; $400 per credit hour for nonresidents. Fees $564 per year full-time, $342 per year part-time. • Dr. Paul Power, Chairman, 301-405-2858. Fax: 301-314-9278. Application contact: John Mollish, Director, Graduate Admissions and Records, 301-405-4198. Fax: 301-314-9305.

University of Massachusetts Amherst, School of Education, Program in Education, Amherst, MA 01003-0001. Offerings include educational administration (M Ed, Ed D, CAGS). Accredited by NCATE. *Degree requirements:* For doctorate, dissertation required, foreign language not required. *Entrance requirements:* For master's and doctorate, GRE General Test. Application deadline: 3/1 (rolling processing; 10/1 for spring admission). Application fee: $40. *Expenses:* Tuition $2640 per year full-time, $110 per credit part-time for state residents; $3690 per year (minimum) full-time, $165 per credit (minimum) part-time for nonresidents. Fees $2856 per year full-time, $422 per semester part-time for state residents; $3204 per year full-time, $480 per semester part-time for nonresidents. • John C. Carey, Director, 413-545-0236.

University of Massachusetts Boston, Graduate College of Education, School Organization, Curriculum and Instruction Department, Program in Educational Administration, Boston, MA 02125-3393. Awards M Ed, CAGS. Students: 1 full-time (0 women), 38 part-time (22 women); includes 11 minority (6 African Americans, 1 Asian American, 4 Hispanics). 32 applicants, 69% accepted. In 1997, 16 master's, 7 CAGSs awarded. *Degree requirements:* Comprehensive exams required, foreign language and thesis not required. *Entrance requirements:* For master's, GRE General Test or MAT, minimum GPA of 2.75, 2 years of teaching experience; for CAGS, minimum GPA of 2.75. Application deadline: 3/1 (priority date; 11/1 for spring admission). Application fee: $25 ($35 for international students). *Expenses:* Tuition $2640 per year full-time, $110 per credit part-time for state residents; $8930 per year full-time, $373 per credit part-time for nonresidents. Fees $2650 per year full-time, $420 per semester (minimum) part-time for state residents; $2736 per year full-time, $420 per semester (minimum) part-time for nonresidents. *Financial aid:* In 1997–98, 1 research assistantship (to a first-year student) averaging $225 per month and totaling $2,000 was awarded; teaching assistantships, administrative assistantships also available. Financial aid application deadline: 3/1; applicants required to submit FAFSA. • Dr. Lee Teitel, Coordinator, 617-287-7612. Application contact: Lisa Lavely, Director of Graduate Admissions and Records, 617-287-6400. Fax: 617-287-6236.

University of Massachusetts Boston, Graduate College of Education, School Organization, Curriculum and Instruction Department, Program in Education, Track in Higher Education Administration, Boston, MA 02125-3393. Awards Ed D. Students: 50 part-time (33 women); includes 15 minority (8 African Americans, 2 Asian Americans, 5 Hispanics). *Degree requirements:* Dissertation, comprehensive exams required, foreign language not required. *Entrance requirements:* GRE General Test or MAT, minimum GPA of 2.75. Application deadline: 3/1. Application fee: $25 ($35 for international students). *Expenses:* Tuition $2640 per year full-time, $110 per credit part-time for state residents; $8930 per year full-time, $373 per credit part-time for nonresidents. Fees $2650 per year full-time, $420 per semester (minimum) part-time for state residents; $2736 per year full-time, $420 per semester (minimum) part-time for nonresidents. *Financial aid:* In 1997–98, 1 research assistantship averaging $225 per month and totaling $2,000 was awarded; teaching assistantships, administrative assistantships also available. Financial aid application deadline: 3/1; applicants required to submit FAFSA. • Dr. Sandra Kanter, Program Coordinator, 617-287-7601. Application contact: Lisa Lavely, Director of Graduate Admissions and Records, 617-287-6400. Fax: 617-287-6236.

University of Massachusetts Boston, Graduate College of Education, School Organization, Curriculum and Instruction Department, Program in Education, Track in Urban School Leadership, Boston, MA 02125-3393. Awards Ed D. Students: 31 part-time (20 women); includes 15 minority (10 African Americans, 3 Asian Americans, 2 Hispanics), 1 international. *Degree requirements:* Dissertation, comprehensive exams required, foreign language not required. *Entrance requirements:* GRE General Test or MAT, minimum GPA of 2.75. Application deadline: 3/1. Application fee: $25 ($35 for international students). *Expenses:* Tuition $2640 per year full-time, $110 per credit part-time for state residents; $8930 per year full-time, $373 per credit part-time for nonresidents. Fees $2650 per year full-time, $420 per semester (minimum) part-time for state residents; $2736 per year full-time, $420 per semester (minimum) part-time for nonresidents. *Financial aid:* In 1997–98, 1 research assistantship averaging $225 per month and totaling $2,000 was awarded; teaching assistantships, administrative assistantships also available. Financial aid application deadline: 3/1; applicants required to submit FAFSA. • Dr. Joseph Check, Program Coordinator, 617-287-7601. Application contact: Lisa Lavely, Director of Graduate Admissions and Records, 617-287-6400. Fax: 617-287-6236.

University of Massachusetts Lowell, College of Education, Program in Educational Administration, 1 University Avenue, Lowell, MA 01854-2881. Awards M Ed, Ed D, CAGS. Accredited by NCATE. Average age 26. 57 applicants, 67% accepted. In 1997, 9 master's awarded. *Degree requirements:* For master's, thesis required (for some programs), foreign language not required; for doctorate, dissertation. *Entrance requirements:* For master's, MAT; for doctorate, GRE General Test. Application deadline: 4/1 (priority date; rolling processing; 10/1 for spring admission). Application fee: $20 ($35 for international students). *Tuition:* $4867 per year full-time, $618 per semester (minimum) part-time for state residents; $10,276 per year full-time, $1294 per semester (minimum) part-time for nonresidents. *Financial aid:* Teaching assistantships and career-related internships or fieldwork available. Financial aid application deadline: 4/1. • Dr. Brenda Jochums, Coordinator, 978-934-4620.

University of Massachusetts Lowell, College of Education, Program in Leadership in Schooling, 1 University Avenue, Lowell, MA 01854-2881. Awards Ed D. Accredited by NCATE. Students: 14 full-time (8 women), 124 part-time (68 women); includes 11 minority (4 African Americans, 5 Asian Americans, 2 Hispanics), 3 international. In 1997, 11 degrees awarded. *Degree requirements:* Dissertation. *Entrance requirements:* GRE General Test. Application deadline: 4/1 (priority date; rolling processing; 10/1 for spring admission). Application fee: $20 ($35 for international students). *Tuition:* $4867 per year full-time, $618 per semester (minimum) part-time for state residents; $10,276 per year full-time, $1294 per semester (minimum) part-time for nonresidents. *Financial aid:* Federal Work-Study, institutionally sponsored loans, and career-related internships or fieldwork available. Aid available to part-time students. Financial aid application deadline: 4/1. • Dr. Brenda Jochums, Coordinator, 978-934-4620.

The University of Memphis, College of Education, Department of Counseling, Educational Psychology and Research, Memphis, TN 38152. Offerings include counseling and personnel services (MS, Ed D), with options in community agency counseling (MS), rehabilitation counseling (MS), school counseling (MS), student personnel services (MS). Accredited by NCATE. Department faculty: 23 full-time (11 women), 17 part-time (8 women). *Degree requirements:* Thesis or alternative, comprehensive exam required, foreign language not required. *Entrance requirements:* GRE General Test or MAT, minimum GPA of 2.5. Application deadline: 8/1 (12/1 for spring admission). Application fee: $25 ($50 for international students). *Tuition:* $2862 per year full-time, $166 per credit hour part-time for state residents; $6696 per year full-time, $379 per credit hour part-time for nonresidents. • Dr. Ronnie Priest, Chair and Coordinator of Graduate Studies, 901-678-2841.

The University of Memphis, College of Education, Department of Leadership, Memphis, TN 38152. Offers programs in adult education (Ed D), community education (Ed D), education (Ed S), educational leadership (Ed D), higher education (Ed D), leadership (MS), policy studies (Ed D), school administration and supervision (MS). Accredited by NCATE. Faculty: 9 full-time (2 women), 23 part-time (9 women). Students: 13 full-time (7 women), 146 part-time (96 women); includes 37 minority (35 African Americans, 1 Asian American, 1 Hispanic), 2 international. Average age 39. 59 applicants, 51% accepted. In 1997, 35 master's, 8 doctorates awarded. *Degree requirements:* For master's, comprehensive exam required, thesis optional, foreign language not required; for doctorate, dissertation, comprehensive exam required, foreign language not required; for Ed S, thesis or alternative, comprehensive exams. *Entrance requirements:* For master's, GRE General Test or MAT (minimum score 30); for doctorate, GRE General Test (minimum combined score of 850), GRE Subject Test, 3 years of teaching experience; for Ed S, GRE General Test (minimum combined score of 800). Application deadline: 8/1 (12/1 for spring admission). Application fee: $25 ($50 for international students). *Tuition:* $2862 per year full-time, $166 per credit hour part-time for state residents; $6696 per year full-time, $379 per credit hour part-time for nonresidents. *Financial aid:* In 1997–98, 3 research assistantships totaling $31,368, 1 teaching assistantship were awarded. *Faculty research:* Team decision making. • Dr. John Petry, Interim Chair, 901-678-2368.

University of Miami, School of Education, Department of Educational and Psychological Studies, Program in Educational Leadership, Coral Gables, FL 33124. Awards MS Ed, Ed D, PhD, Ed S. Accredited by NCATE. Program being phased out; applicants no longer accepted. Students: 16 full-time (7 women), 1 part-time (0 women); includes 9 minority (7 African Americans, 2 Hispanics). Average age 46. In 1997, 5 doctorates awarded. *Degree requirements:* For doctorate, dissertation required, foreign language not required. *Average time to degree:* master's–2 years part-time. *Expenses:* Tuition $815 per credit hour. Fees $174 per year. • Dr. Margaret Crosbie-Burnett, Chairperson, Department of Educational and Psychological Studies, 305-284-2808. Fax: 305-284-3003. E-mail: mcrosbur@umiami.ir.miami.edu.

University of Miami, School of Education, Department of Educational and Psychological Studies, Program in Higher Education/Enrollment Management, Coral Gables, FL 33124. Awards MS Ed. Accredited by NCATE. Program new for fall 1998. *Entrance requirements:* GRE General Test (minimum combined score of 1000), TOEFL (minimum score 550). Application deadline: rolling. Application fee: $35. *Expenses:* Tuition $815 per credit hour. Fees $174 per year. *Financial aid:* Application deadline 3/1. • Dr. Margaret Crosbie-Burnett, Department Chairperson, 305-284-2808. Fax: 305-284-3003. E-mail: mcrosbur@umiami.ir.miami.edu.

University of Michigan, School of Education, Center for the Study of Higher and Postsecondary Education, Ann Arbor, MI 48109. Offers programs in academic affairs (Ed D, PhD); community college administration (AM); community college governance and leadership (Ed D); higher education administration (AM); individually designed studies (Ed D, PhD); organizational behavior (Ed D, PhD); public policy in postsecondary education (AM, Ed D, PhD); research, evaluation, and assessment (PhD); student development and academic support (AM). *Degree requirements:* For doctorate, dissertation, preliminary exam required, foreign language not required. *Entrance requirements:* GRE General Test (minimum combined score of 1800 on three sections), TOEFL (minimum score 600). Application deadline: 1/15 (priority date). Application fee: $55. Electronic applications accepted. • Dr. Janet H. Lawrence, Chairperson, 734-647-1977. Fax: 734-764-2510. E-mail: janlaw@umich.edu. Application contact: Karen Wixson, Associate Dean, 734-764-9470. Fax: 734-763-1229. E-mail: kwixson@umich.edu.

University of Michigan, School of Education, Programs in Educational Studies, Ann Arbor, MI 48109. Offerings include educational administration and policy (AM, PhD). *Degree requirements:* For doctorate, dissertation, preliminary exam required, foreign language not required. *Entrance requirements:* For doctorate, GRE General Test (minimum combined score of 1800 on three sections), TOEFL (minimum score 600). Application deadline: 1/15 (priority date). Application fee: $55. Electronic applications accepted. • Dr. Ronald Marx, Chairperson, 734-763-9497. E-mail: ronmarx@umich.edu. Application contact: Karen Wixson, Associate Dean, 734-764-9470. Fax: 734-763-1229. E-mail: kwixson@umich.edu.

University of Minnesota, Twin Cities Campus, College of Education and Human Development, Department of Educational Policy and Administration, Minneapolis, MN 55455-0213. Offerings include educational administration (Ed D, Ed S), educational policy and administration (MA, PhD), teacher leadership (M Ed). • James Hearn, Chair, 612-624-1006.

University of Mississippi, Graduate School, School of Education, Department of Educational Leadership and Educational Psychology, University, MS 38677-9702. Offers programs in educational leadership (PhD), educational leadership and educational psychology (MA, M Ed, Ed D, Ed S), educational psychology (PhD), higher education/student personnel (MA, M Ed). Accredited by NCATE. Faculty: 11 full-time (4 women). Students: 53 full-time (42 women), 76 part-time (55 women); includes 47 minority (all African Americans), 2 international. In 1997, 66 master's, 3 doctorates awarded. *Degree requirements:* For doctorate, dissertation required, foreign language not required. *Entrance requirements:* For master's, GRE General Test, TOEFL, minimum GPA of 3.0; for doctorate, GRE General Test, TOEFL. Application deadline: 8/1 (rolling processing). Application fee: $0 ($25 for international students). *Financial aid:* Application deadline 3/1. • Dr. William Leary, Acting Chair, 601-232-7195.

University of Missouri–Columbia, College of Education, Department of Educational Leadership and Policy Analysis, Columbia, MO 65211. Offers programs in education administration (MA, M Ed, Ed D, PhD, Ed S), higher and adult education (MA, M Ed, Ed D, PhD, Ed S). Part-time programs available. Faculty: 20 full-time (7 women). Students: 17 full-time (7 women), 133 part-time (75 women); includes 18 minority (17 African Americans, 1 Asian American), 4 international. In 1997, 52 master's, 19 doctorates awarded. Terminal master's awarded for partial completion of doctoral program. *Degree requirements:* For doctorate, variable foreign language requirement, dissertation. *Entrance requirements:* For master's, GRE General Test, minimum GPA of 3.0; for doctorate, GRE General Test, GRE Subject Test, minimum GPA of 3.5; for Ed S, GRE General Test, GRE Subject Test, minimum GPA of 3.25. Application deadline: 6/15 (priority date; rolling processing). Application fee: $25 ($50 for international students). *Expenses:* Tuition $3240 per year full-time, $180 per credit hour part-time for state residents; $9108 per year full-time, $506 per credit hour part-time for nonresidents. Fees $55 per year full-time. *Financial aid:* Career-related internships or fieldwork available. *Faculty research:* Administrative communication and behavior, middle schools leadership, administration of special education. • Dr. Paula Short, Director of Graduate Studies, 573-882-8231.

University of Missouri–Kansas City, School of Education, Division of Urban Leadership and Policy Studies, Kansas City, MO 64110-2499. Awards MA, PhD, Ed S. Accredited by NCATE. PhD offered through the School of Graduate Studies. Part-time and evening/weekend programs available. Students: 36 full-time (24 women), 177 part-time (111 women); includes 49 minority (45 African Americans, 1 Asian American, 2 Hispanics, 1 Native American), 3 international. Average age 37. In 1997, 27 master's, 27 Ed Ss awarded. *Degree requirements:* For master's, final exam, practicum required, foreign language and thesis not required; for doctorate, dissertation, internship, practicum required, foreign language not required; for Ed S, final exam, internship required, foreign language and thesis not required. *Average time to degree:* master's–3 years full-time, 6 years part-time; doctorate–5 years full-time, 7 years part-time; other advanced degree–2 years full-time, 4 years part-time. *Entrance requirements:* For master's, minimum GPA of 2.75; for doctorate, GRE, minimum GPA of 3.0; for Ed S, GRE General Test (minimum combined score of 1500 on three sections), minimum GPA of 3.0. Application deadline: 7/1 (priority date; rolling processing; 12/1 for spring admission). Application fee: $25. *Expenses:* Tuition $182 per credit hour for state residents; $508 per credit hour for nonresidents. Fees $60 per year. *Financial aid:* In 1997–98, 1 research assistantship averaging $858 per month was awarded; teaching assistantships also available. *Faculty research:* Magnet schools/urban education, organizational development/team building/school districts, demographic and financial surveys for school districts, counseling skills of school administrators, alcohol abuse educators. • Dr. Edward Underwood, Chairperson, 816-235-2716.

University of Missouri–St. Louis, School of Education, Program in Educational Administration, St. Louis, MO 63121-4499. Awards M Ed. Accredited by NCATE. Faculty: 17 (5 women). Students: 12 full-time (5 women), 155 part-time (112 women); includes 61 minority (56 African Americans, 2 Asian Americans, 1 Hispanic, 2 Native Americans). In 1997, 81 degrees awarded. *Degree requirements:* Thesis required, foreign language not required. *Application deadline:* 7/1 (priority date; rolling processing; 12/1 for spring admission). *Application fee:* $0. Electronic applications accepted. *Expenses:* Tuition $3903 per year full-time, $167 per credit hour part-time for state residents; $11,745 per year full-time, $489 per credit hour part-time for nonresidents. Fees $816 per year full-time, $34 per credit hour part-time. *Financial aid:* In 1997–98, 1 teaching assistantship was awarded. *Faculty research:* Educational policy research; philosophy of education; higher, adult, and vocational education; school initiatives, change, and reform. • Dr. Edith Young, Chair, 314-516-5944. Application contact: Graduate Admissions, 314-516-5458. Fax: 314-516-6759. E-mail: gradadm@umslvma.umsl.edu.

The University of Montana–Missoula, School of Education, Department of Professional Education, Program in School Administration and Supervision, Missoula, MT 59812-0002. Awards MA, M Ed, Ed S. *Degree requirements:* For Ed S, thesis required, foreign language not required. *Entrance requirements:* For master's, GRE General Test (minimum score 450 on each section), minimum GPA of 3.0; for Ed S, GRE General Test. Application deadline: 3/1 (priority date; 10/1 for spring admission). Application fee: $30. *Tuition:* $2499 per year (minimum) full-time, $376 per semester (minimum) part-time for state residents; $6528 per year (minimum) full-time, $1048 per semester (minimum) part-time for nonresidents. *Financial aid:* Application deadline 3/1. • Chair, Department of Professional Education, 406-243-2032.

University of Montevallo, College of Education, Program in Educational Administration, Montevallo, AL 35115. Awards Ed S. Accredited by NCATE. Part-time and evening/weekend programs available. *Entrance requirements:* Minimum GPA of 3.0. Application deadline: 7/15 (11/15 for spring admission). Application fee: $10.

University of Nebraska at Kearney, College of Education, Department of Educational Administration, Kearney, NE 68849-0001. Offers programs in educational administration (MA Ed, Ed S), supervisor of educational media (MA Ed). Accredited by NCATE. Part-time and evening/weekend programs available. Faculty: 2 full-time (0 women). Students: 11 full-time (8 women), 69 part-time (15 women). In 1997, 20 master's, 5 Ed Ss awarded. *Degree requirements:* For master's, thesis optional. *Entrance requirements:* GRE General Test. Application deadline: 8/1 (priority date; rolling processing; 12/15 for spring admission). Application fee: $35. *Expenses:* Tuition $1494 per year full-time, $83 per credit hour part-time for state residents; $2826 per year full-time, $157 per credit hour part-time for nonresidents. Fees $229 per year full-time, $11.25 per semester (minimum) part-time. *Financial aid:* In 1997–98, 2 research assistantships were awarded; teaching assistantships and career-related internships or fieldwork also available. Aid available to part-time students. Financial aid application deadline: 3/1; applicants required to submit FAFSA. • Dr. Thomas Jacobson, Chair, 308-865-8512.

University of Nebraska at Omaha, College of Education, Department of Counseling, Omaha, NE 68182. Offerings include student affairs practice in higher education (MA, MS). Accredited by NCATE. Department faculty: 5 full-time (1 woman), 1 part-time (0 women). *Degree requirements:* Thesis (for some programs), comprehensive exam required, foreign language not required. *Entrance requirements:* GRE General Test, MAT, or department test, interview, minimum GPA of 3.0. Application deadline: 3/1 (priority date; rolling processing; 10/1 for spring admission). Application fee: $35. *Expenses:* Tuition $1670 per year full-time, $94 per credit hour part-time for state residents; $4082 per year full-time, $227 per credit hour part-time for nonresidents. Fees $302 per year full-time, $108 per semester (minimum) part-time. • Dr. Joseph Davis, Chairperson, 402-554-2306.

University of Nebraska at Omaha, College of Education, Department of Educational Administration and Supervision, Omaha, NE 68182. Awards MS, Ed D, Ed S. Accredited by NCATE. Ed D offered jointly with the University of Nebraska–Lincoln. Part-time and evening/weekend programs available. Faculty: 6 full-time (1 woman). Students: 6 full-time (5 women), 148 part-time (94 women); includes 12 minority (10 African Americans, 2 Asian Americans), 19 international. Average age 34. 71 applicants, 72% accepted. In 1997, 35 master's, 3 doctorates awarded. *Degree requirements:* For master's, comprehensive exam required, foreign language and thesis not required; for doctorate, dissertation required, foreign language not required. *Entrance requirements:* For master's, GRE General Test, MAT, minimum GPA of 3.0; for doctorate, GRE General Test, resume, 3 samples of research/written work. Application deadline: 7/1 (priority date; rolling processing; 11/15 for spring admission). Application fee: $35. *Expenses:* Tuition $1670 per year full-time, $94 per credit hour part-time for state residents; $4082 per year full-time, $227 per credit hour part-time for nonresidents. Fees $302 per year full-time, $108 per semester (minimum) part-time. *Financial aid:* 32 students received aid; research assistantships, full tuition waivers, Federal Work-Study, institutionally sponsored loans available. Aid available to part-time students. Financial aid application deadline: 3/1. • Dr. Martha Bruckner, Chairperson, 402-554-3445.

University of Nebraska–Lincoln, Teachers College, Department of Educational Administration, Lincoln, NE 68588. Awards MA, M Ed, Ed D, Certificate. Accredited by NCATE. Ed D offered jointly with the University of Nebraska at Omaha. Faculty: 8 full-time (2 women). Students: 26 full-time (14 women), 69 part-time (25 women); includes 6 minority (3 African Americans, 1 Asian American, 2 Hispanics), 2 international. Average age 35. 27 applicants, 70% accepted. In 1997, 28 master's, 4 doctorates, 6 Certificates awarded. *Degree requirements:* For master's, thesis optional; for doctorate, dissertation, comprehensive exam. *Average time to degree:* doctorate–3.9 years full-time. *Entrance requirements:* For master's and doctorate, GRE General Test or MAT, TOEFL (minimum score 500). Application deadline: 6/1 (10/1 for spring admission). Application fee: $35. Electronic applications accepted. *Expenses:* Tuition $110 per credit hour for state residents; $270 per credit hour for nonresidents. Fees $480 per year full-time, $110 per semester part-time. *Financial aid:* In 1997–98, 2 fellowships totaling $1,400, 8 teaching assistantships totaling $67,400 were awarded; research assistantships, Federal Work-Study also available. Aid available to part-time students. Financial aid application deadline: 2/15. *Faculty research:* Educational policy, school finance, school law, school restructuring, leadership behavior. • Dr. Larry Dlugosh, Chair, 402-472-3729.

University of Nebraska–Lincoln, Teachers College, Interdepartmental Area of Administration, Curriculum and Instruction, Lincoln, NE 68588. Awards Ed D, PhD, JD/PhD. Accredited by NCATE. Students: 35 full-time (18 women), 145 part-time (87 women); includes 15 minority (4 African Americans, 5 Asian Americans, 3 Hispanics, 3 Native Americans), 15 international. Average age 44. 31 applicants, 55% accepted. In 1997, 42 degrees awarded. *Degree requirements:* Dissertation, comprehensive exam. *Average time to degree:* doctorate–5.6 years full-time. *Entrance requirements:* GRE General Test or MAT, TOEFL (minimum score 500), writing samples. Application deadline: 6/1 (10/1 for spring admission). Application fee: $35. Electronic applications accepted. *Expenses:* Tuition $110 per credit hour for state residents; $270 per credit hour for nonresidents. Fees $480 per year full-time, $110 per semester part-time. *Financial aid:* In 1997–98, 10 fellowships totaling $27,233 were awarded; research assistantships, teaching assistantships, Federal Work-Study also available. Aid available to part-time students. Financial aid application deadline: 2/15. • Dr. Miles Bryant, Graduate Committee Chair, 402-472-3729. E-mail: bryant@unlinfo.unl.edu.

University of Nevada, Las Vegas, College of Education, Department of Educational Leadership, Las Vegas, NV 89154-9900. Offers program in educational administration (M Ed, Ed D, Ed S). Accredited by NCATE. Part-time and evening/weekend programs available. Faculty: 10 full-time (2 women). Students: 11 full-time (5 women), 138 part-time (84 women); includes 18 minority (7 African Americans, 3 Asian Americans, 7 Hispanics, 1 Native American), 3 international. 58 applicants, 78% accepted. In 1997, 47 master's, 6 doctorates awarded. *Degree requirements:* For master's and Ed S, comprehensive exam required, foreign language and thesis not required; for doctorate, dissertation, oral exam required, foreign language not required. *Entrance requirements:* For master's, MAT, minimum GPA of 3.0 during previous 2 years, 2.75 overall; for doctorate, MAT, minimum graduate GPA of 3.5; for Ed S, M Ed or equivalent. Application deadline: 6/15 (priority date; rolling processing; 11/15 for spring admission). Application fee: $40 ($95 for international students). *Expenses:* Tuition $93 per credit for state residents; $93 per credit full-time, $190 per credit part-time for nonresidents. Fees $5570 per year full-time for nonresidents. *Financial aid:* In 1997–98, 3 research assistantships were awarded; teaching assistantships also available. Financial aid application deadline: 3/1. • Dr. Carl Steinhoff, Chair, 702-895-3491. Application contact: Graduate College Admissions Evaluator, 702-895-3320.

University of Nevada, Reno, College of Education, Department of Educational Leadership, Reno, NV 89557. Awards MA, M Ed, MS, Ed D, PhD, Ed S. Accredited by NCATE. Faculty: 7 (2 women). Students: 16 full-time (9 women), 67 part-time (36 women); includes 8 minority (4 African Americans, 1 Asian American, 3 Hispanics). Average age 41. 46 applicants, 70% accepted. In 1997, 17 master's, 3 doctorates awarded. Terminal master's awarded for partial completion of doctoral program. *Degree requirements:* For master's, thesis optional, foreign language not required; for doctorate, dissertation required, foreign language not required. *Entrance requirements:* For master's, GRE, TOEFL (minimum score 500), minimum GPA of 2.75; for doctorate, GRE, TOEFL (minimum score 500), minimum GPA of 3.0. Application deadline: 3/1 (priority date; rolling processing). Application fee: $40. *Expenses:* Tuition $0 for state residents; $5770 per year full-time, $200 per credit part-time for nonresidents. Fees $93 per credit. *Financial aid:* Research assistantships, teaching assistantships, Federal Work-Study, institutionally sponsored loans available. Financial aid application deadline: 3/1. *Faculty research:* Law, finance, supervision, organizational theory, principalship. • Dr. Myrna Matranga, Chair, 702-784-6518. Application contact: Gary L. Peltier, Graduate Director, 702-784-6518 Ext. 2304. E-mail: gpeltier@scs.unr.edu.

University of New Brunswick, Faculty of Education, Division of Educational Foundations, Fredericton, NB E3B 5A3, Canada. Offerings include educational administration (M Ed). *Degree requirements:* Thesis or alternative required, foreign language not required. *Entrance requirements:* TOEFL, TWE, minimum GPA of 3.0. Application deadline: 3/1 (priority date; rolling processing). Application fee: $25.

University of New Hampshire, College of Liberal Arts, Department of Education, Program in Educational Administration, Durham, NH 03824. Awards M Ed, CAGS. Accredited by NCATE. Part-time programs available. Students: 2 full-time (both women), 53 part-time (31 women). Average age 42. 13 applicants, 100% accepted. In 1997, 14 master's, 9 CAGSs awarded. *Degree requirements:* For master's, thesis or alternative required, foreign language not required. *Entrance requirements:* GRE General Test. Application deadline: 4/1 (priority date; rolling processing). Application fee: $50. *Expenses:* Tuition $5440 per year full-time, $302 per credit hour part-time for state residents; $8160 per year (minimum) full-time, $453 per credit hour (minimum) part-time for nonresidents. Fees $868 per year full-time, $15 per year part-time. *Financial aid:* In 1997–98, 4 scholarships (1 to a first-year student) were awarded; research assistantships, teaching assistantships, full and partial tuition waivers, Federal Work-Study, and career-related internships or fieldwork also available. Aid available to part-time students. Financial aid application deadline: 2/15. *Faculty research:* School principalship, supervision, superintendency. • Dr. Charles Ashley, Coordinator, 603-862-3721. Application contact: Dr. Todd DeMitchell, Graduate Coordinator, 603-862-2317.

University of New Mexico, College of Education, Program in Educational Administration, Albuquerque, NM 87131-2039. Offers administration and supervision (Ed D, PhD), educational administration (MA, Ed S). Accredited by NCATE. Part-time programs available. Faculty: 8

Directory: Educational Administration

University of New Mexico (continued)
full-time (3 women), 6 part-time (3 women), 9.50 FTE. Students: 28 full-time (18 women), 33 part-time (23 women); includes 14 minority (1 African American, 2 Asian Americans, 8 Hispanics, 3 Native Americans), 6 international. Average age 39. 20 applicants, 55% accepted. In 1997, 20 master's, 12 Ed Ss awarded. *Degree requirements:* For master's, portfolio or thesis required, foreign language not required; for doctorate, portfolio and project (Ed D), dissertation (PhD) required, foreign language not required. *Entrance requirements:* For master's and Ed S, minimum GPA of 3.0; for doctorate, MAT (Ed D), minimum GPA of 3.0. Application deadline: 2/15. Application fee: $25. *Expenses:* Tuition $2442 per year full-time, $103 per credit hour part-time for state residents; $8691 per year full-time, $103 per credit hour (minimum) part-time for nonresidents. Fees $32 per year. *Financial aid:* In 1997–98, 1 teaching assistantship (to a first-year student) averaging $880 per month and totaling $8,880 was awarded; fellowships, research assistantships, graduate assistantships, and career-related internships or fieldwork also available. *Faculty research:* Group process and adult learning, politics of education, organizational development and leadership, qualitative research methodology. Total annual research expenditures: $111,540. • Dr. Steve Preskill, Graduate Coordinator, 505-277-0441. Fax: 505-277-8427. E-mail: preskill@unm.edu.

University of New Orleans, College of Education, Department of Educational Leadership, Counseling, and Foundations, Program in Educational Leadership and Foundations, New Orleans, LA 70148. Awards M Ed, PhD, Certificate. Accredited by NCATE. Evening/weekend programs available. Students: 198 full-time (144 women), 715 part-time (574 women); includes 247 minority (204 African Americans, 11 Asian Americans, 29 Hispanics, 3 Native Americans), 4 international. Average age 35. 482 applicants, 94% accepted. In 1997, 19 master's, 9 doctorates awarded. Terminal master's awarded for partial completion of doctoral program. *Degree requirements:* For doctorate, variable foreign language requirement, dissertation. *Entrance requirements:* For master's, GRE General Test; for doctorate, GRE General Test (minimum combined score of 1000). Application deadline: 7/1 (priority date; rolling processing). Application fee: $20. *Expenses:* Tuition $2362 per year full-time, $373 per semester (minimum) part-time for state residents; $7888 per year full-time, $1423 per semester (minimum) part-time for nonresidents. Fees $170 per year full-time, $25 per semester (minimum) part-time. *Financial aid:* Fellowships, research assistantships, teaching assistantships, partial tuition waivers, and career-related internships or fieldwork available. • Application contact: Dr. Peggy Kirby, Graduate Coordinator, 504-280-6443. Fax: 504-280-6065. E-mail: pekel@uno.edu.

University of North Alabama, College of Education, Department of Secondary Education, Program in Education Leadership, Florence, AL 35632-0001. Awards Ed S. Accredited by NCATE. Faculty: 8 part-time (2 women). Students: 39 part-time (12 women). Average age 43. In 1997, 9 degrees awarded. *Application deadline:* 7/1 (priority date; rolling processing; 12/1 for spring admission). *Application fee:* $25. *Expenses:* Tuition $2448 per year full-time, $102 per credit hour part-time for state residents; $4896 per year full-time, $204 per credit hour part-time for nonresidents. Fees $3 per semester. *Financial aid:* Application deadline 4/1. • Application contact: Dr. Sue Wilson, Dean of Enrollment Management, 205-765-4316.

University of North Alabama, College of Education, Department of Secondary Education, Programs in Principalship, Superintendency, and Supervision of Instruction, Florence, AL 35632-0001. Offerings in principalship (MA Ed), superintendency (MA Ed), supervision of instruction (MA Ed). Accredited by NCATE. Part-time and evening/weekend programs available. Faculty: 2 part-time (0 women). Students: 2 part-time (0 women). Average age 42. In 1997, 2 degrees awarded. *Degree requirements:* Final written comprehensive exam required, foreign language and thesis not required. *Entrance requirements:* GRE, MAT, or NTE, minimum GPA of 2.5, Alabama Class B Certificate or equivalent, teaching experience. Application deadline: 7/1 (priority date; rolling processing; 12/1 for spring admission). Application fee: $25. *Expenses:* Tuition $2448 per year full-time, $102 per credit hour part-time for state residents; $4896 per year full-time, $204 per credit hour part-time for nonresidents. Fees $3 per semester. *Financial aid:* Federal Work-Study available. Aid available to part-time students. Financial aid application deadline: 4/1. • Application contact: Dr. Sue Wilson, Dean of Enrollment Management, 205-765-4316.

The University of North Carolina at Chapel Hill, School of Education, Programs in Educational Leadership and School Administration, Chapel Hill, NC 27599. Offerings in educational leadership (Ed D), school administration (MSA). Accredited by NCATE. Part-time programs available. Students: 42 full-time (25 women), 25 part-time (16 women). 43 applicants, 77% accepted. *Degree requirements:* For master's, comprehensive exam required, foreign language and thesis not required; for doctorate, dissertation, comprehensive exam required, foreign language not required. *Entrance requirements:* GRE General Test (minimum combined score of 1000), minimum GPA of 3.0 during last 2 years of undergraduate course work. Application deadline: 1/1 (rolling processing). Application fee: $55. *Expenses:* Tuition $1428 per year full-time, $357 per semester (minimum) part-time for state residents; $10,414 per year full-time, $2604 per semester (minimum) part-time for nonresidents. Fees $782 per year full-time, $332 per semester (minimum) part-time. *Financial aid:* Federal Work-Study available. Aid available to part-time students. Financial aid application deadline: 1/1. *Faculty research:* Gender, race, and class issues; school leadership; school finance and reform. • Dr. William Malloy, Coordinator, 919-962-2521. Application contact: Janet Carroll, Registrar, 919-966-1346. Fax: 919-962-1533. E-mail: jscarrol@email.unc.edu.

University of North Carolina at Charlotte, College of Education, Charlotte, NC 28223-0001. Offerings include educational administration (CAS), educational leadership (Ed D), school administration (MSA). One or more programs accredited by NCATE. College faculty: 61 full-time (31 women), 7 part-time (6 women), 62.75 FTE. *Application deadline:* 7/1. *Application fee:* $35. *Tuition:* $1786 per year full-time, $339 per semester (minimum) part-time for state residents; $8914 per year full-time, $2121 per semester (minimum) part-time for nonresidents. • Dr. John M. Nagle, Dean, 704-547-4707. Application contact: Kathy Barringer, Assistant Director of Graduate Admissions, 704-547-3366. Fax: 704-547-3279. E-mail: gradadm@email.uncc.edu.

University of North Carolina at Greensboro, School of Education, Department of Educational Leadership and Cultural Foundations, Greensboro, NC 27412-0001. Offers programs in educational leadership (Ed D, PhD, Ed S), higher education (M Ed), school administration (MSA). Accredited by NCATE. PhD offered jointly with the Program in Curriculum and Teaching. Faculty: 10 full-time (3 women), 8 part-time. Students: 63 full-time (45 women), 28 part-time (11 women); includes 9 minority (7 African Americans, 1 Hispanic, 1 Native American). 55 applicants, 58% accepted. In 1997, 17 master's, 2 doctorates, 1 Ed S awarded. *Degree requirements:* For doctorate, dissertation required, foreign language not required. *Entrance requirements:* GRE General Test. Application deadline: 7/1 (priority date; rolling processing; 11/1 for spring admission). Application fee: $35. *Expenses:* Tuition $1842 per year full-time, $370 per semester (minimum) part-time for state residents; $10,296 per year full-time, $2484 per semester (minimum) part-time for nonresidents. Fees $806 per year full-time, $111 per semester (minimum) part-time. *Financial aid:* In 1997–98, 25 students received aid, including 3 fellowships totaling $5,000, 9 research assistantships totaling $48,500. • Dr. Rick Reitzug, Chair, 336-334-3491.

University of North Carolina at Greensboro, School of Education, Department of Curriculum and Instruction, Program in Supervision, Greensboro, NC 27412-0001. Awards M Ed. Accredited by NCATE. Students: 11 full-time (8 women), 12 part-time (6 women); includes 6 minority (4 African Americans, 1 Hispanic, 1 Native American), 1 international. 13 applicants, 69% accepted. In 1997, 7 degrees awarded. *Entrance requirements:* GRE General Test. Application deadline: 7/1 (priority date; rolling processing; 11/1 for spring admission). Application fee: $35. *Expenses:* Tuition $1842 per year full-time, $370 per semester (minimum) part-time for state residents; $10,296 per year full-time, $2484 per semester (minimum) part-time for nonresidents. Fees $806 per year full-time, $111 per semester (minimum) part-time. *Financial aid:* 3 students received aid; research assistantships available. • Dr. Gerald Ponder, Chair, Department of Curriculum and Instruction, 336-334-3437.

University of North Carolina at Pembroke, Graduate Studies, Department of Education, Program in Educational Administration and Supervision, Pembroke, NC 28372-1510. Awards MA Ed. Accredited by NCATE. Program being phased out; applicants no longer accepted. Part-time and evening/weekend programs available. Faculty: 7 full-time (2 women), 4 part-time (0 women). Students: 1 part-time (0 women); includes 1 minority (Asian American). *Degree requirements:* Comprehensive exam required, thesis optional, foreign language not required. *Average time to degree:* master's–1.5 years full-time, 2.5 years part-time. *Tuition:* $1554 per year full-time, $610 per semester (minimum) part-time for state residents; $8824 per year full-time, $2122 per semester (minimum) part-time for nonresidents. *Financial aid:* Graduate assistantships available. • Dr. Larry Ray Brayboy, Coordinator, 910-521-6283.

University of North Carolina at Pembroke, Graduate Studies, Department of Education, Program in School Administration, Pembroke, NC 28372-1510. Awards MSA. Accredited by NCATE. Program new for fall 1998. *Degree requirements:* Comprehensive exam required, thesis optional, foreign language not required. *Entrance requirements:* GRE General Test or MAT, minimum GPA of 3.0 in major, 2.5 overall. Application deadline: rolling. Application fee: $25. *Tuition:* $1554 per year full-time, $610 per semester (minimum) part-time for state residents; $8824 per year full-time, $2122 per semester (minimum) part-time for nonresidents. *Financial aid:* Application deadline 4/15. • Dr. Larry Ray Brayboy, Coordinator, 910-521-6283.

University of North Carolina at Wilmington, School of Education, Department of Specialty Studies, Wilmington, NC 28403-3201. Offers program in educational administration and supervision (M Ed). Accredited by NCATE. Part-time and evening/weekend programs available. Students: 17 full-time (15 women), 11 part-time (6 women); includes 7 minority (6 African Americans, 1 Native American). Average age 40. 23 applicants, 70% accepted. In 1997, 18 degrees awarded. *Degree requirements:* Comprehensive exam required, foreign language and thesis not required. *Entrance requirements:* GRE General Test, MAT, minimum B average in upper-division undergraduate course work. Application deadline: 7/1 (rolling processing). Application fee: $35. *Tuition:* $1748 per year full-time, $270 per semester (minimum) part-time for state residents; $8882 per year full-time, $2058 per semester (minimum) part-time for nonresidents. *Financial aid:* Assistantships available. Financial aid application deadline: 3/15. • Dr. William Johnston, Chair, 910-962-3719. Application contact: Neil F. Hadley, Dean, Graduate School, 910-962-4117.

University of North Dakota, College of Education and Human Development, Program in Educational Leadership, Grand Forks, ND 58202. Awards M Ed, MS, Ed D, PhD, Ed S. Accredited by NCATE. M Ed offered jointly with North Dakota State University. Part-time and evening/weekend programs available. Postbaccalaureate distance learning degree programs offered (minimal on-campus study). Faculty: 5 full-time (0 women). Students: 9 full-time (5 women), 63 part-time (34 women). 13 applicants, 69% accepted. In 1997, 11 master's, 5 doctorates, 3 Ed Ss awarded. *Degree requirements:* For master's, thesis or alternative; for doctorate, dissertation. *Entrance requirements:* For master's, TOEFL (minimum score 550), minimum GPA of 3.0; for doctorate, TOEFL (minimum score 550), minimum GPA of 3.5. Application deadline: 3/1 (priority date; rolling processing). Application fee: $20. *Financial aid:* In 1997–98, 4 students received aid, including 2 fellowships totaling $4,800, 1 teaching assistantship totaling $3,895, 1 assistantship totaling $7,185; research assistantships, full and partial tuition waivers, Federal Work-Study, institutionally sponsored loans, and career-related internships or fieldwork also available. Financial aid application deadline: 3/15. • Dr. Gerald Bass, Chairperson, 701-777-4255. Fax: 701-777-4393. E-mail: jbass@plains.nodak.edu.

University of Northern Colorado, College of Education, Division of Educational Leadership and Policy Analysis, Program in College Student Personnel Administration, Greeley, CO 80639. Awards PhD. Accredited by NCATE. Faculty: 2 full-time (both women). Students: 24 full-time (14 women), 2 part-time (both women); includes 4 minority (3 African Americans, 1 Hispanic). Average age 35. 9 applicants, 100% accepted. In 1997, 3 degrees awarded. *Degree requirements:* Dissertation, comprehensive exams. *Entrance requirements:* GRE General Test. Application deadline: rolling. Application fee: $35. *Expenses:* Tuition $2327 per year full-time, $129 per credit hour part-time for state residents; $9578 per year full-time, $532 per credit hour part-time for nonresidents. Fees $752 per year full-time, $184 per semester (minimum) part-time. *Financial aid:* In 1997–98, 21 students received aid, including 12 fellowships (3 to first-year students) totaling $12,065, 16 graduate assistantships (4 to first-year students) totaling $166,340; teaching assistantships also available. Financial aid application deadline: 3/1. • Dr. Susan G. Spooner, Coordinator, 970-351-1682.

University of Northern Colorado, College of Education, Division of Educational Leadership and Policy Analysis, Program in Educational Leadership, Greeley, CO 80639. Awards MA, Ed D, Ed S. Accredited by NCATE. Faculty: 7 full-time (5 women), 1 part-time (0 women). Students: 36 full-time (15 women), 41 part-time (20 women); includes 7 minority (1 African American, 4 Hispanics, 2 Native Americans), 1 international. Average age 39. 27 applicants, 78% accepted. In 1997, 24 master's, 9 doctorates, 2 Ed Ss awarded. *Degree requirements:* For master's, thesis or alternative, comprehensive exams; for doctorate and Ed S, thesis/dissertation, comprehensive exams. *Entrance requirements:* For doctorate, GRE General Test. Application deadline: rolling. Application fee: $35. *Expenses:* Tuition $2327 per year full-time, $129 per credit hour part-time for state residents; $9578 per year full-time, $532 per credit hour part-time for nonresidents. Fees $752 per year full-time, $184 per semester (minimum) part-time. *Financial aid:* In 1997–98, 27 students received aid, including 9 fellowships (2 to first-year students) totaling $16,470, 2 teaching assistantships (1 to a first-year student) totaling $22,491, 7 graduate assistantships (2 to first-year students) totaling $70,700. Financial aid application deadline: 3/1. • Dr. Bruce Barnett, Director, Division of Educational Leadership and Policy Analysis, 970-351-2861.

University of Northern Iowa, College of Education, Department of Educational Leadership, Counseling, and Postsecondary Education, Program in Administration and Supervision, Cedar Falls, IA 50614. Offers educational administration (Ed D), elementary principal (MA Ed), secondary principal (MA Ed). Part-time and evening/weekend programs available. Faculty: 10 full-time (3 women). Students: 4 full-time (0 women), 50 part-time (22 women); includes 5 minority (all African Americans), 2 international. Average age 33. 41 applicants, 85% accepted. In 1997, 31 master's, 2 doctorates awarded. *Degree requirements:* For master's, thesis or alternative required, foreign language not required; for doctorate, dissertation required, foreign language not required. *Entrance requirements:* For master's, minimum GPA of 3.5, 3 years of educational experience; for doctorate, minimum GPA of 3.2, 3 years of educational experience, master's degree. Application deadline: 8/1 (priority date; rolling processing). Application fee: $20 ($30 for international students). *Expenses:* Tuition $3166 per year full-time, $176 per hour part-time for state residents; $7805 per year full-time, $176 per hour part-time for nonresidents. Fees $194 per year full-time, $12.50 per semester (minimum) part-time. *Financial aid:* Full and partial tuition waivers, Federal Work-Study, and career-related internships or fieldwork available. Aid available to part-time students. Financial aid application deadline: 3/1. • Dr. Michael D. Waggoner, Head, Department of Educational Leadership, Counseling, and Postsecondary Education, 319-273-2605.

University of Northern Iowa, College of Education, Department of Educational Leadership, Counseling, and Postsecondary Education, Program in College/University Student Services, Cedar Falls, IA 50614. Awards MA Ed. Students: 16 full-time (11 women), 7 part-time (5 women); includes 3 minority (1 African American, 1 Asian American, 1 Native American). Average age 33. 12 applicants, 92% accepted. In 1997, 14 degrees awarded. *Degree requirements:* Comprehensive exams, research paper required, foreign language and thesis not required. *Entrance requirements:* Minimum GPA of 3.5, 3 years of educational experience. Application deadline: 8/1 (priority date; rolling processing). Application fee: $20 ($30 for international students). *Expenses:* Tuition $3166 per year full-time, $176 per hour part-time for state residents; $7805 per year full-time, $176 per hour part-time for nonresidents. Fees $194 per year full-time, $12.50 per semester (minimum) part-time. *Financial aid:* Scholarships, full tuition waivers, Federal Work-Study, and career-related internships or fieldwork available.

Financial aid application deadline: 3/1. • Dr. Michael D. Waggoner, Head, Department of Educational Leadership, Counseling, and Postsecondary Education, 319-273-2605.

University of North Florida, College of Education, Division of Educational Services and Research, Program in Educational Leadership, Jacksonville, FL 32224-2645. Offers administration (M Ed), educational leadership (Ed D). Accredited by NCATE. Part-time and evening/weekend programs available. Students: 24 full-time (13 women), 172 part-time (133 women); includes 43 minority (37 African Americans, 1 Asian American, 5 Hispanics). Average age 39. 17 applicants, 71% accepted. In 1997, 36 master's, 3 doctorates awarded. *Degree requirements:* For doctorate, dissertation required, foreign language not required. *Entrance requirements:* For master's, GRE General Test (minimum combined score of 1000), minimum GPA of 3.0; for doctorate, GRE General Test, master's degree. Application deadline: 3/15 (priority date; rolling processing). Application fee: $20. *Tuition:* $3388 per year full-time, $141 per credit hour part-time for state residents; $11,634 per year full-time, $485 per credit hour part-time for nonresidents. *Financial aid:* Fellowships, research assistantships, Federal Work-Study, institutionally sponsored loans, and career-related internships or fieldwork available. Aid available to part-time students. *Faculty research:* Site-based management, supervision, assessment, policy, finance. • Yiping Wan, Director, 904-646-2990. Fax: 904-646-1025.

University of North Texas, College of Education, Department of Teacher Education and Administration, Program in Educational Administration, Denton, TX 76203-6737. Awards M Ed, Ed D, PhD. Accredited by NCATE. *Degree requirements:* For doctorate, dissertation. *Entrance requirements:* For master's, GRE General Test (minimum score 350 on each section, 800 combined); for doctorate, GRE General Test (minimum score 400 on each section, 1000 combined). Application deadline: 7/17. Application fee: $25 ($50 for international students). *Tuition:* $2063 per year full-time, $815 per year part-time for state residents; $5897 per year full-time, $2100 per year part-time for nonresidents. *Financial aid:* Fellowships, research assistantships, teaching assistantships, Federal Work-Study, institutionally sponsored loans, and career-related internships or fieldwork available. Financial aid application deadline: 4/1. • Application contact: Jane Huffman, Adviser, 940-565-2920.

University of Oklahoma, College of Education, Department of Educational Leadership and Policy Studies, Program in Educational Administration and Curriculum Supervision, Norman, OK 73019-0390. Offers elementary school administration (M Ed, Ed D, PhD), general school administration (M Ed, Ed D, PhD), secondary school administration (M Ed, Ed D, PhD). Accredited by NCATE. Part-time and evening/weekend programs available. Students: 15 full-time (7 women), 82 part-time (55 women); includes 13 minority (5 African Americans, 2 Asian Americans, 1 Hispanic, 5 Native Americans), 2 international. Average age 39. 18 applicants, 89% accepted. In 1997, 50 master's, 9 doctorates awarded. Terminal master's awarded for partial completion of doctoral program. *Degree requirements:* For master's, comprehensive exam required, foreign language and thesis not required; for doctorate, variable foreign language requirement, dissertation, general exam. *Entrance requirements:* For master's, TOEFL (minimum score 550), 12 hours of course work in education; for doctorate, GRE General Test, TOEFL (minimum score 550), master's degree, minimum graduate GPA of 3.25. Application deadline: 6/1 (priority date; 10/1 for spring admission). Application fee: $25. *Expenses:* Tuition $1920 per year full-time, $80 per credit hour part-time for state residents; $6108 per year full-time, $255 per credit hour part-time for nonresidents. Fees $468 per year full-time, $12 per semester (minimum) part-time. *Faculty research:* Education law, policy development, site-based management. Total annual research expenditures: $18,000. • Application contact: Edward Chance, Graduate Liaison, 405-325-4202.

University of Oregon, Graduate School, College of Education, Department of Educational Technology, Leadership and Administration, Department of Educational Policy and Management, Eugene, OR 97403. Offers programs in computer and education (PhD), educational administration (MS, D Ed), educational policy and foundations (MS), foundations and research (PhD), higher education (MS), management and leadership (PhD), organization and governance (PhD). Faculty: 8 full-time (1 woman), 6 part-time (1 woman), 10.29 FTE. Students: 117 full-time (75 women), 45 part-time (18 women); includes 25 minority (2 African Americans, 7 Asian Americans, 12 Hispanics, 4 Native Americans), 23 international. 105 applicants, 64% accepted. In 1997, 47 master's, 7 doctorates awarded. Terminal master's awarded for partial completion of doctoral program. *Degree requirements:* For master's, exam, paper, or project required, foreign language not required; for doctorate, computer language, dissertation, comprehensive exam required, foreign language not required. *Entrance requirements:* MAT, TOEFL (minimum score 550). Application deadline: 3/15. Application fee: $50. *Tuition:* $6429 per year full-time, $873 per quarter (minimum) part-time for state residents; $10,857 per year full-time, $1360 per quarter (minimum) part-time for nonresidents. *Financial aid:* In 1997–98, 35 teaching assistantships (6 to first-year students) were awarded; research assistantships and career-related internships or fieldwork also available. *Faculty research:* Collective bargaining, community colleges, instructional leadership, international education. • Application contact: Tammara Hirte, Graduate Secretary, 541-346-1361. Fax: 541-346-5174.

University of Pennsylvania, Graduate School of Education, Division of Educational Leadership, Program in Educational Policy and Leadership, Philadelphia, PA 19104. Awards MS Ed, Ed D, PhD. Part-time programs available. Faculty: 8 full-time (4 women), 4 part-time (2 women). Students: 165; includes 11 minority (8 African Americans, 1 Asian American, 1 Hispanic, 1 Native American), 4 international. In 1997, 4 master's, 10 doctorates awarded. *Degree requirements:* For master's, thesis, comprehensive exam required, foreign language not required; for doctorate, dissertation, comprehensive and oral exams required, foreign language not required. *Average time to degree:* master's–1 year full-time. *Entrance requirements:* For master's, GRE or MAT; for doctorate, GRE. Application fee: $65. *Expenses:* Tuition $22,716 per year full-time, $2876 per course part-time. Fees $1484 per year full-time, $181 per course part-time. *Financial aid:* Service scholarships, Federal Work-Study, institutionally sponsored loans, and career-related internships or fieldwork available. Aid available to part-time students. Financial aid application deadline: 1/2; applicants required to submit FAFSA. *Faculty research:* Public policy, curriculum and instruction, organization theory/leadership, school reform. • Dr. Harris Sokoloff, Acting Director, 215-898-7371. Fax: 215-898-4399. Application contact: Rona Rosenberg, Administrative Coordinator, 215-898-7364.

University of Phoenix, Graduate Programs, Programs in Education, Specialization in Administration and Supervision, 4615 East Elwood St, PO Box 52069, Phoenix, AZ 85072-2069. Awards MA Ed. Programs offered at campuses in Colorado, Nevada, Phoenix, Puerto Rico, Tucson, Utah, and at the Center for Distance Education. *Degree requirements:* Thesis or alternative. *Entrance requirements:* Comprehensive cognitive assessment (COCA). Application deadline: rolling. Application fee: $50. *Tuition:* $197 per credit hour. • Application contact: Campus Information Center, 602-966-9577.

University of Pittsburgh, School of Education, Department of Administrative and Policy Studies, Program in Educational Leadership, Pittsburgh, PA 15260. Awards MA, M Ed, Ed D. Part-time and evening/weekend programs available. 88 applicants, 98% accepted. *Degree requirements:* Thesis/dissertation required, foreign language not required. *Average time to degree:* master's–2 years full-time, 4 years part-time; doctorate–4 years full-time, 6 years part-time. *Entrance requirements:* GRE General Test, TOEFL (minimum score 650). Application deadline: 2/1 (priority date; rolling processing; 11/15 for spring admission). Application fee: $30 ($40 for international students). *Expenses:* Tuition $8018 per year full-time, $329 per credit part-time for state residents; $16,508 per year full-time, $680 per credit part-time for nonresidents. Fees $480 per year full-time, $180 per year part-time. *Financial aid:* In 1997–98, 4 fellowships were awarded; partial tuition waivers, Federal Work-Study, institutionally sponsored loans also available. Aid available to part-time students. Financial aid application deadline: 5/1; applicants required to submit FAFSA. • Application contact: Jackie Harden, Manager, 412-648-7060. Fax: 412-648-1899. E-mail: jackie@sched.fsl.pitt.edu.

University of Puerto Rico, Río Piedras, College of Education, Program in School Administration, San Juan, PR 00931. Awards M Ed, Ed D. Part-time programs available. *Degree requirements:* Thesis/dissertation required, foreign language not required. *Entrance requirements:* For master's, PAEG, minimum GPA of 3.0; for doctorate, GRE or PAEG, interview, master's degree, minimum GPA of 3.0. Application deadline: 2/21. Application fee: $17.

University of Puget Sound, School of Education, Program in Education, Tacoma, WA 98416-0005. Offerings include educational administration (M Ed). Accredited by NCATE. Program faculty: 12 full-time (9 women), 3 part-time (all women), 12.83 FTE. *Average time to degree:* master's–2 years full-time. *Entrance requirements:* GRE General Test (score in 50th percentile or higher), minimum GPA of 3.0. Application deadline: 2/1. Application fee: $40. *Expenses:* Tuition $19,640 per year full-time, $2480 per course part-time. Fees $155 per year. • Dr. Carol Merz, Dean, School of Education, 253-756-3377.

University of Redlands, Alfred North Whitehead College for Lifelong Learning, Program in Administrative Services, PO Box 3080, Redlands, CA 92373-0999. Awards MA. Students: 17 full-time (11 women); includes 5 minority (1 African American, 4 Hispanics). Average age 41. In 1997, 5 degrees awarded. *Entrance requirements:* Interview. Application deadline: 9/1 (priority date; rolling processing; 3/1 for spring admission). Application fee: $40. Electronic applications accepted. • Dr. Carol Franklin, Director, 909-793-2121 Ext. 4014.

University of Redlands, Alfred North Whitehead College for Lifelong Learning, Program in Pupil Personnel Services, PO Box 3080, Redlands, CA 92373-0999. Awards MA. Students: 66 full-time (43 women); includes 35 minority (9 African Americans, 4 Asian Americans, 20 Hispanics, 2 Native Americans). Average age 36. In 1997, 26 degrees awarded. *Application deadline:* 9/1 (priority date; rolling processing; 3/1 for spring admission). *Application fee:* $40. Electronic applications accepted. • Dr. Drage H. Watson, Director, 909-793-2121 Ext. 4012.

University of Regina, Faculty of Graduate Studies and Research, Faculty of Education, Department of Educational Administration, Regina, SK S4S 0A2, Canada. Awards M Ed, Diploma. Students: 3 full-time, 70 part-time. 25 applicants, 80% accepted. In 1997, 8 master's, 8 Diplomas awarded. *Degree requirements:* For master's, practicum, project, or thesis required, thesis optional, foreign language not required. *Entrance requirements:* For master's, TOEFL (minimum score 580), bachelor's degree in education, 2 years of teaching experience. Application deadline: 3/15 (12/15 for spring admission). Application fee: $0. *Tuition:* $196 per credit for Canadian residents; $383 per credit for nonresidents. *Financial aid:* Fellowships, research assistantships, teaching assistantships available. Financial aid application deadline: 6/15. • Dr. R. Dolmage, Chair, 306-585-4816. Application contact: Dr. M. Taylor, Chair, Graduate Programs, 306-585-4606. Fax: 306-585-4880. E-mail: marlene.taylor@uregina.ca.

University of St. Thomas, School of Education, Program in Educational Leadership and Administration, St. Paul, MN 55105-1096. Awards MA, Ed D, Certificate, Ed S. Accredited by NCATE. Certificate new for fall 1998. Students: 11 full-time (5 women), 277 part-time (200 women). Average age 41. 39 applicants, 95% accepted. In 1997, 24 master's, 16 doctorates, 49 other advanced degrees awarded. *Degree requirements:* For master's, thesis required (for some programs), foreign language not required. *Entrance requirements:* For master's, MAT, minimum GPA of 2.75; for doctorate, MAT, minimum graduate GPA of 3.5; for other advanced degree, MAT, minimum graduate GPA of 3.25. Application deadline: 2/1 (priority date; rolling processing). Application fee: $50. *Tuition:* $375 per credit hour (minimum). *Financial aid:* In 1997–98, 26 grants (4 to first-year students) totaling $61,328 were awarded; research assistantships also available. Financial aid application deadline: 4/1. • Dr. Mary Katherine Hamilton, Director, 612-962-5287. Fax: 612-962-5169.

University of San Diego, School of Education, Division of Educational Leadership, San Diego, CA 92110-2492. Awards MA, M Ed, Ed D. Ed D offered jointly with San Diego State University. Part-time and evening/weekend programs available. Faculty: 2 full-time (both women), 1 part-time (0 women). Students: 13 full-time (10 women), 105 part-time (63 women); includes 22 minority (4 African Americans, 7 Asian Americans, 10 Hispanics, 1 Native American), 15 international. 40 applicants, 83% accepted. In 1997, 13 master's, 9 doctorates awarded. *Degree requirements:* For master's, thesis (for some programs), portfolio required, foreign language not required; for doctorate, dissertation, comprehensive exam required, foreign language not required. *Entrance requirements:* For master's, TOEFL (minimum score 580), TWE, minimum GPA of 2.75; for doctorate, GRE or MAT, master's degree. Application deadline: 5/1 (priority date; rolling processing). Application fee: $45. *Expenses:* Tuition $585 per unit (minimum). Fees $50 per year full-time, $30 per year part-time. *Financial aid:* Fellowships, assistantships, stipends, Federal Work-Study, institutionally sponsored loans, and career-related internships or fieldwork available. Aid available to part-time students. Financial aid application deadline: 5/1; applicants required to submit FAFSA. *Faculty research:* Administrative behavior, management, change, policy making. • Dr. Mary Scherr, Coordinator, 619-260-4600 Ext. 2274. Fax: 619-260-6835. E-mail: scherr@acusd.edu. Application contact: Mary Jane Tiernan, Director of Graduate Admissions, 619-260-4524. Fax: 619-260-4158. E-mail: grads@acusd.edu.

University of San Francisco, School of Education, Department of Organization and Leadership, San Francisco, CA 94117-1080. Awards MA, Ed D. Faculty: 11 full-time (4 women), 10 part-time (5 women). Students: 121 full-time (83 women), 84 part-time (52 women); includes 70 minority (29 African Americans, 14 Asian Americans, 25 Hispanics, 2 Native Americans), 2 international. Average age 37. 91 applicants, 92% accepted. In 1997, 32 master's, 26 doctorates awarded. *Degree requirements:* For doctorate, dissertation required, foreign language not required. *Application fee:* $40. *Tuition:* $658 per unit (minimum). *Financial aid:* 80 students received aid; fellowships, research assistantships, teaching assistantships available. Financial aid application deadline: 3/2. • Dr. Ellen Herda, Chair, 415-422-6551.

University of San Francisco, School of Education, Department of Private School Education, San Francisco, CA 94117-1080. Offers programs in Catholic school teaching (MA), private school administration (MA, Ed D). Faculty: 8 full-time (2 women), 10 part-time (7 women). Students: 13 full-time (4 women), 56 part-time (30 women); includes 15 minority (2 African Americans, 3 Asian Americans, 10 Hispanics), 4 international. Average age 41. 40 applicants, 98% accepted. In 1997, 32 master's, 4 doctorates awarded. *Degree requirements:* For doctorate, dissertation required, foreign language not required. *Application fee:* $40. *Tuition:* $658 per unit (minimum). *Financial aid:* 67 students received aid; fellowships, research assistantships, teaching assistantships available. Financial aid application deadline: 3/2. • Sr. Mary Peter Travis, Chair, 415-422-6226.

University of Sarasota, College of Education, Program in Educational Leadership, Sarasota, FL 34235-8246. Awards MA Ed, Ed D. Part-time and evening/weekend programs available. Postbaccalaureate distance learning degree programs offered (minimal on-campus study). Faculty: 3 full-time (0 women), 10 part-time (5 women). Students: 124 full-time (62 women), 278 part-time (139 women). *Degree requirements:* For master's, thesis optional; for doctorate, dissertation, comprehensive exam. *Average time to degree:* master's–2 years full-time, 3 years part-time; doctorate–3 years full-time, 4 years part-time. *Entrance requirements:* For master's, TOEFL (minimum score 500); for doctorate, TOEFL (minimum score 550), minimum undergraduate GPA of 3.0. Application deadline: rolling. Application fee: $50. *Financial aid:* Available to part-time students. Financial aid applicants required to submit FAFSA. • Application contact: Kathy Ketterer, Admissions Representative, 800-331-5995. Fax: 941-371-8910. E-mail: kathy_ketterer@embanet.com.

University of Saskatchewan, College of Education, Department of Educational Administration, Saskatoon, SK S7N 5A2, Canada. Awards M Ed, PhD, Diploma. Part-time programs available. *Degree requirements:* For doctorate, dissertation. *Entrance requirements:* For master's, CANTEST (minimum score 4.5) or International English Language Testing System (minimum score 6) or Michigan English Language Assessment Battery (minimum score 80), or TOEFL (minimum score 550; average 560); for doctorate, TOEFL; for Diploma, International English Language Testing System (minimum score 6) or Michigan English Language Assessment Battery (minimum score 80), or TOEFL (minimum score 550). Application deadline: 7/1 (priority date; rolling processing). Application fee: $0.

Directory: Educational Administration

University of Scranton, Department of Education, Program in Educational Administration, Scranton, PA 18510-4622. Offers elementary school administration (MS), secondary school administration (MS). Accredited by NCATE. Part-time and evening/weekend programs available. Students: 1 (woman) full-time, 17 part-time (5 women). Average age 30. 12 applicants, 100% accepted. In 1997, 6 degrees awarded. *Degree requirements:* Comprehensive exam required, foreign language and thesis not required. *Entrance requirements:* TOEFL (minimum score 500), minimum GPA of 2.75. Application deadline: rolling. Application fee: $35. *Expenses:* Tuition $465 per credit. Fees $25 per semester. *Financial aid:* Teaching assistantships, Federal Work-Study, and career-related internships or fieldwork available. Aid available to part-time students. Financial aid application deadline: 3/1. • Dr. Robert M. Weir Jr., Director, 717-941-6142. Fax: 717-941-7401.

University of Sioux Falls, Program in Education, Sioux Falls, SD 57105-1699. Offerings include leadership (M Ed). Accredited by NCATE. Summer admission only. Program faculty: 5 full-time (4 women), 7 part-time (4 women). *Entrance requirements:* Minimum GPA of 3.0, 1 year of teaching experience. Application deadline: rolling. Application fee: $25. *Tuition:* $195 per credit hour. • Dr. Donna Goldammer, Chair, 605-331-6713. Application contact: Dr. Nancy Johnson, Director of Graduate Studies, 605-331-6710. Fax: 605-331-6615. E-mail: nancy.johnson@thecoo.edu.

University of South Alabama, College of Education, Department of Educational Leadership and Foundations, Mobile, AL 36688-0002. Awards M Ed, Ed S. Accredited by NCATE. Part-time programs available. Faculty: 6 full-time (1 woman). Students: 10 full-time (2 women), 46 part-time (37 women); includes 12 minority (all African Americans), 1 international. 21 applicants, 95% accepted. In 1997, 6 Ed Ss awarded. *Degree requirements:* For master's, comprehensive exam required, foreign language and thesis not required. *Entrance requirements:* For master's, GRE General Test (minimum combined score of 1000) or MAT (minimum score 37). Application deadline: 9/1 (priority date; rolling processing). Application fee: $25. *Financial aid:* In 1997–98, 1 research assistantship was awarded. Aid available to part-time students. Financial aid application deadline: 4/1. • Dr. Joseph Newman, Chairman, 334-460-7141.

University of South Carolina, Graduate School, College of Education, Department of Educational Leadership and Policies, Program in Educational Administration, Columbia, SC 29208. Awards MA, M Ed, PhD, Ed S. Accredited by NCATE. Part-time and evening/weekend programs available. Students: 156 full-time (94 women), 303 part-time (190 women); includes 110 minority (104 African Americans, 2 Asian Americans, 2 Hispanics, 2 Native Americans), 8 international. Average age 38. In 1997, 77 master's, 17 doctorates, 17 Ed Ss awarded. *Degree requirements:* For master's, thesis (for some programs), comprehensive exam; for doctorate, 1 foreign language (computer language can substitute), dissertation, comprehensive exam. *Entrance requirements:* For master's and Ed S, GRE General Test or MAT; for doctorate, GRE General Test or MAT, interview. Application deadline: 1/15 (priority date; rolling processing). Application fee: $35. Electronic applications accepted. *Expenses:* Tuition $3894 per year full-time, $193 per credit hour part-time for state residents; $8114 per year full-time, $404 per credit hour part-time for nonresidents. Fees $125 per year full-time, $37 per semester (minimum) part-time. *Financial aid:* Assistantships, Federal Work-Study, institutionally sponsored loans, and career-related internships or fieldwork available. • Application contact: Office of Intercollegiate Teacher Education and Student Affairs, 803-777-6732. Fax: 803-777-3068.

University of South Carolina, Graduate School, College of Education, Department of Educational Leadership and Policies, Program in Student and Personnel Services in Higher Education, Columbia, SC 29208. Awards MA, M Ed. Accredited by NCATE. Part-time and evening/weekend programs available. Faculty: 5 full-time (1 woman), 2 part-time (1 woman). Students: 56 full-time (43 women), 19 part-time (12 women); includes 13 minority (10 African Americans, 3 Hispanics). Average age 28. In 1997, 55 degrees awarded (100% found work related to degree). *Degree requirements:* Thesis (for some programs), comprehensive exam required, foreign language not required. *Entrance requirements:* GRE General Test or MAT. Application deadline: 7/15 (priority date; rolling processing). Application fee: $35. Electronic applications accepted. *Expenses:* Tuition $3894 per year full-time, $193 per credit hour part-time for state residents; $8114 per year full-time, $404 per credit hour part-time for nonresidents. Fees $125 per year full-time, $37 per semester (minimum) part-time. *Financial aid:* Teaching assistantships, assistantships, partial tuition waivers, Federal Work-Study, institutionally sponsored loans, and career-related internships or fieldwork available. *Faculty research:* Minorities in higher education, community college transfer problem, federal role in educational research. • Application contact: Office of Intercollegiate Teacher Education and Student Affairs, 803-777-6732. Fax: 803-777-3068.

University of South Dakota, School of Education, Division of Educational Administration, Vermillion, SD 57069-2390. Awards MA, Ed D, Ed S, JD/MA. Accredited by NCATE. Part-time programs available. Faculty: 8 full-time (2 women), 2 part-time (0 women). Students: 74 full-time (36 women), 58 part-time (32 women); includes 13 minority (2 African Americans, 9 Asian Americans, 2 Native Americans), 6 international. 48 applicants, 54% accepted. In 1997, 50 master's, 22 doctorates awarded. *Degree requirements:* For master's, thesis required (for some programs), foreign language not required; for doctorate, dissertation required, foreign language not required. *Entrance requirements:* For master's and doctorate, GRE General Test, MAT. Application deadline: rolling. Application fee: $15. *Expenses:* Tuition $1530 per year full-time, $85 per credit hour part-time for state residents; $4518 per year full-time, $251 per credit hour part-time for nonresidents. Fees $792 per year full-time, $44 per credit hour part-time. *Financial aid:* Teaching assistantships available. • Dr. Phil Vik, Chair, 605-677-5260.

University of Southern California, Graduate School, School of Education, Department of Counseling Psychology, Los Angeles, CA 90089. Offerings include college student personnel services (MS), pupil personnel services (K–12) (MS). *Entrance requirements:* GRE General Test. Application fee: $55. *Expenses:* Tuition $16,944 per year full-time, $706 per unit part-time. Fees $414 per year full-time, $32 per year part-time. • Dr. Michael Newcomb, Chair.

University of Southern California, Graduate School, School of Education, Department of Educational Administration and Policy, Los Angeles, CA 90089. Offers programs in administration and policy (PhD), educational leadership (MS), international and intercultural education (MS). Students: 65 full-time (36 women), 151 part-time (82 women); includes 80 minority (30 African Americans, 20 Asian Americans, 30 Hispanics), 13 international. Average age 36. 122 applicants, 71% accepted. In 1997, 5 master's, 58 doctorates awarded. *Degree requirements:* For doctorate, dissertation. *Entrance requirements:* GRE General Test. Application deadline: 7/1 (priority date; 11/1 for spring admission). Application fee: $55. *Expenses:* Tuition $16,944 per year full-time, $706 per unit part-time. Fees $414 per year full-time, $32 per year part-time. *Financial aid:* In 1997–98, 16 fellowships, 1 research assistantship, 9 teaching assistantships, 12 scholarships were awarded; Federal Work-Study, institutionally sponsored loans also available. Aid available to part-time students. Financial aid application deadline: 2/15; applicants required to submit FAFSA. • Dr. William Tierney, Chair.

University of Southern Maine, College of Education and Human Development, Educational Leadership Program, Portland, ME 04104-9300. Awards MS Ed, CAS. Accredited by NCATE. Part-time and evening/weekend programs available. Faculty: 8 full-time (2 women). Students: 23 full-time (16 women), 103 part-time (57 women). 63 applicants, 94% accepted. In 1997, 20 master's awarded. *Degree requirements:* Thesis or alternative required, foreign language not required. *Entrance requirements:* For master's, GRE General Test (minimum combined score of 900), MAT (minimum score 40), TOEFL (minimum score 550). Application deadline: 2/1 (9/15 for spring admission). Application fee: $25. *Expenses:* Tuition $178 per credit hour for state residents; $267 per credit hour (minimum) for nonresidents. Fees $282 per year full-time, $83 per semester (minimum) part-time. *Financial aid:* Research assistantships, Federal Work-Study, institutionally sponsored loans, and career-related internships or fieldwork available. Financial aid application deadline: 3/1; applicants required to submit FAFSA. • Dr. Margo Wood, Chair, Professional Education Department, 207-780-5400. Application contact: Teresa Belsan, Admissions and Academic Counselor, 207-780-5306. Fax: 207-780-5315. E-mail: belsan@usm.maine.edu.

University of Southern Mississippi, College of Education and Psychology, Department of Educational Leadership and Research, Hattiesburg, MS 39406-5167. Offers programs in adult education (M Ed, Ed D, PhD, Ed S), educational administration (M Ed, Ed D, PhD, Ed S). Faculty: 14 full-time (3 women), 4 part-time (1 woman). Students: 58 full-time (37 women), 164 part-time (95 women); includes 37 minority (34 African Americans, 2 Asian Americans, 1 Native American), 4 international. Average age 40. 86 applicants, 81% accepted. In 1997, 105 master's awarded; 24 doctorates awarded; 26 Ed Ss awarded (100% found work related to degree). *Degree requirements:* For doctorate, 2 foreign languages, dissertation. *Entrance requirements:* For master's, GRE General Test, minimum GPA of 2.75; for doctorate, GRE General Test, minimum GPA of 3.5; for Ed S, GRE General Test, minimum GPA of 3.25. Application deadline: 8/9 (priority date; rolling processing). Application fee: $0 ($25 for international students). *Tuition:* $2870 per year full-time, $137 per credit hour part-time for state residents; $5972 per year full-time, $172 per credit hour part-time for nonresidents. *Financial aid:* Research assistantships, Federal Work-Study, institutionally sponsored loans, and career-related internships or fieldwork available. Financial aid application deadline: 3/15. *Faculty research:* Supervision, learning styles, education finance, higher education organization. • Dr. Arthur Southerland, Chair, 601-266-4579.

University of South Florida, College of Education, Department of Educational Leadership, Program in Educational Leadership, Tampa, FL 33620-9951. Awards M Ed, Ed D, Ed S. Accredited by NCATE. Part-time and evening/weekend programs available. Students: 37 full-time (29 women), 254 part-time (185 women); includes 40 minority (20 African Americans, 3 Asian Americans, 17 Hispanics), 5 international. Average age 37. 72 applicants, 75% accepted. In 1997, 106 master's, 8 doctorates, 1 Ed S awarded. *Degree requirements:* For doctorate, dissertation, 2 tools of research in foreign language, statistics, and/or computers. *Entrance requirements:* For master's, GRE General Test (minimum combined score of 1000), minimum GPA of 3.5 in last 60 hours; for doctorate, GRE General Test (minimum combined score of 1000), minimum GPA of 3.0 (undergraduate) or 3.5 (graduate); for Ed S, GRE General Test (minimum combined score of 1000). Application deadline: 6/1 (10/15 for spring admission). Application fee: $20. Electronic applications accepted. *Tuition:* $142 per credit hour for state residents; $486 per credit hour for nonresidents. *Financial aid:* Federal Work-Study, institutionally sponsored loans available. Aid available to part-time students. Financial aid applicants required to submit FAFSA. • Application contact: Bill Benjamin, Co-Coordinator, 813-974-3420. Fax: 813-974-3366. E-mail: benjamin@tempest.coedu.usf.edu.

University of Southwestern Louisiana, College of Education, Graduate Studies and Research in Education, Program in Administration and Supervision, Lafayette, LA 70503. Awards M Ed. Accredited by NCATE. Faculty: 12 full-time (3 women). Students: 1 (woman) full-time, 47 part-time (31 women); includes 6 minority (all African Americans). 23 applicants, 65% accepted. In 1997, 14 degrees awarded. *Degree requirements:* Thesis or alternative required, foreign language not required. *Entrance requirements:* GRE General Test, teaching certificate. Application deadline: 8/15. Application fee: $5 ($15 for international students). *Tuition:* $2012 per year full-time, $300 per semester (minimum) part-time for state residents; $7244 per year full-time, $300 per semester (minimum) part-time for nonresidents. *Financial aid:* Fellowships, research assistantships, Federal Work-Study available. Financial aid application deadline: 5/1. • Dr. Daniel Jordan, Director, Graduate Studies and Research in Education, 318-482-6747.

University of Tennessee at Chattanooga, School of Education, Education Graduate Studies Division, Chattanooga, TN 37403-2598. Offerings include elementary administration (M Ed), secondary administration (M Ed). One or more programs accredited by NCATE. Division faculty: 15 full-time (5 women), 7 part-time (3 women). *Degree requirements:* Comprehensive exams required, thesis optional, foreign language not required. *Entrance requirements:* GRE General Test or MAT, teaching certificate. Application deadline: rolling. Application fee: $25. *Tuition:* $2864 per year full-time, $160 per credit hour part-time for state residents; $6806 per year full-time, $379 per credit hour part-time for nonresidents. • Dr. Tom Bibler, Acting Head, 423-755-4211. Fax: 423-755-5380. E-mail: tom-bibler@utc.edu. Application contact: Dr. Deborah Arfken, Assistant Provost for Graduate Studies, 423-755-4667. Fax: 423-755-4478.

University of Tennessee, Knoxville, College of Education, Program in Education I, Knoxville, TN 37996. Offerings include educational administration and supervision/higher education (PhD). *Degree requirements:* 1 foreign language (computer language can substitute), dissertation. *Entrance requirements:* GRE General Test, TOEFL (minimum score 550), minimum GPA of 2.7. Application deadline: 2/1 (priority date; rolling processing). Application fee: $35. Electronic applications accepted. *Tuition:* $3354 per year full-time, $181 per semester hour part-time for state residents; $8410 per year full-time, $462 per semester hour part-time for nonresidents. • Dr. Tom George, Associate Dean, 423-974-0907. Fax: 423-974-8718. E-mail: tgeorge1@utk.edu.

University of Tennessee, Knoxville, College of Education, Program in Education II, Knoxville, TN 37996. Offerings include educational administration and supervision (Ed D, Ed S), leadership for teaching and learning (Ed D). One or more programs accredited by NCATE. *Degree requirements:* For doctorate, dissertation required, foreign language not required; for Ed S, thesis optional, foreign language not required. *Entrance requirements:* For doctorate, GRE General Test, TOEFL (minimum score 550), minimum GPA of 2.7; for Ed S, TOEFL (minimum score 550), GRE General Test, minimum GPA of 2.7. Application deadline: 2/1 (priority date; rolling processing). Application fee: $35. Electronic applications accepted. *Tuition:* $3354 per year full-time, $181 per semester hour part-time for state residents; $8410 per year full-time, $462 per semester hour part-time for nonresidents. • Dr. Tom George, Associate Dean, 423-974-0907. Fax: 423-974-8718. E-mail: tgeorge1@utk.edu.

University of Tennessee, Knoxville, College of Education, Program in Leadership Studies in Education, Knoxville, TN 37996. Offers educational administration and supervision (MS). Accredited by NCATE. Part-time and evening/weekend programs available. Postbaccalaureate distance learning degree programs offered (no on-campus study). Students: 13 full-time (6 women), 82 part-time (61 women); includes 11 minority (9 African Americans, 2 Native Americans). 19 applicants, 63% accepted. In 1997, 10 degrees awarded. *Degree requirements:* Thesis optional, foreign language not required. *Entrance requirements:* TOEFL (minimum score 550), minimum GPA of 2.7. Application deadline: 2/1 (priority date; rolling processing). Application fee: $35. Electronic applications accepted. *Tuition:* $3354 per year full-time, $181 per semester hour part-time for state residents; $8410 per year full-time, $462 per semester hour part-time for nonresidents. *Financial aid:* Application deadline 2/1. • Dr. Tom George, Associate Dean, 423-974-0907. Fax: 423-974-8718. E-mail: tgeorge1@utk.edu.

The University of Texas at Austin, Graduate School, College of Education, Department of Educational Administration, Austin, TX 78712. Awards M Ed, Ed D, PhD. Students: 322 (209 women); includes 135 minority (54 African Americans, 3 Asian Americans, 74 Hispanics, 4 Native Americans), 9 international. 154 applicants, 53% accepted. In 1997, 59 master's, 55 doctorates awarded. *Degree requirements:* For doctorate, dissertation. *Entrance requirements:* GRE General Test. Application deadline: 5/1 (priority date). Application fee: $50 ($75 for international students). Electronic applications accepted. *Expenses:* Tuition $2592 per year full-time, $324 per semester (minimum) part-time for state residents; $7704 per year full-time, $963 per semester (minimum) part-time for nonresidents. Fees $778 per year full-time, $161 per semester (minimum) part-time. *Financial aid:* Fellowships available. Financial aid application deadline: 2/1. • Dr. Donald G. Phelps, Chairman, 512-471-7551. E-mail: dphelps@mail.utexas.edu. Application contact: Martha N. Ovando, Graduate Adviser, 512-471-7551.

The University of Texas at Brownsville, Graduate Studies, School of Education, Brownsville, TX 78520-4991. Offerings include educational administration (M Ed), supervision (M Ed). School faculty: 18 full-time (10 women). *Degree requirements:* Thesis optional, foreign language not required. *Entrance requirements:* GRE General Test, TOEFL (minimum score 550). Application deadline: 8/1 (priority date; rolling processing; 1/1 for spring admission). Application fee: $15. *Expenses:* Tuition $648 per year full-time, $120 per semester hour part-time for state residents; $4698 per year full-time, $783 per semester hour part-time for nonresidents. Fees

$593 per year full-time, $109 per year part-time. • Dr. Sylvia C. Peña, Dean, 956-983-7219. Fax: 956-982-0293. E-mail: scpena@utb1.utb.edu.

The University of Texas at El Paso, College of Education, Department of Educational Leadership and Foundations, 500 West University Avenue, El Paso, TX 79968-0001. Awards Ed D. *Degree requirements:* Dissertation optional, foreign language not required. *Entrance requirements:* GRE General Test (minimum combined score of 1400 on three sections), TOEFL (minimum score 550), minimum graduate GPA of 3.0. Application deadline: 7/1 (priority date; 11/1 for spring admission). Application fee: $15 ($65 for international students). Electronic applications accepted. *Tuition:* $1559 per year full-time, $230 per credit hour part-time for state residents; $5393 per year full-time, $405 per credit hour part-time for nonresidents.

The University of Texas at Tyler, School of Education and Psychology, Department of Special Services, Program in Educational Administration, Tyler, TX 75799-0001. Awards M Ed, Certificate. Part-time programs available. Faculty: 2 full-time (0 women). In 1997, 15 master's awarded. *Degree requirements:* For master's, 3 years of teaching experience, comprehensive exam required, foreign language and thesis not required. *Entrance requirements:* For master's, GRE General Test (minimum combined score of 1200). Application fee: $0 ($50 for international students). *Tuition:* $2144 per year full-time, $337 per semester (minimum) part-time for state residents; $7256 per year full-time, $964 per semester (minimum) part-time for nonresidents. *Financial aid:* Application deadline 7/1. *Faculty research:* Effective schools, restructuring of schools, leadership. • Application contact: Martha D. Wheat, Director of Admissions and Student Records, 903-566-7201. Fax: 903-566-7068.

The University of Texas of the Permian Basin, Graduate School, School of Education, Program in Educational Administration, Odessa, TX 79762-0001. Awards MA. *Degree requirements:* Thesis required, foreign language not required. *Entrance requirements:* GRE General Test (minimum combined score of 1200). *Expenses:* Tuition $1314 per year full-time, $73 per hour part-time for state residents; $4896 per year full-time, $272 per hour part-time for nonresidents. Fees $383 per year full-time, $111 per semester (minimum) part-time.

The University of Texas of the Permian Basin, Graduate School, School of Education, Program in Supervision, Odessa, TX 79762-0001. Awards MA. *Degree requirements:* Thesis required, foreign language not required. *Entrance requirements:* GRE General Test (minimum combined score of 1200). *Expenses:* Tuition $1314 per year full-time, $73 per hour part-time for state residents; $4896 per year full-time, $272 per hour part-time for nonresidents. Fees $383 per year full-time, $111 per semester (minimum) part-time.

The University of Texas–Pan American, College of Education, Department of School Administration and Supervision, Edinburg, TX 78539-2999. Offers programs in administration (M Ed), supervision (M Ed). Part-time and evening/weekend programs available. *Degree requirements:* Thesis optional, foreign language not required. *Entrance requirements:* GRE General Test. Application deadline: 7/17 (11/16 for spring admission). Application fee: $0. *Tuition:* $2156 per year full-time, $283 per semester (minimum) part-time for state residents; $6788 per year full-time, $862 per semester (minimum) part-time for nonresidents. *Faculty research:* Community perceptions of education, leadership and gender studies.

University of the Pacific, School of Education, Department of Educational Administration and Foundations, Stockton, CA 95211-0197. Awards MA, Ed D. Accredited by NCATE. Faculty: 2 full-time (0 women). Students: 8 full-time (6 women), 33 part-time (19 women). In 1997, 7 master's, 2 doctorates awarded. *Degree requirements:* For master's, thesis required (for some programs), foreign language not required; for doctorate, dissertation. *Entrance requirements:* GRE General Test, GRE Subject Test. Application deadline: 3/1 (priority date; rolling processing; 10/15 for spring admission). Application fee: $50. *Expenses:* Tuition $19,000 per year full-time, $594 per unit part-time. Fees $30 per year (minimum). *Financial aid:* Application deadline 3/1. • Dr. Dennis Brennan, Chairperson, 209-946-2670. E-mail: dbrennan@uop.edu.

University of Toledo, College of Education and Allied Professions, Department of Educational Leadership, Program in Educational Administration and Supervision, Toledo, OH 43606-3398. Awards M Ed, Ed D, Ed S. Accredited by NCATE. Evening/weekend programs available. Students: 6 full-time (5 women), 97 part-time (45 women); includes 13 minority (10 African Americans, 3 Hispanics), 1 international. Average age 39. 39 applicants, 72% accepted. In 1997, 11 master's, 1 doctorate awarded. *Degree requirements:* For master's, thesis or alternative, comprehensive exam required, foreign language not required; for doctorate, dissertation, comprehensive exams required, foreign language not required; for Ed S, thesis optional, foreign language not required. *Entrance requirements:* For master's, minimum GPA of 2.7; for doctorate, GRE General Test (minimum combined score of 1040), interview; minimum GPA of 2.7 (undergraduate), 3.0 (graduate); for Ed S, minimum GPA of 2.7 (undergraduate), 3.0 (graduate). Application deadline: 8/15 (priority date; rolling processing). Application fee: $30. Electronic applications accepted. *Tuition:* $5907 per year full-time, $246 per hour part-time for state residents; $11,835 per year full-time, $493 per hour part-time for nonresidents. *Financial aid:* Federal Work-Study, institutionally sponsored loans, and career-related internships or fieldwork available. Aid available to part-time students. Financial aid application deadline: 4/1; applicants required to submit FAFSA. *Faculty research:* School learning organizations, equity, access and equality in schools. • Dr. Daniel Merritt, Interim Chair, Department of Educational Leadership, 419-530-2461. Fax: 419-530-7719.

University of Utah, Graduate School of Education, Department of Educational Administration, Salt Lake City, UT 84112-1107. Awards M Ed, Ed D, PhD, MPA/Ed D, MPA/PhD. Faculty: 10 full-time (2 women), 11 part-time (5 women). Students: 17 full-time (9 women), 61 part-time (31 women); includes 7 minority (3 African Americans, 1 Asian American, 3 Hispanics). Average age 40. In 1997, 14 master's, 4 doctorates awarded. *Degree requirements:* For doctorate, dissertation required, foreign language not required. *Entrance requirements:* For master's, GRE or MAT, TOEFL (minimum score 500); for doctorate, GRE, TOEFL (minimum score 500), graduate GPA of 3.25. Application deadline: 7/1. Application fee: $30 ($50 for international students). *Tuition:* $2045 per year full-time, $562 per semester (minimum) part-time for state residents; $6129 per year full-time, $1607 per semester (minimum) part-time for nonresidents. *Financial aid:* In 1997–98, 3 teaching assistantships were awarded; research assistantships and career-related internships or fieldwork also available. *Faculty research:* Organization theory, administration of programs, educational law, leadership, employee relations. • Dr. David J. Sperry, Chair, 801-581-6627. Fax: 801-581-6756. E-mail: sperry@gse.utah.edu. Application contact: Joe Matthews, Academic Adviser, 801-581-3373. E-mail: matthews@gse.utah.edu.

University of Vermont, College of Education and Social Services, Department of Educational Leadership and Policy Studies, Burlington, VT 05405-0160. Awards Ed D. Accredited by NCATE. Students: 74; includes 6 minority (5 African Americans, 1 Hispanic), 1 international. 35 applicants, 74% accepted. In 1997, 13 degrees awarded. *Degree requirements:* Dissertation required, foreign language not required. *Entrance requirements:* GRE General Test, TOEFL (minimum score 550). Application deadline: 6/1 (priority date). Application fee: $25. *Expenses:* Tuition $302 per credit for state residents; $755 per credit for nonresidents. Fees $434 per year full-time, $46 per semester (minimum) part-time. *Financial aid:* Research assistantships, teaching assistantships available. • Dr. S. Hasazi, Chairperson, 802-656-3424.

University of Vermont, College of Education and Social Services, Department of Education, Program in Educational Leadership, Burlington, VT 05405-0160. Awards M Ed. Accredited by NCATE. Students: 10. 10 applicants, 60% accepted. In 1997, 13 degrees awarded. *Degree requirements:* Thesis or alternative required, foreign language not required. *Entrance requirements:* GRE General Test, TOEFL (minimum score 550). Application deadline: 4/1 (priority date). Application fee: $25. *Expenses:* Tuition $302 per credit for state residents; $755 per credit for nonresidents. Fees $434 per year full-time, $46 per semester (minimum) part-time. *Financial aid:* Research assistantships, teaching assistantships, and career-related internships or fieldwork available. Financial aid application deadline: 3/1. • B. Meyers, Chairperson, Department of Education, 802-656-3356.

University of Vermont, College of Education and Social Services, Department of Integrated Professional Studies, Program in Higher Education and Student Affairs Administration, Burlington, VT 05405-0160. Awards M Ed. Accredited by NCATE. Students: 33; includes 5 minority (2 Asian Americans, 3 Hispanics), 1 international. 90 applicants, 27% accepted. In 1997, 13 degrees awarded. *Degree requirements:* Thesis or alternative required, foreign language not required. *Entrance requirements:* GRE General Test, TOEFL (minimum score 550). Application deadline: 2/1 (priority date; rolling processing). Application fee: $25. *Expenses:* Tuition $302 per credit for state residents; $755 per credit for nonresidents. Fees $434 per year full-time, $46 per semester (minimum) part-time. *Financial aid:* Application deadline 2/1. • Dr. D. Hunter, Coordinator, 802-656-2030.

University of Victoria, Faculty of Education, Department of Communication and Social Foundations, Victoria, BC V8W 2Y2, Canada. Offerings include educational administration (MA, M Ed). Postbaccalaureate distance learning degree programs offered (minimal on-campus study). Department faculty: 17 full-time (9 women), 14 part-time (9 women). *Degree requirements:* Thesis, project (M Ed) required, foreign language not required. *Average time to degree:* master's–3.3 years full-time; doctorate–4.4 years full-time. *Entrance requirements:* Minimum B average. Application deadline: 4/30 (rolling processing). Application fee: $50. *Tuition:* $2080 per year full-time, $557 per semester part-time. • Dr. G. Potter, Chair, 250-721-7802. Application contact: Sarah Baylow, Graduate Secretary, 250-721-7882. Fax: 250-721-7767. E-mail: sbaylow@uvic.ca.

University of Virginia, Curry School of Education, Department of Leadership, Foundations and Policy, Program in Administration and Supervision, Charlottesville, VA 22903. Awards M Ed, Ed D, Ed S. Accredited by NCATE. Faculty: 37 full-time (12 women), 1 part-time (0 women). Students: 21 full-time (12 women), 35 part-time (17 women); includes 7 minority (all African Americans). Average age 40. 44 applicants, 68% accepted. In 1997, 21 master's, 9 doctorates, 5 Ed Ss awarded. *Degree requirements:* For doctorate, dissertation required, foreign language not required. *Entrance requirements:* GRE General Test. Application deadline: 3/1 (11/15 for spring admission). Application fee: $40. *Tuition:* $4876 per year full-time, $944 per semester (minimum) part-time for state residents; $15,824 per year full-time, $2748 per semester (minimum) part-time for nonresidents. • Application contact: Linda Berry, Student Enrollment Coordinator, 804-924-0738. E-mail: lrb8e@virginia.edu.

University of Washington, College of Education, Program in Educational Leadership and Policy Studies, Seattle, WA 98195. Awards M Ed, Ed D, PhD. *Degree requirements:* For master's, thesis optional, foreign language not required; for doctorate, dissertation required, foreign language not required. *Entrance requirements:* GRE General Test, TOEFL, minimum GPA of 3.0. Application deadline: 2/15. Application fee: $45. *Tuition:* $5433 per year full-time, $775 per quarter (minimum) part-time for state residents; $13,479 per year full-time, $1925 per quarter (minimum) part-time for nonresidents. *Faculty research:* Evaluation policy, school reform, philosophy, higher education. • Dr. Allen Glenn, Dean, College of Education, 206-543-5390. Fax: 206-685-1713. E-mail: aglenn@u.washington.edu. Application contact: Richard Neel, Associate Dean, 206-543-7833. Fax: 206-543-8439. E-mail: edinfo@u.washington.edu.

The University of West Alabama, College of Education, Department of Instructional Support, Program in School Administration, Livingston, AL 35470. Awards M Ed. Accredited by NCATE. Part-time programs available. *Entrance requirements:* GRE General Test, MAT, minimum GPA of 2.75. Application deadline: 9/10 (priority date; rolling processing; 3/24 for spring admission). Application fee: $15. *Tuition:* $70 per quarter hour.

The University of Western Ontario, Social Sciences Division, Faculty of Education, Program in Educational Studies, London, ON N6A 5B8, Canada. Offerings include educational policy studies (M Ed). Program faculty: 30 full-time (10 women). *Average time to degree:* master's–2 years full-time, 3 years part-time. *Application deadline:* 2/1. *Application fee:* $50. • Dr. S. Haggerty, Graduate Chair, 519-661-2099. E-mail: haggerty@edu.uwo.ca. Application contact: L. Kulak, Graduate Supervisor, 519-661-2099. Fax: 519-661-3833. E-mail: kulak@edu.uwo.ca.

University of West Florida, College of Education, Department of Professional Studies, Educational Foundations, and Technology, Program in Educational Leadership, Pensacola, FL 32514-5750. Awards M Ed, Ed S. Accredited by NCATE. Part-time and evening/weekend programs available. Students: 66 full-time (43 women), 166 part-time (113 women); includes 39 minority (30 African Americans, 6 Asian Americans, 2 Hispanics, 1 Native American), 3 international. Average age 39. In 1997, 89 master's, 8 Ed Ss awarded. *Degree requirements:* For master's, thesis optional, foreign language not required. *Entrance requirements:* For master's, GRE General Test (minimum combined score of 1000) or minimum GPA of 3.0. Application deadline: 7/1 (rolling processing; 11/1 for spring admission). Application fee: $20. *Tuition:* $131 per credit hour (minimum) for state residents; $436 per credit hour (minimum) for nonresidents. *Financial aid:* Fellowships and career-related internships or fieldwork available. • Dr. Janet Pilcher, Interim Chairperson, Department of Professional Studies, Educational Foundations, and Technology, 850-474-2300.

University of Wisconsin–Green Bay, Program in Applied Leadership in Teaching and Learning, Green Bay, WI 54311-7001. Awards MS Ed. Program new for fall 1998. *Degree requirements:* Thesis required, foreign language not required. *Entrance requirements:* Minimum GPA of 3.0. Application deadline: 8/1 (rolling processing; 11/1 for spring admission). Application fee: $35. *Tuition:* $3774 per year full-time, $183 per credit part-time for state residents; $11,418 per year full-time, $425 per credit part-time for nonresidents. *Financial aid:* Application deadline 7/15. • Ronald D. Stieglitz, Associate Dean, Graduate Studies, 920-465-2123. Fax: 920-465-2718.

University of Wisconsin–La Crosse, School of Education, Program in College Student Development and Administration, La Crosse, WI 54601-3742. Awards MS Ed. Accredited by NCATE. Faculty: 15 part-time (5 women), 3.75 FTE. Students: 21 full-time (14 women), 3 part-time (1 woman); includes 2 minority (1 African American, 1 Asian American). Average age 26. 30 applicants, 37% accepted. In 1997, 16 degrees awarded. *Degree requirements:* Comprehensive exams (optional) required, thesis optional, foreign language not required. *Entrance requirements:* Interview, minimum GPA of 2.85, sample of written work. Application deadline: 3/1 (priority date; rolling processing). Application fee: $38. *Tuition:* $3737 per year full-time, $208 per credit part-time for state residents; $11,921 per year full-time, $633 per credit part-time for nonresidents. *Financial aid:* In 1997–98, 21 students received aid, including 21 assistantships (11 to first-year students) averaging $827 per month and totaling $156,303; Federal Work-Study and career-related internships or fieldwork also available. Aid available to part-time students. Financial aid application deadline: 3/15; applicants required to submit FAFSA. *Faculty research:* College student personnel standards, campus ecology, standard testing and admissions, student development theory. • Dr. Larry Ringgenberg, Coordinator, 608-785-8063. Application contact: Tim Lewis, Director of Admissions, 608-785-8939. Fax: 608-785-6695. E-mail: admissions@mail.uwlax.edu.

University of Wisconsin–Madison, School of Education, Department of Educational Administration, Madison, WI 53706-1380. Awards MS, PhD. MS offered jointly with the University of Wisconsin–Oshkosh and the University of Wisconsin–Whitewater. *Degree requirements:* For doctorate, dissertation. *Application fee:* $38. *Tuition:* $4928 per year full-time, $926 per semester (minimum) part-time for state residents; $15,190 per year full-time, $2849 per semester (minimum) part-time for nonresidents.

University of Wisconsin–Milwaukee, School of Education, Department of Administrative Leadership, Milwaukee, WI 53201-0413. Offers program in administrative leadership and supervision in education (MS). Part-time programs available. Faculty: 9 full-time (4 women). Students: 8 full-time (5 women), 148 part-time (98 women); includes 24 minority (16 African Americans, 3 Asian Americans, 3 Hispanics, 2 Native Americans). 37 applicants, 70% accepted. In 1997, 50 degrees awarded. *Degree requirements:* Thesis or alternative required, foreign language not required. *Application deadline:* 1/1 (priority date; rolling processing; 9/1 for spring

Directory: Educational Administration

University of Wisconsin–Milwaukee (continued)
admission). *Application fee:* $45 ($75 for international students). *Tuition:* $4996 per year full-time, $1030 per semester (minimum) part-time for state residents; $15,216 per year full-time, $2947 per semester (minimum) part-time for nonresidents. *Financial aid:* In 1997–98, 2 fellowships were awarded; research assistantships, teaching assistantships, project assistantships, and career-related internships or fieldwork also available. Aid available to part-time students. Financial aid application deadline: 4/15. • Larry Martin, Chair, 414-229-5754.

University of Wisconsin–Oshkosh, College of Education and Human Services, Department of Professional Leadership and Human Services, Oshkosh, WI 54901-8602. Offers program in educational leadership (MS). Accredited by NCATE. Part-time and evening/weekend programs available. Faculty: 8 full-time (6 women), 7 part-time (5 women). Students: 1 (woman) full-time, 80 part-time (54 women); includes 2 minority (both Asian Americans). Average age 34. 9 applicants, 100% accepted. In 1997, 13 degrees awarded. *Degree requirements:* Thesis optional, foreign language not required. *Entrance requirements:* Bachelor's degree in education or related field. Application deadline: rolling. Application fee: $45. *Tuition:* $3638 per year full-time, $609 per semester (minimum) part-time for state residents; $11,282 per year full-time, $1884 per semester (minimum) part-time for nonresidents. *Financial aid:* Application deadline 3/15. *Faculty research:* Supervision models, learning styles, total quality management, cooperative learning, school choice, charters. • Dr. Scherie Lampe, Chair, 920-424-1490. Application contact: Dr. Susan Cramer, Coordinator, 920-424-1490. Fax: 920-424-0858. E-mail: cramer@uwosh.edu.

University of Wisconsin–Stevens Point, College of Professional Studies, School of Education, Program in Educational Administration, Stevens Point, WI 54481-3897. Awards MSE. Offered jointly with the University of Wisconsin–Superior. *Application deadline:* rolling. *Application fee:* $38. *Tuition:* $3702 per year full-time, $664 per semester (minimum) part-time for state residents; $11,346 per year full-time, $1938 per semester (minimum) part-time for nonresidents. *Financial aid:* Application deadline 5/1. • Dr. Leslie McClaine-Ruelle, Head, School of Education, 715-346-2040.

University of Wisconsin–Superior, Department of Educational Administration, Superior, WI 54880-2873. Awards MSE, Ed S. Offered jointly with the University of Wisconsin–Eau Claire and the University of Wisconsin–Stevens Point. Part-time and evening/weekend programs available. Postbaccalaureate distance learning degree programs offered (minimal on-campus study). Students: 88 (41 women). 27 applicants, 81% accepted. In 1997, 24 master's, 3 Ed Ss awarded. *Degree requirements:* For master's, thesis or alternative, research project or position paper, written exam required, foreign language not required; for Ed S, thesis or alternative, internship, oral and written exams required, foreign language not required. *Entrance requirements:* For master's, MAT (minimum score 40) or GRE General Test (minimum score 430 on verbal, 490 on quantitative and analytical), minimum GPA of 2.75; for Ed S, MAT (minimum score 45), master's degree, 3 years of teaching experience. Application deadline: 4/1 (priority date; rolling processing). Application fee: $45. *Tuition:* $3628 per year full-time, $222 per credit hour part-time for state residents; $11,272 per year full-time, $647 per credit hour part-time for nonresidents. *Financial aid:* In 1997–98, 1 research assistantship (to a first-year student) averaging $850 per month and totaling $7,714 was awarded; partial tuition waivers, Federal Work-Study, and career-related internships or fieldwork also available. Aid available to part-time students. Financial aid application deadline: 5/1. • Dr. Michael Wallschlaeger, Chairperson, 715-394-8140. E-mail: mwallsch@staff.uwsuper.edu.

University of Wisconsin–Whitewater, College of Business and Economics, Program in School Business Management, Whitewater, WI 53190-1790. Awards MS Ed. Part-time and evening/weekend programs available. *Degree requirements:* Thesis or alternative required, foreign language not required. *Entrance requirements:* GMAT, minimum GPA of 2.75 or MAT (minimum score 44). Application deadline: rolling. Application fee: $38.

University of Wyoming, College of Education, Division of Leadership and Human Development, Laramie, WY 82071. Awards MA, MS, Ed D, PhD, Ed S. One or more programs accredited by NCATE. Faculty: 31 (10 women). Students: 35 full-time (28 women), 153 part-time (101 women); includes 8 minority (1 African American, 1 Asian American, 5 Hispanics, 1 Native American). 65 applicants, 35% accepted. In 1997, 36 master's, 9 doctorates awarded. *Degree requirements:* For doctorate, dissertation. *Entrance requirements:* GRE General Test, minimum GPA of 3.0. Application deadline: 6/1 (priority date; rolling processing). Application fee: $40. *Expenses:* Tuition $2430 per year full-time, $135 per credit hour part-time for state residents; $7518 per year full-time, $418 per credit hour part-time for nonresidents. Fees $386 per year full-time, $9.25 per credit hour part-time. *Financial aid:* Application deadline 3/1. • Donald Seckinger, Chair, 307-766-2168. Fax: 307-766-2018. E-mail: dseck@uwyo.edu.

Ursuline College, Graduate Studies, Graduate Program in Non-Public Educational Administration, Pepper Pike, OH 44124-4398. Awards MA. Part-time programs available. Students: 15 full-time (12 women), 42 part-time (34 women); includes 5 minority (all African Americans). Average age 42. 17 applicants, 65% accepted. In 1997, 12 degrees awarded. *Degree requirements:* Thesis or alternative required, foreign language not required. *Entrance requirements:* Minimum undergraduate GPA of 3.0, teaching certificate, professional experience. Application deadline: 8/1 (priority date; rolling processing). Application fee: $25. *Expenses:* Tuition $405 per credit hour. Fees $22 per credit hour. *Financial aid:* Federal Work-Study and career-related internships or fieldwork available. Aid available to part-time students. Financial aid application deadline: 3/1; applicants required to submit FAFSA. • Martin Kane, Director, 440-646-8148.

Valdosta State University, College of Education, Department of Educational Leadership, Valdosta, GA 31698. Awards M Ed, Ed D, Ed S. Accredited by NCATE. Faculty: 10 full-time (4 women). Students: 29 full-time (22 women), 83 part-time (54 women); includes 14 minority (all African Americans). 36 applicants, 86% accepted. In 1997, 86 master's awarded. *Entrance requirements:* For master's, GRE General Test (minimum combined score of 800); for doctorate, GRE General Test (minimum combined score of 1000); for Ed S, GRE General Test (minimum combined score of 900). Application deadline: 8/1 (rolling processing; 11/15 for spring admission). Application fee: $10. *Expenses:* Tuition $2472 per year full-time, $83 per semester hour part-time for state residents; $8472 per year full-time, $333 per semester hour part-time for nonresidents. Fees $236 per year full-time. *Faculty research:* Student transition, mentoring in higher education, contemporary issues in higher education, leadership. • Dr. Gerald Seigrist, Head, 912-333-5924. Fax: 912-333-7167. E-mail: gseigrist@grits.valdosta.peachnet.edu.

Vanderbilt University, Graduate School, Program in Education and Human Development, Nashville, TN 37240-1001. Offerings include educational leadership (MS, PhD). Jointly offered with Peabody College. Program faculty: 44 full-time (16 women), 1 (woman) part-time. *Degree requirements:* For master's, thesis required, foreign language not required; for doctorate, dissertation, final and qualifying exams required, foreign language not required. *Entrance requirements:* GRE General Test. Application deadline: 1/15. Application fee: $40. *Expenses:* Tuition $16,452 per year full-time, $914 per semester hour part-time. Fees $236 per year. • Ellen Goldring, Director, 615-322-8265. Fax: 615-322-8501. E-mail: goldrieb@ctrvax.vanderbilt.edu. Application contact: Barbara J. Johnston, Director of Admissions, 615-322-8410. Fax: 615-322-8401. E-mail: johnstbj@ctrvax.vanderbilt.edu.

Vanderbilt University, Peabody College, Department of Educational Leadership, Nashville, TN 37240-1001. Offers programs in general administrative leadership (M Ed, Ed D, Ed S), higher education (M Ed, Ed D, Ed S), school administration (M Ed, Ed D, Ed S). Accredited by NCATE. *Entrance requirements:* For master's and doctorate, GRE General Test, MAT. Application deadline: 3/1 (priority date; rolling processing). Application fee: $35. • Joseph Murphy, Chair, 615-322-8000.

Villanova University, Graduate School of Liberal Arts and Sciences, Department of Education and Human Services, Program in School Administration, Villanova, PA 19085-1699. Awards MA. Part-time and evening/weekend programs available. Students: 14 part-time (10 women); includes 1 minority (Hispanic). Average age 32. 6 applicants, 83% accepted. *Degree requirements:* Comprehensive exam required, foreign language and thesis not required. *Entrance requirements:* GRE or MAT, minimum GPA of 3.0. Application deadline: 8/1 (priority date; 12/1 for spring admission). Application fee: $40. *Expenses:* Tuition $400 per credit. Fees $60 per year. *Financial aid:* Federal Work-Study and career-related internships or fieldwork available. Financial aid application deadline: 4/1. • Dr. Catherine M. Hill, Coordinator, 610-519-4620.

Villanova University, Graduate School of Liberal Arts and Sciences, Department of Education and Human Services, Program in Secondary Administration, Villanova, PA 19085-1699. Offers counseling and human relations (MS). Part-time and evening/weekend programs available. Students: 1 part-time (0 women). Average age 29. *Degree requirements:* Comprehensive exam required, foreign language and thesis not required. *Entrance requirements:* GRE or MAT, minimum GPA of 3.0. Application deadline: 8/1 (priority date; 12/1 for spring admission). Application fee: $40. *Expenses:* Tuition $400 per credit. Fees $60 per year. *Financial aid:* Federal Work-Study and career-related internships or fieldwork available. Financial aid application deadline: 4/1. • Dr. Henry Nichols, Chairperson, Department of Education and Human Services, 610-519-4620.

Virginia Commonwealth University, School of Education, Program in Administration and Supervision, Richmond, VA 23284-9005. Awards M Ed. Accredited by NCATE. Faculty: 5 full-time, 4 part-time. Students: 7 full-time (6 women), 86 part-time (55 women); includes 28 minority (26 African Americans, 2 Hispanics). Average age 35. 34 applicants, 71% accepted. In 1997, 17 degrees awarded. *Entrance requirements:* GRE General Test or MAT. Application deadline: 7/1 (rolling processing; 11/1 for spring admission). Application fee: $30 ($0 for international students). *Tuition:* $4960 per year full-time, $257 per credit part-time for state residents; $12,652 per year full-time, $684 per credit part-time for nonresidents. *Financial aid:* Fellowships, research assistantships, teaching assistantships, partial tuition waivers, Federal Work-Study, institutionally sponsored loans, and career-related internships or fieldwork available. Financial aid application deadline: 3/1. • Dr. John Seyfarth, Division Head, 804-828-1332. Application contact: Dr. Michael D. Davis, Interim Director, Graduate Studies, 804-828-6530. Fax: 804-828-1323. E-mail: mddavis@vcu.edu.

Virginia Polytechnic Institute and State University, College of Human Resources and Education, Department of Educational Leadership and Policy Studies, Program in Administration and Supervision of Special Education, Blacksburg, VA 24061. Awards Ed D, PhD, CAGS. Accredited by NCATE. Students: 11 full-time (7 women), 9 part-time (all women); includes 1 international. 6 applicants, 67% accepted. In 1997, 1 doctorate, 6 CAGSs awarded. *Degree requirements:* For doctorate, dissertation, internship required, foreign language not required. *Entrance requirements:* GRE General Test (minimum combined score of 1000), TOEFL (minimum score 600), teaching experience. Application deadline: 12/1 (priority date; rolling processing). Application fee: $25. *Tuition:* $4927 per year full-time, $792 per semester (minimum) part-time for state residents; $7537 per year full-time, $1227 per semester (minimum) part-time for nonresidents. *Financial aid:* Research assistantships, teaching assistantships, assistantships, and career-related internships or fieldwork available. Financial aid application deadline: 4/1. • Dr. Philip R. Jones, Area Leader, 540-231-5925.

Virginia Polytechnic Institute and State University, College of Human Resources and Education, Department of Educational Leadership and Policy Studies, Program in Educational Administration, Blacksburg, VA 24061. Awards MA Ed, Ed D, PhD, CAGS. Accredited by NCATE. Evening/weekend programs available. Students: 59 full-time (33 women), 220 part-time (131 women); includes 69 minority (66 African Americans, 2 Asian Americans, 1 Native American), 2 international. 22 applicants, 14% accepted. In 1997, 4 master's, 32 doctorates, 47 CAGSs awarded. *Degree requirements:* For doctorate, dissertation required, foreign language not required. *Entrance requirements:* For master's, TOEFL, minimum GPA of 2.75; for doctorate and CAGS, TOEFL. Application deadline: 12/1 (priority date; rolling processing). Application fee: $25. *Tuition:* $4927 per year full-time, $792 per semester (minimum) part-time for state residents; $7537 per year full-time, $1227 per semester (minimum) part-time for nonresidents. *Financial aid:* In 1997–98, 4 teaching assistantships, 12 assistantships were awarded; research assistantships and career-related internships or fieldwork also available. Financial aid application deadline: 4/1. *Faculty research:* Law and finance, policy studies, instructional administration. • Dr. Glen I. Earthman, Area Leader, 540-231-9707.

Virginia Polytechnic Institute and State University, College of Human Resources and Education, Department of Educational Leadership and Policy Studies, Program in Student Personnel Services, Blacksburg, VA 24061. Awards MA Ed, Ed D, PhD, CAGS. Accredited by NCATE. Evening/weekend programs available. Students: 103 full-time (74 women), 135 part-time (112 women); includes 36 minority (28 African Americans, 3 Asian Americans, 4 Hispanics, 1 Native American), 2 international. 124 applicants, 57% accepted. In 1997, 47 master's, 9 doctorates, 3 CAGSs awarded. *Degree requirements:* For doctorate, dissertation required, foreign language not required. *Entrance requirements:* TOEFL. Application deadline: 12/1 (priority date; rolling processing). Application fee: $25. *Tuition:* $4927 per year full-time, $792 per semester (minimum) part-time for state residents; $7537 per year full-time, $1227 per semester (minimum) part-time for nonresidents. *Financial aid:* Application deadline 4/1. • Dr. Carl O. McDaniels, Area Leader, 540-231-6890.

Virginia State University, School of Liberal Arts and Education, Department of Educational Leadership and Community Services, Program in Educational Administration and Supervision, 1 Hayden Drive, Petersburg, VA 23806-2096. Awards M Ed, MS. Accredited by NCATE. Faculty: 2 full-time (0 women). In 1997, 17 degrees awarded. *Application deadline:* 8/15 (rolling processing). *Application fee:* $25. *Tuition:* $3739 per year full-time, $133 per credit hour part-time for state residents; $9056 per year full-time, $364 per credit hour part-time for nonresidents. *Financial aid:* 2 students received aid. Financial aid application deadline: 5/1. • Application contact: Dr. Wayne F. Virag, Dean, Graduate Studies and Continuing Education, 804-524-5985. Fax: 804-524-5104. E-mail: wvirag@vsu.edu.

Walla Walla College, Department of Education and Psychology, Specialization in Educational Leadership, College Place, WA 99324-1198. Awards MA, M Ed. *Degree requirements:* Thesis required (for some programs), foreign language not required. *Entrance requirements:* GRE General Test, minimum GPA of 2.75; undergraduate major in psychology, sociology, or equivalent. Application deadline: 4/1 (priority date; rolling processing). Application fee: $40. *Tuition:* $346 per quarter hour. *Financial aid:* Application deadline 4/1; applicants required to submit FAFSA. *Faculty research:* Instructional psychology. • Application contact: Dr. Joe Galusha, Dean of Graduate Studies, 509-527-2421. Fax: 509-527-2253. E-mail: galujo@wwc.edu.

Washburn University of Topeka, College of Arts and Sciences, Department of Education, Program in Educational Administration, Topeka, KS 66621. Awards M Ed. Accredited by NCATE. Part-time programs available. Faculty: 2 full-time, 4 part-time. Students: 1 full-time (0 women), 37 part-time (15 women); includes 4 minority (3 African Americans, 1 Hispanic), 2 international. Average age 29. In 1997, 5 degrees awarded. *Degree requirements:* Thesis or alternative, comprehensive exam required, foreign language not required. *Entrance requirements:* GRE General Test, minimum GPA of 3.0 during previous 2 years. Application deadline: 5/1. Application fee: $0. *Financial aid:* Application deadline 3/15. • Dr. David Van Cleaf, Chairperson, Department of Education, 785-231-1010 Ext. 1430.

Washington State University, College of Education, Department of Educational Leadership, Program in Educational Leadership, Pullman, WA 99164-1610. Awards MA, M Ed, Ed D, PhD. Accredited by NCATE. *Degree requirements:* For master's, oral exam required, foreign language not required; for doctorate, dissertation, oral exam required, foreign language not required. *Entrance requirements:* GRE General Test, minimum GPA of 3.0. Application deadline: 3/1 (priority date; rolling processing). Application fee: $35. *Tuition:* $5334 per year full-time, $267 per credit hour part-time for state residents; $13,380 per year full-time, $677 per credit hour part-time for nonresidents. *Financial aid:* Application deadline 4/1. • Dr. Donald Reed, Chair, Department of Educational Leadership, 509-335-9117.

Wayne State College, Division of Education, Program in Educational Administration, Wayne, NE 68787. Offers educational administration (Ed S), elementary administration (MSE), secondary administration (MSE). Accredited by NCATE. Students: 4 full-time (1 woman), 41 part-time (14 women); includes 1 minority (Hispanic). Average age 36. In 1997, 10 master's, 1 Ed S awarded. *Degree requirements:* For master's, comprehensive exam, research paper required, foreign language not required. *Entrance requirements:* For master's, GRE General Test, minimum GPA of 2.5; for Ed S, GRE General Test, minimum GPA of 3.2. Application deadline: rolling. Application fee: $10. *Expenses:* Tuition $1788 per year full-time, $75 per credit hour part-time for state residents; $3576 per year full-time, $149 per credit hour part-time for nonresidents. Fees $360 per year full-time, $15 per credit hour part-time. *Financial aid:* Teaching assistantships and career-related internships or fieldwork available. Financial aid application deadline: 5/1; applicants required to submit FAFSA. *Faculty research:* Staff development, peer coaching, instructional leadership. • Dr. Diane Alexander, Head, Division of Education, 402-375-7389.

Wayne State University, College of Education, Division of Administrative and Organizational Studies, Detroit, MI 48202. Offers programs in educational leadership (M Ed), general administration and supervision (Ed D, PhD, Ed S), higher education (Ed D, PhD), instructional technology (M Ed, Ed D, PhD, Ed S). Accredited by NCATE. Faculty: 81. Students: 163 full-time (103 women), 507 part-time (335 women). Average age 35. 178 applicants, 78% accepted. In 1997, 121 master's, 36 doctorates, 147 Ed Ss awarded. *Degree requirements:* For doctorate, dissertation required, foreign language not required. *Entrance requirements:* For doctorate, interview, minimum GPA of 3.0. Application deadline: 7/1. Application fee: $20 ($30 for international students). *Expenses:* Tuition $163 per credit hour for state residents; $355 per credit hour for nonresidents. Fees $498 per year full-time, $114 per semester (minimum) part-time. *Financial aid:* Fellowships, Federal Work-Study, institutionally sponsored loans, and career-related internships or fieldwork available. Aid available to part-time students. *Faculty research:* Total quality management, participatory management, administering educational technology, school improvement, principalship. • Dr. JoAnne Holbert, Assistant Dean, 313-577-0210.

Western Carolina University, College of Education and Allied Professions, Department of Administration, Curriculum and Instruction, Program in Educational Administration, Cullowhee, NC 28723. Awards MA Ed. Accredited by NCATE. Part-time and evening/weekend programs available. Students: 14 part-time (8 women). 35 applicants, 57% accepted. In 1997, 8 degrees awarded. *Degree requirements:* Comprehensive exam required, foreign language and thesis not required. *Entrance requirements:* GRE General Test or MAT. Application deadline: rolling. Application fee: $35. *Tuition:* $1799 per year full-time, $144 per credit hour (minimum) part-time for state residents; $9069 per year full-time, $1053 per credit hour (minimum) part-time for nonresidents. *Financial aid:* In 1997–98, 2 students received aid, including 2 research assistantships (1 to a first-year student) totaling $15,000; fellowships, teaching assistantships, Federal Work-Study, institutionally sponsored loans also available. Financial aid application deadline: 3/15. • Application contact: Kathleen Owen, Assistant to the Dean, 828-227-7398. Fax: 828-227-7480.

Western Carolina University, College of Education and Allied Professions, Department of Administration, Curriculum and Instruction, Program in Educational Leadership, Cullowhee, NC 28723. Awards Ed D, Ed S. Accredited by NCATE. Students: 9 part-time (8 women). 16 applicants, 63% accepted. *Degree requirements:* For doctorate, dissertation, comprehensive exam required, foreign language not required; for Ed S, comprehensive exam required, foreign language and thesis not required. *Entrance requirements:* GRE General Test, minimum graduate GPA of 3.5. Application deadline: rolling. Application fee: $35. *Tuition:* $1799 per year full-time, $144 per credit hour (minimum) part-time for state residents; $9069 per year full-time, $1053 per credit hour (minimum) part-time for nonresidents. *Financial aid:* Research assistantships available. • Application contact: Kathleen Owen, Assistant to the Dean, 828-227-7398. Fax: 828-227-7480.

Western Carolina University, College of Education and Allied Professions, Department of Administration, Curriculum and Instruction, Program in Educational Supervision, Cullowhee, NC 28723. Awards MA Ed. Accredited by NCATE. Students: 11 part-time (7 women). 10 applicants, 40% accepted. In 1997, 1 degree awarded. *Degree requirements:* Comprehensive exam required, foreign language and thesis not required. *Entrance requirements:* GRE General Test or MAT. Application deadline: rolling. Application fee: $35. *Tuition:* $1799 per year full-time, $144 per credit hour (minimum) part-time for state residents; $9069 per year full-time, $1053 per credit hour (minimum) part-time for nonresidents. *Financial aid:* Research assistantships available. Financial aid application deadline: 3/15. • Application contact: Kathleen Owen, Assistant to the Dean, 828-227-7398. Fax: 828-227-7480.

Western Carolina University, College of Education and Allied Professions, Department of Administration, Curriculum and Instruction, Program in School Administration, Cullowhee, NC 28723. Awards MSA. Accredited by NCATE. Students: 11 full-time (6 women), 9 part-time (4 women); includes 3 minority (all African Americans), 1 international. 16 applicants, 56% accepted. *Degree requirements:* Comprehensive exam required, foreign language and thesis not required. *Entrance requirements:* GRE General Test. Application deadline: rolling. Application fee: $35. *Tuition:* $1799 per year full-time, $144 per credit hour (minimum) part-time for state residents; $9069 per year full-time, $1053 per credit hour (minimum) part-time for nonresidents. *Financial aid:* In 1997–98, 2 students received aid, including 2 research assistantships (both to first-year students) totaling $15,000; teaching assistantships also available. Financial aid application deadline: 3/15. • Application contact: Kathleen Owen, Assistant to the Dean, 828-227-7398. Fax: 828-227-7480.

Western Illinois University, College of Education and Human Services, Department of Education Administration and Supervision, Macomb, IL 61455-1390. Awards MS Ed, Ed S. Accredited by NCATE. Part-time programs available. Faculty: 19 full-time (7 women). Students: 7 full-time (4 women), 218 part-time (105 women); includes 10 minority (7 African Americans, 1 Asian American, 2 Hispanics). Average age 38. 9 applicants, 89% accepted. In 1997, 42 master's, 14 Ed Ss awarded. *Degree requirements:* For master's, thesis or alternative required, foreign language not required. *Entrance requirements:* For master's, minimum GPA of 2.75. Application deadline: rolling. Application fee: $0 ($25 for international students). *Expenses:* Tuition $2304 per year full-time, $96 per semester hour part-time for state residents; $6912 per year full-time, $288 per semester hour part-time for nonresidents. Fees $944 per year full-time, $33 per semester hour part-time. *Financial aid:* Research assistantships, full tuition waivers available. Financial aid applicants required to submit FAFSA. *Faculty research:* Business and education partnerships, innovative practices, teacher training, standards-based teaching. • Col. Steve Reinhart, Interim Chairperson, 309-298-1070. Application contact: Barbara Baily, Director of Graduate Studies, 309-298-1806. Fax: 309-298-2245. E-mail: barb_baily@ccmail.wiu.edu.

Western Illinois University, College of Education and Human Services, Department of Counselor Education and College Student Personnel, Program in College Student Personnel, Macomb, IL 61455-1390. Awards MS. Accredited by NCATE. Part-time programs available. Faculty: 16 full-time (4 women). Students: 38 full-time (22 women), 3 part-time (1 woman); includes 7 minority (5 African Americans, 1 Asian American, 1 Hispanic), 5 international. Average age 25. 52 applicants, 37% accepted. In 1997, 18 degrees awarded. *Degree requirements:* Thesis or alternative required, foreign language not required. *Entrance requirements:* Interview. Application deadline: rolling. Application fee: $0 ($25 for international students). *Expenses:* Tuition $2304 per year full-time, $96 per semester hour part-time for state residents; $6912 per year full-time, $288 per semester hour part-time for nonresidents. Fees $944 per year full-time, $33 per semester hour part-time. *Financial aid:* In 1997–98, 36 students received aid, including 36 research assistantships averaging $610 per month; full tuition waivers also available. Financial aid applicants required to submit FAFSA. • Application contact: Barbara Baily, Director of Graduate Studies, 309-298-1806. Fax: 309-298-2245. E-mail: barb_baily@ccmail.wiu.edu.

Western Kentucky University, College of Education, Department of Educational Leadership, Bowling Green, KY 42101-3576. Offers programs in education (PhD, Ed S), guidance and counseling (MA Ed, Ed S), school administration (Ed D, Ed S), school business administration (MA Ed). Accredited by NCATE. PhD offered jointly with the University of Kentucky; Ed D offered jointly with the University of Louisville. Part-time and evening/weekend programs available. Postbaccalaureate distance learning degree programs offered (minimal on-campus study). Faculty: 20. Students: 92 full-time (73 women), 311 part-time (251 women); includes 25 minority (19 African Americans, 2 Asian Americans, 3 Hispanics, 1 Native American), 2 international. Average age 32. 114 applicants, 61% accepted. In 1997, 114 master's, 1 Ed S awarded. *Degree requirements:* For master's, thesis optional, foreign language not required; for Ed S, thesis, oral exam required, foreign language not required. *Entrance requirements:* For master's, GRE General Test (minimum combined score of 1150 on three sections; average 1307), minimum GPA of 2.5; for Ed S, GRE General Test (minimum combined score of 1250 on three sections), minimum GPA of 3.5. Application deadline: 8/1 (priority date; rolling processing; 12/1 for spring admission). Application fee: $20. *Tuition:* $2460 per year full-time, $133 per credit hour part-time for state residents; $6700 per year full-time, $369 per credit hour part-time for nonresidents. *Financial aid:* In 1997–98, 12 service awards (6 to first-year students) averaging $390 per month and totaling $41,600 were awarded; research assistantships, teaching assistantships, Federal Work-Study, institutionally sponsored loans also available. Aid available to part-time students. Financial aid application deadline: 4/1; applicants required to submit FAFSA. • Dr. Stephen B. Schnacke, Head, 502-745-4997. Fax: 502-745-5445.

Western Maryland College, Department of Education, Program in Educational Administration, Westminster, MD 21157-4390. Awards MS. Part-time and evening/weekend programs available. Faculty: 1 full-time (0 women), 5 part-time (0 women). Students: 76 full-time (68 women), 81 part-time (61 women). In 1997, 20 degrees awarded. *Degree requirements:* Thesis optional, foreign language not required. *Entrance requirements:* GRE General Test, MAT, or NTE. Application deadline: rolling. Application fee: $35. *Expenses:* Tuition $210 per credit hour. Fees $30 per semester. *Financial aid:* Career-related internships or fieldwork available. Financial aid application deadline: 3/1. • Dr. Herman Behling, Coordinator. Application contact: Jeanette Witt, Coordinator of Graduate Records, 410-857-2513. Fax: 410-857-2515. E-mail: jwitt@wmdc.edu.

Western Michigan University, College of Education, Department of Educational Leadership, Kalamazoo, MI 49008. Awards MA, Ed D, PhD, Ed S. Accredited by NCATE. Students: 16 full-time (9 women), 270 part-time (160 women); includes 34 minority (26 African Americans, 2 Asian Americans, 5 Hispanics, 1 Native American), 10 international. 86 applicants, 49% accepted. In 1997, 122 master's, 12 doctorates awarded. *Degree requirements:* For doctorate and Ed S, thesis/dissertation, oral exams. *Entrance requirements:* For doctorate and Ed S, GRE General Test. Application deadline: 3/15 (priority date; rolling processing). Application fee: $25. *Expenses:* Tuition $154 per credit hour for state residents; $372 per credit hour for nonresidents. Fees $602 per year full-time, $132 per semester part-time. *Financial aid:* Fellowships, research assistantships, teaching assistantships, Federal Work-Study available. Financial aid application deadline: 2/15; applicants required to submit FAFSA. • Dr. Alonzo Hannaford, Interim Chairperson, 616-387-3879. Application contact: Paula J. Boodt, Coordinator, Graduate Admissions and Recruitment, 616-387-2000. E-mail: paulaboodt@wmich.edu.

Western New Mexico University, School of Education, Silver City, NM 88062-0680. Offerings include school administration (MA). School faculty: 16 full-time (9 women). *Application deadline:* rolling. *Application fee:* $10. *Tuition:* $1516 per year full-time, $55 per credit part-time for state residents; $5604 per year full-time, $55 per credit part-time for nonresidents. • Dr. Bonnie Maldonado, Dean, 505-538-6415.

Western Washington University, Woodring College of Education, Program in Adult Education Administration, Bellingham, WA 98225-5996. Awards M Ed. Accredited by NCATE. Part-time programs available. Students: 27 full-time (20 women), 63 part-time (48 women). 25 applicants, 84% accepted. In 1997, 52 degrees awarded. *Degree requirements:* Thesis optional, foreign language not required. *Entrance requirements:* GRE General Test, TOEFL, minimum GPA of 3.0 in last 60 semester hours or last 90 quarter hours. Application deadline: 6/1 (rolling processing; 2/1 for spring admission). Application fee: $35. *Expenses:* Tuition $4200 per year full-time, $140 per credit part-time for state residents; $12,780 per year full-time, $426 per credit part-time for nonresidents. Fees $249 per year full-time, $83 per quarter part-time. *Financial aid:* Teaching assistantships, partial tuition waivers, Federal Work-Study, institutionally sponsored loans, and career-related internships or fieldwork available. Aid available to part-time students. Financial aid application deadline: 3/31. • Dr. Violet Malone, Adviser, 360-650-7318.

Western Washington University, Woodring College of Education, Program in Elementary and Secondary Educational Administration, Bellingham, WA 98225-5996. Awards M Ed. Accredited by NCATE. Part-time programs available. Students: 28 full-time (12 women), 24 part-time (7 women). 15 applicants, 100% accepted. In 1997, 33 degrees awarded. *Degree requirements:* Thesis optional, foreign language not required. *Entrance requirements:* GRE General Test, TOEFL, minimum GPA of 3.0 in last 60 semester hours or last 90 quarter hours. Application deadline: 6/1 (rolling processing; 2/1 for spring admission). Application fee: $35. *Expenses:* Tuition $4200 per year full-time, $140 per credit part-time for state residents; $12,780 per year full-time, $426 per credit part-time for nonresidents. Fees $249 per year full-time, $83 per quarter part-time. *Financial aid:* Teaching assistantships, partial tuition waivers, Federal Work-Study, institutionally sponsored loans, and career-related internships or fieldwork available. Aid available to part-time students. Financial aid application deadline: 3/31. • Dr. Marv Klein, Adviser, 360-650-3829. Application contact: Judy Gramm, Manager, 360-650-3090.

Western Washington University, Woodring College of Education, Program in Student Personnel Administration, Bellingham, WA 98225-5996. Awards M Ed. Accredited by NCATE. Part-time programs available. Students: 11 full-time (7 women), 3 part-time (2 women). 0 applicants. In 1997, 16 degrees awarded. *Degree requirements:* Thesis optional, foreign language not required. *Entrance requirements:* GRE General Test, TOEFL, minimum GPA of 3.0 in last 60 semester hours or last 90 quarter hours. Application deadline: 6/1. Application fee: $35. *Expenses:* Tuition $4200 per year full-time, $140 per credit part-time for state residents; $12,780 per year full-time, $426 per credit part-time for nonresidents. Fees $249 per year full-time, $83 per quarter part-time. *Financial aid:* Partial tuition waivers, Federal Work-Study, institutionally sponsored loans, and career-related internships or fieldwork available. Aid available to part-time students. Financial aid application deadline: 3/31. • Dr. John Utendale, Graduate Adviser, 360-650-2977.

Westfield State College, Department of Education, Program in School Administration, Westfield, MA 01086. Awards M Ed, CAGS. Part-time and evening/weekend programs available. Faculty: 2 full-time (1 woman), 6 part-time (1 woman). Students: 35 part-time (16 women). Average age 36. In 1997, 5 master's, 8 CAGSs awarded. *Degree requirements:* For master's, comprehensive exam, practicum required, foreign language and thesis not required; for CAGS, research-based field internship required, foreign language and thesis not required. *Entrance requirements:* For master's, GRE General Test or MAT, minimum undergraduate GPA of 2.7; for CAGS, master's degree. Application deadline: rolling. Application fee: $30. *Expenses:* Tuition $145 per credit for state residents; $155 per credit for nonresidents. Fees $90 per semester. *Financial aid:* Research assistantships, teaching assistantships, full and partial tuition waivers, Federal Work-Study, and career-related internships or fieldwork available. Aid available to part-time students. Financial aid application deadline: 4/1; applicants required to submit CSS PROFILE. *Faculty research:* Collaborative teacher education, developmental early childhood education. • Dr. Bernard Fleury, Interim Education Program Director, 413-572-5315. Application contact: Marcia Davio, Graduate Records Clerk, 413-572-8024.

Directory: Educational Administration

Westminster College, Programs in Education, Program in Administration, South Market Street, New Wilmington, PA 16172-0001. Awards M Ed, Certificate. Part-time and evening/weekend programs available. Students: 60 part-time (25 women). In 1997, 5 master's awarded (100% found work related to degree). *Degree requirements:* For master's, computer language required, foreign language and thesis not required. *Average time to degree:* master's–1.5 years full-time, 2.5 years part-time. *Entrance requirements:* For master's, minimum GPA of 2.75. Application deadline: 8/30 (priority date; rolling processing; 1/15 for spring admission). Application fee: $20. *Expenses:* Tuition $1104 per course. Fees $30 per course. *Financial aid:* Grants and career-related internships or fieldwork available. • Dr. Samuel A. Farmerie, Coordinator, 724-946-7181. Fax: 724-946-7171. E-mail: farmersa@westminster.edu.

West Texas A&M University, College of Education and Social Sciences, Division of Education, Program in Administration, Canyon, TX 79016-0001. Awards M Ed. Part-time and evening/weekend programs available. Students: 9 full-time (7 women), 64 part-time (33 women); includes 7 minority (4 African Americans, 3 Hispanics). Average age 34. 18 applicants, 50% accepted. In 1997, 30 degrees awarded. *Degree requirements:* Comprehensive exam required, foreign language and thesis not required. *Average time to degree:* master's–3 years full-time, 6 years part-time. *Entrance requirements:* GRE General Test (combined average 964). Application deadline: rolling. Application fee: $0 ($50 for international students). Electronic applications accepted. *Expenses:* Tuition $46 per semester hour for state residents; $259 per semester hour for nonresidents. Fees $156 per semester (minimum). *Financial aid:* Partial tuition waivers, Federal Work-Study, institutionally sponsored loans, and career-related internships or fieldwork available. Aid available to part-time students. Financial aid applicants required to submit CSS PROFILE or FAFSA. • Application contact: Dr. Mick Stevens, Graduate Adviser, 806-651-2613. E-mail: mick.stevens@wtamu.edu.

West Virginia University, College of Human Resources and Education, Department of Advanced Educational Studies, Program in Educational Leadership Studies, Morgantown, WV 26506. Offers education (Ed D), educational leadership studies (MA). Accredited by NCATE. Ed D offered jointly with West Virginia Graduate College and Marshall University. Part-time programs available. Students: 16 full-time (6 women), 87 part-time (50 women); includes 5 minority (2 African Americans, 1 Asian American, 1 Hispanic, 1 Native American), 1 international. Average age 35. 36 applicants, 50% accepted. In 1997, 51 master's, 18 doctorates awarded. *Degree requirements:* For master's, content exams required, foreign language and thesis not required; for doctorate, dissertation, comprehensive exam required, foreign language not required. *Entrance requirements:* For master's, TOEFL (minimum score 550), minimum GPA of 2.75; for doctorate, GRE General Test (minimum combined score of 1100), MAT (minimum score 50), TOEFL (minimum score 550), minimum GPA of 3.25. Application deadline: rolling. Application fee: $45. *Tuition:* $2820 per year full-time, $149 per credit hour part-time for state residents; $8104 per year full-time, $443 per credit hour part-time for nonresidents. *Financial aid:* In 1997–98, 6 teaching assistantships (1 to a first-year student) were awarded; partial tuition waivers, Federal Work-Study, institutionally sponsored loans, and career-related internships or fieldwork also available. Financial aid application deadline: 2/1; applicants required to submit FAFSA. *Faculty research:* Evaluation, collective bargaining, educational law, international higher education, superintendency, supervision, adult learning. • Dr. David L. McCrory, Chair, Department of Advanced Educational Studies, 304-283-3803 Ext. 1706. Fax: 304-293-2279. E-mail: dmccrory@wvu.edu.

Wheelock College, Graduate School, Program in Leadership and Policy in Early Care and Education, Boston, MA 02215. Awards MS, CAGS. Part-time programs available. Faculty: 2 full-time (0 women), 10 part-time (7 women), 6 FTE. Students: 8 full-time, 35 part-time. *Degree requirements:* For CAGS, thesis. *Entrance requirements:* Interview. Application deadline: rolling. Application fee: $35 ($40 for international students). Electronic applications accepted. *Tuition:* $525 per credit. *Financial aid:* Graduate assistantships, grants, Federal Work-Study, institutionally sponsored loans, and career-related internships or fieldwork available. Aid available to part-time students. Financial aid application deadline: 4/1; applicants required to submit FAFSA. *Faculty research:* Career development in early education, children's play, leadership for community development. • Joan Block, Co-Coordinator, 617-734-5200 Ext. 157. E-mail: jblock@wheelock.edu. Application contact: Martha Sheehan, Director of Graduate Admissions, 617-734-5200 Ext. 212. Fax: 617-232-7127. E-mail: msheehan@wheelock.edu.

Whittier College, Department of Education, Program in Educational Administration, Whittier, CA 90608-0634. Awards MA Ed. Part-time and evening/weekend programs available. Faculty: 7 (2 women). Students: 12 part-time (8 women); includes 6 minority (1 Asian American, 5 Hispanics). Average age 27. 5 applicants, 100% accepted. In 1997, 1 degree awarded (100% found work related to degree). *Degree requirements:* Thesis required, foreign language not required. *Entrance requirements:* GRE General Test, MAT. Application deadline: rolling. Application fee: $60. *Tuition:* $330 per credit. *Financial aid:* Career-related internships or fieldwork available. *Faculty research:* Community relations. • Richard Bartholome, Coordinator of Teacher Education Support Services, 562-907-4200 Ext. 4437. Application contact: Catherine George, Credential Analyst, 562-907-4200 Ext. 4443.

Whitworth College, Graduate Studies in Education, Program in Education Administration, Spokane, WA 99251-0001. Awards M Ed. Accredited by NCATE. Part-time and evening/weekend programs available. *Degree requirements:* Comprehensive exams, internship, practicum, research project, or thesis required, foreign language not required. *Entrance requirements:* GRE General Test. Application deadline: 9/1 (priority date; rolling processing; 2/1 for spring admission). Application fee: $25. *Faculty research:* Rural staff development.

Wichita State University, College of Education, Department of Administration, Counseling, Educational and School Psychology, Wichita, KS 67260. Offerings include education administration (M Ed, Ed D). Accredited by NCATE. Department faculty: 15 full-time (7 women), 71 part-time (33 women). *Degree requirements:* For master's, comprehensive exam required, thesis optional, foreign language not required; for doctorate, 1 foreign language, dissertation. *Entrance requirements:* For master's, TOEFL (minimum score 550), minimum GPA of 2.75; for doctorate, GRE General Test, TOEFL (minimum score 550). Application deadline: 7/1 (priority date; rolling processing; 1/1 for spring admission). Application fee: $25 ($40 for international students). Electronic applications accepted. *Expenses:* Tuition $2303 per year full-time, $96 per credit hour part-time for state residents; $7691 per year full-time, $321 per credit hour part-time for nonresidents. Fees $490 per year full-time, $75 per semester (minimum) part-time. • Dr. Orpha Duell, Chairperson, 316-978-6299. Fax: 316-978-3102. E-mail: oduell@wsuhub.uc.twsu.edu.

Wilkes University, Department of Education, Wilkes-Barre, PA 18766-0002. Offerings include educational leadership (MS Ed). Department faculty: 6 full-time, 14 part-time. *Application deadline:* rolling. *Application fee:* $30. *Expenses:* Tuition $12,552 per year full-time, $523 per credit hour part-time. Fees $240 per year full-time, $10 per credit hour part-time. • Dr. Douglas Lynch, Chair, 717-408-4680.

William Carey College, Department of Education, Concentration in Educational Leadership, Hattiesburg, MS 39401-5499. Awards M Ed. *Entrance requirements:* NTE, minimum GPA of 2.5. Application deadline: 8/15 (priority date; rolling processing). Application fee: $0. *Tuition:* $130 per semester hour. • Dr. William Hetrick, Dean, College of Education and Psychology, Graduate Division, 601-582-6217.

William Woods University, College of Graduate and Adult Studies, Program in Education, Fulton, MO 65251-1098. Offerings include administration (M Ed). Program faculty: 7 full-time (5 women), 20 part-time (9 women). *Degree requirements:* Thesis or alternative required, foreign language not required. *Entrance requirements:* 2 years of teaching experience, minimum GPA of 2.5, teaching certificate. Application deadline: rolling. Application fee: $25. *Tuition:* $240 per credit. • Dr. Larry Ewing, Head, 573-592-4339. Application contact: Mary Henley, Director of Recruitment, 800-995-3199. Fax: 573-592-1164. E-mail: cgas@iris.wmwoods.edu.

Wilmington College, Division of Education, New Castle, DE 19720-6491. Offerings include innovation and leadership (Ed D), school leadership (M Ed). *Degree requirements:* For doctorate, dissertation. *Entrance requirements:* For doctorate, work experience. Application deadline: rolling. Application fee: $25. *Expenses:* Tuition $4410 per year full-time, $735 per course part-time. Fees $50 per year. • Dr. Barbara Raetsch, Chair, 302-328-9401. Application contact: Michael Lee, Director of Admissions and Financial Aid, 302-328-9401 Ext. 102.

Winona State University, Graduate Studies, College of Education, Department of Educational Leadership, Winona, MN 55987-5838. Awards MS, Ed S. Accredited by NCATE. Part-time and evening/weekend programs available. Faculty: 4 full-time (1 woman). Students: 6 full-time (0 women), 47 part-time (19 women). 18 applicants, 100% accepted. In 1997, 9 master's, 2 Ed Ss awarded. *Degree requirements:* For master's, thesis or alternative required, foreign language not required. *Entrance requirements:* For master's, GRE General Test. Application deadline: 8/8 (priority date; rolling processing; 2/17 for spring admission). Application fee: $20. *Financial aid:* Federal Work-Study available. Aid available to part-time students. • Dr. Lee Gray, Chairperson, 507-457-5346. E-mail: lgray@vax2.winona.msus.edu.

Winthrop University, College of Education, Program in Educational Administration, Rock Hill, SC 29733. Awards M Ed, Ed S. Accredited by NCATE. Part-time programs available. Students: 6 full-time (4 women), 68 part-time (45 women); includes 16 minority (15 African Americans, 1 Native American). Average age 33. In 1997, 18 master's, 9 Ed Ss awarded. *Degree requirements:* Comprehensive exam required, foreign language and thesis not required. *Entrance requirements:* For master's, GRE General Test (minimum combined score of 825) or MAT (minimum score 36), South Carolina Class III teaching certificate, 2 years of teaching experience, minimum GPA of 2.5, interview; for Ed S, GRE General Test (minimum combined score of 850) or MAT (minimum score 37), master's degree, teaching or administrative experience, sample of written work, minimum graduate GPA of 3.25, interview. Application deadline: 7/15 (priority date; rolling processing; 12/1 for spring admission). Application fee: $35. *Tuition:* $3928 per year full-time, $164 per credit hour part-time for state residents; $7060 per year full-time, $294 per credit hour part-time for nonresidents. *Financial aid:* Graduate assistantships, graduate scholarships, Federal Work-Study available. Aid available to part-time students. Financial aid application deadline: 2/1; applicants required to submit FAFSA. • Dr. George Reddick, Chairman, 803-323-2151. Fax: 803-323-4755. E-mail: reddickg@winthrop.edu. Application contact: Sharon Johnson, Director of Graduate Studies, 803-323-2204. Fax: 803-323-2292. E-mail: johnsons@winthrop.edu.

Worcester State College, Graduate Studies, Department of Education, Program in Leadership and Administration, Worcester, MA 01602-2597. Awards M Ed. Students: 0. *Degree requirements:* Comprehensive exam. *Entrance requirements:* GRE General Test or MAT. Application fee: $10 ($40 for international students). *Tuition:* $127 per credit hour. • Dr. James Rauker, Graduate Coordinator, 508-929-8071. Application contact: Andrea Wetmore, Graduate Admissions Counselor, 508-929-8120. E-mail: awetmore@worc.mass.edu.

Wright State University, College of Education and Human Services, Department of Educational Leadership, Program in Advanced Educational Leadership, Dayton, OH 45435. Awards Ed S. Accredited by NCATE. Students: 3 full-time (0 women), 18 part-time (11 women); includes 1 minority (African American). Average age 35. 12 applicants, 92% accepted. In 1997, 4 degrees awarded. *Entrance requirements:* GRE General Test, MAT, TOEFL (minimum score 550). Application fee: $25. *Tuition:* $5109 per year full-time, $161 per credit hour part-time for state residents; $9039 per year full-time, $282 per credit hour part-time for nonresidents. *Financial aid:* Available to part-time students. Financial aid applicants required to submit FAFSA. • Dr. Charles W. Ryan, Head, 937-775-3286. Application contact: Gerald C. Malicki, Assistant Dean and Director of Graduate Admissions and Records, 937-775-2976. Fax: 937-775-2357. E-mail: wsugrad@wright.edu.

Wright State University, College of Education and Human Services, Department of Educational Leadership, Programs in Educational Leadership, Dayton, OH 45435. Awards MA, M Ed. Accredited by NCATE. Students: 25 full-time (16 women), 538 part-time (460 women); includes 18 minority (14 African Americans, 2 Hispanics, 2 Native Americans). Average age 33. 216 applicants, 96% accepted. In 1997, 256 degrees awarded. *Degree requirements:* Thesis required (for some programs), foreign language not required. *Entrance requirements:* GRE General Test, MAT, TOEFL (minimum score 550). Application fee: $25. *Tuition:* $5109 per year full-time, $161 per credit hour part-time for state residents; $9039 per year full-time, $282 per credit hour part-time for nonresidents. *Financial aid:* Available to part-time students. Financial aid applicants required to submit FAFSA. • Application contact: Gerald C. Malicki, Assistant Dean and Director of Graduate Admissions and Records, 937-775-2976. Fax: 937-775-2357. E-mail: wsugrad@wright.edu.

Xavier University, College of Social Sciences, Department of Education, Program in Educational Administration, Cincinnati, OH 45207-2111. Awards M Ed. Part-time programs available. Faculty: 3 full-time (0 women), 1 part-time (0 women), 3.25 FTE. Students: 4 full-time (3 women), 30 part-time (19 women); includes 4 minority (2 African Americans, 1 Asian American, 1 Hispanic). Average age 37. 29 applicants, 59% accepted. In 1997, 35 degrees awarded. *Degree requirements:* Comprehensive exam, research project required, foreign language and thesis not required. *Entrance requirements:* GRE or MAT (minimum score 35), minimum GPA of 2.8. Application deadline: 8/15 (priority date; rolling processing). Application fee: $25. *Financial aid:* In 1997–98, 32 students received aid, including 32 scholarships (4 to first-year students). Aid available to part-time students. *Faculty research:* Total quality management for school, ethics in administration, fiscal-social equity in schools. • Dr. Leo Bradley, Director, 513-745-2982. Fax: 513-745-1052. E-mail: bradley@admin.xu.edu. Application contact: Sheila Speth, Director of Graduate Services, 513-745-3360. Fax: 513-745-1048. E-mail: xugrad@admin.xu.edu.

Xavier University of Louisiana, Programs in Education, New Orleans, LA 70125-1098. Offerings include administration and supervision (MA). Accredited by NCATE. Faculty: 9 full-time (6 women), 12 part-time (5 women). *Average time to degree:* master's–3 years full-time, 7 years part-time. *Application deadline:* 7/1 (rolling processing; 12/1 for spring admission). *Application fee:* $30. *Tuition:* $200 per semester hour. • Dr. Rosalind Hale, Chair, Division of Education, 504-483-7536. Fax: 504-485-7909. Application contact: Marlene Robinson, Director of Graduate Admissions, 504-483-7487. Fax: 504-485-7921. E-mail: mrobinso@xula.edu.

Yeshiva University, Azrieli Graduate School of Jewish Education and Administration, New York, NY 10033-3201. Awards MS, Ed D, Specialist. Part-time and evening/weekend programs available. Faculty: 1 full-time (0 women), 18 part-time (4 women). Students: 146 part-time (59 women); includes 8 international. Average age 25. 58 applicants, 83% accepted. In 1997, 27 master's, 1 doctorate, 1 Specialist awarded. Terminal master's awarded for partial completion of doctoral program. *Degree requirements:* For master's, 1 foreign language, student teaching, comprehensive exam or thesis required, thesis optional; for doctorate, 1 foreign language, dissertation, certifying and comprehensive exams, internship; for Specialist, 1 foreign language, certifying and comprehensive exams, internship required, thesis not required. *Entrance requirements:* For master's, GRE General Test (minimum score 500 on each section; average 630), BA in Jewish studies or equivalent; for doctorate, GRE General Test (minimum score 500 on each section), master's degree in Jewish education, 2 years of teaching experience; for Specialist, GRE General Test, master's degree in Jewish education, 2 years of teaching experience. Application deadline: rolling. Application fee: $35. *Expenses:* Tuition $475 per credit. Fees $100 per year. *Financial aid:* In 1997–98, 118 students received aid, including 23 fellowships (all to first-year students), 95 scholarships (35 to first-year students); partial tuition waivers, institutionally sponsored loans also available. Aid available to part-time students. Financial aid application deadline: 4/1. *Faculty research:* Jewish elementary and secondary curriculum development, administration and supervision, effects of day school education on adult attitudes and behavior, adult Jewish education. • Dr. Yitzchak Handel, Director, 212-340-7705. Fax: 212-340-7787.

Youngstown State University, College of Education, Department of Educational Administration, Youngstown, OH 44555-0002. Offers programs in educational administration (MS Ed), educational leadership (Ed D). Accredited by NCATE. Part-time and evening/weekend programs available. Faculty: 12 full-time (4 women), 7 part-time (2 women). Students: 12 full-time (7 women), 194 part-time (89 women); includes 12 minority (all African Americans). 23 applicants, 96% accepted. In 1997, 30 master's awarded. *Degree requirements:* For master's, comprehensive exam required, foreign language and thesis not required; for doctorate, dissertation, comprehensive exam required, foreign language not required. *Entrance requirements:* For master's, TOEFL (minimum score 550), GRE, MAT, or teaching certificate; minimum GPA of 2.5; for doctorate, GRE General Test, GRE Subject Test (score in 50th percentile or higher), interview, minimum GPA of 3.5. Application deadline: 8/15 (priority date; rolling processing; 2/15 for spring admission). Application fee: $30 ($75 for international students). *Expenses:* Tuition $90 per credit hour for state residents; $144 per credit hour (minimum) for nonresidents. Fees $528 per year full-time, $244 per year (minimum) part-time. *Financial aid:* In 1997–98, 18 students received aid, including 1 fellowship totaling $11,715, 1 research assistantship averaging $666 per month and totaling $8,520, 16 scholarships totaling $8,772; teaching assistantships, Federal Work-Study, institutionally sponsored loans also available. Aid available to part-time students. Financial aid application deadline: 3/1. *Faculty research:* Administrative theory, computer applications, education law, school and community relations, finance principalship. • Dr. Linda Wesson, Chair, 330-742-1436. Application contact: Dr. Peter J. Kasvinsky, Dean of Graduate Studies, 330-742-3091. Fax: 330-742-1580. E-mail: amgrad03@ysub.ysu.edu.

Educational Measurement and Evaluation

Abilene Christian University, College of Arts and Sciences, Department of Education, Educational Diagnostician Program, Abilene, TX 79699-9100. Awards M Ed. Part-time programs available. Faculty: 11 part-time (4 women). Students: 1 full-time (0 women), 5 part-time (3 women). 6 applicants, 83% accepted. In 1997, 2 degrees awarded (100% found work related to degree). *Degree requirements:* Comprehensive exam required, foreign language and thesis not required. *Entrance requirements:* GRE General Test or MAT. Application deadline: 4/1 (priority date; rolling processing; 11/1 for spring admission). Application fee: $25 ($45 for international students). *Expenses:* Tuition $308 per credit hour. Fees $430 per year full-time, $85 per semester (minimum) part-time. *Financial aid:* Federal Work-Study available. Aid available to part-time students. Financial aid application deadline: 4/1. • Dr. Roger Gee, Graduate Adviser, 915-674-2122. Application contact: Dr. Carley Dodd, Graduate Dean, 915-674-2354. Fax: 915-674-6717. E-mail: gradinfo@nicanor.acu.edu.

Adelphi University, School of Education, Program in Educational Assessment, Garden City, NY 11530. Awards Certificate. Part-time and evening/weekend programs available. Students: 0. In 1997, 1 degree awarded. *Application deadline:* rolling. *Application fee:* $50. *Expenses:* Tuition $16,000 per year full-time, $485 per credit part-time. Fees $500 per year full-time, $150 per semester part-time. *Financial aid:* Career-related internships or fieldwork available. Financial aid application deadline: 3/1. *Faculty research:* Preparation of educational diagnosticians for schools and clinical settings. • Dr. Sheila Hollander, Chair, 516-877-4085.

Angelo State University, College of Professional Studies, Department of Education, Program in Educational Diagnostics, San Angelo, TX 76909. Awards M Ed. Part-time and evening/weekend programs available. Students: 9 part-time (all women). Average age 35. 3 applicants, 67% accepted. In 1997, 1 degree awarded. *Degree requirements:* Comprehensive exam required, thesis optional, foreign language not required. *Entrance requirements:* GRE General Test, minimum GPA of 2.5. Application deadline: 8/7 (priority date; rolling processing; 1/2 for spring admission). Application fee: $25 ($50 for international students). *Expenses:* Tuition $1022 per year full-time, $36 per semester hour part-time for state residents; $7382 per year full-time, $246 per semester hour part-time for nonresidents. Fees $1140 per year full-time, $165 per semester (minimum) part-time. *Financial aid:* In 1997–98, 1 fellowship was awarded; teaching assistantships, graduate assistantships, partial tuition waivers, Federal Work-Study, and career-related internships or fieldwork also available. Aid available to part-time students. Financial aid application deadline: 8/1. • Dr. James Hademenos, Head, Department of Education, 915-942-2052.

Boston College, Graduate School of Education, Department of Educational Research, Measurement, and Evaluation, Chestnut Hill, MA 02167-9991. Awards M Ed, PhD, CAES. Accredited by NCATE. Students: 19 full-time (12 women), 20 part-time (13 women); includes 6 minority (1 African American, 3 Asian Americans, 2 Hispanics), 5 international. 23 applicants, 78% accepted. In 1997, 2 master's, 2 doctorates awarded. *Degree requirements:* For master's, comprehensive exams required, thesis not required; for doctorate, computer language, dissertation, comprehensive exams; for CAES, comprehensive exam required, thesis not required. *Entrance requirements:* For master's and doctorate, GRE General Test; for CAES, GRE General Test or MAT. Application deadline: 3/15 (11/15 for spring admission). Application fee: $40. *Expenses:* Tuition $626 per semester hour. Fees $80 per year (minimum) full-time, $30 per semester part-time. *Financial aid:* Fellowships, research assistantships, teaching assistantships, administrative assistantships, merit scholarships, Federal Work-Study, and career-related internships or fieldwork available. Aid available to part-time students. *Faculty research:* Classroom assessment, effects and uses of tests in public policy, history of testing, national and international assessment and surveys. • Dr. Walt Haney, Chairperson, 617-552-4710. Application contact: Arline Riordan, Graduate Admissions Director, 617-552-4214. Fax: 617-552-0812. E-mail: riordana@bc.edu.

Bucknell University, College of Arts and Sciences, Department of Education, Specialization in Educational Research, Lewisburg, PA 17837. Awards MS Ed. *Degree requirements:* Thesis or alternative required, foreign language not required. *Entrance requirements:* GRE General Test (minimum combined score of 1000), TOEFL (minimum score 550), minimum GPA of 2.8. Application deadline: 6/1 (priority date; rolling processing; 12/1 for spring admission). Application fee: $25. *Tuition:* $2410 per course. *Financial aid:* Assistantships available. Financial aid application deadline: 3/1. • Dr. Robert Midkiff, Head, Department of Education, 717-524-1133.

Claremont Graduate University, Department of Education, Claremont, CA 91711-6163. Offerings include evaluation and quantitative analysis (MA, PhD). PhD offered jointly with San Diego State University; MA (mathematics education) offered jointly with the Department of Mathematics. Terminal master's awarded for partial completion of doctoral program. Department faculty: 13 full-time (6 women), 13 part-time (10 women). *Degree requirements:* For master's, thesis or alternative; for doctorate, dissertation. *Entrance requirements:* GRE General Test. Application deadline: 2/15 (priority date; rolling processing). Application fee: $40. Electronic applications accepted. *Expenses:* Tuition $20,250 per year full-time, $913 per unit part-time. Fees $130 per year. • David Drew, Chair, 909-621-8075. Application contact: Ethel Rogers, Associate Director, 909-621-8317. Fax: 909-621-8734. E-mail: educ@cgu.edu.

Cleveland State University, College of Education, Department of Curriculum and Foundations, Cleveland, OH 44115-2440. Offerings include educational research (M Ed). Department faculty: 14 full-time (9 women). *Entrance requirements:* GRE General Test or MAT (score in 50th percentile or higher). Application deadline: 9/1 (priority date; rolling processing). Application fee: $25. *Expenses:* Tuition $5252 per year full-time, $202 per credit hour part-time for state residents; $10,504 per year full-time, $404 per credit hour part-time for nonresidents. Fees $2.25 per credit hour (minimum). • Dr. David Adams, Interim Chairperson, 216-687-7128. Fax: 216-687-5370. E-mail: d.adams@csuohio.edu.

Cornell University, Graduate Fields of Agriculture and Life Sciences, Field of Education, Ithaca, NY 14853-0001. Offerings include educational psychology and measurement (MPS, MS, PhD), educational research methodology (MPS, MS, PhD). Terminal master's awarded for partial completion of doctoral program. Faculty: 26 full-time. *Degree requirements:* For doctorate, dissertation required, foreign language not required. *Entrance requirements:* For doctorate, GRE General Test or MAT, TOEFL. Application deadline: 5/1. Application fee: $65. Electronic applications accepted. • Director of Graduate Studies, 607-255-4278. Application contact: Graduate Field Assistant, 607-255-4278. E-mail: edgrfld@cornell.edu.

Florida State University, College of Education, Department of Educational Research, Program in Educational Psychology, Tallahassee, FL 32306. Offerings include measurement and statistics (MS, PhD, Ed S), program evaluation (MS, PhD, Ed S). Program faculty: 7 full-time (1 woman), 2 part-time (0 women). *Degree requirements:* For master's and Ed S, comprehensive exam required, thesis optional; for doctorate, dissertation, comprehensive exam. *Entrance requirements:* GRE General Test (minimum combined score of 1000), minimum GPA of 3.0. Application deadline: 7/1 (priority date; rolling processing; 11/1 for spring admission). Application fee: $20. *Tuition:* $139 per credit hour for state residents; $482 per credit hour for nonresidents. • Dr. Marcy Driscoll, Chair, Department of Educational Research, 850-644-4592. E-mail: driscoll@mail.coe.fsu.edu. Application contact: Admissions Secretary, 850-644-4592. Fax: 850-644-8776.

Gallaudet University, School of Education and Human Services, Department of Educational Foundations and Research, Washington, DC 20002-3625. Offers program in research and evaluation (MA). Accredited by NCATE. *Degree requirements:* Thesis optional. *Entrance requirements:* GRE General Test or MAT. Application deadline: 2/15 (priority date; rolling processing). Application fee: $50. *Expenses:* Tuition $7064 per year full-time, $392 per credit part-time. Fees $50 (one-time charge). *Financial aid:* Application deadline 8/1. • Dr. Thomas N. Kluwin, Chair, 202-651-5545. Application contact: Deborah DeStefano, Director of Admissions, 202-651-5253. Fax: 202-651-5744. E-mail: adm_destefan@gallua.bitnet.

Georgia State University, College of Education, Department of Educational Policy Studies, Program in Educational Research, Atlanta, GA 30303-3083. Offers educational research (MS); research, measurements and statistics (PhD). Accredited by NCATE. Students: 12 full-time (8 women), 8 part-time (5 women); includes 6 minority (3 African Americans, 3 Asian Americans), 5 international. Average age 38. 1 applicant, 0% accepted. In 1997, 1 master's, 2 doctorates awarded. *Degree requirements:* For master's, thesis or project; for doctorate, dissertation, comprehensive exam. *Entrance requirements:* For master's, GRE General Test (minimum combined score of 800), MAT (minimum score 44), minimum GPA of 2.5; for doctorate, GRE General Test (minimum score 500 on verbal section, 500 on either quantitative or analytical sections) or MAT (minimum score 53), minimum GPA of 3.3. Application fee: $25. *Expenses:* Tuition $2673 per year full-time, $99 per semester hour part-time for state residents; $10,692 per year full-time, $396 per semester hour part-time for nonresidents. Fees $228 per year. *Financial aid:* Research assistantships available. *Faculty research:* Educational statistics, item response theory, instructional computing, measurement. • Dr. H. Parker Blount, Chair, Department of Educational Policy Studies, 404-651-2582.

Hofstra University, School of Education and Allied Human Services, Department of Counseling, Research, Special Education and Rehabilitation, Program in Educational Research and Program Evaluation, Hempstead, NY 11549. Offers program evaluation (MS Ed). Accredited by NCATE. Part-time and evening/weekend programs available. Faculty: 2 full-time (both women), 4 part-time (2 women). Students: 0. 0 applicants. In 1997, 1 degree awarded. *Degree requirements:* Thesis, comprehensive exam, departmental qualifying exam required, foreign language not required. *Entrance requirements:* GRE General Test, interview. Application deadline: rolling. Application fee: $40 ($75 for international students). *Expenses:* Tuition $10,968 per year full-time, $457 per credit hour part-time. Fees $670 per year full-time, $112 per semester (minimum) part-time. *Financial aid:* Institutionally sponsored loans and career-related internships or fieldwork available. Aid available to part-time students. Financial aid applicants required to submit FAFSA. *Faculty research:* Evaluation of teaching in higher education. • Application contact: Mary Beth Carey, Dean of Admissions, 516-463-6700. Fax: 516-560-7660. E-mail: hofstra@hofstra.edu.

Houston Baptist University, College of Education and Behavioral Sciences, Programs in Education, Houston, TX 77074-3298. Offerings include educational diagnostician (M Ed). Faculty: 9 full-time (5 women), 4 part-time (3 women). *Degree requirements:* Comprehensive exam required, foreign language and thesis not required. *Entrance requirements:* GRE General Test (minimum combined score of 850), minimum GPA of 2.5, teaching certificate. Application deadline: 7/1 (priority date; rolling processing; 1/1 for spring admission). Application fee: $25 ($85 for international students). *Expenses:* Tuition $280 per semester hour. Fees $235 per quarter. • Dr. John Lutjemeier, Head, 281-649-3000 Ext. 2336. Application contact: Judy Ferguson, Program Assistant, 281-649-3241.

Iowa State University of Science and Technology, College of Education, Department of Educational Leadership and Policy Studies, Program in Research and Evaluation, Ames, IA 50011. Awards MS. *Degree requirements:* Thesis or alternative. *Entrance requirements:* TOEFL. Application fee: $20 ($30 for international students). *Expenses:* Tuition $3166 per year full-time, $176 per credit part-time for state residents; $9324 per year full-time, $518 per credit part-time for nonresidents. Fees $200 per year. • Dr. Mary Huba, Coordinator, 515-294-7358. E-mail: mhuba@iastate.edu.

Kent State University, Graduate School of Education, Department of Educational Foundations and Special Services, Program in Educational Foundations, Kent, OH 44242-0001. Offerings include evaluation and measurement (MA, M Ed, PhD), learning and development (MA, M Ed). One or more programs accredited by NCATE. Program faculty: 8 full-time (3 women), 15 part-time (10 women). *Degree requirements:* For master's, thesis (MA) required, foreign language not required; for doctorate, dissertation required, foreign language not required. *Entrance requirements:* For master's, GRE General Test; for doctorate, GRE General Test (minimum score 550 on verbal section). Application deadline: rolling. Application fee: $30. *Tuition:* $4752 per year full-time, $216 per credit hour part-time for state residents; $9213 per year full-time, $419 per credit hour part-time for nonresidents. • Dr. Averil McClelland, Coordinator, 330-672-2294. Application contact: Deborah Barber, Director, Office of Academic Services, 330-672-2862. Fax: 330-672-3549.

Louisiana State University and Agricultural and Mechanical College, College of Education, Department of Administrative and Foundational Services, Baton Rouge, LA 70803. Offerings include research methodology (PhD). Accredited by NCATE. Terminal master's awarded for partial completion of doctoral program. Department faculty: 16 full-time (5 women), 1 part-time (0 women). *Degree requirements:* Dissertation required, foreign language not required. *Entrance requirements:* GRE General Test (minimum combined score of 1000; average 1100), minimum GPA of 3.0. Application deadline: 1/25 (priority date; rolling processing). Application fee: $25. *Tuition:* $2736 per year full-time, $285 per semester (minimum) part-time for state

Directory: Educational Measurement and Evaluation

Louisiana State University and Agricultural and Mechanical College (continued)

residents; $6636 per year full-time, $460 per semester (minimum) part-time for nonresidents. • Barbara Fuhrmann, Chair, 504-388-6900. Application contact: Jim Fox, Graduate Adviser, 504-388-6933. Fax: 504-388-6918.

Loyola University Chicago, School of Education, Department of Counseling Psychology, Program in Research Methods/Human Development, 820 North Michigan Avenue, Chicago, IL 60611-2196. Awards MA, M Ed, PhD. MA and PhD offered through the Graduate School. Students: 9 full-time (7 women), 11 part-time (7 women); includes 5 minority (1 African American, 3 Asian Americans, 1 Hispanic), 4 international. Average age 25. In 1997, 2 master's awarded (50% found work related to degree, 50% continued full-time study); 1 doctorate awarded (100% entered university research/teaching). *Degree requirements:* For master's, comprehensive exam (M Ed), thesis (MA) required, foreign language not required; for doctorate, 1 foreign language, computer language, dissertation, comprehensive exam. *Average time to degree:* master's–2 years full-time, 5 years part-time; doctorate–5 years full-time. *Entrance requirements:* For master's, GRE General Test; for doctorate, GRE General Test, interview. Application deadline: 8/1 (priority date; rolling processing). Application fee: $35. *Tuition:* $467 per semester hour. *Financial aid:* In 1997–98, 4 research assistantships averaging $800 per month were awarded; fellowships, teaching assistantships also available. Financial aid application deadline: 2/1. *Faculty research:* Circular statistics, program evaluation, psychological measurement, infant attachment, adolescent development. • Dr. Jack Kavanagh, Director, 847-853-3325. Fax: 847-853-3375. E-mail: #w34jkl@cpua.it.luc.edu.

Michigan State University, College of Education, Department of Counseling, Educational Psychology and Special Education, East Lansing, MI 48824-1020. Offerings include measurement and quantitative methods (PhD). Department faculty: 42 (14 women). *Degree requirements:* Dissertation required, foreign language not required. *Entrance requirements:* GRE General Test (combined average 1800 on three sections). Application deadline: rolling. Application fee: $30 ($40 for international students). *Expenses:* Tuition $4609 per year full-time, $223 per credit hour (minimum) part-time for state residents; $8704 per year full-time, $450 per credit hour (minimum) part-time for nonresidents. Fees $576 per year full-time, $476 per year part-time. • Dr. Richard Prawat, Chairperson, 517-353-6417. Application contact: Sharon Anderson, Graduate Secretary, 517-355-6683. Fax: 517-353-6393. E-mail: sharand@msu.edu.

Mississippi State University, College of Education, Department of Counselor Education and Educational Psychology, Mississippi State, MS 39762. Offerings include general education psychology (MS), with option in research and evaluation. Accredited by NCATE. Department faculty: 17 full-time (7 women), 7 part-time (2 women). *Degree requirements:* Comprehensive oral or written exam required, thesis optional, foreign language not required. *Entrance requirements:* GRE, minimum QPA of 3.0 in last 2 years. Application deadline: 3/1. Application fee: $0 ($25 for international students). *Tuition:* $3017 per year full-time, $168 per credit hour part-time for state residents; $6119 per year full-time, $340 per credit hour part-time for nonresidents. • Dr. Tom Hosie, Head, 601-325-3426. Fax: 601-325-3263. E-mail: hosie@colled.msstate.edu.

Morehead State University, College of Education and Behavioral Sciences, Department of Leadership and Secondary Education, Morehead, KY 40351. Offerings include educational policy studies and evaluation (Ed D). Accredited by NCATE. Ed D offered jointly with the University of Kentucky. Department faculty: 12 full-time (6 women), 7 part-time (3 women). *Application deadline:* 8/1 (priority date; rolling processing; 12/1 for spring admission). *Application fee:* $0. *Tuition:* $2470 per year full-time, $138 per semester hour part-time for state residents; $6710 per year full-time, $373 per semester hour part-time for nonresidents. • Dr. Deborah Grubb, Chair, 606-783-5207. Application contact: Betty Cowsert, Graduate Admissions Officer, 606-783-2039. Fax: 606-783-5061.

New York University, School of Education, Department of Applied Psychology, Program in Applied Psychology, New York, NY 10012-1019. Offerings include measurement and evaluation (MA). Program faculty: 12 full-time, 14 part-time. *Degree requirements:* Thesis required (for some programs), foreign language not required. *Entrance requirements:* TOEFL. Application deadline: 2/1 (priority date; rolling processing; 12/1 for spring admission). Application fee: $40 ($60 for international students). • Catherine Tamis-Lemonda, Director, 212-998-5399. Application contact: Office of Graduate Admissions, 212-998-5030. Fax: 212-995-4328.

Northeastern University, Graduate School of Arts and Sciences, Department of Education, Boston, MA 02115-5096. Offerings include educational research (M Ed). Department faculty: 11 full-time (3 women), 3 part-time (2 women). *Average time to degree:* master's–3 years full-time, 5 years part-time. *Entrance requirements:* GRE General Test or MAT. Application deadline: 7/15 (rolling processing; 2/1 for spring admission). Application fee: $50. *Expenses:* Tuition $440 per credit hour. Fees $55 per quarter full-time, $13.25 per quarter part-time. • Dr. James W. Fraser, Acting Chair, 617-373-3302. Application contact: Dr. Mervin Lynch, Director of Graduate Admissions, 617-373-3302. Fax: 617-373-5261.

Northwestern Oklahoma State University, School of Education, Psychology, and Health and Physical Education, Program in Psychometry, Alva, OK 73717. Awards M Ed. Accredited by NCATE. Part-time programs available. Faculty: 5 full-time (3 women). Students: 4 part-time (all women). 2 applicants, 100% accepted. In 1997, 1 degree awarded. *Entrance requirements:* GRE General Test (minimum combined score of 900) or MAT (minimum score 38), minimum GPA of 2.75. Application deadline: rolling. Application fee: $15. *Tuition:* $73 per semester hour for state residents; $175 per semester hour for nonresidents. *Financial aid:* Fellowships, Federal Work-Study available. Aid available to part-time students. Financial aid application deadline: 5/1. • Dr. Nancy Knous, Coordinator, 405-327-8443. Application contact: Dr. Ed Huckeby, Dean of Graduate School, 405-327-8410.

Ohio University, Graduate Studies, College of Education, School of Applied Behavioral Sciences and Educational Leadership, Athens, OH 45701-2979. Offerings include research and evaluation (M Ed, PhD). Accredited by NCATE. Terminal master's awarded for partial completion of doctoral program. School faculty: 12 full-time (3 women), 2 part-time (0 women). *Degree requirements:* For master's, thesis or alternative required, foreign language not required; for doctorate, dissertation. *Entrance requirements:* For master's, GRE General Test (minimum combined score of 1000) or MAT (minimum score 48); for doctorate, GRE General Test (minimum combined score of 1000), MAT (minimum score 45), minimum GPA of 3.0, work experience. Application deadline: rolling. Application fee: $30. *Tuition:* $5430 per year full-time, $216 per quarter hour part-time for state residents; $10,431 per year full-time, $423 per quarter hour part-time for nonresidents. • Dr. Richard Hazler, Director, 740-593-4440. Application contact: Dr. Patricia Beamish, Graduate Chair, 740-593-4440.

Rutgers, The State University of New Jersey, New Brunswick, Graduate School of Education, Department of Educational Psychology, Program in Educational Statistics and Measurement, New Brunswick, NJ 08903. Awards Ed M, Ed D. Faculty: 5 full-time (0 women). Students: 4 full-time, 28 part-time; includes 3 minority (1 Asian American, 2 Hispanics). In 1997, 2 master's, 1 doctorate awarded. *Degree requirements:* For doctorate, dissertation. *Entrance requirements:* GRE General Test. Application deadline: 3/1 (11/1 for spring admission). Application fee: $40. *Expenses:* Tuition $6492 per year full-time, $268 per credit part-time for state residents; $9520 per year full-time, $395 per credit part-time for nonresidents. Fees $208 per year (minimum). *Financial aid:* Application deadline 3/1. • Douglas Penfield, Coordinator, 732-932-7496 Ext. 324.

Seattle University, School of Education, Division of Teaching and Learning, Program in Educational Diagnostics/School Psychology, Seattle, WA 98122. Awards Ed S. Accredited by NCATE. Part-time and evening/weekend programs available. Faculty: 2 full-time (both women). Students: 8 full-time (7 women), 26 part-time (22 women); includes 4 minority (2 Asian Americans, 2 Hispanics). Average age 34. 13 applicants, 46% accepted. In 1997, 4 degrees awarded. *Degree requirements:* Comprehensive exam required, foreign language and thesis not required. *Entrance requirements:* GRE or MAT, interview, 1 year of related experience. Application deadline: 7/1 (rolling processing; 2/20 for spring admission). Application fee: $55. *Expenses:* Tuition $339 per credit hour (minimum). Fees $70 per year. *Financial aid:* Federal Work-Study and career-related internships or fieldwork available. Aid available to part-time students. Financial aid applicants required to submit FAFSA. • Dr. Kristen Guest, Coordinator, 206-296-5776. E-mail: kguest@seattleu.edu.

Southern Connecticut State University, School of Education, Program in Research Measurement and Evaluation, New Haven, CT 06515-1355. Awards MS. Faculty: 2 full-time. Students: 15 full-time (8 women), 13 part-time (4 women); includes 1 international. 37 applicants, 35% accepted. In 1997, 9 degrees awarded. *Entrance requirements:* Interview. Application deadline: 7/15 (priority date; rolling processing). Application fee: $40. *Expenses:* Tuition $2632 per year full-time, $188 per credit part-time for state residents; $7200 per year full-time, $188 per credit part-time for nonresidents. Fees $1806 per year full-time, $45 per semester part-time for state residents; $2703 per year full-time, $45 per semester part-time for nonresidents. • Dr. Michael Martin, Chair, 203-392-5912. Application contact: Dr. Shawky Karas, Coordinator, 203-392-6994.

Southern Illinois University at Carbondale, College of Education, Department of Educational Psychology and Special Education, Program in Educational Psychology, Carbondale, IL 62901-6806. Offerings include measurement and statistics (PhD). Accredited by NCATE. Program faculty: 18 full-time (5 women), 5 part-time (1 woman). *Degree requirements:* Dissertation required, foreign language not required. *Entrance requirements:* TOEFL (minimum score 550), minimum GPA of 3.25. Application deadline: 6/15 (priority date; rolling processing). Application fee: $20. *Expenses:* Tuition $2964 per year full-time, $99 per semester hour part-time for state residents; $8892 per year full-time, $270 per semester hour part-time for nonresidents. Fees $1034 per year full-time, $298 per semester (minimum) part-time. • Application contact: Laurie Viernum, Graduate Secretary, 618-536-7763. Fax: 618-453-7110.

Southwestern Oklahoma State University, School of Education, Program in School Psychometry, Weatherford, OK 73096-3098. Awards M Ed. Accredited by NCATE. M Ed distance learning degree program offered to Oklahoma residents only. Part-time programs available. Postbaccalaureate distance learning degree programs offered. Students: 13 part-time (12 women). 2 applicants, 100% accepted. In 1997, 3 degrees awarded. *Degree requirements:* Exam required, foreign language and thesis not required. *Entrance requirements:* GRE General Test, TOEFL (minimum score 550), minimum GPA of 2.5. Application deadline: rolling. Application fee: $15. *Expenses:* Tuition $60 per credit hour (minimum) for state residents; $147 per credit hour (minimum) for nonresidents. Fees $109 per year full-time, $24 per semester (minimum) part-time. *Financial aid:* Research assistantships, teaching assistantships, partial tuition waivers, Federal Work-Study, institutionally sponsored loans, and career-related internships or fieldwork available. Aid available to part-time students. Financial aid application deadline: 3/1; applicants required to submit FAFSA. • Dr. Lowell Gadberry, Chair, Elementary/Secondary Programs, 580-774-3288. Application contact: Dr. Ronna Vanderslice, Adviser, 580-774-3145.

State University of New York at Albany, School of Education, Department of Educational Psychology and Statistics, Albany, NY 12222-0001. Offerings include measurements and evaluation (Ed D), statistics and research design (Ed D). Department faculty: 14 full-time (6 women), 1 part-time (0 women). *Application fee:* $50. *Expenses:* Tuition $5100 per year full-time, $213 per credit hour part-time for state residents; $8416 per year full-time, $351 per credit hour part-time for nonresidents. Fees $705 per year full-time, $26.85 per credit hour part-time. • Dr. Paul Vogt, Chair, 518-442-5055.

Sul Ross State University, Rio Grande College of Sul Ross State University, Alpine, TX 79832. Offerings include teacher education (M Ed), with options in bilingual education, counseling, educational diagnostics, elementary education, general education, reading, school administration, secondary education. College faculty: 16 full-time (2 women), 2 part-time (1 woman). *Application deadline:* rolling. *Application fee:* $0 ($50 for international students). *Expenses:* Tuition $864 per year full-time, $120 per semester (minimum) part-time for state residents; $5976 per year full-time, $747 per semester (minimum) part-time for nonresidents. Fees $754 per year full-time, $105 per semester (minimum) part-time. • Dr. Frank Abbott, Dean, 512-278-3339. Fax: 512-278-3330.

Sul Ross State University, Department of Teacher Education, Program in Educational Diagnostics, Alpine, TX 79832. Awards M Ed. Part-time and evening/weekend programs available. Students: 1 (woman) full-time, 11 part-time (8 women); includes 8 minority (1 African American, 7 Hispanics). Average age 42. In 1997, 9 degrees awarded. *Degree requirements:* Thesis optional, foreign language not required. *Entrance requirements:* GMAT (minimum score 400) or GRE General Test (minimum combined score of 850), minimum GPA of 2.5 in last 60 hours of undergraduate work. Application deadline: rolling. Application fee: $0 ($50 for international students). *Expenses:* Tuition $864 per year full-time, $120 per semester (minimum) part-time for state residents; $5976 per year full-time, $747 per semester (minimum) part-time for nonresidents. Fees $754 per year full-time, $105 per semester (minimum) part-time. *Financial aid:* Federal Work-Study, institutionally sponsored loans, and career-related internships or fieldwork available. Aid available to part-time students. Financial aid application deadline: 5/1; applicants required to submit FAFSA. • Dr. Mary Ann Weinacht, Director, Department of Teacher Education, 915-837-8170. Fax: 915-837-8390.

Syracuse University, School of Education, Instructional Design, Development, and Evaluation Program, Syracuse, NY 13244-0003. Awards MS, Ed D, PhD, CAS. Part-time programs available. Faculty: 6 full-time (1 woman), 1 part-time (0 women). Students: 46 full-time (33 women), 29 part-time (19 women); includes 4 minority (3 African Americans, 1 Asian American), 16 international. 32 applicants, 75% accepted. In 1997, 21 master's, 5 doctorates awarded. *Degree requirements:* For master's, thesis or alternative required, foreign language not required; for doctorate and CAS, thesis/dissertation required, foreign language not required. *Entrance requirements:* GRE. Application deadline: rolling. Application fee: $40. *Tuition:* $13,320 per year full-time, $555 per credit hour part-time. *Financial aid:* Fellowships, research assistantships, teaching assistantships, administrative assistantships, Federal Work-Study, and career-related internships or fieldwork available. Aid available to part-time students. Financial aid application deadline: 3/1. *Faculty research:* Cultural pluralism and instructional design, corrections training, aging and learning, the University and social change, investigative evaluation. • James Winschel, Chair. Application contact: Donald Ely, Contact, 315-443-3704.

Teachers College, Columbia University, Graduate Faculty of Education, Department of Human Development, Program in Measurement, Evaluation, and Statistics, 525 West 120th Street, New York, NY 10027-6696. Awards MA, MS, Ed D, PhD. Faculty: 4 full-time (2 women), 1 part-time (0 women), 4.2 FTE. Students: 18 full-time (12 women), 39 part-time (26 women); includes 15 minority (4 African Americans, 7 Asian Americans, 4 Hispanics), 8 international. Average age 31. 47 applicants, 57% accepted. In 1997, 19 master's, 2 doctorates awarded. *Entrance requirements:* GRE. Application deadline: 5/15 (12/1 for spring admission). Application fee: $50. *Expenses:* Tuition $640 per credit. Fees $120 per semester. *Financial aid:* Full and partial tuition waivers, Federal Work-Study, institutionally sponsored loans, and career-related internships or fieldwork available. Aid available to part-time students. Financial aid application deadline: 2/1. *Faculty research:* Probability and inference, potentially biased test items, research design, clustering and scaling methods for multivariate data. • Application contact: Barbara Reinhalter, Office of Admissions, 212-678-3710. Fax: 212-678-4171.

Texas A&M University, College of Education, Department of Educational Psychology, College Station, TX 77843. Offerings include research, measurement, and statistics (M Ed, MS, PhD). Accredited by NCATE. Department faculty: 26 full-time (10 women), 2 part-time (both women), 26.9 FTE. *Entrance requirements:* For master's, GRE General Test, TOEFL. Application deadline: 2/1. Application fee: $35 ($75 for international students). • Douglas J. Palmer, Head, 409-845-1831. Fax: 409-862-1256. Application contact: Graduate Adviser, 409-845-1833.

Texas Christian University, School of Education, Department of Educational Foundations and Administration, Program in Educational Research and Collaboration, Fort Worth, TX 76129-0002. Awards M Ed. Part-time and evening/weekend programs available. Students: 15 (10 women); includes 5 minority (1 African American, 2 Asian Americans, 2 Hispanics), 2 international. 6 applicants, 83% accepted. In 1997, 9 degrees awarded. *Entrance requirements:* TOEFL (minimum score 550), interview. Application deadline: 3/1 (rolling processing; 12/1 for spring admission). Application fee: $0. *Expenses:* Tuition $10,350 per year full-time, $345 per credit hour part-time. Fees $1240 per year full-time, $50 per credit hour part-time. *Financial aid:* Graduate assistantships available. Financial aid application deadline: 3/1. • Dr. Cornell Thomas, Chairperson, Department of Educational Foundations and Administration, 817-257-7943.

Université Laval, Faculty of Education, Department of Guidance and Counseling, Administration and Evaluation in Education, Program in Educational Measurement and Testing, Sainte-Foy, PQ G1K 7P4, Canada. Awards MA, PhD. Students: 22 full-time (9 women), 16 part-time (13 women). 20 applicants, 90% accepted. In 1997, 14 master's, 1 doctorate awarded. *Application deadline:* 3/1. *Application fee:* $30. *Expenses:* Tuition $1334 per year (minimum) full-time, $56 per credit (minimum) part-time for Canadian residents; $5966 per year (minimum) full-time, $249 per credit (minimum) part-time for nonresidents. Fees $150 per year full-time, $6.25 per credit part-time. • Jean Plante, Director, 418-656-2131 Ext. 3147. Fax: 418-656-2885. E-mail: jean.plante@ads.ulaval.ca.

The University of Alabama, College of Education, Area of Professional Studies, Program in Educational Research, Tuscaloosa, AL 35487. Awards PhD. Accredited by NCATE. *Degree requirements:* 1 foreign language, computer language, dissertation. *Entrance requirements:* GRE General Test, MAT (score in 50th percentile or higher), or NTE (minimum score 658 on each core battery test), minimum GPA of 3.0. Application deadline: 7/6 (rolling processing). Application fee: $25. *Tuition:* $2684 per year full-time, $594 per semester (minimum) part-time for state residents; $7216 per year full-time, $1248 per semester (minimum) part-time for nonresidents. *Financial aid:* Application deadline 7/14. • Dr. R. Carl Westerfield, Head, Area of Professional Studies, 205-348-8362. Fax: 205-348-0867. E-mail: cwesterf@bamaed.ua.edu.

University of British Columbia, Faculty of Education, Department of Educational Psychology and Special Education, Vancouver, BC V6T 1Z2, Canada. Offerings include measurement, evaluation and research methodology (MA). *Average time to degree:* master's–3 years full-time, 5 years part-time; doctorate–6 years full-time. *Application deadline:* 2/1. *Application fee:* $60.

University of California, Berkeley, School of Education, Division of Policy, Organization, Measurement and Evaluation, Berkeley, CA 94720-1500. Offers programs in educational leadership (Ed D), policy (MA), policy research (PhD), program evaluation and assessment (Ed D), quantitative methods in education (PhD). Terminal master's awarded for partial completion of doctoral program. *Degree requirements:* For master's, exam or thesis required, foreign language not required; for doctorate, dissertation, oral qualifying exam (PhD) required, foreign language not required. *Entrance requirements:* GRE General Test, minimum GPA of 3.0 during last 2 years of undergraduate course work. Application deadline: 12/15 (rolling processing). Application fee: $40. *Expenses:* Tuition $0 for state residents; $9384 per year for nonresidents. Fees $4409 per year. *Financial aid:* Fellowships, research assistantships, teaching assistantships available. Financial aid application deadline: 12/15. • Mark Wilson, Chair, 510-642-0709.

University of Colorado at Boulder, School of Education, Division of Research and Evaluation Methodologies, Boulder, CO 80309. Awards PhD. Accredited by NCATE. Students: 8 full-time (4 women), 2 part-time (both women); includes 1 minority (African American). Average age 35. 9 applicants, 44% accepted. In 1997, 1 degree awarded. *Degree requirements:* 1 foreign language, dissertation. *Entrance requirements:* GRE General Test (minimum combined score of 1500 on three sections), minimum undergraduate GPA of 2.75. Application deadline: 2/1 (priority date; 8/1 for spring admission). Application fee: $40 ($60 for international students). *Expenses:* Tuition $3170 per year full-time, $531 per semester (minimum) part-time for state residents; $14,652 per year full-time, $2442 per semester (minimum) part-time for nonresidents. Fees $667 per year full-time, $130 per semester (minimum) part-time. *Financial aid:* Application deadline 2/1. • Loretta Shepard, Director, 303-492-8108. Fax: 303-492-7090. E-mail: lorrie.shepard@colorado.edu.

University of Connecticut, School of Education, Field of Evaluation and Measurement, Storrs, CT 06269. Awards MA, PhD. Accredited by NCATE. Faculty: 5. Students: 1 full-time (0 women), 2 part-time (1 woman). Average age 40. 0 applicants. In 1997, 1 doctorate awarded. Terminal master's awarded for partial completion of doctoral program. *Degree requirements:* For master's, thesis or alternative; for doctorate, dissertation. *Entrance requirements:* For doctorate, GRE General Test. Application deadline: 6/1 (priority date; rolling processing; 11/1 for spring admission). Application fee: $40 ($45 for international students). *Expenses:* Tuition $5272 per year full-time, $293 per credit part-time for state residents; $13,696 per year full-time, $761 per credit part-time for nonresidents. Fees $948 per year full-time, $640 per year part-time. *Financial aid:* In 1997–98, 1 teaching assistantship totaling $13,500 was awarded; fellowships, research assistantships also available. Financial aid application deadline: 2/15. • Scott W. Brown, Head, 860-486-4031.

University of Delaware, College of Human Resources, Education and Public Policy, School of Education, Newark, DE 19716. Offerings include measurements, statistics, and evaluation (MA, PhD). PhD (exceptionality; cognition, development, and instruction) new for fall 1998. Terminal master's awarded for partial completion of doctoral program. School faculty: 54 (24 women). *Application deadline:* 7/1 (rolling processing; 1/15 for spring admission). *Application fee:* $45. *Expenses:* Tuition $4250 per year full-time, $236 per credit hour part-time for state residents; $12,250 per year full-time, $681 per credit hour part-time for nonresidents. Fees $466 per year full-time, $15 per semester (minimum) part-time. • Dr. Robert Hampel, Director, 302-831-2573.

University of Denver, College of Education, Denver, CO 80208. Offerings include educational psychology (MA, PhD, Ed S), with options in child and family studies (MA, PhD), quantitative research methods (MA, PhD), school psychology (PhD, Ed S). Postbaccalaureate distance learning degree programs offered (no on-campus study). College faculty: 23 full-time (13 women). *Degree requirements:* For master's, comprehensive exam required, foreign language and thesis not required; for doctorate, 2 foreign languages (computer language can substitute for one), dissertation, comprehensive exam. *Entrance requirements:* For master's, GRE General Test (minimum combined score of 870), TOEFL (minimum score 550), TSE (minimum score 230); for doctorate, GRE General Test (minimum combined score of 930), TOEFL (minimum score 550), TSE (minimum score 230). Application deadline: 1/1 (rolling processing). Application fee: $40 ($45 for international students). *Expenses:* Tuition $18,216 per year full-time, $506 per credit hour part-time. Fees $159 per year. • Dr. Elinor Katz, Dean, 303-871-3665. Application contact: Linda McCarthy, 303-871-2509.

University of Florida, College of Education, Department of Foundations of Education, Gainesville, FL 32611. Offerings include statistics, measurement, and evaluation methodology (MAE, M Ed, Ed D, PhD, Ed S). Accredited by NCATE. Terminal master's awarded for partial completion of doctoral program. Department faculty: 23. *Degree requirements:* For master's, thesis (MAE) required, foreign language not required; for doctorate, variable foreign language requirement, dissertation. *Entrance requirements:* For master's and doctorate, GRE General Test, minimum GPA of 3.0; for Ed S, GRE General Test. Application deadline: 6/5 (priority date; rolling processing). Application fee: $20. *Tuition:* $138 per credit hour for state residents; $481 per credit hour for nonresidents. • Dr. James Algina, Chair, 352-392-0723. Application contact: Dr. Barry J. Guinagh, Graduate Coordinator, 352-392-0723. Fax: 352-392-7159. E-mail: guinagh@coe.ufl.edu.

University of Hawaii at Manoa, College of Education, Education Program, Honolulu, HI 96822. Offerings include educational policy studies (Ed D). Program faculty: 53 full-time (25 women). *Degree requirements:* Dissertation required, foreign language not required. *Entrance requirements:* GRE General Test, MAT (optional), TOEFL (minimum score 600), sample of written work. Application deadline: 2/1. Application fee: $0. *Tuition:* $4029 per year full-time, $214 per credit hour part-time for state residents; $9957 per year full-time, $461 per credit hour part-time for nonresidents. • Dr. Royal T. Fruehling, Graduate Chair, 808-956-4243. E-mail: fruehlin@hawaii.edu. Application contact: Melanie Bock, Clerk Typist III, 808-956-7817. Fax: 808-956-9100. E-mail: mbock@hawaii.edu.

The University of Iowa, College of Education, Division of Psychological and Quantitative Foundations, Iowa City, IA 52242-1316. Offers programs in educational media (MA, PhD, Ed S), instructional design and technology (MA, PhD), psychological and quantitative foundations (MA, PhD, Ed S). Faculty: 29 full-time, 1 part-time. Students: 76 full-time (48 women), 110 part-time (66 women); includes 35 minority (16 African Americans, 6 Asian Americans, 11 Hispanics, 2 Native Americans), 34 international. 166 applicants, 26% accepted. In 1997, 14 master's, 17 doctorates, 3 Ed Ss awarded. *Degree requirements:* For master's, exam required, thesis optional, foreign language not required; for doctorate, computer language, dissertation, comprehensive exams required, foreign language not required; for Ed S, computer language, exam required, foreign language not required. *Entrance requirements:* For master's and Ed S, GRE General Test, minimum GPA of 2.5; for doctorate, GRE General Test, minimum GPA of 3.0. Application fee: $30 ($50 for international students). *Expenses:* Tuition $3166 per year full-time, $176 per semester hour part-time for state residents; $10,202 per year full-time, $176 per semester hour part-time for nonresidents. Fees $202 per year full-time, $52 per year (minimum) part-time. *Financial aid:* In 1997–98, 10 fellowships (6 to first-year students), 66 research assistantships (15 to first-year students), 21 teaching assistantships (1 to a first-year student) were awarded. Financial aid applicants required to submit FAFSA. • David F. Lohman, Chair, 319-335-5577. Fax: 319-335-6145.

University of Kentucky, Graduate School Programs from the College of Education, Program in Educational Policy Studies and Evaluation, Lexington, KY 40506-0032. Awards MS Ed U, Ed D, PhD. Accredited by NCATE. Faculty: 18 full-time (5 women), 1 part-time (0 women). Students: 67 full-time (40 women), 51 part-time (32 women); includes 23 minority (20 African Americans, 1 Asian American, 1 Hispanic, 1 Native American), 5 international. 41 applicants, 80% accepted. In 1997, 3 master's, 3 doctorates awarded. Terminal master's awarded for partial completion of doctoral program. *Degree requirements:* For master's, comprehensive exam required, thesis optional, foreign language not required; for doctorate, 1 foreign language, dissertation, comprehensive exam. *Entrance requirements:* For master's, GRE General Test, minimum undergraduate GPA of 2.5; for doctorate, GRE General Test, minimum graduate GPA of 3.0. Application deadline: 7/19 (rolling processing). Application fee: $30 ($35 for international students). *Financial aid:* In 1997–98, 6 fellowships, 3 research assistantships, 3 teaching assistantships, 1 graduate assistantship were awarded; Federal Work-Study, institutionally sponsored loans, and career-related internships or fieldwork also available. Aid available to part-time students. *Faculty research:* Studies in higher education; comparative and international education; evaluation of educational programs, policies, and reform; student, teacher and faculty cultures; gender and education. • Dr. Beth L. Goldstein, Director of Graduate Studies, 606-257-2705. Application contact: Dr. Constance L. Wood, Associate Dean, 606-257-4613. Fax: 606-323-1928.

University of Louisville, School of Education, Department of Administration and Higher Education, Louisville, KY 40292-0001. Offerings include education policy studies and evaluation (Ed D), evaluation (Ed D). One or more programs accredited by NCATE. Ed D (education policy studies and evaluation) offered jointly with the University of Kentucky. Department faculty: 5 full-time (2 women). *Degree requirements:* Dissertation required, foreign language not required. *Entrance requirements:* GRE General Test. Application deadline: rolling. Application fee: $25. • Dr. John L. Strope Jr., Chairman, 502-852-6428.

University of Manitoba, Faculty of Education, Department of Educational Psychology, Winnipeg, MB R3T 2N2, Canada. Offerings include instructional design and evaluation (M Ed). *Degree requirements:* Thesis or alternative required, foreign language not required.

University of Maryland, College Park, College of Education, Measurement, Statistics, and Evaluation Program, College Park, MD 20742-5045. Offers measurement (MA, PhD), program evaluation (MA, PhD), statistics (MA, PhD). Accredited by NCATE. Postbaccalaureate distance learning degree programs offered. Faculty: 7 full-time (0 women), 2 part-time (both women). Students: 9 full-time (6 women), 27 part-time (17 women); includes 5 minority (2 African Americans, 1 Asian American, 2 Hispanics), 7 international. 12 applicants, 33% accepted. In 1997, 1 master's, 1 doctorate awarded. *Degree requirements:* For master's, thesis or alternative; for doctorate, dissertation. *Entrance requirements:* For master's, GRE General Test or MAT, minimum GPA of 3.0; for doctorate, GRE General Test or MAT. Application deadline: rolling. Application fee: $50 ($70 for international students). *Expenses:* Tuition $272 per credit hour for state residents; $400 per credit hour for nonresidents. Fees $564 per year full-time, $342 per year part-time. *Financial aid:* In 1997–98, 3 teaching assistantships were awarded; fellowships, research assistantships also available. • Dr. Robert Lissitz, Chairman, 301-405-3624. Fax: 301-314-9278. Application contact: John Mollish, Director, Graduate Admissions and Records, 301-405-4198. Fax: 301-314-9305.

University of Massachusetts Amherst, School of Education, Program in Education, Amherst, MA 01003-0001. Offerings include research and evaluation methods (M Ed, Ed D, CAGS). Accredited by NCATE. *Degree requirements:* For doctorate, dissertation required, foreign language not required. *Entrance requirements:* For master's and doctorate, GRE General Test. Application deadline: 3/1 (rolling processing; 10/1 for spring admission). Application fee: $40. *Expenses:* Tuition $2640 per year full-time, $110 per credit part-time for state residents; $3690 per year (minimum) full-time, $165 per credit (minimum) part-time for nonresidents. Fees $2856 per year full-time, $422 per semester part-time for state residents; $3204 per year full-time, $480 per semester part-time for nonresidents. • John C. Carey, Director, 413-545-0236.

The University of Memphis, College of Education, Department of Counseling, Educational Psychology and Research, Memphis, TN 38152. Offerings include educational psychology and research (MS, Ed D, PhD), with options in educational psychology (MS, Ed D), educational research (MS, Ed D). Accredited by NCATE. Department faculty: 23 full-time (11 women), 17 part-time (8 women). *Degree requirements:* For master's, thesis or alternative, comprehensive exam required, foreign language not required; for doctorate, dissertation, comprehensive exam required, foreign language not required. *Entrance requirements:* For master's, GRE General Test or MAT, minimum GPA of 2.5; for doctorate, GRE General Test. Application deadline: 8/1 (12/1 for spring admission). Application fee: $25 ($50 for international students). *Tuition:* $2862 per year full-time, $166 per credit hour part-time for state residents; $6696 per year full-time, $379 per credit hour part-time for nonresidents. • Dr. Ronnie Priest, Chair and Coordinator of Graduate Studies, 901-678-2841.

University of Miami, School of Education, Department of Educational and Psychological Studies, Program in Educational Research and Evaluation, Coral Gables, FL 33124. Offers educational research (PhD), research and evaluation (MS Ed). Accredited by NCATE. Faculty: 1 full-time (0 women), 6 part-time (3 women). Students: 9 full-time (5 women), 8 part-time (3 women); includes 5 minority (1 African American, 4 Hispanics), 1 international. Average age 46. 12 applicants, 42% accepted. In 1997, 3 doctorates awarded. Terminal master's awarded for partial completion of doctoral program. *Degree requirements:* For doctorate, dissertation required, foreign language not required. *Entrance requirements:* For master's, GRE General Test (minimum combined score of 1000), GRE Subject Test, TOEFL (minimum score 550); for doctorate, GRE General Test, GRE Subject Test, TOEFL (minimum score 550). Application

Directory: Educational Measurement and Evaluation

University of Miami (continued)

deadline: rolling. Application fee: $35. *Expenses:* Tuition $815 per credit hour. Fees $174 per year. *Financial aid:* In 1997–98, 1 graduate assistantship (to a first-year student) averaging $900 per month and totaling $7,125 was awarded; fellowships, Federal Work-Study, institutionally sponsored loans, and career-related internships or fieldwork also available. Aid available to part-time students. Financial aid application deadline: 3/1. *Faculty research:* Psychometric theory, computer-based testing, quantitative research methods, special education intervention. • Dr. Richard Williams, Coordinator, 305-284-5107. Fax: 305-284-3003. E-mail: rwilliams@umiami.ir.miami.edu.

University of Michigan, School of Education, Center for the Study of Higher and Postsecondary Education, Ann Arbor, MI 48109. Offerings include research, evaluation, and assessment (PhD). *Application deadline:* 1/15 (priority date). *Application fee:* $55. Electronic applications accepted. • Dr. Janet H. Lawrence, Chairperson, 734-647-1977. Fax: 734-764-2510. E-mail: janlaw@umich.edu. Application contact: Karen Wixson, Associate Dean, 734-764-9470. Fax: 734-763-1229. E-mail: kwixson@umich.edu.

University of Minnesota, Twin Cities Campus, College of Education and Human Development, Department of Educational Policy and Administration, Minneapolis, MN 55455-0213. Offerings include evaluation studies (MA, PhD). • James Hearn, Chair, 612-624-1006.

University of Missouri–Kansas City, School of Education, Division of Educational Research and Psychology, Kansas City, MO 64110-2499. Awards MA. Accredited by NCATE. Part-time and evening/weekend programs available. Students: 10 full-time (8 women), 8 part-time (5 women); includes 4 minority (3 African Americans, 1 Hispanic), 2 international. Average age 37. In 1997, 3 degrees awarded. *Degree requirements:* Final project required, thesis optional, foreign language not required. *Average time to degree:* master's–2 years full-time, 4 years part-time. *Entrance requirements:* Minimum GPA of 2.75. Application deadline: 7/1 (priority date; rolling processing; 12/1 for spring admission). Application fee: $25. *Expenses:* Tuition $182 per credit hour for state residents; $508 per credit hour for nonresidents. Fees $60 per year. *Financial aid:* In 1997–98, 1 research assistantship averaging $858 per month was awarded; full and partial tuition waivers, Federal Work-Study, institutionally sponsored loans also available. Aid available to part-time students. *Faculty research:* Reading rate, motivation, metacognitive skills. • Dr. Ann Pace, Chairperson, 816-235-2485.

University of Nevada, Las Vegas, College of Education, Department of Special Education, Las Vegas, NV 89154-9900. Offerings include assessment and evaluation techniques for the exceptional (Ed D). Accredited by NCATE. Department faculty: 13 full-time (5 women). *Degree requirements:* Dissertation, oral exam required, foreign language not required. *Entrance requirements:* GRE General Test, MAT (score in 50th percentile or higher), minimum graduate GPA of 3.5. Application deadline: 6/15 (priority date; rolling processing; 11/15 for spring admission). Application fee: $40 ($95 for international students). *Expenses:* Tuition $93 per credit for state residents; $93 per credit full-time, $190 per credit part-time for nonresidents. Fees $5570 per year full-time for nonresidents. • Dr. William Healey, Chair, 702-895-3205. Application contact: Graduate College Admissions Evaluator, 702-895-3320.

University of North Carolina at Greensboro, School of Education, Department of Educational Research Methodology, Greensboro, NC 27412-0001. Offers program in educational research, measurement and evaluation (M Ed, PhD). Accredited by NCATE. Faculty: 5 full-time (1 woman), 1 (woman) part-time. Students: 16 full-time (9 women), 10 part-time (8 women); includes 6 minority (5 African Americans, 1 Asian American), 2 international. 13 applicants, 38% accepted. In 1997, 4 master's awarded. *Degree requirements:* For doctorate, dissertation. *Entrance requirements:* GRE General Test. Application deadline: 7/1 (priority date; rolling processing; 11/1 for spring admission). Application fee: $35. *Expenses:* Tuition $1842 per year full-time, $370 per semester (minimum) part-time for state residents; $10,296 per year full-time, $2484 per semester (minimum) part-time for nonresidents. Fees $806 per year full-time, $111 per semester (minimum) part-time. *Financial aid:* In 1997–98, 11 students received aid, including 2 fellowships totaling $7,000, 11 research assistantships totaling $89,318; teaching assistantships also available. • Dr. John Hattie, Head, 336-334-3470.

University of North Dakota, College of Education and Human Development, Teaching and Learning Program, Grand Forks, ND 58202. Offerings include measurement and statistics (Ed D, PhD). Accredited by NCATE. Program faculty: 24 full-time (19 women), 22 part-time (21 women). *Degree requirements:* Dissertation. *Entrance requirements:* TOEFL (minimum score 550), minimum GPA of 3.5. Application deadline: 3/1 (priority date; rolling processing). Application fee: $20. • Dr. Mary Harris, Director, 701-777-2674. Fax: 701-777-4393. E-mail: mary_harris@mail.und.nodak.edu.

University of North Texas, College of Education, Department of Technology and Cognition, Program in Educational Research, Denton, TX 76203-6737. Awards PhD. Accredited by NCATE. *Degree requirements:* 1 foreign language (computer language can substitute), dissertation, internship. *Entrance requirements:* GRE General Test, admissions exam. Application deadline: 7/17. Application fee: $25 ($50 for international students). *Tuition:* $2063 per year full-time, $815 per year part-time for state residents; $5897 per year full-time, $2100 per year part-time for nonresidents. *Financial aid:* Fellowships, research assistantships, teaching assistantships, Federal Work-Study, institutionally sponsored loans, and career-related internships or fieldwork available. Financial aid application deadline: 4/1. • Application contact: Jon Young, Adviser, 940-565-2093.

University of Pennsylvania, Graduate School of Education, Division of Psychology in Education, Program in Policy Research, Evaluation, and Measurement, Philadelphia, PA 19104. Awards MS Ed, PhD. Part-time programs available. Students: 18 full-time (11 women), 6 part-time (4 women); includes 3 minority (2 African Americans, 1 Native American), 1 international. In 1997, 2 master's awarded. *Degree requirements:* For master's, exam required, foreign language and thesis not required; for doctorate, dissertation, exam required, foreign language not required. *Entrance requirements:* For master's, GRE General Test (minimum combined score of 1450 on three sections); for doctorate, GRE General Test, GRE Subject Test. Application deadline: 7/15 (rolling processing; 12/1 for spring admission). Application fee: $65. *Expenses:* Tuition $22,716 per year full-time, $2876 per course part-time. Fees $1484 per year full-time, $181 per course part-time. *Financial aid:* Fellowships, scholarships available. Aid available to part-time students. Financial aid application deadline: 1/2; applicants required to submit FAFSA. *Faculty research:* Multivariate analysis of behavioral data, behavioral research design. • Dr. Robert Boruch, Director, 215-898-0409.

University of Pittsburgh, School of Education, Department of Psychology in Education, Program in Research Methodology, Pittsburgh, PA 15260. Awards MA, M Ed, PhD. Part-time and evening/weekend programs available. 30 applicants, 77% accepted. *Degree requirements:* Thesis/dissertation required, foreign language not required. *Average time to degree:* master's–2 years full-time, 4 years part-time; doctorate–4 years full-time, 6 years part-time. *Entrance requirements:* GRE General Test, TOEFL (minimum score 650). Application deadline: 2/1 (11/15 for spring admission). Application fee: $30 ($40 for international students). *Expenses:* Tuition $8018 per year full-time, $329 per credit part-time for state residents; $16,508 per year full-time, $680 per credit part-time for nonresidents. Fees $480 per year full-time, $180 per year part-time. *Financial aid:* In 1997–98, 1 fellowship, 1 research assistantship averaging $1,150 per month, 5 assistantships averaging $1,150 per month were awarded; partial tuition waivers, Federal Work-Study, institutionally sponsored loans also available. Aid available to part-time students. Financial aid application deadline: 5/1; applicants required to submit FAFSA. • Application contact: Jackie Harden, Manager, 412-648-7060. Fax: 412-648-1899. E-mail: jackie@sched.fsl.pitt.edu.

University of Puerto Rico, Río Piedras, College of Education, Program in Educational Research and Evaluation, San Juan, PR 00931. Awards M Ed. Part-time programs available. *Degree requirements:* Thesis required, foreign language not required. *Entrance requirements:* PAEG, interview, minimum GPA of 3.0. Application deadline: 2/21. Application fee: $17.

University of South Carolina, Graduate School, College of Education, Department of Educational Psychology, Program in Educational Research and Measurement, Columbia, SC 29208. Awards MA, M Ed, PhD. Accredited by NCATE. Faculty: 14. Students: 5 full-time (1 woman), 13 part-time (8 women); includes 4 minority (2 Asian Americans, 2 Hispanics), 1 international. Average age 37. In 1997, 2 doctorates awarded. *Degree requirements:* For doctorate, 1 foreign language (computer language can substitute), dissertation, comprehensive exam. *Entrance requirements:* For master's, GRE; for doctorate, GRE General Test. Application deadline: rolling. Application fee: $35. Electronic applications accepted. *Expenses:* Tuition $3894 per year full-time, $193 per credit hour part-time for state residents; $8114 per year full-time, $404 per credit hour part-time for nonresidents. Fees $125 per year full-time, $37 per semester (minimum) part-time. *Faculty research:* Problem solving, higher order thinking skills, psychometric research, methodology. • Margaret Gredler, Coordinator, 803-777-6609. Application contact: Office of Intercollegiate Teacher Education and Student Affairs, 803-777-6732. Fax: 803-777-3068.

University of South Florida, College of Education, Department of Educational Measurement and Research, Tampa, FL 33620-9951. Awards M Ed, PhD, Ed S. Accredited by NCATE. Part-time and evening/weekend programs available. Faculty: 10 full-time (4 women). Students: 9 full-time (5 women), 31 part-time (16 women); includes 7 minority (2 African Americans, 2 Asian Americans, 3 Hispanics), 5 international. Average age 42. 11 applicants, 55% accepted. In 1997, 2 master's, 3 doctorates awarded. *Degree requirements:* For doctorate, dissertation, 2 tools of research in foreign language, statistics, and/or computers. *Entrance requirements:* For master's, GRE General Test (minimum combined score of 1000), minimum GPA of 3.5 in last 60 hours; for doctorate, GRE General Test (minimum combined score of 1000), minimum GPA of 3.0 (undergraduate) or 3.5 (graduate); for Ed S, GRE General Test (minimum combined score of 1000), minimum GPA of 3.0 in last 60 hours. Application deadline: 6/1 (10/15 for spring admission). Application fee: $20. Electronic applications accepted. *Tuition:* $142 per credit hour for state residents; $486 per credit hour for nonresidents. *Financial aid:* Federal Work-Study, institutionally sponsored loans available. Aid available to part-time students. Financial aid applicants required to submit FAFSA. *Total annual research expenditures:* $11,600. • Bruce W. Hall, Chairperson, 813-974-3220. Fax: 813-974-4495. E-mail: bhall@tempest.coedu.usf.edu.

University of Tennessee, Knoxville, College of Education, Program in Education II, Knoxville, TN 37996. Offerings include educational research (Ed D). Accredited by NCATE. *Degree requirements:* Dissertation required, foreign language not required. *Entrance requirements:* GRE General Test, TOEFL (minimum score 550), minimum GPA of 2.7. Application deadline: 2/1 (priority date; rolling processing). Application fee: $35. Electronic applications accepted. *Tuition:* $3354 per year full-time, $181 per semester hour part-time for state residents; $8410 per year full-time, $462 per semester hour part-time for nonresidents. • Dr. Tom George, Associate Dean, 423-974-0907. Fax: 423-974-8718. E-mail: tgeorge1@utk.edu.

The University of Texas–Pan American, College of Education, Department of Educational Psychology, Edinburg, TX 78539-2999. Offerings include educational diagnostics (M Ed). *Application deadline:* 7/17 (11/16 for spring admission). *Application fee:* $0. *Tuition:* $2156 per year full-time, $283 per semester (minimum) part-time for state residents; $6788 per year full-time, $862 per semester (minimum) part-time for nonresidents.

University of the Incarnate Word, School of Graduate Studies, College of Professional Studies, Programs in Education, Program in Educational Diagnostics, San Antonio, TX 78209-6397. Awards MA, M Ed. *Entrance requirements:* GRE, MAT, TOEFL (minimum score 550). Application deadline: 8/15 (priority date; rolling processing; 12/31 for spring admission). Application fee: $20. *Expenses:* Tuition $350 per semester hour. Fees $180 per year full-time, $111 per semester (minimum) part-time. • Application contact: Brian F. Dalton, Dean of Enrollment Services, 210-829-6005. Fax: 210-829-3921.

University of the Pacific, School of Education, Department of Educational and Counseling Psychology, Stockton, CA 95211-0197. Offerings include educational research (MA). Accredited by NCATE. *Degree requirements:* Thesis required (for some programs), foreign language not required. *Entrance requirements:* GRE General Test, GRE Subject Test. Application deadline: 3/1 (priority date; rolling processing; 10/15 for spring admission). Application fee: $50. *Expenses:* Tuition $19,000 per year full-time, $594 per unit part-time. Fees $30 per year (minimum). • Dr. Mari Irvin, Chairperson, 209-946-2559. E-mail: mirvin@uop.edu.

University of Toledo, College of Education and Allied Professions, Department of Educational Psychology, Research, and Social Foundations, Toledo, OH 43606-3398. Offers programs in educational psychology (M Ed), educational theory and social foundations (M Ed), foundations of education (Ed D, PhD), research (M Ed). Accredited by NCATE. Part-time and evening/weekend programs available. Faculty: 17 full-time (7 women). Students: 23 full-time (20 women), 45 part-time (36 women); includes 11 minority (8 African Americans, 3 Asian Americans), 8 international. Average age 38. 34 applicants, 56% accepted. In 1997, 5 master's, 14 doctorates awarded. Terminal master's awarded for partial completion of doctoral program. *Degree requirements:* For master's, project or thesis required, foreign language not required; for doctorate, dissertation, comprehensive exams required, foreign language not required. *Entrance requirements:* For master's, GRE General Test, minimum GPA of 2.7; for doctorate, minimum GPA of 2.7 (undergraduate), 3.0 (graduate). Application deadline: 8/15 (priority date; rolling processing). Application fee: $30. Electronic applications accepted. *Tuition:* $5907 per year full-time, $246 per hour part-time for state residents; $11,835 per year full-time, $493 per hour part-time for nonresidents. *Financial aid:* In 1997–98, 4 research assistantships, 5 teaching assistantships, 2 administrative assistantships, tuition scholarships were awarded; full tuition waivers, Federal Work-Study, institutionally sponsored loans, and career-related internships or fieldwork also available. Aid available to part-time students. Financial aid application deadline: 4/1; applicants required to submit FAFSA. • Dr. Lynne M. Hudson, Chair, 419-530-2475. Fax: 419-530-8447. E-mail: lhudson@utnet.utoledo.edu.

University of Virginia, Curry School of Education, Department of Leadership, Foundations and Policy, Program in Educational Policy Studies, Charlottesville, VA 22903. Awards M Ed, Ed D. Accredited by NCATE. *Application fee:* $40. *Tuition:* $4876 per year full-time, $944 per semester (minimum) part-time for state residents; $15,824 per year full-time, $2748 per semester (minimum) part-time for nonresidents. • Application contact: Linda Berry, Student Enrollment Coordinator, 804-924-0738. E-mail: lrb8e@virginia.edu.

University of Washington, College of Education, Program in School Counseling and School Psychology, Seattle, WA 98195. Offerings include measurement and research (M Ed, PhD). *Degree requirements:* For master's, thesis optional, foreign language not required; for doctorate, dissertation. *Entrance requirements:* GRE General Test, TOEFL, minimum GPA of 3.0. Application fee: $45. *Tuition:* $5433 per year full-time, $775 per quarter (minimum) part-time for state residents; $13,479 per year full-time, $1925 per quarter (minimum) part-time for nonresidents. • Dr. Allen Glenn, Dean, College of Education, 206-543-5390. Fax: 206-685-1713. E-mail: aglenn@u.washington.edu. Application contact: Richard Neel, Associate Dean, 206-543-7833. Fax: 206-543-8439. E-mail: edinfo@u.washington.edu.

Utah State University, College of Education, Doctoral Program in Education, Logan, UT 84322. Offerings include research and evaluation (Ed D, PhD). Program faculty: 65 full-time (17 women). *Degree requirements:* Dissertation required, foreign language not required. *Entrance requirements:* GRE General Test (score in 40th percentile or higher), TOEFL (minimum score 550), minimum GPA of 3.0. Application deadline: 6/15 (priority date; rolling processing; 10/15 for spring admission). Application fee: $40. *Expenses:* Tuition $1448 per year full-time, $624 per year part-time for state residents; $5082 per year full-time, $2192 per year part-time for nonresidents. Fees $421 per year full-time, $165 per year part-time. • Application contact: Louann Parkinson, Administrative Assistant, 435-797-1470. Fax: 435-797-3939. E-mail: luannp@coe.usu.edu.

Vanderbilt University, Graduate School, Program in Education and Human Development, Nashville, TN 37240-1001. Offerings include policy development and program evaluation (MS, PhD). Jointly offered with Peabody College. Program faculty: 44 full-time (16 women), 1 (woman) part-time. *Degree requirements:* For master's, thesis required, foreign language not required; for doctorate, dissertation, final and qualifying exams required, foreign language not required. *Entrance requirements:* GRE General Test. Application deadline: 1/15. Application fee: $40. *Expenses:* Tuition $16,452 per year full-time, $914 per semester hour part-time. Fees $236 per year. • Ellen Goldring, Director, 615-322-8265. Fax: 615-322-8501. E-mail: goldrieb@ctrvax.vanderbilt.edu. Application contact: Barbara J. Johnston, Director of Admissions, 615-322-8410. Fax: 615-322-8401. E-mail: johnstbj@ctrvax.vanderbilt.edu.

Vanderbilt University, Peabody College, Department of Human Resources, Nashville, TN 37240-1001. Offerings include policy development and program evaluation (MPP), with option in policy development and program evaluation. *Application deadline:* 3/1 (priority date; rolling processing). *Application fee:* $35. • Robert B. Innes, Acting Chair, 615-322-6881.

Virginia Polytechnic Institute and State University, College of Human Resources and Education, Department of Educational Leadership and Policy Studies, Program in Educational Research and Evaluation, Blacksburg, VA 24061. Awards PhD. Accredited by NCATE. Students: 6 full-time (3 women), 10 part-time (8 women); includes 2 minority (both African Americans), 3 international. 7 applicants, 43% accepted. In 1997, 2 degrees awarded. *Degree requirements:* Dissertation required, foreign language not required. *Entrance requirements:* TOEFL. Application deadline: 12/1 (priority date; rolling processing). Application fee: $25. *Tuition:* $4927 per year full-time, $792 per semester (minimum) part-time for state residents; $7537 per year full-time, $1227 per semester (minimum) part-time for nonresidents. *Financial aid:* Application deadline 4/1. • Dr. Karl T. Hereford, Area Leader, 540-231-9730.

Washington University in St. Louis, Graduate School of Arts and Sciences, Department of Education, Program in Educational Research, St. Louis, MO 63130-4899. Awards PhD. One or more programs accredited by NCATE. *Entrance requirements:* GRE General Test. Application deadline: 1/15 (priority date; rolling processing). Application fee: $35. *Tuition:* $22,200 per year full-time, $925 per credit hour part-time. *Financial aid:* Application deadline 1/15. • Dr. James Wertsch, Chair, Department of Education, 314-935-6776.

Wayne State University, College of Education, Division of Theoretical and Behavioral Foundations, Detroit, MI 48202. Offerings include educational evaluation and research (M Ed, Ed D, PhD). Accredited by NCATE. PhD (history, philosophy, and sociology of education) admissions temporarily suspended. Division faculty: 90. *Degree requirements:* For doctorate, dissertation required, foreign language not required. *Entrance requirements:* For doctorate, GRE (educational psychology), interview, minimum GPA of 3.0. Application deadline: 7/1. Application fee: $20 ($30 for international students). *Expenses:* Tuition $163 per credit hour for state residents; $355 per credit hour for nonresidents. Fees $498 per year full-time, $114 per semester (minimum) part-time. • Dr. JoAnne Holbert, Associate Dean, 313-577-0210.

West Chester University of Pennsylvania, School of Education, Department of Counselor, Secondary and Professional Education, West Chester, PA 19383. Offerings include educational research (MS). Department faculty: 8 part-time. *Application deadline:* 4/15 (priority date; rolling processing; 10/15 for spring admission). *Application fee:* $25. *Expenses:* Tuition $3468 per year full-time, $193 per credit part-time for state residents; $6236 per year full-time, $346 per credit part-time for nonresidents. Fees $660 per year full-time, $38 per credit part-time. • Dr. John Hynes, Chair, 610-436-2411. Application contact: Dr. Kimberlee Brown, Graduate Coordinator, School Counseling, 610-436-2950.

West Texas A&M University, College of Education and Social Sciences, Division of Education, Program in Educational Diagnostician, Canyon, TX 79016-0001. Awards M Ed. Part-time programs available. Postbaccalaureate distance learning degree programs offered (minimal on-campus study). Students: 1 full-time (0 women), 26 part-time (all women); includes 4 minority (1 African American, 3 Hispanics). Average age 34. 13 applicants, 15% accepted. In 1997, 5 degrees awarded. *Degree requirements:* Comprehensive exam required, foreign language and thesis not required. *Entrance requirements:* GRE General Test (combined average 964). Application deadline: rolling. Application fee: $0 ($50 for international students). Electronic applications accepted. *Expenses:* Tuition $46 per semester hour for state residents; $259 per semester hour for nonresidents. Fees $156 per semester (minimum). *Financial aid:* Partial tuition waivers, Federal Work-Study, institutionally sponsored loans available. Aid available to part-time students. Financial aid applicants required to submit CSS PROFILE or FAFSA. *Faculty research:* Teacher preparation through web-based instruction. • Application contact: Dr. Nella Bea Anderson, Graduate Adviser, 806-651-2906. Fax: 806-651-2601. E-mail: nellabea.anderson@wtamu.edu.

Wilkes University, Department of Education, Wilkes-Barre, PA 18766-0002. Offerings include educational development and strategies (MS Ed). Department faculty: 6 full-time, 14 part-time. *Application deadline:* rolling. *Application fee:* $30. *Expenses:* Tuition $12,552 per year full-time, $523 per credit hour part-time. Fees $240 per year full-time, $10 per credit hour part-time. • Dr. Douglas Lynch, Chair, 717-408-4680.

Educational Media/Instructional Technology

Alabama State University, School of Graduate Studies, College of Education, Department of Instructional Support, Library Educational Media Program, Montgomery, AL 36101-0271. Awards M Ed, Ed S. Students: 5 full-time (all women), 32 part-time (31 women); includes 9 minority (all African Americans). In 1997, 9 master's, 1 Ed S awarded. *Degree requirements:* For master's, comprehensive exam required, thesis optional; for Ed S, thesis. *Entrance requirements:* For master's, GRE General Test, MAT or NTE. Application deadline: 7/15 (rolling processing; 12/15 for spring admission). Application fee: $10. *Expenses:* Tuition $85 per credit hour for state residents; $170 per credit hour for nonresidents. Fees $486 per year. *Faculty research:* Developing research capabilities through media, computer and media usage for teaching young children, use of media for in-service. • Dr. David Okeowo, Acting Head, 334-229-4493. Fax: 334-229-4976. E-mail: dokeowo@asunet.alasu.edu. Application contact: Dr. Fred Dauser, Dean of Graduate Studies, 334-229-4276. Fax: 334-229-4928.

Appalachian State University, College of Education, Department of Curriculum and Instruction, Boone, NC 28608. Offerings include educational media (MA). Accredited by NCATE. Postbaccalaureate distance learning degree programs offered (minimal on-campus study). Department faculty: 19 full-time (9 women), 2 part-time (1 woman). *Degree requirements:* Thesis or alternative, comprehensive exams required, foreign language not required. *Average time to degree:* master's–2 years full-time, 4 years part-time. *Entrance requirements:* GRE General Test or MAT. Application deadline: 7/31 (priority date). Application fee: $35. *Tuition:* $1811 per year full-time, $354 per semester (minimum) part-time for state residents; $9081 per year full-time, $2171 per semester (minimum) part-time for nonresidents. • Dr. Michael Jacobson, Chairperson, 704-262-2224.

Arizona State University, College of Education, Division of Curriculum and Instruction, Academic Program of Educational Media and Computers, Tempe, AZ 85287. Awards M Ed. *Entrance requirements:* GRE General Test or MAT. Application fee: $45. *Expenses:* Tuition $2088 per year full-time, $110 per hour part-time for state residents; $9040 per year full-time, $377 per hour part-time for nonresidents. Fees $72 per year full-time, $18 per semester (minimum) part-time. *Faculty research:* Design of multimedia and computer based instruction; utilization of multimedia, computers. • Dr. Gary Bitter, Coordinator, 602-965-7192. E-mail: eavilez@asu.edu.

Arizona State University, College of Education, Division of Psychology in Education, Academic Program of Learning and Instructional Technology, Tempe, AZ 85287. Awards MA, M Ed, PhD. *Degree requirements:* For master's, thesis or alternative; for doctorate, dissertation. *Entrance requirements:* GRE General Test or MAT. Application fee: $45. *Expenses:* Tuition $2088 per year full-time, $110 per hour part-time for state residents; $9040 per year full-time, $377 per hour part-time for nonresidents. Fees $72 per year full-time, $18 per semester (minimum) part-time. *Faculty research:* Instructional effectiveness, educational motivation, spatial cognition, organization and memory for prose material, knowledge structures. • Application contact: Graduate Secretary, 602-965-5279.

Arkansas Tech University, School of Education, Department of Curriculum and Instruction, Russellville, AR 72801-2222. Offerings include instructional technology (M Ed). Accredited by NCATE. *Application deadline:* 3/1 (priority date; rolling processing; 10/1 for spring admission). *Application fee:* $0 ($30 for international students). *Expenses:* Tuition $98 per credit hour for state residents; $196 per credit hour for nonresidents. Fees $30 per semester. • Head, 501-968-0290. Fax: 501-964-0811.

Auburn University, College of Education, Department of Educational Foundations, Leadership, and Technology, Auburn University, AL 36849-0001. Offerings include media instructional design (MS), media specialist (M Ed). One or more programs accredited by NCATE. Department faculty: 18 full-time (9 women). *Application deadline:* 9/1 (rolling processing; 3/1 for spring admission). *Application fee:* $25 ($50 for international students). *Expenses:* Tuition $2760 per year full-time, $76 per credit hour part-time for state residents; $8280 per year full-time, $228 per credit hour part-time for nonresidents. Fees $30 per year full-time, $160 per quarter part-time for state residents; $30 per year full-time, $480 per quarter part-time for nonresidents. • Dr. James S. Kaminsky, Head, 334-844-4460. Application contact: Dr. John F. Pritchett, Dean of the Graduate School, 334-844-4700.

Azusa Pacific University, School of Education and Behavioral Studies, Department of Education, Program in Educational Technology, Azusa, CA 91702-7000. Awards M Ed. Part-time and evening/weekend programs available. Faculty: 2 full-time (0 women), 14 part-time (5 women). Students: 38. In 1997, 52 degrees awarded. *Degree requirements:* Comprehensive exam, core exam, oral presentation required, foreign language and thesis not required. *Entrance requirements:* 12 units of previous course work in education, minimum GPA of 3.0. Application fee: $45 ($65 for international students). *Expenses:* Tuition $350 per unit. Fees $57 per year. • Application contact: Brian Arnold, Director, 626-815-5355.

Bank Street College of Education, Program in Computers in Education, 610 West 112th Street, New York, NY 10025-1120. Awards MS Ed, Certificate. Program being phased out; applicants no longer accepted. Students: 2. *Degree requirements:* For master's, thesis required, foreign language not required. *Tuition:* $560 per credit. • Dr. Patricia Wasley, Dean, Graduate School, 212-875-4460. Application contact: Ann Morgan, Director of Admissions, 212-875-4404. Fax: 212-875-4678. E-mail: amorgan@bnkst.edu.

Barry University, School of Education, Program in Educational Computing and Technology, Miami Shores, FL 33161-6695. Awards MS, Ed S. Part-time and evening/weekend programs available. Postbaccalaureate distance learning degree programs offered (minimal on-campus study). Faculty: 6 full-time (3 women), 10 part-time (5 women). Students: 26 full-time (20 women), 83 part-time (64 women); includes 61 minority (13 African Americans, 3 Asian Americans, 44 Hispanics, 1 Native American), 2 international. Average age 37. In 1997, 61 master's, 13 Ed Ss awarded. *Degree requirements:* Written comprehensive exam required, foreign language and thesis not required. *Entrance requirements:* For master's, GRE General Test or MAT, minimum GPA of 3.0; for Ed S, GRE General Test, minimum GPA of 3.0. Application deadline: 5/1 (rolling processing). Application fee: $30. *Tuition:* $450 per credit (minimum). *Financial aid:* Partial tuition waivers available. Aid available to part-time students. Financial aid application deadline: 5/1; applicants required to submit FAFSA. • Dr. Joel Levine, Director, 305-899-3608. Fax: 305-899-3718. E-mail: jlevine@aquinas.barry.edu. Application contact: Angela Scott, Enrollment Services, Assistant Dean, 305-899-3112. Fax: 305-899-3149. E-mail: ascott@jeanne.barry.edu.

Barry University, School of Education, Program in Leadership and Education, Miami Shores, FL 33161-6695. Offerings include educational computing and technology (PhD). Program faculty: 1 full-time (0 women), 2 part-time (1 woman), 2 FTE. *Degree requirements:* Dissertation. *Entrance requirements:* GRE General Test, minimum GPA of 3.25. Application deadline: 5/1 (priority date; rolling processing). Application fee: $30. Electronic applications accepted. *Tuition:* $450 per credit (minimum). • Dr. Jack Dezek, Chair, 305-899-3700. Fax: 305-899-3630. E-mail: dezek@aquinas.barry.edu. Application contact: Angela Scott, Enrollment Services, Assistant Dean, 305-899-3112. Fax: 305-899-3149. E-mail: ascott@jeanne.barry.edu.

Beaver College, Department of Education, Glenside, PA 19038-3295. Offerings include school library science (M Ed). *Application fee:* $35. *Expenses:* Tuition $6570 per year full-time, $365 per credit part-time. Fees $35 per year.

Bloomsburg University of Pennsylvania, School of Graduate Studies, College of Arts and Sciences, Department of Mathematics and Computer Sciences, Program in Instructional Technology, Bloomsburg, PA 17815-1905. Awards MS. Faculty: 4 full-time (2 women). Students: 34 full-time (17 women), 54 part-time (21 women); includes 11 minority (6 African Americans, 1 Asian American, 4 Hispanics), 4 international. Average age 29. 36 applicants, 100% accepted. In 1997, 29 degrees awarded. *Degree requirements:* Thesis or alternative required, foreign language not required. *Entrance requirements:* Minimum QPA of 2.5. Application deadline: rolling. Application fee: $25. *Expenses:* Tuition $3468 per year full-time, $193 per credit part-time for state residents; $6236 per year full-time, $346 per credit part-time for nonresidents. Fees $748 per year full-time, $166 per semester (minimum) part-time. *Faculty research:* Instructional design, computer-based instruction, interactive technologies and graphics, design of hypermedia applications, application of learning theory. • Dr. Timothy Phillips, Coordinator, 717-389-4506. Fax: 717-389-3599. E-mail: phil@husky.bloomu.edu.

Boise State University, College of Engineering, Program in Instructional and Performance Technology, Boise, ID 83725-0399. Awards MS. Part-time programs available. Postbaccalaureate distance learning degree programs offered (no on-campus study). Faculty: 3 full-time (0 women), 18 part-time (7 women). Students: 10 full-time (5 women), 115 part-time (58 women); includes 3 minority (1 African American, 1 Asian American, 1 Hispanic), 5 international. Average age 42. 36 applicants, 97% accepted. In 1997, 31 degrees awarded. *Degree requirements:* Thesis. *Entrance requirements:* Minimum GPA of 3.0. Application deadline: 7/26 (priority date; rolling processing; 11/29 for spring admission). Application fee: $20 ($30 for international students). Electronic applications accepted. *Tuition:* $3020 per year full-time, $135 per credit part-time for state residents; $8900 per year full-time, $135 per credit part-time for nonresidents. *Financial aid:* In 1997–98, 3 students received aid, including 3 graduate assistantships; full tuition waivers, Federal Work-Study, institutionally sponsored loans, and

Directory: Educational Media/Instructional Technology

Boise State University (continued)
career-related internships or fieldwork also available. Aid available to part-time students. Financial aid application deadline: 3/1. • Dr. David Cox, Director, 208-385-1312. Fax: 208-385-3637.

Boise State University, College of Education, Programs in Teacher Education, Program in Educational Technology, Boise, ID 83725-0399. Awards MS. Accredited by NCATE. Part-time programs available. Faculty: 3 full-time (1 woman), 3 part-time (1 woman). Students: 8 full-time (3 women), 51 part-time (38 women); includes 3 minority (all Hispanics), 1 international. Average age 38. 16 applicants, 100% accepted. In 1997, 8 degrees awarded. *Degree requirements:* Thesis optional. *Application deadline:* 7/26 (priority date; rolling processing; 11/29 for spring admission). *Application fee:* $20 ($30 for international students). Electronic applications accepted. *Tuition:* $3020 per year full-time, $135 per credit part-time for state residents; $8900 per year full-time, $135 per credit part-time for nonresidents. *Financial aid:* Graduate assistantships, Federal Work-Study, institutionally sponsored loans, and career-related internships or fieldwork available. Aid available to part-time students. Financial aid application deadline: 3/1. • Dr. Roger Stewart, Coordinator, Programs in Teacher Education, 208-385-1731. Fax: 208-385-4365.

Boston University, School of Education, Department of Curriculum and Teaching, Program in Educational Media and Technology, Boston, MA 02215. Awards Ed M, Ed D, CAGS. Students: 11 full-time (10 women), 22 part-time (12 women); includes 7 minority (3 African Americans, 2 Asian Americans, 2 Hispanics), 4 international. Average age 32. In 1997, 18 master's awarded. *Degree requirements:* For doctorate, dissertation, comprehensive exam required, foreign language not required; for CAGS, comprehensive exam required, foreign language and thesis not required. *Entrance requirements:* For master's and CAGS, GRE or MAT, TOEFL; for doctorate, GRE General Test or MAT, TOEFL. Application deadline: 2/15 (priority date; rolling processing). Application fee: $50. *Expenses:* Tuition $22,830 per year full-time, $713 per credit part-time. Fees $218 per year full-time, $40 per semester part-time. *Financial aid:* Application deadline 3/30. *Faculty research:* Facilities design, program evaluation, human factors, computer-based technologies. • Dr. David Whittier, Coordinator, 617-353-3181. E-mail: whittier@bu.edu.

Bridgewater State College, School of Education, Department of Secondary Education and Professional Programs, Program in Library Media, Bridgewater, MA 02325-0001. Awards M Ed. Accredited by NCATE. Evening/weekend programs available. *Entrance requirements:* GRE General Test. Application deadline: 4/1 (10/1 for spring admission). Application fee: $25. *Expenses:* Tuition $1675 per year full-time, $70 per credit part-time for state residents; $6450 per year full-time, $269 per credit part-time for nonresidents. Fees $1588 per year full-time, $66 per credit hour part-time for state residents; $1588 per year full-time, $66 per credit part-time for nonresidents. *Financial aid:* Career-related internships or fieldwork available. • Application contact: Graduate School, 508-697-1300.

Brigham Young University, David O. McKay School of Education, Department of Instructional Psychology and Technology, Provo, UT 84602-1001. Awards MS, PhD. Accredited by NCATE. Faculty: 9 full-time (0 women), 10 part-time (1 woman). Students: 76 full-time (23 women), 3 part-time (0 women); includes 1 minority (Hispanic), 17 international. Average age 30. 35 applicants, 63% accepted. In 1997, 5 master's awarded (20% found work related to degree, 80% continued full-time study); 2 doctorates awarded (100% entered university research/teaching). *Degree requirements:* For master's, thesis or alternative; for doctorate, dissertation. *Entrance requirements:* For master's, GRE General Test, minimum GPA of 3.0 in last 60 hours; for doctorate, GRE General Test, minimum GPA of 3.0. Application deadline: 2/1. Application fee: $30. *Tuition:* $3200 per year full-time, $178 per credit hour part-time for state residents; $4800 per year full-time, $266 per credit hour part-time for nonresidents. *Financial aid:* In 1997–98, 20 students received aid, including 12 research assistantships (4 to first-year students), 9 teaching assistantships (1 to a first-year student); partial tuition waivers and career-related internships or fieldwork also available. Aid available to part-time students. *Faculty research:* Assessment/evaluation. • Dr. Paul F. Merrill, Chair, 801-378-5097. E-mail: paul_merrill@byu.edu. Application contact: Michele Bray, Secretary, 801-378-2746. E-mail: michele_bray@byu.edu.

California State University, Chico, College of Communication and Education, Department of Communication Design, Chico, CA 95929-0722. Offerings include information and communication studies (MA), with option in instructional technology. Department faculty: 13 full-time (3 women), 15 part-time (3 women), 17 FTE. *Entrance requirements:* GRE General Test or MAT, portfolio or sample of written or media work. Application deadline: 4/1 (rolling processing). Application fee: $55. *Expenses:* Tuition $0 for state residents; $246 per unit for nonresidents. Fees $2108 per year full-time, $1442 per year part-time. • Dr. Robert Main, Chair, 530-898-4048. Application contact: Karen Jost, Graduate Coordinator, 530-898-5028.

California State University, Los Angeles, School of Education, Division of Educational Foundations and Interdivisional Studies, Major in Instructional Technology, Los Angeles, CA 90032-8530. Awards MA. Accredited by NCATE. Students: 7 full-time (4 women), 32 part-time (22 women); includes 14 minority (2 African Americans, 6 Asian Americans, 6 Hispanics), 4 international. In 1997, 9 degrees awarded. *Entrance requirements:* TOEFL (minimum score 550), minimum GPA of 2.75 in last 90 units, teaching certificate. Application deadline: 6/30 (rolling processing; 2/1 for spring admission). Application fee: $55. *Expenses:* Tuition $0 for state residents; $164 per unit for nonresidents. Fees $1763 per year full-time, $1097 per year part-time. *Financial aid:* 4 students received aid. Financial aid application deadline: 3/1. • Dr. Simeon Slovacek, Chair, Division of Educational Foundations and Interdivisional Studies, 213-343-4330.

California State University, San Bernardino, Graduate Studies, School of Education, San Bernardino, CA 92407-2397. Offerings include instructional technology (MA). School faculty: 77 full-time (38 women). *Application deadline:* 8/31 (priority date). *Application fee:* $55. *Expenses:* Tuition $0 for state residents; $164 per unit for nonresidents. Fees $1922 per year full-time, $1256 per year part-time. • Patricia Arlin, Dean, 909-880-3600. Fax: 909-880-7011.

California State University, Stanislaus, School of Education, Department of Advanced Studies in Education, Program in Educational Technology, Turlock, CA 95382. Awards MA Ed. Accredited by NCATE. Program new for fall 1998. *Entrance requirements:* MAT. Application fee: $55. *Expenses:* Tuition $0 for state residents; $246 per unit for nonresidents. Fees $1779 per year full-time, $1113 per year part-time. *Financial aid:* Application deadline 3/2. • Dr. Karen Sniezek, Chair, Department of Advanced Studies in Education, 209-667-3364.

Central Connecticut State University, School of Education and Professional Studies, Department of Educational Leadership, Program in Educational Technology and Media, New Britain, CT 06050-4010. Awards MS. Part-time and evening/weekend programs available. Students: 2 full-time (1 woman), 45 part-time (32 women); includes 3 minority (1 African American, 1 Asian American, 1 Hispanic), 2 international. Average age 37. 22 applicants, 95% accepted. In 1997, 6 degrees awarded. *Degree requirements:* Thesis or alternative, comprehensive exam or special project required, foreign language not required. *Entrance requirements:* TOEFL (minimum score 550), minimum GPA of 2.7. Application deadline: 6/1 (priority date; rolling processing; 12/1 for spring admission). Application fee: $40. *Expenses:* Tuition $4458 per year full-time, $175 per credit hour part-time for state residents; $9943 per year full-time, $175 per credit hour part-time for nonresidents. Fees $45 per semester. *Financial aid:* In 1997–98, 1 research assistantship was awarded; Federal Work-Study and career-related internships or fieldwork also available. Financial aid application deadline: 3/15; applicants required to submit FAFSA. *Faculty research:* Design and development of multimedia packages, semiotics, perceptual theories, integrated media presentations, distance teaching. • Dr. Farough Abed, Coordinator, 860-832-2139.

Central Michigan University, College of Education and Human Services, Department of Teacher Education and Professional Development, Program in Library Media, Mount Pleasant, MI 48859. Awards MA. Students: 18 part-time (16 women); includes 1 minority (Hispanic). Average age 34. 4 applicants, 100% accepted. In 1997, 15 degrees awarded. *Degree requirements:* Thesis or alternative required, foreign language not required. *Entrance requirements:* GRE General Test (minimum combined score of 1000), minimum GPA of 2.7. Application deadline: 3/1 (priority date). Application fee: $30. *Expenses:* Tuition $139 per credit hour (minimum) for state residents; $276 per credit hour (minimum) for nonresidents. Fees $260 per year full-time, $150 per semester part-time. *Financial aid:* Fellowships, research assistantships, teaching assistantships, Federal Work-Study available. Financial aid application deadline: 3/7. • Dr. William Merrill, Chairperson, Department of Teacher Education and Professional Development, 517-774-3975. Fax: 517-774-3516. E-mail: 34ltyvi@cmich.edu.

Central State University, Program in Education, Wilberforce, OH 45384. Offerings include educational technology (M Ed). Program faculty: 3 full-time. *Tuition:* $120 per credit hour for state residents; $206 per credit hour for nonresidents. • Constance Robinson, Coordinator, 937-376-6536.

Chestnut Hill College, Program in Applied Technology, Philadelphia, PA 19118-2693. Awards MS. Part-time and evening/weekend programs available. Faculty: 3 full-time (all women), 5 part-time (3 women). Students: 62 part-time (49 women); includes 2 minority (both African Americans). Average age 34. *Average time to degree:* master's–3 years part-time. *Entrance requirements:* GRE or MAT. Application deadline: rolling. Application fee: $35. *Financial aid:* Graduate assistantships available. Aid available to part-time students. • Sr. Louise Mayock, SND, Coordinator of Computer Education, 215-248-7186. Application contact: Regina Raphael Smith, Graduate Admissions, 215-248-7020. Fax: 215-248-7155.

Chicago State University, College of Education, Department of Library Science and Communications Media, Chicago, IL 60628. Awards MS Ed. Accredited by NCATE. *Entrance requirements:* Minimum GPA of 2.75. Application deadline: 7/1 (11/10 for spring admission). *Tuition:* $2268 per year full-time, $95 per credit hour part-time for state residents; $6804 per year full-time, $284 per credit hour part-time for nonresidents.

City University, School of Education, Bellevue, WA 98004-6442. Offerings include education technology (M Ed). Postbaccalaureate distance learning degree programs offered (no on-campus study). School faculty: 21 full-time (13 women), 301 part-time (162 women). *Application deadline:* rolling. *Application fee:* $75 ($175 for international students). Electronic applications accepted. *Tuition:* $280 per credit hour. • Roxanne Kelly, Dean, 425-637-1010 Ext. 3712. Fax: 425-277-2439. Application contact: Nabil El-Khatib, Vice President, Admissions, 800-426-5596. Fax: 425-277-2437. E-mail: nel-khatib@cityu.edu.

Clarke College, Program in Education, Dubuque, IA 52001-3198. Offerings include educational media: elementary and secondary (MA), technology in education (MA). One or more programs accredited by NCATE. Program faculty: 8 part-time (4 women). *Degree requirements:* Comprehensive exam, minimum GPA of 3.25 required, thesis optional, foreign language not required. *Average time to degree:* master's–4 years part-time. *Entrance requirements:* GRE General Test or MAT, minimum GPA of 2.75. Application deadline: rolling. Application fee: $25. Electronic applications accepted. *Expenses:* Tuition $12,688 per year full-time, $315 per credit hour part-time. Fees $240 per year. • Dr. Margaret Feldner, Chair, 319-588-6397. E-mail: mfeldner@clarke.edu. Application contact: Admissions Office, 800-383-2345. Fax: 319-588-6789. E-mail: graduate@clarke.edu.

The College of New Jersey, Graduate Division, School of Education, Department of Elementary/Early Childhood Education, Ewing, NJ 08628. Offerings include instructional computing coordinator (Certificate). *Average time to degree:* master's–2 years full-time. *Application deadline:* 4/15 (10/15 for spring admission). *Application fee:* $50. *Expenses:* Tuition $6892 per year full-time, $287 per credit hour part-time for state residents; $9602 per year full-time, $402 per credit hour part-time for nonresidents. Fees $799 per year full-time, $33 per credit hour part-time. • Lawrence Marcus, Chair, 609-771-3054. Fax: 609-637-5197.

College of Notre Dame, Department of Education, Belmont, CA 94002-1997. Offerings include elementary education (M Ed, Certificate), with options in educational technology (M Ed), elementary education (Certificate), multicultural education (M Ed); secondary education (MAT, M Ed, Certificate), with options in educational technology (M Ed), multicultural education (M Ed), secondary education (MAT, Certificate), teaching art (MAT), teaching biology (MAT), teaching English (MAT), teaching French (MAT), teaching music (MAT), teaching religious studies (MAT), teaching social sciences (MAT). Department faculty: 7 full-time, 24 part-time. *Application deadline:* rolling. *Application fee:* $50 ($500 for international students). *Tuition:* $460 per unit. • Dr. Diane Guay, Chair, 650-508-3701.

College of Saint Elizabeth, Department of Education, Morristown, NJ 07960-6989. Offerings include educational technology (MA). Department faculty: 4 full-time (3 women), 7 part-time (3 women). *Degree requirements:* Thesis or alternative, portfolio required, foreign language not required. *Average time to degree:* master's–2.5 years part-time. *Entrance requirements:* Interview, minimum undergraduate GPA of 3.0. Application deadline: 6/30 (priority date; rolling processing; 11/30 for spring admission). Application fee: $35. *Expenses:* Tuition $364 per credit. Fees $455 per year full-time, $70 per semester part-time. • Dr. Joan T. Walters, SC, Director of Graduate Program, 973-290-4374. Fax: 973-290-4389. E-mail: education@liza.st-elizabeth.edu.

Concordia University, Faculty of Arts and Science, Department of Education, Program in Educational Technology, Montréal, PQ H3G 1M8, Canada. Awards MA, PhD. Students: 90 full-time (57 women), 50 part-time (33 women); includes 7 international. In 1997, 27 master's, 3 doctorates awarded. *Degree requirements:* For master's, 1 foreign language, internship required, thesis optional; for doctorate, dissertation, comprehensive exam. *Entrance requirements:* For doctorate, MA in educational technology or equivalent. Application deadline: 3/31 (priority date; 9/30 for spring admission). Application fee: $30. *Expenses:* Tuition $56 per credit (minimum) for Canadian residents; $249 per credit (minimum) for nonresidents. Fees $158 per year full-time, $117 per year (minimum) part-time. *Financial aid:* Career-related internships or fieldwork available. *Faculty research:* Instructional design and tele-education, educational cybernetics and systems analysis, media research and theory development, distance education. • Application contact: Dr. D. Wells, MA Director, 514-848-2039. Fax: 514-848-4520.

Concordia University, Faculty of Arts and Science, Department of Education, Program in Instructional Technology, Montréal, PQ H3G 1M8, Canada. Awards Diploma. Students: 15 full-time (12 women), 6 part-time (4 women). In 1997, 4 degrees awarded. *Entrance requirements:* BA in related field. Application deadline: 3/31 (priority date; 9/30 for spring admission). Application fee: $30. *Expenses:* Tuition $56 per credit (minimum) for Canadian residents; $249 per credit (minimum) for nonresidents. Fees $158 per year full-time, $117 per year (minimum) part-time. • Application contact: Dr. D. Wells, Director, 514-848-2039. Fax: 514-848-4520.

Dowling College, Professional Program in Educational Administration, Oakdale, NY 11769-1999. Offerings include computers in education (PD). Program faculty: 1 full-time (0 women), 4 part-time (2 women). *Degree requirements:* Comprehensive exam required, foreign language and thesis not required. *Entrance requirements:* Teaching certificate. Application deadline: 9/1 (priority date; rolling processing). Application fee: $0. • Dr. Jerome Traiger, Discipline Coordinator, 516-244-3459. Fax: 516-244-5036. Application contact: Kate Rowe, Director of Admissions, 516-244-3030. Fax: 516-563-3827. E-mail: rowek@dowling.edu.

East Carolina University, School of Education, Department of Library Studies and Educational Technology, Greenville, NC 27858-4353. Offers programs in instruction technology specialist (MA Ed), library science (MLS, CAS). Accredited by NCATE. Part-time and evening/weekend programs available. Faculty: 6 full-time (4 women). Students: 4 full-time (all women), 41 part-time (40 women); includes 1 minority (African American). Average age 39. 21 applicants, 95% accepted. In 1997, 20 master's awarded. *Degree requirements:* For master's, comprehensive exams required, thesis optional, foreign language not required. *Entrance requirements:* For master's, GRE General Test or MAT, TOEFL. Application deadline: 6/1 (priority date; rolling processing). Application fee: $40. *Tuition:* $1886 per year full-time, $472 per semester (minimum) part-time for state residents; $9156 per year full-time, $2289 per semester (minimum) part-time for nonresidents. *Financial aid:* Research assistantships, teaching assistantships, Federal Work-Study available. Aid available to part-time students. Financial aid application deadline: 6/1. • Dr. Gene D. Lanier, Director of Graduate Studies, 252-328-6621. Fax: 252-328-4368. E-mail: lanierg@mail.ecu.edu. Application contact: Dr. Paul D. Tschetter, Associate Dean, 252-328-6012. Fax: 252-328-6071. E-mail: grad@mail.ecu.edu.

Eastern Washington University, College of Education and Human Development, Department of Education, Program in Instructional Communications: Community Services, Cheney, WA 99004-2431. Awards M Ed. Accredited by NCATE. *Degree requirements:* Thesis or alternative, comprehensive exam. *Entrance requirements:* Minimum GPA of 3.0. Application deadline: 4/1 (priority date; rolling processing; 1/15 for spring admission). Application fee: $35. *Tuition:* $4200 per year full-time, $140 per credit part-time for state residents; $12,780 per year full-time, $415 per credit part-time for nonresidents. *Financial aid:* Application deadline 2/1. • Dr. Nancy Todd, Adviser, 509-359-2232.

Eastern Washington University, College of Education and Human Development, Department of Education, Program in School Library Media Administration, Cheney, WA 99004-2431. Awards M Ed. Accredited by NCATE. *Degree requirements:* Thesis or alternative, comprehensive exam. *Entrance requirements:* Minimum GPA of 3.0. Application deadline: 4/1 (priority date; rolling processing; 1/15 for spring admission). Application fee: $35. *Tuition:* $4200 per year full-time, $140 per credit part-time for state residents; $12,780 per year full-time, $415 per credit part-time for nonresidents. *Financial aid:* Application deadline 2/1. • Dr. Nancy Todd, Adviser, 509-359-2232.

East Tennessee State University, College of Education, Department of Curriculum and Instruction, Johnson City, TN 37614-0734. Offerings include media services (M Ed). Accredited by NCATE. Department faculty: 17 full-time (8 women). *Application deadline:* 7/15 (priority date; rolling processing; 12/1 for spring admission). *Application fee:* $25 ($35 for international students). *Tuition:* $2944 per year full-time, $158 per credit hour part-time for state residents; $7770 per year full-time, $369 per credit hour part-time for nonresidents. • Dr. Jack Rhoton, Chair, 423-439-4426. Fax: 423-439-8362.

Emmanuel College, Program in Education Technology, Boston, MA 02115. Awards M Ed. *Degree requirements:* Computer language, internship required, foreign language and thesis not required. *Entrance requirements:* Interview. Application deadline: 9/7 (priority date; rolling processing). Application fee: $50. *Financial aid:* Federal Work-Study and career-related internships or fieldwork available. Aid available to part-time students. *Faculty research:* Development of computer base for teaching autistic children. • Application contact: Lorene Ashton-Reed, Graduate Program Assistant, 617-735-9844.

Emporia State University, School of Graduate Studies, The Teachers College, Division of Instructional Design and Technology, Emporia, KS 66801-5087. Awards MS. Accredited by NCATE. Faculty: 5 full-time (3 women). Students: 5 full-time (3 women), 11 part-time (7 women). 3 applicants, 100% accepted. In 1997, 5 degrees awarded. *Degree requirements:* Comprehensive exam or thesis required, foreign language not required. *Entrance requirements:* GRE General Test or MAT, TOEFL (minimum score 550), written exam. Application deadline: 8/15 (priority date; rolling processing). Application fee: $30 ($75 for international students). Electronic applications accepted. *Tuition:* $2300 per year full-time, $103 per credit hour part-time for state residents; $6012 per year full-time, $258 per credit hour part-time for nonresidents. *Financial aid:* In 1997–98, 1 research assistantship averaging $558 per month, 4 teaching assistantships averaging $522 per month were awarded; Federal Work-Study, institutionally sponsored loans also available. Financial aid application deadline: 3/15; applicants required to submit FAFSA. • Dr. Armand Seguin, Chair, 316-341-5627. E-mail: seguinar@emporia.edu.

Fairfield University, Graduate School of Education and Allied Professions, Department of Curriculum and Instruction, Computers in Education Program, Fairfield, CT 06430-5195. Awards MA, CAS. Part-time and evening/weekend programs available. Faculty: 1 full-time (0 women), 2 part-time (0 women), 2 FTE. Students: 4 full-time (2 women), 36 part-time (25 women); includes 2 minority (1 African American, 1 Asian American). Average age 33. 15 applicants, 100% accepted. In 1997, 6 master's, 1 CAS awarded. *Degree requirements:* For master's, thesis or alternative, comprehensive exam required, foreign language not required. *Entrance requirements:* For master's, TOEFL, minimum QPA of 2.67. Application deadline: 7/10 (priority date; rolling processing). Application fee: $40. *Expenses:* Tuition $350 per credit hour (minimum). Fees $20 per semester (minimum). *Financial aid:* Partial tuition waivers available. Aid available to part-time students. • Dr. John Schurdak, Program Director, 203-254-4000 Ext. 2382. Application contact: Karen Creecy, Assistant Dean, 203-254-4250. Fax: 203-254-4241. E-mail: klcreecy@fair1.fairfield.edu.

Fairfield University, Graduate School of Education and Allied Professions, Department of Curriculum and Instruction, Media/Educational Technology Program, Fairfield, CT 06430-5195. Offers educational media (MA, CAS). Part-time and evening/weekend programs available. Postbaccalaureate distance learning degree programs offered. Faculty: 1 full-time (0 women), 3 part-time (2 women), 2 FTE. Students: 5 full-time (3 women), 28 part-time (21 women); includes 1 minority (African American), 3 international. Average age 32. 13 applicants, 100% accepted. In 1997, 10 master's awarded (100% found work related to degree); 1 CAS awarded (100% found work related to degree). *Degree requirements:* For master's, comprehensive exams required, foreign language and thesis not required. *Entrance requirements:* For master's, PRAXIS I (CBT), TOEFL, minimum QPA of 2.67. Application deadline: 7/10 (priority date; rolling processing). Application fee: $40. *Expenses:* Tuition $350 per credit hour (minimum). Fees $20 per semester (minimum). *Financial aid:* Partial tuition waivers available. Aid available to part-time students. *Faculty research:* Television, advertising, children in television, multimedia applications. • Dr. Ibrahim Hefzallah, Program Director, 203-254-4000 Ext. 2697. Fax: 203-254-4087. Application contact: Karen Creecy, Assistant Dean, 203-254-4250. Fax: 203-254-4241. E-mail: klcreecy@fair1.fairfield.edu.

Florida Atlantic University, College of Education, Department of Educational Technology and Research, Boca Raton, FL 33431-0991. Offers programs in foundations-educational research (M Ed), foundations-educational technology (M Ed). Accredited by NCATE. Part-time programs available. Faculty: 11 full-time (2 women), 2 part-time (1 woman). Students: 6 full-time (3 women), 18 part-time (9 women); includes 6 minority (2 African Americans, 2 Asian Americans, 2 Hispanics). 10 applicants, 70% accepted. In 1997, 2 degrees awarded. *Entrance requirements:* GRE General Test, minimum GPA of 3.0 in last 60 hours. Application deadline: rolling. Application fee: $20. *Expenses:* Tuition $2520 per year full-time, $140 per credit hour part-time for state residents; $8712 per year full-time, $484 per credit hour part-time for nonresidents. Fees $5 per year (minimum). *Financial aid:* Fellowships and career-related internships or fieldwork available. *Faculty research:* Cognition. • Dr. John Morris, Chairperson, 561-297-3600.

Florida State University, College of Education, Department of Educational Research, Program in Instructional Systems, Tallahassee, FL 32306. Awards MS, PhD, Ed S. Faculty: 4 full-time (1 woman), 7 part-time (1 woman). Students: 62 full-time (33 women), 36 part-time (21 women); includes 41 minority (10 African Americans, 26 Asian Americans, 4 Hispanics, 1 Native American). 70 applicants, 67% accepted. In 1997, 35 master's, 5 doctorates awarded. *Degree requirements:* For master's and Ed S, comprehensive exam required, thesis optional; for doctorate, dissertation, comprehensive exam. *Entrance requirements:* GRE General Test (minimum combined score of 1000), minimum GPA of 3.0. Application deadline: 7/1 (priority date; rolling processing; 11/1 for spring admission). Application fee: $20. *Tuition:* $139 per credit hour for state residents; $482 per credit hour for nonresidents. *Financial aid:* Fellowships, research assistantships, teaching assistantships, and career-related internships or fieldwork available. • Dr. Marcy Driscoll, Chair, Department of Educational Research, 850-644-4592. E-mail: driscoll@mail.coe.fsu.edu. Application contact: Admissions Secretary, 850-644-4592. Fax: 850-644-8776.

Fort Hays State University, College of Education, Department of Technology Studies, Hays, KS 67601-4099. Offers program in instructional technology (MS). Accredited by NCATE. Faculty: 1 full-time (0 women). Students: 5 full-time (1 woman), 5 part-time (all women); includes 2 Asian Americans. 3 applicants, 67% accepted. *Entrance requirements:* GRE General Test or MAT. Application deadline: 7/1 (priority date; rolling processing). Application fee: $25 ($35 for international students). *Tuition:* $94 per credit hour for state residents; $249 per credit hour for nonresidents. • Dr. Fred Ruda, Chairperson, 785-628-4315. Fax: 785-628-4267.

Fresno Pacific University, Graduate School, Programs in Education, Division of Foundations, Curriculum and Teaching, Program in School Library Media, Fresno, CA 93702-4709. Awards MA Ed. Faculty: 1 (woman) full-time, 3 part-time (2 women). Students: 34 part-time (31 women). *Application deadline:* 7/31. *Application fee:* $75. *Tuition:* $250 per unit. • Norma Dick, Director, 209-453-2291. Fax: 209-453-2001.

Fresno Pacific University, Graduate School, Programs in Education, Division of Mathematics/Science/Computer Education, Program in Technology, Fresno, CA 93702-4709. Awards MA Ed. Faculty: 8 part-time (0 women). Students: 37 part-time (11 women). *Degree requirements:* Thesis or alternative required, foreign language not required. *Application deadline:* 7/31 (rolling processing). *Application fee:* $75. *Tuition:* $250 per unit. • Scott Smith, Acting Director, 209-453-2024. Fax: 209-453-2001.

Gannon University, School of Graduate Studies, College of Humanities, Business, and Education, School of Education, Program in Educational Computing Technology, Erie, PA 16541. Awards M Ed. Part-time and evening/weekend programs available. Students: 7 part-time (2 women). Average age 31. 6 applicants, 100% accepted. In 1997, 3 degrees awarded. *Degree requirements:* Thesis, comprehensive exam. *Entrance requirements:* GRE or MAT, interview, teaching certificate. Application deadline: rolling. Application fee: $25. *Expenses:* Tuition $405 per credit. Fees $200 per year full-time, $8 per credit part-time. *Financial aid:* Available to part-time students. Financial aid application deadline: 3/1; applicants required to submit FAFSA. • Charles Elliot, Director, 814-871-5348. Application contact: Beth Nemenz, Director of Admissions, 814-871-7240. Fax: 814-871-5803. E-mail: admissions@gannon.edu.

George Mason University, Graduate School of Education, Program in Instructional Technology, Fairfax, VA 22030-4444. Awards M Ed. Accredited by NCATE. Part-time and evening/weekend programs available. Faculty: 42 full-time (24 women), 65 part-time (51 women), 58.73 FTE. Students: 5 full-time (3 women), 61 part-time (42 women); includes 6 minority (4 African Americans, 2 Hispanics), 1 international. Average age 37. 21 applicants, 95% accepted. In 1997, 15 degrees awarded. *Degree requirements:* Computer language required, foreign language not required. *Entrance requirements:* NTE, minimum GPA of 3.0 in last 60 hours. Application deadline: 5/1 (11/1 for spring admission). Application fee: $30. Electronic applications accepted. *Tuition:* $4344 per year full-time, $181 per credit hour part-time for state residents; $12,504 per year full-time, $521 per credit hour part-time for nonresidents. *Financial aid:* Available to part-time students. Financial aid application deadline: 3/1; applicants required to submit FAFSA. • Dr. Michael Bhermann, Director, 703-993-2143. Fax: 703-993-2013.

The George Washington University, Graduate School of Education and Human Development, Department of Educational Leadership, Program in Educational Technology Leadership, Washington, DC 20052. Awards MA Ed. Accredited by NCATE. Part-time and evening/weekend programs available. Faculty: 4 full-time (0 women), 4 part-time (2 women), 5 FTE. Students: 3 full-time (all women), 123 part-time (72 women); includes 12 minority (4 African Americans, 4 Asian Americans, 4 Hispanics), 2 international. Average age 43. 50 applicants, 98% accepted. In 1997, 40 degrees awarded. *Degree requirements:* Thesis or alternative, comprehensive exam required, foreign language not required. *Entrance requirements:* GRE General Test or MAT, minimum GPA of 2.75. Application deadline: 3/1 (priority date; rolling processing; 10/1 for spring admission). Application fee: $50. *Financial aid:* Career-related internships or fieldwork available. *Faculty research:* Interactive multimedia, distance education, federal technology policy. • Dr. William Lynch, Director, 202-994-6862.

Georgia College and State University, School of Education, Department of Special Education and Administration, Program in Instructional Technology, Milledgeville, GA 31061. Awards M Ed. Accredited by NCATE. Students: 20 full-time (16 women), 35 part-time (30 women); includes 7 minority (6 African Americans, 1 Hispanic). Average age 40. In 1997, 17 degrees awarded. *Degree requirements:* Computer language, comprehensive exit exam required, foreign language and thesis not required. *Entrance requirements:* GRE General Test (minimum combined score of 800) or NTE (minimum score 550 on each core battery test), MAT (minimum score 44), minimum GPA of 2.5, NT-4 certificate. Application deadline: 7/31 (priority date; rolling processing). Application fee: $10. *Financial aid:* Assistantships, Federal Work-Study, and career-related internships or fieldwork available. Aid available to part-time students. Financial aid application deadline: 4/15. • Dr. Craig Smith, Chairperson, Department of Special Education and Administration, 912-445-4577.

Georgia Southern University, College of Education, Department of Leadership, Technology, and Human Development, Program in Instructional Media, Statesboro, GA 30460-8126. Awards M Ed, Ed S. Accredited by NCATE. Part-time and evening/weekend programs available. Students: 13 full-time (all women), 23 part-time (20 women); includes 1 minority (African American). Average age 33. 10 applicants, 90% accepted. In 1997, 15 master's, 2 Ed Ss awarded. *Degree requirements:* For master's, exams required, foreign language and thesis not required. *Entrance requirements:* For master's, GRE General Test (minimum score 450 on each section) or MAT (minimum score 44), minimum GPA of 2.5. Application deadline: 7/15 (priority date; rolling processing; 11/15 for spring admission). Application fee: $0. Electronic applications accepted. *Tuition:* $2619 per year full-time, $287 per semester (minimum) part-time for state residents; $8619 per year full-time, $1037 per semester (minimum) part-time for nonresidents. *Financial aid:* Research assistantships, teaching assistantships, Federal Work-Study, and career-related internships or fieldwork available. Aid available to part-time students. Financial aid application deadline: 4/15. • Application contact: Dr. John R. Diebolt, Associate Graduate Dean, 912-681-5384. Fax: 912-681-0740. E-mail: gradschool@gsvms2.cc.gasou.edu.

Georgia State University, College of Education, Department of Middle, Secondary Education and Instructional Technology, Library Science/Media Unit, Atlanta, GA 30303-3083. Offers programs in instructional technology (MS, PhD), library media technology (MLM, PhD, Ed S). Accredited by NCATE. Part-time and evening/weekend programs available. Students: 68 full-time (55 women), 57 part-time (40 women); includes 20 minority (17 African Americans, 2 Asian Americans, 1 Hispanic), 3 international. Average age 37. 41 applicants, 85% accepted. In 1997, 34 master's, 3 doctorates, 13 Ed Ss awarded. *Degree requirements:* For master's, comprehensive exam; for doctorate, dissertation, comprehensive exam; for Ed S, project/exam. *Entrance requirements:* For master's, GRE General Test (minimum combined score of 800) or MAT (minimum score 44), minimum GPA of 2.5; for doctorate, GRE General Test (minimum score 500 on verbal section, 500 on either quantitative or analytical sections) or MAT (minimum score 53), minimum GPA of 3.3; for Ed S, GRE General Test (minimum combined score of 900) or MAT (minimum score 48), minimum graduate GPA of 3.25. Application fee: $25. *Expenses:* Tuition $2673 per year full-time, $99 per semester hour part-time for state residents; $10,692 per year full-time, $396 per semester hour part-time for nonresidents. Fees $228 per year. *Financial aid:* Federal Work-Study, institutionally sponsored loans available. *Faculty research:* Automation, children's literature, cataloging, electronic resources. • Dr. Rosalind Miller, Coordinator, 404-651-2458.

Governors State University, College of Arts and Sciences, Division of Liberal Arts, Program in Communication and Training, University Park, IL 60466. Offerings include instructional and training technology (MA). Program faculty: 3 full-time (2 women), 6 part-time (5 women). *Degree requirements:* Thesis or alternative required, foreign language not required. *Application deadline:* 7/15 (priority date; rolling processing; 11/10 for spring admission). *Application fee:* $0. *Expenses:* Tuition $1140 per trimester full-time, $95 per credit hour part-time for state

Directory: Educational Media/Instructional Technology

Governors State University (continued)

residents; $3420 per trimester full-time, $285 per credit hour part-time for nonresidents. Fees $95 per trimester. • Dr. Sonny Goldenstein, Chairperson, Division of Liberal Arts, 708-534-4010.

Grand Valley State University, School of Education, Programs in General Education, Program in Educational Technology, Allendale, MI 49401-9403. Awards M Ed. Accredited by NCATE. *Degree requirements:* Thesis or alternative, applied research project. *Entrance requirements:* GRE General Test (minimum combined score of 1300) or minimum GPA of 3.0. Application deadline: rolling. Application fee: $20. • Application contact: Admissions Office, 616-895-2025. Fax: 616-895-3081.

Harvard University, Graduate School of Education, Area of Learning and Teaching, Cambridge, MA 02138. Offerings include technology in education (Ed M). Faculty: 7 full-time (5 women), 16 part-time (8 women), 10.3 FTE. *Average time to degree:* master's–1 year full-time, 2.1 years part-time; doctorate–6.3 years full-time, 9 years part-time; other advanced degree–1 year full-time, 2 years part-time. *Entrance requirements:* GRE General Test, TOEFL (minimum score 600), TWE (minimum score 5.0). Application deadline: 1/2. Application fee: $60. • Robert Kegan, Chair, 617-496-2974. Fax: 617-495-7843. Application contact: Roland Hence, Director of Admissions, 617-495-3414. Fax: 617-496-3577. E-mail: gseadmissions@harvard.edu.

Indiana State University, School of Education, Department of Curriculum and Instruction and Media Technology, Terre Haute, IN 47809-1401. Offers programs in business education (MA, MS, PhD, Ed S), curriculum and instruction (M Ed, PhD), educational media (MA, MS, Ed S), industrial arts education (PhD), secondary education (M Ed, MS, PhD, Ed S). Accredited by NCATE. Faculty: 16 full-time (4 women). Students: 13 full-time (6 women), 22 part-time (12 women); includes 2 minority (both African Americans), 5 international. Average age 36. 23 applicants, 65% accepted. In 1997, 12 master's, 2 doctorates awarded. *Degree requirements:* For doctorate, 2 foreign languages, computer language, dissertation. *Entrance requirements:* For master's, minimum undergraduate GPA of 2.5; for doctorate, GRE General Test (minimum score 500 on each section); for Ed S, GRE General Test (minimum combined score of 900), minimum graduate GPA of 3.25. Application deadline: rolling. Application fee: $20. *Tuition:* $143 per credit hour for state residents; $325 per credit hour for nonresidents. *Financial aid:* In 1997–98, 8 fellowships (2 to first-year students), 7 research assistantships (6 to first-year students), 1 teaching assistantship were awarded; partial tuition waivers also available. Financial aid application deadline: 3/1. *Faculty research:* Discipline FERPA reading, teacher strengths and needs. • Dr. Jerry A. Summers, Chairperson, 812-237-2960. Application contact: Dr. Robert Williams, Graduate Adviser, 812-237-2952.

Indiana University Bloomington, School of Education, Department of Instructional Systems Technology, Bloomington, IN 47405. Awards MS, Ed D, PhD, Ed S. Accredited by NCATE. PhD offered through the University Graduate School. Faculty: 9 full-time (1 woman). Students: 105 full-time (58 women), 85 part-time (37 women); includes 13 minority (3 African Americans, 8 Asian Americans, 1 Hispanic, 1 Native American), 61 international. In 1997, 51 master's, 10 doctorates awarded. *Degree requirements:* For master's, computer language required, foreign language and thesis not required; for doctorate, computer language, dissertation required, foreign language not required; for Ed S, comprehensive exam or project required, foreign language not required. *Entrance requirements:* For master's, GRE General Test (minimum combined score of 1350 on three sections); for doctorate and Ed S, GRE General Test (minimum combined score of 1550 on three sections). Application deadline: 6/1. Application fee: $35. *Expenses:* Tuition $153 per credit hour for state residents; $446 per credit hour for nonresidents. Fees $343 per year. *Financial aid:* Fellowships, research assistantships, teaching assistantships, graduate assistantships, Federal Work-Study, institutionally sponsored loans, and career-related internships or fieldwork available. Financial aid application deadline: 2/15. *Faculty research:* Instructional design and development, high technology applications, computer-assisted instruction. • Dr. Thomas Schwen, Chair, 812-856-8451. Application contact: Dr. Dale P. Scannell, Director of Graduate Studies, 812-856-8540.

Inter American University of Puerto Rico, Metropolitan Campus, Division of Science and Technology, Program in Educational Computing, San Juan, PR 00919-1293. Awards MA. Faculty: 3 full-time (1 woman), 5 part-time (2 women), 4.25 FTE. Students: 33 full-time (17 women), 45 part-time (19 women); includes 78 minority (all Hispanics). 22 applicants, 86% accepted. In 1997, 2 degrees awarded (50% entered university research/teaching, 50% found other work related to degree). *Degree requirements:* Computer language, comprehensive exam, portfolio required, foreign language and thesis not required. *Average time to degree:* master's–2 years full-time. *Entrance requirements:* GRE or PAEG, minimum GPA of 2.5. Application deadline: 5/15 (priority date; rolling processing; 11/15 for spring admission). Application fee: $31. Electronic applications accepted. *Expenses:* Tuition $3272 per year full-time, $1740 per year part-time. Fees $328 per year full-time, $176 per year part-time. *Financial aid:* 7 students received aid. Aid available to part-time students. *Faculty research:* Effectiveness of multimedia, World Wide Web for distance learning. • José Vallés, Coordinator, 787-250-1912 Ext. 2144. Fax: 787-250-8736.

Iona College, School of Arts and Science, Program in Educational Computing, 715 North Avenue, New Rochelle, NY 10801-1890. Awards MS, Certificate. Part-time and evening/weekend programs available. Faculty: 4 full-time (3 women), 4 part-time (1 woman). Students: 2 full-time (both women), 24 part-time (21 women); includes 1 minority (Hispanic). Average age 31. In 1997, 32 master's, 2 Certificates awarded. *Degree requirements:* For master's, thesis or alternative. *Entrance requirements:* For master's, minimum GPA of 2.5. Application deadline: rolling. Application fee: $25. *Expenses:* Tuition $455 per credit hour. Fees $25 per semester. *Financial aid:* Graduate assistantships, partial tuition waivers available. Aid available to part-time students. *Faculty research:* Human factors in computing, use of advanced workstations in education, use of authoring languages for educational software, multimedia. • Dr. John Mallozzi, Chair, 914-633-2578. Application contact: Arlene Melillo, Director of Graduate Recruitment, 914-633-2328. Fax: 914-633-2023.

Iowa State University of Science and Technology, College of Education, Department of Curriculum and Instruction, Program in Curriculum and Instruction Technology, Ames, IA 50011. Awards M Ed, MS, PhD. *Degree requirements:* For master's, thesis or alternative; for doctorate, dissertation. *Entrance requirements:* For master's, TOEFL; for doctorate, GRE General Test, TOEFL. Application deadline: 6/1 (priority date; 9/1 for spring admission). Application fee: $20 ($30 for international students). *Expenses:* Tuition $3166 per year full-time, $176 per credit part-time for state residents; $9324 per year full-time, $518 per credit part-time for nonresidents. Fees $200 per year. • Application contact: Daniel Robinson, 515-294-1241.

Jackson State University, School of Education, Department of Educational Foundations and Leadership, Jackson, MS 39217. Offerings include secondary education (MS Ed, Ed S), with option in educational technology (MS Ed). Accredited by NCATE. Department faculty: 21 full-time (10 women), 5 part-time (1 woman). *Degree requirements:* Thesis or alternative, comprehensive exam. *Entrance requirements:* GRE General Test (minimum combined score of 1000), TOEFL (minimum score 550). Application deadline: 3/1 (priority date; rolling processing; 10/1 for spring admission). Application fee: $20. *Tuition:* $2688 per year (minimum) full-time, $150 per semester hour part-time for state residents; $5546 per year (minimum) full-time, $309 per semester hour part-time for nonresidents. • Dr. George Vincent, Chair, 601-968-2351. Fax: 601-968-2213. E-mail: gvincent@ccaix.jsums.edu. Application contact: Mae Robinson, Admissions Coordinator, 601-968-2455. Fax: 601-968-8246. E-mail: mrobinson@ccaix.jsums.edu.

Jacksonville State University, College of Education, Program in Instructional Media, Jacksonville, AL 36265-9982. Awards MS Ed. Accredited by NCATE. Part-time and evening/weekend programs available. Faculty: 2 full-time (1 woman). Students: 2 full-time (both women), 16 part-time (14 women); includes 1 minority (African American). In 1997, 11 degrees awarded. *Degree requirements:* Thesis optional. *Entrance requirements:* GRE General Test or MAT. Application deadline: rolling. Application fee: $20. *Expenses:* Tuition $2140 per year full-time, $107 per semester hour part-time for state residents; $4280 per year full-time, $214 per semester hour part-time for nonresidents. Fees $30 per semester. *Financial aid:* Available to part-time students. Financial aid application deadline: 4/1. • Application contact: College of Graduate Studies and Continuing Education, 205-782-5329.

Jacksonville University, College of Arts and Sciences, Division of Education, Program in Integrated Learning with Educational Technology, 2800 University Boulevard North, Jacksonville, FL 32211-3394. Awards MAT. *Degree requirements:* Computer language, comprehensive exam required, foreign language and thesis not required. *Entrance requirements:* GRE General Test (minimum combined score of 900), TOEFL (minimum score 500), minimum GPA of 3.0. Application deadline: 8/1 (priority date; rolling processing; 11/1 for spring admission). Application fee: $25.

James Madison University, College of Education and Psychology, School of Education, Program in Library Science and Educational Media, Harrisonburg, VA 22807. Awards M Ed. Accredited by NCATE. Part-time and evening/weekend programs available. Students: 6 full-time (5 women), 16 part-time (15 women); includes 1 minority (African American). Average age 30. In 1997, 13 degrees awarded. *Entrance requirements:* GRE General Test. Application deadline: 7/1 (priority date; rolling processing). Application fee: $50. *Tuition:* $134 per credit hour for state residents; $404 per credit hour for nonresidents. *Financial aid:* In 1997–98, 2 assistantships totaling $18,810 were awarded; fellowships, teaching assistantships, Federal Work-Study also available. Financial aid application deadline: 2/15; applicants required to submit FAFSA. • Dr. David Zimmerman, Coordinator, 540-568-6927.

Johns Hopkins University, School of Continuing Studies, Division of Education, Department of Educational Technology, Baltimore, MD 21218-2699. Offers programs in assistive technology (Certificate), computers for educators (CAGS), technology for educators (MS). *Entrance requirements:* For master's, minimum GPA of 3.0, interview; for other advanced degree, master's or doctoral degree. Application fee: $50. • Jacqueline Nunn, Adviser, 410-254-8466.

Johnson & Wales University, Graduate School, Program in Instructional Technology, 8 Abbott Park Place, Providence, RI 02903-3703. Awards MS. Program being phased out; applicants no longer accepted. Part-time and evening/weekend programs available. Faculty: 2 full-time (0 women), 3 part-time (1 woman). Students: 47 part-time (19 women); includes 3 minority (all African Americans), 7 international. Average age 27. *Degree requirements:* Thesis optional. *Expenses:* Tuition $194 per quarter hour (minimum). Fees $477 per year. *Financial aid:* Graduate assistantships, partial tuition waivers available. Aid available to part-time students. • Dr. Paul J. Colbert, Director, 401-598-4738. Fax: 401-598-1125.

Johnson Bible College, Program in Educational Technology, Knoxville, TN 37998-0001. Offers Bible and educational technology (MA). Part-time programs available. Faculty: 7 part-time (1 woman). Students: 1 (woman) full-time, 25 part-time (23 women); includes 1 minority (African American). Average age 41. 18 applicants, 83% accepted. *Degree requirements:* Research project required, thesis not required. *Entrance requirements:* Interview, minimum GPA of 3.0, portfolio, teaching license. Application deadline: 4/1 (4/1 for spring admission). Application fee: $50. Electronic applications accepted. *Tuition:* $125 per hour. *Financial aid:* Career-related internships or fieldwork available. Aid available to part-time students. Financial aid application deadline: 5/1; applicants required to submit FAFSA. • Dr. Chris Templar, Chair, 423-579-2348. Fax: 423-579-2337. E-mail: ctemplar@jbc.edu.

Kent State University, Graduate School of Education, Department of Educational Foundations and Special Services, Program in Instructional Technology, Kent, OH 44242-0001. Awards MA, M Ed, PhD. Accredited by NCATE. Faculty: 5 full-time (1 woman), 10 part-time (2 women). Students: 9 full-time (4 women), 43 part-time (31 women); includes 1 minority (African American), 1 international. In 1997, 16 master's, 12 doctorates awarded. *Degree requirements:* For master's, thesis (MA) required, foreign language not required; for doctorate, dissertation required, foreign language not required. *Entrance requirements:* For master's, GRE General Test; for doctorate, GRE General Test (minimum score 550 on verbal section). Application deadline: rolling. Application fee: $30. *Tuition:* $4752 per year full-time, $216 per credit hour part-time for state residents; $9213 per year full-time, $419 per credit hour part-time for nonresidents. *Financial aid:* Application deadline 4/1. • Dr. Ted Chandler, Coordinator, 330-672-2294. Application contact: Deborah Barber, Director, Office of Academic Services, 330-672-2862. Fax: 330-672-3549.

Lehigh University, College of Education, Department of Education and Human Services, Program in Educational Technology, Bethlehem, PA 18015-3094. Awards MS, Ed D. Part-time and evening/weekend programs available. Faculty: 3 full-time (0 women), 2 part-time (0 women). Students: 6 full-time (3 women), 64 part-time (33 women); includes 2 minority (1 Asian American, 1 Hispanic), 7 international. 21 applicants, 76% accepted. In 1997, 15 master's, 2 doctorates awarded. Terminal master's awarded for partial completion of doctoral program. *Degree requirements:* For doctorate, dissertation required, foreign language not required. *Entrance requirements:* For master's, GRE General Test or MAT, TOEFL, minimum GPA of 2.75; for doctorate, GRE General Test or MAT, TOEFL, minimum graduate GPA of 3.5. Application deadline: 7/15 (rolling processing; 12/1 for spring admission). Application fee: $40. Electronic applications accepted. *Expenses:* Tuition $470 per credit. Fees $12 per semester full-time, $6 per semester part-time. *Financial aid:* Full and partial tuition waivers, Federal Work-Study, institutionally sponsored loans, and career-related internships or fieldwork available. Financial aid application deadline: 1/15. • Dr. Ward M. Cates, Coordinator, 610-758-3231. Fax: 610-758-6223. E-mail: wmc0@leigh.edu.

Long Island University, Brooklyn Campus, School of Education, Department of Educational Leadership and Technology, Brooklyn, NY 11201-8423. Offers programs in computers in education (MS), educational leadership (PD). Part-time and evening/weekend programs available. Faculty: 1 full-time (0 women). Students: 4 full-time (all women), 44 part-time (31 women); includes 32 minority (27 African Americans, 5 Hispanics). 32 applicants, 94% accepted. In 1997, 8 master's, 18 PDs awarded. *Degree requirements:* For master's, thesis optional. *Entrance requirements:* For PD, master's degree in education. Application deadline: rolling. Application fee: $30. Electronic applications accepted. *Expenses:* Tuition $480 per credit. Fees $415 per year full-time, $73 per semester (minimum) part-time. • Dr. Philip Segan, Chair, 718-488-1103. Application contact: Bernard W. Sullivan, Associate Director of Admissions, 718-488-1011.

Longwood College, Department of Education, Farmville, VA 23909-1800. Offerings include library science media specialist (MS). Accredited by NCATE. Department faculty: 34 part-time. *Degree requirements:* Thesis (for some programs), comprehensive exam. *Entrance requirements:* Minimum GPA of 2.5. Application deadline: 5/1 (priority date; rolling processing; 10/15 for spring admission). Application fee: $25. *Expenses:* Tuition $3048 per year full-time, $127 per credit hour part-time for state residents; $8160 per year full-time, $340 per credit hour part-time for nonresidents. Fees $920 per year full-time, $31 per credit hour part-time. • Dr. Frank Howe, Chair, 804-395-2324. Application contact: Admissions Office, 804-395-2060.

Malone College, Graduate School, Program in Education, Canton, OH 44709-3897. Offerings include instructional technology (MA). Program faculty: 10 full-time (6 women), 11 part-time (5 women), 12.68 FTE. *Degree requirements:* Research practicum required, foreign language and thesis not required. *Entrance requirements:* Minimum GPA of 3.0, teaching license. Application deadline: 9/6 (rolling processing; 1/2 for spring admission). Application fee: $20. *Tuition:* $300 per credit hour. • Dr. Marietta Daulton, Director, 330-471-8447. Fax: 330-471-8478. E-mail: mdaulton@malone.edu. Application contact: Dan Depasquale, Director of Graduate Student Services, 800-257-4723. Fax: 330-471-8343. E-mail: depasquale@malone.edu.

Mankato State University, College of Education, Department of Education Technology, South Rd and Ellis Ave, PO Box 8400, Mankato, MN 56002-8400. Awards MS. Accredited by NCATE. Part-time programs available. Faculty: 1 full-time (0 women). Students: 11 full-time (7 women),

10 part-time (5 women); includes 2 minority (1 African American, 1 Asian American). Average age 38. 4 applicants, 50% accepted. In 1997, 6 degrees awarded. *Degree requirements:* Computer language, thesis or alternative, comprehensive exam required, foreign language not required. *Entrance requirements:* Minimum GPA of 3.0 during previous 2 years. Application deadline: 7/10 (priority date; rolling processing; 10/30 for spring admission). Application fee: $20. *Tuition:* $126 per credit (minimum) for state residents; $200 per credit for nonresidents. *Financial aid:* Federal Work-Study and career-related internships or fieldwork available. Aid available to part-time students. Financial aid application deadline: 3/15; applicants required to submit FAFSA. • William Brown, Director, 507-389-5811. Application contact: Joni Roberts, Admissions Coordinator, 507-389-2321. Fax: 507-389-5974. E-mail: grad@mankato.msus.edu.

Mankato State University, College of Education, Department of Library Media Education, South Rd and Ellis Ave, PO Box 8400, Mankato, MN 56002-8400. Awards MS, SP. Accredited by NCATE. Part-time programs available. Faculty: 4 full-time (1 woman). Students: 36 full-time (29 women), 36 part-time (30 women). Average age 40. 9 applicants, 78% accepted. In 1997, 18 master's awarded. *Degree requirements:* For master's, thesis or alternative, comprehensive exam; for SP, thesis, comprehensive exam required, foreign language not required. *Entrance requirements:* For master's, minimum GPA of 3.0 during previous 2 years; for SP, minimum GPA of 3.0. Application deadline: 7/30 (priority date; rolling processing; 10/30 for spring admission). Application fee: $20. *Tuition:* $126 per credit (minimum) for state residents; $200 per credit for nonresidents. *Financial aid:* Research assistantships, teaching assistantships, Federal Work-Study, institutionally sponsored loans, and career-related internships or fieldwork available. Aid available to part-time students. Financial aid application deadline: 3/15; applicants required to submit FAFSA. • Dr. Frank Birmingham, Chairperson, 507-389-5210. Application contact: Joni Roberts, Admissions Coordinator, 507-389-2321. Fax: 507-389-5974. E-mail: grad@mankato.msus.edu.

Marshall University, College of Education, Division of Educational Leadership, Program in Library Science Education, Huntington, WV 25755-2020. Awards MA. Accredited by NCATE. Program being phased out; applicants no longer accepted. Faculty: 1 (0 women). Students: 1 (woman) full-time, 3 part-time (all women). In 1997, 1 degree awarded. *Degree requirements:* Thesis optional. *Tuition:* $2364 per year full-time, $132 per hour part-time for state residents; $6894 per year full-time, $383 per hour part-time for nonresidents. • Dr. Tony L. Williams, Coordinator, 304-696-2858.

Marywood University, Graduate School of Arts and Sciences, Department of Education, Program in Instructional Technology, Scranton, PA 18509-1598. Awards MS. Accredited by NCATE. Part-time and evening/weekend programs available. Students: 1 full-time (0 women), 10 part-time (5 women). Average age 39. 6 applicants, 100% accepted. *Degree requirements:* Thesis or alternative, internship/practicum required, foreign language not required. *Entrance requirements:* GRE or MAT, TOEFL (minimum score 550; average 590). Application deadline: 7/15 (priority date; rolling processing; 12/1 for spring admission). Application fee: $20. *Expenses:* Tuition $449 per credit hour. Fees $530 per year full-time, $180 per year part-time. *Financial aid:* Research assistantships, scholarships/tuition reductions, partial tuition waivers, and career-related internships or fieldwork available. Aid available to part-time students. Financial aid application deadline: 2/15; applicants required to submit FAFSA. *Faculty research:* Integrated thematic instruction. • Sr. Patricia Walsh, IHM, Director, 717-348-6271. Application contact: Deborah M. Flynn, Coordinator of Admissions, 717-340-6002. Fax: 717-961-4745.

McNeese State University, College of Education, Department of Educational Leadership and Instructional Technology, Program in Educational Technology, Lake Charles, LA 70609-2495. Awards M Ed. Evening/weekend programs available. Faculty: 5 full-time (1 woman). Students: 3 full-time (2 women), 46 part-time (40 women). In 1997, 25 degrees awarded. *Entrance requirements:* GRE General Test, teaching certificate. Application deadline: 7/15 (priority date; rolling processing). Application fee: $10 ($25 for international students). *Tuition:* $2118 per year full-time, $344 per semester (minimum) part-time for state residents; $7308 per year full-time, $344 per semester (minimum) part-time for nonresidents. *Financial aid:* Fellowships available. Financial aid application deadline: 5/1. • Joe E. Savoie, Head, Department of Educational Leadership and Instructional Technology, 318-475-5423.

Mercy College, Department of Education, Dobbs Ferry, NY 10522-1189. Offerings include learning technology (MSE). *Entrance requirements:* Teaching certificate. *Tuition:* $390 per credit. • Dr. William Pratella, Chairperson, 914-674-7555.

Mississippi State University, College of Education, Department of Technology and Education, Mississippi State, MS 39762. Offerings include instructional technology (MSIT); technology (MS), with options in business education, industrial technology, instructional technology, vocational education. One or more programs accredited by NCATE. Department faculty: 12 full-time (5 women), 3 part-time (0 women), 13 FTE. *Application deadline:* 7/26 (priority date; rolling processing; 11/10 for spring admission). *Application fee:* $0 ($25 for international students). Electronic applications accepted. *Tuition:* $3017 per year full-time, $168 per credit hour part-time for state residents; $6119 per year full-time, $340 per credit hour part-time for nonresidents. • Dr. John F. Perry Jr., Interim Head, 601-325-2281. Fax: 601-325-7599. E-mail: jfp1@ra.msstate.edu.

Montana State University–Billings, College of Education and Human Services, Department of Curriculum and Instruction, Option in Educational Technology, Billings, MT 59101-9984. Awards M Ed. Accredited by NCATE. Part-time programs available. *Degree requirements:* Professional paper or thesis required, foreign language not required. *Entrance requirements:* GRE General Test (minimum combined score of 1350 on three sections) or MAT (minimum score 38), minimum GPA of 3.0 (undergraduate), 3.25 (graduate). Application deadline: 8/1 (priority date; rolling processing; 1/1 for spring admission). Application fee: $30. *Expenses:* Tuition $2253 per year full-time, $397 per semester (minimum) part-time for state residents; $5313 per year full-time, $907 per semester (minimum) part-time for nonresidents. Fees $378 per year full-time, $105 per semester (minimum) part-time.

National–Louis University, National College of Education, McGaw Graduate School, Program in Technology in Education, 2840 Sheridan Road, Evanston, IL 60201-1730. Awards M Ed, MS Ed, CAS. Part-time and evening/weekend programs available. Students: 131 part-time (108 women); includes 10 minority (4 African Americans, 1 Asian American, 5 Hispanics). Average age 39. In 1997, 32 master's, 10 CASs awarded. *Degree requirements:* For master's, computer language, thesis (for some programs) required, foreign language not required; for CAS, computer language required, foreign language and thesis not required. *Entrance requirements:* For master's, GRE or MAT, minimum GPA of 3.0. Application deadline: rolling. Application fee: $25. *Tuition:* $411 per semester hour. *Financial aid:* Fellowships available. Aid available to part-time students. Financial aid applicants required to submit FAFSA. • Dr. Marianne Handler, Coordinator, 847-475-1100 Ext. 5155. Application contact: Dr. David McCulloch, Vice President for University Services, 800-443-5522 Ext. 5127. Fax: 847-465-0593. E-mail: dmcc@wheeling1.nl.edu.

National University, School of Education and Human Services, Department of Teacher Education and Leadership, La Jolla, CA 92037-1011. Offerings include educational technology (MS). *Application deadline:* rolling. *Application fee:* $60 ($100 for international students). *Tuition:* $7830 per year full-time, $870 per course part-time. • Dr. Helene Mandell, Chair, 619-642-8345. Application contact: Nancy Rohland, Director of Enrollment Management, 619-563-7100. Fax: 619-563-7393.

New York Institute of Technology, School of Education, Program in Instructional Technology, Old Westbury, NY 11568-8000. Awards MS, Certificate. Part-time and evening/weekend programs available. Postbaccalaureate distance learning degree programs offered. Faculty: 6 full-time (2 women), 47 part-time (25 women). Students: 49 full-time (33 women), 642 part-time (443 women); includes 144 minority (98 African Americans, 15 Asian Americans, 30 Hispanics, 1 Native American), 1 international. Average age 37. 150 applicants, 75% accepted. In 1997, 95 master's awarded. *Degree requirements:* For master's, thesis required, foreign language not required. *Average time to degree:* master's–2.5 years full-time, 3 years part-time. *Entrance requirements:* For master's, GRE General Test, TOEFL, minimum QPA of 2.85. Application deadline: 8/1 (priority date; rolling processing). Application fee: $50. *Tuition:* $413 per credit. *Financial aid:* In 1997–98, 4 research assistantships (2 to first-year students) averaging $300 per month and totaling $8,200 were awarded; full and partial tuition waivers, institutionally sponsored loans, and career-related internships or fieldwork also available. Aid available to part-time students. *Faculty research:* Distance learning. • Dr. Davenport Plumer, Chair, 516-686-7777. Fax: 516-686-7655. Application contact: Glenn Berman, Executive Director of Admissions, 516-686-7519. Fax: 516-626-0419. E-mail: gberman@iris.nyit.edu.

New York University, School of Education, Department of Administration, Leadership, and Technology, Program in Educational Communication and Technology, New York, NY 10012-1019. Awards MA, Ed D, PhD, CAS. Part-time and evening/weekend programs available. Faculty: 1 full-time, 9 part-time. Students: 23 full-time, 66 part-time. 66 applicants, 42% accepted. In 1997, 24 master's, 1 doctorate, 1 CAS awarded. Terminal master's awarded for partial completion of doctoral program. *Degree requirements:* For master's, thesis required (for some programs), foreign language not required; for doctorate, dissertation. *Entrance requirements:* For master's, TOEFL; for doctorate, GRE General Test, TOEFL, interview; for CAS, TOEFL, master's degree. Application deadline: 2/1 (priority date; rolling processing; 12/1 for spring admission). Application fee: $40 ($60 for international students). *Financial aid:* Partial tuition waivers, Federal Work-Study, institutionally sponsored loans, and career-related internships or fieldwork available. Aid available to part-time students. Financial aid application deadline: 3/1; applicants required to submit FAFSA. *Faculty research:* Instructional design for video and interactive video programs, critical evaluation of instructional materials, multimedia, cognitive science. • Francine Shuchat-Shaw, Director, 212-998-5220. Application contact: Office of Graduate Admissions, 212-998-5030. Fax: 212-995-4328.

North Carolina Agricultural and Technical State University, Graduate School, School of Education, Department of Curriculum and Instruction, Greensboro, NC 27411. Offerings include educational media (MS). Accredited by NCATE. Department faculty: 20 full-time (11 women). *Degree requirements:* Comprehensive exam, qualifying exam required, foreign language not required. *Entrance requirements:* GRE General Test, minimum GPA of 3.0. Application deadline: 6/1 (priority date; rolling processing; 12/1 for spring admission). Application fee: $35. *Tuition:* $1662 per year full-time, $272 per semester (minimum) part-time for state residents; $8790 per year full-time, $2054 per semester (minimum) part-time for nonresidents. • Dr. Dorothy Leflore, Interim Chairperson, 336-334-7848.

North Carolina Central University, Division of Academic Affairs, School of Education, Program in Educational Technology, Durham, NC 27707-3129. Offers instructional media (MA). Accredited by NCATE. Part-time and evening/weekend programs available. Students: 6 full-time (4 women), 16 part-time (13 women); includes 16 minority (all African Americans). Average age 36. 4 applicants, 100% accepted. In 1997, 5 degrees awarded. *Degree requirements:* Thesis or alternative, comprehensive exam required, foreign language not required. *Entrance requirements:* Minimum GPA of 3.0 in major, 2.5 overall. Application deadline: 8/1. Application fee: $30. *Tuition:* $2027 per year full-time, $508 per semester (minimum) part-time for state residents; $9155 per year full-time, $2290 per semester (minimum) part-time for nonresidents. *Financial aid:* Teaching assistantships, Federal Work-Study, institutionally sponsored loans available. Aid available to part-time students. Financial aid application deadline: 5/1. *Faculty research:* Role of media in school libraries, media and implications for educational gerontology. • Dr. James N. Colt, Director, 919-560-6692. Application contact: Dr. Cecelia Steppe-Jones, Associate Dean of Graduate Studies and Administration, 919-560-6478.

Northern Illinois University, College of Education, Department of Leadership and Educational Policy Studies, Program in Instructional Technology, De Kalb, IL 60115-2854. Awards MS Ed, Ed D. Accredited by NCATE. Part-time and evening/weekend programs available. Faculty: 7 full-time (2 women). Students: 26 full-time (16 women), 159 part-time (106 women); includes 26 minority (22 African Americans, 3 Asian Americans, 1 Hispanic), 11 international. Average age 41. 63 applicants, 54% accepted. In 1997, 18 master's, 4 doctorates awarded. Terminal master's awarded for partial completion of doctoral program. *Degree requirements:* For master's, comprehensive exam required, thesis optional, foreign language not required; for doctorate, candidacy exam, dissertation defense required, foreign language not required. *Entrance requirements:* For master's, GRE General Test, TOEFL (minimum score 550), minimum GPA of 2.75; for doctorate, GRE General Test, TOEFL (minimum score 550), minimum GPA of 2.75 (undergraduate), 3.2 (graduate). Application deadline: 6/1 (rolling processing; 11/1 for spring admission). Application fee: $30. *Tuition:* $3984 per year full-time, $154 per credit hour part-time for state residents; $8160 per year full-time, $328 per credit hour part-time for nonresidents. *Financial aid:* Fellowships, research assistantships, teaching assistantships, staff assistantships, full tuition waivers, Federal Work-Study, and career-related internships or fieldwork available. Aid available to part-time students. • Dr. Margaret Bailey, Faculty Chair, 815-753-9249.

See in-depth description on page 921.

Northwestern Oklahoma State University, School of Education, Psychology, and Health and Physical Education, Library Media Specialist Program, Alva, OK 73717. Awards M Ed. Accredited by NCATE. Part-time programs available. Faculty: 4 full-time (2 women). Students: 2 full-time (both women), 7 part-time (all women). 2 applicants, 100% accepted. In 1997, 2 degrees awarded. *Entrance requirements:* GRE General Test (minimum combined score of 900) or MAT (minimum score 38), minimum GPA of 2.75. Application deadline: rolling. Application fee: $15. *Tuition:* $73 per semester hour for state residents; $175 per semester hour for nonresidents. *Financial aid:* Federal Work-Study available. Aid available to part-time students. Financial aid application deadline: 5/1. • Ray Lau, Director, 405-327-8547. Application contact: Dr. Ed Huckeby, Dean of Graduate School, 405-327-8410.

Northwestern University, School of Education and Social Policy, Program in Education and Social Policy-Learning Sciences, Evanston, IL 60201. Awards MA, PhD. Admissions and degrees offered through The Graduate School. Faculty: 10 full-time (3 women), 3 part-time (0 women). Students: 40 full-time (22 women); includes 12 minority (4 African Americans, 6 Asian Americans, 1 Hispanic, 1 Native American), 2 international. 86 applicants, 28% accepted. In 1997, 23 master's awarded (100% found work related to degree); 3 doctorates awarded. Terminal master's awarded for partial completion of doctoral program. *Degree requirements:* For master's, thesis or alternative, portfolio required, foreign language not required; for doctorate, dissertation, qualifying exam required, foreign language not required. *Average time to degree:* master's–1 year full-time; doctorate–5 years full-time. *Entrance requirements:* For master's, GRE General Test (combined average 1179); for doctorate, GRE General Test (combined average 1223). Application deadline: 2/1 (priority date; rolling processing). Application fee: $50 ($55 for international students). *Tuition:* $2424 per course. *Financial aid:* In 1997–98, 24 students received aid, including 6 fellowships (all to first-year students) averaging $1,169 per month, 17 research assistantships (1 to a first-year student) averaging $1,528 per month, 1 teaching assistantship averaging $1,248 per month; tuition scholarships, Federal Work-Study, institutionally sponsored loans, and career-related internships or fieldwork also available. Financial aid application deadline: 1/15; applicants required to submit FAFSA. *Faculty research:* Technologically supported learning environments; inquiry based learning in math, science, and literacy; learning social contexts; cognitive models of learning and problem solving; changing roles for teachers involved in innovative design and practice. • Dr. Brian J. Reiser, Program Coordinator, 847-491-7494. E-mail: ls-programs@ils.nwu.edu. Application contact: Carolyn Frazier, Department Assistant, 847-491-7494. Fax: 847-491-8999. E-mail: ls-programs@mail.sesp.nwu.edu.

See in-depth description on page 763.

Nova Southeastern University, School of Computer and Information Sciences, Fort Lauderdale, FL 33314-7721. Offerings include computing technology in education (MS, Ed D, PhD). Terminal

Directory: Educational Media/Instructional Technology

Nova Southeastern University (continued)
master's awarded for partial completion of doctoral program. Postbaccalaureate distance learning degree programs offered. School faculty: 15 full-time (4 women), 8 part-time (2 women). *Degree requirements:* For master's, computer language required, thesis optional; for doctorate, computer language, dissertation required, foreign language not required. *Average time to degree:* doctorate–4 years full-time. *Entrance requirements:* For master's, GRE or portfolio; for doctorate, GRE, master's degree, or portfolio. Application deadline: 6/1 (priority date; rolling processing; 1/1 for spring admission). Application fee: $50. *Tuition:* $357 per credit hour (minimum). • Dr. Edward Lieblein, Dean. Application contact: Kimberly Jaggers, Marketing Assistant, 800-986-2247 Ext. 2000. Fax: 954-262-3872. E-mail: scisinfo@scis.nova.edu.

Announcement: MS, PhD, and EdD degrees are available in computing technology in education. Designed for educators and trainers, these programs blend education theory and practice into learning experiences that develop skills applicable to real-world problems. Degrees, on campus or on line, can be earned in 18 months (MS) or 3 years (PhD or EdD).

Nova Southeastern University, Fischler Center for the Advancement of Education, Graduate Teacher Education Program, Fort Lauderdale, FL 33314-7721. Offerings include education technology (MS, Ed S), educational media (MS, Ed S). *Degree requirements:* Thesis, practicum required, foreign language not required. *Entrance requirements:* For master's, teaching certificate; for Ed S, master's degree, teaching certificate. Application deadline: rolling. Application fee: $50. *Tuition:* $245 per credit hour (minimum). • Dr. Deo Nellis, Dean, 954-262-8601. E-mail: deo@fcae.nova.edu. Application contact: Dr. Mark Seldine, Director of Student Affairs, 954-262-8689. Fax: 954-262-3910. E-mail: seldines@fcae.nova.edu.

Nova Southeastern University, Fischler Center for the Advancement of Education, Programs in Education and Technology, Fort Lauderdale, FL 33314-7721. Offering in instructional technology and distance education (MS, Ed D). Postbaccalaureate distance learning degree programs offered. Students: 29 full-time (22 women), 79 part-time (46 women); includes 6 minority (all African Americans), 7 international. *Degree requirements:* For master's, practicum required, foreign language not required; for doctorate, dissertation, practicum required, foreign language not required. *Entrance requirements:* For master's, interview, currently employed in position to use technology; for doctorate, minimum GPA of 3.0, interview, currently employed in position using technology. Application fee: $50. *Tuition:* $245 per credit hour (minimum). • Dr. Abbey Manburg, Dean, 954-262-8555. E-mail: manburg@fcae.nova.edu. Application contact: Dr. Vera Flight, Director of Graduate Student Development and Admissions, 800-986-3223 Ext. 8550. Fax: 954-262-3905. E-mail: flightv@fcae.nova.edu.

Oakland University, School of Education and Human Services, Program in Microcomputer Applications in Education, Rochester, MI 48309-4401. Awards Certificate. Accredited by NCATE. Faculty: 1 full-time. Students: 2 full-time (both women), 8 part-time (7 women); includes 2 minority (1 African American, 1 Hispanic). Average age 40. 12 applicants, 100% accepted. In 1997, 9 degrees awarded. *Application deadline:* 7/15 (3/15 for spring admission). *Application fee:* $30. *Expenses:* Tuition $3852 per year full-time, $214 per credit hour part-time for state residents; $8532 per year full-time, $474 per credit hour part-time for nonresidents. Fees $420 per year. *Financial aid:* Full tuition waivers, Federal Work-Study, institutionally sponsored loans available. Financial aid application deadline: 3/1; applicants required to submit FAFSA. • Dr. Anne Porter, Coordinator, 248-370-3065.

Ohio University, Graduate Studies, College of Education, School of Curriculum and Instruction, Educational Media Program, Athens, OH 45701-2979. Awards M Ed. Accredited by NCATE. Part-time and evening/weekend programs available. Faculty: 3. Students: 19 full-time (10 women), 19 part-time (12 women); includes 2 minority (1 African American, 1 Asian American), 15 international. 34 applicants, 82% accepted. *Degree requirements:* Thesis or alternative required, foreign language not required. *Entrance requirements:* GRE General Test or MAT. Application deadline: rolling. Application fee: $30. *Tuition:* $5430 per year full-time, $216 per quarter hour part-time for state residents; $10,431 per year full-time, $423 per quarter hour part-time for nonresidents. *Financial aid:* Full tuition waivers, Federal Work-Study, institutionally sponsored loans available. Financial aid application deadline: 3/15. • Application contact: Dr. Bonnie Beach, Graduate Chair, 740-593-0523.

Old Dominion University, Darden College of Education, Department of Educational Curriculum and Instruction, Norfolk, VA 23529. Offerings include elementary/middle education (MS Ed), with options in educational media, elementary education; secondary education (MS Ed), with option in instructional technology. One or more programs accredited by NCATE. Postbaccalaureate distance learning degree programs offered (minimal on-campus study). Department faculty: 26 full-time (13 women), 54 part-time (28 women), 33.7 FTE. *Application deadline:* 7/1 (rolling processing). *Application fee:* $30. *Expenses:* Tuition $180 per credit hour for state residents; $477 per credit hour for nonresidents. Fees $140 per year full-time, $32 per semester part-time. • Dr. Rebecca Bowers, Chair, 757-683-4374. Fax: 757-683-5862. E-mail: rbowers@odu.edu.

Our Lady of the Lake University of San Antonio, School of Education and Clinical Studies, Program in Learning Resources, 411 Southwest 24th Street, San Antonio, TX 78207-4689. Awards M Ed. Part-time and evening/weekend programs available. Faculty: 1 (woman) full-time, 3 part-time (2 women). Students: 8 part-time (7 women); includes 4 minority (all Hispanics). Average age 36. In 1997, 3 degrees awarded. *Degree requirements:* Computer language, comprehensive exam required, foreign language and thesis not required. *Entrance requirements:* GRE General Test or MAT. Application deadline: 8/6 (priority date; rolling processing; 1/3 for spring admission). Application fee: $15. *Expenses:* Tuition $371 per credit hour. Fees $57 per semester full-time, $32 per semester part-time. *Financial aid:* Application deadline 4/15. *Faculty research:* Automation and libraries, electronic books. • Dr. Donna D. Staudt, Chair, 210-434-6711 Ext. 306. Fax: 210-436-0824. E-mail: staud@lake.ollusa.edu. Application contact: Debbie Hamilton, Director of Admissions, 210-434-6711 Ext. 314. Fax: 210-436-2314.

Pacific Lutheran University, School of Education, Program in Literacy Education, Tacoma, WA 98447. Offerings include school library media (MA). Accredited by NCATE. Program faculty: 6 full-time (5 women). *Degree requirements:* Comprehensive exam, research project or thesis required, foreign language not required. *Entrance requirements:* GRE General Test or MAT, TOEFL (minimum score 550), interview. Application deadline: rolling. Application fee: $35. *Tuition:* $490 per semester hour. • Dr. Leon Reisberg, Graduate Director, 253-535-7272. Application contact: Marjo Burdick, Office of Admissions, 253-535-7151. Fax: 253-535-8320. E-mail: admissions@plu.edu.

Pennsylvania State University Great Valley School of Graduate Professional Studies, Graduate Studies and Continuing Education, College of Education, Program in Instructional Systems, Malvern, PA 19355-1488. Awards M Ed, MS. Faculty: 9. Students: 8 full-time (7 women), 98 part-time (74 women). Average age 34. In 1997, 29 degrees awarded. *Entrance requirements:* GRE General Test or MAT, TOEFL. Application fee: $40. • Dr. Doris Lee, Coordinator, 610-648-3379.

Pennsylvania State University University Park Campus, College of Education, Department of Curriculum and Instruction, University Park, PA 16802-1503. Offerings include instructional systems (M Ed, MS, D Ed, PhD). Accredited by NCATE. *Degree requirements:* For doctorate, dissertation. *Entrance requirements:* GRE General Test or MAT. Application fee: $40. *Expenses:* Tuition $6534 per year full-time, $276 per credit part-time for state residents; $13,460 per year full-time, $561 per credit part-time for nonresidents. Fees $252 per year (minimum) full-time, $43 per semester (minimum) part-time. • Dr. Peter A. Rubb, Head, 814-865-5433.

Pennsylvania State University University Park Campus, College of Education, Department of Adult Education, Instructional Systems, and Workforce Education and Development, Program in Instructional Systems, University Park, PA 16802-1503. Awards M Ed, MS, D Ed, PhD. Accredited by NCATE. Students: 45 full-time (19 women), 36 part-time (19 women). In 1997, 13 master's, 6 doctorates awarded. *Entrance requirements:* GRE General Test or MAT. Application fee: $40. *Expenses:* Tuition $6534 per year full-time, $276 per credit part-time for state residents; $13,460 per year full-time, $561 per credit part-time for nonresidents. Fees $252 per year (minimum) full-time, $43 per semester (minimum) part-time. • Dr. Barbara Grabowski, Professor in Charge, 814-865-0128.

Pepperdine University, Graduate School of Education and Psychology, Division of Education, Program in Educational Administration, Culver City, CA 90230-7615. Offerings include administration and educational technology (MS). *Entrance requirements:* GRE General Test, TOEFL. Application deadline: 7/1. Application fee: $45. *Tuition:* $540 per unit. • Dr. Robert Paull, Director, 310-568-5738. Application contact: Jo Witte, Coordinator, 310-568-5604.

Pepperdine University, Graduate School of Education and Psychology, Division of Education, Program in Educational Technology, Culver City, CA 90230-7615. Awards Ed D. Students: 20 full-time (9 women), 43 part-time (21 women); includes 11 minority (1 African American, 1 Asian American, 7 Hispanics, 2 Native Americans), 1 international. Average age 44. 52 applicants, 52% accepted. *Entrance requirements:* GMAT, GRE General Test, MAT, TOEFL. Application deadline: 5/1 (priority date). Application fee: $45. *Tuition:* $690 per unit. *Financial aid:* Research assistantships, teaching assistantships, scholarships, institutionally sponsored loans available. Aid available to part-time students. Financial aid application deadline: 7/1; applicants required to submit FAFSA. • Dr. John F. McManus, Director, 310-568-2307. Application contact: Christie Dailo, Administrator, 310-568-5612.

Portland State University, School of Education, Department of Curriculum and Instruction, Program in Educational Media/School Librarianship, Portland, OR 97207-0751. Awards MA, MS. Accredited by NCATE. Part-time programs available. Faculty: 16 full-time (9 women), 6 part-time (4 women), 17 FTE. Students: 1 (woman) full-time, 5 part-time (all women). Average age 42. 7 applicants, 71% accepted. *Degree requirements:* Variable foreign language requirement, special project or thesis, written exam. *Entrance requirements:* California Basic Educational Skills Test, TOEFL (minimum score 550), minimum GPA of 3.0 in upper-division course work or 2.75 overall. Application deadline: 4/1 (priority date; rolling processing; 11/1 for spring admission). Application fee: $50. *Tuition:* $6101 per year full-time, $689 per semester (minimum) part-time for state residents; $10,445 per year full-time, $689 per semester (minimum) part-time for nonresidents. *Financial aid:* Research assistantships, teaching assistantships, Federal Work-Study, institutionally sponsored loans, and career-related internships or fieldwork available. Aid available to part-time students. Financial aid application deadline: 3/1; applicants required to submit FAFSA. *Faculty research:* Teaching/learning in library media, computers and technology in learning, library information skills, children's literature analysis, mainstreaming and special learners. Total annual research expenditures: $10,000. • Application contact: Paul Gregorio, 503-725-4756. Fax: 503-725-5599. E-mail: Paul@ed.pdx.edu.

Prairie View A&M University, College of Education, Department of School Services, Prairie View, TX 77446-0188. Offerings include media technology (M Ed, MS Ed). Accredited by NCATE. Department faculty: 8 full-time (1 woman). *Average time to degree:* master's–2.5 years full-time, 4 years part-time. *Application deadline:* 7/1 (priority date; rolling processing; 11/1 for spring admission). *Application fee:* $10. *Tuition:* $2202 per year full-time, $336 per semester (minimum) part-time for state residents; $6000 per year full-time, $963 per semester (minimum) part-time for nonresidents. • Dr. William H. Parker, Head, 409-857-2312. Fax: 409-857-2911.

Purdue University, School of Education, Department of Curriculum and Instruction, West Lafayette, IN 47907. Offerings include educational technology (MS Ed, PhD, Ed S). Accredited by NCATE. Department faculty: 34 full-time (15 women), 3 part-time (1 woman). *Degree requirements:* For master's, thesis optional; for doctorate, dissertation, oral and written exams; for Ed S, oral presentation, project required, thesis not required. *Entrance requirements:* For master's, TOEFL (minimum score 550), minimum B average; for doctorate, GRE General Test (minimum score 500 on each section), TOEFL (minimum score 550); for Ed S, minimum B average. Application deadline: 1/15 (priority date; 9/15 for spring admission). Application fee: $30. Electronic applications accepted. *Tuition:* $3500 per year full-time, $126 per credit hour part-time for state residents; $11,720 per year full-time, $387 per credit hour part-time for nonresidents. • Dr. J. L. Peters, Head, 765-494-9172. Fax: 765-496-1622. E-mail: peters@purdue.edu. Application contact: Christine Larsen, Coordinator of Graduate Studies, 765-494-2345. Fax: 765-494-5832. E-mail: gradoffice@soe.purdue.edu.

Purdue University Calumet, School of Professional Studies, Department of Education, Program in Media Sciences, Hammond, IN 46323-2094. Awards MS Ed. *Entrance requirements:* TOEFL. Application fee: $30.

Radford University, Graduate College, College of Education and Human Development, Department of Educational Studies, Program in Educational Media, Radford, VA 24142. Awards MS. Accredited by NCATE. Part-time programs available. Postbaccalaureate distance learning degree programs offered (minimal on-campus study). Students: 3 part-time (all women); includes 1 minority (African American). Average age 42. 0 applicants. In 1997, 1 degree awarded. *Degree requirements:* Comprehensive exam required, foreign language and thesis not required. *Entrance requirements:* GMAT, GRE General Test, MAT, or NTE; TOEFL (minimum score 550), minimum GPA of 2.7. Application deadline: 2/1 (priority date; rolling processing; 10/1 for spring admission). Application fee: $25. Electronic applications accepted. *Expenses:* Tuition $2302 per year full-time, $147 per credit hour part-time for state residents; $5672 per year full-time, $287 per credit hour part-time for nonresidents. Fees $1222 per year full-time. *Financial aid:* Fellowships, teaching assistantships, scholarships/grants, Federal Work-Study, institutionally sponsored loans, and career-related internships or fieldwork available. Financial aid application deadline: 2/1; applicants required to submit FAFSA. • Dr. Linda J. Wilson, Coordinator, 540-831-5344. Fax: 540-831-6053. E-mail: lwilson@runet.edu.

The Richard Stockton College of New Jersey, Graduate Programs, Program in Instructional Technology, Pomona, NJ 08240-9988. Awards MA. Part-time programs available. Faculty: 5 full-time (2 women). Students: 21 part-time (12 women); includes 1 minority (Asian American). Average age 36. *Degree requirements:* Project. *Application deadline:* 5/1 (priority date; rolling processing). *Application fee:* $35. Electronic applications accepted. *Financial aid:* Federal Work-Study and career-related internships or fieldwork available. Aid available to part-time students. Financial aid application deadline: 3/1; applicants required to submit FAFSA. *Faculty research:* Ethics, digital imaging, virtual reality in the classroom, 3-D art in multimedia, technology projects for job-skills training, community computing networks. • Ken Tompkins, Head, 609-652-4497. Application contact: Alison Henry, Associate Director of Admissions, 609-652-4261. Fax: 609-748-5541. E-mail: siprod42@pollux.stockton.edu.

Rochester Institute of Technology, College of Applied Science and Technology, Department of Food, Hotel, and Travel Management, Program in Instructional Technology, Rochester, NY 14623-5604. Awards MS. Students: 2 full-time (1 woman), 18 part-time (12 women); includes 1 minority (African American). 7 applicants, 43% accepted. In 1997, 9 degrees awarded. *Entrance requirements:* GRE General Test or GMAT, minimum GPA of 3.0. Application deadline: 3/1 (priority date; rolling processing). Application fee: $40. *Expenses:* Tuition $18,765 per year full-time, $527 per credit hour part-time. Fees $126 per year full-time. *Financial aid:* Assistantships, scholarships available. • Clint Wallington, Coordinator, 716-475-2893.

Rosemont College, College of Graduate Studies, Program in Technology in Education, Rosemont, PA 19010-1699. Offers educational computing and technology literacy (CPS), technology in education (M Ed, CAGS). Part-time and evening/weekend programs available. Faculty: 2 full-time (1 woman), 7 part-time (3 women). Students: 60 (50 women); includes 8 minority (all African Americans), 6 international. Average age 30. 30 applicants, 83% accepted. In 1997, 13 master's awarded (100% found work related to degree). *Degree requirements:* For master's, thesis or alternative required, foreign language not required. *Entrance requirements:* For master's, GRE or MAT. Application deadline: rolling. Application fee: $50. *Tuition:* $375 per credit. *Financial aid:* 15 students received aid; career-related internships or fieldwork available.

Aid available to part-time students. Financial aid application deadline: 3/1. • Dr. Robert J. Siegfried, Director, 610-527-0200 Ext. 2344. E-mail: rsiegfried@rosemont.edu. Application contact: Stan Rostkowski, Enrollment Coordinator, 610-527-0200 Ext. 2187. Fax: 610-526-2964. E-mail: roscolgrad@rosemont.edu.

Rowan University, College of Education, Department of Secondary Education-Education Foundations, Program in School and Public Librarianship, Glassboro, NJ 08028-1701. Awards MA. Accredited by NCATE. Evening/weekend programs available. Students: 48 (46 women); includes 3 minority (all African Americans). 12 applicants, 50% accepted. In 1997, 13 degrees awarded. *Degree requirements:* Thesis, comprehensive exams required, foreign language not required. *Entrance requirements:* GRE General Test, minimum GPA of 2.8. Application deadline: 11/1 (priority date; rolling processing; 4/1 for spring admission). Application fee: $50. *Tuition:* $5728 per year full-time, $258 per credit hour part-time for state residents; $8968 per year full-time, $393 per credit hour part-time for nonresidents. *Financial aid:* Federal Work-Study and career-related internships or fieldwork available. • Dr. Holly Willett, Adviser, 609-256-4759.

Rowan University, College of Education, Department of Secondary Education-Education Foundations, Program in Subject Matter Teaching, Glassboro, NJ 08028-1701. Offerings include education media specialist (Certificate). Accredited by NCATE. *Application deadline:* 11/1 (priority date; rolling processing; 4/1 for spring admission). *Application fee:* $50. *Tuition:* $5728 per year full-time, $258 per credit hour part-time for state residents; $8968 per year full-time, $393 per credit hour part-time for nonresidents. • Dr. John Gallagher, Coordinator, 609-256-4500 Ext. 3858.

St. Cloud State University, College of Education, Center for Information Media, St. Cloud, MN 56301-4498. Awards MS. Accredited by NCATE. Faculty: 11 full-time (6 women), 3 part-time (1 woman). Students: 19 full-time (13 women), 51 part-time (40 women). In 1997, 20 degrees awarded. *Degree requirements:* Thesis or alternative required, foreign language not required. *Entrance requirements:* GRE General Test, minimum GPA of 2.75. Application fee: $20 ($100 for international students). *Expenses:* Tuition $128 per credit for state residents; $203 per credit for nonresidents. Fees $16.32 per credit. *Financial aid:* In 1997–98, 13 graduate assistantships were awarded; Federal Work-Study also available. Financial aid application deadline: 3/1. • Dr. Kristi Tornquist, Director, 320-255-2022. Application contact: Ann Anderson, Graduate Studies Office, 320-255-2113. Fax: 320-654-5371. E-mail: anna@grad.stcloud.msus.edu.

Saint Michael's College, Program in Education, Colchester, VT 05439. Offerings include technology (M Ed). Program faculty: 5 full-time (4 women), 70 part-time (54 women). *Degree requirements:* Computer language, thesis required, foreign language not required. *Entrance requirements:* Minimum GPA of 2.8. Application deadline: rolling. Application fee: $25. • Dr. Aostre Johnson, Director, 802-654-2436. Fax: 802-654-2664.

Salem State College, Department of Education, Program in Library Media Studies, Salem, MA 01970-5353. Awards M Ed. Accredited by NCATE. *Application fee:* $25. *Expenses:* Tuition $140 per credit hour for state residents; $230 per credit hour for nonresidents. Fees $20 per credit hour.

Salisbury State University, Department of Education, Salisbury, MD 21801-6837. Offerings include media and technology (M Ed). Department faculty: 19 full-time (10 women), 2 part-time (1 woman). *Application deadline:* 8/1 (priority date; rolling processing; 1/1 for spring admission). *Application fee:* $30. *Expenses:* Tuition $158 per credit hour for state residents; $310 per credit hour for nonresidents. Fees $4 per credit hour. • Dr. Ellen Whitford, Chair, 410-543-6294. E-mail: evwhitford@ssu.edu. Application contact: Phyllis Meyer, Administrative Aide II, 410-543-6281. Fax: 410-548-2593. E-mail: phmeyer@ssu.edu.

San Diego State University, College of Education, Department of Educational Technology, San Diego, CA 92182. Awards MA. Accredited by NCATE. Evening/weekend programs available. Students: 31 full-time (18 women), 97 part-time (57 women); includes 17 minority (3 African Americans, 4 Asian Americans, 8 Hispanics, 2 Native Americans), 4 international. *Entrance requirements:* GRE General Test (minimum combined score of 950), TOEFL (minimum score 550). Application deadline: 6/1 (priority date; rolling processing; 12/1 for spring admission). Application fee: $55. *Expenses:* Tuition $0 for state residents; $246 per unit for nonresidents. Fees $1932 per year full-time, $1266 per year part-time. *Total annual research expenditures:* $112,000. • Patrick Harrison, Chair, 619-594-6718. Fax: 619-594-6376. E-mail: patrick.harrison@.sdsu.edu.

San Francisco State University, College of Education, Department of Instructional Technologies, San Francisco, CA 94132-1722. Offers programs in educational technology (MA), training systems development (AC). Accredited by NCATE. Part-time programs available. *Entrance requirements:* For master's, minimum GPA of 2.5 in last 60 units. Application deadline: 11/30 (priority date; rolling processing). Application fee: $55. *Expenses:* Tuition $0 for state residents; $246 per unit for nonresidents. Fees $1982 per year full-time, $1316 per year part-time.

San Jose State University, College of Education, Program in Instructional Technology, San Jose, CA 95192-0001. Awards MA, Certificate. Accredited by NCATE. Evening/weekend programs available. Faculty: 9 full-time (1 woman), 6 part-time (2 women). Students: 19 full-time (15 women), 63 part-time (41 women); includes 19 minority (1 African American, 17 Asian Americans, 1 Hispanic). Average age 37. 47 applicants, 74% accepted. In 1997, 42 master's awarded. *Application deadline:* 6/1 (rolling processing). *Application fee:* $59. *Expenses:* Tuition $0 for state residents; $246 per unit for nonresidents. Fees $2017 per year full-time, $1351 per year part-time. *Financial aid:* Career-related internships or fieldwork available. • Jim Cabeceiras, Director, 408-924-3618.

Seton Hall University, College of Education and Human Services, Department of Educational Studies, Program in Instructional Design, South Orange, NJ 07079-2697. Awards MA, Ed S. Program new for fall 1998. *Degree requirements:* For master's, comprehensive exam. *Entrance requirements:* GRE General Test or MAT. Application deadline: rolling. Application fee: $50. *Expenses:* Tuition $500 per credit. Fees $610 per year full-time, $185 per semester part-time. *Financial aid:* Application deadline 2/1. • Dr. Roberta Devlin-Scherer, Chair, Department of Educational Studies, 973-761-7457. E-mail: devlinrb@shu.edu.

Southern Arkansas University–Magnolia, Graduate Program in Education, Program in Library Media, Magnolia, AR 71753. Awards M Ed. Students: 9 part-time (all women). 0 applicants. *Degree requirements:* Comprehensive exam required, foreign language not required. *Average time to degree:* master's–2 years full-time. *Entrance requirements:* GRE, minimum GPA of 2.5. Application deadline: 8/15. Application fee: $0. *Expenses:* Tuition $95 per hour for state residents; $138 per hour for nonresidents. Fees $2 per hour. *Financial aid:* Research assistantships, teaching assistantships available. Financial aid application deadline: 8/15. • Dr. Danield L. Bernard, Dean, Graduate Studies, Graduate Program in Education, 870-235-4055. Fax: 870-235-5035. E-mail: dlbernard@mail.saumag.edu.

Southern Connecticut State University, School of Communication, Information and Library Science, New Haven, CT 06515-1355. Offerings include instructional technology (MS). JD/MLS offered jointly with the University of Connecticut Law School. MLS/MA offered jointly with the Department of History. MLS/MS offered jointly with the Departments of Chemistry, English, and Foreign Languages. *Application deadline:* 7/15 (priority date; rolling processing). *Application fee:* $40. *Expenses:* Tuition $2632 per year full-time, $188 per credit part-time for state residents; $7200 per year full-time, $188 per credit part-time for nonresidents. Fees $1806 per year full-time, $45 per semester part-time for state residents; $2703 per year full-time, $45 per semester part-time for nonresidents. • Dr. Nancy Disbrow, Chairperson, 203-392-5781.

See in-depth description on page 1645.

Southern Illinois University at Edwardsville, School of Education, Department of Educational Administration and Instructional Technology, Program in Instructional Technology, Edwardsville, IL 62026-0001. Awards MS Ed. Accredited by NCATE. Part-time programs available. Students: 31 full-time (24 women), 51 part-time (39 women); includes 1 minority (African American). 32 applicants, 69% accepted. In 1997, 16 degrees awarded. *Degree requirements:* Thesis or alternative, final exam required, foreign language not required. *Entrance requirements:* MAT, interview. Application deadline: 7/24. Application fee: $25. *Expenses:* Tuition $1716 per year full-time, $95 per credit hour part-time for state residents; $5149 per year full-time, $286 per credit hour part-time for nonresidents. Fees $463 per year full-time, $433 per year part-time. *Financial aid:* In 1997–98, 4 assistantships were awarded; fellowships, research assistantships, teaching assistantships, Federal Work-Study, institutionally sponsored loans also available. Aid available to part-time students. • Charles Nelson, Director, 618-692-3291.

Southern University and Agricultural and Mechanical College, College of Education, Department of Curriculum and Instruction, Baton Rouge, LA 70813. Offerings include media (M Ed). Accredited by NCATE. Department faculty: 13 full-time (3 women), 12 part-time (3 women). *Degree requirements:* Thesis optional. *Entrance requirements:* GMAT or GRE General Test, TOEFL. Application deadline: 6/1 (priority date; rolling processing; 11/1 for spring admission). Application fee: $5. *Tuition:* $2226 per year full-time, $267 per semester (minimum) part-time for state residents; $6262 per year full-time, $267 per semester (minimum) part-time for nonresidents. • Dr. Paul Hester, Chairman, 504-771-3871.

Southwestern Oklahoma State University, School of Education, Library Media Program, Weatherford, OK 73096-3098. Awards M Ed. Accredited by NCATE. Program being phased out; applicants no longer accepted. Part-time programs available. Postbaccalaureate distance learning degree programs offered. Students: 2 full-time (1 woman), 13 part-time (all women). In 1997, 11 degrees awarded. *Degree requirements:* Exam required, foreign language and thesis not required. *Expenses:* Tuition $60 per credit hour (minimum) for state residents; $147 per credit hour (minimum) for nonresidents. Fees $109 per year full-time, $24 per semester (minimum) part-time. *Financial aid:* Research assistantships, teaching assistantships, Federal Work-Study, institutionally sponsored loans, and career-related internships or fieldwork available. Aid available to part-time students. Financial aid applicants required to submit FAFSA. • Dr. Greg Moss, Dean, School of Education, 580-774-3285.

State University of New York at Albany, School of Education, Department of Educational Theory and Practice, Albany, NY 12222-0001. Offerings include educational communications (MS, CAS). Department faculty: 13 full-time (7 women), 6 part-time (4 women). *Application fee:* $50. *Expenses:* Tuition $5100 per year full-time, $213 per credit hour part-time for state residents; $8416 per year full-time, $351 per credit hour part-time for nonresidents. Fees $705 per year full-time, $26.85 per credit hour part-time. • Judith Langer, Chair, 518-442-5020.

State University of New York at Stony Brook, School of Professional Development and Continuing Studies, Stony Brook, NY 11794. Offerings include educational computing (Certificate). School faculty: 1 full-time, 101 part-time. *Application deadline:* 1/15. *Application fee:* $50. *Expenses:* Tuition $5100 per year full-time, $213 per credit hour part-time for state residents; $8416 per year full-time, $351 per credit hour part-time for nonresidents. Fees $529 per year full-time, $77 per semester (minimum) part-time. • Dr. Paul J. Edelson, Dean, 516-632-7052. E-mail: paul.edelson@sunysb.edu. Application contact: Sandra Romansky, Director of Admissions and Advisement, 516-632-7050. Fax: 516-632-9046. E-mail: sandra.romansky@sunysb.edu.

State University of New York College at Potsdam, School of Education, Program in Educational Technology, Potsdam, NY 13676. Awards MS Ed. Part-time and evening/weekend programs available. Faculty: 4 full-time (0 women), 4 part-time (1 woman). Students: 65; includes 1 minority (Asian American). *Degree requirements:* Culminating experience required, thesis optional, foreign language not required. *Entrance requirements:* New York State Teachers Certification Exam Liberal Arts and Science Test (minimum score 220), New York State Teachers Certification Exam Assesment of Teaching Skills-Writing (minimum score 220), minimum GPA of 2.75 in last 60 hours. Application deadline: 4/1 (priority date; 10/15 for spring admission). Application fee: $50. *Expenses:* Tuition $5100 per year full-time, $213 per credit hour part-time for state residents; $8416 per year full-time, $351 per credit hour part-time for nonresidents. Fees $315 per year full-time, $12.50 per credit hour part-time. *Financial aid:* Fellowships, teaching assistantships, Federal Work-Study, and career-related internships or fieldwork available. Aid available to part-time students. Financial aid application deadline: 3/1. • Charles Mlynarczyk, Chairperson, Teacher Education Department, 315-267-2535. E-mail: mlynarhc@potsdam.edu. Application contact: Dr. William Amoriell, Dean of Education and Graduate Studies, 315-267-2515. Fax: 315-267-4802.

State University of West Georgia, College of Education, Department of Research, Media and Technology, Carrollton, GA 30118. Offers program in library media (M Ed, Ed S). Accredited by NCATE. Part-time and evening/weekend programs available. Faculty: 6 full-time (5 women). Students: 46 full-time (41 women), 115 part-time (108 women); includes 5 minority (all African Americans). Average age 40. In 1997, 18 master's, 7 Ed Ss awarded. *Degree requirements:* For Ed S, research project required, foreign language and thesis not required. *Entrance requirements:* For master's, GRE General Test (minimum combined score of 800), minimum GPA of 2.5, teaching certificate; for Ed S, GRE General Test (minimum combined score of 800), master's degree, minimum graduate GPA of 3.25. Application deadline: 8/30 (rolling processing). Application fee: $15. *Expenses:* Tuition $2428 per year full-time, $83 per semester hour part-time for state residents; $8428 per year full-time, $250 per semester hour part-time for nonresidents. Fees $428 per year. *Financial aid:* Research assistantships, assistantships, and career-related internships or fieldwork available. Aid available to part-time students. Financial aid applicants required to submit FAFSA. *Faculty research:* Distance learning, multimedia modules. Total annual research expenditures: $19,020. • Dr. Barbara McKenzie, Chair, 770-836-6557. Application contact: Dr. Jack O. Jenkins, Dean, Graduate School, 770-836-6419. Fax: 770-836-2301. E-mail: jjenkins@cob.as.westga.edu.

Teachers College, Columbia University, Graduate Faculty of Education, Department of Scientific Foundations, Program in Educational Media/Instructional Technology, 525 West 120th Street, New York, NY 10027-6696. Awards Ed M, MA, Ed D. Faculty: 5 full-time (1 woman), 13 part-time (0 women), 12.2 FTE. Students: 29 full-time (20 women), 63 part-time (40 women); includes 22 minority (12 African Americans, 5 Asian Americans, 5 Hispanics), 7 international. Average age 36. 64 applicants, 36% accepted. In 1997, 20 master's, 3 doctorates awarded. *Degree requirements:* For doctorate, dissertation required, foreign language not required. *Entrance requirements:* For doctorate, GRE General Test or MAT. Application deadline: 5/15 (12/1 for spring admission). Application fee: $50. *Expenses:* Tuition $640 per credit. Fees $120 per semester. *Financial aid:* Full and partial tuition waivers, Federal Work-Study, institutionally sponsored loans, and career-related internships or fieldwork available. Aid available to part-time students. Financial aid application deadline: 2/1. *Faculty research:* Video and interactive learning. • Application contact: Barbara Reinhalter, Office of Admissions, 212-678-3710. Fax: 212-678-4171.

Tennessee State University, College of Education, Department of Teaching and Learning, Program in Educational Technology, Nashville, TN 37209-1561. Awards M Ed. Accredited by NCATE. *Entrance requirements:* GRE General Test, GRE Subject Test, or MAT (minimum score 44), minimum GPA of 2.5. Application deadline: rolling. Application fee: $15. *Tuition:* $2962 per year full-time, $182 per credit hour part-time for state residents; $7788 per year full-time, $393 per credit hour part-time for nonresidents. *Financial aid:* Application deadline 5/1. • Application contact: Dr. Clinton M. Lipsey, Dean of the Graduate School, 615-963-5901. Fax: 615-963-5963. E-mail: clipsey@picard.tnstate.edu.

Texas A&M University, College of Education, Department of Educational Curriculum and Instruction, Educational Technology Program, College Station, TX 77843. Awards M Ed. Accredited by NCATE. Students: 3 full-time (2 women), 16 part-time (10 women); includes 1 minority (Hispanic), 1 international. Average age 36. 21 applicants, 48% accepted. In 1997, 1 degree awarded (100% found work related to degree). *Entrance requirements:* GRE General Test, TOEFL. Application deadline: 7/15 (priority date; rolling processing). Application fee: $35

Directory: Educational Media/Instructional Technology

Texas A&M University (continued)
($75 for international students). *Financial aid:* In 1997–98, 8 students received aid, including 6 teaching assistantships (4 to first-year students); fellowships, research assistantships, Federal Work-Study, institutionally sponsored loans, and career-related internships or fieldwork also available. *Faculty research:* Role of animation in learning, graphics/maps, computer-based testing. Total annual research expenditures: $10,000. • Ronald Zellner, Coordinator, 409-845-4095.

Texas A&M University–Commerce, College of Education, Department of Secondary and Higher Education, Commerce, TX 75429-3011. Offerings include learning technology and information systems (MA, M Ed, MS), with options in educational computing, library and information science, media and technology. Department faculty: 10 full-time (3 women), 2 part-time (1 woman). *Degree requirements:* Thesis (for some programs), comprehensive exam. *Entrance requirements:* GRE General Test. Application deadline: rolling. Application fee: $0 ($25 for international students). *Tuition:* $2382 per year full-time, $343 per semester (minimum) part-time for state residents; $7518 per year full-time, $343 per semester (minimum) part-time for nonresidents. • Dr. Robert Munday, Head, 903-886-5607. Application contact: Pam Hammonds, Graduate Admissions Adviser, 903-886-5167. Fax: 903-886-5165.

Texas Southern University, School of Technology, Programs in Technology, Houston, TX 77004-4584. Offerings in constructional technology (M Ed), educational technology (M Ed). *Degree requirements:* Comprehensive exam required, foreign language not required. *Entrance requirements:* GRE General Test, TOEFL, minimum GPA of 2.5. Application deadline: 7/15 (priority date; rolling processing). Application fee: $35 ($75 for international students). *Financial aid:* Teaching assistantships, Federal Work-Study, institutionally sponsored loans available. Financial aid application deadline: 5/1. • Dr. Josua Hill, Dean, School of Technology, 713-313-7007.

Texas Tech University, Graduate School, College of Education, Division of Educational Psychology and Leadership, Lubbock, TX 79409. Offerings include instructional technology (M Ed, Ed D). Accredited by NCATE. Division faculty: 28 full-time (13 women), 3 part-time (1 woman), 29.29 FTE. *Degree requirements:* For master's, computer language required, thesis optional, foreign language not required; for doctorate, dissertation required, foreign language not required. *Entrance requirements:* For master's, GRE General Test (combined average 1034); for doctorate, GRE General Test. Application deadline: 4/15 (priority date; rolling processing; 11/1 for spring admission). Application fee: $25 ($50 for international students). Electronic applications accepted. *Expenses:* Tuition $864 per year full-time, $120 per semester (minimum) part-time for state residents; $5976 per year full-time, $747 per semester (minimum) part-time for nonresidents. Fees $2321 per year full-time, $302 per semester (minimum) part-time. • Dr. Loretta J. Bradley, Chair, 806-742-2393.

Towson University, Program in Instructional Technology, Towson, MD 21252-0001. Awards MS. Part-time and evening/weekend programs available. Faculty: 5 full-time (2 women). Students: 9 full-time (5 women), 53 part-time (41 women); includes 9 minority (all African Americans). In 1997, 8 degrees awarded. *Degree requirements:* Thesis optional, foreign language not required. *Application deadline:* 3/1 (priority date; rolling processing; 10/1 for spring admission). *Application fee:* $40. *Expenses:* Tuition $187 per credit hour for state residents; $364 per credit hour for nonresidents. Fees $40 per credit hour. *Financial aid:* Assistantships, Federal Work-Study available. Financial aid application deadline: 4/1; applicants required to submit FAFSA. *Faculty research:* Training and commercial vehicle inspections. Total annual research expenditures: $59,400. • Dr. Gary Rosecrans, Director, 410-830-2194. Fax: 410-830-4227. E-mail: grosecrans@towson.edu. Application contact: Fran Musotto, Office Manager, 410-830-2501. Fax: 410-830-4675. E-mail: fmusotto@towson.edu.

United States International University, College of Arts and Sciences, Department of Education, San Diego, CA 92131-1799. Offerings include technology and learning (MA, Ed D). Terminal master's awarded for partial completion of doctoral program. Department faculty: 10 full-time (7 women), 12 part-time (6 women). *Degree requirements:* Thesis/dissertation. *Average time to degree:* master's–1.5 years full-time, 2.5 years part-time; doctorate–3 years full-time, 5 years part-time. *Entrance requirements:* For master's, TOEFL, minimum GPA of 2.5; for doctorate, GRE General Test or MAT, TOEFL, minimum GPA of 3.0. Application deadline: 8/1 (priority date; rolling processing; 3/1 for spring admission). Application fee: $40. *Expenses:* Tuition $255 per unit. Fees $120 per year full-time, $33 per quarter part-time. • Dr. Mary Ellen Butler-Pascoe, Chair, 619-635-4595. Fax: 619-635-4714. Application contact: Susan Topham, Assistant Director of Admissions, 619-635-4885. Fax: 619-635-4739. E-mail: admissions@usiu.edu.

Université Laval, Faculty of Education, Department of Didactics, Educational Psychology and Instructional Technology, Program in Instructional Technology, Sainte-Foy, PQ G1K 7P4, Canada. Awards MA, PhD. Students: 38 full-time (24 women), 38 part-time (22 women). 30 applicants, 63% accepted. In 1997, 17 master's awarded. *Application deadline:* 3/1. *Application fee:* $30. *Expenses:* Tuition $1334 per year (minimum) full-time, $56 per credit (minimum) part-time for Canadian residents; $5966 per year (minimum) full-time, $249 per credit (minimum) part-time for nonresidents. Fees $150 per year full-time, $6.25 per credit part-time. • Gilles Larin, Director, 418-656-2131 Ext. 5306. Fax: 418-656-2905. E-mail: gilles.larin@fse.ulaval.ca.

University of Alberta, Faculty of Graduate Studies and Research, Department of Educational Psychology, Edmonton, AB T6G 2E1, Canada. Offerings include instructional technology (M Ed). Department faculty: 36 full-time (11 women), 23 part-time (9 women), 41.75 FTE. *Application deadline:* 2/1 (priority date; rolling processing). *Application fee:* $60. *Expenses:* Tuition $390 per course for Canadian residents; $781 per course for nonresidents. Fees $500 per year full-time, $184 per year part-time. • Dr. L. L. Stewin, Chair, 403-492-2389. Fax: 403-492-1318. E-mail: len.stewin@ualberta.ca.

University of Arkansas, College of Education, Department of Educational Leadership, Counseling and Foundations, Program in Educational Technology, Fayetteville, AR 72701-1201. Awards M Ed. Accredited by NCATE. Students: 12 full-time (9 women), 11 part-time (9 women); includes 1 minority (African American), 1 international. 9 applicants, 78% accepted. In 1997, 11 degrees awarded. *Application fee:* $25 ($35 for international students). *Tuition:* $3144 per year full-time, $173 per credit hour part-time for state residents; $7140 per year full-time, $395 per credit hour part-time for nonresidents. *Financial aid:* Research assistantships, teaching assistantships, Federal Work-Study, and career-related internships or fieldwork available. Aid available to part-time students. Financial aid application deadline: 4/1; applicants required to submit FAFSA. • Dr. John Murry, Coordinator, 501-575-2207.

University of Arkansas at Little Rock, College of Education, Department of Educational Leadership, Program in Instructional Resources, Little Rock, AR 72204-1099. Awards M Ed. Students: 3 full-time (2 women), 10 part-time (8 women); includes 1 minority (Hispanic). Average age 36. 7 applicants, 71% accepted. In 1997, 5 degrees awarded. *Degree requirements:* Comprehensive exam or defense of portfolio required, foreign language and thesis not required. *Entrance requirements:* GRE General Test (minimum combined score of 1000 on three sections), interview, minimum GPA of 2.75. Application deadline: rolling. Application fee: $25 ($30 for international students). *Expenses:* Tuition $2466 per year full-time, $137 per credit hour part-time for state residents; $5256 per year full-time, $292 per credit hour part-time for nonresidents. Fees $216 per year full-time, $36 per semester (minimum) part-time. *Financial aid:* Research assistantships, Federal Work-Study, and career-related internships or fieldwork available. *Faculty research:* Instructional program development, educational technology product development, educational technology management. • Dr. David Spillers, Chairperson, Department of Educational Leadership, 501-569-3267.

The University of Calgary, Faculty of Education, Graduate Division of Educational Research, Calgary, AB T2N 1N4, Canada. Offerings include educational technology (MA, M Ed, M Sc, Ed D). Postbaccalaureate distance learning degree programs offered (minimal on-campus study). Division faculty: 60 full-time, 25 part-time. *Degree requirements:* For master's, thesis (for some programs), comprehensive exam required, foreign language not required. *Entrance requirements:* For master's, minimum GPA of 3.0. Application deadline: 2/1. Application fee: $60. Electronic applications accepted. *Expenses:* Tuition $5448 per year full-time, $908 per course part-time for Canadian residents; $10,896 per year full-time, $1816 per course part-time for nonresidents. Fees $285 per year full-time, $119 per semester (minimum) part-time. • Dr. Bryant Griffith, Assistant Dean, 403-220-5675. Fax: 403-282-3005. E-mail: griffith@acs.ucalgary.ca.

University of Central Arkansas, College of Education, Department of Applied Academic Technologies, Program in Education Media and Library Science, Conway, AR 72035-0001. Awards MS. Students: 8 full-time (5 women), 58 part-time (52 women); includes 5 minority (all African Americans), 2 international. 24 applicants, 100% accepted. In 1997, 26 degrees awarded. *Degree requirements:* Comprehensive exam required, foreign language and thesis not required. *Entrance requirements:* GRE General Test, minimum GPA of 2.7. Application deadline: 3/1 (priority date; rolling processing; 10/1 for spring admission). Application fee: $15 ($40 for international students). *Expenses:* Tuition $161 per credit hour for state residents; $298 per credit hour for nonresidents. Fees $50 per year full-time, $30 per year part-time. • Dr. Selvin Royal, Interim Chair, Department of Applied Academic Technologies, 501-450-5463. Fax: 501-450-5680. E-mail: selvinr@mail.uca.edu.

University of Central Florida, College of Education, Department of Educational Services, Educational Media Program, Orlando, FL 32816. Awards M Ed. Accredited by NCATE. Part-time and evening/weekend programs available. Students: 18 full-time (15 women), 7 part-time (all women); includes 1 minority (Hispanic). Average age 40. 2 applicants, 100% accepted. In 1997, 5 degrees awarded. *Degree requirements:* Thesis or alternative required, foreign language not required. *Entrance requirements:* GRE General Test (minimum combined score of 840). Application deadline: 7/15 (12/15 for spring admission). Application fee: $20. *Expenses:* Tuition $3288 per year full-time, $137 per credit hour part-time for state residents; $11,520 per year full-time, $480 per credit hour part-time for nonresidents. Fees $105 per year. *Financial aid:* Teaching assistantships, Federal Work-Study, institutionally sponsored loans, and career-related internships or fieldwork available. Aid available to part-time students. • Application contact: Dr. Judy Lee, Coordinator, 407-823-6139. E-mail: jlee@pegasus.cc.ucf.edu.

University of Central Florida, College of Education, Department of Educational Services, Program in Educational Technology, Orlando, FL 32816. Awards MA, Ed D. Accredited by NCATE. Students: 34 full-time (25 women), 3 part-time (all women). Average age 40. 10 applicants, 100% accepted. In 1997, 25 master's awarded. *Degree requirements:* For master's, thesis or alternative required, foreign language not required; for doctorate, dissertation required, foreign language not required. *Entrance requirements:* For master's, GRE General Test (minimum combined score of 840); for doctorate, GRE General Test (minimum combined score of 1000), GRE Subject Test. Application deadline: 6/30. Application fee: $20. *Expenses:* Tuition $3288 per year full-time, $137 per credit hour part-time for state residents; $11,520 per year full-time, $480 per credit hour part-time for nonresidents. Fees $105 per year. • Application contact: Dr. Gary Orwig, Interim Chair, 407-823-2057. E-mail: orwig@pegasus.cc.ucf.edu.

University of Central Florida, College of Education, Department of Educational Services, Program in Instructional Systems, Orlando, FL 32816. Awards MA. Accredited by NCATE. Students: 34 full-time (18 women), 20 part-time (14 women); includes 7 minority (2 African Americans, 2 Asian Americans, 3 Hispanics), 2 international. Average age 38. 10 applicants, 90% accepted. In 1997, 27 degrees awarded. *Degree requirements:* Thesis or alternative required, foreign language not required. *Entrance requirements:* GRE General Test (minimum combined score of 840). Application deadline: 7/15 (12/15 for spring admission). Application fee: $20. *Expenses:* Tuition $3288 per year full-time, $137 per credit hour part-time for state residents; $11,520 per year full-time, $480 per credit hour part-time for nonresidents. Fees $105 per year. • Application contact: Dr. Richard Cornell, Coordinator, 407-823-2053.

University of Central Oklahoma, College of Education, Department of Curriculum and Instruction, Program in Instructional Media, Edmond, OK 73034-5209. Awards M Ed. Accredited by NCATE. Part-time and evening/weekend programs available. *Entrance requirements:* GRE General Test. Application deadline: 8/18. Application fee: $15. *Tuition:* $76 per credit hour for state residents; $178 per credit hour for nonresidents.

University of Colorado at Denver, School of Education, Program in Information and Learning Technologies, Denver, CO 80217-3364. Awards MA. Accredited by NCATE. Students: 10 full-time (7 women), 61 part-time (44 women); includes 3 minority (1 African American, 1 Asian American, 1 Hispanic), 1 international. Average age 39. 16 applicants, 100% accepted. In 1997, 26 degrees awarded. *Degree requirements:* Thesis or alternative required, foreign language not required. *Entrance requirements:* GRE, MAT, minimum GPA of 2.75. Application deadline: 4/15 (rolling processing; 9/15 for spring admission). Application fee: $50 ($60 for international students). Electronic applications accepted. *Expenses:* Tuition $3530 per year full-time, $199 per semester hour part-time for state residents; $12,722 per year full-time, $764 per semester hour part-time for nonresidents. Fees $252 per year. *Financial aid:* Research assistantships, teaching assistantships, Federal Work-Study available. Financial aid application deadline: 6/1; applicants required to submit FAFSA. • Elizabeth Kozleski, Area Coordinator, 303-556-8449. Application contact: Administrative Assistant, 303-556-6022. Fax: 303-556-4479.

University of Connecticut, School of Education, Field of Instructional Media and Technology, Storrs, CT 06269. Awards MA, PhD. Accredited by NCATE. Faculty: 2. Students: 4 part-time (0 women). Average age 48. 1 applicant, 0% accepted. Terminal master's awarded for partial completion of doctoral program. *Degree requirements:* For master's, thesis or alternative; for doctorate, dissertation. *Entrance requirements:* GRE General Test. Application deadline: 6/1 (priority date; rolling processing; 11/1 for spring admission). Application fee: $40 ($45 for international students). *Expenses:* Tuition $5272 per year full-time, $293 per credit part-time for state residents; $13,696 per year full-time, $761 per credit part-time for nonresidents. Fees $948 per year full-time, $640 per year part-time. *Financial aid:* In 1997–98, 2 research assistantships totaling $23,625 were awarded; fellowships, teaching assistantships also available. Financial aid application deadline: 2/15. • Scott W. Brown, Head, 860-486-4031.

The University of Findlay, College of Professional Studies, Division of Education, 1000 North Main Street, Findlay, OH 45840-3653. Offerings include technology (MA Ed). Accredited by NCATE. Division faculty: 9 full-time (7 women), 8 part-time (4 women), 21 FTE. *Degree requirements:* 4 foreign languages, thesis, cumulative project. *Average time to degree:* master's–1.5 years full-time, 3 years part-time. *Entrance requirements:* Minimum GPA of 3.0. Application deadline: 8/15 (priority date; rolling processing). Application fee: $25. *Tuition:* $236 per semester hour. • Dr. Judith Wahrman, Graduate Program Director, 419-424-4864. Fax: 419-424-4822. E-mail: wahrman@lucy.findlay.edu.

University of Florida, College of Education, Department of Instruction and Curriculum, Gainesville, FL 32611. Offerings include media and instructional design (MAE, M Ed, Ed D, PhD, Ed S). Accredited by NCATE. Department faculty: 42. *Degree requirements:* For master's, thesis optional, foreign language not required; for doctorate, variable foreign language requirement, dissertation. *Entrance requirements:* For master's and doctorate, GRE General Test (minimum combined score of 1000), minimum GPA of 3.0; for Ed S, GRE General Test. Application deadline: 6/5. Application fee: $20. *Tuition:* $138 per credit hour for state residents; $481 per credit hour for nonresidents. • Dr. Mary Grace Kantowski, Chair, 352-392-9191 Ext. 200. E-mail: mgk@coe.ufl.edu. Application contact: Dr. Ben Nelms, Graduate Coordinator, 352-392-9191 Ext. 225. Fax: 352-392-9193. E-mail: bfn@coe.ufl.edu.

University of Georgia, College of Education, Department of Instructional Technology, Athens, GA 30602. Awards M Ed, PhD, Ed S. Accredited by NCATE. Faculty: 10 full-time (2 women). Students: 54 full-time, 45 part-time (33 women); includes 12 minority (7 African Americans, 3 Hispanics, 2 Native Americans), 12 international. 64 applicants, 38% accepted. In 1997, 15 master's, 1 doctorate, 4 Ed Ss awarded. *Degree requirements:* For doctorate, dissertation required, foreign language not required. *Entrance requirements:* For master's and Ed S, GRE General Test or MAT; for doctorate, GRE General Test. Application deadline: 7/1 (priority date; 11/15 for spring admission). Application fee: $30. Electronic applications accepted. *Tuition:* $3290 per year full-time, $643 per semester (minimum) part-time for state residents; $11,300 per year full-time, $1645 per semester (minimum) part-time for nonresidents. *Financial aid:* Fellowships, research assistantships, teaching assistantships, assistantships available. • Dr. Lloyd P. Rieber, Graduate Coordinator, 706-542-3958. Fax: 706-542-4032. E-mail: lrieber@coe.uga.edu.

University of Hartford, College of Education, Nursing, and Health Professions, Program in Educational Computing and Technology, West Hartford, CT 06117-1599. Awards M Ed. Accredited by NCATE. Part-time and evening/weekend programs available. Faculty: 4 full-time (2 women), 1 part-time (0 women). Students: 1 (woman) full-time, 25 part-time (16 women); includes 2 minority (1 Asian American, 1 Hispanic), 2 international. Average age 38. 14 applicants, 93% accepted. In 1997, 16 degrees awarded. *Degree requirements:* Comprehensive exam required, foreign language and thesis not required. *Entrance requirements:* GRE General Test or MAT, interview. Application deadline: 5/15 (priority date; rolling processing; 12/15 for spring admission). Application fee: $40 ($55 for international students). Electronic applications accepted. *Financial aid:* Federal Work-Study available. Aid available to part-time students. Financial aid application deadline: 6/1; applicants required to submit FAFSA. • Dr. Marilyn Schaffer, Director, 860-768-4277. Application contact: Susan Garcia, Coordinator of Student Services, 860-768-5038. E-mail: gettoknow@mail.hartford.edu.

University of Hawaii at Manoa, College of Education, Department of Educational Technology, Honolulu, HI 96822. Awards M Ed. Part-time programs available. Faculty: 3 full-time (2 women), 3 part-time (1 woman). Students: 10 full-time (7 women), 34 part-time (17 women); includes 24 minority (all Asian Americans). Average age 31. 19 applicants, 95% accepted. In 1997, 10 degrees awarded (70% found work related to degree, 30% continued full-time study). *Degree requirements:* Thesis or alternative required, foreign language not required. *Average time to degree:* master's–2 years full-time, 3 years part-time. *Entrance requirements:* TOEFL (minium score of 600). Application deadline: 3/1 (9/1 for spring admission). Application fee: $25 ($50 for international students). *Tuition:* $4029 per year full-time, $214 per credit hour part-time for state residents; $9957 per year full-time, $461 per credit hour part-time for nonresidents. *Financial aid:* In 1997–98, 4 students received aid, including 2 tuition waivers (both to first-year students); full and partial tuition waivers also available. *Faculty research:* Distance education-interaction via electronic means. • Dr. Geoffrey Z. Kucera, Chairman, 808-956-7671. E-mail: etdept-e@hawaii.edu.

University of Houston–Clear Lake, School of Education, Houston, TX 77058-1098. Offerings include instructional technology (MS). Accredited by NCATE. School faculty: 34 full-time (23 women), 17 part-time (12 women), 39 FTE. *Application deadline:* rolling. *Application fee:* $30 ($60 for international students). *Tuition:* $207 per credit hour for state residents; $336 per credit hour for nonresidents. • Dr. Dennis Spuck, Dean, 281-283-3501. Application contact: Dr. Doris L. Prater, Associate Dean, 281-283-3600.

The University of Iowa, College of Education, Division of Psychological and Quantitative Foundations, Iowa City, IA 52242-1316. Offerings include educational media (MA, PhD, Ed S), instructional design and technology (MA, PhD). Division faculty: 29 full-time, 1 part-time. *Degree requirements:* For master's, exam required, thesis optional, foreign language not required; for doctorate, computer language, dissertation, comprehensive exams required, foreign language not required; for Ed S, computer language, exam required, foreign language not required. *Entrance requirements:* For master's and Ed S, GRE General Test, minimum GPA of 2.5; for doctorate, GRE General Test, minimum GPA of 3.0. Application fee: $30 ($50 for international students). *Expenses:* Tuition $3166 per year full-time, $176 per semester hour part-time for state residents; $10,202 per year full-time, $176 per semester hour part-time for nonresidents. Fees $202 per year full-time, $52 per year (minimum) part-time. • David F. Lohman, Chair, 319-335-5577. Fax: 319-335-6145.

University of Manitoba, Faculty of Education, Department of Curriculum: Mathematics and Natural Sciences, Winnipeg, MB R3T 2N2, Canada. Offerings include educational technology (M Ed). *Degree requirements:* Thesis or alternative required, foreign language not required.

University of Maryland, Baltimore County, Graduate School, Department of Education, Baltimore, MD 21250-5398. Offerings include instructional systems development (MA). *Entrance requirements:* GRE General Test, GRE Subject Test, TOEFL, minimum GPA of 3.0. Application deadline: 7/1. Application fee: $40. *Expenses:* Tuition $260 per credit hour for state residents; $468 per credit hour for nonresidents. Fees $39 per credit hour.

University of Maryland, College Park, College of Education, Department of Education Policy, Planning, and Administration, College Park, MD 20742-5045. Offerings include curriculum and educational communications (MA, M Ed, Ed D, PhD). Accredited by NCATE. Postbaccalaureate distance learning degree programs offered. Department faculty: 19 full-time (8 women), 1 (woman) part-time. *Degree requirements:* For master's, thesis or alternative required, foreign language not required; for doctorate, dissertation required, foreign language not required. *Entrance requirements:* For master's, GRE General Test or MAT (score in 40th percentile or higher), minimum GPA of 3.0; for doctorate, GRE General Test or MAT (score in 70th percentile or higher). Application deadline: rolling. Application fee: $50 ($70 for international students). *Expenses:* Tuition $272 per credit hour for state residents; $400 per credit hour for nonresidents. Fees $564 per year full-time, $342 per year part-time. • Dr. James Cibulka, Chairman, 301-405-3589. Fax: 301-314-9278. Application contact: John Mollish, Director, Graduate Admissions and Records, 301-405-4198. Fax: 301-314-9305.

University of Massachusetts Amherst, School of Education, Program in Education, Amherst, MA 01003-0001. Offerings include mathematics, science, and instructional technology (M Ed, Ed D, CAGS). Accredited by NCATE. *Degree requirements:* For doctorate, dissertation required, foreign language not required. *Entrance requirements:* For master's and doctorate, GRE General Test. Application deadline: 3/1 (rolling processing; 10/1 for spring admission). Application fee: $40. *Expenses:* Tuition $2640 per year full-time, $110 per credit part-time for state residents; $3690 per year (minimum) full-time, $165 per credit (minimum) part-time for nonresidents. Fees $2856 per year full-time, $422 per semester part-time for state residents; $3204 per year full-time, $480 per semester part-time for nonresidents. • John C. Carey, Director, 413-545-0236.

The University of Memphis, College of Education, Department of Instruction and Curriculum Leadership, Memphis, TN 38152. Offerings include instruction design and technology (MS, Ed D). Accredited by NCATE. Terminal master's awarded for partial completion of doctoral program. Department faculty: 34 full-time (17 women), 22 part-time (13 women). *Degree requirements:* For doctorate, dissertation, comprehensive exam required, foreign language not required. *Entrance requirements:* For doctorate, GRE General Test, GRE Subject Test, 2 years of teaching experience. Application deadline: 8/1 (12/1 for spring admission). Application fee: $25 ($50 for international students). *Tuition:* $2862 per year full-time, $166 per credit hour part-time for state residents; $6696 per year full-time, $379 per credit hour part-time for nonresidents. • Dr. Dennie Smith, Interim Chair, 901-678-2771. Application contact: Dr. Carole L. Bond, Coordinator of Graduate Studies, 901-678-3490.

University of Nebraska at Kearney, College of Education, Department of Educational Administration, Kearney, NE 68849-0001. Offerings include supervisor of educational media (MA Ed). Accredited by NCATE. Department faculty: 2 full-time (0 women). *Degree requirements:* Thesis optional. *Entrance requirements:* GRE General Test. Application deadline: 8/1 (priority date; rolling processing; 12/15 for spring admission). Application fee: $35. *Expenses:* Tuition $1494 per year full-time, $83 per credit hour part-time for state residents; $2826 per year full-time, $157 per credit hour part-time for nonresidents. Fees $229 per year full-time, $11.25 per semester (minimum) part-time. • Dr. Thomas Jacobson, Chair, 308-865-8512.

University of Nebraska at Kearney, College of Education, Department of Professional Teacher Education, Kearney, NE 68849-0001. Offerings include instructional technology (MS Ed). Accredited by NCATE. Department faculty: 6 full-time (4 women). *Degree requirements:* Thesis optional. *Entrance requirements:* GRE General Test. Application deadline: 8/1 (priority date; rolling processing; 12/15 for spring admission). Application fee: $35. *Expenses:* Tuition $1494 per year full-time, $83 per credit hour part-time for state residents; $2826 per year full-time, $157 per credit hour part-time for nonresidents. Fees $229 per year full-time, $11.25 per semester (minimum) part-time. • Dr. Lynn Johnson, Chair, 308-865-8513.

University of Nevada, Las Vegas, College of Education, Department of Instructional and Curricular Studies, Las Vegas, NV 89154-9900. Offerings include educational computing and technology (M Ed, MS), library science and audiovisual education (M Ed, MS). One or more programs accredited by NCATE. Department faculty: 34 full-time (16 women). *Degree requirements:* Thesis (for some programs), oral or written comprehensive exam required, foreign language not required. *Entrance requirements:* Minimum GPA of 3.0. Application deadline: 2/15 (9/30 for spring admission). Application fee: $40 ($95 for international students). *Expenses:* Tuition $93 per credit for state residents; $93 per credit full-time, $190 per credit part-time for nonresidents. Fees $5570 per year full-time for nonresidents. • Dr. Jan McCarthy, Chair, 702-895-3241. Application contact: Graduate College Admissions Evaluator, 702-895-3320.

University of New Mexico, College of Education, Program in Organizational Learning and Instructional Technologies, Albuquerque, NM 87131-2039. Awards MA, Ed D, PhD, Certificate, Ed S. Accredited by NCATE. Part-time and evening/weekend programs available. Faculty: 2 full-time (1 woman). Students: 48 full-time (26 women), 121 part-time (79 women); includes 40 minority (6 African Americans, 3 Asian Americans, 26 Hispanics, 5 Native Americans), 4 international. Average age 41. 48 applicants, 63% accepted. In 1997, 78 master's, 5 doctorates, 13 other advanced degrees awarded. *Degree requirements:* For master's, thesis optional, foreign language not required; for doctorate, variable foreign language requirement, dissertation. *Application deadline:* 6/15 (10/15 for spring admission). *Application fee:* $25. *Expenses:* Tuition $2442 per year full-time, $103 per credit hour part-time for state residents; $8691 per year full-time, $103 per credit hour (minimum) part-time for nonresidents. Fees $32 per year. *Financial aid:* In 1997–98, fellowships totaling $2,000, 2 teaching assistantships were awarded; career-related internships or fieldwork also available. *Faculty research:* Team development, program education, distance education. • Dr. Hallie Preskill, Graduate Coordinator, 505-277-4131. E-mail: hpreskil@unm.edu. Application contact: Loretta Brown, Program Secretary, 505-277-4131. Fax: 505-277-8427. E-mail: loribrwn@unm.edu.

University of North Carolina at Charlotte, College of Education, Charlotte, NC 28223-0001. Offerings include instructional systems technology (M Ed). Accredited by NCATE. College faculty: 61 full-time (31 women), 7 part-time (6 women), 62.75 FTE. *Application deadline:* 7/1. *Application fee:* $35. *Tuition:* $1786 per year full-time, $339 per semester (minimum) part-time for state residents; $8914 per year full-time, $2121 per semester (minimum) part-time for nonresidents. • Dr. John M. Nagle, Dean, 704-547-4707. Application contact: Kathy Barringer, Assistant Director of Graduate Admissions, 704-547-3366. Fax: 704-547-3279. E-mail: gradadm@email.uncc.edu.

University of Northern Colorado, College of Education, Department of Educational Technology, Program in Educational Media, Greeley, CO 80639. Awards MA. Accredited by NCATE. Students: 1 full-time (0 women), 5 part-time (all women); includes 1 minority (Hispanic). Average age 36. 2 applicants, 100% accepted. In 1997, 7 degrees awarded. *Degree requirements:* Thesis or alternative, comprehensive exams. *Entrance requirements:* GRE General Test. Application deadline: rolling. Application fee: $35. *Expenses:* Tuition $2327 per year full-time, $129 per credit hour part-time for state residents; $9578 per year full-time, $532 per credit hour part-time for nonresidents. Fees $752 per year full-time, $184 per semester (minimum) part-time. *Financial aid:* Fellowships, teaching assistantships, graduate assistantships available. Financial aid application deadline: 3/1. • Dr. Jeff Bauer, Chairperson, Department of Educational Technology, 970-351-2368.

University of Northern Iowa, College of Education, Department of Curriculum and Instruction, Program in Educational Technology, Cedar Falls, IA 50614. Awards MA. Students: 8 full-time (4 women), 29 part-time (20 women); includes 4 international. Average age 33. 22 applicants, 100% accepted. In 1997, 12 degrees awarded. *Degree requirements:* Thesis or alternative required, foreign language not required. *Entrance requirements:* Minimum GPA of 3.5, 3 years of educational experience. Application deadline: 8/1 (priority date; rolling processing). Application fee: $20 ($30 for international students). *Expenses:* Tuition $3166 per year full-time, $176 per hour part-time for state residents; $7805 per year full-time, $176 per hour part-time for nonresidents. Fees $194 per year full-time, $12.50 per semester (minimum) part-time. *Financial aid:* Application deadline 3/1. • Dr. Robert Muffoletto, Acting Head, Department of Curriculum and Instruction, 319-273-2167.

University of Northern Iowa, College of Education, Department of Curriculum and Instruction, Program in Elementary Education, Cedar Falls, IA 50614. Offers communication and training technology (MA Ed), educational media (MA Ed). Part-time and evening/weekend programs available. Students: 5 full-time (4 women), 10 part-time (9 women); includes 2 minority (both African Americans). Average age 33. 7 applicants, 86% accepted. In 1997, 4 degrees awarded. *Degree requirements:* Thesis or alternative required, foreign language not required. *Entrance requirements:* Minimum GPA of 3.5, 3 years of educational experience. Application deadline: 8/1 (priority date; rolling processing). Application fee: $20 ($30 for international students). *Expenses:* Tuition $3166 per year full-time, $176 per hour part-time for state residents; $7805 per year full-time, $176 per hour part-time for nonresidents. Fees $194 per year full-time, $12.50 per semester (minimum) part-time. *Financial aid:* Full and partial tuition waivers, Federal Work-Study, and career-related internships or fieldwork available. Aid available to part-time students. Financial aid application deadline: 3/1. • Dr. Robert Muffoletto, Acting Head, Department of Curriculum and Instruction, 319-273-2167.

University of Northern Iowa, College of Education, Department of Curriculum and Instruction, Program in School Library Media Studies, Cedar Falls, IA 50614. Awards MA. Part-time and evening/weekend programs available. Faculty: 2 full-time (both women). Students: 4 full-time (3 women), 10 part-time (all women). Average age 33. 6 applicants, 100% accepted. In 1997, 15 degrees awarded. *Degree requirements:* Thesis or alternative required, foreign language not required. *Entrance requirements:* Minimum GPA of 3.5, 3 years of educational experience. Application deadline: 8/1 (priority date; rolling processing). Application fee: $20 ($30 for international students). *Expenses:* Tuition $3166 per year full-time, $176 per hour part-time for state residents; $7805 per year full-time, $176 per hour part-time for nonresidents. Fees $194 per year full-time, $12.50 per semester (minimum) part-time. *Financial aid:* Scholarships, full and partial tuition waivers, Federal Work-Study, and career-related internships or fieldwork available. Aid available to part-time students. Financial aid application deadline: 3/1. • Dr. Robert Muffoletto, Acting Head, Department of Curriculum and Instruction, 319-273-2167.

University of Oregon, Graduate School, College of Education, Department of Educational Technology, Leadership and Administration, Department of Educational Policy and Management, Eugene, OR 97403. Offerings include computer and education (PhD). Terminal master's awarded for partial completion of doctoral program. Department faculty: 8 full-time (1 woman), 6 part-time (1 woman), 10.29 FTE. *Application deadline:* 3/15. *Application fee:* $50. *Tuition:* $6429 per year full-time, $873 per quarter (minimum) part-time for state residents; $10,857 per year full-time, $1360 per quarter (minimum) part-time for nonresidents. • Application contact: Tammara Hirte, Graduate Secretary, 541-346-1361. Fax: 541-346-5174.

University of St. Thomas, School of Education, Program in Learning and Human Development Technology, St. Paul, MN 55105-1096. Awards MA, Certificate. Accredited by NCATE. Students: 3 full-time (2 women), 95 part-time (72 women); includes 4 minority (2 African Americans, 2 Asian Americans), 2 international. Average age 34. 28 applicants, 93% accepted. In 1997, 34 master's, 17 Certificates awarded. *Degree requirements:* For master's, thesis (for

Directory: Educational Media/Instructional Technology

University of St. Thomas (continued)
some programs). *Entrance requirements:* For master's, MAT, minimum GPA of 3.0; for Certificate, minimum graduate GPA of 3.25. Application deadline: rolling. Application fee: $50. *Tuition:* $375 per credit hour. *Financial aid:* In 1997–98, 8 grants (1 to a first-year student) totaling $20,377 were awarded; research assistantships also available. Financial aid application deadline: 4/1. • Dr. Mitch Kusy, Director, 612-962-4530. Fax: 612-962-5169.

University of Sioux Falls, Program in Education, Sioux Falls, SD 57105-1699. Offerings include technology (M Ed). Accredited by NCATE. Summer admission only. Program faculty: 5 full-time (4 women), 7 part-time (4 women). *Entrance requirements:* Minimum GPA of 3.0, 1 year of teaching experience. Application deadline: rolling. Application fee: $25. *Tuition:* $195 per credit hour. • Dr. Donna Goldammer, Chair, 605-331-6713. Application contact: Dr. Nancy Johnson, Director of Graduate Studies, 605-331-6710. Fax: 605-331-6615. E-mail: nancy.johnson@thecoo.edu.

University of South Alabama, College of Education, Department of Behavioral Studies and Educational Technology, Mobile, AL 36688-0002. Offers programs in counseling (M Ed, MS, Ed S), educational media (M Ed, MS), instructional design (MS). Accredited by NCATE. Part-time programs available. Faculty: 14 full-time (5 women). Students: 137 full-time (110 women), 137 part-time (112 women); includes 53 minority (48 African Americans, 2 Asian Americans, 2 Hispanics, 1 Native American), 3 international. 103 applicants, 90% accepted. In 1997, 66 master's awarded. *Degree requirements:* For master's, comprehensive exam required, foreign language and thesis not required. *Entrance requirements:* For master's, GRE General Test (minimum combined score of 1000) or MAT (minimum score 37), minimum GPA of 3.0. Application deadline: 9/1 (priority date; rolling processing). Application fee: $25. *Financial aid:* In 1997–98, 5 research assistantships were awarded; career-related internships or fieldwork also available. Aid available to part-time students. Financial aid application deadline: 4/1. *Faculty research:* Agency counseling, rehabilitation counseling, school psychometry. • Dr. John Lane, Chairman, 334-380-2861.

University of South Alabama, College of Education, Program in Instructional Design and Development, Mobile, AL 36688-0002. Awards PhD. Accredited by NCATE. Part-time programs available. Students: 22 full-time (12 women), 37 part-time (17 women); includes 5 minority (3 African Americans, 1 Asian American, 1 Hispanic), 4 international. 9 applicants, 44% accepted. In 1997, 5 degrees awarded. *Degree requirements:* Computer language, dissertation, comprehensive exam required, foreign language not required. *Application deadline:* 9/1 (priority date; rolling processing). *Application fee:* $25. *Financial aid:* Application deadline 4/1. • George E. Uhlig, Dean, College of Education, 334-460-6205.

University of South Carolina, Graduate School, College of Education, Department of Educational Psychology, Program in Instructional Technology, Columbia, SC 29208. Awards M Ed. Accredited by NCATE. Faculty: Students: 1 (woman) full-time, 4 part-time (all women). Average age 38. *Entrance requirements:* GRE. Application deadline: rolling. Application fee: $35. Electronic applications accepted. *Expenses:* Tuition $3894 per year full-time, $193 per credit hour part-time for state residents; $8114 per year full-time, $404 per credit hour part-time for nonresidents. Fees $125 per year full-time, $37 per semester (minimum) part-time. • Dr. Margaret Gredler, Head, 803-777-6609. Application contact: Office of Intercollegiate Teacher Education and Student Affairs, 803-777-6732. Fax: 803-777-3068.

University of Southern California, Graduate School, School of Education, Department of Curriculum and Instruction, Los Angeles, CA 90089. Offerings include instructional technology (MS). *Entrance requirements:* GRE General Test. Application deadline: 7/1 (priority date; 11/1 for spring admission). Application fee: $55. *Expenses:* Tuition $16,944 per year full-time, $706 per unit part-time. Fees $414 per year full-time, $32 per year part-time. • Dr. Edgar Williams, Chair.

University of South Florida, College of Arts and Sciences, School of Library and Information Science, Tampa, FL 33620-9951. Offerings include school library media (MA). Postbaccalaureate distance learning degree programs offered (minimal on-campus study). School faculty: 6 full-time (5 women). *Entrance requirements:* GRE General Test (minimum combined score of 1000), minimum GPA of 3.0 in last 60 hours. Application deadline: 6/1 (10/15 for spring admission). Application fee: $20. Electronic applications accepted. *Tuition:* $142 per credit hour for state residents; $486 per credit hour for nonresidents. • Kathleen de la Pena McCook, Director, 813-974-3520. E-mail: kmccook@chuma.cas.usf.edu. Application contact: Sonia Ramirez Wohlmuth, Assistant Director, 813-974-6837. Fax: 813-974-6840. E-mail: swohlmut@chuma.cas.usf.edu.

University of South Florida, College of Education, Department of Secondary Education, Program in Instructional Computing, Tampa, FL 33620-9951. Awards M Ed, PhD. Accredited by NCATE. Part-time and evening/weekend programs available. Students: 31 full-time (21 women), 107 part-time (78 women); includes 17 minority (4 African Americans, 3 Asian Americans, 10 Hispanics), 8 international. Average age 38. 22 applicants, 64% accepted. In 1997, 43 master's awarded. *Degree requirements:* For doctorate, dissertation, 2 tools of research in foreign language, statistics, and/or computers. *Entrance requirements:* For master's, GRE General Test (minimum combined score of 1000), minimum GPA of 3.5 in last 60 hours; for doctorate, GRE General Test (minimum combined score of 1000), minimum GPA of 3.0 (undergraduate) or 3.5 (graduate). Application deadline: 6/1 (10/15 for spring admission). Application fee: $20. Electronic applications accepted. *Tuition:* $142 per credit hour for state residents; $486 per credit hour for nonresidents. *Financial aid:* Federal Work-Study, institutionally sponsored loans available. Aid available to part-time students. Financial aid applicants required to submit FAFSA. • Application contact: Frank Breit, Coordinator, 813-974-1632. Fax: 813-974-3837. E-mail: breit@tempest.coedu.usf.edu.

University of Tennessee, Knoxville, College of Education, Program in Education I, Knoxville, TN 37996. Offerings include instructional technology/curriculum (PhD). Accredited by NCATE. *Degree requirements:* 1 foreign language (computer language can substitute), dissertation. *Entrance requirements:* GRE General Test, TOEFL (minimum score 550), minimum GPA of 2.7. Application deadline: 2/1 (priority date; rolling processing). Application fee: $35. Electronic applications accepted. *Tuition:* $3354 per year full-time, $181 per semester hour part-time for state residents; $8410 per year full-time, $462 per semester hour part-time for nonresidents. • Dr. Tom George, Associate Dean, 423-974-0907. Fax: 423-974-8718. E-mail: tgeorge1@utk.edu.

University of Tennessee, Knoxville, College of Education, Program in Education II, Knoxville, TN 37996. Offerings include instructional media and technology (MS, Ed D, Ed S). Accredited by NCATE. *Degree requirements:* For master's and Ed S, thesis optional, foreign language not required; for doctorate, dissertation required, foreign language not required. *Entrance requirements:* For master's, TOEFL (minimum score 550), minimum GPA of 2.7; for doctorate, GRE General Test, TOEFL (minimum score 550), minimum GPA of 2.7; for Ed S, TOEFL (minimum score 550), GRE General Test, minimum GPA of 2.7. Application deadline: 2/1 (priority date; rolling processing). Application fee: $35. Electronic applications accepted. *Tuition:* $3354 per year full-time, $181 per semester hour part-time for state residents; $8410 per year full-time, $462 per semester hour part-time for nonresidents. • Dr. Tom George, Associate Dean, 423-974-0907. Fax: 423-974-8718. E-mail: tgeorge1@utk.edu.

The University of Texas at Brownsville, Graduate Studies, School of Education, Brownsville, TX 78520-4991. Offerings include educational technology (M Ed). School faculty: 18 full-time (10 women). *Degree requirements:* Thesis optional, foreign language not required. *Entrance requirements:* GRE General Test, TOEFL (minimum score 550). Application deadline: 8/1 (priority date; rolling processing; 1/1 for spring admission). Application fee: $15. *Expenses:* Tuition $648 per year full-time, $120 per semester hour part-time for state residents; $4698 per year full-time, $783 per semester hour part-time for nonresidents. Fees $593 per year full-time, $109 per year part-time. • Dr. Sylvia C. Peña, Dean, 956-983-7219. Fax: 956-982-0293. E-mail: scpena@utb1.utb.edu.

University of the Sacred Heart, Graduate Programs, Department of Education, Program in Instruction Systems and Education Technology, San Juan, PR 00914-0383. Awards M Ed. Part-time and evening/weekend programs available. Faculty: 1 (woman) full-time, 4 part-time (all women), 2.33 FTE. Students: 2 full-time (1 woman), 51 part-time (42 women). 21 applicants, 57% accepted. In 1997, 13 degrees awarded. *Degree requirements:* Computer language, thesis. *Entrance requirements:* PAEG, minimum undergraduate GPA of 2.5. Application deadline: 5/15. Application fee: $25. *Expenses:* Tuition $150 per credit. Fees $240 per credit. • Prof. Isabel Yamin, Coordinator, 787-728-1515 Ext. 2332. Fax: 787-728-1515 Ext. 2334. E-mail: f_pieras@usca1.usc.clu.edu. Application contact: Dr. Blanca Villamil, Acting Director, Admissions Office, 787-728-1515 Ext. 3237. Fax: 787-728-2066. E-mail: b_villami@uscsi.usc.clu.edu.

University of Toledo, College of Education and Allied Professions, Department of Curriculum and Instruction, Toledo, OH 43606-3398. Offerings include educational technology (M Ed). Accredited by NCATE. Department faculty: 27 full-time (9 women). *Application deadline:* 8/1 (priority date; rolling processing). *Application fee:* $30. *Tuition:* $5907 per year full-time, $246 per hour part-time for state residents; $11,835 per year full-time, $493 per hour part-time for nonresidents. • Dr. James R. Gress, Chair, 419-530-2468. Fax: 419-530-7719. E-mail: jgress@uoft02.utoledo.edu.

The University of West Alabama, College of Education, Department of Foundations, Livingston, AL 35470. Offerings include secondary education (MAT, M Ed), with options in biology with certification (MAT), environmental science with certification (MAT), history with certification (MAT), language arts with certification (MAT), library media with certification (MAT), mathematics with certification (MAT). Accredited by NCATE. *Application deadline:* 9/10 (priority date; rolling processing; 3/24 for spring admission). *Application fee:* $15. *Tuition:* $70 per quarter hour.

The University of West Alabama, College of Liberal Arts, Program in Library Media, Livingston, AL 35470. Awards MAT. Accredited by NCATE. *Tuition:* $70 per quarter hour.

The University of West Alabama, College of Education, Department of Instructional Support, Program in Library Media, Livingston, AL 35470. Awards M Ed. Accredited by NCATE. Part-time programs available. *Average time to degree:* master's–1 year full-time, 2 years part-time. *Entrance requirements:* GRE General Test, MAT, minimum GPA of 2.75. Application deadline: 9/10 (priority date; rolling processing; 3/24 for spring admission). Application fee: $15. *Tuition:* $70 per quarter hour.

University of Wisconsin–Stout, College of Technology, Engineering, and Management, Program in Media Technology, Menomonie, WI 54751. Awards MS. Accredited by NCATE. Program being phased out; applicants no longer accepted. Part-time programs available. Students: 4 part-time (0 women). In 1997, 2 degrees awarded. *Degree requirements:* Thesis required, foreign language not required. *Tuition:* $3284 per year full-time, $183 per credit hour part-time for state residents; $7644 per year full-time, $425 per credit hour part-time for nonresidents. *Financial aid:* Research assistantships, teaching assistantships available. Financial aid applicants required to submit FAFSA. • Dr. Howard Lee, Director, 715-232-1251.

Utah State University, College of Education, Department of Instructional Technology, Logan, UT 84322. Awards M Ed, MS, PhD, Ed S. Accredited by NCATE. Part-time programs available. Postbaccalaureate distance learning degree programs offered (no on-campus study). Faculty: 9 full-time (1 woman), 6 part-time (2 women). Students: 153 full-time (60 women), 45 part-time (19 women). Average age 28. 36 applicants, 69% accepted. In 1997, 42 master's, 3 Ed Ss awarded. *Degree requirements:* For master's, thesis required (for some programs), foreign language not required. *Entrance requirements:* For master's, GRE General Test (score in 40th percentile or higher) or MAT, TOEFL (minimum score 550), minimum GPA of 3.0; for Ed S, GRE General Test (score in 40th percentile or higher), GRE Subject Test, TOEFL (minimum score 550), minimum GPA of 3.0. Application deadline: 6/15 (priority date; rolling processing; 10/15 for spring admission). Application fee: $40. *Expenses:* Tuition $1448 per year full-time, $624 per year part-time for state residents; $5082 per year full-time, $2192 per year part-time for nonresidents. Fees $421 per year full-time, $165 per year part-time. *Financial aid:* Fellowships, research assistantships, teaching assistantships, Federal Work-Study, institutionally sponsored loans, and career-related internships or fieldwork available. Financial aid application deadline: 7/1. *Faculty research:* Interactive instruction, computer-assisted instruction, learning theories, instructional design models, second generation instruction design. Total annual research expenditures: $800,000. • Dr. Don Smellie, Head, 435-797-2694.

Valdosta State University, College of Education, Department of Secondary Education, Valdosta, GA 31698. Offerings include instructional technology (M Ed). Accredited by NCATE. Department faculty: 8 full-time (5 women). *Degree requirements:* Computer language, thesis required, foreign language not required. *Entrance requirements:* GRE General Test (minimum combined score of 800). Application deadline: 8/1 (rolling processing; 11/15 for spring admission). Application fee: $10. *Expenses:* Tuition $2472 per year full-time, $83 per semester hour part-time for state residents; $8472 per year full-time, $333 per semester hour part-time for nonresidents. Fees $236 per year full-time. • Dr. Catherine Price, Head, 912-333-5927. Fax: 912-333-7167. E-mail: cprice@grits.valdosta.peachnet.edu.

Virginia State University, School of Liberal Arts and Education, Department of Education, Program in Educational Media, 1 Hayden Drive, Petersburg, VA 23806-2096. Awards M Ed, MS. Accredited by NCATE. Faculty: 1 full-time (0 women). In 1997, 3 degrees awarded. *Entrance requirements:* GRE, teaching experience. Application deadline: 8/15 (rolling processing). Application fee: $25. *Tuition:* $3739 per year full-time, $133 per credit hour part-time for state residents; $9056 per year full-time, $364 per credit hour part-time for nonresidents. *Financial aid:* Application deadline 5/1. • Application contact: Dr. Wayne F. Virag, Dean, Graduate Studies and Continuing Education, 804-524-5985. Fax: 804-524-5104. E-mail: wvirag@vsu.edu.

Walden University, Graduate Programs, Program in Educational Change and Technology Innovation, 155 Fifth Avenue South, Minneapolis, MN 55401. Awards MS. Part-time programs available. Postbaccalaureate distance learning degree programs offered. *Degree requirements:* Thesis or alternative, brief residency sessions required, foreign language not required. *Entrance requirements:* Minimum of 2 years teaching or equivalent experience in an educational setting. Application deadline: 7/15 (rolling processing). Application fee: $50. Electronic applications accepted. *Tuition:* $230 per credit hour.

Wayne State University, College of Education, Division of Administrative and Organizational Studies, Detroit, MI 48202. Offerings include instructional technology (M Ed, Ed D, PhD, Ed S). Accredited by NCATE. Division faculty: 81. *Degree requirements:* For doctorate, dissertation required, foreign language not required. *Entrance requirements:* For doctorate, interview, minimum GPA of 3.0. Application deadline: 7/1. Application fee: $20 ($30 for international students). *Expenses:* Tuition $163 per credit hour for state residents; $355 per credit hour for nonresidents. Fees $498 per year full-time, $114 per semester (minimum) part-time. • Dr. JoAnne Holbert, Assistant Dean, 313-577-0210.

West Chester University of Pennsylvania, School of Education, Department of Instructional Media, West Chester, PA 19383. Awards M Ed, MS. Accredited by NCATE. Program being phased out; applicants no longer accepted. Faculty: 5 part-time. Students: 3 full-time (all women), 8 part-time (5 women). Average age 37. In 1997, 6 degrees awarded. *Degree requirements:* Comprehensive exam required, foreign language and thesis not required. *Expenses:* Tuition $3468 per year full-time, $193 per credit part-time for state residents; $6236 per year full-time, $346 per credit part-time for nonresidents. Fees $660 per year full-time, $38 per credit part-time. *Financial aid:* Research assistantships available. Aid available to part-time students. • Dr. Nancy Rumfield, Chair, 610-436-1051.

Western Illinois University, College of Education and Human Services, Department of Instructional Technology and Telecommunications, Macomb, IL 61455-1390. Awards MS.

Accredited by NCATE. Faculty: 6 full-time (1 woman). Students: 16 full-time (7 women), 67 part-time (41 women); includes 2 minority (1 African American, 1 Hispanic), 3 international. Average age 39. 7 applicants, 71% accepted. In 1997, 2 degrees awarded. *Degree requirements:* Thesis or alternative required, foreign language not required. *Entrance requirements:* GRE General Test. Application deadline: rolling. Application fee: $0 ($25 for international students). *Expenses:* Tuition $2304 per year full-time, $96 per semester hour part-time for state residents; $6912 per year full-time, $288 per semester hour part-time for nonresidents. Fees $944 per year full-time, $33 per semester hour part-time. *Financial aid:* In 1997–98, 9 students received aid, including 9 research assistantships averaging $610 per month. Financial aid applicants required to submit FAFSA. *Faculty research:* Distance learning, educational technology. • Dr. Mo Hassan, Chairperson, 309-298-1952. Application contact: Barbara Baily, Director of Graduate Studies, 309-298-1806. Fax: 309-298-2245. E-mail: barb_baily@ccmail.wiu.edu.

Western Kentucky University, College of Education, Department of Teacher Education, Program in Library Media Education, Bowling Green, KY 42101-3576. Awards MS. Accredited by NCATE. Part-time and evening/weekend programs available. Faculty: 3 full-time (1 woman). Students: 5 full-time (4 women), 40 part-time (39 women); includes 1 international. Average age 31. 7 applicants, 100% accepted. In 1997, 16 degrees awarded. *Degree requirements:* Thesis or alternative. *Entrance requirements:* GRE General Test (minimum combined score of 1150 on three sections; average 1350), minimum GPA of 2.7 in last 60 hours. Application deadline: 8/1 (priority date; rolling processing; 12/1 for spring admission). Application fee: $20. *Tuition:* $2460 per year full-time, $133 per credit hour part-time for state residents; $6700 per year full-time, $369 per credit hour part-time for nonresidents. *Financial aid:* Federal Work-Study, institutionally sponsored loans available. Aid available to part-time students. Financial aid application deadline: 4/1; applicants required to submit FAFSA. • Dr. Robert Smith, Coordinator, 502-745-3446.

Western Maryland College, Department of Education, Program in Media/Library Science, Westminster, MD 21157-4390. Awards MS. Part-time and evening/weekend programs available. Faculty: 1 (woman) full-time, 3 part-time (all women). Students: 10 full-time (8 women), 145 part-time (141 women). In 1997, 13 degrees awarded. *Degree requirements:* Thesis optional, foreign language not required. *Entrance requirements:* GRE General Test, MAT, or NTE. Application deadline: rolling. Application fee: $35. *Expenses:* Tuition $210 per credit hour. Fees $30 per semester. *Financial aid:* Career-related internships or fieldwork available. Financial aid application deadline: 3/1. • Dr. Ramona Kerby, Coordinator, 410-857-2500. Application contact: Jeanette Witt, Coordinator of Graduate Records, 410-857-2513. Fax: 410-857-2515. E-mail: jwitt@wmdc.edu.

Western Oregon University, School of Education, Department of Information Technology, Monmouth, OR 97361. Awards MS Ed. Accredited by NCATE. Faculty: 1 full-time (0 women), 6 part-time (2 women). Students: 7 full-time (2 women), 11 part-time (7 women); includes 1 minority (Hispanic). Average age 39. 4 applicants, 100% accepted. In 1997, 9 degrees awarded. *Degree requirements:* Written exams required, thesis optional, foreign language not required. *Average time to degree:* master's–1 year full-time, 4 years part-time. *Entrance requirements:* GRE General Test (average 450 on each section) or MAT (minimum score 30), interview, minimum GPA of 3.0, teaching license. Application deadline: rolling. Application fee: $50. *Financial aid:* In 1997–98, 1 research assistantship averaging $2,333 per month was awarded; teaching assistantships, full and partial tuition waivers, and career-related internships or fieldwork also available. Aid available to part-time students. Financial aid application deadline: 3/1; applicants required to submit FAFSA. *Faculty research:* Impact of technology on teaching and learning. • Dr. Randall Engle, Director, 503-838-8471. Fax: 503-838-8228. E-mail: engler@wou.edu. Application contact: Alison Marshall, Director of Admissions, 503-838-8211. Fax: 503-838-8067. E-mail: marshaa@wou.edu.

Western Washington University, Woodring College of Education, Program in Instructional Technology, Bellingham, WA 98225-5996. Awards M Ed. Accredited by NCATE. Part-time programs available. Students: 3 full-time (all women), 3 part-time (2 women). 0 applicants. In 1997, 1 degree awarded. *Degree requirements:* Thesis optional, foreign language not required. *Entrance requirements:* GRE General Test, TOEFL, minimum GPA of 3.0 in last 60 semester hours or last 90 quarter hours. Application deadline: 6/1 (rolling processing; 2/1 for spring admission). Application fee: $35. *Expenses:* Tuition $4200 per year full-time, $140 per credit part-time for state residents; $12,780 per year full-time, $426 per credit part-time for nonresidents. Fees $249 per year full-time, $83 per quarter part-time. *Financial aid:* Teaching assistantships, Federal Work-Study, institutionally sponsored loans, and career-related internships or fieldwork available. Aid available to part-time students. Financial aid application deadline: 3/31. • Dr. Tony Jongejan, Adviser, 360-650-3381.

Westfield State College, Department of Education, Program in Technology for Educators, Westfield, MA 01086. Awards M Ed. *Degree requirements:* Comprehensive exam, practicum required, foreign language and thesis not required. *Entrance requirements:* GRE General Test or MAT, minimum undergraduate GPA of 2.7. Application deadline: rolling. Application fee: $30. *Expenses:* Tuition $145 per credit for state residents; $155 per credit for nonresidents. Fees $90 per semester. *Financial aid:* Application deadline 4/1. • Application contact: Marcia Davio, Graduate Records Clerk, 413-572-8024.

West Texas A&M University, College of Education and Social Sciences, Division of Education, Program in Educational Technology, Canyon, TX 79016-0001. Awards M Ed. Part-time and evening/weekend programs available. Postbaccalaureate distance learning degree programs offered (minimal on-campus study). Students: 2 full-time (1 woman), 6 part-time (5 women); includes 2 minority (1 African American, 1 Hispanic). Average age 34. 12 applicants, 8% accepted. *Degree requirements:* Thesis or alternative, comprehensive exam required, foreign language not required. *Entrance requirements:* GRE General Test (combined average 964). Application deadline: rolling. Application fee: $0 ($50 for international students). Electronic applications accepted. *Expenses:* Tuition $46 per semester hour for state residents; $259 per semester hour for nonresidents. Fees $156 per semester (minimum). *Financial aid:* Teaching assistantships, partial tuition waivers, Federal Work-Study, institutionally sponsored loans, and career-related internships or fieldwork available. Aid available to part-time students. Financial aid applicants required to submit CSS PROFILE or FAFSA. • Dr. George Mann, Head, Division of Education, 806-651-2602. Fax: 806-651-2601. E-mail: george.mann@wtamu.edu.

Winthrop University, College of Education, Program in Educational Media, Rock Hill, SC 29733. Awards M Ed. Accredited by NCATE. Part-time programs available. Students: 8 full-time (7 women), 21 part-time (18 women); includes 1 minority (African American). Average age 33. In 1997, 6 degrees awarded. *Entrance requirements:* GRE General Test (minimum combined score of 800) or NTE, minimum GPA of 3.0, South Carolina Class III teaching certificate. Application deadline: 7/15 (priority date; rolling processing; 12/1 for spring admission). Application fee: $35. *Tuition:* $3928 per year full-time, $164 per credit hour part-time for state residents; $7060 per year full-time, $294 per credit hour part-time for nonresidents. *Financial aid:* Graduate assistantships, graduate scholarships, Federal Work-Study, and career-related internships or fieldwork available. Aid available to part-time students. Financial aid application deadline: 2/1; applicants required to submit FAFSA. • Dr. Richard Ingram, Chairman, 803-323-2151. Fax: 803-323-2585. E-mail: ingramr@winthrop.edu. Application contact: Sharon Johnson, Director of Graduate Studies, 803-323-2204. Fax: 803-323-2292. E-mail: johnsons@winthrop.edu.

Educational Psychology

American International College, Departments of Education and Psychology, Curtis L. Blake Child Development Center, Springfield, MA 01109-3189. Offers program in educational psychology (MA, Ed D). Faculty: 3 full-time (1 woman), 6 part-time (2 women). Students: 13 full-time (11 women), 15 part-time (13 women); includes 2 minority (both African Americans). 2 applicants, 100% accepted. In 1997, 7 master's awarded. Terminal master's awarded for partial completion of doctoral program. *Degree requirements:* For master's, practicum required, foreign language and thesis not required; for doctorate, dissertation required, foreign language not required. *Entrance requirements:* For master's, minimum C average in undergraduate course work; for doctorate, GRE General Test, interview. Application fee: $15 ($25 for international students). *Expenses:* Tuition $363 per credit hour. Fees $25 per semester. • Dr. Paul M. Quinlan, Co-Director, 413-747-6420.

Andrews University, School of Graduate Studies, School of Education, Department of Educational and Counseling Psychology, Berrien Springs, MI 49104. Offerings include educational and developmental psychology (MA), educational psychology (Ed D, PhD). Terminal master's awarded for partial completion of doctoral program. *Degree requirements:* For master's, thesis optional, foreign language not required; for doctorate, dissertation. *Entrance requirements:* For master's, GRE Subject Test, minimum GPA of 2.6; for doctorate, GRE General Test, MA, minimum GPA of 3.5, sample of research. Application deadline: rolling. Application fee: $30. *Expenses:* Tuition $290 per quarter hour (minimum). Fees $75 per quarter. • Dr. Elsie P. Jackson, Chair, 616-471-3113. Application contact: Eileen Lesher, 616-471-3490.

Arizona State University, College of Education, Division of Psychology in Education, Academic Program in Educational Psychology, Tempe, AZ 85287. Awards MA, M Ed, PhD. One or more programs accredited by APA. *Degree requirements:* Thesis/dissertation. *Entrance requirements:* GRE General Test or MAT. Application fee: $45. *Expenses:* Tuition $2088 per year full-time, $110 per hour part-time for state residents; $9040 per year full-time, $377 per hour part-time for nonresidents. Fees $72 per year full-time, $18 per semester (minimum) part-time. *Faculty research:* Lifespan development methodological studies, school psychology, statistics, measurement. • Dr. Raymond Kulhavy, Interim Director, Division of Psychology in Education, 602-965-3384. E-mail: dpe@asu.edu. Application contact: Admissions Secretary, 602-965-5279.

Auburn University, College of Education, Department of Educational Foundations, Leadership, and Technology, Auburn University, AL 36849-0001. Offerings include educational psychology (PhD). Accredited by NCATE. Department faculty: 18 full-time (9 women). *Application deadline:* 9/1 (rolling processing; 3/1 for spring admission). *Application fee:* $25 ($50 for international students). *Expenses:* Tuition $2760 per year full-time, $76 per credit hour part-time for state residents; $8280 per year full-time, $228 per credit hour part-time for nonresidents. Fees $30 per year full-time, $160 per quarter part-time for state residents; $30 per year full-time, $480 per quarter part-time for nonresidents. • Dr. James S. Kaminsky, Head, 334-844-4460. Application contact: Dr. John F. Pritchett, Dean of the Graduate School, 334-844-4700.

Austin Peay State University, College of Education, Department of Education, Clarksville, TN 37044-0001. Offerings include school psychology (Ed S). Accredited by NCATE. Ed S offered jointly with Tennessee State University. *Entrance requirements:* GRE General Test (minimum score 350 on verbal and quantitative sections), master's degree, minimum graduate GPA of 3.0. Application deadline: 7/31 (priority date; rolling processing; 12/4 for spring admission). Application fee: $15. *Expenses:* Tuition $2438 per year full-time, $123 per semester hour part-time for state residents; $7034 per year full-time, $324 per semester hour part-time for nonresidents. Fees $484 per year (minimum) full-time, $154 per semester (minimum) part-time. • J. Ronald Groseclose, Interim Chair, 931-648-7585. Fax: 931-648-5991. E-mail: grosecloseg@apsu.edu.

Ball State University, Teachers College, Department of Educational Psychology, Program in Educational Psychology, 2000 University Avenue, Muncie, IN 47306-1099. Awards MA, PhD, Ed S. Accredited by NCATE. Students: 6 full-time (4 women), 2 part-time (1 woman). Average age 26. 7 applicants, 14% accepted. In 1997, 4 master's awarded. *Degree requirements:* For doctorate, dissertation; for Ed S, thesis required, foreign language not required. *Entrance requirements:* For doctorate, GRE General Test (minimum combined score of 1000), minimum graduate GPA of 3.2; for Ed S, GRE General Test. Application fee: $15 ($25 for international students). *Expenses:* Tuition $3454 per year full-time, $518 per semester (minimum) part-time for state residents; $9316 per year full-time, $1221 per semester (minimum) part-time for nonresidents. Fees $242 per year full-time, $18 per semester (minimum) part-time. • Dr. Gregory Marchant, Head, 785-285-8500.

Baylor University, School of Education, Department of Educational Psychology, Waco, TX 76798. Awards MA, MS Ed, PhD, Ed S. Accredited by NCATE. Part-time programs available. Faculty: 6 full-time (3 women), 2 part-time (1 woman), 6.5 FTE. Students: 27 full-time (19 women), 25 part-time (18 women); includes 7 minority (5 African Americans, 2 Hispanics), 4 international. In 1997, 30 master's, 2 doctorates awarded. *Degree requirements:* For doctorate, dissertation required, foreign language not required. *Entrance requirements:* For master's, GRE General Test; for doctorate, GRE General Test (minimum combined score of 1050), master's degree. Application deadline: 8/1 (rolling processing). Application fee: $25. *Expenses:* Tuition $7392 per year full-time, $308 per semester hour part-time. Fees $1024 per year. *Financial aid:* Federal Work-Study, institutionally sponsored loans available. *Faculty research:* Medical education, cross-cultural learning disabilities, characteristics of an ideal special education teacher, verbal following behavior in adult counseling groups. • Dr. Thomas J. Proctor, Chair, 254-710-3112.

Beaver College, Department of Education, Glenside, PA 19038-3295. Offerings include educational psychology (CAS). *Application fee:* $35. *Expenses:* Tuition $6570 per year full-time, $365 per credit part-time. Fees $35 per year.

Boston College, Graduate School of Education, Department of Counseling Psychology, Developmental and Educational Psychology, Program in Developmental and Educational Psychology, Chestnut Hill, MA 02167-9991. Awards MA, PhD. Accredited by NCATE. Students: 41 full-time (32 women), 39 part-time (28 women); includes 13 minority (5 African Americans, 3 Asian Americans, 5 Hispanics), 5 international. 107 applicants, 50% accepted. In 1997, 13 master's, 5 doctorates awarded. *Degree requirements:* For master's, comprehensive exam required, thesis not required; for doctorate, computer language, dissertation, comprehensive exam. *Entrance requirements:* GRE General Test. Application deadline: 3/15 (11/15 for spring admission). Application fee: $40. *Expenses:* Tuition $626 per semester hour. Fees $80 per year (minimum) full-time, $30 per semester part-time. *Financial aid:* Fellowships, research assistantships, teaching assistantships, administrative assistantships, merit scholarships, Federal Work-Study, and career-related internships or fieldwork available. Aid available to part-time students. *Faculty research:* Facilitating self-control, use of stories in moral development,

Directory: Educational Psychology

Boston College (continued)
changing role of educational psychology, prematurity, development of problem-solving strategies. • Application contact: Arline Riordan, Graduate Admissions Director, 617-552-4214. Fax: 617-552-0812. E-mail: riordana@bc.edu.

Brigham Young University, David O. McKay School of Education, Department of Instructional Psychology and Technology, Provo, UT 84602-1001. Awards MS, PhD. Accredited by NCATE. Faculty: 9 full-time (0 women), 10 part-time (1 woman). Students: 76 full-time (23 women), 3 part-time (0 women); includes 1 minority (Hispanic), 17 international. Average age 30. 35 applicants, 63% accepted. In 1997, 5 master's awarded (20% found work related to degree, 80% continued full-time study); 2 doctorates awarded (100% entered university research/teaching). *Degree requirements:* For master's, thesis or alternative; for doctorate, dissertation. *Entrance requirements:* For master's, GRE General Test, minimum GPA of 3.0 in last 60 hours; for doctorate, GRE General Test, minimum GPA of 3.0. Application deadline: 2/1. Application fee: $30. *Tuition:* $3200 per year full-time, $178 per credit hour part-time for state residents; $4800 per year full-time, $266 per credit hour part-time for nonresidents. *Financial aid:* In 1997–98, 20 students received aid, including 12 research assistantships (4 to first-year students), 9 teaching assistantships (1 to a first-year student); partial tuition waivers and career-related internships or fieldwork also available. Aid available to part-time students. *Faculty research:* Assessment/evaluation. • Dr. Paul F. Merrill, Chair, 801-378-5097. E-mail: paul_merrill@byu.edu. Application contact: Michele Bray, Secretary, 801-378-2746. E-mail: michele_bray@byu.edu.

California State University, Long Beach, College of Education, Department of Educational Psychology and Administration, Program in Educational Psychology, Long Beach, CA 90840-2201. Awards MA. Students: 16 full-time (11 women), 26 part-time (22 women); includes 12 minority (3 African Americans, 1 Asian American, 8 Hispanics), 1 international. Average age 33. 34 applicants, 88% accepted. In 1997, 2 degrees awarded. *Degree requirements:* Thesis required, foreign language not required. *Entrance requirements:* GRE General Test, minimum GPA of 2.75. Application deadline: 8/1 (rolling processing; 12/1 for spring admission). Application fee: $55. *Expenses:* Tuition $0 for state residents; $246 per unit for nonresidents. Fees $1846 per year full-time, $1180 per year part-time. *Financial aid:* Application deadline 3/2. • Dr. Robert Berdan, Chair, Department of Educational Psychology and Administration, 562-985-4517. Fax: 562-985-4534. E-mail: rberdan@csulb.edu.

California State University, Northridge, College of Education, Department of Educational Psychology and Counseling, Northridge, CA 91330. Offers programs in educational psychology and counseling (MA), genetic counseling (MS). Accredited by NCATE. Part-time and evening/weekend programs available. Faculty: 19 full-time, 22 part-time. Students: 10 full-time (9 women), 49 part-time (48 women); includes 17 minority (3 African Americans, 4 Asian Americans, 10 Hispanics), 2 international. Average age 36. 22 applicants, 86% accepted. *Degree requirements:* Thesis or alternative required, foreign language not required. *Entrance requirements:* TOEFL, GRE General Test or minimum GPA of 3.0. Application deadline: 11/30. Application fee: $55. *Expenses:* Tuition $0 for state residents; $246 per unit for nonresidents. Fees $1970 per year full-time, $1304 per year part-time. *Financial aid:* Available to part-time students. Financial aid application deadline: 3/1. *Faculty research:* Motivation, learning development, bilingual education, interpersonal relationships. • Dr. Michael Aver, Chair. Application contact: W. Dean McCafferty, Coordinator, 818-885-2508.

The Catholic University of America, School of Arts and Sciences, Department of Education, Washington, DC 20064. Offerings include educational psychology (PhD). Accredited by NCATE. Department faculty: 13 full-time (8 women), 2 part-time (both women), 14 FTE. *Degree requirements:* 1 foreign language, dissertation, comprehensive exam. *Entrance requirements:* GRE General Test, TOEFL. Application deadline: 8/1 (priority date; rolling processing; 12/1 for spring admission). Application fee: $50. *Expenses:* Tuition $17,325 per year full-time, $668 per credit hour part-time. Fees $680 per year full-time, $360 per year part-time. • Chair, 202-319-5800. Fax: 202-319-5815.

Center for Humanistic Studies, Program in Humanistic, Clinical, and Educational Psychology, Detroit, MI 48202-3802. Awards MA, Psy S. Faculty: 2 full-time (1 woman), 8 part-time (2 women). Students: 71 full-time (51 women), 4 part-time (2 women); includes 10 minority (7 African Americans, 1 Asian American, 2 Hispanics), 1 international. Average age 38. 96 applicants, 57% accepted. In 1997, 34 master's, 18 Psy Ss awarded. *Degree requirements:* For master's, thesis, practicum required, foreign language not required; for Psy S, essay, internship required, thesis not required. *Average time to degree:* master's–1 year full-time; other advanced degree–2 years full-time. *Entrance requirements:* For master's, 1 year of work experience, interview, minimum GPA of 3.0; for Psy S, 5 years of work experience, interview, MA, minimum graduate GPA of 3.0. Application deadline: 9/1 (priority date; rolling processing). Application fee: $75. *Expenses:* Tuition $11,700 per year full-time, $350 per credit hour (minimum) part-time. Fees $175 per year full-time, $100 per year part-time. *Financial aid:* 45 students received aid; career-related internships or fieldwork available. Aid available to part-time students. Financial aid application deadline: 6/30; applicants required to submit FAFSA. *Faculty research:* Qualitative research, existential-phenomenological psychology, applications to clinical practice. • Dr. Kerry Moustakas, President, 313-875-7440. Application contact: Patricia Hagan, Registrar, 313-875-7440. Fax: 313-875-2610.

Chapman University, School of Education, Program in Educational Psychology, Orange, CA 92866. Awards MA. Students: 2. *Degree requirements:* Comprehensive exam required, thesis not required. *Entrance requirements:* GRE General Test (minimum combined score of 900), MAT (minimum score 45), or PRAXIS. Application deadline: rolling. Application fee: $40. *Tuition:* $7020 per year full-time, $390 per credit part-time. *Financial aid:* Application deadline 3/1. • Dr. Michael Hass, Coordinator, 714-997-6781.

Clark Atlanta University, School of Education, Department of Counseling and Psychological Services, Atlanta, GA 30314. Offers programs in counseling (MA, PhD), education psychology (MA). Students: 83 full-time (67 women), 62 part-time (51 women); includes 142 minority (all African Americans), 2 international. In 1997, 59 master's, 3 doctorates awarded. *Degree requirements:* For master's, 1 foreign language (computer language can substitute), thesis; for doctorate, 2 foreign languages (computer language can substitute for one), dissertation. *Entrance requirements:* For master's, GRE General Test, minimum undergraduate GPA of 2.5; for doctorate, GRE General Test, minimum graduate GPA of 3.0. Application deadline: 4/1 (rolling processing; 11/1 for spring admission). Application fee: $30. *Expenses:* Tuition $9672 per year full-time, $403 per credit hour part-time. Fees $200 per year. *Financial aid:* Career-related internships or fieldwork available. Financial aid application deadline: 4/30. • Dr. Lloyd Williams, Interim Chairperson, 404-880-8516. Application contact: Michelle Clark-Davis, Graduate Program Assistant, 404-880-8709.

The College of Saint Rose, School of Education, Educational and School Psychology Department, Program in Educational Psychology, Albany, NY 12203-1419. Awards MS Ed. Part-time and evening/weekend programs available. Faculty: 7 full-time (3 women). Students: 6 full-time (5 women), 46 part-time (35 women); includes 1 minority (Asian American). Average age 31. In 1997, 30 degrees awarded. *Degree requirements:* Thesis or alternative, research seminar project required, foreign language not required. *Entrance requirements:* Minimum undergraduate GPA of 3.0. Application deadline: 7/15 (priority date; rolling processing; 12/1 for spring admission). Application fee: $30. *Expenses:* Tuition $338 per credit. Fees $60 per year. *Financial aid:* Research assistantships, partial tuition waivers, and career-related internships or fieldwork available. Aid available to part-time students. Financial aid application deadline: 3/1; applicants required to submit FAFSA. • Application contact: Graduate Office, 518-454-5136. Fax: 518-458-5479. E-mail: ace@rosnet.strose.edu.

Cornell University, Graduate Fields of Agriculture and Life Sciences, Field of Education, Ithaca, NY 14853-0001. Offerings include educational psychology and measurement (MPS, MS, PhD). Terminal master's awarded for partial completion of doctoral program. Faculty: 26 full-time. *Degree requirements:* For doctorate, dissertation required, foreign language not required. *Entrance requirements:* For doctorate, GRE General Test or MAT, TOEFL. Application deadline: 5/1. Application fee: $65. Electronic applications accepted. • Director of Graduate Studies, 607-255-4278. Application contact: Graduate Field Assistant, 607-255-4278. E-mail: edgrfld@cornell.edu.

Dalhousie University, School of Education, Halifax, NS B3H 3J5, Canada. Offerings include educational psychology (MA, M Ed). Program being phased out; applicants no longer accepted. School faculty: 19 full-time, 12 part-time. *Degree requirements:* Thesis required (for some programs), foreign language not required. • Dr. K. C. Sullivan, Director, 902-494-3724.

Eastern College, Programs in Counseling, Program in Educational Counseling, St. Davids, PA 19087-3696. Offerings include school psychology (MS). *Application deadline:* rolling. *Application fee:* $35. • Lynn Brandsma, Head, 610-341-1484. Application contact: Megan Miscioscia, Graduate Admissions Representative, 610-341-5972. Fax: 610-341-1466.

Eastern Illinois University, College of Education and Professional Studies, Department of Educational Psychology and Guidance, 600 Lincoln Avenue, Charleston, IL 61920-3099. Awards MS Ed, Ed S. Accredited by NCATE. Ed S being phased out; applicants no longer accepted. Part-time and evening/weekend programs available. Faculty: 8 full-time (2 women). Students: 78 full-time (53 women), 137 part-time (108 women); includes 26 minority (24 African Americans, 2 Hispanics). In 1997, 77 master's, 1 Ed S awarded. *Degree requirements:* For master's, comprehensive exam required, foreign language and thesis not required; for Ed S, thesis required, foreign language not required. *Entrance requirements:* For master's, GRE General Test or MAT. Application deadline: 7/31 (priority date; rolling processing). Application fee: $25. *Expenses:* Tuition $3459 per year full-time, $96 per semester hour part-time for state residents; $10,377 per year full-time, $288 per semester hour part-time for nonresidents. Fees $1566 per year full-time, $37 per semester hour part-time. *Financial aid:* In 1997–98, 4 research assistantships were awarded. • Dr. Lynda Kayser, Chairperson, 217-581-2400. Fax: 217-581-7417. E-mail: cflk2@eiu.edu.

Eastern Michigan University, College of Education, Department of Teacher Education, Program in Educational Psychology, Ypsilanti, MI 48197. Awards MA. Accredited by NCATE. Evening/weekend programs available. In 1997, 20 degrees awarded. *Degree requirements:* Thesis or alternative required, foreign language not required. *Entrance requirements:* GRE, TOEFL (minimum score 500). Application deadline: 5/15 (rolling processing; 3/15 for spring admission). Application fee: $30. *Expenses:* Tuition $2691 per year full-time, $150 per credit hour part-time for state residents; $6300 per year full-time, $350 per credit hour part-time for nonresidents. Fees $368 per year full-time, $88 per semester (minimum) part-time. *Financial aid:* Fellowships, teaching assistantships available. Aid available to part-time students. Financial aid application deadline: 3/15; applicants required to submit FAFSA. • Dr. Sarah Huyvaert, Coordinator, 734-487-1410.

Edinboro University of Pennsylvania, School of Education, Department of Special Education and School Psychology, Program in Educational Psychology, Edinboro, PA 16444. Awards M Ed. Evening/weekend programs available. Students: 25 full-time (20 women), 13 part-time (11 women); includes 2 minority (1 African American, 1 Hispanic). Average age 27. In 1997, 12 degrees awarded. *Degree requirements:* Thesis optional, foreign language not required. *Entrance requirements:* GRE or MAT (score in 30th percentile or higher). Application deadline: rolling. Application fee: $25. *Expenses:* Tuition $3468 per year full-time, $193 per credit part-time for state residents; $6236 per year full-time, $346 per credit part-time for nonresidents. Fees $898 per year full-time, $50 per semester (minimum) part-time. *Financial aid:* In 1997–98, 14 assistantships were awarded. • Application contact: Dr. Philip Kerstetter, Dean of Graduate Studies, 814-732-2856. Fax: 814-732-2611. E-mail: kerstetter@edinboro.edu.

Florida State University, College of Education, Department of Educational Research, Program in Educational Psychology, Tallahassee, FL 32306. Offers learning and cognition (MS, PhD, Ed S), measurement and statistics (MS, PhD, Ed S), program evaluation (MS, PhD, Ed S), sports psychology (MS, PhD, Ed S). Faculty: 7 full-time (1 woman), 2 part-time (0 women). Students: 22 full-time (9 women), 29 part-time (15 women); includes 15 minority (3 African Americans, 7 Asian Americans, 4 Hispanics, 1 Native American). 60 applicants, 50% accepted. In 1997, 4 master's, 5 doctorates awarded. *Degree requirements:* For master's and Ed S, comprehensive exam required, thesis optional; for doctorate, dissertation, comprehensive exam. *Entrance requirements:* GRE General Test (minimum combined score of 1000), minimum GPA of 3.0. Application deadline: 7/1 (priority date; rolling processing; 11/1 for spring admission). Application fee: $20. *Tuition:* $139 per credit hour for state residents; $482 per credit hour for nonresidents. *Financial aid:* Fellowships, research assistantships, teaching assistantships, and career-related internships or fieldwork available. • Dr. Marcy Driscoll, Chair, Department of Educational Research, 850-644-4592. E-mail: driscoll@mail.coe.fsu.edu. Application contact: Admissions Secretary, 850-644-4592. Fax: 850-644-8776.

Fordham University, Graduate School of Education, Division of Psychological and Educational Services, New York, NY 10023. Offers programs in counseling and personnel services (MSE, Adv C), counseling psychology (PhD), educational psychology (MSE, PhD), school psychology (PhD), urban and urban bilingual school psychology (Adv C). Accredited by NCATE. One or more programs accredited by APA. Students: 32 full-time (25 women), 319 part-time (249 women); includes 40 minority (32 African Americans, 7 Asian Americans, 1 Hispanic), 8 international. In 1997, 89 master's, 17 doctorates awarded. *Entrance requirements:* For doctorate, GRE General Test. Application fee: $50. • Dr. Giselle Esquivel, Chairman, 212-636-6460.

Georgia State University, College of Education, Department of Educational Psychology and Special Education, Program in Educational Psychology, Atlanta, GA 30303-3083. Awards MS, PhD. One or more programs accredited by APA. Accredited by NCATE. Part-time and evening/weekend programs available. Students: 11 full-time (7 women), 16 part-time (15 women); includes 6 minority (4 African Americans, 1 Asian American, 1 Hispanic), 1 international. Average age 40. 10 applicants, 50% accepted. In 1997, 7 master's, 3 doctorates awarded. *Degree requirements:* For master's, thesis or project; for doctorate, dissertation, comprehensive exam. *Entrance requirements:* For master's, GRE General Test (minimum combined score of 900), minimum GPA of 2.5; for doctorate, GRE General Test (minimum score 500 on verbal section, 500 on either quantitative or analytical sections) or MAT (minimum score 53), minimum GPA of 3.3. Application fee: $25. *Expenses:* Tuition $2673 per year full-time, $99 per semester hour part-time for state residents; $10,692 per year full-time, $396 per semester hour part-time for nonresidents. Fees $228 per year. *Financial aid:* Research assistantships, teaching assistantships available. *Faculty research:* Cognitive and language development, language development of deaf children, reading in adult populations. • Dr. Ron P. Colarusso, Chair, Department of Educational Psychology and Special Education, 404-651-2310.

Graduate School and University Center of the City University of New York, Program in Educational Psychology, New York, NY 10036-8099. Awards PhD. Faculty: 19 full-time (9 women). Students: 68 full-time (50 women), 7 part-time (all women). Average age 38. 102 applicants, 30% accepted. In 1997, 5 doctorates awarded. Terminal master's awarded for partial completion of doctoral program. *Degree requirements:* For doctorate, 2 foreign languages, dissertation. *Entrance requirements:* For doctorate, GRE General Test, interview, minimum GPA of 3.0. Application deadline: 4/1. Application fee: $40. *Expenses:* Tuition $4350 per year full-time, $185 per credit (minimum) part-time for state residents; $7600 per year full-time, $320 per credit (minimum) part-time for nonresidents. Fees $69 per year. *Financial aid:* In 1997–98, 26 students received aid, including 19 fellowships (4 to first-year students); research assistantships, teaching assistantships, full and partial tuition waivers, Federal Work-Study, institutionally sponsored loans, and career-related internships or fieldwork also available. Financial aid application deadline: 2/1; applicants required to submit FAFSA. • Dr. Alan Gross, Executive Officer, 212-642-2261.

Harvard University, Graduate School of Education, Area of Human Development and Psychology, Cambridge, MA 02138. Offers programs in acquisition of language and culture (Ed M), children and adolescents at risk (Ed M), cognitive development (Ed M), human development and psychology (Ed M, Ed D, CAS), individualized program (Ed M), language and literacy (Ed M, Ed D, CAS), methodology in developmental research (Ed M), risk and prevention (CAS). Part-time programs available. Faculty: 13 full-time (7 women), 33 part-time (12 women), 22.9 FTE. Students: 215 full-time (175 women), 49 part-time (38 women); includes 55 minority (18 African Americans, 11 Asian Americans, 20 Hispanics, 6 Native Americans), 35 international. Average age 34. 177 applicants, 20% accepted. In 1997, 102 master's, 28 doctorates, 12 CASs awarded. Terminal master's awarded for partial completion of doctoral program. *Degree requirements:* For doctorate, dissertation required, foreign language not required. *Average time to degree:* master's–1.1 years full-time, 2 years part-time; doctorate–6 years full-time, 7.8 years part-time; other advanced degree–1 year full-time, 3 years part-time. *Entrance requirements:* GRE General Test, TOEFL (minimum score 600), TWE (minimum score 5.0). Application deadline: 1/2. Application fee: $60. *Financial aid:* In 1997–98, 119 students received aid, including 26 fellowships (14 to first-year students) totaling $458,544, 26 research assistantships averaging $588 per month, 72 teaching assistantships averaging $670 per month, 77 need-based scholarships (12 to first-year students) totaling $656,012; Federal Work-Study and career-related internships or fieldwork also available. Aid available to part-time students. Financial aid application deadline: 1/8; applicants required to submit FAFSA. *Faculty research:* Educational technologies; reading, writing, and language; risk and prevention of developmental and educational problems; bilingualism and multicultural education; gender difference in development. • Catherine Snow, Chair, 617-495-3563. Application contact: Roland Hence, Director of Admissions, 617-495-3414. Fax: 617-496-3577. E-mail: gseadmissions@harvard.edu.

Howard University, School of Education, Department of Human Development and Psychoeducational Studies, Program in Educational Psychology, 2400 Sixth Street, NW, Washington, DC 20059-0002. Awards MA, M Ed, Ed D, PhD, CAGS. Accredited by NCATE. MA and PhD offered through the Graduate School of Arts and Sciences. Faculty: 15. Students: 19. In 1997, 1 master's awarded. *Degree requirements:* For master's, thesis or alternative, comprehensive exam, expository writing exam required, foreign language not required; for doctorate, 1 foreign language, dissertation, comprehensive exam, expository writing exam, internship. *Average time to degree:* master's–2 years full-time, 4 years part-time. *Entrance requirements:* For master's, GRE General Test, minimum GPA of 2.7; for doctorate, GRE General Test, minimum GPA of 3.4; for CAGS, GRE General Test, minimum graduate GPA of 3.0. Application deadline: 4/1 (priority date; rolling processing; 11/1 for spring admission). Application fee: $45. *Expenses:* Tuition $10,200 per year full-time, $567 per credit hour part-time. Fees $405 per year. *Financial aid:* Fellowships, research assistantships, teaching assistantships, grants, scholarships, full and partial tuition waivers, Federal Work-Study, institutionally sponsored loans, and career-related internships or fieldwork available. Financial aid application deadline: 4/30. • Dr. James H. Williams, Coordinator, 202-806-7350.

Illinois State University, College of Arts and Sciences, Department of Psychology, Normal, IL 61790-2200. Offerings include psychology (MA, MS), with options in clinical psychology, counseling psychology, developmental psychology, educational psychology, experimental psychology, measurement-evaluation, organizational-industrial psychology. Department faculty: 27 full-time (7 women), 1 part-time (0 women), 27.5 FTE. *Degree requirements:* Thesis or alternative. *Entrance requirements:* GRE General Test, GRE Subject Test, minimum GPA of 3.0 in last 60 hours. Application deadline: rolling. Application fee: $0. *Expenses:* Tuition $2454 per year full-time, $102 per hour part-time for state residents; $7362 per year full-time, $307 per hour part-time for nonresidents. Fees $1048 per year full-time, $44 per hour part-time. • Dr. Larry Alferink, Chairperson, 309-438-8651.

Indiana State University, School of Education, Department of Educational and School Psychology, Terre Haute, IN 47809-1401. Offers programs in educational psychology (MA, MS), school psychology (M Ed, PhD, Ed S). Accredited by NCATE. One or more programs accredited by APA. Faculty: 13 full-time (6 women). Students: 30 full-time (20 women), 15 part-time (10 women); includes 5 minority (3 African Americans, 1 Asian American, 1 Native American), 4 international. Average age 31. 37 applicants, 41% accepted. In 1997, 3 master's, 4 doctorates, 8 Ed Ss awarded. *Degree requirements:* For doctorate, computer language, dissertation required, foreign language not required; for Ed S, individual research project required, foreign language and thesis not required. *Entrance requirements:* For master's, GRE General Test (minimum score 450 on each section), minimum undergraduate GPA of 2.5; for doctorate, GRE General Test (minimum score 500 on each section), minimum graduate GPA of 3.5; for Ed S, GRE General Test (minimum score 450 on each section), minimum graduate GPA of 3.25. Application deadline: rolling. Application fee: $20. *Tuition:* $143 per credit hour for state residents; $325 per credit hour for nonresidents. *Financial aid:* In 1997–98, 11 fellowships (3 to first-year students), 17 research assistantships (2 to first-year students) were awarded; teaching assistantships, assistantships, Federal Work-Study, institutionally sponsored loans, and career-related internships or fieldwork also available. Financial aid application deadline: 3/1. *Faculty research:* Cognitive behavior modification, moral development, emotional handicaps, personality assessments, human development. • Dr. David Andrews, Acting Chairperson, 812-237-2887.

Indiana University Bloomington, School of Education, Department of Counseling and Educational Psychology, Program in Educational Psychology, Bloomington, IN 47405. Offers educational psychology (MS, Ed D, PhD), school psychology (Ed S). PhD offered through the University Graduate School. Students: 40 full-time (29 women), 55 part-time (42 women); includes 11 minority (3 African Americans, 4 Asian Americans, 3 Hispanics, 1 Native American), 19 international. In 1997, 11 master's, 7 doctorates awarded. Terminal master's awarded for partial completion of doctoral program. *Degree requirements:* For master's, thesis optional, foreign language not required; for doctorate, dissertation required, foreign language not required; for Ed S, comprehensive exam or project required, foreign language and thesis not required. *Entrance requirements:* For master's and Ed S, GRE General Test (minimum combined score of 1300 on three sections); for doctorate, GRE General Test (minimum combined score of 1600 on three sections). Application deadline: 6/1. Application fee: $35. *Expenses:* Tuition $153 per credit hour for state residents; $446 per credit hour for nonresidents. Fees $343 per year. *Financial aid:* Fellowships, teaching assistantships, graduate assistantships, full and partial tuition waivers, Federal Work-Study, institutionally sponsored loans, and career-related internships or fieldwork available. Aid available to part-time students. *Faculty research:* Attitude and value measurement, truancy, child art, teacher effectiveness, rural school psychology. • Dr. Jack Cummings, Chairperson, Department of Counseling and Educational Psychology, 812-856-8300. Application contact: Brenda Helms, Administrative Assistant, 812-856-8300. Fax: 812-856-8333.

Indiana University of Pennsylvania, College of Education, Department of Educational and School Psychology, Program in Educational Psychology, Indiana, PA 15705-1087. Awards M Ed, Certificate. Accredited by NCATE. Part-time and evening/weekend programs available. Students: 13 full-time (11 women), 9 part-time (6 women); includes 2 minority (1 African American, 1 Native American). Average age 30. 24 applicants, 54% accepted. In 1997, 12 master's awarded. *Degree requirements:* For master's, thesis optional, foreign language not required. *Entrance requirements:* GRE General Test, GRE Subject Test, TOEFL (minimum score 500). Application deadline: 7/1 (priority date; rolling processing; 11/1 for spring admission). Application fee: $30. *Expenses:* Tuition $3468 per year full-time, $193 per credit part-time for state residents; $6236 per year full-time, $346 per credit part-time for nonresidents. Fees $313 per year (minimum) full-time, $84 per year part-time. *Financial aid:* Research assistantships, Federal Work-Study, and career-related internships or fieldwork available. Aid available to part-time students. Financial aid application deadline: 3/15. • Dr. Mary Ann Rafoth, Graduate Coordinator, 724-357-3784.

John Carroll University, Department of Education and Allied Studies, Program in Educational Psychology, University Heights, OH 44118-4581. Awards MA, M Ed. Accredited by NCATE. Faculty: 6 full-time (3 women), 4 part-time (2 women). Students: 21 full-time (all women), 9 part-time (all women); includes 4 minority (3 African Americans, 1 Asian American). In 1997, 7 degrees awarded. *Degree requirements:* Comprehensive exam, research essay or thesis required, foreign language not required. *Entrance requirements:* GRE General Test or MAT, minimum GPA of 2.75. Application deadline: 8/15 (priority date; rolling processing; 1/3 for spring admission). Application fee: $25 ($35 for international students). *Tuition:* $450 per credit. *Financial aid:* Teaching assistantships, partial tuition waivers available. Financial aid application deadline: 3/1; applicants required to submit FAFSA. • Dr. Christopher M. Faiver, Coordinator, 216-397-3001.

Kansas State University, College of Education, Department of Counseling and Educational Psychology, Manhattan, KS 66506. Offers programs in counselor education (Ed D, PhD), educational psychology (Ed D), school counseling (MS), student affairs in higher education (PhD), student personnel services (MS). Accredited by NCATE. Faculty: 8 full-time (1 woman), 3 part-time (1 woman), 8.9 FTE. Students: 16 full-time (11 women), 72 part-time (51 women); includes 3 minority (1 African American, 2 Hispanics), 3 international. 46 applicants, 57% accepted. *Degree requirements:* For master's, thesis or alternative required, foreign language not required; for doctorate, dissertation required, foreign language not required. *Entrance requirements:* For master's, GRE General Test (minimum combined score of 1000; average 1021), MAT (minimum score 40; average 48), minimum B average; for doctorate, GRE General Test (minimum combined score of 1000; average 1106), minimum B average. Application deadline: 3/1 (priority date; rolling processing; 8/1 for spring admission). Application fee: $0 ($25 for international students). Electronic applications accepted. *Tuition:* $2218 per year full-time, $401 per semester (minimum) part-time for state residents; $6336 per year full-time, $1087 per semester (minimum) part-time for nonresidents. *Financial aid:* In 1997–98, teaching assistantships averaging $850 per month were awarded; research assistantships also available. • Michael Dannells, Chair, 785-532-5541. Application contact: Paul Burden, Assistant Dean, 785-532-5595. Fax: 785-532-7304. E-mail: gradstudy@mail.educ.ksu.edu.

Kean University, School of Liberal Arts, Department of Psychology, Union, NJ 07083. Offerings include educational psychology (MA). Accredited by NCATE. *Degree requirements:* Thesis, comprehensive exams required, foreign language not required. *Entrance requirements:* GRE General Test. Application deadline: 6/15 (11/15 for spring admission). Application fee: $35. *Tuition:* $5926 per year full-time, $248 per credit part-time for state residents; $7312 per year full-time, $304 per credit part-time for nonresidents. • Dr. Henry L. Kaplowitz, Graduate Coordinator, 908-527-2598. Application contact: Joanne Morris, Director of Graduate Admissions, 908-527-2665. Fax: 908-527-2286. E-mail: grad_adm@turbo.kean.edu.

Kent State University, Graduate School of Education, Department of Educational Foundations and Special Services, Program in Educational Foundations, Kent, OH 44242-0001. Offerings include educational psychology (MA, M Ed). Accredited by NCATE. Program faculty: 8 full-time (3 women), 15 part-time (10 women). *Degree requirements:* Thesis (MA) required, foreign language not required. *Entrance requirements:* GRE General Test. Application deadline: rolling. Application fee: $30. *Tuition:* $4752 per year full-time, $216 per credit hour part-time for state residents; $9213 per year full-time, $419 per credit hour part-time for nonresidents. • Dr. Averil McClelland, Coordinator, 330-672-2294. Application contact: Deborah Barber, Director, Office of Academic Services, 330-672-2862. Fax: 330-672-3549.

La Sierra University, School of Education, Department of Educational Psychology and Counseling, Riverside, CA 92515-8247. Offers programs in counseling (MA), educational psychology (Ed S), school psychology (Ed S). Part-time and evening/weekend programs available. Faculty: 3 full-time (1 woman), 4 part-time (2 women), 4 FTE. Students: 27. Average age 35. In 1997, 4 master's, 4 Ed Ss awarded. *Degree requirements:* For master's, thesis optional, foreign language not required; for Ed S, practicum (educational psychology) required, foreign language and thesis not required. *Entrance requirements:* For master's, California Basic Educational Skills Test, NTE, minimum GPA of 3.0; for Ed S, minimum GPA of 3.3. Application deadline: rolling. Application fee: $30. *Financial aid:* Graduate assistantships, Federal Work-Study, institutionally sponsored loans, and career-related internships or fieldwork available. Aid available to part-time students. Financial aid application deadline: 2/10. *Faculty research:* Equivalent score scales, self perception. • Dr. Roger Handysides, Chair, 909-785-2267. Application contact: Myrna Costa-Casado, Director of Admissions, 909-785-2176. Fax: 909-785-2447. E-mail: mcosta@lasierra.edu.

Lindsey Wilson College, Department of Human Services, Columbia, KY 42728-1298. Offerings include counseling and human development (M Ed). Department faculty: 4 full-time (2 women), 1 part-time (0 women). *Application deadline:* rolling. *Application fee:* $30. *Tuition:* $8640 per year full-time, $480 per hour part-time. • Dr. John Rigney, Chair, 800-264-0138. Fax: 502-384-8200.

Loyola Marymount University, School of Education, Program in Educational Psychology, Los Angeles, CA 90045-8350. Offers school psychology (MA). Part-time and evening/weekend programs available. Faculty: 14 full-time (8 women), 25 part-time (20 women). Students: 19 full-time (18 women), 5 part-time (all women); includes 5 minority (3 Asian Americans, 2 Hispanics). In 1997, 8 degrees awarded. *Degree requirements:* Comprehensive exam required, foreign language and thesis not required. *Entrance requirements:* GRE General Test, TOEFL (minimum score 550), interview. Application fee: $35. Electronic applications accepted. *Expenses:* Tuition $500 per unit. Fees $111 per year full-time, $28 per year part-time. *Financial aid:* In 1997–98, 5 students received aid, including 2 grants totaling $3,000. Aid available to part-time students. Financial aid application deadline: 3/2; applicants required to submit FAFSA. • Dr. Scott Kester, Coordinator, 310-338-7308.

Loyola University Chicago, School of Education, Department of Curriculum, Instruction and Educational Psychology, Program in Educational Psychology, 820 North Michigan Avenue, Chicago, IL 60611-2196. Awards MA, M Ed, PhD. MA and PhD offered through the Graduate School. Students: 48. *Degree requirements:* For master's, comprehensive exam required, foreign language not required; for doctorate, computer language, dissertation, comprehensive exam required, foreign language not required. *Average time to degree:* master's–2 years full-time, 3 years part-time; doctorate–3 years full-time, 5 years part-time. *Entrance requirements:* For master's, GRE or MAT; for doctorate, GRE or MAT, interview. Application deadline: 2/15 (10/15 for spring admission). Application fee: $35. *Tuition:* $467 per semester hour. *Financial aid:* Application deadline 5/1. • Dr. Ronald Morgan, Director, 847-853-3332. Application contact: Marie Rosin-Dittmar, Admissions Coordinator, 847-853-3323. Fax: 847-853-3375. E-mail: mrosind@wpo.it.luc.edu.

Marist College, Division of Social/Behavioral Sciences, 290 North Road, Poughkeepsie, NY 12601-1387. Offerings include education psychology (MA). Division faculty: 8 full-time (3 women), 14 part-time (4 women). *Degree requirements:* Thesis optional, foreign language not required. *Entrance requirements:* GRE General Test. Application deadline: 8/1 (priority date; rolling processing; 12/15 for spring admission). Application fee: $30. *Expenses:* Tuition $419 per credit hour. Fees $50 per year (minimum). • Dr. William Eidle, Dean, 914-575-3000 Ext. 2960. Application contact: Dr. H. Griffin Walling, Dean of Graduate and Continuing Education, 914-575-3530. Fax: 914-575-3640.

McGill University, Faculty of Graduate Studies and Research, Faculty of Education, Department of Educational and Counseling Psychology, Program in Educational Psychology, Montréal, PQ H3A 2T5, Canada. Awards MA, M Ed, PhD. Part-time and evening/weekend programs available. Faculty: 25 full-time (13 women), 16 part-time (14 women). Students: 85 full-time (60 women), 123 part-time (103 women); includes 11 international. Average age 32. 67 applicants, 73% accepted. In 1997, 47 master's awarded; 3 doctorates awarded (100% entered university research/teaching). *Degree requirements:* For master's, thesis required (for some programs), foreign language not required; for doctorate, dissertation required, foreign language not required. *Entrance requirements:* For master's, TOEFL (minimum score 550), minimum GPA of 3.0; for doctorate, TOEFL (minimum score 550). Application deadline: 2/1. Application fee: $60. *Expenses:* Tuition $1668 per year for Canadian residents; $8268 per year for nonresidents. Fees $828 per year for Canadian residents; $1216 per year for nonresidents. *Financial aid:* Fellowships, research assistantships, teaching assistantships, full tuition waivers, institutionally sponsored loans, and career-related internships or fieldwork available. *Faculty research:*

Directory: Educational Psychology

McGill University (continued)

Cognitive, instructional design, special education, computers in education. • Evelyn Lusthaus, Director, 514-398-4240 Ext. 3437. E-mail: lusthaue@education.mcgill.ca. Application contact: Geraldine Norton, Secretary, 514-398-4244. Fax: 514-398-6968. E-mail: norton@education.mcgill.ca.

Memorial University of Newfoundland, School of Graduate Studies, Faculty of Education, St. John's, NF A1C 5S7, Canada. Offerings include psychology (M Ed). *Degree requirements:* Comprehensive exam required, foreign language not required. *Application deadline:* 2/1. *Application fee:* $40. *Expenses:* Tuition $1896 per year (minimum). Fees $60 per year for Canadian residents; $621 per year for nonresidents. • Dr. Terry Piper, Dean, 709-737-8588. E-mail: tpiper@kean.ucs.mun.ca. Application contact: Dr. Linda M. Phillips, Associate Dean, 709-737-3402. E-mail: lindap@morgan.ucs.mun.ca.

Miami University, School of Education and Allied Professions, Department of Educational Psychology, Oxford, OH 45056. Offers programs in educational psychology (M Ed), school psychology (MS, Ed S), special education (M Ed). Accredited by NCATE. Faculty: 17. Students: 37 full-time (28 women), 24 part-time (23 women); includes 1 minority (African American). 7 applicants, 100% accepted. In 1997, 2 master's awarded. *Degree requirements:* For master's, thesis or alternative, oral or written exam required, foreign language not required; for Ed S, oral or written exam required, foreign language and thesis not required. *Entrance requirements:* For master's, GRE General Test or MAT, minimum undergraduate GPA of 3.0 during previous 2 years or 2.75 overall; for Ed S, GRE General Test or MAT. Application deadline: 3/1 (priority date; rolling processing; 12/1 for spring admission). Application fee: $35. *Tuition:* $5932 per year full-time, $255 per credit hour part-time for state residents; $12,392 per year full-time, $524 per credit hour part-time for nonresidents. *Financial aid:* Fellowships, research assistantships, teaching assistantships, full tuition waivers, Federal Work-Study, and career-related internships or fieldwork available. Financial aid application deadline: 3/1. • Dr. Alex Thomas, Chair, 513-529-6621.

Michigan State University, College of Education, Department of Counseling, Educational Psychology and Special Education, East Lansing, MI 48824-1020. Offerings include educational psychology (MA, PhD). One or more programs accredited by APA. Department faculty: 42 (14 women). *Degree requirements:* For doctorate, dissertation required, foreign language not required. *Entrance requirements:* For master's, GRE General Test (combined average 1500 on three sections); for doctorate, GRE General Test (combined average 1800 on three sections). Application deadline: rolling. Application fee: $30 ($40 for international students). *Expenses:* Tuition $4609 per year full-time, $223 per credit hour (minimum) part-time for state residents; $8704 per year full-time, $450 per credit hour (minimum) part-time for nonresidents. Fees $576 per year full-time, $476 per year part-time. • Dr. Richard Prawat, Chairperson, 517-353-6417. Application contact: Sharon Anderson, Graduate Secretary, 517-355-6683. Fax: 517-353-6393. E-mail: sharand@msu.edu.

Minot State University, Program in Psychology, Minot, ND 58707-0002. Awards Ed Sp. Faculty: 5 full-time (2 women), 3 part-time (1 woman). Students: 9 full-time (7 women), 9 part-time (all women); includes 3 minority (all Native Americans). Average age 31. 13 applicants, 69% accepted. In 1997, 7 degrees awarded. *Entrance requirements:* GRE General Test (minimum combined score of 1100 rquired) or minimum GPA of 3.0. Application deadline: 3/1 (rolling processing). Application fee: $25. *Tuition:* $2714 per year for state residents; $3235 per year (minimum) for nonresidents. *Financial aid:* In 1997–98, 11 teaching assistantships (9 to first-year students) averaging $571 per month and totaling $132,000 were awarded; research assistantships, institutionally sponsored loans, and career-related internships or fieldwork also available. Aid available to part-time students. Financial aid application deadline: 4/1. *Faculty research:* Oppositional defiance disorder and autism, experimental psychology, statistical genetics, adults with developmental disabilities, psychopharmacology. • Dr. Donald Burke, Chairperson, 701-858-3138. Application contact: Tammy White, Administrative Secretary, 701-858-3250. Fax: 701-839-6933.

Mississippi State University, College of Education, Department of Counselor Education and Educational Psychology, Mississippi State, MS 39762. Offers programs in counselor education (MS), including community counseling, counseling services, rehabilitation, school counseling, student development services; general education psychology (MS), including research and evaluation. Accredited by NCATE. Part-time programs available. Faculty: 17 full-time (7 women), 7 part-time (2 women). Students: 126 full-time (106 women), 85 part-time (70 women); includes 64 minority (63 African Americans, 1 Asian American), 1 international. Average age 33. 158 applicants, 93% accepted. In 1997, 83 degrees awarded. *Degree requirements:* Comprehensive oral or written exam required, thesis optional, foreign language not required. *Entrance requirements:* GRE, minimum QPA of 3.0 in last 2 years. Application deadline: 3/1. Application fee: $0 ($25 for international students). *Tuition:* $3017 per year full-time, $168 per credit hour part-time for state residents; $6119 per year full-time, $340 per credit hour part-time for nonresidents. *Financial aid:* In 1997–98, 2 research assistantships (both to first-year students), 8 teaching assistantships (all to first-year students) were awarded; Federal Work-Study, institutionally sponsored loans, and career-related internships or fieldwork also available. Aid available to part-time students. Financial aid application deadline: 3/1. *Faculty research:* Counselor evaluation, personal development and counselor effectiveness, counselor ethics, disabled work adjustment, substance abuse, school counselor supervison. • Dr. Tom Hosie, Head, 601-325-3426. Fax: 601-325-3263. E-mail: hosie@colled.msstate.edu.

Mississippi State University, College of Education, Program Under Dean of Education, Mississippi State, MS 39762. Offerings include general education psychology (PhD). Accredited by NCATE. *Tuition:* $3017 per year full-time, $168 per credit hour part-time for state residents; $6119 per year full-time, $340 per credit hour part-time for nonresidents. • Dr. William H. Graves, Dean, College of Education, 601-325-3717. Fax: 601-325-8784. E-mail: whg1@ra.msstate.edu.

Montclair State University, College of Humanities and Social Sciences, Department of Psychology, Program in Educational Psychology, Upper Montclair, NJ 07043-1624. Awards MA. Accredited by NCATE. Part-time and evening/weekend programs available. Faculty: 30 full-time. Students: 28 full-time (23 women), 25 part-time (23 women); includes 10 minority (1 African American, 9 Hispanics), 1 international. In 1997, 9 degrees awarded. *Degree requirements:* Comprehensive exam. *Entrance requirements:* GRE General Test (minimum score 400 on each section), GRE Subject Test, MAT, previous course work in psychology. Application deadline: 3/1 (rolling processing; 10/1 for spring admission). Application fee: $40. *Expenses:* Tuition $201 per credit for state residents; $257 per credit for nonresidents. Fees $22.05 per credit. *Financial aid:* Application deadline 3/1; applicants required to submit FAFSA. • Dr. Luis Montesinos, Adviser, 973-655-7634.

Morehead State University, College of Education and Behavioral Sciences, Department of Leadership and Secondary Education, Morehead, KY 40351. Offerings include educational psychology and counseling (Ed D). Accredited by NCATE. Ed D offered jointly with the University of Kentucky. Department faculty: 12 full-time (6 women), 7 part-time (3 women). *Application deadline:* 8/1 (priority date; rolling processing; 12/1 for spring admission). *Application fee:* $0. *Tuition:* $2470 per year full-time, $138 per semester hour part-time for state residents; $6710 per year full-time, $373 per semester hour part-time for nonresidents. • Dr. Deborah Grubb, Chair, 606-783-5207. Application contact: Betty Cowsert, Graduate Admissions Officer, 606-783-2039. Fax: 606-783-5061.

Mount Saint Vincent University, Department of Education, Program in Educational Psychology, Halifax, NS B3M 2J6, Canada. Awards MA, MA Ed, MA(R), M Ed. Part-time and evening/weekend programs available. Students: 9 full-time (6 women), 24 part-time (17 women). Average age 37. 32 applicants, 84% accepted. In 1997, 14 degrees awarded. *Degree requirements:* Thesis. *Entrance requirements:* Bachelor's degree in related field, 1 year of teaching experience. Application deadline: 3/1 (priority date; rolling processing; 9/1 for spring admission). Application fee: $40. *Expenses:* Tuition $1024 per course. Fees $25 per course. *Financial aid:* In 1997–98, 3 fellowships (all to first-year students) totaling $11,500 were awarded. Financial aid application deadline: 5/1. *Faculty research:* Personality measurement, values reasoning, aggression and sexuality, power and control, quantitative and qualitative research methodologies. • Dr. James Manos, Program Head, 902-457-6328. Fax: 902-457-4911. E-mail: james.manos@msvu.ca. Application contact: Susan Tanner, Assistant Registrar, 902-457-6363. Fax: 902-457-6498. E-mail: susan.tanner@msvu.ca.

National–Louis University, National College of Education, McGaw Graduate School, Program in Educational Psychology/Human Learning and Development, 2840 Sheridan Road, Evanston, IL 60201-1730. Offers educational psychology (CAS), educational psychology/human learning and development (M Ed, MS Ed), educational psychology/school psychology (M Ed), school psychology (Ed S). Part-time and evening/weekend programs available. Students: 12 full-time (7 women), 44 part-time (37 women); includes 5 minority (3 African Americans, 1 Asian American, 1 Hispanic). Average age 38. In 1997, 21 master's, 6 other advanced degrees awarded. *Degree requirements:* For master's, thesis required, foreign language not required. *Entrance requirements:* For master's, GRE, minimum GPA of 3.0; for other advanced degree, GRE. Application deadline: 4/15 (rolling processing; 10/15 for spring admission). Application fee: $25. *Tuition:* $411 per semester hour. *Financial aid:* Fellowships, research assistantships available. Aid available to part-time students. Financial aid applicants required to submit FAFSA. • Dr. Philip Garber, Coordinator, 847-475-1100 Ext. 2553. Application contact: Dr. David McCulloch, Vice President for University Services, 800-443-5522 Ext. 5127. Fax: 847-465-0593. E-mail: dmcc@wheeling1.nl.edu.

National–Louis University, National College of Education, McGaw Graduate School, Doctoral Programs in Education, Program in Educational Psychology/Human Learning and Development, 2840 Sheridan Road, Evanston, IL 60201-1730. Awards Ed D. Part-time and evening/weekend programs available. Students: 1 (woman) full-time, 2 part-time (both women). Average age 44. *Degree requirements:* Dissertation, comprehensive exams, internship required, foreign language not required. *Entrance requirements:* GRE General Test, minimum GPA of 3.25. Application deadline: 12/15. Application fee: $25. *Tuition:* $411 per semester hour. *Financial aid:* Fellowships, research assistantships, teaching assistantships, Federal Work-Study, institutionally sponsored loans available. Aid available to part-time students. Financial aid application deadline: 4/15; applicants required to submit FAFSA. • Dr. Diane Salmon, Coordinator, 847-475-1100 Ext. 2726. Application contact: Dr. David McCulloch, Vice President for University Services, 800-443-5522 Ext. 5127. Fax: 847-465-0593. E-mail: dmcc@wheeling1.nl.edu.

New Jersey City University, School of Arts and Sciences, Department of Psychology, Program in Educational Psychology, Jersey City, NJ 07305-1957. Awards MA, PD. *Degree requirements:* For PD, summer internship or externship required, foreign language and thesis not required. *Entrance requirements:* For master's, GRE, TOEFL or MAT; for PD, GRE General Test, TOEFL. Application deadline: 8/1 (priority date; rolling processing; 12/1 for spring admission). Application fee: $0.

Northeastern University, Bouvé College of Pharmacy and Health Sciences Graduate School, Department of Counseling Psychology, Rehabilitation, and Special Education, Program in Applied Educational Psychology, Boston, MA 02115-5096. Offers school counseling (MS), school psychology (MS). Part-time programs available. Faculty: 5 full-time (3 women), 4 part-time (2 women). Students: 60 full-time (51 women), 9 part-time (all women). Average age 27. 117 applicants, 77% accepted. In 1997, 20 degrees awarded. *Entrance requirements:* GRE General Test or MAT. Application deadline: rolling. Application fee: $50. *Expenses:* Tuition $440 per credit hour. Fees $55 per quarter full-time, $13.25 per quarter part-time. *Financial aid:* Research assistantships, administrative assistantships, Federal Work-Study, and career-related internships or fieldwork available. Aid available to part-time students. Financial aid application deadline: 3/1; applicants required to submit FAFSA. *Faculty research:* Multicultural issues, assessment, early intervention, bilingual education. • Dr. Ena Vazquez-Nuttall, Program Director, 617-373-2708. Application contact: Bill Purnell, Director of Graduate Admissions, 617-373-2708. Fax: 617-373-4701. E-mail: w.purnell@nunet.neu.edu.

Northern Arizona University, Center for Excellence in Education, Program in Educational Psychology, Flagstaff, AZ 86011. Awards Ed D. *Degree requirements:* Computer language, dissertation required, foreign language not required. *Entrance requirements:* GRE General Test, GRE Subject Test. Application fee: $45. *Expenses:* Tuition $2088 per year full-time, $330 per semester (minimum) part-time for state residents; $8004 per year full-time, $1002 per semester (minimum) part-time for nonresidents. Fees $72 per year full-time, $18 per semester (minimum) part-time. • Dr. William Martin, Chair, 520-523-6757.

Northern Illinois University, College of Education, Department of Educational Psychology, Counseling, and Special Education, Program in Educational Psychology, De Kalb, IL 60115-2854. Awards MS Ed, Ed D. Accredited by NCATE. Part-time and evening/weekend programs available. Faculty: 14 full-time (6 women), 2 part-time (1 woman). Students: 12 full-time (10 women), 44 part-time (32 women); includes 8 minority (7 African Americans, 1 Hispanic), 5 international. Average age 39. 27 applicants, 44% accepted. In 1997, 7 master's, 3 doctorates awarded. *Degree requirements:* For master's, comprehensive exam required, thesis optional, foreign language not required; for doctorate, candidacy exam, dissertation defense required, foreign language not required. *Entrance requirements:* For master's, GRE General Test, TOEFL (minimum score 550), minimum GPA of 2.75; for doctorate, GRE General Test, TOEFL (minimum score 550), minimum GPA of 2.75 (undergraduate), 3.5 (graduate), master's degree. Application deadline: 6/1 (rolling processing; 11/1 for spring admission). Application fee: $30. *Tuition:* $3984 per year full-time, $154 per credit hour part-time for state residents; $8160 per year full-time, $328 per credit hour part-time for nonresidents. *Financial aid:* Fellowships, research assistantships, teaching assistantships, staff assistantships, full tuition waivers, Federal Work-Study, and career-related internships or fieldwork available. Aid available to part-time students. • Dr. Sarah Peterson, Faculty Chair, 815-753-8470.

Oklahoma State University, College of Education, Department of Applied Behavioral Studies, Stillwater, OK 74078. Offers programs in applied behavioral studies (MS, Ed D, PhD), counseling and student personnel (MS), educational psychology (PhD). Provisionally accredited by APA. Faculty: 23 full-time (11 women). Students: 81 full-time (57 women), 126 part-time (100 women); includes 21 minority (6 African Americans, 2 Asian Americans, 1 Hispanic, 12 Native Americans), 3 international. Average age 36. In 1997, 63 master's, 15 doctorates awarded. *Degree requirements:* For master's, thesis or alternative; for doctorate, dissertation. *Entrance requirements:* TOEFL (minimum score 550). Application deadline: 7/1 (priority date). Application fee: $25. *Financial aid:* In 1997–98, 33 students received aid, including 25 teaching assistantships (7 to first-year students) averaging $819 per month and totaling $184,170; partial tuition waivers, Federal Work-Study, and career-related internships or fieldwork also available. Aid available to part-time students. Financial aid application deadline: 3/1. • Dr. Dale Fuqua, Head, 405-744-6040.

Pennsylvania State University University Park Campus, College of Education, Department of Educational and School Psychology and Special Education, Program in Educational Psychology, University Park, PA 16802-1503. Awards MS, PhD. Accredited by APA and NCATE. Students: 15 full-time (9 women), 11 part-time (7 women). In 1997, 5 master's, 1 doctorate awarded. *Entrance requirements:* GRE General Test. Application fee: $40. *Expenses:* Tuition $6534 per year full-time, $276 per credit part-time for state residents; $13,460 per year full-time, $561 per credit part-time for nonresidents. Fees $252 per year (minimum) full-time, $43 per semester (minimum) part-time. • Dr. Robert J. Stevens, Professor in Charge, 814-863-2417.

Purdue University, School of Education, Department of Educational Studies, West Lafayette, IN 47907. Offerings include educational psychology (MS, MS Ed, PhD). Accredited by NCATE. Department faculty: 26 full-time (13 women), 23 part-time (14 women). *Degree requirements:* For master's, thesis optional; for doctorate, dissertation, oral and written exams. *Entrance* *requirements:* For master's, TOEFL (minimum score 550), minimum B average; for doctorate, GRE General Test (minimum score 500 on each section), TOEFL (minimum score 550). Application deadline: 2/1 (9/15 for spring admission). Application fee: $30. Electronic applications accepted. *Tuition:* $3500 per year full-time, $126 per credit hour part-time for state residents; $11,720 per year full-time, $387 per credit hour part-time for nonresidents. • Dr. D. H. Schunk, Head, 765-494-9170. Fax: 765-496-1228. E-mail: dschunk@purdue.edu. Application contact: Christine Larsen, Coordinator of Graduate Studies, 765-494-2345. Fax: 765-494-5832. E-mail: gradoffice@soe.purdue.edu.

Rhode Island College, School of Graduate Studies, School of Education and Human Development, Department of Counseling and Educational Psychology, Program in Educational Psychology, Providence, RI 02908-1924. Awards MA. Accredited by NCATE. Evening/weekend programs available. Faculty: 9 full-time (2 women), 8 part-time (5 women). Students: 6 full-time (5 women), 16 part-time (11 women). In 1997, 3 degrees awarded. *Entrance requirements:* GRE General Test or MAT. Application deadline: 4/1 (rolling processing). Application fee: $25. *Tuition:* $4064 per year full-time, $214 per credit part-time for state residents; $7658 per year full-time, $376 per credit part-time for nonresidents. *Financial aid:* Application deadline 4/1. • Dr. Mary Wellman, Head, 401-456-8023.

Rutgers, The State University of New Jersey, New Brunswick, Graduate School of Education, Department of Educational Psychology, Program in Learning Cognition and Development, New Brunswick, NJ 08903. Awards Ed M, Ed D. Part-time and evening/weekend programs available. Faculty: 6 full-time (3 women). Students: 8 full-time, 68 part-time; includes 14 minority (6 African Americans, 6 Asian Americans, 2 Hispanics), 4 international. In 1997, 11 master's, 2 doctorates awarded. Terminal master's awarded for partial completion of doctoral program. *Degree requirements:* For doctorate, dissertation. *Entrance requirements:* GRE General Test. Application deadline: 3/1 (11/1 for spring admission). Application fee: $40. *Expenses:* Tuition $6492 per year full-time, $268 per credit part-time for state residents; $9520 per year full-time, $395 per credit part-time for nonresidents. Fees $208 per year (minimum). *Financial aid:* Application deadline 3/1. *Faculty research:* Psychology of sex differences, cognitive development, cooperative learning, learning strategies, development of spatial cognition. • Dr. Angela O'Donnell, Coordinator, 732-932-7496 Ext. 305. Fax: 732-932-6829 Ext. 317.

Simon Fraser University, Faculty of Education, Program in Educational Psychology, Burnaby, BC V5A 1S6, Canada. Awards MA, M Ed, PhD. *Degree requirements:* For master's, thesis (for some programs), project or thesis required, foreign language not required; for doctorate, dissertation. *Entrance requirements:* For master's, TOEFL (minimum score 570), TWE (minimum score 5), or International English Language Test (minimum score 7.5), minimum GPA of 3.0; for doctorate, GRE, TOEFL (minimum score 570), TWE (minimum score 5) or International English Language Test (minimum score 7.5), master's degree or exceptional record in a bachelor's degree, minimum GPA of 3.5. Application fee: $55. *Expenses:* Tuition $768 per trimester. Fees $207 per year full-time, $61 per trimester part-time. • Application contact: Graduate Secretary, 604-291-4787. Fax: 604-291-3203.

Southern Illinois University at Carbondale, College of Education, Department of Educational Psychology and Special Education, Program in Educational Psychology, Carbondale, IL 62901-6806. Offers counselor education (MS Ed, PhD), educational psychology (PhD), human learning and development (MS Ed), measurement and statistics (PhD). Accredited by NCATE. Faculty: 18 full-time (5 women), 5 part-time (1 woman). Students: 97 full-time (63 women), 36 part-time (24 women); includes 17 minority (10 African Americans, 2 Asian Americans, 4 Hispanics, 1 Native American), 8 international. Average age 36. 39 applicants, 41% accepted. In 1997, 20 master's, 8 doctorates awarded. *Degree requirements:* Thesis/dissertation required, foreign language not required. *Entrance requirements:* For master's, GRE General Test, TOEFL (minimum score 550), minimum GPA of 2.7; for doctorate, TOEFL (minimum score 550), minimum GPA of 3.25. Application deadline: 6/15 (priority date; rolling processing). Application fee: $20. *Expenses:* Tuition $2964 per year full-time, $99 per semester hour part-time for state residents; $8892 per year full-time, $270 per semester hour part-time for nonresidents. Fees $1034 per year full-time, $298 per semester (minimum) part-time. *Financial aid:* In 1997–98, 2 fellowships (1 to a first-year student), 4 research assistantships, 43 teaching assistantships (1 to a first-year student) were awarded; full tuition waivers, Federal Work-Study, institutionally sponsored loans, and career-related internships or fieldwork also available. Aid available to part-time students. Financial aid application deadline: 5/1. *Faculty research:* Career development, problem solving, learning and instruction, cognitive development, family assessment. Total annual research expenditures: $10,000. • Application contact: Laurie Viernum, Graduate Secretary, 618-536-7763. Fax: 618-453-7110.

Stanford University, School of Education, Program in Psychological Studies, Stanford, CA 94305-9991. Offers child and adolescent development (PhD), counseling psychology (PhD), educational psychology (PhD), health psychology education (AM). One or more programs accredited by APA. *Degree requirements:* For doctorate, dissertation required, foreign language not required. *Entrance requirements:* GRE General Test. Application deadline: 1/2. Application fee: $65 ($75 for international students). *Expenses:* Tuition $22,110 per year. Fees $156 per year. *Financial aid:* Fellowships available. Financial aid application deadline: 2/1; applicants required to submit FAFSA. • Application contact: Graduate Admissions Office, 650-723-4794.

State University of New York at Albany, School of Education, Department of Educational Psychology and Statistics, Albany, NY 12222-0001. Offers programs in educational psychology (Ed D), educational psychology and statistics (MS), measurements and evaluation (Ed D), school psychology (Psy D, CAS), special education (MS), statistics and research design (Ed D). Evening/weekend programs available. Faculty: 14 full-time (6 women), 1 part-time (0 women). Students: 106 full-time (86 women), 86 part-time (57 women); includes 20 minority (10 African Americans, 2 Asian Americans, 8 Hispanics), 9 international. 102 applicants, 39% accepted. In 1997, 90 master's, 8 doctorates, 13 CASs awarded. *Degree requirements:* For doctorate, 1 foreign language, dissertation. *Entrance requirements:* For doctorate, GRE General Test. Application fee: $50. *Expenses:* Tuition $5100 per year full-time, $213 per credit hour part-time for state residents; $8416 per year full-time, $351 per credit hour part-time for nonresidents. Fees $705 per year full-time, $26.85 per credit hour part-time. *Financial aid:* Fellowships and career-related internships or fieldwork available. • Dr. Paul Vogt, Chair, 518-442-5055.

State University of New York at Buffalo, Graduate School, Graduate School of Education, Department of Counseling and Educational Psychology, Buffalo, NY 14260. Offers programs in counseling psychology (PhD), counselor education (PhD), educational psychology (MA, PhD), rehabilitation counseling (MS), school counseling (Ed M, Certificate), school psychology (MA). Part-time programs available. Faculty: 11 full-time (3 women), 3 part-time (all women). Students: 101 full-time (76 women), 85 part-time (59 women); includes 14 minority (7 African Americans, 1 Asian American, 5 Hispanics, 1 Native American), 7 international. Average age 25. 240 applicants, 23% accepted. In 1997, 43 master's, 17 doctorates awarded. Terminal master's awarded for partial completion of doctoral program. *Degree requirements:* For master's, thesis required (for some programs), foreign language not required; for doctorate, dissertation required, foreign language not required. *Average time to degree:* master's–2 years full-time, 3 years part-time; doctorate–7 years full-time, 10 years part-time. *Entrance requirements:* For master's, GRE General Test, TOEFL (minimum score 550), interview; for doctorate, GRE General Test (minimum combined score of 1100), TOEFL (minimum score 550), interview. Application deadline: 2/1 (priority date). Application fee: $50. *Tuition:* $5970 per year full-time, $288 per credit hour part-time for state residents; $9286 per year full-time, $426 per credit hour part-time for nonresidents. *Financial aid:* In 1997–98, 19 students received aid, including 5 fellowships (2 to first-year students), 12 graduate assistantships (5 to first-year students); research assistantships, teaching assistantships, Federal Work-Study, institutionally sponsored loans, and career-related internships or fieldwork also available. Financial aid application deadline: 2/1. *Faculty research:* Counseling process, vocational psychology, assessment, learning and development, grief counseling. • Dr. Thomas T. Frantz, Chairperson, 716-645-2485. Fax: 716-645-6616. E-mail: ttfranz@acsu.buffalo.edu.

Teachers College, Columbia University, Graduate Faculty of Education, Department of Health and Behavior Studies, Program in Applied Educational Psychology—School Psychology, 525 West 120th Street, New York, NY 10027-6696. Awards Ed M, MA, Ed D, PhD. One or more programs accredited by APA. Faculty: 3 full-time (2 women), 5 part-time (3 women), 4.8 FTE. Students: 38 full-time (35 women), 45 part-time (38 women); includes 17 minority (3 African Americans, 11 Asian Americans, 3 Hispanics), 7 international. Average age 31. 89 applicants, 47% accepted. In 1997, 4 master's, 5 doctorates awarded. *Degree requirements:* For master's, integrative paper required, foreign language not required; for doctorate, dissertation, integrative project. *Entrance requirements:* For doctorate, GRE General Test. Application deadline: 5/15. Application fee: $50. *Expenses:* Tuition $640 per credit. Fees $120 per semester. *Financial aid:* Fellowships, research assistantships, full and partial tuition waivers, Federal Work-Study, institutionally sponsored loans, and career-related internships or fieldwork available. Aid available to part-time students. Financial aid application deadline: 2/1. *Faculty research:* Psychoeducational assessment, observation and concept acquisition in young children, reading, mathematical thinking, memory, cognition and instruction. • Application contact: Ursula Felton, Office of Admissions, 212-678-3710. Fax: 212-678-4171.

Teachers College, Columbia University, Graduate Faculty of Education, Department of Human Development, Program in Educational Psychology-Human Cognition and Learning, 525 West 120th Street, New York, NY 10027-6696. Awards Ed M, MA, Ed D, PhD. One or more programs accredited by APA. Part-time programs available. Faculty: 2 full-time (1 woman). Students: 13 full-time (12 women), 23 part-time (17 women); includes 10 minority (4 African Americans, 3 Asian Americans, 2 Hispanics, 1 Native American), 4 international. Average age 34. 58 applicants, 43% accepted. In 1997, 5 master's, 1 doctorate awarded. Terminal master's awarded for partial completion of doctoral program. *Degree requirements:* For master's, integrative paper required, foreign language not required; for doctorate, dissertation, integrative project. *Entrance requirements:* For doctorate, GRE General Test. Application deadline: 5/15 (12/1 for spring admission). Application fee: $50. *Expenses:* Tuition $640 per credit. Fees $120 per semester. *Financial aid:* Fellowships, research assistantships, full and partial tuition waivers, Federal Work-Study, institutionally sponsored loans, and career-related internships or fieldwork available. Aid available to part-time students. Financial aid application deadline: 2/1. *Faculty research:* Early reading, text comprehension, learning disabilities, mathematical thinking, reasoning. • Application contact: Barbara Reinhalter, Office of Admissions, 212-678-3710. Fax: 212-678-4171.

Temple University, College of Education, Department of Psychological Studies in Education, Program in Educational Psychology, Philadelphia, PA 19122-6096. Awards Ed M, PhD. One or more programs accredited by APA. Accredited by NCATE. Part-time and evening/weekend programs available. Faculty: 9 full-time (2 women). Students: 137 (97 women); includes 8 minority (all African Americans), 2 international. 90 applicants, 59% accepted. In 1997, 10 master's, 2 doctorates awarded. Terminal master's awarded for partial completion of doctoral program. *Degree requirements:* For master's, thesis or alternative required, foreign language not required; for doctorate, dissertation required, foreign language not required. *Entrance requirements:* For master's, GRE General Test (minimum combined score of 1000) or MAT (minimum score 39), minimum GPA of 2.8; for doctorate, GRE General Test (minimum combined score of 1000) or MAT (minimum score 48), minimum GPA of 3.0 during previous 2 years, 2.8 overall. Application deadline: 4/1 (10/1 for spring admission). Application fee: $40. *Expenses:* Tuition $323 per semester hour for state residents; $444 per semester hour for nonresidents. Fees $170 per year full-time, $28 per semester (minimum) part-time. *Financial aid:* Fellowships, research assistantships, teaching assistantships available. *Faculty research:* Computers in education, student motivation, school improvement in city schools, individual differences in learning, teaching strategies. • Dr. Leroy Messinger, Coordinator, 215-204-6116.

Tennessee Technological University, College of Education, Department of School Services Personnel and Psychology, Cookeville, TN 38505. Offers programs in educational psychology (MA, Ed S), educational psychology and student personnel (MA, Ed S). One or more programs accredited by NCATE. Part-time and evening/weekend programs available. Faculty: 24 full-time (6 women). Students: 44 full-time (35 women), 83 part-time (65 women); includes 4 minority (all African Americans). Average age 27. 56 applicants, 89% accepted. In 1997, 38 master's, 7 Ed Ss awarded. *Degree requirements:* For Ed S, thesis or alternative required, foreign language not required. *Entrance requirements:* For master's, MAT, TOEFL (minimum score 525); for Ed S, MAT, NTE. Application deadline: 3/1 (priority date; 8/1 for spring admission). Application fee: $25 ($30 for international students). *Tuition:* $2960 per year full-time, $147 per semester hour part-time for state residents; $7786 per year full-time, $358 per semester hour part-time for nonresidents. *Financial aid:* In 1997–98, 1 fellowship, 12 research assistantships (5 to first-year students), 2 teaching assistantships (1 to a first-year student) were awarded; career-related internships or fieldwork also available. Financial aid application deadline: 4/1. • Dr. Christopher Barton, Interim Chairperson, 615-372-3457. Fax: 615-372-6319. E-mail: cbarton@tntech.edu. Application contact: Dr. Rebecca F. Quattlebaum, Dean of the Graduate School, 615-372-3233. Fax: 615-372-3497. E-mail: rquattlebaum@tntech.edu.

Texas A&M University, College of Education, Department of Educational Psychology, College Station, TX 77843. Offers programs in counseling psychology (PhD); educational psychology (MS), including gifted and talented education; human learning and development (PhD); research, measurement, and statistics (M Ed, MS, PhD); school counseling (PhD), including school psychology; special education (M Ed, PhD); vocational education (Ed D, PhD); vocational education/school counseling (M Ed), including gifted and talented education. One or more programs accredited by APA. Accredited by NCATE. Faculty: 26 full-time (10 women), 2 part-time (both women), 26.9 FTE. Students: 92 full-time (66 women), 84 part-time (71 women); includes 29 minority (13 African Americans, 2 Asian Americans, 14 Hispanics), 9 international. Average age 33. 74 applicants, 57% accepted. In 1997, 26 master's, 7 doctorates awarded. *Degree requirements:* For doctorate, dissertation. *Entrance requirements:* GRE General Test, TOEFL. Application deadline: 2/1. Application fee: $35 ($75 for international students). *Financial aid:* Fellowships, research assistantships, teaching assistantships, and career-related internships or fieldwork available. • Douglas J. Palmer, Head, 409-845-1831. Fax: 409-862-1256. Application contact: Graduate Adviser, 409-845-1833.

Texas A&M University–Commerce, College of Education, Department of Psychology and Special Education, Commerce, TX 75429-3011. Offerings include educational psychology (PhD). Terminal master's awarded for partial completion of doctoral program. Department faculty: 15 full-time (2 women), 4 part-time (2 women). *Degree requirements:* Dissertation, departmental qualifying exam. *Entrance requirements:* GRE General Test. Application deadline: rolling. Application fee: $0 ($25 for international students). *Tuition:* $2382 per year full-time, $343 per semester (minimum) part-time for state residents; $7518 per year full-time, $343 per semester (minimum) part-time for nonresidents. • Dr. Paul Zelhart, Head, 903-886-5594. Application contact: Pam Hammonds, Graduate Admissions Adviser, 903-886-5167. Fax: 903-886-5165.

Texas Tech University, Graduate School, College of Education, Division of Educational Psychology and Leadership, Lubbock, TX 79409. Offers programs in counselor education (M Ed, Ed D, Certificate), early childhood education (M Ed, Certificate), education diagnostician (Certificate), educational leadership (M Ed, Ed D), educational psychology (M Ed, Ed D), higher education (M Ed, Ed D), instructional technology (M Ed, Ed D), principal (Certificate), reading specialist (Certificate), special education (M Ed, Ed D), special education counselor (Certificate), special education supervisor (Certificate), superintendent (Certificate), supervision (M Ed), supervisor (Certificate). Accredited by NCATE. Part-time programs available. Faculty: 28 full-time (13 women), 3 part-time (1 woman), 29.29 FTE. Students: 99 full-time (62 women), 257 part-time (160 women); includes 23 minority (5 African Americans, 4 Asian Americans, 10 Hispanics, 4 Native Americans), 12 international. Average age 37. 136 applicants, 46% accepted. In 1997, 102 master's, 25 doctorates awarded. *Degree requirements:* For

Directory: Educational Psychology

Texas Tech University (continued)

master's, computer language required, thesis optional, foreign language not required; for doctorate, dissertation required, foreign language not required. *Entrance requirements:* For master's, GRE General Test (combined average 1034); for doctorate, GRE General Test. Application deadline: 4/15 (priority date; rolling processing; 11/1 for spring admission). Application fee: $25 ($50 for international students). Electronic applications accepted. *Expenses:* Tuition $864 per year full-time, $120 per semester (minimum) part-time for state residents; $5976 per year full-time, $747 per semester (minimum) part-time for nonresidents. Fees $2321 per year full-time, $302 per semester (minimum) part-time. *Financial aid:* In 1997–98, 162 students received aid, including 1 research assistantship averaging $909 per month; teaching assistantships, Federal Work-Study, institutionally sponsored loans, and career-related internships or fieldwork also available. Aid available to part-time students. Financial aid application deadline: 5/15; applicants required to submit FAFSA. *Faculty research:* Field test of speech/language for visually impaired, medication side effects on handicapped students, adult literacy in visually impaired. • Dr. Loretta J. Bradley, Chair, 806-742-2393.

Université de Moncton, Faculty of Education, Graduate Studies in Education, Moncton, NB E1A 3E9, Canada. Offerings include educational psychology (MA Ed, M Ed). Faculty: 25 full-time (12 women). *Degree requirements:* Proficiency in English and French. *Entrance requirements:* Minimum GPA of 3.0. Application deadline: 6/1 (rolling processing). Application fee: $30. • Léonard Goguen, Director, 506-858-4409. Fax: 506-858-4317. E-mail: goguenl@umoncton.ca. Application contact: Nicole Savoie, Conseillière à l'admission, 506-858-4115. Fax: 506-858-4544. E-mail: savoien@umoncton.ca.

Université de Montréal, Faculty of Arts and Sciences, School of Psychoeducation, Montréal, PQ H3C 3J7, Canada. Awards M Sc. Part-time programs available. Faculty: 12 full-time (4 women), 1 part-time (0 women). Students: 38 full-time (33 women), 5 part-time (all women). 46 applicants, 30% accepted. In 1997, 18 degrees awarded. *Degree requirements:* 1 foreign language, thesis. *Application deadline:* 2/1. *Application fee:* $30. *Financial aid:* Fellowships, research assistantships, teaching assistantships, institutionally sponsored loans, and career-related internships or fieldwork available. Aid available to part-time students. *Faculty research:* Child maladjustment, family, prevention, treatment, antisocial behavior. • Claude Gagnon, Chairman, 514-385-2528. Application contact: Sylvie Normandeau, Program Chair, 514-385-2533.

Université de Montréal, Faculty of Education, Department of Psychopedagogy and Andragogy, Montréal, PQ H3C 3J7, Canada. Awards MA, M Ed, PhD. Part-time and evening/weekend programs available. Faculty: 26 full-time (15 women), 1 (woman) part-time. Students: 135 full-time (93 women), 133 part-time (114 women). 123 applicants, 57% accepted. In 1997, 8 master's awarded. Terminal master's awarded for partial completion of doctoral program. *Degree requirements:* For master's, thesis (for some programs); for doctorate, dissertation, general exam. *Entrance requirements:* For doctorate, MA or M Ed. Application deadline: 2/1 (priority date). Application fee: $30. *Financial aid:* Teaching assistantships available. • Michel Carbonneau, Director, 514-343-7900.

Université du Québec à Hull, Program in Psycho-Education, Hull, PQ J8X 3X7, Canada. Awards M Ed, Diploma. Offered jointly with the Université de Sherbrooke. Part-time programs available. *Entrance requirements:* Appropriate bachelor's degree, proficiency in French. Application deadline: 8/21. Application fee: $30.

Université du Québec à Trois-Rivières, Program in Psycho-education, Trois-Rivières, PQ G9A 5H7, Canada. Awards M Ed, DESS. Offered jointly with the Université de Sherbrooke. Students: 22 full-time (19 women), 4 part-time (3 women). 70 applicants, 43% accepted. *Entrance requirements:* Appropriate bachelor's degree, proficiency in French. Application deadline: 2/1. Application fee: $30. *Financial aid:* Fellowships, research assistantships, teaching assistantships available. • Gaetan Gagnon, Director, 819-376-5085. Fax: 819-376-5127. E-mail: gaetan_gagnon@uqtr.uquebec.ca. Application contact: Suzanne Camirand, Admissions Officer, 819-376-5045 Ext. 2591. Fax: 819-376-5210. E-mail: suzanne_camirand@uqtr.uquebec.ca.

Université Laval, Faculty of Education, Department of Didactics, Educational Psychology and Instructional Technology, Program in Educational Psychology, Sainte-Foy, PQ G1K 7P4, Canada. Awards MA, PhD, Diploma. Students: 70 full-time (56 women), 195 part-time (165 women). 134 applicants, 72% accepted. In 1997, 30 master's, 6 doctorates, 66 Diplomas awarded. *Application deadline:* 3/1. *Application fee:* $30. *Expenses:* Tuition $1334 per year (minimum) full-time, $56 per credit (minimum) part-time for Canadian residents; $5966 per year (minimum) full-time, $249 per credit (minimum) part-time for nonresidents. Fees $150 per year full-time, $6.25 per credit part-time. *Faculty research:* Emotional, social, and cognitive development; learning and motivation in school; language development; reading acquisition; computer and learning strategies. • Jean-Guy Bernard, Director, 418-656-2131 Ext. 3789. Fax: 418-656-2905. E-mail: jean-guy.bernard@did.ulaval.ca.

The University of Alabama, College of Education, Area of Professional Studies, Program in Educational Psychology, Tuscaloosa, AL 35487. Awards MA, Ed D, PhD, Ed S. Accredited by NCATE. *Degree requirements:* For doctorate, 1 foreign language, computer language, dissertation. *Entrance requirements:* For master's and doctorate, GRE General Test, MAT (score in 50th percentile or higher), or NTE (minimum score 658 on each core battery test), minimum GPA of 3.0; for Ed S, minimum GPA of 3.0 during previous 2 years. Application deadline: 7/6 (rolling processing). Application fee: $25. *Tuition:* $2684 per year full-time, $594 per semester (minimum) part-time for state residents; $7216 per year full-time, $1248 per semester (minimum) part-time for nonresidents. *Financial aid:* Application deadline 7/14. • Dr. R. Carl Westerfield, Head, Area of Professional Studies, 205-348-8362. Fax: 205-348-0867. E-mail: cwesterf@bamaed.ua.edu.

University of Alberta, Faculty of Graduate Studies and Research, Department of Educational Psychology, Edmonton, AB T6G 2E1, Canada. Offers programs in counseling psychology (M Ed, PhD), educational psychology (M Ed, PhD), instructional technology (M Ed), school counseling (M Ed), school psychology (M Ed, PhD), special education (M Ed, PhD), special education-deafness studies (M Ed), teaching English as a second language (M Ed). Part-time programs available. Faculty: 36 full-time (11 women), 23 part-time (9 women), 41.75 FTE. Students: 110 full-time (78 women), 132 part-time (90 women); includes 15 international. Average age 35. 231 applicants, 34% accepted. *Degree requirements:* For doctorate, dissertation. *Application deadline:* 2/1 (priority date; rolling processing). *Application fee:* $60. *Expenses:* Tuition $390 per course for Canadian residents; $781 per course for nonresidents. Fees $500 per year full-time, $184 per year part-time. *Financial aid:* In 1997–98, 96 students received aid, including 13 fellowships (1 to a first-year student) averaging $687 per month and totaling $112,172, 39 research assistantships (22 to first-year students) averaging $357 per month and totaling $111,384, 50 teaching assistantships (18 to first-year students) averaging $483 per month and totaling $193,200, 29 research measurements, tuition scholarships averaging $815 per month. *Faculty research:* Human learning, development and assessment. • Dr. L. L. Stewin, Chair, 403-492-2389. Fax: 403-492-1318. E-mail: len.stewin@ualberta.ca.

The University of Arizona, College of Education, Department of Educational Psychology, Tucson, AZ 85721. Awards MA, PhD. Terminal master's awarded for partial completion of doctoral program. *Degree requirements:* For doctorate, dissertation required, foreign language not required. *Entrance requirements:* For master's, TOEFL (minimum score 550); for doctorate, GRE General Test (minimum combined score of 1100), TOEFL (minimum score 550). Application deadline: 3/15 (rolling processing). Application fee: $35. *Tuition:* $2162 per year full-time, $337 per semester (minimum) part-time for state residents; $6860 per year full-time, $1138 per semester (minimum) part-time for nonresidents. *Faculty research:* Human memory and cognition, research on teaching, nondiscriminatory assessment, assessment of learning outcomes, preschool learning and development.

University of British Columbia, Faculty of Education, Department of Educational Psychology and Special Education, Vancouver, BC V6T 1Z2, Canada. Offers programs in educational psychology (M Ed, PhD); general educational psychology (M Ed); human learning, development and instruction (MA); measurement, evaluation and research methodology (MA); school psychology (MA); special education (MA, M Ed, PhD). Part-time and evening/weekend programs available. Terminal master's awarded for partial completion of doctoral program. *Degree requirements:* For master's, thesis, thesis (MA), graduating paper (M Ed) required, foreign language not required; for doctorate, dissertation required, foreign language not required. *Average time to degree:* master's–3 years full-time, 5 years part-time; doctorate–6 years full-time. *Entrance requirements:* For master's, TOEFL (minimum score 590); for doctorate, GRE General Test, TOEFL (minimum score 590). Application deadline: 2/1. Application fee: $60. *Faculty research:* Adolescent/adult cognitive development, learning disabilities in adolescents and adults, school psychology assessment, research design analysis of variance, education of deaf, education of blind, teaching of deaf and hearing impaired.

The University of Calgary, Faculty of Education, Department of Educational Psychology, Calgary, AB T2N 1N4, Canada. Offers programs in community rehabilitation (M Ed, M Sc, PhD), computer applciations (PhD), computer applications (M Ed, M Sc), counseling psychology (M Ed, M Sc, PhD), human development and learning (M Ed, M Sc, PhD), school psychology (M Ed, M Sc, PhD), special education (M Ed, M Sc, PhD). Faculty: 30 full-time, 20 part-time. Students: 143 full-time, 40 part-time; includes 4 international. Average age 36. 222 applicants, 28% accepted. In 1997, 25 master's, 7 doctorates awarded. *Degree requirements:* For master's, thesis required (for some programs), foreign language not required; for doctorate, dissertation, candidacy exam. *Entrance requirements:* For master's, minimum GPA of 3.0; for doctorate, minimum GPA of 3.5. Application deadline: 2/15. Application fee: $60. *Expenses:* Tuition $5448 per year full-time, $908 per course part-time for Canadian residents; $10,896 per year full-time, $1816 per course part-time for nonresidents. Fees $285 per year full-time, $119 per semester (minimum) part-time. *Financial aid:* Fellowships, research assistantships, teaching assistantships available. Financial aid application deadline: 2/1. *Faculty research:* Special education, clinical psychology, counselor education, family life studies, child-computer interaction. • Dr. S. Robertson, Head, 403-220-5651. Fax: 403-282-9244. E-mail: 18601@ucdasvm1.admin.ucalgary.ca.

University of California, Davis, Program in Education, Davis, CA 95616. Offerings include psychological studies (PhD). Program faculty: 19 full-time (9 women). *Application deadline:* 2/15. *Application fee:* $40. *Expenses:* Tuition $0 for state residents; $9384 per year for nonresidents. Fees $4466 per year full-time, $2923 per year part-time. • Johnathan Sandoval, Chair, 530-752-0761. Application contact: Karen Bray, Graduate Adviser, 530-752-0761.

University of Colorado at Boulder, School of Education, Division of Educational and Psychological Studies, Boulder, CO 80309. Awards MA, PhD. Accredited by NCATE. Part-time programs available. Students: 17 full-time (13 women), 7 part-time (4 women); includes 4 minority (1 Asian American, 3 Hispanics), 1 international. Average age 35. 29 applicants, 41% accepted. In 1997, 3 master's, 1 doctorate awarded. *Degree requirements:* For master's, thesis or alternative, comprehensive exam required, foreign language not required; for doctorate, 1 foreign language, dissertation. *Entrance requirements:* For master's, GRE General Test (minimum combined score of 1500 on three sections) or MAT (minimum score 44), minimum undergraduate GPA of 2.75; for doctorate, GRE General Test (minimum combined score of 1500 on three sections). Application deadline: 2/1 (priority date; 8/1 for spring admission). Application fee: $40 ($60 for international students). *Expenses:* Tuition $3170 per year full-time, $531 per semester (minimum) part-time for state residents; $14,652 per year full-time, $2442 per semester (minimum) part-time for nonresidents. Fees $667 per year full-time, $130 per semester (minimum) part-time. *Financial aid:* Application deadline 2/1. • Hilda Borko, Head, 303-492-8399. Fax: 303-492-7090. E-mail: hilda.borko@colorado.edu.

University of Colorado at Denver, School of Education, Program in Educational Psychology, Denver, CO 80217-3364. Awards MA. Accredited by NCATE. Part-time and evening/weekend programs available. Students: 8 full-time (all women), 20 part-time (16 women); includes 2 minority (1 Asian American, 1 Native American). Average age 33. 11 applicants, 55% accepted. In 1997, 18 degrees awarded. *Degree requirements:* Thesis or alternative required, foreign language not required. *Entrance requirements:* GRE, MAT, minimum GPA of 2.75. Application deadline: 4/15 (rolling processing; 9/15 for spring admission). Application fee: $50 ($60 for international students). Electronic applications accepted. *Expenses:* Tuition $3530 per year full-time, $199 per semester hour part-time for state residents; $12,722 per year full-time, $764 per semester hour part-time for nonresidents. Fees $252 per year. *Financial aid:* Research assistantships, teaching assistantships, Federal Work-Study available. Financial aid application deadline: 3/1; applicants required to submit FAFSA. • William Goodwin, Area Coordinator, 303-556-3355. Application contact: Laura Hatcher, Administrative Assistant, 303-556-3535. Fax: 303-556-4479.

University of Connecticut, School of Education, Field of Cognition and Instruction, Storrs, CT 06269. Awards PhD. Accredited by NCATE. Faculty: 8. Students: 11 full-time (8 women), 16 part-time (10 women); includes 3 minority (1 African American, 1 Asian American, 1 Hispanic), 5 international. Average age 37. 16 applicants, 81% accepted. In 1997, 2 degrees awarded. *Degree requirements:* Dissertation. *Entrance requirements:* GRE General Test. Application deadline: 6/1 (priority date; rolling processing; 11/1 for spring admission). Application fee: $40 ($45 for international students). *Expenses:* Tuition $5272 per year full-time, $293 per credit part-time for state residents; $13,696 per year full-time, $761 per credit part-time for nonresidents. Fees $948 per year full-time, $640 per year part-time. *Financial aid:* In 1997–98, research assistantships totaling $7,500, 7 teaching assistantships (1 to a first-year student) totaling $67,389 were awarded; fellowships also available. Financial aid application deadline: 2/15. • Scott W. Brown, Head, 860-486-4031.

University of Connecticut, School of Education, Field of Educational Psychology, Storrs, CT 06269. Awards MA, PhD. Accredited by NCATE. Faculty: 12. Students: 2 part-time (both women). Average age 41. 24 applicants, 0% accepted. In 1997, 1 master's awarded. Terminal master's awarded for partial completion of doctoral program. *Degree requirements:* For master's, thesis or alternative; for doctorate, dissertation. *Entrance requirements:* GRE General Test. Application deadline: 6/1 (priority date; rolling processing; 11/1 for spring admission). Application fee: $40 ($45 for international students). *Expenses:* Tuition $5272 per year full-time, $293 per credit part-time for state residents; $13,696 per year full-time, $761 per credit part-time for nonresidents. Fees $948 per year full-time, $640 per year part-time. *Financial aid:* Fellowships, research assistantships, teaching assistantships available. Financial aid application deadline: 2/15. • Scott W. Brown, Head, 860-486-4031.

University of Florida, College of Education, Department of Foundations of Education, Gainesville, FL 32611. Offerings include educational psychology (MAE, M Ed, Ed D, PhD, Ed S). Accredited by NCATE. Terminal master's awarded for partial completion of doctoral program. Department faculty: 23. *Degree requirements:* For master's, thesis (MAE) required, foreign language not required; for doctorate, variable foreign language requirement, dissertation. *Entrance requirements:* For master's and doctorate, GRE General Test, minimum GPA of 3.0; for Ed S, GRE General Test. Application deadline: 6/5 (priority date; rolling processing). Application fee: $20. *Tuition:* $138 per credit hour for state residents; $481 per credit hour for nonresidents. • Dr. James Algina, Chair, 352-392-0723. Application contact: Dr. Barry J. Guinagh, Graduate Coordinator, 352-392-0723. Fax: 352-392-7159. E-mail: guinagh@coe.ufl.edu.

University of Georgia, College of Education, Department of Educational Psychology, Athens, GA 30602. Offers programs in education of the gifted (Ed D), educational psychology (M Ed, PhD), school psychology and school psychometry (MA, M Ed, Ed S). One or more programs accredited by APA. Accredited by NCATE. Faculty: 18 full-time (8 women). Students: 86 full-time, 50 part-time; includes 10 minority (8 African Americans, 1 Asian American, 1 Hispanic), 13 international. 207 applicants, 24% accepted. In 1997, 13 master's, 5 doctorates, 7 Ed Ss awarded. *Degree requirements:* For master's, thesis (MA) required, foreign language not required; for doctorate, variable foreign language requirement, dissertation. *Entrance requirements:* For master's and Ed S, GRE General Test or MAT; for doctorate, GRE General Test. Application deadline: 7/1 (priority date; 11/15 for spring admission). Application fee: $30. Electronic applications accepted. *Tuition:* $3290 per year full-time, $643 per semester (minimum) part-time for state residents; $11,300 per year full-time, $1645 per semester (minimum) part-time for nonresidents. *Financial aid:* Fellowships, research assistantships, teaching assistantships, assistantships available. • Dr. Joseph M. Wisenbaker, Graduate Coordinator, 706-542-4110. Fax: 706-542-4240. E-mail: joe@coe.uga.edu.

University of Hawaii at Manoa, College of Education, Department of Educational Psychology, Honolulu, HI 96822. Awards M Ed, PhD. Faculty: 7 full-time (3 women), 4 part-time (1 woman). Students: 16 full-time (12 women), 13 part-time (12 women); includes 12 minority (1 African American, 10 Asian Americans, 1 Hispanic), 4 international. 16 applicants, 44% accepted. In 1997, 4 master's awarded (100% continued full-time study); 5 doctorates awarded (100% entered university research/teaching). *Degree requirements:* For master's, thesis (for some programs); for doctorate, computer language, dissertation. *Average time to degree:* master's–2.5 years full-time; doctorate–5 years full-time. *Entrance requirements:* For master's, GRE General Test (average 570 on each section), minimum GPA of 3.0; for doctorate, GRE General Test (average 600 on each section), minimum GPA of 3.0, M Ed, thesis or paper. Application deadline: 2/1 (9/1 for spring admission). Application fee: $25 ($50 for international students). *Tuition:* $4029 per year full-time, $214 per credit hour part-time for state residents; $9957 per year full-time, $461 per credit hour part-time for nonresidents. *Financial aid:* In 1997–98, 11 students received aid, including 1 teaching assistantship averaging $1,066 per month; full tuition waivers, institutionally sponsored loans, and career-related internships or fieldwork also available. Financial aid application deadline: 3/1; applicants required to submit FAFSA. *Faculty research:* Human learning and development, measurement, research methods, statistics. • Dr. Fred Bail, Graduate Chair, 808-956-7775.

University of Houston, College of Education, Department of Educational Psychology, 4800 Calhoun, Houston, TX 77204-2163. Offers programs in counseling psychology (M Ed, PhD), educational psychology (M Ed), educational psychology and individual differences (PhD), special education (M Ed, Ed D). Accredited by NCATE. Part-time and evening/weekend programs available. Faculty: 17 full-time (7 women), 6 part-time (3 women). Students: 92 full-time (76 women), 158 part-time (130 women); includes 48 minority (23 African Americans, 9 Asian Americans, 14 Hispanics, 2 Native Americans), 7 international. Average age 35. In 1997, 61 master's awarded; 15 doctorates awarded (100% found work related to degree). *Degree requirements:* For master's, comprehensive exam or thesis required, foreign language not required; for doctorate, computer language, dissertation, comprehensive exam required, foreign language not required. *Entrance requirements:* For master's, GRE General Test (minimum combined score of 950; average 1100) or MAT (minimum score 45; average 57), interview (counseling psychology); for doctorate, GRE General Test (minimum combined score of 1040; average 1160), interview. Application deadline: 2/1. Application fee: $35 ($75 for international students). *Expenses:* Tuition $1152 per year full-time, $120 per semester (minimum) part-time for state residents; $4482 per year full-time, $249 per credit hour part-time for nonresidents. Fees $977 per year full-time, $119 per semester (minimum) part-time. *Financial aid:* Research assistantships, teaching assistantships available. *Faculty research:* Cross-cultural assessment and counseling, cognitive and psychosocial development, learning and emotional disturbances. • Robert McPherson, Chairperson, 713-743-9827. Fax: 713-743-4989. Application contact: Graduate Adviser, 713-743-5019. Fax: 713-743-4996. E-mail: epsy@uh.edu.

University of Illinois at Urbana–Champaign, College of Education, Department of Educational Psychology, Urbana, IL 61801. Awards AM, Ed M, MS, Ed D, PhD, AC. One or more programs accredited by APA. Faculty: 26 full-time (11 women), 5 part-time (1 woman). Students: 136 full-time (97 women); includes 18 minority (7 African Americans, 7 Asian Americans, 4 Hispanics), 46 international. 166 applicants, 20% accepted. In 1997, 16 master's, 17 doctorates awarded. *Degree requirements:* For doctorate, dissertation. *Entrance requirements:* For master's and doctorate, GRE General Test (minimum score 600 on verbal section, 600 on quantitative). Application deadline: rolling. Application fee: $40 ($50 for international students). *Financial aid:* In 1997–98, 3 fellowships, 77 research assistantships, 35 teaching assistantships were awarded; full and partial tuition waivers also available. Financial aid application deadline: 1/15. • Lenore Harmon, Chair, 217-333-8517. Application contact: Terence J. G. Tracey, Associate Chair, 217-333-2245. Fax: 217-244-7620.

The University of Iowa, College of Education, Division of Psychological and Quantitative Foundations, Iowa City, IA 52242-1316. Offers programs in educational media (MA, PhD, Ed S), instructional design and technology (MA, PhD), psychological and quantitative foundations (MA, PhD, Ed S). Faculty: 29 full-time, 1 part-time. Students: 76 full-time (48 women), 110 part-time (66 women); includes 35 minority (16 African Americans, 6 Asian Americans, 11 Hispanics, 2 Native Americans), 34 international. 166 applicants, 26% accepted. In 1997, 14 master's, 17 doctorates, 3 Ed Ss awarded. *Degree requirements:* For master's, exam required, thesis optional, foreign language not required; for doctorate, computer language, dissertation, comprehensive exams required, foreign language not required; for Ed S, computer language, exam required, foreign language not required. *Entrance requirements:* For master's and Ed S, GRE General Test, minimum GPA of 2.5; for doctorate, GRE General Test, minimum GPA of 3.0. Application fee: $30 ($50 for international students). *Expenses:* Tuition $3166 per year full-time, $176 per semester hour part-time for state residents; $10,202 per year full-time, $176 per semester hour part-time for nonresidents. Fees $202 per year full-time, $52 per year (minimum) part-time. *Financial aid:* In 1997–98, 10 fellowships (6 to first-year students), 66 research assistantships (15 to first-year students), 21 teaching assistantships (1 to a first-year student) were awarded. Financial aid applicants required to submit FAFSA. • David F. Lohman, Chair, 319-335-5577. Fax: 319-335-6145.

University of Kentucky, Graduate School Programs from the College of Education, Program in Educational and Counseling Psychology, Lexington, KY 40506-0032. Awards MA Ed U, MS Ed U, Ed D, PhD, Ed S. One or more programs accredited by APA. Accredited by NCATE. Faculty: 20 full-time (8 women), 4 part-time (0 women). Students: 113 full-time (83 women), 37 part-time (31 women); includes 15 minority (12 African Americans, 2 Asian Americans, 1 Hispanic), 7 international. 191 applicants, 37% accepted. In 1997, 23 master's, 8 doctorates, 4 Ed Ss awarded. *Degree requirements:* For master's, comprehensive exam required, thesis optional, foreign language not required; for doctorate, dissertation, comprehensive exam required, foreign language not required; for Ed S, comprehensive exam required, foreign language and thesis not required. *Entrance requirements:* For master's, GRE General Test, minimum undergraduate GPA of 2.5; for doctorate, GRE General Test, minimum graduate GPA of 3.0; for Ed S, GRE General Test. Application deadline: rolling. Application fee: $30 ($35 for international students). *Financial aid:* In 1997–98, 10 fellowships, 5 research assistantships, 6 teaching assistantships, 3 graduate assistantships were awarded; Federal Work-Study, institutionally sponsored loans, and career-related internships or fieldwork also available. Aid available to part-time students. *Faculty research:* Industrial and agricultural injury prevention, outcome evaluation in counseling and psychology, hypertension and stress in African-American youth, resilience in victims of trauma and violence, achievement motivation during adolescence. • Dr. Charlotte R. Clark, Director of Graduate Studies, 606-257-7928. Application contact: Dr. Constance L. Wood, Associate Dean, 606-257-4613. Fax: 606-323-1928.

University of Mary Hardin–Baylor, School of Education, Belton, TX 76513. Offerings include educational psychology (M Ed). School faculty: 6 full-time (2 women). *Average time to degree:* master's–2 years full-time, 3.5 years part-time. *Entrance requirements:* GRE General Test (minimum combined score of 850), minimum GPA of 2.5. Application deadline: 8/1 (priority date; rolling processing; 1/10 for spring admission). Application fee: $35 ($135 for international students). *Expenses:* Tuition $270 per semester hour. Fees $15 per semester hour. • Dr. Clarence E. Ham, Dean, 254-295-4573. Fax: 254-933-4480. E-mail: ham@tenet.edu.

University of Maryland, College Park, College of Education, Department of Human Development, College Park, MD 20742-5045. Offers programs in early childhood/elementary education (MA, M Ed, Ed D, PhD, CAGS), human development (MA, M Ed, Ed D, PhD, CAGS). Accredited by NCATE. Postbaccalaureate distance learning degree programs offered. Faculty: 36 full-time (21 women), 8 part-time (7 women). Students: 78 full-time (64 women), 75 part-time (66 women); includes 25 minority (15 African Americans, 8 Asian Americans, 2 Hispanics), 12 international. 98 applicants, 53% accepted. In 1997, 21 master's, 21 doctorates awarded. *Degree requirements:* For master's, thesis or alternative, thesis (MA); for doctorate, dissertation. *Entrance requirements:* For master's, GRE General Test or MAT (score in 40th percentile or higher); for doctorate, GRE General Test or MAT (score in 70th percentile or higher); for CAGS, MAT. Application deadline: rolling. Application fee: $50 ($70 for international students). *Expenses:* Tuition $272 per credit hour for state residents; $400 per credit hour for nonresidents. Fees $564 per year full-time, $342 per year part-time. *Financial aid:* In 1997–98, 7 fellowships, 22 teaching assistantships were awarded; research assistantships also available. *Faculty research:* Developmental science, educational psychology. • Dr. Stephen Porges, Chairman/Director, 301-405-2827. Fax: 301-314-9278. Application contact: John Mollish, Director, Graduate Admissions and Records, 301-405-4198. Fax: 301-314-9305.

The University of Memphis, College of Education, Department of Counseling, Educational Psychology and Research, Memphis, TN 38152. Offers programs in counseling and personnel services (MS, Ed D), including community agency counseling (MS), rehabilitation counseling (MS), school counseling (MS), student personnel services (MS); counseling psychology (PhD); educational psychology and research (MS, Ed D, PhD), including educational psychology (MS, Ed D), educational research (MS, Ed D). Accredited by NCATE. One or more programs accredited by APA. Faculty: 23 full-time (11 women), 17 part-time (8 women). Students: 95 full-time (76 women), 172 part-time (129 women); includes 56 minority (53 African Americans, 3 Asian Americans), 4 international. Average age 34. 153 applicants, 37% accepted. In 1997, 58 master's, 24 doctorates awarded. *Degree requirements:* For master's, thesis or alternative, comprehensive exam required, foreign language not required; for doctorate, dissertation, comprehensive exam required, foreign language not required. *Entrance requirements:* For master's, GRE General Test or MAT, minimum GPA of 2.5; for doctorate, GRE General Test. Application deadline: 8/1 (12/1 for spring admission). Application fee: $25 ($50 for international students). *Tuition:* $2862 per year full-time, $166 per credit hour part-time for state residents; $6696 per year full-time, $379 per credit hour part-time for nonresidents. *Financial aid:* In 1997–98, 5 research assistantships totaling $32,992, 10 teaching assistantships totaling $66,336 were awarded; career-related internships or fieldwork also available. *Faculty research:* Anger management, aging and disability, supervision, multicultural counseling. • Dr. Ronnie Priest, Chair and Coordinator of Graduate Studies, 901-678-2841.

University of Minnesota, Duluth, Graduate School, College of Education and Human Service Professions, Program in Counseling Psychology, Duluth, MN 55812-2496. Offers educational psychology (MA). Accredited by NCATE. Faculty: 14 full-time (6 women), 4 part-time (2 women), 16.25 FTE. Students: 32 full-time (25 women); includes 4 minority (2 Asian Americans, 1 Hispanic, 1 Native American), 2 international. Average age 24. 43 applicants, 35% accepted. In 1997, 23 degrees awarded (96% found work related to degree, 4% continued full-time study). *Degree requirements:* Thesis, practicum required, foreign language not required. *Average time to degree:* master's–1.9 years full-time, 4.5 years part-time. *Entrance requirements:* GRE General Test (minimum score 350 on verbal section, 350 on quantitative; average 425 verbal, 535 quantitative), minimum GPA of 3.0, 9 credits in psychology or education, previous undergraduate coursework in inferential statistics. Application deadline: 3/15 (priority date; rolling processing). Application fee: $40 ($50 for international students). *Expenses:* Tuition $5130 per year full-time, $299 per credit part-time for state residents; $10,074 per year full-time, $536 per credit part-time for nonresidents. Fees $612 per year full-time, $76 per quarter part-time. *Financial aid:* In 1997–98, 23 students received aid, including 2 fellowships (both to first-year students) averaging $260 per month and totaling $4,680, 11 teaching assistantships (5 to first-year students) averaging $481 per month and totaling $47,575, 10 grants (5 to first-year students) totaling $3,000; partial tuition waivers, Federal Work-Study, institutionally sponsored loans, and career-related internships or fieldwork also available. Financial aid application deadline: 3/15. *Faculty research:* Adolescent peer relationships, gender equity, group process, mentors, parenting. • Dr. Jane Hovland, Director of Graduate Studies, 218-726-7118. Fax: 218-726-7073. E-mail: jhovland@d.umn.edu.

University of Minnesota, Twin Cities Campus, College of Education and Human Development, Department of Educational Psychology, Minneapolis, MN 55455-0213. Offers programs in educational psychology (MA, PhD, Ed S), special education (M Ed). One or more programs accredited by APA. • Mark Davison, Chairman, 612-624-3543.

University of Mississippi, Graduate School, School of Education, Department of Educational Leadership and Educational Psychology, University, MS 38677-9702. Offers programs in educational leadership (PhD), educational leadership and educational psychology (MA, M Ed, Ed D, Ed S), educational psychology (PhD), higher education/student personnel (MA, M Ed). Accredited by NCATE. Faculty: 11 full-time (4 women). Students: 53 full-time (42 women), 76 part-time (55 women); includes 47 minority (all African Americans), 2 international. In 1997, 66 master's, 3 doctorates awarded. *Degree requirements:* For doctorate, dissertation required, foreign language not required. *Entrance requirements:* For master's, GRE General Test, TOEFL, minimum GPA of 3.0; for doctorate, GRE General Test, TOEFL. Application deadline: 8/1 (rolling processing). Application fee: $0 ($25 for international students). *Financial aid:* Application deadline 3/1. • Dr. William Leary, Acting Chair, 601-232-7195.

University of Missouri–Columbia, College of Education, Department of Educational and Counseling Psychology, Columbia, MO 65211. Awards MA, M Ed, PhD, Ed S. One or more programs accredited by APA. Part-time programs available. Faculty: 24 full-time (8 women), 1 (woman) part-time. Students: 90 full-time (60 women), 62 part-time (42 women); includes 25 minority (13 African Americans, 2 Asian Americans, 7 Hispanics, 3 Native Americans), 3 international. In 1997, 28 master's, 13 doctorates awarded. Terminal master's awarded for partial completion of doctoral program. *Degree requirements:* For doctorate, dissertation. *Entrance requirements:* GRE General Test, minimum GPA of 3.0. Application deadline: rolling. Application fee: $25 ($50 for international students). *Expenses:* Tuition $3240 per year full-time, $180 per credit hour part-time for state residents; $9108 per year full-time, $506 per credit hour part-time for nonresidents. Fees $55 per year full-time. *Financial aid:* Fellowships and career-related internships or fieldwork available. • Dr. Richard Cox, Director of Graduate Studies, 573-882-7601.

University of Missouri–Kansas City, School of Education, Division of Educational Research and Psychology, Kansas City, MO 64110-2499. Awards MA. Accredited by NCATE. Part-time and evening/weekend programs available. Students: 10 full-time (8 women), 8 part-time (5 women); includes 4 minority (3 African Americans, 1 Hispanic), 2 international. Average age 37. In 1997, 3 degrees awarded. *Degree requirements:* Final project required, thesis optional, foreign language not required. *Average time to degree:* master's–2 years full-time, 4 years part-time. *Entrance requirements:* Minimum GPA of 2.75. Application deadline: 7/1 (priority date; rolling processing; 12/1 for spring admission). Application fee: $25. *Expenses:* Tuition $182 per credit hour for state residents; $508 per credit hour for nonresidents. Fees $60 per year. *Financial aid:* In 1997–98, 1 research assistantship averaging $858 per month was awarded; full and partial tuition waivers, Federal Work-Study, institutionally sponsored loans also available. Aid available to part-time students. *Faculty research:* Reading rate, motivation, metacognitive skills. • Dr. Ann Pace, Chairperson, 816-235-2485.

University of Nebraska at Omaha, College of Arts and Sciences, Department of Psychology, Omaha, NE 68182. Offerings include educational psychology (MS). Department faculty: 14 full-time (3 women). *Application deadline:* 2/1 (priority date). *Application fee:* $35. *Expenses:* Tuition $1670 per year full-time, $94 per credit hour part-time for state residents; $4082 per year full-time, $227 per credit hour part-time for nonresidents. Fees $302 per year full-time, $108 per semester (minimum) part-time. • Dr. Kenneth Deffenbacher, Chairperson, 402-554-2419.

Directory: Educational Psychology

University of Nebraska–Lincoln, Teachers College, Department of Educational Psychology, Lincoln, NE 68588. Awards MA, Ed S. Accredited by NCATE. One or more programs accredited by APA. Faculty: 14 full-time (4 women), 2 part-time (both women), 15.50 FTE. Students: 27 full-time (21 women), 26 part-time (20 women); includes 4 minority (1 African American, 3 Asian Americans), 4 international. Average age 30. 67 applicants, 33% accepted. In 1997, 25 master's, 4 Ed Ss awarded. *Degree requirements:* For master's, thesis optional. *Entrance requirements:* For master's, GRE General Test, TOEFL (minimum score 500). Application deadline: 1/15 (10/1 for spring admission). Application fee: $35. Electronic applications accepted. *Expenses:* Tuition $110 per credit hour for state residents; $270 per credit hour for nonresidents. Fees $480 per year full-time, $110 per semester part-time. *Financial aid:* In 1997–98, 1 fellowship totaling $2,500, 13 research assistantships totaling $70,121, 22 teaching assistantships totaling $136,220 were awarded; Federal Work-Study also available. Aid available to part-time students. Financial aid application deadline: 2/15. *Faculty research:* Measurement and assessment, metacognition, academic skills, child development, multicultural education and counseling. Total annual research expenditures: $11,552. • Dr. Harold Keller, Chair, 402-472-2210.

University of Nevada, Las Vegas, College of Education, Department of Educational Psychology, Las Vegas, NV 89154-9900. Awards M Ed, MS. Accredited by NCATE. Part-time and evening/weekend programs available. Faculty: 10 full-time (4 women). Students: 12 full-time (10 women), 32 part-time (29 women); includes 8 minority (4 African Americans, 1 Asian American, 3 Hispanics), 2 international. 28 applicants, 50% accepted. In 1997, 6 degrees awarded. *Degree requirements:* Thesis (for some programs), comprehensive exam required, foreign language not required. *Entrance requirements:* GRE General Test (minimum score 450 on each section), minimum GPA of 3.0 during previous 2 years, 2.75 overall. Application deadline: 4/15 (11/15 for spring admission). Application fee: $40 ($95 for international students). *Expenses:* Tuition $93 per credit for state residents; $93 per credit full-time, $190 per credit part-time for nonresidents. Fees $5570 per year full-time for nonresidents. *Financial aid:* In 1997–98, 5 research assistantships were awarded; teaching assistantships also available. Financial aid application deadline: 3/1. • Dr. Fredrick Krischner, Chair, 702-895-3253. Application contact: Graduate College Admissions Evaluator, 702-895-3320.

University of Nevada, Reno, College of Education, Department of Counseling and Educational Psychology, Reno, NV 89557. Awards MA, M Ed, MS, Ed D, PhD, Ed S. Accredited by NCATE. Faculty: 13 (7 women). Students: 58 full-time (47 women), 79 part-time (58 women); includes 17 minority (6 African Americans, 3 Asian Americans, 6 Hispanics, 2 Native Americans). Average age 38. 54 applicants, 48% accepted. In 1997, 27 master's, 1 doctorate awarded. Terminal master's awarded for partial completion of doctoral program. *Degree requirements:* For master's, thesis optional, foreign language not required; for doctorate, dissertation required, foreign language not required. *Entrance requirements:* For master's, GRE, TOEFL (minimum score 500), minimum GPA of 2.75; for doctorate, GRE, TOEFL (minimum score 500), minimum GPA of 3.0. Application deadline: 2/15 (priority date; 9/15 for spring admission). Application fee: $40. *Expenses:* Tuition $0 for state residents; $5770 per year full-time, $200 per credit part-time for nonresidents. Fees $93 per credit. *Financial aid:* Research assistantships, teaching assistantships, grants, Federal Work-Study, institutionally sponsored loans available. Financial aid application deadline: 3/1. *Faculty research:* Marriage and family counseling, substance abuse attitudes of teachers, current supply of counseling educators, HIV-positive services for patients, family counseling for youth at risk. • Dr. Marlowe Smaby, Chair, 702-784-6637. E-mail: smaby@unr.edu.

University of New Brunswick, Faculty of Education, Division of Educational Foundations, Fredericton, NB E3B 5A3, Canada. Offerings include educational psychology (M Ed). *Degree requirements:* Thesis or alternative required, foreign language not required. *Entrance requirements:* TOEFL, TWE, minimum GPA of 3.0. Application deadline: 3/1 (priority date; rolling processing). Application fee: $25.

University of New Mexico, College of Education, Program in Educational Psychology, Albuquerque, NM 87131-2039. Awards MA, Ed D, PhD. Accredited by NCATE. Part-time programs available. Faculty: 7 full-time (6 women), 4 part-time (all women), 8 FTE. Students: 9 full-time (3 women), 16 part-time (14 women); includes 3 minority (1 African American, 2 Native Americans), 1 international. Average age 43. 5 applicants, 60% accepted. Terminal master's awarded for partial completion of doctoral program. *Degree requirements:* For master's, comprehensive exam or thesis required, foreign language not required; for doctorate, dissertation required, foreign language not required. *Entrance requirements:* For master's, GRE General Test or MAT; for doctorate, GRE General Test or MAT, master's degree in ralated area. Application deadline: 3/15 (10/15 for spring admission). Application fee: $25. *Expenses:* Tuition $2442 per year full-time, $103 per credit hour part-time for state residents; $8691 per year full-time, $103 per credit hour (minimum) part-time for nonresidents. Fees $32 per year. *Financial aid:* In 1997–98, 5 students received aid, including 4 teaching assistantships averaging $850 per month and totaling $19,700; career-related internships or fieldwork also available. Financial aid application deadline: 3/15. *Faculty research:* Alternative assessment, gender roles, phonological awareness, learning strategies, cognitive development. • Dr. Christine McCormick, Graduate Coordinator, 505-277-7222. E-mail: cmccorm@unm.edu. Application contact: Trish Stevens, Division Administrator, 505-277-4535. Fax: 505-277-8361. E-mail: trishste@unm.edu.

The University of North Carolina at Chapel Hill, School of Education, Doctoral Program in Education, Chapel Hill, NC 27599. Offerings include psychological studies in education (PhD). Accredited by NCATE. Program new for fall 1998. *Degree requirements:* Dissertation, comprehensive exams required, foreign language not required. *Entrance requirements:* GRE General Test (minimum combined score of 1000), minimum GPA of 3.0 during last 2 years of undergraduate course work. Application deadline: 1/1 (priority date). *Expenses:* Tuition $1428 per year full-time, $357 per semester (minimum) part-time for state residents; $10,414 per year full-time, $2604 per semester (minimum) part-time for nonresidents. Fees $782 per year full-time, $332 per semester (minimum) part-time. • Dr. Walter Pryzwansky, Director of Graduate Studies, 919-966-7000. Application contact: Janet Carroll, Registrar, 919-966-1346. Fax: 919-962-1533. E-mail: jscarrol@email.unc.edu.

The University of North Carolina at Chapel Hill, School of Education, Program in Educational Psychology, Chapel Hill, NC 27599. Awards MA, M Ed. One or more programs accredited by APA. Accredited by NCATE. Students: 14 full-time (10 women), 14 part-time (9 women). 27 applicants, 30% accepted. *Degree requirements:* Thesis (for some programs), comprehensive exam required, foreign language not required. *Entrance requirements:* GRE General Test (minimum combined score of 1000), minimum GPA of 3.0 during last 2 years of undergraduate course work. Application deadline: 1/1 (priority date; rolling processing). Application fee: $55. *Expenses:* Tuition $1428 per year full-time, $357 per semester (minimum) part-time for state residents; $10,414 per year full-time, $2604 per semester (minimum) part-time for nonresidents. Fees $782 per year full-time, $332 per semester (minimum) part-time. *Financial aid:* Federal Work-Study available. Aid available to part-time students. Financial aid application deadline: 1/1. *Faculty research:* Statistics, measurement, child/adult development, cognitive intervention. • Dr. William Ware, Coordinator, 919-966-5266. Application contact: Janet Carroll, Registrar, 919-966-1346. Fax: 919-962-1533. E-mail: jscarrol@email.unc.edu.

University of Northern Colorado, College of Education, Department of Educational Psychology, Greeley, CO 80639. Awards MA, PhD. One or more programs accredited by APA. Accredited by NCATE. Part-time programs available. Faculty: 5 full-time (2 women), 2 part-time (1 woman). Students: 21 full-time (15 women), 1 (woman) part-time; includes 4 minority (2 African Americans, 1 Asian American, 1 Hispanic), 4 international. Average age 35. 15 applicants, 53% accepted. In 1997, 3 master's, 3 doctorates awarded. *Degree requirements:* For master's, thesis or alternative, comprehensive exams; for doctorate, dissertation, comprehensive exams. *Entrance requirements:* GRE General Test. Application deadline: rolling. Application fee: $35. *Expenses:* Tuition $2327 per year full-time, $129 per credit hour part-time for state residents; $9578 per year full-time, $532 per credit hour part-time for nonresidents. Fees $752 per year full-time, $184 per semester (minimum) part-time. *Financial aid:* In 1997–98, 18 students received aid, including 3 fellowships totaling $3,400, 5 teaching assistantships (1 to a first-year student) totaling $28,858, 3 graduate assistantships (1 to a first-year student) totaling $19,207. Financial aid application deadline: 3/1. • Dr. Randy Lennon, Chairperson, 970-351-2863.

University of Northern Iowa, College of Education, Department of Educational Psychology and Foundations, Cedar Falls, IA 50614. Offers programs in educational psychology (MA Ed), school psychology (Ed S). Part-time and evening/weekend programs available. Faculty: 17 full-time (2 women). Students: 22 full-time (19 women), 15 part-time (8 women); includes 3 international. Average age 33. 25 applicants, 80% accepted. In 1997, 10 master's, 3 Ed Ss awarded. *Degree requirements:* Thesis or alternative required, foreign language not required. *Entrance requirements:* For master's, GRE General Test, GRE Subject Test, minimum GPA of 3.5, 3 years of educational experience; for Ed S, GRE General Test, GRE Subject Test. Application deadline: 8/1 (priority date; rolling processing). Application fee: $20 ($30 for international students). *Expenses:* Tuition $3166 per year full-time, $176 per hour part-time for state residents; $7805 per year full-time, $176 per hour part-time for nonresidents. Fees $194 per year full-time, $12.50 per semester (minimum) part-time. *Financial aid:* Scholarships, full and partial tuition waivers, Federal Work-Study, and career-related internships or fieldwork available. Aid available to part-time students. Financial aid application deadline: 3/1. • Dr. Barry Wilson, Head, 319-273-2694.

University of Oklahoma, College of Education, Department of Educational Psychology, Program in Educational Psychology, Norman, OK 73019-0390. Awards M Ed, PhD. Accredited by NCATE. *Degree requirements:* For doctorate, dissertation. *Entrance requirements:* For master's, TOEFL (minimum score 550), minimum GPA of 3.0, 12 hours of course work in education; for doctorate, GRE General Test, TOEFL (minimum score 550), master's degree, minimum graduate GPA of 3.25. Application fee: $25. *Expenses:* Tuition $1920 per year full-time, $80 per credit hour part-time for state residents; $6108 per year full-time, $255 per credit hour part-time for nonresidents. Fees $468 per year full-time, $12 per semester (minimum) part-time. • Dr. Raymond B. Miller, Chair, Department of Educational Psychology, 405-325-5974.

University of Oklahoma, College of Education, Department of Educational Psychology, Program in Instructional Psychology, Norman, OK 73019-0390. Awards M Ed, Ed D, PhD. Accredited by NCATE. Part-time and evening/weekend programs available. Students: 6 full-time (4 women), 38 part-time (27 women); includes 6 minority (3 African Americans, 1 Asian American, 2 Native Americans), 4 international. In 1997, 28 master's, 11 doctorates awarded. *Degree requirements:* For master's, comprehensive exam required, thesis optional, foreign language not required; for doctorate, computer language, dissertation, general exam. *Entrance requirements:* For master's, TOEFL (minimum score 550), minimum GPA of 3.0, 12 hours of course work in education; for doctorate, GRE General Test, TOEFL (minimum score 550), master's degree, minimum graduate GPA of 3.25. Application fee: $25. *Expenses:* Tuition $1920 per year full-time, $80 per credit hour part-time for state residents; $6108 per year full-time, $255 per credit hour part-time for nonresidents. Fees $468 per year full-time, $12 per semester (minimum) part-time. *Financial aid:* Fellowships, teaching assistantships, Federal Work-Study, institutionally sponsored loans, and career-related internships or fieldwork available. *Faculty research:* Management, organizational change, interactive video, computer-based training, instructional design. • Dr. Raymond B. Miller, Chair, Department of Educational Psychology, 405-325-5974.

University of Pittsburgh, School of Education, Department of Psychology in Education, Program in Developmental/Educational Psychology, Pittsburgh, PA 15260. Awards PhD. 19 applicants, 42% accepted. *Degree requirements:* Dissertation required, foreign language not required. *Average time to degree:* doctorate–6 years full-time. *Entrance requirements:* GRE Subject Test, TOEFL (minimum score 650). Application deadline: 2/1. Application fee: $30 ($40 for international students). *Expenses:* Tuition $8018 per year full-time, $329 per credit part-time for state residents; $16,508 per year full-time, $680 per credit part-time for nonresidents. Fees $480 per year full-time, $180 per year part-time. *Financial aid:* In 1997–98, 2 fellowships, 2 research assistantships averaging $1,150 per month, 4 teaching assistantships averaging $1,250 per month were awarded; partial tuition waivers, Federal Work-Study, institutionally sponsored loans, and career-related internships or fieldwork also available. Financial aid application deadline: 2/1; applicants required to submit FAFSA. • Application contact: Jackie Harden, Manager, 412-648-7060. Fax: 412-648-1899. E-mail: jackie@sched.fsl.pitt.edu.

University of Regina, Faculty of Graduate Studies and Research, Faculty of Education, Department of Educational Psychology, Regina, SK S4S 0A2, Canada. Awards M Ed, PhD, Diploma. Students: 8 full-time, 68 part-time. 33 applicants, 61% accepted. In 1997, 6 master's, 6 Diplomas awarded. *Degree requirements:* For master's, thesis optional, foreign language not required; for doctorate, dissertation required, foreign language not required. *Entrance requirements:* For master's, TOEFL (minimum score 580), bachelor's degree in education, 2 years of teaching experience. Application deadline: 3/15 (12/15 for spring admission). Application fee: $0. *Tuition:* $196 per credit for Canadian residents; $383 per credit for nonresidents. *Financial aid:* Fellowships, research assistantships, teaching assistantships, and career-related internships or fieldwork available. Financial aid application deadline: 6/15. • Dr. N. Kuhns, Chair, 306-585-4612. Application contact: Dr. M. Taylor, Chair, Graduate Programs, 306-585-4606. Fax: 306-585-4880. E-mail: marlene.taylor@uregina.ca.

University of Saskatchewan, College of Education, Department of Educational Psychology, Saskatoon, SK S7N 5A2, Canada. Awards M Ed, PhD, Diploma. *Degree requirements:* For master's, thesis (for some programs); for doctorate, dissertation. *Entrance requirements:* For master's, CANTEST (minimum score 4.5) or International English Language Testing System (minimum score 6) or Michigan English Language Assessment Battery (minimum score 80), or TOEFL (minimum score 550; average 560); for doctorate, TOEFL; for Diploma, International English Language Testing System (minimum score 6) or Michigan English Language Assessment Battery (minimum score 80), or TOEFL (minimum score 550). Application deadline: 7/1 (priority date; rolling processing). Application fee: $0.

University of South Dakota, School of Education, Division of Counseling and Psychology in Education, Vermillion, SD 57069-2390. Awards MA, Ed D, Ed S. Accredited by NCATE. Part-time programs available. Faculty: 10 full-time (3 women), 3 part-time (1 woman). Students: 101 full-time (63 women), 27 part-time (19 women); includes 6 minority (2 Asian Americans, 1 Hispanic, 3 Native Americans), 3 international. 82 applicants, 68% accepted. In 1997, 39 master's, 8 doctorates awarded. *Degree requirements:* For doctorate, dissertation required, foreign language not required. *Entrance requirements:* For master's and doctorate, GRE General Test. Application deadline: rolling. Application fee: $15. *Expenses:* Tuition $1530 per year full-time, $85 per credit hour part-time for state residents; $4518 per year full-time, $251 per credit hour part-time for nonresidents. Fees $792 per year full-time, $44 per credit hour part-time. *Financial aid:* Teaching assistantships and career-related internships or fieldwork available. • Dr. Frank Main, Chair, 605-677-5250.

University of Southern California, Graduate School, School of Education, Department of Counseling Psychology, Los Angeles, CA 90089. Offerings include educational psychology (PhD). *Degree requirements:* Dissertation. *Entrance requirements:* GRE General Test. Application fee: $55. *Expenses:* Tuition $16,944 per year full-time, $706 per unit part-time. Fees $414 per year full-time, $32 per year part-time. • Dr. Michael Newcomb, Chair.

University of Southern California, Graduate School, School of Education, Department of Educational Psychology, Los Angeles, CA 90089. Awards MS, PhD. Students: 57 full-time (37 women), 53 part-time (36 women); includes 24 minority (6 African Americans, 13 Asian Americans, 5 Hispanics), 30 international. Average age 34. 97 applicants, 66% accepted. In 1997, 15 master's, 13 doctorates awarded. *Degree requirements:* For doctorate, dissertation. *Entrance requirements:* GRE General Test. Application deadline: 7/1 (priority date; 11/1 for spring admission). Application fee: $55. *Expenses:* Tuition $16,944 per year full-time, $706 per unit part-time. Fees $414 per year full-time, $32 per year part-time. *Financial aid:* In 1997–98,

7 fellowships, 1 research assistantship, 9 teaching assistantships, 7 scholarships were awarded; Federal Work-Study, institutionally sponsored loans also available. Aid available to part-time students. Financial aid application deadline: 2/15; applicants required to submit FAFSA. • Dr. Robert Rueda, Chair.

University of Tennessee, Knoxville, College of Education, Program in Educational Psychology, Knoxville, TN 37996. Offers adult education (MS), individual and collaborative learning (MS). Accredited by NCATE. Part-time programs available. Students: 33 full-time (25 women), 30 part-time (19 women); includes 6 minority (5 African Americans, 1 Asian American), 4 international. 19 applicants, 74% accepted. In 1997, 22 degrees awarded. *Degree requirements:* Thesis optional, foreign language not required. *Entrance requirements:* TOEFL (minimum score 550), minimum GPA of 2.7. Application deadline: 2/1 (priority date; rolling processing). Application fee: $35. Electronic applications accepted. *Tuition:* $3354 per year full-time, $181 per semester hour part-time for state residents; $8410 per year full-time, $462 per semester hour part-time for nonresidents. *Financial aid:* Application deadline 2/1. • Dr. Tom George, Associate Dean, 423-974-0907. Fax: 423-974-8718. E-mail: tgeorge1@utk.edu.

University of Tennessee, Knoxville, College of Education, Program in Education I, Knoxville, TN 37996. Offerings include educational psychology (PhD). Accredited by NCATE and APA. *Degree requirements:* 1 foreign language (computer language can substitute), dissertation. *Entrance requirements:* GRE General Test, TOEFL (minimum score 550), minimum GPA of 2.7. Application deadline: 2/1 (priority date; rolling processing). Application fee: $35. Electronic applications accepted. *Tuition:* $3354 per year full-time, $181 per semester hour part-time for state residents; $8410 per year full-time, $462 per semester hour part-time for nonresidents. • Dr. Tom George, Associate Dean, 423-974-0907. Fax: 423-974-8718. E-mail: tgeorge1@utk.edu.

University of Tennessee, Knoxville, College of Education, Program in Education II, Knoxville, TN 37996. Offerings include educational psychology: collaborative learning (Ed D). Accredited by NCATE. *Degree requirements:* Dissertation required, foreign language not required. *Entrance requirements:* GRE General Test, TOEFL (minimum score 550), minimum GPA of 2.7. Application deadline: 2/1 (priority date; rolling processing). Application fee: $35. Electronic applications accepted. *Tuition:* $3354 per year full-time, $181 per semester hour part-time for state residents; $8410 per year full-time, $462 per semester hour part-time for nonresidents. • Dr. Tom George, Associate Dean, 423-974-0907. Fax: 423-974-8718. E-mail: tgeorge1@utk.edu.

The University of Texas at Austin, Graduate School, College of Education, Department of Educational Psychology, Austin, TX 78712. Awards MA, M Ed, PhD. Students: 309 (216 women); includes 58 minority (16 African Americans, 6 Asian Americans, 32 Hispanics, 4 Native Americans), 32 international. 326 applicants, 27% accepted. In 1997, 25 master's, 26 doctorates awarded. *Entrance requirements:* GRE General Test. Application deadline: 2/1 (priority date; rolling processing). Application fee: $50 ($75 for international students). Electronic applications accepted. *Expenses:* Tuition $2592 per year full-time, $324 per semester (minimum) part-time for state residents; $7704 per year full-time, $963 per semester (minimum) part-time for nonresidents. Fees $778 per year full-time, $161 per semester (minimum) part-time. *Financial aid:* Fellowships, teaching assistantships available. Financial aid application deadline: 2/1. • Dr. Guy Manaster, Chairman, 512-471-4155. E-mail: guy.manaster@utxvm.cc.utexas.edu. Application contact: Dr. Edmund T. Emmer, Graduate Adviser, 512-471-4155.

The University of Texas at El Paso, College of Education, Department of Educational Psychology and Special Services, 500 West University Avenue, El Paso, TX 79968-0001. Awards M Ed. *Degree requirements:* Thesis optional, foreign language not required. *Entrance requirements:* GRE General Test (minimum combined score of 1400 on three sections), TOEFL (minimum score 550), minimum graduate GPA of 3.0. Application deadline: 7/1 (priority date; rolling processing; 11/1 for spring admission). Application fee: $15 ($65 for international students). Electronic applications accepted. *Tuition:* $1559 per year full-time, $230 per credit hour part-time for state residents; $5393 per year full-time, $405 per credit hour part-time for nonresidents.

The University of Texas–Pan American, College of Education, Department of Educational Psychology, Edinburg, TX 78539-2999. Offers programs in counseling and guidance (M Ed), educational diagnostics (M Ed), gifted and talented education (M Ed), school psychology (MA), special education (M Ed). *Degree requirements:* Thesis optional, foreign language not required. *Entrance requirements:* GRE General Test, interview. Application deadline: 7/17 (11/16 for spring admission). Application fee: $0. *Tuition:* $2156 per year full-time, $283 per semester (minimum) part-time for state residents; $6788 per year full-time, $862 per semester (minimum) part-time for nonresidents. *Faculty research:* Psychoeducational factors of gifted, writing to read, topographic brain mapping, learning disabilities, unbiased testing.

University of the Pacific, School of Education, Department of Educational and Counseling Psychology, Stockton, CA 95211-0197. Offers programs in counseling (MA), counseling psychology (Ed D), educational psychology (MA, Ed D), educational research (MA), school psychology (Ed D). Accredited by NCATE. Students: 25 full-time (22 women), 26 part-time (18 women); includes 3 international. In 1997, 9 master's, 3 doctorates awarded. *Degree requirements:* For master's, thesis required (for some programs), foreign language not required; for doctorate, dissertation. *Entrance requirements:* GRE General Test, GRE Subject Test. Application deadline: 3/1 (priority date; rolling processing; 10/15 for spring admission). Application fee: $50. *Expenses:* Tuition $19,000 per year full-time, $594 per unit part-time. Fees $30 per year (minimum). *Financial aid:* In 1997–98, 6 teaching assistantships were awarded. Financial aid application deadline: 3/1. • Dr. Mari Irvin, Chairperson, 209-946-2559. E-mail: mirvin@uop.edu.

University of Toledo, College of Education and Allied Professions, Department of Educational Psychology, Research, and Social Foundations, Toledo, OH 43606-3398. Offers programs in educational psychology (M Ed), educational theory and social foundations (M Ed), foundations of education (Ed D, PhD), research (M Ed). Accredited by NCATE. Part-time and evening/weekend programs available. Faculty: 17 full-time (7 women). Students: 23 full-time (20 women), 45 part-time (36 women); includes 11 minority (8 African Americans, 3 Asian Americans), 8 international. Average age 38. 34 applicants, 56% accepted. In 1997, 5 master's, 14 doctorates awarded. Terminal master's awarded for partial completion of doctoral program. *Degree requirements:* For master's, project or thesis required, foreign language not required; for doctorate, dissertation, comprehensive exams required, foreign language not required. *Entrance requirements:* For master's, GRE General Test, minimum GPA of 2.7; for doctorate, minimum GPA of 2.7 (undergraduate), 3.0 (graduate). Application deadline: 8/15 (priority date; rolling processing). Application fee: $30. Electronic applications accepted. *Tuition:* $5907 per year full-time, $246 per hour part-time for state residents; $11,835 per year full-time, $493 per hour part-time for nonresidents. *Financial aid:* In 1997–98, 4 research assistantships, 5 teaching assistantships, 2 administrative assistantships, tuition scholarships were awarded; full tuition waivers, Federal Work-Study, institutionally sponsored loans, and career-related internships or fieldwork also available. Aid available to part-time students. Financial aid application deadline: 4/1; applicants required to submit FAFSA. • Dr. Lynne M. Hudson, Chair, 419-530-2475. Fax: 419-530-8447. E-mail: lhudson@utnet.utoledo.edu.

University of Utah, Graduate School of Education, Department of Educational Psychology, Salt Lake City, UT 84112-1107. Awards MA, M Ed, MS, M Stat, PhD. One or more programs accredited by APA. Evening/weekend programs available. Faculty: 17 full-time (4 women), 52 part-time (21 women). Students: 105 full-time (65 women), 52 part-time (34 women); includes 28 minority (4 African Americans, 9 Asian Americans, 11 Hispanics, 4 Native Americans), 4 international. Average age 33. In 1997, 20 master's, 8 doctorates awarded. *Degree requirements:* For master's, variable foreign language requirement, thesis (for some programs), comprehensive exam; for doctorate, variable foreign language requirement, dissertation (for some programs), oral exam. *Entrance requirements:* GRE, TOEFL (minimum score 500), minimum GPA of 3.0. Application deadline: 7/1. Application fee: $30 ($50 for international students). *Tuition:* $2045 per year full-time, $562 per semester (minimum) part-time for state residents; $6129 per year full-time, $1607 per semester (minimum) part-time for nonresidents. *Financial aid:* In 1997–98, 10 teaching assistantships were awarded; Federal Work-Study, institutionally sponsored loans, and career-related internships or fieldwork also available. *Faculty research:* Autism, computer technology and instruction, cognitive behavior, aging, group counseling. • William Jenson, Chair, 801-581-7148. Fax: 801-581-5566. E-mail: jenson@gse.utah.edu. Application contact: Charles H. Gregg, Director of Graduate Studies, 801-581-7361. E-mail: gregg@gse.utah.edu.

University of Victoria, Faculty of Education, Department of Psychological Foundations, Victoria, BC V8W 2Y2, Canada. Offers programs in counseling (MA, M Ed); educational psychology (MA, M Ed, PhD), including counseling psychology (MA, M Ed), learning development (MA), measurement evaluation and computer applications in education (MA, M Ed), special education (M Ed), special eduction (MA). Part-time programs available. Postbaccalaureate distance learning degree programs offered. Faculty: 15 full-time (5 women). Students: 168 full-time (132 women), 15 part-time (11 women); includes 5 international. Average age 37. 110 applicants, 35% accepted. In 1997, 23 master's, 12 doctorates awarded. *Degree requirements:* For master's, thesis (for some programs), comprehensive exam (M Ed) required, foreign language not required; for doctorate, dissertation, candidacy exam required, foreign language not required. *Average time to degree:* master's–2.3 years full-time; doctorate–4.0 years full-time. *Entrance requirements:* 2 years of work experience in relevant field, minimum B average. Application deadline: 4/30 (rolling processing). Application fee: $50. *Tuition:* $2080 per year full-time, $557 per semester part-time. *Financial aid:* In 1997–98, 29 students received aid, including fellowships totaling $22,800; research assistantships, teaching assistantships, institutionally sponsored loans also available. Financial aid application deadline: 2/15. *Faculty research:* Learning and development (child, adolescent and adult), special education and exceptional children, evaluation and measurement. • Dr. Walter Muir, Chair, 250-721-7799. Fax: 250-721-6190. Application contact: Sarah Baylow, Graduate Secretary, 250-721-7882. Fax: 250-721-7767. E-mail: sbaylow@uvic.ca.

University of Virginia, Curry School of Education, Department of Leadership, Foundations and Policy, Program in Educational Psychology, Charlottesville, VA 22903. Awards M Ed, Ed D, Ed S. Accredited by NCATE. Faculty: 37 full-time (12 women), 1 part-time (0 women). Students: 33 full-time (22 women), 13 part-time (10 women); includes 8 minority (5 African Americans, 2 Asian Americans, 1 Hispanic), 2 international. Average age 31. 301 applicants, 24% accepted. In 1997, 61 master's, 2 doctorates awarded. *Entrance requirements:* GRE General Test. Application deadline: 3/1 (11/15 for spring admission). Application fee: $40. *Tuition:* $4876 per year full-time, $944 per semester (minimum) part-time for state residents; $15,824 per year full-time, $2748 per semester (minimum) part-time for nonresidents. • Application contact: Linda Berry, Student Enrollment Coordinator, 804-924-0738. E-mail: lrb8e@virginia.edu.

University of Waterloo, Faculty of Arts, Department of Psychology, Waterloo, ON N2L 3G1, Canada. Offerings include educational psychology (MA Sc). Department faculty: 30 full-time (10 women), 37 part-time (10 women). *Application deadline:* 1/15 (priority date). *Application fee:* $50. *Tuition:* $3220 per year. • Dr. M. P. Zana, Chair, 519-888-4567 Ext. 2546. Application contact: Joyce Fisher, Graduate Secretary, 519-888-4567 Ext. 2043. Fax: 519-746-8631. E-mail: gradpsyc@watarts.uwaterloo.ca.

The University of Western Ontario, Social Sciences Division, Faculty of Education, Program in Educational Studies, London, ON N6A 5B8, Canada. Offerings include educational psychology/special education (M Ed). Program faculty: 30 full-time (10 women). *Average time to degree:* master's–2 years full-time, 3 years part-time. *Application deadline:* 2/1. *Application fee:* $50. • Dr. S. Haggerty, Graduate Chair, 519-661-2099. E-mail: haggerty@edu.uwo.ca. Application contact: L. Kulak, Graduate Supervisor, 519-661-2099. Fax: 519-661-3833. E-mail: kulak@edu.uwo.ca.

University of Wisconsin–Madison, School of Education, Department of Educational Psychology, Madison, WI 53706-1380. Awards MS, PhD. One or more programs accredited by APA. *Degree requirements:* For doctorate, dissertation. *Entrance requirements:* GRE General Test. Application fee: $38. *Tuition:* $4928 per year full-time, $926 per semester (minimum) part-time for state residents; $15,190 per year full-time, $2849 per semester (minimum) part-time for nonresidents.

University of Wisconsin–Milwaukee, School of Education, Program in Educational Psychology, Milwaukee, WI 53201-0413. Awards MS. Part-time programs available. Faculty: 21 full-time (9 women). Students: 53 full-time (39 women), 182 part-time (150 women); includes 34 minority (20 African Americans, 6 Asian Americans, 7 Hispanics, 1 Native American), 1 international. 201 applicants, 65% accepted. In 1997, 68 degrees awarded. *Entrance requirements:* Minimum GPA of 3.0. Application deadline: 1/1 (priority date; rolling processing; 9/1 for spring admission). Application fee: $45 ($75 for international students). *Tuition:* $4996 per year full-time, $1030 per semester (minimum) part-time for state residents; $15,216 per year full-time, $2947 per semester (minimum) part-time for nonresidents. *Financial aid:* In 1997–98, 4 fellowships, 1 teaching assistantship, 4 project assistantships were awarded; research assistantships and career-related internships or fieldwork also available. Aid available to part-time students. Financial aid application deadline: 4/15. • Douglas Mickelson, Chair, 414-229-4767.

Washington State University, College of Education, Department of Teaching and Learning, Pullman, WA 99164-1610. Offerings include educational psychology (MA, MAT, M Ed, MIT, Ed D, PhD). Accredited by NCATE. Department faculty: 24 full-time (10 women). *Degree requirements:* For master's, oral exam required, foreign language not required; for doctorate, dissertation, oral exam required, foreign language not required. *Average time to degree:* master's–2 years full-time; doctorate–4 years full-time. *Entrance requirements:* GRE General Test, minimum GPA of 3.0. Application deadline: 3/1 (priority date; rolling processing). Application fee: $35. *Tuition:* $5334 per year full-time, $267 per credit hour part-time for state residents; $13,380 per year full-time, $677 per credit hour part-time for nonresidents. • Dr. Darcy Miller, Chair, 509-335-7296.

Wayne State University, College of Education, Division of Theoretical and Behavioral Foundations, Detroit, MI 48202. Offerings include educational psychology (M Ed, PhD, Ed S). Accredited by NCATE. PhD (history, philosophy, and sociology of education) admissions temporarily suspended. Division faculty: 90. *Application deadline:* 7/1. *Application fee:* $20 ($30 for international students). *Expenses:* Tuition $163 per credit hour for state residents; $355 per credit hour for nonresidents. Fees $498 per year full-time, $114 per semester (minimum) part-time. • Dr. JoAnne Holbert, Associate Dean, 313-577-0210.

West Virginia University, College of Human Resources and Education, Department of Advanced Educational Studies, Morgantown, WV 26506. Offerings include educational psychology (MA, Ed D), with options in education (Ed D), educational psychology (MA). Accredited by NCATE. *Degree requirements:* For doctorate, dissertation required, foreign language not required. *Entrance requirements:* TOEFL (minimum score 550). Application deadline: rolling. Application fee: $45. *Tuition:* $2820 per year full-time, $149 per credit hour part-time for state residents; $8104 per year full-time, $443 per credit hour part-time for nonresidents. • Dr. David L. McCrory, Chair, 304-283-3803 Ext. 1706. Fax: 304-293-2279. E-mail: dmccrory@wvu.edu.

West Virginia University, College of Human Resources and Education, Program in Educational Psychology, Morgantown, WV 26506. Offers education (Ed D), educational psychology (MA). Accredited by NCATE. Evening/weekend programs available. Students: 6 full-time (3 women), 1 (woman) part-time; includes 1 minority (African American). Average age 25. 25 applicants, 52% accepted. In 1997, 3 master's awarded (67% found work related to degree, 33% continued full-time study); 4 doctorates awarded (20% entered university research/teaching, 80% found other work related to degree). *Degree requirements:* For master's, thesis, content exams required, foreign language not required; for doctorate, computer language, dissertation, comprehensive exam required, foreign language not required. *Average time to degree:* master's–2 years full-time, 3 years part-time; doctorate–4 years full-time, 5.5 years part-time. *Entrance requirements:* For master's, GRE General Test (minimum combined score of 1100)

West Virginia University (continued)
or MAT (minimum score 55), TOEFL (minimum score 550), minimum GPA of 3.0, interview; for doctorate, GRE General Test (minimum combined score of 1100) or MAT (minimum score 55), TOEFL (minimum score 550), minimum graduate GPA of 3.25. Application deadline: rolling. Application fee: $45. *Tuition:* $2820 per year full-time, $149 per credit hour part-time for state residents; $8104 per year full-time, $443 per credit hour part-time for nonresidents. *Financial aid:* In 1997–98, 2 fellowships averaging $1,000 per month, 2 research assistantships averaging $800 per month and totaling $14,400, 3 teaching assistantships averaging $612 per month and totaling $22,032 were awarded; full and partial tuition waivers, Federal Work-Study, institutionally sponsored loans, and career-related internships or fieldwork also available. Financial aid application deadline: 2/1; applicants required to submit FAFSA. *Faculty research:* Learning development, instructional design, stimulus control, rehabilitation, problem solving, meta cognition. • Application contact: Dr. Daniel E. Hursh, Graduate Program Coordinator, 304-293-2515 Ext. 1355. Fax: 304-293-7388. E-mail: dehursh@wvu.edu.

Wichita State University, College of Education, Department of Administration, Counseling, Educational and School Psychology, Wichita, KS 67260. Offerings include educational psychology (M Ed). Accredited by NCATE. Department faculty: 15 full-time (7 women), 71 part-time (33 women). *Degree requirements:* Comprehensive exam required, thesis optional, foreign language not required. *Entrance requirements:* TOEFL (minimum score 550), minimum GPA of 2.75. Application deadline: 7/1 (priority date; rolling processing; 1/1 for spring admission). Application fee: $25 ($40 for international students). Electronic applications accepted. *Expenses:* Tuition $2303 per year full-time, $96 per credit hour part-time for state residents; $7691 per year full-time, $321 per credit hour part-time for nonresidents. Fees $490 per year full-time, $75 per semester (minimum) part-time. • Dr. Orpha Duell, Chairperson, 316-978-6299. Fax: 316-978-3102. E-mail: oduell@wsuhub.uc.twsu.edu.

Foundations and Philosophy of Education

Antioch New England Graduate School, Graduate School, Department of Education, Experienced Educators Program, 40 Avon Street, Keene, NH 03431-3516. Offers education by design (M Ed), professional development (M Ed). Faculty: 7 full-time (2 women), 12 part-time (11 women). Students: 49 full-time (37 women), 28 part-time (22 women). 57 applicants, 98% accepted. In 1997, 34 degrees awarded. *Degree requirements:* Thesis, practicum required, foreign language not required. *Entrance requirements:* Previous course work and work experience in education. Application deadline: 5/1 (rolling processing). Application fee: $40. *Expenses:* Tuition $12,700 per year full-time, $330 per credit part-time. Fees $165 per year. *Financial aid:* 10 students received aid; Federal Work-Study and career-related internships or fieldwork available. *Faculty research:* Classroom action research, school restructuring, problem-based learning, brain-based learning. • Dr. Talu Robertson, Director, 603-357-3122 Ext. 359. E-mail: trobertson@antiochne.edu. Application contact: Diane K. Hewitt, Co-Director of Admissions, 603-357-6265 Ext. 286. Fax: 603-357-0718. E-mail: dhewitt@antiochne.edu.

Appalachian State University, College of Education, Department of Human Development and Psychological Counseling, Boone, NC 28608. Offerings include community counseling (MA). Accredited by NCATE. Department faculty: 17 full-time (7 women), 5 part-time (4 women). *Degree requirements:* Thesis or alternative, comprehensive exams required, foreign language not required. *Entrance requirements:* GRE General Test. Application deadline: 2/1 (priority date; rolling processing). Application fee: $35. *Tuition:* $1811 per year full-time, $354 per semester (minimum) part-time for state residents; $9081 per year full-time, $2171 per semester (minimum) part-time for nonresidents. • Dr. Lee Baruth, Chairman, 704-262-2055.

Arizona State University, College of Education, Division of Educational Leadership and Policy Studies, Academic Program in Social and Philosophical Foundations of Education, Tempe, AZ 85287. Awards MA. *Degree requirements:* Thesis or alternative. *Entrance requirements:* GRE General Test or MAT. Application fee: $45. *Expenses:* Tuition $2088 per year full-time, $110 per hour part-time for state residents; $9040 per year full-time, $377 per hour part-time for nonresidents. Fees $72 per year full-time, $18 per semester (minimum) part-time. *Faculty research:* Minority education, theory of evaluation and educational policy. • Dr. Mary Lee Smith, Coordinator, 602-965-6357. E-mail: delps@asu.edu.

Brigham Young University, David O. McKay School of Education, Department of Educational Leadership and Foundations, Provo, UT 84602-1001. Awards M Ed, Ed D, PhD. Accredited by NCATE. Faculty: 11 full-time (1 woman). Students: 57 full-time (23 women), 60 part-time (25 women); includes 24 minority (3 African Americans, 15 Asian Americans, 5 Hispanics, 1 Native American), 12 international. Average age 35. 88 applicants, 55% accepted. In 1997, 40 master's, 15 doctorates awarded. *Degree requirements:* For doctorate, 1 foreign language, dissertation. *Entrance requirements:* For master's, minimum GPA of 3.0 in last 60 hours; for doctorate, minimum GPA of 3.25 in last 60 hours. Application deadline: 2/15. Application fee: $30. *Tuition:* $3200 per year full-time, $178 per credit hour part-time for state residents; $4800 per year full-time, $266 per credit hour part-time for nonresidents. *Financial aid:* In 1997–98, 4 research assistantships were awarded; career-related internships or fieldwork also available. *Faculty research:* Cognition, mentoring, pre-service training of administrators, policy development. • Dr. E. Vance Randall, Chair, 801-378-5073. Fax: 801-378-7740. E-mail: vance_randall@byu.edu.

California State University, Long Beach, College of Education, Department of Educational Psychology and Administration, Program in the Social and Philosophical Foundations of Education, Long Beach, CA 90840-2201. Awards MA. Students: 1 full-time (0 women), 8 part-time (all women); includes 3 minority (2 Asian Americans, 1 Hispanic), 2 international. Average age 32. 9 applicants, 89% accepted. In 1997, 2 degrees awarded. *Degree requirements:* Comprehensive exam or thesis required, foreign language not required. *Entrance requirements:* GRE General Test, minimum GPA of 2.75. Application deadline: 8/1 (rolling processing; 12/1 for spring admission). Application fee: $55. *Expenses:* Tuition $0 for state residents; $246 per unit for nonresidents. Fees $1846 per year full-time, $1180 per year part-time. *Financial aid:* Application deadline 3/2. • Dr. Robert Berdan, Chair, Department of Educational Psychology and Administration, 562-985-4517. Fax: 562-985-4534. E-mail: rberdan@csulb.edu.

California State University, Los Angeles, School of Education, Division of Educational Foundations and Interdivisional Studies, Major in Educational Foundations, Los Angeles, CA 90032-8530. Offers programs in psychological foundations (MA), social foundations (MA). Accredited by NCATE. Part-time and evening/weekend programs available. Students: 6 full-time (4 women), 15 part-time (9 women); includes 14 minority (1 Asian American, 13 Hispanics), 1 international. In 1997, 3 degrees awarded. *Degree requirements:* Comprehensive exam, project, or thesis required, foreign language not required. *Entrance requirements:* TOEFL (minimum score 550), minimum GPA of 2.75 in last 90 units, teaching certificate. Application deadline: 6/30 (rolling processing; 2/1 for spring admission). Application fee: $55. *Expenses:* Tuition $0 for state residents; $164 per unit for nonresidents. Fees $1763 per year full-time, $1097 per year part-time. *Financial aid:* 3 students received aid; Federal Work-Study and career-related internships or fieldwork available. Aid available to part-time students. Financial aid application deadline: 3/1. • Dr. Simeon Slovacek, Chair, Division of Educational Foundations and Interdivisional Studies, 213-343-4330.

California State University, Northridge, College of Education, Department of Educational Leadership and Policy Studies, Program in Administration and Supervision, Northridge, CA 91330. Offerings include educational foundations (MA). Accredited by NCATE. *Entrance requirements:* GRE General Test, MAT, TOEFL. Application deadline: 11/30. Application fee: $55. *Expenses:* Tuition $0 for state residents; $246 per unit for nonresidents. Fees $1970 per year full-time, $1304 per year part-time. • Application contact: John Schulte, Graduate Coordinator, 818-677-2517.

Central Connecticut State University, School of Education and Professional Studies, Department of Teacher Education, Program in Educational Foundations, New Britain, CT 06050-4010. Offers educational foundation and policy studies (MS). Part-time and evening/weekend programs available. Students: 1 (woman) full-time, 16 part-time (12 women); includes 1 minority (African American). Average age 34. 5 applicants, 60% accepted. In 1997, 2 degrees awarded. *Degree requirements:* Thesis or alternative, comprehensive exam required, foreign language not required. *Entrance requirements:* TOEFL (minimum score 550), minimum GPA of 2.7. Application deadline: 6/1 (priority date; rolling processing; 12/1 for spring admission). Application fee: $40. *Expenses:* Tuition $4458 per year full-time, $175 per credit hour part-time for state residents; $9943 per year full-time, $175 per credit hour part-time for nonresidents. Fees $45 per semester. *Financial aid:* Federal Work-Study available. Financial aid application deadline: 3/15; applicants required to submit FAFSA. • Dr. Lawrence Klein, Coordinator, 860-832-2424.

Clemson University, College of Health, Education, and Human Development, Department of Foundations and Special Education, Clemson, SC 29634. Awards M Ed. Accredited by NCATE. Part-time and evening/weekend programs available. Students: 4 full-time (3 women), 42 part-time (39 women); includes 1 minority (African American), 1 international. 11 applicants, 55% accepted. In 1997, 24 degrees awarded. *Average time to degree:* master's–1.5 years full-time, 5 years part-time. *Entrance requirements:* TOEFL, GRE or minimum GPA of 3.0, teaching certificate. Application deadline: 6/1. Application fee: $35. *Expenses:* Tuition $3154 per year full-time, $130 per credit hour part-time for state residents; $6452 per year full-time, $264 per credit hour part-time for nonresidents. Fees $190 per year. *Financial aid:* Research assistantships, teaching assistantships, graduate stipends, full tuition waivers, Federal Work-Study, and career-related internships or fieldwork available. Aid available to part-time students. Financial aid application deadline: 6/1; applicants required to submit FAFSA. *Faculty research:* Field-based teacher training transition, assessment, national policy outcome. Total annual research expenditures: $250,000. • Dr. William Fisk, Chair, 864-656-5119. E-mail: bill252@clemson.edu. Application contact: Dr. Janie Hodge, Coordinator, 864-656-1613. Fax: 864-656-1322. E-mail: hodge@clemson.edu.

College of Mount St. Joseph, Education Department, Program in Educational Foundations, Cincinnati, OH 45233-1670. Awards MA Ed. Part-time and evening/weekend programs available. *Degree requirements:* Comprehensive exam required, foreign language and thesis not required. *Entrance requirements:* GRE General Test (minimum combined score of 825), minimum GPA of 2.7. Application deadline: rolling. Application fee: $0. *Tuition:* $320 per credit hour. *Financial aid:* Application deadline 6/1. • Application contact: Jean Abrams, Graduate Secretary, 513-244-4812.

Dalhousie University, School of Education, Halifax, NS B3H 3J5, Canada. Offerings include foundations of education (MA, M Ed, PhD). Program being phased out; applicants no longer accepted. School faculty: 19 full-time, 12 part-time. *Degree requirements:* For master's, thesis required (for some programs), foreign language not required; for doctorate, dissertation required, foreign language not required. • Dr. K. C. Sullivan, Director, 902-494-3724.

Duquesne University, School of Education, Department of Foundations and Leadership, Program in Educational Studies, Pittsburgh, PA 15282-0001. Awards MS Ed. Part-time programs available. Faculty: 4 full-time (2 women), 3 part-time (1 woman). Students: 52. 20 applicants, 75% accepted. In 1997, 16 degrees awarded. *Average time to degree:* master's–1.5 years full-time, 2.5 years part-time. *Entrance requirements:* MAT. Application deadline: 8/1 (rolling processing; 12/1 for spring admission). Application fee: $40. *Expenses:* Tuition $481 per credit. Fees $39 per credit. • Dr. Rick McCown, Chair, Department of Foundations and Leadership, 412-396-5856. Fax: 412-396-5585.

Eastern Michigan University, College of Education, Department of Teacher Education, Program in Social Foundations of Education, Ypsilanti, MI 48197. Awards MA. Accredited by NCATE. Evening/weekend programs available. In 1997, 4 degrees awarded. *Entrance requirements:* GRE, TOEFL (minimum score 500). Application deadline: 5/15 (rolling processing; 3/15 for spring admission). Application fee: $30. *Expenses:* Tuition $2691 per year full-time, $150 per credit hour part-time for state residents; $6300 per year full-time, $350 per credit hour part-time for nonresidents. Fees $368 per year full-time, $88 per semester (minimum) part-time. *Financial aid:* Fellowships, teaching assistantships available. Aid available to part-time students. Financial aid application deadline: 3/15; applicants required to submit FAFSA. • Dr. Maureen McCormack, Coordinator, 734-487-1446.

Eastern Washington University, College of Education and Human Development, Department of Education, Program in Foundations of Education, Cheney, WA 99004-2431. Awards M Ed. Accredited by NCATE. *Degree requirements:* Comprehensive exam required, thesis not required. *Entrance requirements:* Minimum GPA of 3.0. Application deadline: 4/1 (priority date; rolling processing; 1/15 for spring admission). Application fee: $35. *Tuition:* $4200 per year full-time, $140 per credit part-time for state residents; $12,780 per year full-time, $415 per credit part-time for nonresidents. *Financial aid:* Application deadline 2/1. • Dr. Rita Seedorf, Adviser, 509-359-7029.

Fairfield University, Graduate School of Education and Allied Professions, Department of Curriculum and Instruction, Program in Teaching and Foundation, Fairfield, CT 06430-5195. Awards MA, CAS. *Degree requirements:* For master's, comprehensive exams required, foreign language not required. *Entrance requirements:* For master's, PRAXIS I (CBT), TOEFL, minimum QPA of 2.67. Application deadline: 7/10 (rolling processing). Application fee: $40. *Expenses:* Tuition $350 per credit hour (minimum). Fees $20 per semester (minimum). • Application contact: Karen Creecy, Assistant Dean, 203-254-4250. Fax: 203-254-4241. E-mail: klcreecy@fair1.fairfield.edu.

Florida Atlantic University, College of Education, Department of Teacher Education, Boca Raton, FL 33431-0991. Offerings include foundations of education (M Ed). Department faculty: 24 full-time (18 women), 6 part-time (4 women). *Entrance requirements:* GRE General Test. Application deadline: rolling. Application fee: $20. *Expenses:* Tuition $2520 per year full-time, $140 per credit hour part-time for state residents; $8712 per year full-time, $484 per credit hour part-time for nonresidents. Fees $5 per year (minimum). • Dr. Valerie Bristor, Chairperson, 561-297-3584. Application contact: University Registrar, 561-297-3040.

Florida State University, College of Education, Department of Educational Foundations and Policy Studies, Program in Foundations of Education, Tallahassee, FL 32306. Offers history and philosophy of education (MS, PhD, Ed S), international and intercultural education (MS,

PhD, Ed S), social science and education (PhD, Ed S). Faculty: 8 full-time (3 women). Students: 24 full-time (17 women), 25 part-time (10 women); includes 11 minority (3 African Americans, 6 Asian Americans, 2 Hispanics). 33 applicants, 58% accepted. In 1997, 2 master's, 2 doctorates awarded. *Degree requirements:* For master's and Ed S, comprehensive exam required, thesis optional; for doctorate, dissertation, comprehensive exam. *Entrance requirements:* GRE General Test (minimum combined score of 1000), minimum GPA of 3.0. Application deadline: 7/1 (priority date; rolling processing; 11/1 for spring admission). Application fee: $20. *Tuition:* $139 per credit hour for state residents; $482 per credit hour for nonresidents. *Financial aid:* Fellowships, research assistantships, teaching assistantships, and career-related internships or fieldwork available. • Dr. Sande Milton, Chair, Department of Educational Foundations and Policy Studies, 850-644-4594. E-mail: milton@mail.coe.fsu.edu. Application contact: Brendetta Douglas, Admissions Secretary, 850-644-4594. Fax: 850-644-6401.

The George Washington University, Graduate School of Education and Human Development, Department of Educational Leadership, Program in Education Policy Studies, Washington, DC 20052. Awards MA Ed. Accredited by NCATE. Students: 2 full-time (both women), 7 part-time (6 women); includes 1 minority (Hispanic). Average age 25. 14 applicants, 79% accepted. In 1997, 3 degrees awarded. *Degree requirements:* Comprehensive exam required, foreign language and thesis not required. *Entrance requirements:* GRE General Test or MAT, interview, minimum GPA of 2.75. Application deadline: 3/1 (priority date; rolling processing; 10/1 for spring admission). Application fee: $50. *Expenses:* Tuition $680 per semester hour. Fees $35 per semester hour. *Financial aid:* Fellowships, partial tuition waivers, Federal Work-Study, and career-related internships or fieldwork available. • Dr. John Boswell, Director, 202-994-7117.

Georgia College and State University, School of Education, Department of Foundations and Secondary Education, Milledgeville, GA 31061. Awards MAT, M Ed, Ed S. Accredited by NCATE. Students: 30 full-time (22 women), 30 part-time (15 women); includes 10 minority (all African Americans). Average age 31. In 1997, 13 master's, 6 Ed Ss awarded. *Degree requirements:* For master's, computer language, comprehensive exit exam required, foreign language and thesis not required; for Ed S, computer language, comprehensive exit exam, oral exam, research project required, foreign language and thesis not required. *Entrance requirements:* For master's, GRE General Test (minimum combined score of 800) or NTE (minimum score 550 on each core battery test), MAT (minimum score 44), minimum GPA of 2.5, NT-4 certificate; for Ed S, GRE General Test (minimum combined score of 900) or NTE (minimum score 575 on each core battery test), MAT (minimum score 48), master's degree, minimum graduate GPA of 3.25, NT-5 certificate, 2 years of teaching experience. Application deadline: 7/31 (priority date; rolling processing). Application fee: $10. *Financial aid:* Federal Work-Study and career-related internships or fieldwork available. Aid available to part-time students. Financial aid application deadline: 4/15. • Dr. Charlotte Harris, Chair, 912-471-2898.

Georgia State University, College of Education, Department of Educational Policy Studies, Program in Social Foundations of Education, Atlanta, GA 30303-3083. Awards MS, PhD. Accredited by NCATE. Part-time and evening/weekend programs available. Students: 5 full-time (3 women), 10 part-time (4 women); includes 2 minority (both African Americans), 1 international. Average age 38. 7 applicants, 86% accepted. In 1997, 2 master's awarded. *Degree requirements:* For master's, thesis or project; for doctorate, dissertation, comprehensive exam. *Entrance requirements:* For master's, GRE General Test (minimum combined score of 800) or MAT (minimum score 44), minimum GPA of 2.5; for doctorate, GRE General Test (minimum score 500 on verbal section, 500 on either quantitative or analytical sections) or MAT (minimum score 53), minimum GPA of 3.3. Application fee: $25. *Expenses:* Tuition $2673 per year full-time, $99 per semester hour part-time for state residents; $10,692 per year full-time, $396 per semester hour part-time for nonresidents. Fees $228 per year. *Financial aid:* Teaching assistantships and career-related internships or fieldwork available. *Faculty research:* Teacher unionism, African and African-American history and culture, multicultural and workplace education, teacher autonomy and epistemology. • Dr. H. Parker Blount, Chair, Department of Educational Policy Studies, 404-651-2582.

Harvard University, Graduate School of Education, Area of Learning and Teaching, Cambridge, MA 02138. Offers programs in arts in education (Ed M); education in the community (Ed D); experienced teachers program (Ed M, CAS); individualized program (Ed M); learning and teaching (Ed M, Ed D), including curriculum development and evaluation (Ed D), study of teaching (Ed D); mid-career mathematics and science (teaching certification) (Ed M, CAS); philosophy of education and curriculum theory (Ed D); schools and schooling (Ed D); teaching and curriculum (teaching certification) (Ed M); technology in education (Ed M). Part-time programs available. Faculty: 7 full-time (5 women), 16 part-time (8 women), 10.3 FTE. Students: 176 full-time (111 women), 48 part-time (32 women); includes 62 minority (20 African Americans, 25 Asian Americans, 13 Hispanics, 4 Native Americans), 13 international. Average age 35. 136 applicants, 17% accepted. In 1997, 218 master's, 11 doctorates, 5 CASs awarded. Terminal master's awarded for partial completion of doctoral program. *Degree requirements:* For doctorate, dissertation required, foreign language not required. *Average time to degree:* master's–1 year full-time, 2.1 years part-time; doctorate–6.3 years full-time, 9 years part-time; other advanced degree–1 year full-time, 2 years part-time. *Entrance requirements:* GRE General Test, TOEFL (minimum score 600), TWE (minimum score 5.0). Application deadline: 1/2. Application fee: $60. *Financial aid:* In 1997–98, 67 students received aid, including 21 fellowships (10 to first-year students) totaling $344,113, 8 research assistantships averaging $588 per month, 60 teaching assistantships averaging $670 per month, 49 need-based scholarships (3 to first-year students) totaling $416,012; Federal Work-Study and career-related internships or fieldwork also available. Aid available to part-time students. Financial aid application deadline: 1/8; applicants required to submit FAFSA. *Faculty research:* Science education, philosophy of education, community education, perceived and actual participation in secondary school classrooms. • Robert Kegan, Chair, 617-496-2974. Fax: 617-495-7843. Application contact: Roland Hence, Director of Admissions, 617-495-3414. Fax: 617-496-3577. E-mail: gseadmissions@harvard.edu.

Hofstra University, School of Education and Allied Human Services, Department of Administration and Policy Studies, Specialization in Foundations of Education, Hempstead, NY 11549. Awards MS Ed, CAS. Accredited by NCATE. Part-time and evening/weekend programs available. Faculty: 3 full-time (1 woman), 4 part-time (2 women). Students: 12 part-time (7 women). Average age 30. 10 applicants, 60% accepted. In 1997, 5 master's awarded. *Degree requirements:* For master's, comprehensive exam required, foreign language not required. *Entrance requirements:* For CAS, minimum GPA of 2.9. Application deadline: rolling. Application fee: $40 ($75 for international students). *Expenses:* Tuition $10,968 per year full-time, $457 per credit hour part-time. Fees $670 per year full-time, $112 per semester (minimum) part-time. *Financial aid:* In 1997–98, 3 students received aid, including 3 grants totaling $1,500; institutionally sponsored loans also available. Aid available to part-time students. Financial aid application deadline: 4/1. *Faculty research:* Seventeenth-century Dutch paintings, aesthetic issues in education, alternative schools. • Dr. Timothy H. Smith, Director, 516-463-5758. Fax: 516-463-6503. E-mail: edaths@hofstra.edu. Application contact: Mary Beth Carey, Dean of Admissions, 516-463-6700. Fax: 516-560-7660. E-mail: hofstra@hofstra.edu.

Indiana University Bloomington, School of Education, Department of Educational Leadership and Policy Studies, Program in History, Philosophy, and Policy Studies in Education, Bloomington, IN 47405. Offers history and philosophy of education (MS); history, philosophy, and policy studies in education (PhD); international and comparative education (MS). Accredited by NCATE. PhD offered through the University Graduate School. Students: 22 full-time (13 women), 17 part-time (8 women); includes 6 minority (5 African Americans, 1 Asian American), 5 international. In 1997, 1 master's, 1 doctorate awarded. *Degree requirements:* For doctorate, dissertation required, foreign language not required. *Entrance requirements:* For master's, GRE General Test (minimum combined score of 1300 on three sections); for doctorate, GRE General Test (minimum combined score of 1500 on three sections). Application deadline: 6/1. Application fee: $35. *Expenses:* Tuition $153 per credit hour for state residents; $446 per credit hour for nonresidents. Fees $343 per year. *Financial aid:* Fellowships, teaching assistantships, full and partial tuition waivers, Federal Work-Study available. *Faculty research:* Policy development, Third World literacy, history of American high schools, history of curriculum, philanthropy. • Head, 812-856-8374. Application contact: Dr. Dale P. Scannell, Director of Graduate Studies, 812-856-8540.

Iowa State University of Science and Technology, College of Education, Department of Educational Leadership and Policy Studies, Program in Historical, Philosophical and Comparative Studies in Education, Ames, IA 50011. Awards M Ed, MS. *Degree requirements:* Thesis or alternative. *Entrance requirements:* TOEFL. Application fee: $20 ($30 for international students). *Expenses:* Tuition $3166 per year full-time, $176 per credit part-time for state residents; $9324 per year full-time, $518 per credit part-time for nonresidents. Fees $200 per year. • Coordinator, 515-294-1241.

Kansas State University, College of Education, Department of Foundations and Adult Education, Manhattan, KS 66506. Awards MS, Ed D, PhD. Accredited by NCATE. Faculty: 8 full-time (3 women). Students: 23 full-time (15 women), 89 part-time (60 women); includes 10 minority (8 African Americans, 1 Asian American, 1 Hispanic), 8 international. 29 applicants, 86% accepted. *Degree requirements:* For master's, thesis or alternative required, foreign language not required; for doctorate, dissertation required, foreign language not required. *Entrance requirements:* For master's, minimum B average; for doctorate, GRE General Test (minimum combined score of 1000; average 1010), minimum B average, writing sample. Application deadline: 4/1 (priority date; rolling processing; 9/1 for spring admission). Application fee: $0 ($25 for international students). Electronic applications accepted. *Tuition:* $2218 per year full-time, $401 per semester (minimum) part-time for state residents; $6336 per year full-time, $1087 per semester (minimum) part-time for nonresidents. *Financial aid:* Career-related internships or fieldwork available. • Robert Newhouse, Chair, 785-532-5535. Application contact: Paul Burden, Assistant Dean, 785-532-5595. Fax: 785-532-7304. E-mail: gradstudy@mail.educ.ksu.edu.

Kent State University, Graduate School of Education, Department of Educational Foundations and Special Services, Program in Educational Foundations, Kent, OH 44242-0001. Offers cultural foundations (MA, M Ed, PhD), educational psychology (MA, M Ed), evaluation and measurement (MA, M Ed, PhD), learning and development (MA, M Ed). Faculty: 8 full-time (3 women), 15 part-time (10 women). Students: 33 full-time (18 women), 33 part-time (19 women); includes 10 minority (8 African Americans, 2 Asian Americans), 3 international. In 1997, 1 master's, 1 doctorate awarded. *Degree requirements:* For master's, thesis (MA) required, foreign language not required; for doctorate, dissertation required, foreign language not required. *Entrance requirements:* For master's, GRE General Test; for doctorate, GRE General Test (minimum score 550 on verbal section). Application deadline: rolling. Application fee: $30. *Tuition:* $4752 per year full-time, $216 per credit hour part-time for state residents; $9213 per year full-time, $419 per credit hour part-time for nonresidents. *Financial aid:* Application deadline 4/1. • Dr. Averil McClelland, Coordinator, 330-672-2294. Application contact: Deborah Barber, Director, Office of Academic Services, 330-672-2862. Fax: 330-672-3549.

Loyola College, College of Arts and Sciences, Department of Education, Program in Foundations of Education, Baltimore, MD 21210-2699. Awards MA, M Ed, CAS. Part-time and evening/weekend programs available. Students: 2 part-time (both women). *Entrance requirements:* For CAS, master's degree. Application deadline: 8/1 (rolling processing; 12/1 for spring admission). Application fee: $35. *Tuition:* $222 per credit (minimum). *Financial aid:* Career-related internships or fieldwork available. • Dr. Beatrice Sarlos, Coordinator, 410-617-2492.

Loyola University Chicago, School of Education, Department of Educational Leadership and Policy Studies, Program in Cultural and Educational Policy Studies, 820 North Michigan Avenue, Chicago, IL 60611-2196. Offers comparative-international education (MA, M Ed, Ed D, PhD), history of education (MA, M Ed, Ed D, PhD), philosophy of education (MA, M Ed, Ed D, PhD), sociology of education (MA, M Ed, Ed D, PhD). Part-time programs available. Faculty: 4 full-time (0 women), 6 part-time (3 women). Students: 23 (8 women); includes 3 African Americans, 2 Hispanics, 1 international. Average age 30. In 1997, 1 master's awarded; 3 doctorates awarded (100% found work related to degree). *Degree requirements:* For master's, comprehensive exam (M Ed), thesis (MA) required, foreign language not required; for doctorate, dissertation, comprehensive exam, oral candidacy exam required, foreign language not required. *Entrance requirements:* For master's, GRE General Test; for doctorate, GRE General Test, interview. Application deadline: 8/1 (rolling processing; 12/1 for spring admission). Application fee: $35. *Tuition:* $467 per semester hour. *Financial aid:* 3 students received aid; fellowships, research assistantships, partial tuition waivers, Federal Work-Study, institutionally sponsored loans, and career-related internships or fieldwork available. Aid available to part-time students. Financial aid application deadline: 2/1; applicants required to submit FAFSA. *Faculty research:* Politics of education, cultural foundations, policy studies, qualitative research methods, multicultural diversity. • Dr. Steven Miller, Director, 847-853-3331. Application contact: Marie Rosin-Dittmar, Admissions Coordinator, 847-853-3323. Fax: 847-853-3375. E-mail: mrosind@wpo.it.luc.edu.

Maharishi University of Management, Department of Education, Fairfield, IA 52557. Offerings include foundations of education (MA). Department faculty: 11 (2 women). *Degree requirements:* Thesis or alternative required, foreign language not required. *Entrance requirements:* GRE, TOEFL (minimum score 550), minimum GPA of 3.0. Application deadline: 4/15 (priority date; rolling processing). Application fee: $40. • Dr. Christopher Jones, Associate Chairperson, 515-472-1105. Application contact: Harry Bright, Director of Admissions, 515-472-1166.

McGill University, Faculty of Graduate Studies and Research, Faculty of Education, Department of Culture and Values in Education, Montréal, PQ H3A 2T5, Canada. Offers programs in art education (M Ed), culture and values in education (MA, PhD). M Ed and PhD new for fall 1998. Part-time and evening/weekend programs available. Faculty: 11 full-time (4 women), 8 part-time (3 women). Students: 41 full-time (22 women), 20 part-time (15 women). 23 applicants, 91% accepted. In 1997, 9 master's awarded. *Degree requirements:* For master's, thesis (for some programs); for doctorate, dissertation. *Entrance requirements:* For master's, TOEFL (minimum score 550), minimum GPA of 3.0. Application deadline: 3/1 (priority date; rolling processing). Application fee: $60. *Expenses:* Tuition $1668 per year for Canadian residents; $8268 per year for nonresidents. Fees $828 per year for Canadian residents; $1216 per year for nonresidents. *Financial aid:* In 1997–98, 2 teaching assistantships were awarded. *Faculty research:* Comparative and international education, moral and religious education, peace education, art and aesthetics education, values education. • D. C. Smith, Chair, 514-398-3328. E-mail: smith@education.mcgill.ca. Application contact: R. Ghosh, Director of Graduate Studies, 514-398-4493. Fax: 514-398-4642. E-mail: ghosh@education.mcgill.ca.

Mount Saint Vincent University, Department of Education, Program in Educational Foundations, Halifax, NS B3M 2J6, Canada. Awards MA, MA Ed, MA(R), M Ed. Faculty: 7 full-time (3 women), 2 part-time (1 woman). Students: 5. 5 applicants, 60% accepted. *Degree requirements:* Thesis. *Entrance requirements:* Bachelor's degree in related field, minimum B average. Application deadline: 3/1 (priority date; rolling processing; 9/1 for spring admission). Application fee: $40. *Expenses:* Tuition $1024 per course. Fees $25 per course. *Financial aid:* In 1997–98, 1 fellowship (to a first-year student) totaling $500 was awarded. Financial aid application deadline: 5/1. *Faculty research:* Research paradigms, moral aspects of education and teaching, private/independent schools, theory of critical thinking, teachers as workers and as agents of social change. • Dr. Blye Frank, Head, 902-457-6184. Fax: 902-457-4911. E-mail: blye.frank@msvu.ca. Application contact: Susan Tanner, Assistant Registrar, 902-457-6363. Fax: 902-457-6498. E-mail: susan.tanner@msvu.ca.

New York University, School of Education, Department of Culture and Communication, Program in History of Education, New York, NY 10012-1019. Awards MA, PhD. Part-time and evening/weekend programs available. Faculty: 2 full-time, 2 part-time. Students: 1 full-time, 10 part-time. 4 applicants, 100% accepted. In 1997, 1 doctorate awarded. Terminal master's

Directory: Foundations and Philosophy of Education

New York University (continued)

awarded for partial completion of doctoral program. *Degree requirements:* For master's, thesis required (for some programs), foreign language not required; for doctorate, dissertation. *Entrance requirements:* For master's, TOEFL; for doctorate, GRE General Test, TOEFL, interview. Application deadline: 2/1 (priority date; rolling processing; 12/1 for spring admission). Application fee: $40 ($60 for international students). *Financial aid:* Partial tuition waivers, Federal Work-Study, institutionally sponsored loans available. Aid available to part-time students. Financial aid application deadline: 3/1; applicants required to submit FAFSA. *Faculty research:* American educational thought, foundations in education, history of philanthropy. • Dr. Ellen Condliffe Lagemann, Director, 212-998-5631. Application contact: Office of Graduate Admissions, 212-998-5030. Fax: 212-995-4328.

New York University, School of Education, Department of Culture and Communication, Program in Philosophy of Education, New York, NY 10012-1019. Awards MA, PhD. Faculty: 2 full-time, 2 part-time. Students: 3 part-time. 3 applicants, 33% accepted. *Degree requirements:* For master's, thesis required (for some programs), foreign language not required; for doctorate, dissertation. *Entrance requirements:* For master's, TOEFL; for doctorate, GRE General Test, TOEFL, interview. Application deadline: 2/1 (priority date; rolling processing; 12/1 for spring admission). Application fee: $40 ($60 for international students). *Financial aid:* Partial tuition waivers, Federal Work-Study, institutionally sponsored loans available. Aid available to part-time students. Financial aid application deadline: 3/1; applicants required to submit FAFSA. *Faculty research:* Feminist theory, foundations in education, moral education. • Dr. Thomas Colwell, Co-Director, 212-998-5637. Application contact: Office of Graduate Admissions, 212-998-5030. Fax: 212-995-4328.

Niagara University, Graduate Division of Education, Concentration in Foundations and Teaching, Niagara University, NY 14109. Awards MA, MS Ed. Accredited by NCATE. Part-time and evening/weekend programs available. Faculty: 1 full-time (0 women), 7 part-time (4 women). Students: 10 full-time (7 women), 53 part-time (39 women); includes 2 minority (1 African American, 1 Hispanic), 1 international. In 1997, 21 degrees awarded. *Degree requirements:* Thesis required, foreign language not required. *Entrance requirements:* GRE General Test or MAT. Application deadline: 8/1 (rolling processing). Application fee: $30. *Expenses:* Tuition $4950 per year full-time, $275 per credit hour part-time. Fees $25 per semester. *Financial aid:* Application deadline 3/15. • Dr. Paul J. Vermette, Chairman, 716-286-8550. Application contact: Rev. Daniel F. O'Leary, OMI, Dean of Education, 716-286-8560.

Northern Illinois University, College of Education, Department of Leadership and Educational Policy Studies, Program in Foundations of Education, De Kalb, IL 60115-2854. Awards MS Ed. Accredited by NCATE. Part-time and evening/weekend programs available. Faculty: 7 full-time (3 women). Students: 4 full-time (2 women), 8 part-time (6 women); includes 4 international. Average age 37. 6 applicants, 100% accepted. In 1997, 4 degrees awarded. *Degree requirements:* Comprehensive exam required, thesis optional, foreign language not required. *Entrance requirements:* GRE General Test, TOEFL (minimum score 550), minimum GPA of 2.75. Application deadline: 6/1 (rolling processing; 11/1 for spring admission). Application fee: $0. *Tuition:* $3984 per year full-time, $154 per credit hour part-time for state residents; $8160 per year full-time, $328 per credit hour part-time for nonresidents. *Financial aid:* Fellowships, research assistantships, teaching assistantships, staff assistantships, full tuition waivers, Federal Work-Study, and career-related internships or fieldwork available. Aid available to part-time students. • Dr. Wilma Miranda, Faculty Chair, 815-753-1562.

See in-depth description on page 921.

The Ohio State University, College of Education, School of Teaching and Learning, Program in Educational Theory and Practice, Columbus, OH 43210. Awards MA, M Ed, PhD. Accredited by NCATE. Faculty: 71. Students: 159 full-time (118 women), 389 part-time (343 women); includes 54 minority (44 African Americans, 4 Asian Americans, 5 Hispanics, 1 Native American), 21 international. 141 applicants, 54% accepted. In 1997, 329 master's, 18 doctorates awarded. *Degree requirements:* For master's, thesis optional, foreign language not required; for doctorate, dissertation required, foreign language not required. *Application deadline:* 8/15 (rolling processing). *Application fee:* $30 ($40 for international students). *Tuition:* $5472 per year full-time, $554 per quarter (minimum) part-time for state residents; $14,172 per year full-time, $1424 per quarter (minimum) part-time for nonresidents. *Financial aid:* Fellowships, research assistantships, teaching assistantships, Federal Work-Study, institutionally sponsored loans available. Aid available to part-time students. • Dr. Robert J. Tierney, Director, School of Teaching and Learning, 614-292-1257. Fax: 614-292-7695. E-mail: tierney.4@osu.edu.

Pennsylvania State University University Park Campus, College of Education, Department of Education Policy Studies, Program in Educational Theory and Policy, University Park, PA 16802-1503. Awards MA, PhD. Accredited by NCATE. Students: 17 full-time (15 women), 8 part-time (6 women). *Entrance requirements:* GRE General Test or MAT. Application fee: $40. *Expenses:* Tuition $6534 per year full-time, $276 per credit part-time for state residents; $13,460 per year full-time, $561 per credit part-time for nonresidents. Fees $252 per year (minimum) full-time, $43 per semester (minimum) part-time. • Dr. David Baker, Professor in Charge, 814-865-1488.

Purdue University, School of Education, Department of Educational Studies, West Lafayette, IN 47907. Offerings include foundations of education (MS Ed). Accredited by NCATE. Department faculty: 26 full-time (13 women), 23 part-time (14 women). *Application deadline:* 2/1 (9/15 for spring admission). *Application fee:* $30. Electronic applications accepted. *Tuition:* $3500 per year full-time, $126 per credit hour part-time for state residents; $11,720 per year full-time, $387 per credit hour part-time for nonresidents. • Dr. D. H. Schunk, Head, 765-494-9170. Fax: 765-496-1228. E-mail: dschunk@purdue.edu. Application contact: Christine Larsen, Coordinator of Graduate Studies, 765-494-2345. Fax: 765-494-5832. E-mail: gradoffice@soe.purdue.edu.

Rutgers, The State University of New Jersey, New Brunswick, Graduate School of Education, Department of Educational Theory, Policy and Administration, Program in Social and Philosophical Foundations of Education, New Brunswick, NJ 08903. Awards Ed M, Ed D, Ed S. Part-time programs available. Faculty: 9 full-time. Students: 7 full-time, 17 part-time; includes 8 minority (3 African Americans, 5 Asian Americans). In 1997, 8 master's, 11 doctorates, 2 Ed Ss awarded. Terminal master's awarded for partial completion of doctoral program. *Degree requirements:* For doctorate, dissertation. *Entrance requirements:* GRE General Test. Application deadline: 3/1 (11/1 for spring admission). Application fee: $40. *Expenses:* Tuition $6492 per year full-time, $268 per credit part-time for state residents; $9520 per year full-time, $395 per credit part-time for nonresidents. Fees $208 per year (minimum). *Financial aid:* Application deadline 3/1. • Nobuo Shimahara, Coordinator, 732-932-7496 Ext. 233.

Saint Louis University, Institute for Leadership and Public Service, Programs in Education, Department of Educational Studies, St. Louis, MO 63103-2097. Offerings include foundations (MA, Ed D, PhD). Accredited by NCATE. *Degree requirements:* For master's, comprehensive oral exam required, foreign language and thesis not required; for doctorate, dissertation, preliminary oral and written exams. *Entrance requirements:* For master's, GRE General Test or MAT; for doctorate, GRE General Test. Application deadline: 7/1 (rolling processing; 11/1 for spring admission). Application fee: $40. *Tuition:* $542 per credit hour. • Dr. Ann Rule, Director, 314-977-2486. Application contact: Dr. Marcia Buresch, Assistant Dean of the Graduate School, 314-977-2240. Fax: 314-977-3943.

Southern Connecticut State University, School of Education, Department of Educational Foundations, New Haven, CT 06515-1355. Offers program in foundational studies (Diploma). Faculty: 3 full-time, 2 part-time. Students: 3 full-time (all women), 68 part-time (57 women); includes 2 minority (both African Americans). 54 applicants, 65% accepted. In 1997, 43 degrees awarded. *Entrance requirements:* Master's degree. Application deadline: 7/15 (priority date; rolling processing). Application fee: $40. *Expenses:* Tuition $2632 per year full-time, $188 per credit part-time for state residents; $7200 per year full-time, $188 per credit part-time for nonresidents. Fees $1806 per year full-time, $45 per semester part-time for state residents; $2703 per year full-time, $45 per semester part-time for nonresidents. *Financial aid:* Teaching assistantships available. • Dr. Gilbert Noble, Coordinator, 203-392-5894.

Stanford University, School of Education, Program in Social Sciences in Educational Practice, Stanford, CA 94305-9991. Offerings include history of education (PhD), philosophy of education (PhD). *Application deadline:* 1/2. *Application fee:* $65 ($75 for international students). *Expenses:* Tuition $22,110 per year. Fees $156 per year. • Application contact: Graduate Admissions Office, 650-723-4794.

State University of New York at Binghamton, School of Education and Human Development, Program in Educational Theory and Practice, Binghamton, NY 13902-6000. Awards Ed D. Students: 13 full-time (9 women), 32 part-time (23 women); includes 3 minority (2 African Americans, 1 Hispanic), 3 international. Average age 44. 13 applicants, 69% accepted. In 1997, 1 degree awarded. *Degree requirements:* Dissertation. *Entrance requirements:* GRE General Test, TOEFL, writing sample. Application deadline: 3/15 (priority date; rolling processing; 11/1 for spring admission). Application fee: $50. Electronic applications accepted. *Expenses:* Tuition $5100 per year full-time, $213 per credit hour part-time for state residents; $8416 per year full-time, $351 per credit hour part-time for nonresidents. Fees $654 per year full-time, $75 per semester (minimum) part-time. *Financial aid:* In 1997–98, 3 fellowships averaging $810 per month and totaling $24,300, 2 teaching assistantships averaging $810 per month and totaling $16,200, 6 graduate assistantships (2 to first-year students) averaging $810 per month and totaling $42,700 were awarded; research assistantships, Federal Work-Study, institutionally sponsored loans, and career-related internships or fieldwork also available. Aid available to part-time students. Financial aid application deadline: 2/15. • Dr. Kenneth Teitelbaum, Coordinator, 607-777-6769.

State University of New York at Buffalo, Graduate School, Graduate School of Education, Department of Educational Leadership and Policy, Buffalo, NY 14260. Offerings include social, philosophical, and historical foundations (Ed D, PhD). Terminal master's awarded for partial completion of doctoral program. Department faculty: 17 full-time (3 women), 1 (woman) part-time. *Degree requirements:* Dissertation required, foreign language not required. *Entrance requirements:* GRE General Test or MAT, TOEFL (minimum score 550), sample of written work. Application deadline: 3/1 (rolling processing; 11/15 for spring admission). Application fee: $50. *Tuition:* $5970 per year full-time, $288 per credit hour part-time for state residents; $9286 per year full-time, $426 per credit hour part-time for nonresidents. • Dr. Robert B. Stevenson, Chairman, 716-645-2471. Fax: 716-645-2481. E-mail: eoastevo@acsu.buffalo.edu.

Syracuse University, School of Education, Program in Cultural Foundations of Education and Curriculum, Syracuse, NY 13244-0003. Awards MS, PhD, CAS. Faculty: 7 full-time (3 women), 1 part-time (0 women). Students: 33 full-time (20 women), 9 part-time (5 women); includes 5 minority (4 African Americans, 1 Native American), 6 international. 22 applicants, 64% accepted. In 1997, 5 doctorates awarded. *Degree requirements:* For master's, thesis or alternative required, foreign language not required; for doctorate, dissertation required, foreign language not required; for CAS, thesis. *Entrance requirements:* GRE. Application deadline: rolling. Application fee: $40. *Tuition:* $13,320 per year full-time, $555 per credit hour part-time. *Financial aid:* Fellowships, research assistantships, teaching assistantships, administrative assistantships, Federal Work-Study, and career-related internships or fieldwork available. Aid available to part-time students. Financial aid application deadline: 3/1. *Faculty research:* Gender and education, history of women's education, the role of science in liberal education, student attrition. • Dr. Sari Biklen, Chair, 315-443-9074.

Teachers College, Columbia University, Graduate Faculty of Education, Department of Arts and Humanities, Program in Philosophy and Education, 525 West 120th Street, New York, NY 10027-6696. Awards Ed M, MA, Ed D, PhD. Faculty: 4 full-time (1 woman). Students: 11 full-time (5 women), 39 part-time (19 women); includes 7 minority (2 African Americans, 4 Asian Americans, 1 Hispanic), 10 international. Average age 37. 20 applicants, 45% accepted. In 1997, 3 master's, 3 doctorates awarded. *Degree requirements:* For doctorate, dissertation. *Entrance requirements:* For master's, previous course work in philosophy; for doctorate, previous course work in philosophy (Ed D), undergraduate degree in philosophy (PhD). Application deadline: 5/15 (12/1 for spring admission). Application fee: $50. *Expenses:* Tuition $640 per credit. Fees $120 per semester. *Financial aid:* Full and partial tuition waivers, Federal Work-Study, institutionally sponsored loans, and career-related internships or fieldwork available. Aid available to part-time students. Financial aid application deadline: 2/1. *Faculty research:* Philosophy and its relationship to educational thought, ethics and education, social theory and ideology. • Application contact: Amy Rotheim, Office of Admissions, 212-678-3710. Fax: 212-678-4171.

Texas A&M University, College of Education, Department of Educational Curriculum and Instruction, Unit in Social Foundation, College Station, TX 77843. Awards M Ed, MS, Ed D, PhD. Accredited by NCATE. *Degree requirements:* For doctorate, dissertation required, foreign language not required. *Entrance requirements:* GRE General Test, TOEFL. Application fee: $35 ($75 for international students). *Financial aid:* Fellowships, research assistantships, teaching assistantships available. • Patricia Larke, Coordinator, 409-845-6436.

Troy State University, Graduate School, School of Education, Program in Foundations of Education, Troy, AL 36082. Awards MS. Accredited by NCATE. Also offered through the University College. Part-time and evening/weekend programs available. Students: 73 full-time (37 women), 98 part-time (66 women); includes 30 minority (25 African Americans, 1 Asian American, 3 Hispanics, 1 Native American), 1 international. Average age 30. In 1997, 18 degrees awarded. *Degree requirements:* Thesis, comprehensive exam. *Entrance requirements:* Minimum GPA of 2.5. Application deadline: rolling. Application fee: $20. Electronic applications accepted. *Expenses:* Tuition $2040 per year full-time, $68 per hour part-time for state residents; $4200 per year full-time, $140 per hour part-time for nonresidents. Fees $240 per year full-time, $27 per quarter (minimum) part-time. *Financial aid:* Available to part-time students. Financial aid applicants required to submit FAFSA. • Dr. Saramma Mathew, Chair, 334-670-3362. Fax: 334-670-3474. E-mail: smathew@trojan.troyst.edu. Application contact: Teresa Rodgers, Director of Graduate Admissions, 334-670-3188. Fax: 334-670-3733. E-mail: trodgers@trojan.troyst.edu.

Troy State University Dothan, School of Education, Dothan, AL 36304-0368. Offerings include foundations of education (MS). Accredited by NCATE. *Application fee:* $20. *Expenses:* Tuition $68 per credit hour for state residents; $140 per credit hour for nonresidents. Fees $2 per credit hour. • Dr. Betty Anderson, Dean, 334-983-6556. Application contact: Reta Cordell, Director of Admissions and Records, 334-983-6556. Fax: 334-983-6322. E-mail: rcordell@tsud.edu.

Université du Québec à Montréal, Program in Research Integration in Educational Practice, Montréal, PQ H3C 3P8, Canada. Awards Diploma. Program being phased out; applicants no longer accepted. Part-time programs available. *Degree requirements:* Research report required, thesis not required.

University of Alberta, Faculty of Graduate Studies and Research, Department of Educational Policy Studies, Edmonton, AB T6G 2E1, Canada. Offers programs in administration of postsecondary education (M Ed, PhD), adult education (M Ed), educational administration (M Ed, Ed D, PhD, Postgraduate Diploma), educational leadership (M Ed), First Nations education (M Ed, PhD), international and global education (M Ed, PhD), social and cultural education (M Ed, PhD). Part-time programs available. Faculty: 25 full-time (7 women), 3 part-time (1 woman). Students: 109 full-time (61 women), 259 part-time (166 women); includes 17 international. In 1997, 53 master's, 18 doctorates awarded. *Degree requirements:* For master's, thesis (for some programs); for doctorate, dissertation. *Average time to degree:* master's–1 year full-time, 3 years part-time; doctorate–2 years full-time, 4 years part-time. *Entrance requirements:* For master's and doctorate, TOEFL (minimum score 580). Application deadline: 8/1 (priority date; rolling processing; 4/1 for spring admission). Application fee: $60. *Expenses:*

Tuition $390 per course for Canadian residents; $781 per course for nonresidents. Fees $500 per year full-time, $184 per year part-time. *Financial aid:* In 1997–98, 10 tuition scholarships were awarded. • Dr. D. M. Richards, Chair, 403-492-3679. E-mail: don.richards@ualberta.ca. Application contact: Joan White, Graduate Secretary, 403-492-3679. Fax: 403-492-2024. E-mail: joan.white@ualberta.ca.

University of British Columbia, Faculty of Education, Department of Educational Studies, Vancouver, BC V6T 1Z2, Canada. Offerings include educational studies (MA, M Ed, PhD), with options in history of education (MA, M Ed), philosophy of education (MA, M Ed), sociology of education (MA, M Ed). Terminal master's awarded for partial completion of doctoral program. *Degree requirements:* For master's, thesis (MA) required, foreign language not required. *Entrance requirements:* For master's, TOEFL (minimum score 550). Application fee: $60.

University of California, Berkeley, School of Education, Division of Social and Cultural Studies in Education, Berkeley, CA 94720-1500. Awards MA, PhD, PhD/MA. Program in social and cultural analysis and social theory (MA, PhD). *Degree requirements:* For master's, exam or thesis required, foreign language not required; for doctorate, dissertation, oral qualifying exam required, foreign language not required. *Entrance requirements:* GRE General Test, minimum GPA of 3.0 during last 2 years of undergraduate course work. Application deadline: 12/15 (rolling processing). Application fee: $40. *Expenses:* Tuition $0 for state residents; $9384 per year for nonresidents. Fees $4409 per year. *Financial aid:* Application deadline 12/15. • Dr. Harley Shaiken, Professor.

University of Cincinnati, College of Education, Division of Educational Studies, Department of Educational Foundations, Cincinnati, OH 45221. Awards M Ed, Ed D. Accredited by NCATE. Part-time programs available. Students: 26 full-time (25 women), 26 part-time (14 women); includes 24 minority (21 African Americans, 2 Asian Americans, 1 Hispanic), 5 international. 43 applicants, 16% accepted. In 1997, 5 master's, 10 doctorates awarded. *Degree requirements:* For master's, thesis or alternative required, foreign language not required; for doctorate, dissertation required, foreign language not required. *Average time to degree:* master's–3.9 years full-time; doctorate–6.6 years full-time. *Entrance requirements:* For master's, GRE General Test; for doctorate, GRE General Test, GRE Subject Test. Application deadline: 2/1. Application fee: $30. *Tuition:* $7228 per year full-time, $185 per credit hour part-time for state residents; $13,812 per year full-time, $352 per credit hour part-time for nonresidents. *Financial aid:* Fellowships, graduate assistantships, full tuition waivers available. Aid available to part-time students. Financial aid application deadline: 3/1. • Application contact: Dr. Mary Anne Pitman, Graduate Program Coordinator, 513-556-3609. Fax: 513-556-2483. E-mail: maryanne.pitman@uc.edu.

University of Connecticut, School of Education, Field of Educational Studies, Storrs, CT 06269. Awards MA, PhD. Accredited by NCATE. Faculty: 6. Students: 3 full-time (2 women), 14 part-time (8 women); includes 4 minority (2 African Americans, 1 Asian American, 1 Hispanic), 4 international. Average age 44. 2 applicants, 50% accepted. In 1997, 6 doctorates awarded. Terminal master's awarded for partial completion of doctoral program. *Degree requirements:* For master's, thesis or alternative; for doctorate, dissertation. *Entrance requirements:* For doctorate, GRE General Test. Application deadline: 6/1 (priority date; rolling processing; 11/1 for spring admission). Application fee: $40 ($45 for international students). *Expenses:* Tuition $5272 per year full-time, $293 per credit part-time for state residents; $13,696 per year full-time, $761 per credit part-time for nonresidents. Fees $948 per year full-time, $640 per year part-time. *Financial aid:* In 1997–98, 1 fellowship totaling $1,200, 2 research assistantships (1 to a first-year student) totaling $19,575, 1 teaching assistantship totaling $6,750 were awarded. Financial aid application deadline: 2/15. • Patrick B. Mullarney, Head, 860-486-6278.

University of Florida, College of Education, Department of Foundations of Education, Gainesville, FL 32611. Offers programs in comparative education (MAE, M Ed, Ed D, PhD, Ed S); educational psychology (MAE, M Ed, Ed D, PhD, Ed S); history, philosophy, and sociology of education (MAE, M Ed, Ed D, PhD, Ed S); school psychology (MAE, PhD, Ed S); statistics, measurement, and evaluation methodology (MAE, M Ed, Ed D, PhD, Ed S). Accredited by NCATE. Faculty: 23. Students: 59 full-time (43 women), 44 part-time (31 women); includes 10 minority (1 African American, 1 Asian American, 7 Hispanics, 1 Native American), 7 international. Average age 30. 90 applicants, 51% accepted. In 1997, 1 master's, 1 doctorate, 1 Ed S awarded. Terminal master's awarded for partial completion of doctoral program. *Degree requirements:* For master's, thesis (MAE) required, foreign language not required; for doctorate, variable foreign language requirement, dissertation. *Entrance requirements:* For master's and doctorate, GRE General Test, minimum GPA of 3.0; for Ed S, GRE General Test. Application deadline: 6/5 (priority date; rolling processing). Application fee: $20. *Tuition:* $138 per credit hour for state residents; $481 per credit hour for nonresidents. *Financial aid:* In 1997–98, 39 students received aid, including 6 fellowships averaging $798 per month, 9 research assistantships averaging $734 per month, 23 teaching assistantships averaging $480 per month, 1 graduate assistantship averaging $534 per month; career-related internships or fieldwork also available. Financial aid application deadline: 4/30. *Faculty research:* School improvement, teaching and learning, item response theory. • Dr. James Algina, Chair, 352-392-0723. Application contact: Dr. Barry J. Guinagh, Graduate Coordinator, 352-392-0723. Fax: 352-392-7159. E-mail: guinagh@coe.ufl.edu.

University of Hawaii at Manoa, College of Education, Department of Educational Foundations, Honolulu, HI 96822. Awards M Ed. Evening/weekend programs available. Faculty: 5 full-time (2 women), 3 part-time (1 woman). Students: 12 full-time (6 women), 42 part-time (28 women); includes 32 minority (1 African American, 27 Asian Americans, 4 Native Americans), 7 international. Average age 35. In 1997, 8 degrees awarded (100% found work related to degree). *Degree requirements:* Thesis or alternative required, foreign language not required. *Average time to degree:* master's–2 years full-time. *Entrance requirements:* TOEFL (minimum score 540). Application deadline: 1/15 (rolling processing; 8/1 for spring admission). *Tuition:* $4029 per year full-time, $214 per credit hour part-time for state residents; $9957 per year full-time, $461 per credit hour part-time for nonresidents. *Financial aid:* Full and partial tuition waivers, institutionally sponsored loans available. Aid available to part-time students. Financial aid application deadline: 9/26. *Faculty research:* Multicultural-ethnic education, comparative education, educational policy, interdisciplinary inquiry, moral/political education. • Dr. David P. Ericson, Chairperson, 808-956-7901. E-mail: ericson@hawaii.edu. Application contact: Dr. Royal T. Fruehling, Graduate Field Chairperson, 808-956-4243. Fax: 808-956-9100. E-mail: fruehlin@hawaii.edu.

University of Hawaii at Manoa, College of Education, Education Program, Honolulu, HI 96822. Offerings include educational foundations (Ed D). Program faculty: 53 full-time (25 women). *Degree requirements:* Dissertation required, foreign language not required. *Entrance requirements:* GRE General Test, MAT (optional), TOEFL (minimum score 600), sample of written work. Application deadline: 2/1. Application fee: $0. *Tuition:* $4029 per year full-time, $214 per credit hour part-time for state residents; $9957 per year full-time, $461 per credit hour part-time for nonresidents. • Dr. Royal T. Fruehling, Graduate Chair, 808-956-4243. E-mail: fruehlin@hawaii.edu. Application contact: Melanie Bock, Clerk Typist III, 808-956-7817. Fax: 808-956-9100. E-mail: mbock@hawaii.edu.

University of Houston, College of Education, Department of Educational Leadership and Cultural Studies, 4800 Calhoun, Houston, TX 77204-2163. Offers programs in educational administration (M Ed, Ed D); higher education (M Ed); historical, social, and cultural foundations of education (M Ed, Ed D). Accredited by NCATE. Part-time and evening/weekend programs available. Faculty: 15 full-time (9 women), 10 part-time (3 women), 20 FTE. Students: 53 full-time (41 women), 287 part-time (206 women); includes 96 minority (51 African Americans, 8 Asian Americans, 37 Hispanics), 1 international. Average age 39. 75 applicants, 61% accepted. In 1997, 48 master's, 24 doctorates awarded. *Degree requirements:* For master's, comprehensive exam or thesis required, foreign language not required; for doctorate, dissertation, comprehensive exam required, foreign language not required. *Average time to degree:* master's–1.5 years full-time, 3 years part-time; doctorate–3 years full-time, 6 years part-time. *Entrance requirements:* For master's, GRE General Test (minimum score 460 on verbal section) or MAT (minimum score 43), minimum GPA of 3.0 in last 60 hours; for doctorate, GRE General Test (minimum score 500 on verbal section), interview, minimum GPA of 3.0 in last 60 hours. Application deadline: 7/18 (priority date; rolling processing; 12/18 for spring admission). Application fee: $35 ($75 for international students). *Expenses:* Tuition $1152 per year full-time, $120 per semester (minimum) part-time for state residents; $4482 per year full-time, $249 per credit hour part-time for nonresidents. Fees $977 per year full-time, $119 per semester (minimum) part-time. *Financial aid:* Research assistantships, teaching assistantships, Federal Work-Study, institutionally sponsored loans, and career-related internships or fieldwork available. Aid available to part-time students. Financial aid application deadline: 4/1; applicants required to submit FAFSA. *Faculty research:* Change, supervision, multiculturalism, evaluation, policy. • Richard L. Hooker, Chairperson, 713-743-5035. Application contact: Rose L. Hernandez, Office Assistant, 713-743-5044. Fax: 713-743-4979.

University of Illinois at Urbana–Champaign, College of Education, Department of Educational Policy Studies, Urbana, IL 61801. Awards AM, Ed M, MS, Ed D, PhD, AC. Faculty: 13 full-time (5 women). Students: 80 full-time (55 women); includes 45 minority (31 African Americans, 4 Asian Americans, 10 Hispanics), 6 international. 65 applicants, 18% accepted. In 1997, 8 master's, 6 doctorates awarded. *Degree requirements:* For doctorate, dissertation. *Application deadline:* rolling. *Application fee:* $40 ($50 for international students). *Financial aid:* In 1997–98, 29 fellowships, 27 research assistantships, 13 teaching assistantships were awarded; full and partial tuition waivers also available. Financial aid application deadline: 2/15. • James D. Anderson, Head, 217-333-7404. Fax: 217-244-7064. E-mail: anderson@uiuc.edu.

The University of Iowa, College of Education, Division of Foundations, Post-Secondary, and Continuing Education, Program in Social Foundations, Iowa City, IA 52242-1316. Awards MA, PhD, JD/MA. Faculty: 3 full-time. Students: 16 full-time (13 women), 21 part-time (13 women); includes 12 minority (8 African Americans, 3 Asian Americans, 1 Hispanic). 11 applicants, 73% accepted. In 1997, 2 master's, 1 doctorate awarded. *Degree requirements:* For master's, exam required, thesis optional, foreign language not required; for doctorate, computer language, dissertation, comprehensive exams required, foreign language not required. *Entrance requirements:* For master's, GRE General Test, minimum GPA of 2.5; for doctorate, GRE General Test, minimum GPA of 3.0. Application deadline: rolling. Application fee: $30 ($50 for international students). *Expenses:* Tuition $3166 per year full-time, $176 per semester hour part-time for state residents; $10,202 per year full-time, $176 per semester hour part-time for nonresidents. Fees $202 per year full-time, $52 per year (minimum) part-time. *Financial aid:* In 1997–98, 2 fellowships, 6 research assistantships (1 to a first-year student), 11 teaching assistantships were awarded. Financial aid applicants required to submit FAFSA. • David B. Bills, Coordinator, 319-335-5366. Fax: 319-384-0587.

University of Kansas, School of Education, Department of Teaching and Leadership, Program in Foundations of Education, Lawrence, KS 66045. Awards MS Ed, Ed D, PhD. Accredited by NCATE. Students: 1 full-time (0 women), 7 part-time (3 women); includes 1 minority (Asian American), 1 international. *Degree requirements:* For master's, thesis required, foreign language not required; for doctorate, variable foreign language requirement, dissertation. *Entrance requirements:* For master's, minimum GPA of 3.0; for doctorate, GRE General Test (combined average 1000), minimum graduate GPA of 3.5. Application deadline: 7/1. Application fee: $25. *Expenses:* Tuition $2400 per year full-time, $100 per credit hour part-time for state residents; $7890 per year full-time, $329 per credit hour part-time for nonresidents. Fees $428 per year full-time, $31 per credit hour part-time. *Faculty research:* History of childhood, ethics in education, communicative virtue. • James Hillesheim, Director, 785-864-4432.

University of Kentucky, Graduate School Programs from the College of Education, Program in Educational Policy Studies and Evaluation, Lexington, KY 40506-0032. Awards MS Ed U, Ed D, PhD. Accredited by NCATE. Faculty: 18 full-time (5 women), 1 part-time (0 women). Students: 67 full-time (40 women), 51 part-time (32 women); includes 23 minority (20 African Americans, 1 Asian American, 1 Hispanic, 1 Native American), 5 international. 41 applicants, 80% accepted. In 1997, 3 master's, 3 doctorates awarded. Terminal master's awarded for partial completion of doctoral program. *Degree requirements:* For master's, comprehensive exam required, thesis optional, foreign language not required; for doctorate, 1 foreign language, dissertation, comprehensive exam. *Entrance requirements:* For master's, GRE General Test, minimum undergraduate GPA of 2.5; for doctorate, GRE General Test, minimum graduate GPA of 3.0. Application deadline: 7/19 (rolling processing). Application fee: $30 ($35 for international students). *Financial aid:* In 1997–98, 6 fellowships, 3 research assistantships, 3 teaching assistantships, 1 graduate assistantship were awarded; Federal Work-Study, institutionally sponsored loans, and career-related internships or fieldwork also available. Aid available to part-time students. *Faculty research:* Studies in higher education; comparative and international education; evaluation of educational programs, policies, and reform; student, teacher and faculty cultures; gender and education. • Dr. Beth L. Goldstein, Director of Graduate Studies, 606-257-2705. Application contact: Dr. Constance L. Wood, Associate Dean, 606-257-4613. Fax: 606-323-1928.

University of Manitoba, Faculty of Education, Department of Educational Administration and Foundations, Winnipeg, MB R3T 2N2, Canada. Offerings include educational foundations (M Ed). *Degree requirements:* Thesis or alternative required, foreign language not required.

University of Maryland, College Park, College of Education, Department of Education Policy, Planning, and Administration, College Park, MD 20742-5045. Offerings include social foundations of education (MA, M Ed, Ed D, PhD, CAGS). Accredited by NCATE. Postbaccalaureate distance learning degree programs offered. Department faculty: 19 full-time (8 women), 1 (woman) part-time. *Degree requirements:* For master's, thesis or alternative required, foreign language not required; for doctorate, dissertation required, foreign language not required. *Entrance requirements:* For master's, GRE General Test or MAT (score in 40th percentile or higher), minimum GPA of 3.0; for doctorate, GRE General Test or MAT (score in 70th percentile or higher). Application deadline: rolling. Application fee: $50 ($70 for international students). *Expenses:* Tuition $272 per credit hour for state residents; $400 per credit hour for nonresidents. Fees $564 per year full-time, $342 per year part-time. • Dr. James Cibulka, Chairman, 301-405-3589. Fax: 301-314-9278. Application contact: John Mollish, Director, Graduate Admissions and Records, 301-405-4198. Fax: 301-314-9305.

University of Michigan, School of Education, Programs in Educational Studies, Ann Arbor, MI 48109. Offerings include educational foundations and policy (AM, PhD). *Degree requirements:* For doctorate, dissertation, preliminary exam required, foreign language not required. *Entrance requirements:* For doctorate, GRE General Test (minimum combined score of 1800 on three sections), TOEFL (minimum score 600). Application deadline: 1/15 (priority date). Application fee: $55. Electronic applications accepted. • Dr. Ronald Marx, Chairperson, 734-763-9497. E-mail: ronmarx@umich.edu. Application contact: Karen Wixson, Associate Dean, 734-764-9470. Fax: 734-763-1229. E-mail: kwixson@umich.edu.

University of New Mexico, College of Education, Program in Educational Thought and Sociocultural Studies, Albuquerque, NM 87131-2039. Offers educational foundations (MA), educational thought and sociocultural studies (Ed D, PhD). Accredited by NCATE. Part-time programs available. Faculty: 12 full-time (9 women). Students: 10 full-time (6 women), 20 part-time (14 women); includes 5 minority (3 Hispanics, 2 Native Americans), 4 international. Average age 44. 19 applicants, 74% accepted. In 1997, 2 doctorates awarded. Terminal master's awarded for partial completion of doctoral program. *Degree requirements:* For doctorate, dissertation required, foreign language not required. *Entrance requirements:* For doctorate, GRE General Test. Application deadline: 3/30 (10/15 for spring admission). Application fee: $25. *Expenses:* Tuition $2442 per year full-time, $103 per credit hour part-time for state residents; $8691 per year full-time, $103 per credit hour (minimum) part-time for nonresidents. Fees $32 per year. *Financial aid:* In 1997–98, 1 fellowship (to a first-year student) averaging $400 per month and totaling $2,000, 7 teaching assistantships (5 to first-year students) averaging $400 per month and totaling $19,600 were awarded; Federal Work-Study, institutionally sponsored loans, and career-related internships or fieldwork also available. Aid available

Directory: Foundations and Philosophy of Education

University of New Mexico (continued)

to part-time students. Financial aid application deadline: 5/30; applicants required to submit FAFSA. *Faculty research:* School reform, professional development, history of education, Native American education, politics of education, feminism and issues of sexual identity. • Dr. Ann Nihlen, Graduate Coordinator, 505-277-5979. E-mail: anihlen@unm.edu. Application contact: Paula Pascetti, Division Administrator, 505-277-0437. Fax: 505-277-8362. E-mail: pascetti@unm.edu.

University of New Orleans, College of Education, Department of Educational Leadership, Counseling, and Foundations, Program in Educational Leadership and Foundations, New Orleans, LA 70148. Awards M Ed, PhD, Certificate. Accredited by NCATE. Evening/weekend programs available. Students: 198 full-time (144 women), 715 part-time (574 women); includes 247 minority (204 African Americans, 11 Asian Americans, 29 Hispanics, 3 Native Americans), 4 international. Average age 35. 482 applicants, 94% accepted. In 1997, 19 master's, 9 doctorates awarded. Terminal master's awarded for partial completion of doctoral program. *Degree requirements:* For doctorate, variable foreign language requirement, dissertation. *Entrance requirements:* For master's, GRE General Test; for doctorate, GRE General Test (minimum combined score of 1000). Application deadline: 7/1 (priority date; rolling processing). Application fee: $20. *Expenses:* Tuition $2362 per year full-time, $373 per semester (minimum) part-time for state residents; $7888 per year full-time, $1423 per semester (minimum) part-time for nonresidents. Fees $170 per year full-time, $25 per semester (minimum) part-time. *Financial aid:* Fellowships, research assistantships, teaching assistantships, partial tuition waivers, and career-related internships or fieldwork available. • Application contact: Dr. Peggy Kirby, Graduate Coordinator, 504-280-6443. Fax: 504-280-6065. E-mail: pekel@uno.edu.

University of Oklahoma, College of Education, Department of Educational Leadership and Policy Studies, Program in Foundations of Education, Norman, OK 73019-0390. Awards M Ed, Ed D, PhD. Accredited by NCATE. Part-time and evening/weekend programs available. Students: 3 full-time (all women), 12 part-time (6 women); includes 3 minority (2 African Americans, 1 Native American), 1 international. Average age 35. In 1997, 1 master's awarded. Terminal master's awarded for partial completion of doctoral program. *Degree requirements:* For master's, comprehensive exam required, foreign language and thesis not required; for doctorate, variable foreign language requirement, dissertation, general exam. *Entrance requirements:* For master's, TOEFL (minimum score 550), 12 hours of course work in education; for doctorate, GRE General Test, TOEFL (minimum score 550), master's degree, minimum graduate GPA of 3.25. Application deadline: 6/1 (10/1 for spring admission). Application fee: $25. *Expenses:* Tuition $1920 per year full-time, $80 per credit hour part-time for state residents; $6108 per year full-time, $255 per credit hour part-time for nonresidents. Fees $468 per year full-time, $12 per semester (minimum) part-time. *Financial aid:* Full tuition waivers, Federal Work-Study, institutionally sponsored loans available. *Faculty research:* Educational history, educational philosophy, comparative and international education, multicultural education, gender studies. • Application contact: Edward Chance, Graduate Liaison, 405-325-4202.

University of Oregon, Graduate School, College of Education, Department of Educational Technology, Leadership and Administration, Department of Educational Policy and Management, Eugene, OR 97403. Offerings include educational policy and foundations (MS), foundations and research (PhD). Terminal master's awarded for partial completion of doctoral program. Department faculty: 8 full-time (1 woman), 6 part-time (1 woman), 10.29 FTE. *Degree requirements:* For master's, exam, paper, or project required, foreign language not required. *Entrance requirements:* For master's, MAT, TOEFL (minimum score 550). Application deadline: 3/15. Application fee: $50. *Tuition:* $6429 per year full-time, $873 per quarter (minimum) part-time for state residents; $10,857 per year full-time, $1360 per quarter (minimum) part-time for nonresidents. • Application contact: Tammara Hirte, Graduate Secretary, 541-346-1361. Fax: 541-346-5174.

University of Pennsylvania, Graduate School of Education, Division of Educational Leadership, Program in Education, Culture, and Society, Philadelphia, PA 19104. Awards MS Ed, Ed D, PhD. Part-time programs available. Students: 95; includes 13 minority (9 African Americans, 2 Asian Americans, 2 Native Americans), 7 international. In 1997, 6 master's, 5 doctorates awarded. *Degree requirements:* For master's, thesis, comprehensive exam required, foreign language not required; for doctorate, dissertation, comprehensive and oral exams required, foreign language not required. *Average time to degree:* doctorate–1 year full-time. *Entrance requirements:* For master's, GRE General Test or MAT; for doctorate, GRE General Test. Application fee: $65. *Expenses:* Tuition $22,716 per year full-time, $2876 per course part-time. Fees $1484 per year full-time, $181 per course part-time. *Financial aid:* Federal Work-Study, institutionally sponsored loans, and career-related internships or fieldwork available. Aid available to part-time students. Financial aid application deadline: 1/2; applicants required to submit FAFSA. *Faculty research:* Anthropology of education, history of education, bicultural education, identity and gender education. • Application contact: Rona Rosenberg, Administrative Coordinator, 215-898-7364.

University of Pittsburgh, School of Education, Department of Administrative and Policy Studies, Program in Social and Comparative Analysis, Pittsburgh, PA 15260. Offers international development education (MA, PhD); international developmental education (M Ed); social, philosophical, and historical foundations of education (MA, M Ed, PhD). Part-time programs available. 54 applicants, 94% accepted. *Degree requirements:* Thesis/dissertation required, foreign language not required. *Average time to degree:* master's–2 years full-time, 4 years part-time; doctorate–4 years full-time, 6 years part-time. *Entrance requirements:* For master's, TOEFL (minimum score 650); for doctorate, GRE General Test, TOEFL (minimum score 650). Application deadline: 2/1 (priority date; rolling processing; 11/15 for spring admission). Application fee: $30 ($40 for international students). *Expenses:* Tuition $8018 per year full-time, $329 per credit part-time for state residents; $16,508 per year full-time, $680 per credit part-time for nonresidents. Fees $480 per year full-time, $180 per year part-time. *Financial aid:* In 1997–98, 15 research assistantships (5 to first-year students) averaging $1,100 per month, 4 teaching assistantships averaging $1,250 per month were awarded; partial tuition waivers, Federal Work-Study, institutionally sponsored loans also available. Aid available to part-time students. Financial aid application deadline: 5/1; applicants required to submit FAFSA. • Application contact: Jackie Harden, Manager, 412-648-7060. Fax: 412-648-1899. E-mail: jackie@sched.fsl.pitt.edu.

University of Saskatchewan, College of Education, Department of Educational Foundations, Saskatoon, SK S7N 5A2, Canada. Awards MC Ed, M Ed, PhD, Diploma. Part-time programs available. *Degree requirements:* For master's, thesis (for some programs); for doctorate, dissertation. *Entrance requirements:* For master's, CANTEST (minimum score 4.5) or International English Language Testing System (minimum score 6) or Michigan English Language Assessment Battery (minimum score 80), or TOEFL (minimum score 550; average 560); for doctorate, TOEFL; for Diploma, International English Language Testing System (minimum score 6) or Michigan English Language Assessment Battery (minimum score 80), or TOEFL (minimum score 550). Application deadline: 7/1 (priority date; rolling processing). Application fee: $0. *Faculty research:* Indian and northern education, adult and continuing education, international education.

University of South Alabama, College of Education, Department of Educational Leadership and Foundations, Mobile, AL 36688-0002. Awards M Ed, Ed S. Accredited by NCATE. Part-time programs available. Faculty: 6 full-time (1 woman). Students: 10 full-time (2 women), 46 part-time (37 women); includes 12 minority (all African Americans), 1 international. 21 applicants, 95% accepted. In 1997, 6 Ed Ss awarded. *Degree requirements:* For master's, comprehensive exam required, foreign language and thesis not required. *Entrance requirements:* For master's, GRE General Test (minimum combined score of 1000) or MAT (minimum score 37). Application deadline: 9/1 (priority date; rolling processing). Application fee: $25. *Financial aid:* In 1997–98, 1 research assistantship was awarded. Aid available to part-time students. Financial aid application deadline: 4/1. • Dr. Joseph Newman, Chairman, 334-460-7141.

University of South Carolina, Graduate School, College of Education, Department of Educational Psychology, Program in Foundations in Education, Columbia, SC 29208. Awards PhD. Accredited by NCATE. Faculty: 3 full-time (0 women), 1 part-time (0 women). Students: 6 full-time (3 women), 20 part-time (14 women); includes 2 minority (both African Americans), 1 international. Average age 41. In 1997, 3 degrees awarded. *Degree requirements:* 1 foreign language (computer language can substitute), dissertation, comprehensive exam. *Entrance requirements:* GRE General Test. Application deadline: rolling. Application fee: $35. Electronic applications accepted. *Expenses:* Tuition $3894 per year full-time, $193 per credit hour part-time for state residents; $8114 per year full-time, $404 per credit hour part-time for nonresidents. Fees $125 per year full-time, $37 per semester (minimum) part-time. *Faculty research:* Oral history, educational biography, home schooling, international education. • Dr. Margaret Gredler, Head, 803-777-6609. Application contact: Office of Intercollegiate Teacher Education and Student Affairs, 803-777-6732. Fax: 803-777-3068.

University of Tennessee, Knoxville, College of Education, Program in Education II, Knoxville, TN 37996. Offerings include social foundations (MS). Accredited by NCATE. *Degree requirements:* Thesis optional, foreign language not required. *Entrance requirements:* TOEFL (minimum score 550), minimum GPA of 2.7. Application deadline: 2/1 (priority date; rolling processing). Application fee: $35. Electronic applications accepted. *Tuition:* $3354 per year full-time, $181 per semester hour part-time for state residents; $8410 per year full-time, $462 per semester hour part-time for nonresidents. • Dr. Tom George, Associate Dean, 423-974-0907. Fax: 423-974-8718. E-mail: tgeorge1@utk.edu.

The University of Texas at El Paso, College of Education, Department of Educational Leadership and Foundations, 500 West University Avenue, El Paso, TX 79968-0001. Awards Ed D. *Degree requirements:* Dissertation optional, foreign language not required. *Entrance requirements:* GRE General Test (minimum combined score of 1400 on three sections), TOEFL (minimum score 550), minimum graduate GPA of 3.0. Application deadline: 7/1 (priority date; 11/1 for spring admission). Application fee: $15 ($65 for international students). Electronic applications accepted. *Tuition:* $1559 per year full-time, $230 per credit hour part-time for state residents; $5393 per year full-time, $405 per credit hour part-time for nonresidents.

University of the Pacific, School of Education, Department of Educational Administration and Foundations, Stockton, CA 95211-0197. Awards MA, Ed D. Accredited by NCATE. Faculty: 2 full-time (0 women). Students: 8 full-time (6 women), 33 part-time (19 women). In 1997, 7 master's, 2 doctorates awarded. *Degree requirements:* For master's, thesis required (for some programs), foreign language not required; for doctorate, dissertation. *Entrance requirements:* GRE General Test, GRE Subject Test. Application deadline: 3/1 (priority date; rolling processing; 10/15 for spring admission). Application fee: $50. *Expenses:* Tuition $19,000 per year full-time, $594 per unit part-time. Fees $30 per year (minimum). *Financial aid:* Application deadline 3/1. • Dr. Dennis Brennan, Chairperson, 209-946-2670. E-mail: dbrennan@uop.edu.

University of Toledo, College of Education and Allied Professions, Department of Educational Psychology, Research, and Social Foundations, Toledo, OH 43606-3398. Offers programs in educational psychology (M Ed), educational theory and social foundations (M Ed), foundations of education (Ed D, PhD), research (M Ed). Accredited by NCATE. Part-time and evening/weekend programs available. Faculty: 17 full-time (7 women). Students: 23 full-time (20 women), 45 part-time (36 women); includes 11 minority (8 African Americans, 3 Asian Americans), 8 international. Average age 38. 34 applicants, 56% accepted. In 1997, 5 master's, 14 doctorates awarded. Terminal master's awarded for partial completion of doctoral program. *Degree requirements:* For master's, project or thesis required, foreign language not required; for doctorate, dissertation, comprehensive exams required, foreign language not required. *Entrance requirements:* For master's, GRE General Test, minimum GPA of 2.7; for doctorate, minimum GPA of 2.7 (undergraduate), 3.0 (graduate). Application deadline: 8/15 (priority date; rolling processing). Application fee: $30. Electronic applications accepted. *Tuition:* $5907 per year full-time, $246 per hour part-time for state residents; $11,835 per year full-time, $493 per hour part-time for nonresidents. *Financial aid:* In 1997–98, 4 research assistantships, 5 teaching assistantships, 2 administrative assistantships, tuition scholarships were awarded; full tuition waivers, Federal Work-Study, institutionally sponsored loans, and career-related internships or fieldwork also available. Aid available to part-time students. Financial aid application deadline: 4/1; applicants required to submit FAFSA. • Dr. Lynne M. Hudson, Chair, 419-530-2475. Fax: 419-530-8447. E-mail: lhudson@utnet.utoledo.edu.

University of Utah, Graduate School of Education, Department of Educational Studies, Program in Cultural Foundations, Salt Lake City, UT 84112-1107. Awards M Ed, PhD. Students: 1 full-time (0 women), 1 part-time (0 women); includes 1 international. Average age 42. In 1997, 3 doctorates awarded. *Degree requirements:* For master's, professional experience required, foreign language and thesis not required; for doctorate, dissertation required, foreign language not required. *Entrance requirements:* For master's, GRE General Test or MAT, TOEFL (minimum score 540), minimum GPA of 3.0; for doctorate, GRE General Test, TOEFL (minimum score 540), minimum GPA of 3.5. Application deadline: 7/1. Application fee: $30 ($50 for international students). *Tuition:* $2045 per year full-time, $562 per semester (minimum) part-time for state residents; $6129 per year full-time, $1607 per semester (minimum) part-time for nonresidents. *Financial aid:* Career-related internships or fieldwork available. • Application contact: Harvey Kantor, Director of Graduate Studies, 801-581-7158.

The University of West Alabama, College of Education, Department of Foundations, Livingston, AL 35470. Offers programs in continuing education (MSCE); secondary education (MAT, M Ed), including biology with certification (MAT), environmental science with certification (MAT), history with certification (MAT), language arts with certification (MAT), library media with certification (MAT), mathematics with certification (MAT). Accredited by NCATE. Part-time programs available. *Degree requirements:* Comprehensive exam required, foreign language and thesis not required. *Entrance requirements:* GRE General Test, MAT, minimum GPA of 2.75. Application deadline: 9/10 (priority date; rolling processing; 3/24 for spring admission). Application fee: $15. *Tuition:* $70 per quarter hour.

University of Wisconsin–Madison, School of Education, Department of Educational Policy Studies, Madison, WI 53706-1380. Awards MA, PhD. *Degree requirements:* For doctorate, dissertation. *Application fee:* $38. *Tuition:* $4928 per year full-time, $926 per semester (minimum) part-time for state residents; $15,190 per year full-time, $2849 per semester (minimum) part-time for nonresidents.

University of Wisconsin–Milwaukee, School of Education, Department of Educational Policy and Community Studies, Milwaukee, WI 53201-0413. Offers program in cultural foundations of education (MS). Part-time programs available. Faculty: 10 full-time (2 women). Students: 6 full-time (4 women), 20 part-time (15 women); includes 10 minority (7 African Americans, 1 Asian American, 2 Hispanics), 1 international. 15 applicants, 67% accepted. In 1997, 7 degrees awarded. *Degree requirements:* Thesis or alternative required, foreign language not required. *Application deadline:* 1/1 (priority date; rolling processing; 9/1 for spring admission). *Application fee:* $45 ($75 for international students). *Tuition:* $4996 per year full-time, $1030 per semester (minimum) part-time for state residents; $15,216 per year full-time, $2947 per semester (minimum) part-time for nonresidents. *Financial aid:* In 1997–98, 1 fellowship was awarded; research assistantships, teaching assistantships, and career-related internships or fieldwork also available. Aid available to part-time students. Financial aid application deadline: 4/15. *Faculty research:* Human relations in education, international and multicultural education. • Walter Farrell, Representative, 414-229-4323.

Wayne State University, College of Education, Division of Theoretical and Behavioral Foundations, Detroit, MI 48202. Offerings include history, philosophy, and sociology of education (PhD). Accredited by NCATE. PhD (history, philosophy, and sociology of education) admissions temporarily suspended. Division faculty: 90. *Application deadline:* 7/1. *Application fee:* $20 ($30 for international students). *Expenses:* Tuition $163 per credit hour for state residents; $355 per credit hour for nonresidents. Fees $498 per year full-time, $114 per semester (minimum) part-time. • Dr. JoAnne Holbert, Associate Dean, 313-577-0210.

Western Illinois University, College of Education and Human Services, Department of Educational Foundations, Macomb, IL 61455-1390. Offers program in interdisciplinary studies (MS Ed). Accredited by NCATE. Part-time programs available. Faculty: 15 full-time (3 women). Students: 11 full-time (6 women), 60 part-time (49 women); includes 9 minority (2 African Americans, 1 Asian American, 6 Hispanics), 3 international. Average age 38. 4 applicants, 25% accepted. In 1997, 23 degrees awarded. *Degree requirements:* Thesis or alternative required, foreign language not required. *Entrance requirements:* Minimum GPA of 2.75. Application deadline: rolling. Application fee: $0 ($25 for international students). *Expenses:* Tuition $2304 per year full-time, $96 per semester hour part-time for state residents; $6912 per year full-time, $288 per semester hour part-time for nonresidents. Fees $944 per year full-time, $33 per semester hour part-time. *Financial aid:* In 1997–98, 6 students received aid, including 6 research assistantships averaging $610 per month; full tuition waivers also available. Financial aid applicants required to submit FAFSA. *Faculty research:* Expanding cultural diversity, contractual agreement for student workers, bilingual education. • Sandra Nelson, Chairperson, 309-298-1183. Application contact: Barbara Baily, Director of Graduate Studies, 309-298-1806. Fax: 309-298-2245. E-mail: barb_baily@ccmail.wiu.edu.

International and Comparative Education

American University, College of Arts and Sciences, Department of Sociology, International Training and Education Program, Washington, DC 20016-8001. Awards MA. Part-time and evening/weekend programs available. Faculty: 9 full-time (4 women), 5 part-time (4 women), 11 FTE. Students: 16 full-time (13 women), 12 part-time (11 women); includes 5 minority (3 African Americans, 1 Asian American, 1 Hispanic), 2 international. 27 applicants, 89% accepted. *Degree requirements:* Comprehensive exams required, thesis optional, foreign language not required. *Entrance requirements:* GRE, TOEFL. Application deadline: 2/1 (priority date; rolling processing; 10/1 for spring admission). Application fee: $50. *Expenses:* Tuition $687 per credit hour. Fees $180 per year full-time, $110 per year part-time. *Financial aid:* In 1997–98, 5 students received aid, including 4 research assistantships (2 to first-year students); Federal Work-Study, institutionally sponsored loans, and career-related internships or fieldwork also available. Aid available to part-time students. Financial aid application deadline: 2/1. *Faculty research:* African studies, nonformal education, education sector analysis, global and multicultural education. • Dr. Leon Clark, Director, 202-885-3723. Fax: 202-885-2477. E-mail: itep@american.edu. Application contact: Director of Graduate Studies, 202-885-2479.

Boston University, School of Education, Department of Administration, Training, and Policy Studies, International Educational Development Program, Boston, MA 02215. Awards Ed M. Students: 6 full-time (5 women), 4 part-time (2 women); includes 1 international. Average age 28. In 1997, 9 degrees awarded. *Entrance requirements:* GRE or MAT, TOEFL. Application deadline: 2/15 (priority date; rolling processing). Application fee: $50. *Expenses:* Tuition $22,830 per year full-time, $713 per credit part-time. Fees $218 per year full-time, $40 per semester part-time. *Financial aid:* Application deadline 3/30. *Faculty research:* Formal and nonformal education for social and economic development, industrialized and agrarian societies. • Karen Boatman, Coordinator, 617-353-3187. E-mail: kboats@bu.edu.

Claremont Graduate University, Department of Education, Claremont, CA 91711-6163. Offerings include comparative and intercultural studies (MA, PhD), cross-cultural studies (MA, PhD). PhD offered jointly with San Diego State University; MA (mathematics education) offered jointly with the Department of Mathematics. Terminal master's awarded for partial completion of doctoral program. Department faculty: 13 full-time (6 women), 13 part-time (10 women). *Degree requirements:* For master's, thesis or alternative; for doctorate, dissertation. *Entrance requirements:* GRE General Test. Application deadline: 2/15 (priority date; rolling processing). Application fee: $40. Electronic applications accepted. *Expenses:* Tuition $20,250 per year full-time, $913 per unit part-time. Fees $130 per year. • David Drew, Chair, 909-621-8075. Application contact: Ethel Rogers, Associate Director, 909-621-8317. Fax: 909-621-8734. E-mail: educ@cgu.edu.

Florida International University, College of Education, Department of Educational Leadership and Policy Studies, Program in International Development Education, Miami, FL 33199. Awards MS. Accredited by NCATE. Part-time and evening/weekend programs available. Students: 3 full-time (2 women), 2 part-time (0 women); includes 3 minority (all Hispanics). Average age 33. 4 applicants, 75% accepted. In 1997, 1 degree awarded. *Degree requirements:* Thesis required, foreign language not required. *Entrance requirements:* GRE General Test (minimum combined score of 1000) or minimum GPA of 3.0 in last 60 credits of baccalaureate. Application deadline: 4/1 (priority date; rolling processing; 10/1 for spring admission). Application fee: $20. *Expenses:* Tuition $138 per credit hour for state residents; $482 per credit hour for nonresidents. Fees $46 per semester. • Dr. Kingsley Banya, Chairperson, Department of Educational Leadership and Policy Studies, 305-348-2724. Fax: 305-348-2081. E-mail: banyak@fiu.edu.

Florida State University, College of Education, Department of Educational Foundations and Policy Studies, Program in Foundations of Education, Tallahassee, FL 32306. Offerings include international and intercultural education (MS, PhD, Ed S). Program faculty: 8 full-time (3 women). *Degree requirements:* For master's and Ed S, comprehensive exam required, thesis optional; for doctorate, dissertation, comprehensive exam. *Entrance requirements:* GRE General Test (minimum combined score of 1000), minimum GPA of 3.0. Application deadline: 7/1 (priority date; rolling processing; 11/1 for spring admission). Application fee: $20. *Tuition:* $139 per credit hour for state residents; $482 per credit hour for nonresidents. • Dr. Sande Milton, Chair, Department of Educational Foundations and Policy Studies, 850-644-4594. E-mail: milton@mail.coe.fsu.edu. Application contact: Brendetta Douglas, Admissions Secretary, 850-644-4594. Fax: 850-644-6401.

The George Washington University, Graduate School of Education and Human Development, Department of Educational Leadership, Program in International Education, Washington, DC 20052. Awards MA Ed. Accredited by NCATE. Faculty: 1 (woman) full-time. Students: 6 full-time (4 women), 15 part-time (14 women); includes 1 minority (African American), 4 international. Average age 30. 24 applicants, 88% accepted. In 1997, 7 degrees awarded. *Degree requirements:* Comprehensive exam required, foreign language and thesis not required. *Entrance requirements:* GRE General Test or MAT, minimum GPA of 2.75. Application deadline: 3/1 (priority date; rolling processing; 10/1 for spring admission). Application fee: $50. *Expenses:* Tuition $680 per semester hour. Fees $35 per semester hour. *Financial aid:* Federal Work-Study and career-related internships or fieldwork available. Financial aid applicants required to submit FAFSA. *Faculty research:* Education and development. • Dr. Dorothy Moore, Faculty Coordinator, 202-994-7138.

Harvard University, Graduate School of Education, Area of Administration, Planning and Social Policy, Cambridge, MA 02138. Offerings include international education (Ed M, Ed D). Terminal master's awarded for partial completion of doctoral program. Faculty: 14 full-time (6 women), 21 part-time (8 women), 15.7 FTE. *Degree requirements:* For doctorate, dissertation required, foreign language not required. *Average time to degree:* master's–1 year full-time, 2 years part-time; doctorate–6.3 years full-time, 7.2 years part-time; other advanced degree–1 year full-time, 4.7 years part-time. *Entrance requirements:* GRE General Test, TOEFL (minimum score 600), TWE (minimum score 5.0). Application deadline: 1/2. Application fee: $60. • Richard Murnane, Chair, 617-496-4813. Application contact: Roland Hence, Director of Admissions, 617-495-3414. Fax: 617-496-3577. E-mail: gseadmissions@harvard.edu.

Howard University, School of Education, Department of Educational Administration and Policy, Program in International Development Education, 2400 Sixth Street, NW, Washington, DC 20059-0002. Awards MA, M Ed, CAGS. Accredited by NCATE. MA offered through the Graduate School of Arts and Sciences. Admissions temporarily suspended. Faculty: 1 full-time. Students: 4. *Degree requirements:* For master's, comprehensive exam required, thesis optional, foreign language not required; for CAGS, thesis. *Expenses:* Tuition $10,200 per year full-time, $567 per credit hour part-time. Fees $405 per year. *Financial aid:* Fellowships, research assistantships, teaching assistantships, grants, scholarships, full and partial tuition waivers, Federal Work-Study, institutionally sponsored loans available. • Dr. Edwin Hamilton Jr., Chairman, Department of Educational Administration and Policy, 202-806-7347. Fax: 202-806-7018.

Indiana University Bloomington, School of Education, Department of Educational Leadership and Policy Studies, Program in History, Philosophy, and Policy Studies in Education, Bloomington, IN 47405. Offerings include international and comparative education (MS). Accredited by NCATE. *Entrance requirements:* GRE General Test (minimum combined score of 1300 on three sections). Application deadline: 6/1. Application fee: $35. *Expenses:* Tuition $153 per credit hour for state residents; $446 per credit hour for nonresidents. Fees $343 per year. • Head, 812-856-8374. Application contact: Dr. Dale P. Scannell, Director of Graduate Studies, 812-856-8540.

Iowa State University of Science and Technology, College of Education, Department of Educational Leadership and Policy Studies, Program in Historical, Philosophical and Comparative Studies in Education, Ames, IA 50011. Awards M Ed, MS. *Degree requirements:* Thesis or alternative. *Entrance requirements:* TOEFL. Application fee: $20 ($30 for international students). *Expenses:* Tuition $3166 per year full-time, $176 per credit part-time for state residents; $9324 per year full-time, $518 per credit part-time for nonresidents. Fees $200 per year. • Coordinator, 515-294-1241.

Lesley College, Graduate School of Arts and Social Sciences, Cambridge, MA 02138-2790. Offerings include intercultural relations (MA, CAGS), with options in development project administration (MA), individually designed (MA), intercultural conflict resolution (MA), intercultural health and human services (MA), intercultural training and consulting (MA), international education exchange (MA), international student advising (MA), managing culturally diverse human resources (MA), multicultural education (MA). Postbaccalaureate distance learning degree programs offered (minimal on-campus study). School faculty: 24 full-time (14 women), 344 part-time (225 women). *Application deadline:* rolling. *Application fee:* $45. *Tuition:* $425 per credit. • Dr. Martha B. McKenna, Dean, 617-349-8467. Application contact: Graduate Admissions, 617-349-8300. Fax: 617-349-8366.

Louisiana State University and Agricultural and Mechanical College, College of Agriculture, School of Vocational Education, Baton Rouge, LA 70803. Offerings include extension and international education (MS, PhD). Accredited by NCATE. Terminal master's awarded for partial completion of doctoral program. School faculty: 11 full-time (3 women). *Degree requirements:* For master's, thesis required (for some programs), foreign language not required; for doctorate, dissertation required, foreign language not required. *Entrance requirements:* GRE General Test (minimum combined score of 1000), minimum GPA of 3.0. Application deadline: 1/25 (priority date; rolling processing). Application fee: $25. *Tuition:* $2736 per year full-time, $285 per semester (minimum) part-time for state residents; $6636 per year full-time, $460 per semester (minimum) part-time for nonresidents. • Dr. Michael F. Burnett, Director, 504-388-5748.

Loyola University Chicago, School of Education, Department of Educational Leadership and Policy Studies, Program in Cultural and Educational Policy Studies, 820 North Michigan Avenue, Chicago, IL 60611-2196. Offerings include comparative-international education (MA, M Ed, Ed D, PhD). Program faculty: 4 full-time (0 women), 6 part-time (3 women). *Degree requirements:* For master's, comprehensive exam (M Ed), thesis (MA) required, foreign language not required; for doctorate, dissertation, comprehensive exam, oral candidacy exam required, foreign language not required. *Entrance requirements:* For master's, GRE General Test; for doctorate, GRE General Test, interview. Application deadline: 8/1 (rolling processing; 12/1 for spring admission). Application fee: $35. *Tuition:* $467 per semester hour. • Dr. Steven Miller, Director, 847-853-3331. Application contact: Marie Rosin-Dittmar, Admissions Coordinator, 847-853-3323. Fax: 847-853-3375. E-mail: mrosind@wpo.it.luc.edu.

Lynn University, School of Graduate Studies, College of Education, Boca Raton, FL 33431-5598. Offerings include educational leadership with a global perspective (PhD). College faculty: 5 full-time (4 women), 3 part-time (all women). *Degree requirements:* Dissertation. *Average time to degree:* master's–1.8 years full-time. *Entrance requirements:* GRE General Test (minimum combined score of 1000) or MAT (score in 50th percentile or higher). Application deadline: rolling. Application fee: $50. Electronic applications accepted. *Expenses:* Tuition $375 per credit hour. Fees $60 per year. • Dr. Carole Warshaw, Dean, 561-994-0770 Ext. 247. Fax: 561-241-3939. E-mail: admission@lynn.edu. Application contact: Peter Gallo, Graduate Admissions Counselor, 800-544-8035. Fax: 561-241-3552. E-mail: admission@lynn.edu.

New York University, School of Education, Department of Teaching and Learning, Program in International and Social Studies Education, New York, NY 10012-1019. Offers international education (MA, PhD), including Asian studies (MA); social studies (MA). Part-time and evening/weekend programs available. Faculty: 2 full-time (0 women), 4 part-time. Students: 31 full-time, 47 part-time. 99 applicants, 68% accepted. In 1997, 26 master's awarded. Terminal master's awarded for partial completion of doctoral program. *Degree requirements:* For master's, thesis required (for some programs), foreign language not required; for doctorate, dissertation. *Entrance requirements:* For master's, TOEFL; for doctorate, GRE General Test, TOEFL, interview. Application deadline: 2/1 (priority date; rolling processing; 12/1 for spring admission). Application fee: $40 ($60 for international students). *Financial aid:* Partial tuition waivers, Federal Work-Study, institutionally sponsored loans, and career-related internships or fieldwork available. Aid available to part-time students. Financial aid application deadline: 3/1; applicants required to submit FAFSA. • Dr. Donald J. Johnson, Director, 212-998-5498. Application contact: Office of Graduate Admissions, 212-998-5030. Fax: 212-995-4328.

Stanford University, School of Education, Program in Social Sciences in Educational Practice, Stanford, CA 94305-9991. Offerings include international comparative education (AM, PhD), international education administration and policy analysis (AM). *Entrance requirements:* For master's, GRE General Test. Application deadline: 1/2. Application fee: $65 ($75 for international students). *Expenses:* Tuition $22,110 per year. Fees $156 per year. • Application contact: Graduate Admissions Office, 650-723-4794.

Teachers College, Columbia University, Graduate Faculty of Education, Department of International and Transcultural Studies, Program in Comparative and International Education, 525 West 120th Street, New York, NY 10027-6696. Awards Ed M, MA, Ed D, PhD. Faculty: 6 full-time (5 women), 3 part-time (2 women), 7 FTE. Students: 16 full-time (11 women), 52 part-time (39 women); includes 21 minority (10 African Americans, 4 Asian Americans, 7 Hispanics), 15 international. Average age 34. 48 applicants, 63% accepted. In 1997, 7 master's,

Directory: International and Comparative Education

Teachers College, Columbia University (continued)
1 doctorate awarded. *Degree requirements:* For doctorate, dissertation. *Application deadline:* 5/15 (12/1 for spring admission). *Application fee:* $50. *Expenses:* Tuition $640 per credit. Fees $120 per semester. *Financial aid:* Full and partial tuition waivers, Federal Work-Study, institutionally sponsored loans, and career-related internships or fieldwork available. Aid available to part-time students. Financial aid application deadline: 2/1. *Faculty research:* Comparative analysis of national educational systems, identity and community in local and trans-cultural settings. • Application contact: Ursula Felton, Office of Admissions, 212-678-3710. Fax: 212-678-4171.

Teachers College, Columbia University, Graduate Faculty of Education, Department of International and Transcultural Studies, Program in International Educational Development, 525 West 120th Street, New York, NY 10027-6696. Awards Ed M, MA, Ed D, PhD. Faculty: 6 full-time (5 women), 3 part-time (2 women), 7 FTE. Students: 34 full-time (25 women), 98 part-time (67 women); includes 44 minority (23 African Americans, 16 Asian Americans, 5 Hispanics), 32 international. Average age 34. 86 applicants, 91% accepted. In 1997, 13 master's, 7 doctorates awarded. *Degree requirements:* For doctorate, dissertation. *Application deadline:* 5/15 (12/1 for spring admission). *Application fee:* $50. *Expenses:* Tuition $640 per credit. Fees $120 per semester. *Financial aid:* Full and partial tuition waivers, Federal Work-Study, institutionally sponsored loans, and career-related internships or fieldwork available. Aid available to part-time students. Financial aid application deadline: 2/1. *Faculty research:* Application of formal and nonformal education to programs of social and economic development in Third World countries. • Application contact: Ursula Felton, Office of Admissions, 212-678-3710. Fax: 212-678-4171.

University of Alberta, Faculty of Graduate Studies and Research, Department of Educational Policy Studies, Edmonton, AB T6G 2E1, Canada. Offerings include international and global education (M Ed, PhD). Department faculty: 25 full-time (7 women), 3 part-time (1 woman). *Degree requirements:* For master's, thesis (for some programs). *Average time to degree:* master's–1 year full-time, 3 years part-time; doctorate–2 years full-time, 4 years part-time. *Entrance requirements:* For master's, TOEFL (minimum score 580). Application deadline: 8/1 (priority date; rolling processing; 4/1 for spring admission). Application fee: $60. *Expenses:* Tuition $390 per course for Canadian residents; $781 per course for nonresidents. Fees $500 per year full-time, $184 per year part-time. • Dr. D. M. Richards, Chair, 403-492-3679. E-mail: don.richards@ualberta.ca. Application contact: Joan White, Graduate Secretary, 403-492-3679. Fax: 403-492-2024. E-mail: joan.white@ualberta.ca.

University of Bridgeport, College of Graduate and Undergraduate Studies, School of Education and Human Resources, Division of Education, Program in Secondary Education, 380 University Avenue, Bridgeport, CT 06601. Offerings include international education (MS, Diploma). Program faculty: 8 full-time (2 women), 57 part-time (26 women), 27 FTE. *Degree requirements:* For master's, computer language, final exam, final project, or thesis required, foreign language not required; for Diploma, thesis or alternative, final project required, foreign language not required. *Entrance requirements:* For master's, GRE General Test, MAT (score in 35th percentile or higher), minimum undergraduate QPA of 2.5; for Diploma, GRE General Test or MAT (score in 40th percentile or higher), minimum graduate QPA of 3.0. Application deadline: rolling. Application fee: $35 ($50 for international students). *Tuition:* $340 per credit. • Dr. Allen P. Cook, Associate Dean, Division of Education, 203-576-4206.

University of Florida, College of Education, Department of Foundations of Education, Gainesville, FL 32611. Offerings include comparative education (MAE, M Ed, Ed D, PhD, Ed S). Accredited by NCATE. Terminal master's awarded for partial completion of doctoral program. Department faculty: 23. *Degree requirements:* For master's, thesis (MAE) required, foreign language not required; for doctorate, variable foreign language requirement, dissertation. *Entrance requirements:* For master's and doctorate, GRE General Test, minimum GPA of 3.0; for Ed S, GRE General Test. Application deadline: 6/5 (priority date; rolling processing). Application fee: $20. *Tuition:* $138 per credit hour for state residents; $481 per credit hour for nonresidents. • Dr. James Algina, Chair, 352-392-0723. Application contact: Dr. Barry J. Guinagh, Graduate Coordinator, 352-392-0723. Fax: 352-392-7159. E-mail: guinagh@coe.ufl.edu.

University of Massachusetts Amherst, School of Education, Program in Education, Amherst, MA 01003-0001. Offerings include international education (M Ed, Ed D, CAGS). Accredited by NCATE. *Degree requirements:* For doctorate, dissertation required, foreign language not required. *Entrance requirements:* For master's and doctorate, GRE General Test. Application deadline: 3/1 (rolling processing; 10/1 for spring admission). Application fee: $40. *Expenses:* Tuition $2640 per year full-time, $110 per credit part-time for state residents; $3690 per year (minimum) full-time, $165 per credit (minimum) part-time for nonresidents. Fees $2856 per year full-time, $422 per semester part-time for state residents; $3204 per year full-time, $480 per semester part-time for nonresidents. • John C. Carey, Director, 413-545-0236.

University of Minnesota, Twin Cities Campus, College of Education and Human Development, Department of Educational Policy and Administration, Minneapolis, MN 55455-0213. Offerings include comparative and international development education (MA, PhD). • James Hearn, Chair, 612-624-1006.

University of Pittsburgh, School of Education, Department of Administrative and Policy Studies, Program in Social and Comparative Analysis, Pittsburgh, PA 15260. Offers international development education (MA, PhD); international developmental education (M Ed); social, philosophical, and historical foundations of education (MA, M Ed, PhD). Part-time programs available. 54 applicants, 94% accepted. *Degree requirements:* Thesis/dissertation required, foreign language not required. *Average time to degree:* master's–2 years full-time, 4 years part-time; doctorate–4 years full-time, 6 years part-time. *Entrance requirements:* For master's, TOEFL (minimum score 650); for doctorate, GRE General Test, TOEFL (minimum score 650). Application deadline: 2/1 (priority date; rolling processing; 11/15 for spring admission). Application fee: $30 ($40 for international students). *Expenses:* Tuition $8018 per year full-time, $329 per credit part-time for state residents; $16,508 per year full-time, $680 per credit part-time for nonresidents. Fees $480 per year full-time, $180 per year part-time. *Financial aid:* In 1997–98, 15 research assistantships (5 to first-year students) averaging $1,100 per month, 4 teaching assistantships averaging $1,250 per month were awarded; partial tuition waivers, Federal Work-Study, institutionally sponsored loans also available. Aid available to part-time students. Financial aid application deadline: 5/1; applicants required to submit FAFSA. • Application contact: Jackie Harden, Manager, 412-648-7060. Fax: 412-648-1899. E-mail: jackie@sched.fsl.pitt.edu.

University of San Francisco, School of Education, Department of International and Multicultural Education, San Francisco, CA 94117-1080. Offers programs in international and multicultural education (MA, Ed D), teaching English as a second language (MA). Faculty: 8 full-time (5 women), 9 part-time (5 women). Students: 105 full-time (81 women), 59 part-time (44 women); includes 78 minority (32 African Americans, 23 Asian Americans, 22 Hispanics, 1 Native American), 13 international. Average age 41. 124 applicants, 89% accepted. In 1997, 24 master's, 11 doctorates awarded. *Degree requirements:* For doctorate, dissertation required, foreign language not required. *Application fee:* $40. *Tuition:* $658 per unit (minimum). *Financial aid:* 73 students received aid; fellowships, research assistantships, teaching assistantships available. Financial aid application deadline: 3/2. • Dr. Rosita Galang, Chair, 415-422-6878.

University of Southern California, Graduate School, School of Education, Department of Educational Administration and Policy, Los Angeles, CA 90089. Offerings include international and intercultural education (MS). *Entrance requirements:* GRE General Test. Application deadline: 7/1 (priority date; 11/1 for spring admission). Application fee: $55. *Expenses:* Tuition $16,944 per year full-time, $706 per unit part-time. Fees $414 per year full-time, $32 per year part-time. • Dr. William Tierney, Chair.

NORTHERN ILLINOIS UNIVERSITY

College of Education
Department of Leadership and Educational Policy Studies

Programs of Study

The department offers programs that lead to the degrees of Master of Science in Education (M.S.Ed.) and Doctor of Education (Ed.D.). The Educational Specialist (Ed.S.) degree is also offered.

The M.S.Ed. is available with specializations in adult continuing education, educational administration, foundations of education, instructional technology, and school business management. Master's program course work requirements range from 30 to 39 semester hours. A thesis is required for the major in foundations of education; it is optional in the other programs.

The Ed.D. requires 93 hours beyond the bachelor's degree, including a minimum of 15 hours for the dissertation. Areas of specialization for the doctorate are adult continuing education, educational administration, and instructional technology.

The Ed.S. is a post-master's program offered in educational administration.

Research Facilities

The University library system has 1.9 million volumes and receives 9,000 active journal titles as well as 63 daily newspapers. Students have access to ample computer facilities.

The History of Education Collection in the College of Education is probably the most extensive collection of education artifacts to be found anywhere. It contains nineteenth-century and earlier texts, as well as other educational materials.

Many schools and other educational institutions in the Chicago area can be, and frequently are, used for graduate research projects.

Financial Aid

Graduate teaching, research, and staff assistantships are available to qualified graduate students. Also, Graduate School Fellowships are available to a limited number of outstanding students. Northern Illinois University participates in the Student Loan Program of the National Defense Act of 1958. In addition, the Federal Work-Study Program, the Federal Stafford Student Loan Program, Federal Supplemental Loans for Students, and Short-Term Loan Funds are available for students. There are several scholarship opportunities for minority students, including the two-year Carter G. Woodson Scholar's Program.

Cost of Study

For Illinois residents, graduate tuition and fees in fall 1997 were $142.82 per semester hour. For out-of-state students, tuition and fees were $354.82 per semester hour. Major medical insurance cost $138 per semester. (Tuition and fees are subject to change.)

Living and Housing Costs

Room and board in a residence hall on campus cost approximately $1846 for a double ($2482 for a single) for the 1997–98 academic year. Off-campus, privately owned apartments are available. Reasonably priced dining facilities are available on campus.

Student Group

There are more than 3,000 students pursuing advanced degrees in the College of Education. The LEPS department has about 900 graduate students, of whom 29 percent are members of minority groups. There are about 80 international students pursuing advanced work. At the spring commencement of 1997, the department conferred 11 doctoral degrees and 62 master's degrees.

Location

Northern Illinois University is located 65 miles west of Chicago in the town of DeKalb, Illinois, which has a population of 33,000. DeKalb was named for Baron Johann DeKalb, a Revolutionary War general. This town entered the history books as the place where barbed wire was invented.

DeKalb has an excellent public school system. A comprehensive park district gives residents a choice of many recreational activities. Churches, financial institutions, stores, and restaurants round out the town's attractions.

The University and The Department

Northern Illinois University was established in 1895. It is accredited in all its degree programs (baccalaureate through doctorate) by the North Central Association of Colleges and Schools. It is also accredited by the National Council for Accreditation of Teacher Education in the programs in education leading to bachelor's and master's degrees, the sixth-year Educational Specialist degree, and the doctorate. The College of Education is one of the ten largest colleges in the country preparing educators, and the Department of Leadership and Educational Policy Studies is one of the largest instructional units in the College.

The department houses three educational journals and an educational press. Formal international exchange programs with the Lahti Research Center in Finland, the Shanghai Second Institute of Education in the People's Republic of China, and Universidad Metropolitana de Ciencias de la Education and Universidad Bolivariana in Santiago, Chile, provide a base for experiencing global education. Cooperative programs with the City Colleges of Chicago and community-based organizations ensure cross-cultural interaction with an array of ethnic and racial groups.

Applying

All applicants must submit the University Graduate School application form, a $30 application fee, transcripts of undergraduate work and any graduate work undertaken, a writing sample, and letters of recommendation (two for applicants to the M.S.Ed. program and three for Ed.D. applicants). Applicants may submit scores on the General Test of the Graduate Record Examinations. Application deadlines for U.S. citizens are June 1 for the fall semester, November 1 for the spring semester, and April 1 for the summer term. International students must apply by May 1 for fall and October 1 for spring. There is no deadline for applications for nonmatriculated study. Students seeking financial aid should apply by February 1; some awards require completed admission status. Interviews are strongly recommended for all applicants.

Correspondence and Information

Gary L. McConeghy, Chair
Department of Leadership and Educational Policy Studies
Gabel Hall 208
Northern Illinois University
DeKalb, Illinois 60115
Telephone: 815-753-9339
Fax: 815-753-9388

Northern Illinois University

THE FACULTY AND THEIR RESEARCH

Gary L. McConeghy, Professor and Chair; Ed.D., Wayne State. Technology applications/administration, technology in society.
Margaret L. Bailey, Assistant Professor; Ph.D., Kansas State. Performance technology, instructional design and development.
Keith M. Collins, Professor and Director, Media Services; Ph.D., Michigan State. Facility design, instructional development.
G. Robb Cooper, Associate Professor; Ph.D., J.D., Loyola (Chicago). Education law, education policy, personnel and collective bargaining.
Phyllis M. Cunningham, Presidential Teaching Professor; Ph.D., Chicago. Educational policy critique, critical pedagogy, community-based education.
Ronald E. Everett, Professor and Executive Director, Illinois Association of School Business Officials (IASBO); Ph.D., Utah. School finance, property tax reform, school business management, preparation program/certification, cash management in PSD.
Connie L. Fulmer, Associate Professor and Associate Chair; Ph.D., Penn State. Educational technology, organizational theory, instructional leadership.
Thomas E. Glass, Professor; Ed.D., Wayne State. Executive leadership, labor management relations, policy analysis.
David G. Gueulette, Professor; Ph.D., Ohio State. Instructional technologies, adult learning, cross-cultural training.
LaVerne Gyant, Assistant Professor and Assistant Director, Center for Black Studies; Ph.D., Penn State. Black studies, African-American historiography, adult education.
Paul J. Ilsley, Professor; Ed.D., Northern Illinois. Ethnographic methodologies, phenomenology, future studies.
Jorge Jeria, Associate Professor; Ph.D., Iowa State. Formal and nonformal education, popular education, educational planning, Latin America.
Donald Johnson, Associate Professor; Ed.D., Northern Illinois. School finance, superintendency, school business management.
Marshall G. Jones, Assistant Professor; Ed.D., Georgia. Instructional design, authoring software, computer-based instruction.
Robert M. Lang, Professor; Ed.D., Indiana. Educational biography, international education, history of American education.
James A. Lockard, Presidential Teaching Professor and Technology Coordinator, College of Education; Ph.D., Iowa State. Computer-based learning, interactive technologies, hypermedia, artificial intelligence.
Richard W. MacFeely, Associate Professor; Ed.D., Illinois at Urbana–Champaign. Leadership and organizational theory, principalship, superintendency.
Muriel E. Mackett, Professor; Ph.D., Ohio State. Organizational theory, information technology, policy studies, ethnographic research.
Rosita L. Marcano, Assistant Professor; Ed.D., Northern Illinois. Educational policy, bilingual and multicultural issues in leadership.
Robert C. Mason, Professor and Director, Research and Evaluation in Adult and Continuing Education (RE/ACE); Ed.D., Nebraska–Lincoln. Leadership and evaluation of adult continuing education.
Wilma R. Miranda, Professor; Ph.D., SUNY at Buffalo. Philosophy, women's studies.
Diann Musial, Professor; Ed.D., Northern Illinois. Sociology of education, social theory.
John A. Niemi, Distinguished Teaching Professor; Ed.D., UCLA. Comparative education, human resource development, distance education.
Jeri M. Nowakowski, Associate Professor; Ed.D., Western Michigan. Program evaluation, planning and decision making, educational reform. (On leave)
Richard A. Orem, Professor; Ed.D., Georgia. English as a second language, policy studies, organizational culture changes.
David B. Ripley, Professor; Ph.D., Iowa. Educational biography, colonial education, transcendentalism, intellectual history.
Rhonda S. Robinson, Professor; Ph.D., Wisconsin–Madison. Visual literacy, film and video, naturalistic inquiry, K–12, educational technology policy.
Amy D. Rose, Professor; Ed.D., Columbia. History, adult and higher education, nontraditional higher education, policy studies.
Gene L. Roth, Professor; Ph.D., Southern Illinois. Workplace education, adult education.
Leslie A. Sassone, Assistant Professor; Ph.D., Purdue. Philosophy, critical pedagogy.
L. Glenn Smith, Professor; Ph.D., Oklahoma. Historiography, educational biography, research ontologies, policy studies.
Susan Stratton, Assistant Professor; Ph.D., Iowa. School-business partnership, continuing professional development for practitioners, gender equity in school administration.
Manfred Thullen, Professor and Executive Director, International Programs; Ph.D., LSU. International education.
Alfonzo Thurman, Professor and Dean, College of Education; Ph.D., Wisconsin–Madison. Educational opportunity, organizational behavior, policy studies, leadership.
Andrew G. Torok, Associate Professor; Ph.D., Case Western Reserve. Information technology, network administration.
Lucy F. Townsend, Associate Professor; Ph.D., Loyola (Chicago). Women in education history, educational biography, the teaching profession.
Brent E. Wholeben, Professor; Ph.D., Wisconsin–Madison. Systems analysis and operations research, strategic planning, policy validation.
William H. Young, Professor; Ed.D., Penn State. Community college leadership, continuing professional education, continuing education administration.

Section 23
Instructional Levels

This section contains directories of institutions offering graduate work in adult education, community college education, early childhood education, elementary education, higher education, middle school education, and secondary education, followed by in-depth entries submitted by institutions that chose to prepare detailed program descriptions. Additional information about programs listed in the directories but not augmented by an in-depth entry may be obtained by writing directly to the dean of a graduate school or chair of a department at the address given in the directory.

For programs offering related work, see also in this book Administration, Instruction, and Theory; Education; Health-Related Professions; Leisure Studies and Recreation; Physical Education and Kinesiology; Special Focus; and Subject Areas; and in Book 2, Psychology and Counseling (School Psychology).

CONTENTS

Program Directories

Announcements

In-Depth Descriptions

See also:

Adult Education

Appalachian State University, College of Education, Department of Leadership and Educational Studies, Program in Adult Education, Boone, NC 28608. Awards MA, Ed S. Accredited by NCATE. 0 applicants. *Degree requirements:* For master's, thesis or alternative, comprehensive exams required, foreign language not required; for Ed S, comprehensive exams required, thesis optional, foreign language not required. *Entrance requirements:* GRE General Test. Application deadline: 7/31 (priority date). Application fee: $35. *Tuition:* $1811 per year full-time, $354 per semester (minimum) part-time for state residents; $9081 per year full-time, $2171 per semester (minimum) part-time for nonresidents. *Financial aid:* Fellowships, research assistantships, teaching assistantships available. • Chairman, Department of Leadership and Educational Studies, 704-262-6041.

Auburn University, College of Education, Department of Vocational and Adult Education, Auburn University, AL 36849-0001. Awards M Ed, MS, Ed D, Ed S. Accredited by NCATE. Part-time programs available. Faculty: 7 full-time (4 women). Students: 27 full-time (14 women), 59 part-time (36 women); includes 17 minority (16 African Americans, 1 Hispanic). 28 applicants, 43% accepted. In 1997, 24 master's, 2 doctorates awarded. *Degree requirements:* For master's, thesis (MS) required, foreign language not required; for doctorate, dissertation required, foreign language not required; for Ed S, research project required, foreign language and thesis not required. *Entrance requirements:* For master's and Ed S, GRE General Test; for doctorate, GRE General Test (minimum score 400 on each section), 3 years of experience. Application deadline: 9/1 (rolling processing; 3/1 for spring admission). Application fee: $25 ($50 for international students). *Expenses:* Tuition $2760 per year full-time, $76 per credit hour part-time for state residents; $8280 per year full-time, $228 per credit hour part-time for nonresidents. Fees $30 per year full-time, $160 per quarter part-time for state residents; $30 per year full-time, $480 per quarter part-time for nonresidents. *Financial aid:* Research assistantships, teaching assistantships, Federal Work-Study available. Aid available to part-time students. Financial aid application deadline: 3/15. *Faculty research:* Agriculture education, business education, home economics education, industrial arts education. • Dr. Bonnie J. White, Interim Head, 334-844-3800. Application contact: Dr. John F. Pritchett, Dean of the Graduate School, 334-844-4700.

Ball State University, Teachers College, Department of Educational Leadership, Program in Adult Education, 2000 University Avenue, Muncie, IN 47306-1099. Awards MA, Ed D. Accredited by NCATE. Students: 13 full-time (8 women), 63 part-time (46 women); includes 5 minority (2 African Americans, 2 Asian Americans, 1 Hispanic), 3 international. Average age 37. 25 applicants, 64% accepted. In 1997, 15 master's, 10 doctorates awarded. *Degree requirements:* For doctorate, dissertation required, foreign language not required. *Entrance requirements:* For doctorate, GRE General Test (minimum combined score of 1000), minimum graduate GPA of 3.2. Application fee: $15 ($25 for international students). *Expenses:* Tuition $3454 per year full-time, $518 per semester (minimum) part-time for state residents; $9316 per year full-time, $1221 per semester (minimum) part-time for nonresidents. Fees $242 per year full-time, $18 per semester (minimum) part-time. *Financial aid:* Research assistantships and career-related internships or fieldwork available. *Faculty research:* Community education, executive development for public services, applied gerontology. • James McElhinney, Director of Doctoral Program, 765-285-5348.

Boston University, School of Education, Department of Curriculum and Teaching, Program in Adult and Continuing Education, Boston, MA 02215. Awards Ed M, Ed D, CAGS. There is a moratorium on admissions for the 1998/1999 and 1999/2000 academic years. Students: 0. *Degree requirements:* For doctorate, dissertation, comprehensive exam required, foreign language not required; for CAGS, comprehensive exam required, foreign language and thesis not required. *Entrance requirements:* GRE or MAT, TOEFL. Application deadline: 2/15 (priority date; rolling processing). Application fee: $50. *Expenses:* Tuition $22,830 per year full-time, $713 per credit part-time. Fees $218 per year full-time, $40 per semester part-time. *Financial aid:* Application deadline 3/30. *Faculty research:* Adult illiteracy, teaching adult learners. • Dr. Stephan Ellenwood, Coordinator, 617-353-3238. E-mail: ellenwoo@bu.edu.

California State University, Los Angeles, School of Education, Division of Educational Foundations and Interdivisional Studies, Major in Adult and Continuing Education, Los Angeles, CA 90032-8530. Awards MA. Accredited by NCATE. Students: 1 (woman) part-time; includes 1 minority (Hispanic). *Entrance requirements:* TOEFL (minimum score 550), minimum GPA of 2.75 in last 90 units, teaching certificate. Application deadline: 6/30 (rolling processing; 2/1 for spring admission). Application fee: $55. *Expenses:* Tuition $0 for state residents; $164 per unit for nonresidents. Fees $1763 per year full-time, $1097 per year part-time. *Financial aid:* Application deadline 3/1. • Dr. Simeon Slovacek, Chair, Division of Educational Foundations and Interdivisional Studies, 213-343-4330.

Central Missouri State University, College of Education and Human Services, Department of Curriculum and Instruction, Warrensburg, MO 64093. Offerings include adult education (MSE). Accredited by NCATE. Department faculty: 20 full-time. *Degree requirements:* Comprehensive exam or thesis. *Entrance requirements:* GRE General Test, minimum GPA of 2.75, teaching certificate. Application deadline: 6/30 (priority date; rolling processing). Application fee: $25 ($50 for international students). *Tuition:* $3288 per year full-time, $137 per credit hour part-time for state residents; $5928 per year full-time, $274 per credit hour part-time for nonresidents. • Dr. Ted Garten, Chair, 660-543-4235. Fax: 660-543-4167.

Cheyney University of Pennsylvania, Program in Adult and Continuing Education, Cheyney, PA 19319. Awards MS. Part-time and evening/weekend programs available. Faculty: 5 full-time (3 women), 7 part-time (4 women). Students: 10 full-time (9 women), 8 part-time (6 women); includes 18 minority (all African Americans). Average age 39. In 1997, 7 degrees awarded. *Degree requirements:* Thesis or alternative required, foreign language not required. *Entrance requirements:* GRE General Test, MAT, minimum GPA of 2.75. Application deadline: 8/1 (priority date; rolling processing; 12/15 for spring admission). Application fee: $25. *Tuition:* $3848 per year full-time, $193 per credit hour part-time for state residents; $6616 per year full-time, $346 per credit hour part-time for nonresidents. *Financial aid:* Assistantships, institutionally sponsored loans, and career-related internships or fieldwork available. Financial aid application deadline: 5/1. • Dr. Velma Mitchell, Coordinator, 610-399-2387. Application contact: Dean of Graduate Studies, 610-399-2400. Fax: 610-399-2118.

Cleveland State University, College of Education, Department of Counseling, Administration, Supervision and Adult Learning, Program in Adult Learning and Development, Cleveland, OH 44115-2440. Awards M Ed. Part-time programs available. Students: 3 full-time (all women), 17 part-time (10 women); includes 6 minority (5 African Americans, 1 Hispanic). Average age 38. In 1997, 31 degrees awarded. *Degree requirements:* Thesis or alternative, comprehensive exam, internship required, foreign language not required. *Entrance requirements:* GRE General Test or MAT (score in 50th percentile or higher). Application deadline: 9/1 (priority date; rolling processing). Application fee: $25. *Expenses:* Tuition $5252 per year full-time, $202 per credit hour part-time for state residents; $10,504 per year full-time, $404 per credit hour part-time for nonresidents. Fees $2.25 per credit hour (minimum). *Financial aid:* Research assistantships and career-related internships or fieldwork available. *Faculty research:* Human resource development, instruction, burnout, career development. • Dr. Ernest M. Schuttenberg, Coordinator, 216-523-7134.

Concordia University, Faculty of Arts and Science, Department of Education, Program in Adult Education, Montréal, PQ H3G 1M8, Canada. Awards Diploma. Students: 7 full-time (5 women), 26 part-time (21 women). In 1997, 17 degrees awarded. *Degree requirements:* Internship. *Entrance requirements:* Interview. Application fee: $30. *Expenses:* Tuition $56 per credit (minimum) for Canadian residents; $249 per credit (minimum) for nonresidents. Fees $158 per year full-time, $117 per year (minimum) part-time. *Faculty research:* Staff development, human relations training, adult learning, professional development, learning in the workplace. • Application contact: Dr. Riva Heft, Director, 514-848-2029. Fax: 514-848-4520.

Coppin State College, Division of Education, Department of Adult and General Education, Baltimore, MD 21216-3698. Awards M Ed, MS. Part-time and evening/weekend programs available. Faculty: 4 full-time (2 women), 2 part-time (both women). Students: 6 full-time (5 women), 42 part-time (35 women); includes 46 minority (all African Americans), 2 international. Average age 35. In 1997, 19 degrees awarded. *Degree requirements:* Thesis or alternative required, foreign language not required. *Entrance requirements:* Minimum GPA of 2.5. Application deadline: 7/15 (12/15 for spring admission). Application fee: $20. *Expenses:* Tuition $140 per credit for state residents; $240 per credit for nonresidents. Fees $504 per year. *Financial aid:* Federal Work-Study, institutionally sponsored loans, and career-related internships or fieldwork available. Aid available to part-time students. Financial aid application deadline: 4/1; applicants required to submit FAFSA. • Dr. Geraldine Waters, Chair, 410-383-5670. Fax: 410-669-2861. Application contact: Allen Mosley, Director of Admissions, 410-383-5990.

Cornell University, Graduate Fields of Agriculture and Life Sciences, Field of Education, Ithaca, NY 14853-0001. Offerings include agricultural, extension, and adult education (MPS, MS, PhD). Terminal master's awarded for partial completion of doctoral program. Faculty: 26 full-time. *Degree requirements:* For doctorate, dissertation required, foreign language not required. *Entrance requirements:* For doctorate, GRE General Test or MAT, TOEFL. Application deadline: 5/1. Application fee: $65. Electronic applications accepted. • Director of Graduate Studies, 607-255-4278. Application contact: Graduate Field Assistant, 607-255-4278. E-mail: edgrfld@cornell.edu.

Curry College, Graduate Program in Education, Milton, MA 02186-9984. Offerings include adult education (M Ed, Certificate). Certificate (learning disabilities across the lifespan, adult education) new for fall 1998. College faculty: 10. *Degree requirements:* For master's, research project required, foreign language and thesis not required. *Application deadline:* 8/1 (priority date; 1/1 for spring admission). *Application fee:* $50. Electronic applications accepted. *Tuition:* $325 per credit. • Dr. Jane Utley Adelizzi, Director, 617-333-2130. Fax: 617-333-9722. E-mail: jutleyad@curry.edu.

Dalhousie University, School of Education, Halifax, NS B3H 3J5, Canada. Offerings include continuing education (MA, M Ed). Program being phased out; applicants no longer accepted. School faculty: 19 full-time, 12 part-time. *Degree requirements:* Thesis required (for some programs), foreign language not required. • Dr. K. C. Sullivan, Director, 902-494-3724.

Drake University, School of Education, Department of Leadership and Adult Development, Program in Adult Education, Des Moines, IA 50311-4516. Offers adult education (MSE, Ed D, Ed S), including adult education (Ed S); adult education, training and development (MS). Faculty: 2 full-time (0 women), 2 part-time (0 women). Students: 70 part-time (57 women). 65 applicants, 74% accepted. In 1997, 22 master's, 1 doctorate awarded. *Degree requirements:* For master's, thesis or alternative required, foreign language not required; for doctorate, dissertation; for Ed S, thesis or alternative. *Entrance requirements:* For master's, GRE General Test (minimum combined score of 1000) or MAT (minimum score 36); for doctorate and Ed S, GRE General Test (minimum combined score of 1000) or MAT (minimum score 43). Application deadline: rolling. Application fee: $25. *Tuition:* $16,000 per year full-time, $260 per hour (minimum) part-time. *Financial aid:* Career-related internships or fieldwork available. Aid available to part-time students. • Dr. Thomas Westbrook, Coordinator, 515-271-3078. Application contact: Ann J. Martin, Graduate Coordinator, 515-271-3871. Fax: 515-271-2831. E-mail: ajm@admin.drake.edu.

East Carolina University, School of Education, Department of Counselor Education, Greenville, NC 27858-4353. Offerings include adult education (MA Ed). Accredited by NCATE. Department faculty: 5 full-time (1 woman). *Degree requirements:* Comprehensive exams. *Entrance requirements:* GRE General Test or MAT, TOEFL, interview. Application deadline: 5/15 (priority date; rolling processing). Application fee: $40. *Tuition:* $1886 per year full-time, $472 per semester (minimum) part-time for state residents; $9156 per year full-time, $2289 per semester (minimum) part-time for nonresidents. • Dr. John Schmidt, Chairperson, 252-328-6856. Fax: 252-328-4219. E-mail: edjschmi@ecuvm.cis.ecu.edu.

Eastern Washington University, College of Education and Human Development, Department of Education, Program in Adult Education, Cheney, WA 99004-2431. Awards M Ed. Accredited by NCATE. *Degree requirements:* Thesis or alternative, comprehensive exam. *Entrance requirements:* Minimum GPA of 3.0. Application deadline: 4/1 (priority date; rolling processing; 1/15 for spring admission). Application fee: $35. *Tuition:* $4200 per year full-time, $140 per credit part-time for state residents; $12,780 per year full-time, $415 per credit part-time for nonresidents. *Financial aid:* Application deadline 2/1. • Dr. Nancy Todd, Adviser, 509-359-2232.

Elmira College, Graduate Programs in Education, Program in Adult Education, Elmira, NY 14901. Awards MS Ed. Part-time and evening/weekend programs available. Faculty: 25. Students: 17. *Degree requirements:* Thesis or alternative required, foreign language not required. *Application fee:* $35. *Tuition:* $344 per credit hour. *Financial aid:* Career-related internships or fieldwork available. Aid available to part-time students. • Application contact: Judith B. Clack, Associate Dean for Graduate Studies, 607-735-1825.

Florida Agricultural and Mechanical University, Division of Graduate Studies, Research, and Continuing Education, College of Education, Department of Educational Leadership and Human Services, Tallahassee, FL 32307-3200. Offerings include adult education (M Ed, MS Ed). Accredited by NCATE. *Entrance requirements:* GRE General Test (minimum combined score of 1000), minimum GPA of 3.0. Application deadline: 5/13. Application fee: $20. *Expenses:* Tuition $140 per credit hour for state residents; $484 per credit hour for nonresidents. Fees $130 per year. • Dr. Ada Burnette, Chairperson, 850-599-3191. Fax: 850-561-2211.

Florida Atlantic University, College of Education, Department of Educational Leadership, Program in Adult/Community Education, Boca Raton, FL 33431-0991. Awards M Ed, Ed D, Ed S. Accredited by NCATE. Part-time programs available. Faculty: 4 full-time (2 women), 1 (woman) part-time. Students: 12 full-time (10 women), 65 part-time (37 women); includes 16 minority (9 African Americans, 2 Asian Americans, 5 Hispanics). Average age 30. 52 applicants, 73% accepted. In 1997, 24 master's awarded. *Degree requirements:* For doctorate, dissertation required, foreign language not required; for Ed S, departmental qualifying exam required, foreign language and thesis not required. *Entrance requirements:* For master's, GRE General Test (minimum combined score of 1000), minimum GPA of 3.0 during previous 2 years; for doctorate and Ed S, GRE General Test, GRE Subject Test. Application deadline: rolling. Application fee: $20. *Expenses:* Tuition $2520 per year full-time, $140 per credit hour part-time for state residents; $8712 per year full-time, $484 per credit hour part-time for nonresidents. Fees $5 per year (minimum). *Financial aid:* In 1997–98, 1 fellowship was awarded; career-related internships or fieldwork also available. *Faculty research:* Self-direction in learning, mentorship, programs and service for older adults, exemplary adult/community education programs. Total annual research expenditures: $115,000. • Dr. Lucy Guglielmino, Coordinator, 561-367-3550.

Florida International University, College of Education, Department of Educational Leadership and Policy Studies, Program in Adult Education, Miami, FL 33199. Awards MS. Accredited by NCATE. Part-time and evening/weekend programs available. Students: 5 full-time (all women), 20 part-time (15 women). Average age 39. 14 applicants, 50% accepted. *Entrance requirements:* GRE General Test (minimum combined score of 1000) or minimum GPA of 3.0 in last 60 credits of baccalaureate. Application deadline: 4/1 (priority date; rolling processing; 10/1 for spring admission). Application fee: $20. *Expenses:* Tuition $138 per credit hour for state residents; $482 per credit hour for nonresidents. Fees $46 per semester. *Financial aid:* In 1997–98, 3 teaching assistantships were awarded; research assistantships also available.

• Dr. Kingsley Banya, Chairperson, Department of Educational Leadership and Policy Studies, 305-348-2724. Fax: 305-348-2081. E-mail: banyak@fiu.edu.

Florida State University, College of Education, Department of Educational Foundations and Policy Studies, Program in Adult Education, Tallahassee, FL 32306. Awards MS, Ed D, PhD, Ed S. Faculty: 2 full-time (0 women). Students: 6 full-time (3 women), 22 part-time (13 women); includes 4 minority (1 African American, 2 Asian Americans, 1 Hispanic). 18 applicants, 50% accepted. In 1997, 6 master's, 2 doctorates awarded. *Degree requirements:* For master's and Ed S, comprehensive exam required, thesis optional; for doctorate, dissertation, comprehensive exam. *Entrance requirements:* For master's, GRE General Test (minimum combined score of 1000), minimum GPA of 3.0; for doctorate and Ed S, GRE General Test (minimum combined score of 1000), minimum graduate GPA of 3.0. Application deadline: 7/1 (priority date; rolling processing; 11/1 for spring admission). Application fee: $20. *Tuition:* $139 per credit hour for state residents; $482 per credit hour for nonresidents. *Financial aid:* Fellowships, research assistantships, teaching assistantships, and career-related internships or fieldwork available. • Application contact: Irwin Jahns, Coordinator, 904-644-4594. Fax: 904-644-6401.

Fordham University, Graduate School of Education, Division of Curriculum and Teaching, New York, NY 10023. Offerings include adult education (MS, MSE). Accredited by NCATE. *Application fee:* $50. • Dr. Angela Carrasquillo, Chairperson, 212-636-6427.

Georgia Southern University, College of Education, Department of Leadership, Technology, and Human Development, Program in Adult and Vocational Education, Statesboro, GA 30460-8126. Awards M Ed. Accredited by NCATE. Part-time and evening/weekend programs available. Students: 7 full-time (4 women), 9 part-time (7 women); includes 2 minority (both African Americans). Average age 40. 4 applicants, 100% accepted. In 1997, 11 degrees awarded. *Degree requirements:* Exams required, foreign language and thesis not required. *Entrance requirements:* GRE General Test (minimum score 450 on each section) or MAT (minimum score 44), minimum GPA of 2.5. Application deadline: 7/15 (priority date; rolling processing; 11/15 for spring admission). Application fee: $0. Electronic applications accepted. *Tuition:* $2619 per year full-time, $287 per semester (minimum) part-time for state residents; $8619 per year full-time, $1037 per semester (minimum) part-time for nonresidents. *Financial aid:* Research assistantships, teaching assistantships, Federal Work-Study, and career-related internships or fieldwork available. Aid available to part-time students. Financial aid application deadline: 4/15. • Dr. Catherine Hansman, Coordinator, 912-681-0032. Fax: 912-486-7104. E-mail: chansman@gsvm2.cc.gasou.edu. Application contact: Dr. John R. Diebolt, Associate Graduate Dean, 912-681-5384. Fax: 912-681-0740. E-mail: gradschool@gsvms2.cc.gasou.edu.

Harvard University, Graduate School of Education, Area of Administration, Planning and Social Policy, Cambridge, MA 02138. Offerings include community and lifelong learning (Ed D). Terminal master's awarded for partial completion of doctoral program. Faculty: 14 full-time (6 women), 21 part-time (8 women), 15.7 FTE. *Degree requirements:* Dissertation required, foreign language not required. *Average time to degree:* master's–1 year full-time, 2 years part-time; doctorate–6.3 years full-time, 7.2 years part-time; other advanced degree–1 year full-time, 4.7 years part-time. *Entrance requirements:* GRE General Test, TOEFL (minimum score 600), TWE (minimum score 5.0). Application deadline: 1/2. Application fee: $60. • Richard Murnane, Chair, 617-496-4813. Application contact: Roland Hence, Director of Admissions, 617-495-3414. Fax: 617-496-3577. E-mail: gseadmissions@harvard.edu.

Indiana University of Pennsylvania, College of Education, Department of Adult and Community Education, Indiana, PA 15705-1087. Awards MA. Accredited by NCATE. Students: 11 full-time (5 women), 58 part-time (47 women); includes 11 minority (10 African Americans, 1 Native American), 3 international. Average age 36. 37 applicants, 95% accepted. In 1997, 23 degrees awarded. *Degree requirements:* Thesis optional, foreign language not required. *Entrance requirements:* TOEFL (minimum score 500). Application deadline: 7/1 (priority date; rolling processing; 11/1 for spring admission). Application fee: $30. *Expenses:* Tuition $3468 per year full-time, $193 per credit part-time for state residents; $6236 per year full-time, $346 per credit part-time for nonresidents. Fees $313 per year (minimum) full-time, $84 per year part-time. *Financial aid:* Research assistantships, Federal Work-Study, and career-related internships or fieldwork available. Aid available to part-time students. Financial aid application deadline: 3/15. • Dr. Gary Dean, Chairperson, 724-357-2470. Application contact: Dr. Trenton Ferro, Graduate Coordinator, 724-357-2470. E-mail: trferro@grove.iup.edu.

Iowa State University of Science and Technology, College of Education, Department of Educational Leadership and Policy Studies, Program in Adult and Extension Education, Ames, IA 50011. Awards M Ed, MS, PhD. *Degree requirements:* For master's, thesis or alternative. *Entrance requirements:* For master's, TOEFL; for doctorate, TOEFL, GRE General Test. Application fee: $20 ($30 for international students). *Expenses:* Tuition $3166 per year full-time, $176 per credit part-time for state residents; $9324 per year full-time, $518 per credit part-time for nonresidents. Fees $200 per year. • Coordinator, 515-294-1241.

Kansas State University, College of Education, Department of Foundations and Adult Education, Manhattan, KS 66506. Awards MS, Ed D, PhD. Accredited by NCATE. Faculty: 8 full-time (3 women). Students: 23 full-time (15 women), 89 part-time (60 women); includes 10 minority (8 African Americans, 1 Asian American, 1 Hispanic), 8 international. 29 applicants, 86% accepted. *Degree requirements:* For master's, thesis or alternative required, foreign language not required; for doctorate, dissertation required, foreign language not required. *Entrance requirements:* For master's, minimum B average; for doctorate, GRE General Test (minimum combined score of 1000; average 1010), minimum B average, writing sample. Application deadline: 4/1 (priority date; rolling processing; 9/1 for spring admission). Application fee: $0 ($25 for international students). Electronic applications accepted. *Tuition:* $2218 per year full-time, $401 per semester (minimum) part-time for state residents; $6336 per year full-time, $1087 per semester (minimum) part-time for nonresidents. *Financial aid:* Career-related internships or fieldwork available. • Robert Newhouse, Chair, 785-532-5535. Application contact: Paul Burden, Assistant Dean, 785-532-5595. Fax: 785-532-7304. E-mail: gradstudy@mail.educ.ksu.edu.

Marshall University, College of Education, Division of Human Development and Allied Technology, Program in Adult and Technical Education, Huntington, WV 25755-2020. Awards MS. Accredited by NCATE. Evening/weekend programs available. Faculty: 4 (2 women). Students: 16 full-time (11 women), 71 part-time (52 women); includes 5 minority (all African Americans), 3 international. In 1997, 19 degrees awarded. *Degree requirements:* Thesis optional. *Entrance requirements:* GRE General Test (minimum combined score of 1200). *Tuition:* $2364 per year full-time, $132 per hour part-time for state residents; $6894 per year full-time, $383 per hour part-time for nonresidents. • Dr. Laura Wyant, Director, 304-696-3073. Application contact: Dr. James Harless, Director of Admissions, 304-696-3160.

Memorial University of Newfoundland, School of Graduate Studies, Faculty of Education, St. John's, NF A1C 5S7, Canada. Offerings include post-secondary education (M Ed). *Degree requirements:* Comprehensive exam required, foreign language not required. *Application deadline:* 2/1. *Application fee:* $40. *Expenses:* Tuition $1896 per year (minimum). Fees $60 per year for Canadian residents; $621 per year for nonresidents. • Dr. Terry Piper, Dean, 709-737-8588. E-mail: tpiper@kean.ucs.mun.ca. Application contact: Dr. Linda M. Phillips, Associate Dean, 709-737-3402. E-mail: lindap@morgan.ucs.mun.ca.

Michigan State University, College of Education, Department of Educational Administration, East Lansing, MI 48824-1020. Offerings include adult and continuing education (MA); higher, adult and lifelong education (PhD). Department faculty: 17 (6 women). *Degree requirements:* For doctorate, dissertation required, foreign language not required. *Application deadline:* rolling. *Application fee:* $30 ($40 for international students). *Expenses:* Tuition $4609 per year full-time, $223 per credit hour (minimum) part-time for state residents; $8704 per year full-time, $450 per credit hour (minimum) part-time for nonresidents. Fees $576 per year full-time, $476 per year part-time. • Dr. Philip Cusick, Chairperson, 517-355-4538.

Morehead State University, College of Education and Behavioral Sciences, Department of Leadership and Secondary Education, Program in Adult and Higher Education, Morehead, KY 40351. Awards MA, Ed S. Accredited by NCATE. Part-time and evening/weekend programs available. Faculty: 2 full-time (0 women), 1 (woman) part-time. Students: 9 full-time (3 women), 39 part-time (28 women); includes 3 minority (2 African Americans, 1 Asian American), 3 international. Average age 25. 16 applicants, 94% accepted. In 1997, 13 master's, 1 Ed S awarded. *Degree requirements:* For master's, oral and/or written comprehensive exams required, foreign language and thesis not required; for Ed S, thesis, oral exam required, foreign language not required. *Entrance requirements:* For master's, GRE General Test (minimum combined score of 1050), minimum GPA of 2.5, 2 years of work experience; for Ed S, GRE General Test (minimum combined score of 1200), interview, master's degree, minimum GPA of 3.5, work experience. Application deadline: 8/1 (priority date; rolling processing; 12/1 for spring admission). Application fee: $0. *Tuition:* $2470 per year full-time, $138 per semester hour part-time for state residents; $6710 per year full-time, $373 per semester hour part-time for nonresidents. *Financial aid:* Research assistantships, teaching assistantships, Federal Work-Study, and career-related internships or fieldwork available. Financial aid application deadline: 4/1; applicants required to submit FAFSA. *Faculty research:* Self-directed learning projects for nontraditional students, evaluation of adult educational programs, adult literacy, evaluation of homeless. • Application contact: Betty Cowsert, Graduate Admissions Officer, 606-783-2039. Fax: 606-783-5061.

Mount Saint Vincent University, Department of Education, Program in Adult Education, Halifax, NS B3M 2J6, Canada. Awards MA, MA Ed, MA(R), M Ed. Faculty: 2 full-time (0 women), 2 part-time (1 woman). Students: 1 full-time (0 women), 63 part-time (47 women). Average age 35. 39 applicants, 87% accepted. In 1997, 2 degrees awarded. *Degree requirements:* Thesis. *Entrance requirements:* Bachelor's degree in related field. Application deadline: 3/1 (priority date; rolling processing; 9/1 for spring admission). Application fee: $40. *Expenses:* Tuition $1024 per course. Fees $25 per course. *Financial aid:* In 1997–98, 2 fellowships (both to first-year students) totaling $1,000 were awarded. Financial aid application deadline: 5/1. *Faculty research:* Cultural studies, critical pedagogy, sociology of education, distance education. • Dr. Michael Welton, Head, 902-457-6147. Fax: 902-457-4911. E-mail: michael.welton@msvu.ca. Application contact: Susan Tanner, Assistant Registrar, 902-457-6363. Fax: 902-457-6498. E-mail: susan.tanner@msvu.ca.

National–Louis University, College of Arts and Sciences, Department of Adult and Continuing Education, Doctoral Program in Adult Education, 2840 Sheridan Road, Evanston, IL 60201-1730. Awards Ed D. Students: 20 full-time (15 women), 3 part-time (all women); includes 7 minority (2 African Americans, 2 Asian Americans, 3 Hispanics). Average age 47. *Degree requirements:* Dissertation, comprehensive exams, internship required, foreign language not required. *Entrance requirements:* GRE General Test, MAT, or Watson-Glaser Critical Thinking Appraisal, interview, master's degree, 3 years of experience in field. Application deadline: 12/15 (priority date). Application fee: $25. *Tuition:* $411 per semester hour. *Financial aid:* Fellowships, Federal Work-Study, institutionally sponsored loans available. Aid available to part-time students. Financial aid application deadline: 4/15; applicants required to submit FAFSA. • Dr. Thomas Heaney, Coordinator, 847-475-1100 Ext. 3274. Application contact: Dr. David McCulloch, Vice President for University Services, 800-443-5522 Ext. 5127. Fax: 847-465-0593. E-mail: dmcc@wheeling1.nl.edu.

National–Louis University, College of Arts and Sciences, Department of Adult and Continuing Education, Master's Program in Adult Education, 2840 Sheridan Road, Evanston, IL 60201-1730. Awards M Ad Ed, Certificate. Students: 3 full-time (all women), 39 part-time (33 women); includes 12 minority (9 African Americans, 3 Hispanics). Average age 41. *Degree requirements:* For master's, thesis or alternative, internship required, foreign language not required. *Entrance requirements:* For master's, GRE General Test, MAT, or Watson-Glaser Critical Thinking Appraisal, interview, minimum GPA of 3.0. Application deadline: 12/15 (rolling processing). Application fee: $25. *Tuition:* $411 per semester hour. *Financial aid:* Fellowships, research assistantships, Federal Work-Study, institutionally sponsored loans available. Aid available to part-time students. Financial aid application deadline: 4/15; applicants required to submit FAFSA. • Dr. Randee Lawrence, Coordinator, 847-475-1100 Ext. 4388. Application contact: Dr. David McCulloch, Vice President for University Services, 800-443-5522 Ext. 5127. Fax: 847-465-0593. E-mail: dmcc@wheeling1.nl.edu.

National–Louis University, College of Arts and Sciences, Department of Adult and Continuing Education, Program in Adult Education and Developmental Studies, 2840 Sheridan Road, Evanston, IL 60201-1730. Offers adult education (M Ad Ed), adult education and developmental studies (Certificate), developmental studies (M Ad Ed). Part-time and evening/weekend programs available. Students: 11 full-time (all women), 4 part-time (3 women); includes 4 minority (3 African Americans, 1 Hispanic). Average age 40. In 1997, 5 master's awarded. *Entrance requirements:* For master's, GRE General Test, MAT, or Watson-Glaser Critical Thinking Appraisal, interview, minimum GPA of 3.0. Application deadline: 12/15 (rolling processing). Application fee: $25. *Tuition:* $411 per semester hour. *Financial aid:* Fellowships and career-related internships or fieldwork available. Aid available to part-time students. Financial aid application deadline: 4/15; applicants required to submit FAFSA. *Faculty research:* Adult learning and development, learner-centered development, political and social foundations, reading development, curricular processes. • Application contact: Dr. David McCulloch, Vice President for University Services, 800-443-5522 Ext. 5127. Fax: 847-465-0593. E-mail: dmcc@wheeling1.nl.edu.

National University, School of Education and Human Services, Department of Teacher Education and Leadership, La Jolla, CA 92037-1011. Offerings include instructional leadership for adult learners (MS). *Application deadline:* rolling. *Application fee:* $60 ($100 for international students). *Tuition:* $7830 per year full-time, $870 per course part-time. • Dr. Helene Mandell, Chair, 619-642-8345. Application contact: Nancy Rohland, Director of Enrollment Management, 619-563-7100. Fax: 619-563-7393.

Newman University, Program in Education, Wichita, KS 67213-2084. Offerings include adult education (MS Ed). Program faculty: 5 full-time, 9 part-time. *Degree requirements:* Thesis or alternative. *Average time to degree:* master's–3 years part-time. *Application deadline:* 8/15 (priority date; rolling processing; 1/10 for spring admission). *Application fee:* $25. *Tuition:* $257 per credit hour. • Dr. Laura McLemore, Division Chair of Institute for Teacher Education, 316-942-4291 Ext. 253. Fax: 316-942-4483.

North Carolina Agricultural and Technical State University, Graduate School, School of Education, Department of Educational Leadership and Policy, Program in Adult Education, Greensboro, NC 27411. Awards MS. Accredited by NCATE. Part-time and evening/weekend programs available. Faculty: 2 full-time (0 women). Students: 3 full-time (all women), 25 part-time (20 women); includes 23 minority (all African Americans). Average age 32. In 1997, 6 degrees awarded. *Degree requirements:* Thesis or alternative, comprehensive exam, qualifying exam required, foreign language not required. *Entrance requirements:* GRE General Test, minimum GPA of 2.6. Application deadline: 6/1 (priority date; rolling processing; 12/1 for spring admission). Application fee: $35. *Tuition:* $1662 per year full-time, $272 per semester (minimum) part-time for state residents; $8790 per year full-time, $2054 per semester (minimum) part-time for nonresidents. *Financial aid:* Career-related internships or fieldwork available. Financial aid application deadline: 6/1. • Dr. Fred Wood, Interim Chairperson, Department of Educational Leadership and Policy, 336-334-7522. E-mail: woodf@ncat.edu.

North Carolina State University, Colleges of Education and Psychology and Agriculture and Life Sciences, Department of Adult and Community College Education, Raleigh, NC 27695. Awards M Ed, MS, Ed D. Accredited by NCATE. Faculty: 31 full-time (10 women), 38 part-time (15 women). Students: 55 full-time (38 women), 310 part-time (187 women); includes 92 minority (82 African Americans, 6 Asian Americans, 1 Hispanic, 3 Native Americans), 4

Directory: Adult Education

North Carolina State University (continued)
international. Average age 42. 107 applicants, 61% accepted. In 1997, 29 master's, 60 doctorates awarded. *Degree requirements:* Thesis/dissertation, comprehensive exam required, foreign language not required. *Entrance requirements:* GRE General Test or MAT, minimum GPA of 3.0 in major. Application deadline: 6/1 (priority date; rolling processing; 11/1 for spring admission). Application fee: $45. *Tuition:* $2370 per year full-time, $517 per semester (minimum) part-time for state residents; $11,536 per year full-time, $2809 per semester (minimum) part-time for nonresidents. *Financial aid:* In 1997–98, 32 research assistantships (8 to first-year students) averaging $969 per month and totaling $139,536 were awarded; fellowships, teaching assistantships also available. *Faculty research:* Techniques in education, organization/development in higher education, historical and philosophical foundations of adult education, adult learning and development, educational gerontology. Total annual research expenditures: $495,653. • Dr. William L. Deegan, Head, 919-515-6240. E-mail: deegan@poe.coe.ncsu.edu. Application contact: Dr. J. Conrad Glass, Director of Graduate Programs, 919-515-6241. Fax: 919-515-4039. E-mail: glass@poe.coe.ncsu.edu.

Northern Illinois University, College of Education, Department of Leadership and Educational Policy Studies, Program in Adult Continuing Education, De Kalb, IL 60115-2854. Awards MS Ed, Ed D. Accredited by NCATE. Part-time and evening/weekend programs available. Faculty: 9 full-time (2 women), 4 part-time (2 women). Students: 40 full-time (28 women), 168 part-time (103 women); includes 57 minority (43 African Americans, 4 Asian Americans, 10 Hispanics), 12 international. Average age 44. 69 applicants, 46% accepted. In 1997, 47 master's, 17 doctorates awarded. Terminal master's awarded for partial completion of doctoral program. *Degree requirements:* For master's, comprehensive exam required, thesis optional, foreign language not required; for doctorate, candidacy exam, dissertation defense required, foreign language not required. *Entrance requirements:* For master's, GRE General Test, TOEFL (minimum score 550), minimum GPA of 2.75; for doctorate, GRE General Test, TOEFL (minimum score 550), minimum GPA of 2.75 (undergraduate), 3.2 (graduate). Application deadline: 6/1 (rolling processing; 11/1 for spring admission). Application fee: $30. *Tuition:* $3984 per year full-time, $154 per credit hour part-time for state residents; $8160 per year full-time, $328 per credit hour part-time for nonresidents. *Financial aid:* Fellowships, research assistantships, teaching assistantships, staff assistantships, full tuition waivers, Federal Work-Study, and career-related internships or fieldwork available. Aid available to part-time students. • Dr. Richard Orem, Faculty Chair, 815-753-9316.

See in-depth description on page 921.

Nova Southeastern University, Fischler Center for the Advancement of Education, Programs in Higher Education, Fort Lauderdale, FL 33314-7721. Offerings include adult education (Ed D). *Degree requirements:* Dissertation, practicum required, foreign language not required. *Entrance requirements:* Master's degree, work experience in field. Application deadline: rolling. Application fee: $50. *Tuition:* $8460 per year. • Dr. Ross E. Moreton, Dean, 954-262-8526. E-mail: moreton@fcae.nova.edu. Application contact: Dr. Delores Smiley, 800-986-3223 Ext. 8527. Fax: 954-262-3903. E-mail: smiley@fcae.nova.edu.

Oregon State University, Graduate School, College of Home Economics and Education, School of Education, Program in Adult Education, Corvallis, OR 97331. Awards Ed M, MAIS. Accredited by NCATE. Part-time programs available. Students: 41 part-time; includes 1 international. Average age 39. In 1997, 16 degrees awarded. *Degree requirements:* Thesis or alternative, minimum GPA of 3.0 required, foreign language not required. *Entrance requirements:* TOEFL (minimum score 550), minimum GPA of 3.0 in last 90 hours. Application deadline: 3/1 (rolling processing). Application fee: $50. *Tuition:* $6207 per year full-time, $810 per quarter (minimum) part-time for state residents; $10,551 per year full-time, $1293 per quarter (minimum) part-time for nonresidents. *Financial aid:* Research assistantships, teaching assistantships, Federal Work-Study, institutionally sponsored loans, and career-related internships or fieldwork available. Aid available to part-time students. Financial aid application deadline: 2/1. *Faculty research:* Adult training and developmental psychology, cross-cultural communication, leadership development and human relations, adult literacy. • Dr. Lance Haddon, Coordinator, 541-737-5956.

Pennsylvania State University Harrisburg Campus of the Capital College, Division of Behavioral Sciences and Education, Program in Adult Education, Middletown, PA 17057-4898. Awards D Ed. Part-time programs available. Students: 23 part-time (14 women). Average age 33. In 1997, 2 degrees awarded. *Entrance requirements:* GRE General Test or MAT. Application deadline: 7/26. Application fee: $40. *Expenses:* Tuition $6534 per year full-time, $276 per credit part-time for state residents; $12,516 per year full-time, $523 per credit part-time for nonresidents. Fees $232 per year (minimum) full-time, $40 per semester (minimum) part-time. • Dr. Andrea Ellinger, Head, 717-948-6213.

Pennsylvania State University University Park Campus, College of Education, Department of Adult Education, Instructional Systems, and Workforce Education and Development, Program in Adult Education, University Park, PA 16802-1503. Awards M Ed, D Ed. Accredited by NCATE. Students: 23 full-time (18 women), 93 part-time (68 women). In 1997, 19 master's, 4 doctorates awarded. *Entrance requirements:* GRE General Test or MAT. Application fee: $40. *Expenses:* Tuition $6534 per year full-time, $276 per credit part-time for state residents; $13,460 per year full-time, $561 per credit part-time for nonresidents. Fees $252 per year (minimum) full-time, $43 per semester (minimum) part-time. • Dr. Eunice N. Askov, Head, Department of Adult Education, Instructional Systems, and Workforce Education and Development, 814-865-0625.

Portland State University, School of Education, Department of Educational Policy, Foundations, and Administrative Studies, Program in Postsecondary Education, Portland, OR 97207-0751. Offers educational leadership/postsecondary adult and continuing education (Ed D). Accredited by NCATE. Part-time and evening/weekend programs available. Faculty: 11 full-time (6 women), 2 part-time (1 woman), 12 FTE. Students: 5 full-time (2 women), 19 part-time (14 women); includes 1 minority (African American), 1 international. Average age 43. 9 applicants, 67% accepted. *Degree requirements:* Dissertation, comprehensive exam required, foreign language not required. *Entrance requirements:* GRE General Test or MAT, TOEFL (minimum score 550). Application deadline: 4/1 (rolling processing; 11/1 for spring admission). Application fee: $50. *Tuition:* $6101 per year full-time, $689 per semester (minimum) part-time for state residents; $10,445 per year full-time, $689 per semester (minimum) part-time for nonresidents. *Financial aid:* Research assistantships, teaching assistantships, Federal Work-Study, institutionally sponsored loans, and career-related internships or fieldwork available. Aid available to part-time students. Financial aid application deadline: 3/1; applicants required to submit FAFSA. *Faculty research:* Adult learning and development, learning communities assessment, college teaching, urban postsecondary education. Total annual research expenditures: $15,000. • Dr. Douglas L. Robertson, Head, 503-725-4753. Fax: 503-725-8475. E-mail: doug@ed.pdx.edu.

Rutgers, The State University of New Jersey, New Brunswick, Graduate School of Education, Department of Educational Theory, Policy and Administration, Program in Adult and Continuing Education, New Brunswick, NJ 08903. Awards Ed M, Ed D. Part-time and evening/weekend programs available. Faculty: 2 full-time (0 women), 3 part-time (1 woman), 3 FTE. Students: 15 full-time, 33 part-time. 16 applicants, 75% accepted. In 1997, 3 master's, 2 doctorates awarded. Terminal master's awarded for partial completion of doctoral program. *Degree requirements:* For doctorate, dissertation required, foreign language not required. *Entrance requirements:* GRE General Test. Application deadline: 3/1 (11/1 for spring admission). Application fee: $40. *Expenses:* Tuition $6492 per year full-time, $268 per credit part-time for state residents; $9520 per year full-time, $395 per credit part-time for nonresidents. Fees $208 per year (minimum). *Financial aid:* Scholarships, Federal Work-Study, institutionally sponsored loans, and career-related internships or fieldwork available. Financial aid application deadline: 3/1. *Faculty research:* Adult literacy, popular education, continuing higher education, training and development. Total annual research expenditures: $30,000. • Dr. Gordon Darkenwald, Coordinator, 732-932-7496 Ext. 203. Fax: 732-932-6803. E-mail: darkenwa@rci.rutgers.edu.

St. Francis Xavier University, Program in Adult Education, Antigonish, NS B2G 2W5, Canada. Awards M Ad Ed. Part-time programs available. Postbaccalaureate distance learning degree programs offered (minimal on-campus study). Faculty: 3 full-time (2 women), 1 part-time (0 women). Students: 154 part-time (118 women). Average age 35. 82 applicants, 54% accepted. In 1997, 23 degrees awarded. *Degree requirements:* Thesis required, foreign language not required. *Average time to degree:* master's–3.5 years part-time. *Entrance requirements:* Minimum B average in undergraduate course work, 2 years of work experience in field. Application deadline: rolling. Application fee: $30. *Tuition:* $4365 per year for Canadian residents; $7365 per year for nonresidents. *Faculty research:* Adult learning and development, religious education, women's issues, literacy, action research. • Dr. Marie Gillen, Chair, 902-867-2393. Fax: 902-867-3765. E-mail: mgillen@stfx.ca. Application contact: Admissions Office, 902-867-2219. Fax: 902-867-2329. E-mail: admit@stfx.ca.

Saint Joseph's University, Department of Education, Program in Training and Development, Philadelphia, PA 19131-1395. Awards MS. Part-time and evening/weekend programs available. Students: 65 (50 women). *Entrance requirements:* 2 years of experience with adult learners; GRE General Test, MAT, or minimum undergraduate GPA of 2.7. Application deadline: 7/15. Application fee: $30. *Tuition:* $510 per credit hour. *Financial aid:* Fellowships, research assistantships, Federal Work-Study, and career-related internships or fieldwork available. Aid available to part-time students. • Dr. Mary DeKonty Applegate, Director, Department of Education, 610-660-1583.

San Francisco State University, College of Education, Department of Administration and Interdisciplinary Studies, Program in Adult Education, San Francisco, CA 94132-1722. Awards MA, AC. Accredited by NCATE. Part-time programs available. *Entrance requirements:* For master's, minimum GPA of 2.5 in last 60 units. Application deadline: 11/30 (priority date; rolling processing). Application fee: $55. *Expenses:* Tuition $0 for state residents; $246 per unit for nonresidents. Fees $1982 per year full-time, $1316 per year part-time.

Seattle University, School of Education, Division of Leadership and Service, Program in Adult Education and Training, Seattle, WA 98122. Awards MA, M Ed. Accredited by NCATE. Part-time and evening/weekend programs available. Students: 5 full-time (all women), 41 part-time (32 women); includes 5 minority (1 African American, 2 Asian Americans, 1 Hispanic, 1 Native American), 3 international. Average age 39. 14 applicants, 64% accepted. In 1997, 16 degrees awarded. *Degree requirements:* Comprehensive exam required, foreign language and thesis not required. *Entrance requirements:* GRE, MAT, or minimum GPA of 2.75; 1 year of related experience. Application deadline: 8/20 (priority date; rolling processing; 2/20 for spring admission). Application fee: $55. *Expenses:* Tuition $339 per credit hour (minimum). Fees $70 per year. *Financial aid:* Federal Work-Study and career-related internships or fieldwork available. Aid available to part-time students. Financial aid applicants required to submit FAFSA. • Dr. Carol L. Weaver, Chairperson, Division of Leadership and Service, 206-296-6170. E-mail: cweaver@seattleu.edu.

Suffolk University, College of Liberal Arts and Sciences, Department of Education and Human Services, Program in Adult and Organizational Learning, Boston, MA 02108-2770. Awards MS, CAGS. Part-time and evening/weekend programs available. Faculty: 2 full-time (both women), 2 part-time (1 woman). *Entrance requirements:* For master's, GRE General Test (average 500 on each section) or MAT (average 50). Application deadline: 6/15 (priority date; rolling processing; 11/15 for spring admission). Application fee: $50. *Expenses:* Tuition $14,544 per year full-time, $1452 per course part-time. Fees $20 per year full-time, $10 per year part-time. *Financial aid:* Fellowships available. Financial aid application deadline: 4/1. *Faculty research:* Adult training methods, adult learning theory, instructional design, learning and teaching styles, systems thinking. • Dr. Barbara F. Ash, Director, 617-573-8280. Fax: 617-722-9440. Application contact: Judy Reynolds, Acting Director of Graduate Admissions, 617-573-8302. Fax: 617-523-0116. E-mail: grad.admission@admin.suffolk.edu.

Teachers College, Columbia University, Graduate Faculty of Education, Department of Organization and Leadership, Program in Adult Education, 525 West 120th Street, New York, NY 10027-6696. Awards MA, Ed D. Faculty: 3 full-time (2 women), 4 part-time (2 women), 5 FTE. Students: 52 full-time (37 women), 60 part-time (45 women); includes 19 minority (14 African Americans, 3 Asian Americans, 2 Hispanics), 2 international. Average age 46. 17 applicants, 35% accepted. In 1997, 6 master's, 5 doctorates awarded. *Degree requirements:* For doctorate, variable foreign language requirement, dissertation. *Entrance requirements:* For doctorate, master's degree, 3-5 years of professional experience. Application deadline: 5/15. Application fee: $50. *Expenses:* Tuition $640 per credit. Fees $120 per semester. *Financial aid:* Full and partial tuition waivers, Federal Work-Study, institutionally sponsored loans, and career-related internships or fieldwork available. Aid available to part-time students. Financial aid application deadline: 2/1. *Faculty research:* Adult learning, perspective transformation, training and evaluation, workplace learning, theory to practice, international models of management. • Application contact: Christine Souders, Office of Admissions, 212-678-3710. Fax: 212-678-4171.

Tennessee State University, College of Education, Department of Teaching and Learning, Program in Adult Education, Nashville, TN 37209-1561. Offers curriculum and instruction (M Ed), including adult education, secondary instruction. Accredited by NCATE. *Degree requirements:* Thesis (for some programs). *Entrance requirements:* GRE General Test, GRE Subject Test, or MAT (minimum score 44), minimum GPA of 2.5. Application deadline: rolling. Application fee: $15. *Tuition:* $2962 per year full-time, $182 per credit hour part-time for state residents; $7788 per year full-time, $393 per credit hour part-time for nonresidents. *Financial aid:* Application deadline 5/1. *Faculty research:* Post-retirement as a time for self-resignation or self-actualization, educator's role in ensuring diversity, relationship of homework to parent's absence in student achievement, multiculturism in adult education. • Application contact: Dr. Clinton M. Lipsey, Dean of the Graduate School, 615-963-5901. Fax: 615-963-5963. E-mail: clipsey@picard.tnstate.edu.

Texas A&M University, College of Education, Department of Educational Human Resource Development, College Station, TX 77843. Offerings include adult education (M Ed, MS, Ed D, PhD). Accredited by NCATE. Department faculty: 14 full-time (5 women). *Degree requirements:* For doctorate, dissertation required, foreign language not required. *Entrance requirements:* GRE General Test, TOEFL. Application fee: $35 ($75 for international students). • Lloyd Korhonan, Head, 409-845-3016. E-mail: lloyd@summa.tamu.edu. Application contact: Anne Koppa, Graduate Admissions Supervisor, 409-862-4154. Fax: 409-845-0409. E-mail: cak5866@zeys.tamu.edu.

Texas A&M University–Kingsville, College of Education, Department of Education, Program in Adult Education, Kingsville, TX 78363. Awards M Ed. Offered jointly with Texas A&M University. Part-time and evening/weekend programs available. Faculty: 3 part-time (0 women). *Degree requirements:* Comprehensive exam, mini-thesis required, foreign language not required. *Entrance requirements:* GRE General Test (minimum combined score of 1000), MAT (minimum score 34), minimum GPA of 3.0. Application deadline: 6/1 (rolling processing; 11/15 for spring admission). Application fee: $15 ($25 for international students). *Tuition:* $1822 per year full-time, $281 per semester (minimum) part-time for state residents; $6934 per year full-time, $908 per semester (minimum) part-time for nonresidents. *Financial aid:* Federal Work-Study, institutionally sponsored loans available. Aid available to part-time students. Financial aid application deadline: 5/15. *Faculty research:* Continuing education efforts in south Texas, adult education methodologies. • Dr. Travis Polk, Chair, Department of Education, 512-593-3204.

Troy State University Montgomery, Division of Counseling, Education, and Psychology, Program in Adult Education, PO Drawer 4419, Montgomery, AL 36103-4419. Awards MS. Part-time and evening/weekend programs available. In 1997, 14 degrees awarded. *Degree requirements:* Thesis or alternative. *Entrance requirements:* GRE, MAT, or NTE; TOEFL.

Application deadline: rolling. Application fee: $20. Electronic applications accepted. *Expenses:* Tuition $52 per quarter hour for state residents; $104 per quarter hour for nonresidents. Fees $30 per year. • Dr. James Macey, Coordinator, 334-241-9553. Fax: 334-240-7320. E-mail: jmacey@tsum.edu.

Tusculum College, Graduate School, Program in Education, Greeneville, TN 37743-9997. Offerings include adult education (MA Ed). *Degree requirements:* Thesis or alternative required, foreign language not required. *Average time to degree:* master's–1.3 years full-time. *Entrance requirements:* GRE or MAT, NTE, minimum GPA of 2.75, 3 years of work experience. Application fee: $0. *Tuition:* $190 per credit hour (minimum). • Application contact: Don Stout, Executive Director of Professional Studies, 423-636-7330 Ext. 612. Fax: 423-638-5181.

Université de Sherbrooke, Faculty of Education, Program in Adult Education Training, Sherbrooke, PQ J1K 2R1, Canada. Awards Diploma. Part-time and evening/weekend programs available. *Application deadline:* 6/1. *Application fee:* $15.

Université du Québec à Hull, Program in Adult Education, Hull, PQ J8X 3X7, Canada. Awards Diploma. Part-time programs available. *Entrance requirements:* Appropriate bachelor's degree, proficiency in French. Application deadline: 8/21. Application fee: $30.

University of Alaska Anchorage, College of Health, Education and Social Welfare, School of Education, Program in Adult Education, Anchorage, AK 99508-8060. Awards M Ed. Part-time programs available. Students: 3 full-time (2 women), 15 part-time (9 women); includes 4 minority (1 African American, 3 Native Americans). 4 applicants, 50% accepted. In 1997, 5 degrees awarded. *Degree requirements:* Thesis required, foreign language not required. *Entrance requirements:* GRE Subject Test, interview. Application deadline: 5/1 (rolling processing). Application fee: $45. *Expenses:* Tuition $2988 per year full-time, $1990 per year part-time for state residents; $5814 per year full-time, $3876 per year part-time for nonresidents. Fees $298 per year. *Financial aid:* Federal Work-Study and career-related internships or fieldwork available. Aid available to part-time students. Financial aid application deadline: 4/1. • Dr. Chris Jensen, Head, 907-786-4415. Fax: 907-786-4444. Application contact: Linda Berg Smith, Associate Vice Chancellor for Enrollment Services, 907-786-1529.

University of Alberta, Faculty of Graduate Studies and Research, Department of Educational Policy Studies, Edmonton, AB T6G 2E1, Canada. Offerings include adult education (M Ed). Department faculty: 25 full-time (7 women), 3 part-time (1 woman). *Degree requirements:* Thesis (for some programs). *Average time to degree:* master's–1 year full-time, 3 years part-time; doctorate–2 years full-time, 4 years part-time. *Entrance requirements:* TOEFL (minimum score 580). Application deadline: 8/1 (priority date; rolling processing; 4/1 for spring admission). Application fee: $60. *Expenses:* Tuition $390 per course for Canadian residents; $781 per course for nonresidents. Fees $500 per year full-time, $184 per year part-time. • Dr. D. M. Richards, Chair, 403-492-3679. E-mail: don.richards@ualberta.ca. Application contact: Joan White, Graduate Secretary, 403-492-3679. Fax: 403-492-2024. E-mail: joan.white@ualberta.ca.

University of Arkansas, College of Education, Department of Vocational and Adult Education, Program in Adult Education, Fayetteville, AR 72701-1201. Awards M Ed, Ed D, Ed S. Accredited by NCATE. Students: 30 full-time (22 women), 27 part-time (18 women); includes 5 minority (4 African Americans, 1 Native American), 5 international. 14 applicants, 43% accepted. In 1997, 10 master's, 6 doctorates, 4 Ed Ss awarded. *Degree requirements:* For doctorate, dissertation. *Entrance requirements:* For master's, GRE General Test or MAT. Application fee: $25 ($35 for international students). *Tuition:* $3144 per year full-time, $173 per credit hour part-time for state residents; $7140 per year full-time, $395 per credit hour part-time for nonresidents. *Financial aid:* Federal Work-Study and career-related internships or fieldwork available. Financial aid application deadline: 4/1. • Dr. B. R. Lyle, Coordinator, 501-575-4759.

University of Arkansas at Little Rock, College of Education, Department of Teacher Education, Program in Adult Education, Little Rock, AR 72204-1099. Awards M Ed. Accredited by NCATE. Part-time programs available. Students: 5 full-time (3 women), 29 part-time (24 women); includes 7 minority (6 African Americans, 1 Asian American), 2 international. Average age 38. 20 applicants, 85% accepted. In 1997, 14 degrees awarded. *Degree requirements:* Comprehensive exam required, foreign language and thesis not required. *Entrance requirements:* Interview, minimum GPA of 2.75, GRE General Test (minimum combined score of 1000 on three sections) or teaching certificate. Application deadline: rolling. Application fee: $25 ($30 for international students). *Expenses:* Tuition $2466 per year full-time, $137 per credit hour part-time for state residents; $5256 per year full-time, $292 per credit hour part-time for nonresidents. Fees $216 per year full-time, $36 per semester (minimum) part-time. *Financial aid:* Research assistantships, teaching assistantships, Federal Work-Study, institutionally sponsored loans, and career-related internships or fieldwork available. Aid available to part-time students. *Faculty research:* Adult literacy, volunteer training, in-services education. • Dr. Howard Stephens, Adviser, 501-569-3124.

University of British Columbia, Faculty of Education, Department of Educational Studies, Program in Adult Education, Vancouver, BC V6T 1Z2, Canada. Awards MA, M Ed. Evening/weekend programs available. *Degree requirements:* Thesis (MA) required, foreign language not required. *Entrance requirements:* TOEFL (minimum score 550). Application fee: $60. *Faculty research:* Adult basic education, lifelong education, program planning, health promotion, policy, transfer of learning.

The University of Calgary, Faculty of Education, Graduate Division of Educational Research, Calgary, AB T2N 1N4, Canada. Offerings include adult education (MA, M Sc, Ed D, PhD). Postbaccalaureate distance learning degree programs offered (minimal on-campus study). Division faculty: 60 full-time, 25 part-time. *Degree requirements:* For doctorate, dissertation. *Entrance requirements:* For doctorate, minimum GPA of 3.5. Application deadline: 2/1. Application fee: $60. Electronic applications accepted. *Expenses:* Tuition $5448 per year full-time, $908 per course part-time for Canadian residents; $10,896 per year full-time, $1816 per course part-time for nonresidents. Fees $285 per year full-time, $119 per semester (minimum) part-time. • Dr. Bryant Griffith, Assistant Dean, 403-220-5675. Fax: 403-282-3005. E-mail: griffith@acs.ucalgary.ca.

University of Central Oklahoma, College of Education, Department of Occupational and Technical Education, Program in Adult Education, Edmond, OK 73034-5209. Offers community services (M Ed), gerontology (M Ed). Accredited by NCATE. M Ed (gerontology) offered jointly through the Department of Psychology. Part-time and evening/weekend programs available. *Entrance requirements:* GRE General Test. Application deadline: 8/18. Application fee: $15. *Tuition:* $76 per credit hour for state residents; $178 per credit hour for nonresidents.

University of Connecticut, School of Education, Field of Adult and Vocational Education, Storrs, CT 06269. Awards MA, PhD. Accredited by NCATE. Faculty: 5. Students: 6 full-time (5 women), 36 part-time (24 women); includes 1 minority (African American), 3 international. Average age 43. 10 applicants, 60% accepted. In 1997, 2 master's, 7 doctorates awarded. Terminal master's awarded for partial completion of doctoral program. *Degree requirements:* For master's, thesis or alternative required, foreign language not required; for doctorate, dissertation. *Entrance requirements:* GRE General Test. Application deadline: 6/1 (priority date; rolling processing; 11/1 for spring admission). Application fee: $40 ($45 for international students). *Expenses:* Tuition $5272 per year full-time, $293 per credit part-time for state residents; $13,696 per year full-time, $761 per credit part-time for nonresidents. Fees $948 per year full-time, $640 per year part-time. *Financial aid:* In 1997–98, 3 fellowships totaling $3,185, 2 research assistantships totaling $27,000, 3 teaching assistantships totaling $27,750 were awarded. • Patrick B. Mullarney, Head, 860-486-6278.

University of Denver, College of Education, Denver, CO 80208. Offerings include higher education and adult studies (MA, PhD). Postbaccalaureate distance learning degree programs offered (no on-campus study). College faculty: 23 full-time (13 women). *Degree requirements:* For master's, comprehensive exam required, foreign language and thesis not required; for doctorate, 2 foreign languages (computer language can substitute for one), dissertation, comprehensive exam. *Entrance requirements:* For master's, GRE General Test (minimum combined score of 870), TOEFL (minimum score 550), TSE (minimum score 230); for doctorate, GRE General Test (minimum combined score of 930), TOEFL (minimum score 550), TSE (minimum score 230). Application deadline: 1/1 (rolling processing). Application fee: $40 ($45 for international students). *Expenses:* Tuition $18,216 per year full-time, $506 per credit hour part-time. Fees $159 per year. • Dr. Elinor Katz, Dean, 303-871-3665. Application contact: Linda McCarthy, 303-871-2509.

University of Georgia, College of Education, Department of Adult Education, Athens, GA 30602. Offers programs in adult education (MA, M Ed, Ed D, PhD, Ed S), human resource and organization development (M Ed). Accredited by NCATE. Faculty: 9 full-time (4 women). Students: 61 full-time, 78 part-time (57 women); includes 18 minority (13 African Americans, 2 Asian Americans, 3 Hispanics), 18 international. 46 applicants, 57% accepted. In 1997, 18 master's, 11 doctorates, 1 Ed S awarded. *Degree requirements:* For master's, thesis (MA) required, foreign language not required; for doctorate, dissertation. *Entrance requirements:* For master's and Ed S, GRE General Test or MAT; for doctorate, GRE General Test. Application deadline: 7/1 (priority date; 11/15 for spring admission). Application fee: $30. Electronic applications accepted. *Tuition:* $3290 per year full-time, $643 per semester (minimum) part-time for state residents; $11,300 per year full-time, $1645 per semester (minimum) part-time for nonresidents. *Financial aid:* Fellowships, research assistantships, teaching assistantships, assistantships available. • Dr. Ronald M. Cervero, Graduate Coordinator, 706-542-4011. Fax: 706-542-4204.

University of Idaho, College of Graduate Studies, College of Education, Division of Adult, Counselor, and Technology Education, Program in Adult Education, Moscow, ID 83844-4140. Awards M Ed, MS, Ed D, PhD. Accredited by NCATE. Ed D and PhD offered through the College of Education. Students: 5 full-time (4 women), 23 part-time (20 women); includes 1 minority (Native American). *Degree requirements:* For doctorate, dissertation. *Entrance requirements:* For master's, minimum GPA of 2.8; for doctorate, minimum undergraduate GPA of 2.8, 3.0 graduate. Application deadline: 8/1 (12/15 for spring admission). Application fee: $35 ($45 for international students). *Expenses:* Tuition $0 for state residents; $6000 per year full-time, $95 per credit part-time for nonresidents. Fees $2676 per year full-time, $134 per credit part-time. *Financial aid:* Application deadline 2/15. • Dr. Gerald Tuchscherer, Director, Division of Adult, Counselor, and Technology Education, 208-885-6556.

The University of Memphis, College of Education, Department of Leadership, Memphis, TN 38152. Offerings include adult education (Ed D). Accredited by NCATE. Department faculty: 9 full-time (2 women), 23 part-time (9 women). *Degree requirements:* Dissertation, comprehensive exam required, foreign language not required. *Entrance requirements:* GRE General Test (minimum combined score of 850), GRE Subject Test, 3 years of teaching experience. Application deadline: 8/1 (12/1 for spring admission). Application fee: $25 ($50 for international students). *Tuition:* $2862 per year full-time, $166 per credit hour part-time for state residents; $6696 per year full-time, $379 per credit hour part-time for nonresidents. • Dr. John Petry, Interim Chair, 901-678-2368.

University of Michigan–Dearborn, School of Education, Program in Adult Instruction and Performance Technology, 4901 Evergreen Road, Dearborn, MI 48128-1491. Awards MA. Part-time programs available. Faculty: 2 full-time (1 woman). Students: 113 part-time (96 women); includes 25 minority (22 African Americans, 1 Asian American, 1 Hispanic, 1 Native American), 1 international. Average age 35. 36 applicants, 100% accepted. In 1997, 10 degrees awarded. *Average time to degree:* master's–2 years part-time. *Entrance requirements:* Minimum GPA of 3.0, writing sample. Application deadline: 8/30 (rolling processing). Application fee: $30. *Expenses:* Tuition $4536 per year full-time, $252 per credit hour part-time for state residents; $13,086 per year full-time, $727 per credit hour part-time for nonresidents. Fees $480 per year (minimum). *Financial aid:* Application deadline 3/15. *Faculty research:* Distance learning, organizational learning, trends in performance technology. Total annual research expenditures: $7600. • Dr. Joseph Lapides, Head, 313-593-5133. E-mail: jlapides@fob-f1.umd.umich.edu. Application contact: Rachel Chapman, Academic Services Secretary II, 313-593-5091. E-mail: rchapman@fob-f1.umd.umich.edu.

University of Minnesota, Twin Cities Campus, College of Education and Human Development, Department of Work, Community, and Family Education, Minneapolis, MN 55455-0213. Offerings include adult education (M Ed). • Jane Plihal, Chair, 612-624-3069.

University of Missouri–Columbia, College of Education, Department of Educational Leadership and Policy Analysis, Columbia, MO 65211. Offerings include higher and adult education (MA, M Ed, Ed D, PhD, Ed S). Terminal master's awarded for partial completion of doctoral program. Department faculty: 20 full-time (7 women). *Degree requirements:* For doctorate, variable foreign language requirement, dissertation. *Entrance requirements:* For master's, GRE General Test, minimum GPA of 3.0; for doctorate, GRE General Test, GRE Subject Test, minimum GPA of 3.5; for Ed S, GRE General Test, GRE Subject Test, minimum GPA of 3.25. Application deadline: 6/15 (priority date; rolling processing). Application fee: $25 ($50 for international students). *Expenses:* Tuition $3240 per year full-time, $180 per credit hour part-time for state residents; $9108 per year full-time, $506 per credit hour part-time for nonresidents. Fees $55 per year full-time. • Dr. Paula Short, Director of Graduate Studies, 573-882-8231.

University of Nebraska–Lincoln, Teachers College, Department of Vocational and Adult Education, Lincoln, NE 68588. Awards MA, M Ed. Accredited by NCATE. Faculty: 7 full-time (2 women). Students: 6 full-time (2 women), 25 part-time (21 women); includes 1 international. Average age 35. 7 applicants, 43% accepted. In 1997, 19 degrees awarded. *Degree requirements:* Thesis optional. *Entrance requirements:* TOEFL (minimum score 500). Application deadline: 3/1 (priority date; rolling processing). Application fee: $35. Electronic applications accepted. *Expenses:* Tuition $110 per credit hour for state residents; $270 per credit hour for nonresidents. Fees $480 per year full-time, $110 per semester part-time. *Financial aid:* In 1997–98, 5 research assistantships totaling $27,661, 3 teaching assistantships totaling $16,250 were awarded; fellowships, Federal Work-Study also available. Aid available to part-time students. Financial aid application deadline: 2/15. *Faculty research:* Leadership, technology, adult learning, curriculum and instruction, human resource development. • Dr. Steven Eggland, Graduate Committee Chair, 402-472-2552.

University of New Brunswick, Faculty of Education, Division of Vocational Education, Fredericton, NB E3B 5A3, Canada. Offerings include adult education (M Ed). *Entrance requirements:* TOEFL, TWE, minimum GPA of 3.0. Application deadline: 3/1 (priority date; rolling processing). Application fee: $25.

University of Oklahoma, College of Education, Department of Educational Leadership and Policy Studies, Program in Adult and Higher Education, Norman, OK 73019-0390. Awards M Ed, Ed D, PhD. Accredited by NCATE. Part-time and evening/weekend programs available. Students: 19 full-time (13 women), 66 part-time (38 women); includes 18 minority (9 African Americans, 9 Native Americans). Average age 41. 23 applicants, 83% accepted. In 1997, 53 master's, 8 doctorates awarded. Terminal master's awarded for partial completion of doctoral program. *Degree requirements:* For master's, comprehensive exam required, foreign language and thesis not required; for doctorate, variable foreign language requirement, dissertation, general exam. *Entrance requirements:* For master's, TOEFL (minimum score 550), 12 hours of course work in education; for doctorate, GRE General Test, TOEFL (minimum score 550), master's degree, minimum graduate GPA of 3.25. Application deadline: 6/1 (10/1 for spring admission). Application fee: $25. *Expenses:* Tuition $1920 per year full-time, $80 per credit hour part-time for state residents; $6108 per year full-time, $255 per credit hour part-time for nonresidents. Fees $468 per year full-time, $12 per semester (minimum) part-time. *Faculty research:* Higher education administration, training and development, distance education, evaluation, gerontology. Total annual research expenditures: $125,000. • Application contact: Edward Chance, Graduate Liaison, 405-325-4202.

Directories: Adult Education; Community College Education

University of Rhode Island, College of Human Science and Services, Department of Education, Program in Adult Education, Kingston, RI 02881. Awards MA. Accredited by NCATE. Evening/weekend programs available. *Entrance requirements:* MAT or GRE, TOEFL (minimum score 600). Application deadline: 4/15 (priority date; rolling processing; 11/15 for spring admission). Application fee: $35. *Expenses:* Tuition $3446 per year full-time, $191 per credit part-time for state residents; $9850 per year full-time, $547 per credit part-time for nonresidents. Fees $1276 per year full-time, $135 per semester (minimum) part-time.

University of Southern Maine, College of Education and Human Development, Program in Adult Education, Portland, ME 04104-9300. Awards MS, CAS. Accredited by NCATE. Part-time and evening/weekend programs available. Faculty: 3 full-time (1 woman). Students: 24 full-time (20 women), 47 part-time (38 women). 25 applicants, 92% accepted. In 1997, 17 master's awarded. *Degree requirements:* For master's, thesis or alternative, comprehensive exam, portfolio required, foreign language not required; for CAS, thesis or alternative required, foreign language not required. *Average time to degree:* master's–2 years full-time, 3 years part-time. *Entrance requirements:* For master's, GRE General Test (minimum combined score of 900), MAT (minimum score 40), TOEFL, interview. Application deadline: 2/1 (9/15 for spring admission). Application fee: $25. *Expenses:* Tuition $178 per credit hour for state residents; $267 per credit hour (minimum) for nonresidents. Fees $282 per year full-time, $83 per semester (minimum) part-time. *Financial aid:* Research assistantships, scholarships, Federal Work-Study, institutionally sponsored loans, and career-related internships or fieldwork available. Aid available to part-time students. Financial aid application deadline: 3/1; applicants required to submit FAFSA. • Dr. C. E. VanZandt, Chair, Human Resource Development Department, 207-780-5316. Application contact: Teresa Belsan, Admissions and Academic Counselor, 207-780-5306. Fax: 207-780-5315. E-mail: belsan@usm.maine.edu.

University of Southern Mississippi, College of Education and Psychology, Department of Educational Leadership and Research, Hattiesburg, MS 39406-5167. Offerings include adult education (M Ed, Ed D, PhD, Ed S). Department faculty: 14 full-time (3 women), 4 part-time (1 woman). *Degree requirements:* For doctorate, 2 foreign languages, dissertation. *Entrance requirements:* For master's, GRE General Test, minimum GPA of 2.75; for doctorate, GRE General Test, minimum GPA of 3.5; for Ed S, GRE General Test, minimum GPA of 3.25. Application deadline: 8/9 (priority date; rolling processing). Application fee: $0 ($25 for international students). *Tuition:* $2870 per year full-time, $137 per credit hour part-time for state residents; $5972 per year full-time, $172 per credit hour part-time for nonresidents. • Dr. Arthur Southerland, Chair, 601-266-4579.

University of South Florida, College of Education, Department of Adult and Vocational Education, Program in Adult Education, Tampa, FL 33620-9951. Awards MA, Ed D, PhD, Ed S. Accredited by NCATE. Part-time and evening/weekend programs available. Students: 24 full-time (16 women), 81 part-time (62 women); includes 19 minority (12 African Americans, 5 Hispanics, 2 Native Americans). Average age 41. 19 applicants, 74% accepted. In 1997, 15 master's, 13 doctorates, 1 Ed S awarded. *Degree requirements:* For doctorate, dissertation, 2 tools of research in foreign language, statistics, and/or computers. *Entrance requirements:* For master's, GRE General Test (minimum combined score of 1000), minimum GPA of 3.5 in last 60 hours; for doctorate, GRE General Test (minimum combined score of 1000), minimum GPA of 3.0 (undergraduate) or 3.5 (graduate); for Ed S, GRE General Test (minimum combined score of 1000). Application deadline: 6/1 (10/15 for spring admission). Application fee: $20. Electronic applications accepted. *Tuition:* $142 per credit hour for state residents; $486 per credit hour for nonresidents. *Financial aid:* Teaching assistantships, Federal Work-Study, institutionally sponsored loans, and career-related internships or fieldwork available. Aid available to part-time students. Financial aid applicants required to submit FAFSA. *Faculty research:* Learning styles, adult social roles, adult learning and development, staff development, human resource development. • Application contact: Dan Gardner, Coordinator, 813-974-3455. Fax: 813-974-5423. E-mail: gardner@tempest.coedu.usf.edu.

University of Tennessee, Knoxville, College of Education, Program in Educational Psychology, Knoxville, TN 37996. Offerings include adult education (MS). Accredited by NCATE. *Degree requirements:* Thesis optional, foreign language not required. *Entrance requirements:* TOEFL (minimum score 550), minimum GPA of 2.7. Application deadline: 2/1 (priority date; rolling processing). Application fee: $35. Electronic applications accepted. *Tuition:* $3354 per year full-time, $181 per semester hour part-time for state residents; $8410 per year full-time, $462 per semester hour part-time for nonresidents. • Dr. Tom George, Associate Dean, 423-974-0907. Fax: 423-974-8718. E-mail: tgeorge1@utk.edu.

University of Tennessee, Knoxville, College of Education, Program in Education I, Knoxville, TN 37996. Offerings include adult education (PhD). Accredited by NCATE. *Degree requirements:* 1 foreign language (computer language can substitute), dissertation. *Entrance requirements:* GRE General Test, TOEFL (minimum score 550), minimum GPA of 2.7. Application deadline: 2/1 (priority date; rolling processing). Application fee: $35. Electronic applications accepted. *Tuition:* $3354 per year full-time, $181 per semester hour part-time for state residents; $8410 per year full-time, $462 per semester hour part-time for nonresidents. • Dr. Tom George, Associate Dean, 423-974-0907. Fax: 423-974-8718. E-mail: tgeorge1@utk.edu.

University of Tennessee, Knoxville, College of Education, Program in Education II, Knoxville, TN 37996. Offerings include adult education (Ed D). Accredited by NCATE. *Degree requirements:* Dissertation required, foreign language not required. *Entrance requirements:* GRE General Test, TOEFL (minimum score 550), minimum GPA of 2.7. Application deadline: 2/1 (priority date; rolling processing). Application fee: $35. Electronic applications accepted. *Tuition:* $3354 per year full-time, $181 per semester hour part-time for state residents; $8410 per year full-time, $462 per semester hour part-time for nonresidents. • Dr. Tom George, Associate Dean, 423-974-0907. Fax: 423-974-8718. E-mail: tgeorge1@utk.edu.

University of the Incarnate Word, School of Graduate Studies, College of Professional Studies, Program in Adult Education, San Antonio, TX 78209-6397. Awards MA, M Ed. Evening/weekend programs available. Faculty: 7 full-time (4 women), 4 part-time (3 women). *Entrance requirements:* GRE, MAT, TOEFL (minimum score 550). Application deadline: 8/15 (priority date; rolling processing; 12/31 for spring admission). Application fee: $20. *Expenses:* Tuition $350 per semester hour. Fees $180 per year full-time, $111 per semester (minimum) part-time. • Victor Prosper, Coordinator, 210-829-3185. Fax: 210-829-3169. Application contact: Brian F. Dalton, Dean of Enrollment Services, 210-829-6005. Fax: 210-829-3921. E-mail: briand@the-college.iwctx.edu.

The University of West Alabama, College of Education, Department of Foundations, Program in Continuing Education, Livingston, AL 35470. Awards MSCE. Accredited by NCATE. Part-time programs available. *Degree requirements:* Comprehensive exam required, foreign language and thesis not required. *Entrance requirements:* GRE General Test, MAT, minimum GPA of 2.75. Application deadline: 9/10 (priority date; rolling processing; 3/24 for spring admission). Application fee: $15. *Tuition:* $70 per quarter hour.

The University of West Alabama, College of Education, Department of Instructional Support, Program in Guidance and Counseling, Livingston, AL 35470. Offerings include continuing education (MSCE). Accredited by NCATE. *Average time to degree:* master's–1 year full-time, 2 years part-time. *Application deadline:* 9/10 (priority date; rolling processing; 3/21 for spring admission). *Application fee:* $15. *Tuition:* $70 per quarter hour.

University of Wisconsin–Madison, Schools of Education and Human Ecology and College of Agricultural and Life Sciences, Department of Continuing and Vocational Education, Madison, WI 53706-1380. Awards MS, PhD. *Degree requirements:* For doctorate, dissertation. *Application fee:* $38. *Tuition:* $4928 per year full-time, $926 per semester (minimum) part-time for state residents; $15,190 per year full-time, $2849 per semester (minimum) part-time for nonresidents.

University of Wisconsin–Platteville, College of Liberal Arts and Education, School of Education, Platteville, WI 53818-3099. Offerings include adult education (MSE). Accredited by NCATE. School faculty: 8 part-time (3 women). *Degree requirements:* Thesis or alternative, comprehensive exam required, foreign language not required. *Entrance requirements:* TOEFL (minimum score 500). Application deadline: 7/1 (priority date; rolling processing; 11/1 for spring admission). Application fee: $45. • Dr. Sally Standiford, Director, 608-342-1131. Fax: 608-342-1133. E-mail: standiford@uwplatt.edu.

University of Wyoming, College of Education, Division of Lifelong Learning and Instruction, Laramie, WY 82071. Awards MA, MS, Ed D, PhD, Ed S. Accredited by NCATE. Faculty: 20 (8 women). Students: 28 full-time (15 women), 138 part-time (83 women); includes 10 minority (5 African Americans, 1 Asian American, 4 Hispanics), 2 international. 133 applicants, 48% accepted. In 1997, 23 master's, 3 doctorates awarded. *Degree requirements:* For doctorate, dissertation. *Entrance requirements:* GRE General Test, minimum GPA of 3.0. Application deadline: 6/1 (priority date; rolling processing). Application fee: $40. *Expenses:* Tuition $2430 per year full-time, $135 per credit hour part-time for state residents; $7518 per year full-time, $418 per credit hour part-time for nonresidents. Fees $386 per year full-time, $9.25 per credit hour part-time. *Financial aid:* Application deadline 3/1. • Dr. Patricia McClurg, Chair, 307-766-6353. Fax: 307-766-6668. E-mail: patmc@uwyo.edu.

Valdosta State University, College of Education, Department of Business and Vocational Education, Valdosta, GA 31698. Offerings include adult and vocational education (Ed D). Accredited by NCATE. Department faculty: 9 full-time (2 women). *Entrance requirements:* GRE General Test (minimum combined score of 1000). Application deadline: 8/1 (rolling processing; 11/15 for spring admission). Application fee: $10. *Expenses:* Tuition $2472 per year full-time, $83 per semester hour part-time for state residents; $8472 per year full-time, $333 per semester hour part-time for nonresidents. Fees $236 per year full-time. • Donnie McGahee, Head, 912-333-5928.

Virginia Commonwealth University, School of Education, Program in Adult Education and Human Resource Development, Richmond, VA 23284-9005. Awards M Ed. Accredited by NCATE. Part-time programs available. Faculty: 3 full-time (1 woman). Students: 12 full-time (10 women), 41 part-time (34 women); includes 13 minority (11 African Americans, 2 Native Americans). Average age 37. 24 applicants, 83% accepted. In 1997, 13 degrees awarded. *Degree requirements:* Thesis optional, foreign language not required. *Entrance requirements:* GRE General Test or MAT. Application deadline: 7/1 (rolling processing; 11/1 for spring admission). Application fee: $30 ($0 for international students). *Tuition:* $4960 per year full-time, $257 per credit part-time for state residents; $12,652 per year full-time, $684 per credit part-time for nonresidents. *Financial aid:* Federal Work-Study and career-related internships or fieldwork available. Financial aid application deadline: 3/1. *Faculty research:* Adult development and learning, program planning and evaluation. • Dr. John Seyfarth, Division Head, 804-828-1332. Application contact: Dr. Michael D. Davis, Interim Director, Graduate Studies, 804-828-6530. Fax: 804-828-1323. E-mail: mddavis@vcu.edu.

Virginia Polytechnic Institute and State University, College of Human Resources and Education, Department of Educational Leadership and Policy Studies, Program in Adult and Continuing Education, Blacksburg, VA 24061. Awards MA Ed, MS Ed, Ed D, PhD, CAGS. One or more programs accredited by NCATE. *Degree requirements:* For doctorate, dissertation required, foreign language not required. *Entrance requirements:* TOEFL. Application deadline: 12/1 (priority date; rolling processing). Application fee: $25. *Tuition:* $4927 per year full-time, $792 per semester (minimum) part-time for state residents; $7537 per year full-time, $1227 per semester (minimum) part-time for nonresidents. *Financial aid:* Application deadline 4/1. • Dr. David Alexander, Head, Department of Educational Leadership and Policy Studies, 540-231-5642.

Virginia Polytechnic Institute and State University, College of Human Resources and Education, Department of Family and Child Development, Program in Adult Learning and Human Resource Development, Blacksburg, VA 24061. Awards MS, PhD. Accredited by NCATE. Offered jointly with Northern Virginia campus. *Degree requirements:* Thesis/dissertation required, foreign language not required. *Entrance requirements:* For master's, GRE General Test (minimum combined score of 900), TOEFL (minimum score 600), minimum GPA of 3.0; for doctorate, GRE General Test (minimum combined score of 900), TOEFL (minimum score 600), minimum GPA of 3.5. Application deadline: 12/1 (priority date; rolling processing). Application fee: $25. *Tuition:* $4927 per year full-time, $792 per semester (minimum) part-time for state residents; $7537 per year full-time, $1227 per semester (minimum) part-time for nonresidents. *Financial aid:* Application deadline 4/1. • Dr. Michael Sporakowski, Head, Department of Family and Child Development, 540-231-4794. E-mail: fed@vt.edu.

Western Washington University, Woodring College of Education, Program in Adult Education Administration, Bellingham, WA 98225-5996. Awards M Ed. Accredited by NCATE. Part-time programs available. Students: 27 full-time (20 women), 63 part-time (48 women). 25 applicants, 84% accepted. In 1997, 52 degrees awarded. *Degree requirements:* Thesis optional, foreign language not required. *Entrance requirements:* GRE General Test, TOEFL, minimum GPA of 3.0 in last 60 semester hours or last 90 quarter hours. Application deadline: 6/1 (rolling processing; 2/1 for spring admission). Application fee: $35. *Expenses:* Tuition $4200 per year full-time, $140 per credit part-time for state residents; $12,780 per year full-time, $426 per credit part-time for nonresidents. Fees $249 per year full-time, $83 per quarter part-time. *Financial aid:* Teaching assistantships, partial tuition waivers, Federal Work-Study, institutionally sponsored loans, and career-related internships or fieldwork available. Aid available to part-time students. Financial aid application deadline: 3/31. • Dr. Violet Malone, Adviser, 360-650-7318.

Community College Education

Eastern Washington University, College of Education and Human Development, Department of Education, Program in College Instruction, Cheney, WA 99004-2431. Awards MA, MS. Accredited by NCATE. Faculty: 3 full-time. *Degree requirements:* Comprehensive exam, internship required, thesis not required. *Entrance requirements:* Minimum GPA of 3.0. Application deadline: 4/1 (priority date; rolling processing; 1/15 for spring admission). Application fee: $35. *Tuition:* $4200 per year full-time, $140 per credit part-time for state residents; $12,780 per year full-time, $415 per credit part-time for nonresidents. *Financial aid:* Federal Work-Study, institutionally sponsored loans, and career-related internships or fieldwork available. Financial aid application deadline: 2/1. • Dr. Russell Hubbard, Adviser, 509-359-7021.

Florida International University, College of Education, Department of Educational Leadership and Policy Studies, Program in Community College Teaching, Miami, FL 33199. Awards

Ed D. Accredited by NCATE. Part-time and evening/weekend programs available. Students: 7 full-time (4 women), 38 part-time (23 women); includes 10 minority (2 African Americans, 2 Asian Americans, 6 Hispanics). Average age 44. 27 applicants, 30% accepted. In 1997, 4 degrees awarded. *Degree requirements:* Dissertation required, foreign language not required. *Entrance requirements:* GRE General Test (minimum combined score of 1000). Application deadline: 4/1 (priority date; rolling processing; 10/1 for spring admission). Application fee: $20. *Expenses:* Tuition $138 per credit hour for state residents; $482 per credit hour for nonresidents. Fees $46 per semester. *Financial aid:* In 1997–98, 3 teaching assistantships were awarded; research assistantships also available. • Dr. Kingsley Banya, Chairperson, Department of Educational Leadership and Policy Studies, 305-348-2724. Fax: 305-348-2081. E-mail: banyak@fiu.edu.

George Mason University, Graduate School of Education, The National Center for Community College Education, Fairfax, VA 22030-4444. Awards DA Ed. Faculty: 4 part-time (2 women), 1.25 FTE. Students: 12 full-time (4 women), 118 part-time (48 women); includes 37 minority (25 African Americans, 4 Asian Americans, 7 Hispanics, 1 Native American), 2 international. Average age 48. 60 applicants, 77% accepted. In 1997, 13 degrees awarded. *Degree requirements:* Computer language, dissertation, comprehensive exam, final project, internship required, foreign language not required. *Entrance requirements:* GRE or MAT, appropriate master's degree, interview. Application deadline: 5/1 (11/1 for spring admission). Application fee: $30. Electronic applications accepted. *Tuition:* $4344 per year full-time, $181 per credit hour part-time for state residents; $12,504 per year full-time, $521 per credit hour part-time for nonresidents. *Financial aid:* Fellowships available. Aid available to part-time students. Financial aid application deadline: 3/1; applicants required to submit FAFSA. • Dr. Gustavo A. Mellander, Director, 703-993-2004. Fax: 703-993-2307.

Michigan State University, College of Arts and Letters, Department of English, East Lansing, MI 48824-1020. Offerings include secondary school/community college teaching (MA). Department faculty: 51 (17 women). *Degree requirements:* Thesis (for some programs). *Entrance requirements:* GRE General Test, GRE Subject Test. Application deadline: 1/10 (priority date; rolling processing). Application fee: $30 ($40 for international students). *Expenses:* Tuition $4609 per year full-time, $223 per credit hour (minimum) part-time for state residents; $8704 per year full-time, $450 per credit hour (minimum) part-time for nonresidents. Fees $576 per year full-time, $476 per year part-time. • Dr. Patrick O'Donnell, Interim Chairperson, 517-355-7570. Application contact: Dr. Robert Uphaus, Associate Chairperson, Graduate Studies, 517-355-7570. Fax: 517-353-3755. E-mail: uphaus@pilot.msu.edu.

North Carolina State University, Colleges of Education and Psychology and Agriculture and Life Sciences, Department of Adult and Community College Education, Raleigh, NC 27695. Awards M Ed, MS, Ed D. Accredited by NCATE. Faculty: 31 full-time (10 women), 38 part-time (15 women). Students: 55 full-time (38 women), 310 part-time (187 women); includes 92 minority (82 African Americans, 6 Asian Americans, 1 Hispanic, 3 Native Americans), 4 international. Average age 42. 107 applicants, 61% accepted. In 1997, 29 master's, 60 doctorates awarded. *Degree requirements:* Thesis/dissertation, comprehensive exam required, foreign language not required. *Entrance requirements:* GRE General Test or MAT, minimum GPA of 3.0 in major. Application deadline: 6/1 (priority date; rolling processing; 11/1 for spring admission). Application fee: $45. *Tuition:* $2370 per year full-time, $517 per semester (minimum) part-time for state residents; $11,536 per year full-time, $2809 per semester (minimum) part-time for nonresidents. *Financial aid:* In 1997–98, 32 research assistantships (8 to first-year students) averaging $969 per month and totaling $139,536 were awarded; fellowships, teaching assistantships also available. *Faculty research:* Techniques in education, organization/development in higher education, historical and philosophical foundations of adult education, adult learning and development, educational gerontology. Total annual research expenditures: $495,653. • Dr. William L. Deegan, Head, 919-515-6240. E-mail: deegan@poe.coe.ncsu.edu. Application contact: Dr. J. Conrad Glass, Director of Graduate Programs, 919-515-6241. Fax: 919-515-4039. E-mail: glass@poe.coe.ncsu.edu.

Pittsburg State University, School of Education, Department of Special Services and Leadership Studies, Program in Community College Teaching, Pittsburg, KS 66762-5880. Awards Ed S. Accredited by NCATE. Students: 8 full-time (5 women), 22 part-time (17 women). *Application fee:* $40. *Tuition:* $2418 per year full-time, $103 per credit hour part-time for state residents; $6130 per year full-time, $258 per credit hour part-time for nonresidents. *Financial aid:* Teaching assistantships, Federal Work-Study, and career-related internships or fieldwork available. • Dr. Steve Scott, Chairman, Department of Special Services and Leadership Studies, 316-235-4487.

Princeton University, Department of History, Princeton, NJ 08544-1019. Offerings include community college history teaching (PhD). Department faculty: 44 full-time (16 women). *Degree requirements:* Variable foreign language requirement, dissertation. *Average time to degree:* doctorate–6.2 years full-time. *Entrance requirements:* GRE General Test, sample of written work. Application deadline: 1/4. Application fee: $55 ($60 for international students). *Tuition:* $24,330 per year. • Director of Graduate Studies, 609-258-5529. Application contact: Director of Graduate Admissions, 609-258-3034.

University of South Florida, College of Education, Department of Educational Leadership, Program in Junior College Teaching, Tampa, FL 33620-9951. Awards MA. Accredited by NCATE. Part-time and evening/weekend programs available. Students: 2 full-time (1 woman), 10 part-time (6 women); includes 1 minority (Hispanic), 1 international. Average age 40. 8 applicants, 38% accepted. In 1997, 2 degrees awarded. *Entrance requirements:* GRE General Test (minimum combined score of 1000), minimum GPA of 3.5 in last 60 hours. Application deadline: 6/1 (10/15 for spring admission). Application fee: $20. *Tuition:* $142 per credit hour for state residents; $486 per credit hour for nonresidents. *Financial aid:* Federal Work-Study, institutionally sponsored loans available. Aid available to part-time students. Financial aid applicants required to submit FAFSA. • Application contact: Mel Villeme, Coordinator, 813-974-3420. Fax: 813-974-3366. E-mail: villeme@tempest.coedu.usf.edu.

Western Carolina University, College of Education and Allied Professions, Department of Administration, Curriculum and Instruction, Program in Community College Education, Cullowhee, NC 28723. Awards MA Ed. Accredited by NCATE. Part-time and evening/weekend programs available. Students: 6 full-time (3 women), 13 part-time (9 women); includes 1 minority (African American), 1 international. 10 applicants, 50% accepted. In 1997, 3 degrees awarded. *Degree requirements:* Comprehensive exam required, foreign language and thesis not required. *Entrance requirements:* GRE General Test. Application deadline: rolling. Application fee: $35. *Tuition:* $1799 per year full-time, $144 per credit hour (minimum) part-time for state residents; $9069 per year full-time, $1053 per credit hour (minimum) part-time for nonresidents. *Financial aid:* In 1997–98, 3 students received aid, including 3 research assistantships (2 to first-year students) totaling $11,889; fellowships, teaching assistantships, Federal Work-Study, institutionally sponsored loans also available. Financial aid application deadline: 3/15. • Application contact: Kathleen Owen, Assistant to the Dean, 828-227-7398. Fax: 828-227-7480.

Early Childhood Education

Adelphi University, School of Education, Program in Early Childhood/Elementary Education, Garden City, NY 11530. Awards MA. Part-time and evening/weekend programs available. Students: 76 full-time (65 women), 255 part-time (225 women); includes 73 minority (41 African Americans, 3 Asian Americans, 28 Hispanics, 1 Native American), 4 international. Average age 35. In 1997, 171 degrees awarded. *Application deadline:* rolling. *Application fee:* $50. *Expenses:* Tuition $16,000 per year full-time, $485 per credit part-time. Fees $500 per year full-time, $150 per semester part-time. *Financial aid:* Research assistantships available. Financial aid application deadline: 3/1. *Faculty research:* Critical thinking, cognition, teacher as researcher, methods of mathematics in elementary education, mentor-intern programs. • Director, 516-877-4080. Application contact: Marilyn Nissensohn, Director of Graduate Admissions, 516-663-3020.

Alabama Agricultural and Mechanical University, School of Education, Department of Curriculum and Instruction, Area in Elementary and Early Childhood Education, PO Box 1357, Normal, AL 35762-1357. Offers programs in early childhood education (M Ed, MS, Ed S), elementary education (M Ed, MS, Ed S). Accredited by NCATE. Evening/weekend programs available. Faculty: 8 full-time (all women), 1 (woman) part-time. *Degree requirements:* For master's, comprehensive exam required, foreign language not required; for Ed S, thesis. *Entrance requirements:* For master's, GRE General Test. Application deadline: 5/1. Application fee: $15 ($20 for international students). *Expenses:* Tuition $2782 per year full-time, $565 per semester (minimum) part-time for state residents; $5164 per year full-time, $1015 per semester (minimum) part-time for nonresidents. Fees $560 per year full-time, $390 per year part-time. *Financial aid:* Fellowships and career-related internships or fieldwork available. Financial aid application deadline: 4/1. *Faculty research:* Multicultural education, learning styles, diagnostic-prescriptive instruction. • Dr. Earnest Dees, Chair, Department of Curriculum and Instruction, 205-851-5520. Fax: 205-851-5526.

Alabama State University, School of Graduate Studies, College of Education, Department of Curriculum and Instruction, Program in Early Childhood Education, Montgomery, AL 36101-0271. Awards M Ed, Ed S. Faculty: 2 full-time (both women). Students: 9 full-time (8 women), 22 part-time (all women); includes 24 minority (23 African Americans, 1 Asian American). In 1997, 22 master's awarded. *Degree requirements:* For master's, comprehensive exam required, thesis optional; for Ed S, thesis. *Entrance requirements:* For master's, GRE General Test, MAT or NTE. Application deadline: 7/15 (rolling processing; 12/15 for spring admission). Application fee: $10. *Expenses:* Tuition $85 per credit hour for state residents; $170 per credit hour for nonresidents. Fees $486 per year. • Dr. Jeanne Blevins, Coordinator, 334-229-4896. Fax: 334-229-4904. Application contact: Dr. Fred Dauser, Dean of Graduate Studies, 334-229-4276. Fax: 334-229-4928.

Albany State University, School of Education, Program in Early Childhood Education, Albany, GA 31705-2717. Awards M Ed. Accredited by NCATE. Part-time programs available. Faculty: 1 (woman) part-time. Students: 21 part-time (all women); includes 1 international. 11 applicants, 45% accepted. In 1997, 10 degrees awarded (100% found work related to degree). *Degree requirements:* Comprehensive exam. *Entrance requirements:* GRE General Test (minimum combined score of 800), MAT (minimum score 44) or NTE (minimum score 550 required. Application deadline: 9/1. Application fee: $10. *Financial aid:* Federal Work-Study and career-related internships or fieldwork available. Aid available to part-time students. Financial aid application deadline: 4/1. • Dr. Claude Perkins, Dean, School of Education, 912-430-4715. Fax: 912-430-4993. E-mail: cperkins@fld94.alsnet.peachnet.edu.

Antioch New England Graduate School, Graduate School, Department of Education, Program in Elementary Education/Early Childhood Education, 40 Avon Street, Keene, NH 03431-3516. Offers integrated day education (M Ed), science and environmental education (M Ed). Faculty: 7 full-time (2 women), 12 part-time (11 women). Students: 41 full-time (31 women), 4 part-time (all women); includes 1 minority (Native American). Average age 32. 32 applicants, 97% accepted. In 1997, 29 degrees awarded. *Degree requirements:* Internship required, foreign language and thesis not required. *Application fee:* $40. *Expenses:* Tuition $12,700 per year full-time, $330 per credit part-time. Fees $165 per year. *Financial aid:* Federal Work-Study and career-related internships or fieldwork available. Financial aid applicants required to submit FAFSA. *Faculty research:* Mathematics education, ecological literacy, democratic classrooms, arts education. • David Sobel, Director, 603-357-3122 Ex. 358. E-mail: dsobel@antiochne.edu. Application contact: Diane K. Hewitt, Co-Director of Admissions, 603-357-6265 Ext. 286. Fax: 603-357-0718. E-mail: dhewitt@antiochne.edu.

Appalachian State University, College of Education, Department of Curriculum and Instruction, Boone, NC 28608. Offerings include early childhood education (MA). Accredited by NCATE. Postbaccalaureate distance learning degree programs offered (minimal on-campus study). Department faculty: 19 full-time (9 women), 2 part-time (1 woman). *Degree requirements:* Thesis or alternative, comprehensive exams required, foreign language not required. *Average time to degree:* master's–2 years full-time, 4 years part-time. *Entrance requirements:* GRE General Test or MAT. Application deadline: 7/31 (priority date). Application fee: $35. *Tuition:* $1811 per year full-time, $354 per semester (minimum) part-time for state residents; $9081 per year full-time, $2171 per semester (minimum) part-time for nonresidents. • Dr. Michael Jacobson, Chairperson, 704-262-2224.

Arkansas State University, College of Education, Department of Elementary Education, State University, AR 72467. Offerings include early childhood education (MSE), early childhood services (MS). One or more programs accredited by NCATE. Department faculty: 10 full-time (8 women). *Application deadline:* 7/1 (priority date; rolling processing; 11/15 for spring admission). *Application fee:* $15 ($25 for international students). *Expenses:* Tuition $2760 per year full-time, $115 per credit hour part-time for state residents; $6936 per year full-time, $289 per credit hour part-time for nonresidents. Fees $506 per year full-time, $44 per semester (minimum) part-time. • Dr. Roberta Daniels, Interim Chair, 870-972-3059. Fax: 870-972-3828. E-mail: rdaniels@kiowa.astate.edu.

Ashland University, College of Education, Graduate Studies in Teacher Education, Program in Curriculum and Instruction, Ashland, OH 44805-3702. Offerings include early childhood education (M Ed). Accredited by NCATE. Program faculty: 8 full-time (4 women), 24 part-time (9 women). *Degree requirements:* Practicum or thesis. *Entrance requirements:* GRE General Test or MAT, teaching certificate. Application deadline: rolling. Application fee: $15. *Tuition:* $275 per credit hour. • Carl Walley, Program Team Leader, 419-289-5355. E-mail: cwalley@ashland.edu. Application contact: Dr. Joe Bailey, Director, 419-289-5377. Fax: 419-289-5097. E-mail: jbailey@ashland.edu.

Auburn University, College of Education, Department of Curriculum and Teaching, Auburn University, AL 36849-0001. Offerings include early childhood education (M Ed, MS, PhD, Ed S). Accredited by NCATE. Department faculty: 20 full-time (11 women). *Degree requirements:* For master's, thesis (MS) required, foreign language not required; for doctorate, dissertation required, foreign language not required; for Ed S, field project required, foreign language and thesis not required. *Entrance requirements:* For master's and Ed S, GRE General Test; for doctorate, GRE General Test (minimum score 450 on each section, 1000 combined). Application deadline: 9/1 (rolling processing; 3/1 for spring admission). Application fee: $25 ($50 for international students). *Expenses:* Tuition $2760 per year full-time, $76 per credit hour part-time for state residents; $8280 per year full-time, $228 per credit hour part-time for nonresidents.

Directory: Early Childhood Education

Auburn University (continued)

Fees $30 per year full-time, $160 per quarter part-time for state residents; $30 per year full-time, $480 per quarter part-time for nonresidents. • Dr. Andrew M. Weaver, Head, 334-844-4434. E-mail: weavearn@mail.auburn.edu. Application contact: Dr. John F. Pritchett, Dean of the Graduate School, 334-844-4700.

Auburn University Montgomery, School of Education, Department of Early Childhood, Elementary, and Reading Education, Montgomery, AL 36124-4023. Offers programs in early childhood education (M Ed, Ed S), elementary education (M Ed, Ed S), reading education (M Ed, Ed S). Accredited by NCATE. Part-time and evening/weekend programs available. Students: 71 full-time (65 women), 58 part-time (49 women); includes 46 minority (45 African Americans, 1 Hispanic), 1 international. Average age 32. In 1997, 77 master's, 3 Ed Ss awarded. *Degree requirements:* Comprehensive exam required, foreign language and thesis not required. *Entrance requirements:* For master's, GRE General Test or MAT, certification, BS in teaching; for Ed S, GRE General Test or MAT, certification. Application deadline: 9/1 (priority date; rolling processing; 3/28 for spring admission). Application fee: $25. Electronic applications accepted. *Tuition:* $2664 per year full-time, $85 per quarter hour part-time for state residents; $7080 per year full-time, $255 per quarter hour part-time for nonresidents. *Financial aid:* In 1997–98, 3 teaching assistantships were awarded; career-related internships or fieldwork also available. • Dr. Janet Warren, Head, 334-244-3422.

Augusta State University, College of Education, Program in Early Childhood Education, Augusta, GA 30904-2200. Awards M Ed, Ed S. Accredited by NCATE. Part-time and evening/weekend programs available. Faculty: 8 full-time (3 women). Students: 12 full-time (all women), 26 part-time (all women); includes 3 minority (all African Americans). Average age 35. 10 applicants, 100% accepted. In 1997, 13 master's, 1 Ed S awarded. *Degree requirements:* Thesis, comprehensive exam. *Entrance requirements:* GRE, MAT. Application deadline: 7/26 (priority date; rolling processing). Application fee: $10. *Tuition:* $2260 per year full-time, $83 per credit hour part-time for state residents; $8260 per year full-time, $333 per credit hour part-time for nonresidents. *Financial aid:* Graduate assistantships, Federal Work-Study, institutionally sponsored loans, and career-related internships or fieldwork available. Aid available to part-time students. Financial aid application deadline: 4/15; applicants required to submit FAFSA. *Faculty research:* Whole language, computers in teaching. • Dr. Mary Gendernalik Cooper, Chair, 706-737-1496. E-mail: mcooper@aug.edu. Application contact: Elfredia Phillips, Degree Program Assistant, 706-737-1496. Fax: 706-667-4706. E-mail: ephillips@aug.edu.

Ball State University, Teachers College, Department of Elementary Education, Program in Early Childhood Education, 2000 University Avenue, Muncie, IN 47306-1099. Awards MAE, Ed D. Accredited by NCATE. Students: 1 (woman) full-time, 9 part-time (all women); includes 1 international. Average age 27. 7 applicants, 71% accepted. In 1997, 2 master's, 2 doctorates awarded. *Degree requirements:* For doctorate, dissertation required, foreign language not required. *Entrance requirements:* For doctorate, GRE General Test (minimum combined score of 1000), minimum graduate GPA of 3.2. Application fee: $15 ($25 for international students). *Expenses:* Tuition $3454 per year full-time, $518 per semester (minimum) part-time for state residents; $9316 per year full-time, $1221 per semester (minimum) part-time for nonresidents. Fees $242 per year full-time, $18 per semester (minimum) part-time. • James Stroud, Head, 785-286-8560.

Bank Street College of Education, Program in Early Childhood and Elementary Teacher Education, 610 West 112th Street, New York, NY 10025-1120. Awards MS Ed, MSW/MS Ed. Offerings include early adolescence education (MS Ed), early childhood and elementary teacher education (MS Ed), infant and parent development (MS Ed), museum education (MS Ed), museum special education (MS Ed), reading/literacy (MS Ed). MSW/MS Ed (infant and parent development) offered jointly with Hunter College of the City University of New York. *Degree requirements:* 1 foreign language, thesis. *Entrance requirements:* TOEFL (minimum score 550). Application deadline: 3/1 (priority date; rolling processing; 11/1 for spring admission). Application fee: $50. *Tuition:* $560 per credit. *Financial aid:* Career-related internships or fieldwork available. Financial aid application deadline: 3/1. • Linda Levine, Chairperson, 212-875-4480. Application contact: Ann Morgan, Director of Admissions, 212-875-4404. Fax: 212-875-4678. E-mail: amorgan@bnkst.edu.

Bank Street College of Education, Program in Educational Leadership, 610 West 112th Street, New York, NY 10025-1120. Offerings include early child leadership (MS Ed). MS Ed (supervision and administration in the visual arts) offered jointly with Parsons School of Design, New School of Social Research. *Application deadline:* 3/1 (priority date; rolling processing; 11/1 for spring admission). *Application fee:* $50. *Tuition:* $560 per credit. • Dr. Frank Pignatelli, Chairperson, 212-875-4710. Application contact: Ann Morgan, Director of Admissions, 212-875-4404. Fax: 212-875-4678. E-mail: amorgan@bnkst.edu.

Barry University, School of Education, Program in Pre-Kindergarten and Primary Education, Miami Shores, FL 33161-6695. Awards MS. Part-time and evening/weekend programs available. Students: 20 full-time (19 women), 7 part-time (all women); includes 15 minority (5 African Americans, 10 Hispanics). In 1997, 18 degrees awarded. *Degree requirements:* Practicum, written comprehensive exam required, foreign language and thesis not required. *Entrance requirements:* GRE General Test or MAT, minimum GPA of 3.0. Application deadline: 5/1 (priority date; rolling processing). Application fee: $30. Electronic applications accepted. *Tuition:* $450 per credit (minimum). *Financial aid:* Career-related internships or fieldwork available. Aid available to part-time students. Financial aid application deadline: 5/1. • Dr. Deanna Radeloff, Coordinator, 305-899-3700. Fax: 305-899-3630. E-mail: radeloff@aquinas.barry.edu. Application contact: Angela Scott, Enrollment Services, Assistant Dean, 305-899-3112. Fax: 305-899-3149. E-mail: ascott@jeanne.barry.edu.

Baruch College of the City University of New York, Department of Education, 17 Lexington Avenue, New York, NY 10010-5585. Offerings include early childhood education (MS Ed). Program being phased out; applicants no longer accepted. Department faculty: 5 full-time (2 women), 4 part-time (2 women), 6.25 FTE. *Expenses:* Tuition $4350 per year full-time, $185 per credit part-time for state residents; $7600 per year full-time, $320 per credit part-time for nonresidents. Fees $53 per year. • Dr. Jeffrey H. Golland, Chairperson, 212-389-1731. Fax: 212-387-1748. E-mail: jegbb@cunyvm.cuny.edu.

Beaver College, Department of Education, Glenside, PA 19038-3295. Offerings include early childhood education (M Ed, CAS), with options in individualized (M Ed), master teacher (M Ed), research in child development (M Ed). *Application fee:* $35. *Expenses:* Tuition $6570 per year full-time, $365 per credit part-time. Fees $35 per year.

Bellarmine College, College of Arts and Sciences, Graduate Programs in Education, Louisville, KY 40205-0671. Offerings include early elementary education (MA, MAT). Accredited by NCATE. Faculty: 2 full-time (both women). *Application deadline:* 8/1 (priority date; rolling processing; 12/15 for spring admission). *Application fee:* $25. Electronic applications accepted. *Tuition:* $360 per credit hour. • Dr. Doris Tegart, Director, 502-452-8191.

Berry College, Graduate Programs in Education, Program in Early Childhood Education, Mount Berry, GA 30149-0159. Awards M Ed. Accredited by NCATE. Part-time programs available. Faculty: 6 part-time (2 women), 1 FTE. Students: 5 full-time (all women), 40 part-time (39 women). Average age 31. 25 applicants, 84% accepted. In 1997, 39 degrees awarded (100% found work related to degree). *Degree requirements:* Oral exams required, thesis optional, foreign language not required. *Average time to degree:* master's–2 years full-time, 3 years part-time. *Entrance requirements:* GRE General Test, MAT, or NTE, minimum GPA of 2.5. Application deadline: 7/29 (rolling processing; 12/16 for spring admission). Application fee: $25 ($30 for international students). *Tuition:* $146 per semester hour. *Financial aid:* Assistantships available. Aid available to part-time students. Financial aid application deadline: 4/1; applicants required to submit FAFSA. • Application contact: George Gaddie, Dean of Admissions, 706-236-2215. Fax: 706-290-2178.

Bloomsburg University of Pennsylvania, School of Graduate Studies, College of Professional Studies, School of Education, Department of Curriculum and Foundations, Program in Early Childhood Education, Bloomsburg, PA 17815-1905. Awards MS. Accredited by NCATE. Faculty: 6 full-time (4 women). Students: 6 full-time (5 women), 10 part-time (all women); includes 3 minority (2 African Americans, 1 Asian American). Average age 32. 4 applicants, 100% accepted. In 1997, 7 degrees awarded. *Degree requirements:* Thesis optional, foreign language not required. *Entrance requirements:* MAT, minimum QPA of 2.5. Application deadline: rolling. Application fee: $25. *Expenses:* Tuition $3468 per year full-time, $193 per credit part-time for state residents; $6236 per year full-time, $346 per credit part-time for nonresidents. Fees $748 per year full-time, $166 per semester (minimum) part-time. *Faculty research:* Child development, children's literature, theory, administration. • Dr. John Hranitz, Chair, Department of Curriculum and Foundations, 717-389-4025. Fax: 717-389-3894. E-mail: hral@bf486.bloomu.edu.

Boise State University, College of Education, Programs in Teacher Education, Program in Early Childhood Education, Boise, ID 83725-0399. Awards MA. Accredited by NCATE. Part-time programs available. Faculty: 2 full-time (both women), 4 part-time (all women). Students: 3 full-time (all women), 42 part-time (41 women); includes 1 minority (Asian American), 1 international. Average age 38. 8 applicants, 100% accepted. In 1997, 8 degrees awarded. *Degree requirements:* Thesis optional. *Application deadline:* 7/26 (priority date; rolling processing; 11/29 for spring admission). *Application fee:* $20 ($30 for international students). Electronic applications accepted. *Tuition:* $3020 per year full-time, $135 per credit part-time for state residents; $8900 per year full-time, $135 per credit part-time for nonresidents. *Financial aid:* Graduate assistantships, Federal Work-Study, institutionally sponsored loans, and career-related internships or fieldwork available. Aid available to part-time students. Financial aid application deadline: 3/1. • Dr. Roger Stewart, Coordinator, Programs in Teacher Education, 208-385-1731. Fax: 208-385-4365.

Boston College, Graduate School of Education, Department of Counseling Psychology, Developmental and Educational Psychology, Program in Early Childhood/Specialist Option, Chestnut Hill, MA 02167-9991. Awards MA. Accredited by NCATE. Students: 2 full-time (both women), 1 (woman) part-time; includes 1 minority (Asian American). 3 applicants, 100% accepted. In 1997, 3 degrees awarded. *Degree requirements:* Comprehensive exam required, thesis not required. *Entrance requirements:* GRE General Test. Application deadline: 3/15 (11/15 for spring admission). Application fee: $40. *Expenses:* Tuition $626 per semester hour. Fees $80 per year (minimum) full-time, $30 per semester part-time. • Application contact: Arline Riordan, Graduate Admissions Director, 617-552-4214. Fax: 617-552-0812. E-mail: riordana@bc.edu.

Boston College, Graduate School of Education, Department of Teacher Education/Special Education and Curriculum and Instruction, Early Childhood Education/Teacher Option Program, Chestnut Hill, MA 02167-9991. Awards M Ed. Accredited by NCATE. Students: 8 full-time (all women), 12 part-time (all women); includes 5 international. 37 applicants, 76% accepted. In 1997, 7 degrees awarded. *Degree requirements:* Comprehensive exam required, thesis not required. *Entrance requirements:* GRE General Test. Application deadline: 3/15 (11/15 for spring admission). Application fee: $40. *Expenses:* Tuition $626 per semester hour. Fees $80 per year (minimum) full-time, $30 per semester part-time. *Financial aid:* Fellowships, research assistantships, teaching assistantships, administrative assistantships, merit scholarships, partial tuition waivers, Federal Work-Study, and career-related internships or fieldwork available. *Faculty research:* Early childhood testing and assessment, selective attention abilities in children, play therapy, problem-solving. • Application contact: Arline Riordan, Graduate Admissions Director, 617-552-4214. Fax: 617-552-0812. E-mail: riordana@bc.edu.

Boston University, School of Education, Department of Curriculum and Teaching, Program in Early Childhood Education, Boston, MA 02215. Awards Ed M, Ed D, CAGS. Students: 6 full-time (all women), 1 (woman) part-time. Average age 25. In 1997, 5 master's awarded. *Degree requirements:* For doctorate, dissertation, comprehensive exam required, foreign language not required; for CAGS, comprehensive exam required, foreign language and thesis not required. *Entrance requirements:* For master's and CAGS, GRE or MAT, TOEFL; for doctorate, GRE General Test or MAT, TOEFL. Application deadline: 2/15 (priority date; rolling processing). Application fee: $50. *Expenses:* Tuition $22,830 per year full-time, $713 per credit part-time. Fees $218 per year full-time, $40 per semester part-time. *Financial aid:* Application deadline 3/30. *Faculty research:* Language acquisition, child development, needs of handicapped children. • Dr. Jane Lannak, Coordinator, 617-353-7258. E-mail: jlannak@bu.edu.

Brenau University, School of Education and Human Development, Gainesville, GA 30501-3697. Offerings include early childhood education (M Ed, Ed S), with option in behavior disorders (M Ed). *Degree requirements:* For master's, comprehensive exam (M Ed) required, foreign language and thesis not required. *Average time to degree:* master's–2 years part-time; other advanced degree–1.5 years part-time. *Entrance requirements:* For master's, GRE, MAT. Application deadline: rolling. Application fee: $30. *Tuition:* $198 per semester hour. • Dr. William B. Ware, Dean, 770-534-6220. Application contact: Kathy Cobb, Director of Graduate Admissions, 770-534-6162. Fax: 770-538-4306. E-mail: kcobb@lib.brenau.edu.

Bridgewater State College, School of Education, Department of Elementary and Early Childhood Education, Program in Early Childhood Education, Bridgewater, MA 02325-0001. Awards M Ed. Accredited by NCATE. Evening/weekend programs available. *Entrance requirements:* GRE General Test. Application deadline: 4/1 (10/1 for spring admission). Application fee: $25. *Expenses:* Tuition $1675 per year full-time, $70 per credit part-time for state residents; $6450 per year full-time, $269 per credit part-time for nonresidents. Fees $1588 per year full-time, $66 per credit hour part-time for state residents; $1588 per year full-time, $66 per credit part-time for nonresidents. *Financial aid:* Career-related internships or fieldwork available. • Application contact: Graduate School, 508-697-1300.

Brooklyn College of the City University of New York, School of Education, Division of Early Childhood Education, 2900 Bedford Avenue, Brooklyn, NY 11210-2889. Awards MS Ed. Part-time and evening/weekend programs available. Students: 4 full-time (all women), 180 part-time (176 women); includes 86 minority (62 African Americans, 7 Asian Americans, 17 Hispanics), 2 international. In 1997, 67 degrees awarded. *Entrance requirements:* GRE, TOEFL (minimum score 500), bachelor's degree in early childhood education. Application deadline: 3/1 (11/1 for spring admission). Application fee: $40. *Expenses:* Tuition $4350 per year full-time, $185 per credit part-time for state residents; $7600 per year full-time, $320 per credit part-time for nonresidents. Fees $500 per year for state residents; $806 per year for nonresidents. *Financial aid:* Institutionally sponsored loans and career-related internships or fieldwork available. Financial aid application deadline: 5/1; applicants required to submit FAFSA. • Dr. Lorraine Harner, Coordinator, 718-951-5517.

California State University, Bakersfield, School of Education, Program in Early Childhood Education, 9001 Stockdale Highway, Bakersfield, CA 93311-1099. Awards MA. Accredited by NCATE. *Degree requirements:* Thesis or alternative, culminating projects. *Application deadline:* rolling. *Application fee:* $55. *Expenses:* Tuition $0 for state residents; $246 per unit full-time, $164 per unit part-time for nonresidents. Fees $1584 per year full-time, $918 per year part-time. • Dr. Lon Kellenberger, Interim Dean, School of Education, 805-664-2219. Application contact: Dr. Dianne Turner, Graduate Coordinator, 805-664-2422. Fax: 805-664-2063.

California State University, Fresno, Division of Graduate Studies, School of Education and Human Development, Department of Literacy and Early Education, 5241 North Maple Avenue, Fresno, CA 93740. Offerings include education (MA), with options in early childhood education, reading/language arts. Accredited by NCATE. Department faculty: 6 full-time (4 women). *Degree requirements:* Thesis or alternative. *Average time to degree:* master's–3.5 years full-time. *Entrance requirements:* GRE General Test, TOEFL (minimum score 550), MAT, minimum GPA of 2.75. Application deadline: 4/1 (priority date; rolling processing; 11/1 for spring admission). Application fee: $55. Electronic applications accepted. *Expenses:* Tuition

$0 for state residents; $246 per unit for nonresidents. Fees $1872 per year full-time, $1206 per year part-time. • Jacques Benninga, Chair, 209-278-0250. Fax: 209-278-0404.

California State University, Northridge, College of Education, Department of Educational Leadership and Policy Studies, Program in Early Childhood Education, Northridge, CA 91330. Awards MA. Accredited by NCATE. Part-time and evening/weekend programs available. 28 applicants, 89% accepted. *Entrance requirements:* TOEFL, GRE General Test, MAT, or minimum GPA of 3.0. Application deadline: 11/30. Application fee: $55. *Expenses:* Tuition $0 for state residents; $246 per unit for nonresidents. Fees $1970 per year full-time, $1304 per year part-time. *Financial aid:* Application deadline 3/1. *Faculty research:* Infant and child care. • Application contact: Dr. Rose Bromwich, Graduate Coordinator, 818-677-2542 Ext. 2599.

California State University, Sacramento, School of Education, Department of Teacher Education, Program in Early Childhood Education, Sacramento, CA 95819-6048. Awards MA. Part-time programs available. *Degree requirements:* Thesis or alternative, writing proficiency exam. *Entrance requirements:* TOEFL (minimum score 550), minimum GPA of 2.75, experience with children. Application deadline: 4/15 (11/1 for spring admission). Application fee: $55. *Expenses:* Tuition $0 for state residents; $246 per unit for nonresidents. Fees $2012 per year full-time, $1346 per year part-time. *Financial aid:* Federal Work-Study and career-related internships or fieldwork available. Aid available to part-time students. Financial aid application deadline: 3/1. • Dr. Ed Arnsdorf, Chair, Department of Teacher Education, 916-278-6155. Application contact: Dr. Robert Edwards, Graduate Coordinator, 916-278-5559.

California University of Pennsylvania, School of Education, Department of Elementary Education, Program in Early Childhood Education, 250 University Avenue, California, PA 15419-1394. Awards M Ed. Accredited by NCATE. Part-time and evening/weekend programs available. Faculty: 2 part-time (both women). Students: 5 full-time (all women), 7 part-time (6 women); includes 1 international. 1 applicant, 100% accepted. In 1997, 1 degree awarded. *Degree requirements:* Comprehensive exam required, thesis optional, foreign language not required. *Entrance requirements:* MAT (minimum score 35), TOEFL (minimum score 550), minimum GPA of 3.0, teaching certificate. Application deadline: rolling. Application fee: $25. *Expenses:* Tuition $3468 per year full-time, $193 per credit part-time for state residents; $6236 per year full-time, $346 per credit part-time for nonresidents. Fees $886 per year full-time, $153 per semester (minimum) part-time. • Dr. Phyllis McIlwain, Coordinator, 724-938-4135.

Carlow College, Division of Education, Program in Early Childhood Education, Pittsburgh, PA 15213-3165. Awards M Ed. Part-time and evening/weekend programs available. Faculty: 2 full-time (both women), 7 part-time (6 women). Students: 44 part-time (all women); includes 2 minority (both African Americans), 2 international. Average age 30. 8 applicants, 100% accepted. In 1997, 7 degrees awarded (100% found work related to degree). *Degree requirements:* Thesis required, foreign language not required. *Average time to degree:* master's–7 years part-time. *Entrance requirements:* Interview, minimum GPA of 3.0. Application deadline: 4/1 (priority date; rolling processing; 10/30 for spring admission). Application fee: $35. *Financial aid:* 6 students received aid; Federal Work-Study and career-related internships or fieldwork available. Aid available to part-time students. Financial aid application deadline: 3/15. *Faculty research:* Conflict resolution, child care training, play, infant-toddler issues, attitudes toward inclusion, school age child care, early Head Start. • Dr. Roberta Schomburg, Director, 412-578-6312. Application contact: Bonnie Potthoff, Office Manager, Graduate Studies, 412-578-8764. Fax: 412-578-8822.

Carlow College, Division of Education, Program in Early Childhood Supervision, Pittsburgh, PA 15213-3165. Awards M Ed. Part-time and evening/weekend programs available. Faculty: 2 full-time (both women). Students: 2 part-time (both women). Average age 36. In 1997, 1 degree awarded (100% found work related to degree). *Degree requirements:* Thesis or alternative required, foreign language not required. *Average time to degree:* master's–2 years part-time. *Entrance requirements:* Interview, minimum GPA of 3.0. Application deadline: 4/1 (priority date; rolling processing; 10/15 for spring admission). Application fee: $35. *Financial aid:* Federal Work-Study available. Aid available to part-time students. Financial aid application deadline: 3/15. *Faculty research:* Adult education, training and supervision. • Dr. Roberta Schomburg, Director, 412-578-6312. Application contact: Bonnie Potthoff, Office Manager, Graduate Studies, 412-578-8764. Fax: 412-578-8822.

Central Connecticut State University, School of Education and Professional Studies, Department of Teacher Education, Program in Early Childhood Education, New Britain, CT 06050-4010. Awards MS. Part-time and evening/weekend programs available. Students: 1 (woman) full-time, 33 part-time (32 women); includes 4 minority (1 African American, 2 Asian Americans, 1 Hispanic). Average age 34. 12 applicants, 92% accepted. In 1997, 8 degrees awarded. *Degree requirements:* Thesis or alternative, comprehensive exam or special project required, foreign language not required. *Entrance requirements:* TOEFL (minimum score 550), minimum GPA of 2.7. Application deadline: 6/1 (priority date; rolling processing; 12/1 for spring admission). Application fee: $40. *Expenses:* Tuition $4458 per year full-time, $175 per credit hour part-time for state residents; $9943 per year full-time, $175 per credit hour part-time for nonresidents. Fees $45 per semester. *Financial aid:* Federal Work-Study available. Financial aid application deadline: 3/15; applicants required to submit FAFSA. *Faculty research:* Pre-kindergarten and early learning research, early learning environments. • Dr. Susan Seider, Coordinator, 860-832-2418.

Central Michigan University, College of Education and Human Services, Department of Teacher Education and Professional Development, Program in Elementary Education, Concentration in Early Childhood Education, Mount Pleasant, MI 48859. Awards MA. Accredited by NCATE. Students: 2 full-time (both women), 13 part-time (12 women). Average age 33. In 1997, 28 degrees awarded. *Degree requirements:* Thesis or alternative required, foreign language not required. *Entrance requirements:* GRE General Test (minimum combined score of 1000), minimum GPA of 2.7. Application deadline: 3/1 (priority date). Application fee: $30. *Expenses:* Tuition $139 per credit hour (minimum) for state residents; $276 per credit hour (minimum) for nonresidents. Fees $260 per year full-time, $150 per semester part-time. *Financial aid:* Federal Work-Study available. Financial aid application deadline: 3/7. • Dr. William Merrill, Chairperson, Department of Teacher Education and Professional Development, 517-774-3975. Fax: 517-774-3516. E-mail: 34ltyvi@cmich.edu.

Chestnut Hill College, Program in Early Childhood Education, Philadelphia, PA 19118-2693. Awards M Ed. Part-time and evening/weekend programs available. Faculty: 6 full-time (5 women), 8 part-time (5 women). Students: 21 part-time (20 women); includes 1 minority (African American). Average age 32. *Average time to degree:* master's–3 years part-time. *Application deadline:* rolling. *Application fee:* $35. *Financial aid:* Graduate assistantships and career-related internships or fieldwork available. Aid available to part-time students. *Faculty research:* Children's literature, humor. • Dr. Dominic Cotugno SSJ, Coordinator, 215-248-7078. Application contact: Regina Raphael Smith, Graduate Admissions, 215-248-7020. Fax: 215-248-7155.

Chicago State University, Departments of Early Childhood and Elementary Education and Curriculum and Instruction, Program in Early Childhood Education, Chicago, IL 60628. Awards MS Ed. Accredited by NCATE. *Degree requirements:* Thesis optional, foreign language not required. *Entrance requirements:* Minimum GPA of 2.75. Application deadline: 7/1 (11/10 for spring admission). *Tuition:* $2268 per year full-time, $95 per credit hour part-time for state residents; $6804 per year full-time, $284 per credit hour part-time for nonresidents.

City College of the City University of New York, Graduate School, School of Education, Department of Elementary Education, Program in Early Childhood Education, Convent Avenue at 138th Street, New York, NY 10031-6977. Awards MS. In 1997, 87 degrees awarded. *Degree requirements:* Thesis required, foreign language not required. *Entrance requirements:* TOEFL (minimum score 500). Application fee: $40. *Expenses:* Tuition $4350 per year full-time, $185 per credit part-time for state residents; $7600 per year full-time, $320 per credit part-time for nonresidents. Fees $41 per year. *Financial aid:* Career-related internships or fieldwork available. • Director, 212-650-7262.

Cleveland State University, College of Education, Department of Specialized Instructional Programs, Cleveland, OH 44115-2440. Offerings include curriculum and instruction (M Ed), with options in bilingual education, early childhood education, early childhood/special education, education of emerging adolescents, elementary education, English as a second language, learning disabilities, Montessori education, multihandicapped, reading, secondary education. Department faculty: 18 full-time (12 women). *Entrance requirements:* GRE General Test or MAT (score in 50th percentile or higher). Application deadline: 9/1 (priority date; rolling processing). Application fee: $25. *Expenses:* Tuition $5252 per year full-time, $202 per credit hour part-time for state residents; $10,504 per year full-time, $404 per credit hour part-time for nonresidents. Fees $2.25 per credit hour (minimum). • Dr. Jane Zaharias, Chairperson, 216-687-4585. Fax: 216-687-5379. E-mail: j.zaharias@csuohio.edu.

Coastal Carolina University, School of Education, Program in Education, Conway, SC 29528-6054. Offerings include early childhood education (M Ed). Program faculty: 6 full-time (3 women). *Entrance requirements:* GRE General Test (minimum combined score of 800), MAT (minimum score 35), teacher certification. Application deadline: 8/15 (priority date; rolling processing). Application fee: $25. Electronic applications accepted. • Dr. Sandra Bowden, Head, 843-349-2606.

College of Mount St. Joseph, Education Department, Program in Inclusive Early Childhood Education, Cincinnati, OH 45233-1670. Awards MA Ed. *Degree requirements:* Comprehensive exam required, foreign language and thesis not required. *Entrance requirements:* GRE General Test (minimum combined score of 825), minimum GPA of 2.7. Application deadline: rolling. Application fee: $0. *Tuition:* $320 per credit hour. *Financial aid:* Application deadline 6/1. • Application contact: Jean Abrams, Graduate Secretary, 513-244-4812.

College of New Rochelle, Division of Education, Program in Elementary Education/Early Childhood Education, New Rochelle, NY 10805-2308. Awards MS Ed. Part-time programs available. Faculty: 2 full-time (both women), 5 part-time (3 women), 4 FTE. Students: 13 full-time (11 women), 121 part-time (109 women); includes 11 minority (5 African Americans, 6 Hispanics). 45 applicants, 84% accepted. In 1997, 43 degrees awarded. *Degree requirements:* Practicum required, foreign language not required. *Average time to degree:* master's–1.5 years full-time, 3 years part-time. *Entrance requirements:* Interview; minimum GPA of 3.0 in field, 2.7 overall. Application deadline: 8/1 (priority date; rolling processing). Application fee: $35. *Tuition:* $329 per credit. *Financial aid:* In 1997–98, 12 students received aid, including 1 assistantship totaling $4,050; research assistantships and career-related internships or fieldwork also available. • Dr. Melanie Hannigan, Division Head, Division of Education, 914-654-5330.

College of Notre Dame, Department of Education, Emphasis in Montessori Teaching, Belmont, CA 94002-1997. Awards M Ed. Part-time programs available. Faculty: 7 part-time. Students: 1 (woman) full-time, 16 part-time (all women); includes 1 minority (Hispanic), 4 international. Average age 29. 7 applicants, 71% accepted. In 1997, 5 degrees awarded. *Entrance requirements:* TOEFL (minimum score 550), interview, minimum GPA of 2.5. Application deadline: rolling. Application fee: $50 ($500 for international students). *Tuition:* $460 per unit. *Financial aid:* Career-related internships or fieldwork available. Aid available to part-time students. • Beverly Farrell, Program Director, 650-508-3705.

College of Our Lady of the Elms, Department of Education, Chicopee, MA 01013-2839. Offerings include early childhood education (MAT). Department faculty: 7 full-time (all women), 6 part-time (5 women). *Application deadline:* rolling. *Application fee:* $30. *Expenses:* Tuition $320 per credit. Fees $40 per year. • Sr. Kathleen M. Kirley, Dean of Continuing Education and Graduate Studies, 413-594-2761. Fax: 413-592-4871. Application contact: Dr. Mary Janeczek, Director, 413-594-2761.

The College of Saint Rose, School of Education, Teacher Education Department, Program in Early Childhood Education, Albany, NY 12203-1419. Awards MS Ed. Part-time and evening/weekend programs available. Faculty: 10 full-time (6 women), 1 (woman) part-time. Students: 18 part-time (all women). Average age 31. In 1997, 5 degrees awarded. *Degree requirements:* Thesis or alternative, comprehensive exam required, foreign language not required. *Entrance requirements:* Minimum undergraduate GPA of 3.0. Application deadline: 7/15 (priority date; rolling processing; 12/1 for spring admission). Application fee: $30. *Expenses:* Tuition $338 per credit. Fees $60 per year. *Financial aid:* Research assistantships, partial tuition waivers, and career-related internships or fieldwork available. Aid available to part-time students. Financial aid application deadline: 3/1; applicants required to submit FAFSA. • Application contact: Graduate Office, 518-454-5136. Fax: 518-458-5479. E-mail: ace@rosnet.strose.edu.

Columbus State University, College of Education, Department of Curriculum and Instruction, Columbus, GA 31907-5645. Offerings include early childhood education (M Ed, Ed S). Accredited by NCATE. Ed S (mathematics) offered jointly with Georgia Southwestern University. M Ed (political science) being phased out; applicants no longer accepted. *Degree requirements:* For master's, exit exam required, foreign language and thesis not required; for Ed S, thesis or alternative required, foreign language not required. *Entrance requirements:* For master's, GRE General Test (minimum combined score of 800), MAT (minimum score 44); for Ed S, GRE General Test (minimum combined score of 900), MAT (minimum score 44). Application deadline: 7/10 (priority date; rolling processing; 10/23 for spring admission). Application fee: $20. *Tuition:* $1718 per year full-time, $151 per semester hour part-time for state residents; $6218 per year full-time, $401 per semester hour part-time for nonresidents. • Dr. David Shoemaker, Chair, 706-568-2255. Fax: 706-568-3134. E-mail: shoemaker_david@colstate.edu. Application contact: Katie Thornton, Graduate Admissions, 706-568-2279. Fax: 706-568-2462. E-mail: thornton_katie@colstate.edu.

Concordia University, Program in Early Childhood Education, River Forest, IL 60305-1499. Awards MA, CAS. Part-time and evening/weekend programs available. Faculty: 11 full-time (6 women), 6 part-time (5 women). Students: 41 (40 women); includes 4 minority (all African Americans), 1 international. In 1997, 11 master's awarded. *Degree requirements:* For master's, thesis, comprehensive exam required, foreign language not required; for CAS, thesis, final project required, foreign language not required. *Entrance requirements:* For master's, minimum GPA of 2.9; for CAS, master's degree. Application deadline: rolling. Application fee: $0. *Tuition:* $372 per semester hour. *Financial aid:* Research assistantships, institutionally sponsored loans available. Aid available to part-time students. *Faculty research:* Child care training project, "Children in Workship" project, ethical development of children. Total annual research expenditures: $155,000. • Dr. Shirley Morgenthaler, Coordinator, 708-209-3076. Application contact: Mary Betancourt, Admissions Secretary, 708-209-4093. Fax: 708-209-3454. E-mail: crfdngrad@curf.edu.

Concordia University, Graduate Programs in Education, Program in Early Childhood Education, Seward, NE 68434-1599. Awards M Ed. Accredited by NCATE. Part-time programs available. Faculty: 6 full-time (2 women), 4 part-time (all women). Students: 32 part-time (all women). 3 applicants, 100% accepted. *Degree requirements:* Thesis or alternative required, foreign language not required. *Entrance requirements:* GRE, MAT, or NTE, minimum GPA of 3.0, BS in education or equivalent. Application deadline: 8/1 (priority date; rolling processing; 12/1 for spring admission). Application fee: $15. *Tuition:* $127 per hour. *Financial aid:* Federal Work-Study, institutionally sponsored loans available. Aid available to part-time students. Financial aid applicants required to submit FAFSA. • Prof. Leah Serck, Coordinator, 402-643-7300.

Concordia University, Faculty of Arts and Science, Department of Education, Program in Early Childhood Education, Montréal, PQ H3G 1M8, Canada. Awards Diploma. Admissions temporarily suspended. Students: 0. *Degree requirements:* Internship required, thesis not required. *Expenses:* Tuition $56 per credit (minimum) for Canadian residents; $249 per credit (minimum) for nonresidents. Fees $158 per year full-time, $117 per year (minimum) part-time. *Financial aid:* Career-related internships or fieldwork available. • Dr. R. Schmid, Chair, Depart-

Directory: Early Childhood Education

Concordia University (continued)
ment of Education, 514-848-2033. Application contact: Dr. Steven Shaw, Director, 514-848-2044. Fax: 514-848-4520.

Concordia University at St. Paul, Program in Education, St. Paul, MN 55104-5494. Offerings include early childhood education (MA Ed). Postbaccalaureate distance learning degree programs offered (minimal on-campus study). Program faculty: 13 full-time (6 women), 8 part-time (4 women), 15 FTE. *Degree requirements:* Thesis or alternative required, foreign language not required. *Application deadline:* rolling. *Application fee:* $20. *Tuition:* $220 per semester hour. • Dr. Robert DeWerff, Dean of Graduate and Continuing Studies, 612-641-8277. Fax: 612-659-0207. E-mail: dewerff@luther.csp.edu.

Concordia University Wisconsin, Division of Graduate Studies, Education Department, Program in Early Childhood, Mequon, WI 53097-2402. Awards MS Ed. *Degree requirements:* Thesis or alternative, comprehensive exam. *Entrance requirements:* TOEFL (minimum score 550), minimum GPA of 3.0, teaching license. Application fee: $25. *Tuition:* $250 per credit. *Financial aid:* Application deadline 8/1. • Application contact: Brooke Tireman, Graduate Admissions, 414-243-4248. Fax: 414-243-4428. E-mail: btireman@back.cuw.edu.

Cumberland College, Program in Early Childhood Education, 6178 College Station Drive, Williamsburg, KY 40769-1372. Awards MA Ed. Part-time and evening/weekend programs available. Faculty: 4 full-time (2 women), 5 part-time (2 women). *Degree requirements:* Comprehensive exam required, foreign language and thesis not required. *Entrance requirements:* GRE or NTE, Kentucky teaching certificate. Application deadline: 8/26 (rolling processing). Application fee: $25. *Tuition:* $175 per credit. • Application contact: Erica Harris, Admissions Office, 606-539-4241.

Dallas Baptist University, Dorothy M. Bush College of Education, Education Program, Dallas, TX 75211-9299. Offerings include early childhood education (M Ed). Program faculty: 15 full-time (4 women), 5 part-time (3 women). *Entrance requirements:* GRE General Test, TOEFL (minimum score 550). Application deadline: rolling. Application fee: $25. *Tuition:* $285 per hour. • Dr. Bill Gilbert, Director, 214-333-5404. Fax: 214-333-5551. Application contact: Travis Bundrick, Director of Graduate Programs, 214-333-5243. Fax: 214-333-5579. E-mail: graduate@dbu.edu.

Dominican University, Graduate School of Education, River Forest, IL 60305-1099. Offerings include early childhood education (MS). School faculty: 9 full-time (7 women), 14 part-time (11 women), 14 FTE. *Application deadline:* 8/15 (priority date; rolling processing; 1/16 for spring admission). *Application fee:* $25. *Expenses:* Tuition $6120 per year full-time, $1020 per course part-time. Fees $10 per course. • Sr. Colleen McNicholas, Dean, 708-524-6830. E-mail: educate@email.dom.edu. Application contact: Deborah Davison, Coordinator of Admissions, 708-524-6922. Fax: 708-524-6665. E-mail: educate@email.dom.edu.

Eastern Connecticut State University, School of Education and Professional Studies/Graduate Division, Program in Early Childhood Education, Willimantic, CT 06226-2295. Awards MS. Part-time and evening/weekend programs available. Faculty: 6 full-time (5 women), 1 (woman) part-time. Students: 1 (woman) full-time, 18 part-time (15 women); includes 1 minority (Hispanic). Average age 33. 14 applicants, 100% accepted. In 1997, 7 degrees awarded. *Degree requirements:* Comprehensive exam or thesis required, foreign language not required. *Entrance requirements:* Minimum GPA of 2.7. Application fee: $40. *Expenses:* Tuition $2632 per year full-time, $175 per credit hour part-time for state residents; $7220 per year full-time, $175 per credit hour part-time for nonresidents. Fees $1851 per year full-time, $20 per semester part-time for state residents; $2748 per year full-time, $20 per semester part-time for nonresidents. *Financial aid:* In 1997–98, 1 fellowship (to a first-year student) totaling $1,653 was awarded; career-related internships or fieldwork also available. Financial aid application deadline: 3/15. • Dr. Jeffrey Trawick-Smith, Adviser, 860-465-5232. E-mail: trawick@ecsuc.ctstateu.edu. Application contact: Edith Mavor, Graduate Division Director, 860-465-4543. E-mail: mavor@ecsuc.ctstateu.edu.

Eastern Michigan University, College of Education, Department of Teacher Education, Program in Early Childhood Education, Ypsilanti, MI 48197. Awards MA. Accredited by NCATE. Evening/weekend programs available. In 1997, 47 degrees awarded. *Degree requirements:* Thesis optional, foreign language not required. *Entrance requirements:* GRE, TOEFL (minimum score 500). Application deadline: 5/15 (rolling processing; 3/15 for spring admission). Application fee: $30. *Expenses:* Tuition $2691 per year full-time, $150 per credit hour part-time for state residents; $6300 per year full-time, $350 per credit hour part-time for nonresidents. Fees $368 per year full-time, $88 per semester (minimum) part-time. *Financial aid:* Fellowships, teaching assistantships available. Aid available to part-time students. Financial aid application deadline: 3/15; applicants required to submit FAFSA. • Dr. Leah Adams, Coordinator, 734-487-1424.

Eastern Nazarene College, Graduate Studies, Division of Education, Quincy, MA 02170-2999. Offerings include early childhood education (M Ed, Certificate). M Ed and Certificate also available through weekend program for administration, special needs, and reading only. Division faculty: 9 full-time (5 women), 11 part-time (5 women). *Entrance requirements:* For master's, TOEFL (minimum score 500). Application deadline: rolling. Application fee: $35. *Expenses:* Tuition $350 per credit. Fees $125 per semester full-time, $15 per semester part-time. • Dr. Lorne Ranstrom, Chair, 617-745-3528. Application contact: Cleo P. Cakridas, Graduate Enrollment Counselor, 617-745-3870. Fax: 617-745-3907. E-mail: cakridac@enc.edu.

Eastern Washington University, College of Education and Human Development, Department of Education, Program in Early Childhood Education, Cheney, WA 99004-2431. Awards M Ed. Accredited by NCATE. *Degree requirements:* Comprehensive exam required, thesis not required. *Entrance requirements:* Minimum GPA of 3.0. Application deadline: 4/1 (priority date; rolling processing; 1/15 for spring admission). Application fee: $35. *Tuition:* $4200 per year full-time, $140 per credit part-time for state residents; $12,780 per year full-time, $415 per credit part-time for nonresidents. *Financial aid:* Application deadline 2/1. • Dr. Judy Leach, Adviser, 509-359-6095.

East Tennessee State University, College of Education, Department of Human Development and Learning, Johnson City, TN 37614-0734. Offerings include early childhood learning and development (MA, M Ed). Accredited by NCATE. Department faculty: 22 full-time (8 women). *Degree requirements:* Thesis (for some programs), comprehensive exam required, foreign language not required. *Entrance requirements:* GRE General Test, TOEFL (minimum score 550), minimum GPA of 3.0. Application deadline: 7/15 (priority date; rolling processing; 11/1 for spring admission). Application fee: $25 ($35 for international students). *Tuition:* $2944 per year full-time, $158 per credit hour part-time for state residents; $7770 per year full-time, $369 per credit hour part-time for nonresidents. • Dr. James Bitter, Chair, 423-439-4194. Fax: 423-439-5764. E-mail: bitterj@etsu-tn.edu.

Edinboro University of Pennsylvania, School of Education, Department of Elementary Education, Program in Elementary Education, Edinboro, PA 16444. Offerings include early childhood (M Ed). *Degree requirements:* Thesis or alternative required, foreign language not required. *Entrance requirements:* GRE or MAT (score in 30th percentile or higher). Application deadline: rolling. Application fee: $25. *Expenses:* Tuition $3468 per year full-time, $193 per credit part-time for state residents; $6236 per year full-time, $346 per credit part-time for nonresidents. Fees $898 per year full-time, $50 per semester (minimum) part-time. • Application contact: Dr. Philip Kerstetter, Dean of Graduate Studies, 814-732-2856. Fax: 814-732-2611. E-mail: kerstetter@edinboro.edu.

Emory University, Graduate School of Arts and Sciences, Division of Educational Studies, Atlanta, GA 30322-1100. Offerings include early childhood teaching (MAT, M Ed). Division faculty: 13. *Application deadline:* 1/20 (3/15 for spring admission). *Application fee:* $45. *Expenses:* Tuition $21,770 per year. Fees $300 per year. • Dr. Robert Jensen, Acting Director, 404-727-0606. Fax: 404-727-2799. E-mail: rjensen@emory.edu. Application contact: Dr. Glen Avant, Program Development Coordinator, 404-727-0612.

Emporia State University, School of Graduate Studies, The Teachers College, Division of Early Childhood/Elementary Teacher Education, Program in Early Childhood Education, Emporia, KS 66801-5087. Awards MS. Accredited by NCATE. Students: 4 full-time (all women), 18 part-time (17 women). 1 applicant, 100% accepted. In 1997, 9 degrees awarded. *Degree requirements:* Comprehensive exam or thesis required, foreign language not required. *Entrance requirements:* GRE General Test or MAT, TOEFL (minimum score 550), written exam. Application deadline: 8/15 (priority date; rolling processing). Application fee: $30 ($75 for international students). Electronic applications accepted. *Tuition:* $2300 per year full-time, $103 per credit hour part-time for state residents; $6012 per year full-time, $258 per credit hour part-time for nonresidents. *Financial aid:* Federal Work-Study, institutionally sponsored loans available. Financial aid application deadline: 3/15; applicants required to submit FAFSA. • Dr. Eileen Hogan, Chair, Division of Early Childhood/Elementary Teacher Education, 316-341-5751. E-mail: hoganeil@emporia.edu.

Fairfield University, Graduate School of Education and Allied Professions, Department of Curriculum and Instruction, Program in Early Childhood Education, Fairfield, CT 06430-5195. Awards MA, CAS. *Degree requirements:* For master's, comprehensive exams required, foreign language not required. *Entrance requirements:* For master's, PRAXIS I (CBT), TOEFL, minimum QPA of 2.67. Application deadline: 7/10 (rolling processing). Application fee: $40. *Expenses:* Tuition $350 per credit hour (minimum). Fees $20 per semester (minimum). • Application contact: Karen Creecy, Assistant Dean, 203-254-4250. Fax: 203-254-4241. E-mail: klcreecy@fair1.fairfield.edu.

Fitchburg State College, Program in Early Childhood Education, Fitchburg, MA 01420-2697. Awards M Ed. Accredited by NCATE. Part-time and evening/weekend programs available. *Entrance requirements:* GRE General Test or MAT (minimum score 47), interview, teaching certificate. Application deadline: rolling. Application fee: $10. *Expenses:* Tuition $147 per credit. Fees $55 per semester. *Financial aid:* Graduate assistantships, Federal Work-Study available. Aid available to part-time students. Financial aid application deadline: 3/30; applicants required to submit FAFSA. • Dr. Patricia Barbaresi, Chair, 978-665-3510. Fax: 978-665-3658. E-mail: dgce@fsc.edu. Application contact: James DuPont, Director of Admissions, 978-665-3144. Fax: 978-665-4540. E-mail: admissions@fsc.edu.

Florida Agricultural and Mechanical University, Division of Graduate Studies, Research, and Continuing Education, College of Education, Program in Elementary Education, Tallahassee, FL 32307-3200. Offers early childhood and elementary education (M Ed, MS Ed). Accredited by NCATE. Students: 57 (50 women); includes 32 minority (all African Americans). In 1997, 20 degrees awarded. *Entrance requirements:* GRE General Test (minimum combined score of 1000), minimum GPA of 3.0. Application deadline: 5/13. Application fee: $20. *Expenses:* Tuition $140 per credit hour for state residents; $484 per credit hour for nonresidents. Fees $130 per year. • Dr. Robert Lemons, Chairperson, 850-599-3397. Fax: 850-561-2211.

Florida Atlantic University, College of Education, Department of Teacher Education, Program in Early Childhood Education, Boca Raton, FL 33431-0991. Awards M Ed. Accredited by NCATE. Part-time and evening/weekend programs available. Faculty: 1 (woman) full-time. Students: 5 full-time (all women), 14 part-time (all women); includes 3 minority (1 African American, 2 Hispanics). Average age 27. 6 applicants, 50% accepted. In 1997, 14 degrees awarded. *Entrance requirements:* GRE General Test, minimum GPA of 3.0 during previous 2 years. Application deadline: rolling. Application fee: $20. *Expenses:* Tuition $2520 per year full-time, $140 per credit hour part-time for state residents; $8712 per year full-time, $484 per credit hour part-time for nonresidents. Fees $5 per year (minimum). • Dr. Rhoda Chalker, Coordinator, 561-367-3579.

Florida International University, College of Education, Department of Elementary Education, Program in Early Childhood Education, Miami, FL 33199. Awards MS. Accredited by NCATE. Part-time and evening/weekend programs available. Students: 11 part-time (all women); includes 8 minority (all Hispanics). Average age 33. 10 applicants, 30% accepted. In 1997, 14 degrees awarded. *Entrance requirements:* GRE General Test (minimum combined score of 1000) or minimum GPA of 3.0, teaching certificate. Application deadline: 4/1 (priority date; rolling processing; 10/1 for spring admission). Application fee: $20. *Expenses:* Tuition $138 per credit hour for state residents; $482 per credit hour for nonresidents. Fees $46 per semester. *Faculty research:* Children's literature, parental involvement. • Dr. George O'Brien, Chairperson, Department of Elementary Education, 305-348-2561. E-mail: obrieng@fiu.edu.

Florida State University, College of Education, Department of Educational Theory and Practice, Program in Early Childhood Education, Tallahassee, FL 32306. Awards MS, Ed D, PhD, Ed S. Part-time programs available. Faculty: 2 full-time (1 woman). Students: 15 full-time (14 women), 17 part-time (14 women); includes 8 minority (4 African Americans, 1 Asian American, 3 Hispanics). 30 applicants, 73% accepted. In 1997, 11 master's, 3 doctorates awarded. *Degree requirements:* For master's and Ed S, comprehensive exams required, thesis optional; for doctorate, dissertation, comprehensive exams. *Entrance requirements:* GRE General Test (minimum combined score of 1000), minimum GPA of 3.0. Application deadline: 7/1 (priority date; rolling processing; 11/1 for spring admission). Application fee: $20. *Tuition:* $139 per credit hour for state residents; $482 per credit hour for nonresidents. *Financial aid:* Fellowships, research assistantships, teaching assistantships, and career-related internships or fieldwork available. • Dr. Charles Wolfgang, Chair, Department of Educational Theory and Practice, 850-644-5458. E-mail: wolfgang@mail.coe.fsu.edu. Application contact: Admissions Secretary, 850-644-5458. Fax: 850-644-7736.

Fordham University, Graduate School of Education, Division of Curriculum and Teaching, New York, NY 10023. Offerings include early childhood education (MSE). Accredited by NCATE. *Application fee:* $50. • Dr. Angela Carrasquillo, Chairperson, 212-636-6427.

Fort Valley State University, Department of Curriculum and Instruction, Program in Early Childhood Education, Fort Valley, GA 31030-3298. Awards MS. Accredited by NCATE. Part-time programs available. Faculty: 1 full-time (0 women), 3 part-time (1 woman). Students: 34. *Degree requirements:* Thesis optional, foreign language not required. *Entrance requirements:* GRE General Test (minimum combined score of 800) or MAT (minimum score 44). Application deadline: 8/23. Application fee: $20. *Tuition:* $2486 per year full-time, $83 per semester hour part-time for state residents; $8486 per year full-time, $333 per semester hour part-time for nonresidents. *Financial aid:* Federal Work-Study available. Aid available to part-time students. Financial aid application deadline: 5/1; applicants required to submit FAFSA. • Head, Department of Curriculum and Instruction, 912-825-6250.

Francis Marion University, School of Education, Florence, SC 29501-0547. Offerings include early childhood education (M Ed). School faculty: 65 full-time (14 women). *Application deadline:* 8/21 (priority date; rolling processing). *Application fee:* $25. • Dr. Wayne Pruitt, Coordinator, 803-661-1462.

Gallaudet University, School of Education and Human Services, Department of Education, Washington, DC 20002-3625. Offerings include early childhood education (MA, Ed S), parent/infant specialty (MA, Ed S). One or more programs accredited by NCATE. *Degree requirements:* For master's, thesis optional. *Entrance requirements:* For master's, GRE General Test or MAT. Application deadline: 2/15 (priority date; rolling processing). Application fee: $50. *Expenses:* Tuition $7064 per year full-time, $392 per credit part-time. Fees $50 (one-time charge). • Dr. Barbara Bodner-Johnson, Chair, 202-651-5530. Application contact: Deborah DeStefano, Director of Admissions, 202-651-5253. Fax: 202-651-5744. E-mail: adm_destefan@gallua.bitnet.

Gannon University, School of Graduate Studies, College of Humanities, Business, and Education, School of Education, Program in Early Intervention, Erie, PA 16541. Awards MS, Certificate. Part-time and evening/weekend programs available. Students: 1 (woman) full-time, 5 part-time (all women). Average age 30. 1 applicant, 100% accepted. *Degree requirements:*

For master's, thesis, comprehensive exam, practicum. *Entrance requirements:* For master's, GRE or MAT, interview, teaching certificate. Application deadline: rolling. Application fee: $25. *Expenses:* Tuition $405 per credit. Fees $200 per year full-time, $8 per credit part-time. *Financial aid:* Career-related internships or fieldwork available. Aid available to part-time students. Financial aid application deadline: 3/1; applicants required to submit FAFSA. • Application contact: Beth Nemenz, Director of Admissions, 814-871-7240. Fax: 814-871-5803. E-mail: admissions@gannon.edu.

George Mason University, Graduate School of Education, Program in Early Childhood Education, Fairfax, VA 22030-4444. Awards M Ed. Accredited by NCATE. Part-time and evening/weekend programs available. Faculty: 42 full-time (24 women), 65 part-time (51 women), 58.73 FTE. Students: 78 full-time (72 women), 103 part-time (95 women); includes 34 minority (11 African Americans, 9 Asian Americans, 14 Hispanics), 2 international. Average age 31. 190 applicants, 68% accepted. In 1997, 58 degrees awarded. *Degree requirements:* Computer language required, foreign language not required. *Entrance requirements:* NTE, minimum GPA of 3.0 in last 60 hours. Application deadline: 5/1 (11/1 for spring admission). Application fee: $30. Electronic applications accepted. *Tuition:* $4344 per year full-time, $181 per credit hour part-time for state residents; $12,504 per year full-time, $521 per credit hour part-time for nonresidents. *Financial aid:* Career-related internships or fieldwork available. Aid available to part-time students. Financial aid application deadline: 3/1; applicants required to submit FAFSA. • Dr. Joan Isenberg, Coordinator, 703-993-4648. Fax: 703-993-2013.

The George Washington University, Graduate School of Education and Human Development, Department of Teacher Preparation and Special Education, Program in Infant Special Education, Washington, DC 20052. Awards MA Ed. Accredited by NCATE. Faculty: 2 full-time (both women), 2 part-time (both women), 3 FTE. Students: 6 full-time (all women), 5 part-time (all women); includes 2 minority (1 African American, 1 Asian American). Average age 27. 5 applicants, 100% accepted. In 1997, 10 degrees awarded. *Degree requirements:* Comprehensive exam required, foreign language and thesis not required. *Entrance requirements:* GRE General Test or MAT, minimum GPA of 2.75. Application deadline: 3/1 (priority date; rolling processing; 10/1 for spring admission). Application fee: $50. *Expenses:* Tuition $680 per semester hour. Fees $35 per semester hour. *Financial aid:* Fellowships, research assistantships, full tuition waivers, Federal Work-Study, and career-related internships or fieldwork available. Financial aid applicants required to submit FAFSA. *Faculty research:* Assessment, early intervention. • Dr. Barbara Brown, Faculty Coordinator, 202-994-6170.

The George Washington University, Graduate School of Education and Human Development, Department of Teacher Preparation and Special Education, Program in Special Education/Early Childhood, Washington, DC 20052. Awards MA Ed. Accredited by NCATE. Faculty: 3 full-time, 4 part-time, 4 FTE. Students: 8 full-time (all women), 28 part-time (27 women); includes 8 minority (7 African Americans, 1 Asian American), 1 international. Average age 34. 35 applicants, 91% accepted. In 1997, 7 degrees awarded. *Degree requirements:* Comprehensive exam required, foreign language and thesis not required. *Entrance requirements:* GRE General Test or MAT, minimum GPA of 2.75. Application deadline: 3/1 (priority date; rolling processing; 10/1 for spring admission). Application fee: $50. *Expenses:* Tuition $680 per semester hour. Fees $35 per semester hour. *Financial aid:* Fellowships, full tuition waivers, Federal Work-Study, and career-related internships or fieldwork available. Financial aid applicants required to submit FAFSA. *Faculty research:* Computer-assisted instruction and learning, disabled learner assessment of preschool, handicapped children. • Dr. Michael Castleberry, Faculty Coordinator, 202-994-6170.

Georgia College and State University, School of Education, Department of Early Childhood Education, Milledgeville, GA 31061. Awards M Ed, Ed S. Accredited by NCATE. Students: 23 full-time (22 women), 64 part-time (62 women); includes 7 minority (all African Americans). Average age 31. In 1997, 37 master's, 20 Ed Ss awarded. *Degree requirements:* For master's, computer language, comprehensive exit exam required, foreign language and thesis not required; for Ed S, computer language, comprehensive exit exam, oral exam, research project required, foreign language and thesis not required. *Entrance requirements:* For master's, GRE General Test (minimum combined score of 800) or NTE (minimum score 550 on each core battery test), MAT (minimum score 44), minimum GPA of 2.5, NT-4 certificate; for Ed S, GRE General Test (minimum combined score of 900) or NTE (minimum score 575 on each core battery test), MAT (minimum score 48), master's degree, minimum graduate GPA of 3.25, NT-5 certificate, 2 years of teaching experience. Application deadline: 7/31 (priority date; rolling processing). Application fee: $10. *Financial aid:* Assistantships, Federal Work-Study, and career-related internships or fieldwork available. Aid available to part-time students. Financial aid application deadline: 4/15. • Dr. Charles Love, Acting Chair, 912-445-5479.

Georgia Southern University, College of Education, Department of Early Childhood Education and Reading, Program in Early Childhood Education, Statesboro, GA 30460-8126. Awards M Ed, Ed S. Accredited by NCATE. Part-time and evening/weekend programs available. Students: 22 full-time (21 women), 34 part-time (33 women); includes 3 minority (all African Americans). Average age 34. 16 applicants, 50% accepted. In 1997, 28 master's, 10 Ed Ss awarded. *Degree requirements:* For master's, comprehensive written exams required, foreign language and thesis not required; for Ed S, oral exams required, foreign language and thesis not required. *Entrance requirements:* For master's, GRE General Test (minimum score 450 on each section) or MAT (minimum score 44), minimum GPA of 2.5; for Ed S, GRE General Test (minimum score 450 on each section) or MAT (minimum score 49), minimum graduate GPA of 3.25. Application deadline: 7/15 (priority date; rolling processing; 11/15 for spring admission). Application fee: $0. Electronic applications accepted. *Tuition:* $2619 per year full-time, $287 per semester (minimum) part-time for state residents; $8619 per year full-time, $1037 per semester (minimum) part-time for nonresidents. *Financial aid:* Research assistantships, Federal Work-Study, and career-related internships or fieldwork available. Aid available to part-time students. Financial aid application deadline: 4/15. *Faculty research:* Technology, effective instructional strategies, addressing needs of diverse learners, teacher effectiveness. • Application contact: Dr. John R. Diebolt, Associate Graduate Dean, 912-681-5384. Fax: 912-681-0740. E-mail: gradschool@gsvms2.cc.gasou.edu.

Georgia Southwestern State University, School of Education, Americus, GA 31709-4693. Offerings include early childhood education (M Ed, Ed S). Accredited by NCATE. *Entrance requirements:* For master's, GRE General Test (minimum score 400 on each section) or MAT (minimum score 44), minimum GPA of 2.5; for Ed S, GRE General Test (minimum score 450 on each section) or MAT (minimum score 48), minimum GPA of 3.25. Application deadline: 9/1 (rolling processing; 3/15 for spring admission). Application fee: $10. • Dr. Kurt Myers, Chair, 912-931-2145. Application contact: Chris Laney, Graduate Admissions Specialist, 912-931-2027. Fax: 912-931-2059. E-mail: claney@gsw1500.gsw.peachnet.edu.

Georgia State University, College of Education, Department of Early Childhood Education, Atlanta, GA 30303-3083. Awards M Ed, PhD, Ed S. Accredited by NCATE. Part-time and evening/weekend programs available. Faculty: 24 full-time (21 women), 24 part-time (23 women). Students: 86 full-time (78 women), 5 part-time (4 women); includes 18 minority (9 African Americans, 5 Asian Americans, 3 Hispanics, 1 Native American). Average age 29. 4 applicants, 75% accepted. In 1997, 52 master's, 3 Ed Ss awarded. *Degree requirements:* For master's, comprehensive exams; for doctorate, dissertation, comprehensive exams; for Ed S, project. *Entrance requirements:* For master's, GRE General Test (minimum combined score of 800) or MAT (minimum score 44), minimum GPA of 2.5; for doctorate, GRE General Test (minimum score 500 on verbal section, 500 on either quantitative or analytical sections) or MAT (minimum score 53), minimum GPA of 3.3; for Ed S, GRE General Test (minimum combined score of 900) or MAT (minimum score 48), minimum graduate GPA of 3.25. Application fee: $25. *Expenses:* Tuition $2673 per year full-time, $99 per semester hour part-time for state residents; $10,692 per year full-time, $396 per semester hour part-time for nonresidents. Fees $228 per year. *Financial aid:* In 1997–98, 28 research assistantships, 3 teaching assistantships were awarded; career-related internships or fieldwork also available. *Faculty research:* Teacher training program evaluation, pre-kindergarten program evaluation, literacy development, children's literature, alternative assessment strategies, children in poverty. Total annual research expenditures: $1.5 million. • Dr. Brenda M. Galina, Chair, 404-651-2584.

Grambling State University, College of Education, Program in Early Childhood Education, Grambling, LA 71245. Awards MS. Accredited by NCATE. Faculty: 2 part-time (both women). Students: 3 full-time (2 women), 8 part-time (all women); includes 11 minority (all African Americans). Average age 25. 2 applicants, 100% accepted. *Entrance requirements:* GRE, NTE. Application deadline: 8/1 (priority date; rolling processing; 1/2 for spring admission). Application fee: $15. *Tuition:* $1960 per year full-time, $297 per semester (minimum) part-time for state residents; $7110 per year full-time, $297 per semester (minimum) part-time for nonresidents. *Financial aid:* Research assistantships, full and partial tuition waivers, institutionally sponsored loans, and career-related internships or fieldwork available. Financial aid application deadline: 5/31; applicants required to submit FAFSA. *Faculty research:* Self-evaluation, field-based experience, curriculum revision, multiculturalism. • Dr. Mary Minter, Head, 318-274-3155. Fax: 318-274-3161.

Grand Valley State University, School of Education, Programs in General Education, Program in Early Childhood Education, Allendale, MI 49401-9403. Awards M Ed. Accredited by NCATE. *Degree requirements:* Thesis or alternative, applied research project. *Entrance requirements:* GRE General Test (minimum combined score of 1300) or minimum GPA of 3.0. Application deadline: rolling. Application fee: $20. • Application contact: Admissions Office, 616-895-2025. Fax: 616-895-3081.

Henderson State University, School of Education, Department of Special Education, Arkadelphia, AR 71999-0001. Offerings include early childhood/special education (MSE). Accredited by NCATE. Postbaccalaureate distance learning degree programs offered (minimal on-campus study). *Entrance requirements:* GRE General Test or MAT, minimum GPA of 2.7. Application deadline: 7/31 (priority date; rolling processing). Application fee: $0. Electronic applications accepted. *Expenses:* Tuition $120 per credit hour for state residents; $240 per credit hour for nonresidents. Fees $105 per semester (minimum) full-time, $52 per semester (minimum) part-time. • Kenneth Harris, Chairperson, 870-230-5203. Fax: 870-230-5455. E-mail: harris@holly.hsu.edu.

Heritage College, Graduate Program in Education, Program in Professional Development, Toppenish, WA 98948-9599. Offerings include early childhood education (M Ed). *Degree requirements:* Comprehensive exam required, thesis optional, foreign language not required. *Application deadline:* rolling. *Application fee:* $35 ($75 for international students). *Tuition:* $270 per credit. • Application contact: Dr. Robert Plumb, Chair, 509-865-2244.

Hofstra University, School of Education and Allied Human Services, Department of Curriculum and Teaching, Programs in Elementary and Early Childhood Education, Hempstead, NY 11549. Offerings in art education (MA, MS Ed), early childhood education (MA), elementary education (MA, MS Ed), music education (MA, MS Ed). Accredited by NCATE. Part-time and evening/weekend programs available. Faculty: 10 full-time (all women), 52 part-time (37 women). Students: 70 full-time (57 women), 200 part-time (176 women); includes 9 minority (6 African Americans, 1 Asian American, 2 Hispanics). Average age 29. 278 applicants, 65% accepted. In 1997, 113 degrees awarded. *Degree requirements:* Thesis (for some programs), comprehensive exam, departmental qualifying exam required, foreign language not required. *Entrance requirements:* Minimum GPA of 2.5. Application deadline: rolling. Application fee: $40 ($75 for international students). *Expenses:* Tuition $10,968 per year full-time, $457 per credit hour part-time. Fees $670 per year full-time, $112 per semester (minimum) part-time. *Financial aid:* In 1997–98, 33 students received aid, including scholarships, grants, graduate assistantships totaling $27,132; research assistantships, teaching assistantships, and career-related internships or fieldwork also available. Financial aid application deadline: 9/1. *Faculty research:* Gender equity, social studies education, teacher education, play, culturally relevant pedagogy, integrated dynamic themes. • Application contact: Mary Beth Carey, Dean of Admissions, 516-463-6700. Fax: 516-560-7660. E-mail: hofstra@hofstra.edu.

Hood College, Department of Education, Frederick, MD 21701-8575. Offerings include curriculum and instruction (MS), with options in early childhood education, elementary education, elementary school science and mathematics, reading, secondary education, special education. *Entrance requirements:* Minimum GPA of 2.5. Application deadline: rolling. Application fee: $30. *Tuition:* $285 per credit. • Dr. Patricia Bartlett, Chairperson, 301-696-3471. E-mail: bartlett@nimue.hood.edu. Application contact: Hood College Graduate School, 301-696-3600. Fax: 301-696-3597. E-mail: postmaster@nimue.hood.edu.

Howard University, School of Education, Department of Curriculum and Instruction, Program in Early Childhood Education, 2400 Sixth Street, NW, Washington, DC 20059-0002. Awards MA, MAT, M Ed, CAGS. Accredited by NCATE. MA offered through the Graduate School of Arts and Sciences. Faculty: 1 (woman) full-time. Students: 13. In 1997, 8 master's awarded. *Degree requirements:* For master's, thesis (for some programs), comprehensive exam, expository writing exam, internships, practicum required, foreign language not required; for CAGS, thesis optional, foreign language not required. *Entrance requirements:* For master's, GRE General Test, minimum GPA of 2.7; for CAGS, GRE General Test, minimum graduate GPA of 3.0. Application deadline: 4/1 (priority date; rolling processing; 11/1 for spring admission). Application fee: $45. *Expenses:* Tuition $10,200 per year full-time, $567 per credit hour part-time. Fees $405 per year. *Financial aid:* Fellowships, research assistantships, teaching assistantships, grants, scholarships, full and partial tuition waivers, Federal Work-Study, institutionally sponsored loans, and career-related internships or fieldwork available. Financial aid application deadline: 4/1. • Dr. Rosa Trapp-Dail, Coordinator, 202-806-7343.

Hunter College of the City University of New York, Division of Education, Department of Curriculum and Teaching, 695 Park Avenue, New York, NY 10021-5085. Offerings include early childhood education (MS Ed). *Application deadline:* /1 (rolling processing). *Application fee:* $40. *Expenses:* Tuition $4350 per year full-time, $185 per credit part-time for state residents; $7600 per year full-time, $320 per credit part-time for nonresidents. Fees $26 per year.

Idaho State University, College of Education, Division I, Pocatello, ID 83209. Offerings include human exceptionality–early childhood education (M Ed). Accredited by NCATE. Postbaccalaureate distance learning degree programs offered (no on-campus study). Division faculty: 19 full-time (8 women), 4 part-time (0 women). *Degree requirements:* Oral exam, written exam required, thesis optional, foreign language not required. *Average time to degree:* master's–2 years full-time, 4 years part-time; other advanced degree–1 year full-time, 2 years part-time. *Entrance requirements:* GRE General Test (score in 35th percentile or higher on one section) or MAT (minimum score 48), minimum undergraduate GPA of 3.0. Application deadline: 7/1 (priority date; rolling processing; 12/1 for spring admission). Application fee: $30. *Tuition:* $3130 per year full-time, $136 per credit hour part-time for state residents; $9370 per year full-time, $226 per credit hour part-time for nonresidents. • Dr. Peter Denner, Director, 208-236-4230. E-mail: dennpete@isu.edu. Application contact: Dr. Stephanie Salzman, Director, Office of Standards and Assessment, 208-236-3114. Fax: 208-236-4697. E-mail: salzstep@isu.edu.

Indiana State University, School of Education, Department of Elementary and Early Childhood Education, Terre Haute, IN 47809-1401. Offers programs in early childhood education (M Ed, PhD, Ed S), elementary education (M Ed, PhD, Ed S), reading education (M Ed, PhD, Ed S). Accredited by NCATE. Faculty: 13 full-time (10 women). Students: 5 full-time (4 women), 54 part-time (50 women); includes 2 minority (both African Americans), 1 international. Average age 35. 19 applicants, 53% accepted. In 1997, 22 master's, 2 doctorates awarded. *Degree requirements:* For doctorate, 2 foreign languages, computer language, dissertation. *Entrance requirements:* For master's, minimum undergraduate GPA of 2.5; for doctorate, GRE General Test (minimum score 500 on each section), minimum undergraduate GPA of 3.5; for Ed S, GRE General Test (minimum combined score of 900), minimum graduate GPA of 3.25. Application deadline: rolling. Application fee: $20. *Tuition:* $143 per credit hour for state

Directory: Early Childhood Education

Indiana State University (continued)
residents; $325 per credit hour for nonresidents. *Financial aid:* In 1997–98, 3 fellowships (1 to a first-year student), 3 research assistantships (1 to a first-year student), 2 teaching assistantships (both to first-year students) were awarded. Financial aid application deadline: 3/1. • Dr. Sandra DeCosta, Chairperson, 812-237-2852.

Indiana University Bloomington, School of Education, Department of Curriculum and Instruction, Program in Early Childhood Education, Bloomington, IN 47405. Awards MS, Ed S. Accredited by NCATE. *Degree requirements:* For master's, internship or thesis required, foreign language not required; for Ed S, comprehensive exam or project required, foreign language and thesis not required. *Entrance requirements:* For master's, GRE General Test (minimum combined score of 1300 on three sections); for Ed S, GRE General Test (minimum combined score of 1500 on three sections). Application deadline: 3/1 (priority date; rolling processing). Application fee: $35. *Expenses:* Tuition $153 per credit hour for state residents; $446 per credit hour for nonresidents. Fees $343 per year. *Financial aid:* Fellowships, research assistantships, teaching assistantships, partial tuition waivers, Federal Work-Study, institutionally sponsored loans, and career-related internships or fieldwork available. *Faculty research:* Social comparison, staff development, school effectiveness, career ladders, whole language learning. • Dr. Judith Chafel, Coordinator, 812-856-8105. Application contact: Cary Buzzelli, 812-856-8105.

Indiana University of Pennsylvania, College of Education, Department of Professional Studies in Education, Program in Early Childhood Education, Indiana, PA 15705-1087. Awards M Ed. Accredited by NCATE. Students: 18 part-time (all women). Average age 29. 4 applicants, 75% accepted. In 1997, 2 degrees awarded. *Degree requirements:* Thesis optional, foreign language not required. *Entrance requirements:* TOEFL (minimum score 500). Application deadline: 7/1 (priority date; rolling processing; 11/1 for spring admission). Application fee: $30. *Expenses:* Tuition $3468 per year full-time, $193 per credit part-time for state residents; $6236 per year full-time, $346 per credit part-time for nonresidents. Fees $313 per year (minimum) full-time, $84 per year part-time. *Financial aid:* Research assistantships, Federal Work-Study, and career-related internships or fieldwork available. Financial aid application deadline: 3/15. • Dr. Mary R. Jalongo, Graduate Coordinator, 724-357-2417. E-mail: mjalongo@grove.iup.edu.

Jackson State University, School of Education, Department of Curriculum and Instruction, Jackson, MS 39217. Offers programs in early childhood education (MS Ed, Ed D), elementary education (MS Ed, Ed S). Accredited by NCATE. Evening/weekend programs available. Faculty: 10 full-time (7 women), 1 (woman) part-time. Students: 17 full-time (15 women), 51 part-time (45 women); includes 57 minority (56 African Americans, 1 Native American). 39 applicants, 77% accepted. In 1997, 20 master's, 1 Ed S awarded. Terminal master's awarded for partial completion of doctoral program. *Degree requirements:* For master's, thesis or alternative, comprehensive exam; for doctorate, dissertation, comprehensive exam. *Entrance requirements:* For master's, GRE General Test (minimum combined score of 1000), TOEFL (minimum score 550); for doctorate, MAT (minimum score 45), teaching experience. Application deadline: 3/1 (priority date; rolling processing; 10/1 for spring admission). Application fee: $20. *Tuition:* $2688 per year (minimum) full-time, $150 per semester hour part-time for state residents; $5546 per year (minimum) full-time, $309 per semester hour part-time for nonresidents. *Financial aid:* Federal Work-Study available. Financial aid application deadline: 3/1. • Dr. Anita Hall, Chair, 601-968-2336. Fax: 601-968-2178. Application contact: Mae Robinson, Admissions Coordinator, 601-968-2455. Fax: 601-968-8246. E-mail: mrobinson@ccaix.jsums.edu.

Jacksonville State University, College of Education, Program in Early Childhood Education, Jacksonville, AL 36265-9982. Awards MS Ed. Accredited by NCATE. Faculty: 2 full-time (both women). Students: 3 full-time (all women), 27 part-time (25 women); includes 3 minority (all African Americans). In 1997, 24 degrees awarded. *Degree requirements:* Thesis optional. *Entrance requirements:* GRE General Test or MAT. Application deadline: rolling. Application fee: $20. *Expenses:* Tuition $2140 per year full-time, $107 per semester hour part-time for state residents; $4280 per year full-time, $214 per semester hour part-time for nonresidents. Fees $30 per semester. *Financial aid:* Available to part-time students. Financial aid application deadline: 4/1. • Application contact: College of Graduate Studies and Continuing Education, 205-782-5329.

Jacksonville University, College of Arts and Sciences, Division of Education, 2800 University Boulevard North, Jacksonville, FL 32211-3394. Offerings include early childhood education (Certificate). *Average time to degree:* master's–1.5 years full-time, 2.5 years part-time. *Entrance requirements:* TOEFL (minimum score 500). Application deadline: 8/1 (priority date; rolling processing; 11/1 for spring admission). Application fee: $25.

James Madison University, College of Education and Psychology, School of Education, Program in Early Childhood Education, Harrisonburg, VA 22807. Awards M Ed. Accredited by NCATE. Program being phased out; applicants no longer accepted. Part-time programs available. Students: 1 (woman) full-time, 3 part-time (all women). Average age 30. In 1997, 8 degrees awarded. *Tuition:* $134 per credit hour for state residents; $404 per credit hour for nonresidents. *Financial aid:* Fellowships, teaching assistantships, assistantships, and career-related internships or fieldwork available. Financial aid applicants required to submit FAFSA. • Dr. Diane Fuqua, Coordinator, 540-568-6292.

Johns Hopkins University, School of Continuing Studies, Division of Education, Department of Teacher Development and Leadership, Baltimore, MD 21218-2699. Offerings include early childhood education (MAT). *Application fee:* $50. • Rochelle Ingram, Chair, 410-516-4957.

Johnson State College, Graduate Program in Education, Program in Early Childhood Education, Johnson, VT 05656-9405. Awards MA Ed. Part-time programs available. Students: 1 (woman) full-time, 4 part-time (all women). *Degree requirements:* Thesis or alternative, comprehensive exam required, foreign language not required. *Entrance requirements:* Interview. Application deadline: 7/15 (priority date; rolling processing; 11/1 for spring admission). Application fee: $30. *Expenses:* Tuition $164 per credit for state residents; $383 per credit for nonresidents. Fees $15.90 per credit. *Financial aid:* Federal Work-Study, institutionally sponsored loans, and career-related internships or fieldwork available. Aid available to part-time students. Financial aid application deadline: 3/1; applicants required to submit FAFSA. • Application contact: Catherine H. Higley, Administrative Assistant, 802-635-2356 Ext. 1244. Fax: 802-635-1248. E-mail: higleyc@badger.jsc.vsc.edu.

Kean University, School of Education, Department of Early Childhood Education, Union, NJ 07083. Offers programs in administration in early childhood and family studies (MA), advanced curriculum and teaching (MA), education for family living (MA). Accredited by NCATE. Part-time programs available. Students: 6 full-time (all women), 43 part-time (42 women); includes 7 minority (5 African Americans, 2 Hispanics). Average age 32. In 1997, 21 degrees awarded. *Degree requirements:* Thesis, comprehensive exams required, foreign language not required. *Entrance requirements:* GRE General Test or MAT. Application deadline: 6/15 (11/15 for spring admission). Application fee: $35. *Tuition:* $5926 per year full-time, $248 per credit part-time for state residents; $7312 per year full-time, $304 per credit part-time for nonresidents. *Financial aid:* Graduate assistantships available. • Dr. Polly Ashelman, Coordinator, 908-527-2561. Application contact: Joanne Morris, Director of Graduate Admissions, 908-527-2665. Fax: 908-527-2286. E-mail: grad_adm@turbo.kean.edu.

Kennesaw State University, Leland and Clarice C. Bagwell College of Education, Program in Elementary Education, Kennesaw, GA 30144-5591. Offerings include early childhood (M Ed). Accredited by NCATE. Program faculty: 38 full-time (24 women), 2 part-time (both women). *Degree requirements:* Thesis or alternative required, foreign language not required. *Entrance requirements:* GRE General Test (minimum combined score of 800), T-4 state certification, minimum GPA of 2.5. Application deadline: 7/1 (2/20 for spring admission). Application fee: $20. *Expenses:* Tuition $2398 per year full-time, $83 per credit hour part-time for state residents; $8398 per year full-time, $333 per credit hour part-time for nonresidents. Fees $338 per year. • Dr. David Martin, Director, 770-423-6117. Fax: 770-423-6527. E-mail: dmartin1@ksumail.kennesaw.edu. Application contact: Susan N. Barrett, Administrative Specialist, Admissions, 770-423-6500. Fax: 770-423-6541. E-mail: sbarrett@ksumail.kennesaw.edu.

Kent State University, Graduate School of Education, Department of Teaching, Leadership, and Curriculum Studies, Program in Early Childhood Education, Kent, OH 44242-0001. Awards MA, M Ed. Accredited by NCATE. Faculty: 6 full-time (5 women), 4 part-time (all women). Students: 9 full-time (all women), 55 part-time (54 women); includes 5 minority (all African Americans). In 1997, 27 degrees awarded. *Degree requirements:* Thesis (MA) required, foreign language not required. *Entrance requirements:* GRE General Test. Application deadline: rolling. Application fee: $30. *Tuition:* $4752 per year full-time, $216 per credit hour part-time for state residents; $9213 per year full-time, $419 per credit hour part-time for nonresidents. *Financial aid:* Application deadline 4/1. • Carol Bersani, Coordinator, 330-672-2559. Application contact: Deborah Barber, Director, Office of Academic Services, 330-672-2862. Fax: 330-672-3549.

LaGrange College, Department of Education, LaGrange, GA 30240-2999. Offerings include early childhood education (M Ed). Department faculty: 1 (woman) full-time, 6 part-time (4 women). *Degree requirements:* Comprehensive exam required, thesis not required. *Entrance requirements:* GRE, MAT, or NTE, minimum GPA of 2.5. Application deadline: 8/1 (priority date; rolling processing). Application fee: $20 ($25 for international students). *Expenses:* Tuition $219 per quarter hour. Fees $80 per quarter hour. • Dr. Evelyn Jordan, Chair, 706-812-7276. Application contact: Andy Geeter, Director of Admissions, 706-812-7260. Fax: 706-812-7348. E-mail: ageeter@mentor.lgc.peachnet.edu.

Lehman College of the City University of New York, Division of Education, Department of Early Childhood and Elementary Education, Program in Early Childhood Education, 250 Bedford Park Boulevard West, Bronx, NY 10468-1589. Awards MS Ed. Students: 8 full-time (7 women), 323 part-time (271 women). *Entrance requirements:* Minimum GPA of 2.7. Application deadline: 4/1 (rolling processing; 11/1 for spring admission). Application fee: $40. *Expenses:* Tuition $4350 per year full-time, $185 per credit part-time for state residents; $7600 per year full-time, $320 per credit part-time for nonresidents. Fees $120 per year full-time, $80 per year part-time. *Financial aid:* Full and partial tuition waivers, Federal Work-Study available. Aid available to part-time students. Financial aid application deadline: 5/15; applicants required to submit FAFSA. • Application contact: Abigail McNamee, Adviser, 718-960-7873.

Lenoir–Rhyne College, Division of Graduate Programs, Department of Education, Program in Early Childhood Education, Hickory, NC 28601. Awards MA. Part-time and evening/weekend programs available. Students: 1 (woman) full-time, 16 part-time (all women). In 1997, 6 degrees awarded (100% found work related to degree). *Degree requirements:* Thesis optional, foreign language not required. *Entrance requirements:* GRE General Test (minimum score 450 on verbal section, 1350 combined), minimum GPA of 2.7. Application deadline: 8/1 (12/1 for spring admission). Application fee: $25. *Tuition:* $190 per credit hour. *Financial aid:* Career-related internships or fieldwork available. • Dr. Gail Summer, Head, 828-328-7243. Application contact: Dr. Thomas W. Fauquet, Dean of Graduate Studies, 828-328-7275. Fax: 828-328-7368. E-mail: fauquet@lrc.edu.

Lesley College, School of Education, Cambridge, MA 02138-2790. Offerings include early childhood education (M Ed). Postbaccalaureate distance learning degree programs offered (no on-campus study). School faculty: 36 full-time (31 women), 340 part-time (220 women). *Degree requirements:* Computer language required, foreign language and thesis not required. *Entrance requirements:* TOEFL (minimum score 550). Application deadline: rolling. Application fee: $45. *Tuition:* $425 per credit. • Dr. William L. Dandridge, Dean, 617-349-8375. Application contact: Graduate Admissions, 617-349-8300. Fax: 617-349-8366.

Loyola University Chicago, School of Education, Erikson Institute, 820 North Michigan Avenue, Chicago, IL 60611-2196. Offers program in early childhood education (M Ed, PhD). PhD offered through the Graduate School. Faculty: 8 full-time (7 women), 7 part-time (all women), 11 FTE. Students: 128 full-time (123 women), 13 part-time (all women); includes 41 minority (28 African Americans, 4 Asian Americans, 9 Hispanics), 3 international. Average age 33. 89 applicants, 69% accepted. In 1997, 22 master's awarded (100% found work related to degree); 3 doctorates awarded. *Degree requirements:* For master's, comprehensive exam required, foreign language and thesis not required; for doctorate, 1 foreign language (computer language can substitute), dissertation, comprehensive exam. *Average time to degree:* master's–3 years part-time; doctorate–6 years full-time. *Entrance requirements:* For doctorate, GRE General Test, interview. Application deadline: 4/1 (priority date; rolling processing). Application fee: $30. *Tuition:* $467 per semester hour. *Financial aid:* In 1997–98, 47 students received aid, including 3 project assistantships; partial tuition waivers, Federal Work-Study, institutionally sponsored loans, and career-related internships or fieldwork also available. Aid available to part-time students. Financial aid application deadline: 3/1; applicants required to submit FAFSA. *Faculty research:* Early childhood development, development of cognitives, academic skills in sociocultural context. • Barbara T. Bowman, President, 773-755-2250. E-mail: bbowman@luc.edu. Application contact: Bernard A. Lalor, Registrar, 773-755-2290. Fax: 773-755-2255. E-mail: blalor@luc.edu.

Loyola University Chicago, School of Education, Department of Curriculum, Instruction and Educational Psychology, Program in Early Childhood Development, 820 North Michigan Avenue, Chicago, IL 60611-2196. Awards Ed D. Students: 78. *Degree requirements:* Computer language, dissertation, comprehensive exam required, foreign language not required. *Entrance requirements:* GRE or MAT, interview. Application fee: $35. *Tuition:* $467 per semester hour. *Financial aid:* Application deadline 5/1. • Janet Pierce-Ritter, Assistant Dean, 847-853-3336. Application contact: Marie Rosin-Dittmar, Admissions Coordinator, 847-853-3323. Fax: 847-853-3375. E-mail: mrosind@wpo.it.luc.edu.

Lynchburg College, School of Education and Human Development, Program in Early Childhood Education, Lynchburg, VA 24501-3199. Offerings include curriculum and instruction: early childhood education (M Ed). *Entrance requirements:* Minimum GPA of 3.0 (undergraduate). Application fee: $20.

Malone College, Graduate School, Program in Education, Canton, OH 44709-3897. Offerings include early childhood education (MA). Program faculty: 10 full-time (6 women), 11 part-time (5 women), 12.68 FTE. *Degree requirements:* Research practicum required, foreign language and thesis not required. *Entrance requirements:* Minimum GPA of 3.0, teaching license. Application deadline: 9/6 (rolling processing; 1/2 for spring admission). Application fee: $20. *Tuition:* $300 per credit hour. • Dr. Marietta Daulton, Director, 330-471-8447. Fax: 330-471-8478. E-mail: mdaulton@malone.edu. Application contact: Dan Depasquale, Director of Graduate Student Services, 800-257-4723. Fax: 330-471-8343. E-mail: depasquale@malone.edu.

Mankato State University, College of Education, Department of Curriculum and Instruction, Program in Early Childhood Education, South Rd and Ellis Ave, PO Box 8400, Mankato, MN 56002-8400. Awards MS. Accredited by NCATE. Part-time programs available. Students: 1 (woman) full-time, 2 part-time (both women). Average age 32. 0 applicants. In 1997, 4 degrees awarded. *Degree requirements:* Thesis or alternative, comprehensive exam required, foreign language not required. *Entrance requirements:* GRE General Test or MAT, minimum GPA of 3.0 during previous 2 years. Application deadline: 7/10 (priority date; rolling processing; 10/30 for spring admission). Application fee: $20. *Tuition:* $126 per credit (minimum) for state residents; $200 per credit for nonresidents. *Financial aid:* Application deadline 3/15; applicants required to submit FAFSA. • Dr. Howard Schroeder, Coordinator, 507-389-5713. Application contact: Joni Roberts, Admissions Coordinator, 507-389-2321. Fax: 507-389-5974. E-mail: grad@mankato.msus.edu.

Marshall University, College of Education, Division of Teacher Education, Program in Early Childhood Education, Huntington, WV 25755-2020. Awards MA. Accredited by NCATE. Evening/weekend programs available. Faculty: 2 (both women). Students: 7 full-time (6 women), 18 part-time (all women); includes 2 minority (both African Americans). In 1997, 5 degrees awarded. *Degree requirements:* Thesis optional. *Entrance requirements:* GRE General Test (minimum combined score of 1200). *Tuition:* $2364 per year full-time, $132 per hour part-time for state residents; $6894 per year full-time, $383 per hour part-time for nonresidents. • Dr. Boots Dilley, Coordinator, 304-696-3101. Application contact: Dr. James Harless, Director of Admissions, 304-696-3160.

Marycrest International University, Division of Education, Davenport, IA 52804-4096. Offerings include early childhood education (MA, MS). Division faculty: 4 full-time (all women), 3 part-time (0 women), 4.8 FTE. *Average time to degree:* master's–2.5 years part-time. *Application deadline:* 4/15 (priority date; rolling processing; 12/1 for spring admission). *Application fee:* $25. *Expenses:* Tuition of $198 per credit hour for students holding a valid teaching certificate (for MA in education and reading specialist only); $413 per credit hour for other degree programs. • Dr. Michelle Schiffgens, Chair, 319-326-9241. Fax: 319-326-9250.

Marygrove College, Division of Education, Program in Early Childhood Education, Detroit, MI 48221-2599. Awards M Ed. Accredited by NCATE. Part-time and evening/weekend programs available. *Degree requirements:* Internship, research project required, foreign language and thesis not required. *Average time to degree:* master's–2 years full-time, 3 years part-time. *Entrance requirements:* MAT, elementary teaching certificate, interview, minimum undergraduate GPA of 3.0. Application deadline: 8/15 (rolling processing). Application fee: $25.

Maryville University of Saint Louis, School of Education, St. Louis, MO 63141-7299. Offerings include early childhood education (MA). Accredited by NCATE. School faculty: 9 full-time (7 women), 15 part-time (9 women). *Degree requirements:* Thesis, project required, foreign language not required. *Average time to degree:* master's–2 years full-time, 4 years part-time. *Entrance requirements:* Minimum GPA of 3.0. Application deadline: rolling. Application fee: $20. Electronic applications accepted. *Expenses:* Tuition $11,480 per year full-time, $345 per credit hour part-time. Fees $120 per year full-time, $60 per year part-time. • Dr. Kathe Rasch, Dean, 314-529-9466. Fax: 314-529-9921. E-mail: krasch@maryville.edu.

Marywood University, Graduate School of Arts and Sciences, Department of Education, Program in Early Childhood Education, Scranton, PA 18509-1598. Awards MS. Accredited by NCATE. Part-time and evening/weekend programs available. Students: 1 (woman) full-time, 5 part-time (all women). Average age 35. 1 applicant, 0% accepted. In 1997, 4 degrees awarded. *Degree requirements:* Thesis or alternative, comprehensive exam required, foreign language not required. *Entrance requirements:* GRE or MAT, TOEFL (minimum score 550; average 590). Application deadline: 7/15 (priority date; rolling processing; 12/1 for spring admission). Application fee: $20. *Expenses:* Tuition $449 per credit hour. Fees $530 per year full-time, $180 per year part-time. *Financial aid:* Research assistantships, scholarships/tuition reductions, partial tuition waivers, and career-related internships or fieldwork available. Aid available to part-time students. Financial aid application deadline: 2/15; applicants required to submit FAFSA. *Faculty research:* Montessori education, developmentally appropriate practice, child care environment. • Dr. Fintan Kavanaugh, Head, 717-348-6211 Ext. 2321. Application contact: Deborah M. Flynn, Coordinator of Admissions, 717-340-6002. Fax: 717-961-4745.

McNeese State University, College of Education, Department of Curriculum and Instruction, Program in Early Childhood Education, Lake Charles, LA 70609-2495. Awards M Ed. Evening/weekend programs available. Faculty: 8 full-time (3 women). Students: 2 full-time (both women), 13 part-time (all women). In 1997, 7 degrees awarded. *Entrance requirements:* GRE General Test, teaching certificate, 24 hours in professional education. Application deadline: 7/15 (priority date; rolling processing). Application fee: $10 ($25 for international students). *Tuition:* $2118 per year full-time, $344 per semester (minimum) part-time for state residents; $7308 per year full-time, $344 per semester (minimum) part-time for nonresidents. *Financial aid:* Application deadline 5/1. • Dr. Everett Waddell Burge, Head, Department of Curriculum and Instruction, 318-475-5404.

Mercer University, School of Education, 1400 Coleman Avenue, Macon, GA 31207-0003. Offerings include early childhood education (M Ed, Ed S). School faculty: 11 full-time (5 women), 17 part-time (11 women). *Degree requirements:* Research project report required, foreign language and thesis not required. *Entrance requirements:* For master's, GRE, MAT, NTE, minimum GPA of 2.75; for Ed S, GRE, MAT, NTE, minimum GPA of 3.25, 3 years of teaching experience. Application deadline: 8/1 (priority date; rolling processing; 12/1 for spring admission). Application fee: $25. *Tuition:* $180 per credit hour. • Dr. Anne Hathaway, Dean, 912-752-5397. Fax: 912-752-2280. E-mail: hathaway_ha@mercer.edu. Application contact: Dr. Louis Gallien, Chair, Department of Teacher Education, 912-752-2585. Fax: 912-752-2576. E-mail: gallien_lb@mercer.edu.

Mercer University, Cecil B. Day Campus, Graduate Education Programs, 3001 Mercer University Drive, Atlanta, GA 30341-4155. Offerings include early childhood education (M Ed, Ed S). Faculty: 8 full-time (4 women), 33 part-time (17 women). *Degree requirements:* Research project required, foreign language and thesis not required. *Entrance requirements:* For master's, GRE, MAT, or NTE, minimum undergraduate GPA of 2.75; for Ed S, GRE, MAT, or NTE, minimum GPA of 3.25, 3 years of teaching experience. Application deadline: 8/1 (priority date; rolling processing; 12/1 for spring admission). Application fee: $25. *Tuition:* $220 per semester hour. • Dr. Anne Hathaway, Dean, 912-752-5397. Fax: 912-752-2280. E-mail: hathaway_ha@mercer.edu. Application contact: Dr. Allison Gilmore, Associate Dean and Director of Graduate Education, 770-986-3330. Fax: 770-986-3292. E-mail: gilmore_a@mercer.edu.

Middle Tennessee State University, College of Education, Department of Elementary and Special Education, Major in Curriculum and Instruction, Murfreesboro, TN 37132. Offerings include early childhood education (M Ed). Accredited by NCATE. *Degree requirements:* Comprehensive exams required, foreign language and thesis not required. *Entrance requirements:* Cooperative English Test, GRE, MAT (minimum score 25). Application deadline: 8/1 (priority date). Application fee: $5. *Expenses:* Tuition $2560 per year full-time, $129 per semester hour part-time for state residents; $7386 per year full-time, $340 per semester hour part-time for nonresidents. Fees $486 per year full-time, $17 per semester (minimum) part-time. • Dr. Charles Babb, Chair, Department of Elementary and Special Education, 615-898-2680. Fax: 615-898-5309. E-mail: cwbabb@mtsu.edu.

Mills College, Education Department, Oakland, CA 94613-1000. Offerings include early childhood education (MA). Department faculty: 8 full-time (6 women), 13 part-time (11 women), 11 FTE. *Degree requirements:* Comprehensive exam required, thesis not required. *Average time to degree:* master's–2 years full-time. *Entrance requirements:* TOEFL (minimum score 550). Application deadline: 2/1 (priority date; rolling processing; 11/1 for spring admission). Application fee: $50. Electronic applications accepted. *Expenses:* Tuition $10,600 per year full-time, $2560 per year part-time. Fees $468 per year. • Jane Bowyer, Chairperson, 510-430-2118. Fax: 510-430-3314. E-mail: grad-studies@mills.edu. Application contact: La Vonna S. Brown, Coordinator of Graduate Studies, 510-430-3309. Fax: 510-430-2159. E-mail: grad-studies@mills.edu.

Montana State University–Billings, College of Education and Human Services, Department of Special Education and Reading, Option in Early Childhood Education, Billings, MT 59101-9984. Awards M Ed. Accredited by NCATE. Part-time programs available. *Degree requirements:* Thesis or professional paper and/or field experience required, foreign language not required. *Entrance requirements:* GRE General Test (minimum combined score of 1350 on three sections) or MAT (minimum score 38), minimum GPA of 3.0 (undergraduate), 3.25 (graduate). Application deadline: 8/1 (priority date; rolling processing; 1/1 for spring admission). Application fee: $30. *Expenses:* Tuition $2253 per year full-time, $397 per semester (minimum) part-time for state residents; $5313 per year full-time, $907 per semester (minimum) part-time for nonresidents. Fees $378 per year full-time, $105 per semester (minimum) part-time. *Faculty research:* Bilingual education.

Mount Vernon College, Graduate School, Washington, DC 20007. Offerings include early childhood program administration (MA). *Average time to degree:* master's–1.5 years full-time, 3 years part-time. *Application deadline:* rolling. *Application fee:* $35.

Murray State University, College of Education, Interdisciplinary Program in Early Childhood Education, Murray, KY 42071-0009. Awards MS. Accredited by NCATE. Students: 3 full-time (all women), 21 part-time (all women); includes 3 African Americans. 10 applicants, 100% accepted. *Entrance requirements:* TOEFL (minimum score 500). Application deadline: rolling. Application fee: $20. *Expenses:* Tuition $2500 per year full-time, $124 per hour part-time for state residents; $6740 per year full-time, $357 per hour part-time for nonresidents. Fees $360 per year full-time, $180 per year part-time. *Financial aid:* Application deadline 4/1. • Dr. Allan Beane, Director, 502-762-6819. Fax: 502-762-6803.

National–Louis University, National College of Education, McGaw Graduate School, Program in Early Childhood Administration, 2840 Sheridan Road, Evanston, IL 60201-1730. Awards M Ed, CAS. Program new for fall 1998. *Entrance requirements:* For master's, GRE or MAT, minimum GPA of 3.0. Application fee: $25. *Tuition:* $411 per semester hour. • Dr. Paula Jorde-Bloom, Coordinator, 847-475-1100 Ext. 5551. Application contact: Dr. David McCulloch, Vice President for University Services, 800-443-5522 Ext. 5127. Fax: 847-465-0593. E-mail: dmcc@wheeling1.nl.edu.

National–Louis University, National College of Education, McGaw Graduate School, Program in Early Childhood Education, 2840 Sheridan Road, Evanston, IL 60201-1730. Offers early childhood curriculum and instruction specialist (M Ed, MS Ed, CAS), early childhood education (MAT, CAS). Part-time and evening/weekend programs available. Students: 9 full-time (all women), 99 part-time (96 women); includes 16 minority (11 African Americans, 3 Asian Americans, 1 Hispanic, 1 Native American). Average age 36. In 1997, 23 master's awarded. *Degree requirements:* For master's, thesis required (for some programs), foreign language not required. *Entrance requirements:* For master's, GRE or MAT, minimum GPA of 3.0; for CAS, GRE or MAT. Application deadline: rolling. Application fee: $25. *Tuition:* $411 per semester hour. *Financial aid:* Fellowships available. Aid available to part-time students. Financial aid applicants required to submit FAFSA. *Faculty research:* Head Start training. Total annual research expenditures: $719,067. • Dr. Betty Hutchinson, Coordinator, 847-475-1100 Ext. 2227. Application contact: Dr. David McCulloch, Vice President for University Services, 800-443-5522 Ext. 5127. Fax: 847-465-0593. E-mail: dmcc@wheeling1.nl.edu.

National–Louis University, National College of Education, McGaw Graduate School, Program in Early Childhood Leadership and Advocacy, 2840 Sheridan Road, Evanston, IL 60201-1730. Awards M Ed. Students: 25 full-time (all women), 3 part-time (all women); includes 2 minority (both African Americans). In 1997, 62 degrees awarded. *Entrance requirements:* GRE or MAT, minimum GPA of 3.0. Application fee: $25. *Tuition:* $411 per semester hour. *Financial aid:* Fellowships, Federal Work-Study, institutionally sponsored loans available. Aid available to part-time students. Financial aid applicants required to submit FAFSA. • Dr. Marjorie Lee, Coordinator, 847-475-1100 Ext. 3523. Application contact: Dr. David McCulloch, Vice President for University Services, 800-443-5522 Ext. 5127. Fax: 847-465-0593. E-mail: dmcc@wheeling1.nl.edu.

Nazareth College of Rochester, Graduate Studies, Department of Education, Program in Early Childhood Education, Rochester, NY 14618-3790. Awards MS Ed. Part-time and evening/weekend programs available. Faculty: 1 (woman) full-time, 6 part-time (5 women). Students: 2 full-time (both women), 15 part-time (14 women); includes 1 minority (African American). 7 applicants, 86% accepted. In 1997, 7 degrees awarded. *Degree requirements:* Comprehensive exam required, foreign language and thesis not required. *Entrance requirements:* Minimum GPA of 2.7. Application deadline: 6/1 (rolling processing; 11/1 for spring admission). Application fee: $40. *Expenses:* Tuition $436 per credit hour. Fees $20 per semester. • Dr. Leigh O'Brien, Director, 716-389-2599. Application contact: Dr. Kay F. Marshman, Dean, 716-389-2815. Fax: 716-389-2452.

New Jersey City University, School of Professional Studies and Education, Program in Early Childhood Education, Jersey City, NJ 07305-1957. Awards MA. Evening/weekend programs available. *Entrance requirements:* GRE General Test or MAT, TOEFL. Application deadline: 8/1 (priority date; rolling processing; 12/1 for spring admission). Application fee: $0.

New Jersey City University, School of Professional Studies and Education, Programs in Urban Education, Jersey City, NJ 07305-1957. Offerings include administration, curriculum and instruction (MA), with options in early childhood education, urban education; early childhood education (MA). *Entrance requirements:* GRE General Test, TOEFL or MAT. Application deadline: 8/1 (priority date; rolling processing; 12/1 for spring admission). Application fee: $0.

New York University, School of Education, Department of Teaching and Learning, Program in Early Childhood and Elementary Education, New York, NY 10012-1019. Awards MA, Ed D, PhD, CAS. Part-time and evening/weekend programs available. Faculty: 9 full-time, 5 part-time. Students: 105 full-time, 95 part-time. 223 applicants, 61% accepted. In 1997, 92 master's, 1 doctorate, 3 CASs awarded. Terminal master's awarded for partial completion of doctoral program. *Degree requirements:* For master's, thesis required (for some programs), foreign language not required; for doctorate, dissertation. *Entrance requirements:* For master's, TOEFL; for doctorate, GRE General Test, TOEFL, interview; for CAS, TOEFL, master's degree. Application deadline: 2/1 (priority date; rolling processing; 12/1 for spring admission). Application fee: $40 ($60 for international students). *Financial aid:* Partial tuition waivers, Federal Work-Study, institutionally sponsored loans, and career-related internships or fieldwork available. Aid available to part-time students. Financial aid application deadline: 3/1; applicants required to submit FAFSA. *Faculty research:* Teacher evaluation and beliefs about teaching, early literacy development, language arts, child development and education. • Stephen Weiss, Director, 212-998-5460. Application contact: Office of Graduate Admissions, 212-998-5030. Fax: 212-995-4328.

Norfolk State University, School of Education, Department of Early Childhood and Elementary Education, 2401 Corprew Avenue, Norfolk, VA 23504-3907. Offers programs in early childhood education (MA), pre-elementary education (MA). Accredited by NCATE. Part-time programs available. Faculty: 7 full-time. Students: 13 full-time (11 women), 7 part-time (6 women); includes 17 minority (all African Americans), 3 international. In 1997, 5 degrees awarded. *Degree requirements:* Thesis or alternative required, foreign language not required. *Entrance requirements:* GRE General Test, minimum GPA of 2.5. Application deadline: 8/1. Application fee: $30. *Tuition:* $3718 per year full-time, $198 per credit hour part-time for state residents; $7668 per year full-time, $404 per credit hour part-time for nonresidents. *Financial aid:* Fellowships and career-related internships or fieldwork available. *Faculty research:* Parent involvement in education. • Dr. Barbara Graham, Head, 757-683-8702.

North Carolina Agricultural and Technical State University, Graduate School, School of Education, Department of Curriculum and Instruction, Greensboro, NC 27411. Offerings include early childhood education (MS). Accredited by NCATE. Department faculty: 20 full-time (11 women). *Degree requirements:* Comprehensive exam, qualifying exam required, foreign language not required. *Entrance requirements:* GRE General Test, minimum GPA of 3.0. Application deadline: 6/1 (priority date; rolling processing; 12/1 for spring admission). Application fee: $35. *Tuition:* $1662 per year full-time, $272 per semester (minimum) part-time for state residents; $8790 per year full-time, $2054 per semester (minimum) part-time for nonresidents. • Dr. Dorothy Leflore, Interim Chairperson, 336-334-7848.

Northeastern State University, College of Education, Department of Curriculum and Instruction, Program in Early Childhood Education, Tahlequah, OK 74464-2399. Awards M Ed. Students: 87 (86 women); includes 1 international. In 1997, 35 degrees awarded. *Degree requirements:* Thesis or alternative required, foreign language not required. *Entrance requirements:* GRE General Test (minimum combined score of 900) or MAT (minimum score 35), minimum GPA of 2.5. Application deadline: 6/1 (priority date; rolling processing). Application fee: $0. *Expenses:* Tuition $74 per credit hour for state residents; $176 per credit hour for nonresidents. Fees $30 per year. *Financial aid:* Teaching assistantships, Federal Work-Study available. Financial aid application deadline: 3/1. • Dr. Mary Johnson, Coordinator, 918-456-5511 Ext. 3392.

Northern Arizona University, Center for Excellence in Education, Program in Early Childhood Education, Flagstaff, AZ 86011. Awards M Ed. Part-time programs available. Students: 9

Directory: Early Childhood Education

Northern Arizona University (continued)
full-time (all women), 89 part-time (88 women); includes 12 minority (6 Hispanics, 6 Native Americans). Average age 22. 32 applicants, 81% accepted. In 1997, 28 degrees awarded. *Degree requirements:* Thesis or alternative required, foreign language not required. *Entrance requirements:* GRE Subject Test or minimum GPA of 3.0. Application deadline: 3/15 (priority date; rolling processing). Application fee: $45. *Expenses:* Tuition $2088 per year full-time, $330 per semester (minimum) part-time for state residents; $8004 per year full-time, $1002 per semester (minimum) part-time for nonresidents. Fees $72 per year full-time, $18 per semester (minimum) part-time. *Financial aid:* Research assistantships, teaching assistantships, full and partial tuition waivers, Federal Work-Study, and career-related internships or fieldwork available. *Faculty research:* Multi-age education, early literacy, mathematical concepts development, integration of the arts, developmentally appropriate practices. • Dr. Lynda Hatch, Interim Chair, 520-523-5342.

Northern Illinois University, College of Education, Department of Curriculum and Instruction, Program in Early Childhood Education, De Kalb, IL 60115-2854. Awards MS Ed. Accredited by NCATE. Part-time and evening/weekend programs available. Faculty: 2 full-time (both women). Students: 2 full-time (both women), 21 part-time (19 women); includes 2 minority (both African Americans). Average age 31. 14 applicants, 50% accepted. In 1997, 5 degrees awarded. *Degree requirements:* Comprehensive exam required, thesis optional, foreign language not required. *Entrance requirements:* GRE General Test or MAT, TOEFL (minimum score 550), minimum GPA of 2.75. Application deadline: 6/1 (rolling processing; 11/1 for spring admission). Application fee: $30. *Tuition:* $3984 per year full-time, $154 per credit hour part-time for state residents; $8160 per year full-time, $328 per credit hour part-time for nonresidents. *Financial aid:* Fellowships, research assistantships, teaching assistantships, staff assistantships, full tuition waivers, Federal Work-Study, and career-related internships or fieldwork available. Aid available to part-time students. • Dr. Norman Stahl, Chair, Department of Curriculum and Instruction, 815-753-9032.

North Georgia College & State University, Graduate School, Program in Education, Dahlonega, GA 30597-1001. Offerings include early childhood education (M Ed). Accredited by NCATE. Program faculty: 57 full-time (15 women), 7 part-time (4 women). *Degree requirements:* Comprehensive exam required, thesis optional, foreign language not required. *Entrance requirements:* GRE General Test (minimum combined score of 800) or MAT (minimum score 44), minimum GPA of 2.75. Application deadline: 9/1 (priority date; rolling processing). Application fee: $25. • Dr. Bob Michael, Dean, School of Education, 706-864-1533. Application contact: Mai-Lan Ledbetter, Coordinator of Graduate Admissions, 706-864-1543. Fax: 706-864-1668. E-mail: mledbetter@nugget.ngc.peachnet.edu.

Northwestern State University of Louisiana, Division of Education, Emphasis in Early Childhood Education, Natchitoches, LA 71497. Awards M Ed. Accredited by NCATE. Faculty: 2 full-time (both women). Students: 3 full-time (all women), 21 part-time (all women); includes 6 minority (5 African Americans, 1 Asian American). Average age 32. In 1997, 7 degrees awarded. *Entrance requirements:* GRE General Test (minimum combined score of 800), GRE Subject Test, minimum undergraduate GPA of 2.5. Application deadline: 8/1 (priority date; rolling processing; 1/10 for spring admission). Application fee: $15 ($25 for international students). *Tuition:* $2147 per year full-time, $336 per semester (minimum) part-time for state residents; $6437 per year full-time, $336 per semester (minimum) part-time for nonresidents. *Financial aid:* Application deadline 7/15. *Faculty research:* Early childhood program administration, cognitive development in early childhood. • Dr. Celia Decker, Head, 318-357-5067. Application contact: Dr. Tom Hanson, Dean, Graduate Studies and Research, 318-357-5851. Fax: 318-357-5019.

Northwest Missouri State University, College of Education and Human Services, Department of Curriculum and Instruction, Program in Early Childhood Education, 800 University Drive, Maryville, MO 64468-6001. Awards MS Ed. Accredited by NCATE. Part-time programs available. Faculty: 14 full-time (12 women). Students: 1 (woman) full-time, 16 part-time (all women). 3 applicants, 100% accepted. In 1997, 8 degrees awarded. *Degree requirements:* Comprehensive exam required, foreign language and thesis not required. *Entrance requirements:* GRE General Test (minimum combined score of 700), TOEFL (minimum score 550), teaching certificate, minimum undergraduate GPA of 2.5, writing sample. Application deadline: rolling. Application fee: $0 ($50 for international students). *Expenses:* Tuition $113 per credit hour for state residents; $197 per credit hour for nonresidents. Fees $3 per credit hour. *Financial aid:* In 1997–98, 3 teaching assistantships averaging $585 per month were awarded. Financial aid application deadline: 3/1. • Dr. Preeti Suppal, Director, 816-562-1236. Application contact: Dr. Frances Shipley, Dean of Graduate School, 816-562-1145. E-mail: gradsch@acad.nwmissouri.edu.

Nova Southeastern University, Fischler Center for the Advancement of Education, Graduate Teacher Education Program, Fort Lauderdale, FL 33314-7721. Offerings include prekindergarten/primary (Ed S), prekindergarten/primary (MS). *Degree requirements:* Thesis, practicum required, foreign language not required. *Entrance requirements:* For master's, teaching certificate; for Ed S, master's degree, teaching certificate. Application deadline: rolling. Application fee: $50. *Tuition:* $245 per credit hour (minimum). • Dr. Deo Nellis, Dean, 954-262-8601. E-mail: deo@fcae.nova.edu. Application contact: Dr. Mark Seldine, Director of Student Affairs, 954-262-8689. Fax: 954-262-3910. E-mail: seldines@fcae.nova.edu.

Nova Southeastern University, Fischler Center for the Advancement of Education, Program in Child and Youth Studies, Fort Lauderdale, FL 33314-7721. Awards Ed D. Part-time and evening/weekend programs available. Postbaccalaureate distance learning degree programs offered. Students: 34 full-time (27 women), 362 part-time (280 women); includes 89 minority (69 African Americans, 1 Asian American, 16 Hispanics, 3 Native Americans), 10 international. In 1997, 107 degrees awarded. *Degree requirements:* Dissertation, practicum required, foreign language not required. *Entrance requirements:* Master's degree, 3 years of work experience, interview, minimum GPA of 3.0. Application deadline: rolling. Application fee: $50. *Tuition:* $8460 per year. *Financial aid:* Federal Work-Study and career-related internships or fieldwork available. Aid available to part-time students. • Dr. Abbey Manburg, Dean, 954-262-8555. E-mail: manburg@fcae.nova.edu. Application contact: Dr. Vera Flight, Director of Student Development and Admissions, 800-986-3223 Ext. 8550. Fax: 954-262-3905. E-mail: flightr@fcae.nova.edu.

Nova Southeastern University, Fischler Center for the Advancement of Education, Program in Life-Span Care and Administration, Fort Lauderdale, FL 33314-7721. Offerings include early childhood education administration (MS). MS (applied gerontology administration) new for fall 1998. Postbaccalaureate distance learning degree programs offered. *Degree requirements:* Thesis, practicum required, foreign language not required. *Entrance requirements:* Work experience in field. Application deadline: rolling. Application fee: $50. *Tuition:* $300 per credit hour. • Dr. Norman Powell, Dean, 954-262-8701. E-mail: powell@fcae.nova.edu. Application contact: Sara Sauceda, Program Secretary, 800-986-3223 Ext. 8302. Fax: 954-262-3907. E-mail: powell@fcae.nova.edu.

Oakland University, School of Education and Human Services, Program in Early Childhood Education, Rochester, MI 48309-4401. Awards M Ed, Certificate. Accredited by NCATE. Faculty: 14 full-time. Students: 5 full-time (all women), 212 part-time (207 women); includes 21 minority (13 African Americans, 2 Asian Americans, 5 Hispanics, 1 Native American), 2 international. Average age 37. 58 applicants, 76% accepted. In 1997, 74 master's awarded. *Entrance requirements:* For master's, minimum GPA of 3.0 for unconditional admission. Application deadline: 6/1 (2/1 for spring admission). Application fee: $30. *Expenses:* Tuition $3852 per year full-time, $214 per credit hour part-time for state residents; $8532 per year full-time, $474 per credit hour part-time for nonresidents. Fees $420 per year. *Financial aid:* Full tuition waivers, Federal Work-Study, institutionally sponsored loans, and career-related internships or fieldwork available. Financial aid application deadline: 3/1; applicants required to submit FAFSA. • Dr. Ronald Swartz, Chair, 248-377-3077. Application contact: Dr. Andrew Gunsberg, Coordinator, 248-377-3077.

Oglethorpe University, Division of Education, Atlanta, GA 30319-2797. Offerings include early childhood education (MA). Division faculty: 4 full-time (3 women), 3 part-time (all women), 5 FTE. *Degree requirements:* Comprehensive exam required, foreign language and thesis not required. *Entrance requirements:* GRE General Test (minimum combined score of 800), MAT (minimum score 44), PRAXIS, minimum GPA of 2.5. Application deadline: rolling. Application fee: $30. *Tuition:* $500 per course. • Dr. Vienna K. Volante, Chair, 404-261-1441 Ext. 385. Application contact: Bill Price, Graduate Admissions Counselor, 404-364-8307. Fax: 404-364-8500.

Ohio University, Graduate Studies, College of Health and Human Services, School of Human and Consumer Sciences, Program in Child Development and Family Life, Athens, OH 45701-2979. Offerings include early childhood education (MSHCS). Accredited by NCATE. *Degree requirements:* Thesis required, foreign language not required. *Entrance requirements:* GRE. Application deadline: 8/30 (priority date; rolling processing). Application fee: $30. *Tuition:* $5430 per year full-time, $216 per quarter hour part-time for state residents; $10,431 per year full-time, $423 per quarter hour part-time for nonresidents. • Application contact: Dr. June Varner, Graduate Chair, 740-593-2877.

Oklahoma City University, Petree College of Arts and Sciences, Division of Education, Program in Early Childhood Education, Oklahoma City, OK 73106-1402. Awards M Ed. Part-time and evening/weekend programs available. Students: 1 (woman) full-time, 9 part-time (all women). Average age 27. *Degree requirements:* Thesis or alternative required, foreign language not required. *Average time to degree:* master's–1.5 years full-time, 3.3 years part-time. *Entrance requirements:* Minimum GPA of 3.0. Application deadline: 8/25 (priority date; rolling processing; 1/15 for spring admission). Application fee: $35 ($55 for international students). *Expenses:* Tuition $318 per hour. Fees $124 per year. *Financial aid:* Fellowships, partial tuition waivers, and career-related internships or fieldwork available. Aid available to part-time students. Financial aid application deadline: 8/1; applicants required to submit FAFSA. • Dr. Donna C. Richardson, Director, 405-521-5371. Application contact: Laura L. Rahhal, Director of Graduate Admissions, 800-633-7242 Ext. 2. Fax: 405-521-5356. E-mail: lrahhal1@froda.okcu.edu.

Old Dominion University, Darden College of Education, Department of Early Childhood, Speech-Language Pathology, and Special Education, Program in Early Childhood Education, Norfolk, VA 23529. Awards MS Ed. Accredited by NCATE. Part-time and evening/weekend programs available. Students: 42 full-time (36 women), 62 part-time (56 women); includes 12 minority (8 African Americans, 2 Asian Americans, 1 Hispanic, 1 Native American), 3 international. Average age 31. 67 applicants, 60% accepted. In 1997, 43 degrees awarded. *Degree requirements:* Thesis or alternative, comprehensive and written exams required, foreign language not required. *Entrance requirements:* GRE General Test (minimum combined score of 900), minimum undergraduate GPA of 2.5. Application deadline: 7/1 (rolling processing). Application fee: $30. *Expenses:* Tuition $180 per credit hour for state residents; $477 per credit hour for nonresidents. Fees $140 per year full-time, $32 per semester part-time. *Financial aid:* In 1997–98, 35 students received aid, including 2 research assistantships totaling $9,000, 3 tuition grants totaling $2,982; teaching assistantships, partial tuition waivers, and career-related internships or fieldwork also available. Aid available to part-time students. Financial aid application deadline: 2/15; applicants required to submit FAFSA. *Faculty research:* Child abuse, day care, parenting. • Dr. Katherine Clark Kersey, Chair, Department of Early Childhood, Speech-Language Pathology, and Special Education, 757-683-4121. Fax: 757-683-5593. E-mail: kck100f@oduvm.cc.odu.edu.

Oral Roberts University, School of Education, Tulsa, OK 74171-0001. Offerings include early childhood education (MA Ed). Postbaccalaureate distance learning degree programs offered (minimal on-campus study). School faculty: 7 full-time (2 women), 13 part-time (3 women). *Degree requirements:* Thesis (for some programs), comprehensive exam. *Average time to degree:* master's–1.5 years full-time, 3 years part-time. *Entrance requirements:* GRE General Test (minimum combined score of 1000) or MAT, minimum GPA of 3.0. Application deadline: rolling. Application fee: $35. • Dr. David Hand, Dean, 918-495-7084. Fax: 918-495-6050. Application contact: David H. Fulmer III, Coordinator of Graduate Admissions, 918-495-6058. Fax: 918-495-7214. E-mail: dhfulmer@oru.edu.

Pacific University, School of Education, Forest Grove, OR 97116-1797. Offerings include early childhood education/elementary education (MAT). School faculty: 11 full-time, 8 part-time. *Application deadline:* 3/15 (priority date; rolling processing; 10/15 for spring admission). *Application fee:* $35. • Dr. Willard Kniep, Program Director, 503-359-2205. Application contact: Joel Albin, Admissions Counselor, 503-359-2958. Fax: 503-359-2975. E-mail: admissions@pacificu.edu.

Pennsylvania State University University Park Campus, College of Education, Department of Curriculum and Instruction, University Park, PA 16802-1503. Offerings include early childhood education (M Ed, MS, D Ed, PhD). Accredited by NCATE. *Degree requirements:* For doctorate, dissertation. *Entrance requirements:* GRE General Test or MAT. Application fee: $40. *Expenses:* Tuition $6534 per year full-time, $276 per credit part-time for state residents; $13,460 per year full-time, $561 per credit part-time for nonresidents. Fees $252 per year (minimum) full-time, $43 per semester (minimum) part-time. • Dr. Peter A. Rubb, Head, 814-865-5433.

Piedmont College, Division of Education, Demorest, GA 30535-0010. Offerings include early childhood education (MAT). Postbaccalaureate distance learning degree programs offered (no on-campus study). Division faculty: 24 full-time (12 women), 25 part-time (13 women), 30 FTE. *Degree requirements:* Computer language, thesis, field experience in the teaching classroom required, foreign language not required. *Average time to degree:* master's–1.3 years full-time, 1.5 years part-time. *Entrance requirements:* GRE General Test (minimum combined score of 800; average 835), MAT (minimum score 30; average 45), minimum undergraduate GPA of 2.5. Application deadline: 8/1 (12/1 for spring admission). Application fee: $30. *Tuition:* $2880 per year full-time, $160 per hour part-time. • Dr. Jane McFerrin, Chair, 706-778-3000 Ext. 201. Fax: 706-776-9608. E-mail: jmcferrin@piedmont.edu. Application contact: James L. Clement, Associate Dean for Admissions and Financial Aid, 800-277-7020. Fax: 706-776-6635. E-mail: jclement@piedmont.edu.

Pine Manor College, Program in Education, Chestnut Hill, MA 02167-2332. Offerings include early childhood education (M Ed). College faculty: 5 full-time (all women). *Degree requirements:* Clinical experience, fieldwork. *Application deadline:* rolling. *Application fee:* $25. • Dr. Joanna S. Hall, Director of Graduate Studies, 617-731-7075. Application contact: Pat Dunbar, Graduate Admissions, 617-731-7111. Fax: 617-731-7199.

Portland State University, School of Education, Department of Curriculum and Instruction, Program in Early Childhood Education, Portland, OR 97207-0751. Awards MA, MS. Accredited by NCATE. *Degree requirements:* Special project or thesis, written exam. *Entrance requirements:* California Basic Educational Skills Test, TOEFL (minimum score 550), minimum GPA of 3.0 in upper-division course work or 2.75 overall. Application deadline: 4/1 (rolling processing; 11/1 for spring admission). Application fee: $50. *Tuition:* $6101 per year full-time, $689 per semester (minimum) part-time for state residents; $10,445 per year full-time, $689 per semester (minimum) part-time for nonresidents. *Financial aid:* Research assistantships, teaching assistantships, Federal Work-Study, institutionally sponsored loans, and career-related internships or fieldwork available. Financial aid application deadline: 3/1; applicants required to submit FAFSA. • Dr. Ulrich Hardt, Head, Department of Curriculum and Instruction, 503-725-4756. Fax: 503-725-8475. E-mail: hardtu@ed.pdx.edu.

Rhode Island College, School of Graduate Studies, School of Education and Human Development, Department of Elementary Education, Program in Early Childhood Education, Providence, RI 02908-1924. Awards M Ed. Accredited by NCATE. Evening/weekend programs available. Faculty: 19 full-time (9 women), 9 part-time (7 women). Students: 1 (woman) full-time, 33 part-time (all women); includes 1 minority (African American). In 1997, 9 degrees awarded. *Entrance requirements:* GRE General Test or MAT. Application deadline: 4/1 (rolling processing). Application fee: $25. *Tuition:* $4064 per year full-time, $214 per credit part-time for state residents; $7658 per year full-time, $376 per credit part-time for nonresidents. *Financial aid:* Application deadline 4/1. • Dr. Patricia Cordeiro, Chair, Department of Elementary Education, 401-456-8016.

Rivier College, Graduate Education Department, Program in Early Childhood Education, Nashua, NH 03060-5086. Awards M Ed. *Entrance requirements:* GRE General Test or MAT. Application deadline: rolling. Application fee: $25.

Roosevelt University, College of Education, Chicago, IL 60605-1394. Offerings include early childhood education (MA). Accredited by NCATE. *Application deadline:* 6/1 (priority date; rolling processing). *Application fee:* $25 ($35 for international students). *Expenses:* Tuition $445 per credit hour. Fees $100 per year. • Dr. George Lowery, Dean, 312-341-3700. Application contact: Joanne Canyon-Heller, Coordinator of Graduate Admissions, 312-341-3612.

Rutgers, The State University of New Jersey, New Brunswick, Graduate School of Education, Department of Learning and Teaching, Program in Early Childhood/Elementary Education, New Brunswick, NJ 08903. Awards Ed M, Ed D, Ed S. Part-time programs available. Faculty: 4 full-time (all women), 2 part-time (both women). Students: 102; includes 18 minority (10 African Americans, 6 Asian Americans, 2 Hispanics). 141 applicants, 45% accepted. In 1997, 42 master's, 1 doctorate awarded. Terminal master's awarded for partial completion of doctoral program. *Degree requirements:* For master's, comprehensive exam required, thesis not required; for doctorate, dissertation, qualifying exam. *Entrance requirements:* For master's, GRE General Test (minimum combined score of 1000), minimum GPA of 3.0; for doctorate, GRE General Test (minimum combined score of 1100), minimum GPA of 3.5; for Ed S, GRE General Test. Application deadline: 3/1 (11/1 for spring admission). Application fee: $40. *Expenses:* Tuition $6492 per year full-time, $268 per credit part-time for state residents; $9520 per year full-time, $395 per credit part-time for nonresidents. Fees $208 per year (minimum). *Financial aid:* Fellowships, teaching assistantships, scholarships available. Financial aid application deadline: 3/1. • Dr. Lesley M. Morrow, Coordinator, 732-932-7496 Ext. 119.

Saginaw Valley State University, College of Education, Program in Early Childhood Education, University Center, MI 48710. Awards MAT. Accredited by NCATE. Part-time and evening/weekend programs available. Faculty: 12 full-time (9 women). Students: 156 part-time (153 women); includes 2 minority (1 African American, 1 Hispanic). In 1997, 41 degrees awarded. *Entrance requirements:* Minimum GPA of 3.0, teaching certificate. Application deadline: rolling. Application fee: $25. *Expenses:* Tuition $159 per credit hour for state residents; $311 per credit hour for nonresidents. Fees $8.70 per credit hour. • Application contact: Dr. Sally Edgerton, Coordinator, 517-790-4377. E-mail: edge@tardis.svsu.edu.

Saint Joseph College, Education Programs and Department of Special Education, Program in Early Childhood Education/Special Education, West Hartford, CT 06117-2700. Awards MA. Faculty: 2 full-time (1 woman), 3 part-time (2 women). Students: 21 (all women). Average age 27. In 1997, 8 degrees awarded. *Degree requirements:* Thesis or alternative required, foreign language not required. *Application deadline:* 8/29 (rolling processing). *Application fee:* $25. *Tuition:* $395 per credit. *Financial aid:* Application deadline 8/31. • Dr. Lois Davis, Chairman, 860-232-4571 Ext. 341.

St. Joseph's College, Suffolk Campus, Infant/Toddler Therapeutic Education Major, Patchogue, NY 11772-2399. Awards MA. Faculty: 6 full-time (all women), 6 part-time (5 women). Students: 43 part-time (all women). Average age 31. 42 applicants, 60% accepted. *Degree requirements:* Thesis. *Entrance requirements:* Minimum undergraduate GPA of 3.0, previous course work in child study and special education. Application deadline: 8/15 (priority date; rolling processing). Application fee: $25. *Expenses:* Tuition $360 per credit. Fees $304 per year. • Sr. Frances Solano Carmody, Co-Director, 516-447-3307. Application contact: Marion E. Salgado, Director of Admissions, 516-447-3219. Fax: 516-447-1734.

Saint Mary's College of California, School of Education, Program in Early Childhood Education and Montessori Teacher Training, Moraga, CA 94575. Awards MA, M Ed. Part-time and evening/weekend programs available. Faculty: 3 full-time (all women), 4 part-time (all women). Students: 3 full-time (2 women), 15 part-time (all women); includes 4 international. 6 applicants, 83% accepted. In 1997, 2 degrees awarded. *Degree requirements:* Thesis or alternative required, foreign language not required. *Entrance requirements:* Interview, minimum GPA of 3.0. Application deadline: rolling. Application fee: $50. *Tuition:* $1319 per course. *Financial aid:* Career-related internships or fieldwork available. Aid available to part-time students. Financial aid application deadline: 2/15. • Carole Swain, Director, 925-631-4700.

Salem College, Department of Education, PO Box 10548, Winston-Salem, NC 27108-0548. Offerings include early education and leadership (MAT). Accredited by NCATE. College faculty: 10 full-time (7 women), 2 part-time (both women). *Average time to degree:* master's–1.5 years full-time, 3 years part-time. *Application deadline:* rolling. *Application fee:* $35. *Tuition:* $195 per hour. • Dr. Robin L. Smith, Director of Graduate Studies, 336-721-2656. Fax: 336-721-2683. E-mail: smith@salem.edu.

Salem State College, Department of Education, Program in Early Childhood Education, Salem, MA 01970-5353. Awards M Ed. Accredited by NCATE. *Entrance requirements:* GRE General Test. Application deadline: rolling. Application fee: $25. *Expenses:* Tuition $140 per credit hour for state residents; $230 per credit hour for nonresidents. Fees $20 per credit hour.

Salisbury State University, Department of Education, Concentration in Early Childhood Education, Salisbury, MD 21801-6837. Awards M Ed. 9 applicants, 56% accepted. *Application deadline:* 8/1 (rolling processing; 1/1 for spring admission). *Application fee:* $30. *Expenses:* Tuition $158 per credit hour for state residents; $310 per credit hour for nonresidents. Fees $4 per credit hour. • Dr. Ellen Whitford, Chair, Department of Education, 410-543-6294. E-mail: evwhitford@ssu.edu. Application contact: Phyllis Meyer, Administrative Aide II, 410-543-6281. Fax: 410-548-2593. E-mail: phmeyer@ssu.edu.

Samford University, School of Education, Program in Early Childhood Education, Birmingham, AL 35229-0002. Awards MS Ed, Ed S, M Div/MS Ed. Accredited by NCATE. 10 applicants, 100% accepted. In 1997, 14 master's awarded. *Entrance requirements:* For master's, GRE or MAT, minimum GPA of 2.75; for Ed S, master's degree, teaching certificate. Application deadline: 8/1 (priority date; rolling processing; 4/1 for spring admission). Application fee: $25. *Tuition:* $344 per credit hour. • Dr. Jean Ann Box, Chair, 205-870-2566. Application contact: Dr. Alyce Golowash, Counselor, 205-870-2121.

Sam Houston State University, College of Education and Applied Science, Department of Language, Literacy, and Special Populations, Early Childhood Education Program, Huntsville, TX 77341. Awards M Ed. Accredited by NCATE. Part-time and evening/weekend programs available. Students: 1 (woman) full-time, 5 part-time (all women). In 1997, 5 degrees awarded. *Entrance requirements:* GRE General Test (minimum combined score of 800), minimum GPA of 2.5. Application deadline: 9/1. Application fee: $15. *Tuition:* $1810 per year full-time, $297 per semester (minimum) part-time for state residents; $6922 per year full-time, $924 per semester (minimum) part-time for nonresidents. *Financial aid:* Teaching assistantships available. • Dr. Hollis Lowery-Moore, Chair, Department of Language, Literacy, and Special Populations, 409-294-1595. Fax: 409-294-1131. E-mail: edu_lap@shsu.edu.

San Francisco State University, College of Education, Department of Elementary Education, Program in Early Childhood Education, San Francisco, CA 94132-1722. Awards MA. Accredited by NCATE. Part-time programs available. *Degree requirements:* Thesis or alternative. *Entrance requirements:* Minimum GPA of 2.5 in last 60 units. Application deadline: 11/30 (priority date; rolling processing). Application fee: $55. *Expenses:* Tuition $0 for state residents; $246 per unit for nonresidents. Fees $1982 per year full-time, $1316 per year part-time. *Faculty research:* Play, social development, language and culture.

Siena Heights University, Program in Teacher Education, Concentration in Early Childhood Education, Adrian, MI 49221-1796. Offers program in Montessori education (MA). Part-time programs available. *Degree requirements:* Computer language, thesis, presentation required, foreign language not required. *Entrance requirements:* Minimum GPA of 3.0, interview. Application deadline: 7/1 (priority date; rolling processing; 12/1 for spring admission). Application fee: $25.

Slippery Rock University of Pennsylvania, College of Education, Department of Elementary Education and Early Childhood, Program in Early Childhood Education, Slippery Rock, PA 16057. Awards M Ed. Accredited by NCATE. Part-time and evening/weekend programs available. *Degree requirements:* Comprehensive exams required, thesis optional. *Entrance requirements:* GRE, minimum GPA of 2.75. Application deadline: 7/1 (priority date; rolling processing; 11/1 for spring admission). Application fee: $25. *Tuition:* $4484 per year full-time, $247 per credit part-time for state residents; $7667 per year full-time, $423 per credit part-time for nonresidents.

Smith College, Department of Education and Child Study, Program in Elementary Education, Northampton, MA 01063. Offerings include preschool education (Ed M). Program faculty: 7 full-time (3 women), 1 (woman) part-time, 7.2 FTE. *Degree requirements:* 1 foreign language required, thesis not required. *Average time to degree:* master's–1 year full-time, 4 years part-time. *Entrance requirements:* GRE General Test or MAT. Application deadline: 4/15 (12/1 for spring admission). Application fee: $50. *Tuition:* $21,680 per year full-time, $2720 per course part-time. • Alan Rudnitsky, Chair, Department of Education and Child Study, 413-585-3261. E-mail: arudnits@sophia.smith.edu.

Sonoma State University, School of Education, Program in Early Childhood Education, Rohnert Park, CA 94928-3609. Awards MA. Part-time and evening/weekend programs available. Students: 5 full-time (all women), 14 part-time (all women); includes 3 minority (1 African American, 1 Asian American, 1 Hispanic), 1 international. Average age 42. 0 applicants. In 1997, 3 degrees awarded. *Degree requirements:* Thesis or alternative required, foreign language not required. *Entrance requirements:* GRE General Test, minimum GPA of 2.5. Application fee: $55. *Expenses:* Tuition $0 for state residents; $246 per unit for nonresidents. Fees $2130 per year full-time, $1464 per year part-time. *Financial aid:* Application deadline 3/2. • Patricia Nourot, Advocate, 707-664-2628. E-mail: patricia.nourot@sonoma.edu.

South Carolina State University, School of Education, Department of Teacher Education, 300 College Street Northeast, Orangeburg, SC 29117-0001. Offerings include early childhood and special education (M Ed), early childhood education (MAT). One or more programs accredited by NCATE. Department faculty: 7 full-time (3 women), 2 part-time (1 woman). *Average time to degree:* master's–2 years full-time, 4 years part-time. *Application deadline:* 7/15 (priority date; rolling processing; 11/10 for spring admission). *Application fee:* $25. *Tuition:* $2974 per year full-time, $165 per credit hour part-time. • Dr. Jesse Kinard, Chairman, 803-536-8934. Application contact: Dr. Gail Joyner-Fleming, Interim Associate Dean and Director, Graduate Teacher Education, 803-536-8824. Fax: 803-536-8492.

Southern Connecticut State University, School of Education, Department of Education, Program in Early Childhood Education, New Haven, CT 06515-1355. Awards MS Ed. Students: 38 full-time (35 women), 139 part-time (129 women). In 1997, 48 degrees awarded. *Entrance requirements:* Interview, minimum QPA of 2.5. Application deadline: 7/15. Application fee: $40. *Expenses:* Tuition $2632 per year full-time, $188 per credit part-time for state residents; $7200 per year full-time, $188 per credit part-time for nonresidents. Fees $1806 per year full-time, $45 per semester part-time for state residents; $2703 per year full-time, $45 per semester part-time for nonresidents. • Application contact: Dr. David Levande, Graduate Coordinator, 203-392-6429.

Southern Oregon University, School of Social Science, Health and Physical Education, Department of Education, Ashland, OR 97520. Offerings include elementary education (MA Ed, MS Ed), with options in classroom teacher, early childhood, handicapped learner, reading, supervision. *Application deadline:* 2/1. *Application fee:* $50. *Tuition:* $5187 per year full-time, $586 per quarter (minimum) part-time for state residents; $9228 per year full-time, $586 per quarter (minimum) part-time for nonresidents. • Dr. Mary-Curtis Gramley, Associate Dean of Education, 541-552-6918.

Southwestern Oklahoma State University, School of Education, Program in Early Childhood Education, Weatherford, OK 73096-3098. Awards M Ed. Accredited by NCATE. M Ed distance learning degree program offered to Oklahoma residents only. Part-time and evening/weekend programs available. Postbaccalaureate distance learning degree programs offered. Students: 2 full-time (1 woman), 6 part-time (5 women). 2 applicants, 100% accepted. In 1997, 5 degrees awarded. *Degree requirements:* Exam required, foreign language and thesis not required. *Entrance requirements:* GRE General Test, TOEFL (minimum score 550), minimum GPA of 2.5. Application deadline: rolling. Application fee: $15. *Expenses:* Tuition $60 per credit hour (minimum) for state residents; $147 per credit hour (minimum) for nonresidents. Fees $109 per year full-time, $24 per semester (minimum) part-time. *Financial aid:* Research assistantships, teaching assistantships, partial tuition waivers, Federal Work-Study, institutionally sponsored loans, and career-related internships or fieldwork available. Aid available to part-time students. Financial aid application deadline: 3/1; applicants required to submit FAFSA. • Dr. Lowell Gadberry, Chair, Elementary/Secondary Programs, 580-774-3288.

Spring Hill College, Graduate Programs, Program in Education, Mobile, AL 36608-1791. Offerings include early childhood education (MAT, MS Ed). Program faculty: 5 full-time (3 women), 5 part-time (1 woman). *Degree requirements:* Comprehensive exam required, thesis optional, foreign language not required. *Average time to degree:* master's–2 years part-time. *Entrance requirements:* GRE, MAT, or NTE, minimum undergraduate GPA of 3.0. Application deadline: rolling. Application fee: $25. • Dr. B. C. Algero, Chair, 334-380-3477.

State University of New York at Binghamton, School of Education and Human Development, Program in Early Childhood and Elementary Education, Binghamton, NY 13902-6000. Awards MS Ed. Part-time and evening/weekend programs available. Students: 22 full-time (18 women), 19 part-time (15 women); includes 3 minority (1 African American, 2 Hispanics), 1 international. Average age 28. 42 applicants, 57% accepted. In 1997, 8 degrees awarded. *Entrance requirements:* GRE General Test, TOEFL. Application deadline: 4/15 (priority date; rolling processing; 11/1 for spring admission). Application fee: $50. Electronic applications accepted. *Expenses:* Tuition $5100 per year full-time, $213 per credit hour part-time for state residents; $8416 per year full-time, $351 per credit hour part-time for nonresidents. Fees $654 per year full-time, $75 per semester (minimum) part-time. *Financial aid:* In 1997–98, 1 research assistantship (to a first-year student) averaging $400 per month and totaling $4,000, 4 graduate assistantships (3 to first-year students) averaging $500 per month and totaling $19,962 were awarded; fellowships, Federal Work-Study, institutionally sponsored loans, and career-related internships or fieldwork also available. Aid available to part-time students. Financial aid application deadline: 2/15. • Dr. Judy Kugelmass, Coordinator, 607-777-4696.

State University of New York at Buffalo, Graduate School, Graduate School of Education, Department of Learning and Instruction, Buffalo, NY 14260. Offerings include elementary education (Ed M, Ed D, PhD), with options in early childhood education (Ed M, Ed D), elementary education (Ed M, Ed D). Terminal master's awarded for partial completion of doctoral program. Department faculty: 20 full-time (9 women), 7 part-time (2 women). *Degree requirements:* For master's, comprehensive exam required, foreign language and thesis not required. *Entrance requirements:* For master's, GRE General Test, TOEFL (minimum score 590). Application deadline: 2/1 (11/15 for spring admission). Application fee: $50. *Tuition:* $5970 per year full-time, $288 per credit hour part-time for state residents; $9286 per year full-time, $426 per credit hour part-time for nonresidents. • Dr. Michael Kibby, Chair, 716-645-2455. Application contact: Barbara Cracchiolo, Admissions Secretary, 716-645-2457. Fax: 716-645-3161.

State University of New York at New Paltz, Faculty of Education, Department of Elementary Education, New Paltz, NY 12561-2499. Offerings include early childhood education (MS Ed). *Application deadline:* 3/15 (priority date; rolling processing). *Application fee:* $50. *Expenses:*

Directory: Early Childhood Education

State University of New York at New Paltz (continued)
Tuition $5100 per year full-time, $213 per credit hour part-time for state residents; $8416 per year full-time, $351 per credit hour part-time for nonresidents. Fees $493 per year full-time, $48 per semester (minimum) part-time. • Dr. Rose Rudnitski, Chair, 914-257-2860.

State University of West Georgia, College of Education, Department of Early Childhood Education and Reading, Program in Early Childhood Education, Carrollton, GA 30118. Awards M Ed, Ed S. Accredited by NCATE. M Ed offered jointly with Dalton College. Part-time and evening/weekend programs available. Faculty: 9 full-time (7 women). Students: 105 full-time (101 women), 186 part-time (182 women); includes 33 minority (31 African Americans, 1 Asian American, 1 Hispanic). Average age 33. In 1997, 105 master's, 44 Ed Ss awarded. *Degree requirements:* For Ed S, research project required, foreign language and thesis not required. *Entrance requirements:* For master's, GRE General Test (minimum combined score of 800), minimum GPA of 2.5; for Ed S, GRE General Test (minimum combined score of 800), master's degree, minimum graduate GPA of 3.25. Application deadline: 8/30 (rolling processing). Application fee: $15. *Expenses:* Tuition $2428 per year full-time, $83 per semester hour part-time for state residents; $8428 per year full-time, $250 per semester hour part-time for nonresidents. Fees $428 per year. *Financial aid:* Research assistantships, assistantships, and career-related internships or fieldwork available. Aid available to part-time students. Financial aid applicants required to submit FAFSA. • Application contact: Dr. Jack O. Jenkins, Dean, Graduate School, 770-836-6419. Fax: 770-836-2301.

Stephen F. Austin State University, College of Education, Department of Elementary Education, Program in Early Childhood Education, Nacogdoches, TX 75962. Awards M Ed. Accredited by NCATE. Faculty: 2 full-time (both women). Students: 4 part-time (all women). 3 applicants, 100% accepted. In 1997, 1 degree awarded. *Degree requirements:* Comprehensive exam required, foreign language and thesis not required. *Entrance requirements:* GRE General Test (minimum combined score of 1000). Application deadline: 8/1 (priority date; rolling processing; 12/15 for spring admission). Application fee: $0 ($25 for international students). *Tuition:* $1465 per year full-time, $263 per semester (minimum) part-time for state residents; $5299 per year full-time, $890 per semester (minimum) part-time for nonresidents. *Financial aid:* Application deadline 3/1. • Dr. Elvia Rodriguez, Chair, Department of Elementary Education, 409-468-2904.

Syracuse University, School of Education, Programs in Special Education, Program in Educating Infants and Young Children with Special Needs, Syracuse, NY 13244-0003. Awards MS. Students: 5 full-time (all women), 10 part-time (9 women); includes 1 minority (African American), 3 international. 11 applicants, 100% accepted. In 1997, 8 degrees awarded. *Degree requirements:* Thesis or alternative required, foreign language not required. *Entrance requirements:* GRE General Test, interview. Application fee: $40. *Tuition:* $13,320 per year full-time, $555 per credit hour part-time. *Financial aid:* Application deadline 3/1. • Dr. Gail Ensher, Chair, 315-443-9659.

Teachers College, Columbia University, Graduate Faculty of Education, Department of Curriculum and Teaching, Program in Early Childhood Education, 525 West 120th Street, New York, NY 10027-6696. Awards Ed M, MA, Ed D. Faculty: 2 full-time (1 woman), 4 part-time (3 women), 3.4 FTE. Students: 13 full-time (11 women), 36 part-time (32 women); includes 11 minority (6 African Americans, 3 Asian Americans, 2 Hispanics), 9 international. Average age 38. 23 applicants, 65% accepted. In 1997, 14 master's, 2 doctorates awarded. *Degree requirements:* For doctorate, variable foreign language requirement, dissertation. *Entrance requirements:* For doctorate, GRE General Test or MAT. Application deadline: 5/15 (12/1 for spring admission). Application fee: $50. *Expenses:* Tuition $640 per credit. Fees $120 per semester. *Financial aid:* Full and partial tuition waivers, Federal Work-Study, institutionally sponsored loans, and career-related internships or fieldwork available. Aid available to part-time students. Financial aid application deadline: 2/1. *Faculty research:* Infancy, child development, children and family, policy and program, childhood bilingualism. • Application contact: Victor Singletary, Office of Admissions, 212-678-3710. Fax: 212-678-4171.

Teachers College, Columbia University, Graduate Faculty of Education, Department of Curriculum and Teaching, Program in Early Childhood Special Education, 525 West 120th Street, New York, NY 10027-6696. Awards Ed M, MA. Evening/weekend programs available. Faculty: 1 (woman) full-time, 4 part-time (2 women), 2.2 FTE. Students: 6 full-time (all women), 27 part-time (26 women); includes 8 minority (1 African American, 3 Asian Americans, 4 Hispanics), 3 international. Average age 30. 29 applicants, 62% accepted. In 1997, 17 degrees awarded. *Application deadline:* 5/15 (12/1 for spring admission). *Application fee:* $50. *Expenses:* Tuition $640 per credit. Fees $120 per semester. *Financial aid:* Research assistantships, teaching assistantships, full and partial tuition waivers, Federal Work-Study, institutionally sponsored loans, and career-related internships or fieldwork available. Aid available to part-time students. Financial aid application deadline: 2/1. *Faculty research:* Curriculum development, infants, urban education, visually impaired infants. Total annual research expenditures: $80,000. • Application contact: Victor Singletary, Office of Admissions, 212-678-3710. Fax: 212-678-4171.

Teachers College, Columbia University, Graduate Faculty of Education, Department of Curriculum and Teaching, Program in Elementary/Childhood Education, Preservice, 525 West 120th Street, New York, NY 10027-6696. Awards MA. Faculty: 3 full-time (all women), 9 part-time (7 women), 8.6 FTE. Students: 55 full-time (48 women), 111 part-time (100 women); includes 42 minority (14 African Americans, 22 Asian Americans, 6 Hispanics), 3 international. Average age 27. 181 applicants, 73% accepted. In 1997, 76 degrees awarded. *Application deadline:* 5/15 (12/1 for spring admission). *Application fee:* $50. *Expenses:* Tuition $640 per credit. Fees $120 per semester. *Financial aid:* Full and partial tuition waivers, Federal Work-Study, and career-related internships or fieldwork available. Financial aid application deadline: 2/1. *Faculty research:* Teaching of reading and writing, reforming schools, urban education, curriculum development. • Application contact: Victor Singletary, Office of Admissions, 212-678-3710. Fax: 212-678-4171.

Temple University, College of Education, Department of Curriculum, Instruction, and Technology in Education, Philadelphia, PA 19122-6096. Offerings include early childhood education (Certificate), early childhood education and elementary education (Ed M, MS). One or more programs accredited by NCATE. Department faculty: 33 full-time (14 women). *Degree requirements:* For master's, thesis or alternative required, foreign language not required. *Entrance requirements:* For master's, GRE General Test (minimum combined score of 1000) or MAT (minimum score 39), minimum GPA of 2.8. Application deadline: 2/15 (10/1 for spring admission). Application fee: $40. *Expenses:* Tuition $323 per semester hour for state residents; $444 per semester hour for nonresidents. Fees $170 per year full-time, $28 per semester (minimum) part-time. • Dr. Raymond Lolla, Chair, 215-204-6387. Fax: 215-204-1414.

Tennessee Technological University, College of Education, Department of Curriculum and Instruction, Program in Early Childhood Education, Cookeville, TN 38505. Awards MA, Ed S. Accredited by NCATE. Part-time and evening/weekend programs available. Faculty: 2 full-time (both women). Students: 5 full-time (all women), 12 part-time (11 women). Average age 27. 3 applicants, 100% accepted. In 1997, 5 master's awarded. *Degree requirements:* For Ed S, thesis or alternative required, foreign language not required. *Entrance requirements:* For master's, MAT, TOEFL (minimum score 525); for Ed S, MAT, NTE. Application deadline: 3/1 (8/1 for spring admission). Application fee: $25 ($30 for international students). *Tuition:* $2960 per year full-time, $147 per semester hour part-time for state residents; $7786 per year full-time, $358 per semester hour part-time for nonresidents. *Financial aid:* In 1997–98, 1 student received aid, including 1 research assistantship (to a first-year student); fellowships, teaching assistantships, and career-related internships or fieldwork also available. Financial aid application deadline: 4/1. • Application contact: Dr. Rebecca F. Quattlebaum, Dean of the Graduate School, 615-372-3233. Fax: 615-372-3497. E-mail: rquattlebaum@tntech.edu.

Texas A&M International University, Division of Teacher Education and Psychology, 5201 University Boulevard, Laredo, TX 78041-1900. Offerings include early childhood education (MS Ed). *Degree requirements:* Thesis required (for some programs), foreign language not required. *Entrance requirements:* GRE General Test. Application deadline: 7/15 (priority date; rolling processing; 11/12 for spring admission). Application fee: $0.

Texas A&M University–Commerce, College of Education, Department of Elementary Education, Commerce, TX 75429-3011. Offerings include early childhood education (MA, M Ed, MS). MA, M Ed, and MS (early childhood education) offered jointly with Texas Woman's University and the University of North Texas. Department faculty: 15 full-time (6 women), 4 part-time (2 women). *Degree requirements:* Thesis (for some programs), comprehensive exam. *Entrance requirements:* GRE General Test. Application deadline: rolling. Application fee: $0 ($25 for international students). *Tuition:* $2382 per year full-time, $343 per semester (minimum) part-time for state residents; $7518 per year full-time, $343 per semester (minimum) part-time for nonresidents. • Dr. Wayne Linek, Head, 903-886-5537. Application contact: Pam Hammonds, Graduate Admissions Adviser, 903-886-5167. Fax: 903-886-5165.

Texas A&M University–Kingsville, College of Education, Department of Education, Program in Early Childhood Education, Kingsville, TX 78363. Awards M Ed. Part-time and evening/weekend programs available. Faculty: 1 full-time, 1 part-time (0 women). *Degree requirements:* Comprehensive exam, mini-thesis required, foreign language not required. *Entrance requirements:* GRE General Test (minimum combined score of 1000), MAT (minimum score 34), minimum GPA of 3.0. Application deadline: 6/1 (rolling processing; 11/15 for spring admission). Application fee: $15 ($25 for international students). *Tuition:* $1822 per year full-time, $281 per semester (minimum) part-time for state residents; $6934 per year full-time, $908 per semester (minimum) part-time for nonresidents. *Financial aid:* Application deadline 5/15. • Director, 512-593-3203.

Texas Southern University, College of Education, Area of Curriculum and Instruction, Houston, TX 77004-4584. Offerings include early childhood education (M Ed). Faculty: 15 full-time (7 women), 4 part-time (all women). *Degree requirements:* Comprehensive exam required, foreign language not required. *Entrance requirements:* GRE General Test, TOEFL, minimum GPA of 2.5. Application deadline: 7/15 (priority date; rolling processing). Application fee: $35 ($75 for international students). • Dr. Claudette Ligon, Chairperson, 713-313-7775.

Texas Tech University, Graduate School, College of Education, Division of Educational Psychology and Leadership, Lubbock, TX 79409. Offerings include early childhood education (M Ed, Certificate). Accredited by NCATE. Division faculty: 28 full-time (13 women), 3 part-time (1 woman), 29.29 FTE. *Degree requirements:* For master's, computer language required, thesis optional, foreign language not required. *Entrance requirements:* For master's, GRE General Test (combined average 1034). Application deadline: 4/15 (priority date; rolling processing; 11/1 for spring admission). Application fee: $25 ($50 for international students). Electronic applications accepted. *Expenses:* Tuition $864 per year full-time, $120 per semester (minimum) part-time for state residents; $5976 per year full-time, $747 per semester (minimum) part-time for nonresidents. Fees $2321 per year full-time, $302 per semester (minimum) part-time. • Dr. Loretta J. Bradley, Chair, 806-742-2393.

Texas Woman's University, College of Education and Human Ecology, Department of Early Childhood and Special Education, Program in Early Childhood Education, Denton, TX 76204. Awards MA, M Ed, MS, Ed D. Part-time programs available. Faculty: 4 full-time (all women). Students: 9 full-time (all women), 49 part-time (48 women); includes 14 minority (5 African Americans, 3 Asian Americans, 5 Hispanics, 1 Native American), 3 international. Average age 36. 30 applicants, 90% accepted. In 1997, 5 master's, 3 doctorates awarded. Terminal master's awarded for partial completion of doctoral program. *Degree requirements:* For master's, thesis, professional paper (M Ed) required, foreign language not required; for doctorate, computer language, dissertation. *Average time to degree:* master's–1 year full-time, 9 years part-time; doctorate–1 year full-time, 3 years part-time. *Entrance requirements:* For master's, GRE General Test (minimum combined score of 700), minimum GPA of 3.0; for doctorate, GRE General Test (minimum combined score of 1000), minimum graduate GPA of 3.5. Application fee: $25. *Financial aid:* Research assistantships, teaching assistantships, Federal Work-Study, institutionally sponsored loans, and career-related internships or fieldwork available. Aid available to part-time students. Financial aid application deadline: 4/1. *Faculty research:* Early literacy, reading and writing, whole language, international education, teacher education. • Dr. Lloyd R. Kinnison, Chair, Department of Early Childhood and Special Education, 940-898-2271. Fax: 940-898-2209. E-mail: d_kinnison@twu.edu.

Towson University, Program in Early Childhood Education, Towson, MD 21252-0001. Awards M Ed, Spec. Part-time and evening/weekend programs available. Faculty: 4 full-time (3 women), 1 (woman) part-time. Students: 4 full-time (all women), 95 part-time (93 women); includes 7 minority (5 African Americans, 1 Hispanic, 1 Native American). In 1997, 19 master's awarded. *Degree requirements:* For master's, thesis optional, foreign language not required. *Application deadline:* 3/1 (priority date; rolling processing; 10/1 for spring admission). *Application fee:* $40. *Expenses:* Tuition $187 per credit hour for state residents; $364 per credit hour for nonresidents. Fees $40 per credit hour. *Financial aid:* Assistantships, Federal Work-Study available. Financial aid application deadline: 4/1; applicants required to submit FAFSA. *Faculty research:* Developmental programs, training caregivers for HIV/AIDS children. • Dr. Joan Hildebrand, Director, 410-830-2460. Fax: 410-830-2733. E-mail: jhildebrand@towson.edu. Application contact: Fran Musotto, Office Manager, 410-830-2501. Fax: 410-830-4675. E-mail: fmusotto@towson.edu.

Trinity College, School of Professional Studies, Programs in Education, Washington, DC 20017-1094. Offerings include early childhood education (MAT). Faculty: 6 full-time (5 women), 18 part-time (13 women). *Application deadline:* rolling. *Application fee:* $35. *Tuition:* $460 per credit hour. • Sr. Rosemarie Bosler, Division Chair, 202-884-9557. Application contact: Karen Goodwin, Director of Graduate Admissions, 202-884-9400. Fax: 202-884-9229.

Troy State University, Graduate School, School of Education, Program in Early Childhood Education, Troy, AL 36082. Awards MS, Ed S. Accredited by NCATE. Students: 8 full-time (all women), 18 part-time (all women); includes 4 minority (2 Asian Americans, 2 Native Americans), 1 international. Average age 30. In 1997, 12 master's awarded. *Degree requirements:* For master's, thesis, comprehensive exam. *Entrance requirements:* For master's, minimum GPA of 2.5; for Ed S, GRE General Test (minimum combined score of 850) or MAT (minimum score 33), Alabama Class A certificate or equivalent, minimum graduate GPA of 3.0. Application deadline: rolling. Application fee: $20. Electronic applications accepted. *Expenses:* Tuition $2040 per year full-time, $68 per hour part-time for state residents; $4200 per year full-time, $140 per hour part-time for nonresidents. Fees $240 per year full-time, $27 per quarter (minimum) part-time. • Application contact: Teresa Rodgers, Director of Graduate Admissions, 334-670-3188. Fax: 334-670-3733. E-mail: trodgers@trojan.troyst.edu.

Troy State University Dothan, School of Education, Dothan, AL 36304-0368. Offerings include pre-elementary education (MS Ed, Ed S). Accredited by NCATE. *Application fee:* $20. *Expenses:* Tuition $68 per credit hour for state residents; $140 per credit hour for nonresidents. Fees $2 per credit hour. • Dr. Betty Anderson, Dean, 334-983-6556. Application contact: Reta Cordell, Director of Admissions and Records, 334-983-6556. Fax: 334-983-6322. E-mail: rcordell@tsud.edu.

Tufts University, Division of Graduate and Continuing Studies and Research, Graduate School of Arts and Sciences, Department of Child Development, Medford, MA 02155. Offerings include early childhood education (MAT). Department faculty: 11 full-time, 8 part-time. *Application deadline:* 1/15 (rolling processing). *Application fee:* $50. *Expenses:* Tuition $20,859 per year. Fees $1200 per year. • Francine Jacobs, Chair, 617-627-3355. Application contact: Ann Easterbrooks, 617-627-3355.

The University of Alabama, College of Education, Area of Teacher Education, Tuscaloosa, AL 35487. Offerings include early childhood education (MA, Ed S). Accredited by NCATE.

Faculty: 32 full-time (18 women), 8 part-time (4 women). *Degree requirements:* For Ed S, thesis required, foreign language not required. *Entrance requirements:* For master's, GRE General Test, MAT (score in 50th percentile or higher), or NTE (minimum score 658 on each core battery test), minimum GPA of 3.0; for Ed S, minimum GPA of 3.0 during previous 2 years. Application deadline: 7/6 (priority date; rolling processing). Application fee: $25. *Tuition:* $2684 per year full-time, $594 per semester (minimum) part-time for state residents; $7216 per year full-time, $1248 per semester (minimum) part-time for nonresidents. • Dr. Lea McGee, Head, 205-348-1196. Fax: 205-348-9863. E-mail: lmcgee@bamaed.ua.edu.

The University of Alabama at Birmingham, Graduate School, School of Education, Department of Curriculum and Instruction, Program in Early Childhood Education, Birmingham, AL 35294. Awards MA Ed, PhD, Ed S. Accredited by NCATE. Students: 22 full-time (20 women), 33 part-time (32 women); includes 11 minority (10 African Americans, 1 Asian American). 42 applicants, 88% accepted. In 1997, 40 master's, 3 doctorates awarded. *Degree requirements:* For master's, comprehensive exam required, thesis optional; for doctorate, dissertation; for Ed S, comprehensive exam. *Entrance requirements:* For master's, GRE General Test, MAT, or NTE, minimum GPA of 3.0. Application deadline: rolling. Application fee: $30 ($60 for international students). Electronic applications accepted. *Expenses:* Tuition $99 per credit hour for state residents; $198 per credit hour for nonresidents. Fees $516 per year (minimum) full-time, $73 per quarter (minimum) part-time for state residents; $516 per year (minimum) full-time, $73 per unit (minimum) part-time for nonresidents. • Dr. Joseph C. Burns, Chair, Department of Curriculum and Instruction, 205-934-5371.

University of Alaska Southeast, Program in Education, Juneau, AK 99801-8625. Offerings include early childhood education (M Ed). *Application deadline:* 8/15 (priority date; rolling processing; 2/15 for spring admission). *Application fee:* $35. Electronic applications accepted. *Tuition:* $162 per credit for state residents; $316 per credit for nonresidents. • Application contact: Greg Wagner, Recruiter, 907-465-6239. Fax: 907-465-6365. E-mail: jngaw@acad1.alaska.edu.

University of Arkansas, College of Education, Department of Curriculum and Instruction, Program in Childhood Education, Fayetteville, AR 72701-1201. Awards MAT. Accredited by NCATE. Students: 45 full-time (40 women). 13 applicants, 100% accepted. In 1997, 30 degrees awarded. *Tuition:* $3144 per year full-time, $173 per credit hour part-time for state residents; $7140 per year full-time, $395 per credit hour part-time for nonresidents. • Dr. Jerry Ford, Coordinator, 501-575-6676.

University of Arkansas at Little Rock, College of Education, Department of Teacher Education, Program in Elementary Education, Little Rock, AR 72204-1099. Offerings include early childhood education (M Ed, Ed S). Accredited by NCATE. *Degree requirements:* For master's, thesis or alternative, Arkansas Department of Education certification, comprehensive exam required, foreign language not required; for Ed S, comprehensive exams, oral defense of thesis required, foreign language not required. *Entrance requirements:* For master's, minimum GPA of 2.75, teaching certificate; for Ed S, GRE General Test (minimum combined score of 1350 on three sections) or MAT (minimum score 40), Arkansas teaching certificate, interview, M Ed, minimum GPA of 3.3. Application deadline: rolling. Application fee: $25 ($30 for international students). *Expenses:* Tuition $2466 per year full-time, $137 per credit hour part-time for state residents; $5256 per year full-time, $292 per credit hour part-time for nonresidents. Fees $216 per year full-time, $36 per semester (minimum) part-time. • Dr. Jamie Foster, Adviser, 501-569-3124.

University of Bridgeport, College of Graduate and Undergraduate Studies, School of Education and Human Resources, Division of Education, Program in Elementary Education, 380 University Avenue, Bridgeport, CT 06601. Offerings include early childhood education (MS, Diploma). Program faculty: 8 full-time (2 women), 57 part-time (26 women), 27 FTE. *Degree requirements:* For master's, computer language, final exam, final project, or thesis required, foreign language not required; for Diploma, thesis or alternative, final project required, foreign language not required. *Entrance requirements:* For master's, GRE General Test, MAT (score in 35th percentile or higher), minimum undergraduate QPA of 2.5; for Diploma, GRE General Test or MAT (score in 40th percentile or higher), minimum graduate QPA of 3.0. Application deadline: rolling. Application fee: $35 ($50 for international students). *Tuition:* $340 per credit. • Dr. Allen P. Cook, Associate Dean, Division of Education, 203-576-4206.

University of British Columbia, Faculty of Education, Centre for the Study of Curriculum and Instruction, Vancouver, BC V6T 1Z4, Canada. Offerings include early childhood education (MA, M Ed). *Degree requirements:* Thesis (MA) required, foreign language not required. *Entrance requirements:* TOEFL. Application deadline: 4/30 (2/1 for spring admission). Application fee: $60.

University of Central Arkansas, College of Education, Department of Childhood and Special Education, Program in Early Childhood Education, Conway, AR 72035-0001. Awards MSE. Accredited by NCATE. Students: 4 full-time (all women), 13 part-time (all women). 9 applicants, 100% accepted. In 1997, 5 degrees awarded. *Degree requirements:* Comprehensive exam required, thesis optional. *Entrance requirements:* GRE General Test, minimum GPA of 2.7. Application deadline: 3/1 (priority date; rolling processing; 10/1 for spring admission). Application fee: $15 ($40 for international students). *Expenses:* Tuition $161 per credit hour for state residents; $298 per credit hour for nonresidents. Fees $50 per year full-time, $30 per year part-time. *Financial aid:* Federal Work-Study available. Financial aid application deadline: 2/15. • Dr. Sidney Mitchell, Coordinator, 501-450-5455. E-mail: sidneym@mail.uca.edu.

University of Central Oklahoma, College of Education, Department of Curriculum and Instruction, Program in Early Childhood Education, Edmond, OK 73034-5209. Awards M Ed. Accredited by NCATE. Part-time and evening/weekend programs available. *Entrance requirements:* GRE General Test. Application deadline: 8/18. Application fee: $15. *Tuition:* $76 per credit hour for state residents; $178 per credit hour for nonresidents.

University of Charleston, South Carolina, School of Education, Department of Elementary and Early Childhood Education, Program in Early Childhood Education, Charleston, SC 29424-0001. Awards MAT, M Ed. Part-time and evening/weekend programs available. Faculty: 13 full-time (8 women), 5 part-time (3 women), 14.5 FTE. Students: 25 full-time (24 women), 29 part-time (all women); includes 4 minority (3 African Americans, 1 Hispanic). Average age 32. 35 applicants, 91% accepted. In 1997, 29 degrees awarded. *Degree requirements:* Thesis or alternative, written qualifying exam, student teaching (MAT) required, foreign language not required. *Entrance requirements:* GRE (score in 50th percentile or higher), MAT (score in 50th percentile or higher), or NTE; South Carolina Education Entrance Exam (MAT); TOEFL, teaching certificate (M Ed). Application deadline: rolling. Application fee: $35. *Expenses:* Tuition $2568 per year full-time, $438 per semester (minimum) part-time for state residents; $4596 per year full-time, $876 per semester (minimum) part-time for nonresidents. Fees $51 per year full-time, $21 per semester (minimum) part-time. *Financial aid:* Research assistantships, teaching assistantships, Federal Work-Study available. Aid available to part-time students. Financial aid application deadline: 4/1. *Faculty research:* Teacher education and creative arts, integrated curriculum, multicultural awareness, teaching models, cooperative learning. • Application contact: Laura H. Hines, Graduate School Coordinator, 843-953-5614. Fax: 843-953-1434. E-mail: hinesl@cofc.edu.

University of Cincinnati, College of Education, Division of Teacher Education, Department of Early Childhood and Special Education, Program in Early Childhood Education, Cincinnati, OH 45221. Awards M Ed. Accredited by NCATE. Part-time programs available. Students: 16 full-time (15 women), 26 part-time (all women); includes 10 minority (all African Americans), 1 international. 32 applicants, 59% accepted. In 1997, 8 degrees awarded. *Degree requirements:* Thesis or alternative required, foreign language not required. *Average time to degree:* master's–3.4 years full-time. *Entrance requirements:* GRE General Test. Application deadline: 2/1. Application fee: $30. *Tuition:* $7228 per year full-time, $185 per credit hour part-time for state residents; $13,812 per year full-time, $352 per credit hour part-time for nonresidents. *Financial aid:* Fellowships, graduate assistantships, full tuition waivers available. Aid available to part-time students. Financial aid application deadline: 5/1. • Application contact: Anne Dorsey, Coordinator, 513-556-4537. Fax: 513-556-3764.

University of Colorado at Denver, School of Education, Program in Early Childhood Education, Denver, CO 80217-3364. Awards MA. Accredited by NCATE. Part-time and evening/weekend programs available. Students: 12 full-time (11 women), 33 part-time (all women); includes 4 minority (2 African Americans, 2 Hispanics), 1 international. Average age 38. 12 applicants, 100% accepted. In 1997, 20 degrees awarded. *Degree requirements:* Thesis or alternative required, foreign language not required. *Entrance requirements:* GRE, MAT, minimum GPA of 2.75. Application deadline: 4/15 (rolling processing; 9/15 for spring admission). Application fee: $50 ($60 for international students). Electronic applications accepted. *Expenses:* Tuition $3530 per year full-time, $199 per semester hour part-time for state residents; $12,722 per year full-time, $764 per semester hour part-time for nonresidents. Fees $252 per year. *Financial aid:* Research assistantships, teaching assistantships, Federal Work-Study available. Financial aid application deadline: 3/1; applicants required to submit FAFSA. • William Goodwin, Area Coordinator, 303-556-3355. Application contact: Agnes Romero, Administrative Assistant, 303-556-4366. Fax: 303-556-4479.

University of Detroit Mercy, College of Education and Human Services, Department of Education, Program in Early Childhood Education, Detroit, MI 48219-0900. Awards MA. *Degree requirements:* Thesis or alternative. *Entrance requirements:* Minimum GPA of 2.75. Application deadline: 8/1. Application fee: $25.

The University of Findlay, College of Professional Studies, Division of Education, 1000 North Main Street, Findlay, OH 45840-3653. Offerings include early childhood (MA Ed). Accredited by NCATE. Division faculty: 9 full-time (7 women), 8 part-time (4 women), 21 FTE. *Degree requirements:* 4 foreign languages, thesis, cumulative project. *Average time to degree:* master's–1.5 years full-time, 3 years part-time. *Entrance requirements:* Minimum GPA of 3.0. Application deadline: 8/15 (priority date; rolling processing). Application fee: $25. *Tuition:* $236 per semester hour. • Dr. Judith Wahrman, Graduate Program Director, 419-424-4864. Fax: 419-424-4822. E-mail: wahrman@lucy.findlay.edu.

University of Florida, College of Education, Department of Instruction and Curriculum, Gainesville, FL 32611. Offerings include early childhood education (MAE, M Ed, Ed D, PhD, Ed S). Accredited by NCATE. Department faculty: 42. *Degree requirements:* For master's, thesis optional, foreign language not required; for doctorate, variable foreign language requirement, dissertation. *Entrance requirements:* For master's and doctorate, GRE General Test (minimum combined score of 1000), minimum GPA of 3.0; for Ed S, GRE General Test. Application deadline: 6/5. Application fee: $20. *Tuition:* $138 per credit hour for state residents; $481 per credit hour for nonresidents. • Dr. Mary Grace Kantowski, Chair, 352-392-9191 Ext. 200. E-mail: mgk@coe.ufl.edu. Application contact: Dr. Ben Nelms, Graduate Coordinator, 352-392-9191 Ext. 225. Fax: 352-392-9193. E-mail: bfn@coe.ufl.edu.

University of Georgia, College of Education, Department of Elementary Education, Program in Early Childhood Education, Athens, GA 30602. Awards M Ed, Ed D, Ed S. Accredited by NCATE. Faculty: 15 full-time (11 women). Students: 18 full-time (all women), 63 part-time; includes 3 minority (all African Americans), 1 international. 54 applicants, 61% accepted. In 1997, 48 master's, 2 doctorates, 7 Ed Ss awarded. *Degree requirements:* For doctorate, dissertation required, foreign language not required. *Entrance requirements:* For master's and Ed S, GRE General Test or MAT; for doctorate, GRE General Test. Application deadline: 7/1 (priority date; 11/15 for spring admission). Application fee: $30. Electronic applications accepted. *Tuition:* $3290 per year full-time, $643 per semester (minimum) part-time for state residents; $11,300 per year full-time, $1645 per semester (minimum) part-time for nonresidents. *Financial aid:* Fellowships, research assistantships, teaching assistantships, assistantships available. • Dr. Judith C. Reiff, Graduate Coordinator, Department of Elementary Education, 706-542-4268. Fax: 706-542-4277.

University of Hartford, College of Education, Nursing, and Health Professions, Program in Early Childhood Education, West Hartford, CT 06117-1599. Awards M Ed. Accredited by NCATE. Part-time and evening/weekend programs available. Faculty: 8 full-time (3 women). Students: 1 (woman) full-time, 9 part-time (8 women); includes 1 minority (African American). Average age 32. 4 applicants, 25% accepted. In 1997, 6 degrees awarded. *Degree requirements:* Comprehensive exam required, foreign language and thesis not required. *Entrance requirements:* GRE General Test or MAT, PRAXIS I, interview. Application deadline: 5/15 (priority date; rolling processing; 12/15 for spring admission). Application fee: $40 ($55 for international students). Electronic applications accepted. *Financial aid:* Graduate assistantships, Federal Work-Study available. Aid available to part-time students. Financial aid application deadline: 6/1; applicants required to submit FAFSA. • Dr. Regina Miller, Director, 860-768-4553. Application contact: Susan Garcia, Coordinator of Student Services, 860-768-5038. E-mail: gettoknow@mail.hartford.edu.

University of Houston, College of Education, Department of Curriculum and Instruction, 4800 Calhoun, Houston, TX 77204-2163. Offerings include early childhood education (M Ed). Accredited by NCATE. Department faculty: 37 full-time (19 women), 10 part-time (7 women). *Degree requirements:* Comprehensive exam or thesis required, foreign language not required. *Entrance requirements:* GRE General Test or MAT. Application deadline: 7/3 (priority date; rolling processing). Application fee: $35 ($75 for international students). *Expenses:* Tuition $1152 per year full-time, $120 per semester (minimum) part-time for state residents; $4482 per year full-time, $249 per credit hour part-time for nonresidents. Fees $977 per year full-time, $119 per semester (minimum) part-time. • Wilford Weber, Chair, 713-743-4970. Fax: 713-743-9870. E-mail: wweber@uh.edu.

University of Houston–Clear Lake, School of Education, Houston, TX 77058-1098. Offerings include early childhood education (MS). Accredited by NCATE. School faculty: 34 full-time (23 women), 17 part-time (12 women), 39 FTE. *Application deadline:* rolling. *Application fee:* $30 ($60 for international students). *Tuition:* $207 per credit hour for state residents; $336 per credit hour for nonresidents. • Dr. Dennis Spuck, Dean, 281-283-3501. Application contact: Dr. Doris L. Prater, Associate Dean, 281-283-3600.

The University of Iowa, College of Education, Division of Early Childhood and Elementary Education, Iowa City, IA 52242-1316. Offers programs in curriculum and instruction (Ed S), early childhood and elementary education (MA), early childhood education (MA), elementary education (PhD). Faculty: 12 full-time. Students: 14 full-time (12 women), 60 part-time (54 women); includes 5 minority (3 African Americans, 1 Asian American, 1 Hispanic), 11 international. 31 applicants, 68% accepted. In 1997, 16 master's, 8 doctorates, 1 Ed S awarded. *Degree requirements:* For master's, exam required, thesis optional, foreign language not required; for doctorate, computer language, dissertation, comprehensive exams required, foreign language not required. *Entrance requirements:* For master's, minimum GPA of 2.5; for doctorate, minimum GPA of 3.0. Application deadline: rolling. Application fee: $30 ($50 for international students). *Expenses:* Tuition $3166 per year full-time, $176 per semester hour part-time for state residents; $10,202 per year full-time, $176 per semester hour part-time for nonresidents. Fees $202 per year full-time, $52 per year (minimum) part-time. *Financial aid:* In 1997–98, 5 research assistantships (1 to a first-year student), 12 teaching assistantships (4 to first-year students) were awarded; fellowships also available. Financial aid applicants required to submit FAFSA. • William Nibbelink, Chair, 319-335-5324. Fax: 319-335-5608.

University of Kansas, College of Liberal Arts and Sciences, Department of Human Development and Family Life, Program in Early Childhood Education, Lawrence, KS 66045. Awards MA, PhD. Accredited by NCATE. *Degree requirements:* For master's, thesis or alternative required, foreign language not required; for doctorate, dissertation, comprehensive oral and written exams. *Entrance requirements:* For master's, TOEFL (minimum score 570), minimum GPA of 3.0; for doctorate, GRE, TOEFL (minimum score 570). Application deadline: 2/15 (priority date). Application fee: $25. *Expenses:* Tuition $2400 per year full-time, $100 per credit

Directory: Early Childhood Education

University of Kansas (continued)
hour part-time for state residents; $7890 per year full-time, $329 per credit hour part-time for nonresidents. Fees $428 per year full-time, $31 per credit hour part-time. • Jan Sheldon, Director, 785-864-4840.

University of Louisville, School of Education, Department of Early and Middle Childhood Education, Program in Early Childhood Education, Louisville, KY 40292-0001. Awards M Ed. Students: 5 full-time (all women), 14 part-time (all women); includes 3 minority (all African Americans), 1 international. Average age 29. In 1997, 6 degrees awarded. *Entrance requirements:* GRE General Test. Application deadline: rolling. Application fee: $25. • Dr. Diane W. Kyle, Chair, Department of Early and Middle Childhood Education, 502-852-6431.

University of Manitoba, Faculty of Education, Department of Educational Psychology, Winnipeg, MB R3T 2N2, Canada. Offerings include early childhood education (M Ed). *Degree requirements:* Thesis or alternative required, foreign language not required.

University of Maryland, College Park, College of Education, Department of Human Development, College Park, MD 20742-5045. Offers programs in early childhood/elementary education (MA, M Ed, Ed D, PhD, CAGS), human development (MA, M Ed, Ed D, PhD, CAGS). Accredited by NCATE. Postbaccalaureate distance learning degree programs offered. Faculty: 36 full-time (21 women), 8 part-time (7 women). Students: 78 full-time (64 women), 75 part-time (66 women); includes 25 minority (15 African Americans, 8 Asian Americans, 2 Hispanics), 12 international. 98 applicants, 53% accepted. In 1997, 21 master's, 21 doctorates awarded. *Degree requirements:* For master's, thesis or alternative, thesis (MA); for doctorate, dissertation. *Entrance requirements:* For master's, GRE General Test or MAT (score in 40th percentile or higher); for doctorate, GRE General Test or MAT (score in 70th percentile or higher); for CAGS, MAT. Application deadline: rolling. Application fee: $50 ($70 for international students). *Expenses:* Tuition $272 per credit hour for state residents; $400 per credit hour for nonresidents. Fees $564 per year full-time, $342 per year part-time. *Financial aid:* In 1997–98, 7 fellowships, 22 teaching assistantships were awarded; research assistantships also available. *Faculty research:* Developmental science, educational psychology. • Dr. Stephen Porges, Chairman/Director, 301-405-2827. Fax: 301-314-9278. Application contact: John Mollish, Director, Graduate Admissions and Records, 301-405-4198. Fax: 301-314-9305.

University of Massachusetts Amherst, School of Education, Program in Education, Amherst, MA 01003-0001. Offerings include early childhood education and development (M Ed, Ed D, CAGS). Accredited by NCATE. *Degree requirements:* For doctorate, dissertation required, foreign language not required. *Entrance requirements:* For master's and doctorate, GRE General Test. Application deadline: 3/1 (rolling processing; 10/1 for spring admission). Application fee: $40. *Expenses:* Tuition $2640 per year full-time, $110 per credit part-time for state residents; $3690 per year (minimum) full-time, $165 per credit (minimum) part-time for nonresidents. Fees $2856 per year full-time, $422 per semester part-time for state residents; $3204 per year full-time, $480 per semester part-time for nonresidents. • John C. Carey, Director, 413-545-0236.

The University of Memphis, College of Education, Department of Instruction and Curriculum Leadership, Memphis, TN 38152. Offerings include early childhood education (MAT, MS, Ed D). Accredited by NCATE. Terminal master's awarded for partial completion of doctoral program. Department faculty: 34 full-time (17 women), 22 part-time (13 women). *Degree requirements:* For master's, thesis or alternative, comprehensive exam required, foreign language not required; for doctorate, dissertation, comprehensive exam required, foreign language not required. *Entrance requirements:* For master's, GRE General Test or MAT, minimum GPA of 2.5; for doctorate, GRE General Test, GRE Subject Test, 2 years of teaching experience. Application deadline: 8/1 (12/1 for spring admission). Application fee: $25 ($50 for international students). *Tuition:* $2862 per year full-time, $166 per credit hour part-time for state residents; $6696 per year full-time, $379 per credit hour part-time for nonresidents. • Dr. Dennie Smith, Interim Chair, 901-678-2771. Application contact: Dr. Carole L. Bond, Coordinator of Graduate Studies, 901-678-3490.

University of Miami, School of Education, Department of Teaching and Learning, Program in Early Childhood Special Education, Coral Gables, FL 33124. Awards MS Ed, Ed S. Accredited by NCATE. Faculty: 8 full-time (6 women), 4 part-time (all women). Students: 9 full-time (all women), 25 part-time (24 women); includes 20 minority (11 African Americans, 9 Hispanics). Average age 29. 12 applicants, 50% accepted. In 1997, 11 master's awarded. *Degree requirements:* For Ed S, thesis optional, foreign language not required. *Entrance requirements:* For master's, GRE General Test (minimum combined score of 1000), TOEFL (minimum score 550); for Ed S, GRE General Test, TOEFL (minimum score 550). Application deadline: rolling. Application fee: $35. *Expenses:* Tuition $815 per credit hour. Fees $174 per year. *Financial aid:* Application deadline 3/1. *Faculty research:* Technology, social skills, inclusion. • Dr. Marie Hughes, Adviser, 305-284-2470. Fax: 305-284-6998. E-mail: svaughn@umiami.ir.miami.edu.

University of Michigan, School of Education, Programs in Educational Studies, Ann Arbor, MI 48109. Offerings include early childhood education (AM, PhD). *Degree requirements:* For doctorate, dissertation, preliminary exam required, foreign language not required. *Entrance requirements:* For doctorate, GRE General Test (minimum combined score of 1800 on three sections), TOEFL (minimum score 600). Application deadline: 1/15 (priority date). Application fee: $55. Electronic applications accepted. • Dr. Ronald Marx, Chairperson, 734-763-9497. E-mail: ronmarx@umich.edu. Application contact: Karen Wixson, Associate Dean, 734-764-9470. Fax: 734-763-1229. E-mail: kwixson@umich.edu.

University of Minnesota, Twin Cities Campus, College of Education and Human Development, Institute of Child Development, Minneapolis, MN 55455-0213. Awards PhD. *Faculty research:* Cognitive development, psychobiology psychopathology, perceptual development. • Richard Weinberg, Director, 612-624-3575. Application contact: Claudia Johnston, 612-624-2576. Fax: 612-624-6373. E-mail: johnstc@staff.tc.umn.edu.

University of Minnesota, Twin Cities Campus, College of Education and Human Development, Department of Curriculum and Instruction, Program in Early Childhood Education, Minneapolis, MN 55455-0213. Awards MA, M Ed, PhD. • Harlan Hansen, Head, 612-624-3575.

University of Montevallo, College of Education, Program in Early Childhood Education, Montevallo, AL 35115. Awards M Ed, Ed S. Accredited by NCATE. Part-time and evening/weekend programs available. *Entrance requirements:* For master's, GRE General Test (minimum combined score of 850), MAT (minimum score 35), minimum undergraduate GPA of 2.75 in last 60 hours or 2.5 overall. Application deadline: 7/15 (11/15 for spring admission). Application fee: $10.

University of Nebraska at Kearney, College of Education, Department of Elementary/Early Childhood Education, Kearney, NE 68849-0001. Offerings include early childhood education (MA Ed). Accredited by NCATE. Department faculty: 4 full-time (1 woman). *Degree requirements:* Thesis optional. *Entrance requirements:* GRE General Test. Application deadline: 8/1 (priority date; rolling processing; 12/15 for spring admission). Application fee: $35. *Expenses:* Tuition $1494 per year full-time, $83 per credit hour part-time for state residents; $2826 per year full-time, $157 per credit hour part-time for nonresidents. Fees $229 per year full-time, $11.25 per semester (minimum) part-time. • Dr. Ed Walker, Chair, 308-865-8513.

University of New Hampshire, College of Liberal Arts, Department of Education, Program in Early Childhood Education, Durham, NH 03824. Awards M Ed. Accredited by NCATE. Part-time programs available. Students: 2 full-time (both women), 8 part-time (all women). Average age 32. 5 applicants, 60% accepted. *Degree requirements:* Thesis or alternative required, foreign language not required. *Entrance requirements:* GRE General Test. Application deadline: 4/1 (priority date; rolling processing). Application fee: $50. *Expenses:* Tuition $5440 per year full-time, $302 per credit hour part-time for state residents; $8160 per year (minimum) full-time, $453 per credit hour (minimum) part-time for nonresidents. Fees $868 per year full-time, $15 per year part-time. *Financial aid:* Research assistantships, teaching assistantships, scholarships, full and partial tuition waivers, Federal Work-Study, and career-related internships or fieldwork available. Aid available to part-time students. Financial aid application deadline: 2/15. *Faculty research:* Young children with special needs. • Dr. Rebecca New, Chairperson, 603-862-3720. Application contact: Dr. Todd DeMitchell, Graduate Coordinator, 603-862-2317.

University of North Alabama, College of Education, Department of Elementary Education, Program in Early Childhood Education, Florence, AL 35632-0001. Awards MA Ed. Accredited by NCATE. Part-time and evening/weekend programs available. Faculty: 1 (woman) part-time. Students: 1 (woman) full-time, 22 part-time (all women); includes 1 minority (African American). Average age 30. In 1997, 10 degrees awarded. *Degree requirements:* Final written comprehensive exam required, foreign language and thesis not required. *Entrance requirements:* GRE, MAT, or NTE, minimum GPA of 2.5, Alabama Class B Certificate or equivalent, teaching experience. Application deadline: 7/1 (priority date; rolling processing; 12/1 for spring admission). Application fee: $25. *Expenses:* Tuition $2448 per year full-time, $102 per credit hour part-time for state residents; $4896 per year full-time, $204 per credit hour part-time for nonresidents. Fees $3 per semester. *Financial aid:* Federal Work-Study available. Aid available to part-time students. Financial aid application deadline: 4/1. • Application contact: Dr. Sue Wilson, Dean of Enrollment Management, 205-765-4316.

The University of North Carolina at Chapel Hill, School of Education, Doctoral Program in Education, Chapel Hill, NC 27599. Offerings include early childhood, family, and literacy studies (PhD). Accredited by NCATE. Program new for fall 1998. *Degree requirements:* Dissertation, comprehensive exams required, foreign language not required. *Entrance requirements:* GRE General Test (minimum combined score of 1000), minimum GPA of 3.0 during last 2 years of undergraduate course work. Application deadline: 1/1 (priority date). *Expenses:* Tuition $1428 per year full-time, $357 per semester (minimum) part-time for state residents; $10,414 per year full-time, $2604 per semester (minimum) part-time for nonresidents. Fees $782 per year full-time, $332 per semester (minimum) part-time. • Dr. Walter Pryzwansky, Director of Graduate Studies, 919-966-7000. Application contact: Janet Carroll, Registrar, 919-966-1346. Fax: 919-962-1533. E-mail: jscarrol@email.unc.edu.

University of North Dakota, College of Education and Human Development, Program in Early Childhood Education, Grand Forks, ND 58202. Awards MS. Accredited by NCATE. Part-time programs available. Faculty: 6 full-time (4 women). Students: 7 full-time (all women). 2 applicants, 100% accepted. In 1997, 1 degree awarded. *Degree requirements:* Thesis or alternative. *Entrance requirements:* TOEFL (minimum score 550), minimum GPA of 3.0. Application deadline: 3/1 (priority date; rolling processing). Application fee: $20. *Financial aid:* In 1997–98, 2 students received aid, including 2 fellowships totaling $4,800; research assistantships, teaching assistantships, assistantships, full and partial tuition waivers, Federal Work-Study, institutionally sponsored loans also available. Financial aid application deadline: 3/15. • Dr. Glenn Olsen, Director, 701-777-3239. Fax: 701-777-4393. E-mail: golsen@plains.nodak.edu.

University of Northern Colorado, College of Education, School for the Study of Teaching and Teacher Education, Program in Early Childhood Education, Greeley, CO 80639. Awards MA. Accredited by NCATE. Part-time programs available. Faculty: 1 full-time (0 women). Students: 10 full-time (all women), 18 part-time (all women); includes 4 minority (1 African American, 2 Asian Americans, 1 Hispanic), 3 international. Average age 36. 10 applicants, 80% accepted. In 1997, 4 degrees awarded. *Degree requirements:* Thesis or alternative, comprehensive exams. *Entrance requirements:* GRE General Test. Application deadline: rolling. Application fee: $35. *Expenses:* Tuition $2327 per year full-time, $129 per credit hour part-time for state residents; $9578 per year full-time, $532 per credit hour part-time for nonresidents. Fees $752 per year full-time, $184 per semester (minimum) part-time. *Financial aid:* In 1997–98, 7 students received aid, including 1 graduate assistantship totaling $3,600; fellowships, teaching assistantships also available. Financial aid application deadline: 3/1. • Dr. Phillip Wishon, Coordinator, 970-351-2537.

University of Northern Iowa, College of Education, Department of Curriculum and Instruction, Program in Early Childhood Education, Cedar Falls, IA 50614. Awards MA Ed. *Degree requirements:* Thesis or alternative required, foreign language not required. *Entrance requirements:* Minimum GPA of 3.5, 3 years of educational experience. Application deadline: 8/1 (priority date; rolling processing). Application fee: $20 ($30 for international students). *Expenses:* Tuition $3166 per year full-time, $176 per hour part-time for state residents; $7805 per year full-time, $176 per hour part-time for nonresidents. Fees $194 per year full-time, $12.50 per semester (minimum) part-time. *Financial aid:* Application deadline 3/1. • Dr. Robert Muffoletto, Acting Head, Department of Curriculum and Instruction, 319-273-2167.

University of North Texas, College of Education, Department of Teacher Education and Administration, Program in Early Childhood Education, Denton, TX 76203-6737. Awards M Ed, MS, PhD. Accredited by NCATE. PhD offered jointly with Texas Woman's University. *Degree requirements:* For doctorate, dissertation. *Entrance requirements:* For master's, GRE General Test (minimum score 350 on each section, 800 combined); for doctorate, GRE General Test (minimum score 400 on each section, 1000 combined). Application deadline: 7/17. Application fee: $25 ($50 for international students). *Tuition:* $2063 per year full-time, $815 per year part-time for state residents; $5897 per year full-time, $2100 per year part-time for nonresidents. *Financial aid:* Fellowships, research assistantships, teaching assistantships, Federal Work-Study, institutionally sponsored loans, and career-related internships or fieldwork available. Financial aid application deadline: 4/1. • Application contact: George Morrison, Adviser, 940-565-2920.

University of Oklahoma, College of Education, Department of Instructional Leadership and Academic Curriculum, Program in Instructional Leadership and Academic Curriculum, Norman, OK 73019-0390. Offerings include early childhood education (M Ed, PhD). Accredited by NCATE. Program faculty: 19 full-time (12 women), 12 part-time (11 women). *Degree requirements:* For doctorate, variable foreign language requirement, dissertation. *Entrance requirements:* For master's, TOEFL (minimum score 550), 12 hours of course work in education; for doctorate, GRE General Test (minimum combined score of 1000), TOEFL (minimum score 500), master's degree, minimum graduate GPA of 3.0. Application deadline: 6/1 (priority date; rolling processing). Application fee: $25. *Expenses:* Tuition $1920 per year full-time, $80 per credit hour part-time for state residents; $6108 per year full-time, $255 per credit hour part-time for nonresidents. Fees $468 per year full-time, $12 per semester (minimum) part-time. • Dr. Bonnie Konopak, Chair, Department of Instructional Leadership and Academic Curriculum, 405-325-1498.

University of Pennsylvania, Graduate School of Education, Division of Educational Leadership, Program in Early Childhood Education, Philadelphia, PA 19104. Awards MS Ed. Part-time programs available. Students: 15 full-time (all women), 7 part-time (6 women); includes 9 minority (5 African Americans, 4 Asian Americans), 1 international. In 1997, 11 degrees awarded. *Degree requirements:* Thesis/project required, foreign language not required. *Average time to degree:* master's–2 years full-time. *Entrance requirements:* GRE General Test or MAT. Application deadline: 7/15 (rolling processing; 12/15 for spring admission). Application fee: $65. *Expenses:* Tuition $22,716 per year full-time, $2876 per course part-time. Fees $1484 per year full-time, $181 per course part-time. *Financial aid:* Federal Work-Study and career-related internships or fieldwork available. Financial aid applicants required to submit FAFSA. *Faculty research:* Early intervention, classification, and assessment on behalf of developmentally disabled children. • Dr. Joan Goodman, Chair, 215-898-5677.

University of Pittsburgh, School of Education, Department of Instruction and Learning, Program in Early Childhood Education, Pittsburgh, PA 15260. Awards M Ed. Part-time and evening/weekend programs available. 212 applicants, 83% accepted. *Degree requirements:* Thesis required, foreign language not required. *Average time to degree:* master's–2 years full-time, 4 years part-time. *Entrance requirements:* TOEFL (minimum score 650). Application deadline: 2/1. Application fee: $30 ($40 for international students). *Expenses:* Tuition $8018 per year full-time, $329 per credit part-time for state residents; $16,508 per year full-time, $680 per credit part-time for nonresidents. Fees $480 per year full-time, $180 per year part-time. *Financial aid:* In 1997–98, 10 fellowships (9 to first-year students) were awarded; partial tuition waivers, Federal Work-Study, institutionally sponsored loans, and career-related internships or fieldwork also available. Aid available to part-time students. Financial aid application deadline: 5/1; applicants required to submit FAFSA. • Application contact: Jackie Harden, Manager, 412-648-7060. Fax: 412-648-1899. E-mail: jackie@sched.fsl.pitt.edu.

University of Portland, School of Education, Department of Elementary Education, Portland, OR 97203-5798. Offers program in early childhood education (MA, MAT, M Ed). *Degree requirements:* Thesis optional, foreign language not required. *Entrance requirements:* GRE General Test (MA), California Basic Educational Skills Test, PRAXIS (MAT), GRE General Test or MAT (M Ed), TOEFL (minimum score 550), minimum GPA of 3.0, teaching certificate. Application deadline: 8/1 (priority date; rolling processing; 12/1 for spring admission). Application fee: $40. *Tuition:* $515 per semester hour. *Financial aid:* Federal Work-Study available. Financial aid application deadline: 3/15. • Dr. Tom Greene, Director, 503-283-7135. E-mail: greene@up.edu.

University of Puerto Rico, Río Piedras, College of Education, Program in Child Education, San Juan, PR 00931. Awards M Ed. *Degree requirements:* Thesis. *Entrance requirements:* PAEG, interview, minimum GPA of 3.0. Application deadline: 2/21. Application fee: $17.

University of Richmond, Department of Education, Program in Early Childhood Education, University of Richmond, VA 23173. Awards M Ed. Part-time and evening/weekend programs available. Faculty: 2 full-time (both women). *Degree requirements:* Comprehensive exam required, foreign language and thesis not required. *Entrance requirements:* GRE General Test, PRAXIS I, teaching certificate. Application deadline: 5/15 (priority date; 12/1 for spring admission). Application fee: $30. *Tuition:* $18,695 per year full-time, $320 per credit hour part-time. *Financial aid:* Fellowships, research assistantships, tuition awards, partial tuition waivers, Federal Work-Study, institutionally sponsored loans, and career-related internships or fieldwork available. Financial aid application deadline: 3/15. • Dr. Mavis Brown, Coordinator, Department of Education, 804-289-8429.

University of South Alabama, College of Education, Department of Curriculum and Instruction, Mobile, AL 36688-0002. Offerings include early childhood education (M Ed). Accredited by NCATE. Department faculty: 13 full-time (6 women). *Degree requirements:* Comprehensive exams required, foreign language and thesis not required. *Entrance requirements:* GRE General Test (minimum combined score of 1000) or MAT (minimum score 37), minimum GPA of 3.0. Application deadline: 9/1 (priority date; rolling processing). Application fee: $25. • Dr. Walter S. Hopkins, Chairman, 334-380-2893.

University of South Alabama, College of Education, Department of Interdepartmental Education, Mobile, AL 36688-0002. Offerings include early childhood education (Ed S). Accredited by NCATE. *Application deadline:* 9/1 (priority date; rolling processing). *Application fee:* $25. • George E. Uhlig, Dean, College of Education, 334-460-6205.

University of South Carolina, Graduate School, College of Education, Department of Instruction and Teacher Education, Program in Early Childhood Education, Columbia, SC 29208. Awards MA, MAT, M Ed, PhD. Accredited by NCATE. Faculty: 8 full-time (5 women). Students: 9 full-time (all women), 329 part-time (305 women); includes 63 minority (59 African Americans, 2 Asian Americans, 2 Native Americans), 2 international. Average age 36. In 1997, 147 master's, 2 doctorates awarded. *Degree requirements:* For master's, 1 foreign language (computer language can substitute), thesis (for some programs); for doctorate, 1 foreign language, dissertation, comprehensive exam. *Entrance requirements:* For master's, GRE General Test, MAT, teaching certificate; for doctorate, GRE General Test, MAT, teaching experience. Application deadline: rolling. Application fee: $35. Electronic applications accepted. *Expenses:* Tuition $3894 per year full-time, $193 per credit hour part-time for state residents; $8114 per year full-time, $404 per credit hour part-time for nonresidents. Fees $125 per year full-time, $37 per semester (minimum) part-time. *Financial aid:* In 1997–98, 2 research assistantships (1 to a first-year student), 4 teaching assistantships (2 to first-year students) were awarded. *Faculty research:* Parent involvement, play, multicultural education, global education. • Dr. Mac H. Brown, Coordinator, 803-777-5129. Application contact: Office of Intercollegiate Teacher Education and Student Affairs, 803-777-6732. Fax: 803-777-3068.

University of South Carolina Spartanburg, Graduate Programs, Spartanburg, SC 29303-4999. Offerings include early childhood development (M Ed). Postbaccalaureate distance learning degree programs offered. Faculty: 9 full-time (5 women). *Entrance requirements:* GRE General Test (minimum combined score of 800), MAT (minimum score 35), minimum GPA of 2.5. Application deadline: rolling. Application fee: $25. *Expenses:* Tuition $193 per hour for state residents; $404 per hour for nonresidents. Fees $120 per year full-time, $5 per hour part-time. • Dr. Linda Randolph, Director, 864-503-5573. Fax: 864-503-5574.

University of Southern Mississippi, College of Education and Psychology, Department of Curriculum and Instruction, Hattiesburg, MS 39406-5167. Offerings include early childhood education (M Ed, Ed S). Department faculty: 11 full-time (7 women), 1 part-time (0 women). *Degree requirements:* For Ed S, thesis required, foreign language not required. *Entrance requirements:* For Ed S, GRE General Test, minimum GPA of 3.25. Application deadline: 8/9 (priority date; rolling processing). Application fee: $0 ($25 for international students). *Tuition:* $2870 per year full-time, $137 per credit hour part-time for state residents; $5972 per year full-time, $172 per credit hour part-time for nonresidents. • Dr. Carolyn Reeves-Kazelskis, Acting Chair, 601-266-4547. Fax: 601-266-4175.

University of South Florida, College of Education, Department of Childhood/Language Arts/Reading Education, Program in Early Childhood Education, Tampa, FL 33620-9951. Awards M Ed, PhD. Accredited by NCATE. Part-time and evening/weekend programs available. Students: 8 full-time (all women), 9 part-time (all women); includes 3 minority (1 African American, 2 Hispanics). Average age 32. 14 applicants, 50% accepted. In 1997, 1 master's awarded. *Degree requirements:* For doctorate, dissertation, 2 tools of research in foreign language, statistics, and/or computers. *Entrance requirements:* For master's, GRE General Test (minimum combined score of 1000), minimum GPA of 3.5 in last 60 hours; for doctorate, GRE General Test (minimum combined score of 1000), minimum GPA of 3.0 (undergraduate) or 3.5 (graduate). Application deadline: 6/1 (10/15 for spring admission). Application fee: $20. Electronic applications accepted. *Tuition:* $142 per credit hour for state residents; $486 per credit hour for nonresidents. *Financial aid:* Federal Work-Study, institutionally sponsored loans available. Aid available to part-time students. Financial aid applicants required to submit FAFSA. *Faculty research:* Developmentally appropriate practice. • Application contact: Nancy Ratcliff, Coordinator, 813-974-1029. Fax: 813-974-0938. E-mail: ratcliff@tempest.coedu.usf.edu.

University of Tennessee at Chattanooga, School of Education, Education Graduate Studies Division, Chattanooga, TN 37403-2598. Offerings include early childhood education (M Ed). Accredited by NCATE. Division faculty: 15 full-time (5 women), 7 part-time (3 women). *Degree requirements:* Comprehensive exams required, thesis optional, foreign language not required. *Entrance requirements:* GRE General Test or MAT, teaching certificate. Application deadline: rolling. Application fee: $25. *Tuition:* $2864 per year full-time, $160 per credit hour part-time for state residents; $6806 per year full-time, $379 per credit hour part-time for nonresidents. • Dr. Tom Bibler, Acting Head, 423-755-4211. Fax: 423-755-5380. E-mail: tom-bibler@utc.edu. Application contact: Dr. Deborah Arfken, Assistant Provost for Graduate Studies, 423-755-4667. Fax: 423-755-4478.

University of Tennessee, Knoxville, College of Education, Program in Education I, Knoxville, TN 37996. Offerings include early childhood education (PhD). Accredited by NCATE. *Degree requirements:* 1 foreign language (computer language can substitute), dissertation. *Entrance requirements:* GRE General Test, TOEFL (minimum score 550), minimum GPA of 2.7. Application deadline: 2/1 (priority date; rolling processing). Application fee: $35. Electronic applications accepted. *Tuition:* $3354 per year full-time, $181 per semester hour part-time for state residents; $8410 per year full-time, $462 per semester hour part-time for nonresidents. • Dr. Tom George, Associate Dean, 423-974-0907. Fax: 423-974-8718. E-mail: tgeorge1@utk.edu.

University of Tennessee, Knoxville, College of Education, Program in Education II, Knoxville, TN 37996. Offerings include early childhood special education (MS). Accredited by NCATE. *Degree requirements:* Thesis optional, foreign language not required. *Entrance requirements:* TOEFL (minimum score 550), minimum GPA of 2.7. Application deadline: 2/1 (priority date; rolling processing). Application fee: $35. Electronic applications accepted. *Tuition:* $3354 per year full-time, $181 per semester hour part-time for state residents; $8410 per year full-time, $462 per semester hour part-time for nonresidents. • Dr. Tom George, Associate Dean, 423-974-0907. Fax: 423-974-8718. E-mail: tgeorge1@utk.edu.

The University of Texas at Brownsville, Graduate Studies, School of Education, Brownsville, TX 78520-4991. Offerings include early childhood education (M Ed). School faculty: 18 full-time (10 women). *Degree requirements:* Thesis optional, foreign language not required. *Entrance requirements:* GRE General Test, TOEFL (minimum score 550). Application deadline: 8/1 (priority date; rolling processing; 1/1 for spring admission). Application fee: $15. *Expenses:* Tuition $648 per year full-time, $120 per semester hour part-time for state residents; $4698 per year full-time, $783 per semester hour part-time for nonresidents. Fees $593 per year full-time, $109 per year part-time. • Dr. Sylvia C. Peña, Dean, 956-983-7219. Fax: 956-982-0293. E-mail: scpena@utb1.utb.edu.

The University of Texas at Tyler, School of Education and Psychology, Department of Curriculum and Instruction, Program in Early Childhood Education, Tyler, TX 75799-0001. Awards MA, M Ed. Part-time programs available. Faculty: 3 full-time (all women). In 1997, 2 degrees awarded. *Degree requirements:* Comprehensive and departmental qualifying exams required, foreign language not required. *Entrance requirements:* GRE General Test (score in 25th percentile or higher). Application deadline: 11/1 (rolling processing). Application fee: $0 ($50 for international students). *Tuition:* $2144 per year full-time, $337 per semester (minimum) part-time for state residents; $7256 per year full-time, $964 per semester (minimum) part-time for nonresidents. *Financial aid:* Application deadline 7/1. *Faculty research:* Evolving self-concept in beginning teachers, effectiveness of transitional classes and four year-old programs, new program development in schools, factors related to readiness. • Dr. Lisa Starnes, Team Leader, 903-566-7133. Application contact: Martha D. Wheat, Director of Admissions and Student Records, 903-566-7201. Fax: 903-566-7068.

The University of Texas of the Permian Basin, Graduate School, School of Education, Program in Early Childhood Education, Odessa, TX 79762-0001. Awards MA. *Degree requirements:* Thesis required, foreign language not required. *Entrance requirements:* GRE General Test (minimum combined score of 1200). *Expenses:* Tuition $1314 per year full-time, $73 per hour part-time for state residents; $4896 per year full-time, $272 per hour part-time for nonresidents. Fees $383 per year full-time, $111 per semester (minimum) part-time.

The University of Texas–Pan American, College of Education, Department of Curriculum and Instruction: Elementary and Secondary, Edinburg, TX 78539-2999. Offerings include early childhood education (M Ed). *Degree requirements:* Thesis optional. *Entrance requirements:* GRE General Test. Application deadline: 7/17 (11/16 for spring admission). Application fee: $0. *Tuition:* $2156 per year full-time, $283 per semester (minimum) part-time for state residents; $6788 per year full-time, $862 per semester (minimum) part-time for nonresidents.

University of the District of Columbia, College of Arts and Sciences, School of Arts and Education, Division of Education, Program in Early Childhood Education, 4200 Connecticut Avenue, NW, Washington, DC 20008-1175. Awards MA. *Degree requirements:* Comprehensive exam, research paper required, foreign language and thesis not required. *Entrance requirements:* GRE General Test, writing proficiency exam, minimum GPA of 3.0. Application deadline: 6/14 (priority date; rolling processing; 11/15 for spring admission). Application fee: $20. *Expenses:* Tuition $3564 per year full-time, $198 per credit part-time for district residents; $5922 per year full-time, $329 per credit part-time for nonresidents. Fees $990 per year full-time, $55 per credit part-time.

University of the Incarnate Word, School of Graduate Studies, College of Professional Studies, Programs in Education, Program in Early Childhood Education, San Antonio, TX 78209-6397. Awards MA, M Ed. Evening/weekend programs available. *Entrance requirements:* GRE, MAT, TOEFL (minimum score 550). Application deadline: 8/15 (priority date; rolling processing; 12/31 for spring admission). Application fee: $20. *Expenses:* Tuition $350 per semester hour. Fees $180 per year full-time, $111 per semester (minimum) part-time. *Faculty research:* Play and play environments. • Application contact: Brian F. Dalton, Dean of Enrollment Services, 210-829-6005. Fax: 210-829-3921.

University of Toledo, College of Education and Allied Professions, Department of Curriculum and Instruction, Toledo, OH 43606-3398. Offerings include early childhood education (M Ed). Accredited by NCATE. Department faculty: 27 full-time (9 women). *Application deadline:* 8/1 (priority date; rolling processing). *Application fee:* $30. *Tuition:* $5907 per year full-time, $246 per hour part-time for state residents; $11,835 per year full-time, $493 per hour part-time for nonresidents. • Dr. James R. Gress, Chair, 419-530-2468. Fax: 419-530-7719. E-mail: jgress@uoft02.utoledo.edu.

The University of West Alabama, College of Education, Department of Elementary and Early Childhood Education, Program in Early Childhood Education, Livingston, AL 35470. Awards M Ed. Accredited by NCATE. Part-time programs available. *Entrance requirements:* GRE General Test, MAT, minimum GPA of 2.75. Application deadline: 9/10 (priority date; rolling processing; 3/24 for spring admission). Application fee: $15. *Tuition:* $70 per quarter hour.

University of West Florida, College of Education, Division of Teacher Education, Program in Primary Education, Pensacola, FL 32514-5750. Awards M Ed. Accredited by NCATE. Part-time and evening/weekend programs available. Students: 1 (woman) full-time, 3 part-time (all women); includes 1 minority (African American). Average age 34. In 1997, 1 degree awarded. *Degree requirements:* Thesis or alternative required, foreign language not required. *Entrance requirements:* GRE General Test (minimum combined score of 1000) or minimum GPA of 3.0. Application deadline: 7/1 (rolling processing; 11/1 for spring admission). Application fee: $20. *Tuition:* $131 per credit hour (minimum) for state residents; $436 per credit hour (minimum) for nonresidents. *Financial aid:* Fellowships and career-related internships or fieldwork available. *Faculty research:* Diagnostic/prescriptive teaching, in-service teacher education, curriculum design and teaching methodology. • Dr. William Evans, Chairperson, Division of Teacher Education, 850-474-2891.

University of Wisconsin–Milwaukee, School of Education, Department of Curriculum and Instruction, Milwaukee, WI 53201-0413. Offerings include early childhood education (MS). Offered jointly with University of Wisconsin–Green Bay. Department faculty: 28 full-time (17 women). *Degree requirements:* Thesis or alternative required, foreign language not required. *Application deadline:* 1/1 (priority date; rolling processing; 9/1 for spring admission). *Application fee:* $45 ($75 for international students). *Tuition:* $4996 per year full-time, $1030 per semester (minimum) part-time for state residents; $15,216 per year full-time, $2947 per semester (minimum) part-time for nonresidents. • Linda Post, Chair, 414-229-4884.

University of Wisconsin–Oshkosh, College of Education and Human Services, Department of Special Education, Oshkosh, WI 54901-8602. Offerings include early childhood: exceptional education needs (MSE). Accredited by NCATE. Department faculty: 12 full-time (4 women), 7 part-time (4 women). *Degree requirements:* Thesis or extra course work, comprehensive exam required, foreign language not required. *Entrance requirements:* Minimum GPA of 2.75, interview. Application deadline: rolling. Application fee: $45. *Tuition:* $3638 per year full-time, $609 per semester (minimum) part-time for state residents; $11,282 per year full-time, $1884 per

Directory: Early Childhood Education

University of Wisconsin–Oshkosh (continued)
semester (minimum) part-time for nonresidents. • Dr. Craig Fiedler, Chair, 920-424-3421. Application contact: Dr. Bert Chiang, Graduate Coordinator, 920-424-2246. E-mail: chiang@uwosh.edu.

Valdosta State University, College of Education, Department of Early Childhood and Reading Education, Valdosta, GA 31698. Offerings include early childhood education (M Ed, Ed S). Accredited by NCATE. Department faculty: 11 full-time (9 women). *Entrance requirements:* For master's, GRE General Test (minimum combined score of 800); for Ed S, GRE General Test (minimum combined score of 900). Application deadline: 8/1 (rolling processing; 11/15 for spring admission). Application fee: $10. *Expenses:* Tuition $2472 per year full-time, $83 per semester hour part-time for state residents; $8472 per year full-time, $333 per semester hour part-time for nonresidents. Fees $236 per year full-time. • Dr. Brenda Dixey, Head, 912-333-5929. Fax: 912-333-7167. E-mail: bdixey@grits.valdosta.peachnet.edu.

Vanderbilt University, Peabody College, Department of Teaching and Learning, Nashville, TN 37240-1001. Offerings include early childhood education (M Ed, Ed D). Accredited by NCATE. *Entrance requirements:* GRE General Test, MAT. Application deadline: 3/1 (priority date; rolling processing). Application fee: $35. • Carolyn Evertson, Chair, 615-322-8100.

Virginia Commonwealth University, School of Education, Program in Teaching, Richmond, VA 23284-9005. Offerings include early education (MT). Accredited by NCATE. *Entrance requirements:* GRE General Test or MAT. Application deadline: 3/1 (rolling processing; 10/15 for spring admission). Application fee: $30 ($0 for international students). *Tuition:* $4960 per year full-time, $257 per credit part-time for state residents; $12,652 per year full-time, $684 per credit part-time for nonresidents. • Dr. Alan M. McLeod, Division Head, 804-828-1305. E-mail: ammcleod@vcu.edu. Application contact: Dr. Michael D. Davis, Interim Director, Graduate Studies, 804-828-6530. Fax: 804-828-1323. E-mail: mddavis@vcu.edu.

Washington University in St. Louis, Graduate School of Arts and Sciences, Department of Education, Program in Early Childhood Education, St. Louis, MO 63130-4899. Awards MA Ed, AGC. One or more programs accredited by NCATE. *Degree requirements:* Thesis or alternative required, foreign language not required. *Entrance requirements:* GRE General Test or MAT. Application deadline: 1/15 (priority date; rolling processing). Application fee: $35. *Tuition:* $22,200 per year full-time, $925 per credit hour part-time. *Financial aid:* Career-related internships or fieldwork available. Financial aid application deadline: 1/15. • Dr. James Wertsch, Chair, Department of Education, 314-935-6776.

Webster University, School of Education, Department of Learning and Communication Arts, St. Louis, MO 63119-3194. Offerings include early childhood education (MAT). Department faculty: 7 full-time (6 women). *Entrance requirements:* 2 years of work experience in education, interview, min GPA of 2.5. Application deadline: rolling. Application fee: $25 ($50 for international students). *Tuition:* $350 per credit hour. • Theresa Prosser, Chair, 314-968-7652. Fax: 314-968-7118. E-mail: prosseth@webster.edu. Application contact: Beth Russell, Director of Graduate Admissions, 314-968-7089. Fax: 314-968-7166. E-mail: russelmb@webster.edu.

Wesleyan College, Department of Education, Program in Early Childhood Education, Macon, GA 31210-4462. Awards MA. Program new for spring 1999. *Degree requirements:* Practicum, professional portfolio required, thesis optional, foreign language not required. *Entrance requirements:* TOEFL (minimum score 550), interview, teaching certificate. *Tuition:* $150 per semester hour. • Application contact: Patricia R. Hardeman, Assistant Dean and Registrar, 912-477-1110. Fax: 912-757-4030.

Western Kentucky University, College of Education, Department of Teacher Education, Interdisciplinary Program in Early Childhood Education, Bowling Green, KY 42101-3576. Awards MA Ed. Accredited by NCATE. Part-time programs available. Faculty: 2 full-time (both women), 8 part-time (4 women). Students: 28 part-time (all women); includes 1 minority (African American). Average age 29. 18 applicants, 78% accepted. *Entrance requirements:* GRE General Test (minimum combined score of 1250 on three sections), minimum GPA of 2.5. Application deadline: 8/1 (priority date; rolling processing). Application fee: $20. *Tuition:* $2460 per year full-time, $133 per credit hour part-time for state residents; $6700 per year full-time, $369 per credit hour part-time for nonresidents. *Financial aid:* Federal Work-Study, institutionally sponsored loans available. Aid available to part-time students. Financial aid application deadline: 4/1; applicants required to submit FAFSA. • Dr. Louella Fong, Head, 502-745-4111.

Western Michigan University, College of Education, Department of Education and Professional Development, Program in Early Childhood Education, Kalamazoo, MI 49008. Awards MA. Accredited by NCATE. Students: 105 part-time (104 women); includes 2 minority (1 African American, 1 Hispanic), 2 international. 35 applicants, 66% accepted. In 1997, 26 degrees awarded. *Application deadline:* 2/15 (priority date; rolling processing). *Application fee:* $25. *Expenses:* Tuition $154 per credit hour for state residents; $372 per credit hour for nonresidents. Fees $602 per year full-time, $132 per semester part-time. *Financial aid:* Fellowships, research assistantships, teaching assistantships, Federal Work-Study available. Financial aid application deadline: 2/15; applicants required to submit FAFSA. • Application contact: Paula J. Boodt, Coordinator, Graduate Admissions and Recruitment, 616-387-2000. E-mail: paulaboodt@wmich.edu.

Western Oregon University, School of Education, Department of Elementary Education, Program in Early Childhood Education, Monmouth, OR 97361. Awards MS Ed. Accredited by NCATE. Faculty: 1 full-time (0 women), 1 (woman) part-time. Students: 1 (woman) full-time, 3 part-time (all women); includes 1 minority (Native American). Average age 35. In 1997, 5 degrees awarded. *Degree requirements:* Written exam required, thesis optional, foreign language not required. *Average time to degree:* master's–1 year full-time, 5 years part-time. *Entrance requirements:* GRE General Test (average 450 on each section) or MAT (minimum score 30), minimum GPA of 3.0, teaching license. Application deadline: rolling. Application fee: $50. *Financial aid:* Research assistantships, teaching assistantships, full and partial tuition waivers, and career-related internships or fieldwork available. Aid available to part-time students. Financial aid application deadline: 3/1; applicants required to submit FAFSA. *Faculty research:* Articulation, retention. • Dr. David Wright, Director, 503-838-8330. Fax: 503-838-8228. E-mail: wrightd@wou.edu. Application contact: Alison Marshall, Director of Admissions, 503-838-8211. Fax: 503-838-8067. E-mail: marshaa@wou.edu.

Westfield State College, Department of Education, Program in Early Childhood Education, Westfield, MA 01086. Awards M Ed. *Degree requirements:* Comprehensive exam, practicum required, foreign language and thesis not required. *Entrance requirements:* GRE General Test or MAT, minimum undergraduate GPA of 2.7. Application deadline: rolling. Application fee: $30. *Expenses:* Tuition $145 per credit for state residents; $155 per credit for nonresidents. Fees $90 per semester. *Financial aid:* Application deadline 4/1. • Application contact: Marcia Davio, Graduate Records Clerk, 413-572-8024.

Wheelock College, Graduate School, Program in Child Development and Early Childhood Education, Boston, MA 02215. Awards MS, CAGS. One or more programs accredited by NCATE. Part-time and evening/weekend programs available. Postbaccalaureate distance learning degree programs offered (minimal on-campus study). Faculty: Students: 6 full-time (all women), 127 part-time (125 women); includes 35 international. *Degree requirements:* For CAGS, thesis. *Entrance requirements:* For CAGS, interview. Application deadline: rolling. Application fee: $35 ($40 for international students). Electronic applications accepted. *Tuition:* $525 per credit. *Financial aid:* Graduate assistantships, grants, Federal Work-Study, institutionally sponsored loans, and career-related internships or fieldwork available. Aid available to part-time students. Financial aid application deadline: 4/1; applicants required to submit FAFSA. *Faculty research:* Cultural influences on early development and parenting, design of learning environments for young children. • Mary Ann Ferrara, Coordinator, 617-734-5200 Ext. 240. E-mail: maferrara@wheelock.edu. Application contact: Martha Sheehan, Director of Graduate Admissions, 617-734-5200 Ext. 212. Fax: 617-232-7127. E-mail: msheehan@wheelock.edu.

Wheelock College, Graduate School, Program in Teaching: Early Childhood and Elementary Education, Boston, MA 02215. Awards MS. Accredited by NCATE. Evening/weekend programs available. Postbaccalaureate distance learning degree programs offered (minimal on-campus study). Students: 57 full-time (51 women), 42 part-time (38 women). *Application deadline:* rolling. *Application fee:* $35 ($40 for international students). Electronic applications accepted. *Tuition:* $525 per credit. *Financial aid:* Grants, Federal Work-Study, institutionally sponsored loans, and career-related internships or fieldwork available. Aid available to part-time students. Financial aid application deadline: 4/1; applicants required to submit FAFSA. *Faculty research:* Academic achievement for students of color, mentoring, teacher development. • Cheryl Render-Brown, Coordinator, 617-734-5200 Ext. 125. E-mail: cbrown@wheelock.edu. Application contact: Martha Sheehan, Director of Graduate Admissions, 617-734-5200 Ext. 212. Fax: 617-232-7127. E-mail: msheehan@wheelock.edu.

Whittier College, Department of Education, Program in Early Childhood Education, Whittier, CA 90608-0634. Awards MA Ed. Evening/weekend programs available. Faculty: 2 full-time (both women). Students: 4 part-time (3 women); includes 1 minority (Hispanic). Average age 22. 4 applicants, 100% accepted. In 1997, 4 degrees awarded (100% found work related to degree). *Degree requirements:* Thesis required, foreign language not required. *Entrance requirements:* GRE General Test, MAT. Application deadline: rolling. Application fee: $60. *Tuition:* $330 per credit. *Financial aid:* In 1997–98, 1 fellowship was awarded; career-related internships or fieldwork also available. *Faculty research:* Conflict resolution, peer relationships. • Judith Wagner, Director, Broadoaks School, 562-907-4200 Ext. 4250. Application contact: Catherine George, Credential Analyst, 562-907-4200 Ext. 4443.

Winona State University, Graduate Studies, College of Education, Education Program, Winona, MN 55987-5838. Offerings include early childhood education (MS). Accredited by NCATE. *Entrance requirements:* GRE General Test. Application deadline: 8/8 (priority date; rolling processing; 2/17 for spring admission). Application fee: $20. • Dr. Robert Clay, Chairperson, 507-457-5353. E-mail: rclay@vax2.winona.msus.edu.

Worcester State College, Graduate Studies, Department of Education, Program in Early Childhood Education, Worcester, MA 01602-2597. Awards M Ed. Part-time and evening/weekend programs available. Students: 35 part-time (all women); includes 2 minority (1 Asian American, 1 Hispanic). Average age 35. 7 applicants, 86% accepted. In 1997, 10 degrees awarded. *Degree requirements:* Comprehensive exam required, thesis not required. *Entrance requirements:* GRE General Test or MAT. Application deadline: rolling. Application fee: $10 ($40 for international students). *Tuition:* $127 per credit hour. *Financial aid:* Career-related internships or fieldwork available. • Dr. Josephine S. Bunuan, Coordinator, 508-929-8609. Application contact: Andrea Wetmore, Graduate Admissions Counselor, 508-929-8120. E-mail: awetmore@worc.mass.edu.

Wright State University, College of Education and Human Services, Department of Teacher Education, Program in Early Childhood Education, Dayton, OH 45435. Awards MA, M Ed. Accredited by NCATE. Students: 3 full-time (all women), 19 part-time (all women); includes 1 minority (Native American). Average age 37. 9 applicants, 56% accepted. In 1997, 19 degrees awarded. *Degree requirements:* Thesis required (for some programs), foreign language not required. *Entrance requirements:* GRE General Test, MAT, TOEFL (minimum score 550). Application fee: $25. *Tuition:* $5109 per year full-time, $161 per credit hour part-time for state residents; $9039 per year full-time, $282 per credit hour part-time for nonresidents. *Financial aid:* Available to part-time students. Financial aid applicants required to submit FAFSA. • Dr. Sam Harris, Coordinator, 937-775-3285. Fax: 937-775-3301. Application contact: Gerald C. Malicki, Assistant Dean and Director of Graduate Admissions and Records, 937-775-2976. Fax: 937-775-2357. E-mail: wsugrad@wright.edu.

Xavier University, College of Social Sciences, Department of Education, Montessori Program, Cincinnati, OH 45207-2111. Awards M Ed. Faculty: 2 full-time (both women), 5 part-time (all women), 3.25 FTE. Students: 28 full-time (27 women), 57 part-time (52 women); includes 10 minority (7 African Americans, 2 Asian Americans, 1 Hispanic), 11 international. Average age 33. 19 applicants, 68% accepted. In 1997, 47 degrees awarded. *Degree requirements:* Comprehensive exam, research project required, foreign language and thesis not required. *Entrance requirements:* GRE or MAT (minimum score 35), minimum GPA of 2.8. Application deadline: 8/15 (priority date; rolling processing). Application fee: $25. *Financial aid:* In 1997–98, 26 students received aid, including 26 scholarships (3 to first-year students). Aid available to part-time students. *Faculty research:* Language development, curriculum development, multiple age groupings. • Elizabeth Bronsil, Director, 513-745-1072. Fax: 513-745-4378. E-mail: bronsile@admin.xu.edu. Application contact: Sheila Speth, Director of Graduate Services, 513-745-3360. Fax: 513-745-1048. E-mail: xugrad@admin.xu.edu.

Youngstown State University, College of Education, Department of Teacher Education, Program in Early and Middle Childhood Education, Youngstown, OH 44555-0002. Offers teaching—elementary education (MS Ed), teaching—secondary reading (MS Ed). Accredited by NCATE. Part-time and evening/weekend programs available. Faculty: 9 full-time (6 women), 8 part-time (all women). Students: 3 full-time (2 women), 144 part-time (132 women); includes 1 minority (African American). 29 applicants, 100% accepted. In 1997, 44 degrees awarded. *Degree requirements:* Comprehensive exam required, foreign language and thesis not required. *Entrance requirements:* TOEFL (minimum score 550), GRE, MAT, or teaching certificate; minimum GPA of 2.5. Application deadline: 8/15 (priority date; rolling processing; 2/15 for spring admission). Application fee: $30 ($75 for international students). *Expenses:* Tuition $90 per credit hour for state residents; $144 per credit hour (minimum) for nonresidents. Fees $528 per year full-time, $244 per year (minimum) part-time. *Financial aid:* In 1997–98, 40 students received aid, including 4 research assistantships averaging $666 per month and totaling $34,080, 36 scholarships totaling $17,974; teaching assistantships, Federal Work-Study, institutionally sponsored loans also available. Aid available to part-time students. Financial aid application deadline: 3/1. • Application contact: Dr. Peter J. Kasvinsky, Dean of Graduate Studies, 330-742-3091. Fax: 330-742-1580. E-mail: amgrad03@ysub.ysu.edu.

Elementary Education

Abilene Christian University, College of Arts and Sciences, Department of Education, Program in Elementary Teaching, Abilene, TX 79699-9100. Awards M Ed. Part-time programs available. Faculty: 11 part-time (4 women). Students: 2 part-time (1 woman). 3 applicants, 100% accepted. In 1997, 1 degree awarded. *Degree requirements:* Comprehensive exam required, foreign language and thesis not required. *Entrance requirements:* GRE General Test or MAT. Application deadline: 4/1 (priority date; rolling processing; 11/1 for spring admission). Application fee: $25 ($45 for international students). *Expenses:* Tuition $308 per credit hour. Fees $430 per year full-time, $85 per semester (minimum) part-time. *Financial aid:* Federal Work-Study available. Aid available to part-time students. Financial aid application deadline: 4/1. • Dr. Roger Gee, Graduate Adviser, 915-674-2122. Application contact: Dr. Carley Dodd, Graduate Dean, 915-674-2354. Fax: 915-674-6717. E-mail: gradinfo@nicanor.acu.edu.

Adams State College, School of Education and Graduate Studies, Department of Teacher Education, Program in Elementary Education, Alamosa, CO 81102. Awards MA. Accredited by NCATE. Offered jointly with the University of Southern Colorado. Part-time programs available. *Degree requirements:* Qualifying exam required, foreign language and thesis not required. *Entrance requirements:* GRE General Test or MAT, minimum undergraduate GPA of 2.75. Application deadline: 5/15 (priority date; rolling processing; 10/15 for spring admission). Application fee: $25. *Tuition:* $2164 per year full-time, $111 per credit part-time for state residents; $7284 per year full-time, $377 per credit part-time for nonresidents. *Financial aid:* In 1997–98, 1 graduate assistantship (to a first-year student) averaging $500 per month and totaling $4,000 was awarded; Federal Work-Study, institutionally sponsored loans, and career-related internships or fieldwork also available. Aid available to part-time students. Financial aid application deadline: 4/15; applicants required to submit FAFSA. • Dr. John Cross, Head, Department of Teacher Education, 719-587-7776.

Adelphi University, School of Education, Program in Early Childhood/Elementary Education, Garden City, NY 11530. Awards MA. Part-time and evening/weekend programs available. Students: 76 full-time (65 women), 255 part-time (225 women); includes 73 minority (41 African Americans, 3 Asian Americans, 28 Hispanics, 1 Native American), 4 international. Average age 35. In 1997, 171 degrees awarded. *Application deadline:* rolling. *Application fee:* $50. *Expenses:* Tuition $16,000 per year full-time, $485 per credit part-time. Fees $500 per year full-time, $150 per semester part-time. *Financial aid:* Research assistantships available. Financial aid application deadline: 3/1. *Faculty research:* Critical thinking, cognition, teacher as researcher, methods of mathematics in elementary education, mentor-intern programs. • Director, 516-877-4080. Application contact: Marilyn Nissensohn, Director of Graduate Admissions, 516-663-3020.

Adelphi University, School of Education, Specialization in Bilingual Education, Garden City, NY 11530. Offerings include elementary education (MA). *Application deadline:* rolling. *Application fee:* $50. *Expenses:* Tuition $16,000 per year full-time, $485 per credit part-time. Fees $500 per year full-time, $150 per semester part-time. • Eva Roca, Director, 516-877-4070.

Alabama Agricultural and Mechanical University, School of Education, Department of Curriculum and Instruction, Area in Elementary and Early Childhood Education, PO Box 1357, Normal, AL 35762-1357. Offers programs in early childhood education (M Ed, MS, Ed S), elementary education (M Ed, MS, Ed S). Accredited by NCATE. Evening/weekend programs available. Faculty: 8 full-time (all women), 1 (woman) part-time. *Degree requirements:* For master's, comprehensive exam required, foreign language not required; for Ed S, thesis. *Entrance requirements:* For master's, GRE General Test. Application deadline: 5/1. Application fee: $15 ($20 for international students). *Expenses:* Tuition $2782 per year full-time, $565 per semester (minimum) part-time for state residents; $5164 per year full-time, $1015 per semester (minimum) part-time for nonresidents. Fees $560 per year full-time, $390 per year part-time. *Financial aid:* Fellowships and career-related internships or fieldwork available. Financial aid application deadline: 4/1. *Faculty research:* Multicultural education, learning styles, diagnostic-prescriptive instruction. • Dr. Earnest Dees, Chair, Department of Curriculum and Instruction, 205-851-5520. Fax: 205-851-5526.

Alabama State University, School of Graduate Studies, College of Education, Department of Curriculum and Instruction, Program in Elementary Education, Montgomery, AL 36101-0271. Awards M Ed, Ed S. Faculty: 4 full-time (2 women). Students: 21 full-time (18 women), 83 part-time (73 women); includes 75 minority (74 African Americans, 1 Hispanic). In 1997, 36 master's, 8 Ed Ss awarded. *Degree requirements:* For master's, comprehensive exam required, thesis optional; for Ed S, thesis. *Entrance requirements:* For master's, GRE General Test, MAT or NTE. Application deadline: 7/15 (rolling processing; 12/15 for spring admission). Application fee: $10. *Expenses:* Tuition $85 per credit hour for state residents; $170 per credit hour for nonresidents. Fees $486 per year. • Dr. Martha Poole Simmons, Coordinator, 334-229-4327. Fax: 334-229-4904. Application contact: Dr. Fred Dauser, Dean of Graduate Studies, 334-229-4276. Fax: 334-229-4928.

Alaska Pacific University, Graduate Programs, Education Department, 4101 University Drive, Anchorage, AK 99508-4672. Offerings include teaching (MAT), with option in K–8. Department faculty: 5 full-time (4 women), 2 part-time (both women), 5.6 FTE. *Degree requirements:* Comprehensive exam or thesis required, foreign language not required. *Entrance requirements:* GRE or MAT, minimum GPA of 3.0. Application deadline: 4/15 (rolling processing; 12/15 for spring admission). Application fee: $25. *Expenses:* Tuition $6600 per year full-time, $370 per credit hour part-time. Fees $80 per year. • Diane Hoffbauer, Director, 907-564-8271. Fax: 907-562-4276. Application contact: Kirsty Gladkoff, Associate Director of Admissions, 907-564-8248. Fax: 907-564-8317. E-mail: apu@corecom.net.

Alcorn State University, School of Psychology and Education, Lorman, MS 39096-9402. Offerings include elementary education (MS Ed, Ed S). Accredited by NCATE. *Degree requirements:* For master's, thesis optional, foreign language not required. *Application deadline:* 7/1 (priority date; rolling processing; 12/1 for spring admission). *Application fee:* $10. *Tuition:* $2470 per year full-time, $378 per semester (minimum) part-time for state residents; $5331 per year full-time, $855 per semester (minimum) part-time for nonresidents.

Alfred University, Graduate School, Division of Education, Alfred, NY 14802-1205. Offerings include elementary education (MS Ed). Division faculty: 45 full-time (12 women). *Degree requirements:* Thesis required (for some programs), foreign language not required. *Entrance requirements:* TOEFL. Application deadline: rolling. Application fee: $50. *Expenses:* Tuition $20,376 per year full-time, $390 per credit hour (minimum) part-time. Fees $546 per year. • Dr. Katherine D. Wiesendanger, Chair, 607-871-2219. E-mail: fwiesendange@bigvax.alfred.edu. Application contact: Cathleen R. Johnson, Assistant Director of Admissions, 607-871-2141. Fax: 607-871-2198. E-mail: johnsonc@bigvax.alfred.edu.

American International College, School of Continuing Education and Graduate Studies, School of Psychology and Education, Department of Education, Springfield, MA 01109-3189. Offerings include elementary education (M Ed, CAGS). Department faculty: 5 full-time (3 women), 15 part-time (9 women). *Degree requirements:* For CAGS, practicum required, foreign language not required. *Application fee:* $15 ($25 for international students). *Expenses:* Tuition $363 per credit hour. Fees $25 per semester. • C. Gerald Weaver, Dean, School of Psychology and Education, 413-747-6338.

American University, College of Arts and Sciences, School of Education, Program in Elementary Education, Washington, DC 20016-8001. Awards MAT. Faculty: 8 full-time (5 women), 10 part-time (8 women), 11.3 FTE. Students: 14 full-time (12 women), 2 part-time (both women); includes 1 minority (Asian American). 30 applicants, 90% accepted. In 1997, 13 degrees awarded. *Degree requirements:* Thesis or alternative required, foreign language not required. *Entrance requirements:* GRE General Test or MAT, minimum GPA of 3.0. Application deadline: 2/1 (10/1 for spring admission). Application fee: $50. *Expenses:* Tuition $687 per credit hour. Fees $180 per year full-time, $110 per year part-time. *Financial aid:* Application deadline 2/1. • Application contact: Tim Willmot, Academic Coordinator, 202-885-3716. Fax: 202-885-1187. E-mail: tw7106a@american.edu.

Andrews University, School of Graduate Studies, School of Education, Department of Teaching/Learning/Administration, Berrien Springs, MI 49104. Offerings include elementary education (MAT). *Application deadline:* 8/15 (rolling processing). *Application fee:* $30. *Expenses:* Tuition $290 per quarter hour (minimum). Fees $75 per quarter. • Dr. William H. Green, Chair, 616-471-3465.

Antioch New England Graduate School, Graduate School, Department of Education, Program in Elementary Education/Early Childhood Education, 40 Avon Street, Keene, NH 03431-3516. Offers integrated day education (M Ed), science and environmental education (M Ed). Faculty: 7 full-time (2 women), 12 part-time (11 women). Students: 41 full-time (31 women), 4 part-time (all women); includes 1 minority (Native American). Average age 32. 32 applicants, 97% accepted. In 1997, 29 degrees awarded. *Degree requirements:* Internship required, foreign language and thesis not required. *Application fee:* $40. *Expenses:* Tuition $12,700 per year full-time, $330 per credit part-time. Fees $165 per year. *Financial aid:* Federal Work-Study and career-related internships or fieldwork available. Financial aid applicants required to submit FAFSA. *Faculty research:* Mathematics education, ecological literacy, democratic classrooms, arts education. • David Sobel, Director, 603-357-3122 Ex. 358. E-mail: dsobel@antiochne.edu. Application contact: Diane K. Hewitt, Co-Director of Admissions, 603-357-6265 Ext. 286. Fax: 603-357-0718. E-mail: dhewitt@antiochne.edu.

Appalachian State University, College of Education, Department of Curriculum and Instruction, Boone, NC 28608. Offerings include elementary education (MA). Accredited by NCATE. Postbaccalaureate distance learning degree programs offered (minimal on-campus study). Department faculty: 19 full-time (9 women), 2 part-time (1 woman). *Degree requirements:* Thesis or alternative, comprehensive exams required, foreign language not required. *Average time to degree:* master's–2 years full-time, 4 years part-time. *Entrance requirements:* GRE General Test or MAT. Application deadline: 7/31 (priority date). Application fee: $35. *Tuition:* $1811 per year full-time, $354 per semester (minimum) part-time for state residents; $9081 per year full-time, $2171 per semester (minimum) part-time for nonresidents. • Dr. Michael Jacobson, Chairperson, 704-262-2224.

Arizona State University West, College of Education, Phoenix, AZ 85069-7100. Offerings include elementary education (M Ed). College faculty: 19 full-time (13 women), 12 part-time (7 women), 24.23 FTE. *Degree requirements:* Comprehensive exams required, thesis not required. *Entrance requirements:* GRE or MAT, TOEFL. Application deadline: rolling. Application fee: $40. *Expenses:* Tuition $2088 per year full-time, $330 per course part-time for state residents; $9040 per year full-time, $1131 per course part-time for nonresidents. Fees $10 per year (minimum). • Dr. William S. Svoboda, Dean, 602-543-6300. Application contact: Ray Buss, Assistant Dean, 602-543-6300. Fax: 602-543-6350.

Arkansas State University, College of Education, Department of Elementary Education, State University, AR 72467. Offers programs in early childhood education (MSE), early childhood services (MS), elementary education (MSE), reading (MSE, SCCT). Accredited by NCATE. Part-time programs available. Faculty: 10 full-time (8 women). Students: 3 full-time (all women), 58 part-time (55 women); includes 5 minority (all African Americans). Average age 37. In 1997, 30 master's, 1 SCCT awarded. *Degree requirements:* For master's, thesis or alternative, comprehensive exam; for SCCT, comprehensive exam required, thesis not required. *Entrance requirements:* For master's, GRE General Test or MAT, appropriate bachelor's degree; for SCCT, GRE General Test or MAT, master's degree. Application deadline: 7/1 (priority date; rolling processing; 11/15 for spring admission). Application fee: $15 ($25 for international students). *Expenses:* Tuition $2760 per year full-time, $115 per credit hour part-time for state residents; $6936 per year full-time, $289 per credit hour part-time for nonresidents. Fees $506 per year full-time, $44 per semester (minimum) part-time. *Financial aid:* Teaching assistantships and career-related internships or fieldwork available. Aid available to part-time students. Financial aid application deadline: 7/1; applicants required to submit FAFSA. • Dr. Roberta Daniels, Interim Chair, 870-972-3059. Fax: 870-972-3828. E-mail: rdaniels@kiowa.astate.edu.

Arkansas Tech University, School of Education, Department of Curriculum and Instruction, Russellville, AR 72801-2222. Offerings include elementary education (M Ed). Accredited by NCATE. *Application deadline:* 3/1 (priority date; rolling processing; 10/1 for spring admission). *Application fee:* $0 ($30 for international students). *Expenses:* Tuition $98 per credit hour for state residents; $196 per credit hour for nonresidents. Fees $30 per semester. • Head, 501-968-0290. Fax: 501-964-0811.

Armstrong Atlantic State University, School of Graduate Studies, Program in Education, Savannah, GA 31419-1997. Offerings include elementary education (M Ed). Accredited by NCATE. Program faculty: 25. *Expenses:* Tuition $83 per quarter hour for state residents; $250 per quarter hour for nonresidents. Fees $145 per quarter hour for state residents; $228 per quarter hour for nonresidents. • Dr. Bettye Anne Battiste, Department Head, 912-927-5281.

Auburn University, College of Education, Department of Curriculum and Teaching, Auburn University, AL 36849-0001. Offerings include elementary education (M Ed, MS, PhD, Ed S). Accredited by NCATE. Department faculty: 20 full-time (11 women). *Degree requirements:* For master's, thesis (MS) required, foreign language not required; for doctorate, dissertation required, foreign language not required; for Ed S, field project required, foreign language and thesis not required. *Entrance requirements:* For master's and Ed S, GRE General Test; for doctorate, GRE General Test (minimum score 450 on each section, 1000 combined). Application deadline: 9/1 (rolling processing; 3/1 for spring admission). Application fee: $25 ($50 for international students). *Expenses:* Tuition $2760 per year full-time, $76 per credit hour part-time for state residents; $8280 per year full-time, $228 per credit hour part-time for nonresidents. Fees $30 per year full-time, $160 per quarter part-time for state residents; $30 per year full-time, $480 per quarter part-time for nonresidents. • Dr. Andrew M. Weaver, Head, 334-844-4434. E-mail: weaveam@mail.auburn.edu. Application contact: Dr. John F. Pritchett, Dean of the Graduate School, 334-844-4700.

Auburn University Montgomery, School of Education, Department of Early Childhood, Elementary, and Reading Education, Montgomery, AL 36124-4023. Offers programs in early childhood education (M Ed, Ed S), elementary education (M Ed, Ed S), reading education (M Ed, Ed S). Accredited by NCATE. Part-time and evening/weekend programs available. Students: 71 full-time (65 women), 58 part-time (49 women); includes 46 minority (45 African Americans, 1 Hispanic), 1 international. Average age 32. In 1997, 77 master's, 3 Ed Ss awarded. *Degree requirements:* Comprehensive exam required, foreign language and thesis not required. *Entrance requirements:* For master's, GRE General Test or MAT, certification, BS in teaching; for Ed S, GRE General Test or MAT, certification. Application deadline: 9/1 (priority date; rolling processing; 3/28 for spring admission). Application fee: $25. Electronic applications accepted. *Tuition:* $2664 per year full-time, $85 per quarter hour part-time for state residents; $7080 per year full-time, $255 per quarter hour part-time for nonresidents. *Financial aid:* In 1997–98, 3 teaching assistantships were awarded; career-related internships or fieldwork also available. • Dr. Janet Warren, Head, 334-244-3422.

Austin College, Sherman, TX 75090-4440. Offerings include teacher education (MA), with options in elementary education, secondary education. Applicants must meet Austin College's undergraduate curriculum requirements. College faculty: 5 full-time (3 women). *Degree requirements:* 1 foreign language, computer language, thesis or alternative. *Average time to degree:* master's–5 years full-time. *Entrance requirements:* Texas Academic Skills Program (minimum score 220 required on reading, writing, and math sections). Application deadline: 5/1

Directory: Elementary Education

Austin College (continued)
(priority date; rolling processing). Application fee: $35. Electronic applications accepted. *Expenses:* Tuition $14,080 per year full-time, $2010 per course part-time. Fees $125 per year full-time. • Dr. John White, Director, 903-813-2459. Fax: 903-813-2326.

Austin Peay State University, College of Education, Department of Education, Clarksville, TN 37044-0001. Offerings include elementary education (MA Ed, Ed S). Accredited by NCATE. Ed S offered jointly with Tennessee State University. *Entrance requirements:* For Ed S, GRE General Test (minimum score 350 on verbal and quantitative sections), master's degree, minimum graduate GPA of 3.0. Application deadline: 7/31 (priority date; rolling processing; 12/4 for spring admission). Application fee: $15. *Expenses:* Tuition $2438 per year full-time, $123 per semester hour part-time for state residents; $7034 per year full-time, $324 per semester hour part-time for nonresidents. Fees $484 per year (minimum) full-time, $154 per semester (minimum) part-time. • J. Ronald Groseclose, Interim Chair, 931-648-7585. Fax: 931-648-5991. E-mail: groseclosеg@apsu.edu.

Ball State University, Teachers College, Department of Elementary Education, Program in Elementary Education, 2000 University Avenue, Muncie, IN 47306-1099. Awards MAE, Ed D, PhD. Accredited by NCATE. Students: 10 full-time (6 women), 66 part-time (62 women); includes 3 minority (2 African Americans, 1 Hispanic). Average age 31. 30 applicants, 73% accepted. In 1997, 36 master's, 1 doctorate awarded. *Degree requirements:* For doctorate, 2 foreign languages, dissertation. *Entrance requirements:* For doctorate, GRE General Test (minimum combined score of 1000), minimum graduate GPA of 3.2. Application fee: $15 ($25 for international students). *Expenses:* Tuition $3454 per year full-time, $518 per semester (minimum) part-time for state residents; $9316 per year full-time, $1221 per semester (minimum) part-time for nonresidents. Fees $242 per year full-time, $18 per semester (minimum) part-time. • James Stroud, Head, 785-286-8560.

Bank Street College of Education, Program in Early Childhood and Elementary Teacher Education, 610 West 112th Street, New York, NY 10025-1120. Awards MS Ed, MSW/MS Ed. Offerings include early adolescence education (MS Ed), early childhood and elementary teacher education (MS Ed), infant and parent development (MS Ed), museum education (MS Ed), museum special education (MS Ed), reading/literacy (MS Ed). MSW/MS Ed (infant and parent development) offered jointly with Hunter College of the City University of New York. *Degree requirements:* 1 foreign language, thesis. *Entrance requirements:* TOEFL (minimum score 550). Application deadline: 3/1 (priority date; rolling processing; 11/1 for spring admission). Application fee: $50. *Tuition:* $560 per credit. *Financial aid:* Career-related internships or fieldwork available. Financial aid application deadline: 3/1. • Linda Levine, Chairperson, 212-875-4480. Application contact: Ann Morgan, Director of Admissions, 212-875-4404. Fax: 212-875-4678. E-mail: amorgan@bnkst.edu.

Bank Street College of Education, Program in Elementary Education and Special Education, 610 West 112th Street, New York, NY 10025-1120. Awards MS Ed. *Degree requirements:* Thesis. *Entrance requirements:* TOEFL (minimum score 550). Application deadline: 3/1 (priority date; rolling processing; 11/1 for spring admission). Application fee: $50. *Tuition:* $560 per credit. *Financial aid:* Application deadline 3/1. • Linda Levine, Chairperson, 212-875-4480. Application contact: Ann Morgan, Director of Admissions, 212-875-4404. Fax: 212-875-4678. E-mail: amorgan@bnkst.edu.

Barry University, School of Education, Program in Elementary Education, Miami Shores, FL 33161-6695. Awards MS. Part-time and evening/weekend programs available. Faculty: 1 (woman) full-time, 6 part-time (4 women). Students: 29 full-time (23 women), 40 part-time (34 women); includes 48 minority (17 African Americans, 2 Asian Americans, 29 Hispanics), 1 international. Average age 34. In 1997, 7 degrees awarded. *Degree requirements:* Practicum, written comprehensive exam. *Entrance requirements:* GRE General Test or MAT, minimum GPA of 3.0. Application deadline: 5/1 (priority date; rolling processing). Application fee: $30. Electronic applications accepted. *Tuition:* $450 per credit (minimum). *Financial aid:* Partial tuition waivers and career-related internships or fieldwork available. Aid available to part-time students. Financial aid application deadline: 5/1; applicants required to submit FAFSA. • Dr. Gerry Bohning, Director, 305-899-3700. Fax: 305-899-3630. E-mail: bohning@aquinas.barry.edu. Application contact: Angela Scott, Enrollment Services, Assistant Dean, 305-899-3112. Fax: 305-899-3149. E-mail: ascott@jeanne.barry.edu.

Baruch College of the City University of New York, Department of Education, 17 Lexington Avenue, New York, NY 10010-5585. Offerings include elementary education (MS Ed). Program being phased out; applicants no longer accepted. Department faculty: 5 full-time (2 women), 4 part-time (2 women), 6.25 FTE. *Expenses:* Tuition $4350 per year full-time, $185 per credit part-time for state residents; $7600 per year full-time, $320 per credit part-time for nonresidents. Fees $53 per year. • Dr. Jeffrey H. Golland, Chairperson, 212-389-1731. Fax: 212-387-1748. E-mail: jegbb@cunyvm.cuny.edu.

Beaver College, Department of Education, Glenside, PA 19038-3295. Offerings include elementary education (M Ed, CAS). *Application fee:* $35. *Expenses:* Tuition $6570 per year full-time, $365 per credit part-time. Fees $35 per year.

Bellarmine College, College of Arts and Sciences, Graduate Programs in Education, Louisville, KY 40205-0671. Offerings include elementary education (MA). Accredited by NCATE. Faculty: 2 full-time (both women). *Application deadline:* 8/1 (priority date; rolling processing; 12/15 for spring admission). *Application fee:* $25. Electronic applications accepted. *Tuition:* $360 per credit hour. • Dr. Doris Tegart, Director, 502-452-8191.

Belmont Abbey College, School of Graduate Studies, Division of Education, Belmont, NC 28012-1802. Offerings include elementary education (MA). MA (special education) being phased out; applicants no longer accepted. *Application deadline:* 6/1 (rolling processing; 11/1 for spring admission). *Application fee:* $20. *Expenses:* Tuition $530 per course (minimum). Fees $43 per semester (minimum). • Dr. Sandra Loehr, Director, 704-825-6728. Application contact: Julia Gunter, Director of Adult Admissions, 704-825-6671. Fax: 704-825-6658.

Belmont University, Graduate Studies in Education, Nashville, TN 37212-3757. Offerings include elementary education (M Ed). Accredited by NCATE. Faculty: 31 full-time (16 women), 1 (woman) part-time. *Average time to degree:* master's–2 years full-time, 5 years part-time. *Application deadline:* 7/15 (priority date; rolling processing; 11/15 for spring admission). *Application fee:* $50. • Dr. Norma Stevens, Associate Dean, 615-460-6233. E-mail: stevensn@belmont.edu. Application contact: Lois Smith, Admissions Counselor, 615-460-5483. Fax: 615-385-5084. E-mail: smithl@belmont.edu.

Benedictine University, Program in Education, Lisle, IL 60532-0900. Offerings include elementary education (MA Ed). Program faculty: 4 full-time (3 women), 3 part-time (1 woman). *Application fee:* $30. • Dr. Eileen M. Kolich, Director, 630-829-6280. Fax: 630-960-1126. E-mail: ekolich@ben.edu.

Bloomsburg University of Pennsylvania, School of Graduate Studies, College of Professional Studies, School of Education, Department of Curriculum and Foundations, Program in Elementary Education, Bloomsburg, PA 17815-1905. Awards M Ed. Accredited by NCATE. Faculty: 27 full-time (12 women). Students: 2 full-time (0 women), 37 part-time (33 women); includes 2 minority (1 African American, 1 Asian American). Average age 34. 4 applicants, 100% accepted. In 1997, 26 degrees awarded. *Degree requirements:* Thesis or alternative required, foreign language not required. *Entrance requirements:* MAT (minimum score 30), teaching certificate, minimum QPA of 2.5. Application deadline: rolling. Application fee: $25. *Expenses:* Tuition $3468 per year full-time, $193 per credit part-time for state residents; $6236 per year full-time, $346 per credit part-time for nonresidents. Fees $748 per year full-time, $166 per semester (minimum) part-time. *Faculty research:* Supervision, computing, measurement, mathematics, school law, foundations. • Dr. John Hranitz, Chair, Department of Curriculum and Foundations, 717-389-4025. Fax: 717-389-3894. E-mail: hral@bf486.bloomu.edu.

Boston College, Graduate School of Education, Department of Teacher Education/Special Education and Curriculum and Instruction, Specialization in Elementary Teaching, Chestnut Hill, MA 02167-9991. Awards M Ed. Accredited by NCATE. Students: 19 full-time (15 women), 54 part-time (43 women); includes 8 minority (3 African Americans, 1 Asian American, 4 Hispanics), 2 international. 140 applicants, 79% accepted. In 1997, 33 degrees awarded. *Degree requirements:* Comprehensive exam required, thesis not required. *Entrance requirements:* GRE General Test. Application deadline: 3/15 (11/15 for spring admission). Application fee: $40. *Expenses:* Tuition $626 per semester hour. Fees $80 per year (minimum) full-time, $30 per semester part-time. *Financial aid:* Fellowships, research assistantships, teaching assistantships, Federal Work-Study, and career-related internships or fieldwork available. Aid available to part-time students. *Faculty research:* Cross-cultural studies in teaching, learning or supervision, curriculum design. • Application contact: Arline Riordan, Graduate Admissions Director, 617-552-4214. Fax: 617-552-0812. E-mail: riordana@bc.edu.

Boston University, School of Education, Department of Curriculum and Teaching, Program in Elementary Education, Boston, MA 02215. Awards Ed M. Students: 15 full-time (6 women), 2 part-time (0 women); includes 2 minority (both Asian Americans). Average age 25. In 1997, 13 degrees awarded. *Entrance requirements:* GRE or MAT, TOEFL. Application deadline: 2/15 (priority date; rolling processing). Application fee: $50. *Expenses:* Tuition $22,830 per year full-time, $713 per credit part-time. Fees $218 per year full-time, $40 per semester part-time. *Financial aid:* Application deadline 3/30. *Faculty research:* Learning theory, program evaluation, preservice field experiences. • Dr. Carol Jenkins, Coordinator, 617-353-7103. E-mail: cbj@bu.edu.

Bowie State University, Programs in Education, Program in Elementary Education, 14000 Jericho Park Road, Bowie, MD 20715. Awards M Ed. Part-time and evening/weekend programs available. *Degree requirements:* Research paper, written comprehensive exam required, thesis optional. *Average time to degree:* master's–2 years full-time, 4 years part-time. *Entrance requirements:* Minimum GPA of 2.5, teaching certificate, teaching experience. Application deadline: 8/16 (priority date; rolling processing). Application fee: $30. *Expenses:* Tuition $169 per credit hour for state residents; $304 per credit hour for nonresidents. Fees $171 per year.

Bowling Green State University, College of Education and Allied Professions, Department of Educational Curriculum and Instruction, Program in Elementary Education, Bowling Green, OH 43403. Awards M Ed. Accredited by NCATE. Part-time programs available. Faculty: 14 full-time (8 women), 1 part-time (0 women). Students: 4 full-time (2 women), 27 part-time (24 women); includes 1 minority (Hispanic), 1 international. 21 applicants, 86% accepted. In 1997, 4 degrees awarded. *Degree requirements:* Thesis or alternative required, foreign language not required. *Entrance requirements:* GRE General Test, TOEFL (minimum score 580). Application deadline: rolling. Application fee: $30. *Tuition:* $6070 per year full-time, $284 per credit hour part-time for state residents; $11,358 per year full-time, $536 per credit hour part-time for nonresidents. *Financial aid:* Institutionally sponsored loans available. Financial aid application deadline: 2/15; applicants required to submit FAFSA. *Faculty research:* Teaching and learning in disciplines, impact of professional development schools on pre-service teacher training, technology and education, teaching of reading, pre-service and in-servicce teacher education. • Dr. Rosalind Hammond, Chair, Department of Educational Curriculum and Instruction, 419-372-7320.

Bridgewater State College, School of Education, Department of Elementary and Early Childhood Education, Program in Elementary Education, Bridgewater, MA 02325-0001. Awards M Ed. Accredited by NCATE. Evening/weekend programs available. *Entrance requirements:* GRE General Test. Application deadline: 4/1 (10/1 for spring admission). Application fee: $25. *Expenses:* Tuition $1675 per year full-time, $70 per credit part-time for state residents; $6450 per year full-time, $269 per credit part-time for nonresidents. Fees $1588 per year full-time, $66 per credit hour part-time for state residents; $1588 per year full-time, $66 per credit part-time for nonresidents. *Financial aid:* Career-related internships or fieldwork available. • Application contact: Graduate School, 508-697-1300.

Brigham Young University, David O. McKay School of Education, Department of Teacher Education, Provo, UT 84602-1001. Offerings include teaching and learning (MA, M Ed). Accredited by NCATE. Department faculty: 15 full-time (1 woman). *Degree requirements:* Thesis (MA). *Average time to degree:* master's–2 years full-time, 3 years part-time. *Entrance requirements:* GRE General Test (minimum combined score of 900), valid teaching credential, minimum 1 year of teaching experience, minimum GPA of 3.0 in last 60 hours. Application deadline: 2/15 (rolling processing). Application fee: $30. *Tuition:* $3200 per year full-time, $178 per credit hour part-time for state residents; $4800 per year full-time, $266 per credit hour part-time for nonresidents. • Dr. M. Winston Egan, Chair, 801-378-4077. E-mail: winn_egan@byu.edu. Application contact: Eual E. Monroe, Graduate Coordinator, 801-378-4843. Fax: 801-378-3570. E-mail: eula_monroe@byu.edu.

Brooklyn College of the City University of New York, School of Education, Division of Elementary School Education, 2900 Bedford Avenue, Brooklyn, NY 11210-2889. Offers programs in art education (MS Ed), bilingual education (MS Ed), elementary mathematics education (MS Ed), humanities education (MS Ed), music education (MS Ed), science and environmental education (MS Ed), social science (MS Ed). Part-time and evening/weekend programs available. Students: 16 full-time (13 women), 404 part-time (337 women); includes 147 minority (100 African Americans, 11 Asian Americans, 36 Hispanics), 1 international. Average age 27. 530 applicants, 90% accepted. In 1997, 159 degrees awarded (98% entered university research/teaching, 2% found other work related to degree). *Average time to degree:* master's–1.5 years full-time, 3 years part-time. *Entrance requirements:* TOEFL (minimum score 500), interview, previous course work in education, writing sample. Application deadline: 3/1 (rolling processing; 11/1 for spring admission). Application fee: $40. *Expenses:* Tuition $4350 per year full-time, $185 per credit part-time for state residents; $7600 per year full-time, $320 per credit part-time for nonresidents. Fees $500 per year for state residents; $806 per year for nonresidents. *Financial aid:* Partial tuition waivers, Federal Work-Study, institutionally sponsored loans, and career-related internships or fieldwork available. Aid available to part-time students. Financial aid application deadline: 5/1; applicants required to submit FAFSA. *Faculty research:* Emotional intelligence, multiculturalism, arts immersion, the Holocaust. Total annual research expenditures: $20,000. • Dr. Milga Morales, Coordinator, 718-951-5933.

Brown University, Department of Education, Providence, RI 02912. Offerings include elementary education K–6 (MAT). MAT (elementary education K–6) new for fall 1998. Department faculty: 4 full-time (2 women), 20 part-time (15 women). *Average time to degree:* master's–1 year full-time. *Entrance requirements:* GRE (score in 95th percentile or higher). Application deadline: 1/2 (priority date). Application fee: $60. *Expenses:* Tuition $23,616 per year. Fees $436 per year. • Lawrence Wakeford, Chairman, 401-863-2407. Application contact: Yvette Nachmias, Teacher Education Coordinator, 401-863-3364. Fax: 401-863-1276. E-mail: yvette_nachmias@brown.edu.

Butler University, College of Education, Indianapolis, IN 46208-3485. Offerings include elementary education (MS). Accredited by NCATE. College faculty: 10 full-time (3 women), 22 part-time (8 women), 22.5 FTE. *Average time to degree:* master's–7 years part-time; other advanced degree–5 years part-time. *Entrance requirements:* GRE General Test, MAT (minimum score 40), interview. Application deadline: 8/15 (priority date; rolling processing). Application fee: $25. *Tuition:* $220 per credit hour. • Dr. Saundra Tracy, Dean, 317-940-9514. Fax: 317-940-6481. E-mail: stracy@butler.edu.

California State University, Fullerton, School of Human Development and Community Service, Department of Elementary and Bilingual Education, PO Box 34080, Fullerton, CA 92834-9480. Offers programs in bilingual/bicultural education (MS), elementary curriculum and instruction (MS). Accredited by NCATE. Part-time programs available. Faculty: 19 full-time (16 women), 54 part-time, 30 FTE. Students: 4 full-time (all women), 131 part-time (125 women); includes 28 minority (10 Asian Americans, 17 Hispanics, 1 Native American). Average age 32. 61 applicants, 79% accepted. In 1997, 33 degrees awarded. *Degree requirements:* Project or thesis. *Entrance requirements:* Minimum GPA of 2.5, teaching certificate. Application fee: $55. *Expenses:* Tuition $0 for state residents; $246 per unit for nonresidents. Fees $1947 per year full-time, $1281 per year part-time. *Financial aid:* Teaching assistantships, state grants, Federal Work-Study, institutionally sponsored loans, and career-related internships or fieldwork available. Aid available to part-time students. Financial aid application deadline: 3/1. *Faculty research:* Teacher training and tracking, model for improvement of teaching. • Dr. Tom Savage, Head, 714-278-3411. Application contact: Hallie Yopp, Adviser, 714-278-3411.

California State University, Long Beach, College of Education, Department of Teacher Education, Program in Elementary Education, Long Beach, CA 90840-2201. Awards MA. Faculty: 6 full-time (5 women), 1 (woman) part-time. Students: 4 full-time (all women), 118 part-time (110 women); includes 27 minority (5 African Americans, 9 Asian Americans, 12 Hispanics, 1 Native American). Average age 33. 46 applicants, 83% accepted. In 1997, 37 degrees awarded. *Degree requirements:* Comprehensive exam or thesis required, foreign language not required. *Entrance requirements:* GRE General Test, minimum GPA of 2.75. Application deadline: 8/1 (rolling processing; 12/1 for spring admission). Application fee: $55. *Expenses:* Tuition $0 for state residents; $246 per unit for nonresidents. Fees $1846 per year full-time, $1180 per year part-time. *Financial aid:* Application deadline 3/2. • Dr. John Attinasi, Chair, Department of Teacher Education, 562-985-4506. Fax: 562-985-1774. E-mail: jattinas@csulb.edu.

California State University, Los Angeles, School of Education, Division of Curriculum and Instruction, Major in Elementary Teaching, Los Angeles, CA 90032-8530. Awards MA. Accredited by NCATE. Part-time and evening/weekend programs available. Students: 6 full-time (4 women), 16 part-time (14 women); includes 15 minority (2 Asian Americans, 13 Hispanics). *Degree requirements:* Comprehensive exam required, foreign language and thesis not required. *Entrance requirements:* TOEFL (minimum score 550), minimum GPA of 2.75 in last 90 units, teaching certificate. Application deadline: 6/30 (rolling processing; 2/1 for spring admission). Application fee: $55. *Expenses:* Tuition $0 for state residents; $164 per unit for nonresidents. Fees $1763 per year full-time, $1097 per year part-time. *Financial aid:* 4 students received aid; Federal Work-Study available. Aid available to part-time students. Financial aid application deadline: 3/1. • Dr. Judith Washburn, Chair, Division of Curriculum and Instruction, 213-343-4350.

California State University, Northridge, College of Education, Department of Elementary Education, Northridge, CA 91330. Awards MA. Accredited by NCATE. Part-time and evening/weekend programs available. Faculty: 21 full-time, 31 part-time. Students: 7 full-time (6 women), 58 part-time (55 women); includes 24 minority (2 African Americans, 6 Asian Americans, 15 Hispanics, 1 Native American). Average age 34. 27 applicants, 85% accepted. *Degree requirements:* Comprehensive exam required, foreign language and thesis not required. *Entrance requirements:* TOEFL, GRE General Test or minimum GPA of 3.0. Application deadline: 11/30. Application fee: $55. *Expenses:* Tuition $0 for state residents; $246 per unit for nonresidents. Fees $1970 per year full-time, $1304 per year part-time. *Financial aid:* Federal Work-Study available. Financial aid application deadline: 3/1. • Dr. Arlinda J. Eaton, Chair, 818-677-2621. Application contact: Thomas Potter, Graduate Coordinator, 818-677-2621.

California State University, San Bernardino, Graduate Studies, School of Education, San Bernardino, CA 92407-2397. Offerings include elementary education (MA). School faculty: 77 full-time (38 women). *Application deadline:* 8/31 (priority date). *Application fee:* $55. *Expenses:* Tuition $0 for state residents; $164 per unit for nonresidents. Fees $1922 per year full-time, $1256 per year part-time. • Patricia Arlin, Dean, 909-880-3600. Fax: 909-880-7011.

California State University, Stanislaus, School of Education, Department of Teacher Education, Program in Curriculum and Instruction, Specialization in Elementary Education, Turlock, CA 95382. Awards MA Ed. Part-time and evening/weekend programs available. Students: 1 (woman). In 1997, 5 degrees awarded. *Degree requirements:* Thesis required, foreign language not required. *Entrance requirements:* MAT. Application fee: $55. *Expenses:* Tuition $0 for state residents; $246 per unit for nonresidents. Fees $1779 per year full-time, $1113 per year part-time. *Financial aid:* Application deadline 3/2; applicants required to submit FAFSA. • Dr. Armin Schulz, Coordinator.

California University of Pennsylvania, School of Education, Department of Elementary Education, Program in Elementary Education, 250 University Avenue, California, PA 15419-1394. Awards M Ed. Accredited by NCATE. Part-time and evening/weekend programs available. Faculty: 10 part-time (2 women). Students: 46 full-time (30 women), 56 part-time (47 women); includes 3 minority (all African Americans). 48 applicants, 71% accepted. In 1997, 33 degrees awarded. *Degree requirements:* Comprehensive exam required, thesis optional, foreign language not required. *Entrance requirements:* MAT (minimum score 35), TOEFL (minimum score 550), minimum GPA of 3.0, teaching certificate. Application deadline: rolling. Application fee: $25. *Expenses:* Tuition $3468 per year full-time, $193 per credit part-time for state residents; $6236 per year full-time, $346 per credit part-time for nonresidents. Fees $886 per year full-time, $153 per semester (minimum) part-time. *Financial aid:* Graduate assistantships available. • Dr. Richard Wyman, Chairperson, Department of Elementary Education, 724-938-4135.

Campbell University, School of Education, Buies Creek, NC 27506. Offerings include elementary education (M Ed). Accredited by NCATE. School faculty: 8 full-time (6 women), 6 part-time (0 women). *Application deadline:* 8/1 (priority date; rolling processing; 1/2 for spring admission). *Application fee:* $25. *Tuition:* $168 per credit hour (minimum). • Dr. Margaret Giesbrecht, Dean, 910-893-1630. Fax: 910-893-1999. E-mail: giesbrec@mailcenter.campbell.edu. Application contact: James S. Farthing, Director of Graduate Admissions, 910-893-1200 Ext. 1318. Fax: 910-893-1288.

Carson-Newman College, Graduate Program in Education, Jefferson City, TN 37760. Offerings include elementary education (MAT). Accredited by NCATE. College faculty: 18 full-time (8 women), 7 part-time (5 women). *Application deadline:* 7/15 (priority date; rolling processing). *Application fee:* $25 ($50 for international students). *Expenses:* Tuition $190 per credit hour. Fees $10 per year. • Dr. Margaret A. Hypes, Chair, 423-471-3461. Application contact: Jane W. McGill, Graduate Admissions and Services Adviser, 423-471-3460. Fax: 423-471-3475.

Centenary College of Louisiana, Department of Education, Shreveport, LA 71134-1188. Offerings include elementary education (M Ed). Department faculty: 5 full-time (2 women), 6 part-time (1 woman). *Average time to degree:* master's–2 years full-time, 4 years part-time. *Entrance requirements:* GRE. Application fee: $30. *Tuition:* $360 per course. • Dr. E. John Turner, Chairman, 318-869-5223.

Central Connecticut State University, School of Education and Professional Studies, Department of Teacher Education, Program in Elementary Education, New Britain, CT 06050-4010. Awards MS. Part-time and evening/weekend programs available. Students: 37 full-time (29 women), 133 part-time (107 women); includes 9 minority (5 African Americans, 2 Asian Americans, 2 Hispanics). Average age 32. 142 applicants, 65% accepted. In 1997, 25 degrees awarded. *Degree requirements:* Thesis or alternative, comprehensive exam or special project required, foreign language not required. *Entrance requirements:* TOEFL (minimum score 550), minimum GPA of 2.7. Application deadline: 6/1 (priority date; rolling processing; 12/1 for spring admission). Application fee: $40. *Expenses:* Tuition $4458 per year full-time, $175 per credit hour part-time for state residents; $9943 per year full-time, $175 per credit hour part-time for nonresidents. Fees $45 per semester. *Financial aid:* Federal Work-Study available. Financial aid application deadline: 3/15; applicants required to submit FAFSA. *Faculty research:* Elementary school curriculum, changing school populations, multicultural education, professional development. • Dr. Susan Seider, Coordinator, 860-832-2418.

Central Michigan University, College of Education and Human Services, Department of Teacher Education and Professional Development, Program in Elementary Education, Concentration in Elementary Education, Mount Pleasant, MI 48859. Awards MA. Accredited by NCATE. Students: 26 part-time (25 women); includes 1 minority (African American). Average age 36. In 1997, 20 degrees awarded. *Degree requirements:* Thesis or alternative required, foreign language not required. *Entrance requirements:* GRE General Test (minimum combined score of 1000), minimum GPA of 2.7. Application deadline: 3/1 (priority date). Application fee: $30. *Expenses:* Tuition $139 per credit hour (minimum) for state residents; $276 per credit hour (minimum) for nonresidents. Fees $260 per year full-time, $150 per semester part-time. *Financial aid:* Federal Work-Study available. Financial aid application deadline: 3/7. • Dr. William Merrill, Chairperson, Department of Teacher Education and Professional Development, 517-774-3975. Fax: 517-774-3516. E-mail: 34ltyvi@cmich.edu.

Central Missouri State University, College of Education and Human Services, Department of Curriculum and Instruction, Warrensburg, MO 64093. Offerings include elementary education (MSE). Accredited by NCATE. Department faculty: 20 full-time. *Degree requirements:* Comprehensive exam or thesis. *Entrance requirements:* GRE General Test, minimum GPA of 2.75, teaching certificate. Application deadline: 6/30 (priority date; rolling processing). Application fee: $25 ($50 for international students). *Tuition:* $3288 per year full-time, $137 per credit hour part-time for state residents; $5928 per year full-time, $274 per credit hour part-time for nonresidents. • Dr. Ted Garten, Chair, 660-543-4235. Fax: 660-543-4167.

Central Washington University, College of Education and Professional Studies, Department of Curriculum and Supervision, Program in Elementary Education, Ellensburg, WA 98926. Awards M Ed. Part-time programs available. Faculty: 14 full-time (4 women). Students: 27 full-time (14 women), 31 part-time (26 women); includes 5 minority (1 Asian American, 2 Hispanics, 2 Native Americans). 44 applicants, 84% accepted. In 1997, 23 degrees awarded. *Degree requirements:* Thesis or alternative required, foreign language not required. *Entrance requirements:* Minimum GPA of 3.0. Application deadline: 4/1 (priority date; rolling processing; 1/1 for spring admission). Application fee: $35. *Expenses:* Tuition $4200 per year full-time, $140 per credit hour part-time for state residents; $12,780 per year full-time, $426 per credit hour part-time for nonresidents. Fees $240 per year. *Financial aid:* In 1997–98, 1 research assistantship (to a first-year student) averaging $1,108 per month and totaling $9,972, 2 teaching assistantships (1 to a first-year student) averaging $1,108 per month and totaling $19,944 were awarded; Federal Work-Study also available. Financial aid application deadline: 2/15. • Application contact: Christie A. Fevergeon, Program Coordinator, Graduate Studies and Research, 509-963-3103. Fax: 509-963-1799. E-mail: masters@cwu.edu.

Chadron State College, Department of Education, Chadron, NE 69337. Offerings include elementary education (MS Ed). Accredited by NCATE. *Application deadline:* rolling. *Application fee:* $15. *Expenses:* Tuition $1788 per year full-time, $75 per credit hour part-time for state residents; $3588 per year full-time, $149 per credit hour part-time for nonresidents. Fees $388 per year full-time, $1232 per year part-time. • Dr. Pat Colgate, Dean, School of Graduate Studies, 308-432-6330. Fax: 308-432-6454. E-mail: pcolgate@csc1.csc.edu.

Charleston Southern University, Programs in Education, Charleston, SC 29423-8087. Offerings include elementary education (M Ed). Faculty: 16 full-time (5 women), 5 part-time (3 women), 17.6 FTE. *Application deadline:* rolling. *Application fee:* $25. *Tuition:* $9821 per year full-time, $173 per hour (minimum) part-time. • Dr. Martha Watson, Director of Graduate Programs, 803-863-7555.

Chestnut Hill College, Program in Elementary Education, Philadelphia, PA 19118-2693. Awards M Ed. Part-time and evening/weekend programs available. Faculty: 6 full-time (5 women), 8 part-time (5 women). Students: 142 part-time (125 women); includes 23 minority (20 African Americans, 1 Asian American, 2 Hispanics), 1 international. Average age 32. *Average time to degree:* master's–3 years part-time. *Application deadline:* rolling. *Application fee:* $35. *Financial aid:* Graduate assistantships and career-related internships or fieldwork available. Aid available to part-time students. • Dr. Dominic Cotugno SSJ, Coordinator, 215-248-7078. Application contact: Regina Raphael Smith, Graduate Admissions, 215-248-7020. Fax: 215-248-7155.

Cheyney University of Pennsylvania, Program in Elementary Education, Cheyney, PA 19319. Awards M Ed. Accredited by NCATE. Part-time and evening/weekend programs available. Faculty: 5 full-time (3 women), 7 part-time (4 women). Students: 16 full-time (10 women), 73 part-time (48 women); includes 79 minority (77 African Americans, 2 Hispanics). Average age 39. In 1997, 43 degrees awarded. *Degree requirements:* Thesis or alternative required, foreign language not required. *Entrance requirements:* GRE General Test, MAT, minimum GPA of 2.75. Application deadline: 8/1 (priority date; rolling processing; 12/15 for spring admission). Application fee: $25. *Tuition:* $3848 per year full-time, $193 per credit hour part-time for state residents; $6616 per year full-time, $346 per credit hour part-time for nonresidents. *Financial aid:* Assistantships, institutionally sponsored loans, and career-related internships or fieldwork available. Financial aid application deadline: 5/1. • E. Sonny Harris, Coordinator, 610-399-2262. Application contact: Dean of Graduate Studies, 610-399-2400. Fax: 610-399-2118.

Chicago State University, Departments of Early Childhood and Elementary Education and Curriculum and Instruction, Program in Elementary Education, Chicago, IL 60628. Awards MS Ed. Accredited by NCATE. *Degree requirements:* Thesis optional, foreign language not required. *Entrance requirements:* Minimum GPA of 2.75. Application deadline: 7/1 (11/10 for spring admission). *Tuition:* $2268 per year full-time, $95 per credit hour part-time for state residents; $6804 per year full-time, $284 per credit hour part-time for nonresidents.

City College of the City University of New York, Graduate School, School of Education, Department of Elementary Education, Program in Elementary Education, Convent Avenue at 138th Street, New York, NY 10031-6977. Awards MS. Students: 10 full-time (9 women), 132 part-time (100 women). In 1997, 64 degrees awarded. *Degree requirements:* Thesis required, foreign language not required. *Entrance requirements:* TOEFL (minimum score 500). Application fee: $40. *Expenses:* Tuition $4350 per year full-time, $185 per credit part-time for state residents; $7600 per year full-time, $320 per credit part-time for nonresidents. Fees $41 per year. *Financial aid:* Career-related internships or fieldwork available. • Head, 212-650-6253.

Clarion University of Pennsylvania, College of Education and Human Services, Department of Education, Program in Elementary Education, Clarion, PA 16214. Awards M Ed. Accredited by NCATE. Part-time programs available. Faculty: 15 full-time (9 women). Students: 1 (woman) full-time, 13 part-time (11 women); includes 1 international. 6 applicants, 67% accepted. In 1997, 2 degrees awarded. *Degree requirements:* Thesis or alternative required, foreign language not required. *Entrance requirements:* Minimum QPA of 2.75. Application deadline: 8/1 (priority date; rolling processing). Application fee: $25. *Expenses:* Tuition $3468 per year full-time, $193 per credit hour part-time for state residents; $6236 per year full-time, $346 per credit hour part-time for nonresidents. Fees $921 per year full-time, $90 per credit hour part-time for state residents; $921 per year full-time, $89 per credit hour part-time for nonresidents. *Financial aid:* In 1997–98, 3 research assistantships (1 to a first-year student) averaging $533 per month were awarded. Aid available to part-time students. Financial aid application deadline: 5/1. • Application contact: Dr. Gail Grejda, Graduate Coordinator, 814-226-2058.

Clemson University, College of Health, Education, and Human Development, Department of Curriculum and Instruction, Program in Elementary Education, Clemson, SC 29634. Awards M Ed. Accredited by NCATE. Students: 1 (woman) full-time, 43 part-time (40 women); includes 5 minority (4 African Americans, 1 Hispanic). 27 applicants, 74% accepted. In 1997, 29 degrees awarded. *Degree requirements:* Written comprehensive exam required, foreign language and thesis not required. *Entrance requirements:* TOEFL, teaching certificate. Application deadline: 6/1. Application fee: $35. *Expenses:* Tuition $3154 per year full-time, $130 per credit hour part-time for state residents; $6452 per year full-time, $264 per credit hour part-time for nonresidents. Fees $190 per year. *Financial aid:* Teaching assistantships available. Financial aid application deadline: 6/1. • Dr. Robert Green, Chair, Department of Curriculum and Instruction, 864-656-5108. Fax: 864-656-1322. E-mail: rpgreen@clemson.edu.

Cleveland State University, College of Education, Department of Specialized Instructional Programs, Cleveland, OH 44115-2440. Offerings include curriculum and instruction (M Ed), with options in bilingual education, early childhood education, early childhood/special education, education of emerging adolescents, elementary education, English as a second language, learning disabilities, Montessori education, multihandicapped, reading, secondary education.

Directory: Elementary Education

Cleveland State University (continued)
Department faculty: 18 full-time (12 women). *Entrance requirements:* GRE General Test or MAT (score in 50th percentile or higher). Application deadline: 9/1 (priority date; rolling processing). Application fee: $25. *Expenses:* Tuition $5252 per year full-time, $202 per credit hour part-time for state residents; $10,504 per year full-time, $404 per credit hour part-time for nonresidents. Fees $2.25 per credit hour (minimum). • Dr. Jane Zaharias, Chairperson, 216-687-4585. Fax: 216-687-5379. E-mail: j.zaharias@csuohio.edu.

Coastal Carolina University, School of Education, Program in Education, Conway, SC 29528-6054. Offerings include elementary education (M Ed). Program faculty: 6 full-time (3 women). *Entrance requirements:* GRE General Test (minimum combined score of 800), MAT (minimum score 35), teacher certification. Application deadline: 8/15 (priority date; rolling processing). Application fee: $25. Electronic applications accepted. • Dr. Sandra Bowden, Head, 843-349-2606.

College of Mount St. Joseph, Education Department, Program in Elementary Education, Cincinnati, OH 45233-1670. Awards MA Ed. Program being phased out; applicants no longer accepted. Part-time and evening/weekend programs available. Faculty: 3 full-time, 3 part-time. *Degree requirements:* Comprehensive exam required, foreign language and thesis not required. *Application deadline:* rolling. *Tuition:* $320 per credit hour. • Dr. Barbara Reid, Chairperson, Education Department, 513-244-4812. Fax: 513-244-4222. Application contact: Jean Abrams, Graduate Secretary, 513-244-4812.

The College of New Jersey, Graduate Division, School of Education, Department of Elementary/Early Childhood Education, Program in Elementary Education, Ewing, NJ 08628. Awards MAT, M Ed. Accredited by NCATE. Part-time and evening/weekend programs available. Students: 26 full-time (19 women), 110 part-time (90 women); includes 21 minority (3 African Americans, 2 Asian Americans, 15 Hispanics, 1 Native American), 5 international. Average age 27. In 1997, 47 degrees awarded. *Degree requirements:* Comprehensive exam required, foreign language and thesis not required. *Average time to degree:* master's–2 years full-time. *Entrance requirements:* GRE General Test, minimum GPA of 3.0 in field or 2.75 overall. Application deadline: 4/15 (10/15 for spring admission). Application fee: $50. *Expenses:* Tuition $6892 per year full-time, $287 per credit hour part-time for state residents; $9602 per year full-time, $402 per credit hour part-time for nonresidents. Fees $799 per year full-time, $33 per credit hour part-time. *Financial aid:* Graduate assistantships available. Financial aid application deadline: 5/1; applicants required to submit FAFSA. • Dr. Brenda Leake, Coordinator of M Ed Program, 609-771-2219. Application contact: Dr. Anthony Conte, Coordinator of MAT Program, 609-771-2991. Fax: 609-637-5197.

College of New Rochelle, Division of Education, Program in Elementary Education/Early Childhood Education, New Rochelle, NY 10805-2308. Awards MS Ed. Part-time programs available. Faculty: 2 full-time (both women), 5 part-time (3 women), 4 FTE. Students: 13 full-time (11 women), 121 part-time (109 women); includes 11 minority (5 African Americans, 6 Hispanics). 45 applicants, 84% accepted. In 1997, 43 degrees awarded. *Degree requirements:* Practicum required, foreign language not required. *Average time to degree:* master's–1.5 years full-time, 3 years part-time. *Entrance requirements:* Interview; minimum GPA of 3.0 in field, 2.7 overall. Application deadline: 8/1 (priority date; rolling processing). Application fee: $35. *Tuition:* $329 per credit. *Financial aid:* In 1997–98, 12 students received aid, including 1 assistantship totaling $4,050; research assistantships and career-related internships or fieldwork also available. • Dr. Melanie Hannigan, Division Head, Division of Education, 914-654-5330.

College of Notre Dame, Department of Education, Emphasis in Elementary Education, Belmont, CA 94002-1997. Offers programs in educational technology (M Ed), elementary education (Certificate), multicultural education (M Ed). Faculty: 6 full-time, 16 part-time. Students: 88 full-time (82 women), 98 part-time (88 women). Average age 31. In 1997, 4 master's awarded. *Entrance requirements:* For master's, PRAXIS, TOEFL (minimum score 550), interview, minimum GPA of 2.5. Application deadline: rolling. Application fee: $50 ($500 for international students). *Tuition:* $460 per unit. *Financial aid:* Career-related internships or fieldwork available. Aid available to part-time students. • Dr. Carla Eide, Program Director of Multiple Subject Credential, 650-508-3706.

College of Our Lady of the Elms, Department of Education, Chicopee, MA 01013-2839. Offerings include elementary education (MAT). Department faculty: 7 full-time (all women), 6 part-time (5 women). *Application deadline:* rolling. *Application fee:* $30. *Expenses:* Tuition $320 per credit. Fees $40 per year. • Sr. Kathleen M. Kirley, Dean of Continuing Education and Graduate Studies, 413-594-2761. Fax: 413-592-4871. Application contact: Dr. Mary Janeczek, Director, 413-594-2761.

College of St. Joseph, Division of Education, Program in Elementary Education, Rutland, VT 05701-3899. Awards M Ed. Part-time and evening/weekend programs available. Faculty: 3 full-time (2 women), 9 part-time (7 women). Students: 7 full-time (5 women), 14 part-time (11 women). *Degree requirements:* Comprehensive exams required, foreign language and thesis not required. *Entrance requirements:* GRE General Test (combined average 1100), interview. Application deadline: rolling. Application fee: $25. *Tuition:* $7950 per year full-time, $220 per credit part-time. *Financial aid:* Federal Work-Study and career-related internships or fieldwork available. Aid available to part-time students. Financial aid application deadline: 3/1. • Application contact: Steve Soba, Director of Admissions, 802-773-5900 Ext. 206. Fax: 802-773-5900 Ext. 258. E-mail: suite9@aol.com.

The College of Saint Rose, School of Education, Teacher Education Department, Program in Elementary Education, Albany, NY 12203-1419. Awards MS Ed. Part-time and evening/weekend programs available. Faculty: 10 full-time (6 women), 1 (woman) part-time. Students: 27 full-time (20 women), 104 part-time (88 women); includes 3 minority (2 African Americans, 1 Asian American). Average age 31. In 1997, 47 degrees awarded. *Degree requirements:* Thesis or alternative, comprehensive exam required, foreign language not required. *Entrance requirements:* Minimum undergraduate GPA of 3.0. Application deadline: 7/15 (priority date; rolling processing; 12/1 for spring admission). Application fee: $30. *Expenses:* Tuition $338 per credit. Fees $60 per year. *Financial aid:* Research assistantships, partial tuition waivers, and career-related internships or fieldwork available. Aid available to part-time students. Financial aid application deadline: 3/1; applicants required to submit FAFSA. • Application contact: Graduate Office, 518-454-5136. Fax: 518-458-5479. E-mail: ace@rosnet.strose.edu.

College of Staten Island of the City University of New York, Department of Education, Program in Elementary Education, Staten Island, NY 10314-6600. Awards MS Ed. Evening/weekend programs available. Faculty: 10 full-time (2 women), 8 part-time (5 women). Students: 13 full-time (all women), 342 part-time (322 women); includes 13 minority (5 African Americans, 1 Asian American, 6 Hispanics, 1 Native American). Average age 31. In 1997, 160 degrees awarded. *Entrance requirements:* Teaching certificate. Application deadline: 6/1 (priority date; rolling processing; 12/1 for spring admission). Application fee: $40. *Expenses:* Tuition $4350 per year full-time, $185 per credit part-time for state residents; $7600 per year full-time, $320 per credit part-time for nonresidents. Fees $106 per year full-time, $54 per year part-time. • Dr. Jed Luchow, Coordinator, 718-982-3740. Application contact: Earl Teasley, Director of Admissions, 718-982-2010. Fax: 718-982-2500.

The Colorado College, Programs for Experienced Teachers, Colorado Springs, CO 80903-3294. Offerings include liberal arts for elementary school teachers and administrators (MAT). Offered during summer only. *Degree requirements:* Thesis, oral exam, 30-50 page paper required, foreign language not required. *Entrance requirements:* Minimum undergraduate GPA of 2.75. Application deadline: rolling. Application fee: $30.

The Colorado College, Department of Education, Program in Elementary Education, Colorado Springs, CO 80903-3294. Offers elementary school teaching (MAT). Faculty: 2 full-time (1 woman), 12 part-time (9 women). Students: 16 full-time (12 women); includes 1 minority (Hispanic). Average age 28. 37 applicants, 43% accepted. In 1997, 21 degrees awarded (100% found work related to degree). *Degree requirements:* Thesis, internship required, foreign language not required. *Entrance requirements:* GRE Subject Test, Program for Licensing Assessments for Colorado Educators Basic Skills Test. Application deadline: 3/1. Application fee: $40. *Financial aid:* In 1997–98, 15 fellowships (all to first-year students) were awarded; institutionally sponsored loans and career-related internships or fieldwork also available. Financial aid application deadline: 3/1; applicants required to submit CSS PROFILE or FAFSA. • Application contact: Marsha Unruh, Educational Services Coordinator, 719-389-6472. Fax: 719-389-6473.

Columbia College, Department of Educational Studies, 600 South Michigan Avenue, Chicago, IL 60605-1997. Offerings include elementary (MAT). *Application deadline:* 7/15 (rolling processing; 12/4 for spring admission). *Application fee:* $35. *Expenses:* Tuition $392 per credit hour. Fees $170 per year full-time, $150 per year part-time.

Columbia College, Department of Elementary Education, Columbia, SC 29203-5998. Awards M Ed. Part-time programs available. Faculty: 22 full-time (10 women). Students: 38 part-time (29 women); includes 5 minority (all African Americans). Average age 30. In 1997, 12 degrees awarded (100% found work related to degree). *Degree requirements:* Thesis or alternative, comprehensive exam required, foreign language not required. *Average time to degree:* master's–4 years part-time. *Entrance requirements:* NTE, minimum B average, teaching certificate. Application deadline: rolling. Application fee: $20. *Tuition:* $200 per credit hour. *Financial aid:* Career-related internships or fieldwork available. Aid available to part-time students. Financial aid applicants required to submit FAFSA. • Dr. Barbara Gottesman, Chair, 803-786-3747. Fax: 803-786-3034. E-mail: bgottesman@colacoll.edu. Application contact: Laura McElwaine, Director of Graduate Admissions, 803-786-3871. Fax: 803-786-3674. E-mail: lmcelwaine@colacoll.edu.

Concordia University, Graduate Programs in Education, Program in Elementary Education, Seward, NE 68434-1599. Awards M Ed. Accredited by NCATE. Part-time programs available. Faculty: 14 full-time (2 women). Students: 3 full-time (all women), 56 part-time (37 women); includes 4 minority (3 Asian Americans, 1 Native American), 2 international. 13 applicants, 100% accepted. In 1997, 3 degrees awarded (100% found work related to degree). *Degree requirements:* Thesis or alternative required, foreign language not required. *Entrance requirements:* GRE, MAT, or NTE, minimum GPA of 3.0, BS in education or equivalent. Application deadline: 8/1 (priority date; rolling processing; 12/1 for spring admission). Application fee: $15. *Tuition:* $127 per hour. *Financial aid:* Federal Work-Study, institutionally sponsored loans available. Aid available to part-time students. Financial aid applicants required to submit FAFSA. • Dr. William Preuss, Coordinator, 402-643-7480.

Concordia University, College of Education, Portland, OR 97211-6099. Offerings include elementary education (MAT). College faculty: 8 part-time (3 women). *Application deadline:* rolling. *Application fee:* $35. *Tuition:* $350 per credit. • Dr. Joseph Mannion, Dean, 503-493-6233. Application contact: Dr. Peter Johnson, Director of Admissions, 503-280-8501.

Concordia University at St. Paul, Program in Education, St. Paul, MN 55104-5494. Offerings include elementary education (MA Ed). Postbaccalaureate distance learning degree programs offered (minimal on-campus study). Program faculty: 13 full-time (6 women), 8 part-time (4 women), 15 FTE. *Degree requirements:* Thesis or alternative required, foreign language not required. *Application deadline:* rolling. *Application fee:* $20. *Tuition:* $220 per semester hour. • Dr. Robert DeWerff, Dean of Graduate and Continuing Studies, 612-641-8277. Fax: 612-659-0207. E-mail: dewerff@luther.csp.edu.

Connecticut College, Programs in Education, Program in Elementary Education, New London, CT 06320-4196. Awards MAT. Part-time programs available. *Entrance requirements:* MAT. Application deadline: 2/2. Application fee: $35.

Converse College, Department of Education, Program in Elementary Education, Spartanburg, SC 29302-0006. Awards M Ed. Part-time programs available. Faculty: 2 full-time, 4 part-time. Students: 213 (153 women); includes 35 minority (30 African Americans, 3 Asian Americans, 2 Hispanics). Average age 35. 36 applicants, 97% accepted. In 1997, 76 degrees awarded. *Entrance requirements:* NTE, minimum GPA of 2.5. Application deadline: 5/1 (priority date; rolling processing; 1/30 for spring admission). Application fee: $35. *Tuition:* $185 per credit. *Financial aid:* Available to part-time students. Financial aid applicants required to submit FAFSA. • Dr. Anita P. Davis, Director, 864-596-9017.

Cumberland College, Program in Elementary Education, 6178 College Station Drive, Williamsburg, KY 40769-1372. Offers early elementary K–4 (MA Ed), middle school 5–8 (MA Ed). Part-time and evening/weekend programs available. Faculty: 4 full-time (2 women), 5 part-time (2 women). *Degree requirements:* Comprehensive exam required, foreign language and thesis not required. *Entrance requirements:* GRE or NTE, Kentucky teaching certificate. Application deadline: 8/26 (rolling processing). Application fee: $25. *Tuition:* $175 per credit. • Application contact: Erica Harris, Admissions Office, 606-539-4241.

Cumberland College, Program in Elementary/Secondary Teaching, 6178 College Station Drive, Williamsburg, KY 40769-1372. Awards Certificate. Faculty: 4 full-time (2 women), 5 part-time (2 women). *Entrance requirements:* Master's degree, 3 years of teaching experience. Application deadline: 8/26 (rolling processing). Application fee: $25. *Tuition:* $175 per credit. • Application contact: Erica Harris, Admissions Office, 606-539-4241.

Dallas Baptist University, Dorothy M. Bush College of Education, Education Program, Dallas, TX 75211-9299. Offerings include general elementary education (M Ed). Program faculty: 15 full-time (4 women), 5 part-time (3 women). *Entrance requirements:* GRE General Test, TOEFL (minimum score 550). Application deadline: rolling. Application fee: $25. *Tuition:* $285 per hour. • Dr. Bill Gilbert, Director, 214-333-5404. Fax: 214-333-5551. Application contact: Travis Bundrick, Director of Graduate Programs, 214-333-5243. Fax: 214-333-5579. E-mail: graduate@dbu.edu.

Delta State University, School of Education, Division of Curriculum, Instruction, Leadership and Research, Program in Elementary Education, Cleveland, MS 38733-0001. Awards M Ed, Ed S. Accredited by NCATE. Part-time and evening/weekend programs available. *Degree requirements:* For master's, thesis optional, foreign language not required. *Entrance requirements:* For master's, GRE General Test (minimum combined score of 800) or MAT (minimum score 34); for Ed S, master's degree, teaching certificate. Application deadline: 8/1 (priority date; rolling processing). Application fee: $0. *Tuition:* $2596 per year full-time, $121 per semester hour part-time for state residents; $5546 per year full-time, $285 per semester hour part-time for nonresidents. *Financial aid:* Research assistantships, Federal Work-Study, institutionally sponsored loans, and career-related internships or fieldwork available. Aid available to part-time students. Financial aid application deadline: 6/1. • Application contact: Dr. John Thornell, Dean of Graduate Studies and Continuing Education, 601-846-4310. Fax: 601-846-4016.

DePaul University, School of Education, Program in Curriculum Development, Chicago, IL 60604-2287. Offerings include elementary education (MA, M Ed). Accredited by NCATE. *Degree requirements:* Oral exam or thesis required, foreign language not required. *Entrance requirements:* Interview, minimum GPA of 2.75, work experience. Application deadline: rolling. Application fee: $25. *Expenses:* Tuition $320 per credit hour. Fees $30 per year. • Dr. Barbara Sizemore, Dean, School of Education, 312-325-7000 Ext. 1666. Fax: 312-325-7748. Application contact: Director of Graduate Admissions, 312-325-7000 Ext. 1666. E-mail: mmurphy@wppost.depaul.edu.

DePaul University, School of Education, Program in Human Services and Counseling, Chicago, IL 60604-2287. Offerings include elementary schools (MA, M Ed). Accredited by NCATE. Program faculty: 3 full-time (1 woman). *Degree requirements:* Oral exam or thesis required, foreign language not required. *Entrance requirements:* Interview, minimum GPA of 2.75, work experience. Application deadline: rolling. Application fee: $25. *Expenses:* Tuition $320 per credit hour. Fees $30 per year. • Dr. Barbara Sizemore, Dean, School of Education, 312-325-7000 Ext. 1666. Fax: 312-325-7748. Application contact: Director of Graduate Admissions, 312-325-7000 Ext. 1666. E-mail: mmurphy@wppost.depaul.edu.

Dowling College, Programs in Elementary Education, Oakdale, NY 11769-1999. Awards MS Ed. Part-time and evening/weekend programs available. Faculty: 5 full-time (all women), 12 part-time (5 women). Students: 10 full-time (8 women), 487 part-time (378 women); includes 14 minority (4 African Americans, 4 Asian Americans, 6 Hispanics). Average age 32. In 1997, 128 degrees awarded. *Degree requirements:* Comprehensive exam required, foreign language and thesis not required. *Entrance requirements:* Provisional teaching certificate. Application deadline: 9/1 (priority date; rolling processing). Application fee: $0. *Financial aid:* General graduate assistantships, Federal Work-Study, and career-related internships or fieldwork available. Aid available to part-time students. Financial aid application deadline: 4/30. • Dr. Jerome Traiger, Discipline Coordinator, 516-244-3459. Fax: 516-244-5036. Application contact: Kate Rowe, Director of Admissions, 516-244-3030. Fax: 516-563-3827. E-mail: rowek@dowling.edu.

Drake University, School of Education, Department of Teaching and Learning, Program in Elementary Education, Des Moines, IA 50311-4516. Awards MST. Faculty: 8 full-time (2 women), 5 part-time (4 women). Students: 2 full-time (1 woman), 14 part-time (13 women); includes 1 minority (Asian American). 13 applicants, 85% accepted. In 1997, 6 degrees awarded. *Entrance requirements:* GRE General Test (minimum combined score of 1000) or MAT (minimum score 36). Application deadline: rolling. Application fee: $25. *Tuition:* $16,000 per year full-time, $260 per hour (minimum) part-time. *Financial aid:* Career-related internships or fieldwork available. Aid available to part-time students. • Dr. Lloyd Stjernberg, Coordinator, 515-271-3992. Application contact: Ann J. Martin, Graduate Coordinator, 515-271-3871. Fax: 515-271-2831. E-mail: ajm@admin.drake.edu.

Drury College, Graduate Programs in Education, Program in Elementary Education, Springfield, MO 65802-3791. Awards M Ed. Accredited by NCATE. Part-time and evening/weekend programs available. Faculty: 25 applicants, 100% accepted. In 1997, 54 degrees awarded. *Degree requirements:* Thesis required, foreign language not required. *Average time to degree:* master's–1.5 years full-time, 3 years part-time. *Entrance requirements:* MAT (minimum score 35), minimum GPA of 2.75. Application fee: $15. *Tuition:* $170 per credit hour. *Financial aid:* Career-related internships or fieldwork available. • Dr. Melissa Hartley-Montgomery, Head, 417-873-7266.

Duquesne University, School of Education, Department of Elementary, Secondary, and Reading Education, Program in Elementary Education, Pittsburgh, PA 15282-0001. Awards MS Ed. Faculty: 5 full-time (2 women), 2 part-time (1 woman). Students: 120. 66 applicants, 68% accepted. In 1997, 74 degrees awarded. *Average time to degree:* master's–1.5 years full-time, 2.5 years part-time. *Entrance requirements:* MAT. Application deadline: 8/1 (rolling processing; 12/1 for spring admission). Application fee: $40. *Expenses:* Tuition $481 per credit. Fees $39 per credit. • Application contact: Dr. Joseph T. Brennan, Coordinator, 412-396-6089. Fax: 412-396-5585.

D'Youville College, Division of Education, Buffalo, NY 14201-1084. Offerings include elementary education (MS Ed). Division faculty: 5 full-time (4 women), 8 part-time (2 women). *Degree requirements:* Computer language, thesis required, foreign language not required. *Entrance requirements:* Minimum GPA of 3.0. Application deadline: rolling. Application fee: $25. *Expenses:* Tuition $357 per credit hour. Fees $350 per year. • Dr. Robert DiSibio, Graduate Director, 716-881-3200. Application contact: Joseph Syracuse, Graduate Admissions Director, 716-881-7676. Fax: 716-881-7790.

East Carolina University, School of Education, Department of Elementary Education, Greenville, NC 27858-4353. Offers programs in elementary education (MA Ed), middle grade education (MA Ed), reading education (MA Ed). Accredited by NCATE. Part-time and evening/weekend programs available. Faculty: 8 full-time (5 women). Students: 13 full-time (10 women), 72 part-time (68 women); includes 8 minority (all African Americans). Average age 32. 58 applicants, 76% accepted. In 1997, 30 degrees awarded. *Degree requirements:* Comprehensive exams required, thesis optional. *Entrance requirements:* GRE General Test or MAT, TOEFL. Application deadline: 6/1 (priority date; rolling processing). Application fee: $40. *Tuition:* $1886 per year full-time, $472 per semester (minimum) part-time for state residents; $9156 per year full-time, $2289 per semester (minimum) part-time for nonresidents. *Financial aid:* Research assistantships, teaching assistantships, Federal Work-Study available. Aid available to part-time students. Financial aid application deadline: 6/1. • Dr. Parmalee Hawk, Acting Chair, 252-328-6271. Fax: 252-328-4219. E-mail: hawkp@mail.ecu.edu.

Eastern Connecticut State University, School of Education and Professional Studies/Graduate Division, Program in Elementary Education, Willimantic, CT 06226-2295. Awards MS. Faculty: 5 full-time (3 women), 4 part-time (3 women). Students: 12 full-time (7 women), 69 part-time (61 women). Average age 35. 13 applicants, 100% accepted. In 1997, 20 degrees awarded. *Degree requirements:* Comprehensive exam or thesis required, foreign language not required. *Entrance requirements:* Minimum GPA of 2.7, teaching certificate. Application fee: $40. *Expenses:* Tuition $2632 per year full-time, $175 per credit hour part-time for state residents; $7220 per year full-time, $175 per credit hour part-time for nonresidents. Fees $1851 per year full-time, $20 per semester part-time for state residents; $2748 per year full-time, $20 per semester part-time for nonresidents. *Financial aid:* Career-related internships or fieldwork available. Financial aid application deadline: 3/15. • Dr. Leslie Ricklin, Head, 860-465-5229. E-mail: ricklinl@ecsuc.ctstateu.edu. Application contact: Edith Mavor, Graduate Division Director, 860-465-4543. E-mail: mavor@ecsuc.ctstateu.edu.

Eastern Illinois University, College of Education and Professional Studies, Department of Elementary and Junior High School Education, 600 Lincoln Avenue, Charleston, IL 61920-3099. Offers programs in elementary education (MS Ed), junior high education (MS Ed). Accredited by NCATE. Part-time programs available. Faculty: 14 full-time (6 women). Students: 15 full-time (12 women), 129 part-time (115 women). In 1997, 29 degrees awarded. *Degree requirements:* Comprehensive exam required, foreign language and thesis not required. *Application deadline:* 7/31 (priority date; rolling processing). *Application fee:* $25. *Expenses:* Tuition $3459 per year full-time, $96 per semester hour part-time for state residents; $10,377 per year full-time, $288 per semester hour part-time for nonresidents. Fees $1566 per year full-time, $37 per semester hour part-time. *Financial aid:* In 1997–98, 1 research assistantship, 4 teaching assistantships were awarded. • Dr. Carol Helwig, Chairperson, 217-581-5728. E-mail: cfcmh2@eiu.edu.

Eastern Kentucky University, College of Education, Department of Curriculum and Instruction, Richmond, KY 40475-3101. Offerings include elementary education general (MA Ed), with options in early elementary education, elementary education general, reading. Accredited by NCATE. *Entrance requirements:* GRE General Test, minimum GPA of 2.5. Application fee: $0. *Tuition:* $2390 per year full-time, $133 per credit hour part-time for state residents; $6630 per year full-time, $365 per credit hour part-time for nonresidents. • Dr. Imogene Ramsey, Chair, 606-622-2154.

Eastern Michigan University, College of Education, Department of Teacher Education, Program in Elementary Education, Ypsilanti, MI 48197. Awards MA. Accredited by NCATE. Evening/weekend programs available. In 1997, 61 degrees awarded. *Entrance requirements:* GRE, TOEFL (minimum score 500). Application deadline: 5/15 (rolling processing; 3/15 for spring admission). Application fee: $30. *Expenses:* Tuition $2691 per year full-time, $150 per credit hour part-time for state residents; $6300 per year full-time, $350 per credit hour part-time for nonresidents. Fees $368 per year full-time, $88 per semester (minimum) part-time. *Financial aid:* Fellowships, teaching assistantships available. Aid available to part-time students. Financial aid application deadline: 3/15; applicants required to submit FAFSA. • Dr. Leah Adams, Coordinator, 734-487-1424.

Eastern Nazarene College, Graduate Studies, Division of Education, Quincy, MA 02170-2999. Offerings include elementary education (M Ed, Certificate). M Ed and Certificate also available through weekend program for administration, special needs, and reading only. Division faculty: 9 full-time (5 women), 11 part-time (5 women). *Entrance requirements:* For master's, TOEFL (minimum score 500). Application deadline: rolling. Application fee: $35. *Expenses:* Tuition $350 per credit. Fees $125 per semester full-time, $15 per semester part-time. • Dr. Lorne Ranstrom, Chair, 617-745-3528. Application contact: Cleo P. Cakridas, Graduate Enrollment Counselor, 617-745-3870. Fax: 617-745-3907. E-mail: cakridac@enc.edu.

Eastern Oregon University, School of Education, Program in Elementary Education, La Grande, OR 97850-2899. Awards MTE. Part-time programs available. Postbaccalaureate distance learning degree programs offered (minimal on-campus study). Faculty: 12 full-time (3 women), 8 part-time (4 women). Students: 50 full-time (45 women), 110 part-time (70 women); includes 7 minority (all Hispanics). In 1997, 27 degrees awarded. *Degree requirements:* Thesis required, foreign language not required. *Average time to degree:* master's–1 year full-time. *Entrance requirements:* NTE. Application deadline: 1/15 (priority date; rolling processing). Application fee: $50. *Expenses:* Tuition $4371 per year for state residents; $8379 per year for nonresidents. Fees $957 per year. *Financial aid:* Full and partial tuition waivers, Federal Work-Study available. Aid available to part-time students. • Dr. Michael Jaeger, Dean, 541-962-3682. Fax: 541-962-3701. E-mail: mjaeger@eou.edu.

Eastern Washington University, College of Education and Human Development, Department of Education, Program in Elementary Teaching, Cheney, WA 99004-2431. Awards M Ed. Accredited by NCATE. *Degree requirements:* Comprehensive exam required, thesis not required. *Entrance requirements:* Minimum GPA of 3.0. Application deadline: 4/1 (priority date; rolling processing; 1/15 for spring admission). Application fee: $35. *Tuition:* $4200 per year full-time, $140 per credit part-time for state residents; $12,780 per year full-time, $415 per credit part-time for nonresidents. *Financial aid:* Application deadline 2/1. • Dr. Charles Miller, Adviser, 509-359-7024.

East Stroudsburg University of Pennsylvania, School of Professional Studies, Program in Elementary Education, East Stroudsburg, PA 18301-2999. Awards M Ed. Part-time and evening/weekend programs available. *Degree requirements:* Comprehensive exam required, foreign language and thesis not required. *Application deadline:* 7/31 (priority date; rolling processing; 11/30 for spring admission). *Application fee:* $15 ($25 for international students). *Expenses:* Tuition $3468 per year full-time, $193 per credit part-time for state residents; $6236 per year full-time, $346 per credit part-time for nonresidents. Fees $700 per year full-time, $39 per credit part-time.

East Tennessee State University, College of Education, Department of Curriculum and Instruction, Johnson City, TN 37614-0734. Offerings include elementary education (MAT, M Ed). Accredited by NCATE. Department faculty: 17 full-time (8 women). *Application deadline:* 7/15 (priority date; rolling processing; 12/1 for spring admission). *Application fee:* $25 ($35 for international students). *Tuition:* $2944 per year full-time, $158 per credit hour part-time for state residents; $7770 per year full-time, $369 per credit hour part-time for nonresidents. • Dr. Jack Rhoton, Chair, 423-439-4426. Fax: 423-439-8362.

Edinboro University of Pennsylvania, School of Education, Department of Elementary Education, Program in Elementary Education, Edinboro, PA 16444. Offers early childhood (M Ed), elementary education (M Ed), elementary education clinical (M Ed), language arts (M Ed), mathematics (M Ed), science (M Ed), social studies (M Ed). Students: 25 full-time (19 women), 36 part-time (32 women); includes 1 minority (African American). Average age 31. In 1997, 22 degrees awarded. *Degree requirements:* Thesis or alternative required, foreign language not required. *Entrance requirements:* GRE or MAT (score in 30th percentile or higher). Application deadline: rolling. Application fee: $25. *Expenses:* Tuition $3468 per year full-time, $193 per credit part-time for state residents; $6236 per year full-time, $346 per credit part-time for nonresidents. Fees $898 per year full-time, $50 per semester (minimum) part-time. *Financial aid:* In 1997–98, 10 assistantships were awarded. • Application contact: Dr. Philip Kerstetter, Dean of Graduate Studies, 814-732-2856. Fax: 814-732-2611. E-mail: kerstetter@edinboro.edu.

Elmira College, Graduate Programs in Education, Program in Elementary Education, Elmira, NY 14901. Awards MS Ed. Part-time and evening/weekend programs available. Faculty: 5 full-time (3 women), 31 part-time (12 women). Students: 40. *Degree requirements:* Thesis or alternative required, foreign language not required. *Entrance requirements:* Provisional New York state certification. Application fee: $35. *Tuition:* $344 per credit hour. *Financial aid:* Career-related internships or fieldwork available. Aid available to part-time students. • Dr. John Madison, Director of Education, 607-735-1912. Application contact: Judith B. Clack, Associate Dean for Graduate Studies, 607-735-1825.

Elon College, Program in Education, Elon College, NC 27244. Offerings include elementary education (M Ed). Accredited by NCATE. Program faculty: 15 full-time (10 women). *Entrance requirements:* GRE, MAT, NTE (special education). Application deadline: 8/15 (priority date; rolling processing). Application fee: $25. *Tuition:* $210 per credit hour. • Dr. Glenda W. Beamon, Director, 336-584-2126. Fax: 336-538-2609. E-mail: beamon@vax1.elon.edu. Application contact: Alice N. Essen, Director of Graduate Admissions, 800-334-8448. Fax: 336-538-3986. E-mail: essen@numen.elon.edu.

Emporia State University, School of Graduate Studies, The Teachers College, Division of Early Childhood/Elementary Teacher Education, Program in Elementary Education, Emporia, KS 66801-5087. Awards MS. Accredited by NCATE. Students: 3 full-time (all women), 11 part-time (10 women); includes 1 international. 1 applicant, 100% accepted. In 1997, 4 degrees awarded. *Degree requirements:* Comprehensive exam or thesis required, foreign language not required. *Entrance requirements:* GRE General Test or MAT, TOEFL (minimum score 550), written exam. Application deadline: 8/15 (priority date; rolling processing). Application fee: $30 ($75 for international students). Electronic applications accepted. *Tuition:* $2300 per year full-time, $103 per credit hour part-time for state residents; $6012 per year full-time, $258 per credit hour part-time for nonresidents. *Financial aid:* Federal Work-Study, institutionally sponsored loans available. Financial aid application deadline: 3/15; applicants required to submit FAFSA. • Dr. Eileen Hogan, Chair, Division of Early Childhood/Elementary Teacher Education, 316-341-5751. E-mail: hoganeil@emporia.edu.

Endicott College, School of Continuing Education and Graduate Studies, Program in Elementary Education, Beverly, MA 01915-2096. Awards M Ed. Part-time and evening/weekend programs available. Postbaccalaureate distance learning degree programs offered (minimal on-campus study). Faculty: 9 part-time (7 women). Students: 21 full-time (16 women); includes 2 Hispanics. Average age 35. 13 applicants, 100% accepted. *Degree requirements:* Written comprehensive exams required, foreign language and thesis not required. *Entrance requirements:* MAT (minimum score 50). Application deadline: rolling. Application fee: $50. Electronic applications accepted. *Tuition:* $585 per course. *Financial aid:* Federal Work-Study, institutionally sponsored loans, and career-related internships or fieldwork available. • Dr. Paul J. Tortolani, Dean, School of Continuing Education and Graduate Studies, 978-232-2199. Fax: 978-232-3000. E-mail: ptortola@endicott.edu.

Fairfield University, Graduate School of Education and Allied Professions, Department of Curriculum and Instruction, Program in Elementary Education, Fairfield, CT 06430-5195. Awards MA. *Degree requirements:* Comprehensive exams required, foreign language not required. *Entrance requirements:* PRAXIS I (CBT), TOEFL, minimum QPA of 2.67. Application deadline: 7/10 (rolling processing). Application fee: $40. *Expenses:* Tuition $350 per credit hour (minimum). Fees $20 per semester (minimum). • Application contact: Karen Creecy, Assistant Dean, 203-254-4250. Fax: 203-254-4241. E-mail: klcreecy@fair1.fairfield.edu.

Fairleigh Dickinson University, Teaneck–Hackensack Campus, University College: Arts, Sciences, and Professional Studies, Peter Sammartino School of Education, Program in

Directory: Elementary Education

Fairleigh Dickinson University, Teaneck–Hackensack Campus (continued)
Elementary Education, 1000 River Road, Teaneck, NJ 07666-1914. Awards MAT. Faculty: 11 full-time (8 women), 27 part-time (10 women). *Degree requirements:* Research project required, thesis not required. *Application deadline:* rolling. *Application fee:* $35. *Expenses:* Tuition $522 per credit. Fees $302 per year full-time, $138 per year part-time. *Faculty research:* Mathematics for students with learning disabilities, gender issues in education, social problem-solving and conflict resolution in the classroom, multicultural education in the elementary classroom, problems encountered by international students in college programs. • Dr. Eloise Forster, Interim Director, Peter Sammartino School of Education, 201-692-2834. Fax: 201-692-2603.

Fayetteville State University, Program in Elementary Education, 1200 Murchison Road, Fayetteville, NC 28301-4298. Awards MA Ed. Accredited by NCATE. Part-time and evening/weekend programs available. *Degree requirements:* Comprehensive exams, internships required, foreign language and thesis not required. *Entrance requirements:* GRE or MAT, minimum GPA of 2.5, professional certification or waiver permission. Application deadline: 8/1 (rolling processing; 12/15 for spring admission). Application fee: $20. *Tuition:* $1498 per year full-time, $327 per semester (minimum) part-time for state residents; $8768 per year full-time, $2144 per semester (minimum) part-time for nonresidents.

Fitchburg State College, Program in Elementary Education, Fitchburg, MA 01420-2697. Awards M Ed. Accredited by NCATE. Part-time and evening/weekend programs available. *Entrance requirements:* GRE General Test or MAT (minimum score 47), interview, teaching certificate. Application deadline: rolling. Application fee: $10. *Expenses:* Tuition $147 per credit. Fees $55 per semester. *Financial aid:* Graduate assistantships, Federal Work-Study available. Aid available to part-time students. Financial aid application deadline: 3/30; applicants required to submit FAFSA. • Dr. Robert Greene, Chair, 978-665-3512. Fax: 978-665-3658. E-mail: dgce@fsc.edu. Application contact: James DuPont, Director of Admissions, 978-665-3144. Fax: 978-665-4540. E-mail: admissions@fsc.edu.

Florida Agricultural and Mechanical University, Division of Graduate Studies, Research, and Continuing Education, College of Education, Program in Elementary Education, Tallahassee, FL 32307-3200. Offers early childhood and elementary education (M Ed, MS Ed). Accredited by NCATE. Students: 57 (50 women); includes 32 minority (all African Americans). In 1997, 20 degrees awarded. *Entrance requirements:* GRE General Test (minimum combined score of 1000), minimum GPA of 3.0. Application deadline: 5/13. Application fee: $20. *Expenses:* Tuition $140 per credit hour for state residents; $484 per credit hour for nonresidents. Fees $130 per year. • Dr. Robert Lemons, Chairperson, 850-599-3397. Fax: 850-561-2211.

Florida Atlantic University, College of Education, Department of Teacher Education, Program in Elementary Education, Boca Raton, FL 33431-0991. Awards M Ed, Ed D. Accredited by NCATE. Part-time and evening/weekend programs available. Faculty: 15 full-time (11 women). Students: 49 full-time (48 women), 109 part-time (97 women); includes 23 minority (10 African Americans, 3 Asian Americans, 10 Hispanics), 2 international. Average age 27. 90 applicants, 67% accepted. In 1997, 39 master's awarded. *Degree requirements:* For doctorate, dissertation, departmental qualifying exam required, foreign language not required. *Entrance requirements:* For master's, minimum GPA of 3.0 in last 60 hours and GRE General Test (minimum combined score of 800) or bachelor's degree with minimum GPA of 2.5 in last 60 hours and GRE General Test (minimum combined score of 1000); for doctorate, GRE General Test (minimum combined score of 1000), GRE Subject Test (score in 50th percentile or higher), minimum graduate GPA of 3.25, 3.0 in last 2 years of undergraduate course work. Application deadline: rolling. Application fee: $20. *Expenses:* Tuition $2520 per year full-time, $140 per credit hour part-time for state residents; $8712 per year full-time, $484 per credit hour part-time for nonresidents. Fees $5 per year (minimum). *Financial aid:* Fellowships and career-related internships or fieldwork available. *Faculty research:* Reading, curriculum. • Dr. Valerie Bristor, Coordinator, 561-297-3583.

Florida Gulf Coast University, College of Professional Studies, School of Education, Program in Elementary Education, Fort Myers, FL 33965-6565. Awards MA, M Ed. Part-time and evening/weekend programs available. Postbaccalaureate distance learning degree programs offered (minimal on-campus study). Faculty: 7 full-time (4 women). Students: 2 full-time (both women), 40 part-time (37 women); includes 1 minority (Hispanic). Average age 33. 19 applicants, 74% accepted. *Degree requirements:* Thesis or alternative, comprehensive exam, final project required, foreign language not required. *Entrance requirements:* GRE General Test (minimum combined score of 900), MAT (minimum score 42), minimum GPA of 3.0. Application fee: $20. Electronic applications accepted. *Faculty research:* Language acquisition, impact of literature on reading. • Application contact: Carolyn Spillman, Coordinator, 941-590-7791. E-mail: carolyns@fgcu.edu.

Florida International University, College of Education, Department of Elementary Education, Program in Elementary Education, Miami, FL 33199. Awards MS. Accredited by NCATE. Part-time and evening/weekend programs available. Students: 8 full-time (5 women), 44 part-time (40 women); includes 43 minority (5 African Americans, 38 Hispanics). Average age 28. 23 applicants, 39% accepted. In 1997, 29 degrees awarded. *Entrance requirements:* GRE General Test (minimum combined score of 1000) or minimum GPA of 3.0. Application deadline: 4/1 (priority date; rolling processing; 10/1 for spring admission). Application fee: $20. *Expenses:* Tuition $138 per credit hour for state residents; $482 per credit hour for nonresidents. Fees $46 per semester. *Faculty research:* Social studies, aerospace education, teacher training. • Dr. George O'Brien, Chairperson, Department of Elementary Education, 305-348-2561. E-mail: obrieng@fiu.edu.

Florida State University, College of Education, Department of Educational Theory and Practice, Program in Elementary Education, Tallahassee, FL 32306. Awards MS, Ed D, PhD, Ed S. Part-time programs available. Faculty: 7 full-time (6 women), 1 part-time (0 women). Students: 37 full-time (29 women), 29 part-time (25 women); includes 13 minority (5 African Americans, 1 Asian American, 7 Hispanics). 33 applicants, 91% accepted. In 1997, 25 master's awarded. *Degree requirements:* For master's and Ed S, comprehensive exams required, thesis optional; for doctorate, dissertation, comprehensive exams. *Entrance requirements:* GRE General Test (minimum combined score of 1000), minimum GPA of 3.0. Application deadline: 7/1 (priority date; rolling processing; 11/1 for spring admission). Application fee: $20. *Tuition:* $139 per credit hour for state residents; $482 per credit hour for nonresidents. *Financial aid:* Fellowships, research assistantships, teaching assistantships, and career-related internships or fieldwork available. • Dr. Charles Wolfgang, Chair, Department of Educational Theory and Practice, 850-644-5458. E-mail: wolfgang@mail.coe.fsu.edu. Application contact: Admissions Secretary, 850-644-5458. Fax: 850-644-7736.

Fordham University, Graduate School of Education, Division of Curriculum and Teaching, New York, NY 10023. Offerings include elementary education (MST). Accredited by NCATE. *Application fee:* $50. • Dr. Angela Carrasquillo, Chairperson, 212-636-6427.

Fort Hays State University, College of Education, Department of Teacher Education, Program in Elementary Education, Hays, KS 67601-4099. Awards MS. Accredited by NCATE. Faculty: 11 full-time (7 women). Students: 3 full-time (all women), 58 part-time (56 women); includes 6 minority (1 African American, 4 Hispanics, 1 Native American). Average age 37. 9 applicants, 89% accepted. In 1997, 13 degrees awarded. *Application deadline:* 7/1 (priority date; rolling processing). *Application fee:* $25 ($35 for international students). *Tuition:* $94 per credit hour for state residents; $249 per credit hour for nonresidents. *Financial aid:* Research assistantships, teaching assistantships available. *Faculty research:* Metric measurement (elementary and middle school), rural special education strategies for arithmetic mastery, word reading efficiency, textbooks on Great Plains, exceptional children. • Dr. Wally Guyot, Chair, Department of Teacher Education, 785-628-4212.

Francis Marion University, School of Education, Florence, SC 29501-0547. Offerings include elementary education (M Ed). School faculty: 65 full-time (14 women). *Application deadline:* 8/21 (priority date; rolling processing). *Application fee:* $25. • Dr. Wayne Pruitt, Coordinator, 803-661-1462.

Friends University, Graduate Programs, College of Arts and Sciences, Program in Teaching, Wichita, KS 67213. Offerings include elementary education (MAT). Accredited by NCATE. *Application deadline:* rolling. *Application fee:* $45. *Expenses:* Tuition $326 per credit hour (minimum). Fees $215 per year. • Dr. Dona Coleman, Director, 800-794-6945 Ext. 5826. Application contact: Director of Graduate Admissions, 800-794-6945 Ext. 5583.

Frostburg State University, School of Education, Department of Educational Professions, Program in Curriculum and Instruction, Frostburg, MD 21532-1099. Offerings include elementary education (M Ed). *Application deadline:* 7/15 (rolling processing). *Application fee:* $30.

Furman University, Department of Education, Greenville, SC 29613. Offerings include elementary education (MA Ed). *Degree requirements:* Comprehensive written exam. *Application deadline:* rolling. *Application fee:* $25. *Tuition:* $185 per credit hour. • Dr. Hazel W. Harris, Director, 864-294-2213.

Gallaudet University, School of Education and Human Services, Department of Education, Washington, DC 20002-3625. Offerings include elementary education (MA, Ed S). Accredited by NCATE. *Degree requirements:* For master's, thesis optional. *Entrance requirements:* For master's, GRE General Test or MAT. Application deadline: 2/15 (priority date; rolling processing). Application fee: $50. *Expenses:* Tuition $7064 per year full-time, $392 per credit part-time. Fees $50 (one-time charge). • Dr. Barbara Bodner-Johnson, Chair, 202-651-5530. Application contact: Deborah DeStefano, Director of Admissions, 202-651-5253. Fax: 202-651-5744. E-mail: adm_destefan@gallua.bitnet.

Gardner–Webb University, Department of Education, Program in Elementary Education, Boiling Springs, NC 28017. Awards MA. Accredited by NCATE. Part-time and evening/weekend programs available. Faculty: 6 full-time (3 women), 2 part-time (both women). Students: 2 full-time (both women), 60 part-time (all women); includes 2 minority (both African Americans). Average age 30. 47 applicants, 94% accepted. In 1997, 16 degrees awarded. *Degree requirements:* Comprehensive exam required, foreign language and thesis not required. *Entrance requirements:* GRE General Test (minimum combined score of 900), MAT (minimum score 35), or NTE, minimum GPA of 2.5. Application deadline: 8/1. Application fee: $25. *Tuition:* $178 per semester hour full-time, $220 per semester hour part-time. *Financial aid:* In 1997–98, 2 assistantships (both to first-year students) averaging $450 per month were awarded. • Dr. Ben Carson, Chair, Department of Education, 704-434-4406. Fax: 704-434-3921. E-mail: bcarson@gardner-webb.edu.

The George Washington University, Graduate School of Education and Human Development, Department of Teacher Preparation and Special Education, Program in Elementary Education, Washington, DC 20052. Awards M Ed. Accredited by NCATE. Part-time programs available. Faculty: 7. Students: 21 full-time (18 women), 6 part-time (all women); includes 7 minority (5 African Americans, 2 Asian Americans). Average age 28. 56 applicants, 91% accepted. In 1997, 34 degrees awarded. *Degree requirements:* Comprehensive exam required, foreign language and thesis not required. *Entrance requirements:* GRE General Test or MAT, minimum GPA of 2.75. Application deadline: 3/1 (priority date; rolling processing; 10/1 for spring admission). Application fee: $50. *Expenses:* Tuition $680 per semester hour. Fees $35 per semester hour. *Financial aid:* Fellowships, partial tuition waivers, Federal Work-Study, and career-related internships or fieldwork available. Financial aid applicants required to submit FAFSA. *Faculty research:* Issues in teacher training. • Dr. Sylven Beck, Faculty Coordinator, 202-994-6170.

Grambling State University, College of Education, Program in Elementary Education, Grambling, LA 71245. Awards MS. Accredited by NCATE. Part-time and evening/weekend programs available. Faculty: 5 full-time (3 women), 3 part-time (all women). Students: 5 full-time (all women), 16 part-time (10 women); includes 21 minority (all African Americans). Average age 25. 2 applicants, 100% accepted. In 1997, 9 degrees awarded. *Average time to degree:* master's–1.5 years full-time, 3 years part-time. *Entrance requirements:* GRE, NTE. Application deadline: 8/1 (rolling processing). Application fee: $15. *Tuition:* $1960 per year full-time, $297 per semester (minimum) part-time for state residents; $7110 per year full-time, $297 per semester (minimum) part-time for nonresidents. *Financial aid:* In 1997–98, 3 students received aid, including 3 research assistantships (1 to a first-year student) averaging $500 per month and totaling $13,500; full and partial tuition waivers, institutionally sponsored loans, and career-related internships or fieldwork also available. Financial aid application deadline: 5/31. *Faculty research:* Self-evaluation, field-based experience, curriculum revision, multiculturalism. • Dr. Mary Minter, Head, 318-274-3155. Fax: 318-274-3161.

Grand Canyon University, College of Education, Phoenix, AZ 85017-3030. Offerings include elementary education (MA, M Ed). College faculty: 8 full-time (5 women), 2 part-time (1 woman). *Application deadline:* rolling. *Application fee:* $25. • Dr. Betz Fredrick, Director, 602-589-2472.

Grand Valley State University, School of Education, Programs in General Education, Program in Elementary Education, Allendale, MI 49401-9403. Awards M Ed. Accredited by NCATE. *Degree requirements:* Thesis or alternative, applied research project. *Entrance requirements:* GRE General Test (minimum combined score of 1300) or minimum GPA of 3.0. Application deadline: rolling. Application fee: $20. • Application contact: Admissions Office, 616-895-2025. Fax: 616-895-3081.

Hampton University, Department of Education, Program in Elementary Education, Hampton, VA 23668. Awards MA. Accredited by NCATE. Part-time and evening/weekend programs available. Faculty: 5 full-time (all women), 2 part-time (both women). Students: 10 full-time (8 women), 11 part-time (8 women); includes 19 minority (18 African Americans, 1 Native American). In 1997, 11 degrees awarded. *Entrance requirements:* GRE General Test (minimum score 450 on verbal section). Application deadline: 6/1 (priority date; rolling processing; 11/1 for spring admission). Application fee: $25. *Expenses:* Tuition $9038 per year full-time, $220 per credit part-time. Fees $70 per year. *Financial aid:* Fellowships, research assistantships, teaching assistantships, scholarships, Federal Work-Study, institutionally sponsored loans, and career-related internships or fieldwork available. Aid available to part-time students. Financial aid application deadline: 5/1; applicants required to submit FAFSA. • Dr. Helen Stiff, Coordinator, 757-727-5793. Application contact: Erika Henderson, Director, Graduate Programs, 757-727-5454. Fax: 757-727-5084.

Harding University, School of Education, Program in Elementary Education, Searcy, AR 72149-0001. Awards M Ed. Accredited by NCATE. Part-time programs available. Faculty: 8 part-time (4 women), 1 FTE. Students: 22 full-time (18 women), 17 part-time (all women); includes 1 minority (Native American). Average age 30. 20 applicants, 100% accepted. In 1997, 19 degrees awarded. *Degree requirements:* Comprehensive exam required, foreign language and thesis not required. *Average time to degree:* master's–1 year full-time, 3 years part-time. *Entrance requirements:* GRE, MAT, or NTE. Application deadline: 8/27 (rolling processing). Application fee: $25. *Expenses:* Tuition $212 per credit hour. Fees $39 per credit hour. *Financial aid:* Graduate assistantships, scholarships available. • Dr. Dee Carson, Director, School of Education, 501-279-4315. Fax: 501-279-4685. E-mail: dcarson@harding.edu.

Hardin–Simmons University, Irvin School of Education, Department of Elementary and Secondary Education, Program in Elementary Education, Abilene, TX 79698-0001. Offers psychology (M Ed), reading (M Ed), Spanish (M Ed), speech (M Ed). Part-time programs available. Faculty: 5 full-time (2 women), 4 part-time (3 women). Students: 1 (woman) part-time. Average age 30. *Degree requirements:* Project required, foreign language and thesis not required. *Application deadline:* 8/15 (priority date; rolling processing; 1/5 for spring admission). *Application fee:* $25. *Expenses:* Tuition $280 per semester hour. Fees $630 per year full-time. *Financial aid:* In 1997–98, 1 student received aid, including 1 fellowship; full and partial tuition waivers, Federal Work-Study, and career-related internships or fieldwork also available. Aid available to part-time students. Financial aid application deadline: 3/15; applicants required to submit FAFSA. *Faculty research:* Professional development schools, emergent literacy. • Application contact: Dr. J. Paul Sorrels, Dean of Graduate Studies, 915-670-1298. Fax: 915-670-1564.

Harvard University, Graduate School of Education, Area of Administration, Planning and Social Policy, Cambridge, MA 02138. Offerings include elementary and secondary education (Ed D). Terminal master's awarded for partial completion of doctoral program. Faculty: 14 full-time (6 women), 21 part-time (8 women), 15.7 FTE. *Degree requirements:* Dissertation required, foreign language not required. *Average time to degree:* master's–1 year full-time, 2 years part-time; doctorate–6.3 years full-time, 7.2 years part-time; other advanced degree–1 year full-time, 4.7 years part-time. *Entrance requirements:* GRE General Test, TOEFL (minimum score 600), TWE (minimum score 5.0). Application deadline: 1/2. Application fee: $60. • Richard Murnane, Chair, 617-496-4813. Application contact: Roland Hence, Director of Admissions, 617-495-3414. Fax: 617-496-3577. E-mail: gseadmissions@harvard.edu.

Henderson State University, School of Education, Department of Elementary Education, Arkadelphia, AR 71999-0001. Offers programs in elementary school administration (MSE), general elementary education (MSE). Accredited by NCATE. Part-time programs available. Students: 30 part-time (all women); includes 1 minority (African American). Average age 33. 30 applicants, 100% accepted. In 1997, 9 degrees awarded. *Entrance requirements:* GRE General Test or MAT, minimum GPA of 2.7, teacher certification. Application deadline: 7/31 (priority date; rolling processing). Application fee: $0. Electronic applications accepted. *Expenses:* Tuition $120 per credit hour for state residents; $240 per credit hour for nonresidents. Fees $105 per semester (minimum) full-time, $52 per semester (minimum) part-time. *Financial aid:* Research assistantships, Federal Work-Study, institutionally sponsored loans available. Aid available to part-time students. Financial aid application deadline: 7/31. • Dr. Kenneth Harris, Chairperson, 870-230-5203. Fax: 870-230-5455. E-mail: harris@holly.hsu.edu.

Hofstra University, School of Education and Allied Human Services, Department of Curriculum and Teaching, Programs in Elementary and Early Childhood Education, Hempstead, NY 11549. Offerings in art education (MA, MS Ed), early childhood education (MA), elementary education (MA, MS Ed), music education (MA, MS Ed). Accredited by NCATE. Part-time and evening/weekend programs available. Faculty: 10 full-time (all women), 52 part-time (37 women). Students: 70 full-time (57 women), 200 part-time (176 women); includes 9 minority (6 African Americans, 1 Asian American, 2 Hispanics). Average age 29. 278 applicants, 65% accepted. In 1997, 113 degrees awarded. *Degree requirements:* Thesis (for some programs), comprehensive exam, departmental qualifying exam required, foreign language not required. *Entrance requirements:* Minimum GPA of 2.5. Application deadline: rolling. Application fee: $40 ($75 for international students). *Expenses:* Tuition $10,968 per year full-time, $457 per credit hour part-time. Fees $670 per year full-time, $112 per semester (minimum) part-time. *Financial aid:* In 1997–98, 33 students received aid, including scholarships, grants, graduate assistantships totaling $27,132; research assistantships, teaching assistantships, and career-related internships or fieldwork also available. Financial aid application deadline: 9/1. *Faculty research:* Gender equity, social studies education, teacher education, play, culturally relevant pedagogy, integrated dynamic themes. • Application contact: Mary Beth Carey, Dean of Admissions, 516-463-6700. Fax: 516-560-7660. E-mail: hofstra@hofstra.edu.

Holy Family College, Graduate Studies, Program in Education, Philadelphia, PA 19114-2094. Offerings include elementary education (M Ed). Program faculty: 11 full-time (6 women), 22 part-time (10 women), 16.5 FTE. *Average time to degree:* master's–3.5 years part-time. *Entrance requirements:* GRE or MAT, interview. Application deadline: 4/30 (priority date; rolling processing; 11/15 for spring admission). Application fee: $25. *Expenses:* Tuition $320 per credit hour. Fees $65 per semester. • Leonard Soroka, Chair, 215-637-7700 Ext. 3565. Fax: 215-824-2438. Application contact: Joseph Canaday, Graduate Coordinator, 215-637-7203. Fax: 215-637-1478. E-mail: jcanaday@hfc.edu.

Hood College, Department of Education, Frederick, MD 21701-8575. Offerings include curriculum and instruction (MS), with options in early childhood education, elementary education, elementary school science and mathematics, reading, secondary education, special education. *Entrance requirements:* Minimum GPA of 2.5. Application deadline: rolling. Application fee: $30. *Tuition:* $285 per credit. • Dr. Patricia Bartlett, Chairperson, 301-696-3471. E-mail: bartlett@nimue.hood.edu. Application contact: Hood College Graduate School, 301-696-3600. Fax: 301-696-3597. E-mail: postmaster@nimue.hood.edu.

Houston Baptist University, College of Education and Behavioral Sciences, Programs in Education, Houston, TX 77074-3298. Offerings include elementary education (M Ed). Faculty: 9 full-time (5 women), 4 part-time (3 women). *Degree requirements:* Comprehensive exam required, foreign language and thesis not required. *Entrance requirements:* GRE General Test (minimum combined score of 850), minimum GPA of 2.5, teaching certificate. Application deadline: 7/1 (priority date; rolling processing; 1/1 for spring admission). Application fee: $25 ($85 for international students). *Expenses:* Tuition $280 per semester hour. Fees $235 per quarter. • Dr. John Lutjemeier, Head, 281-649-3000 Ext. 2336. Application contact: Judy Ferguson, Program Assistant, 281-649-3241.

Howard University, School of Education, Department of Curriculum and Instruction, Program in Elementary Education, 2400 Sixth Street, NW, Washington, DC 20059-0002. Awards M Ed. Accredited by NCATE. Faculty: 4 full-time (3 women). Students: 29. In 1997, 25 degrees awarded. *Degree requirements:* Comprehensive exam, expository writing exam, internships, seminar paper required, foreign language and thesis not required. *Entrance requirements:* GRE General Test, minimum GPA of 2.7. Application deadline: 4/1 (priority date; rolling processing; 11/1 for spring admission). Application fee: $45. *Expenses:* Tuition $10,200 per year full-time, $567 per credit hour part-time. Fees $405 per year. *Financial aid:* Scholarships available. Financial aid application deadline: 4/1. • Melissa Hinkson, Director, 202-806-7343.

Hunter College of the City University of New York, Departments of Curriculum and Teaching and Educational Foundations and Counseling Programs, Program in Elementary Education, 695 Park Avenue, New York, NY 10021-5085. Awards MS. *Degree requirements:* Research seminar required, foreign language not required. *Entrance requirements:* TOEFL (minimum score 575). Application deadline: 4/7 (11/7 for spring admission). Application fee: $40. *Expenses:* Tuition $4350 per year full-time, $185 per credit part-time for state residents; $7600 per year full-time, $320 per credit part-time for nonresidents. Fees $26 per year. *Faculty research:* Urban education, multicultural education, gifted education, educational technology, cultural cognition.

Immaculata College, Graduate Division, Program in Educational Leadership and Administration, Immaculata, PA 19345-0500. Offerings include elementary education (Certificate). *Application fee:* $25. *Expenses:* Tuition $345 per credit (minimum). Fees $60 per year. • Sr. Anne Marie Burton, Chair, 610-647-4400 Ext. 3280. Application contact: Office of Graduate Admission, 610-647-4400 Ext. 3211.

Indiana State University, School of Education, Department of Elementary and Early Childhood Education, Terre Haute, IN 47809-1401. Offers programs in early childhood education (M Ed, PhD, Ed S), elementary education (M Ed, PhD, Ed S), reading education (M Ed, PhD, Ed S). Accredited by NCATE. Faculty: 13 full-time (10 women). Students: 5 full-time (4 women), 54 part-time (50 women); includes 2 minority (both African Americans), 1 international. Average age 35. 19 applicants, 53% accepted. In 1997, 22 master's, 2 doctorates awarded. *Degree requirements:* For doctorate, 2 foreign languages, computer language, dissertation. *Entrance requirements:* For master's, minimum undergraduate GPA of 2.5; for doctorate, GRE General Test (minimum score 500 on each section), minimum undergraduate GPA of 3.5; for Ed S, GRE General Test (minimum combined score of 900), minimum graduate GPA of 3.25. Application deadline: rolling. Application fee: $20. *Tuition:* $143 per credit hour for state residents; $325 per credit hour for nonresidents. *Financial aid:* In 1997–98, 3 fellowships (1 to a first-year student), 3 research assistantships (1 to a first-year student), 2 teaching assistantships (both to first-year students) were awarded. Financial aid application deadline: 3/1. • Dr. Sandra DeCosta, Chairperson, 812-237-2852.

Indiana University Bloomington, School of Education, Department of Curriculum and Instruction, Program in Elementary Education, Bloomington, IN 47405. Awards MS, Ed S. Accredited by NCATE. Students: 47 full-time (36 women), 33 part-time (29 women); includes 3 African Americans, 5 Asian Americans, 5 international. In 1997, 16 master's awarded. *Degree requirements:* For master's, internship or thesis required, foreign language not required; for Ed S, comprehensive exam or project required, foreign language and thesis not required. *Entrance requirements:* For master's, GRE General Test (minimum combined score of 1300 on three sections); for Ed S, GRE General Test (minimum combined score of 1500 on three sections). Application deadline: 3/1 (priority date; rolling processing). Application fee: $35. *Expenses:* Tuition $153 per credit hour for state residents; $446 per credit hour for nonresidents. Fees $343 per year. *Financial aid:* Fellowships, research assistantships, teaching assistantships, partial tuition waivers, Federal Work-Study, institutionally sponsored loans, and career-related internships or fieldwork available. • Dr. Terrence Mason, Coordinator, 812-856-8106.

Indiana University Kokomo, Division of Education, Program in Elementary Education, Kokomo, IN 46904-9003. Awards MS. Accredited by NCATE. Part-time and evening/weekend programs available. Faculty: 5 full-time (1 woman). Average age 30. *Degree requirements:* Research project required, thesis optional, foreign language not required. *Entrance requirements:* GRE General Test, minimum GPA of 2.5. Application deadline: 8/1 (rolling processing; 12/1 for spring admission). Application fee: $30 ($50 for international students). *Financial aid:* Minority teacher scholarships available. *Faculty research:* Reading, science education, teaching effectiveness, textbook adoptions. • Application contact: Cindy Metsker, Counselor, 765-455-9419. Fax: 765-455-9503. E-mail: lmetsker@iuk.edu.

Indiana University Northwest, Division of Education, Program in Elementary Education, Gary, IN 46408-1197. Awards MS Ed. Part-time and evening/weekend programs available. Faculty: 14. Students: 101 part-time; includes 48 minority (33 African Americans, 15 Hispanics). Average age 32. *Degree requirements:* Thesis. *Entrance requirements:* GRE General Test or MAT, minimum GPA of 3.0. Application deadline: 7/15 (priority date; 11/15 for spring admission). Application fee: $25. • Dr. William May, Interim Dean, Division of Education, 219-981-4278. Application contact: John Burson, Director of Education Student Services, 219-980-6514. Fax: 219-981-4208. E-mail: jburson@iunhaw1.iun.indiana.edu.

Indiana University of Pennsylvania, College of Education, Department of Professional Studies in Education, Program in Elementary Education, Indiana, PA 15705-1087. Awards D Ed. Accredited by NCATE. Offered jointly with Bloomsburg University of Pennsylvania and Edinboro University of Pennsylvania. Students: 11 full-time (6 women), 22 part-time (15 women); includes 5 minority (2 African Americans, 3 Asian Americans), 9 international. Average age 41. 10 applicants, 70% accepted. In 1997, 3 degrees awarded. *Degree requirements:* 1 foreign language (computer language can substitute), dissertation. *Entrance requirements:* TOEFL (minimum score 500). Application deadline: 7/1 (priority date; rolling processing; 11/1 for spring admission). Application fee: $30. *Expenses:* Tuition $3468 per year full-time, $193 per credit part-time for state residents; $6236 per year full-time, $346 per credit part-time for nonresidents. Fees $313 per year (minimum) full-time, $84 per year part-time. *Financial aid:* Federal Work-Study and career-related internships or fieldwork available. Aid available to part-time students. Financial aid application deadline: 3/15. • Dr. George Bieger, Graduate Coordinator, 724-357-2400. E-mail: grbieger@grove.iup.edu.

Indiana University–Purdue University Fort Wayne, School of Education, Program in Elementary Education, Fort Wayne, IN 46805-1499. Awards MS Ed. Accredited by NCATE. Part-time and evening/weekend programs available. Faculty: 9 full-time (5 women), 4 part-time (1 woman), 10 FTE. Students: 2 full-time (both women), 78 part-time (72 women); includes 2 minority (both African Americans). Average age 38. 50 applicants, 100% accepted. In 1997, 40 degrees awarded (100% found work related to degree). *Entrance requirements:* Minimum GPA of 2.5. Application deadline: 8/1 (priority date; rolling processing; 12/1 for spring admission). Application fee: $30. *Expenses:* Tuition $2356 per year full-time, $131 per credit hour part-time for state residents; $5253 per year full-time, $292 per credit hour part-time for nonresidents. Fees $183 per year full-time, $10.15 per credit hour part-time. *Financial aid:* Application deadline 3/1. • Betty Steffy, Dean, School of Education, 219-481-6456. Fax: 219-481-6083.

Indiana University–Purdue University Indianapolis, School of Education, Department of Elementary Education, Indianapolis, IN 46202-2896. Awards MS. Evening/weekend programs available. Faculty: 7 full-time (5 women), 4 part-time (3 women). Students: 8 full-time (5 women), 40 part-time (33 women); includes 3 minority (2 African Americans, 1 Hispanic). Average age 32. In 1997, 21 degrees awarded. *Degree requirements:* Thesis optional, foreign language not required. *Entrance requirements:* GRE General Test (minimum combined score of 1300), minimum GPA of 3.0. Application deadline: 3/1 (priority date; 11/1 for spring admission). Application fee: $35. *Expenses:* Tuition $3602 per year full-time, $150 per credit hour part-time for state residents; $10,392 per year full-time, $433 per credit hour part-time for nonresidents. Fees $100 per year (minimum) full-time, $40 per year (minimum) part-time. *Financial aid:* Federal Work-Study available. *Faculty research:* Professional development schools, emergent literacy, field-based training for teachers. • Michael Cohen, Director, Teacher Education, 317-274-6814. Application contact: Dr. O. Gilbert Brown, Assistant Dean for Education Student Services, 317-274-0649. Fax: 317-274-6864. E-mail: ogbrown@iupui.edu.

Indiana University South Bend, Division of Education, Department of Elementary Education, South Bend, IN 46634-7111. Awards MS Ed. Accredited by NCATE. Part-time and evening/weekend programs available. Faculty: 7 full-time (5 women), 6 part-time (4 women), 9 FTE. Students: 57 full-time (43 women), 115 part-time (95 women); includes 7 minority (5 African Americans, 1 Asian American, 1 Hispanic), 1 international. Average age 33. 50 applicants, 100% accepted. In 1997, 23 degrees awarded (100% found work related to degree). *Degree requirements:* Thesis or alternative, exit project required, foreign language not required. *Entrance requirements:* TOEFL (minimum score 550). Application deadline: rolling. Application fee: $35 ($40 for international students). *Expenses:* Tuition $3024 per year full-time, $126 per credit hour part-time for state residents; $7320 per year full-time, $305 per credit hour part-time for nonresidents. Fees $222 per year full-time, $34 per semester (minimum) part-time. *Financial aid:* Federal Work-Study available. Financial aid application deadline: 3/1. *Faculty research:* Reading methods, early childhood education. • Director, 219-237-4576. Fax: 219-237-4550. Application contact: Graduate Director, 219-237-4183. Fax: 219-237-6549.

Indiana University Southeast, Division of Education, Program in Elementary Education, New Albany, IN 47150-6405. Awards MS Ed. Accredited by NCATE. Part-time and evening/weekend programs available. Students: 199 part-time (160 women); includes 6 minority (all African Americans). Average age 26. 44 applicants, 100% accepted. In 1997, 43 degrees awarded (100% found work related to degree). *Degree requirements:* Thesis or alternative required, foreign language not required. *Entrance requirements:* Appropriate bachelor's degree, minimum GPA of 2.5. Application deadline: rolling. Application fee: $28. *Expenses:* Tuition $125 per credit hour (minimum) for state residents; $284 per credit hour (minimum) for nonresidents. Fees $33 per year full-time, $2.75 per credit hour part-time. *Faculty research:* Service learning, calculator applications. • Dr. Teesue H. Fields, Director of Graduate Studies, 812-941-2658. Fax: 812-941-2667. E-mail: thfields@iusmail.indiana.edu.

Inter American University of Puerto Rico, Metropolitan Campus, Division of Education, Program in Elementary Education, San Juan, PR 00919-1293. Awards MA. Students: 3 full-time (all women), 23 part-time (15 women); includes 26 minority (all Hispanics). In 1997, 4 degrees awarded. *Degree requirements:* Comprehensive exam required, foreign language and thesis not required. *Entrance requirements:* GRE or PAEG, interview. Application deadline: 5/15 (priority date; rolling processing; 11/15 for spring admission). Application fee: $31. Electronic applications accepted. *Expenses:* Tuition $3272 per year full-time, $1740 per year part-time. Fees $328 per year full-time, $176 per year part-time. • Dr. Amalia Charneco, Director,

Directory: Elementary Education

Inter American University of Puerto Rico, Metropolitan Campus (continued)
Division of Education, 787-758-5652. Application contact: Jenny Maldonado, Administrative Assistant, 787-250-1912 Ext. 2393. Fax: 787-250-1197.

Iona College, School of Arts and Science, Program in Elementary Education, 715 North Avenue, New Rochelle, NY 10801-1890. Awards MST. Faculty: 5 full-time (1 woman), 13 part-time (3 women). Students: 6 full-time (5 women), 102 part-time (90 women); includes 8 minority (5 African Americans, 1 Asian American, 2 Hispanics). Average age 30. In 1997, 49 degrees awarded. *Entrance requirements:* GRE or minimum GPA of 2.5. Application deadline: rolling. Application fee: $25. *Expenses:* Tuition $455 per credit hour. Fees $25 per semester. *Financial aid:* Graduate assistantships available. *Faculty research:* Reading/writing assessment, multicultural education, administration, technology and education. • Dr. Lucy Murphy, Chair, 914-633-2210. Fax: 914-633-2608. Application contact: Arlene Melillo, Director of Graduate Recruitment, 914-633-2328. Fax: 914-633-2023.

Iowa State University of Science and Technology, College of Education, Department of Curriculum and Instruction, Program in Elementary and Secondary Education, Ames, IA 50011. Awards M Ed, MS. *Degree requirements:* Thesis or alternative. *Entrance requirements:* TOEFL. Application deadline: 6/1 (priority date; 9/1 for spring admission). Application fee: $20 ($30 for international students). *Expenses:* Tuition $3166 per year full-time, $176 per credit part-time for state residents; $9324 per year full-time, $518 per credit part-time for nonresidents. Fees $200 per year. • Application contact: Daniel Robinson, 515-294-1241.

Jackson State University, School of Education, Department of Curriculum and Instruction, Jackson, MS 39217. Offers programs in early childhood education (MS Ed, Ed D), elementary education (MS Ed, Ed S). Accredited by NCATE. Evening/weekend programs available. Faculty: 10 full-time (7 women), 1 (woman) part-time. Students: 17 full-time (15 women), 51 part-time (45 women); includes 57 minority (56 African Americans, 1 Native American). 39 applicants, 77% accepted. In 1997, 20 master's, 1 Ed S awarded. Terminal master's awarded for partial completion of doctoral program. *Degree requirements:* For master's, thesis or alternative, comprehensive exam; for doctorate, dissertation, comprehensive exam. *Entrance requirements:* For master's, GRE General Test (minimum combined score of 1000), TOEFL (minimum score 550); for doctorate, MAT (minimum score 45), teaching experience. Application deadline: 3/1 (priority date; rolling processing; 10/1 for spring admission). Application fee: $20. *Tuition:* $2688 per year (minimum) full-time, $150 per semester hour part-time for state residents; $5546 per year (minimum) full-time, $309 per semester hour part-time for nonresidents. *Financial aid:* Federal Work-Study available. Financial aid application deadline: 3/1. • Dr. Anita Hall, Chair, 601-968-2336. Fax: 601-968-2178. Application contact: Mae Robinson, Admissions Coordinator, 601-968-2455. Fax: 601-968-8246. E-mail: mrobinson@ccaix.jsums.edu.

Jacksonville State University, College of Education, Program in Elementary Education, Jacksonville, AL 36265-9982. Awards MS Ed. Accredited by NCATE. Faculty: 5 full-time (all women). Students: 20 full-time (all women), 50 part-time (42 women); includes 9 minority (8 African Americans, 1 Native American). In 1997, 36 degrees awarded. *Degree requirements:* Thesis optional. *Entrance requirements:* GRE General Test or MAT. Application deadline: rolling. Application fee: $20. *Expenses:* Tuition $2140 per year full-time, $107 per semester hour part-time for state residents; $4280 per year full-time, $214 per semester hour part-time for nonresidents. Fees $30 per semester. *Financial aid:* Available to part-time students. Financial aid application deadline: 4/1. • Application contact: College of Graduate Studies and Continuing Education, 205-782-5329.

Jacksonville University, College of Arts and Sciences, Division of Education, Program in Elementary Education, 2800 University Boulevard North, Jacksonville, FL 32211-3394. Awards MAT. Part-time and evening/weekend programs available. *Degree requirements:* Comprehensive exam required, foreign language and thesis not required. *Entrance requirements:* GRE General Test (minimum combined score of 900), TOEFL (minimum score 500), minimum GPA of 3.0. Application deadline: 8/1 (priority date; rolling processing; 11/1 for spring admission). Application fee: $25.

John Carroll University, Department of Education and Allied Studies, Program in School Based Elementary Education, University Heights, OH 44118-4581. Awards M Ed. Accredited by NCATE. Faculty: 3 full-time (2 women), 6 part-time (4 women). Students: 39 full-time (31 women), 3 part-time (2 women); includes 8 minority (6 African Americans, 2 Asian Americans). In 1997, 41 degrees awarded. *Degree requirements:* Comprehensive exam, research essay or thesis required, foreign language not required. *Entrance requirements:* GRE General Test or MAT, minimum GPA of 2.75. Application deadline: rolling. Application fee: $25 ($35 for international students). *Tuition:* $450 per credit. *Financial aid:* Partial tuition waivers available. Financial aid application deadline: 3/1; applicants required to submit FAFSA. • Carola Drosdeck, Coordinator, 216-397-3070.

Johns Hopkins University, School of Continuing Studies, Division of Education, Department of Teacher Development and Leadership, Baltimore, MD 21218-2699. Offerings include elementary education (MAT). *Application fee:* $50. • Rochelle Ingram, Chair, 410-516-4957.

Kansas State University, College of Education, Department of Elementary Education, Manhattan, KS 66506. Awards MS. Accredited by NCATE. Part-time and evening/weekend programs available. Faculty: 10 full-time (4 women), 1 (woman) part-time. Students: 13 full-time (12 women), 53 part-time (48 women); includes 13 minority (all African Americans). 20 applicants, 75% accepted. *Degree requirements:* Thesis or alternative required, foreign language not required. *Entrance requirements:* Minimum B average. Application deadline: 4/1 (priority date; rolling processing; 10/1 for spring admission). Application fee: $0 ($25 for international students). Electronic applications accepted. *Tuition:* $2218 per year full-time, $401 per semester (minimum) part-time for state residents; $6336 per year full-time, $1087 per semester (minimum) part-time for nonresidents. *Financial aid:* In 1997–98, teaching assistantships averaging $850 per month were awarded; Federal Work-Study, institutionally sponsored loans, and career-related internships or fieldwork also available. Financial aid application deadline: 3/1. *Faculty research:* Language arts/reading education, mathematics/science education, social studies/primary education. • Ray Kurtz, Chair, 785-532-5550. Application contact: Paul Burden, Assistant Dean, 785-532-5595. Fax: 785-532-7304. E-mail: gradstudy@mail.educ.ksu.edu.

Kennesaw State University, Leland and Clarice C. Bagwell College of Education, Program in Elementary Education, Kennesaw, GA 30144-5591. Offers early childhood (M Ed), middle grades (M Ed), special education (M Ed). Accredited by NCATE. Part-time programs available. Faculty: 38 full-time (24 women), 2 part-time (both women). Students: 81 full-time (71 women), 194 part-time (170 women); includes 17 minority (15 African Americans, 1 Asian American, 1 Hispanic). Average age 34. 193 applicants, 80% accepted. In 1997, 50 degrees awarded. *Degree requirements:* Thesis or alternative required, foreign language not required. *Entrance requirements:* GRE General Test (minimum combined score of 800), T-4 state certification, minimum GPA of 2.5. Application deadline: 7/1 (2/20 for spring admission). Application fee: $20. *Expenses:* Tuition $2398 per year full-time, $83 per credit hour part-time for state residents; $8398 per year full-time, $333 per credit hour part-time for nonresidents. Fees $338 per year. *Financial aid:* Federal Work-Study available. Financial aid application deadline: 6/15; applicants required to submit FAFSA. • Dr. David Martin, Director, 770-423-6117. Fax: 770-423-6527. E-mail: dmartin1@ksumail.kennesaw.edu. Application contact: Susan N. Barrett, Administrative Specialist, Admissions, 770-423-6500. Fax: 770-423-6541. E-mail: sbarrett@ksumail.kennesaw.edu.

Kent State University, Graduate School of Education, Department of Teaching, Leadership, and Curriculum Studies, Program in Elementary Education, Kent, OH 44242-0001. Awards MA, MAT, M Ed. Accredited by NCATE. Faculty: 8 full-time (4 women), 7 part-time (6 women). Students: 47 full-time (33 women), 14 part-time (all women); includes 8 minority (all African Americans). In 1997, 28 degrees awarded. *Degree requirements:* Thesis (MA) required, foreign language not required. *Entrance requirements:* GRE General Test. Application deadline: rolling. Application fee: $30. *Tuition:* $4752 per year full-time, $216 per credit hour part-time for state residents; $9213 per year full-time, $419 per credit hour part-time for nonresidents. *Financial aid:* Application deadline 4/1. • Dr. Sandra Hornick, Coordinator, 330-672-2580. Application contact: Deborah Barber, Director, Office of Academic Services, 330-672-2862. Fax: 330-672-3549.

Kutztown University of Pennsylvania, Graduate School, College of Education, Program in Elementary Education, Kutztown, PA 19530. Awards M Ed. Accredited by NCATE. Part-time and evening/weekend programs available. Faculty: 15 full-time (8 women). Students: 15 full-time (9 women), 172 part-time (152 women); includes 3 Hispanics. Average age 33. In 1997, 56 degrees awarded. *Degree requirements:* Comprehensive project required, thesis optional, foreign language not required. *Entrance requirements:* GRE General Test, TOEFL, TSE. Application deadline: 3/1 (8/1 for spring admission). Application fee: $25. *Tuition:* $4111 per year full-time, $225 per credit hour part-time for state residents; $6879 per year full-time, $393 per credit hour part-time for nonresidents. *Financial aid:* Graduate assistantships, partial tuition waivers, Federal Work-Study, and career-related internships or fieldwork available. Financial aid application deadline: 3/15; applicants required to submit FAFSA. *Faculty research:* Whole language, middle schools, cooperative learning discussion techniques, oral reading techniques, hemisphericity. • Elsa Geskus, Chairperson, 610-683-4262.

Lamar University, College of Education and Human Development, Department of Professional Pedagogy, Program in Elementary Education, Beaumont, TX 77710. Awards M Ed, Certificate. Faculty: 8 full-time (3 women). Students: 1 (woman) full-time, 3 part-time (all women). Average age 40. In 1997, 3 master's awarded. *Degree requirements:* For master's, thesis optional, foreign language not required. *Entrance requirements:* For master's, GRE General Test (minimum combined score of 950), TOEFL (minimum score 500), minimum GPA of 2.5. Application deadline: 8/1 (rolling processing; 12/1 for spring admission). Application fee: $0. *Expenses:* Tuition $1296 per year full-time, $360 per year part-time for state residents; $6432 per year full-time, $1608 per year part-time for nonresidents. Fees $238 per year full-time, $103 per year part-time. *Financial aid:* Application deadline 4/1. • Application contact: Alicia Satre, Graduate Admissions Coordinator, 409-880-8350. Fax: 409-880-8414.

Lander University, School of Education, Greenwood, SC 29649-2099. Offerings include elementary education (M Ed). School faculty: 9 full-time (5 women). *Application deadline:* rolling. *Application fee:* $25. *Tuition:* $3700 per year full-time, $148 per semester hour part-time for state residents; $6326 per year full-time, $253 per semester hour part-time for nonresidents. • Dr. Phil Bennett, Dean, 864-388-8225.

Lehigh University, College of Education, Department of Education and Human Services, Program in Teacher Education and Reading, Bethlehem, PA 18015-3094. Offerings include elementary education (M Ed, Ed D, Certificate). Program faculty: 4 full-time (1 woman), 4 part-time (0 women). *Degree requirements:* For doctorate, dissertation required, foreign language not required. *Entrance requirements:* For doctorate, GRE General Test, TOEFL, minimum graduate GPA of 3.3; for Certificate, TOEFL (minimum score 550). Application deadline: rolling. Application fee: $40. *Expenses:* Tuition $470 per credit. Fees $12 per semester full-time, $6 per semester part-time. • Dr. H. Lynn Columba, Coordinator, 610-758-3230. Fax: 610-758-6223. E-mail: hlc0@lehigh.edu.

Lehman College of the City University of New York, Division of Education, Department of Early Childhood and Elementary Education, Program in Elementary Education, 250 Bedford Park Boulevard West, Bronx, NY 10468-1589. Awards MS Ed. Students: 0. *Entrance requirements:* Minimum GPA of 2.7. Application deadline: 4/1 (rolling processing; 11/1 for spring admission). Application fee: $40. *Expenses:* Tuition $4350 per year full-time, $185 per credit part-time for state residents; $7600 per year full-time, $320 per credit part-time for nonresidents. Fees $120 per year full-time, $80 per year part-time. *Financial aid:* Application deadline 5/15. • Ronald Manyin, Adviser, 718-960-8167.

Lenoir–Rhyne College, Division of Graduate Programs, Department of Education, Program in Elementary Education, Hickory, NC 28601. Awards MA. Part-time and evening/weekend programs available. Students: 11 part-time (all women). In 1997, 3 degrees awarded (100% found work related to degree). *Degree requirements:* Thesis optional, foreign language not required. *Entrance requirements:* GRE General Test (minimum score 450 on verbal section, 1350 combined), minimum GPA of 2.7. Application deadline: 8/1 (12/1 for spring admission). Application fee: $25. *Tuition:* $190 per credit hour. • Dr. Becky Watson, Coordinator, 828-328-7192. Application contact: Dr. Thomas W. Fauquet, Dean of Graduate Studies, 828-328-7275. Fax: 828-328-7368. E-mail: fauquet@lrc.edu.

Lesley College, School of Education, Cambridge, MA 02138-2790. Offerings include elementary education (M Ed). Postbaccalaureate distance learning degree programs offered (no on-campus study). School faculty: 36 full-time (31 women), 340 part-time (220 women). *Degree requirements:* Computer language required, foreign language and thesis not required. *Entrance requirements:* TOEFL (minimum score 550). Application deadline: rolling. Application fee: $45. *Tuition:* $425 per credit. • Dr. William L. Dandridge, Dean, 617-349-8375. Application contact: Graduate Admissions, 617-349-8300. Fax: 617-349-8366.

Lewis & Clark College, Department of Education, Program in Elementary Education, Portland, OR 97219-7899. Awards MAT. Part-time and evening/weekend programs available. *Degree requirements:* Thesis optional, foreign language not required. *Entrance requirements:* California Basic Educational Skills Test (preservice), GRE General Test or MAT; NTE, minimum GPA of 2.75. Application deadline: 1/15. Application fee: $45. *Faculty research:* Classroom ethnography, assessing student learning, reading, moral development, language arts.

Liberty University, School of Education, 1971 University Road, Lynchburg, VA 24502. Offerings include elementary education (M Ed). School faculty: 3 full-time (1 woman), 4 part-time (2 women). *Degree requirements:* Thesis optional, foreign language not required. *Entrance requirements:* GRE General Test (minimum combined score of 900). Application deadline: 8/15 (priority date; rolling processing). Application fee: $35. *Tuition:* $280 per credit hour. • Dr. Pauline Donaldson, Dean, 804-582-2314. Application contact: Bill Wegert, Coordinator of Graduate Admissions, 804-582-2175.

Lincoln University, Graduate School, College of Arts and Sciences, Department of Education, Jefferson City, MO 65102. Offerings include elementary and secondary teaching (M Ed), with options in elementary, secondary; guidance and counseling (M Ed), with options in agency, elementary, secondary. One or more programs accredited by NCATE. Department faculty: 2 full-time (0 women), 10 part-time (6 women). *Entrance requirements:* GRE General Test or MAT, minimum GPA of 2.75 in major, 2.5 overall. Application deadline: 7/25 (rolling processing; 12/15 for spring admission). Application fee: $17. *Expenses:* Tuition $117 per credit hour for state residents; $234 per credit hour for nonresidents. Fees $552 per year (minimum) for state residents; $1104 per year (minimum) for nonresidents. • Dr. Marilyn Hofmann, Acting Head, 573-681-5250.

Long Island University, Brooklyn Campus, School of Education, Department of Education, Program in Elementary Education, Brooklyn, NY 11201-8423. Awards MS Ed. Part-time and evening/weekend programs available. 51 applicants, 86% accepted. In 1997, 20 degrees awarded. *Degree requirements:* Thesis optional, foreign language not required. *Application deadline:* rolling. *Application fee:* $30. Electronic applications accepted. *Expenses:* Tuition $480 per credit. Fees $415 per year full-time, $73 per semester (minimum) part-time. • Application contact: Bernard W. Sullivan, Associate Director of Admissions, 718-488-1011.

Long Island University, C.W. Post Campus, School of Education, Department of Curriculum and Instruction, Brookville, NY 11548-1300. Offerings include elementary education (MS Ed). Department faculty: 10 full-time (5 women), 46 part-time (19 women). *Application deadline:* rolling. *Application fee:* $30. Electronic applications accepted. *Expenses:* Tuition $480 per credit. Fees $316 per year full-time, $71 per semester (minimum) part-time. • Dr. Anthony De Falco, Chairperson, 516-299-2372. Application contact: Camille Marziliano, Academic Counselor, 516-299-2123. Fax: 516-299-4167. E-mail: cmarzili@eagle.liunet.edu.

Long Island University, Southampton College, Education Division, Program in Elementary Education, Southampton, NY 11968-9822. Awards MS Ed. Faculty: 4 full-time (2 women), 6 part-time (3 women). *Degree requirements:* Computer language, thesis. *Entrance requirements:* MAT. Application deadline: 4/15 (priority date; 11/30 for spring admission). Application fee: $30. • Dr. R. Lawrence McCann, Director, Education Division, 516-287-8211 Ext. 211.

Longwood College, Department of Education, Farmville, VA 23909-1800. Offerings include curriculum and instruction specialist-elementary (MS), with options in English (MS), mild disabilities (MS), modern language (MS), physical education (MS), speech and drama (MS). Accredited by NCATE. Department faculty: 34 part-time. *Degree requirements:* Thesis (for some programs), comprehensive exam. *Entrance requirements:* Minimum GPA of 2.5. Application deadline: 5/1 (priority date; rolling processing; 10/15 for spring admission). Application fee: $25. *Expenses:* Tuition $3048 per year full-time, $127 per credit hour part-time for state residents; $8160 per year full-time, $340 per credit hour part-time for nonresidents. Fees $920 per year full-time, $31 per credit hour part-time. • Dr. Frank Howe, Chair, 804-395-2324. Application contact: Admissions Office, 804-395-2060.

Louisiana State University and Agricultural and Mechanical College, College of Education, Department of Curriculum and Instruction, Baton Rouge, LA 70803. Offerings include elementary education (M Ed). Accredited by NCATE. Department faculty: 27 full-time (15 women), 1 (woman) part-time. *Application deadline:* 1/25 (priority date; rolling processing). *Application fee:* $25. *Tuition:* $2736 per year full-time, $285 per semester (minimum) part-time for state residents; $6636 per year full-time, $460 per semester (minimum) part-time for nonresidents. • Dr. Robert Lafayette, Interim Chair, 504-388-6867. Application contact: Dr. Earl Cheek, Professor, 504-388-6867. Fax: 504-388-1045.

Loyola Marymount University, School of Education, Program in Elementary Education, Los Angeles, CA 90045-8350. Awards MA. Part-time and evening/weekend programs available. Faculty: 14 full-time (8 women), 25 part-time (20 women). Students: 32 full-time (29 women), 35 part-time (28 women); includes 24 minority (4 African Americans, 3 Asian Americans, 17 Hispanics), 2 international. In 1997, 15 degrees awarded. *Degree requirements:* Comprehensive exam required, foreign language and thesis not required. *Entrance requirements:* GRE General Test, TOEFL (minimum score 550), interview. Application fee: $35. Electronic applications accepted. *Expenses:* Tuition $500 per unit. Fees $111 per year full-time, $28 per year part-time. *Financial aid:* In 1997–98, 42 students received aid, including 26 grants, scholarships (2 to first-year students) totaling $27,809; Federal Work-Study also available. Aid available to part-time students. Financial aid application deadline: 3/2; applicants required to submit FAFSA. • Dr. Irene Oliver, Coordinator, 310-338-7302.

Loyola University New Orleans, College of Arts and Sciences, Department of Education, Program in Elementary Education, New Orleans, LA 70118-6195. Awards MS. Part-time and evening/weekend programs available. Faculty: 3 full-time (all women), 4 part-time (all women). Students: 3 full-time (all women), 8 part-time (all women); includes 1 international. Average age 29. 11 applicants, 91% accepted. In 1997, 5 degrees awarded. *Degree requirements:* Comprehensive exams required, foreign language and thesis not required. *Entrance requirements:* GRE, MAT (preferred), interview, sample of written work. Application deadline: 8/1 (priority date; rolling processing; 12/1 for spring admission). Application fee: $20. Electronic applications accepted. *Expenses:* Tuition $247 per credit hour. Fees $556 per year full-time, $164 per year part-time. *Financial aid:* 1 student received aid; research assistantships, partial tuition waivers, Federal Work-Study, and career-related internships or fieldwork available. Aid available to part-time students. Financial aid application deadline: 5/1; applicants required to submit FAFSA. *Faculty research:* Mathematics in school settings. • Dr. Janet Melanson, Director, 504-865-3540. Fax: 504-865-3571.

Maharishi University of Management, Department of Education, Fairfield, IA 52557. Offerings include elementary education (MA). Department faculty: 11 (2 women). *Degree requirements:* Thesis or alternative required, foreign language not required. *Entrance requirements:* GRE, TOEFL (minimum score 550), minimum GPA of 3.0. Application deadline: 4/15 (priority date; rolling processing). Application fee: $40. • Dr. Christopher Jones, Associate Chairperson, 515-472-1105. Application contact: Harry Bright, Director of Admissions, 515-472-1166.

Manhattanville College, School of Education, Program in Elementary Education, Purchase, NY 10577-2132. Awards MAT. *Degree requirements:* Thesis, comprehensive exam or research project required, foreign language not required. *Entrance requirements:* Minimum undergraduate GPA of 3.0. Application deadline: rolling. Application fee: $40. *Expenses:* Tuition $410 per credit (minimum). Fees $25 per semester. • Application contact: Carol Messar, Director of Admissions, 914-323-5142. Fax: 914-323-5493.

Manhattanville College, School of Education, Program in Special Education, Purchase, NY 10577-2132. Offerings include elementary education and special education (MPS). *Application deadline:* rolling. *Application fee:* $40. *Expenses:* Tuition $410 per credit (minimum). Fees $25 per semester. • Dr. Rebecca Rich, Coordinator, 914-323-5143. Application contact: Carol Messar, Director of Admissions, 914-323-5142. Fax: 914-323-5493.

Mankato State University, College of Education, Department of Elementary Education, South Rd and Ellis Ave, PO Box 8400, Mankato, MN 56002-8400. Awards MS, SP. Accredited by NCATE. Part-time programs available. Students: 49 full-time (45 women), 51 part-time (45 women); includes 2 minority (both Asian Americans). Average age 32. 40 applicants, 73% accepted. In 1997, 29 master's, 3 SPs awarded. *Degree requirements:* For master's, thesis or alternative, comprehensive exam required, foreign language not required; for SP, thesis, comprehensive exam required, foreign language not required. *Entrance requirements:* For master's, GRE General Test or MAT, minimum GPA of 3.0 during previous 2 years; for SP, GRE, minimum GPA of 3.0. Application deadline: 7/10 (priority date; rolling processing; 10/30 for spring admission). Application fee: $20. *Tuition:* $126 per credit (minimum) for state residents; $200 per credit for nonresidents. *Financial aid:* Teaching assistantships available. Financial aid application deadline: 3/15; applicants required to submit FAFSA. • Dr. Howard Schroeder, Coordinator, 507-389-5713. Application contact: Joni Roberts, Admissions Coordinator, 507-389-2321. Fax: 507-389-5974. E-mail: grad@mankato.msus.edu.

Mansfield University of Pennsylvania, Department of Education, Program in Elementary Education, Mansfield, PA 16933. Awards M Ed. Accredited by NCATE. Part-time and evening/weekend programs available. Faculty: 12 part-time (6 women). Students: 8 full-time (7 women), 29 part-time (25 women); includes 1 minority (Hispanic). Average age 32. 11 applicants, 100% accepted. In 1997, 13 degrees awarded. *Degree requirements:* Thesis optional, foreign language not required. *Entrance requirements:* GRE General Test, MAT, NTE, or minimum GPA of 3.0. Application deadline: rolling. Application fee: $25. *Expenses:* Tuition $3468 per year full-time, $193 per credit part-time for state residents; $6236 per year full-time, $346 per credit part-time for nonresidents. Fees $236 per year full-time, $18.25 per semester (minimum) part-time for state residents; $266 per year full-time, $18.25 per semester (minimum) part-time for nonresidents. *Financial aid:* In 1997–98, 1 graduate assistantship was awarded; career-related internships or fieldwork also available. Aid available to part-time students. Financial aid application deadline: 5/1; applicants required to submit FAFSA. • Dr. Robert Putt, Chairperson, Department of Education, 717-662-4562.

Marshall University, Graduate School of Education and Professional Studies, Program in Elementary Education, South Charleston, WV 25303-1600. Awards MA. Accredited by NCATE. Part-time and evening/weekend programs available. Faculty: 3 full-time (1 woman), 8 part-time (2 women), 4.9 FTE. Students: 9 full-time (8 women), 136 part-time (113 women); includes 6 minority (4 African Americans, 1 Hispanic, 1 Native American). Average age 40. In 1997, 33 degrees awarded. *Degree requirements:* Comprehensive or oral exam, research project required, foreign language and thesis not required. *Entrance requirements:* GRE General Test, minimum undergraduate GPA of 2.5. Application deadline: 8/1 (priority date; rolling processing). Application fee: $0. *Tuition:* $2364 per year full-time, $132 per hour part-time for state residents; $6894 per year full-time, $383 per hour part-time for nonresidents. *Financial aid:* Full tuition waivers available. Aid available to part-time students. Financial aid applicants required to submit FAFSA. • Dr. James Ranson, Dean, Graduate School of Education and Professional Studies, 304-746-1998. Fax: 304-746-1942.

Marshall University, College of Education, Division of Teacher Education, Program in Elementary Education, Huntington, WV 25755-2020. Awards MA. Accredited by NCATE. Evening/weekend programs available. Faculty: 6 (3 women). Students: 4 full-time (3 women), 51 part-time (48 women). In 1997, 10 degrees awarded. *Degree requirements:* Thesis optional, foreign language not required. *Entrance requirements:* GRE General Test (minimum combined score of 1200). *Tuition:* $2364 per year full-time, $132 per hour part-time for state residents; $6894 per year full-time, $383 per hour part-time for nonresidents. • Dr. Boots Dilley, Coordinator, 304-696-3101. Application contact: Dr. James Harless, Director of Admissions, 304-696-3160.

Mary Baldwin College, Graduate Studies, Staunton, VA 24401. Offerings include elementary education (MAT). College faculty: 1 (woman) full-time, 38 part-time (24 women). *Degree requirements:* Final paper, student teaching required, foreign language and thesis not required. *Average time to degree:* master's–2 years full-time, 4 years part-time. *Entrance requirements:* Previous course work in college algebra, English composition. Application deadline: 7/1 (priority date; rolling processing; 12/15 for spring admission). Application fee: $35. *Expenses:* Tuition $305 per credit hour. Fees $250 per year. • Dr. Beth Roberts, Director, 540-887-7333.

Marymount University, School of Education and Human Services, Program in Elementary Education, Arlington, VA 22207-4299. Awards M Ed. Accredited by NCATE. Part-time and evening/weekend programs available. Students: 146. In 1997, 118 degrees awarded. *Degree requirements:* Thesis or alternative required, foreign language not required. *Entrance requirements:* GRE General Test or MAT, interview. Application deadline: rolling. Application fee: $35. *Expenses:* Tuition $465 per credit hour. Fees $120 per year full-time, $5 per credit hour part-time. *Financial aid:* Career-related internships or fieldwork available. Aid available to part-time students. Financial aid applicants required to submit FAFSA. • Dr. Shirley Smith, Chair, 703-284-1620. Fax: 703-284-1631. E-mail: shirley.smith@marymount.edu.

Maryville University of Saint Louis, School of Education, St. Louis, MO 63141-7299. Offerings include elementary education (MA). Accredited by NCATE. School faculty: 9 full-time (7 women), 15 part-time (9 women). *Degree requirements:* Thesis, project required, foreign language not required. *Average time to degree:* master's–2 years full-time, 4 years part-time. *Entrance requirements:* Minimum GPA of 3.0. Application deadline: rolling. Application fee: $20. Electronic applications accepted. *Expenses:* Tuition $11,480 per year full-time, $345 per credit hour part-time. Fees $120 per year full-time, $60 per year part-time. • Dr. Kathe Rasch, Dean, 314-529-9466. Fax: 314-529-9921. E-mail: krasch@maryville.edu.

Marywood University, Graduate School of Arts and Sciences, Department of Education, Program in Elementary Education, Scranton, PA 18509-1598. Awards MAT, MS. Accredited by NCATE. Part-time and evening/weekend programs available. Students: 16 full-time (7 women), 32 part-time (28 women). Average age 31. 22 applicants, 86% accepted. In 1997, 14 degrees awarded. *Degree requirements:* Thesis or alternative, internship/practicum required, foreign language not required. *Entrance requirements:* GRE or MAT, TOEFL (minimum score 550; average 590). Application deadline: 7/15 (priority date; rolling processing; 12/1 for spring admission). Application fee: $20. *Expenses:* Tuition $449 per credit hour. Fees $530 per year full-time, $180 per year part-time. *Financial aid:* Research assistantships, scholarships/tuition reductions, partial tuition waivers, and career-related internships or fieldwork available. Aid available to part-time students. Financial aid application deadline: 2/15; applicants required to submit FAFSA. *Faculty research:* Pre-service teacher education, classroom computer applications. • Application contact: Deborah M. Flynn, Coordinator of Admissions, 717-340-6002. Fax: 717-961-4745.

McNeese State University, College of Education, Department of Curriculum and Instruction, Program in Elementary Education, Lake Charles, LA 70609-2495. Awards M Ed. Evening/weekend programs available. Faculty: 8 full-time (3 women). Students: 17 part-time (all women). In 1997, 12 degrees awarded. *Entrance requirements:* GRE General Test, teaching certificate, 24 hours in professional education. Application deadline: 7/15 (priority date; rolling processing). Application fee: $10 ($25 for international students). *Tuition:* $2118 per year full-time, $344 per semester (minimum) part-time for state residents; $7308 per year full-time, $344 per semester (minimum) part-time for nonresidents. *Financial aid:* Application deadline 5/1. • Dr. Everett Waddell Burge, Head, Department of Curriculum and Instruction, 318-475-5404.

Miami University, School of Education and Allied Professions, Department of Teacher Education, Program in Elementary Education, Oxford, OH 45056. Awards MAT, M Ed. Accredited by NCATE. Part-time programs available. Faculty: 21. Students: 49 full-time (48 women), 14 part-time (13 women); includes 4 minority (all African Americans), 1 international. 47 applicants, 89% accepted. In 1997, 37 degrees awarded. *Degree requirements:* Final exam required, foreign language and thesis not required. *Entrance requirements:* MAT, minimum undergraduate GPA of 3.0 during previous 2 years or 2.75 overall. Application deadline: 3/1 (priority date; rolling processing; 12/1 for spring admission). Application fee: $35. *Tuition:* $5932 per year full-time, $255 per credit hour part-time for state residents; $12,392 per year full-time, $524 per credit hour part-time for nonresidents. *Financial aid:* Research assistantships, teaching assistantships, full tuition waivers, Federal Work-Study, and career-related internships or fieldwork available. Financial aid application deadline: 3/1. • Dr. Robert Shearer, Director of Graduate Study, 513-529-5708.

Middle Tennessee State University, College of Education, Department of Elementary and Special Education, Major in Curriculum and Instruction, Murfreesboro, TN 37132. Offerings include elementary education (M Ed, Ed S). Accredited by NCATE. *Degree requirements:* Comprehensive exams required, foreign language and thesis not required. *Entrance requirements:* For master's, Cooperative English Test, GRE, MAT (minimum score 25); for Ed S, Cooperative English Test, GRE, MAT (minimum score 38), master's degree, teaching certificate. Application deadline: 8/1 (priority date). Application fee: $5. *Expenses:* Tuition $2560 per year full-time, $129 per semester hour part-time for state residents; $7386 per year full-time, $340 per semester hour part-time for nonresidents. Fees $486 per year full-time, $17 per semester (minimum) part-time. • Dr. Charles Babb, Chair, Department of Elementary and Special Education, 615-898-2680. Fax: 615-898-5309. E-mail: cwbabb@mtsu.edu.

Midwestern State University, Division of Education, Program in Elementary Education, Wichita Falls, TX 76308-2096. Awards M Ed. Part-time and evening/weekend programs available. *Entrance requirements:* GRE General Test, MAT (average 46), TOEFL (minimum score 550). Application deadline: 8/7 (12/15 for spring admission). Application fee: $0 ($50 for international students). *Expenses:* Tuition $44 per hour for state residents; $259 per hour for nonresidents. Fees $90 per year (minimum) full-time, $9 per semester (minimum) part-time. *Financial aid:* Teaching assistantships, assistantships, partial tuition waivers, Federal Work-Study, institutionally sponsored loans, and career-related internships or fieldwork available. Aid available to part-time students. • Dr. Emerson Capps, Director, Division of Education, 940-397-4313.

Millersville University of Pennsylvania, School of Education, Department of Elementary and Early Childhood Education, Program in Elementary Education, Millersville, PA 17551-0302. Awards M Ed. Accredited by NCATE. Part-time and evening/weekend programs available. Faculty: 19 full-time (13 women), 11 part-time (5 women). Students: 28 full-time (19 women), 78 part-time (64 women); includes 2 minority (1 Asian American, 1 Hispanic), 1 international. Average age 30. 40 applicants, 95% accepted. In 1997, 42 degrees awarded. *Degree requirements:* Thesis optional, foreign language not required. *Entrance requirements:* MAT (minimum score 35), instructional certificate, minimum undergraduate GPA of 2.75. Application deadline: 5/1 (priority date; rolling processing). Application fee: $25. *Tuition:* $3468 per year full-time, $234 per credit part-time for state residents; $6236 per year full-time, $387 per credit

Directory: Elementary Education

Millersville University of Pennsylvania (continued)

part-time for nonresidents. *Financial aid:* In 1997–98, 7 graduate assistantships (3 to first-year students) averaging $445 per month and totaling $28,000 were awarded; Federal Work-Study, institutionally sponsored loans, and career-related internships or fieldwork also available. Aid available to part-time students. Financial aid application deadline: 5/1. *Faculty research:* Learning styles, cooperative learning styles, whole language approach. • Application contact: Dr. Robert J. Labriola, Dean of Graduate Studies, 717-872-3030. Fax: 717-871-2022.

Mills College, Education Department, Oakland, CA 94613-1000. Offerings include education (MA), with options in curriculum and instruction, elementary education, English education, mathematics education, science education, secondary education, social sciences education, teaching. Department faculty: 8 full-time (6 women), 13 part-time (11 women), 11 FTE. *Degree requirements:* Comprehensive exam required, thesis not required. *Average time to degree:* master's–2 years full-time. *Entrance requirements:* TOEFL (minimum score 550). Application deadline: 2/1 (priority date; rolling processing; 11/1 for spring admission). Application fee: $50. Electronic applications accepted. *Expenses:* Tuition $10,600 per year full-time, $2560 per year part-time. Fees $468 per year. • Jane Bowyer, Chairperson, 510-430-2118. Fax: 510-430-3314. E-mail: grad-studies@mills.edu. Application contact: La Vonna S. Brown, Coordinator of Graduate Studies, 510-430-3309. Fax: 510-430-2159. E-mail: grad-studies@mills.edu.

Minot State University, Program in Elementary Education, Minot, ND 58707-0002. Awards MS. Faculty: 12 full-time (9 women), 9 part-time (3 women). Students: 0. In 1997, 16 degrees awarded (100% found work related to degree). *Degree requirements:* Thesis or alternative. *Entrance requirements:* GRE General Test (minimum combined score of 1000) or minimum GPA of 3.0, bachelor's in secondary education, 2 years of teaching experience. Application deadline: rolling. Application fee: $25. *Tuition:* $2714 per year for state residents; $3235 per year (minimum) for nonresidents. *Faculty research:* Technology, pergonel-teaching efficacy, reflective teaching. • Dr. Neil Nordquist, Chairperson, 701-858-3028. Application contact: Tammy White, Administrative Secretary, 701-858-3250. Fax: 701-839-6933.

Mississippi College, School of Education, Program in Elementary Education, Clinton, MS 39058. Awards M Ed. Accredited by NCATE. Part-time and evening/weekend programs available. *Degree requirements:* Comprehensive exam required, foreign language and thesis not required. *Entrance requirements:* GRE or NTE, minimum GPA of 2.5, Class A Certificate. Application deadline: 8/15 (priority date; rolling processing). Application fee: $25 ($75 for international students). *Expenses:* Tuition $6624 per year full-time, $276 per hour part-time. Fees $230 per year full-time, $35 per semester (minimum) part-time. *Financial aid:* Professional development scholarships and career-related internships or fieldwork available. Aid available to part-time students. Financial aid application deadline: 4/1. • Dr. Thomas Taylor, Dean, School of Education, 601-925-3402.

Mississippi State University, College of Education, Department of Curriculum and Instruction, Mississippi State, MS 39762. Offerings include elementary education (MS). Accredited by NCATE. Department faculty: 26 full-time (13 women). *Degree requirements:* Comprehensive written exam required, foreign language and thesis not required. *Entrance requirements:* Minimum QPA of 2.75 in last 2 years. Application deadline: 7/26 (priority date; rolling processing; 11/10 for spring admission). Application fee: $0 ($25 for international students). Electronic applications accepted. *Tuition:* $3017 per year full-time, $168 per credit hour part-time for state residents; $6119 per year full-time, $340 per credit hour part-time for nonresidents. • Dr. James S. Turner, Interim Head, 601-325-3747. Application contact: Dr. Dwight Hare, Graduate Coordinator, 601-325-3747. Fax: 601-325-8784. E-mail: rdh1@ra.msstate.edu.

Mississippi State University, College of Education, Program Under Dean of Education, Mississippi State, MS 39762. Offerings include elementary education (Ed D, PhD, Ed S). Accredited by NCATE. *Degree requirements:* For doctorate, computer language (for some programs), dissertation required, foreign language not required; for Ed S, thesis or alternative required, foreign language not required. *Entrance requirements:* For Ed S, minimum QPA of 3.2 in graduate course work. *Tuition:* $3017 per year full-time, $168 per credit hour part-time for state residents; $6119 per year full-time, $340 per credit hour part-time for nonresidents. • Dr. William H. Graves, Dean, College of Education, 601-325-3717. Fax: 601-325-8784. E-mail: whg1@ra.msstate.edu.

Mississippi Valley State University, Department of Education, Itta Bena, MS 38941-1400. Offerings include elementary education (MA). MAT new for fall 1998. Department faculty: 5. *Application deadline:* rolling. *Application fee:* $0. *Expenses:* Tuition $97 per hour for state residents; $139 per hour for nonresidents. Fees $30 per hour. • Dr. O. Edward Jack, Chair, 601-254-3619. Application contact: Office of Admissions, 601-254-3344.

Monmouth University, School of Education, West Long Branch, NJ 07764-1898. Offerings include elementary education (MAT), with options in certified teachers, non-certified teachers. School faculty: 9 full-time (7 women), 14 part-time (9 women). *Application deadline:* 8/1 (priority date; rolling processing; 12/1 for spring admission). *Application fee:* $35. *Expenses:* Tuition $459 per credit. Fees $274 per semester full-time, $137 per semester part-time. • Dr. Bernice Willis, Dean, 732-571-7518. Fax: 732-263-5277. Application contact: Office of Graduate Admissions, 732-571-3452. Fax: 732-571-5123.

Montana State University–Northern, Option in Elementary Education, Havre, MT 59501-7751. Awards M Ed. Faculty: 4 full-time (3 women). Students: 15 full-time (11 women), 28 part-time (20 women); includes 2 minority (both Native Americans). Average age 40. *Degree requirements:* Comprehensive and oral exams required, thesis optional, foreign language not required. *Entrance requirements:* GRE General Test, minimum GPA of 3.0. Application deadline: 9/20 (priority date; rolling processing). Application fee: $30. *Tuition:* $3090 per year full-time, $696 per semester (minimum) part-time for state residents; $8044 per year full-time, $1758 per semester (minimum) part-time for nonresidents. *Financial aid:* Teaching assistantships, Federal Work-Study, institutionally sponsored loans available. Aid available to part-time students. Financial aid application deadline: 4/1; applicants required to submit FAFSA. • Dr. Ben Johnson, Director of Education and Graduate Programs, Department of Education, 406-265-3738. Fax: 406-265-3570. E-mail: johnson@nmcl.nmclites.edu.

Moorhead State University, Department of Education, Program in Elementary Education, Moorhead, MN 56563-0002. Awards MS. Accredited by NCATE. Program being phased out; applicants no longer accepted. Part-time and evening/weekend programs available. Faculty: 6 full-time (4 women). Students: 1 (woman) full-time, 2 part-time (both women). In 1997, 1 degree awarded. *Degree requirements:* Final oral exam, project or thesis, written comprehensive exam required, foreign language not required. *Tuition:* $145 per credit hour for state residents; $220 per credit hour for nonresidents. *Financial aid:* In 1997–98, 1 administrative assistantship was awarded; Federal Work-Study also available. Financial aid applicants required to submit FAFSA. • Sandra Gordon, Chairperson, 218-236-3580.

Morehead State University, College of Education and Behavioral Sciences, Department of Elementary, Reading, and Special Education, Program in Elementary Education, Morehead, KY 40351. Offers elementary teaching (MA Ed), middle school education (MA Ed), reading (MA Ed). Accredited by NCATE. Part-time and evening/weekend programs available. Faculty: 15 full-time (8 women), 1 part-time (0 women). Students: 7 full-time (3 women), 169 part-time (144 women); includes 1 international. Average age 25. 46 applicants, 96% accepted. In 1997, 78 degrees awarded. *Degree requirements:* Written comprehensive exams required, foreign language and thesis not required. *Entrance requirements:* GRE General Test (minimum combined score of 1200), minimum GPA of 2.75, teaching certificate. Application deadline: 8/1 (priority date; rolling processing; 12/1 for spring admission). Application fee: $0. *Tuition:* $2470 per year full-time, $138 per semester hour part-time for state residents; $6710 per year full-time, $373 per semester hour part-time for nonresidents. *Financial aid:* In 1997–98, 3 teaching assistantships (1 to a first-year student) averaging $471 per month and totaling $12,000 were awarded; research assistantships, Federal Work-Study also available. Financial aid application deadline: 4/1; applicants required to submit FAFSA. *Faculty research:* Teaching through journal writing, gifted children, reading instruction in elementary schools, teaching social studies in elementary schools, ungraded elementary schools. • Application contact: Betty Cowsert, Graduate Admissions Officer, 606-783-2039. Fax: 606-783-5061.

Morgan State University, School of Education and Urban Studies, Department of Teacher Education and Administration, Program in Elementary and Middle School Education, Baltimore, MD 21251. Awards MS. Accredited by NCATE. Part-time and evening/weekend programs available. Faculty: 5 full-time (1 woman), 4 part-time (1 woman). Students: 1 (woman) full-time, 2 part-time (both women); includes 3 minority (all African Americans). Average age 30. 3 applicants, 0% accepted. In 1997, 3 degrees awarded. *Degree requirements:* Comprehensive exam required, thesis optional, foreign language not required. *Average time to degree:* master's–3 years part-time. *Application deadline:* 7/1 (rolling processing; 11/1 for spring admission). *Application fee:* $0. *Expenses:* Tuition $160 per credit hour for state residents; $286 per credit hour for nonresidents. Fees $326 per year. *Financial aid:* Application deadline 4/1. *Faculty research:* Multicultural education, cooperative learning, psychology of cognition. • Dr. Dennis Brown, Coordinator, 410-319-3356. Fax: 410-319-3871. Application contact: James E. Waller, Admissions and Programs Officer, 410-319-3186. Fax: 410-319-3837.

Morningside College, Department of Education, Program in Elementary Education, Sioux City, IA 51106-1751. Awards MAT. Accredited by NCATE. Part-time and evening/weekend programs available. Faculty: 20 full-time (7 women), 7 part-time (6 women). *Entrance requirements:* MAT, writing sample. Application deadline: rolling. Application fee: $15. *Tuition:* $245 per credit hour. *Financial aid:* Tuition rebates, partial tuition waivers, institutionally sponsored loans available. Aid available to part-time students. • Dr. Glenna Tevis, Director, Graduate Division, 712-274-5375.

Mount Saint Mary College, Division of Education, Program in Elementary Education, Newburgh, NY 12550-3494. Awards MS Ed. Part-time and evening/weekend programs available. Students: 6 full-time (5 women), 111 part-time (96 women); includes 5 minority (3 African Americans, 1 Asian American, 1 Hispanic). Average age 33. In 1997, 25 degrees awarded. *Degree requirements:* Comprehensive exam, practicum required, foreign language and thesis not required. *Application deadline:* rolling. *Application fee:* $20. *Expenses:* Tuition $367 per credit. Fees $30 per year. *Financial aid:* Application deadline 9/30. *Faculty research:* Learning and teaching styles, language development, computers. • Application contact: Sr. Frances Berski, Coordinator, 914-569-3267. Fax: 914-562-6762. E-mail: berski@msmc.edu.

Mount Saint Mary College, Division of Education, Program in Elementary/Special Education, Newburgh, NY 12550-3494. Awards MS Ed. Part-time and evening/weekend programs available. Students: 7 full-time (all women), 80 part-time (63 women); includes 7 minority (3 African Americans, 1 Asian American, 3 Hispanics). Average age 32. In 1997, 25 degrees awarded. *Degree requirements:* Comprehensive exam, practicum required, foreign language and thesis not required. *Application deadline:* rolling. *Application fee:* $20. *Expenses:* Tuition $367 per credit. Fees $30 per year. *Financial aid:* Federal Work-Study and career-related internships or fieldwork available. Financial aid application deadline: 9/30. • Application contact: Sr. Frances Berski, Coordinator, 914-569-3267. Fax: 914-562-6762. E-mail: berski@msmc.edu.

Mount St. Mary's College, Department of Education, Specialization in Elementary Education, Los Angeles, CA 90049-1597. Awards MS. *Degree requirements:* Thesis, research project required, foreign language not required. *Entrance requirements:* MAT, minimum GPA of 3.0. Application fee: $50.

Mount Saint Vincent University, Department of Education, Program in Elementary Education, Halifax, NS B3M 2J6, Canada. Awards MA, MA Ed, MA(R), M Ed. Part-time and evening/weekend programs available. Faculty: 3 full-time (1 woman), 4 part-time (1 woman). Students: 1 (woman) full-time, 34 part-time (30 women). Average age 33. In 1997, 10 degrees awarded. *Degree requirements:* Thesis. *Entrance requirements:* Bachelor's degree in education, 1 year of teaching experience. Application deadline: 3/1 (priority date; rolling processing; 9/1 for spring admission). Application fee: $40. *Expenses:* Tuition $1024 per course. Fees $25 per course. *Financial aid:* Fellowships available. Financial aid application deadline: 5/1. *Faculty research:* Curriculum theory, critical/feminist pedagogy and curriculum, collaborative teaching of mathematics, philosophy in teacher education. • Dr. Yvonne Pothier, Head, 902-457-6183. Fax: 902-457-4911. E-mail: yvonne.pothier@msvu.ca. Application contact: Susan Tanner, Assistant Registrar, 902-457-6363. Fax: 902-457-6498. E-mail: susan.tanner@msvu.ca.

Murray State University, College of Education, Department of Elementary, Middle School, and Secondary Education, Program in Elementary Education, Murray, KY 42071-0009. Awards MA Ed, Ed S. Accredited by NCATE. Part-time programs available. Faculty: 11 full-time (4 women). Students: 2 full-time (1 woman), 123 part-time (122 women); includes 5 African Americans, 1 international. 24 applicants, 100% accepted. In 1997, 19 master's awarded. *Entrance requirements:* For master's, TOEFL (minimum score 500); for Ed S, GRE General Test or MAT. Application deadline: rolling. Application fee: $20. *Expenses:* Tuition $2500 per year full-time, $124 per hour part-time for state residents; $6740 per year full-time, $357 per hour part-time for nonresidents. Fees $360 per year full-time, $180 per year part-time. *Financial aid:* Research assistantships, teaching assistantships, Federal Work-Study available. Financial aid application deadline: 4/1. • Dr. Chuck Hulick, Director, 502-762-2496. Fax: 502-762-2540.

National–Louis University, National College of Education, McGaw Graduate School, Program in Elementary Education, 2840 Sheridan Road, Evanston, IL 60201-1730. Awards MAT. Part-time and evening/weekend programs available. Students: 72 full-time (62 women), 454 part-time (395 women); includes 53 minority (24 African Americans, 14 Asian Americans, 15 Hispanics), 2 international. Average age 35. In 1997, 209 degrees awarded. *Degree requirements:* Pre-clinical, clinical, student teaching required, foreign language and thesis not required. *Entrance requirements:* MAT, minimum GPA of 3.0. Application deadline: rolling. Application fee: $25. *Tuition:* $411 per semester hour. *Financial aid:* Fellowships available. Aid available to part-time students. Financial aid applicants required to submit FAFSA. • Dr. Pennie Olson, Coordinator, 847-475-1100 Ext. 3403. Application contact: Dr. David McCulloch, Vice President for University Services, 800-443-5522 Ext. 5127. Fax: 847-465-0593. E-mail: dmcc@wheeling1.nl.edu.

Nazareth College of Rochester, Graduate Studies, Department of Education, Program in Elementary Education, Rochester, NY 14618-3790. Awards MS Ed. Part-time programs available. Faculty: 1 (woman) full-time, 9 part-time (2 women). Students: 26 full-time (23 women), 103 part-time (83 women); includes 9 minority (7 African Americans, 2 Hispanics). 58 applicants, 84% accepted. In 1997, 66 degrees awarded. *Degree requirements:* Comprehensive exam required, foreign language and thesis not required. *Entrance requirements:* Minimum GPA of 2.7. Application deadline: 3/1 (9/15 for spring admission). Application fee: $40. *Expenses:* Tuition $436 per credit hour. Fees $20 per semester. • Jill Zulauf, Director, 716-389-2608. Application contact: Dr. Kay F. Marshman, Dean, 716-389-2815. Fax: 716-389-2452.

Newman University, Program in Education, Wichita, KS 67213-2084. Offerings include elementary/middle-level education (MS Ed). Program faculty: 5 full-time, 9 part-time. *Degree requirements:* Thesis or alternative. *Average time to degree:* master's–3 years part-time. *Application deadline:* 8/15 (priority date; rolling processing; 1/10 for spring admission). *Application fee:* $25. *Tuition:* $257 per credit hour. • Dr. Laura McLemore, Division Chair of Institute for Teacher Education, 316-942-4291 Ext. 253. Fax: 316-942-4483.

New York Institute of Technology, School of Education, Program in Elementary Education, Old Westbury, NY 11568-8000. Awards MS. Part-time and evening/weekend programs available. Faculty: 5 full-time (2 women), 14 part-time (9 women). Students: 15 full-time (9 women), 154 part-time (118 women); includes 40 minority (27 African Americans, 3 Asian Americans, 10 Hispanics), 2 international. Average age 33. 37 applicants, 65% accepted. In 1997, 19 degrees awarded. *Degree requirements:* Thesis required, foreign language not required. *Average time to degree:* master's–2 years full-time, 3 years part-time. *Entrance requirements:* GRE General Test, TOEFL, minimum QPA of 2.85. Application deadline: 8/1 (priority date; rolling processing). Application fee: $50. *Tuition:* $413 per credit. *Financial aid:* In 1997–98, 1 research assistantship (to a first-year student) averaging $300 per month and totaling $3,000 was awarded. • Dr. Davenport Plumer, Chair, 516-686-7777. Fax: 516-686-7655. Application contact: Glenn Berman, Executive Director of Admissions, 516-686-7519. Fax: 516-626-0419. E-mail: gberman@iris.nyit.edu.

New York University, School of Education, Department of Teaching and Learning, Program in Early Childhood and Elementary Education, New York, NY 10012-1019. Awards MA, Ed D, PhD, CAS. Part-time and evening/weekend programs available. Faculty: 9 full-time, 5 part-time. Students: 105 full-time, 95 part-time. 223 applicants, 61% accepted. In 1997, 92 master's, 1 doctorate, 3 CASs awarded. Terminal master's awarded for partial completion of doctoral program. *Degree requirements:* For master's, thesis required (for some programs), foreign language not required; for doctorate, dissertation. *Entrance requirements:* For master's, TOEFL; for doctorate, GRE General Test, TOEFL, interview; for CAS, TOEFL, master's degree. Application deadline: 2/1 (priority date; rolling processing; 12/1 for spring admission). Application fee: $40 ($60 for international students). *Financial aid:* Partial tuition waivers, Federal Work-Study, institutionally sponsored loans, and career-related internships or fieldwork available. Aid available to part-time students. Financial aid application deadline: 3/1; applicants required to submit FAFSA. *Faculty research:* Teacher evaluation and beliefs about teaching, early literacy development, language arts, child development and education. • Stephen Weiss, Director, 212-998-5460. Application contact: Office of Graduate Admissions, 212-998-5030. Fax: 212-995-4328.

Niagara University, Graduate Division of Education, Concentration in Teacher Education, Niagara University, NY 14109. Offerings include elementary education (MS Ed). Accredited by NCATE. Faculty: 4 full-time (1 woman), 6 part-time (4 women). *Entrance requirements:* GRE General Test or MAT. Application deadline: 8/1 (rolling processing). Application fee: $30. *Expenses:* Tuition $6048 per year full-time, $336 per credit hour part-time. Fees $25 per semester. • Dr. Paul J. Vermette, Chairman, 716-286-8550. Application contact: Rev. Daniel F. O'Leary, OMI, Dean of Education, 716-286-8560.

North Carolina Agricultural and Technical State University, Graduate School, School of Education, Department of Curriculum and Instruction, Program in Elementary Education, Greensboro, NC 27411. Awards MS. Accredited by NCATE. Part-time and evening/weekend programs available. Faculty: 2 full-time (both women). Students: 31 full-time (30 women), 40 part-time (37 women); includes 52 minority (all African Americans). Average age 33. 53 applicants, 81% accepted. In 1997, 12 degrees awarded. *Degree requirements:* Thesis or alternative, comprehensive exam, qualifying exam required, foreign language not required. *Entrance requirements:* GRE General Test, minimum GPA of 3.0. Application deadline: 6/1 (priority date; rolling processing; 12/1 for spring admission). Application fee: $35. *Tuition:* $1662 per year full-time, $272 per semester (minimum) part-time for state residents; $8790 per year full-time, $2054 per semester (minimum) part-time for nonresidents. *Financial aid:* Fellowships available. Financial aid application deadline: 6/1. • Dr. Dorothy Leflore, Interim Chairperson, Department of Curriculum and Instruction, 336-334-7848.

North Carolina Central University, Division of Academic Affairs, School of Education, Program in Elementary Education, Durham, NC 27707-3129. Awards MA, M Ed. Accredited by NCATE. Part-time and evening/weekend programs available. Students: 1 full-time (0 women), 15 part-time (all women); includes 9 minority (all African Americans). Average age 39. 9 applicants, 100% accepted. In 1997, 6 degrees awarded. *Degree requirements:* Thesis or alternative, comprehensive exam required, foreign language not required. *Entrance requirements:* Minimum GPA of 3.0 in major, 2.5 overall. Application deadline: 8/1. Application fee: $30. *Tuition:* $2027 per year full-time, $508 per semester (minimum) part-time for state residents; $9155 per year full-time, $2290 per semester (minimum) part-time for nonresidents. *Financial aid:* Fellowships, teaching assistantships, Federal Work-Study, institutionally sponsored loans, and career-related internships or fieldwork available. Aid available to part-time students. Financial aid application deadline: 5/1. *Faculty research:* Building self-image through contest application in middle grades education. • Dr. Vicki S. Fuller, Licensure Officer, 919-560-6417. Application contact: Dr. Cecelia Steppe-Jones, Associate Dean of Graduate Studies and Administration, 919-560-6478.

Northeastern State University, College of Education, Department of Curriculum and Instruction, Program in Elementary Education, Tahlequah, OK 74464-2399. Awards M Ed. Faculty: 17 part-time (3 women). Students: 16 (14 women). *Degree requirements:* Thesis or alternative required, foreign language not required. *Entrance requirements:* GRE General Test (minimum combined score of 900) or MAT (minimum score 35), minimum GPA of 2.5. Application deadline: 6/1 (priority date; rolling processing). Application fee: $0. *Expenses:* Tuition $74 per credit hour for state residents; $176 per credit hour for nonresidents. Fees $30 per year. *Financial aid:* Teaching assistantships, Federal Work-Study available. Financial aid application deadline: 3/1. • Dr. Louis White, Head, Department of Curriculum and Instruction, 918-456-5511 Ext. 3737.

Northeast Louisiana University, College of Education, Department of Curriculum and Instruction, Program in Elementary Education, Monroe, LA 71209-0001. Awards M Ed, Ed S. Accredited by NCATE. Part-time and evening/weekend programs available. *Degree requirements:* For master's, thesis optional, foreign language not required. *Entrance requirements:* For master's, GRE General Test, minimum GPA of 2.5. Application deadline: 7/1 (11/1 for spring admission). Application fee: $15 ($25 for international students). *Tuition:* $2028 per year full-time, $240 per semester (minimum) part-time for state residents; $6852 per year full-time, $240 per semester (minimum) part-time for nonresidents. *Faculty research:* Student attitudes.

Northern Arizona University, Center for Excellence in Education, Program in Elementary Education, Flagstaff, AZ 86011. Awards M Ed. Part-time and evening/weekend programs available. Students: 55 full-time (45 women), 742 part-time (664 women); includes 94 minority (14 African Americans, 4 Asian Americans, 63 Hispanics, 13 Native Americans). Average age 22. 248 applicants, 83% accepted. In 1997, 392 degrees awarded. *Degree requirements:* Thesis or alternative required, foreign language not required. *Entrance requirements:* GRE General Test, GRE Subject Test, or minimum GPA of 3.0. Application deadline: 3/15 (priority date; rolling processing). Application fee: $45. *Expenses:* Tuition $2088 per year full-time, $330 per semester (minimum) part-time for state residents; $8004 per year full-time, $1002 per semester (minimum) part-time for nonresidents. Fees $72 per year full-time, $18 per semester (minimum) part-time. *Financial aid:* Career-related internships or fieldwork available. *Faculty research:* Science/environmental education, whole language/literacy issues, technology education, school/university partnerships, school/museum partnerships. • Dr. Lynda Hatch, Interim Chair, 520-523-5342.

Northern Illinois University, College of Education, Department of Curriculum and Instruction, Program in Elementary Education, De Kalb, IL 60115-2854. Awards MS Ed. Accredited by NCATE. Part-time and evening/weekend programs available. Faculty: 6 full-time (4 women). Students: 7 full-time (2 women), 96 part-time (87 women); includes 5 minority (4 African Americans, 1 Hispanic). Average age 34. 27 applicants, 44% accepted. In 1997, 32 degrees awarded. *Degree requirements:* Comprehensive exam required, thesis optional, foreign language not required. *Entrance requirements:* GRE General Test or MAT, TOEFL (minimum score 550), minimum GPA of 2.75. Application deadline: 6/1 (rolling processing; 11/1 for spring admission). Application fee: $30. *Tuition:* $3984 per year full-time, $154 per credit hour part-time for state residents; $8160 per year full-time, $328 per credit hour part-time for nonresidents. *Financial aid:* Fellowships, research assistantships, teaching assistantships, staff assistantships, full tuition waivers, Federal Work-Study, and career-related internships or fieldwork available. Aid available to part-time students. • Dr. Norman Stahl, Chair, Department of Curriculum and Instruction, 815-753-9032.

Northern Kentucky University, Department of Education, Highland Heights, KY 41099. Offerings include elementary education (MA Ed). Accredited by NCATE. Department faculty: 16 full-time (11 women). *Entrance requirements:* GRE, teaching certificate. Application deadline: 8/15 (priority date; rolling processing). Application fee: $25. *Tuition:* $2420 per year full-time, $132 per semester hour part-time for state residents; $6660 per year full-time, $368 per semester hour part-time for nonresidents. • Dr. Darrell Garber, Chairperson, 606-572-5365. Application contact: Peg Griffin, Coordinator, Graduate Program, 606-572-6364.

Northern Michigan University, College of Behavioral Sciences and Human Services, Department of Education, Program in Elementary Education, Marquette, MI 49855-5301. Awards MA Ed. Accredited by NCATE. Part-time programs available. Students: 29 full-time (all women), 3 part-time (1 woman). 12 applicants, 100% accepted. In 1997, 7 degrees awarded. *Degree requirements:* Thesis or alternative required, foreign language not required. *Entrance requirements:* GRE General Test (minimum combined score of 900), minimum GPA of 2.75. Application deadline: 7/1 (priority date; rolling processing; 11/1 for spring admission). Application fee: $25. *Expenses:* Tuition $135 per credit hour for state residents; $215 per credit hour for nonresidents. Fees $183 per year full-time, $94 per year (minimum) part-time. *Financial aid:* Federal Work-Study, institutionally sponsored loans available. Aid available to part-time students. Financial aid application deadline: 3/1. *Faculty research:* Whole language research, literature-based reading, essential elements of instruction, supervision and improvement of instruction. • Dr. James D. Hendricks, Head, Department of Education, 906-227-2728.

Northern State University, Division of Graduate Studies in Education, Program in Teaching and Learning, Aberdeen, SD 57401-7198. Offerings include elementary classroom teaching (MS Ed). Accredited by NCATE. Offered jointly with Huron University, Jamestown College, and the University of Mary. Program faculty: 98 full-time (28 women). *Degree requirements:* Thesis required, foreign language not required. *Average time to degree:* master's–1.5 years full-time. *Entrance requirements:* Minimum GPA of 2.75. Application deadline: 8/15 (priority date; rolling processing; 12/15 for spring admission). Application fee: $15. *Expenses:* Tuition $1999 per year full-time, $83 per credit hour part-time for state residents; $6034 per year full-time, $251 per credit hour part-time for nonresidents. Fees $954 per year full-time, $40 per credit hour part-time. • Dr. Paul Deputy, Head, 605-626-2415. Application contact: Dr. Sharon Tebben, Director of Graduate Studies, 605-626-2558. Fax: 605-626-2542.

Northwestern Oklahoma State University, School of Education, Psychology, and Health and Physical Education, Program in Elementary Education, Alva, OK 73717. Awards M Ed. Accredited by NCATE. Part-time programs available. Faculty: 6 full-time (4 women). Students: 8 full-time (6 women), 18 part-time (15 women); includes 1 minority (African American). 9 applicants, 89% accepted. In 1997, 8 degrees awarded. *Entrance requirements:* GRE General Test (minimum combined score of 900) or MAT (minimum score 38), minimum GPA of 2.75. Application deadline: rolling. Application fee: $15. *Tuition:* $73 per semester hour for state residents; $175 per semester hour for nonresidents. *Financial aid:* Federal Work-Study available. Aid available to part-time students. Financial aid application deadline: 5/1. • Dr. Bob Cason, Coordinator, 405-327-8452. Application contact: Dr. Ed Huckeby, Dean of Graduate School, 405-327-8410.

Northwestern State University of Louisiana, Division of Education, Emphasis in Elementary Teaching, Natchitoches, LA 71497. Awards M Ed, Ed S. Accredited by NCATE. Faculty: 2 full-time (1 woman), 2 part-time (0 women). Students: 14 part-time (all women); includes 2 minority (both African Americans). Average age 36. In 1997, 4 master's awarded. *Entrance requirements:* For master's, GRE General Test (minimum combined score of 800), GRE Subject Test, minimum undergraduate GPA of 2.5. Application deadline: 8/1 (priority date; rolling processing; 1/10 for spring admission). Application fee: $15 ($25 for international students). *Tuition:* $2147 per year full-time, $336 per semester (minimum) part-time for state residents; $6437 per year full-time, $336 per semester (minimum) part-time for nonresidents. *Financial aid:* Career-related internships or fieldwork available. Financial aid application deadline: 7/15. • Application contact: Dr. Tom Hanson, Dean, Graduate Studies and Research, 318-357-5851. Fax: 318-357-5019.

Northwestern University, School of Education and Social Policy, Evanston, IL 60208. Offerings include elementary teaching (MS). School faculty: 19 full-time (5 women), 6 part-time (1 woman). *Tuition:* $2424 per course. • Jean Egmon, Assistant Dean, 847-491-3790. Fax: 847-461-2495. E-mail: egmon@nwu.edu. Application contact: Andrew Ager, Office of Student Affairs, 847-491-3790. Fax: 847-467-2495. E-mail: andrew-ager@nwu.edu.

Northwest Missouri State University, College of Education and Human Services, Department of Curriculum and Instruction, Program in Elementary Education, 800 University Drive, Maryville, MO 64468-6001. Awards MS Ed. Accredited by NCATE. Part-time programs available. Faculty: 14 full-time (12 women). Students: 2 full-time (both women), 16 part-time (all women). 9 applicants, 100% accepted. In 1997, 12 degrees awarded. *Degree requirements:* Comprehensive exam required, foreign language and thesis not required. *Entrance requirements:* GRE General Test (minimum combined score of 700), TOEFL (minimum score 550), minimum undergraduate GPA of 2.5, teaching certificate, writing sample. Application deadline: rolling. Application fee: $0 ($50 for international students). *Expenses:* Tuition $113 per credit hour for state residents; $197 per credit hour for nonresidents. Fees $3 per credit hour. *Financial aid:* In 1997–98, 6 students received aid, including 1 teaching assistantship averaging $585 per month, 1 administrative assistantship averaging $585 per month. Financial aid application deadline: 3/1. • Dr. Jean Bouas, Director, 816-562-1359. Application contact: Dr. Frances Shipley, Dean of Graduate School, 816-562-1145. E-mail: gradsch@acad.nwmissouri.edu.

Notre Dame College, Education Division, Program in Elementary Teaching, Manchester, NH 03104-2299. Awards M Ed. Faculty: 1 (woman) full-time, 9 part-time (7 women). Students: 42 full-time (33 women), 53 part-time (45 women). Average age 34. 39 applicants, 79% accepted. In 1997, 12 degrees awarded. *Degree requirements:* Computer language, comprehensive exams, portfolio, or thesis required, foreign language not required. *Entrance requirements:* GRE General Test or MAT. Application deadline: rolling. Application fee: $35. *Tuition:* $299 per credit. *Financial aid:* Fellowships available. • Dr. Denise Marchionda, Director, 603-669-4298 Ext. 122.

Nova Southeastern University, Fischler Center for the Advancement of Education, Graduate Teacher Education Program, Fort Lauderdale, FL 33314-7721. Offerings include elementary education (MS, Ed S). *Degree requirements:* Thesis, practicum required, foreign language not required. *Entrance requirements:* For master's, teaching certificate; for Ed S, master's degree, teaching certificate. Application deadline: rolling. Application fee: $50. *Tuition:* $245 per credit hour (minimum). • Dr. Deo Nellis, Dean, 954-262-8601. E-mail: deo@fcae.nova.edu. Application contact: Dr. Mark Seldine, Director of Student Affairs, 954-262-8689. Fax: 954-262-3910. E-mail: seldines@fcae.nova.edu.

Occidental College, Department of Education, Program in Elementary Education, Los Angeles, CA 90041-3392. Offers liberal studies (MAT). Part-time programs available. Faculty: 4 full-time (1 woman). Students: 12 full-time (all women); includes 9 minority (2 Asian Americans, 7 Hispanics). Average age 24. 16 applicants, 94% accepted. *Degree requirements:* Internship required, foreign language and thesis not required. *Entrance requirements:* GRE General Test (minimum score 550 on each section or combined score of 1650 on three sections), TOEFL (minimum score 600), minimum GPA of 3.0. Application deadline: 3/1 (priority date; rolling processing; 10/1 for spring admission). Application fee: $40. *Expenses:* Tuition $21,256 per year full-time, $865 per unit part-time. Fees $314 per year. *Financial aid:* Fellowships, institutionally sponsored loans, and career-related internships or fieldwork available. Aid available to part-time students. Financial aid application deadline: 3/1. • Application contact: Susan Molik, Administrative Assistant, Graduate Office, 213-259-2921.

Ohio University, Graduate Studies, College of Education, School of Curriculum and Instruction, Program in Elementary Education, Athens, OH 45701-2979. Awards M Ed. Accredited by NCATE. Part-time and evening/weekend programs available. Students: 11 full-time (all women), 13 part-time (12 women); includes 2 international. 25 applicants, 60% accepted. *Degree requirements:* Thesis or alternative required, foreign language not required. *Entrance requirements:* GRE General Test or MAT. Application deadline: rolling. Application fee: $30. *Tuition:* $5430 per year full-time, $216 per quarter hour part-time for state residents; $10,431 per year full-time, $423 per quarter hour part-time for nonresidents. *Financial aid:* In 1997–98,

Directory: Elementary Education

Ohio University (continued)

1 assistantship (to a first-year student) was awarded; full tuition waivers, Federal Work-Study, institutionally sponsored loans also available. Financial aid application deadline: 3/15. • Application contact: Dr. Bonnie Beach, Graduate Chair, 740-593-0523.

Oklahoma City University, Petree College of Arts and Sciences, Division of Education, Program in Elementary Education, Oklahoma City, OK 73106-1402. Awards M Ed. Part-time and evening/weekend programs available. Students: 3 full-time (2 women), 3 part-time (2 women); includes 3 international. Average age 29. *Degree requirements:* Thesis or alternative required, foreign language not required. *Average time to degree:* master's–1.5 years full-time, 3.3 years part-time. *Entrance requirements:* Minimum GPA of 3.0. Application deadline: 8/25 (priority date; rolling processing; 1/15 for spring admission). Application fee: $35 ($55 for international students). *Expenses:* Tuition $318 per hour. Fees $124 per year. *Financial aid:* Fellowships, partial tuition waivers, Federal Work-Study, institutionally sponsored loans, and career-related internships or fieldwork available. Aid available to part-time students. Financial aid application deadline: 8/1; applicants required to submit FAFSA. • Dr. Donna C. Richardson, Director, 405-521-5371. Application contact: Laura L. Rahhal, Director of Graduate Admissions, 800-633-7242 Ext. 2. Fax: 405-521-5356. E-mail: lrahhal1@froda.okcu.edu.

Old Dominion University, Darden College of Education, Department of Educational Curriculum and Instruction, Program in Elementary/Middle Education, Norfolk, VA 23529. Offers educational media (MS Ed), elementary education (MS Ed). Accredited by NCATE. Part-time and evening/weekend programs available. Students: 212 full-time (149 women), 334 part-time (216 women); includes 89 minority (74 African Americans, 4 Asian Americans, 7 Hispanics, 4 Native Americans). Average age 36. In 1997, 260 degrees awarded. *Degree requirements:* Comprehensive exam required, foreign language and thesis not required. *Entrance requirements:* GRE General Test, MAT, minimum GPA of 3.0, teaching certificate. Application deadline: 7/1 (rolling processing). Application fee: $30. *Expenses:* Tuition $180 per credit hour for state residents; $477 per credit hour for nonresidents. Fees $140 per year full-time, $32 per semester part-time. *Financial aid:* In 1997–98, 195 students received aid, including 4 fellowships totaling $7,814, 10 research assistantships totaling $43,414, 89 tuition grants (5 to first-year students) totaling $81,906; teaching assistantships, partial tuition waivers, Federal Work-Study, institutionally sponsored loans, and career-related internships or fieldwork also available. Aid available to part-time students. Financial aid application deadline: 2/15; applicants required to submit FAFSA. • Dr. Katherine Bucher, Director, 757-683-3284. Fax: 757-683-5862. E-mail: kbucher@odu.edu.

Olivet Nazarene University, Division of Education, Program in Elementary Education, Kankakee, IL 60901-0592. Awards MAT. Evening/weekend programs available. *Degree requirements:* Thesis or alternative required, foreign language not required. *Application deadline:* rolling. *Application fee:* $20.

Oregon State University, Graduate School, College of Home Economics and Education, School of Education, Program in Elementary Education, Corvallis, OR 97331. Awards MAT. Accredited by NCATE. Students: 46 full-time; includes 4 minority (2 Asian Americans, 2 Hispanics). Average age 28. 115 applicants, 44% accepted. In 1997, 29 degrees awarded (100% found work related to degree). *Degree requirements:* Minimum GPA of 3.0 required, foreign language and thesis not required. *Entrance requirements:* NTE, TOEFL (minimum score 550), minimum GPA of 3.0 in last 90 hours. Application deadline: 3/1 (priority date; rolling processing). Application fee: $50. *Tuition:* $6207 per year full-time, $810 per quarter (minimum) part-time for state residents; $10,551 per year full-time, $1293 per quarter (minimum) part-time for nonresidents. *Financial aid:* In 1997–98, 15 fellowships (all to first-year students) were awarded; Federal Work-Study, institutionally sponsored loans also available. Aid available to part-time students. Financial aid application deadline: 2/1. *Faculty research:* Kindergarten curriculum, the reading-writing connection, authentic assessment, classroom management. • Dr. R. Lance Haddon, Coordinator, 541-737-5956.

Pacific Lutheran University, School of Education, Program in Classroom Teaching, Tacoma, WA 98447. Offerings include elementary education (MA). Accredited by NCATE. Program faculty: 2 full-time (1 woman). *Degree requirements:* Comprehensive exam, research project or thesis required, foreign language not required. *Entrance requirements:* GRE General Test or MAT, TOEFL (minimum score 550), interview. Application deadline: rolling. Application fee: $35. *Tuition:* $490 per semester hour. • Dr. Leon Reisberg, Graduate Director, 253-535-7272. Application contact: Marjo Burdick, Office of Admissions, 253-535-7151. Fax: 253-535-8320. E-mail: admissions@plu.edu.

Pacific Union College, Department of Education, Angwin, CA 94508. Offerings include elementary education (MA). Department faculty: 4 full-time (3 women), 1 (woman) part-time. *Degree requirements:* Thesis required, foreign language not required. *Average time to degree:* master's–1 year full-time, 4 years part-time. *Entrance requirements:* GRE, California Basic Educational Skills Test, MSAT, interview, teaching credential. Application deadline: 6/1 (priority date; rolling processing). Application fee: $30. Electronic applications accepted. • Dr. Jean Buller, Chair, 707-965-7265. E-mail: jbuller@puc.edu. Application contact: Marsha Crow, Credential Analyst, 707-965-6643. Fax: 707-965-6645. E-mail: mcrow@puc.edu.

Pacific University, School of Education, Forest Grove, OR 97116-1797. Offerings include early childhood education/elementary education (MAT), elementary/middle school education (MAT). School faculty: 11 full-time, 8 part-time. *Application deadline:* 3/15 (priority date; rolling processing; 10/15 for spring admission). *Application fee:* $35. • Dr. Willard Kniep, Program Director, 503-359-2205. Application contact: Joel Albin, Admissions Counselor, 503-359-2958. Fax: 503-359-2975. E-mail: admissions@pacificu.edu.

Palm Beach Atlantic College, School of Education and Behavioral Studies, Program in Elementary Education, West Palm Beach, FL 33416-4708. Awards M Ed. Faculty: 1 (woman) full-time, 2 part-time (both women). Students: 5 full-time (4 women), 19 part-time (17 women); includes 6 minority (3 African Americans, 2 Asian Americans, 1 Hispanic), 1 international. Average age 32. 19 applicants, 68% accepted. In 1997, 11 degrees awarded. *Entrance requirements:* GRE General Test (combined average 1000), minimum GPA of 3.0 in last 60 hours. Application deadline: 7/15 (priority date; rolling processing; 11/15 for spring admission). Application fee: $35. *Tuition:* $280 per credit hour. • Dr. Karen Rumbley, Director, 561-803-2353. Fax: 561-803-2186. E-mail: rumbleyk@pbac.edu. Application contact: Carolanne M. Brown, Director of Graduate Admissions, 800-281-3466. Fax: 561-803-2115. E-mail: grad@pbac.edu.

Pennsylvania State University University Park Campus, College of Education, Department of Curriculum and Instruction, University Park, PA 16802-1503. Offerings include elementary education (M Ed, MS, D Ed, PhD). Accredited by NCATE. *Degree requirements:* For doctorate, dissertation. *Entrance requirements:* GRE General Test or MAT. Application fee: $40. *Expenses:* Tuition $6534 per year full-time, $276 per credit part-time for state residents; $13,460 per year full-time, $561 per credit part-time for nonresidents. Fees $252 per year (minimum) full-time, $43 per semester (minimum) part-time. • Dr. Peter A. Rubb, Head, 814-865-5433.

Phillips University, School of Education, 100 South University Avenue, Enid, OK 73701-6439. Offerings include elementary education (M Ed). School faculty: 5 full-time (2 women), 4 part-time (2 women). *Degree requirements:* Thesis required (for some programs), foreign language not required. *Entrance requirements:* Minimum GPA of 2.5. Application deadline: 8/1 (1/1 for spring admission). Application fee: $20. *Expenses:* Tuition $97 per credit hour. Fees $10 per credit hour. • Dr. Donna Payne, Dean, 405-237-4433 Ext. 207.

Pine Manor College, Program in Education, Chestnut Hill, MA 02167-2332. Offerings include elementary education (M Ed). College faculty: 5 full-time (all women). *Degree requirements:* Clinical experience, fieldwork. *Application deadline:* rolling. *Application fee:* $25. • Dr. Joanna S. Hall, Director of Graduate Studies, 617-731-7075. Application contact: Pat Dunbar, Graduate Admissions, 617-731-7111. Fax: 617-731-7199.

Pittsburg State University, School of Education, Department of Curriculum and Instruction, Pittsburg, KS 66762-5880. Offerings include elementary education (MS), elementary teaching (Ed S). One or more programs accredited by NCATE. *Degree requirements:* For master's, thesis or alternative required, foreign language not required. *Entrance requirements:* For master's, GRE or MAT. Application fee: $40. *Tuition:* $2418 per year full-time, $103 per credit hour part-time for state residents; $6130 per year full-time, $258 per credit hour part-time for nonresidents. • Dr. Sandra Greer, Chairperson, 316-235-4496.

Plattsburgh State University of New York, Faculty of Professional Studies, Center for Educational Studies and Services, Program in Elementary Education, Plattsburgh, NY 12901-2681. Awards MS, MST. Students: 38 full-time (29 women), 49 part-time (39 women); includes 1 minority (Hispanic). 41 applicants, 76% accepted. In 1997, 52 degrees awarded. *Degree requirements:* Comprehensive exam or research project required, thesis optional. *Entrance requirements:* GRE General Test or MAT, minimum GPA of 2.5. Application deadline: rolling. Application fee: $50. *Expenses:* Tuition $5100 per year full-time, $213 per credit hour part-time for state residents; $8416 per year full-time, $351 per credit hour part-time for nonresidents. Fees $395 per year full-time, $15.10 per credit hour part-time. *Financial aid:* 30 students received aid; Federal Work-Study available. Aid available to part-time students. Financial aid application deadline: 4/15; applicants required to submit FAFSA. • Dr. Raymond Domenico, Director and Associate Dean, Center for Educational Studies and Services, 518-564-2122.

Plymouth State College of the University System of New Hampshire, Department of Education, Program in Elementary Education, Plymouth, NH 03264-1595. Awards M Ed. Accredited by NCATE. Part-time and evening/weekend programs available. Students: 12 full-time (10 women), 15 part-time (14 women). Average age 37. 12 applicants, 75% accepted. In 1997, 10 degrees awarded. *Entrance requirements:* GRE General Test (average 500 on each section) or MAT (minimum score 50), minimum GPA of 3.0. Application deadline: 9/1 (priority date; rolling processing). Application fee: $25 ($35 for international students). *Tuition:* $232 per credit for state residents; $254 per credit for nonresidents. *Financial aid:* Graduate assistantships, institutionally sponsored loans, and career-related internships or fieldwork available. Aid available to part-time students. Financial aid application deadline: 3/15; applicants required to submit FAFSA. • Dr. Dennise Bartelo, Adviser, 603-535-2286. Application contact: Maryann Szabadics, Administrative Assistant, 603-535-2636. Fax: 603-535-2572. E-mail: for.grad@psc.plymouth.edu.

Portland State University, School of Education, Department of Curriculum and Instruction, Program in Elementary Education, Portland, OR 97207-0751. Awards MAT, M Ed, MST. Accredited by NCATE. Faculty: 51 full-time (28 women), 9 part-time (5 women), 52 FTE. Students: 82 full-time (68 women), 11 part-time (9 women); includes 24 minority (12 African Americans, 4 Asian Americans, 4 Hispanics, 4 Native Americans). Average age 30. 61 applicants, 97% accepted. *Degree requirements:* Special project or thesis, written exam. *Entrance requirements:* California Basic Educational Skills Test, TOEFL (minimum score 550), minimum GPA of 3.0 in upper-division course work or 2.75 overall. Application deadline: 4/1 (rolling processing; 11/1 for spring admission). Application fee: $50. *Tuition:* $6101 per year full-time, $689 per semester (minimum) part-time for state residents; $10,445 per year full-time, $689 per semester (minimum) part-time for nonresidents. *Financial aid:* Research assistantships, teaching assistantships, Federal Work-Study, institutionally sponsored loans, and career-related internships or fieldwork available. Financial aid application deadline: 3/1; applicants required to submit FAFSA. • Dr. Ulrich Hardt, Head, Department of Curriculum and Instruction, 503-725-4756. Fax: 503-725-8475. E-mail: hardtu@ed.pdx.edu.

Purdue University, School of Education, Department of Curriculum and Instruction, West Lafayette, IN 47907. Offerings include elementary education (MS Ed). Accredited by NCATE. Department faculty: 34 full-time (15 women), 3 part-time (1 woman). *Degree requirements:* Thesis optional. *Entrance requirements:* TOEFL (minimum score 550), minimum B average. Application deadline: 1/15 (priority date; 9/15 for spring admission). Application fee: $30. Electronic applications accepted. *Tuition:* $3500 per year full-time, $126 per credit hour part-time for state residents; $11,720 per year full-time, $387 per credit hour part-time for nonresidents. • Dr. J. L. Peters, Head, 765-494-9172. Fax: 765-496-1622. E-mail: peters@purdue.edu. Application contact: Christine Larsen, Coordinator of Graduate Studies, 765-494-2345. Fax: 765-494-5832. E-mail: gradoffice@soe.purdue.edu.

Purdue University Calumet, School of Professional Studies, Department of Education, Program in Elementary Education, Hammond, IN 46323-2094. Awards MS Ed. *Entrance requirements:* TOEFL. Application fee: $30.

Purdue University North Central, Graduate Program in Education, Westville, IN 46391-9528. Offers elementary education (MS Ed). Part-time and evening/weekend programs available. Students: 40 part-time. • Dr. Edward Hackett, Chair, 219-785-5485. Fax: 219-785-5516. E-mail: ehackett@purduenc.edu.

Queens College, Hayworth College, Department of Education, 1900 Selwyn Avenue, Charlotte, NC 28274-0002. Offerings include elementary education (MAT). Accredited by NCATE. Department faculty: 4 full-time (all women), 2 part-time (both women). *Degree requirements:* Comprehensive written exam required, foreign language and thesis not required. *Entrance requirements:* GRE General Test (minimum combined score of 850). Application deadline: rolling. Application fee: $25. *Expenses:* Tuition $225 per credit hour. Fees $40 per year. • Dr. Joyce Eckart, Chairperson, 704-337-2565. Application contact: Anne Duplessis, Director of Admissions, 704-337-2314. Fax: 704-337-2415.

Queens College of the City University of New York, Social Science Division, School of Education, Department of Elementary and Early Childhood Education, 65-30 Kissena Boulevard, Flushing, NY 11367-1597. Offers programs in bilingual education (MS Ed), elementary education (MS Ed, AC). Part-time and evening/weekend programs available. Students: 103 full-time (90 women), 730 part-time (671 women); includes 103 minority (41 African Americans, 20 Asian Americans, 40 Hispanics, 2 Native Americans). 418 applicants, 70% accepted. In 1997, 186 master's awarded. *Degree requirements:* For master's, research project required, foreign language and thesis not required; for AC, thesis optional, foreign language not required. *Entrance requirements:* For master's, TOEFL (minimum score 600), minimum GPA of 3.0; for AC, TOEFL (minimum score 600). Application deadline: 4/1 (rolling processing; 11/1 for spring admission). Application fee: $40. *Expenses:* Tuition $4350 per year full-time, $185 per credit part-time for state residents; $7600 per year full-time, $320 per credit part-time for nonresidents. Fees $104 per year. *Financial aid:* Partial tuition waivers, Federal Work-Study, institutionally sponsored loans, and career-related internships or fieldwork available. Aid available to part-time students. Financial aid application deadline: 4/1; applicants required to submit FAFSA. • Dr. Glenna Sloan, Chairperson, 718-997-5300. Application contact: Dr. Janet Ezair, Graduate Adviser, 718-997-5304.

Rhode Island College, School of Graduate Studies, School of Education and Human Development, Department of Elementary Education, Program in Elementary Education, Providence, RI 02908-1924. Awards MAT, M Ed. Accredited by NCATE. Evening/weekend programs available. Faculty: 19 full-time (9 women), 9 part-time (7 women). Students: 77 full-time (72 women), 97 part-time (91 women); includes 4 minority (1 African American, 2 Asian Americans, 1 Native American). In 1997, 51 degrees awarded. *Entrance requirements:* GRE General Test or MAT. Application deadline: 4/1 (rolling processing). Application fee: $25. *Tuition:* $4064 per year full-time, $214 per credit part-time for state residents; $7658 per year full-time, $376 per credit part-time for nonresidents. *Financial aid:* Application deadline 4/1. • Dr. Patricia Cordeiro, Chair, Department of Elementary Education, 401-456-8016.

Rivier College, Graduate Education Department, Program in Elementary Education, Nashua, NH 03060-5086. Awards M Ed. Part-time and evening/weekend programs available. *Entrance requirements:* GRE General Test or MAT. Application deadline: rolling. Application fee: $25.

Rockford College, Department of Education, Program in Elementary Education, Rockford, IL 61108-2393. Awards MAT. Part-time and evening/weekend programs available. Faculty: 17 full-time (7 women), 17 part-time (14 women), 21 FTE. Students: 26 full-time (17 women), 96 part-time (78 women); includes 8 minority (6 African Americans, 2 Hispanics). Average age 33. 23 applicants, 96% accepted. In 1997, 23 degrees awarded. *Degree requirements:* Thesis optional, foreign language not required. *Entrance requirements:* GRE General Test (minimum combined score of 1000). Application deadline: rolling. Application fee: $35. *Tuition:* $15,500 per year full-time, $400 per credit part-time. • Barbara Heal, Chair, Department of Education, 815-394-5201.

Rollins College, Program in Education, Winter Park, FL 32789-4499. Offerings include elementary education (MAT, M Ed). Program faculty: 13 full-time (8 women), 11 part-time (4 women), 17 FTE. *Degree requirements:* Comprehensive exam required, foreign language and thesis not required. *Entrance requirements:* Interview. Application deadline: rolling. Application fee: $50. *Tuition:* $190 per hour. • Dr. Nancy McAleer, Director, 407-646-2305. Application contact: Laura Pfister, Coordinator of Records and Registration, 407-646-2416. Fax: 407-646-1551.

Roosevelt University, College of Education, Chicago, IL 60605-1394. Offerings include elementary education (MA). Accredited by NCATE. *Application deadline:* 6/1 (priority date; rolling processing). *Application fee:* $25 ($35 for international students). *Expenses:* Tuition $445 per credit hour. Fees $100 per year. • Dr. George Lowery, Dean, 312-341-3700. Application contact: Joanne Canyon-Heller, Coordinator of Graduate Admissions, 312-341-3612.

Rowan University, College of Education, Department of Elementary Education, Glassboro, NJ 08028-1701. Offers programs in computers in education (Certificate), elementary education (MA, MST), elementary mathematics achievement (Certificate). Accredited by NCATE. Part-time and evening/weekend programs available. Students: 54 (45 women); includes 3 minority (2 African Americans, 1 Hispanic). 53 applicants, 64% accepted. In 1997, 14 master's awarded. *Degree requirements:* For master's, thesis, comprehensive exams required, foreign language not required. *Entrance requirements:* For master's, GRE General Test (minimum combined score of 800), interview, minimum GPA of 2.8. Application deadline: 11/1 (priority date; rolling processing; 4/1 for spring admission). Application fee: $50. *Tuition:* $5728 per year full-time, $258 per credit hour part-time for state residents; $8968 per year full-time, $393 per credit hour part-time for nonresidents. *Financial aid:* Federal Work-Study available. Aid available to part-time students. • Dr. Carl Calliari, Adviser, 609-256-4763.

Rutgers, The State University of New Jersey, New Brunswick, Graduate School of Education, Department of Learning and Teaching, Program in Early Childhood/Elementary Education, New Brunswick, NJ 08903. Awards Ed M, Ed D, Ed S. Part-time programs available. Faculty: 4 full-time (all women), 2 part-time (both women). Students: 102; includes 18 minority (10 African Americans, 6 Asian Americans, 2 Hispanics). 141 applicants, 45% accepted. In 1997, 42 master's, 1 doctorate awarded. Terminal master's awarded for partial completion of doctoral program. *Degree requirements:* For master's, comprehensive exam required, thesis not required; for doctorate, dissertation, qualifying exam. *Entrance requirements:* For master's, GRE General Test (minimum combined score of 1000), minimum GPA of 3.0; for doctorate, GRE General Test (minimum combined score of 1100), minimum GPA of 3.5; for Ed S, GRE General Test. Application deadline: 3/1 (11/1 for spring admission). Application fee: $40. *Expenses:* Tuition $6492 per year full-time, $268 per credit part-time for state residents; $9520 per year full-time, $395 per credit part-time for nonresidents. Fees $208 per year (minimum). *Financial aid:* Fellowships, teaching assistantships, scholarships available. Financial aid application deadline: 3/1. • Dr. Lesley M. Morrow, Coordinator, 732-932-7496 Ext. 119.

Sacred Heart University, College of Education and Health Professions, Faculty of Education and Psychology, 5151 Park Avenue, Fairfield, CT 06432-1000. Offerings include elementary education (MAT). *Degree requirements:* Thesis or alternative required, foreign language not required. *Application deadline:* rolling. *Application fee:* $40 ($100 for international students). *Expenses:* Tuition $335 per credit. Fees $78 per semester. • Dr. A. Harris Stone, Director, 203-371-7800. Application contact: Linda B. Kirby, Dean of Graduate Admissions, 203-371-7880. Fax: 203-365-4732. E-mail: gradstudies@sacredheart.edu.

Sage Graduate School, Graduate School, Division of Education, Program in Elementary Education, Troy, NY 12180-4115. Awards MS Ed. Part-time and evening/weekend programs available. Students: 27 full-time (16 women), 60 part-time (38 women). *Degree requirements:* Thesis required, foreign language not required. *Entrance requirements:* Minimum GPA of 2.75. Application deadline: 8/1 (rolling processing; 12/15 for spring admission). Application fee: $25. *Expenses:* Tuition $360 per credit hour. Fees $50 per semester. *Financial aid:* Research assistantships and career-related internships or fieldwork available. Aid available to part-time students. Financial aid application deadline: 7/1; applicants required to submit FAFSA. *Faculty research:* The effects of teachers' personal characteristics on the instructional process. • Dr. Connell Frazer, Adviser, 518-244-2403. Fax: 518-244-2334. E-mail: frazec@sage.edu. Application contact: Melissa Robertson, Associate Director of Admissions, 518-244-6878. Fax: 518-244-6880. E-mail: sgsadm@sage.edu.

Saginaw Valley State University, College of Education, Program in Elementary Classroom Teaching, University Center, MI 48710. Awards MAT. Accredited by NCATE. Part-time and evening/weekend programs available. Faculty: 12 full-time (9 women). Students: 4 full-time (all women), 130 part-time (116 women); includes 3 minority (1 African American, 2 Asian Americans). In 1997, 23 degrees awarded. *Entrance requirements:* Minimum GPA of 3.0, teaching certificate. Application deadline: rolling. Application fee: $25. *Expenses:* Tuition $159 per credit hour for state residents; $311 per credit hour for nonresidents. Fees $8.70 per credit hour. • Application contact: Dr. Susie Emond, Coordinator, 517-790-4331.

St. Cloud State University, College of Education, Department of Teacher Development, Elementary Education Track, St. Cloud, MN 56301-4498. Awards MS. Accredited by NCATE. Faculty: 12 full-time (5 women). Students: 1 (woman) part-time. In 1997, 21 degrees awarded. *Degree requirements:* Thesis or alternative required, foreign language not required. *Entrance requirements:* GRE General Test, minimum GPA of 2.75. Application fee: $20 ($100 for international students). *Expenses:* Tuition $128 per credit for state residents; $203 per credit for nonresidents. Fees $16.32 per credit. *Financial aid:* Graduate assistantships, Federal Work-Study available. Financial aid application deadline: 3/1. • Application contact: Ann Anderson, Graduate Studies Office, 320-255-2113. Fax: 320-654-5371. E-mail: anna@grad.stcloud.msus.edu.

St. John's University, School of Education and Human Services, Division of Administration and Instructional Leadership, Program in Elementary Education, Jamaica, NY 11439. Awards MS Ed. Part-time and evening/weekend programs available. Students: 26 full-time (24 women), 153 part-time (133 women); includes 25 minority (5 African Americans, 4 Asian Americans, 14 Hispanics, 2 Native Americans), 1 international. Average age 29. 110 applicants, 95% accepted. In 1997, 65 degrees awarded. *Entrance requirements:* Minimum GPA of 3.0. Application deadline: 6/1 (rolling processing; 10/1 for spring admission). Application fee: $40. *Expenses:* Tuition $525 per credit. Fees $150 per year. *Financial aid:* Teaching assistantships, administrative assistantship, Federal Work-Study, and career-related internships or fieldwork available. Aid available to part-time students. Financial aid application deadline: 3/1; applicants required to submit FAFSA. *Faculty research:* Early childhood. • Application contact: Shamus J. McGrenra, TOR, Associate Director, Graduate Admissions, 718-990-6107. Fax: 718-990-5736. E-mail: mcgrenrs@stjohns.edu.

Saint Joseph College, Field of Education and Counseling, Education Programs, Program in Elementary Education, West Hartford, CT 06117-2700. Awards MA. *Degree requirements:* Thesis or alternative required, foreign language not required. *Application deadline:* 8/29 (rolling processing). *Application fee:* $25. *Tuition:* $395 per credit. *Financial aid:* Application deadline 8/31. • Dr. Gerard Thibodeau, Co-Chair, Education Department, Field of Education and Counseling, 860-232-4571 Ext. 331.

Saint Peter's College, Graduate Programs in Education, Program in Teaching, 2641 Kennedy Boulevard, Jersey City, NJ 07306-5997. Offerings include elementary teacher (Certificate). Program faculty: 2 full-time (0 women), 10 part-time (4 women). *Application deadline:* 8/1 (priority date; rolling processing). *Application fee:* $20. *Tuition:* $516 per credit. • Dr. Joseph McLaughlin, Director, Graduate Programs in Education, 201-915-9254. Fax: 201-915-9074. Application contact: Nancy P. Campbell, Associate Vice President for Enrollment, 201-915-9213. Fax: 201-432-5860. E-mail: admissions@spcvxa.spc.edu.

St. Thomas Aquinas College, Division of Teacher Education, Program in Elementary Education, Sparkill, NY 10976. Awards MS Ed. Faculty: 6 full-time (4 women), 6 part-time (3 women). *Degree requirements:* Comprehensive professional portfolio required, thesis not required. *Entrance requirements:* New York State Qualifying Exam, GRE General Test or minimum GPA of 3.0, teaching certificate. Application deadline: 7/31 (priority date; rolling processing; 12/1 for spring admission). Application fee: $35. Electronic applications accepted. *Expenses:* Tuition $390 per credit. Fees $10 per year. *Financial aid:* In 1997–98, 2 assistantships (both to first-year students) were awarded; partial tuition waivers also available. Financial aid application deadline: 2/15. *Faculty research:* Infusing technology in education, curriculum development and evaluation. • Application contact: Joseph L. Chillo, Executive Director of Enrollment Services, 914-398-4100. Fax: 914-398-4224. E-mail: joestacenroll@rockland.net.

St. Thomas University, School of Graduate Studies, Department of Education, Program in Elementary Education, Miami, FL 33054-6459. Awards MS. Part-time and evening/weekend programs available. *Degree requirements:* Comprehensive exam required, foreign language and thesis not required. *Average time to degree:* master's–2.5 years full-time. *Entrance requirements:* TOEFL (minimum score 550), interview, minimum GPA of 3.0 or GRE, teaching certificate. Application deadline: 6/15 (priority date; rolling processing; 11/15 for spring admission). Application fee: $30. *Tuition:* $410 per credit.

Salem College, Department of Education, PO Box 10548, Winston-Salem, NC 27108-0548. Offerings include elementary education (MAT). Accredited by NCATE. College faculty: 10 full-time (7 women), 2 part-time (both women). *Average time to degree:* master's–1.5 years full-time, 3 years part-time. *Application deadline:* rolling. *Application fee:* $35. *Tuition:* $195 per hour. • Dr. Robin L. Smith, Director of Graduate Studies, 336-721-2656. Fax: 336-721-2683. E-mail: smith@salem.edu.

Salem State College, Department of Education, Program in Elementary Education, Salem, MA 01970-5353. Awards M Ed. Accredited by NCATE. *Entrance requirements:* GRE General Test. Application deadline: rolling. Application fee: $25. *Expenses:* Tuition $140 per credit hour for state residents; $230 per credit hour for nonresidents. Fees $20 per credit hour.

Salem–Teikyo University, Department of Education, Salem, WV 26426-0500. Offerings include elementary education (MA). Department faculty: 1 (woman) full-time, 6 part-time (1 woman). *Degree requirements:* Thesis required, foreign language not required. *Average time to degree:* master's–2 years full-time, 5 years part-time. *Entrance requirements:* GRE, MAT, NTE. Application deadline: rolling. Application fee: $25. Electronic applications accepted. *Tuition:* $160 per credit hour. • Dr. E. G. vander Giessen, Director of Graduate Education, 304-782-5258. Fax: 304-782-5588. E-mail: gabby@salem.wvnet.edu. Application contact: Carolyn Sue Ritter, Director of Admissions, 304-782-5336. Fax: 304-782-5592. E-mail: admiss_new@salem.wvnet.edu.

Salisbury State University, Department of Education, Salisbury, MD 21801-6837. Offerings include elementary education (M Ed). Department faculty: 19 full-time (10 women), 2 part-time (1 woman). *Application deadline:* 8/1 (priority date; rolling processing; 1/1 for spring admission). *Application fee:* $30. *Expenses:* Tuition $158 per credit hour for state residents; $310 per credit hour for nonresidents. Fees $4 per credit hour. • Dr. Ellen Whitford, Chair, 410-543-6294. E-mail: evwhitford@ssu.edu. Application contact: Phyllis Meyer, Administrative Aide II, 410-543-6281. Fax: 410-548-2593. E-mail: phmeyer@ssu.edu.

Samford University, School of Education, Program in Elementary Education, Birmingham, AL 35229-0002. Awards MS Ed, Ed S, M Div/MS Ed. Offerings include elementary education (MS Ed, Ed S), music education (MS Ed). Accredited by NCATE. 21 applicants, 100% accepted. In 1997, 14 master's awarded. *Entrance requirements:* For master's, GRE or MAT, minimum GPA of 2.75; for Ed S, master's degree, teaching certificate. Application deadline: rolling. Application fee: $25. *Tuition:* $344 per credit hour. • Dr. David Little, Coordinator, 205-870-2371. Application contact: Dr. Alyce Golowash, Counselor, 205-870-2121.

Sam Houston State University, College of Education and Applied Science, Department of Education and Applied Science, Department of Curriculum and Instruction, Elementary Education Program, Huntsville, TX 77341. Awards M Ed, Certificate. Accredited by NCATE. Part-time and evening/weekend programs available. Students: 1 (woman) full-time, 23 part-time (all women); includes 4 minority (1 African American, 3 Hispanics). Average age 35. In 1997, 9 master's awarded. *Entrance requirements:* For master's, GRE General Test (minimum combined score of 800). Application fee: $15. *Tuition:* $1810 per year full-time, $297 per semester (minimum) part-time for state residents; $6922 per year full-time, $924 per semester (minimum) part-time for nonresidents. *Financial aid:* Teaching assistantships, institutionally sponsored loans available. *Faculty research:* Teacher appraisal, effective teaching, teacher education, outcome evaluation. • Dr. John C. Huber, Chair, Department of Curriculum and Instruction, 409-294-1146.

San Diego State University, College of Education, School of Teacher Education, Program in Elementary Curriculum and Instruction, San Diego, CA 92182. Awards MA. Accredited by NCATE. Evening/weekend programs available. Students: 6 full-time (all women), 69 part-time (61 women); includes 29 minority (2 African Americans, 7 Asian Americans, 18 Hispanics, 2 Native Americans). Average age 29. *Entrance requirements:* GRE General Test (minimum combined score of 950), TOEFL (minimum score 550). Application deadline: 6/1 (priority date; rolling processing; 12/1 for spring admission). Application fee: $55. *Expenses:* Tuition $0 for state residents; $246 per unit for nonresidents. Fees $1932 per year full-time, $1266 per year part-time. *Total annual research expenditures:* $150,000. • Larry Shaw, Graduate Adviser, 619-594-1379. Fax: 619-594-7828. E-mail: lshaw@mail.sdsu.edu.

San Francisco State University, College of Education, Department of Elementary Education, Program in Elementary Education, San Francisco, CA 94132-1722. Awards MA. Accredited by NCATE. Part-time programs available. *Degree requirements:* Thesis or alternative. *Entrance requirements:* Minimum GPA of 2.5 in last 60 units. Application deadline: 11/30 (priority date; rolling processing). Application fee: $55. *Expenses:* Tuition $0 for state residents; $246 per unit for nonresidents. Fees $1982 per year full-time, $1316 per year part-time.

San Jose State University, College of Education, Program in Elementary Education, San Jose, CA 95192-0001. Awards MA. Accredited by NCATE. Students: 10 full-time (8 women), 41 part-time (39 women); includes 14 minority (1 African American, 5 Asian Americans, 8 Hispanics). Average age 35. 29 applicants, 52% accepted. In 1997, 12 degrees awarded. *Degree requirements:* Thesis or alternative. *Application deadline:* 6/1 (rolling processing). *Application fee:* $59. *Expenses:* Tuition $0 for state residents; $246 per unit for nonresidents. Fees $2017 per year full-time, $1351 per year part-time. *Financial aid:* Career-related internships or fieldwork available. • Dr. Lynne Gray, Chair, 408-924-3771.

Seton Hall University, College of Education and Human Services, Department of Educational Studies, Program in Elementary Education, South Orange, NJ 07079-2697. Awards MA. Evening/weekend programs available. *Degree requirements:* Thesis or alternative, comprehensive exam required, foreign language not required. *Entrance requirements:* GRE or MAT, minimum GPA of 3.0. Application deadline: rolling. Application fee: $50. *Expenses:* Tuition $500 per credit. Fees $610 per year full-time, $185 per semester part-time. *Financial aid:* Application deadline 2/1. • Dr. Roberta Devlin-Scherer, Chair, Department of Educational Studies, 973-761-7457. E-mail: devlinrb@shu.edu.

Directory: Elementary Education

Seton Hill College, Program in Elementary Education, Greensburg, PA 15601. Awards MA, Teaching Certificate. Part-time programs available. Faculty: 2 full-time (0 women), 2 part-time (1 woman). Students: 5 full-time (all women), 20 part-time (19 women); includes 1 minority (African American), 1 international. Average age 35. 5 applicants, 100% accepted. *Degree requirements:* For master's, thesis required, foreign language not required. *Entrance requirements:* For master's, minimum GPA of 3.0. Application deadline: 8/15 (priority date; rolling processing; 12/15 for spring admission). Application fee: $30. *Tuition:* $360 per credit for state residents; $360 per credit full-time, $360 per year part-time for nonresidents. *Financial aid:* Scholarships, partial tuition waivers available. Aid available to part-time students. Financial aid application deadline: 8/1. • Dr. Terrance E. DePasquale, Director, 724-838-4256. E-mail: depasqua@setonhill.edu. Application contact: Mary Kay Cooper, Graduate Adviser, 800-826-6234. Fax: 724-830-1294. E-mail: coope91@setonhill.edu.

Announcement: The Master of Arts in elementary education—with or without certification—is designed to help teachers read, critique, and evaluate educational theory and research and enhance pedagogical skills. Both evening and summer intensive courses are available. For more information, please see our in-depth description in volume one of this series.

Shippensburg University of Pennsylvania, College of Education and Human Services, Department of Teacher Education, Shippensburg, PA 17257-2299. Offerings include elementary education (M Ed). Accredited by NCATE. Department faculty: 16 full-time (11 women), 10 part-time (7 women). *Application deadline:* rolling. *Application fee:* $25. Electronic applications accepted. *Expenses:* Tuition $3468 per year full-time, $193 per credit hour part-time for state residents; $6236 per year full-time, $346 per credit hour part-time for nonresidents. Fees $678 per year full-time, $108 per semester (minimum) part-time. • Dr. Audrey Sprenger, Chairperson, 717-532-1688.

Siena Heights University, Program in Teacher Education, Concentration in Elementary Education, Adrian, MI 49221-1796. Offers program in elementary education/reading (MA). Part-time programs available. *Degree requirements:* Computer language, thesis, presentation required, foreign language not required. *Entrance requirements:* Minimum GPA of 3.0, interview. Application deadline: 7/1 (priority date; rolling processing; 12/1 for spring admission). Application fee: $25.

Sierra Nevada College, Program in Teacher Education, Incline Village, NV 89450-4269. Offerings include elementary education (Certificate). College faculty: 4 full-time, 17 part-time. *Entrance requirements:* Minimum GPA of 2.75. Application deadline: rolling. Application fee: $35. *Expenses:* Tuition $360 per unit full-time, $250 per unit (minimum) part-time. Fees $50 per year. • Dr. Skip Wenda, Director, 800-332-8666.

Simmons College, Department of Education, Program in Teacher Preparation, Boston, MA 02115. Offers elementary school education (MAT). Faculty: 4 full-time (3 women), 14 part-time (8 women). Students: 48 full-time (38 women), 29 part-time (24 women); includes 9 minority (6 African Americans, 1 Asian American, 2 Hispanics), 1 international. Average age 24. 77 applicants, 88% accepted. In 1997, 53 degrees awarded. *Degree requirements:* Student teaching experience required, foreign language and thesis not required. *Entrance requirements:* GRE General Test or MAT, interview. Application deadline: 8/1 (priority date; rolling processing; 12/15 for spring admission). Application fee: $35. *Expenses:* Tuition $587 per credit hour. Fees $20 per year. *Financial aid:* In 1997–98, 3 teaching assistantships (all to first-year students) totaling $3,276 were awarded; partial tuition waivers, Federal Work-Study, institutionally sponsored loans, and career-related internships or fieldwork also available. Aid available to part-time students. Financial aid application deadline: 3/1; applicants required to submit FAFSA. *Faculty research:* Putting standards/frameworks into practice, restructuring middle and high schools, interactive teaching and learning developing curriculum for Third World countries. • Lynda Johnson, Director, 617-521-2576. Fax: 617-521-3174. Application contact: Director, Graduate Studies Admission, 617-521-2910. Fax: 617-521-3058. E-mail: gsa@simmons.edu.

Sinte Gleska University, Graduate Education Program, Rosebud, SD 57570-0490. Offerings include elementary education (M Ed). Program faculty: 1 full-time (0 women), 4 part-time (3 women). *Degree requirements:* Thesis required, foreign language not required. *Average time to degree:* master's–2 years full-time. *Entrance requirements:* Minimum GPA of 2.5, 2 years experience in elementary education. Application deadline: rolling. Application fee: $0. • Dr. Archie Beauvais, Chair, 605-747-2263. Fax: 605-747-2098. E-mail: abbeau@rosebud.sinte.edu.

Slippery Rock University of Pennsylvania, College of Education, Department of Elementary Education and Early Childhood, Slippery Rock, PA 16057. Offers programs in early childhood education (M Ed), elementary education (M Ed), reading (M Ed). Accredited by NCATE. M Ed (elementary education) being phased out; applicants no longer accepted. Part-time and evening/weekend programs available. *Degree requirements:* Thesis or alternative, comprehensive exams required, foreign language not required. *Entrance requirements:* GRE, minimum GPA of 2.75. Application deadline: 7/1 (priority date; rolling processing; 11/1 for spring admission). Application fee: $25. *Tuition:* $4484 per year full-time, $247 per credit part-time for state residents; $7667 per year full-time, $423 per credit part-time for nonresidents.

Smith College, Department of Education and Child Study, Program in Elementary Education, Northampton, MA 01063. Offers elementary education (Ed M), preschool education (Ed M). Part-time programs available. Faculty: 7 full-time (3 women), 1 (woman) part-time, 7.2 FTE. Students: 21 full-time (19 women), 5 part-time (4 women); includes 1 Asian American, 3 international. Average age 22. 32 applicants, 91% accepted. In 1997, 19 degrees awarded. *Degree requirements:* 1 foreign language required, thesis not required. *Average time to degree:* master's–1 year full-time, 4 years part-time. *Entrance requirements:* GRE General Test or MAT. Application deadline: 4/15 (12/1 for spring admission). Application fee: $50. *Tuition:* $21,680 per year full-time, $2720 per course part-time. *Financial aid:* In 1997–98, 6 teaching assistantships (all to first-year students) totaling $53,820, 13 scholarships (12 to first-year students) totaling $153,792 were awarded; fellowships, research assistantships, institutionally sponsored loans also available. Aid available to part-time students. Financial aid application deadline: 1/15. • Alan Rudnitsky, Chair, Department of Education and Child Study, 413-585-3261. E-mail: arudnits@sophia.smith.edu.

South Carolina State University, School of Education, Department of Teacher Education, 300 College Street Northeast, Orangeburg, SC 29117-0001. Offerings include elementary education (MAT, M Ed). Accredited by NCATE. Department faculty: 7 full-time (3 women), 2 part-time (1 woman). *Degree requirements:* Departmental qualifying exam required, thesis optional. *Average time to degree:* master's–2 years full-time, 4 years part-time. *Entrance requirements:* GRE General Test (minimum combined score of 850) or MAT (minimum score 35), NTE (minimum score 650 on each core battery test), interview, teaching certificate. Application deadline: 7/15 (priority date; rolling processing; 11/10 for spring admission). Application fee: $25. *Tuition:* $2974 per year full-time, $165 per credit hour part-time. • Dr. Jesse Kinard, Chairman, 803-536-8934. Application contact: Dr. Gail Joyner-Fleming, Interim Associate Dean and Director, Graduate Teacher Education, 803-536-8824. Fax: 803-536-8492.

Southeastern Louisiana University, College of Education, Department of Teacher Education, Hammond, LA 70402. Offerings include elementary teaching (M Ed, Ed S). Accredited by NCATE. Ed S being phased out; applicants no longer accepted. Department faculty: 22 full-time, 14 part-time. *Degree requirements:* For Ed S, thesis required, foreign language not required. *Entrance requirements:* For master's, GRE, teaching certificate. Application deadline: 7/15 (priority date; rolling processing; 12/15 for spring admission). Application fee: $10 ($25 for international students). Electronic applications accepted. *Expenses:* Tuition $2010 per year full-time, $287 per semester (minimum) part-time for state residents; $5232 per year full-time, $287 per semester (minimum) part-time for nonresidents. Fees $5 per year. • Dr. Martha Head, Head, 504-549-2221. E-mail: mhead@selu.edu. Application contact: Dr. Jeanne Burns, Graduate Coordinator, 504-549-2221. Fax: 504-549-5009. E-mail: jburns@selu.edu.

Southeastern Oklahoma State University, School of Education, Department of Elementary Education, Durant, OK 74701-0609. Awards M Ed. Accredited by NCATE. Part-time and evening/weekend programs available. Faculty: 6 full-time (all women). Students: 6 full-time (5 women), 51 part-time (50 women); includes 5 minority (1 African American, 4 Native Americans). Average age 38. 16 applicants, 94% accepted. In 1997, 20 degrees awarded. *Degree requirements:* Thesis optional, foreign language not required. *Entrance requirements:* Minimum GPA of 3.0 in last 60 hours or 2.75 overall. Application deadline: 8/1. *Tuition:* $76 per credit hour for state residents; $178 per credit hour for nonresidents. *Financial aid:* 40 students received aid; Federal Work-Study, institutionally sponsored loans available. Aid available to part-time students. Financial aid application deadline: 6/15. • Dr. Mary Hitchcock, Chairperson, 580-924-0121 Ext. 2261. Fax: 580-920-7473.

Southeast Missouri State University, Department of Elementary and Special Education, Program in Elementary Education, Cape Girardeau, MO 63701-4799. Awards MA. Accredited by NCATE. Evening/weekend programs available. *Degree requirements:* Thesis or alternative required, foreign language not required. *Entrance requirements:* GRE General Test (score in 50th percentile or higher), minimum GPA of 2.75. Application deadline: 4/1 (priority date; rolling processing; 11/21 for spring admission). Application fee: $20 ($100 for international students). *Tuition:* $2034 per year full-time, $113 per credit hour part-time for state residents; $3672 per year full-time, $204 per credit hour part-time for nonresidents. *Financial aid:* Research assistantships and career-related internships or fieldwork available. • Application contact: Office of Graduate Studies, 573-651-2192.

Southern Arkansas University–Magnolia, Graduate Program in Education, Program in Elementary Education, Magnolia, AR 71753. Offers elementary counseling (M Ed), elementary education (M Ed), reading education (M Ed). Faculty: 5 part-time. Students: 5 full-time (3 women), 46 part-time (all women); includes 6 minority (5 African Americans, 1 Hispanic). Average age 32. 11 applicants, 100% accepted. *Degree requirements:* Thesis or alternative, comprehensive exam required, foreign language not required. *Average time to degree:* master's–2 years full-time. *Entrance requirements:* GRE, minimum GPA of 2.5. Application deadline: 8/15 (rolling processing). Application fee: $0. *Expenses:* Tuition $95 per hour for state residents; $138 per hour for nonresidents. Fees $2 per hour. *Financial aid:* Research assistantships, teaching assistantships available. Financial aid application deadline: 8/15. • Dr. Danield L. Bernard, Dean, Graduate Studies, Graduate Program in Education, 870-235-4055. Fax: 870-235-5035. E-mail: dlbernard@mail.saumag.edu.

Southern Connecticut State University, School of Education, Department of Education, Program in Elementary Education, New Haven, CT 06515-1355. Awards MS Ed. Faculty: 10 full-time. Students: 3 full-time (all women), 26 part-time (22 women). 368 applicants, 30% accepted. In 1997, 71 degrees awarded. *Degree requirements:* Thesis optional, foreign language not required. *Entrance requirements:* Connecticut Competency Exam for Prospective Teachers, interview, minimum QPA of 2.5. Application deadline: 7/15 (priority date; rolling processing). Application fee: $40. *Expenses:* Tuition $2632 per year full-time, $188 per credit part-time for state residents; $7200 per year full-time, $188 per credit part-time for nonresidents. Fees $1806 per year full-time, $45 per semester part-time for state residents; $2703 per year full-time, $45 per semester part-time for nonresidents. • Application contact: Dr. David Levande, Graduate Coordinator, 203-392-6429.

Southern Illinois University at Edwardsville, School of Education, Department of Curriculum and Instruction, Program in Elementary Education, Edwardsville, IL 62026-0001. Awards MS Ed. Accredited by NCATE. Part-time programs available. Students: 44 full-time (43 women), 213 part-time (202 women); includes 15 minority (all African Americans). 56 applicants, 77% accepted. In 1997, 94 degrees awarded. *Degree requirements:* Thesis or alternative, final exam required, foreign language not required. *Entrance requirements:* MAT, teaching certificate. Application deadline: 7/24. Application fee: $25. *Expenses:* Tuition $1716 per year full-time, $95 per credit hour part-time for state residents; $5149 per year full-time, $286 per credit hour part-time for nonresidents. Fees $463 per year full-time, $433 per year part-time. *Financial aid:* In 1997–98, 2 assistantships were awarded; fellowships, research assistantships, teaching assistantships, Federal Work-Study, institutionally sponsored loans also available. Aid available to part-time students. • Dr. Lela M. De Toye, Director, 618-692-3433.

Southern Oregon University, School of Social Science, Health and Physical Education, Department of Education, Ashland, OR 97520. Offerings include elementary education (MA Ed, MS Ed), with options in classroom teacher, early childhood, handicapped learner, reading, supervision. *Application deadline:* 2/1. *Application fee:* $50. *Tuition:* $5187 per year full-time, $586 per quarter (minimum) part-time for state residents; $9228 per year full-time, $586 per quarter (minimum) part-time for nonresidents. • Dr. Mary-Curtis Gramley, Associate Dean of Education, 541-552-6918.

Southern University and Agricultural and Mechanical College, College of Education, Department of Curriculum and Instruction, Baton Rouge, LA 70813. Offerings include elementary education (M Ed). Accredited by NCATE. Department faculty: 13 full-time (3 women), 12 part-time (3 women). *Degree requirements:* Thesis optional. *Entrance requirements:* GMAT or GRE General Test, TOEFL. Application deadline: 6/1 (priority date; rolling processing; 11/1 for spring admission). Application fee: $5. *Tuition:* $2226 per year full-time, $267 per semester (minimum) part-time for state residents; $6262 per year full-time, $267 per semester (minimum) part-time for nonresidents. • Dr. Paul Hester, Chairman, 504-771-3871.

Southern Utah University, School of Education, Cedar City, UT 84720-2498. Offerings include elementary education (M Ed). School faculty: 1 full-time (0 women), 18 part-time (3 women). *Degree requirements:* Thesis or alternative required, foreign language not required. *Entrance requirements:* MAT (minimum score 43). Application deadline: 8/1 (rolling processing; 12/1 for spring admission). Application fee: $30. • Dr. Paul Wilford, Director, 435-865-8149.

Southwestern Adventist University, Graduate School of Education, Keene, TX 76059. Offers program in elementary education (M Ed). Part-time and evening/weekend programs available. Faculty: 10 full-time (3 women). Students: 1 (woman) full-time, 10 part-time (7 women); includes 6 minority (4 African Americans, 1 Asian American, 1 Native American). Average age 38. 4 applicants, 75% accepted. In 1997, 4 degrees awarded. *Degree requirements:* Thesis or alternative, professional paper required, foreign language not required. *Average time to degree:* master's–4 years part-time. *Entrance requirements:* GRE General Test (minimum combined score of 750). Application deadline: 8/24 (priority date; rolling processing; 12/28 for spring admission). Application fee: $0. *Tuition:* $3300 per year full-time, $275 per hour part-time. *Financial aid:* Federal Work-Study, institutionally sponsored loans available. Aid available to part-time students. Financial aid application deadline: 5/1. • Dee Anderson, Director, 817-645-3921. E-mail: andersonde@swau.edu. Application contact: Marie Redwine, Graduate Dean, 817-645-3921 Ext. 211. Fax: 817-556-4744. E-mail: redwinem@swau.edu.

Southwestern Oklahoma State University, School of Education, Program in Elementary Education, Weatherford, OK 73096-3098. Awards M Ed. Accredited by NCATE. M Ed distance learning degree program offered to Oklahoma residents only. Part-time programs available. Postbaccalaureate distance learning degree programs offered. Students: 3 full-time (2 women), 9 part-time (all women); includes 2 minority (1 African American, 1 Hispanic). 1 applicant, 100% accepted. In 1997, 6 degrees awarded. *Degree requirements:* Exam required, foreign language and thesis not required. *Entrance requirements:* GRE General Test, TOEFL (minimum score 550), minimum GPA of 2.5. Application deadline: rolling. Application fee: $15. *Expenses:* Tuition $60 per credit hour (minimum) for state residents; $147 per credit hour (minimum) for nonresidents. Fees $109 per year full-time, $24 per semester (minimum) part-time. *Financial aid:* Research assistantships, teaching assistantships, partial tuition waivers, Federal Work-Study, institutionally sponsored loans available. Aid available to part-time students. Financial aid application deadline: 3/1; applicants required to submit FAFSA. • Dr. Lowell Gadberry, Chair, Elementary/Secondary Programs, 580-774-3288.

Southwest Missouri State University, College of Education, Department of Early Childhood, Elementary, and Middle School Education, Springfield, MO 65804-0094. Offers program in elementary education (MS Ed). Part-time and evening/weekend programs available. Faculty: 8 full-time (3 women). Students: 3 full-time (all women), 187 part-time (184 women); includes 3 minority (1 African American, 2 Native Americans). Average age 35. In 1997, 52 degrees awarded. *Degree requirements:* Thesis or alternative, comprehensive exam required, foreign language not required. *Entrance requirements:* Minimum GPA of 2.75, teaching certificate. Application deadline: 8/7 (priority date; rolling processing; 12/17 for spring admission). Application fee: $25. *Expenses:* Tuition $1980 per year full-time, $110 per credit hour part-time for state residents; $3960 per year full-time, $220 per credit hour part-time for nonresidents. Fees $274 per year full-time, $73 per semester part-time. • Dr. David Brown, Head, 417-836-5796. Fax: 417-836-4884. E-mail: dwb638f@wpgate.smsu.edu.

Southwest Texas State University, School of Education, Department of Curriculum and Instruction, Program in Elementary Education, San Marcos, TX 78666. Awards MA, M Ed. Part-time and evening/weekend programs available. Students: 73 full-time (62 women), 151 part-time (137 women); includes 37 minority (5 African Americans, 4 Asian Americans, 28 Hispanics). Average age 31. In 1997, 57 degrees awarded. *Degree requirements:* Thesis (for some programs), comprehensive exam required, foreign language not required. *Entrance requirements:* GRE General Test (minimum combined score of 900), TOEFL (minimum score 550), minimum GPA of 2.75 in last 60 hours, teaching experience. Application deadline: 7/15 (priority date; rolling processing; 11/15 for spring admission). Application fee: $25 ($50 for international students). *Expenses:* Tuition $648 per year full-time, $120 per semester (minimum) part-time for state residents; $4500 per year full-time, $750 per semester (minimum) part-time for nonresidents. Fees $1264 per year full-time, $314 per semester (minimum) part-time. *Financial aid:* Federal Work-Study, institutionally sponsored loans, and career-related internships or fieldwork available. Aid available to part-time students. Financial aid application deadline: 4/1; applicants required to submit FAFSA. *Faculty research:* Bilingual, general elementary, and early childhood education; gifted and talented education. • Dr. Shirley Beck, Graduate Adviser, 512-245-3701. E-mail: sb20@swt.edu.

Spalding University, School of Education, Programs in Teacher Education and Administration, Louisville, KY 40203-2188. Offerings include K–4 (MA, MAT). Accredited by NCATE. Faculty: 7 full-time (5 women), 5 part-time (4 women). *Entrance requirements:* GRE General Test, interview, portfolio. Application deadline: 8/15 (priority date; rolling processing). Application fee: $30. *Expenses:* Tuition $350 per credit hour (minimum). Fees $48 per year full-time, $4 per credit hour part-time. • Application contact: Jeanne Anderson, Assistant to the Provost and Director of Graduate Office, 502-585-7105. Fax: 502-585-7158. E-mail: gradoffc@spalding6.win.net.

Spring Hill College, Graduate Programs, Program in Education, Mobile, AL 36608-1791. Offerings include elementary education (MAT, MS Ed). Program faculty: 5 full-time (3 women), 5 part-time (1 woman). *Degree requirements:* Comprehensive exam required, thesis optional, foreign language not required. *Average time to degree:* master's–2 years part-time. *Entrance requirements:* GRE, MAT, or NTE, minimum undergraduate GPA of 3.0. Application deadline: rolling. Application fee: $25. • Dr. B. C. Algero, Chair, 334-380-3477.

State University of New York at Binghamton, School of Education and Human Development, Program in Early Childhood and Elementary Education, Binghamton, NY 13902-6000. Awards MS Ed. Part-time and evening/weekend programs available. Students: 22 full-time (18 women), 19 part-time (15 women); includes 3 minority (1 African American, 2 Hispanics), 1 international. Average age 28. 42 applicants, 57% accepted. In 1997, 8 degrees awarded. *Entrance requirements:* GRE General Test, TOEFL. Application deadline: 4/15 (priority date; rolling processing; 11/1 for spring admission). Application fee: $50. Electronic applications accepted. *Expenses:* Tuition $5100 per year full-time, $213 per credit hour part-time for state residents; $8416 per year full-time, $351 per credit hour part-time for nonresidents. Fees $654 per year full-time, $75 per semester (minimum) part-time. *Financial aid:* In 1997–98, 1 research assistantship (to a first-year student) averaging $400 per month and totaling $4,000, 4 graduate assistantships (3 to first-year students) averaging $500 per month and totaling $19,962 were awarded; fellowships, Federal Work-Study, institutionally sponsored loans, and career-related internships or fieldwork also available. Aid available to part-time students. Financial aid application deadline: 2/15. • Dr. Judy Kugelmass, Coordinator, 607-777-4696.

State University of New York at Buffalo, Graduate School, Graduate School of Education, Department of Learning and Instruction, Buffalo, NY 14260. Offerings include elementary education (Ed M, Ed D, PhD), with options in early childhood education (Ed M, Ed D), elementary education (Ed M, Ed D). Terminal master's awarded for partial completion of doctoral program. Department faculty: 20 full-time (9 women), 7 part-time (2 women). *Degree requirements:* For master's, comprehensive exam required, foreign language and thesis not required; for doctorate, dissertation, research analysis exam required, foreign language not required. *Entrance requirements:* For master's, GRE General Test, TOEFL (minimum score 590); for doctorate, GRE General Test, TOEFL (minimum score 600), interview. Application deadline: 2/1 (11/15 for spring admission). Application fee: $50. *Tuition:* $5970 per year full-time, $288 per credit hour part-time for state residents; $9286 per year full-time, $426 per credit hour part-time for nonresidents. • Dr. Michael Kibby, Chair, 716-645-2455. Application contact: Barbara Cracchiolo, Admissions Secretary, 716-645-2457. Fax: 716-645-3161.

State University of New York at New Paltz, Faculty of Education, Department of Elementary Education, New Paltz, NY 12561-2499. Offers programs in early childhood education (MS Ed), elementary education (MST), environmental education (MS Ed), general education (MS Ed), reading (MS Ed). Students: 48 full-time (39 women), 205 part-time (180 women); includes 6 minority (1 African American, 2 Asian Americans, 2 Hispanics, 1 Native American), 2 international. In 1997, 120 degrees awarded. *Entrance requirements:* GRE General Test or MAT, minimum GPA of 3.0, teaching certificate. Application deadline: 3/15 (priority date; rolling processing). Application fee: $50. *Expenses:* Tuition $5100 per year full-time, $213 per credit hour part-time for state residents; $8416 per year full-time, $351 per credit hour part-time for nonresidents. Fees $493 per year full-time, $48 per semester (minimum) part-time. *Financial aid:* Federal Work-Study, institutionally sponsored loans available. • Dr. Rose Rudnitski, Chair, 914-257-2860.

State University of New York at Oswego, School of Education, Department of Curriculum and Instruction, Oswego, NY 13126. Offerings include elementary education (MS Ed). MS Ed (special education) offered jointly with the State University of New York College at Geneseo. Department faculty: 17 full-time, 5 part-time. *Application deadline:* 7/1. *Application fee:* $50. *Expenses:* Tuition $5100 per year full-time, $213 per credit hour part-time for state residents; $8416 per year full-time, $351 per credit hour part-time for nonresidents. Fees $135 per year (minimum). • Dr. Frank Bickel, Chairman, 315-341-4052. Application contact: Dr. Terrance Lindenberg, Coordinator, Graduate Education, 315-341-4052.

State University of New York College at Brockport, School of Professions, Department of Education and Human Development, Program in Elementary Education, Brockport, NY 14420-2997. Awards MS Ed. Part-time and evening/weekend programs available. Students: 47 full-time (37 women), 95 part-time (82 women); includes 16 minority (13 African Americans, 3 Hispanics). Average age 31. 42 applicants, 81% accepted. In 1997, 60 degrees awarded. *Degree requirements:* Thesis or alternative required, foreign language not required. *Entrance requirements:* Minimum GPA of 3.0. Application deadline: 1/15 (priority date; 9/15 for spring admission). Application fee: $50. *Expenses:* Tuition $5100 per year full-time, $213 per credit hour part-time for state residents; $8416 per year full-time, $351 per credit hour part-time for nonresidents. Fees $440 per year full-time, $22.60 per credit hour part-time. *Financial aid:* Federal Work-Study and career-related internships or fieldwork available. Aid available to part-time students. Financial aid application deadline: 4/1; applicants required to submit FAFSA. *Faculty research:* Bilingual education, curriculum materials, special needs diagnosis. • William Veenis, Chairperson, Department of Education and Human Development, 716-395-2205.

State University of New York College at Buffalo, Faculty of Applied Science and Education, Department of Elementary Education and Reading, Program in Elementary and Early Secondary Education, Buffalo, NY 14222-1095. Offers elementary education (MS Ed), English education (MS Ed), general science education (MS Ed), mathematics education (MS Ed), social studies education (MS Ed). Accredited by NCATE. Part-time and evening/weekend programs available. Students: 17 full-time (16 women), 245 part-time (225 women); includes 15 minority (11 African Americans, 3 Hispanics, 1 Native American). Average age 30. 45 applicants, 93% accepted. In 1997, 73 degrees awarded. *Degree requirements:* Thesis or project required, foreign language not required. *Entrance requirements:* Minimum GPA of 2.5 in last 60 hours, New York teaching certificate. Application deadline: 5/1 (10/1 for spring admission). Application fee: $50. *Expenses:* Tuition $5100 per year full-time, $213 per credit hour part-time for state residents; $8416 per year full-time, $351 per credit hour part-time for nonresidents. Fees $195 per year full-time, $8.60 per credit hour part-time. *Financial aid:* Fellowships, assistantships, Federal Work-Study available. Aid available to part-time students. Financial aid application deadline: 3/1. • Dr. Maria Ceprano, Chairperson, Department of Elementary Education and Reading, 716-878-5916.

State University of New York College at Cortland, Division of Professional Studies, Department of Education, Programs in Elementary Education, Cortland, NY 13045. Offerings in English education (MS Ed), general science education (MS Ed), mathematics education (MS Ed), social studies education (MS Ed). Part-time and evening/weekend programs available. In 1997, 241 degrees awarded. *Degree requirements:* 1 foreign language, computer language, thesis (for some programs), comprehensive exams. *Entrance requirements:* Provisional certification. Application deadline: rolling. Application fee: $50. *Expenses:* Tuition $5100 per year full-time, $213 per credit hour part-time for state residents; $8416 per year full-time, $351 per credit hour part-time for nonresidents. Fees $644 per year full-time, $79 per semester (minimum) part-time. *Financial aid:* Partial tuition waivers, Federal Work-Study, and career-related internships or fieldwork available. Aid available to part-time students. Financial aid applicants required to submit CSS PROFILE or FAFSA. • Application contact: Jeanne M. Bechtel, Director of Admissions, 607-753-4711. Fax: 607-753-5998.

State University of New York College at Fredonia, Department of Education, Program in Elementary Education, Fredonia, NY 14063. Awards MS Ed. Part-time and evening/weekend programs available. Faculty: 2 full-time (1 woman), 2 part-time (1 woman). Students: 5 full-time (4 women), 76 part-time (61 women); includes 1 minority (Hispanic). 52 applicants, 87% accepted. In 1997, 53 degrees awarded. *Degree requirements:* Thesis or alternative required, foreign language not required. *Application deadline:* 7/5. *Application fee:* $50. *Expenses:* Tuition $5100 per year full-time, $213 per credit hour part-time for state residents; $8416 per year full-time, $351 per credit hour part-time for nonresidents. Fees $725 per year full-time, $30 per credit hour part-time. *Financial aid:* Research assistantships, teaching assistantships, full and partial tuition waivers, and career-related internships or fieldwork available. Aid available to part-time students. Financial aid application deadline: 3/15. • Dr. Julius Adams, Chair, Department of Education, 716-673-3311.

State University of New York College at Geneseo, School of Education, Program in Elementary Education, Geneseo, NY 14454-1401. Awards MS Ed. Part-time and evening/weekend programs available. Faculty: 13 full-time (8 women). Students: 7 full-time (all women), 55 part-time (50 women); includes 1 minority (Hispanic). Average age 24. 45 applicants, 96% accepted. In 1997, 33 degrees awarded. *Degree requirements:* Thesis optional, foreign language not required. *Entrance requirements:* GRE General Test. Application deadline: 6/1 (priority date; 10/1 for spring admission). Application fee: $35. *Expenses:* Tuition $5100 per year full-time, $213 per credit hour part-time for state residents; $8416 per year full-time, $351 per credit hour part-time for nonresidents. Fees $375 per year full-time, $15.35 per credit hour part-time. *Financial aid:* In 1997–98, 1 fellowship (to a first-year student), 3 teaching assistantships (all to first-year students) were awarded; Federal Work-Study, institutionally sponsored loans, and career-related internships or fieldwork also available. Financial aid application deadline: 4/1; applicants required to submit FAFSA. • Dr. Gary DeBolt, Head, School of Education, 716-245-5558. Fax: 716-245-5220. E-mail: debolt@uno.cc.geneseo.edu.

State University of New York College at Oneonta, Department of Education, Program in Elementary Education, Oneonta, NY 13820-4015. Offers early secondary English (N–9) (MS Ed), early secondary math (N–9) (MS Ed), early secondary social science (N–9) (MS Ed), general science (N–9) (MS Ed). Part-time and evening/weekend programs available. Students: 3 full-time (2 women), 32 part-time (27 women). In 1997, 24 degrees awarded. *Entrance requirements:* GRE General Test. Application deadline: 4/15. Application fee: $50. *Expenses:* Tuition $5100 per year full-time, $213 per credit hour part-time for state residents; $8416 per year full-time, $351 per credit hour part-time for nonresidents. Fees $482 per year full-time, $6.85 per credit hour part-time. • Dr. Ronald Cromwell, Chair, Department of Education, 607-436-2538.

State University of New York College at Potsdam, School of Education, Program in Elementary Education, Potsdam, NY 13676. Awards MS Ed, MST. Part-time programs available. Faculty: 9 full-time (2 women), 6 part-time (2 women). Students: 114; includes 4 minority (1 African American, 1 Asian American, 2 Hispanics), 17 international. *Degree requirements:* Variable foreign language requirement, culminating experience required, thesis optional. *Entrance requirements:* New York State Teachers Certification Exam Liberal Arts and Science Test (minimum score 220), New York State Teachers Certification Exam Assesment of Teaching Skills-Writing (minimum score 220), minimum GPA of 2.75 in last 60 hours. Application deadline: 4/1 (priority date; 10/15 for spring admission). Application fee: $50. *Expenses:* Tuition $5100 per year full-time, $213 per credit hour part-time for state residents; $8416 per year full-time, $351 per credit hour part-time for nonresidents. Fees $315 per year full-time, $12.50 per credit hour part-time. *Financial aid:* Fellowships, teaching assistantships, Federal Work-Study, and career-related internships or fieldwork available. Aid available to part-time students. Financial aid application deadline: 3/1. • Charles Mlynarczyk, Chairperson, Teacher Education Department, 315-267-2535. E-mail: mlynarhc@potsdam.edu. Application contact: Dr. William Amoriell, Dean of Education and Graduate Studies, 315-267-2515. Fax: 315-267-4802.

Stephen F. Austin State University, College of Education, Department of Elementary Education, Program in Elementary Education, Nacogdoches, TX 75962. Awards M Ed. Accredited by NCATE. Students: 24 full-time (17 women), 61 part-time (59 women); includes 10 minority (1 African American, 9 Hispanics). 29 applicants, 100% accepted. In 1997, 18 degrees awarded. *Degree requirements:* Comprehensive exam required, foreign language and thesis not required. *Entrance requirements:* GRE General Test (minimum combined score of 1000). Application deadline: 8/1 (priority date; rolling processing; 12/15 for spring admission). Application fee: $0 ($25 for international students). *Tuition:* $1465 per year full-time, $263 per semester (minimum) part-time for state residents; $5299 per year full-time, $890 per semester (minimum) part-time for nonresidents. *Financial aid:* Application deadline 3/1. • Dr. Elvia Rodriguez, Chair, Department of Elementary Education, 409-468-2904.

Stetson University, College of Arts and Sciences, Division of Education, Department of Teacher Education, Program in Elementary Education, 421 North Woodland Boulevard, DeLand, FL 32720-3781. Awards M Ed. Accredited by NCATE. Evening/weekend programs available. Students: 1 (woman) full-time, 6 part-time (all women); includes 1 minority (Hispanic). Average age 31. 1 applicant, 100% accepted. In 1997, 5 degrees awarded. *Degree requirements:* Comprehensive exam required, foreign language and thesis not required. *Entrance requirements:* GRE General Test (minimum combined score of 1000) or MAT. Application deadline: 3/1 (priority date; rolling processing; 11/1 for spring admission). Application fee: $25. *Tuition:* $370 per credit hour. *Financial aid:* Career-related internships or fieldwork available. *Faculty research:* Cooperative learning, whole language, reading, parental involvement in schools. • Dr. Adrienne Perry, Coordinator, 904-822-7075. Application contact: Pat LeClaire, Office of Graduate Studies, 904-822-7075.

Directory: Elementary Education

Sul Ross State University, Rio Grande College of Sul Ross State University, Alpine, TX 79832. Offerings include teacher education (M Ed), with options in bilingual education, counseling, educational diagnostics, elementary education, general education, reading, school administration, secondary education. College faculty: 16 full-time (2 women), 2 part-time (1 woman). *Application deadline:* rolling. *Application fee:* $0 ($50 for international students). *Expenses:* Tuition $864 per year full-time, $120 per semester (minimum) part-time for state residents; $5976 per year full-time, $747 per semester (minimum) part-time for nonresidents. Fees $754 per year full-time, $105 per semester (minimum) part-time. • Dr. Frank Abbott, Dean, 512-278-3339. Fax: 512-278-3330.

Sul Ross State University, Department of Teacher Education, Program in Elementary Education, Alpine, TX 79832. Awards M Ed. Part-time and evening/weekend programs available. Students: 2 full-time (both women), 11 part-time (all women); includes 6 minority (all Hispanics). Average age 41. In 1997, 3 degrees awarded. *Degree requirements:* Thesis optional, foreign language not required. *Entrance requirements:* GMAT (minimum score 400) or GRE General Test (minimum combined score of 850), minimum GPA of 2.5 in last 60 hours of undergraduate work. Application deadline: rolling. Application fee: $0 ($50 for international students). *Expenses:* Tuition $864 per year full-time, $120 per semester (minimum) part-time for state residents; $5976 per year full-time, $747 per semester (minimum) part-time for nonresidents. Fees $754 per year full-time, $105 per semester (minimum) part-time. *Financial aid:* Federal Work-Study, institutionally sponsored loans, and career-related internships or fieldwork available. Aid available to part-time students. Financial aid application deadline: 5/1; applicants required to submit FAFSA. • Dr. Mary Ann Weinacht, Director, Department of Teacher Education, 915-837-8170. Fax: 915-837-8390.

Syracuse University, School of Education, Teaching and Leadership Programs, Program in Elementary Education, Syracuse, NY 13244-0003. Awards MS, CAS. Students: 23 full-time (18 women), 11 part-time (7 women); includes 3 minority (2 African Americans, 1 Asian American). 6 applicants, 50% accepted. In 1997, 23 master's awarded. *Degree requirements:* For master's, thesis or alternative; for CAS, thesis. *Entrance requirements:* GRE. Application fee: $40. *Tuition:* $13,320 per year full-time, $555 per credit hour part-time. *Financial aid:* Application deadline 3/1. • Pat Tinto, Coordinator. Application contact: Dr. Frank Broadbent, Contact, 315-443-2684.

Tarleton State University, College of Education, Department of Education and Psychology, Program in Elementary Education, Stephenville, TX 76402. Awards M Ed, Certificate. Part-time and evening/weekend programs available. Students: 3 full-time (all women), 73 part-time (60 women); includes 9 minority (2 African Americans, 7 Hispanics). 9 applicants, 100% accepted. In 1997, 5 master's awarded. *Degree requirements:* For master's, comprehensive exam required, foreign language and thesis not required. *Entrance requirements:* For master's, GRE General Test, minimum GPA of 2.9 during last 60 hours. Application deadline: 8/5 (priority date; rolling processing; 12/1 for spring admission). Application fee: $25 ($100 for international students). *Expenses:* Tuition $46 per hour for state residents; $249 per hour for nonresidents. Fees $49 per hour. *Financial aid:* Teaching assistantships, Federal Work-Study, institutionally sponsored loans, and career-related internships or fieldwork available. Aid available to part-time students. Financial aid application deadline: 5/1; applicants required to submit FAFSA. • Dr. Virginia Kennedy, Coordinator, 254-968-9821.

Teachers College, Columbia University, Graduate Faculty of Education, Department of Curriculum and Teaching, Program in Elementary/Childhood Education, Preservice, 525 West 120th Street, New York, NY 10027-6696. Awards MA. Faculty: 3 full-time (all women), 9 part-time (7 women), 8.6 FTE. Students: 55 full-time (48 women), 111 part-time (100 women); includes 42 minority (14 African Americans, 22 Asian Americans, 6 Hispanics), 3 international. Average age 27. 181 applicants, 73% accepted. In 1997, 76 degrees awarded. *Application deadline:* 5/15 (12/1 for spring admission). *Application fee:* $50. *Expenses:* Tuition $640 per credit. Fees $120 per semester. *Financial aid:* Full and partial tuition waivers, Federal Work-Study, and career-related internships or fieldwork available. Financial aid application deadline: 2/1. *Faculty research:* Teaching of reading and writing, reforming schools, urban education, curriculum development. • Application contact: Victor Singletary, Office of Admissions, 212-678-3710. Fax: 212-678-4171.

Temple University, College of Education, Department of Curriculum, Instruction, and Technology in Education, Philadelphia, PA 19122-6096. Offerings include early childhood education and elementary education (Ed M, MS), elementary education (Certificate). One or more programs accredited by NCATE. Department faculty: 33 full-time (14 women). *Degree requirements:* For master's, thesis or alternative required, foreign language not required. *Entrance requirements:* For master's, GRE General Test (minimum combined score of 1000) or MAT (minimum score 39), minimum GPA of 2.8. Application deadline: 2/15 (10/1 for spring admission). Application fee: $40. *Expenses:* Tuition $323 per semester hour for state residents; $444 per semester hour for nonresidents. Fees $170 per year full-time, $28 per semester (minimum) part-time. • Dr. Raymond Lolla, Chair, 215-204-6387. Fax: 215-204-1414.

Tennessee State University, College of Education, Department of Teaching and Learning, Program in Elementary Education, Nashville, TN 37209-1561. Awards MA Ed, M Ed, Ed D. Accredited by NCATE. *Degree requirements:* For master's, computer language, project required, foreign language not required; for doctorate, dissertation, comprehensive exam. *Entrance requirements:* For master's, GRE General Test, GRE Subject Test, or MAT, minimum GPA of 2.5; for doctorate, GRE General Test (minimum combined score of 870), GRE Subject Test, or MAT (minimum score 25), master's degree, minimum GPA of 3.25, teaching certificate. Application deadline: rolling. Application fee: $15. *Tuition:* $2962 per year full-time, $182 per credit hour part-time for state residents; $7788 per year full-time, $393 per credit hour part-time for nonresidents. *Financial aid:* Fellowships available. Financial aid application deadline: 5/1. *Faculty research:* Multicultural education, middle school education, curriculum development. • Application contact: Dr. Clinton M. Lipsey, Dean of the Graduate School, 615-963-5901. Fax: 615-963-5963. E-mail: clipsey@picard.tnstate.edu.

Tennessee Technological University, College of Education, Department of Curriculum and Instruction, Program in Elementary Education, Cookeville, TN 38505. Awards MA, Ed S. Accredited by NCATE. Part-time and evening/weekend programs available. Faculty: 8 full-time (2 women). Students: 18 full-time (15 women), 63 part-time (58 women); includes 1 minority (Hispanic). Average age 27. 30 applicants, 97% accepted. In 1997, 32 master's, 1 Ed S awarded. *Degree requirements:* For Ed S, thesis or alternative required, foreign language not required. *Entrance requirements:* For master's, MAT, TOEFL (minimum score 525); for Ed S, MAT, NTE. Application deadline: 3/1 (priority date; 8/1 for spring admission). Application fee: $25 ($30 for international students). *Tuition:* $2960 per year full-time, $147 per semester hour part-time for state residents; $7786 per year full-time, $358 per semester hour part-time for nonresidents. *Financial aid:* In 1997–98, 2 students received aid, including 2 teaching assistantships (1 to a first-year student); fellowships, research assistantships, and career-related internships or fieldwork also available. Financial aid application deadline: 4/1. *Faculty research:* Educational television art program. • Application contact: Dr. Rebecca F. Quattlebaum, Dean of the Graduate School, 615-372-3233. Fax: 615-372-3497. E-mail: rquattlebaum@tntech.edu.

Texas A&M International University, Division of Teacher Education and Psychology, 5201 University Boulevard, Laredo, TX 78041-1900. Offerings include elementary education (MS Ed). *Degree requirements:* Thesis required (for some programs), foreign language not required. *Entrance requirements:* GRE General Test. Application deadline: 7/15 (priority date; rolling processing; 11/12 for spring admission). Application fee: $0.

Texas A&M University–Commerce, College of Education, Department of Elementary Education, Commerce, TX 75429-3011. Offers programs in early childhood education (MA, M Ed, MS), elementary education (M Ed, MS), reading (MA, M Ed, MS), supervision of curriculum and instruction: elementary education (Ed D). MA, M Ed, and MS (early childhood education) offered jointly with Texas Woman's University and the University of North Texas. Faculty: 15 full-time (6 women), 4 part-time (2 women). Students: 7 full-time (6 women), 101 part-time (95 women); includes 15 minority (11 African Americans, 1 Asian American, 2 Hispanics, 1 Native American). In 1997, 70 master's, 5 doctorates awarded. Terminal master's awarded for partial completion of doctoral program. *Degree requirements:* For master's, thesis (for some programs), comprehensive exam; for doctorate, 2 foreign languages (computer language can substitute for one), dissertation, departmental qualifying exam. *Entrance requirements:* GRE General Test. Application deadline: rolling. Application fee: $0 ($25 for international students). *Tuition:* $2382 per year full-time, $343 per semester (minimum) part-time for state residents; $7518 per year full-time, $343 per semester (minimum) part-time for nonresidents. *Financial aid:* Research assistantships, teaching assistantships, Federal Work-Study, institutionally sponsored loans available. *Faculty research:* Literacy and learning. • Dr. Wayne Linek, Head, 903-886-5537. Application contact: Pam Hammonds, Graduate Admissions Adviser, 903-886-5167. Fax: 903-886-5165.

Texas A&M University–Corpus Christi, College of Education, Program in Elementary Education, Corpus Christi, TX 78412-5503. Awards MS. Part-time and evening/weekend programs available. Faculty: 10 full-time. Students: 11 full-time (10 women), 8 part-time (7 women); includes 9 minority (all Hispanics). Average age 32. *Entrance requirements:* GRE General Test. Application deadline: 7/15 (priority date; rolling processing; 11/15 for spring admission). Application fee: $10 ($30 for international students). *Expenses:* Tuition $648 per year full-time, $120 per semester (minimum) part-time for state residents; $4482 per year full-time, $747 per semester (minimum) part-time for nonresidents. Fees $1010 per year full-time, $205 per semester part-time. *Financial aid:* Federal Work-Study, institutionally sponsored loans, and career-related internships or fieldwork available. Aid available to part-time students. Financial aid application deadline: 3/15; applicants required to submit FAFSA. • Dr. Arturo Medina, Graduate Adviser, 512-994-2667. E-mail: adedu005@tamucc.edu. Application contact: Mary Margaret Dechant, Director of Admissions, 512-994-2624. Fax: 512-994-5887.

Texas A&M University–Kingsville, College of Education, Department of Education, Program in Elementary Education, Kingsville, TX 78363. Awards MA, MS. Part-time and evening/weekend programs available. Faculty: 4 full-time. *Degree requirements:* Thesis or alternative, comprehensive exam required, foreign language not required. *Entrance requirements:* GRE General Test (minimum combined score of 1000), MAT (minimum score 34), minimum GPA of 3.0. Application deadline: 6/1 (rolling processing; 11/15 for spring admission). Application fee: $15 ($25 for international students). *Tuition:* $1822 per year full-time, $281 per semester (minimum) part-time for state residents; $6934 per year full-time, $908 per semester (minimum) part-time for nonresidents. *Financial aid:* Scholarships, Federal Work-Study, institutionally sponsored loans available. Aid available to part-time students. Financial aid application deadline: 5/15. *Faculty research:* Strategies in elementary science, manipulatives in the classroom, latest developments. • Dr. Travis Polk, Chair, Department of Education, 512-593-3204.

Texas A&M University–Texarkana, Division of Arts and Sciences and Education, Texarkana, TX 75505-5518. Offerings include elementary education (MA, M Ed, MS). Division faculty: 9 full-time (3 women), 5 part-time (3 women). *Degree requirements:* Thesis or alternative required, foreign language not required. *Average time to degree:* master's–1.5 years full-time. *Entrance requirements:* GRE General Test, bachelor's degree from a regionally accredited institution, minimum GPA of 3.0, teaching certificate (M Ed). Application deadline: rolling. Application fee: $0 ($25 for international students). *Tuition:* $2136 per year for state residents; $7248 per year for nonresidents. • Dr. John Anderson, Interim Head, 903-223-3003. Application contact: Pat Black, Registrar, 903-223-3068. Fax: 903-832-8890. E-mail: pat.black@tamut.edu.

Texas Christian University, School of Education, Department of Curriculum and Instruction, Program in Elementary Education, Fort Worth, TX 76129-0002. Awards M Ed. Part-time and evening/weekend programs available. Students: 49 (44 women); includes 7 minority (2 African Americans, 1 Asian American, 4 Hispanics). 37 applicants, 76% accepted. In 1997, 24 degrees awarded. *Degree requirements:* Thesis optional, foreign language not required. *Entrance requirements:* TOEFL (minimum score 550). Application deadline: 3/1 (rolling processing; 12/1 for spring admission). Application fee: $0. *Expenses:* Tuition $10,350 per year full-time, $345 per credit hour part-time. Fees $1240 per year full-time, $50 per credit hour part-time. *Financial aid:* Application deadline 3/1. • Dr. Luther Clegg, Chairperson, Department of Curriculum and Instruction, 817-257-7660.

Texas Southern University, College of Education, Area of Curriculum and Instruction, Houston, TX 77004-4584. Offerings include elementary education (M Ed). Faculty: 15 full-time (7 women), 4 part-time (all women). *Degree requirements:* Comprehensive exam required, foreign language not required. *Entrance requirements:* GRE General Test, TOEFL, minimum GPA of 2.5. Application deadline: 7/15 (priority date; rolling processing). Application fee: $35 ($75 for international students). • Dr. Claudette Ligon, Chairperson, 713-313-7775.

Texas Tech University, Graduate School, College of Education, Division of Curriculum and Instruction, Lubbock, TX 79409. Offerings include elementary education (M Ed, Ed D, Certificate). Accredited by NCATE. Division faculty: 23 full-time (12 women). *Degree requirements:* For master's, computer language required, thesis optional, foreign language not required; for doctorate, dissertation required, foreign language not required. *Entrance requirements:* For master's, GRE General Test (combined average 992); for doctorate, GRE General Test. Application deadline: 4/15 (priority date; rolling processing; 11/1 for spring admission). Application fee: $25 ($50 for international students). Electronic applications accepted. *Expenses:* Tuition $864 per year full-time, $120 per semester (minimum) part-time for state residents; $5976 per year full-time, $747 per semester (minimum) part-time for nonresidents. Fees $2321 per year full-time, $302 per semester (minimum) part-time. • Dr. William E. Sparkman, Chair, 805-742-2371.

Texas Woman's University, College of Education and Human Ecology, Department of Reading and Bilingual Education, Program in General Elementary Education, Denton, TX 76204. Awards MA, M Ed. Part-time programs available. Faculty: 9 full-time (6 women), 6 part-time (5 women). Students: 16 full-time (14 women), 74 part-time (68 women); includes 22 minority (6 African Americans, 2 Asian Americans, 14 Hispanics), 3 international. Average age 34. In 1997, 10 degrees awarded. *Degree requirements:* Thesis required, foreign language not required. *Entrance requirements:* GRE General Test (minimum combined score of 750), minimum GPA of 3.0. Application fee: $25. *Financial aid:* In 1997–98, 45 students received aid, including 35 fellowships (15 to first-year students); research assistantships, teaching assistantships, Federal Work-Study, institutionally sponsored loans, and career-related internships or fieldwork also available. Aid available to part-time students. Financial aid application deadline: 4/1. *Faculty research:* Early literacy, learning styles, discourse analysis, minority education, multicultural education, bilingual education. Total annual research expenditures: $50,000. • Rodolfo Rodriguez, Chair, Department of Reading and Bilingual Education, 940-898-2227. Fax: 940-898-2224. E-mail: d_rodriguez@twu.edu.

Towson University, Program in Elementary Education, Towson, MD 21252-0001. Awards M Ed, Spec. Part-time and evening/weekend programs available. Faculty: 6 full-time (2 women), 1 part-time (0 women). Students: 3 full-time (all women), 167 part-time (153 women); includes 23 minority (18 African Americans, 2 Asian Americans, 3 Hispanics). In 1997, 35 master's awarded. *Degree requirements:* For master's, thesis optional, foreign language not required. *Application deadline:* 3/1 (priority date; rolling processing; 10/1 for spring admission). *Application fee:* $40. *Expenses:* Tuition $187 per credit hour for state residents; $364 per credit hour for nonresidents. Fees $40 per credit hour. *Financial aid:* Assistantships, Federal Work-Study available. Financial aid application deadline: 4/1; applicants required to submit FAFSA. *Faculty research:* Professional development schools, values education, teacher development, reading. • Dr. Roxana Della Vecchia, Director, 410-830-2422. Fax: 410-830-3434. E-mail: rdellavecchia@towson.edu. Application contact: Fran Musotto, Office Manager, 410-830-2501. Fax: 410-830-4675. E-mail: fmusotto@towson.edu.

Trevecca Nazarene University, Division of Education, Major in Elementary Education, Nashville, TN 37210-2834. Awards M Ed. Students: 0. *Degree requirements:* Exit assessment required, foreign language and thesis not required. *Entrance requirements:* GRE General Test, MAT, minimum GPA of 2.7. Application deadline: 8/31 (rolling processing; 1/18 for spring admission). Application fee: $25. *Expenses:* Tuition $230 per hour. Fees $60 per year. • Dr. Melvin Welch, Dean of Education, Division of Education, 615-248-1201. Fax: 615-248-7728. E-mail: mwelch@trevecca.edu.

Trinity College, School of Professional Studies, Programs in Education, Washington, DC 20017-1094. Offerings include elementary education (MAT). Faculty: 6 full-time (5 women), 18 part-time (13 women). *Application deadline:* rolling. *Application fee:* $35. *Tuition:* $460 per credit hour. • Sr. Rosemarie Bosler, Division Chair, 202-884-9557. Application contact: Karen Goodwin, Director of Graduate Admissions, 202-884-9400. Fax: 202-884-9229.

Troy State University, Graduate School, School of Education, Program in Elementary Education, Troy, AL 36082. Awards MS, Ed S. Accredited by NCATE. Part-time and evening/weekend programs available. Students: 226 full-time (186 women), 143 part-time (121 women); includes 185 minority (174 African Americans, 3 Asian Americans, 6 Hispanics, 2 Native Americans), 2 international. Average age 30. In 1997, 107 master's awarded. *Degree requirements:* For master's, thesis, comprehensive exam. *Entrance requirements:* For master's, minimum GPA of 2.5; for Ed S, GRE General Test (minimum combined score of 850) or MAT (minimum score 33), Alabama Class A certificate or equivalent, minimum graduate GPA of 3.0. Application deadline: rolling. Application fee: $20. Electronic applications accepted. *Expenses:* Tuition $2040 per year full-time, $68 per hour part-time for state residents; $4200 per year full-time, $140 per hour part-time for nonresidents. Fees $240 per year full-time, $27 per quarter (minimum) part-time. *Financial aid:* Available to part-time students. Financial aid applicants required to submit FAFSA. • Dr. Shirley Fischer, Chair, 334-670-3365. Fax: 334-670-3474. E-mail: sfischer@trojan.troyst.edu. Application contact: Teresa Rodgers, Director of Graduate Admissions, 334-670-3188. Fax: 334-670-3733. E-mail: trodgers@trojan.troyst.edu.

Troy State University Dothan, School of Education, Dothan, AL 36304-0368. Offerings include elementary education (MS Ed, Ed S). Accredited by NCATE. *Application fee:* $20. *Expenses:* Tuition $68 per credit hour for state residents; $140 per credit hour for nonresidents. Fees $2 per credit hour. • Dr. Betty Anderson, Dean, 334-983-6556. Application contact: Reta Cordell, Director of Admissions and Records, 334-983-6556. Fax: 334-983-6322. E-mail: rcordell@tsud.edu.

Troy State University Montgomery, Division of Counseling, Education, and Psychology, Program in Elementary Education, PO Drawer 4419, Montgomery, AL 36103-4419. Awards MS. Part-time and evening/weekend programs available. Faculty: 2 full-time, 4 part-time. In 1997, 24 degrees awarded. *Degree requirements:* Thesis or alternative. *Entrance requirements:* TOEFL. Application deadline: rolling. Application fee: $20. Electronic applications accepted. *Expenses:* Tuition $52 per quarter hour for state residents; $104 per quarter hour for nonresidents. Fees $30 per year. • Dr. Vicki Lauderdale, Coordinator, 334-241-9578. Fax: 334-241-9586. E-mail: vlaud@tsum.edu.

Tufts University, Division of Graduate and Continuing Studies and Research, Graduate School of Arts and Sciences, Department of Education, Medford, MA 02155. Offerings include elementary education (MAT). Department faculty: 9 full-time, 7 part-time. *Application deadline:* 2/15 (rolling processing). *Application fee:* $50. • Kathleen Camara, Chair, 617-627-3244.

Union College, Department of Education, Program in Elementary Education, Barbourville, KY 40906-1499. Awards MA Ed. *Degree requirements:* Thesis optional, foreign language not required. *Entrance requirements:* GRE General Test, NTE. Application deadline: rolling. Application fee: $15. *Tuition:* $220 per hour. • Dr. Frieda Kalb, Assistant Professor of Education, 606-546-1263. Fax: 606-546-1217.

Université de Sherbrooke, Faculty of Education, Program in Elementary Education, Sherbrooke, PQ J1K 2R1, Canada. Awards M Ed, Diploma. Part-time and evening/weekend programs available. *Degree requirements:* For master's, thesis. *Application deadline:* 6/1. *Application fee:* $15.

Université du Québec à Montréal, Program in Elementary Education, Montréal, PQ H3C 3P8, Canada. Awards M Ed. Program being phased out; applicants no longer accepted. Part-time programs available.

The University of Akron, College of Education, Department of Curricular and Instructional Studies, Program in Elementary Education, Akron, OH 44325-0001. Awards MA, PhD. Accredited by NCATE. Students: 13 full-time (11 women), 114 part-time (105 women); includes 16 minority (11 African Americans, 4 Asian Americans, 1 Hispanic), 2 international. Average age 36. In 1997, 21 master's, 3 doctorates awarded. *Degree requirements:* For master's, written comprehensive exam required, foreign language not required; for doctorate, variable foreign language requirement, dissertation, written and oral exams. *Entrance requirements:* For master's, MAT, minimum GPA of 2.75; for doctorate, MAT, interview, minimum GPA of 3.25. Application deadline: 8/15 (rolling processing). Application fee: $25 ($50 for international students). *Expenses:* Tuition $178 per credit hour for state residents; $333 per credit hour for nonresidents. Fees $145 per year full-time, $32 per semester (minimum) part-time. • Application contact: Dr. Robert Eley, Director of Student Services, 330-972-7750. E-mail: reley@uakron.edu.

The University of Akron, College of Education, Department of Curricular and Instructional Studies, Program in Elementary Education with Certification, Akron, OH 44325-0001. Awards MS. Accredited by NCATE. *Degree requirements:* Written comprehensive exam required, foreign language not required. *Entrance requirements:* MAT, minimum GPA of 2.75. Application deadline: 8/15 (rolling processing). Application fee: $25 ($50 for international students). *Expenses:* Tuition $178 per credit hour for state residents; $333 per credit hour for nonresidents. Fees $145 per year full-time, $32 per semester (minimum) part-time. • Application contact: Dr. Robert Eley, Director of Student Services, 330-972-7750. E-mail: reley@uakron.edu.

The University of Alabama, College of Education, Area of Teacher Education, Tuscaloosa, AL 35487. Offerings include elementary education (MA, Ed D, PhD, Ed S). Accredited by NCATE. Faculty: 32 full-time (18 women), 8 part-time (4 women). *Degree requirements:* For doctorate, 1 foreign language (computer language can substitute), dissertation, residency; for Ed S, thesis required, foreign language not required. *Entrance requirements:* For master's and doctorate, GRE General Test, MAT (score in 50th percentile or higher), or NTE (minimum score 658 on each core battery test), minimum GPA of 3.0; for Ed S, minimum GPA of 3.0 during previous 2 years. Application deadline: 7/6 (priority date; rolling processing). Application fee: $25. *Tuition:* $2684 per year full-time, $594 per semester (minimum) part-time for state residents; $7216 per year full-time, $1248 per semester (minimum) part-time for nonresidents. • Dr. Lea McGee, Head, 205-348-1196. Fax: 205-348-9863. E-mail: lmcgee@bamaed.ua.edu.

The University of Alabama at Birmingham, Graduate School, School of Education, Department of Curriculum and Instruction, Program in Elementary Education, Birmingham, AL 35294. Awards MA Ed, Ed S. Accredited by NCATE. Students: 45 full-time (40 women), 44 part-time (41 women); includes 22 minority (19 African Americans, 2 Asian Americans, 1 Native American). 56 applicants, 96% accepted. In 1997, 97 master's awarded. *Degree requirements:* For master's, thesis optional; for Ed S, comprehensive exam. *Entrance requirements:* For master's, GRE General Test, MAT, or NTE, minimum GPA of 3.0. Application deadline: rolling. Application fee: $30 ($60 for international students). Electronic applications accepted. *Expenses:* Tuition $99 per credit hour for state residents; $198 per credit hour for nonresidents. Fees $516 per year (minimum) full-time, $73 per quarter (minimum) part-time for state residents; $516 per year (minimum) full-time, $73 per unit (minimum) part-time for nonresidents. • Dr. Joseph C. Burns, Chair, Department of Curriculum and Instruction, 205-934-5371.

University of Alaska Southeast, Program in Education, Juneau, AK 99801-8625. Offerings include elementary education (MAT, M Ed). *Degree requirements:* Comprehensive exam or project required, foreign language and thesis not required. *Entrance requirements:* Minimum GPA of 3.0. Application deadline: 8/15 (priority date; rolling processing; 2/15 for spring admission). Application fee: $35. Electronic applications accepted. *Tuition:* $162 per credit for state residents; $316 per credit for nonresidents. • Application contact: Greg Wagner, Recruiter, 907-465-6239. Fax: 907-465-6365. E-mail: jngaw@acad1.alaska.edu.

University of Alberta, Faculty of Graduate Studies and Research, Department of Elementary Education, Edmonton, AB T6G 2E1, Canada. Awards M Ed, Ed D, PhD. Part-time programs available. Faculty: 21 full-time (15 women). Students: 38 full-time (30 women), 65 part-time (53 women); includes 9 international. Average age 38. 37 applicants, 84% accepted. In 1997, 9 master's awarded (75% found work related to degree, 25% continued full-time study); 4 doctorates awarded (75% entered university research/teaching, 25% found other work related to degree). *Degree requirements:* For master's, thesis required (for some programs), foreign language not required; for doctorate, dissertation required, foreign language not required. *Entrance requirements:* For master's, 1 year of teaching experience, minimum GPA of 6.5 (on a 9.0 scale). Application deadline: 6/1 (priority date; rolling processing; 2/1 for spring admission). Application fee: $60. *Expenses:* Tuition $390 per course for Canadian residents; $781 per course for nonresidents. Fees $500 per year full-time, $184 per year part-time. *Financial aid:* In 1997–98, 23 students received aid, including 13 fellowships averaging $900 per month, 18 teaching assistantships (7 to first-year students) averaging $850 per month, 7 tuition scholarships; research assistantships and career-related internships or fieldwork also available. Financial aid application deadline: 6/1. *Faculty research:* Literacy education, early childhood education, teacher education, curriculum studies, instructional studies. Total annual research expenditures: $100,000. • Dr. R. K. Jackson, Chair, 403-492-4273 Ext. 225. Application contact: Gwen Parker, 403-492-4273 Ext. 225. Fax: 403-492-7622. E-mail: educ.elem@ualberta.ca.

The University of Arizona, College of Education, Department of Teaching and Teacher Education, Concentration in Elementary Education, Tucson, AZ 85721. Awards M Ed, MT, Ed D. *Degree requirements:* For master's, thesis optional, foreign language not required; for doctorate, dissertation required, foreign language not required. *Entrance requirements:* For master's, TOEFL (minimum score 550), minimum GPA of 3.0, 5 units of education course work; for doctorate, GRE General Test, TOEFL (minimum score 550), minimum graduate GPA of 3.0, 15 units of education course work, 2 years teaching experience. Application deadline: 4/12 (rolling processing). Application fee: $35. *Tuition:* $2162 per year full-time, $337 per semester (minimum) part-time for state residents; $6860 per year full-time, $1138 per semester (minimum) part-time for nonresidents. *Faculty research:* Mathematics diagnosis, middle schools, teacher effectiveness, curriculum design.

University of Arkansas, College of Education, Department of Curriculum and Instruction, Program in Elementary Education, Fayetteville, AR 72701-1201. Awards M Ed. Accredited by NCATE. Students: 8 full-time (all women), 8 part-time (7 women). 18 applicants, 94% accepted. In 1997, 14 degrees awarded. *Entrance requirements:* GRE General Test or MAT. Application fee: $25 ($35 for international students). *Tuition:* $3144 per year full-time, $173 per credit hour part-time for state residents; $7140 per year full-time, $395 per credit hour part-time for nonresidents. *Financial aid:* Federal Work-Study and career-related internships or fieldwork available. Aid available to part-time students. Financial aid application deadline: 4/1; applicants required to submit FAFSA. • Dr. Jerry Ford, Coordinator, 501-575-6676.

University of Arkansas at Little Rock, College of Education, Department of Teacher Education, Program in Elementary Education, Little Rock, AR 72204-1099. Offers early childhood education (M Ed, Ed S), elementary education (M Ed, Ed S), reading (M Ed, Ed S). Accredited by NCATE. Part-time and evening/weekend programs available. Students: 10 full-time (all women), 50 part-time (48 women); includes 8 minority (7 African Americans, 1 Hispanic). Average age 35. 45 applicants, 71% accepted. In 1997, 18 master's, 3 Ed Ss awarded. *Degree requirements:* For master's, thesis or alternative, Arkansas Department of Education certification, comprehensive exam required, foreign language not required; for Ed S, comprehensive exams, oral defense of thesis required, foreign language not required. *Entrance requirements:* For master's, minimum GPA of 2.75, teaching certificate; for Ed S, GRE General Test (minimum combined score of 1350 on three sections) or MAT (minimum score 40), Arkansas teaching certificate, interview, M Ed, minimum GPA of 3.3. Application deadline: rolling. Application fee: $25 ($30 for international students). *Expenses:* Tuition $2466 per year full-time, $137 per credit hour part-time for state residents; $5256 per year full-time, $292 per credit hour part-time for nonresidents. Fees $216 per year full-time, $36 per semester (minimum) part-time. *Financial aid:* Research assistantships, teaching assistantships, Federal Work-Study, institutionally sponsored loans available. Aid available to part-time students. • Dr. Jamie Foster, Adviser, 501-569-3124.

University of Arkansas at Monticello, School of Education, Monticello, AR 71656. Offerings include elementary education (M Ed). School faculty: 13 full-time (4 women). *Degree requirements:* Comprehensive exam required, foreign language and thesis not required. *Entrance requirements:* Minimum GPA of 2.75, teaching certificate. Application deadline: 8/22 (priority date). Application fee: $0. • Dr. Gerald Norris, Dean, 870-460-1062. Fax: 870-460-1563.

University of Arkansas at Pine Bluff, Program in Education, Pine Bluff, AR 71601-2799. Offerings include elementary education (M Ed). Accredited by NCATE. Program faculty: 51. *Entrance requirements:* GRE, minimum GPA of 2.75; NTE or Standard Arkansas Teaching Certificate. Application deadline: rolling. Application fee: $0. *Expenses:* Tuition $82 per credit hour for state residents; $192 per credit hour for nonresidents. Fees $25 per year. • Dr. Calvin Johnson, Dean, 870-543-8256.

University of Bridgeport, College of Graduate and Undergraduate Studies, School of Education and Human Resources, Division of Education, Program in Elementary Education, 380 University Avenue, Bridgeport, CT 06601. Offers early childhood education (MS, Diploma), elementary education (MS, Diploma). Evening/weekend programs available. Faculty: 8 full-time (2 women), 57 part-time (26 women), 27 FTE. Students: 2 full-time (both women), 7 part-time (6 women); includes 1 minority (Hispanic). 6 applicants, 67% accepted. In 1997, 10 Diplomas awarded. *Degree requirements:* For master's, computer language, final exam, final project, or thesis required, foreign language not required; for Diploma, thesis or alternative, final project required, foreign language not required. *Entrance requirements:* For master's, GRE General Test, MAT (score in 35th percentile or higher), minimum undergraduate QPA of 2.5; for Diploma, GRE General Test or MAT (score in 40th percentile or higher), minimum graduate QPA of 3.0. Application deadline: rolling. Application fee: $35 ($50 for international students). *Tuition:* $340 per credit. *Financial aid:* Federal Work-Study, institutionally sponsored loans, and career-related internships or fieldwork available. Aid available to part-time students. Financial aid application deadline: 6/1; applicants required to submit FAFSA. *Faculty research:* Self-concept, internship assessment, stress and situational development, follow-up of graduation. • Dr. Allen P. Cook, Associate Dean, Division of Education, 203-576-4206.

University of Central Arkansas, College of Education, Department of Administration and Secondary Education, Programs in Elementary and Secondary School Leadership, Conway, AR 72035-0001. Offerings include elementary school leadership (MSE). Accredited by NCATE. *Degree requirements:* Comprehensive exam required, thesis not required. *Entrance requirements:* GRE General Test, minimum GPA of 2.7. Application deadline: 3/1 (priority date; rolling processing; 10/1 for spring admission). Application fee: $15 ($40 for international students). *Expenses:* Tuition $161 per credit hour for state residents; $298 per credit hour for nonresidents. Fees $50 per year full-time, $30 per year part-time. • Dr. David Skotko, Interim Chairperson, Department of Administration and Secondary Education, 501-450-5407. Fax: 501-450-5671. E-mail: davids@mail.uca.edu.

University of Central Arkansas, College of Education, Department of Childhood and Special Education, Program in Elementary Education, Conway, AR 72035-0001. Awards MSE. Accredited by NCATE. Students: 3 full-time (all women), 14 part-time (all women). 22 applicants, 100% accepted. In 1997, 11 degrees awarded. *Degree requirements:* Comprehensive exam required, thesis optional. *Entrance requirements:* GRE General Test, minimum GPA of 2.7. Application deadline: 3/1 (priority date; rolling processing; 10/1 for spring admission). Application fee: $15 ($40 for international students). *Expenses:* Tuition $161 per credit hour for state residents;

Directory: Elementary Education

University of Central Arkansas (continued)
$298 per credit hour for nonresidents. Fees $50 per year full-time, $30 per year part-time. *Financial aid:* Federal Work-Study available. Financial aid application deadline: 2/15. • Dr. David Naylor, Coordinator, 501-450-5403. E-mail: davidn@mail.uca.edu.

University of Central Florida, College of Education, Department of Instructional Programs, Special Programs in Elementary and Secondary Education, Orlando, FL 32816. Offerings in elementary and secondary education (MA, M Ed), elementary education (MA, M Ed). Accredited by NCATE. Part-time and evening/weekend programs available. Students: 72 full-time (66 women), 94 part-time (81 women); includes 16 minority (7 African Americans, 1 Asian American, 7 Hispanics, 1 Native American). Average age 34. 44 applicants, 57% accepted. In 1997, 34 degrees awarded. *Degree requirements:* Thesis or alternative required, foreign language not required. *Entrance requirements:* GRE General Test (minimum combined score of 840). Application deadline: 7/12 (12/15 for spring admission). Application fee: $20. *Expenses:* Tuition $3288 per year full-time, $137 per credit hour part-time for state residents; $11,520 per year full-time, $480 per credit hour part-time for nonresidents. Fees $105 per year. *Financial aid:* Teaching assistantships, Federal Work-Study, institutionally sponsored loans, and career-related internships or fieldwork available. Aid available to part-time students. • Application contact: Dr. Martha Hopkins, Coordinator, 407-823-2039. E-mail: marthah@pegasus.cc.ucf.edu.

University of Central Oklahoma, College of Education, Department of Curriculum and Instruction, Program in Elementary Education, Edmond, OK 73034-5209. Awards M Ed. Accredited by NCATE. Part-time and evening/weekend programs available. *Entrance requirements:* GRE General Test. Application deadline: 8/18. Application fee: $15. *Tuition:* $76 per credit hour for state residents; $178 per credit hour for nonresidents.

University of Charleston, South Carolina, School of Education, Department of Elementary and Early Childhood Education, Program in Elementary Education, Charleston, SC 29424-0001. Awards MAT, M Ed. Part-time and evening/weekend programs available. Faculty: 13 full-time (8 women), 5 part-time (3 women), 14.5 FTE. Students: 46 full-time (36 women), 42 part-time (38 women); includes 5 minority (all African Americans). Average age 31. 64 applicants, 94% accepted. In 1997, 28 degrees awarded. *Degree requirements:* Thesis or alternative, written qualifying exam, student teaching (MAT) required, foreign language not required. *Entrance requirements:* GRE (score in 50th percentile or higher), MAT (score in 50th percentile or higher), or NTE; South Carolina Education Entrance Exam (MAT); TOEFL, teaching certificate (M Ed). Application deadline: rolling. Application fee: $35. *Expenses:* Tuition $2568 per year full-time, $438 per semester (minimum) part-time for state residents; $4596 per year full-time, $876 per semester (minimum) part-time for nonresidents. Fees $51 per year full-time, $21 per semester (minimum) part-time. *Financial aid:* Research assistantships, teaching assistantships, Federal Work-Study available. Aid available to part-time students. Financial aid application deadline: 4/1; applicants required to submit FAFSA. • Application contact: Laura H. Hines, Graduate School Coordinator, 843-953-5614. Fax: 843-953-1434. E-mail: hinesl@cofc.edu.

University of Cincinnati, College of Education, Division of Teacher Education, Department of Curriculum and Instruction, Program in Elementary Education, Cincinnati, OH 45221. Awards M Ed, Ed D. Accredited by NCATE. Part-time programs available. Students: 120; includes 31 minority (29 African Americans, 2 Hispanics), 1 international. 18 applicants, 11% accepted. In 1997, 19 master's, 1 doctorate awarded. *Degree requirements:* For master's, thesis or alternative required, foreign language not required; for doctorate, dissertation required, foreign language not required. *Average time to degree:* master's–3.6 years full-time; doctorate–3.3 years full-time. *Entrance requirements:* For master's, GRE General Test. Application deadline: 2/1. Application fee: $30. *Tuition:* $7228 per year full-time, $185 per credit hour part-time for state residents; $13,812 per year full-time, $352 per credit hour part-time for nonresidents. *Financial aid:* Fellowships, graduate assistantships, full tuition waivers available. Aid available to part-time students. Financial aid application deadline: 2/15. • Application contact: Dr. Glenn Markle, Graduate Program Director, 513-556-3582. Fax: 513-556-2483. E-mail: glenn.markle@uc.edu.

University of Connecticut, School of Education, Field of Elementary Education, Storrs, CT 06269. Awards MA, PhD. Accredited by NCATE. Faculty: 9. Students: 56 full-time (47 women), 9 part-time (8 women); includes 4 minority (1 African American, 3 Hispanics). Average age 25. 63 applicants, 87% accepted. In 1997, 53 master's, 1 doctorate awarded. Terminal master's awarded for partial completion of doctoral program. *Degree requirements:* For master's, thesis or alternative; for doctorate, dissertation. *Entrance requirements:* For doctorate, GRE General Test. Application deadline: 6/1 (priority date; rolling processing; 11/1 for spring admission). Application fee: $40 ($45 for international students). *Expenses:* Tuition $5272 per year full-time, $293 per credit part-time for state residents; $13,696 per year full-time, $761 per credit part-time for nonresidents. Fees $948 per year full-time, $640 per year part-time. *Financial aid:* In 1997–98, 1 fellowship totaling $200, 5 research assistantships (3 to first-year students) totaling $22,444, 1 teaching assistantship totaling $15,000 were awarded. Financial aid application deadline: 2/15. • Thomas P. Weinland, Head, 860-486-2433.

The University of Findlay, College of Professional Studies, Division of Education, 1000 North Main Street, Findlay, OH 45840-3653. Offerings include elementary education (MA Ed). Accredited by NCATE. Division faculty: 9 full-time (7 women), 8 part-time (4 women), 21 FTE. *Degree requirements:* 4 foreign languages, thesis, cumulative project. *Average time to degree:* master's–1.5 years full-time, 3 years part-time. *Entrance requirements:* Minimum GPA of 3.0. Application deadline: 8/15 (priority date; rolling processing). Application fee: $25. *Tuition:* $236 per semester hour. • Dr. Judith Wahrman, Graduate Program Director, 419-424-4864. Fax: 419-424-4822. E-mail: wahrman@lucy.findlay.edu.

University of Florida, College of Education, Department of Instruction and Curriculum, Gainesville, FL 32611. Offerings include elementary education (MAE, M Ed, Ed D, PhD, Ed S). Accredited by NCATE. Department faculty: 42. *Degree requirements:* For master's, thesis optional, foreign language not required; for doctorate, variable foreign language requirement, dissertation. *Entrance requirements:* For master's and doctorate, GRE General Test (minimum combined score of 1000), minimum GPA of 3.0; for Ed S, GRE General Test. Application deadline: 6/5. Application fee: $20. *Tuition:* $138 per credit hour for state residents; $481 per credit hour for nonresidents. • Dr. Mary Grace Kantowski, Chair, 352-392-9191 Ext. 200. E-mail: mgk@coe.ufl.edu. Application contact: Dr. Ben Nelms, Graduate Coordinator, 352-392-9191 Ext. 225. Fax: 352-392-9193. E-mail: bfn@coe.ufl.edu.

University of Georgia, College of Education, Department of Elementary Education, Programs in Elementary and Middle School Education, Athens, GA 30602. Offerings in elementary and middle school education (M Ed, Ed D, Ed S), middle school education (PhD). Accredited by NCATE. Faculty: 15 full-time (11 women). Students: 19 full-time (15 women), 77 part-time; includes 4 minority (3 African Americans, 1 Hispanic), 1 international. 51 applicants, 63% accepted. In 1997, 39 master's, 3 doctorates, 7 Ed Ss awarded. *Degree requirements:* For doctorate, dissertation required, foreign language not required. *Entrance requirements:* For master's and Ed S, GRE General Test or MAT; for doctorate, GRE General Test. Application fee: $30. *Tuition:* $3290 per year full-time, $643 per semester (minimum) part-time for state residents; $11,300 per year full-time, $1645 per semester (minimum) part-time for nonresidents. *Financial aid:* Fellowships, research assistantships, teaching assistantships, assistantships available. • Dr. Judith C. Reiff, Graduate Coordinator, Department of Elementary Education, 706-542-4268. Fax: 706-542-4277.

University of Great Falls, Graduate Studies Division, Master of Arts in Teaching Program, Great Falls, MT 59405. Offerings include elementary education (MAT). Postbaccalaureate distance learning degree programs offered (minimal on-campus study). Program faculty: 5 full-time (all women), 6 part-time (4 women), 6 FTE. *Degree requirements:* Thesis or alternative required, foreign language not required. *Entrance requirements:* GRE General Test (minimum score 500 on each section; combined average 1000), bachelor's degree in teaching, teaching certificate, 3 years of teaching experience. Application deadline: 8/15 (priority date; rolling processing). Application fee: $35. *Expenses:* Tuition $327 per credit. Fees $150 per year full-time, $45 per semester (minimum) part-time. • Dr. Eleanore Gowen, Head. E-mail: agowen@ugf.edu.

University of Hartford, College of Education, Nursing, and Health Professions, Program in Elementary Education, West Hartford, CT 06117-1599. Awards M Ed. Accredited by NCATE. Part-time and evening/weekend programs available. Faculty: 10 full-time (5 women), 7 part-time (3 women). Students: 14 full-time (8 women), 38 part-time (30 women); includes 2 minority (both African Americans). Average age 31. 24 applicants, 50% accepted. In 1997, 36 degrees awarded. *Degree requirements:* Comprehensive exam required, foreign language and thesis not required. *Entrance requirements:* GRE General Test or MAT, PRAXIS I, interview. Application deadline: 5/15 (priority date; rolling processing; 12/15 for spring admission). Application fee: $40 ($55 for international students). Electronic applications accepted. *Financial aid:* Graduate assistantships, Federal Work-Study available. Aid available to part-time students. Financial aid application deadline: 6/1; applicants required to submit FAFSA. • Dr. S. Edward Weinswig, Director, 860-768-4529. Application contact: Susan Garcia, Coordinator of Student Services, 860-768-5038. E-mail: gettoknow@mail.hartford.edu.

University of Hawaii at Manoa, College of Education, Department of Teacher Education and Curriculum Studies, Program in Elementary Education, Honolulu, HI 96822. Awards M Ed. Faculty: 44 full-time (21 women), 1 (woman) part-time, 44.5 FTE. Students: 97 (94 women). 56 applicants, 63% accepted. *Application deadline:* 3/1 (9/1 for spring admission). *Tuition:* $4029 per year full-time, $214 per credit hour part-time for state residents; $9957 per year full-time, $461 per credit hour part-time for nonresidents. *Financial aid:* 10 students received aid. • Dr. Richard Johnson, Graduate Chairperson, 808-956-4410. E-mail: rich@hawaii.edu. Application contact: Myrna Nakasato, Secretary, 808-956-4401. Fax: 808-956-3918.

University of Houston, College of Education, Department of Curriculum and Instruction, 4800 Calhoun, Houston, TX 77204-2163. Offerings include elementary education (M Ed). Accredited by NCATE. Department faculty: 37 full-time (19 women), 10 part-time (7 women). *Degree requirements:* Comprehensive exam or thesis required, foreign language not required. *Entrance requirements:* GRE General Test or MAT. Application deadline: 7/3 (priority date; rolling processing). Application fee: $35 ($75 for international students). *Expenses:* Tuition $1152 per year full-time, $120 per semester (minimum) part-time for state residents; $4482 per year full-time, $249 per credit hour part-time for nonresidents. Fees $977 per year full-time, $119 per semester (minimum) part-time. • Wilford Weber, Chair, 713-743-4970. Fax: 713-743-9870. E-mail: wweber@uh.edu.

University of Idaho, College of Graduate Studies, College of Education, Division of Teacher Education, Department of Teacher Education, Moscow, ID 83844-4140. Offerings include elementary education (M Ed). Accredited by NCATE. *Application deadline:* 8/1 (12/15 for spring admission). *Application fee:* $35 ($45 for international students). *Expenses:* Tuition $0 for state residents; $6000 per year full-time, $95 per credit part-time for nonresidents. Fees $2676 per year full-time, $134 per credit part-time. • Dr. Grace Goc Karp, Acting Head, Division of Teacher Education, 208-885-6586.

University of Illinois at Chicago, College of Education, Department of Curriculum and Instruction, Chicago, IL 60607-7128. Offerings include instructional leadership (M Ed), with options in elementary education, reading, secondary education. Department faculty: 28 full-time (13 women), 1 part-time (0 women). *Entrance requirements:* TOEFL (minimum score 550), minimum GPA of 3.75 on a 5.0 scale. Application deadline: 2/15. Application fee: $40 ($50 for international students). • Dr. John Smart, Area Chair, 312-996-4526. Application contact: Victoria Hare, Director of Graduate Studies, 312-996-4520.

University of Indianapolis, School of Education, Indianapolis, IN 46227-3697. Offerings include elementary education (MA). Accredited by NCATE. *Average time to degree:* master's–5 years part-time. *Entrance requirements:* GRE Subject Test. Application deadline: rolling. Application fee: $30.

The University of Iowa, College of Education, Division of Early Childhood and Elementary Education, Iowa City, IA 52242-1316. Offers programs in curriculum and instruction (Ed S), early childhood and elementary education (MA), early childhood education (MA), elementary education (PhD). Faculty: 12 full-time. Students: 14 full-time (12 women), 60 part-time (54 women); includes 5 minority (3 African Americans, 1 Asian American, 1 Hispanic), 11 international. 31 applicants, 68% accepted. In 1997, 16 master's, 8 doctorates, 1 Ed S awarded. *Degree requirements:* For master's, exam required, thesis optional, foreign language not required; for doctorate, computer language, dissertation, comprehensive exams required, foreign language not required. *Entrance requirements:* For master's, minimum GPA of 2.5; for doctorate, minimum GPA of 3.0. Application deadline: rolling. Application fee: $30 ($50 for international students). *Expenses:* Tuition $3166 per year full-time, $176 per semester hour part-time for state residents; $10,202 per year full-time, $176 per semester hour part-time for nonresidents. Fees $202 per year full-time, $52 per year (minimum) part-time. *Financial aid:* In 1997–98, 5 research assistantships (1 to a first-year student), 12 teaching assistantships (4 to first-year students) were awarded; fellowships also available. Financial aid applicants required to submit FAFSA. • William Nibbelink, Chair, 319-335-5324. Fax: 319-335-5608.

University of Louisville, School of Education, Department of Early and Middle Childhood Education, Program in Early Elementary Education, Louisville, KY 40292-0001. Awards MAT. Accredited by NCATE. Students: 26 full-time (21 women), 48 part-time (46 women); includes 9 minority (8 African Americans, 1 Asian American). Average age 30. In 1997, 59 degrees awarded. *Entrance requirements:* GRE General Test. Application deadline: rolling. Application fee: $25. • Dr. Diane W. Kyle, Chair, Department of Early and Middle Childhood Education, 502-852-6431.

University of Louisville, School of Education, Department of Early and Middle Childhood Education, Program in Elementary Education, Louisville, KY 40292-0001. Awards MA, MAT, M Ed, Ed S. Accredited by NCATE. Students: 10 full-time (9 women), 42 part-time (40 women); includes 5 minority (all African Americans). Average age 33. In 1997, 3 master's, 1 Ed S awarded. *Entrance requirements:* GRE General Test. Application deadline: rolling. Application fee: $25. • Dr. Diane W. Kyle, Chair, Department of Early and Middle Childhood Education, 502-852-6431.

University of Maine, College of Education and Human Development, Program in Elementary Education, Orono, ME 04469. Awards M Ed, MS, CAS. Accredited by NCATE. Part-time and evening/weekend programs available. *Degree requirements:* For master's, thesis or alternative required, foreign language not required. *Entrance requirements:* For master's, MAT, TOEFL (minimum score 550); for CAS, MA, M Ed, or MS. Application deadline: 2/1 (priority date; rolling processing; 10/15 for spring admission). Application fee: $50. *Expenses:* Tuition $194 per credit hour for state residents; $548 per credit hour for nonresidents. Fees $378 per year full-time, $33 per semester (minimum) part-time. *Financial aid:* Research assistantships, teaching assistantships, and career-related internships or fieldwork available. Financial aid application deadline: 3/1. • Application contact: Scott Delcourt, Director of the Graduate School, 207-581-3218. Fax: 207-581-3232. E-mail: graduate@maine.edu.

University of Mary, Program in Education, 7500 University Drive, Bismarck, ND 58504-9652. Offerings include elementary education (MS). Program faculty: 5 full-time (3 women), 6 part-time (4 women). *Average time to degree:* master's–3 years part-time. *Application deadline:* 8/1 (12/1 for spring admission). *Application fee:* $15. *Tuition:* $265 per credit. • Ramona Klein, Director, 701-255-7500. Application contact: Dr. Diane Fladeland, Director, Graduate Programs, 701-255-7500. Fax: 701-255-7687.

University of Massachusetts Amherst, School of Education, Program in Education, Amherst, MA 01003-0001. Offerings include elementary teacher education (M Ed, Ed D, CAGS). Accredited by NCATE. *Degree requirements:* For doctorate, dissertation required, foreign language not required. *Entrance requirements:* For master's and doctorate, GRE General Test. Application deadline: 3/1 (rolling processing; 10/1 for spring admission). Application fee: $40. *Expenses:* Tuition $2640 per year full-time, $110 per credit part-time for state residents; $3690 per year (minimum) full-time, $165 per credit (minimum) part-time for nonresidents. Fees $2856 per year full-time, $422 per semester part-time for state residents; $3204 per year full-time, $480 per semester part-time for nonresidents. • John C. Carey, Director, 413-545-0236.

University of Massachusetts Boston, Graduate College of Education, School Organization, Curriculum and Instruction Department, Program in Education, Track in Elementary and Secondary Education, Boston, MA 02125-3393. Awards M Ed. Students: 90 full-time (63 women), 222 part-time (139 women); includes 41 minority (19 African Americans, 8 Asian Americans, 14 Hispanics), 2 international. 209 applicants, 70% accepted. In 1997, 97 degrees awarded. *Degree requirements:* Comprehensive exams required, foreign language and thesis not required. *Entrance requirements:* GRE General Test or MAT, minimum GPA of 2.75, 2 years of teaching experience. Application deadline: 3/1 (priority date; 11/1 for spring admission). Application fee: $25 ($35 for international students). *Expenses:* Tuition $2640 per year full-time, $110 per credit part-time for state residents; $8930 per year full-time, $373 per credit part-time for nonresidents. Fees $2650 per year full-time, $420 per semester (minimum) part-time for state residents; $2736 per year full-time, $420 per semester (minimum) part-time for nonresidents. *Financial aid:* In 1997–98, 10 research assistantships (9 to first-year students) averaging $225 per month and totaling $20,000 were awarded; teaching assistantships, administrative assistantships also available. Financial aid application deadline: 3/1; applicants required to submit FAFSA. • Dr. Denise Patmon, Program Coordinator, 617-287-7625. Application contact: Lisa Lavely, Director of Graduate Admissions and Records, 617-287-6400. Fax: 617-287-6236.

The University of Memphis, College of Education, Department of Instruction and Curriculum Leadership, Memphis, TN 38152. Offerings include elementary education (MAT). Accredited by NCATE. Department faculty: 34 full-time (17 women), 22 part-time (13 women). *Application deadline:* 8/1 (12/1 for spring admission). *Application fee:* $25 ($50 for international students). *Tuition:* $2862 per year full-time, $166 per credit hour part-time for state residents; $6696 per year full-time, $379 per credit hour part-time for nonresidents. • Dr. Dennie Smith, Interim Chair, 901-678-2771. Application contact: Dr. Carole L. Bond, Coordinator of Graduate Studies, 901-678-3490.

University of Miami, School of Education, Department of Teaching and Learning, Program in Elementary Education, Coral Gables, FL 33124. Awards MS Ed, Ed S. Accredited by NCATE. Part-time and evening/weekend programs available. Faculty: 9 full-time (5 women). Students: 12 full-time (10 women), 70 part-time (61 women); includes 38 minority (10 African Americans, 1 Asian American, 26 Hispanics, 1 Native American). Average age 31. 70 applicants, 94% accepted. In 1997, 24 master's, 1 Ed S awarded. *Degree requirements:* For Ed S, thesis optional, foreign language not required. *Entrance requirements:* For master's, GRE General Test (minimum combined score of 1000), TOEFL (minimum score 550); for Ed S, GRE General Test, TOEFL (minimum score 550). Application deadline: rolling. Application fee: $35. *Expenses:* Tuition $815 per credit hour. Fees $174 per year. *Financial aid:* Application deadline 3/1. *Faculty research:* Mathematics, technology. • Dr. Harry Forgan, Adviser, 305-284-4962. Fax: 305-284-6998. E-mail: hforgan@umiami.ir.miami.edu.

University of Minnesota, Twin Cities Campus, College of Education and Human Development, Department of Curriculum and Instruction, Program in Elementary Education, Minneapolis, MN 55455-0213. Awards MA, M Ed, PhD. • Roger Johnson, Director of Graduate Studies, 612-624-7031.

University of Missouri–Kansas City, School of Education, Division of Curriculum and Instruction, Kansas City, MO 64110-2499. Offerings include elementary education (MA). Accredited by NCATE. *Degree requirements:* Thesis optional, foreign language not required. *Entrance requirements:* Minimum GPA of 2.75. Application deadline: 7/1 (priority date; rolling processing; 12/1 for spring admission). Application fee: $25. *Expenses:* Tuition $182 per credit hour for state residents; $508 per credit hour for nonresidents. Fees $60 per year. • Dr. Cheryl Grossman, Chairperson, 816-235-2245.

University of Missouri–St. Louis, School of Education, Program in Elementary Education, St. Louis, MO 63121-4499. Awards M Ed. Accredited by NCATE. Part-time and evening/weekend programs available. Faculty: 14 (7 women). Students: 9 full-time (6 women), 165 part-time (151 women); includes 23 minority (20 African Americans, 1 Asian American, 1 Hispanic, 1 Native American). In 1997, 56 degrees awarded. *Degree requirements:* Thesis or alternative required, foreign language not required. *Entrance requirements:* Minimum GPA of 2.75. Application deadline: 7/1 (priority date; rolling processing; 12/1 for spring admission). Application fee: $0. Electronic applications accepted. *Expenses:* Tuition $3903 per year full-time, $167 per credit hour part-time for state residents; $11,745 per year full-time, $489 per credit hour part-time for nonresidents. Fees $816 per year full-time, $34 per credit hour part-time. *Financial aid:* In 1997–98, 6 teaching assistantships averaging $833 per month were awarded. *Faculty research:* Literacy, mathematics remediation, language development, K–8 science methods, field experiences. • Dr. Helene Sherman, Chair, 314-516-5796. Application contact: Graduate Admissions, 314-516-5458. Fax: 314-516-6759. E-mail: gradadm@umslvma.umsl.edu.

University of Montevallo, College of Education, Program in Elementary Education, Montevallo, AL 35115. Awards M Ed, Ed S. Accredited by NCATE. Part-time and evening/weekend programs available. *Entrance requirements:* For master's, GRE General Test (minimum combined score of 850), MAT (minimum score 35), minimum undergraduate GPA of 2.75 in last 60 hours or 2.5 overall. Application deadline: 7/15 (11/15 for spring admission). Application fee: $10.

University of Nebraska at Kearney, College of Education, Department of Elementary/Early Childhood Education, Kearney, NE 68849-0001. Offerings include elementary education (MA Ed). Accredited by NCATE. Department faculty: 4 full-time (1 woman). *Degree requirements:* Thesis optional. *Entrance requirements:* GRE General Test. Application deadline: 8/1 (priority date; rolling processing; 12/15 for spring admission). Application fee: $35. *Expenses:* Tuition $1494 per year full-time, $83 per credit hour part-time for state residents; $2826 per year full-time, $157 per credit hour part-time for nonresidents. Fees $229 per year full-time, $11.25 per semester (minimum) part-time. • Dr. Ed Walker, Chair, 308-865-8513.

University of Nebraska at Omaha, College of Education, Department of Teacher Education, Program in Elementary Education, Omaha, NE 68182. Awards MA, MS. Accredited by NCATE. Part-time and evening/weekend programs available. Faculty: 9 full-time (6 women). Students: 6 full-time (all women), 113 part-time (107 women); includes 5 minority (4 African Americans, 1 Hispanic). Average age 34. 43 applicants, 93% accepted. In 1997, 49 degrees awarded. *Degree requirements:* Thesis (for some programs), comprehensive exam required, foreign language not required. *Entrance requirements:* GRE General Test (minimum combined score of 840) or MAT (minimum score 35), minimum GPA of 3.0. Application deadline: 7/1 (priority date; rolling processing; 12/1 for spring admission). Application fee: $35. *Expenses:* Tuition $1670 per year full-time, $94 per credit hour part-time for state residents; $4082 per year full-time, $227 per credit hour part-time for nonresidents. Fees $302 per year full-time, $108 per semester (minimum) part-time. *Financial aid:* 46 students received aid; fellowships, teaching assistantships, full tuition waivers, Federal Work-Study, institutionally sponsored loans available. Aid available to part-time students. Financial aid application deadline: 3/1. • Dr. Kathy Danielson, Adviser, 402-554-3452.

University of Nevada, Las Vegas, College of Education, Department of Instructional and Curricular Studies, Las Vegas, NV 89154-9900. Offerings include general elementary curriculum (M Ed, MS). Accredited by NCATE. Department faculty: 34 full-time (16 women). *Degree requirements:* Thesis (for some programs), oral or written comprehensive exam required, foreign language not required. *Entrance requirements:* Minimum GPA of 3.0. Application deadline: 2/15 (9/30 for spring admission). Application fee: $40 ($95 for international students). *Expenses:* Tuition $93 per credit for state residents; $93 per credit full-time, $190 per credit part-time for nonresidents. Fees $5570 per year full-time for nonresidents. • Dr. Jan McCarthy, Chair, 702-895-3241. Application contact: Graduate College Admissions Evaluator, 702-895-3320.

University of Nevada, Reno, College of Education, Department of Curriculum and Instruction, Reno, NV 89557. Offerings include elementary education (MA, M Ed, MS). Accredited by NCATE. Department faculty: 19 (7 women). *Degree requirements:* Thesis optional, foreign language not required. *Entrance requirements:* GRE, TOEFL (minimum score 500), minimum GPA of 2.75. Application deadline: 3/1 (priority date; rolling processing; 10/1 for spring admission). Application fee: $40. *Expenses:* Tuition $0 for state residents; $5770 per year full-time, $200 per credit part-time for nonresidents. Fees $93 per credit. • Dr. Vernon D. Luft, Chair, 702-784-4961. Application contact: Dr. J. Randall Koetting, Graduate Director, 702-784-4961 Ext. 2008. E-mail: koetting@unr.edu.

University of New Hampshire, College of Liberal Arts, Department of Education, Program in Elementary Education, Durham, NH 03824. Awards MAT, M Ed. Accredited by NCATE. Part-time programs available. Students: 50 full-time (45 women), 95 part-time (84 women). Average age 29. 60 applicants, 73% accepted. In 1997, 58 degrees awarded. *Degree requirements:* Thesis or alternative required, foreign language not required. *Entrance requirements:* GRE General Test. Application deadline: 4/1 (priority date; rolling processing). Application fee: $50. *Expenses:* Tuition $5440 per year full-time, $302 per credit hour part-time for state residents; $8160 per year (minimum) full-time, $453 per credit hour (minimum) part-time for nonresidents. Fees $868 per year full-time, $15 per year part-time. *Financial aid:* In 1997–98, 10 scholarships (2 to first-year students) were awarded; research assistantships, teaching assistantships, full and partial tuition waivers, Federal Work-Study, and career-related internships or fieldwork also available. Aid available to part-time students. Financial aid application deadline: 2/15. *Faculty research:* Pre-service teacher education. • Dr. Michael D. Andrew, Coordinator, 603-862-2371. Application contact: Dr. Todd DeMitchell, Graduate Coordinator, 603-862-2317.

University of New Mexico, College of Education, Program in Elementary Education, Albuquerque, NM 87131-2039. Awards MA. Accredited by NCATE. Students: 56 full-time (50 women), 116 part-time (104 women); includes 54 minority (2 African Americans, 5 Asian Americans, 42 Hispanics, 5 Native Americans), 1 international. Average age 35. 56 applicants, 93% accepted. In 1997, 121 degrees awarded. *Degree requirements:* Comprehensive exam or thesis required, thesis optional, foreign language not required. *Entrance requirements:* Elementary teaching certificate. Application deadline: 3/31 (10/10 for spring admission). Application fee: $25. *Expenses:* Tuition $2442 per year full-time, $103 per credit hour part-time for state residents; $8691 per year full-time, $103 per credit hour (minimum) part-time for nonresidents. Fees $32 per year. *Financial aid:* In 1997–98, 6 students received aid, including 2 research assistantships (both to first-year students) averaging $880 per month and totaling $17,600, 4 teaching assistantships (1 to a first-year student) averaging $880 per month and totaling $35,200; fellowships, Federal Work-Study, institutionally sponsored loans, and career-related internships or fieldwork also available. Aid available to part-time students. Financial aid applicants required to submit FAFSA. *Faculty research:* Bilingualism, math, science, language and literacy, special education. • Dr. Peter Winograd, Graduate Coordinator, 505-277-4533. E-mail: winograd@unm.edu. Application contact: Irene Martinez, Division Administrator, 505-277-4533. Fax: 505-277-4166. E-mail: icmartin@unm.edu.

University of North Alabama, College of Education, Department of Elementary Education, Program in Elementary Education, Florence, AL 35632-0001. Awards MA Ed. Accredited by NCATE. Part-time and evening/weekend programs available. Students: 5 full-time (2 women), 68 part-time (51 women); includes 4 minority (all African Americans). Average age 30. In 1997, 42 degrees awarded. *Degree requirements:* Final written comprehensive exam required, foreign language and thesis not required. *Entrance requirements:* GRE, MAT, or NTE, minimum GPA of 2.5, Alabama Class B Certificate or equivalent, teaching experience. Application deadline: 7/1 (priority date; rolling processing; 12/1 for spring admission). Application fee: $25. *Expenses:* Tuition $2448 per year full-time, $102 per credit hour part-time for state residents; $4896 per year full-time, $204 per credit hour part-time for nonresidents. Fees $3 per semester. *Financial aid:* Federal Work-Study available. Aid available to part-time students. Financial aid application deadline: 4/1. • Application contact: Dr. Sue Wilson, Dean of Enrollment Management, 205-765-4316.

The University of North Carolina at Chapel Hill, School of Education, Programs in Teacher Education, Program in Elementary Education, Chapel Hill, NC 27599. Awards M Ed. Accredited by NCATE. Students: 5 full-time (all women), 8 part-time (all women). 21 applicants, 52% accepted. *Degree requirements:* Comprehensive exam required, foreign language and thesis not required. *Entrance requirements:* GRE General Test (minimum combined score of 1000), minimum GPA of 3.0 during last 2 years of undergraduate course work. Application deadline: 1/1 (rolling processing). Application fee: $55. *Expenses:* Tuition $1428 per year full-time, $357 per semester (minimum) part-time for state residents; $10,414 per year full-time, $2604 per semester (minimum) part-time for nonresidents. Fees $782 per year full-time, $332 per semester (minimum) part-time. *Financial aid:* Federal Work-Study available. Aid available to part-time students. Financial aid application deadline: 1/1. *Faculty research:* Early childhood and intermediate education, teacher education, supervision, teachers as researchers, moral dimensions of teaching. • Dr. Richard A. Brice, Coordinator, 919-966-3291. Application contact: Janet Carroll, Registrar, 919-966-1346. Fax: 919-962-1533. E-mail: jscarrol@email.unc.edu.

University of North Carolina at Charlotte, College of Education, Charlotte, NC 28223-0001. Offerings include elementary education (M Ed). Accredited by NCATE. College faculty: 61 full-time (31 women), 7 part-time (6 women), 62.75 FTE. *Application deadline:* 7/1. *Application fee:* $35. *Tuition:* $1786 per year full-time, $339 per semester (minimum) part-time for state residents; $8914 per year full-time, $2121 per semester (minimum) part-time for nonresidents. • Dr. John M. Nagle, Dean, 704-547-4707. Application contact: Kathy Barringer, Assistant Director of Graduate Admissions, 704-547-3366. Fax: 704-547-3279. E-mail: gradadm@email.uncc.edu.

University of North Carolina at Greensboro, School of Education, Department of Curriculum and Instruction, Program in Elementary Curriculum and Teaching, Greensboro, NC 27412-0001. Awards M Ed. Accredited by NCATE. Part-time programs available. Students: 41 full-time (40 women), 40 part-time (39 women); includes 6 minority (2 African Americans, 2 Asian Americans, 2 Hispanics). 46 applicants, 46% accepted. In 1997, 43 degrees awarded. *Entrance requirements:* GRE General Test, TOEFL. Application deadline: 7/1 (priority date; rolling processing; 11/1 for spring admission). Application fee: $35. *Expenses:* Tuition $1842 per year full-time, $370 per semester (minimum) part-time for state residents; $10,296 per year full-time, $2484 per semester (minimum) part-time for nonresidents. Fees $806 per year full-time, $111 per semester (minimum) part-time. *Financial aid:* 19 students received aid; research assistantships, teaching assistantships, and career-related internships or fieldwork available. • Dr. Gerald Ponder, Chair, Department of Curriculum and Instruction, 336-334-3437.

University of North Carolina at Pembroke, Graduate Studies, Department of Education, Program in Elementary Education, Pembroke, NC 28372-1510. Awards MA Ed. Accredited by NCATE. Part-time and evening/weekend programs available. Faculty: 10 full-time (6 women). Students: 1 full-time (0 women), 74 part-time (66 women); includes 26 minority (9 African Americans, 1 Asian American, 16 Native Americans). In 1997, 35 degrees awarded. *Degree requirements:* Comprehensive exam required, thesis optional, foreign language not required. *Average time to degree:* master's–1.5 years full-time, 2.5 years part-time. *Entrance requirements:* GRE General Test or MAT, minimum GPA of 3.0 in major, 2.5 overall. Application deadline: rolling. Application fee: $25. *Tuition:* $1554 per year full-time, $610 per semester (minimum) part-time for state residents; $8824 per year full-time, $2122 per semester (minimum) part-time for nonresidents. *Financial aid:* Graduate assistantships available. Aid available to part-

Directory: Elementary Education

University of North Carolina at Pembroke (continued)
time students. Financial aid application deadline: 4/15. • Dr. Swannee Dickson, Coordinator, 910-521-6628. Application contact: Director of Graduate Studies, 910-521-6271. Fax: 910-521-6497.

University of North Carolina at Wilmington, School of Education, Department of Curricular Studies, Program in Elementary Education, Wilmington, NC 28403-3201. Awards M Ed. Accredited by NCATE. Part-time and evening/weekend programs available. Students: 3 full-time (all women), 7 part-time (6 women). Average age 35. 19 applicants, 21% accepted. In 1997, 9 degrees awarded. *Degree requirements:* Comprehensive exams required, foreign language and thesis not required. *Entrance requirements:* GRE General Test, MAT, minimum B average in upper-division undergraduate course work, bachelor's degree in elementary education. Application deadline: 7/1 (rolling processing). Application fee: $35. *Tuition:* $1748 per year full-time, $270 per semester (minimum) part-time for state residents; $8882 per year full-time, $2058 per semester (minimum) part-time for nonresidents. *Financial aid:* Assistantships, Federal Work-Study, and career-related internships or fieldwork available. Aid available to part-time students. Financial aid application deadline: 3/15. • Application contact: Neil F. Hadley, Dean, Graduate School, 910-962-4117.

University of North Dakota, College of Education and Human Development, Program in Elementary Education, Grand Forks, ND 58202. Awards M Ed, MS. Accredited by NCATE. Part-time programs available. Faculty: 7 full-time (6 women). Students: 7 full-time (all women), 10 part-time (all women). 4 applicants, 100% accepted. In 1997, 9 degrees awarded. *Degree requirements:* Thesis or alternative. *Entrance requirements:* TOEFL (minimum score 550), minimum GPA of 3.0. Application deadline: 3/1 (priority date; rolling processing). Application fee: $20. *Financial aid:* In 1997–98, 7 students received aid, including 7 assistantships totaling $61,083; fellowships, research assistantships, teaching assistantships, full and partial tuition waivers, Federal Work-Study, institutionally sponsored loans, and career-related internships or fieldwork also available. Financial aid application deadline: 3/15. *Faculty research:* Whole language, multicultural education, child-focused learning, experiential science, cooperative learning. • Dr. Shelby Barrentine, Director, 701-777-3239. Fax: 701-777-4393. E-mail: sbarrent@badlands.nodak.edu.

University of North Dakota, College of Education and Human Development, Teaching and Learning Program, Grand Forks, ND 58202. Offerings include elementary education (Ed D, PhD). Accredited by NCATE. Program faculty: 24 full-time (19 women), 22 part-time (21 women). *Degree requirements:* Dissertation. *Entrance requirements:* TOEFL (minimum score 550), minimum GPA of 3.5. Application deadline: 3/1 (priority date; rolling processing). Application fee: $20. • Dr. Mary Harris, Director, 701-777-2674. Fax: 701-777-4393. E-mail: mary_harris@mail.und.nodak.edu.

University of Northern Colorado, College of Education, School for the Study of Teaching and Teacher Education, Program in Elementary Education, Greeley, CO 80639. Awards MA, Ed D. Accredited by NCATE. Part-time programs available. Faculty: 9 full-time (5 women). Students: 65 full-time (52 women), 12 part-time (11 women); includes 5 minority (2 Asian Americans, 3 Hispanics), 5 international. Average age 33. 32 applicants, 66% accepted. In 1997, 29 master's, 2 doctorates awarded. *Degree requirements:* For master's, thesis or alternative, comprehensive exams; for doctorate, dissertation, comprehensive exams. *Entrance requirements:* GRE General Test. Application deadline: rolling. Application fee: $35. *Expenses:* Tuition $2327 per year full-time, $129 per credit hour part-time for state residents; $9578 per year full-time, $532 per credit hour part-time for nonresidents. Fees $752 per year full-time, $184 per semester (minimum) part-time. *Financial aid:* In 1997–98, 34 students received aid, including 4 fellowships totaling $3,500, 1 graduate assistantship totaling $6,000; teaching assistantships also available. Financial aid application deadline: 3/1. • Dr. Debbie Powell, Coordinator, 970-351-1345.

University of North Florida, College of Education, Department of Elementary and Secondary Education, Program in Elementary Education, Jacksonville, FL 32224-2645. Awards M Ed. Accredited by NCATE. Faculty: 23 full-time (13 women). Students: 23 full-time (21 women), 123 part-time (117 women); includes 19 minority (15 African Americans, 2 Asian Americans, 2 Hispanics). Average age 37. 1 applicant, 100% accepted. In 1997, 101 degrees awarded. *Entrance requirements:* GRE General Test (minimum combined score of 1000), minimum GPA of 3.0. Application deadline: rolling. Application fee: $20. *Tuition:* $3388 per year full-time, $141 per credit hour part-time for state residents; $11,634 per year full-time, $485 per credit hour part-time for nonresidents. • Dr. Dennis Holt, Chairperson, Department of Elementary and Secondary Education, 904-646-2610.

University of North Texas, College of Education, Department of Teacher Education and Administration, Program in Elementary Education, Denton, TX 76203-6737. Awards M Ed, MS. Accredited by NCATE. *Entrance requirements:* GRE General Test (minimum score 350 on each section, 800 combined). Application deadline: 7/17. Application fee: $25 ($50 for international students). *Tuition:* $2063 per year full-time, $815 per year part-time for state residents; $5897 per year full-time, $2100 per year part-time for nonresidents. *Financial aid:* Fellowships, research assistantships, teaching assistantships, Federal Work-Study, institutionally sponsored loans, and career-related internships or fieldwork available. Financial aid application deadline: 4/1. • Application contact: Frances van Tassell, Adviser, 940-565-2920.

University of Oklahoma, College of Education, Department of Instructional Leadership and Academic Curriculum, Program in Instructional Leadership and Academic Curriculum, Norman, OK 73019-0390. Offerings include elementary education (M Ed, PhD). Accredited by NCATE. Program faculty: 19 full-time (12 women), 12 part-time (11 women). *Degree requirements:* For doctorate, variable foreign language requirement, dissertation. *Entrance requirements:* For master's, TOEFL (minimum score 550), 12 hours of course work in education; for doctorate, GRE General Test (minimum combined score of 1000), TOEFL (minimum score 500), master's degree, minimum graduate GPA of 3.0. Application deadline: 6/1 (priority date; rolling processing). Application fee: $25. *Expenses:* Tuition $1920 per year full-time, $80 per credit hour part-time for state residents; $6108 per year full-time, $255 per credit hour part-time for nonresidents. Fees $468 per year full-time, $12 per semester (minimum) part-time. • Dr. Bonnie Konopak, Chair, Department of Instructional Leadership and Academic Curriculum, 405-325-1498.

University of Pennsylvania, Graduate School of Education, Division of Educational Leadership, Program in Elementary Education, Philadelphia, PA 19104. Awards MS Ed. Students: 36 full-time (32 women), 1 (woman) part-time; includes 9 minority (5 African Americans, 3 Asian Americans, 1 Hispanic). In 1997, 42 degrees awarded. *Degree requirements:* Comprehensive exam or portfolio required, foreign language not required. *Average time to degree:* master's–1 year full-time. *Entrance requirements:* GRE General Test, MAT. Application fee: $65. *Expenses:* Tuition $22,716 per year full-time, $2876 per course part-time. Fees $1484 per year full-time, $181 per course part-time. *Financial aid:* Fellowships, Federal Work-Study, institutionally sponsored loans available. Financial aid applicants required to submit FAFSA. • Dr. Kenneth Tobin, Director, 215-898-7370. Application contact: Evelyn Williams, Coordinator, 215-898-5690.

University of Pittsburgh, School of Education, Department of Instruction and Learning, Program in Elementary Education, Pittsburgh, PA 15260. Awards MAT, M Ed. Part-time and evening/weekend programs available. *Degree requirements:* Thesis required, foreign language not required. *Average time to degree:* master's–2 years full-time, 4 years part-time. *Entrance requirements:* GRE General Test, TOEFL (minimum score 650). Application deadline: 2/1. Application fee: $30 ($40 for international students). *Expenses:* Tuition $8018 per year full-time, $329 per credit part-time for state residents; $16,508 per year full-time, $680 per credit part-time for nonresidents. Fees $480 per year full-time, $180 per year part-time. *Financial aid:* Partial tuition waivers, Federal Work-Study, institutionally sponsored loans, and career-related internships or fieldwork available. Aid available to part-time students. Financial aid application deadline: 5/1; applicants required to submit FAFSA. • Application contact: Jackie Harden, Manager, 412-648-7060. Fax: 412-648-1899. E-mail: jackie@sched.fsl.pitt.edu.

University of Puerto Rico, Río Piedras, College of Education, Program in Elementary Education, San Juan, PR 00931. Awards M Ed. *Degree requirements:* Thesis. *Entrance requirements:* PAEG, minimum GPA of 3.0. Application deadline: 2/21. Application fee: $17.

University of Puget Sound, School of Education, Program in Education, Tacoma, WA 98416-0005. Offerings include improvement of instruction (M Ed), with options in elementary education, reading, secondary education. Accredited by NCATE. Program faculty: 12 full-time (9 women), 3 part-time (all women), 12.83 FTE. *Average time to degree:* master's–2 years full-time. *Entrance requirements:* GRE General Test (score in 50th percentile or higher), minimum GPA of 3.0. Application deadline: 2/1. Application fee: $40. *Expenses:* Tuition $19,640 per year full-time, $2480 per course part-time. Fees $155 per year. • Dr. Carol Merz, Dean, School of Education, 253-756-3377.

University of Puget Sound, School of Education, Program in Teaching, Tacoma, WA 98416-0005. Offerings include elementary education (MAT). Accredited by NCATE. Program faculty: 12 full-time (9 women), 3 part-time (all women), 12.83 FTE. *Average time to degree:* master's–2 years full-time. *Entrance requirements:* GRE General Test (score in 50th percentile or higher), minimum GPA of 3.0. Application deadline: 2/1. Application fee: $40. *Expenses:* Tuition $19,640 per year full-time, $2480 per course part-time. Fees $155 per year. • Dr. Carol Merz, Dean, School of Education, 253-756-3377.

University of Rhode Island, College of Human Science and Services, Department of Education, Program in Elementary Education, Kingston, RI 02881. Awards MA. Accredited by NCATE. *Entrance requirements:* MAT or GRE, TOEFL (minimum score 600). Application deadline: 4/15 (priority date; rolling processing; 11/15 for spring admission). Application fee: $35. *Expenses:* Tuition $3446 per year full-time, $191 per credit part-time for state residents; $9850 per year full-time, $547 per credit part-time for nonresidents. Fees $1276 per year full-time, $135 per semester (minimum) part-time.

University of Richmond, Department of Education, Master of Teaching Program, University of Richmond, VA 23173. Offerings include elementary education (MT). MT (learning disabled) being phased out; applicants no longer accepted. Program faculty: 5 full-time (3 women). *Entrance requirements:* GRE General Test, PRAXIS I. Application deadline: 6/1 (priority date; 12/1 for spring admission). Application fee: $30. *Tuition:* $18,695 per year full-time, $320 per credit hour part-time. • Dr. Mavis Brown, Coordinator, Department of Education, 804-289-8429.

University of Scranton, Department of Education, Program in Elementary Education, Scranton, PA 18510-4622. Awards MS. Accredited by NCATE. Part-time and evening/weekend programs available. Students: 6 full-time (4 women), 9 part-time (all women). Average age 30. 5 applicants, 100% accepted. In 1997, 6 degrees awarded. *Degree requirements:* Comprehensive exam required, foreign language and thesis not required. *Entrance requirements:* TOEFL (minimum score 500), minimum GPA of 2.75. Application deadline: rolling. Application fee: $35. *Expenses:* Tuition $465 per credit. Fees $25 per semester. *Financial aid:* Teaching assistantships, teaching fellowships, Federal Work-Study, and career-related internships or fieldwork available. Aid available to part-time students. Financial aid application deadline: 3/1. • Dr. David A. Wiley, Chair, Department of Education, 717-941-4032. Fax: 717-941-7401. E-mail: daw315@uofs.edu.

University of South Alabama, College of Education, Department of Curriculum and Instruction, Mobile, AL 36688-0002. Offerings include elementary education (M Ed). Accredited by NCATE. Department faculty: 13 full-time (6 women). *Degree requirements:* Comprehensive exams required, foreign language and thesis not required. *Entrance requirements:* GRE General Test (minimum combined score of 1000) or MAT (minimum score 37), minimum GPA of 3.0. Application deadline: 9/1 (priority date; rolling processing). Application fee: $25. • Dr. Walter S. Hopkins, Chairman, 334-380-2893.

University of South Alabama, College of Education, Department of Interdepartmental Education, Mobile, AL 36688-0002. Offerings include elementary education (Ed S). Accredited by NCATE. *Application deadline:* 9/1 (priority date; rolling processing). *Application fee:* $25. • George E. Uhlig, Dean, College of Education, 334-460-6205.

University of South Carolina, Graduate School, College of Education, Department of Instruction and Teacher Education, Program in Elementary Education, Columbia, SC 29208. Awards MA, MAT, M Ed, PhD. Accredited by NCATE. Faculty: 7 full-time (4 women), 3 part-time. Students: 78 full-time (69 women), 521 part-time (476 women); includes 110 minority (103 African Americans, 4 Asian Americans, 3 Hispanics), 1 international. Average age 39. In 1997, 70 master's, 3 doctorates awarded. *Degree requirements:* For master's, variable foreign language requirement, thesis (for some programs); for doctorate, 1 foreign language (computer language can substitute), dissertation, comprehensive exam. *Entrance requirements:* For master's, GRE General Test, MAT, teaching certificate (M Ed); for doctorate, GRE General Test or MAT. Application deadline: rolling. Application fee: $35. Electronic applications accepted. *Expenses:* Tuition $3894 per year full-time, $193 per credit hour part-time for state residents; $8114 per year full-time, $404 per credit hour part-time for nonresidents. Fees $125 per year full-time, $37 per semester (minimum) part-time. *Financial aid:* In 1997–98, 2 research assistantships (1 to a first-year student), 6 teaching assistantships (4 to first-year students) were awarded; Federal Work-Study, institutionally sponsored loans also available. *Faculty research:* Children's conception of science, whole language, middle school curriculum. • Dr. David Whitin, Coordinator, 803-777-4265. Application contact: Office of Intercollegiate Teacher Education and Student Affairs, 803-777-6732. Fax: 803-777-3068.

University of South Carolina–Aiken, Program in Elementary Education, 471 University Parkway, Aiken, SC 29801-6309. Awards M Ed. Part-time and evening/weekend programs available. Faculty: 3 part-time (2 women). Students: 3 full-time (all women), 46 part-time (44 women); includes 7 minority (all African Americans). Average age 33. 12 applicants, 100% accepted. In 1997, 15 degrees awarded. *Degree requirements:* Comprehensive exam required, foreign language and thesis not required. *Entrance requirements:* GRE General Test (minimum score 400 on verbal section, 400 on quantitative) or MAT (minimum score 35). Application deadline: 8/1 (priority date; rolling processing). Application fee: $35. Electronic applications accepted. *Expenses:* Tuition $3894 per year full-time, $193 per credit hour part-time for state residents; $8114 per year full-time, $404 per credit hour part-time for nonresidents. Fees $120 per year full-time, $32 per semester (minimum) part-time. *Financial aid:* Federal Work-Study, institutionally sponsored loans available. Aid available to part-time students. Financial aid application deadline: 3/15; applicants required to submit FAFSA. • Dr. Margaret Riedell, Head, 803-648-6851. Fax: 803-641-3698. Application contact: Karen Morris, Graduate Studies Coordinator, 803-641-3489.

University of South Carolina Spartanburg, Graduate Programs, Spartanburg, SC 29303-4999. Offerings include elementary education (M Ed). Postbaccalaureate distance learning degree programs offered. Faculty: 9 full-time (5 women). *Entrance requirements:* GRE General Test (minimum combined score of 800), MAT (minimum score 35), minimum GPA of 2.5. Application deadline: rolling. Application fee: $25. *Expenses:* Tuition $193 per hour for state residents; $404 per hour for nonresidents. Fees $120 per year full-time, $5 per hour part-time. • Dr. Linda Randolph, Director, 864-503-5573. Fax: 864-503-5574.

University of South Dakota, School of Education, Division of Curriculum and Instruction, Program in Elementary Education, Vermillion, SD 57069-2390. Awards MA. Accredited by NCATE. Students: 4 full-time (all women), 9 part-time (8 women). 6 applicants, 33% accepted. In 1997, 28 degrees awarded. *Entrance requirements:* GRE General Test, MAT. Application deadline: rolling. Application fee: $15. *Expenses:* Tuition $1530 per year full-time, $85 per credit hour part-time for state residents; $4518 per year full-time, $251 per credit hour part-time for nonresidents. Fees $792 per year full-time, $44 per credit hour part-time. *Financial* *aid:* Teaching assistantships, Federal Work-Study available. • Dr. Linda Reetz, Chair, Division of Curriculum and Instruction, 605-677-5210.

University of Southern Indiana, Graduate Studies, School of Education and Human Services, Department of Teacher Education, Program in Elementary Education, Evansville, IN 47712-3590. Awards MS. Accredited by NCATE. Part-time and evening/weekend programs available. Faculty: 6 full-time (2 women). Students: 1 (woman) full-time, 46 part-time (41 women); includes 1 minority (African American). Average age 33. 11 applicants, 100% accepted. In 1997, 17 degrees awarded. *Entrance requirements:* GRE General Test, NTE, minimum GPA of 3.0. Application deadline: rolling. Application fee: $25. *Tuition:* $129 per credit hour for state residents; $260 per credit hour for nonresidents. • Dr. Annette Lamb, Head, 812-465-7148.

University of Southern Mississippi, College of Education and Psychology, Department of Curriculum and Instruction, Hattiesburg, MS 39406-5167. Offerings include elementary education (M Ed, Ed D, PhD, Ed S). Department faculty: 11 full-time (7 women), 1 part-time (0 women). *Degree requirements:* For doctorate, 2 foreign languages, dissertation; for Ed S, thesis required, foreign language not required. *Entrance requirements:* For doctorate and Ed S, GRE General Test, minimum GPA of 3.25. Application deadline: 8/9 (priority date; rolling processing). Application fee: $0 ($25 for international students). *Tuition:* $2870 per year full-time, $137 per credit hour part-time for state residents; $5972 per year full-time, $172 per credit hour part-time for nonresidents. • Dr. Carolyn Reeves-Kazelskis, Acting Chair, 601-266-4547. Fax: 601-266-4175.

University of South Florida, College of Education, Department of Childhood/Language Arts/Reading Education, Program in Elementary Education, Tampa, FL 33620-9951. Awards MA, Ed D, PhD, Ed S. Accredited by NCATE. Part-time and evening/weekend programs available. Students: 84 full-time (75 women), 179 part-time (165 women); includes 11 minority (1 African American, 1 Asian American, 8 Hispanics, 1 Native American), 2 international. Average age 34. 63 applicants, 89% accepted. In 1997, 55 master's, 1 doctorate, 2 Ed Ss awarded. *Degree requirements:* For doctorate, dissertation, 2 tools of research in foreign language, statistics, and/or computers. *Entrance requirements:* For master's, GRE General Test (minimum combined score of 1000), minimum GPA of 3.5 in last 60 hours; for doctorate, GRE General Test (minimum combined score of 1000), minimum GPA of 3.0 (undergraduate) or 3.5 (graduate); for Ed S, GRE General Test (minimum combined score of 1000). Application deadline: 6/1 (10/15 for spring admission). Application fee: $20. Electronic applications accepted. *Tuition:* $142 per credit hour for state residents; $486 per credit hour for nonresidents. *Financial aid:* Federal Work-Study, institutionally sponsored loans available. Aid available to part-time students. Financial aid applicants required to submit FAFSA. *Faculty research:* Professional development school, case method instruction. • Application contact: Nancy Anderson, Coordinator, 813-974-1025. Fax: 813-974-0938. E-mail: nanderso@tempest.coedu.usf.edu.

University of Tennessee, Knoxville, College of Education, Program in Education I, Knoxville, TN 37996. Offerings include elementary education (PhD). Accredited by NCATE. *Degree requirements:* 1 foreign language (computer language can substitute), dissertation. *Entrance requirements:* GRE General Test, TOEFL (minimum score 550), minimum GPA of 2.7. Application deadline: 2/1 (priority date; rolling processing). Application fee: $35. Electronic applications accepted. *Tuition:* $3354 per year full-time, $181 per semester hour part-time for state residents; $8410 per year full-time, $462 per semester hour part-time for nonresidents. • Dr. Tom George, Associate Dean, 423-974-0907. Fax: 423-974-8718. E-mail: tgeorge1@utk.edu.

University of Tennessee, Knoxville, College of Education, Program in Education II, Knoxville, TN 37996. Offerings include elementary education (MS, Ed D, Ed S). Accredited by NCATE. *Degree requirements:* For master's and Ed S, thesis optional, foreign language not required; for doctorate, dissertation required, foreign language not required. *Entrance requirements:* For master's, TOEFL (minimum score 550), minimum GPA of 2.7; for doctorate, GRE General Test, TOEFL (minimum score 550), minimum GPA of 2.7; for Ed S, TOEFL (minimum score 550), GRE General Test, minimum GPA of 2.7. Application deadline: 2/1 (priority date; rolling processing). Application fee: $35. Electronic applications accepted. *Tuition:* $3354 per year full-time, $181 per semester hour part-time for state residents; $8410 per year full-time, $462 per semester hour part-time for nonresidents. • Dr. Tom George, Associate Dean, 423-974-0907. Fax: 423-974-8718. E-mail: tgeorge1@utk.edu.

The University of Texas at Brownsville, Graduate Studies, School of Education, Brownsville, TX 78520-4991. Offerings include elementary education (M Ed). School faculty: 18 full-time (10 women). *Degree requirements:* Thesis optional, foreign language not required. *Entrance requirements:* GRE General Test, TOEFL (minimum score 550). Application deadline: 8/1 (priority date; rolling processing; 1/1 for spring admission). Application fee: $15. *Expenses:* Tuition $648 per year full-time, $120 per semester hour part-time for state residents; $4698 per year full-time, $783 per semester hour part-time for nonresidents. Fees $593 per year full-time, $109 per year part-time. • Dr. Sylvia C. Peña, Dean, 956-983-7219. Fax: 956-982-0293. E-mail: scpena@utb1.utb.edu.

The University of Texas at Tyler, School of Education and Psychology, Department of Curriculum and Instruction, Program in Elementary Education, Tyler, TX 75799-0001. Offers biology (M Ed, Certificate), English (M Ed, Certificate), history (M Ed, Certificate), reading (M Ed, Certificate). Part-time programs available. *Degree requirements:* For master's, comprehensive and departmental qualifying exams required, foreign language not required. *Entrance requirements:* For master's, GRE General Test. Application fee: $0 ($50 for international students). *Tuition:* $2144 per year full-time, $337 per semester (minimum) part-time for state residents; $7256 per year full-time, $964 per semester (minimum) part-time for nonresidents. *Financial aid:* Application deadline 7/1. • Application contact: Martha D. Wheat, Director of Admissions and Student Records, 903-566-7201. Fax: 903-566-7068.

The University of Texas of the Permian Basin, Graduate School, School of Education, Program in Elementary Education, Odessa, TX 79762-0001. Awards MA. *Degree requirements:* Thesis required, foreign language not required. *Entrance requirements:* GRE General Test (minimum combined score of 1200). *Expenses:* Tuition $1314 per year full-time, $73 per hour part-time for state residents; $4896 per year full-time, $272 per hour part-time for nonresidents. Fees $383 per year full-time, $111 per semester (minimum) part-time.

The University of Texas–Pan American, College of Education, Department of Curriculum and Instruction: Elementary and Secondary, Edinburg, TX 78539-2999. Offers programs in early childhood education (M Ed), elementary bilingual education (M Ed), elementary education (M Ed), reading (M Ed), secondary education (M Ed). Part-time and evening/weekend programs available. *Degree requirements:* Thesis optional. *Entrance requirements:* GRE General Test. Application deadline: 7/17 (11/16 for spring admission). Application fee: $0. *Tuition:* $2156 per year full-time, $283 per semester (minimum) part-time for state residents; $6788 per year full-time, $862 per semester (minimum) part-time for nonresidents. *Faculty research:* Language minority children, reading education for non-English speakers, alternative teacher certification degree program, English as a second language, bilingual education.

University of the Incarnate Word, School of Graduate Studies, College of Professional Studies, Programs in Education, Program in Elementary Education, San Antonio, TX 78209-6397. Awards MA, M Ed. *Entrance requirements:* GRE, MAT, TOEFL (minimum score 550). Application deadline: 8/15 (priority date; rolling processing; 12/31 for spring admission). Application fee: $20. *Expenses:* Tuition $350 per semester hour. Fees $180 per year full-time, $111 per semester (minimum) part-time. *Faculty research:* Play and play environments, elementary pedagogy. • Application contact: Brian F. Dalton, Dean of Enrollment Services, 210-829-6005. Fax: 210-829-3921.

University of Toledo, College of Education and Allied Professions, Department of Curriculum and Instruction, Toledo, OH 43606-3398. Offerings include elementary education (M Ed). Accredited by NCATE. Department faculty: 27 full-time (9 women). *Application deadline:* 8/1 (priority date; rolling processing). *Application fee:* $30. *Tuition:* $5907 per year full-time, $246 per hour part-time for state residents; $11,835 per year full-time, $493 per hour part-time for nonresidents. • Dr. James R. Gress, Chair, 419-530-2468. Fax: 419-530-7719. E-mail: jgress@uoft02.utoledo.edu.

University of Utah, Graduate School of Education, Department of Educational Studies, Program in Elementary and Secondary Education, Salt Lake City, UT 84112-1107. Awards M Ed. *Entrance requirements:* GRE General Test or MAT, TOEFL (minimum score 540), minimum GPA of 3.0. Application deadline: 7/1. Application fee: $30 ($50 for international students). *Tuition:* $2045 per year full-time, $562 per semester (minimum) part-time for state residents; $6129 per year full-time, $1607 per semester (minimum) part-time for nonresidents. • Application contact: Harvey Kantor, Director of Graduate Studies, 801-581-7158.

The University of West Alabama, College of Education, Department of Elementary and Early Childhood Education, Program in Elementary Education, Livingston, AL 35470. Awards M Ed. Accredited by NCATE. Part-time programs available. *Entrance requirements:* GRE General Test, MAT, minimum GPA of 2.75. Application deadline: 9/10 (priority date; rolling processing; 3/24 for spring admission). Application fee: $15. *Tuition:* $70 per quarter hour.

University of West Florida, College of Education, Division of Teacher Education, Program in Elementary Education, Pensacola, FL 32514-5750. Awards M Ed. Accredited by NCATE. Part-time and evening/weekend programs available. Students: 21 full-time (19 women), 38 part-time (35 women); includes 12 minority (9 African Americans, 1 Asian American, 1 Hispanic, 1 Native American). Average age 36. In 1997, 13 degrees awarded. *Degree requirements:* Thesis or alternative required, foreign language not required. *Entrance requirements:* GRE General Test (minimum combined score of 1000) or minimum GPA of 3.0. Application deadline: 7/1 (rolling processing; 11/1 for spring admission). Application fee: $20. *Tuition:* $131 per credit hour (minimum) for state residents; $436 per credit hour (minimum) for nonresidents. *Financial aid:* Fellowships and career-related internships or fieldwork available. *Faculty research:* Curriculum development, in-service teacher education, teaching methodologies. • Dr. William Evans, Chairperson, Division of Teacher Education, 850-474-2891.

University of Wisconsin–Eau Claire, College of Professional Studies, School of Education, Program in Elementary Education, Eau Claire, WI 54702-4004. Awards MST. Students: 1 (woman) full-time, 10 part-time (7 women). In 1997, 8 degrees awarded. *Degree requirements:* Oral and written comprehensive exams required, thesis optional, foreign language not required. *Application deadline:* 7/1 (rolling processing; 12/1 for spring admission). *Application fee:* $45. *Tuition:* $3651 per year full-time, $611 per semester (minimum) part-time for state residents; $11,295 per year full-time, $1886 per semester (minimum) part-time for nonresidents. *Financial aid:* Federal Work-Study and career-related internships or fieldwork available. Financial aid application deadline: 3/1. • Stephen Kurth, Associate Dean, School of Education, 715-836-3671.

University of Wisconsin–La Crosse, School of Education, Professional Development Program, La Crosse, WI 54601-3742. Offerings include elementary education (MEPD), with options in grades 1 through 6, grades 1 through 9. Accredited by NCATE. MEPD (K–12) new for fall 1998. Program faculty: 27 full-time (15 women), 6 part-time (2 women), 28.69 FTE. *Degree requirements:* Thesis, seminar paper, or comprehensive exam required, foreign language not required. *Entrance requirements:* Minimum GPA of 2.85. Application fee: $45. *Tuition:* $3737 per year full-time, $208 per credit part-time for state residents; $11,921 per year full-time, $633 per credit part-time for nonresidents. • Dr. Ronald S. Rochon, Director, 608-785-8138. E-mail: rochon@mail.uwlax.edu. Application contact: Tim Lewis, Director of Admissions, 608-785-8939. Fax: 608-785-6695. E-mail: admissions@mail.uwlax.edu.

University of Wisconsin–Milwaukee, School of Education, Department of Curriculum and Instruction, Milwaukee, WI 53201-0413. Offerings include elementary education (MS). Offered jointly with University of Wisconsin–Green Bay. Department faculty: 28 full-time (17 women). *Degree requirements:* Thesis or alternative required, foreign language not required. *Application deadline:* 1/1 (priority date; rolling processing; 9/1 for spring admission). *Application fee:* $45 ($75 for international students). *Tuition:* $4996 per year full-time, $1030 per semester (minimum) part-time for state residents; $15,216 per year full-time, $2947 per semester (minimum) part-time for nonresidents. • Linda Post, Chair, 414-229-4884.

University of Wisconsin–Platteville, College of Liberal Arts and Education, School of Education, Platteville, WI 53818-3099. Offerings include elementary education (MSE). Accredited by NCATE. School faculty: 8 part-time (3 women). *Degree requirements:* Thesis or alternative, comprehensive exam required, foreign language not required. *Entrance requirements:* TOEFL (minimum score 500). Application deadline: 7/1 (priority date; rolling processing; 11/1 for spring admission). Application fee: $45. • Dr. Sally Standiford, Director, 608-342-1131. Fax: 608-342-1133. E-mail: standiford@uwplatt.edu.

University of Wisconsin–River Falls, College of Education and Graduate Studies, Department of Teacher Education, Program in Elementary Education, River Falls, WI 54022-5001. Awards MSE. Accredited by NCATE. *Application deadline:* 3/1. *Application fee:* $45. *Financial aid:* Research assistantships, Federal Work-Study, and career-related internships or fieldwork available. Financial aid application deadline: 3/1. • Tim Holleran, Chair, Department of Teacher Education, 715-425-3230. E-mail: tim.k.holleran@uwrf.edu. Application contact: Graduate Admissions, 715-425-3843.

University of Wisconsin–Stevens Point, College of Professional Studies, School of Education, Program in Elementary Education, Stevens Point, WI 54481-3897. Awards MSE. Students: 15 part-time (14 women). In 1997, 4 degrees awarded. *Degree requirements:* Thesis or alternative required, foreign language not required. *Application deadline:* rolling. *Application fee:* $38. *Tuition:* $3702 per year full-time, $664 per semester (minimum) part-time for state residents; $11,346 per year full-time, $1938 per semester (minimum) part-time for nonresidents. *Financial aid:* Application deadline 5/1. • Dr. Leslie McClaine-Ruelle, Head, School of Education, 715-346-2040.

Utah State University, College of Education, Department of Elementary Education, Logan, UT 84322. Awards MA, M Ed, MS. Accredited by NCATE. Part-time programs available. Postbaccalaureate distance learning degree programs offered (no on-campus study). Faculty: 14 full-time (6 women). Students: 45 full-time (37 women), 68 part-time (55 women). Average age 39. 26 applicants, 73% accepted. In 1997, 49 degrees awarded. *Degree requirements:* Thesis (for some programs). *Entrance requirements:* GRE General Test (score in 40th percentile or higher) or MAT, TOEFL (minimum score 550), minimum GPA of 3.0, teaching certificate. Application deadline: 6/15 (priority date; rolling processing; 10/15 for spring admission). Application fee: $40. *Expenses:* Tuition $1448 per year full-time, $624 per year part-time for state residents; $5082 per year full-time, $2192 per year part-time for nonresidents. Fees $421 per year full-time, $165 per year part-time. *Financial aid:* In 1997–98, 6 teaching assistantships were awarded; fellowships, research assistantships, full and partial tuition waivers, institutionally sponsored loans, and career-related internships or fieldwork also available. *Faculty research:* Teacher education, supervision, gifted and talented education, language arts/writing, early childhood education. Total annual research expenditures: $330,000. • Dr. Jay A. Monson, Head, 435-797-0385.

Vanderbilt University, Peabody College, Department of Teaching and Learning, Nashville, TN 37240-1001. Offerings include elementary education (M Ed, Ed D). Accredited by NCATE. *Entrance requirements:* GRE General Test, MAT. Application deadline: 3/1 (priority date; rolling processing). Application fee: $35. • Carolyn Evertson, Chair, 615-322-8100.

Villanova University, Graduate School of Liberal Arts and Sciences, Department of Education and Human Services, Program in Elementary Education, Villanova, PA 19085-1699. Awards MA. Part-time and evening/weekend programs available. Students: 8 part-time (all women). Average age 27. *Degree requirements:* Comprehensive exam required, foreign language and thesis not required. *Entrance requirements:* GRE or MAT, minimum GPA of 3.0. Application deadline: 8/1 (priority date; 12/1 for spring admission). Application fee: $40.

Directory: Elementary Education

Villanova University (continued)

Expenses: Tuition $400 per credit. Fees $60 per year. *Financial aid:* Federal Work-Study and career-related internships or fieldwork available. Financial aid application deadline: 4/1. • Dr. Gerald Flood, Coordinator, 610-519-4620.

Virginia State University, School of Liberal Arts and Education, Department of Education, Program in Elementary Education, 1 Hayden Drive, Petersburg, VA 23806-2096. Awards M Ed, MS. Offerings include). Accredited by NCATE. Faculty: 2 full-time (both women). In 1997, 2 degrees awarded. *Application deadline:* 8/15 (rolling processing). *Application fee:* $25. *Tuition:* $3739 per year full-time, $133 per credit hour part-time for state residents; $9056 per year full-time, $364 per credit hour part-time for nonresidents. *Financial aid:* Application deadline 5/1. • Application contact: Dr. Wayne F. Virag, Dean, Graduate Studies and Continuing Education, 804-524-5985. Fax: 804-524-5104. E-mail: wvirag@vsu.edu.

Wagner College, Department of Education, Program in Elementary Education, Staten Island, NY 10301. Awards MS Ed. Part-time and evening/weekend programs available. Faculty: 5 full-time (4 women), 6 part-time (3 women). Students: 45 full-time (33 women), 58 part-time (49 women); includes 1 minority (Hispanic). 44 applicants, 80% accepted. In 1997, 37 degrees awarded. *Degree requirements:* Thesis optional, foreign language not required. *Entrance requirements:* Minimum GPA of 2.75. Application deadline: 8/1 (priority date; rolling processing; 12/10 for spring admission). Application fee: $50 ($65 for international students). *Tuition:* $580 per credit. *Financial aid:* In 1997–98, 8 teaching assistantships (4 to first-year students) averaging $300 per month and totaling $19,200, 9 alumni fellowships (3 to first-year students) were awarded; partial tuition waivers also available. • Application contact: Admissions Office, 718-390-3411.

Washington State University, College of Education, Department of Teaching and Learning, Pullman, WA 99164-1610. Offerings include elementary education (MA, MAT, M Ed, MIT, Ed D, PhD). Accredited by NCATE. Department faculty: 24 full-time (10 women). *Degree requirements:* For master's, oral exam required, foreign language not required; for doctorate, dissertation, oral exam required, foreign language not required. *Average time to degree:* master's–2 years full-time; doctorate–4 years full-time. *Entrance requirements:* GRE General Test, minimum GPA of 3.0. Application deadline: 3/1 (priority date; rolling processing). Application fee: $35. *Tuition:* $5334 per year full-time, $267 per credit hour part-time for state residents; $13,380 per year full-time, $677 per credit hour part-time for nonresidents. • Dr. Darcy Miller, Chair, 509-335-7296.

Washington University in St. Louis, Graduate School of Arts and Sciences, Department of Education, Program in Elementary Education, St. Louis, MO 63130-4899. Awards MA Ed, AGC. One or more programs accredited by NCATE. *Degree requirements:* Thesis or alternative required, foreign language not required. *Entrance requirements:* GRE General Test or MAT. Application deadline: 1/15 (priority date; rolling processing). Application fee: $35. *Tuition:* $22,200 per year full-time, $925 per credit hour part-time. *Financial aid:* Career-related internships or fieldwork available. Financial aid application deadline: 1/15. • Dr. James Wertsch, Chair, Department of Education, 314-935-6776.

Wayne State College, Division of Education, Program in Curriculum and Instruction, Wayne, NE 68787. Offerings include elementary education (MSE). Accredited by NCATE. *Degree requirements:* Comprehensive exam, research paper required, foreign language not required. *Entrance requirements:* GRE General Test. Application deadline: rolling. Application fee: $10. *Expenses:* Tuition $1788 per year full-time, $75 per credit hour part-time for state residents; $3576 per year full-time, $149 per credit hour part-time for nonresidents. Fees $360 per year full-time, $15 per credit hour part-time. • Dr. Diane Alexander, Head, Division of Education, 402-375-7389.

Wayne State University, College of Education, Division of Teacher Education, Detroit, MI 48202. Offerings include elementary education (MAT, M Ed). Accredited by NCATE. Division faculty: 53. *Entrance requirements:* Minimum GPA of 2.6. Application deadline: 7/1. Application fee: $20 ($30 for international students). *Expenses:* Tuition $163 per credit hour for state residents; $355 per credit hour for nonresidents. Fees $498 per year full-time, $114 per semester (minimum) part-time. • Dr. Sharon Elliott, Assistant Dean, 313-577-0902.

West Chester University of Pennsylvania, School of Education, Department of Childhood Studies and Reading, West Chester, PA 19383. Offers programs in elementary education (M Ed), reading (M Ed). Accredited by NCATE. Faculty: 10 part-time. Students: 10 full-time (9 women), 129 part-time (122 women); includes 2 minority (1 African American, 1 Hispanic). Average age 33. 95 applicants, 77% accepted. In 1997, 61 degrees awarded. *Degree requirements:* Comprehensive exam required, thesis optional, foreign language not required. *Entrance requirements:* GRE or MAT, instructional certificate, minimum GPA of 3.0. Application deadline: 4/15 (priority date; rolling processing; 10/15 for spring admission). Application fee: $25. *Expenses:* Tuition $3468 per year full-time, $193 per credit part-time for state residents; $6236 per year full-time, $346 per credit part-time for nonresidents. Fees $660 per year full-time, $38 per credit part-time. *Financial aid:* In 1997–98, 2 research assistantships were awarded. Aid available to part-time students. Financial aid application deadline: 2/15. • Mary Ann Maggitti, Chair, 610-436-2944. Application contact: Dr. Dave Brown, Graduate Coordinator, 610-436-3225.

Western Carolina University, College of Education and Allied Professions, Department of Elementary and Middle Grades Education, Program in Elementary Education, Cullowhee, NC 28723. Awards MA Ed. Accredited by NCATE. Part-time and evening/weekend programs available. Students: 2 full-time (both women), 26 part-time (25 women). 14 applicants, 64% accepted. In 1997, 7 degrees awarded. *Degree requirements:* Comprehensive exam required, foreign language and thesis not required. *Entrance requirements:* GRE General Test. Application deadline: rolling. Application fee: $35. *Tuition:* $1799 per year full-time, $144 per credit hour (minimum) part-time for state residents; $9069 per year full-time, $1053 per credit hour (minimum) part-time for nonresidents. *Financial aid:* In 1997–98, 3 students received aid, including 3 research assistantships (2 to first-year students) totaling $9,000; fellowships, teaching assistantships, Federal Work-Study, institutionally sponsored loans also available. Financial aid application deadline: 3/15. • Application contact: Kathleen Owen, Assistant to the Dean, 828-227-7398. Fax: 828-227-7480.

Western Connecticut State University, School of Professional Studies, Department of Education and Educational Psychology, Program in Elementary Education, Danbury, CT 06810-6885. Awards MS. Part-time and evening/weekend programs available. Students: 51 part-time (48 women); includes 2 minority (1 African American, 1 Hispanic). In 1997, 16 degrees awarded. *Degree requirements:* Thesis or research project required, foreign language not required. *Entrance requirements:* Minimum GPA of 2.67. Application deadline: 8/1 (priority date; rolling processing). Application fee: $40. *Expenses:* Tuition $4127 per year (minimum) full-time, $178 per credit hour part-time for state residents; $9581 per year (minimum) full-time, $178 per credit hour part-time for nonresidents. Fees $25 per year part-time. *Financial aid:* Federal Work-Study and career-related internships or fieldwork available. Aid available to part-time students. Financial aid application deadline: 5/1. • Dr. Thomas Cordy, Chair, Department of Education and Educational Psychology, 203-837-8520.

Western Illinois University, College of Education and Human Services, Department of Elementary Education and Reading, Program in Elementary Education, Macomb, IL 61455-1390. Awards MS Ed. Accredited by NCATE. Part-time programs available. Faculty: 21 full-time (9 women). Students: 12 full-time (10 women), 221 part-time (208 women); includes 5 minority (2 African Americans, 3 Hispanics), 1 international. Average age 36. 19 applicants, 58% accepted. In 1997, 67 degrees awarded. *Degree requirements:* Thesis or alternative required, foreign language not required. *Application deadline:* rolling. *Application fee:* $0 ($25 for international students). *Expenses:* Tuition $2304 per year full-time, $96 per semester hour part-time for state residents; $6912 per year full-time, $288 per semester hour part-time for nonresidents. Fees $944 per year full-time, $33 per semester hour part-time. *Financial aid:* In 1997–98, 7 students received aid, including 7 research assistantships averaging $610 per month; full tuition waivers also available. Financial aid applicants required to submit FAFSA. *Faculty research:* Assistive technology capsule, expressive art projects, childcare, preschool education, early childhood education. • Dr. Kevin Finson, Graduate Committee Chairperson, 309-298-1961. Application contact: Barbara Baily, Director of Graduate Studies, 309-298-1806. Fax: 309-298-2245. E-mail: barb_baily@ccmail.wiu.edu.

Western Kentucky University, College of Education, Department of Teacher Education, Program in Elementary Education, Bowling Green, KY 42101-3576. Awards MA Ed, Ed S. Accredited by NCATE. Part-time and evening/weekend programs available. Postbaccalaureate distance learning degree programs offered (minimal on-campus study). Faculty: 29 full-time (16 women), 2 part-time (1 woman), 30 FTE. Students: 9 full-time (all women), 273 part-time (260 women); includes 6 minority (5 African Americans, 1 Hispanic). Average age 31. 61 applicants, 72% accepted. In 1997, 107 master's awarded. *Degree requirements:* For Ed S, thesis, oral comprehensive exam required, foreign language not required. *Entrance requirements:* For master's, GRE General Test (minimum combined score of 1150 on three sections; average 1400), minimum GPA of 2.5; for Ed S, GRE General Test (minimum combined score of 1250 on three sections), minimum GPA of 3.5. Application deadline: 8/1 (priority date; rolling processing; 12/1 for spring admission). Application fee: $20. *Tuition:* $2460 per year full-time, $133 per credit hour part-time for state residents; $6700 per year full-time, $369 per credit hour part-time for nonresidents. *Financial aid:* Teaching assistantships, Federal Work-Study, institutionally sponsored loans available. Aid available to part-time students. Financial aid application deadline: 4/1; applicants required to submit FAFSA. • Dr. Vicki Stayton, Head, Department of Teacher Education, 502-745-5414.

Western Maryland College, Department of Education, Program in Elementary and Secondary Education, Westminster, MD 21157-4390. Awards MS. Part-time and evening/weekend programs available. Faculty: 1 full-time (0 women). Students: 186 full-time (164 women), 427 part-time (285 women). In 1997, 122 degrees awarded. *Degree requirements:* Thesis optional, foreign language not required. *Entrance requirements:* GRE General Test, MAT, or NTE. Application deadline: rolling. Application fee: $35. *Expenses:* Tuition $210 per credit hour. Fees $30 per semester. *Financial aid:* Application deadline 3/1. • Dr. Francis M. Fennell, Coordinator, 410-857-2500. Application contact: Jeanette Witt, Coordinator of Graduate Records, 410-857-2513. Fax: 410-857-2515. E-mail: jwitt@wmdc.edu.

Western Michigan University, College of Education, Department of Education and Professional Development, Program in Elementary Education, Kalamazoo, MI 49008. Awards MA. Accredited by NCATE. Students: 2 full-time (both women), 136 part-time (125 women); includes 2 minority (both African Americans), 1 international. 59 applicants, 32% accepted. In 1997, 96 degrees awarded. *Application deadline:* 2/15 (priority date; rolling processing). *Application fee:* $25. *Expenses:* Tuition $154 per credit hour for state residents; $372 per credit hour for nonresidents. Fees $602 per year full-time, $132 per semester part-time. *Financial aid:* Fellowships, research assistantships, teaching assistantships, Federal Work-Study available. Financial aid application deadline: 2/15; applicants required to submit FAFSA. • Application contact: Paula J. Boodt, Coordinator, Graduate Admissions and Recruitment, 616-387-2000. E-mail: paulaboodt@wmich.edu.

Western New Mexico University, School of Education, Silver City, NM 88062-0680. Offerings include elementary education (MAT). School faculty: 16 full-time (9 women). *Application deadline:* rolling. *Application fee:* $10. *Tuition:* $1516 per year full-time, $55 per credit part-time for state residents; $5604 per year full-time, $55 per credit part-time for nonresidents. • Dr. Bonnie Maldonado, Dean, 505-538-6415.

Western Oregon University, School of Education, Department of Elementary Education, Program in Elementary Education, Monmouth, OR 97361. Offers middle school education (MS Ed). Faculty: 5 full-time (4 women), 9 part-time (5 women), 6 FTE. In 1997, 14 degrees awarded. *Degree requirements:* Written exam required, thesis optional, foreign language not required. *Average time to degree:* master's–1 year full-time, 5 years part-time. *Entrance requirements:* California Basic Educational Skills Test, GRE General Test (average 450 on each section) or MAT (30), minimum GPA of 3.0, teaching license. Application deadline: rolling. Application fee: $50. *Financial aid:* Research assistantships, teaching assistantships, full and partial tuition waivers, and career-related internships or fieldwork available. Aid available to part-time students. Financial aid application deadline: 3/1; applicants required to submit FAFSA. • Application contact: Alison Marshall, Director of Admissions, 503-838-8211. Fax: 503-838-8807. E-mail: marshaa@wou.edu.

Western Washington University, Woodring College of Education, Program in Elementary Education, Bellingham, WA 98225-5996. Awards M Ed. Accredited by NCATE. Part-time programs available. Students: 6 full-time (all women), 18 part-time (17 women). 0 applicants. In 1997, 35 degrees awarded. *Degree requirements:* Thesis optional, foreign language not required. *Entrance requirements:* GRE General Test, TOEFL, minimum GPA of 3.0 in last 60 semester hours or last 90 quarter hours. Application deadline: 6/1 (rolling processing; 2/1 for spring admission). Application fee: $35. *Expenses:* Tuition $4200 per year full-time, $140 per credit part-time for state residents; $12,780 per year full-time, $426 per credit part-time for nonresidents. Fees $249 per year full-time, $83 per quarter part-time. *Financial aid:* Teaching assistantships, partial tuition waivers, Federal Work-Study, institutionally sponsored loans, and career-related internships or fieldwork available. Aid available to part-time students. Financial aid application deadline: 3/31. • Dr. Phil Riner, Adviser, 360-650-3416.

Westfield State College, Department of Education, Program in Elementary Education, Westfield, MA 01086. Awards M Ed. *Degree requirements:* Comprehensive exam, practicum required, foreign language and thesis not required. *Entrance requirements:* GRE General Test or MAT, minimum undergraduate GPA of 2.7. Application deadline: rolling. Application fee: $30. *Expenses:* Tuition $145 per credit for state residents; $155 per credit for nonresidents. Fees $90 per semester. *Financial aid:* Application deadline 4/1. • Application contact: Marcia Davio, Graduate Records Clerk, 413-572-8024.

Westminster College, Programs in Education, Program in Elementary Education, South Market Street, New Wilmington, PA 16172-0001. Awards M Ed, Certificate. Part-time and evening/weekend programs available. Students: 7 part-time (4 women). In 1997, 1 master's awarded (100% found work related to degree). *Degree requirements:* For master's, computer language required, foreign language and thesis not required. *Average time to degree:* master's–1.5 years full-time, 2.5 years part-time. *Entrance requirements:* For master's, minimum GPA of 2.75. Application deadline: 8/30 (priority date; rolling processing; 1/15 for spring admission). Application fee: $20. *Expenses:* Tuition $1104 per course. Fees $30 per course. *Financial aid:* Grants and career-related internships or fieldwork available. • Dr. Allen C. Johnston, Coordinator, 724-946-7188.

West Texas A&M University, College of Education and Social Sciences, Division of Education, Program in Elementary Education, Canyon, TX 79016-0001. Awards MA, M Ed. MA being phased out; applicants no longer accepted. Part-time and evening/weekend programs available. Postbaccalaureate distance learning degree programs offered (minimal on-campus study). Students: 1 (woman) full-time, 21 part-time (19 women); includes 6 minority (1 African American, 1 Asian American, 4 Hispanics). Average age 34. 5 applicants, 80% accepted. *Degree requirements:* Thesis (for some programs), comprehensive exam required, foreign language not required. *Entrance requirements:* GRE General Test (combined average 964). Application deadline: rolling. Application fee: $0 ($50 for international students). Electronic applications accepted. *Expenses:* Tuition $46 per semester hour for state residents; $259 per semester hour for nonresidents. Fees $156 per semester (minimum). *Financial aid:* Federal Work-Study, institutionally sponsored loans available. Aid available to part-time students. Financial aid applicants required to submit FAFSA. • Dr. George Mann, Head, Division of Education, 806-651-2602. Fax: 806-651-2601. E-mail: george.mann@wtamu.edu.

West Virginia University, College of Human Resources and Education, Department of Educational Theory and Practice, Program in Elementary Education, Morgantown, WV 26506. Awards MA. Accredited by NCATE. Students enter program as undergraduates. Part-time programs available. Students: 20 full-time (all women), 103 part-time (93 women); includes 3 minority (2 African Americans, 1 Asian American), 2 international. Average age 36. 11 applicants, 100% accepted. In 1997, 33 degrees awarded (100% found work related to degree). *Degree requirements:* Content exams required, thesis optional, foreign language not required. *Average time to degree:* master's–3 years full-time, 8 years part-time. *Entrance requirements:* TOEFL (minimum score 550), minimum GPA of 2.75. Application deadline: rolling. Application fee: $45. *Tuition:* $2820 per year full-time, $149 per credit hour part-time for state residents; $8104 per year full-time, $443 per credit hour part-time for nonresidents. *Financial aid:* In 1997–98, 1 teaching assistantship was awarded; full and partial tuition waivers, Federal Work-Study, institutionally sponsored loans, and career-related internships or fieldwork also available. Financial aid application deadline: 2/1; applicants required to submit FAFSA. *Faculty research:* Teacher education, school reform, teacher and student attitudes, curriculum development, education technology. • Dr. Jerrald Shive, Chair, Department of Educational Theory and Practice, 304-293-3441. Fax: 304-293-3802.

Wheelock College, Graduate School, Program in Teaching: Early Childhood and Elementary Education, Boston, MA 02215. Awards MS. Accredited by NCATE. Evening/weekend programs available. Postbaccalaureate distance learning degree programs offered (minimal on-campus study). Students: 57 full-time (51 women), 42 part-time (38 women). *Application deadline:* rolling. *Application fee:* $35 ($40 for international students). Electronic applications accepted. *Tuition:* $525 per credit. *Financial aid:* Grants, Federal Work-Study, institutionally sponsored loans, and career-related internships or fieldwork available. Aid available to part-time students. Financial aid application deadline: 4/1; applicants required to submit FAFSA. • *Faculty research:* Academic achievement for students of color, mentoring, teacher development. • Cheryl Render-Brown, Coordinator, 617-734-5200 Ext. 125. E-mail: cbrown@wheelock.edu. Application contact: Martha Sheehan, Director of Graduate Admissions, 617-734-5200 Ext. 212. Fax: 617-232-7127. E-mail: msheehan@wheelock.edu.

Wheelock College, Graduate School, Program in Urban Teaching, Boston, MA 02215. Offers elementary education (MS). Offered during summer only. Students: 25 (20 women); includes 1 international. *Entrance requirements:* Interview. Application deadline: rolling. Application fee: $35 ($40 for international students). Electronic applications accepted. *Tuition:* $525 per credit. *Financial aid:* In 1997–98, 25 grants (all to first-year students) totaling $118,000 were awarded. Financial aid application deadline: 4/1. *Faculty research:* Mentor relationship. • Dr. Shirley Malone-Fenner, Coordinator, 617-734-5200 Ext. 248. E-mail: sfenner@wheelock.edu. Application contact: Martha Sheehan, Director of Graduate Admissions, 617-734-5200 Ext. 212. Fax: 617-232-7127. E-mail: msheehan@wheelock.edu.

Whittier College, Department of Education, Program in Elementary Education, Whittier, CA 90608-0634. Awards MA Ed. Part-time and evening/weekend programs available. Faculty: 2 full-time (both women), 4 part-time (all women), 2.5 FTE. Students: 32 part-time (29 women); includes 12 minority (2 African Americans, 2 Asian Americans, 8 Hispanics). Average age 24. 41 applicants, 78% accepted. In 1997, 28 degrees awarded (100% found work related to degree). *Degree requirements:* Thesis required, foreign language not required. *Entrance requirements:* GRE General Test, MAT. Application deadline: rolling. Application fee: $60. *Tuition:* $330 per credit. *Financial aid:* In 1997–98, 13 fellowships were awarded; career-related internships or fieldwork also available. • Application contact: Catherine George, Credential Analyst, 562-907-4200 Ext. 4443.

Wilkes University, Department of Education, Wilkes-Barre, PA 18766-0002. Offerings include elementary education (MS Ed). Department faculty: 6 full-time, 14 part-time. *Application deadline:* rolling. *Application fee:* $30. *Expenses:* Tuition $12,552 per year full-time, $523 per credit hour part-time. Fees $240 per year full-time, $10 per credit hour part-time. • Dr. Douglas Lynch, Chair, 717-408-4680.

William Carey College, Department of Education, Concentration in Elementary Education, Hattiesburg, MS 39401-5499. Awards M Ed. *Entrance requirements:* NTE, minimum GPA of 2.5. Application deadline: 8/15 (priority date; rolling processing). Application fee: $0. *Tuition:* $130 per semester hour. • Dr. William Hetrick, Dean, College of Education and Psychology, Graduate Division, 601-582-6217.

William Paterson University of New Jersey, College of Education, Department of Curriculum and Instruction, Program in Elementary Education, Wayne, NJ 07470-8420. Awards MAT, M Ed. Accredited by NCATE. Students: 5 full-time (all women), 163 part-time (152 women); includes 5 minority (1 African American, 1 Asian American, 3 Hispanics). Average age 34. 80 applicants, 60% accepted. In 1997, 39 degrees awarded. *Degree requirements:* Comprehensive exam, research design required, foreign language and thesis not required. *Entrance requirements:* GRE General Test (minimum combined score of 850), MAT (minimum score 42), minimum GPA of 2.75, teaching certificate. Application deadline: 4/1 (rolling processing; 10/15 for spring admission). Application fee: $35. *Expenses:* Tuition $230 per credit for state residents; $327 per credit for nonresidents. Fees $3.25 per credit. *Financial aid:* 17 students received aid; graduate assistantships and career-related internships or fieldwork available. Aid available to part-time students. Financial aid application deadline: 4/1; applicants required to submit FAFSA. • Dr. Rochelle Kaplan, Coordinator, 973-720-2598. Application contact: Office of Graduate Studies, 973-720-2237. Fax: 973-720-2035.

Wilmington College, Division of Education, New Castle, DE 19720-6491. Offerings include elementary special education (M Ed), elementary studies (M Ed). *Application deadline:* rolling. *Application fee:* $25. *Expenses:* Tuition $4410 per year full-time, $735 per course part-time. Fees $50 per year. • Dr. Barbara Raetsch, Chair, 302-328-9401. Application contact: Michael Lee, Director of Admissions and Financial Aid, 302-328-9401 Ext. 102.

Wingate University, Program in Education, Wingate, NC 28174. Offerings include elementary education (MA Ed). Accredited by NCATE. Program faculty: 13 part-time (3 women). *Average time to degree:* master's–2 years part-time. *Application deadline:* 8/15 (priority date; rolling processing). *Application fee:* $0. • Dr. Robert A. Shaw, Dean, 704-233-8078. Fax: 704-233-8192. Application contact: Phyllis Starnes, Secretary, School of Education, 704-233-8075. Fax: 704-233-8285.

Winona State University, Graduate Studies, College of Education, Education Program, Winona, MN 55987-5838. Offerings include elementary education (MS). Accredited by NCATE. *Entrance requirements:* GRE General Test. Application deadline: 8/8 (priority date; rolling processing; 2/17 for spring admission). Application fee: $20. • Dr. Robert Clay, Chairperson, 507-457-5353. E-mail: rclay@vax2.winona.msus.edu.

Winthrop University, College of Education, Program in Curriculum and Instruction, Rock Hill, SC 29733. Offerings include curriculum development (Ed S), with options in elementary education, secondary education, special education. Accredited by NCATE. *Entrance requirements:* NTE, master's degree, 2 years of teaching experience, minimum GPA of 3.0. Application deadline: 7/15 (priority date; rolling processing; 12/1 for spring admission). Application fee: $35. *Tuition:* $3928 per year full-time, $164 per credit hour part-time for state residents; $7060 per year full-time, $294 per credit hour part-time for nonresidents. • Dr. Richard Ingram, Chairman, 803-323-2151. Fax: 803-323-2585. E-mail: ingramr@winthrop.edu. Application contact: Sharon Johnson, Director of Graduate Studies, 803-323-2204. Fax: 803-323-2292. E-mail: johnsons@winthrop.edu.

Winthrop University, College of Education, Program in Elementary Education, Rock Hill, SC 29733. Awards M Ed. Accredited by NCATE. Part-time programs available. Students: 1 (woman) full-time, 17 part-time (16 women); includes 4 minority (3 African Americans, 1 Native American). Average age 33. In 1997, 4 degrees awarded. *Entrance requirements:* NTE, minimum GPA of 3.0, teaching certificate in elementary or early childhood education. Application deadline: 7/15 (priority date; rolling processing; 12/1 for spring admission). Application fee: $35. *Tuition:* $3928 per year full-time, $164 per credit hour part-time for state residents; $7060 per year full-time, $294 per credit hour part-time for nonresidents. *Financial aid:* Graduate assistantships, graduate scholarships, Federal Work-Study, and career-related internships or fieldwork available. Aid available to part-time students. Financial aid application deadline: 2/1; applicants required to submit FAFSA. • Dr. Richard Ingram, Chairman, 803-323-2151. Fax: 803-323-2585. E-mail: ingramr@winthrop.edu. Application contact: Sharon Johnson, Director of Graduate Studies, 803-323-2204. Fax: 803-323-2292. E-mail: johnsons@winthrop.edu.

Worcester State College, Graduate Studies, Department of Education, Program in Elementary Education, Worcester, MA 01602-2597. Awards M Ed. Part-time and evening/weekend programs available. Students: 1 (woman) full-time, 52 part-time (49 women); includes 2 minority (1 African American, 1 Hispanic). Average age 37. 5 applicants, 60% accepted. In 1997, 22 degrees awarded. *Degree requirements:* Comprehensive exam. *Entrance requirements:* GRE General Test or MAT, elementary teaching certificate. Application deadline: rolling. Application fee: $10 ($40 for international students). *Tuition:* $127 per credit hour. *Financial aid:* Career-related internships or fieldwork available. *Faculty research:* Contemporary elementary education, social studies in the elementary school. • Dr. Nancy Harris, Coordinator, 508-929-8850. Application contact: Andrea Wetmore, Graduate Admissions Counselor, 508-929-8120. E-mail: awetmore@worc.mass.edu.

Wright State University, College of Education and Human Services, Department of Teacher Education, Programs in Classroom Teacher Education, Dayton, OH 45435. Awards MA, M Ed. Accredited by NCATE. Students: 57 full-time (38 women), 39 part-time (36 women); includes 12 minority (9 African Americans, 2 Hispanics, 1 Native American). Average age 34. 38 applicants, 79% accepted. In 1997, 34 degrees awarded. *Degree requirements:* Thesis required (for some programs), foreign language not required. *Entrance requirements:* GRE General Test, MAT, TOEFL (minimum score 550). Application fee: $25. *Tuition:* $5109 per year full-time, $161 per credit hour part-time for state residents; $9039 per year full-time, $282 per credit hour part-time for nonresidents. *Financial aid:* Available to part-time students. Financial aid applicants required to submit FAFSA. • Dr. Donna Cole, Coordinator, 937-775-3273. Fax: 937-775-3301. Application contact: Gerald C. Malicki, Assistant Dean and Director of Graduate Admissions and Records, 937-775-2976. Fax: 937-775-2357. E-mail: wsugrad@wright.edu.

Xavier University, College of Social Sciences, Department of Education, Program in Elementary Education, Cincinnati, OH 45207-2111. Awards M Ed. Faculty: 4 full-time (all women), 3 part-time (all women), 4.75 FTE. Students: 30 full-time (24 women), 32 part-time (28 women); includes 8 minority (7 African Americans, 1 Hispanic). Average age 33. 30 applicants, 60% accepted. In 1997, 18 degrees awarded. *Degree requirements:* Comprehensive exam, research project required, foreign language and thesis not required. *Entrance requirements:* GRE or MAT (minimum score 35), minimum GPA of 2.8. Application deadline: 8/15 (priority date; rolling processing). Application fee: $25. *Financial aid:* In 1997–98, 29 students received aid, including 29 scholarships (8 to first-year students). Aid available to part-time students. *Faculty research:* Reading/language arts, multicultural elementary education, special needs/inclusion. • Mary Lisa Vertuca, Director, 513-745-2981. Fax: 513-745-1052. E-mail: vertuca@admin.xu.edu. Application contact: Sheila Speth, Director of Graduate Services, 513-745-3360. Fax: 513-745-1048. E-mail: xugrad@admin.xu.edu.

Youngstown State University, College of Education, Department of Teacher Education, Program in Early and Middle Childhood Education, Youngstown, OH 44555-0002. Offerings include teaching—elementary education (MS Ed). Accredited by NCATE. Program faculty: 9 full-time (6 women), 8 part-time (all women). *Degree requirements:* Comprehensive exam required, foreign language and thesis not required. *Entrance requirements:* TOEFL (minimum score 550), GRE, MAT, or teaching certificate; minimum GPA of 2.5. Application deadline: 8/15 (priority date; rolling processing; 2/15 for spring admission). Application fee: $30 ($75 for international students). *Expenses:* Tuition $90 per credit hour for state residents; $144 per credit hour (minimum) for nonresidents. Fees $528 per year full-time, $244 per year (minimum) part-time. • Application contact: Dr. Peter J. Kasvinsky, Dean of Graduate Studies, 330-742-3091. Fax: 330-742-1580. E-mail: amgrad03@ysub.ysu.edu.

Higher Education

Appalachian State University, College of Education, Department of Leadership and Educational Studies, Program in Higher Education, Boone, NC 28608. Awards MA, Ed S. Accredited by NCATE. Faculty: 12 full-time, 3 part-time. Students: 27 full-time (15 women), 40 part-time (24 women); includes 6 minority (all African Americans). In 1997, 28 master's awarded. *Degree requirements:* For master's, thesis or alternative, comprehensive exams required, foreign language not required; for Ed S, comprehensive exams required, thesis optional, foreign language not required. *Entrance requirements:* GRE General Test. Application deadline: 7/31 (priority date). Application fee: $35. *Tuition:* $1811 per year full-time, $354 per semester (minimum) part-time for state residents; $9081 per year full-time, $2171 per semester (minimum) part-time for nonresidents. *Financial aid:* Fellowships, research assistantships, teaching assistantships available. • Chairman, Department of Leadership and Educational Studies, 704-262-6041.

Arizona State University, College of Education, Division of Educational Leadership and Policy Studies, Academic Program of Higher and Post-Secondary Education, Tempe, AZ 85287. Awards M Ed, Ed D. *Degree requirements:* For doctorate, dissertation required, foreign language not required. *Entrance requirements:* GRE General Test or MAT. Application fee: $45. *Expenses:* Tuition $2088 per year full-time, $110 per hour part-time for state residents; $9040 per year full-time, $377 per hour part-time for nonresidents. Fees $72 per year full-time, $18 per semester (minimum) part-time. *Faculty research:* Student access and retention, student financial assistance, marketing/institutional advancement in higher education, Hispanic studies, legal aspects of higher education. • Dr. Howard Simmons, Coordinator, 602-965-6248. E-mail: hlsimmons@asu.edu.

Auburn University, College of Education, Department of Curriculum and Teaching, Auburn University, AL 36849-0001. Offerings include postsecondary education (PhD). Accredited by NCATE. Department faculty: 20 full-time (11 women). *Degree requirements:* Dissertation required, foreign language not required. *Entrance requirements:* GRE General Test (minimum score 450 on each section, 1000 combined). Application deadline: 9/1 (rolling processing; 3/1 for spring admission). Application fee: $25 ($50 for international students). *Expenses:* Tuition $2760 per year full-time, $76 per credit hour part-time for state residents; $8280 per year full-time, $228 per credit hour part-time for nonresidents. Fees $30 per year full-time, $160 per

Directory: Higher Education

Auburn University (continued)

quarter part-time for state residents; $30 per year full-time, $480 per quarter part-time for nonresidents. • Dr. Andrew M. Weaver, Head, 334-844-4434. E-mail: weaveam@mail.auburn.edu. Application contact: Dr. John F. Pritchett, Dean of the Graduate School, 334-844-4700.

Auburn University, College of Education, Department of Educational Foundations, Leadership, and Technology, Auburn University, AL 36849-0001. Offerings include higher education administration (M Ed, MS, Ed D, Ed S). Department faculty: 18 full-time (9 women). *Degree requirements:* For master's, thesis (MS) required, foreign language not required; for Ed S, field project required, foreign language and thesis not required. *Entrance requirements:* For master's and Ed S, GRE General Test. Application deadline: 9/1 (rolling processing; 3/1 for spring admission). Application fee: $25 ($50 for international students). *Expenses:* Tuition $2760 per year full-time, $76 per credit hour part-time for state residents; $8280 per year full-time, $228 per credit hour part-time for nonresidents. Fees $30 per year full-time, $160 per quarter part-time for state residents; $30 per year full-time, $480 per quarter part-time for nonresidents. • Dr. James S. Kaminsky, Head, 334-844-4460. Application contact: Dr. John F. Pritchett, Dean of the Graduate School, 334-844-4700.

Azusa Pacific University, School of Education and Behavioral Studies, Department of College Student Affairs and Leadership Studies, Program in College Student Affairs and Leadership Studies, Azusa, CA 91702-7000. Offers college student affairs (M Ed), social science leadership studies (MA). Part-time and evening/weekend programs available. Faculty: 3 full-time (1 woman), 5 part-time (1 woman). Students: 84. In 1997, 15 degrees awarded. *Degree requirements:* Exam required, foreign language and thesis not required. *Entrance requirements:* 12 units of previous course work in social science, minimum GPA of 3.0. Application fee: $45 ($65 for international students). *Expenses:* Tuition $350 per unit. Fees $57 per year. • Application contact: Grace Barnes, Coordinator, 626-815-3848. Fax: 626-815-3868.

Barry University, School of Education, Program in Higher Education Administration, Miami Shores, FL 33161-6695. Awards MS. Part-time and evening/weekend programs available. Students: 6 full-time (5 women), 16 part-time (12 women); includes 8 minority (3 African Americans, 5 Hispanics), 1 international. Average age 39. In 1997, 8 degrees awarded. *Degree requirements:* Written comprehensive exam required, foreign language and thesis not required. *Entrance requirements:* GRE General Test or MAT, minimum GPA of 3.0. Application deadline: 5/1 (priority date; rolling processing). Application fee: $30. Electronic applications accepted. *Tuition:* $450 per credit (minimum). *Financial aid:* Partial tuition waivers and career-related internships or fieldwork available. Aid available to part-time students. Financial aid application deadline: 5/1; applicants required to submit FAFSA. • Dr. George Wanko, Director, 305-899-3085. Fax: 305-899-3959. E-mail: wanko@jeanne.barry.edu. Application contact: Angela Scott, Enrollment Services, Assistant Dean, 305-899-3112. Fax: 305-899-3149. E-mail: ascott@jeanne.barry.edu.

Barry University, School of Education, Program in Leadership and Education, Miami Shores, FL 33161-6695. Offerings include higher education administration (PhD). Program faculty: 1 full-time (0 women), 2 part-time (1 woman), 2 FTE. *Degree requirements:* Dissertation. *Entrance requirements:* GRE General Test, minimum GPA of 3.25. Application deadline: 5/1 (priority date; rolling processing). Application fee: $30. Electronic applications accepted. *Tuition:* $450 per credit (minimum). • Dr. Jack Dezek, Chair, 305-899-3700. Fax: 305-899-3630. E-mail: dezek@aquinas.barry.edu. Application contact: Angela Scott, Enrollment Services, Assistant Dean, 305-899-3112. Fax: 305-899-3149. E-mail: ascott@jeanne.barry.edu.

Baruch College of the City University of New York, School of Public Affairs, Program in Higher Education Administration, 17 Lexington Avenue, New York, NY 10010-5585. Awards MS Ed. Part-time programs available. Faculty: 1 full-time, 2 part-time. Students: 1 (woman) full-time, 47 part-time (30 women); includes 1 international. Average age 35. 26 applicants, 85% accepted. In 1997, 12 degrees awarded. *Degree requirements:* Internship required, foreign language and thesis not required. *Entrance requirements:* GRE General Test, minimum GPA of 3.0. Application deadline: 7/15 (priority date; rolling processing; 12/15 for spring admission). Application fee: $40. *Expenses:* Tuition $4350 per year full-time, $185 per credit part-time for state residents; $7600 per year full-time, $320 per credit part-time for nonresidents. Fees $53 per year. *Financial aid:* Research assistantships, full tuition waivers, and career-related internships or fieldwork available. Financial aid application deadline: 5/3. • Application contact: Pamela S. Ferner, Director of Admissions, 212-802-5912. Fax: 212-802-5928. E-mail: spa_admissions@baruch.cuny.edu.

Boston College, Graduate School of Education, Department of Educational Administration and Higher Education Administration, Higher Education Administration Specialization, Chestnut Hill, MA 02167-9991. Awards MA, PhD, JD/MA. Accredited by NCATE. Students: 40 full-time (24 women), 58 part-time (36 women); includes 11 minority (7 African Americans, 2 Asian Americans, 2 Hispanics), 6 international. 128 applicants, 57% accepted. In 1997, 38 master's, 6 doctorates awarded. *Degree requirements:* For master's, comprehensive exam required, thesis not required; for doctorate, computer language, dissertation, comprehensive exam. *Entrance requirements:* GRE General Test. Application deadline: 3/15 (11/15 for spring admission). Application fee: $40. *Expenses:* Tuition $626 per semester hour. Fees $80 per year (minimum) full-time, $30 per semester part-time. *Financial aid:* Fellowships, research assistantships, teaching assistantships, administrative assistantships, merit scholarships, partial tuition waivers, Federal Work-Study, and career-related internships or fieldwork available. *Faculty research:* Administration and leadership theory, change process in policy making, organizational analysis, comparative education, higher education in developing countries. • Application contact: Arline Riordan, Graduate Admissions Director, 617-552-4214. Fax: 617-552-0812. E-mail: riordana@bc.edu.

Boston University, School of Education, Department of Administration, Training, and Policy Studies, Program in Policy, Planning, and Administration, Boston, MA 02215. Offerings include higher education administration (Ed M). *Entrance requirements:* GRE or MAT, TOEFL. Application deadline: 2/15 (priority date; rolling processing). Application fee: $50. *Expenses:* Tuition $22,830 per year full-time, $713 per credit part-time. Fees $218 per year full-time, $40 per semester part-time. • Dr. Charles Glenn, Coordinator, 617-353-7108. E-mail: glennsed@bu.edu.

Bowling Green State University, College of Education and Allied Professions, Department of Higher Education and Student Affairs, Program in Higher Education Administration, Bowling Green, OH 43403. Awards PhD. Accredited by NCATE. Part-time programs available. Students: 32 full-time (17 women), 20 part-time (12 women); includes 12 minority (10 African Americans, 1 Hispanic, 1 Native American), 7 international. 24 applicants, 54% accepted. In 1997, 6 degrees awarded. *Degree requirements:* Dissertation, global higher education research required, foreign language not required. *Entrance requirements:* GRE General Test, TOEFL (minimum score 600). Application deadline: 3/31 (rolling processing). Application fee: $30. *Tuition:* $6070 per year full-time, $284 per credit hour part-time for state residents; $11,358 per year full-time, $536 per credit hour part-time for nonresidents. *Financial aid:* In 1997–98, 23 assistantships were awarded; Federal Work-Study, institutionally sponsored loans, and career-related internships or fieldwork also available. Aid available to part-time students. Financial aid application deadline: 2/15; applicants required to submit FAFSA. • Dr. Donald Gehring, Director, 419-372-7305.

Briercrest Biblical Seminary, Program in Leadership and Management, Caronport, SK S0H 0S0, Canada. Offerings include higher education (MA). *Degree requirements:* Thesis optional, foreign language not required. *Application fee:* $25. *Tuition:* $471 per course. • Application contact: Michael Penner, Enrollment Management Officer, 306-756-3200. Fax: 306-756-7366.

Claremont Graduate University, Department of Education, Claremont, CA 91711-6163. Offerings include higher education (MA, PhD). PhD offered jointly with San Diego State University; MA (mathematics education) offered jointly with the Department of Mathematics. Terminal master's awarded for partial completion of doctoral program. Department faculty: 13 full-time (6 women), 13 part-time (10 women). *Degree requirements:* For master's, thesis or alternative; for doctorate, dissertation. *Entrance requirements:* GRE General Test. Application deadline: 2/15 (priority date; rolling processing). Application fee: $40. Electronic applications accepted. *Expenses:* Tuition $20,250 per year full-time, $913 per unit part-time. Fees $130 per year. • David Drew, Chair, 909-621-8075. Application contact: Ethel Rogers, Associate Director, 909-621-8317. Fax: 909-621-8734. E-mail: educ@cgu.edu.

Dallas Baptist University, Dorothy M. Bush College of Education, Higher Education Program, Dallas, TX 75211-9299. Awards M Ed. Part-time and evening/weekend programs available. Faculty: 15 full-time (4 women), 5 part-time (3 women). Students: 3 full-time (2 women), 10 part-time (4 women). Average age 28. 9 applicants, 56% accepted. In 1997, 10 degrees awarded. *Entrance requirements:* GRE General Test, TOEFL (minimum score 550). Application deadline: rolling. Application fee: $25. *Tuition:* $285 per hour. *Financial aid:* In 1997–98, 8 scholarships (4 to first-year students) totaling $24,170 were awarded. *Faculty research:* Enrollment management, portfolio assessment, servant leadership. • Dr. Mike Rosato, Director, 214-333-5200. Fax: 214-333-5551. Application contact: Travis Bundrick, Director of Graduate Programs, 214-333-5243. Fax: 214-333-5579. E-mail: graduate@dbu.edu.

DePaul University, School of Education, Program in Human Services and Counseling, Chicago, IL 60604-2287. Offerings include agencies, family concerns, and higher education (MA, M Ed). Accredited by NCATE. Program faculty: 3 full-time (1 woman). *Degree requirements:* Oral exam or thesis required, foreign language not required. *Entrance requirements:* Interview, minimum GPA of 2.75, work experience. Application deadline: rolling. Application fee: $25. *Expenses:* Tuition $320 per credit hour. Fees $30 per year. • Dr. Barbara Sizemore, Dean, School of Education, 312-325-7000 Ext. 1666. Fax: 312-325-7748. Application contact: Director of Graduate Admissions, 312-325-7000 Ext. 1666. E-mail: mmurphy@wppost.depaul.edu.

Drake University, School of Education, Department of Leadership and Adult Development, Program in Higher Education, Des Moines, IA 50311-4516. Awards MSE, Ed D, Ed S. Faculty: 1 full-time (0 women), 2 part-time (1 woman). Students: 30 part-time (15 women). 21 applicants, 71% accepted. In 1997, 8 master's, 4 doctorates awarded. *Degree requirements:* For master's and Ed S, thesis or alternative; for doctorate, dissertation. *Entrance requirements:* For master's, GRE General Test (minimum combined score of 1000) or MAT (minimum score 36); for doctorate and Ed S, GRE General Test (minimum combined score of 1000) or MAT (minimum score 43). Application deadline: rolling. Application fee: $25. *Tuition:* $16,000 per year full-time, $260 per hour (minimum) part-time. *Financial aid:* Career-related internships or fieldwork available. Aid available to part-time students. • Dr. Thomas Westbrook, Coordinator, 515-271-3078. Application contact: Ann J. Martin, Graduate Coordinator, 515-271-3871. Fax: 515-271-2831. E-mail: ajm@admin.drake.edu.

Eastern Kentucky University, College of Education, Department of Curriculum and Instruction, Program in Secondary and Higher Education, Richmond, KY 40475-3101. Offers agricultural education (MA Ed), allied health sciences education (MA Ed), art education (MA Ed), biological sciences education (MA Ed), business education (MA Ed), chemistry education (MA Ed), earth science education (MA Ed), English education (MA Ed), general science education (MA Ed), geography education (MA Ed), history education (MA Ed), home economics education (MA Ed), industrial education (MA Ed), mathematical sciences education (MA Ed), physical education (MA Ed), physics education (MA Ed), political science education (MA Ed), psychology education (MA Ed), reading (MA Ed), school health education (MA Ed), sociology education (MA Ed). Accredited by NCATE. Part-time programs available. *Entrance requirements:* GRE General Test, minimum GPA of 2.5. Application fee: $0. *Tuition:* $2390 per year full-time, $133 per credit hour part-time for state residents; $6630 per year full-time, $365 per credit hour part-time for nonresidents. *Financial aid:* Research assistantships, teaching assistantships, Federal Work-Study available. Aid available to part-time students. • Dr. Imogene Ramsey, Chair, Department of Curriculum and Instruction, 606-622-2154.

Eastern Washington University, College of Education and Human Development, Department of Education, Program in College Instruction, Cheney, WA 99004-2431. Awards MA, MS. Accredited by NCATE. Faculty: 3 full-time. *Degree requirements:* Comprehensive exam, internship required, thesis not required. *Entrance requirements:* Minimum GPA of 3.0. Application deadline: 4/1 (priority date; rolling processing; 1/15 for spring admission). Application fee: $35. *Tuition:* $4200 per year full-time, $140 per credit part-time for state residents; $12,780 per year full-time, $415 per credit part-time for nonresidents. *Financial aid:* Federal Work-Study, institutionally sponsored loans, and career-related internships or fieldwork available. Financial aid application deadline: 2/1. • Dr. Russell Hubbard, Adviser, 509-359-7021.

Florida State University, College of Education, Department of Educational Leadership, Program in Higher Education, Tallahassee, FL 32306. Offers higher education (MS, Ed D, PhD, Ed S), institutional research (MS, Ed D, PhD, Ed S). Faculty: 3 full-time (2 women), 5 part-time (0 women). Students: 67 full-time (47 women), 40 part-time (20 women); includes 19 minority (12 African Americans, 2 Asian Americans, 4 Hispanics, 1 Native American), 1 international. 112 applicants, 85% accepted. In 1997, 33 master's, 4 doctorates awarded. Terminal master's awarded for partial completion of doctoral program. *Degree requirements:* For master's and Ed S, comprehensive exam required, thesis optional; for doctorate, dissertation, comprehensive exam. *Entrance requirements:* For master's, GRE General Test (minimum combined score of 1000), minimum GPA of 3.0; for doctorate and Ed S, GRE General Test (minimum combined score of 1000), minimum graduate GPA of 3.0. Application deadline: 7/1 (priority date; rolling processing; 11/1 for spring admission). Application fee: $20. *Tuition:* $139 per credit hour for state residents; $482 per credit hour for nonresidents. *Financial aid:* Fellowships, research assistantships, teaching assistantships, and career-related internships or fieldwork available. • Dr. Hollie Thomas, Head, Department of Educational Leadership, 850-644-6777. E-mail: thomas@mail.coe.fsu.edu. Application contact: Admissions Secretary, 850-644-6777. Fax: 850-644-1258.

Geneva College, Department of Education, Beaver Falls, PA 15010-3599. Offers program in higher education (MA). Part-time and evening/weekend programs available. Postbaccalaureate distance learning degree programs offered (minimal on-campus study). Faculty: 11 part-time (2 women). Students: 55 part-time (25 women); includes 1 minority (African American), 1 international. Average age 24. 17 applicants, 100% accepted. In 1997, 17 degrees awarded. *Degree requirements:* Integrative seminar, practicum required, foreign language and thesis not required. *Average time to degree:* master's–3 years part-time. *Entrance requirements:* Minimum GPA of 2.8. Application deadline: 9/15 (priority date; rolling processing). Application fee: $15. *Financial aid:* Career-related internships or fieldwork available. Financial aid applicants required to submit FAFSA. *Faculty research:* Student development and learning theories, college student popular culture use. • Dr. David S. Guthrie, Director, 724-847-5564. E-mail: hed@geneva.edu. Application contact: Debbie Michalik, Administrative Assistant, 724-847-5564. Fax: 724-847-6696. E-mail: hed@geneva.edu.

Announcement: The Master of Arts in higher education program seeks to provide a vision for higher education that is driven by a consideration of foundational issues and shaped by an integrated Christian worldview. The program equips students with the professional skills needed to make an impact in the field. Contextualized learning is a participation requirement with 600 hours of related field work during each student's tenure as a full-time student. The program requires 36 credit hours, taught in weekly evening classes in a modular style, over an 85-week period. Elective classes allow for concentration in either student affairs administration or educational leadership. For detailed information, contact Geneva College, Master of Arts in Higher Education, 3200 College Avenue, Beaver Falls, PA 15010; 724-847-5564 (e-mail: hed@geneva.edu).

The George Washington University, Graduate School of Education and Human Development, Department of Educational Leadership, Program in Higher Education Administration, Washington, DC 20052. Offers higher education (Ed D, Ed S), higher education administration (MA Ed). Accredited by NCATE. Faculty: 3 full-time (1 woman), 3 part-time (1 woman), 4 FTE.

Students: 41 full-time (27 women), 84 part-time (46 women); includes 44 minority (38 African Americans, 2 Asian Americans, 2 Hispanics, 2 Native Americans), 14 international. Average age 40. 66 applicants, 94% accepted. In 1997, 27 master's, 15 doctorates awarded. *Degree requirements:* For master's and Ed S, comprehensive exam required, foreign language and thesis not required; for doctorate, dissertation, comprehensive exam required, foreign language not required. *Entrance requirements:* For master's, GRE General Test or MAT, minimum GPA of 2.75; for doctorate, GRE General Test or MAT, interview, minimum GPA of 3.3; for Ed S, GRE General Test or MAT, minimum GPA of 3.3. Application deadline: 3/1 (priority date; rolling processing; 10/1 for spring admission). Application fee: $50. *Expenses:* Tuition $680 per semester hour. Fees $35 per semester hour. *Financial aid:* Fellowships, research assistantships, partial tuition waivers, Federal Work-Study, and career-related internships or fieldwork available. Financial aid applicants required to submit FAFSA. *Faculty research:* Technology in higher education administration. • Dr. Reynolds Ferrante, Faculty Coordinator, 202-994-2767.

Georgia State University, College of Education, Department of Educational Policy Studies, Program in Higher Education, Atlanta, GA 30303-3083. Awards PhD. Accredited by NCATE. Part-time and evening/weekend programs available. Students: 19 full-time (16 women), 20 part-time (10 women); includes 11 minority (10 African Americans, 1 Asian American), 1 international. Average age 38. 8 applicants, 13% accepted. In 1997, 11 degrees awarded. *Degree requirements:* Dissertation, comprehensive exam. *Entrance requirements:* GRE General Test (minimum score 500 on verbal section, 500 on either quantitative or analytical sections) or MAT (minimum score 53), minimum GPA of 3.3. Application deadline: 4/1 (10/1 for spring admission). Application fee: $25. *Expenses:* Tuition $2673 per year full-time, $99 per semester hour part-time for state residents; $10,692 per year full-time, $396 per semester hour part-time for nonresidents. Fees $228 per year. *Financial aid:* Federal Work-Study, institutionally sponsored loans available. *Faculty research:* Organization leadership faculty, students, governance and history. • Dr. H. Parker Blount, Chair, Department of Educational Policy Studies, 404-651-2582.

Harvard University, Graduate School of Education, Area of Administration, Planning and Social Policy, Cambridge, MA 02138. Offerings include higher education (Ed D). Terminal master's awarded for partial completion of doctoral program. Faculty: 14 full-time (6 women), 21 part-time (8 women), 15.7 FTE. *Degree requirements:* Dissertation required, foreign language not required. *Average time to degree:* master's–1 year full-time, 2 years part-time; doctorate–6.3 years full-time, 7.2 years part-time; other advanced degree–1 year full-time, 4.7 years part-time. *Entrance requirements:* GRE General Test, TOEFL (minimum score 600), TWE (minimum score 5.0). Application deadline: 1/2. Application fee: $60. • Richard Murnane, Chair, 617-496-4813. Application contact: Roland Hence, Director of Admissions, 617-495-3414. Fax: 617-496-3577. E-mail: gseadmissions@harvard.edu.

Illinois State University, College of Education, Department of Curriculum and Instruction, Normal, IL 61790-2200. Offerings include postsecondary education (Ed D). Accredited by NCATE. Department faculty: 28 full-time (11 women), 3 part-time (1 woman), 28.78 FTE. *Degree requirements:* Variable foreign language requirement, dissertation, 2 terms of residency, internship. *Entrance requirements:* GRE General Test. Application deadline: rolling. Application fee: $0. *Expenses:* Tuition $2454 per year full-time, $102 per hour part-time for state residents; $7362 per year full-time, $307 per hour part-time for nonresidents. Fees $1048 per year full-time, $44 per hour part-time. • Dr. John Godbold, Acting Chairperson, 309-438-5425.

Indiana State University, School of Education, Department of Counseling, Terre Haute, IN 47809-1401. Offerings include higher education (MA, MS). Accredited by NCATE. Department faculty: 14 full-time (3 women), 1 (woman) part-time. *Application deadline:* 2/15 (rolling processing). *Application fee:* $20. *Tuition:* $143 per credit hour for state residents; $325 per credit hour for nonresidents. • Dr. William Osmon, Chairperson, 812-237-2868.

Indiana University Bloomington, School of Education, Department of Educational Leadership and Policy Studies, Program in Higher Education and College Student Personnel Administration, Bloomington, IN 47405. Offers college student personnel administration (MS), higher education (Ed D, PhD). Accredited by NCATE. PhD offered through the University Graduate School. Evening/weekend programs available. Students: 49 full-time (29 women), 12 part-time (10 women); includes 12 minority (6 African Americans, 2 Asian Americans, 4 Hispanics), 2 international. In 1997, 30 doctorates awarded. *Degree requirements:* For doctorate, dissertation required, foreign language not required. *Entrance requirements:* For master's, GRE General Test (minimum combined score of 1300 on three sections); for doctorate, GRE General Test (minimum combined score of 1500 on three sections). Application deadline: 6/1. Application fee: $35. *Expenses:* Tuition $153 per credit hour for state residents; $446 per credit hour for nonresidents. Fees $343 per year. *Financial aid:* Fellowships, research assistantships, full tuition waivers, Federal Work-Study, institutionally sponsored loans, and career-related internships or fieldwork available. Aid available to part-time students. • Dr. Michael D. Parsons, Chair, 812-856-8364. Fax: 812-856-8394. Application contact: Dr. Dale P. Scannell, Director of Graduate Studies, 812-856-8540.

Indiana University of Pennsylvania, College of Education, Department of Student Affairs in Higher Education, Indiana, PA 15705-1087. Offers programs in student affairs in higher education (MA), student personnel services (MA). Accredited by NCATE. Part-time programs available. Students: 56 full-time (37 women), 18 part-time (9 women); includes 11 minority (9 African Americans, 1 Hispanic, 1 Native American). Average age 25. 52 applicants, 79% accepted. In 1997, 24 degrees awarded. *Degree requirements:* Thesis optional, foreign language not required. *Entrance requirements:* TOEFL (minimum score 500). Application deadline: 7/1 (priority date; rolling processing; 11/1 for spring admission). Application fee: $30. *Expenses:* Tuition $3468 per year full-time, $193 per credit part-time for state residents; $6236 per year full-time, $346 per credit part-time for nonresidents. Fees $313 per year (minimum) full-time, $84 per year part-time. *Financial aid:* Research assistantships, Federal Work-Study, and career-related internships or fieldwork available. Aid available to part-time students. Financial aid application deadline: 3/15. • Dr. Ronald W. Thomas, Chairperson and Graduate Coordinator, 724-357-1251. E-mail: rwt@grove.iup.edu.

Inter American University of Puerto Rico, Metropolitan Campus, Division of Education, Program in Higher Education, San Juan, PR 00919-1293. Awards MA Ed. *Degree requirements:* Comprehensive exam. *Entrance requirements:* GRE or PAEG, interview. Application deadline: 5/15 (priority date; rolling processing; 11/15 for spring admission). Application fee: $31. Electronic applications accepted. *Expenses:* Tuition $3272 per year full-time, $1740 per year part-time. Fees $328 per year full-time, $176 per year part-time. • Application contact: Jenny Maldonado, Administrative Assistant, 787-250-1912 Ext. 2393. Fax: 787-250-1197.

Inter American University of Puerto Rico, San Germán Campus, Department of Education, Program in Administration of Higher Education Institutions, San Germán, PR 00683-5008. Awards MA. Part-time and evening/weekend programs available. Faculty: 8 full-time (1 woman), 13 part-time (7 women). In 1997, 10 degrees awarded. *Degree requirements:* Comprehensive exam required, foreign language and thesis not required. *Entrance requirements:* Minimum GPA of 3.0, GRE General Test, or PAEG. Application deadline: 4/30 (priority date; rolling processing; 11/15 for spring admission). Application fee: $31. *Expenses:* Tuition $150 per credit. Fees $177 per semester. *Financial aid:* Teaching assistantships available. • Application contact: Mildred Camacho, Admissions Director, 787-892-3090. Fax: 787-892-6350.

Iowa State University of Science and Technology, College of Education, Department of Educational Leadership and Policy Studies, Program in Higher Education, Ames, IA 50011. Awards MS, PhD. *Degree requirements:* For master's, thesis or alternative; for doctorate, dissertation. *Entrance requirements:* For master's, TOEFL; for doctorate, GRE General Test, TOEFL. Application fee: $20 ($30 for international students). *Expenses:* Tuition $3166 per year full-time, $176 per credit part-time for state residents; $9324 per year full-time, $518 per credit part-time for nonresidents. Fees $200 per year. • Dr. John Schuh, Coordinator, 515-294-6393. E-mail: jschuh@iastate.edu.

Kent State University, Graduate School of Education, Department of Teaching, Leadership, and Curriculum Studies, Program in Higher Education Administration and Student Personnel, Kent, OH 44242-0001. Awards MA, M Ed, PhD, Ed S. Accredited by NCATE. Faculty: 3 full-time (0 women). Students: 52 full-time (30 women), 29 part-time (19 women); includes 11 minority (10 African Americans, 1 Hispanic), 1 international. In 1997, 14 master's, 2 doctorates, 2 Ed Ss awarded. *Degree requirements:* For master's, thesis (MA) required, foreign language not required; for doctorate, dissertation required, foreign language not required. *Entrance requirements:* For doctorate, GRE General Test (minimum score 550 on verbal section); for Ed S, MAT or minimum graduate GPA of 3.5. Application deadline: rolling. Application fee: $30. *Tuition:* $4752 per year full-time, $216 per credit hour part-time for state residents; $9213 per year full-time, $419 per credit hour part-time for nonresidents. *Financial aid:* Application deadline 4/1. • Dr. William Konnert, Coordinator, 330-672-2477. Application contact: Deborah Barber, Director, Office of Academic Services, 330-672-2862. Fax: 330-672-3549.

Loyola University Chicago, School of Education, Department of Educational Leadership and Policy Studies, Program in Higher Education, 820 North Michigan Avenue, Chicago, IL 60611-2196. Awards Ed D, PhD. PhD offered through the Graduate School. Part-time programs available. Faculty: 3 full-time (1 woman), 3 part-time (2 women). Students: 4 full-time (3 women), 55 part-time (38 women); includes 9 minority (5 African Americans, 1 Asian American, 3 Hispanics). Average age 40. 12 applicants, 75% accepted. In 1997, 6 degrees awarded (33% entered university research/teaching, 67% found other work related to degree). *Degree requirements:* Comprehensive exam, dissertation defense, oral candidacy exam required, foreign language not required. *Average time to degree:* doctorate–5 years full-time, 7 years part-time. *Entrance requirements:* GMAT, GRE General Test, or MAT, 2 years of higher education work experience, interview. Application deadline: 4/1 (rolling processing; 11/1 for spring admission). Application fee: $35. *Tuition:* $467 per semester hour. *Financial aid:* 4 students received aid; fellowships, research assistantships, Federal Work-Study, and career-related internships or fieldwork available. Financial aid application deadline: 2/1; applicants required to submit FAFSA. *Faculty research:* Church-affiliated higher education, enrollment management, academic programs, program evaluation/quality. • Dr. Terry Williams, Director, 847-853-3354. E-mail: twillia@orion.it.luc.edu. Application contact: Marie Rosin-Dittmar, Admissions Coordinator, 847-853-3323. Fax: 847-853-3375. E-mail: mrosind@wpo.it.luc.edu.

Mankato State University, College of Education, Department of Educational Administration, Program in Educational Leadership, South Rd and Ellis Ave, PO Box 8400, Mankato, MN 56002-8400. Offerings include higher education administration (MS). Program faculty: 6 full-time (2 women). *Degree requirements:* Thesis or alternative, comprehensive exam required, foreign language not required. *Entrance requirements:* Minimum GPA of 3.0 during previous 2 years. Application deadline: 7/10 (priority date; rolling processing; 10/30 for spring admission). Application fee: $20. *Tuition:* $126 per credit (minimum) for state residents; $200 per credit for nonresidents. • Application contact: Joni Roberts, Admissions Coordinator, 507-389-2321. Fax: 507-389-5974. E-mail: grad@mankato.msus.edu.

Morehead State University, College of Education and Behavioral Sciences, Department of Leadership and Secondary Education, Program in Adult and Higher Education, Morehead, KY 40351. Awards MA, Ed S. Accredited by NCATE. Part-time and evening/weekend programs available. Faculty: 2 full-time (0 women), 1 (woman) part-time. Students: 9 full-time (3 women), 39 part-time (28 women); includes 3 minority (2 African Americans, 1 Asian American), 3 international. Average age 25. 16 applicants, 94% accepted. In 1997, 13 master's, 1 Ed S awarded. *Degree requirements:* For master's, oral and/or written comprehensive exams required, foreign language and thesis not required; for Ed S, thesis, oral exam required, foreign language not required. *Entrance requirements:* For master's, GRE General Test (minimum combined score of 1050), minimum GPA of 2.5, 2 years of work experience; for Ed S, GRE General Test (minimum combined score of 1200), interview, master's degree, minimum GPA of 3.5, work experience. Application deadline: 8/1 (priority date; rolling processing; 12/1 for spring admission). Application fee: $0. *Tuition:* $2470 per year full-time, $138 per semester hour part-time for state residents; $6710 per year full-time, $373 per semester hour part-time for nonresidents. *Financial aid:* Research assistantships, teaching assistantships, Federal Work-Study, and career-related internships or fieldwork available. Financial aid application deadline: 4/1; applicants required to submit FAFSA. *Faculty research:* Self-directed learning projects for nontraditional students, evaluation of adult educational programs, adult literacy, evaluation of homeless. • Application contact: Betty Cowsert, Graduate Admissions Officer, 606-783-2039. Fax: 606-783-5061.

New York University, School of Education, Department of Administration, Leadership, and Technology, Program in Higher Education, New York, NY 10012-1019. Offers higher education (Ed D, PhD), student personnel administration in higher education (MA). Part-time and evening/weekend programs available. Faculty: 4 full-time, 10 part-time. Students: 56 full-time, 61 part-time. 93 applicants, 52% accepted. In 1997, 31 master's, 4 doctorates awarded. Terminal master's awarded for partial completion of doctoral program. *Degree requirements:* For master's, thesis required (for some programs), foreign language not required; for doctorate, dissertation. *Entrance requirements:* For master's, TOEFL; for doctorate, GRE General Test, TOEFL, interview. Application deadline: 2/1 (priority date; rolling processing; 12/1 for spring admission). Application fee: $40 ($60 for international students). *Financial aid:* In 1997–98, fellowships averaging $850 per month were awarded; partial tuition waivers, Federal Work-Study, institutionally sponsored loans, and career-related internships or fieldwork also available. Aid available to part-time students. Financial aid application deadline: 3/1; applicants required to submit FAFSA. *Faculty research:* Organizational theory applied to colleges and universities, leadership development, community college leadership and administration. • Joshua Smith, Director, 212-998-5656. Application contact: Office of Graduate Admissions, 212-998-5030. Fax: 212-995-4328.

Northeastern State University, College of Education, Department of Education, Program in College Teaching, Tahlequah, OK 74464-2399. Awards MS. Faculty: 4 part-time (0 women). Students: 75 (43 women); includes 1 international. In 1997, 24 degrees awarded. *Degree requirements:* Thesis or alternative required, foreign language not required. *Entrance requirements:* GRE General Test (minimum combined score of 900) or MAT (minimum score 35), minimum GPA of 2.5. Application deadline: 6/1 (priority date; rolling processing). Application fee: $0. *Expenses:* Tuition $74 per credit hour for state residents; $176 per credit hour for nonresidents. Fees $30 per year. *Financial aid:* Federal Work-Study available. Financial aid application deadline: 3/1. • Dr. Jay Munsell, Head, 918-456-5511 Ext. 3723.

Northwestern University, School of Education and Social Policy, Evanston, IL 60208. Offerings include higher education administration (MS). School faculty: 19 full-time (5 women), 6 part-time (1 woman). *Tuition:* $2424 per course. • Jean Egmon, Assistant Dean, 847-491-3790. Fax: 847-461-2495. E-mail: egmon@nwu.edu. Application contact: Andrew Ager, Office of Student Affairs, 847-491-3790. Fax: 847-467-2495. E-mail: andrew-ager@nwu.edu.

Nova Southeastern University, Fischler Center for the Advancement of Education, Programs in Higher Education, Fort Lauderdale, FL 33314-7721. Offerings in adult education (Ed D); computing and information technology (Ed D); health care education (Ed D); higher education (Ed D); vocational, occupational and technical education (Ed D). Part-time and evening/weekend programs available. Students: 8 full-time (5 women), 631 part-time (382 women). In 1997, 112 degrees awarded. *Degree requirements:* Dissertation, practicum required, foreign language not required. *Entrance requirements:* Master's degree, work experience in field. Application deadline: rolling. Application fee: $50. *Tuition:* $8460 per year. *Financial aid:* Fellowships and career-related internships or fieldwork available. • Dr. Ross E. Moreton, Dean, 954-262-8526. E-mail: moreton@fcae.nova.edu. Application contact: Dr. Delores Smiley, 800-986-3223 Ext. 8527. Fax: 954-262-3903. E-mail: smiley@fcae.nova.edu.

Ohio University, Graduate Studies, College of Education, School of Applied Behavioral Sciences and Educational Leadership, Athens, OH 45701-2979. Offerings include higher education (M Ed, PhD). Accredited by NCATE. Terminal master's awarded for partial completion of doctoral program. School faculty: 12 full-time (3 women), 2 part-time (0 women).

Directory: Higher Education

Ohio University (continued)

Degree requirements: For master's, thesis or alternative required, foreign language not required; for doctorate, dissertation. *Entrance requirements:* For master's, GRE General Test (minimum combined score of 1000) or MAT (minimum score 48); for doctorate, GRE General Test (minimum combined score of 1000), MAT (minimum score 45), minimum GPA of 3.0, work experience. Application deadline: rolling. Application fee: $30. *Tuition:* $5430 per year full-time, $216 per quarter hour part-time for state residents; $10,431 per year full-time, $423 per quarter hour part-time for nonresidents. • Dr. Richard Hazler, Director, 740-593-4440. Application contact: Dr. Patricia Beamish, Graduate Chair, 740-593-4440.

Oklahoma State University, College of Education, Department of Educational Administration and Higher Education, Stillwater, OK 74078. Offers programs in educational administration (MS, Ed S), higher education (MS, Ed D). Faculty: 11 full-time (3 women). Students: 17 full-time (7 women), 144 part-time (79 women); includes 28 minority (17 African Americans, 2 Asian Americans, 3 Hispanics, 6 Native Americans), 3 international. Average age 42. In 1997, 2 master's, 16 doctorates awarded. *Degree requirements:* For master's, thesis or alternative; for doctorate, dissertation. *Entrance requirements:* For master's and doctorate, TOEFL (minimum score 550). Application deadline: 7/1 (priority date). Application fee: $25. *Financial aid:* 1 student received aid; partial tuition waivers, Federal Work-Study, and career-related internships or fieldwork available. Aid available to part-time students. Financial aid application deadline: 3/1. • Dr. Joseph Licata, Head, 405-744-7244.

Pennsylvania State University University Park Campus, College of Education, Department of Education Policy Studies, Program in Higher Education, University Park, PA 16802-1503. Awards M Ed, D Ed, PhD. Accredited by NCATE. Students: 31 full-time (20 women), 39 part-time (20 women). In 1997, 2 master's, 6 doctorates awarded. *Entrance requirements:* GRE General Test or MAT. Application fee: $40. *Expenses:* Tuition $6534 per year full-time, $276 per credit part-time for state residents; $13,460 per year full-time, $561 per credit part-time for nonresidents. Fees $252 per year (minimum) full-time, $43 per semester (minimum) part-time. • Dr. Rober L. Geiger, Professor in Charge, 814-863-2690.

Portland State University, School of Education, Department of Educational Policy, Foundations, and Administrative Studies, Program in Postsecondary Education, Portland, OR 97207-0751. Offers educational leadership/postsecondary adult and continuing education (Ed D). Accredited by NCATE. Part-time and evening/weekend programs available. Faculty: 11 full-time (6 women), 2 part-time (1 woman), 12 FTE. Students: 5 full-time (2 women), 19 part-time (14 women); includes 1 minority (African American), 1 international. Average age 43. 9 applicants, 67% accepted. *Degree requirements:* Dissertation, comprehensive exam required, foreign language not required. *Entrance requirements:* GRE General Test or MAT, TOEFL (minimum score 550). Application deadline: 4/1 (rolling processing; 11/1 for spring admission). Application fee: $50. *Tuition:* $6101 per year full-time, $689 per semester (minimum) part-time for state residents; $10,445 per year full-time, $689 per semester (minimum) part-time for nonresidents. *Financial aid:* Research assistantships, teaching assistantships, Federal Work-Study, institutionally sponsored loans, and career-related internships or fieldwork available. Aid available to part-time students. Financial aid application deadline: 3/1; applicants required to submit FAFSA. *Faculty research:* Adult learning and development, learning communities assessment, college teaching, urban postsecondary education. Total annual research expenditures: $15,000. • Dr. Douglas L. Robertson, Head, 503-725-4753. Fax: 503-725-8475. E-mail: doug@ed.pdx.edu.

Rowan University, College of Education, Department of Educational Leadership, Program in Higher Education Administration, Glassboro, NJ 08028-1701. Awards MA. Accredited by NCATE. Part-time and evening/weekend programs available. Students: 14 (9 women). 4 applicants, 25% accepted. In 1997, 7 degrees awarded. *Degree requirements:* Thesis, comprehensive exams required, foreign language not required. *Entrance requirements:* GRE General Test (minimum combined score of 840), minimum GPA of 2.8, 2 years of teaching experience. Application deadline: 11/1 (priority date; rolling processing; 4/1 for spring admission). Application fee: $50. *Tuition:* $5728 per year full-time, $258 per credit hour part-time for state residents; $8968 per year full-time, $393 per credit hour part-time for nonresidents. *Financial aid:* Career-related internships or fieldwork available. • Dr. Richard Smith, Adviser, 609-256-4500 Ext. 3820.

St. John's University, School of Education and Human Services, Division of Human Services and Counseling, Program in Student Development Practice in Higher Education, Jamaica, NY 11439. Awards MS Ed. Students: 2 full-time (1 woman), 18 part-time (12 women); includes 9 minority (5 African Americans, 4 Hispanics). Average age 33. 9 applicants, 100% accepted. In 1997, 7 degrees awarded. *Entrance requirements:* Interview, minimum GPA of 3.0, 18 credits in behavioral sciences. Application deadline: 6/1 (rolling processing; 10/1 for spring admission). Application fee: $40. *Expenses:* Tuition $525 per credit. Fees $150 per year. *Financial aid:* Administrative assistantships, Federal Work-Study, and career-related internships or fieldwork available. Aid available to part-time students. Financial aid application deadline: 3/1; applicants required to submit FAFSA. *Faculty research:* Counseling techniques, communication skills, American college student, college retention. • Dr. Shirley Griggs, Coordinator, 718-990-1559. Fax: 718-990-1614. Application contact: Shamus J. McGrenra, TOR, Associate Director, Graduate Admissions, 718-990-6107. Fax: 718-990-5736. E-mail: mcgrenrs@stjohns.edu.

Saint Louis University, Institute for Leadership and Public Service, Programs in Education, Department of Leadership and Higher Education, St. Louis, MO 63103-2097. Offers programs in educational administration (MA, Ed D, PhD, Ed S), higher education (MA, Ed D, PhD, Ed S). Accredited by NCATE. *Degree requirements:* For master's, comprehensive oral exam required, foreign language and thesis not required; for doctorate, dissertation, preliminary oral and written exams. *Entrance requirements:* For master's, GRE General Test or MAT; for doctorate and Ed S, GRE General Test. Application deadline: 7/1 (rolling processing; 11/1 for spring admission). Application fee: $40. *Tuition:* $542 per credit hour. *Financial aid:* Application deadline 4/1. *Faculty research:* Urban leadership, executive leadership development ethics, mediation and arbitration, comparative systems in higher education. • Dr. William T. Rebore, Director, 314-977-2510. Application contact: Dr. Marcia Buresch, Assistant Dean of the Graduate School, 314-977-2240. Fax: 314-977-3943.

San Jose State University, College of Education, Program in Administration/Higher Education, San Jose, CA 95192-0001. Awards MA, Certificate. Accredited by NCATE. Faculty: 6 full-time (2 women), 1 part-time (0 women). Students: 28 full-time (17 women), 66 part-time (40 women); includes 34 minority (6 African Americans, 7 Asian Americans, 21 Hispanics). Average age 36. 68 applicants, 84% accepted. In 1997, 24 master's awarded. *Degree requirements:* For master's, thesis or alternative required, foreign language not required. *Application deadline:* 6/1 (rolling processing). *Application fee:* $59. *Expenses:* Tuition $0 for state residents; $246 per unit for nonresidents. Fees $2017 per year full-time, $1351 per year part-time. *Financial aid:* Career-related internships or fieldwork available. • Dr. Marsha Speck, Director, 408-924-3625.

Seton Hall University, College of Education and Human Services, Department of Educational Administration and Supervision, Program in Higher Education Administration, South Orange, NJ 07079-2697. Awards Ed D, Exec Ed D, PhD, Ed S. PhD new for fall 1998. Evening/weekend programs available. Faculty: 6 full-time. *Degree requirements:* For doctorate, dissertation, comprehensive exam, internship required, foreign language not required; for Ed S, internship, research project required, foreign language not required. *Entrance requirements:* For doctorate, GRE or MAT, interview, minimum GPA of 3.5; for Ed S, GRE or MAT, minimum GPA of 3.5. Application deadline: 2/1 (priority date; rolling processing; 10/1 for spring admission). Application fee: $50. *Expenses:* Tuition $500 per credit. Fees $610 per year full-time, $185 per semester part-time. *Financial aid:* Application deadline 2/1. • Dr. Charles Mitchell, Chairman, Department of Educational Administration and Supervision, 973-761-9397. E-mail: mitcheca@shu.edu.

Southern Illinois University at Carbondale, College of Education, Department of Educational Administration and Higher Education, Program in Higher Education, Carbondale, IL 62901-6806. Awards MS Ed. Accredited by NCATE. Part-time programs available. Faculty: 3 full-time (1 woman). Students: 31 full-time (20 women), 7 part-time (4 women); includes 3 minority (2 African Americans, 1 Asian American). Average age 26. 23 applicants, 48% accepted. In 1997, 19 degrees awarded. *Degree requirements:* Thesis or alternative required, foreign language not required. *Entrance requirements:* GRE General Test or MAT, TOEFL (minimum score 550), minimum GPA of 2.7. Application deadline: rolling. Application fee: $20. *Expenses:* Tuition $2964 per year full-time, $99 per semester hour part-time for state residents; $8892 per year full-time, $270 per semester hour part-time for nonresidents. Fees $1034 per year full-time, $298 per semester (minimum) part-time. *Financial aid:* Fellowships, research assistantships, teaching assistantships, administrative assistantships, full tuition waivers, Federal Work-Study, institutionally sponsored loans available. Aid available to part-time students. Financial aid application deadline: 4/1. *Faculty research:* Student affairs administration, international education, community college teaching. • Application contact: Debra Mibb, Admissions Secretary, 618-536-4434. Fax: 618-453-4338. E-mail: dmibb@siu.edu.

Spalding University, School of Education, Programs in Teacher Education and Administration, Louisville, KY 40203-2188. Offerings include 9–12 (MA, MAT). Accredited by NCATE. Faculty: 7 full-time (5 women), 5 part-time (4 women). *Entrance requirements:* GRE General Test, interview, portfolio. Application deadline: 8/15 (priority date; rolling processing). Application fee: $30. *Expenses:* Tuition $350 per credit hour (minimum). Fees $48 per year full-time, $4 per credit hour part-time. • Application contact: Jeanne Anderson, Assistant to the Provost and Director of Graduate Office, 502-585-7105. Fax: 502-585-7158. E-mail: gradoffc@spalding6.win.net.

Stanford University, School of Education, Program in Social Sciences in Educational Practice, Stanford, CA 94305-9991. Offerings include higher education administration (AM, Ed D, PhD). *Degree requirements:* For doctorate, dissertation required, foreign language not required. *Entrance requirements:* GRE General Test. Application deadline: 1/2. Application fee: $65 ($75 for international students). *Expenses:* Tuition $22,110 per year. Fees $156 per year. • Application contact: Graduate Admissions Office, 650-723-4794.

Syracuse University, School of Education, Higher Education Program, Syracuse, NY 13244-0003. Awards MS, Ed D, PhD, CAS. Part-time programs available. Faculty: 3 full-time (0 women). Students: 24 full-time (11 women), 18 part-time (13 women); includes 3 minority (all African Americans), 3 international. 45 applicants, 84% accepted. In 1997, 18 master's, 2 doctorates awarded. *Degree requirements:* For master's, thesis or alternative required, foreign language not required; for doctorate, dissertation; for CAS, thesis required, foreign language not required. *Entrance requirements:* GRE. Application fee: $40. *Tuition:* $13,320 per year full-time, $555 per credit hour part-time. *Financial aid:* Fellowships, research assistantships, teaching assistantships, administrative assistantships, Federal Work-Study, and career-related internships or fieldwork available. Aid available to part-time students. Financial aid application deadline: 3/1. *Faculty research:* Faculty evaluation, teaching portfolios, student culture, college student personnel development, organizational culture. • Dr. John Centra, Chair, 315-443-4763.

Teachers College, Columbia University, Graduate Faculty of Education, Department of Organization and Leadership, Program in College Teaching and Academic Leadership, 525 West 120th Street, New York, NY 10027-6696. Awards Ed D. Part-time and evening/weekend programs available. Faculty: 2 full-time (1 woman), 5 part-time (3 women). Terminal master's awarded for partial completion of doctoral program. *Degree requirements:* For doctorate, dissertation. *Entrance requirements:* For doctorate, master's degree, 2 years of professional experience. Application deadline: 5/15. Application fee: $50. *Expenses:* Tuition $640 per credit. Fees $120 per semester. *Financial aid:* Full and partial tuition waivers, Federal Work-Study, institutionally sponsored loans, and career-related internships or fieldwork available. Aid available to part-time students. Financial aid application deadline: 2/1. *Faculty research:* Scholarship of race, class, and gender in higher education; faculty careers and evaluation; theories of intellectual and moral development; curriculum transformation. • Application contact: Christine Souders, Office of Admissions, 212-678-3710. Fax: 212-678-4171.

Teachers College, Columbia University, Graduate Faculty of Education, Department of Organization and Leadership, Program in Higher Education, 525 West 120th Street, New York, NY 10027-6696. Awards Ed M, MA, Ed D, PhD. Faculty: 2 full-time (both women), 6 part-time (1 woman), 4.6 FTE. Students: 32 full-time (24 women), 97 part-time (71 women); includes 49 minority (38 African Americans, 4 Asian Americans, 7 Hispanics), 5 international. Average age 37. 72 applicants, 57% accepted. In 1997, 15 master's, 8 doctorates awarded. *Degree requirements:* For doctorate, variable foreign language requirement, dissertation. *Entrance requirements:* For doctorate, master's degree, 2 years of professional experience. Application deadline: 5/15. Application fee: $50. *Expenses:* Tuition $640 per credit. Fees $120 per semester. *Financial aid:* Full and partial tuition waivers, Federal Work-Study, institutionally sponsored loans, and career-related internships or fieldwork available. Aid available to part-time students. Financial aid application deadline: 2/1. *Faculty research:* Educational leadership, general management issues, finance and planning, organizational analysis and development, higher education issues. • Application contact: Christine Souders, Office of Admissions, 212-678-3710. Fax: 212-678-4171.

Texas A&M University–Commerce, College of Education, Department of Secondary and Higher Education, Commerce, TX 75429-3011. Offers programs in higher education (MS), including administration, teaching; learning technology and information systems (MA, M Ed, MS), including educational computing, library and information science, media and technology; secondary education (MA, M Ed, MS); supervision of curriculum and instruction: higher education (PhD); training and development (MS); vocational/technical education (MA, M Ed, MS). Faculty: 10 full-time (3 women), 2 part-time (1 woman). Students: 53 full-time (32 women), 129 part-time (71 women); includes 18 minority (14 African Americans, 3 Hispanics, 1 Native American), 4 international. In 1997, 48 master's, 14 doctorates awarded. Terminal master's awarded for partial completion of doctoral program. *Degree requirements:* For master's, thesis (for some programs), comprehensive exam; for doctorate, dissertation, departmental qualifying exam. *Entrance requirements:* GRE General Test. Application deadline: rolling. Application fee: $0 ($25 for international students). *Tuition:* $2382 per year full-time, $343 per semester (minimum) part-time for state residents; $7518 per year full-time, $343 per semester (minimum) part-time for nonresidents. *Financial aid:* Research assistantships, teaching assistantships, Federal Work-Study, institutionally sponsored loans, and career-related internships or fieldwork available. • Dr. Robert Munday, Head, 903-886-5607. Application contact: Pam Hammonds, Graduate Admissions Adviser, 903-886-5167. Fax: 903-886-5165.

Texas A&M University–Kingsville, College of Education, Department of Education, Program in Higher Education Administration, Kingsville, TX 78363. Awards PhD. Offered jointly with Texas A&M University. *Degree requirements:* 1 foreign language, dissertation, comprehensive exam. *Entrance requirements:* GRE General Test (minimum combined score of 1000), MAT (minimum score 50), minimum GPA of 3.25. Application deadline: 6/1 (rolling processing; 11/15 for spring admission). Application fee: $15 ($25 for international students). *Tuition:* $1822 per year full-time, $281 per semester (minimum) part-time for state residents; $6934 per year full-time, $908 per semester (minimum) part-time for nonresidents. *Financial aid:* Application deadline 5/15. • Dr. Travis Polk, Chair, Department of Education, 512-593-3204.

Texas Southern University, College of Education, Department of Administration and Higher Education, Houston, TX 77004-4584. Offers programs in educational administration (M Ed, Ed D), higher education administration (Ed D). Faculty: 12 full-time (4 women), 3 part-time (0 women). Students: 5 full-time (all women), 13 part-time (2 women); includes 19 international. Average age 30. 110 applicants, 55% accepted. In 1997, 4 doctorates awarded (100% found work related to degree). *Degree requirements:* For master's, comprehensive exam; for doctorate, dissertation, comprehensive exam required, foreign language not required. *Entrance requirements:* For master's, GRE General Test, TOEFL, minimum GPA of 2.5; for doctorate,

GRE General Test or MAT, master's degree, minimum B+ average. Application deadline: 7/15 (priority date; rolling processing). Application fee: $35 ($75 for international students). *Financial aid:* Federal Work-Study, institutionally sponsored loans available. Financial aid application deadline: 5/1. • Dr. Lonnie Sadberry, Chairperson, 713-313-7256.

Texas Tech University, Graduate School, College of Education, Division of Educational Psychology and Leadership, Lubbock, TX 79409. Offerings include higher education (M Ed, Ed D). Accredited by NCATE. Division faculty: 28 full-time (13 women), 3 part-time (1 woman), 29.29 FTE. *Degree requirements:* For master's, computer language required, thesis optional, foreign language not required; for doctorate, dissertation required, foreign language not required. *Entrance requirements:* For master's, GRE General Test (combined average 1034); for doctorate, GRE General Test. Application deadline: 4/15 (priority date; rolling processing; 11/1 for spring admission). Application fee: $25 ($50 for international students). Electronic applications accepted. *Expenses:* Tuition $864 per year full-time, $120 per semester (minimum) part-time for state residents; $5976 per year full-time, $747 per semester (minimum) part-time for nonresidents. Fees $2321 per year full-time, $302 per semester (minimum) part-time. • Dr. Loretta J. Bradley, Chair, 806-742-2393.

Université de Sherbrooke, Faculty of Education, Program in Postsecondary Education Training, Sherbrooke, PQ J1K 2R1, Canada. Awards M Ed, Diploma. *Degree requirements:* For master's, thesis. *Application deadline:* 6/1. *Application fee:* $15.

The University of Akron, College of Education, Department of Educational Foundations and Leadership, Program in Higher Education Administration, Akron, OH 44325-0001. Awards MA, MS. Accredited by NCATE. Admissions temporarily suspended. Students: 22 full-time (12 women), 40 part-time (17 women); includes 17 minority (15 African Americans, 1 Asian American, 1 Hispanic). Average age 37. In 1997, 7 degrees awarded. *Application deadline:* 8/15 (rolling processing). *Application fee:* $25 ($50 for international students). *Expenses:* Tuition $178 per credit hour for state residents; $333 per credit hour for nonresidents. Fees $145 per year full-time, $32 per semester (minimum) part-time. *Financial aid:* Fellowships, research assistantships, teaching assistantships, administrative assistantships, and career-related internships or fieldwork available. • Application contact: Dr. Robert Eley, Director of Student Services, 330-972-7750. E-mail: reley@uakron.edu.

The University of Alabama, College of Education, Area of Professional Studies, Program in Higher Education Administration, Tuscaloosa, AL 35487. Awards MA, Ed D, PhD, Ed S. Accredited by NCATE. *Degree requirements:* For doctorate, 1 foreign language, computer language, dissertation. *Entrance requirements:* For master's and doctorate, GRE General Test, MAT (score in 50th percentile or higher), or NTE (minimum score 658 on each core battery test), minimum GPA of 3.0; for Ed S, minimum GPA of 3.0 during previous 2 years. Application deadline: 7/6 (rolling processing). Application fee: $25. *Tuition:* $2684 per year full-time, $594 per semester (minimum) part-time for state residents; $7216 per year full-time, $1248 per semester (minimum) part-time for nonresidents. *Financial aid:* Application deadline 7/14. • Dr. R. Carl Westerfield, Head, Area of Professional Studies, 205-348-8362. Fax: 205-348-0867. E-mail: cwesterf@bamaed.ua.edu.

The University of Arizona, College of Education, Department of Educational Administration and Higher Education, Program in Higher Education, Tucson, AZ 85721. Awards MA, M Ed, Ed D, PhD. Terminal master's awarded for partial completion of doctoral program. *Degree requirements:* For master's, thesis (MA) required, foreign language not required; for doctorate, dissertation required, foreign language not required. *Entrance requirements:* GRE General Test (minimum combined score of 1100) or MAT (minimum score 60), TOEFL (minimum score 550). Application deadline: 4/15 (rolling processing). Application fee: $35. *Tuition:* $2162 per year full-time, $337 per semester (minimum) part-time for state residents; $6860 per year full-time, $1138 per semester (minimum) part-time for nonresidents. *Faculty research:* Technology transfer, higher education policy, finance, curricular change.

University of Arkansas, College of Education, Department of Educational Leadership, Counseling and Foundations, Program in Higher Education, Fayetteville, AR 72701-1201. Awards M Ed, Ed D, Ed S. Accredited by NCATE. Students: 29 full-time (18 women), 13 part-time (6 women); includes 4 minority (2 African Americans, 2 Native Americans), 1 international. 13 applicants, 46% accepted. In 1997, 13 master's, 5 doctorates awarded. *Degree requirements:* For master's, thesis optional, foreign language not required; for doctorate, dissertation. *Application fee:* $25 ($35 for international students). *Tuition:* $3144 per year full-time, $173 per credit hour part-time for state residents; $7140 per year full-time, $395 per credit hour part-time for nonresidents. *Financial aid:* Research assistantships, teaching assistantships, Federal Work-Study, and career-related internships or fieldwork available. Aid available to part-time students. Financial aid application deadline: 4/1; applicants required to submit FAFSA. • Dr. John Murry, Coordinator, 501-575-2207.

University of Arkansas at Little Rock, College of Education, Department of Educational Leadership, Program in Higher Education Administration, Little Rock, AR 72204-1099. Awards Ed D. Students: 16 full-time (11 women), 102 part-time (68 women); includes 18 minority (15 African Americans, 1 Asian American, 2 Hispanics), 4 international. Average age 42. 91 applicants, 84% accepted. In 1997, 13 degrees awarded. *Degree requirements:* Comprehensive exam, oral defense of dissertation, residency required, foreign language not required. *Entrance requirements:* GRE General Test (minimum combined score of 1500 on three sections) or MAT (minimum score 55), interview, minimum graduate GPA of 3.0, teaching certificate, work experience. Application deadline: 8/1 (priority date). Application fee: $25 ($30 for international students). *Expenses:* Tuition $2466 per year full-time, $137 per credit hour part-time for state residents; $5256 per year full-time, $292 per credit hour part-time for nonresidents. Fees $216 per year full-time, $36 per semester (minimum) part-time. *Financial aid:* Research assistantships available. • Dr. David Spillers, Chairperson, Department of Educational Leadership, 501-569-3267.

University of British Columbia, Faculty of Education, Department of Educational Studies, Program in Higher Education, Vancouver, BC V6T 1Z2, Canada. Awards MA, M Ed. Part-time programs available. *Degree requirements:* Thesis (MA), major paper (M Ed) required, foreign language not required. *Entrance requirements:* TOEFL (minimum score 550). Application deadline: 5/31 (priority date). Application fee: $60. *Faculty research:* Comparative and international higher education, postsecondary structures, postsecondary education and training and the economy.

University of Central Oklahoma, College of Education, Department of Occupational and Technical Education, Program in General Education, Edmond, OK 73034-5209. Awards M Ed. Accredited by NCATE. *Entrance requirements:* GRE General Test. Application deadline: 8/18. Application fee: $15. *Tuition:* $76 per credit hour for state residents; $178 per credit hour for nonresidents.

University of Connecticut, School of Education, Field of Professional Higher Education Administration, Storrs, CT 06269. Awards MA, PhD. Accredited by NCATE. Faculty: 7. Students: 7 full-time (5 women), 24 part-time (16 women); includes 3 minority (2 African Americans, 1 Asian American), 1 international. Average age 40. 4 applicants, 0% accepted. In 1997, 14 master's, 7 doctorates awarded. Terminal master's awarded for partial completion of doctoral program. *Degree requirements:* For master's, thesis or alternative; for doctorate, dissertation. *Entrance requirements:* For doctorate, GRE General Test. Application deadline: 6/1 (priority date; rolling processing; 11/1 for spring admission). Application fee: $40 ($45 for international students). *Expenses:* Tuition $5272 per year full-time, $293 per credit part-time for state residents; $13,696 per year full-time, $761 per credit part-time for nonresidents. Fees $948 per year full-time, $640 per year part-time. *Financial aid:* In 1997–98, 1 fellowship totaling $1,910, 11 research assistantships (3 to first-year students) totaling $110,148, 2 teaching assistantships (1 to a first-year student) totaling $16,875 were awarded. Financial aid application deadline: 2/15. • Patrick B. Mullarney, Head, 860-486-6278.

University of Delaware, College of Human Resources, Education and Public Policy, Program in College Counseling and Student Affairs, Newark, DE 19716. Offers college counseling (M Ed), student affairs practice in higher education (M Ed). *Entrance requirements:* GRE. Application fee: $45. *Expenses:* Tuition $4250 per year full-time, $236 per credit hour part-time for state residents; $12,250 per year full-time, $681 per credit hour part-time for nonresidents. Fees $466 per year full-time, $15 per semester (minimum) part-time. • Don Bishop, Director and Assistant Vice President, Student Life, 302-831-8107.

University of Denver, College of Education, Denver, CO 80208. Offerings include higher education and adult studies (MA, PhD). Postbaccalaureate distance learning degree programs offered (no on-campus study). College faculty: 23 full-time (13 women). *Degree requirements:* For master's, comprehensive exam required, foreign language and thesis not required; for doctorate, 2 foreign languages (computer language can substitute for one), dissertation, comprehensive exam. *Entrance requirements:* For master's, GRE General Test (minimum combined score of 870), TOEFL (minimum score 550), TSE (minimum score 230); for doctorate, GRE General Test (minimum combined score of 930), TOEFL (minimum score 550), TSE (minimum score 230). Application deadline: 1/1 (rolling processing). Application fee: $40 ($45 for international students). *Expenses:* Tuition $18,216 per year full-time, $506 per credit hour part-time. Fees $159 per year. • Dr. Elinor Katz, Dean, 303-871-3665. Application contact: Linda McCarthy, 303-871-2509.

University of Florida, College of Education, Department of Educational Leadership, Gainesville, FL 32611. Offerings include higher education (Ed D, PhD, Ed S). Accredited by NCATE. Department faculty: 18. *Degree requirements:* For doctorate, variable foreign language requirement, dissertation. *Entrance requirements:* GRE General Test, minimum GPA of 3.0. Application deadline: 6/5 (priority date; rolling processing). Application fee: $20. *Tuition:* $138 per credit hour for state residents; $481 per credit hour for nonresidents. • Dr. James L. Doud, Chair, 352-392-2391 Ext. 263. E-mail: jldoud@coe.ufl.edu. Application contact: Dr. Walter Smith, Graduate Coordinator, 352-392-2391 Ext. 274. Fax: 352-392-0038. E-mail: wis@coe.ufl.edu.

University of Georgia, College of Education, Program in Higher Education, Athens, GA 30602. Awards Ed D, PhD. Accredited by NCATE. Faculty: 4 full-time (1 woman). Students: 13 full-time, 18 part-time; includes 3 minority (all African Americans). 17 applicants, 35% accepted. In 1997, 4 degrees awarded. *Degree requirements:* Dissertation required, foreign language not required. *Entrance requirements:* GRE General Test. Application deadline: 7/1 (priority date; 11/15 for spring admission). Application fee: $30. Electronic applications accepted. *Tuition:* $3290 per year full-time, $643 per semester (minimum) part-time for state residents; $11,300 per year full-time, $1645 per semester (minimum) part-time for nonresidents. *Financial aid:* Fellowships, research assistantships, teaching assistantships, assistantships available. • Dr. Ronald D. Simpson, Graduate Coordinator, 706-542-0575. Fax: 706-542-7588. E-mail: rsimpson@arches.uga.edu.

University of Houston, College of Education, Department of Educational Leadership and Cultural Studies, 4800 Calhoun, Houston, TX 77204-2163. Offerings include higher education (M Ed). Accredited by NCATE. Department faculty: 15 full-time (9 women), 10 part-time (3 women), 20 FTE. *Degree requirements:* Comprehensive exam or thesis required, foreign language not required. *Average time to degree:* master's–1.5 years full-time, 3 years part-time; doctorate–3 years full-time, 6 years part-time. *Entrance requirements:* GRE General Test (minimum score 460 on verbal section) or MAT (minimum score 43), minimum GPA of 3.0 in last 60 hours. Application deadline: 7/18 (priority date; rolling processing; 12/18 for spring admission). Application fee: $35 ($75 for international students). *Expenses:* Tuition $1152 per year full-time, $120 per semester (minimum) part-time for state residents; $4482 per year full-time, $249 per credit hour part-time for nonresidents. Fees $977 per year full-time, $119 per semester (minimum) part-time. • Richard L. Hooker, Chairperson, 713-743-5035. Application contact: Rose L. Hernandez, Office Assistant, 713-743-5044. Fax: 713-743-4979.

The University of Iowa, College of Education, Division of Foundations, Post-Secondary, and Continuing Education, Program in Higher Education, Iowa City, IA 52242-1316. Awards MA, PhD, Ed S. Faculty: 8 full-time. Students: 24 full-time (11 women), 61 part-time (34 women); includes 9 minority (6 African Americans, 1 Asian American, 2 Hispanics), 8 international. 21 applicants, 67% accepted. In 1997, 17 master's, 13 doctorates, 2 Ed Ss awarded. *Degree requirements:* For master's, exam required, foreign language and thesis not required; for doctorate, computer language, dissertation, comprehensive exams required, foreign language not required; for Ed S, computer language, exam required, foreign language not required. *Entrance requirements:* For master's and Ed S, GRE General Test, minimum GPA of 2.5; for doctorate, GRE General Test, minimum GPA of 3.0. Application deadline: 4/1. Application fee: $30 ($50 for international students). *Expenses:* Tuition $3166 per year full-time, $176 per semester hour part-time for state residents; $10,202 per year full-time, $176 per semester hour part-time for nonresidents. Fees $202 per year full-time, $52 per year (minimum) part-time. *Financial aid:* In 1997–98, 2 fellowships (1 to a first-year student), 11 research assistantships (2 to first-year students), 7 teaching assistantships (2 to first-year students) were awarded; career-related internships or fieldwork also available. Financial aid applicants required to submit FAFSA. • Chet Rzonca, Coordinator, 319-335-5392. Fax: 319-384-0587.

University of Kansas, School of Education, Department of Teaching and Leadership, Program in Higher Education, Lawrence, KS 66045. Awards MS Ed, Ed D, PhD. Accredited by NCATE. Students: 18 full-time (11 women), 23 part-time (13 women); includes 5 minority (4 African Americans, 1 Hispanic), 1 international. *Degree requirements:* For master's, project required, foreign language not required; for doctorate, variable foreign language requirement, dissertation. *Entrance requirements:* For master's, minimum GPA of 3.0; for doctorate, GRE General Test (combined average 1000), minimum graduate GPA of 3.5. Application deadline: 7/1. Application fee: $25. *Expenses:* Tuition $2400 per year full-time, $100 per credit hour part-time for state residents; $7890 per year full-time, $329 per credit hour part-time for nonresidents. Fees $428 per year full-time, $31 per credit hour part-time. *Faculty research:* Leadership, comparative education, faculty issues, diversity in higher education. • Marc Mahlios, Chair, Department of Teaching and Leadership, 785-864-4435.

University of Kentucky, Graduate School Programs from the College of Education, Program in Curriculum and Instruction, Lexington, KY 40506-0032. Offerings include clinical and college teaching (MS Ed U). Accredited by NCATE. Program faculty: 22 full-time (13 women), 3 part-time (1 woman). *Degree requirements:* Comprehensive exam required, thesis optional, foreign language not required. *Entrance requirements:* GRE General Test, minimum undergraduate GPA of 2.5. Application deadline: 7/19 (rolling processing; 12/15 for spring admission). Application fee: $30 ($35 for international students). • Dr. Douglas C. Smith, Director of Graduate Studies, 606-257-1643. Application contact: Dr. Constance L. Wood, Associate Dean, 606-257-4613. Fax: 606-323-1928.

University of Louisville, School of Education, Department of Administration and Higher Education, Program in Higher Education, Louisville, KY 40292-0001. Awards MA, Ed S. Accredited by NCATE. Students: 48 full-time (30 women), 63 part-time (46 women); includes 17 minority (11 African Americans, 3 Asian Americans, 3 Hispanics), 3 international. Average age 40. In 1997, 1 master's awarded. *Degree requirements:* For Ed S, thesis required, foreign language not required. *Entrance requirements:* For Ed S, GRE General Test. Application deadline: rolling. Application fee: $25. • Dr. John L. Strope Jr., Chairman, Department of Administration and Higher Education, 502-852-6428.

University of Maine, College of Education and Human Development, Program in Higher Education, Orono, ME 04469. Awards MAT, M Ed, MS, CAS. Accredited by NCATE. Part-time and evening/weekend programs available. *Degree requirements:* For master's, thesis or alternative. *Entrance requirements:* For master's, TOEFL (minimum score 550); for CAS, MA, M Ed, or MS. Application deadline: 2/1 (priority date; rolling processing; 10/15 for spring admission). Application fee: $50. *Expenses:* Tuition $194 per credit hour for state residents; $548 per credit hour for nonresidents. Fees $378 per year full-time, $33 per semester (minimum)

Directory: Higher Education

University of Maine (continued)

part-time. *Financial aid:* Application deadline 3/1. • Application contact: Scott Delcourt, Director of the Graduate School, 207-581-3218. Fax: 207-581-3232. E-mail: graduate@maine.edu.

University of Mary, Program in Education, 7500 University Drive, Bismarck, ND 58504-9652. Offerings include higher education (MS Ed). Program faculty: 5 full-time (3 women), 6 part-time (4 women). *Average time to degree:* master's–3 years part-time. *Application deadline:* 8/1 (12/1 for spring admission). *Application fee:* $15. *Tuition:* $265 per credit. • Ramona Klein, Director, 701-255-7500. Application contact: Dr. Diane Fladeland, Director, Graduate Programs, 701-255-7500. Fax: 701-255-7687.

University of Massachusetts Amherst, School of Education, Program in Education, Amherst, MA 01003-0001. Offerings include higher education (M Ed, Ed D, CAGS). Accredited by NCATE. *Degree requirements:* For doctorate, dissertation required, foreign language not required. *Entrance requirements:* For master's and doctorate, GRE General Test. Application deadline: 3/1 (rolling processing; 10/1 for spring admission). Application fee: $40. *Expenses:* Tuition $2640 per year full-time, $110 per credit part-time for state residents; $3690 per year (minimum) full-time, $165 per credit (minimum) part-time for nonresidents. Fees $2856 per year full-time, $422 per semester part-time for state residents; $3204 per year full-time, $480 per semester part-time for nonresidents. • John C. Carey, Director, 413-545-0236.

University of Massachusetts Boston, Graduate College of Education, School Organization, Curriculum and Instruction Department, Program in Education, Track in Higher Education Administration, Boston, MA 02125-3393. Awards Ed D. Students: 50 part-time (33 women); includes 15 minority (8 African Americans, 2 Asian Americans, 5 Hispanics). *Degree requirements:* Dissertation, comprehensive exams required, foreign language not required. *Entrance requirements:* GRE General Test or MAT, minimum GPA of 2.75. Application deadline: 3/1. Application fee: $25 ($35 for international students). *Expenses:* Tuition $2640 per year full-time, $110 per credit part-time for state residents; $8930 per year full-time, $373 per credit part-time for nonresidents. Fees $2650 per year full-time, $420 per semester (minimum) part-time for state residents; $2736 per year full-time, $420 per semester (minimum) part-time for nonresidents. *Financial aid:* In 1997–98, 1 research assistantship averaging $225 per month and totaling $2,000 was awarded; teaching assistantships, administrative assistantships also available. Financial aid application deadline: 3/1; applicants required to submit FAFSA. • Dr. Sandra Kanter, Program Coordinator, 617-287-7601. Application contact: Lisa Lavely, Director of Graduate Admissions and Records, 617-287-6400. Fax: 617-287-6236.

The University of Memphis, College of Education, Department of Leadership, Memphis, TN 38152. Offerings include higher education (Ed D). Accredited by NCATE. Department faculty: 9 full-time (2 women), 23 part-time (9 women). *Degree requirements:* Dissertation, comprehensive exam required, foreign language not required. *Entrance requirements:* GRE General Test (minimum combined score of 850), GRE Subject Test, 3 years of teaching experience. Application deadline: 8/1 (12/1 for spring admission). Application fee: $25 ($50 for international students). *Tuition:* $2862 per year full-time, $166 per credit hour part-time for state residents; $6696 per year full-time, $379 per credit hour part-time for nonresidents. • Dr. John Petry, Interim Chair, 901-678-2368.

University of Miami, School of Education, Department of Educational and Psychological Studies, Program in Higher Education, Coral Gables, FL 33124. Offers higher education (MS Ed), higher education/sports administration (Ed D, PhD). Accredited by NCATE. Program being phased out; applicants no longer accepted. Faculty: 2 full-time (1 woman), 4 part-time (3 women). Students: 23 full-time (14 women), 27 part-time (22 women); includes 22 minority (10 African Americans, 2 Asian Americans, 10 Hispanics). Average age 36. In 1997, 1 master's awarded; 4 doctorates awarded (100% entered university research/teaching). *Degree requirements:* For doctorate, dissertation required, foreign language not required. *Average time to degree:* master's–2.5 years part-time; doctorate–5 years part-time. *Expenses:* Tuition $815 per credit hour. Fees $174 per year. *Financial aid:* In 1997–98, 2 graduate assistantships (1 to a first-year student) averaging $900 per month and totaling $14,000 were awarded; fellowships, full and partial tuition waivers, Federal Work-Study, institutionally sponsored loans, and career-related internships or fieldwork also available. Aid available to part-time students. *Faculty research:* College teaching and learning, student affairs, college administration, classroom assessment. • Dr. Thomas Angelo, Coordinator, 305-284-2968. Fax: 305-284-3003. E-mail: tangelo@umiami.ir.miami.edu.

University of Michigan, School of Education, Center for the Study of Higher and Postsecondary Education, Ann Arbor, MI 48109. Offerings include higher education administration (AM). *Entrance requirements:* GRE General Test (minimum combined score of 1800 on three sections), TOEFL (minimum score 600). Application deadline: 1/15 (priority date). Application fee: $55. Electronic applications accepted. • Dr. Janet H. Lawrence, Chairperson, 734-647-1977. Fax: 734-764-2510. E-mail: janlaw@umich.edu. Application contact: Karen Wixson, Associate Dean, 734-764-9470. Fax: 734-763-1229. E-mail: kwixson@umich.edu.

University of Minnesota, Twin Cities Campus, College of Education and Human Development, Department of Educational Policy and Administration, Minneapolis, MN 55455-0213. Offerings include higher education (MA, PhD). • James Hearn, Chair, 612-624-1006.

University of Minnesota, Twin Cities Campus, College of Education and Human Development, Program in Higher Education, Minneapolis, MN 55455-0213. Awards MA, PhD. • Darrell Lewis, Director of Graduate Studies, 612-624-1006.

University of Mississippi, Graduate School, School of Education, Department of Educational Leadership and Educational Psychology, Program in Higher Education/Student Personnel, University, MS 38677-9702. Awards MA, M Ed. Accredited by NCATE. Students: 26 full-time (17 women), 10 part-time (5 women); includes 24 minority (22 African Americans, 1 Asian American, 1 Native American). In 1997, 15 degrees awarded. *Entrance requirements:* GRE General Test, TOEFL, minimum GPA of 3.0. Application deadline: 8/1 (rolling processing). Application fee: $0 ($25 for international students). *Financial aid:* Application deadline 3/1. • Dr. William Leary, Acting Chair, Department of Educational Leadership and Educational Psychology, 601-232-7195.

University of Missouri–Columbia, College of Education, Department of Educational Leadership and Policy Analysis, Columbia, MO 65211. Offerings include higher and adult education (MA, M Ed, Ed D, PhD, Ed S). Terminal master's awarded for partial completion of doctoral program. Department faculty: 20 full-time (7 women). *Degree requirements:* For doctorate, variable foreign language requirement, dissertation. *Entrance requirements:* For master's, GRE General Test, minimum GPA of 3.0; for doctorate, GRE General Test, GRE Subject Test, minimum GPA of 3.5; for Ed S, GRE General Test, GRE Subject Test, minimum GPA of 3.25. Application deadline: 6/15 (priority date; rolling processing). Application fee: $25 ($50 for international students). *Expenses:* Tuition $3240 per year full-time, $180 per credit hour part-time for state residents; $9108 per year full-time, $506 per credit hour part-time for nonresidents. Fees $55 per year full-time. • Dr. Paula Short, Director of Graduate Studies, 573-882-8231.

University of Nevada, Las Vegas, College of Education, Department of Instructional and Curricular Studies, Las Vegas, NV 89154-9900. Offerings include postsecondary education (M Ed, MS). Accredited by NCATE. Department faculty: 34 full-time (16 women). *Degree requirements:* Thesis (for some programs), oral or written comprehensive exam required, foreign language not required. *Entrance requirements:* Minimum GPA of 3.0. Application deadline: 2/15 (9/30 for spring admission). Application fee: $40 ($95 for international students). *Expenses:* Tuition $93 per credit for state residents; $93 per credit full-time, $190 per credit part-time for nonresidents. Fees $5570 per year full-time for nonresidents. • Dr. Jan McCarthy, Chair, 702-895-3241. Application contact: Graduate College Admissions Evaluator, 702-895-3320.

University of North Carolina at Greensboro, School of Education, Department of Educational Leadership and Cultural Foundations, Greensboro, NC 27412-0001. Offerings include higher education (M Ed). Accredited by NCATE. Department faculty: 10 full-time (3 women), 8 part-time. *Application deadline:* 7/1 (priority date; rolling processing; 11/1 for spring admission). *Application fee:* $35. *Expenses:* Tuition $1842 per year full-time, $370 per semester (minimum) part-time for state residents; $10,296 per year full-time, $2484 per semester (minimum) part-time for nonresidents. Fees $806 per year full-time, $111 per semester (minimum) part-time. • Dr. Rick Reitzug, Chair, 336-334-3491.

University of North Texas, College of Education, Department of Counseling, Development and Higher Education, Program in Higher Education, Denton, TX 76203-6737. Awards Ed D, PhD. Accredited by NCATE. Evening/weekend programs available. Terminal master's awarded for partial completion of doctoral program. *Degree requirements:* For doctorate, dissertation. *Entrance requirements:* For doctorate, GRE General Test, admissions exam. Application deadline: 7/17. Application fee: $25 ($50 for international students). *Tuition:* $2063 per year full-time, $815 per year part-time for state residents; $5897 per year full-time, $2100 per year part-time for nonresidents. *Financial aid:* Teaching assistantships, Federal Work-Study, institutionally sponsored loans, and career-related internships or fieldwork available. Financial aid application deadline: 4/1. • Application contact: Ron Newsom, Adviser, 940-565-2910.

University of Oklahoma, College of Education, Department of Educational Leadership and Policy Studies, Program in Adult and Higher Education, Norman, OK 73019-0390. Awards M Ed, Ed D, PhD. Accredited by NCATE. Part-time and evening/weekend programs available. Students: 19 full-time (13 women), 66 part-time (38 women); includes 18 minority (9 African Americans, 9 Native Americans). Average age 41. 23 applicants, 83% accepted. In 1997, 53 master's, 8 doctorates awarded. Terminal master's awarded for partial completion of doctoral program. *Degree requirements:* For master's, comprehensive exam required, foreign language and thesis not required; for doctorate, variable foreign language requirement, dissertation, general exam. *Entrance requirements:* For master's, TOEFL (minimum score 550), 12 hours of course work in education; for doctorate, GRE General Test, TOEFL (minimum score 550), master's degree, minimum graduate GPA of 3.25. Application deadline: 6/1 (10/1 for spring admission). Application fee: $25. *Expenses:* Tuition $1920 per year full-time, $80 per credit hour part-time for state residents; $6108 per year full-time, $255 per credit hour part-time for nonresidents. Fees $468 per year full-time, $12 per semester (minimum) part-time. *Faculty research:* Higher education administration, training and development, distance education, evaluation, gerontology. Total annual research expenditures: $125,000. • Application contact: Edward Chance, Graduate Liaison, 405-325-4202.

University of Oregon, Graduate School, College of Education, Department of Educational Technology, Leadership and Administration, Department of Educational Policy and Management, Eugene, OR 97403. Offerings include higher education (MS). Department faculty: 8 full-time (1 woman), 6 part-time (1 woman), 10.29 FTE. *Degree requirements:* Exam, paper, or project required, foreign language not required. *Entrance requirements:* MAT, TOEFL (minimum score 550). Application deadline: 3/15. Application fee: $50. *Tuition:* $6429 per year full-time, $873 per quarter (minimum) part-time for state residents; $10,857 per year full-time, $1360 per quarter (minimum) part-time for nonresidents. • Application contact: Tammara Hirte, Graduate Secretary, 541-346-1361. Fax: 541-346-5174.

University of Pennsylvania, Graduate School of Education, Division of Higher Education, Philadelphia, PA 19104. Awards MS Ed, Ed D, PhD. Part-time programs available. Faculty: 3 full-time (0 women), 7 part-time (2 women). Students: 78 full-time (47 women), 36 part-time (23 women); includes 26 minority (16 African Americans, 5 Asian Americans, 3 Hispanics, 2 Native Americans), 4 international. In 1997, 18 master's, 3 doctorates awarded. Terminal master's awarded for partial completion of doctoral program. *Degree requirements:* For master's, comprehensive exam required, foreign language not required; for doctorate, dissertation, comprehensive exam required, foreign language not required. *Entrance requirements:* GRE. Application fee: $65. *Expenses:* Tuition $22,716 per year full-time, $2876 per course part-time. Fees $1484 per year full-time, $181 per course part-time. *Financial aid:* Fellowships, service scholarships, Federal Work-Study, institutionally sponsored loans, and career-related internships or fieldwork available. Aid available to part-time students. Financial aid application deadline: 1/2; applicants required to submit FAFSA. *Faculty research:* Institutional research, strategic planning, governance and administration, public policy, budgeting and finance. • Dr. Robert Zemsky, Chair, 215-898-2444. Fax: 215-573-2109. Application contact: Steve Feld, 215-898-2444.

University of South Carolina, Graduate School, College of Education, Department of Educational Leadership and Policies, Program in Student and Personnel Services in Higher Education, Columbia, SC 29208. Awards MA, M Ed. Accredited by NCATE. Part-time and evening/weekend programs available. Faculty: 5 full-time (1 woman), 2 part-time (1 woman). Students: 56 full-time (43 women), 19 part-time (12 women); includes 13 minority (10 African Americans, 3 Hispanics). Average age 28. In 1997, 55 degrees awarded (100% found work related to degree). *Degree requirements:* Thesis (for some programs), comprehensive exam required, foreign language not required. *Entrance requirements:* GRE General Test or MAT. Application deadline: 7/15 (priority date; rolling processing). Application fee: $35. Electronic applications accepted. *Expenses:* Tuition $3894 per year full-time, $193 per credit hour part-time for state residents; $8114 per year full-time, $404 per credit hour part-time for nonresidents. Fees $125 per year full-time, $37 per semester (minimum) part-time. *Financial aid:* Teaching assistantships, assistantships, partial tuition waivers, Federal Work-Study, institutionally sponsored loans, and career-related internships or fieldwork available. *Faculty research:* Minorities in higher education, community college transfer problem, federal role in educational research. • Application contact: Office of Intercollegiate Teacher Education and Student Affairs, 803-777-6732. Fax: 803-777-3068.

University of South Florida, College of Education, Department of College Student Affairs, Tampa, FL 33620-9951. Awards MA. Accredited by NCATE. Students: 3 full-time (all women), 5 part-time (3 women); includes 4 minority (all African Americans), 2 international. Average age 27. 24 applicants, 63% accepted. *Entrance requirements:* GRE General Test (minimum combined score of 1000), minimum GPA of 3.5 in last 60 hours. Application fee: $20. *Tuition:* $142 per credit hour for state residents; $486 per credit hour for nonresidents. • Arthur Shapiro, Chairperson, 813-974-3420. Fax: 813-974-8360. E-mail: shapiro@tempest.coedu.usf.edu.

University of South Florida, College of Education, Department of Educational Leadership, Program in Higher Education, Tampa, FL 33620-9951. Awards PhD, Ed S. Accredited by NCATE. Part-time and evening/weekend programs available. Students: 2 part-time (0 women); includes 2 minority (1 African American, 1 Hispanic). Average age 39. 3 applicants, 100% accepted. *Degree requirements:* For doctorate, dissertation, 2 tools of research in foreign language, statistics, and/or computers. *Entrance requirements:* For doctorate, GRE General Test (minimum combined score of 1000), minimum GPA of 3.0 (undergraduate) or 3.5 (graduate); for Ed S, GRE General Test (minimum combined score of 1000), minimum GPA of 3.0 in last 60 hours. Application deadline: 6/1 (10/15 for spring admission). Application fee: $20. Electronic applications accepted. *Tuition:* $142 per credit hour for state residents; $486 per credit hour for nonresidents. *Financial aid:* Federal Work-Study, institutionally sponsored loans available. Aid available to part-time students. Financial aid applicants required to submit FAFSA. • Arthur Shapiro, Chairperson, 813-974-3420. Fax: 813-974-3661. E-mail: shapiro@tempest.coedu.usf.edu.

University of Tennessee, Knoxville, College of Education, Program in College Student Personnel, Knoxville, TN 37996. Awards MS. Accredited by NCATE. Part-time programs available. Students: 19 full-time (14 women), 13 part-time (4 women); includes 3 minority (2 African Americans, 1 Hispanic). 31 applicants, 71% accepted. In 1997, 14 degrees awarded. *Degree requirements:* Thesis optional, foreign language not required. *Entrance requirements:* GRE General Test, TOEFL (minimum score 550), minimum GPA of 2.7. Application deadline: 2/1 (priority date; rolling processing). Application fee: $35. Electronic applications accepted. *Tuition:* $3354 per year full-time, $181 per semester hour part-time for state residents; $8410 per year full-time, $462 per semester hour part-time for nonresidents. *Financial aid:* Application deadline 2/1. • Dr. Tom George, Associate Dean, 423-974-0907. Fax: 423-974-8718. E-mail: tgeorge1@utk.edu.

University of Tennessee, Knoxville, College of Education, Program in Education I, Knoxville, TN 37996. Offerings include educational administration and supervision/higher education (PhD). *Degree requirements:* 1 foreign language (computer language can substitute), dissertation. *Entrance requirements:* GRE General Test, TOEFL (minimum score 550), minimum GPA of 2.7. Application deadline: 2/1 (priority date; rolling processing). Application fee: $35. Electronic applications accepted. *Tuition:* $3354 per year full-time, $181 per semester hour part-time for state residents; $8410 per year full-time, $462 per semester hour part-time for nonresidents. • Dr. Tom George, Associate Dean, 423-974-0907. Fax: 423-974-8718. E-mail: tgeorge1@utk.edu.

University of Tennessee, Knoxville, College of Education, Program in Education II, Knoxville, TN 37996. Offerings include higher education (Ed D). Accredited by NCATE. *Degree requirements:* Dissertation required, foreign language not required. *Entrance requirements:* GRE General Test, TOEFL (minimum score 550), minimum GPA of 2.7. Application deadline: 2/1 (priority date; rolling processing). Application fee: $35. Electronic applications accepted. *Tuition:* $3354 per year full-time, $181 per semester hour part-time for state residents; $8410 per year full-time, $462 per semester hour part-time for nonresidents. • Dr. Tom George, Associate Dean, 423-974-0907. Fax: 423-974-8718. E-mail: tgeorge1@utk.edu.

University of Toledo, College of Education and Allied Professions, Department of Educational Leadership, Program in Higher Education, Toledo, OH 43606-3398. Awards M Ed, PhD. Accredited by NCATE. Students: 15 full-time (5 women), 69 part-time (40 women); includes 10 minority (all African Americans), 4 international. Average age 36. 31 applicants, 77% accepted. In 1997, 6 master's, 5 doctorates awarded. *Degree requirements:* For master's, thesis or alternative, comprehensive exam required, foreign language not required; for doctorate, dissertation, comprehensive exams required, foreign language not required. *Entrance requirements:* For master's, minimum GPA of 2.7; for doctorate, GRE General Test (minimum combined score of 1040), minimum GPA of 2.7 (undergraduate), 3.0 (graduate). Application deadline: 8/15 (priority date; rolling processing). Application fee: $30. *Tuition:* $5907 per year full-time, $246 per hour part-time for state residents; $11,835 per year full-time, $493 per hour part-time for nonresidents. *Financial aid:* Federal Work-Study, institutionally sponsored loans, and career-related internships or fieldwork available. Aid available to part-time students. Financial aid application deadline: 4/1; applicants required to submit FAFSA. • Dr. Daniel Merritt, Interim Chair, Department of Educational Leadership, 419-530-2461. Fax: 419-530-7719.

University of Virginia, Curry School of Education, Department of Leadership, Foundations and Policy, Program in Higher Education, Charlottesville, VA 22903. Awards Ed D, Ed S. Accredited by NCATE. Faculty: 37 full-time (12 women), 1 part-time (0 women). Students: 12 full-time (5 women), 5 part-time (4 women); includes 2 minority (both African Americans). Average age 39. 12 applicants, 75% accepted. In 1997, 3 doctorates awarded. *Entrance requirements:* GRE General Test. Application deadline: 3/1 (11/15 for spring admission). Application fee: $40. *Tuition:* $4876 per year full-time, $944 per semester (minimum) part-time for state residents; $15,824 per year full-time, $2748 per semester (minimum) part-time for nonresidents. • Application contact: Linda Berry, Student Enrollment Coordinator, 804-924-0738. E-mail: lrb8e@virginia.edu.

Vanderbilt University, Peabody College, Department of Educational Leadership, Nashville, TN 37240-1001. Offerings include higher education (M Ed, Ed D, Ed S). Accredited by NCATE. *Entrance requirements:* For master's and doctorate, GRE General Test, MAT. Application deadline: 3/1 (priority date; rolling processing). Application fee: $35. • Joseph Murphy, Chair, 615-322-8000.

Wayne State University, College of Education, Division of Administrative and Organizational Studies, Detroit, MI 48202. Offerings include higher education (Ed D, PhD). Accredited by NCATE. Division faculty: 81. *Degree requirements:* Dissertation required, foreign language not required. *Entrance requirements:* Interview, minimum GPA of 3.0. Application deadline: 7/1. Application fee: $20 ($30 for international students). *Expenses:* Tuition $163 per credit hour for state residents; $355 per credit hour for nonresidents. Fees $498 per year full-time, $114 per semester (minimum) part-time. • Dr. JoAnne Holbert, Assistant Dean, 313-577-0210.

Middle School Education

Alaska Pacific University, Graduate Programs, Education Department, 4101 University Drive, Anchorage, AK 99508-4672. Offerings include teaching (MAT), with option in K–8. Department faculty: 5 full-time (4 women), 2 part-time (both women), 5.6 FTE. *Degree requirements:* Comprehensive exam or thesis required, foreign language not required. *Entrance requirements:* GRE or MAT, minimum GPA of 3.0. Application deadline: 4/15 (rolling processing; 12/15 for spring admission). Application fee: $25. *Expenses:* Tuition $6600 per year full-time, $370 per credit hour part-time. Fees $80 per year. • Diane Hoffbauer, Director, 907-564-8271. Fax: 907-562-4276. Application contact: Kirsty Gladkoff, Associate Director of Admissions, 907-564-8248. Fax: 907-564-8317. E-mail: apu@corecom.net.

Albany State University, School of Education, Program in Middle Childhood Education, Albany, GA 31705-2717. Awards M Ed. Accredited by NCATE. Faculty: 1 full-time (0 women), 1 (woman) part-time. Students: 27 full-time (21 women), 14 part-time (12 women). In 1997, 9 degrees awarded. *Degree requirements:* Comprehensive exam. *Entrance requirements:* GRE General Test (minimum combined score of 800), MAT (minimum score 44) or NTE (minimum score 550 required. Application deadline: 9/1. Application fee: $10. *Financial aid:* Application deadline 4/1. • Dr. Claude Perkins, Dean, School of Education, 912-430-4715. Fax: 912-430-4993. E-mail: cperkins@fld94.alsnet.peachnet.edu.

Armstrong Atlantic State University, School of Graduate Studies, Program in Education, Savannah, GA 31419-1997. Offerings include middle grades education (M Ed). Accredited by NCATE. Program faculty: 25. *Expenses:* Tuition $83 per quarter hour for state residents; $250 per quarter hour for nonresidents. Fees $145 per quarter hour for state residents; $228 per quarter hour for nonresidents. • Dr. Bettye Anne Battiste, Department Head, 912-927-5281.

Augusta State University, College of Education, Program in Middle Grades Education, Augusta, GA 30904-2200. Awards M Ed, Ed S. Accredited by NCATE. Part-time and evening/weekend programs available. Faculty: 10 full-time (4 women). Students: 7 full-time (6 women), 13 part-time (12 women); includes 4 minority (all African Americans). Average age 35. 6 applicants, 100% accepted. In 1997, 14 master's, 5 Ed Ss awarded. *Degree requirements:* Thesis, comprehensive exam. *Entrance requirements:* GRE, MAT. Application deadline: 7/26 (priority date; rolling processing). Application fee: $10. *Tuition:* $2260 per year full-time, $83 per credit hour part-time for state residents; $8260 per year full-time, $333 per credit hour part-time for nonresidents. *Financial aid:* Federal Work-Study, institutionally sponsored loans, and career-related internships or fieldwork available. Aid available to part-time students. Financial aid application deadline: 4/15; applicants required to submit FAFSA. • Dr. Mary Gendernalik Cooper, Chair, 706-737-1496. E-mail: mcooper@aug.edu. Application contact: Elfredia Phillips, Degree Program Assistant, 706-737-1496. Fax: 706-667-4706. E-mail: ephillips@aug.edu.

Ball State University, Teachers College, Department of Secondary, Higher, and Foundations of Education, Program in Junior High/Middle School Education, 2000 University Avenue, Muncie, IN 47306-1099. Awards MAE. Accredited by NCATE. Students: 1 full-time (0 women), 2 part-time (both women). 3 applicants, 100% accepted. In 1997, 1 degree awarded. *Application fee:* $15 ($25 for international students). *Expenses:* Tuition $3454 per year full-time, $518 per semester (minimum) part-time for state residents; $9316 per year full-time, $1221 per semester (minimum) part-time for nonresidents. Fees $242 per year full-time, $18 per semester (minimum) part-time. • Dr. Lane Binkel, Chairman, Department of Secondary, Higher, and Foundations of Education, 765-285-5460.

Bellarmine College, College of Arts and Sciences, Graduate Programs in Education, Louisville, KY 40205-0671. Offerings include middle school education (MA, MAT). Accredited by NCATE. Faculty: 2 full-time (both women). *Application deadline:* 8/1 (priority date; rolling processing; 12/15 for spring admission). *Application fee:* $25. Electronic applications accepted. *Tuition:* $360 per credit hour. • Dr. Doris Tegart, Director, 502-452-8191.

Belmont Abbey College, School of Graduate Studies, Division of Education, Belmont, NC 28012-1802. Offerings include middle grades education (MA). Accredited by NCATE. MA (special education) being phased out; applicants no longer accepted. *Application deadline:* 6/1 (rolling processing; 11/1 for spring admission). *Application fee:* $20. *Expenses:* Tuition $530 per course (minimum). Fees $43 per semester (minimum). • Dr. Sandra Loehr, Director, 704-825-6728. Application contact: Julia Gunter, Director of Adult Admissions, 704-825-6671. Fax: 704-825-6658.

Berry College, Graduate Programs in Education, Program in Middle-Grades Education, Mount Berry, GA 30149-0159. Awards M Ed. Accredited by NCATE. Part-time programs available. Faculty: 10 part-time (8 women), 2.6 FTE. Students: 10 full-time (9 women), 36 part-time (22 women); includes 1 minority (African American). Average age 35. 17 applicants, 71% accepted. In 1997, 25 degrees awarded (100% found work related to degree). *Degree requirements:* Oral exams required, thesis optional, foreign language not required. *Average time to degree:* master's–2 years full-time, 3 years part-time. *Entrance requirements:* GRE General Test, MAT, or NTE, minimum GPA of 2.5. Application deadline: 7/29 (rolling processing; 12/16 for spring admission). Application fee: $25 ($30 for international students). *Tuition:* $146 per semester hour. *Financial aid:* In 1997–98, 22 students received aid, including 4 assistantships (2 to first-year students) averaging $600 per month and totaling $14,850. Aid available to part-time students. Financial aid application deadline: 4/1; applicants required to submit FAFSA. • Application contact: George Gaddie, Dean of Admissions, 706-236-2215. Fax: 706-290-2178.

Brenau University, School of Education and Human Development, Gainesville, GA 30501-3697. Offerings include middle grades education (M Ed, Ed S). *Degree requirements:* For master's, comprehensive exam (M Ed) required, foreign language and thesis not required. *Average time to degree:* master's–2 years part-time; other advanced degree–1.5 years part-time. *Entrance requirements:* For master's, GRE, MAT. Application deadline: rolling. Application fee: $30. *Tuition:* $198 per semester hour. • Dr. William B. Ware, Dean, 770-534-6220. Application contact: Kathy Cobb, Director of Graduate Admissions, 770-534-6162. Fax: 770-538-4306. E-mail: kcobb@lib.brenau.edu.

Campbell University, School of Education, Buies Creek, NC 27506. Offerings include middle grades education (M Ed). Accredited by NCATE. School faculty: 8 full-time (6 women), 6 part-time (0 women). *Application deadline:* 8/1 (priority date; rolling processing; 1/2 for spring admission). *Application fee:* $25. *Tuition:* $168 per credit hour (minimum). • Dr. Margaret Giesbrecht, Dean, 910-893-1630. Fax: 910-893-1999. E-mail: giesbrec@mailcenter.campbell.edu. Application contact: James S. Farthing, Director of Graduate Admissions, 910-893-1200 Ext. 1318. Fax: 910-893-1288.

Central Michigan University, College of Education and Human Services, Department of Teacher Education and Professional Development, Program in Middle Level Education, Mount Pleasant, MI 48859. Awards MA. Accredited by NCATE. *Degree requirements:* Thesis or alternative required, foreign language not required. *Entrance requirements:* GRE General Test (minimum combined score of 1000), minimum GPA of 2.7. Application deadline: 3/1 (priority date). Application fee: $30. *Expenses:* Tuition $139 per credit hour (minimum) for state residents; $276 per credit hour (minimum) for nonresidents. Fees $260 per year full-time, $150 per semester part-time. *Financial aid:* Application deadline 3/7. • Dr. William Merrill, Chairperson, Department of Teacher Education and Professional Development, 517-774-3975. Fax: 517-774-3516. E-mail: 34ltyvi@cmich.edu.

Cleveland State University, College of Education, Department of Specialized Instructional Programs, Cleveland, OH 44115-2440. Offerings include curriculum and instruction (M Ed), with options in bilingual education, early childhood education, early childhood/special education, education of emerging adolescents, elementary education, English as a second language, learning disabilities, Montessori education, multihandicapped, reading, secondary education. Department faculty: 18 full-time (12 women). *Entrance requirements:* GRE General Test or MAT (score in 50th percentile or higher). Application deadline: 9/1 (priority date; rolling processing). Application fee: $25. *Expenses:* Tuition $5252 per year full-time, $202 per credit hour part-time for state residents; $10,504 per year full-time, $404 per credit hour part-time for nonresidents. Fees $2.25 per credit hour (minimum). • Dr. Jane Zaharias, Chairperson, 216-687-4585. Fax: 216-687-5379. E-mail: j.zaharias@csuohio.edu.

Columbus State University, College of Education, Department of Curriculum and Instruction, Columbus, GA 31907-5645. Offerings include middle grades education (M Ed, Ed S). Accredited by NCATE. Ed S (mathematics) offered jointly with Georgia Southwestern University. M Ed (political science) being phased out; applicants no longer accepted. *Degree requirements:* For master's, exit exam required, foreign language and thesis not required; for Ed S, thesis or alternative required, foreign language not required. *Entrance requirements:* For master's, GRE General Test (minimum combined score of 800), MAT (minimum score 44); for Ed S, GRE General Test (minimum combined score of 900), MAT (minimum score 44). Application deadline: 7/10 (priority date; rolling processing; 10/23 for spring admission). Application fee: $20. *Tuition:* $1718 per year full-time, $151 per semester hour part-time for state residents; $6218 per year full-time, $401 per semester hour part-time for nonresidents. • Dr. David Shoemaker, Chair, 706-568-2255. Fax: 706-568-3134. E-mail: shoemaker_david@colstate.edu. Application contact: Katie Thornton, Graduate Admissions, 706-568-2279. Fax: 706-568-2462. E-mail: thornton_katie@colstate.edu.

Cumberland College, Program in Middle School Education, 6178 College Station Drive, Williamsburg, KY 40769-1372. Awards MA Ed. Faculty: 4 full-time (2 women), 5 part-time (2 women). *Degree requirements:* Comprehensive exam required, foreign language and thesis not required. *Entrance requirements:* GRE or NTE, Kentucky teaching certificate. Application deadline: 8/26 (rolling processing). Application fee: $25. *Tuition:* $175 per credit. • Application contact: Erica Harris, Admissions Office, 606-539-4241.

Drury College, Graduate Programs in Education, Program in Middle School Teaching, Springfield, MO 65802-3791. Awards M Ed. Accredited by NCATE. Part-time and evening/

Directory: Middle School Education

Drury College (continued)

weekend programs available. Faculty: 1 full-time (0 women), 3 part-time (1 woman), 2.5 FTE. Students: 55 part-time (40 women); includes 3 minority (all African Americans). Average age 28. 18 applicants, 100% accepted. *Degree requirements:* Thesis required, foreign language not required. *Entrance requirements:* MAT (minimum score 35), minimum GPA of 2.75. Application deadline: 8/15 (rolling processing). Application fee: $15. *Tuition:* $170 per credit hour. *Financial aid:* Career-related internships or fieldwork available. • Dr. Terry Hudson, Head, 417-873-7530.

East Carolina University, School of Education, Department of Elementary Education, Greenville, NC 27858-4353. Offerings include middle grade education (MA Ed). Accredited by NCATE. Department faculty: 8 full-time (5 women). *Degree requirements:* Comprehensive exams required, thesis optional. *Entrance requirements:* GRE General Test or MAT, TOEFL. Application deadline: 6/1 (priority date; rolling processing). Application fee: $40. *Tuition:* $1886 per year full-time, $472 per semester (minimum) part-time for state residents; $9156 per year full-time, $2289 per semester (minimum) part-time for nonresidents. • Dr. Parmalee Hawk, Acting Chair, 252-328-6271. Fax: 252-328-4219. E-mail: hawkp@mail.ecu.edu.

Eastern Illinois University, College of Education and Professional Studies, Department of Elementary and Junior High School Education, 600 Lincoln Avenue, Charleston, IL 61920-3099. Offers programs in elementary education (MS Ed), junior high education (MS Ed). Accredited by NCATE. Part-time programs available. Faculty: 14 full-time (6 women). Students: 15 full-time (12 women), 129 part-time (115 women). In 1997, 29 degrees awarded. *Degree requirements:* Comprehensive exam required, foreign language and thesis not required. *Application deadline:* 7/31 (priority date; rolling processing). *Application fee:* $25. *Expenses:* Tuition $3459 per year full-time, $96 per semester hour part-time for state residents; $10,377 per year full-time, $288 per semester hour part-time for nonresidents. Fees $1566 per year full-time, $37 per semester hour part-time. *Financial aid:* In 1997–98, 1 research assistantship, 4 teaching assistantships were awarded. • Dr. Carol Helwig, Chairperson, 217-581-5728. E-mail: cfcmh2@eiu.edu.

Eastern Michigan University, College of Education, Department of Teacher Education, Program in Middle School Education, Ypsilanti, MI 48197. Awards MA. Accredited by NCATE. In 1997, 4 degrees awarded. *Entrance requirements:* GRE, TOEFL (minimum score 500). Application deadline: 5/15 (rolling processing; 3/15 for spring admission). Application fee: $30. *Expenses:* Tuition $2691 per year full-time, $150 per credit hour part-time for state residents; $6300 per year full-time, $350 per credit hour part-time for nonresidents. Fees $368 per year full-time, $88 per semester (minimum) part-time. *Financial aid:* Fellowships, teaching assistantships available. Aid available to part-time students. Financial aid application deadline: 3/15; applicants required to submit FAFSA. • Dr. Georgea Langer, Coordinator, 734-487-3185.

Eastern Nazarene College, Graduate Studies, Division of Education, Quincy, MA 02170-2999. Offerings include middle school education (M Ed, Certificate). M Ed and Certificate also available through weekend program for administration, special needs, and reading only. Division faculty: 9 full-time (5 women), 11 part-time (5 women). *Entrance requirements:* For master's, TOEFL (minimum score 500). Application deadline: rolling. Application fee: $35. *Expenses:* Tuition $350 per credit. Fees $125 per semester full-time, $15 per semester part-time. • Dr. Lorne Ranstrom, Chair, 617-745-3528. Application contact: Cleo P. Cakridas, Graduate Enrollment Counselor, 617-745-3870. Fax: 617-745-3907. E-mail: cakridac@enc.edu.

Edinboro University of Pennsylvania, School of Education, Department of Educational Services, Program in Middle and Secondary Instruction, Edinboro, PA 16444. Awards M Ed. Students: 2 full-time (1 woman), 3 part-time (all women). Average age 31. *Degree requirements:* Thesis or alternative required, foreign language not required. *Entrance requirements:* GRE or MAT (score in 30th percentile or higher). Application deadline: rolling. Application fee: $25. *Expenses:* Tuition $3468 per year full-time, $193 per credit part-time for state residents; $6236 per year full-time, $346 per credit part-time for nonresidents. Fees $898 per year full-time, $50 per semester (minimum) part-time. *Financial aid:* In 1997–98, 1 assistantship was awarded. • Application contact: Dr. Philip Kerstetter, Dean of Graduate Studies, 814-732-2856. Fax: 814-732-2611. E-mail: kerstetter@edinboro.edu.

Emory University, Graduate School of Arts and Sciences, Division of Educational Studies, Atlanta, GA 30322-1100. Offerings include middle grades teaching (MAT, M Ed). Division faculty: 13. *Application deadline:* 1/20 (3/15 for spring admission). *Application fee:* $45. *Expenses:* Tuition $21,770 per year. Fees $300 per year. • Dr. Robert Jensen, Acting Director, 404-727-0606. Fax: 404-727-2799. E-mail: rjensen@emory.edu. Application contact: Dr. Glen Avant, Program Development Coordinator, 404-727-0612.

Fayetteville State University, Program in Middle Grades Education, 1200 Murchison Road, Fayetteville, NC 28301-4298. Awards MA Ed. Accredited by NCATE. Part-time and evening/weekend programs available. *Degree requirements:* Comprehensive exams, internship required, foreign language and thesis not required. *Application deadline:* 8/1 (rolling processing; 12/15 for spring admission). *Application fee:* $20. *Tuition:* $1498 per year full-time, $327 per semester (minimum) part-time for state residents; $8768 per year full-time, $2144 per semester (minimum) part-time for nonresidents.

Fitchburg State College, Program in Middle School Education, Fitchburg, MA 01420-2697. Awards M Ed. Accredited by NCATE. Part-time and evening/weekend programs available. *Entrance requirements:* GRE General Test or MAT (minimum score 47), interview, teaching certificate. Application deadline: rolling. Application fee: $10. *Expenses:* Tuition $147 per credit. Fees $55 per semester. *Financial aid:* Graduate assistantships, Federal Work-Study available. Aid available to part-time students. Financial aid application deadline: 3/30; applicants required to submit FAFSA. • Dr. Patricia Barbaresi, Chair, 978-665-3510. Fax: 978-665-3658. E-mail: dgce@fsc.edu. Application contact: James DuPont, Director of Admissions, 978-665-3144. Fax: 978-665-4540. E-mail: admissions@fsc.edu.

Fort Valley State University, Department of Curriculum and Instruction, Program in Middle Grades Education, Fort Valley, GA 31030-3298. Awards MS. Accredited by NCATE. Part-time programs available. Faculty: 2 full-time (0 women), 3 part-time (1 woman). Students: 32 full-time (22 women), 34 part-time (19 women); includes 53 minority (all African Americans). *Degree requirements:* Thesis optional, foreign language not required. *Entrance requirements:* GRE General Test (minimum combined score of 800) or MAT (minimum score 44). Application deadline: 8/23. Application fee: $20. *Tuition:* $2486 per year full-time, $83 per semester hour part-time for state residents; $8486 per year full-time, $333 per semester hour part-time for nonresidents. *Financial aid:* Federal Work-Study available. Aid available to part-time students. Financial aid application deadline: 5/1; applicants required to submit FAFSA. • Head, Department of Curriculum and Instruction, 912-825-6250.

Gardner–Webb University, Department of Education, Program in Middle Grades Education, Boiling Springs, NC 28017. Awards MA. Accredited by NCATE. Part-time and evening/weekend programs available. Faculty: 4 full-time (2 women). Students: 3 part-time (all women). Average age 34. 3 applicants, 100% accepted. *Degree requirements:* Comprehensive exam required, foreign language and thesis not required. *Entrance requirements:* GRE General Test (minimum combined score of 900), MAT (minimum score 35), or NTE, minimum GPA of 2.5. Application deadline: 8/1. Application fee: $25. *Tuition:* $178 per semester hour full-time, $220 per semester hour part-time. *Financial aid:* In 1997–98, 1 graduate assistantship (to a first-year student) averaging $450 per month was awarded. • Dr. Jeffrey Peck, Head, 704-434-4403. Fax: 704-434-3921. E-mail: jpeck@gardner-webb.edu.

George Mason University, Graduate School of Education, Program in Middle Education, Fairfax, VA 22030-4444. Awards M Ed. Accredited by NCATE. Part-time and evening/weekend programs available. Faculty: 42 full-time (24 women), 65 part-time (51 women), 58.73 FTE. Students: 41 full-time (32 women), 104 part-time (74 women); includes 20 minority (8 African Americans, 5 Asian Americans, 6 Hispanics, 1 Native American). Average age 33. 113 applicants, 87% accepted. In 1997, 49 degrees awarded. *Degree requirements:* Computer language required, foreign language not required. *Entrance requirements:* NTE, minimum GPA of 3.0 in last 60 hours. Application deadline: 5/1 (11/1 for spring admission). Application fee: $30. Electronic applications accepted. *Tuition:* $4344 per year full-time, $181 per credit hour part-time for state residents; $12,504 per year full-time, $521 per credit hour part-time for nonresidents. *Financial aid:* Available to part-time students. Financial aid application deadline: 3/1; applicants required to submit FAFSA. • Dr. Robert Gilstrap, Co-Coordinator, 703-993-4648. Fax: 703-993-2013.

Georgia College and State University, School of Education, Department of Middle Grades Education, Milledgeville, GA 31061. Awards M Ed, Ed S. Accredited by NCATE. Students: 15 full-time (all women), 51 part-time (45 women); includes 5 minority (all African Americans). Average age 33. In 1997, 17 master's, 7 Ed Ss awarded. *Degree requirements:* For master's, computer language, comprehensive exit exam required, foreign language and thesis not required; for Ed S, computer language, comprehensive exit exam, oral exam, research project required, foreign language and thesis not required. *Entrance requirements:* For master's, GRE General Test (minimum combined score of 800) or NTE (minimum score 550 on each core battery test), MAT (minimum score 44), minimum GPA of 2.5, NT-4 certificate; for Ed S, GRE General Test (minimum combined score of 900) or NTE (minimum score 575 on each core battery test), MAT (minimum score 48), master's degree, minimum graduate GPA of 3.25, NT-5 certificate, 2 years of teaching experience. Application deadline: 7/31 (priority date; rolling processing). Application fee: $10. *Financial aid:* Assistantships, Federal Work-Study, and career-related internships or fieldwork available. Aid available to part-time students. Financial aid application deadline: 4/15. *Faculty research:* Performance skills of middle school principals in Georgia. • Dr. Charles Love, Chair, 912-445-5479.

Georgia Southern University, College of Education, Department of Middle Grades and Secondary Education, Program in Middle Grades Education, Statesboro, GA 30460-8126. Awards M Ed, Ed S. Accredited by NCATE. Part-time and evening/weekend programs available. Students: 27 full-time (21 women), 50 part-time (41 women); includes 5 minority (all African Americans). Average age 34. 32 applicants, 66% accepted. In 1997, 31 master's, 11 Ed Ss awarded. *Degree requirements:* Exams required, foreign language and thesis not required. *Entrance requirements:* For master's, GRE General Test (minimum score 450 on each section) or MAT (minimum score 44), minimum GPA of 2.5; for Ed S, GRE General Test (minimum score 450 on each section) or MAT (minimum score 49), minimum graduate GPA of 3.25. Application deadline: 7/15 (priority date; rolling processing; 11/15 for spring admission). Application fee: $0. Electronic applications accepted. *Tuition:* $2619 per year full-time, $287 per semester (minimum) part-time for state residents; $8619 per year full-time, $1037 per semester (minimum) part-time for nonresidents. *Financial aid:* Research assistantships, teaching assistantships, Federal Work-Study, and career-related internships or fieldwork available. Aid available to part-time students. Financial aid application deadline: 4/15. • Application contact: Dr. John R. Diebolt, Associate Graduate Dean, 912-681-5384. Fax: 912-681-0740. E-mail: gradschool@gsvms2.cc.gasou.edu.

Georgia Southwestern State University, School of Education, Americus, GA 31709-4693. Offerings include middle grades education (M Ed, Ed S). Accredited by NCATE. *Entrance requirements:* For master's, GRE General Test (minimum score 400 on each section) or MAT (minimum score 44), minimum GPA of 2.5; for Ed S, GRE General Test (minimum score 450 on each section) or MAT (minimum score 48), minimum GPA of 3.25. Application deadline: 9/1 (rolling processing; 3/15 for spring admission). Application fee: $10. • Dr. Kurt Myers, Chair, 912-931-2145. Application contact: Chris Laney, Graduate Admissions Specialist, 912-931-2027. Fax: 912-931-2059. E-mail: claney@gsw1500.gsw.peachnet.edu.

Georgia State University, College of Education, Department of Middle, Secondary Education and Instructional Technology, Program in Middle Childhood Education, Atlanta, GA 30303-3083. Awards M Ed, Ed S. Accredited by NCATE. Part-time and evening/weekend programs available. Students: 17 full-time (15 women), 61 part-time (52 women); includes 15 minority (13 African Americans, 1 Asian American, 1 Hispanic), 1 international. Average age 33. 20 applicants, 85% accepted. In 1997, 31 master's, 5 Ed Ss awarded. *Degree requirements:* For master's, comprehensive exam; for Ed S, project/exam. *Entrance requirements:* For master's, GRE General Test (minimum combined score of 800) or MAT (minimum score 44), minimum GPA of 2.5; for Ed S, GRE General Test (minimum combined score of 900) or MAT (minimum score 48), minimum graduate GPA of 3.25. Application deadline: 7/15 (1/15 for spring admission). Application fee: $25. *Expenses:* Tuition $2673 per year full-time, $99 per semester hour part-time for state residents; $10,692 per year full-time, $396 per semester hour part-time for nonresidents. Fees $228 per year. *Financial aid:* Federal Work-Study, institutionally sponsored loans available. • Dr. Beverly J. Armento, Chair, Department of Middle, Secondary Education and Instructional Technology, 404-651-2510.

James Madison University, College of Education and Psychology, School of Education, Program in Middle School Education, Harrisonburg, VA 22807. Awards M Ed. Accredited by NCATE. Part-time and evening/weekend programs available. Students: 13 full-time (9 women), 12 part-time (8 women); includes 1 minority (Asian American), 1 international. Average age 30. In 1997, 18 degrees awarded. *Entrance requirements:* GRE General Test. Application deadline: 7/1 (priority date; rolling processing). Application fee: $50. *Tuition:* $134 per credit hour for state residents; $404 per credit hour for nonresidents. *Financial aid:* In 1997–98, 1 assistantship totaling $8,640 was awarded; fellowships, teaching assistantships, Federal Work-Study also available. Financial aid application deadline: 2/15; applicants required to submit FAFSA. • Dr. Gerald Green, Coordinator, 540-568-6255.

Kennesaw State University, Leland and Clarice C. Bagwell College of Education, Program in Elementary Education, Kennesaw, GA 30144-5591. Offerings include middle grades (M Ed). Accredited by NCATE. Program faculty: 38 full-time (24 women), 2 part-time (both women). *Degree requirements:* Thesis or alternative required, foreign language not required. *Entrance requirements:* GRE General Test (minimum combined score of 800), T-4 state certification, minimum GPA of 2.5. Application deadline: 7/1 (2/20 for spring admission). Application fee: $20. *Expenses:* Tuition $2398 per year full-time, $83 per credit hour part-time for state residents; $8398 per year full-time, $333 per credit hour part-time for nonresidents. Fees $338 per year. • Dr. David Martin, Director, 770-423-6117. Fax: 770-423-6527. E-mail: dmartin1@ksumail.kennesaw.edu. Application contact: Susan N. Barrett, Administrative Specialist, Admissions, 770-423-6500. Fax: 770-423-6541. E-mail: sbarrett@ksumail.kennesaw.edu.

LaGrange College, Department of Education, LaGrange, GA 30240-2999. Offerings include middle childhood education (M Ed). Department faculty: 1 (woman) full-time, 6 part-time (4 women). *Degree requirements:* Comprehensive exam required, thesis not required. *Entrance requirements:* GRE, MAT, or NTE, minimum GPA of 2.5. Application deadline: 8/1 (priority date; rolling processing). Application fee: $20 ($25 for international students). *Expenses:* Tuition $219 per quarter hour. Fees $80 per quarter hour. • Dr. Evelyn Jordan, Chair, 706-812-7276. Application contact: Andy Geeter, Director of Admissions, 706-812-7260. Fax: 706-812-7348. E-mail: ageeter@mentor.lgc.peachnet.edu.

Lenoir–Rhyne College, Division of Graduate Programs, Department of Education, Program in Middle School Education, Hickory, NC 28601. Awards MA. Part-time and evening/weekend programs available. Students: 0. In 1997, 4 degrees awarded (100% found work related to degree). *Degree requirements:* Thesis optional, foreign language not required. *Entrance requirements:* GRE General Test (minimum score 450 on verbal section, 1350 combined), minimum GPA of 2.7. Application deadline: 8/1 (12/1 for spring admission). Application fee: $25. *Tuition:* $190 per credit hour. *Financial aid:* Federal Work-Study and career-related internships or fieldwork available. Aid available to part-time students. • Dr. Lorene Painter, Head, 828-328-7193. Application contact: Dr. Thomas W. Fauquet, Dean of Graduate Studies, 828-328-7275. Fax: 828-328-7368. E-mail: fauquet@lrc.edu.

Lesley College, School of Education, Cambridge, MA 02138-2790. Offerings include middle school education (M Ed). Postbaccalaureate distance learning degree programs offered (no on-campus study). School faculty: 36 full-time (31 women), 340 part-time (220 women). *Degree requirements:* Computer language required, foreign language and thesis not required. *Entrance requirements:* TOEFL (minimum score 550). Application deadline: rolling. Application fee: $45. *Tuition:* $425 per credit. • Dr. William L. Dandridge, Dean, 617-349-8375. Application contact: Graduate Admissions, 617-349-8300. Fax: 617-349-8366.

Long Island University, C.W. Post Campus, School of Education, Department of Curriculum and Instruction, Brookville, NY 11548-1300. Offerings include middle school education (MS). Department faculty: 10 full-time (5 women), 46 part-time (19 women). *Application deadline:* rolling. *Application fee:* $30. Electronic applications accepted. *Expenses:* Tuition $480 per credit. Fees $316 per year full-time, $71 per semester (minimum) part-time. • Dr. Anthony De Falco, Chairperson, 516-299-2372. Application contact: Camille Marziliano, Academic Counselor, 516-299-2123. Fax: 516-299-4167. E-mail: cmarzili@eagle.liunet.edu.

Lynchburg College, School of Education and Human Development, Lynchburg, VA 24501-3199. Offerings include early childhood education (M Ed), with options in curriculum and instruction: early childhood education, curriculum and instruction: middle education; middle school education (M Ed). M Ed (adapted physical education, physical education) admissions temporarily suspended. *Entrance requirements:* Minimum GPA of 3.0 (undergraduate). Application fee: $20.

Malone College, Graduate School, Program in Education, Canton, OH 44709-3897. Offerings include middle school (MA). Program faculty: 10 full-time (6 women), 11 part-time (5 women), 12.68 FTE. *Degree requirements:* Research practicum required, foreign language and thesis not required. *Entrance requirements:* Minimum GPA of 3.0, teaching license. Application deadline: 9/6 (rolling processing; 1/2 for spring admission). Application fee: $20. *Tuition:* $300 per credit hour. • Dr. Marietta Daulton, Director, 330-471-8447. Fax: 330-471-8478. E-mail: mdaulton@malone.edu. Application contact: Dan Depasquale, Director of Graduate Student Services, 800-257-4723. Fax: 330-471-8343. E-mail: depasquale@malone.edu.

Maryville University of Saint Louis, School of Education, St. Louis, MO 63141-7299. Offerings include middle grades education (MA). Accredited by NCATE. School faculty: 9 full-time (7 women), 15 part-time (9 women). *Degree requirements:* Thesis, project required, foreign language not required. *Average time to degree:* master's–2 years full-time, 4 years part-time. *Entrance requirements:* Minimum GPA of 3.0. Application deadline: rolling. Application fee: $20. Electronic applications accepted. *Expenses:* Tuition $11,480 per year full-time, $345 per credit hour part-time. Fees $120 per year full-time, $60 per year part-time. • Dr. Kathe Rasch, Dean, 314-529-9466. Fax: 314-529-9921. E-mail: krasch@maryville.edu.

Mercer University, School of Education, 1400 Coleman Avenue, Macon, GA 31207-0003. Offerings include middle grades education (M Ed, Ed S). School faculty: 11 full-time (5 women), 17 part-time (11 women). *Degree requirements:* Research project report required, foreign language and thesis not required. *Entrance requirements:* For master's, GRE, MAT, NTE, minimum GPA of 2.75; for Ed S, GRE, MAT, NTE, minimum GPA of 3.25, 3 years of teaching experience. Application deadline: 8/1 (priority date; rolling processing; 12/1 for spring admission). Application fee: $25. *Tuition:* $180 per credit hour. • Dr. Anne Hathaway, Dean, 912-752-5397. Fax: 912-752-2280. E-mail: hathaway_ha@mercer.edu. Application contact: Dr. Louis Gallien, Chair, Department of Teacher Education, 912-752-2585. Fax: 912-752-2576. E-mail: gallien_lb@mercer.edu.

Mercer University, Cecil B. Day Campus, Graduate Education Programs, 3001 Mercer University Drive, Atlanta, GA 30341-4155. Offerings include middle grades education (M Ed, Ed S). Faculty: 8 full-time (4 women), 33 part-time (17 women). *Degree requirements:* Research project required, foreign language and thesis not required. *Entrance requirements:* For master's, GRE, MAT, or NTE, minimum undergraduate GPA of 2.75; for Ed S, GRE, MAT, or NTE, minimum GPA of 3.25, 3 years of teaching experience. Application deadline: 8/1 (priority date; rolling processing; 12/1 for spring admission). Application fee: $25. *Tuition:* $220 per semester hour. • Dr. Anne Hathaway, Dean, 912-752-5397. Fax: 912-752-2280. E-mail: hathaway_ha@mercer.edu. Application contact: Dr. Allison Gilmore, Associate Dean and Director of Graduate Education, 770-986-3330. Fax: 770-986-3292. E-mail: gilmore_a@mercer.edu.

Middle Tennessee State University, College of Education, Department of Elementary and Special Education, Major in Curriculum and Instruction, Murfreesboro, TN 37132. Offerings include middle school education (M Ed). Accredited by NCATE. *Degree requirements:* Comprehensive exams required, foreign language and thesis not required. *Entrance requirements:* Cooperative English Test, GRE, MAT (minimum score 25). Application deadline: 8/1 (priority date). Application fee: $5. *Expenses:* Tuition $2560 per year full-time, $129 per semester hour part-time for state residents; $7386 per year full-time, $340 per semester hour part-time for nonresidents. Fees $486 per year full-time, $17 per semester (minimum) part-time. • Dr. Charles Babb, Chair, Department of Elementary and Special Education, 615-898-2680. Fax: 615-898-5309. E-mail: cwbabb@mtsu.edu.

Morehead State University, College of Education and Behavioral Sciences, Department of Elementary, Reading, and Special Education, Program in Elementary Education, Morehead, KY 40351. Offerings include middle school education (MA Ed). Accredited by NCATE. Program faculty: 15 full-time (8 women), 1 part-time (0 women). *Degree requirements:* Written comprehensive exams required, foreign language and thesis not required. *Entrance requirements:* GRE General Test (minimum combined score of 1200), minimum GPA of 2.75, teaching certificate. Application deadline: 8/1 (priority date; rolling processing; 12/1 for spring admission). Application fee: $0. *Tuition:* $2470 per year full-time, $138 per semester hour part-time for state residents; $6710 per year full-time, $373 per semester hour part-time for nonresidents. • Application contact: Betty Cowsert, Graduate Admissions Officer, 606-783-2039. Fax: 606-783-5061.

Morgan State University, School of Education and Urban Studies, Department of Teacher Education and Administration, Program in Elementary and Middle School Education, Baltimore, MD 21251. Awards MS. Accredited by NCATE. Part-time and evening/weekend programs available. Faculty: 5 full-time (1 woman), 4 part-time (1 woman). Students: 1 (woman) full-time, 2 part-time (both women); includes 3 minority (all African Americans). Average age 30. 3 applicants, 0% accepted. In 1997, 3 degrees awarded. *Degree requirements:* Comprehensive exam required, thesis optional, foreign language not required. *Average time to degree:* master's–3 years part-time. *Application deadline:* 7/1 (rolling processing; 11/1 for spring admission). *Application fee:* $0. *Expenses:* Tuition $160 per credit hour for state residents; $286 per credit hour for nonresidents. Fees $326 per year. *Financial aid:* Application deadline 4/1. *Faculty research:* Multicultural education, cooperative learning, psychology of cognition. • Dr. Dennis Brown, Coordinator, 410-319-3356. Fax: 410-319-3871. Application contact: James E. Waller, Admissions and Programs Officer, 410-319-3186. Fax: 410-319-3837.

Murray State University, College of Education, Department of Elementary, Middle School, and Secondary Education, Program in Middle School Education, Murray, KY 42071-0009. Awards MA Ed, Ed S. Accredited by NCATE. Students: 25 part-time (15 women); includes 1 minority (African American). 4 applicants, 100% accepted. In 1997, 2 master's awarded. *Entrance requirements:* For master's, TOEFL (minimum score 500). Application deadline: rolling. Application fee: $20. *Expenses:* Tuition $2500 per year full-time, $124 per hour part-time for state residents; $6740 per year full-time, $357 per hour part-time for nonresidents. Fees $360 per year full-time, $180 per year part-time. *Financial aid:* Research assistantships, teaching assistantships, Federal Work-Study available. Financial aid application deadline: 4/1. • Dr. Chuck Hulick, Director, 502-762-2496. Fax: 502-762-2540.

Newman University, Program in Education, Wichita, KS 67213-2084. Offerings include elementary/middle-level education (MS Ed). Program faculty: 5 full-time, 9 part-time. *Degree requirements:* Thesis or alternative. *Average time to degree:* master's–3 years part-time. *Application deadline:* 8/15 (priority date; rolling processing; 1/10 for spring admission). *Application fee:* $25. *Tuition:* $257 per credit hour. • Dr. Laura McLemore, Division Chair of Institute for Teacher Education, 316-942-4291 Ext. 253. Fax: 316-942-4483.

North Carolina Agricultural and Technical State University, Graduate School, School of Education, Department of Curriculum and Instruction, Program in Intermediate Education, Greensboro, NC 27411. Offers biology education (MS), chemistry education (MS), English education (MS), history education (MS), social science education (MS). Accredited by NCATE. Part-time and evening/weekend programs available. Students: 0. *Degree requirements:* Thesis (for some programs), comprehensive exam, qualifying exam required, foreign language not required. *Entrance requirements:* GRE General Test, minimum GPA of 3.0. Application deadline: 6/1 (priority date; rolling processing; 12/1 for spring admission). Application fee: $35. *Tuition:* $1662 per year full-time, $272 per semester (minimum) part-time for state residents; $8790 per year full-time, $2054 per semester (minimum) part-time for nonresidents. *Financial aid:* Fellowships, research assistantships, teaching assistantships available. Financial aid application deadline: 6/1. • Dr. Dorothy Leflore, Interim Chairperson, Department of Curriculum and Instruction, 336-334-7848.

North Carolina State University, College of Education and Psychology, Department of Curriculum and Instruction, Program in Middle Years Education, Raleigh, NC 27695. Awards M Ed, MS. Accredited by NCATE. Students: 9 full-time (8 women), 11 part-time (6 women); includes 3 minority (2 African Americans, 1 Asian American). Average age 31. 11 applicants, 73% accepted. In 1997, 7 degrees awarded. *Degree requirements:* Thesis required (for some programs), foreign language not required. *Entrance requirements:* GRE General Test or MAT, minimum GPA of 3.0 in major. Application deadline: 2/26 (10/30 for spring admission). Application fee: $45. *Tuition:* $2370 per year full-time, $517 per semester (minimum) part-time for state residents; $11,536 per year full-time, $2809 per semester (minimum) part-time for nonresidents. *Financial aid:* Fellowships, research assistantships available. • Dr. Barbara J. Fox, Director of Graduate Programs, 919-515-1781. Fax: 919-515-6978. E-mail: fox@poe.coe.ncsu.edu.

North Georgia College & State University, Graduate School, Program in Education, Dahlonega, GA 30597-1001. Offerings include middle grades education (M Ed). Accredited by NCATE. Program faculty: 57 full-time (15 women), 7 part-time (4 women). *Degree requirements:* Comprehensive exam required, thesis optional, foreign language not required. *Entrance requirements:* GRE General Test (minimum combined score of 800) or MAT (minimum score 44), minimum GPA of 2.75. Application deadline: 9/1 (priority date; rolling processing). Application fee: $25. • Dr. Bob Michael, Dean, School of Education, 706-864-1533. Application contact: Mai-Lan Ledbetter, Coordinator of Graduate Admissions, 706-864-1543. Fax: 706-864-1668. E-mail: mledbetter@nugget.ngc.peachnet.edu.

Northwest Missouri State University, College of Education and Human Services, Department of Curriculum and Instruction, Program in Middle School Education, 800 University Drive, Maryville, MO 64468-6001. Awards MS Ed. Accredited by NCATE. Faculty: 14 full-time (12 women). Students: 1 (woman) full-time, 4 part-time (all women). 0 applicants. In 1997, 1 degree awarded. *Degree requirements:* Comprehensive exam required, foreign language and thesis not required. *Entrance requirements:* GRE General Test (minimum combined score of 700), TOEFL (minimum score 550), minimum undergraduate GPA of 2.5, teaching certificate, writing sample. Application deadline: rolling. Application fee: $0 ($50 for international students). *Expenses:* Tuition $113 per credit hour for state residents; $197 per credit hour for nonresidents. Fees $3 per credit hour. *Financial aid:* In 1997–98, 2 teaching assistantships averaging $585 per month were awarded. Financial aid application deadline: 3/1. • Pat Thompson, Director, 816-562-1775. Application contact: Dr. Frances Shipley, Dean of Graduate School, 816-562-1145. E-mail: gradsch@acad.nwmissouri.edu.

Nova Southeastern University, Fischler Center for the Advancement of Education, Program in Child and Youth Studies, Fort Lauderdale, FL 33314-7721. Awards Ed D. Part-time and evening/weekend programs available. Postbaccalaureate distance learning degree programs offered. Students: 34 full-time (27 women), 362 part-time (280 women); includes 89 minority (69 African Americans, 1 Asian American, 16 Hispanics, 3 Native Americans), 10 international. In 1997, 107 degrees awarded. *Degree requirements:* Dissertation, practicum required, foreign language not required. *Entrance requirements:* Master's degree, 3 years of work experience, interview, minimum GPA of 3.0. Application deadline: rolling. Application fee: $50. *Tuition:* $8460 per year. *Financial aid:* Federal Work-Study and career-related internships or fieldwork available. Aid available to part-time students. • Dr. Abbey Manburg, Dean, 954-262-8555. E-mail: manburg@fcae.nova.edu. Application contact: Dr. Vera Flight, Director of Student Development and Admissions, 800-986-3223 Ext. 8550. Fax: 954-262-3905. E-mail: flightr@fcae.nova.edu.

Oglethorpe University, Division of Education, Atlanta, GA 30319-2797. Offerings include middle grades education (MA). Division faculty: 4 full-time (3 women), 3 part-time (all women), 5 FTE. *Degree requirements:* Comprehensive exam required, foreign language and thesis not required. *Entrance requirements:* GRE General Test (minimum combined score of 800), MAT (minimum score 44), PRAXIS, minimum GPA of 2.5. Application deadline: rolling. Application fee: $30. *Tuition:* $500 per course. • Dr. Vienna K. Volante, Chair, 404-261-1441 Ext. 385. Application contact: Bill Price, Graduate Admissions Counselor, 404-364-8307. Fax: 404-364-8500.

Ohio University, Graduate Studies, College of Education, School of Curriculum and Instruction, Athens, OH 45701-2979. Offerings include middle school education (M Ed). Accredited by NCATE. School faculty: 21 full-time (7 women), 16 part-time (11 women). *Application deadline:* rolling. *Application fee:* $30. *Tuition:* $5430 per year full-time, $216 per quarter hour part-time for state residents; $10,431 per year full-time, $423 per quarter hour part-time for nonresidents. • Dr. Ralph Martin, Director, 740-593-4422. Application contact: Dr. Bonnie Beach, Graduate Chair, 740-593-0523.

Pacific University, School of Education, Forest Grove, OR 97116-1797. Offerings include elementary/middle school education (MAT). School faculty: 11 full-time, 8 part-time. *Application deadline:* 3/15 (priority date; rolling processing; 10/15 for spring admission). *Application fee:* $35. • Dr. Willard Kniep, Program Director, 503-359-2205. Application contact: Joel Albin, Admissions Counselor, 503-359-2958. Fax: 503-359-2975. E-mail: admissions@pacificu.edu.

Quinnipiac College, School of Liberal Arts, Program in Secondary and Middle School Teaching, Hamden, CT 06518-1904. Offers biology (MAT), chemistry (MAT), English (MAT), French (MAT), history/social studies (MAT), mathematics (MAT), physics (MAT), Spanish (MAT). Part-time programs available. Faculty: 21 full-time (5 women), 16 part-time (9 women). Students: 55 full-time (35 women), 42 part-time (20 women); includes 4 minority (3 African Americans, 1 Native American). Average age 28. 79 applicants, 91% accepted. In 1997, 48 degrees awarded. *Degree requirements:* Thesis. *Average time to degree:* master's–1.5 years full-time, 3 years part-time. *Entrance requirements:* PRAXIS I, minimum GPA of 2.67. Application deadline: rolling. Application fee: $45. Electronic applications accepted. *Expenses:* Tuition $395 per credit hour. Fees $380 per year full-time. *Financial aid:* Fellowships, partial tuition waivers, and career-related internships or fieldwork available. Aid available to part-time students. Financial aid applicants required to submit FAFSA. • Carol Orticari, Director, 203-281-8978. Fax: 203-281-8709. E-mail: orticari@quinnipiac.edu. Application contact: Scott Farber, Director of Graduate Admissions, 203-281-8795. Fax: 203-287-5238. E-mail: qcgradadmi@quinnipiac.edu.

See in-depth description on page 775.

Rosemont College, College of Graduate Studies, Program in Middle School Education, Rosemont, PA 19010-1699. Awards M Ed. Program new for fall 1998. *Degree requirements:* Thesis or alternative required, foreign language not required. *Entrance requirements:* GRE or MAT. Application deadline: rolling. Application fee: $50. *Tuition:* $6300 per year full-time, $350 per credit part-time. • Application contact: Stan Rostkowski, Enrollment Coordinator, 610-527-0200 Ext. 2187. Fax: 610-526-2964. E-mail: roscolgrad@rosemont.edu.

Directory: Middle School Education

Saginaw Valley State University, College of Education, Program in Middle School Classroom Teaching, University Center, MI 48710. Awards MAT. Accredited by NCATE. Faculty: 12 full-time (9 women). Students: 45 part-time (36 women); includes 2 minority (1 African American, 1 Hispanic). In 1997, 6 degrees awarded. *Entrance requirements:* Minimum GPA of 3.0, teaching certificate. Application deadline: rolling. Application fee: $25. *Expenses:* Tuition $159 per credit hour for state residents; $311 per credit hour for nonresidents. Fees $8.70 per credit hour. • Application contact: Dr. Ervin F. Sparapani, Coordinator, 517-790-4395.

St. Cloud State University, College of Education, Department of Teacher Development, Junior High/Middle School Education Track, St. Cloud, MN 56301-4498. Awards MS. Accredited by NCATE. Faculty: 2 full-time (0 women). Students: 16 part-time (8 women). In 1997, 9 degrees awarded. *Degree requirements:* Thesis or alternative required, foreign language not required. *Entrance requirements:* GRE General Test, minimum GPA of 2.75. Application fee: $20 ($100 for international students). *Expenses:* Tuition $128 per credit for state residents; $203 per credit for nonresidents. Fees $16.32 per credit. *Financial aid:* Graduate assistantships, Federal Work-Study available. Financial aid application deadline: 3/1. • Application contact: Ann Anderson, Graduate Studies Office, 320-255-2113. Fax: 320-654-5371. E-mail: anna@grad.stcloud.msus.edu.

Siena Heights University, Program in Teacher Education, Concentration in Middle School Education, Adrian, MI 49221-1796. Awards MA. Part-time programs available. *Degree requirements:* Computer language, thesis, presentation required, foreign language not required. *Entrance requirements:* Minimum GPA of 3.0, interview. Application deadline: 7/1 (priority date; rolling processing; 12/1 for spring admission). Application fee: $25.

Simmons College, Department of Education, Program in Middle School and High School Teaching, Boston, MA 02115. Awards MAT. Faculty: 3 full-time (2 women), 13 part-time (8 women). Students: 48 full-time (39 women), 28 part-time (23 women); includes 9 minority (5 African Americans, 2 Asian Americans, 2 Hispanics). Average age 24. 78 applicants, 87% accepted. In 1997, 53 degrees awarded. *Degree requirements:* Student teaching experience required, foreign language and thesis not required. *Entrance requirements:* GRE General Test or MAT, interview. Application deadline: 8/1 (priority date; rolling processing; 12/15 for spring admission). Application fee: $35. *Expenses:* Tuition $587 per credit hour. Fees $20 per year. *Financial aid:* Partial tuition waivers, Federal Work-Study, institutionally sponsored loans, and career-related internships or fieldwork available. Aid available to part-time students. Financial aid application deadline: 3/1; applicants required to submit FAFSA. • Lynda Johnson, Director, 617-521-2576. Fax: 617-521-3174. Application contact: Director, Graduate Studies Admission, 617-521-2910. Fax: 617-521-3058. E-mail: gsa@simmons.edu.

Southeast Missouri State University, Department of Secondary Education, Cape Girardeau, MO 63701-4799. Offerings include middle level education (MA). *Degree requirements:* Thesis or alternative required, foreign language not required. *Entrance requirements:* GRE General Test (score in 50th percentile or higher), minimum GPA of 2.75. Application deadline: 4/1 (priority date; rolling processing; 11/21 for spring admission). Application fee: $20 ($100 for international students). *Tuition:* $2034 per year full-time, $113 per credit hour part-time for state residents; $3672 per year full-time, $204 per credit hour part-time for nonresidents. • Dalton Curtis, Chairperson, 573-651-5965. Application contact: Office of Graduate Studies, 573-651-2192.

Spalding University, School of Education, Programs in Teacher Education and Administration, Louisville, KY 40203-2188. Offerings include 5–8 (MA, MAT). Accredited by NCATE. Faculty: 7 full-time (5 women), 5 part-time (4 women). *Entrance requirements:* GRE General Test, interview, portfolio. Application deadline: 8/15 (priority date; rolling processing). Application fee: $30. *Expenses:* Tuition $350 per credit hour (minimum). Fees $48 per year full-time, $4 per credit hour part-time. • Application contact: Jeanne Anderson, Assistant to the Provost and Director of Graduate Office, 502-585-7105. Fax: 502-585-7158. E-mail: gradoffc@spalding6.win.net.

State University of West Georgia, College of Education, Department of Middle Grades Education and Secondary Education, Program in Middle Grades Education, Carrollton, GA 30118. Awards M Ed, Ed S. Accredited by NCATE. M Ed offered jointly with Dalton College. Part-time and evening/weekend programs available. Faculty: 7 full-time (4 women). Students: 115 full-time (91 women), 140 part-time (112 women); includes 46 minority (45 African Americans, 1 Asian American). Average age 37. In 1997, 46 master's, 42 Ed Ss awarded. *Degree requirements:* For Ed S, research project required, foreign language and thesis not required. *Entrance requirements:* For master's, GRE General Test (minimum combined score of 800), minimum GPA of 2.5; for Ed S, GRE General Test (minimum combined score of 800), master's degree, minimum graduate GPA of 3.25. Application deadline: 8/30 (rolling processing). Application fee: $15. *Expenses:* Tuition $2428 per year full-time, $83 per semester hour part-time for state residents; $8428 per year full-time, $250 per semester hour part-time for nonresidents. Fees $428 per year. *Financial aid:* Assistantships and career-related internships or fieldwork available. Aid available to part-time students. Financial aid applicants required to submit FAFSA. *Total annual research expenditures:* $510. • Application contact: Dr. Jack O. Jenkins, Dean, Graduate School, 770-836-6419. Fax: 770-836-2301. E-mail: jjenkins@cob.as.westga.edu.

Tufts University, Division of Graduate and Continuing Studies and Research, Graduate School of Arts and Sciences, Department of Education, Medford, MA 02155. Offerings include middle and secondary education (MA, MAT). Department faculty: 9 full-time, 7 part-time. *Entrance requirements:* GRE General Test, TOEFL (minimum score 550). Application deadline: 2/15 (rolling processing). Application fee: $50. • Kathleen Camara, Chair, 617-627-3244.

Union College, Department of Education, Program in Middle Grades, Barbourville, KY 40906-1499. Awards MA Ed. *Degree requirements:* Thesis optional, foreign language not required. *Entrance requirements:* GRE General Test, NTE. Application deadline: rolling. Application fee: $15. *Tuition:* $220 per hour. • Dr. William E. Bernhardt, Dean of Graduate Academic Affairs, Graduate Programs, 606-546-1210. Fax: 606-546-2217.

University of Arkansas, College of Education, Department of Curriculum and Instruction, Fayetteville, AR 72701-1201. Offerings include middle-level education (MAT). Accredited by NCATE. Department faculty: 26 full-time (16 women). *Application fee:* $25 ($35 for international students). *Tuition:* $3144 per year full-time, $173 per credit hour part-time for state residents; $7140 per year full-time, $395 per credit hour part-time for nonresidents. • Dr. John Helfeldt, Head, 501-575-4209.

University of Florida, College of Education, Department of Instruction and Curriculum, Gainesville, FL 32611. Offerings include middle school education (MAE, M Ed, Ed D, PhD, Ed S). Accredited by NCATE. Department faculty: 42. *Degree requirements:* For master's, thesis optional, foreign language not required; for doctorate, variable foreign language requirement, dissertation. *Entrance requirements:* For master's and doctorate, GRE General Test (minimum combined score of 1000), minimum GPA of 3.0; for Ed S, GRE General Test. Application deadline: 6/5. Application fee: $20. *Tuition:* $138 per credit hour for state residents; $481 per credit hour for nonresidents. • Dr. Mary Grace Kantowski, Chair, 352-392-9191 Ext. 200. E-mail: mgk@coe.ufl.edu. Application contact: Dr. Ben Nelms, Graduate Coordinator, 352-392-9191 Ext. 225. Fax: 352-392-9193. E-mail: bfn@coe.ufl.edu.

University of Georgia, College of Education, Department of Elementary Education, Programs in Elementary and Middle School Education, Athens, GA 30602. Offerings in elementary and middle school education (M Ed, Ed D, Ed S), middle school education (PhD). Accredited by NCATE. Faculty: 15 full-time (11 women). Students: 19 full-time (15 women), 77 part-time; includes 4 minority (3 African Americans, 1 Hispanic), 1 international. 51 applicants, 63% accepted. In 1997, 39 master's, 3 doctorates, 7 Ed Ss awarded. *Degree requirements:* For doctorate, dissertation required, foreign language not required. *Entrance requirements:* For master's and Ed S, GRE General Test or MAT; for doctorate, GRE General Test. Application fee: $30. *Tuition:* $3290 per year full-time, $643 per semester (minimum) part-time for state residents; $11,300 per year full-time, $1645 per semester (minimum) part-time for nonresidents. *Financial aid:* Fellowships, research assistantships, teaching assistantships, assistantships available. • Dr. Judith C. Reiff, Graduate Coordinator, Department of Elementary Education, 706-542-4268. Fax: 706-542-4277.

University of Louisville, School of Education, Department of Early and Middle Childhood Education, Program in Middle School Education, Louisville, KY 40292-0001. Awards M Ed. Accredited by NCATE. Students: 4 full-time (2 women), 35 part-time (27 women); includes 4 minority (3 African Americans, 1 Hispanic). Average age 33. In 1997, 18 degrees awarded. *Entrance requirements:* GRE General Test. Application deadline: rolling. Application fee: $25. • Dr. Diane W. Kyle, Chair, Department of Early and Middle Childhood Education, 502-852-6431.

University of Nebraska at Kearney, College of Education, Department of Elementary/Early Childhood Education, Kearney, NE 68849-0001. Offerings include middle school education (MA Ed). Accredited by NCATE. Department faculty: 4 full-time (1 woman). *Degree requirements:* Thesis optional. *Entrance requirements:* GRE General Test. Application deadline: 8/1 (priority date; rolling processing; 12/15 for spring admission). Application fee: $35. *Expenses:* Tuition $1494 per year full-time, $83 per credit hour part-time for state residents; $2826 per year full-time, $157 per credit hour part-time for nonresidents. Fees $229 per year full-time, $11.25 per semester (minimum) part-time. • Dr. Ed Walker, Chair, 308-865-8513.

University of Nevada, Las Vegas, College of Education, Department of Instructional and Curricular Studies, Las Vegas, NV 89154-9900. Offerings include middle school education (M Ed, MS). Accredited by NCATE. Department faculty: 34 full-time (16 women). *Degree requirements:* Thesis (for some programs), oral or written comprehensive exam required, foreign language not required. *Entrance requirements:* Minimum GPA of 3.0. Application deadline: 2/15 (9/30 for spring admission). Application fee: $40 ($95 for international students). *Expenses:* Tuition $93 per credit for state residents; $93 per credit full-time, $190 per credit part-time for nonresidents. Fees $5570 per year full-time for nonresidents. • Dr. Jan McCarthy, Chair, 702-895-3241. Application contact: Graduate College Admissions Evaluator, 702-895-3320.

University of North Carolina at Charlotte, College of Education, Charlotte, NC 28223-0001. Offerings include middle school education (M Ed). Accredited by NCATE. College faculty: 61 full-time (31 women), 7 part-time (6 women), 62.75 FTE. *Application deadline:* 7/1. *Application fee:* $35. *Tuition:* $1786 per year full-time, $339 per semester (minimum) part-time for state residents; $8914 per year full-time, $2121 per semester (minimum) part-time for nonresidents. • Dr. John M. Nagle, Dean, 704-547-4707. Application contact: Kathy Barringer, Assistant Director of Graduate Admissions, 704-547-3366. Fax: 704-547-3279. E-mail: gradadm@email.uncc.edu.

University of North Carolina at Greensboro, School of Education, Department of Curriculum and Instruction, Program in Middle Grades Education, Greensboro, NC 27412-0001. Awards M Ed. Accredited by NCATE. Part-time programs available. Students: 23 full-time (21 women), 7 part-time (6 women); includes 3 minority (all African Americans), 6 international. 9 applicants, 67% accepted. In 1997, 11 degrees awarded. *Entrance requirements:* GRE General Test. Application fee: $35. *Expenses:* Tuition $1842 per year full-time, $370 per semester (minimum) part-time for state residents; $10,296 per year full-time, $2484 per semester (minimum) part-time for nonresidents. Fees $806 per year full-time, $111 per semester (minimum) part-time. *Financial aid:* 4 students received aid. • Dr. Gerald Ponder, Chair, Department of Curriculum and Instruction, 336-334-3437.

University of North Carolina at Pembroke, Graduate Studies, Department of Education, Program in Middle Grades Education, Pembroke, NC 28372-1510. Awards MA Ed. Accredited by NCATE. Part-time and evening/weekend programs available. Faculty: 18 full-time (6 women). Students: 0. *Degree requirements:* Comprehensive exam required, thesis optional, foreign language not required. *Average time to degree:* master's–2 years full-time, 3 years part-time. *Entrance requirements:* GRE General Test or MAT, minimum GPA of 3.0 in major, 2.5 overall. Application deadline: rolling. Application fee: $25. *Tuition:* $1554 per year full-time, $610 per semester (minimum) part-time for state residents; $8824 per year full-time, $2122 per semester (minimum) part-time for nonresidents. *Financial aid:* Graduate assistantships available. Aid available to part-time students. Financial aid application deadline: 4/15. • Dr. Rhoda Collins, Coordinator, 910-521-6354. Application contact: Director of Graduate Studies, 910-521-6271. Fax: 910-521-6497.

University of Northern Iowa, College of Education, Department of Curriculum and Instruction, Program in Middle School/Junior High Education, Cedar Falls, IA 50614. Awards MA. *Degree requirements:* Thesis or alternative required, foreign language not required. *Entrance requirements:* Minimum GPA of 3.5, 3 years of educational experience. Application deadline: 8/1 (priority date; rolling processing). Application fee: $20 ($30 for international students). *Expenses:* Tuition $3166 per year full-time, $176 per hour part-time for state residents; $7805 per year full-time, $176 per hour part-time for nonresidents. Fees $194 per year full-time, $12.50 per semester (minimum) part-time. *Financial aid:* Application deadline 3/1. • Dr. Robert Muffoletto, Acting Head, Department of Curriculum and Instruction, 319-273-2167.

University of St. Francis, Graduate Studies, Program in Curriculum in Instruction in Middle Schools, Joliet, IL 60435-6188. Awards MS. Faculty: 1 (woman) full-time, 6 part-time (2 women). Students: 31 part-time (29 women). *Degree requirements:* Computer language. *Entrance requirements:* Minimum GPA of 2.75, valid teaching certificate. Application fee: $25. *Tuition:* $285 per credit hour. • Dr. F. William Kelley Jr., Dean, Graduate Studies, 800-735-4723. Fax: 815-740-3537. E-mail: grdinfo@stfrancis.edu.

University of South Florida, College of Education, Department of Secondary Education, Program in Middle School Education, Tampa, FL 33620-9951. Awards M Ed. Accredited by NCATE. Part-time and evening/weekend programs available. Students: 1 full-time (0 women), 4 part-time (all women). Average age 37. 2 applicants, 100% accepted. In 1997, 1 degree awarded. *Entrance requirements:* GRE General Test (minimum combined score of 1000), minimum GPA of 3.5 in last 60 hours. Application deadline: 6/1 (10/15 for spring admission). Application fee: $20. Electronic applications accepted. *Tuition:* $142 per credit hour for state residents; $486 per credit hour for nonresidents. *Financial aid:* Federal Work-Study, institutionally sponsored loans available. Aid available to part-time students. Financial aid applicants required to submit FAFSA. • Application contact: Howard Johnston, Coordinator, 813-974-3398. Fax: 813-974-3837. E-mail: johnston@tempest.coedu.usf.edu.

University of West Florida, College of Education, Division of Teacher Education, Program in Middle Level Education, Pensacola, FL 32514-5750. Awards M Ed. Accredited by NCATE. Part-time and evening/weekend programs available. Students: 12 full-time (8 women), 14 part-time (8 women); includes 8 minority (7 African Americans, 1 Hispanic). Average age 38. In 1997, 8 degrees awarded. *Degree requirements:* Thesis or alternative required, foreign language not required. *Entrance requirements:* GRE General Test (minimum combined score of 1000) or minimum GPA of 3.0. Application deadline: 7/1 (rolling processing; 11/1 for spring admission). Application fee: $20. *Tuition:* $131 per credit hour (minimum) for state residents; $436 per credit hour (minimum) for nonresidents. • Dr. William Evans, Chairperson, Division of Teacher Education, 850-474-2891.

University of Wisconsin–Milwaukee, School of Education, Department of Curriculum and Instruction, Milwaukee, WI 53201-0413. Offerings include junior high/middle school education (MS). Offered jointly with University of Wisconsin–Green Bay. Department faculty: 28 full-time (17 women). *Degree requirements:* Thesis or alternative required, foreign language not required. *Application deadline:* 1/1 (priority date; rolling processing; 9/1 for spring admission). *Application fee:* $45 ($75 for international students). *Tuition:* $4996 per year full-time, $1030 per semester (minimum) part-time for state residents; $15,216 per year full-time, $2947 per semester (minimum) part-time for nonresidents. • Linda Post, Chair, 414-229-4884.

University of Wisconsin–Platteville, College of Liberal Arts and Education, School of Education, Platteville, WI 53818-3099. Offerings include middle school education (MSE). Accredited by NCATE. School faculty: 8 part-time (3 women). *Degree requirements:* Thesis or alternative, comprehensive exam required, foreign language not required. *Entrance requirements:* TOEFL (minimum score 500). Application deadline: 7/1 (priority date; rolling processing; 11/1 for spring admission). Application fee: $45. • Dr. Sally Standiford, Director, 608-342-1131. Fax: 608-342-1133. E-mail: standiford@uwplatt.edu.

Valdosta State University, College of Education, Department of Middle Grades Education, Valdosta, GA 31698. Awards M Ed, Ed S. Accredited by NCATE. Faculty: 5 full-time (3 women). Students: 14 full-time (11 women), 37 part-time (32 women); includes 5 minority (4 African Americans, 1 Asian American). 14 applicants, 86% accepted. In 1997, 25 master's awarded. *Entrance requirements:* For master's, GRE General Test (minimum combined score of 800); for Ed S, GRE General Test (minimum combined score of 900). Application deadline: 8/1 (rolling processing). Application fee: $10. *Expenses:* Tuition $2472 per year full-time, $83 per semester hour part-time for state residents; $8472 per year full-time, $333 per semester hour part-time for nonresidents. Fees $236 per year full-time. *Faculty research:* Learning styles of pre-service teachers, school reform, science teaching practices. • Dr. Frances A. Ducharme, Head, 912-333-5611.

Virginia Commonwealth University, School of Education, Program in Teaching, Richmond, VA 23284-9005. Offerings include middle education (MT). Accredited by NCATE. *Entrance requirements:* GRE General Test or MAT. Application deadline: 3/1 (rolling processing; 10/15 for spring admission). Application fee: $30 ($0 for international students). *Tuition:* $4960 per year full-time, $257 per credit part-time for state residents; $12,652 per year full-time, $684 per credit part-time for nonresidents. • Dr. Alan M. McLeod, Division Head, 804-828-1305. E-mail: ammcleod@vcu.edu. Application contact: Dr. Michael D. Davis, Interim Director, Graduate Studies, 804-828-6530. Fax: 804-828-1323. E-mail: mddavis@vcu.edu.

Wesleyan College, Department of Education, Program in Middle-Level Mathematics and Middle-Level Science Education, Macon, GA 31210-4462. Awards MA. Offered during summer only. Part-time programs available. Faculty: 10 full-time (4 women), 3 part-time (2 women). Students: 7 full-time (all women). Average age 32. 12 applicants, 75% accepted. *Degree requirements:* Practicum, professional portfolio required, thesis optional, foreign language not required. *Average time to degree:* master's–3 years full-time, 6 years part-time. *Entrance requirements:* TOEFL (minimum score 550), interview, teaching certificate. Application deadline: rolling. Application fee: $25. *Tuition:* $150 per semester hour. *Financial aid:* Federal Work-Study available. Financial aid application deadline: 4/15; applicants required to submit FAFSA. *Faculty research:* Instructional technology, cognitive development, verbal classroom interactions. • Application contact: Dr. Patricia R. Hardeman, Assistant Dean and Registrar, 912-477-1110. Fax: 912-757-4030.

Wesley College, Division of Education and Psychology, Dover, DE 19901. Offerings include middle childhood education (M Ed). Division faculty: 5 full-time (4 women), 1 part-time (0 women). *Degree requirements:* Thesis optional, foreign language not required. *Entrance requirements:* GRE. Application deadline: rolling. Application fee: $20. • Dr. B. Patricia Patterson, Chair, 302-736-2448. E-mail: patterpa@mail.wesley.edu. Application contact: Dr. J. Thomas Sturgis, Director of Graduate Studies, 302-736-2414. Fax: 302-736-2301. E-mail: sturgisto@mail.wesley.edu.

Western Carolina University, College of Education and Allied Professions, Department of Elementary and Middle Grades Education, Program in Middle Grades Education, Cullowhee, NC 28723. Awards MA Ed. Accredited by NCATE. Part-time and evening/weekend programs available. Students: 2 full-time (1 woman), 8 part-time (7 women). 3 applicants, 67% accepted. In 1997, 3 degrees awarded. *Degree requirements:* Comprehensive exam required, foreign language and thesis not required. *Entrance requirements:* GRE General Test. Application deadline: rolling. Application fee: $35. *Tuition:* $1799 per year full-time, $144 per credit hour (minimum) part-time for state residents; $9069 per year full-time, $1053 per credit hour (minimum) part-time for nonresidents. *Financial aid:* In 1997–98, 3 students received aid, including 3 research assistantships (2 to first-year students) totaling $7,500; fellowships, teaching assistantships, Federal Work-Study, institutionally sponsored loans also available. Financial aid application deadline: 3/15. • Application contact: Kathleen Owen, Assistant to the Dean, 828-227-7398. Fax: 828-227-7480.

Western Kentucky University, College of Education, Department of Teacher Education, Program in Middle Grades Education, Bowling Green, KY 42101-3576. Awards MA Ed. Accredited by NCATE. Part-time and evening/weekend programs available. Postbaccalaureate distance learning degree programs offered (minimal on-campus study). Faculty: 29 full-time (16 women), 2 part-time (1 woman), 30 FTE. Students: 1 (woman) full-time, 64 part-time (41 women). Average age 31. 11 applicants, 91% accepted. In 1997, 38 degrees awarded. *Entrance requirements:* GRE General Test (minimum combined score of 1150 on three sections; average 1265), minimum GPA of 2.5. Application deadline: 8/1 (priority date; rolling processing; 12/1 for spring admission). Application fee: $20. *Tuition:* $2460 per year full-time, $133 per credit hour part-time for state residents; $6700 per year full-time, $369 per credit hour part-time for nonresidents. *Financial aid:* Federal Work-Study, institutionally sponsored loans available. Aid available to part-time students. Financial aid application deadline: 4/1; applicants required to submit FAFSA. • Dr. Vicki Stayton, Head, Department of Teacher Education, 502-745-5414.

Western Michigan University, College of Education, Department of Education and Professional Development, Program in Middle School Education, Kalamazoo, MI 49008. Awards MA. Accredited by NCATE. Students: 47 part-time (43 women); includes 2 minority (both African Americans), 2 international. 13 applicants, 8% accepted. In 1997, 8 degrees awarded. *Application deadline:* 2/15 (priority date; rolling processing). *Application fee:* $25. *Expenses:* Tuition $154 per credit hour for state residents; $372 per credit hour for nonresidents. Fees $602 per year full-time, $132 per semester part-time. *Financial aid:* Fellowships, research assistantships, teaching assistantships, Federal Work-Study available. Financial aid application deadline: 2/15; applicants required to submit FAFSA. • Application contact: Paula J. Boodt, Coordinator, Graduate Admissions and Recruitment, 616-387-2000. E-mail: paulaboodt@wmich.edu.

Western Oregon University, School of Education, Department of Elementary Education, Program in Elementary Education, Monmouth, OR 97361. Offerings include middle school education (MS Ed). Accredited by NCATE. Program faculty: 5 full-time (4 women), 9 part-time (5 women), 6 FTE. *Degree requirements:* Written exam required, thesis optional, foreign language not required. *Average time to degree:* master's–1 year full-time, 5 years part-time. *Entrance requirements:* California Basic Educational Skills Test, GRE General Test (average 450 on each section) or MAT (30), minimum GPA of 3.0, teaching license. Application deadline: rolling. Application fee: $50. • Application contact: Alison Marshall, Director of Admissions, 503-838-8211. Fax: 503-838-8807. E-mail: marshaa@wou.edu.

Westfield State College, Department of Education, Program in Middle School Education, Westfield, MA 01086. Awards M Ed. *Degree requirements:* Comprehensive exam, practicum required, foreign language and thesis not required. *Entrance requirements:* GRE General Test or MAT, minimum undergraduate GPA of 2.7. Application deadline: rolling. Application fee: $30. *Expenses:* Tuition $145 per credit for state residents; $155 per credit for nonresidents. Fees $90 per semester. *Financial aid:* Application deadline 4/1. • Application contact: Marcia Davio, Graduate Records Clerk, 413-572-8024.

Worcester State College, Graduate Studies, Department of Education, Program in Middle School Education, Worcester, MA 01602-2597. Awards M Ed, Certificate. *Degree requirements:* For master's, comprehensive exam. *Entrance requirements:* For master's, GRE General Test or MAT. Application fee: $10 ($40 for international students). *Tuition:* $127 per credit hour. • Dr. Joshua Aisiku, Coordinator, 508-929-8668. Application contact: Andrea Wetmore, Graduate Admissions Counselor, 508-929-8120. E-mail: awetmore@worc.mass.edu.

Youngstown State University, College of Education, Department of Teacher Education, Program in Early and Middle Childhood Education, Youngstown, OH 44555-0002. Offers teaching—elementary education (MS Ed), teaching—secondary reading (MS Ed). Accredited by NCATE. Part-time and evening/weekend programs available. Faculty: 9 full-time (6 women), 8 part-time (all women). Students: 3 full-time (2 women), 144 part-time (132 women); includes 1 minority (African American). 29 applicants, 100% accepted. In 1997, 44 degrees awarded. *Degree requirements:* Comprehensive exam required, foreign language and thesis not required. *Entrance requirements:* TOEFL (minimum score 550), GRE, MAT, or teaching certificate; minimum GPA of 2.5. Application deadline: 8/15 (priority date; rolling processing; 2/15 for spring admission). Application fee: $30 ($75 for international students). *Expenses:* Tuition $90 per credit hour for state residents; $144 per credit hour (minimum) for nonresidents. Fees $528 per year full-time, $244 per year (minimum) part-time. *Financial aid:* In 1997–98, 40 students received aid, including 4 research assistantships averaging $666 per month and totaling $34,080, 36 scholarships totaling $17,974; teaching assistantships, Federal Work-Study, institutionally sponsored loans also available. Aid available to part-time students. Financial aid application deadline: 3/1. • Application contact: Dr. Peter J. Kasvinsky, Dean of Graduate Studies, 330-742-3091. Fax: 330-742-1580. E-mail: amgrad03@ysub.ysu.edu.

Secondary Education

Abilene Christian University, College of Arts and Sciences, Department of Education, Program in Secondary Teaching, Abilene, TX 79699-9100. Awards M Ed. Part-time programs available. Faculty: 11 part-time (4 women). Students: 3 full-time (2 women), 2 part-time (0 women); includes 1 minority (African American). 8 applicants, 63% accepted. In 1997, 4 degrees awarded (100% found work related to degree). *Degree requirements:* Comprehensive exam required, foreign language and thesis not required. *Entrance requirements:* GRE General Test or MAT. Application deadline: 4/1 (priority date; rolling processing; 11/1 for spring admission). Application fee: $25 ($45 for international students). *Expenses:* Tuition $308 per credit hour. Fees $430 per year full-time, $85 per semester (minimum) part-time. *Financial aid:* Federal Work-Study available. Aid available to part-time students. Financial aid application deadline: 4/1. • Dr. Roger Gee, Graduate Adviser, 915-674-2122. Application contact: Dr. Carley Dodd, Graduate Dean, 915-674-2354. Fax: 915-674-6717. E-mail: gradinfo@nicanor.acu.edu.

Adams State College, School of Education and Graduate Studies, Department of Teacher Education, Program in Secondary Education, Alamosa, CO 81102. Awards MA. Accredited by NCATE. Part-time programs available. *Degree requirements:* Qualifying exam required, foreign language and thesis not required. *Entrance requirements:* GRE General Test or MAT, minimum undergraduate GPA of 2.75. Application deadline: 5/15 (priority date; rolling processing; 10/15 for spring admission). Application fee: $25. *Tuition:* $2164 per year full-time, $111 per credit part-time for state residents; $7284 per year full-time, $377 per credit part-time for nonresidents. *Financial aid:* In 1997–98, 1 graduate assistantship averaging $400 per month and totaling $4,000 was awarded; Federal Work-Study, institutionally sponsored loans, and career-related internships or fieldwork also available. Aid available to part-time students. Financial aid application deadline: 4/15; applicants required to submit FAFSA. • Dr. John Cross, Head, Department of Teacher Education, 719-587-7776.

Adelphi University, School of Education, Program in Secondary Education, Garden City, NY 11530. Offers art (MA), biology (MA), chemistry (MA), English (MA), mathematics (MA), music (MA), physics (MA), social studies (MA), Spanish (MA). Part-time and evening/weekend programs available. Students: 21 full-time (14 women), 87 part-time (56 women); includes 13 minority (7 African Americans, 6 Hispanics). Average age 33. In 1997, 44 degrees awarded. *Application deadline:* rolling. *Application fee:* $50. *Expenses:* Tuition $16,000 per year full-time, $485 per credit part-time. Fees $500 per year full-time, $150 per semester part-time. *Financial aid:* Assistantships available. Financial aid application deadline: 3/1. *Faculty research:* Education and inequality, gender and education, history of progressive education, secondary social studies curriculum issues, school histories. • Director, 516-877-4090. Application contact: Jennifer Spiegel, Associate Director of Graduate Admissions, 516-877-3055.

Adelphi University, School of Education, Specialization in Bilingual Education, Garden City, NY 11530. Offerings include secondary education (MA). *Application deadline:* rolling. *Application fee:* $50. *Expenses:* Tuition $16,000 per year full-time, $485 per credit part-time. Fees $500 per year full-time, $150 per semester part-time. • Eva Roca, Director, 516-877-4070.

Alabama Agricultural and Mechanical University, School of Education, Department of Curriculum and Instruction, Area in Secondary Education, PO Box 1357, Normal, AL 35762-1357. Offers programs in education (M Ed, Ed S), higher administration (MS). Accredited by NCATE. Evening/weekend programs available. Faculty: 7 full-time (2 women), 2 part-time (0 women). *Degree requirements:* For master's, comprehensive exam required, foreign language not required; for Ed S, thesis required, foreign language not required. *Entrance requirements:* For master's, GRE General Test. Application deadline: 5/1. Application fee: $15 ($20 for international students). *Expenses:* Tuition $2782 per year full-time, $565 per semester (minimum) part-time for state residents; $5164 per year full-time, $1015 per semester (minimum) part-time for nonresidents. Fees $560 per year full-time, $390 per year part-time. *Financial aid:* Fellowships and career-related internships or fieldwork available. Financial aid application deadline: 4/1. *Faculty research:* World peace through education, computer-assisted instruction. • Dr. Earnest Dees, Chair, Department of Curriculum and Instruction, 205-851-5520. Fax: 205-851-5526.

Alabama State University, School of Graduate Studies, College of Education, Department of Curriculum and Instruction, Program in Secondary Education, Montgomery, AL 36101-0271. Offers biology education (M Ed), English education (M Ed), history education (M Ed), mathematics education (M Ed), secondary education (Ed S). Faculty: 2 full-time (1 woman). Students: 5 full-time (3 women), 19 part-time (12 women); includes 15 minority (all African Americans). In 1997, 33 master's awarded. *Degree requirements:* For master's, comprehensive exam required, thesis optional; for Ed S, thesis. *Entrance requirements:* For master's, GRE General Test, MAT or NTE. Application deadline: 7/15 (rolling processing; 12/15 for spring admission). Application fee: $10. *Expenses:* Tuition $85 per credit hour for state residents; $170 per credit hour for nonresidents. Fees $486 per year. • Dr. Linda Bradford, Coordinator, 334-229-4485. Fax: 334-229-4904. E-mail: lbradford@asunet.alasu.edu. Application contact: Dr. Fred Dauser, Dean of Graduate Studies, 334-229-4276. Fax: 334-229-4928.

Albany State University, School of Education, Program in Secondary Education, Albany, GA 31705-2717. Awards M Ed. Accredited by NCATE. *Degree requirements:* Comprehensive exam. *Entrance requirements:* GRE General Test (minimum combined score of 800), MAT (minimum score 44) or NTE (minimum score 550). Application deadline: 9/1. Application fee:

Directory: Secondary Education

Albany State University (continued)
$10. *Financial aid:* Application deadline 4/1. • Dr. Claude Perkins, Dean, School of Education, 912-430-4715. Fax: 912-430-4993. E-mail: cperkins@fld94.alsnet.peachnet.edu.

Alcorn State University, School of Psychology and Education, Lorman, MS 39096-9402. Offerings include secondary education (MS Ed), with option in health and physical education. Accredited by NCATE. *Degree requirements:* Thesis optional, foreign language not required. *Application deadline:* 7/1 (priority date; rolling processing; 12/1 for spring admission). *Application fee:* $10. *Tuition:* $2470 per year full-time, $378 per semester (minimum) part-time for state residents; $5331 per year full-time, $855 per semester (minimum) part-time for nonresidents.

Alfred University, Graduate School, Division of Education, Alfred, NY 14802-1205. Offerings include secondary education (MS Ed), with options in biology education, chemistry education, earth science education, English education, mathematics education, physics education, social studies education. Division faculty: 45 full-time (12 women). *Degree requirements:* Thesis required (for some programs), foreign language not required. *Entrance requirements:* TOEFL. Application deadline: rolling. Application fee: $50. *Expenses:* Tuition $20,376 per year full-time, $390 per credit hour (minimum) part-time. Fees $546 per year. • Dr. Katherine D. Wiesendanger, Chair, 607-871-2219. E-mail: fwiesendange@bigvax.alfred.edu. Application contact: Cathleen R. Johnson, Assistant Director of Admissions, 607-871-2141. Fax: 607-871-2198. E-mail: johnsonc@bigvax.alfred.edu.

American International College, School of Continuing Education and Graduate Studies, School of Psychology and Education, Department of Education, Springfield, MA 01109-3189. Offerings include secondary education (M Ed, CAGS). Department faculty: 5 full-time (3 women), 15 part-time (9 women). *Degree requirements:* For CAGS, practicum required, foreign language not required. *Application fee:* $15 ($25 for international students). *Expenses:* Tuition $363 per credit hour. Fees $25 per semester. • C. Gerald Weaver, Dean, School of Psychology and Education, 413-747-6338.

American University, College of Arts and Sciences, School of Education, Program in Secondary Teaching, Washington, DC 20016-8001. Awards MAT. Faculty: 8 full-time (5 women), 10 part-time (8 women), 11.3 FTE. Students: 8 full-time (6 women), 15 part-time (12 women); includes 1 minority (Hispanic). 27 applicants, 89% accepted. In 1997, 22 degrees awarded. *Degree requirements:* Thesis or alternative, comprehensive exam required, foreign language not required. *Entrance requirements:* GRE General Test or MAT, minimum GPA of 3.0. Application deadline: 2/1 (10/1 for spring admission). Application fee: $50. *Expenses:* Tuition $687 per credit hour. Fees $180 per year full-time, $110 per year part-time. *Financial aid:* Application deadline 2/1. • Application contact: Tim Willmot, Academic Coordinator, 202-885-3716. Fax: 202-885-1187. E-mail: tw7106a@american.edu.

Andrews University, School of Graduate Studies, School of Education, Department of Teaching/Learning/Administration, Berrien Springs, MI 49104. Offerings include secondary education (MAT), with options in biology, education, English, English as a second language, French, history, physics. *Application deadline:* 8/15 (rolling processing). *Application fee:* $30. *Expenses:* Tuition $290 per quarter hour (minimum). Fees $75 per quarter. • Dr. William H. Green, Chair, 616-471-3465.

Appalachian State University, College of Education, Department of Curriculum and Instruction, Boone, NC 28608. Offerings include secondary education (MA). Accredited by NCATE. Postbaccalaureate distance learning degree programs offered (minimal on-campus study). Department faculty: 19 full-time (9 women), 2 part-time (1 woman). *Degree requirements:* Thesis or alternative, comprehensive exams required, foreign language not required. *Average time to degree:* master's–2 years full-time, 4 years part-time. *Entrance requirements:* GRE General Test or MAT. Application deadline: 7/31 (priority date). Application fee: $35. *Tuition:* $1811 per year full-time, $354 per semester (minimum) part-time for state residents; $9081 per year full-time, $2171 per semester (minimum) part-time for nonresidents. • Dr. Michael Jacobson, Chairperson, 704-262-2224.

Arizona State University West, College of Education, Phoenix, AZ 85069-7100. Offerings include secondary education (M Ed). College faculty: 19 full-time (13 women), 12 part-time (7 women), 24.23 FTE. *Degree requirements:* Comprehensive exams required, thesis not required. *Entrance requirements:* GRE or MAT, TOEFL. Application deadline: rolling. Application fee: $40. *Expenses:* Tuition $2088 per year full-time, $330 per course part-time for state residents; $9040 per year full-time, $1131 per course part-time for nonresidents. Fees $10 per year (minimum). • Dr. William S. Svoboda, Dean, 602-543-6300. Application contact: Ray Buss, Assistant Dean, 602-543-6300. Fax: 602-543-6350.

Arkansas State University, College of Education, Department of Educational Administration and Secondary Education, State University, AR 72467. Offers programs in curriculum and instruction (MSE, Ed S), educational administration (MSE, Ed S), educational leadership (Ed D), secondary education teaching (MSE). Accredited by NCATE. Part-time programs available. Faculty: 12 full-time (3 women), 2 part-time (both women). Students: 16 full-time (9 women), 140 part-time (76 women); includes 21 minority (all African Americans). Average age 39. In 1997, 32 master's, 5 doctorates, 3 Ed Ss awarded. *Degree requirements:* For master's, thesis or alternative, comprehensive exam; for doctorate, dissertation, comprehensive exam; for Ed S, 2 years of professional experience, oral and written comprehensive exams required, thesis not required. *Entrance requirements:* For master's, GRE General Test or MAT, appropriate bachelor's degree; for doctorate and Ed S, GRE General Test or MAT, master's degree. Application deadline: 7/1 (priority date; rolling processing; 11/15 for spring admission). Application fee: $15 ($25 for international students). *Expenses:* Tuition $2760 per year full-time, $115 per credit hour part-time for state residents; $6936 per year full-time, $289 per credit hour part-time for nonresidents. Fees $506 per year full-time, $44 per semester (minimum) part-time. *Financial aid:* Teaching assistantships and career-related internships or fieldwork available. Aid available to part-time students. Financial aid application deadline: 7/1; applicants required to submit FAFSA. • Dr. David Cox, Chair, 870-972-3062. Fax: 870-972-3945. E-mail: dwcox@pawnee.astate.edu.

Armstrong Atlantic State University, School of Graduate Studies, Program in Education, Savannah, GA 31419-1997. Offerings include secondary education (M Ed). Accredited by NCATE. Program faculty: 25. *Expenses:* Tuition $83 per quarter hour for state residents; $250 per quarter hour for nonresidents. Fees $145 per quarter hour for state residents; $228 per quarter hour for nonresidents. • Dr. Bettye Anne Battiste, Department Head, 912-927-5281.

Auburn University, College of Education, Department of Curriculum and Teaching, Auburn University, AL 36849-0001. Offerings include secondary education (M Ed, MS, PhD, Ed S), with options in English language arts, mathematics, science, social studies. Accredited by NCATE. Department faculty: 20 full-time (11 women). *Degree requirements:* For master's, thesis (MS) required, foreign language not required; for doctorate, dissertation required, foreign language not required; for Ed S, field project required, foreign language and thesis not required. *Entrance requirements:* For master's and Ed S, GRE General Test; for doctorate, GRE General Test (minimum score 450 on each section, 1000 combined). Application deadline: 9/1 (rolling processing; 3/1 for spring admission). Application fee: $25 ($50 for international students). *Expenses:* Tuition $2760 per year full-time, $76 per credit hour part-time for state residents; $8280 per year full-time, $228 per credit hour part-time for nonresidents. Fees $30 per year full-time, $160 per quarter part-time for state residents; $30 per year full-time, $480 per quarter part-time for nonresidents. • Dr. Andrew M. Weaver, Head, 334-844-4434. E-mail: weaveam@mail.auburn.edu. Application contact: Dr. John F. Pritchett, Dean of the Graduate School, 334-844-4700.

Auburn University Montgomery, School of Education, Department of Foundations, Secondary, and Physical Education, Montgomery, AL 36124-4023. Offers programs in physical education (M Ed), secondary education (M Ed, Ed S). Accredited by NCATE. Part-time and evening/weekend programs available. Students: 64 full-time (36 women), 34 part-time (22 women); includes 26 minority (25 African Americans, 1 Native American). Average age 31. In 1997, 73 master's, 12 Ed Ss awarded. *Degree requirements:* Comprehensive exam required, thesis optional, foreign language not required. *Entrance requirements:* For master's, GRE General Test or MAT, certification, BS in teaching; for Ed S, GRE General Test or MAT, certification. Application deadline: 9/1 (priority date; rolling processing; 3/28 for spring admission). Application fee: $25. Electronic applications accepted. *Tuition:* $2664 per year full-time, $85 per quarter hour part-time for state residents; $7080 per year full-time, $255 per quarter hour part-time for nonresidents. *Financial aid:* In 1997–98, 3 teaching assistantships were awarded. • Dr. Jennifer Brown, Head, 334-244-3545.

Augusta State University, College of Education, Program in Secondary Education, Augusta, GA 30904-2200. Awards M Ed, Ed S. Accredited by NCATE. Part-time and evening/weekend programs available. Faculty: 6 full-time (3 women). Students: 6 full-time (4 women), 13 part-time (11 women); includes 2 minority (both African Americans). Average age 35. 5 applicants, 100% accepted. In 1997, 6 master's, 1 Ed S awarded. *Degree requirements:* Thesis, comprehensive exam. *Entrance requirements:* For master's, GRE, MAT, minimum GPA of 2.5; for Ed S, GRE, MAT. Application deadline: 7/26 (priority date; rolling processing). Application fee: $10. *Tuition:* $2260 per year full-time, $83 per credit hour part-time for state residents; $8260 per year full-time, $333 per credit hour part-time for nonresidents. *Financial aid:* Federal Work-Study, institutionally sponsored loans, and career-related internships or fieldwork available. Aid available to part-time students. Financial aid application deadline: 4/15; applicants required to submit FAFSA. *Faculty research:* Effective teaching practices. • Dr. Mary Gendernalik Cooper, Chair, 706-737-1496. E-mail: mcooper@aug.edu. Application contact: Heather Eakin, Secretary to the Dean, 706-737-1499. Fax: 706-667-4706. E-mail: heakin@aug.edu.

Austin College, Sherman, TX 75090-4440. Offerings include teacher education (MA), with options in elementary education, secondary education. Applicants must meet Austin College's undergraduate curriculum requirements. College faculty: 5 full-time (3 women). *Degree requirements:* 1 foreign language, computer language, thesis or alternative. *Average time to degree:* master's–5 years full-time. *Entrance requirements:* Texas Academic Skills Program (minimum score 220 required on reading, writing, and math sections). Application deadline: 5/1 (priority date; rolling processing). Application fee: $35. Electronic applications accepted. *Expenses:* Tuition $14,080 per year full-time, $2010 per course part-time. Fees $125 per year full-time. • Dr. John White, Director, 903-813-2459. Fax: 903-813-2326.

Austin Peay State University, College of Education, Department of Education, Clarksville, TN 37044-0001. Offerings include secondary education (Ed S). Accredited by NCATE. Ed S offered jointly with Tennessee State University. *Entrance requirements:* GRE General Test (minimum score 350 on verbal and quantitative sections), master's degree, minimum graduate GPA of 3.0. Application deadline: 7/31 (priority date; rolling processing; 12/4 for spring admission). Application fee: $15. *Expenses:* Tuition $2438 per year full-time, $123 per semester hour part-time for state residents; $7034 per year full-time, $324 per semester hour part-time for nonresidents. Fees $484 per year (minimum) full-time, $154 per semester (minimum) part-time. • J. Ronald Groseclose, Interim Chair, 931-648-7585. Fax: 931-648-5991. E-mail: groseclosег@apsu.edu.

Ball State University, Teachers College, Department of Secondary, Higher, and Foundations of Education, Program in Secondary Education, 2000 University Avenue, Muncie, IN 47306-1099. Awards MA. Accredited by NCATE. Students: 12 full-time (6 women), 25 part-time (17 women); includes 4 minority (all African Americans). Average age 30. 27 applicants, 89% accepted. In 1997, 34 degrees awarded. *Application fee:* $15 ($25 for international students). *Expenses:* Tuition $3454 per year full-time, $518 per semester (minimum) part-time for state residents; $9316 per year full-time, $1221 per semester (minimum) part-time for nonresidents. Fees $242 per year full-time, $18 per semester (minimum) part-time. • Thomas Fiala, Head, 765-285-5460.

Beaver College, Department of Education, Glenside, PA 19038-3295. Offerings include secondary education (M Ed, CAS). *Application fee:* $35. *Expenses:* Tuition $6570 per year full-time, $365 per credit part-time. Fees $35 per year.

Boston College, Graduate School of Education, Department of Teacher Education/Special Education and Curriculum and Instruction, Program in Secondary Education, Chestnut Hill, MA 02167-9991. Offers biology (MST), chemistry (MST), English (MAT), geology (MST), history (MAT), Latin and classics (MAT), mathematics (MST), physics (MST), religious education (M Ed), Romance languages (MAT), secondary teaching (M Ed). Accredited by NCATE. Students: 52 full-time (32 women), 73 part-time (45 women); includes 18 minority (7 African Americans, 5 Asian Americans, 6 Hispanics), 3 international. 262 applicants, 71% accepted. In 1997, 63 degrees awarded. *Degree requirements:* Comprehensive exam required, thesis not required. *Entrance requirements:* GRE General Test. Application deadline: 3/15 (11/15 for spring admission). Application fee: $40. *Expenses:* Tuition $626 per semester hour. Fees $80 per year (minimum) full-time, $30 per semester part-time. *Financial aid:* Fellowships, research assistantships, teaching assistantships, administrative assistantships, merit scholarships, partial tuition waivers, Federal Work-Study, and career-related internships or fieldwork available. Aid available to part-time students. *Faculty research:* Curriculum theory and practice, teacher preparation, learning styles. • Application contact: Arline Riordan, Graduate Admissions Director, 617-552-4214. Fax: 617-552-0812. E-mail: riordana@bc.edu.

Bowie State University, Programs in Education, Program in Secondary Education, 14000 Jericho Park Road, Bowie, MD 20715. Awards M Ed. Part-time and evening/weekend programs available. *Degree requirements:* Research paper, written comprehensive exam required, thesis optional. *Entrance requirements:* Minimum undergraduate GPA of 3.0, bachelor's degree in education, teaching certificate, teaching experience. Application deadline: 8/16 (priority date; rolling processing). Application fee: $30. *Expenses:* Tuition $169 per credit hour for state residents; $304 per credit hour for nonresidents. Fees $171 per year.

Bowling Green State University, College of Education and Allied Professions, Department of Educational Curriculum and Instruction, Program in Secondary Education, Bowling Green, OH 43403. Awards M Ed. Accredited by NCATE. Part-time programs available. Faculty: 14 full-time (8 women), 1 part-time (0 women). Students: 2 full-time (0 women), 13 part-time (9 women). 11 applicants, 55% accepted. In 1997, 11 degrees awarded. *Degree requirements:* Thesis or alternative required, foreign language not required. *Entrance requirements:* GRE General Test, TOEFL (minimum score 580). Application deadline: rolling. Application fee: $30. Electronic applications accepted. *Tuition:* $6070 per year full-time, $284 per credit hour part-time for state residents; $11,358 per year full-time, $536 per credit hour part-time for nonresidents. *Financial aid:* Federal Work-Study available. Financial aid application deadline: 2/15; applicants required to submit FAFSA. • Dr. Rosalind Hammond, Chair, Department of Educational Curriculum and Instruction, 419-372-7320.

Bridgewater State College, School of Education, Department of Secondary Education and Professional Programs, Program in Secondary Education, Bridgewater, MA 02325-0001. Awards MAT. Accredited by NCATE. *Entrance requirements:* GRE General Test. Application deadline: 4/1 (10/1 for spring admission). Application fee: $25. *Expenses:* Tuition $1675 per year full-time, $70 per credit part-time for state residents; $6450 per year full-time, $269 per credit part-time for nonresidents. Fees $1588 per year full-time, $66 per credit hour part-time for state residents; $1588 per year full-time, $66 per credit part-time for nonresidents. • Application contact: Graduate School, 508-697-1300.

Brooklyn College of the City University of New York, School of Education, Division of Secondary Education, 2900 Bedford Avenue, Brooklyn, NY 11210-2889. Offers programs in art education (MA), biology education (MA), chemistry education (MA), English education (MA), French (MA), general science education (MA), health and nutrition sciences (MS Ed), home economics education (MS Ed), mathematics education (MA), music (MS Ed), physics education (MA), social studies education (MA), Spanish education (MA), speech (MA), speech and hearing handicapped education (MS Ed). Part-time and evening/weekend programs available. Students: 5 full-time (2 women), 204 part-time (115 women); includes 52 minority (30 African Americans, 7 Asian Americans, 15 Hispanics), 4 international. In 1997, 57 degrees awarded. *Entrance requirements:* GRE, TOEFL (minimum score 500), previous course work in education. Application deadline: 3/1 (11/1 for spring admission). Application fee: $40. *Expenses:* Tuition $4350 per year full-time, $185 per credit part-time for state residents; $7600 per year full-time, $320 per credit part-time for nonresidents. Fees $500 per year for state residents; $806 per year for nonresidents. *Financial aid:* Full and partial tuition waivers, Federal Work-Study, institutionally sponsored loans, and career-related internships or fieldwork available. Financial aid application deadline: 5/1; applicants required to submit FAFSA. *Faculty research:* Interdisciplinary education, semiotics, discourse analysis, autobiography, teacher identity. • Dr. Peter Taubman, Coordinator, 718-951-5218. Fax: 718-951-4816. E-mail: ptaubman@brooklyn.cuny.edu.

Brown University, Department of Education, Providence, RI 02912. Offerings include secondary biology (MAT), secondary English (MAT), secondary social studies (MAT). MAT (elementary education K–6) new for fall 1998. Department faculty: 4 full-time (2 women), 20 part-time (15 women). *Average time to degree:* master's–1 year full-time. *Entrance requirements:* GRE (score in 95th percentile or higher). Application deadline: 1/2 (priority date). Application fee: $60. *Expenses:* Tuition $23,616 per year. Fees $436 per year. • Lawrence Wakeford, Chairman, 401-863-2407. Application contact: Yvette Nachmias, Teacher Education Coordinator, 401-863-3364. Fax: 401-863-1276. E-mail: yvette_nachmias@brown.edu.

Butler University, College of Education, Indianapolis, IN 46208-3485. Offerings include secondary education (MS). Accredited by NCATE. College faculty: 10 full-time (3 women), 22 part-time (8 women), 22.5 FTE. *Average time to degree:* master's–7 years part-time; other advanced degree–5 years part-time. *Entrance requirements:* GRE General Test, MAT (minimum score 40), interview. Application deadline: 8/15 (priority date; rolling processing). Application fee: $25. *Tuition:* $220 per credit hour. • Dr. Saundra Tracy, Dean, 317-940-9514. Fax: 317-940-6481. E-mail: stracy@butler.edu.

California State University, Long Beach, College of Education, Department of Teacher Education, Program in Secondary Education, Long Beach, CA 90840-2201. Awards MA. Faculty: 3 full-time (2 women). Students: 2 full-time (1 woman), 10 part-time (7 women); includes 4 minority (1 African American, 3 Asian Americans). Average age 35. 6 applicants, 33% accepted. In 1997, 3 degrees awarded. *Degree requirements:* Comprehensive exam or thesis required, foreign language not required. *Entrance requirements:* GRE General Test, minimum GPA of 2.75. Application deadline: 8/1 (rolling processing; 12/1 for spring admission). Application fee: $55. *Expenses:* Tuition $0 for state residents; $246 per unit for nonresidents. Fees $1846 per year full-time, $1180 per year part-time. *Financial aid:* Application deadline 3/2. • Dr. John Attinasi, Chair, Department of Teacher Education, 562-985-4506. Fax: 562-985-1774. E-mail: jattinas@csulb.edu.

California State University, Los Angeles, School of Education, Division of Curriculum and Instruction, Major in Secondary Teaching, Los Angeles, CA 90032-8530. Awards MA. Accredited by NCATE. Part-time and evening/weekend programs available. Students: 6 full-time (3 women), 9 part-time (7 women); includes 8 minority (2 Asian Americans, 6 Hispanics), 1 international. *Degree requirements:* Comprehensive exam, project, or thesis required, foreign language not required. *Entrance requirements:* TOEFL (minimum score 550), minimum GPA of 2.75 in last 90 units, teaching certificate. Application deadline: 6/30 (rolling processing; 2/1 for spring admission). Application fee: $55. *Expenses:* Tuition $0 for state residents; $164 per unit for nonresidents. Fees $1763 per year full-time, $1097 per year part-time. *Financial aid:* 3 students received aid; Federal Work-Study available. Aid available to part-time students. Financial aid application deadline: 3/1. *Faculty research:* Computer education, teaching effectiveness, diagnosis and treatment of reading disabilities, library science, language acquisition. • Dr. Judith Washburn, Chair, Division of Curriculum and Instruction, 213-343-4350.

California State University, Northridge, College of Education, Department of Secondary Education, Northridge, CA 91330. Awards MA. Accredited by NCATE. Part-time programs available. Faculty: 11 full-time, 16 part-time. Students: 16 full-time (6 women), 64 part-time (39 women); includes 23 minority (4 African Americans, 6 Asian Americans, 11 Hispanics, 2 Native Americans), 2 international. Average age 35. 50 applicants, 86% accepted. *Degree requirements:* Thesis optional, foreign language not required. *Entrance requirements:* TOEFL, GRE General Test, MAT, or minimum GPA of 3.0. Application deadline: 11/30. Application fee: $55. *Expenses:* Tuition $0 for state residents; $246 per unit for nonresidents. Fees $1970 per year full-time, $1304 per year part-time. *Financial aid:* Application deadline 3/1. • Dr. James Cunningham, Chair, 818-677-2580. Application contact: Barnabas Hughes, Graduate Coordinator, 818-677-2581.

California State University, San Bernardino, Graduate Studies, School of Education, Program in Secondary Education, San Bernardino, CA 92407-2397. Awards MA. Part-time and evening/weekend programs available. Faculty: 17 full-time (7 women), 9 part-time (4 women). Students: 56 full-time (41 women), 109 part-time (67 women); includes 17 minority (7 Asian Americans, 10 Hispanics). 103 applicants, 100% accepted. *Degree requirements:* Thesis or alternative required, foreign language not required. *Entrance requirements:* GRE General Test, minimum GPA of 3.0 in education. Application deadline: 8/31 (priority date). Application fee: $55. *Expenses:* Tuition $0 for state residents; $164 per unit for nonresidents. Fees $1922 per year full-time, $1256 per year part-time. *Financial aid:* Federal Work-Study and career-related internships or fieldwork available. Aid available to part-time students. • Dr. Alvin Wolf, Coordinator, Secondary Interns, 909-880-5643.

California State University, Stanislaus, School of Education, Department of Teacher Education, Program in Curriculum and Instruction, Specialization in Secondary Education, Turlock, CA 95382. Awards MA Ed. Accredited by NCATE. Part-time programs available. Faculty: 12 full-time (8 women). Students: 0. Average age 28. *Degree requirements:* Thesis required, foreign language not required. *Entrance requirements:* MAT. Application fee: $55. *Expenses:* Tuition $0 for state residents; $246 per unit for nonresidents. Fees $1779 per year full-time, $1113 per year part-time. *Financial aid:* Application deadline 3/2; applicants required to submit FAFSA. *Faculty research:* Adolescence, secondary school, significant adults, teacher education. • Dr. Melissa M. Aronson, Coordinator, 209-667-3217.

Campbell University, School of Education, Buies Creek, NC 27506. Offerings include secondary education (M Ed). Accredited by NCATE. School faculty: 8 full-time (6 women), 6 part-time (0 women). *Application deadline:* 8/1 (priority date; rolling processing; 1/2 for spring admission). *Application fee:* $25. *Tuition:* $168 per credit hour (minimum). • Dr. Margaret Giesbrecht, Dean, 910-893-1630. Fax: 910-893-1999. E-mail: giesbrec@mailcenter.campbell.edu. Application contact: James S. Farthing, Director of Graduate Admissions, 910-893-1200 Ext. 1318. Fax: 910-893-1288.

Canisius College, School of Education and Human Services, Program in Secondary Education, Buffalo, NY 14208-1098. Awards MS. Part-time and evening/weekend programs available. Faculty: 1 full-time (0 women), 19 part-time (4 women). Students: 8 full-time (5 women), 8 part-time (5 women). 10 applicants, 80% accepted. *Degree requirements:* Research project required, foreign language and thesis not required. *Entrance requirements:* GRE General Test, minimum GPA of 2.5. Application deadline: 8/15 (priority date; rolling processing). Application fee: $20. *Expenses:* Tuition $415 per credit hour. Fees $15 per credit hour. *Financial aid:* In 1997–98, 1 graduate assistantship was awarded; Federal Work-Study, institutionally sponsored loans, and career-related internships or fieldwork also available. Aid available to part-time students. • Rev. Paul Nochelski, SJ, Chairman, 716-888-3292. Application contact: Kevin Smith, Graduate Recruitment and Admissions, 716-888-2544. Fax: 716-888-3290.

Carson-Newman College, Graduate Program in Education, Jefferson City, TN 37760. Offerings include secondary education (MAT). Accredited by NCATE. College faculty: 18 full-time (8 women), 7 part-time (5 women). *Application deadline:* 7/15 (priority date; rolling processing). *Application fee:* $25 ($50 for international students). *Expenses:* Tuition $190 per credit hour. Fees $10 per year. • Dr. Margaret A. Hypes, Chair, 423-471-3461. Application contact: Jane W. McGill, Graduate Admissions and Services Adviser, 423-471-3460. Fax: 423-471-3475.

Central Connecticut State University, School of Education and Professional Studies, Department of Teacher Education, Program in Secondary Education, New Britain, CT 06050-4010. Awards MS. Part-time and evening/weekend programs available. 22 applicants, 91% accepted. *Degree requirements:* Thesis or alternative required, foreign language not required. *Entrance requirements:* TOEFL (minimum score 550), minimum GPA of 2.7. Application deadline: 6/1 (priority date; rolling processing; 12/1 for spring admission). Application fee: $40. *Expenses:* Tuition $4458 per year full-time, $175 per credit hour part-time for state residents; $9943 per year full-time, $175 per credit hour part-time for nonresidents. Fees $45 per semester. *Financial aid:* Federal Work-Study available. Financial aid application deadline: 3/15; applicants required to submit FAFSA. *Faculty research:* Secondary curriculum and instructional issues. • Dr. Carole Shmurak, Coordinator, 860-832-2429.

Central Michigan University, College of Education and Human Services, Department of Teacher Education and Professional Development, Program in Secondary Education, Mount Pleasant, MI 48859. Awards MA. Accredited by NCATE. Students: 23 part-time (11 women); includes 1 international. Average age 31. In 1997, 17 degrees awarded. *Degree requirements:* Thesis or alternative required, foreign language not required. *Entrance requirements:* GRE General Test (minimum combined score of 1000), minimum GPA of 2.7. Application deadline: 3/1 (priority date; rolling processing). Application fee: $30. *Expenses:* Tuition $139 per credit hour (minimum) for state residents; $276 per credit hour (minimum) for nonresidents. Fees $260 per year full-time, $150 per semester part-time. *Financial aid:* Fellowships, research assistantships, teaching assistantships, Federal Work-Study available. Financial aid application deadline: 3/7. *Faculty research:* Curriculum development and supervision. • Dr. William Merrill, Chairperson, Department of Teacher Education and Professional Development, 517-774-3975. Fax: 517-774-3516. E-mail: 34ltyvi@cmich.edu.

Central Missouri State University, College of Education and Human Services, Department of Curriculum and Instruction, Warrensburg, MO 64093. Offerings include secondary education (MSE). Accredited by NCATE. Department faculty: 20 full-time. *Degree requirements:* Comprehensive exam or thesis. *Entrance requirements:* GRE General Test, minimum GPA of 2.75, teaching certificate. Application deadline: 6/30 (priority date; rolling processing). Application fee: $25 ($50 for international students). *Tuition:* $3288 per year full-time, $137 per credit hour part-time for state residents; $5928 per year full-time, $274 per credit hour part-time for nonresidents. • Dr. Ted Garten, Chair, 660-543-4235. Fax: 660-543-4167.

Chadron State College, Department of Education, Chadron, NE 69337. Offerings include secondary education (MS Ed). Accredited by NCATE. *Application deadline:* rolling. *Application fee:* $15. *Expenses:* Tuition $1788 per year full-time, $75 per credit hour part-time for state residents; $3588 per year full-time, $149 per credit hour part-time for nonresidents. Fees $388 per year full-time, $1232 per year part-time. • Dr. Pat Colgate, Dean, School of Graduate Studies, 308-432-6330. Fax: 308-432-6454. E-mail: pcolgate@csc1.csc.edu.

Charleston Southern University, Programs in Education, Charleston, SC 29423-8087. Offerings include secondary education (M Ed). Faculty: 16 full-time (5 women), 5 part-time (3 women), 17.6 FTE. *Application deadline:* rolling. *Application fee:* $25. *Tuition:* $9821 per year full-time, $173 per hour (minimum) part-time. • Dr. Martha Watson, Director of Graduate Programs, 803-863-7555.

Chicago State University, College of Education, Department of Curriculum and Instruction, Program in Secondary Education, Chicago, IL 60628. Awards MS Ed. Accredited by NCATE. *Degree requirements:* Comprehensive exams required, thesis optional, foreign language not required. *Entrance requirements:* Minimum GPA of 2.75. Application deadline: 7/1 (11/10 for spring admission). *Tuition:* $2268 per year full-time, $95 per credit hour part-time for state residents; $6804 per year full-time, $284 per credit hour part-time for nonresidents.

The Citadel, The Military College of South Carolina, Department of Education, Program in Secondary Education, Charleston, SC 29409. Awards MAT. Accredited by NCATE. Faculty: 8 full-time. Students: 44 full-time (25 women), 81 part-time (45 women); includes 17 minority (16 African Americans, 1 Asian American), 2 international. In 1997, 47 degrees awarded. *Entrance requirements:* GRE, MAT, or 12 hours of graduate course work with a minimum GPA of 3.0. Application deadline: rolling. Application fee: $25. *Expenses:* Tuition $130 per credit hour for state residents; $260 per credit hour for nonresidents. Fees $30 per semester. • Dr. Robert Carter, Head, Department of Education, 803-953-5097.

City College of the City University of New York, Graduate School, School of Education, Department of Secondary and Continuing Education, Convent Avenue at 138th Street, New York, NY 10031-6977. Offers programs in art education (MA), English education (MA), environmental education (MA), mathematics education (MA), secondary science education (MA), social studies education (MA), technology education (MA). Part-time and evening/weekend programs available. Students: 11 full-time (5 women), 179 part-time (67 women). In 1997, 117 degrees awarded. *Degree requirements:* Thesis required, foreign language not required. *Entrance requirements:* TOEFL (minimum score 500). Application fee: $40. *Expenses:* Tuition $4350 per year full-time, $185 per credit part-time for state residents; $7600 per year full-time, $320 per credit part-time for nonresidents. Fees $41 per year. *Financial aid:* Federal Work-Study and career-related internships or fieldwork available. Aid available to part-time students. Financial aid application deadline: 5/1. • Hope Hartman, Chair, 212-650-7954.

Clemson University, College of Health, Education, and Human Development, Department of Curriculum and Instruction, Program in Secondary Education, Clemson, SC 29634. Offers English (M Ed), history and government (M Ed), mathematics (M Ed), natural sciences (M Ed). Accredited by NCATE. Students: 7 full-time (5 women), 18 part-time (13 women); includes 3 minority (all African Americans). 15 applicants, 73% accepted. In 1997, 19 degrees awarded. *Entrance requirements:* TOEFL, teaching certificate. Application deadline: 6/1. Application fee: $35. *Expenses:* Tuition $3154 per year full-time, $130 per credit hour part-time for state residents; $6452 per year full-time, $264 per credit hour part-time for nonresidents. Fees $190 per year. *Financial aid:* Application deadline 6/1. • Dr. Robert Green, Chair, Department of Curriculum and Instruction, 864-656-5108. Fax: 864-656-1322. E-mail: rpgreen@clemson.edu.

Cleveland State University, College of Education, Department of Specialized Instructional Programs, Cleveland, OH 44115-2440. Offerings include curriculum and instruction (M Ed), with options in bilingual education, early childhood education, early childhood/special education, education of emerging adolescents, elementary education, English as a second language, learning disabilities, Montessori education, multihandicapped, reading, secondary education. Department faculty: 18 full-time (12 women). *Entrance requirements:* GRE General Test or MAT (score in 50th percentile or higher). Application deadline: 9/1 (priority date; rolling processing). Application fee: $25. *Expenses:* Tuition $5252 per year full-time, $202 per credit hour part-time for state residents; $10,504 per year full-time, $404 per credit hour part-time for nonresidents. Fees $2.25 per credit hour (minimum). • Dr. Jane Zaharias, Chairperson, 216-687-4585. Fax: 216-687-5379. E-mail: j.zaharias@csuohio.edu.

Coastal Carolina University, School of Education, Program in Education, Conway, SC 29528-6054. Offerings include secondary education (M Ed). Program faculty: 6 full-time (3 women). *Entrance requirements:* GRE General Test (minimum combined score of 800), MAT (minimum score 35), teacher certification. Application deadline: 8/15 (priority date; rolling processing). Application fee: $25. Electronic applications accepted. • Dr. Sandra Bowden, Head, 843-349-2606.

Colgate University, Department of Education, Hamilton, NY 13346-1386. Offerings include secondary education (MAT). Department faculty: 10 full-time (5 women). *Degree requirements:*

Directory: Secondary Education

Colgate University (continued)

1 foreign language, special project or thesis. *Entrance requirements:* GRE General Test. Application deadline: 3/15 (priority date; rolling processing; 9/1 for spring admission). Application fee: $155. *Expenses:* Tuition $2635 per course. Fees $165 per year. • Dr. D. K. Johnston, Chair, 315-228-7256. Application contact: Joan Thompson, Secretary, 315-228-7256. Fax: 315-228-7857. E-mail: jthompson@mail.colgate.edu.

The College of New Jersey, Graduate Division, School of Education, Department of Educational Administration and Secondary Education, Ewing, NJ 08628. Offers programs in educational leadership (M Ed), secondary education (MAT). Accredited by NCATE. Part-time and evening/weekend programs available. Students: 20 full-time (8 women), 103 part-time (57 women); includes 26 minority (10 African Americans, 1 Asian American, 14 Hispanics, 1 Native American), 5 international. Average age 28. In 1997, 47 degrees awarded. *Degree requirements:* Comprehensive exam required, foreign language and thesis not required. *Average time to degree:* master's–2 years full-time. *Entrance requirements:* GRE General Test, minimum GPA of 3.0 in field or 2.75 overall. Application deadline: 4/15 (10/15 for spring admission). Application fee: $50. *Expenses:* Tuition $6892 per year full-time, $287 per credit hour part-time for state residents; $9602 per year full-time, $402 per credit hour part-time for nonresidents. Fees $799 per year full-time, $33 per credit hour part-time. *Financial aid:* Graduate assistantships available. Financial aid application deadline: 5/1; applicants required to submit FAFSA. • Dr. Richard Farber, Chair, 609-771-3470. Fax: 609-637-5197.

College of Notre Dame, Department of Education, Emphasis in Secondary Education, Belmont, CA 94002-1997. Offers programs in educational technology (M Ed), multicultural education (M Ed), secondary education (MAT, Certificate), teaching art (MAT), teaching biology (MAT), teaching English (MAT), teaching French (MAT), teaching music (MAT), teaching religious studies (MAT), teaching social sciences (MAT). Faculty: 5 full-time, 8 part-time. Students: 43 full-time (29 women), 47 part-time (25 women). Average age 31. *Entrance requirements:* For master's, PRAXIS, TOEFL (minimum score 550), interview, minimum GPA of 2.5. Application deadline: rolling. Application fee: $50 ($500 for international students). *Tuition:* $460 per unit. *Financial aid:* Career-related internships or fieldwork available. Aid available to part-time students. • Dr. Kim Tolley, Program Director, 650-508-3456.

College of Our Lady of the Elms, Department of Education, Chicopee, MA 01013-2839. Offerings include secondary education (MAT), with options in biology education, English education, Spanish education. Department faculty: 7 full-time (all women), 6 part-time (5 women). *Application deadline:* rolling. *Application fee:* $30. *Expenses:* Tuition $320 per credit. Fees $40 per year. • Sr. Kathleen M. Kirley, Dean of Continuing Education and Graduate Studies, 413-594-2761. Fax: 413-592-4871. Application contact: Dr. Mary Janeczek, Director, 413-594-2761.

The College of Saint Rose, School of Education, Teacher Education Department, Program in Secondary Education, Albany, NY 12203-1419. Awards MS Ed. Part-time and evening/weekend programs available. Faculty: 10 full-time (6 women), 1 (woman) part-time. Students: 15 full-time (9 women), 48 part-time (26 women); includes 3 minority (1 African American, 1 Asian American, 1 Hispanic). Average age 31. In 1997, 30 degrees awarded. *Degree requirements:* Thesis or alternative, comprehensive exam required, foreign language not required. *Entrance requirements:* Minimum undergraduate GPA of 3.0. Application deadline: 7/15 (priority date; rolling processing; 12/1 for spring admission). Application fee: $30. *Expenses:* Tuition $338 per credit. Fees $60 per year. *Financial aid:* Research assistantships, partial tuition waivers, and career-related internships or fieldwork available. Aid available to part-time students. Financial aid application deadline: 3/1; applicants required to submit FAFSA. • Application contact: Graduate Office, 518-454-5136. Fax: 518-458-5479. E-mail: ace@rosnet.strose.edu.

College of Staten Island of the City University of New York, Department of Education, Program in Secondary Education, Staten Island, NY 10314-6600. Awards MS Ed. Evening/weekend programs available. Faculty: 9 full-time (1 woman), 7 part-time (5 women). Students: 3 full-time (2 women), 88 part-time (53 women); includes 3 minority (2 African Americans, 1 Hispanic). Average age 32. In 1997, 37 degrees awarded. *Degree requirements:* Thesis or alternative required, foreign language not required. *Entrance requirements:* Teaching certificate. Application deadline: 6/1 (priority date; rolling processing; 12/1 for spring admission). Application fee: $40. *Expenses:* Tuition $4350 per year full-time, $185 per credit part-time for state residents; $7600 per year full-time, $320 per credit part-time for nonresidents. Fees $106 per year full-time, $54 per year part-time. • Dr. Jed Luchow, Coordinator, 718-982-3740. Application contact: Earl Teasley, Director of Admissions, 718-982-2010. Fax: 718-982-2500.

The Colorado College, Programs for Experienced Teachers, Colorado Springs, CO 80903-3294. Offerings include humanities for secondary school teachers and administrators (MAT). Offered during summer only. *Degree requirements:* Thesis, oral exam, 30-50 page paper required, foreign language not required. *Entrance requirements:* Minimum undergraduate GPA of 2.75. Application deadline: rolling. Application fee: $30.

The Colorado College, Department of Education, Program in Secondary Education, Colorado Springs, CO 80903-3294. Offers mathematics teaching (MAT), science teaching (MAT). Faculty: 2 full-time (1 woman), 3 part-time (2 women). Students: 9 full-time (8 women); includes 1 minority (Hispanic). Average age 28. 14 applicants, 64% accepted. In 1997, 5 degrees awarded (100% found work related to degree). *Degree requirements:* Thesis, internship required, foreign language not required. *Entrance requirements:* GRE Subject Test (score in 50th percentile or higher), Program for Licensing Assessments for Colorado Educators Basic Skills Test. Application deadline: 3/1. Application fee: $40. *Financial aid:* In 1997–98, 8 fellowships (all to first-year students) were awarded; institutionally sponsored loans and career-related internships or fieldwork also available. Financial aid application deadline: 3/1; applicants required to submit CSS PROFILE or FAFSA. • Paul J. Kuerbis, Director, 719-389-6726. Application contact: Marsha Unruh, Educational Services Coordinator, 719-389-6472. Fax: 719-389-6473.

Columbus State University, College of Education, Department of Curriculum and Instruction, Columbus, GA 31907-5645. Offerings include secondary education (M Ed, Ed S), with options in biology (M Ed), English (M Ed, Ed S), general science (M Ed), history (M Ed), mathematics (M Ed, Ed S), political science (M Ed), science/biology (Ed S), social science (M Ed, Ed S). Accredited by NCATE. Ed S (mathematics) offered jointly with Georgia Southwestern University. M Ed (political science) being phased out; applicants no longer accepted. *Degree requirements:* For master's, exit exam required, foreign language and thesis not required; for Ed S, thesis or alternative, foreign language not required. *Entrance requirements:* For master's, GRE General Test (minimum combined score of 800), MAT (minimum score 44); for Ed S, GRE General Test (minimum combined score of 900), MAT (minimum score 44). Application deadline: 7/10 (priority date; rolling processing; 10/23 for spring admission). Application fee: $20. *Tuition:* $1718 per year full-time, $151 per semester hour part-time for state residents; $6218 per year full-time, $401 per semester hour part-time for nonresidents. • Dr. David Shoemaker, Chair, 706-568-2255. Fax: 706-568-3134. E-mail: shoemaker_david@colstate.edu. Application contact: Katie Thornton, Graduate Admissions, 706-568-2279. Fax: 706-568-2462. E-mail: thornton_katie@colstate.edu.

Concordia University, College of Education, Portland, OR 97211-6099. Offerings include secondary education (MAT). College faculty: 8 part-time (3 women). *Application deadline:* rolling. *Application fee:* $35. *Tuition:* $350 per credit. • Dr. Joseph Mannion, Dean, 503-493-6233. Application contact: Dr. Peter Johnson, Director of Admissions, 503-280-8501.

Connecticut College, Programs in Education, Program in Secondary Education, New London, CT 06320-4196. Awards MAT. Part-time programs available. *Entrance requirements:* MAT. Application deadline: 2/2. Application fee: $35.

Converse College, Department of Education, Program in Secondary Education, Spartanburg, SC 29302-0006. Awards M Ed. Part-time programs available. Faculty: 49 full-time, 3 part-time. Students: 75 (55 women); includes 16 minority (12 African Americans, 1 Asian American, 3 Hispanics). Average age 35. 25 applicants, 92% accepted. In 1997, 48 degrees awarded. *Entrance requirements:* NTE, minimum GPA of 2.5. Application deadline: 5/1 (priority date; rolling processing; 1/30 for spring admission). Application fee: $35. *Tuition:* $185 per credit. *Financial aid:* Available to part-time students. Financial aid applicants required to submit FAFSA. • Dr. Martha T. Lovett, Dean of Graduate Education and Special Programs, Department of Education, 864-596-9082. Fax: 864-596-9221. E-mail: martylovett@converse.edu.

Cumberland College, Program in Elementary/Secondary Teaching, 6178 College Station Drive, Williamsburg, KY 40769-1372. Awards Certificate. Faculty: 4 full-time (2 women), 5 part-time (2 women). *Entrance requirements:* Master's degree, 3 years of teaching experience. Application deadline: 8/26 (rolling processing). Application fee: $25. *Tuition:* $175 per credit. • Application contact: Erica Harris, Admissions Office, 606-539-4241.

Cumberland College, Program in Secondary General Education, 6178 College Station Drive, Williamsburg, KY 40769-1372. Awards MA Ed. Faculty: 4 full-time (2 women), 5 part-time (2 women). *Degree requirements:* Comprehensive exam required, foreign language and thesis not required. *Entrance requirements:* GRE or NTE, Kentucky teaching certificate. Application deadline: 8/26 (rolling processing). Application fee: $25. *Tuition:* $175 per credit. • Application contact: Erica Harris, Admissions Office, 606-539-4241.

DePaul University, School of Education, Program in Curriculum Development, Chicago, IL 60604-2287. Offerings include secondary education (MA, M Ed). Accredited by NCATE. *Degree requirements:* Oral exam or thesis required, foreign language not required. *Entrance requirements:* Interview, minimum GPA of 2.75, work experience. Application deadline: rolling. Application fee: $25. *Expenses:* Tuition $320 per credit hour. Fees $30 per year. • Dr. Barbara Sizemore, Dean, School of Education, 312-325-7000 Ext. 1666. Fax: 312-325-7748. Application contact: Director of Graduate Admissions, 312-325-7000 Ext. 1666. E-mail: mmurphy@wppost.depaul.edu.

DePaul University, School of Education, Program in Human Services and Counseling, Chicago, IL 60604-2287. Offerings include secondary schools (MA, M Ed). Accredited by NCATE. Program faculty: 3 full-time (1 woman). *Degree requirements:* Oral exam or thesis required, foreign language not required. *Entrance requirements:* Interview, minimum GPA of 2.75, work experience. Application deadline: rolling. Application fee: $25. *Expenses:* Tuition $320 per credit hour. Fees $30 per year. • Dr. Barbara Sizemore, Dean, School of Education, 312-325-7000 Ext. 1666. Fax: 312-325-7748. Application contact: Director of Graduate Admissions, 312-325-7000 Ext. 1666. E-mail: mmurphy@wppost.depaul.edu.

Dowling College, Programs in Secondary Education, Oakdale, NY 11769-1999. Awards MS Ed. Part-time and evening/weekend programs available. Faculty: 2 full-time (1 woman), 11 part-time (3 women). Students: 4 full-time (0 women), 312 part-time (169 women); includes 15 minority (2 African Americans, 3 Asian Americans, 9 Hispanics, 1 Native American). Average age 32. In 1997, 54 degrees awarded. *Degree requirements:* Comprehensive exam required, foreign language and thesis not required. *Entrance requirements:* Provisional teaching certificate. Application deadline: 9/1 (priority date; rolling processing). Application fee: $0. *Financial aid:* General graduate assistantships, Federal Work-Study, and career-related internships or fieldwork available. Aid available to part-time students. Financial aid application deadline: 4/30. • Dr. Ira Finkel, Discipline Coordinator, 516-244-3304. Fax: 516-244-5036. Application contact: Kate Rowe, Director of Admissions, 516-244-3030. Fax: 516-563-3827. E-mail: rowek@dowling.edu.

Drake University, School of Education, Department of Teaching and Learning, Program in Secondary Education, Des Moines, IA 50311-4516. Awards MAT. Faculty: 7 full-time (2 women), 2 part-time (1 woman). Students: 3 full-time (2 women), 24 part-time (19 women). 22 applicants, 82% accepted. In 1997, 8 degrees awarded. *Entrance requirements:* GRE General Test (minimum combined score of 1000) or MAT (minimum score 36). Application deadline: rolling. Application fee: $25. *Tuition:* $16,000 per year full-time, $260 per hour (minimum) part-time. *Financial aid:* Career-related internships or fieldwork available. Aid available to part-time students. • Application contact: Ann J. Martin, Graduate Coordinator, 515-271-3871. Fax: 515-271-2831. E-mail: ajm@admin.drake.edu.

Drury College, Graduate Programs in Education, Program in Secondary Education, Springfield, MO 65802-3791. Awards M Ed. Accredited by NCATE. Part-time and evening/weekend programs available. Faculty: 7 full-time (5 women), 6 part-time (2 women). Students: 29; includes 2 minority (both African Americans), 1 international. Average age 30. 18 applicants, 89% accepted. *Degree requirements:* Thesis required, foreign language not required. *Average time to degree:* master's–1.5 years full-time, 3 years part-time. *Entrance requirements:* MAT (minimum score 35), minimum GPA of 2.75. Application fee: $15. *Tuition:* $170 per credit hour. *Financial aid:* Career-related internships or fieldwork available. • Dr. Maggie Payne, Head, 417-873-7344.

Duquesne University, School of Education, Department of Elementary, Secondary, and Reading Education, Program in Secondary Education, Pittsburgh, PA 15282-0001. Awards MS Ed. Faculty: 4 full-time (1 woman), 1 part-time (0 women). Students: 135. 42 applicants, 69% accepted. In 1997, 57 degrees awarded. *Average time to degree:* master's–1.5 years full-time, 2.5 years part-time. *Entrance requirements:* MAT. Application deadline: 8/1 (rolling processing; 12/1 for spring admission). Application fee: $40. *Expenses:* Tuition $481 per credit. Fees $39 per credit. • Application contact: Dr. Robert Agostino, Coordinator, 412-396-6104. Fax: 412-396-5585.

D'Youville College, Division of Education, Buffalo, NY 14201-1084. Offerings include secondary education (MS Ed). Division faculty: 5 full-time (4 women), 8 part-time (2 women). *Degree requirements:* Computer language, thesis required, foreign language not required. *Entrance requirements:* Minimum GPA of 3.0. Application deadline: rolling. Application fee: $25. *Expenses:* Tuition $357 per credit hour. Fees $350 per year. • Dr. Robert DiSibio, Graduate Director, 716-881-3200. Application contact: Joseph Syracuse, Graduate Admissions Director, 716-881-7676. Fax: 716-881-7790.

Eastern Kentucky University, College of Education, Department of Curriculum and Instruction, Program in Secondary and Higher Education, Richmond, KY 40475-3101. Offers agricultural education (MA Ed), allied health sciences education (MA Ed), art education (MA Ed), biological sciences education (MA Ed), business education (MA Ed), chemistry education (MA Ed), earth science education (MA Ed), English education (MA Ed), general science education (MA Ed), geography education (MA Ed), history education (MA Ed), home economics education (MA Ed), industrial education (MA Ed), mathematical sciences education (MA Ed), physical education (MA Ed), physics education (MA Ed), political science education (MA Ed), psychology education (MA Ed), reading (MA Ed), school health education (MA Ed), sociology education (MA Ed). Accredited by NCATE. Part-time programs available. *Entrance requirements:* GRE General Test, minimum GPA of 2.5. Application fee: $0. *Tuition:* $2390 per year full-time, $133 per credit hour part-time for state residents; $6630 per year full-time, $365 per credit hour part-time for nonresidents. *Financial aid:* Research assistantships, teaching assistantships, Federal Work-Study available. Aid available to part-time students. • Dr. Imogene Ramsey, Chair, Department of Curriculum and Instruction, 606-622-2154.

Eastern Michigan University, College of Education, Department of Teacher Education, Program in Secondary Curriculum, Ypsilanti, MI 48197. Awards MA. Accredited by NCATE. *Entrance requirements:* GRE, TOEFL (minimum score 500). Application deadline: 5/15 (rolling processing; 3/15 for spring admission). Application fee: $30. *Expenses:* Tuition $2691 per year full-time, $150 per credit hour part-time for state residents; $6300 per year full-time, $350 per credit hour part-time for nonresidents. Fees $368 per year full-time, $88 per semester (minimum) part-time. *Financial aid:* Fellowships, teaching assistantships available. Aid available to part-time students. Financial aid application deadline: 3/15; applicants required to submit FAFSA. • Dr. Georgea Langer, Coordinator, 734-487-3185.

Eastern Michigan University, College of Education, Department of Teacher Education, Program in Secondary School Teaching, Ypsilanti, MI 48197. Awards MA. Accredited by NCATE. Evening/weekend programs available. In 1997, 15 degrees awarded. *Entrance requirements:* GRE, TOEFL (minimum score 500). Application deadline: 5/15 (rolling processing; 3/15 for spring admission). Application fee: $30. *Expenses:* Tuition $2691 per year full-time, $150 per credit hour part-time for state residents; $6300 per year full-time, $350 per credit hour part-time for nonresidents. Fees $368 per year full-time, $88 per semester (minimum) part-time. *Financial aid:* Fellowships, teaching assistantships available. Aid available to part-time students. Financial aid application deadline: 3/15; applicants required to submit FAFSA. • Dr. Georgea Langer, Coordinator, 734-487-3185.

Eastern Nazarene College, Graduate Studies, Division of Education, Quincy, MA 02170-2999. Offerings include secondary education (M Ed, Certificate). M Ed and Certificate also available through weekend program for administration, special needs, and reading only. Division faculty: 9 full-time (5 women), 11 part-time (5 women). *Entrance requirements:* For master's, TOEFL (minimum score 500). Application deadline: rolling. Application fee: $35. *Expenses:* Tuition $350 per credit. Fees $125 per semester full-time, $15 per semester part-time. • Dr. Lorne Ranstrom, Chair, 617-745-3528. Application contact: Cleo P. Cakridas, Graduate Enrollment Counselor, 617-745-3870. Fax: 617-745-3907. E-mail: cakridac@enc.edu.

Eastern Oregon University, School of Education, Program in Secondary Education, La Grande, OR 97850-2899. Awards MTE. Part-time programs available. Postbaccalaureate distance learning degree programs offered (minimal on-campus study). Faculty: 12 full-time (3 women), 8 part-time (4 women). Students: 16 full-time (3 women), 8 part-time (3 women); includes 1 Hispanic. In 1997, 8 degrees awarded. *Degree requirements:* Thesis required, foreign language not required. *Average time to degree:* master's–1 year full-time. *Entrance requirements:* NTE. Application deadline: 1/15 (priority date; rolling processing). Application fee: $50. *Expenses:* Tuition $4371 per year for state residents; $8379 per year for nonresidents. Fees $957 per year. *Financial aid:* Full and partial tuition waivers, Federal Work-Study available. Aid available to part-time students. • Dr. Margo Mack, Professor of Education, 541-962-3586. Fax: 541-962-3701. E-mail: mmack@eou.edu.

East Stroudsburg University of Pennsylvania, School of Professional Studies, Department of Professional and Secondary Education, East Stroudsburg, PA 18301-2999. Awards M Ed. Part-time and evening/weekend programs available. *Degree requirements:* Comprehensive exam required, foreign language and thesis not required. *Application deadline:* 7/31 (priority date; rolling processing; 11/30 for spring admission). *Application fee:* $15 ($25 for international students). *Expenses:* Tuition $3468 per year full-time, $193 per credit part-time for state residents; $6236 per year full-time, $346 per credit part-time for nonresidents. Fees $700 per year full-time, $39 per credit part-time.

East Tennessee State University, College of Education, Department of Curriculum and Instruction, Johnson City, TN 37614-0734. Offerings include secondary education (MAT, M Ed). Accredited by NCATE. Department faculty: 17 full-time (8 women). *Application deadline:* 7/15 (priority date; rolling processing; 12/1 for spring admission). *Application fee:* $25 ($35 for international students). *Tuition:* $2944 per year full-time, $158 per credit hour part-time for state residents; $7770 per year full-time, $369 per credit hour part-time for nonresidents. • Dr. Jack Rhoton, Chair, 423-439-4426. Fax: 423-439-8362.

Edinboro University of Pennsylvania, School of Education, Department of Educational Services, Program in Middle and Secondary Instruction, Edinboro, PA 16444. Awards M Ed. Students: 2 full-time (1 woman), 3 part-time (all women). Average age 31. *Degree requirements:* Thesis or alternative required, foreign language not required. *Entrance requirements:* GRE or MAT (score in 30th percentile or higher). Application deadline: rolling. Application fee: $25. *Expenses:* Tuition $3468 per year full-time, $193 per credit part-time for state residents; $6236 per year full-time, $346 per credit part-time for nonresidents. Fees $898 per year full-time, $50 per semester (minimum) part-time. *Financial aid:* In 1997–98, 1 assistantship was awarded. • Application contact: Dr. Philip Kerstetter, Dean of Graduate Studies, 814-732-2856. Fax: 814-732-2611. E-mail: kerstetter@edinboro.edu.

Elmira College, Graduate Programs in Education, Program in Secondary Education, Elmira, NY 14901. Awards MS Ed. Part-time and evening/weekend programs available. Faculty: 14 full-time (3 women), 8 part-time (3 women). Students: 10. *Degree requirements:* Thesis or alternative required, foreign language not required. *Entrance requirements:* Provisional New York state certification. Application fee: $35. *Tuition:* $344 per credit hour. *Financial aid:* Career-related internships or fieldwork available. Aid available to part-time students. • Dr. John Madison, Director of Education, 607-735-1912. Application contact: Judith B. Clack, Dean for Graduate Studies, 607-735-1825.

Emory University, Graduate School of Arts and Sciences, Division of Educational Studies, Atlanta, GA 30322-1100. Offerings include secondary teaching (MAT, M Ed). Division faculty: 13. *Application deadline:* 1/20 (3/15 for spring admission). *Application fee:* $45. *Expenses:* Tuition $21,770 per year. Fees $300 per year. • Dr. Robert Jensen, Acting Director, 404-727-0606. Fax: 404-727-2799. E-mail: rjensen@emory.edu. Application contact: Dr. Glen Avant, Program Development Coordinator, 404-727-0612.

Emporia State University, School of Graduate Studies, The Teachers College, Division of School Leadership/Middle and Secondary Teacher Education, Program in Secondary Education, Emporia, KS 66801-5087. Awards MS. Accredited by NCATE. Students: 1 (woman) full-time, 9 part-time (8 women). 2 applicants, 0% accepted. In 1997, 4 degrees awarded. *Degree requirements:* Comprehensive exam or thesis required, foreign language not required. *Entrance requirements:* GRE General Test (minimum score 480 on each section) or MAT (minimum score 42), TOEFL (minimum score 550). Application deadline: 8/15 (priority date; rolling processing). Application fee: $30 ($75 for international students). Electronic applications accepted. *Tuition:* $2300 per year full-time, $103 per credit hour part-time for state residents; $6012 per year full-time, $258 per credit hour part-time for nonresidents. *Financial aid:* Federal Work-Study, institutionally sponsored loans available. Financial aid application deadline: 3/15; applicants required to submit FAFSA. • Dr. Jerry Will, Chair, Division of School Leadership/Middle and Secondary Teacher Education, 316-341-5777.

Fayetteville State University, Programs in Educational Leadership and Secondary Education, 1200 Murchison Road, Fayetteville, NC 28301-4298. Offerings in biology (MAT), educational leadership and secondary education (MA Ed), history (MAT), mathematics (MAT), political science (MAT), sociology (MAT). One or more programs accredited by NCATE. Part-time and evening/weekend programs available. *Degree requirements:* Internship, written and oral exams required, foreign language and thesis not required. *Entrance requirements:* GRE or MAT, minimum GPA of 2.5. Application deadline: 8/1 (rolling processing; 12/15 for spring admission). Application fee: $20. *Tuition:* $1498 per year full-time, $327 per semester (minimum) part-time for state residents; $8768 per year full-time, $2144 per semester (minimum) part-time for nonresidents.

Fitchburg State College, Program in Secondary Education, Fitchburg, MA 01420-2697. Awards M Ed. Accredited by NCATE. Part-time and evening/weekend programs available. *Entrance requirements:* GRE General Test or MAT (minimum score 47). Application deadline: rolling. Application fee: $10. *Expenses:* Tuition $147 per credit. Fees $55 per semester. *Financial aid:* Graduate assistantships, Federal Work-Study available. Aid available to part-time students. Financial aid application deadline: 3/30; applicants required to submit FAFSA. • Dr. Ronald Colbert, Chair, 978-665-3493. Fax: 978-665-3658. E-mail: dgce@fsc.edu. Application contact: James DuPont, Director of Admissions, 978-665-3144. Fax: 978-665-4540. E-mail: admissions@fsc.edu.

Florida Agricultural and Mechanical University, Division of Graduate Studies, Research, and Continuing Education, College of Education, Program in Secondary Education, Tallahassee, FL 32307-3200. Awards M Ed, MS Ed. Accredited by NCATE. Students: 0. *Entrance requirements:* GRE General Test (minimum combined score of 1000), minimum GPA of 3.0. Application deadline: 5/13. Application fee: $20. *Expenses:* Tuition $140 per credit hour for state residents; $484 per credit hour for nonresidents. Fees $130 per year. • Dr. V. E. Evans, Chairperson, 850-599-3123.

Fordham University, Graduate School of Education, Division of Curriculum and Teaching, New York, NY 10023. Offerings include secondary education (MAT, MSE). Accredited by NCATE. *Application fee:* $50. • Dr. Angela Carrasquillo, Chairperson, 212-636-6427.

Fort Hays State University, College of Education, Department of Education, Administration and Counseling, Program in Secondary Education, Hays, KS 67601-4099. Awards MS. Accredited by NCATE. Faculty: 10 full-time (1 woman). Students: 17 part-time (11 women). Average age 35. 8 applicants, 88% accepted. In 1997, 7 degrees awarded. *Entrance requirements:* GRE General Test or MAT. Application deadline: 7/1 (priority date; rolling processing). Application fee: $25 ($35 for international students). *Tuition:* $94 per credit hour for state residents; $249 per credit hour for nonresidents. *Financial aid:* Research assistantships, teaching assistantships available. *Faculty research:* Special education, testing out secondary gifted, effect of parent attitudes on student performances, severe behavior disorders (treatments), consulting. • Dr. Allan Miller, Coordinator, 785-628-5849.

Francis Marion University, School of Education, Florence, SC 29501-0547. Offerings include secondary education (M Ed). School faculty: 65 full-time (14 women). *Application deadline:* 8/21 (priority date; rolling processing). *Application fee:* $25. • Dr. Wayne Pruitt, Coordinator, 803-661-1462.

Friends University, Graduate Programs, College of Arts and Sciences, Program in Teaching, Wichita, KS 67213. Offerings include secondary education (MAT). Accredited by NCATE. *Application deadline:* rolling. *Application fee:* $45. *Expenses:* Tuition $326 per credit hour (minimum). Fees $215 per year. • Dr. Dona Coleman, Director, 800-794-6945 Ext. 5826. Application contact: Director of Graduate Admissions, 800-794-6945 Ext. 5583.

Frostburg State University, School of Education, Department of Educational Professions, Program in Curriculum and Instruction, Frostburg, MD 21532-1099. Offerings include secondary education (M Ed). *Application deadline:* 7/15 (rolling processing). *Application fee:* $30.

Gallaudet University, School of Education and Human Services, Department of Education, Washington, DC 20002-3625. Offerings include secondary education (MA, Ed S). Accredited by NCATE. *Degree requirements:* For master's, thesis optional. *Entrance requirements:* For master's, GRE General Test or MAT. Application deadline: 2/15 (priority date; rolling processing). Application fee: $50. *Expenses:* Tuition $7064 per year full-time, $392 per credit part-time. Fees $50 (one-time charge). • Dr. Barbara Bodner-Johnson, Chair, 202-651-5530. Application contact: Deborah DeStefano, Director of Admissions, 202-651-5253. Fax: 202-651-5744. E-mail: adm_destefan@gallua.bitnet.

Gannon University, School of Graduate Studies, College of Humanities, Business, and Education, School of Education, Programs in Secondary Education, Erie, PA 16541. Awards M Ed. Part-time and evening/weekend programs available. Students: 0. 0 applicants. *Degree requirements:* Thesis, comprehensive exam. *Entrance requirements:* GRE or MAT, interview, teaching certificate. Application deadline: rolling. Application fee: $25. *Expenses:* Tuition $405 per credit. Fees $200 per year full-time, $8 per credit part-time. *Financial aid:* Available to part-time students. Financial aid application deadline: 3/1; applicants required to submit FAFSA. *Faculty research:* English, natural sciences, environmental education. • Application contact: Beth Nemenz, Director of Admissions, 814-871-7240. Fax: 814-871-5803. E-mail: admissions@gannon.edu.

George Mason University, Graduate School of Education, Program in Secondary Education, Fairfax, VA 22030-4444. Awards M Ed. Accredited by NCATE. Part-time and evening/weekend programs available. Faculty: 42 full-time (24 women), 65 part-time (51 women), 58.73 FTE. Students: 73 full-time (46 women), 128 part-time (85 women); includes 27 minority (9 African Americans, 3 Asian Americans, 15 Hispanics). Average age 32. 132 applicants, 80% accepted. In 1997, 77 degrees awarded. *Degree requirements:* Computer language required, foreign language not required. *Entrance requirements:* NTE, minimum GPA of 3.0 in last 60 hours. Application deadline: 5/1 (11/1 for spring admission). Application fee: $30. Electronic applications accepted. *Tuition:* $4344 per year full-time, $181 per credit hour part-time for state residents; $12,504 per year full-time, $521 per credit hour part-time for nonresidents. *Financial aid:* Career-related internships or fieldwork available. Aid available to part-time students. Financial aid application deadline: 3/1; applicants required to submit FAFSA. • Dr. Mary Anne Lecos, Interim Coordinator, 703-993-4648. Fax: 703-993-2082.

The George Washington University, Graduate School of Education and Human Development, Department of Teacher Preparation and Special Education, Program in Secondary Education, Washington, DC 20052. Awards M Ed. Accredited by NCATE. Faculty: 6 full-time (5 women), 3 part-time (all women), 7 FTE. Students: 38 full-time (20 women), 121 part-time (63 women); includes 24 minority (16 African Americans, 2 Asian Americans, 6 Hispanics), 3 international. Average age 34. 119 applicants, 89% accepted. In 1997, 65 degrees awarded. *Degree requirements:* Comprehensive exam required, foreign language and thesis not required. *Entrance requirements:* GRE General Test or MAT, interview, minimum GPA of 2.75. Application deadline: 3/1 (priority date; rolling processing; 10/1 for spring admission). Application fee: $50. *Expenses:* Tuition $680 per semester hour. Fees $35 per semester hour. *Financial aid:* Fellowships, stipends, full and partial tuition waivers, Federal Work-Study, and career-related internships or fieldwork available. Financial aid applicants required to submit FAFSA. • Dr. Harriet Hunter-Boykin, Faculty Coordinator, 202-994-4516.

Georgia College and State University, School of Education, Department of Foundations and Secondary Education, Milledgeville, GA 31061. Awards MAT, M Ed, Ed S. Accredited by NCATE. Students: 30 full-time (22 women), 30 part-time (15 women); includes 10 minority (all African Americans). Average age 31. In 1997, 13 master's, 6 Ed Ss awarded. *Degree requirements:* For master's, computer language, comprehensive exit exam required, foreign language and thesis not required; for Ed S, computer language, comprehensive exit exam, oral exam, research project required, foreign language and thesis not required. *Entrance requirements:* For master's, GRE General Test (minimum combined score of 800) or NTE (minimum score 550 on each core battery test), MAT (minimum score 44), minimum GPA of 2.5, NT-4 certificate; for Ed S, GRE General Test (minimum combined score of 900) or NTE (minimum score 575 on each core battery test), MAT (minimum score 48), master's degree, minimum graduate GPA of 3.25, NT-5 certificate, 2 years of teaching experience. Application deadline: 7/31 (priority date; rolling processing). Application fee: $10. *Financial aid:* Federal Work-Study and career-related internships or fieldwork available. Aid available to part-time students. Financial aid application deadline: 4/15. • Dr. Charlotte Harris, Chair, 912-471-2898.

Georgia Southwestern State University, School of Education, Americus, GA 31709-4693. Offerings include secondary education (M Ed). Accredited by NCATE. *Entrance requirements:* GRE General Test (minimum score 400 on each section) or MAT (minimum score 44), minimum GPA of 2.5. Application deadline: 9/1 (rolling processing; 3/15 for spring admission). Application fee: $10. • Dr. Kurt Myers, Chair, 912-931-2145. Application contact: Chris Laney, Graduate Admissions Specialist, 912-931-2027. Fax: 912-931-2059. E-mail: claney@gsw1500.gsw.peachnet.edu.

Grand Canyon University, College of Education, Phoenix, AZ 85017-3030. Offerings include secondary education (M Ed). College faculty: 8 full-time (5 women), 2 part-time (1 woman). *Application deadline:* rolling. *Application fee:* $25. • Dr. Betz Fredrick, Director, 602-589-2472.

Harding University, School of Education, Program in Secondary Education, Searcy, AR 72149-0001. Awards M Ed, MSE. Accredited by NCATE. Part-time programs available. Faculty: 11 part-time (1 woman), 2 FTE. Students: 56 full-time (28 women), 63 part-time (35 women); includes 3 minority (2 African Americans, 1 Hispanic). Average age 30. 18 applicants, 100%

Directory: Secondary Education

Harding University (continued)

accepted. In 1997, 44 degrees awarded. *Degree requirements:* Comprehensive exam required, foreign language and thesis not required. *Average time to degree:* master's–1 year full-time, 3 years part-time. *Entrance requirements:* GRE, MAT, or NTE. Application deadline: 8/27 (rolling processing). Application fee: $25. *Expenses:* Tuition $212 per credit hour. Fees $39 per credit hour. *Financial aid:* Graduate assistantships, scholarships available. • Dr. Dee Carson, Director, School of Education, 501-279-4315. Fax: 501-279-4685. E-mail: dcarson@harding.edu.

Hardin–Simmons University, Irvin School of Education, Department of Elementary and Secondary Education, Program in Secondary Education, Abilene, TX 79698-0001. Offers psychology (M Ed), reading (M Ed), Spanish (M Ed), speech (M Ed). Part-time programs available. Faculty: 6 full-time (3 women), 5 part-time (3 women). Students: 0. In 1997, 1 degree awarded. *Application deadline:* 8/15 (priority date; rolling processing; 1/5 for spring admission). *Application fee:* $25. *Expenses:* Tuition $280 per semester hour. Fees $630 per year full-time. *Financial aid:* Fellowships, full and partial tuition waivers, Federal Work-Study, and career-related internships or fieldwork available. Aid available to part-time students. Financial aid application deadline: 3/15; applicants required to submit FAFSA. *Faculty research:* Professional development schools. • Application contact: Dr. J. Paul Sorrels, Dean of Graduate Studies, 915-670-1298. Fax: 915-670-1564.

Harvard University, Graduate School of Education, Area of Administration, Planning and Social Policy, Cambridge, MA 02138. Offerings include elementary and secondary education (Ed D). Terminal master's awarded for partial completion of doctoral program. Faculty: 14 full-time (6 women), 21 part-time (8 women), 15.7 FTE. *Degree requirements:* Dissertation required, foreign language not required. *Average time to degree:* master's–1 year full-time, 2 years part-time; doctorate–6.3 years full-time, 7.2 years part-time; other advanced degree–1 year full-time, 4.7 years part-time. *Entrance requirements:* GRE General Test, TOEFL (minimum score 600), TWE (minimum score 5.0). Application deadline: 1/2. Application fee: $60. • Richard Murnane, Chair, 617-496-4813. Application contact: Roland Hence, Director of Admissions, 617-495-3414. Fax: 617-496-3577. E-mail: gseadmissions@harvard.edu.

Henderson State University, School of Education, Department of Secondary Education, Arkadelphia, AR 71999-0001. Offers programs in art education (MSE), biology education (MSE), English education (MSE), mathematics education (MSE), physical education (MSE), secondary school administration (MSE), social sciences education (MSE). Accredited by NCATE. Part-time programs available. Postbaccalaureate distance learning degree programs offered (minimal on-campus study). Students: 9 full-time (2 women), 55 part-time (29 women); includes 7 minority (all African Americans). Average age 34. In 1997, 24 degrees awarded. *Degree requirements:* Thesis optional, foreign language not required. *Entrance requirements:* GRE General Test or MAT, minimum GPA of 2.7, teacher certification. Application deadline: 7/31 (priority date; rolling processing). Application fee: $15. Electronic applications accepted. *Expenses:* Tuition $120 per credit hour for state residents; $240 per credit hour for nonresidents. Fees $105 per semester (minimum) full-time, $52 per semester (minimum) part-time. *Financial aid:* Research assistantships, teaching assistantships, Federal Work-Study, institutionally sponsored loans available. Aid available to part-time students. Financial aid application deadline: 7/31. • Dr. Charles Weiner, Chairperson, 870-230-5163. Fax: 870-230-5455. E-mail: weinerc@holly.hsu.edu.

Hofstra University, School of Education and Allied Human Services, Department of Curriculum and Teaching, Program in Secondary Education, Hempstead, NY 11549. Offers art education (MA), music education (MA), secondary education (MA, MS Ed). Accredited by NCATE. Evening/weekend programs available. Faculty: 6 full-time (4 women), 25 part-time (8 women). Students: 42 full-time (28 women), 136 part-time (91 women); includes 6 minority (3 African Americans, 1 Asian American, 2 Hispanics), 1 international. Average age 28. 148 applicants, 66% accepted. In 1997, 81 degrees awarded. *Degree requirements:* Thesis, departmental qualifying exam required, foreign language not required. *Entrance requirements:* Minimum GPA of 2.5. Application deadline: rolling. Application fee: $40 ($75 for international students). *Expenses:* Tuition $10,968 per year full-time, $457 per credit hour part-time. Fees $670 per year full-time, $112 per semester (minimum) part-time. *Financial aid:* Fellowships, research assistantships, teaching assistantships, Federal Work-Study, institutionally sponsored loans, and career-related internships or fieldwork available. Aid available to part-time students. Financial aid application deadline: 9/1. *Faculty research:* Middle level mathematics; curriculum development; mathematics and educational computing; integrating mathematics, science and technology. Total annual research expenditures: $4.6 million. • Dr. Sabrina Hope King, Coordinator, 516-463-5768. Fax: 516-463-6503. E-mail: catshk@hofstra.edu. Application contact: Mary Beth Carey, Dean of Admissions, 516-463-6700. Fax: 516-560-7660. E-mail: hofstra@hofstra.edu.

Holy Family College, Graduate Studies, Program in Education, Philadelphia, PA 19114-2094. Offerings include secondary education (M Ed). Program faculty: 11 full-time (6 women), 22 part-time (10 women), 16.5 FTE. *Average time to degree:* master's–3.5 years part-time. *Entrance requirements:* GRE or MAT, interview. Application deadline: 4/30 (priority date; rolling processing; 11/15 for spring admission). Application fee: $25. *Expenses:* Tuition $320 per credit hour. Fees $65 per semester. • Leonard Soroka, Chair, 215-637-7700 Ext. 3565. Fax: 215-824-2438. Application contact: Joseph Canaday, Graduate Coordinator, 215-637-7203. Fax: 215-637-1478. E-mail: jcanaday@hfc.edu.

Hood College, Department of Education, Frederick, MD 21701-8575. Offerings include curriculum and instruction (MS), with options in early childhood education, elementary education, elementary school science and mathematics, reading, secondary education, special education. *Entrance requirements:* Minimum GPA of 2.5. Application deadline: rolling. Application fee: $30. *Tuition:* $285 per credit. • Dr. Patricia Bartlett, Chairperson, 301-696-3471. E-mail: bartlett@nimue.hood.edu. Application contact: Hood College Graduate School, 301-696-3600. Fax: 301-696-3597. E-mail: postmaster@nimue.hood.edu.

Houston Baptist University, College of Education and Behavioral Sciences, Programs in Education, Houston, TX 77074-3298. Offerings include secondary education (M Ed). Faculty: 9 full-time (5 women), 4 part-time (3 women). *Degree requirements:* Comprehensive exam required, foreign language and thesis not required. *Entrance requirements:* GRE General Test (minimum combined score of 850), minimum GPA of 2.5, teaching certificate. Application deadline: 7/1 (priority date; rolling processing; 1/1 for spring admission). Application fee: $25 ($85 for international students). *Expenses:* Tuition $280 per semester hour. Fees $235 per quarter. • Dr. John Lutjemeier, Head, 281-649-3000 Ext. 2336. Application contact: Judy Ferguson, Program Assistant, 281-649-3241.

Howard University, School of Education, Department of Curriculum and Instruction, Program in Secondary Curriculum and Instruction, 2400 Sixth Street, NW, Washington, DC 20059-0002. Awards MA, MAT, M Ed, CAGS. Accredited by NCATE. MA offered through the Graduate School of Arts and Sciences. Faculty: 2 full-time (both women). Students: 54. In 1997, 11 master's awarded. *Degree requirements:* For master's, thesis (for some programs), comprehensive exam, expository writing exam, internships, practicum required, foreign language not required. *Entrance requirements:* For master's, GRE General Test, minimum GPA of 2.7; for CAGS, GRE General Test. Application deadline: 4/1 (priority date; rolling processing; 11/1 for spring admission). Application fee: $45. *Expenses:* Tuition $10,200 per year full-time, $567 per credit hour part-time. Fees $405 per year. *Financial aid:* Research assistantships, grants, scholarships available. Financial aid application deadline: 4/1. • Dr. Mary R. Hoover, Coordinator, 202-806-7343.

Hunter College of the City University of New York, Division of Education, Secondary Education Curriculum, 695 Park Avenue, New York, NY 10021-5085. Offers programs in biology and general science education (MA), English education (MA), French education (MA), Italian education (MA), mathematics education (MA), social studies education (MA), Spanish education (MA). Part-time and evening/weekend programs available. *Degree requirements:* Comprehensive exam required, foreign language not required. *Entrance requirements:* TOEFL (minimum score 575). Application fee: $40. *Expenses:* Tuition $4350 per year full-time, $185 per credit part-time for state residents; $7600 per year full-time, $320 per credit part-time for nonresidents. Fees $26 per year.

Indiana State University, School of Education, Department of Curriculum and Instruction and Media Technology, Terre Haute, IN 47809-1401. Offerings include secondary education (M Ed, MS, PhD, Ed S). Accredited by NCATE. Department faculty: 16 full-time (4 women). *Degree requirements:* For doctorate, 2 foreign languages, computer language, dissertation. *Entrance requirements:* For doctorate, GRE General Test (minimum score 500 on each section); for Ed S, GRE General Test (minimum combined score of 900), minimum graduate GPA of 3.25. Application deadline: rolling. Application fee: $20. *Tuition:* $143 per credit hour for state residents; $325 per credit hour for nonresidents. • Dr. Jerry A. Summers, Chairperson, 812-237-2960. Application contact: Dr. Robert Williams, Graduate Adviser, 812-237-2952.

Indiana University Bloomington, School of Education, Department of Curriculum and Instruction, Program in Secondary Education, Bloomington, IN 47405. Awards MS, Ed S. Accredited by NCATE. Students: 36 full-time (18 women), 30 part-time (23 women); includes 4 minority (all African Americans), 2 international. In 1997, 14 master's awarded. *Degree requirements:* For master's, internship or thesis required, foreign language not required; for Ed S, comprehensive exam or project required, foreign language and thesis not required. *Entrance requirements:* For master's, GRE General Test (minimum combined score of 1300 on three sections); for Ed S, GRE General Test (minimum combined score of 1500 on three sections). Application deadline: 3/1 (priority date; rolling processing). Application fee: $35. *Expenses:* Tuition $153 per credit hour for state residents; $446 per credit hour for nonresidents. Fees $343 per year. *Financial aid:* Fellowships, research assistantships, teaching assistantships, partial tuition waivers, Federal Work-Study, institutionally sponsored loans, and career-related internships or fieldwork available. *Faculty research:* Student/teacher attitudes, classroom management, individualized instruction, school evaluation. • Dr. David Flinders, Coordinator, 812-856-8109.

Indiana University Northwest, Division of Education, Program in Secondary Education, Gary, IN 46408-1197. Awards MS Ed. Part-time and evening/weekend programs available. Faculty: 14. Students: 43 part-time; includes 22 minority (13 African Americans, 1 Asian American, 8 Hispanics). Average age 32. *Degree requirements:* Thesis. *Entrance requirements:* GRE General Test or MAT, minimum GPA of 3.0. Application deadline: 7/15 (priority date; 11/15 for spring admission). Application fee: $25. • Dr. William May, Interim Dean, Division of Education, 219-981-4278. Application contact: John Burson, Director of Education Student Services, 219-980-6514. Fax: 219-981-4208. E-mail: jburson@iunhaw1.iun.indiana.edu.

Indiana University–Purdue University Fort Wayne, School of Education, Program in Secondary Education, Fort Wayne, IN 46805-1499. Awards MS Ed. Accredited by NCATE. Part-time and evening/weekend programs available. Faculty: 3 full-time (2 women), 2 part-time (1 woman), 3.5 FTE. Students: 2 full-time (1 woman), 77 part-time (45 women); includes 2 minority (both African Americans), 1 international. Average age 38. 30 applicants, 100% accepted. In 1997, 29 degrees awarded (100% found work related to degree). *Entrance requirements:* Minimum GPA of 2.5. Application deadline: 8/1 (priority date; rolling processing; 12/1 for spring admission). Application fee: $30. *Expenses:* Tuition $2356 per year full-time, $131 per credit hour part-time for state residents; $5253 per year full-time, $292 per credit hour part-time for nonresidents. Fees $183 per year full-time, $10.15 per credit hour part-time. *Financial aid:* Application deadline 3/1. • Betty Steffy, Dean, School of Education, 219-481-6456. Fax: 219-481-6083.

Indiana University–Purdue University Indianapolis, School of Education, Department of Secondary Education, Indianapolis, IN 46202-2896. Awards MS. Evening/weekend programs available. Faculty: 7 full-time (0 women), 8 part-time (2 women). Students: 3 full-time (all women), 25 part-time (12 women); includes 1 minority (African American). Average age 35. In 1997, 10 degrees awarded. *Degree requirements:* Thesis optional, foreign language not required. *Entrance requirements:* GRE General Test (minimum combined score of 1300), minimum GPA of 3.0. Application deadline: 3/1 (priority date; 11/1 for spring admission). Application fee: $35. *Expenses:* Tuition $3602 per year full-time, $150 per credit hour part-time for state residents; $10,392 per year full-time, $433 per credit hour part-time for nonresidents. Fees $100 per year (minimum) full-time, $40 per year (minimum) part-time. *Financial aid:* Federal Work-Study and career-related internships or fieldwork available. *Faculty research:* Shared information system for gifted and talented education, professional development schools, field-based teacher training. Total annual research expenditures: $76,500. • Michael Cohen, Director, Teacher Education, 317-274-6814. Application contact: Dr. O. Gilbert Brown, Assistant Dean for Education Student Services, 317-274-0649. Fax: 317-274-6864. E-mail: ogbrown@iupui.edu.

Indiana University South Bend, Division of Education, Department of Secondary Education, South Bend, IN 46634-7111. Awards MS Ed. Accredited by NCATE. Part-time and evening/weekend programs available. Faculty: 10 full-time (4 women), 7 part-time (3 women), 12 FTE. Students: 61 full-time (35 women), 87 part-time (57 women); includes 8 minority (5 African Americans, 1 Asian American, 2 Hispanics), 1 international. Average age 35. 59 applicants, 100% accepted. In 1997, 26 degrees awarded. *Degree requirements:* Thesis or alternative, exit exam required, foreign language not required. *Entrance requirements:* TOEFL (minimum score 550). Application deadline: rolling. Application fee: $35 ($40 for international students). *Expenses:* Tuition $3024 per year full-time, $126 per credit hour part-time for state residents; $7320 per year full-time, $305 per credit hour part-time for nonresidents. Fees $222 per year full-time, $34 per semester (minimum) part-time. *Financial aid:* Federal Work-Study available. Aid available to part-time students. Financial aid application deadline: 3/1. *Faculty research:* Science objectives, free and inexpensive materials. • Dr. Floyd Urbach, Director, 219-237-4486. Fax: 219-237-4550. E-mail: furbach@vines.iusb.edu. Application contact: Graduate Director, 219-237-4183. Fax: 219-237-6549.

Indiana University Southeast, Division of Education, Program in Secondary Education, New Albany, IN 47150-6405. Awards MS Ed. Accredited by NCATE. Part-time and evening/weekend programs available. Students: 1 (woman) full-time, 127 part-time (69 women); includes 8 minority (7 African Americans, 1 Native American), 1 international. Average age 26. 22 applicants, 100% accepted. In 1997, 23 degrees awarded (100% found work related to degree). *Degree requirements:* Thesis or alternative required, foreign language not required. *Entrance requirements:* Appropriate bachelor's degree, minimum GPA of 2.5. Application deadline: rolling. Application fee: $28. *Expenses:* Tuition $125 per credit hour (minimum) for state residents; $284 per credit hour (minimum) for nonresidents. Fees $33 per year full-time, $2.75 per credit hour part-time. *Faculty research:* Distance learning-vocational education. • Dr. Teesue H. Fields, Director of Graduate Studies, 812-941-2658. Fax: 812-941-2667. E-mail: thfields@iusmail.indiana.edu.

Iona College, School of Arts and Science, Program in Secondary School Subjects, 715 North Avenue, New Rochelle, NY 10801-1890. Offers biology education (MS Ed, MST), business education (MST), English education (MS Ed, MST), mathematics education (MS Ed, MST), multicultural education (MS Ed), social studies education (MS Ed, MST), Spanish education (MS Ed, MST). Part-time and evening/weekend programs available. Faculty: 4 full-time (1 woman), 8 part-time (2 women). Students: 3 full-time (2 women), 75 part-time (53 women); includes 3 minority (1 African American, 2 Hispanics). Average age 32. In 1997, 35 degrees awarded. *Degree requirements:* Thesis or alternative required, foreign language not required. *Entrance requirements:* Minimum GPA of 2.5 (MST), New York teaching certificate (MS Ed). Application deadline: rolling. Application fee: $25. *Expenses:* Tuition $455 per credit hour. Fees $25 per semester. *Financial aid:* Graduate assistantships available. Aid available to part-time students. *Faculty research:* Reading/writing, educational technology, administration. • Dr. Lucy Murphy, Chair, 914-633-2210. Fax: 914-633-2608. Application contact: Arlene Melillo, Director of Graduate Recruitment, 914-633-2328. Fax: 914-633-2023.

Iowa State University of Science and Technology, College of Education, Department of Curriculum and Instruction, Program in Elementary and Secondary Education, Ames, IA 50011. Awards M Ed, MS. *Degree requirements:* Thesis or alternative. *Entrance requirements:* TOEFL. Application deadline: 6/1 (priority date; 9/1 for spring admission). Application fee: $20 ($30 for international students). *Expenses:* Tuition $3166 per year full-time, $176 per credit part-time for state residents; $9324 per year full-time, $518 per credit part-time for nonresidents. Fees $200 per year. • Application contact: Daniel Robinson, 515-294-1241.

Jackson State University, School of Education, Department of Educational Foundations and Leadership, Jackson, MS 39217. Offerings include secondary education (MS Ed, Ed S), with option in educational technology (MS Ed). Accredited by NCATE. Department faculty: 21 full-time (10 women), 5 part-time (1 woman). *Degree requirements:* For master's, thesis or alternative, comprehensive exam; for Ed S, thesis, comprehensive exam. *Entrance requirements:* For master's, GRE General Test (minimum combined score of 1000), TOEFL (minimum score 550). Application deadline: 3/1 (priority date; rolling processing; 10/1 for spring admission). Application fee: $20. *Tuition:* $2688 per year (minimum) full-time, $150 per semester hour part-time for state residents; $5546 per year (minimum) full-time, $309 per semester hour part-time for nonresidents. • Dr. George Vincent, Chair, 601-968-2351. Fax: 601-968-2213. E-mail: gvincent@ccaix.jsums.edu. Application contact: Mae Robinson, Admissions Coordinator, 601-968-2455. Fax: 601-968-8246. E-mail: mrobinson@ccaix.jsums.edu.

Jacksonville State University, College of Education, Program in Secondary Education, Jacksonville, AL 36265-9982. Awards MS Ed. Accredited by NCATE. Faculty: 6 full-time (3 women). Students: 34 full-time (21 women), 58 part-time (28 women); includes 19 minority (17 African Americans, 2 Asian Americans). In 1997, 41 degrees awarded. *Degree requirements:* Thesis optional. *Entrance requirements:* GRE General Test or MAT. Application deadline: rolling. Application fee: $20. *Expenses:* Tuition $2140 per year full-time, $107 per semester hour part-time for state residents; $4280 per year full-time, $214 per semester hour part-time for nonresidents. Fees $30 per semester. *Financial aid:* Available to part-time students. Financial aid application deadline: 4/1. • Application contact: College of Graduate Studies and Continuing Education, 205-782-5329.

Jacksonville University, College of Arts and Sciences, Division of Education, Program in Secondary Education, 2800 University Boulevard North, Jacksonville, FL 32211-3394. Awards Certificate. *Entrance requirements:* TOEFL (minimum score 500). Application deadline: 8/1 (priority date; rolling processing; 11/1 for spring admission). Application fee: $25.

James Madison University, College of Education and Psychology, School of Education, Program in Secondary Education, Harrisonburg, VA 22807. Awards M Ed. Accredited by NCATE. Program being phased out; applicants no longer accepted. Part-time and evening/weekend programs available. Students: 2 part-time (1 woman). Average age 30. In 1997, 6 degrees awarded. *Tuition:* $134 per credit hour for state residents; $404 per credit hour for nonresidents. *Financial aid:* Fellowships, teaching assistantships, assistantships, Federal Work-Study available. Financial aid applicants required to submit FAFSA. • Dr. Alvin M. Pettus, Coordinator, 540-568-6486.

John Carroll University, Department of Education and Allied Studies, Program in School Based Secondary Education, University Heights, OH 44118-4581. Awards M Ed. Accredited by NCATE. Faculty: 3 full-time (2 women), 5 part-time (1 woman). Students: 28 full-time (13 women); includes 2 minority (both African Americans). In 1997, 13 degrees awarded. *Degree requirements:* Comprehensive exam, research essay or thesis required, foreign language not required. *Entrance requirements:* GRE General Test or MAT, minimum GPA of 2.75. Application deadline: rolling. Application fee: $25 ($35 for international students). *Tuition:* $450 per credit. *Financial aid:* Partial tuition waivers available. Financial aid application deadline: 3/1; applicants required to submit FAFSA. • Dr. Kathleen Manning, Coordinator, 216-397-4331.

Johns Hopkins University, School of Continuing Studies, Division of Education, Department of Teacher Development and Leadership, Baltimore, MD 21218-2699. Offerings include secondary education (MAT). *Application fee:* $50. • Rochelle Ingram, Chair, 410-516-4957.

Kansas State University, College of Education, Department of Secondary Education, Manhattan, KS 66506. Awards MS. Accredited by NCATE. Part-time and evening/weekend programs available. Faculty: 10 full-time (2 women), 2 part-time (1 woman). Students: 12 full-time (9 women), 46 part-time (34 women). 25 applicants, 72% accepted. *Degree requirements:* Thesis or alternative required, foreign language not required. *Entrance requirements:* Minimum B average. Application deadline: 4/1 (priority date; rolling processing; 10/1 for spring admission). Application fee: $0 ($25 for international students). Electronic applications accepted. *Tuition:* $2218 per year full-time, $401 per semester (minimum) part-time for state residents; $6336 per year full-time, $1087 per semester (minimum) part-time for nonresidents. *Financial aid:* In 1997–98, teaching assistantships averaging $850 per month were awarded; career-related internships or fieldwork also available. • Lawrence C. Scharmann, Chair, 785-532-5904. Application contact: Paul Burden, Assistant Dean, 785-532-5595. Fax: 785-532-7304. E-mail: gradstudy@mail.educ.ksu.edu.

Kent State University, Graduate School of Education, Department of Teaching, Leadership, and Curriculum Studies, Program in Secondary Education, Kent, OH 44242-0001. Awards MA, MAT, M Ed. Accredited by NCATE. Faculty: 4 full-time (2 women), 7 part-time (4 women). Students: 42 full-time (26 women), 3 part-time (2 women); includes 2 minority (both African Americans). In 1997, 43 degrees awarded. *Degree requirements:* Thesis (MA) required, foreign language not required. *Entrance requirements:* GRE General Test. Application deadline: rolling. Application fee: $30. *Tuition:* $4752 per year full-time, $216 per credit hour part-time for state residents; $9213 per year full-time, $419 per credit hour part-time for nonresidents. *Financial aid:* Application deadline 4/1. • Dr. Bill Wilen, Coordinator, 330-672-2580. Application contact: Deborah Barber, Director, Office of Academic Services, 330-672-2862. Fax: 330-672-3549.

Kutztown University of Pennsylvania, Graduate School, College of Education, Program in Secondary Education, Kutztown, PA 19530. Offers biology (M Ed), curriculum and instruction (M Ed), English (M Ed), mathematics (M Ed), social studies (M Ed). Accredited by NCATE. Part-time and evening/weekend programs available. Faculty: 7 full-time (1 woman). Students: 29 full-time (18 women), 66 part-time (40 women); includes 7 minority (4 African Americans, 1 Asian American, 1 Hispanic, 1 Native American). Average age 33. In 1997, 21 degrees awarded. *Degree requirements:* Comprehensive exam required, thesis optional, foreign language not required. *Entrance requirements:* GRE General Test, TOEFL, TSE. Application deadline: 3/1 (8/1 for spring admission). Application fee: $25. *Tuition:* $4111 per year full-time, $225 per credit hour part-time for state residents; $6879 per year full-time, $393 per credit hour part-time for nonresidents. *Financial aid:* Graduate assistantships, partial tuition waivers, Federal Work-Study, and career-related internships or fieldwork available. Financial aid application deadline: 3/15; applicants required to submit FAFSA. • Kathleen Dolgos, Chairperson, 610-683-4259.

Lamar University, College of Education and Human Development, Department of Professional Pedagogy, Program in Secondary Education, Beaumont, TX 77710. Awards M Ed, Certificate. Faculty: 8 full-time (3 women). Students: 1 full-time (0 women); includes 1 minority (African American). Average age 45. In 1997, 1 master's awarded. *Degree requirements:* For master's, thesis optional, foreign language not required. *Entrance requirements:* For master's, GRE General Test (minimum combined score of 950), TOEFL (minimum score 500), minimum GPA of 2.5. Application deadline: 8/1 (rolling processing; 12/1 for spring admission). Application fee: $0. *Expenses:* Tuition $1296 per year full-time, $360 per year part-time for state residents; $6432 per year full-time, $1608 per year part-time for nonresidents. Fees $238 per year full-time, $103 per year part-time. *Financial aid:* Application deadline 4/1. • Application contact: Alicia Satre, Graduate Admissions Coordinator, 409-880-8350. Fax: 409-880-8414.

Lehigh University, College of Education, Department of Education and Human Services, Program in Teacher Education and Reading, Bethlehem, PA 18015-3094. Offerings include secondary education (MA, M Ed, Certificate). Program faculty: 4 full-time (1 woman), 4 part-time (0 women). *Entrance requirements:* For master's, GRE General Test, MAT, TOEFL, minimum GPA of 2.75; for Certificate, TOEFL (minimum score 550). Application deadline: rolling. Application fee: $40. *Expenses:* Tuition $470 per credit. Fees $12 per semester full-time, $6 per semester part-time. • Dr. H. Lynn Columba, Coordinator, 610-758-3230. Fax: 610-758-6223. E-mail: hlc0@lehigh.edu.

Lewis & Clark College, Department of Education, Program in Secondary Education, Portland, OR 97219-7899. Awards MAT. Part-time and evening/weekend programs available. *Degree requirements:* Thesis optional, foreign language not required. *Entrance requirements:* California Basic Educational Skills Test (preservice), GRE General Test or MAT; NTE, minimum GPA of 2.75. Application deadline: 1/15 (rolling processing). Application fee: $45. *Faculty research:* Classroom management, classroom assessment, science education, classroom ethnography, moral development.

Liberty University, School of Education, 1971 University Road, Lynchburg, VA 24502. Offerings include secondary education (M Ed). School faculty: 3 full-time (1 woman), 4 part-time (2 women). *Degree requirements:* Thesis optional, foreign language not required. *Entrance requirements:* GRE General Test (minimum combined score of 900). Application deadline: 8/15 (priority date; rolling processing). Application fee: $35. *Tuition:* $280 per credit hour. • Dr. Pauline Donaldson, Dean, 804-582-2314. Application contact: Bill Wegert, Coordinator of Graduate Admissions, 804-582-2175.

Lincoln University, Graduate School, College of Arts and Sciences, Department of Education, Jefferson City, MO 65102. Offerings include elementary and secondary teaching (M Ed), with options in elementary, secondary; guidance and counseling (M Ed), with options in agency, elementary, secondary. One or more programs accredited by NCATE. Department faculty: 2 full-time (0 women), 10 part-time (6 women). *Entrance requirements:* GRE General Test or MAT, minimum GPA of 2.75 in major, 2.5 overall. Application deadline: 7/25 (rolling processing; 12/15 for spring admission). Application fee: $17. *Expenses:* Tuition $117 per credit hour for state residents; $234 per credit hour for nonresidents. Fees $552 per year (minimum) for state residents; $1104 per year (minimum) for nonresidents. • Dr. Marilyn Hofmann, Acting Head, 573-681-5250.

Long Island University, C.W. Post Campus, School of Education, Department of Curriculum and Instruction, Brookville, NY 11548-1300. Offerings include secondary education (MS). Department faculty: 10 full-time (5 women), 46 part-time (19 women). *Application deadline:* rolling. *Application fee:* $30. Electronic applications accepted. *Expenses:* Tuition $480 per credit. Fees $316 per year full-time, $71 per semester (minimum) part-time. • Dr. Anthony De Falco, Chairperson, 516-299-2372. Application contact: Camille Marziliano, Academic Counselor, 516-299-2123. Fax: 516-299-4167. E-mail: cmarzili@eagle.liunet.edu.

Louisiana State University and Agricultural and Mechanical College, College of Education, Department of Curriculum and Instruction, Baton Rouge, LA 70803. Offerings include secondary education (M Ed). Accredited by NCATE. Department faculty: 27 full-time (15 women), 1 (woman) part-time. *Application deadline:* 1/25 (priority date; rolling processing). *Application fee:* $25. *Tuition:* $2736 per year full-time, $285 per semester (minimum) part-time for state residents; $6636 per year full-time, $460 per semester (minimum) part-time for nonresidents. • Dr. Robert Lafayette, Interim Chair, 504-388-6867. Application contact: Dr. Earl Cheek, Professor, 504-388-6867. Fax: 504-388-1045.

Louisiana Tech University, College of Education, Department of Curriculum, Instruction and Leadership, Ruston, LA 71272. Offerings include secondary education (M Ed), with options in business education, English education, foreign language education, health and physical education, mathematics education, science education, social studies education, speech education. Accredited by NCATE. Department faculty: 16 full-time (11 women). *Application deadline:* 7/29 (2/3 for spring admission). *Application fee:* $20 ($30 for international students). *Tuition:* $2382 per year full-time, $223 per quarter (minimum) part-time for state residents; $5307 per year full-time, $223 per quarter (minimum) part-time for nonresidents. • Dr. Samuel V. Dauzat, Head, 318-257-4609.

Loyola Marymount University, School of Education, Program in Secondary Education, Los Angeles, CA 90045-8350. Awards MA. Part-time and evening/weekend programs available. Faculty: 14 full-time (8 women), 25 part-time (20 women). Students: 26 full-time (18 women), 30 part-time (17 women); includes 18 minority (2 African Americans, 3 Asian Americans, 13 Hispanics). In 1997, 9 degrees awarded. *Degree requirements:* Comprehensive exam required, foreign language and thesis not required. *Entrance requirements:* GRE General Test, TOEFL (minimum score 550), interview. Application fee: $35. Electronic applications accepted. *Expenses:* Tuition $500 per unit. Fees $111 per year full-time, $28 per year part-time. *Financial aid:* In 1997–98, 32 students received aid, including 4 research assistantships (3 to first-year students) totaling $5,650, grants, scholarships totaling $44,465; Federal Work-Study also available. Aid available to part-time students. Financial aid application deadline: 3/2; applicants required to submit FAFSA. • Dr. Albert P. Koppes, Coordinator, 310-338-7301.

Loyola University New Orleans, College of Arts and Sciences, Department of Education, Program in Secondary Education, New Orleans, LA 70118-6195. Awards MS. Part-time and evening/weekend programs available. Faculty: 4 full-time (3 women), 4 part-time (all women). Students: 1 (woman) full-time, 16 part-time (10 women); includes 1 minority (African American). Average age 34. 13 applicants, 54% accepted. In 1997, 1 degree awarded. *Degree requirements:* Comprehensive exam required, foreign language and thesis not required. *Entrance requirements:* GRE, MAT (preferred), interview, sample of written work. Application deadline: 8/1 (priority date; rolling processing; 12/1 for spring admission). Application fee: $20. Electronic applications accepted. *Expenses:* Tuition $247 per credit hour. Fees $556 per year full-time, $164 per year part-time. *Financial aid:* Research assistantships, partial tuition waivers, Federal Work-Study, and career-related internships or fieldwork available. Aid available to part-time students. Financial aid application deadline: 5/1; applicants required to submit FAFSA. *Faculty research:* Moral development, curriculum. • Dr. Mary Ann Doyle, Director, 504-865-3540. Fax: 504-865-3571.

Lynchburg College, School of Education and Human Development, Program in Secondary Education, Lynchburg, VA 24501-3199. Awards M Ed. *Entrance requirements:* Minimum GPA of 3.0 (undergraduate). Application fee: $20.

Maharishi University of Management, Department of Education, Fairfield, IA 52557. Offerings include secondary education (MA). Department faculty: 11 (2 women). *Degree requirements:* Thesis or alternative required, foreign language not required. *Entrance requirements:* GRE, TOEFL (minimum score 550), minimum GPA of 3.0. Application deadline: 4/15 (priority date; rolling processing). Application fee: $40. • Dr. Christopher Jones, Associate Chairperson, 515-472-1105. Application contact: Harry Bright, Director of Admissions, 515-472-1166.

Manhattanville College, School of Education, Program in Secondary Education, Purchase, NY 10577-2132. Offers English (MAT); languages (MAT), including French, Spanish; mathematics (MAT); science (MAT), including biology, chemistry; social studies (MAT). *Degree requirements:* Thesis, comprehensive exam or research project required, foreign language not required. *Entrance requirements:* Minimum undergraduate GPA of 3.0. Application deadline: rolling. Application fee: $40. *Expenses:* Tuition $410 per credit (minimum). Fees $25 per semester. • Application contact: Carol Messar, Director of Admissions, 914-323-5142. Fax: 914-323-5493.

Manhattanville College, School of Education, Program in Secondary and Special Education, Purchase, NY 10577-2132. Awards MPS. *Degree requirements:* Thesis, comprehensive exam or research project required, foreign language not required. *Entrance requirements:* Minimum undergraduate GPA of 3.0. Application deadline: rolling. Application fee: $40. *Expenses:* Tuition $410 per credit (minimum). Fees $25 per semester. • Application contact: Carol Messar, Director of Admissions, 914-323-5142. Fax: 914-323-5493.

Directory: Secondary Education

Mankato State University, College of Education, Department of Curriculum and Instruction, Program in Secondary Teaching, South Rd and Ellis Ave, PO Box 8400, Mankato, MN 56002-8400. Awards MA, MS, SP. Accredited by NCATE. *Degree requirements:* For master's, thesis or alternative, comprehensive exam required, foreign language not required; for SP, thesis, comprehensive exam required, foreign language not required. *Entrance requirements:* For master's, GRE General Test or MAT, minimum GPA of 3.0 during previous 2 years; for SP, GRE, minimum GPA of 3.0. Application deadline: 7/10 (priority date; rolling processing; 10/30 for spring admission). Application fee: $20. *Tuition:* $126 per credit (minimum) for state residents; $200 per credit for nonresidents. *Financial aid:* Application deadline 3/15. • Application contact: Joni Roberts, Admissions Coordinator, 507-389-2321. Fax: 507-389-5974. E-mail: grad@mankato.msus.edu.

Mansfield University of Pennsylvania, Department of Education, Program in Secondary Education, Mansfield, PA 16933. Awards MS. Accredited by NCATE. Part-time and evening/weekend programs available. Faculty: 12 part-time (6 women). Students: 17 full-time (7 women), 15 part-time (8 women); includes 2 minority (1 African American, 1 Asian American), 1 international. Average age 31. 18 applicants, 100% accepted. In 1997, 19 degrees awarded. *Degree requirements:* Thesis optional, foreign language not required. *Entrance requirements:* GRE General Test, MAT, NTE, or minimum GPA of 3.0. Application deadline: rolling. Application fee: $25. *Expenses:* Tuition $3468 per year full-time, $193 per credit part-time for state residents; $6236 per year full-time, $346 per credit part-time for nonresidents. Fees $236 per year full-time, $18.25 per semester (minimum) part-time for state residents; $266 per year full-time, $18.25 per semester (minimum) part-time for nonresidents. *Financial aid:* In 1997–98, 2 graduate assistantships (1 to a first-year student) were awarded; career-related internships or fieldwork also available. Financial aid application deadline: 5/1; applicants required to submit FAFSA. • Dr. Robert Putt, Chairperson, Department of Education, 717-662-4562.

Marshall University, Graduate School of Education and Professional Studies, Program in Secondary Education, South Charleston, WV 25303-1600. Awards MA. Accredited by NCATE. Part-time and evening/weekend programs available. Faculty: 2 full-time (1 woman), 8 part-time (2 women), 4.1 FTE. Students: 9 full-time (6 women), 30 part-time (19 women). Average age 39. In 1997, 12 degrees awarded. *Degree requirements:* Comprehensive or oral exam, research project required, foreign language and thesis not required. *Entrance requirements:* GRE General Test, minimum undergraduate GPA of 2.5. Application deadline: 8/1 (priority date; rolling processing). Application fee: $0. *Tuition:* $2364 per year full-time, $132 per hour part-time for state residents; $6894 per year full-time, $383 per hour part-time for nonresidents. *Financial aid:* Full tuition waivers available. Aid available to part-time students. Financial aid applicants required to submit FAFSA. • Dr. James Ranson, Dean, Graduate School of Education and Professional Studies, 304-746-1998. Fax: 304-746-1942.

Marshall University, College of Education, Division of Teacher Education, Program in Secondary Education, Huntington, WV 25755-2020. Awards MA. Accredited by NCATE. Evening/weekend programs available. Faculty: 7 (2 women). Students: 4 full-time (3 women), 26 part-time (18 women). In 1997, 4 degrees awarded. *Degree requirements:* Thesis optional. *Entrance requirements:* GRE General Test (minimum combined score of 1200). *Tuition:* $2364 per year full-time, $132 per hour part-time for state residents; $6894 per year full-time, $383 per hour part-time for nonresidents. • Dr. Harry E. Sowards, Director, 304-696-2333. Application contact: Dr. James Harless, Director of Admissions, 304-696-3160.

Marymount University, School of Education and Human Services, Program in Secondary Education, Arlington, VA 22207-4299. Awards M Ed. Accredited by NCATE. Part-time and evening/weekend programs available. In 1997, 26 degrees awarded. *Degree requirements:* Thesis or alternative required, foreign language not required. *Entrance requirements:* GRE General Test or MAT, interview. Application deadline: rolling. Application fee: $35. *Expenses:* Tuition $465 per credit hour. Fees $120 per year full-time, $5 per credit hour part-time. *Financial aid:* Career-related internships or fieldwork available. Aid available to part-time students. Financial aid applicants required to submit FAFSA. • Dr. Shirley Smith, Chair, 703-284-1620. Fax: 703-284-1631. E-mail: shirley.smith@marymount.edu.

Maryville University of Saint Louis, School of Education, St. Louis, MO 63141-7299. Offerings include secondary education (MA). Accredited by NCATE. School faculty: 9 full-time (7 women), 15 part-time (9 women). *Degree requirements:* Thesis, project required, foreign language not required. *Average time to degree:* master's–2 years full-time, 4 years part-time. *Entrance requirements:* Minimum GPA of 3.0. Application deadline: rolling. Application fee: $20. Electronic applications accepted. *Expenses:* Tuition $11,480 per year full-time, $345 per credit hour part-time. Fees $120 per year full-time, $60 per year part-time. • Dr. Kathe Rasch, Dean, 314-529-9466. Fax: 314-529-9921. E-mail: krasch@maryville.edu.

McNeese State University, College of Education, Department of Curriculum and Instruction, Program in Secondary Education, Lake Charles, LA 70609-2495. Offers biology education (M Ed), business education (M Ed), English education (M Ed), mathematics education (M Ed), social science education (M Ed), speech education (M Ed). Evening/weekend programs available. Faculty: 8 full-time (3 women). Students: 14 part-time (12 women). In 1997, 5 degrees awarded. *Entrance requirements:* GRE General Test, teaching certificate. Application deadline: 7/15 (priority date; rolling processing). Application fee: $10 ($25 for international students). *Tuition:* $2118 per year full-time, $344 per semester (minimum) part-time for state residents; $7308 per year full-time, $344 per semester (minimum) part-time for nonresidents. *Financial aid:* Application deadline 5/1. • Dr. Everett Waddell Burge, Head, Department of Curriculum and Instruction, 318-475-5404.

Miami University, School of Education and Allied Professions, Department of Teacher Education, Program in Secondary Education, Oxford, OH 45056. Awards MAT, M Ed. Accredited by NCATE. Part-time programs available. Students: 38 full-time (20 women), 11 part-time (6 women); includes 8 minority (all African Americans). 47 applicants, 85% accepted. In 1997, 24 degrees awarded. *Degree requirements:* Thesis (for some programs), final exam required, foreign language not required. *Entrance requirements:* MAT, minimum undergraduate GPA of 3.0 during previous 2 years or 2.75 overall. Application deadline: 3/1 (priority date; rolling processing; 12/1 for spring admission). Application fee: $35. *Tuition:* $5932 per year full-time, $255 per credit hour part-time for state residents; $12,392 per year full-time, $524 per credit hour part-time for nonresidents. *Financial aid:* Research assistantships, teaching assistantships, full tuition waivers, Federal Work-Study, and career-related internships or fieldwork available. Financial aid application deadline: 3/1. *Faculty research:* Teacher effectiveness, collaboration models. • Dr. Robert Shearer, Director of Graduate Study, 513-529-5708.

Middle Tennessee State University, College of Education, Department of Educational Leadership, Major in Curriculum and Instruction, Murfreesboro, TN 37132. Offerings include secondary education (M Ed, Ed S). Accredited by NCATE. *Degree requirements:* Comprehensive exams required, foreign language and thesis not required. *Entrance requirements:* Cooperative English Test, MAT. Application deadline: 8/1 (priority date). Application fee: $5. *Expenses:* Tuition $2560 per year full-time, $129 per semester hour part-time for state residents; $7386 per year full-time, $340 per semester hour part-time for nonresidents. Fees $486 per year full-time, $17 per semester (minimum) part-time. • Dr. Nancy Keese, Chair, Department of Educational Leadership, 615-898-2855. Fax: 615-898-2859. E-mail: nkeese@mtsu.edu.

Midwestern State University, Division of Education, Program in Secondary Education, Wichita Falls, TX 76308-2096. Awards M Ed. Part-time and evening/weekend programs available. Students: 1. *Entrance requirements:* GRE General Test, TOEFL (minimum score 550). Application deadline: 8/7 (12/15 for spring admission). Application fee: $0 ($50 for international students). *Expenses:* Tuition $44 per hour for state residents; $259 per hour for nonresidents. Fees $90 per year (minimum) full-time, $9 per semester (minimum) part-time. *Financial aid:* Teaching assistantships available. • Dr. Emerson Capps, Director, Division of Education, 940-397-4313.

Mills College, Education Department, Oakland, CA 94613-1000. Offerings include education (MA), with options in curriculum and instruction, elementary education, English education, mathematics education, science education, secondary education, social sciences education, teaching. Department faculty: 8 full-time (6 women), 13 part-time (11 women), 11 FTE. *Degree requirements:* Comprehensive exam required, thesis not required. *Average time to degree:* master's–2 years full-time. *Entrance requirements:* TOEFL (minimum score 550). Application deadline: 2/1 (priority date; rolling processing; 11/1 for spring admission). Application fee: $50. Electronic applications accepted. *Expenses:* Tuition $10,600 per year full-time, $2560 per year part-time. Fees $468 per year. • Jane Bowyer, Chairperson, 510-430-2118. Fax: 510-430-3314. E-mail: grad-studies@mills.edu. Application contact: La Vonna S. Brown, Coordinator of Graduate Studies, 510-430-3309. Fax: 510-430-2159. E-mail: grad-studies@mills.edu.

Mississippi College, School of Education, Programs in Secondary Education, Program in Secondary Education, Clinton, MS 39058. Awards M Ed. Accredited by NCATE. *Degree requirements:* Comprehensive exam required, foreign language and thesis not required. *Entrance requirements:* GRE or NTE, minimum GPA of 2.5, Class A Certificate. Application deadline: 8/15 (priority date; rolling processing). Application fee: $25 ($75 for international students). *Expenses:* Tuition $6624 per year full-time, $276 per hour part-time. Fees $228 per year full-time, $35 per semester (minimum) part-time. *Financial aid:* Application deadline 4/1. • Dr. Thomas Taylor, Dean, School of Education, 601-925-3402.

Mississippi State University, College of Education, Department of Curriculum and Instruction, Mississippi State, MS 39762. Offerings include secondary education (MS). Accredited by NCATE. Department faculty: 26 full-time (13 women). *Degree requirements:* Comprehensive written exam required, foreign language and thesis not required. *Entrance requirements:* Minimum QPA of 2.75 in last 2 years. Application deadline: 7/26 (priority date; rolling processing; 11/10 for spring admission). Application fee: $0 ($25 for international students). Electronic applications accepted. *Tuition:* $3017 per year full-time, $168 per credit hour part-time for state residents; $6119 per year full-time, $340 per credit hour part-time for nonresidents. • Dr. James S. Turner, Interim Head, 601-325-3747. Application contact: Dr. Dwight Hare, Graduate Coordinator, 601-325-3747. Fax: 601-325-8784. E-mail: rdh1@ra.msstate.edu.

Mississippi State University, College of Education, Program Under Dean of Education, Mississippi State, MS 39762. Offerings include secondary education (Ed D, PhD, Ed S). Accredited by NCATE. *Degree requirements:* For doctorate, computer language (for some programs), dissertation required, foreign language not required; for Ed S, thesis or alternative required, foreign language not required. *Entrance requirements:* For Ed S, minimum QPA of 3.2 in graduate course work. *Tuition:* $3017 per year full-time, $168 per credit hour part-time for state residents; $6119 per year full-time, $340 per credit hour part-time for nonresidents. • Dr. William H. Graves, Dean, College of Education, 601-325-3717. Fax: 601-325-8784. E-mail: whg1@ra.msstate.edu.

Montana State University–Billings, College of Education and Human Services, Department of Curriculum and Instruction, Option in Secondary Education, Billings, MT 59101-9984. Offers program in teaching as a second career (M Ed), including K–12 education, secondary education. Accredited by NCATE. Part-time programs available. *Degree requirements:* Professional paper or thesis required, foreign language not required. *Entrance requirements:* GRE General Test (minimum combined score of 1350 on three sections) or MAT (minimum score 38), minimum GPA of 3.0 (undergraduate), 3.25 (graduate). Application deadline: 8/1 (priority date; rolling processing; 1/1 for spring admission). Application fee: $30. *Expenses:* Tuition $2253 per year full-time, $397 per semester (minimum) part-time for state residents; $5313 per year full-time, $907 per semester (minimum) part-time for nonresidents. Fees $378 per year full-time, $105 per semester (minimum) part-time.

Morehead State University, College of Education and Behavioral Sciences, Department of Leadership and Secondary Education, Program in Secondary Education, Morehead, KY 40351. Offers secondary teaching (MA Ed). Accredited by NCATE. Part-time and evening/weekend programs available. Faculty: 4 full-time (3 women), 2 part-time (0 women). Students: 8 full-time (5 women), 96 part-time (45 women). Average age 25. 33 applicants, 100% accepted. In 1997, 52 degrees awarded. *Degree requirements:* Oral and/or written comprehensive exams required, foreign language and thesis not required. *Entrance requirements:* GRE General Test (minimum combined score of 1000), minimum GPA of 2.5, teaching certificate. Application deadline: 8/1 (priority date; rolling processing; 12/1 for spring admission). Application fee: $0. *Tuition:* $2470 per year full-time, $138 per semester hour part-time for state residents; $6710 per year full-time, $373 per semester hour part-time for nonresidents. *Financial aid:* In 1997–98, 3 teaching assistantships (all to first-year students) averaging $471 per month and totaling $12,000 were awarded; research assistantships, Federal Work-Study also available. Financial aid application deadline: 4/1; applicants required to submit FAFSA. *Faculty research:* Critical thinking techniques, student ability concepts, instructional applications of microcomputers, dropout prevention. • Application contact: Betty Cowsert, Graduate Admissions Officer, 606-783-2039. Fax: 606-783-5061.

Mount Saint Mary College, Division of Education, Program in Secondary Education, Newburgh, NY 12550-3494. Awards MS Ed. Part-time and evening/weekend programs available. Students: 5 full-time (4 women), 24 part-time (17 women); includes 2 minority (1 African American, 1 Asian American). Average age 32. In 1997, 1 degree awarded. *Degree requirements:* Comprehensive exam, practicum required, foreign language and thesis not required. *Application deadline:* rolling. *Application fee:* $20. *Expenses:* Tuition $367 per credit. Fees $30 per year. *Financial aid:* Application deadline 9/30. • Application contact: Sr. Frances Berski, Coordinator, 914-569-3267. Fax: 914-562-6762. E-mail: berski@msmc.edu.

Mount St. Mary's College, Department of Education, Specialization in Secondary Education, Los Angeles, CA 90049-1597. Awards MS. *Degree requirements:* Thesis, research project required, foreign language not required. *Entrance requirements:* MAT, minimum GPA of 3.0. Application fee: $50.

Murray State University, College of Education, Department of Elementary, Middle School, and Secondary Education, Program in Secondary Education, Murray, KY 42071-0009. Awards MA Ed, Ed S. Accredited by NCATE. Part-time programs available. Faculty: 10 full-time (3 women). Students: 3 full-time (2 women), 93 part-time (63 women); includes 3 minority (all African Americans). 17 applicants, 100% accepted. In 1997, 15 master's awarded. *Entrance requirements:* For master's, TOEFL (minimum score 500). Application deadline: rolling. Application fee: $20. *Expenses:* Tuition $2500 per year full-time, $124 per hour part-time for state residents; $6740 per year full-time, $357 per hour part-time for nonresidents. Fees $360 per year full-time, $180 per year part-time. *Financial aid:* Research assistantships, teaching assistantships, Federal Work-Study available. Financial aid application deadline: 4/1. • Dr. Chuck Hulick, Director, 502-762-2496. Fax: 502-762-2540.

National–Louis University, National College of Education, McGaw Graduate School, Program in Secondary Education, 2840 Sheridan Road, Evanston, IL 60201-1730. Awards MAT. Program new for fall 1998. *Entrance requirements:* GRE or MAT, minimum GPA of 3.0. Application fee: $25. *Tuition:* $411 per semester hour. • Dr. David Freitas, Coordinator, 847-475-1100 Ext. 5201. Application contact: Dr. David McCulloch, Vice President for University Services, 800-443-5522 Ext. 5127. Fax: 847-465-0593. E-mail: dmcc@wheeling1.nl.edu.

Nazareth College of Rochester, Graduate Studies, Department of Education, Program in General Secondary Education, Rochester, NY 14618-3790. Awards MS Ed. Part-time and evening/weekend programs available. Faculty: 4 full-time (1 woman), 5 part-time (2 women). Students: 4 full-time (all women), 55 part-time (37 women); includes 1 minority (African American). 13 applicants, 100% accepted. In 1997, 30 degrees awarded. *Degree requirements:* Comprehensive exam required, foreign language and thesis not required. *Entrance requirements:* Minimum GPA of 2.7. Application deadline: 6/1 (11/1 for spring admission). Application fee:

$40. *Expenses:* Tuition $436 per credit hour. Fees $20 per semester. • Dr. Robert C. Marino, Director, 716-389-2604. Application contact: Dr. Kay F. Marshman, Dean, 716-389-2815. Fax: 716-389-2452.

New School University, Adult Division, Teacher Education Program, New York, NY 10011-8603. Awards MST. Faculty: 8 part-time (7 women). Students: 43 full-time (32 women); includes 11 minority (9 African Americans, 2 Hispanics). Average age 32. 79 applicants, 68% accepted. In 1997, 44 degrees awarded. *Entrance requirements:* Interview, portfolio. Application deadline: 5/1 (rolling processing). Application fee: $30. *Tuition:* $616 per credit. *Financial aid:* Departmental scholarships, full and partial tuition waivers, Federal Work-Study, institutionally sponsored loans, and career-related internships or fieldwork available. Financial aid application deadline: 5/1; applicants required to submit FAFSA. • Carolina Mancuso, Acting Director, 212-229-5881. Application contact: Gerianne Brusati, Director, Educational Advising and Admissions, 212-229-5630. Fax: 212-989-3887. E-mail: admissions@dialnsa.edu.

See in-depth description on page 995.

Niagara University, Graduate Division of Education, Concentration in Teacher Education, Niagara University, NY 14109. Offerings include secondary education (MS Ed). Accredited by NCATE. Faculty: 4 full-time (1 woman), 6 part-time (4 women). *Entrance requirements:* GRE General Test or MAT. Application deadline: 8/1 (rolling processing). Application fee: $30. *Expenses:* Tuition $6048 per year full-time, $336 per credit hour part-time. Fees $25 per semester. • Dr. Paul J. Vermette, Chairman, 716-286-8550. Application contact: Rev. Daniel F. O'Leary, OMI, Dean of Education, 716-286-8560.

Norfolk State University, School of Education, Department of Secondary Education and School Management, 2401 Corprew Avenue, Norfolk, VA 23504-3907. Offers programs in principal preparation (MA), secondary education (MAT), urban education/administration (MA). Accredited by NCATE. Part-time programs available. Faculty: 3 full-time, 1 part-time. Students: 78 full-time (60 women), 55 part-time (41 women); includes 100 minority (98 African Americans, 2 Asian Americans), 31 international. Average age 35. In 1997, 62 degrees awarded. *Entrance requirements:* GRE General Test, minimum GPA of 3.0 in major, 2.5 overall. Application deadline: 8/1. Application fee: $30. *Tuition:* $3718 per year full-time, $198 per credit hour part-time for state residents; $7668 per year full-time, $404 per credit hour part-time for nonresidents. *Financial aid:* Fellowships and career-related internships or fieldwork available. • Dr. Mary Kimble, Acting Head, 757-683-8178.

Northeastern State University, College of Education, Department of Education, Program in Secondary Education, Tahlequah, OK 74464-2399. Awards M Ed. Students: 20 (12 women). In 1997, 16 degrees awarded. *Degree requirements:* Thesis or alternative required, foreign language not required. *Entrance requirements:* GRE General Test (minimum combined score of 900) or MAT (minimum score 35), minimum GPA of 3.0. Application deadline: 6/1 (priority date; rolling processing). Application fee: $0. *Expenses:* Tuition $74 per credit hour for state residents; $176 per credit hour for nonresidents. Fees $30 per year. *Financial aid:* Teaching assistantships, Federal Work-Study available. Financial aid application deadline: 3/1. • Dr. James Bond, Head, 918-456-5511 Ext. 3747.

Northeast Louisiana University, College of Education, Department of Curriculum and Instruction, Program in Secondary Education, Monroe, LA 71209-0001. Awards M Ed, Ed S. Accredited by NCATE. Part-time and evening/weekend programs available. *Degree requirements:* For Ed S, thesis. *Entrance requirements:* For master's, GRE General Test, minimum GPA of 2.5. Application deadline: 6/1 (priority date; rolling processing; 11/1 for spring admission). Application fee: $15 ($25 for international students). *Tuition:* $2028 per year full-time, $240 per semester (minimum) part-time for state residents; $6852 per year full-time, $240 per semester (minimum) part-time for nonresidents.

Northern Arizona University, Center for Excellence in Education, Program in Secondary Education, Flagstaff, AZ 86011. Awards M Ed. Students: 30 full-time (19 women), 204 part-time (123 women); includes 36 minority (5 African Americans, 4 Asian Americans, 26 Hispanics, 1 Native American). Average age 22. 103 applicants, 77% accepted. In 1997, 91 degrees awarded. *Degree requirements:* Thesis or alternative required, foreign language not required. *Entrance requirements:* GRE General Test or minimum GPA of 3.0. Application deadline: 3/15 (priority date; rolling processing). Application fee: $45. *Expenses:* Tuition $2088 per year full-time, $330 per semester (minimum) part-time for state residents; $8004 per year full-time, $1002 per semester (minimum) part-time for nonresidents. Fees $72 per year full-time, $18 per semester (minimum) part-time. *Financial aid:* Career-related internships or fieldwork available. *Faculty research:* Early adolescent stress, vocational education, portfolio assessment, school-to-work, gender issues. • Dr. Lynda Hatch, Interim Coordinator, 520-523-5854.

Northern Kentucky University, Department of Education, Highland Heights, KY 41099. Offerings include secondary education (MA Ed). Accredited by NCATE. Department faculty: 16 full-time (11 women). *Entrance requirements:* GRE, teaching certificate. Application deadline: 8/15 (priority date; rolling processing). Application fee: $25. *Tuition:* $2420 per year full-time, $132 per semester hour part-time for state residents; $6660 per year full-time, $368 per semester hour part-time for nonresidents. • Dr. Darrell Garber, Chairperson, 606-572-5365. Application contact: Peg Griffin, Coordinator, Graduate Program, 606-572-6364.

Northern Michigan University, College of Behavioral Sciences and Human Services, Department of Education, Program in Secondary Education, Marquette, MI 49855-5301. Awards MA Ed. Accredited by NCATE. Part-time programs available. Students: 30 part-time (17 women); includes 1 minority (Native American). 2 applicants, 100% accepted. In 1997, 11 degrees awarded. *Degree requirements:* Thesis or alternative required, foreign language not required. *Entrance requirements:* GRE General Test (minimum combined score of 900), minimum GPA of 2.75. Application deadline: 7/1 (priority date; rolling processing; 11/1 for spring admission). Application fee: $25. *Expenses:* Tuition $135 per credit hour for state residents; $215 per credit hour for nonresidents. Fees $183 per year full-time, $94 per year (minimum) part-time. *Financial aid:* Federal Work-Study, institutionally sponsored loans available. Aid available to part-time students. Financial aid application deadline: 3/1. *Faculty research:* Supervision and improvement of instruction. • Dr. James D. Hendricks, Head, Department of Education, 906-227-2728.

Northern State University, Division of Graduate Studies in Education, Program in Teaching and Learning, Aberdeen, SD 57401-7198. Offerings include secondary classroom teaching (MS Ed). Accredited by NCATE. Offered jointly with Huron University, Jamestown College, and the University of Mary. Program faculty: 98 full-time (28 women). *Degree requirements:* Thesis required, foreign language not required. *Average time to degree:* master's–1.5 years full-time. *Entrance requirements:* Minimum GPA of 2.75. Application deadline: 8/15 (priority date; rolling processing; 12/15 for spring admission). Application fee: $15. *Expenses:* Tuition $1999 per year full-time, $83 per credit hour part-time for state residents; $6034 per year full-time, $251 per credit hour part-time for nonresidents. Fees $954 per year full-time, $40 per credit hour part-time. • Dr. Paul Deputy, Head, 605-626-2415. Application contact: Dr. Sharon Tebben, Director of Graduate Studies, 605-626-2558. Fax: 605-626-2542.

North Georgia College & State University, Graduate School, Program in Education, Dahlonega, GA 30597-1001. Offerings include secondary education (M Ed), with options in art education, biology education, chemistry education, English education, mathematics education, modern languages education, physical education, science education, social science education. Accredited by NCATE. Program faculty: 57 full-time (15 women), 7 part-time (4 women). *Degree requirements:* Comprehensive exam required, thesis optional, foreign language not required. *Entrance requirements:* GRE General Test (minimum combined score of 800) or MAT (minimum score 44), minimum GPA of 2.75. Application deadline: 9/1 (priority date; rolling processing). Application fee: $25. • Dr. Bob Michael, Dean, School of Education, 706-864-1533. Application contact: Mai-Lan Ledbetter, Coordinator of Graduate Admissions, 706-864-1543. Fax: 706-864-1668. E-mail: mledbetter@nugget.ngc.peachnet.edu.

Northwestern Oklahoma State University, School of Education, Psychology, and Health and Physical Education, Program in Secondary Education, Alva, OK 73717. Awards M Ed. Accredited by NCATE. Part-time programs available. Faculty: 4 full-time (2 women). Students: 10 full-time (1 woman), 22 part-time (10 women); includes 2 minority (1 African American, 1 Hispanic). 21 applicants, 90% accepted. In 1997, 3 degrees awarded (100% found work related to degree). *Entrance requirements:* GRE General Test (minimum combined score of 900) or MAT (minimum score 38), minimum GPA of 2.75. Application deadline: rolling. Application fee: $15. *Tuition:* $73 per semester hour for state residents; $175 per semester hour for nonresidents. *Financial aid:* Federal Work-Study available. Aid available to part-time students. Financial aid application deadline: 5/1. *Faculty research:* Teacher education, professional school models of pedagogy, competency exams for teachers, teacher accreditation/certification. • Application contact: Dr. Ed Huckeby, Dean of Graduate School, 405-327-8410.

Northwestern State University of Louisiana, Division of Education, Emphasis in Secondary Teaching, Natchitoches, LA 71497. Awards M Ed, Ed S. Accredited by NCATE. Faculty: 1 full-time (0 women), 2 part-time (1 woman). Students: 2 part-time (both women). Average age 30. In 1997, 1 master's awarded. *Degree requirements:* For Ed S, thesis required, foreign language not required. *Entrance requirements:* For master's, GRE General Test (minimum combined score of 800), GRE Subject Test, minimum undergraduate GPA of 2.5; for Ed S, GRE General Test, GRE Subject Test. Application deadline: 8/1 (priority date; rolling processing; 1/10 for spring admission). Application fee: $15 ($25 for international students). *Tuition:* $2147 per year full-time, $336 per semester (minimum) part-time for state residents; $6437 per year full-time, $336 per semester (minimum) part-time for nonresidents. *Financial aid:* Career-related internships or fieldwork available. Financial aid application deadline: 7/15. • Application contact: Dr. Tom Hanson, Dean, Graduate Studies and Research, 318-357-5851. Fax: 318-357-5019.

Northwestern University, School of Education and Social Policy, Evanston, IL 60208. Offerings include secondary teaching (MS). School faculty: 19 full-time (5 women), 6 part-time (1 woman). *Tuition:* $2424 per course. • Jean Egmon, Assistant Dean, 847-491-3790. Fax: 847-461-2495. E-mail: egmon@nwu.edu. Application contact: Andrew Ager, Office of Student Affairs, 847-491-3790. Fax: 847-467-2495. E-mail: andrew-ager@nwu.edu.

Northwest Missouri State University, College of Education and Human Services, Department of Curriculum and Instruction, 800 University Drive, Maryville, MO 64468-6001. Offerings include secondary education (MS Ed). Accredited by NCATE. Department faculty: 14 full-time (12 women). *Degree requirements:* Comprehensive exam required, foreign language and thesis not required. *Entrance requirements:* GRE General Test (minimum combined score of 700), TOEFL (minimum score 550), minimum undergraduate GPA of 2.5, teaching certificate, writing sample. Application deadline: rolling. Application fee: $0 ($50 for international students). *Expenses:* Tuition $113 per credit hour for state residents; $197 per credit hour for nonresidents. Fees $3 per credit hour. • Dr. Betty Bush, Chairperson, 816-562-1359. Application contact: Dr. Frances Shipley, Dean of Graduate School, 816-562-1145. E-mail: gradsch@acad.nwmissouri.edu.

Notre Dame College, Education Division, Program in Secondary Teaching, Manchester, NH 03104-2299. Awards M Ed. Faculty: 1 (woman) full-time, 4 part-time (3 women). Students: 9 full-time (4 women), 9 part-time (4 women). Average age 32. 12 applicants, 67% accepted. In 1997, 5 degrees awarded. *Degree requirements:* Computer language, comprehensive exams, portfolio, or thesis required, foreign language not required. *Entrance requirements:* GRE General Test or MAT. Application fee: $35. *Tuition:* $299 per credit. *Financial aid:* Fellowships available. • Dr. Denise Marchionda, Director, 603-669-4298 Ext. 122.

Occidental College, Department of Education, Program in Secondary Education, Los Angeles, CA 90041-3392. Offers English and comparative literary studies (MAT), French (MAT), history (MAT), life science (MAT), mathematics (MAT), music (MAT), physical science (MAT), Spanish (MAT). Part-time programs available. Faculty: 4 full-time (1 woman). Students: 19 full-time (13 women); includes 9 minority (1 African American, 3 Asian Americans, 5 Hispanics). Average age 24. 23 applicants, 91% accepted. *Degree requirements:* Internship required, foreign language and thesis not required. *Entrance requirements:* GRE General Test (minimum score 550 on each section or combined score of 1650 on three sections), TOEFL (minimum score 600), minimum GPA of 3.0. Application deadline: 3/1 (priority date; rolling processing; 10/1 for spring admission). Application fee: $40. *Expenses:* Tuition $21,256 per year full-time, $865 per unit part-time. Fees $314 per year. *Financial aid:* Fellowships, Federal Work-Study, institutionally sponsored loans, and career-related internships or fieldwork available. Aid available to part-time students. Financial aid application deadline: 3/1. • Application contact: Susan Molik, Administrative Assistant, Graduate Office, 213-259-2921.

Ohio University, Graduate Studies, College of Education, School of Curriculum and Instruction, Program in Secondary Education, Athens, OH 45701-2979. Awards M Ed. Accredited by NCATE. Evening/weekend programs available. Faculty: 16. Students: 70 full-time (30 women), 41 part-time (17 women); includes 2 minority (1 African American, 1 Hispanic), 48 international. 80 applicants, 61% accepted. *Degree requirements:* Thesis or alternative required, foreign language not required. *Entrance requirements:* GRE General Test or MAT. Application deadline: rolling. Application fee: $30. *Tuition:* $5430 per year full-time, $216 per quarter hour part-time for state residents; $10,431 per year full-time, $423 per quarter hour part-time for nonresidents. *Financial aid:* Full tuition waivers, Federal Work-Study, institutionally sponsored loans available. Financial aid application deadline: 3/15. • Application contact: Dr. Bonnie Beach, Graduate Chair, 740-593-0523.

Oklahoma City University, Petree College of Arts and Sciences, Division of Education, Program in Secondary Education, Oklahoma City, OK 73106-1402. Awards M Ed. Part-time and evening/weekend programs available. Students: 14 full-time (12 women), 5 part-time (2 women); includes 4 minority (3 African Americans, 1 Asian American), 2 international. Average age 32. *Degree requirements:* Thesis or alternative required, foreign language not required. *Average time to degree:* master's–1.5 years full-time, 3.3 years part-time. *Entrance requirements:* GRE, minimum GPA of 3.0. Application deadline: 8/25 (priority date; rolling processing; 1/15 for spring admission). Application fee: $35 ($55 for international students). *Expenses:* Tuition $318 per hour. Fees $124 per year. *Financial aid:* Fellowships, partial tuition waivers, Federal Work-Study, institutionally sponsored loans, and career-related internships or fieldwork available. Aid available to part-time students. Financial aid application deadline: 8/1; applicants required to submit FAFSA. • Application contact: Laura L. Rahhal, Director of Graduate Admissions, 800-633-7242 Ext. 2. Fax: 405-521-5356. E-mail: lrahhal1@froda.okcu.edu.

Old Dominion University, Darden College of Education, Department of Curriculum and Instruction, Programs in Secondary Education, Norfolk, VA 23529. Offering in instructional technology (MS Ed). Accredited by NCATE. Part-time and evening/weekend programs available. Postbaccalaureate distance learning degree programs offered (minimal on-campus study). Students: 61 full-time (29 women), 136 part-time (90 women); includes 32 minority (24 African Americans, 5 Asian Americans, 3 Hispanics), 1 international. Average age 36. In 1997, 78 degrees awarded. *Degree requirements:* Candidacy exam required, thesis optional, foreign language not required. *Entrance requirements:* GRE General Test, MAT, minimum GPA of 3.0, teaching certificate. Application deadline: 7/1 (rolling processing). Application fee: $30. *Expenses:* Tuition $180 per credit hour for state residents; $477 per credit hour for nonresidents. Fees $140 per year full-time, $32 per semester part-time. *Financial aid:* In 1997–98, 72 students received aid, including 2 fellowships totaling $4,300, 5 research assistantships (4 to first-year students) totaling $24,464, 42 tuition grants (3 to first-year students) totaling $48,246; teaching assistantships, partial tuition waivers, Federal Work-Study, institutionally sponsored loans, and career-related internships or fieldwork also available. Aid available to part-time students. Financial aid application deadline: 2/15; applicants required to submit FAFSA. *Faculty research:* Mathematics retraining, writing project for teachers, geography teaching, reading. • Dr. Murray Rudisill, Director, 757-683-3300. Fax: 757-683-5862. E-mail: mrudisil@odu.edu.

Directory: Secondary Education

Olivet Nazarene University, Division of Education, Program in Secondary Education, Kankakee, IL 60901-0592. Awards MAT. Evening/weekend programs available. *Degree requirements:* Thesis or alternative required, foreign language not required. *Application deadline:* rolling. *Application fee:* $20.

Pacific Lutheran University, School of Education, Program in Classroom Teaching, Tacoma, WA 98447. Offerings include secondary education (MA). Accredited by NCATE. Program faculty: 2 full-time (1 woman). *Degree requirements:* Comprehensive exam, research project or thesis required, foreign language not required. *Entrance requirements:* GRE General Test or MAT, TOEFL (minimum score 550), interview. Application deadline: rolling. Application fee: $35. *Tuition:* $490 per semester hour. • Dr. Leon Reisberg, Graduate Director, 253-535-7272. Application contact: Marjo Burdick, Office of Admissions, 253-535-7151. Fax: 253-535-8320. E-mail: admissions@plu.edu.

Pacific University, School of Education, Forest Grove, OR 97116-1797. Offerings include secondary education (MAT). School faculty: 11 full-time, 8 part-time. *Application deadline:* 3/15 (priority date; rolling processing; 10/15 for spring admission). *Application fee:* $35. • Dr. Willard Kniep, Program Director, 503-359-2205. Application contact: Joel Albin, Admissions Counselor, 503-359-2958. Fax: 503-359-2975. E-mail: admissions@pacificu.edu.

Phillips University, School of Education, 100 South University Avenue, Enid, OK 73701-6439. Offerings include secondary education (M Ed). School faculty: 5 full-time (2 women), 4 part-time (2 women). *Degree requirements:* Thesis required (for some programs), foreign language not required. *Entrance requirements:* Minimum GPA of 2.5. Application deadline: 8/1 (1/1 for spring admission). Application fee: $20. *Expenses:* Tuition $97 per credit hour. Fees $10 per credit hour. • Dr. Donna Payne, Dean, 405-237-4433 Ext. 207.

Piedmont College, Division of Education, Demorest, GA 30535-0010. Offerings include secondary education (MAT). Postbaccalaureate distance learning degree programs offered (no on-campus study). Division faculty: 24 full-time (12 women), 25 part-time (13 women), 30 FTE. *Degree requirements:* Computer language, thesis, field experience in the teaching classroom required, foreign language not required. *Average time to degree:* master's–1.3 years full-time, 1.5 years part-time. *Entrance requirements:* GRE General Test (minimum combined score of 800; average 835), MAT (minimum score 30; average 45), minimum undergraduate GPA of 2.5. Application deadline: 8/1 (12/1 for spring admission). Application fee: $30. *Tuition:* $2880 per year full-time, $160 per hour part-time. • Dr. Jane McFerrin, Chair, 706-778-3000 Ext. 201. Fax: 706-776-9608. E-mail: jmcferrin@piedmont.edu. Application contact: James L. Clement, Associate Dean for Admissions and Financial Aid, 800-277-7020. Fax: 706-776-6635. E-mail: jclement@piedmont.edu.

Pittsburg State University, School of Education, Department of Special Services and Leadership Studies, Program in Secondary Education, Pittsburg, KS 66762-5880. Offers secondary education (MS), secondary reading (Ed S), secondary school administration (Ed S). Accredited by NCATE. Students: 10 part-time (7 women); includes 1 minority (Asian American). In 1997, 3 master's awarded. *Degree requirements:* For master's, thesis or alternative required, foreign language not required. *Entrance requirements:* For master's, GRE General Test or MAT. Application fee: $40. *Tuition:* $2418 per year full-time, $103 per credit hour part-time for state residents; $6130 per year full-time, $258 per credit hour part-time for nonresidents. *Financial aid:* Teaching assistantships, Federal Work-Study, and career-related internships or fieldwork available. • Dr. Steve Scott, Chairman, Department of Special Services and Leadership Studies, 316-235-4487.

Plattsburgh State University of New York, Faculty of Professional Studies, Center for Educational Studies and Services, Program in Secondary Education, Plattsburgh, NY 12901-2681. Offers biology (MST), earth sciences (MST), English (MS Ed, MST), French (MST), mathematics (MST), physics (MST), social studies (MS Ed, MST), Spanish (MST). Students: 32 full-time (18 women), 20 part-time (13 women); includes 1 minority (Hispanic). 19 applicants, 79% accepted. In 1997, 27 degrees awarded. *Degree requirements:* Comprehensive exam or research project required, thesis optional. *Entrance requirements:* GRE General Test or MAT, minimum GPA of 2.5. Application deadline: rolling. Application fee: $50. *Expenses:* Tuition $5100 per year full-time, $213 per credit hour part-time for state residents; $8416 per year full-time, $351 per credit hour part-time for nonresidents. Fees $395 per year full-time, $15.10 per credit hour part-time. *Financial aid:* 23 students received aid; Federal Work-Study available. Aid available to part-time students. Financial aid application deadline: 4/15; applicants required to submit FAFSA. • Dr. Raymond Domenico, Director and Associate Dean, Center for Educational Studies and Services, 518-564-2122.

Plymouth State College of the University System of New Hampshire, Department of Education, Program in Secondary Education (Teacher Certification), Plymouth, NH 03264-1595. Awards M Ed. Accredited by NCATE. Part-time and evening/weekend programs available. Students: 16 full-time (9 women), 22 part-time (16 women); includes 1 minority (Asian American), 1 international. Average age 35. 10 applicants, 70% accepted. In 1997, 32 degrees awarded. *Entrance requirements:* GRE General Test (average 500 on each section) or MAT (minimum score 50), minimum GPA of 3.0. Application deadline: 9/1 (priority date; rolling processing). Application fee: $25 ($35 for international students). *Tuition:* $232 per credit for state residents; $254 per credit for nonresidents. *Financial aid:* Graduate assistantships, institutionally sponsored loans, and career-related internships or fieldwork available. Aid available to part-time students. Financial aid application deadline: 3/15; applicants required to submit FAFSA. • Dr. Lynn Davis, Adviser, 603-535-2862. Application contact: Maryann Szabadics, Administrative Assistant, 603-535-2636. Fax: 603-535-2572. E-mail: for.grad@psc.plymouth.edu.

Portland State University, School of Education, Department of Curriculum and Instruction, Programs in Secondary Education, Portland, OR 97207-0751. Awards MAT, M Ed, MST. Accredited by NCATE. Part-time programs available. Students: 47 full-time (23 women), 8 part-time (3 women); includes 5 minority (3 Asian Americans, 1 Hispanic, 1 Native American). Average age 30. 30 applicants, 90% accepted. *Degree requirements:* Variable foreign language requirement, special project or thesis, written exam. *Entrance requirements:* California Basic Educational Skills Test, TOEFL (minimum score 550), minimum GPA of 3.0 in upper-division course work or 2.75 overall. Application deadline: 4/1 (rolling processing; 11/1 for spring admission). Application fee: $50. *Tuition:* $6101 per year full-time, $689 per semester (minimum) part-time for state residents; $10,445 per year full-time, $689 per semester (minimum) part-time for nonresidents. *Financial aid:* Research assistantships, teaching assistantships, Federal Work-Study, institutionally sponsored loans available. Aid available to part-time students. Financial aid application deadline: 3/1; applicants required to submit FAFSA. *Faculty research:* Multicultural education; workforce issues; technology, teaching, and learning; urban issues. • Application contact: M. Carrol Tama, Professor, 503-725-4756. Fax: 503-725-8475. E-mail: carrol@ed.pdx.edu.

Purdue University Calumet, School of Professional Studies, Department of Education, Program in Secondary Education, Hammond, IN 46323-2094. Awards MS Ed. *Entrance requirements:* TOEFL. Application fee: $30.

Queens College of the City University of New York, Social Science Division, School of Education, Department of Secondary Education, 65-30 Kissena Boulevard, Flushing, NY 11367-1597. Offers programs in art (MS Ed), biology (MS Ed, AC), chemistry (MS Ed, AC), earth sciences (MS Ed, AC), English (MS Ed, AC), French (MS Ed, AC), Italian (MS Ed, AC), mathematics (MS Ed, AC), music (MS Ed, AC), physics (MS Ed, AC), social studies (MS Ed, AC), Spanish (MS Ed, AC). Part-time and evening/weekend programs available. Students: 37 full-time (16 women), 556 part-time (303 women); includes 90 minority (33 African Americans, 19 Asian Americans, 38 Hispanics). 306 applicants, 82% accepted. In 1997, 126 master's awarded. *Degree requirements:* For master's, research project required, foreign language and thesis not required; for AC, thesis optional, foreign language not required. *Entrance requirements:* For master's, TOEFL (minimum score 600), minimum GPA of 3.0; for AC, TOEFL (minimum score 600). Application deadline: 4/1 (rolling processing; 11/1 for spring admission). Application fee: $40. *Expenses:* Tuition $4350 per year full-time, $185 per credit part-time for state residents; $7600 per year full-time, $320 per credit part-time for nonresidents. Fees $104 per year. *Financial aid:* Partial tuition waivers, Federal Work-Study, institutionally sponsored loans, and career-related internships or fieldwork available. Aid available to part-time students. Financial aid application deadline: 4/1; applicants required to submit FAFSA. • Dr. Philip Anderson, Chairperson, 718-997-5150. Application contact: Mario Caruso, Director of Graduate Admissions, 718-997-5200. Fax: 718-997-5193. E-mail: graduate%queens.bitnet@cunyvm.cuny.edu.

Quinnipiac College, School of Liberal Arts, Program in Secondary and Middle School Teaching, Hamden, CT 06518-1904. Offers biology (MAT), chemistry (MAT), English (MAT), French (MAT), history/social studies (MAT), mathematics (MAT), physics (MAT), Spanish (MAT). Part-time programs available. Faculty: 21 full-time (5 women), 16 part-time (9 women). Students: 55 full-time (35 women), 42 part-time (20 women); includes 4 minority (3 African Americans, 1 Native American). Average age 28. 79 applicants, 91% accepted. In 1997, 48 degrees awarded. *Degree requirements:* Thesis. *Average time to degree:* master's–1.5 years full-time, 3 years part-time. *Entrance requirements:* PRAXIS I, minimum GPA of 2.67. Application deadline: rolling. Application fee: $45. Electronic applications accepted. *Expenses:* Tuition $395 per credit hour. Fees $380 per year full-time. *Financial aid:* Fellowships, partial tuition waivers, and career-related internships or fieldwork available. Aid available to part-time students. Financial aid applicants required to submit FAFSA. • Carol Orticari, Director, 203-281-8978. Fax: 203-281-8709. E-mail: orticari@quinnipiac.edu. Application contact: Scott Farber, Director of Graduate Admissions, 203-281-8795. Fax: 203-287-5238. E-mail: qcgradadmi@quinnipiac.edu.

See in-depth description on page 775.

Rhode Island College, School of Graduate Studies, School of Education and Human Development, Department of Educational Studies, Program in Secondary Education, Providence, RI 02908-1924. Awards M Ed. Accredited by NCATE. Faculty: 4 full-time (0 women), 1 part-time (0 women). Students: 7 part-time (5 women). In 1997, 2 degrees awarded. *Entrance requirements:* GRE General Test or MAT. Application deadline: 4/1 (rolling processing). Application fee: $25. *Tuition:* $4064 per year full-time, $214 per credit part-time for state residents; $7658 per year full-time, $376 per credit part-time for nonresidents. *Financial aid:* Application deadline 4/1. • Dr. Carolyn Panofsky, Chair, Department of Educational Studies, 401-456-8170.

Rivier College, Graduate Education Department, Program in Secondary Education, Nashua, NH 03060-5086. Awards M Ed. Part-time and evening/weekend programs available. *Entrance requirements:* GRE General Test or MAT. Application deadline: rolling. Application fee: $25.

Rochester Institute of Technology, National Technical Institute for the Deaf, Department of Graduate Secondary Education, Rochester, NY 14623-5604. Awards MS. Students: 11 full-time (5 women), 5 part-time (4 women); includes 1 minority (African American). 13 applicants, 92% accepted. In 1997, 5 degrees awarded. *Application deadline:* 3/1 (priority date; rolling processing). *Application fee:* $40. Electronic applications accepted. *Expenses:* Tuition $18,765 per year full-time, $527 per credit hour part-time. Fees $126 per year full-time. • Gerald Bateman, Director, 716-475-6480.

Rockford College, Department of Education, Program in Secondary Education, Rockford, IL 61108-2393. Offers art education (MAT), English (MAT), history (MAT), political science (MAT), secondary education (MAT), social sciences (MAT). Part-time and evening/weekend programs available. Faculty: 15 full-time (2 women), 8 part-time (6 women), 17 FTE. Students: 14 full-time (7 women), 28 part-time (15 women); includes 4 minority (all African Americans). Average age 31. 9 applicants, 89% accepted. In 1997, 12 degrees awarded. *Degree requirements:* Thesis optional, foreign language not required. *Entrance requirements:* GRE General Test (minimum combined score of 1000). Application deadline: rolling. Application fee: $35. *Tuition:* $15,500 per year full-time, $400 per credit part-time. • Dr. Debra Dew, Head, 815-392-5202. Fax: 815-226-4119.

Rollins College, Program in Education, Winter Park, FL 32789-4499. Offerings include secondary education (MAT), with options in English, mathematics, music. Program faculty: 13 full-time (8 women), 11 part-time (4 women), 17 FTE. *Application deadline:* rolling. *Application fee:* $50. *Tuition:* $190 per hour. • Dr. Nancy McAleer, Director, 407-646-2305. Application contact: Laura Pfister, Coordinator of Records and Registration, 407-646-2416. Fax: 407-646-1551.

Roosevelt University, College of Education, Chicago, IL 60605-1394. Offerings include secondary education (MA). Accredited by NCATE. *Application deadline:* 6/1 (priority date; rolling processing). *Application fee:* $25 ($35 for international students). *Expenses:* Tuition $445 per credit hour. Fees $100 per year. • Dr. George Lowery, Dean, 312-341-3700. Application contact: Joanne Canyon-Heller, Coordinator of Graduate Admissions, 312-341-3612.

Rowan University, College of Education, Department of Secondary Education-Education Foundations, Program in Teaching-Secondary, Glassboro, NJ 08028-1701. Awards MST. Accredited by NCATE. Students: 6 (3 women). 0 applicants. In 1997, 7 degrees awarded. *Degree requirements:* Thesis, comprehensive exams required, foreign language not required. *Entrance requirements:* GRE General Test, minimum GPA of 2.8. Application deadline: 11/1 (priority date; rolling processing; 4/1 for spring admission). Application fee: $50. *Tuition:* $5728 per year full-time, $258 per credit hour part-time for state residents; $8968 per year full-time, $393 per credit hour part-time for nonresidents. • Dr. John Gallagher, Adviser, Department of Secondary Education-Education Foundations, 609-256-4500 Ext. 3858.

Sacred Heart University, College of Education and Health Professions, Faculty of Education and Psychology, 5151 Park Avenue, Fairfield, CT 06432-1000. Offerings include secondary education (MAT). *Degree requirements:* Thesis or alternative required, foreign language not required. *Application deadline:* rolling. *Application fee:* $40 ($100 for international students). *Expenses:* Tuition $335 per credit. Fees $78 per semester. • Dr. A. Harris Stone, Director, 203-371-7800. Application contact: Linda B. Kirby, Dean of Graduate Admissions, 203-371-7880. Fax: 203-365-4732. E-mail: gradstudies@sacredheart.edu.

Sage Graduate School, Graduate School, Division of Education, Program in Secondary Education, Troy, NY 12180-4115. Awards MS Ed, PMC. Part-time programs available. Students: 15 full-time (9 women), 42 part-time (21 women). *Entrance requirements:* For master's, minimum GPA of 2.75. Application deadline: 8/1 (rolling processing; 12/15 for spring admission). Application fee: $25. *Expenses:* Tuition $360 per credit hour. Fees $50 per semester. *Financial aid:* Research assistantships and career-related internships or fieldwork available. Aid available to part-time students. Financial aid application deadline: 7/1; applicants required to submit FAFSA. • Dr. Connell Frazer, Adviser, 518-244-2403. Fax: 518-244-2334. E-mail: frazec@sage.edu. Application contact: Melissa Robertson, Associate Director of Admissions, 518-244-6878. Fax: 518-244-6880. E-mail: sgsadm@sage.edu.

Saginaw Valley State University, College of Education, Program in Secondary Classroom Teaching, University Center, MI 48710. Awards MAT. Accredited by NCATE. Part-time and evening/weekend programs available. Faculty: 12 full-time (9 women). Students: 2 full-time (1 woman), 63 part-time (45 women); includes 1 minority (African American). In 1997, 13 degrees awarded. *Entrance requirements:* Minimum GPA of 3.0, teaching certificate. Application deadline: rolling. Application fee: $25. *Expenses:* Tuition $159 per credit hour for state residents; $311 per credit hour for nonresidents. Fees $8.70 per credit hour. • Application contact: Dr. Ervin F. Sparapani, Coordinator, 517-790-4395.

St. Bonaventure University, School of Education, Program in Secondary Education, St. Bonaventure, NY 14778-2284. Awards MS Ed. Program new for fall 1998. Part-time and evening/weekend programs available. Faculty: 2 full-time (0 women). *Degree requirements:* Written comprehensive exams required, thesis optional, foreign language not required. *Entrance requirements:* TOEFL (minimum score 600). Application deadline: 8/1 (rolling processing). Application fee: $35. *Tuition:* $8100 per year full-time, $450 per credit hour part-time. *Financial* *aid:* Federal Work-Study and career-related internships or fieldwork available. Aid available to part-time students. *Faculty research:* Foundations, reading, health, media. • Dr. Richard Gates, Director, 716-375-2371.

St. Cloud State University, College of Education, Department of Teacher Development, Secondary Education Track, St. Cloud, MN 56301-4498. Awards MS. Accredited by NCATE. Faculty: 7 full-time (3 women). Students: 6 part-time (4 women). In 1997, 1 degree awarded. *Degree requirements:* Thesis or alternative required, foreign language not required. *Entrance requirements:* GRE General Test, minimum GPA of 2.75. Application fee: $20 ($100 for international students). *Expenses:* Tuition $128 per credit for state residents; $203 per credit for nonresidents. Fees $16.32 per credit. *Financial aid:* Graduate assistantships, Federal Work-Study available. Financial aid application deadline: 3/1. • Application contact: Ann Anderson, Graduate Studies Office, 320-255-2113. Fax: 320-654-5371. E-mail: anna@grad.stcloud.msus.edu.

St. John's University, School of Education and Human Services, Division of Administration and Instructional Leadership, Program in Secondary Education, Jamaica, NY 11439. Awards MS Ed. Part-time and evening/weekend programs available. Students: 19 full-time (11 women), 82 part-time (49 women); includes 14 minority (10 African Americans, 1 Asian American, 3 Hispanics), 5 international. Average age 29. 58 applicants, 91% accepted. In 1997, 28 degrees awarded. *Degree requirements:* Variable foreign language requirement, thesis not required. *Entrance requirements:* Minimum GPA of 3.0. Application deadline: 6/1 (rolling processing; 10/1 for spring admission). Application fee: $40. *Expenses:* Tuition $525 per credit. Fees $150 per year. *Financial aid:* Teaching assistantships, administrative assistantship, Federal Work-Study, and career-related internships or fieldwork available. Aid available to part-time students. Financial aid application deadline: 3/1; applicants required to submit FAFSA. *Faculty research:* Gifted parenting, human relations, mathematics, science, technology. • Application contact: Shamus J. McGrenra, TOR, Associate Director, Graduate Admissions, 718-990-6107. Fax: 718-990-5736. E-mail: mcgrenrs@stjohns.edu.

Saint Joseph College, Field of Education and Counseling, Education Programs, Program in Secondary Education, West Hartford, CT 06117-2700. Awards MA. *Degree requirements:* Thesis or alternative required, foreign language not required. *Application deadline:* 8/29 (rolling processing). *Application fee:* $25. *Tuition:* $395 per credit. *Financial aid:* Application deadline 8/31. • Dr. Gerard Thibodeau, Co-Chair, Education Department, Field of Education and Counseling, 860-232-4571 Ext. 331.

Saint Joseph's University, Department of Education, Program in Secondary Education, Philadelphia, PA 19131-1395. Awards MS. Evening/weekend programs available. Students: 104 (63 women). *Degree requirements:* Computer language required, foreign language and thesis not required. *Entrance requirements:* TOEFL. Application deadline: 7/15. Application fee: $30. *Tuition:* $510 per credit hour. *Financial aid:* Fellowships available. • Dr. Mary DeKonty Applegate, Director, Department of Education, 610-660-1583.

St. Thomas Aquinas College, Division of Teacher Education, Program in Secondary Education, Sparkill, NY 10976. Awards MS Ed. *Degree requirements:* Comprehensive professional portfolio required, thesis not required. *Entrance requirements:* New York State Qualifying Exam, GRE General Test or minimum GPA of 3.0, teaching certificate. Application deadline: 7/31 (priority date; rolling processing; 12/1 for spring admission). Application fee: $35. Electronic applications accepted. *Expenses:* Tuition $390 per credit. Fees $10 per year. *Financial aid:* In 1997–98, 2 assistantships (both to first-year students) were awarded; partial tuition waivers also available. Financial aid application deadline: 2/15. *Faculty research:* Curriculum development and assessment, technology infused instruction. • Application contact: Joseph L. Chillo, Executive Director of Enrollment Services, 914-398-4100. Fax: 914-398-4224. E-mail: joestacenroll@rockland.net.

Salem-Teikyo University, Department of Education, Salem, WV 26426-0500. Offerings include secondary education (MA). Department faculty: 1 (woman) full-time, 6 part-time (1 woman). *Degree requirements:* Thesis required, foreign language not required. *Average time to degree:* master's–2 years full-time, 5 years part-time. *Entrance requirements:* GRE, MAT, NTE. Application deadline: rolling. Application fee: $25. Electronic applications accepted. *Tuition:* $160 per credit hour. • Dr. E. G. vander Giessen, Director of Graduate Education, 304-782-5258. Fax: 304-782-5588. E-mail: gabby@salem.wvnet.edu. Application contact: Carolyn Sue Ritter, Director of Admissions, 304-782-5336. Fax: 304-782-5592. E-mail: admiss_new@salem.wvnet.edu.

Salisbury State University, Department of Education, Concentration in Secondary Education, Salisbury, MD 21801-6837. Awards M Ed. 26 applicants, 58% accepted. *Application deadline:* 8/1 (rolling processing; 1/1 for spring admission). *Application fee:* $30. *Expenses:* Tuition $158 per credit hour for state residents; $310 per credit hour for nonresidents. Fees $4 per credit hour. • Dr. Ellen Whitford, Chair, Department of Education, 410-543-6294. E-mail: evwhitford@ssu.edu. Application contact: Phyllis Meyer, Administrative Aide II, 410-543-6281. Fax: 410-548-2593. E-mail: phmeyer@ssu.edu.

Sam Houston State University, College of Education and Applied Science, Department of Education and Applied Science, Department of Curriculum and Instruction, Programs in Secondary Education, Huntsville, TX 77341. Awards MA, M Ed, Certificate. Accredited by NCATE. Part-time and evening/weekend programs available. Students: 1 full-time (0 women), 16 part-time (14 women); includes 1 international. Average age 35. In 1997, 6 master's awarded. *Entrance requirements:* For master's, GRE General Test (minimum combined score of 800). Application fee: $15. *Tuition:* $1810 per year full-time, $297 per semester (minimum) part-time for state residents; $6922 per year full-time, $924 per semester (minimum) part-time for nonresidents. *Financial aid:* Teaching assistantships, institutionally sponsored loans available. *Faculty research:* Teacher education, effective teaching, teacher evaluation. • Application contact: Dr. Leonard Breen, Coordinator, 409-294-1146.

San Diego State University, College of Education, School of Teacher Education, Program in Secondary Curriculum and Instruction, San Diego, CA 92182. Awards MA. Accredited by NCATE. Students: 3 full-time (0 women), 45 part-time (31 women); includes 7 minority (1 African American, 3 Asian Americans, 3 Hispanics). Average age 29. *Entrance requirements:* GRE General Test (minimum combined score of 950), TOEFL (minimum score 550). Application deadline: 6/1 (priority date; rolling processing; 12/1 for spring admission). Application fee: $55. *Expenses:* Tuition $0 for state residents; $246 per unit for nonresidents. Fees $1932 per year full-time, $1266 per year part-time. • Larry Shaw, Graduate Adviser, 619-594-1379. Fax: 619-594-7828. E-mail: lshaw@mail.sdsu.edu.

San Francisco State University, College of Education, Department of Secondary Education, San Francisco, CA 94132-1722. Awards MA, AC. Accredited by NCATE. Part-time and evening/weekend programs available. *Entrance requirements:* For master's, minimum GPA of 2.5 in last 60 units. Application deadline: 11/30 (priority date; rolling processing; 3/15 for spring admission). Application fee: $55. *Expenses:* Tuition $0 for state residents; $246 per unit for nonresidents. Fees $1982 per year full-time, $1316 per year part-time. *Faculty research:* Science education, substance abuse, impact of television on adolescents, middle schools.

San Jose State University, College of Education, Program in Secondary Education, San Jose, CA 95192-0001. Awards MA. Accredited by NCATE. Evening/weekend programs available. Faculty: 11 full-time (3 women), 1 part-time (0 women). Students: 5 full-time (3 women), 2 part-time (both women). Average age 31. 2 applicants, 100% accepted. In 1997, 3 degrees awarded. *Degree requirements:* Thesis or alternative required, foreign language not required. *Application deadline:* 6/1 (rolling processing). *Application fee:* $59. *Expenses:* Tuition $0 for state residents; $246 per unit for nonresidents. Fees $2017 per year full-time, $1351 per year part-time. *Financial aid:* Career-related internships or fieldwork available. • Dr. David Bond, Chair, 408-924-3755.

Seattle Pacific University, School of Education, Program in Secondary Teaching, Seattle, WA 98119-1997. Awards MAT. Accredited by NCATE. Students: 52 part-time (34 women); includes 9 minority (3 African Americans, 3 Asian Americans, 2 Hispanics, 1 Native American), 7 international. 27 applicants, 85% accepted. In 1997, 11 degrees awarded. *Average time to degree:* master's–3 years part-time. *Entrance requirements:* MAT (minimum score 35) or GRE General Test (minimum score 300 on verbal section, 350 on quantitative, 950 combined), minimum GPA of 3.0. Application deadline: 9/24 (4/15 for spring admission). Application fee: $50. *Tuition:* $274 per credit. • Linda Montgomery, Head, 206-281-2214. Fax: 206-281-2756.

Seton Hall University, College of Education and Human Services, Department of Educational Studies, Program in Secondary Education, South Orange, NJ 07079-2697. Awards MA, Ed S. *Degree requirements:* For master's, thesis or alternative, comprehensive exam required, foreign language not required; for Ed S, thesis or alternative, internship required, foreign language not required. *Entrance requirements:* GRE or MAT. Application deadline: rolling. Application fee: $50. *Expenses:* Tuition $500 per credit. Fees $610 per year full-time, $185 per semester part-time. *Financial aid:* Fellowships, assistantships available. Financial aid application deadline: 2/1. • Dr. James Daly, Coordinator, 732-761-2726. E-mail: dalyjame@shu.edu.

Siena Heights University, Program in Teacher Education, Concentration in Secondary Education, Adrian, MI 49221-1796. Offers program in secondary education/reading (MA). Part-time programs available. *Degree requirements:* Computer language, thesis, presentation required, foreign language not required. *Entrance requirements:* Minimum GPA of 3.0, interview. Application deadline: 7/1 (priority date; rolling processing; 12/1 for spring admission). Application fee: $25.

Sierra Nevada College, Program in Teacher Education, Incline Village, NV 89450-4269. Offerings include secondary education (Certificate). College faculty: 4 full-time, 17 part-time. *Entrance requirements:* Minimum GPA of 2.75. Application deadline: rolling. Application fee: $35. *Expenses:* Tuition $360 per unit full-time, $250 per unit (minimum) part-time. Fees $50 per year. • Dr. Skip Wenda, Director, 800-332-8666.

Simmons College, Department of Education, Program in Middle School and High School Teaching, Boston, MA 02115. Awards MAT. Faculty: 3 full-time (2 women), 13 part-time (8 women). Students: 48 full-time (39 women), 28 part-time (23 women); includes 9 minority (5 African Americans, 2 Asian Americans, 2 Hispanics). Average age 24. 78 applicants, 87% accepted. In 1997, 53 degrees awarded. *Degree requirements:* Student teaching experience required, foreign language and thesis not required. *Entrance requirements:* GRE General Test or MAT, interview. Application deadline: 8/1 (priority date; rolling processing; 12/15 for spring admission). Application fee: $35. *Expenses:* Tuition $587 per credit hour. Fees $20 per year. *Financial aid:* Partial tuition waivers, Federal Work-Study, institutionally sponsored loans, and career-related internships or fieldwork available. Aid available to part-time students. Financial aid application deadline: 3/1; applicants required to submit FAFSA. • Lynda Johnson, Director, 617-521-2576. Fax: 617-521-3174. Application contact: Director, Graduate Studies Admission, 617-521-2910. Fax: 617-521-3058. E-mail: gsa@simmons.edu.

Slippery Rock University of Pennsylvania, College of Education, Department of Secondary Education/Foundations of Education, Slippery Rock, PA 16057. Offers program in secondary education in math/science (M Ed). Accredited by NCATE. *Degree requirements:* Comprehensive exams. *Entrance requirements:* GRE, minimum GPA of 2.75. Application deadline: 7/1 (priority date; rolling processing; 11/1 for spring admission). Application fee: $25. *Tuition:* $4484 per year full-time, $247 per credit part-time for state residents; $7667 per year full-time, $423 per credit part-time for nonresidents.

Smith College, Department of Education and Child Study, Program in Secondary Education, Northampton, MA 01063. Offers art education (MAT), biological sciences education (MAT), chemistry education (MAT), classics education (MAT), English education (MAT), French education (MAT), history education (MAT), mathematics education (MAT), music education (MAT), physics education (MAT), Spanish education (MAT). Part-time programs available. Faculty: 6 full-time (3 women), 3 part-time (2 women). Students: 8 full-time (7 women), 1 (woman) part-time. Average age 22. 24 applicants, 79% accepted. In 1997, 5 degrees awarded. *Degree requirements:* 1 foreign language required, thesis not required. *Average time to degree:* master's–1 year full-time, 4 years part-time. *Entrance requirements:* GRE General Test or MAT. Application deadline: 4/15 (12/1 for spring admission). Application fee: $50. *Tuition:* $21,680 per year full-time, $2720 per course part-time. *Financial aid:* In 1997–98, 7 students received aid, including 7 scholarships (5 to first-year students) totaling $94,212; institutionally sponsored loans also available. Aid available to part-time students. Financial aid application deadline: 1/15; applicants required to submit CSS PROFILE or FAFSA. • Rosetta Cohen, Head, 413-585-3266. E-mail: rcohen@sophia.smith.edu.

South Carolina State University, School of Education, Department of Teacher Education, 300 College Street Northeast, Orangeburg, SC 29117-0001. Offerings include secondary education (M Ed), with options in biology education, business education, counselor education, English education, home economics education, industrial education, mathematics education, science education, social studies education. Accredited by NCATE. Department faculty: 7 full-time (3 women), 2 part-time (1 woman). *Average time to degree:* master's–2 years full-time, 4 years part-time. *Application deadline:* 7/15 (priority date; rolling processing; 11/10 for spring admission). *Application fee:* $25. *Tuition:* $2974 per year full-time, $165 per credit hour part-time. • Dr. Jesse Kinard, Chairman, 803-536-8934. Application contact: Dr. Gail Joyner-Fleming, Interim Associate Dean and Director, Graduate Teacher Education, 803-536-8824. Fax: 803-536-8492.

Southeastern Louisiana University, College of Education, Department of Teacher Education, Hammond, LA 70402. Offerings include secondary teaching (M Ed). Accredited by NCATE. Department faculty: 22 full-time, 14 part-time. *Entrance requirements:* GRE, teaching certificate. Application deadline: 7/15 (priority date; rolling processing; 12/15 for spring admission). Application fee: $10 ($25 for international students). Electronic applications accepted. *Expenses:* Tuition $2010 per year full-time, $287 per semester (minimum) part-time for state residents; $5232 per year full-time, $287 per semester (minimum) part-time for nonresidents. Fees $5 per year. • Dr. Martha Head, Head, 504-549-2221. E-mail: mhead@selu.edu. Application contact: Dr. Jeanne Burns, Graduate Coordinator, 504-549-2221. Fax: 504-549-5009. E-mail: jburns@selu.edu.

Southeastern Oklahoma State University, School of Education, Durant, OK 74701-0609. Offerings include secondary education (M Ed). Accredited by NCATE. School faculty: 69 full-time (23 women), 3 part-time (0 women), 69.7 FTE. *Application deadline:* 8/1. *Tuition:* $76 per credit hour for state residents; $178 per credit hour for nonresidents. • Dr. Barbara Decker, Dean, 580-924-0121 Ext. 2251. Fax: 580-920-7473.

Southeast Missouri State University, Department of Secondary Education, Cape Girardeau, MO 63701-4799. Offers programs in business education (MA), middle level education (MA), physical education (MA). One or more programs accredited by NCATE. Part-time and evening/weekend programs available. *Degree requirements:* Thesis or alternative required, foreign language not required. *Entrance requirements:* GRE General Test (score in 50th percentile or higher), minimum GPA of 2.75. Application deadline: 4/1 (priority date; rolling processing; 11/21 for spring admission). Application fee: $20 ($100 for international students). *Tuition:* $2034 per year full-time, $113 per credit hour part-time for state residents; $3672 per year full-time, $204 per credit hour part-time for nonresidents. *Financial aid:* Teaching assistantships available. • Dalton Curtis, Chairperson, 573-651-5965. Application contact: Office of Graduate Studies, 573-651-2192.

Southern Connecticut State University, School of Education, Programs in Secondary Education, New Haven, CT 06515-1355. Awards MS Ed. *Degree requirements:* Thesis or alternative. *Entrance requirements:* Connecticut Competency Exam for Prospective Teachers, interview. Application deadline: 7/15. Application fee: $40. *Expenses:* Tuition $2632 per year full-time, $188 per credit part-time for state residents; $7200 per year full-time, $188 per credit part-time

Directory: Secondary Education

Southern Connecticut State University (continued)
for nonresidents. Fees $1806 per year full-time, $45 per semester part-time for state residents; $2703 per year full-time, $45 per semester part-time for nonresidents. • Dr. Susan Hageman, Coordinator, 203-392-6610.

Southern Illinois University at Edwardsville, School of Education, Department of Curriculum and Instruction, Program in Secondary Education, Edwardsville, IL 62026-0001. Awards MS Ed. Accredited by NCATE. Part-time programs available. Students: 15 full-time (10 women), 31 part-time (21 women); includes 5 minority (1 African American, 1 Asian American, 3 Hispanics). 25 applicants, 44% accepted. In 1997, 29 degrees awarded. *Degree requirements:* Thesis or alternative, final exam required, foreign language not required. *Entrance requirements:* GRE General Test or MAT. Application deadline: 7/24. Application fee: $25. *Expenses:* Tuition $1716 per year full-time, $95 per credit hour part-time for state residents; $5149 per year full-time, $286 per credit hour part-time for nonresidents. Fees $463 per year full-time, $433 per year part-time. *Financial aid:* In 1997–98, 6 assistantships were awarded; fellowships, research assistantships, teaching assistantships, Federal Work-Study, institutionally sponsored loans also available. Aid available to part-time students. • David Winnett, Director, 618-692-3442.

Southern Oregon University, School of Social Science, Health and Physical Education, Department of Education, Ashland, OR 97520. Offerings include secondary education (MA Ed, MS Ed), with options in classroom teacher, handicapped learner, reading, supervision. *Application deadline:* 2/1. *Application fee:* $50. *Tuition:* $5187 per year full-time, $586 per quarter (minimum) part-time for state residents; $9228 per year full-time, $586 per quarter (minimum) part-time for nonresidents. • Dr. Mary-Curtis Gramley, Associate Dean of Education, 541-552-6918.

Southern University and Agricultural and Mechanical College, College of Education, Department of Curriculum and Instruction, Baton Rouge, LA 70813. Offerings include secondary education (M Ed). Accredited by NCATE. Department faculty: 13 full-time (3 women), 12 part-time (3 women). *Degree requirements:* Thesis optional. *Entrance requirements:* GMAT or GRE General Test, TOEFL. Application deadline: 6/1 (priority date; rolling processing; 11/1 for spring admission). Application fee: $5. *Tuition:* $2226 per year full-time, $267 per semester (minimum) part-time for state residents; $6262 per year full-time, $267 per semester (minimum) part-time for nonresidents. • Dr. Paul Hester, Chairman, 504-771-3871.

Southern Utah University, School of Education, Cedar City, UT 84720-2498. Offerings include secondary education (M Ed). School faculty: 1 full-time (0 women), 18 part-time (3 women). *Degree requirements:* Thesis or alternative required, foreign language not required. *Entrance requirements:* MAT (minimum score 43). Application deadline: 8/1 (rolling processing; 12/1 for spring admission). Application fee: $30. • Dr. Paul Wilford, Director, 435-865-8149.

Southwestern Oklahoma State University, School of Education, Program in Secondary Education, Weatherford, OK 73096-3098. Awards M Ed. Accredited by NCATE. M Ed distance learning degree program offered to Oklahoma residents only. Part-time programs available. Postbaccalaureate distance learning degree programs offered. Students: 5 full-time (3 women), 19 part-time (7 women). 1 applicant, 100% accepted. In 1997, 6 degrees awarded. *Degree requirements:* Exam required, foreign language and thesis not required. *Entrance requirements:* GRE General Test, TOEFL (minimum score 550), minimum GPA of 2.5. Application deadline: rolling. Application fee: $15. *Expenses:* Tuition $60 per credit hour (minimum) for state residents; $147 per credit hour (minimum) for nonresidents. Fees $109 per year full-time, $24 per semester (minimum) part-time. *Financial aid:* Research assistantships, teaching assistantships, partial tuition waivers, Federal Work-Study, institutionally sponsored loans available. Aid available to part-time students. Financial aid application deadline: 3/1; applicants required to submit FAFSA. • Dr. Lowell Gadberry, Chair, Elementary/Secondary Programs, 580-774-3288.

Southwest Missouri State University, College of Education, Department of Secondary Education, Foundations, and Educational Technology, Springfield, MO 65804-0094. Offers program in secondary education (MS Ed). Part-time and evening/weekend programs available. Faculty: 8 full-time (2 women). Students: 8 full-time (4 women), 96 part-time (72 women); includes 3 minority (1 African American, 2 Asian Americans), 3 international. In 1997, 22 degrees awarded. *Degree requirements:* Thesis or alternative, comprehensive exam required, foreign language not required. *Entrance requirements:* Minimum GPA of 2.75, teaching certificate. Application deadline: 8/7 (priority date; rolling processing; 12/17 for spring admission). Application fee: $25. *Expenses:* Tuition $1980 per year full-time, $110 per credit hour part-time for state residents; $3960 per year full-time, $220 per credit hour part-time for nonresidents. Fees $274 per year full-time, $73 per semester part-time. • Dr. Stefan Broidy, Head, 417-836-6721. Fax: 417-836-4884. E-mail: sjb289f@wpgate.smsu.edu.

Southwest Texas State University, School of Education, Department of Curriculum and Instruction, Program in Secondary Education, San Marcos, TX 78666. Awards MA, M Ed. Part-time and evening/weekend programs available. Students: 7 full-time (4 women), 24 part-time (19 women); includes 6 minority (1 African American, 1 Asian American, 4 Hispanics), 1 international. Average age 33. In 1997, 4 degrees awarded. *Degree requirements:* Thesis (for some programs), comprehensive exam required, foreign language not required. *Entrance requirements:* GRE General Test (minimum combined score of 900), TOEFL (minimum score 550), minimum GPA of 2.75 in last 60 hours, teaching experience. Application deadline: 7/15 (priority date; rolling processing; 11/15 for spring admission). Application fee: $25 ($50 for international students). *Expenses:* Tuition $648 per year full-time, $120 per semester (minimum) part-time for state residents; $4500 per year full-time, $750 per semester (minimum) part-time for nonresidents. Fees $1264 per year full-time, $314 per semester (minimum) part-time. *Financial aid:* Federal Work-Study, institutionally sponsored loans, and career-related internships or fieldwork available. Aid available to part-time students. Financial aid application deadline: 4/1; applicants required to submit FAFSA. *Faculty research:* Gifted and talented education, general secondary education, induction of first-year teachers. • Dr. Thomas Mandeville, Graduate Adviser, 512-245-2157. E-mail: tm08@swt.edu.

Springfield College, Program in Education, Springfield, MA 01109-3797. Offerings include counseling and secondary education (M Ed, MS). Program faculty: 7 full-time (4 women), 2 part-time (both women), 8 FTE. *Degree requirements:* Comprehensive exam required, foreign language and thesis not required. *Application deadline:* (12/1 for spring admission). *Application fee:* $40. *Expenses:* Tuition $474 per credit. Fees $25 per year. • Dr. Thomas L. Bernard, Director, 413-748-3251. Application contact: Donald J. Shaw Jr., Director of Graduate Admissions, 413-748-3225. Fax: 413-748-3694. E-mail: dshaw@spfldcol.edu.

State University of New York at Albany, College of Arts and Sciences, Department of Mathematics and Statistics, Albany, NY 12222-0001. Offerings include secondary teaching (MA). Department faculty: 29 full-time (2 women), 1 part-time (0 women). *Application fee:* $50. *Expenses:* Tuition $5100 per year full-time, $213 per credit hour part-time for state residents; $8416 per year full-time, $351 per credit hour part-time for nonresidents. Fees $705 per year full-time, $26.85 per credit hour part-time. • Timothy Lance, Chair, 518-442-4602.

State University of New York at Binghamton, School of Education and Human Development, Program in Secondary Education, Binghamton, NY 13902-6000. Offers biology education (MAT, MS Ed, MST), earth science education (MAT, MS Ed, MST), English education (MAT, MS Ed, MST), French education (MAT, MST), mathematical sciences education (MAT, MS Ed, MST), physics (MAT, MS Ed, MST), social studies (MAT, MS Ed, MST), Spanish education (MAT, MST). Part-time and evening/weekend programs available. Students: 83 full-time (47 women), 33 part-time (21 women); includes 11 minority (2 African Americans, 8 Hispanics, 1 Native American), 2 international. Average age 28. 88 applicants, 53% accepted. In 1997, 46 degrees awarded. *Entrance requirements:* GRE General Test, TOEFL. Application deadline: 4/15 (priority date; rolling processing; 11/1 for spring admission). Application fee: $50. Electronic applications accepted. *Expenses:* Tuition $5100 per year full-time, $213 per credit hour part-time for state residents; $8416 per year full-time, $351 per credit hour part-time for nonresidents. Fees $654 per year full-time, $75 per semester (minimum) part-time. *Financial aid:* In 1997–98, 3 fellowships (1 to a first-year student) averaging $823 per month and totaling $16,000, 4 teaching assistantships (1 to a first-year student) averaging $810 per month and totaling $24,063, 11 graduate assistantships (6 to first-year students) averaging $474 per month and totaling $43,882 were awarded; research assistantships, Federal Work-Study, institutionally sponsored loans, and career-related internships or fieldwork also available. Aid available to part-time students. Financial aid application deadline: 2/15. • Dr. Wayne Ross, Coordinator, 607-777-2478.

State University of New York at Buffalo, Graduate School, Graduate School of Education, Department of Learning and Instruction, Buffalo, NY 14260. Offerings include secondary education (Ed M, Ed D, PhD), with options in English education (Ed D, PhD), foreign language education (Ed D, PhD), mathematics education (Ed D, PhD), science education (PhD). Terminal master's awarded for partial completion of doctoral program. Department faculty: 20 full-time (9 women), 7 part-time (2 women). *Degree requirements:* For master's, comprehensive exam required, foreign language and thesis not required; for doctorate, dissertation, research analysis exam required, foreign language not required. *Entrance requirements:* For master's, GRE General Test, TOEFL (minimum score 590); for doctorate, GRE General Test, TOEFL (minimum score 600), interview. Application deadline: 2/1 (11/15 for spring admission). Application fee: $50. *Tuition:* $5970 per year full-time, $288 per credit hour part-time for state residents; $9286 per year full-time, $426 per credit hour part-time for nonresidents. • Dr. Michael Kibby, Chair, 716-645-2455. Application contact: Barbara Cracchiolo, Admissions Secretary, 716-645-2457. Fax: 716-645-3161.

State University of New York at New Paltz, Faculty of Education, Department of Secondary Education, New Paltz, NY 12561-2499. Awards MAT, MS Ed. Students: 41 full-time (18 women), 85 part-time (52 women); includes 4 minority (1 African American, 3 Hispanics), 3 international. In 1997, 84 degrees awarded. *Degree requirements:* Comprehensive exam. *Entrance requirements:* GRE General Test or MAT, minimum GPA of 3.0, teaching certificate. Application deadline: 3/15 (priority date; rolling processing). Application fee: $50. *Expenses:* Tuition $5100 per year full-time, $213 per credit hour part-time for state residents; $8416 per year full-time, $351 per credit hour part-time for nonresidents. Fees $493 per year full-time, $48 per semester (minimum) part-time. *Financial aid:* Federal Work-Study, institutionally sponsored loans available. • Dr. Michael Whelan, Chairman, 914-257-2850.

State University of New York at Oswego, School of Education, Department of Curriculum and Instruction, Oswego, NY 13126. Offerings include secondary education (MS Ed). MS Ed (special education) offered jointly with the State University of New York College at Geneseo. Department faculty: 17 full-time, 5 part-time. *Application deadline:* 7/1. *Application fee:* $50. *Expenses:* Tuition $5100 per year full-time, $213 per credit hour part-time for state residents; $8416 per year full-time, $351 per credit hour part-time for nonresidents. Fees $135 per year (minimum). • Dr. Frank Bickel, Chairman, 315-341-4052. Application contact: Dr. Terrance Lindenberg, Coordinator, Graduate Education, 315-341-4052.

State University of New York College at Brockport, School of Professions, Department of Education and Human Development, Programs in Secondary Education, Brockport, NY 14420-2997. Offerings in biology education (MS Ed), chemistry education (MS Ed), earth science education (MS Ed), English education (MS Ed), mathematics education (MS Ed), physics education (MS Ed), social studies education (MS Ed). Part-time and evening/weekend programs available. Students: 44 full-time (22 women), 101 part-time (55 women); includes 10 minority (9 African Americans, 1 Native American), 1 international. Average age 31. 55 applicants, 96% accepted. In 1997, 33 degrees awarded. *Degree requirements:* Thesis or alternative required, foreign language not required. *Entrance requirements:* Minimum GPA of 3.0. Application deadline: 1/15 (priority date; 9/15 for spring admission). Application fee: $50. *Expenses:* Tuition $5100 per year full-time, $213 per credit hour part-time for state residents; $8416 per year full-time, $351 per credit hour part-time for nonresidents. Fees $440 per year full-time, $22.60 per credit hour part-time. *Financial aid:* Teaching assistantships, Federal Work-Study, and career-related internships or fieldwork available. Aid available to part-time students. Financial aid application deadline: 4/1; applicants required to submit FAFSA. *Faculty research:* Whole language, literature response, portfolio assessment, middle schools. • William Veenis, Chairperson, Department of Education and Human Development, 716-395-2205.

State University of New York College at Cortland, Division of Arts and Sciences, Program in Secondary Education, Cortland, NY 13045. Offers biology (MAT, MS Ed), chemistry (MAT, MS Ed), earth science (MAT, MS Ed), French (MS Ed), mathematics (MAT, MS Ed), physics (MAT, MS Ed), social studies (MS Ed). Part-time and evening/weekend programs available. *Degree requirements:* 1 foreign language, thesis (for some programs), comprehensive exam. *Application deadline:* rolling. *Application fee:* $50. *Expenses:* Tuition $5100 per year full-time, $213 per credit hour part-time for state residents; $8416 per year full-time, $351 per credit hour part-time for nonresidents. Fees $644 per year full-time, $79 per semester (minimum) part-time. *Financial aid:* Partial tuition waivers, Federal Work-Study, and career-related internships or fieldwork available. Aid available to part-time students. Financial aid applicants required to submit FAFSA. • Roger Sipher, Head, 607-753-2723. Application contact: Jeanne M. Bechtel, Director of Admissions, 607-753-4711. Fax: 607-753-5998.

State University of New York College at Cortland, Division of Professional Studies, Department of Education, Cortland, NY 13045. Offerings include secondary education (MS Ed), with options in biology, chemistry, earth science, French, mathematics, physics. *Application deadline:* rolling. *Application fee:* $50. *Expenses:* Tuition $5100 per year full-time, $213 per credit hour part-time for state residents; $8416 per year full-time, $351 per credit hour part-time for nonresidents. Fees $644 per year full-time, $79 per semester (minimum) part-time. • Mary Ware, Chair, 607-753-2705. Application contact: Jeanne M. Bechtel, Director of Admissions, 607-753-4711. Fax: 607-753-5998.

State University of New York College at Fredonia, Department of Education, Program in Secondary Education, Fredonia, NY 14063. Awards MS Ed. Part-time and evening/weekend programs available. Students: 24 part-time (15 women); includes 1 minority (Native American). 4 applicants, 100% accepted. In 1997, 3 degrees awarded. *Degree requirements:* Thesis or alternative required, foreign language not required. *Application deadline:* 7/5. *Application fee:* $50. *Expenses:* Tuition $5100 per year full-time, $213 per credit hour part-time for state residents; $8416 per year full-time, $351 per credit hour part-time for nonresidents. Fees $725 per year full-time, $30 per credit hour part-time. *Financial aid:* Research assistantships, teaching assistantships, full and partial tuition waivers, and career-related internships or fieldwork available. Aid available to part-time students. Financial aid application deadline: 3/15. • Dr. Julius Adams, Chair, Department of Education, 716-673-3311.

State University of New York College at Geneseo, School of Education, Program in Secondary Education, Geneseo, NY 14454-1401. Awards MS Ed. Part-time and evening/weekend programs available. Faculty: 6 full-time (0 women). Students: 4 full-time (3 women), 32 part-time (22 women); includes 1 minority (Asian American). Average age 24. 22 applicants, 82% accepted. In 1997, 14 degrees awarded. *Degree requirements:* Thesis optional, foreign language not required. *Entrance requirements:* GRE General Test. Application deadline: 6/1 (priority date; 10/1 for spring admission). Application fee: $35. *Expenses:* Tuition $5100 per year full-time, $213 per credit hour part-time for state residents; $8416 per year full-time, $351 per credit hour part-time for nonresidents. Fees $375 per year full-time, $15.35 per credit hour part-time. *Financial aid:* 2 students received aid; Federal Work-Study, institutionally sponsored loans, and career-related internships or fieldwork available. Financial aid application deadline: 4/1; applicants required to submit FAFSA. • Dr. Gary DeBolt, Head, School of Education, 716-245-5558. Fax: 716-245-5220. E-mail: debolt@uno.cc.geneseo.edu.

State University of New York College at Oneonta, Department of Education, Program in Secondary Education, Oneonta, NY 13820-4015. Offers biology education (MS Ed), chemistry education (MS Ed), earth science education (MS Ed), English education (MS Ed), home economics education (MS Ed), mathematics education (MS Ed), physics education (MS Ed), social science education (MS Ed). Part-time and evening/weekend programs available. Students: 4 full-time (3 women), 16 part-time (9 women). In 1997, 13 degrees awarded. *Entrance requirements:* GRE General Test. Application deadline: 4/15. Application fee: $50. *Expenses:* Tuition $5100 per year full-time, $213 per credit hour part-time for state residents; $8416 per year full-time, $351 per credit hour part-time for nonresidents. Fees $482 per year full-time, $6.85 per credit hour part-time. • Dr. John Clow, Coordinator, 607-436-3275.

State University of New York College at Potsdam, School of Education, Program in Secondary Education, Potsdam, NY 13676. Awards MS Ed, MST. Part-time programs available. Faculty: 10 full-time (2 women), 5 part-time (2 women). Students: 75. *Degree requirements:* Variable foreign language requirement, culminating experience required, thesis optional. *Entrance requirements:* New York State Teachers Certification Exam Liberal Arts and Science Test (minimum score 220), New York State Teachers Certification Exam Assesment of Teaching Skills-Writing (minimum score 220), minimum GPA of 2.75 in last 60 hours. Application deadline: 4/1 (priority date; 10/15 for spring admission). Application fee: $50. *Expenses:* Tuition $5100 per year full-time, $213 per credit hour part-time for state residents; $8416 per year full-time, $351 per credit hour part-time for nonresidents. Fees $315 per year full-time, $12.50 per credit hour part-time. *Financial aid:* Fellowships, teaching assistantships, Federal Work-Study, and career-related internships or fieldwork available. Aid available to part-time students. Financial aid application deadline: 3/1. • Charles Mlynarczyk, Chairperson, Teacher Education Department, 315-267-2535. E-mail: mlynarhc@potsdam.edu. Application contact: Dr. William Amoriell, Dean of Education and Graduate Studies, 315-267-2515. Fax: 315-267-4802.

State University of West Georgia, College of Education, Department of Middle Grades Education and Secondary Education, Program in Secondary Education, Carrollton, GA 30118. Awards M Ed, Ed S. Accredited by NCATE. Part-time and evening/weekend programs available. Faculty: 6 full-time (3 women). Students: 79 full-time (49 women), 106 part-time (73 women); includes 29 minority (23 African Americans, 2 Asian Americans, 3 Hispanics, 1 Native American), 2 international. Average age 34. In 1997, 48 master's, 5 Ed Ss awarded. *Degree requirements:* For Ed S, research project required, foreign language and thesis not required. *Entrance requirements:* For master's, GRE General Test (minimum combined score of 800), minimum GPA of 2.5; for Ed S, GRE General Test (minimum combined score of 800), master's degree, minimum graduate GPA of 3.25. Application deadline: 8/30 (rolling processing). Application fee: $15. *Expenses:* Tuition $2428 per year full-time, $83 per semester hour part-time for state residents; $8428 per year full-time, $250 per semester hour part-time for nonresidents. Fees $428 per year. *Financial aid:* Research assistantships, assistantships, and career-related internships or fieldwork available. Aid available to part-time students. Financial aid applicants required to submit FAFSA. *Total annual research expenditures:* $1679. • Application contact: Dr. Jack O. Jenkins, Dean, Graduate School, 770-836-6419. Fax: 770-836-2301. E-mail: jjenkins@cob.as.westga.edu.

Stephen F. Austin State University, College of Education, Department of Secondary Education and Educational Leadership, Nacogdoches, TX 75962. Offers programs in educational leadership (Ed D), secondary education (M Ed). Accredited by NCATE. Faculty: 12 full-time (4 women), 4 part-time (0 women). Students: 154 full-time (98 women), 425 part-time (261 women); includes 92 minority (71 African Americans, 1 Asian American, 17 Hispanics, 3 Native Americans). Average age 33. 425 applicants, 98% accepted. In 1997, 175 master's awarded. *Degree requirements:* For master's, comprehensive exam required, foreign language and thesis not required; for doctorate, dissertation required, foreign language not required. *Entrance requirements:* For master's, GRE General Test (minimum combined score of 1000); for doctorate, GRE General Test (minimum combined score of 1000), TOEFL. Application deadline: 8/1 (priority date; rolling processing; 12/15 for spring admission). Application fee: $0 ($25 for international students). *Tuition:* $1465 per year full-time, $263 per semester (minimum) part-time for state residents; $5299 per year full-time, $890 per semester (minimum) part-time for nonresidents. *Financial aid:* Teaching assistantships available. Financial aid application deadline: 3/1. • Dr. Patrick Jenlink, Chair, 409-468-2908.

Suffolk University, College of Liberal Arts and Sciences, Department of Education and Human Services, Program in Secondary School Teaching, Boston, MA 02108-2770. Awards MS. Part-time and evening/weekend programs available. *Entrance requirements:* GRE General Test (average 500 on each section) or MAT (average 50). Application deadline: 6/15 (priority date; rolling processing; 11/15 for spring admission). Application fee: $50. *Expenses:* Tuition $14,544 per year full-time, $1452 per course part-time. Fees $20 per year full-time, $10 per year part-time. *Financial aid:* Fellowships, Federal Work-Study, institutionally sponsored loans, and career-related internships or fieldwork available. Aid available to part-time students. Financial aid application deadline: 4/1; applicants required to submit FAFSA. • Dr. Stephen Shatkin, Director, 617-573-8269. Fax: 617-722-9440. Application contact: Judy Reynolds, Acting Director of Graduate Admissions, 617-573-8302. Fax: 617-523-0116. E-mail: grad.admission@admin.suffolk.edu.

Sul Ross State University, Rio Grande College of Sul Ross State University, Alpine, TX 79832. Offerings include teacher education (M Ed), with options in bilingual education, counseling, educational diagnostics, elementary education, general education, reading, school administration, secondary education. College faculty: 16 full-time (2 women), 2 part-time (1 woman). *Application deadline:* rolling. *Application fee:* $0 ($50 for international students). *Expenses:* Tuition $864 per year full-time, $120 per semester (minimum) part-time for state residents; $5976 per year full-time, $747 per semester (minimum) part-time for nonresidents. Fees $754 per year full-time, $105 per semester (minimum) part-time. • Dr. Frank Abbott, Dean, 512-278-3339. Fax: 512-278-3330.

Sul Ross State University, Department of Teacher Education, Program in Secondary Education, Alpine, TX 79832. Awards M Ed. Part-time and evening/weekend programs available. Students: 5 full-time (4 women). Average age 43. In 1997, 4 degrees awarded. *Degree requirements:* Thesis optional, foreign language not required. *Entrance requirements:* GMAT (minimum score 400) or GRE General Test (minimum combined score of 850), minimum GPA of 2.5 in last 60 hours of undergraduate work. Application deadline: rolling. Application fee: $0 ($50 for international students). *Expenses:* Tuition $864 per year full-time, $120 per semester (minimum) part-time for state residents; $5976 per year full-time, $747 per semester (minimum) part-time for nonresidents. Fees $754 per year full-time, $105 per semester (minimum) part-time. *Financial aid:* Federal Work-Study, institutionally sponsored loans, and career-related internships or fieldwork available. Aid available to part-time students. Financial aid application deadline: 5/1; applicants required to submit FAFSA. • Dr. Mary Ann Weinacht, Director, Department of Teacher Education, 915-837-8170. Fax: 915-837-8390.

Tarleton State University, College of Education, Department of Education and Psychology, Program in Secondary Education, Stephenville, TX 76402. Awards M Ed, Certificate. Part-time and evening/weekend programs available. Students: 4 full-time (2 women), 56 part-time (33 women); includes 2 minority (both African Americans). 5 applicants, 80% accepted. In 1997, 2 master's awarded. *Degree requirements:* For master's, comprehensive exam required, foreign language and thesis not required. *Entrance requirements:* For master's, GRE General Test, minimum GPA of 2.9 during last 60 hours. Application deadline: 8/5 (priority date; rolling processing; 12/1 for spring admission). Application fee: $25 ($100 for international students). *Expenses:* Tuition $46 per hour for state residents; $249 per hour for nonresidents. Fees $49 per hour. *Financial aid:* Teaching assistantships, Federal Work-Study, institutionally sponsored loans, and career-related internships or fieldwork available. Aid available to part-time students. Financial aid application deadline: 5/1; applicants required to submit FAFSA. • Dr. Laurie Hawke, Coordinator, 254-968-9948.

Temple University, College of Education, Department of Curriculum, Instruction, and Technology in Education, Philadelphia, PA 19122-6096. Offerings include secondary education (Ed M, MS, Certificate). Accredited by NCATE. Department faculty: 33 full-time (14 women). *Degree requirements:* For master's, thesis or alternative required, foreign language not required. *Entrance requirements:* For master's, GRE General Test (minimum combined score of 1000) or MAT (minimum score 39), minimum GPA of 2.8. Application deadline: 2/15 (10/1 for spring admission). Application fee: $40. *Expenses:* Tuition $323 per semester hour for state residents; $444 per semester hour for nonresidents. Fees $170 per year full-time, $28 per semester (minimum) part-time. • Dr. Raymond Lolla, Chair, 215-204-6387. Fax: 215-204-1414.

Tennessee State University, College of Education, Department of Teaching and Learning, Program in Adult Education, Nashville, TN 37209-1561. Offerings include curriculum and instruction (M Ed), with options in adult education, secondary instruction. Accredited by NCATE. *Degree requirements:* Thesis (for some programs). *Entrance requirements:* GRE General Test, GRE Subject Test, or MAT (minimum score 44), minimum GPA of 2.5. Application deadline: rolling. Application fee: $15. *Tuition:* $2962 per year full-time, $182 per credit hour part-time for state residents; $7788 per year full-time, $393 per credit hour part-time for nonresidents. • Application contact: Dr. Clinton M. Lipsey, Dean of the Graduate School, 615-963-5901. Fax: 615-963-5963. E-mail: clipsey@picard.tnstate.edu.

Tennessee State University, College of Education, Department of Teaching and Learning, Program in Secondary Education, Nashville, TN 37209-1561. Offers reading (M Ed), secondary education (MA Ed, Ed D). Accredited by NCATE. *Degree requirements:* For doctorate, dissertation. *Entrance requirements:* For master's, GRE General Test, GRE Subject Test, or MAT (minimum score 44), minimum GPA of 2.5; for doctorate, GRE General Test (minimum score 870), GRE Subject Test, or MAT (minimum score 25), minimum GPA of 3.25. Application deadline: rolling. Application fee: $15. *Tuition:* $2962 per year full-time, $182 per credit hour part-time for state residents; $7788 per year full-time, $393 per credit hour part-time for nonresidents. *Financial aid:* Fellowships available. Financial aid application deadline: 5/1. *Faculty research:* Diversity, cooperative learning and multiculturism. • Application contact: Dr. Clinton M. Lipsey, Dean of the Graduate School, 615-963-5901. Fax: 615-963-5963. E-mail: clipsey@picard.tnstate.edu.

Tennessee Technological University, College of Education, Department of Curriculum and Instruction, Program in Secondary Education, Cookeville, TN 38505. Awards MA, Ed S. Accredited by NCATE. Part-time and evening/weekend programs available. Faculty: 7 full-time (0 women). Students: 18 full-time (5 women), 19 part-time (8 women); includes 1 minority (Hispanic). Average age 27. 11 applicants, 100% accepted. In 1997, 10 master's awarded. *Degree requirements:* For Ed S, thesis or alternative required, foreign language not required. *Entrance requirements:* For master's, MAT, TOEFL (minimum score 525); for Ed S, MAT, NTE. Application deadline: 3/1 (priority date; 8/1 for spring admission). Application fee: $25 ($30 for international students). *Tuition:* $2960 per year full-time, $147 per semester hour part-time for state residents; $7786 per year full-time, $358 per semester hour part-time for nonresidents. *Financial aid:* In 1997–98, 6 students received aid, including 5 research assistantships (4 to first-year students), 1 teaching assistantship; fellowships and career-related internships or fieldwork also available. Financial aid application deadline: 4/1. • Application contact: Dr. Rebecca F. Quattlebaum, Dean of the Graduate School, 615-372-3233. Fax: 615-372-3497. E-mail: rquattlebaum@tntech.edu.

Texas A&M International University, Division of Teacher Education and Psychology, 5201 University Boulevard, Laredo, TX 78041-1900. Offerings include secondary education (MS Ed), with options in business education, secondary education. *Degree requirements:* Thesis required (for some programs), foreign language not required. *Entrance requirements:* GRE General Test. Application deadline: 7/15 (priority date; rolling processing; 11/12 for spring admission). Application fee: $0.

Texas A&M University–Commerce, College of Education, Department of Secondary and Higher Education, Commerce, TX 75429-3011. Offers programs in higher education (MS), including administration, teaching; learning technology and information systems (MA, M Ed, MS), including educational computing, library and information science, media and technology; secondary education (MA, M Ed, MS); supervision of curriculum and instruction: higher education (PhD); training and development (MS); vocational/technical education (MA, M Ed, MS). Faculty: 10 full-time (3 women), 2 part-time (1 woman). Students: 53 full-time (32 women), 129 part-time (71 women); includes 18 minority (14 African Americans, 3 Hispanics, 1 Native American), 4 international. In 1997, 48 master's, 14 doctorates awarded. Terminal master's awarded for partial completion of doctoral program. *Degree requirements:* For master's, thesis (for some programs), comprehensive exam; for doctorate, dissertation, departmental qualifying exam. *Entrance requirements:* GRE General Test. Application deadline: rolling. Application fee: $0 ($25 for international students). *Tuition:* $2382 per year full-time, $343 per semester (minimum) part-time for state residents; $7518 per year full-time, $343 per semester (minimum) part-time for nonresidents. *Financial aid:* Research assistantships, teaching assistantships, Federal Work-Study, institutionally sponsored loans, and career-related internships or fieldwork available. • Dr. Robert Munday, Head, 903-886-5607. Application contact: Pam Hammonds, Graduate Admissions Adviser, 903-886-5167. Fax: 903-886-5165.

Texas A&M University–Corpus Christi, College of Education, Program in Secondary Education, Corpus Christi, TX 78412-5503. Awards MS. Part-time and evening/weekend programs available. Faculty: 10 full-time. Students: 8 full-time (4 women), 9 part-time (5 women); includes 3 minority (1 African American, 2 Hispanics). Average age 35. In 1997, 5 degrees awarded. *Entrance requirements:* GRE General Test. Application deadline: 7/15 (priority date; rolling processing; 11/15 for spring admission). Application fee: $10 ($30 for international students). *Expenses:* Tuition $648 per year full-time, $120 per semester (minimum) part-time for state residents; $4482 per year full-time, $747 per semester (minimum) part-time for nonresidents. Fees $1010 per year full-time, $205 per semester part-time. *Financial aid:* Federal Work-Study, institutionally sponsored loans available. Aid available to part-time students. Financial aid application deadline: 3/15; applicants required to submit FAFSA. • Dr. Arturo Medina, Graduate Adviser, 512-994-2667. E-mail: adedu005@tamucc.edu. Application contact: Mary Margaret Dechant, Director of Admissions, 512-994-2624. Fax: 512-994-5887.

Texas A&M University–Kingsville, College of Education, Department of Education, Program in Secondary Education, Kingsville, TX 78363. Awards MA, MS. Part-time and evening/weekend programs available. Faculty: 5 full-time, 1 part-time (0 women). *Degree requirements:* Thesis or alternative, comprehensive exam, research report required, foreign language not required. *Entrance requirements:* GRE General Test (minimum combined score of 1000), MAT (minimum score 34), minimum GPA of 3.0. Application deadline: 6/1 (rolling processing; 11/15 for spring admission). Application fee: $15 ($25 for international students). *Tuition:* $1822 per year full-time, $281 per semester (minimum) part-time for state residents; $6934 per year full-time, $908 per semester (minimum) part-time for nonresidents. *Financial aid:* Application deadline 5/15. *Faculty research:* Professional development/technology, interdisciplinary teaming, educational restructuring. • Dr. Glenna Cannon, Director, 512-593-2899.

Texas A&M University–Texarkana, Division of Arts and Sciences and Education, Texarkana, TX 75505-5518. Offerings include secondary education (MA, M Ed, MS). Division faculty: 9 full-time (3 women), 5 part-time (3 women). *Degree requirements:* Thesis or alternative required, foreign language not required. *Average time to degree:* master's–1.5 years full-time. *Entrance requirements:* GRE General Test, bachelor's degree from a regionally accredited institution, minimum GPA of 3.0, teaching certificate (M Ed). Application deadline: rolling. Application fee: $0 ($25 for international students). *Tuition:* $2136 per year for state residents; $7248 per year for nonresidents. • Dr. John Anderson, Interim Head, 903-223-3003. Application contact: Pat Black, Registrar, 903-223-3068. Fax: 903-832-8890. E-mail: pat.black@tamut.edu.

Texas Christian University, School of Education, Department of Curriculum and Instruction, Program in Secondary Education, Fort Worth, TX 76129-0002. Awards M Ed. Part-time and evening/weekend programs available. Students: 26 (24 women); includes 6 minority (1 African American, 1 Asian American, 3 Hispanics, 1 Native American). 21 applicants, 62% accepted. In 1997, 6 degrees awarded. *Degree requirements:* Thesis optional, foreign language not required. *Entrance requirements:* TOEFL (minimum score 550). Application deadline: 3/1 (rolling processing; 12/1 for spring admission). Application fee: $0. *Expenses:* Tuition $10,350

Directory: Secondary Education

Texas Christian University (continued)
per year full-time, $345 per credit hour part-time. Fees $1240 per year full-time, $50 per credit hour part-time. *Financial aid:* Graduate assistantships and career-related internships or fieldwork available. Financial aid application deadline: 3/1. • Dr. Luther Clegg, Chairperson, Department of Curriculum and Instruction, 817-257-7660.

Texas Southern University, College of Education, Area of Curriculum and Instruction, Houston, TX 77004-4584. Offerings include secondary education (M Ed). Faculty: 15 full-time (7 women), 4 part-time (all women). *Degree requirements:* Comprehensive exam required, foreign language not required. *Entrance requirements:* GRE General Test, TOEFL, minimum GPA of 2.5. Application deadline: 7/15 (priority date; rolling processing). Application fee: $35 ($75 for international students). • Dr. Claudette Ligon, Chairperson, 713-313-7775.

Texas Tech University, Graduate School, College of Education, Division of Curriculum and Instruction, Lubbock, TX 79409. Offerings include secondary education (M Ed, Ed D, Certificate). Accredited by NCATE. Division faculty: 23 full-time (12 women). *Degree requirements:* For master's, computer language required, thesis optional, foreign language not required; for doctorate, dissertation required, foreign language not required. *Entrance requirements:* For master's, GRE General Test (combined average 992); for doctorate, GRE General Test. Application deadline: 4/15 (priority date; rolling processing; 11/1 for spring admission). Application fee: $25 ($50 for international students). Electronic applications accepted. *Expenses:* Tuition $864 per year full-time, $120 per semester (minimum) part-time for state residents; $5976 per year full-time, $747 per semester (minimum) part-time for nonresidents. Fees $2321 per year full-time, $302 per semester (minimum) part-time. • Dr. William E. Sparkman, Chair, 805-742-2371.

Towson University, Program in Secondary Education, Towson, MD 21252-0001. Awards M Ed, Spec. Part-time and evening/weekend programs available. Faculty: 6 full-time (3 women). Students: 2 full-time (1 woman), 87 part-time (54 women); includes 3 minority (all African Americans). In 1997, 19 master's awarded. *Degree requirements:* For master's, thesis optional, foreign language not required. *Application deadline:* 3/1 (priority date; rolling processing; 10/1 for spring admission). *Application fee:* $40. *Expenses:* Tuition $187 per credit hour for state residents; $364 per credit hour for nonresidents. Fees $40 per credit hour. *Financial aid:* Assistantships, Federal Work-Study available. Financial aid application deadline: 4/1; applicants required to submit FAFSA. *Faculty research:* Assessment, learning disabilities. • Dr. Margaret Kiley, Director, 410-830-3184. Fax: 410-830-3434. E-mail: mkiley@towson.edu. Application contact: Fran Musotto, Office Manager, 410-830-2501. Fax: 410-830-4675. E-mail: fmusotto@towson.edu.

Trinity College, School of Professional Studies, Programs in Education, Washington, DC 20017-1094. Offerings include secondary education (MAT). Faculty: 6 full-time (5 women), 18 part-time (13 women). *Application deadline:* rolling. *Application fee:* $35. *Tuition:* $460 per credit hour. • Sr. Rosemarie Bosler, Division Chair, 202-884-9557. Application contact: Karen Goodwin, Director of Graduate Admissions, 202-884-9400. Fax: 202-884-9229.

Troy State University, Graduate School, School of Education, Program in Secondary Education, Troy, AL 36082. Awards MS, Ed S. Accredited by NCATE. Part-time and evening/weekend programs available. Students: 34 full-time (24 women), 59 part-time (47 women); includes 42 minority (41 African Americans, 1 Native American), 2 international. Average age 30. In 1997, 21 master's awarded. *Degree requirements:* For master's, thesis, comprehensive exam. *Entrance requirements:* For master's, minimum GPA of 2.5; for Ed S, GRE General Test (minimum combined score of 850) or MAT (minimum score 33), Alabama Class A certificate or equivalent, minimum graduate GPA of 3.0. Application deadline: rolling. Application fee: $20. Electronic applications accepted. *Expenses:* Tuition $2040 per year full-time, $68 per hour part-time for state residents; $4200 per year full-time, $140 per hour part-time for nonresidents. Fees $240 per year full-time, $27 per quarter (minimum) part-time. *Financial aid:* Career-related internships or fieldwork available. Aid available to part-time students. Financial aid applicants required to submit FAFSA. • Dr. Perry A. Castelli, Chairman, 334-670-3545. Fax: 334-670-3474. E-mail: pcastelli@trojan.troyst.edu. Application contact: Teresa Rodgers, Director of Graduate Admissions, 334-670-3188. Fax: 334-670-3733. E-mail: trodgers@trojan.troyst.edu.

Troy State University Dothan, School of Education, Dothan, AL 36304-0368. Offerings include secondary education (MS Ed). Accredited by NCATE. *Application fee:* $20. *Expenses:* Tuition $68 per credit hour for state residents; $140 per credit hour for nonresidents. Fees $2 per credit hour. • Dr. Betty Anderson, Dean, 334-983-6556. Application contact: Reta Cordell, Director of Admissions and Records, 334-983-6556. Fax: 334-983-6322. E-mail: rcordell@tsud.edu.

Tufts University, Division of Graduate and Continuing Studies and Research, Graduate School of Arts and Sciences, Department of Education, Medford, MA 02155. Offerings include middle and secondary education (MA, MAT), secondary education (MA). Department faculty: 9 full-time, 7 part-time. *Entrance requirements:* GRE General Test, TOEFL (minimum score 550). Application deadline: 2/15 (rolling processing). Application fee: $50. • Kathleen Camara, Chair, 617-627-3244.

Union College, Department of Education, Program in Secondary Education, Barbourville, KY 40906-1499. Awards MA Ed. *Degree requirements:* Thesis optional, foreign language not required. *Entrance requirements:* GRE General Test, NTE. Application deadline: rolling. Application fee: $15. *Tuition:* $220 per hour. • Dr. Robert Swanson, Head, 666-546-1296.

The University of Akron, College of Education, Department of Curricular and Instructional Studies, Program in Secondary Education, Akron, OH 44325-0001. Awards MA, PhD. Accredited by NCATE. Students: 22 full-time (12 women), 76 part-time (53 women); includes 12 minority (9 African Americans, 1 Asian American, 1 Hispanic, 1 Native American), 1 international. Average age 38. *Degree requirements:* For master's, written comprehensive exam required, foreign language not required; for doctorate, variable foreign language requirement, dissertation, written and oral exams. *Entrance requirements:* For master's, MAT, minimum GPA of 2.75; for doctorate, MAT, interview, minimum GPA of 3.25. Application deadline: 8/15 (rolling processing). Application fee: $25 ($50 for international students). *Expenses:* Tuition $178 per credit hour for state residents; $333 per credit hour for nonresidents. Fees $145 per year full-time, $32 per semester (minimum) part-time. • Application contact: Dr. Robert Eley, Director of Student Services, 330-972-7750. E-mail: reley@uakron.edu.

The University of Akron, College of Education, Department of Curricular and Instructional Studies, Program in Secondary Education with Certification, Akron, OH 44325-0001. Awards MS. Accredited by NCATE. *Degree requirements:* Written comprehensive exam required, foreign language not required. *Entrance requirements:* MAT, minimum GPA of 2.75. Application deadline: 8/15 (rolling processing). Application fee: $25 ($50 for international students). *Expenses:* Tuition $178 per credit hour for state residents; $333 per credit hour for nonresidents. Fees $145 per year full-time, $32 per semester (minimum) part-time. • Application contact: Dr. Robert Eley, Director of Student Services, 330-972-7750. E-mail: reley@uakron.edu.

The University of Alabama, College of Education, Area of Teacher Education, Tuscaloosa, AL 35487. Offerings include secondary education (MA, Ed D, PhD, Ed S). Accredited by NCATE. Faculty: 32 full-time (18 women), 8 part-time (4 women). *Degree requirements:* For doctorate, 1 foreign language (computer language can substitute), dissertation, residency; for Ed S, thesis required, foreign language not required. *Entrance requirements:* For master's and doctorate, GRE General Test, MAT (score in 50th percentile or higher), or NTE (minimum score 658 on each core battery test), minimum GPA of 3.0; for Ed S, minimum GPA of 3.0 during previous 2 years. Application deadline: 7/6 (priority date; rolling processing). Application fee: $25. *Tuition:* $2684 per year full-time, $594 per semester (minimum) part-time for state residents; $7216 per year full-time, $1248 per semester (minimum) part-time for nonresidents. • Dr. Lea McGee, Head, 205-348-1196. Fax: 205-348-9863. E-mail: lmcgee@bamaed.ua.edu.

The University of Alabama at Birmingham, Graduate School, School of Education, Department of Curriculum and Instruction, Program in High School Education, Birmingham, AL 35294. Awards MA Ed, Ed S. Accredited by NCATE. Students: 53 full-time (37 women), 53 part-time (37 women); includes 12 minority (10 African Americans, 2 Native Americans). 68 applicants, 99% accepted. In 1997, 94 master's awarded. *Degree requirements:* For master's, thesis optional; for Ed S, comprehensive exam. *Entrance requirements:* For master's, GRE General Test, MAT, or NTE, minimum GPA of 3.0. Application deadline: rolling. Application fee: $30 ($60 for international students). Electronic applications accepted. *Expenses:* Tuition $99 per credit hour for state residents; $198 per credit hour for nonresidents. Fees $516 per year (minimum) full-time, $73 per quarter (minimum) part-time for state residents; $516 per year (minimum) full-time, $73 per unit (minimum) part-time for nonresidents. *Faculty research:* Soviet education, religious education, cultural pluralism. • Dr. Joseph C. Burns, Chair, Department of Curriculum and Instruction, 205-934-5371.

University of Alaska Southeast, Program in Education, Juneau, AK 99801-8625. Offerings include secondary education (MAT, M Ed). *Degree requirements:* Comprehensive exam or project required, foreign language and thesis not required. *Entrance requirements:* Minimum GPA of 3.0. Application deadline: 8/15 (priority date; rolling processing; 2/15 for spring admission). Application fee: $35. Electronic applications accepted. *Tuition:* $162 per credit for state residents; $316 per credit for nonresidents. • Application contact: Greg Wagner, Recruiter, 907-465-6239. Fax: 907-465-6365. E-mail: jngaw@acad1.alaska.edu.

University of Alberta, Faculty of Graduate Studies and Research, Department of Secondary Education, Edmonton, AB T6G 2E1, Canada. Awards M Ed, Ed D, PhD. Part-time programs available. Faculty: 17 full-time (7 women). Students: 32 full-time (21 women), 47 part-time (22 women). 34 applicants, 88% accepted. In 1997, 5 master's awarded (100% found work related to degree); 6 doctorates awarded (80% entered university research/teaching, 20% found other work related to degree). *Degree requirements:* For master's, thesis or alternative, 1 year of residency required, foreign language not required; for doctorate, dissertation, 2 years of residency (PhD), 1 year of residency (Ed D) required, foreign language not required. *Average time to degree:* master's–6 years full-time, 8 years part-time; doctorate–9 years full-time, 11 years part-time. *Entrance requirements:* For master's, teaching certificate, 2 years of teaching experience; for doctorate, master's degree. Application deadline: 4/1 (priority date; 10/1 for spring admission). Application fee: $60. *Expenses:* Tuition $390 per course for Canadian residents; $781 per course for nonresidents. Fees $500 per year full-time, $184 per year part-time. *Financial aid:* In 1997–98, 32 students received aid, including 2 fellowships, 10 research assistantships, 20 teaching assistantships (12 to first-year students), 10 graduate teaching awards, tuition scholarships. Financial aid application deadline: 6/1. *Faculty research:* Curriculum studies, teacher education, subject area specializations. Total annual research expenditures: $100,000. • Dr. W. Brouwer, Graduate Coordinator, 403-492-5613. E-mail: educ.sec@ualberta.ca. Application contact: Barb Keppy, Graduate Secretary, 403-492-2688. Fax: 403-492-9402. E-mail: barb.keppy@ualberta.ca.

The University of Arizona, College of Education, Department of Teaching and Teacher Education, Concentration in Secondary Education, Tucson, AZ 85721. Awards M Ed, MT, Ed D, Ed S. *Degree requirements:* For master's, thesis (MA) required, foreign language not required; for doctorate, 1 foreign language (computer language can substitute), dissertation. *Entrance requirements:* For master's, TOEFL (minimum score 550), minimum GPA of 3.0, 5 units of education course work; for doctorate, GRE General Test (minimum combined score of 1500 on three sections), TOEFL (minimum score 550), minimum graduate GPA of 3.0, 15 units of education course work, 2 years teaching experience; for Ed S, GRE General Test (minimum combined score of 1500 on three sections), TOEFL (minimum score 550). Application deadline: 4/12 (rolling processing). Application fee: $35. *Tuition:* $2162 per year full-time, $337 per semester (minimum) part-time for state residents; $6860 per year full-time, $1138 per semester (minimum) part-time for nonresidents. *Faculty research:* Teacher effectiveness, experimental curriculum design, middle schools.

University of Arkansas, College of Education, Department of Curriculum and Instruction, Program in Secondary Education, Fayetteville, AR 72701-1201. Awards MAT, M Ed. Accredited by NCATE. Students: 38 full-time (22 women), 9 part-time (8 women); includes 3 minority (2 African Americans, 1 Asian American), 1 international. 16 applicants, 88% accepted. In 1997, 31 degrees awarded. *Entrance requirements:* GRE General Test or MAT. Application fee: $25 ($35 for international students). *Tuition:* $3144 per year full-time, $173 per credit hour part-time for state residents; $7140 per year full-time, $395 per credit hour part-time for nonresidents. *Financial aid:* Federal Work-Study and career-related internships or fieldwork available. Aid available to part-time students. Financial aid application deadline: 4/1; applicants required to submit FAFSA. *Faculty research:* Mathematics. • Dr. Jerry Ford, Coordinator, 501-575-6676.

University of Arkansas at Little Rock, College of Education, Department of Teacher Education, Program in Secondary Education, Little Rock, AR 72204-1099. Awards M Ed. Accredited by NCATE. Part-time programs available. Students: 31 full-time (19 women), 21 part-time (17 women); includes 15 minority (12 African Americans, 1 Asian American, 2 Hispanics). Average age 30. 50 applicants, 66% accepted. In 1997, 27 degrees awarded. *Degree requirements:* Comprehensive exam required, foreign language and thesis not required. *Entrance requirements:* Interview, minimum GPA of 2.75, GRE General Test (minimum combined score of 1000 on three sections) or teaching certificate. Application deadline: rolling. Application fee: $25 ($30 for international students). *Expenses:* Tuition $2466 per year full-time, $137 per credit hour part-time for state residents; $5256 per year full-time, $292 per credit hour part-time for nonresidents. Fees $216 per year full-time, $36 per semester (minimum) part-time. *Financial aid:* Research assistantships, teaching assistantships, Federal Work-Study, institutionally sponsored loans available. Aid available to part-time students. • Dr. Robert Johns, Adviser, 501-569-3124.

University of Arkansas at Monticello, School of Education, Monticello, AR 71656. Offerings include secondary education (M Ed). School faculty: 13 full-time (4 women). *Degree requirements:* Comprehensive exam required, foreign language and thesis not required. *Entrance requirements:* Minimum GPA of 2.75, teaching certificate. Application deadline: 8/22 (priority date). Application fee: $0. • Dr. Gerald Norris, Dean, 870-460-1062. Fax: 870-460-1563.

University of Arkansas at Pine Bluff, Program in Education, Pine Bluff, AR 71601-2799. Offerings include secondary education (M Ed), with options in aquaculture, English, general science, mathematics, physical education, social studies. Accredited by NCATE. Program faculty: 51. *Entrance requirements:* GRE, minimum GPA of 2.75; NTE or Standard Arkansas Teaching Certificate. Application deadline: rolling. Application fee: $0. *Expenses:* Tuition $82 per credit hour for state residents; $192 per credit hour for nonresidents. Fees $25 per year. • Dr. Calvin Johnson, Dean, 870-543-8256.

University of Bridgeport, College of Graduate and Undergraduate Studies, School of Education and Human Resources, Division of Education, Program in Secondary Education, 380 University Avenue, Bridgeport, CT 06601. Offers computer specialist (MS, Diploma), international education (MS, Diploma), reading specialist (MS, Diploma), secondary education (MS, Diploma). Part-time and evening/weekend programs available. Faculty: 8 full-time (2 women), 57 part-time (26 women), 27 FTE. Students: 6 part-time (5 women); includes 1 minority (African American). 2 applicants, 100% accepted. In 1997, 3 Diplomas awarded. *Degree requirements:* For master's, computer language, final exam, final project, or thesis required, foreign language not required; for Diploma, thesis or alternative, final project required, foreign language not required. *Entrance requirements:* For master's, GRE General Test, MAT (score in 35th percentile or higher), minimum undergraduate QPA of 2.5; for Diploma, GRE General Test or MAT (score in 40th percentile or higher), minimum graduate QPA of 3.0. Application deadline: rolling. Application fee: $35 ($50 for international students). *Tuition:* $340 per credit. *Financial aid:* Federal Work-Study, institutionally sponsored loans, and career-related internships or fieldwork available. Aid available to part-time students. Financial aid application deadline: 6/1; applicants required to submit FAFSA. *Faculty research:* Self-concept, internship assessment, stress and situational development, follow-up of graduation, trend analysis. • Dr. Allen P. Cook, Associate Dean, Division of Education, 203-576-4206.

University of Central Arkansas, College of Education, Department of Administration and Secondary Education, Programs in Elementary and Secondary School Leadership, Conway, AR 72035-0001. Offerings include secondary school leadership (MSE). Accredited by NCATE. *Degree requirements:* Comprehensive exam required, thesis not required. *Entrance requirements:* GRE General Test, minimum GPA of 2.7. Application deadline: 3/1 (priority date; rolling processing; 10/1 for spring admission). Application fee: $15 ($40 for international students). *Expenses:* Tuition $161 per credit hour for state residents; $298 per credit hour for nonresidents. Fees $50 per year full-time, $30 per year part-time. • Dr. David Skotko, Interim Chairperson, Department of Administration and Secondary Education, 501-450-5407. Fax: 501-450-5671. E-mail: davids@mail.uca.edu.

University of Central Florida, College of Education, Department of Instructional Programs, Special Programs in Elementary and Secondary Education, Orlando, FL 32816. Offerings in elementary and secondary education (MA, M Ed), elementary education (MA, M Ed). Accredited by NCATE. Part-time and evening/weekend programs available. Students: 72 full-time (66 women), 94 part-time (81 women); includes 16 minority (7 African Americans, 1 Asian American, 7 Hispanics, 1 Native American). Average age 34. 44 applicants, 57% accepted. In 1997, 34 degrees awarded. *Degree requirements:* Thesis or alternative required, foreign language not required. *Entrance requirements:* GRE General Test (minimum combined score of 840). Application deadline: 7/12 (12/15 for spring admission). Application fee: $20. *Expenses:* Tuition $3288 per year full-time, $137 per credit hour part-time for state residents; $11,520 per year full-time, $480 per credit hour part-time for nonresidents. Fees $105 per year. *Financial aid:* Teaching assistantships, Federal Work-Study, institutionally sponsored loans, and career-related internships or fieldwork available. Aid available to part-time students. • Application contact: Dr. Martha Hopkins, Coordinator, 407-823-2039. E-mail: marthah@pegasus.cc.ucf.edu.

University of Central Oklahoma, College of Education, Department of Professional Teacher Education, Program in Secondary Education, Edmond, OK 73034-5209. Awards M Ed. Accredited by NCATE. Part-time and evening/weekend programs available. *Entrance requirements:* GRE General Test. Application deadline: 8/18. Application fee: $15. *Tuition:* $76 per credit hour for state residents; $178 per credit hour for nonresidents.

University of Cincinnati, College of Education, Division of Teacher Education, Department of Curriculum and Instruction, Program in Secondary Education, Cincinnati, OH 45221. Awards M Ed. Accredited by NCATE. Part-time programs available. Students: 71; includes 8 minority (7 African Americans, 1 Hispanic), 2 international. 10 applicants, 0% accepted. In 1997, 4 degrees awarded. *Degree requirements:* Thesis or alternative required, foreign language not required. *Average time to degree:* master's–3.3 years full-time. *Entrance requirements:* GRE General Test. Application deadline: 2/1. Application fee: $30. *Tuition:* $7228 per year full-time, $185 per credit hour part-time for state residents; $13,812 per year full-time, $352 per credit hour part-time for nonresidents. *Financial aid:* Fellowships, graduate assistantships, full tuition waivers available. Aid available to part-time students. Financial aid application deadline: 5/1. • Application contact: Dr. Glenn Markle, Graduate Program Director, 513-556-3582. Fax: 513-556-2483. E-mail: glenn.markle@uc.edu.

University of Connecticut, School of Education, Field of Secondary Education, Storrs, CT 06269. Awards MA, PhD. Accredited by NCATE. Faculty: 7. Students: 4 full-time (2 women), 11 part-time (6 women); includes 1 minority (African American). Average age 35. 14 applicants, 57% accepted. In 1997, 8 master's, 2 doctorates awarded. Terminal master's awarded for partial completion of doctoral program. *Degree requirements:* For master's, thesis or alternative; for doctorate, dissertation. *Entrance requirements:* For doctorate, GRE General Test. Application deadline: 6/1 (priority date; rolling processing; 11/1 for spring admission). Application fee: $40 ($45 for international students). *Expenses:* Tuition $5272 per year full-time, $293 per credit part-time for state residents; $13,696 per year full-time, $761 per credit part-time for nonresidents. Fees $948 per year full-time, $640 per year part-time. *Financial aid:* In 1997–98, 1 fellowship totaling $1,200, 2 research assistantships (both to first-year students) totaling $9,619, 7 teaching assistantships (1 to a first-year student) totaling $6,750 were awarded. Financial aid application deadline: 2/15. • Thomas P. Weinland, Head, 860-486-2433.

University of Delaware, College of Human Resources, Education and Public Policy, School of Education, Newark, DE 19716. Offerings include secondary education (M Ed). School faculty: 54 (24 women). *Application deadline:* 7/1 (rolling processing; 1/15 for spring admission). *Application fee:* $45. *Expenses:* Tuition $4250 per year full-time, $236 per credit hour part-time for state residents; $12,250 per year full-time, $681 per credit hour part-time for nonresidents. Fees $466 per year full-time, $15 per semester (minimum) part-time. • Dr. Robert Hampel, Director, 302-831-2573.

University of Florida, College of Education, Department of Instruction and Curriculum, Gainesville, FL 32611. Offerings include secondary education (MAE, M Ed, Ed D, PhD, Ed S). Accredited by NCATE. Department faculty: 42. *Degree requirements:* For master's, thesis optional, foreign language not required; for doctorate, variable foreign language requirement, dissertation. *Entrance requirements:* For master's and doctorate, GRE General Test (minimum combined score of 1000), minimum GPA of 3.0; for Ed S, GRE General Test. Application deadline: 6/5. Application fee: $20. *Tuition:* $138 per credit hour for state residents; $481 per credit hour for nonresidents. • Dr. Mary Grace Kantowski, Chair, 352-392-9191 Ext. 200. E-mail: mgk@coe.ufl.edu. Application contact: Dr. Ben Nelms, Graduate Coordinator, 352-392-9191 Ext. 225. Fax: 352-392-9193. E-mail: bfn@coe.ufl.edu.

University of Georgia, College of Education, Programs in Secondary Education, Athens, GA 30602. Offerings in education (MA), English education (M Ed, Ed S), language education (M Ed, PhD, Ed S), mathematics education (M Ed, Ed D, PhD, Ed S), science education (M Ed, Ed D, PhD, Ed S), social science education (PhD), social sciences education (M Ed, Ed D, Ed S), speech education (M Ed, Ed S). Accredited by NCATE. Faculty: 46 full-time (17 women). Students: 187 full-time, 145 part-time (97 women); includes 22 minority (17 African Americans, 2 Asian Americans, 3 Hispanics), 36 international. 192 applicants, 53% accepted. In 1997, 90 master's, 15 doctorates, 12 Ed Ss awarded. *Degree requirements:* For master's, thesis (MA) required, foreign language not required; for doctorate, dissertation required, foreign language not required. *Entrance requirements:* For master's and Ed S, GRE General Test or MAT; for doctorate, GRE General Test. Application deadline: 7/1 (priority date; 11/15 for spring admission). Application fee: $30. Electronic applications accepted. *Tuition:* $3290 per year full-time, $643 per semester (minimum) part-time for state residents; $11,300 per year full-time, $1645 per semester (minimum) part-time for nonresidents. *Financial aid:* Fellowships, research assistantships, teaching assistantships, assistantships available. • Dr. Russell H. Yeany, Dean, 706-542-3866. Fax: 706-542-0360.

University of Great Falls, Graduate Studies Division, Master of Arts in Teaching Program, Great Falls, MT 59405. Offerings include secondary education (MAT). Postbaccalaureate distance learning degree programs offered (minimal on-campus study). Program faculty: 5 full-time (all women), 6 part-time (4 women), 6 FTE. *Degree requirements:* Thesis or alternative required, foreign language not required. *Entrance requirements:* GRE General Test (minimum score 500 on each section; combined average 1000), bachelor's degree in teaching, teaching certificate, 3 years of teaching experience. Application deadline: 8/15 (priority date; rolling processing). Application fee: $35. *Expenses:* Tuition $327 per credit. Fees $150 per year full-time, $45 per semester (minimum) part-time. • Dr. Eleanore Gowen, Head. E-mail: agowen@ugf.edu.

University of Guam, College of Education, Program in Secondary Education, 303 University Drive, UOG Station, Mangilao, GU 96923. Awards M Ed. *Degree requirements:* Thesis, comprehensive oral and written exams required, foreign language not required. *Entrance requirements:* GRE General Test. Application deadline: 5/31. Application fee: $31 ($56 for international students).

University of Hartford, College of Education, Nursing, and Health Professions, Program in Secondary Education, West Hartford, CT 06117-1599. Awards M Ed. Accredited by NCATE. Part-time and evening/weekend programs available. Faculty: 6 full-time (2 women), 4 part-time (2 women). Students: 7 full-time (2 women), 13 part-time (8 women); includes 1 minority (Asian American). Average age 29. 7 applicants, 43% accepted. In 1997, 9 degrees awarded. *Degree requirements:* Comprehensive exam required, foreign language and thesis not required. *Entrance requirements:* GRE General Test or MAT, PRAXIS I, interview. Application deadline: 5/15 (priority date; rolling processing; 12/15 for spring admission). Application fee: $40 ($55 for international students). Electronic applications accepted. *Financial aid:* Graduate assistantships, Federal Work-Study available. Aid available to part-time students. Financial aid application deadline: 6/1; applicants required to submit FAFSA. • Dr. A. Cheryl Curtis, Director, 860-768-4927. Application contact: Susan Garcia, Coordinator of Student Services, 860-768-5038. E-mail: gettoknow@mail.hartford.edu.

University of Hawaii at Manoa, College of Education, Department of Teacher Education and Curriculum Studies, Program in Secondary Education, Honolulu, HI 96822. Awards M Ed. Faculty: 44 full-time (21 women), 1 (woman) part-time, 44.5 FTE. Students: 76 (57 women). 23 applicants, 74% accepted. *Application deadline:* 3/1 (9/1 for spring admission). *Tuition:* $4029 per year full-time, $214 per credit hour part-time for state residents; $9957 per year full-time, $461 per credit hour part-time for nonresidents. *Financial aid:* In 1997–98, 10 students received aid, including 5 teaching assistantships; full tuition waivers, Federal Work-Study also available. • Dr. Richard Johnson, Graduate Chairperson, 808-956-4410. E-mail: rich@hawaii.edu. Application contact: Myrna Nakasato, Secretary, 808-956-4401. Fax: 808-956-3918.

University of Houston, College of Education, Department of Curriculum and Instruction, 4800 Calhoun, Houston, TX 77204-2163. Offerings include secondary education (M Ed). Accredited by NCATE. Department faculty: 37 full-time (19 women), 10 part-time (7 women). *Degree requirements:* Comprehensive exam or thesis required, foreign language not required. *Entrance requirements:* GRE General Test or MAT. Application deadline: 7/3 (priority date; rolling processing). Application fee: $35 ($75 for international students). *Expenses:* Tuition $1152 per year full-time, $120 per semester (minimum) part-time for state residents; $4482 per year full-time, $249 per credit hour part-time for nonresidents. Fees $977 per year full-time, $119 per semester (minimum) part-time. • Wilford Weber, Chair, 713-743-4970. Fax: 713-743-9870. E-mail: wweber@uh.edu.

University of Houston–Clear Lake, School of Education, Houston, TX 77058-1098. Offerings include secondary education (MA). Accredited by NCATE. School faculty: 34 full-time (23 women), 17 part-time (12 women), 39 FTE. *Application deadline:* rolling. *Application fee:* $30 ($60 for international students). *Tuition:* $207 per credit hour for state residents; $336 per credit hour for nonresidents. • Dr. Dennis Spuck, Dean, 281-283-3501. Application contact: Dr. Doris L. Prater, Associate Dean, 281-283-3600.

University of Idaho, College of Graduate Studies, College of Education, Division of Teacher Education, Department of Teacher Education, Moscow, ID 83844-4140. Offerings include secondary education (M Ed, MS). Accredited by NCATE. *Application deadline:* 8/1 (12/15 for spring admission). *Application fee:* $35 ($45 for international students). *Expenses:* Tuition $0 for state residents; $6000 per year full-time, $95 per credit part-time for nonresidents. Fees $2676 per year full-time, $134 per credit part-time. • Dr. Grace Goc Karp, Acting Head, Division of Teacher Education, 208-885-6586.

University of Illinois at Chicago, College of Education, Department of Curriculum and Instruction, Chicago, IL 60607-7128. Offerings include instructional leadership (M Ed), with options in elementary education, reading, secondary education. Department faculty: 28 full-time (13 women), 1 part-time (0 women). *Entrance requirements:* TOEFL (minimum score 550), minimum GPA of 3.75 on a 5.0 scale. Application deadline: 2/15. Application fee: $40 ($50 for international students). • Dr. John Smart, Area Chair, 312-996-4526. Application contact: Victoria Hare, Director of Graduate Studies, 312-996-4520.

University of Indianapolis, School of Education, Indianapolis, IN 46227-3697. Offerings include secondary education (MA), with options in art education, education, English education, social studies education. Accredited by NCATE. *Average time to degree:* master's–5 years part-time. *Entrance requirements:* GRE Subject Test. Application deadline: rolling. Application fee: $30.

The University of Iowa, College of Education, Division of Secondary Education, Iowa City, IA 52242-1316. Offers programs in art education (MA, PhD), curriculum and supervision (Ed S), music education (MA, MAT, PhD). Faculty: 21 full-time. Students: 99 full-time (62 women), 69 part-time (51 women); includes 18 minority (9 African Americans, 4 Asian Americans, 4 Hispanics, 1 Native American), 24 international. 71 applicants, 73% accepted. In 1997, 41 master's, 10 doctorates awarded. *Degree requirements:* For master's, exam required, foreign language not required; for doctorate, computer language, dissertation, comprehensive exams required, foreign language not required. *Entrance requirements:* For master's, minimum GPA of 2.5; for doctorate, minimum GPA of 3.0. Application fee: $30 ($50 for international students). *Expenses:* Tuition $3166 per year full-time, $176 per semester hour part-time for state residents; $10,202 per year full-time, $176 per semester hour part-time for nonresidents. Fees $202 per year full-time, $52 per year (minimum) part-time. *Financial aid:* In 1997–98, 4 fellowships (1 to a first-year student), 13 research assistantships (3 to first-year students), 49 teaching assistantships (16 to first-year students) were awarded; Federal Work-Study, institutionally sponsored loans, and career-related internships or fieldwork also available. Financial aid applicants required to submit FAFSA. • William Nibbelink, Chair, 319-335-5324. Fax: 319-335-5608.

University of Louisville, School of Education, Department of Secondary Education, Program in Secondary Education, Louisville, KY 40292-0001. Awards MA, MAT, M Ed, Ed S. Accredited by NCATE. Students: 85 full-time (51 women), 78 part-time (52 women); includes 10 minority (8 African Americans, 2 Hispanics). Average age 32. In 1997, 106 master's awarded. *Entrance requirements:* GRE General Test. Application deadline: rolling. Application fee: $25. • Dr. Allan E. Dittmer, Chair, Department of Secondary Education, 502-852-6591.

University of Maine, College of Education and Human Development, Program in Secondary Education, Orono, ME 04469. Awards M Ed, MS, CAS. Accredited by NCATE. Part-time and evening/weekend programs available. *Degree requirements:* For master's, thesis or alternative. *Entrance requirements:* For master's, MAT, TOEFL (minimum score 550); for CAS, MAT, MA, M Ed, or MS. Application deadline: 2/1 (priority date; rolling processing; 10/15 for spring admission). Application fee: $50. *Expenses:* Tuition $194 per credit hour for state residents; $548 per credit hour for nonresidents. Fees $378 per year full-time, $33 per semester (minimum) part-time. *Financial aid:* Teaching assistantships and career-related internships or fieldwork available. Aid available to part-time students. Financial aid application deadline: 3/1. • Application contact: Scott Delcourt, Director of the Graduate School, 207-581-3218. Fax: 207-581-3232. E-mail: graduate@maine.edu.

University of Mary, Program in Education, 7500 University Drive, Bismarck, ND 58504-9652. Offerings include secondary teaching (MS Ed). Program faculty: 5 full-time (3 women), 6 part-time (4 women). *Average time to degree:* master's–3 years part-time. *Application deadline:* 8/1 (12/1 for spring admission). *Application fee:* $15. *Tuition:* $265 per credit. • Ramona Klein, Director, 701-255-7500. Application contact: Dr. Diane Fladeland, Director, Graduate Programs, 701-255-7500. Fax: 701-255-7687.

University of Maryland, College Park, College of Education, Department of Curriculum and Instruction, College Park, MD 20742-5045. Offerings include secondary education (MA, M Ed, Ed D, PhD, CAGS). Accredited by NCATE. Postbaccalaureate distance learning degree programs offered. Department faculty: 29 full-time (14 women), 11 part-time (8 women). *Degree requirements:* For doctorate, dissertation. *Entrance requirements:* For master's, GRE

Directory: Secondary Education

University of Maryland, College Park (continued)
General Test or MAT, minimum GPA of 3.0; for doctorate, GRE General Test or MAT, minimum GPA of 3.5. Application deadline: rolling. Application fee: $50 ($70 for international students). *Expenses:* Tuition $272 per credit hour for state residents; $400 per credit hour for nonresidents. Fees $564 per year full-time, $342 per year part-time. • Dr. Martin Johnson, Chairman, 301-405-3117. Fax: 301-314-9278. Application contact: John Mollish, Director, Graduate Admissions and Records, 301-405-4198. Fax: 301-314-9305.

University of Massachusetts Amherst, School of Education, Program in Education, Amherst, MA 01003-0001. Offerings include secondary teacher education (M Ed, Ed D, CAGS). Accredited by NCATE. *Degree requirements:* For doctorate, dissertation required, foreign language not required. *Entrance requirements:* For master's and doctorate, GRE General Test. Application deadline: 3/1 (rolling processing; 10/1 for spring admission). Application fee: $40. *Expenses:* Tuition $2640 per year full-time, $110 per credit part-time for state residents; $3690 per year (minimum) full-time, $165 per credit (minimum) part-time for nonresidents. Fees $2856 per year full-time, $422 per semester part-time for state residents; $3204 per year full-time, $480 per semester part-time for nonresidents. • John C. Carey, Director, 413-545-0236.

University of Massachusetts Boston, Graduate College of Education, School Organization, Curriculum and Instruction Department, Program in Education, Track in Elementary and Secondary Education, Boston, MA 02125-3393. Awards M Ed. Students: 90 full-time (63 women), 222 part-time (139 women); includes 41 minority (19 African Americans, 8 Asian Americans, 14 Hispanics), 2 international. 209 applicants, 70% accepted. In 1997, 97 degrees awarded. *Degree requirements:* Comprehensive exams required, foreign language and thesis not required. *Entrance requirements:* GRE General Test or MAT, minimum GPA of 2.75, 2 years of teaching experience. Application deadline: 3/1 (priority date; 11/1 for spring admission). Application fee: $25 ($35 for international students). *Expenses:* Tuition $2640 per year full-time, $110 per credit part-time for state residents; $8930 per year full-time, $373 per credit part-time for nonresidents. Fees $2650 per year full-time, $420 per semester (minimum) part-time for state residents; $2736 per year full-time, $420 per semester (minimum) part-time for nonresidents. *Financial aid:* In 1997–98, 10 research assistantships (9 to first-year students) averaging $225 per month and totaling $20,000 were awarded; teaching assistantships, administrative assistantships also available. Financial aid application deadline: 3/1; applicants required to submit FAFSA. • Dr. Denise Patmon, Program Coordinator, 617-287-7625. Application contact: Lisa Lavely, Director of Graduate Admissions and Records, 617-287-6400. Fax: 617-287-6236.

The University of Memphis, College of Education, Department of Instruction and Curriculum Leadership, Memphis, TN 38152. Offerings include secondary education (MAT). Accredited by NCATE. Department faculty: 34 full-time (17 women), 22 part-time (13 women). *Application deadline:* 8/1 (12/1 for spring admission). *Application fee:* $25 ($50 for international students). *Tuition:* $2862 per year full-time, $166 per credit hour part-time for state residents; $6696 per year full-time, $379 per credit hour part-time for nonresidents. • Dr. Dennie Smith, Interim Chair, 901-678-2771. Application contact: Dr. Carole L. Bond, Coordinator of Graduate Studies, 901-678-3490.

University of Mississippi, Graduate School, School of Education, Department of Curriculum and Instruction, University, MS 38677-9702. Offerings include secondary education (MA). Accredited by NCATE. Department faculty: 19 full-time (15 women). *Application deadline:* 8/1 (rolling processing). *Application fee:* $0 ($25 for international students). • Dr. Peggy Emerson, Acting Chair, 601-232-7123.

University of Missouri–Kansas City, School of Education, Division of Curriculum and Instruction, Kansas City, MO 64110-2499. Offerings include secondary education (MA). Accredited by NCATE. *Degree requirements:* Thesis optional, foreign language not required. *Entrance requirements:* Minimum GPA of 2.75. Application deadline: 7/1 (priority date; rolling processing; 12/1 for spring admission). Application fee: $25. *Expenses:* Tuition $182 per credit hour for state residents; $508 per credit hour for nonresidents. Fees $60 per year. • Dr. Cheryl Grossman, Chairperson, 816-235-2245.

University of Missouri–St. Louis, School of Education, Program in Secondary Education, St. Louis, MO 63121-4499. Awards M Ed. Accredited by NCATE. Faculty: 17 (5 women). Students: 31 full-time (18 women), 148 part-time (109 women); includes 36 minority (33 African Americans, 1 Asian American, 2 Hispanics), 3 international. In 1997, 40 degrees awarded. *Degree requirements:* Thesis required, foreign language not required. *Application deadline:* 7/1 (priority date; rolling processing; 12/1 for spring admission). *Application fee:* $0. Electronic applications accepted. *Expenses:* Tuition $3903 per year full-time, $167 per credit hour part-time for state residents; $11,745 per year full-time, $489 per credit hour part-time for nonresidents. Fees $816 per year full-time, $34 per credit hour part-time. *Faculty research:* Middle-level schools, staff development, pre-service and in-service training, curriculum development, effect of wait time on student achievement. • Dr. Edith Young, Chair, 314-516-5944. Application contact: Graduate Admissions, 314-516-5458. Fax: 314-516-6759. E-mail: gradadm@umslvma.umsl.edu.

University of Montevallo, College of Education, Program in Secondary Education, Montevallo, AL 35115. Awards M Ed, Ed S. Accredited by NCATE. Part-time and evening/weekend programs available. *Entrance requirements:* For master's, GRE General Test (minimum combined score of 850), MAT (minimum score 35), minimum undergraduate GPA of 2.75 in last 60 hours or 2.5 overall. Application deadline: 7/15 (11/15 for spring admission). Application fee: $10.

University of Nebraska at Omaha, College of Education, Department of Teacher Education, Program in Secondary Education, Omaha, NE 68182. Awards MA, MS. Accredited by NCATE. Part-time and evening/weekend programs available. Faculty: 9 full-time (1 woman), 1 part-time (0 women). Students: 14 full-time (9 women), 79 part-time (52 women); includes 3 minority (2 African Americans, 1 Asian American), 1 international. Average age 34. 28 applicants, 82% accepted. In 1997, 28 degrees awarded. *Degree requirements:* Thesis (for some programs), comprehensive exam required, foreign language not required. *Entrance requirements:* GRE General Test (minimum combined score of 840) or MAT (minimum score 35), minimum GPA of 3.0. Application deadline: 7/1 (priority date; rolling processing; 12/1 for spring admission). Application fee: $35. *Expenses:* Tuition $1670 per year full-time, $94 per credit hour part-time for state residents; $4082 per year full-time, $227 per credit hour part-time for nonresidents. Fees $302 per year full-time, $108 per semester (minimum) part-time. *Financial aid:* 21 students received aid; fellowships, teaching assistantships, full tuition waivers, Federal Work-Study, institutionally sponsored loans available. Aid available to part-time students. Financial aid application deadline: 3/1. • Dr. Raymond Ziebarth, Adviser, 402-554-3666.

University of Nevada, Las Vegas, College of Education, Department of Instructional and Curricular Studies, Las Vegas, NV 89154-9900. Offerings include general secondary education (M Ed, MS). Accredited by NCATE. Department faculty: 34 full-time (16 women). *Degree requirements:* Thesis (for some programs), oral or written comprehensive exam required, foreign language not required. *Entrance requirements:* Minimum GPA of 3.0. Application deadline: 2/15 (9/30 for spring admission). Application fee: $40 ($95 for international students). *Expenses:* Tuition $93 per credit for state residents; $93 per credit full-time, $190 per credit part-time for nonresidents. Fees $5570 per year full-time for nonresidents. • Dr. Jan McCarthy, Chair, 702-895-3241. Application contact: Graduate College Admissions Evaluator, 702-895-3320.

University of Nevada, Reno, College of Education, Department of Curriculum and Instruction, Reno, NV 89557. Offerings include secondary education (MA, M Ed, MS). Accredited by NCATE. Department faculty: 19 (7 women). *Degree requirements:* Thesis optional, foreign language not required. *Entrance requirements:* GRE, TOEFL (minimum score 500), minimum GPA of 2.75. Application deadline: 3/1 (priority date; rolling processing; 10/1 for spring admission). Application fee: $40. *Expenses:* Tuition $0 for state residents; $5770 per year full-time, $200 per credit part-time for nonresidents. Fees $93 per credit. • Dr. Vernon D. Luft, Chair, 702-784-4961. Application contact: Dr. J. Randall Koetting, Graduate Director, 702-784-4961 Ext. 2008. E-mail: koetting@unr.edu.

University of New Hampshire, College of Liberal Arts, Department of Education, Program in Secondary Education, Durham, NH 03824. Awards MAT, M Ed. Accredited by NCATE. Part-time programs available. Students: 53 full-time (34 women), 105 part-time (53 women); includes 3 minority (1 African American, 1 Asian American, 1 Hispanic), 1 international. Average age 28. 73 applicants, 82% accepted. In 1997, 63 degrees awarded. *Degree requirements:* Thesis or alternative required, foreign language not required. *Entrance requirements:* GRE General Test. Application deadline: 4/1 (priority date; rolling processing). Application fee: $50. *Expenses:* Tuition $5440 per year full-time, $302 per credit hour part-time for state residents; $8160 per year (minimum) full-time, $453 per credit hour (minimum) part-time for nonresidents. Fees $868 per year full-time, $15 per year part-time. *Financial aid:* In 1997–98, 1 research assistantship, 3 teaching assistantships (all to first-year students), 13 scholarships (4 to first-year students) were awarded; full and partial tuition waivers, Federal Work-Study, and career-related internships or fieldwork also available. Aid available to part-time students. Financial aid application deadline: 2/15. *Faculty research:* Pre-service teacher education. • Dr. Michael D. Andrew, Coordinator, 603-862-2371. Application contact: Dr. Todd DeMitchell, Graduate Coordinator, 603-862-2317.

University of New Mexico, College of Education, Program in Secondary Education, Albuquerque, NM 87131-2039. Awards MA. Accredited by NCATE. Faculty: 11 full-time (5 women), 28 part-time (18 women), 18.72 FTE. Students: 24 full-time (15 women), 45 part-time (26 women); includes 15 minority (1 African American, 13 Hispanics, 1 Native American), 1 international. Average age 35. 32 applicants, 81% accepted. In 1997, 86 degrees awarded. *Degree requirements:* Comprehensive exam or thesis required, foreign language not required. *Entrance requirements:* Secondary teaching certificate. Application deadline: 3/31 (10/10 for spring admission). Application fee: $25. *Expenses:* Tuition $2442 per year full-time, $103 per credit hour part-time for state residents; $8691 per year full-time, $103 per credit hour (minimum) part-time for nonresidents. Fees $32 per year. *Financial aid:* In 1997–98, 6 students received aid, including research assistantships averaging $880 per month and totaling $8,800, teaching assistantships averaging $880 per month and totaling $44,000; Federal Work-Study, institutionally sponsored loans, and career-related internships or fieldwork also available. *Faculty research:* Bilingualism, math, science, language and literacy, social studies. • Dr. Peter Winograd, Graduate Coordinator, 505-277-4553. E-mail: winograd@unm.edu. Application contact: Irene Martinez, Division Administrator, 505-277-4533. Fax: 505-277-4116. E-mail: icmartin@unm.edu.

University of North Alabama, College of Education, Department of Secondary Education, Program in Secondary Education, Florence, AL 35632-0001. Awards MA Ed. Accredited by NCATE. Part-time and evening/weekend programs available. Faculty: 11 part-time (3 women). Students: 30 full-time (20 women), 100 part-time (55 women); includes 5 minority (4 African Americans, 1 Asian American). Average age 33. In 1997, 72 degrees awarded. *Degree requirements:* Final written comprehensive exam required, foreign language and thesis not required. *Entrance requirements:* GRE, MAT, or NTE, minimum GPA of 2.5, Alabama Class B Certificate or equivalent, teaching experience. Application deadline: 7/1 (priority date; rolling processing; 12/1 for spring admission). Application fee: $25. *Expenses:* Tuition $2448 per year full-time, $102 per credit hour part-time for state residents; $4896 per year full-time, $204 per credit hour part-time for nonresidents. Fees $3 per semester. *Financial aid:* Federal Work-Study available. Aid available to part-time students. Financial aid application deadline: 4/1. • Application contact: Dr. Sue Wilson, Dean of Enrollment Management, 205-765-4316.

The University of North Carolina at Chapel Hill, School of Education, Programs in Teacher Education, Program in Secondary Education, Chapel Hill, NC 27599. Offers English (MAT), French (MAT), German (MAT), Japanese (MAT), Latin (MAT), mathematics (MAT), music (MAT), science (MAT), social studies/social science (MAT), Spanish (MAT). Accredited by NCATE. Students: 20 full-time (16 women), 10 part-time (8 women). 97 applicants, 49% accepted. *Degree requirements:* Comprehensive exam required, foreign language and thesis not required. *Entrance requirements:* GRE General Test (minimum combined score of 1000), minimum GPA of 3.0 during last 2 years of undergraduate course work. Application deadline: 1/1 (rolling processing). Application fee: $55. *Expenses:* Tuition $1428 per year full-time, $357 per semester (minimum) part-time for state residents; $10,414 per year full-time, $2604 per semester (minimum) part-time for nonresidents. Fees $782 per year full-time, $332 per semester (minimum) part-time. *Financial aid:* Federal Work-Study available. Aid available to part-time students. Financial aid application deadline: 1/1. *Faculty research:* Curriculum and instruction, teacher education per subject. • Dr. Walter Pryzwansky, Director of Graduate Studies, 919-966-7000. Application contact: Janet Carroll, Registrar, 919-966-1346. Fax: 919-962-1533. E-mail: jscarrol@email.unc.edu.

University of North Carolina at Charlotte, College of Education, Charlotte, NC 28223-0001. Offerings include secondary education (M Ed). Accredited by NCATE. College faculty: 61 full-time (31 women), 7 part-time (6 women), 62.75 FTE. *Application deadline:* 7/1. *Application fee:* $35. *Tuition:* $1786 per year full-time, $339 per semester (minimum) part-time for state residents; $8914 per year full-time, $2121 per semester (minimum) part-time for nonresidents. • Dr. John M. Nagle, Dean, 704-547-4707. Application contact: Kathy Barringer, Assistant Director of Graduate Admissions, 704-547-3366. Fax: 704-547-3279. E-mail: gradadm@email.uncc.edu.

University of North Carolina at Greensboro, School of Education, Department of Curriculum and Instruction, Program in Secondary Curriculum and Teaching, Greensboro, NC 27412-0001. Awards M Ed. Accredited by NCATE. Students: 9 full-time (4 women), 31 part-time (26 women); includes 4 minority (2 African Americans, 2 Hispanics). 38 applicants, 53% accepted. In 1997, 2 degrees awarded. *Entrance requirements:* GRE General Test, TOEFL. Application deadline: 7/1 (priority date; rolling processing; 11/1 for spring admission). Application fee: $35. *Expenses:* Tuition $1842 per year full-time, $370 per semester (minimum) part-time for state residents; $10,296 per year full-time, $2484 per semester (minimum) part-time for nonresidents. Fees $806 per year full-time, $111 per semester (minimum) part-time. *Financial aid:* Research assistantships, teaching assistantships available. • Dr. Gerald Ponder, Chair, Department of Curriculum and Instruction, 336-334-3437.

University of North Dakota, College of Education and Human Development, Teaching and Learning Program, Grand Forks, ND 58202. Offerings include secondary education (Ed D, PhD). Accredited by NCATE. Program faculty: 24 full-time (19 women), 22 part-time (21 women). *Degree requirements:* Dissertation. *Entrance requirements:* TOEFL (minimum score 550), minimum GPA of 3.5. Application deadline: 3/1 (priority date; rolling processing). Application fee: $20. • Dr. Mary Harris, Director, 701-777-2674. Fax: 701-777-4393. E-mail: mary_harris@mail.und.nodak.edu.

University of North Florida, College of Education, Department of Elementary and Secondary Education, Program in Secondary Education, Jacksonville, FL 32224-2645. Awards M Ed. Accredited by NCATE. Part-time and evening/weekend programs available. Faculty: 23 full-time (11 women). Students: 11 part-time (6 women); includes 1 minority (African American). Average age 35. 0 applicants. In 1997, 2 degrees awarded. *Entrance requirements:* GRE General Test (minimum combined score of 1000), minimum GPA of 3.0. Application deadline: rolling. Application fee: $20. *Tuition:* $3388 per year full-time, $141 per credit hour part-time for state residents; $11,634 per year full-time, $485 per credit hour part-time for nonresidents. *Financial aid:* Career-related internships or fieldwork available. *Faculty research:* Learning, memory, testing. • Dr. Dennis Holt, Chairperson, Department of Elementary and Secondary Education, 904-646-2610.

University of North Texas, College of Education, Department of Teacher Education and Administration, Program in Secondary Education, Denton, TX 76203-6737. Awards M Ed, MS. Accredited by NCATE. *Entrance requirements:* GRE General Test (minimum score 350 on each section, 800 combined). Application deadline: 7/17. Application fee: $25 ($50 for international students). *Tuition:* $2063 per year full-time, $815 per year part-time for state residents; $5897 per year full-time, $2100 per year part-time for nonresidents. *Financial aid:* Fellowships, research assistantships, teaching assistantships, Federal Work-Study, institutionally sponsored loans, and career-related internships or fieldwork available. Financial aid application deadline: 4/1. • Application contact: Lloyd Campbell, Adviser, 940-565-2920.

University of Oklahoma, College of Education, Department of Instructional Leadership and Academic Curriculum, Program in Instructional Leadership and Academic Curriculum, Norman, OK 73019-0390. Offerings include secondary education (M Ed, PhD). Accredited by NCATE. Program faculty: 19 full-time (12 women), 12 part-time (11 women). *Degree requirements:* For doctorate, variable foreign language requirement, dissertation. *Entrance requirements:* For master's, TOEFL (minimum score 550), 12 hours of course work in education; for doctorate, GRE General Test (minimum combined score of 1000), TOEFL (minimum score 500), master's degree, minimum graduate GPA of 3.0. Application deadline: 6/1 (priority date; rolling processing). Application fee: $25. *Expenses:* Tuition $1920 per year full-time, $80 per credit hour part-time for state residents; $6108 per year full-time, $255 per credit hour part-time for nonresidents. Fees $468 per year full-time, $12 per semester (minimum) part-time. • Dr. Bonnie Konopak, Chair, Department of Instructional Leadership and Academic Curriculum, 405-325-1498.

University of Pennsylvania, Graduate School of Education, Division of Educational Leadership, Programs in Secondary Education, Philadelphia, PA 19104. Awards MS Ed. Students: 36 full-time (21 women), 1 part-time (0 women); includes 8 minority (4 African Americans, 3 Asian Americans, 1 Native American). In 1997, 45 degrees awarded. *Degree requirements:* Comprehensive exam or portfolio required, foreign language not required. *Average time to degree:* master's–1 year full-time. *Entrance requirements:* GRE, MAT. Application fee: $65. *Expenses:* Tuition $22,716 per year full-time, $2876 per course part-time. Fees $1484 per year full-time, $181 per course part-time. *Financial aid:* Federal Work-Study, institutionally sponsored loans available. Financial aid applicants required to submit FAFSA. • Dr. Kenneth Tobin, Director, 215-898-7370. Application contact: Evelyn Williams, Coordinator, 215-898-5690.

University of Pittsburgh, School of Education, Department of Instruction and Learning, Program in Secondary Education, Pittsburgh, PA 15260. Offers English/communications education (MAT, M Ed, Ed D, PhD), foreign languages education (MA, MAT, M Ed, Ed D, PhD), mathematics education (MAT, M Ed, Ed D), reading education (M Ed, Ed D, PhD), science education (MAT, M Ed, MS, Ed D, PhD), social studies education (MAT, M Ed, Ed D, PhD). Part-time and evening/weekend programs available. 325 applicants, 82% accepted. *Degree requirements:* Thesis/dissertation required, foreign language not required. *Average time to degree:* master's–2 years full-time, 4 years part-time; doctorate–4 years full-time, 6 years part-time. *Entrance requirements:* GRE General Test, TOEFL (minimum score 650). Application deadline: 2/1. Application fee: $30 ($40 for international students). *Expenses:* Tuition $8018 per year full-time, $329 per credit part-time for state residents; $16,508 per year full-time, $680 per credit part-time for nonresidents. Fees $480 per year full-time, $180 per year part-time. *Financial aid:* In 1997–98, 2 fellowships, 6 teaching assistantships averaging $1,250 per month, 13 assistantships averaging $1,150 per month were awarded; partial tuition waivers, Federal Work-Study, institutionally sponsored loans, and career-related internships or fieldwork also available. Aid available to part-time students. Financial aid application deadline: 5/1; applicants required to submit FAFSA. • Application contact: Jackie Harden, Manager, 412-648-7060. Fax: 412-648-1899. E-mail: jackie@sched.fsl.pitt.edu.

University of Portland, School of Education, Department of Secondary Education, Portland, OR 97203-5798. Awards MA, MAT, M Ed. Part-time and evening/weekend programs available. *Degree requirements:* Thesis optional, foreign language not required. *Entrance requirements:* GRE General Test (MA), California Basic Educational Skills Test, PRAXIS (MAT), GRE General Test or MAT (M Ed), TOEFL (minimum score 550), minimum GPA of 3.0, teaching certificate. Application deadline: 8/1 (priority date; rolling processing; 12/1 for spring admission). Application fee: $40. *Tuition:* $515 per semester hour. *Financial aid:* Federal Work-Study available. Financial aid application deadline: 3/15. • Dr. Ellyn Arwood, Director, 503-283-7325. E-mail: arwood@up.edu.

University of Puerto Rico, Río Piedras, College of Education, Program in Curriculum and Teaching, San Juan, PR 00931. Offerings include secondary education (M Ed). *Degree requirements:* Thesis required, foreign language not required. *Entrance requirements:* PAEG, minimum GPA of 3.0. Application deadline: 2/21. Application fee: $17.

University of Puget Sound, School of Education, Program in Education, Tacoma, WA 98416-0005. Offerings include improvement of instruction (M Ed), with options in elementary education, reading, secondary education. Accredited by NCATE. Program faculty: 12 full-time (9 women), 3 part-time (all women), 12.83 FTE. *Average time to degree:* master's–2 years full-time. *Entrance requirements:* GRE General Test (score in 50th percentile or higher), minimum GPA of 3.0. Application deadline: 2/1. Application fee: $40. *Expenses:* Tuition $19,640 per year full-time, $2480 per course part-time. Fees $155 per year. • Dr. Carol Merz, Dean, School of Education, 253-756-3377.

University of Puget Sound, School of Education, Program in Teaching, Tacoma, WA 98416-0005. Offerings include secondary education (MAT). Accredited by NCATE. Program faculty: 12 full-time (9 women), 3 part-time (all women), 12.83 FTE. *Average time to degree:* master's–2 years full-time. *Entrance requirements:* GRE General Test (score in 50th percentile or higher), minimum GPA of 3.0. Application deadline: 2/1. Application fee: $40. *Expenses:* Tuition $19,640 per year full-time, $2480 per course part-time. Fees $155 per year. • Dr. Carol Merz, Dean, School of Education, 253-756-3377.

University of Rhode Island, College of Human Science and Services, Department of Education, Program in Secondary Education, Kingston, RI 02881. Awards MA. Accredited by NCATE. Evening/weekend programs available. *Entrance requirements:* MAT or GRE, TOEFL (minimum score 600). Application deadline: 4/15 (priority date; rolling processing; 11/15 for spring admission). Application fee: $35. *Expenses:* Tuition $3446 per year full-time, $191 per credit part-time for state residents; $9850 per year full-time, $547 per credit part-time for nonresidents. Fees $1276 per year full-time, $135 per semester (minimum) part-time.

University of Richmond, Department of Education, Master of Teaching Program, University of Richmond, VA 23173. Offerings include secondary education (MT). MT (learning disabled) being phased out; applicants no longer accepted. Program faculty: 5 full-time (3 women). *Entrance requirements:* GRE General Test, PRAXIS I. Application deadline: 6/1 (priority date; 12/1 for spring admission). Application fee: $30. *Tuition:* $18,695 per year full-time, $320 per credit hour part-time. • Dr. Mavis Brown, Coordinator, Department of Education, 804-289-8429.

University of Richmond, Department of Education, Program in Secondary Education, University of Richmond, VA 23173. Awards M Ed. Part-time and evening/weekend programs available. Faculty: 2 full-time (0 women), 2 part-time (1 woman). *Degree requirements:* Comprehensive exam required, foreign language and thesis not required. *Entrance requirements:* GRE General Test, PRAXIS I, teaching certificate. Application deadline: 5/15 (priority date; 12/1 for spring admission). Application fee: $30. *Tuition:* $18,695 per year full-time, $320 per credit hour part-time. *Financial aid:* Fellowships, research assistantships, partial tuition waivers, Federal Work-Study, institutionally sponsored loans, and career-related internships or fieldwork available. Financial aid application deadline: 3/15. • Dr. Mavis Brown, Coordinator, Department of Education, 804-289-8429.

University of Scranton, Department of Education, Program in Secondary Education, Scranton, PA 18510-4622. Awards MS. Accredited by NCATE. Part-time and evening/weekend programs available. Students: 4 full-time (1 woman), 19 part-time (11 women); includes 1 minority (African American), 1 international. Average age 30. 23 applicants, 100% accepted. In 1997, 13 degrees awarded. *Degree requirements:* Comprehensive exam required, foreign language and thesis not required. *Entrance requirements:* TOEFL (minimum score 500), minimum GPA of 2.75. Application deadline: rolling. Application fee: $35. *Expenses:* Tuition $465 per credit. Fees $25 per semester. *Financial aid:* Teaching assistantships, Federal Work-Study, and career-related internships or fieldwork available. Aid available to part-time students. Financial aid application deadline: 3/1. • Dr. David A. Wiley, Chair, Department of Education, 717-941-4032. Fax: 717-941-7401. E-mail: daw315@uofs.edu.

University of South Alabama, College of Education, Department of Curriculum and Instruction, Mobile, AL 36688-0002. Offerings include secondary education (M Ed). Accredited by NCATE. Department faculty: 13 full-time (6 women). *Degree requirements:* Comprehensive exams required, foreign language and thesis not required. *Entrance requirements:* GRE General Test (minimum combined score of 1000) or MAT (minimum score 37), minimum GPA of 3.0. Application deadline: 9/1 (priority date; rolling processing). Application fee: $25. • Dr. Walter S. Hopkins, Chairman, 334-380-2893.

University of South Alabama, College of Education, Department of Interdepartmental Education, Mobile, AL 36688-0002. Offerings include secondary education (Ed S). Accredited by NCATE. *Application deadline:* 9/1 (priority date; rolling processing). *Application fee:* $25. • George E. Uhlig, Dean, College of Education, 334-460-6205.

University of South Carolina, Graduate School, College of Education, Department of Instruction and Teacher Education, Program in Secondary Education, Columbia, SC 29208. Awards IMA, MA, MAT, M Ed, MT, Ed D, PhD. Accredited by NCATE. IMA and MAT offered jointly with the subject areas. Faculty: 5 full-time (1 woman). Students: 31 full-time (21 women), 484 part-time (340 women); includes 97 minority (93 African Americans, 3 Hispanics, 1 Native American), 4 international. Average age 39. In 1997, 29 master's, 3 doctorates awarded. *Degree requirements:* For master's, 1 foreign language (computer language can substitute), thesis (for some programs); for doctorate, 1 foreign language (computer language can substitute), dissertation, comprehensive exam. *Entrance requirements:* For master's, GRE General Test or MAT, teaching certificate; for doctorate, GRE General Test. Application deadline: 8/1 (priority date; rolling processing). Application fee: $35. Electronic applications accepted. *Expenses:* Tuition $3894 per year full-time, $193 per credit hour part-time for state residents; $8114 per year full-time, $404 per credit hour part-time for nonresidents. Fees $125 per year full-time, $37 per semester (minimum) part-time. *Financial aid:* Research assistantships, teaching assistantships available. *Faculty research:* Middle school programs, professional development, school collaboration. • Dr. Elizabeth Burnett, Coordinator, 803-777-6242.

University of South Dakota, School of Education, Division of Curriculum and Instruction, Program in Secondary Education, Vermillion, SD 57069-2390. Awards MA. Accredited by NCATE. Part-time programs available. Students: 15 full-time (4 women), 3 part-time (2 women); includes 1 minority (Hispanic). 10 applicants, 60% accepted. In 1997, 18 degrees awarded. *Entrance requirements:* GRE General Test, MAT. Application deadline: rolling. Application fee: $15. *Expenses:* Tuition $1530 per year full-time, $85 per credit hour part-time for state residents; $4518 per year full-time, $251 per credit hour part-time for nonresidents. Fees $792 per year full-time, $44 per credit hour part-time. *Financial aid:* Teaching assistantships, Federal Work-Study available. • Dr. Linda Reetz, Chair, Division of Curriculum and Instruction, 605-677-5210.

University of Southern Indiana, Graduate Studies, School of Education and Human Services, Department of Teacher Education, Program in Secondary Education, Evansville, IN 47712-3590. Awards MS. Accredited by NCATE. Part-time and evening/weekend programs available. Faculty: 6 full-time (1 woman). Students: 38 part-time (20 women). Average age 33. 16 applicants, 56% accepted. In 1997, 21 degrees awarded. *Entrance requirements:* GRE General Test, NTE, minimum GPA of 3.0. Application fee: $25. *Tuition:* $129 per credit hour for state residents; $260 per credit hour for nonresidents. • Dr. Annette Lamb, Head, 812-465-7148.

University of Southern Mississippi, College of Education and Psychology, Department of Curriculum and Instruction, Hattiesburg, MS 39406-5167. Offerings include secondary education (M Ed, MS, Ed D, PhD, Ed S). Department faculty: 11 full-time (7 women), 1 part-time (0 women). *Degree requirements:* For master's, thesis or alternative required, foreign language not required; for doctorate, 2 foreign languages, dissertation; for Ed S, thesis required, foreign language not required. *Entrance requirements:* For master's, GRE General Test, minimum GPA of 2.75; for doctorate and Ed S, GRE General Test, minimum GPA of 3.25. Application deadline: 8/9 (priority date; rolling processing). Application fee: $0 ($25 for international students). *Tuition:* $2870 per year full-time, $137 per credit hour part-time for state residents; $5972 per year full-time, $172 per credit hour part-time for nonresidents. • Dr. Carolyn Reeves-Kazelskis, Acting Chair, 601-266-4547. Fax: 601-266-4175.

University of South Florida, College of Education, Department of Secondary Education, Program in Secondary Education, Tampa, FL 33620-9951. Awards PhD. Accredited by NCATE. Part-time and evening/weekend programs available. Students: 2 full-time (1 woman), 5 part-time (all women). Average age 44. 4 applicants, 100% accepted. *Degree requirements:* Dissertation, 2 tools of research in foreign language, statistics, and/or computers. *Entrance requirements:* GRE General Test (minimum combined score of 1000), minimum GPA of 3.0 (undergraduate) or 3.5 (graduate). Application deadline: 6/1 (10/15 for spring admission). Application fee: $20. Electronic applications accepted. *Tuition:* $142 per credit hour for state residents; $486 per credit hour for nonresidents. *Financial aid:* Federal Work-Study, institutionally sponsored loans available. Aid available to part-time students. Financial aid applicants required to submit FAFSA. • Application contact: Howard Johnston, Coordinator, 813-974-3398. Fax: 813-974-3837. E-mail: johnston@tempest.coedu.usf.edu.

University of Tennessee at Chattanooga, School of Education, Education Graduate Studies Division, Chattanooga, TN 37403-2598. Offerings include secondary education (M Ed). Accredited by NCATE. Division faculty: 15 full-time (5 women), 7 part-time (3 women). *Degree requirements:* Comprehensive exams required, thesis optional, foreign language not required. *Entrance requirements:* GRE General Test or MAT, teaching certificate. Application deadline: rolling. Application fee: $25. *Tuition:* $2864 per year full-time, $160 per credit hour part-time for state residents; $6806 per year full-time, $379 per credit hour part-time for nonresidents. • Dr. Tom Bibler, Acting Head, 423-755-4211. Fax: 423-755-5380. E-mail: tom-bibler@utc.edu. Application contact: Dr. Deborah Arfken, Assistant Provost for Graduate Studies, 423-755-4667. Fax: 423-755-4478.

The University of Texas at Tyler, School of Education and Psychology, Department of Curriculum and Instruction, Program in Secondary Education, Tyler, TX 75799-0001. Offers biology (M Ed, Certificate), English (M Ed, Certificate), history (M Ed, Certificate), mathematics (M Ed, Certificate). Part-time programs available. *Degree requirements:* For master's, comprehensive and departmental qualifying exams required, foreign language not required. *Entrance requirements:* For master's, GRE General Test. Application fee: $0 ($50 for international students). *Tuition:* $2144 per year full-time, $337 per semester (minimum) part-time for state residents; $7256 per year full-time, $964 per semester (minimum) part-time for nonresidents. *Financial aid:* Application deadline 7/1. • Application contact: Martha D. Wheat, Director of Admissions and Student Records, 903-566-7201. Fax: 903-566-7068.

The University of Texas at Tyler, School of Education and Psychology, Department of Curriculum and Instruction, Program in Secondary Teaching, Tyler, TX 75799-0001. Awards MAT. Program new for fall 1998. Part-time programs available. *Degree requirements:* Thesis required, foreign language not required. *Entrance requirements:* GRE General Test. Application fee: $0 ($50 for international students). *Tuition:* $2144 per year full-time, $337 per semester (minimum) part-time for state residents; $7256 per year full-time, $964 per semester (minimum) part-time for nonresidents. *Financial aid:* Application deadline 7/1. • Application contact: Martha D. Wheat, Director of Admissions and Student Records, 903-566-7201. Fax: 903-566-7068.

The University of Texas of the Permian Basin, Graduate School, School of Education, Program in Secondary Education, Odessa, TX 79762-0001. Awards MA. *Degree requirements:* Thesis required, foreign language not required. *Entrance requirements:* GRE General Test (minimum combined score of 1200). *Expenses:* Tuition $1314 per year full-time, $73 per hour

Directory: Secondary Education

The University of Texas of the Permian Basin (continued)

part-time for state residents; $4896 per year full-time, $272 per hour part-time for nonresidents. Fees $383 per year full-time, $111 per semester (minimum) part-time.

The University of Texas–Pan American, College of Education, Department of Curriculum and Instruction: Elementary and Secondary, Edinburg, TX 78539-2999. Offers programs in early childhood education (M Ed), elementary bilingual education (M Ed), elementary education (M Ed), reading (M Ed), secondary education (M Ed). Part-time and evening/weekend programs available. *Degree requirements:* Thesis optional. *Entrance requirements:* GRE General Test. Application deadline: 7/17 (11/16 for spring admission). Application fee: $0. *Tuition:* $2156 per year full-time, $283 per semester (minimum) part-time for state residents; $6788 per year full-time, $862 per semester (minimum) part-time for nonresidents. *Faculty research:* Language minority children, reading education for non-English speakers, alternative teacher certification degree program, English as a second language, bilingual education.

University of the Incarnate Word, School of Graduate Studies, College of Professional Studies, Programs in Education, Program in Secondary Teaching, San Antonio, TX 78209-6397. Awards MA, M Ed. *Entrance requirements:* GRE, MAT, TOEFL (minimum score 550). Application deadline: 8/15 (priority date; rolling processing; 12/31 for spring admission). Application fee: $20. *Expenses:* Tuition $350 per semester hour. Fees $180 per year full-time, $111 per semester (minimum) part-time. • Application contact: Brian F. Dalton, Dean of Enrollment Services, 210-829-6005. Fax: 210-829-3921.

University of Toledo, College of Education and Allied Professions, Department of Curriculum and Instruction, Toledo, OH 43606-3398. Offerings include secondary education (M Ed). Accredited by NCATE. Department faculty: 27 full-time (9 women). *Application deadline:* 8/1 (priority date; rolling processing). *Application fee:* $30. *Tuition:* $5907 per year full-time, $246 per hour part-time for state residents; $11,835 per year full-time, $493 per hour part-time for nonresidents. • Dr. James R. Gress, Chair, 419-530-2468. Fax: 419-530-7719. E-mail: jgress@uoft02.utoledo.edu.

University of Utah, Graduate School of Education, Department of Educational Studies, Program in Elementary and Secondary Education, Salt Lake City, UT 84112-1107. Awards M Ed. *Entrance requirements:* GRE General Test or MAT, TOEFL (minimum score 540), minimum GPA of 3.0. Application deadline: 7/1. Application fee: $30 ($50 for international students). *Tuition:* $2045 per year full-time, $562 per semester (minimum) part-time for state residents; $6129 per year full-time, $1607 per semester (minimum) part-time for nonresidents. • Application contact: Harvey Kantor, Director of Graduate Studies, 801-581-7158.

The University of West Alabama, College of Education, Department of Foundations, Livingston, AL 35470. Offerings include secondary education (MAT, M Ed), with options in biology with certification (MAT), environmental science with certification (MAT), history with certification (MAT), language arts with certification (MAT), library media with certification (MAT), mathematics with certification (MAT). Accredited by NCATE. *Application deadline:* 9/10 (priority date; rolling processing; 3/24 for spring admission). *Application fee:* $15. *Tuition:* $70 per quarter hour.

University of Wisconsin–Eau Claire, College of Professional Studies, School of Education, Program in Secondary Education, Eau Claire, WI 54702-4004. Offers biology (MAT, MST), education and professional development (MEPD), English (MAT, MST), history (MAT, MST), mathematics (MAT, MST). Students: 6 full-time (3 women), 38 part-time (28 women); includes 1 minority (Native American). In 1997, 34 degrees awarded. *Degree requirements:* Oral and written comprehensive exams required, thesis optional, foreign language not required. *Entrance requirements:* 2 years of teaching experience or equivalent. Application deadline: 7/1 (rolling processing; 12/1 for spring admission). Application fee: $45. *Tuition:* $3651 per year full-time, $611 per semester (minimum) part-time for state residents; $11,295 per year full-time, $1886 per semester (minimum) part-time for nonresidents. *Financial aid:* Federal Work-Study available. Financial aid application deadline: 3/1. • Stephen Kurth, Associate Dean, School of Education, 715-836-3671.

University of Wisconsin–La Crosse, School of Education, Professional Development Program, La Crosse, WI 54601-3742. Offerings include secondary education (MEPD), with option in grades 6 through 12. Accredited by NCATE. MEPD (K–12) new for fall 1998. Program faculty: 27 full-time (15 women), 6 part-time (2 women), 28.69 FTE. *Degree requirements:* Thesis, seminar paper, or comprehensive exam required, foreign language not required. *Entrance requirements:* Minimum GPA of 2.85. Application fee: $45. *Tuition:* $3737 per year full-time, $208 per credit part-time for state residents; $11,921 per year full-time, $633 per credit part-time for nonresidents. • Dr. Ronald S. Rochon, Director, 608-785-8138. E-mail: rochon@mail.uwlax.edu. Application contact: Tim Lewis, Director of Admissions, 608-785-8939. Fax: 608-785-6695. E-mail: admissions@mail.uwlax.edu.

University of Wisconsin–Milwaukee, School of Education, Department of Curriculum and Instruction, Milwaukee, WI 53201-0413. Offerings include secondary education (MS). Offered jointly with University of Wisconsin–Green Bay. Department faculty: 28 full-time (17 women). *Degree requirements:* Thesis or alternative required, foreign language not required. *Application deadline:* 1/1 (priority date; rolling processing; 9/1 for spring admission). *Application fee:* $45 ($75 for international students). *Tuition:* $4996 per year full-time, $1030 per semester (minimum) part-time for state residents; $15,216 per year full-time, $2947 per semester (minimum) part-time for nonresidents. • Linda Post, Chair, 414-229-4884.

University of Wisconsin–Platteville, College of Liberal Arts and Education, School of Education, Platteville, WI 53818-3099. Offerings include secondary education (MSE). Accredited by NCATE. School faculty: 8 part-time (3 women). *Degree requirements:* Thesis or alternative, comprehensive exam required, foreign language not required. *Entrance requirements:* TOEFL (minimum score 500). Application deadline: 7/1 (priority date; rolling processing; 11/1 for spring admission). Application fee: $45. • Dr. Sally Standiford, Director, 608-342-1131. Fax: 608-342-1133. E-mail: standiford@uwplatt.edu.

Utah State University, College of Education, Department of Secondary Education, Logan, UT 84322. Awards MA, M Ed, MS. Accredited by NCATE. Part-time and evening/weekend programs available. Faculty: 7 full-time (2 women), 4 part-time (0 women). Students: 22 full-time (11 women), 38 part-time (14 women). Average age 33. 15 applicants, 67% accepted. In 1997, 13 degrees awarded. *Degree requirements:* Thesis (for some programs). *Entrance requirements:* GRE General Test (score in 40th percentile or higher) or MAT, TOEFL (minimum score 550), minimum GPA of 3.0. Application deadline: 6/15 (priority date; 10/15 for spring admission). Application fee: $40. *Expenses:* Tuition $1448 per year full-time, $624 per year part-time for state residents; $5082 per year full-time, $2192 per year part-time for nonresidents. Fees $421 per year full-time, $165 per year part-time. *Financial aid:* Fellowships, research assistantships, teaching assistantships, partial tuition waivers, and career-related internships or fieldwork available. Financial aid application deadline: 4/15. *Faculty research:* Learning theory, reading/writing skills, educational measurement, social studies education, science education. • Dr. William Strong, Head, 435-797-2221. Fax: 435-797-1441. E-mail: bills@coe.usu.edu.

Valdosta State University, College of Education, Department of Secondary Education, Valdosta, GA 31698. Offers programs in curriculum and instruction (Ed D), instructional technology (M Ed), secondary education (M Ed, Ed S). Accredited by NCATE. Part-time and evening/weekend programs available. Faculty: 8 full-time (5 women). Students: 31 full-time (21 women), 116 part-time (91 women); includes 27 minority (24 African Americans, 3 Hispanics). 90 applicants, 71% accepted. In 1997, 34 master's awarded. *Degree requirements:* Computer language, thesis/dissertation required, foreign language not required. *Entrance requirements:* For master's, GRE General Test (minimum combined score of 800); for doctorate, GRE General Test (minimum combined score of 1000); for Ed S, GRE General Test (minimum combined score of 900). Application deadline: 8/1 (rolling processing; 11/15 for spring admission). Application fee: $10. *Expenses:* Tuition $2472 per year full-time, $83 per semester hour part-time for state residents; $8472 per year full-time, $333 per semester hour part-time for nonresidents. Fees $236 per year full-time. *Faculty research:* Distance education, learning styles, alternative assessment methods, interactive teaching strategies. • Dr. Catherine Price, Head, 912-333-5927. Fax: 912-333-7167. E-mail: cprice@grits.valdosta.peachnet.edu.

Vanderbilt University, Peabody College, Department of Teaching and Learning, Nashville, TN 37240-1001. Offerings include secondary education (M Ed). Accredited by NCATE. *Entrance requirements:* GRE General Test, MAT. Application deadline: 3/1 (priority date; rolling processing). Application fee: $35. • Carolyn Evertson, Chair, 615-322-8100.

Villanova University, Graduate School of Liberal Arts and Sciences, Department of Education and Human Services, Program in Secondary Education, Villanova, PA 19085-1699. Awards MA. Part-time and evening/weekend programs available. Students: 1 (woman) full-time, 7 part-time (6 women). Average age 33. 8 applicants, 100% accepted. *Degree requirements:* Comprehensive exam required, foreign language and thesis not required. *Entrance requirements:* GRE or MAT, minimum GPA of 3.0. Application deadline: 8/1 (priority date; 12/1 for spring admission). Application fee: $40. *Expenses:* Tuition $400 per credit. Fees $60 per year. *Financial aid:* Federal Work-Study and career-related internships or fieldwork available. Financial aid application deadline: 4/1. • Dr. Gerald Flood, Coordinator, 610-519-4620.

Virginia Commonwealth University, School of Education, Program in Teaching, Richmond, VA 23284-9005. Offerings include secondary education (MT, Certificate). Accredited by NCATE. *Entrance requirements:* For master's, GRE General Test or MAT. Application deadline: 3/1 (rolling processing; 10/15 for spring admission). Application fee: $30 ($0 for international students). *Tuition:* $4960 per year full-time, $257 per credit part-time for state residents; $12,652 per year full-time, $684 per credit part-time for nonresidents. • Dr. Alan M. McLeod, Division Head, 804-828-1305. E-mail: ammcleod@vcu.edu. Application contact: Dr. Michael D. Davis, Interim Director, Graduate Studies, 804-828-6530. Fax: 804-828-1323. E-mail: mddavis@vcu.edu.

Wagner College, Department of Education, Program in Secondary Education, Staten Island, NY 10301. Awards MS Ed. Part-time and evening/weekend programs available. Faculty: 3 full-time (2 women), 4 part-time (1 woman). Students: 13 full-time (7 women), 10 part-time (5 women). 28 applicants, 86% accepted. In 1997, 14 degrees awarded. *Degree requirements:* Thesis optional, foreign language not required. *Entrance requirements:* Minimum GPA of 2.75. Application deadline: 8/1 (priority date; rolling processing; 12/10 for spring admission). Application fee: $50 ($65 for international students). *Tuition:* $580 per credit. *Financial aid:* In 1997–98, 3 teaching assistantships averaging $300 per month and totaling $7,200, 9 alumni fellowships (6 to first-year students) were awarded; partial tuition waivers also available. • Dr. Geoffry Coward, Head, Department of Education, 718-390-3472. Application contact: Admissions Office, 718-390-3411.

Wake Forest University, Department of Education, Winston-Salem, NC 27109. Offerings include secondary education (MA Ed). Accredited by NCATE. Department faculty: 10 full-time (5 women), 3 part-time (2 women). *Degree requirements:* Thesis optional, foreign language not required. *Entrance requirements:* GRE General Test. Application deadline: 2/15. Application fee: $25. *Tuition:* $17,150 per year full-time, $550 per hour part-time. • Dr. Joseph O. Milner, Chairman, 336-759-5341. Application contact: Loraine Stewart, Certification Officer, 336-759-5990. Fax: 336-759-4591.

Washington State University, College of Education, Department of Teaching and Learning, Pullman, WA 99164-1610. Offerings include secondary education (MA, MAT, M Ed, MIT, Ed D, PhD). Accredited by NCATE. Department faculty: 24 full-time (10 women). *Degree requirements:* For master's, oral exam required, foreign language not required; for doctorate, dissertation, oral exam required, foreign language not required. *Average time to degree:* master's–2 years full-time; doctorate–4 years full-time. *Entrance requirements:* GRE General Test, minimum GPA of 3.0. Application deadline: 3/1 (priority date; rolling processing). Application fee: $35. *Tuition:* $5334 per year full-time, $267 per credit hour part-time for state residents; $13,380 per year full-time, $677 per credit hour part-time for nonresidents. • Dr. Darcy Miller, Chair, 509-335-7296.

Washington University in St. Louis, Graduate School of Arts and Sciences, Department of Education, Program in Secondary Education, St. Louis, MO 63130-4899. Awards MA Ed, MAT. One or more programs accredited by NCATE. *Degree requirements:* Thesis or alternative required, foreign language not required. *Entrance requirements:* GRE General Test or MAT. Application deadline: 1/15 (priority date; rolling processing). Application fee: $35. *Tuition:* $22,200 per year full-time, $925 per credit hour part-time. *Financial aid:* Career-related internships or fieldwork available. Financial aid application deadline: 1/15. • Dr. James Wertsch, Chair, Department of Education, 314-935-6776.

Wayne State University, College of Education, Division of Teacher Education, Detroit, MI 48202. Offerings include secondary education (MAT, M Ed). Accredited by NCATE. Division faculty: 53. *Entrance requirements:* Minimum GPA of 2.6. Application deadline: 7/1. Application fee: $20 ($30 for international students). *Expenses:* Tuition $163 per credit hour for state residents; $355 per credit hour for nonresidents. Fees $498 per year full-time, $114 per semester (minimum) part-time. • Dr. Sharon Elliott, Assistant Dean, 313-577-0902.

Wesley College, Division of Education and Psychology, Dover, DE 19901. Offerings include secondary education (M Ed). Division faculty: 5 full-time (4 women), 1 part-time (0 women). *Degree requirements:* Thesis optional, foreign language not required. *Entrance requirements:* GRE. Application deadline: rolling. Application fee: $20. • Dr. B. Patricia Patterson, Chair, 302-736-2448. E-mail: patterpa@mail.wesley.edu. Application contact: Dr. J. Thomas Sturgis, Director of Graduate Studies, 302-736-2414. Fax: 302-736-2301. E-mail: sturgisto@mail.wesley.edu.

West Chester University of Pennsylvania, School of Education, Department of Counselor, Secondary and Professional Education, West Chester, PA 19383. Offers programs in educational research (MS), school counseling (M Ed, MS), secondary education (M Ed). Accredited by NCATE. Faculty: 8 part-time. Students: 55 full-time (39 women), 154 part-time (127 women); includes 16 minority (11 African Americans, 5 Asian Americans), 2 international. Average age 33. 98 applicants, 71% accepted. In 1997, 69 degrees awarded. *Degree requirements:* Comprehensive exam required, foreign language and thesis not required. *Entrance requirements:* GRE or MAT. Application deadline: 4/15 (priority date; rolling processing; 10/15 for spring admission). Application fee: $25. *Expenses:* Tuition $3468 per year full-time, $193 per credit part-time for state residents; $6236 per year full-time, $346 per credit part-time for nonresidents. Fees $660 per year full-time, $38 per credit part-time. *Financial aid:* Research assistantships available. Aid available to part-time students. Financial aid application deadline: 2/15. • Dr. John Hynes, Chair, 610-436-2411. Application contact: Dr. Kimberlee Brown, Graduate Coordinator, School Counseling, 610-436-2950.

Western Carolina University, College of Education and Allied Professions, Department of Administration, Curriculum and Instruction, Programs in Secondary Education, Cullowhee, NC 28723. Offerings in art education (MAT), biology (MAT), chemistry (MAT), English (MAT), family and consumer sciences (MAT), mathematics (MAT), physical education (MAT), reading (MAT), social sciences (MAT). One or more programs accredited by NCATE. Part-time and evening/weekend programs available. Students: 3 full-time (2 women), 11 part-time (8 women). 9 applicants, 78% accepted. In 1997, 14 degrees awarded. *Degree requirements:* Comprehensive exam required, foreign language and thesis not required. *Entrance requirements:* GRE General Test. Application deadline: rolling. Application fee: $35. *Tuition:* $1799 per year full-time, $144 per credit hour (minimum) part-time for state residents; $9069 per year full-time, $1053 per credit hour (minimum) part-time for nonresidents. *Financial aid:* In 1997–98, 2 students received aid, including 2 research assistantships (1 to a first-year student) totaling $6,567; fellowships, teaching assistantships, Federal Work-Study, institutionally sponsored loans also available. Financial aid application deadline: 3/15. • Application contact: Kathleen Owen, Assistant to the Dean, 828-227-7398. Fax: 828-227-7480.

Western Connecticut State University, School of Professional Studies, Department of Education and Educational Psychology, Program in Secondary Education, Danbury, CT 06810-6885. Awards MS. Part-time and evening/weekend programs available. Students: 7 part-time (5 women). *Degree requirements:* Thesis or research project required, foreign language not required. *Entrance requirements:* Minimum GPA of 2.67. Application deadline: 8/1 (priority date; rolling processing). Application fee: $40. *Expenses:* Tuition $4127 per year (minimum) full-time, $178 per credit hour part-time for state residents; $9581 per year (minimum) full-time, $178 per credit hour part-time for nonresidents. Fees $25 per year part-time. *Financial aid:* Fellowships, Federal Work-Study, and career-related internships or fieldwork available. Aid available to part-time students. Financial aid application deadline: 5/1. • Dr. Thomas Cordy, Chair, Department of Education and Educational Psychology, 203-837-8520.

Western Kentucky University, College of Education, Department of Teacher Education, Programs in Secondary Education, Bowling Green, KY 42101-3576. Awards MA Ed, Ed S. Accredited by NCATE. Part-time and evening/weekend programs available. Postbaccalaureate distance learning degree programs offered (minimal on-campus study). Faculty: 29 full-time (16 women), 2 part-time (1 woman), 30 FTE. Students: 4 full-time (0 women), 75 part-time (45 women). Average age 30. 23 applicants, 57% accepted. In 1997, 25 master's awarded. *Degree requirements:* For Ed S, thesis, oral exam required, foreign language not required. *Entrance requirements:* For master's, GRE General Test (minimum combined score of 1150 on three sections; average 1660), minimum GPA of 2.5; for Ed S, GRE General Test (minimum combined score of 1250 on three sections), minimum GPA of 3.5. Application deadline: 8/1 (priority date; rolling processing; 12/1 for spring admission). Application fee: $20. *Tuition:* $2460 per year full-time, $133 per credit hour part-time for state residents; $6700 per year full-time, $369 per credit hour part-time for nonresidents. *Financial aid:* Federal Work-Study, institutionally sponsored loans available. Aid available to part-time students. Financial aid application deadline: 4/1; applicants required to submit FAFSA. • Dr. Vicki Stayton, Head, Department of Teacher Education, 502-745-5414.

Western Maryland College, Department of Education, Program in Elementary and Secondary Education, Westminster, MD 21157-4390. Awards MS. Part-time and evening/weekend programs available. Faculty: 1 full-time (0 women). Students: 186 full-time (164 women), 427 part-time (285 women). In 1997, 122 degrees awarded. *Degree requirements:* Thesis optional, foreign language not required. *Entrance requirements:* GRE General Test, MAT, or NTE. Application deadline: rolling. Application fee: $35. *Expenses:* Tuition $210 per credit hour. Fees $30 per semester. *Financial aid:* Application deadline 3/1. • Dr. Francis M. Fennell, Coordinator, 410-857-2500. Application contact: Jeanette Witt, Coordinator of Graduate Records, 410-857-2513. Fax: 410-857-2515. E-mail: jwitt@wmdc.edu.

Western New Mexico University, School of Education, Silver City, NM 88062-0680. Offerings include secondary education (MAT). School faculty: 16 full-time (9 women). *Application deadline:* rolling. *Application fee:* $10. *Tuition:* $1516 per year full-time, $55 per credit part-time for state residents; $5604 per year full-time, $55 per credit part-time for nonresidents. • Dr. Bonnie Maldonado, Dean, 505-538-6415.

Western Oregon University, School of Education, Department of Secondary Education, Monmouth, OR 97361. Offers programs in humanities (MAT, MS Ed), mathematics (MAT, MS Ed), science (MAT, MS Ed), social science (MAT, MS Ed). Accredited by NCATE. Faculty: 83 full-time (28 women), 26 part-time (11 women), 92.81 FTE. Students: 7 full-time (4 women), 15 part-time (6 women). Average age 38. In 1997, 42 degrees awarded. *Degree requirements:* Written exam required, thesis optional, foreign language not required. *Average time to degree:* master's–1 year full-time, 4 years part-time. *Entrance requirements:* GRE General (average 450 on each section) or MAT (minimum score 30), minimum GPA of 3.0, teaching license. Application deadline: rolling. Application fee: $50. *Financial aid:* In 1997–98, 1 research assistantship averaging $800 per month, 11 teaching assistantships (7 to first-year students) averaging $720 per month were awarded; full and partial tuition waivers and career-related internships or fieldwork also available. Aid available to part-time students. Financial aid application deadline: 3/1; applicants required to submit FAFSA. *Faculty research:* Literacy, science in primary grades, geography education, retention, teacher burnout, work sample methodology, bilingual/English as a second language technology and literacy, classroom discipline, inclusion, media and literacy, interdisciplinary methodology. • Dr. George Cabrera, Chair, 503-838-8471. Fax: 503-838-8228. E-mail: cabrerg@wou.edu. Application contact: Alison Marshall, Director of Admissions, 503-838-8211. Fax: 503-838-8067. E-mail: marshaa@wou.edu.

Western Washington University, Woodring College of Education, Program in Secondary Education, Bellingham, WA 98225-5996. Awards M Ed. Accredited by NCATE. Part-time programs available. Students: 102 full-time (48 women), 24 part-time (12 women). 39 applicants, 79% accepted. In 1997, 45 degrees awarded. *Degree requirements:* Comprehensive exam required, thesis optional, foreign language not required. *Entrance requirements:* GRE General Test, TOEFL, minimum GPA of 3.0 in last 60 semester hours or last 90 quarter hours. Application deadline: 4/1 (2/1 for spring admission). Application fee: $35. *Expenses:* Tuition $4200 per year full-time, $140 per credit part-time for state residents; $12,780 per year full-time, $426 per credit part-time for nonresidents. Fees $249 per year full-time, $83 per quarter part-time. *Financial aid:* Teaching assistantships, partial tuition waivers, Federal Work-Study, institutionally sponsored loans, and career-related internships or fieldwork available. Aid available to part-time students. Financial aid application deadline: 3/31. • Dr. Robert Keiper, Graduate Adviser, 360-650-3986.

Westfield State College, Department of Education, Program in Secondary Education, Westfield, MA 01086. Awards M Ed. *Degree requirements:* Comprehensive exam, practicum required, foreign language and thesis not required. *Entrance requirements:* GRE General Test or MAT, minimum undergraduate GPA of 2.7. Application deadline: rolling. Application fee: $30. *Expenses:* Tuition $145 per credit for state residents; $155 per credit for nonresidents. Fees $90 per semester. *Financial aid:* Application deadline 4/1. • Application contact: Marcia Davio, Graduate Records Clerk, 413-572-8024.

West Texas A&M University, College of Education and Social Sciences, Division of Education, Program in Secondary Education, Canyon, TX 79016-0001. Awards MA, M Ed. Part-time and evening/weekend programs available. Students: 2 full-time (1 woman), 3 part-time (1 woman). Average age 36. 2 applicants, 0% accepted. *Degree requirements:* Thesis (for some programs), comprehensive exam required, foreign language not required. *Average time to degree:* master's–3 years full-time, 6 years part-time. *Entrance requirements:* GRE General Test (combined average 964). Application deadline: rolling. Application fee: $0 ($50 for international students). Electronic applications accepted. *Expenses:* Tuition $46 per semester hour for state residents; $259 per semester hour for nonresidents. Fees $156 per semester (minimum). *Financial aid:* Federal Work-Study available. Aid available to part-time students. • Dr. George Mann, Head, Division of Education, 806-651-2602. Fax: 806-651-2601. E-mail: george.mann@wtamu.edu.

West Virginia University, College of Human Resources and Education, Department of Educational Theory and Practice, Program in Secondary Education, Morgantown, WV 26506. Awards MA. Accredited by NCATE. Students enter program as undergraduates. Part-time programs available. Students: 66 full-time (31 women), 72 part-time (54 women); includes 4 minority (2 African Americans, 1 Asian American, 1 Hispanic), 2 international. Average age 34. 12 applicants, 100% accepted. In 1997, 50 degrees awarded (100% found work related to degree). *Degree requirements:* Content exams required, thesis optional, foreign language not required. *Average time to degree:* master's–3 years full-time, 8 years part-time. *Entrance requirements:* TOEFL (minimum score 550), minimum GPA of 2.75. Application deadline: rolling. Application fee: $45. *Tuition:* $2820 per year full-time, $149 per credit hour part-time for state residents; $8104 per year full-time, $443 per credit hour part-time for nonresidents. *Financial aid:* In 1997–98, 12 teaching assistantships (2 to first-year students) were awarded; full and partial tuition waivers, Federal Work-Study, institutionally sponsored loans, and career-related internships or fieldwork also available. Financial aid application deadline: 2/1; applicants required to submit FAFSA. *Faculty research:* Teacher education, school reform, curriculum development, education technology. • Dr. Jerrald Shive, Chair, Department of Educational Theory and Practice, 304-293-3441. Fax: 304-293-3802.

Wheaton College, Department of Education, Wheaton, IL 60187-5593. Offerings include secondary level (MAT). Accredited by NCATE. *Degree requirements:* Thesis or alternative. *Entrance requirements:* GRE General Test (minimum combined score of 1100; average 1250), MAT (minimum score 50; average 65). Application deadline: 3/1 (priority date; rolling processing; 10/15 for spring admission). Application fee: $20. *Tuition:* $365 per credit hour (minimum).

Whittier College, Department of Education, Program in Secondary Education, Whittier, CA 90608-0634. Awards MA Ed. Part-time and evening/weekend programs available. Faculty: 3 full-time (0 women), 2 part-time (0 women), 3.5 FTE. Students: 10 part-time (2 women); includes 2 minority (both Hispanics). Average age 24. 12 applicants, 83% accepted. In 1997, 6 degrees awarded (100% found work related to degree). *Degree requirements:* Thesis required, foreign language not required. *Entrance requirements:* GRE General Test, MAT. Application deadline: rolling. Application fee: $60. *Tuition:* $330 per credit. *Financial aid:* In 1997–98, 5 fellowships were awarded; career-related internships or fieldwork also available. • Application contact: Catherine George, Credential Analyst, 562-907-4200 Ext. 4443.

Wilkes University, Department of Education, Wilkes-Barre, PA 18766-0002. Offerings include secondary education (MS Ed), with options in biology, chemistry, English, history. Department faculty: 6 full-time, 14 part-time. *Application deadline:* rolling. *Application fee:* $30. *Expenses:* Tuition $12,552 per year full-time, $523 per credit hour part-time. Fees $240 per year full-time, $10 per credit hour part-time. • Dr. Douglas Lynch, Chair, 717-408-4680.

William Carey College, Department of Education, Concentration in Secondary Education, Hattiesburg, MS 39401-5499. Awards M Ed. Faculty: 21 full-time (9 women), 11 part-time (4 women). *Entrance requirements:* NTE, minimum GPA of 2.5. Application deadline: 8/15 (priority date; rolling processing). Application fee: $0. *Tuition:* $130 per semester hour. • Dr. William Hetrick, Dean, College of Education and Psychology, Graduate Division, 601-582-6217.

Wingate University, Program in Education, Wingate, NC 28174. Offerings include secondary education (MA Ed). Accredited by NCATE. Program faculty: 13 part-time (3 women). *Average time to degree:* master's–2 years part-time. *Application deadline:* 8/15 (priority date; rolling processing). *Application fee:* $0. • Dr. Robert A. Shaw, Dean, 704-233-8078. Fax: 704-233-8192. Application contact: Phyllis Starnes, Secretary, School of Education, 704-233-8075. Fax: 704-233-8285.

Winthrop University, College of Education, Program in Curriculum and Instruction, Rock Hill, SC 29733. Offerings include curriculum development (Ed S), with options in elementary education, secondary education, special education. Accredited by NCATE. *Entrance requirements:* NTE, master's degree, 2 years of teaching experience, minimum GPA of 3.0. Application deadline: 7/15 (priority date; rolling processing; 12/1 for spring admission). Application fee: $35. *Tuition:* $3928 per year full-time, $164 per credit hour part-time for state residents; $7060 per year full-time, $294 per credit hour part-time for nonresidents. • Dr. Richard Ingram, Chairman, 803-323-2151. Fax: 803-323-2585. E-mail: ingramr@winthrop.edu. Application contact: Sharon Johnson, Director of Graduate Studies, 803-323-2204. Fax: 803-323-2292. E-mail: johnsons@winthrop.edu.

Winthrop University, College of Education, Program in Secondary Education, Rock Hill, SC 29733. Awards MAT, M Ed. Accredited by NCATE. Part-time programs available. Students: 33 full-time (18 women), 25 part-time (20 women); includes 6 minority (5 African Americans, 1 Hispanic). Average age 33. In 1997, 13 degrees awarded. *Entrance requirements:* GRE General Test (minimum combined score of 800) or NTE (M Ed); GRE General Test or MAT, South Carolina Education Entrance Exam (MAT), minimum GPA of 3.0, sample of written work, South Carolina Class III teaching certificate (M Ed). Application deadline: 7/15 (priority date; rolling processing; 12/1 for spring admission). Application fee: $35. *Tuition:* $3928 per year full-time, $164 per credit hour part-time for state residents; $7060 per year full-time, $294 per credit hour part-time for nonresidents. *Financial aid:* Graduate assistantships, graduate scholarships, Federal Work-Study, and career-related internships or fieldwork available. Aid available to part-time students. Financial aid application deadline: 2/1; applicants required to submit FAFSA. • Dr. Richard Ingram, Chairman, 803-323-2151. Fax: 803-323-2585. E-mail: ingramr@winthrop.edu. Application contact: Sharon Johnson, Director of Graduate Studies, 803-323-2204. Fax: 803-323-2292. E-mail: johnsons@winthrop.edu.

Worcester State College, Graduate Studies, Department of Education, Program in Secondary Education, Worcester, MA 01602-2597. Awards M Ed, Certificate. Part-time and evening/weekend programs available. Students: 4 full-time (0 women), 44 part-time (28 women); includes 1 minority (Native American). Average age 38. In 1997, 18 master's awarded. *Degree requirements:* For master's, comprehensive exam. *Entrance requirements:* For master's, GRE General Test or MAT. Application deadline: rolling. Application fee: $10 ($40 for international students). *Tuition:* $127 per credit hour. *Financial aid:* Career-related internships or fieldwork available. • Dr. Joshua Aisiku, Coordinator, 508-929-8668. Application contact: Andrea Wetmore, Graduate Admissions Counselor, 508-929-8120. E-mail: awetmore@worc.mass.edu.

Wright State University, College of Education and Human Services, Department of Teacher Education, Programs in Classroom Teacher Education, Dayton, OH 45435. Awards MA, M Ed. Accredited by NCATE. Students: 57 full-time (38 women), 39 part-time (36 women); includes 12 minority (9 African Americans, 2 Hispanics, 1 Native American). Average age 34. 38 applicants, 79% accepted. In 1997, 34 degrees awarded. *Degree requirements:* Thesis required (for some programs), foreign language not required. *Entrance requirements:* GRE General Test, MAT, TOEFL (minimum score 550). Application fee: $25. *Tuition:* $5109 per year full-time, $161 per credit hour part-time for state residents; $9039 per year full-time, $282 per credit hour part-time for nonresidents. *Financial aid:* Available to part-time students. Financial aid applicants required to submit FAFSA. • Dr. Donna Cole, Coordinator, 937-775-3273. Fax: 937-775-3301. Application contact: Gerald C. Malicki, Assistant Dean and Director of Graduate Admissions and Records, 937-775-2976. Fax: 937-775-2357. E-mail: wsugrad@wright.edu.

Xavier University, College of Social Sciences, Department of Education, Program in Secondary Education, Cincinnati, OH 45207-2111. Awards M Ed. Part-time programs available. Faculty: 2 full-time (0 women), 5 part-time (3 women), 3.25 FTE. Students: 63 full-time (39 women), 55 part-time (41 women); includes 12 minority (10 African Americans, 1 Asian American, 1 Hispanic). Average age 31. 62 applicants, 65% accepted. In 1997, 47 degrees awarded. *Degree requirements:* Comprehensive exam, research project required, foreign language and thesis not required. *Entrance requirements:* GRE or MAT (minimum score 35), minimum GPA of 2.7. Application deadline: 8/15 (priority date; rolling processing). Application fee: $25. *Financial aid:* In 1997–98, 60 students received aid, including 60 scholarships (20 to first-year students). Aid available to part-time students. *Faculty research:* Ethics, school violence, teaching methods. • Jeff Hutton, Director, 513-745-3702. Fax: 513-745-1052. E-mail: hutton@admin.xu.edu. Application contact: Sheila Speth, Director of Graduate Services, 513-745-3360. Fax: 513-745-1048. E-mail: xugrad@admin.xu.edu.

Youngstown State University, College of Education, Department of Teacher Education, Program in Secondary Education, Youngstown, OH 44555-0002. Awards MS Ed. Accredited by NCATE. Part-time and evening/weekend programs available. Faculty: 9 full-time (5 women), 4 part-time (1 women). Students: 2 full-time (both women), 49 part-time (40 women); includes 1 minority (Hispanic), 2 international. 6 applicants, 67% accepted. In 1997, 24 degrees awarded. *Degree requirements:* Comprehensive exam required, thesis optional, foreign language

Directory: Secondary Education

Youngstown State University (continued)

not required. *Entrance requirements:* TOEFL (minimum score 550), GRE, MAT, or teaching certificate; minimum GPA of 2.5. Application deadline: 8/15 (priority date; rolling processing; 2/15 for spring admission). Application fee: $30 ($75 for international students). *Expenses:* Tuition $90 per credit hour for state residents; $144 per credit hour (minimum) for nonresidents. Fees $528 per year full-time, $244 per year (minimum) part-time. *Financial aid:* In 1997–98, 19 students received aid, including 4 research assistantships averaging $666 per month and totaling $34,080, 15 scholarships totaling $5,762; teaching assistantships, Federal Work-Study, institutionally sponsored loans also available. Aid available to part-time students. Financial aid application deadline: 3/1. *Faculty research:* Critical reflectivity, gender issues in classroom instruction, collaborative research and analysis, literacy methodology. • Application contact: Dr. Peter J. Kasvinsky, Dean of Graduate Studies, 330-742-3091. Fax: 330-742-1580. E-mail: amgrad03@ysub.ysu.edu.

NEW SCHOOL UNIVERSITY

Master of Science in Teaching

Program of Study

The New School offers a Master of Science in Teaching (M.S.T.) program for students who have completed their undergraduate study in the liberal arts and wish to teach on the secondary school level (grades 7–12) in one of the major academic subject areas. Students are educated to be agents of change in urban public schools.

The M.S.T. is an intensive 36-credit program, which students complete within eleven months. Students are accepted into cohort groups who study, research, and teach together. The program's goals focus on preparing students for the kinds of schools that are emerging from the current school reform movement—schools that are small, caring communities, with interdisciplinary and multicultural curricula, where teachers and students have a voice in governance.

Students work with young people both in and out of classrooms from the first semester of the program. They observe, tutor, conduct collaborative classroom-based research, and team teach throughout the year. The program focuses on uniting theory and practice in order to develop teachers capable of transforming traditional schooling.

Upon completion of the program, students receive provisional New York State certification in a secondary school academic subject (e.g., English, math, science, social science, a language other than English) and the master's degree required for permanent certification.

Research Facilities

The Raymond Fogelman Library contains books, standard references, pamphlets, and periodicals essential to the program of study. Matriculated students have access to the Elmer Holmes Bobst Library at New York University and the Cooper Union Library, which are members, with the New School, of the Research Libraries Association of Southern Manhattan. The Academic Computing Center, which has both Macintosh and IBM-compatible platforms, is available to students for their research and writing. Collaborations with alternative secondary schools throughout the city provide off-campus sites for student teaching and observation.

Financial Aid

Scholarships and awards are available to all matriculated students. The Financial Aid Committee considers both merit and need in granting available funds. The University Scholars fund provides added financial support for African-American and Latino students. An extended payment plan allows students to pay tuition in installments throughout the academic year.

Cost of Study

Tuition for the 1998–99 academic year is $612 per credit. A $100 registration fee is charged each semester.

Living and Housing Costs

The University Housing Office maintains a comprehensive resource center with apartment listings. In addition, the office maintains a building where students over 21 years of age may rent apartments, subject to availability. The cost of housing, food, transportation, and living expenses ranges between $8000 and $10,000 per year.

Student Group

Teacher education students in the current cohorts have either come directly from college or are people with varied work backgrounds who want to make a career change. All share a commitment to change and the school reform efforts. They are a diverse group in age, gender, race, and background.

Location

New York City provides students with access to a varied, multicultural, multiethnic environment in which to teach and learn.

The School and The Department

Since its founding in 1919, New School University (formerly the New School for Social Research) has defined its central mission as identifying and illuminating the larger social and political issues of the times through open discussion and instruction. America's first university for adults now consists of seven divisions: the New School, the Graduate Faculty of Political and Social Science, the Milano Graduate School of Management and Urban Policy, Parsons School of Design, the Eugene Lang College, Mannes College of Music, and the School of Dramatic Arts. The New School, the university's adult education division, aims to nurture the widest possible range of thought and offers hundreds of courses in dozens of subjects each term to adult learners in nondegree, degree, and certificate programs. The teacher education program, a graduate program in media studies, a graduate program in creative writing, and an undergraduate program for adults are part of the division. The graduate program in teacher education offers special workshops and classes for teaching professionals and has sponsored public forums and lectures on current trends and issues surrounding the school reform movement.

Applying

Applications from students in liberal arts disciplines are invited. Recent graduates as well as those changing careers are encouraged to apply. In addition to official transcripts, letters of recommendation, and an application fee of $30, each applicant must submit a portfolio of learning and teaching experiences. The portfolio is a significant component of the application and enables a student to individualize and personalize her or his application by providing a fuller picture than might be evident from either a transcript or reference letters. A personal interview is conducted after the application and portfolio have been reviewed. Applications for both admissions and financial aid must be received by May 1 at the latest; earlier applications are invited.

Correspondence and Information

Office of Admissions
Teacher Education Program
New School University
66 West 12 Street, Room 401
New York, New York 10011
Telephone: 212-229-5630
E-mail: admissions@dialnsa.edu

New School University

THE FACULTY

Donna Andrade, Ed.D., Fordham. Director of Student Services at Fairfield College Preparatory School, Connecticut, and National Director of Diversity for the Jesuit Secondary Education Association, Washington, D.C. Ms. Andrade has worked as a consultant to schools on diversity issues, has taught at Fordham and Fairfield universities, and was an English teacher in secondary schools in Connecticut.

Sandra Bowie, Ph.D. candidate, NYU. Former director of the Acting Program at Howard University. Ms. Bowie has taught at Howard and Yale universities and has served as educational director for the Apollo Theater's Arts in Education Program.

Gregory Hamilton, Ed.D. candidate, Columbia Teachers College. Currently full-time faculty, English education, Columbia Teachers College, and middle school language arts and humanities teacher. Formerly, Mr. Hamilton coordinated an ESL adult literacy program for the Consortium for Worker Education. He has worked as a consultant for New York City public schools and presented research on teacher education at the National Council for the Teachers of English. Mr. Hamilton is currently writing his first young adult novel set in India.

Rosana Wong Hiu, Ph.D. candidate, NYU. Former director, ACTWU Worker Education Program of the Consortium for Worker Education. Ms. Hiu has taught native language literacy and ESL for students with minimal literacy proficiency in their native language. She is an adjunct instructor at New York University.

Carolina Mancuso, Ph.D. candidate, NYU. Instructor and writing consultant at NYU and former writer-in-residence at Eugene Lang College. Ms. Mancuso has taught reading workshops in the Department of Educational Services at Brooklyn College. She is the author of works of nonfiction, fiction, poetry, and plays.

Petriana Monize, Ph.D. candidate, NYU. Adjunct Reading and Writing Professor at CUNY; full-time English professor at Indian River Community College in Florida; high school English/language arts teacher at Lemon Bay High School in Florida.

Susan Sutton, Ph.D. candidate, NYU. Former junior and senior high school teacher, field supervisor of student teachers, and academic adviser at NYU. Current research interests include curriculum theory, practitioner research, and critical reflection.

Section 24
Special Focus

This section contains directories of institutions offering graduate work in education of the gifted, education of the multiply handicapped, English as a second language, multilingual and multicultural education, special education, and urban education, followed by in-depth entries submitted by institutions that chose to prepare detailed program descriptions. Additional information about programs listed in the directories but not augmented by an in-depth entry may be obtained by writing directly to the dean of a graduate school or chair of a department at the address given in the directory.

For programs offering related work, see also in this book Administration, Instruction, and Theory; Education; Health-Related Professions; Instructional Levels; Leisure Studies and Recreation; Physical Education and Kinesiology; and Subject Areas; and in Book 2, Psychology and Counseling (School Psychology) and Public, Regional, and Industrial Affairs (Urban Studies).

CONTENTS

Program Directories

Announcements

Cross-Discipline Announcement

In-Depth Descriptions

See also:

Education of the Gifted

Arkansas State University, College of Education, Department of Special Education, State University, AR 72467. Offerings include gifted and talented education (MSE). Accredited by NCATE. Department faculty: 5 full-time (1 woman). *Degree requirements:* Thesis or alternative, comprehensive exam. *Entrance requirements:* GRE General Test or MAT, appropriate bachelor's degree. Application deadline: 7/1 (priority date; rolling processing; 11/15 for spring admission). Application fee: $15 ($25 for international students). *Expenses:* Tuition $2760 per year full-time, $115 per credit hour part-time for state residents; $6936 per year full-time, $289 per credit hour part-time for nonresidents. Fees $506 per year full-time, $44 per semester (minimum) part-time. • Dr. Roberta Daniels, Interim Chair, 870-972-3061. Fax: 870-972-3828. E-mail: rdaniels@kiowa.astate.edu.

Arkansas Tech University, School of Education, Department of Curriculum and Instruction, Russellville, AR 72801-2222. Offerings include gifted education (MSE). Accredited by NCATE. *Application deadline:* 3/1 (priority date; rolling processing; 10/1 for spring admission). *Application fee:* $0 ($30 for international students). *Expenses:* Tuition $98 per credit hour for state residents; $196 per credit hour for nonresidents. Fees $30 per semester. • Head, 501-968-0290. Fax: 501-964-0811.

Ashland University, College of Education, Graduate Studies in Teacher Education, Program in Curriculum and Instruction, Ashland, OH 44805-3702. Offerings include gifted education (M Ed). Accredited by NCATE. Program faculty: 8 full-time (4 women), 24 part-time (9 women). *Degree requirements:* Practicum or thesis. *Entrance requirements:* GRE General Test or MAT, teaching certificate. Application deadline: rolling. Application fee: $15. *Tuition:* $275 per credit hour. • Carl Walley, Program Team Leader, 419-289-5355. E-mail: cwalley@ashland.edu. Application contact: Dr. Joe Bailey, Director, 419-289-5377. Fax: 419-289-5097. E-mail: jbailey@ashland.edu.

Barry University, School of Education, Program in Exceptional Student Education, Miami Shores, FL 33161-6695. Awards MS, Ed S. Part-time and evening/weekend programs available. Faculty: 1 (woman) full-time, 1 part-time (0 women). Students: 71 full-time (67 women), 26 part-time (19 women); includes 32 minority (16 African Americans, 16 Hispanics), 1 international. Average age 38. In 1997, 20 master's awarded. *Degree requirements:* For master's, written comprehensive exam required, foreign language and thesis not required; for Ed S, practicum required, foreign language and thesis not required. *Entrance requirements:* For master's, GRE General Test or MAT, minimum GPA of 3.0; for Ed S, GRE General Test, minimum GPA of 3.0. Application deadline: 5/1 (priority date; rolling processing). Application fee: $30. Electronic applications accepted. *Tuition:* $450 per credit (minimum). *Financial aid:* Partial tuition waivers and career-related internships or fieldwork available. Aid available to part-time students. Financial aid application deadline: 5/1; applicants required to submit FAFSA. • Dr. Clara Wolman, Director, 305-899-3700. Fax: 305-899-3630. E-mail: wolman@aquinas.barry.edu. Application contact: Angela Scott, Enrollment Services, Assistant Dean, 305-899-3112. Fax: 305-899-3149. E-mail: ascott@jeanne.barry.edu.

Barry University, School of Education, Program in Leadership and Education, Miami Shores, FL 33161-6695. Offerings include exceptional student education (PhD). Program faculty: 1 full-time (0 women), 2 part-time (1 woman), 2 FTE. *Degree requirements:* Dissertation. *Entrance requirements:* GRE General Test, minimum GPA of 3.25. Application deadline: 5/1 (priority date; rolling processing). Application fee: $30. Electronic applications accepted. *Tuition:* $450 per credit (minimum). • Dr. Jack Dezek, Chair, 305-899-3700. Fax: 305-899-3630. E-mail: dezek@aquinas.barry.edu. Application contact: Angela Scott, Enrollment Services, Assistant Dean, 305-899-3112. Fax: 305-899-3149. E-mail: ascott@jeanne.barry.edu.

California State University, Los Angeles, School of Education, Division of Special Education, Los Angeles, CA 90032-8530. Offerings include gifted education (MA). Accredited by NCATE. Division faculty: 16 full-time, 11 part-time. *Degree requirements:* Comprehensive exam, project, or thesis required, foreign language not required. *Entrance requirements:* TOEFL (minimum score 550), minimum GPA of 2.75 in last 90 units, teaching certificate. Application deadline: 6/30 (rolling processing; 2/1 for spring admission). Application fee: $55. *Expenses:* Tuition $0 for state residents; $164 per unit for nonresidents. Fees $1763 per year full-time, $1097 per year part-time. • Dr. Philip Chinn, Chair, 213-343-4400.

California State University, Northridge, College of Education, Department of Special Education, Northridge, CA 91330. Offerings include education of the gifted (MA). Accredited by NCATE. Department faculty: 16 full-time, 15 part-time. *Application deadline:* 11/30. *Application fee:* $55. *Expenses:* Tuition $0 for state residents; $246 per unit for nonresidents. Fees $1970 per year full-time, $1304 per year part-time. • Dr. Claire Cavallaro, Chair, 818-677-2596. Application contact: Dr. Ellen Schneiderman, Graduate Coordinator, 818-677-2528.

Carthage College, Division of Teacher Education, Kenosha, WI 53140-1994. Offerings include gifted and talented children (M Ed). College faculty: 6 full-time (4 women), 13 part-time (8 women). *Degree requirements:* Thesis optional, foreign language not required. *Average time to degree:* master's–5 years part-time. *Entrance requirements:* MAT, minimum B average. Application deadline: rolling. Application fee: $25. • Dr. Judith B. Schaumberg, Director of Graduate Programs, 414-551-5876. Fax: 414-551-5704.

Clark Atlanta University, School of Education, Department of Exceptional Student Education, Atlanta, GA 30314. Awards MA, Ed S. Students: 17 full-time (14 women), 30 part-time (22 women); includes 45 minority (all African Americans), 1 international. In 1997, 10 master's awarded. *Degree requirements:* For master's, 1 foreign language (computer language can substitute), thesis; for Ed S, thesis. *Entrance requirements:* For master's, GRE General Test, minimum undergraduate GPA of 2.5; for Ed S, GRE General Test, minimum graduate GPA of 3.0. Application deadline: 4/1 (rolling processing; 11/1 for spring admission). Application fee: $30. *Expenses:* Tuition $9672 per year full-time, $403 per credit hour part-time. Fees $200 per year. *Financial aid:* Application deadline 4/30. • Dr. Brenda Rogers, Chairperson, 404-880-8508. Application contact: Michelle Clark-Davis, Graduate Program Assistant, 404-880-8709.

Cleveland State University, College of Education, Department of Curriculum and Foundations, Cleveland, OH 44115-2440. Offerings include gifted education (M Ed). Department faculty: 14 full-time (9 women). *Entrance requirements:* GRE General Test or MAT (score in 50th percentile or higher). Application deadline: 9/1 (priority date; rolling processing). Application fee: $25. *Expenses:* Tuition $5252 per year full-time, $202 per credit hour part-time for state residents; $10,504 per year full-time, $404 per credit hour part-time for nonresidents. Fees $2.25 per credit hour (minimum). • Dr. David Adams, Interim Chairperson, 216-687-7128. Fax: 216-687-5370. E-mail: d.adams@csuohio.edu.

College of New Rochelle, Division of Education, Program in Gifted Education, New Rochelle, NY 10805-2308. Awards MS Ed, Certificate. Part-time programs available. Faculty: 1 (woman) part-time.5 FTE. Students: 6 part-time (5 women). 3 applicants, 67% accepted. In 1997, 7 master's awarded. *Degree requirements:* For master's, practicum required, foreign language not required. *Average time to degree:* master's–1.2 years full-time, 2.5 years part-time. *Entrance requirements:* For master's, interview; minimum GPA of 3.0 in field, 2.7 overall. Application deadline: 8/1 (priority date; rolling processing). Application fee: $35. *Tuition:* $329 per credit. *Financial aid:* In 1997–98, 3 students received aid, including 2 research assistantships totaling $5,096, 1 assistantship totaling $1,896; career-related internships or fieldwork also available. Aid available to part-time students. • Dr. Melanie Hannigan, Division Head, Division of Education, 914-654-5330.

College of William and Mary, School of Education, Specialization in Gifted Education, Williamsburg, VA 23187-8795. Awards MA Ed. Accredited by NCATE. Part-time programs available. Students: 2 full-time (both women), 6 part-time (5 women); includes 1 minority (Hispanic). Average age 30. 5 applicants, 80% accepted. In 1997, 6 degrees awarded. *Entrance requirements:* GRE or MAT, minimum GPA of 2.5. Application deadline: 2/15 (priority date; 10/1 for spring admission). Application fee: $30. *Tuition:* $5262 per year full-time, $165 per semester hour part-time for state residents; $16,138 per year full-time, $500 per semester hour part-time for nonresidents. *Financial aid:* In 1997–98, graduate assistantships averaging $693 per month were awarded; research assistantships also available. Financial aid application deadline: 2/15. *Faculty research:* National Council of Teachers of Mathematics standards, counseling, self concept, special education, curriculum development. • Dr. George Bass, Coordinator, 757-221-4300. E-mail: gmbass@facstaff.wm.edu.

Converse College, Department of Education, Program in Gifted Education, Spartanburg, SC 29302-0006. Awards M Ed. Part-time programs available. Faculty: 1 full-time, 1 part-time. Students: 23 part-time (20 women); includes 2 minority (both African Americans). Average age 35. 1 applicant, 100% accepted. In 1997, 14 degrees awarded. *Entrance requirements:* NTE, minimum GPA of 2.5, teaching certificate. Application deadline: 5/1 (priority date; rolling processing; 1/30 for spring admission). Application fee: $35. *Tuition:* $185 per credit. *Financial aid:* Career-related internships or fieldwork available. Aid available to part-time students. Financial aid applicants required to submit FAFSA. *Faculty research:* Identification of gifted minorities, arts in gifted education. Total annual research expenditures: $50,000. • Dr. Nancy Breard, Assistant Director of Graduate Education, 864-596-9732.

Drury College, Graduate Programs in Education, Program in Gifted Education, Springfield, MO 65802-3791. Awards M Ed. Accredited by NCATE. Part-time and evening/weekend programs available. Faculty: 3 full-time (2 women), 1 (woman) part-time. Students: 45; includes 1 minority (Asian American), 1 international. Average age 32. 20 applicants, 100% accepted. In 1997, 15 degrees awarded. *Degree requirements:* Thesis required, foreign language not required. *Average time to degree:* master's–1.5 years full-time, 3 years part-time. *Entrance requirements:* MAT (minimum score 35; average 52), minimum GPA of 2.75. Application fee: $15. *Tuition:* $170 per credit hour. *Financial aid:* Career-related internships or fieldwork available. • Bob Roach, Coordinator of Center for Gifted Education, 417-873-7271.

Emporia State University, School of Graduate Studies, The Teachers College, Division of Psychology and Special Education, Program in Special Education, Emporia, KS 66801-5087. Offerings include teaching of the gifted, talented, and creative (MS). Accredited by NCATE. *Degree requirements:* Comprehensive exam or thesis required, foreign language not required. *Entrance requirements:* GRE General Test or MAT, TOEFL (minimum score 550), written exam. Application deadline: 8/15 (priority date; rolling processing). Application fee: $30 ($75 for international students). Electronic applications accepted. *Tuition:* $2300 per year full-time, $103 per credit hour part-time for state residents; $6012 per year full-time, $258 per credit hour part-time for nonresidents. • Dr. Kenneth A. Weaver, Chair, Division of Psychology and Special Education, 316-341-5317. E-mail: weaverke@emporia.edu.

Grand Valley State University, School of Education, Programs in General Education, Program in Education of the Gifted and Talented, Allendale, MI 49401-9403. Awards M Ed. Accredited by NCATE. *Degree requirements:* Thesis or alternative, applied research project. *Entrance requirements:* GRE General Test (minimum combined score of 1300) or minimum GPA of 3.0. Application deadline: rolling. Application fee: $20. • Application contact: Admissions Office, 616-895-2025. Fax: 616-895-3081.

Hardin–Simmons University, Irvin School of Education, Department of Elementary and Secondary Education, Program in Gifted Education, Abilene, TX 79698-0001. Awards M Ed. Part-time programs available. Faculty: 4 full-time (all women), 1 (woman) part-time. Students: 29 part-time (28 women); includes 2 minority (1 African American, 1 Hispanic). Average age 41. In 1997, 21 degrees awarded. *Application deadline:* 8/15 (priority date; rolling processing; 1/5 for spring admission). *Application fee:* $25. *Expenses:* Tuition $280 per semester hour. Fees $630 per year full-time. *Financial aid:* In 1997–98, 13 students received aid, including 5 fellowships (2 to first-year students) averaging $250 per month and totaling $4,500; full and partial tuition waivers, Federal Work-Study, and career-related internships or fieldwork also available. Aid available to part-time students. Financial aid application deadline: 3/15; applicants required to submit FAFSA. *Faculty research:* Authentic assessment, identification, differentiation. • Application contact: Dr. J. Paul Sorrels, Dean of Graduate Studies, 915-670-1298. Fax: 915-670-1564.

Indiana State University, School of Education, Department of Communication Disorders and Special Education, Terre Haute, IN 47809-1401. Offerings include gifted/talented education (MA, MS, Ed S). Accredited by NCATE. Department faculty: 14 full-time (8 women). *Degree requirements:* For Ed S, computer language, thesis. *Entrance requirements:* For Ed S, GRE General Test (minimum combined score of 900), minimum graduate GPA of 3.25. Application deadline: rolling. Application fee: $20. *Tuition:* $143 per credit hour for state residents; $325 per credit hour for nonresidents. • Dr. Raymond Quist, Chairperson, 812-237-3585.

Jacksonville University, College of Arts and Sciences, Division of Education, 2800 University Boulevard North, Jacksonville, FL 32211-3394. Offerings include gifted education (Certificate). *Average time to degree:* master's–1.5 years full-time, 2.5 years part-time. *Entrance requirements:* TOEFL (minimum score 500). Application deadline: 8/1 (priority date; rolling processing; 11/1 for spring admission). Application fee: $25.

Johns Hopkins University, School of Continuing Studies, Division of Education, Department of Teacher Development and Leadership, Baltimore, MD 21218-2699. Offerings include gifted education (MS, Certificate). *Application fee:* $50. • Rochelle Ingram, Chair, 410-516-4957.

Johnson State College, Graduate Program in Education, Program in Education of the Gifted, Johnson, VT 05656-9405. Awards MA Ed. Part-time programs available. Students: 5 part-time (3 women). *Degree requirements:* Thesis or alternative, comprehensive exam required, foreign language not required. *Entrance requirements:* Interview. Application deadline: 7/15 (priority date; rolling processing; 11/1 for spring admission). Application fee: $30. *Expenses:* Tuition $164 per credit for state residents; $383 per credit for nonresidents. Fees $15.90 per credit. *Financial aid:* Federal Work-Study, institutionally sponsored loans, and career-related internships or fieldwork available. Aid available to part-time students. Financial aid application deadline: 3/1; applicants required to submit FAFSA. • Application contact: Catherine H. Higley, Administrative Assistant, 802-635-2356 Ext. 1244. Fax: 802-635-1248. E-mail: higleyc@badger.jsc.vsc.edu.

Kent State University, Graduate School of Education, Department of Educational Foundations and Special Services, Program in Special Education, Kent, OH 44242-0001. Offerings include gifted education (MA, M Ed). Accredited by NCATE. Program faculty: 12 full-time (8 women), 16 part-time (10 women). *Degree requirements:* Thesis (MA) required, foreign language not required. *Entrance requirements:* GRE General Test. Application deadline: rolling. Application fee: $30. *Tuition:* $4752 per year full-time, $216 per credit hour part-time for state residents; $9213 per year full-time, $419 per credit hour part-time for nonresidents. • Dr. Melody Tankersley, Coordinator, 330-672-2477. Application contact: Deborah Barber, Director, Office of Academic Services, 330-672-2862. Fax: 330-672-3549.

Lenoir–Rhyne College, Division of Graduate Programs, Department of Education, Program in Academically Gifted, Hickory, NC 28601. Awards MA. Students: 1 (woman) full-time, 2 part-time (both women). In 1997, 1 degree awarded (100% found work related to degree). *Degree requirements:* Thesis optional, foreign language not required. *Entrance requirements:* GRE General Test (minimum score 450 on verbal section, 1350 combined), minimum GPA of 2.7. Application deadline: 8/1 (12/1 for spring admission). Application fee: $25. *Tuition:* $190 per credit hour. • Dr. Don Hayes, Head, 828-328-7191. Application contact: Dr. Thomas W. Fauquet, Dean of Graduate Studies, 828-328-7275. Fax: 828-328-7368. E-mail: fauquet@lrc.edu.

Mankato State University, College of Education, Department of Curriculum and Instruction, Program in Education of the Gifted and Talented, South Rd and Ellis Ave, PO Box 8400, Mankato, MN 56002-8400. Awards MS. Accredited by NCATE. Students: 0. 0 applicants. *Degree requirements:* Thesis or alternative, comprehensive exam required, foreign language not required. *Entrance requirements:* GRE General Test or MAT, minimum GPA of 3.0 during previous 2 years. Application deadline: 7/10 (priority date; rolling processing; 10/30 for spring admission). Application fee: $20. *Tuition:* $126 per credit (minimum) for state residents; $200 per credit for nonresidents. *Financial aid:* Application deadline 3/15. • Application contact: Joni Roberts, Admissions Coordinator, 507-389-2321. Fax: 507-389-5974. E-mail: grad@mankato.msus.edu.

Maryville University of Saint Louis, School of Education, St. Louis, MO 63141-7299. Offerings include gifted education (MA). Accredited by NCATE. School faculty: 9 full-time (7 women), 15 part-time (9 women). *Degree requirements:* Thesis, project required, foreign language not required. *Average time to degree:* master's–2 years full-time, 4 years part-time. *Entrance requirements:* Minimum GPA of 3.0. Application deadline: rolling. Application fee: $20. Electronic applications accepted. *Expenses:* Tuition $11,480 per year full-time, $345 per credit hour part-time. Fees $120 per year full-time, $60 per year part-time. • Dr. Kathe Rasch, Dean, 314-529-9466. Fax: 314-529-9921. E-mail: krasch@maryville.edu.

Millersville University of Pennsylvania, School of Education, Department of Elementary and Early Childhood Education, Program in Gifted Education, Millersville, PA 17551-0302. Awards M Ed. Accredited by NCATE. Part-time and evening/weekend programs available. Students: 5 part-time (all women). Average age 29. 3 applicants, 100% accepted. In 1997, 2 degrees awarded. *Degree requirements:* Departmental exam, practicum required, foreign language and thesis not required. *Entrance requirements:* MAT (minimum score 35), minimum undergraduate GPA of 2.75, teaching certificate in elementary education. Application deadline: 5/1 (priority date; rolling processing). Application fee: $25. *Tuition:* $3468 per year full-time, $234 per credit part-time for state residents; $6236 per year full-time, $387 per credit part-time for nonresidents. *Financial aid:* In 1997–98, 3 graduate assistantships (2 to first-year students) averaging $445 per month and totaling $12,000 were awarded; Federal Work-Study, institutionally sponsored loans, and career-related internships or fieldwork also available. Aid available to part-time students. Financial aid application deadline: 5/1. *Faculty research:* Instructional strategies, state and federal definitions. • Dr. W. Jack Cassidy, Coordinator, 717-872-3745. Fax: 717-872-3856. Application contact: Dr. Robert J. Labriola, Dean of Graduate Studies, 717-872-3030. Fax: 717-871-2022.

Mississippi University for Women, Division of Education and Human Sciences, Columbus, MS 39701-9998. Offerings include gifted studies (M Ed). Accredited by NCATE. Division faculty: 13 full-time (11 women). *Application deadline:* 4/1 (priority date; rolling processing). *Application fee:* $0 ($25 for international students). *Tuition:* $2556 per year full-time, $142 per hour part-time for state residents; $5546 per year full-time, $308 per hour part-time for nonresidents. • Dr. Suzanne Bean, Head, 601-329-7175. Fax: 601-329-8515. E-mail: sbean@muw.edu.

Norfolk State University, School of Education, Department of Special Education, Program in Education of the Gifted, 2401 Corprew Avenue, Norfolk, VA 23504-3907. Awards MA. Accredited by NCATE. Part-time programs available. Faculty: 7 full-time. Students: 10 full-time (7 women), 7 part-time (all women); includes 10 minority (all African Americans), 7 international. Average age 32. In 1997, 8 degrees awarded. *Degree requirements:* Thesis or alternative required, foreign language not required. *Entrance requirements:* GRE General Test, minimum GPA of 3.0 in major, 2.5 overall. Application deadline: 8/1. Application fee: $30. *Tuition:* $3718 per year full-time, $198 per credit hour part-time for state residents; $7668 per year full-time, $404 per credit hour part-time for nonresidents. *Financial aid:* Fellowships and career-related internships or fieldwork available. *Faculty research:* Identification of gifted minority children. • Dr. Gae Golembiewski, Coordinator, 757-683-8736.

Northeastern Illinois University, College of Education, Department of Special Education, Program in Gifted Education, Chicago, IL 60625-4699. Awards MA. Part-time and evening/weekend programs available. Faculty: 15 full-time (9 women), 3 part-time (all women). Students: 1 (woman) full-time, 20 part-time (18 women); includes 3 minority (1 Asian American, 2 Hispanics). Average age 37. 11 applicants, 45% accepted. In 1997, 4 degrees awarded. *Degree requirements:* Thesis or alternative, comprehensive exam required, foreign language not required. *Entrance requirements:* Teaching certificate or course work in history or philosophy of education, minimum GPA of 2.75. Application deadline: 3/18 (priority date; rolling processing; 9/30 for spring admission). Application fee: $0. *Expenses:* Tuition $2226 per year full-time, $93 per credit hour part-time for state residents; $6678 per year full-time, $278 per credit hour part-time for nonresidents. Fees $358 per year full-time, $14.90 per credit hour part-time. *Financial aid:* 6 students received aid; research assistantships, full and partial tuition waivers, Federal Work-Study, institutionally sponsored loans, and career-related internships or fieldwork available. Aid available to part-time students. *Faculty research:* Effect of inclusion in public school gifted programs, social and emotional needs of gifted children, problem-based learning strategies. • Dr. Edmund Hunt, Coordinator, 773-794-2810. Application contact: Dr. Mohan K. Sood, Dean of Graduate College, 773-583-4050 Ext. 6143. Fax: 773-794-6670.

Ohio University, Graduate Studies, College of Education, School of Curriculum and Instruction, Athens, OH 45701-2979. Offerings include education of the gifted (M Ed). Accredited by NCATE. School faculty: 21 full-time (7 women), 16 part-time (11 women). *Application deadline:* rolling. *Application fee:* $30. *Tuition:* $5430 per year full-time, $216 per quarter hour part-time for state residents; $10,431 per year full-time, $423 per quarter hour part-time for nonresidents. • Dr. Ralph Martin, Director, 740-593-4422. Application contact: Dr. Bonnie Beach, Graduate Chair, 740-593-0523.

Oklahoma City University, Petree College of Arts and Sciences, Division of Education, Program in Gifted and Talented Education, Oklahoma City, OK 73106-1402. Awards M Ed. Part-time and evening/weekend programs available. Students: 1 (woman) full-time, 5 part-time (all women). Average age 33. *Degree requirements:* Thesis or alternative required, foreign language not required. *Entrance requirements:* Minimum GPA of 3.0. Application deadline: 8/25 (priority date; rolling processing; 1/15 for spring admission). Application fee: $35 ($55 for international students). *Expenses:* Tuition $318 per hour. Fees $124 per year. *Financial aid:* Fellowships, partial tuition waivers, Federal Work-Study, institutionally sponsored loans, and career-related internships or fieldwork available. Aid available to part-time students. Financial aid application deadline: 8/1; applicants required to submit FAFSA. • Dr. Cathy Kass, Head, 405-521-5371. E-mail: ckass@lec.okcu.edu. Application contact: Laura L. Rahhal, Director of Graduate Admissions, 800-633-7242 Ext. 2. Fax: 405-521-5356. E-mail: lrahhal1@froda.okcu.edu.

Purdue University, School of Education, Department of Educational Studies, West Lafayette, IN 47907. Offerings include education of the gifted (MS Ed). Accredited by NCATE. Department faculty: 26 full-time (13 women), 23 part-time (14 women). *Application deadline:* 2/1 (9/15 for spring admission). *Application fee:* $30. Electronic applications accepted. *Tuition:* $3500 per year full-time, $126 per credit hour part-time for state residents; $11,720 per year full-time, $387 per credit hour part-time for nonresidents. • Dr. D. H. Schunk, Head, 765-494-9170. Fax: 765-496-1228. E-mail: dschunk@purdue.edu. Application contact: Christine Larsen, Coordinator of Graduate Studies, 765-494-2345. Fax: 765-494-5832. E-mail: gradoffice@soe.purdue.edu.

St. Cloud State University, College of Education, Department of Special Education, St. Cloud, MN 56301-4498. Offerings include gifted and talented (MS). Accredited by NCATE. Department faculty: 9 full-time (4 women), 4 part-time (2 women). *Degree requirements:* Thesis or alternative required, foreign language not required. *Entrance requirements:* GRE General Test, minimum GPA of 2.75. Application fee: $20 ($100 for international students). *Expenses:* Tuition $128 per credit for state residents; $203 per credit for nonresidents. Fees $16.32 per credit. • Dr. Joan Kellet, Chairperson, 320-255-2041. Application contact: Ann Anderson, Graduate Studies Office, 320-255-2113. Fax: 320-654-5371. E-mail: anna@grad.stcloud.msus.edu.

Southern Arkansas University–Magnolia, Graduate Program in Education, Program in Secondary Education, Magnolia, AR 71753. Offerings include gifted and talented education (M Ed). *Degree requirements:* Thesis or alternative, comprehensive exam required, foreign language not required. *Average time to degree:* master's–2 years full-time. *Entrance requirements:* GRE, minimum GPA of 2.5. Application deadline: 8/15. Application fee: $0. *Expenses:* Tuition $95 per hour for state residents; $138 per hour for nonresidents. Fees $2 per hour. • Dr. Danield L. Bernard, Dean, Graduate Studies, Graduate Program in Education, 870-235-4055. Fax: 870-235-5035. E-mail: dlbernard@mail.saumag.edu.

Teachers College, Columbia University, Graduate Faculty of Education, Department of Curriculum and Teaching, Program in Giftedness, 525 West 120th Street, New York, NY 10027-6696. Awards MA, Ed D. Part-time programs available. Faculty: 1 full-time (0 women), 2 part-time (1 woman), 2.2 FTE. Students: 9 full-time (8 women), 36 part-time (30 women); includes 7 minority (3 African Americans, 2 Asian Americans, 2 Hispanics), 4 international. Average age 42. 12 applicants, 67% accepted. In 1997, 2 master's, 1 doctorate awarded. Terminal master's awarded for partial completion of doctoral program. *Degree requirements:* For master's, thesis or alternative required, foreign language not required; for doctorate, dissertation. *Entrance requirements:* For doctorate, GRE General Test or MAT. Application deadline: 5/15 (12/1 for spring admission). Application fee: $50. *Expenses:* Tuition $640 per credit. Fees $120 per semester. *Financial aid:* Research assistantships, full and partial tuition waivers, Federal Work-Study, institutionally sponsored loans, and career-related internships or fieldwork available. Aid available to part-time students. Financial aid application deadline: 2/1. *Faculty research:* Urban and economically disadvantaged gifted children, identification issues with regard to gifted and early childhood giftedness. • Application contact: Victor Singletary, Office of Admissions, 212-678-3710. Fax: 212-678-4171.

Texas A&M International University, Division of Teacher Education and Psychology, 5201 University Boulevard, Laredo, TX 78041-1900. Offerings include gifted and talented (MS Ed). *Degree requirements:* Thesis required (for some programs), foreign language not required. *Entrance requirements:* GRE General Test. Application deadline: 7/15 (priority date; rolling processing; 11/12 for spring admission). Application fee: $0.

Texas A&M University, College of Education, Department of Educational Psychology, College Station, TX 77843. Offerings include educational psychology (MS), with option in gifted and talented education; vocational education/school counseling (M Ed), with option in gifted and talented education. One or more programs accredited by NCATE. Department faculty: 26 full-time (10 women), 2 part-time (both women), 26.9 FTE. *Application deadline:* 2/1. *Application fee:* $35 ($75 for international students). • Douglas J. Palmer, Head, 409-845-1831. Fax: 409-862-1256. Application contact: Graduate Adviser, 409-845-1833.

University of Arkansas at Little Rock, College of Education, Department of Teacher Education, Program in Teaching the Gifted and Talented, Little Rock, AR 72204-1099. Awards M Ed. Accredited by NCATE. Part-time and evening/weekend programs available. Students: 3 full-time (all women), 22 part-time (20 women); includes 1 minority (African American). Average age 34. 16 applicants, 81% accepted. In 1997, 8 degrees awarded. *Degree requirements:* Comprehensive exam required, foreign language and thesis not required. *Entrance requirements:* Interview, minimum GPA of 2.75, GRE General Test (minimum combined score of 1000 on three sections) or teaching certificate. Application deadline: rolling. Application fee: $25 ($30 for international students). *Expenses:* Tuition $2466 per year full-time, $137 per credit hour part-time for state residents; $5256 per year full-time, $292 per credit hour part-time for nonresidents. Fees $216 per year full-time, $36 per semester (minimum) part-time. *Financial aid:* Research assistantships, teaching assistantships, Federal Work-Study, institutionally sponsored loans, and career-related internships or fieldwork available. Aid available to part-time students. Financial aid application deadline: 6/1. • Dr. Mary Prentice, Adviser, 501-569-3124.

University of Connecticut, School of Education, Field of Gifted and Talented, Storrs, CT 06269. Awards MA, PhD. Accredited by NCATE. Faculty: 3. Students: 18 full-time (14 women), 40 part-time (35 women); includes 3 minority (1 African American, 1 Asian American, 1 Hispanic), 11 international. Average age 39. 32 applicants, 100% accepted. In 1997, 17 master's, 3 doctorates awarded. Terminal master's awarded for partial completion of doctoral program. *Degree requirements:* For master's, thesis or alternative; for doctorate, dissertation. *Entrance requirements:* GRE General Test. Application deadline: 6/1 (priority date; rolling processing; 11/1 for spring admission). Application fee: $40 ($45 for international students). *Expenses:* Tuition $5272 per year full-time, $293 per credit part-time for state residents; $13,696 per year full-time, $761 per credit part-time for nonresidents. Fees $948 per year full-time, $640 per year part-time. *Financial aid:* In 1997–98, 4 research assistantships totaling $40,885, 4 teaching assistantships totaling $40,470 were awarded. Financial aid application deadline: 2/15. • Richard L. Schwab, Dean, School of Education, 860-486-3813. Application contact: Judith A. Meagher, Chairperson, 860-486-3815.

University of Georgia, College of Education, Department of Educational Psychology, Athens, GA 30602. Offerings include education of the gifted (Ed D). Accredited by NCATE. Department faculty: 18 full-time (8 women). *Application deadline:* 7/1 (priority date; 11/15 for spring admission). *Application fee:* $30. Electronic applications accepted. *Tuition:* $3290 per year full-time, $643 per semester (minimum) part-time for state residents; $11,300 per year full-time, $1645 per semester (minimum) part-time for nonresidents. • Dr. Joseph M. Wisenbaker, Graduate Coordinator, 706-542-4110. Fax: 706-542-4240. E-mail: joe@coe.uga.edu.

University of Houston, College of Education, Department of Curriculum and Instruction, 4800 Calhoun, Houston, TX 77204-2163. Offerings include education of the gifted (M Ed). Accredited by NCATE. Department faculty: 37 full-time (19 women), 10 part-time (7 women). *Degree requirements:* Comprehensive exam or thesis required, foreign language not required. *Entrance requirements:* GRE General Test or MAT. Application deadline: 7/3 (priority date; rolling processing). Application fee: $35 ($75 for international students). *Expenses:* Tuition $1152 per year full-time, $120 per semester (minimum) part-time for state residents; $4482 per year full-time, $249 per credit hour part-time for nonresidents. Fees $977 per year full-time, $119 per semester (minimum) part-time. • Wilford Weber, Chair, 713-743-4970. Fax: 713-743-9870. E-mail: wweber@uh.edu.

University of Kansas, School of Education, Department of Psychology and Research in Education, Program in Education for the Gifted, Talented and Creative, Lawrence, KS 66045. Awards MS Ed, Ed D, PhD, Ed S. Accredited by NCATE. *Degree requirements:* For doctorate, variable foreign language requirement, dissertation. *Entrance requirements:* For master's, GRE General Test, minimum GPA of 3.0; for doctorate, GRE General Test, minimum graduate GPA of 3.5; for Ed S, minimum GPA of 3.0. Application deadline: 2/15. Application fee: $25. *Expenses:* Tuition $2400 per year full-time, $100 per credit hour part-time for state residents; $7890 per year full-time, $329 per credit hour part-time for nonresidents. Fees $428 per year full-time, $31 per credit hour part-time. • Reva Jenkins-Friedman, Coordinator, 785-864-4526.

University of Nebraska at Kearney, College of Education, Department of Special Education and Communication Disorders, Kearney, NE 68849-0001. Offerings include education of the gifted and talented (MA Ed). Accredited by NCATE. Department faculty: 5 full-time (4 women). *Application deadline:* 8/1 (priority date; rolling processing; 12/15 for spring admission). *Application fee:* $35. *Expenses:* Tuition $1494 per year full-time, $83 per credit hour part-time for state residents; $2826 per year full-time, $157 per credit hour part-time for nonresidents. Fees $229 per year full-time, $11.25 per semester (minimum) part-time. • Dr. Lillian Larson, Chair, 308-865-8314.

University of Northern Iowa, College of Education, Department of Curriculum and Instruction, Program in Education of the Gifted, Cedar Falls, IA 50614. Awards MA Ed. Part-time and

Directories: Education of the Gifted; Education of the Multiply Handicapped

University of Northern Iowa (continued)
evening/weekend programs available. Faculty: 1 full-time. Students: 1 (woman) full-time, 2 part-time (both women); includes 1 international. Average age 33. 3 applicants, 100% accepted. In 1997, 4 degrees awarded. *Degree requirements:* Thesis or alternative required, foreign language not required. *Entrance requirements:* Minimum GPA of 3.5, 3 years of educational experience. Application deadline: 8/1 (priority date; rolling processing). Application fee: $20 ($30 for international students). *Expenses:* Tuition $3166 per year full-time, $176 per hour part-time for state residents; $7805 per year full-time, $176 per hour part-time for nonresidents. Fees $194 per year full-time, $12.50 per semester (minimum) part-time. *Financial aid:* Full and partial tuition waivers, Federal Work-Study, and career-related internships or fieldwork available. Aid available to part-time students. Financial aid application deadline: 3/1. • Dr. William Waack, Director of Teacher Education, 319-273-2265.

University of St. Thomas, School of Education, St. Paul, MN 55105-1096. Offerings include gifted, creative and talented education (MA). Postbaccalaureate distance learning degree programs offered (no on-campus study). School faculty: 32 full-time (18 women), 47 part-time (27 women). *Entrance requirements:* MAT. Application deadline: rolling. Application fee: $50. *Tuition:* $375 per credit hour. • Dr. Richard Podemski, Dean, 612-962-5435. Application contact: Myrna Engebretson, Admissions Counselor, 612-962-5430. Fax: 612-962-5169.

University of South Alabama, College of Education, Department of Special Education, Mobile, AL 36688-0002. Offerings include education of the gifted (M Ed). Accredited by NCATE. Department faculty: 6 full-time (3 women). *Degree requirements:* Comprehensive exam required, foreign language and thesis not required. *Entrance requirements:* GRE General Test (minimum combined score of 1000) or MAT (minimum score 46), minimum GPA of 3.0. Application deadline: 9/1 (priority date; rolling processing). Application fee: $25. • Dr. Terry Cronis, Chairman, 334-460-6460.

University of Southern Mississippi, College of Education and Psychology, Department of Special Education, Hattiesburg, MS 39406-5167. Offerings include education of the gifted (M Ed, Ed D, PhD, Ed S). Department faculty: 7 full-time (4 women). *Degree requirements:* For doctorate, 2 foreign languages, computer language, dissertation. *Entrance requirements:* For master's, GRE General Test, minimum GPA of 2.75; for doctorate, GRE General Test, experience in field, minimum GPA of 3.5; for Ed S, GRE General Test, minimum GPA of 3.25. Application deadline: 8/9 (priority date; rolling processing). Application fee: $0 ($25 for international students). *Tuition:* $2870 per year full-time, $137 per credit hour part-time for state residents; $5972 per year full-time, $172 per credit hour part-time for nonresidents. • Dr. April Miller, Chair, 601-266-5236. Application contact: Director of Graduate Admissions, 601-266-4369.

University of South Florida, College of Education, Department of Special Education, Program in Gifted Education, Tampa, FL 33620-9951. Awards MA. Accredited by NCATE. Part-time and evening/weekend programs available. Faculty: 4 full-time. Students: 1 (woman) full-time, 11 part-time (10 women). Average age 39. 1 applicant, 100% accepted. In 1997, 1 degree awarded. *Entrance requirements:* GRE General Test (minimum combined score of 1000), minimum GPA of 3.5 in last 60 hours. Application deadline: 6/1 (10/15 for spring admission). Application fee: $20. Electronic applications accepted. *Tuition:* $142 per credit hour for state residents; $486 per credit hour for nonresidents. *Financial aid:* 1 student received aid; Federal Work-Study, institutionally sponsored loans available. Aid available to part-time students. Financial aid applicants required to submit FAFSA. *Faculty research:* Ethics, teaching cases, early intervention, systems and program evaluation, school restructuring, social skills, inclusion. • Betty Epanchin, Chairperson, Department of Special Education, 813-974-3760. Fax: 813-974-5542. E-mail: epanchin@tempest.coedu.usf.edu.

University of Southwestern Louisiana, College of Education, Graduate Studies and Research in Education, Program in Education of the Gifted, Lafayette, LA 70503. Awards M Ed. Accredited by NCATE. Faculty: 4 full-time (1 woman). Students: 3 full-time (all women), 18 part-time (14 women); includes 3 minority (all African Americans). 3 applicants, 67% accepted. In 1997, 4 degrees awarded. *Degree requirements:* Thesis or alternative required, foreign language not required. *Entrance requirements:* GRE General Test, teaching certificate. Application deadline: 8/15. Application fee: $5 ($15 for international students). *Tuition:* $2012 per year full-time, $300 per semester (minimum) part-time for state residents; $7244 per year full-time, $300 per semester (minimum) part-time for nonresidents. *Financial aid:* Federal Work-Study available. Financial aid application deadline: 5/1. • Dr. Jeanette Parker, Coordinator, 318-482-6701.

The University of Texas–Pan American, College of Education, Department of Educational Psychology, Edinburg, TX 78539-2999. Offerings include gifted and talented education (M Ed). *Application deadline:* 7/17 (11/16 for spring admission). *Application fee:* $0. *Tuition:* $2156 per year full-time, $283 per semester (minimum) part-time for state residents; $6788 per year full-time, $862 per semester (minimum) part-time for nonresidents.

Whitworth College, Graduate Studies in Education, Program in Gifted and Talented, Spokane, WA 99251-0001. Awards MAT. Accredited by NCATE. Part-time and evening/weekend programs available. *Degree requirements:* Comprehensive exams, internship, practicum, research project, or thesis required, foreign language not required. *Entrance requirements:* GRE General Test. Application deadline: 9/1 (priority date; rolling processing; 2/1 for spring admission). Application fee: $25.

William Carey College, Department of Education, Concentration in Gifted Education, Hattiesburg, MS 39401-5499. Awards M Ed. *Entrance requirements:* NTE, minimum GPA of 2.5. Application deadline: 8/15 (priority date; rolling processing). Application fee: $0. *Tuition:* $130 per semester hour. • Dr. William Hetrick, Dean, College of Education and Psychology, Graduate Division, 601-582-6217.

Wright State University, College of Education and Human Services, Department of Teacher Education, Programs in Special Education, Dayton, OH 45435. Offerings include gifted (MA, M Ed). Accredited by NCATE. *Degree requirements:* Thesis required (for some programs), foreign language not required. *Entrance requirements:* GRE General Test, MAT, TOEFL (minimum score 550). Application fee: $25. *Tuition:* $5109 per year full-time, $161 per credit hour part-time for state residents; $9039 per year full-time, $282 per credit hour part-time for nonresidents. • Dr. Michael Williams, Coordinator, 937-775-2678. Fax: 937-775-3301. Application contact: Gerald C. Malicki, Assistant Dean and Director of Graduate Admissions and Records, 937-775-2976. Fax: 937-775-2357. E-mail: wsugrad@wright.edu.

Xavier University, College of Social Sciences, Department of Education, Program in Special Education, Cincinnati, OH 45207-2111. Offerings include gifted (M Ed). Program faculty: 2 full-time (both women), 9 part-time (6 women), 4.25 FTE. *Degree requirements:* Comprehensive exam, research project required, foreign language and thesis not required. *Entrance requirements:* GRE or MAT (minimum score 35), minimum GPA of 2.7. Application deadline: 8/15 (priority date; rolling processing). Application fee: $25. • Dr. Sharon A. Merrill, Director, 513-745-1078. Fax: 513-745-2920. E-mail: merrill@admin.xu.edu. Application contact: Sheila Speth, Director of Graduate Services, 513-745-3360. Fax: 513-745-1048. E-mail: xugrad@admin.xu.edu.

Youngstown State University, College of Education, Department of Teacher Education, Program in Special Education, Youngstown, OH 44555-0002. Offerings include gifted and talented education (MS Ed). Accredited by NCATE. Program faculty: 4 full-time (3 women), 14 part-time (13 women). *Degree requirements:* Comprehensive exam required, foreign language and thesis not required. *Entrance requirements:* TOEFL (minimum score 550), GRE, MAT, or teaching certificate; interview; minimum GPA of 2.5. Application deadline: 8/15 (priority date; rolling processing; 2/15 for spring admission). Application fee: $30 ($75 for international students). *Expenses:* Tuition $90 per credit hour for state residents; $144 per credit hour (minimum) for nonresidents. Fees $528 per year full-time, $244 per year (minimum) part-time. • Application contact: Dr. Peter J. Kasvinsky, Dean of Graduate Studies, 330-742-3091. Fax: 330-742-1580. E-mail: amgrad03@ysub.ysu.edu.

Education of the Multiply Handicapped

Boston College, Graduate School of Education, Department of Teacher Education/Special Education and Curriculum and Instruction, Multihandicapped and Deaf/Blind Program, Chestnut Hill, MA 02167-9991. Awards M Ed. Accredited by NCATE. Students: 8 full-time (7 women), 10 part-time (9 women); includes 1 minority (Hispanic). 15 applicants, 73% accepted. In 1997, 11 degrees awarded. *Degree requirements:* Comprehensive exam required, thesis not required. *Entrance requirements:* GRE General Test. Application deadline: 3/15 (11/15 for spring admission). Application fee: $40. *Expenses:* Tuition $626 per semester hour. Fees $80 per year (minimum) full-time, $30 per semester part-time. *Financial aid:* Fellowships, research assistantships, teaching assistantships, administrative assistantships, merit scholarships, Federal Work-Study, and career-related internships or fieldwork available. Aid available to part-time students. *Faculty research:* Inclusion, delivery of services for children with special needs. • Application contact: Arline Riordan, Graduate Admissions Director, 617-552-4214. Fax: 617-552-0812. E-mail: riordana@bc.edu.

Cleveland State University, College of Education, Department of Specialized Instructional Programs, Cleveland, OH 44115-2440. Offerings include curriculum and instruction (M Ed), with options in bilingual education, early childhood education, early childhood/special education, education of emerging adolescents, elementary education, English as a second language, learning disabilities, Montessori education, multihandicapped, reading, secondary education. Department faculty: 18 full-time (12 women). *Entrance requirements:* GRE General Test or MAT (score in 50th percentile or higher). Application deadline: 9/1 (priority date; rolling processing). Application fee: $25. *Expenses:* Tuition $5252 per year full-time, $202 per credit hour part-time for state residents; $10,504 per year full-time, $404 per credit hour part-time for nonresidents. Fees $2.25 per credit hour (minimum). • Dr. Jane Zaharias, Chairperson, 216-687-4585. Fax: 216-687-5379. E-mail: j.zaharias@csuohio.edu.

Fresno Pacific University, Graduate School, Programs in Education, Division of Special Education, Fresno, CA 93702-4709. Offerings include severely handicapped (MA Ed). Division faculty: 2 full-time (0 women), 15 part-time (11 women). *Degree requirements:* Thesis or alternative. *Application deadline:* 7/31 (rolling processing). *Application fee:* $75. *Tuition:* $250 per unit. • Dr. Peter Kopriva, Head, 209-453-2202. Fax: 209-453-2001.

Gallaudet University, School of Education and Human Services, Department of Education, Washington, DC 20002-3625. Offerings include education of deaf and hard of hearing students and multihandicapped deaf and hard of hearing students (MA, Ed S). Accredited by NCATE. *Degree requirements:* For master's, thesis optional. *Entrance requirements:* For master's, GRE General Test or MAT. Application deadline: 2/15 (priority date; rolling processing). Application fee: $50. *Expenses:* Tuition $7064 per year full-time, $392 per credit part-time. Fees $50 (one-time charge). • Dr. Barbara Bodner-Johnson, Chair, 202-651-5530. Application contact: Deborah DeStefano, Director of Admissions, 202-651-5253. Fax: 202-651-5744. E-mail: adm_destefan@gallua.bitnet.

Georgia State University, College of Education, Department of Educational Psychology and Special Education, Program in Multiple/Severe Disabilities, Atlanta, GA 30303-3083. Awards M Ed. Accredited by NCATE. Students: 21 full-time (20 women), 23 part-time (21 women); includes 4 minority (all African Americans). Average age 32. 14 applicants, 71% accepted. In 1997, 23 degrees awarded. *Degree requirements:* Comprehensive exams. *Entrance requirements:* GRE General Test (minimum combined score of 800) or MAT (minimum score 44), minimum GPA of 2.5. Application deadline: 7/15 (1/15 for spring admission). Application fee: $25. *Expenses:* Tuition $2673 per year full-time, $99 per semester hour part-time for state residents; $10,692 per year full-time, $396 per semester hour part-time for nonresidents. Fees $228 per year. *Financial aid:* Research assistantships available. *Faculty research:* Cognition, discipline, curriculum development, social maladjustment. • Dr. Ron P. Colarusso, Chair, Department of Educational Psychology and Special Education, 404-651-2310.

Kent State University, Graduate School of Education, Department of Educational Foundations and Special Services, Program in Special Education, Kent, OH 44242-0001. Offerings include multiply handicapped/orthopedically handicapped education (MA, M Ed). Accredited by NCATE. Program faculty: 12 full-time (8 women), 16 part-time (10 women). *Degree requirements:* Thesis (MA) required, foreign language not required. *Entrance requirements:* GRE General Test. Application deadline: rolling. Application fee: $30. *Tuition:* $4752 per year full-time, $216 per credit hour part-time for state residents; $9213 per year full-time, $419 per credit hour part-time for nonresidents. • Dr. Melody Tankersley, Coordinator, 330-672-2477. Application contact: Deborah Barber, Director, Office of Academic Services, 330-672-2862. Fax: 330-672-3549.

Mankato State University, College of Education, Department of Special Education, South Rd and Ellis Ave, PO Box 8400, Mankato, MN 56002-8400. Offerings include severely handicapped (MS). Department faculty: 6 full-time (2 women). *Degree requirements:* Thesis or alternative, comprehensive exam required, foreign language not required. *Entrance requirements:* Minimum GPA of 3.0 during previous 2 years. Application deadline: 7/10 (priority date; rolling processing; 10/30 for spring admission). Application fee: $20. *Tuition:* $126 per credit (minimum) for state residents; $200 per credit for nonresidents. • Dr. Raphael Kudela, Chairperson, 507-389-5650. Application contact: Joni Roberts, Admissions Coordinator, 507-389-2321. Fax: 507-389-5974. E-mail: grad@mankato.msus.edu.

Minot State University, Program in Special Education, Minot, ND 58707-0002. Offerings include special education (MS), with options in infant/toddler, severely multihandicapped. Program faculty: 11 full-time (7 women). *Degree requirements:* Thesis or alternative required, foreign language not required. *Entrance requirements:* GRE General Test (minimum combined score of 1100 rquired) or minimum GPA of 3.0. Application fee: $25. *Tuition:* $2714 per year for state residents; $3235 per year (minimum) for nonresidents. • Dr. David K. Williams, Chairperson, 701-858-3031. E-mail: williamd@warple.cs.misu.nodak.edu. Application contact: Tammy White, Administrative Secretary, 701-858-3250. Fax: 701-839-6933.

Montana State University–Billings, College of Education and Human Services, Department of Special Education and Reading, Program in Special Education, Billings, MT 59101-9984. Offerings include multiply handicapped (MS Sp Ed). Accredited by NCATE. *Degree requirements:* Thesis or professional paper and/or field experience required, foreign language not required. *Entrance requirements:* GRE General Test (minimum combined score of 1350 on three sections) or MAT (minimum score 38), minimum GPA of 3.0 (undergraduate), 3.25 (graduate). Application deadline: 8/1 (priority date; rolling processing; 1/1 for spring admission). Application fee: $30. *Expenses:* Tuition $2253 per year full-time, $397 per semester (minimum) part-time for state residents; $5313 per year full-time, $907 per semester (minimum) part-time for nonresidents. Fees $378 per year full-time, $105 per semester (minimum) part-time.

Norfolk State University, School of Education, Department of Special Education, Program in Orthopedic Education and Education of the Multiply Handicapped and Health Impaired, 2401 Corprew Avenue, Norfolk, VA 23504-3907. Awards MA. Accredited by NCATE. Part-time programs available. Faculty: 7 full-time, 1 part-time. Students: 17 full-time (13 women), 3 part-time (all women); includes 18 minority (17 African Americans, 1 Asian American), 1 international. Average age 35. In 1997, 14 degrees awarded. *Degree requirements:* Thesis or alternative required, foreign language not required. *Entrance requirements:* GRE, minimum GPA of 3.0 in major, 2.5 overall. Application deadline: 8/1. Application fee: $30. *Tuition:* $3718 per year full-time, $198 per credit hour part-time for state residents; $7668 per year full-time, $404 per credit hour part-time for nonresidents. *Financial aid:* In 1997–98, 2 fellowships were awarded; career-related internships or fieldwork also available. • Dr. Helen Bessant-Byrd, Coordinator, 757-683-8733.

University of Arkansas at Little Rock, College of Education, Department of Teacher Education, Program in Special Education, Little Rock, AR 72204-1099. Offerings include teaching persons with severe disabilities (M Ed). Accredited by NCATE. *Degree requirements:* Comprehensive exam, portfolio or thesis required, foreign language not required. *Entrance requirements:* Interview, minimum GPA of 2.75, GRE General Test (minimum combined score of 1000 on three sections) or teaching certificate. Application deadline: rolling. Application fee: $25 ($30 for international students). *Expenses:* Tuition $2466 per year full-time, $137 per credit hour part-time for state residents; $5256 per year full-time, $292 per credit hour part-time for nonresidents. Fees $216 per year full-time, $36 per semester (minimum) part-time. • Application contact: Dr. Mary Hendricks, Adviser, 501-569-3335.

University of South Alabama, College of Education, Department of Special Education, Mobile, AL 36688-0002. Offerings include multihandicapped education (M Ed). Accredited by NCATE. Department faculty: 6 full-time (3 women). *Degree requirements:* Comprehensive exam required, foreign language and thesis not required. *Entrance requirements:* GRE General Test (minimum combined score of 1000) or MAT (minimum score 46), minimum GPA of 3.0. Application deadline: 9/1 (priority date; rolling processing). Application fee: $25. • Dr. Terry Cronis, Chairman, 334-460-6460.

Valdosta State University, College of Education, Department of Special Education, Valdosta, GA 31698. Offerings include education of the multiply handicapped (M Ed, Ed S). Accredited by NCATE. Department faculty: 14 full-time (6 women). *Entrance requirements:* For master's, GRE General Test (minimum combined score of 800); for Ed S, GRE General Test (minimum combined score of 900). Application deadline: 8/1 (rolling processing; 11/15 for spring admission). Application fee: $10. *Expenses:* Tuition $2472 per year full-time, $83 per semester hour part-time for state residents; $8472 per year full-time, $333 per semester hour part-time for nonresidents. Fees $236 per year full-time. • Dr. Phillip Gunter, Head, 912-333-5932. E-mail: pgunter@grits.valdosta.peachnet.edu.

Western Oregon University, School of Education, Department of Special Education, Monmouth, OR 97361. Offerings include multihandicapped education (MS Ed). Accredited by NCATE. Department faculty: 15 full-time (11 women), 8 part-time (5 women), 19.04 FTE. *Degree requirements:* Oral exam, portfolio, written exam required, thesis optional, foreign language not required. *Average time to degree:* master's–1 year full-time, 5 years part-time. *Entrance requirements:* GRE General Test (average 450 on each section) or MAT (minimum score 30), interview, minimum GPA of 3.0. Application deadline: rolling. Application fee: $50. • Dr. Joseph Sendelbaugh, Chair, 503-838-8730. Fax: 503-838-8228. E-mail: sedelj@wou.edu. Application contact: Alison Marshall, Director of Admissions, 503-838-8211. Fax: 503-838-8067. E-mail: marshaa@wou.edu.

Wright State University, College of Education and Human Services, Department of Teacher Education, Programs in Special Education, Dayton, OH 45435. Offerings include multiple handicapped (MA, M Ed). Accredited by NCATE. *Degree requirements:* Thesis required (for some programs), foreign language not required. *Entrance requirements:* GRE General Test, MAT, TOEFL (minimum score 550). Application fee: $25. *Tuition:* $5109 per year full-time, $161 per credit hour part-time for state residents; $9039 per year full-time, $282 per credit hour part-time for nonresidents. • Dr. Michael Williams, Coordinator, 937-775-2678. Fax: 937-775-3301. Application contact: Gerald C. Malicki, Assistant Dean and Director of Graduate Admissions and Records, 937-775-2976. Fax: 937-775-2357. E-mail: wsugrad@wright.edu.

Xavier University, College of Social Sciences, Department of Education, Program in Special Education, Cincinnati, OH 45207-2111. Offerings include multiple handicapped (M Ed). Program faculty: 2 full-time (both women), 9 part-time (6 women), 4.25 FTE. *Degree requirements:* Comprehensive exam, research project required, foreign language and thesis not required. *Entrance requirements:* GRE or MAT (minimum score 35), minimum GPA of 2.7. Application deadline: 8/15 (priority date; rolling processing). Application fee: $25. • Dr. Sharon A. Merrill, Director, 513-745-1078. Fax: 513-745-2920. E-mail: merrill@admin.xu.edu. Application contact: Sheila Speth, Director of Graduate Services, 513-745-3360. Fax: 513-745-1048. E-mail: xugrad@admin.xu.edu.

English as a Second Language

Adelphi University, School of Education, Program in Teaching English to Speakers of Other Languages, Garden City, NY 11530. Awards MA, Certificate. Part-time and evening/weekend programs available. Students: 23 full-time (20 women), 97 part-time (75 women); includes 32 minority (9 African Americans, 5 Asian Americans, 18 Hispanics), 1 international. Average age 35. In 1997, 72 master's awarded. *Application deadline:* rolling. *Application fee:* $50. *Expenses:* Tuition $16,000 per year full-time, $485 per credit part-time. Fees $500 per year full-time, $150 per semester part-time. *Financial aid:* Research assistantships available. Financial aid application deadline: 3/1. *Faculty research:* Theories of language acquisition, English as a second language in the content areas, apprenticeship in English as a second language instruction. • Dr. Billie Robbins, Director, 516-877-4080. Application contact: Jennifer Spiegel, Associate Director of Graduate Admissions, 516-877-3055.

American University, College of Arts and Sciences, Department of Language and Foreign Studies, Program in Teaching English to Speakers of Other Languages, Washington, DC 20016-8001. Awards MA, Certificate. Faculty: 2 full-time (both women), 4 part-time (3 women). Students: 15 full-time (11 women), 14 part-time (13 women); includes 7 minority (4 African Americans, 2 Asian Americans, 1 Hispanic), 8 international. 63 applicants, 83% accepted. In 1997, 20 master's awarded. *Degree requirements:* For master's, 1 foreign language, thesis or alternative, comprehensive exams. *Entrance requirements:* For master's, TOEFL (minimum score 600). Application deadline: 2/1 (10/1 for spring admission). Application fee: $50. *Expenses:* Tuition $687 per credit hour. Fees $180 per year full-time, $110 per year part-time. *Financial aid:* Application deadline 2/1. • Application contact: Prof. Terry Waldspunger, Graduate Adviser, 202-885-2245. E-mail: twaldsp@american.edu.

American University, College of Arts and Sciences, School of Education, Program in English for Speakers of Other Languages, Washington, DC 20016-8001. Awards MAT. Faculty: 8 full-time (5 women), 10 part-time (8 women), 11.3 FTE. Students: 1 (woman) full-time, 3 part-time (all women); includes 2 minority (both Asian Americans). 5 applicants, 80% accepted. *Degree requirements:* Thesis or alternative required, foreign language not required. *Entrance requirements:* GRE General Test or MAT, minimum GPA of 3.0. Application deadline: 2/1 (10/1 for spring admission). Application fee: $50. *Expenses:* Tuition $687 per credit hour. Fees $180 per year full-time, $110 per year part-time. *Financial aid:* Application deadline 2/1. • Application contact: Tim Willmot, Academic Coordinator, 202-885-3716. Fax: 202-885-1187. E-mail: tw7106a@american.edu.

American University in Cairo, Graduate Studies, School of Humanities and Social Sciences, English Language Institute, Cairo, Egypt. Offers program in teaching English as a foreign language (MA, Diploma). Part-time programs available. *Degree requirements:* For master's, 1 foreign language required, thesis optional. *Entrance requirements:* For master's, English entrance exam and/or TOEFL. Application fee: $35.

Andrews University, School of Graduate Studies, School of Education, Department of Teaching/Learning/Administration, Berrien Springs, MI 49104. Offerings include secondary education (MAT), with options in biology, education, English, English as a second language, French, history, physics. *Application deadline:* 8/15 (rolling processing). *Application fee:* $30. *Expenses:* Tuition $290 per quarter hour (minimum). Fees $75 per quarter. • Dr. William H. Green, Chair, 616-471-3465.

Arizona State University, College of Liberal Arts and Sciences, Department of English, Program in Teaching English as a Second Language, Tempe, AZ 85287. Awards MTESL. *Entrance requirements:* GRE. Application fee: $45. *Expenses:* Tuition $2088 per year full-time, $110 per hour part-time for state residents; $9040 per year full-time, $377 per hour part-time for nonresidents. Fees $72 per year full-time, $18 per semester (minimum) part-time. • Dr. Roy Major, Director, 602-965-3364.

Azusa Pacific University, College of Liberal Arts and Sciences, Department of Global Studies and Sociology, Azusa, CA 91702-7000. Offers program in teaching English to speakers of other languages (MA, Certificate). Part-time programs available. Postbaccalaureate distance learning degree programs offered (minimal on-campus study). Faculty: 3 full-time (0 women), 2 part-time (both women). Students: 30; includes 5 minority (1 African American, 2 Asian Americans, 2 Hispanics), 20 international. Average age 25. In 1997, 17 master's awarded. *Degree requirements:* For master's, thesis optional, foreign language not required. *Entrance requirements:* For master's, TOEFL (minimum score 550), 8 units of a foreign language or equivalent. Application deadline: 9/5 (rolling processing; 2/5 for spring admission). Application fee: $45 ($65 for international students). *Expenses:* Tuition $350 per unit. Fees $57 per year. *Financial aid:* Career-related internships or fieldwork available. Financial aid application deadline: 3/2. *Faculty research:* E-mail as a tool for English as a Foreign Language pedagogy, language program design, English as a Foreign Language in China, second language acquisition. • Dr. Richard Slimbach, Chairman, 626-969-3434. E-mail: slimbach@apu.edu. Application contact: Ann Grave, Director, Graduate Admissions, 626-815-5470. Fax: 626-815-5445. E-mail: gradcenter@apu.edu.

Azusa Pacific University, School of Education and Behavioral Studies, Department of Education, Program in Language Development, Azusa, CA 91702-7000. Awards MA. Faculty: 2 full-time (1 woman), 22 part-time (17 women). Students: 30. *Degree requirements:* Comprehensive exam or thesis, core exams, oral presentation required, foreign language not required. *Entrance requirements:* 12 units of previous course work in education, minimum GPA of 3.0. Application fee: $45 ($65 for international students). *Expenses:* Tuition $350 per unit. Fees $57 per year. *Faculty research:* Biliteracy development, home-school connections, integrated curriculum. • Application contact: Dr. Dan Doorn, Director, 626-815-5371.

Biola University, School of Intercultural Studies, La Mirada, CA 90639-0001. Offerings include teaching English to speakers of other languages (MA, Certificate). School faculty: 9 full-time (3 women). *Average time to degree:* master's–2 years full-time, 4 years part-time; doctorate–5 years full-time, 7 years part-time. *Application deadline:* 6/1 (rolling processing; 1/1 for spring admission). *Application fee:* $35. *Expenses:* Tuition $9810 per year full-time, $327 per unit part-time. Fees $40 per year full-time. • Dr. Donald Douglas, Dean, 562-903-4844. Fax: 562-903-4748. Application contact: Roy Allinson, Director of Graduate Admissions, 562-903-4752. Fax: 562-903-4709. E-mail: admissions@biola.edu.

Bishop's University, School of Education, Lennoxville, PQ J1M 1Z7, Canada. Offerings include teaching English as a second language (Certificate). Postbaccalaureate distance learning degree programs offered (minimal on-campus study). School faculty: 4 full-time (3 women), 3 part-time (1 woman). *Average time to degree:* master's–4 years part-time. *Application deadline:* 3/1 (priority date). *Application fee:* $40. • Dr. W. Duffie Van Balkom, Director, 819-822-9658. Application contact: Jane Wilson, Director of Admissions, 819-822-9600 Ext. 2220. Fax: 819-822-9661. E-mail: jwilson@ubishops.ca.

Boston University, School of Education, Department of Developmental Studies and Counseling, Teaching of English to Speakers of Other Languages Program, Boston, MA 02215. Awards Ed M, CAGS. Students: 14 full-time (all women), 22 part-time (18 women); includes 2 minority (1 Asian American, 1 Native American), 5 international. Average age 31. In 1997, 29 master's awarded. *Degree requirements:* For CAGS, comprehensive exam required, foreign language and thesis not required. *Entrance requirements:* GRE or MAT, TOEFL. Application deadline: 2/15 (priority date; rolling processing). Application fee: $50. *Expenses:* Tuition $22,830 per year full-time, $713 per credit part-time. Fees $218 per year full-time, $40 per semester part-time. *Financial aid:* Application deadline 3/30. *Faculty research:* Second language acquisition, innovative approaches to language teaching. • Dr. Steven Molinsky, Coordinator, 617-353-3233. E-mail: tesol@bu.edu.

Bowling Green State University, College of Arts and Sciences, Department of English, Program in English, Bowling Green, OH 43403. Offerings include teaching English as a second language (MA). *Degree requirements:* Thesis required (for some programs), foreign language not required. *Entrance requirements:* GRE General Test, TOEFL (minimum score 580). Application fee: $30. *Tuition:* $6070 per year full-time, $284 per credit hour part-time for state residents; $11,358 per year full-time, $536 per credit hour part-time for nonresidents. • Dr. Thomas Wymer, Graduate Coordinator, 419-372-6864.

Brigham Young University, College of Humanities, Department of Linguistics, Provo, UT 84602-6278. Offerings include teaching English as a second language (MA, Certificate). Department faculty: 12 full-time (3 women), 3 part-time (1 woman), 13 FTE. *Degree requirements:* For master's, variable foreign language requirement, thesis; for Certificate, 1 foreign language required, thesis not required. *Average time to degree:* master's–2.5 years full-time, 3.5 years part-time; other advanced degree–1 year full-time, 2 years part-time. *Entrance requirements:* GRE General Test, TOEFL (minimum score 580), minimum GPA of 3.6 in last 60 hours. Application deadline: 2/1 (2/1 for spring admission). Application fee: $30. *Tuition:* $3200 per

Directory: English as a Second Language

Brigham Young University (continued)
year full-time, $178 per credit hour part-time for state residents; $4800 per year full-time, $266 per credit hour part-time for nonresidents. • Dr. John S. Robertson, Chair, 801-378-2937. E-mail: john_robertson@byu.edu. Application contact: Belva Burgess, Secretary, 801-378-2937. Fax: 801-378-8295. E-mail: belva_burgess@byu.edu.

Brigham Young University, David O. McKay School of Education, Department of Teacher Education, Provo, UT 84602-1001. Offerings include teaching English to speakers of other languages (Certificate). Accredited by NCATE. Certificate new for fall 1998. Department faculty: 15 full-time (1 woman). *Average time to degree:* master's–2 years full-time, 3 years part-time. *Application deadline:* 2/15 (rolling processing). *Application fee:* $30. *Tuition:* $3200 per year full-time, $178 per credit hour part-time for state residents; $4800 per year full-time, $266 per credit hour part-time for nonresidents. • Dr. M. Winston Egan, Chair, 801-378-4077. E-mail: winn_egan@byu.edu. Application contact: Eual E. Monroe, Graduate Coordinator, 801-378-4843. Fax: 801-378-3570. E-mail: eula_monroe@byu.edu.

Brock University, Faculty of Education, St. Catharines, ON L2S 3A1, Canada. Offerings include teaching English as a second language (M Ed). M Ed (teaching English as a second language) new for fall 1998. Faculty: 37 full-time (14 women), 24 part-time (15 women). *Degree requirements:* Thesis optional, foreign language not required. *Average time to degree:* master's–2 years full-time, 5 years part-time. *Entrance requirements:* B Ed, 1 year of teaching experience. Application deadline: 4/12 (rolling processing). Application fee: $35. *Expenses:* Tuition $5185 per year full-time, $2074 per year part-time for Canadian residents; $10,800 per year for nonresidents. Fees $90 per year. • Victor D. Cicci, Acting Dean, 905-688-5550 Ext. 3712. Fax: 905-685-4131. E-mail: vcicci@dewey.ed.brocku.ca. Application contact: Ellie Koop, Assistant Registrar, Graduate Studies, 905-688-5550 Ext. 4467. Fax: 905-988-5488. E-mail: ekoop@spartan.ac.brocku.ca.

California State University, Dominguez Hills, Department of English, Carson, CA 90747-0001. Offerings include teaching English as a second language (Certificate). *Application deadline:* 6/1. *Application fee:* $55. *Expenses:* Tuition $0 for state residents; $246 per unit for nonresidents. Fees $1896 per year full-time, $1230 per year part-time. • Dr. Agnes Yamada, Chair, 310-243-3322. Application contact: Admissions Office, 310-243-3600.

California State University, Fresno, Division of Graduate Studies, School of Arts and Humanities, Department of Linguistics, 5241 North Maple Avenue, Fresno, CA 93740. Offerings include linguistics (MA), with options in English as a second language, general linguistics. Department faculty: 7 full-time (2 women). *Average time to degree:* master's–3.5 years full-time. *Entrance requirements:* GRE General Test, TOEFL (minimum score 550), minimum GPA of 3.0. Application deadline: 8/1 (priority date; rolling processing; 12/1 for spring admission). Application fee: $55. Electronic applications accepted. *Expenses:* Tuition $0 for state residents; $246 per unit for nonresidents. Fees $1872 per year full-time, $1206 per year part-time. • Dr. George Raney, Chair, 209-278-2441. E-mail: george_raney@csufresno.edu. Application contact: Graham Thurgood, Graduate Program Coordinator, 209-278-2136. Fax: 209-278-7299. E-mail: graham_thurgood@csufresno.edu.

California State University, Fullerton, School of Humanities and Social Sciences, Department of Foreign Languages and Literatures, PO Box 34080, Fullerton, CA 92834-9480. Offerings include teaching English to speakers of other languages (MS). Department faculty: 19 full-time (10 women), 18 part-time, 24.5 FTE. *Application fee:* $55. *Expenses:* Tuition $0 for state residents; $246 per unit for nonresidents. Fees $1947 per year full-time, $1281 per year part-time. • Dr. Lee Gilbert, Chair, 714-278-3534.

California State University, Los Angeles, School of Education, Division of Educational Foundations and Interdivisional Studies, Major in Teaching English to Speakers of Other Languages, Los Angeles, CA 90032-8530. Awards MA. Accredited by NCATE. Students: 27 full-time (18 women), 71 part-time (53 women); includes 47 minority (2 African Americans, 28 Asian Americans, 17 Hispanics), 23 international. In 1997, 41 degrees awarded. *Entrance requirements:* TOEFL (minimum score 550), minimum GPA of 2.75 in last 90 units, teaching certificate. Application deadline: 6/30 (rolling processing; 2/1 for spring admission). Application fee: $55. *Expenses:* Tuition $0 for state residents; $164 per unit for nonresidents. Fees $1763 per year full-time, $1097 per year part-time. *Financial aid:* 17 students received aid. Financial aid application deadline: 3/1. • Dr. Simeon Slovacek, Chair, Division of Educational Foundations and Interdivisional Studies, 213-343-4330.

California State University, Sacramento, School of Arts and Letters, Department of English, Sacramento, CA 95819-6048. Offerings include teaching English to speakers of other languages (MA). *Degree requirements:* Thesis, project, or comprehensive exam; writing proficiency exam required, foreign language not required. *Entrance requirements:* TOEFL (minimum score 600), portfolio (creative writing); minimum GPA of 3.0 in English, 2.75 overall during previous 2 years. Application deadline: 4/15 (11/1 for spring admission). Application fee: $55. *Expenses:* Tuition $0 for state residents; $246 per unit for nonresidents. Fees $2012 per year full-time, $1346 per year part-time. • Dr. Mark Hennelly, Chairman, 916-278-5745. Application contact: Dr. David Madden, Coordinator, 916-278-6247.

California State University, San Bernardino, Graduate Studies, School of Education, San Bernardino, CA 92407-2397. Offerings include English as a second language (MA). School faculty: 77 full-time (38 women). *Application deadline:* 8/31 (priority date). *Application fee:* $55. *Expenses:* Tuition $0 for state residents; $164 per unit for nonresidents. Fees $1922 per year full-time, $1256 per year part-time. • Patricia Arlin, Dean, 909-880-3600. Fax: 909-880-7011.

California State University, San Bernardino, Graduate Studies, School of Humanities, Department of English, San Bernardino, CA 92407-2397. Offerings include English as a second language/linguistics (MA). Department faculty: 14 full-time (6 women), 1 (woman) part-time. *Degree requirements:* 1 foreign language, thesis. *Entrance requirements:* BA in English or linguistics, minimum GPA of 3.0. Application deadline: 8/31 (priority date). Application fee: $55. *Expenses:* Tuition $0 for state residents; $164 per unit for nonresidents. Fees $1922 per year full-time, $1256 per year part-time. • Sandra Kamusikiri, Chair, 909-880-5834. Fax: 909-880-7086.

California State University, Stanislaus, College of Arts, Letters, and Sciences, Department of English, Foreign Languages, and Philosophy, Turlock, CA 95382. Offerings include teaching English to speakers of other languages (MA). *Degree requirements:* 1 foreign language, thesis or alternative, comprehensive exam. *Entrance requirements:* GRE General Test, GRE Subject Test, bachelor's degree in English. Application fee: $55. *Expenses:* Tuition $0 for state residents; $246 per unit for nonresidents. Fees $1779 per year full-time, $1113 per year part-time. • Dr. George Settera, Chair, 209-667-3361. Application contact: Susan Marshall, Coordinator, Graduate Program, 209-667-3361.

Cardinal Stritch University, College of Education, Department of Education, Milwaukee, WI 53217-3985. Offerings include professional development (ME), with options in English as a second language, teaching. Accredited by NCATE. ME (Catholic urban educator) offered in collaboration with the Archdiocese of Milwaukee. *Application deadline:* 4/1 (priority date; rolling processing). *Application fee:* $20. *Expenses:* Tuition $338 per credit. Fees $25 per semester. • Dr. Nancy Blair, Chair, 414-410-4367. Application contact: Amy Knox, Graduate Admissions Officer, 414-410-4042.

Carson-Newman College, Graduate Program in Education, Jefferson City, TN 37760. Offerings include teaching English as a second language (MATESL). Accredited by NCATE. College faculty: 18 full-time (8 women), 7 part-time (5 women). *Application deadline:* 7/15 (priority date; rolling processing). *Application fee:* $25 ($50 for international students). *Expenses:* Tuition $190 per credit hour. Fees $10 per year. • Dr. Margaret A. Hypes, Chair, 423-471-3461. Application contact: Jane W. McGill, Graduate Admissions and Services Adviser, 423-471-3460. Fax: 423-471-3475.

The Catholic University of America, School of Arts and Sciences, Department of Education, Washington, DC 20064. Offerings include English as a second language (MA). Accredited by NCATE. MA (English as a second language) new for fall 1998. Department faculty: 13 full-time (8 women), 2 part-time (both women), 14 FTE. *Degree requirements:* Comprehensive exam required, foreign language not required. *Entrance requirements:* GRE General Test, TOEFL. Application deadline: 8/1 (priority date; rolling processing; 12/1 for spring admission). Application fee: $50. *Expenses:* Tuition $17,325 per year full-time, $668 per credit hour part-time. Fees $680 per year full-time, $360 per year part-time. • Chair, 202-319-5800. Fax: 202-319-5815.

Central Connecticut State University, School of Arts and Sciences, Department of English, Program in Teaching English to Speakers of Other Languages, New Britain, CT 06050-4010. Awards MS. Part-time and evening/weekend programs available. Students: 12 full-time (8 women), 21 part-time (14 women); includes 2 minority (1 Hispanic, 1 Native American), 5 international. Average age 36. 47 applicants, 40% accepted. In 1997, 12 degrees awarded. *Degree requirements:* Thesis or alternative, comprehensive exam required, foreign language not required. *Entrance requirements:* TOEFL (minimum score 550), minimum GPA of 2.7, knowledge of second language (preferred). Application deadline: 6/1 (priority date; rolling processing; 12/1 for spring admission). Application fee: $40. *Expenses:* Tuition $4458 per year full-time, $175 per credit hour part-time for state residents; $9943 per year full-time, $175 per credit hour part-time for nonresidents. Fees $45 per semester. *Financial aid:* Federal Work-Study available. Financial aid application deadline: 3/15; applicants required to submit FAFSA. *Faculty research:* Phonology, general linguistics, second language writing, East Asian languages, English language structure. • Dr. Andrea Osburne, Coordinator, Department of English, 860-832-2748.

Central Michigan University, College of Humanities and Social and Behavioral Sciences, Department of English Language and Literature, Mount Pleasant, MI 48859. Offerings include teaching English to speakers of other languages (MA). Department faculty: 41 full-time (22 women). *Degree requirements:* Thesis or alternative required, foreign language not required. *Entrance requirements:* Michigan English Language Assessment Battery (minimum score 85), TOEFL (minimum score 550), minimum GPA of 2.7, portfolio. Application deadline: 3/1 (priority date; rolling processing). Application fee: $30. *Expenses:* Tuition $139 per credit hour (minimum) for state residents; $276 per credit hour (minimum) for nonresidents. Fees $260 per year full-time, $150 per semester part-time. • Dr. Stephen Holder, Chairperson, 517-774-3171. Fax: 517-774-7106.

Central Missouri State University, College of Arts and Sciences, Department of English and Philosophy, Warrensburg, MO 64093. Offerings include teaching English as a second language (MA). Department faculty: 30 full-time. *Application deadline:* 6/30 (priority date; rolling processing). *Application fee:* $25 ($50 for international students). *Tuition:* $3288 per year full-time, $137 per credit hour part-time for state residents; $5928 per year full-time, $274 per credit hour part-time for nonresidents. • Dr. David Smith, Chair, 660-543-4425. Fax: 660-543-8544. E-mail: mxs51750@cmsu2.cmsu.edu.

Central Washington University, College of Arts and Humanities, Department of English, Ellensburg, WA 98926. Offerings include teaching English as a foreign language (MA), teaching English as a second language (MA). Department faculty: 21 full-time (7 women). *Degree requirements:* Thesis or alternative required, foreign language not required. *Entrance requirements:* GRE General Test, minimum GPA of 3.0, sample of written work. Application deadline: 4/1 (priority date; rolling processing; 1/1 for spring admission). Application fee: $35. *Expenses:* Tuition $4200 per year full-time, $140 per credit hour part-time for state residents; $12,780 per year full-time, $426 per credit hour part-time for nonresidents. Fees $240 per year. • Dr. Patricia Callaghan, Chair, 509-963-1546. Application contact: Christie A. Fevergeon, Program Coordinator, Graduate Studies and Research, 509-963-3103. Fax: 509-963-1799. E-mail: masters@cwu.edu.

Chapman University, School of Communication Arts, Program in English, Orange, CA 92866. Offerings include teaching English as a second language (MA). Program faculty: 22 full-time (12 women). *Degree requirements:* Comprehensive exam required, thesis not required. *Entrance requirements:* GRE General Test (minimum combined score of 900), MAT (minimum score 52). Application deadline: rolling. Application fee: $40. *Tuition:* $460 per credit. • Dr. Matthew Schneider, Coordinator, 714-997-6750.

City University, School of Education, Bellevue, WA 98004-6442. Offerings include ESL counseling (Certificate), ESL instructional methods (M Ed). Postbaccalaureate distance learning degree programs offered (no on-campus study). School faculty: 21 full-time (13 women), 301 part-time (162 women). *Application deadline:* rolling. *Application fee:* $75 ($175 for international students). Electronic applications accepted. *Tuition:* $280 per credit hour. • Roxanne Kelly, Dean, 425-637-1010 Ext. 3712. Fax: 425-277-2439. Application contact: Nabil El-Khatib, Vice President, Admissions, 800-426-5596. Fax: 425-277-2437. E-mail: nel-khatib@cityu.edu.

Cleveland State University, College of Education, Department of Specialized Instructional Programs, Cleveland, OH 44115-2440. Offerings include curriculum and instruction (M Ed), with options in bilingual education, early childhood education, early childhood/special education, education of emerging adolescents, elementary education, English as a second language, learning disabilities, Montessori education, multihandicapped, reading, secondary education. Department faculty: 18 full-time (12 women). *Entrance requirements:* GRE General Test or MAT (score in 50th percentile or higher). Application deadline: 9/1 (priority date; rolling processing). Application fee: $25. *Expenses:* Tuition $5252 per year full-time, $202 per credit hour part-time for state residents; $10,504 per year full-time, $404 per credit hour part-time for nonresidents. Fees $2.25 per credit hour (minimum). • Dr. Jane Zaharias, Chairperson, 216-687-4585. Fax: 216-687-5379. E-mail: j.zaharias@csuohio.edu.

The College of New Jersey, Graduate Division, School of Education, Department of Language and Communication Sciences, Program in English as a Second Language, Ewing, NJ 08628. Offers English as a second language (M Ed), teaching English as a second language (Certificate). Accredited by NCATE. Students: 2 full-time (1 woman), 40 part-time (34 women); includes 10 minority (1 African American, 3 Asian Americans, 6 Hispanics), 3 international. Average age 27. In 1997, 10 master's awarded. *Degree requirements:* For master's, comprehensive exam required, foreign language and thesis not required. *Average time to degree:* master's–2 years full-time. *Entrance requirements:* For master's, GRE General Test, minimum GPA of 3.0 in field or 2.75 overall. Application deadline: 4/15 (10/15 for spring admission). Application fee: $50. *Expenses:* Tuition $6892 per year full-time, $287 per credit hour part-time for state residents; $9602 per year full-time, $402 per credit hour part-time for nonresidents. Fees $799 per year full-time, $33 per credit hour part-time. *Financial aid:* Application deadline 5/1; applicants required to submit FAFSA. • Dr. Yiqiang Wu, Coordinator, 609-771-2808.

College of New Rochelle, Division of Education, Program in Teaching English as a Second Language, New Rochelle, NY 10805-2308. Awards MS Ed. Part-time and evening/weekend programs available. Faculty: 1 full-time (0 women), 4 part-time (3 women), 2 FTE. Students: 3 full-time (2 women), 59 part-time (52 women); includes 49 minority (11 African Americans, 3 Asian Americans, 35 Hispanics). 48 applicants, 77% accepted. In 1997, 45 degrees awarded. *Degree requirements:* Practicum required, foreign language not required. *Average time to degree:* master's–1.2 years full-time, 2.5 years part-time. *Entrance requirements:* Interview; minimum GPA of 3.0 in field, 2.7 overall. Application deadline: 8/1 (priority date; rolling processing). Application fee: $35. *Tuition:* $329 per credit. *Financial aid:* In 1997–98, 2 students received aid, including 1 research assistantship totaling $948; scholarships also available. • Dr. Melanie Hannigan, Division Head, Division of Education, 914-654-5330.

College of Our Lady of the Elms, Department of Education, Chicopee, MA 01013-2839. Offerings include English as a second language (MAT). Department faculty: 7 full-time (all women), 6 part-time (5 women). *Application deadline:* rolling. *Application fee:* $30. *Expenses:*

Tuition $320 per credit. Fees $40 per year. • Sr. Kathleen M. Kirley, Dean of Continuing Education and Graduate Studies, 413-594-2761. Fax: 413-592-4871. Application contact: Dr. Mary Janeczek, Director, 413-594-2761.

Columbia International University, Columbia Biblical Seminary and Graduate School of Missions, Columbia, SC 29230-3122. Offerings include teaching English as a foreign language (MA). MACE offered jointly with Erskine Theological Seminary; PhD offered jointly with the University of South Carolina. Seminary faculty: 36 full-time (3 women), 38 part-time (1 woman). *Application deadline:* rolling. *Application fee:* $25. *Expenses:* Tuition $7410 per year full-time, $285 per semester hour part-time. Fees $150 per year. • Dr. Ken B. Mulholland, Dean, 803-754-4100. E-mail: kenm@ciu.edu. Application contact: Brian O'Donnell, Director of Admissions, 803-754-4100. Fax: 803-786-4209. E-mail: bodonell@ciu.edu.

Eastern College, Graduate Education Programs, Program in English as a Second or Foreign Language, St. Davids, PA 19087-3696. Awards Certificate. *Application deadline:* rolling. *Application fee:* $35. • Application contact: Megan Miscioscia, Graduate Admissions Representative, 610-341-5972. Fax: 610-341-1466.

Eastern Michigan University, College of Arts and Sciences, Department of Foreign Languages and Bilingual Studies, Program in Teaching English to Speakers of Other Languages, Ypsilanti, MI 48197. Awards MA. Evening/weekend programs available. In 1997, 12 degrees awarded. *Degree requirements:* 1 foreign language required, thesis not required. *Entrance requirements:* TOEFL (minimum score 520). Application deadline: 5/15 (rolling processing; 3/15 for spring admission). Application fee: $30. *Expenses:* Tuition $2691 per year full-time, $150 per credit hour part-time for state residents; $6300 per year full-time, $350 per credit hour part-time for nonresidents. Fees $368 per year full-time, $88 per semester (minimum) part-time. *Financial aid:* Fellowships, teaching assistantships available. Aid available to part-time students. Financial aid application deadline: 3/15; applicants required to submit FAFSA. • Dr. JoAnn Aebersold, Coordinator, 734-487-0130.

Eastern Nazarene College, Graduate Studies, Division of Education, Quincy, MA 02170-2999. Offerings include English as a second language (M Ed, Certificate). M Ed and Certificate also available through weekend program for administration, special needs, and reading only. Division faculty: 9 full-time (5 women), 11 part-time (5 women). *Entrance requirements:* For master's, TOEFL (minimum score 500). Application deadline: rolling. Application fee: $35. *Expenses:* Tuition $350 per credit. Fees $125 per semester full-time, $15 per semester part-time. • Dr. Lorne Ranstrom, Chair, 617-745-3528. Application contact: Cleo P. Cakridas, Graduate Enrollment Counselor, 617-745-3870. Fax: 617-745-3907. E-mail: cakridac@enc.edu.

Fairfield University, Graduate School of Education and Allied Professions, Department of TESOL, Foreign Language and Bilingual/Multicultural Education, Fairfield, CT 06430-5195. Awards MA, CAS. Part-time and evening/weekend programs available. Faculty: 1 (woman) full-time, 3 part-time (1 woman), 2 FTE. Students: 5 full-time (4 women), 52 part-time (42 women); includes 19 minority (2 Asian Americans, 17 Hispanics), 3 international. Average age 34. 14 applicants, 100% accepted. In 1997, 2 master's, 1 CAS awarded. *Entrance requirements:* For master's, PRAXIS I (CBT), TOEFL. Application deadline: 7/1 (priority date; rolling processing). Application fee: $40. *Expenses:* Tuition $350 per credit hour (minimum). Fees $20 per semester (minimum). *Financial aid:* Partial tuition waivers available. Aid available to part-time students. *Faculty research:* Teacher education. • Sr. Juliann Poole, Assistant Professor, 203-254-4000 Ext. 2873. Application contact: Karen Creecy, Assistant Dean, 203-254-4250. Fax: 203-254-4241. E-mail: klcreecy@fair1.fairfield.edu.

Fairleigh Dickinson University, Teaneck–Hackensack Campus, University College: Arts, Sciences, and Professional Studies, Peter Sammartino School of Education, Program in Teaching English as a Second Language, 1000 River Road, Teaneck, NJ 07666-1914. Awards MAT. Faculty: 11 full-time (8 women), 27 part-time (10 women). *Degree requirements:* Research project required, thesis not required. *Application deadline:* rolling. *Application fee:* $35. *Expenses:* Tuition $522 per credit. Fees $302 per year full-time, $138 per year part-time. *Faculty research:* Mathematics for students with learning disabilities, gender issues in education, social problem-solving and conflict resolution in the classroom, multicultural education in the elementary classroom, problems encountered by international students in college programs. • Dr. Eloise Forster, Interim Director, Peter Sammartino School of Education, 201-692-2834. Fax: 201-692-2603.

Florida International University, College of Education, Department of Foundations and Professional Studies, Program in English for Non-English Speakers, Miami, FL 33199. Awards MS. Accredited by NCATE. Part-time and evening/weekend programs available. Students: 27 full-time (19 women), 99 part-time (83 women); includes 85 minority (13 African Americans, 3 Asian Americans, 69 Hispanics), 3 international. Average age 32. 49 applicants, 82% accepted. In 1997, 38 degrees awarded. *Entrance requirements:* GRE General Test (minimum combined score of 1000) or minimum GPA of 3.0 in last 60 credits of baccalaureate. Application deadline: 4/1 (priority date; rolling processing; 10/1 for spring admission). Application fee: $20. *Expenses:* Tuition $138 per credit hour for state residents; $482 per credit hour for nonresidents. Fees $46 per semester. *Financial aid:* Research assistantships, Federal Work-Study, and career-related internships or fieldwork available. *Faculty research:* Methodology, applied languages. • Dr. Robert Farrell, Chairperson, Department of Foundations and Professional Studies, 305-348-3418. Fax: 305-348-3996. E-mail: farrellr@fiu.edu.

Fordham University, Graduate School of Education, Division of Curriculum and Teaching, New York, NY 10023. Offerings include teaching English as a second language (MSE). Accredited by NCATE. *Application fee:* $50. • Dr. Angela Carrasquillo, Chairperson, 212-636-6427.

Fresno Pacific University, Graduate School, Program in Teaching English to Speakers of Other Languages, Fresno, CA 93702-4709. Awards MA. Faculty: 4 full-time (3 women), 6 part-time (4 women). Students: 7 full-time (5 women), 17 part-time (12 women). *Application fee:* $75. *Tuition:* $250 per unit. • Dr. David Freeman, Director, 209-453-2201. Fax: 209-453-2001.

Fresno Pacific University, Graduate School, Programs in Education, Division of Language, Literacy, and Culture, Program in Reading, Fresno, CA 93702-4709. Offerings include reading/English as a second language (MA Ed). Program faculty: 4 full-time (3 women), 6 part-time (4 women). *Degree requirements:* Thesis or alternative. *Application deadline:* 7/31. *Application fee:* $75. *Tuition:* $250 per unit. • Jean Fennacy, Head, Division of Language, Literacy, and Culture, 209-453-2203. Fax: 209-453-2001.

George Mason University, Graduate School of Education, Programs in Bilingual/Multicultural/English as a Second Language Education, Fairfax, VA 22030-4444. Awards M Ed. Accredited by NCATE. Part-time and evening/weekend programs available. Faculty: 42 full-time (24 women), 65 part-time (51 women), 58.73 FTE. Students: 2 full-time (1 woman), 12 part-time (10 women); includes 8 minority (2 Asian Americans, 6 Hispanics), 2 international. Average age 37. 38 applicants, 84% accepted. In 1997, 11 degrees awarded. *Degree requirements:* Computer language required, foreign language not required. *Entrance requirements:* NTE, minimum GPA of 3.0 in last 60 hours. Application deadline: 5/1 (11/1 for spring admission). Application fee: $30. Electronic applications accepted. *Tuition:* $4344 per year full-time, $181 per credit hour part-time for state residents; $12,504 per year full-time, $521 per credit hour part-time for nonresidents. *Financial aid:* Available to part-time students. Financial aid application deadline: 3/1; applicants required to submit FAFSA. • Dr. Harold Chu, Director, 703-993-3688. Fax: 703-993-3336.

Georgetown University, Department of Linguistics, Washington, DC 20057. Offerings include bilingual education (Certificate), teaching English as a second language (MAT, Certificate). *Application deadline:* 2/1 (10/15 for spring admission). *Application fee:* $50 ($55 for international students). *Expenses:* Tuition $19,128 per year full-time, $797 per credit part-time. Fees $99 (one-time charge).

Georgia State University, College of Arts and Sciences, Department of Applied Linguistics/Teaching English as a Second Language, Atlanta, GA 30303-3083. Awards MS. Part-time and evening/weekend programs available. Faculty: 5 full-time (4 women), 2 part-time (0 women). Students: 45 full-time (38 women); includes 13 minority (2 African Americans, 10 Asian Americans, 1 Hispanic), 11 international. Average age 36. 42 applicants, 55% accepted. In 1997, 17 degrees awarded. *Entrance requirements:* GRE General Test or MAT. Application fee: $25. *Expenses:* Tuition $2673 per year full-time, $99 per semester hour part-time for state residents; $10,692 per year full-time, $396 per semester hour part-time for nonresidents. Fees $228 per year. *Financial aid:* Research assistantships, teaching assistantships, scholarships, institutionally sponsored loans available. Aid available to part-time students. Financial aid applicants required to submit FAFSA. *Faculty research:* Native language and second language, literature acquisition, intercultural communication, classroom-centered research, learning styles/strategies. • Dr. Joan Carson, Chair, 404-651-3650. E-mail: esljgc@panther.gsu.edu. Application contact: Dr. Gayle Nelson, Director of Graduate Studies, 404-651-3650. Fax: 404-651-3652. E-mail: gnelson@gsu.edu.

Grand Canyon University, College of Education, Phoenix, AZ 85017-3030. Offerings include teaching English as a second language (MA). College faculty: 8 full-time (5 women), 2 part-time (1 woman). *Application deadline:* rolling. *Application fee:* $25. • Dr. Betz Fredrick, Director, 602-589-2472.

Heritage College, Graduate Program in Education, Program in Professional Development, Toppenish, WA 98948-9599. Offerings include bilingual education/ESL (M Ed). *Degree requirements:* Comprehensive exam required, thesis optional, foreign language not required. *Application deadline:* rolling. *Application fee:* $35 ($75 for international students). *Tuition:* $270 per credit. • Application contact: Dr. Robert Plumb, Chair, 509-865-2244.

Hofstra University, School of Education and Allied Human Services, Department of Curriculum and Teaching, Program in Teaching English as a Second Language, Hempstead, NY 11549. Awards MS Ed. Accredited by NCATE. Part-time and evening/weekend programs available. Students: 2 full-time (both women), 33 part-time (30 women); includes 2 minority (1 African American, 1 Hispanic). Average age 28. 25 applicants, 56% accepted. In 1997, 13 degrees awarded. *Degree requirements:* Departmental qualifying exam. *Entrance requirements:* Minimum GPA of 2.5. Application deadline: rolling. Application fee: $40 ($75 for international students). *Expenses:* Tuition $10,968 per year full-time, $457 per credit hour part-time. Fees $670 per year full-time, $112 per semester (minimum) part-time. *Financial aid:* 8 students received aid. Financial aid application deadline: 9/1. *Faculty research:* Roles and responsibility of English as a second language teachers, acculturation, special needs students. • Dr. Mary Savage, Co-Director, 516-463-5348. Fax: 516-463-6503. E-mail: catmcs@hofstra.edu. Application contact: Mary Beth Carey, Dean of Admissions, 516-463-6700. Fax: 516-560-7660. E-mail: hofstra@hofstra.edu.

Holy Names College, Department of Education, Program in Teaching English as a Second Language, 3500 Mountain Boulevard, Oakland, CA 94619-1699. Awards Certificate. Part-time programs available. Faculty: 1 (woman) full-time. Students: 2 full-time (both women), 3 part-time (1 woman); includes 3 minority (1 African American, 2 Asian Americans). 4 applicants, 100% accepted. *Average time to degree:* other advanced degree–1 year full-time, 2 years part-time. *Application deadline:* 8/1 (rolling processing; 12/1 for spring admission). *Application fee:* $35. *Tuition:* $7650 per year full-time, $425 per unit part-time. *Financial aid:* 3 students received aid; Federal Work-Study available. Aid available to part-time students. Financial aid application deadline: 3/2; applicants required to submit FAFSA. *Faculty research:* Second language acquisition. • Meryl Siegal, Contact Person, 510-436-1329. Application contact: Graduate Admissions Office, 800-430-1321. Fax: 510-436-1317. E-mail: garner@admin.hnc.edu.

Hunter College of the City University of New York, Division of Education, Department of Curriculum and Teaching, Program in Teaching English as a Second Language, 695 Park Avenue, New York, NY 10021-5085. Awards MA. Part-time and evening/weekend programs available. *Degree requirements:* 1 foreign language, comprehensive exam. *Entrance requirements:* TOEFL (minimum score 575), minimum GPA of 2.7, 4 years of foreign language experience. Application deadline: 4/28 (rolling processing). Application fee: $40. *Expenses:* Tuition $4350 per year full-time, $185 per credit part-time for state residents; $7600 per year full-time, $320 per credit part-time for nonresidents. Fees $26 per year.

Indiana University Bloomington, College of Arts and Sciences, Program in Teaching English as a Second Language and Applied Linguistics, Bloomington, IN 47405. Offers applied linguistics (teaching English as a second language) (MA, Certificate), linguistics (PhD). PhD offered through the University Graduate School. Students: 36 full-time (29 women); includes 11 international. *Degree requirements:* For master's, 1 foreign language required, thesis optional; for doctorate, 2 foreign languages, oral defense of dissertation, qualifying exam. *Entrance requirements:* For master's and doctorate, GRE General Test, TOEFL (minimum score 573). Application deadline: 1/15 (priority date; 9/1 for spring admission). Application fee: $35. *Expenses:* Tuition $153 per credit hour for state residents; $446 per credit hour for nonresidents. Fees $343 per year. *Financial aid:* Research assistantships, teaching assistantships, partial tuition waivers, Federal Work-Study, and career-related internships or fieldwork available. *Faculty research:* Second language acquisition, interlanguage pragmatics, world Englishes, language testing, language learner backgrounds. • Harry L. Gradman, Chair, 812-855-7951. E-mail: gradman@ucs.indiana.edu. Application contact: Karla J. Bastin, Departmental Secretary, 812-855-7951. Fax: 812-855-5605. E-mail: kjbastin@ucs.indiana.edu.

Indiana University of Pennsylvania, College of Humanities and Social Sciences, Department of English, Program in Rhetoric and Linguistics, Indiana, PA 15705-1087. Offerings include teaching English to speakers of other languages (MA). *Application deadline:* 7/1 (priority date; rolling processing; 11/1 for spring admission). *Application fee:* $30. *Expenses:* Tuition $3468 per year full-time, $193 per credit part-time for state residents; $6236 per year full-time, $346 per credit part-time for nonresidents. Fees $313 per year (minimum) full-time, $84 per year part-time. • Dr. Dan Tannacito, Graduate Coordinator, 724-357-7675. E-mail: djt@grove.iup.edu.

Inter American University of Puerto Rico, Metropolitan Campus, Division of Humanities, Program in English, San Juan, PR 00919-1293. Offers teaching English as a second language (MA). Part-time and evening/weekend programs available. Faculty: 6 full-time, 1 part-time. Students: 23 part-time (16 women); includes 23 minority (all Hispanics). In 1997, 4 degrees awarded. *Degree requirements:* Thesis or alternative, comprehensive exam required, foreign language not required. *Average time to degree:* master's–1.5 years full-time, 2.5 years part-time. *Entrance requirements:* GRE General Test or PAEG, minimum GPA of 2.5. Application deadline: 5/15 (priority date; rolling processing; 11/15 for spring admission). Application fee: $31. Electronic applications accepted. *Expenses:* Tuition $3272 per year full-time, $1740 per year part-time. Fees $328 per year full-time, $176 per year part-time. *Financial aid:* In 1997–98, 2 teaching assistantships (both to first-year students) averaging $150 per month were awarded; graduate assistantships, Federal Work-Study also available. Aid available to part-time students. *Faculty research:* Contemporary American fiction, feminine discourse, teaching of literature, use of multimedia in the teaching of language, social dimensions of language acquisition. • Application contact: Dr. Robert Van Trieste, Director, 787-250-1912 Ext. 2492. Fax: 787-765-6965.

Inter American University of Puerto Rico, San Germán Campus, Department of English, San Germán, PR 00683-5008. Offers program in teaching English as a second language (MA). Part-time and evening/weekend programs available. Faculty: 4 full-time (1 woman). In 1997, 5 degrees awarded. *Degree requirements:* Comprehensive exam required, foreign

Directory: English as a Second Language

Inter American University of Puerto Rico, San Germán Campus (continued)
language and thesis not required. *Entrance requirements:* Minimum GPA of 3.0, GRE General Test, or PAEG. Application deadline: 4/30 (priority date; rolling processing; 11/15 for spring admission). Application fee: $31. *Expenses:* Tuition $150 per credit. Fees $177 per semester. *Financial aid:* Teaching assistantships available. • Dr. Olena Saciuk, Coordinator of Graduate Programs, 787-264-1912 Ext. 7540. Application contact: Mildred Camacho, Admissions Director, 787-892-3090. Fax: 787-892-6350.

Kean University, School of Education, Department of Instruction, Curriculum and Administration, Instruction and Curriculum Program, Union, NJ 07083. Offerings include English as a second language (Certificate), teaching English as a second language (MA). One or more programs accredited by NCATE. *Degree requirements:* For master's, thesis, comprehensive exams required, foreign language not required. *Entrance requirements:* For master's, GRE General Test or MAT. Application deadline: 6/15 (rolling processing; 11/15 for spring admission). Application fee: $35. *Tuition:* $5926 per year full-time, $248 per credit part-time for state residents; $7312 per year full-time, $304 per credit part-time for nonresidents. • Dr. Janet Prince, Coordinator, 908-527-2525. Application contact: Joanne Morris, Director of Graduate Admissions, 908-527-2665. Fax: 908-527-2286. E-mail: grad_adm@turbo.kean.edu.

Lehman College of the City University of New York, Division of Education, Department of Secondary, Adult and Business Education, Program in Teaching English to Speakers of Other Languages, 250 Bedford Park Boulevard West, Bronx, NY 10468-1589. Awards MS Ed. Students: 1 (woman) full-time, 90 part-time (71 women). *Degree requirements:* Thesis. *Entrance requirements:* Minimum GPA of 3.0. Application deadline: 4/1 (rolling processing; 11/1 for spring admission). Application fee: $40. *Expenses:* Tuition $4350 per year full-time, $185 per credit part-time for state residents; $7600 per year full-time, $320 per credit part-time for nonresidents. Fees $120 per year full-time, $80 per year part-time. *Financial aid:* Full and partial tuition waivers, Federal Work-Study available. Aid available to part-time students. Financial aid application deadline: 5/15; applicants required to submit FAFSA. • Joye Smith, Adviser, 718-960-8171.

Long Island University, Brooklyn Campus, School of Education, Department of Education, Program in Teaching English to Speakers of Other Languages, Brooklyn, NY 11201-8423. Awards MS Ed. Part-time and evening/weekend programs available. 25 applicants, 84% accepted. In 1997, 9 degrees awarded. *Degree requirements:* Thesis optional. *Application deadline:* rolling. *Application fee:* $30. Electronic applications accepted. *Expenses:* Tuition $480 per credit. Fees $415 per year full-time, $73 per semester (minimum) part-time. • Application contact: Bernard W. Sullivan, Associate Director of Admissions, 718-488-1011.

Long Island University, C.W. Post Campus, School of Education, Department of Curriculum and Instruction, Brookville, NY 11548-1300. Offerings include teaching English as a second language (MS). Department faculty: 10 full-time (5 women), 46 part-time (19 women). *Application deadline:* rolling. *Application fee:* $30. Electronic applications accepted. *Expenses:* Tuition $480 per credit. Fees $316 per year full-time, $71 per semester (minimum) part-time. • Dr. Anthony De Falco, Chairperson, 516-299-2372. Application contact: Camille Marziliano, Academic Counselor, 516-299-2123. Fax: 516-299-4167. E-mail: cmarzili@eagle.liunet.edu.

Loyola Marymount University, School of Education, Program in Teaching English as a Second Language/Multicultural Education, Los Angeles, CA 90045-8350. Awards MA. Part-time and evening/weekend programs available. Faculty: 14 full-time (8 women), 25 part-time (20 women). Students: 3 full-time (all women), 4 part-time (3 women); includes 3 minority (1 African American, 2 Hispanics). *Degree requirements:* Comprehensive exam required, foreign language and thesis not required. *Entrance requirements:* GRE General Test, TOEFL (minimum score 550), interview; minimum GPA of 2.7 (undergraduate), 3.0 (graduate). Application fee: $35. Electronic applications accepted. *Expenses:* Tuition $500 per unit. Fees $111 per year full-time, $28 per year part-time. *Financial aid:* In 1997–98, 2 students received aid, including 1 grant totaling $1,300; Federal Work-Study also available. Aid available to part-time students. Financial aid application deadline: 3/2; applicants required to submit FAFSA. • Dr. Magaly Lavandez, Coordinator, 310-338-2924.

Lynn University, School of Graduate Studies, College of Education, Boca Raton, FL 33431-5598. Offerings include ESOL and varying exceptionalities (M Ed). College faculty: 5 full-time (4 women), 3 part-time (all women). *Degree requirements:* Thesis (for some programs), comprehensive exam (ESOL and varying exceptionalities), (varying exceptionalities) required, foreign language not required. *Average time to degree:* master's–1.8 years full-time. *Entrance requirements:* MAT, minimum undergraduate GPA of 3.0. Application deadline: rolling. Application fee: $50. Electronic applications accepted. *Expenses:* Tuition $375 per credit hour. Fees $60 per year. • Dr. Carole Warshaw, Dean, 561-994-0770 Ext. 247. Fax: 561-241-3939. E-mail: admission@lynn.edu. Application contact: Peter Gallo, Graduate Admissions Counselor, 800-544-8035. Fax: 561-241-3552. E-mail: admission@lynn.edu.

Manhattanville College, School of Education, Program in English as a Second Language, Purchase, NY 10577-2132. Offers teaching English as a second language (MPS). *Degree requirements:* Thesis, comprehensive exam or research project required, foreign language not required. *Entrance requirements:* Minimum undergraduate GPA of 3.0. Application deadline: rolling. Application fee: $40. *Expenses:* Tuition $410 per credit (minimum). Fees $25 per semester. • Dr. Laurence Krute, Coordinator, 914-323-5141. Fax: 914-694-2386. Application contact: Carol Messar, Director of Admissions, 914-323-5142. Fax: 914-323-5493.

Marymount University, School of Education and Human Services, Program in English as a Second Language, Arlington, VA 22207-4299. Awards M Ed. Accredited by NCATE. Part-time and evening/weekend programs available. Students: 21. In 1997, 19 degrees awarded. *Degree requirements:* Thesis or alternative required, foreign language not required. *Entrance requirements:* GRE General Test or MAT, interview. Application deadline: rolling. Application fee: $35. *Expenses:* Tuition $465 per credit hour. Fees $120 per year full-time, $5 per credit hour part-time. • Dr. Shirley Smith, Chair, 703-284-1620. Fax: 703-284-1631. E-mail: shirley.smith@marymount.edu.

McGill University, Faculty of Graduate Studies and Research, Faculty of Education, Department of Second Language Education, Program in Teaching English as a Second Language, Montréal, PQ H3A 2T5, Canada. Awards M Ed. Part-time programs available. Faculty: 8 full-time (6 women). Students: 5 full-time (all women), 20 part-time (all women). Average age 25. 50 applicants, 56% accepted. In 1997, 7 degrees awarded. *Degree requirements:* Monograph required, thesis not required. *Entrance requirements:* TOEFL (minimum score 550), mastery of spoken and written English, minimum GPA of 3.0. Application deadline: 3/1 (priority date; rolling processing). Application fee: $60. *Expenses:* Tuition $1668 per year for Canadian residents; $8268 per year for nonresidents. Fees $828 per year for Canadian residents; $1216 per year for nonresidents. *Financial aid:* In 1997–98, 2 students received aid, including 2 teaching assistantships (both to first-year students); fellowships, full tuition waivers also available. *Faculty research:* Classroom-centered research in L2 learning, testing evaluation, second language acquisition, discourse analysis, literacy development. • Application contact: Joyce Gaul, Administrative Assistant, 514-398-6982. Fax: 514-398-5595. E-mail: gaul@education.mcgill.ca.

Michigan State University, College of Arts and Letters, Department of English, East Lansing, MI 48824-1020. Offerings include teaching of English to speakers of other languages (MA). Department faculty: 51 (17 women). *Degree requirements:* Thesis (for some programs). *Entrance requirements:* GRE General Test, GRE Subject Test. Application deadline: 1/10 (priority date; rolling processing). Application fee: $30 ($40 for international students). *Expenses:* Tuition $4609 per year full-time, $223 per credit hour (minimum) part-time for state residents; $8704 per year full-time, $450 per credit hour (minimum) part-time for nonresidents. Fees $576 per year full-time, $476 per year part-time. • Dr. Patrick O'Donnell, Interim Chairperson, 517-355-7570. Application contact: Dr. Robert Uphaus, Associate Chairperson, Graduate Studies, 517-355-7570. Fax: 517-353-3755. E-mail: uphaus@pilot.msu.edu.

Monterey Institute of International Studies, Graduate School of Language and Educational Linguistics, Program in Peace Corps Master's Internationalist in TESOL, 425 Van Buren Street, Monterey, CA 93940-2691. Awards MATESOL. *Degree requirements:* Portfolio and oral defense. *Entrance requirements:* TOEFL (minimum score 600), minimum GPA of 3.0. Application deadline: 8/1 (priority date; rolling processing; 12/1 for spring admission). Application fee: $50. *Expenses:* Tuition $18,200 per year full-time, $760 per semester hour part-time. Fees $45 per year. *Financial aid:* Federal Work-Study, institutionally sponsored loans available. Aid available to part-time students. Financial aid application deadline: 3/15; applicants required to submit FAFSA. • Application contact: Admissions Office, 408-647-4123. Fax: 408-647-6405. E-mail: admit@miis.edu.

Monterey Institute of International Studies, Graduate School of Language and Educational Linguistics, Program in Teaching English to Speakers of Other Languages, 425 Van Buren Street, Monterey, CA 93940-2691. Awards MATESOL. Faculty: 9 full-time (5 women), 2 part-time (1 woman). Students: 55 full-time (43 women), 31 part-time (28 women); includes 6 minority (3 Asian Americans, 3 Hispanics), 15 international. Average age 26. 90 applicants, 77% accepted. In 1997, 35 degrees awarded. *Degree requirements:* Portfolio and oral defense. *Average time to degree:* master's–1.5 years full-time, 2 years part-time. *Entrance requirements:* TOEFL (minimum score 600), minimum GPA of 3.0. Application deadline: 8/1 (priority date; rolling processing; 12/1 for spring admission). Application fee: $50. *Expenses:* Tuition $18,200 per year full-time, $760 per semester hour part-time. Fees $45 per year. *Financial aid:* Federal Work-Study, institutionally sponsored loans available. Aid available to part-time students. Financial aid application deadline: 3/15; applicants required to submit FAFSA. • Application contact: Admissions Office, 408-647-4123. Fax: 408-647-6405. E-mail: admit@miis.edu.

Mount Vernon College, Graduate School, Washington, DC 20007. Offerings include teaching English to speakers of other languages (MA). *Average time to degree:* master's–1.5 years full-time, 3 years part-time. *Application deadline:* rolling. *Application fee:* $35.

Murray State University, College of Humanistic Studies, Department of English, Murray, KY 42071-0009. Offerings include teaching English to speakers of other languages (MA). Department faculty: 29 full-time (7 women). *Degree requirements:* 1 foreign language. *Entrance requirements:* GRE General Test, TOEFL (minimum score 500). Application deadline: rolling. Application fee: $20. *Expenses:* Tuition $2500 per year full-time, $124 per hour part-time for state residents; $6740 per year full-time, $357 per hour part-time for nonresidents. Fees $360 per year full-time, $180 per year part-time. • Dr. Thayle Anderson, Director, 502-762-4532. Fax: 502-762-2540.

Nazareth College of Rochester, Graduate Studies, Department of Education, Program in Teaching English to Speakers of Other Languages, Rochester, NY 14618-3790. Awards MS Ed. Faculty: 1 (woman) full-time, 4 part-time (1 woman). Students: 2 full-time (both women), 36 part-time (35 women); includes 3 minority (1 African American, 2 Hispanics). 19 applicants, 79% accepted. In 1997, 21 degrees awarded. *Degree requirements:* Comprehensive exam required, foreign language and thesis not required. *Entrance requirements:* Minimum GPA of 2.7. Application deadline: 3/1 (priority date; 9/15 for spring admission). Application fee: $40. *Expenses:* Tuition $436 per credit hour. Fees $20 per semester. • Dr. Brett Blake, Adviser, 716-389-2612. Application contact: Dr. Kay F. Marshman, Dean, 716-389-2815. Fax: 716-389-2452.

New Jersey City University, School of Professional Studies and Education, Programs in Urban Education, Concentration in Bilingual/Bicultural Education and English as a Second Language, Jersey City, NJ 07305-1957. Awards MA. *Entrance requirements:* GRE General Test, TOEFL or MAT. Application deadline: 8/1 (priority date; rolling processing; 12/1 for spring admission). Application fee: $0.

New Jersey City University, School of Professional Studies and Education, Programs in Urban Education, Program in Administration, Curriculum and Instruction, Jersey City, NJ 07305-1957. Offerings include urban education (MA), with options in administration and supervision, basics and urban studies, bilingual/bicultural education and English as a second language. Accredited by NCATE. *Entrance requirements:* GRE General Test, MAT or TOEFL. Application deadline: 8/1 (priority date; rolling processing; 12/1 for spring admission). Application fee: $0.

Newman University, Program in Education, Wichita, KS 67213-2084. Offerings include English as a second language (MS Ed). Program faculty: 5 full-time, 9 part-time. *Degree requirements:* Thesis or alternative. *Average time to degree:* master's–3 years part-time. *Application deadline:* 8/15 (priority date; rolling processing; 1/10 for spring admission). *Application fee:* $25. *Tuition:* $257 per credit hour. • Dr. Laura McLemore, Division Chair of Institute for Teacher Education, 316-942-4291 Ext. 253. Fax: 316-942-4483.

New York University, School of Education, Department of Teaching and Learning, Program in Multilingual/Multicultural Studies, New York, NY 10012-1019. Offerings include teaching English to speakers of other languages (MA, PhD, CAS). Terminal master's awarded for partial completion of doctoral program. Program faculty: 3 full-time, 7 part-time. *Degree requirements:* For master's, thesis required (for some programs), foreign language not required; for doctorate, dissertation. *Entrance requirements:* For master's, TOEFL; for doctorate, GRE General Test, TOEFL, interview; for CAS, TOEFL, master's degree. Application deadline: 2/1 (priority date; rolling processing; 12/1 for spring admission). Application fee: $40 ($60 for international students). • Harvey Nadler, Director, 212-998-5494. Application contact: Office of Graduate Admissions, 212-998-5030. Fax: 212-995-4328.

Northern Arizona University, College of Arts and Sciences, Department of English, Program in Teaching English as a Second Language/Applied Linguistics, Flagstaff, AZ 86011. Offers applied linguistics (PhD), teaching English as a second language (MAT). Students: 55 full-time (39 women), 21 part-time (15 women); includes 8 minority (2 African Americans, 4 Asian Americans, 2 Hispanics), 19 international. 93 applicants, 55% accepted. In 1997, 25 master's, 2 doctorates awarded. *Degree requirements:* For master's, departmental qualifying exam required, foreign language not required; for doctorate, dissertation. *Entrance requirements:* GRE General Test, GRE Subject Test. Application deadline: 2/15. Application fee: $45. *Expenses:* Tuition $2088 per year full-time, $330 per semester (minimum) part-time for state residents; $8004 per year full-time, $1002 per semester (minimum) part-time for nonresidents. Fees $72 per year full-time, $18 per semester (minimum) part-time. • Dr. William Grabe, Coordinator, 520-523-9011.

Notre Dame College, Education Division, Program in Teaching English as a Second Language, Manchester, NH 03104-2299. Awards M Ed. Faculty: 1 (woman) full-time, 3 part-time (all women). Students: 6 full-time (all women), 19 part-time (16 women); includes 2 international. Average age 38. 3 applicants, 67% accepted. In 1997, 8 degrees awarded. *Degree requirements:* Comprehensive exams or thesis required, foreign language not required. *Entrance requirements:* GRE General Test or MAT. Application deadline: rolling. Application fee: $35. *Tuition:* $299 per credit. • Director, 603-669-4298.

Nova Southeastern University, Fischler Center for the Advancement of Education, Graduate Teacher Education Program, Fort Lauderdale, FL 33314-7721. Offerings include teaching English to speakers of other languages (MS, Ed S). *Degree requirements:* Thesis, practicum required, foreign language not required. *Entrance requirements:* For master's, teaching certificate; for Ed S, master's degree, teaching certificate. Application deadline: rolling. Application fee: $50. *Tuition:* $245 per credit hour (minimum). • Dr. Deo Nellis, Dean, 954-262-8601. E-mail: deo@fcae.nova.edu. Application contact: Dr. Mark Seldine, Director of Student Affairs, 954-262-8689. Fax: 954-262-3910. E-mail: seldines@fcae.nova.edu.

Oklahoma City University, Petree College of Arts and Sciences, Division of Education, Program in Teaching English as a Second Language, Oklahoma City, OK 73106-1402. Awards M Ed. Part-time and evening/weekend programs available. Students: 44 full-time (33 women), 18 part-time (13 women); includes 5 minority (all Asian Americans), 44 international. Average age 39. *Degree requirements:* Thesis or alternative required, foreign language not required.

Average time to degree: master's–1.5 years full-time, 3.3 years part-time. *Entrance requirements:* Minimum GPA of 3.0. Application deadline: 8/25 (priority date; rolling processing; 1/15 for spring admission). Application fee: $35 ($55 for international students). *Expenses:* Tuition $318 per hour. Fees $124 per year. *Financial aid:* Fellowships, partial tuition waivers, Federal Work-Study, institutionally sponsored loans, and career-related internships or fieldwork available. Aid available to part-time students. Financial aid application deadline: 8/1. • Dr. Dilin Liu, Head, 405-521-5371. E-mail: dliu@lec.okcu.edu. Application contact: Laura L. Rahhal, Director of Graduate Admissions, 800-633-7242 Ext. 2. Fax: 405-521-5356. E-mail: lrahhal1@froda.okcu.edu.

Oral Roberts University, School of Education, Tulsa, OK 74171-0001. Offerings include teaching English as a second language (MA Ed). Postbaccalaureate distance learning degree programs offered (minimal on-campus study). School faculty: 7 full-time (2 women), 13 part-time (3 women). *Degree requirements:* Thesis (for some programs), comprehensive exam. *Average time to degree:* master's–1.5 years full-time, 3 years part-time. *Entrance requirements:* GRE General Test (minimum combined score of 1000) or MAT, minimum GPA of 3.0. Application deadline: rolling. Application fee: $35. • Dr. David Hand, Dean, 918-495-7084. Fax: 918-495-6050. Application contact: David H. Fulmer III, Coordinator of Graduate Admissions, 918-495-6058. Fax: 918-495-7214. E-mail: dhfulmer@oru.edu.

Pennsylvania State University University Park Campus, College of Liberal Arts, Department of Speech Communications, Program in Teaching English as a Second Language, University Park, PA 16802-1503. Awards MA. Students: 18 full-time (12 women), 2 part-time (both women). In 1997, 15 degrees awarded. *Entrance requirements:* GRE General Test. Application fee: $40. *Expenses:* Tuition $6534 per year full-time, $276 per credit part-time for state residents; $13,460 per year full-time, $561 per credit part-time for nonresidents. Fees $252 per year (minimum) full-time, $43 per semester (minimum) part-time. • Dr. Sandra Savignon, Head, 814-865-7365.

Portland State University, College of Liberal Arts and Sciences, Department of Applied Linguistics, Portland, OR 97207-0751. Offers program in teaching English to speakers of other languages (MA). Part-time programs available. Faculty: 6 full-time (4 women), 1 (woman) part-time, 6.2 FTE. Students: 32 full-time (26 women), 34 part-time (25 women); includes 5 minority (3 Asian Americans, 2 Hispanics), 12 international. Average age 33. 38 applicants, 55% accepted. In 1997, 19 degrees awarded. *Degree requirements:* 1 foreign language, thesis, written comprehensive exams. *Entrance requirements:* TOEFL (minimum score 600), minimum GPA of 3.0 in upper-division course work or 2.75 overall. Application deadline: 2/1 (priority date; rolling processing; 11/1 for spring admission). Application fee: $50. *Tuition:* $6101 per year full-time, $689 per semester (minimum) part-time for state residents; $10,445 per year full-time, $689 per semester (minimum) part-time for nonresidents. *Financial aid:* In 1997–98, 7 teaching assistantships (3 to first-year students) were awarded; research assistantships, Federal Work-Study, institutionally sponsored loans, and career-related internships or fieldwork also available. Aid available to part-time students. Financial aid application deadline: 3/1; applicants required to submit FAFSA. *Faculty research:* Sociolinguistics, linguistics and cognitive science, language proficiency testing, lexical phrases and language teaching, teaching English as a second language methodology. Total annual research expenditures: $30,000. • Dr. Jeanette DeCarrico, Head, 503-725-4088. E-mail: jan@nh1.nh.pdx.edu. Application contact: Karen Tittelbach-Goodwin, Office Coordinator, 503-725-4098. Fax: 503-725-4139. E-mail: goodwin@nh1.pdx.edu.

Prescott College, Graduate Programs, Program in Education, Prescott, AZ 86301-2990. Offerings include bilingual education (MA), with options in English as a second language, Native American bilingual teacher education. Postbaccalaureate distance learning degree programs offered (minimal on-campus study). *Degree requirements:* Thesis, fieldwork or internship, practicum required, foreign language not required. *Application deadline:* 6/1 (11/1 for spring admission). *Application fee:* $40. *Tuition:* $9000 per year. • Dr. Gene Hanson, Head, 520-319-9868. Application contact: Joan Clingan, Graduate Director, 520-776-5130. Fax: 520-776-5137. E-mail: mapmail@northlink.com.

Providence College and Theological Seminary, Theological Seminary, Otterburne, MB R0A 1G0, Canada. Offerings include teaching English to speakers of other languages (Certificate). Seminary faculty: 13 full-time (4 women), 8 part-time (2 women), 17 FTE. *Average time to degree:* master's–2 years full-time; first professional–3 years full-time. *Application deadline:* 8/25 (priority date; rolling processing). *Application fee:* $25. • Dr. David L. Smith, Vice President of Seminary Academics, 204-433-7488. E-mail: dsmith@providence.mb.ca. Application contact: Dewey Thiele, Director of Enrollment Management, 204-433-7488. Fax: 204-433-7158. E-mail: dthiele@providence.mb.ca.

Queens College of the City University of New York, Arts Division, Department of Linguistics, Program in Teaching English to Speakers of Other Languages, 65-30 Kissena Boulevard, Flushing, NY 11367-1597. Awards MS Ed. Part-time and evening/weekend programs available. Students: 10 full-time (9 women), 88 part-time (76 women); includes 14 minority (8 Asian Americans, 6 Hispanics). 74 applicants, 68% accepted. In 1997, 20 degrees awarded. *Degree requirements:* Thesis optional, foreign language not required. *Entrance requirements:* TOEFL (minimum score 650), minimum GPA of 3.0. Application deadline: 4/1 (rolling processing; 11/1 for spring admission). Application fee: $40. *Expenses:* Tuition $4350 per year full-time, $185 per credit part-time for state residents; $7600 per year full-time, $320 per credit part-time for nonresidents. Fees $104 per year. *Financial aid:* Partial tuition waivers, Federal Work-Study, institutionally sponsored loans, and career-related internships or fieldwork available. Aid available to part-time students. Financial aid application deadline: 4/1; applicants required to submit FAFSA. • Dr. Herbert Seliger, Graduate Adviser, 718-997-5720. Application contact: Mario Caruso, Director of Graduate Admissions, 718-997-5200. Fax: 718-997-5193. E-mail: graduate%queens.bitnet@cunyvm.cuny.edu.

Rhode Island College, School of Graduate Studies, School of Education and Human Development, Department of Educational Studies, Program in English as a Second Language, Providence, RI 02908-1924. Awards M Ed. Accredited by NCATE. Faculty: 4 full-time (0 women), 1 part-time (0 women). Students: 8 full-time (6 women), 27 part-time (18 women); includes 4 minority (all Asian Americans). In 1997, 8 degrees awarded. *Entrance requirements:* GRE General Test or MAT. Application deadline: 4/1 (rolling processing). Application fee: $25. *Tuition:* $4064 per year full-time, $214 per credit part-time for state residents; $7658 per year full-time, $376 per credit part-time for nonresidents. *Financial aid:* Application deadline 4/1. • Willis Poole, Head, 401-456-8018.

Rowan University, College of Education, Department of Secondary Education-Education Foundations, Program in Subject Matter Teaching, Program in English as a Second Language/Bilingual, Glassboro, NJ 08028-1701. Awards Certificate. Accredited by NCATE. Part-time and evening/weekend programs available. Students: 14 (11 women); includes 8 minority (2 African Americans, 1 Asian American, 5 Hispanics). 13 applicants, 69% accepted. *Application deadline:* 11/1 (priority date; rolling processing; 4/1 for spring admission). *Application fee:* $50. *Tuition:* $5728 per year full-time, $258 per credit hour part-time for state residents; $8968 per year full-time, $393 per credit hour part-time for nonresidents. • Dr. Jacqueline Benevento, Adviser, 609-256-4649.

Rutgers, The State University of New Jersey, New Brunswick, Graduate School of Education, Department of Learning and Teaching, Program in Language Education, New Brunswick, NJ 08903. Offerings include English as a second language education (Ed M, Ed D). Terminal master's awarded for partial completion of doctoral program. Program faculty: 3 full-time (2 women). *Degree requirements:* For master's, comprehensive exam required, thesis not required; for doctorate, dissertation, concept paper and qualifying exam. *Average time to degree:* master's–1.5 years full-time, 3 years part-time; doctorate–4 years full-time, 7 years part-time. *Entrance requirements:* For master's, GRE General Test (minimum combined score of 1000; average 1100), TOEFL (minimum score 600), minimum GPA of 3.0; for doctorate, GRE General Test (minimum combined score of 1100; average 1150), TOEFL (minimum score 600), minimum GPA of 3.5. Application deadline: 3/1 (11/1 for spring admission). Application fee: $40. *Expenses:* Tuition $6492 per year full-time, $268 per credit part-time for state residents; $9520 per year full-time, $395 per credit part-time for nonresidents. Fees $208 per year (minimum). • Dr. Eliane C. Condon, Coordinator, 732-932-7496 Ext. 123. Fax: 732-932-7552. E-mail: condon@rci.rutgers.edu.

St. Cloud State University, College of Fine Arts and Humanities, Department of English, St. Cloud, MN 56301-4498. Offerings include teaching English as a second language (MA). Department faculty: 28 full-time (12 women). *Application fee:* $20 ($100 for international students). *Expenses:* Tuition $128 per credit for state residents; $203 per credit for nonresidents. Fees $16.32 per credit. • Dr. Robert Inkster, Chairperson, 320-255-3061. Application contact: Ann Anderson, Graduate Studies Office, 320-255-2113. Fax: 320-654-5371. E-mail: anna@grad.stcloud.msus.edu.

St. John's University, School of Education and Human Services, Division of Human Services and Counseling, Program in Bilingual/Multicultural Education/Teaching English to Speakers of Other Languages, Jamaica, NY 11439. Awards MS Ed. Part-time and evening/weekend programs available. Students: 9 full-time (8 women), 37 part-time (34 women); includes 12 minority (3 African Americans, 1 Asian American, 8 Hispanics), 5 international. Average age 35. 28 applicants, 93% accepted. In 1997, 6 degrees awarded. *Entrance requirements:* Minimum GPA of 3.0, New York teaching certificate. Application deadline: 6/1 (rolling processing; 10/1 for spring admission). Application fee: $40. *Expenses:* Tuition $525 per credit. Fees $150 per year. *Financial aid:* Administrative assistantships, Federal Work-Study, and career-related internships or fieldwork available. Aid available to part-time students. Financial aid application deadline: 3/1; applicants required to submit FAFSA. *Faculty research:* Second language learning, cross-cultural studies. • Dr. J. Spiridakis, Coordinator, 718-990-6407. Fax: 718-990-1614. Application contact: Shamus J. McGrenra, TOR, Associate Director, Graduate Admissions, 718-990-6107. Fax: 718-990-5736. E-mail: mcgrenrs@stjohns.edu.

Saint Michael's College, Program in Teaching English as a Second Language, Colchester, VT 05439. Awards MATESL. Part-time and evening/weekend programs available. Faculty: 9 full-time (5 women), 4 part-time (all women). Students: 44 full-time (34 women), 72 part-time (52 women); includes 32 minority (1 African American, 20 Asian Americans, 11 Hispanics). Average age 29. 32 applicants, 100% accepted. In 1997, 59 degrees awarded. *Entrance requirements:* TOEFL (minimum score 550), minimum GPA of 3.0. Application deadline: 6/1 (priority date; rolling processing). Application fee: $25. *Financial aid:* In 1997–98, 2 research assistantships (1 to a first-year student) were awarded; Federal Work-Study, institutionally sponsored loans, and career-related internships or fieldwork also available. Aid available to part-time students. Financial aid applicants required to submit FAFSA. *Faculty research:* Language teaching methodology, discourse analysis, second language acquisition, language assessment, sociolinguistics, K–12 English as a second language for children. • Dr. Mahmound T. Arani, Director, 802-654-2700. E-mail: marani@smcvt.edu. Application contact: Erin Stehmeyer, Administrative Assistant, 802-654-2684. Fax: 802-654-2595. E-mail: estehmeyer@smcvt.edu.

Salem State College, Department of English, Salem, MA 01970-5353. Offerings include English as a second language (MAT). MAT (English as a second language) offered jointly with the Department of Education. *Application deadline:* rolling. *Application fee:* $25. *Expenses:* Tuition $140 per credit hour for state residents; $230 per credit hour for nonresidents. Fees $20 per credit hour.

Salem State College, Department of Education, Program in Teaching English as a Second Language K–9, Salem, MA 01970-5353. Awards M Ed. Accredited by NCATE. *Application fee:* $25. *Expenses:* Tuition $140 per credit hour for state residents; $230 per credit hour for nonresidents. Fees $20 per credit hour.

Salisbury State University, Program in English, Salisbury, MD 21801-6837. Offerings include teaching English to speakers of other languages (MA). Program faculty: 16 full-time (5 women). *Degree requirements:* Thesis optional, foreign language not required. *Entrance requirements:* GRE General Test, GRE Subject Test. Application deadline: 8/1 (rolling processing; 1/1 for spring admission). Application fee: $30. *Expenses:* Tuition $158 per credit hour for state residents; $310 per credit hour for nonresidents. Fees $4 per credit hour. • Dr. William C. Horne, Graduate Director, 410-543-6447. Fax: 410-543-6063. E-mail: wchorne@ssu.edu.

Sam Houston State University, College of Education and Applied Science, Department of Language, Literacy, and Special Populations, Program in Bilingual Education and English as a Second Language, Huntsville, TX 77341. Awards Certificate. Accredited by NCATE. Students: 0. *Application fee:* $15. *Tuition:* $1810 per year full-time, $297 per semester (minimum) part-time for state residents; $6922 per year full-time, $924 per semester (minimum) part-time for nonresidents. • Dr. Hollis Lowery-Moore, Chair, Department of Language, Literacy, and Special Populations, 409-294-1595. Fax: 409-294-1131. E-mail: edu_lap@shsu.edu.

San Francisco State University, College of Humanities, Department of English Language and Literature, Program in English as a Foreign/Second Language, San Francisco, CA 94132-1722. Awards MA. Part-time programs available. *Degree requirements:* Thesis (for some programs). *Entrance requirements:* Minimum GPA of 2.5 in last 60 units. Application deadline: rolling. Application fee: $55. *Expenses:* Tuition $0 for state residents; $246 per unit for nonresidents. Fees $1982 per year full-time, $1316 per year part-time.

San Jose State University, College of Humanities and Arts, Department of Linguistics and Language Development, San Jose, CA 95192-0001. Offerings include teaching English as a second language (MA). *Application deadline:* 6/1 (rolling processing). *Application fee:* $59. *Expenses:* Tuition $0 for state residents; $246 per unit for nonresidents. Fees $2017 per year full-time, $1351 per year part-time. • Dr. Denise Murray, Chair, 408-924-4413. Application contact: Dr. Martha Bean, Graduate Coordinator, 408-924-4707.

School for International Training, Program in Teaching, Brattleboro, VT 05302-0676. Offers endorsement in bilingual-multicultural education (MAT), English for speakers of other languages (MAT), French (MAT), Spanish (MAT). Faculty: 20 full-time (12 women), 4 part-time (3 women). Students: 79 full-time (56 women), 71 part-time (54 women). Average age 26. In 1997, 97 degrees awarded. *Degree requirements:* 1 foreign language, thesis, practice teaching. *Entrance requirements:* TOEFL (minimum score 550). Application deadline: rolling. Application fee: $45. *Expenses:* Tuition $18,000 per year (minimum). Fees $1283 per year (minimum). *Financial aid:* In 1997–98, 67 students received aid, including 49 grants, scholarships (all to first-year students); Federal Work-Study, institutionally sponsored loans, and career-related internships or fieldwork also available. Financial aid application deadline: 4/1; applicants required to submit FAFSA. • Claire Stanley, Director, 802-257-7751 Ext.3300. Application contact: Fiona Cook, Admissions Counselor, 802-258-3270. Fax: 802-258-3500.

Seattle Pacific University, College of Arts and Sciences, Program in Teaching English as a Second Language, Seattle, WA 98119-1997. Awards MA. Part-time programs available. Faculty: 9 full-time (4 women), 5 part-time (all women). Students: 9 full-time (7 women), 21 part-time (15 women); includes 8 Asian Americans, 5 international. Average age 26. 31 applicants, 58% accepted. In 1997, 16 degrees awarded. *Degree requirements:* 1 foreign language, practicum. *Average time to degree:* master's–1.5 years full-time, 3 years part-time. *Entrance requirements:* GRE General Test (minimum combined score of 950; average 1200) or MAT (minimum score 35), TOEFL (minimum score of 600), minimum GPA of 3.0. Application deadline: 8/11 (priority date; rolling processing; 3/11 for spring admission). Application fee: $35. *Tuition:* $268 per credit. *Financial aid:* In 1997–98, 20 students received aid, including 2 research assistantships totaling $4,319; Federal Work-Study and career-related internships or fieldwork also available. Financial aid application deadline: 6/1; applicants required to submit FAFSA. *Faculty research:* Second language acquisition. • Dr. Kathryn Bartholomew, Chair, 206-281-3533. Fax: 206-281-2500. Application contact: Teri Owens, Assistant, 206-281-2670. Fax: 206-281-2771. E-mail: tesol@spu.edu.

Directory: English as a Second Language

Seattle University, School of Education, Division of Leadership and Service, Program in Teaching English to Speakers of Other Languages, Seattle, WA 98122. Awards MA, M Ed. Accredited by NCATE. Part-time programs available. Students: 10 full-time (7 women), 36 part-time (26 women); includes 6 minority (all Asian Americans), 3 international. Average age 34. 35 applicants, 77% accepted. In 1997, 11 degrees awarded. *Degree requirements:* Thesis, comprehensive exam required, foreign language not required. *Entrance requirements:* GRE, MAT, or minimum GPA of 3.0. Application deadline: 8/20 (priority date; rolling processing; 2/20 for spring admission). Application fee: $55. *Expenses:* Tuition $339 per credit hour (minimum). Fees $70 per year. *Financial aid:* Federal Work-Study and career-related internships or fieldwork available. Aid available to part-time students. Financial aid applicants required to submit FAFSA. • Dr. Brita Butler-Wahe, Coordinator, 209-296-5750.

Seton Hall University, College of Education and Human Services, Teacher Training Program in English as a Second Language, South Orange, NJ 07079-2697. Awards MA, Ed S. *Degree requirements:* For master's, 2 foreign languages, comprehensive exam, project; for Ed S, 2 foreign languages, comprehensive exam, cumulative project. *Entrance requirements:* MAT, interview. Application deadline: 5/1 (priority date; rolling processing; 11/1 for spring admission). Application fee: $50. *Expenses:* Tuition $500 per credit. Fees $610 per year full-time, $185 per semester part-time. *Financial aid:* Application deadline 2/1. *Faculty research:* Spanish, Mandarin and Cantonese Chinese, Japanese, Korean, school supervision and administration. • Dr. Juan Cobarrubias, Director, 973-761-9617. Fax: 973-761-7642. E-mail: cobarrju@shu.edu.

Simmons College, Department of Education, Program in English as a Second Language, Boston, MA 02115. Awards MAT. Faculty: 2 full-time (1 woman), 2 part-time (both women). Students: 11 full-time (9 women), 21 part-time (19 women); includes 3 minority (2 Asian Americans, 1 Hispanic), 2 international. Average age 33. 18 applicants, 72% accepted. In 1997, 15 degrees awarded (100% found work related to degree). *Degree requirements:* 1 foreign language, teaching practica required, thesis not required. *Entrance requirements:* GRE General Test or MAT, interview. Application deadline: 8/1 (priority date; rolling processing; 12/15 for spring admission). Application fee: $35. *Expenses:* Tuition $587 per credit hour. Fees $20 per year. *Financial aid:* In 1997–98, 13 students received aid, including 3 teaching assistantships (all to first-year students) totaling $3,372; partial tuition waivers, Federal Work-Study, institutionally sponsored loans, and career-related internships or fieldwork also available. Aid available to part-time students. Financial aid application deadline: 3/1; applicants required to submit FAFSA. • Dr. Paul Abraham, Director, 617-521-2575. E-mail: pabraham@simmons.edu. Application contact: Director, Graduate Studies Admission, 617-521-2910. Fax: 617-521-3058. E-mail: gsa@simmons.edu.

Southeast Missouri State University, Department of English, Cape Girardeau, MO 63701-4799. Offerings include teaching English to speakers of other languages (MA). *Degree requirements:* Thesis or alternative required, foreign language not required. *Entrance requirements:* Minimum GPA of 2.5. Application deadline: 4/1 (priority date; rolling processing; 11/21 for spring admission). Application fee: $20 ($100 for international students). *Tuition:* $2034 per year full-time, $113 per credit hour part-time for state residents; $3672 per year full-time, $204 per credit hour part-time for nonresidents. • Carol Scates, Chairperson, 573-651-2156. Application contact: Office of Graduate Studies, 573-651-2192.

Southern Connecticut State University, School of Arts and Sciences, Department of Foreign Languages, New Haven, CT 06515-1355. Offerings include multicultural-bilingual education/ teaching English to speakers of other languages (MS). MLS/MS offered jointly with the College of Communication, Information and Library Science. Department faculty: 9 full-time. *Application deadline:* 7/15 (priority date; rolling processing). *Application fee:* $40. *Expenses:* Tuition $2632 per year full-time, $188 per credit part-time for state residents; $7200 per year full-time, $188 per credit part-time for nonresidents. Fees $1806 per year full-time, $45 per semester part-time for state residents; $2703 per year full-time, $45 per semester part-time for nonresidents. • Dr. Joseph Solodow, Chairperson, 203-392-6770.

Southern Illinois University at Carbondale, College of Liberal Arts, Department of Linguistics, Carbondale, IL 62901-6806. Offerings include teaching English as a second language (MA). Department faculty: 8 full-time (5 women), 3 part-time (2 women). *Degree requirements:* 1 foreign language, thesis. *Entrance requirements:* TOEFL (minimum score 570), minimum GPA of 3.0. Application deadline: 4/1 (priority date; rolling processing). Application fee: $20. *Expenses:* Tuition $2964 per year full-time, $99 per semester hour part-time for state residents; $8892 per year full-time, $270 per semester hour part-time for nonresidents. Fees $1034 per year full-time, $298 per semester (minimum) part-time. • Paul J. Angelis, Chair, 618-536-3385. E-mail: ling@siu.edu. Application contact: Diane Korando, Departmental Secretary, 618-536-3385. Fax: 618-453-6527. E-mail: ling@siu.edu.

Southern Illinois University at Edwardsville, College of Arts and Sciences, Department of English Language and Literature, Program in Teaching English as a Second Language, Edwardsville, IL 62026-0001. Awards MA. Part-time programs available. Students: 13 full-time (9 women), 5 part-time (1 woman); includes 2 minority (1 African American, 1 Asian American), 8 international. 20 applicants, 30% accepted. In 1997, 3 degrees awarded. *Degree requirements:* 1 foreign language, thesis or alternative, final exam. *Application deadline:* 7/24. *Application fee:* $25. *Expenses:* Tuition $1716 per year full-time, $95 per credit hour part-time for state residents; $5149 per year full-time, $286 per credit hour part-time for nonresidents. Fees $463 per year full-time, $433 per year part-time. *Financial aid:* In 1997–98, 1 teaching assistantship was awarded; fellowships, research assistantships, institutionally sponsored loans also available. Aid available to part-time students. • Application contact: Ronald Schafer, Director, 618-692-2060.

State University of New York at Buffalo, Graduate School, Graduate School of Education, Department of Learning and Instruction, Buffalo, NY 14260. Offerings include bilingual education/ teaching English to speakers of other languages (Ed M), teaching English as a second language (Ed D, PhD). Terminal master's awarded for partial completion of doctoral program. Department faculty: 20 full-time (9 women), 7 part-time (2 women). *Degree requirements:* For master's, comprehensive exam required, foreign language and thesis not required; for doctorate, dissertation, research analysis exam required, foreign language not required. *Entrance requirements:* For master's, GRE General Test, TOEFL (minimum score 590); for doctorate, GRE General Test, TOEFL (minimum score 600), interview. Application deadline: 2/1 (11/15 for spring admission). Application fee: $50. *Tuition:* $5970 per year full-time, $288 per credit hour part-time for state residents; $9286 per year full-time, $426 per credit hour part-time for nonresidents. • Dr. Michael Kibby, Chair, 716-645-2455. Application contact: Barbara Cracchiolo, Admissions Secretary, 716-645-2457. Fax: 716-645-3161.

State University of New York at New Paltz, Faculty of Education, Program in Secondary Language Education, New Paltz, NY 12561-2499. Offers English as a second language (MS Ed). Students: 20 full-time (14 women), 19 part-time (15 women); includes 6 minority (2 African Americans, 4 Hispanics), 2 international. *Entrance requirements:* Minimum GPA of 3.0. Application deadline: 3/15 (priority date; rolling processing). Application fee: $50. *Expenses:* Tuition $5100 per year full-time, $213 per credit hour part-time for state residents; $8416 per year full-time, $351 per credit hour part-time for nonresidents. Fees $493 per year full-time, $48 per semester (minimum) part-time. • Vern Todd, Coordinator, 914-257-2818.

State University of New York at Stony Brook, College of Arts and Sciences, Department of Linguistics, Program in Teaching English to Speakers of Other Languages, Stony Brook, NY 11794. Offers foreign languages (DA), including teaching English to speakers of other languages; teaching English to speakers of other languages (MA). Students: 24 full-time (16 women), 12 part-time (all women); includes 5 minority (1 African American, 1 Asian American, 3 Hispanics), 12 international. 57 applicants, 70% accepted. In 1997, 18 master's awarded. *Application deadline:* 1/15. *Application fee:* $50. *Expenses:* Tuition $5100 per year full-time, $213 per credit hour part-time for state residents; $8416 per year full-time, $351 per credit hour part-time for nonresidents. Fees $529 per year full-time, $77 per semester (minimum) part-time. *Financial aid:* Fellowships, research assistantships, teaching assistantships available. • Application contact: Dr. Frank Anshen, Director, 516-632-7776.

Teachers College, Columbia University, Graduate Faculty of Education, Department of Arts and Humanities, Program in Teaching English to Speakers of Other Languages, 525 West 120th Street, New York, NY 10027-6696. Awards Ed M, MA, Ed D. Part-time programs available. Faculty: 2 full-time (1 woman), 13 part-time (10 women), 7.8 FTE. Students: 18 full-time (12 women), 138 part-time (118 women); includes 42 minority (6 African Americans, 27 Asian Americans, 9 Hispanics), 39 international. Average age 30. 212 applicants, 58% accepted. In 1997, 67 master's, 3 doctorates awarded. *Degree requirements:* For doctorate, dissertation. *Entrance requirements:* For master's, TOEFL; for doctorate, MA in teaching English to speakers of other languages. Application deadline: 2/1 (priority date). Application fee: $50. *Expenses:* Tuition $640 per credit. Fees $120 per semester. *Financial aid:* Full and partial tuition waivers, Federal Work-Study, institutionally sponsored loans, and career-related internships or fieldwork available. Aid available to part-time students. Financial aid application deadline: 2/1. *Faculty research:* Classroom-centered research, electronic media, K–12 English as a second language, second language acquisition. • Application contact: Amy Rotheim, Office of Admissions, 212-678-3710. Fax: 212-678-4171.

Texas A&M University–Kingsville, College of Education, Department of Education, Program in English as a Second Language, Kingsville, TX 78363. Awards M Ed. *Degree requirements:* Comprehensive exam required, foreign language not required. *Entrance requirements:* GRE General Test (minimum combined score of 1000), MAT (minimum score 34), minimum GPA of 3.0. Application deadline: 6/1 (rolling processing; 11/15 for spring admission). Application fee: $15 ($25 for international students). *Tuition:* $1822 per year full-time, $281 per semester (minimum) part-time for state residents; $6934 per year full-time, $908 per semester (minimum) part-time for nonresidents. *Financial aid:* Application deadline 5/15. • Dr. Travis Polk, Chair, Department of Education, 512-593-3204.

United States International University, College of Arts and Sciences, Department of Education, San Diego, CA 92131-1799. Offerings include teaching English to speakers of other languages (MA, Ed D). Terminal master's awarded for partial completion of doctoral program. Department faculty: 10 full-time (7 women), 12 part-time (6 women). *Degree requirements:* Thesis/dissertation. *Average time to degree:* master's–1.5 years full-time, 2.5 years part-time; doctorate–3 years full-time, 5 years part-time. *Entrance requirements:* For master's, TOEFL, minimum GPA of 2.5; for doctorate, GRE General Test or MAT, TOEFL, minimum GPA of 3.0. Application deadline: 8/1 (priority date; rolling processing; 3/1 for spring admission). Application fee: $40. *Expenses:* Tuition $255 per unit. Fees $120 per year full-time, $33 per quarter part-time. • Dr. Mary Ellen Butler-Pascoe, Chair, 619-635-4595. Fax: 619-635-4714. Application contact: Susan Topham, Assistant Director of Admissions, 619-635-4885. Fax: 619-635-4739. E-mail: admissions@usiu.edu.

Universidad del Turabo, Programs in Education, Program in Teaching English as a Second Language, Gurabo, PR 00778-3030. Awards MA. *Entrance requirements:* GRE, PAEG, interview. Application deadline: 8/5. Application fee: $25.

The University of Alabama, College of Arts and Sciences, Department of English, Tuscaloosa, AL 35487. Offerings include teaching English to speakers of other languages (MA). Department faculty: 33 full-time (11 women), 2 part-time (1 woman), 34 FTE. *Average time to degree:* master's–3 years full-time; doctorate–6 years full-time. *Application deadline:* 2/21 (priority date). *Application fee:* $25. Electronic applications accepted. *Tuition:* $2684 per year full-time, $594 per semester (minimum) part-time for state residents; $7216 per year full-time, $1248 per semester (minimum) part-time for nonresidents. • Sara D. Davis, Chairperson, 205-348-5065. Application contact: Joseph A. Hornsby, Director, 205-348-9493.

University of Alberta, Faculty of Graduate Studies and Research, Department of Educational Psychology, Edmonton, AB T6G 2E1, Canada. Offerings include teaching English as a second language (M Ed). Department faculty: 36 full-time (11 women), 23 part-time (9 women), 41.75 FTE. *Application deadline:* 2/1 (priority date; rolling processing). *Application fee:* $60. *Expenses:* Tuition $390 per course for Canadian residents; $781 per course for nonresidents. Fees $500 per year full-time, $184 per year part-time. • Dr. L. L. Stewin, Chair, 403-492-2389. Fax: 403-492-1318. E-mail: len.stewin@ualberta.ca.

The University of Arizona, Graduate Interdisciplinary Programs, Graduate Interdisciplinary Program in Second Language Acquisition and Teaching, Tucson, AZ 85721. Awards PhD. *Degree requirements:* Dissertation. *Entrance requirements:* TOEFL. Application deadline: 8/1 (rolling processing). Application fee: $35. *Tuition:* $2162 per year full-time, $337 per semester (minimum) part-time for state residents; $6860 per year full-time, $1138 per semester (minimum) part-time for nonresidents.

The University of Arizona, College of Humanities, Department of English, Program in English as a Second Language, Tucson, AZ 85721. Awards MA. Part-time programs available. *Degree requirements:* 1 foreign language, comprehensive exam required, thesis not required. *Entrance requirements:* GRE General Test, GRE Subject Test (literature), TOEFL (minimum score 600), foreign language, sample of written work, teaching experience. Application deadline: 2/1 (rolling processing). Application fee: $35. *Tuition:* $2162 per year full-time, $337 per semester (minimum) part-time for state residents; $6860 per year full-time, $1138 per semester (minimum) part-time for nonresidents. *Faculty research:* First and second language acquisition, writing in ESL, sociolinguistics of second language learning, linguistic universals.

University of British Columbia, Faculty of Education, Department of Language Education, Vancouver, BC V6T 1Z2, Canada. Offers programs in English education (MA, M Ed, PhD), library education (MA, M Ed, PhD), modern language education (MA, M Ed, PhD), reading education (MA, M Ed, Ed D, PhD), teaching English as a second language (MA, M Ed, PhD). Part-time and evening/weekend programs available. *Degree requirements:* For master's, thesis (MA) required, foreign language not required; for doctorate, dissertation required, foreign language not required. *Entrance requirements:* TOEFL (minimum score 550), minimum B average in most recent 2 years of study with minimum of two courses at A standing. Application deadline: 2/28 (priority date; rolling processing; 8/1 for spring admission). Application fee: $60. *Faculty research:* Language and literacy development, second language acquisition, Asia Pacific language curriculum, children's literature, whole language instruction.

University of California, Los Angeles, College of Letters and Science, Department of Applied Linguistics and Teaching English as a Second Language, Los Angeles, CA 90095. Offers programs in applied linguistics and teaching English as a second language (MA), teaching English as a second language (Certificate). Certificate admissions temporarily suspended. Faculty: 6 (2 women). Students: 12 full-time (10 women); includes 2 minority (1 Asian American, 1 Hispanic), 5 international. 43 applicants, 49% accepted. *Degree requirements:* For master's, thesis. *Entrance requirements:* For master's, GRE General Test, minimum GPA of 3.0, sample of research writing. Application deadline: 12/15. Application fee: $40. Electronic applications accepted. *Expenses:* Tuition $0 for state residents; $9384 per year for nonresidents. Fees $4551 per year. *Financial aid:* In 1997–98, 11 students received aid, including fellowships totaling $42,238, research assistantships totaling $52,953, teaching assistantships totaling $109,851, federal fellowships and scholarships totaling $15,243; full and partial tuition waivers, Federal Work-Study, institutionally sponsored loans also available. Financial aid application deadline: 3/1. • Dr. John Schumann, Chair, 310-825-4631. Application contact: Departmental Office, 310-825-4631. Fax: 310-206-4118. E-mail: lyn@humnet.ucla.edu.

University of Central Florida, Colleges of Arts and Sciences and Education, Program in Teaching English as a Second Language, Orlando, FL 32816. Awards MA. Students: 12 full-time (8 women), 10 part-time (9 women); includes 7 minority (all Hispanics), 1 international. Average age 38. 33 applicants, 67% accepted. *Degree requirements:* Thesis or alternative required, foreign language not required. *Entrance requirements:* GRE General Test. Application deadline: 6/15 (11/1 for spring admission). Application fee: $20. *Expenses:* Tuition $3288 per year full-time, $137 per credit hour part-time for state residents; $11,520 per year full-time,

$480 per credit hour part-time for nonresidents. Fees $105 per year. • Dr. Consuelo D. Stebbins, Chair, 407-823-0088.

University of Colorado at Denver, College of Liberal Arts and Sciences, Department of English, Program in Teaching English as a Second Language, Denver, CO 80217-3364. Awards MA. Accredited by NCATE. *Degree requirements:* Thesis optional. *Entrance requirements:* GRE General Test, TOEFL, minimum GPA of 3.0. Application deadline: 6/1 (rolling processing; 11/1 for spring admission). Application fee: $50. Electronic applications accepted. *Expenses:* Tuition $2996 per year full-time, $181 per semester hour part-time for state residents; $11,954 per year full-time, $717 per semester hour part-time for nonresidents. Fees $252 per year. *Financial aid:* Research assistantships, teaching assistantships, and career-related internships or fieldwork available. Financial aid application deadline: 3/1; applicants required to submit FAFSA. • Dr. Rex Burns, Chair, Department of English, 303-556-8304.

Announcement: Master's program in teaching English as a second language (ESL) prepares students to be effective classroom teachers at colleges and language schools in the U.S. and overseas. Assistantships and paid overseas internships are available on a competitive basis. MA without thesis offered; 30 credit hours required. For more information, visit the Web site at http://www.cudenver.edu/public/english

University of Delaware, College of Human Resources, Education and Public Policy, School of Education, Newark, DE 19716. Offerings include English as a second language/bilingualism (MA). School faculty: 54 (24 women). *Application deadline:* 7/1 (rolling processing; 1/15 for spring admission). *Application fee:* $45. *Expenses:* Tuition $4250 per year full-time, $236 per credit hour part-time for state residents; $12,250 per year full-time, $681 per credit hour part-time for nonresidents. Fees $466 per year full-time, $15 per semester (minimum) part-time. • Dr. Robert Hampel, Director, 302-831-2573.

The University of Findlay, College of Professional Studies, Program in Teaching English to Speakers of Other Languages and Bilingual and Multicultural Education, 1000 North Main Street, Findlay, OH 45840-3653. Offers bilingual and multicultural education (MA), teaching English to speakers of other languages (MA). Faculty: 4 full-time (3 women), 3 part-time (2 women). Students: 24 full-time (21 women), 53 part-time (51 women); includes 30 minority (2 African Americans, 25 Asian Americans, 3 Hispanics). Average age 30. In 1997, 23 degrees awarded. *Degree requirements:* Cumulative project. *Application deadline:* rolling. *Application fee:* $25. *Tuition:* $236 per semester hour. *Financial aid:* Teaching assistantships available. Aid available to part-time students. Financial aid applicants required to submit FAFSA. • Dr. Irma A. Hanson, Director, 419-424-4826. Fax: 419-424-4822. E-mail: hanson@hewey.findlay.edu.

University of Florida, College of Liberal Arts and Sciences, Program in Linguistics, Gainesville, FL 32611. Offerings include teaching English as a second language (Certificate). Program faculty: 26. *Entrance requirements:* TOEFL (minimum score 600). Application deadline: 6/5 (priority date; rolling processing). Application fee: $20. *Tuition:* $138 per credit hour for state residents; $481 per credit hour for nonresidents. • Dr. Marie Nelson, Director, 352-392-0639. E-mail: mnelson@lin.ufl.edu. Application contact: Dr. William J. Sullivan, Graduate Coordinator, 352-392-0639. Fax: 352-392-8480. E-mail: wjs@nervm.nerdc.ufl.edu.

University of Guam, College of Education, Program in Teaching English to Speakers of Other Languages, 303 University Drive, UOG Station, Mangilao, GU 96923. Awards M Ed. *Degree requirements:* Comprehensive oral and written exams, special project or thesis required, foreign language not required. *Entrance requirements:* GRE General Test. Application deadline: 5/31. Application fee: $31 ($56 for international students).

University of Hawaii at Manoa, College of Arts and Sciences, College of Language, Linguistics and Literature, Department of English as a Second Language, Honolulu, HI 96822. Offers programs in English as a second language (MA), second language acquisition (PhD). Faculty: 13 full-time (4 women). Students: 83 full-time (50 women), 29 part-time (22 women); includes 42 international. 107 applicants, 53% accepted. In 1997, 19 master's awarded; 1 doctorate awarded (100% entered university research/teaching). *Degree requirements:* For master's, 1 foreign language, thesis or alternative; for doctorate, 2 foreign languages (computer language can substitute for one), dissertation, comprehensive exams. *Average time to degree:* master's–2 years full-time, 3.5 years part-time; doctorate–5 years full-time. *Entrance requirements:* For master's, GRE General Test, TOEFL (minimum score 600), minimum GPA of 3.0; for doctorate, GRE General Test, TOEFL (minimum score 600), MA, scholarly publications. Application deadline: rolling. Application fee: $25 ($50 for international students). *Tuition:* $4029 per year full-time, $214 per credit hour part-time for state residents; $9957 per year full-time, $461 per credit hour part-time for nonresidents. *Financial aid:* In 1997–98, 48 students received aid, including 2 fellowships averaging $450 per month, 5 research assistantships averaging $985 per month, 19 teaching assistantships averaging $985 per month, 4 grants (2 to first-year students); full and partial tuition waivers, Federal Work-Study, institutionally sponsored loans, and career-related internships or fieldwork also available. Financial aid application deadline: 2/1; applicants required to submit FAFSA. *Faculty research:* Second language use, second language analysis, second language pedagogy and testing, second language learning, qualitative and quantitative research methods for second languages. • Dr. Roderick A. Jacobs, Chairperson, 808-956-8610. E-mail: rjacobs@hawaii.edu. Application contact: Graduate Chair, 808-956-8610. Fax: 808-956-2802. E-mail: desl@hawaii.edu.

University of Houston, College of Education, Department of Curriculum and Instruction, 4800 Calhoun, Houston, TX 77204-2163. Offerings include second language education (M Ed). Accredited by NCATE. Department faculty: 37 full-time (19 women), 10 part-time (7 women). *Degree requirements:* Comprehensive exam or thesis required, foreign language not required. *Entrance requirements:* GRE General Test or MAT. Application deadline: 7/3 (priority date; rolling processing). Application fee: $35 ($75 for international students). *Expenses:* Tuition $1152 per year full-time, $120 per semester (minimum) part-time for state residents; $4482 per year full-time, $249 per credit hour part-time for nonresidents. Fees $977 per year full-time, $119 per semester (minimum) part-time. • Wilford Weber, Chair, 713-743-4970. Fax: 713-743-9870. E-mail: wweber@uh.edu.

University of Idaho, College of Graduate Studies, College of Letters and Science, Department of English, Program in Teaching English as a Second Language, Moscow, ID 83844-4140. Awards MA. Students: 13 full-time (6 women), 1 part-time (0 women); includes 4 international. In 1997, 12 degrees awarded. *Entrance requirements:* Minimum GPA of 2.8. Application deadline: 8/1 (12/15 for spring admission). Application fee: $35 ($45 for international students). *Expenses:* Tuition $0 for state residents; $6000 per year full-time, $95 per credit part-time for nonresidents. Fees $2676 per year full-time, $134 per credit part-time. *Financial aid:* Application deadline 2/15. • Dr. Douglas Q. Adams, Chair, Department of English, 208-885-6156.

University of Illinois at Chicago, College of Liberal Arts and Sciences, Department of English, Program in Linguistics, Chicago, IL 60607-7128. Offerings include applied linguistics (teaching English as a second language) (MA). *Degree requirements:* 1 foreign language, thesis (for some programs), comprehensive exam. *Entrance requirements:* GRE General Test, TOEFL (minimum score 580), TSE (minimum score 230), minimum GPA of 4.0 on a 5.0 scale. Application deadline: 7/3 (11/8 for spring admission). Application fee: $40 ($50 for international students). • Dr. Elliott Judd, Director of Graduate Studies, 312-996-2370.

University of Illinois at Urbana–Champaign, College of Liberal Arts and Sciences, Division of English as an International Language, Urbana, IL 61801. Awards AM. Faculty: 8 full-time (3 women). Students: 85 full-time (62 women); includes 6 minority (2 African Americans, 3 Asian Americans, 1 Hispanic), 37 international. 141 applicants, 36% accepted. In 1997, 44 degrees awarded. *Entrance requirements:* Minimum GPA of 4.0 on a 5.0 scale. Application deadline: rolling. Application fee: $40 ($50 for international students). *Financial aid:* In 1997–98, 3 fellowships, 7 research assistantships, 45 teaching assistantships were awarded; full and partial tuition waivers also available. Financial aid application deadline: 2/15. • Dr. Lawrence Bouton, Acting Director, 217-333-1506.

University of Kansas, School of Education, Department of Teaching and Leadership, Program in Teaching English as a Second Language, Lawrence, KS 66045. Awards MA, MS Ed, Ed D, PhD. Accredited by NCATE. *Degree requirements:* For master's, 1 foreign language, thesis or alternative; for doctorate, variable foreign language requirement, dissertation. *Entrance requirements:* For master's, TOEFL (minimum score 590), minimum GPA of 3.0, teaching certificate; for doctorate, GRE General Test, minimum graduate GPA of 3.5. Application deadline: 7/1. Application fee: $25. *Expenses:* Tuition $2400 per year full-time, $100 per credit hour part-time for state residents; $7890 per year full-time, $329 per credit hour part-time for nonresidents. Fees $428 per year full-time, $31 per credit hour part-time. • Paul Markham, Director, 785-864-9677.

University of Manitoba, Faculty of Education, Department of Curriculum: Humanities and Social Sciences, Winnipeg, MB R3T 2N2, Canada. Offerings include English as a second language (M Ed). *Degree requirements:* Thesis or alternative required, foreign language not required.

University of Maryland, College Park, College of Education, Department of Curriculum and Instruction, College Park, MD 20742-5045. Offerings include teaching English to speakers of other languages (M Ed). Accredited by NCATE. Postbaccalaureate distance learning degree programs offered. Department faculty: 29 full-time (14 women), 11 part-time (8 women). *Application deadline:* rolling. *Application fee:* $50 ($70 for international students). *Expenses:* Tuition $272 per credit hour for state residents; $400 per credit hour for nonresidents. Fees $564 per year full-time, $342 per year part-time. • Dr. Martin Johnson, Chairman, 301-405-3117. Fax: 301-314-9278. Application contact: John Mollish, Director, Graduate Admissions and Records, 301-405-4198. Fax: 301-314-9305.

University of Massachusetts Boston, College of Arts and Sciences, Faculty of Arts, Program in English as a Second Language, Boston, MA 02125-3393. Awards MA. Students: 23 full-time (15 women), 105 part-time (82 women); includes 14 minority (5 African Americans, 3 Asian Americans, 6 Hispanics), 16 international. 73 applicants, 64% accepted. In 1997, 64 degrees awarded. *Degree requirements:* Comprehensive exams required, thesis optional, foreign language not required. *Entrance requirements:* Minimum GPA of 2.75. Application deadline: 2/1 (priority date; 10/15 for spring admission). Application fee: $25 ($35 for international students). *Expenses:* Tuition $2640 per year full-time, $110 per credit part-time for state residents; $8930 per year full-time, $373 per credit part-time for nonresidents. Fees $2650 per year full-time, $420 per semester (minimum) part-time for state residents; $2736 per year full-time, $420 per semester (minimum) part-time for nonresidents. *Financial aid:* Research assistantships, teaching assistantships, administrative assistantships available. Financial aid application deadline: 3/1; applicants required to submit FAFSA. • Dr. Donaldo Macedo, Director, 617-287-5760. Application contact: Lisa Lavely, Director of Graduate Admissions and Records, 617-287-6400. Fax: 617-287-6236.

University of Miami, School of Education, Department of Teaching and Learning, Program in Teaching English to Speakers of Other Languages, Coral Gables, FL 33124. Awards MS Ed, Ed S. Accredited by NCATE. Part-time programs available. Faculty: 5 full-time (3 women), 1 part-time (0 women). Students: 2 full-time (1 woman), 5 part-time (4 women); includes 2 minority (both African Americans), 3 international. Average age 29. 27 applicants, 70% accepted. In 1997, 16 master's awarded. *Degree requirements:* For master's, thesis optional, foreign language not required. *Average time to degree:* master's–2 years part-time. *Entrance requirements:* For master's, GRE General Test (minimum combined score of 1000), TOEFL (minimum score 550). Application deadline: rolling. Application fee: $35. *Expenses:* Tuition $815 per credit hour. Fees $174 per year. *Financial aid:* Full tuition waivers, Federal Work-Study, institutionally sponsored loans, and career-related internships or fieldwork available. Financial aid application deadline: 3/1. *Faculty research:* Cognitive strategies, language development and science learning, second language acquisition, second language assessment. Total annual research expenditures: $15,000. • Dr. Janette Klingner, Coordinator, 305-284-5937. Fax: 305-284-3003. E-mail: jklingner@miami.ir.miami.edu.

University of Nevada, Las Vegas, College of Education, Department of Instructional and Curricular Studies, Las Vegas, NV 89154-9900. Offerings include teaching English as a second language (M Ed, MS). Accredited by NCATE. Department faculty: 34 full-time (16 women). *Degree requirements:* Thesis (for some programs), oral or written comprehensive exam required, foreign language not required. *Entrance requirements:* Minimum GPA of 3.0. Application deadline: 2/15 (9/30 for spring admission). Application fee: $40 ($95 for international students). *Expenses:* Tuition $93 per credit for state residents; $93 per credit full-time, $190 per credit part-time for nonresidents. Fees $5570 per year full-time for nonresidents. • Dr. Jan McCarthy, Chair, 702-895-3241. Application contact: Graduate College Admissions Evaluator, 702-895-3320.

University of Nevada, Reno, College of Arts and Science, Department of English, Reno, NV 89557. Offerings include teaching English as a second language (MA). Accredited by NCATE. Department faculty: 21 (7 women). *Application deadline:* 2/1. *Application fee:* $40. *Expenses:* Tuition $0 for state residents; $5770 per year full-time, $200 per credit part-time for nonresidents. Fees $93 per credit. • Dr. Stephen Tchudi, Chair, 702-784-6689. Application contact: Dr. Stacy Burton, Director of Graduate Studies, 702-784-6689. E-mail: sburton@unr.edu.

University of North Carolina at Charlotte, College of Education, Charlotte, NC 28223-0001. Offerings include teaching English as a second language (M Ed). Accredited by NCATE. College faculty: 61 full-time (31 women), 7 part-time (6 women), 62.75 FTE. *Application deadline:* 7/1. *Application fee:* $35. *Tuition:* $1786 per year full-time, $339 per semester (minimum) part-time for state residents; $8914 per year full-time, $2121 per semester (minimum) part-time for nonresidents. • Dr. John M. Nagle, Dean, 704-547-4707. Application contact: Kathy Barringer, Assistant Director of Graduate Admissions, 704-547-3366. Fax: 704-547-3279. E-mail: gradadm@email.uncc.edu.

University of Northern Iowa, College of Humanities and Fine Arts, Department of English Language and Literature, Cedar Falls, IA 50614. Offerings include teaching English to speakers of other languages (MA). Department faculty: 25 full-time (10 women). *Degree requirements:* 1 foreign language. *Entrance requirements:* GRE General Test, GRE Subject Test. Application deadline: 8/1 (priority date; rolling processing). Application fee: $20 ($30 for international students). *Expenses:* Tuition $3166 per year full-time, $176 per hour part-time for state residents; $7805 per year full-time, $176 per hour part-time for nonresidents. Fees $194 per year full-time, $12.50 per semester (minimum) part-time. • Dr. Jeffrey Copeland, Head, 319-273-2822.

University of Northern Iowa, College of Humanities and Fine Arts, Department of Modern Languages, Cedar Falls, IA 50614. Offerings include teaching English to speakers of other languages (MA), with options in French, German, Spanish. Department faculty: 13 full-time (1 woman). *Degree requirements:* 1 foreign language, thesis or alternative. *Application deadline:* 8/1 (priority date; rolling processing). *Application fee:* $20 ($30 for international students). *Expenses:* Tuition $3166 per year full-time, $176 per hour part-time for state residents; $7805 per year full-time, $176 per hour part-time for nonresidents. Fees $194 per year full-time, $12.50 per semester (minimum) part-time. • Dr. Ann Marie Basom, Head, 319-273-2749.

University of Pennsylvania, Graduate School of Education, Division of Language in Education, Programs in Educational Linguistics, Teaching English to Speakers of Other Languages and Intercultural Communication, Philadelphia, PA 19104. Offerings in educational linguistics (PhD), intercultural communication (MS Ed), teaching English to speakers of other languages (MS Ed). Part-time programs available. Postbaccalaureate distance learning degree programs offered (minimal on-campus study). Students: 95 full-time (81 women), 22 part-time (17 women). In 1997, 33 master's, 6 doctorates awarded. Terminal master's awarded for partial completion of doctoral program. *Degree requirements:* For master's, thesis (for some programs),

Directory: English as a Second Language

University of Pennsylvania (continued)
comprehensive exam required, foreign language not required; for doctorate, 1 foreign language, dissertation, preliminary exam. *Entrance requirements:* GRE General Test or MAT, TOEFL (minimum score 550). Application fee: $65. Electronic applications accepted. *Expenses:* Tuition $22,716 per year full-time, $2876 per course part-time. Fees $1484 per year full-time, $181 per course part-time. *Financial aid:* Fellowships, research assistantships, Federal Work-Study, institutionally sponsored loans, and career-related internships or fieldwork available. Financial aid application deadline: 1/2; applicants required to submit FAFSA. *Faculty research:* Second language acquisition, social linguistics, English as a second language. • Dr. Nancy Hornberger, Director, 215-898-4800. Application contact: Keith Watanabe, Coordinator, 215-898-3245. Fax: 215-573-2109.

University of Puerto Rico, Río Piedras, College of Education, Program in Teaching English as a Second Language, San Juan, PR 00931. Awards M Ed. Part-time programs available. *Degree requirements:* 1 foreign language, thesis. *Entrance requirements:* PAEG, minimum GPA of 3.0. Application deadline: 2/21. Application fee: $17.

University of San Francisco, School of Education, Department of International and Multicultural Education, San Francisco, CA 94117-1080. Offerings include teaching English as a second language (MA). Department faculty: 8 full-time (5 women), 9 part-time (5 women). *Application fee:* $40. *Tuition:* $658 per unit (minimum). • Dr. Rosita Galang, Chair, 415-422-6878.

University of South Carolina, Graduate School, College of Liberal Arts, Interdepartmental Program in Linguistics, Columbia, SC 29208. Offerings include teaching English as a foreign language (Certificate). Program faculty: 12 full-time (6 women), 18 part-time (9 women). *Average time to degree:* master's–2 years full-time; doctorate–4 years full-time; other advanced degree–1 year full-time. *Entrance requirements:* GRE General Test (minimum combined score of 800), TOEFL (minimum score 560), minimum GPA of 3.0. Application deadline: 7/15 (priority date; rolling processing). Application fee: $35. Electronic applications accepted. *Expenses:* Tuition $3894 per year full-time, $193 per credit hour part-time for state residents; $8114 per year full-time, $404 per credit hour part-time for nonresidents. Fees $125 per year full-time, $37 per semester (minimum) part-time. • Dr. Carol Myers-Scotton, Director, 803-777-2258. Fax: 803-777-9064. E-mail: linguistics@sc.edu.

University of Southern California, Graduate School, School of Education, Department of Curriculum and Instruction, Los Angeles, CA 90089. Offerings include teaching English as a second language (MS). *Entrance requirements:* GRE General Test. Application deadline: 7/1 (priority date; 11/1 for spring admission). Application fee: $55. *Expenses:* Tuition $16,944 per year full-time, $706 per unit part-time. Fees $414 per year full-time, $32 per year part-time. • Dr. Edgar Williams, Chair.

University of Southern Maine, College of Education and Human Development, English as a Second Language Program, Portland, ME 04104-9300. Awards MS Ed, CAS. Accredited by NCATE. Part-time and evening/weekend programs available. Faculty: 1 part-time (0 women). Students: 4 full-time (3 women), 8 part-time (7 women); includes 1 minority (Asian American), 1 international. 11 applicants, 91% accepted. In 1997, 2 master's awarded. *Degree requirements:* For master's, thesis or alternative, comprehensive exam required, foreign language not required; for CAS, thesis or alternative required, foreign language not required. *Entrance requirements:* For master's, GRE General Test (minimum combined score of 900), MAT (minimum score 40), TOEFL (minimum score 550). Application deadline: 2/1 (9/15 for spring admission). Application fee: $25. *Expenses:* Tuition $178 per credit hour for state residents; $267 per credit hour (minimum) for nonresidents. Fees $282 per year full-time, $83 per semester (minimum) part-time. *Financial aid:* Research assistantships, Federal Work-Study, institutionally sponsored loans, and career-related internships or fieldwork available. Financial aid application deadline: 3/1; applicants required to submit FAFSA. • Dr. Margo Wood, Chair, Professional Education Department, 207-780-5400. Application contact: Teresa Belsan, Admissions and Academic Counselor, 207-780-5306. Fax: 207-780-5315. E-mail: belsan@usm.maine.edu.

University of South Florida, College of Arts and Sciences, Division of Languages and Linguistics, Program in Applied Linguistics, Tampa, FL 33620-9951. Offers teaching English as a second language (MA). Accredited by NCATE. Part-time and evening/weekend programs available. *Entrance requirements:* GRE General Test (minimum combined score of 1000), minimum GPA of 3.0 in last 60 hours. Application deadline: 6/1 (10/15 for spring admission). Application fee: $20. *Tuition:* $142 per credit hour for state residents; $486 per credit hour for nonresidents. • Application contact: Roger Cole, Director, 813-974-2548. Fax: 813-974-1718. E-mail: rogrcole@chuma1.cas.usf.edu.

University of Tennessee, Knoxville, College of Education, Program in Education I, Knoxville, TN 37996. Offerings include English, foreign language and ESL education (PhD). Accredited by NCATE. *Degree requirements:* 1 foreign language (computer language can substitute), dissertation. *Entrance requirements:* GRE General Test, TOEFL (minimum score 550), minimum GPA of 2.7. Application deadline: 2/1 (priority date; rolling processing). Application fee: $35. Electronic applications accepted. *Tuition:* $3354 per year full-time, $181 per semester hour part-time for state residents; $8410 per year full-time, $462 per semester hour part-time for nonresidents. • Dr. Tom George, Associate Dean, 423-974-0907. Fax: 423-974-8718. E-mail: tgeorge1@utk.edu.

University of Tennessee, Knoxville, College of Education, Program in Education II, Knoxville, TN 37996. Offerings include foreign language/ESL education (MS, Ed D, Ed S). Accredited by NCATE. *Degree requirements:* For master's and Ed S, thesis optional, foreign language not required; for doctorate, dissertation required, foreign language not required. *Entrance requirements:* For master's, TOEFL (minimum score 550), minimum GPA of 2.7; for doctorate, GRE General Test, TOEFL (minimum score 550), minimum GPA of 2.7; for Ed S, TOEFL (minimum score 550), GRE General Test, minimum GPA of 2.7. Application deadline: 2/1 (priority date; rolling processing). Application fee: $35. Electronic applications accepted. *Tuition:* $3354 per year full-time, $181 per semester hour part-time for state residents; $8410 per year full-time, $462 per semester hour part-time for nonresidents. • Dr. Tom George, Associate Dean, 423-974-0907. Fax: 423-974-8718. E-mail: tgeorge1@utk.edu.

The University of Texas at Brownsville, Graduate Studies, School of Education, Brownsville, TX 78520-4991. Offerings include English as a second language (M Ed). School faculty: 18 full-time (10 women). *Degree requirements:* Thesis optional, foreign language not required. *Entrance requirements:* GRE General Test, TOEFL (minimum score 550). Application deadline: 8/1 (priority date; rolling processing; 1/1 for spring admission). Application fee: $15. *Expenses:* Tuition $648 per year full-time, $120 per semester hour part-time for state residents; $4698 per year full-time, $783 per semester hour part-time for nonresidents. Fees $593 per year full-time, $109 per year part-time. • Dr. Sylvia C. Peña, Dean, 956-983-7219. Fax: 956-982-0293. E-mail: scpena@utb1.utb.edu.

The University of Texas at San Antonio, College of Social and Behavioral Sciences, Division of Bicultural-Bilingual Studies, San Antonio, TX 78249-0617. Offerings include teaching English as a second language (MA). Division faculty: 9 full-time (3 women), 12 part-time (7 women). *Degree requirements:* 1 foreign language, thesis or alternative, comprehensive exam. *Entrance requirements:* GRE General Test. Application deadline: 7/1 (rolling processing). Application fee: $20. *Expenses:* Tuition $2476 per year full-time, $309 per semester (minimum) part-time for state residents; $7584 per year full-time, $948 per semester (minimum) part-time for nonresidents. Fees $361 per year full-time, $133 per semester (minimum) part-time. • Dr. Robert Milk, Director, 210-458-4426.

The University of Texas–Pan American, College of Liberal and Performing Arts, Department of English, Program in English as a Second Language, Edinburg, TX 78539-2999. Awards MA. *Degree requirements:* Comprehensive exam required, thesis optional, foreign language not required. *Average time to degree:* master's–2 years full-time, 4 years part-time. *Entrance requirements:* GRE General Test (minimum score 500 on verbal section), minimum GPA of 3.0. Application deadline: rolling. Application fee: $0. *Tuition:* $2156 per year full-time, $283 per semester (minimum) part-time for state residents; $6788 per year full-time, $862 per semester (minimum) part-time for nonresidents.

University of Toledo, College of Arts and Sciences, Department of English Language and Literature, Toledo, OH 43606-3398. Offerings include English as a second language (MA Ed). Department faculty: 22 full-time (7 women). *Application deadline:* 8/1 (priority date; rolling processing). *Application fee:* $30. Electronic applications accepted. *Tuition:* $5907 per year full-time, $246 per hour part-time for state residents; $11,835 per year full-time, $493 per hour part-time for nonresidents. • Dr. Russell Reising, Chair, 419-530-2318. Application contact: Dr. Thomas Barden, Director, 419-530-2318. Fax: 419-530-4440. E-mail: tbarden@uoft02.utoledo.edu.

University of Washington, College of Arts and Sciences, Department of English, Seattle, WA 98195. Offerings include English as a second language (MAT). Department faculty: 60 full-time (24 women), 2 part-time (0 women). *Average time to degree:* master's–2 years full-time; doctorate–6 years full-time. *Application deadline:* 1/15. *Application fee:* $45. *Tuition:* $5433 per year full-time, $775 per quarter (minimum) part-time for state residents; $13,479 per year full-time, $1925 per quarter (minimum) part-time for nonresidents. • Thomas Lockwood, Chairperson, 206-543-2690. Application contact: John Coldewey, Director of Graduate Studies, 206-543-6077. E-mail: englgrad@u.washington.edu.

Wayne State College, Division of Education, Program in Curriculum and Instruction, Wayne, NE 68787. Offerings include English as a second language (MSE). Accredited by NCATE. *Degree requirements:* Comprehensive exam, research paper required, foreign language not required. *Entrance requirements:* GRE General Test. Application deadline: rolling. Application fee: $10. *Expenses:* Tuition $1788 per year full-time, $75 per credit hour part-time for state residents; $3576 per year full-time, $149 per credit hour part-time for nonresidents. Fees $360 per year full-time, $15 per credit hour part-time. • Dr. Diane Alexander, Head, Division of Education, 402-375-7389.

West Chester University of Pennsylvania, College of Arts and Sciences, Program in Teaching English as a Second Language, West Chester, PA 19383. Awards MA. *Degree requirements:* Comprehensive exam. *Application deadline:* 4/15 (priority date; rolling processing; 10/15 for spring admission). *Application fee:* $25. *Expenses:* Tuition $3468 per year full-time, $193 per credit part-time for state residents; $6236 per year full-time, $346 per credit part-time for nonresidents. Fees $660 per year full-time, $38 per credit part-time. *Financial aid:* Application deadline 2/15. • Application contact: Cherie Micheau, Graduate Coordinator, 610-436-2898. E-mail: cmicheau@wcupa.edu.

Western Kentucky University, Potter College of Arts and Humanities, Department of English, Bowling Green, KY 42101-3576. Offerings include teaching English as a second language (MA). Accredited by NCATE. Department faculty: 24 full-time (13 women). *Application deadline:* 8/1 (priority date; rolling processing; 12/1 for spring admission). *Application fee:* $20. *Tuition:* $2460 per year full-time, $133 per credit hour part-time for state residents; $6700 per year full-time, $369 per credit hour part-time for nonresidents. • Dr. Mary Ellen Pitts, Head, 502-745-3043. Fax: 502-745-2533.

Western Oregon University, School of Education, Program in English for Speakers of Other Languages, Monmouth, OR 97361. Awards MS Ed. Accredited by NCATE. Faculty: 1 (woman) full-time, 9 part-time (6 women). Students: 5 full-time (4 women), 12 part-time (11 women); includes 4 minority (3 Asian Americans, 1 Hispanic). Average age 35. *Degree requirements:* Written exam required, thesis optional, foreign language not required. *Entrance requirements:* GRE General Test (average 450 on each section) or MAT (minimum score 30), NTE, minimum GPA of 3.0, teaching license. Application deadline: rolling. Application fee: $50. *Financial aid:* Research assistantships, teaching assistantships, full and partial tuition waivers, and career-related internships or fieldwork available. Aid available to part-time students. Financial aid application deadline: 3/1; applicants required to submit FAFSA. • Dr. Dovie Trevino, Coordinator, 503-838-8834. Fax: 503-838-8228. E-mail: trevid@wou.edu. Application contact: Alison Marshall, Director of Admissions, 503-838-8211. Fax: 503-838-8067. E-mail: marshaa@wou.edu.

West Virginia University, Eberly College of Arts and Sciences, Department of Foreign Languages, Morgantown, WV 26506. Offerings include teaching English to speakers of other languages (MA). Department faculty: 21 full-time (11 women), 31 part-time (24 women). *Degree requirements:* Variable foreign language requirement, thesis optional. *Entrance requirements:* GRE, TOEFL (minimum score 550), minimum GPA of 3.0. Application deadline: 2/1 (priority date; rolling processing; 10/1 for spring admission). Application fee: $45. *Tuition:* $2820 per year full-time, $149 per credit hour part-time for state residents; $8104 per year full-time, $443 per credit hour part-time for nonresidents. • Frank W. Medley Jr., Chair, 304-293-5121. Fax: 304-393-7655. E-mail: fmedley@wvu.edu.

Wheaton College, Department of Missions/Intercultural Studies, Wheaton, IL 60187-5593. Offerings include teaching English as a second language (Certificate). *Application deadline:* 3/1 (priority date; rolling processing; 10/15 for spring admission). *Application fee:* $20. *Tuition:* $365 per credit hour (minimum).

Whitworth College, Graduate Studies in Education, Program in English as a Second Language, Spokane, WA 99251-0001. Awards MAT. Accredited by NCATE. *Degree requirements:* Comprehensive exams, internship, practicum, research project, or thesis required, foreign language not required. *Entrance requirements:* GRE General Test. Application deadline: 9/1 (priority date; rolling processing; 2/1 for spring admission). Application fee: $25.

Wright State University, College of Liberal Arts, Department of English Language and Literatures, Dayton, OH 45435. Offerings include teaching students of other languages (MA). *Degree requirements:* Thesis (for some programs), portfolio required, foreign language not required. *Entrance requirements:* TOEFL (minimum score 600), 20 hours in upper-level English. Application deadline: rolling. Application fee: $25. *Tuition:* $5109 per year full-time, $161 per credit hour part-time for state residents; $9039 per year full-time, $282 per credit hour part-time for nonresidents. • Dr. Henry S. Limouze, Chair, 937-775-3136. Application contact: Dr. Donald R. Swanson, Graduate Program Adviser, 937-775-2268. Fax: 937-775-2707.

Multilingual and Multicultural Education

Adelphi University, School of Education, Specialization in Bilingual Education, Garden City, NY 11530. Offers programs in elementary education (MA), secondary education (MA), special education (MS). Part-time and evening/weekend programs available. Students: 3 full-time (all women), 7 part-time (5 women); includes 7 minority (all Hispanics). Average age 35. *Application deadline:* rolling. *Application fee:* $50. *Expenses:* Tuition $16,000 per year full-time, $485 per credit part-time. Fees $500 per year full-time, $150 per semester part-time. *Financial aid:* Assistantships, full tuition waivers, Federal Work-Study, institutionally sponsored loans, and career-related internships or fieldwork available. Aid available to part-time students. Financial aid application deadline: 3/1. • Eva Roca, Director, 516-877-4070.

Azusa Pacific University, School of Education and Behavioral Studies, Department of Education, Program in Language Development, Azusa, CA 91702-7000. Awards MA. Faculty: 2 full-time (1 woman), 22 part-time (17 women). Students: 30. *Degree requirements:* Comprehensive exam or thesis, core exams, oral presentation required, foreign language not required. *Entrance requirements:* 12 units of previous course work in education, minimum GPA of 3.0. Application fee: $45 ($65 for international students). *Expenses:* Tuition $350 per unit. Fees $57 per year. *Faculty research:* Biliteracy development, home-school connections, integrated curriculum. • Application contact: Dr. Dan Doorn, Director, 626-815-5371.

Bank Street College of Education, Program in Bilingual Education, 610 West 112th Street, New York, NY 10025-1120. Awards Ed M, MS Ed. *Degree requirements:* 1 foreign language, thesis. *Entrance requirements:* TOEFL (minimum score 550). Application deadline: 3/1 (priority date; rolling processing; 11/1 for spring admission). Application fee: $50. *Tuition:* $560 per credit. *Financial aid:* Application deadline 3/1. • Dr. Olga Romero, Chairperson, 212-875-4468. Application contact: Ann Morgan, Director of Admissions, 212-875-4404. Fax: 212-875-4678. E-mail: amorgan@bnkst.edu.

Boston University, School of Education, Department of Developmental Studies and Counseling, Program in Bilingual Education, Boston, MA 02215. Awards Ed M, Ed D, CAGS. Part-time programs available. Students: 3 full-time (all women), 3 part-time (all women); includes 1 minority (Hispanic), 4 international. Average age 32. In 1997, 6 master's awarded. *Degree requirements:* For doctorate, dissertation, comprehensive exam; for CAGS, comprehensive exam required, foreign language and thesis not required. *Entrance requirements:* GRE or MAT, TOEFL. Application deadline: 2/15 (priority date; rolling processing). Application fee: $50. *Expenses:* Tuition $22,830 per year full-time, $713 per credit part-time. Fees $218 per year full-time, $40 per semester part-time. *Financial aid:* Application deadline 3/30. *Faculty research:* Use of computers in second language acquisition, cross-cultural communication, reading and language development. • Dr. Maria Estela Brisk, Coordinator, 617-353-3260. E-mail: brisk@bu.edu.

Brooklyn College of the City University of New York, School of Education, Program in Special Education, 2900 Bedford Avenue, Brooklyn, NY 11210-2889. Offerings include bilingual special education (MS Ed). *Degree requirements:* Practicum required, foreign language and thesis not required. *Entrance requirements:* TOEFL (minimum score 550), interview; previous course work in education and psychology; minimum GPA of 3.0 in education, 2.8 overall. Application deadline: 3/1 (11/1 for spring admission). Application fee: $40. *Expenses:* Tuition $4350 per year full-time, $185 per credit part-time for state residents; $7600 per year full-time, $320 per credit part-time for nonresidents. Fees $500 per year for state residents; $806 per year for nonresidents. • Dr. Kathleen McSorley, Head, 718-951-5995. Fax: 718-951-4816. E-mail: mcsorley@brooklyn.cuny.edu.

Brooklyn College of the City University of New York, School of Education, Division of Elementary School Education, Program in Bilingual Education, 2900 Bedford Avenue, Brooklyn, NY 11210-2889. Awards MS Ed. Part-time programs available. Students: 3 full-time (all women), 45 part-time (34 women); includes 26 minority (8 African Americans, 4 Asian Americans, 14 Hispanics). Average age 25. 50 applicants, 80% accepted. In 1997, 13 degrees awarded. *Degree requirements:* 1 foreign language required, thesis not required. *Average time to degree:* master's–2 years full-time, 3 years part-time. *Entrance requirements:* TOEFL (minimum score 500), interview, previous course work in education, writing sample. Application deadline: 3/1 (rolling processing; 11/1 for spring admission). Application fee: $40. *Expenses:* Tuition $4350 per year full-time, $185 per credit part-time for state residents; $7600 per year full-time, $320 per credit part-time for nonresidents. Fees $500 per year for state residents; $806 per year for nonresidents. *Financial aid:* Partial tuition waivers, Federal Work-Study, institutionally sponsored loans, and career-related internships or fieldwork available. Aid available to part-time students. Financial aid application deadline: 5/1; applicants required to submit FAFSA. *Faculty research:* Academic achievement of LEP children, education of Latinos in public schools, social action projects for minority children. • Dr. Milga Morales, Coordinator, Division of Elementary School Education, 718-951-5933.

Brown University, Center for Portuguese and Brazilian Studies, Providence, RI 02912. Offerings include Portuguese studies and bilingual education (AM). Center faculty: 3 full-time (0 women). *Application deadline:* 1/2 (priority date; rolling processing). *Application fee:* $60. *Expenses:* Tuition $23,616 per year. Fees $436 per year. • Onesimo Almeida, Chair, 401-863-3042. Application contact: Nelson Vieira, Graduate Representative, 401-863-3042.

California Baptist College, Graduate Program in Education, Riverside, CA 92504-3206. Offerings include cross-cultural language academic development (MA Ed). Program faculty: 8 full-time (7 women), 4 part-time (2 women). *Application deadline:* rolling. *Application fee:* $40. *Expenses:* Tuition $275 per unit. Fees $100 per year. • Dr. Marsha Savage, Chair, 909-689-5771. Application contact: Gail Ronveaux, Director of Graduate Services, 909-343-4249. Fax: 909-351-1808. E-mail: gradser@cal.baptist.edu.

California State University, Bakersfield, School of Education, 9001 Stockdale Highway, Bakersfield, CA 93311-1099. Offerings include bilingual/bicultural education (MA). Accredited by NCATE. *Application deadline:* rolling. *Application fee:* $55. *Expenses:* Tuition $0 for state residents; $246 per unit full-time, $164 per unit part-time for nonresidents. Fees $1584 per year full-time, $918 per year part-time. • Dr. Lon Kellenberger, Interim Dean, 805-664-2219. Application contact: Dr. Dianne Turner, Graduate Coordinator, 805-664-2422. Fax: 805-664-2063.

California State University, Chico, College of Communication and Education, School of Education, Department of Professional Studies in Education, Chico, CA 95929-0722. Offerings include education (MA), with options in linguistically and culturally diverse learners, reading and language arts, special education. *Application deadline:* 4/1 (rolling processing). *Application fee:* $55. *Expenses:* Tuition $0 for state residents; $246 per unit for nonresidents. Fees $2108 per year full-time, $1442 per year part-time. • Dr. James Richmond, Chair, 530-898-5398.

California State University, Dominguez Hills, School of Education, Department of Graduate Education, Program in Multicultural Education, Carson, CA 90747-0001. Awards MA. *Entrance requirements:* Minimum GPA of 2.75. Application deadline: 6/1. Application fee: $55. *Expenses:* Tuition $0 for state residents; $246 per unit for nonresidents. Fees $1896 per year full-time, $1230 per year part-time. • Application contact: Admissions Office, 310-243-3600.

California State University, Fullerton, School of Human Development and Community Service, Department of Elementary and Bilingual Education, PO Box 34080, Fullerton, CA 92834-9480. Offers programs in bilingual/bicultural education (MS), elementary curriculum and instruction (MS). Accredited by NCATE. Part-time programs available. Faculty: 19 full-time (16 women), 54 part-time, 30 FTE. Students: 4 full-time (all women), 131 part-time (125 women); includes 28 minority (10 Asian Americans, 17 Hispanics, 1 Native American). Average age 32. 61 applicants, 79% accepted. In 1997, 33 degrees awarded. *Degree requirements:* Project or thesis. *Entrance requirements:* Minimum GPA of 2.5, teaching certificate. Application fee: $55. *Expenses:* Tuition $0 for state residents; $246 per unit for nonresidents. Fees $1947 per year full-time, $1281 per year part-time. *Financial aid:* Teaching assistantships, state grants, Federal Work-Study, institutionally sponsored loans, and career-related internships or fieldwork available. Aid available to part-time students. Financial aid application deadline: 3/1. *Faculty research:* Teacher training and tracking, model for improvement of teaching. • Dr. Tom Savage, Head, 714-278-3411. Application contact: Hallie Yopp, Adviser, 714-278-3411.

California State University, Los Angeles, School of Education, Division of Special Education, Los Angeles, CA 90032-8530. Offerings include multicultural and multilingual special education (MA). Accredited by NCATE. Division faculty: 16 full-time, 11 part-time. *Degree requirements:* Comprehensive exam, project, or thesis required, foreign language not required. *Entrance requirements:* TOEFL (minimum score 550), minimum GPA of 2.75 in last 90 units, teaching certificate. Application deadline: 6/30 (rolling processing; 2/1 for spring admission). Application fee: $55. *Expenses:* Tuition $0 for state residents; $164 per unit for nonresidents. Fees $1763 per year full-time, $1097 per year part-time. • Dr. Philip Chinn, Chair, 213-343-4400.

California State University, Sacramento, School of Education, Department of Teacher Education, Program in Bilingual/Cross-Cultural Education, Sacramento, CA 95819-6048. Awards MA. Part-time programs available. *Degree requirements:* Thesis or alternative, writing proficiency exam. *Entrance requirements:* TOEFL (minimum score 550), minimum GPA of 2.5. Application deadline: 4/15 (11/1 for spring admission). Application fee: $55. *Expenses:* Tuition $0 for state residents; $246 per unit for nonresidents. Fees $2012 per year full-time, $1346 per year part-time. *Financial aid:* Federal Work-Study and career-related internships or fieldwork available. Aid available to part-time students. Financial aid application deadline: 3/1. • Dr. Ed Arnsdorf, Chair, Department of Teacher Education, 916-278-6155. Application contact: Dr. Robert Edwards, Graduate Coordinator, 916-278-5559.

California State University, San Bernardino, Graduate Studies, School of Education, San Bernardino, CA 92407-2397. Offerings include bilingual/cross-cultural education (MA). School faculty: 77 full-time (38 women). *Application deadline:* 8/31 (priority date). *Application fee:* $55. *Expenses:* Tuition $0 for state residents; $164 per unit for nonresidents. Fees $1922 per year full-time, $1256 per year part-time. • Patricia Arlin, Dean, 909-880-3600. Fax: 909-880-7011.

California State University, Stanislaus, School of Education, Department of Teacher Education, Program in Curriculum and Instruction, Concentration in Multilingual Education, Turlock, CA 95382. Awards MA Ed. Accredited by NCATE. Part-time and evening/weekend programs available. Students: 8 (6 women); includes 3 minority (1 Asian American, 2 Hispanics). In 1997, 9 degrees awarded. *Degree requirements:* Thesis or alternative required, foreign language not required. *Entrance requirements:* MAT. Application fee: $55. *Expenses:* Tuition $0 for state residents; $246 per unit for nonresidents. Fees $1779 per year full-time, $1113 per year part-time. *Financial aid:* Federal Work-Study available. Financial aid application deadline: 3/2; applicants required to submit FAFSA. • Dr. Joan Wink, Coordinator, 209-667-3471.

Chicago State University, College of Education, Department of Curriculum and Instruction, Program in Bilingual/Bicultural Education, Chicago, IL 60628. Awards MS Ed. Accredited by NCATE. *Degree requirements:* Comprehensive exams required, thesis optional, foreign language not required. *Entrance requirements:* Minimum GPA of 2.75. Application deadline: 7/1 (11/10 for spring admission). *Tuition:* $2268 per year full-time, $95 per credit hour part-time for state residents; $6804 per year full-time, $284 per credit hour part-time for nonresidents.

City College of the City University of New York, Graduate School, School of Education, Department of Elementary Education, Program in Bilingual Education, Convent Avenue at 138th Street, New York, NY 10031-6977. Awards MS. Part-time programs available. Students: 1 (woman) full-time, 243 part-time (184 women). In 1997, 82 degrees awarded. *Degree requirements:* Thesis required, foreign language not required. *Entrance requirements:* TOEFL (minimum score 500). Application fee: $40. *Expenses:* Tuition $4350 per year full-time, $185 per credit part-time for state residents; $7600 per year full-time, $320 per credit part-time for nonresidents. Fees $41 per year. *Financial aid:* Career-related internships or fieldwork available. • Head, 212-650-7215.

Cleveland State University, College of Education, Department of Specialized Instructional Programs, Cleveland, OH 44115-2440. Offerings include curriculum and instruction (M Ed), with options in bilingual education, early childhood education, early childhood/special education, education of emerging adolescents, elementary education, English as a second language, learning disabilities, Montessori education, multihandicapped, reading, secondary education. Department faculty: 18 full-time (12 women). *Entrance requirements:* GRE General Test or MAT (score in 50th percentile or higher). Application deadline: 9/1 (priority date; rolling processing). Application fee: $25. *Expenses:* Tuition $5252 per year full-time, $202 per credit hour part-time for state residents; $10,504 per year full-time, $404 per credit hour part-time for nonresidents. Fees $2.25 per credit hour (minimum). • Dr. Jane Zaharias, Chairperson, 216-687-4585. Fax: 216-687-5379. E-mail: j.zaharias@csuohio.edu.

College of Mount Saint Vincent, Program in Education, Riverdale, NY 10471-1093. Offerings include urban and multicultural education (MS). *Application deadline:* rolling. *Application fee:* $50.

College of Notre Dame, Department of Education, Belmont, CA 94002-1997. Offerings include elementary education (M Ed, Certificate), with options in educational technology (M Ed), elementary education (Certificate), multicultural education (M Ed); secondary education (MAT, M Ed, Certificate), with options in educational technology (M Ed), multicultural education (M Ed), secondary education (MAT, Certificate), teaching art (MAT), teaching biology (MAT), teaching English (MAT), teaching French (MAT), teaching music (MAT), teaching religious studies (MAT), teaching social sciences (MAT). Department faculty: 7 full-time, 24 part-time. *Application deadline:* rolling. *Application fee:* $50 ($500 for international students). *Tuition:* $460 per unit. • Dr. Diane Guay, Chair, 650-508-3701.

College of Santa Fe, Department of Education, Program in At-Risk Youth, Santa Fe, NM 87505-7634. Offerings include bilingual/multicultural education (MA). Program faculty: 7 full-time (5 women), 14 part-time (10 women). *Entrance requirements:* Minimum GPA of 3.0. Application deadline: rolling. Application fee: $25. *Expenses:* Tuition $237 per credit hour. Fees $25 per year. • Dr. Barbara Reider, Chair, Department of Education, 800-246-2673. Fax: 505-473-6510.

College of Santa Fe, Department of Education, Program in Multicultural Special Education, Santa Fe, NM 87505-7634. Awards MA. Part-time and evening/weekend programs available. Faculty: 1 (woman) full-time, 4 part-time (3 women). Students: 41 part-time (29 women); includes 12 minority (1 African American, 7 Hispanics, 4 Native Americans). 54 applicants, 98% accepted. In 1997, 3 degrees awarded. *Degree requirements:* Comprehensive exams, portfolio presentation required, foreign language not required. *Average time to degree:* master's–1 year full-time, 1.5 years part-time. *Entrance requirements:* Interview, minimum GPA of 3.0. Application deadline: rolling. Application fee: $25. *Expenses:* Tuition $237 per credit hour. Fees $25 per year. *Financial aid:* Institutionally sponsored loans and career-related internships or fieldwork available. Aid available to part-time students. Financial aid application deadline: 3/1; applicants required to submit FAFSA. • Dr. Kate Friesner, Director of Teacher Education, 505-880-8259. Application contact: Clarissa Rosas, Coordinator, 505-880-8254. Fax: 505-880-8262.

Columbia College, Department of Educational Studies, 600 South Michigan Avenue, Chicago, IL 60605-1997. Offerings include multicultural education (MA). *Application deadline:* 7/15 (rolling processing; 12/4 for spring admission). *Application fee:* $35. *Expenses:* Tuition $392 per credit hour. Fees $170 per year full-time, $150 per year part-time.

Directory: Multilingual and Multicultural Education

DePaul University, School of Education, Program in Reading and Learning Disabilities, Chicago, IL 60604-2287. Offerings include bilingual multicultural learning disabilities (MA, M Ed). Accredited by NCATE. Program faculty: 3 full-time (all women), 2 part-time (both women). *Degree requirements:* Oral exam or thesis required, foreign language not required. *Entrance requirements:* Interview, minimum GPA of 2.75, work experience. Application deadline: rolling. Application fee: $25. *Expenses:* Tuition $320 per credit hour. Fees $30 per year. • Dr. Barbara Sizemore, Dean, School of Education, 312-325-7000 Ext. 1666. Fax: 312-325-7748. Application contact: Director of Graduate Admissions, 312-325-7000 Ext. 1666. E-mail: mmurphy@wppost.depaul.edu.

Eastern College, Graduate Education Programs, Program in Multicultural Education, St. Davids, PA 19087-3696. Awards M Ed. In 1997, 37 degrees awarded. *Entrance requirements:* TOEFL, minimum GPA of 2.5. Application deadline: rolling. Application fee: $35. *Financial aid:* Research assistantships, teaching assistantships available. • Application contact: Megan Miscioscia, Graduate Admissions Representative, 610-341-5972. Fax: 610-341-1466.

Eastern Michigan University, College of Arts and Sciences, Department of Foreign Languages and Bilingual Studies, Program in Spanish (Bilingual-Bicultural Education), Ypsilanti, MI 48197. Awards MA. Evening/weekend programs available. *Degree requirements:* 1 foreign language required, thesis not required. *Entrance requirements:* TOEFL (minimum score 500). Application deadline: 5/15 (rolling processing; 3/15 for spring admission). Application fee: $30. *Expenses:* Tuition $2691 per year full-time, $150 per credit hour part-time for state residents; $6300 per year full-time, $350 per credit hour part-time for nonresidents. Fees $368 per year full-time, $88 per semester (minimum) part-time. *Financial aid:* Fellowships, teaching assistantships available. Aid available to part-time students. Financial aid application deadline: 3/15; applicants required to submit FAFSA. • Dr. Phyllis Noda, Coordinator, 734-487-0370.

Eastern Nazarene College, Graduate Studies, Division of Education, Quincy, MA 02170-2999. Offerings include bilingual education (M Ed, Certificate). M Ed and Certificate also available through weekend program for administration, special needs, and reading only. Division faculty: 9 full-time (5 women), 11 part-time (5 women). *Entrance requirements:* For master's, TOEFL (minimum score 500). Application deadline: rolling. Application fee: $35. *Expenses:* Tuition $350 per credit. Fees $125 per semester full-time, $15 per semester part-time. • Dr. Lorne Ranstrom, Chair, 617-745-3528. Application contact: Cleo P. Cakridas, Graduate Enrollment Counselor, 617-745-3870. Fax: 617-745-3907. E-mail: cakridac@enc.edu.

Fairfield University, Graduate School of Education and Allied Professions, Department of TESOL, Foreign Language and Bilingual/Multicultural Education, Fairfield, CT 06430-5195. Awards MA, CAS. Part-time and evening/weekend programs available. Faculty: 1 (woman) full-time, 3 part-time (1 woman), 2 FTE. Students: 5 full-time (4 women), 52 part-time (42 women); includes 19 minority (2 Asian Americans, 17 Hispanics), 3 international. Average age 34. 14 applicants, 100% accepted. In 1997, 2 master's, 1 CAS awarded. *Entrance requirements:* For master's, PRAXIS I (CBT), TOEFL. Application deadline: 7/1 (priority date; rolling processing). Application fee: $40. *Expenses:* Tuition $350 per credit hour (minimum). Fees $20 per semester (minimum). *Financial aid:* Partial tuition waivers available. Aid available to part-time students. *Faculty research:* Teacher education. • Sr. Juliann Poole, Assistant Professor, 203-254-4000 Ext. 2873. Application contact: Karen Creecy, Assistant Dean, 203-254-4250. Fax: 203-254-4241. E-mail: klcreecy@fair1.fairfield.edu.

Fairleigh Dickinson University, Teaneck–Hackensack Campus, University College: Arts, Sciences, and Professional Studies, Peter Sammartino School of Education, Program in Bilingual/Bicultural Education, 1000 River Road, Teaneck, NJ 07666-1914. Awards MAT. Faculty: 11 full-time (8 women), 27 part-time (10 women). *Degree requirements:* Research project required, thesis not required. *Application deadline:* rolling. *Application fee:* $35. *Expenses:* Tuition $522 per credit. Fees $302 per year full-time, $138 per year part-time. *Faculty research:* Mathematics for students with learning disabilities, gender issues in education, social problem-solving and conflict resolution in the classroom, multicultural education in the elementary classroom, problems encountered by international students in college programs. • Dr. Eloise Forster, Interim Director, Peter Sammartino School of Education, 201-692-2834. Fax: 201-692-2603.

Fairleigh Dickinson University, Teaneck–Hackensack Campus, University College: Arts, Sciences, and Professional Studies, Peter Sammartino School of Education, Program in Multilingual Education, 1000 River Road, Teaneck, NJ 07666-1914. Awards MA. Faculty: 11 full-time (8 women), 27 part-time (10 women). Students: 19 full-time (17 women), 12 part-time (11 women); includes 28 international. Average age 31. In 1997, 7 degrees awarded. *Degree requirements:* 1 foreign language required, thesis not required. *Entrance requirements:* MAT, PRAXIS, certification. Application deadline: rolling. Application fee: $35. *Expenses:* Tuition $522 per credit. Fees $302 per year full-time, $138 per year part-time. *Faculty research:* Mathematics for students with learning disabilities, gender issues in education, social problem-solving and conflict resolution in the classroom, multicultural education in the elementary classroom, problems encountered by international students in college programs. • Dr. Lillian Gaffney, Coordinator, 201-692-2839. Fax: 201-692-2603.

Florida State University, College of Education, Department of Curriculum and Instruction, Program in Multilingual-Multicultural Education, Tallahassee, FL 32306. Awards MS, PhD, Ed S. Part-time programs available. Faculty: 4 full-time (1 woman). Students: 17 full-time (12 women), 13 part-time (5 women); includes 11 minority (1 African American, 8 Asian Americans, 2 Hispanics). 46 applicants, 83% accepted. In 1997, 14 master's, 3 doctorates awarded. *Degree requirements:* For master's and Ed S, comprehensive exam required, thesis optional; for doctorate, dissertation, comprehensive exam. *Entrance requirements:* GRE General Test (minimum combined score of 1000), minimum GPA of 3.0. Application deadline: 7/1 (priority date; rolling processing; 11/1 for spring admission). Application fee: $20. *Tuition:* $139 per credit hour for state residents; $482 per credit hour for nonresidents. *Financial aid:* Fellowships, research assistantships, teaching assistantships, and career-related internships or fieldwork available. • Dr. David Foulk, Chair, Department of Curriculum and Instruction, 850-644-6553. E-mail: foulk@mail.coe.fsu.edu. Application contact: Admissions Secretary, 850-644-6553. Fax: 850-644-1880.

Fordham University, Graduate School of Education, Division of Curriculum and Teaching, New York, NY 10023. Offerings include bilingual teacher education (MSE). Accredited by NCATE. *Application fee:* $50. • Dr. Angela Carrasquillo, Chairperson, 212-636-6427.

Fresno Pacific University, Graduate School, Programs in Education, Division of Language, Literacy, and Culture, Program in Bilingual/Cross-Culture Education, Fresno, CA 93702-4709. Awards MA Ed. Faculty: 5 full-time (4 women), 6 part-time (4 women). Students: 44 part-time (38 women). *Degree requirements:* Thesis or alternative. *Application deadline:* 7/31. *Application fee:* $75. *Tuition:* $250 per unit. • Dr. Yvonne Freeman, Director, 209-453-2054. Fax: 209-453-2001.

George Mason University, Graduate School of Education, Programs in Bilingual/Multicultural/English as a Second Language Education, Fairfax, VA 22030-4444. Awards M Ed. Accredited by NCATE. Part-time and evening/weekend programs available. Faculty: 42 full-time (24 women), 65 part-time (51 women), 58.73 FTE. Students: 2 full-time (1 woman), 12 part-time (10 women); includes 8 minority (2 Asian Americans, 6 Hispanics), 2 international. Average age 37. 38 applicants, 84% accepted. In 1997, 11 degrees awarded. *Degree requirements:* Computer language required, foreign language not required. *Entrance requirements:* NTE, minimum GPA of 3.0 in last 60 hours. Application deadline: 5/1 (11/1 for spring admission). Application fee: $30. Electronic applications accepted. *Tuition:* $4344 per year full-time, $181 per credit hour part-time for state residents; $12,504 per year full-time, $521 per credit hour part-time for nonresidents. *Financial aid:* Available to part-time students. Financial aid application deadline: 3/1; applicants required to submit FAFSA. • Dr. Harold Chu, Director, 703-993-3688. Fax: 703-993-3336.

Georgetown University, Department of Linguistics, Washington, DC 20057. Offerings include bilingual education (Certificate). *Application deadline:* 2/1 (10/15 for spring admission). *Application fee:* $50 ($55 for international students). *Expenses:* Tuition $19,128 per year full-time, $797 per credit part-time. Fees $99 (one-time charge).

Heritage College, Graduate Program in Education, Program in Professional Development, Toppenish, WA 98948-9599. Offerings include bilingual education/ESL (M Ed). *Degree requirements:* Comprehensive exam required, thesis optional, foreign language not required. *Application deadline:* rolling. *Application fee:* $35 ($75 for international students). *Tuition:* $270 per credit. • Application contact: Dr. Robert Plumb, Chair, 509-865-2244.

Hofstra University, College of Liberal Arts and Sciences, Division of Humanities, Program in Bilingualism, Hempstead, NY 11549. Awards MA. Accredited by NCATE. Part-time and evening/weekend programs available. Faculty: 3 full-time (2 women), 1 part-time (0 women). Students: 0. 4 applicants, 100% accepted. *Degree requirements:* 1 foreign language, departmental comprehensive exam required, thesis not required. *Application deadline:* rolling. *Application fee:* $40 ($75 for international students). *Expenses:* Tuition $10,968 per year full-time, $457 per credit hour part-time. Fees $670 per year full-time, $112 per semester (minimum) part-time. *Financial aid:* Fellowships available. *Faculty research:* Bilingual cultures, linguistics, Spanish-American literature. • Dr. Nora de Marval-McNair, Coordinator, 516-463-5501. E-mail: spnndm@hofstra.edu. Application contact: Mary Beth Carey, Dean of Admissions, 516-463-6700. Fax: 516-560-7660. E-mail: hofstra@hofstra.edu.

Hofstra University, School of Education and Allied Human Services, Department of Curriculum and Teaching, Program in Bilingual Education, Hempstead, NY 11549. Awards MS Ed. Accredited by NCATE. Part-time and evening/weekend programs available. Students: 4 part-time (all women); includes 3 minority (all Hispanics). Average age 29. 4 applicants, 25% accepted. *Degree requirements:* Thesis, departmental qualifying exam. *Entrance requirements:* Interview, provisional elementary education certificate, Spanish/English linguistic skills. Application deadline: rolling. Application fee: $40 ($75 for international students). *Expenses:* Tuition $10,968 per year full-time, $457 per credit hour part-time. Fees $670 per year full-time, $112 per semester (minimum) part-time. *Financial aid:* 2 students received aid; fellowships available. Financial aid application deadline: 9/1. *Faculty research:* Acculturation and adjustment, special education needs of language minority children. • Dr. Mary Savage, Coordinator, 516-463-5348. Fax: 516-463-6503. E-mail: catmcs@hofstra.edu. Application contact: Mary Beth Carey, Dean of Admissions, 516-463-6700. Fax: 516-560-7660. E-mail: hofstra@hofstra.edu.

Houston Baptist University, College of Education and Behavioral Sciences, Programs in Education, Houston, TX 77074-3298. Offerings include bilingual education (M Ed). Faculty: 9 full-time (5 women), 4 part-time (3 women). *Degree requirements:* Comprehensive exam required, foreign language and thesis not required. *Entrance requirements:* GRE General Test (minimum combined score of 850), minimum GPA of 2.5, teaching certificate. Application deadline: 7/1 (priority date; rolling processing; 1/1 for spring admission). Application fee: $25 ($85 for international students). *Expenses:* Tuition $280 per semester hour. Fees $235 per quarter. • Dr. John Lutjemeier, Head, 281-649-3000 Ext. 2336. Application contact: Judy Ferguson, Program Assistant, 281-649-3241.

Hunter College of the City University of New York, Division of Education, Department of Curriculum and Teaching, Program in Bilingual Education, 695 Park Avenue, New York, NY 10021-5085. Awards MS. Part-time and evening/weekend programs available. *Degree requirements:* 1 foreign language, research seminar. *Entrance requirements:* TOEFL (minimum score 575), minimum GPA of 2.7. Application deadline: 4/1 (rolling processing; 11/21 for spring admission). Application fee: $40. *Expenses:* Tuition $4350 per year full-time, $185 per credit part-time for state residents; $7600 per year full-time, $320 per credit part-time for nonresidents. Fees $26 per year. *Faculty research:* Teacher effectiveness, language development, Spanish language and linguistics and multicultural education.

Immaculata College, Graduate Division, Program in Cultural and Linguistic Diversity, Immaculata, PA 19345-0500. Awards MA. Part-time and evening/weekend programs available. Students: 13 part-time (12 women). Average age 31. 2 applicants, 100% accepted. In 1997, 3 degrees awarded. *Degree requirements:* 1 foreign language, comprehensive exam, professional experience required, thesis optional. *Entrance requirements:* GRE or MAT, proficiency in Spanish or Asian language, minimum GPA of 3.0. Application deadline: rolling. Application fee: $25. *Expenses:* Tuition $345 per credit (minimum). Fees $60 per year. *Financial aid:* Application deadline 5/1. *Faculty research:* Cognitive learning, Caribbean literature and culture, English as a second language, teaching English to speakers of other languages. • Sr. Grace Schiavone, Chair, 610-647-4400 Ext. 3635. Application contact: Office of Graduate Admission, 610-647-4400 Ext. 3211.

Iona College, School of Arts and Science, Program in Multicultural Education, 715 North Avenue, New Rochelle, NY 10801-1890. Awards MS Ed. Part-time and evening/weekend programs available. Faculty: 1 full-time (0 women), 2 part-time (1 woman). Students: 1 (woman) full-time, 27 part-time (20 women); includes 3 minority (all African Americans). Average age 32. In 1997, 25 degrees awarded. *Entrance requirements:* New York teaching certificate. Application deadline: rolling. Application fee: $25. *Expenses:* Tuition $455 per credit hour. Fees $25 per semester. *Financial aid:* Graduate assistantships, partial tuition waivers, and career-related internships or fieldwork available. Aid available to part-time students. • Dr. Lucy Murphy, Chair, 914-633-2210. Fax: 914-633-2608. Application contact: Arlene Melillo, Director of Graduate Recruitment, 914-633-2328. Fax: 914-633-2023.

Iona College, School of Arts and Science, Program in Secondary School Subjects, 715 North Avenue, New Rochelle, NY 10801-1890. Offerings include multicultural education (MS Ed). Program faculty: 4 full-time (1 woman), 8 part-time (2 women). *Application deadline:* rolling. *Application fee:* $25. *Expenses:* Tuition $455 per credit hour. Fees $25 per semester. • Dr. Lucy Murphy, Chair, 914-633-2210. Fax: 914-633-2608. Application contact: Arlene Melillo, Director of Graduate Recruitment, 914-633-2328. Fax: 914-633-2023.

Kean University, School of Education, Department of Instruction, Curriculum and Administration, Instruction and Curriculum Program, Union, NJ 07083. Offerings include bilingual education (Certificate), bilingual/bicultural education (MA). One or more programs accredited by NCATE. *Degree requirements:* For master's, thesis, comprehensive exams required, foreign language not required. *Entrance requirements:* For master's, GRE General Test or MAT. Application deadline: 6/15 (rolling processing; 11/15 for spring admission). Application fee: $35. *Tuition:* $5926 per year full-time, $248 per credit part-time for state residents; $7312 per year full-time, $304 per credit part-time for nonresidents. • Dr. Janet Prince, Coordinator, 908-527-2525. Application contact: Joanne Morris, Director of Graduate Admissions, 908-527-2665. Fax: 908-527-2286. E-mail: grad_adm@turbo.kean.edu.

Lehigh University, College of Education, Department of Education and Human Services, Bethlehem, PA 18015-3094. Offerings include bilingual/bicultural education (M Ed). M Ed (bilingual/bicultural education) being phased out; applicants no longer accepted. Postbaccalaureate distance learning degree programs offered (minimal on-campus study). Department faculty: 22 full-time (8 women), 12 part-time (4 women). *Application fee:* $40. Electronic applications accepted. *Expenses:* Tuition $470 per credit. Fees $12 per semester full-time, $6 per semester part-time. • Raymond Bell, Chairman, 610-758-3241. Fax: 610-758-6223. E-mail: rb02@lehigh.edu.

Lehman College of the City University of New York, Division of Education, Department of Specialized Services in Education, Teachers of Special Education Program, Option in Bilingual Special Education, 250 Bedford Park Boulevard West, Bronx, NY 10468-1589. Awards MS Ed. Faculty: 1 (woman) full-time. Students: 2 full-time (both women), 31 part-time (16 women). *Entrance requirements:* Minimum GPA of 3.0. Application deadline: 4/1 (rolling processing; 11/1 for spring admission). Application fee: $40. *Expenses:* Tuition $4350 per year full-time, $185 per credit part-time for state residents; $7600 per year full-time, $320 per credit part-time for nonresidents. Fees $120 per year full-time, $80 per year part-time. *Financial aid:* Full and partial tuition waivers, Federal Work-Study available. Aid available to part-time students. Financial aid application deadline: 5/15; applicants required to submit FAFSA. • Susan Polirstok, Adviser, 718-960-8173.

Lesley College, Graduate School of Arts and Social Sciences, Cambridge, MA 02138-2790. Offerings include creative arts in learning (M Ed, CAGS), with options in individually designed (M Ed), multicultural education (M Ed), storytelling (M Ed), theater studies (M Ed); intercultural relations (MA, CAGS), with options in development project administration (MA), individually designed (MA), intercultural conflict resolution (MA), intercultural health and human services (MA), intercultural training and consulting (MA), international education exchange (MA), international student advising (MA), managing culturally diverse human resources (MA), multicultural education (MA). Postbaccalaureate distance learning degree programs offered (minimal on-campus study). School faculty: 24 full-time (14 women), 344 part-time (225 women). *Application deadline:* rolling. *Application fee:* $45. *Tuition:* $425 per credit. • Dr. Martha B. McKenna, Dean, 617-349-8467. Application contact: Graduate Admissions, 617-349-8300. Fax: 617-349-8366.

Long Island University, Brooklyn Campus, School of Education, Department of Education, Program in Bilingual Education, Brooklyn, NY 11201-8423. Awards MS Ed. Part-time and evening/weekend programs available. 30 applicants, 80% accepted. In 1997, 24 degrees awarded. *Degree requirements:* 1 foreign language required, thesis optional. *Application deadline:* rolling. *Application fee:* $30. Electronic applications accepted. *Expenses:* Tuition $480 per credit. Fees $415 per year full-time, $73 per semester (minimum) part-time. • Dr. Joann Floyd, Director, 718-488-1384. Application contact: Bernard W. Sullivan, Associate Director of Admissions, 718-488-1011.

Long Island University, C.W. Post Campus, School of Education, Department of Curriculum and Instruction, Brookville, NY 11548-1300. Offerings include bilingual education (MS). Department faculty: 10 full-time (5 women), 46 part-time (19 women). *Application deadline:* rolling. *Application fee:* $30. Electronic applications accepted. *Expenses:* Tuition $480 per credit. Fees $316 per year full-time, $71 per semester (minimum) part-time. • Dr. Anthony De Falco, Chairperson, 516-299-2372. Application contact: Camille Marziliano, Academic Counselor, 516-299-2123. Fax: 516-299-4167. E-mail: cmarzili@eagle.liunet.edu.

Loyola Marymount University, School of Education, Program in Bilingual and Bicultural Education, Los Angeles, CA 90045-8350. Awards MA. Part-time and evening/weekend programs available. Faculty: 14 full-time (8 women), 25 part-time (20 women). Students: 6 full-time (all women), 6 part-time (4 women); includes 12 minority (all Hispanics). In 1997, 8 degrees awarded. *Degree requirements:* Comprehensive exam required, foreign language and thesis not required. *Entrance requirements:* GRE General Test, TOEFL (minimum score 550), competency in Spanish, interview, minimum GPA of 2.7 (undergraduate), 3.0 (graduate). Application fee: $35. Electronic applications accepted. *Expenses:* Tuition $500 per unit. Fees $111 per year full-time, $28 per year part-time. *Financial aid:* In 1997–98, 4 students received aid, including 2 research assistantships totaling $1,450, 1 teaching assistantship totaling $600, 1 grant totaling $3,000; Federal Work-Study also available. Aid available to part-time students. Financial aid application deadline: 3/2; applicants required to submit FAFSA. • Dr. Magaly Lavandez, Coordinator, 310-338-2924.

Loyola Marymount University, School of Education, Program in Teaching English as a Second Language/Multicultural Education, Los Angeles, CA 90045-8350. Awards MA. Part-time and evening/weekend programs available. Faculty: 14 full-time (8 women), 25 part-time (20 women). Students: 3 full-time (all women), 4 part-time (3 women); includes 3 minority (1 African American, 2 Hispanics). *Degree requirements:* Comprehensive exam required, foreign language and thesis not required. *Entrance requirements:* GRE General Test, TOEFL (minimum score 550), interview; minimum GPA of 2.7 (undergraduate), 3.0 (graduate). Application fee: $35. Electronic applications accepted. *Expenses:* Tuition $500 per unit. Fees $111 per year full-time, $28 per year part-time. *Financial aid:* In 1997–98, 2 students received aid, including 1 grant totaling $1,300; Federal Work-Study also available. Aid available to part-time students. Financial aid application deadline: 3/2; applicants required to submit FAFSA. • Dr. Magaly Lavandez, Coordinator, 310-338-2924.

Mankato State University, College of Education, Department of Curriculum and Instruction, Program in Bilingual/Bicultural Education, South Rd and Ellis Ave, PO Box 8400, Mankato, MN 56002-8400. Awards MS. Accredited by NCATE. *Degree requirements:* Thesis or alternative, comprehensive exam required, foreign language not required. *Entrance requirements:* GRE General Test or MAT, minimum GPA of 3.0 during previous 2 years. Application deadline: 7/10 (priority date; rolling processing; 10/30 for spring admission). Application fee: $20. *Tuition:* $126 per credit (minimum) for state residents; $200 per credit for nonresidents. *Financial aid:* Application deadline 3/15. • Application contact: Joni Roberts, Admissions Coordinator, 507-389-2321. Fax: 507-389-5974. E-mail: grad@mankato.msus.edu.

Maryville University of Saint Louis, School of Education, St. Louis, MO 63141-7299. Offerings include multicultural education (MA). Accredited by NCATE. School faculty: 9 full-time (7 women), 15 part-time (9 women). *Degree requirements:* Thesis, project required, foreign language not required. *Average time to degree:* master's–2 years full-time, 4 years part-time. *Entrance requirements:* Minimum GPA of 3.0. Application deadline: rolling. Application fee: $20. Electronic applications accepted. *Expenses:* Tuition $11,480 per year full-time, $345 per credit hour part-time. Fees $120 per year full-time, $60 per year part-time. • Dr. Kathe Rasch, Dean, 314-529-9466. Fax: 314-529-9921. E-mail: krasch@maryville.edu.

Mercyhurst College, Program in Special Education, 501 East 38th Street, Erie, PA 16546. Offerings include bilingual/bicultural special education (MS). Program faculty: 2 full-time (1 woman), 2 part-time (both women), 3 FTE. *Degree requirements:* Thesis required, foreign language not required. *Average time to degree:* master's–1.5 years full-time, 2.5 years part-time. *Entrance requirements:* GRE General Test, MAT, or minimum GPA of 3.0; interview. Application deadline: 8/1 (priority date; rolling processing; 3/1 for spring admission). Application fee: $35. Electronic applications accepted. *Expenses:* Tuition $681 per course. Fees $250 per year. • Dr. Phillip J. Belfiore, Coordinator, 814-824-2267. Fax: 814-824-2438. E-mail: belfiore@mercyhurst.edu. Application contact: Mary Ellen Dahlkemper, Director, Office of Adult and Graduate Programs, 814-824-2294. Fax: 814-824-2055. E-mail: medahlk@mercyhurst.edu.

National University, School of Education and Human Services, Department of Teacher Education and Leadership, La Jolla, CA 92037-1011. Offerings include bilingual crosscultural teaching (ME), cross-cultural teaching (ME). *Application deadline:* rolling. *Application fee:* $60 ($100 for international students). *Tuition:* $7830 per year full-time, $870 per course part-time. • Dr. Helene Mandell, Chair, 619-642-8345. Application contact: Nancy Rohland, Director of Enrollment Management, 619-563-7100. Fax: 619-563-7393.

New Jersey City University, School of Professional Studies and Education, Programs in Urban Education, Concentration in Bilingual/Bicultural Education and English as a Second Language, Jersey City, NJ 07305-1957. Awards MA. *Entrance requirements:* GRE General Test, TOEFL or MAT. Application deadline: 8/1 (priority date; rolling processing; 12/1 for spring admission). Application fee: $0.

New Jersey City University, School of Professional Studies and Education, Programs in Urban Education, Program in Administration, Curriculum and Instruction, Jersey City, NJ 07305-1957. Offerings include urban education (MA), with options in administration and supervision, basics and urban studies, bilingual/bicultural education and English as a second language. Accredited by NCATE. *Entrance requirements:* GRE General Test, MAT or TOEFL. Application deadline: 8/1 (priority date; rolling processing; 12/1 for spring admission). Application fee: $0.

New York University, School of Education, Department of Teaching and Learning, Program in Multilingual/Multicultural Studies, New York, NY 10012-1019. Offers bilingual education (MA, PhD, CAS), foreign language education (MA, CAS), teaching English to speakers of other languages (MA, PhD, CAS). Part-time and evening/weekend programs available. Faculty: 3 full-time, 7 part-time. Students: 108 full-time, 109 part-time. 227 applicants, 64% accepted. In 1997, 73 master's, 2 doctorates awarded. Terminal master's awarded for partial completion of doctoral program. *Degree requirements:* For master's, thesis required (for some programs), foreign language not required; for doctorate, dissertation. *Entrance requirements:* For master's, TOEFL; for doctorate, GRE General Test, TOEFL, interview; for CAS, TOEFL, master's degree. Application deadline: 2/1 (priority date; rolling processing; 12/1 for spring admission). Application fee: $40 ($60 for international students). *Financial aid:* Partial tuition waivers, Federal Work-Study, institutionally sponsored loans, and career-related internships or fieldwork available. Aid available to part-time students. Financial aid application deadline: 3/1; applicants required to submit FAFSA. • Harvey Nadler, Director, 212-998-5494. Application contact: Office of Graduate Admissions, 212-998-5030. Fax: 212-995-4328.

Northeastern Illinois University, College of Education, Department of Teacher Education, Program in Bilingual/Bicultural, Chicago, IL 60625-4699. Awards MAT, MSI. Program new for fall 1998. Faculty: 21 full-time (13 women), 9 part-time (7 women). *Entrance requirements:* Minimum GPA of 2.75. Application deadline: 3/18 (priority date; rolling processing; 9/30 for spring admission). Application fee: $0. *Expenses:* Tuition $2226 per year full-time, $93 per credit hour part-time for state residents; $6678 per year full-time, $278 per credit hour part-time for nonresidents. Fees $358 per year full-time, $14.90 per credit hour part-time. • Dr. Maria Korkatsch-Grozko, Coordinator, 773-794-2955. Application contact: Dr. Mohan K. Sood, Dean of Graduate College, 773-583-4050 Ext. 6143. Fax: 773-794-6670.

Northern Arizona University, Center for Excellence in Education, Program in Bilingual/Multicultural Education, Flagstaff, AZ 86011. Awards M Ed. Part-time and evening/weekend programs available. Students: 55 full-time (45 women), 216 part-time (183 women); includes 125 minority (3 African Americans, 2 Asian Americans, 90 Hispanics, 30 Native Americans), 5 international. Average age 30. 115 applicants, 69% accepted. In 1997, 105 degrees awarded. *Entrance requirements:* GRE Subject Test or minimum GPA of 3.0. Application deadline: 3/15 (priority date; rolling processing). Application fee: $45. *Expenses:* Tuition $2088 per year full-time, $330 per semester (minimum) part-time for state residents; $8004 per year full-time, $1002 per semester (minimum) part-time for nonresidents. Fees $72 per year full-time, $18 per semester (minimum) part-time. *Financial aid:* Assistantships available. *Faculty research:* Second language literacy; biliteracy and metalinguistic awareness; language shift, maintenance, and revitalization; American Indian education; minority student retention. • Dr. Malathi Sandhu, Interim Chair, 520-523-5342.

Pennsylvania State University University Park Campus, College of Education, Department of Curriculum and Instruction, University Park, PA 16802-1503. Offerings include bilingual education (M Ed, MS, D Ed, PhD). Accredited by NCATE. *Degree requirements:* For doctorate, dissertation. *Entrance requirements:* GRE General Test or MAT. Application fee: $40. *Expenses:* Tuition $6534 per year full-time, $276 per credit part-time for state residents; $13,460 per year full-time, $561 per credit part-time for nonresidents. Fees $252 per year (minimum) full-time, $43 per semester (minimum) part-time. • Dr. Peter A. Rubb, Head, 814-865-5433.

Prescott College, Graduate Programs, Program in Education, Prescott, AZ 86301-2990. Offerings include bilingual education (MA), with options in English as a second language, Native American bilingual teacher education; multicultural education (MA). Postbaccalaureate distance learning degree programs offered (minimal on-campus study). *Degree requirements:* Thesis, fieldwork or internship, practicum required, foreign language not required. *Application deadline:* 6/1 (11/1 for spring admission). *Application fee:* $40. *Tuition:* $9000 per year. • Dr. Gene Hanson, Head, 520-319-9868. Application contact: Joan Clingan, Graduate Director, 520-776-5130. Fax: 520-776-5137. E-mail: mapmail@northlink.com.

Queens College of the City University of New York, Social Science Division, School of Education, Department of Elementary and Early Childhood Education, 65-30 Kissena Boulevard, Flushing, NY 11367-1597. Offerings include bilingual education (MS Ed). *Degree requirements:* Research project required, foreign language and thesis not required. *Entrance requirements:* TOEFL (minimum score 600), minimum GPA of 3.0. Application deadline: 4/1 (rolling processing; 11/1 for spring admission). Application fee: $40. *Expenses:* Tuition $4350 per year full-time, $185 per credit part-time for state residents; $7600 per year full-time, $320 per credit part-time for nonresidents. Fees $104 per year. • Dr. Glenna Sloan, Chairperson, 718-997-5300. Application contact: Dr. Janet Ezair, Graduate Adviser, 718-997-5304.

Rhode Island College, School of Graduate Studies, School of Education and Human Development, Department of Educational Studies, Program in Bilingual/Bicultural Education, Providence, RI 02908-1924. Awards M Ed. Accredited by NCATE. Faculty: 4 full-time (0 women), 1 part-time (0 women). Students: 1 (woman) full-time, 8 part-time (6 women); includes 1 minority (African American). In 1997, 4 degrees awarded. *Entrance requirements:* GRE General Test or MAT. Application deadline: 4/1 (rolling processing). Application fee: $25. *Tuition:* $4064 per year full-time, $214 per credit part-time for state residents; $7658 per year full-time, $376 per credit part-time for nonresidents. *Financial aid:* Application deadline 4/1. • Dr. Joao Botelho, Head, 401-456-8173.

St. John's University, School of Education and Human Services, Division of Human Services and Counseling, Program in Bilingual/Multicultural Education/Teaching English to Speakers of Other Languages, Jamaica, NY 11439. Awards MS Ed. Part-time and evening/weekend programs available. Students: 9 full-time (8 women), 37 part-time (34 women); includes 12 minority (3 African Americans, 1 Asian American, 8 Hispanics), 5 international. Average age 35. 28 applicants, 93% accepted. In 1997, 6 degrees awarded. *Entrance requirements:* Minimum GPA of 3.0, New York teaching certificate. Application deadline: 6/1 (rolling processing; 10/1 for spring admission). Application fee: $40. *Expenses:* Tuition $525 per credit. Fees $150 per year. *Financial aid:* Administrative assistantships, Federal Work-Study, and career-related internships or fieldwork available. Aid available to part-time students. Financial aid application deadline: 3/1; applicants required to submit FAFSA. *Faculty research:* Second language learning, cross-cultural studies. • Dr. J. Spiridakis, Coordinator, 718-990-6407. Fax: 718-990-1614. Application contact: Shamus J. McGrenra, TOR, Associate Director, Graduate Admissions, 718-990-6107. Fax: 718-990-5736. E-mail: mcgrenrs@stjohns.edu.

Sam Houston State University, College of Education and Applied Science, Department of Language, Literacy, and Special Populations, Program in Bilingual Education and English as a Second Language, Huntsville, TX 77341. Awards Certificate. Accredited by NCATE. Students: 0. *Application fee:* $15. *Tuition:* $1810 per year full-time, $297 per semester (minimum) part-time for state residents; $6922 per year full-time, $924 per semester (minimum) part-time for nonresidents. • Dr. Hollis Lowery-Moore, Chair, Department of Language, Literacy, and Special Populations, 409-294-1595. Fax: 409-294-1131. E-mail: edu_lap@shsu.edu.

San Diego State University, College of Education, Department of Policy Studies in Language and Cross Cultural Education, San Diego, CA 92182. Awards MA. Accredited by NCATE. Students: 4 full-time (3 women), 16 part-time (11 women); includes 9 minority (2 Asian Americans, 7 Hispanics), 3 international. *Entrance requirements:* GRE General Test (minimum combined score of 950), TOEFL (minimum score 550). Application deadline: rolling. Application fee: $55. *Expenses:* Tuition $0 for state residents; $246 per unit for nonresidents. Fees $1932 per year full-time, $1266 per year part-time. • Natalie Kuhlman, Interim Chair, 619-594-5155. Fax: 619-594-7082. E-mail: nkuhlman@mail.sdsu.edu.

School for International Training, Program in Teaching, Brattleboro, VT 05302-0676. Offerings include endorsement in bilingual-multicultural education (MAT). Program faculty: 20 full-time (12 women), 4 part-time (3 women). *Degree requirements:* 1 foreign language, thesis, practice teaching. *Entrance requirements:* TOEFL (minimum score 550). Application deadline: rolling. Application fee: $45. *Expenses:* Tuition $18,000 per year (minimum). Fees $1283 per year (minimum). • Claire Stanley, Director, 802-257-7751 Ext.3300. Application contact: Fiona Cook, Admissions Counselor, 802-258-3270. Fax: 802-258-3500.

Directory: Multilingual and Multicultural Education

Seton Hall University, College of Education and Human Services, Department of Educational Studies, Teacher Training Program in Bilingual Education, South Orange, NJ 07079-2697. Awards MA, Ed S. *Degree requirements:* For master's, 2 foreign languages, comprehensive exam, project; for Ed S, 2 foreign languages, comprehensive exam, cumulative project. *Entrance requirements:* GRE or MAT. Application deadline: rolling. Application fee: $50. *Expenses:* Tuition $500 per credit. Fees $610 per year full-time, $185 per semester part-time. *Financial aid:* Fellowships, assistantships available. Financial aid application deadline: 2/1. *Faculty research:* Spanish, Mandarin and Cantonese Chinese, Japanese, Korean, school administration and supervision. • Dr. Juan Cobarrubias, Director, 973-761-9617. E-mail: cobarrju@shu.edu.

Southern Connecticut State University, School of Arts and Sciences, Department of Foreign Languages, New Haven, CT 06515-1355. Offerings include multicultural-bilingual education/teaching English to speakers of other languages (MS). MLS/MS offered jointly with the College of Communication, Information and Library Science. Department faculty: 9 full-time. *Application deadline:* 7/15 (priority date; rolling processing). *Application fee:* $40. *Expenses:* Tuition $2632 per year full-time, $188 per credit part-time for state residents; $7200 per year full-time, $188 per credit part-time for nonresidents. Fees $1806 per year full-time, $45 per semester part-time for state residents; $2703 per year full-time, $45 per semester part-time for nonresidents. • Dr. Joseph Solodow, Chairperson, 203-392-6770.

Stanford University, School of Education, Program in Language, Literacy, and Culture, Stanford, CA 94305-9991. Awards AM, PhD. *Degree requirements:* For doctorate, dissertation required, foreign language not required. *Entrance requirements:* GRE General Test. Application deadline: 1/2. Application fee: $65 ($75 for international students). *Expenses:* Tuition $22,110 per year. Fees $156 per year. *Financial aid:* Fellowships available. Financial aid application deadline: 2/1; applicants required to submit FAFSA. • Administrator, 650-723-2115. Application contact: Graduate Admissions Office, 650-723-4794.

State University of New York at Buffalo, Graduate School, Graduate School of Education, Department of Learning and Instruction, Buffalo, NY 14260. Offerings include bilingual education/teaching English to speakers of other languages (Ed M). Department faculty: 20 full-time (9 women), 7 part-time (2 women). *Degree requirements:* Comprehensive exam required, foreign language and thesis not required. *Entrance requirements:* GRE General Test, TOEFL (minimum score 590). Application deadline: 2/1 (11/15 for spring admission). Application fee: $50. *Tuition:* $5970 per year full-time, $288 per credit hour part-time for state residents; $9286 per year full-time, $426 per credit hour part-time for nonresidents. • Dr. Michael Kibby, Chair, 716-645-2455. Application contact: Barbara Cracchiolo, Admissions Secretary, 716-645-2457. Fax: 716-645-3161.

State University of New York College at Brockport, School of Professions, Department of Education and Human Development, Program in Bilingual Education, Brockport, NY 14420-2997. Awards MS Ed. Students: 1 (woman) full-time, 4 part-time (3 women); includes 2 minority (both Hispanics). Average age 30. 3 applicants, 100% accepted. In 1997, 7 degrees awarded. *Entrance requirements:* Minimum GPA of 3.0. Application deadline: 1/15 (priority date; 9/15 for spring admission). Application fee: $50. *Expenses:* Tuition $5100 per year full-time, $213 per credit hour part-time for state residents; $8416 per year full-time, $351 per credit hour part-time for nonresidents. Fees $440 per year full-time, $22.60 per credit hour part-time. *Financial aid:* Federal Work-Study and career-related internships or fieldwork available. Financial aid application deadline: 4/1; applicants required to submit FAFSA. • William Veenis, Chairperson, Department of Education and Human Development, 716-395-2205.

State University of New York College at Buffalo, Faculty of Applied Science and Education, Department of Exceptional Education, Program in Teaching Bilingual Exceptional Individuals, Buffalo, NY 14222-1095. Awards MS Ed. Accredited by NCATE. Students: 9 full-time (8 women), 7 part-time (all women); includes 10 minority (9 Hispanics, 1 Native American), 1 international. Average age 29. 6 applicants, 100% accepted. In 1997, 7 degrees awarded. *Degree requirements:* Project required, foreign language not required. *Entrance requirements:* Minimum GPA of 2.5. Application deadline: 5/1 (10/1 for spring admission). Application fee: $50. *Expenses:* Tuition $5100 per year full-time, $213 per credit hour part-time for state residents; $8416 per year full-time, $351 per credit hour part-time for nonresidents. Fees $195 per year full-time, $8.60 per credit hour part-time. *Financial aid:* In 1997–98, 1 assistantship was awarded; fellowships also available. Financial aid application deadline: 3/1. • Dr. Sarita Samora, Coordinator, 716-878-3038.

Sul Ross State University, Rio Grande College of Sul Ross State University, Alpine, TX 79832. Offerings include teacher education (M Ed), with options in bilingual education, counseling, educational diagnostics, elementary education, general education, reading, school administration, secondary education. College faculty: 16 full-time (2 women), 2 part-time (1 woman). *Application deadline:* rolling. *Application fee:* $0 ($50 for international students). *Expenses:* Tuition $864 per year full-time, $120 per semester (minimum) part-time for state residents; $5976 per year full-time, $747 per semester (minimum) part-time for nonresidents. Fees $754 per year full-time, $105 per semester (minimum) part-time. • Dr. Frank Abbott, Dean, 512-278-3339. Fax: 512-278-3330.

Sul Ross State University, Department of Teacher Education, Program in Bilingual Education, Alpine, TX 79832. Awards M Ed. Part-time and evening/weekend programs available. Students: 2 full-time (1 woman), 5 part-time (4 women); includes 7 minority (all Hispanics). Average age 31. *Degree requirements:* Thesis optional, foreign language not required. *Entrance requirements:* GMAT (minimum score 400) or GRE General Test (minimum combined score of 850), minimum GPA of 2.5 in last 60 hours of undergraduate work. Application deadline: rolling. Application fee: $0 ($50 for international students). *Expenses:* Tuition $864 per year full-time, $120 per semester (minimum) part-time for state residents; $5976 per year full-time, $747 per semester (minimum) part-time for nonresidents. Fees $754 per year full-time, $105 per semester (minimum) part-time. *Financial aid:* Federal Work-Study, institutionally sponsored loans, and career-related internships or fieldwork available. Aid available to part-time students. Financial aid application deadline: 5/1; applicants required to submit FAFSA. • Dr. Mary Ann Weinacht, Director, Department of Teacher Education, 915-837-8170. Fax: 915-837-8390.

Teachers College, Columbia University, Graduate Faculty of Education, Department of International and Transcultural Studies, Program in Bilingual and Bicultural Education, 525 West 120th Street, New York, NY 10027-6696. Awards MA. Part-time programs available. Faculty: 2 full-time (both women), 4 part-time (2 women), 3.4 FTE. Students: 4 full-time (2 women), 31 part-time (29 women); includes 21 minority (5 African Americans, 2 Asian Americans, 14 Hispanics), 1 international. Average age 29. 31 applicants, 52% accepted. In 1997, 6 degrees awarded. *Degree requirements:* 1 foreign language. *Application deadline:* 5/15. *Application fee:* $50. *Expenses:* Tuition $640 per credit. Fees $120 per semester. *Financial aid:* Research assistantships, grants, full and partial tuition waivers, Federal Work-Study, institutionally sponsored loans, and career-related internships or fieldwork available. Aid available to part-time students. Financial aid application deadline: 2/1. *Faculty research:* Cross-cultural research in bilingual and bicultural school settings, diversity and teacher education. • Application contact: Ursula Felton, Office of Admissions, 212-678-3710. Fax: 212-678-4171.

Texas A&M International University, Division of Teacher Education and Psychology, 5201 University Boulevard, Laredo, TX 78041-1900. Offerings include bilingual education (MS Ed). *Degree requirements:* Thesis required (for some programs), foreign language not required. *Entrance requirements:* GRE General Test. Application deadline: 7/15 (priority date; rolling processing; 11/12 for spring admission). Application fee: $0.

Texas A&M University, College of Education, Department of Educational Curriculum and Instruction, Unit in Bilingual Education, College Station, TX 77843. Awards M Ed, MS, PhD. Accredited by NCATE. *Degree requirements:* For doctorate, dissertation required, foreign language not required. *Entrance requirements:* GRE General Test, TOEFL. Application fee: $35 ($75 for international students). *Financial aid:* Fellowships, research assistantships, teaching assistantships available. • Viola Florez, Coordinator, 409-845-0854.

Texas A&M University–Kingsville, College of Education, Department of Bilingual Education, Kingsville, TX 78363. Awards MA, MS, Ed D. Faculty: 4 full-time (2 women), 4 part-time (2 women). *Degree requirements:* For master's, 1 foreign language, thesis or alternative, comprehensive exam; for doctorate, 1 foreign language, dissertation, comprehensive exam. *Entrance requirements:* For master's, GRE General Test (minimum combined score of 1000), minimum GPA of 3.0; for doctorate, GRE General Test (minimum combined score of 1000), MAT (minimum score 50), minimum GPA of 3.25. Application deadline: 6/1 (rolling processing; 11/15 for spring admission). Application fee: $15 ($25 for international students). *Tuition:* $1822 per year full-time, $281 per semester (minimum) part-time for state residents; $6934 per year full-time, $908 per semester (minimum) part-time for nonresidents. *Financial aid:* Fellowships, Federal Work-Study, institutionally sponsored loans available. Financial aid application deadline: 5/15. *Faculty research:* Language acquisition, acculturation in minority communities, English as a second language strategies. • Dr. Gustavo Gonzalez, Chair, 512-593-2871.

Texas Southern University, College of Education, Area of Curriculum and Instruction, Houston, TX 77004-4584. Offerings include bilingual education (M Ed). Faculty: 15 full-time (7 women), 4 part-time (all women). *Degree requirements:* Comprehensive exam required, foreign language not required. *Entrance requirements:* GRE General Test, TOEFL, minimum GPA of 2.5. Application deadline: 7/15 (priority date; rolling processing). Application fee: $35 ($75 for international students). • Dr. Claudette Ligon, Chairperson, 713-313-7775.

Texas Tech University, Graduate School, College of Education, Division of Curriculum and Instruction, Lubbock, TX 79409. Offerings include bilingual education (M Ed, Ed D). Accredited by NCATE. Division faculty: 23 full-time (12 women). *Degree requirements:* For master's, computer language required, thesis optional, foreign language not required; for doctorate, dissertation required, foreign language not required. *Entrance requirements:* For master's, GRE General Test (combined average 992); for doctorate, GRE General Test. Application deadline: 4/15 (priority date; rolling processing; 11/1 for spring admission). Application fee: $25 ($50 for international students). Electronic applications accepted. *Expenses:* Tuition $864 per year full-time, $120 per semester (minimum) part-time for state residents; $5976 per year full-time, $747 per semester (minimum) part-time for nonresidents. Fees $2321 per year full-time, $302 per semester (minimum) part-time. • Dr. William E. Sparkman, Chair, 805-742-2371.

Universidad del Turabo, Programs in Education, Program in Bilingual Education, Gurabo, PR 00778-3030. Awards MA. *Entrance requirements:* GRE, PAEG, interview. Application deadline: 8/5. Application fee: $25.

University of Alaska Fairbanks, Graduate School, School of Education, Fairbanks, AK 99775-7480. Offerings include cross-cultural education (M Ed, Ed S). School faculty: 23 full-time (13 women), 2 part-time (both women). *Degree requirements:* For master's, thesis or alternative, comprehensive exam required, foreign language not required. *Entrance requirements:* For master's, GRE General Test, TOEFL (minimum score 550). Application deadline: 4/1 (10/1 for spring admission). Application fee: $35. *Expenses:* Tuition $162 per credit for state residents; $316 per credit for nonresidents. Fees $520 per year full-time, $45 per semester (minimum) part-time. • Dr. Joe Kan, Director, 907-474-7341.

University of Alberta, Faculty of Graduate Studies and Research, Department of Educational Policy Studies, Edmonton, AB T6G 2E1, Canada. Offerings include international and global education (M Ed, PhD). Department faculty: 25 full-time (7 women), 3 part-time (1 woman). *Degree requirements:* For master's, thesis (for some programs). *Average time to degree:* master's–1 year full-time, 3 years part-time; doctorate–2 years full-time, 4 years part-time. *Entrance requirements:* For master's, TOEFL (minimum score 580). Application deadline: 8/1 (priority date; rolling processing; 4/1 for spring admission). Application fee: $60. *Expenses:* Tuition $390 per course for Canadian residents; $781 per course for nonresidents. Fees $500 per year full-time, $184 per year part-time. • Dr. D. M. Richards, Chair, 403-492-3679. E-mail: don.richards@ualberta.ca. Application contact: Joan White, Graduate Secretary, 403-492-3679. Fax: 403-492-2024. E-mail: joan.white@ualberta.ca.

University of Alberta, Faculty of Graduate Studies and Research, Faculté Saint. Jean, Edmonton, AB T6G 2E1, Canada. Awards M Ed. Part-time and evening/weekend programs available. Faculty: 11 part-time (7 women). Students: 5 full-time (3 women), 9 part-time (8 women). Average age 35. 3 applicants, 100% accepted. In 1997, 1 degree awarded (100% found work related to degree). *Degree requirements:* Thesis (for some programs). *Average time to degree:* master's–3 years part-time. *Entrance requirements:* Proficiency in French. Application fee: $60. *Expenses:* Tuition $390 per course for Canadian residents; $781 per course for nonresidents. Fees $500 per year full-time, $184 per year part-time. *Financial aid:* In 1997–98, 3 students received aid, including 3 fellowships, 2 teaching assistantships, 1 tuition scholarship. *Faculty research:* First and second language acquisition, first and second language learning through subject matter, cultural transmission. • Yvette Mah&e, Coordinator, 403-465-8770. Application contact: Lise Desbiens, Department Office, 403-465-8703. Fax: 403-465-8760. E-mail: ldesbien@gpu.srv.ualberta.ca.

The University of Arizona, College of Education, Department of Language, Reading, and Culture, Tucson, AZ 85721. Offers programs in bilingual education (M Ed); bilingual/multicultural education (MA); language, reading and culture (MA, Ed D, PhD, Ed S); reading (MA, M Ed, Ed D, PhD, Ed S). *Degree requirements:* For master's, thesis (MA) required, foreign language not required; for doctorate, dissertation required, foreign language not required. *Entrance requirements:* For master's, TOEFL (minimum score 550); for doctorate, GRE, TOEFL (minimum score 550); for Ed S, TOEFL (minimun score of 550). Application deadline: 4/15 (rolling processing). Application fee: $35. *Tuition:* $2162 per year full-time, $337 per semester (minimum) part-time for state residents; $6860 per year full-time, $1138 per semester (minimum) part-time for nonresidents. *Faculty research:* Bilingual/bicultural literacy, influence of original and adapted texts on readers, readability, bilingual reading.

University of California, Berkeley, School of Education, Division of Education in Language, Literature, and Culture, Berkeley, CA 94720-1500. Offers programs in advanced reading and language leadership (MA), including reading/reading and language arts; English (Certificate); language, literacy, and culture (MA, Ed D, PhD), including athletes and academic achievement (MA), language, literacy, and culture (MA). Faculty: 10 full-time (5 women), 5 part-time (2 women). *Degree requirements:* For master's, exam or thesis required, foreign language not required; for doctorate, dissertation, oral qualifying exam (PhD) required, foreign language not required. *Entrance requirements:* For master's and doctorate, GRE General Test, minimum GPA of 3.0 during last 2 years of undergraduate course work. Application deadline: 12/15. Application fee: $40. *Expenses:* Tuition $0 for state residents; $9384 per year for nonresidents. Fees $4409 per year. *Financial aid:* Fellowships, research assistantships, teaching assistantships available. Financial aid application deadline: 12/15. *Faculty research:* Literature, English education, reading education, second language teaching and learning, teacher education. • Robert B. Ruddell, Chair, 510-642-0746. Application contact: Admissions Office, 510-642-0841.

University of Colorado at Boulder, School of Education, Division of Social MultiCultural and Bilingual Foundations, Boulder, CO 80309. Awards MA, PhD. Accredited by NCATE. Part-time programs available. Students: 24 full-time (20 women), 23 part-time (18 women); includes 17 minority (14 Hispanics, 3 Native Americans), 1 international. Average age 37. 25 applicants, 44% accepted. In 1997, 22 master's, 2 doctorates awarded. *Degree requirements:* For master's, thesis or alternative, comprehensive exam required, foreign language not required; for doctorate, 1 foreign language, dissertation. *Entrance requirements:* For master's, GRE General Test (minimum combined score of 1500 on three sections) or MAT (minimum score 44), minimum undergraduate GPA of 2.75; for doctorate, GRE General Test (minimum combined score of 1500 on three sections). Application deadline: 2/1 (priority date; 8/1 for spring admission).

Application fee: $40 ($60 for international students). *Expenses:* Tuition $3170 per year full-time, $531 per semester (minimum) part-time for state residents; $14,652 per year full-time, $2442 per semester (minimum) part-time for nonresidents. Fees $667 per year full-time, $130 per semester (minimum) part-time. *Financial aid:* Application deadline 2/1. • Leonard Baca, Director, 303-492-5416. E-mail: leonard.baca@colorado.edu. Application contact: Office of Graduate Studies, 303-492-8430. Fax: 303-492-7090. E-mail: ed.advise@colorado.edu.

University of Connecticut, School of Education, Field of Bilingual and Bicultural Education, Storrs, CT 06269. Awards MA, PhD. Accredited by NCATE. Faculty: 4. Students: 15 full-time (8 women), 20 part-time (17 women); includes 18 minority (all Hispanics), 4 international. Average age 39. 12 applicants, 67% accepted. In 1997, 20 master's, 1 doctorate awarded. Terminal master's awarded for partial completion of doctoral program. *Degree requirements:* For doctorate, dissertation. *Entrance requirements:* For doctorate, GRE General Test. Application deadline: 6/1 (priority date; rolling processing; 11/1 for spring admission). Application fee: $40 ($45 for international students). *Expenses:* Tuition $5272 per year full-time, $293 per credit part-time for state residents; $13,696 per year full-time, $761 per credit part-time for nonresidents. Fees $948 per year full-time, $640 per year part-time. *Financial aid:* Fellowships, teaching assistantships available. Financial aid application deadline: 2/15. • Thomas P. Weinland, Head, 860-486-2433.

University of Delaware, College of Human Resources, Education and Public Policy, School of Education, Newark, DE 19716. Offerings include English as a second language/bilingualism (MA). School faculty: 54 (24 women). *Application deadline:* 7/1 (rolling processing; 1/15 for spring admission). *Application fee:* $45. *Expenses:* Tuition $4250 per year full-time, $236 per credit hour part-time for state residents; $12,250 per year full-time, $681 per credit hour part-time for nonresidents. Fees $466 per year full-time, $15 per semester (minimum) part-time. • Dr. Robert Hampel, Director, 302-831-2573.

The University of Findlay, College of Professional Studies, Program in Teaching English to Speakers of Other Languages and Bilingual and Multicultural Education, 1000 North Main Street, Findlay, OH 45840-3653. Offers bilingual and multicultural education (MA), teaching English to speakers of other languages (MA). Faculty: 4 full-time (3 women), 3 part-time (2 women). Students: 24 full-time (21 women), 53 part-time (51 women); includes 30 minority (2 African Americans, 25 Asian Americans, 3 Hispanics). Average age 30. In 1997, 23 degrees awarded. *Degree requirements:* Cumulative project. *Application deadline:* rolling. *Application fee:* $25. *Tuition:* $236 per semester hour. *Financial aid:* Teaching assistantships available. Aid available to part-time students. Financial aid applicants required to submit FAFSA. • Dr. Irma A. Hanson, Director, 419-424-4826. Fax: 419-424-4822. E-mail: hanson@hewey.findlay.edu.

University of Florida, College of Education, Department of Instruction and Curriculum, Gainesville, FL 32611. Offerings include bilingual education (MAE, M Ed, Ed D, PhD, Ed S). Accredited by NCATE. Department faculty: 42. *Degree requirements:* For master's, thesis optional, foreign language not required; for doctorate, variable foreign language requirement, dissertation. *Entrance requirements:* For master's and doctorate, GRE General Test (minimum combined score of 1000), minimum GPA of 3.0; for Ed S, GRE General Test. Application deadline: 6/5. Application fee: $20. *Tuition:* $138 per credit hour for state residents; $481 per credit hour for nonresidents. • Dr. Mary Grace Kantowski, Chair, 352-392-9191 Ext. 200. E-mail: mgk@coe.ufl.edu. Application contact: Dr. Ben Nelms, Graduate Coordinator, 352-392-9191 Ext. 225. Fax: 352-392-9193. E-mail: bfn@coe.ufl.edu.

University of Houston, College of Education, Department of Curriculum and Instruction, 4800 Calhoun, Houston, TX 77204-2163. Offerings include bilingual education (M Ed). Accredited by NCATE. Department faculty: 37 full-time (19 women), 10 part-time (7 women). *Degree requirements:* Comprehensive exam or thesis required, foreign language not required. *Entrance requirements:* GRE General Test or MAT. Application deadline: 7/3 (priority date; rolling processing). Application fee: $35 ($75 for international students). *Expenses:* Tuition $1152 per year full-time, $120 per semester (minimum) part-time for state residents; $4482 per year full-time, $249 per credit hour part-time for nonresidents. Fees $977 per year full-time, $119 per semester (minimum) part-time. • Wilford Weber, Chair, 713-743-4970. Fax: 713-743-9870. E-mail: wweber@uh.edu.

University of Houston–Clear Lake, School of Education, Houston, TX 77058-1098. Offerings include multicultural education (MS). Accredited by NCATE. School faculty: 34 full-time (23 women), 17 part-time (12 women), 39 FTE. *Application deadline:* rolling. *Application fee:* $30 ($60 for international students). *Tuition:* $207 per credit hour for state residents; $336 per credit hour for nonresidents. • Dr. Dennis Spuck, Dean, 281-283-3501. Application contact: Dr. Doris L. Prater, Associate Dean, 281-283-3600.

University of Massachusetts Amherst, School of Education, Program in Education, Amherst, MA 01003-0001. Offerings include cultural diversity and curriculum reform (M Ed, Ed D, CAGS). Accredited by NCATE. *Degree requirements:* For doctorate, dissertation required, foreign language not required. *Entrance requirements:* For master's and doctorate, GRE General Test. Application deadline: 3/1 (rolling processing; 10/1 for spring admission). Application fee: $40. *Expenses:* Tuition $2640 per year full-time, $110 per credit part-time for state residents; $3690 per year (minimum) full-time, $165 per credit (minimum) part-time for nonresidents. Fees $2856 per year full-time, $422 per semester part-time for state residents; $3204 per year full-time, $480 per semester part-time for nonresidents. • John C. Carey, Director, 413-545-0236.

University of Massachusetts Boston, College of Arts and Sciences, Faculty of Arts, Program in Bilingual Education, Boston, MA 02125-3393. Awards MA. Students: 9 full-time (4 women), 44 part-time (36 women); includes 26 minority (6 African Americans, 2 Asian Americans, 18 Hispanics), 7 international. 26 applicants, 77% accepted. In 1997, 9 degrees awarded. *Degree requirements:* Comprehensive exams required, thesis optional, foreign language not required. *Entrance requirements:* Minimum GPA of 2.75. Application deadline: 2/1 (priority date; 10/15 for spring admission). Application fee: $25 ($35 for international students). *Expenses:* Tuition $2640 per year full-time, $110 per credit part-time for state residents; $8930 per year full-time, $373 per credit part-time for nonresidents. Fees $2650 per year full-time, $420 per semester (minimum) part-time for state residents; $2736 per year full-time, $420 per semester (minimum) part-time for nonresidents. *Financial aid:* In 1997–98, 6 research assistantships (3 to first-year students) averaging $225 per month and totaling $13,331, 4 teaching assistantships (all to first-year students) averaging $309 per month and totaling $11,000 were awarded; administrative assistantships also available. Financial aid application deadline: 3/1; applicants required to submit FAFSA. • Dr. Donaldo Macedo, Director, 617-287-5760. Application contact: Lisa Lavely, Director of Graduate Admissions and Records, 617-287-6400. Fax: 617-287-6236.

University of Minnesota, Twin Cities Campus, College of Education and Human Development, Department of Curriculum and Instruction, Minneapolis, MN 55455-0213. Offerings include second languages and cultures (MA, M Ed, PhD). • Fred Finley, Chairman, 612-625-2545.

University of New Mexico, College of Education, Program in Multicultural Teacher and Childhood Education, Albuquerque, NM 87131-2039. Awards Ed D, PhD, Ed S. Offerings include curriculum and instruction (Ed S), multicultural teacher and childhood education (PhD, Ed S). Accredited by NCATE. Faculty: 11 full-time (5 women), 28 part-time (18 women), 18.72 FTE. Students: 22 full-time (17 women), 45 part-time (35 women); includes 19 minority (1 African American, 13 Hispanics, 5 Native Americans), 2 international. Average age 45. 10 applicants, 60% accepted. In 1997, 12 doctorates awarded. Terminal master's awarded for partial completion of doctoral program. *Degree requirements:* For doctorate, dissertation required, foreign language not required. *Entrance requirements:* For doctorate, GRE or MAT, 3 years of teaching experience. Application deadline: 3/31 (10/10 for spring admission). Application fee: $25. *Expenses:* Tuition $2442 per year full-time, $103 per credit hour part-time for state residents; $8691 per year full-time, $103 per credit hour (minimum) part-time for nonresidents. Fees $32 per year. *Financial aid:* Research assistantships, teaching assistantships, Federal Work-Study, institutionally sponsored loans, and career-related internships or fieldwork available. Aid available to part-time students. Financial aid application deadline: 3/31. *Faculty research:* Bilingualism, teacher development, language and literacy, mathematics, science, technology. • Dr. Peter Winograd, Graduate Coordinator, 505-277-4533. E-mail: winograd@unm.edu. Application contact: Irene Martinez, Division Administrator, 505-277-4533. Fax: 505-277-4166. E-mail: icmartin@unm.edu.

University of Pennsylvania, Graduate School of Education, Division of Language in Education, Programs in Educational Linguistics, Teaching English to Speakers of Other Languages and Intercultural Communication, Philadelphia, PA 19104. Offerings include intercultural communication (MS Ed). Postbaccalaureate distance learning degree programs offered (minimal on-campus study). *Degree requirements:* Thesis (for some programs), comprehensive exam required, foreign language not required. *Entrance requirements:* GRE General Test or MAT, TOEFL (minimum score 550). Application fee: $65. Electronic applications accepted. *Expenses:* Tuition $22,716 per year full-time, $2876 per course part-time. Fees $1484 per year full-time, $181 per course part-time. • Dr. Nancy Hornberger, Director, 215-898-4800. Application contact: Keith Watanabe, Coordinator, 215-898-3245. Fax: 215-573-2109.

University of San Francisco, School of Education, Department of International and Multicultural Education, San Francisco, CA 94117-1080. Offers programs in international and multicultural education (MA, Ed D), teaching English as a second language (MA). Faculty: 8 full-time (5 women), 9 part-time (5 women). Students: 105 full-time (81 women), 59 part-time (44 women); includes 78 minority (32 African Americans, 23 Asian Americans, 22 Hispanics, 1 Native American), 13 international. Average age 41. 124 applicants, 89% accepted. In 1997, 24 master's, 11 doctorates awarded. *Degree requirements:* For doctorate, dissertation required, foreign language not required. *Application fee:* $40. *Tuition:* $658 per unit (minimum). *Financial aid:* 73 students received aid; fellowships, research assistantships, teaching assistantships available. Financial aid application deadline: 3/2. • Dr. Rosita Galang, Chair, 415-422-6878.

University of Tennessee, Knoxville, College of Education, Program in Education I, Knoxville, TN 37996. Offerings include cultural studies in education (PhD). Accredited by NCATE. *Degree requirements:* 1 foreign language (computer language can substitute), dissertation. *Entrance requirements:* GRE General Test, TOEFL (minimum score 550), minimum GPA of 2.7. Application deadline: 2/1 (priority date; rolling processing). Application fee: $35. Electronic applications accepted. *Tuition:* $3354 per year full-time, $181 per semester hour part-time for state residents; $8410 per year full-time, $462 per semester hour part-time for nonresidents. • Dr. Tom George, Associate Dean, 423-974-0907. Fax: 423-974-8718. E-mail: tgeorge1@utk.edu.

University of Tennessee, Knoxville, College of Education, Program in Education II, Knoxville, TN 37996. Offerings include cultural studies in education (MS). Accredited by NCATE. *Degree requirements:* Thesis optional, foreign language not required. *Entrance requirements:* TOEFL (minimum score 550), minimum GPA of 2.7. Application deadline: 2/1 (priority date; rolling processing). Application fee: $35. Electronic applications accepted. *Tuition:* $3354 per year full-time, $181 per semester hour part-time for state residents; $8410 per year full-time, $462 per semester hour part-time for nonresidents. • Dr. Tom George, Associate Dean, 423-974-0907. Fax: 423-974-8718. E-mail: tgeorge1@utk.edu.

The University of Texas at San Antonio, College of Social and Behavioral Sciences, Division of Bicultural-Bilingual Studies, San Antonio, TX 78249-0617. Offers programs in bicultural studies (MA), bicultural-bilingual studies (MA), teaching English as a second language (MA). Faculty: 9 full-time (3 women), 12 part-time (7 women). Students: 22 full-time (18 women), 70 part-time (59 women); includes 54 minority (2 African Americans, 3 Asian Americans, 48 Hispanics, 1 Native American), 3 international. Average age 34. 43 applicants, 63% accepted. In 1997, 41 degrees awarded. *Degree requirements:* 1 foreign language, thesis or alternative, comprehensive exam. *Entrance requirements:* GRE General Test. Application deadline: 7/1 (rolling processing). Application fee: $20. *Expenses:* Tuition $2476 per year full-time, $309 per semester (minimum) part-time for state residents; $7584 per year full-time, $948 per semester (minimum) part-time for nonresidents. Fees $361 per year full-time, $133 per semester (minimum) part-time. *Financial aid:* Federal Work-Study and career-related internships or fieldwork available. Aid available to part-time students. *Faculty research:* Spanish-English bilingualism, cultural transmission in bilingual communities, literacy in bilingual settings, content-based ESL, second language acquisition in classroom contexts. • Dr. Robert Milk, Director, 210-458-4426.

The University of Texas–Pan American, College of Education, Department of Curriculum and Instruction: Elementary and Secondary, Edinburg, TX 78539-2999. Offerings include elementary bilingual education (M Ed). *Degree requirements:* Thesis optional. *Entrance requirements:* GRE General Test. Application deadline: 7/17 (11/16 for spring admission). Application fee: $0. *Tuition:* $2156 per year full-time, $283 per semester (minimum) part-time for state residents; $6788 per year full-time, $862 per semester (minimum) part-time for nonresidents.

Xavier University, College of Social Sciences, Department of Education, Program in Multicultural Literature for Children, Cincinnati, OH 45207-2111. Awards M Ed. Part-time programs available. Faculty: 2 full-time (both women), 3 part-time (2 women), 2.75 FTE. Students: 7 part-time (all women); includes 1 minority (African American). Average age 34. 3 applicants, 100% accepted. In 1997, 1 degree awarded. *Degree requirements:* Comprehensive exam required, foreign language and thesis not required. *Average time to degree:* master's–1.5 years full-time, 2.5 years part-time. *Entrance requirements:* MAT (minimum score 35), minimum GPA of 2.8. Application deadline: 8/15 (priority date; rolling processing). Application fee: $25. *Financial aid:* In 1997–98, 3 scholarships (all to first-year students) were awarded. Aid available to part-time students. *Faculty research:* Analysis of Canadian children's literature, adolescent literature, gender issues in literature for children. • Dr. Leslie Prosak-Beres, Director, 513-745-3652. Fax: 513-745-1052. E-mail: prosak@xavier.xu.edu. Application contact: Sheila Speth, Director of Graduate Services, 513-745-3360. Fax: 513-745-1048. E-mail: xugrad@admin.xu.edu.

Special Education

Acadia University, Faculty of Professional Studies, School of Education, Program in Special Education, Wolfville, NS B0P 1X0, Canada. Awards M Ed. *Degree requirements:* Thesis required, foreign language not required. *Entrance requirements:* Bachelor's degree in education, minimum B average in undergraduate course work, previous course work in special education. Application deadline: 2/1 (rolling processing). Application fee: $25. *Expenses:* Tuition $4095 per year for Canadian residents; $8190 per year for nonresidents. Fees $145 per year. *Financial aid:* Teaching assistantships available. Financial aid application deadline: 2/1. • Dr. Bryant Griffith, Director, School of Education, 902-585-1229. E-mail: bryant.griffith@acadiau.ca. Application contact: Sheila Langille, Secretary, 902-585-1229. Fax: 902-585-1071.

Adams State College, School of Education and Graduate Studies, Department of Teacher Education, Program in Special Education, Alamosa, CO 81102. Awards MA. Accredited by NCATE. Part-time programs available. Postbaccalaureate distance learning degree programs offered. *Degree requirements:* Practicum, qualifying exam required, foreign language and thesis not required. *Entrance requirements:* GRE General Test or MAT, minimum undergraduate GPA of 2.75. Application deadline: 5/15 (priority date; rolling processing; 10/15 for spring admission). Application fee: $25. *Tuition:* $2164 per year full-time, $111 per credit part-time for state residents; $7284 per year full-time, $377 per credit part-time for nonresidents. *Financial aid:* In 1997–98, 2 graduate assistantships (1 to a first-year student) averaging $500 per month and totaling $8,000 were awarded; Federal Work-Study, institutionally sponsored loans, and career-related internships or fieldwork also available. Aid available to part-time students. Financial aid application deadline: 4/15; applicants required to submit FAFSA. • Dr. John Cross, Head, Department of Teacher Education, 719-587-7776.

Adelphi University, School of Education, Department of Physical Education, Recreation, and Human Performance Science, Garden City, NY 11530. Offerings include special physical education (Certificate). *Application deadline:* rolling. *Application fee:* $50. *Expenses:* Tuition $16,000 per year full-time, $485 per credit part-time. Fees $500 per year full-time, $150 per semester part-time. • Dr. Ronald Feingold, Chairperson, 516-877-4260.

Adelphi University, School of Education, Program in Special Education, Garden City, NY 11530. Offers early childhood special education (MS), early childhood/elementary education-special education (MS), special education (MS). Part-time and evening/weekend programs available. Students: 71 full-time (60 women), 207 part-time (173 women); includes 38 minority (25 African Americans, 1 Asian American, 12 Hispanics), 1 international. Average age 34. In 1997, 171 degrees awarded. *Degree requirements:* Thesis required, foreign language not required. *Application deadline:* rolling. *Application fee:* $50. *Expenses:* Tuition $16,000 per year full-time, $485 per credit part-time. Fees $500 per year full-time, $150 per semester part-time. *Financial aid:* Fellowships, research assistantships, teaching assistantships, assistantships, and career-related internships or fieldwork available. Financial aid application deadline: 3/1. • Dr. Sheila Hollander, Director, 516-877-4085.

Adelphi University, School of Education, Programs in Speech Pathology and Audiology and Education of the Deaf, Garden City, NY 11530. Offerings include education of the speech and hearing handicapped (MS). *Degree requirements:* Comprehensive exam required, foreign language and thesis not required. *Entrance requirements:* GRE General Test. Application deadline: 4/15. Application fee: $50. *Expenses:* Tuition $16,000 per year full-time, $485 per credit part-time. Fees $500 per year full-time, $150 per semester part-time. • Dr. Elaine Sands, Chairperson, 516-877-4770.

Adelphi University, School of Education, Specialization in Bilingual Education, Garden City, NY 11530. Offerings include special education (MS). *Application deadline:* rolling. *Application fee:* $50. *Expenses:* Tuition $16,000 per year full-time, $485 per credit part-time. Fees $500 per year full-time, $150 per semester part-time. • Eva Roca, Director, 516-877-4070.

Alabama Agricultural and Mechanical University, School of Education, Department of Counseling and Special Education, Area in Special Education, PO Box 1357, Normal, AL 35762-1357. Awards M Ed, MS. Accredited by NCATE. Part-time and evening/weekend programs available. Faculty: 6 full-time (2 women). *Degree requirements:* Comprehensive exam required, foreign language and thesis not required. *Entrance requirements:* GRE General Test, minimum GPA of 2.5. Application deadline: 5/1 (rolling processing). Application fee: $15 ($20 for international students). *Expenses:* Tuition $2782 per year full-time, $565 per semester (minimum) part-time for state residents; $5164 per year full-time, $1015 per semester (minimum) part-time for nonresidents. Fees $560 per year full-time, $390 per year part-time. *Financial aid:* Fellowships, research assistantships, and career-related internships or fieldwork available. Aid available to part-time students. Financial aid application deadline: 4/1. *Faculty research:* Minority retention and recruitment, etiology and treatment of the mentally retarded. • Dr. Annie Grace Robinson, Chair, Department of Counseling and Special Education, 205-851-5533.

Alabama State University, School of Graduate Studies, College of Education, Department of Curriculum and Instruction, Program in Special Education, Montgomery, AL 36101-0271. Awards M Ed. Faculty: 3 full-time (1 woman), 2 part-time (0 women). Students: 17 full-time (9 women), 60 part-time (39 women); includes 65 minority (64 African Americans, 1 Hispanic). In 1997, 18 degrees awarded. *Degree requirements:* Comprehensive exam required, thesis optional. *Entrance requirements:* GRE General Test, MAT or NTE. Application deadline: 7/15 (rolling processing; 12/15 for spring admission). Application fee: $10. *Expenses:* Tuition $85 per credit hour for state residents; $170 per credit hour for nonresidents. Fees $486 per year. • Dr. Willa B. Harris, Coordinator, 334-229-4394. Fax: 334-229-4904. Application contact: Dr. Fred Dauser, Dean of Graduate Studies, 334-229-4276. Fax: 334-229-4928.

Albany State University, School of Education, Program in Special Education, Albany, GA 31705-2717. Awards M Ed. Accredited by NCATE. Part-time programs available. Faculty: 2 full-time (both women), 2 part-time (1 woman). Students: 34 part-time (29 women). 8 applicants, 100% accepted. In 1997, 13 degrees awarded. *Degree requirements:* Comprehensive exam. *Entrance requirements:* GRE General Test (minimum combined score of 800), MAT (minimum score 44) or NTE (minimum score 550). Application deadline: 9/1. Application fee: $10. *Financial aid:* Federal Work-Study and career-related internships or fieldwork available. Aid available to part-time students. Financial aid application deadline: 4/1. • Dr. Claude Perkins, Dean, School of Education, 912-430-4715. Fax: 912-430-4993. E-mail: cperkins@fld94.alsnet.peachnet.edu.

Alcorn State University, School of Psychology and Education, Lorman, MS 39096-9402. Offerings include special education (MS Ed). Accredited by NCATE. *Degree requirements:* Thesis optional, foreign language not required. *Application deadline:* 7/1 (priority date; rolling processing; 12/1 for spring admission). *Application fee:* $10. *Tuition:* $2470 per year full-time, $378 per semester (minimum) part-time for state residents; $5331 per year full-time, $855 per semester (minimum) part-time for nonresidents.

American International College, School of Continuing Education and Graduate Studies, School of Psychology and Education, Department of Education, Springfield, MA 01109-3189. Offerings include special education (M Ed, CAGS). Department faculty: 5 full-time (3 women), 15 part-time (9 women). *Degree requirements:* For CAGS, practicum required, foreign language not required. *Application fee:* $15 ($25 for international students). *Expenses:* Tuition $363 per credit hour. Fees $25 per semester. • C. Gerald Weaver, Dean, School of Psychology and Education, 413-747-6338.

American University, College of Arts and Sciences, School of Education, Programs in Special Education, Washington, DC 20016-8001. Offering in learning disabilities (MA). Part-time and evening/weekend programs available. Faculty: 8 full-time (5 women), 10 part-time (8 women), 11.3 FTE. Students: 22 full-time (21 women), 16 part-time (13 women); includes 4 minority (1 African American, 1 Asian American, 1 Hispanic, 1 Native American), 4 international. 32 applicants, 91% accepted. In 1997, 16 degrees awarded. *Degree requirements:* Thesis or alternative, comprehensive exam required, foreign language not required. *Entrance requirements:* GRE General Test or MAT, minimum GPA of 3.0. Application deadline: 2/1 (10/1 for spring admission). Application fee: $50. *Expenses:* Tuition $687 per credit hour. Fees $180 per year full-time, $110 per year part-time. *Financial aid:* Fellowships, research assistantships, teaching assistantships, Federal Work-Study, institutionally sponsored loans, and career-related internships or fieldwork available. Aid available to part-time students. Financial aid application deadline: 2/1. • Dr. Sally Smith, Director, 202-885-3731. Fax: 202-885-1187. E-mail: educate@american.edu.

Appalachian State University, College of Education, Department of Language, Reading and Exceptionalities, Boone, NC 28608. Offerings include special education (MA). Accredited by NCATE. Department faculty: 25 full-time (12 women), 13 part-time (11 women). *Degree requirements:* Thesis or alternative, comprehensive exams required, foreign language not required. *Average time to degree:* master's–2 years full-time, 4 years part-time. *Entrance requirements:* GRE General Test. Application deadline: 7/31 (priority date). Application fee: $35. *Tuition:* $1811 per year full-time, $354 per semester (minimum) part-time for state residents; $9081 per year full-time, $2171 per semester (minimum) part-time for nonresidents. • Dr. Tim Harris, Chairperson, 704-262-2182.

Arizona State University, College of Education, Division of Curriculum and Instruction, Academic Program of Special Education, Tempe, AZ 85287. Awards MA, M Ed. *Degree requirements:* Thesis or alternative. *Entrance requirements:* GRE General Test or MAT. Application fee: $45. *Expenses:* Tuition $2088 per year full-time, $110 per hour part-time for state residents; $9040 per year full-time, $377 per hour part-time for nonresidents. Fees $72 per year full-time, $18 per semester (minimum) part-time. *Faculty research:* Gifted, mildly handicapped, multicultural exceptional, severely/multiply handicapped. • Dr. Alfonso G. Prieto, Coordinator, 602-965-1458.

Arizona State University West, College of Education, Phoenix, AZ 85069-7100. Offerings include special education (M Ed). College faculty: 19 full-time (13 women), 12 part-time (7 women), 24.23 FTE. *Degree requirements:* Comprehensive exams required, thesis not required. *Entrance requirements:* GRE or MAT, TOEFL. Application deadline: rolling. Application fee: $40. *Expenses:* Tuition $2088 per year full-time, $330 per course part-time for state residents; $9040 per year full-time, $1131 per course part-time for nonresidents. Fees $10 per year (minimum). • Dr. William S. Svoboda, Dean, 602-543-6300. Application contact: Ray Buss, Assistant Dean, 602-543-6300. Fax: 602-543-6350.

Arkansas State University, College of Education, Department of Special Education, State University, AR 72467. Offers programs in gifted and talented education (MSE), special education (MSE). Part-time programs available. Faculty: 5 full-time (1 woman). Students: 7 full-time (all women), 34 part-time (all women); includes 3 minority (1 African American, 1 Asian American, 1 Hispanic). Average age 36. In 1997, 13 degrees awarded. *Degree requirements:* Thesis or alternative, comprehensive exam. *Entrance requirements:* GRE General Test or MAT, appropriate bachelor's degree. Application deadline: 7/1 (priority date; rolling processing; 11/15 for spring admission). Application fee: $15 ($25 for international students). *Expenses:* Tuition $2760 per year full-time, $115 per credit hour part-time for state residents; $6936 per year full-time, $289 per credit hour part-time for nonresidents. Fees $506 per year full-time, $44 per semester (minimum) part-time. *Financial aid:* Teaching assistantships and career-related internships or fieldwork available. Aid available to part-time students. Financial aid application deadline: 7/1; applicants required to submit FAFSA. • Dr. Roberta Daniels, Interim Chair, 870-972-3061. Fax: 870-972-3828. E-mail: rdaniels@kiowa.astate.edu.

Armstrong Atlantic State University, School of Graduate Studies, Program in Education, Savannah, GA 31419-1997. Offerings include special education (M Ed). Accredited by NCATE. Program faculty: 25. *Expenses:* Tuition $83 per quarter hour for state residents; $250 per quarter hour for nonresidents. Fees $145 per quarter hour for state residents; $228 per quarter hour for nonresidents. • Dr. Bettye Anne Battiste, Department Head, 912-927-5281.

Ashland University, College of Education, Graduate Studies in Teacher Education, Program in Curriculum and Instruction, Ashland, OH 44805-3702. Offerings include developmentally handicapped education (M Ed), early education of the handicapped child (M Ed), multihandicapped education (M Ed), special education (M Ed), specific learning disabled education (M Ed). One or more programs accredited by NCATE. Program faculty: 8 full-time (4 women), 24 part-time (9 women). *Degree requirements:* Practicum or thesis. *Entrance requirements:* GRE General Test or MAT, teaching certificate. Application deadline: rolling. Application fee: $15. *Tuition:* $275 per credit hour. • Carl Walley, Program Team Leader, 419-289-5355. E-mail: cwalley@ashland.edu. Application contact: Dr. Joe Bailey, Director, 419-289-5377. Fax: 419-289-5097. E-mail: jbailey@ashland.edu.

Assumption College, Institute for Social and Rehabilitation Services, Program in Special Education, 500 Salisbury Street, PO Box 15005, Worcester, MA 01615-0005. Awards MA. Part-time and evening/weekend programs available. *Degree requirements:* Internship, oral comprehensive exam, practicum. *Entrance requirements:* TOEFL. Application deadline: rolling. Application fee: $20. *Expenses:* Tuition $297 per credit hour. Fees $10 per semester.

Auburn University, College of Education, Department of Rehabilitation and Special Education, Auburn University, AL 36849-0001. Awards M Ed, MS, PhD, Ed S. Accredited by NCATE. Part-time programs available. Faculty: 10 full-time (3 women). Students: 81 full-time (65 women), 47 part-time (41 women); includes 22 minority (19 African Americans, 3 Native Americans), 1 international. 68 applicants, 71% accepted. In 1997, 36 master's, 6 doctorates awarded. *Degree requirements:* For master's, thesis (MS) required, foreign language not required; for doctorate, dissertation required, foreign language not required. *Entrance requirements:* For master's, GRE General Test; for doctorate, GRE General Test (minimum score 400 on each section), interview; for Ed S, GRE General Test, interview. Application deadline: 9/1 (rolling processing; 3/1 for spring admission). Application fee: $25 ($50 for international students). *Expenses:* Tuition $2760 per year full-time, $76 per credit hour part-time for state residents; $8280 per year full-time, $228 per credit hour part-time for nonresidents. Fees $30 per year full-time, $160 per quarter part-time for state residents; $30 per year full-time, $480 per quarter part-time for nonresidents. *Financial aid:* Research assistantships, teaching assistantships, Federal Work-Study available. Aid available to part-time students. Financial aid application deadline: 3/15. *Faculty research:* Emotional conflict/behavior disorders, gifted and talented, learning disabilities, mental retardation, multihandicapped. • Dr. Philip L. Browning, Head, 334-844-5943. Application contact: Dr. John F. Pritchett, Dean of the Graduate School, 334-844-4700.

Auburn University Montgomery, School of Education, Department of Counselor Leadership and Special Education, Montgomery, AL 36124-4023. Offers programs in counseling (M Ed, Ed S), education administration (M Ed, Ed S), special education (M Ed, Ed S). Accredited by NCATE. Part-time and evening/weekend programs available. Students: 72 full-time (56 women), 61 part-time (55 women); includes 56 minority (53 African Americans, 3 Hispanics). Average age 34. In 1997, 16 master's, 12 Ed Ss awarded. *Degree requirements:* For master's, comprehensive exam required, foreign language and thesis not required; for Ed S, comprehensive exam required, foreign language not required. *Entrance requirements:* For master's, GRE General Test or MAT, certification, BS in teaching; for Ed S, GRE General Test or MAT, certification. Application deadline: 9/1 (priority date; rolling processing; 3/28 for spring admission). Application fee: $25. Electronic applications accepted. *Tuition:* $2664 per year full-time, $85 per quarter hour part-time for state residents; $7080 per year full-time, $255 per quarter hour part-time for nonresidents. *Financial aid:* In 1997–98, 1 teaching assistantship was awarded. • Dr. James Wright, Head, 334-244-3457.

Directory: Special Education

Augustana College, Department of Education, Program in Special Education, Sioux Falls, SD 57197. Offers computer applications in special education (MA), education of the emotionally disturbed (MA), education of the learning disabled (MA), education of the mentally retarded (MA), education of the physically handicapped (MA), educator/child and youth services (MA), special education (MA). Accredited by NCATE. Part-time programs available. Faculty: 6 full-time. Students: 37 part-time (35 women); includes 1 international. Average age 35. *Degree requirements:* Comprehensive and oral exams required, foreign language and thesis not required. *Entrance requirements:* Appropriate bachelor's degree, minimum GPA of 3.0. Application deadline: 6/1 (priority date; rolling processing). Application fee: $50. *Tuition:* $14,726 per year full-time, $250 per credit hour part-time. *Financial aid:* Application deadline 2/1. • Application contact: Kay West, Secretary, 605-336-4126. Fax: 605-336-4450.

Augusta State University, College of Education, Program in Special Education, Augusta, GA 30904-2200. Awards M Ed, Ed S. Accredited by NCATE. Part-time and evening/weekend programs available. Faculty: 4 full-time (3 women). Students: 23 full-time (21 women), 16 part-time (14 women); includes 7 minority (6 African Americans, 1 Hispanic). Average age 35. 13 applicants, 100% accepted. In 1997, 17 master's, 2 Ed Ss awarded. *Degree requirements:* Thesis, comprehensive exam. *Entrance requirements:* GRE, MAT. Application deadline: 7/26 (priority date; rolling processing). Application fee: $10. *Tuition:* $2260 per year full-time, $83 per credit hour part-time for state residents; $8260 per year full-time, $333 per credit hour part-time for nonresidents. *Financial aid:* In 1997–98, 1 graduate assistantship (to a first-year student) was awarded; Federal Work-Study, institutionally sponsored loans, and career-related internships or fieldwork also available. Aid available to part-time students. Financial aid application deadline: 4/15; applicants required to submit FAFSA. *Faculty research:* Behavior disorders, gifted programs. • Dr. C. Jay Hertzog, Acting Chair, 706-737-1497. E-mail: jhertzog@aug.edu. Application contact: Heather Eakin, Secretary to the Dean, 706-737-1499. Fax: 706-667-4706. E-mail: heakin@aug.edu.

Austin Peay State University, College of Education, Department of Education, Clarksville, TN 37044-0001. Offerings include special education (MA). Accredited by NCATE. *Application deadline:* 7/31 (priority date; rolling processing; 12/4 for spring admission). *Application fee:* $15. *Expenses:* Tuition $2438 per year full-time, $123 per semester hour part-time for state residents; $7034 per year full-time, $324 per semester hour part-time for nonresidents. Fees $484 per year (minimum) full-time, $154 per semester (minimum) part-time. • J. Ronald Groseclose, Interim Chair, 931-648-7585. Fax: 931-648-5991. E-mail: grosecloseg@apsu.edu.

Azusa Pacific University, School of Education and Behavioral Studies, Department of Education, Program in Special Education, Azusa, CA 91702-7000. Awards MA. Part-time and evening/weekend programs available. Faculty: 1 full-time, 9 part-time. Students: 40. In 1997, 55 degrees awarded. *Degree requirements:* Core exams, oral presentations required, foreign language and thesis not required. *Entrance requirements:* 12 units of previous course work in education, minimum GPA of 3.0. Application fee: $45 ($65 for international students). *Expenses:* Tuition $350 per unit. Fees $57 per year. • Dr. Bruce Simmerok, Director, 626-815-5362.

Baldwin-Wallace College, Division of Education, Specialization in Specific Learning Disabilities, Berea, OH 44017-2088. Awards MA Ed. Accredited by NCATE. Part-time and evening/weekend programs available. *Entrance requirements:* Bachelor's degree in field, MAT or minimum GPA of 2.75. Application fee: $15. *Financial aid:* Career-related internships or fieldwork available. • Dr. Patrick F. Cosiano, Chairman, Division of Education, 440-826-2168. Fax: 440-826-3779. E-mail: pcosiano@bw.edu. Application contact: Dr. Jane F. Cavanaugh, Director of Continuing Education, 440-826-2222. Fax: 440-826-3640. E-mail: admission@bw.edu.

Ball State University, Teachers College, Department of Special Education, 2000 University Avenue, Muncie, IN 47306-1099. Awards MA, MAE, Ed D, Ed S. Accredited by NCATE. Faculty: 11. Students: 15 full-time (14 women), 63 part-time (59 women); includes 2 minority (1 African American, 1 Asian American), 1 international. Average age 35. 31 applicants, 71% accepted. In 1997, 48 master's, 1 Ed S awarded. *Degree requirements:* For doctorate and Ed S, thesis/dissertation required, foreign language not required. *Entrance requirements:* For doctorate, GRE General Test (minimum combined score of 1000), minimum graduate GPA of 3.2; for Ed S, GRE General Test. Application fee: $15 ($25 for international students). *Expenses:* Tuition $3454 per year full-time, $518 per semester (minimum) part-time for state residents; $9316 per year full-time, $1221 per semester (minimum) part-time for nonresidents. Fees $242 per year full-time, $18 per semester (minimum) part-time. *Financial aid:* Research assistantships and career-related internships or fieldwork available. *Faculty research:* Language development and utilization in the handicapped (preschool through adult). • John Merbler, Chairperson, 765-285-5700.

Bank Street College of Education, Program in Elementary Education and Special Education, 610 West 112th Street, New York, NY 10025-1120. Awards MS Ed. *Degree requirements:* Thesis. *Entrance requirements:* TOEFL (minimum score 550). Application deadline: 3/1 (priority date; rolling processing; 11/1 for spring admission). Application fee: $50. *Tuition:* $560 per credit. *Financial aid:* Application deadline 3/1. • Linda Levine, Chairperson, 212-875-4480. Application contact: Ann Morgan, Director of Admissions, 212-875-4404. Fax: 212-875-4678. E-mail: amorgan@bnkst.edu.

Bank Street College of Education, Program in Special Education, 610 West 112th Street, New York, NY 10025-1120. Awards Ed M, MS Ed, MSW/MS Ed. MSW/MS Ed offered jointly with Columbia University. *Degree requirements:* Thesis required, foreign language not required. *Entrance requirements:* TOEFL (minimum score 550). Application deadline: 3/15 (priority date; rolling processing; 11/1 for spring admission). Application fee: $50. *Tuition:* $560 per credit. *Financial aid:* Career-related internships or fieldwork available. Financial aid application deadline: 3/1. • Claire Wurtzel, Chairperson, 212-875-4708. Application contact: Ann Morgan, Director of Admissions, 212-875-4404. Fax: 212-875-4678. E-mail: amorgan@bnkst.edu.

Barry University, School of Education, Program in Exceptional Student Education, Miami Shores, FL 33161-6695. Awards MS, Ed S. Part-time and evening/weekend programs available. Faculty: 1 (woman) full-time, 1 part-time (0 women). Students: 71 full-time (67 women), 26 part-time (19 women); includes 32 minority (16 African Americans, 16 Hispanics), 1 international. Average age 38. In 1997, 20 master's awarded. *Degree requirements:* For master's, written comprehensive exam required, foreign language and thesis not required; for Ed S, practicum required, foreign language and thesis not required. *Entrance requirements:* For master's, GRE General Test or MAT, minimum GPA of 3.0; for Ed S, GRE General Test, minimum GPA of 3.0. Application deadline: 5/1 (priority date; rolling processing). Application fee: $30. Electronic applications accepted. *Tuition:* $450 per credit (minimum). *Financial aid:* Partial tuition waivers and career-related internships or fieldwork available. Aid available to part-time students. Financial aid application deadline: 5/1; applicants required to submit FAFSA. • Dr. Clara Wolman, Director, 305-899-3700. Fax: 305-899-3630. E-mail: wolman@aquinas.barry.edu. Application contact: Angela Scott, Enrollment Services, Assistant Dean, 305-899-3112. Fax: 305-899-3149. E-mail: ascott@jeanne.barry.edu.

Barry University, School of Education, Program in Leadership and Education, Miami Shores, FL 33161-6695. Offerings include exceptional student education (PhD). Program faculty: 1 full-time (0 women), 2 part-time (1 woman), 2 FTE. *Degree requirements:* Dissertation. *Entrance requirements:* GRE General Test, minimum GPA of 3.25. Application deadline: 5/1 (priority date; rolling processing). Application fee: $30. Electronic applications accepted. *Tuition:* $450 per credit (minimum). • Dr. Jack Dezek, Chair, 305-899-3700. Fax: 305-899-3630. E-mail: dezek@aquinas.barry.edu. Application contact: Angela Scott, Enrollment Services, Assistant Dean, 305-899-3112. Fax: 305-899-3149. E-mail: ascott@jeanne.barry.edu.

Beaver College, Department of Education, Glenside, PA 19038-3295. Offerings include special education (M Ed, CAS). *Application fee:* $35. *Expenses:* Tuition $6570 per year full-time, $365 per credit part-time. Fees $35 per year.

Bellarmine College, College of Arts and Sciences, Graduate Programs in Education, Louisville, KY 40205-0671. Offerings include learning and behavior disorders (MA). Accredited by NCATE. Faculty: 2 full-time (both women). *Application deadline:* 8/1 (priority date; rolling processing; 12/15 for spring admission). *Application fee:* $25. Electronic applications accepted. *Tuition:* $360 per credit hour. • Dr. Doris Tegart, Director, 502-452-8191.

Belmont Abbey College, School of Graduate Studies, Division of Education, Belmont, NC 28012-1802. Offerings include special education (MA). MA (special education) being phased out; applicants no longer accepted. *Application deadline:* 6/1 (rolling processing; 11/1 for spring admission). *Application fee:* $20. *Expenses:* Tuition $530 per course (minimum). Fees $43 per semester (minimum). • Dr. Sandra Loehr, Director, 704-825-6728. Application contact: Julia Gunter, Director of Adult Admissions, 704-825-6671. Fax: 704-825-6658.

Bemidji State University, Division of Professional Studies, Program in Special Education, Bemidji, MN 56601-2699. Awards MS Ed. Accredited by NCATE. Part-time programs available. Students: 1 full-time (0 women), 15 part-time (12 women). Average age 42. In 1997, 2 degrees awarded. *Degree requirements:* Thesis required, foreign language not required. *Application deadline:* 5/1. *Application fee:* $20. *Expenses:* Tuition $128 per credit for state residents; $134 per credit (minimum) for nonresidents. Fees $517 per year full-time, $35 per credit (minimum) part-time. *Financial aid:* Federal Work-Study and career-related internships or fieldwork available. Aid available to part-time students. Financial aid application deadline: 5/1. • Dr. Karen Lee Alexander, Director, 218-755-3767. E-mail: karenlee@vax1.bemidji.msus.edu.

Benedictine University, Program in Education, Lisle, IL 60532-0900. Offerings include special education (MA Ed). Program faculty: 4 full-time (3 women), 3 part-time (1 woman). *Application fee:* $30. • Dr. Eileen M. Kolich, Director, 630-829-6280. Fax: 630-960-1126. E-mail: ekolich@ben.edu.

Bloomsburg University of Pennsylvania, School of Graduate Studies, College of Professional Studies, School of Education, Department of Communication Disorders and Special Education, Program in Special Education, Bloomsburg, PA 17815-1905. Awards MS. Accredited by NCATE. Faculty: 8 full-time (3 women). Students: 24 full-time (19 women), 27 part-time (19 women). Average age 29. 22 applicants, 100% accepted. In 1997, 24 degrees awarded. *Degree requirements:* Thesis or alternative required, foreign language not required. *Entrance requirements:* GRE General Test, teaching certificate, minimum QPA of 2.5. Application deadline: rolling. Application fee: $25. *Expenses:* Tuition $3468 per year full-time, $193 per credit part-time for state residents; $6236 per year full-time, $346 per credit part-time for nonresidents. Fees $748 per year full-time, $166 per semester (minimum) part-time. *Faculty research:* Exceptionalities, learning disabilities, behavior disorders, gifted, early childhood, transition, mainstreaming mildly handicapped. • Dr. Carroll J. Redfern, Chair, Department of Communication Disorders and Special Education, 717-389-4119. Fax: 717-389-3980. E-mail: redfern@planetx.bloomu.edu.

Boise State University, College of Education, Programs in Teacher Education, Program in Special Education, Boise, ID 83725-0399. Awards MA. Accredited by NCATE. Faculty: 5 full-time (3 women). Students: 10 full-time (8 women), 25 part-time (24 women); includes 3 minority (1 Asian American, 1 Hispanic, 1 Native American). Average age 39. 14 applicants, 93% accepted. In 1997, 4 degrees awarded. *Degree requirements:* Thesis optional. *Application deadline:* 7/26 (priority date; rolling processing; 11/29 for spring admission). *Application fee:* $20 ($30 for international students). Electronic applications accepted. *Tuition:* $3020 per year full-time, $135 per credit part-time for state residents; $8900 per year full-time, $135 per credit part-time for nonresidents. *Financial aid:* Graduate assistantships, Federal Work-Study, institutionally sponsored loans, and career-related internships or fieldwork available. Aid available to part-time students. Financial aid application deadline: 3/1. • Dr. Roger Stewart, Coordinator, Programs in Teacher Education, 208-385-1731. Fax: 208-385-4365.

Boston College, Graduate School of Education, Department of Teacher Education/Special Education and Curriculum and Instruction, Moderate Special Needs Program, Chestnut Hill, MA 02167-9991. Awards M Ed, CAES. Accredited by NCATE. Students: 36 full-time (35 women), 54 part-time (50 women); includes 8 minority (1 African American, 3 Asian Americans, 4 Hispanics), 2 international. 69 applicants, 87% accepted. In 1997, 30 master's awarded. *Degree requirements:* Comprehensive exam required, thesis not required. *Entrance requirements:* For master's, GRE General Test; for CAES, GRE General Test or MAT. Application deadline: 3/15 (11/15 for spring admission). Application fee: $40. *Expenses:* Tuition $626 per semester hour. Fees $80 per year (minimum) full-time, $30 per semester part-time. *Financial aid:* Fellowships, research assistantships, teaching assistantships, administrative assistantships, merit scholarships, Federal Work-Study, and career-related internships or fieldwork available. Aid available to part-time students. *Faculty research:* Application of cognitive and metacognitive learning strategies within regular curriculum, strategies for supporting learning-disabled college students. • Application contact: Arline Riordan, Graduate Admissions Director, 617-552-4214. Fax: 617-552-0812. E-mail: riordana@bc.edu.

Boston College, Graduate School of Education, Department of Teacher Education/Special Education and Curriculum and Instruction, Program in Special Education and Rehabilitation, Chestnut Hill, MA 02167-9991. Awards PhD. Accredited by NCATE. Program being phased out; applicants no longer accepted. Students: 3 full-time (2 women), 3 part-time (2 women). In 1997, 1 degree awarded. *Degree requirements:* Computer language, dissertation, comprehensive exam. *Expenses:* Tuition $626 per semester hour. Fees $80 per year (minimum) full-time, $30 per semester part-time. • Dr. Marilyn Cochran-Smith, Chairperson, Department of Teacher Education/Special Education and Curriculum and Instruction, 617-552-4180. Application contact: Arline Riordan, Graduate Admissions Director, 617-552-4214. Fax: 617-552-0812. E-mail: riordana@bc.edu.

Boston College, Graduate School of Education, Department of Teacher Education/Special Education and Curriculum and Instruction, Severe Special Needs Program, Chestnut Hill, MA 02167-9991. Awards M Ed. Accredited by NCATE. Students: 6 full-time (5 women), 11 part-time (9 women); includes 1 minority (Asian American). 14 applicants, 79% accepted. In 1997, 3 degrees awarded. *Degree requirements:* Comprehensive exam required, thesis not required. *Entrance requirements:* GRE General Test. Application deadline: 3/15 (11/15 for spring admission). Application fee: $40. *Expenses:* Tuition $626 per semester hour. Fees $80 per year (minimum) full-time, $30 per semester part-time. *Financial aid:* Fellowships, research assistantships, teaching assistantships, Federal Work-Study, and career-related internships or fieldwork available. Aid available to part-time students. • Application contact: Arline Riordan, Graduate Admissions Director, 617-552-4214. Fax: 617-552-0812. E-mail: riordana@bc.edu.

Boston College, Graduate School of Education, Department of Teacher Education/Special Education and Curriculum and Instruction, Visually Handicapped Studies Program, Chestnut Hill, MA 02167-9991. Awards M Ed. Accredited by NCATE. Students: 7 full-time (5 women), 10 part-time (8 women); includes 1 minority (Asian American). 11 applicants, 73% accepted. In 1997, 7 degrees awarded. *Degree requirements:* Comprehensive exam required, thesis not required. *Entrance requirements:* GRE General Test. Application deadline: 3/15 (11/15 for spring admission). Application fee: $40. *Expenses:* Tuition $626 per semester hour. Fees $80 per year (minimum) full-time, $30 per semester part-time. *Financial aid:* Fellowships, research assistantships, teaching assistantships, administrative assistantships, merit scholarships, Federal Work-Study, and career-related internships or fieldwork available. Aid available to part-time students. *Faculty research:* VDT access for low-vision individuals, access technology for the handicapped, multimedia courseware development. • Application contact: Arline Riordan, Graduate Admissions Director, 617-552-4214. Fax: 617-552-0812. E-mail: riordana@bc.edu.

Boston University, School of Education, Department of Special Education, Boston, MA 02215. Offers programs in special education (Ed M, Ed D, CAGS), including alternative community settings (Ed D, CAGS), learning and behavioral disabilities (Ed D, CAGS), severe disabilities (Ed D, CAGS), therapeutic recreation (Ed D, CAGS), young children with special needs (Ed D, CAGS); special education and social work (MSW/Ed D, MSW/Ed M). Students:

Directory: Special Education

Boston University (continued)
33 full-time (28 women), 29 part-time (25 women); includes 4 minority (1 African American, 1 Asian American, 2 Hispanics), 4 international. Average age 30. In 1997, 29 master's, 1 doctorate awarded. *Degree requirements:* For doctorate, dissertation, comprehensive exam required, foreign language not required; for CAGS, comprehensive exam required, foreign language and thesis not required. *Entrance requirements:* GRE or MAT, TOEFL. Application deadline: 2/15 (priority date; rolling processing). Application fee: $50. *Expenses:* Tuition $22,830 per year full-time, $713 per credit part-time. Fees $218 per year full-time, $40 per semester part-time. *Financial aid:* Application deadline 3/30. • Dr. Gerald Fain, Coordinator, 617-353-4478. E-mail: fain@bu.edu.

Boston University, School of Social Work and Department of Special Education, Dual Degree Program in Special Education and Social Work, Boston, MA 02215. Awards MSW/Ed D, MSW/Ed M. Students: 2 full-time (both women). Average age 24. *Application fee:* $50. *Expenses:* Tuition $18,024 per year full-time, $563 per credit part-time. Fees $218 per year full-time, $40 per semester part-time. • Dr. Gerald Fain, Coordinator, 617-353-4478. E-mail: fain@bu.edu.

Boston University, School of Education, Department of Developmental Studies and Counseling, Program in Education of the Deaf, Boston, MA 02215. Awards Ed M, CAGS. Part-time programs available. Students: 12 full-time (10 women), 11 part-time (10 women). Average age 27. In 1997, 4 master's awarded. *Degree requirements:* For CAGS, comprehensive exam required, foreign language and thesis not required. *Entrance requirements:* GRE or MAT, TOEFL. Application deadline: 2/15 (priority date; rolling processing). Application fee: $50. *Expenses:* Tuition $22,830 per year full-time, $713 per credit part-time. Fees $218 per year full-time, $40 per semester part-time. *Financial aid:* Application deadline 3/30. *Faculty research:* Structure of American Sign Language, acquisition of American Sign Language, problems in educating the deaf, impact of legislation on the deaf, relations between hearing parents and deaf children. • Dr. Robert Hoffmeister, Coordinator, 617-353-3275. E-mail: rhoff@bu.edu.

Bowie State University, Programs in Education, Program in Special Education, 14000 Jericho Park Road, Bowie, MD 20715. Awards M Ed. Part-time and evening/weekend programs available. *Degree requirements:* Research paper, written comprehensive exam required, thesis optional. *Entrance requirements:* Teaching experience. Application deadline: 8/16 (priority date; rolling processing). Application fee: $30. *Expenses:* Tuition $169 per credit hour for state residents; $304 per credit hour for nonresidents. Fees $171 per year.

Bowling Green State University, College of Education and Allied Professions, Department of Special Education, Program in Special Education, Bowling Green, OH 43403. Awards M Ed. Accredited by NCATE. Students: 19 full-time (18 women), 50 part-time (48 women); includes 1 minority (African American). 39 applicants, 64% accepted. In 1997, 12 degrees awarded. *Degree requirements:* Thesis or alternative required, foreign language not required. *Entrance requirements:* GRE General Test, TOEFL (minimum score 550). Application deadline: rolling. Application fee: $30. Electronic applications accepted. *Tuition:* $6070 per year full-time, $284 per credit hour part-time for state residents; $11,358 per year full-time, $536 per credit hour part-time for nonresidents. *Financial aid:* In 1997–98, 15 assistantships were awarded; Federal Work-Study also available. Financial aid application deadline: 2/15; applicants required to submit FAFSA. *Faculty research:* Reading and special populations, deafness, early childhood, gifted and talented, behavior disorders. • Dr. Richard Wilson, Chair, Department of Special Education, 419-372-7293. Application contact: Dr. Eric Jones, Graduate Coordinator, 419-372-7287.

Bradley University, College of Education and Health Sciences, Department of Education and Learning Disabilities, Peoria, IL 61625-0002. Awards MA. Accredited by NCATE. Part-time and evening/weekend programs available. *Degree requirements:* Comprehensive exams required, thesis not required. *Entrance requirements:* MAT, TOEFL (minimum score 500). Application deadline: 7/1 (priority date; rolling processing; 11/1 for spring admission). Application fee: $35. *Tuition:* $13,240 per year full-time, $359 per semester hour (minimum) part-time.

Brandon University, Faculty of Education, Brandon, MB R7A 6A9, Canada. Offerings include special education (M Ed). Faculty: 27 full-time (3 women), 1 part-time (0 women). *Degree requirements:* Thesis. *Average time to degree:* master's–2 years full-time; other advanced degree–1 year full-time. *Entrance requirements:* TOEFL (minimum score 550), minimum GPA of 3.0, teaching certificate or equivalent. Application deadline: 3/1. Application fee: $30. *Expenses:* Tuition $421 per course (minimum). Fees $24.95 per year. • Dean, 204-728-9520. Application contact: Faye Douglas, Admissions Director, 204-727-7352. Fax: 204-725-2143. E-mail: douglas@brandonu.ca.

Brenau University, School of Education and Human Development, Gainesville, GA 30501-3697. Offerings include early childhood education (M Ed, Ed S), with option in behavior disorders (M Ed); learning disabilities (M Ed), with option in special education interrelated. *Degree requirements:* Comprehensive exam (M Ed) required, foreign language and thesis not required. *Average time to degree:* master's–2 years part-time; other advanced degree–1.5 years part-time. *Entrance requirements:* GRE, MAT. Application deadline: rolling. Application fee: $30. *Tuition:* $198 per semester hour. • Dr. William B. Ware, Dean, 770-534-6220. Application contact: Kathy Cobb, Director of Graduate Admissions, 770-534-6162. Fax: 770-538-4306. E-mail: kcobb@lib.brenau.edu.

Bridgewater State College, School of Education, Department of Special Education, Bridgewater, MA 02325-0001. Awards M Ed. Accredited by NCATE. Evening/weekend programs available. *Entrance requirements:* GRE General Test, teaching certificate. Application deadline: 4/1 (10/1 for spring admission). Application fee: $25. *Expenses:* Tuition $1675 per year full-time, $70 per credit part-time for state residents; $6450 per year full-time, $269 per credit part-time for nonresidents. Fees $1588 per year full-time, $66 per credit hour part-time for state residents; $1588 per year full-time, $66 per credit part-time for nonresidents. *Financial aid:* Career-related internships or fieldwork available. • Application contact: Graduate School, 508-697-1300.

Brigham Young University, David O. McKay School of Education, Department of Counseling and Special Education, Provo, UT 84602-1001. Offers programs in counseling and school psychology (MS), counseling psychology (PhD), special education (MS). Faculty: 10 full-time (2 women), 12 part-time (7 women). Students: 73 full-time (29 women); includes 1 minority (Hispanic), 5 international. Average age 34. 106 applicants, 33% accepted. In 1997, 28 master's, 3 doctorates awarded. *Degree requirements:* For master's, written comprehensive exams required, thesis not required; for doctorate, dissertation, written comprehensive exams. *Entrance requirements:* For master's, GRE General Test, minimum GPA of 3.0 in last 60 hours; for doctorate, GRE General Test, minimum GPA of 3.4 in last 60 hours. Application deadline: 2/1. Application fee: $30. *Tuition:* $3200 per year full-time, $178 per credit hour part-time for state residents; $4800 per year full-time, $266 per credit hour part-time for nonresidents. *Financial aid:* In 1997–98, 38 students received aid, including 6 research assistantships (3 to first-year students) averaging $407 per month, 10 teaching assistantships (5 to first-year students) averaging $407 per month; partial tuition waivers, institutionally sponsored loans, and career-related internships or fieldwork also available. *Faculty research:* Learning, hardiness, values and mental health, distance education. • Dr. Ronald D. Bingham, Chair, 801-378-3857. E-mail: ron_bingham@byu.edu. Application contact: Diane Hancock, Secretary, 801-378-3859. E-mail: diane_hancock@byu.edu.

Brooklyn College of the City University of New York, School of Education, Division of Secondary Education, 2900 Bedford Avenue, Brooklyn, NY 11210-2889. Offerings include speech and hearing handicapped education (MS Ed). *Application deadline:* 3/1 (11/1 for spring admission). *Application fee:* $40. *Expenses:* Tuition $4350 per year full-time, $185 per credit part-time for state residents; $7600 per year full-time, $320 per credit part-time for nonresidents. Fees $500 per year for state residents; $806 per year for nonresidents. • Dr. Peter Taubman, Coordinator, 718-951-5218. Fax: 718-951-4816. E-mail: ptaubman@brooklyn.cuny.edu.

Brooklyn College of the City University of New York, School of Education, Program in Special Education, 2900 Bedford Avenue, Brooklyn, NY 11210-2889. Offers bilingual special education (MS Ed), children with emotional handicaps (MS Ed), children with neuropsychological learning disabilities (MS Ed), children with retarded mental development (MS Ed). Part-time programs available. Students: 175 part-time (144 women); includes 51 minority (32 African Americans, 4 Asian Americans, 15 Hispanics). Average age 32. 38 applicants, 71% accepted. In 1997, 70 degrees awarded. *Degree requirements:* Practicum required, foreign language and thesis not required. *Entrance requirements:* TOEFL (minimum score 550), interview; previous course work in education and psychology; minimum GPA of 3.0 in education, 2.8 overall. Application deadline: 3/1 (11/1 for spring admission). Application fee: $40. *Expenses:* Tuition $4350 per year full-time, $185 per credit part-time for state residents; $7600 per year full-time, $320 per credit part-time for nonresidents. Fees $500 per year for state residents; $806 per year for nonresidents. *Financial aid:* Application deadline 5/1; applicants required to submit FAFSA. *Faculty research:* School reform, conflict resolution, curriculum for inclusive settings, urban issues in special education. • Dr. Kathleen McSorley, Head, 718-951-5995. Fax: 718-951-4816. E-mail: mcsorley@brooklyn.cuny.edu.

Butler University, College of Education, Indianapolis, IN 46208-3485. Offerings include special education (MS). Accredited by NCATE. College faculty: 10 full-time (3 women), 22 part-time (8 women), 22.5 FTE. *Average time to degree:* master's–7 years part-time; other advanced degree–5 years part-time. *Entrance requirements:* GRE General Test, MAT (minimum score 40), interview. Application deadline: 8/15 (priority date; rolling processing). Application fee: $25. *Tuition:* $220 per credit hour. • Dr. Saundra Tracy, Dean, 317-940-9514. Fax: 317-940-6481. E-mail: stracy@butler.edu.

California Baptist College, Graduate Program in Education, Riverside, CA 92504-3206. Offerings include special education (MS Ed). Program faculty: 8 full-time (7 women), 4 part-time (2 women). *Application deadline:* rolling. *Application fee:* $40. *Expenses:* Tuition $275 per unit. Fees $100 per year. • Dr. Marsha Savage, Chair, 909-689-5771. Application contact: Gail Ronveaux, Director of Graduate Services, 909-343-4249. Fax: 909-351-1808. E-mail: gradser@cal.baptist.edu.

California Lutheran University, School of Education, Emphasis in Special Education, Thousand Oaks, CA 91360-2787. Awards MS. Students: 18 full-time (14 women), 104 part-time (87 women). Average age 35. 20 applicants, 65% accepted. In 1997, 12 degrees awarded. *Degree requirements:* Thesis or comprehensive exam required, foreign language not required. *Entrance requirements:* GRE General Test, minimum GPA of 3.0. Application deadline: 8/1 (priority date; rolling processing; 12/1 for spring admission). Application fee: $50. *Tuition:* $335 per unit. • Dr. Carol Genrich, Head, 805-493-3420.

California Polytechnic State University, San Luis Obispo, Center for Teacher Education, Program in Special Education, San Luis Obispo, CA 93407. Awards MA. Part-time and evening/weekend programs available. In 1997, 7 degrees awarded. *Degree requirements:* Comprehensive exam required, thesis optional, foreign language not required. *Entrance requirements:* Minimum GPA of 3.0. Application deadline: 4/1 (12/15 for spring admission). Application fee: $55. *Expenses:* Tuition $0 for state residents; $164 per unit for nonresidents. Fees $2102 per year full-time, $1632 per year part-time. *Faculty research:* Early childhood special education assessment, social development. • Howard Drucker, Coordinator, 805-756-1575.

California State University, Bakersfield, School of Education, Program in Special Education, 9001 Stockdale Highway, Bakersfield, CA 93311-1099. Awards MA. Accredited by NCATE. *Degree requirements:* Thesis or alternative, culminating projects. *Application deadline:* rolling. *Application fee:* $55. *Expenses:* Tuition $0 for state residents; $246 per unit full-time, $164 per unit part-time for nonresidents. Fees $1584 per year full-time, $918 per year part-time. • Dr. Lon Kellenberger, Interim Dean, School of Education, 805-664-2219. Application contact: Dr. Dianne Turner, Graduate Coordinator, 805-664-2422. Fax: 805-664-2063.

California State University, Chico, College of Communication and Education, School of Education, Department of Professional Studies in Education, Chico, CA 95929-0722. Offerings include education (MA), with options in linguistically and culturally diverse learners, reading and language arts, special education. *Application deadline:* 4/1 (rolling processing). *Application fee:* $55. *Expenses:* Tuition $0 for state residents; $246 per unit for nonresidents. Fees $2108 per year full-time, $1442 per year part-time. • Dr. James Richmond, Chair, 530-898-5398.

California State University, Dominguez Hills, School of Education, Department of Graduate Education, Program in Special Education, Carson, CA 90747-0001. Offers learning handicapped (MA), severely handicapped (MA). Faculty: 20. Students: 123 full-time (93 women), 173 part-time (130 women); includes 150 minority (75 African Americans, 30 Asian Americans, 43 Hispanics, 2 Native Americans), 2 international. Average age 37. 78 applicants, 100% accepted. In 1997, 49 degrees awarded. *Entrance requirements:* Minimum GPA of 2.75. Application deadline: 6/1. Application fee: $55. *Expenses:* Tuition $0 for state residents; $246 per unit for nonresidents. Fees $1896 per year full-time, $1230 per year part-time. • Dr. Karl Skindrund, Coordinator, 310-243-3524. Application contact: Admissions Office, 310-243-3600.

California State University, Fresno, Division of Graduate Studies, School of Education and Human Development, Department of Counseling and Special Education, Program in Special Education, 5241 North Maple Avenue, Fresno, CA 93740. Awards MA. Accredited by NCATE. Part-time and evening/weekend programs available. Faculty: 5 full-time (all women). Students: 43 full-time (35 women), 55 part-time (40 women); includes 23 minority (1 African American, 6 Asian Americans, 15 Hispanics, 1 Native American). Average age 31. 36 applicants, 89% accepted. In 1997, 25 degrees awarded. *Degree requirements:* Thesis or alternative required, foreign language not required. *Average time to degree:* master's–3.5 years full-time. *Entrance requirements:* GRE General Test, TOEFL (minimum score 550), MAT, minimum GPA of 3.4. Application deadline: 4/1 (priority date; rolling processing; 11/1 for spring admission). Application fee: $55. Electronic applications accepted. *Expenses:* Tuition $0 for state residents; $246 per unit for nonresidents. Fees $1872 per year full-time, $1206 per year part-time. *Financial aid:* In 1997–98, 46 research awards, travel grants, scholarships totaling $89,375 were awarded; fellowships, Federal Work-Study, and career-related internships or fieldwork also available. Financial aid application deadline: 3/1; applicants required to submit FAFSA. • Dr. Leslie Farlow, Coordinator, 209-278-0289.

California State University, Fullerton, School of Human Development and Community Service, Department of Special Education, PO Box 34080, Fullerton, CA 92834-9480. Awards MS. Accredited by NCATE. Part-time programs available. Faculty: 5 full-time (4 women), 15 part-time, 9 FTE. Students: 30 full-time (24 women), 63 part-time (55 women); includes 15 minority (7 African Americans, 3 Asian Americans, 4 Hispanics, 1 Native American), 2 international. Average age 36. 72 applicants, 90% accepted. In 1997, 16 degrees awarded. *Degree requirements:* Comprehensive exam, project or thesis required, foreign language not required. *Entrance requirements:* Minimum GPA of 2.75. Application fee: $55. *Expenses:* Tuition $0 for state residents; $246 per unit for nonresidents. Fees $1947 per year full-time, $1281 per year part-time. *Financial aid:* Teaching assistantships, state grants, Federal Work-Study, institutionally sponsored loans, and career-related internships or fieldwork available. Aid available to part-time students. Financial aid application deadline: 3/1. • Dr. Belinda Karge, Head, 714-278-3395.

California State University, Hayward, School of Education, Department of Educational Psychology, Program in Special Education, Hayward, CA 94542-3000. Awards MS. Accredited by NCATE. Students: 24 full-time (20 women), 38 part-time (31 women); includes 12 minority (3 African Americans, 3 Asian Americans, 5 Hispanics, 1 Native American). 10 applicants, 60% accepted. In 1997, 13 degrees awarded. *Degree requirements:* Project or thesis required, foreign language not required. *Entrance requirements:* GRE or MAT, interview, minimum GPA of 2.5 during previous 2 years. Application deadline: 4/19 (priority date; rolling processing; 1/5 for spring admission). Application fee: $55. *Expenses:* Tuition $0 for state residents; $164 per unit for nonresidents. Fees $1827 per year full-time, $1161 per year part-time. *Financial aid:* Federal Work-Study, institutionally sponsored loans, and career-related internships or fieldwork available. Aid available to part-time students. Financial aid application deadline: 3/1. • Dr. Jacki L. Anderson, Coordinator, 510-885-3332. Application contact: Dr. Maria De Anda-Ramos, Executive Director, Admissions and Outreach, 510-885-2624.

California State University, Long Beach, College of Education, Department of Educational Psychology and Administration, Program in Special Education, Long Beach, CA 90840-2201. Awards MS. Students: 13 full-time (10 women), 31 part-time (23 women); includes 14 minority (2 African Americans, 5 Asian Americans, 7 Hispanics), 1 international. Average age 34. 20 applicants, 85% accepted. In 1997, 14 degrees awarded. *Degree requirements:* Comprehensive exam or thesis required, foreign language not required. *Entrance requirements:* GRE General Test, minimum GPA of 2.75. Application deadline: 8/1 (rolling processing; 12/1 for spring admission). Application fee: $55. *Expenses:* Tuition $0 for state residents; $246 per unit for nonresidents. Fees $1846 per year full-time, $1180 per year part-time. *Financial aid:* Application deadline 3/2. • Dr. Charles Kokaska, Coordinator, 562-985-4438. Fax: 562-985-4534.

California State University, Los Angeles, School of Education, Division of Special Education, Los Angeles, CA 90032-8530. Offers programs in early childhood education for the handicapped (MA), education of handicapped adolescents and young adults (MA), education of the communication handicapped (MA), education of the learning handicapped (MA), education of the physically handicapped (MA), education of the severely handicapped (MA), education of the visually handicapped (MA), gifted education (MA), multicultural and multilingual special education (MA), orientation and mobility specialist for the blind (MA), resource specialist (MA), special education (PhD). Accredited by NCATE. PhD offered jointly with the University of California, Los Angeles. Part-time and evening/weekend programs available. Faculty: 16 full-time, 11 part-time. Students: 51 full-time (41 women), 155 part-time (107 women); includes 83 minority (20 African Americans, 20 Asian Americans, 43 Hispanics), 4 international. In 1997, 37 master's awarded. *Degree requirements:* For master's, comprehensive exam, project, or thesis required, foreign language not required; for doctorate, dissertation. *Entrance requirements:* For master's, TOEFL (minimum score 550), minimum GPA of 2.75 in last 90 units, teaching certificate; for doctorate, GRE General Test (minimum combined score of 1000), TOEFL (minimum score 550), master's degree; minimum GPA of 3.0 (undergraduate), 3.5 (graduate). Application deadline: 6/30 (rolling processing; 2/1 for spring admission). Application fee: $55. *Expenses:* Tuition $0 for state residents; $164 per unit for nonresidents. Fees $1763 per year full-time, $1097 per year part-time. *Financial aid:* 53 students received aid; Federal Work-Study available. Aid available to part-time students. Financial aid application deadline: 3/1. *Faculty research:* Early childhood development, computer application in special education, recovery for postpartum substance abuse. • Dr. Philip Chinn, Chair, 213-343-4400.

California State University, Northridge, College of Education, Department of Special Education, Northridge, CA 91330. Offers programs in early childhood special education (MA), education of the deaf and hard of hearing (MA), education of the gifted (MA), education of the learning handicapped (MA), education of the severely handicapped (MA), educational therapy (MA), genetic counseling (MS). Accredited by NCATE. Faculty: 16 full-time, 15 part-time. Students: 90 full-time (74 women), 158 part-time (135 women); includes 53 minority (13 African Americans, 19 Asian Americans, 20 Hispanics, 1 Native American). Average age 36. 80 applicants, 91% accepted. *Entrance requirements:* GRE General Test, TOEFL. Application deadline: 11/30. Application fee: $55. *Expenses:* Tuition $0 for state residents; $246 per unit for nonresidents. Fees $1970 per year full-time, $1304 per year part-time. *Financial aid:* Application deadline 3/1. *Faculty research:* Teacher training, classroom aide training. • Dr. Claire Cavallaro, Chair, 818-677-2596. Application contact: Dr. Ellen Schneiderman, Graduate Coordinator, 818-677-2528.

California State University, Sacramento, School of Education, Department of Special Education and Rehabilitation, Sacramento, CA 95819-6048. Offers program in special education (MA). Part-time programs available. *Degree requirements:* Thesis or alternative, writing proficiency exam. *Entrance requirements:* TOEFL (minimum score 550), minimum GPA of 2.5. Application deadline: 4/15 (11/1 for spring admission). Application fee: $55. *Expenses:* Tuition $0 for state residents; $246 per unit for nonresidents. Fees $2012 per year full-time, $1346 per year part-time. *Financial aid:* Federal Work-Study and career-related internships or fieldwork available. Aid available to part-time students. Financial aid application deadline: 3/1. • Dr. Michael Lewis, Chair, 916-278-6622.

California State University, San Bernardino, Graduate Studies, School of Education, Program in Special Education and Rehabilitation Counseling, San Bernardino, CA 92407-2397. Offers rehabilitation counseling (MA), special education (MA). Part-time and evening/weekend programs available. Faculty: 10 full-time (7 women), 4 part-time (1 woman). Students: 98 full-time (79 women), 53 part-time (41 women); includes 34 minority (19 African Americans, 2 Asian Americans, 11 Hispanics, 2 Native Americans), 3 international. 52 applicants, 96% accepted. In 1997, 18 degrees awarded. *Degree requirements:* Thesis or alternative required, foreign language not required. *Entrance requirements:* Minimum GPA of 3.0 in education. Application deadline: 8/31 (priority date). Application fee: $55. *Expenses:* Tuition $0 for state residents; $164 per unit for nonresidents. Fees $1922 per year full-time, $1256 per year part-time. *Financial aid:* Federal Work-Study and career-related internships or fieldwork available. Aid available to part-time students. • Dr. Jeff McNair, Coordinator, 909-880-5685.

California State University, Stanislaus, School of Education, Department of Advanced Studies in Education, Program in Special Education, Turlock, CA 95382. Awards MA Ed. Accredited by NCATE. Part-time programs available. Faculty: 3 full-time (2 women). Students: 2 (both women); includes 2 minority (1 Hispanic, 1 Native American). 3 applicants, 100% accepted. In 1997, 1 degree awarded. *Degree requirements:* Thesis required, foreign language not required. *Entrance requirements:* MAT. Application fee: $55. *Expenses:* Tuition $0 for state residents; $246 per unit for nonresidents. Fees $1779 per year full-time, $1113 per year part-time. *Financial aid:* Application deadline 3/2; applicants required to submit FAFSA. • Dr. Karen Sniezek, Coordinator, 209-667-3364.

California University of Pennsylvania, School of Education, Department of Special Education, 250 University Avenue, California, PA 15419-1394. Offers program in mentally and/or physically handicapped education (M Ed). Accredited by NCATE. Part-time and evening/weekend programs available. Faculty: 7 part-time (1 woman). Students: 58 full-time (38 women), 61 part-time (53 women); includes 6 minority (5 African Americans, 1 Native American), 1 international. 40 applicants, 100% accepted. In 1997, 54 degrees awarded. *Degree requirements:* Comprehensive exam required, thesis optional, foreign language not required. *Entrance requirements:* MAT (minimum score 35), TOEFL (minimum score 550), minimum GPA of 2.5, teaching certificate. Application deadline: rolling. Application fee: $25. *Expenses:* Tuition $3468 per year full-time, $193 per credit part-time for state residents; $6236 per year full-time, $346 per credit part-time for nonresidents. Fees $886 per year full-time, $153 per semester (minimum) part-time. *Financial aid:* Graduate assistantships available. • Dr. Peter Belch, Coordinator, 724-938-4142.

Calvin College, Graduate Programs in Education, Grand Rapids, MI 49546-4388. Offerings include learning disabilities (M Ed). Accredited by NCATE. M Ed (reading, school administration) admissions temporarily suspended. Faculty: 1 (woman) full-time, 15 part-time (6 women). *Degree requirements:* Thesis required, foreign language not required. *Entrance requirements:* GRE General Test, TOEFL, teaching certificate. Application deadline: 8/15 (priority date; rolling processing; 1/15 for spring admission). Application fee: $0. Electronic applications accepted. *Tuition:* $250 per semester hour. • Dr. Robert S. Fortner, Director of Graduate Studies, 616-957-8533. Fax: 616-957-8551. E-mail: forr@calvin.edu.

Canisius College, School of Education and Human Services, Program in Special Education—Preparation of Teachers of the Deaf, Buffalo, NY 14208-1098. Awards MS. Offered jointly with St. Mary's School for the Deaf. Part-time and evening/weekend programs available. Faculty: 2 full-time (1 woman), 9 part-time (6 women). Students: 11 full-time (10 women), 4 part-time (3 women). 25 applicants, 80% accepted. *Degree requirements:* Research project required, foreign language and thesis not required. *Entrance requirements:* GRE General Test, minimum GPA of 2.5. Application deadline: 5/30 (priority date; rolling processing). Application fee: $20. *Expenses:* Tuition $415 per credit hour. Fees $15 per credit hour. *Financial aid:* Graduate assistantships, Federal Work-Study, institutionally sponsored loans, and career-related internships or fieldwork available. Financial aid application deadline: 5/30. • Sr. Virginia Young, Acting Director, 716-888-2261. Application contact: Kevin Smith, Graduate Recruitment and Admissions, 716-888-2544. Fax: 716-888-3290.

Cardinal Stritch University, College of Education, Department of Special Education, Milwaukee, WI 53217-3985. Awards MA. Accredited by NCATE. Students: 155. *Application deadline:* 4/1 (priority date; rolling processing). *Application fee:* $20. *Expenses:* Tuition $338 per credit. Fees $25 per semester. *Financial aid:* Federal Work-Study available. Financial aid applicants required to submit FAFSA. • Chair, 414-410-4434. Application contact: Amy Knox, Graduate Admissions Officer, 414-410-4042.

Castleton State College, Department of Education, Program in Special Education, Castleton, VT 05735. Awards MA Ed. Part-time and evening/weekend programs available. Faculty: 9 full-time (5 women), 7 part-time (4 women). *Degree requirements:* Thesis or written exams required, foreign language not required. *Entrance requirements:* GRE General Test (minimum combined score of 1000), MAT (minimum score 50), interview, minimum undergraduate GPA of 3.0. Application deadline: 7/1 (10/1 for spring admission). Application fee: $30. *Expenses:* Tuition $3924 per year full-time, $164 per credit part-time for state residents; $9192 per year full-time, $383 per credit part-time for nonresidents. Fees $902 per year full-time, $26 per credit part-time. *Financial aid:* Federal Work-Study and career-related internships or fieldwork available. • Application contact: Mary Frucelli, Graduate Assistant, 802-468-1441. Fax: 802-468-5237.

Central Connecticut State University, School of Education and Professional Studies, Department of Special Education, New Britain, CT 06050-4010. Awards MS. Part-time and evening/weekend programs available. Faculty: 5 full-time (2 women), 12 part-time (10 women), 9 FTE. Students: 24 full-time (22 women), 115 part-time (94 women); includes 2 minority (1 African American, 1 Hispanic). Average age 33. 82 applicants, 74% accepted. In 1997, 11 degrees awarded. *Degree requirements:* Thesis or alternative, comprehensive exam required, foreign language not required. *Entrance requirements:* TOEFL (minimum score 550), minimum GPA of 2.7. Application deadline: 6/1 (priority date; rolling processing; 12/1 for spring admission). Application fee: $40. *Expenses:* Tuition $4458 per year full-time, $175 per credit hour part-time for state residents; $9943 per year full-time, $175 per credit hour part-time for nonresidents. Fees $45 per semester. *Financial aid:* In 1997–98, 1 research assistantship (to a first-year student) was awarded; Federal Work-Study also available. Financial aid application deadline: 3/15; applicants required to submit FAFSA. *Faculty research:* Learning disabilities/language development, consulting teacher practice, occupational/special education, teaching emotionally disturbed students. • Dr. Mitchell Beck, Chair, 860-832-2400.

Central Michigan University, College of Extended Learning, Program in Humanities, Mount Pleasant, MI 48859. Offerings include special education (MA). Postbaccalaureate distance learning degree programs offered. *Entrance requirements:* Minimum GPA of 2.5 in major. Application fee: $50. *Tuition:* $211 per credit hour. • Dr. Ronald Primeau, Director, 517-774-3117. Application contact: Marketing Office, 800-950-1144. Fax: 517-774-2461.

Central Michigan University, College of Education and Human Services, Department of Counseling and Special Education, Program in Special Education, Mount Pleasant, MI 48859. Awards MA. Accredited by NCATE. Students: 3 full-time (all women), 21 part-time (20 women). Average age 32. In 1997, 7 degrees awarded. *Degree requirements:* Thesis or alternative required, foreign language not required. *Entrance requirements:* MAT, teaching certificate. Application deadline: 2/1 (9/1 for spring admission). Application fee: $30. *Expenses:* Tuition $139 per credit hour (minimum) for state residents; $276 per credit hour (minimum) for nonresidents. Fees $260 per year full-time, $150 per semester part-time. *Financial aid:* Federal Work-Study available. Financial aid application deadline: 3/7. *Faculty research:* Mainstreaming, learning disabled, attention and organization disorders. • Dr. D. Terry Rawls, Chairperson, Department of Counseling and Special Education, 517-774-3205. Fax: 517-774-4374. E-mail: d.terry.rawls@cmich.edu.

Central Missouri State University, College of Education and Human Services, Department of Special Education, Warrensburg, MO 64093. Offers programs in special education (MSE), special education/human services (Ed S). Accredited by NCATE. Part-time programs available. Faculty: 5 full-time. Students: 6 full-time (3 women), 78 part-time (74 women). In 1997, 41 master's awarded. *Degree requirements:* For master's, internship; for Ed S, thesis or alternative. *Entrance requirements:* For master's, GRE General Test, minimum GPA of 2.75, teaching certificate, 2 years of teaching experience; for Ed S, GRE General Test, master's degree, minimum GPA of 3.25. Application deadline: 6/30 (priority date; rolling processing). Application fee: $25 ($50 for international students). *Tuition:* $3288 per year full-time, $137 per credit hour part-time for state residents; $5928 per year full-time, $274 per credit hour part-time for nonresidents. *Financial aid:* In 1997–98, 1 teaching assistantship was awarded; Federal Work-Study and career-related internships or fieldwork also available. Aid available to part-time students. Financial aid application deadline: 3/1; applicants required to submit FAFSA. • Dr. Gordon Warren, Chair, 660-543-4341. Fax: 660-543-4167. E-mail: gcw8803@cmsu2.cmsu.edu.

Central Washington University, College of Education and Professional Studies, Department of Teacher Education, Program in Special Education, Ellensburg, WA 98926. Awards M Ed. Part-time programs available. Faculty: 21 full-time (10 women). Students: 3 part-time (2 women). 5 applicants, 40% accepted. In 1997, 1 degree awarded. *Degree requirements:* Thesis or alternative required, foreign language not required. *Entrance requirements:* Minimum GPA of 3.0. Application deadline: 4/1 (priority date; rolling processing; 1/1 for spring admission). Application fee: $35. *Expenses:* Tuition $4200 per year full-time, $140 per credit hour part-time for state residents; $12,780 per year full-time, $426 per credit hour part-time for nonresidents. Fees $240 per year. *Financial aid:* In 1997–98, 1 teaching assistantship (to a first-year student) averaging $1,108 per month and totaling $9,972 was awarded; research assistantships, Federal Work-Study also available. Financial aid application deadline: 2/15. • Application contact: Christie A. Fevergeon, Program Coordinator, Graduate Studies and Research, 509-963-3103. Fax: 509-963-1799. E-mail: masters@cwu.edu.

Chapman University, School of Education, Program in Special Education, Orange, CA 92866. Offers learning handicapped (MA), severely handicapped (MA), special education (MA). Evening/weekend programs available. Faculty: 10 full-time (8 women). Students: 12. *Degree requirements:* Comprehensive exam required, thesis not required. *Entrance requirements:* GRE General Test (minimum combined score of 900), MAT (minimum score 45), or PRAXIS. Application deadline: rolling. Application fee: $40. *Tuition:* $7020 per year full-time, $390 per credit part-time. *Financial aid:* Application deadline 3/1. • Dr. Don Cardinal, Coordinator, 714-997-6781.

Cheyney University of Pennsylvania, Program in Special Education, Cheyney, PA 19319. Awards M Ed, MS. Accredited by NCATE. Part-time and evening/weekend programs available. Faculty: 5 full-time (3 women), 7 part-time (4 women). Students: 8 full-time (7 women), 40 part-time (24 women); includes 43 minority (42 African Americans, 1 Hispanic). Average age 39. In 1997, 25 degrees awarded. *Degree requirements:* Thesis or alternative required, foreign language not required. *Entrance requirements:* GRE General Test, MAT, minimum GPA of 2.75. Application deadline: 8/1 (priority date; rolling processing; 12/15 for spring admission). Application fee: $25. *Tuition:* $3848 per year full-time, $193 per credit hour part-time for state residents; $6616 per year full-time, $346 per credit hour part-time for nonresidents. *Financial aid:* Assistantships, institutionally sponsored loans, and career-related internships or fieldwork

Directory: Special Education

Cheyney University of Pennsylvania (continued)
available. Financial aid application deadline: 5/1. • Gloria Stone Mitchell, Coordinator, 610-399-2029. Application contact: Dean of Graduate Studies, 610-399-2400. Fax: 610-399-2118.

Chicago State University, College of Education, Department of Special Education, Chicago, IL 60628. Awards MS Ed. Accredited by NCATE. *Degree requirements:* Thesis optional, foreign language not required. *Entrance requirements:* Minimum GPA of 2.75. Application deadline: 7/1 (11/10 for spring admission). *Tuition:* $2268 per year full-time, $95 per credit hour part-time for state residents; $6804 per year full-time, $284 per credit hour part-time for nonresidents.

The Citadel, The Military College of South Carolina, Department of Education, Program in Special Education, Charleston, SC 29409. Awards M Ed. Accredited by NCATE. Offered jointly with the University of Charleston, South Carolina. Faculty: 6 full-time, 1 part-time. Students: 2 full-time (1 woman), 10 part-time (all women); includes 1 minority (African American). In 1997, 4 degrees awarded. *Entrance requirements:* GRE, MAT, or 12 hours of graduate course work with a minimum GPA of 3.0. Application deadline: rolling. Application fee: $25. *Expenses:* Tuition $130 per credit hour for state residents; $260 per credit hour for nonresidents. Fees $30 per semester. *Financial aid:* Fellowships available. • Dr. Robert Carter, Head, Department of Education, 803-953-5097.

City College of the City University of New York, Graduate School, School of Education, Department of School Services, Program in Special Education, Convent Avenue at 138th Street, New York, NY 10031-6977. Awards MS. Students: 8 full-time (6 women), 245 part-time (182 women). In 1997, 32 degrees awarded. *Degree requirements:* Thesis, research paper required, foreign language not required. *Entrance requirements:* TOEFL (minimum score 500), interview, minimum GPA of 2.5 overall, 3.0 in major. Application fee: $40. *Expenses:* Tuition $4350 per year full-time, $185 per credit part-time for state residents; $7600 per year full-time, $320 per credit part-time for nonresidents. Fees $41 per year. *Financial aid:* Career-related internships or fieldwork available. Financial aid application deadline: 5/1. • Head, 212-650-7986.

City University, School of Education, Bellevue, WA 98004-6442. Offerings include special education (M Ed). Postbaccalaureate distance learning degree programs offered (no on-campus study). School faculty: 21 full-time (13 women), 301 part-time (162 women). *Application deadline:* rolling. *Application fee:* $75 ($175 for international students). Electronic applications accepted. *Tuition:* $280 per credit hour. • Roxanne Kelly, Dean, 425-637-1010 Ext. 3712. Fax: 425-277-2439. Application contact: Nabil El-Khatib, Vice President, Admissions, 800-426-5596. Fax: 425-277-2437. E-mail: nel-khatib@cityu.edu.

Clarion University of Pennsylvania, College of Education and Human Services, Department of Special Education, Clarion, PA 16214. Awards MS. Accredited by NCATE. Part-time programs available. Faculty: 8 full-time (2 women). Students: 15 full-time (9 women), 31 part-time (18 women); includes 1 minority (African American), 1 international. 23 applicants, 83% accepted. In 1997, 11 degrees awarded. *Degree requirements:* Thesis or alternative required, foreign language not required. *Entrance requirements:* Minimum QPA of 2.75. Application deadline: 8/1 (priority date; rolling processing). Application fee: $25. *Expenses:* Tuition $3468 per year full-time, $193 per credit hour part-time for state residents; $6236 per year full-time, $346 per credit hour part-time for nonresidents. Fees $921 per year full-time, $90 per credit hour part-time for state residents; $921 per year full-time, $89 per credit hour part-time for nonresidents. *Financial aid:* In 1997–98, 3 research assistantships (1 to a first-year student) averaging $533 per month were awarded. Aid available to part-time students. Financial aid application deadline: 5/1. • Dr. Bryan Huwar, Chairman, 814-226-2463. Application contact: Dr. Lisa Turner, Graduate Coordinator, 814-226-2589.

Clemson University, College of Health, Education, and Human Development, Department of Foundations and Special Education, Clemson, SC 29634. Awards M Ed. Accredited by NCATE. Part-time and evening/weekend programs available. Students: 4 full-time (3 women), 42 part-time (39 women); includes 1 minority (African American), 1 international. 11 applicants, 55% accepted. In 1997, 24 degrees awarded. *Average time to degree:* master's–1.5 years full-time, 5 years part-time. *Entrance requirements:* TOEFL, GRE or minimum GPA of 3.0, teaching certificate. Application deadline: 6/1. Application fee: $35. *Expenses:* Tuition $3154 per year full-time, $130 per credit hour part-time for state residents; $6452 per year full-time, $264 per credit hour part-time for nonresidents. Fees $190 per year. *Financial aid:* Research assistantships, teaching assistantships, graduate stipends, full tuition waivers, Federal Work-Study, and career-related internships or fieldwork available. Aid available to part-time students. Financial aid application deadline: 6/1; applicants required to submit FAFSA. *Faculty research:* Field-based teacher training transition, assessment, national policy outcome. Total annual research expenditures: $250,000. • Dr. William Fisk, Chair, 864-656-5119. E-mail: bill252@clemson.edu. Application contact: Dr. Janie Hodge, Coordinator, 864-656-1613. Fax: 864-656-1322. E-mail: hodge@clemson.edu.

Cleveland State University, College of Education, Department of Specialized Instructional Programs, Cleveland, OH 44115-2440. Offerings include curriculum and instruction (M Ed), with options in bilingual education, early childhood education, early childhood/special education, education of emerging adolescents, elementary education, English as a second language, learning disabilities, Montessori education, multihandicapped, reading, secondary education. Department faculty: 18 full-time (12 women). *Entrance requirements:* GRE General Test or MAT (score in 50th percentile or higher). Application deadline: 9/1 (priority date; rolling processing). Application fee: $25. *Expenses:* Tuition $5252 per year full-time, $202 per credit hour part-time for state residents; $10,504 per year full-time, $404 per credit hour part-time for nonresidents. Fees $2.25 per credit hour (minimum). • Dr. Jane Zaharias, Chairperson, 216-687-4585. Fax: 216-687-5379. E-mail: j.zaharias@csuohio.edu.

College of Mount St. Joseph, Education Department, Program in Special Education, Cincinnati, OH 45233-1670. Awards MA Ed. Part-time and evening/weekend programs available. *Degree requirements:* Comprehensive exam required, foreign language and thesis not required. *Entrance requirements:* GRE General Test (minimum combined score of 825), minimum GPA of 2.7. Application deadline: rolling. Application fee: $0. *Tuition:* $320 per credit hour. *Financial aid:* Application deadline 6/1. • Application contact: Jean Abrams, Graduate Secretary, 513-244-4812.

The College of New Jersey, Graduate Division, School of Education, Department of Special Education, Program in Special Education, Ewing, NJ 08628. Awards MAT, M Ed. Accredited by NCATE. Students: 4 full-time (all women), 125 part-time (108 women); includes 16 minority (2 African Americans, 3 Asian Americans, 11 Hispanics), 6 international. Average age 26. In 1997, 30 degrees awarded. *Degree requirements:* Comprehensive exam required, foreign language and thesis not required. *Average time to degree:* master's–2 years full-time. *Entrance requirements:* GRE General Test, minimum GPA of 3.0 in field or 2.75 overall. Application deadline: 4/15 (10/15 for spring admission). Application fee: $50. *Expenses:* Tuition $6892 per year full-time, $287 per credit hour part-time for state residents; $9602 per year full-time, $402 per credit hour part-time for nonresidents. Fees $799 per year full-time, $33 per credit hour part-time. *Financial aid:* Graduate assistantships available. Financial aid application deadline: 5/1; applicants required to submit FAFSA. • Dr. Phyllis Weisberg, Coordinator, 609-771-2992. Fax: 609-637-5172.

The College of New Jersey, Graduate Division, School of Education, Department of Special Education, Program in Special Education with Learning Disabilities, Ewing, NJ 08628. Awards M Ed. Accredited by NCATE. Students: 10 part-time (9 women); includes 2 international. Average age 28. In 1997, 1 degree awarded. *Degree requirements:* Comprehensive exam required, foreign language and thesis not required. *Average time to degree:* master's–2 years full-time. *Entrance requirements:* GRE General Test, minimum GPA of 3.0 in field or 2.75 overall. Application deadline: 4/15 (10/15 for spring admission). Application fee: $50. *Expenses:* Tuition $6892 per year full-time, $287 per credit hour part-time for state residents; $9602 per year full-time, $402 per credit hour part-time for nonresidents. Fees $799 per year full-time, $33 per credit hour part-time. *Financial aid:* Application deadline 5/1; applicants required to submit FAFSA. • Dr. Phyllis Weisberg, Coordinator, 609-771-2992. Fax: 609-637-5172.

College of New Rochelle, Division of Education, Program in Special Education/Therapeutic Education, New Rochelle, NY 10805-2308. Offers special education (MS Ed), therapeutic education (MS Ed). Part-time programs available. Faculty: 4 full-time (2 women), 12 part-time (8 women), 8 FTE. Students: 23 full-time (20 women), 224 part-time (189 women); includes 26 minority (21 African Americans, 4 Hispanics, 1 Native American), 6 international. 64 applicants, 100% accepted. In 1997, 124 degrees awarded. *Degree requirements:* Practicum required, foreign language not required. *Average time to degree:* master's–1.2 years full-time, 2.5 years part-time. *Entrance requirements:* Interview; minimum GPA of 3.0 in field, 2.7 overall. Application deadline: 8/1 (priority date; rolling processing). Application fee: $35. *Tuition:* $329 per credit. *Financial aid:* In 1997–98, 10 students received aid, including 4 research assistantships totaling $12,150; assistantships, scholarships also available. • Dr. Melanie Hannigan, Division Head, Division of Education, 914-654-5330.

College of Our Lady of the Elms, Department of Education, Chicopee, MA 01013-2839. Offerings include special education (MAT). Department faculty: 7 full-time (all women), 6 part-time (5 women). *Application deadline:* rolling. *Application fee:* $30. *Expenses:* Tuition $320 per credit. Fees $40 per year. • Sr. Kathleen M. Kirley, Dean of Continuing Education and Graduate Studies, 413-594-2761. Fax: 413-592-4871. Application contact: Dr. Mary Janeczek, Director, 413-594-2761.

College of St. Joseph, Division of Education, Program in Special Education, Rutland, VT 05701-3899. Awards M Ed. Part-time and evening/weekend programs available. Faculty: 3 full-time (2 women), 9 part-time (7 women). Students: 6 full-time (3 women), 5 part-time (all women). *Degree requirements:* Comprehensive exams required, foreign language and thesis not required. *Entrance requirements:* GRE General Test (combined average 1100), interview. Application deadline: rolling. Application fee: $25. *Tuition:* $7950 per year full-time, $220 per credit part-time. *Financial aid:* Federal Work-Study and career-related internships or fieldwork available. Aid available to part-time students. Financial aid application deadline: 3/1. • Application contact: Steve Soba, Director of Admissions, 802-773-5900 Ext. 206. Fax: 802-773-5900 Ext. 258. E-mail: suite9@aol.com.

The College of Saint Rose, School of Education, Reading/Special Education Department, Program in Special Education, Albany, NY 12203-1419. Awards MS Ed. Part-time and evening/weekend programs available. Faculty: 7 full-time (4 women), 7 part-time (4 women). Students: 28 full-time (26 women), 225 part-time (194 women); includes 1 minority (Hispanic). Average age 31. In 1997, 124 degrees awarded. *Degree requirements:* Thesis or alternative, comprehensive exam required, foreign language not required. *Entrance requirements:* Minimum undergraduate GPA of 3.0. Application deadline: 7/15 (priority date; rolling processing; 12/1 for spring admission). Application fee: $30. *Expenses:* Tuition $338 per credit. Fees $60 per year. *Financial aid:* Research assistantships, partial tuition waivers, and career-related internships or fieldwork available. Aid available to part-time students. Financial aid application deadline: 3/1; applicants required to submit FAFSA. • Application contact: Graduate Office, 518-454-5136. Fax: 518-458-5479. E-mail: ace@rosnet.strose.edu.

College of Santa Fe, Department of Education, Program in Multicultural Special Education, Santa Fe, NM 87505-7634. Awards MA. Part-time and evening/weekend programs available. Faculty: 1 (woman) full-time, 4 part-time (3 women). Students: 41 part-time (29 women); includes 12 minority (1 African American, 7 Hispanics, 4 Native Americans). 54 applicants, 98% accepted. In 1997, 3 degrees awarded. *Degree requirements:* Comprehensive exams, portfolio presentation required, foreign language not required. *Average time to degree:* master's–1 year full-time, 1.5 years part-time. *Entrance requirements:* Interview, minimum GPA of 3.0. Application deadline: rolling. Application fee: $25. *Expenses:* Tuition $237 per credit hour. Fees $25 per year. *Financial aid:* Institutionally sponsored loans and career-related internships or fieldwork available. Aid available to part-time students. Financial aid application deadline: 3/1; applicants required to submit FAFSA. • Dr. Kate Friesner, Director of Teacher Education, 505-880-8259. Application contact: Clarissa Rosas, Coordinator, 505-880-8254. Fax: 505-880-8262.

College of Staten Island of the City University of New York, Department of Education, Program in Special Education, Staten Island, NY 10314-6600. Awards MS Ed. Part-time and evening/weekend programs available. Faculty: 3 full-time (1 woman), 13 part-time (9 women). Students: 5 full-time (4 women), 151 part-time (137 women); includes 10 minority (3 African Americans, 7 Hispanics). Average age 34. In 1997, 130 degrees awarded. *Degree requirements:* Thesis or alternative required, foreign language not required. *Entrance requirements:* Teaching certificate or previous course work in psychology. Application deadline: 6/1 (priority date; rolling processing; 12/1 for spring admission). Application fee: $40. *Expenses:* Tuition $4350 per year full-time, $185 per credit part-time for state residents; $7600 per year full-time, $320 per credit part-time for nonresidents. Fees $106 per year full-time, $54 per year part-time. *Faculty research:* Strategies and reading for the learning disabled, special education referrals, sexual abuse and the mentally retarded. • Dr. Effie P. M. Simmonds, Coordinator, 718-982-3741. Application contact: Earl Teasley, Director of Admissions, 718-982-2010. Fax: 718-982-2500.

College of William and Mary, School of Education, Specialization in Special Education, Williamsburg, VA 23187-8795. Awards MA Ed. Accredited by NCATE. Students: 6 full-time (5 women), 20 part-time (17 women); includes 5 minority (3 African Americans, 2 Asian Americans). Average age 32. 39 applicants, 77% accepted. In 1997, 27 degrees awarded. *Entrance requirements:* GRE or MAT, minimum GPA of 2.5. Application deadline: 2/15 (priority date). Application fee: $30. *Tuition:* $5262 per year full-time, $165 per semester hour part-time for state residents; $16,138 per year full-time, $500 per semester hour part-time for nonresidents. *Financial aid:* In 1997–98, 6 graduate assistantships (1 to a first-year student) averaging $1,115 per month and totaling $73,948 were awarded; research assistantships and career-related internships or fieldwork also available. Financial aid application deadline: 2/15. *Faculty research:* Collaboration, gifted African-American education, multicultural education, women, learning disabled. • Dr. George Bass, Coordinator, 757-221-4300. E-mail: gmbass@facstaff.wm.edu.

Columbus State University, College of Education, Department of Counseling and Clinical Programs, Columbus, GA 31907-5645. Offerings include special education (M Ed, Ed S), with options in behavioral disorders (M Ed), learning disabilities (M Ed), mental retardation (M Ed). Accredited by NCATE. M Ed (reading), Ed S (special education) being phased out; applicants no longer accepted. *Degree requirements:* For Ed S, thesis or alternative required, foreign language not required. *Entrance requirements:* For Ed S, GRE General Test (minimum combined score of 900), MAT (minimum score 44). Application deadline: 7/10 (priority date; rolling processing; 10/23 for spring admission). Application fee: $20. *Tuition:* $1718 per year full-time, $151 per semester hour part-time for state residents; $6218 per year full-time, $401 per semester hour part-time for nonresidents. • Dr. Joyce Hickson, Chair, 706-568-2222. Fax: 706-569-3134. E-mail: hickson_joyce@colstate.edu. Application contact: Katie Thornton, Graduate Admissions, 706-568-2279. Fax: 706-568-2462. E-mail: thornton_katie@colstate.edu.

Converse College, Department of Education, Program in Special Education, Spartanburg, SC 29302-0006. Awards M Ed. Part-time programs available. Faculty: 3 full-time, 1 part-time. Students: 92 (62 women); includes 12 minority (10 African Americans, 1 Asian American, 1 Hispanic). Average age 35. 16 applicants, 100% accepted. In 1997, 31 degrees awarded. *Entrance requirements:* NTE, minimum GPA of 2.5. Application deadline: 5/1 (priority date; rolling processing; 1/30 for spring admission). Application fee: $35. *Tuition:* $185 per credit. *Financial aid:* Available to part-time students. Financial aid applicants required to submit FAFSA. • Dr. Ansley H. Boggs, Director, 864-596-9017.

Coppin State College, Division of Education, Department of Special Education, Baltimore, MD 21216-3698. Awards M Ed. Part-time and evening/weekend programs available. Faculty:

5 full-time (2 women), 5 part-time (3 women). Students: 10 full-time (8 women), 146 part-time (107 women); includes 133 minority (129 African Americans, 4 Hispanics), 3 international. Average age 35. In 1997, 54 degrees awarded. *Degree requirements:* Thesis or alternative required, foreign language not required. *Entrance requirements:* Minimum GPA of 2.5. Application deadline: 7/15 (12/15 for spring admission). Application fee: $20. *Expenses:* Tuition $140 per credit for state residents; $240 per credit for nonresidents. Fees $504 per year. *Financial aid:* Federal Work-Study, institutionally sponsored loans, and career-related internships or fieldwork available. Aid available to part-time students. Financial aid application deadline: 4/1; applicants required to submit FAFSA. *Faculty research:* Survey of colleges and universities in Maryland with programs for the learning disabled. • George Taylor, Chair, 410-383-5949. Fax: 410-669-2861. Application contact: Allen Mosley, Director of Admissions, 410-383-5990.

Cumberland College, Program in Special Education, 6178 College Station Drive, Williamsburg, KY 40769-1372. Awards MA Ed. Evening/weekend programs available. Faculty: 4 full-time (2 women), 5 part-time (2 women). *Degree requirements:* Comprehensive exam required, foreign language and thesis not required. *Entrance requirements:* GRE or NTE, Kentucky teaching certificate. Application deadline: 8/26 (rolling processing). Application fee: $25. *Tuition:* $175 per credit. • Application contact: Erica Harris, Admissions Office, 606-539-4241.

Curry College, Graduate Program in Education, Milton, MA 02186-9984. Offerings include learning disabilities across the lifespan (Certificate), post-secondary learning disabilities (M Ed). Certificate (learning disabilities across the lifespan, adult education) new for fall 1998. College faculty: 10. *Degree requirements:* For master's, research project required, foreign language and thesis not required. *Application deadline:* 8/1 (priority date; 1/1 for spring admission). *Application fee:* $50. Electronic applications accepted. *Tuition:* $325 per credit. • Dr. Jane Utley Adelizzi, Director, 617-333-2130. Fax: 617-333-9722. E-mail: jutleyad@curry.edu.

Daemen College, Program in Special Education, Amherst, NY 14226-3592. Offers education (MS). Part-time and evening/weekend programs available. Faculty: 3 full-time (1 woman), 1 (woman) part-time. Students: 6 part-time (all women). Average age 34. *Degree requirements:* Thesis. *Entrance requirements:* Minimum GPA of 2.85, teaching certificate. Application deadline: 3/1 (priority date; rolling processing; 10/1 for spring admission). Application fee: $25. *Expenses:* Tuition $430 per credit. Fees $13 per credit. *Financial aid:* Available to part-time students. Financial aid application deadline: 2/15; applicants required to submit FAFSA. *Faculty research:* Reading remediation, portfolio and other assessments. • Dr. Patrick J. Hartwick, Chair, 716-839-8349. E-mail: phartwic@daemen.edu. Application contact: Deborah Fargo, Associate Director of Admissions, 716-839-8225. Fax: 716-839-8516. E-mail: dfargo@daemen.edu.

Delaware State University, Department of Education, Program in Special Education, Dover, DE 19901-2277. Awards MA. Part-time and evening/weekend programs available. *Degree requirements:* Comprehensive exam required, thesis optional, foreign language not required. *Entrance requirements:* GRE General Test, minimum GPA of 3.0 in field, 2.75 overall. Application deadline: 6/30 (priority date; rolling processing). Application fee: $10. *Faculty research:* Curriculum and instruction, distributive education.

Delta State University, School of Education, Division of Behavioral Sciences, Program in Special Education, Cleveland, MS 38733-0001. Awards M Ed. Accredited by NCATE. Part-time and evening/weekend programs available. *Degree requirements:* Practicum required, thesis optional, foreign language not required. *Entrance requirements:* GRE General Test (minimum combined score of 800) or MAT (minimum score 34). Application deadline: 8/1 (priority date; rolling processing). Application fee: $0. *Tuition:* $2596 per year full-time, $121 per semester hour part-time for state residents; $5546 per year full-time, $285 per semester hour part-time for nonresidents. *Financial aid:* Research assistantships, Federal Work-Study, institutionally sponsored loans, and career-related internships or fieldwork available. Aid available to part-time students. Financial aid application deadline: 6/1. • Application contact: Dr. John Thornell, Dean of Graduate Studies and Continuing Education, 601-846-4310. Fax: 601-846-4016.

DePaul University, School of Education, Program in Reading and Learning Disabilities, Chicago, IL 60604-2287. Offers adolescent learning disabilities (MA, M Ed), bilingual multicultural learning disabilities (MA, M Ed), reading and learning disabilities (MA, M Ed). Accredited by NCATE. Faculty: 3 full-time (all women), 2 part-time (both women). Students: 34 full-time (32 women), 46 part-time (42 women); includes 13 minority (7 African Americans, 6 Hispanics), 1 international. Average age 29. 34 applicants, 85% accepted. In 1997, 19 degrees awarded. *Degree requirements:* Oral exam or thesis required, foreign language not required. *Entrance requirements:* Interview, minimum GPA of 2.75, work experience. Application deadline: rolling. Application fee: $25. *Expenses:* Tuition $320 per credit hour. Fees $30 per year. *Financial aid:* Teaching assistantships and career-related internships or fieldwork available. *Faculty research:* Reading specialist theory, behavior disorders. • Dr. Barbara Sizemore, Dean, School of Education, 312-325-7000 Ext. 1666. Fax: 312-325-7748. Application contact: Director of Graduate Admissions, 312-325-7000 Ext. 1666. E-mail: mmurphy@wppost.depaul.edu.

Dominican College of Blauvelt, Division of Teacher Education, Orangeburg, NY 10962-1210. Offerings include special education (MS Ed). *Degree requirements:* Practicum, research project required, foreign language and thesis not required. *Entrance requirements:* Interview. Application deadline: rolling. Application fee: $50. *Expenses:* Tuition $400 per credit hour. Fees $155 per year.

Dominican University, Graduate School of Education, River Forest, IL 60305-1099. Offerings include special education (MS). School faculty: 9 full-time (7 women), 14 part-time (11 women), 14 FTE. *Application deadline:* 8/15 (priority date; rolling processing; 1/16 for spring admission). *Application fee:* $25. *Expenses:* Tuition $6120 per year full-time, $1020 per course part-time. Fees $10 per course. • Sr. Colleen McNicholas, Dean, 708-524-6830. E-mail: educate@email.dom.edu. Application contact: Deborah Davison, Coordinator of Admissions, 708-524-6922. Fax: 708-524-6665. E-mail: educate@email.dom.edu.

Dowling College, Program in Reading/Special Education, Oakdale, NY 11769-1999. Awards MS Ed. Part-time and evening/weekend programs available. Students: 3 full-time (all women), 185 part-time (172 women); includes 17 minority (7 African Americans, 1 Asian American, 9 Hispanics). Average age 32. In 1997, 55 degrees awarded. *Degree requirements:* Comprehensive exam required, foreign language and thesis not required. *Entrance requirements:* Provisional teaching certificate. Application deadline: 9/1 (priority date; rolling processing). Application fee: $0. *Financial aid:* General graduate assistantships available. Financial aid application deadline: 4/30. • Application contact: Kate Rowe, Director of Admissions, 516-244-3030. Fax: 516-563-3827. E-mail: rowek@dowling.edu.

Dowling College, Program in Special Education, Oakdale, NY 11769-1999. Awards MS Ed. Part-time and evening/weekend programs available. Faculty: 3 full-time (2 women), 10 part-time (6 women). Students: 3 full-time (all women), 311 part-time (231 women); includes 19 minority (6 African Americans, 3 Asian Americans, 9 Hispanics, 1 Native American). Average age 32. In 1997, 128 degrees awarded. *Degree requirements:* Comprehensive exam required, foreign language and thesis not required. *Entrance requirements:* Provisional teaching certificate. Application deadline: 9/1 (priority date; rolling processing). Application fee: $0. *Financial aid:* General graduate assistantships, Federal Work-Study, and career-related internships or fieldwork available. Aid available to part-time students. Financial aid application deadline: 4/30. • Dr. Barry McNamara, Discipline Coordinator, 516-244-3448. Fax: 516-244-5036. Application contact: Kate Rowe, Director of Admissions, 516-244-3030. Fax: 516-563-3827. E-mail: rowek@dowling.edu.

Drake University, School of Education, Department of Special Education, Counseling and Vocational Rehabilitation, Program in Special Education, Des Moines, IA 50311-4516. Awards MSE. Faculty: 2 full-time (both women), 8 part-time (5 women). Students: 39 part-time (33 women); includes 1 minority (Hispanic). 21 applicants, 71% accepted. In 1997, 16 degrees awarded. *Entrance requirements:* GRE General Test (minimum combined score of 1000) or MAT (minimum score 36). Application deadline: rolling. Application fee: $25. *Tuition:* $16,000 per year full-time, $260 per hour (minimum) part-time. *Financial aid:* Career-related internships or fieldwork available. Aid available to part-time students. • Application contact: Ann J. Martin, Graduate Coordinator, 515-271-3871. Fax: 515-271-2831. E-mail: ajm@admin.drake.edu.

Duquesne University, School of Education, Department of Counseling, Psychology, and Special Education, Program in Special Education, Pittsburgh, PA 15282-0001. Awards MS Ed. Faculty: 3 full-time (all women), 1 (woman) part-time. Students: 71. 15 applicants, 67% accepted. In 1997, 21 degrees awarded. *Average time to degree:* master's–1.5 years full-time, 2.5 years part-time. *Entrance requirements:* MAT. Application deadline: 8/1 (rolling processing; 12/1 for spring admission). Application fee: $40. *Expenses:* Tuition $481 per credit. Fees $39 per credit. • Application contact: Dr. Julia Hartzog, Coordinator, 412-396-5710. Fax: 412-396-5585.

D'Youville College, Division of Education, Buffalo, NY 14201-1084. Offerings include special education (MS Ed). Division faculty: 5 full-time (4 women), 8 part-time (2 women). *Degree requirements:* Computer language, thesis required, foreign language not required. *Entrance requirements:* Minimum GPA of 3.0. Application deadline: rolling. Application fee: $25. *Expenses:* Tuition $357 per credit hour. Fees $350 per year. • Dr. Robert DiSibio, Graduate Director, 716-881-3200. Application contact: Joseph Syracuse, Graduate Admissions Director, 716-881-7676. Fax: 716-881-7790.

East Carolina University, School of Education, Department of Special Education, Greenville, NC 27858-4353. Offers programs in learning disabilities (MA Ed), mental retardation (MA Ed). Accredited by NCATE. Faculty: 4 full-time (2 women). Students: 6 full-time (all women), 24 part-time (22 women); includes 4 minority (all African Americans). Average age 33. 13 applicants, 62% accepted. In 1997, 17 degrees awarded. *Degree requirements:* Comprehensive exams. *Application deadline:* 6/1 (priority date; rolling processing). *Application fee:* $40. *Tuition:* $1886 per year full-time, $472 per semester (minimum) part-time for state residents; $9156 per year full-time, $2289 per semester (minimum) part-time for nonresidents. *Financial aid:* Research assistantships, teaching assistantships, Federal Work-Study available. Aid available to part-time students. Financial aid application deadline: 6/1. • Dr. John T. Richards, Chairperson, 252-328-6181. Fax: 252-328-4219. E-mail: richardsj@mail.ecu.edu. Application contact: Dr. Paul D. Tschetter, Associate Dean, 252-328-6012. Fax: 252-328-6071. E-mail: grad@mail.ecu.edu.

Eastern Illinois University, College of Education and Professional Studies, Department of Special Education, 600 Lincoln Avenue, Charleston, IL 61920-3099. Awards MS Ed. Accredited by NCATE. Part-time programs available. Faculty: 4 full-time (all women). Students: 14 full-time (10 women), 16 part-time (14 women). In 1997, 16 degrees awarded. *Degree requirements:* Comprehensive exam required, foreign language and thesis not required. *Entrance requirements:* GRE General Test or MAT. Application deadline: 7/31 (priority date; rolling processing). Application fee: $25. *Expenses:* Tuition $3459 per year full-time, $96 per semester hour part-time for state residents; $10,377 per year full-time, $288 per semester hour part-time for nonresidents. Fees $1566 per year full-time, $37 per semester hour part-time. *Financial aid:* In 1997–98, 3 research assistantships were awarded. • Dr. Kathlene Shank, Chairperson, 217-581-5315. E-mail: cfkss@eiu.edu.

Eastern Kentucky University, College of Education, Department of Special Education, Richmond, KY 40475-3101. Awards MA Ed, Ed S. Accredited by NCATE. Ed S being phased out; applicants no longer accepted. Part-time programs available. Faculty: 15 full-time (12 women), 15 part-time (13 women), 19.25 FTE. Students: 45. In 1997, 9 master's awarded. *Entrance requirements:* For master's, GRE General Test, minimum GPA of 2.5. Application fee: $0. *Tuition:* $2390 per year full-time, $133 per credit hour part-time for state residents; $6630 per year full-time, $365 per credit hour part-time for nonresidents. *Financial aid:* Fellowships, research assistantships, teaching assistantships, Federal Work-Study available. Aid available to part-time students. *Faculty research:* Personnel needs in communication disorders, education needs of people who stutter, variables importing on interpreting for the deaf. • Dr. Martin Diebold, Chair, 606-622-4442.

Eastern Michigan University, College of Education, Department of Special Education, Program in Special Education, Ypsilanti, MI 48197. Awards MA, SPA. Accredited by NCATE. Average age 37. *Entrance requirements:* For master's, GRE General Test, TOEFL (minimum score 570). Application deadline: 5/15 (rolling processing; 3/15 for spring admission). Application fee: $30. *Expenses:* Tuition $2691 per year full-time, $150 per credit hour part-time for state residents; $6300 per year full-time, $350 per credit hour part-time for nonresidents. Fees $368 per year full-time, $88 per semester (minimum) part-time. *Financial aid:* Fellowships, teaching assistantships available. Aid available to part-time students. Financial aid application deadline: 3/15; applicants required to submit FAFSA. • Dr. Roberta Anderson, Coordinator, 734-487-3302.

Eastern Nazarene College, Graduate Studies, Division of Education, Quincy, MA 02170-2999. Offerings include moderate special needs education (M Ed, Certificate), special education administrator (Certificate). M Ed and Certificate also available through weekend program for administration, special needs, and reading only. Division faculty: 9 full-time (5 women), 11 part-time (5 women). *Entrance requirements:* For master's, TOEFL (minimum score 500). Application deadline: rolling. Application fee: $35. *Expenses:* Tuition $350 per credit. Fees $125 per semester full-time, $15 per semester part-time. • Dr. Lorne Ranstrom, Chair, 617-745-3528. Application contact: Cleo P. Cakridas, Graduate Enrollment Counselor, 617-745-3870. Fax: 617-745-3907. E-mail: cakridac@enc.edu.

Eastern New Mexico University, College of Education and Technology, School of Education, Program in Special Education, Portales, NM 88130. Awards M Sp Ed. Part-time programs available. Faculty: 3 full-time (1 woman). Students: 7 full-time (6 women), 21 part-time (17 women); includes 6 minority (2 African Americans, 3 Hispanics, 1 Native American). 0 applicants. In 1997, 8 degrees awarded. *Degree requirements:* Thesis optional, foreign language not required. *Entrance requirements:* Minimum GPA of 2.5. Application deadline: rolling. Application fee: $10. *Tuition:* $1956 per year full-time, $82 per credit hour part-time for state residents; $6702 per year full-time, $280 per credit hour part-time for nonresidents. *Financial aid:* Research assistantships, teaching assistantships, Federal Work-Study, and career-related internships or fieldwork available. Aid available to part-time students. Financial aid application deadline: 4/1. • Dr. Sherrie Bettenhausen, Graduate Coordinator, School of Education, 505-562-2603.

Eastern Washington University, College of Education and Human Development, Department of Applied Psychology, Cheney, WA 99004-2431. Offerings include special education (M Ed). Accredited by NCATE. Department faculty: 14 full-time (2 women). *Application deadline:* 2/1 (rolling processing). *Application fee:* $35. *Tuition:* $4200 per year full-time, $140 per credit part-time for state residents; $12,780 per year full-time, $415 per credit part-time for nonresidents. • Dr. Armin Arndt, Chair, 509-359-2827.

East Stroudsburg University of Pennsylvania, School of Professional Studies, Department of Special Education, East Stroudsburg, PA 18301-2999. Awards M Ed. Part-time and evening/weekend programs available. *Degree requirements:* Comprehensive exam required, foreign language and thesis not required. *Application deadline:* 7/31 (priority date; rolling processing; 11/30 for spring admission). *Application fee:* $15 ($25 for international students). *Expenses:* Tuition $3468 per year full-time, $193 per credit part-time for state residents; $6236 per year full-time, $346 per credit part-time for nonresidents. Fees $700 per year full-time, $39 per credit part-time.

East Tennessee State University, College of Education, Department of Human Development and Learning, Johnson City, TN 37614-0734. Offerings include special education (MA, M Ed). Accredited by NCATE. Department faculty: 22 full-time (8 women). *Degree requirements:* Thesis (for some programs), comprehensive exam required, foreign language not required. *Entrance requirements:* GRE General Test, TOEFL (minimum score 550), minimum GPA of 3.0. Application deadline: 7/15 (priority date; rolling processing; 11/1 for spring admission).

Directory: Special Education

East Tennessee State University (continued)

Application fee: $25 ($35 for international students). *Tuition:* $2944 per year full-time, $158 per credit hour part-time for state residents; $7770 per year full-time, $369 per credit hour part-time for nonresidents. • Dr. James Bitter, Chair, 423-439-4194. Fax: 423-439-5764. E-mail: bitterj@etsu-tn.edu.

Edgewood College, Program in Education, Madison, WI 53711-1998. Offerings include director of special education and pupil services (Certificate), emotional disturbances (MA, Certificate), learning disabilities (MA, Certificate), learning disabilities and emotional disturbances (MA, Certificate). One or more programs accredited by NCATE. Program faculty: 6 full-time (3 women), 3 part-time (0 women), 7 FTE. *Application deadline:* 8/1 (priority date; rolling processing). *Application fee:* $25. *Tuition:* $330 per credit. • Dr. Joseph Schmiedicke, Chair, 608-257-4861 Ext. 2293. Application contact: Sr. Lucille Marie Frost, Assistant Dean of Graduate Programs, 608-254-4861 Ext. 2382. Fax: 608-257-1455.

Edinboro University of Pennsylvania, School of Education, Department of Special Education and School Psychology, Program in Special Education, Edinboro, PA 16444. Awards M Ed. Evening/weekend programs available. Students: 18 full-time (15 women), 39 part-time (29 women); includes 2 minority (both African Americans). Average age 33. In 1997, 20 degrees awarded. *Degree requirements:* Thesis or alternative required, foreign language not required. *Entrance requirements:* GRE or MAT (score in 30th percentile or higher). Application deadline: rolling. Application fee: $25. *Expenses:* Tuition $3468 per year full-time, $193 per credit part-time for state residents; $6236 per year full-time, $346 per credit part-time for nonresidents. Fees $898 per year full-time, $50 per semester (minimum) part-time. *Financial aid:* In 1997–98, 9 assistantships were awarded. • Dr. Sondra Dastoli, Head, 814-732-2766. E-mail: dastoli@edinboro.edu. Application contact: Dr. Philip Kerstetter, Dean of Graduate Studies, 814-732-2856. Fax: 814-732-2611. E-mail: kerstetter@edinboro.edu.

Elon College, Program in Education, Elon College, NC 27244. Offerings include special education (M Ed). Accredited by NCATE. Program faculty: 15 full-time (10 women). *Entrance requirements:* GRE, MAT, NTE (special education). Application deadline: 8/15 (priority date; rolling processing). Application fee: $25. *Tuition:* $210 per credit hour. • Dr. Glenda W. Beamon, Director, 336-584-2126. Fax: 336-538-2609. E-mail: beamon@vax1.elon.edu. Application contact: Alice N. Essen, Director of Graduate Admissions, 800-334-8448. Fax: 336-538-3986. E-mail: essen@numen.elon.edu.

Emporia State University, School of Graduate Studies, The Teachers College, Division of Psychology and Special Education, Program in Special Education, Emporia, KS 66801-5087. Offers behavior disorders (MS); interrelated special education (MS); learning disabilities (MS); mental retardation (MS); teaching of the gifted, talented, and creative (MS). Accredited by NCATE. Students: 3 full-time (2 women), 19 part-time (17 women); includes 1 minority (Hispanic). 5 applicants, 0% accepted. In 1997, 19 degrees awarded. *Degree requirements:* Comprehensive exam or thesis required, foreign language not required. *Entrance requirements:* GRE General Test or MAT, TOEFL (minimum score 550), written exam. Application deadline: 8/15 (priority date; rolling processing). Application fee: $30 ($75 for international students). Electronic applications accepted. *Tuition:* $2300 per year full-time, $103 per credit hour part-time for state residents; $6012 per year full-time, $258 per credit hour part-time for nonresidents. *Financial aid:* Federal Work-Study, institutionally sponsored loans available. Financial aid application deadline: 3/15; applicants required to submit FAFSA. • Dr. Kenneth A. Weaver, Chair, Division of Psychology and Special Education, 316-341-5317. E-mail: weaverke@emporia.edu.

Endicott College, School of Continuing Education and Graduate Studies, Program in Special Education, Beverly, MA 01915-2096. Awards M Ed. Part-time and evening/weekend programs available. Postbaccalaureate distance learning degree programs offered (minimal on-campus study). Faculty: 4 part-time (3 women). Students: 11 full-time (all women). Average age 35. 11 applicants, 100% accepted. *Degree requirements:* Written comprehensive exams required, foreign language and thesis not required. *Entrance requirements:* MAT (minimum score 50). Application deadline: rolling. Application fee: $80. Electronic applications accepted. *Tuition:* $585 per course. *Financial aid:* Federal Work-Study, institutionally sponsored loans, and career-related internships or fieldwork available. *Faculty research:* Literacy, parent education, inclusion, school reform, technology in education. • Dr. Paul J. Tortolani, Dean, School of Continuing Education and Graduate Studies, 978-232-2199. Fax: 978-232-3000. E-mail: ptortola@endicott.edu.

Fairfield University, Graduate School of Education and Allied Professions, Department of Psychology and Special Education, Fairfield, CT 06430-5195. Offerings include special education (MA, CAS). Department faculty: 5 full-time (2 women), 10 part-time (3 women), 8 FTE. *Degree requirements:* For master's, thesis or alternative, comprehensive exams. *Entrance requirements:* For master's, PRAXIS I (CBT), TOEFL, minimum QPA of 2.67. Application deadline: 7/10 (rolling processing). Application fee: $40. *Expenses:* Tuition $350 per credit hour (minimum). Fees $20 per semester (minimum). • Dr. Margaret Deignan, Chair, 203-254-4000 Ext. 2483. Application contact: Karen Creecy, Assistant Dean, 203-254-4250. Fax: 203-254-4241. E-mail: klcreecy@fair1.fairfield.edu.

Fairleigh Dickinson University, Teaneck–Hackensack Campus, University College: Arts, Sciences, and Professional Studies, Peter Sammartino School of Education, Program in Learning Disabilities, 1000 River Road, Teaneck, NJ 07666-1914. Awards MA. Faculty: 11 full-time (8 women), 27 part-time (10 women). Students: 22 part-time (21 women); includes 1 minority (African American). Average age 39. In 1997, 6 degrees awarded. *Entrance requirements:* GRE General Test or PRAXIS, MAT. Application deadline: rolling. Application fee: $35. *Expenses:* Tuition $522 per credit. Fees $302 per year full-time, $138 per year part-time. *Faculty research:* Mathematics for students with learning disabilities, gender issues in education, social problem-solving and conflict resolution in the classroom, multicultural education in the elementary classroom, problems encountered by international students in college programs. • Dr. Mary Farrell, Director, 201-692-2808. Fax: 201-692-2813.

Fayetteville State University, Program in Special Education, 1200 Murchison Road, Fayetteville, NC 28301-4298. Awards MA Ed. Accredited by NCATE. Part-time and evening/weekend programs available. *Degree requirements:* Internship, comprehensive exam required, foreign language and thesis not required. *Entrance requirements:* GRE or MAT, minimum GPA of 3.0 during previous 2 years, 2.5 overall. Application deadline: 8/1 (rolling processing; 12/15 for spring admission). Application fee: $20. *Tuition:* $1498 per year full-time, $327 per semester (minimum) part-time for state residents; $8768 per year full-time, $2144 per semester (minimum) part-time for nonresidents.

Fitchburg State College, Program in Special Education, Fitchburg, MA 01420-2697. Offers guided study (M Ed), teaching students with intensive special needs (M Ed), teaching students with special needs (M Ed). Accredited by NCATE. Part-time and evening/weekend programs available. *Degree requirements:* Practicum required, foreign language and thesis not required. *Entrance requirements:* GRE General Test or MAT (minimum score 47), interview. Application deadline: rolling. Application fee: $10. *Expenses:* Tuition $147 per credit. Fees $55 per semester. *Financial aid:* Graduate assistantships, Federal Work-Study available. Aid available to part-time students. Financial aid application deadline: 3/30; applicants required to submit FAFSA. • Dr. Elaine Francis, Chair, 978-665-3501. Fax: 978-665-3658. E-mail: dgce@fsc.edu. Application contact: James DuPont, Director of Admissions, 978-665-3144. Fax: 978-665-4540. E-mail: admissions@fsc.edu.

Florida Atlantic University, College of Education, Department of Exceptional Student Education, Boca Raton, FL 33431-0991. Offers programs in learning disabilities, mental retardation, and emotional disturbance (M Ed); special education (Ed D); special education administration (Ed D). Accredited by NCATE. Faculty: 10 full-time (7 women), 4 part-time (2 women). Students: 13 full-time (12 women), 113 part-time (105 women). Average age 26. 130 applicants, 50% accepted. In 1997, 23 master's, 1 doctorate awarded. *Degree requirements:* For master's, written comprehensive exam required, foreign language and thesis not required; for doctorate, computer language, dissertation required, foreign language not required. *Entrance requirements:* For master's, GRE General Test (minimum combined score of 1000), minimum GPA of 3.0 during previous 2 years; for doctorate, GRE General Test (minimum combined score of 1000), GRE Subject Test. Application deadline: rolling. Application fee: $20. *Expenses:* Tuition $2520 per year full-time, $140 per credit hour part-time for state residents; $8712 per year full-time, $484 per credit hour part-time for nonresidents. Fees $5 per year (minimum). *Financial aid:* In 1997–98, 1 fellowship, 2 teaching assistantships averaging $500 per month and totaling $7,000 were awarded; career-related internships or fieldwork also available. *Faculty research:* Instructional design, assessment, educational reform, evoked potential. • Dr. Mary Lou Caldwell, Chairperson, 561-297-3280.

Florida Gulf Coast University, College of Professional Studies, School of Education, Program in Special Education, Fort Myers, FL 33965-6565. Offers behavior disorders (MA), mental retardation (MA), specific learning disabilities (MA), varying exceptionalities (MA). Faculty: 3 full-time (all women), 3 part-time (all women). Students: 40 part-time (36 women). Average age 34. In 1997, 14 degrees awarded. *Degree requirements:* Thesis or alternative required, foreign language not required. *Entrance requirements:* GRE General Test (minimum combined score of 800; average 1000), MAT (minimum score 35; average 55), minimum GPA of 3.0. Application fee: $20. Electronic applications accepted. *Faculty research:* Inclusion, portfolio assessment, professional development schools. • Application contact: Marci Green, Coordinator, 941-590-7781. E-mail: mgreene@fgcu.edu.

Florida International University, College of Education, Department of Educational Psychology and Special Education, Program in Emotional Disturbances, Miami, FL 33199. Awards MS. Accredited by NCATE. Part-time and evening/weekend programs available. Students: 0. 0 applicants. *Entrance requirements:* GRE General Test (minimum combined score of 1000) or minimum GPA of 3.0. Application deadline: 4/1 (priority date; rolling processing; 10/1 for spring admission). Application fee: $20. *Expenses:* Tuition $138 per credit hour for state residents; $482 per credit hour for nonresidents. Fees $46 per semester. *Faculty research:* Autism. • Dr. Wendy Cheyney, Chairperson, Department of Educational Psychology and Special Education, 305-348-2551. Fax: 305-348-4125.

Florida International University, College of Education, Department of Educational Psychology and Special Education, Program in Exceptional Student Education, Miami, FL 33199. Awards Ed D. Accredited by NCATE. Part-time and evening/weekend programs available. Students: 2 full-time (1 woman), 13 part-time (11 women); includes 6 minority (2 African Americans, 4 Hispanics), 1 international. Average age 39. 4 applicants, 0% accepted. In 1997, 2 degrees awarded. *Degree requirements:* Dissertation, comprehensive and qualifying exams required, foreign language not required. *Entrance requirements:* GRE General Test (minimum combined score of 1000), interview. Application deadline: 4/1 (priority date; rolling processing; 10/1 for spring admission). Application fee: $20. *Expenses:* Tuition $138 per credit hour for state residents; $482 per credit hour for nonresidents. Fees $46 per semester. *Faculty research:* Handicapped adolescents and young adults, learning disabilities. • Dr. Wendy Cheyney, Chairperson, Department of Educational Psychology and Special Education, 305-348-2551. Fax: 305-348-4125.

Florida International University, College of Education, Department of Educational Psychology and Special Education, Program in Specific Learning Disabilities, Miami, FL 33199. Awards MS. Accredited by NCATE. Part-time and evening/weekend programs available. Students: 26 full-time (22 women), 64 part-time (58 women); includes 59 minority (11 African Americans, 2 Asian Americans, 46 Hispanics), 2 international. Average age 32. 44 applicants, 39% accepted. In 1997, 45 degrees awarded. *Entrance requirements:* GRE General Test (minimum combined score of 1000) or minimum GPA of 3.0. Application deadline: 4/1 (priority date; rolling processing; 10/1 for spring admission). Application fee: $20. *Expenses:* Tuition $138 per credit hour for state residents; $482 per credit hour for nonresidents. Fees $46 per semester. *Faculty research:* Reading, brain disorders, language arts. • Dr. Wendy Cheyney, Chairperson, Department of Educational Psychology and Special Education, 305-348-2551. Fax: 305-348-4125.

Florida State University, College of Education, Department of Special Education, Tallahassee, FL 32306. Offers programs in emotional disturbance/learning disabilities (MS), mental retardation (MS), special education (PhD, Ed S), visual disabilities (MS). Faculty: 12 full-time (6 women). Students: 79 full-time (70 women), 66 part-time (53 women); includes 17 minority (10 African Americans, 2 Asian Americans, 4 Hispanics, 1 Native American). 60 applicants, 92% accepted. In 1997, 59 master's, 2 doctorates awarded. *Degree requirements:* For master's, comprehensive exam required, thesis optional; for doctorate, dissertation, comprehensive exam; for Ed S, comprehensive exam required, thesis not required. *Entrance requirements:* GRE General Test (minimum combined score of 1000), minimum GPA of 3.0. Application deadline: 7/1 (rolling processing; 11/1 for spring admission). Application fee: $20. *Tuition:* $139 per credit hour for state residents; $482 per credit hour for nonresidents. *Financial aid:* Fellowships, research assistantships, teaching assistantships, traineeships, and career-related internships or fieldwork available. *Total annual research expenditures:* $979,736. • Dr. Mark Koorland, Chair, 850-644-4880. E-mail: koorland@mail.coe.fsu.edu. Application contact: Admission Secretary, 850-644-4880. Fax: 850-644-8715.

Fordham University, Graduate School of Education, Division of Curriculum and Teaching, New York, NY 10023. Offerings include special education (MSE, Adv C). Accredited by NCATE. *Degree requirements:* For Adv C, thesis required, foreign language not required. *Application fee:* $50. • Dr. Angela Carrasquillo, Chairperson, 212-636-6427.

Fort Hays State University, College of Education, Department of Teacher Education, Program in Special Education, Hays, KS 67601-4099. Awards MS. Accredited by NCATE. Faculty: 11 full-time (7 women). Students: 2 full-time (both women), 95 part-time (91 women); includes 2 minority (both Hispanics). Average age 36. 13 applicants, 92% accepted. In 1997, 20 degrees awarded. *Entrance requirements:* GRE General Test. Application deadline: 7/1 (priority date; rolling processing). Application fee: $25 ($35 for international students). *Tuition:* $94 per credit hour for state residents; $249 per credit hour for nonresidents. *Financial aid:* Research assistantships, teaching assistantships available. *Faculty research:* Severe behavior disorders, early childhood language, multicultural speech. • Dr. Wally Guyot, Chair, Department of Teacher Education, 785-628-4212.

Framingham State College, Graduate Programs, Department of Education, Program in Special Education, Framingham, MA 01701-9101. Awards M Ed. Part-time and evening/weekend programs available. Faculty: 2 part-time. Students: 113 part-time. In 1997, 24 degrees awarded. *Entrance requirements:* MAT, interview. *Tuition:* $4184 per year full-time, $523 per course part-time for state residents; $4848 per year full-time, $606 per course part-time for nonresidents. • Application contact: Graduate Office, 508-626-4550.

Francis Marion University, School of Education, Florence, SC 29501-0547. Offerings include learning disabilities (MAT, M Ed). School faculty: 65 full-time (14 women). *Entrance requirements:* GRE General Test, MAT, or NTE. Application deadline: 8/21 (priority date; rolling processing). Application fee: $25. • Dr. Wayne Pruitt, Coordinator, 803-661-1462.

Fresno Pacific University, Graduate School, Programs in Education, Division of Special Education, Fresno, CA 93702-4709. Offers programs in learning handicapped (MA Ed), physical and health impairments (MA Ed), severely handicapped (MA Ed). Part-time and evening/weekend programs available. Faculty: 2 full-time (0 women), 15 part-time (11 women). Students: 127 part-time (91 women). *Degree requirements:* Thesis or alternative. *Application deadline:* 7/31 (rolling processing). *Application fee:* $75. *Tuition:* $250 per unit. • Dr. Peter Kopriva, Head, 209-453-2202. Fax: 209-453-2001.

Furman University, Department of Education, Greenville, SC 29613. Offerings include special education (MA Ed). *Degree requirements:* Comprehensive written exam. *Application deadline:* rolling. *Application fee:* $25. *Tuition:* $185 per credit hour. • Dr. Hazel W. Harris, Director, 864-294-2213.

Gallaudet University, School of Education and Human Services, Department of Education, Washington, DC 20002-3625. Offerings include education of deaf and hard of hearing students and multihandicapped deaf and hard of hearing students (MA, Ed S). Accredited by NCATE. *Degree requirements:* For master's, thesis optional. *Entrance requirements:* For master's, GRE General Test or MAT. Application deadline: 2/15 (priority date; rolling processing). Application fee: $50. *Expenses:* Tuition $7064 per year full-time, $392 per credit part-time. Fees $50 (one-time charge). • Dr. Barbara Bodner-Johnson, Chair, 202-651-5530. Application contact: Deborah DeStefano, Director of Admissions, 202-651-5253. Fax: 202-651-5744. E-mail: adm_destefan@gallua.bitnet.

Gallaudet University, School of Education and Human Services, Department of Administration and Supervision, Program in Special Education Administration, Washington, DC 20002-3625. Awards PhD. Accredited by NCATE. Students: 71 full-time, 37 part-time; includes 12 minority (9 African Americans, 2 Asian Americans, 1 Hispanic), 12 international. *Degree requirements:* 2 foreign languages, computer language, dissertation. *Entrance requirements:* GRE General Test or MAT, interview. Application deadline: 2/15 (priority date; rolling processing). Application fee: $50. *Expenses:* Tuition $7064 per year full-time, $392 per credit part-time. Fees $50 (one-time charge). *Financial aid:* Application deadline 8/1. • Application contact: Deborah DeStefano, Director of Admissions, 202-651-5253. Fax: 202-651-5744. E-mail: adm_destefan@gallua.bitnet.

George Mason University, Graduate School of Education, Program in Special Education, Fairfax, VA 22030-4444. Awards M Ed. Accredited by NCATE. Part-time and evening/weekend programs available. Faculty: 42 full-time (24 women), 65 part-time (51 women), 58.73 FTE. Students: 81 full-time (73 women), 260 part-time (232 women); includes 34 minority (18 African Americans, 11 Asian Americans, 3 Hispanics, 2 Native Americans), 5 international. Average age 34. 135 applicants, 85% accepted. In 1997, 81 degrees awarded. *Degree requirements:* Computer language, comprehensive exam required, foreign language and thesis not required. *Entrance requirements:* Interview, minimum GPA of 3.0 in last 60 hours. Application deadline: 5/1 (11/1 for spring admission). Application fee: $30. Electronic applications accepted. *Tuition:* $4344 per year full-time, $181 per credit hour part-time for state residents; $12,504 per year full-time, $521 per credit hour part-time for nonresidents. *Financial aid:* Career-related internships or fieldwork available. Aid available to part-time students. Financial aid application deadline: 3/1; applicants required to submit FAFSA. • Dr. Michael Behrmann, Coordinator, 703-993-2143. Fax: 703-993-2013.

The George Washington University, Graduate School of Education and Human Development, Department of Teacher Preparation and Special Education, Program in Infant Special Education, Washington, DC 20052. Awards MA Ed. Accredited by NCATE. Faculty: 2 full-time (both women), 2 part-time (both women), 3 FTE. Students: 6 full-time (all women), 5 part-time (all women); includes 2 minority (1 African American, 1 Asian American). Average age 27. 5 applicants, 100% accepted. In 1997, 10 degrees awarded. *Degree requirements:* Comprehensive exam required, foreign language and thesis not required. *Entrance requirements:* GRE General Test or MAT, minimum GPA of 2.75. Application deadline: 3/1 (priority date; rolling processing; 10/1 for spring admission). Application fee: $50. *Expenses:* Tuition $680 per semester hour. Fees $35 per semester hour. *Financial aid:* Fellowships, research assistantships, full tuition waivers, Federal Work-Study, and career-related internships or fieldwork available. Financial aid applicants required to submit FAFSA. *Faculty research:* Assessment, early intervention. • Dr. Barbara Brown, Faculty Coordinator, 202-994-6170.

The George Washington University, Graduate School of Education and Human Development, Department of Teacher Preparation and Special Education, Program in Special Education, Washington, DC 20052. Awards Ed D, Ed S. Accredited by NCATE. Faculty: 9 full-time (7 women), 4 part-time (all women), 10 FTE. Students: 7 full-time (5 women), 65 part-time (53 women); includes 19 minority (9 African Americans, 4 Asian Americans, 5 Hispanics, 1 Native American), 1 international. Average age 41. 19 applicants, 84% accepted. In 1997, 1 doctorate, 6 Ed Ss awarded. *Degree requirements:* For doctorate, dissertation, comprehensive exam required, foreign language not required; for Ed S, comprehensive exam required, thesis not required. *Entrance requirements:* GRE General Test or MAT, interview, minimum GPA of 3.3. Application deadline: 3/1 (priority date; rolling processing; 10/1 for spring admission). Application fee: $50. *Expenses:* Tuition $680 per semester hour. Fees $35 per semester hour. *Financial aid:* Fellowships, research assistantships, partial tuition waivers, Federal Work-Study, and career-related internships or fieldwork available. Financial aid applicants required to submit FAFSA. • Dr. Carol Kochhar, Faculty Coordinator, 202-994-6170.

The George Washington University, Graduate School of Education and Human Development, Department of Teacher Preparation and Special Education, Program in Special Education of Seriously Emotionally Disturbed Students, Washington, DC 20052. Awards MA Ed. Accredited by NCATE. Faculty: 2 full-time (both women), 1 (woman) part-time. Students: 15 full-time (11 women), 4 part-time (1 woman); includes 3 minority (all African Americans), 1 international. Average age 30. 11 applicants, 91% accepted. In 1997, 3 degrees awarded. *Degree requirements:* Comprehensive exam required, foreign language and thesis not required. *Entrance requirements:* GRE General Test or MAT, interview, minimum GPA of 2.75. Application deadline: 3/1 (priority date; rolling processing; 10/1 for spring admission). Application fee: $50. *Expenses:* Tuition $680 per semester hour. Fees $35 per semester hour. *Financial aid:* Fellowships, Federal Work-Study, and career-related internships or fieldwork available. Financial aid applicants required to submit FAFSA. *Faculty research:* Action research on the act of teaching emotionally disturbed students, teacher training. • Dr. Rita K. Ives, Faculty Co-Coordinator, 202-994-6170. Fax: 202-994-3365. Application contact: Dr. Nancy Belknap, Faculty Co-Coordinator, 202-994-6170.

The George Washington University, Graduate School of Education and Human Development, Department of Teacher Preparation and Special Education, Program in Special Education/Early Childhood, Washington, DC 20052. Awards MA Ed. Accredited by NCATE. Faculty: 3 full-time, 4 part-time, 4 FTE. Students: 8 full-time (all women), 28 part-time (27 women); includes 8 minority (7 African Americans, 1 Asian American), 1 international. Average age 34. 35 applicants, 91% accepted. In 1997, 7 degrees awarded. *Degree requirements:* Comprehensive exam required, foreign language and thesis not required. *Entrance requirements:* GRE General Test or MAT, minimum GPA of 2.75. Application deadline: 3/1 (priority date; rolling processing; 10/1 for spring admission). Application fee: $50. *Expenses:* Tuition $680 per semester hour. Fees $35 per semester hour. *Financial aid:* Fellowships, full tuition waivers, Federal Work-Study, and career-related internships or fieldwork available. Financial aid applicants required to submit FAFSA. *Faculty research:* Computer-assisted instruction and learning, disabled learner assessment of preschool, handicapped children. • Dr. Michael Castleberry, Faculty Coordinator, 202-994-6170.

The George Washington University, Graduate School of Education and Human Development, Department of Teacher Preparation and Special Education, Program in Transitional Special Education, Washington, DC 20052. Awards MA Ed, Certificate. Accredited by NCATE. Evening/weekend programs available. Faculty: 3 full-time (2 women). Students: 7 full-time (6 women), 21 part-time (16 women); includes 3 minority (2 African Americans, 1 Hispanic). Average age 33. 4 applicants, 100% accepted. In 1997, 16 master's awarded. *Degree requirements:* For master's, comprehensive exam required, foreign language and thesis not required. *Entrance requirements:* For master's, GRE General Test or MAT, interview, minimum GPA of 2.75. Application deadline: 3/1 (priority date; rolling processing; 10/1 for spring admission). Application fee: $50. *Expenses:* Tuition $680 per semester hour. Fees $35 per semester hour. *Financial aid:* Fellowships, research assistantships, stipends, full and partial tuition waivers, Federal Work-Study, and career-related internships or fieldwork available. *Faculty research:* Computer applications for transition, transition follow-up research, curriculum-based vocational assessment, traumatic brain injury. • Dr. Carol Kochhar, Faculty Coordinator, 202-994-6170.

Georgia College and State University, School of Education, Department of Special Education and Administration, Program in Special Education, Milledgeville, GA 31061. Offers behavior disorders (M Ed). Accredited by NCATE. Students: 52 full-time (46 women), 51 part-time (48 women); includes 21 minority (all African Americans), 1 international. Average age 34. In 1997, 36 degrees awarded. *Degree requirements:* Computer language, comprehensive exit exam required, foreign language and thesis not required. *Entrance requirements:* GRE General Test (minimum combined score of 800) or NTE (minimum score 550 on each core battery test), MAT (minimum score 44), minimum GPA of 2.5, NT-4 certificate. Application deadline: 7/31 (priority date; rolling processing). Application fee: $10. *Financial aid:* Assistantships, Federal Work-Study, and career-related internships or fieldwork available. Aid available to part-time students. Financial aid application deadline: 4/15. • Dr. Craig Smith, Chairperson, Department of Special Education and Administration, 912-445-4577.

Georgian Court College, Program in Education, Lakewood, NJ 08701-2697. Offerings include special education (MA). *Application deadline:* 8/25 (rolling processing; 1/15 for spring admission). *Application fee:* $30. *Tuition:* $350 per credit. • Application contact: Renee Loew, Director of Graduate Admissions and Records, 732-367-1717. Fax: 732-364-4516.

Georgia Southern University, College of Education, Department of Leadership, Technology, and Human Development, Program in Special Education for Exceptional Children, Statesboro, GA 30460-8126. Awards M Ed, Ed S. Accredited by NCATE. Part-time and evening/weekend programs available. Students: 28 full-time (26 women), 38 part-time (35 women); includes 8 minority (6 African Americans, 1 Hispanic, 1 Native American). Average age 33. 28 applicants, 71% accepted. In 1997, 25 master's, 5 Ed Ss awarded. *Degree requirements:* Exams required, foreign language and thesis not required. *Entrance requirements:* For master's, GRE General Test (minimum score 450 on each section) or MAT (minimum score 44), minimum GPA of 2.5; for Ed S, GRE General Test (minimum score 450 on each section) or MAT (minimum score 49), minimum graduate GPA of 3.25. Application deadline: 7/15 (priority date; rolling processing; 11/15 for spring admission). Application fee: $0. Electronic applications accepted. *Tuition:* $2619 per year full-time, $287 per semester (minimum) part-time for state residents; $8619 per year full-time, $1037 per semester (minimum) part-time for nonresidents. *Financial aid:* Research assistantships, teaching assistantships, Federal Work-Study, and career-related internships or fieldwork available. Aid available to part-time students. Financial aid application deadline: 4/15. *Faculty research:* Learning disorders, behavior disorders, education of the mentally retarded. • Application contact: Dr. John R. Diebolt, Associate Graduate Dean, 912-681-5384. Fax: 912-681-0740. E-mail: gradschool@gsvms2.cc.gasou.edu.

Georgia State University, College of Education, Department of Educational Psychology and Special Education, Program in Communication Disorders, Atlanta, GA 30303-3083. Awards M Ed. Students: 37 full-time (36 women), 14 part-time (all women); includes 6 minority (all African Americans). Average age 26. 201 applicants, 9% accepted. In 1997, 15 degrees awarded. *Degree requirements:* Comprehensive exams. *Entrance requirements:* GRE General Test (minimum combined score of 885), minimum GPA of 3.0. Application deadline: 2/15. Application fee: $25. *Expenses:* Tuition $2673 per year full-time, $99 per semester hour part-time for state residents; $10,692 per year full-time, $396 per semester hour part-time for nonresidents. Fees $228 per year. *Financial aid:* Research assistantships available. *Faculty research:* Language development, minority students. • Dr. Ron P. Colarusso, Chair, Department of Educational Psychology and Special Education, 404-651-2310.

Georgia State University, College of Education, Department of Educational Psychology and Special Education, Program in Education of Behavior/Learning Disabled, Atlanta, GA 30303-3083. Awards M Ed. Accredited by NCATE. Students: 77 full-time (62 women), 96 part-time (81 women); includes 23 minority (21 African Americans, 1 Asian American, 1 Native American), 2 international. Average age 31. 77 applicants, 55% accepted. In 1997, 85 degrees awarded. *Entrance requirements:* GRE General Test (minimum combined score of 800) or MAT (minimum score 44). Application deadline: 7/15 (1/15 for spring admission). Application fee: $25. *Expenses:* Tuition $2673 per year full-time, $99 per semester hour part-time for state residents; $10,692 per year full-time, $396 per semester hour part-time for nonresidents. Fees $228 per year. *Financial aid:* Research assistantships available. *Faculty research:* Inclusion, behavior management, basic teaching strategies. • Dr. Ron P. Colarusso, Chair, Department of Educational Psychology and Special Education, 404-651-2310.

Georgia State University, College of Education, Department of Educational Psychology and Special Education, Program in Education of the Hearing Impaired, Atlanta, GA 30303-3083. Awards M Ed. Students: 10 full-time (9 women), 7 part-time (all women); includes 2 minority (both African Americans). Average age 27. 11 applicants, 91% accepted. In 1997, 10 degrees awarded. *Degree requirements:* Comprehensive exams. *Entrance requirements:* GRE General Test (minimum combined score of 800) or MAT (minimum score 44), minimum GPA of 2.5. Application deadline: 7/15 (1/15 for spring admission). Application fee: $25. *Expenses:* Tuition $2673 per year full-time, $99 per semester hour part-time for state residents; $10,692 per year full-time, $396 per semester hour part-time for nonresidents. Fees $228 per year. *Faculty research:* Language acquisition in deaf children. • Dr. Ron P. Colarusso, Chair, Department of Educational Psychology and Special Education, 404-651-2310.

Georgia State University, College of Education, Department of Educational Psychology and Special Education, Program in Exceptionalities, Atlanta, GA 30303-3083. Offers exceptionalities (PhD). Accredited by NCATE. Students: 5 full-time (all women), 10 part-time (9 women); includes 3 minority (all African Americans). Average age 37. 1 applicant, 100% accepted. In 1997, 5 degrees awarded. *Degree requirements:* Dissertation, comprehensive exam. *Entrance requirements:* GRE General Test (minimum score 500 on verbal section, 500 on either quantitative or analytical sections) or MAT (minimum score 53), minimum GPA of 3.3. Application deadline: 4/1 (10/1 for spring admission). Application fee: $25. *Expenses:* Tuition $2673 per year full-time, $99 per semester hour part-time for state residents; $10,692 per year full-time, $396 per semester hour part-time for nonresidents. Fees $228 per year. • Dr. Ron P. Colarusso, Chair, Department of Educational Psychology and Special Education, 404-651-2310.

Georgia State University, College of Education, Department of Educational Psychology and Special Education, Program in Special Education, Atlanta, GA 30303-3083. Awards Ed S. Accredited by NCATE. Students: 3 full-time (all women), 21 part-time (18 women); includes 2 minority (1 African American, 1 Hispanic). Average age 42. 12 applicants, 75% accepted. In 1997, 9 degrees awarded. *Degree requirements:* Comprehensive exams, project. *Entrance requirements:* GRE General Test (minimum combined score of 900) or MAT (minimum score 48), minimum graduate GPA of 3.25. Application deadline: 7/15 (1/15 for spring admission). Application fee: $25. *Expenses:* Tuition $2673 per year full-time, $99 per semester hour part-time for state residents; $10,692 per year full-time, $396 per semester hour part-time for nonresidents. Fees $228 per year. *Financial aid:* Research assistantships, Federal Work-Study, institutionally sponsored loans, and career-related internships or fieldwork available. Aid available to part-time students. • Dr. Ron P. Colarusso, Chair, Department of Educational Psychology and Special Education, 404-651-2310.

Gonzaga University, Graduate School, School of Education, Program in Special Education, Spokane, WA 99258-0001. Awards MES. Accredited by NCATE. Faculty: 5 full-time (1 woman), 4 part-time (1 woman). Students: 14 full-time (11 women); includes 3 international. Average age 38. 9 applicants, 56% accepted. In 1997, 5 degrees awarded. *Degree requirements:* Comprehensive exam required, foreign language and thesis not required. *Entrance requirements:* GRE General Test or MAT, TOEFL (minimum score 550), minimum B average in undergraduate course work. Application deadline: 7/20 (priority date; rolling processing; 11/1 for spring admission). Application fee: $40. *Tuition:* $7380 per year (minimum) full-time, $410 per credit (minimum) part-time. *Financial aid:* Teaching assistantships available. Aid available to part-time students. Financial aid application deadline: 3/1. • Dr. Thomas F. McLaughlin, Chairman, 509-328-4220 Ext. 3508.

Governors State University, College of Education, Division of Education, Program in Multi-Categorical Special Education, University Park, IL 60466. Awards MA. Part-time and evening/weekend programs available. Faculty: 2 full-time (both women), 3 part-time (1 woman). Average age 35. In 1997, 11 degrees awarded. *Degree requirements:* Computer language, comprehensive exam, practicum required, foreign language and thesis not required. *Entrance*

Directory: Special Education

Governors State University (continued)
requirements: Minimum GPA of 2.75 in last 60 hours of undergraduate course work, 3.0 in any graduate work attempted. Application deadline: 7/15 (priority date; rolling processing; 11/10 for spring admission). Application fee: $0. *Expenses:* Tuition $1140 per trimester full-time, $95 per credit hour part-time for state residents; $3420 per trimester full-time, $285 per credit hour part-time for nonresidents. Fees $95 per trimester. *Financial aid:* Full and partial tuition waivers, Federal Work-Study, institutionally sponsored loans, and career-related internships or fieldwork available. Aid available to part-time students. Financial aid application deadline: 5/1. • Application contact: Nick Battaglia, Adviser, 708-534-4393.

Grand Valley State University, School of Education, Program in Special Education, Allendale, MI 49401-9403. Offers learning disabilities (M Ed), pre-primary impaired (M Ed), special education administration (M Ed). Accredited by NCATE. Part-time and evening/weekend programs available. Faculty: 4 full-time (1 woman), 23 part-time (9 women). Students: 12 full-time (10 women), 161 part-time (132 women); includes 3 minority (1 African American, 2 Native Americans). Average age 35. 85 applicants, 93% accepted. In 1997, 46 degrees awarded (100% found work related to degree). *Degree requirements:* Thesis or alternative, applied research project. *Entrance requirements:* GRE General Test (minimum combined score of 1300) or minimum GPA of 3.0. Application deadline: rolling. Application fee: $20. *Financial aid:* In 1997–98, 1 research assistantship was awarded; career-related internships or fieldwork also available. *Faculty research:* Evaluation of special education program effects, adaptive behavior assessment, language development, writing disorders, comparative effects of presentation methods. • Dr. James Grant, Coordinator, 616-771-6650. Application contact: Admissions Office, 616-895-2025. Fax: 616-895-3081.

Hampton University, Department of Education, Program in Special Education, Hampton, VA 23668. Awards MA. Accredited by NCATE. Part-time and evening/weekend programs available. Faculty: 6 full-time (5 women), 2 part-time (0 women). Students: 4 full-time (2 women), 2 part-time (1 woman); includes 4 minority (all African Americans). In 1997, 8 degrees awarded. *Entrance requirements:* GRE General Test (minimum score 450 on verbal section). Application deadline: 6/1 (priority date; rolling processing; 11/1 for spring admission). Application fee: $25. *Expenses:* Tuition $9038 per year full-time, $220 per credit part-time. Fees $70 per year. *Financial aid:* Fellowships, research assistantships, teaching assistantships, scholarships, Federal Work-Study, institutionally sponsored loans, and career-related internships or fieldwork available. Aid available to part-time students. Financial aid application deadline: 5/1; applicants required to submit FAFSA. • Dr. Joann Haysbert, Coordinator, 757-727-5793. Application contact: Erika Henderson, Director, Graduate Programs, 757-727-5454. Fax: 757-727-5084.

Henderson State University, School of Education, Department of Special Education, Arkadelphia, AR 71999-0001. Offers programs in early childhood/special education (MSE), education of the mildly handicapped (MSE). Accredited by NCATE. Part-time programs available. Postbaccalaureate distance learning degree programs offered (minimal on-campus study). Students: 12 full-time (8 women), 16 part-time (13 women); includes 6 minority (5 African Americans, 1 Native American). Average age 33. In 1997, 17 degrees awarded. *Entrance requirements:* GRE General Test or MAT, minimum GPA of 2.7. Application deadline: 7/31 (priority date; rolling processing). Application fee: $0. Electronic applications accepted. *Expenses:* Tuition $120 per credit hour for state residents; $240 per credit hour for nonresidents. Fees $105 per semester (minimum) full-time, $52 per semester (minimum) part-time. *Financial aid:* Research assistantships, Federal Work-Study, institutionally sponsored loans available. Aid available to part-time students. Financial aid application deadline: 7/31. • Kenneth Harris, Chairperson, 870-230-5203. Fax: 870-230-5455. E-mail: harris@holly.hsu.edu.

Heritage College, Graduate Program in Education, Program in Professional Development, Toppenish, WA 98948-9599. Offerings include special education (M Ed). *Degree requirements:* Comprehensive exam required, thesis optional, foreign language not required. *Application deadline:* rolling. *Application fee:* $35 ($75 for international students). *Tuition:* $270 per credit. • Application contact: Dr. Robert Plumb, Chair, 509-865-2244.

Hofstra University, School of Education and Allied Human Services, Department of Counseling, Research, Special Education and Rehabilitation, Program in Special Education, Hempstead, NY 11549. Offers consultation in special education (CAS), early childhood special education (MS Ed, CAS), emotional disturbance (MS Ed), learning disability (MS Ed), mental retardation (MS Ed), physical disability (MS Ed), special education (MA, MPS, PD), special education and reading (PD), special education assessment and diagnosis (CAS). Accredited by NCATE. Part-time and evening/weekend programs available. Faculty: 5 full-time (2 women), 9 part-time (6 women). Students: 23 full-time (21 women), 142 part-time (132 women); includes 3 minority (1 African American, 1 Asian American, 1 Native American), 1 international. Average age 30. 111 applicants, 50% accepted. In 1997, 67 master's awarded. *Degree requirements:* For master's, comprehensive exam, departmental qualifying exam, thesis (MA) required, foreign language not required; for other advanced degree, comprehensive exam. *Entrance requirements:* For master's, interview, minimum GPA of 2.9; for other advanced degree, interview, minimum GPA of 2.9, 1 year of professional experience. Application deadline: rolling. Application fee: $40 ($75 for international students). *Expenses:* Tuition $10,968 per year full-time, $457 per credit hour part-time. Fees $670 per year full-time, $112 per semester (minimum) part-time. *Financial aid:* 15 students received aid; fellowships, research assistantships, scholarships, partial tuition waivers, institutionally sponsored loans, and career-related internships or fieldwork available. Aid available to part-time students. Financial aid applicants required to submit FAFSA. *Faculty research:* Portfolio assessment, mediated learning, technology and disability. • Dr. Frank Bowe, Coordinator, 516-463-5782. Fax: 516-463-6502. E-mail: serfgb@hofstra.edu. Application contact: Mary Beth Carey, Dean of Admissions, 516-463-6700. Fax: 516-560-7660. E-mail: hofstra@hofstra.edu.

Hood College, Department of Education, Frederick, MD 21701-8575. Offerings include curriculum and instruction (MS), with options in early childhood education, elementary education, elementary school science and mathematics, reading, secondary education, special education. *Entrance requirements:* Minimum GPA of 2.5. Application deadline: rolling. Application fee: $30. *Tuition:* $285 per credit. • Dr. Patricia Bartlett, Chairperson, 301-696-3471. E-mail: bartlett@nimue.hood.edu. Application contact: Hood College Graduate School, 301-696-3600. Fax: 301-696-3597. E-mail: postmaster@nimue.hood.edu.

Houston Baptist University, College of Education and Behavioral Sciences, Programs in Education, Houston, TX 77074-3298. Offerings include generic special education (M Ed). Faculty: 9 full-time (5 women), 4 part-time (3 women). *Degree requirements:* Comprehensive exam required, foreign language and thesis not required. *Entrance requirements:* GRE General Test (minimum combined score of 850), minimum GPA of 2.5, teaching certificate. Application deadline: 7/1 (priority date; rolling processing; 1/1 for spring admission). Application fee: $25 ($85 for international students). *Expenses:* Tuition $280 per semester hour. Fees $235 per quarter. • Dr. John Lutjemeier, Head, 281-649-3000 Ext. 2336. Application contact: Judy Ferguson, Program Assistant, 281-649-3241.

Howard University, School of Education, Department of Curriculum and Instruction, Program in Special Education, 2400 Sixth Street, NW, Washington, DC 20059-0002. Awards MA, M Ed, CAGS. Accredited by NCATE. MA offered through the Graduate School of Arts and Sciences. Part-time programs available. Faculty: 3 full-time (2 women). Students: 7. In 1997, 1 master's awarded. *Degree requirements:* For master's, thesis (for some programs), comprehensive exam, expository writing exam, internships, practicum required, foreign language not required. *Entrance requirements:* For master's, GRE General Test, minimum GPA of 2.7; for CAGS, GRE General Test, minimum graduate GPA of 3.0. Application deadline: 4/1 (priority date; rolling processing; 11/1 for spring admission). Application fee: $45. *Expenses:* Tuition $10,200 per year full-time, $567 per credit hour part-time. Fees $405 per year. *Financial aid:* Fellowships, research assistantships, teaching assistantships, grants, scholarships, full and partial tuition waivers, Federal Work-Study, institutionally sponsored loans, and career-related internships or fieldwork available. Financial aid application deadline: 4/1. • Dr. Will Johnson, Coordinator, 202-806-7343.

Hunter College of the City University of New York, Division of Education, Department of Special Education, 695 Park Avenue, New York, NY 10021-5085. Awards MS Ed. Part-time and evening/weekend programs available. *Degree requirements:* Comprehensive exam required, foreign language and thesis not required. *Entrance requirements:* TOEFL (minimum score 600), minimum GPA of 2.7. Application deadline: 4/28 (rolling processing; 11/21 for spring admission). Application fee: $40. *Expenses:* Tuition $4350 per year full-time, $185 per credit part-time for state residents; $7600 per year full-time, $320 per credit part-time for nonresidents. Fees $26 per year. *Faculty research:* Mathematics learning disabilities; street behavior; assessment; bilingual special education; families, diversity, and disabilities.

Idaho State University, College of Education, Division I, Pocatello, ID 83209. Offerings include human exceptionality–special education (M Ed), special education (Ed S). One or more programs accredited by NCATE. Postbaccalaureate distance learning degree programs offered (no on-campus study). Division faculty: 19 full-time (8 women), 4 part-time (0 women). *Degree requirements:* Oral exam, written exam required, thesis optional, foreign language not required. *Average time to degree:* master's–2 years full-time, 4 years part-time; other advanced degree–1 year full-time, 2 years part-time. *Entrance requirements:* For master's, GRE General Test (score in 35th percentile or higher on one section) or MAT (minimum score 48), minimum undergraduate GPA of 3.0; for Ed S, GRE, minimum graduate GPA of 3.0. Application deadline: 7/1 (priority date; rolling processing; 12/1 for spring admission). Application fee: $30. *Tuition:* $3130 per year full-time, $136 per credit hour part-time for state residents; $9370 per year full-time, $226 per credit hour part-time for nonresidents. • Dr. Peter Denner, Director, 208-236-4230. E-mail: dennpete@isu.edu. Application contact: Dr. Stephanie Salzman, Director, Office of Standards and Assessment, 208-236-3114. Fax: 208-236-4697. E-mail: salzstep@isu.edu.

Idaho State University, College of Health Professions, Department of Speech Pathology and Audiology, Pocatello, ID 83209. Offerings include deaf education (MS). Department faculty: 15 full-time (8 women), 5 part-time (3 women). *Degree requirements:* Thesis optional, foreign language not required. *Entrance requirements:* GRE General Test, minimum GPA of 3.0. Application deadline: 2/1 (priority date). Application fee: $30. *Tuition:* $3130 per year full-time, $136 per credit hour part-time for state residents; $9370 per year full-time, $226 per credit hour part-time for nonresidents. • Dr. David Sorensen, Chairman, 208-236-3495. Fax: 208-236-4571. Application contact: Dr. Thayne Smedley, Director of Graduate Studies, 208-236-2190.

Illinois State University, College of Education, Department of Specialized Educational Development, Program in Special Education, Normal, IL 61790-2200. Awards MA, MS, MS Ed, Ed D. Accredited by NCATE. Students: 44 full-time (37 women), 107 part-time (90 women); includes 14 minority (11 African Americans, 3 Hispanics), 1 international. 35 applicants, 91% accepted. In 1997, 46 master's, 4 doctorates awarded. *Degree requirements:* For master's, thesis or alternative; for doctorate, variable foreign language requirement, dissertation, 2 terms of residency. *Entrance requirements:* For master's, GRE General Test (minimum combined score of 800), minimum GPA of 3.0 in last 60 hours; for doctorate, GRE General Test. Application deadline: rolling. Application fee: $0. *Expenses:* Tuition $2454 per year full-time, $102 per hour part-time for state residents; $7362 per year full-time, $307 per hour part-time for nonresidents. Fees $1048 per year full-time, $44 per hour part-time. *Financial aid:* Full tuition waivers available. Financial aid application deadline: 4/1. • Dr. Paula Smith, Chairperson, Department of Specialized Educational Development, 309-438-5419.

Indiana State University, School of Education, Department of Communication Disorders and Special Education, Terre Haute, IN 47809-1401. Offers programs in director of special education (M Ed), gifted/talented education (MA, MS, Ed S), special education (MA, MS, PhD), speech pathology and audiology (MA, MS). One or more programs accredited by NCATE. Part-time and evening/weekend programs available. Faculty: 14 full-time (8 women). Students: 28 full-time (all women), 9 part-time (7 women); includes 1 international. Average age 31. 52 applicants, 21% accepted. In 1997, 14 master's awarded. Terminal master's awarded for partial completion of doctoral program. *Degree requirements:* For doctorate, 2 foreign languages, computer language, dissertation; for Ed S, computer language, thesis. *Entrance requirements:* For master's, minimum undergraduate GPA of 2.5; for doctorate, GRE General Test (minimum score 500 on each section), minimum undergraduate GPA of 3.5; for Ed S, GRE General Test (minimum combined score of 900), minimum graduate GPA of 3.25. Application deadline: rolling. Application fee: $20. *Tuition:* $143 per credit hour for state residents; $325 per credit hour for nonresidents. *Financial aid:* In 1997–98, 6 research assistantships (5 to first-year students) were awarded; fellowships, teaching assistantships, institutionally sponsored loans also available. Aid available to part-time students. Financial aid application deadline: 3/1. *Faculty research:* Vocational/transitional programs, social adjustment, consultation with regular education, microcomputers, stuttering. • Dr. Raymond Quist, Chairperson, 812-237-3585.

Indiana University Bloomington, School of Education, Department of Curriculum and Instruction, Program in Special Education, Bloomington, IN 47405. Awards MS, Ed D, PhD, Ed S. Accredited by NCATE. PhD offered through the University Graduate School. Part-time and evening/weekend programs available. Faculty: 7 full-time (3 women). Students: 15 full-time (14 women), 28 part-time (22 women); includes 6 international. 2 applicants. In 1997, 18 master's, 1 doctorate awarded. Terminal master's awarded for partial completion of doctoral program. *Degree requirements:* For master's, thesis optional, foreign language not required; for doctorate, dissertation required, foreign language not required; for Ed S, comprehensive exam or project required, foreign language not required. *Entrance requirements:* For master's, GRE General Test (minimum combined score of 1300 on three sections), teaching experience; for doctorate and Ed S, GRE General Test (minimum combined score of 1500 on three sections). Application deadline: 3/1 (priority date; rolling processing). Application fee: $35. *Expenses:* Tuition $153 per credit hour for state residents; $446 per credit hour for nonresidents. Fees $343 per year. *Financial aid:* Fellowships, research assistantships, teaching assistantships, Federal Work-Study available. Aid available to part-time students. Financial aid application deadline: 3/1. *Faculty research:* Learning disabilities, emotional/behavioral disturbances, microcomputer technology, severe disabilities and gifted/talented. • Dr. James McLeskey, Chair, 812-856-8111.

Indiana University of Pennsylvania, College of Education, Department of Special Education and Clinical Services, Program in Education of Exceptional Persons, Indiana, PA 15705-1087. Awards M Ed. Accredited by NCATE. Students: 5 full-time (all women), 12 part-time (11 women). Average age 26. 10 applicants, 70% accepted. In 1997, 3 degrees awarded. *Degree requirements:* Thesis optional, foreign language not required. *Entrance requirements:* TOEFL (minimum score 500). Application deadline: 7/1 (priority date; rolling processing; 11/1 for spring admission). Application fee: $30. *Expenses:* Tuition $3468 per year full-time, $193 per credit part-time for state residents; $6236 per year full-time, $346 per credit part-time for nonresidents. Fees $313 per year (minimum) full-time, $84 per year part-time. *Financial aid:* Research assistantships, Federal Work-Study, and career-related internships or fieldwork available. Aid available to part-time students. Financial aid application deadline: 3/15. • Dr. Dianne Ferrell, Graduate Coordinator, 724-357-5677. E-mail: dferrell@grove.iup.edu.

Indiana University–Purdue University Indianapolis, School of Education, Department of Special Education, Indianapolis, IN 46202-2896. Awards MS. Faculty: 3 full-time (1 woman), 4 part-time (1 woman). Students: 1 (woman) full-time, 32 part-time (26 women); includes 2 minority (1 African American, 1 Hispanic), 2 international. Average age 32. In 1997, 15 degrees awarded. *Degree requirements:* Thesis optional, foreign language not required. *Entrance requirements:* GRE General Test (minimum combined score of 1300), minimum GPA of 3.0. Application deadline: 3/1 (priority date; 11/1 for spring admission). Application fee: $35. *Expenses:* Tuition $3602 per year full-time, $150 per credit hour part-time for state residents; $10,392 per year full-time, $433 per credit hour part-time for nonresidents. Fees $100 per year (minimum) full-time, $40 per year (minimum) part-time. *Financial aid:* Federal Work-Study available. *Faculty research:* Statewide system change, personnel training for low-incidence handicapped students, school-to-work transitions. Total annual research expenditures: $150,501. • Marilyn Friend, Coordinator, 317-274-6807. Application contact: Dr. O. Gilbert Brown, Assistant Dean for Education Student Services, 317-274-0649. Fax: 317-274-6864. E-mail: ogbrown@iupui.edu.

Indiana University South Bend, Division of Education, Department of Special Education, South Bend, IN 46634-7111. Awards MS Ed. Accredited by NCATE. Part-time and evening/weekend programs available. Faculty: 3 full-time (0 women), 2 part-time (1 woman), 4 FTE. Students: 42 full-time (38 women), 113 part-time (92 women); includes 5 minority (4 African Americans, 1 Native American). Average age 36. 34 applicants, 100% accepted. In 1997, 37 degrees awarded. *Degree requirements:* Thesis or alternative, exit project required, foreign language not required. *Entrance requirements:* TOEFL (minimum score 550). Application deadline: rolling. Application fee: $35 ($40 for international students). *Expenses:* Tuition $3024 per year full-time, $126 per credit hour part-time for state residents; $7320 per year full-time, $305 per credit hour part-time for nonresidents. Fees $222 per year full-time, $34 per semester (minimum) part-time. *Financial aid:* Federal Work-Study available. Aid available to part-time students. Financial aid application deadline: 3/1. • Dr. Curtis Leggett, Director, 219-237-4328. Fax: 219-237-4550. E-mail: cleggett@iusb.edu. Application contact: Graduate Director, 219-237-4183. Fax: 219-237-6549.

Inter American University of Puerto Rico, Metropolitan Campus, Division of Education, Program in Special Education, San Juan, PR 00919-1293. Awards MA Ed. *Degree requirements:* Comprehensive exam. *Entrance requirements:* GRE or PAEG, interview. Application deadline: 5/15 (priority date; rolling processing; 11/15 for spring admission). Application fee: $31. Electronic applications accepted. *Expenses:* Tuition $3272 per year full-time, $1740 per year part-time. Fees $328 per year full-time, $176 per year part-time. • Application contact: Jenny Maldonado, Administrative Assistant, 787-250-1912 Ext. 2393. Fax: 787-250-1197.

Inter American University of Puerto Rico, San Germán Campus, Department of Education, Program in Special Education, San Germán, PR 00683-5008. Awards MS Ed. Part-time and evening/weekend programs available. Faculty: 8 full-time (1 woman), 13 part-time (7 women). In 1997, 6 degrees awarded. *Degree requirements:* Comprehensive exam required, foreign language and thesis not required. *Entrance requirements:* Minimum GPA of 3.0, GRE General Test, or PAEG. Application deadline: 4/30 (priority date; rolling processing; 11/15 for spring admission). Application fee: $31. *Expenses:* Tuition $150 per credit. Fees $177 per semester. *Financial aid:* Teaching assistantships available. • Application contact: Mildred Camacho, Admissions Director, 787-892-3090. Fax: 787-892-6350.

Iowa State University of Science and Technology, College of Education, Department of Curriculum and Instruction, Program in Special Education, Ames, IA 50011. Awards MS. *Degree requirements:* Thesis or alternative. *Entrance requirements:* TOEFL. Application deadline: 6/1 (priority date; 9/1 for spring admission). Application fee: $20 ($30 for international students). *Expenses:* Tuition $3166 per year full-time, $176 per credit part-time for state residents; $9324 per year full-time, $518 per credit part-time for nonresidents. Fees $200 per year. • Application contact: Daniel Robinson, 515-294-1241.

Jackson State University, School of Education, Department of Special Education and Rehabilitative Services, Jackson, MS 39217. Awards MS Ed, Ed S. Accredited by NCATE. Evening/weekend programs available. Faculty: 9 full-time (7 women), 3 part-time (1 woman). Students: 7 full-time (4 women), 17 part-time (12 women); includes 22 minority (all African Americans). 38 applicants, 63% accepted. In 1997, 10 master's awarded. *Degree requirements:* For master's, thesis or alternative, comprehensive exam. *Entrance requirements:* For master's, GRE General Test (minimum combined score of 1000), TOEFL (minimum score 550). Application deadline: 3/1 (priority date; rolling processing; 10/1 for spring admission). Application fee: $20. *Tuition:* $2688 per year (minimum) full-time, $150 per semester hour part-time for state residents; $5546 per year (minimum) full-time, $309 per semester hour part-time for nonresidents. *Financial aid:* Federal Work-Study available. Financial aid application deadline: 3/1. • Dr. Celestine R. Jefferson, Chair, 601-968-2370. Fax: 601-968-2213. Application contact: Mae Robinson, Admissions Coordinator, 601-968-2455. Fax: 601-968-8246. E-mail: mrobinson@ccaix.jsums.edu.

Jacksonville State University, College of Education, Program in Special Education, Jacksonville, AL 36265-9982. Awards MS Ed. Accredited by NCATE. Faculty: 3 full-time (2 women). Students: 23 full-time (22 women), 47 part-time (38 women); includes 18 minority (all African Americans). In 1997, 29 degrees awarded. *Degree requirements:* Thesis optional. *Entrance requirements:* GRE General Test or MAT. Application deadline: rolling. Application fee: $20. *Expenses:* Tuition $2140 per year full-time, $107 per semester hour part-time for state residents; $4280 per year full-time, $214 per semester hour part-time for nonresidents. Fees $30 per semester. *Financial aid:* Available to part-time students. Financial aid application deadline: 4/1. • Application contact: College of Graduate Studies and Continuing Education, 205-782-5329.

Jacksonville University, College of Arts and Sciences, Division of Education, 2800 University Boulevard North, Jacksonville, FL 32211-3394. Offerings include exceptional child education (Certificate). *Average time to degree:* master's–1.5 years full-time, 2.5 years part-time. *Entrance requirements:* TOEFL (minimum score 500). Application deadline: 8/1 (priority date; rolling processing; 11/1 for spring admission). Application fee: $25.

James Madison University, College of Education and Psychology, School of Education, Program in Special Education, Harrisonburg, VA 22807. Awards M Ed. Accredited by NCATE. Part-time programs available. Students: 23 full-time (19 women), 28 part-time (23 women); includes 1 minority (Asian American), 1 international. Average age 30. In 1997, 34 degrees awarded. *Entrance requirements:* GRE General Test. Application deadline: 7/1 (priority date; rolling processing). Application fee: $50. *Tuition:* $134 per credit hour for state residents; $404 per credit hour for nonresidents. *Financial aid:* In 1997–98, 8 assistantships totaling $63,332 were awarded; fellowships, teaching assistantships, Federal Work-Study also available. Financial aid application deadline: 2/15; applicants required to submit FAFSA. • Dr. J. Gerald Minskoff, Coordinator, 540-568-6193.

Johns Hopkins University, School of Continuing Studies, Division of Education, Department of Special Education, Baltimore, MD 21218-2699. Offers programs in autism (Certificate), inclusion (Certificate), learning disabilities (CAGS), severely and profoundly handicapped (CAGS), special education (MS, Ed D). *Degree requirements:* For doctorate, dissertation, comprehensive exam required, foreign language not required. *Entrance requirements:* For master's, minimum GPA of 3.0, interview; for doctorate, MAT, interview, master's degree, minimum GPA of 3.25; for other advanced degree, master's or doctoral degree. Application fee: $50. • Michael Rosenberg, Chair, 410-516-8275.

Johnson State College, Graduate Program in Education, Programs in Special Education, Johnson, VT 05656-9405. Awards MA Ed. Part-time programs available. Students: 11 part-time (7 women). *Degree requirements:* Thesis or alternative, comprehensive exam required, foreign language not required. *Entrance requirements:* Interview. Application deadline: 7/15 (priority date; rolling processing; 11/1 for spring admission). Application fee: $30. *Expenses:* Tuition $164 per credit for state residents; $383 per credit for nonresidents. Fees $15.90 per credit. *Financial aid:* Federal Work-Study, institutionally sponsored loans, and career-related internships or fieldwork available. Aid available to part-time students. Financial aid application deadline: 3/1; applicants required to submit FAFSA. • Application contact: Catherine H. Higley, Administrative Assistant, 802-635-2356 Ext. 1244. Fax: 802-635-1248. E-mail: higleyc@badger.jsc.vsc.edu.

Kansas State University, College of Education, Department of Special Education, Manhattan, KS 66506. Awards MS, Ed D. Accredited by NCATE. Part-time programs available. Faculty: 5 full-time (3 women), 1 (woman) part-time. Students: 10 full-time (8 women), 43 part-time (35 women); includes 3 minority (1 Asian American, 2 Hispanics), 1 international. Average age 30. 13 applicants, 62% accepted. *Degree requirements:* For master's, thesis or alternative required, foreign language not required; for doctorate, dissertation required, foreign language not required. *Entrance requirements:* For master's, GRE General Test (minimum combined score of 960; average 961) or MAT (minimum score 45; average 48), teaching experience, BS in education, minimum B average; for doctorate, GRE General Test (minimum combined score of 1000; average 1023), teaching experience, BS in education, minimum B average. Application deadline: 5/1 (priority date; rolling processing; 11/1 for spring admission). Application fee: $0 ($25 for international students). Electronic applications accepted. *Tuition:* $2218 per year full-time, $401 per semester (minimum) part-time for state residents; $6336 per year full-time, $1087 per semester (minimum) part-time for nonresidents. *Financial aid:* Federal Work-Study and career-related internships or fieldwork available. *Faculty research:* Consulting, inclusion, burnout, transition. • Mary Kay Zabel, Chair, 785-532-5836. Application contact: Paul Burden, Assistant Dean, 785-532-5595. Fax: 785-532-7304. E-mail: gradstudy@mail.educ.ksu.edu.

Kean University, School of Education, Department of Special Education and Individualized Services, Program in Special Education, Union, NJ 07083. Offers developmental disabilities (MA), emotionally disturbed and socially maladjusted (MA), learning disabilities (MA), preschool handicapped (MA). Accredited by NCATE. Part-time programs available. Students: 10 full-time (8 women), 133 part-time (121 women); includes 11 minority (7 African Americans, 4 Hispanics). Average age 33. In 1997, 31 degrees awarded. *Degree requirements:* Thesis, comprehensive exams required, foreign language not required. *Entrance requirements:* GRE General Test or MAT, teaching certificate. Application deadline: 6/15 (11/15 for spring admission). Application fee: $35. *Tuition:* $5926 per year full-time, $248 per credit part-time for state residents; $7312 per year full-time, $304 per credit part-time for nonresidents. *Financial aid:* Graduate assistantships and career-related internships or fieldwork available. • Beverly Kling, Coordinator, 908-527-2292. Application contact: Joanne Morris, Director of Graduate Admissions, 908-527-2665. Fax: 908-527-2286. E-mail: grad_adm@turbo.kean.edu.

Keene State College, Program in Special Education, Keene, NH 03435. Awards M Ed. Part-time and evening/weekend programs available. Students: 16 part-time (all women). Average age 39. 4 applicants, 100% accepted. In 1997, 1 degree awarded. *Degree requirements:* Thesis, project required, foreign language not required. *Entrance requirements:* Resume. Application deadline: 6/15 (rolling processing; 10/15 for spring admission). Application fee: $25 ($35 for international students). *Financial aid:* Application deadline 3/1. • Evie Gleckel, Coordinator, 603-358-2297. Application contact: Peter Tandy, Academic Counselor, 603-358-2332. Fax: 603-358-2257. E-mail: ptandy@keene.edu.

Kennesaw State University, Leland and Clarice C. Bagwell College of Education, Program in Elementary Education, Kennesaw, GA 30144-5591. Offerings include special education (M Ed). Program faculty: 38 full-time (24 women), 2 part-time (both women). *Degree requirements:* Thesis or alternative required, foreign language not required. *Entrance requirements:* GRE General Test (minimum combined score of 800), T-4 state certification, minimum GPA of 2.5. Application deadline: 7/1 (2/20 for spring admission). Application fee: $20. *Expenses:* Tuition $2398 per year full-time, $83 per credit hour part-time for state residents; $8398 per year full-time, $333 per credit hour part-time for nonresidents. Fees $338 per year. • Dr. David Martin, Director, 770-423-6117. Fax: 770-423-6527. E-mail: dmartin1@ksumail.kennesaw.edu. Application contact: Susan N. Barrett, Administrative Specialist, Admissions, 770-423-6500. Fax: 770-423-6541. E-mail: sbarrett@ksumail.kennesaw.edu.

Kent State University, Graduate School of Education, Department of Educational Foundations and Special Services, Program in Special Education, Kent, OH 44242-0001. Offers developmentally handicapped education (MA, M Ed), gifted education (MA, M Ed), hearing impaired education (MA, M Ed), multiply handicapped/orthopedically handicapped education (MA, M Ed), severe behavior disordered education (MA, M Ed), special education (PhD, Ed S), specific learning disabled education (MA, M Ed). Accredited by NCATE. Faculty: 12 full-time (8 women), 16 part-time (10 women). Students: 69 full-time (58 women), 138 part-time (108 women); includes 12 minority (7 African Americans, 3 Asian Americans, 2 Hispanics), 5 international. In 1997, 5 doctorates awarded. *Degree requirements:* For master's, thesis (MA) required, foreign language not required; for doctorate, dissertation required, foreign language not required. *Entrance requirements:* For master's, GRE General Test; for doctorate, GRE General Test (minimum score 550 on verbal section). Application deadline: rolling. Application fee: $30. *Tuition:* $4752 per year full-time, $216 per credit hour part-time for state residents; $9213 per year full-time, $419 per credit hour part-time for nonresidents. *Financial aid:* Application deadline 4/1. • Dr. Melody Tankersley, Coordinator, 330-672-2477. Application contact: Deborah Barber, Director, Office of Academic Services, 330-672-2862. Fax: 330-672-3549.

Lamar University, College of Education and Human Development, Department of Professional Pedagogy, Program in Special Education, Beaumont, TX 77710. Awards M Ed, Certificate. Faculty: 8 full-time (3 women). Students: 4 full-time (3 women), 9 part-time (7 women); includes 1 minority (African American). Average age 38. In 1997, 4 master's awarded. *Degree requirements:* For master's, thesis optional, foreign language not required. *Entrance requirements:* For master's, GRE General Test (minimum combined score of 950), TOEFL (minimum score 500), minimum GPA of 2.5. Application deadline: 8/1 (rolling processing; 12/1 for spring admission). Application fee: $0. *Expenses:* Tuition $1296 per year full-time, $360 per year part-time for state residents; $6432 per year full-time, $1608 per year part-time for nonresidents. Fees $238 per year full-time, $103 per year part-time. *Financial aid:* Application deadline 4/1. • Application contact: Alicia Satre, Graduate Admissions Coordinator, 409-880-8350. Fax: 409-880-8414.

Lamar University, College of Fine Arts and Communication, Department of Communication Disorders, Program in Deaf Education, Beaumont, TX 77710. Awards MS, Ed D. Faculty: 4 full-time (1 woman). Students: 26 full-time (15 women), 4 part-time (3 women); includes 6 minority (1 African American, 4 Hispanics, 1 Native American), 1 international. Average age 22. In 1997, 8 master's awarded (100% found work related to degree). *Degree requirements:* For master's, thesis optional, foreign language not required; for doctorate, dissertation required, foreign language not required. *Entrance requirements:* For master's, GRE General Test (minimum combined score of 950), TOEFL (minimum score 550), minimum GPA of 2.5, Performance IQ score of 115 required for deaf students; for doctorate, GRE General Test (minimum combined score of 1100), TOEFL, Performance IQ score of 115 required for deaf students. Application deadline: 8/1 (rolling processing; 12/1 for spring admission). Application fee: $0. *Expenses:* Tuition $1072 per year full-time, $748 per year part-time for state residents; $4924 per year full-time, $3316 per year part-time for nonresidents. Fees $458 per year full-time, $332 per year part-time. *Financial aid:* In 1997–98, fellowships totaling $63,550 were awarded; research assistantships also available. Financial aid application deadline: 4/1. *Faculty research:* Sign language, reading, language development, multicultural and deaf teacher training. • Application contact: Dr. Jean Andrews, Coordinator, 409-880-8177. Fax: 409-880-2265.

La Sierra University, School of Education, Department of Curriculum and Instruction, Riverside, CA 92515-8247. Offerings include special education (MA). Department faculty: 4 full-time (3 women), 7 part-time (3 women), 5 FTE. *Degree requirements:* Computer language required, foreign language and thesis not required. *Entrance requirements:* Minimum GPA of 3.0. Application deadline: rolling. Application fee: $30. • Dr. Anita Oliver, Chair, 909-785-2203. Fax: 909-785-2205. Application contact: Myrna Costa-Casado, Director of Admissions, 909-785-2176. Fax: 909-785-2447. E-mail: mcosta@lasierra.edu.

Lehigh University, College of Education, Department of Education and Human Services, Program in Special Education, Bethlehem, PA 18015-3094. Awards M Ed, PhD, Certificate. Faculty: 3 full-time (all women). Students: 7 full-time (all women), 68 part-time (52 women); includes 6 minority (1 African American, 5 Hispanics), 5 international. 23 applicants, 83% accepted. In 1997, 28 master's, 2 doctorates awarded. *Degree requirements:* For doctorate, dissertation required, foreign language not required. *Entrance requirements:* For master's,

Directory: Special Education

Lehigh University (continued)

GRE General Test or MAT, TOEFL, minimum GPA of 2.75; for doctorate, GRE General Test or MAT, TOEFL; for Certificate, TOEFL (minimum score 550). Application fee: $40. *Expenses:* Tuition $470 per credit. Fees $12 per semester full-time, $6 per semester part-time. *Financial aid:* Research assistantships, field-based positions, full and partial tuition waivers, Federal Work-Study, institutionally sponsored loans, and career-related internships or fieldwork available. Financial aid application deadline: 1/15. • Dr. Linda Bambara, Coordinator, 610-758-3256. Fax: 610-758-6223. E-mail: lmb1@lehigh.edu.

Lehman College of the City University of New York, Division of Education, Department of Specialized Services in Education, Teachers of Special Education Program, Option in Bilingual Special Education, 250 Bedford Park Boulevard West, Bronx, NY 10468-1589. Awards MS Ed. Faculty: 1 (woman) full-time. Students: 2 full-time (both women), 31 part-time (16 women). *Entrance requirements:* Minimum GPA of 3.0. Application deadline: 4/1 (rolling processing; 11/1 for spring admission). Application fee: $40. *Expenses:* Tuition $4350 per year full-time, $185 per credit part-time for state residents; $7600 per year full-time, $320 per credit part-time for nonresidents. Fees $120 per year full-time, $80 per year part-time. *Financial aid:* Full and partial tuition waivers, Federal Work-Study available. Aid available to part-time students. Financial aid application deadline: 5/15; applicants required to submit FAFSA. • Susan Polirstok, Adviser, 718-960-8173.

Lehman College of the City University of New York, Division of Education, Department of Specialized Services in Education, Teachers of Special Education Program, Option in Early Special Education, 250 Bedford Park Boulevard West, Bronx, NY 10468-1589. Awards MS Ed. Students: 0. *Entrance requirements:* Minimum GPA of 3.0. Application deadline: 4/1 (rolling processing; 11/1 for spring admission). Application fee: $40. *Expenses:* Tuition $4350 per year full-time, $185 per credit part-time for state residents; $7600 per year full-time, $320 per credit part-time for nonresidents. Fees $120 per year full-time, $80 per year part-time. *Financial aid:* Application deadline 5/15. • Victoria Rodriguez, Adviser, 718-960-7882.

Lehman College of the City University of New York, Division of Education, Department of Specialized Services in Education, Teachers of Special Education Program, Option in Emotional Handicaps, 250 Bedford Park Boulevard West, Bronx, NY 10468-1589. Awards MS Ed. Part-time and evening/weekend programs available. Faculty: 1 (woman) full-time, 1 part-time (0 women). Students: 28 part-time (22 women). *Entrance requirements:* Minimum GPA of 2.7. Application deadline: 4/1 (rolling processing; 11/1 for spring admission). Application fee: $40. *Expenses:* Tuition $4350 per year full-time, $185 per credit part-time for state residents; $7600 per year full-time, $320 per credit part-time for nonresidents. Fees $120 per year full-time, $80 per year part-time. *Financial aid:* Full and partial tuition waivers, Federal Work-Study available. Aid available to part-time students. Financial aid application deadline: 5/15; applicants required to submit FAFSA. *Faculty research:* Behavioral disorders, self-evaluation, applied behavior analysis. • Susan Polirstok, Adviser, 718-960-8173.

Lehman College of the City University of New York, Division of Education, Department of Specialized Services in Education, Teachers of Special Education Program, Option in Learning Disabilities, 250 Bedford Park Boulevard West, Bronx, NY 10468-1589. Awards MS Ed. Part-time and evening/weekend programs available. Faculty: 1 (woman) full-time, 2 part-time (1 woman). Students: 1 (woman) full-time, 122 part-time (90 women). *Entrance requirements:* Interview, minimum GPA of 2.7. Application deadline: 4/1 (rolling processing; 11/1 for spring admission). Application fee: $40. *Expenses:* Tuition $4350 per year full-time, $185 per credit part-time for state residents; $7600 per year full-time, $320 per credit part-time for nonresidents. Fees $120 per year full-time, $80 per year part-time. *Financial aid:* Full and partial tuition waivers, Federal Work-Study available. Aid available to part-time students. Financial aid application deadline: 5/15; applicants required to submit FAFSA. *Faculty research:* Emergent literacy, language-based classrooms, primary and secondary social contexts of language and literacy, innovative in-service education models, adult literacy. • Barbara Gottlieb, Adviser, 718-960-8173.

Lehman College of the City University of New York, Division of Education, Department of Specialized Services in Education, Teachers of Special Education Program, Option in Mental Retardation, 250 Bedford Park Boulevard West, Bronx, NY 10468-1589. Awards MS Ed. Part-time and evening/weekend programs available. Faculty: 1 (woman) full-time, 2 part-time (1 woman). Students: 15 part-time (12 women). Average age 30. *Entrance requirements:* Minimum GPA of 2.7. Application deadline: 4/1 (rolling processing; 11/1 for spring admission). Application fee: $40. *Expenses:* Tuition $4350 per year full-time, $185 per credit part-time for state residents; $7600 per year full-time, $320 per credit part-time for nonresidents. Fees $120 per year full-time, $80 per year part-time. *Financial aid:* Full and partial tuition waivers, Federal Work-Study available. Aid available to part-time students. Financial aid application deadline: 5/15; applicants required to submit FAFSA. *Faculty research:* Conductive education, homeless infants and their families, infant stimulation, hospitalizing infants with AIDS, legislation PL99-457. • Susan Polirstok, Adviser, 718-960-8173.

Lesley College, School of Education, Cambridge, MA 02138-2790. Offerings include intensive special needs (M Ed), special needs (M Ed, CAGS). Postbaccalaureate distance learning degree programs offered (no on-campus study). School faculty: 36 full-time (31 women), 340 part-time (220 women). *Degree requirements:* Computer language required, foreign language and thesis not required. *Entrance requirements:* For master's, TOEFL (minimum score 550); for CAGS, interview, master's degree. Application deadline: rolling. Application fee: $45. *Tuition:* $425 per credit. • Dr. William L. Dandridge, Dean, 617-349-8375. Application contact: Graduate Admissions, 617-349-8300. Fax: 617-349-8366.

Lewis & Clark College, Department of Special Education—Hearing Impaired, Portland, OR 97219-7899. Awards M Ed. Part-time programs available. *Entrance requirements:* GRE General Test or MAT, interview. Application deadline: rolling. Application fee: $45. *Faculty research:* Language development, learning disabilities, parent support, sign communication, international perspectives.

Long Island University, Brooklyn Campus, School of Education, Department of Education, Program in Special Education, Brooklyn, NY 11201-8423. Awards MS Ed. Part-time and evening/weekend programs available. 113 applicants, 87% accepted. In 1997, 80 degrees awarded. *Degree requirements:* Thesis optional. *Application deadline:* rolling. *Application fee:* $30. Electronic applications accepted. *Expenses:* Tuition $480 per credit. Fees $415 per year full-time, $73 per semester (minimum) part-time. • Application contact: Bernard W. Sullivan, Associate Director of Admissions, 718-488-1011.

Long Island University, C.W. Post Campus, School of Education, Department of Special Education and Reading, Brookville, NY 11548-1300. Offers programs in reading (MS), special education (MS). Part-time and evening/weekend programs available. Faculty: 11 full-time (4 women), 14 part-time (4 women). Students: 3 full-time, 362 part-time. 135 applicants, 91% accepted. In 1997, 215 degrees awarded. *Degree requirements:* Research project, comprehensive exam or thesis required, foreign language not required. *Entrance requirements:* Writing proficiency test, interview. Application deadline: rolling. Application fee: $30. Electronic applications accepted. *Expenses:* Tuition $480 per credit. Fees $316 per year full-time, $71 per semester (minimum) part-time. *Financial aid:* In 1997–98, 5 research assistantships were awarded; career-related internships or fieldwork also available. Aid available to part-time students. Financial aid application deadline: 5/15; applicants required to submit FAFSA. *Faculty research:* Autism, mainstreaming, robotics and microcomputers in special education, transition from school to work. • Dr. Alvin Kravitz, Chairperson, 516-299-2245. Application contact: Linda D'Agostino, Academic Counselor, 516-299-2199. Fax: 516-299-4167.

Longwood College, Department of Education, Farmville, VA 23909-1800. Offerings include curriculum and instruction specialist-elementary (MS), with options in English (MS), mild disabilities (MS), modern language (MS), physical education (MS), speech and drama (MS). Accredited by NCATE. Department faculty: 34 part-time. *Degree requirements:* Thesis (for some programs), comprehensive exam. *Entrance requirements:* Minimum GPA of 2.5. Application deadline: 5/1 (priority date; rolling processing; 10/15 for spring admission). Application fee: $25. *Expenses:* Tuition $3048 per year full-time, $127 per credit hour part-time for state residents; $8160 per year full-time, $340 per credit hour part-time for nonresidents. Fees $920 per year full-time, $31 per credit hour part-time. • Dr. Frank Howe, Chair, 804-395-2324. Application contact: Admissions Office, 804-395-2060.

Louisiana Tech University, College of Education, Department of Behavioral Sciences, Ruston, LA 71272. Offerings include special education (MA). Accredited by NCATE. Department faculty: 14 full-time (4 women). *Degree requirements:* Computer language, thesis or alternative required, foreign language not required. *Entrance requirements:* GRE General Test. Application deadline: 7/29 (2/3 for spring admission). Application fee: $20 ($30 for international students). *Tuition:* $2382 per year full-time, $223 per quarter (minimum) part-time for state residents; $5307 per year full-time, $223 per quarter (minimum) part-time for nonresidents. • Dr. JoAnn Dauzat, Acting Head, 318-257-4315.

Loyola College, College of Arts and Sciences, Department of Education, Program in Special Education, Baltimore, MD 21210-2699. Awards MA, M Ed, CAS. Part-time and evening/weekend programs available. Students: 5 full-time (all women), 161 part-time (143 women); includes 8 minority (5 African Americans, 1 Asian American, 2 Hispanics). In 1997, 32 master's, 1 CAS awarded. *Entrance requirements:* For CAS, master's degree. Application deadline: 8/1 (rolling processing; 12/1 for spring admission). Application fee: $35. *Tuition:* $222 per credit (minimum). *Financial aid:* Career-related internships or fieldwork available. • Dr. Sharyn Rhodes, Coordinator, 410-617-2546.

Loyola Marymount University, School of Education, Program in Special Education Specialist in Mild and Moderate Disabilities, Los Angeles, CA 90045-8350. Awards MA. Part-time and evening/weekend programs available. Faculty: 14 full-time (8 women), 25 part-time (20 women). Students: 14 full-time (13 women), 7 part-time (5 women); includes 5 minority (2 African Americans, 1 Asian American, 2 Hispanics). In 1997, 3 degrees awarded. *Degree requirements:* Comprehensive exam required, foreign language and thesis not required. *Entrance requirements:* GRE General Test, TOEFL (minimum score 550), interview. Application fee: $35. Electronic applications accepted. *Expenses:* Tuition $500 per unit. Fees $111 per year full-time, $28 per year part-time. *Financial aid:* In 1997–98, 20 students received aid, including 1 research assistantship totaling $2,120, grants, scholarships totaling $42,326; Federal Work-Study also available. Aid available to part-time students. Financial aid application deadline: 3/2; applicants required to submit FAFSA. • Dr. Victoria L. Graf, Coordinator, 310-338-7305.

Loyola University Chicago, School of Education, Department of Curriculum, Instruction and Educational Psychology, Program in Special Education, 820 North Michigan Avenue, Chicago, IL 60611-2196. Awards M Ed. Students: 12. *Degree requirements:* Comprehensive exam required, foreign language not required. *Average time to degree:* master's–2 years full-time, 3 years part-time. *Application fee:* $35. *Tuition:* $467 per semester hour. *Financial aid:* Application deadline 5/1. • Dr. Pamela Fenning, Director, 847-853-3334. Application contact: Marie Rosin-Dittmar, Admissions Coordinator, 847-853-3323. Fax: 847-853-3375. E-mail: mrosind@wpo.it.luc.edu.

Lynchburg College, School of Education and Human Development, Program in Special Education, Lynchburg, VA 24501-3199. Offers early childhood special education (M Ed), mental retardation (M Ed), severely/profoundly handicapped education (M Ed), teaching children with learning disabilities (M Ed), teaching the emotionally disturbed (M Ed). *Entrance requirements:* Minimum GPA of 3.0 (undergraduate). Application fee: $20.

Lyndon State College, Graduate Programs in Education, Department of Education, Lyndonville, VT 05851. Offerings include special education (M Ed). *Degree requirements:* Exam or major field project required, foreign language and thesis not required. *Entrance requirements:* GRE General Test or MAT. Application deadline: 2/28 (priority date; 10/31 for spring admission). Application fee: $30. *Expenses:* Tuition $3924 per year full-time, $164 per credit part-time for state residents; $9192 per year full-time, $383 per credit part-time for nonresidents. Fees $632 per year. • Application contact: Elaine L. Turner, Administrative Secretary, 802-626-6497. Fax: 802-626-9770. E-mail: turnere@king.lsc.vsc.edu.

Lynn University, School of Graduate Studies, College of Education, Boca Raton, FL 33431-5598. Offerings include ESOL and varying exceptionalities (M Ed), varying exceptionalities (M Ed). College faculty: 5 full-time (4 women), 3 part-time (all women). *Degree requirements:* Thesis (for some programs), comprehensive exam (ESOL and varying exceptionalities), (varying exceptionalities) required, foreign language not required. *Average time to degree:* master's–1.8 years full-time. *Entrance requirements:* MAT, minimum undergraduate GPA of 3.0. Application deadline: rolling. Application fee: $50. Electronic applications accepted. *Expenses:* Tuition $375 per credit hour. Fees $60 per year. • Dr. Carole Warshaw, Dean, 561-994-0770 Ext. 247. Fax: 561-241-3939. E-mail: admission@lynn.edu. Application contact: Peter Gallo, Graduate Admissions Counselor, 800-544-8035. Fax: 561-241-3552. E-mail: admission@lynn.edu.

Madonna University, Programs in Education, Livonia, MI 48150-1173. Offerings include learning disabilities (MAT). Accredited by NCATE. Faculty: 7 full-time (4 women), 3 part-time (2 women). *Application deadline:* 8/1 (priority date; rolling processing). *Application fee:* $0. *Expenses:* Tuition $260 per credit hour (minimum). Fees $50 per semester. • Dr. Robert Kimball, Chair, Education Department, 734-432-5652. E-mail: kimball@smtp.munet.edu. Application contact: Sandra Kellums, Coordinator of Graduate Admissions, 734-432-5666. Fax: 734-432-5393. E-mail: kellums@smtp.munet.edu.

Malone College, Graduate School, Program in Education, Canton, OH 44709-3897. Offerings include early childhood special education (MA), specific learning disabilities (MA). Program faculty: 10 full-time (6 women), 11 part-time (5 women), 12.68 FTE. *Degree requirements:* Research practicum required, foreign language and thesis not required. *Entrance requirements:* Minimum GPA of 3.0, teaching license. Application deadline: 9/6 (rolling processing; 1/2 for spring admission). Application fee: $20. *Tuition:* $300 per credit hour. • Dr. Marietta Daulton, Director, 330-471-8447. Fax: 330-471-8478. E-mail: mdaulton@malone.edu. Application contact: Dan Depasquale, Director of Graduate Student Services, 800-257-4723. Fax: 330-471-8343. E-mail: depasquale@malone.edu.

Manhattan College, School of Education, Program in Special Education, Riverdale, NY 10471. Awards MS Ed, Diploma. Part-time programs available. Faculty: 1 (woman) full-time, 8 part-time (5 women). Students: 6 full-time (5 women), 60 part-time (46 women); includes 16 minority (7 African Americans, 1 Asian American, 8 Hispanics), 1 international. Average age 32. 54 applicants, 91% accepted. In 1997, 28 master's awarded (100% entered university research/teaching). *Degree requirements:* For master's, thesis, internship. *Entrance requirements:* For master's, minimum GPA of 3.0. Application deadline: 8/10 (priority date; rolling processing; 1/7 for spring admission). Application fee: $50. *Expenses:* Tuition $385 per credit. Fees $100 per year. *Financial aid:* In 1997–98, 11 scholarships were awarded. Financial aid application deadline: 2/1. *Faculty research:* Adapted physical education. • Application contact: William J. Bisset Jr., Dean of Admissions/Financial Aid, 718-862-7200. Fax: 718-863-8019. E-mail: admit@manhattan.edu.

Manhattanville College, School of Education, Program in Secondary and Special Education, Purchase, NY 10577-2132. Awards MPS. *Degree requirements:* Thesis, comprehensive exam or research project required, foreign language not required. *Entrance requirements:* Minimum undergraduate GPA of 3.0. Application deadline: rolling. Application fee: $40. *Expenses:* Tuition $410 per credit (minimum). Fees $25 per semester. • Application contact: Carol Messar, Director of Admissions, 914-323-5142. Fax: 914-323-5493.

Manhattanville College, School of Education, Program in Special Education, Purchase, NY 10577-2132. Offers elementary education and special education (MPS), leadership and strategic management (MS), special education (MPS), special education and reading (MPS). *Degree requirements:* Thesis, comprehensive exam or research project required, foreign language not required. *Entrance requirements:* Minimum undergraduate GPA of 3.0. Application deadline: rolling. Application fee: $40. *Expenses:* Tuition $410 per credit (minimum). Fees $25 per semester. • Dr. Rebecca Rich, Coordinator, 914-323-5143. Application contact: Carol Messar, Director of Admissions, 914-323-5142. Fax: 914-323-5493.

Mankato State University, College of Education, Department of Special Education, South Rd and Ellis Ave, PO Box 8400, Mankato, MN 56002-8400. Offers programs in early education for exceptional children (MS), emotional disturbance (MS), learning disabilities (MS), mental retardation (MS), severely handicapped (MS). Accredited by NCATE. Part-time programs available. Faculty: 6 full-time (2 women). Students: 46 full-time (37 women), 118 part-time (100 women); includes 1 minority (Native American). Average age 36. 25 applicants, 84% accepted. In 1997, 29 degrees awarded. *Degree requirements:* Thesis or alternative, comprehensive exam required, foreign language not required. *Entrance requirements:* Minimum GPA of 3.0 during previous 2 years. Application deadline: 7/10 (priority date; rolling processing; 10/30 for spring admission). Application fee: $20. *Tuition:* $126 per credit (minimum) for state residents; $200 per credit for nonresidents. *Financial aid:* Teaching assistantships, Federal Work-Study, institutionally sponsored loans, and career-related internships or fieldwork available. Aid available to part-time students. Financial aid application deadline: 3/15; applicants required to submit FAFSA. • Dr. Raphael Kudela, Chairperson, 507-389-5650. Application contact: Joni Roberts, Admissions Coordinator, 507-389-2321. Fax: 507-389-5974. E-mail: grad@mankato.msus.edu.

Mansfield University of Pennsylvania, Department of Special Education, Mansfield, PA 16933. Offers programs in mentally/physically handicapped (M Ed), special education (M Ed, MS). Accredited by NCATE. Part-time and evening/weekend programs available. Faculty: 5 part-time (2 women). Students: 22 full-time (15 women), 45 part-time (31 women). Average age 31. 15 applicants, 100% accepted. In 1997, 35 degrees awarded. *Degree requirements:* Thesis optional, foreign language not required. *Entrance requirements:* GRE, MAT, NTE, Pennsylvania teaching certificate, or minimum GPA of 3.0. Application deadline: rolling. Application fee: $25. *Expenses:* Tuition $3468 per year full-time, $193 per credit part-time for state residents; $6236 per year full-time, $346 per credit part-time for nonresidents. Fees $236 per year full-time, $18.25 per semester (minimum) part-time for state residents; $266 per year full-time, $18.25 per semester (minimum) part-time for nonresidents. *Financial aid:* In 1997–98, 4 graduate assistantships (2 to first-year students) were awarded; career-related internships or fieldwork also available. Financial aid application deadline: 5/1; applicants required to submit FAFSA. • Dr. Ronald Straub, Chairperson, 717-662-4796.

Marshall University, Graduate School of Education and Professional Studies, Program in Special Education, South Charleston, WV 25303-1600. Awards MA. Accredited by NCATE. Part-time and evening/weekend programs available. Faculty: 5 full-time (1 woman), 5 part-time (all women), 6.3 FTE. Students: 12 full-time (6 women), 205 part-time (149 women); includes 9 minority (all African Americans). Average age 39. In 1997, 49 degrees awarded. *Degree requirements:* Comprehensive or oral exam, research project required, foreign language and thesis not required. *Entrance requirements:* GRE General Test, minimum undergraduate GPA of 2.5. Application deadline: 8/1 (priority date; rolling processing). Application fee: $0. *Tuition:* $2364 per year full-time, $132 per hour part-time for state residents; $6894 per year full-time, $383 per hour part-time for nonresidents. *Financial aid:* Full tuition waivers available. Aid available to part-time students. Financial aid applicants required to submit FAFSA. *Faculty research:* Teaching the severely handicapped, career/vocational education, education of the gifted. • Dr. James Ranson, Dean, Graduate School of Education and Professional Studies, 304-746-1998. Fax: 304-746-1942.

Marshall University, College of Education, Division of Teacher Education, Program in Special Education, Huntington, WV 25755-2020. Awards MA. Accredited by NCATE. Evening/weekend programs available. Faculty: 7 (4 women). Students: 20 full-time (17 women), 133 part-time (118 women); includes 4 minority (3 African Americans, 1 Native American), 2 international. In 1997, 40 degrees awarded. *Degree requirements:* Thesis optional. *Entrance requirements:* GRE General Test (minimum combined score of 1200). *Tuition:* $2364 per year full-time, $132 per hour part-time for state residents; $6894 per year full-time, $383 per hour part-time for nonresidents. *Financial aid:* Career-related internships or fieldwork available. • Dr. Daryll Bauer, Coordinator, 304-696-2340. Application contact: Dr. James Harless, Director of Admissions, 304-696-3160.

Marygrove College, Division of Education, Program in Special Education, Detroit, MI 48221-2599. Offers education of the emotionally impaired (M Ed). Accredited by NCATE. Part-time programs available. *Degree requirements:* Research project required, foreign language and thesis not required. *Average time to degree:* master's–2 years full-time, 3 years part-time. *Entrance requirements:* MAT, interview, minimum undergraduate GPA of 3.0, teaching certificate. Application deadline: 8/15 (rolling processing). Application fee: $25.

Marymount University, School of Education and Human Services, Program in Learning Disabilities, Arlington, VA 22207-4299. Awards M Ed. Accredited by NCATE. Part-time and evening/weekend programs available. Students: 30. In 1997, 21 degrees awarded. *Degree requirements:* Thesis or alternative required, foreign language not required. *Entrance requirements:* GRE General Test or MAT, interview. Application deadline: rolling. Application fee: $35. *Expenses:* Tuition $465 per credit hour. Fees $120 per year full-time, $5 per credit hour part-time. • Dr. Shirley Smith, Chair, 703-284-1620. Fax: 703-284-1631. E-mail: shirley.smith@marymount.edu.

Marywood University, Graduate School of Arts and Sciences, Department of Special Education, Program in Special Education, Scranton, PA 18509-1598. Awards MS. Accredited by NCATE. Students: 5 full-time (4 women), 33 part-time (29 women). Average age 32. 9 applicants, 100% accepted. *Degree requirements:* Thesis or alternative required, foreign language not required. *Entrance requirements:* MAT, TOEFL (minimum score 550; average 590). Application deadline: 7/15 (priority date; rolling processing; 12/1 for spring admission). Application fee: $20. *Expenses:* Tuition $449 per credit hour. Fees $530 per year full-time, $180 per year part-time. *Financial aid:* Research assistantships, scholarships/tuition reductions, partial tuition waivers, and career-related internships or fieldwork available. Aid available to part-time students. Financial aid application deadline: 2/15; applicants required to submit FAFSA. • Application contact: Deborah M. Flynn, Coordinator of Admissions, 717-340-6002. Fax: 717-961-4745. E-mail: gsas_adm@ac.marywood.edu.

Marywood University, Graduate School of Arts and Sciences, Department of Special Education, Program in Special Education Administration and Supervision, Scranton, PA 18509-1598. Awards MS. Accredited by NCATE. Students: 2 part-time (both women). Average age 31. 2 applicants, 100% accepted. *Degree requirements:* Thesis or alternative required, foreign language not required. *Entrance requirements:* MAT, TOEFL (minimum score 550; average 590). Application deadline: 7/15 (priority date; rolling processing; 12/1 for spring admission). Application fee: $20. *Expenses:* Tuition $449 per credit hour. Fees $530 per year full-time, $180 per year part-time. *Financial aid:* Research assistantships, scholarships/tuition reductions, partial tuition waivers, and career-related internships or fieldwork available. Aid available to part-time students. Financial aid application deadline: 2/15; applicants required to submit FAFSA. • Application contact: Deborah M. Flynn, Coordinator of Admissions, 717-340-6002. Fax: 717-961-4745. E-mail: gsas_adm@ac.marywood.edu.

Massachusetts College of Liberal Arts, Graduate Program in Education, North Adams, MA 01247-4100. Offerings include special education (M Ed). Program faculty: 8 full-time (5 women), 4 part-time (2 women). *Degree requirements:* Thesis required, foreign language not required. *Average time to degree:* master's–3 years part-time. *Entrance requirements:* Writing sample. Application deadline: rolling. Application fee: $0. *Expenses:* Tuition $130 per credit. Fees $15 per credit. • Dr. Susanne Chandler, Chair, 413-662-5381.

McNeese State University, College of Education, Department of Special Education, Lake Charles, LA 70609-2495. Awards M Ed. Evening/weekend programs available. Faculty: 5 full-time (1 woman). Students: 4 full-time (all women), 1 (woman) part-time. In 1997, 1 degree awarded. *Degree requirements:* Comprehensive exam required, foreign language and thesis not required. *Entrance requirements:* GRE General Test (minimum combined score of 900), minimum undergraduate GPA of 2.5, teaching certificate. Application deadline: 7/15 (priority date; rolling processing). Application fee: $10 ($25 for international students). *Tuition:* $2118 per year full-time, $344 per semester (minimum) part-time for state residents; $7308 per year full-time, $344 per semester (minimum) part-time for nonresidents. *Financial aid:* Application deadline 5/1. • Dr. Kirby Detraz, Head, 318-478-5471.

Mercyhurst College, Program in Special Education, 501 East 38th Street, Erie, PA 16546. Offers bilingual/bicultural special education (MS), special education (MS). Part-time and evening/weekend programs available. Faculty: 2 full-time (1 woman), 2 part-time (both women), 3 FTE. Students: 15 full-time (14 women), 35 part-time (29 women); includes 4 minority (1 African American, 3 Hispanics). Average age 30. 20 applicants, 75% accepted. In 1997, 4 degrees awarded. *Degree requirements:* Thesis required, foreign language not required. *Average time to degree:* master's–1.5 years full-time, 2.5 years part-time. *Entrance requirements:* GRE General Test, MAT, or minimum GPA of 3.0; interview. Application deadline: 8/1 (priority date; rolling processing; 3/1 for spring admission). Application fee: $35. Electronic applications accepted. *Expenses:* Tuition $681 per course. Fees $250 per year. *Financial aid:* In 1997–98, 10 research assistantships (9 to first-year students) averaging $333 per month and totaling $40,000 were awarded; institutionally sponsored loans also available. Aid available to part-time students. Financial aid application deadline: 5/15. *Faculty research:* College age learning disabled program, functional communication program, teacher preparation/collaboration, supported employment. • Dr. Phillip J. Belfiore, Coordinator, 814-824-2267. Fax: 814-824-2438. E-mail: belfiore@mercyhurst.edu. Application contact: Mary Ellen Dahlkemper, Director, Office of Adult and Graduate Programs, 814-824-2294. Fax: 814-824-2055. E-mail: medahlk@mercyhurst.edu.

Miami University, School of Education and Allied Professions, Department of Educational Psychology, Program in Special Education, Oxford, OH 45056. Awards M Ed. Accredited by NCATE. Faculty: 17. Students: 7 full-time (6 women), 15 part-time (all women); includes 1 minority (African American). 15 applicants, 73% accepted. In 1997, 4 degrees awarded. *Degree requirements:* Thesis or alternative, oral or written final exam required, foreign language not required. *Entrance requirements:* GRE General Test or MAT, minimum undergraduate GPA of 3.0 during previous 2 years or 2.75 overall. Application deadline: 3/1 (priority date; rolling processing; 12/1 for spring admission). Application fee: $35. *Tuition:* $5932 per year full-time, $255 per credit hour part-time for state residents; $12,392 per year full-time, $524 per credit hour part-time for nonresidents. *Financial aid:* Fellowships, research assistantships, teaching assistantships, full tuition waivers, Federal Work-Study, and career-related internships or fieldwork available. Financial aid application deadline: 3/1. *Faculty research:* Language development, teacher effectiveness, intervention. • Dr. Alex Thomas, Chair, Department of Educational Psychology, 513-529-6621.

Michigan State University, College of Education, Department of Counseling, Educational Psychology and Special Education, East Lansing, MI 48824-1020. Offerings include special education (MA, PhD). Department faculty: 42 (14 women). *Degree requirements:* For doctorate, dissertation required, foreign language not required. *Entrance requirements:* For master's, GRE General Test (combined average 1500 on three sections); for doctorate, GRE General Test (combined average 1800 on three sections). Application deadline: rolling. Application fee: $30 ($40 for international students). *Expenses:* Tuition $4609 per year full-time, $223 per credit hour (minimum) part-time for state residents; $8704 per year full-time, $450 per credit hour (minimum) part-time for nonresidents. Fees $576 per year full-time, $476 per year part-time. • Dr. Richard Prawat, Chairperson, 517-353-6417. Application contact: Sharon Anderson, Graduate Secretary, 517-355-6683. Fax: 517-353-6393. E-mail: sharand@msu.edu.

Middle Tennessee State University, College of Education, Department of Elementary and Special Education, Major in Special Education, Murfreesboro, TN 37132. Awards M Ed. Accredited by NCATE. Students: 11 full-time (9 women), 33 part-time (31 women); includes 5 minority (all African Americans). Average age 34. 17 applicants, 29% accepted. In 1997, 19 degrees awarded. *Degree requirements:* Comprehensive exams required, foreign language and thesis not required. *Entrance requirements:* Cooperative English Test, MAT. Application deadline: 8/1 (priority date). Application fee: $5. *Expenses:* Tuition $2560 per year full-time, $129 per semester hour part-time for state residents; $7386 per year full-time, $340 per semester hour part-time for nonresidents. Fees $486 per year full-time, $17 per semester (minimum) part-time. *Financial aid:* Teaching assistantships available. Financial aid application deadline: 5/1. • Dr. Charles Babb, Chair, Department of Elementary and Special Education, 615-898-2680. Fax: 615-898-5309. E-mail: cwbabb@mtsu.edu.

Midwestern State University, Division of Education, Program in Special Education, Wichita Falls, TX 76308-2096. Awards M Ed. Part-time and evening/weekend programs available. Faculty: 2 full-time (0 women). Students: 9. Average age 35. In 1997, 3 degrees awarded. *Entrance requirements:* GRE General Test, MAT (average 46), TOEFL (minimum score 550). Application deadline: 8/7 (12/15 for spring admission). Application fee: $0 ($50 for international students). *Expenses:* Tuition $44 per hour for state residents; $259 per hour for nonresidents. Fees $90 per year (minimum) full-time, $9 per semester (minimum) part-time. *Financial aid:* Teaching assistantships available. *Faculty research:* Fragile-X syndrome, phenylketonuria and other causes of handicapping conditions. • Dr. Emerson Capps, Director, Division of Education, 940-397-4313.

Millersville University of Pennsylvania, School of Education, Department of Special Education, Millersville, PA 17551-0302. Awards M Ed. Accredited by NCATE. Part-time and evening/weekend programs available. Faculty: 6 full-time (4 women), 8 part-time (5 women). Students: 16 full-time (9 women), 64 part-time (51 women); includes 2 minority (1 African American, 1 Hispanic). Average age 32. 22 applicants, 55% accepted. In 1997, 19 degrees awarded. *Degree requirements:* Departmental exam required, thesis optional, foreign language not required. *Entrance requirements:* GRE General Test (minimum score 450 on each of three sections) or MAT (minimum score 35), minimum undergraduate GPA of 2.75. Application deadline: 5/1 (priority date; rolling processing). Application fee: $25. *Tuition:* $3468 per year full-time, $234 per credit part-time for state residents; $6236 per year full-time, $387 per credit part-time for nonresidents. *Financial aid:* In 1997–98, 4 graduate assistantships (1 to a first-year student) averaging $445 per month and totaling $16,000 were awarded; Federal Work-Study, institutionally sponsored loans, and career-related internships or fieldwork also available. Aid available to part-time students. Financial aid application deadline: 5/1. • Dr. Edward Ottinger, Coordinator, 717-872-3851. Fax: 717-872-3856. Application contact: Dr. Robert J. Labriola, Dean of Graduate Studies, 717-872-3030. Fax: 717-871-2022.

Minot State University, Program in Special Education, Minot, ND 58707-0002. Offers education of the deaf (MS); learning disabilities (MS); special education (MS), including infant/toddler, severely multihandicapped. Faculty: 11 full-time (7 women). Students: 9 full-time (8 women), 15 part-time (14 women); includes 1 minority (Native American). In 1997, 15 degrees awarded. *Degree requirements:* Thesis or alternative required, foreign language not required. *Entrance requirements:* GRE General Test (minimum combined score of 1100 rquired) or minimum GPA of 3.0. Application fee: $25. *Tuition:* $2714 per year for state residents; $3235 per year (minimum) for nonresidents. *Financial aid:* Research assistantships, teaching assistantships, institutionally sponsored loans, and career-related internships or fieldwork available. Aid available to part-time students. Financial aid application deadline: 4/1. *Faculty research:* Special education team diagnostic unit; individual diagnostic assessments of mentally retarded, learning-disabled, hearing-impaired, and speech-impaired youth; educational programming for the hearing impaired. • Dr. David K. Williams, Chairperson, 701-858-3031. E-mail: williamd@warple.cs.misu.nodak.edu. Application contact: Tammy White, Administrative Secretary, 701-858-3250. Fax: 701-839-6933.

Directory: Special Education

Mississippi State University, College of Education, Department of Curriculum and Instruction, Mississippi State, MS 39762. Offerings include special education (MS). Accredited by NCATE. Department faculty: 26 full-time (13 women). *Degree requirements:* Comprehensive written exam required, foreign language and thesis not required. *Entrance requirements:* Minimum QPA of 2.75 in last 2 years. Application deadline: 7/26 (priority date; rolling processing; 11/10 for spring admission). Application fee: $0 ($25 for international students). Electronic applications accepted. *Tuition:* $3017 per year full-time, $168 per credit hour part-time for state residents; $6119 per year full-time, $340 per credit hour part-time for nonresidents. • Dr. James S. Turner, Interim Head, 601-325-3747. Application contact: Dr. Dwight Hare, Graduate Coordinator, 601-325-3747. Fax: 601-325-8784. E-mail: rdh1@ra.msstate.edu.

Mississippi State University, College of Education, Program Under Dean of Education, Mississippi State, MS 39762. Offerings include special education (PhD, Ed S). Accredited by NCATE. *Degree requirements:* For Ed S, thesis or alternative required, foreign language not required. *Entrance requirements:* For Ed S, minimum QPA of 3.2 in graduate course work. *Tuition:* $3017 per year full-time, $168 per credit hour part-time for state residents; $6119 per year full-time, $340 per credit hour part-time for nonresidents. • Dr. William H. Graves, Dean, College of Education, 601-325-3717. Fax: 601-325-8784. E-mail: whg1@ra.msstate.edu.

Monmouth University, School of Education, West Long Branch, NJ 07764-1898. Offerings include learning disabilities-teacher consultant (Certificate), special education (MS Ed, Certificate). Certificate (learning disabilities-teacher consultant, reading specialist, supervision) new for fall 1998. School faculty: 9 full-time (7 women), 14 part-time (9 women). *Application deadline:* 8/1 (priority date; rolling processing; 12/1 for spring admission). *Application fee:* $35. *Expenses:* Tuition $459 per credit. Fees $274 per semester full-time, $137 per semester part-time. • Dr. Bernice Willis, Dean, 732-571-7518. Fax: 732-263-5277. Application contact: Office of Graduate Admissions, 732-571-3452. Fax: 732-571-5123.

Montana State University–Billings, College of Education and Human Services, Department of Special Education and Reading, Program in Special Education, Billings, MT 59101-9984. Offers community counseling (MS Sp Ed), emotionally disturbed (MS Sp Ed), learning disabilities (MS Sp Ed), mental retardation (MS Sp Ed), multiply handicapped (MS Sp Ed), special education generalist (MS Sp Ed). Accredited by NCATE. Part-time programs available. *Degree requirements:* Thesis or professional paper and/or field experience required, foreign language not required. *Entrance requirements:* GRE General Test (minimum combined score of 1350 on three sections) or MAT (minimum score 38), minimum GPA of 3.0 (undergraduate), 3.25 (graduate). Application deadline: 8/1 (priority date; rolling processing; 1/1 for spring admission). Application fee: $30. *Expenses:* Tuition $2253 per year full-time, $397 per semester (minimum) part-time for state residents; $5313 per year full-time, $907 per semester (minimum) part-time for nonresidents. Fees $378 per year full-time, $105 per semester (minimum) part-time.

Montclair State University, College of Humanities and Social Sciences, Department of Communication Sciences and Disorders, Upper Montclair, NJ 07043-1624. Offerings include early childhood special education (MA), learning disabilities (MA). Department faculty: 9 full-time. *Degree requirements:* Comprehensive exam or fieldwork/project required, foreign language and thesis not required. *Entrance requirements:* GRE General Test. Application deadline: 4/1 (rolling processing; 11/1 for spring admission). Application fee: $40. *Expenses:* Tuition $201 per credit for state residents; $257 per credit for nonresidents. Fees $22.05 per credit. • Dr. Warren Heiss, Chairperson, 973-655-4232.

Moorhead State University, Department of Education, Program in Special Education, Moorhead, MN 56563-0002. Awards MS. Accredited by NCATE. Part-time and evening/weekend programs available. Faculty: 7 full-time (4 women). Students: 5 full-time (all women), 15 part-time (all women); includes 1 minority (Hispanic), 1 international. 8 applicants, 88% accepted. In 1997, 10 degrees awarded. *Degree requirements:* Final oral exam, project or thesis, written comprehensive exam required, foreign language not required. *Entrance requirements:* GRE General Test, TOEFL (minimum score 550), minimum GPA of 3.0, 1 year of teaching experience. Application deadline: 5/1 (priority date; rolling processing; 9/1 for spring admission). Application fee: $20 ($35 for international students). Electronic applications accepted. *Tuition:* $145 per credit hour for state residents; $220 per credit hour for nonresidents. *Financial aid:* In 1997–98, 4 administrative assistantships were awarded; Federal Work-Study and career-related internships or fieldwork also available. Financial aid application deadline: 7/15; applicants required to submit FAFSA. • Dr. Linda Svobodny, Chairperson, 218-236-2005. Application contact: Dr. Paul Beare, Coordinator, 218-236-2004.

Morehead State University, College of Education and Behavioral Sciences, Department of Elementary, Reading, and Special Education, Program in Special Education, Morehead, KY 40351. Awards MA Ed, Ed D. Accredited by NCATE. Ed D offered jointly with the University of Kentucky. Part-time programs available. Faculty: 5 full-time (2 women), 1 (woman) part-time. Students: 1 (woman) full-time, 25 part-time (20 women). Average age 25. 16 applicants, 94% accepted. In 1997, 12 master's awarded. *Degree requirements:* For master's, written comprehensive exams required, foreign language and thesis not required. *Entrance requirements:* For master's, GRE General Test (minimum combined score of 1200), minimum GPA of 2.75, teaching certificate. Application deadline: 8/1 (priority date; rolling processing; 12/1 for spring admission). Application fee: $0. *Tuition:* $2470 per year full-time, $138 per semester hour part-time for state residents; $6710 per year full-time, $373 per semester hour part-time for nonresidents. *Financial aid:* Research assistantships, teaching assistantships, Federal Work-Study available. Financial aid application deadline: 4/1; applicants required to submit FAFSA. *Faculty research:* Communicative competence of learning-disabled students, study skills. • Application contact: Betty Cowsert, Graduate Admissions Officer, 606-783-2039. Fax: 606-783-5061.

Morningside College, Department of Education, Program in Special Education, Sioux City, IA 51106-1751. Awards MAT. Accredited by NCATE. Part-time and evening/weekend programs available. Faculty: 6 full-time (2 women), 7 part-time (6 women). *Entrance requirements:* MAT, writing sample. Application deadline: rolling. Application fee: $15. *Tuition:* $245 per credit hour. *Financial aid:* Partial tuition waivers, institutionally sponsored loans available. Aid available to part-time students. • Dr. Glenna Tevis, Director, Graduate Division, 712-274-5375.

Mount Saint Mary College, Division of Education, Program in Elementary/Special Education, Newburgh, NY 12550-3494. Awards MS Ed. Part-time and evening/weekend programs available. Students: 7 full-time (all women), 80 part-time (63 women); includes 7 minority (3 African Americans, 1 Asian American, 3 Hispanics). Average age 32. In 1997, 25 degrees awarded. *Degree requirements:* Comprehensive exam, practicum required, foreign language and thesis not required. *Application deadline:* rolling. *Application fee:* $20. *Expenses:* Tuition $367 per credit. Fees $30 per year. *Financial aid:* Federal Work-Study and career-related internships or fieldwork available. Financial aid application deadline: 9/30. • Application contact: Sr. Frances Berski, Coordinator, 914-569-3267. Fax: 914-562-6762. E-mail: berski@msmc.edu.

Mount Saint Mary College, Division of Education, Program in Special Education, Newburgh, NY 12550-3494. Awards MS Ed. Part-time programs available. Students: 78 part-time (70 women); includes 4 minority (1 African American, 3 Hispanics). Average age 31. In 1997, 35 degrees awarded. *Degree requirements:* Practicum or research project required, foreign language and thesis not required. *Entrance requirements:* Provisional teaching certificate. Application deadline: rolling. Application fee: $20. *Expenses:* Tuition $367 per credit. Fees $30 per year. *Financial aid:* Federal Work-Study and career-related internships or fieldwork available. Aid available to part-time students. Financial aid application deadline: 9/30. *Faculty research:* Learning and teaching styles, computers in special education, language development. • Application contact: Sr. Frances Berski, Coordinator, 914-569-3267. Fax: 914-562-6762. E-mail: berski@msmc.edu.

Mount St. Mary's College, Department of Education, Specialization in Special Education, Los Angeles, CA 90049-1597. Awards MS. Part-time and evening/weekend programs available. *Degree requirements:* Thesis, research project required, foreign language not required. *Entrance requirements:* MAT, minimum GPA of 3.0. Application fee: $50.

Murray State University, College of Education, Department of Special Education, Program in Learning Disabilities, Murray, KY 42071-0009. Awards MA Ed. Accredited by NCATE. Part-time programs available. Faculty: 3 full-time (1 woman). Students: 6 full-time (all women), 72 part-time (65 women); includes 6 minority (all African Americans), 1 international. 9 applicants, 100% accepted. In 1997, 13 degrees awarded. *Entrance requirements:* GRE General Test or MAT, TOEFL (minimum score 500). Application deadline: rolling. Application fee: $20. *Expenses:* Tuition $2500 per year full-time, $124 per hour part-time for state residents; $6740 per year full-time, $357 per hour part-time for nonresidents. Fees $360 per year full-time, $180 per year part-time. *Financial aid:* Research assistantships, teaching assistantships, Federal Work-Study available. Financial aid application deadline: 4/1. • Dr. Elizabeth Blodgett, Interim Director, 502-762-3084. Fax: 502-762-6803.

National–Louis University, National College of Education, McGaw Graduate School, Programs in Special Education, 2840 Sheridan Road, Evanston, IL 60201-1730. Offerings in general special education (M Ed, MS Ed, CAS), learning disabilities (M Ed, MS Ed, CAS), learning disabilities/behavior disorders (MAT, M Ed, MS Ed, CAS). Part-time and evening/weekend programs available. Students: 19 full-time (15 women), 145 part-time (127 women); includes 11 minority (8 African Americans, 2 Hispanics, 1 Native American), 1 international. Average age 33. In 1997, 48 master's, 2 CASs awarded. *Degree requirements:* For master's, thesis (for some programs), practicum required, foreign language not required; for CAS, practicum required, foreign language and thesis not required. *Entrance requirements:* For master's, MAT, minimum GPA of 3.0. Application deadline: rolling. Application fee: $25. *Tuition:* $411 per semester hour. *Financial aid:* Fellowships available. Aid available to part-time students. Financial aid applicants required to submit FAFSA. • Dr. Peter Schwartz, Coordinator, 847-475-1100 Ext. 5379. Application contact: Dr. David McCulloch, Vice President for University Services, 800-443-5522 Ext. 5127. Fax: 847-465-0593. E-mail: dmcc@wheeling1.nl.edu.

National University, School of Education and Human Services, Department of Special Education and Pupil Personnel Services, La Jolla, CA 92037-1011. Offers programs in educational administration (MS), educational counseling (MS), school psychology (MS), special education (MS). Students: 301 full-time (196 women), 182 part-time (122 women); includes 169 minority (62 African Americans, 18 Asian Americans, 83 Hispanics, 6 Native Americans). Average age 36. In 1997, 237 degrees awarded. *Entrance requirements:* Interview, minimum GPA of 2.5. Application deadline: rolling. Application fee: $60 ($100 for international students). *Tuition:* $7830 per year full-time, $870 per course part-time. *Financial aid:* Application deadline 5/1. • Dr. Judy Mantel, Chair, 619-642-8347. Application contact: Nancy Rohland, Director of Enrollment Management, 619-563-7100. Fax: 619-563-7393.

Nazareth College of Rochester, Graduate Studies, Department of Education, Program in Special Education, Rochester, NY 14618-3790. Awards MS Ed. Part-time and evening/weekend programs available. Faculty: 4 full-time (3 women), 18 part-time (11 women). Students: 86 full-time (81 women), 255 part-time (213 women); includes 14 minority (11 African Americans, 2 Asian Americans, 1 Hispanic). 88 applicants, 91% accepted. In 1997, 131 degrees awarded. *Degree requirements:* Comprehensive exam required, foreign language and thesis not required. *Entrance requirements:* Minimum GPA of 2.7. Application deadline: 6/1 (priority date; 11/1 for spring admission). Application fee: $40. *Expenses:* Tuition $436 per credit hour. Fees $20 per semester. • Dr. James W. Black, Director, 716-389-2619. Application contact: Dr. Kay F. Marshman, Dean, 716-389-2815. Fax: 716-389-2452.

New Jersey City University, School of Professional Studies and Education, Department of Special Education, Jersey City, NJ 07305-1957. Awards MA. Evening/weekend programs available. *Entrance requirements:* GRE General Test, TOEFL or MAT. Application deadline: 8/1 (priority date; rolling processing; 12/1 for spring admission). Application fee: $0. *Faculty research:* Mainstreaming the handicapped child and the autistic child.

New Mexico Highlands University, School of Education, Las Vegas, NM 87701. Offerings include special education (MA). School faculty: 32 full-time (14 women). *Degree requirements:* Thesis or alternative required, foreign language not required. *Entrance requirements:* Minimum undergraduate GPA of 3.0. Application deadline: 8/1 (priority date; rolling processing). Application fee: $15. *Expenses:* Tuition $1816 per year full-time, $227 per hour part-time for state residents; $7468 per year full-time, $227 per hour part-time for nonresidents. Fees $10 per year. • Dr. James Abreu, Dean, 505-454-3357. Application contact: Dr. Glen W. Davidson, Academic Vice President, 505-454-3311. Fax: 505-454-3558. E-mail: glendavidson@venus.nmhu.edu.

New Mexico State University, College of Education, Department of Special Education/Communication Disorders, Las Cruces, NM 88003-8001. Awards MA. Accredited by NCATE. Part-time programs available. Faculty: 12 full-time (7 women). 111 applicants, 30% accepted. In 1997, 164 degrees awarded. *Degree requirements:* Thesis or alternative. *Entrance requirements:* GRE General Test or MAT. Application deadline: 3/1 (priority date; rolling processing). Application fee: $15 ($35 for international students). Electronic applications accepted. *Tuition:* $2514 per year full-time, $105 per credit hour part-time for state residents; $7848 per year full-time, $327 per credit hour part-time for nonresidents. *Financial aid:* Research assistantships, teaching assistantships, Federal Work-Study, and career-related internships or fieldwork available. Aid available to part-time students. Financial aid application deadline: 3/1. *Faculty research:* Multicultural special education, multicultural communication disorders, mild handicaps, augmentative and alternative communication, transdisciplinary training. • Dr. Gerard Giordano, Head, 505-646-2402. Fax: 505-646-7712. E-mail: ggiordan@nmsu.edu.

New York University, School of Education, Department of Health Studies, Program in Deafness Rehabilitation, New York, NY 10012-1019. Awards MA. Part-time and evening/weekend programs available. Faculty: 1 full-time (0 women), 7 part-time. Students: 9 full-time, 10 part-time. 15 applicants, 73% accepted. In 1997, 4 degrees awarded. *Degree requirements:* Thesis required (for some programs), foreign language not required. *Entrance requirements:* TOEFL. Application deadline: 2/1 (priority date; rolling processing; 12/1 for spring admission). Application fee: $40 ($60 for international students). *Financial aid:* Partial tuition waivers, Federal Work-Study, institutionally sponsored loans, and career-related internships or fieldwork available. Aid available to part-time students. Financial aid application deadline: 3/1; applicants required to submit FAFSA. • Randolph Mowry, Director, 212-998-5224. Application contact: Office of Graduate Admissions, 212-998-5030. Fax: 212-995-4328.

New York University, School of Education, Department of Teaching and Learning, Program in Special Education, New York, NY 10012-1019. Offers bilingual special education (MA), early childhood special education (MA), special education (MA), special education learning consultant (CAS). Part-time and evening/weekend programs available. Faculty: 6 full-time, 7 part-time. Students: 36 full-time, 32 part-time. 99 applicants, 66% accepted. In 1997, 41 master's, 8 CASs awarded. *Degree requirements:* For master's, thesis required (for some programs), foreign language not required. *Entrance requirements:* For master's, TOEFL, interview; for CAS, TOEFL, master's degree. Application deadline: 2/1 (priority date; rolling processing; 12/1 for spring admission). Application fee: $40 ($60 for international students). *Financial aid:* Partial tuition waivers, Federal Work-Study, institutionally sponsored loans, and career-related internships or fieldwork available. Aid available to part-time students. Financial aid application deadline: 3/1; applicants required to submit FAFSA. *Faculty research:* Special education referrals, attention deficit disorders in children, mainstreaming, curriculum-based assessment and program implementation. • Lisa Fleisher, Director, 212-998-5200. Application contact: Office of Graduate Admissions, 212-998-5030. Fax: 212-995-4328.

North Carolina Central University, Division of Academic Affairs, School of Education, Special Education Program, Durham, NC 27707-3129. Offers education of the emotionally handicapped (M Ed), education of the mentally handicapped (M Ed). Accredited by NCATE. Part-time and evening/weekend programs available. Students: 6 full-time (all women), 36 part-time (30 women); includes 22 minority (all African Americans). Average age 34. 15 applicants, 87% accepted. In 1997, 12 degrees awarded. *Degree requirements:* Thesis or alternative, comprehensive exam required, foreign language not required. *Entrance requirements:* Minimum GPA of 3.0 in major, 2.5 overall. Application deadline: 8/1. Application fee: $30. *Tuition:* $2027 per year full-time, $508 per semester (minimum) part-time for state residents; $9155 per year full-time, $2290 per semester (minimum) part-time for nonresidents. *Financial aid:* Fellowships, teaching assistantships, Federal Work-Study, institutionally sponsored loans, and career-related internships or fieldwork available. Aid available to part-time students. Financial aid application deadline: 5/1. *Faculty research:* Vocational programs for special needs learners. • Dr. Virginia East, Director, 919-560-6478. Application contact: Dr. Cecelia Steppe-Jones, Associate Dean of Graduate Studies and Administration, 919-560-6478.

North Carolina State University, College of Education and Psychology, Department of Curriculum and Instruction, Program in Special Education, Raleigh, NC 27695. Awards M Ed, MS. Accredited by NCATE. Students: 12 full-time (all women), 49 part-time (45 women); includes 5 minority (3 African Americans, 2 Asian Americans). Average age 32. 38 applicants, 66% accepted. In 1997, 26 degrees awarded. *Degree requirements:* Thesis required (for some programs), foreign language not required. *Entrance requirements:* GRE General Test or MAT, minimum GPA of 3.0 in major. Application deadline: 3/1 (11/1 for spring admission). Application fee: $45. *Tuition:* $2370 per year full-time, $517 per semester (minimum) part-time for state residents; $11,536 per year full-time, $2809 per semester (minimum) part-time for nonresidents. *Financial aid:* Fellowships, research assistantships, teaching assistantships, and career-related internships or fieldwork available. • Dr. Barbara J. Fox, Director of Graduate Programs, 919-515-1781. Fax: 919-515-6978. E-mail: fox@poe.coe.ncsu.edu.

Northeastern Illinois University, College of Education, Department of Special Education, Program in Special Education, Chicago, IL 60625-4699. Offers early childhood special education (MA), educating children with behavior disorders (MA), educating individuals with mental retardation (MA), teaching children with learning disabilities (MA). Part-time and evening/weekend programs available. Faculty: 15 full-time (9 women), 3 part-time (all women). Students: 44 full-time (30 women), 291 part-time (231 women); includes 52 minority (25 African Americans, 8 Asian Americans, 19 Hispanics), 1 international. Average age 34. 145 applicants, 85% accepted. In 1997, 93 degrees awarded. *Degree requirements:* Project required, thesis optional, foreign language not required. *Entrance requirements:* Teaching certificate or course work in history or philosophy of education, minimum GPA of 2.75. Application deadline: 3/18 (priority date; rolling processing; 9/30 for spring admission). Application fee: $0. *Expenses:* Tuition $2226 per year full-time, $93 per credit hour part-time for state residents; $6678 per year full-time, $278 per credit hour part-time for nonresidents. Fees $358 per year full-time, $14.90 per credit hour part-time. *Financial aid:* In 1997–98, 62 students received aid, including 5 research assistantships averaging $450 per month; full and partial tuition waivers, Federal Work-Study, institutionally sponsored loans, and career-related internships or fieldwork also available. Aid available to part-time students. *Faculty research:* Bilingual special education, use of technology in the classroom, teachers' attitudes towards inclusion. • Application contact: Dr. Mohan K. Sood, Dean of Graduate College, 773-583-4050 Ext. 6143. Fax: 773-794-6670.

Northeastern State University, College of Education, Department of Special Education, Tahlequah, OK 74464-2399. Awards M Ed. Part-time and evening/weekend programs available. Faculty: 4 (0 women). Students: 78 (73 women). In 1997, 35 degrees awarded. *Degree requirements:* Thesis or alternative required, foreign language not required. *Entrance requirements:* GRE General Test (minimum combined score of 900) or MAT (minimum score 33), minimum GPA of 2.75. Application deadline: 6/1 (priority date; rolling processing). Application fee: $0. *Expenses:* Tuition $74 per credit hour for state residents; $176 per credit hour for nonresidents. Fees $30 per year. *Financial aid:* Teaching assistantships, Federal Work-Study, and career-related internships or fieldwork available. Financial aid application deadline: 3/1. • Dr. Lillian Young, Head, 918-456-5511 Ext. 3781.

Northeastern University, Bouvé College of Pharmacy and Health Sciences Graduate School, Department of Counseling Psychology, Rehabilitation, and Special Education, Program in Special Needs and Intensive Special Needs, Boston, MA 02115-5096. Awards MS Ed. Part-time programs available. Faculty: 2 full-time (both women), 2 part-time (both women). Students: 9 full-time (7 women), 7 part-time (5 women). Average age 28. 22 applicants, 86% accepted. In 1997, 7 degrees awarded. *Entrance requirements:* GRE General Test or MAT. Application deadline: rolling. Application fee: $40. *Expenses:* Tuition $440 per credit hour. Fees $55 per quarter full-time, $13.25 per quarter part-time. *Financial aid:* Research assistantships, teaching assistantships, administrative assistantships, graduate assistantships, Federal Work-Study, and career-related internships or fieldwork available. Aid available to part-time students. Financial aid application deadline: 3/1; applicants required to submit FAFSA. *Faculty research:* Bilingual special education, early intervention, language development. • Dr. Karin Lifter, Co-Director, 617-373-3276. Fax: 617-373-6756. Application contact: Bill Purnell, Director of Graduate Admissions, 617-373-2708. Fax: 617-373-4701. E-mail: w.purnell@nunet.neu.edu.

Announcement: Master's-level special education programs leading to certification in special needs and intensive special needs are offered on both a full- and part-time basis. Programs are designed to meet the Interstate Certification Compact (ICC) and Massachusetts Department of Education regulations for certification. A variety of practicum sites are available in urban and suburban areas in private and public settings that range from substantially separate to fully integrated programs. Course work emphasizes a life-span management approach from early intervention through transitional planning. Courses are scheduled during the late afternoon and evening to accommodate students who are working.

See in-depth description on page 1797.

Northeast Louisiana University, College of Education, Department of Curriculum and Instruction, Program in Special Education, Monroe, LA 71209-0001. Awards M Ed. Accredited by NCATE. Part-time and evening/weekend programs available. *Entrance requirements:* GRE General Test, minimum GPA of 2.5. Application deadline: 6/1 (priority date; rolling processing; 11/1 for spring admission). Application fee: $15 ($25 for international students). *Tuition:* $2028 per year full-time, $240 per semester (minimum) part-time for state residents; $6852 per year full-time, $240 per semester (minimum) part-time for nonresidents.

Northern Arizona University, Center for Excellence in Education, Program in Reading and Learning Disabilities, Flagstaff, AZ 86011. Awards M Ed. Students: 1 (woman) full-time, 4 part-time (all women). Average age 29. 3 applicants, 33% accepted. In 1997, 1 degree awarded. *Degree requirements:* Thesis optional, foreign language not required. *Entrance requirements:* GRE General Test or minimum GPA of 3.0. Application deadline: 3/15 (priority date; rolling processing). Application fee: $45. *Expenses:* Tuition $2088 per year full-time, $330 per semester (minimum) part-time for state residents; $8004 per year full-time, $1002 per semester (minimum) part-time for nonresidents. Fees $72 per year full-time, $18 per semester (minimum) part-time. *Financial aid:* Full and partial tuition waivers, Federal Work-Study, and career-related internships or fieldwork available. *Faculty research:* Mild to moderate disabilities. • Dr. Malathi Sandhu, Interim Chair, 520-523-5342.

Northern Arizona University, Center for Excellence in Education, Program in Special Education, Flagstaff, AZ 86011. Awards M Ed. Part-time programs available. Students: 20 full-time (18 women), 52 part-time (49 women); includes 8 minority (3 Hispanics, 5 Native Americans), 1 international. Average age 28. 28 applicants, 75% accepted. In 1997, 37 degrees awarded. *Degree requirements:* Thesis or alternative required, foreign language not required. *Entrance requirements:* GRE General Test or minimum GPA of 3.0. Application deadline: 3/15 (priority date; rolling processing). Application fee: $45. *Expenses:* Tuition $2088 per year full-time, $330 per semester (minimum) part-time for state residents; $8004 per year full-time, $1002 per semester (minimum) part-time for nonresidents. Fees $72 per year full-time, $18 per semester (minimum) part-time. *Financial aid:* Assistantships and career-related internships or fieldwork available. *Faculty research:* Special education teacher training, mainstreaming, assessing and teaching mildly disabled, emotional disturbance, parent involvement. • Dr. Malathi Sandhu, Interim Chair, 520-523-5342.

Northern Illinois University, College of Education, Department of Educational Psychology, Counseling, and Special Education, Program in Special Education, De Kalb, IL 60115-2854. Awards MS Ed, Ed D. Accredited by NCATE. Part-time and evening/weekend programs available. Faculty: 14 full-time (8 women), 1 part-time (0 women). Students: 52 full-time (41 women), 73 part-time (61 women); includes 2 minority (1 African American, 1 Hispanic). Average age 33. 70 applicants, 54% accepted. In 1997, 60 master's, 2 doctorates awarded. *Degree requirements:* For master's, comprehensive exam required, thesis optional, foreign language not required; for doctorate, candidacy exam, dissertation defense required, foreign language not required. *Entrance requirements:* For master's, GRE General Test, TOEFL (minimum score 550), minimum GPA of 2.75; for doctorate, GRE General Test, TOEFL (minimum score 550), minimum GPA of 2.75 (undergraduate), 3.2 (graduate), master's degree. Application deadline: 6/1 (rolling processing; 11/1 for spring admission). Application fee: $30. *Tuition:* $3984 per year full-time, $154 per credit hour part-time for state residents; $8160 per year full-time, $328 per credit hour part-time for nonresidents. *Financial aid:* Fellowships, research assistantships, teaching assistantships, staff assistantships, full tuition waivers, Federal Work-Study, and career-related internships or fieldwork available. Aid available to part-time students. • Dr. Diane Deitz, Faculty Chair, 815-753-8458.

Northern Michigan University, College of Behavioral Sciences and Human Services, Department of Education, Program in Special Education, Marquette, MI 49855-5301. Awards MA Ed. Accredited by NCATE. Part-time programs available. Students: 6 full-time (5 women), 32 part-time (30 women). 4 applicants, 100% accepted. In 1997, 6 degrees awarded. *Degree requirements:* Thesis or alternative required, foreign language not required. *Entrance requirements:* GRE General Test (minimum combined score of 900), minimum GPA of 2.75. Application deadline: 7/1 (priority date; rolling processing; 11/1 for spring admission). Application fee: $25. *Expenses:* Tuition $135 per credit hour for state residents; $215 per credit hour for nonresidents. Fees $183 per year full-time, $94 per year (minimum) part-time. *Financial aid:* Federal Work-Study, institutionally sponsored loans available. Aid available to part-time students. Financial aid application deadline: 3/1. *Faculty research:* Interdisciplinary approaches to learning disabilities, neurological bases for cognitive processing of information. • Application contact: Dr. Marjorie McKee, Coordinator, 906-227-2145.

Northern State University, Division of Graduate Studies in Education, Program in Teaching and Learning, Aberdeen, SD 57401-7198. Offerings include special education (MS Ed). Accredited by NCATE. Offered jointly with Huron University, Jamestown College, and the University of Mary. Program faculty: 98 full-time (28 women). *Degree requirements:* Thesis required, foreign language not required. *Average time to degree:* master's–1.5 years full-time. *Entrance requirements:* Minimum GPA of 2.75. Application deadline: 8/15 (priority date; rolling processing; 12/15 for spring admission). Application fee: $15. *Expenses:* Tuition $1999 per year full-time, $83 per credit hour part-time for state residents; $6034 per year full-time, $251 per credit hour part-time for nonresidents. Fees $954 per year full-time, $40 per credit hour part-time. • Dr. Paul Deputy, Head, 605-626-2415. Application contact: Dr. Sharon Tebben, Director of Graduate Studies, 605-626-2558. Fax: 605-626-2542.

North Georgia College & State University, Graduate School, Program in Education, Dahlonega, GA 30597-1001. Offerings include special education (M Ed), with options in behavior disorders, interrelated special education, learning disabilities, mental retardation. Accredited by NCATE. Program faculty: 57 full-time (15 women), 7 part-time (4 women). *Degree requirements:* Comprehensive exam required, thesis optional, foreign language not required. *Entrance requirements:* GRE General Test (minimum combined score of 800) or MAT (minimum score 44), minimum GPA of 2.75. Application deadline: 9/1 (priority date; rolling processing). Application fee: $25. • Dr. Bob Michael, Dean, School of Education, 706-864-1533. Application contact: Mai-Lan Ledbetter, Coordinator of Graduate Admissions, 706-864-1543. Fax: 706-864-1668. E-mail: mledbetter@nugget.ngc.peachnet.edu.

Northwestern State University of Louisiana, Division of Education, Program in Human Services, Natchitoches, LA 71497. Offerings include special education (M Ed, Ed S). Accredited by NCATE. Program faculty: 3 full-time (2 women), 2 part-time (1 woman). *Application deadline:* 8/1 (priority date; rolling processing; 1/10 for spring admission). *Application fee:* $15 ($25 for international students). *Tuition:* $2147 per year full-time, $336 per semester (minimum) part-time for state residents; $6437 per year full-time, $336 per semester (minimum) part-time for nonresidents. • Dr. Hurst Hall, Head, 318-357-4169. Application contact: Dr. Tom Hanson, Dean, Graduate Studies and Research, 318-357-5851. Fax: 318-357-5019.

Northwestern University, School of Speech, Department of Communication Sciences and Disorders, Program in Learning Disabilities, Evanston, IL 60208. Awards MA, PhD. Admissions and degrees offered through The Graduate School. Part-time programs available. Faculty: 5 full-time (1 woman). Students: 29 full-time (22 women), 3 part-time (all women); includes 6 minority (3 African Americans, 2 Asian Americans, 1 Native American), 2 international. 25 applicants, 68% accepted. In 1997, 12 master's, 4 doctorates awarded. Terminal master's awarded for partial completion of doctoral program. *Degree requirements:* For master's, comprehensive exams required, thesis optional, foreign language not required; for doctorate, dissertation, pre-dissertation research project, qualifying exam required, foreign language not required. *Entrance requirements:* For master's, GRE General Test (minimum combined score of 1000), minimum GPA of 3.2; for doctorate, GRE General Test (minimum combined score of 1200), minimum GPA of 3.2. Application deadline: 8/30. Application fee: $50 ($55 for international students). *Tuition:* $20,430 per year full-time, $2424 per course part-time. *Financial aid:* In 1997–98, 12 students received aid, including 3 fellowships averaging $1,256 per month, 1 research assistantship averaging $1,592 per month, 4 teaching assistantships averaging $1,296 per month, 1 traineeship; Federal Work-Study, institutionally sponsored loans, and career-related internships or fieldwork also available. Financial aid application deadline: 1/15; applicants required to submit FAFSA. *Faculty research:* Reading and writing disabilities, inter-relations of oral and written language, social context of atypical development, attention deficit disorder, neuroscience of learning disorders. Total annual research expenditures: $15,000. • Dr. C. Addison Stone, Director, 847-491-3183. E-mail: a-stone@nwu.edu. Application contact: Betty Stafford, Admission Contact, 847-491-3971. Fax: 847-491-2494. E-mail: elstaff@nwu.edu.

See in-depth description on page 1047.

Northwestern University, School of Speech, Department of Communication Sciences and Disorders, Program in Speech and Language Pathology and Learning Disabilities, Evanston, IL 60208. Awards MA. Admissions and degree offered through The Graduate School. Students: 4 full-time (all women); includes 1 international. 15 applicants, 47% accepted. *Degree requirements:* Seminar paper required, foreign language not required. *Entrance requirements:* GRE General Test. Application deadline: 8/30. Application fee: $50 ($55 for international students). *Tuition:* $20,430 per year full-time, $2424 per course part-time. *Financial aid:* Partial tuition scholarships, institutionally sponsored loans available. Financial aid application deadline: 1/15; applicants required to submit FAFSA. *Faculty research:* Language and cognitive development, phonological and reading development. • Dr. Bruce L. Smith, Director, 847-491-5073. E-mail: b-smith2@nwu.edu. Application contact: Cindy Coy, Admission Contact, 847-491-5073. Fax: 847-467-2776. E-mail: ccoy@nwu.edu.

Northwest Missouri State University, College of Education and Human Services, Department of Curriculum and Instruction, Program in the Learning Disabled and Mentally Handicapped, 800 University Drive, Maryville, MO 64468-6001. Offers elementary education of the learning disabled (MS Ed), elementary education of the mentally handicapped (MS Ed), secondary education of the learning disabled (MS Ed), secondary education of the mentally handicapped (MS Ed). Accredited by NCATE. Part-time programs available. Faculty: 14 full-time (12 women). Students: 2 full-time (both women), 28 part-time (26 women). 2 applicants, 100% accepted. In 1997, 8 degrees awarded. *Degree requirements:* Comprehensive exam required, foreign

Directory: Special Education

Northwest Missouri State University (continued)

language and thesis not required. *Entrance requirements:* GRE General Test (minimum combined score of 700), TOEFL (minimum score 550), minimum undergraduate GPA of 2.5, teaching certificate, writing sample. Application deadline: rolling. Application fee: $0 ($50 for international students). *Expenses:* Tuition $113 per credit hour for state residents; $197 per credit hour for nonresidents. Fees $3 per credit hour. *Financial aid:* In 1997–98, 2 students received aid, including 1 teaching assistantship averaging $585 per month. Financial aid application deadline: 3/1. • Dr. Nancy Riley, Adviser, 816-562-1774. Application contact: Dr. Frances Shipley, Dean of Graduate School, 816-562-1145. E-mail: gradsch@acad.nwmissouri.edu.

Notre Dame College, Education Division, Program in Emotional and Behavioral Disorders, Manchester, NH 03104-2299. Awards M Ed. Faculty: 1 (woman) full-time, 3 part-time (2 women). Students: 6 full-time (5 women), 30 part-time (26 women). Average age 33. 20 applicants, 85% accepted. In 1997, 1 degree awarded. *Degree requirements:* Comprehensive exams or thesis required, foreign language not required. *Entrance requirements:* GRE General Test or MAT, teaching certificate. Application fee: $35. *Tuition:* $299 per credit. *Financial aid:* Assistantships available. • Laura Wasielewski, Director, 603-669-4298 Ext. 159.

Notre Dame College, Education Division, Program in Learning and Language Disabilities, Manchester, NH 03104-2299. Awards M Ed. Part-time programs available. Faculty: 1 (woman) full-time, 6 part-time (5 women). Students: 18 full-time (16 women), 67 part-time (55 women). Average age 33. 35 applicants, 74% accepted. In 1997, 16 degrees awarded. *Degree requirements:* Comprehensive exams, portfolio, or thesis required, foreign language not required. *Entrance requirements:* GRE General Test or MAT, teaching certificate. Application deadline: rolling. Application fee: $35. *Tuition:* $299 per credit. *Financial aid:* Assistantships available. • Kelly Moore Dunn, Director, 603-669-4298 Ext. 153.

Nova Southeastern University, Fischler Center for the Advancement of Education, Graduate Teacher Education Program, Fort Lauderdale, FL 33314-7721. Offerings include emotionally handicapped (MS, Ed S), mentally handicapped (MS, Ed S), specific learning disabilities (MS, Ed S). *Degree requirements:* Thesis, practicum required, foreign language not required. *Entrance requirements:* For master's, teaching certificate; for Ed S, master's degree, teaching certificate. Application deadline: rolling. Application fee: $50. *Tuition:* $245 per credit hour (minimum). • Dr. Deo Nellis, Dean, 954-262-8601. E-mail: deo@fcae.nova.edu. Application contact: Dr. Mark Seldine, Director of Student Affairs, 954-262-8689. Fax: 954-262-3910. E-mail: seldines@fcae.nova.edu.

Oakland University, School of Education and Human Services, Program in Special Education, Rochester, MI 48309-4401. Awards M Ed, Certificate. Accredited by NCATE. Faculty: 13 full-time. Students: 21 full-time (16 women), 101 part-time (90 women); includes 1 minority (Asian American). Average age 36. In 1997, 4 master's awarded. *Entrance requirements:* For master's, minimum GPA of 3.0 for unconditional admission, interview. Application deadline: 6/1. Application fee: $30. *Expenses:* Tuition $3852 per year full-time, $214 per credit hour part-time for state residents; $8532 per year full-time, $474 per credit hour part-time for nonresidents. Fees $420 per year. *Financial aid:* Full tuition waivers, Federal Work-Study, institutionally sponsored loans, and career-related internships or fieldwork available. Financial aid application deadline: 3/1; applicants required to submit FAFSA. • Dr. Ronald Swartz, Chair, 248-370-3077. Application contact: Dr. Carol Swift, Coordinator, 248-370-3077.

Ohio University, Graduate Studies, College of Education, School of Curriculum and Instruction, Program in Special Education, Athens, OH 45701-2979. Awards M Ed. Accredited by NCATE. Evening/weekend programs available. Students: 17 full-time (14 women), 36 part-time (27 women); includes 1 minority (African American), 3 international. 34 applicants, 65% accepted. *Degree requirements:* Thesis or alternative required, foreign language not required. *Entrance requirements:* GRE General Test or MAT. Application deadline: rolling. Application fee: $30. *Tuition:* $5430 per year full-time, $216 per quarter hour part-time for state residents; $10,431 per year full-time, $423 per quarter hour part-time for nonresidents. *Financial aid:* In 1997–98, 4 assistantships (2 to first-year students) were awarded; teaching assistantships, full tuition waivers, Federal Work-Study, institutionally sponsored loans also available. Financial aid application deadline: 3/15. • Application contact: Dr. Bonnie Beach, Graduate Chair, 740-593-0523.

Old Dominion University, Darden College of Education, Department of Early Childhood, Speech-Language Pathology, and Special Education, Program in Special Education, Norfolk, VA 23529. Awards MS Ed. Accredited by NCATE. Part-time and evening/weekend programs available. Postbaccalaureate distance learning degree programs offered (no on-campus study). Students: 93 full-time (77 women), 203 part-time (168 women); includes 35 minority (26 African Americans, 4 Asian Americans, 1 Hispanic, 4 Native Americans), 1 international. Average age 34. 170 applicants, 75% accepted. In 1997, 94 degrees awarded. *Degree requirements:* Comprehensive and written exams required, thesis optional, foreign language not required. *Entrance requirements:* GRE General Test (minimum combined score of 1350 on three sections), minimum GPA of 3.0 in major, 2.75 overall. Application deadline: 7/1 (rolling processing; 4/1 for spring admission). Application fee: $30. Electronic applications accepted. *Expenses:* Tuition $180 per credit hour for state residents; $477 per credit hour for nonresidents. Fees $140 per year full-time, $32 per semester part-time. *Financial aid:* In 1997–98, 80 students received aid, including 1 fellowship totaling $3,000, 3 research assistantships (1 to a first-year student) totaling $14,314, 21 tution grants (2 to first-year students) totaling $17,428; partial tuition waivers and career-related internships or fieldwork also available. Aid available to part-time students. Financial aid application deadline: 2/15; applicants required to submit FAFSA. *Faculty research:* Mainstreaming/inclusion, clinical practice, infant and preschool handicapped, distance learning. • Dr. Cheryl S. Baker, Director, 757-683-3226. Fax: 757-683-5593. E-mail: csbaker@odu.edu.

Our Lady of the Lake University of San Antonio, School of Education and Clinical Studies, Program in Special Education, 411 Southwest 24th Street, San Antonio, TX 78207-4689. Awards MA. Part-time and evening/weekend programs available. Postbaccalaureate distance learning degree programs offered (minimal on-campus study). Faculty: 4 full-time (all women), 3 part-time (1 woman). Students: 4 full-time (3 women), 19 part-time (17 women); includes 11 minority (2 African Americans, 9 Hispanics). Average age 35. In 1997, 14 degrees awarded. *Degree requirements:* Comprehensive exam/Examination for the Certification of Education in Texas required, thesis optional, foreign language not required. *Entrance requirements:* GRE General Test or MAT, interview. Application deadline: rolling. Application fee: $15. *Expenses:* Tuition $371 per credit hour. Fees $57 per semester full-time, $32 per semester part-time. *Financial aid:* Partial tuition waivers and career-related internships or fieldwork available. Financial aid application deadline: 4/15. • Dr. Consuelo Bossey, Coordinator, 210-434-6711 Ext. 303. Application contact: Debbie Hamilton, Director of Admissions, 210-434-6711 Ext. 314. Fax: 210-436-2314.

Pacific Lutheran University, School of Education, Program in Special Education, Tacoma, WA 98447. Offers early childhood (MA), kindergarten through twelfth grade (MA). Accredited by NCATE. Part-time and evening/weekend programs available. Faculty: 7 full-time (3 women). Students: 1 (woman) full-time, 1 (woman) part-time. Average age 43. 2 applicants, 100% accepted. In 1997, 8 degrees awarded. *Degree requirements:* Comprehensive exam, research project or thesis required, foreign language not required. *Entrance requirements:* GRE General Test or MAT, TOEFL (minimum score 550), interview. Application deadline: rolling. Application fee: $35. *Tuition:* $490 per semester hour. *Financial aid:* Fellowships, research assistantships, scholarships, Federal Work-Study available. Financial aid application deadline: 3/1. • Dr. Leon Reisberg, Graduate Director, 253-535-7272. Application contact: Marjo Burdick, Office of Admissions, 253-535-7151. Fax: 253-535-8320. E-mail: admissions@plu.edu.

Pennsylvania College of Optometry, Department of Vision Impairment, 8360 Old York Road, Elkins Park, PA 19027. Offerings include education of children and youth with visual and multiple impairments (M Ed). Department faculty: 5 full-time (all women), 10 part-time (8 women). *Average time to degree:* master's–1 year full-time, 2.5 years part-time. *Application deadline:* 6/16 (rolling processing). *Application fee:* $50. • Dr. Kathleen M. Huebner, Assistant Dean, 215-276-6093. Fax: 215-276-6292. E-mail: kathyh@pco.edu. Application contact: Diane Wormsley, Recruitment Committee Chair, 215-780-1366. Fax: 215-780-1357. E-mail: lwormsley@pco.edu.

Pennsylvania State University Great Valley School of Graduate Professional Studies, Graduate Studies and Continuing Education, College of Education, Program in Special Education, Malvern, PA 19355-1488. Awards M Ed, MS. Students: 11 full-time (10 women), 56 part-time (45 women). Average age 34. In 1997, 10 degrees awarded. *Entrance requirements:* GRE General Test or MAT. Application fee: $40. • Dr. Mary C. Scheeler, Coordinator, 610-648-3284. Application contact: Dr. James McAfee, 610-889-1300.

Pennsylvania State University University Park Campus, College of Education, Department of Educational and School Psychology and Special Education, Program in Special Education, University Park, PA 16802-1503. Awards M Ed, MS, PhD. Accredited by NCATE. Students: 27 full-time (23 women), 12 part-time (11 women). In 1997, 14 master's, 1 doctorate awarded. *Entrance requirements:* GRE General Test or MAT. Application fee: $40. *Expenses:* Tuition $6534 per year full-time, $276 per credit part-time for state residents; $13,460 per year full-time, $561 per credit part-time for nonresidents. Fees $252 per year (minimum) full-time, $43 per semester (minimum) part-time. • Dr. Charles Hughes, Professor in Charge, 814-863-1699.

Pittsburg State University, School of Education, Department of Special Services and Leadership Studies, Program in Special Education Teaching, Pittsburg, KS 66762-5880. Offers behavioral disorders (MS), learning disabilities (MS), mentally retarded (MS). Accredited by NCATE. Students: 6 full-time (all women), 55 part-time (47 women); includes 1 minority (Native American), 1 international. In 1997, 39 degrees awarded. *Degree requirements:* Thesis or alternative required, foreign language not required. *Entrance requirements:* GRE General Test or MAT. Application fee: $40. *Tuition:* $2418 per year full-time, $103 per credit hour part-time for state residents; $6130 per year full-time, $258 per credit hour part-time for nonresidents. *Financial aid:* Teaching assistantships, Federal Work-Study, and career-related internships or fieldwork available. • Dr. Steve Scott, Chairman, Department of Special Services and Leadership Studies, 316-235-4487.

Plattsburgh State University of New York, Faculty of Professional Studies, Center for Educational Studies and Services, Program in Special Education, Plattsburgh, NY 12901-2681. Awards MS. Students: 18 full-time (15 women), 21 part-time (18 women); includes 3 minority (1 African American, 1 Asian American, 1 Hispanic). 7 applicants, 43% accepted. In 1997, 24 degrees awarded. *Degree requirements:* Comprehensive exam or research project required, thesis optional, foreign language not required. *Entrance requirements:* GRE General Test or MAT, minimum GPA of 2.5. Application deadline: rolling. Application fee: $50. *Expenses:* Tuition $5100 per year full-time, $213 per credit hour part-time for state residents; $8416 per year full-time, $351 per credit hour part-time for nonresidents. Fees $395 per year full-time, $15.10 per credit hour part-time. *Financial aid:* 11 students received aid; Federal Work-Study available. Aid available to part-time students. Financial aid application deadline: 4/15; applicants required to submit FAFSA. • Dr. Raymond Domenico, Director and Associate Dean, Center for Educational Studies and Services, 518-564-2122.

Portland State University, School of Education, Department of Special Education and Counselor Education, Program in Special Education, Portland, OR 97207-0751. Awards MA, MS. Accredited by NCATE. Part-time and evening/weekend programs available. Faculty: 24 full-time (13 women), 1 part-time (0 women), 24.2 FTE. Students: 67 full-time (53 women), 42 part-time (30 women); includes 9 minority (2 African Americans, 1 Asian American, 4 Hispanics, 2 Native Americans), 2 international. Average age 33. 89 applicants, 80% accepted. *Degree requirements:* Thesis or alternative required, foreign language not required. *Entrance requirements:* California Basic Educational Skills Test, TOEFL (minimum score 550), minimum GPA of 3.0 in upper-division course work or 2.75 overall. Application deadline: 4/1. Application fee: $50. *Tuition:* $6101 per year full-time, $689 per semester (minimum) part-time for state residents; $10,445 per year full-time, $689 per semester (minimum) part-time for nonresidents. *Financial aid:* Research assistantships, teaching assistantships, Federal Work-Study, institutionally sponsored loans, and career-related internships or fieldwork available. Aid available to part-time students. Financial aid application deadline: 3/1; applicants required to submit FAFSA. *Faculty research:* Autism, severe handicaps, functional curriculum, inclusive education, outcome-based assessment. Total annual research expenditures: $400,000. • Application contact: Amber Jones, Graduate Secretary, 503-725-4632. Fax: 503-725-5599. E-mail: amber@ed.pdx.edu.

Prairie View A&M University, College of Education, Department of Curriculum and Instruction, Prairie View, TX 77446-0188. Offerings include special education (M Ed, MS Ed). Accredited by NCATE. Department faculty: 8 full-time (5 women). *Degree requirements:* Seminar paper required, thesis optional, foreign language not required. *Average time to degree:* master's–2.5 years full-time, 4 years part-time. *Entrance requirements:* GRE General Test. Application deadline: 7/1 (priority date; rolling processing; 11/1 for spring admission). Application fee: $10. *Tuition:* $2202 per year full-time, $336 per semester (minimum) part-time for state residents; $6000 per year full-time, $963 per semester (minimum) part-time for nonresidents. • Dr. Joan B. Clark, Head, 409-857-3921. Fax: 409-857-2911.

Pratt Institute, School of Art and Design, Department of Creative Arts Therapy, Brooklyn, NY 11205-3899. Offerings include art therapy-special education (MPS). *Degree requirements:* Thesis required, foreign language not required. *Entrance requirements:* TOEFL (minimum score 550). Application deadline: 3/1 (priority date; rolling processing). Application fee: $35 ($80 for international students). *Expenses:* Tuition $15,288 per year full-time, $637 per credit part-time. Fees $480 per year.

Providence College, Department of Education, Program in Special Education, Providence, RI 02918. Awards M Ed. Faculty: 8 full-time (7 women), 15 part-time (10 women). Students: 7 full-time (6 women), 145 part-time (129 women); includes 3 minority (2 African Americans, 1 Hispanic). Average age 32. 33 applicants, 94% accepted. In 1997, 65 degrees awarded (100% entered university research/teaching). *Degree requirements:* Comprehensive exam required, foreign language and thesis not required. *Entrance requirements:* GRE General Test (minimum combined score of 1000) or MAT (minimum score 45), TOEFL. Application deadline: 8/12 (priority date; rolling processing; 12/1 for spring admission). Application fee: $40. *Tuition:* $621 per course. *Financial aid:* Graduate assistantships and career-related internships or fieldwork available. Aid available to part-time students. Financial aid applicants required to submit FAFSA. • Dr. Thomas F. Flaherty, Dean, Graduate School, 401-865-2247. Fax: 401-865-2057.

Purdue University, School of Education, Department of Educational Studies, West Lafayette, IN 47907. Offerings include special education (MS Ed). Accredited by NCATE. Department faculty: 26 full-time (13 women), 23 part-time (14 women). *Application deadline:* 2/1 (9/15 for spring admission). *Application fee:* $30. Electronic applications accepted. *Tuition:* $3500 per year full-time, $126 per credit hour part-time for state residents; $11,720 per year full-time, $387 per credit hour part-time for nonresidents. • Dr. D. H. Schunk, Head, 765-494-9170. Fax: 765-496-1228. E-mail: dschunk@purdue.edu. Application contact: Christine Larsen, Coordinator of Graduate Studies, 765-494-2345. Fax: 765-494-5832. E-mail: gradoffice@soe.purdue.edu.

Queens College of the City University of New York, Social Science Division, School of Education, Department of Educational and Community Programs, Program in Special Education, 65-30 Kissena Boulevard, Flushing, NY 11367-1597. Awards MS Ed. Part-time programs available. Students: 11 full-time (10 women), 170 part-time (147 women); includes 31 minority (14 African Americans, 6 Asian Americans, 11 Hispanics), 1 international. 202 applicants, 58% accepted. In 1997, 38 degrees awarded. *Degree requirements:* Research project required, foreign language and thesis not required. *Entrance requirements:* TOEFL (minimum score

600), minimum GPA of 3.0. Application deadline: 4/1 (rolling processing; 11/1 for spring admission). Application fee: $40. *Expenses:* Tuition $4350 per year full-time, $185 per credit part-time for state residents; $7600 per year full-time, $320 per credit part-time for nonresidents. Fees $104 per year. *Financial aid:* Partial tuition waivers, Federal Work-Study, institutionally sponsored loans, and career-related internships or fieldwork available. Aid available to part-time students. Financial aid application deadline: 4/1; applicants required to submit FAFSA. • Dr. Fredda Brown, Coordinator and Graduate Adviser, 718-997-5240. Application contact: Mario Caruso, Director of Graduate Admissions, 718-997-5200. Fax: 718-997-5193. E-mail: graduate%queens.bitnet@cunyvm.cuny.edu.

Radford University, Graduate College, College of Education and Human Development, Department of Special Education, Radford, VA 24142. Offers programs in education of the emotionally disturbed (MS), learning disabilities (MS), mentally retarded (MS). Accredited by NCATE. Part-time programs available. Postbaccalaureate distance learning degree programs offered (minimal on-campus study). Faculty: 6 full-time (all women). Students: 17 full-time (16 women), 25 part-time (23 women); includes 1 minority (African American). Average age 31. 26 applicants, 69% accepted. In 1997, 9 degrees awarded. *Degree requirements:* Comprehensive exam required, foreign language and thesis not required. *Entrance requirements:* GMAT, GRE General Test, MAT, or NTE; TOEFL (minimum score 550), minimum GPA of 2.7. Application deadline: 2/1 (priority date; rolling processing; 10/1 for spring admission). Application fee: $25. Electronic applications accepted. *Expenses:* Tuition $2302 per year full-time, $147 per credit hour part-time for state residents; $5672 per year full-time, $287 per credit hour part-time for nonresidents. Fees $1222 per year full-time. *Financial aid:* In 1997–98, 3 fellowships totaling $11,220, 5 research assistantships totaling $10,400, 23 scholarships/grants totaling $90,745 were awarded; teaching assistantships, Federal Work-Study, institutionally sponsored loans, and career-related internships or fieldwork also available. Financial aid application deadline: 2/1; applicants required to submit FAFSA. • Dr. Judy B. Engelhard, Chairperson, 540-831-6425. Fax: 540-831-6053. E-mail: jengelha@runet.edu.

Rhode Island College, School of Graduate Studies, School of Education and Human Development, Department of Special Education, Providence, RI 02908-1924. Offers programs in special education (M Ed, CAGS), teaching of the handicapped (M Ed, CAGS). Accredited by NCATE. Evening/weekend programs available. Faculty: 10 full-time (2 women), 7 part-time (6 women). Students: 12 full-time (10 women), 67 part-time (62 women); includes 3 minority (1 African American, 2 Asian Americans). In 1997, 37 master's awarded. *Degree requirements:* For CAGS, thesis required, foreign language not required. *Entrance requirements:* For master's, GRE General Test or MAT, 1 year of special education experience. Application deadline: 4/1 (rolling processing). Application fee: $25. *Tuition:* $4064 per year full-time, $214 per credit part-time for state residents; $7658 per year full-time, $376 per credit part-time for nonresidents. *Financial aid:* In 1997–98, 12 fellowships were awarded. Financial aid application deadline: 4/1. *Faculty research:* Early detection, handicapped infants. • Dr. John Gleason, Chair, 401-456-8024.

Rivier College, Graduate Education Department, Program in Learning Disabilities, Nashua, NH 03060-5086. Awards M Ed. Part-time and evening/weekend programs available. *Entrance requirements:* GRE General Test or MAT. Application deadline: rolling. Application fee: $25.

Rochester Institute of Technology, College of Liberal Arts, Department of Behavioral Science, Rochester, NY 14623-5604. Offerings include school psychology and deafness (AC). *Application deadline:* 3/1 (priority date; rolling processing). *Application fee:* $40. *Expenses:* Tuition $18,765 per year full-time, $527 per credit hour part-time. Fees $126 per year full-time. • Paul Grebinger, Director, 716-475-6763.

Rochester Institute of Technology, National Technical Institute for the Deaf, Department of Graduate Secondary Education, Rochester, NY 14623-5604. Awards MS. Students: 11 full-time (5 women), 5 part-time (4 women); includes 1 minority (African American). 13 applicants, 92% accepted. In 1997, 5 degrees awarded. *Application deadline:* 3/1 (priority date; rolling processing). *Application fee:* $40. Electronic applications accepted. *Expenses:* Tuition $18,765 per year full-time, $527 per credit hour part-time. Fees $126 per year full-time. • Gerald Bateman, Director, 716-475-6480.

Rockford College, Department of Education, Program in Learning Disabilities, Rockford, IL 61108-2393. Awards MAT. Part-time and evening/weekend programs available. Faculty: 3 full-time (2 women), 8 part-time (6 women), 5 FTE. Students: 20 part-time (17 women). Average age 33. 3 applicants, 100% accepted. In 1997, 4 degrees awarded. *Degree requirements:* Thesis optional, foreign language not required. *Entrance requirements:* GRE General Test (minimum combined score of 1000). Application deadline: rolling. Application fee: $35. *Tuition:* $15,500 per year full-time, $400 per credit part-time. • Dr. Christy Lendman, Head, 815-226-4181.

Rowan University, College of Education, Department of Special Educational Services/Instruction, Program in Learning Disabilities, Glassboro, NJ 08028-1701. Awards MA, Certificate. Accredited by NCATE. Evening/weekend programs available. Students: 59 (57 women); includes 3 minority (1 African American, 2 Hispanics). 16 applicants, 50% accepted. In 1997, 22 master's awarded. *Degree requirements:* For master's, thesis, comprehensive exams required, foreign language not required; for Certificate, thesis or alternative required, foreign language not required. *Entrance requirements:* For master's, GRE General Test (minimum combined score of 800), minimum GPA of 2.8, 1 year of teaching experience; for Certificate, GRE General Test. Application deadline: 11/1 (priority date; rolling processing; 4/1 for spring admission). Application fee: $50. *Tuition:* $5728 per year full-time, $258 per credit hour part-time for state residents; $8968 per year full-time, $393 per credit hour part-time for nonresidents. *Financial aid:* Federal Work-Study and career-related internships or fieldwork available. Aid available to part-time students. • Dr. Sharon Davis, Adviser, 609-256-4500 Ext. 3796.

Rowan University, College of Education, Department of Special Educational Services/Instruction, Program in Special Education, Glassboro, NJ 08028-1701. Awards MA, MST. Accredited by NCATE. Part-time and evening/weekend programs available. Students: 47 (39 women); includes 6 minority (4 African Americans, 2 Asian Americans). 26 applicants, 58% accepted. In 1997, 12 degrees awarded. *Degree requirements:* Thesis, comprehensive exams required, foreign language not required. *Entrance requirements:* GRE General Test (minimum combined score of 800), minimum GPA of 2.8. Application deadline: 11/1 (priority date; rolling processing; 4/1 for spring admission). Application fee: $50. *Tuition:* $5728 per year full-time, $258 per credit hour part-time for state residents; $8968 per year full-time, $393 per credit hour part-time for nonresidents. *Financial aid:* Federal Work-Study and career-related internships or fieldwork available. Aid available to part-time students. • Dr. Stanley Urban, MA Adviser, 609-256-4500 Ext. 3795. Application contact: Dr. Donna Hathaway, MST Adviser, 609-256-4500 Ext. 3794.

Rutgers, The State University of New Jersey, New Brunswick, Graduate School of Education, Department of Educational Psychology, Program in Special Education, New Brunswick, NJ 08903. Awards Ed M, Ed D. Faculty: 4 full-time (2 women). Students: 63; includes 7 minority (6 Asian Americans, 1 Hispanic), 3 international. In 1997, 8 master's, 2 doctorates awarded. *Degree requirements:* For doctorate, dissertation. *Entrance requirements:* GRE General Test. Application deadline: 3/1 (11/1 for spring admission). Application fee: $40. *Expenses:* Tuition $6492 per year full-time, $268 per credit part-time for state residents; $9520 per year full-time, $395 per credit part-time for nonresidents. Fees $208 per year (minimum). *Financial aid:* Application deadline 3/1. *Faculty research:* Cross-cultural research in mental retardation, cognitive development, inclusive education, developmental dyslexia. • Stanley Vitello, Coordinator, 732-932-7496 Ext. 326.

Sage Graduate School, Graduate School, Division of Education, Program in Reading/Special Education, Troy, NY 12180-4115. Awards MS Ed. Part-time and evening/weekend programs available. *Entrance requirements:* Minimum GPA of 2.75. Application deadline: 8/1 (rolling processing; 12/15 for spring admission). Application fee: $25. *Expenses:* Tuition $360 per credit hour. Fees $50 per semester. *Financial aid:* Research assistantships and career-related internships or fieldwork available. Aid available to part-time students. Financial aid application deadline: 7/1; applicants required to submit FAFSA. *Faculty research:* Commonalities in the roles of reading specialists and resource/consultant teachers. • Dr. Connell Frazer, Adviser, 518-244-2403. Fax: 518-244-2334. E-mail: frazec@sage.edu. Application contact: Melissa Robertson, Associate Director of Admissions, 518-244-6878. Fax: 518-244-6880. E-mail: sgsadm@sage.edu.

Sage Graduate School, Graduate School, Division of Education, Program in Special Education, Troy, NY 12180-4115. Awards MS Ed. Part-time and evening/weekend programs available. Students: 30 full-time (25 women), 71 part-time (45 women). *Degree requirements:* Thesis optional, foreign language not required. *Entrance requirements:* Minimum GPA of 2.75. Application deadline: 8/1 (rolling processing; 12/15 for spring admission). Application fee: $25. *Expenses:* Tuition $360 per credit hour. Fees $50 per semester. *Financial aid:* Research assistantships and career-related internships or fieldwork available. Aid available to part-time students. Financial aid application deadline: 7/1; applicants required to submit FAFSA. *Faculty research:* Effective behavioral strategies for classroom instruction. • Dr. Connell Frazer, Adviser, 518-244-2403. Fax: 518-244-2334. E-mail: frazec@sage.edu. Application contact: Melissa Robertson, Associate Director of Admissions, 518-244-6878. Fax: 518-244-6880. E-mail: sgsadm@sage.edu.

Saginaw Valley State University, College of Education, Program in Learning and Behavioral Disorders, University Center, MI 48710. Awards MAT. Accredited by NCATE. Faculty: 3 full-time (2 women). Students: 4 full-time (3 women), 64 part-time (53 women); includes 5 minority (4 African Americans, 1 Native American), 1 international. In 1997, 31 degrees awarded. *Entrance requirements:* Minimum GPA of 3.0, teaching certificate. Application deadline: rolling. Application fee: $25. *Expenses:* Tuition $159 per credit hour for state residents; $311 per credit hour for nonresidents. Fees $8.70 per credit hour. • Application contact: Dr. Melissa Hayden, 517-790-4350. E-mail: mhayden@tardis.svsu.edu.

St. Ambrose University, College of Human Services, Program in Special Education, Davenport, IA 52803-2898. Awards M Ed. Part-time and evening/weekend programs available. Postbaccalaureate distance learning degree programs offered (no on-campus study). *Degree requirements:* Thesis, oral and written comprehensive exams required, foreign language not required. *Average time to degree:* master's–4.5 years part-time. *Entrance requirements:* GRE General Test (minimum combined score of 1000) or MAT (minimum score 20), minimum GPA of 2.75. Application deadline: 8/15 (priority date; rolling processing; 11/1 for spring admission). Application fee: $25. Electronic applications accepted. *Faculty research:* Disabilities and postsecondary career avenues, self-determination.

St. Bonaventure University, School of Education, Program in Special Education, St. Bonaventure, NY 14778-2284. Awards MS Ed. Faculty: 2 full-time (1 woman), 3 part-time (all women). Students: 32 full-time (28 women), 29 part-time (22 women); includes 2 minority (both African Americans). 75 applicants, 84% accepted. *Degree requirements:* Comprehensive exam required, foreign language not required. *Entrance requirements:* TOEFL (minimum score 600). Application deadline: 8/1 (rolling processing). Application fee: $35. *Tuition:* $8100 per year full-time, $450 per credit hour part-time. • Dr. Kim Riggs, Director, 716-375-2366.

St. Cloud State University, College of Education, Department of Special Education, St. Cloud, MN 56301-4498. Offers programs in administration of special education (Spt), educable mentally handicapped (MS), emotionally disturbed (MS), gifted and talented (MS), learning disabled (MS), special education (MS), trainable mentally retarded (MS). Accredited by NCATE. Faculty: 9 full-time (4 women), 4 part-time (2 women). Students: 11 full-time (7 women), 55 part-time (42 women). In 1997, 30 master's awarded. *Degree requirements:* For master's, thesis or alternative required, foreign language not required; for Spt, thesis, field study required, foreign language not required. *Entrance requirements:* For master's, GRE General Test, minimum GPA of 2.75; for Spt, GRE General Test, minimum GPA of 3.25. Application fee: $20 ($100 for international students). *Expenses:* Tuition $128 per credit for state residents; $203 per credit for nonresidents. Fees $16.32 per credit. *Financial aid:* In 1997–98, 7 graduate assistantships were awarded; Federal Work-Study also available. Financial aid application deadline: 3/1. • Dr. Joan Kellet, Chairperson, 320-255-2041. Application contact: Ann Anderson, Graduate Studies Office, 320-255-2113. Fax: 320-654-5371. E-mail: anna@grad.stcloud.msus.edu.

St. John's University, School of Education and Human Services, Division of Human Services and Counseling, Program in Special Education/Bilingual Special Education, Jamaica, NY 11439. Awards MS Ed, PD. Part-time and evening/weekend programs available. Students: 10 full-time (8 women), 88 part-time (77 women); includes 11 minority (3 African Americans, 1 Asian American, 7 Hispanics), 1 international. Average age 31. 47 applicants, 89% accepted. In 1997, 40 master's awarded. *Entrance requirements:* For master's, minimum GPA of 3.0, previous course work in education; for PD, minimum GPA of 3.0, MS Ed. Application deadline: 6/1 (rolling processing; 10/1 for spring admission). Application fee: $40. *Expenses:* Tuition $525 per credit. Fees $150 per year. *Financial aid:* Administrative assistantships, Federal Work-Study, and career-related internships or fieldwork available. Aid available to part-time students. Financial aid application deadline: 3/1; applicants required to submit FAFSA. *Faculty research:* Constructivist education, alternate assessments in mathematics and science, relationship between assessment and instructions, African-American boys in special education. • Dr. Joan Benevento, Coordinator, 718-990-1569. Fax: 718-990-1614. Application contact: Shamus J. McGrenra, TOR, Associate Director, Graduate Admissions, 718-990-6107. Fax: 718-990-5736. E-mail: mcgrenrs@stjohns.edu.

Saint Joseph College, Field of Education and Counseling, Department of Special Education, West Hartford, CT 06117-2700. Offers programs in early childhood education/special education (MA), special education (MA), special education/counseling (MA). Faculty: 11 full-time (9 women), 24 part-time (18 women). Students: 78 (64 women); includes 4 minority (all African Americans). Average age 27. In 1997, 48 degrees awarded. *Degree requirements:* Thesis or alternative required, foreign language not required. *Application deadline:* 8/29 (rolling processing). *Application fee:* $25. *Tuition:* $395 per credit. *Financial aid:* Application deadline 8/31. • Dr. Gerard Thibodeau, Co-Chair, Education Department, Field of Education and Counseling, 860-232-4571 Ext. 331.

Saint Joseph College, Education Programs and Department of Special Education, Program in Early Childhood Education/Special Education, West Hartford, CT 06117-2700. Awards MA. Faculty: 2 full-time (1 woman), 3 part-time (2 women). Students: 21 (all women). Average age 27. In 1997, 8 degrees awarded. *Degree requirements:* Thesis or alternative required, foreign language not required. *Application deadline:* 8/29 (rolling processing). *Application fee:* $25. *Tuition:* $395 per credit. *Financial aid:* Application deadline 8/31. • Dr. Lois Davis, Chairman, 860-232-4571 Ext. 341.

Saint Joseph's University, Department of Education, Program in Special Education, Philadelphia, PA 19131-1395. Awards MS. Students: 12 full-time (all women). *Application deadline:* 7/15. *Application fee:* $30. *Tuition:* $510 per credit hour. • Dr. Sheila Macrie, Director, 610-660-1580.

Saint Louis University, Institute for Leadership and Public Service, Programs in Education, Department of Educational Studies, St. Louis, MO 63103-2097. Offerings include special education (MA). Accredited by NCATE. *Degree requirements:* Comprehensive oral exam required, foreign language and thesis not required. *Entrance requirements:* GRE General Test or MAT. Application deadline: 7/1 (rolling processing; 11/1 for spring admission). Application fee: $40. *Tuition:* $542 per credit hour. • Dr. Ann Rule, Director, 314-977-2486. Application contact: Dr. Marcia Buresch, Assistant Dean of the Graduate School, 314-977-2240. Fax: 314-977-3943.

Directory: Special Education

Saint Martin's College, Graduate Programs, Department of Education, Lacey, WA 98503-7500. Offerings include special education (M Ed). Department faculty: 8 full-time (3 women), 5 part-time (2 women). *Application deadline:* 7/1 (priority date; rolling processing; 12/1 for spring admission). *Application fee:* $25. • Dr. Paul Nelson, Director, 360-438-4529. Application contact: Michelle Roman, Administrative Assistant, 360-438-4333.

Saint Mary's College of California, School of Education, Program in Special Education, Moraga, CA 94575. Awards MA, M Ed. Faculty: 2 full-time (1 woman), 11 part-time (10 women). Students: 3 full-time (2 women), 26 part-time (23 women); includes 2 minority (1 Asian American, 1 Native American). Average age 37. 4 applicants, 75% accepted. In 1997, 6 degrees awarded (100% found work related to degree). *Degree requirements:* Thesis or alternative required, foreign language not required. *Entrance requirements:* Interview, minimum GPA of 3.0, teaching experience. Application deadline: rolling. Application fee: $50. *Tuition:* $1319 per course. *Financial aid:* Career-related internships or fieldwork available. Aid available to part-time students. Financial aid application deadline: 2/15. *Faculty research:* Consultation model, impact of gifted model on special education. • Dr. Mary Parish, Director, 925-631-4054. Fax: 925-376-8379.

Saint Mary's University of Minnesota, Program in Developmental Disabilities, Minneapolis, MN 55404. Awards MA, MA/MA. MA/MA offered jointly with the Program in Counseling and Psychological Services. Part-time and evening/weekend programs available. *Degree requirements:* Thesis or alternative required, foreign language not required. *Entrance requirements:* Interview, minimum GPA of 2.75. Application deadline: rolling. Application fee: $20.

Saint Michael's College, Program in Education, Colchester, VT 05439. Offerings include special education (M Ed, CAGS). Program faculty: 5 full-time (4 women), 70 part-time (54 women). *Degree requirements:* For master's, computer language, thesis required, foreign language not required. *Entrance requirements:* For master's, minimum GPA of 2.8. Application deadline: rolling. Application fee: $25. • Dr. Aostre Johnson, Director, 802-654-2436. Fax: 802-654-2664.

St. Thomas Aquinas College, Division of Teacher Education, Program in Special Education, Sparkill, NY 10976. Awards MS Ed. Part-time and evening/weekend programs available. *Degree requirements:* Comprehensive professional portfolio required, thesis not required. *Entrance requirements:* New York State Qualifying Exam, GRE General Test or minimum GPA of 3.0, teaching certificate with special education background. Application deadline: 7/31 (priority date; rolling processing; 12/1 for spring admission). Application fee: $35. Electronic applications accepted. *Expenses:* Tuition $390 per credit. Fees $10 per year. *Financial aid:* Assistantships, partial tuition waivers available. Financial aid application deadline: 2/15. *Faculty research:* Computer applications in education, adolescent special education students. • Application contact: Joseph L. Chillo, Executive Director of Enrollment Services, 914-398-4100. Fax: 914-398-4224. E-mail: joestacenroll@rockland.net.

Saint Xavier University, School of Education, Chicago, IL 60655-3105. Offerings include learning disabilities (MA). School faculty: 16 full-time (12 women), 3 part-time (1 woman). *Degree requirements:* Thesis or project required, thesis optional. *Entrance requirements:* MAT, minimum GPA of 3.0. Application deadline: 8/15 (priority date; rolling processing). Application fee: $35. *Expenses:* Tuition $435 per hour. Fees $50 per year. • Dr. Beverly Gulley, Dean, 773-298-3221. Fax: 773-779-9061. E-mail: gulley@sxu.edu. Application contact: Sr. Evelyn McKenna, Vice President of Enrollment Management, 773-298-3050. Fax: 773-298-3076. E-mail: mckenna@sxu.edu.

Salem College, Department of Education, PO Box 10548, Winston-Salem, NC 27108-0548. Offerings include learning disabilities (MAT). Accredited by NCATE. College faculty: 10 full-time (7 women), 2 part-time (both women). *Average time to degree:* master's–1.5 years full-time, 3 years part-time. *Application deadline:* rolling. *Application fee:* $35. *Tuition:* $195 per hour. • Dr. Robin L. Smith, Director of Graduate Studies, 336-721-2656. Fax: 336-721-2683. E-mail: smith@salem.edu.

Salem State College, Department of Education, Program in Special Education, Salem, MA 01970-5353. Awards M Ed. Accredited by NCATE. *Entrance requirements:* GRE General Test or MAT. Application deadline: rolling. Application fee: $25. *Expenses:* Tuition $140 per credit hour for state residents; $230 per credit hour for nonresidents. Fees $20 per credit hour.

Sam Houston State University, College of Education and Applied Science, Department of Language, Literacy, and Special Populations, Special Education Program, Huntsville, TX 77341. Awards M Ed. Accredited by NCATE. Part-time and evening/weekend programs available. Students: 2 full-time (both women), 34 part-time (31 women); includes 2 minority (1 Asian American, 1 Hispanic), 1 international. In 1997, 12 degrees awarded. *Entrance requirements:* GRE General Test (minimum combined score of 800), minimum GPA of 2.5. Application deadline: 9/1. Application fee: $15. *Tuition:* $1810 per year full-time, $297 per semester (minimum) part-time for state residents; $6922 per year full-time, $924 per semester (minimum) part-time for nonresidents. *Financial aid:* Teaching assistantships available. • Dr. Hollis Lowery-Moore, Chair, Department of Language, Literacy, and Special Populations, 409-294-1595. Fax: 409-294-1131. E-mail: edu_lap@shsu.edu.

San Diego State University, College of Education, Department of Special Education, San Diego, CA 92182. Awards MA. Accredited by NCATE. Evening/weekend programs available. Students: 15 full-time (13 women), 79 part-time (62 women); includes 16 minority (5 African Americans, 3 Asian Americans, 7 Hispanics, 1 Native American), 1 international. Average age 29. *Entrance requirements:* GRE General Test (minimum combined score of 950), TOEFL (minimum score 550). Application deadline: 4/1 (priority date; rolling processing; 12/1 for spring admission). Application fee: $55. *Expenses:* Tuition $0 for state residents; $246 per unit for nonresidents. Fees $1932 per year full-time, $1266 per year part-time. *Financial aid:* Fellowships and career-related internships or fieldwork available. *Total annual research expenditures:* $3.1 million. • Eleanor Lynch, Interim Chair, 619-594-6665. E-mail: eleanor.lynch@sdsu.edu. Application contact: Dan Doorlag, Graduate Coordinator, 619-594-4899. Fax: 619-594-6628. E-mail: doorlag@mail.sdsu.edu.

San Francisco State University, College of Education, Department of Special Education, Program in Special Education, San Francisco, CA 94132-1722. Awards MA, Ed D, PhD, AC. Accredited by NCATE. Ed D and PhD offered jointly with the University of California, Berkeley. Part-time programs available. *Degree requirements:* For doctorate, dissertation. *Entrance requirements:* For master's, minimum GPA of 2.5 in last 60 units; for doctorate, GRE General Test. Application deadline: 11/30 (priority date; rolling processing). Application fee: $55. *Expenses:* Tuition $0 for state residents; $246 per unit for nonresidents. Fees $1982 per year full-time, $1316 per year part-time.

San Jose State University, College of Education, Program in Learning Assistance, San Jose, CA 95192-0001. Offers learning handicapped (MA), special education (MA). Accredited by NCATE. Evening/weekend programs available. Faculty: 8 full-time (4 women), 2 part-time (1 woman). Students: 4 full-time (3 women), 38 part-time (33 women); includes 9 minority (2 African Americans, 5 Asian Americans, 2 Hispanics), 4 international. Average age 36. 48 applicants, 81% accepted. In 1997, 14 degrees awarded. *Application deadline:* 6/1 (rolling processing). *Application fee:* $59. *Expenses:* Tuition $0 for state residents; $246 per unit for nonresidents. Fees $2017 per year full-time, $1351 per year part-time. *Financial aid:* Career-related internships or fieldwork available. • Louis Denti, Coordinator, 408-924-3687.

San Jose State University, College of Education, Program in Sensory and Severe Disabilities, San Jose, CA 95192-0001. Offers education for the hearing impaired (MA), education for the severely handicapped (MA). Accredited by NCATE. Evening/weekend programs available. Faculty: 3 full-time (1 woman), 2 part-time (0 women). Students: 1 full-time (0 women), 7 part-time (all women); includes 1 minority (Asian American). Average age 43. 2 applicants, 100% accepted. In 1997, 2 degrees awarded. *Degree requirements:* Thesis or alternative required, foreign language not required. *Entrance requirements:* GRE General Test. Application deadline: 6/1 (rolling processing). Application fee: $59. *Expenses:* Tuition $0 for state residents; $246 per unit for nonresidents. Fees $2017 per year full-time, $1351 per year part-time. *Financial aid:* Career-related internships or fieldwork available. • Sharon Sacks, Coordinator, 408-924-3695.

Santa Clara University, Division of Counseling Psychology and Education, Program in Special Education, Santa Clara, CA 95053-0001. Awards MA. Part-time and evening/weekend programs available. Students: 4 full-time (all women), 23 part-time (21 women); includes 5 minority (3 Asian Americans, 2 Hispanics), 2 international. Average age 37. 3 applicants, 67% accepted. In 1997, 14 degrees awarded. *Degree requirements:* Comprehensive exam required, foreign language and thesis not required. *Entrance requirements:* GRE or MAT, TOEFL, minimum GPA of 3.0. Application deadline: 5/1 (2/1 for spring admission). Application fee: $30. *Financial aid:* Fellowships, teaching assistantships, Federal Work-Study, and career-related internships or fieldwork available. Aid available to part-time students. Financial aid application deadline: 2/1. • Dr. Ruth E. Cook, Director, 408-554-4119. Application contact: Barbara F. Simmons, Assistant to the Dean, 408-554-4355. Fax: 408-554-2392.

Seton Hill College, Program in Special Education, Greensburg, PA 15601. Awards MA, Teaching Certificate. Part-time programs available. Faculty: 2 full-time (both women), 2 part-time (1 woman). Students: 2 full-time (both women), 14 part-time (13 women). Average age 32. 8 applicants, 88% accepted. *Degree requirements:* For master's, thesis required, foreign language not required. *Entrance requirements:* For master's, minimum GPA of 3.0. Application deadline: 8/15 (priority date; rolling processing; 12/15 for spring admission). Application fee: $30. *Tuition:* $360 per credit for state residents; $360 per credit full-time, $360 per year part-time for nonresidents. *Financial aid:* 11 students received aid; scholarships, partial tuition waivers available. Aid available to part-time students. Financial aid application deadline: 8/1. • Dr. Sondra Lettrich, Director, 724-830-1010. E-mail: lettrich@setonhill.edu. Application contact: Mary Kay Cooper, Graduate Adviser, 800-826-6234. Fax: 724-830-1294. E-mail: coope91@setonhill.edu.

Announcement: In the Master of Arts in special education, theory and skills are presented to help teachers address the educational needs of children and youth who have a variety of mental and/or physical disabilities. For more information, please see our in-depth description in volume one of this series.

Shippensburg University of Pennsylvania, College of Education and Human Services, Department of Teacher Education, Shippensburg, PA 17257-2299. Offerings include special education (M Ed). Accredited by NCATE. Department faculty: 16 full-time (11 women), 10 part-time (7 women). *Application deadline:* rolling. *Application fee:* $25. Electronic applications accepted. *Expenses:* Tuition $3468 per year full-time, $193 per credit hour part-time for state residents; $6236 per year full-time, $346 per credit hour part-time for nonresidents. Fees $678 per year full-time, $108 per semester (minimum) part-time. • Dr. Audrey Sprenger, Chairperson, 717-532-1688.

Simmons College, Department of Education, Program in Special Education, Boston, MA 02115. Offers inclusion specialist (MS Ed), intensive special needs (MS Ed), special needs (MS Ed). Faculty: 9 full-time (7 women), 20 part-time (16 women). Students: 98 full-time (87 women), 338 part-time (260 women); includes 12 minority (7 African Americans, 1 Asian American, 3 Hispanics, 1 Native American), 2 international. Average age 28. 171 applicants, 83% accepted. In 1997, 104 degrees awarded. *Degree requirements:* Practicum, student teaching experience required, foreign language not required. *Entrance requirements:* Interview. Application deadline: 8/1 (priority date; rolling processing; 12/15 for spring admission). Application fee: $35. *Expenses:* Tuition $587 per credit hour. Fees $20 per year. *Financial aid:* 71 students received aid; partial tuition waivers, Federal Work-Study, institutionally sponsored loans, and career-related internships or fieldwork available. Aid available to part-time students. Financial aid application deadline: 3/1; applicants required to submit FAFSA. • Elizabeth Fleming, Director, 617-521-2558. Fax: 617-521-3174. Application contact: Director, Graduate Studies Admission, 617-521-2910. Fax: 617-521-3058. E-mail: gsa@simmons.edu.

Slippery Rock University of Pennsylvania, College of Education, Department of Special Education, Slippery Rock, PA 16057. Awards M Ed. Accredited by NCATE. Part-time and evening/weekend programs available. *Degree requirements:* Comprehensive exams required, thesis optional. *Entrance requirements:* GRE, minimum GPA of 2.75. Application deadline: 7/1 (priority date; rolling processing; 11/1 for spring admission). Application fee: $25. *Tuition:* $4484 per year full-time, $247 per credit part-time for state residents; $7667 per year full-time, $423 per credit part-time for nonresidents. *Faculty research:* In-service teacher education, contemporary issues in special education, education for developmentally disabled, educational assessment.

Smith College, Department of Education and Child Study, Program in the Education of the Deaf, Northampton, MA 01063. Awards MA, MED. Part-time programs available. Faculty: 13 full-time (11 women), 2 part-time (both women). Students: 11 full-time (10 women); includes 2 international. Average age 22. 20 applicants, 85% accepted. In 1997, 13 degrees awarded. *Average time to degree:* master's–1 year full-time, 4 years part-time. *Entrance requirements:* GRE General Test or MAT. Application deadline: 4/1. Application fee: $50. *Tuition:* $21,680 per year full-time, $2720 per course part-time. *Financial aid:* In 1997–98, 11 students received aid, including 11 scholarships (all to first-year students) totaling $194,040; institutionally sponsored loans also available. Aid available to part-time students. Financial aid application deadline: 1/15; applicants required to submit CSS PROFILE or FAFSA. • Alan Rudnitsky, Chair, Department of Education and Child Study, 413-585-3261. E-mail: arudnits@sophia.smith.edu.

Sonoma State University, School of Education, Program in Special Education, Rohnert Park, CA 94928-3609. Awards MA. Part-time and evening/weekend programs available. Students: 3 full-time (1 woman), 5 part-time (all women). Average age 45. 8 applicants, 75% accepted. In 1997, 1 degree awarded. *Degree requirements:* Thesis or alternative required, foreign language not required. *Entrance requirements:* GRE General Test, minimum GPA of 2.5. Application fee: $55. *Expenses:* Tuition $0 for state residents; $246 per unit for nonresidents. Fees $2130 per year full-time, $1464 per year part-time. *Financial aid:* Application deadline 3/2. • Dr. Kevin Feldman, Coordinator, 707-664-2515. E-mail: kevin.feldman@sonoma.edu.

South Carolina State University, School of Education, Department of Teacher Education, 300 College Street Northeast, Orangeburg, SC 29117-0001. Offerings include early childhood and special education (M Ed); special education (M Ed), with options in emotionally handicapped, learning disabilities, mentally handicapped. One or more programs accredited by NCATE. Department faculty: 7 full-time (3 women), 2 part-time (1 woman). *Average time to degree:* master's–2 years full-time, 4 years part-time. *Application deadline:* 7/15 (priority date; rolling processing; 11/10 for spring admission). *Application fee:* $25. *Tuition:* $2974 per year full-time, $165 per credit hour part-time. • Dr. Jesse Kinard, Chairman, 803-536-8934. Application contact: Dr. Gail Joyner-Fleming, Interim Associate Dean and Director, Graduate Teacher Education, 803-536-8824. Fax: 803-536-8492.

Southeastern Louisiana University, College of Education, Department of Special Education, Hammond, LA 70402. Awards M Ed, MS. Accredited by NCATE. Part-time programs available. Faculty: 14 full-time, 16 part-time. Students: 33 full-time (28 women), 63 part-time (60 women); includes 4 minority (3 African Americans, 1 Asian American). Average age 33. In 1997, 40 degrees awarded. *Entrance requirements:* GRE General Test (minimum combined score of 850). Application deadline: 7/15 (priority date; rolling processing; 12/15 for spring admission). Application fee: $10 ($25 for international students). Electronic applications accepted. *Expenses:* Tuition $2010 per year full-time, $287 per semester (minimum) part-time for state residents; $5232 per year full-time, $287 per semester (minimum) part-time for nonresidents. Fees $5 per year. *Financial aid:* Research assistantships, teaching assistantships, administrative assistantships, Federal Work-Study, and career-related internships or fieldwork available. Aid available to part-time students. Financial aid application deadline: 5/1; applicants required to submit FAFSA. *Faculty research:* Classroom organization and management, impact of multicultural education on teacher training, instructional and assistive technology, reading comprehension-cognitive/metacognitive, instructional design. Total annual research expenditures: $1500. • Dr. W. Glenn Morgan, Head, 504-549-2214. Application contact: Dr. Sonya Carr, Graduate Coordinator, 504-549-2214. Fax: 504-549-5030. E-mail: scarr@selu.edu.

Southeast Missouri State University, Department of Elementary and Special Education, Program in Special Education, Cape Girardeau, MO 63701-4799. Awards MA. Accredited by NCATE. Evening/weekend programs available. *Degree requirements:* Thesis or alternative required, foreign language not required. *Entrance requirements:* GRE General Test (score in 50th percentile or higher), minimum GPA of 2.75. Application deadline: 4/1 (priority date; rolling processing; 11/21 for spring admission). Application fee: $20 ($100 for international students). *Tuition:* $2034 per year full-time, $113 per credit hour part-time for state residents; $3672 per year full-time, $204 per credit hour part-time for nonresidents. *Financial aid:* Career-related internships or fieldwork available. • Application contact: Office of Graduate Studies, 573-651-2192.

Southern Arkansas University–Magnolia, Graduate Program in Education, Program in Secondary Education, Magnolia, AR 71753. Offerings include special education (M Ed). *Degree requirements:* Thesis or alternative, comprehensive exam required, foreign language not required. *Average time to degree:* master's–2 years full-time. *Entrance requirements:* GRE, minimum GPA of 2.5. Application deadline: 8/15. Application fee: $0. *Expenses:* Tuition $95 per hour for state residents; $138 per hour for nonresidents. Fees $2 per hour. • Dr. Danield L. Bernard, Dean, Graduate Studies, Graduate Program in Education, 870-235-4055. Fax: 870-235-5035. E-mail: dlbernard@mail.saumag.edu.

Southern Connecticut State University, School of Education, Department of Exercise Science, New Haven, CT 06515-1355. Offerings include physical education and recreation for the handicapped (MS Ed). Department faculty: 7 full-time, 1 part-time. *Degree requirements:* Thesis or alternative required, foreign language not required. *Entrance requirements:* Interview. Application deadline: 7/15 (priority date; rolling processing). Application fee: $40. *Expenses:* Tuition $2632 per year full-time, $188 per credit part-time for state residents; $7200 per year full-time, $188 per credit part-time for nonresidents. Fees $1806 per year full-time, $45 per semester part-time for state residents; $2703 per year full-time, $45 per semester part-time for nonresidents. • Dr. Joan Barbarich, Chair, 203-392-6088. Application contact: Dr. Robert Axtell, Coordinator, 203-392-6037.

Southern Connecticut State University, School of Education, Department of Special Education, New Haven, CT 06515-1355. Awards MS Ed, Diploma. Faculty: 13 full-time. Students: 31 full-time (24 women), 327 part-time (289 women); includes 12 minority (7 African Americans, 1 Asian American, 3 Hispanics, 1 Native American), 1 international. 359 applicants, 30% accepted. In 1997, 144 master's awarded. *Degree requirements:* For master's, thesis or alternative required, foreign language not required. *Entrance requirements:* For master's, interview; for Diploma, 3 years of teaching experience, master's degree, teacher certification, interview. Application deadline: 7/15. Application fee: $40. *Expenses:* Tuition $2632 per year full-time, $188 per credit part-time for state residents; $7200 per year full-time, $188 per credit part-time for nonresidents. Fees $1806 per year full-time, $45 per semester part-time for state residents; $2703 per year full-time, $45 per semester part-time for nonresidents. *Financial aid:* Career-related internships or fieldwork available. • Dr. Irving Newman, Chair, 203-392-5925. Application contact: Dr. Steven Feldman, Coordinator, 203-392-5925.

Southern Illinois University at Carbondale, College of Education, Department of Educational Psychology and Special Education, Program in Special Education, Carbondale, IL 62901-6806. Awards MS Ed. Accredited by NCATE. Part-time programs available. Faculty: 9 full-time (4 women), 3 part-time (1 woman). Students: 23 full-time (21 women), 13 part-time (10 women); includes 4 minority (3 African Americans, 1 Hispanic), 1 international. Average age 28. 13 applicants, 69% accepted. In 1997, 10 degrees awarded. *Degree requirements:* Thesis required, foreign language not required. *Entrance requirements:* GRE General Test, TOEFL (minimum score 550), minimum GPA of 2.7. Application deadline: rolling. Application fee: $20. *Expenses:* Tuition $2964 per year full-time, $99 per semester hour part-time for state residents; $8892 per year full-time, $270 per semester hour part-time for nonresidents. Fees $1034 per year full-time, $298 per semester (minimum) part-time. *Financial aid:* In 1997–98, 5 research assistantships, 20 administrative assistantships were awarded; fellowships, teaching assistantships, full tuition waivers, Federal Work-Study, institutionally sponsored loans, and career-related internships or fieldwork also available. Aid available to part-time students. *Faculty research:* Applied and action research; scientific methods used to evaluate effectiveness of products and programs for the handicapped; scientific methods used to develop generalizations about instructional, motivational, and learning processes of the handicapped. • John Pohlmann, Chairperson, Department of Educational Psychology and Special Education, 618-536-7763.

Southern Illinois University at Edwardsville, School of Education, Department of Special Education, Edwardsville, IL 62026-0001. Awards MS Ed. Accredited by NCATE. Students: 15 full-time (13 women), 22 part-time (20 women); includes 3 minority (all African Americans), 1 international. 13 applicants, 77% accepted. In 1997, 9 degrees awarded. *Degree requirements:* Thesis or alternative, final exam required, foreign language not required. *Entrance requirements:* MAT, teaching certificate. Application deadline: 7/24. Application fee: $25. *Expenses:* Tuition $1716 per year full-time, $95 per credit hour part-time for state residents; $5149 per year full-time, $286 per credit hour part-time for nonresidents. Fees $463 per year full-time, $433 per year part-time. *Financial aid:* In 1997–98, 1 assistantship was awarded; fellowships, research assistantships, teaching assistantships, Federal Work-Study, institutionally sponsored loans also available. Aid available to part-time students. • Dr. Nikki Murdick, Chair, 618-692-3940.

Southern Oregon University, School of Social Science, Health and Physical Education, Department of Education, Ashland, OR 97520. Offerings include elementary education (MA Ed, MS Ed), with options in classroom teacher, early childhood, handicapped learner, reading, supervision; secondary education (MA Ed, MS Ed), with options in classroom teacher, handicapped learner, reading, supervision. *Application deadline:* 2/1. *Application fee:* $50. *Tuition:* $5187 per year full-time, $586 per quarter (minimum) part-time for state residents; $9228 per year full-time, $586 per quarter (minimum) part-time for nonresidents. • Dr. Mary-Curtis Gramley, Associate Dean of Education, 541-552-6918.

Southern University and Agricultural and Mechanical College, Special Education Institute, Baton Rouge, LA 70813. Awards M Ed, PhD. Accredited by NCATE. Faculty: 8 full-time (5 women), 3 part-time (2 women). Students: 35 full-time (33 women), 41 part-time (35 women); includes 64 minority (all African Americans), 2 international. 27 applicants, 63% accepted. In 1997, 10 master's awarded. *Degree requirements:* For master's, thesis optional; for doctorate, dissertation. *Entrance requirements:* For master's, GMAT or GRE General Test, TOEFL; for doctorate, GRE General Test, TOEFL. Application deadline: 6/1 (priority date; rolling processing; 11/1 for spring admission). Application fee: $5. *Tuition:* $2226 per year full-time, $267 per semester (minimum) part-time for state residents; $6262 per year full-time, $267 per semester (minimum) part-time for nonresidents. *Financial aid:* Research assistantships available. Financial aid application deadline: 4/15. • Dr. Carolyn Person, Director, 504-771-3950.

Southwestern Oklahoma State University, School of Education, Program in Special Education, Weatherford, OK 73096-3098. Awards M Ed. Accredited by NCATE. M Ed distance learning degree program offered to Oklahoma residents only. Part-time programs available. Postbaccalaureate distance learning degree programs offered. Students: 5 full-time (all women), 15 part-time (all women); includes 2 minority (both African Americans). 1 applicant, 100% accepted. In 1997, 1 degree awarded. *Degree requirements:* Exam required, foreign language and thesis not required. *Entrance requirements:* GRE General Test, TOEFL (minimum score 550), minimum GPA of 2.5. Application deadline: rolling. Application fee: $15. *Expenses:* Tuition $60 per credit hour (minimum) for state residents; $147 per credit hour (minimum) for nonresidents. Fees $109 per year full-time, $24 per semester (minimum) part-time. *Financial aid:* Research assistantships, partial tuition waivers, Federal Work-Study, institutionally sponsored loans, and career-related internships or fieldwork available. Aid available to part-time students. Financial aid application deadline: 3/1; applicants required to submit FAFSA. • Dr. Lowell Gladberry, Chair, Elementary/Secondary Programs, 580-774-3288. Application contact: Dr. Ronna Vanderslice, Adviser, 580-774-3145.

Southwest Missouri State University, College of Education, Department of Reading and Special Education, Springfield, MO 65804-0094. Awards MS Ed. Part-time and evening/weekend programs available. Faculty: 7 full-time (5 women). Students: 7 full-time (all women), 81 part-time (75 women); includes 2 minority (1 African American, 1 Native American), 2 international. In 1997, 28 degrees awarded. *Degree requirements:* Thesis or alternative, comprehensive exam required, foreign language not required. *Entrance requirements:* Minimum GPA of 2.75, teaching certificate. Application deadline: 8/7 (priority date; rolling processing; 12/17 for spring admission). Application fee: $25. *Expenses:* Tuition $1980 per year full-time, $110 per credit hour part-time for state residents; $3960 per year full-time, $220 per credit hour part-time for nonresidents. Fees $274 per year full-time, $73 per semester part-time. • Dr. Christopher Craig, Head, 417-836-6769. Fax: 417-836-4884. E-mail: cjc886@wpgate.smsu.edu.

Southwest Texas State University, School of Education, Department of Curriculum and Instruction, Program in Special Education, San Marcos, TX 78666. Awards M Ed. Part-time programs available. Students: 12 full-time (7 women), 63 part-time (45 women); includes 24 minority (15 African Americans, 1 Asian American, 8 Hispanics), 1 international. Average age 38. In 1997, 34 degrees awarded. *Degree requirements:* Comprehensive exam required, foreign language and thesis not required. *Entrance requirements:* GRE General Test (minimum combined score of 900), TOEFL (minimum score 550), minimum GPA of 2.75 in last 60 hours, teaching experience. Application deadline: 7/15 (priority date; rolling processing; 11/15 for spring admission). Application fee: $25 ($50 for international students). *Expenses:* Tuition $648 per year full-time, $120 per semester (minimum) part-time for state residents; $4500 per year full-time, $750 per semester (minimum) part-time for nonresidents. Fees $1264 per year full-time, $314 per semester (minimum) part-time. *Financial aid:* Fellowships, Federal Work-Study, institutionally sponsored loans, and career-related internships or fieldwork available. Aid available to part-time students. Financial aid application deadline: 4/1; applicants required to submit FAFSA. *Faculty research:* Educational diagnostics; generic, severely handicapped, emotionally disturbed, and autistic education. • Dr. Larry J. Wheeler, Graduate Adviser, 512-245-2157. E-mail: lw06@swt.edu.

State University of New York at Albany, School of Education, Department of Educational Psychology and Statistics, Program in Special Education, Albany, NY 12222-0001. Awards MS. *Application fee:* $50. *Expenses:* Tuition $5100 per year full-time, $213 per credit hour part-time for state residents; $8416 per year full-time, $351 per credit hour part-time for nonresidents. Fees $705 per year full-time, $26.85 per credit hour part-time. *Financial aid:* Fellowships and career-related internships or fieldwork available. • Debbie May, Chair, 516-442-5074.

State University of New York at Binghamton, School of Education and Human Development, Program in Special Education, Binghamton, NY 13902-6000. Awards MS Ed. Part-time and evening/weekend programs available. Students: 8 full-time (6 women), 50 part-time (39 women). Average age 31. 19 applicants, 47% accepted. In 1997, 13 degrees awarded. *Entrance requirements:* GRE General Test, TOEFL. Application deadline: 4/15 (priority date; rolling processing; 11/1 for spring admission). Application fee: $50. Electronic applications accepted. *Expenses:* Tuition $5100 per year full-time, $213 per credit hour part-time for state residents; $8416 per year full-time, $351 per credit hour part-time for nonresidents. Fees $654 per year full-time; $75 per semester (minimum) part-time. *Financial aid:* Fellowships, research assistantships, teaching assistantships, graduate assistantships, Federal Work-Study, institutionally sponsored loans, and career-related internships or fieldwork available. Aid available to part-time students. Financial aid application deadline: 2/15. • Dr. Beverly Rainforth, Coordinator, 607-777-2277.

State University of New York at New Paltz, Faculty of Education, Department of Educational Studies, Program in Special Education, New Paltz, NY 12561-2499. Awards MS Ed. Students: 45 full-time (37 women), 131 part-time (111 women); includes 16 minority (8 African Americans, 7 Hispanics, 1 Native American), 1 international. In 1997, 81 degrees awarded. *Entrance requirements:* Minimum GPA of 3.0. Application deadline: 3/15 (priority date; rolling processing). Application fee: $50. *Expenses:* Tuition $5100 per year full-time, $213 per credit hour part-time for state residents; $8416 per year full-time, $351 per credit hour part-time for nonresidents. Fees $493 per year full-time, $48 per semester (minimum) part-time. *Financial aid:* Federal Work-Study, institutionally sponsored loans, and career-related internships or fieldwork available. • Dr. Spencer Salend, Coordinator, 914-257-2830.

State University of New York at Oswego, School of Education, Department of Curriculum and Instruction, Oswego, NY 13126. Offerings include special education (MS Ed). MS Ed (special education) offered jointly with the State University of New York College at Geneseo. Department faculty: 17 full-time, 5 part-time. *Application deadline:* 7/1. *Application fee:* $50. *Expenses:* Tuition $5100 per year full-time, $213 per credit hour part-time for state residents; $8416 per year full-time, $351 per credit hour part-time for nonresidents. Fees $135 per year (minimum). • Dr. Frank Bickel, Chairman, 315-341-4052. Application contact: Dr. Terrance Lindenberg, Coordinator, Graduate Education, 315-341-4052.

State University of New York College at Buffalo, Faculty of Applied Science and Education, Department of Exceptional Education, Program in Special Education, Buffalo, NY 14222-1095. Awards MS Ed. Accredited by NCATE. Part-time and evening/weekend programs available. Students: 39 full-time (34 women), 250 part-time (220 women); includes 11 minority (7 African Americans, 1 Asian American, 2 Hispanics, 1 Native American), 1 international. Average age 31. 67 applicants, 69% accepted. In 1997, 129 degrees awarded. *Degree requirements:* Thesis or project required, foreign language not required. *Entrance requirements:* Minimum GPA of 2.5. Application deadline: 5/1 (10/1 for spring admission). Application fee: $50. *Expenses:* Tuition $5100 per year full-time, $213 per credit hour part-time for state residents; $8416 per year full-time, $351 per credit hour part-time for nonresidents. Fees $195 per year full-time, $8.60 per credit hour part-time. *Financial aid:* Fellowships, assistantships, Federal Work-Study available. Aid available to part-time students. Financial aid application deadline: 3/1. • Linda Gleckel, Coordinator, 716-878-3038.

State University of New York College at Geneseo, School of Education, Program in Special Education, Geneseo, NY 14454-1401. Awards MS Ed. Part-time and evening/weekend programs available. Faculty: 8 full-time (4 women), 8 part-time (4 women), 10 FTE. Students: 2 full-time (1 woman), 88 part-time (73 women); includes 1 minority (African American). Average age 24. 57 applicants, 88% accepted. In 1997, 25 degrees awarded. *Entrance requirements:* GRE General Test. Application deadline: 6/1 (priority date; 10/1 for spring admission). Application fee: $35. *Expenses:* Tuition $5100 per year full-time, $213 per credit hour part-time for state residents; $8416 per year full-time, $351 per credit hour part-time for nonresidents. Fees $375 per year full-time, $15.35 per credit hour part-time. *Financial aid:* 1 student received aid; fellowships, Federal Work-Study, institutionally sponsored loans, and career-related internships or fieldwork available. Financial aid application deadline: 4/1; applicants required to submit FAFSA. *Faculty research:* Transition of individuals with handicaps. • Dr. Gary DeBolt, Head, School of Education, 716-245-5558. Fax: 716-245-5220. E-mail: debolt@uno.cc.geneseo.edu.

State University of New York College at Potsdam, School of Education, Program in Special Education, Potsdam, NY 13676. Awards MS Ed. Part-time programs available. Students: 71. *Degree requirements:* Culminating experience. *Entrance requirements:* New York State Teachers Certification Exam Liberal Arts and Science Test (minimum score 220), New York State Teachers Certification Exam Assesment of Teaching Skills-Writing (minimum score 220), minimum GPA of 2.75 in last 60 hours. Application deadline: 4/1 (priority date; 10/15 for spring

Directory: Special Education

State University of New York College at Potsdam (continued)
admission). Application fee: $50. *Expenses:* Tuition $5100 per year full-time, $213 per credit hour part-time for state residents; $8416 per year full-time, $351 per credit hour part-time for nonresidents. Fees $315 per year full-time, $12.50 per credit hour part-time. *Financial aid:* Application deadline 3/1. • Application contact: Dr. William Amoriell, Dean of Education and Graduate Studies, 315-267-2515. Fax: 315-267-4802.

State University of West Georgia, College of Education, Department of Special Education, Carrollton, GA 30118. Awards M Ed, Ed S. Accredited by NCATE. Part-time and evening/weekend programs available. Faculty: 5 full-time (2 women), 4 part-time (2 women). Students: 184 full-time (152 women), 216 part-time (195 women); includes 64 minority (62 African Americans, 2 Hispanics), 1 international. Average age 35. In 1997, 121 master's, 27 Ed Ss awarded. *Degree requirements:* For Ed S, research project required, foreign language and thesis not required. *Entrance requirements:* For master's, GRE General Test (minimum combined score of 800), minimum GPA of 2.5; for Ed S, GRE General Test (minimum combined score of 800), master's degree, minimum graduate GPA of 3.25. Application deadline: 8/30 (rolling processing). Application fee: $15. *Expenses:* Tuition $2428 per year full-time, $83 per semester hour part-time for state residents; $8428 per year full-time, $250 per semester hour part-time for nonresidents. Fees $428 per year. *Financial aid:* Research assistantships, assistantships, and career-related internships or fieldwork available. Aid available to part-time students. Financial aid applicants required to submit FAFSA. • Dr. Suzanne Cobb, Chair, 770-836-6567. Application contact: Dr. Jack O. Jenkins, Dean, Graduate School, 770-836-6419. Fax: 770-836-2301. E-mail: jjenkins@cob.as.westga.edu.

Stephen F. Austin State University, College of Education, Department of Counseling and Special Education, Nacogdoches, TX 75962. Offers programs in counseling (MA), school psychology (MA), special education (M Ed), speech pathology (MS). Faculty: 13 full-time (2 women), 3 part-time (1 woman). Students: 60 full-time (51 women), 127 part-time (109 women); includes 14 minority (11 African Americans, 1 Asian American, 2 Hispanics). 71 applicants, 52% accepted. In 1997, 55 degrees awarded. *Degree requirements:* Comprehensive exam required, foreign language and thesis not required. *Entrance requirements:* GRE General Test (minimum combined score of 1000), minimum GPA of 2.8. Application deadline: 3/1 (10/1 for spring admission). Application fee: $0 ($25 for international students). *Tuition:* $1465 per year full-time, $263 per semester (minimum) part-time for state residents; $5299 per year full-time, $890 per semester (minimum) part-time for nonresidents. *Financial aid:* Research assistantships, teaching assistantships, Federal Work-Study, institutionally sponsored loans, and career-related internships or fieldwork available. Financial aid application deadline: 3/1. • Dr. Anna Bradfield, Chair, 409-468-2906.

Stephens College, School of Graduate and Continuing Education, Department of Elementary and Secondary Education, Program in Inclusion, 1200 East Broadway, Columbia, MO 65215-0002. Awards M Ed. Part-time programs available. Faculty: 5 full-time (4 women). Students: 5 part-time (all women). *Degree requirements:* Thesis or alternative required, foreign language not required. *Entrance requirements:* GRE, TOEFL (minimum score 550), minimum GPA of 3.0 in last 60 hours. Application deadline: rolling. Application fee: $25. *Tuition:* $690 per course. *Financial aid:* Available to part-time students. • Dr. Joan Vaughan, Director, 573-442-2211 Ext. 591. Fax: 573-876-7223. E-mail: vaughn@wc.stephens.edu. Application contact: Dr. Joan T. Rines, Director of Graduate Programs, 800-338-7579. Fax: 573-876-7248. E-mail: grad@wc.stephens.edu.

Stetson University, College of Arts and Sciences, Division of Education, Department of Teacher Education, Program in Varying Exceptionalities, 421 North Woodland Boulevard, DeLand, FL 32720-3781. Offers exceptional student education (M Ed). Accredited by NCATE. Students: 8 part-time (all women); includes 1 minority (African American). Average age 39. 5 applicants, 100% accepted. In 1997, 5 degrees awarded. *Entrance requirements:* GRE General Test (minimum combined score of 1000) or MAT. Application deadline: 3/1 (priority date; rolling processing; 11/1 for spring admission). Application fee: $25. *Tuition:* $370 per credit hour. • Dr. Kathy Piechura-Couture, Coordinator, 904-822-7075. Application contact: Pat LeClaire, Office of Graduate Studies, 904-822-7075.

Syracuse University, School of Education, Department of Reading and Language Arts, Program in Learning Disabilities, Syracuse, NY 13244-0003. Awards MS. Students: 4 full-time (3 women), 11 part-time (all women); includes 1 minority (African American). 11 applicants, 64% accepted. In 1997, 7 degrees awarded. *Degree requirements:* Thesis or alternative required, foreign language not required. *Entrance requirements:* GRE General Test, interview. Application fee: $40. *Tuition:* $13,320 per year full-time, $555 per credit hour part-time. *Financial aid:* Application deadline 3/1. • Dr. Benita Blachman, Chair, 315-443-9644.

Syracuse University, School of Education, Programs in Special Education, Program in Educating Infants and Young Children with Special Needs, Syracuse, NY 13244-0003. Awards MS. Students: 5 full-time (all women), 10 part-time (9 women); includes 1 minority (African American), 3 international. 11 applicants, 100% accepted. In 1997, 8 degrees awarded. *Degree requirements:* Thesis or alternative required, foreign language not required. *Entrance requirements:* GRE General Test, interview. Application fee: $40. *Tuition:* $13,320 per year full-time, $555 per credit hour part-time. *Financial aid:* Application deadline 3/1. • Dr. Gail Ensher, Chair, 315-443-9659.

Syracuse University, School of Education, Programs in Special Education, Program in Special Education (Emotional Disorders and Severe Disabilities), Syracuse, NY 13244-0003. Awards MS, Ed D, PhD. Students: 37 full-time (28 women), 49 part-time (38 women); includes 5 minority (3 African Americans, 1 Hispanic, 1 Native American), 6 international. 32 applicants, 72% accepted. In 1997, 28 master's, 2 doctorates awarded. *Degree requirements:* For master's, thesis or alternative required, foreign language not required; for doctorate, dissertation required, foreign language not required. *Entrance requirements:* GRE General Test, interview. Application fee: $40. *Tuition:* $13,320 per year full-time, $555 per credit hour part-time. *Financial aid:* Application deadline 3/1. • Doug Biklen, Chair, Programs in Special Education, 315-443-9659. Application contact: Peter Knoblock, Contact, 315-443-9654.

Tarleton State University, College of Education, Department of Education and Psychology, Stephenville, TX 76402. Offerings include special education (Certificate). Postbaccalaureate distance learning degree programs offered. Department faculty: 28 full-time (9 women). *Application deadline:* 8/5 (priority date; rolling processing; 12/1 for spring admission). *Application fee:* $25 ($100 for international students). *Expenses:* Tuition $46 per hour for state residents; $249 per hour for nonresidents. Fees $49 per hour. • Dr. Bob Newby, Head, 254-968-9091.

Teachers College, Columbia University, Graduate Faculty of Education, Program in Cross Categorical Studies in Special Education, 525 West 120th Street, New York, NY 10027-6696. Awards Ed M, MA, Ed D, PhD. Faculty: 1 full-time (0 women), 2 part-time (both women), 1.6 FTE. Students: 13 full-time (11 women), 45 part-time (40 women); includes 9 minority (5 African Americans, 2 Asian Americans, 2 Hispanics), 1 international. Average age 38. 7 applicants, 57% accepted. In 1997, 5 doctorates awarded. *Degree requirements:* For doctorate, dissertation. *Application deadline:* 5/15. *Application fee:* $50. *Expenses:* Tuition $640 per credit. Fees $120 per semester. *Financial aid:* Full and partial tuition waivers, Federal Work-Study, institutionally sponsored loans, and career-related internships or fieldwork available. Aid available to part-time students. Financial aid application deadline: 2/1. *Faculty research:* Cognition and comprehension, disability studies, self-determination, literacy development. • Application contact: Urusla Felton, Office of Admissions, 212-678-3710. Fax: 212-678-4171.

Teachers College, Columbia University, Graduate Faculty of Education, Program in Reading/Learning Disability, 525 West 120th Street, New York, NY 10027-6696. Awards Ed M. Students: 3 full-time (all women), 6 part-time (5 women); includes 1 minority (Hispanic), 1 international. Average age 31. 7 applicants, 86% accepted. In 1997, 4 degrees awarded. *Application deadline:* 5/15. *Application fee:* $50. *Expenses:* Tuition $640 per credit. Fees $120 per semester. *Financial aid:* Partial tuition waivers, Federal Work-Study, institutionally sponsored loans, and career-related internships or fieldwork available. Aid available to part-time students. Financial aid application deadline: 2/1. *Faculty research:* Reading and spelling disorders, workplace literacy, reading and writing among children and adults. • Arthur Levine, President, Graduate Faculty of Education, 212-678-3050. Application contact: John Fisher, Executive Director of Admissions and Financial Aid, 212-678-3710. Fax: 212-678-4171.

Teachers College, Columbia University, Graduate Faculty of Education, Department of Curriculum and Teaching, Program in Early Childhood Special Education, 525 West 120th Street, New York, NY 10027-6696. Awards Ed M, MA. Evening/weekend programs available. Faculty: 1 (woman) full-time, 4 part-time (2 women), 2.2 FTE. Students: 6 full-time (all women), 27 part-time (26 women); includes 8 minority (1 African American, 3 Asian Americans, 4 Hispanics), 3 international. Average age 30. 29 applicants, 62% accepted. In 1997, 17 degrees awarded. *Application deadline:* 5/15 (12/1 for spring admission). *Application fee:* $50. *Expenses:* Tuition $640 per credit. Fees $120 per semester. *Financial aid:* Research assistantships, teaching assistantships, full and partial tuition waivers, Federal Work-Study, institutionally sponsored loans, and career-related internships or fieldwork available. Aid available to part-time students. Financial aid application deadline: 2/1. *Faculty research:* Curriculum development, infants, urban education, visually impaired infants. Total annual research expenditures: $80,000. • Application contact: Victor Singletary, Office of Admissions, 212-678-3710. Fax: 212-678-4171.

Teachers College, Columbia University, Graduate Faculty of Education, Department of Curriculum and Teaching, Program in Learning Disabilities, 525 West 120th Street, New York, NY 10027-6696. Awards Ed M, MA, Ed D. Faculty: 1 (woman) full-time, 4 part-time (3 women), 3 FTE. Students: 29 full-time (25 women), 72 part-time (62 women); includes 14 minority (8 African Americans, 2 Asian Americans, 4 Hispanics), 5 international. Average age 31. 53 applicants, 81% accepted. In 1997, 33 master's, 1 doctorate awarded. *Degree requirements:* For doctorate, dissertation required, foreign language not required. *Entrance requirements:* For doctorate, GRE General Test or MAT. Application deadline: 5/15 (12/1 for spring admission). Application fee: $50. *Expenses:* Tuition $640 per credit. Fees $120 per semester. *Financial aid:* Fellowships, teaching assistantships, full and partial tuition waivers, Federal Work-Study, institutionally sponsored loans, and career-related internships or fieldwork available. Aid available to part-time students. Financial aid application deadline: 2/1. *Faculty research:* Reading and mathematics disorders in students with learning disabilities, special education curriculum development. • Application contact: Victor Singletary, Office of Admissions, 212-678-3710. Fax: 212-678-4171.

Teachers College, Columbia University, Graduate Faculty of Education, Department of Curriculum and Teaching, Programs in Physical Disabilities, 525 West 120th Street, New York, NY 10027-6696. Awards MA, Ed D, PhD. Part-time and evening/weekend programs available. Faculty: 1 (woman) full-time, 4 part-time (3 women), 3 FTE. Students: 4 full-time (2 women), 4 part-time (all women); includes 2 minority (1 African American, 1 Hispanic). Average age 39. 3 applicants, 67% accepted. In 1997, 1 master's, 1 doctorate awarded. *Degree requirements:* For doctorate, variable foreign language requirement, dissertation. *Entrance requirements:* For doctorate, GRE General Test or MAT. Application deadline: 5/15 (priority date; rolling processing; 12/1 for spring admission). Application fee: $50. *Expenses:* Tuition $640 per credit. Fees $120 per semester. *Financial aid:* Fellowships, teaching assistantships, full and partial tuition waivers, Federal Work-Study, institutionally sponsored loans, and career-related internships or fieldwork available. Aid available to part-time students. Financial aid application deadline: 2/1. *Faculty research:* Students with traumatic brain injury, health impairments, learning disabilities. • Application contact: Victor Singletary, Office of Admissions, 212-678-3710. Fax: 212-678-4171.

Teachers College, Columbia University, Graduate Faculty of Education, Department of Health and Behavior Studies, Program in Behavioral Disorders, 525 West 120th Street, New York, NY 10027-6696. Awards MA, Ed D, PhD. Part-time programs available. Faculty: 1 full-time (0 women), 2 part-time (1 woman), 1.6 FTE. Students: 3 full-time (all women), 54 part-time (46 women); includes 8 minority (5 African Americans, 3 Asian Americans), 5 international. Average age 29. 33 applicants, 79% accepted. In 1997, 9 master's, 1 doctorate awarded. Terminal master's awarded for partial completion of doctoral program. *Degree requirements:* For doctorate, computer language, dissertation. *Application deadline:* 5/15 (12/1 for spring admission). *Application fee:* $50. *Expenses:* Tuition $640 per credit. Fees $120 per semester. *Financial aid:* Fellowships, research assistantships, full and partial tuition waivers, Federal Work-Study, institutionally sponsored loans, and career-related internships or fieldwork available. Aid available to part-time students. Financial aid application deadline: 2/1. *Faculty research:* Functional analysis of behavior, comprehensive analysis, comprehensive application of behavior analysis to schooling. • Application contact: Ursula Felton, Office of Admissions, 212-678-3710. Fax: 212-678-4171.

Teachers College, Columbia University, Graduate Faculty of Education, Department of Health and Behavior Studies, Program in Blind and Visual Impairment, 525 West 120th Street, New York, NY 10027-6696. Awards MA, Ed D. Faculty: 4 part-time (all women), 2 FTE. Students: 3 full-time (all women), 12 part-time (11 women); includes 2 minority (1 African American, 1 Hispanic). Average age 38. 6 applicants, 50% accepted. In 1997, 7 master's, 1 doctorate awarded. *Degree requirements:* For doctorate, dissertation. *Application deadline:* 5/15 (12/1 for spring admission). *Application fee:* $50. *Expenses:* Tuition $640 per credit. Fees $120 per semester. *Financial aid:* Full and partial tuition waivers, Federal Work-Study, institutionally sponsored loans, and career-related internships or fieldwork available. Aid available to part-time students. Financial aid application deadline: 2/1. *Faculty research:* Cross-modality transfer, issues in early childhood. • Application contact: Ursula Felton, Office of Admissions, 212-678-3710. Fax: 212-678-4171.

Teachers College, Columbia University, Graduate Faculty of Education, Department of Health and Behavior Studies, Program in Hearing Impairment, 525 West 120th Street, New York, NY 10027-6696. Awards MA, Ed D. Faculty: 1 full-time (0 women), 4 part-time (3 women), 3.1 FTE. Students: 5 full-time (4 women), 42 part-time (33 women); includes 11 minority (3 African Americans, 3 Asian Americans, 5 Hispanics), 1 international. Average age 31. 32 applicants, 75% accepted. In 1997, 14 master's awarded. *Degree requirements:* For doctorate, dissertation. *Application deadline:* 5/15 (12/1 for spring admission). *Application fee:* $50. *Expenses:* Tuition $640 per credit. Fees $120 per semester. *Financial aid:* Fellowships, full and partial tuition waivers, Federal Work-Study, institutionally sponsored loans, and career-related internships or fieldwork available. Aid available to part-time students. Financial aid application deadline: 2/1. *Faculty research:* Language development, reading/writing, cognitive abilities, text analysis, auditory streaming, teaching the deaf and hard of hearing. • Application contact: Ursula Felton, Office of Admissions, 212-678-3710. Fax: 212-678-4171.

Teachers College, Columbia University, Graduate Faculty of Education, Department of Health and Behavior Studies, Program in Mental Retardation, 525 West 120th Street, New York, NY 10027-6696. Awards MA, Ed D, PhD. Part-time programs available. Faculty: 1 (woman) full-time, 3 part-time (all women), 1.9 FTE. Students: 3 full-time (2 women), 25 part-time (20 women); includes 10 minority (4 African Americans, 4 Asian Americans, 2 Hispanics), 2 international. Average age 33. 14 applicants, 71% accepted. In 1997, 5 master's, 1 doctorate awarded. Terminal master's awarded for partial completion of doctoral program. *Degree requirements:* For doctorate, dissertation. *Application deadline:* 5/15 (12/1 for spring admission). *Application fee:* $50. *Expenses:* Tuition $640 per credit. Fees $120 per semester. *Financial aid:* Fellowships, research assistantships, teaching assistantships, full and partial tuition waivers, Federal Work-Study, institutionally sponsored loans, and career-related internships or fieldwork available. Aid available to part-time students. Financial aid application deadline: 2/1. *Faculty research:* Information processing, memory comprehension and problem-solving issues related to mental retardation, transition issues, cognition and comprehension. • Application contact: Ursula Felton, Office of Admissions, 212-678-3710. Fax: 212-678-4171.

Teachers College, Columbia University, Graduate Faculty of Education, Department of Health and Behavior Studies, Program in Research in Special Education, 525 West 120th

Street, New York, NY 10027-6696. Awards Ed D. Faculty: 1 full-time (0 women), 3 part-time (2 women). Students: 2 part-time (both women); includes 1 international. Average age 33. 2 applicants, 100% accepted. *Degree requirements:* Dissertation. *Application deadline:* 5/15. *Application fee:* $50. *Expenses:* Tuition $640 per credit. Fees $120 per semester. *Financial aid:* Full and partial tuition waivers, Federal Work-Study, institutionally sponsored loans, and career-related internships or fieldwork available. Aid available to part-time students. Financial aid application deadline: 2/1. • Application contact: Ursula Felton, Office of Admissions, 212-678-3710. Fax: 212-678-4171.

Teachers College, Columbia University, Graduate Faculty of Education, Department of Health and Behavior Studies, Program in Special Education Administration and Supervision, Instructional Practice, 525 West 120th Street, New York, NY 10027-6696. Awards Ed M, MA, Ed D. Part-time and evening/weekend programs available. Faculty: 1 full-time (0 women), 3 part-time (2 women), 2.2 FTE. Students: 1 (woman) full-time, 25 part-time (18 women); includes 2 minority (1 African American, 1 Native American), 4 international. Average age 35. 9 applicants, 78% accepted. In 1997, 8 master's, 1 doctorate awarded. Terminal master's awarded for partial completion of doctoral program. *Application deadline:* 5/15 (12/1 for spring admission). *Application fee:* $50. *Expenses:* Tuition $640 per credit. Fees $120 per semester. *Financial aid:* Full and partial tuition waivers, Federal Work-Study, institutionally sponsored loans, and career-related internships or fieldwork available. Aid available to part-time students. Financial aid application deadline: 2/1. • Application contact: Ursula Felton, Office of Admissions, 212-678-3710. Fax: 212-678-4171.

Temple University, College of Education, Department of Curriculum, Instruction, and Technology in Education, Philadelphia, PA 19122-6096. Offerings include special education (Ed M, MS). Accredited by NCATE. Department faculty: 33 full-time (14 women). *Degree requirements:* Thesis or alternative required, foreign language not required. *Entrance requirements:* GRE General Test (minimum combined score of 1000) or MAT (minimum score 39), minimum GPA of 2.8. Application deadline: 2/15 (10/1 for spring admission). Application fee: $40. *Expenses:* Tuition $323 per semester hour for state residents; $444 per semester hour for nonresidents. Fees $170 per year full-time, $28 per semester (minimum) part-time. • Dr. Raymond Lolla, Chair, 215-204-6387. Fax: 215-204-1414.

Tennessee State University, College of Education, Department of Teaching and Learning, Program in Special Education, Nashville, TN 37209-1561. Awards MA Ed, M Ed, Ed D. Accredited by NCATE. *Degree requirements:* For master's, comprehensive exam (M Ed), thesis (MA Ed) required, foreign language not required; for doctorate, dissertation. *Entrance requirements:* For master's, GRE General Test, GRE Subject Test, or MAT (minimum score 44), minimum GPA of 2.5; for doctorate, GRE General Test (minimum score 870), GRE Subject Test, or MAT (minimum score 25), minimum GPA of 3.25. Application deadline: rolling. Application fee: $15. *Tuition:* $2962 per year full-time, $182 per credit hour part-time for state residents; $7788 per year full-time, $393 per credit hour part-time for nonresidents. *Financial aid:* Fellowships available. Financial aid application deadline: 5/1. • Application contact: Dr. Clinton M. Lipsey, Dean of the Graduate School, 615-963-5901. Fax: 615-963-5963. E-mail: clipsey@picard.tnstate.edu.

Tennessee Technological University, College of Education, Department of Curriculum and Instruction, Program in Special Education, Cookeville, TN 38505. Awards MA, Ed S. Accredited by NCATE. Part-time programs available. Faculty: 6 full-time (3 women). Students: 3 full-time (2 women), 24 part-time (19 women). Average age 27. 10 applicants, 100% accepted. In 1997, 20 master's, 1 Ed S awarded. *Degree requirements:* For Ed S, thesis or alternative required, foreign language not required. *Entrance requirements:* For master's, MAT, TOEFL (minimum score 525); for Ed S, MAT, NTE. Application deadline: 3/1 (priority date; 8/1 for spring admission). Application fee: $25 ($30 for international students). *Tuition:* $2960 per year full-time, $147 per semester hour part-time for state residents; $7786 per year full-time, $358 per semester hour part-time for nonresidents. *Financial aid:* In 1997–98, 2 students received aid, including 2 teaching assistantships (both to first-year students); fellowships, research assistantships, and career-related internships or fieldwork also available. Financial aid application deadline: 4/1. • Application contact: Dr. Rebecca F. Quattlebaum, Dean of the Graduate School, 615-372-3233. Fax: 615-372-3497. E-mail: rquattlebaum@tntech.edu.

Texas A&M University, College of Education, Department of Educational Psychology, Specialization in Special Education, College Station, TX 77843. Awards M Ed, PhD. Accredited by NCATE. *Degree requirements:* For doctorate, dissertation. *Entrance requirements:* GRE General Test, TOEFL. Application deadline: 2/1. Application fee: $35 ($75 for international students). *Financial aid:* Fellowships, research assistantships, teaching assistantships available. • Douglas J. Palmer, Head, Department of Educational Psychology, 409-845-1831. Fax: 409-862-1256. Application contact: Graduate Adviser, 409-845-1833.

Texas A&M University–Commerce, College of Education, Department of Psychology and Special Education, Commerce, TX 75429-3011. Offers programs in educational psychology (PhD), psychology (MA, MS), special education (MA, M Ed, MS). Faculty: 15 full-time (2 women), 4 part-time (2 women). Students: 31 full-time (22 women), 69 part-time (53 women); includes 14 minority (6 African Americans, 3 Asian Americans, 1 Hispanic, 4 Native Americans), 2 international. In 1997, 32 master's, 2 doctorates awarded. Terminal master's awarded for partial completion of doctoral program. *Degree requirements:* For master's, thesis (for some programs), comprehensive exam required, foreign language not required; for doctorate, dissertation, departmental qualifying exam. *Entrance requirements:* GRE General Test. Application deadline: rolling. Application fee: $0 ($25 for international students). *Tuition:* $2382 per year full-time, $343 per semester (minimum) part-time for state residents; $7518 per year full-time, $343 per semester (minimum) part-time for nonresidents. *Financial aid:* Research assistantships, teaching assistantships, Federal Work-Study, institutionally sponsored loans, and career-related internships or fieldwork available. *Faculty research:* Human learning, study skills, Delphi, Minnesota Multiphasic Personality Inventory, anxiety. • Dr. Paul Zelhart, Head, 903-886-5594. Application contact: Pam Hammonds, Graduate Admissions Adviser, 903-886-5167. Fax: 903-886-5165.

Texas A&M University–Corpus Christi, College of Education, Program in Special Education, Corpus Christi, TX 78412-5503. Awards MS. Students: 1 (woman) full-time, 7 part-time (5 women); includes 2 minority (1 Asian American, 1 Hispanic), 1 international. Average age 34. In 1997, 6 degrees awarded. *Entrance requirements:* GRE General Test. Application deadline: 7/15 (priority date; rolling processing; 11/15 for spring admission). Application fee: $10 ($30 for international students). *Expenses:* Tuition $648 per year full-time, $120 per semester (minimum) part-time for state residents; $4482 per year full-time, $747 per semester (minimum) part-time for nonresidents. Fees $1010 per year full-time, $205 per semester part-time. *Financial aid:* Application deadline 3/15. • Dr. Arturo Medina, Graduate Adviser, 512-994-2667. E-mail: adedu005@tamucc.edu. Application contact: Mary Margaret Dechant, Director of Admissions, 512-994-2624. Fax: 512-994-5887.

Texas A&M University–Kingsville, College of Education, Department of Education, Program in Special Education, Kingsville, TX 78363. Awards M Ed. Part-time and evening/weekend programs available. Faculty: 2 full-time, 2 part-time. *Degree requirements:* Comprehensive exam, mini-thesis required, foreign language not required. *Entrance requirements:* GRE General Test (minimum combined score of 1000), MAT (minimum score 34), minimum GPA of 3.0. Application deadline: 6/1 (rolling processing; 11/15 for spring admission). Application fee: $15 ($25 for international students). *Tuition:* $1822 per year full-time, $281 per semester (minimum) part-time for state residents; $6934 per year full-time, $908 per semester (minimum) part-time for nonresidents. *Financial aid:* Federal Work-Study, institutionally sponsored loans available. Financial aid application deadline: 5/15. *Faculty research:* Training for trainers of the disabled. • Dr. Grace Hopkins, Director, 512-593-2843.

Texas A&M University–Texarkana, Division of Arts and Sciences and Education, Texarkana, TX 75505-5518. Offerings include special education (MA, M Ed, MS). Division faculty: 9 full-time (3 women), 5 part-time (3 women). *Degree requirements:* Thesis or alternative required, foreign language not required. *Average time to degree:* master's–1.5 years full-time. *Entrance requirements:* GRE General Test, bachelor's degree from a regionally accredited institution, minimum GPA of 3.0, teaching certificate (M Ed). Application deadline: rolling. Application fee: $0 ($25 for international students). *Tuition:* $2136 per year for state residents; $7248 per year for nonresidents. • Dr. John Anderson, Interim Head, 903-223-3003. Application contact: Pat Black, Registrar, 903-223-3068. Fax: 903-832-8890. E-mail: pat.black@tamut.edu.

Texas Christian University, School of Education, Department of Curriculum and Instruction, Program in Special Education, Fort Worth, TX 76129-0002. Awards M Ed. Part-time and evening/weekend programs available. Students: 10 (9 women); includes 2 minority (1 African American, 1 Hispanic), 1 international. 4 applicants, 75% accepted. In 1997, 6 degrees awarded. *Degree requirements:* Thesis optional, foreign language not required. *Entrance requirements:* TOEFL (minimum score 550). Application deadline: 3/1 (rolling processing; 12/1 for spring admission). Application fee: $0. *Expenses:* Tuition $10,350 per year full-time, $345 per credit hour part-time. Fees $1240 per year full-time, $50 per credit hour part-time. *Financial aid:* Graduate assistantships and career-related internships or fieldwork available. Financial aid application deadline: 3/1. • Dr. Luther Clegg, Chairperson, Department of Curriculum and Instruction, 817-257-7660.

Texas Southern University, College of Education, Area of Curriculum and Instruction, Houston, TX 77004-4584. Offerings include special education (M Ed). Faculty: 15 full-time (7 women), 4 part-time (all women). *Degree requirements:* Comprehensive exam required, foreign language not required. *Entrance requirements:* GRE General Test, TOEFL, minimum GPA of 2.5. Application deadline: 7/15 (priority date; rolling processing). Application fee: $35 ($75 for international students). • Dr. Claudette Ligon, Chairperson, 713-313-7775.

Texas Tech University, Graduate School, College of Education, Division of Educational Psychology and Leadership, Lubbock, TX 79409. Offerings include special education (M Ed, Ed D), special education counselor (Certificate), special education supervisor (Certificate). One or more programs accredited by NCATE. Division faculty: 28 full-time (13 women), 3 part-time (1 woman), 29.29 FTE. *Degree requirements:* For master's, computer language required, thesis optional, foreign language not required; for doctorate, dissertation required, foreign language not required. *Entrance requirements:* For master's, GRE General Test (combined average 1034); for doctorate, GRE General Test. Application deadline: 4/15 (priority date; rolling processing; 11/1 for spring admission). Application fee: $25 ($50 for international students). Electronic applications accepted. *Expenses:* Tuition $864 per year full-time, $120 per semester (minimum) part-time for state residents; $5976 per year full-time, $747 per semester (minimum) part-time for nonresidents. Fees $2321 per year full-time, $302 per semester (minimum) part-time. • Dr. Loretta J. Bradley, Chair, 806-742-2393.

Texas Woman's University, College of Education and Human Ecology, Department of Early Childhood and Special Education, Program in Special Education, Denton, TX 76204. Awards MA, M Ed, PhD. Faculty: 8 full-time (4 women), 2 part-time (both women). Students: 12 full-time (10 women), 119 part-time (108 women); includes 11 minority (7 African Americans, 2 Asian Americans, 2 Hispanics), 1 international. Average age 37. 75 applicants, 91% accepted. In 1997, 14 master's, 5 doctorates awarded. *Degree requirements:* For master's, thesis, professional paper (M Ed) required, foreign language not required; for doctorate, 1 foreign language, computer language, dissertation. *Average time to degree:* master's–3 years part-time; doctorate–8 years part-time. *Entrance requirements:* For master's, GRE General Test (minimum combined score of 700), minimum GPA of 3.0; for doctorate, GRE General Test (minimum combined score of 1000), minimum graduate GPA of 3.5. Application fee: $25. *Financial aid:* Fellowships, research assistantships, teaching assistantships, partial tuition waivers, and career-related internships or fieldwork available. Aid available to part-time students. Financial aid application deadline: 4/1. *Faculty research:* Assessment of the handicapped, at-risk students, learning-disabled, gifted, teacher education. • Dr. Lloyd R. Kinnison, Chair, Department of Early Childhood and Special Education, 940-898-2271. Fax: 940-898-2209. E-mail: d_kinnison@twu.edu.

Trinity College, School of Professional Studies, Programs in Education, Washington, DC 20017-1094. Offerings include special education (MAT). Faculty: 6 full-time (5 women), 18 part-time (13 women). *Application deadline:* rolling. *Application fee:* $35. *Tuition:* $460 per credit hour. • Sr. Rosemarie Bosler, Division Chair, 202-884-9557. Application contact: Karen Goodwin, Director of Graduate Admissions, 202-884-9400. Fax: 202-884-9229.

Troy State University, Graduate School, School of Education, Program in Special Education, Troy, AL 36082. Offers emotional conflict (MS), learning disabilities (MS), mental retardation (MS), mild learning handicapped (MS, Ed S). Accredited by NCATE. Part-time and evening/weekend programs available. Students: 21 full-time (17 women), 47 part-time (38 women); includes 32 minority (all African Americans). Average age 30. In 1997, 26 master's awarded. *Degree requirements:* For master's, thesis, comprehensive exam. *Entrance requirements:* For master's, minimum GPA of 2.5; for Ed S, GRE General Test (minimum combined score of 850) or MAT (minimum score 33), Alabama Class A certificate or equivalent, minimum graduate GPA of 3.0. Application deadline: rolling. Application fee: $20. Electronic applications accepted. *Expenses:* Tuition $2040 per year full-time, $68 per hour part-time for state residents; $4200 per year full-time, $140 per hour part-time for nonresidents. Fees $240 per year full-time, $27 per quarter (minimum) part-time. *Financial aid:* Available to part-time students. Financial aid applicants required to submit FAFSA. • Dr. Patricia Hardin, Chair, 334-670-3354. Fax: 334-670-3474. E-mail: phardin@trojan.troyst.edu. Application contact: Teresa Rodgers, Director of Graduate Admissions, 334-670-3188. Fax: 334-670-3733. E-mail: trodgers@trojan.troyst.edu.

Troy State University Dothan, School of Education, Dothan, AL 36304-0368. Offerings include special education (MS Ed). Accredited by NCATE. *Application fee:* $20. *Expenses:* Tuition $68 per credit hour for state residents; $140 per credit hour for nonresidents. Fees $2 per credit hour. • Dr. Betty Anderson, Dean, 334-983-6556. Application contact: Reta Cordell, Director of Admissions and Records, 334-983-6556. Fax: 334-983-6322. E-mail: rcordell@tsud.edu.

Union College, Department of Education, Program in Special Education, Barbourville, KY 40906-1499. Awards MA Ed. *Degree requirements:* Thesis optional, foreign language not required. *Entrance requirements:* GRE General Test, NTE. Application deadline: rolling. Application fee: $15. *Tuition:* $220 per hour. • Dr. William E. Bernhardt, Dean of Graduate Academic Affairs, Graduate Programs, 606-546-1210. Fax: 606-546-2217.

Universidad del Turabo, Programs in Education, Program in Special Education, Gurabo, PR 00778-3030. Awards MA. *Entrance requirements:* GRE, PAEG, interview. Application deadline: 8/5. Application fee: $25.

Université de Sherbrooke, Faculty of Education, Program in Special Education, Sherbrooke, PQ J1K 2R1, Canada. Awards M Ed, Diploma. Part-time and evening/weekend programs available. *Degree requirements:* For master's, thesis. *Application deadline:* 6/1. *Application fee:* $15.

The University of Akron, College of Education, Department of Counseling and Special Education, Program in Special Education, Akron, OH 44325-0001. Awards MA Ed, MS Ed. Accredited by NCATE. Students: 5 full-time (all women), 27 part-time (24 women); includes 3 minority (2 African Americans, 1 Native American). Average age 36. In 1997, 4 degrees awarded. *Degree requirements:* Thesis or alternative, written comprehensive exam required, foreign language not required. *Entrance requirements:* MAT (minimum score 35), minimum GPA of 2.75. Application deadline: 8/15 (rolling processing). Application fee: $25 ($50 for international students). *Expenses:* Tuition $178 per credit hour for state residents; $333 per credit hour for nonresidents. Fees $145 per year full-time, $32 per semester (minimum) part-time. *Financial aid:* Fellowships, research assistantships, teaching assistantships, administrative assistantships, and career-related internships or fieldwork available. • Dr. Bridgie Ford, Coordinator, 330-972-8150. Application contact: Dr. Robert Eley, Director of Student Services, 330-972-7750. E-mail: reley@uakron.edu.

Directory: Special Education

The University of Alabama, College of Education, Area of Teacher Education, Tuscaloosa, AL 35487. Offerings include special education (MA, Ed D, PhD, Ed S). Accredited by NCATE. Faculty: 32 full-time (18 women), 8 part-time (4 women). *Degree requirements:* For doctorate, 1 foreign language (computer language can substitute), dissertation, residency; for Ed S, thesis required, foreign language not required. *Entrance requirements:* For master's and doctorate, GRE General Test, MAT (score in 50th percentile or higher), or NTE (minimum score 658 on each core battery test), minimum GPA of 3.0; for Ed S, minimum GPA of 3.0 during previous 2 years. Application deadline: 7/6 (priority date; rolling processing). Application fee: $25. *Tuition:* $2684 per year full-time, $594 per semester (minimum) part-time for state residents; $7216 per year full-time, $1248 per semester (minimum) part-time for nonresidents. • Dr. Lea McGee, Head, 205-348-1196. Fax: 205-348-9863. E-mail: lmcgee@bamaed.ua.edu.

The University of Alabama at Birmingham, Graduate School, School of Education, Department of Leadership, Special Education and Foundations, Program in Special Education, Birmingham, AL 35294. Awards MA Ed, Ed S. Accredited by NCATE. Students: 23 full-time (20 women), 36 part-time (31 women); includes 10 minority (9 African Americans, 1 Asian American). 43 applicants, 93% accepted. In 1997, 40 master's awarded. *Degree requirements:* For master's, thesis optional; for Ed S, comprehensive exam. *Entrance requirements:* For master's, GRE General Test (minimum combined score of 1000), MAT (minimum score 35), or NTE (minimum score 620), minimum GPA of 3.0. Application deadline: rolling. Application fee: $30 ($60 for international students). Electronic applications accepted. *Expenses:* Tuition $99 per credit hour for state residents; $198 per credit hour for nonresidents. Fees $516 per year (minimum) full-time, $73 per quarter (minimum) part-time for state residents; $516 per year (minimum) full-time, $73 per unit (minimum) part-time for nonresidents. • Dr. W. Boyd Rogan, Chair, Department of Leadership, Special Education and Foundations, 205-934-4892.

University of Alaska Anchorage, College of Health, Education and Social Welfare, School of Education, Program in Special Education, Anchorage, AK 99508-8060. Awards M Ed. Part-time programs available. Students: 6 full-time (5 women), 30 part-time (26 women); includes 2 minority (both Native Americans). 22 applicants, 86% accepted. In 1997, 16 degrees awarded. *Entrance requirements:* GRE Subject Test, interview. Application deadline: 3/1 (priority date). Application fee: $45. *Expenses:* Tuition $2988 per year full-time, $1990 per year part-time for state residents; $5814 per year full-time, $3876 per year part-time for nonresidents. Fees $298 per year. *Financial aid:* Federal Work-Study and career-related internships or fieldwork available. Aid available to part-time students. Financial aid application deadline: 4/1. *Faculty research:* Mild disabilities. • Dr. Claudia Dybdahl, Head, 907-786-4422. Fax: 907-786-4444. Application contact: Linda Berg Smith, Associate Vice Chancellor for Enrollment Services, 907-786-1529.

University of Alberta, Faculty of Graduate Studies and Research, Department of Educational Psychology, Edmonton, AB T6G 2E1, Canada. Offerings include special education (M Ed, PhD). Department faculty: 36 full-time (11 women), 23 part-time (9 women), 41.75 FTE. *Degree requirements:* For doctorate, dissertation. *Application deadline:* 2/1 (priority date; rolling processing). *Application fee:* $60. *Expenses:* Tuition $390 per course for Canadian residents; $781 per course for nonresidents. Fees $500 per year full-time, $184 per year part-time. • Dr. L. L. Stewin, Chair, 403-492-2389. Fax: 403-492-1318. E-mail: len.stewin@ualberta.ca.

The University of Arizona, College of Education, Department of Special Education and Rehabilitation, Tucson, AZ 85721. Awards MA, M Ed, MS, Ed D, PhD, Ed S. Part-time programs available. Terminal master's awarded for partial completion of doctoral program. *Degree requirements:* For doctorate, dissertation required, foreign language not required. *Entrance requirements:* For master's, TOEFL (minimum score 550); for doctorate, GRE General Test or MAT, TOEFL (minimum score 550); for Ed S, TOEFL (minimun score of 550). Application deadline: 4/15 (rolling processing). Application fee: $35. *Tuition:* $2162 per year full-time, $337 per semester (minimum) part-time for state residents; $6860 per year full-time, $1138 per semester (minimum) part-time for nonresidents. *Faculty research:* Teacher assistant teams, self-advocacy, language development in preschool, the deaf, comprehension of the learning disabled.

University of Arkansas, College of Education, Department of Curriculum and Instruction, Program in Special Education, Fayetteville, AR 72701-1201. Awards MAT, M Ed. Accredited by NCATE. Students: 19 full-time (18 women), 11 part-time (10 women); includes 2 minority (both African Americans), 1 international. 16 applicants, 88% accepted. In 1997, 10 degrees awarded. *Entrance requirements:* GRE General Test or MAT. Application fee: $25 ($35 for international students). *Tuition:* $3144 per year full-time, $173 per credit hour part-time for state residents; $7140 per year full-time, $395 per credit hour part-time for nonresidents. *Financial aid:* Federal Work-Study and career-related internships or fieldwork available. Aid available to part-time students. Financial aid application deadline: 4/1; applicants required to submit FAFSA. • Dr. Jerry Ford, Coordinator, 501-575-6676.

University of Arkansas at Little Rock, College of Education, Department of Rehabilitation, Little Rock, AR 72204-1099. Offers program in rehabilitation for the blind (MA), including orientation and mobility, rehabilitation teaching. Accredited by NCATE. Part-time programs available. Students: 11 full-time (10 women), 11 part-time (10 women); includes 5 minority (all African Americans), 3 international. Average age 36. 20 applicants, 75% accepted. In 1997, 15 degrees awarded. *Entrance requirements:* GRE General Test (minimum combined score of 1000 on three sections), interview, minimum GPA of 2.75. Application deadline: rolling. Application fee: $25 ($30 for international students). *Expenses:* Tuition $2466 per year full-time, $137 per credit hour part-time for state residents; $5256 per year full-time, $292 per credit hour part-time for nonresidents. Fees $216 per year full-time, $36 per semester (minimum) part-time. *Financial aid:* Teaching assistantships, full tuition waivers, Federal Work-Study, institutionally sponsored loans, and career-related internships or fieldwork available. Aid available to part-time students. Financial aid application deadline: 6/30. *Faculty research:* Low vision, orientation and mobility instruction. • Dr. Patricia Smith, Chairperson, 501-569-3169.

University of Arkansas at Little Rock, College of Education, Department of Teacher Education, Program in Special Education, Little Rock, AR 72204-1099. Offers early childhood special education (M Ed), education of hearing impaired children (M Ed), teaching of the mildly disabled student (M Ed), teaching persons with severe disabilities (M Ed), teaching the visually impaired child (M Ed). Accredited by NCATE. Part-time and evening/weekend programs available. Students: 33 full-time (31 women), 49 part-time (45 women); includes 14 minority (all African Americans), 2 international. Average age 32. 46 applicants, 83% accepted. In 1997, 41 degrees awarded. *Degree requirements:* Comprehensive exam, portfolio or thesis required, foreign language not required. *Entrance requirements:* Interview, minimum GPA of 2.75, GRE General Test (minimum combined score of 1000 on three sections) or teaching certificate. Application deadline: rolling. Application fee: $25 ($30 for international students). *Expenses:* Tuition $2466 per year full-time, $137 per credit hour part-time for state residents; $5256 per year full-time, $292 per credit hour part-time for nonresidents. Fees $216 per year full-time, $36 per semester (minimum) part-time. *Financial aid:* Research assistantships, Federal Work-Study, institutionally sponsored loans, and career-related internships or fieldwork available. Aid available to part-time students. • Application contact: Dr. Mary Hendricks, Adviser, 501-569-3335.

University of British Columbia, Faculty of Education, Department of Educational Psychology and Special Education, Vancouver, BC V6T 1Z2, Canada. Offers programs in educational psychology (M Ed, PhD); general educational psychology (M Ed); human learning, development and instruction (MA); measurement, evaluation and research methodology (MA); school psychology (MA); special education (MA, M Ed, PhD). Part-time and evening/weekend programs available. Terminal master's awarded for partial completion of doctoral program. *Degree requirements:* For master's, thesis, thesis (MA), graduating paper (M Ed) required, foreign language not required; for doctorate, dissertation required, foreign language not required. *Average time to degree:* master's–3 years full-time, 5 years part-time; doctorate–6 years full-time. *Entrance requirements:* For master's, TOEFL (minimum score 590); for doctorate, GRE General Test, TOEFL (minimum score 590). Application deadline: 2/1. Application fee: $60. *Faculty research:* Adolescent/adult cognitive development, learning disabilities in adolescents and adults, school psychology assessment, research design analysis of variance, education of deaf, education of blind, teaching of deaf and hearing impaired.

The University of Calgary, Faculty of Education, Department of Educational Psychology, Calgary, AB T2N 1N4, Canada. Offerings include special education (M Ed, M Sc, PhD). Department faculty: 30 full-time, 20 part-time. *Degree requirements:* For master's, thesis required (for some programs), foreign language not required; for doctorate, dissertation, candidacy exam. *Entrance requirements:* For master's, minimum GPA of 3.0; for doctorate, minimum GPA of 3.5. Application deadline: 2/15. Application fee: $60. *Expenses:* Tuition $5448 per year full-time, $908 per course part-time for Canadian residents; $10,896 per year full-time, $1816 per course part-time for nonresidents. Fees $285 per year full-time, $119 per semester (minimum) part-time. • Dr. S. Robertson, Head, 403-220-5651. Fax: 403-282-9244. E-mail: 18601@ucdasvm1.admin.ucalgary.ca.

University of California, Berkeley, School of Education, Division of Cognition and Development, Joint Doctoral Program in Special Education, Berkeley, CA 94720-1500. Awards PhD. Offered jointly with San Francisco State University; applicants must apply to both the University of California, Berkeley and San Francisco State University. Students: 27 full-time (22 women); includes 5 minority (3 African Americans, 2 Asian Americans), 1 international. 15 applicants, 27% accepted. In 1997, 3 degrees awarded. *Degree requirements:* Dissertation, oral qualifying exam required, foreign language not required. *Entrance requirements:* GRE General Test, minimum GPA of 3.0 during last 2 years of undergraduate course work. Application deadline: 12/15 (rolling processing). Application fee: $40. *Expenses:* Tuition $0 for state residents; $9384 per year for nonresidents. Fees $4409 per year. *Financial aid:* Fellowships available. Financial aid application deadline: 12/15. • Anne Cunningham, Coordinator. Application contact: Melissa Quilter, Program Assistant, 510-643-6871. E-mail: gse_info@uclink4.berkeley.edu.

University of California, Los Angeles, Graduate School of Education and Information Studies, Program in Special Education, Los Angeles, CA 90095. Awards PhD. Offered jointly with California State University, Los Angeles. Students: 0. *Degree requirements:* Dissertation, oral and written qualifying exams required, foreign language not required. *Entrance requirements:* GRE General Test (minimum combined score of 1000), MAT, or Doppelt Math Reasoning Test, minimum undergraduate GPA of 3.0. Application deadline: 12/15. Application fee: $40. Electronic applications accepted. *Expenses:* Tuition $0 for state residents; $9384 per year for nonresidents. Fees $4551 per year. *Financial aid:* Research assistantships, teaching assistantships, full and partial tuition waivers, Federal Work-Study, institutionally sponsored loans available. Financial aid application deadline: 3/1. • Application contact: Departmental Office, 310-206-1673. E-mail: nobody@bert.gse.ucla.edu.

University of Central Arkansas, College of Education, Department of Childhood and Special Education, Program in Special Education, Conway, AR 72035-0001. Offers early childhood special education (MSE), mildly handicapped (MSE), moderately/profoundly handicapped (MSE), seriously emotionally disturbed (MSE). Accredited by NCATE. Students: 12 full-time (10 women), 42 part-time (38 women); includes 13 minority (12 African Americans, 1 Hispanic). 34 applicants, 94% accepted. In 1997, 24 degrees awarded. *Degree requirements:* Comprehensive exam required, thesis optional. *Entrance requirements:* GRE General Test, minimum GPA of 2.7. Application deadline: 3/1 (priority date; rolling processing; 10/1 for spring admission). Application fee: $15 ($40 for international students). *Expenses:* Tuition $161 per credit hour for state residents; $298 per credit hour for nonresidents. Fees $50 per year full-time, $30 per year part-time. *Financial aid:* In 1997–98, 3 assistantships were awarded; Federal Work-Study also available. Financial aid application deadline: 2/15. • Dr. Jim Mainord, Interim Chairperson, Department of Childhood and Special Education, 501-450-5442. Fax: 501-450-5358. E-mail: jamesm@mail.uca.edu.

University of Central Florida, College of Education, Department of Exceptional and Physical Education, Program in Exceptional Child Education, Orlando, FL 32816. Awards M Ed. Accredited by NCATE. Part-time and evening/weekend programs available. Students: 59 full-time (52 women), 37 part-time (31 women); includes 9 minority (8 African Americans, 1 Hispanic), 1 international. Average age 34. 42 applicants, 55% accepted. In 1997, 30 degrees awarded. *Degree requirements:* Thesis or alternative required, foreign language not required. *Entrance requirements:* GRE General Test (minimum combined score of 840). Application deadline: 7/15 (12/15 for spring admission). Application fee: $20. *Expenses:* Tuition $3288 per year full-time, $137 per credit hour part-time for state residents; $11,520 per year full-time, $480 per credit hour part-time for nonresidents. Fees $105 per year. *Financial aid:* Teaching assistantships, Federal Work-Study, institutionally sponsored loans, and career-related internships or fieldwork available. Aid available to part-time students. • Application contact: Dr. Lee Cross, Coordinator, 407-823-2402. E-mail: lcross@pegasus.cc.ucf.edu.

University of Central Oklahoma, College of Education, Department of Curriculum and Instruction, Program in Special Education, Edmond, OK 73034-5209. Awards M Ed. Accredited by NCATE. Part-time and evening/weekend programs available. *Entrance requirements:* GRE General Test. Application deadline: 8/18. Application fee: $15. *Tuition:* $76 per credit hour for state residents; $178 per credit hour for nonresidents.

University of Charleston, South Carolina, School of Education, Department of Educational Foundations and Specializations, Charleston, SC 29424-0001. Offers program in special education (MAT, M Ed). M Ed offered jointly with The Citadel, The Military College of South Carolina. Part-time and evening/weekend programs available. Faculty: 13 full-time (9 women), 1 (woman) part-time, 13.75 FTE. Students: 30 full-time (24 women), 36 part-time (32 women); includes 2 minority (both African Americans), 3 international. Average age 33. 38 applicants, 92% accepted. In 1997, 34 degrees awarded. *Degree requirements:* Thesis or alternative, practicum, written qualifying exam, student teaching (MAT) required, foreign language not required. *Entrance requirements:* GRE (score in 50th percentile or higher), MAT (score in 50th percentile or higher), or NTE; South Carolina Education Entrance Exam (MAT); TOEFL, teaching certificate (M Ed). Application deadline: rolling. Application fee: $35. *Expenses:* Tuition $2568 per year full-time, $438 per semester (minimum) part-time for state residents; $4596 per year full-time, $876 per semester (minimum) part-time for nonresidents. Fees $51 per year full-time, $21 per semester (minimum) part-time. *Financial aid:* Research assistantships, teaching assistantships, Federal Work-Study available. Aid available to part-time students. Financial aid application deadline: 4/1; applicants required to submit FAFSA. *Faculty research:* Applied behavioral analysis, classroom management, substance abuse in special needs learning. • Dr. Frances Welch, Program Director, 843-953-5613. Fax: 843-953-5407. E-mail: welchf@cofc.edu. Application contact: Laura H. Hines, Graduate School Coordinator, 843-953-5614. Fax: 843-953-1434. E-mail: hinesl@cofc.edu.

University of Cincinnati, College of Education, Division of Teacher Education, Department of Early Childhood and Special Education, Program in Special Education, Cincinnati, OH 45221. Awards M Ed, Ed D. Accredited by NCATE. Part-time programs available. Students: 35 full-time (31 women), 37 part-time (34 women); includes 8 minority (7 African Americans, 1 Asian American), 10 international. 46 applicants, 50% accepted. In 1997, 29 master's, 4 doctorates awarded. *Degree requirements:* For master's, thesis or alternative required, foreign language not required; for doctorate, dissertation required, foreign language not required. *Average time to degree:* master's–2.5 years full-time; doctorate–6.9 years full-time. *Entrance requirements:* For master's, GRE General Test; for doctorate, GRE General Test, GRE Subject Test. Application deadline: 2/1. Application fee: $30. *Tuition:* $7228 per year full-time, $185 per credit hour part-time for state residents; $13,812 per year full-time, $352 per credit hour part-time for nonresidents. *Financial aid:* Fellowships, graduate assistantships, full tuition waivers available. Aid available to part-time students. Financial aid application deadline: 5/1. • Application contact: Jerald Etienne, Graduate Coordinator, 513-556-4538. Fax: 513-556-1581.

University of Colorado at Colorado Springs, School of Education, Colorado Springs, CO 80933-7150. Offerings include special education (MA). Accredited by NCATE. School faculty: 13 full-time (6 women). *Degree requirements:* Thesis or alternative, comprehensive exams, microcomputer proficiency required, foreign language not required. *Entrance requirements:* GRE General Test, MAT. Application deadline: rolling. Application fee: $40 ($50 for international students). *Expenses:* Tuition $2760 per year full-time, $115 per credit hour part-time for state residents; $9960 per year full-time, $415 per credit hour part-time for nonresidents. Fees $399 per year (minimum) full-time, $106 per year (minimum) part-time. • Dr. Greg R. Weisenstein, Dean, 719-262-4103. E-mail: gweisens@mail.uccs.edu. Application contact: Connie Wroten, Academic Adviser, 719-262-3268. Fax: 719-262-3554. E-mail: cwroten@mail.uccs.edu.

University of Colorado at Denver, School of Education, Program in Special Education, Denver, CO 80217-3364. Awards MA. Accredited by NCATE. Part-time and evening/weekend programs available. Students: 26 full-time (24 women), 71 part-time (62 women); includes 12 minority (3 African Americans, 3 Asian Americans, 6 Hispanics). Average age 32. 39 applicants, 62% accepted. In 1997, 22 degrees awarded. *Degree requirements:* Thesis or alternative required, foreign language not required. *Entrance requirements:* GRE or MAT, minimum GPA of 2.75. Application deadline: 4/15 (rolling processing; 9/15 for spring admission). Application fee: $50 ($60 for international students). Electronic applications accepted. *Expenses:* Tuition $3530 per year full-time, $199 per semester hour part-time for state residents; $12,722 per year full-time, $764 per semester hour part-time for nonresidents. Fees $252 per year. *Financial aid:* Research assistantships, teaching assistantships, Federal Work-Study available. Financial aid application deadline: 6/1; applicants required to submit FAFSA. • Elizabeth Kozelski, Area Coordinator, 303-556-8449. Application contact: Administrative Assistant, 303-556-6022. Fax: 303-556-4479.

University of Connecticut, School of Education, Field of Special Education, Storrs, CT 06269. Awards MA, PhD. Accredited by NCATE. Faculty: 15. Students: 29 full-time (26 women), 37 part-time (32 women); includes 7 minority (4 African Americans, 2 Asian Americans, 1 Native American), 3 international. Average age 35. 42 applicants, 79% accepted. In 1997, 35 master's, 4 doctorates awarded. Terminal master's awarded for partial completion of doctoral program. *Degree requirements:* For master's, thesis or alternative; for doctorate, dissertation. *Entrance requirements:* For doctorate, GRE General Test. Application deadline: 6/1 (priority date; rolling processing; 11/1 for spring admission). Application fee: $40 ($45 for international students). *Expenses:* Tuition $5272 per year full-time, $293 per credit part-time for state residents; $13,696 per year full-time, $761 per credit part-time for nonresidents. Fees $948 per year full-time, $640 per year part-time. *Financial aid:* In 1997–98, 3 fellowships totaling $7,641, 3 research assistantships (1 to a first-year student) totaling $18,225, 24 teaching assistantships (11 to first-year students) totaling $148,232 were awarded. Financial aid application deadline: 2/15. • Scott W. Brown, Head, 860-486-4031.

University of Delaware, College of Human Resources, Education and Public Policy, School of Education, Newark, DE 19716. Offerings include exceptional children (M Ed). School faculty: 54 (24 women). *Application deadline:* 7/1 (rolling processing; 1/15 for spring admission). *Application fee:* $45. *Expenses:* Tuition $4250 per year full-time, $236 per credit hour part-time for state residents; $12,250 per year full-time, $681 per credit hour part-time for nonresidents. Fees $466 per year full-time, $15 per semester (minimum) part-time. • Dr. Robert Hampel, Director, 302-831-2573.

University of Detroit Mercy, College of Education and Human Services, Department of Education, Program in Special Education, Detroit, MI 48219-0900. Offers emotionally impaired (MA), learning disabilities (MA). Part-time programs available. *Degree requirements:* Thesis or alternative, practicum. *Entrance requirements:* Minimum GPA of 2.75. Application deadline: 8/1. Application fee: $25. *Faculty research:* Emerging roles of special education, inclusionary education, high potential underachievers in secondary schools.

University of Dubuque, Program in Education, 2000 University Avenue, Dubuque, IA 52001-5050. Offerings include special education: multicategorical, elementary and secondary (MA). Program faculty: 3 full-time (2 women), 3 part-time (2 women), 5 FTE. *Degree requirements:* Comprehensive exam required, thesis optional, foreign language not required. *Average time to degree:* master's–2 years full-time, 4 years part-time. *Entrance requirements:* GRE or MAT. Application deadline: 8/15 (priority date; rolling processing). Application fee: $25. • Dr. Sally Naylor, Director of Graduate Education, 319-589-3000. Application contact: Clifford D. Bunting, Dean of Admission and Records, 319-589-3270. Fax: 319-589-3690.

University of Evansville, Graduate Programs, School of Education, Program in Special Education, Evansville, IN 47722-0002. Awards MA. Accredited by NCATE. Faculty: 1 (woman) full-time. Students: 1 (woman) part-time. Average age 28. *Entrance requirements:* GRE, NTE. Application deadline: 7/1. Application fee: $20. *Expenses:* Tuition $395 per credit hour. Fees $30 per year. *Financial aid:* Research assistantships available. Financial aid application deadline: 7/1. • Dr. Marlaine Chase, Director, 812-479-2386.

The University of Findlay, College of Professional Studies, Division of Education, 1000 North Main Street, Findlay, OH 45840-3653. Offerings include special education (MA Ed). Accredited by NCATE. Division faculty: 9 full-time (7 women), 8 part-time (4 women), 21 FTE. *Degree requirements:* 4 foreign languages, thesis, cumulative project. *Average time to degree:* master's–1.5 years full-time, 3 years part-time. *Entrance requirements:* Minimum GPA of 3.0. Application deadline: 8/15 (priority date; rolling processing). Application fee: $25. *Tuition:* $236 per semester hour. • Dr. Judith Wahrman, Graduate Program Director, 419-424-4864. Fax: 419-424-4822. E-mail: wahrman@lucy.findlay.edu.

University of Florida, College of Education, Department of Special Education, Gainesville, FL 32611. Awards MAE, M Ed, Ed D, PhD, Ed S. Accredited by NCATE. Faculty: 13. Students: 60 full-time (52 women), 35 part-time (30 women); includes 11 minority (1 African American, 3 Asian Americans, 6 Hispanics, 1 Native American), 3 international. 56 applicants, 77% accepted. In 1997, 55 master's, 8 doctorates, 2 Ed Ss awarded. *Degree requirements:* For master's, thesis (MAE) required, foreign language not required; for doctorate, variable foreign language requirement, dissertation. *Entrance requirements:* For master's and doctorate, GRE General Test, minimum GPA of 3.0; for Ed S, GRE General Test. Application deadline: 6/5 (priority date; rolling processing). Application fee: $20. *Tuition:* $138 per credit hour for state residents; $481 per credit hour for nonresidents. *Financial aid:* In 1997–98, 24 students received aid, including 7 fellowships averaging $460 per month, 7 research assistantships averaging $828 per month, 10 teaching assistantships averaging $672 per month; graduate assistantships and career-related internships or fieldwork also available. *Faculty research:* Teacher attrition, school restructuring, Latino families. Total annual research expenditures: $306,542. • Vivian Correa, Chairperson, 352-392-0701 Ext. 300. E-mail: vcorrea@coe.ufl.edu. Application contact: Cary L. Reichard, Graduate Coordinator, 352-392-0701 Ext. 0755. Fax: 352-392-2655. E-mail: creichd@coe.ufl.edu.

University of Georgia, College of Education, Department of Special Education, Athens, GA 30602. Awards MA, M Ed, Ed D, PhD, Ed S. Accredited by NCATE. Faculty: 8 full-time (3 women). Students: 42 full-time, 51 part-time; includes 4 minority (3 African Americans, 1 Hispanic), 4 international. 62 applicants, 39% accepted. In 1997, 33 master's, 2 doctorates, 6 Ed Ss awarded. *Degree requirements:* For master's, thesis (MA) required, foreign language not required; for doctorate, variable foreign language requirement, dissertation. *Entrance requirements:* GRE General Test. Application deadline: 7/1 (priority date; 11/15 for spring admission). Application fee: $30. Electronic applications accepted. *Tuition:* $3290 per year full-time, $643 per semester (minimum) part-time for state residents; $11,300 per year full-time, $1645 per semester (minimum) part-time for nonresidents. *Financial aid:* Fellowships, research assistantships, teaching assistantships, assistantships available. • Dr. David L. Gast, Graduate Coordinator, 706-542-4617. Fax: 706-542-5877.

University of Guam, College of Education, Program in Special Education, 303 University Drive, UOG Station, Mangilao, GU 96923. Awards M Ed. *Degree requirements:* Comprehensive oral and written exams, special project or thesis required, foreign language not required. *Entrance requirements:* GRE General Test. Application deadline: 5/31. Application fee: $31 ($56 for international students). *Faculty research:* Mainstreaming, multiculturalism.

University of Hartford, College of Education, Nursing, and Health Professions, Program in Special Education, West Hartford, CT 06117-1599. Awards M Ed. Accredited by NCATE. Part-time and evening/weekend programs available. Faculty: 8 full-time (4 women), 1 part-time (0 women). Students: 10 full-time (8 women), 35 part-time (27 women). Average age 33. 27 applicants, 74% accepted. In 1997, 19 degrees awarded. *Degree requirements:* Comprehensive exam required, foreign language and thesis not required. *Entrance requirements:* GRE General Test or MAT, PRAXIS I, interview. Application deadline: 5/15 (priority date; rolling processing; 12/15 for spring admission). Application fee: $40 ($55 for international students). Electronic applications accepted. *Financial aid:* Graduate assistantships, Federal Work-Study available. Aid available to part-time students. Financial aid application deadline: 6/1; applicants required to submit FAFSA. • Dr. Victoria Day, Director, 860-768-4562. Application contact: Susan Garcia, Coordinator of Student Services, 860-768-5038. E-mail: gettoknow@mail.hartford.edu.

University of Hawaii at Manoa, College of Education, Department of Special Education, Honolulu, HI 96822. Awards M Ed. Part-time and evening/weekend programs available. Faculty: 9 full-time (7 women). Students: 42 full-time (36 women), 20 part-time (17 women); includes 30 minority (2 African Americans, 27 Asian Americans, 1 Native American), 6 international. Average age 30. 28 applicants, 75% accepted. In 1997, 16 degrees awarded (100% entered university research/teaching). *Entrance requirements:* GRE General Test (minimum combined score of 900), interview, minimum GPA of 3.0. Application deadline: 3/1 (9/1 for spring admission). Application fee: $0. *Tuition:* $4029 per year full-time, $214 per credit hour part-time for state residents; $9957 per year full-time, $461 per credit hour part-time for nonresidents. *Financial aid:* 3 students received aid; full and partial tuition waivers, institutionally sponsored loans, and career-related internships or fieldwork available. Aid available to part-time students. Financial aid application deadline: 3/1. *Faculty research:* Mild/moderate/severe disabilities, early childhood interventions, inclusion, transition. • Dr. Mary Anne Prater, Chairperson, 808-956-7956. Fax: 808-956-4345. E-mail: prater@hawaii.edu.

University of Hawaii at Manoa, College of Education, Education Program, Honolulu, HI 96822. Offerings include exceptionalities (Ed D). Program faculty: 53 full-time (25 women). *Degree requirements:* Dissertation required, foreign language not required. *Entrance requirements:* GRE General Test, MAT (optional), TOEFL (minimum score 600), sample of written work. Application deadline: 2/1. Application fee: $0. *Tuition:* $4029 per year full-time, $214 per credit hour part-time for state residents; $9957 per year full-time, $461 per credit hour part-time for nonresidents. • Dr. Royal T. Fruehling, Graduate Chair, 808-956-4243. E-mail: fruehlin@hawaii.edu. Application contact: Melanie Bock, Clerk Typist III, 808-956-7817. Fax: 808-956-9100. E-mail: mbock@hawaii.edu.

University of Houston, College of Education, Department of Educational Psychology, 4800 Calhoun, Houston, TX 77204-2163. Offerings include special education (M Ed, Ed D). Accredited by NCATE. Department faculty: 17 full-time (7 women), 6 part-time (3 women). *Degree requirements:* For master's, comprehensive exam or thesis required, foreign language not required. *Entrance requirements:* For master's, GRE General Test (minimum combined score of 950; average 1100) or MAT (minimum score 45; average 57), interview (counseling psychology). Application deadline: 2/1. Application fee: $35 ($75 for international students). *Expenses:* Tuition $1152 per year full-time, $120 per semester (minimum) part-time for state residents; $4482 per year full-time, $249 per credit hour part-time for nonresidents. Fees $977 per year full-time, $119 per semester (minimum) part-time. • Robert McPherson, Chairperson, 713-743-9827. Fax: 713-743-4989. Application contact: Graduate Adviser, 713-743-5019. Fax: 713-743-4996. E-mail: epsy@uh.edu.

University of Idaho, College of Graduate Studies, College of Education, Division of Teacher Education, Department of Special Education, Moscow, ID 83844-4140. Awards M Ed, MS, Sp Ed S. Accredited by NCATE. Students: 6 full-time (3 women), 26 part-time (23 women); includes 1 minority (Asian American), 2 international. In 1997, 5 master's, 1 Sp Ed S awarded. *Entrance requirements:* For master's, minimum GPA of 2.8. Application deadline: 8/1 (12/15 for spring admission). Application fee: $35 ($45 for international students). *Expenses:* Tuition $0 for state residents; $6000 per year full-time, $95 per credit part-time for nonresidents. Fees $2676 per year full-time, $134 per credit part-time. *Financial aid:* Research assistantships, teaching assistantships available. Financial aid application deadline: 2/15. • Dr. Jeanne Christiansen, Head, 208-885-6556.

University of Illinois at Chicago, College of Education, Program in Special Education, Chicago, IL 60607-7128. Awards M Ed, PhD. Part-time programs available. Faculty: 28 full-time (13 women), 1 part-time (0 women). Students: 29 full-time (27 women), 86 part-time (74 women); includes 24 minority (18 African Americans, 3 Asian Americans, 3 Hispanics), 1 international. 54 applicants, 56% accepted. In 1997, 29 master's, 6 doctorates awarded. Terminal master's awarded for partial completion of doctoral program. *Degree requirements:* For doctorate, dissertation required, foreign language not required. *Entrance requirements:* For master's, TOEFL (minimum score 550), minimum GPA of 3.75 on a 5.0 scale; for doctorate, GRE General Test (minimum combined score of 1000) or MAT (minimum score 55), TOEFL (minimum score 550), minimum GPA of 3.75 on a 5.0 scale. Application deadline: 2/15. Application fee: $40 ($50 for international students). *Financial aid:* In 1997–98, 11 research assistantships, 2 teaching assistantships were awarded; fellowships, traineeships, full tuition waivers, and career-related internships or fieldwork also available. Financial aid application deadline: 6/1. *Faculty research:* Teaching and learning for special learners, individual differences. • Dr. Mavis Donahue, Area Chair, 312-996-8139. Application contact: Victoria Hare, Director of Graduate Studies, 312-996-4520.

University of Illinois at Urbana–Champaign, College of Education, Department of Special Education, Urbana, IL 61801. Awards AM, Ed M, MS, Ed D, PhD, AC. Faculty: 10 full-time (8 women), 6 part-time (4 women). Students: 72 full-time (61 women), 31 part-time (all women); includes 12 minority (10 African Americans, 2 Asian Americans), 11 international. 75% of applicants accepted. In 1997, 44 master's, 10 doctorates, 1 AC awarded. *Degree requirements:* For master's and doctorate, thesis/dissertation. *Entrance requirements:* For master's and doctorate, GRE General Test or MAT. Application deadline: rolling. Application fee: $40 ($50 for international students). *Financial aid:* In 1997–98, 2 fellowships, 61 research assistantships, 13 teaching assistantships were awarded; full and partial tuition waivers also available. Financial aid application deadline: 2/15. • Adelle Renzaglia, Head, 217-333-0260.

The University of Iowa, College of Education, Division of Special Education, Iowa City, IA 52242-1316. Awards MA, PhD, Ed S. Faculty: 7 full-time. Students: 23 full-time (15 women), 54 part-time (41 women); includes 1 minority (Hispanic), 9 international. 25 applicants, 56% accepted. In 1997, 22 master's, 2 doctorates awarded. *Degree requirements:* For master's, exam required, thesis optional, foreign language not required; for doctorate, computer language, dissertation, comprehensive exams required, foreign language not required; for Ed S, computer language, exam required, foreign language not required. *Entrance requirements:* For master's and Ed S, GRE General Test, minimum GPA of 2.5; for doctorate, GRE General Test, minimum GPA of 3.0. Application deadline: rolling. Application fee: $30 ($50 for international students). *Expenses:* Tuition $3166 per year full-time, $176 per semester hour part-time for state residents; $10,202 per year full-time, $176 per semester hour part-time for nonresidents. Fees $202 per year full-time, $52 per year (minimum) part-time. *Financial aid:* In 1997–98, 6 research assistantships (2 to first-year students), 8 teaching assistantships were awarded; fellowships also available. Financial aid applicants required to submit FAFSA. • William Nibbelink, Chair, 319-335-5324. Fax: 319-335-5608.

University of Kansas, School of Education, Department of Special Education, Lawrence, KS 66045. Awards MS Ed, Ed D, PhD, Ed S. Accredited by NCATE. MS Ed, Ed D, and PhD offered jointly with the Kansas City campus. Faculty: 18 full-time. Students: 66 full-time (56 women), 161 part-time (150 women); includes 14 minority (4 African Americans, 2 Asian Americans, 4 Hispanics, 4 Native Americans), 8 international. In 1997, 55 master's, 11 doctorates awarded. *Degree requirements:* For doctorate, variable foreign language requirement, dissertation. *Entrance requirements:* For master's and Ed S, minimum GPA of 3.0; for doctor-

Directory: Special Education

University of Kansas (continued)
ate, GRE General Test, minimum graduate GPA of 3.5. Application deadline: 7/1. Application fee: $25. *Expenses:* Tuition $2400 per year full-time, $100 per credit hour part-time for state residents; $7890 per year full-time, $329 per credit hour part-time for nonresidents. Fees $428 per year full-time, $31 per credit hour part-time. *Financial aid:* Fellowships, research assistantships, teaching assistantships available. • Nancy Peterson, Chair, 785-864-4954. Application contact: Douglas Guess, Graduate Director.

University of Kansas, School of Allied Health, Department of Hearing and Speech, Kansas City, KS 66160. Offerings include education of the deaf (MS). Accredited by NCATE. Offered jointly with the Department of Speech-Language-Hearing: Sciences and Disorders at the Lawrence campus. Department faculty: 11 full-time (7 women), 3 part-time (all women). *Application deadline:* 2/15 (priority date; rolling processing; 10/1 for spring admission). *Application fee:* $25. *Expenses:* Tuition $2400 per year full-time, $100 per credit hour part-time for state residents; $7890 per year full-time, $329 per credit hour part-time for nonresidents. Fees $428 per year full-time, $31 per credit hour part-time. • Dr. John A. Ferraro, Chairman, 913-588-5937. E-mail: jferraro@kumc.edu. Application contact: Diane Wright, Secretary, 913-588-5730. Fax: 913-588-5923. E-mail: dswright@kumc.edu.

University of Kentucky, Graduate School Programs from the College of Education, Program in Special Education, Lexington, KY 40506-0032. Awards MA Ed U, MS Ed U, Ed D, Ed S. Accredited by NCATE. Faculty: 16 full-time (8 women). Students: 17 full-time (15 women), 70 part-time (64 women); includes 2 minority (1 African American, 1 Native American), 2 international. 15 applicants, 80% accepted. In 1997, 18 master's awarded. Terminal master's awarded for partial completion of doctoral program. *Degree requirements:* For master's, comprehensive exam required, thesis optional, foreign language not required; for doctorate, dissertation, comprehensive exam required, foreign language not required; for Ed S, comprehensive exam required, foreign language and thesis not required. *Entrance requirements:* For master's, GRE General Test, minimum undergraduate GPA of 2.5; for doctorate, GRE General Test, minimum graduate GPA of 3.0; for Ed S, GRE General Test. Application deadline: 7/19 (rolling processing). Application fee: $30 ($35 for international students). *Financial aid:* In 1997–98, 4 research assistantships were awarded; fellowships, graduate assistantships, Federal Work-Study, institutionally sponsored loans, and career-related internships or fieldwork also available. Aid available to part-time students. *Faculty research:* Applied behavior analysis applications in special education, single subject research design in classroom settings, transition research across life span, rural special education personnel. Total annual research expenditures: $1.6 million. • Dr. Belva C. Collins, Director of Graduate Studies, 606-257-8591. Application contact: Dr. Constance L. Wood, Associate Dean, 606-257-4613. Fax: 606-323-1928.

University of La Verne, Department of Education, Program in Special Education, La Verne, CA 91750-4443. Awards MS. *Degree requirements:* Thesis or alternative required, foreign language not required. *Entrance requirements:* TOEFL (minimum score 550), minimum GPA of 2.5. Application fee: $25. *Expenses:* Tuition $370 per unit (minimum). Fees $60 per year.

University of Louisville, School of Education, Department of Special Education, Louisville, KY 40292-0001. Awards M Ed, Ed D, Ed S. Accredited by NCATE. Faculty: 9 full-time (4 women), 4 part-time (3 women), 10 FTE. Students: 38 full-time (34 women), 73 part-time (63 women); includes 12 minority (10 African Americans, 1 Hispanic, 1 Native American), 2 international. Average age 35. In 1997, 26 master's awarded. *Degree requirements:* For doctorate, dissertation. *Entrance requirements:* GRE General Test. Application deadline: rolling. Application fee: $25. • Dr. Denzil Edge, Chair, 502-852-6421.

University of Maine, College of Education and Human Development, Program in Special Education, Orono, ME 04469. Awards M Ed, CAS. Accredited by NCATE. Part-time and evening/weekend programs available. *Degree requirements:* For master's, thesis or alternative required, foreign language not required. *Entrance requirements:* For master's, MAT, TOEFL (minimum score 550); for CAS, MA, M Ed, or MS. Application deadline: 2/1 (priority date; rolling processing; 10/15 for spring admission). Application fee: $50. *Expenses:* Tuition $194 per credit hour for state residents; $548 per credit hour for nonresidents. Fees $378 per year full-time, $33 per semester (minimum) part-time. *Financial aid:* Career-related internships or fieldwork available. Aid available to part-time students. Financial aid application deadline: 3/1. • Application contact: Scott Delcourt, Director of the Graduate School, 207-581-3218. Fax: 207-581-3232. E-mail: graduate@maine.edu.

University of Manitoba, Faculty of Education, Department of Educational Psychology, Winnipeg, MB R3T 2N2, Canada. Offerings include special education (M Ed). *Degree requirements:* Thesis or alternative required, foreign language not required.

University of Mary, Program in Education, 7500 University Drive, Bismarck, ND 58504-9652. Offerings include special education (MS). Program faculty: 5 full-time (3 women), 6 part-time (4 women). *Average time to degree:* master's–3 years part-time. *Application deadline:* 8/1 (12/1 for spring admission). *Application fee:* $15. *Tuition:* $265 per credit. • Ramona Klein, Director, 701-255-7500. Application contact: Dr. Diane Fladeland, Director, Graduate Programs, 701-255-7500. Fax: 701-255-7687.

University of Maryland, College Park, College of Education, Department of Special Education, College Park, MD 20742-5045. Awards MA, M Ed, Ed D, PhD, CAGS. Accredited by NCATE. Faculty: 18 full-time (11 women), 22 part-time (all women). Students: 33 full-time (29 women), 92 part-time (79 women); includes 27 minority (22 African Americans, 4 Asian Americans, 1 Hispanic), 4 international. 83 applicants, 65% accepted. In 1997, 44 master's, 8 doctorates awarded. *Degree requirements:* For master's, thesis required (for some programs), foreign language not required; for doctorate, dissertation required, foreign language not required. *Entrance requirements:* For master's and doctorate, GRE General Test or MAT (score in 40th percentile or higher), minimum GPA of 3.0. Application deadline: rolling. Application fee: $50 ($70 for international students). *Expenses:* Tuition $272 per credit hour for state residents; $400 per credit hour for nonresidents. Fees $564 per year full-time, $342 per year part-time. *Financial aid:* In 1997–98, 4 fellowships, 28 research assistantships, 3 teaching assistantships were awarded; career-related internships or fieldwork also available. *Faculty research:* Educational diagnosis and prescription, mental retardation, severely/profoundly handicapped. • Dr. Philip Burke, Chairman, 301-405-6515. Fax: 301-314-9278. Application contact: John Mollish, Director, Graduate Admissions and Records, 301-405-4198. Fax: 301-314-9305.

University of Maryland Eastern Shore, Department of Education, Program in Special Education, Princess Anne, MD 21853-1299. Awards M Ed. Faculty: 3 full-time (all women). Students: 3 full-time (2 women), 11 part-time (9 women); includes 1 international. Average age 35. 10 applicants, 80% accepted. In 1997, 10 degrees awarded (100% found work related to degree). *Degree requirements:* Comprehensive exams, seminar paper required, foreign language and thesis not required. *Average time to degree:* master's–2 years full-time, 3.5 years part-time. *Entrance requirements:* GRE or NTE (passing scores on each core battery test), TOEFL (minimum score 550), interview, minimum GPA of 3.0. Application deadline: 5/1 (priority date; rolling processing; 11/1 for spring admission). Application fee: $30. *Expenses:* Tuition $143 per credit hour for state residents; $253 per credit hour for nonresidents. Fees $50 per year. *Financial aid:* In 1997–98, 3 students received aid, including 1 research assistantship, 2 teaching assistantships; Federal Work-Study and career-related internships or fieldwork also available. Aid available to part-time students. Financial aid application deadline: 3/1. *Faculty research:* Learning disabilities, mental retardation, assessment, gifted/talented education. • Dr. Karen Verbeke, Coordinator, 410-651-6220. Fax: 410-651-7962. E-mail: kverbeke@umes3.umd.edu.

University of Massachusetts Amherst, School of Education, Program in Education, Amherst, MA 01003-0001. Offerings include special education (M Ed, Ed D, CAGS). Accredited by NCATE. *Degree requirements:* For doctorate, dissertation required, foreign language not required. *Entrance requirements:* For master's and doctorate, GRE General Test. Application deadline: 3/1 (rolling processing; 10/1 for spring admission). Application fee: $40. *Expenses:* Tuition $2640 per year full-time, $110 per credit part-time for state residents; $3690 per year (minimum) full-time, $165 per credit (minimum) part-time for nonresidents. Fees $2856 per year full-time, $422 per semester part-time for state residents; $3204 per year full-time, $480 per semester part-time for nonresidents. • John C. Carey, Director, 413-545-0236.

University of Massachusetts Boston, Graduate College of Education, School Organization, Curriculum and Instruction Department, Program in Special Education, Boston, MA 02125-3393. Awards M Ed. Students: 24 full-time (16 women), 68 part-time (54 women); includes 9 minority (6 African Americans, 2 Asian Americans, 1 Hispanic). 57 applicants, 75% accepted. In 1997, 17 degrees awarded. *Degree requirements:* Comprehensive exams required, foreign language and thesis not required. *Entrance requirements:* GRE General Test or MAT, minimum GPA of 2.75. Application deadline: 3/1 (priority date; 11/1 for spring admission). Application fee: $25 ($35 for international students). *Expenses:* Tuition $2640 per year full-time, $110 per credit part-time for state residents; $8930 per year full-time, $373 per credit part-time for nonresidents. Fees $2650 per year full-time, $420 per semester (minimum) part-time for state residents; $2736 per year full-time, $420 per semester (minimum) part-time for nonresidents. *Financial aid:* In 1997–98, 3 research assistantships totaling $6,000, 1 teaching assistantship totaling $2,000 were awarded; administrative assistantships also available. Financial aid application deadline: 3/1; applicants required to submit FAFSA. • Dr. Doris Norman, Coordinator, 617-287-7621. Application contact: Lisa Lavely, Director of Graduate Admissions and Records, 617-287-6400. Fax: 617-287-6236.

The University of Memphis, College of Education, Department of Instruction and Curriculum Leadership, Memphis, TN 38152. Offerings include special education (MAT, MS, Ed D). Accredited by NCATE. Terminal master's awarded for partial completion of doctoral program. Department faculty: 34 full-time (17 women), 22 part-time (13 women). *Degree requirements:* For master's, thesis or alternative, comprehensive exam required, foreign language not required; for doctorate, dissertation, comprehensive exam required, foreign language not required. *Entrance requirements:* For master's, GRE General Test or MAT, minimum GPA of 2.5; for doctorate, GRE General Test, GRE Subject Test, 2 years of teaching experience. Application deadline: 8/1 (12/1 for spring admission). Application fee: $25 ($50 for international students). *Tuition:* $2862 per year full-time, $166 per credit hour part-time for state residents; $6696 per year full-time, $379 per credit hour part-time for nonresidents. • Dr. Dennie Smith, Interim Chair, 901-678-2771. Application contact: Dr. Carole L. Bond, Coordinator of Graduate Studies, 901-678-3490.

University of Miami, School of Education, Department of Teaching and Learning, Program in Early Childhood Special Education, Coral Gables, FL 33124. Awards MS Ed, Ed S. Accredited by NCATE. Faculty: 8 full-time (6 women), 4 part-time (all women). Students: 9 full-time (all women), 25 part-time (24 women); includes 20 minority (11 African Americans, 9 Hispanics). Average age 29. 12 applicants, 50% accepted. In 1997, 11 master's awarded. *Degree requirements:* For Ed S, thesis optional, foreign language not required. *Entrance requirements:* For master's, GRE General Test (minimum combined score of 1000), TOEFL (minimum score 550); for Ed S, GRE General Test, TOEFL (minimum score 550). Application deadline: rolling. Application fee: $35. *Expenses:* Tuition $815 per credit hour. Fees $174 per year. *Financial aid:* Application deadline 3/1. *Faculty research:* Technology, social skills, inclusion. • Dr. Marie Hughes, Adviser, 305-284-2470. Fax: 305-284-6998. E-mail: svaughn@umiami.ir.miami.edu.

University of Miami, School of Education, Department of Teaching and Learning, Program in Special Education and Reading, Coral Gables, FL 33124. Awards MS Ed, PhD, Ed S. Accredited by NCATE. Faculty: 8 full-time (5 women), 1 (woman) part-time. Students: 17 full-time (13 women), 18 part-time (17 women); includes 14 minority (5 African Americans, 3 Asian Americans, 6 Hispanics), 3 international. Average age 32. 14 applicants, 57% accepted. In 1997, 11 master's, 2 Ed Ss awarded. *Degree requirements:* For doctorate, dissertation required, foreign language not required; for Ed S, thesis optional, foreign language not required. *Entrance requirements:* For master's, GRE General Test (minimum combined score of 1000), TOEFL (minimum score 550); for doctorate, GRE General Test, GRE Subject Test, TOEFL (minimum score 550); for Ed S, GRE General Test, TOEFL (minimum score 550). Application deadline: rolling. Application fee: $35. *Expenses:* Tuition $815 per credit hour. Fees $174 per year. *Financial aid:* In 1997–98, 6 graduate assistantships were awarded. Financial aid application deadline: 3/1. *Faculty research:* Inclusion, behavior disorders, learning disabilities, literacy. • Dr. Marjorie Montague, Coordinator, 305-284-2902. Fax: 305-284-3003. E-mail: mmontagu@umiami.ir.miami.edu.

University of Michigan, School of Education, Programs in Educational Studies, Concentration in Learning Disabilities and Literacy, Ann Arbor, MI 48109. Awards AM. *Entrance requirements:* GRE General Test (minimum combined score of 1800 on three sections), TOEFL (minimum score 600). Application deadline: 1/15 (priority date). Application fee: $55. Electronic applications accepted. • Application contact: Karen Wixson, Associate Dean, 734-764-9470. Fax: 734-763-1229. E-mail: kwixson@umich.edu.

Announcement: Literacy, language, and learning disabilities master's degree programs are designed for practicing K–12 teachers to study literacy, language, and learning in typical and atypical learners. Graduates are eligible for Michigan K–12 reading and learning disability endorsements. Contact the Office of Student Services, 1033 School of Education Building, University of Michigan, 610 East University, Ann Arbor, MI 48109-1259 (telephone: 734-764-7563; e-mail: ed.grad.admit@umich.edu).

University of Michigan–Dearborn, School of Education, Division of Special Education, 4901 Evergreen Road, Dearborn, MI 48128-1491. Awards M Ed. Part-time and evening/weekend programs available. Faculty: 2 full-time (both women), 2 part-time (both women). Students: 58 part-time (52 women). 17 applicants, 100% accepted. In 1997, 22 degrees awarded. *Application deadline:* 11/1 (priority date; rolling processing). *Application fee:* $30. *Expenses:* Tuition $4536 per year full-time, $252 per credit hour part-time for state residents; $13,086 per year full-time, $727 per credit hour part-time for nonresidents. Fees $480 per year (minimum). *Financial aid:* Federal Work-Study and career-related internships or fieldwork available. Aid available to part-time students. Financial aid application deadline: 3/15. • Dr. Belinda Lazarus, Associate Professor, 313-436-9136. E-mail: blazarus@fob-f1.umd.umich.edu. Application contact: Carol Hudak, Academic Services Secretary II, 313-436-9135. Fax: 313-593-9961. E-mail: chudak@fob-f1.umd.umich.edu.

University of Minnesota, Twin Cities Campus, College of Education and Human Development, Department of Educational Psychology, Minneapolis, MN 55455-0213. Offerings include special education (M Ed). • Mark Davison, Chairman, 612-624-3543.

University of Missouri–Columbia, College of Education, Department of Special Education, Columbia, MO 65211. Awards MA, M Ed, Ed D, PhD, Ed S. Part-time programs available. Faculty: 13 full-time (8 women). Students: 21 full-time (13 women), 29 part-time (23 women); includes 3 minority (1 African American, 2 Asian Americans), 1 international. In 1997, 32 master's, 4 doctorates awarded. *Degree requirements:* For doctorate, dissertation. *Entrance requirements:* GRE General Test, minimum GPA of 3.0. Application deadline: 7/1 (priority date; rolling processing). Application fee: $25 ($50 for international students). *Expenses:* Tuition $3240 per year full-time, $180 per credit hour part-time for state residents; $9108 per year full-time, $506 per credit hour part-time for nonresidents. Fees $55 per year full-time. *Faculty research:* Teacher education, needs assessments. • Dr. Michael Pullis, Director of Graduate Studies, 573-882-3741.

University of Missouri–Kansas City, School of Education, Division of Curriculum and Instruction, Kansas City, MO 64110-2499. Offerings include special education (MA). Accredited by NCATE. *Degree requirements:* Thesis optional, foreign language not required. *Entrance requirements:* Minimum GPA of 2.75. Application deadline: 7/1 (priority date; rolling processing; 12/1 for spring admission). Application fee: $25. *Expenses:* Tuition $182 per credit hour for state residents; $508 per credit hour for nonresidents. Fees $60 per year. • Dr. Cheryl Grossman, Chairperson, 816-235-2245.

University of Missouri–St. Louis, School of Education, Program in Special Education, St. Louis, MO 63121-4499. Awards M Ed. Accredited by NCATE. Faculty: 23 (8 women). Students: 13 full-time (12 women), 79 part-time (75 women); includes 9 minority (7 African Americans, 2 Asian Americans), 1 international. In 1997, 32 degrees awarded. *Degree requirements:* Thesis required, foreign language not required. *Application deadline:* 7/1 (priority date; rolling processing; 12/1 for spring admission). *Application fee:* $0. Electronic applications accepted. *Expenses:* Tuition $3903 per year full-time, $167 per credit hour part-time for state residents; $11,745 per year full-time, $489 per credit hour part-time for nonresidents. Fees $816 per year full-time, $34 per credit hour part-time. *Financial aid:* In 1997–98, 3 teaching assistantships (1 to a first-year student) averaging $833 per month were awarded. *Faculty research:* Multicultural education, autism, inclusion, behavior disorders/emotional disturbance. • Dr. George Yard, Chair, 314-516-5782. Application contact: Graduate Admissions, 314-516-5458. Fax: 314-516-6759. E-mail: gradadm@umslvma.umsl.edu.

University of Nebraska at Kearney, College of Education, Department of Special Education and Communication Disorders, Kearney, NE 68849-0001. Offers programs in early childhood special education (MA Ed), education of behaviorally disordered (MA Ed), education of the gifted and talented (MA Ed), mild/moderate handicapped (MA Ed), special education (MA Ed), specific learning disabilities (MA Ed), speech pathology (MS Ed). Accredited by NCATE. Part-time and evening/weekend programs available. Faculty: 5 full-time (4 women). Students: 30 full-time (28 women), 25 part-time (24 women); includes 2 minority (1 Asian American, 1 Hispanic), 2 international. In 1997, 21 degrees awarded. *Degree requirements:* Thesis optional. *Entrance requirements:* GRE General Test. Application deadline: 8/1 (priority date; rolling processing; 12/15 for spring admission). Application fee: $35. *Expenses:* Tuition $1494 per year full-time, $83 per credit hour part-time for state residents; $2826 per year full-time, $157 per credit hour part-time for nonresidents. Fees $229 per year full-time, $11.25 per semester (minimum) part-time. *Financial aid:* In 1997–98, 2 research assistantships, 3 teaching assistantships were awarded; career-related internships or fieldwork also available. Aid available to part-time students. Financial aid application deadline: 3/1; applicants required to submit FAFSA. • Dr. Lillian Larson, Chair, 308-865-8314.

University of Nebraska at Omaha, College of Education, Department of Special Education and Communication Disorders, Omaha, NE 68182. Offers programs in behavioral disorders (MS), mental retardation (MA), resource teaching and learning disabilities (MS), speech-language pathology (MA, MS), teaching the hearing impaired (MS), teaching the mentally retarded (MS). Accredited by NCATE. Part-time and evening/weekend programs available. Faculty: 10 full-time (2 women). Students: 5 full-time (all women), 48 part-time (47 women); includes 1 minority (African American). Average age 34. 17 applicants, 47% accepted. In 1997, 28 degrees awarded. *Degree requirements:* Thesis (for some programs), comprehensive exam required, foreign language not required. *Entrance requirements:* GRE General Test or MAT, minimum GPA of 3.0. Application deadline: 2/1 (priority date; rolling processing; 9/1 for spring admission). Application fee: $35. *Expenses:* Tuition $1670 per year full-time, $94 per credit hour part-time for state residents; $4082 per year full-time, $227 per credit hour part-time for nonresidents. Fees $302 per year full-time, $108 per semester (minimum) part-time. *Financial aid:* 17 students received aid; fellowships, research assistantships, full tuition waivers, Federal Work-Study, institutionally sponsored loans, and career-related internships or fieldwork available. Aid available to part-time students. Financial aid application deadline: 3/1. • Dr. John Christensen, Chairperson, 402-554-2203. Application contact: Dr. John Hill, Adviser, 402-554-2203.

University of Nebraska–Lincoln, Teachers College, Department of Special Education and Communication Disorders, Program in Special Education, Lincoln, NE 68588. Awards MA, M Ed. Accredited by NCATE. Students: 26 full-time (22 women), 22 part-time (21 women); includes 3 minority (all Hispanics), 3 international. Average age 30. 14 applicants, 64% accepted. In 1997, 30 degrees awarded. *Degree requirements:* Thesis optional. *Entrance requirements:* GRE General Test, TOEFL (minimum score 500). Application deadline: 2/15 (10/15 for spring admission). Application fee: $35. Electronic applications accepted. *Expenses:* Tuition $110 per credit hour for state residents; $270 per credit hour for nonresidents. Fees $480 per year full-time, $110 per semester part-time. *Financial aid:* In 1997–98, 5 fellowships totaling $2,300 were awarded; research assistantships, teaching assistantships, Federal Work-Study also available. Aid available to part-time students. Financial aid application deadline: 2/15. • Dr. Stanley Vasa, Graduate Committee Chair, 402-472-5494. E-mail: svasa@unl.edu.

University of Nevada, Las Vegas, College of Education, Department of Special Education, Las Vegas, NV 89154-9900. Offers programs in assessment and evaluation techniques for the exceptional (Ed D), emotional disturbance (Ed D), general special education (Ed D), learning disabilities (Ed D), mental retardation (Ed D), school psychology (Ed S), special education (MA, M Ed, MS, Ed S). Accredited by NCATE. Part-time and evening/weekend programs available. Faculty: 13 full-time (5 women). Students: 53 full-time (42 women), 122 part-time (102 women); includes 28 minority (15 African Americans, 8 Asian Americans, 2 Hispanics, 3 Native Americans), 1 international. 54 applicants, 91% accepted. In 1997, 69 master's, 1 doctorate awarded. *Degree requirements:* For master's, thesis (for some programs), comprehensive exam required, foreign language not required; for doctorate, dissertation, oral exam required, foreign language not required; for Ed S, comprehensive exam required, foreign language and thesis not required. *Entrance requirements:* For master's, GRE General Test, GRE Subject Test, minimum GPA of 3.0; for doctorate, GRE General Test, MAT (score in 50th percentile or higher), minimum graduate GPA of 3.5. Application deadline: 6/15 (priority date; rolling processing; 11/15 for spring admission). Application fee: $40 ($95 for international students). *Expenses:* Tuition $93 per credit for state residents; $93 per credit full-time, $190 per credit part-time for nonresidents. Fees $5570 per year full-time for nonresidents. *Financial aid:* In 1997–98, 10 teaching assistantships were awarded; research assistantships also available. Financial aid application deadline: 3/1. • Dr. William Healey, Chair, 702-895-3205. Application contact: Graduate College Admissions Evaluator, 702-895-3320.

University of Nevada, Reno, College of Education, Department of Curriculum and Instruction, Reno, NV 89557. Offerings include special education (MA, M Ed, MS). Accredited by NCATE. Department faculty: 19 (7 women). *Degree requirements:* Thesis optional, foreign language not required. *Entrance requirements:* GRE, TOEFL (minimum score 500), minimum GPA of 2.75. Application deadline: 3/1 (priority date; rolling processing; 10/1 for spring admission). Application fee: $40. *Expenses:* Tuition $0 for state residents; $5770 per year full-time, $200 per credit part-time for nonresidents. Fees $93 per credit. • Dr. Vernon D. Luft, Chair, 702-784-4961. Application contact: Dr. J. Randall Koetting, Graduate Director, 702-784-4961 Ext. 2008. E-mail: koetting@unr.edu.

University of New Brunswick, Faculty of Education, Division of Educational Foundations, Fredericton, NB E3B 5A3, Canada. Offerings include special education (M Ed). *Degree requirements:* Thesis or alternative required, foreign language not required. *Entrance requirements:* TOEFL, TWE, minimum GPA of 3.0. Application deadline: 3/1 (priority date; rolling processing). Application fee: $25.

University of New Hampshire, College of Liberal Arts, Department of Education, Program in Special Education, Durham, NH 03824. Awards M Ed. Accredited by NCATE. Part-time programs available. Students: 8 full-time (5 women), 18 part-time (16 women). Average age 33. 16 applicants, 88% accepted. In 1997, 6 degrees awarded. *Degree requirements:* Thesis or alternative required, foreign language not required. *Entrance requirements:* GRE General Test. Application deadline: 4/1 (priority date; rolling processing). Application fee: $50. *Expenses:* Tuition $5440 per year full-time, $302 per credit hour part-time for state residents; $8160 per year (minimum) full-time, $453 per credit hour (minimum) part-time for nonresidents. Fees $868 per year full-time, $15 per year part-time. *Financial aid:* In 1997–98, 1 fellowship was awarded; research assistantships, teaching assistantships, scholarships, full and partial tuition waivers, Federal Work-Study, and career-related internships or fieldwork also available. Aid available to part-time students. Financial aid application deadline: 2/15. • Dr. Georgia Kerns, Coordinator, 603-862-2310. Application contact: Dr. Todd DeMitchell, Graduate Coordinator, 603-862-2317.

University of New Mexico, College of Education, Program in Special Education, Albuquerque, NM 87131-2039. Awards MA, Ed D, PhD, Ed S. Accredited by NCATE. Part-time programs available. Faculty: 12 full-time (9 women), 15 part-time (11 women), 15.48 FTE. Students: 54 full-time (38 women), 88 part-time (74 women); includes 37 minority (3 African Americans, 5 Asian Americans, 26 Hispanics, 3 Native Americans). Average age 44. 46 applicants, 83% accepted. In 1997, 64 master's awarded. Terminal master's awarded for partial completion of doctoral program. *Degree requirements:* For doctorate, dissertation required, foreign language not required. *Entrance requirements:* For master's, GRE General Test or NTE; for doctorate and Ed S, GRE General Test or NTE, degree in special education, 2 years of teaching experience with the disabled. Application fee: $25. *Expenses:* Tuition $2442 per year full-time, $103 per credit hour part-time for state residents; $8691 per year full-time, $103 per credit hour (minimum) part-time for nonresidents. Fees $32 per year. *Financial aid:* Fellowships, teaching assistantships, stipends, full and partial tuition waivers, Federal Work-Study, institutionally sponsored loans, and career-related internships or fieldwork available. Aid available to part-time students. Financial aid application deadline: 2/28. *Faculty research:* Mathematics instruction, bilingual special education, parent training. Total annual research expenditures: $11,957. • Dr. M. Elizabeth Nielsen, Graduate Coordinator, 505-277-6652. Fax: 505-277-8679. E-mail: enielsen@unm.edu. Application contact: Jo Sanchez, Student Adviser, 505-277-5018. Fax: 505-277-8674. E-mail: jsanchez@unm.edu.

University of New Orleans, College of Education, Department of Special Education, New Orleans, LA 70148. Awards M Ed, PhD, Certificate. Accredited by NCATE. Evening/weekend programs available. Faculty: 12 full-time (6 women), 1 (woman) part-time. Students: 20 full-time (18 women), 100 part-time (84 women); includes 24 minority (20 African Americans, 1 Asian American, 3 Hispanics), 2 international. Average age 34. 18 applicants, 67% accepted. In 1997, 34 master's, 3 doctorates awarded. *Degree requirements:* For doctorate, variable foreign language requirement, dissertation. *Entrance requirements:* For master's, GRE General Test (minimum combined score of 750); for doctorate, GRE General Test (minimum combined score of 1000), GRE Subject Test (minimum score 500). Application deadline: 7/1 (priority date; rolling processing). Application fee: $20. *Expenses:* Tuition $2362 per year full-time, $373 per semester (minimum) part-time for state residents; $7888 per year full-time, $1423 per semester (minimum) part-time for nonresidents. Fees $170 per year full-time, $25 per semester (minimum) part-time. *Financial aid:* Research assistantships, teaching assistantships, grants, partial tuition waivers, and career-related internships or fieldwork available. Financial aid application deadline: 4/15. *Faculty research:* Inclusion, transition, early childhood, mild/moderate, severe/profound. Total annual research expenditures: $909,221. • Dr. James Miller, Chairperson, 504-280-6541. E-mail: jhmse@uno.edu. Application contact: Dr. Randall Scott, Graduate Coordinator, 504-280-7162. Fax: 504-280-5588. E-mail: klsse@uno.edu.

University of North Alabama, College of Education, Department of Elementary Education, Programs in Special Education, Florence, AL 35632-0001. Offerings in learning disabilities (MA Ed), mentally retarded (MA Ed), mild learning handicapped (MA Ed). Accredited by NCATE. Part-time and evening/weekend programs available. Faculty: 2 part-time (1 woman). Students: 1 (woman) full-time, 34 part-time (30 women). Average age 31. In 1997, 10 degrees awarded. *Degree requirements:* Final written comprehensive exam required, foreign language and thesis not required. *Entrance requirements:* GRE, MAT, or NTE, minimum GPA of 2.5, Alabama Class B Certificate or equivalent, teaching experience. Application deadline: 7/1 (priority date; rolling processing; 12/1 for spring admission). Application fee: $25. *Expenses:* Tuition $2448 per year full-time, $102 per credit hour part-time for state residents; $4896 per year full-time, $204 per credit hour part-time for nonresidents. Fees $3 per semester. *Financial aid:* Federal Work-Study available. Aid available to part-time students. Financial aid application deadline: 4/1. • Application contact: Dr. Sue Wilson, Dean of Enrollment Management, 205-765-4316.

The University of North Carolina at Chapel Hill, School of Education, Programs in Special Education, Learning Disabilities Training Program, Chapel Hill, NC 27599. Awards M Ed. Accredited by NCATE. *Degree requirements:* Comprehensive exam required, foreign language not required. *Entrance requirements:* GRE General Test (minimum combined score of 1000), minimum GPA of 3.0 during last 2 years of undergraduate course work. Application deadline: 1/1 (rolling processing). Application fee: $55. *Expenses:* Tuition $1428 per year full-time, $357 per semester (minimum) part-time for state residents; $10,414 per year full-time, $2604 per semester (minimum) part-time for nonresidents. Fees $782 per year full-time, $332 per semester (minimum) part-time. *Financial aid:* Application deadline 1/1. *Faculty research:* Special education, individualized instruction, teacher preparation. • Dr. David Lillie, Coordinator, 919-966-7001. Application contact: Janet Carroll, Registrar, 919-966-1346. Fax: 919-962-1533. E-mail: jscarrol@email.unc.edu.

The University of North Carolina at Chapel Hill, School of Education, Programs in Special Education, Program in Early Intervention and Family Support, Chapel Hill, NC 27599. Awards M Ed. Accredited by NCATE. *Degree requirements:* Comprehensive exam required, foreign language not required. *Entrance requirements:* GRE General Test (minimum combined score of 1000), minimum GPA of 3.0 during last 2 years of undergraduate course work. Application deadline: 1/1 (rolling processing). Application fee: $55. *Expenses:* Tuition $1428 per year full-time, $357 per semester (minimum) part-time for state residents; $10,414 per year full-time, $2604 per semester (minimum) part-time for nonresidents. Fees $782 per year full-time, $332 per semester (minimum) part-time. *Financial aid:* Application deadline 1/1. *Faculty research:* Families of young children, ethics and early intervention, exceptional child development, assessment and evaluation. • Dr. Harriet Boone, Coordinator, 919-962-9371. Application contact: Janet Carroll, Registrar, 919-966-1346. Fax: 919-962-1533. E-mail: jscarrol@email.unc.edu.

The University of North Carolina at Chapel Hill, School of Education, Programs in Special Education, Program in Special Education, Chapel Hill, NC 27599. Awards MA, M Ed. Accredited by NCATE. *Degree requirements:* Comprehensive exam required, foreign language not required. *Entrance requirements:* GRE General Test (minimum combined score of 1000), minimum GPA of 3.0 during last 2 years of undergraduate course work. Application deadline: 1/1 (rolling processing). Application fee: $55. *Expenses:* Tuition $1428 per year full-time, $357 per semester (minimum) part-time for state residents; $10,414 per year full-time, $2604 per semester (minimum) part-time for nonresidents. Fees $782 per year full-time, $332 per semester (minimum) part-time. *Financial aid:* Federal Work-Study available. Aid available to part-time students. Financial aid application deadline: 1/1. • Dr. Samuel Odom, Coordinator, 919-962-5579. Application contact: Janet Carroll, Registrar, 919-966-1346. Fax: 919-962-1533. E-mail: jscarrol@email.unc.edu.

University of North Carolina at Charlotte, College of Education, Charlotte, NC 28223-0001. Offerings include special education (M Ed). Accredited by NCATE. College faculty: 61 full-time (31 women), 7 part-time (6 women), 62.75 FTE. *Application deadline:* 7/1. *Application fee:* $35. *Tuition:* $1786 per year full-time, $339 per semester (minimum) part-time for state residents; $8914 per year full-time, $2121 per semester (minimum) part-time for nonresidents. • Dr. John M. Nagle, Dean, 704-547-4707. Application contact: Kathy Barringer, Assistant Director of Graduate Admissions, 704-547-3366. Fax: 704-547-3279. E-mail: gradadm@email.uncc.edu.

University of North Carolina at Greensboro, School of Education, Department of Curriculum and Instruction, Program in Education and Welfare of Exceptional Individuals, Greensboro, NC 27412-0001. Awards M Ed. Accredited by NCATE. Students: 25 full-time (23 women), 12 part-time (8 women); includes 1 international. 19 applicants, 58% accepted. In 1997, 9 degrees awarded. *Entrance requirements:* GRE General Test, TOEFL. Application deadline: 5/1 (10/15 for spring admission). Application fee: $35. *Expenses:* Tuition $1842 per year full-time, $370 per semester (minimum) part-time for state residents; $10,296 per year

Directory: Special Education

University of North Carolina at Greensboro (continued)
full-time, $2484 per semester (minimum) part-time for nonresidents. Fees $806 per year full-time, $111 per semester (minimum) part-time. *Financial aid:* 23 students received aid; research assistantships and career-related internships or fieldwork available. • Dr. Gerald Ponder, Chair, Department of Curriculum and Instruction, 336-334-3437.

University of North Carolina at Greensboro, School of Education, Department of Specialized Education Services, Program in Deaf Education, Greensboro, NC 27412-0001. Awards MA, M Ed. Accredited by NCATE. Admissions temporarily suspended. *Degree requirements:* Thesis or alternative required, foreign language not required. *Entrance requirements:* GRE General Test. Application deadline: 2/15. Application fee: $35. *Expenses:* Tuition $1842 per year full-time, $370 per semester (minimum) part-time for state residents; $10,296 per year full-time, $2484 per semester (minimum) part-time for nonresidents. Fees $806 per year full-time, $111 per semester (minimum) part-time. • Dr. Edgar Shroyer, Chair, Department of Specialized Education Services, 336-334-5843.

University of North Carolina at Wilmington, School of Education, Department of Curricular Studies, Program in Special Education, Wilmington, NC 28403-3201. Awards M Ed. Accredited by NCATE. Part-time and evening/weekend programs available. Students: 4 full-time (3 women), 5 part-time (3 women). Average age 32. 7 applicants, 29% accepted. In 1997, 3 degrees awarded. *Degree requirements:* Comprehensive exam required, foreign language and thesis not required. *Entrance requirements:* GRE General Test, MAT, minimum B average in upper-division undergraduate course work, bachelor's degree in special education. Application deadline: 7/1 (rolling processing). Application fee: $35. *Tuition:* $1748 per year full-time, $270 per semester (minimum) part-time for state residents; $8882 per year full-time, $2058 per semester (minimum) part-time for nonresidents. *Financial aid:* Application deadline 3/15. • Application contact: Neil F. Hadley, Dean, Graduate School, 910-962-4117.

University of North Dakota, College of Education and Human Development, Program in Special Education, Grand Forks, ND 58202. Awards M Ed, MS. Accredited by NCATE. Part-time programs available. Postbaccalaureate distance learning degree programs offered (minimal on-campus study). Faculty: 5 full-time (3 women). Students: 7 full-time (all women), 38 part-time (33 women). 12 applicants, 92% accepted. In 1997, 23 degrees awarded. *Degree requirements:* Thesis or alternative. *Entrance requirements:* TOEFL (minimum score 550), minimum GPA of 3.0. Application deadline: 3/1 (priority date; rolling processing). Application fee: $20. *Financial aid:* In 1997–98, 7 students received aid, including 7 assistantships totaling $69,625; fellowships, research assistantships, teaching assistantships, full and partial tuition waivers, Federal Work-Study, institutionally sponsored loans, and career-related internships or fieldwork also available. Financial aid application deadline: 3/15. *Faculty research:* Visual, emotional, and mental disabilities; early childhood. • Dr. Myrna Olson, Director, 701-777-3239. Fax: 701-777-4393. E-mail: myolson@badlands.nodak.edu.

University of North Dakota, College of Education and Human Development, Teaching and Learning Program, Grand Forks, ND 58202. Offerings include special education (Ed D, PhD). Accredited by NCATE. Program faculty: 24 full-time (19 women), 22 part-time (21 women). *Degree requirements:* Dissertation. *Entrance requirements:* TOEFL (minimum score 550), minimum GPA of 3.5. Application deadline: 3/1 (priority date; rolling processing). Application fee: $20. • Dr. Mary Harris, Director, 701-777-2674. Fax: 701-777-4393. E-mail: mary_harris@mail.und.nodak.edu.

University of Northern Colorado, College of Education, Division of Special Education, Program in Special Education, Greeley, CO 80639. Awards MA, Ed D. Accredited by NCATE. Part-time programs available. Faculty: 19 full-time (9 women), 2 part-time (1 woman). Students: 250 full-time (203 women), 106 part-time (86 women); includes 30 minority (4 African Americans, 7 Asian Americans, 15 Hispanics, 4 Native Americans), 8 international. Average age 34. 128 applicants, 88% accepted. In 1997, 133 master's, 6 doctorates awarded. *Degree requirements:* For master's, thesis or alternative, comprehensive exams; for doctorate, dissertation, comprehensive exams. *Entrance requirements:* For doctorate, GRE General Test. Application deadline: rolling. Application fee: $35. *Expenses:* Tuition $2327 per year full-time, $129 per credit hour part-time for state residents; $9578 per year full-time, $532 per credit hour part-time for nonresidents. Fees $752 per year full-time, $184 per semester (minimum) part-time. *Financial aid:* In 1997–98, 144 students received aid, including 2 teaching assistantships totaling $17,399, 7 graduate assistantships (1 to a first-year student) totaling $34,140; fellowships also available. Financial aid application deadline: 3/1. • Dr. James DeRuiter, Interim Director, Division of Special Education, 970-351-2691.

University of Northern Iowa, College of Education, Department of Special Education, Cedar Falls, IA 50614. Awards MA Ed. Part-time and evening/weekend programs available. Faculty: 11 full-time (4 women). Students: 15 full-time (12 women), 63 part-time (56 women); includes 1 minority (African American). Average age 33. 20 applicants, 80% accepted. In 1997, 27 degrees awarded. *Degree requirements:* Thesis or alternative required, foreign language not required. *Entrance requirements:* Minimum GPA of 3.5, 3 years of educational experience. Application deadline: 8/1 (priority date; rolling processing). Application fee: $20 ($30 for international students). *Expenses:* Tuition $3166 per year full-time, $176 per hour part-time for state residents; $7805 per year full-time, $176 per hour part-time for nonresidents. Fees $194 per year full-time, $12.50 per semester (minimum) part-time. *Financial aid:* Scholarships, full and partial tuition waivers, Federal Work-Study, and career-related internships or fieldwork available. Aid available to part-time students. Financial aid application deadline: 3/1. • Dr. Sandra Alper, Head, 319-273-6061.

University of North Florida, College of Education, Division of Educational Services and Research, Program in Special Education, Jacksonville, FL 32224-2645. Awards M Ed. Accredited by NCATE. Faculty: 9 full-time (3 women). Students: 19 full-time (16 women), 39 part-time (36 women); includes 8 minority (5 African Americans, 2 Asian Americans, 1 Native American). Average age 33. 6 applicants, 100% accepted. In 1997, 25 degrees awarded. *Entrance requirements:* GRE General Test (minimum combined score of 1000), minimum GPA of 3.0. Application deadline: rolling. Application fee: $20. *Tuition:* $3388 per year full-time, $141 per credit hour part-time for state residents; $11,634 per year full-time, $485 per credit hour part-time for nonresidents. *Financial aid:* Career-related internships or fieldwork available. *Faculty research:* Counseling for the handicapped, education for the gifted, assessment, deaf education. • Thomas Serwatka, Director, 904-646-2930.

University of North Texas, College of Education, Department of Technology and Cognition, Program in Special Education, Denton, TX 76203-6737. Awards M Ed, MS, PhD. Accredited by NCATE. PhD offered jointly with Texas Woman's University. *Degree requirements:* For doctorate, 1 foreign language (computer language can substitute), dissertation, internship. *Entrance requirements:* For master's, GRE General Test; for doctorate, GRE General Test, admissions exam. Application deadline: 7/17. Application fee: $25 ($50 for international students). *Tuition:* $2063 per year full-time, $815 per year part-time for state residents; $5897 per year full-time, $2100 per year part-time for nonresidents. *Financial aid:* Fellowships, research assistantships, teaching assistantships, Federal Work-Study, institutionally sponsored loans, and career-related internships or fieldwork available. Financial aid application deadline: 4/1. • Application contact: Tandra Tyler-Wood, Adviser, 940-565-2093.

University of Oklahoma, College of Education, Department of Educational Psychology, Program in Special Education, Norman, OK 73019-0390. Awards M Ed, Ed D, PhD. Accredited by NCATE. Part-time programs available. Students: 10 full-time (9 women), 25 part-time (21 women); includes 3 minority (1 Asian American, 1 Hispanic, 1 Native American), 1 international. Average age 35. In 1997, 2 master's, 4 doctorates awarded. Terminal master's awarded for partial completion of doctoral program. *Degree requirements:* For doctorate, variable foreign language requirement, dissertation. *Entrance requirements:* For master's, TOEFL (minimum score 550), minimum GPA of 3.0, 12 hours of course work in education; for doctorate, GRE General Test, TOEFL (minimum score 550), master's degree, minimum graduate GPA of 3.25. Application fee: $25. *Expenses:* Tuition $1920 per year full-time, $80 per credit hour part-time for state residents; $6108 per year full-time, $255 per credit hour part-time for nonresidents. Fees $468 per year full-time, $12 per semester (minimum) part-time. *Financial aid:* 6 students received aid; research assistantships, teaching assistantships, institutionally sponsored loans, and career-related internships or fieldwork available. *Faculty research:* Attitudes and the handicapped, consultation in special education, infant exceptionalities, gifted/talented education, special education technology. • Application contact: Dr. David Lovett, Coordinator, 405-325-5974.

University of Oklahoma Health Sciences Center, College of Allied Health, Department of Communication Sciences and Disorders, Oklahoma City, OK 73190. Offerings include education of the deaf (MS). Department faculty: 19 full-time (12 women), 13 part-time (11 women). *Degree requirements:* Comprehensive exam required, thesis optional, foreign language not required. *Entrance requirements:* GRE General Test, TOEFL (minimum score 550). Application deadline: 7/1 (rolling processing; 12/1 for spring admission). Application fee: $25 ($50 for international students). • Application contact: Dr. Ann Owens, Graduate Liaison, 405-271-4214. Fax: 405-271-1153. E-mail: ann-owens@uokhsc.edu.

University of Oregon, Graduate School, College of Education, Department of Special Education and Community Resources, Program in Developmental Disabilities, Eugene, OR 97403. Awards MA, MS, PhD. Students: 22 full-time (15 women), 13 part-time (all women); includes 3 minority (2 African Americans, 1 Asian American), 5 international. 8 applicants, 100% accepted. In 1997, 9 master's, 3 doctorates awarded. *Degree requirements:* For master's, exam, paper, or project required, foreign language not required; for doctorate, dissertation, comprehensive exam required, foreign language not required. *Entrance requirements:* GRE General Test, TOEFL (minimum score 550). Application deadline: 5/15. Application fee: $50. *Tuition:* $6429 per year full-time, $873 per quarter (minimum) part-time for state residents; $10,857 per year full-time, $1360 per quarter (minimum) part-time for nonresidents. *Financial aid:* In 1997–98, 9 teaching assistantships (3 to first-year students) were awarded. • Rob Horner, Head, 541-346-2462. Application contact: Claudia Vincent, Graduate Secretary, 541-346-1638.

University of Oregon, Graduate School, College of Education, Department of Special Education and Community Resources, Program in Early Intervention, Eugene, OR 97403. Awards MA, M Ed, MS, D Ed, PhD. Students: 34 full-time (32 women), 16 part-time (15 women); includes 1 minority (Native American), 3 international. 37 applicants, 81% accepted. In 1997, 29 master's, 2 doctorates awarded. *Degree requirements:* For master's, exam, paper, or project required, foreign language not required; for doctorate, dissertation, comprehensive exam required, foreign language not required. *Entrance requirements:* GRE General Test, TOEFL (minimum score 550). Application deadline: 1/15. Application fee: $50. *Tuition:* $6429 per year full-time, $873 per quarter (minimum) part-time for state residents; $10,857 per year full-time, $1360 per quarter (minimum) part-time for nonresidents. *Financial aid:* In 1997–98, 1 teaching assistantship was awarded. • Diane Bricker, Coordinator, 541-346-0807. Application contact: Claudia Vincent, Graduate Secretary, 541-346-1638.

University of Oregon, Graduate School, College of Education, Department of Special Education and Community Resources, Program in Exceptional Learner, Eugene, OR 97403. Awards MA, M Ed, MS, D Ed, PhD. Students: 47 full-time (31 women), 13 part-time (8 women); includes 8 minority (2 African Americans, 1 Asian American, 4 Hispanics, 1 Native American), 5 international. 40 applicants, 75% accepted. In 1997, 45 master's, 7 doctorates awarded. *Degree requirements:* For master's, exam, paper, or project required, foreign language not required; for doctorate, dissertation, comprehensive exam required, foreign language not required. *Entrance requirements:* GRE General Test, TOEFL (minimum score 550). Application deadline: 3/15. Application fee: $50. *Tuition:* $6429 per year full-time, $873 per quarter (minimum) part-time for state residents; $10,857 per year full-time, $1360 per quarter (minimum) part-time for nonresidents. *Financial aid:* In 1997–98, 5 teaching assistantships (1 to a first-year student) were awarded. • Kathy Jungjohann, Coordinator, 541-346-1643. Application contact: Claudia Vincent, Graduate Secretary, 541-346-1638.

University of Oregon, Graduate School, College of Education, Department of Special Education and Community Resources, Program in Special Education, Eugene, OR 97403. Awards MA, M Ed, MS, D Ed, PhD. Students: 0. 8 applicants, 0% accepted. *Degree requirements:* For master's, exam, paper, or project required, foreign language not required; for doctorate, dissertation, comprehensive exam required, foreign language not required. *Entrance requirements:* GRE General Test, TOEFL (minimum score 550). Application deadline: 3/15. Application fee: $50. *Tuition:* $6429 per year full-time, $873 per quarter (minimum) part-time for state residents; $10,857 per year full-time, $1360 per quarter (minimum) part-time for nonresidents. *Financial aid:* Teaching assistantships available. • Cindy Herr, Head, 541-346-1410. Application contact: Claudia Vincent, Graduate Secretary, 541-346-1638.

University of Pittsburgh, School of Education, Department of Instruction and Learning, Program in Special Education, Pittsburgh, PA 15260. Offers deaf and hard of hearing (M Ed), early education of disabled students (M Ed), education of students with mental and physical disabilities (M Ed), education of the visually impaired (M Ed), general special education (M Ed), special education (Ed D, PhD). Part-time and evening/weekend programs available. 145 applicants, 85% accepted. *Degree requirements:* Thesis/dissertation required, foreign language not required. *Average time to degree:* master's–2 years full-time, 4 years part-time; doctorate–4 years full-time, 6 years part-time. *Entrance requirements:* GRE General Test, TOEFL (minimum score 650). Application deadline: 2/1. Application fee: $30 ($40 for international students). *Expenses:* Tuition $8018 per year full-time, $329 per credit part-time for state residents; $16,508 per year full-time, $680 per credit part-time for nonresidents. Fees $480 per year full-time, $180 per year part-time. *Financial aid:* In 1997–98, 14 research assistantships averaging $1,150 per month, 4 teaching assistantships averaging $1,250 per month were awarded; partial tuition waivers, Federal Work-Study, institutionally sponsored loans, and career-related internships or fieldwork also available. Aid available to part-time students. Financial aid application deadline: 5/15; applicants required to submit FAFSA. • Application contact: Jackie Harden, Manager, 412-648-7060. Fax: 412-648-1899. E-mail: jackie@sched.fsl.pitt.edu.

University of Portland, School of Education, Department of Special Education, Portland, OR 97203-5798. Awards MA, M Ed. Part-time and evening/weekend programs available. *Degree requirements:* Thesis optional, foreign language not required. *Entrance requirements:* GRE General Test (MA), GRE General Test or MAT (M Ed), TOEFL (minimum score 550), minimum GPA of 3.0, teaching certificate. Application deadline: 8/1 (priority date; rolling processing; 12/1 for spring admission). Application fee: $40. *Tuition:* $515 per semester hour. *Financial aid:* Federal Work-Study available. Financial aid application deadline: 3/15. • Dr. Maria Ciriello, OP, Dean, School of Education, 503-283-7135. Fax: 503-283-8042. E-mail: ciriello@up.edu.

University of Puerto Rico, Medical Sciences Campus, Graduate School of Public Health, Department of Human Development, Program in Developmental Disabilities-Early Intervention, San Juan, PR 00936-5067. Awards Certificate. Students: 11 (10 women). *Application deadline:* 3/3. *Application fee:* $15. *Financial aid:* Application deadline 4/30. • Dr. Annie Alonso, Coordinator, 787-758-2525 Ext. 1447. Application contact: Mayra E. Santiago-Vargas, Counselor, 787-756-5244. Fax: 787-759-6719.

University of Puerto Rico, Río Piedras, College of Education, Graduate Program in Special Education, San Juan, PR 00931. Awards M Ed. *Degree requirements:* Thesis. *Entrance requirements:* PAEG, interview, minimum GPA of 3.0. Application deadline: 2/21. Application fee: $17.

University of Richmond, Department of Education, Master of Teaching Program, University of Richmond, VA 23173. Offerings include learning disabled (MT). MT (learning disabled) being phased out; applicants no longer accepted. Program faculty: 5 full-time (3 women). *Entrance requirements:* GRE General Test, PRAXIS I. Application deadline: 6/1 (priority date;

12/1 for spring admission). Application fee: $30. *Tuition:* $18,695 per year full-time, $320 per credit hour part-time. • Dr. Mavis Brown, Coordinator, Department of Education, 804-289-8429.

University of Richmond, Department of Education, Program in Learning Disabilities, University of Richmond, VA 23173. Awards M Ed. Program being phased out; applicants no longer accepted. Part-time and evening/weekend programs available. Faculty: 4 full-time (2 women). *Degree requirements:* Comprehensive exam required, foreign language and thesis not required. *Tuition:* $18,695 per year full-time, $320 per credit hour part-time. *Financial aid:* Fellowships, tuition awards, partial tuition waivers, Federal Work-Study, institutionally sponsored loans, and career-related internships or fieldwork available. • Dr. Mavis Brown, Coordinator, Department of Education, 804-289-8429.

University of Rio Grande, Graduate School, Rio Grande, OH 45674. Offerings include classroom teaching (M Ed), with options in fine arts, learning disabilities, mathematics, reading education. School faculty: 9 full-time (3 women), 6 part-time (2 women). *Degree requirements:* Final research project, portfolio required, foreign language and thesis not required. *Entrance requirements:* Minimum GPA of 2.7 in major, 2.5 overall. Application deadline: rolling. Application fee: $20. • Dr. Greg Miller, Coordinator, 740-245-7364. Application contact: Dr. Mark Abell, Director of Administration, 740-245-5353.

University of Saint Francis, Department of Education, Fort Wayne, IN 46808-3994. Offerings include special education (MS Ed). Accredited by NCATE. Department faculty: 4 full-time, 9 part-time. *Entrance requirements:* MAT (average 40), minimum GPA of 2.5. Application deadline: 7/1 (priority date; rolling processing; 11/1 for spring admission). Application fee: $20. *Expenses:* Tuition $350 per semester hour. Fees $390 per year full-time, $69 per semester (minimum) part-time. • Dr. Nancy Clements, Chair, 219-434-3271. E-mail: nclements@sfc.edu. Application contact: Scott Flanagan, Director of Admissions, 219-434-3264. Fax: 219-434-3183. E-mail: sflanagan@sfc.edu.

University of St. Thomas, School of Education, Program in Special Education, St. Paul, MN 55105-1096. Awards MA. Accredited by NCATE. Students: 14 full-time (12 women), 96 part-time (84 women); includes 2 minority (both African Americans). Average age 34. 51 applicants, 90% accepted. In 1997, 30 degrees awarded. *Degree requirements:* Thesis (for some programs). *Entrance requirements:* MAT, minimum GPA of 2.75. Application deadline: rolling. Application fee: $50. *Tuition:* $375 per credit hour. *Financial aid:* In 1997–98, 3 grants totaling $3,420 were awarded; research assistantships also available. Financial aid application deadline: 4/1. • Dr. Ann Ryan, Director, 612-962-5388. Fax: 612-962-5169.

University of San Diego, School of Education, Program in Special Education, San Diego, CA 92110-2492. Awards M Ed. Part-time and evening/weekend programs available. Faculty: 2 full-time (1 woman), 1 part-time (0 women). Students: 14 full-time (13 women), 13 part-time (all women); includes 9 minority (3 Asian Americans, 6 Hispanics). 15 applicants, 100% accepted. In 1997, 12 degrees awarded. *Degree requirements:* Portfolio required, foreign language and thesis not required. *Entrance requirements:* TOEFL (minimum score 580), TWE, minimum GPA of 2.75, preliminary teaching credential. Application deadline: 5/1 (priority date; rolling processing; 11/15 for spring admission). Application fee: $45. *Expenses:* Tuition $585 per unit (minimum). Fees $50 per year full-time, $30 per year part-time. *Financial aid:* Fellowships, stipends, Federal Work-Study, institutionally sponsored loans, and career-related internships or fieldwork available. Aid available to part-time students. Financial aid application deadline: 5/1; applicants required to submit FAFSA. *Faculty research:* Competencies for special and regular educators, education of the orthopedically handicapped, specialized programs for the severely handicapped. • Dr. Edward Kujawa, Coordinator, 619-260-4286. Fax: 619-260-6835. Application contact: Mary Jane Tiernan, Director of Graduate Admissions, 619-260-4524. Fax: 619-260-4158. E-mail: grads@acusd.edu.

University of Saskatchewan, College of Education, Department of Education of Exceptional Children, Saskatoon, SK S7N 5A2, Canada. Awards M Ed, PhD, Diploma. Part-time programs available. *Degree requirements:* For master's, thesis (for some programs); for doctorate, dissertation. *Entrance requirements:* For master's, CANTEST (minimum score 4.5) or International English Language Testing System (minimum score 6) or Michigan English Language Assessment Battery (minimum score 80), or TOEFL (minimum score 550; average 560); for doctorate, TOEFL; for Diploma, International English Language Testing System (minimum score 6) or Michigan English Language Assessment Battery (minimum score 80), or TOEFL (minimum score 550). Application deadline: 7/1 (priority date; rolling processing). Application fee: $0.

University of South Alabama, College of Education, Department of Interdepartmental Education, Mobile, AL 36688-0002. Offerings include special education (Ed S). Accredited by NCATE. *Application deadline:* 9/1 (priority date; rolling processing). *Application fee:* $25. • George E. Uhlig, Dean, College of Education, 334-460-6205.

University of South Alabama, College of Education, Department of Special Education, Mobile, AL 36688-0002. Offers programs in education of the emotionally disturbed (M Ed), education of the gifted (M Ed), learning disability (M Ed), mentally retarded (M Ed), multihandicapped education (M Ed), special education (M Ed). Accredited by NCATE. Part-time programs available. Faculty: 6 full-time (3 women). Students: 22 full-time (21 women), 73 part-time (64 women); includes 14 minority (13 African Americans, 1 Native American). 42 applicants, 90% accepted. In 1997, 19 degrees awarded. *Degree requirements:* Comprehensive exam required, foreign language and thesis not required. *Entrance requirements:* GRE General Test (minimum combined score of 1000) or MAT (minimum score 46), minimum GPA of 3.0. Application deadline: 9/1 (priority date; rolling processing). Application fee: $25. *Financial aid:* In 1997–98, 4 research assistantships were awarded; career-related internships or fieldwork also available. Aid available to part-time students. Financial aid application deadline: 4/1. • Dr. Terry Cronis, Chairman, 334-460-6460.

University of South Carolina, Graduate School, College of Education, Department of Educational Psychology, Program in Special Education, Columbia, SC 29208. Awards MAT, PhD. Accredited by NCATE. Faculty: 7 full-time (4 women), 4 part-time (3 women). Students: 39 full-time (36 women), 55 part-time (49 women); includes 15 minority (11 African Americans, 2 Asian Americans, 1 Hispanic, 1 Native American), 1 international. Average age 33. In 1997, 34 master's awarded (100% found work related to degree). *Degree requirements:* For master's, comprehensive and oral exams; for doctorate, 1 foreign language (computer language can substitute), dissertation, comprehensive exam. *Entrance requirements:* For master's, GRE or MAT, sample of written work; for doctorate, GRE General Test, sample of written work. Application deadline: rolling. Application fee: $35. Electronic applications accepted. *Expenses:* Tuition $3894 per year full-time, $193 per credit hour part-time for state residents; $8114 per year full-time, $404 per credit hour part-time for nonresidents. Fees $125 per year full-time, $37 per semester (minimum) part-time. *Financial aid:* In 1997–98, 1 research assistantship (to a first-year student), 2 teaching assistantships (both to first-year students) were awarded; fellowships also available. *Faculty research:* Strategy training, transition, technology, rural special education, behavior management. • Dr. Cheryl Wissick, Coordinator, 803-777-8859. Application contact: Office of Intercollegiate Teacher Education and Student Affairs, 803-777-6732. Fax: 803-777-3068.

University of South Dakota, School of Education, Division of Curriculum and Instruction, Program in Special Education, Vermillion, SD 57069-2390. Awards MA. Accredited by NCATE. Students: 10 full-time (all women), 11 part-time (10 women); includes 1 minority (Native American). 14 applicants, 43% accepted. In 1997, 12 degrees awarded. *Entrance requirements:* GRE General Test, MAT. Application deadline: rolling. Application fee: $15. *Expenses:* Tuition $1530 per year full-time, $85 per credit hour part-time for state residents; $4518 per year full-time, $251 per credit hour part-time for nonresidents. Fees $792 per year full-time, $44 per credit hour part-time. *Financial aid:* Teaching assistantships available. • Dr. Linda Reetz, Chair, Division of Curriculum and Instruction, 605-677-5210.

University of Southern California, Graduate School, School of Education, Department of Curriculum and Instruction, Los Angeles, CA 90089. Offerings include communication handicapped (MS), learning handicapped (MS). *Entrance requirements:* GRE General Test. Application deadline: 7/1 (priority date; 11/1 for spring admission). Application fee: $55. *Expenses:* Tuition $16,944 per year full-time, $706 per unit part-time. Fees $414 per year full-time, $32 per year part-time. • Dr. Edgar Williams, Chair.

University of Southern Maine, College of Education and Human Development, Program in Special Education, Portland, ME 04104-9300. Awards MS. Accredited by NCATE. Part-time and evening/weekend programs available. Faculty: 4 full-time (2 women), 2 part-time (1 woman). Students: 19 full-time (14 women), 56 part-time (45 women); includes 1 minority (Native American). 67 applicants, 81% accepted. In 1997, 26 degrees awarded. *Degree requirements:* Thesis or alternative, portfolio required, foreign language not required. *Entrance requirements:* GRE General Test (minimum combined score of 900), MAT (minimum score 40), TOEFL. Application deadline: 2/1 (9/15 for spring admission). Application fee: $25. *Expenses:* Tuition $178 per credit hour for state residents; $267 per credit hour (minimum) for nonresidents. Fees $282 per year full-time, $83 per semester (minimum) part-time. *Financial aid:* Research assistantships, scholarships, Federal Work-Study, institutionally sponsored loans, and career-related internships or fieldwork available. Aid available to part-time students. Financial aid application deadline: 3/1; applicants required to submit FAFSA. • Dr. Margo Wood, Chair, Professional Education Department, 207-780-5400. Application contact: Teresa Belsan, Admissions and Academic Counselor, 207-780-5306. Fax: 207-780-5315. E-mail: belsan@usm.maine.edu.

University of Southern Mississippi, College of Education and Psychology, Department of Special Education, Hattiesburg, MS 39406-5167. Offers programs in education of the gifted (M Ed, Ed D, PhD, Ed S), special education (M Ed, Ed D, PhD, Ed S). Faculty: 7 full-time (4 women). Students: 16 full-time (13 women), 72 part-time (69 women); includes 11 minority (all African Americans), 1 international. Average age 36. 34 applicants, 79% accepted. In 1997, 70 master's, 2 Ed Ss awarded. *Degree requirements:* For doctorate, 2 foreign languages, computer language, dissertation. *Entrance requirements:* For master's, GRE General Test, minimum GPA of 2.75; for doctorate, GRE General Test, experience in field, minimum GPA of 3.5; for Ed S, GRE General Test, minimum GPA of 3.25. Application deadline: 8/9 (priority date; rolling processing). Application fee: $0 ($25 for international students). *Tuition:* $2870 per year full-time, $137 per credit hour part-time for state residents; $5972 per year full-time, $172 per credit hour part-time for nonresidents. *Financial aid:* Teaching assistantships, Federal Work-Study, and career-related internships or fieldwork available. Financial aid application deadline: 3/15. *Faculty research:* Certification policy. Total annual research expenditures: $140,000. • Dr. April Miller, Chair, 601-266-5236. Application contact: Director of Graduate Admissions, 601-266-4369.

University of South Florida, College of Education, Department of Special Education, Program in Education of the Emotionally Disturbed, Tampa, FL 33620-9951. Awards MA. Accredited by NCATE. Part-time and evening/weekend programs available. Students: 21 part-time (16 women); includes 2 minority (both African Americans). Average age 37. 3 applicants, 67% accepted. In 1997, 7 degrees awarded. *Entrance requirements:* GRE General Test (minimum combined score of 1000), minimum GPA of 3.5 in last 60 hours. Application deadline: 6/1 (10/15 for spring admission). Application fee: $20. Electronic applications accepted. *Tuition:* $142 per credit hour for state residents; $486 per credit hour for nonresidents. *Financial aid:* 3 students received aid; Federal Work-Study, institutionally sponsored loans available. Aid available to part-time students. Financial aid applicants required to submit FAFSA. *Faculty research:* Ethics, teaching cases, early intervention, systems and program evaluation, school restructuring, social skills, models of collaborative and co-teaching. • Betty Epanchin, Chairperson, Department of Special Education, 813-974-3760. Fax: 813-974-5542. E-mail: epanchin@tempest.coedu.usf.edu.

University of South Florida, College of Education, Department of Special Education, Program in Education of the Mentally Handicapped, Tampa, FL 33620-9951. Awards MA. Accredited by NCATE. Part-time and evening/weekend programs available. Students: 7 part-time (6 women); includes 1 minority (African American). Average age 35. 1 applicant, 100% accepted. In 1997, 4 degrees awarded. *Entrance requirements:* GRE General Test (minimum combined score of 1000), minimum GPA of 3.5 in last 60 hours. Application deadline: 6/1 (10/15 for spring admission). Application fee: $20. Electronic applications accepted. *Tuition:* $142 per credit hour for state residents; $486 per credit hour for nonresidents. *Financial aid:* 2 students received aid; Federal Work-Study, institutionally sponsored loans available. Aid available to part-time students. Financial aid applicants required to submit FAFSA. *Faculty research:* Ethics, teaching cases, early intervention, systems and program evaluation, school restructuring, social skills, inclusion. • Betty Epanchin, Chairperson, Department of Special Education, 813-974-3760. Fax: 813-974-5542. E-mail: epanchin@tempest.coedu.usf.edu.

University of South Florida, College of Education, Department of Special Education, Program in Learning Disabilities, Tampa, FL 33620-9951. Awards MA. Accredited by NCATE. Part-time and evening/weekend programs available. Students: 9 full-time (8 women), 19 part-time (17 women); includes 3 minority (2 African Americans, 1 Hispanic), 1 international. Average age 37. 12 applicants, 67% accepted. In 1997, 15 degrees awarded. *Entrance requirements:* GRE General Test (minimum combined score of 1000), minimum GPA of 3.5 in last 60 hours. Application deadline: 6/1 (10/15 for spring admission). Application fee: $20. Electronic applications accepted. *Tuition:* $142 per credit hour for state residents; $486 per credit hour for nonresidents. *Financial aid:* Federal Work-Study, institutionally sponsored loans available. Aid available to part-time students. Financial aid applicants required to submit FAFSA. *Faculty research:* Ethics, teaching cases, early intervention, systems and program evaluation, school restructuring, social skills, inclusion. • Betty Epanchin, Chairperson, Department of Special Education, 813-974-3760. Fax: 813-974-5542. E-mail: epanchin@tempest.coedu.usf.edu.

University of South Florida, College of Education, Department of Special Education, Program in Special Education, Tampa, FL 33620-9951. Awards Ed D, PhD, Ed S. Accredited by NCATE. Part-time and evening/weekend programs available. Students: 19 full-time (16 women), 31 part-time (26 women); includes 9 minority (7 African Americans, 1 Asian American, 1 Native American), 5 international. Average age 41. 9 applicants, 33% accepted. In 1997, 5 doctorates awarded. *Degree requirements:* For doctorate, dissertation, 2 tools of research in foreign language, statistics, and/or computers. *Entrance requirements:* For doctorate, GRE General Test (minimum combined score of 1000), minimum GPA of 3.0 (undergraduate) or 3.5 (graduate); for Ed S, GRE General Test (minimum combined score of 1000), minimum GPA of 3.0 in last 60 hours. Application deadline: 6/1 (10/15 for spring admission). Application fee: $20. Electronic applications accepted. *Tuition:* $142 per credit hour for state residents; $486 per credit hour for nonresidents. *Financial aid:* Federal Work-Study, institutionally sponsored loans available. Aid available to part-time students. Financial aid applicants required to submit FAFSA. *Faculty research:* Ethics, teaching cases, early intervention, system and program evaluation, school restructuring, social skills, inclusion. • Application contact: Kofi Marfo, Coordinator, 813-974-3460. Fax: 813-974-5542. E-mail: marfo@tempest.coedu.usf.edu.

University of South Florida, College of Education, Department of Special Education, Program in Varying Exceptionalities, Tampa, FL 33620-9951. Awards MA. Accredited by NCATE. Part-time and evening/weekend programs available. Students: 56 full-time (50 women), 172 part-time (141 women); includes 29 minority (13 African Americans, 1 Asian American, 14 Hispanics, 1 Native American), 2 international. Average age 34. 32 applicants, 69% accepted. In 1997, 70 degrees awarded. *Entrance requirements:* GRE General Test (minimum combined score of 1000), minimum GPA of 3.5 in last 60 hours. Application deadline: 6/1 (10/15 for spring admission). Application fee: $20. Electronic applications accepted. *Tuition:* $142 per credit hour for state residents; $486 per credit hour for nonresidents. *Financial aid:* Federal Work-Study, institutionally sponsored loans available. Aid available to part-time students. Financial aid applicants required to submit FAFSA. *Faculty research:* Ethics, teaching cases, early intervention, systems and program evaluation, school restructuring, social skills, inclusion.

Directory: Special Education

University of South Florida (continued)

• Betty Epanchin, Chairperson, Department of Special Education, 813-974-3760. Fax: 813-974-5542. E-mail: epanchin@tempest.coedu.usf.edu.

University of Tennessee at Chattanooga, School of Education, Education Graduate Studies Division, Chattanooga, TN 37403-2598. Offerings include special education (M Ed). Accredited by NCATE. Division faculty: 15 full-time (5 women), 7 part-time (3 women). *Degree requirements:* Comprehensive exams required, thesis optional, foreign language not required. *Entrance requirements:* GRE General Test or MAT, teaching certificate. Application deadline: rolling. Application fee: $25. *Tuition:* $2864 per year full-time, $160 per credit hour part-time for state residents; $6806 per year full-time, $379 per credit hour part-time for nonresidents. • Dr. Tom Bibler, Acting Head, 423-755-4211. Fax: 423-755-5380. E-mail: tom-bibler@utc.edu. Application contact: Dr. Deborah Arfken, Assistant Provost for Graduate Studies, 423-755-4667. Fax: 423-755-4478.

University of Tennessee, Knoxville, College of Education, Program in Education I, Knoxville, TN 37996. Offerings include rehabilitation and special education (PhD). Accredited by NCATE. *Degree requirements:* 1 foreign language (computer language can substitute), dissertation. *Entrance requirements:* GRE General Test, TOEFL (minimum score 550), minimum GPA of 2.7. Application deadline: 2/1 (priority date; rolling processing). Application fee: $35. Electronic applications accepted. *Tuition:* $3354 per year full-time, $181 per semester hour part-time for state residents; $8410 per year full-time, $462 per semester hour part-time for nonresidents. • Dr. Tom George, Associate Dean, 423-974-0907. Fax: 423-974-8718. E-mail: tgeorge1@utk.edu.

University of Tennessee, Knoxville, College of Education, Program in Education II, Knoxville, TN 37996. Offerings include early childhood special education (MS), education of deaf and hard of hearing (MS), modified and comprehensive special education (MS). One or more programs accredited by NCATE. *Degree requirements:* Thesis optional, foreign language not required. *Entrance requirements:* TOEFL (minimum score 550), minimum GPA of 2.7. Application deadline: 2/1 (priority date; rolling processing). Application fee: $35. Electronic applications accepted. *Tuition:* $3354 per year full-time, $181 per semester hour part-time for state residents; $8410 per year full-time, $462 per semester hour part-time for nonresidents. • Dr. Tom George, Associate Dean, 423-974-0907. Fax: 423-974-8718. E-mail: tgeorge1@utk.edu.

The University of Texas at Austin, Graduate School, College of Education, Department of Special Education, Austin, TX 78712. Awards MA, M Ed, Ed D, PhD. Students: 140 (108 women); includes 41 minority (15 African Americans, 6 Asian Americans, 19 Hispanics, 1 Native American), 17 international. 62 applicants, 69% accepted. In 1997, 32 master's, 6 doctorates awarded. *Entrance requirements:* GRE General Test. Application fee: $50 ($75 for international students). *Expenses:* Tuition $2592 per year full-time, $324 per semester (minimum) part-time for state residents; $7704 per year full-time, $963 per semester (minimum) part-time for nonresidents. Fees $778 per year full-time, $161 per semester (minimum) part-time. *Financial aid:* Application deadline 2/1. • Herbert J. Rieth Jr., Chairman, 512-471-4161. Application contact: Keith Turner, Graduate Adviser, 512-471-4161.

The University of Texas at Brownsville, Graduate Studies, School of Education, Brownsville, TX 78520-4991. Offerings include special education (M Ed). School faculty: 18 full-time (10 women). *Degree requirements:* Thesis optional, foreign language not required. *Entrance requirements:* GRE General Test, TOEFL (minimum score 550). Application deadline: 8/1 (priority date; rolling processing; 1/1 for spring admission). Application fee: $15. *Expenses:* Tuition $648 per year full-time, $120 per semester hour part-time for state residents; $4698 per year full-time, $783 per semester hour part-time for nonresidents. Fees $593 per year full-time, $109 per year part-time. • Dr. Sylvia C. Peña, Dean, 956-983-7219. Fax: 956-982-0293. E-mail: scpena@utb1.utb.edu.

The University of Texas at Tyler, School of Education and Psychology, Department of Special Services, Program in Special Education, Tyler, TX 75799-0001. Awards MA, M Ed, Certificate. Part-time programs available. Faculty: 3 full-time (2 women), 1 part-time (0 women). In 1997, 9 master's awarded. *Degree requirements:* For master's, comprehensive exam and/or thesis required, foreign language not required. *Entrance requirements:* For master's, GRE General Test (minimum combined score of 1200). Application fee: $0 ($50 for international students). *Tuition:* $2144 per year full-time, $337 per semester (minimum) part-time for state residents; $7256 per year full-time, $964 per semester (minimum) part-time for nonresidents. *Financial aid:* Application deadline 7/1. *Faculty research:* Social skills, behavior disorders, autism, attention deficit disorders, inclusion. • Dr. Brenda Gilliam, Head, 903-566-7055. Application contact: Martha D. Wheat, Director of Admissions and Student Records, 903-566-7201. Fax: 903-566-7068.

The University of Texas of the Permian Basin, Graduate School, School of Education, Program in Special Education, Odessa, TX 79762-0001. Awards MA. *Degree requirements:* Thesis required, foreign language not required. *Entrance requirements:* GRE General Test (minimum combined score of 1200). *Expenses:* Tuition $1314 per year full-time, $73 per hour part-time for state residents; $4896 per year full-time, $272 per hour part-time for nonresidents. Fees $383 per year full-time, $111 per semester (minimum) part-time.

The University of Texas–Pan American, College of Education, Department of Educational Psychology, Edinburg, TX 78539-2999. Offerings include special education (M Ed). *Application deadline:* 7/17 (11/16 for spring admission). *Application fee:* $0. *Tuition:* $2156 per year full-time, $283 per semester (minimum) part-time for state residents; $6788 per year full-time, $862 per semester (minimum) part-time for nonresidents.

University of the Incarnate Word, School of Graduate Studies, College of Professional Studies, Programs in Education, Program in Deaf Education, San Antonio, TX 78209-6397. Awards M Ed. *Entrance requirements:* GRE, MAT, TOEFL (minimum score 550). Application deadline: 8/15 (priority date; rolling processing; 12/31 for spring admission). Application fee: $20. *Expenses:* Tuition $350 per semester hour. Fees $180 per year full-time, $111 per semester (minimum) part-time. • Application contact: Brian F. Dalton, Dean of Enrollment Services, 210-829-6005. Fax: 210-829-3921.

University of the Incarnate Word, School of Graduate Studies, College of Professional Studies, Programs in Education, Program in Special Education, San Antonio, TX 78209-6397. Awards MA, M Ed. Evening/weekend programs available. *Entrance requirements:* GRE, MAT, TOEFL (minimum score 550). Application deadline: 8/15 (priority date; rolling processing; 12/31 for spring admission). Application fee: $20. *Expenses:* Tuition $350 per semester hour. Fees $180 per year full-time, $111 per semester (minimum) part-time. • Application contact: Brian F. Dalton, Dean of Enrollment Services, 210-829-6005. Fax: 210-829-3921.

University of the Pacific, School of Education, Department of Special Education, Stockton, CA 95211-0197. Awards MA, M Ed, Ed D. Accredited by NCATE. M Ed and Ed D being phased out; applicants no longer accepted. Students: 3 full-time (2 women), 6 part-time (5 women). In 1997, 8 master's, 2 doctorates awarded. *Degree requirements:* For master's, thesis required (for some programs), foreign language not required; for doctorate, dissertation. *Entrance requirements:* For master's, GRE General Test, GRE Subject Test. Application deadline: 3/1 (priority date; rolling processing; 10/15 for spring admission). Application fee: $50. *Expenses:* Tuition $19,000 per year full-time, $594 per unit part-time. Fees $30 per year (minimum). *Financial aid:* Teaching assistantships available. Financial aid application deadline: 3/1. • Dr. Marilyn Draheim, Chairperson, 209-946-2167. E-mail: awinczer@uop.edu.

University of Toledo, College of Education and Allied Professions, Department of Special Education Services, Toledo, OH 43606-3398. Offers programs in special education services (M Ed), speech-language pathology (M Ed). Accredited by NCATE. Faculty: 9 full-time (5 women). Students: 24 full-time (20 women), 145 part-time (131 women); includes 17 minority (15 African Americans, 1 Hispanic, 1 Native American). Average age 35. 129 applicants, 36% accepted. In 1997, 40 degrees awarded. *Degree requirements:* Thesis, comprehensive exam required, foreign language not required. *Entrance requirements:* Minimum GPA of 2.7. Application deadline: 8/1 (priority date; rolling processing). Application fee: $30. *Tuition:* $5907 per year full-time, $246 per hour part-time for state residents; $11,835 per year full-time, $493 per hour part-time for nonresidents. *Financial aid:* In 1997–98, 6 research assistantships, 6 teaching assistantships were awarded; fellowships, administrative assistantships, tuition scholarships, and career-related internships or fieldwork also available. Aid available to part-time students. Financial aid application deadline: 4/1. • Dr. Martha Carroll, Chair, 419-530-2055. E-mail: mcarrol@utnet.utoledo.edu.

University of Utah, Graduate School of Education, Department of Special Education, Salt Lake City, UT 84112-1107. Awards M Ed, MS, PhD. Evening/weekend programs available. Faculty: 10 full-time (5 women), 95 part-time (79 women). Students: 54 full-time (42 women), 35 part-time (30 women); includes 1 minority (Native American), 1 international. Average age 36. In 1997, 44 master's, 1 doctorate awarded. *Degree requirements:* Thesis/dissertation required (for some programs), foreign language not required. *Entrance requirements:* For master's, GRE General Test or MAT, TOEFL (minimum score 500), minimum GPA of 3.0; for doctorate, GRE, TOEFL (minimum score 500), minimum GPA of 3.0. Application deadline: 7/1. Application fee: $30 ($50 for international students). *Tuition:* $2045 per year full-time, $562 per semester (minimum) part-time for state residents; $6129 per year full-time, $1607 per semester (minimum) part-time for nonresidents. *Financial aid:* In 1997–98, 1 teaching assistantship was awarded; fellowships and career-related internships or fieldwork also available. *Faculty research:* Learning disability, mental retardation, school psychology, learning and retention, diagnosis. • John McDonnell, Chair, 801-581-8122. Fax: 801-581-5223. Application contact: Patty Davis, Director of Graduate Studies, 801-581-4764.

University of Vermont, College of Education and Social Services, Department of Education, Program in Special Education, Burlington, VT 05405-0160. Awards M Ed. Accredited by NCATE. Students: 37; includes 1 international. 31 applicants, 65% accepted. In 1997, 21 degrees awarded. *Degree requirements:* Thesis or alternative required, foreign language not required. *Entrance requirements:* GRE General Test, TOEFL (minimum score 550). Application deadline: 3/15 (priority date; rolling processing). Application fee: $25. *Expenses:* Tuition $302 per credit for state residents; $755 per credit for nonresidents. Fees $434 per year full-time, $46 per semester (minimum) part-time. *Financial aid:* Research assistantships, teaching assistantships, and career-related internships or fieldwork available. Financial aid application deadline: 3/1. • Dr. W. Fox, Chairperson, 802-656-2936. Application contact: W. Williams, Coordinator, 802-656-2936.

University of Victoria, Faculty of Education, Department of Psychological Foundations, Victoria, BC V8W 2Y2, Canada. Offerings include educational psychology (MA, M Ed, PhD), with options in counseling psychology (MA, M Ed), learning development (MA), measurement evaluation and computer applications in education (MA, M Ed), special education (M Ed), special eduction (MA). Postbaccalaureate distance learning degree programs offered. Department faculty: 15 full-time (5 women). *Average time to degree:* master's–2.3 years full-time; doctorate–4.0 years full-time. *Application deadline:* 4/30 (rolling processing). *Application fee:* $50. *Tuition:* $2080 per year full-time, $557 per semester part-time. • Dr. Walter Muir, Chair, 250-721-7799. Fax: 250-721-6190. Application contact: Sarah Baylow, Graduate Secretary, 250-721-7882. Fax: 250-721-7767. E-mail: sbaylow@uvic.ca.

University of Virginia, Curry School of Education, Department of Curriculum, Instruction, and Special Education, Program in Special Education, Charlottesville, VA 22903. Awards M Ed, Ed D, Ed S. Accredited by NCATE. Faculty: 27 full-time (12 women), 2 part-time (both women), 28 FTE. Students: 14 full-time (13 women), 6 part-time (all women). Average age 28. 31 applicants, 84% accepted. In 1997, 9 master's awarded. *Degree requirements:* For doctorate, dissertation required, foreign language not required. *Entrance requirements:* GRE General Test. Application deadline: 3/1 (11/15 for spring admission). Application fee: $40. *Tuition:* $4876 per year full-time, $944 per semester (minimum) part-time for state residents; $15,824 per year full-time, $2748 per semester (minimum) part-time for nonresidents. • Application contact: Linda Berry, Student Enrollment Coordinator, 804-924-0738. E-mail: lrb8e@virginia.edu.

University of Washington, College of Education, Program in Special Education, Seattle, WA 98195. Awards M Ed, Ed D, PhD. *Degree requirements:* For master's, thesis optional, foreign language not required; for doctorate, dissertation required, foreign language not required. *Entrance requirements:* GRE General Test, TOEFL, minimum GPA of 3.0. Application deadline: 7/1 (rolling processing; 2/1 for spring admission). Application fee: $45. *Tuition:* $5433 per year full-time, $775 per quarter (minimum) part-time for state residents; $13,479 per year full-time, $1925 per quarter (minimum) part-time for nonresidents. *Faculty research:* Early childhood, elementary special education, severe disabilities. • Dr. Allen Glenn, Dean, College of Education, 206-543-5390. Fax: 206-685-1713. E-mail: aglenn@u.washington.edu. Application contact: Richard Neel, Associate Dean, 206-543-7833. Fax: 206-543-8439. E-mail: edinfo@u.washington.edu.

The University of West Alabama, College of Education, Department of Instructional Support, Program in Special Education, Livingston, AL 35470. Awards M Ed. Accredited by NCATE. Part-time programs available. *Average time to degree:* master's–2 years full-time, 3 years part-time. *Entrance requirements:* GRE General Test, MAT, minimum GPA of 2.75. Application deadline: 9/10 (priority date; rolling processing; 3/24 for spring admission). Application fee: $15. *Tuition:* $70 per quarter hour. *Faculty research:* Learning strategies/reading; imagine, discuss, and decide; transition; at-risk students.

The University of Western Ontario, Social Sciences Division, Faculty of Education, Program in Educational Studies, London, ON N6A 5B8, Canada. Offerings include educational psychology/special education (M Ed). Program faculty: 30 full-time (10 women). *Average time to degree:* master's–2 years full-time, 3 years part-time. *Application deadline:* 2/1. *Application fee:* $50. • Dr. S. Haggerty, Graduate Chair, 519-661-2099. E-mail: haggerty@edu.uwo.ca. Application contact: L. Kulak, Graduate Supervisor, 519-661-2099. Fax: 519-661-3833. E-mail: kulak@edu.uwo.ca.

University of West Florida, College of Education, Division of Teacher Education, Program in Special Education-Clinical Teaching, Pensacola, FL 32514-5750. Offers clinical teaching (MA), including emotionally handicapped, learning disabled, mentally handicapped; habilitative science (MA). Accredited by NCATE. Part-time and evening/weekend programs available. Students: 19 full-time (15 women), 27 part-time (21 women); includes 10 minority (9 African Americans, 1 Asian American), 1 international. Average age 38. 23 applicants, 96% accepted. In 1997, 19 degrees awarded. *Entrance requirements:* GRE General Test (minimum combined score of 1000) or minimum GPA of 3.0, 1 year of teaching experience. Application deadline: 7/1 (rolling processing; 11/1 for spring admission). Application fee: $20. *Tuition:* $131 per credit hour (minimum) for state residents; $436 per credit hour (minimum) for nonresidents. *Financial aid:* Fellowships and career-related internships or fieldwork available. *Faculty research:* Memory, semantic structure, remedial programming. • Dr. William Evans, Chairperson, Division of Teacher Education, 850-474-2891.

University of Wisconsin–Eau Claire, College of Professional Studies, School of Education, Programs in Special Education, Eau Claire, WI 54702-4004. Awards MSE. Students: 14 full-time (12 women), 35 part-time (33 women); includes 1 minority (Native American). In 1997, 18 degrees awarded. *Degree requirements:* Oral and written comprehensive exams required, thesis optional, foreign language not required. *Application deadline:* 7/1 (rolling processing; 12/1 for spring admission). *Application fee:* $45. *Tuition:* $3651 per year full-time, $611 per semester (minimum) part-time for state residents; $11,295 per year full-time, $1886 per semester (minimum) part-time for nonresidents. *Financial aid:* Federal Work-Study available. Financial aid application deadline: 3/1. • Stephen Kurth, Associate Dean, School of Education, 715-836-3671.

University of Wisconsin–La Crosse, School of Education, Program in Special Education, La Crosse, WI 54601-3742. Awards MS Ed. Accredited by NCATE. Faculty: 5 full-time (1 woman), 1 (woman) part-time, 5.5 FTE. Students: 2 full-time (both women), 13 part-time (10 women). Average age 39. 25 applicants, 92% accepted. In 1997, 3 degrees awarded (100% found work related to degree). *Degree requirements:* Seminar paper required, foreign language and thesis not required. *Average time to degree:* master's–2 years full-time, 4 years part-time. *Entrance requirements:* GRE General Test, minimum GPA of 3.0, certificate in education, interview. Application deadline: 5/1 (priority date; 11/1 for spring admission). Application fee: $38. *Tuition:* $3737 per year full-time, $208 per credit part-time for state residents; $11,921 per year full-time, $633 per credit part-time for nonresidents. *Financial aid:* In 1997–98, 4 students received aid, including 3 research assistantships (2 to first-year students) averaging $546 per month and totaling $14,742; assistantships, Federal Work-Study, and career-related internships or fieldwork also available. Financial aid application deadline: 3/15; applicants required to submit FAFSA. *Faculty research:* Inclusive schools, legal aspects of special education, collaborative practices. • Charlotte Erickson, Coordinator, 608-785-6894. E-mail: erick_cl@mail.uwlax.edu. Application contact: Tim Lewis, Director of Admissions, 608-785-8067.

University of Wisconsin–La Crosse, College of Health, Physical Education and Recreation, Department of Exercise and Sport Science, Program in Special Adaptive Physical Education, La Crosse, WI 54601-3742. Awards MS. Part-time programs available. Faculty: 3 full-time (0 women). Students: 4 full-time (2 women); includes 1 minority (Asian American). Average age 24. 15 applicants, 80% accepted. In 1997, 5 degrees awarded (80% found work related to degree, 20% continued full-time study). *Degree requirements:* Critical analysis project or thesis required, foreign language not required. *Average time to degree:* master's–1.2 years full-time, 4.5 years part-time. *Entrance requirements:* Minimum GPA of 3.0 during previous 2 years, 2.85 overall. Application deadline: 7/1 (priority date; rolling processing). Application fee: $38. *Tuition:* $3737 per year full-time, $208 per credit part-time for state residents; $11,921 per year full-time, $633 per credit part-time for nonresidents. *Financial aid:* In 1997–98, 3 students received aid, including 3 federal training stipends averaging $772 per month and totaling $23,160; partial tuition waivers, Federal Work-Study, institutionally sponsored loans, and career-related internships or fieldwork also available. Aid available to part-time students. Financial aid application deadline: 3/15; applicants required to submit FAFSA. *Faculty research:* Physical fitness of the physically disabled, teacher preparation in adapted physical education, motor development of the disabled. • Dr. Patrick DiRocco, Coordinator, 608-785-8695. Fax: 608-785-8206. E-mail: dirocco@mail.uwlax.edu. Application contact: Tim Lewis, Director of Admissions, 608-785-8939. Fax: 608-785-6695. E-mail: admissions@mail.uwlax.edu.

University of Wisconsin–Madison, School of Education, Department of Rehabilitation Psychology and Special Education, Program in Special Education, Madison, WI 53706-1380. Awards MA, MS, PhD. *Degree requirements:* For doctorate, dissertation. *Application fee:* $38. *Tuition:* $4928 per year full-time, $926 per semester (minimum) part-time for state residents; $15,190 per year full-time, $2849 per semester (minimum) part-time for nonresidents.

University of Wisconsin–Milwaukee, School of Education, Department of Exceptional Education, Milwaukee, WI 53201-0413. Awards MS. Part-time programs available. Faculty: 10 full-time (7 women). Students: 3 full-time (all women), 21 part-time (all women); includes 6 minority (2 African Americans, 3 Hispanics, 1 Native American). 11 applicants, 27% accepted. In 1997, 8 degrees awarded. *Degree requirements:* Thesis required, foreign language not required. *Application deadline:* 1/1 (priority date; rolling processing; 9/1 for spring admission). *Application fee:* $45 ($75 for international students). *Tuition:* $4996 per year full-time, $1030 per semester (minimum) part-time for state residents; $15,216 per year full-time, $2947 per semester (minimum) part-time for nonresidents. *Financial aid:* In 1997–98, 1 fellowship was awarded; research assistantships, teaching assistantships, project assistantships, and career-related internships or fieldwork also available. Aid available to part-time students. Financial aid application deadline: 4/15. *Faculty research:* Emotional disturbance, hearing impairment, learning disabilities, mental retardation. • Ann Hains, Chair, 414-229-5251.

University of Wisconsin–Oshkosh, College of Education and Human Services, Department of Special Education, Oshkosh, WI 54901-8602. Offers programs in early childhood: exceptional education needs (MSE), emotionally disturbed (MSE), learning disabilities (MSE), mental retardation (MSE), special education (MSE). Accredited by NCATE. Evening/weekend programs available. Faculty: 12 full-time (4 women), 7 part-time (4 women). Students: 37 full-time (26 women), 151 part-time (113 women); includes 5 minority (1 African American, 2 Asian Americans, 2 Native Americans), 2 international. Average age 28. 37 applicants, 92% accepted. In 1997, 20 degrees awarded (100% found work related to degree). *Degree requirements:* Thesis or extra course work, comprehensive exam required, foreign language not required. *Entrance requirements:* Minimum GPA of 2.75, interview. Application deadline: rolling. Application fee: $45. *Tuition:* $3638 per year full-time, $609 per semester (minimum) part-time for state residents; $11,282 per year full-time, $1884 per semester (minimum) part-time for nonresidents. *Financial aid:* Federal Work-Study, institutionally sponsored loans available. Aid available to part-time students. Financial aid application deadline: 3/15. *Faculty research:* Private agency contributions to the disabled, graduation requirements for exceptional education needs students, direct instruction in spelling for learning disabled, effects of behavioral parent training, secondary education programming issues. • Dr. Craig Fiedler, Chair, 920-424-3421. Application contact: Dr. Bert Chiang, Graduate Coordinator, 920-424-2246. E-mail: chiang@uwosh.edu.

University of Wisconsin–Superior, Department of Teacher Education, Program in Special Education, Superior, WI 54880-2873. Offers emotionally disturbed learners (MSE), learning disabilities (MSE). Part-time and evening/weekend programs available. Postbaccalaureate distance learning degree programs offered (minimal on-campus study). Students: 39 (27 women). 13 applicants, 100% accepted. In 1997, 18 degrees awarded. *Degree requirements:* Research project required, foreign language not required. *Entrance requirements:* Minimum GPA of 2.75, teaching certificate. Application deadline: 4/1 (priority date; rolling processing). Application fee: $45. *Tuition:* $3628 per year full-time, $222 per credit hour part-time for state residents; $11,272 per year full-time, $647 per credit hour part-time for nonresidents. *Financial aid:* In 1997–98, 1 research assistantship (to a first-year student) averaging $850 per month and totaling $7,714 was awarded; partial tuition waivers, Federal Work-Study, and career-related internships or fieldwork also available. Aid available to part-time students. Financial aid application deadline: 5/1. • Dr. Gail Peterson Craig, Coordinator, 715-394-8144. E-mail: gcraig@staff.uwsuper.edu.

University of Wisconsin–Whitewater, College of Education, Department of Special Education, Whitewater, WI 53190-1790. Awards MS Ed. Accredited by NCATE. Part-time and evening/weekend programs available. *Degree requirements:* Thesis or alternative required, foreign language not required. *Application deadline:* rolling. *Application fee:* $38.

Utah State University, College of Education, Department of Special Education and Rehabilitation, Logan, UT 84322. Offers program in special education (M Ed, MS, Ed D, PhD). One or more programs accredited by NCATE. Faculty: 16 full-time (5 women), 8 part-time (3 women). Students: 105 full-time (74 women), 25 part-time (23 women). Average age 36. 43 applicants, 70% accepted. In 1997, 30 master's, 1 doctorate awarded. *Degree requirements:* Thesis/dissertation required, foreign language not required. *Entrance requirements:* GRE General Test (score in 40th percentile or higher) or MAT, TOEFL (minimum score 550), minimum GPA of 3.0. Application deadline: 5/15 (priority date; rolling processing; 10/15 for spring admission). Application fee: $40. *Expenses:* Tuition $1448 per year full-time, $624 per year part-time for state residents; $5082 per year full-time, $2192 per year part-time for nonresidents. Fees $421 per year full-time, $165 per year part-time. *Financial aid:* Fellowships, research assistantships, teaching assistantships, Federal Work-Study, institutionally sponsored loans, and career-related internships or fieldwork available. *Faculty research:* Applied behavior analysis, effective instructional practices, transitional/supported employment, early childhood teacher training research, substance abuse prevention. Total annual research expenditures: $3.5 million. • Dr. Charles L. Salzberg, Head, 435-797-3234. Application contact: Dr. K. Richard Young, Chair, Graduate Committee, 435-797-3244. Fax: 435-797-3572.

Utah State University, College of Education, Doctoral Program in Education, Logan, UT 84322. Offerings include special education (Ed D). Program faculty: 65 full-time (17 women). *Application deadline:* 6/15 (priority date; rolling processing; 10/15 for spring admission). *Application fee:* $40. *Expenses:* Tuition $1448 per year full-time, $624 per year part-time for state residents; $5082 per year full-time, $2192 per year part-time for nonresidents. Fees $421 per year full-time, $165 per year part-time. • Application contact: Louann Parkinson, Administrative Assistant, 435-797-1470. Fax: 435-797-3939. E-mail: luannp@coe.usu.edu.

Valdosta State University, College of Education, Department of Special Education, Valdosta, GA 31698. Offers programs in education of the multiply handicapped (M Ed, Ed S), special education (M Ed, Ed S), speech-language pathology (M Ed). Accredited by NCATE. Faculty: 14 full-time (6 women). Students: 209 full-time (193 women), 178 part-time (171 women); includes 27 minority (25 African Americans, 1 Asian American, 1 Native American). 300 applicants, 35% accepted. In 1997, 85 master's awarded. *Entrance requirements:* For master's, GRE General Test (minimum combined score of 800); for Ed S, GRE General Test (minimum combined score of 900). Application deadline: 8/1 (rolling processing; 11/15 for spring admission). Application fee: $10. *Expenses:* Tuition $2472 per year full-time, $83 per semester hour part-time for state residents; $8472 per year full-time, $333 per semester hour part-time for nonresidents. Fees $236 per year full-time. • Dr. Phillip Gunter, Head, 912-333-5932. E-mail: pgunter@grits.valdosta.peachnet.edu.

Valparaiso University, Department of Education, Program in Special Education, Valparaiso, IN 46383-6493. Offers emotionally handicapped (M Ed, MS Sp Ed), learning disabilities (MS Sp Ed), learning disability (M Ed), mild disabilities (M Ed, MS Sp Ed), mild mentally handicapped (M Ed, MS Sp Ed). Accredited by NCATE. Faculty: 6 full-time (4 women). Students: 24 part-time (21 women); includes 1 minority (African American). Average age 41. In 1997, 5 degrees awarded. *Degree requirements:* Thesis (for some programs). *Entrance requirements:* Minimum GPA of 3.0. Application deadline: 8/15 (rolling processing). Application fee: $30. *Tuition:* $3870 per year full-time, $215 per credit hour part-time. • Dr. Barbara Livdahl, Chair, Department of Education, 219-464-5078.

Vanderbilt University, Graduate School, Program in Education and Human Development, Nashville, TN 37240-1001. Offerings include special education (MS, PhD). Jointly offered with Peabody College. Program faculty: 44 full-time (16 women), 1 (woman) part-time. *Degree requirements:* For master's, thesis required, foreign language not required; for doctorate, dissertation, final and qualifying exams required, foreign language not required. *Entrance requirements:* GRE General Test. Application deadline: 1/15. Application fee: $40. *Expenses:* Tuition $16,452 per year full-time, $914 per semester hour part-time. Fees $236 per year. • Ellen Goldring, Director, 615-322-8265. Fax: 615-322-8501. E-mail: goldrieb@ctrvax.vanderbilt.edu. Application contact: Barbara J. Johnston, Director of Admissions, 615-322-8410. Fax: 615-322-8401. E-mail: johnstbj@ctrvax.vanderbilt.edu.

Vanderbilt University, Peabody College, Department of Special Education, Nashville, TN 37240-1001. Awards M Ed, MS, Ed D, PhD, Ed S. Accredited by NCATE. MS and PhD offered through the Graduate School. *Entrance requirements:* For master's and doctorate, GRE General Test, MAT. Application deadline: 3/1 (priority date; rolling processing). Application fee: $35. • Ann Kaiser, Chair, 615-322-8150.

Virginia Commonwealth University, School of Education, Program in Special Education, Richmond, VA 23284-9005. Offers emotionally disturbed (M Ed, MT), learning disabilities (M Ed), mentally retarded (M Ed, MT), preschool handicapped (M Ed), severely/profoundly handicapped (M Ed). Accredited by NCATE. Faculty: 10 full-time. Students: 19 full-time (16 women), 7 part-time (6 women); includes 5 African Americans, 1 international. Average age 30. 13 applicants, 77% accepted. In 1997, 17 degrees awarded. *Entrance requirements:* GRE General Test or MAT. Application deadline: 7/1 (rolling processing; 11/15 for spring admission). Application fee: $30 ($0 for international students). *Tuition:* $4960 per year full-time, $257 per credit part-time for state residents; $12,652 per year full-time, $684 per credit part-time for nonresidents. *Financial aid:* Partial tuition waivers available. Financial aid application deadline: 3/1. • Dr. Alan M. McLeod, Division Head, 804-828-1305. Application contact: Dr. Michael D. Davis, Interim Director, Graduate Studies, 804-828-6530. Fax: 804-828-1323. E-mail: mddavis@vcu.edu.

Virginia Polytechnic Institute and State University, College of Human Resources and Education, Department of Educational Leadership and Policy Studies, Program in Administration and Supervision of Special Education, Blacksburg, VA 24061. Awards Ed D, PhD, CAGS. Accredited by NCATE. Students: 11 full-time (7 women), 9 part-time (all women); includes 1 international. 6 applicants, 67% accepted. In 1997, 1 doctorate, 6 CAGSs awarded. *Degree requirements:* For doctorate, dissertation, internship required, foreign language not required. *Entrance requirements:* GRE General Test (minimum combined score of 1000), TOEFL (minimum score 600), teaching experience. Application deadline: 12/1 (priority date; rolling processing). Application fee: $25. *Tuition:* $4927 per year full-time, $792 per semester (minimum) part-time for state residents; $7537 per year full-time, $1227 per semester (minimum) part-time for nonresidents. *Financial aid:* Research assistantships, teaching assistantships, assistantships, and career-related internships or fieldwork available. Financial aid application deadline: 4/1. • Dr. Philip R. Jones, Area Leader, 540-231-5925.

Virginia State University, School of Liberal Arts and Education, Department of Education, Program in Special Education, 1 Hayden Drive, Petersburg, VA 23806-2096. Awards M Ed, MS. Accredited by NCATE. Faculty: 2 full-time (1 woman). In 1997, 14 degrees awarded. *Application deadline:* 8/15 (rolling processing). *Application fee:* $25. *Tuition:* $3739 per year full-time, $133 per credit hour part-time for state residents; $9056 per year full-time, $364 per credit hour part-time for nonresidents. *Financial aid:* 2 students received aid. Financial aid application deadline: 5/1. • Application contact: Dr. Wayne F. Virag, Dean, Graduate Studies and Continuing Education, 804-524-5985. Fax: 804-524-5104. E-mail: wvirag@vsu.edu.

Wagner College, Department of Education, Program in Special Education, Staten Island, NY 10301. Awards MS Ed. Part-time and evening/weekend programs available. Faculty: 2 full-time (both women), 2 part-time (0 women). Students: 9 full-time (8 women), 1 (woman) part-time. 12 applicants, 83% accepted. In 1997, 4 degrees awarded. *Degree requirements:* Thesis optional, foreign language not required. *Entrance requirements:* Minimum GPA of 2.75. Application deadline: 8/1 (priority date; rolling processing; 12/10 for spring admission). Application fee: $50 ($65 for international students). *Tuition:* $580 per credit. *Financial aid:* In 1997–98, 1 teaching assistantship averaging $300 per month and totaling $2,400, 4 alumni fellowships (1 to a first-year student) were awarded; partial tuition waivers also available. • Application contact: Admissions Office, 718-390-3411.

Walla Walla College, Department of Education and Psychology, Specialization in Special Education, College Place, WA 99324-1198. Awards MA, M Ed. *Degree requirements:* Thesis required (for some programs), foreign language not required. *Entrance requirements:* GRE General Test, minimum GPA of 2.75. Application deadline: 4/1 (priority date; rolling processing). Application fee: $40. *Tuition:* $346 per quarter hour. *Financial aid:* Application deadline 4/1; applicants required to submit FAFSA. • Application contact: Dr. Joe Galusha, Dean of Graduate Studies, 509-527-2421. Fax: 509-527-2253. E-mail: galujo@wwc.edu.

Walla Walla College, Department of Education and Psychology, Specialization in Students at Risk, College Place, WA 99324-1198. Awards MA, M Ed. *Degree requirements:* Thesis required (for some programs), foreign language not required. *Entrance requirements:* GRE General Test, minimum GPA of 2.75. Application deadline: 4/1 (priority date; rolling processing). Application fee: $40. *Tuition:* $346 per quarter hour. *Financial aid:* Application deadline 4/1; applicants required to submit FAFSA. • Application contact: Dr. Joe Galusha, Dean of Graduate Studies, 509-527-2421. Fax: 509-527-2253. E-mail: galujo@wwc.edu.

Washburn University of Topeka, College of Arts and Sciences, Department of Education, Program in Special Education, Topeka, KS 66621. Awards M Ed. Accredited by NCATE. Part-time programs available. Faculty: 2 full-time, 5 part-time. Students: 5 full-time (4 women),

Directory: Special Education

Washburn University of Topeka (continued)

63 part-time (47 women); includes 2 minority (both African Americans). Average age 27. In 1997, 15 degrees awarded. *Degree requirements:* Thesis or alternative, comprehensive exam required, foreign language not required. *Entrance requirements:* GRE General Test, minimum GPA of 3.0 during previous 2 years. Application deadline: 5/1. Application fee: $0. *Financial aid:* Application deadline 3/15. • Dr. David Van Cleaf, Chairperson, Department of Education, 785-231-1010 Ext. 1430.

Wayne State College, Division of Education, Program in Special Education, Wayne, NE 68787. Awards MSE. Accredited by NCATE. Students: 7 part-time (all women). Average age 32. In 1997, 6 degrees awarded. *Degree requirements:* Comprehensive exam, research paper required, thesis optional, foreign language not required. *Entrance requirements:* GRE General Test, minimum GPA of 2.8. Application deadline: rolling. Application fee: $10. *Expenses:* Tuition $1788 per year full-time, $75 per credit hour part-time for state residents; $3576 per year full-time, $149 per credit hour part-time for nonresidents. Fees $360 per year full-time, $15 per credit hour part-time. *Financial aid:* Teaching assistantships and career-related internships or fieldwork available. Financial aid application deadline: 5/1; applicants required to submit FAFSA. • Carolyn Linster, Coordinator, 402-375-7373.

Wayne State University, College of Education, Division of Teacher Education, Detroit, MI 48202. Offerings include special education (M Ed, Ed D, PhD, Ed S). Accredited by NCATE. Division faculty: 53. *Degree requirements:* For doctorate, dissertation required, foreign language not required. *Entrance requirements:* For doctorate, minimum GPA of 3.0 (undergraduate), 3.5 (graduate); interview. Application deadline: 7/1. Application fee: $20 ($30 for international students). *Expenses:* Tuition $163 per credit hour for state residents; $355 per credit hour for nonresidents. Fees $498 per year full-time, $114 per semester (minimum) part-time. • Dr. Sharon Elliott, Assistant Dean, 313-577-0902.

Webster University, School of Education, Department of Multidisciplinary Studies, St. Louis, MO 63119-3194. Offerings include special education (MAT). Department faculty: 7 full-time (5 women). *Entrance requirements:* 2 years of work experience in education, interview, min GPA of 2.5. Application deadline: rolling. Application fee: $25 ($50 for international students). *Tuition:* $350 per credit hour. • Roy Tamashiro, Chair, 314-968-7098. Fax: 314-968-7118. E-mail: tamashro@webster.edu. Application contact: Beth Russell, Director of Graduate Admissions, 314-968-7089. Fax: 314-968-7166. E-mail: russelmb@webster.edu.

West Chester University of Pennsylvania, School of Education, Department of Special Education, West Chester, PA 19383. Awards M Ed. Accredited by NCATE. Faculty: 3 part-time. Students: 2 full-time (both women), 15 part-time (14 women). Average age 33. 23 applicants, 70% accepted. In 1997, 2 degrees awarded. *Degree requirements:* Comprehensive exam required, thesis optional, foreign language not required. *Entrance requirements:* MAT, interview, teaching certificate. Application deadline: 4/15 (priority date; rolling processing; 10/15 for spring admission). Application fee: $25. *Expenses:* Tuition $3468 per year full-time, $193 per credit part-time for state residents; $6236 per year full-time, $346 per credit part-time for nonresidents. Fees $660 per year full-time, $38 per credit part-time. *Financial aid:* In 1997–98, 1 research assistantship was awarded. Aid available to part-time students. Financial aid application deadline: 2/15. • Dr. Judith Finkel, Chair, 610-436-2579. Application contact: Dr. Martin Zlotowski, Graduate Coordinator, 610-436-2579.

Western Carolina University, College of Education and Allied Professions, Department of Human Services, Programs in General Special Education, Cullowhee, NC 28723. Offerings in behavioral disorders (MA Ed), learning disabilities (MA Ed), mental retardation (MA Ed). Accredited by NCATE. Part-time and evening/weekend programs available. Students: 6 full-time (5 women), 20 part-time (18 women); includes 1 minority (Native American). 10 applicants, 70% accepted. In 1997, 9 degrees awarded. *Degree requirements:* Comprehensive exam required, foreign language and thesis not required. *Entrance requirements:* GRE General Test. Application deadline: rolling. Application fee: $35. *Tuition:* $1799 per year full-time, $144 per credit hour (minimum) part-time for state residents; $9069 per year full-time, $1053 per credit hour (minimum) part-time for nonresidents. *Financial aid:* In 1997–98, 5 students received aid, including 5 research assistantships (3 to first-year students) totaling $20,000; fellowships, teaching assistantships, Federal Work-Study, institutionally sponsored loans also available. Financial aid application deadline: 3/15. • Application contact: Kathleen Owen, Assistant to the Dean, 828-227-7398. Fax: 828-227-7480.

Western Illinois University, College of Education and Human Services, Department of Special Education, Macomb, IL 61455-1390. Awards MS Ed. Accredited by NCATE. Part-time programs available. Faculty: 7 full-time (3 women). Students: 11 full-time (10 women), 53 part-time (49 women); includes 4 minority (3 African Americans, 1 Hispanic). Average age 34. 5 applicants, 80% accepted. In 1997, 20 degrees awarded. *Degree requirements:* Thesis or alternative required, foreign language not required. *Application deadline:* rolling. *Application fee:* $0 ($25 for international students). *Expenses:* Tuition $2304 per year full-time, $96 per semester hour part-time for state residents; $6912 per year full-time, $288 per semester hour part-time for nonresidents. Fees $944 per year full-time, $33 per semester hour part-time. *Financial aid:* In 1997–98, 6 students received aid, including 6 research assistantships averaging $610 per month; full tuition waivers also available. Financial aid applicants required to submit FAFSA. *Faculty research:* Training personnel, training for families of infants and toddlers. • Dr. Lyman W. Boomer, Chairperson, 309-298-1909. Application contact: Barbara Baily, Director of Graduate Studies, 309-298-1806. Fax: 309-298-2245. E-mail: barb_baily@ccmail.wiu.edu.

Western Kentucky University, College of Education, Department of Teacher Education, Program in Exceptional Child Education, Bowling Green, KY 42101-3576. Awards MA Ed. Accredited by NCATE. Part-time and evening/weekend programs available. Faculty: 5 full-time (3 women). Students: 37 full-time (36 women), 22 part-time (20 women). Average age 27. 97 applicants, 22% accepted. In 1997, 25 degrees awarded. *Entrance requirements:* GRE General Test (minimum combined score of 1150 on three sections), minimum GPA of 2.5. Application deadline: 8/1 (priority date; rolling processing; 12/1 for spring admission). Application fee: $20. *Tuition:* $2460 per year full-time, $133 per credit hour part-time for state residents; $6700 per year full-time, $369 per credit hour part-time for nonresidents. *Financial aid:* Teaching assistantships, Federal Work-Study, institutionally sponsored loans available. Aid available to part-time students. Financial aid application deadline: 4/1; applicants required to submit FAFSA. • Dr. John Vokurka, Coordinator, 502-745-4541.

Western Maryland College, Department of Education, Program in Education of the Deaf, Westminster, MD 21157-4390. Offers education of the deaf (MS), sensory impairment (MS). Part-time and evening/weekend programs available. Faculty: 2 full-time (1 woman), 6 part-time (3 women). Students: 2 full-time (both women), 191 part-time (169 women). In 1997, 41 degrees awarded. *Degree requirements:* Thesis optional, foreign language not required. *Entrance requirements:* GRE General Test, MAT, or NTE. Application deadline: rolling. Application fee: $35. *Expenses:* Tuition $210 per credit hour. Fees $30 per semester. *Financial aid:* Scholarships, institutionally sponsored loans, and career-related internships or fieldwork available. Aid available to part-time students. Financial aid application deadline: 3/1. *Faculty research:* Mainstreaming of multihandicapped children. • Dr. Judy Coryell, Director, 410-857-2506. Application contact: Jeanette Witt, Coordinator of Graduate Records, 410-857-2513. Fax: 410-857-2515. E-mail: jwitt@wmdc.edu.

Western Maryland College, Department of Education, Program in Special Education, Westminster, MD 21157-4390. Awards MS. Evening/weekend programs available. Faculty: 2 full-time (0 women), 5 part-time (3 women). Students: 2 full-time (both women), 191 part-time (169 women). In 1997, 21 degrees awarded. *Degree requirements:* Thesis optional, foreign language not required. *Entrance requirements:* GRE General Test, MAT, or NTE. Application deadline: rolling. Application fee: $35. *Expenses:* Tuition $210 per credit hour. Fees $30 per semester. *Financial aid:* Application deadline 3/1. • Dr. Henry Reiff, Chairman, 410-857-2506. Application contact: Jeanette Witt, Coordinator of Graduate Records, 410-857-2513. Fax: 410-857-2515. E-mail: jwitt@wmdc.edu.

Western Michigan University, College of Education, Department of Health, Physical Education and Recreation, Kalamazoo, MI 49008. Offerings include special education for handicapped children (MA). Accredited by NCATE. *Application deadline:* 2/15 (priority date; rolling processing). *Application fee:* $25. *Expenses:* Tuition $154 per credit hour for state residents; $372 per credit hour for nonresidents. Fees $602 per year full-time, $132 per semester part-time. • Dr. Debra Berkey, Chair, 616-387-2705. Application contact: Paula J. Boodt, Coordinator, Graduate Admissions and Recruitment, 616-387-2000. E-mail: paulaboodt@wmich.edu.

Western Michigan University, College of Education, Department of Special Education, Kalamazoo, MI 49008. Awards MA, Ed D. Accredited by NCATE. Students: 11 full-time (8 women), 69 part-time (62 women); includes 2 minority (1 African American, 1 Asian American), 1 international. 29 applicants, 28% accepted. In 1997, 11 master's, 1 doctorate awarded. *Degree requirements:* For master's, written exams required, thesis not required; for doctorate, dissertation. *Entrance requirements:* For doctorate, GRE General Test. Application deadline: 2/15 (priority date; rolling processing). Application fee: $25. *Expenses:* Tuition $154 per credit hour for state residents; $372 per credit hour for nonresidents. Fees $602 per year full-time, $132 per semester part-time. *Financial aid:* Fellowships, research assistantships, teaching assistantships, Federal Work-Study available. Financial aid application deadline: 2/15; applicants required to submit FAFSA. • Dr. Elizabeth Whitten, Interim Chair, 616-387-5935. Application contact: Paula J. Boodt, Coordinator, Graduate Admissions and Recruitment, 616-387-2000. E-mail: paulaboodt@wmich.edu.

Western New Mexico University, School of Education, Silver City, NM 88062-0680. Offerings include special education (MAT). School faculty: 16 full-time (9 women). *Application deadline:* rolling. *Application fee:* $10. *Tuition:* $1516 per year full-time, $55 per credit part-time for state residents; $5604 per year full-time, $55 per credit part-time for nonresidents. • Dr. Bonnie Maldonado, Dean, 505-538-6415.

Western Oregon University, School of Education, Department of Socially and Educationally Different, Monmouth, OR 97361. Awards MS Ed. Accredited by NCATE. Faculty: 1 full-time (0 women). Students: 1 (woman) full-time, 1 (woman) part-time. Average age 30. In 1997, 1 degree awarded. *Degree requirements:* Written exam required, thesis optional, foreign language not required. *Average time to degree:* master's–1 year full-time, 3 years part-time. *Entrance requirements:* GRE General Test (average 450 on each section) or MAT (minimum score 30), minimum GPA of 3.0. Application deadline: rolling. Application fee: $50. *Financial aid:* Research assistantships, teaching assistantships, full and partial tuition waivers, and career-related internships or fieldwork available. Aid available to part-time students. Financial aid application deadline: 3/1; applicants required to submit FAFSA. • Dr. Carl Stevenson, Director, 503-838-8854. Fax: 503-838-8474. E-mail: stevenc@wou.edu. Application contact: Alison Marshall, Director of Admissions, 503-838-8211. Fax: 503-838-8067. E-mail: marshaa@wou.edu.

Western Oregon University, School of Education, Department of Special Education, Monmouth, OR 97361. Offers programs in learning disabilities (MS Ed), multihandicapped education (MS Ed), teacher preparation: deafness (MS Ed). Accredited by NCATE. Faculty: 15 full-time (11 women), 8 part-time (5 women), 19.04 FTE. Students: 29 full-time (22 women), 21 part-time (15 women); includes 5 minority (2 Asian Americans, 3 Hispanics). Average age 35. In 1997, 46 degrees awarded. *Degree requirements:* Oral exam, portfolio, written exam required, thesis optional, foreign language not required. *Average time to degree:* master's–1 year full-time, 5 years part-time. *Entrance requirements:* GRE General Test (average 450 on each section) or MAT (minimum score 30), interview, minimum GPA of 3.0. Application deadline: rolling. Application fee: $50. *Financial aid:* In 1997–98, 2 research assistantships averaging $634 per month were awarded; teaching assistantships, full and partial tuition waivers, and career-related internships or fieldwork also available. Aid available to part-time students. Financial aid application deadline: 3/1; applicants required to submit FAFSA. *Faculty research:* Interpreter teacher training, special education, deafness, hearing disabilities, disabilities, mental retardation. • Dr. Joseph Sendelbaugh, Chair, 503-838-8730. Fax: 503-838-8228. E-mail: sedelj@wou.edu. Application contact: Alison Marshall, Director of Admissions, 503-838-8211. Fax: 503-838-8067. E-mail: marshaa@wou.edu.

Western Oregon University, School of Education, Program in Early Intervention/Special Education, Monmouth, OR 97361. Awards MS Ed. Accredited by NCATE. Faculty: 1 (woman) full-time. 15 applicants, 73% accepted. *Entrance requirements:* GRE General Test (average 450 on each section) or MAT (minimum score 30), NTE, interview, minimum GPA of 3.0, teaching license. Application deadline: rolling. Application fee: $50. *Financial aid:* Research assistantships, teaching assistantships, full and partial tuition waivers, and career-related internships or fieldwork available. Aid available to part-time students. Financial aid application deadline: 3/1; applicants required to submit FAFSA. *Faculty research:* Effects of infant massage on the interactions between high-risk infants and their caregivers. • Dr. Mickey Pardew, Coordinator, 503-838-8765. Fax: 503-838-8228. E-mail: pardewm@wou.edu. Application contact: Alison Marshall, Director of Admissions, 503-838-8211. Fax: 503-838-8067. E-mail: marshaa@wou.edu.

Western Washington University, Woodring College of Education, Program in Special Education, Bellingham, WA 98225-5996. Awards M Ed. Accredited by NCATE. Part-time programs available. Students: 19 full-time (17 women), 6 part-time (5 women). 8 applicants, 75% accepted. In 1997, 10 degrees awarded. *Degree requirements:* Comprehensive exams required, thesis optional, foreign language not required. *Entrance requirements:* GRE General Test, TOEFL, minimum GPA of 3.0 in last 60 semester hours or last 90 quarter hours. Application deadline: 6/1 (rolling processing; 2/1 for spring admission). Application fee: $35. *Expenses:* Tuition $4200 per year full-time, $140 per credit part-time for state residents; $12,780 per year full-time, $426 per credit part-time for nonresidents. Fees $249 per year full-time, $83 per quarter part-time. *Financial aid:* Teaching assistantships, partial tuition waivers, Federal Work-Study, institutionally sponsored loans available. Aid available to part-time students. Financial aid application deadline: 3/31. • Dr. Ken Howell, Graduate Adviser, 360-650-3971.

Westfield State College, Department of Education, Program in Intensive Special Needs Education, Westfield, MA 01086. Awards M Ed. *Degree requirements:* Comprehensive exam, practicum required, foreign language and thesis not required. *Entrance requirements:* GRE General Test or MAT, minimum undergraduate GPA of 2.7. Application deadline: rolling. Application fee: $30. *Expenses:* Tuition $145 per credit for state residents; $155 per credit for nonresidents. Fees $90 per semester. *Financial aid:* Application deadline 4/1. • Application contact: Marcia Davio, Graduate Records Clerk, 413-572-8024.

Westfield State College, Department of Education, Program in Special Education, Westfield, MA 01086. Awards M Ed. *Degree requirements:* Comprehensive exam, practicum required, foreign language and thesis not required. *Entrance requirements:* GRE General Test or MAT, minimum undergraduate GPA of 2.7. Application deadline: rolling. Application fee: $30. *Expenses:* Tuition $145 per credit for state residents; $155 per credit for nonresidents. Fees $90 per semester. *Financial aid:* Application deadline 4/1. • Application contact: Marcia Davio, Graduate Records Clerk, 413-572-8024.

Westfield State College, Department of Education, Program in Special Needs Education, Westfield, MA 01086. Awards M Ed. *Degree requirements:* Comprehensive exam, practicum required, foreign language and thesis not required. *Entrance requirements:* GRE General Test or MAT, minimum undergraduate GPA of 2.7. Application deadline: rolling. Application fee: $30. *Expenses:* Tuition $145 per credit for state residents; $155 per credit for nonresidents. Fees $90 per semester. *Financial aid:* Application deadline 4/1. • Application contact: Marcia Davio, Graduate Records Clerk, 413-572-8024.

West Virginia University, College of Human Resources and Education, Department of Educational Theory and Practice, Program in Special Education, Morgantown, WV 26506. Offers education (Ed D), special education (MA). Accredited by NCATE. Part-time and evening/

weekend programs available. Students: 69 full-time (51 women), 313 part-time (270 women); includes 14 minority (9 African Americans, 2 Asian Americans, 1 Hispanic, 2 Native Americans), 1 international. Average age 34. 32 applicants, 100% accepted. In 1997, 146 master's, 3 doctorates awarded. *Degree requirements:* For master's, culminating project required, foreign language and thesis not required; for doctorate, dissertation, comprehensive exam required, foreign language not required. *Entrance requirements:* For master's, TOEFL (minimum score 550), minimum GPA of 2.75; for doctorate, GRE General Test (minimum combined score of 1000) or MAT (minimum score 50), TOEFL (minimum score 550), interview. Application deadline: rolling. Application fee: $5. *Tuition:* $2820 per year full-time, $149 per credit hour part-time for state residents; $8104 per year full-time, $443 per credit hour part-time for nonresidents. *Financial aid:* In 1997–98, 5 research assistantships (1 to a first-year student), 2 teaching assistantships (1 to a first-year student), 1 graduate resident hall assistantship were awarded; full and partial tuition waivers, Federal Work-Study, institutionally sponsored loans, and career-related internships or fieldwork also available. Financial aid application deadline: 2/1; applicants required to submit FAFSA. *Faculty research:* Learning behavioral disorders, inclusion, severely-disabled education, gifted education, infant/preschool disabilities. • Dr. Jerrald Shire, Chair, 304-293-3441. Fax: 304-293-3802.

Wheelock College, Graduate School, Program in Early Intervention: Infants and Toddlers with Special Needs, Boston, MA 02215. Awards MS, CAGS. Students: 13 full-time, 17 part-time. 17 applicants, 71% accepted. *Degree requirements:* For CAGS, thesis. *Entrance requirements:* Interview. Application deadline: 7/1 (priority date; rolling processing). Application fee: $35 ($40 for international students). Electronic applications accepted. *Tuition:* $525 per credit. *Financial aid:* Graduate assistantships, grants, Federal Work-Study, institutionally sponsored loans, and career-related internships or fieldwork available. Aid available to part-time students. Financial aid application deadline: 4/1; applicants required to submit FAFSA. *Faculty research:* Cultural influences on early childhood and parenting, cross-cultural perspectives on families. • Catherine Finn, Coordinator, 617-734-5200 Ext. 160. E-mail: cfinn@wheelock.edu. Application contact: Martha Sheehan, Director of Graduate Admissions, 617-734-5200 Ext. 212. Fax: 617-232-7127. E-mail: msheehan@wheelock.edu.

Wheelock College, Graduate School, Program in Teaching Students with Special Needs, Boston, MA 02215. Awards MS, CAGS. Accredited by NCATE. 14-month program starting in summer only. Students: 50 full-time (45 women). 88 applicants, 57% accepted. *Degree requirements:* For CAGS, thesis. *Entrance requirements:* Interview. Application deadline: rolling. Application fee: $35 ($40 for international students). Electronic applications accepted. *Tuition:* $525 per credit. *Financial aid:* In 1997–98, 50 students received aid, including 50 teaching assistantships (all to first-year students) totaling $500,000; Federal Work-Study, institutionally sponsored loans, and career-related internships or fieldwork also available. Aid available to part-time students. Financial aid application deadline: 4/1; applicants required to submit FAFSA. • Dr. Joseph Cambone, Coordinator, 617-734-5200 Ext. 160. E-mail: jcambone@wheelock.edu. Application contact: Martha Sheehan, Director of Graduate Admissions, 617-734-5200 Ext. 212. Fax: 617-232-7127. E-mail: msheehan@wheelock.edu.

Whitworth College, Graduate Studies in Education, Program in Special Education, Spokane, WA 99251-0001. Awards MAT. Accredited by NCATE. Part-time and evening/weekend programs available. *Degree requirements:* Comprehensive exams, internship, practicum, research project, or thesis required, foreign language not required. *Entrance requirements:* GRE General Test. Application deadline: 9/1 (priority date; rolling processing; 2/1 for spring admission). Application fee: $25.

Wichita State University, College of Education, Department of Curriculum and Instruction, Program in Special Education, Wichita, KS 67260. Awards M Ed. Accredited by NCATE. *Degree requirements:* Comprehensive exam required, thesis optional, foreign language not required. *Entrance requirements:* MAT, TOEFL (minimum score 550), minimum GPA of 2.75. Application deadline: 3/1 (priority date; rolling processing; 1/1 for spring admission). Application fee: $0 ($40 for international students). *Expenses:* Tuition $2303 per year full-time, $96 per credit hour part-time for state residents; $7691 per year full-time, $321 per credit hour part-time for nonresidents. Fees $490 per year full-time, $75 per semester (minimum) part-time. *Financial aid:* Application deadline 4/1. • Application contact: Dr. Bryant Fillion, Graduate Coordinator, 316-978-3322. Fax: 316-978-3302. E-mail: fillion@wsuhub.uc.twsu.edu.

William Carey College, Department of Education, Concentration in Special Education, Hattiesburg, MS 39401-5499. Awards M Ed. *Entrance requirements:* NTE, minimum GPA of 2.5. Application deadline: 8/15 (priority date; rolling processing). Application fee: $0. *Tuition:* $130 per semester hour. • Dr. William Hetrick, Dean, College of Education and Psychology, Graduate Division, 601-582-6217.

William Paterson University of New Jersey, College of Education, Department of Special Education and Counseling Services, Program in Special Education, Wayne, NJ 07470-8420. Awards M Ed. Accredited by NCATE. Students: 76 part-time (69 women); includes 2 minority (1 Asian American, 1 Hispanic). Average age 31. 45 applicants, 53% accepted. In 1997, 33 degrees awarded. *Degree requirements:* Thesis, comprehensive exam required, foreign language not required. *Entrance requirements:* GRE General Test (minimum combined score of 850), MAT (minimum score 42), minimum GPA of 2.75, teaching certificate. Application deadline: 4/1 (rolling processing; 10/15 for spring admission). Application fee: $35. *Expenses:* Tuition $230 per credit for state residents; $327 per credit for nonresidents. Fees $3.25 per credit. *Financial aid:* 12 students received aid. Financial aid application deadline: 4/1. • Application contact: Office of Graduate Studies, 973-720-2237. Fax: 973-720-2035.

Wilmington College, Division of Education, New Castle, DE 19720-6491. Offerings include elementary special education (M Ed). *Application deadline:* rolling. *Application fee:* $25. *Expenses:* Tuition $4410 per year full-time, $735 per course part-time. Fees $50 per year. • Dr. Barbara Raetsch, Chair, 302-328-9401. Application contact: Michael Lee, Director of Admissions and Financial Aid, 302-328-9401 Ext. 102.

Winona State University, Graduate Studies, College of Education, Department of Special Education, Winona, MN 55987-5838. Awards MS. Accredited by NCATE. Faculty: 4 full-time (2 women). Students: 3 part-time (2 women); includes 1 international. 5 applicants, 100% accepted. In 1997, 4 degrees awarded. *Degree requirements:* Thesis or alternative required, foreign language not required. *Entrance requirements:* GRE General Test. Application deadline: 8/8 (priority date; rolling processing; 2/17 for spring admission). Application fee: $20. *Financial aid:* Assistantships, Federal Work-Study, and career-related internships or fieldwork available. Aid available to part-time students. • Dr. Carol Long, Chairperson, 507-457-5535.

Winthrop University, College of Education, Program in Curriculum and Instruction, Rock Hill, SC 29733. Offerings include curriculum development (Ed S), with options in elementary education, secondary education, special education. Accredited by NCATE. *Entrance requirements:* NTE, master's degree, 2 years of teaching experience, minimum GPA of 3.0. Application deadline: 7/15 (priority date; rolling processing; 12/1 for spring admission). Application fee: $35. *Tuition:* $3928 per year full-time, $164 per credit hour part-time for state residents; $7060 per year full-time, $294 per credit hour part-time for nonresidents. • Dr. Richard Ingram, Chairman, 803-323-2151. Fax: 803-323-2585. E-mail: ingramr@winthrop.edu. Application contact: Sharon Johnson, Director of Graduate Studies, 803-323-2204. Fax: 803-323-2292. E-mail: johnsons@winthrop.edu.

Winthrop University, College of Education, Program in Special Education, Rock Hill, SC 29733. Awards M Ed. Accredited by NCATE. Part-time programs available. Students: 1 full-time (0 women), 16 part-time (all women); includes 2 minority (both African Americans). Average age 33. In 1997, 3 degrees awarded. *Entrance requirements:* NTE or South Carolina Area Teaching Exam, South Carolina Class III teaching certificate, sample of written work. Application deadline: 7/15 (priority date; rolling processing; 12/1 for spring admission). Application fee: $35. *Tuition:* $3928 per year full-time, $164 per credit hour part-time for state residents; $7060 per year full-time, $294 per credit hour part-time for nonresidents. *Financial aid:* Graduate assistantships, graduate scholarships, Federal Work-Study, and career-related internships or fieldwork available. Aid available to part-time students. Financial aid application deadline: 2/1; applicants required to submit FAFSA. • Dr. Richard Ingram, Chairman, 803-323-2151. Fax: 803-323-2585. E-mail: ingramr@winthrop.edu. Application contact: Sharon Johnson, Director of Graduate Studies, 803-323-2204. Fax: 803-323-2292. E-mail: johnsons@winthrop.edu.

Wright State University, College of Education and Human Services, Department of Teacher Education, Programs in Special Education, Dayton, OH 45435. Offerings in developmentally handicapped (MA, M Ed), gifted (MA, M Ed), multiple handicapped (MA, M Ed), orthopedically handicapped (MA, M Ed), severe behavior handicapped (MA, M Ed), specific learning disabilities (MA, M Ed). Accredited by NCATE. Students: 13 full-time (9 women), 54 part-time (42 women); includes 3 minority (all African Americans), 1 international. Average age 34. 22 applicants, 91% accepted. In 1997, 28 degrees awarded. *Degree requirements:* Thesis required (for some programs), foreign language not required. *Entrance requirements:* GRE General Test, MAT, TOEFL (minimum score 550). Application fee: $25. *Tuition:* $5109 per year full-time, $161 per credit hour part-time for state residents; $9039 per year full-time, $282 per credit hour part-time for nonresidents. *Financial aid:* Available to part-time students. Financial aid applicants required to submit FAFSA. • Dr. Michael Williams, Coordinator, 937-775-2678. Fax: 937-775-3301. Application contact: Gerald C. Malicki, Assistant Dean and Director of Graduate Admissions and Records, 937-775-2976. Fax: 937-775-2357. E-mail: wsugrad@wright.edu.

Xavier University, College of Social Sciences, Department of Education, Program in Special Education, Cincinnati, OH 45207-2111. Offers developmentally handicapped (M Ed), early childhood education of handicapped (M Ed), gifted (M Ed), multiple handicapped (M Ed), severe behavior handicapped (M Ed), specific learning disabilities (M Ed). Part-time programs available. Faculty: 2 full-time (both women), 9 part-time (6 women), 4.25 FTE. Students: 7 full-time (all women), 53 part-time (48 women); includes 4 minority (all African Americans), 1 international. Average age 38. 17 applicants, 65% accepted. In 1997, 15 degrees awarded. *Degree requirements:* Comprehensive exam, research project required, foreign language and thesis not required. *Entrance requirements:* GRE or MAT (minimum score 35), minimum GPA of 2.7. Application deadline: 8/15 (priority date; rolling processing). Application fee: $25. *Financial aid:* In 1997–98, 22 students received aid, including 22 scholarships (3 to first-year students). Aid available to part-time students. *Faculty research:* School and community relationship, professional development, inclusion, tutoring, student teaching field experiences. • Dr. Sharon A. Merrill, Director, 513-745-1078. Fax: 513-745-2920. E-mail: merrill@admin.xu.edu. Application contact: Sheila Speth, Director of Graduate Services, 513-745-3360. Fax: 513-745-1048. E-mail: xugrad@admin.xu.edu.

Youngstown State University, College of Education, Department of Teacher Education, Program in Special Education, Youngstown, OH 44555-0002. Offers gifted and talented education (MS Ed), special education (MS Ed). Accredited by NCATE. Part-time and evening/weekend programs available. Faculty: 4 full-time (3 women), 14 part-time (13 women). Students: 2 full-time (1 woman), 70 part-time (65 women); includes 4 minority (3 African Americans, 1 Native American), 1 international. 16 applicants, 88% accepted. In 1997, 18 degrees awarded. *Degree requirements:* Comprehensive exam required, foreign language and thesis not required. *Entrance requirements:* TOEFL (minimum score 550), GRE, MAT, or teaching certificate; interview; minimum GPA of 2.5. Application deadline: 8/15 (priority date; rolling processing; 2/15 for spring admission). Application fee: $30 ($75 for international students). *Expenses:* Tuition $90 per credit hour for state residents; $144 per credit hour (minimum) for nonresidents. Fees $528 per year full-time, $244 per year (minimum) part-time. *Financial aid:* In 1997–98, 31 students received aid, including 3 research assistantships averaging $666 per month and totaling $25,560, 28 scholarships totaling $13,588; teaching assistantships, Federal Work-Study, institutionally sponsored loans also available. Aid available to part-time students. Financial aid application deadline: 3/1. *Faculty research:* Learning disabilities, learning styles, developing self-esteem and social skills of severe behaviorally handicapped students, gifted education, inclusion. • Application contact: Dr. Peter J. Kasvinsky, Dean of Graduate Studies, 330-742-3091. Fax: 330-742-1580. E-mail: amgrad03@ysub.ysu.edu.

Urban Education

Cleveland State University, College of Education, Program in Urban Education, Cleveland, OH 44115-2440. Awards PhD. Part-time programs available. Students: 22 full-time (18 women), 61 part-time (39 women); includes 19 minority (14 African Americans, 2 Asian Americans, 3 Hispanics), 1 international. Average age 43. 24 applicants, 29% accepted. In 1997, 4 degrees awarded. *Degree requirements:* 1 foreign language (computer language can substitute), dissertation. *Entrance requirements:* GRE General Test, minimum graduate GPA of 3.25. Application deadline: 3/15 (priority date). Application fee: $25. *Expenses:* Tuition $5252 per year full-time, $202 per credit hour part-time for state residents; $10,504 per year full-time, $404 per credit hour part-time for nonresidents. Fees $2.25 per credit hour (minimum). *Financial aid:* In 1997–98, 3 teaching assistantships, 2 assistantships were awarded; research assistantships also available. *Faculty research:* Equity issues (race, ethnicity, and gender), education development consequences for special needs of urban populations, urban education programming. • Dr. Lewis Patterson, Director, 216-687-4697. Application contact: Toni Foster, Administrative Assistant, 216-687-4697.

College of Mount Saint Vincent, Program in Education, Riverdale, NY 10471-1093. Offerings include urban and multicultural education (MS). *Application deadline:* rolling. *Application fee:* $50.

Columbia College, Department of Educational Studies, 600 South Michigan Avenue, Chicago, IL 60605-1997. Offerings include urban teaching (MA). *Application deadline:* 7/15 (rolling processing; 12/4 for spring admission). *Application fee:* $35. *Expenses:* Tuition $392 per credit hour. Fees $170 per year full-time, $150 per year part-time.

Concordia University, Program in Curriculum and Instruction, River Forest, IL 60305-1499. Offerings include urban teaching (MA). MA offered jointly with the Chicago Consortium of Colleges and Universities. Program faculty: 11 full-time (4 women), 42 part-time (26 women). *Degree requirements:* Thesis, comprehensive exams required, foreign language not required. *Entrance requirements:* Minimum GPA of 2.9. Application deadline: rolling. Application fee: $0. *Tuition:* $372 per semester hour. • Dr. Daniel Tomal, Coordinator, 708-209-3476. Application

Directory: Urban Education

Concordia University (continued)

contact: Mary Betancourt, Admissions Secretary, 708-209-4093. Fax: 708-209-3454. E-mail: crfdngrad@curf.edu.

Concordia University, Program in Urban Teaching, River Forest, IL 60305-1499. Awards MA. *Entrance requirements:* Minimum GPA of 2.9. Application deadline: rolling. Application fee: $0. *Tuition:* $372 per semester hour. *Financial aid:* Research assistantships, institutionally sponsored loans available. Aid available to part-time students. • Dr. Curtis Arthur, Coordinator, 708-209-3192. Application contact: Mary Betancourt, Admissions Secretary, 708-209-4093. Fax: 708-209-3454. E-mail: crfdngrad@curf.edu.

DePaul University, School of Education, Program in Urban Education, Chicago, IL 60604-2287. Offers curriculum development (MA, M Ed). Accredited by NCATE. Faculty: 1 full-time (0 women). Students: 13 full-time (7 women), 9 part-time (6 women); includes 11 minority (5 African Americans, 2 Asian Americans, 3 Hispanics, 1 Native American). Average age 35. 18 applicants, 89% accepted. *Degree requirements:* Thesis optional, foreign language not required. *Entrance requirements:* Interview, minimum GPA of 2.75, work experience. Application deadline: rolling. Application fee: $25. *Expenses:* Tuition $320 per credit hour. Fees $30 per year. *Financial aid:* Career-related internships or fieldwork available. • Barbara Radner, Chairperson, 312-362-8828.

Florida International University, College of Education, Department of Foundations and Professional Studies, Program in Urban Education, Miami, FL 33199. Awards MS. Accredited by NCATE. Part-time and evening/weekend programs available. Students: 10 full-time (8 women), 35 part-time (32 women); includes 35 minority (13 African Americans, 22 Hispanics). Average age 37. 15 applicants, 100% accepted. *Entrance requirements:* GRE General Test (minimum combined score of 1000) or minimum GPA of 3.0 in last 60 credits of baccalaureate. Application deadline: 4/1 (priority date; rolling processing; 10/1 for spring admission). Application fee: $20. *Expenses:* Tuition $138 per credit hour for state residents; $482 per credit hour for nonresidents. Fees $46 per semester. *Financial aid:* Fellowships available. • Dr. Robert Farrell, Chairperson, Department of Foundations and Professional Studies, 305-348-3418. Fax: 305-348-3996. E-mail: farrellr@fiu.edu.

Harvard University, Graduate School of Education, Area of Administration, Planning and Social Policy, Cambridge, MA 02138. Offerings include urban superintendency (Ed D). Terminal master's awarded for partial completion of doctoral program. Faculty: 14 full-time (6 women), 21 part-time (8 women), 15.7 FTE. *Degree requirements:* Dissertation required, foreign language not required. *Average time to degree:* master's–1 year full-time, 2 years part-time; doctorate–6.3 years full-time, 7.2 years part-time; other advanced degree–1 year full-time, 4.7 years part-time. *Entrance requirements:* GRE General Test, TOEFL (minimum score 600), TWE (minimum score 5.0). Application deadline: 1/2. Application fee: $60. • Richard Murnane, Chair, 617-496-4813. Application contact: Roland Hence, Director of Admissions, 617-495-3414. Fax: 617-496-3577. E-mail: gseadmissions@harvard.edu.

Morgan State University, School of Education and Urban Studies, Department of Teacher Education and Administration, Program in Urban Educational Leadership, Baltimore, MD 21251. Awards Ed D. Accredited by NCATE. Part-time and evening/weekend programs available. Faculty: 5 full-time (1 woman), 4 part-time (1 woman). Students: 2 full-time (0 women), 47 part-time (27 women); includes 43 minority (42 African Americans, 1 Asian American). Average age 40. 29 applicants, 28% accepted. In 1997, 5 degrees awarded (100% found work related to degree). *Degree requirements:* Dissertation, comprehensive exam required, foreign language not required. *Average time to degree:* doctorate–7 years part-time. *Entrance requirements:* GRE General Test or MAT. Application deadline: 7/1 (rolling processing). Application fee: $0. *Expenses:* Tuition $160 per credit hour for state residents; $286 per credit hour for nonresidents. Fees $326 per year. *Financial aid:* Application deadline 4/1. *Faculty research:* Multicultural education, cooperative learning, psychology of cognition. • Dr. Iola Ragins Smith, Chair, 410-319-3292. Application contact: James E. Waller, Admissions and Programs Officer, 410-319-3186. Fax: 410-319-3837.

New Jersey City University, School of Professional Studies and Education, Programs in Urban Education, Jersey City, NJ 07305-1957. Offerings in administration and supervision (MA); administration, curriculum and instruction (MA), including early childhood education, urban education; basics and urban studies (MA); bilingual/bicultural education and English as a second language (MA); early childhood education (MA). Evening/weekend programs available. *Entrance requirements:* GRE General Test, TOEFL or MAT. Application deadline: 8/1 (priority date; rolling processing; 12/1 for spring admission). Application fee: $0.

Norfolk State University, School of Education, Department of Secondary Education and School Management, Program in Urban Education/Administration, 2401 Corprew Avenue, Norfolk, VA 23504-3907. Awards MA. Accredited by NCATE. Part-time programs available. Faculty: 3 full-time, 1 part-time. Students: 46 full-time (39 women), 47 part-time (33 women); includes 68 minority (67 African Americans, 1 Asian American), 23 international. Average age 35. In 1997, 43 degrees awarded. *Entrance requirements:* GRE General Test, minimum GPA of 3.0 in major, 2.5 overall. Application deadline: 8/1. Application fee: $30. *Tuition:* $3718 per year full-time, $198 per credit hour part-time for state residents; $7668 per year full-time, $404 per credit hour part-time for nonresidents. *Financial aid:* Fellowships and career-related internships or fieldwork available. • Dr. Mary Kimble, Acting Head, Department of Secondary Education and School Management, 757-683-8178.

Northeastern Illinois University, College of Education, Department of Educational Leadership and Development, Program in Inner City Studies, Chicago, IL 60625-4699. Awards MA. Part-time and evening/weekend programs available. Faculty: 6 full-time (1 woman), 2 part-time (0 women). Students: 4 full-time (2 women), 29 part-time (19 women); includes 30 minority (29 African Americans, 1 Hispanic). Average age 40. 16 applicants, 56% accepted. In 1997, 16 degrees awarded. *Degree requirements:* Thesis or alternative, oral comprehensive exams required, foreign language not required. *Entrance requirements:* Minimum GPA of 2.75. Application deadline: 3/18 (priority date; rolling processing; 9/30 for spring admission). Application fee: $0. *Expenses:* Tuition $2226 per year full-time, $93 per credit hour part-time for state residents; $6678 per year full-time, $278 per credit hour part-time for nonresidents. Fees $358 per year full-time, $14.90 per credit hour part-time. *Financial aid:* 12 students received aid; full and partial tuition waivers, Federal Work-Study, institutionally sponsored loans, and career-related internships or fieldwork available. Aid available to part-time students. • Dr. Conrad Worrill, Coordinator, 773-268-7500 Ext. 144. Application contact: Dr. Mohan K. Sood, Dean of Graduate College, 773-583-4050 Ext. 6143. Fax: 773-794-6670.

Old Dominion University, Darden College of Education, Program in Urban Services/Urban Education, Norfolk, VA 23529. Awards PhD. Accredited by NCATE. Students: 22 full-time (15 women), 78 part-time (42 women); includes 27 minority (25 African Americans, 1 Hispanic, 1 Native American), 3 international. Average age 43. In 1997, 6 degrees awarded. *Degree requirements:* Dissertation, comprehensive exams required, foreign language not required. *Entrance requirements:* GRE General Test (minimum combined score of 1350 on three sections), master's degree, minimum GPA of 3.5. Application deadline: 7/1 (4/1 for spring admission). Application fee: $30. *Expenses:* Tuition $180 per credit hour for state residents; $477 per credit hour for nonresidents. Fees $140 per year full-time, $32 per semester part-time. *Financial aid:* In 1997–98, 27 students received aid, including 17 research assistantships (2 to first-year students) totaling $146,688, 5 tuition grants totaling $8,332; teaching assistantships, institutionally sponsored loans, and career-related internships or fieldwork also available. Financial aid application deadline: 2/15; applicants required to submit FAFSA. *Faculty research:* Race relations, effective schools, comparative education, expert teaching. • Dr. Rebecca Bowers, Director, 757-683-4374. Fax: 757-683-5862. E-mail: rbowers@odu.edu.

Saint Peter's College, Graduate Programs in Education, Program in Urban Education, 2641 Kennedy Boulevard, Jersey City, NJ 07306-5997. Awards MA. Part-time and evening/weekend programs available. Faculty: 3 full-time (0 women), 4 part-time (1 woman). Students: 17 part-time (13 women); includes 3 minority (2 African Americans, 1 Asian American). Average age 40. In 1997, 2 degrees awarded. *Degree requirements:* Departmental qualifying exam required, foreign language and thesis not required. *Entrance requirements:* GRE or MAT (minimum score 40). Application deadline: 8/1 (priority date; rolling processing). Application fee: $20. *Tuition:* $516 per credit. *Financial aid:* Career-related internships or fieldwork available. Aid available to part-time students. Financial aid application deadline: 7/1. • Dr. Joseph McLaughlin, Director, Graduate Programs in Education, 201-915-9254. Fax: 201-915-9074. Application contact: Nancy P. Campbell, Associate Vice President for Enrollment, 201-915-9213. Fax: 201-432-5860. E-mail: admissions@spcvxa.spc.edu.

Temple University, College of Education, Department of Educational Leadership and Policy Studies, Philadelphia, PA 19122-6096. Offerings include urban education (Ed M, Ed D). Accredited by NCATE. Terminal master's awarded for partial completion of doctoral program. Department faculty: 14 full-time (8 women). *Degree requirements:* For master's, thesis or alternative, comprehensive exam required, foreign language not required; for doctorate, dissertation, preliminary exam required, foreign language not required. *Entrance requirements:* For master's, GRE General Test (minimum combined score of 1000) or MAT (minimum score 39), minimum GPA of 2.8; for doctorate, GRE General Test (minimum combined score of 1000) or MAT (minimum score 48), minimum GPA of 2.8 undergraduate, 3.0 graduate. Application deadline: 7/1 (11/1 for spring admission). Application fee: $40. *Expenses:* Tuition $323 per semester hour for state residents; $444 per semester hour for nonresidents. Fees $170 per year full-time, $28 per semester (minimum) part-time. • Dr. Donald Walters, Chair, 215-204-6169. Application contact: Dr. Stiles Seay, Director of Advising, 215-204-8011. Fax: 215-204-5622.

Texas Southern University, College of Education, Area of Curriculum and Instruction, Houston, TX 77004-4584. Offerings include curriculum, instruction, and urban education (Ed D). Faculty: 15 full-time (7 women), 4 part-time (all women). *Degree requirements:* Dissertation, comprehensive exam required, foreign language not required. *Entrance requirements:* GRE General Test or MAT, master's degree, minimum B+ average. Application deadline: 7/15 (priority date; rolling processing). Application fee: $35 ($75 for international students). • Dr. Claudette Ligon, Chairperson, 713-313-7775.

Trinity College, School of Professional Studies, Programs in Education, Washington, DC 20017-1094. Offerings include curriculum and instruction (M Ed), with options in literacy, urban learner. Faculty: 6 full-time (5 women), 18 part-time (13 women). *Application deadline:* rolling. *Application fee:* $35. *Tuition:* $460 per credit hour. • Sr. Rosemarie Bosler, Division Chair, 202-884-9557. Application contact: Karen Goodwin, Director of Graduate Admissions, 202-884-9400. Fax: 202-884-9229.

University of Massachusetts Boston, Graduate College of Education, School Organization, Curriculum and Instruction Department, Program in Education, Track in Urban School Leadership, Boston, MA 02125-3393. Awards Ed D. Students: 31 part-time (20 women); includes 15 minority (10 African Americans, 3 Asian Americans, 2 Hispanics), 1 international. *Degree requirements:* Dissertation, comprehensive exams required, foreign language not required. *Entrance requirements:* GRE General Test or MAT, minimum GPA of 2.75. Application deadline: 3/1. Application fee: $25 ($35 for international students). *Expenses:* Tuition $2640 per year full-time, $110 per credit hour for state residents; $8930 per year full-time, $373 per credit part-time for nonresidents. Fees $2650 per year full-time, $420 per semester (minimum) part-time for state residents; $2736 per year full-time, $420 per semester (minimum) part-time for nonresidents. *Financial aid:* In 1997–98, 1 research assistantship averaging $225 per month and totaling $2,000 was awarded; teaching assistantships, administrative assistantships also available. Financial aid application deadline: 3/1; applicants required to submit FAFSA. • Dr. Joseph Check, Program Coordinator, 617-287-7601. Application contact: Lisa Lavely, Director of Graduate Admissions and Records, 617-287-6400. Fax: 617-287-6236.

University of Nebraska at Omaha, College of Education, Department of Teacher Education, Program in Urban Education, Omaha, NE 68182. Awards MS. Accredited by NCATE. Part-time and evening/weekend programs available. Students: 6 full-time (3 women), 13 part-time (6 women); includes 7 minority (6 African Americans, 1 Asian American). Average age 34. In 1997, 4 degrees awarded. *Degree requirements:* Comprehensive exam required, foreign language and thesis not required. *Entrance requirements:* GRE General Test (minimum combined score of 840) or MAT (minimum score 35), minimum GPA of 3.0. Application deadline: 7/1 (priority date; rolling processing; 12/1 for spring admission). Application fee: $35. *Expenses:* Tuition $1670 per year full-time, $94 per credit hour part-time for state residents; $4082 per year full-time, $227 per credit hour part-time for nonresidents. Fees $302 per year full-time, $108 per semester (minimum) part-time. *Financial aid:* 7 students received aid; Federal Work-Study, institutionally sponsored loans available. Aid available to part-time students. Financial aid application deadline: 3/1; applicants required to submit FAFSA. • Dr. John Langan, Chairperson, Department of Teacher Education, 402-554-2717.

University of Wisconsin–Milwaukee, School of Education, Department of Curriculum and Instruction, Milwaukee, WI 53201-0413. Offerings include teaching in an urban setting (MS). Offered jointly with University of Wisconsin–Green Bay. Department faculty: 28 full-time (17 women). *Degree requirements:* Thesis or alternative required, foreign language not required. *Application deadline:* 1/1 (priority date; rolling processing; 9/1 for spring admission). *Application fee:* $45 ($75 for international students). *Tuition:* $4996 per year full-time, $1030 per semester (minimum) part-time for state residents; $15,216 per year full-time, $2947 per semester (minimum) part-time for nonresidents. • Linda Post, Chair, 414-229-4884.

University of Wisconsin–Milwaukee, School of Education, Program in Urban Education, Milwaukee, WI 53201-0413. Awards PhD. Students: 29 full-time (22 women), 115 part-time (77 women); includes 33 minority (24 African Americans, 1 Asian American, 6 Hispanics, 2 Native Americans), 1 international. 69 applicants, 45% accepted. In 1997, 9 degrees awarded. *Degree requirements:* Dissertation required, foreign language not required. *Entrance requirements:* GRE General Test. Application deadline: 1/1 (priority date; rolling processing; 9/1 for spring admission). Application fee: $45 ($75 for international students). *Tuition:* $4996 per year full-time, $1030 per semester (minimum) part-time for state residents; $15,216 per year full-time, $2947 per semester (minimum) part-time for nonresidents. *Financial aid:* In 1997–98, 1 fellowship, 2 research assistantships, 5 teaching assistantships, 9 project assistantships were awarded; career-related internships or fieldwork also available. Aid available to part-time students. Financial aid application deadline: 4/15. • Dr. Diane Pollard, Representative, 414-229-4729.

Virginia Commonwealth University, School of Education, Program in Urban Services, Richmond, VA 23284-9005. Awards PhD. Accredited by NCATE. Part-time programs available. Faculty: 12 full-time, 13 part-time. Students: 16 full-time (12 women), 72 part-time (48 women); includes 21 minority (18 African Americans, 2 Asian Americans, 1 Hispanic), 3 international. Average age 42. 35 applicants, 71% accepted. In 1997, 15 degrees awarded. *Degree requirements:* Dissertation required, foreign language not required. *Entrance requirements:* GRE, interview, master's degree. Application deadline: 3/15 (10/15 for spring admission). Application fee: $30 ($0 for international students). *Tuition:* $4960 per year full-time, $257 per credit part-time for state residents; $12,652 per year full-time, $684 per credit part-time for nonresidents. *Financial aid:* Fellowships, research assistantships, Federal Work-Study, institutionally sponsored loans, and career-related internships or fieldwork available. Financial aid application deadline: 3/1. • Dr. Michael D. Davis, Coordinator, 804-828-6530. Fax: 804-828-1323. E-mail: mddavis@vcu.edu.

Cross-Discipline Announcement

Washington University in St. Louis, Graduate School of Arts and Sciences, Department of Speech and Hearing, St. Louis, MO 63130-4899.

MS program in education of the hearing-impaired. NCATE and CED certified. Students take all classes and practicum at Central Institute for the Deaf, with 2 full semesters of practice teaching. Tuition scholarships are available for qualified students who are accepted into the graduate program. See in-depth program description in the Allied Health section of this volume.

NORTHWESTERN UNIVERSITY

Graduate Programs in Learning Disabilities

Programs of Study

The program in the field of learning disabilities is one of three programs in the Department of Communication Sciences and Disorders. In recent years, cognitive and linguistic disturbances among atypical learners have emerged as an important field of study for professionals in many disciplines, including psychology, special education, linguistics, neurology, and neuropsychology. The field of learning disabilities is an area of special education that has been enhanced by interdisciplinary studies and collaborative research. By definition, individuals with learning disabilities have no primary sensory, intellectual, or emotional deficits, but there is a discrepancy between their potential and their achievement in one or more such areas as spoken language, reading, written language, mathematics, and nonverbal functions. These disturbances are related to deficits in certain processes, such as attention, perception, memory, symbolization, and conceptualization.

Graduate study at Northwestern involves courses in both normal and atypical development, clinical investigations, and research pertaining to the nature of learning disabilities. The faculty is interdisciplinary; faculty members have backgrounds in such areas as learning disabilities; developmental, cognitive, and clinical psychology; neuropsychology; speech and language pathology; and linguistics. In addition, faculty members from other departments serve as cognate professors for students enrolled in learning disabilities programs.

The one-year M.A. program and the first year of the Ph.D. program include theoretical, research, and clinical courses. The second year of the doctoral program involves study of advanced theories in learning, language, cognition, statistics, and research design as well as a research apprenticeship. The third year is devoted to completion of the dissertation. Opportunities for formal interdisciplinary study are also available. A joint M.A. degree is offered in conjunction with the program in speech and language pathology. Ph.D. students may also opt to become affiliated with the interdepartmental Program on Language and Cognition.

Graduates of the M.A. program are typically employed in roles involving the diagnosis and remediation of learning-disabled students in schools, clinics, and hospitals. Advanced M.A. students assume consultant and supervisory roles. Graduates of the doctoral program are employed in universities; research centers; medical schools; local, state, and federal educational agencies; and private medical and educational facilities.

Research Facilities

The Learning Disabilities Center on Northwestern's Evanston campus has extensive facilities for diagnostic and remedial work as well as research. Children, adolescents, and young adults come to this campus for two days of comprehensive psychoeducational studies. Laboratories for individual faculty research are on the Evanston campus. There are opportunities for collaborative research with professionals on both the Evanston and Chicago campuses, in hospitals, and in local public and private schools. An outstanding computing center is located on the Evanston campus. Excellent libraries are available on both campuses and in the Chicago area.

Financial Aid

Various types of financial aid are offered, including fellowships and scholarships from the University, assistantships, and special departmental awards. Funding from some private foundations is also available.

Cost of Study

Tuition and fees in 1998–99 are $7747 per quarter. After the Ph.D. student is admitted to candidacy, these costs are reduced. In 1998–99, the reduced rate is $3207 per quarter.

Living and Housing Costs

The University has a limited number of living units for single and married students on the Chicago and Evanston campuses. University housing rates range from $502 to $875 per month. Many students find satisfactory accommodations in private homes and in apartments in the vicinities of the campuses; rents vary widely.

Student Group

Students from many disciplines are encouraged to apply, since the faculty and student body welcome interdisciplinary discussions and research. Students in the learning disabilities program work closely with those in the audiology and hearing sciences and the speech and language pathology programs, the other programs offered within the Department of Communicative Sciences and Disorders.

Location

The main campus of the University is located in Evanston, on the shore of Lake Michigan. The Chicago campus, about 12 miles south of Evanston, is also on the lakeshore near the center of the business district, one of Chicago's most attractive areas. An immense variety of cultural, social, and recreational activities are to be found on and near both campuses.

The University

Northwestern University, one of the nation's largest private universities, was founded in 1851. The College of Arts and Sciences; the Technological Institute; the Schools of Education and Social Policy, Journalism, Music, and Speech; and the Graduate School of Management are located on the Evanston campus. The Medical and Dental Schools and the School of Law are located on the Chicago campus.

Applying

Applications are solicited from highly qualified students from many fields of study. The program typically admits students at the beginning of the fall term. Although there is no deadline for the receipt of applications, students are urged to apply early in the fall. In order to be eligible for University scholarships and fellowships, applications should be completed as early as possible and no later than March 15. The General Test of the Graduate Record Examinations is required. Application forms may be obtained from the Northwestern University Graduate School in Evanston or from the program head.

Correspondence and Information

C. Addison Stone, Professor and Program Head
Graduate Programs in Learning Disabilities
Frances Searle Building
Northwestern University
2299 North Campus Drive
Evanston, Illinois 60208-3560
Telephone: 847-491-3183
E-mail: a-stone@nwu.edu

Northwestern University

THE DEPARTMENT FACULTY AND THEIR RESEARCH

Margaret Aylesworth, M.A., Northwestern. Cerebral palsy, alternative systems of communication.
Elaine Brown-Grant (Emerita), M.A., Northwestern. Clinical supervision.
Gerald Canter (Emeritus), Ph.D., Northwestern. Neurology of speech and language.
Joanne Carlisle, Ph.D., Connecticut. Reading and written language.
Mary Ann Cheatham, Ph.D., Northwestern. Physiology of the cochlea.
Peter Dallos, Ph.D., Northwestern. Biophysics and physiology of the cochlea.
Hilda Fisher (Emerita), Ph.D., LSU. Vocal physiology and pathologies.
Kimberly Fisher, Ph.D., Oklahoma. Voice disorders, motor speech disorders.
Dean C. Garstecki, Chairman; Ph.D., Illinois at Urbana–Champaign. Hearing loss and aging.
Hugo H. Gregory (Emeritus), Ph.D., Northwestern. Speech fluency and stuttering.
Doris J. Johnson, Ph.D., Northwestern. Relationship between auditory disorders and higher levels of learning.
Dawn B. Koch, Ph.D., Northwestern. Speech processing and cochlea implantation.
Nina Kraus, Ph.D., Northwestern. Evoked potentials.
Charles R. Larson, Ph.D., Washington (Seattle). Motor speech control.
Jerilyn Ann Logemann, Ph.D., Northwestern. Structural anomalies of the vocal tract, dysphagia.
Karla McGregor, Ph.D., Purdue. Child language disorders.
Mario A. Ruggero, Ph.D., Chicago. Biophysics and physiology of the cochlea.
David Rutherford, Ph.D., Northwestern. Speech perception and production, word retrieval skills.
Jonathan Siegel, Ph.D., Washington (St. Louis). Biophysics and physiology of the cochlea.
Bruce Smith, Ph.D., Texas at Austin. Phonological and phonetic development.
Laszlo Stein, Ph.D., Northwestern. Pediatric audiology.
C. Addison Stone, Ph.D., Chicago. Cognitive development in normal and exceptional populations, language-learning disabilities.
Tom W. Tillman (Emeritus), Ph.D., Northwestern. Speech intelligibility testing.
Cynthia Thompson, Ph.D., Kansas. Neurological disorders of language and cognition.
Donna Whitlon, Ph.D., Wisconsin–Madison. Development of the cochlea and its innervation.
Laura Ann Wilber, Ph.D., Northwestern. Pediatric audiology, audiologic instrumentation.
Beverly Wright, Ph.D., Texas at Austin. Psychoacoustics.
Yi Xu, Ph.D., Connecticut. Speech acoustics, speech perception.
Steven Zecker, Ph.D., Wayne State. Lexical coding and reading disorders, attention deficits.

Lecturers and Clinical Faculty

Margaret Beeman, Ph.D., Northwestern. Bilingualism, early literacy.
Frances Block, M.A., Northwestern. Supervision, language disorders in older children.
Janet Bornhoeft, M.A., Northwestern. Supervision, learning disabilities.
Pamela Fiebig, M.A., Northwestern. Audiologic assessment and rehabilitation of adults and children.
Diane Hill, M.A., Northwestern. Stuttering problems in preschool children, differential evaluation and treatment.
Cathy Lazarus, M.A., Northwestern. Swallowing disorders, speech problems after treatment of head and neck cancer.
Monica Maso, M.A., Wisconsin. Habilitation/rehabilitation of children with impaired hearing.
Susan Mulhern, M.A., Northwestern. Articulation and language problems in children.
Barbara Nathanson, M.S., Illinois. Developmental delay, pediatric neurological disorders, preschool speech and language disorders.
Ann Oehring, M.A., Northwestern. Adult neurological disorders of speech and language.
Melinda Rice, B.A., Northwestern. Educational intervention, reading comprehension.
Jane Rosenberg, Ph.D., Northwestern. Educational programs in learning disabilities.
Amy Soifer, M.A., Northwestern. Swallowing, speech and language disorders.
Carrie Stangl, M.S., Wisconsin. Dysphagia, speech, language disorders after neurologic injury.
Sharon Veis, M.A., Northwestern. Swallowing disorders, language disorders after neurosurgery.

Adjunct Faculty

Martha Burns, Ph.D., Northwestern. Aphasia and adult neurological disorders.
David Hanson, M.D., Washington (Seattle). Physiology and objective measurement of laryngeal function and dysfunction.
Michael McCanna, Ph.D., DePaul. Behavior therapy, assessment of behavior disorders and learning disabilities, children's social skill development, parenting skills.
Harold Pelzer, M.D., Northwestern. Treatment for head and neck cancer.

Section 25
Subject Areas

This section contains directories of institutions offering graduate work in the following areas of education: agricultural, art, business, computer, counselor, English, foreign languages, health, home economics, mathematics, music, reading, religious, science, social sciences, and vocational and technical, followed by in-depth entries submitted by institutions that chose to prepare detailed program descriptions. Additional information about programs listed in the directories but not augmented by an in-depth entry may be obtained by writing directly to the dean of a graduate school or chair of a department at the address given in the directory.

For programs offering related work, see also in this book Administration, Instruction, and Theory; Business Administration and Management; Education; Health-Related Professions; Instructional Levels; Leisure Studies and Recreation; Physical Education and Kinesiology; and Special Focus. In Book 2, see Art and Art History; Home Economics and Family Studies; Language and Literature; Performing Arts; Psychology and Counseling (School Psychology); Public, Regional, and Industrial Affairs (Urban Studies); Religious Studies; and Social Sciences; in Book 4, see Mathematical Sciences; and in Book 5, see Computer Science and Information Technology.

CONTENTS

Program Directories

Cross-Discipline Announcements

In-Depth Descriptions

See also:

Agricultural Education

Alcorn State University, School of Psychology and Education, Lorman, MS 39096-9402. Offerings include agricultural education (MS Ed). Accredited by NCATE. *Degree requirements:* Thesis optional, foreign language not required. *Application deadline:* 7/1 (priority date; rolling processing; 12/1 for spring admission). *Application fee:* $10. *Tuition:* $2470 per year full-time, $378 per semester (minimum) part-time for state residents; $5331 per year full-time, $855 per semester (minimum) part-time for nonresidents.

Clemson University, College of Agriculture, Forestry and Life Sciences, School of Applied Science and Agribusiness, Faculty of Agricultural Education, Clemson, SC 29634. Awards M Ag Ed. Accredited by NCATE. Part-time programs available. Students: 7 full-time (0 women), 7 part-time (1 woman); includes 1 minority (African American). Average age 28. 6 applicants, 100% accepted. In 1997, 2 degrees awarded (100% found work related to degree). *Average time to degree:* master's–1 year full-time. *Entrance requirements:* GRE General Test, TOEFL. Application deadline: 6/1. Application fee: $35. *Expenses:* Tuition $3154 per year full-time, $130 per credit hour part-time for state residents; $6452 per year full-time, $264 per credit hour part-time for nonresidents. Fees $190 per year. *Financial aid:* Teaching assistantships, grants, Federal Work-Study, institutionally sponsored loans, and career-related internships or fieldwork available. Financial aid application deadline: 4/1. *Faculty research:* Adaption and change, curriculum assessment and innovation, career development, adult and extension education, technology transfer. • Dr. Curtis D. White, Interim Chair, 864-656-3300. Fax: 864-656-5675. E-mail: cdwhite@clemson.edu.

Cornell University, Graduate Fields of Agriculture and Life Sciences, Field of Education, Ithaca, NY 14853-0001. Offerings include agricultural education (MAT); agricultural, extension, and adult education (MPS, MS, PhD). Terminal master's awarded for partial completion of doctoral program. Faculty: 26 full-time. *Degree requirements:* For master's, thesis (MS) required, foreign language not required; for doctorate, dissertation required, foreign language not required. *Entrance requirements:* GRE General Test or MAT, TOEFL. Application deadline: 5/1. Application fee: $65. Electronic applications accepted. • Director of Graduate Studies, 607-255-4278. Application contact: Graduate Field Assistant, 607-255-4278. E-mail: edgrfld@cornell.edu.

Eastern Kentucky University, College of Education, Department of Curriculum and Instruction, Program in Secondary and Higher Education, Richmond, KY 40475-3101. Offerings include agricultural education (MA Ed). Accredited by NCATE. *Entrance requirements:* GRE General Test, minimum GPA of 2.5. Application fee: $0. *Tuition:* $2390 per year full-time, $133 per credit hour part-time for state residents; $6630 per year full-time, $365 per credit hour part-time for nonresidents. • Dr. Imogene Ramsey, Chair, Department of Curriculum and Instruction, 606-622-2154.

Florida Agricultural and Mechanical University, Division of Graduate Studies, Research, and Continuing Education, College of Engineering Science, Technology, and Agriculture, Division of Agricultural Sciences, Tallahassee, FL 32307-3200. Offers program in agricultural and extension education (M Ed, MS Ed). Students: 15 (5 women); includes 8 minority (6 African Americans, 1 Asian American, 1 Hispanic). In 1997, 1 degree awarded. *Degree requirements:* Thesis required, foreign language not required. *Entrance requirements:* GRE General Test (minimum combined score of 1000), minimum GPA of 3.0. Application deadline: 5/13. Application fee: $20. *Expenses:* Tuition $140 per credit hour for state residents; $484 per credit hour for nonresidents. Fees $130 per year. *Financial aid:* Application deadline 2/15. • Dr. Robert Bradford, Dean, College of Engineering Science, Technology, and Agriculture, 850-561-2644. Fax: 850-561-2794.

Iowa State University of Science and Technology, College of Agriculture, Department of Agricultural Education and Studies, Ames, IA 50011. Awards MS, PhD. Faculty: 12 full-time. Students: 11 full-time (6 women), 25 part-time (6 women); includes 4 minority (all African Americans), 9 international. 21 applicants, 62% accepted. In 1997, 2 master's, 4 doctorates awarded. *Degree requirements:* For master's, thesis or alternative; for doctorate, dissertation. *Entrance requirements:* TOEFL, GRE General Test, sample of written work. Application deadline: 6/15 (priority date; rolling processing; 11/15 for spring admission). Application fee: $20 ($30 for international students). *Expenses:* Tuition $3166 per year full-time, $176 per credit part-time for state residents; $9324 per year full-time, $518 per credit part-time for nonresidents. Fees $200 per year. *Financial aid:* In 1997–98, 14 research assistantships (3 to first-year students), 13 teaching assistantships (2 to first-year students), 2 scholarships (1 to a first-year student) were awarded; fellowships also available. • Dr. Richard I. Carter, Head, 515-294-5904. E-mail: agedsinfo@iastate.edu. Application contact: Robert A. Martin, 515-294-0896. E-mail: agedsinfo@iastate.edu.

Louisiana State University and Agricultural and Mechanical College, College of Agriculture, School of Vocational Education, Baton Rouge, LA 70803. Offerings include vocational agriculture education (MS, PhD). Terminal master's awarded for partial completion of doctoral program. School faculty: 11 full-time (3 women). *Degree requirements:* For master's, thesis required (for some programs), foreign language not required; for doctorate, dissertation required, foreign language not required. *Entrance requirements:* GRE General Test (minimum combined score of 1000), minimum GPA of 3.0. Application deadline: 1/25 (priority date; rolling processing). Application fee: $25. *Tuition:* $2736 per year full-time, $285 per semester (minimum) part-time for state residents; $6636 per year full-time, $460 per semester (minimum) part-time for nonresidents. • Dr. Michael F. Burnett, Director, 504-388-5748.

Michigan State University, College of Agriculture and Natural Resources, Department of Agricultural and Extension Education, East Lansing, MI 48824-1020. Offers programs in agricultural education (MS, PhD), extension education (MS, PhD). Part-time and evening/weekend programs available. Postbaccalaureate distance learning degree programs offered (minimal on-campus study). Faculty: 6 (0 women). Students: 41 (20 women); includes 9 minority (7 African Americans, 1 Asian American, 1 Hispanic), 6 international. Average age 29. In 1997, 14 master's, 2 doctorates awarded. *Degree requirements:* For doctorate, dissertation. *Entrance requirements:* GRE. Application deadline: rolling. Application fee: $30 ($40 for international students). *Expenses:* Tuition $4609 per year full-time, $223 per credit hour (minimum) part-time for state residents; $8704 per year full-time, $450 per credit hour (minimum) part-time for nonresidents. Fees $576 per year full-time, $476 per year part-time. *Financial aid:* Teaching assistantships, Federal Work-Study, institutionally sponsored loans available. Aid available to part-time students. *Faculty research:* Evaluative research, distance learning/leadership development, agriscience curriculum development. Total annual research expenditures: $78,000. • Dr. Kirk L. Heinze, Interim Chairperson, 517-355-6580. Application contact: Mary Pierce, Departmental Secretary/Graduate Records, 517-355-6580. Fax: 517-353-4981. E-mail: piercem@pilot.msu.edu.

Mississippi State University, College of Agriculture and Life Sciences, Department of Agriculture Education and Experimental Statistics, Mississippi State, MS 39762. Offers programs in agriculture and extension education (ME Ed), agriculture education and experimental statistics (MS, Ed D, PhD, Ed S). One or more programs accredited by NCATE. MS, Ed D, PhD, Ed S offered jointly with the College of Education. Faculty: 4 full-time (1 woman), 4 part-time (0 women), 5.54 FTE. Students: 3 full-time (all women), 4 part-time (3 women). Average age 28. In 1997, 8 master's awarded. Terminal master's awarded for partial completion of doctoral program. *Degree requirements:* For master's, thesis (for some programs), comprehensive oral or written exam required, foreign language not required; for doctorate, dissertation, comprehensive oral or written exam; for Ed S, special project. *Entrance requirements:* For master's, minimum QPA of 2.75, GRE General Test (minimum combined score of 800), or MAT (minimum score 30); for doctorate, minimum QPA of 3.4; for Ed S, minimum QPA of 3.0. Application deadline: 7/1 (priority date; rolling processing; 11/1 for spring admission). Application fee: $0 ($25 for international students). *Tuition:* $3017 per year full-time, $168 per credit hour part-time for state residents; $6119 per year full-time, $340 per credit hour part-time for nonresidents. *Financial aid:* In 1997–98, 4 students received aid, including 4 research assistantships (2 to first-year students) averaging $900 per month and totaling $30,000; Federal Work-Study and career-related internships or fieldwork also available. Aid available to part-time students. Financial aid application deadline: 4/1. *Faculty research:* Animal welfare, agriscience, information technology, learning styles, problem solving. Total annual research expenditures: $15,000. • Dr. Walter Taylor, Head, 601-325-3326. E-mail: wtaylor@ra.msstate.edu. Application contact: Dr. Michael Newman, Graduate Coordinator, 601-325-3326. Fax: 601-325-7832. E-mail: men1@ra.msstate.edu.

New Mexico State University, College of Agriculture and Home Economics, Department of Agriculture and Extension Education, Las Cruces, NM 88003-8001. Awards MA. Accredited by NCATE. Part-time programs available. Faculty: 7 full-time (2 women). Students: 14 full-time (9 women), 10 part-time (6 women); includes 3 minority (all Hispanics). Average age 32. 5 applicants, 80% accepted. In 1997, 9 degrees awarded. *Degree requirements:* Thesis or alternative required, foreign language not required. *Application deadline:* 7/1 (priority date; rolling processing; 11/1 for spring admission). *Application fee:* $15 ($35 for international students). Electronic applications accepted. *Tuition:* $2514 per year full-time, $105 per credit hour part-time for state residents; $7848 per year full-time, $327 per credit hour part-time for nonresidents. *Financial aid:* Research assistantships, teaching assistantships, Federal Work-Study, and career-related internships or fieldwork available. Aid available to part-time students. Financial aid application deadline: 3/1. *Faculty research:* Youth leadership development, learning styles and cognition, adult organizations in agricultural education, technology education. • Dr. Thomas J. Dormody, Head, 505-646-4511. Fax: 505-646-4082. E-mail: tdormody@nmsu.edu.

North Carolina Agricultural and Technical State University, Graduate School, School of Agriculture, Department of Agricultural Education, Economics, and Rural Sociology, Greensboro, NC 27411. Offers programs in agricultural economics (MS), agricultural education (MS). One or more programs accredited by NCATE. Part-time and evening/weekend programs available. Faculty: 8 full-time (0 women). Students: 21 full-time (10 women), 19 part-time (9 women); includes 36 minority (35 African Americans, 1 Asian American), 2 international. Average age 33. 22 applicants, 86% accepted. In 1997, 10 degrees awarded. *Degree requirements:* Thesis or alternative, comprehensive exam, qualifying exam required, foreign language not required. *Entrance requirements:* GRE General Test, minimum GPA of 3.0. Application deadline: 6/1 (priority date; rolling processing; 12/1 for spring admission). Application fee: $35. *Tuition:* $1662 per year full-time, $272 per semester (minimum) part-time for state residents; $8790 per year full-time, $2054 per semester (minimum) part-time for nonresidents. *Financial aid:* Fellowships, research assistantships, teaching assistantships, and career-related internships or fieldwork available. Financial aid application deadline: 6/1. *Faculty research:* Aid for small farmers, agricultural technology resources, labor force mobility, agrology. • Dr. Alton Thompson, Chairperson, 336-334-7943. Fax: 336-334-7793. E-mail: altont@garfield.ncat.edu.

North Carolina State University, College of Agriculture and Life Sciences, Department of Agricultural and Extension Education, Raleigh, NC 27695. Awards MS. Accredited by NCATE. Faculty: 10 full-time (2 women), 2 part-time (0 women). Students: 7 full-time (3 women), 18 part-time (9 women); includes 1 minority (African American). Average age 34. 15 applicants, 80% accepted. In 1997, 11 degrees awarded. *Entrance requirements:* GRE. Application fee: $45. *Tuition:* $2370 per year full-time, $517 per semester (minimum) part-time for state residents; $11,536 per year full-time, $2809 per semester (minimum) part-time for nonresidents. *Financial aid:* In 1997–98, 1 research assistantship (to a first-year student) averaging $1,008 per month and totaling $4,537, 1 teaching assistantship (to a first-year student) averaging $1,120 per month and totaling $5,041 were awarded. *Faculty research:* Instructional methodology, program and curriculum development, evaluation, leadership development, accountability. Total annual research expenditures: $1.884 million. • Dr. Ronald W. Shearon, Head, 919-515-2707. Fax: 919-515-1965. E-mail: rshearon@ricks.ces.ncsu.edu. Application contact: Dr. Gary E. Moore, Director of Graduate Programs, 919-515-1756. Fax: 919-515-1956. E-mail: gary_moore@ncsu.edu/.

North Carolina State University, College of Education and Psychology, Department of Mathematics, Science, and Technology Education, Program in Occupational Education, Raleigh, NC 27695. Offerings include agricultural education (M Ed, MS, CAGS). Accredited by NCATE. Program faculty: 1 full-time (0 women), 7 part-time (0 women). *Degree requirements:* For master's, oral exam required, foreign language not required. *Entrance requirements:* For master's, GRE General Test or MAT, minimum GPA of 3.0 in major; for CAGS, GRE General Test, MAT, minimum GPA of 3.0 in major. Application deadline: 4/15 (priority date; rolling processing; 11/15 for spring admission). Application fee: $45. *Tuition:* $2370 per year full-time, $517 per semester (minimum) part-time for state residents; $11,536 per year full-time, $2809 per semester (minimum) part-time for nonresidents. • Dr. Robert E. Wenig, Director of Graduate Programs, 919-515-1742. Fax: 919-515-6892. E-mail: wenig@poe.coe.ncsu.edu. Application contact: Linda Trogdon, Graduate Secretary, 919-515-1740. Fax: 919-515-7634. E-mail: trogdon@poe.coe.ncsu.edu.

North Dakota State University, College of Human Development and Education, School of Education, Program in Agricultural Education, Fargo, ND 58105. Offers agricultural education (M Ed, MS), agricultural extension education (MS). Accredited by NCATE. Part-time programs available. Faculty: 1 part-time (0 women). Students: 1 full-time (0 women), 6 part-time (0 women). Average age 32. 6 applicants, 100% accepted. In 1997, 9 degrees awarded (100% found work related to degree). *Degree requirements:* Thesis or alternative required, foreign language not required. *Entrance requirements:* MAT, TOEFL (minimum score 525). Application deadline: rolling. Application fee: $25. *Tuition:* $2572 per year full-time, $107 per credit part-time for state residents; $6868 per year full-time, $286 per credit part-time for nonresidents. *Financial aid:* Research assistantships, full tuition waivers, Federal Work-Study, institutionally sponsored loans, and career-related internships or fieldwork available. Financial aid application deadline: 4/15. *Faculty research:* Vocational and cooperative extension education, rural leadership, rural education, international extension. • Dr. James Wigtil, Education Coordinator, 701-231-7104. Fax: 701-231-7416. Application contact: Dr. Diane Jackman, Assistant Professor, 701-231-7102. Fax: 701-231-9685. E-mail: jackman@plains.nodak.edu.

Northwest Missouri State University, College of Arts and Sciences, Department of Agriculture, 800 University Drive, Maryville, MO 64468-6001. Offerings include teaching secondary agriculture education (MS Ed). Department faculty: 11 full-time (1 woman). *Application deadline:* rolling. *Application fee:* $0 ($50 for international students). *Expenses:* Tuition $113 per credit hour for state residents; $197 per credit hour for nonresidents. Fees $3 per credit hour. • Dr. Arley Larson, Chairperson, 816-562-1161. Application contact: Dr. Frances Shipley, Dean of Graduate School, 816-562-1145. E-mail: gradsch@acad.nwmissouri.edu.

The Ohio State University, College of Food, Agricultural, and Environmental Sciences, Department of Agricultural Education, Columbus, OH 43210. Offers programs in agricultural education (MS, PhD), vocational education (PhD). Faculty: 29. Students: 47 full-time (21 women), 53 part-time (31 women); includes 6 minority (4 African Americans, 2 Hispanics), 14 international. 50 applicants, 62% accepted. In 1997, 21 master's, 6 doctorates awarded. *Degree requirements:* For master's, thesis optional, foreign language not required; for doctorate, dissertation required, foreign language not required. *Application deadline:* 8/15 (rolling processing). *Application fee:* $30 ($40 for international students). *Tuition:* $5472 per year full-time, $554 per quarter (minimum) part-time for state residents; $14,172 per year full-time, $1424 per quarter (minimum) part-time for nonresidents. *Financial aid:* Fellowships, research assistantships, teaching assistantships, administrative assistantships, Federal Work-Study, institutionally sponsored loans available. Aid available to part-time students. • N. L. McCaslin, Chairman, 614-292-6321. Fax: 614-292-7007. E-mail: mccaslin.2@osu.edu.

Oklahoma State University, College of Agricultural Sciences and Natural Resources, Department of Agricultural Education, Communication and 4H, Stillwater, OK 74078. Awards M Ag,

MS, Ed D, PhD. Faculty: 11 full-time (3 women). Students: 33 full-time (15 women), 33 part-time (7 women); includes 7 minority (2 African Americans, 1 Hispanic, 4 Native Americans), 5 international. Average age 33. In 1997, 16 master's, 7 doctorates awarded. *Degree requirements:* For doctorate, dissertation. *Entrance requirements:* TOEFL (minimum score 550). Application deadline: 7/1 (priority date). Application fee: $25. *Financial aid:* In 1997–98, 10 students received aid, including 6 research assistantships (3 to first-year students) totaling $64,962, 3 teaching assistantships (2 to first-year students) totaling $35,040; partial tuition waivers, Federal Work-Study, and career-related internships or fieldwork also available. Aid available to part-time students. Financial aid application deadline: 3/1. • Dr. James Leising, Head, 405-744-5129.

Oregon State University, Graduate School, College of Agricultural Sciences, Department of Agricultural Education and General Agriculture, Corvallis, OR 97331. Offers programs in agricultural education (M Agr, MAIS, MAT, MS), agriculture (M Agr). Part-time programs available. Faculty: 2 full-time (both women). Students: 0. In 1997, 8 degrees awarded. *Degree requirements:* Thesis (MS), minimum GPA of 3.0 required, foreign language not required. *Entrance requirements:* GRE General Test, TOEFL (minimum score 550), minimum GPA of 3.0 in last 90 hours. Application deadline: rolling. Application fee: $50. *Tuition:* $6207 per year full-time, $810 per quarter (minimum) part-time for state residents; $10,551 per year full-time, $1293 per quarter (minimum) part-time for nonresidents. *Financial aid:* Fellowships, research assistantships, teaching assistantships, Federal Work-Study, institutionally sponsored loans, and career-related internships or fieldwork available. Aid available to part-time students. Financial aid application deadline: 2/1. *Faculty research:* Curriculum development and vocational education program evaluation, agricultural extension education. • Dr. Richard L. Cole, Head, 541-737-2661.

Pennsylvania State University University Park Campus, College of Agricultural Sciences, Department of Extension and Agricultural Education, Program in Agricultural Education, University Park, PA 16802-1503. Awards M Ed, MS, D Ed, PhD. Accredited by NCATE. Students: 15 full-time (7 women), 7 part-time (3 women). In 1997, 4 master's, 9 doctorates awarded. *Entrance requirements:* GRE General Test. Application fee: $40. *Expenses:* Tuition $6534 per year full-time, $276 per credit part-time for state residents; $13,460 per year full-time, $561 per credit part-time for nonresidents. Fees $252 per year (minimum) full-time, $43 per semester (minimum) part-time. • Dr. Edgar P. Yoder, Chair, 814-865-1688.

Pennsylvania State University University Park Campus, College of Agricultural Sciences, Department of Extension and Agricultural Education, Program in Extension Education, University Park, PA 16802-1503. Awards M Agr, M Ed. Students: 1 full-time (0 women), 1 part-time (0 women). *Entrance requirements:* GRE General Test. Application fee: $40. *Expenses:* Tuition $6534 per year full-time, $276 per credit part-time for state residents; $13,460 per year full-time, $561 per credit part-time for nonresidents. Fees $252 per year (minimum) full-time, $43 per semester (minimum) part-time. • Dr. Edgar P. Yoder, Chair, 814-865-1688.

Purdue University, School of Education, Department of Curriculum and Instruction, West Lafayette, IN 47907. Offerings include agricultural and extension education (PhD, Ed S), agriculture and extension education (MS Ed). One or more programs accredited by NCATE. Department faculty: 34 full-time (15 women), 3 part-time (1 woman). *Degree requirements:* For master's, thesis optional; for doctorate, dissertation, oral and written exams; for Ed S, oral presentation, project required, thesis not required. *Entrance requirements:* For master's, TOEFL (minimum score 550), minimum B average; for doctorate, GRE General Test (minimum score 500 on each section), TOEFL (minimum score 550); for Ed S, minimum B average. Application deadline: 1/15 (priority date; 9/15 for spring admission). Application fee: $30. Electronic applications accepted. *Tuition:* $3500 per year full-time, $126 per credit hour part-time for state residents; $11,720 per year full-time, $387 per credit hour part-time for nonresidents. • Dr. J. L. Peters, Head, 765-494-9172. Fax: 765-496-1622. E-mail: peters@purdue.edu. Application contact: Christine Larsen, Coordinator of Graduate Studies, 765-494-2345. Fax: 765-494-5832. E-mail: gradoffice@soe.purdue.edu.

Sam Houston State University, College of Education and Applied Science, Department of Agricultural Sciences and Vocational Education, Program in Agricultural Education, Huntsville, TX 77341. Awards M Ed. Accredited by NCATE. Part-time programs available. Students: 10 full-time (2 women), 14 part-time (1 woman); includes 1 international. Average age 29. In 1997, 8 degrees awarded (100% found work related to degree). *Degree requirements:* Thesis optional, foreign language not required. *Entrance requirements:* GRE General Test (minimum combined score of 800), minimum GPA of 2.5. Application deadline: 5/1. Application fee: $15. *Tuition:* $1810 per year full-time, $297 per semester (minimum) part-time for state residents; $6922 per year full-time, $924 per semester (minimum) part-time for nonresidents. *Financial aid:* Career-related internships or fieldwork available. Financial aid application deadline: 5/1. • Dr. Herbert Schumann, Coordinator, 409-294-1186. Fax: 409-294-1232. E-mail: agr_hbs@shsu.edu.

Southwest Texas State University, School of Applied Arts and Technology, Department of Agriculture Education, San Marcos, TX 78666. Awards M Ed. Part-time and evening/weekend programs available. Faculty: 2 full-time (0 women). Students: 5 full-time (3 women), 6 part-time (2 women). Average age 33. In 1997, 1 degree awarded. *Degree requirements:* Thesis (for some programs), comprehensive exam required, foreign language not required. *Entrance requirements:* GRE General Test (minimum combined score of 900), TOEFL (minimum score 550), minimum GPA of 2.75 in last 60 hours. Application deadline: 7/15 (priority date; rolling processing; 11/15 for spring admission). Application fee: $25 ($50 for international students). *Expenses:* Tuition $648 per year full-time, $120 per semester (minimum) part-time for state residents; $4500 per year full-time, $750 per semester (minimum) part-time for nonresidents. Fees $1264 per year full-time, $314 per semester (minimum) part-time. *Financial aid:* In 1997–98, 3 research assistantships (all to first-year students) averaging $650 per month and totaling $23,400 were awarded; Federal Work-Study, institutionally sponsored loans, and career-related internships or fieldwork also available. Aid available to part-time students. Financial aid application deadline: 4/1; applicants required to submit FAFSA. *Faculty research:* Computerized monitoring of tractor fuel efficiency, safety research, technical preparation program integration, internationalization of secondary curriculum, e-mail networking of secondary teachers. • Dr. Bob Davis Jr., Chair, 512-245-2130. E-mail: bd01@swt.edu. Application contact: Dr. Aditi Angirasa, Graduate Adviser, 512-245-2130. Fax: 512-245-3338. E-mail: aa05@swt.edu.

Stephen F. Austin State University, College of Education, Department of Agriculture, Nacogdoches, TX 75962. Awards MS. Accredited by NCATE. Faculty: 9 full-time (1 woman). Students: 12 full-time (3 women), 6 part-time (3 women); includes 1 minority (African American). 6 applicants, 100% accepted. In 1997, 11 degrees awarded (100% found work related to degree). *Degree requirements:* Thesis (for some programs), comprehensive exam required, foreign language not required. *Entrance requirements:* GRE General Test (minimum combined score of 1000), minimum GPA of 2.8 in last half of major, 2.5 overall. Application deadline: 8/1 (priority date; rolling processing; 12/15 for spring admission). Application fee: $0 ($25 for international students). *Tuition:* $1465 per year full-time, $263 per semester (minimum) part-time for state residents; $5299 per year full-time, $890 per semester (minimum) part-time for nonresidents. *Financial aid:* Research assistantships, teaching assistantships, Federal Work-Study, institutionally sponsored loans available. Financial aid application deadline: 3/1. *Faculty research:* Asian vegetables, soil fertility, animal breeding, animal nutrition. • Dr. Dale Perritt, Chair, 409-468-3705.

Texas A&M University, College of Agriculture and Life Sciences, Department of Agricultural Education, College Station, TX 77843. Awards M Ed, MS, Ed D, PhD. Accredited by NCATE. Faculty: 12 full-time (1 woman). Students: 40 (15 women); includes 5 minority (1 African American, 4 Hispanics), 1 international. Average age 29. 12 applicants, 83% accepted. In 1997, 15 master's, 3 doctorates awarded. *Degree requirements:* For master's, computer language required, thesis optional, foreign language not required; for doctorate, computer language, dissertation required, foreign language not required. *Entrance requirements:* GRE General Test, TOEFL. Application deadline: 4/15 (priority date; rolling processing; 11/1 for spring admission). Application fee: $35 ($75 for international students). *Financial aid:* Fellowships, research assistantships, teaching assistantships, and career-related internships or fieldwork available. • Glen Shinn, Head, 409-862-3012. E-mail: 9-shinn@tamu.edu. Application contact: Don Herring, Coordinator, 409-862-3006. Fax: 409-845-6296. E-mail: d-herring@tamum1.tamu.edu.

Texas A&M University–Commerce, College of Arts and Sciences, Department of Agriculture, Commerce, TX 75429-3011. Offerings include agricultural education (M Ed, MS). Department faculty: 5 full-time (0 women). *Degree requirements:* Thesis (for some programs), comprehensive exam. *Entrance requirements:* GRE General Test. Application deadline: rolling. Application fee: $0 ($25 for international students). *Tuition:* $2382 per year full-time, $343 per semester (minimum) part-time for state residents; $7518 per year full-time, $343 per semester (minimum) part-time for nonresidents. • Dr. Donald Cawthon, Head, 903-886-5358. Application contact: Pam Hammonds, Graduate Admissions Adviser, 903-886-5167. Fax: 903-886-5165.

Texas A&M University–Kingsville, College of Agriculture and Home Economics, Program in Agricultural Education, Kingsville, TX 78363. Awards MS. Faculty: 1 full-time (0 women), 1 part-time (0 women). Students: 2 full-time (1 woman), 5 part-time (1 woman); includes 4 minority (all Hispanics). In 1997, 4 degrees awarded. *Degree requirements:* Thesis or alternative, comprehensive exam required, foreign language not required. *Entrance requirements:* GRE General Test (minimum combined score of 800), TOEFL (minimum score 525), minimum GPA of 3.0. Application deadline: 6/1 (rolling processing; 11/15 for spring admission). Application fee: $15 ($25 for international students). *Tuition:* $1822 per year full-time, $281 per semester (minimum) part-time for state residents; $6934 per year full-time, $908 per semester (minimum) part-time for nonresidents. *Financial aid:* Application deadline 5/15. • Dr. James D. Arnold, Graduate Coordinator, 512-593-3711.

Texas Tech University, Graduate School, College of Agricultural Sciences and Natural Resources, Department of Agricultural Education and Communications, Lubbock, TX 79409. Offers program in agricultural education (M Agr, MS). Part-time programs available. Faculty: 4 full-time (0 women). Students: 13 full-time (4 women), 5 part-time (2 women); includes 1 minority (Native American). Average age 24. 11 applicants, 82% accepted. In 1997, 21 degrees awarded. *Entrance requirements:* GRE General Test (combined average 838). Application deadline: 4/15 (priority date; rolling processing; 11/1 for spring admission). Application fee: $25 ($50 for international students). Electronic applications accepted. *Expenses:* Tuition $864 per year full-time, $120 per semester (minimum) part-time for state residents; $5976 per year full-time, $747 per semester (minimum) part-time for nonresidents. Fees $2321 per year full-time, $302 per semester (minimum) part-time. *Financial aid:* In 1997–98, 9 research assistantships averaging $700 per month and totaling $56,700 were awarded; fellowships, teaching assistantships, Federal Work-Study, institutionally sponsored loans also available. Aid available to part-time students. Financial aid application deadline: 5/15; applicants required to submit FAFSA. *Faculty research:* Classroom mechanics laboratory safety, agricultural literacy, youth leadership and personal development. Total annual research expenditures: $157,705. • Dr. Paul Vaughn, Chairman, 806-742-2816. Fax: 806-742-2880.

The University of Arizona, College of Agriculture, Department of Agricultural Education, Tucson, AZ 85721. Awards M Ag Ed, MS. *Degree requirements:* Thesis required, foreign language not required. *Entrance requirements:* TOEFL (minimum score 550), teaching/extension experience or equivalent. Application deadline: 4/15 (rolling processing). Application fee: $35. *Tuition:* $2162 per year full-time, $337 per semester (minimum) part-time for state residents; $6860 per year full-time, $1138 per semester (minimum) part-time for nonresidents. *Faculty research:* Career placement, learning styles, noise impact on learning, computer technology, vocational education.

University of Arkansas, Dale Bumpers College of Agricultural, Food and Life Sciences, Department of Agricultural and Extension Education, Fayetteville, AR 72701-1201. Awards MAT, MS. Accredited by NCATE. Faculty: 5 full-time (0 women). Students: 1 part-time (0 women). 3 applicants, 67% accepted. In 1997, 3 degrees awarded. *Application fee:* $25 ($35 for international students). *Tuition:* $3144 per year full-time, $173 per credit hour part-time for state residents; $7140 per year full-time, $395 per credit hour part-time for nonresidents. *Financial aid:* Federal Work-Study and career-related internships or fieldwork available. Aid available to part-time students. Financial aid application deadline: 4/1; applicants required to submit FAFSA. • Don Herring, Chair, 501-575-2035.

University of Florida, College of Agriculture, Department of Agricultural Education and Communication, Gainesville, FL 32611. Awards M Ag, MS. Faculty: 17. Students: 15 full-time (9 women), 10 part-time (4 women); includes 2 minority (both Hispanics), 1 international. 12 applicants, 83% accepted. In 1997, 12 degrees awarded. *Degree requirements:* Thesis optional. *Entrance requirements:* GRE General Test, minimum GPA of 3.0. Application deadline: 6/5 (priority date; rolling processing). Application fee: $20. *Tuition:* $138 per credit hour for state residents; $481 per credit hour for nonresidents. *Financial aid:* In 1997–98, 14 students received aid, including 1 fellowship averaging $480 per month, 7 research assistantships averaging $622 per month, 2 teaching assistantships averaging $506 per month, 4 graduate assistantships averaging $530 per month. *Faculty research:* Cooperative extension service, including home economics, agriculture, Four-H, foods, housing, and nutrition. • Dr. E. W. Osborne, Chair, 352-392-0502. E-mail: aee@gnv.ifas.ufl.edu. Application contact: Dr. Mathew T. Baker, Graduate Coordinator, 352-392-0502. Fax: 352-392-9585. E-mail: mtb@gnv.ifas.ufl.edu.

University of Georgia, College of Agricultural and Environmental Sciences, Program in Agricultural Extension, Athens, GA 30602. Awards MA Ext. Faculty: 2 full-time (1 woman). Students: 1 full-time (0 women), 4 part-time (1 woman). 1 applicant, 0% accepted. In 1997, 4 degrees awarded. *Entrance requirements:* GRE General Test. Application deadline: 7/1 (priority date; 11/15 for spring admission). Application fee: $30. Electronic applications accepted. *Tuition:* $3290 per year full-time, $643 per semester (minimum) part-time for state residents; $11,300 per year full-time, $1645 per semester (minimum) part-time for nonresidents. *Financial aid:* Fellowships, research assistantships, teaching assistantships, assistantships available. • Dr. Richard Rohs, Graduate Coordinator, 706-542-2713. Fax: 706-542-8820.

University of Georgia, College of Education, Department of Occupational Studies, Athens, GA 30602. Offerings include agricultural education (M Ed). Accredited by NCATE. Department faculty: 12 full-time (4 women). *Degree requirements:* Thesis required (for some programs), foreign language not required. *Entrance requirements:* GRE General Test, MAT. Application deadline: 7/1 (priority date; 11/15 for spring admission). Application fee: $30. Electronic applications accepted. *Tuition:* $3290 per year full-time, $643 per semester (minimum) part-time for state residents; $11,300 per year full-time, $1645 per semester (minimum) part-time for nonresidents. • Dr. Robert C. Wicklein, Graduate Coordinator, 706-542-3132. Fax: 706-542-1765.

University of Idaho, College of Graduate Studies, College of Agriculture, Department of Agricultural and Extension Education, Moscow, ID 83844-4140. Awards MS. Accredited by NCATE. Faculty: 5 full-time (0 women). Students: 1 (woman) full-time, 21 part-time (2 women). In 1997, 7 degrees awarded. *Entrance requirements:* Minimum GPA of 2.8. Application deadline: 8/1 (12/15 for spring admission). Application fee: $35 ($45 for international students). *Expenses:* Tuition $0 for state residents; $6000 per year full-time, $95 per credit part-time for nonresidents. Fees $2676 per year full-time, $134 per credit part-time. *Financial aid:* Application deadline 2/15. • Dr. Louis Riesenberg, Head, 208-885-6358.

University of Illinois at Urbana–Champaign, College of Agricultural, Consumer and Environmental Sciences, Department of Human and Community Development, Program in Extension Education, Urbana, IL 61801. Awards MS. Faculty: 3 full-time (0 women). Students: 16 full-time (10 women); includes 1 minority (Asian American), 1 international. 6 applicants, 50% accepted. In 1997, 2 degrees awarded. *Entrance requirements:* Minimum GPA of 4.0 on a 5.0 scale. Application deadline: rolling. Application fee: $40 ($50 for international students).

Directories: Agricultural Education; Art Education

University of Illinois at Urbana–Champaign (continued)
Financial aid: Research assistantships, teaching assistantships available. Financial aid application deadline: 2/15. • Constance H. Shapiro, Head, Department of Human and Community Development, 217-333-3790.

University of Maryland, College Park, College of Agriculture and Natural Resources, Department of Agricultural and Extension Education, College Park, MD 20742-5045. Offers programs in agriculture education (MS, PhD, AGSC); environmental education (MS, PhD, AGSC); extension, adult, and continuing education (MS, PhD, AGSC). Program being phased out; applicants no longer accepted. Faculty: 1 (0 women). Students: 2 part-time (1 woman). In 1997, 2 master's, 3 doctorates awarded. *Degree requirements:* For doctorate, dissertation. *Expenses:* Tuition $272 per credit hour for state residents; $400 per credit hour for nonresidents. Fees $564 per year full-time, $342 per year part-time. *Financial aid:* In 1997–98, 2 teaching assistantships were awarded; research assistantships also available. • Ronald Seibel, Director, Applied Agriculture, 301-405-4685. Fax: 301-314-9300. E-mail: grschool@deans.umd.edu.

University of Maryland Eastern Shore, Department of Agriculture, Program in Agriculture Education and Extension, Princess Anne, MD 21853-1299. Awards MS. Faculty: 10 full-time (1 woman), 3 part-time (0 women). Students: 3 full-time (0 women), 6 part-time (3 women); includes 6 minority (all African Americans), 2 international. Average age 33. 6 applicants, 33% accepted. *Degree requirements:* Thesis required (for some programs), foreign language not required. *Average time to degree:* master's–2 years full-time, 3.5 years part-time. *Entrance requirements:* GRE, TOEFL (minimum score 550), interview, minimum GPA of 3.0. Application deadline: 4/15 (priority date; rolling processing; 10/30 for spring admission). Application fee: $30. *Expenses:* Tuition $143 per credit hour for state residents; $253 per credit hour for nonresidents. Fees $50 per year. *Financial aid:* In 1997–98, 1 student received aid, including 1 research assistantship; grants, Federal Work-Study, and career-related internships or fieldwork also available. Aid available to part-time students. Financial aid application deadline: 3/1. *Faculty research:* Poultry and swine nutrition and management, soybean specialty products, farm management practices, agriculture technology. Total annual research expenditures: $2.486 million. • Dr. George Shorter, Coordinator, 410-651-6193. Fax: 410-651-7931. E-mail: gshorter@umes-bird.umd.edu.

University of Minnesota, Twin Cities Campus, Department of Work, Community, and Family Education and College of Agricultural, Food, and Environmental Sciences, Program in Agricultural Education, Minneapolis, MN 55455-0213. Awards M Ed. • Roland Peterson, Coordinator, 612-624-2221.

University of Nebraska–Lincoln, College of Agricultural Sciences and Natural Resources, Department of Agricultural Leadership, Education and Communication, Lincoln, NE 68588. Awards MS. Faculty: 9 full-time (3 women), 1 part-time (0 women), 10 FTE. Students: 3 full-time (0 women), 6 part-time (3 women); includes 1 minority (Hispanic), 1 international. Average age 32. 5 applicants, 60% accepted. In 1997, 2 degrees awarded. *Degree requirements:* Thesis optional, foreign language not required. *Entrance requirements:* TOEFL (minimum score 550). Application deadline: 3/1 (priority date; rolling processing). Application fee: $35. Electronic applications accepted. *Expenses:* Tuition $110 per credit hour for state residents; $270 per credit hour for nonresidents. Fees $480 per year full-time, $110 per semester part-time. *Financial aid:* In 1997–98, 2 teaching assistantships totaling $16,091 were awarded; fellowships, research assistantships, Federal Work-Study also available. Aid available to part-time students. Financial aid application deadline: 2/15. *Faculty research:* Teaching and instruction, extension education, leadership and human resource development, international agricultural education. • Dr. Earl Russell, Head, 402-472-2807.

University of Puerto Rico, Mayagüez Campus, College of Agricultural Sciences, Department of Agricultural Education and Agricultural Extension, Mayagüez, PR 00681-5000. Offers programs in agricultural education (MS), agricultural extension (MS). Part-time programs available. Faculty: 10 (5 women). Students: 22 full-time (13 women), 12 part-time (8 women); includes 34 minority (all Hispanics). 14 applicants, 64% accepted. *Degree requirements:* Thesis, comprehensive exam required, foreign language not required. *Application deadline:* 2/28 (rolling processing; 9/15 for spring admission). *Application fee:* $15. *Expenses:* Tuition $75 per credit for commonwealth residents; $75 per credit (minimum) for nonresidents. Fees $35 per semester (minimum). *Financial aid:* In 1997–98, 3 fellowships (2 to first-year students) averaging $200 per month, 5 teaching assistantships averaging $350 per month were awarded. *Faculty research:* Curricular development and supervision, youth education, rural sociology. • Dr. Jose Villamil, Director, 787-832-4040 Ext. 3855.

University of Tennessee, Knoxville, College of Agricultural Sciences and Natural Resources, Department of Agricultural and Extension Education, Knoxville, TN 37901. Offers programs in agricultural education (MS), agricultural extension education (MS). One or more programs accredited by NCATE. Part-time programs available. Postbaccalaureate distance learning degree programs offered (minimal on-campus study). Faculty: 4 full-time (0 women). Students: 2 full-time (1 woman), 16 part-time (4 women). 4 applicants, 100% accepted. In 1997, 10 degrees awarded. *Degree requirements:* Thesis or alternative required, foreign language not required. *Entrance requirements:* TOEFL (minimum score 550), minimum GPA of 2.7. Application deadline: 2/1 (priority date; rolling processing). Application fee: $35. Electronic applications accepted. *Tuition:* $3354 per year full-time, $181 per semester hour part-time for state residents; $8410 per year full-time, $462 per semester hour part-time for nonresidents. *Financial aid:* Research assistantships, graduate assistantships, Federal Work-Study, institutionally sponsored loans, and career-related internships or fieldwork available. Financial aid application deadline: 2/1. • Dr. Roy R. Lessly, Head, 423-974-7308. Fax: 423-974-7448. E-mail: rlessly@utk.edu.

University of Wisconsin–River Falls, College of Agriculture, Food, and Environmental Sciences, Department of Agricultural Education, River Falls, WI 54022-5001. Awards MS. Accredited by NCATE. Students: 2 (both women). *Degree requirements:* Thesis required, foreign language not required. *Application deadline:* 3/1. *Application fee:* $45. *Financial aid:* Federal Work-Study available. Financial aid application deadline: 3/1. • Richard Jensen, Chair, 715-425-3555. E-mail: richard.a.jensen@uwrf.edu. Application contact: Graduate Admissions, 715-425-3843.

Utah State University, College of Agriculture, Department of Agricultural Systems Technology and Education, Logan, UT 84322. Offers program in agricultural systems technology (MA, MS), including agricultural extension education (MS), agricultural mechanization (MS), farm systems research (MS), international agricultural extension (MS), secondary and postsecondary agricultural education (MS). Part-time programs available. Postbaccalaureate distance learning degree programs offered (minimal on-campus study). Faculty: 7 full-time (1 woman), 1 part-time (0 women). Students: 4 full-time (2 women), 4 part-time (1 woman). Average age 30. 3 applicants, 0% accepted. In 1997, 1 degree awarded. *Degree requirements:* Thesis required (for some programs), foreign language not required. *Entrance requirements:* GRE General Test (score in 40th percentile or higher), MAT, TOEFL (minimum score 550), BS in agricultural education, agricultural extension, or related discipline; minimum GPA of 3.0. Application deadline: 6/15 (priority date; rolling processing; 10/15 for spring admission). Application fee: $40. *Expenses:* Tuition $1448 per year full-time, $624 per year part-time for state residents; $5082 per year full-time, $2192 per year part-time for nonresidents. Fees $421 per year full-time, $165 per year part-time. *Financial aid:* In 1997–98, 3 research assistantships (all to first-year students) totaling $2,550, 1 teaching assistantship (to a first-year student) totaling $800 were awarded; partial tuition waivers, Federal Work-Study, institutionally sponsored loans, and career-related internships or fieldwork also available. Aid available to part-time students. Financial aid application deadline: 3/1. *Faculty research:* Extension and adult education; structures and environment; low-input agriculture; farm safety, systems, and mechanizations. Total annual research expenditures: $161,000. • Gary S. Straquadine, Head, 435-797-3521. Fax: 435-797-4002. E-mail: garys@cc.usu.edu. Application contact: Bruce Miller, Graduate Adviser, 435-797-2232. E-mail: bemiller@cc.usu.edu.

West Virginia University, College of Agriculture, Forestry and Consumer Sciences, Division of Resource Management, Program in Agricultural and Environmental Education, Morgantown, WV 26506. Awards MS. Accredited by NCATE. Part-time programs available. Students: 9 full-time (6 women), 5 part-time (1 woman); includes 1 international. Average age 28. 7 applicants, 86% accepted. In 1997, 4 degrees awarded. *Degree requirements:* Thesis required, foreign language not required. *Entrance requirements:* GRE General Test, TOEFL (minimum score 550), minimum GPA of 2.75. Application deadline: 7/1 (priority date; rolling processing). Application fee: $45. *Tuition:* $2820 per year full-time, $149 per credit hour part-time for state residents; $8104 per year full-time, $443 per credit hour part-time for nonresidents. *Financial aid:* In 1997–98, 1 teaching assistantship was awarded; full and partial tuition waivers, Federal Work-Study, institutionally sponsored loans also available. Financial aid application deadline: 2/1; applicants required to submit FAFSA. *Faculty research:* Program development in vocational agriculture, agricultural extension. • Dr. Layle D. Lawrence, Chair, 304-293-3740. E-mail: llawrenc@wvu.edu.

Art Education

Adelphi University, School of Education, Program in Secondary Education, Garden City, NY 11530. Offerings include art (MA). *Application deadline:* rolling. *Application fee:* $50. *Expenses:* Tuition $16,000 per year full-time, $485 per credit part-time. Fees $500 per year full-time, $150 per semester part-time. • Director, 516-877-4090. Application contact: Jennifer Spiegel, Associate Director of Graduate Admissions, 516-877-3055.

Alabama Agricultural and Mechanical University, School of Education, Department of Curriculum and Instruction, Area in Art and Art Education, PO Box 1357, Normal, AL 35762-1357. Awards M Ed. Accredited by NCATE. Evening/weekend programs available. Faculty: 3 full-time (0 women). *Degree requirements:* Thesis or alternative, comprehensive exam required, foreign language not required. *Entrance requirements:* GRE General Test. Application deadline: 5/1. Application fee: $15 ($20 for international students). *Expenses:* Tuition $2782 per year full-time, $565 per semester (minimum) part-time for state residents; $5164 per year full-time, $1015 per semester (minimum) part-time for nonresidents. Fees $560 per year full-time, $390 per year part-time. *Financial aid:* Fellowships and career-related internships or fieldwork available. Financial aid application deadline: 4/1. *Faculty research:* Aesthetics and art criticism, teaching art to children, medieval jewelry techniques and processes. • Dr. Earnest Dees, Chair, Department of Curriculum and Instruction, 205-851-5520. Fax: 205-851-5526.

Art Academy of Cincinnati, Program in Art Education, Cincinnati, OH 45202-1700. Awards MA. Accredited by NASAD. Offered during summer only. Part-time programs available. Faculty: 5 full-time (2 women), 7 part-time (all women). Students: 14 full-time (10 women), 5 part-time (all women); includes 2 minority (both African Americans). 29 applicants, 28% accepted. *Degree requirements:* Thesis, portfolio/exhibit required, foreign language not required. *Average time to degree:* master's–3 years full-time, 5 years part-time. *Entrance requirements:* Portfolio. Application deadline: rolling. Application fee: $25. *Financial aid:* In 1997–98, 13 students received aid, including 13 scholarships (5 to first-year students) totaling $5,000; institutionally sponsored loans also available. Aid available to part-time students. Financial aid applicants required to submit FAFSA. • Paige Williams, Chair, 513-562-8777. Application contact: Sarah Colby, Director of Enrollment Services, 513-562-8754. Fax: 513-562-8778.

Ball State University, College of Fine Arts, Department of Art, 2000 University Avenue, Muncie, IN 47306-1099. Offerings include art education (MA, MAE). Accredited by NASAD and NCATE. Department faculty: 17. *Application fee:* $15 ($25 for international students). *Expenses:* Tuition $3454 per year full-time, $518 per semester (minimum) part-time for state residents; $9316 per year full-time, $1221 per semester (minimum) part-time for nonresidents. Fees $242 per year full-time, $18 per semester (minimum) part-time. • Thomas Spoerner, Head, 765-285-5838.

Beaver College, Department of Education, Glenside, PA 19038-3295. Offerings include art education (MA Ed, M Ed). *Application fee:* $35. *Expenses:* Tuition $6570 per year full-time, $365 per credit part-time. Fees $35 per year.

Boise State University, College of Education, Programs in Teacher Education, Program in Art Education, Boise, ID 83725-0399. Awards MA. Accredited by NCATE. Part-time programs available. Students: 5 full-time (all women), 5 part-time (4 women); includes 1 minority (Asian American). Average age 38. 4 applicants, 100% accepted. In 1997, 2 degrees awarded. *Degree requirements:* Thesis optional. *Entrance requirements:* Portfolio. Application deadline: 7/26 (priority date; rolling processing; 11/29 for spring admission). Application fee: $20 ($30 for international students). Electronic applications accepted. *Tuition:* $3020 per year full-time, $135 per credit part-time for state residents; $8900 per year full-time, $135 per credit part-time for nonresidents. *Financial aid:* Graduate assistantships, Federal Work-Study, institutionally sponsored loans, and career-related internships or fieldwork available. Aid available to part-time students. Financial aid application deadline: 3/1. • Dr. Heather Hanlon, Coordinator, 208-385-3873. Fax: 208-385-1524. Application contact: Dr. Roger Stewart, Coordinator, 208-385-1731. Fax: 208-385-4365.

Boston University, School for the Arts, Division of Visual Arts, Program in Art Education, Boston, MA 02215. Awards MFA. Students: 1 full-time (0 women), 2 part-time (1 woman). Average age 32. In 1997, 6 degrees awarded. *Entrance requirements:* TOEFL (minimum score 550), portfolio. Application deadline: 3/1 (priority date; rolling processing). Application fee: $50. *Expenses:* Tuition $22,830 per year full-time, $713 per credit part-time. Fees $218 per year full-time, $40 per semester part-time. *Financial aid:* Fellowships, teaching assistantships available. Financial aid application deadline: 2/15. • Janet Olson, Chairman, 617-353-3373. Application contact: Patricia Mitro, Assistant Dean for Enrollment Services, 617-353-3350.

Boston University, School for the Arts, Division of Visual Arts, Program in Studio Teaching, Boston, MA 02215. Awards MFA. Students: 6 full-time (5 women), 1 (woman) part-time; includes 1 minority (Native American), 1 international. Average age 27. *Entrance requirements:* TOEFL (minimum score 550), portfolio. Application deadline: 3/1 (rolling processing). Application fee: $50. *Expenses:* Tuition $22,830 per year full-time, $713 per credit part-time. Fees $218 per year full-time, $40 per semester part-time. *Financial aid:* Fellowships, teaching assistantships available. Financial aid application deadline: 2/15. • Janet Olson, Chairman, 617-353-3373. Application contact: Patricia Mitro, Assistant Dean for Enrollment Services, 617-353-3350.

Bridgewater State College, School of Arts and Sciences, Department of Art, Bridgewater, MA 02325-0001. Awards MAT. Evening/weekend programs available. *Degree requirements:*

Comprehensive exam. *Entrance requirements:* GRE General Test. Application deadline: 4/1 (10/1 for spring admission). Application fee: $25. *Expenses:* Tuition $1675 per year full-time, $70 per credit part-time for state residents; $6450 per year full-time, $269 per credit part-time for nonresidents. Fees $1588 per year full-time, $66 per credit hour part-time for state residents; $1588 per year full-time, $66 per credit part-time for nonresidents. *Financial aid:* Career-related internships or fieldwork available. • Application contact: Graduate School, 508-697-1300.

Brigham Young University, College of Fine Arts and Communications, Department of Visual Arts, Provo, UT 84602-1001. Offerings include art education (MA). Accredited by NASAD. Department faculty: 19 full-time (3 women). *Average time to degree:* master's–3 years full-time. *Application deadline:* 2/1. *Application fee:* $30. *Tuition:* $3200 per year full-time, $178 per credit hour part-time for state residents; $4800 per year full-time, $266 per credit hour part-time for nonresidents. • Dr. Mark J. Johnson, Chair, 801-378-4429. Fax: 801-378-5964.

Brooklyn College of the City University of New York, School of Education, Division of Elementary School Education, 2900 Bedford Avenue, Brooklyn, NY 11210-2889. Offerings include art education (MS Ed). *Average time to degree:* master's–1.5 years full-time, 3 years part-time. *Entrance requirements:* TOEFL (minimum score 500), interview, previous course work in education, writing sample. Application deadline: 3/1 (rolling processing; 11/1 for spring admission). Application fee: $40. *Expenses:* Tuition $4350 per year full-time, $185 per credit part-time for state residents; $7600 per year full-time, $320 per credit part-time for nonresidents. Fees $500 per year for state residents; $806 per year for nonresidents. • Dr. Milga Morales, Coordinator, 718-951-5933.

Brooklyn College of the City University of New York, School of Education, Division of Secondary Education, 2900 Bedford Avenue, Brooklyn, NY 11210-2889. Offerings include art education (MA). *Application deadline:* 3/1 (11/1 for spring admission). *Application fee:* $40. *Expenses:* Tuition $4350 per year full-time, $185 per credit part-time for state residents; $7600 per year full-time, $320 per credit part-time for nonresidents. Fees $500 per year for state residents; $806 per year for nonresidents. • Dr. Peter Taubman, Coordinator, 718-951-5218. Fax: 718-951-4816. E-mail: ptaubman@brooklyn.cuny.edu.

California State University, Long Beach, College of the Arts, Department of Art, Long Beach, CA 90840-3501. Offerings include art education (MA). Accredited by NASAD. *Application deadline:* 8/1 (rolling processing; 12/1 for spring admission). *Application fee:* $55. *Expenses:* Tuition $0 for state residents; $246 per unit for nonresidents. Fees $1846 per year full-time, $1180 per year part-time. • James S. Kvapil, Chair, 562-985-7819. Application contact: Cynthia Osborne, Graduate Coordinator, 562-985-4376. Fax: 562-985-1650.

California State University, Los Angeles, School of Arts and Letters, Department of Art, Los Angeles, CA 90032-8530. Offerings include art (MA), with options in art education, art history, art therapy, ceramics, metals, and textiles, design, painting, sculpture, and graphic arts, photography. Accredited by NASAD. Department faculty: 18 full-time, 25 part-time. *Application deadline:* 6/30 (rolling processing; 2/1 for spring admission). *Application fee:* $55. *Expenses:* Tuition $0 for state residents; $164 per unit for nonresidents. Fees $1763 per year full-time, $1097 per year part-time. • Dr. Joseph Soldate, Chair, 213-343-4010.

Carlow College, Division of Education, Program in Art Education, Pittsburgh, PA 15213-3165. Awards M Ed. Faculty: 4 part-time (3 women). Students: 1 (woman) part-time. 1 applicant, 100% accepted. *Degree requirements:* Thesis or alternative required, foreign language not required. *Entrance requirements:* Interview, minimum GPA of 3.0, portfolio review. Application deadline: 6/30 (rolling processing; 4/25 for spring admission). Application fee: $35. *Financial aid:* Federal Work-Study available. Aid available to part-time students. Financial aid application deadline: 3/15. • Dr. Julie Agar, Director, 412-578-8761. Application contact: Bonnie Potthoff, Office Manager, Graduate Studies, 412-578-8764. Fax: 412-578-8822.

Carthage College, Division of Teacher Education, Kenosha, WI 53140-1994. Offerings include creative arts (M Ed). College faculty: 6 full-time (4 women), 13 part-time (8 women). *Degree requirements:* Thesis optional, foreign language not required. *Average time to degree:* master's–5 years part-time. *Entrance requirements:* MAT, minimum B average. Application deadline: rolling. Application fee: $25. • Dr. Judith B. Schaumberg, Director of Graduate Programs, 414-551-5876. Fax: 414-551-5704.

Case Western Reserve University, Department of Art History and Art, Program in Art Education, Cleveland, OH 44106. Awards MA. Accredited by NASAD. Offered jointly with the Cleveland Institute of Art. Part-time programs available. Faculty: 1 full-time (0 women), 4 part-time (2 women). Students: 7 full-time (5 women), 2 part-time (1 woman); includes 2 minority (1 African American, 1 Asian American). Average age 30. 10 applicants, 80% accepted. In 1997, 3 degrees awarded (100% found work related to degree). *Degree requirements:* Thesis (for some programs), art exhibit required, foreign language not required. *Average time to degree:* master's–1.5 years full-time. *Entrance requirements:* NTE, TOEFL (minimum score 550), interview, portfolio. Application deadline: 7/10 (rolling processing). Application fee: $25. *Tuition:* $18,400 per year full-time, $767 per credit hour part-time. *Financial aid:* Partial tuition waivers, Federal Work-Study, and career-related internships or fieldwork available. Financial aid application deadline: 7/10. *Faculty research:* Visual and aesthetic education, ethnographic arts, multiculturalism. • Tim Shuckerow, Director, 216-368-2714. Fax: 216-368-2715. E-mail: txs10@po.cwru.edu.

Central Connecticut State University, School of Arts and Sciences, Department of Art, New Britain, CT 06050-4010. Offers program in art education (MS). Part-time and evening/weekend programs available. Faculty: 12 full-time (7 women), 17 part-time (9 women), 20 FTE. Students: 16 full-time (12 women), 48 part-time (44 women); includes 3 minority (1 African American, 1 Asian American, 1 Hispanic). Average age 34. 34 applicants, 79% accepted. In 1997, 10 degrees awarded. *Degree requirements:* Thesis or alternative, exhibit or special project required, foreign language not required. *Entrance requirements:* TOEFL (minimum score 550), minimum GPA of 2.7. Application deadline: 6/1 (priority date; rolling processing; 12/1 for spring admission). Application fee: $40. *Expenses:* Tuition $4458 per year full-time, $175 per credit hour part-time for state residents; $9943 per year full-time, $175 per credit hour part-time for nonresidents. Fees $45 per semester. *Financial aid:* In 1997–98, 1 research assistantship (to a first-year student) was awarded; Federal Work-Study also available. Financial aid application deadline: 3/15; applicants required to submit FAFSA. *Faculty research:* Visual arts. • Prof. Sherinatu Fafunwa-Ndibe, Acting Chair, 860-832-2620.

Central Missouri State University, College of Arts and Sciences, Department of Art, Warrensburg, MO 64093. Offerings include art education (MSE). Department faculty: 14 full-time. *Application deadline:* 6/30 (priority date; rolling processing). *Application fee:* $25 ($50 for international students). *Tuition:* $3288 per year full-time, $137 per credit hour part-time for state residents; $5928 per year full-time, $274 per credit hour part-time for nonresidents. • Dr. Jerry Miller, Chair, 660-543-4594. Fax: 660-543-8006.

City College of the City University of New York, Graduate School, School of Education, Department of Secondary and Continuing Education, Convent Avenue at 138th Street, New York, NY 10031-6977. Offerings include art education (MA). *Degree requirements:* Thesis required, foreign language not required. *Entrance requirements:* TOEFL (minimum score 500). Application fee: $40. *Expenses:* Tuition $4350 per year full-time, $185 per credit part-time for state residents; $7600 per year full-time, $320 per credit part-time for nonresidents. Fees $41 per year. • Hope Hartman, Chair, 212-650-7954.

College of Mount St. Joseph, Education Department, Program in Art, Cincinnati, OH 45233-1670. Awards MA Ed. *Degree requirements:* Comprehensive exam required, foreign language and thesis not required. *Entrance requirements:* GRE General Test (minimum combined score of 825), minimum GPA of 2.7, portfolio. Application deadline: rolling. Application fee: $0. *Tuition:* $320 per credit hour. *Financial aid:* Application deadline 6/1. • Dan Mader, Chair, 513-244-4942. Fax: 513-244-4222. E-mail: dan_mader@mail.msj.edu. Application contact: Jean Abrams, Graduate Secretary, 513-244-4812.

College of New Rochelle, Programs in Art, Program in Art Education, New Rochelle, NY 10805-2308. Awards MA. Part-time and evening/weekend programs available. Faculty: 6 part-time (all women), 2 FTE. Students: 1 full-time (0 women), 24 part-time (22 women); includes 1 minority (Hispanic). 16 applicants, 100% accepted. In 1997, 13 degrees awarded. *Degree requirements:* Thesis required, foreign language not required. *Average time to degree:* master's–1.2 years full-time, 2.5 years part-time. *Entrance requirements:* Interview; minimum GPA of 3.0 in field, 2.7 overall; portfolio; 36 credits in studio art. Application deadline: 8/1 (priority date; rolling processing). Application fee: $35. *Tuition:* $329 per credit. *Financial aid:* In 1997–98, 4 assistantships, scholarships (1 to a first-year student) totaling $3,792 were awarded; research assistantships, partial tuition waivers, and career-related internships or fieldwork also available. Aid available to part-time students. *Faculty research:* Developmental stages in art, assessment and evaluation, curriculum development, multicultural education, art museum education. • Dr. Patricia St. John, Division Head, Programs in Art, 914-654-5279.

College of Notre Dame, Department of Education, Emphasis in Secondary Education, Belmont, CA 94002-1997. Offerings include teaching art (MAT). Faculty: 5 full-time, 8 part-time. *Application deadline:* rolling. *Application fee:* $50 ($500 for international students). *Tuition:* $460 per unit. • Dr. Kim Tolley, Program Director, 650-508-3456.

The College of Saint Rose, School of Arts and Humanities, Program in Art Education, Albany, NY 12203-1419. Awards MS Ed. Accredited by NASAD. Part-time and evening/weekend programs available. Faculty: 9 full-time (6 women), 1 part-time (0 women). Students: 2 full-time (1 woman), 22 part-time (14 women). Average age 31. In 1997, 5 degrees awarded. *Degree requirements:* Thesis or alternative, final project. *Entrance requirements:* Minimum undergraduate GPA of 3.0, slide portfolio. Application deadline: 7/15 (priority date; rolling processing; 12/1 for spring admission). Application fee: $30. *Expenses:* Tuition $338 per credit. Fees $60 per year. *Financial aid:* Research assistantships, partial tuition waivers available. Aid available to part-time students. Financial aid application deadline: 3/1; applicants required to submit FAFSA. • Karene Faul, Head, 518-485-3901. Application contact: Graduate Office, 518-454-5136. Fax: 518-458-5479. E-mail: ace@rosnet.strose.edu.

Columbus State University, College of Arts and Letters, Program in Art Education, Columbus, GA 31907-5645. Awards M Ed. Accredited by NCATE. *Application deadline:* 7/10 (priority date; rolling processing; 10/23 for spring admission). *Application fee:* $20. *Tuition:* $1718 per year full-time, $151 per semester hour part-time for state residents; $6218 per year full-time, $401 per semester hour part-time for nonresidents. *Financial aid:* Research assistantships, teaching assistantships, full tuition waivers, Federal Work-Study, institutionally sponsored loans, and career-related internships or fieldwork available. Aid available to part-time students. Financial aid application deadline: 7/15; applicants required to submit FAFSA. • Jeff Burden, Chair, 706-568-2047. Fax: 706-569-3123. E-mail: burden_jeff@colstate.edu. Application contact: Katie Thornton, Graduate Admissions, 706-568-2279. Fax: 706-568-2462. E-mail: thornton_katie@colstate.edu.

Concordia University, Faculty of Fine Arts, Department of Art Education and Art Therapy, Montréal, PQ H3G 1M8, Canada. Offers programs in art education (MA, PhD, Diploma), including art in education (MA), art in therapy (MA); creative arts therapies (MA), including art therapy, drama therapy. Students: 78 full-time (62 women), 17 part-time (16 women); includes 4 international. In 1997, 14 master's, 14 Diplomas awarded. *Degree requirements:* For master's, thesis (for some programs), practicum; for doctorate, dissertation, comprehensive exam; for Diploma, comprehensive exam or research paper. *Entrance requirements:* For master's, teaching experience; for doctorate, teaching or related professional experience; for Diploma, portfolio. Application deadline: 1/15. Application fee: $30. *Expenses:* Tuition $56 per credit (minimum) for Canadian residents; $249 per credit (minimum) for nonresidents. Fees $158 per year full-time, $117 per year (minimum) part-time. *Financial aid:* Fellowships available. Financial aid application deadline: 2/1. *Faculty research:* Vernacular culture, museum education, psychotic art, adults and families. • Dr. A. Fairchild, Chair, 514-848-4639. Application contact: Dr. L. Peterson, Director, 514-848-4790. Fax: 514-848-8627.

Eastern Kentucky University, College of Education, Department of Curriculum and Instruction, Program in Secondary and Higher Education, Richmond, KY 40475-3101. Offerings include art education (MA Ed). Accredited by NCATE. *Entrance requirements:* GRE General Test, minimum GPA of 2.5. Application fee: $0. *Tuition:* $2390 per year full-time, $133 per credit hour part-time for state residents; $6630 per year full-time, $365 per credit hour part-time for nonresidents. • Dr. Imogene Ramsey, Chair, Department of Curriculum and Instruction, 606-622-2154.

Eastern Michigan University, College of Arts and Sciences, Department of Art, Program in Art Education, Ypsilanti, MI 48197. Awards MA. Accredited by NCATE. Part-time and evening/weekend programs available. In 1997, 6 degrees awarded. *Entrance requirements:* TOEFL (minimum score 560). Application deadline: 5/15 (rolling processing; 3/15 for spring admission). Application fee: $30. *Expenses:* Tuition $2691 per year full-time, $150 per credit hour part-time for state residents; $6300 per year full-time, $350 per credit hour part-time for nonresidents. Fees $368 per year full-time, $88 per semester (minimum) part-time. *Financial aid:* Fellowships, teaching assistantships available. Aid available to part-time students. Financial aid application deadline: 3/15; applicants required to submit FAFSA. • Christopher Bocklage, Coordinator, 734-487-3388.

Eastern Washington University, College of Letters and Social Sciences, Program in Art, Cheney, WA 99004-2431. Offers college instruction (MA). One or more programs accredited by NCATE. Faculty: 8 full-time (2 women). Students: 1 full-time (0 women); includes 1 international. 2 applicants, 0% accepted. In 1997, 1 degree awarded. *Degree requirements:* Thesis or alternative, comprehensive oral exam. *Entrance requirements:* Minimum GPA of 3.0, portfolio. Application deadline: 4/1 (priority date; rolling processing; 1/15 for spring admission). Application fee: $35. *Tuition:* $4200 per year full-time, $140 per credit part-time for state residents; $12,780 per year full-time, $415 per credit part-time for nonresidents. *Financial aid:* Teaching assistantships, Federal Work-Study, institutionally sponsored loans available. Financial aid application deadline: 2/1. • Richard Twedt, Chair, 509-359-2493.

Endicott College, School of Continuing Education and Graduate Studies, Program in Arts and Learning, Beverly, MA 01915-2096. Awards M Ed. Program new for spring 1998. Part-time and evening/weekend programs available. Postbaccalaureate distance learning degree programs offered (minimal on-campus study). Faculty: 6 part-time (3 women). *Degree requirements:* Portfolio, written comprehensive exams required, foreign language and thesis not required. *Entrance requirements:* MAT (minimum score 80). Application deadline: rolling. Application fee: $80. *Tuition:* $585 per course. *Financial aid:* Career-related internships or fieldwork available. *Faculty research:* Linkage of creative processes to effective teaching and learning. • Dr. Paul J. Tortolani, Dean, School of Continuing Education and Graduate Studies, 978-232-2199. Fax: 978-232-3000. E-mail: ptortola@endicott.edu.

Fitchburg State College, Program in Arts in Education, Fitchburg, MA 01420-2697. Awards M Ed. Accredited by NCATE. Program new for fall 1998. Part-time and evening/weekend programs available. *Entrance requirements:* GRE General Test or MAT. Application deadline: rolling. Application fee: $10. *Expenses:* Tuition $147 per credit. Fees $55 per semester. *Financial aid:* Graduate assistantships, Federal Work-Study available. Aid available to part-time students. Financial aid application deadline: 3/30; applicants required to submit FAFSA. • Dr. Harry Semerjian, Chair, Humanities, 978-665-3279. Fax: 978-665-3658. E-mail: dgce@fsc.edu. Application contact: James DuPont, Director of Admissions, 978-665-3144. Fax: 978-665-4540. E-mail: admissions@fsc.edu.

Florida Atlantic University, College of Arts and Letters, Department of Art, Boca Raton, FL 33431-0991. Offerings include art education (MAT). Department faculty: 12 full-time (4 women). *Application deadline:* 6/1 (priority date; rolling processing; 11/1 for spring admission). *Applica-*

Directory: Art Education

Florida Atlantic University (continued)

tion fee: $15. *Expenses:* Tuition $2520 per year full-time, $140 per credit hour part-time for state residents; $8712 per year full-time, $484 per credit hour part-time for nonresidents. Fees $5 per year (minimum). • Dr. Kathleen Russo, Chair, 561-297-3870. Fax: 561-297-2752. E-mail: russok@fau.edu.

Florida International University, College of Education, Department of Subject Specializations, Program in Art Education, Miami, FL 33199. Awards MS. Accredited by NCATE. Part-time and evening/weekend programs available. Students: 8 full-time (7 women), 21 part-time (18 women); includes 13 minority (all Hispanics). Average age 38. 10 applicants, 0% accepted. In 1997, 17 degrees awarded. *Entrance requirements:* GRE General Test (minimum combined score of 1000) or minimum GPA of 3.0. Application deadline: 4/1 (priority date; rolling processing; 10/1 for spring admission). Application fee: $20. *Expenses:* Tuition $138 per credit hour for state residents; $482 per credit hour for nonresidents. Fees $46 per semester. *Faculty research:* Elementary art, macramé, stained glass works. • Dr. Dean Hauenstein, Chairperson, Department of Subject Specializations, 305-348-2005. Fax: 305-348-2086.

Florida State University, School of Visual Arts and Dance, Department of Art Education, Tallahassee, FL 32306. Awards MA, MS, Ed D, PhD, Ed S. One or more programs accredited by NASAD. Part-time programs available. Faculty: 6 full-time (4 women), 3 part-time (2 women). Students: 74 full-time (56 women), 7 part-time (5 women); includes 28 minority (10 African Americans, 3 Asian Americans, 13 Hispanics, 2 Native Americans), 4 international. Average age 34. 34 applicants, 62% accepted. In 1997, 12 master's, 5 doctorates awarded. *Degree requirements:* For master's, thesis required (for some programs), foreign language not required; for doctorate, dissertation required, foreign language not required. *Entrance requirements:* For master's, GRE General Test (minimum combined score of 1000) or minimum GPA of 3.0 in last 2 years; for doctorate, GRE General Test (minimum combined score of 1000) or minimum GPA of 3.5. Application deadline: 4/17 (priority date; rolling processing). Application fee: $20. *Tuition:* $139 per credit hour for state residents; $482 per credit hour for nonresidents. *Financial aid:* In 1997–98, 9 students received aid, including 1 fellowship (to a first-year student), 4 research assistantships, 6 teaching assistantships (2 to first-year students); full tuition waivers, Federal Work-Study, and career-related internships or fieldwork also available. *Faculty research:* Teaching and learning in art, museum education, art therapy, arts administration, discipline-based art education. • Sally McRorie, Chairman, 850-664-1915. Fax: 850-644-5067. E-mail: smcrorie@mailer.fsu.edu.

Georgia Southern University, College of Education, Department of Middle Grades and Secondary Education, Program in Art, Statesboro, GA 30460-8126. Offers art education (M Ed, Ed S). One or more programs accredited by NCATE. Accredited by NASAD. Part-time and evening/weekend programs available. Students: 1 (woman) full-time, 4 part-time (all women). Average age 29. 0 applicants. In 1997, 2 master's awarded. *Degree requirements:* For master's, exams required, foreign language and thesis not required. *Entrance requirements:* For master's, GRE General Test (minimum score 450 on each section) or MAT (minimum score 44), minimum GPA of 2.5. Application deadline: 7/15 (priority date; rolling processing; 11/15 for spring admission). Application fee: $0. Electronic applications accepted. *Tuition:* $2619 per year full-time, $287 per semester (minimum) part-time for state residents; $8619 per year full-time, $1037 per semester (minimum) part-time for nonresidents. *Financial aid:* Federal Work-Study and career-related internships or fieldwork available. Aid available to part-time students. Financial aid application deadline: 4/15. • Application contact: Dr. John R. Diebolt, Associate Graduate Dean, 912-681-5384. Fax: 912-681-0740. E-mail: gradschool@gsvms2.cc.gasou.edu.

Georgia State University, College of Education, Department of Middle, Secondary Education and Instructional Technology, Atlanta, GA 30303-3083. Offerings include art education (Ed S); secondary education (M Ed, PhD, Ed S), with options in art education (Ed S), English education (M Ed, Ed S), language and literacy education (PhD), mathematics education (M Ed, PhD, Ed S), music education (Ed S), science education (M Ed, PhD, Ed S), social science education (Ed S), social studies education (M Ed, PhD), vocational education (M Ed). One or more programs accredited by NCATE. Department faculty: 26 full-time (16 women), 7 part-time (3 women). *Degree requirements:* Project/exam. *Entrance requirements:* GRE General Test (minimum combined score of 900) or MAT (minimum score 48), minimum graduate GPA of 3.25. Application fee: $25. *Expenses:* Tuition $2673 per year full-time, $99 per semester hour part-time for state residents; $10,692 per year full-time, $396 per semester hour part-time for nonresidents. Fees $228 per year. • Dr. Beverly J. Armento, Chair, 404-651-2510.

Georgia State University, College of Arts and Sciences, School of Art and Design, Program in Art Education, Atlanta, GA 30303-3083. Awards MA Ed. Accredited by NASAD. Part-time programs available. Faculty: 3 full-time (1 woman). Students: 15 full-time (12 women); includes 2 minority (both African Americans). Average age 34. 5 applicants, 60% accepted. In 1997, 5 degrees awarded (100% found work related to degree). *Degree requirements:* 1 foreign language, thesis, studio exhibit. *Average time to degree:* master's–2.5 years full-time, 4 years part-time. *Entrance requirements:* GRE General Test or MAT, TOEFL (minimum score 550), portfolio, minimum GPA of 3.0. Application fee: $25. *Expenses:* Tuition $2673 per year full-time, $99 per semester hour part-time for state residents; $10,692 per year full-time, $396 per semester hour part-time for nonresidents. Fees $228 per year. *Financial aid:* Research assistantships, Federal Work-Study, institutionally sponsored loans, and career-related internships or fieldwork available. Aid available to part-time students. *Faculty research:* Art–maturing adults, computer instruction in art. • Application contact: George Beasley, Director of Graduate Studies, 404-651-2257. Fax: 404-651-1779. E-mail: gbeasley@gsu.edu.

Gonzaga University, Graduate School, College of Arts and Sciences, Program in Art, Spokane, WA 99258-0001. Awards MAT. *Degree requirements:* Comprehensive exam. *Entrance requirements:* GRE General Test or MAT, TOEFL (minimum score 550), minimum GPA of 3.0. Application deadline: 7/20 (priority date; rolling processing; 11/1 for spring admission). Application fee: $40. *Tuition:* $7380 per year (minimum) full-time, $410 per credit (minimum) part-time. *Financial aid:* Application deadline 3/1. • Dr. Terry Gieber, Chairperson. Application contact: Dr. Leonard Doohan, Dean of the Graduate School, 509-328-4220 Ext. 3546. Fax: 509-324-5399.

Harvard University, Graduate School of Education, Area of Learning and Teaching, Cambridge, MA 02138. Offerings include arts in education (Ed M). Faculty: 7 full-time (5 women), 16 part-time (8 women), 10.3 FTE. *Average time to degree:* master's–1 year full-time, 2.1 years part-time; doctorate–6.3 years full-time, 9 years part-time; other advanced degree–1 year full-time, 2 years part-time. *Entrance requirements:* GRE General Test, TOEFL (minimum score 600), TWE (minimum score 5.0). Application deadline: 1/2. Application fee: $60. • Robert Kegan, Chair, 617-496-2974. Fax: 617-495-7843. Application contact: Roland Hence, Director of Admissions, 617-495-3414. Fax: 617-496-3577. E-mail: gseadmissions@harvard.edu.

Henderson State University, School of Education, Department of Secondary Education, Arkadelphia, AR 71999-0001. Offerings include art education (MSE). Accredited by NCATE. Postbaccalaureate distance learning degree programs offered (minimal on-campus study). *Degree requirements:* Thesis optional, foreign language not required. *Entrance requirements:* GRE General Test or MAT, minimum GPA of 2.7, teacher certification. Application deadline: 7/31 (priority date; rolling processing). Application fee: $15. Electronic applications accepted. *Expenses:* Tuition $120 per credit hour for state residents; $240 per credit hour for nonresidents. Fees $105 per semester (minimum) full-time, $52 per semester (minimum) part-time. • Dr. Charles Weiner, Chairperson, 870-230-5163. Fax: 870-230-5455. E-mail: weinerc@holly.hsu.edu.

Hofstra University, School of Education and Allied Human Services, Department of Curriculum and Teaching, Hempstead, NY 11549. Offerings include elementary and early childhood education (MA, MS Ed), with options in art education (MA, MS Ed), early childhood education (MA), elementary education (MA, MS Ed), music education (MA, MS Ed); secondary education (MA, MS Ed), with options in art education (MA), music education (MA), secondary education (MA, MS Ed). One or more programs accredited by NCATE. Department faculty: 24 full-time (20 women), 77 part-time (45 women). *Degree requirements:* Departmental qualifying exam. *Application deadline:* rolling. *Application fee:* $40 ($75 for international students). *Expenses:* Tuition $10,968 per year full-time, $457 per credit hour part-time. Fees $670 per year full-time, $112 per semester (minimum) part-time. • Dr. Doris Fromberg, Chairperson, 516-463-5749. Fax: 516-463-6503. E-mail: catdpf@hofstra.edu. Application contact: Mary Beth Carey, Dean of Admissions, 516-463-6700. Fax: 516-560-7660. E-mail: hofstra@hofstra.edu.

Illinois State University, College of Fine Arts, Department of Art, Program in Art Education, Normal, IL 61790-2200. Offers aesthetics (Ed D), art administration (Ed D), art education research (Ed D), arts for special needs (Ed D), instructional technology (Ed D). Program being phased out; applicants no longer accepted. Students: 1 full-time (0 women), 1 (woman) part-time. *Degree requirements:* Dissertation, 2 terms of residency, comprehensive exams required, foreign language not required. *Expenses:* Tuition $2454 per year full-time, $102 per hour part-time for state residents; $7362 per year full-time, $307 per hour part-time for nonresidents. Fees $1048 per year full-time, $44 per hour part-time. *Financial aid:* Research assistantships, teaching assistantships, full tuition waivers available. • Dr. Ron Mottram, Chairperson, Department of Art, 309-438-5621.

Indiana University Bloomington, School of Fine Arts, Bloomington, IN 47405. Offerings include art education (MAT). School faculty: 21 full-time (9 women). *Application deadline:* 1/15 (priority date; 9/1 for spring admission). *Application fee:* $35. *Expenses:* Tuition $153 per credit hour for state residents; $446 per credit hour for nonresidents. Fees $343 per year. • Jefferey Wolin, Director, 812-855-7766. Application contact: Daryl King, Graduate Secretary, 812-855-9556. E-mail: dalking@indiana.edu.

Indiana University Bloomington, School of Education, Department of Curriculum and Instruction, Bloomington, IN 47405. Offerings include art education (MS). Accredited by NASAD and NCATE. Department faculty: 23 full-time (9 women). *Entrance requirements:* GRE General Test (minimum combined score of 1300 on three sections). Application deadline: 3/1 (priority date; rolling processing). Application fee: $35. *Expenses:* Tuition $153 per credit hour for state residents; $446 per credit hour for nonresidents. Fees $343 per year. • Peter Kloosterman, Chairperson, 812-856-8100. Application contact: Sara White, 812-856-8100.

Indiana University–Purdue University Indianapolis, Herron School of Art, Indianapolis, IN 46202-2896. Offers program in art education (MAE). Accredited by NASAD. Part-time and evening/weekend programs available. Students: 1 (woman) full-time, 11 part-time (9 women); includes 1 African American. 67% of applicants accepted. *Entrance requirements:* Portfolio, 44 hours in art history and studio art. Application deadline: 7/15 (priority date; rolling processing; 10/11 for spring admission). Application fee: $25. *Expenses:* Tuition $3602 per year full-time, $150 per credit hour part-time for state residents; $10,392 per year full-time, $433 per credit hour part-time for nonresidents. Fees $100 per year (minimum) full-time, $40 per year (minimum) part-time. *Financial aid:* Federal Work-Study available. • Robert Shay, Dean, 317-920-2403. E-mail: rshay@indyvax.iupui.edu. Application contact: Cindy Borgmann, Program Coordinator, 317-920-2451. Fax: 317-920-2401. E-mail: cborgman@champion.iupui.edu.

Jacksonville University, College of Arts and Sciences, Division of Education, Program in Art, 2800 University Boulevard North, Jacksonville, FL 32211-3394. Awards MAT. Part-time and evening/weekend programs available. *Degree requirements:* Comprehensive exam required, foreign language and thesis not required. *Entrance requirements:* GRE General Test (minimum combined score of 900), TOEFL (minimum score 500), minimum GPA of 3.0. Application deadline: 8/1 (priority date; rolling processing; 11/1 for spring admission). Application fee: $25.

James Madison University, College of Arts and Letters, School of Art and Art History, Harrisonburg, VA 22807. Offerings include art education (MA). Accredited by NASAD and NCATE. School faculty: 5 full-time (3 women). *Application deadline:* 7/1 (priority date; rolling processing). *Application fee:* $50. *Tuition:* $134 per credit hour for state residents; $404 per credit hour for nonresidents. • Dr. Cole Welter, Director, 540-568-6216.

Kean University, School of Liberal Arts, Department of Fine Arts, Union, NJ 07083. Offers program in fine arts education (MA). Accredited by NASAD. Part-time programs available. Students: 14 full-time (11 women), 30 part-time (21 women); includes 4 minority (2 African Americans, 2 Hispanics). Average age 37. In 1997, 4 degrees awarded. *Degree requirements:* Thesis or alternative required, foreign language not required. *Entrance requirements:* GRE General Test, portfolio. Application deadline: 6/15 (11/15 for spring admission). Application fee: $35. *Tuition:* $5926 per year full-time, $248 per credit part-time for state residents; $7312 per year full-time, $304 per credit part-time for nonresidents. *Financial aid:* Graduate assistantships available. • Richard Buncamper, Coordinator, 908-527-2691. Application contact: Joanne Morris, Director of Graduate Admissions, 908-527-2665. Fax: 908-527-2286. E-mail: grad_adm@turbo.kean.edu.

Kent State University, College of Fine and Professional Arts, School of Art, Program in Art Education, Kent, OH 44242-0001. Awards MA. Accredited by NASAD and NCATE. *Degree requirements:* Thesis required, foreign language not required. *Entrance requirements:* Minimum GPA of 2.5. Application deadline: 7/12 (rolling processing; 11/29 for spring admission). Application fee: $30. *Tuition:* $4752 per year full-time, $216 per credit hour part-time for state residents; $9213 per year full-time, $419 per credit hour part-time for nonresidents. *Financial aid:* Research assistantships, teaching assistantships, full tuition waivers, Federal Work-Study available. Financial aid application deadline: 2/1. • William Quinn, Director, School of Art, 330-672-2192. Application contact: Frank Susi, Graduate Coordinator, 330-672-2192. Fax: 330-672-4729.

Kutztown University of Pennsylvania, Graduate School, College of Education, Program in Art Education, Kutztown, PA 19530. Awards M Ed. Accredited by NCATE. Part-time programs available. Faculty: 1 (woman) full-time. Students: 11 full-time (7 women), 24 part-time (23 women); includes 2 minority (both Hispanics). Average age 32. In 1997, 6 degrees awarded. *Degree requirements:* Comprehensive exams required, thesis optional, foreign language not required. *Entrance requirements:* GRE, TOEFL, TSE, teacher certification. Application deadline: 3/1 (8/1 for spring admission). Application fee: $25. *Tuition:* $4111 per year full-time, $225 per credit hour part-time for state residents; $6879 per year full-time, $393 per credit hour part-time for nonresidents. *Financial aid:* Graduate assistantships, partial tuition waivers, Federal Work-Study, and career-related internships or fieldwork available. Financial aid application deadline: 3/15; applicants required to submit FAFSA. *Faculty research:* Teaching of art history, child development in art, aesthetics and criticism curriculum, multicultural education, assessment in art. • Dr. Mary Burkett, Chairperson, 610-683-4520.

Lander University, School of Education, Greenwood, SC 29649-2099. Offerings include art (MAT). School faculty: 9 full-time (5 women). *Application deadline:* rolling. *Application fee:* $25. *Tuition:* $3700 per year full-time, $148 per semester hour part-time for state residents; $6326 per year full-time, $253 per semester hour part-time for nonresidents. • Dr. Phil Bennett, Dean, 864-388-8225.

Lesley College, Graduate School of Arts and Social Sciences, Cambridge, MA 02138-2790. Offerings include creative arts in learning (M Ed, CAGS), with options in individually designed (M Ed), multicultural education (M Ed), storytelling (M Ed), theater studies (M Ed). Postbaccalaureate distance learning degree programs offered (minimal on-campus study). School faculty: 24 full-time (14 women), 344 part-time (225 women). *Degree requirements:* For CAGS, thesis, internship (clinical mental health counseling, counseling psychology, expressive therapies). *Entrance requirements:* For CAGS, interview, master's degree. Application deadline: rolling. Application fee: $45. *Tuition:* $425 per credit. • Dr. Martha B. McKenna, Dean, 617-349-8467. Application contact: Graduate Admissions, 617-349-8300. Fax: 617-349-8366.

Long Island University, C.W. Post Campus, School of Education, Department of Curriculum and Instruction, Brookville, NY 11548-1300. Offerings include art education (MS). Department faculty: 10 full-time (5 women), 46 part-time (19 women). *Application deadline:* rolling. *Applica-*

tion fee: $30. Electronic applications accepted. *Expenses:* Tuition $480 per credit. Fees $316 per year full-time, $71 per semester (minimum) part-time. • Dr. Anthony De Falco, Chairperson, 516-299-2372. Application contact: Camille Marziliano, Academic Counselor, 516-299-2123. Fax: 516-299-4167. E-mail: cmarzili@eagle.liunet.edu.

Long Island University, C.W. Post Campus, School of Visual and Performing Arts, Department of Art, Brookville, NY 11548-1300. Offerings include art education (MS). Department faculty: 14 full-time (7 women), 15 part-time (7 women). *Average time to degree:* master's–2 years full-time, 3 years part-time. *Application deadline:* rolling. *Application fee:* $30. Electronic applications accepted. *Expenses:* Tuition $480 per credit. Fees $316 per year full-time, $71 per semester (minimum) part-time. • Jerome Zimmerman, Chair, 516-299-2464. Application contact: Andrew Ruhren, Graduate Adviser, 516-299-3844.

Manhattanville College, School of Education, Program in Art Education, Purchase, NY 10577-2132. Awards MAT. *Degree requirements:* Thesis, comprehensive exam or research project required, foreign language not required. *Entrance requirements:* Minimum undergraduate GPA of 3.0. Application deadline: rolling. Application fee: $40. *Expenses:* Tuition $410 per credit (minimum). Fees $25 per semester. • Application contact: Carol Messar, Director of Admissions, 914-323-5142. Fax: 914-323-5493.

Mankato State University, College of Arts and Humanities, Department of Art, South Rd and Ellis Ave, PO Box 8400, Mankato, MN 56002-8400. Offerings include art education (MS), teaching art (MAT, MT). One or more programs accredited by NASAD. Department faculty: 12 full-time (4 women). *Application deadline:* 7/10 (priority date; rolling processing; 10/30 for spring admission). *Application fee:* $20. *Tuition:* $126 per credit (minimum) for state residents; $200 per credit for nonresidents. • Dr. Bob Finkler, Chairman, 507-389-6412. Application contact: Joni Roberts, Admissions Coordinator, 507-389-2321. Fax: 507-389-5974. E-mail: grad@mankato.msus.edu.

Mansfield University of Pennsylvania, Department of Art, Mansfield, PA 16933. Offers program in art education (M Ed). Part-time programs available. Faculty: 6 part-time (1 woman). Students: 5 full-time (4 women), 2 part-time (1 woman); includes 1 minority (Asian American). Average age 31. 1 applicant, 100% accepted. In 1997, 2 degrees awarded. *Degree requirements:* Thesis optional, foreign language not required. *Entrance requirements:* GRE or MAT, minimum GPA of 3.0. Application deadline: 8/1 (priority date; rolling processing). Application fee: $25. *Expenses:* Tuition $3468 per year full-time, $193 per credit part-time for state residents; $6236 per year full-time, $346 per credit part-time for nonresidents. Fees $236 per year full-time, $18.25 per semester (minimum) part-time for state residents; $266 per year full-time, $18.25 per semester (minimum) part-time for nonresidents. *Financial aid:* In 1997–98, 1 graduate assistantship (to a first-year student) was awarded. Aid available to part-time students. Financial aid application deadline: 5/1; applicants required to submit FAFSA. • Dr. Harold Carter, Chairperson, 717-662-4503.

Maryland Institute, College of Art, Program in Art Education, Baltimore, MD 21217-4192. Awards MAT, MFA. Accredited by NASAD. Part-time programs available. Faculty: 3 full-time (2 women), 2 part-time (1 woman), 4.7 FTE. Students: 50 full-time (37 women), 3 part-time (1 woman); includes 9 minority (5 African Americans, 2 Asian Americans, 2 Hispanics), 1 international. In 1997, 18 degrees awarded. *Degree requirements:* Exhibit required, foreign language and thesis not required. *Average time to degree:* master's–1 year full-time, 4 years part-time. *Entrance requirements:* 40 studio credits, 6 credits in art history, portfolio, professional certification (MFA). Application deadline: 3/1 (10/1 for spring admission). Application fee: $50. *Expenses:* Tuition $17,250 per year. Fees $220 per year. *Financial aid:* Fellowships, teaching assistantships, and career-related internships or fieldwork available. Financial aid application deadline: 3/1; applicants required to submit FAFSA. • Dr. Karen Carroll, Director, 410-225-2297. Application contact: Sandra D. Ray, Assistant to the Dean, 410-225-2255. Fax: 410-225-2408.

Maryville University of Saint Louis, School of Education, St. Louis, MO 63141-7299. Offerings include art education (MA). Accredited by NCATE. School faculty: 9 full-time (7 women), 15 part-time (9 women). *Degree requirements:* Thesis, project required, foreign language not required. *Average time to degree:* master's–2 years full-time, 4 years part-time. *Entrance requirements:* Minimum GPA of 3.0. Application deadline: rolling. Application fee: $20. Electronic applications accepted. *Expenses:* Tuition $11,480 per year full-time, $345 per credit hour part-time. Fees $120 per year full-time, $60 per year part-time. • Dr. Kathe Rasch, Dean, 314-529-9466. Fax: 314-529-9921. E-mail: krasch@maryville.edu.

Marywood University, Graduate School of Arts and Sciences, Art Department, Program in Art Education, Scranton, PA 18509-1598. Awards MA. Accredited by NASAD and NCATE. Part-time and evening/weekend programs available. Students: 2 full-time (both women), 4 part-time (all women). Average age 36. 0 applicants. *Degree requirements:* Thesis or alternative, comprehensive exam required, foreign language not required. *Entrance requirements:* GRE or MAT, TOEFL (minimum score 500; average 590), portfolio. Application deadline: 7/15 (priority date; rolling processing; 12/1 for spring admission). Application fee: $20. *Expenses:* Tuition $449 per credit hour. Fees $530 per year full-time, $180 per year part-time. *Financial aid:* Research assistantships, scholarships/tuition reductions, partial tuition waivers available. Aid available to part-time students. Financial aid application deadline: 2/15; applicants required to submit FAFSA. *Faculty research:* Current trends in art education, color theories, research in Mariology. • Sr. Rosemary Ludwick, IHM, Coordinator, 717-348-6211 Ext. 2606. Application contact: Deborah M. Flynn, Coordinator of Admissions, 717-340-6002. Fax: 717-961-4745.

Massachusetts College of Art, Program in Art Education, Boston, MA 02115-5882. Awards MSAE. Accredited by NASAD. Part-time programs available. Faculty: 2 full-time (1 woman), 5 part-time (all women). Students: 60. *Degree requirements:* Thesis required, foreign language not required. *Entrance requirements:* Portfolio. Application deadline: 3/15 (11/1 for spring admission). Application fee: $50. *Tuition:* $6000 per year full-time, $225 per credit part-time. *Financial aid:* Teaching assistantships, administrative assistantships, Federal Work-Study, and career-related internships or fieldwork available. Aid available to part-time students. Financial aid application deadline: 5/1. *Faculty research:* Museum education, history of visual arts education, teaching studio art K–12. • Claudine Bing, Chairperson, 617-232-1555 Ext. 411. Application contact: Kay Ransdell, Associate Dean for Admissions and Retention, 617-232-1555 Ext. 235. Fax: 617-566-4034.

McGill University, Faculty of Graduate Studies and Research, Faculty of Education, Department of Culture and Values in Education, Montréal, PQ H3A 2T5, Canada. Offerings include art education (M Ed). M Ed and PhD new for fall 1998. Department faculty: 11 full-time (4 women), 8 part-time (3 women). *Application deadline:* 3/1 (priority date; rolling processing). *Application fee:* $60. *Expenses:* Tuition $1668 per year for Canadian residents; $8268 per year for nonresidents. Fees $828 per year for Canadian residents; $1216 per year for nonresidents. • D. C. Smith, Chair, 514-398-3328. E-mail: smith@education.mcgill.ca. Application contact: R. Ghosh, Director of Graduate Studies, 514-398-4493. Fax: 514-398-4642. E-mail: ghosh@education.mcgill.ca.

Miami University, School of Fine Arts, Department of Art, Program in Art Education, Oxford, OH 45056. Awards MA, M Ed. One or more programs accredited by NASAD. Accredited by NCATE. Students: 8 full-time (6 women), 7 part-time (4 women); includes 1 minority (African American). 13 applicants, 77% accepted. In 1997, 3 degrees awarded. *Degree requirements:* Thesis or alternative, exhibit, speech, article, or oral exam required, foreign language not required. *Entrance requirements:* Minimum undergraduate GPA of 3.0 during previous 2 years or 2.75 overall. Application deadline: 3/1 (priority date; rolling processing; 10/15 for spring admission). Application fee: $35. *Tuition:* $5932 per year full-time, $255 per credit hour part-time for state residents; $12,392 per year full-time, $524 per credit hour part-time for nonresidents. *Financial aid:* Fellowships, research assistantships, teaching assistantships, full tuition waivers, Federal Work-Study available. Financial aid application deadline: 3/1. • Ralph Raunft, Director of Graduate Study, 513-529-2900.

Millersville University of Pennsylvania, School of Humanities and Social Sciences, Department of Art, Millersville, PA 17551-0302. Awards M Ed. Accredited by NCATE. Part-time and evening/weekend programs available. Faculty: 11 full-time (5 women), 5 part-time (3 women). Students: 13 full-time (11 women), 9 part-time (5 women). Average age 32. 9 applicants, 89% accepted. In 1997, 3 degrees awarded. *Degree requirements:* Thesis or alternative, departmental exam required, foreign language not required. *Entrance requirements:* GRE or MAT, minimum QPA of 3.25 in art, 2.75 overall, portfolio review. Application deadline: 5/1 (priority date; rolling processing). Application fee: $25. *Tuition:* $3468 per year full-time, $234 per credit part-time for state residents; $6236 per year full-time, $387 per credit part-time for nonresidents. *Financial aid:* In 1997–98, 1 graduate assistantship (to a first-year student) averaging $445 per month and totaling $4,000 was awarded; Federal Work-Study, institutionally sponsored loans also available. Aid available to part-time students. Financial aid application deadline: 5/1. *Faculty research:* Researching historical photographs of Lancaster County. • Dr. Ronald Sykes, Coordinator, 717-872-3300. Fax: 717-871-2003. Application contact: Dr. Robert J. Labriola, Dean of Graduate Studies, 717-872-3030. Fax: 717-871-2022.

Mississippi College, School of Education, Programs in Secondary Education, Program in Art Education, Clinton, MS 39058. Awards M Ed. Accredited by NCATE. Part-time and evening/weekend programs available. *Degree requirements:* Comprehensive exam required, foreign language and thesis not required. *Entrance requirements:* GRE or NTE, minimum GPA of 2.5, Class A Certificate. Application deadline: 8/15 (priority date; rolling processing). Application fee: $25 ($75 for international students). *Expenses:* Tuition $6624 per year full-time, $276 per hour part-time. Fees $230 per year full-time, $35 per semester (minimum) part-time. *Financial aid:* Teaching assistantships, professional development scholarships, and career-related internships or fieldwork available. Aid available to part-time students. Financial aid application deadline: 4/1. • Dr. Ruth Glaze, Head, 601-925-3807.

Moorhead State University, Department of Art, Moorhead, MN 56563-0002. Offerings include art education (MS). Accredited by NASAD. Program being phased out; applicants no longer accepted. Department faculty: 5 full-time (1 woman). *Tuition:* $145 per credit hour for state residents; $220 per credit hour for nonresidents. • Allen Sheets, Chairperson, 218-236-2369.

Morehead State University, Caudill College of Humanities, Department of Art, Program in Art Education, Morehead, KY 40351. Awards MA. Accredited by NCATE. Part-time and evening/weekend programs available. Students: 0. 0 applicants. *Degree requirements:* Thesis, oral and qualifying exams required, foreign language not required. *Entrance requirements:* GRE General Test (minimum combined score of 1000 on three sections), minimum GPA of 3.0 in major, 2.5 overall; portfolio; bachelor's degree in art. Application deadline: 8/1 (priority date; rolling processing; 12/1 for spring admission). Application fee: $0. *Tuition:* $2470 per year full-time, $138 per semester hour part-time for state residents; $6710 per year full-time, $373 per semester hour part-time for nonresidents. *Financial aid:* Research assistantships, teaching assistantships, Federal Work-Study available. Financial aid application deadline: 4/1; applicants required to submit FAFSA. *Faculty research:* Computer-assisted instruction in elementary school art. • Application contact: Betty Cowsert, Graduate Admissions Officer, 606-783-2039. Fax: 606-783-5061.

Nazareth College of Rochester, Graduate Studies, Department of Art, Program in Art Education, Rochester, NY 14618-3790. Awards MS Ed. Part-time and evening/weekend programs available. Faculty: 5 full-time (3 women), 2 part-time (1 woman). Students: 19 part-time (14 women); includes 2 minority (1 Hispanic, 1 Native American). 7 applicants, 100% accepted. In 1997, 7 degrees awarded. *Degree requirements:* Comprehensive exam required, foreign language and thesis not required. *Entrance requirements:* Minimum GPA of 2.7. Application deadline: 6/1 (11/1 for spring admission). Application fee: $40. *Expenses:* Tuition $436 per credit hour. Fees $20 per semester. • Dr. Karen Trickey, Director, 716-389-2537. Application contact: Dr. Kay F. Marshman, Dean, 716-389-2815. Fax: 716-389-2452.

New Jersey City University, School of Arts and Sciences, Department of Art, Jersey City, NJ 07305-1957. Offerings include art education (MA). Accredited by NASAD. *Degree requirements:* Thesis or alternative, exhibit required, foreign language not required. *Entrance requirements:* GRE General Test, TOEFL or MAT, portfolio. Application deadline: 8/1 (priority date; rolling processing; 12/1 for spring admission). Application fee: $0.

New York University, School of Education, Department of Art and Art Professions, Program in Art Education, New York, NY 10012-1019. Awards MA, Ed D, PhD. Part-time and evening/weekend programs available. Faculty: 2 full-time (1 woman), 3 part-time. Students: 16 full-time, 27 part-time. 50 applicants, 48% accepted. In 1997, 13 master's awarded. Terminal master's awarded for partial completion of doctoral program. *Degree requirements:* For master's, thesis required (for some programs), foreign language not required; for doctorate, dissertation. *Entrance requirements:* For master's, TOEFL; for doctorate, GRE General Test, TOEFL, interview. Application deadline: 2/1 (priority date; rolling processing; 12/1 for spring admission). Application fee: $40 ($60 for international students). *Financial aid:* Partial tuition waivers, Federal Work-Study, institutionally sponsored loans, and career-related internships or fieldwork available. Aid available to part-time students. Financial aid application deadline: 3/1; applicants required to submit FAFSA. *Faculty research:* Multicultural aesthetic inquiry, urban art education. • Director, 212-998-5700. Application contact: Office of Graduate Admissions, 212-998-5030. Fax: 212-995-4328.

North Carolina Agricultural and Technical State University, Graduate School, College of Arts and Sciences, Department of Art, Greensboro, NC 27411. Offers program in art education (MS). One or more programs accredited by NCATE. Part-time and evening/weekend programs available. Faculty: 2 full-time (0 women). Students: 1 full-time (0 women); includes 1 minority (African American). Average age 25. 0 applicants. *Degree requirements:* Thesis or alternative, comprehensive exam, qualifying exam required, foreign language not required. *Entrance requirements:* GRE General Test, minimum GPA of 2.6. Application deadline: 6/1 (priority date; rolling processing; 12/1 for spring admission). Application fee: $35. *Tuition:* $1662 per year full-time, $272 per semester (minimum) part-time for state residents; $8790 per year full-time, $2054 per semester (minimum) part-time for nonresidents. *Financial aid:* Application deadline 6/1. • Dr. Timothy Hicks, Chairman, 336-334-7933.

North Georgia College & State University, Graduate School, Program in Education, Dahlonega, GA 30597-1001. Offerings include secondary education (M Ed), with options in art education, biology education, chemistry education, English education, mathematics education, modern languages education, physical education, science education, social science education. Accredited by NCATE. Program faculty: 57 full-time (15 women), 7 part-time (4 women). *Degree requirements:* Comprehensive exam required, thesis optional, foreign language not required. *Entrance requirements:* GRE General Test (minimum combined score of 800) or MAT (minimum score 44), minimum GPA of 2.75. Application deadline: 9/1 (priority date; rolling processing). Application fee: $25. • Dr. Bob Michael, Dean, School of Education, 706-864-1533. Application contact: Mai-Lan Ledbetter, Coordinator of Graduate Admissions, 706-864-1543. Fax: 706-864-1668. E-mail: mledbetter@nugget.ngc.peachnet.edu.

Northwest Missouri State University, College of Arts and Sciences, Department of Art, 800 University Drive, Maryville, MO 64468-6001. Offers program in teaching art (MS Ed). Faculty: 8 full-time (0 women). Students: 1 (woman) full-time. 1 applicant, 100% accepted. In 1997, 1 degree awarded. *Degree requirements:* Comprehensive exam required, foreign language and thesis not required. *Entrance requirements:* GRE General Test (minimum combined score of 700), TOEFL (minimum score 550), minimum undergraduate GPA of 2.5, writing sample. Application deadline: rolling. Application fee: $0 ($50 for international students). *Expenses:* Tuition $113 per credit hour for state residents; $197 per credit hour for nonresidents. Fees $3 per credit hour. *Financial aid:* In 1997–98, 1 research assistantship averaging $585 per month was awarded; teaching assistantships also available. Financial aid application deadline: 3/1. • Lee Hageman, Chairperson, 816-562-1314. Application contact: Dr. Frances Shipley, Dean of Graduate School, 816-562-1145. E-mail: gradsch@acad.nwmissouri.edu.

Directory: Art Education

Nova Scotia College of Art and Design, Program in Art Education, Halifax, NS B3J 3J6, Canada. Awards MAAE. Students: 2 full-time (1 woman), 2 part-time (both women). *Degree requirements:* Thesis, exhibit. *Entrance requirements:* BA in art education or equivalent, 1 year of teaching experience, portfolio. Application deadline: 6/3 (10/2 for spring admission). Application fee: $25. *Financial aid:* Teaching assistantships, institutionally sponsored loans available. Aid available to part-time students. *Faculty research:* Philosophical and psychological issues in art education, child art. • Dr. Nick Webb, Chair, 902-494-8149.

The Ohio State University, College of the Arts, Department of Art Education, Columbus, OH 43210. Offers programs in art education (MA, PhD), arts policy and administration (MA). Accredited by NASAD and NCATE. Faculty: 16. Students: 63 full-time (48 women), 51 part-time (41 women); includes 10 minority (4 African Americans, 4 Asian Americans, 2 Native Americans), 20 international. 69 applicants, 57% accepted. In 1997, 11 master's, 7 doctorates awarded. *Degree requirements:* Thesis/dissertation. *Application deadline:* 8/15 (rolling processing). *Application fee:* $30 ($40 for international students). *Tuition:* $5472 per year full-time, $554 per quarter (minimum) part-time for state residents; $14,172 per year full-time, $1424 per quarter (minimum) part-time for nonresidents. *Financial aid:* Fellowships, research assistantships, teaching assistantships, Federal Work-Study, institutionally sponsored loans, and career-related internships or fieldwork available. Aid available to part-time students. Financial aid applicants required to submit FAFSA. • James W. Hutchens, Chairman, 614-292-7183. Fax: 614-688-4483. E-mail: hutchens.1@osu.edu.

Ohio University, Graduate Studies, College of Fine Arts, School of Art, Athens, OH 45701-2979. Offerings include art education (MA). Accredited by NCATE. School faculty: 32 full-time (16 women), 4 part-time (2 women). *Application deadline:* 3/1. *Application fee:* $30. *Tuition:* $5430 per year full-time, $216 per quarter hour part-time for state residents; $10,431 per year full-time, $423 per quarter hour part-time for nonresidents. • Judith Perani, Interim Director, 740-593-4290. Application contact: Michael Harper, Assistant Director of Graduate Affairs, 740-593-0274. Fax: 740-593-0457. E-mail: harper@art.ohiou.edu.

Pennsylvania State University University Park Campus, College of Arts and Architecture, School of Visual Arts, Program in Art Education, University Park, PA 16802-1503. Awards M Ed, MS, D Ed, PhD. Accredited by NASAD and NCATE. Students: 27 full-time (21 women), 14 part-time (12 women). *Entrance requirements:* GRE General Test or MAT. Application fee: $40. *Expenses:* Tuition $6534 per year full-time, $276 per credit part-time for state residents; $13,460 per year full-time, $561 per credit part-time for nonresidents. Fees $252 per year (minimum) full-time, $43 per semester (minimum) part-time. • Dr. Brent G. Wilson, Head, 814-865-6570.

Plymouth State College of the University System of New Hampshire, Department of Education, Program in Integrated Arts, Plymouth, NH 03264-1595. Awards M Ed. Part-time and evening/weekend programs available. Students: 7 part-time (6 women). Average age 43. 2 applicants, 50% accepted. In 1997, 6 degrees awarded. *Entrance requirements:* GRE General Test (average 500 on each section) or MAT (minimum score 50), minimum GPA of 3.0. Application deadline: 9/1 (priority date; rolling processing). Application fee: $25 ($35 for international students). *Tuition:* $232 per credit for state residents; $254 per credit for nonresidents. *Financial aid:* Graduate assistantships, institutionally sponsored loans, and career-related internships or fieldwork available. Aid available to part-time students. Financial aid application deadline: 3/15; applicants required to submit FAFSA. • Dr. Patricia Lindberg, Adviser, 603-535-2647. Application contact: Maryann Szabadics, Administrative Assistant, 603-535-2636. Fax: 603-535-2572. E-mail: for.grad@psc.plymouth.edu.

Pratt Institute, School of Art and Design, Program in Art and Design Education, Brooklyn, NY 11205-3899. Awards MS. Accredited by NASAD. *Degree requirements:* Thesis required, foreign language not required. *Entrance requirements:* TOEFL (minimum score 550). Application deadline: 3/1. Application fee: $35 ($80 for international students). *Expenses:* Tuition $15,288 per year full-time, $637 per credit part-time. Fees $480 per year.

Purdue University, School of Education, Department of Curriculum and Instruction, West Lafayette, IN 47907. Offerings include art education (PhD). Accredited by NCATE. Department faculty: 34 full-time (15 women), 3 part-time (1 woman). *Degree requirements:* Dissertation, oral and written exams. *Entrance requirements:* GRE General Test (minimum score 500 on each section), TOEFL (minimum score 550). Application deadline: 1/15 (priority date; 9/15 for spring admission). Application fee: $30. Electronic applications accepted. *Tuition:* $3500 per year full-time, $126 per credit hour part-time for state residents; $11,720 per year full-time, $387 per credit hour part-time for nonresidents. • Dr. J. L. Peters, Head, 765-494-9172. Fax: 765-496-1622. E-mail: peters@purdue.edu. Application contact: Christine Larsen, Coordinator of Graduate Studies, 765-494-2345. Fax: 765-494-5832. E-mail: gradoffice@soe.purdue.edu.

Queens College of the City University of New York, Social Science Division, School of Education, Department of Secondary Education, 65-30 Kissena Boulevard, Flushing, NY 11367-1597. Offerings include art (MS Ed). *Degree requirements:* Research project required, foreign language and thesis not required. *Entrance requirements:* TOEFL (minimum score 600), minimum GPA of 3.0. Application deadline: 4/1 (rolling processing; 11/1 for spring admission). Application fee: $40. *Expenses:* Tuition $4350 per year full-time, $185 per credit part-time for state residents; $7600 per year full-time, $320 per credit part-time for nonresidents. Fees $104 per year. • Dr. Philip Anderson, Chairperson, 718-997-5150. Application contact: Mario Caruso, Director of Graduate Admissions, 718-997-5200. Fax: 718-997-5193. E-mail: graduate%queens.bitnet@cunyvm.cuny.edu.

Radford University, Graduate College, College of Visual and Performing Arts, Department of Art, Radford, VA 24142. Offerings include art education (MS). Accredited by NCATE. Postbaccalaureate distance learning degree programs offered (minimal on-campus study). Department faculty: 13 full-time (6 women). *Application deadline:* 2/1 (priority date; rolling processing; 10/1 for spring admission). *Application fee:* $25. Electronic applications accepted. *Expenses:* Tuition $2302 per year full-time, $147 per credit hour part-time for state residents; $5672 per year full-time, $287 per credit hour part-time for nonresidents. Fees $1222 per year full-time. • Dr. Arthur F. Jones, Chairperson, 540-831-5475. Fax: 540-831-6313. E-mail: ajones@runet.edu.

Rhode Island College, School of Graduate Studies, Faculty of Arts and Sciences, Department of Art, Program in Art Education and Studio Art, Providence, RI 02908-1924. Offers art education (MAT), art studio (MA). Accredited by NASAD. Faculty: 12 full-time (3 women), 7 part-time (4 women). Students: 14 full-time (11 women), 11 part-time (10 women); includes 1 minority (Hispanic). In 1997, 3 degrees awarded. *Degree requirements:* Thesis. *Entrance requirements:* GRE General Test or MAT, portfolio (MA). Application deadline: 4/1 (rolling processing). Application fee: $25. *Tuition:* $4064 per year full-time, $214 per credit part-time for state residents; $7658 per year full-time, $376 per credit part-time for nonresidents. *Financial aid:* Career-related internships or fieldwork available. Financial aid application deadline: 4/1. • Dr. Mary Ball Howkins, Chair, Department of Art, 401-456-8054.

Rhode Island School of Design, Program in Art Education, Providence, RI 02903-2784. Awards MA, MAT. Accredited by NASAD. *Degree requirements:* Thesis, exhibit required, foreign language not required. *Entrance requirements:* Portfolio. Application deadline: 2/1. Application fee: $35.

Rochester Institute of Technology, College of Imaging Arts and Sciences, School of Art and Design, Programs in Art Education, Rochester, NY 14623-5604. Awards MST. Accredited by NASAD. Students: 12 full-time (6 women), 1 (woman) part-time. 17 applicants, 94% accepted. In 1997, 11 degrees awarded. *Entrance requirements:* Portfolio, minimum GPA of 3.0. Application deadline: 3/1 (priority date; rolling processing). Application fee: $40. *Expenses:* Tuition $18,765 per year full-time, $527 per credit hour part-time. Fees $126 per year full-time. • David Dickinson, Chairperson, 716-475-6125.

Rockford College, Department of Education, Program in Secondary Education, Rockford, IL 61108-2393. Offerings include art education (MAT). Program faculty: 15 full-time (2 women), 8 part-time (6 women), 17 FTE. *Degree requirements:* Thesis optional, foreign language not required. *Entrance requirements:* GRE General Test (minimum combined score of 1000). Application deadline: rolling. Application fee: $35. *Tuition:* $15,500 per year full-time, $400 per credit part-time. • Dr. Debra Dew, Head, 815-392-5202. Fax: 815-226-4119.

Rowan University, College of Education, Department of Secondary Education-Education Foundations, Program in Subject Matter Teaching, Program in Art Education, Glassboro, NJ 08028-1701. Awards MA. Accredited by NASAD and NCATE. Part-time and evening/weekend programs available. Students: 2 (both women). 1 applicant, 100% accepted. In 1997, 1 degree awarded. *Degree requirements:* Thesis, comprehensive exams required, foreign language not required. *Entrance requirements:* GRE General Test (minimum combined score of 800), minimum GPA of 2.8. Application deadline: 11/1 (priority date; rolling processing; 4/1 for spring admission). Application fee: $50. *Tuition:* $5728 per year full-time, $258 per credit hour part-time for state residents; $8968 per year full-time, $393 per credit hour part-time for nonresidents. *Financial aid:* Federal Work-Study and career-related internships or fieldwork available. • Dr. Byron Young, Adviser, 609-256-4020.

St. Cloud State University, College of Fine Arts and Humanities, Department of Art, St. Cloud, MN 56301-4498. Offerings include art education (MS). Accredited by NASAD. Department faculty: 11 full-time (6 women). *Application fee:* $20 ($100 for international students). *Expenses:* Tuition $128 per credit for state residents; $203 per credit for nonresidents. Fees $16.32 per credit. • Dr. Virginia Bradley, Chairperson, 320-255-4283. Application contact: Ann Anderson, Graduate Studies Office, 320-255-2113. Fax: 320-654-5371. E-mail: anna@grad.stcloud.msus.edu.

Sam Houston State University, College of Arts and Sciences, Department of Art, Huntsville, TX 77341. Offerings include art education (M Ed). Accredited by NCATE. *Application deadline:* 4/15 (priority date; 10/15 for spring admission). *Application fee:* $15. *Tuition:* $1810 per year full-time, $297 per semester (minimum) part-time for state residents; $6922 per year full-time, $924 per semester (minimum) part-time for nonresidents. • Martin Amorous, Chair, 409-294-1315. E-mail: art_mfa@shsu.edu. Application contact: Gene Eastman, Graduate Adviser, 409-294-1318.

San Jose State University, College of Humanities and Arts, School of Art and Design, San Jose, CA 95192-0001. Offerings include art education (MA). Accredited by NASAD and NCATE. School faculty: 41 full-time (10 women), 25 part-time (5 women). *Application deadline:* 6/1 (rolling processing). *Application fee:* $59. *Expenses:* Tuition $0 for state residents; $246 per unit for nonresidents. Fees $2017 per year full-time, $1351 per year part-time. • Dr. Robert Milnes, Chair, 408-924-4320. Application contact: Dr. Paul Staiger, Graduate Adviser, 408-924-4345.

School of the Art Institute of Chicago, Program in Art Education, Chicago, IL 60603-3103. Awards MAAE, Certificate. Accredited by NASAD. Students: 45. 35 applicants, 74% accepted. *Entrance requirements:* For master's, TOEFL (minimum score 550). Application fee: $45. *Tuition:* $19,980 per year full-time, $666 per credit part-time. *Financial aid:* Partial tuition waivers, Federal Work-Study, and career-related internships or fieldwork available. Aid available to part-time students. Financial aid application deadline: 3/15; applicants required to submit FAFSA. • Drea Howenstein, Chairperson, 312-899-7482.

Smith College, Department of Education and Child Study, Program in Secondary Education, Northampton, MA 01063. Offerings include art education (MAT). Program faculty: 6 full-time (3 women), 3 part-time (2 women). *Degree requirements:* 1 foreign language required, thesis not required. *Average time to degree:* master's–1 year full-time, 4 years part-time. *Entrance requirements:* GRE General Test or MAT. Application deadline: 4/15 (12/1 for spring admission). Application fee: $50. *Tuition:* $21,680 per year full-time, $2720 per course part-time. • Rosetta Cohen, Head, 413-585-3266. E-mail: rcohen@sophia.smith.edu.

Southern Connecticut State University, School of Arts and Sciences, Department of Art, New Haven, CT 06515-1355. Offers program in art education (MS). Faculty: 9 full-time. Students: 3 full-time (2 women), 30 part-time (23 women). 60 applicants, 13% accepted. In 1997, 7 degrees awarded. *Degree requirements:* Thesis or alternative. *Entrance requirements:* Interview. Application deadline: 5/1 (priority date; rolling processing; 12/1 for spring admission). Application fee: $40. *Expenses:* Tuition $2632 per year full-time, $188 per credit part-time for state residents; $7200 per year full-time, $188 per credit part-time for nonresidents. Fees $1806 per year full-time, $45 per semester part-time for state residents; $2703 per year full-time, $45 per semester part-time for nonresidents. • Keith Hatcher, Chairman, 203-392-6654. Application contact: Dr. Kathleen Connors, Graduate Coordinator, 203-392-6659.

State University of New York at New Paltz, Faculty of Fine and Performing Arts, Department of Art Education, New Paltz, NY 12561-2499. Awards MS. Accredited by NASAD. Students: 22 part-time (20 women). In 1997, 11 degrees awarded. *Degree requirements:* Thesis required, foreign language not required. *Entrance requirements:* Art education certificate, minimum GPA of 3.0. Application deadline: 3/15 (priority date; rolling processing). Application fee: $50. *Expenses:* Tuition $5100 per year full-time, $213 per credit hour part-time for state residents; $8416 per year full-time, $351 per credit hour part-time for nonresidents. Fees $493 per year full-time, $48 per semester (minimum) part-time. • Francois Deschamps, Chair, 914-257-3850.

State University of New York at Oswego, School of Education, Department of Curriculum and Instruction, Oswego, NY 13126. Offerings include art education (MAT). Department faculty: 17 full-time, 5 part-time. *Application deadline:* 7/1. *Application fee:* $50. *Expenses:* Tuition $5100 per year full-time, $213 per credit hour part-time for state residents; $8416 per year full-time, $351 per credit hour part-time for nonresidents. Fees $135 per year (minimum). • Dr. Frank Bickel, Chairman, 315-341-4052. Application contact: Dr. Terrance Lindenberg, Coordinator, Graduate Education, 315-341-4052.

State University of New York College at Buffalo, Faculty of Arts and Humanities, Department of Art Education, Buffalo, NY 14222-1095. Awards MS Ed. Accredited by NCATE. Part-time and evening/weekend programs available. Faculty: 7 full-time (4 women). Students: 3 full-time (2 women), 50 part-time (41 women); includes 2 minority (both African Americans). Average age 32. 15 applicants, 80% accepted. In 1997, 18 degrees awarded. *Degree requirements:* Thesis or alternative, project required, foreign language not required. *Entrance requirements:* New York teaching certificate, interview, minimum GPA of 3.0. Application deadline: 5/1 (10/1 for spring admission). Application fee: $50. *Expenses:* Tuition $5100 per year full-time, $213 per credit hour part-time for state residents; $8416 per year full-time, $351 per credit hour part-time for nonresidents. Fees $195 per year full-time, $8.60 per credit hour part-time. *Financial aid:* Fellowships, assistantships, Federal Work-Study, and career-related internships or fieldwork available. Aid available to part-time students. Financial aid application deadline: 3/1. • Dr. Michael Parks, Chairperson, 716-878-4106.

State University of West Georgia, College of Arts and Sciences, Department of Art, Carrollton, GA 30118. Offers program in art education (M Ed). Accredited by NCATE. Part-time programs available. Faculty: 6 full-time (2 women). Students: 2 full-time (both women), 6 part-time (5 women); includes 2 minority (both African Americans). Average age 30. In 1997, 1 degree awarded (100% found work related to degree). *Entrance requirements:* GRE General Test (minimum combined score of 800) or MAT (minimum score 44), minimum GPA of 2.5, portfolio. Application deadline: 8/30. Application fee: $15. *Expenses:* Tuition $2428 per year full-time, $83 per semester hour part-time for state residents; $8428 per year full-time, $250 per semester hour part-time for nonresidents. Fees $428 per year. *Financial aid:* Career-related internships or fieldwork available. Aid available to part-time students. Financial aid applicants required to submit FAFSA. *Faculty research:* Digital imaging technology. Total annual research expenditures: $19,978. • J. Bruce Bobick, Chairman, 770-836-6521. Application contact: Dr. Jack O. Jenkins, Dean, Graduate School, 770-836-6419. Fax: 770-836-2301. E-mail: jjenkins@cob.as.westga.edu.

Sul Ross State University, School of Arts and Sciences, Department of Fine Arts and Communication, Alpine, TX 79832. Offerings include art education (M Ed). Department faculty: 3 full-time (1 woman). *Degree requirements:* Oral or written exam required, foreign language and thesis not required. *Entrance requirements:* GRE General Test (minimum combined score of 850), minimum GPA of 2.5 in last 60 hours of undergraduate work. Application deadline: rolling. Application fee: $0 ($50 for international students). *Expenses:* Tuition $864 per year full-time, $120 per semester (minimum) part-time for state residents; $5976 per year full-time, $747 per semester (minimum) part-time for nonresidents. Fees $754 per year full-time, $105 per semester (minimum) part-time. • Dr. George Bradley, Chair, 915-837-8221.

Syracuse University, School of Education, Teaching and Leadership Programs, Program in Art Education, Syracuse, NY 13244-0003. Awards MS, CAS. Students: 14 full-time (12 women), 10 part-time (6 women). 17 applicants, 100% accepted. In 1997, 10 master's awarded. *Degree requirements:* For master's, thesis or alternative; for CAS, thesis. *Entrance requirements:* GRE. Application fee: $40. *Tuition:* $13,320 per year full-time, $555 per credit hour part-time. *Financial aid:* Application deadline 3/1. • Dr. Hope Irvine, Chair, 315-443-2355.

Teachers College, Columbia University, Graduate Faculty of Education, Department of Arts and Humanities, Program in Art and Art Education, 525 West 120th Street, New York, NY 10027-6696. Awards Ed M, MA, Ed D, Ed DCT. Part-time and evening/weekend programs available. Faculty: 2 full-time (1 woman), 16 part-time (13 women), 8 FTE. Students: 30 full-time (26 women), 102 part-time (87 women); includes 11 minority (3 African Americans, 5 Asian Americans, 3 Hispanics), 12 international. Average age 38. 53 applicants, 83% accepted. In 1997, 23 master's awarded. Terminal master's awarded for partial completion of doctoral program. *Degree requirements:* For doctorate, variable foreign language requirement, dissertation. *Entrance requirements:* For doctorate, portfolio. Application deadline: 5/15 (12/1 for spring admission). Application fee: $50. *Expenses:* Tuition $640 per credit. Fees $120 per semester. *Financial aid:* Research assistantships, teaching assistantships, full and partial tuition waivers, Federal Work-Study, institutionally sponsored loans, and career-related internships or fieldwork available. Aid available to part-time students. Financial aid application deadline: 2/1. *Faculty research:* Technology and creativity with respect to pedagogy and curriculum, artistic-aesthetic development in children and adolescents. • Application contact: Amy Rotheim, Office of Admissions, 212-678-3710. Fax: 212-678-4171.

Temple University, Tyler School of Art, Department of Art Education, Philadelphia, PA 19122-6096. Awards M Ed. Accredited by NASAD. Faculty: 2 full-time (1 woman). Students: 11 (8 women). 11 applicants, 64% accepted. In 1997, 8 degrees awarded. *Degree requirements:* Paper, portfolio review required, foreign language and thesis not required. *Entrance requirements:* GRE or MAT, TOEFL (minimum score 600), minimum GPA of 2.8, slide portfolio, 40 credits in studio art, 12 credits in art history. Application deadline: 2/15. Application fee: $40. *Expenses:* Tuition $323 per semester hour for state residents; $444 per semester hour for nonresidents. Fees $170 per year full-time, $28 per semester (minimum) part-time. *Financial aid:* Research assistantships, teaching assistantships, Federal Work-Study available. Aid available to part-time students. Financial aid application deadline: 3/31; applicants required to submit FAFSA. • Dr. Jo Anna Moore, Coordinator, 215-782-2730. Application contact: Carmina Cianciulli, Assistant Dean for Admissions, 215-782-2875. Fax: 215-782-2711.

Texas Tech University, Graduate School, College of Arts and Sciences, Department of Art, Lubbock, TX 79409. Offerings include art education (MAE). Accredited by NASAD. Department faculty: 24 full-time (10 women), 1 (woman) part-time, 24.75 FTE. *Application deadline:* 4/15 (priority date; rolling processing; 11/1 for spring admission). *Application fee:* $25 ($50 for international students). Electronic applications accepted. *Expenses:* Tuition $864 per year full-time, $120 per semester (minimum) part-time for state residents; $5976 per year full-time, $747 per semester (minimum) part-time for nonresidents. Fees $1961 per year full-time, $257 per semester (minimum) part-time. • Dr. Melody Weiler, Chairperson, 806-742-3825. Fax: 806-742-1971.

Texas Tech University, Graduate School, College of Education, Division of Curriculum and Instruction, Lubbock, TX 79409. Offerings include art education (Certificate). Accredited by NCATE. Division faculty: 23 full-time (12 women). *Application deadline:* 4/15 (priority date; rolling processing; 11/1 for spring admission). *Application fee:* $25 ($50 for international students). Electronic applications accepted. *Expenses:* Tuition $864 per year full-time, $120 per semester (minimum) part-time for state residents; $5976 per year full-time, $747 per semester (minimum) part-time for nonresidents. Fees $2321 per year full-time, $302 per semester (minimum) part-time. • Dr. William E. Sparkman, Chair, 805-742-2371.

Texas Woman's University, College of Arts and Sciences, Department of Visual Arts, Program in Art Education, Denton, TX 76204. Awards MA. Faculty: 9 full-time (5 women), 4 part-time (3 women). Students: 1 (woman) full-time, 2 part-time (both women). Average age 41. 9 applicants, 100% accepted. *Degree requirements:* Thesis, oral exam, professional paper required, foreign language not required. *Entrance requirements:* GRE General Test (minimum combined score of 750), minimum GPA of 3.0, portfolio. Application deadline: 2/15 (priority date; rolling processing; 10/15 for spring admission). Application fee: $25. *Financial aid:* In 1997–98, 1 scholarship was awarded; Federal Work-Study and career-related internships or fieldwork also available. Aid available to part-time students. Financial aid application deadline: 4/1. *Faculty research:* Relationship of perceptual style to teaching, arts for the handicapped, mainstreaming curriculum design. • Gary Washman, Chair, Department of Visual Arts, 940-898-2530. Fax: 940-898-2496.

Towson University, Program in Art Education, Towson, MD 21252-0001. Awards M Ed. Part-time and evening/weekend programs available. Faculty: 13 full-time (3 women), 2 part-time (1 woman). Students: 33 part-time (28 women). In 1997, 8 degrees awarded. *Degree requirements:* Exam required, thesis optional. *Application deadline:* 3/1 (priority date; rolling processing; 10/1 for spring admission). *Application fee:* $40. *Expenses:* Tuition $187 per credit hour for state residents; $364 per credit hour for nonresidents. Fees $40 per credit hour. *Financial aid:* Assistantships, Federal Work-Study available. Financial aid application deadline: 4/1; applicants required to submit FAFSA. • Jane Bates, Director, 410-830-2797. Fax: 410-830-2810. E-mail: jbates@towson.edu. Application contact: Fran Musotto, Office Manager, 410-830-2501. Fax: 410-830-4675. E-mail: fmusotto@towson.edu.

The University of Alabama, College of Arts and Sciences, Department of Art, Tuscaloosa, AL 35487. Offerings include art education (MA). Accredited by NASAD and NCATE. MA (art history) offered jointly with the University of Alabama at Birmingham. Department faculty: 11 full-time (5 women). *Average time to degree:* master's–2 years full-time, 4 years part-time. *Application deadline:* 4/14 (priority date; rolling processing; 11/1 for spring admission). *Application fee:* $25. *Tuition:* $2684 per year full-time, $594 per semester (minimum) part-time for state residents; $7216 per year full-time, $1248 per semester (minimum) part-time for nonresidents. • W. Lowell Baker, Chairperson, 205-348-1889.

The University of Alabama at Birmingham, Graduate School, School of Education, Department of Curriculum and Instruction, Program in Arts Education, Birmingham, AL 35294. Awards MA Ed, Ed S. One or more programs accredited by NASAD. Accredited by NCATE. Students: 4 full-time (3 women), 2 part-time (1 woman); includes 3 minority (2 African Americans, 1 Hispanic). 4 applicants, 50% accepted. In 1997, 6 master's awarded. *Degree requirements:* For master's, thesis optional; for Ed S, comprehensive exam. *Entrance requirements:* For master's, GRE General Test, MAT, or NTE, minimum GPA of 3.0. Application deadline: rolling. Application fee: $30 ($60 for international students). Electronic applications accepted. *Expenses:* Tuition $99 per credit hour for state residents; $198 per credit hour for nonresidents. Fees $516 per year (minimum) full-time, $73 per quarter (minimum) part-time for state residents; $516 per year (minimum) full-time, $73 per unit (minimum) part-time for nonresidents. • Dr. Joseph C. Burns, Chair, Department of Curriculum and Instruction, 205-934-5371.

The University of Arizona, College of Fine Arts, Department of Art, Program in Art Education, Tucson, AZ 85721. Awards MA. *Degree requirements:* Thesis required, foreign language not required. *Entrance requirements:* TOEFL (minimum score 650), minimum GPA of 3.0, teaching certificate. Application deadline: 2/1 (rolling processing). Application fee: $35. *Tuition:* $2162 per year full-time, $337 per semester (minimum) part-time for state residents; $6860 per year full-time, $1138 per semester (minimum) part-time for nonresidents. *Faculty research:* Artistic styles, visual perception, integration of arts into elementary curricula, aesthetics of the vanishing roadsides of America.

University of Arkansas at Little Rock, College of Arts, Humanities, and Social Science, Department of Art, Little Rock, AR 72204-1099. Offerings include art education (MA). Accredited by NCATE. *Degree requirements:* 4 foreign languages, oral exam, oral defense of thesis or exhibit. *Entrance requirements:* GRE, portfolio review or term paper evaluation, minimum GPA of 2.7. Application deadline: 5/31 (priority date; rolling processing; 11/1 for spring admission). Application fee: $25 ($30 for international students). *Expenses:* Tuition $2466 per year full-time, $137 per credit hour part-time for state residents; $5256 per year full-time, $292 per credit hour part-time for nonresidents. Fees $216 per year full-time, $36 per semester (minimum) part-time. • Dr. Jane Brown, Chairperson, 501-569-3182. Application contact: Marjorie Williams-Smith, Coordinator, 501-569-3182.

University of British Columbia, Faculty of Education, Department of Curriculum Studies, Vancouver, BC V6T 1Z2, Canada. Offerings include art education (MA, M Ed, PhD). *Degree requirements:* For master's, thesis (MA) required, foreign language not required; for doctorate, dissertation required, foreign language not required. *Entrance requirements:* TOEFL (minimum score 550). Application deadline: 3/1 (12/1 for spring admission). Application fee: $60.

University of Central Florida, College of Education, Department of Instructional Programs, Program in Art Education, Orlando, FL 32816. Awards MA, M Ed. Accredited by NCATE. Part-time and evening/weekend programs available. Students: 12 full-time (11 women), 6 part-time (all women); includes 1 international. Average age 30. 3 applicants, 100% accepted. In 1997, 3 degrees awarded. *Degree requirements:* Thesis or alternative required, foreign language not required. *Entrance requirements:* GRE General Test (minimum combined score of 840). Application deadline: 7/15 (12/15 for spring admission). Application fee: $20. *Expenses:* Tuition $3288 per year full-time, $137 per credit hour part-time for state residents; $11,520 per year full-time, $480 per credit hour part-time for nonresidents. Fees $105 per year. *Financial aid:* Teaching assistantships, Federal Work-Study, institutionally sponsored loans, and career-related internships or fieldwork available. Aid available to part-time students. • Application contact: Dr. Thomas Brewer, Coordinator, 407-823-3714.

University of Cincinnati, College of Design, Architecture, Art and Planning, School of Art, Program in Art Education, Cincinnati, OH 45221. Awards MA. Accredited by NASAD and NCATE. Faculty: 3 full-time. Students: 8 full-time (all women), 7 part-time (all women); includes 1 minority (African American). 3 applicants, 67% accepted. In 1997, 2 degrees awarded. *Average time to degree:* master's–1.8 years full-time. *Entrance requirements:* MAT. Application deadline: 2/1. Application fee: $30. *Tuition:* $7228 per year full-time, $185 per credit hour part-time for state residents; $13,812 per year full-time, $352 per credit hour part-time for nonresidents. *Financial aid:* Fellowships, graduate assistantships, full tuition waivers available. Aid available to part-time students. Financial aid application deadline: 3/1. • Dr. Robert Russell, Director, 513-556-0265. Fax: 513-556-2887. E-mail: robert.russell@uc.edu.

University of Florida, College of Fine Arts, School of Art and Art History, Gainesville, FL 32611. Offerings include art education (MA). Accredited by NASAD and NCATE. School faculty: 31. *Application deadline:* 1/15 (priority date; rolling processing). *Application fee:* $20. *Tuition:* $138 per credit hour for state residents; $481 per credit hour for nonresidents. • Barbara Jo Revelle, Chair, 352-392-0211. Application contact: Linda Arbuckle, Graduate Adviser, 352-392-0201 Ext. 219. Fax: 352-392-8453. E-mail: arbuck@nerum.nerdc.ufl.edu.

University of Georgia, College of Education, Program in Art Education, Athens, GA 30602. Awards MA Ed, Ed D, Ed S. Accredited by NASAD and NCATE. Faculty: 31 full-time (10 women). Students: 8 full-time (all women), 11 part-time (10 women); includes 2 international. 10 applicants, 50% accepted. In 1997, 5 master's awarded. *Degree requirements:* For doctorate, dissertation required, foreign language not required. *Entrance requirements:* For master's, GRE General Test, MAT; for doctorate, GRE General Test; for Ed S, GRE General Test or MAT. Application deadline: 7/1 (priority date; 11/15 for spring admission). Application fee: $30. Electronic applications accepted. *Tuition:* $3290 per year full-time, $643 per semester (minimum) part-time for state residents; $11,300 per year full-time, $1645 per semester (minimum) part-time for nonresidents. *Financial aid:* Fellowships, research assistantships, teaching assistantships, assistantships available. • Dr. William T. Squires Jr., Graduate Coordinator, 706-542-1636. Fax: 706-542-0226. E-mail: bandrews@arches.uga.edu.

University of Houston, College of Education, Department of Curriculum and Instruction, 4800 Calhoun, Houston, TX 77204-2163. Offerings include art education (M Ed). Accredited by NCATE. Department faculty: 37 full-time (19 women), 10 part-time (7 women). *Degree requirements:* Comprehensive exam or thesis required, foreign language not required. *Entrance requirements:* GRE General Test or MAT. Application deadline: 7/3 (priority date; rolling processing). Application fee: $35 ($75 for international students). *Expenses:* Tuition $1152 per year full-time, $120 per semester (minimum) part-time for state residents; $4482 per year full-time, $249 per credit hour part-time for nonresidents. Fees $977 per year full-time, $119 per semester (minimum) part-time. • Wilford Weber, Chair, 713-743-4970. Fax: 713-743-9870. E-mail: wweber@uh.edu.

University of Idaho, College of Graduate Studies, College of Art and Architecture, Department of Art, Moscow, ID 83844-4140. Offerings include art education (MAT). Accredited by NCATE. Department faculty: 9 full-time (3 women), 6 part-time (4 women), 12.4 FTE. *Application deadline:* 8/1 (12/15 for spring admission). *Application fee:* $35 ($45 for international students). *Expenses:* Tuition $0 for state residents; $6000 per year full-time, $95 per credit part-time for nonresidents. Fees $2676 per year full-time, $134 per credit part-time. • Dr. Jill Dacey, Chair, 208-885-6851.

University of Illinois at Urbana–Champaign, College of Fine and Applied Arts, School of Art and Design, Program in Art Education, Urbana, IL 61801. Awards AM, Ed D. Accredited by NASAD. Faculty: 4 full-time (3 women). Students: 43 full-time (29 women); includes 8 minority (2 African Americans, 3 Asian Americans, 3 Hispanics), 10 international. 28 applicants, 64% accepted. In 1997, 32 master's awarded. *Degree requirements:* For doctorate, dissertation. *Entrance requirements:* For master's, minimum GPA of 4.0 on a 5.0 scale, portfolio. Application deadline: rolling. Application fee: $40 ($50 for international students). *Financial aid:* Application deadline 2/15. • Christine Thompson, Chairman, 217-244-6555.

University of Indianapolis, School of Education, Indianapolis, IN 46227-3697. Offerings include secondary education (MA), with options in art education, education, English education, social studies education. Accredited by NCATE. *Average time to degree:* master's–5 years part-time. *Entrance requirements:* GRE Subject Test. Application deadline: rolling. Application fee: $30.

The University of Iowa, College of Education, Division of Secondary Education, Iowa City, IA 52242-1316. Offerings include art education (MA, PhD). Division faculty: 21 full-time. *Degree requirements:* For doctorate, computer language, dissertation, comprehensive exams required, foreign language not required. *Entrance requirements:* For doctorate, minimum GPA of 3.0. Application fee: $30 ($50 for international students). *Expenses:* Tuition $3166 per year full-time, $176 per semester hour part-time for state residents; $10,202 per year full-time, $176 per semester hour part-time for nonresidents. Fees $202 per year full-time, $52 per year (minimum) part-time. • William Nibbelink, Chair, 319-335-5324. Fax: 319-335-5608.

University of Kansas, School of Fine Arts, Department of Design, Lawrence, KS 66045. Offerings include visual arts education (MA). Accredited by NASAD. Department faculty: 26 full-time. *Application deadline:* 2/15. *Application fee:* $25. *Expenses:* Tuition $2400 per year full-time, $100 per credit hour part-time for state residents; $7890 per year full-time, $329 per

Directory: Art Education

University of Kansas (continued)

credit hour part-time for nonresidents. Fees $428 per year full-time, $31 per credit hour part-time. • Joseph Zeller, Chairperson, 785-864-4401. Application contact: Cima Katz, Director, 785-864-4401. Fax: 785-864-4404.

University of Kentucky, Graduate School Programs from the College of Fine Arts, Program in Art Education, Lexington, KY 40506-0032. Awards MA. Faculty: 5 full-time (2 women). Students: 1 (woman) full-time, 2 part-time (both women). 3 applicants, 67% accepted. In 1997, 4 degrees awarded. *Degree requirements:* Thesis optional, foreign language not required. *Entrance requirements:* GRE General Test, minimum undergraduate GPA of 2.5. Application deadline: 7/19 (rolling processing). Application fee: $30 ($35 for international students). *Financial aid:* In 1997–98, 1 fellowship, 1 teaching assistantship were awarded; research assistantships also available. *Faculty research:* Multicultural art education, women's issues in art education, lifelong learning in the arts, the artist-teacher, art teaching as a form of art, place and art, children's home art and creativity as a basis for school art instruction. • Dr. George Szekely, Director of Graduate Studies, 606-257-8151. Application contact: Dr. Constance L. Wood, Associate Dean, 606-257-4613. Fax: 606-323-1928.

University of Louisville, School of Education, Department of Early and Middle Childhood Education, Program in Art Education, Louisville, KY 40292-0001. Awards M Ed. Accredited by NCATE. Students: 4 full-time (all women), 3 part-time (all women). Average age 30. In 1997, 8 degrees awarded. *Entrance requirements:* GRE General Test. Application deadline: rolling. Application fee: $25. • Dr. Diane W. Kyle, Chair, Department of Early and Middle Childhood Education, 502-852-6431.

University of Manitoba, Faculty of Education, Department of Curriculum: Humanities and Social Sciences, Winnipeg, MB R3T 2N2, Canada. Offerings include art education (M Ed). *Degree requirements:* Thesis or alternative required, foreign language not required.

University of Massachusetts Dartmouth, Graduate School, College of Visual and Performing Arts, Program in Art Education, North Dartmouth, MA 02747-2300. Awards MAE, MAT. Accredited by NASAD. Part-time programs available. Faculty: 3 full-time (1 woman). Students: 7 full-time (all women), 23 part-time (19 women); includes 1 minority (African American). 13 applicants, 100% accepted. In 1997, 3 degrees awarded. *Degree requirements:* Thesis required, foreign language not required. *Entrance requirements:* TOEFL, interview, portfolio. Application deadline: 4/20 (priority date; rolling processing; 11/15 for spring admission). Application fee: $40. *Expenses:* Tuition $2950 per year full-time, $82 per credit part-time for state residents; $10,249 per year full-time, $285 per credit part-time for nonresidents. Fees $5002 per year full-time, $143 per credit part-time for state residents; $6830 per year full-time, $194 per credit part-time for nonresidents. *Financial aid:* In 1997–98, 1 research assistantship totaling $2,000 was awarded; Federal Work-Study also available. Aid available to part-time students. Financial aid application deadline: 3/15; applicants required to submit FAFSA. *Faculty research:* Creativity in a humanistic context. • Dr. Arleen Mollo, Director, 508-999-9204. Application contact: Carol A. Novo, Graduate Admissions Office, 508-999-8604. Fax: 508-999-8375. E-mail: graduate@umassd.edu.

University of Minnesota, Twin Cities Campus, College of Education and Human Development, Department of Curriculum and Instruction, Program in Art Education, Minneapolis, MN 55455-0213. Awards MA, M Ed, PhD. • M. K. DiBlasio, Director of Graduate Studies, 612-625-2545.

University of Mississippi, Graduate School, College of Liberal Arts, Department of Art, University, MS 38677-9702. Offerings include art education (MA). Accredited by NASAD. Department faculty: 11 full-time (4 women). *Application deadline:* 8/1 (rolling processing). *Application fee:* $0 ($25 for international students). • Janice Murray, Chair, 601-232-7193.

University of Nebraska at Kearney, College of Fine Arts and Humanities, Department of Art, Kearney, NE 68849-0001. Offers program in art education (MA Ed). One or more programs accredited by NCATE. Part-time and evening/weekend programs available. Faculty: 7 full-time (1 woman). Students: 1 (woman) full-time, 8 part-time (5 women). In 1997, 4 degrees awarded. *Degree requirements:* Thesis optional. *Entrance requirements:* GRE General Test. Application deadline: 8/1 (priority date; rolling processing; 12/15 for spring admission). Application fee: $35. *Expenses:* Tuition $1494 per year full-time, $83 per credit hour part-time for state residents; $2826 per year full-time, $157 per credit hour part-time for nonresidents. Fees $229 per year full-time, $11.25 per semester (minimum) part-time. *Financial aid:* In 1997–98, 2 teaching assistantships were awarded; research assistantships and career-related internships or fieldwork also available. Aid available to part-time students. Financial aid application deadline: 3/1; applicants required to submit FAFSA. • John Dinsmore, Chair, 308-865-8353.

University of New Mexico, College of Education, Program in Art Education, Albuquerque, NM 87131-2039. Awards MA. Accredited by NCATE. Part-time and evening/weekend programs available. Faculty: 2 full-time (1 woman). Students: 19 full-time (18 women), 15 part-time (13 women); includes 6 minority (1 African American, 1 Asian American, 3 Hispanics, 1 Native American). Average age 33. 12 applicants, 92% accepted. In 1997, 29 degrees awarded. *Degree requirements:* Comprehensive exams required, thesis optional, foreign language not required. *Entrance requirements:* 24 credit hours of previous course work in art. Application deadline: 7/1 (11/1 for spring admission). Application fee: $25. *Expenses:* Tuition $2442 per year full-time, $103 per credit hour part-time for state residents; $8691 per year full-time, $103 per credit hour (minimum) part-time for nonresidents. Fees $32 per year. *Financial aid:* Fellowships, teaching assistantships, full tuition waivers, Federal Work-Study, institutionally sponsored loans, and career-related internships or fieldwork available. Aid available to part-time students. Financial aid application deadline: 3/31. *Faculty research:* Porcelain ceramics, archetypal psychology, early childhood art, history of art education, multiculturalism. Total annual research expenditures: $1172. • Dr. Peter Smith, Coordinator, 505-277-4112. E-mail: kolms@unm.edu. Application contact: Karen Olmsted, Office Manager, 505-277-4112. Fax: 505-277-8427. E-mail: kolms@unm.edu.

University of North Carolina at Greensboro, College of Arts and Sciences, Department of Art, Greensboro, NC 27412-0001. Offerings include art (M Ed). Department faculty: 15 full-time (4 women), 1 (woman) part-time. *Application deadline:* 2/6. *Application fee:* $35. *Expenses:* Tuition $1842 per year full-time, $370 per semester (minimum) part-time for state residents; $10,296 per year full-time, $2484 per semester (minimum) part-time for nonresidents. Fees $806 per year full-time, $111 per semester (minimum) part-time. • Patricia Wasserboehr, Head, 336-334-5248.

University of Northern Iowa, College of Humanities and Fine Arts, Department of Art, Cedar Falls, IA 50614. Offerings include art education (MA). Accredited by NASAD. Department faculty: 12 full-time (4 women). *Entrance requirements:* GRE (art education). Application deadline: 8/1 (priority date; rolling processing). Application fee: $20 ($30 for international students). *Expenses:* Tuition $3166 per year full-time, $176 per hour part-time for state residents; $7805 per year full-time, $176 per hour part-time for nonresidents. Fees $194 per year full-time, $12.50 per semester (minimum) part-time. • Dr. William Lew, Head, 319-273-2077.

University of North Texas, School of Visual Arts, Denton, TX 76203-6737. Offerings include art education (MA, MFA, PhD). School faculty: 37 full-time (10 women). *Degree requirements:* For master's, variable foreign language requirement, thesis (for some programs); for doctorate, dissertation. *Entrance requirements:* For master's, GRE General Test (minimum combined score of 800), portfolio; for doctorate, GRE General Test (minimum combined score of 1000), portfolio. Application deadline: 7/17 (priority date; rolling processing; 10/1 for spring admission). Application fee: $25 ($50 for international students). *Tuition:* $2063 per year full-time, $815 per year part-time for state residents; $5897 per year full-time, $2100 per year part-time for nonresidents. • Dr. D. Jack Davis, Dean, 940-565-4001. Fax: 940-565-4717. E-mail: davis@abn.unt.edu. Application contact: Dr. Connie Newton, Director, Graduate Program, 940-565-4004.

University of Rio Grande, Graduate School, Rio Grande, OH 45674. Offerings include classroom teaching (M Ed), with options in fine arts, learning disabilities, mathematics, reading education. School faculty: 9 full-time (3 women), 6 part-time (2 women). *Degree requirements:* Final research project, portfolio required, foreign language and thesis not required. *Entrance requirements:* Minimum GPA of 2.7 in major, 2.5 overall. Application deadline: rolling. Application fee: $20. • Dr. Greg Miller, Coordinator, 740-245-7364. Application contact: Dr. Mark Abell, Director of Administration, 740-245-5353.

University of South Alabama, College of Education, Department of Curriculum and Instruction, Mobile, AL 36688-0002. Offerings include art/music education (M Ed). Accredited by NCATE. Department faculty: 13 full-time (6 women). *Degree requirements:* Comprehensive exams required, foreign language and thesis not required. *Entrance requirements:* GRE General Test (minimum combined score of 1000) or MAT (minimum score 37), minimum GPA of 3.0. Application deadline: 9/1 (priority date; rolling processing). Application fee: $25. • Dr. Walter S. Hopkins, Chairman, 334-380-2893.

University of South Carolina, Graduate School, College of Liberal Arts, Department of Art, Program in Art Education, Columbia, SC 29208. Awards IMA, MA, MAT. Accredited by NCATE. IMA and MAT offered in cooperation with the College of Education. Faculty: 4 full-time (2 women), 4 part-time (all women). Students: 25 full-time (18 women), 12 part-time (10 women); includes 4 minority (3 African Americans, 1 Hispanic). Average age 50. In 1997, 7 degrees awarded. *Degree requirements:* Thesis required (for some programs), foreign language not required. *Entrance requirements:* GRE General Test (minimum combined score of 900) or MAT (minimum score 35), portfolio. Application deadline: 3/1 (11/1 for spring admission). Application fee: $35. Electronic applications accepted. *Expenses:* Tuition $3894 per year full-time, $193 per credit hour part-time for state residents; $8114 per year full-time, $404 per credit hour part-time for nonresidents. Fees $125 per year full-time, $37 per semester (minimum) part-time. *Financial aid:* Teaching assistantships and career-related internships or fieldwork available. • Cynthia Colbert, Division Chair, Art Education, 803-777-6223. Application contact: Mary Kay Hall, Graduate Studies Admissions Specialist, 803-777-6438. Fax: 803-777-0535.

University of Southern Mississippi, College of the Arts, Department of Art, Hattiesburg, MS 39406-5167. Offers program in art education (MAE). Accredited by NASAD. Faculty: 8 full-time (2 women). Students: 3 full-time (all women), 6 part-time (5 women); includes 1 minority (African American). Average age 40. 3 applicants, 67% accepted. In 1997, 1 degree awarded. *Degree requirements:* Comprehensive exam, exhibit required, foreign language not required. *Entrance requirements:* GRE General Test, BFA, minimum GPA of 3.0, portfolio. Application deadline: 8/9 (priority date; rolling processing). Application fee: $0 ($25 for international students). *Tuition:* $2870 per year full-time, $137 per credit hour part-time for state residents; $5972 per year full-time, $172 per credit hour part-time for nonresidents. *Financial aid:* Teaching assistantships, Federal Work-Study, and career-related internships or fieldwork available. Financial aid application deadline: 3/15. • H. Ward, Chairman, 601-266-4972.

University of South Florida, College of Education, Program in Art Education, Tampa, FL 33620-9951. Awards MA. Accredited by NCATE. Part-time and evening/weekend programs available. *Entrance requirements:* GRE General Test (minimum combined score of 1000), minimum GPA of 3.0 in last 60 hours. Application fee: $20. *Tuition:* $142 per credit hour for state residents; $486 per credit hour for nonresidents. • Jane Applegate, Dean, College of Education, 813-974-3406. Fax: 813-974-3826. E-mail: applegat@tempest.coedu.usf.edu. Application contact: Diane Briscoe, Graduate Adviser, 813-974-0544. Fax: 813-974-3391. E-mail: briscoe@tempest.coedu.usf.edu.

University of Tennessee, Knoxville, College of Education, Program in Education II, Knoxville, TN 37996. Offerings include art education (MS). Accredited by NASAD and NCATE. *Degree requirements:* Thesis optional, foreign language not required. *Entrance requirements:* TOEFL (minimum score 550), minimum GPA of 2.7. Application deadline: 2/1 (priority date; rolling processing). Application fee: $35. Electronic applications accepted. *Tuition:* $3354 per year full-time, $181 per semester hour part-time for state residents; $8410 per year full-time, $462 per semester hour part-time for nonresidents. • Dr. Tom George, Associate Dean, 423-974-0907. Fax: 423-974-8718. E-mail: tgeorge1@utk.edu.

The University of Texas at Austin, Graduate School, College of Fine Arts, Department of Art and Art History, Program in Art Education, Austin, TX 78712. Awards MA. Part-time programs available. Faculty: 7 full-time (5 women). Students: 19 full-time; includes 2 minority (both Hispanics), 2 international. Average age 24. 10 applicants, 50% accepted. *Degree requirements:* Thesis, oral and written exam required, foreign language not required. *Average time to degree:* master's–3 years full-time. *Entrance requirements:* GRE General Test, slide portfolio or 3 samples of written work. Application deadline: 2/1 (10/1 for spring admission). Application fee: $50 ($75 for international students). Electronic applications accepted. *Expenses:* Tuition $2592 per year full-time, $324 per semester (minimum) part-time for state residents; $7704 per year full-time, $963 per semester (minimum) part-time for nonresidents. Fees $778 per year full-time, $161 per semester (minimum) part-time. *Financial aid:* In 1997–98, 6 teaching assistantships were awarded; partial tuition waivers and career-related internships or fieldwork also available. *Faculty research:* Museum education; community-based, environmental, and multicultural art education; interdisciplinary art education. • Dr. Kenneth J. Hale, Acting Chairman, Department of Art and Art History, 512-471-3382. Application contact: Don Herron, Graduate Adviser, 512-471-3377. E-mail: don.herron@mail.utexas.edu.

University of the Arts, Philadelphia College of Art and Design, Department of Art Education, 320 South Broad Street, Philadelphia, PA 19102-4944. Offers programs in art education (MA), museum education (MA), visual arts (MAT). Accredited by NASAD. Part-time programs available. *Degree requirements:* Thesis required, foreign language not required. *Entrance requirements:* TOEFL (minimum score 500), portfolio. Application deadline: 3/1 (priority date; rolling processing; 12/15 for spring admission). Application fee: $30 ($50 for international students).

University of Toledo, College of Education and Allied Professions, Department of Art Education, Toledo, OH 43606-3398. Awards M Ed. Accredited by NCATE. Faculty: 3 full-time (2 women). Students: 1 (woman) full-time, 18 part-time (15 women). Average age 38. 5 applicants, 60% accepted. In 1997, 10 degrees awarded. *Degree requirements:* Thesis or alternative, comprehensive exam required, foreign language not required. *Entrance requirements:* Minimum GPA of 2.7. Application deadline: 8/1 (priority date; rolling processing). Application fee: $30. Electronic applications accepted. *Tuition:* $5907 per year full-time, $246 per hour part-time for state residents; $11,835 per year full-time, $493 per hour part-time for nonresidents. *Financial aid:* Teaching assistantships, Federal Work-Study, institutionally sponsored loans, and career-related internships or fieldwork available. Aid available to part-time students. Financial aid application deadline: 4/1; applicants required to submit FAFSA. • Dr. David Guip, Director, 419-530-8306. Fax: 419-530-8337.

University of Utah, College of Fine Arts, Department of Art, Salt Lake City, UT 84112-1107. Offerings include art education (MA). Department faculty: 20 full-time (7 women), 9 part-time (2 women). *Application deadline:* 2/15. *Application fee:* $30 ($50 for international students). *Tuition:* $2045 per year full-time, $562 per semester (minimum) part-time for state residents; $6129 per year full-time, $1607 per semester (minimum) part-time for nonresidents. • Nathan B. Winters, Chair, 801-581-8677. Application contact: Joseph Marotta, Director of Graduate Studies, 801-581-8677.

University of Victoria, Faculty of Education, Department of Arts in Education, Victoria, BC V8W 2Y2, Canada. Offers programs in art education (M Ed), music education (MA, M Ed). Part-time programs available. Faculty: 7 full-time (3 women), 4 part-time (2 women). Students: 14 full-time (11 women), 15 part-time (all women); includes 2 international. Average age 39. 3 applicants, 33% accepted. In 1997, 3 degrees awarded. *Degree requirements:* Thesis (for some programs), project (M Ed). *Average time to degree:* master's–3.1 years full-time. *Entrance requirements:* Minimum B average. Application deadline: 5/31 (priority date; rolling processing). Application fee: $50. *Tuition:* $2080 per year full-time, $557 per semester part-time. *Financial aid:* In 1997–98, 3 students received aid, including 1 fellowship (to a first-year student); teaching assistantships, institutionally sponsored loans also available. Financial aid application deadline: 2/15. *Faculty research:* Multicultural and first nations art, multimedia performance artistry, gender issues in art education, critical thinking, reflective practice. • Dr. B. Hanley, Chair, 250-721-7836. Fax: 250-721-6589. E-mail: bhanley@uvic.ca. Application contact: Sarah Baylow, Graduate Secretary, 250-721-7882. Fax: 250-721-7767. E-mail: sbaylow@uvic.ca.

University of Wisconsin–Madison, Departments of Art and Curriculum and Instruction, Program in Art Education, Madison, WI 53706-1380. Awards MA. Accredited by NASAD. *Application fee:* $38. *Tuition:* $4928 per year full-time, $926 per semester (minimum) part-time for state residents; $15,190 per year full-time, $2849 per semester (minimum) part-time for nonresidents.

University of Wisconsin–Milwaukee, School of Fine Arts, Department of Art, Milwaukee, WI 53201-0413. Offerings include art education (MA, MFA, MS). Department faculty: 27 full-time (11 women). *Degree requirements:* Thesis or alternative required, foreign language not required. *Entrance requirements:* Portfolio. Application deadline: 1/1 (priority date; rolling processing; 9/1 for spring admission). Application fee: $45 ($75 for international students). *Tuition:* $4996 per year full-time, $1030 per semester (minimum) part-time for state residents; $15,216 per year full-time, $2947 per semester (minimum) part-time for nonresidents. • Richard Zauft, Chair, 414-229-6052.

University of Wisconsin–Superior, Department of Visual Arts, Superior, WI 54880-2873. Offerings include art education (MA). *Degree requirements:* Comprehensive exam, exhibit required, foreign language not required. *Entrance requirements:* Minimum GPA of 2.75, portfolio. Application deadline: 4/1 (priority date; rolling processing). Application fee: $45. *Tuition:* $3628 per year full-time, $222 per credit hour part-time for state residents; $11,272 per year full-time, $647 per credit hour part-time for nonresidents. • James R. Grittner, Chairperson, 715-394-8368.

Valdosta State University, Colleges of Fine Arts and Education, Department of Art, Valdosta, GA 31698. Offers program in art education (MAE). Students: 1 (woman) full-time, 5 part-time (4 women); includes 1 minority (African American). 7 applicants, 100% accepted. In 1997, 1 degree awarded. *Entrance requirements:* GRE General Test (minimum combined score of 800). Application deadline: 8/1 (rolling processing). Application fee: $10. *Expenses:* Tuition $2472 per year full-time, $83 per semester hour part-time for state residents; $8472 per year full-time, $333 per semester hour part-time for nonresidents. Fees $236 per year full-time. • Dr. J. Stephen Lahr, Acting Head, 912-333-5835. Fax: 912-245-3799. E-mail: jslahr@valdosta.edu.

Virginia Commonwealth University, School of the Arts, Department of Art Education, Richmond, VA 23284-9005. Awards MAE. Accredited by NASAD. Faculty: 7 full-time (2 women). Students: 10 full-time (9 women), 17 part-time (15 women); includes 7 minority (1 African American, 3 Asian Americans, 3 Hispanics), 1 international. Average age 36. 20 applicants, 65% accepted. In 1997, 4 degrees awarded. *Degree requirements:* Thesis optional. *Entrance requirements:* GRE or MAT, portfolio. Application deadline: 7/1 (12/1 for spring admission). Application fee: $30 ($0 for international students). *Tuition:* $4960 per year full-time, $257 per credit part-time for state residents; $12,652 per year full-time, $684 per credit part-time for nonresidents. *Financial aid:* Fellowships, Federal Work-Study, institutionally sponsored loans, and career-related internships or fieldwork available. Financial aid application deadline: 3/15. *Faculty research:* Teaching methods. • Dr. James Wright, Acting Chair, 804-828-1995. E-mail: awright@saturn.vcu.edu. Application contact: Dr. Daniel J. Reeves, Assistant Dean and Director, Graduate Studies, 804-828-2787. Fax: 804-828-6469. E-mail: djreeves@vcu.edu.

Wayne State College, Division of Fine Arts, Wayne, NE 68787. Offers program in art education (MSE). One or more programs accredited by NCATE. Faculty: 3 part-time (1 woman). Students: 1 full-time (0 women). Average age 29. In 1997, 4 degrees awarded. *Degree requirements:* Comprehensive exam, research paper required, thesis optional. *Application deadline:* rolling. *Application fee:* $10. *Expenses:* Tuition $1788 per year full-time, $75 per credit hour part-time for state residents; $3576 per year full-time, $149 per credit hour part-time for nonresidents. Fees $360 per year full-time, $15 per credit hour part-time. *Financial aid:* In 1997–98, 1 teaching assistantship (to a first-year student) was awarded. Financial aid application deadline: 5/1; applicants required to submit FAFSA. • Dr. James O'Leary, Head, 402-375-7359.

Wayne State College, Division of Education, Program in Curriculum and Instruction, Wayne, NE 68787. Offerings include art education (MSE). Accredited by NCATE. *Degree requirements:* Comprehensive exam, research paper required, foreign language not required. *Entrance requirements:* GRE General Test. Application deadline: rolling. Application fee: $10. *Expenses:* Tuition $1788 per year full-time, $75 per credit hour part-time for state residents; $3576 per year full-time, $149 per credit hour part-time for nonresidents. Fees $360 per year full-time, $15 per credit hour part-time. • Dr. Diane Alexander, Head, Division of Education, 402-375-7389.

Western Carolina University, College of Arts and Sciences, Department of Art, Program in Art Education, Cullowhee, NC 28723. Awards MAT. Accredited by NCATE. *Degree requirements:* Thesis, comprehensive exam, exhibit required, foreign language not required. *Entrance requirements:* GRE General Test, portfolio. Application deadline: rolling. Application fee: $35. *Tuition:* $1799 per year full-time, $144 per credit hour (minimum) part-time for state residents; $9069 per year full-time, $1053 per credit hour (minimum) part-time for nonresidents. *Financial aid:* Application deadline 3/15. • Application contact: Kathleen Owen, Assistant to the Dean, 828-227-7398. Fax: 828-227-7480.

Western Carolina University, College of Education and Allied Professions, Department of Administration, Curriculum and Instruction, Programs in Secondary Education, Cullowhee, NC 28723. Offerings include art education (MAT). Accredited by NCATE. *Degree requirements:* Comprehensive exam required, foreign language and thesis not required. *Entrance requirements:* GRE General Test. Application deadline: rolling. Application fee: $35. *Tuition:* $1799 per year full-time, $144 per credit hour (minimum) part-time for state residents; $9069 per year full-time, $1053 per credit hour (minimum) part-time for nonresidents. • Application contact: Kathleen Owen, Assistant to the Dean, 828-227-7398. Fax: 828-227-7480.

Western Kentucky University, Potter College of Arts and Humanities, Department of Art, Bowling Green, KY 42101-3576. Offers program in art education (MA Ed). Accredited by NASAD and NCATE. Part-time programs available. Faculty: 5 full-time (2 women). Students: 4 part-time (3 women). Average age 35. 2 applicants, 50% accepted. In 1997, 1 degree awarded. *Degree requirements:* Thesis or alternative, final exam required, foreign language not required. *Entrance requirements:* GRE General Test (minimum combined score of 1150 on three sections), minimum GPA of 2.5, portfolio. Application deadline: 8/1 (priority date; rolling processing; 12/1 for spring admission). Application fee: $20. *Tuition:* $2460 per year full-time, $133 per credit hour part-time for state residents; $6700 per year full-time, $369 per credit hour part-time for nonresidents. *Financial aid:* Service awards, Federal Work-Study, institutionally sponsored loans available. Aid available to part-time students. Financial aid application deadline: 4/1; applicants required to submit FAFSA. • Leo Fernandez, Head, 502-745-3944. Fax: 502-745-5932.

Western Washington University, College of Fine and Performing Arts, Department of Art, Bellingham, WA 98225-5996. Offers program in art education (M Ed). Accredited by NCATE. Part-time programs available. Faculty: 11 (1 woman). Students: 4 full-time (3 women). 2 applicants, 100% accepted. In 1997, 4 degrees awarded. *Degree requirements:* Thesis optional, foreign language not required. *Entrance requirements:* GRE General Test, TOEFL, audition, portfolio, minimum GPA of 3.0 in last 60 semester hours or last 90 quarter hours. Application deadline: 6/1 (rolling processing; 2/1 for spring admission). Application fee: $35. *Expenses:* Tuition $4200 per year full-time, $140 per credit part-time for state residents; $12,780 per year full-time, $426 per credit part-time for nonresidents. Fees $249 per year full-time, $83 per quarter part-time. *Financial aid:* Teaching assistantships, partial tuition waivers, Federal Work-Study, institutionally sponsored loans available. Aid available to part-time students. Financial aid application deadline: 3/31. • Dr. Elsi Vassdal-Ellis, Chairperson, 360-650-3660. Application contact: Dr. Gaye Leigh-Green, Graduate Adviser, 360-650-3672.

West Virginia University, College of Creative Arts, Division of Art, Morgantown, WV 26506. Offerings include art (MA), with options in art education, art history. Accredited by NASAD and NCATE. Division faculty: 14 full-time (5 women), 2 part-time (both women). *Average time to degree:* master's–2 years full-time. *Application deadline:* 3/1 (priority date; 11/1 for spring admission). *Application fee:* $45. *Tuition:* $2820 per year full-time, $149 per credit hour part-time for state residents; $8104 per year full-time, $443 per credit hour part-time for nonresidents. • Sergio Soave, Chair, 304-293-3140 Ext. 3140. Fax: 304-293-5731. Application contact: Paul Krainak, Coordinator of Graduate Students, 304-293-2140.

Wichita State University, College of Fine Arts, School of Art and Design, Wichita, KS 67260. Offerings include art education (MA). School faculty: 11 full-time (4 women), 13 part-time (8 women). *Application deadline:* 7/1 (priority date; rolling processing; 1/1 for spring admission). *Application fee:* $25 ($40 for international students). Electronic applications accepted. *Expenses:* Tuition $2303 per year full-time, $96 per credit hour part-time for state residents; $7691 per year full-time, $321 per credit hour part-time for nonresidents. Fees $490 per year full-time, $75 per semester (minimum) part-time. • Dr. Don Byrum, Chair, 316-978-3551. E-mail: byrum@twsuvm.uc.twsu.edu. Application contact: Ron Christ, Graduate Coordinator, 316-978-3555. E-mail: christ@twsuvm.uc.twsu.edu.

Winthrop University, School of Visual and Performing Arts, Department of Art and Design, Rock Hill, SC 29733. Offerings include art education (MA). Accredited by NASAD and NCATE. Department faculty: 18 full-time (5 women). *Application deadline:* 3/1 (priority date; rolling processing; 9/1 for spring admission). *Application fee:* $35. *Tuition:* $3928 per year full-time, $164 per credit hour part-time for state residents; $7060 per year full-time, $294 per credit hour part-time for nonresidents. • Jerry Walden, Chairman, 803-323-2126. E-mail: waldenj@winthrop.edu. Application contact: Sharon Johnson, Director of Graduate Studies, 803-323-2204. Fax: 803-323-2292. E-mail: johnsons@winthrop.edu.

Xavier University, College of Social Sciences, Department of Education, Cincinnati, OH 45207-2111. Offerings include art (M Ed). Department faculty: 32 full-time (14 women), 49 part-time (31 women), 44.25 FTE. *Application deadline:* rolling. *Application fee:* $25. • Dr. James Boothe, Chair, 513-745-2951. Fax: 513-745-1052. E-mail: boothe@admin.xu.edu. Application contact: Sheila Speth, Director of Graduate Services, 513-745-3360. Fax: 513-745-1048. E-mail: xugrad@admin.xu.edu.

Business Education

Albany State University, School of Education, Program in Business Education, Albany, GA 31705-2717. Awards M Ed. Accredited by NCATE. Faculty: 3 full-time (all women). Students: 3 part-time (all women). Average age 30. 1 applicant, 100% accepted. In 1997, 2 degrees awarded (100% found work related to degree). *Degree requirements:* Comprehensive exam required, foreign language not required. *Entrance requirements:* GRE General Test (minimum combined score of 800), MAT (minimum score 44) or NTE (minimum score 550). Application deadline: 9/1. Application fee: $10. *Financial aid:* Career-related internships or fieldwork available. Financial aid application deadline: 4/1. • Dr. Mollie B. Brown, Chairperson, 912-430-4788. Fax: 912-430-5119. E-mail: mbrown@fld94.alsnet.peachnet.edu.

Alfred University, Graduate School, Division of Education, Alfred, NY 14802-1205. Offerings include business education (MS Ed). Division faculty: 45 full-time (12 women). *Degree requirements:* Thesis required (for some programs), foreign language not required. *Entrance requirements:* TOEFL. Application deadline: rolling. Application fee: $50. *Expenses:* Tuition $20,376 per year full-time, $390 per credit hour (minimum) part-time. Fees $546 per year. • Dr. Katherine D. Wiesendanger, Chair, 607-871-2219. E-mail: fwiesendange@bigvax.alfred.edu. Application contact: Cathleen R. Johnson, Assistant Director of Admissions, 607-871-2141. Fax: 607-871-2198. E-mail: johnsonc@bigvax.alfred.edu.

Arkansas State University, College of Business, Department of Management, Marketing, and Business Systems, State University, AR 72467. Offers program in business education (MSE, SCCT). Accredited by NCATE. Offered jointly with the College of Education. Part-time programs available. Faculty: 14 full-time (6 women). Students: 1 (woman) full-time, 14 part-time (all women); includes 1 minority (African American). Average age 37. In 1997, 5 master's, 1 SCCT awarded. *Degree requirements:* For master's, thesis or alternative, comprehensive exam required, foreign language not required; for SCCT, comprehensive exam required, thesis not required. *Entrance requirements:* For master's, GRE General Test or MAT, appropriate bachelor's degree; for SCCT, GRE General Test or MAT, master's degree. Application deadline: 7/1 (priority date; rolling processing; 11/15 for spring admission). Application fee: $15 ($25 for international students). *Expenses:* Tuition $2760 per year full-time, $115 per credit hour part-time for state residents; $6936 per year full-time, $289 per credit hour part-time for nonresidents. Fees $506 per year full-time, $44 per semester (minimum) part-time. *Financial aid:* Teaching assistantships available. Aid available to part-time students. Financial aid application deadline: 7/1; applicants required to submit FAFSA. • Dr. Emelda Williams, Chair, 870-972-3430. Fax: 870-972-3868. E-mail: ewms@cherokee.astate.edu.

Ashland University, College of Education, Graduate Studies in Teacher Education, Program in Curriculum and Instruction, Ashland, OH 44805-3702. Offerings include economics education (M Ed). Accredited by NCATE. Program faculty: 8 full-time (4 women), 24 part-time (9 women). *Degree requirements:* Practicum or thesis. *Entrance requirements:* GRE General Test or MAT, teaching certificate. Application deadline: rolling. Application fee: $15. *Tuition:* $275 per credit hour. • Carl Walley, Program Team Leader, 419-289-5355. E-mail: cwalley@ashland.edu. Application contact: Dr. Joe Bailey, Director, 419-289-5377. Fax: 419-289-5097. E-mail: jbailey@ashland.edu.

Ball State University, College of Business, Department of Business Education and Office Administration, 2000 University Avenue, Muncie, IN 47306-1099. Awards MAE. One or more programs accredited by NCATE. Faculty: 10. Students: 3 part-time (all women). Average age

Directory: Business Education

Ball State University (continued)
30. 2 applicants, 100% accepted. In 1997, 4 degrees awarded. *Entrance requirements:* GMAT. Application fee: $15 ($25 for international students). *Expenses:* Tuition $3454 per year full-time, $518 per semester (minimum) part-time for state residents; $9316 per year full-time, $1221 per semester (minimum) part-time for nonresidents. Fees $242 per year full-time, $18 per semester (minimum) part-time. *Financial aid:* Teaching assistantships available. • Dr. Rodney Davis, Chairman, 765-285-5227.

Bloomsburg University of Pennsylvania, School of Graduate Studies, College of Business, Department of Business Education/Office Administration, Program in Business Education, Bloomsburg, PA 17815-1905. Awards M Ed. Faculty: 7 full-time (4 women). Students: 9 full-time (7 women), 8 part-time (6 women); includes 3 minority (1 Asian American, 2 Hispanics). Average age 29. 4 applicants, 100% accepted. In 1997, 11 degrees awarded. *Degree requirements:* Thesis optional, foreign language not required. *Entrance requirements:* GRE General Test, minimum QPA of 2.5. Application deadline: rolling. Application fee: $25. *Expenses:* Tuition $3468 per year full-time, $193 per credit part-time for state residents; $6236 per year full-time, $346 per credit part-time for nonresidents. Fees $748 per year full-time, $166 per semester (minimum) part-time. *Faculty research:* Records and information management, training and development, ergonomics, methodology, business and international communications, software applications. • Dr. Roger W. Ellis, Chair, Department of Business Education/Office Administration, 717-389-4109. Fax: 717-389-3892. E-mail: re@neptune.bloomu.edu.

Bowling Green State University, College of Education and Allied Professions, Department of Business Education, Bowling Green, OH 43403. Awards M Ed. Accredited by NCATE. Part-time programs available. Faculty: 1 full-time (0 women). Students: 8 full-time (5 women), 12 part-time (8 women); includes 1 minority (African American). 11 applicants, 55% accepted. In 1997, 8 degrees awarded. *Degree requirements:* Thesis or alternative required, foreign language not required. *Entrance requirements:* GRE General Test, TOEFL (minimum score 565). Application deadline: rolling. Application fee: $30. Electronic applications accepted. *Tuition:* $6070 per year full-time, $284 per credit hour part-time for state residents; $11,358 per year full-time, $536 per credit hour part-time for nonresidents. *Financial aid:* In 1997–98, 4 assistantships were awarded; Federal Work-Study and career-related internships or fieldwork also available. Financial aid application deadline: 2/15; applicants required to submit FAFSA. *Faculty research:* School to work, workforce education, marketing education, contextual teaching and learning. • Dr. Robert Berns, Chair, 419-372-2901.

California State University, Northridge, College of Business Administration and Economics, Department of Office Systems and Business Education, Northridge, CA 91330. Offers programs in administrative/office management (MBA), business education (MBA, MS). Part-time programs available. Faculty: 8 full-time, 3 part-time. 4 applicants, 50% accepted. *Degree requirements:* Thesis or alternative required, foreign language not required. *Entrance requirements:* GMAT (score in 50th percentile or higher), TOEFL, minimum GPA of 3.0 in last 60 units. Application deadline: 11/30. Application fee: $55. *Expenses:* Tuition $0 for state residents; $246 per unit for nonresidents. Fees $1970 per year full-time, $1304 per year part-time. *Financial aid:* Application deadline 3/1. • Dr. Susan Plutsky, Acting Chair. Application contact: Dr. Richard Moore, Director of Graduate Programs, 818-677-2467.

Central Connecticut State University, School of Business, Department of Business Education, New Britain, CT 06050-4010. Awards MS. Part-time and evening/weekend programs available. Students: 8 full-time (6 women), 20 part-time (14 women); includes 1 minority (Native American). Average age 35. 28 applicants, 64% accepted. In 1997, 3 degrees awarded. *Degree requirements:* Thesis or alternative, comprehensive exam required, foreign language not required. *Entrance requirements:* TOEFL (minimum score 550), minimum GPA of 2.7, bachelor's degree in business or equivalent. Application deadline: 6/1 (priority date; rolling processing; 12/1 for spring admission). Application fee: $40. *Expenses:* Tuition $4458 per year full-time, $175 per credit hour part-time for state residents; $9943 per year full-time, $175 per credit hour part-time for nonresidents. Fees $45 per semester. *Financial aid:* Federal Work-Study available. Financial aid application deadline: 3/15; applicants required to submit FAFSA. *Faculty research:* Marketing education, office systems education, accounting education for secondary schools. • Dr. George Claffey, Coordinator, 860-832-3210.

Central Michigan University, College of Business Administration, Department of Business Information Systems, Mount Pleasant, MI 48859. Offers program in business education (MBE). Faculty: 15 full-time (4 women). Students: 1 (woman) full-time, 1 (woman) part-time; includes 1 minority (African American). Average age 39. In 1997, 4 degrees awarded. *Degree requirements:* Thesis or alternative required, foreign language not required. *Entrance requirements:* GMAT. Application deadline: 3/1 (priority date; rolling processing). Application fee: $30. *Expenses:* Tuition $139 per credit hour (minimum) for state residents; $276 per credit hour (minimum) for nonresidents. Fees $260 per year full-time, $150 per semester part-time. *Financial aid:* Teaching assistantships, Federal Work-Study, and career-related internships or fieldwork available. Financial aid application deadline: 3/7. *Faculty research:* Business teacher education, office systems, management information systems, decision support systems. • Dr. Frank Andera, Chairperson, 517-774-3554. Fax: 517-774-2372. E-mail: 3zcl2xv@cmich.edu.

Central Washington University, College of Education and Professional Studies, Department of Business Education and Administrative Management, Ellensburg, WA 98926. Offers program in business and distributive education (M Ed). Accredited by NCATE. Part-time programs available. Faculty: 9 full-time (4 women). Students: 2 full-time (1 woman), 2 part-time (both women). 2 applicants, 0% accepted. In 1997, 7 degrees awarded. *Degree requirements:* Thesis or alternative. *Entrance requirements:* Minimum GPA of 3.0. Application deadline: 4/1 (priority date; rolling processing; 1/1 for spring admission). Application fee: $35. *Expenses:* Tuition $4200 per year full-time, $140 per credit hour part-time for state residents; $12,780 per year full-time, $426 per credit hour part-time for nonresidents. Fees $240 per year. *Financial aid:* In 1997–98, 2 teaching assistantships (both to first-year students) averaging $1,108 per month and totaling $19,944 were awarded; research assistantships, Federal Work-Study also available. Financial aid application deadline: 2/15. • Dr. Ross Byrd, Chairman, 509-963-2611. Application contact: Christie A. Fevergeon, Program Coordinator, Graduate Studies and Research, 509-963-3103. Fax: 509-963-1799. E-mail: masters@cwu.edu.

Chadron State College, Department of Education, Chadron, NE 69337. Offerings include business (MA Ed). Accredited by NCATE. *Application deadline:* rolling. *Application fee:* $15. *Expenses:* Tuition $1788 per year full-time, $75 per credit hour part-time for state residents; $3588 per year full-time, $149 per credit hour part-time for nonresidents. Fees $388 per year full-time, $1232 per year part-time. • Dr. Pat Colgate, Dean, School of Graduate Studies, 308-432-6330. Fax: 308-432-6454. E-mail: pcolgate@csc1.csc.edu.

College of Mount St. Joseph, Education Department, Program in Professional Effectiveness, Cincinnati, OH 45233-1670. Awards MA Ed. Part-time and evening/weekend programs available. *Degree requirements:* Comprehensive exam required, foreign language and thesis not required. *Entrance requirements:* GRE General Test (minimum combined score of 825), minimum GPA of 2.7. Application deadline: rolling. Application fee: $0. *Tuition:* $320 per credit hour. *Financial aid:* Application deadline 6/1. • Application contact: Jean Abrams, Graduate Secretary, 513-244-4812.

Eastern Illinois University, Lumpkin College of Business and Applied Sciences and College of Education and Professional Studies, Program in Business Education, 600 Lincoln Avenue, Charleston, IL 61920-3099. Awards MS Ed. Program being phased out; applicants no longer accepted. Part-time programs available. Faculty: 9 full-time (6 women). In 1997, 3 degrees awarded. *Expenses:* Tuition $3459 per year full-time, $96 per semester hour part-time for state residents; $10,377 per year full-time, $288 per semester hour part-time for nonresidents. Fees $1566 per year full-time, $37 per semester hour part-time. *Financial aid:* Research assistantships available. • Dr. Lillian Greathouse, Chairperson, 217-581-2627. Fax: 217-581-6642. E-mail: cflrg@eiu.edu.

Eastern Kentucky University, College of Education, Department of Curriculum and Instruction, Program in Secondary and Higher Education, Richmond, KY 40475-3101. Offerings include business education (MA Ed). Accredited by NCATE. *Entrance requirements:* GRE General Test, minimum GPA of 2.5. Application fee: $0. *Tuition:* $2390 per year full-time, $133 per credit hour part-time for state residents; $6630 per year full-time, $365 per credit hour part-time for nonresidents. • Dr. Imogene Ramsey, Chair, Department of Curriculum and Instruction, 606-622-2154.

Eastern Michigan University, College of Technology, Department of Business and Technology Education, Program in Business Education, Ypsilanti, MI 48197. Awards MBE. Accredited by NCATE. Evening/weekend programs available. In 1997, 5 degrees awarded. *Degree requirements:* Thesis optional, foreign language not required. *Entrance requirements:* GRE General Test, TOEFL (minimum score 500). Application deadline: 5/15 (rolling processing; 3/15 for spring admission). Application fee: $30. *Expenses:* Tuition $2691 per year full-time, $150 per credit hour part-time for state residents; $6300 per year full-time, $350 per credit hour part-time for nonresidents. Fees $368 per year full-time, $88 per semester (minimum) part-time. *Financial aid:* Fellowships, teaching assistantships available. Aid available to part-time students. Financial aid application deadline: 3/15; applicants required to submit FAFSA. • Dr. Earl Meyer, Coordinator, 734-487-4330.

Eastern Washington University, College of Business Administration, Department of Management Information Systems, Cheney, WA 99004-2431. Offerings include business education (M Ed). Accredited by NCATE. Admissions temporarily suspended. *Degree requirements:* Comprehensive exam required, thesis optional, foreign language not required. *Tuition:* $4200 per year full-time, $140 per credit part-time for state residents; $12,780 per year full-time, $415 per credit part-time for nonresidents. • Dr. John Zurenko, Chair, 509-358-2285.

Emporia State University, School of Graduate Studies, Division of Business Education and General Business, Emporia, KS 66801-5087. Awards MS. One or more programs accredited by NCATE. Faculty: 4 full-time (2 women). Students: 1 (woman) full-time, 5 part-time (4 women). 1 applicant, 100% accepted. In 1997, 2 degrees awarded. *Degree requirements:* Comprehensive exam or thesis required, foreign language not required. *Entrance requirements:* GRE General Test (minimum combined score of 1000), TOEFL (minimum score 550). Application deadline: 8/15 (priority date; rolling processing). Application fee: $30 ($75 for international students). Electronic applications accepted. *Tuition:* $2300 per year full-time, $103 per credit hour part-time for state residents; $6012 per year full-time, $258 per credit hour part-time for nonresidents. *Financial aid:* In 1997–98, 4 teaching assistantships averaging $522 per month were awarded; research assistantships, Federal Work-Study, institutionally sponsored loans, and career-related internships or fieldwork also available. Financial aid application deadline: 3/15; applicants required to submit FAFSA. • Dr. Nancy Groneman, Chair, 316-341-5345. E-mail: groneman@emporia.edu.

Florida Agricultural and Mechanical University, Division of Graduate Studies, Research, and Continuing Education, College of Education, Department of Industrial Arts and Vocational Education, Tallahassee, FL 32307-3200. Offerings include business education (MBE). Accredited by NCATE. *Application deadline:* 5/13. *Application fee:* $20. *Expenses:* Tuition $140 per credit hour for state residents; $484 per credit hour for nonresidents. Fees $130 per year. • Dr. Jerrlyne Jackson, Chairperson, 850-599-3061.

Georgia Southern University, College of Education, Department of Middle Grades and Secondary Education, Program in Business Education, Statesboro, GA 30460-8126. Awards M Ed. Accredited by NCATE. Part-time and evening/weekend programs available. Faculty: 1 (woman) full-time. Students: 5 part-time (all women). Average age 29. 4 applicants, 50% accepted. In 1997, 3 degrees awarded. *Degree requirements:* Exams required, foreign language and thesis not required. *Entrance requirements:* GRE General Test (minimum score 450 on each section) or MAT (minimum score 44), minimum GPA of 2.5. Application deadline: 7/15 (priority date; rolling processing; 11/15 for spring admission). Application fee: $0. Electronic applications accepted. *Tuition:* $2619 per year full-time, $287 per semester (minimum) part-time for state residents; $8619 per year full-time, $1037 per semester (minimum) part-time for nonresidents. *Financial aid:* Application deadline 4/15. • Application contact: Dr. John R. Diebolt, Associate Graduate Dean, 912-681-5384. Fax: 912-681-0740. E-mail: gradschool@gsvms2.cc.gasou.edu.

Georgia Southwestern State University, School of Education, Americus, GA 31709-4693. Offerings include business education (M Ed). Accredited by NCATE. *Entrance requirements:* GRE General Test (minimum score 400 on each section) or MAT (minimum score 44), minimum GPA of 2.5. Application deadline: 9/1 (rolling processing; 3/15 for spring admission). Application fee: $10. • Dr. Kurt Myers, Chair, 912-931-2145. Application contact: Chris Laney, Graduate Admissions Specialist, 912-931-2027. Fax: 912-931-2059. E-mail: claney@gsw1500.gsw.peachnet.edu.

Georgia State University, College of Education, Department of Middle, Secondary Education and Instructional Technology, Program in Comprehensive Business Education, Atlanta, GA 30303-3083. Awards MBE. Accredited by NCATE. Program being phased out; applicants no longer accepted. Part-time and evening/weekend programs available. Students: 5 part-time (4 women). Average age 49. *Degree requirements:* Comprehensive exam. *Expenses:* Tuition $2673 per year full-time, $99 per semester hour part-time for state residents; $10,692 per year full-time, $396 per semester hour part-time for nonresidents. Fees $228 per year. *Financial aid:* Research assistantships, teaching assistantships available. *Faculty research:* Business and management issues, business communications, instruction in business applications. • Dr. Beverly J. Armento, Chair, Department of Middle, Secondary Education and Instructional Technology, 404-651-2510.

Indiana State University, Department of Curriculum and Instruction and Media Technology and School of Business, Program in Business Education, Terre Haute, IN 47809-1401. Awards MA, MS, PhD, Ed S. Accredited by NCATE. Students: 1 (woman) full-time, 3 part-time (all women); includes 1 international. Average age 30. 1 applicant, 100% accepted. *Degree requirements:* For doctorate, 2 foreign languages, computer language, dissertation. *Entrance requirements:* For master's, minimum undergraduate GPA of 2.5; for doctorate, GRE General Test (minimum score 500 on each section), minimum undergraduate GPA of 2.5, 3.5 graduate; for Ed S, GRE General Test (minimum combined score of 900), minimum graduate GPA of 3.25. Application deadline: rolling. Application fee: $20. *Tuition:* $143 per credit hour for state residents; $325 per credit hour for nonresidents. *Financial aid:* Teaching assistantships available. Financial aid application deadline: 3/1. • Dr. Sandra Nelson, Acting Chairperson.

Indiana University of Pennsylvania, College of Business, Program in Business Education, Indiana, PA 15705-1087. Awards M Ed. Students: 3 full-time (2 women), 5 part-time (3 women); includes 2 minority (both Hispanics). Average age 45. 8 applicants, 75% accepted. In 1997, 2 degrees awarded. *Degree requirements:* Thesis optional, foreign language not required. *Entrance requirements:* TOEFL (minimum score 500). Application deadline: 7/1 (priority date; rolling processing; 11/1 for spring admission). Application fee: $30. *Expenses:* Tuition $3468 per year full-time, $193 per credit part-time for state residents; $6236 per year full-time, $346 per credit part-time for nonresidents. Fees $313 per year (minimum) full-time, $84 per year part-time. *Financial aid:* Research assistantships, Federal Work-Study, and career-related internships or fieldwork available. Aid available to part-time students. Financial aid application deadline: 3/15. • Dr. Wayne Moore, Graduate Coordinator, 724-357-3003. E-mail: moore@grove.iup.edu.

Inter American University of Puerto Rico, Metropolitan Campus, Division of Economics and Business Administration, Program in Business Education, San Juan, PR 00919-1293. Awards MA. *Degree requirements:* Comprehensive exam required, foreign language and thesis not required. *Entrance requirements:* GRE or PAEG, interview. Application deadline: 5/15 (priority date; rolling processing; 11/15 for spring admission). Application fee: $31. Electronic applications accepted. *Expenses:* Tuition $3272 per year full-time, $1740 per year part-time.

Fees $328 per year full-time, $176 per year part-time. • Application contact: Dr. Antonio Llorens, Director, 787-250-1912 Ext. 2320. Fax: 787-250-0361.

Inter American University of Puerto Rico, San Germán Campus, Department of Business Administration, Program in Business Education, San Germán, PR 00683-5008. Awards MA. Part-time and evening/weekend programs available. Students: 0. In 1997, 6 degrees awarded. *Degree requirements:* Comprehensive exam required, foreign language and thesis not required. *Entrance requirements:* Minimum GPA of 3.0, GRE General Test, or PAEG. Application deadline: 4/30 (priority date; rolling processing; 11/15 for spring admission). Application fee: $31. *Expenses:* Tuition $150 per credit. Fees $177 per semester. • Application contact: Mildred Camacho, Admissions Director, 787-892-3090. Fax: 787-892-6350.

Iona College, School of Arts and Science, Program in Secondary School Subjects, 715 North Avenue, New Rochelle, NY 10801-1890. Offerings include business education (MST). Program faculty: 4 full-time (1 woman), 8 part-time (2 women). *Application deadline:* rolling. *Application fee:* $25. *Expenses:* Tuition $455 per credit hour. Fees $25 per semester. • Dr. Lucy Murphy, Chair, 914-633-2210. Fax: 914-633-2608. Application contact: Arlene Melillo, Director of Graduate Recruitment, 914-633-2328. Fax: 914-633-2023.

Jackson State University, School of Business, Department of Business Education and Administrative Services, Jackson, MS 39217. Offers program in business education (M Bus Ed). Part-time and evening/weekend programs available. Faculty: 5 full-time (all women). Students: 4 full-time (3 women), 8 part-time (all women); includes 12 minority (all African Americans). 7 applicants, 86% accepted. In 1997, 1 degree awarded. *Degree requirements:* Comprehensive exam required, thesis optional. *Entrance requirements:* GRE General Test (minimum combined score of 1000), TOEFL (minimum score 550). Application deadline: 3/1 (priority date; rolling processing; 10/1 for spring admission). Application fee: $20. *Tuition:* $2688 per year (minimum) full-time, $150 per semester hour part-time for state residents; $5546 per year (minimum) full-time, $309 per semester hour part-time for nonresidents. *Financial aid:* Federal Work-Study available. Financial aid application deadline: 3/1. • Dr. Mary M. White, Chair, 601-968-2541. Application contact: Mae Robinson, Admissions Coordinator, 601-968-2455. Fax: 601-968-8246. E-mail: mrobinson@ccaix.jsums.edu.

Johnson & Wales University, Graduate School, Program in Teacher Education, 8 Abbott Park Place, Providence, RI 02903-3703. Offerings include business administration (MAT). Program faculty: 2 full-time (1 woman), 5 part-time (0 women). *Average time to degree:* master's–2.5 years part-time. *Entrance requirements:* MAT, minimum GPA of 2.75. Application deadline: 8/21 (priority date; rolling processing). Application fee: $0. *Expenses:* Tuition $194 per quarter hour (minimum). Fees $477 per year. • Application contact: Dr. Allan G. Freedman, Director of Graduate Admissions, 401-598-1015. Fax: 401-598-4773. E-mail: clifb@jwu.edu.

Lehman College of the City University of New York, Division of Education, Department of Secondary, Adult and Business Education, Program in Business Education, 250 Bedford Park Boulevard West, Bronx, NY 10468-1589. Awards MS Ed. Part-time and evening/weekend programs available. Faculty: 10 full-time. Students: 3 full-time (2 women), 35 part-time (22 women). *Degree requirements:* Thesis. *Entrance requirements:* Minimum GPA of 2.7. Application deadline: 4/1 (rolling processing; 11/1 for spring admission). Application fee: $40. *Expenses:* Tuition $4350 per year full-time, $185 per credit part-time for state residents; $7600 per year full-time, $320 per credit part-time for nonresidents. Fees $120 per year full-time, $80 per year part-time. *Financial aid:* Full and partial tuition waivers, Federal Work-Study available. Aid available to part-time students. Financial aid application deadline: 5/15; applicants required to submit FAFSA. • Nathan Avani, Adviser, 718-960-8171.

Louisiana State University and Agricultural and Mechanical College, College of Agriculture, School of Vocational Education, Baton Rouge, LA 70803. Offerings include vocational business education (MS). Accredited by NCATE. School faculty: 11 full-time (3 women). *Degree requirements:* Thesis required (for some programs), foreign language not required. *Entrance requirements:* GRE General Test (minimum combined score of 1000), minimum GPA of 3.0. Application deadline: 1/25 (priority date; rolling processing). Application fee: $25. *Tuition:* $2736 per year full-time, $285 per semester (minimum) part-time for state residents; $6636 per year full-time, $460 per semester (minimum) part-time for nonresidents. • Dr. Michael F. Burnett, Director, 504-388-5748.

Louisiana Tech University, College of Education, Department of Curriculum, Instruction and Leadership, Ruston, LA 71272. Offerings include secondary education (M Ed), with options in business education, English education, foreign language education, health and physical education, mathematics education, science education, social studies education, speech education. Accredited by NCATE. Department faculty: 16 full-time (11 women). *Application deadline:* 7/29 (2/3 for spring admission). *Application fee:* $20 ($30 for international students). *Tuition:* $2382 per year full-time, $223 per quarter (minimum) part-time for state residents; $5307 per year full-time, $223 per quarter (minimum) part-time for nonresidents. • Dr. Samuel V. Dauzat, Head, 318-257-4609.

Mankato State University, College of Education, Department of Business and Technology Education, South Rd and Ellis Ave, PO Box 8400, Mankato, MN 56002-8400. Offers programs in business education (MS, MT), technology education (MS, MT). Accredited by NCATE. Faculty: 1 full-time (0 women). Students: 3 part-time (0 women). Average age 45. 0 applicants. In 1997, 1 degree awarded. *Degree requirements:* Thesis or alternative, comprehensive exam required, foreign language not required. *Entrance requirements:* GRE General Test, minimum GPA of 3.0 during previous 2 years. Application deadline: 7/10 (priority date; rolling processing; 10/30 for spring admission). Application fee: $20. *Tuition:* $126 per credit (minimum) for state residents; $200 per credit for nonresidents. *Financial aid:* Teaching assistantships, Federal Work-Study, and career-related internships or fieldwork available. Aid available to part-time students. Financial aid application deadline: 3/15; applicants required to submit FAFSA. *Faculty research:* Longitudinal studies of business communications. • Dr. Janet Adams, Chairperson, 507-389-6116. Application contact: Joni Roberts, Admissions Coordinator, 507-389-2321. Fax: 507-389-5974. E-mail: grad@mankato.msus.edu.

McNeese State University, College of Education, Department of Curriculum and Instruction, Program in Secondary Education, Lake Charles, LA 70609-2495. Offerings include business education (M Ed). Program faculty: 8 full-time (3 women). *Entrance requirements:* GRE General Test, teaching certificate. Application deadline: 7/15 (priority date; rolling processing). Application fee: $10 ($25 for international students). *Tuition:* $2118 per year full-time, $344 per semester (minimum) part-time for state residents; $7308 per year full-time, $344 per semester (minimum) part-time for nonresidents. • Dr. Everett Waddell Burge, Head, Department of Curriculum and Instruction, 318-475-5404.

Middle Tennessee State University, College of Business, Program in Business Administration, Murfreesboro, TN 37132. Offerings include business education (MBE). Accredited by NCATE. MBE offered jointly with the Department of Educational Leadership. Program faculty: 26 full-time (9 women). *Application deadline:* 8/1 (priority date). *Application fee:* $5. *Expenses:* Tuition $2560 per year full-time, $129 per semester hour part-time for state residents; $7386 per year full-time, $340 per semester hour part-time for nonresidents. Fees $486 per year full-time, $17 per semester (minimum) part-time. • Dr. Jill Austin, Chair, 615-898-2736. Fax: 615-898-5308. E-mail: jaustin@mtsu.edu.

Middle Tennessee State University, College of Education, Department of Educational Leadership, Murfreesboro, TN 37132. Offerings include business education (MBE). Accredited by NCATE. MBE offered jointly with the Program in Business Administration. Department faculty: 20 full-time (9 women), 7 part-time (3 women). *Application deadline:* 8/1 (priority date). *Application fee:* $5. *Expenses:* Tuition $2560 per year full-time, $129 per semester hour part-time for state residents; $7386 per year full-time, $340 per semester hour part-time for nonresidents. Fees $486 per year full-time, $17 per semester (minimum) part-time. • Dr. Nancy Keese, Chair, 615-898-2855. Fax: 615-898-2859. E-mail: nkeese@mtsu.edu.

Mississippi College, School of Education, Programs in Secondary Education, Program in Business Education, Clinton, MS 39058. Awards M Ed. Accredited by NCATE. *Degree requirements:* Comprehensive exam required, foreign language and thesis not required. *Entrance requirements:* GRE or NTE, minimum GPA of 2.5, Class A Certificate. Application deadline: 8/15 (priority date; rolling processing). Application fee: $25 ($75 for international students). *Expenses:* Tuition $6624 per year full-time, $276 per hour part-time. Fees $230 per year full-time, $35 per semester (minimum) part-time. *Financial aid:* Application deadline 4/1. • Dr. Thomas Taylor, Dean, School of Education, 601-925-3402.

Mississippi State University, College of Education, Department of Technology and Education, Mississippi State, MS 39762. Offerings include technology (MS), with options in business education, industrial technology, instructional technology, vocational education. Accredited by NCATE. Department faculty: 12 full-time (5 women), 3 part-time (0 women), 13 FTE. *Application deadline:* 7/26 (priority date; rolling processing; 11/10 for spring admission). *Application fee:* $0 ($25 for international students). Electronic applications accepted. *Tuition:* $3017 per year full-time, $168 per credit hour part-time for state residents; $6119 per year full-time, $340 per credit hour part-time for nonresidents. • Dr. John F. Perry Jr., Interim Head, 601-325-2281. Fax: 601-325-7599. E-mail: jfp1@ra.msstate.edu.

Montana State University–Bozeman, College of Business, 211 Montana Hall, Bozeman, MT 59717. Offerings include business education (MS). Accredited by NCATE. MS offered during summer only. College faculty: 21 full-time (3 women), 2 part-time (both women). *Application deadline:* 6/1 (priority date; rolling processing; 11/1 for spring admission). *Application fee:* $50. *Tuition:* $3994 per year full-time, $367 per semester (minimum) part-time for state residents; $9507 per year full-time, $957 per semester (minimum) part-time for nonresidents. • Michael Owen, Dean, 406-994-4421. Fax: 406-994-6206. E-mail: busgrad@montana.edu.

Montclair State University, School of Business, Department of Information and Decision Sciences, Upper Montclair, NJ 07043-1624. Offers program in distributive education (MA). Part-time and evening/weekend programs available. Faculty: 11 full-time. Students: 1 (woman) part-time. In 1997, 1 degree awarded. *Degree requirements:* Comprehensive exam required, thesis not required. *Entrance requirements:* GRE General Test (minimum score 400 on each section), minimum GPA of 2.75. Application deadline: 4/1 (rolling processing; 11/1 for spring admission). Application fee: $40. *Expenses:* Tuition $201 per credit for state residents; $257 per credit for nonresidents. Fees $22.05 per credit. *Financial aid:* Research assistantships available. Aid available to part-time students. Financial aid application deadline: 3/1; applicants required to submit FAFSA. • Application contact: Dr. Rosemary McCauley, Adviser, 973-655-7039.

Nazareth College of Rochester, Graduate Studies, Department of Business, Program in Business Education, Rochester, NY 14618-3790. Awards MS Ed. Part-time and evening/weekend programs available. Faculty: 1 full-time (0 women), 2 part-time (0 women). Students: 5 part-time (4 women); includes 1 minority (Hispanic). 1 applicant, 100% accepted. In 1997, 3 degrees awarded. *Degree requirements:* Comprehensive exam required, foreign language and thesis not required. *Entrance requirements:* Minimum GPA of 2.7. Application deadline: 6/1 (11/1 for spring admission). Application fee: $40. *Expenses:* Tuition $436 per credit hour. Fees $20 per semester. • Dr. Robert C. Marino, Director, 716-389-2604. Application contact: Dr. Kay F. Marshman, Dean, 716-389-2815. Fax: 716-389-2452.

New Hampshire College, Graduate School of Business, Program in Business Education, Manchester, NH 03106-1045. Awards MS. Part-time and evening/weekend programs available. Faculty: 1 full-time (0 women), 10 part-time (3 women), 4 FTE. Students: 105. In 1997, 45 degrees awarded. *Degree requirements:* Thesis or alternative required, foreign language not required. *Average time to degree:* master's–1.2 years full-time, 3.5 years part-time. *Entrance requirements:* Minimum GPA of 2.7 during previous 2 years, 2.5 overall. Application deadline: rolling. Application fee: $0. *Expenses:* Tuition $17,044 per year full-time, $945 per course part-time. Fees $530 per year full-time, $80 per year part-time. *Financial aid:* In 1997–98, 1 fellowship (to a first-year student) was awarded; Federal Work-Study, institutionally sponsored loans, and career-related internships or fieldwork also available. Aid available to part-time students. • Dr. Paul Schneiderman, Acting Dean, Graduate School of Business, 603-644-3102. Fax: 603-644-3150.

New York University, School of Education, Department of Administration, Leadership, and Technology, Program in Business Education, New York, NY 10012-1019. Offers teachers of business subjects in higher education (MA, Ed D, PhD, CAS). Part-time and evening/weekend programs available. Faculty: 2 full-time (1 woman), 2 part-time. Students: 3 full-time, 46 part-time. 24 applicants, 79% accepted. In 1997, 12 master's, 4 doctorates awarded. Terminal master's awarded for partial completion of doctoral program. *Degree requirements:* For master's, thesis required (for some programs), foreign language not required; for doctorate, dissertation. *Entrance requirements:* For master's, TOEFL; for doctorate, GRE General Test, TOEFL, interview; for CAS, TOEFL, master's degree. Application deadline: 2/1 (priority date; rolling processing; 12/1 for spring admission). Application fee: $40 ($60 for international students). *Financial aid:* Partial tuition waivers, Federal Work-Study, institutionally sponsored loans available. Aid available to part-time students. Financial aid application deadline: 3/1; applicants required to submit FAFSA. *Faculty research:* Applications of technology to instruction, end user information systems. • Bridget N. O'Connor, Director, 212-998-5488. Application contact: Office of Graduate Admissions, 212-998-5030. Fax: 212-995-4328.

Northwestern State University of Louisiana, Division of Education, Natchitoches, LA 71497. Offerings include business and distributive education (M Ed). Accredited by NCATE. Division faculty: 10 full-time (7 women), 4 part-time (2 women). *Application deadline:* 8/1 (priority date; rolling processing; 1/10 for spring admission). *Application fee:* $15 ($25 for international students). *Tuition:* $2147 per year full-time, $336 per semester (minimum) part-time for state residents; $6437 per year full-time, $336 per semester (minimum) part-time for nonresidents. • Dr. Sue Weaver, Chair, 318-357-5195. Application contact: Dr. Tom Hanson, Dean, Graduate Studies and Research, 318-357-5851. Fax: 318-357-5019.

Northwest Missouri State University, College of Professional and Applied Studies, Program in Secondary Business Education, 800 University Drive, Maryville, MO 64468-6001. Awards MS Ed. Students: 2 full-time (0 women). 1 applicant, 100% accepted. *Degree requirements:* Comprehensive exam required, foreign language and thesis not required. *Entrance requirements:* GRE General Test (minimum combined score of 700), TOEFL (minimum score 550), minimum GPA of 2.5. Application deadline: 7/1 (rolling processing; 12/1 for spring admission). Application fee: $0 ($50 for international students). *Expenses:* Tuition $113 per credit hour for state residents; $197 per credit hour for nonresidents. Fees $3 per credit hour. *Financial aid:* Application deadline 3/1. • Application contact: Dr. Frances Shipley, Dean of Graduate School, 816-562-1145. E-mail: gradsch@acad.nwmissouri.edu.

Old Dominion University, Darden College of Education, Department of Occupational and Technical Studies, Program in Business and Distributive Education, Norfolk, VA 23529. Awards MS Ed. Accredited by NCATE. Part-time and evening/weekend programs available. Students: 1 (woman) full-time, 3 part-time (0 women); includes 1 minority (African American). Average age 36. 4 applicants, 100% accepted. In 1997, 1 degree awarded. *Degree requirements:* Thesis, comprehensive exams required, foreign language not required. *Entrance requirements:* GRE General Test (minimum combined score of 900), BS in field; minimum GPA of 3.0 in major, 2.5 overall. Application deadline: 7/1 (rolling processing; 12/1 for spring admission). Application fee: $30. *Expenses:* Tuition $180 per credit hour for state residents; $477 per credit hour for nonresidents. Fees $140 per year full-time, $32 per semester part-time. *Financial aid:* In 1997–98, 1 student received aid, including 1 teaching assistantship (to a first-year student) totaling $5,328; research assistantships, tuition grants, partial tuition waivers, and career-related internships or fieldwork also available. Aid available to part-time students. Financial aid application deadline: 2/15; applicants required to submit FAFSA. *Faculty research:*

Directory: Business Education

Old Dominion University (continued)
Marketing and business education, special populations. • Dr. John M. Ritz, Chair, Department of Occupational and Technical Studies, 757-683-4305. Fax: 757-683-5227. E-mail: jritz@odu.edu.

Rider University, School of Graduate Education and Human Services, Program in Business Education, Lawrenceville, NJ 08648-3001. Awards MA. Accredited by NCATE. Part-time and evening/weekend programs available. Faculty: 1 part-time (0 women).33 FTE. Students: 11 part-time (5 women). Average age 36. 0 applicants. In 1997, 5 degrees awarded. *Degree requirements:* Comprehensive exams, research project required, foreign language and thesis not required. *Entrance requirements:* Interview, minimum GPA of 2.5. Application deadline: 8/15 (priority date; rolling processing; 12/15 for spring admission). Application fee: $35. *Tuition:* $329 per credit hour. *Financial aid:* Career-related internships or fieldwork available. Aid available to part-time students. *Faculty research:* Information processing, teaching via microcomputers, teaching methodologies. • Dr. Peter Yacyk, Adviser, 609-895-5449. Application contact: Dr. John Carpenter, Dean, Continuing Studies, 609-896-5036. Fax: 609-896-5261.

Robert Morris College, Program in Business Education, 881 Narrows Run Road, Moon Township, PA 15108-1189. Awards MS. Only part-time programs offered. Part-time and evening/weekend programs available. Faculty: 35 full-time (6 women), 35 part-time (5 women). Students: 33 part-time. In 1997, 3 degrees awarded. *Entrance requirements:* MAT (minimum score 32), minimum GPA of 2.5. Application deadline: 8/1 (priority date; rolling processing; 11/30 for spring admission). Application fee: $25 ($35 for international students). *Expenses:* Tuition $298 per credit. Fees $15 per credit. *Financial aid:* Assistantships available. Aid available to part-time students. Financial aid application deadline: 5/1; applicants required to submit FAFSA. • Dr. Jon A. Shank, Dean, School of Applied Sciences and Education, 412-262-8279. Fax: 412-262-8494. E-mail: shank@robert-morris.edu. Application contact: Vincent J. Kane, Recruiting Coordinator, 412-262-8535. Fax: 412-299-2425.

Shippensburg University of Pennsylvania, College of Business, Department of Business Education/Office Administration, Shippensburg, PA 17257-2299. Offers program in business education (M Ed). Faculty: 2 full-time (1 woman). Students: 0. In 1997, 6 degrees awarded. *Degree requirements:* Thesis optional, foreign language not required. *Entrance requirements:* MAT or minimum GPA of 2.5. Application deadline: rolling. Application fee: $25. Electronic applications accepted. *Expenses:* Tuition $3468 per year full-time, $193 per credit hour part-time for state residents; $6236 per year full-time, $346 per credit hour part-time for nonresidents. Fees $678 per year full-time, $108 per semester (minimum) part-time. *Financial aid:* Graduate assistantships available. Financial aid application deadline: 3/1. • Dr. Francis R. Cannon, Chairperson, 717-532-1438.

South Carolina State University, School of Education, Department of Teacher Education, 300 College Street Northeast, Orangeburg, SC 29117-0001. Offerings include secondary education (M Ed), with options in biology education, business education, counselor education, English education, home economics education, industrial education, mathematics education, science education, social studies education. Accredited by NCATE. Department faculty: 7 full-time (3 women), 2 part-time (1 woman). *Average time to degree:* master's–2 years full-time, 4 years part-time. *Application deadline:* 7/15 (priority date; rolling processing; 11/10 for spring admission). *Application fee:* $25. *Tuition:* $2974 per year full-time, $165 per credit hour part-time. • Dr. Jesse Kinard, Chairman, 803-536-8934. Application contact: Dr. Gail Joyner-Fleming, Interim Associate Dean and Director, Graduate Teacher Education, 803-536-8824. Fax: 803-536-8492.

Southeast Missouri State University, Department of Secondary Education, Cape Girardeau, MO 63701-4799. Offerings include business education (MA). *Degree requirements:* Thesis or alternative required, foreign language not required. *Entrance requirements:* GRE General Test (score in 50th percentile or higher), minimum GPA of 2.75. Application deadline: 4/1 (priority date; rolling processing; 11/21 for spring admission). Application fee: $20 ($100 for international students). *Tuition:* $2034 per year full-time, $113 per credit hour part-time for state residents; $3672 per year full-time, $204 per credit hour part-time for nonresidents. • Dalton Curtis, Chairperson, 573-651-5965. Application contact: Office of Graduate Studies, 573-651-2192.

Southern Illinois University at Edwardsville, Schools of Education and Business, Program in Business Education, Edwardsville, IL 62026-0001. Awards MS Ed. Accredited by NCATE. Part-time programs available. Students: 0. 0 applicants. *Degree requirements:* Final exam, project required, foreign language and thesis not required. *Entrance requirements:* GMAT. Application deadline: 7/24. Application fee: $25. *Expenses:* Tuition $1716 per year full-time, $95 per credit hour part-time for state residents; $5149 per year full-time, $286 per credit hour part-time for nonresidents. Fees $463 per year full-time, $433 per year part-time. *Financial aid:* Fellowships, research assistantships, teaching assistantships, assistantships, Federal Work-Study, institutionally sponsored loans available. Aid available to part-time students. • Application contact: Dr. David Winnett, Director, 618-692-3439.

State University of New York College at Buffalo, Faculty of Applied Science and Education, Department of Business Studies, Program in Business Education, Buffalo, NY 14222-1095. Awards MS Ed. Accredited by NCATE. Faculty: 9 full-time (1 woman). Students: 4 part-time (all women). Average age 36. 2 applicants, 50% accepted. In 1997, 4 degrees awarded. *Degree requirements:* Thesis or alternative, project required, foreign language not required. *Entrance requirements:* Minimum GPA of 2.5 in last 60 hours, New York teaching certificate. Application deadline: 5/1 (10/1 for spring admission). Application fee: $50. *Expenses:* Tuition $5100 per year full-time, $213 per credit hour part-time for state residents; $8416 per year full-time, $351 per credit hour part-time for nonresidents. Fees $195 per year full-time, $8.60 per credit hour part-time. *Financial aid:* In 1997–98, 1 assistantship was awarded; fellowships also available. Financial aid application deadline: 3/1. • Dr. Mary Davis, Chairperson, Department of Business Studies, 716-878-4239.

State University of New York College at Buffalo, Faculty of Applied Science and Education, Department of Business Studies, Program in Business and Distributive Education, Buffalo, NY 14222-1095. Awards MS Ed. Faculty: 9 full-time (1 woman). Students: 1 full-time (0 women), 7 part-time (6 women); includes 2 minority (both African Americans). Average age 38. 1 applicant, 100% accepted. In 1997, 1 degree awarded. *Degree requirements:* Thesis or alternative, project required, foreign language not required. *Entrance requirements:* Minimum GPA of 2.5 in last 60 hours, New York teaching certificate. Application deadline: 5/1 (10/1 for spring admission). Application fee: $50. *Expenses:* Tuition $5100 per year full-time, $213 per credit hour part-time for state residents; $8416 per year full-time, $351 per credit hour part-time for nonresidents. Fees $195 per year full-time, $8.60 per credit hour part-time. *Financial aid:* Fellowships available. Financial aid application deadline: 3/1. • Dr. Mary Davis, Chairperson, Department of Business Studies, 716-878-4239.

State University of West Georgia, College of Business, Department of Management and Business Systems, Carrollton, GA 30118. Offers program in business education (M Ed, Ed S). One or more programs accredited by NCATE. Part-time programs available. Faculty: 4 full-time (3 women). Students: 16 full-time (4 women), 42 part-time (29 women); includes 13 minority (all African Americans). Average age 36. In 1997, 11 master's, 1 Ed S awarded. *Degree requirements:* For master's, comprehensive exam, research paper required, foreign language and thesis not required; for Ed S, oral exam, research project required, foreign language and thesis not required. *Entrance requirements:* For master's, GRE General Test (minimum combined score of 800), minimum GPA of 2.5; for Ed S, GRE General Test (minimum combined score of 800), master's degree, minimum graduate GPA of 3.25. Application deadline: 8/30 (rolling processing). Application fee: $15. *Expenses:* Tuition $2428 per year full-time, $83 per semester hour part-time for state residents; $8428 per year full-time, $250 per semester hour part-time for nonresidents. Fees $428 per year. *Financial aid:* Research assistantships and career-related internships or fieldwork available. Aid available to part-time students. Financial aid applicants required to submit FAFSA. • Dr. Jack Johnson, Director of Business Education, 770-836-6475. Fax: 770-836-6774. E-mail: jjohnson@sbf.bus.westga.edu. Application contact: Dr. Jack O. Jenkins, Dean, Graduate School, 770-836-6419. Fax: 770-836-2301. E-mail: jjenkins@cob.as.westga.edu.

Texas A&M International University, Division of Teacher Education and Psychology, 5201 University Boulevard, Laredo, TX 78041-1900. Offerings include secondary education (MS Ed), with options in business education, secondary education. *Degree requirements:* Thesis required (for some programs), foreign language not required. *Entrance requirements:* GRE General Test. Application deadline: 7/15 (priority date; rolling processing; 11/12 for spring admission). Application fee: $0.

Texas Southern University, School of Business, Department of Business Education, Houston, TX 77004-4584. Awards M Ed. Faculty: 3 full-time (2 women), 1 (woman) part-time. Students: 6 full-time (4 women), 6 part-time (4 women); includes 5 international. Average age 26. *Degree requirements:* Computer language, comprehensive exam required, foreign language and thesis not required. *Entrance requirements:* GRE General Test, TOEFL, minimum GPA of 2.5. Application deadline: 7/15 (priority date; rolling processing). Application fee: $35 ($75 for international students). *Financial aid:* Teaching assistantships, Federal Work-Study available. Financial aid application deadline: 5/1. • Dr. Priscilla Slade, Dean, School of Business, 713-313-7215.

Troy State University Dothan, School of Business, Department of Computer Information Systems and Business Education, Dothan, AL 36304-0368. Offers programs in business education (MS), computer information systems (MS). *Entrance requirements:* GMAT, GRE General Test, or MAT, minimum GPA of 2.5. Application deadline: rolling. Application fee: $20. *Expenses:* Tuition $68 per credit hour for state residents; $140 per credit hour for nonresidents. Fees $2 per credit hour. • Dr. Gary Buchanan, Chair. Application contact: Reta Cordell, Director of Admissions and Records, 334-983-6556. Fax: 334-983-6322. E-mail: rcordell@tsud.edu.

University of British Columbia, Faculty of Education, Department of Curriculum Studies, Vancouver, BC V6T 1Z2, Canada. Offerings include business education (MA, M Ed). *Degree requirements:* Thesis (MA) required, foreign language not required. *Entrance requirements:* TOEFL (minimum score 550). Application deadline: 3/1 (12/1 for spring admission). Application fee: $60.

University of Central Arkansas, College of Education, Department of Applied Academic Technologies, Program in Business Education, Conway, AR 72035-0001. Awards MSE. Accredited by NCATE. Part-time programs available. Students: 22 part-time (17 women); includes 1 minority (African American). 5 applicants, 100% accepted. In 1997, 4 degrees awarded. *Degree requirements:* Comprehensive exam required, thesis not required. *Entrance requirements:* GRE General Test, minimum GPA of 2.7. Application deadline: 3/1 (priority date; rolling processing; 10/1 for spring admission). Application fee: $15 ($40 for international students). *Expenses:* Tuition $161 per credit hour for state residents; $298 per credit hour for nonresidents. Fees $50 per year full-time, $30 per year part-time. *Financial aid:* Application deadline 2/15. • Dr. Joseph Arn, Coordinator, 501-450-3177. Fax: 501-450-5680. E-mail: joea@mail.uca.edu.

University of Central Florida, College of Education, Department of Instructional Programs, Program in Business Education, Orlando, FL 32816. Awards MA, M Ed. Accredited by NCATE. Part-time and evening/weekend programs available. Students: 1 (woman) part-time. Average age 47. In 1997, 4 degrees awarded. *Degree requirements:* Thesis or alternative required, foreign language not required. *Entrance requirements:* GRE General Test (minimum combined score of 840). Application deadline: 7/15 (12/15 for spring admission). Application fee: $20. *Expenses:* Tuition $3288 per year full-time, $137 per credit hour part-time for state residents; $11,520 per year full-time, $480 per credit hour part-time for nonresidents. Fees $105 per year. • Application contact: Dr. Barry Siebert, Coordinator, 407-823-2009. E-mail: siebert@pegasus.cc.ucf.edu.

University of Georgia, College of Education, Department of Occupational Studies, Athens, GA 30602. Offerings include business education (M Ed), marketing education (M Ed). One or more programs accredited by NCATE. Department faculty: 12 full-time (4 women). *Degree requirements:* Thesis required (for some programs), foreign language not required. *Entrance requirements:* GRE General Test, MAT. Application deadline: 7/1 (priority date; 11/15 for spring admission). Application fee: $30. Electronic applications accepted. *Tuition:* $3290 per year full-time, $643 per semester (minimum) part-time for state residents; $11,300 per year full-time, $1645 per semester (minimum) part-time for nonresidents. • Dr. Robert C. Wicklein, Graduate Coordinator, 706-542-3132. Fax: 706-542-1765.

University of Idaho, College of Graduate Studies, College of Education, Division of Adult, Counselor, and Technology Education, Program in Business Education, Moscow, ID 83844-4140. Awards M Ed. Accredited by NCATE. Students: 3 full-time (all women), 6 part-time (4 women). *Entrance requirements:* Minimum GPA of 2.8. Application deadline: 8/1 (12/15 for spring admission). Application fee: $35 ($45 for international students). *Expenses:* Tuition $0 for state residents; $6000 per year full-time, $95 per credit part-time for nonresidents. Fees $2676 per year full-time, $134 per credit part-time. *Financial aid:* Application deadline 2/15. • Dr. Gerald Tuchscherer, Director, Division of Adult, Counselor, and Technology Education, 208-885-6556.

University of Louisville, School of Education, Department of Secondary Education, Program in Business Education, Louisville, KY 40292-0001. Awards MAT. Accredited by NCATE. Students: 0. *Entrance requirements:* GRE General Test, TOEFL. Application deadline: rolling. Application fee: $25. • Dr. Randall Wells, Director.

University of Manitoba, Faculty of Education, Department of Curriculum: Mathematics and Natural Sciences, Winnipeg, MB R3T 2N2, Canada. Offerings include industrial/vocational/business education (M Ed). *Degree requirements:* Thesis or alternative required, foreign language not required.

University of Maryland, College Park, College of Education, Department of Industrial, Technological, and Occupational Education, College Park, MD 20742-5045. Offerings include business education (MA, M Ed, Ed D, PhD, CAGS). Accredited by NCATE. Program being phased out; applicants no longer accepted. *Degree requirements:* For doctorate, dissertation. *Application deadline:* rolling. *Expenses:* Tuition $272 per credit hour for state residents; $400 per credit hour for nonresidents. Fees $564 per year full-time, $342 per year part-time. • Dr. Willis Hawley, Dean, College of Education, 301-405-2334. Fax: 301-314-9890. Application contact: John Mollish, Director, Graduate Admissions and Records, 301-405-4198. Fax: 301-314-9305.

University of Minnesota, Twin Cities Campus, College of Education and Human Development, Department of Work, Community, and Family Education, Program in Business and Marketing Education, Minneapolis, MN 55455-0213. Awards M Ed. • David Pucel, Coordinator, 612-624-3004.

University of Nebraska at Kearney, College of Business and Technology, Department of Business Administration/Education, Kearney, NE 68849-0001. Awards MS Ed. One or more programs accredited by NCATE. Part-time and evening/weekend programs available. Faculty: 9 full-time (4 women). Students: 4 part-time (3 women). In 1997, 1 degree awarded. *Degree requirements:* Thesis optional. *Entrance requirements:* GRE General Test. Application deadline: 8/1 (priority date; rolling processing; 12/15 for spring admission). Application fee: $35. *Expenses:* Tuition $1494 per year full-time, $83 per credit hour part-time for state residents; $2826 per year full-time, $157 per credit hour part-time for nonresidents. Fees $229 per year full-time, $11.25 per semester (minimum) part-time. *Financial aid:* In 1997–98, 1 research assistantship was awarded; teaching assistantships and career-related internships or fieldwork also available.

Aid available to part-time students. Financial aid application deadline: 3/1; applicants required to submit FAFSA. • Dale Zikmund, Chair, 308-865-8468.

University of North Carolina at Greensboro, Joseph M. Bryan School of Business and Economics, Division of Business Marketing Education, Greensboro, NC 27412-0001. Awards MSBE. Part-time programs available. Students: 8 full-time (7 women), 12 part-time (9 women); includes 4 minority (3 African Americans, 1 Native American). 8 applicants, 50% accepted. In 1997, 9 degrees awarded. *Degree requirements:* Comprehensive exam required, foreign language and thesis not required. *Entrance requirements:* GMAT, GRE General Test, MAT, or PRAXIS. Application deadline: 7/1 (priority date; rolling processing; 11/1 for spring admission). Application fee: $35. *Expenses:* Tuition $1842 per year full-time, $370 per semester (minimum) part-time for state residents; $10,296 per year full-time, $2484 per semester (minimum) part-time for nonresidents. Fees $806 per year full-time, $111 per semester (minimum) part-time. *Financial aid:* 8 students received aid; research assistantships available. *Faculty research:* Computer simulation. • Dr. Stephen R. Lucas, Head, 336-334-5691.

University of North Dakota, College of Business and Public Administration, Department of Business and Vocational Education, Grand Forks, ND 58202. Offers programs in business education (MS), vocational education (MS). Part-time programs available. Faculty: 4 full-time (1 woman). Students: 3 full-time (1 woman), 2 part-time (1 woman). 1 applicant, 100% accepted. In 1997, 8 degrees awarded. *Degree requirements:* Thesis or alternative required, foreign language not required. *Entrance requirements:* TOEFL (minimum score 550), minimum GPA of 3.0. Application deadline: 3/1 (priority date; rolling processing). Application fee: $20. *Financial aid:* In 1997–98, 5 teaching assistantships totaling $36,250, 1 assistantship totaling $3,625 were awarded; fellowships, research assistantships, full and partial tuition waivers, Federal Work-Study, institutionally sponsored loans also available. Financial aid application deadline: 3/15. • Dr. James Navara, Chairperson, 701-777-2517. Fax: 701-777-5099. E-mail: navara@badlands.nodak.edu.

University of South Alabama, College of Education, Department of Curriculum and Instruction, Mobile, AL 36688-0002. Offerings include business education (M Ed). Accredited by NCATE. Department faculty: 13 full-time (6 women). *Degree requirements:* Comprehensive exams required, foreign language and thesis not required. *Entrance requirements:* GRE General Test (minimum combined score of 1000) or MAT (minimum score 37), minimum GPA of 3.0. Application deadline: 9/1 (priority date; rolling processing). Application fee: $25. • Dr. Walter S. Hopkins, Chairman, 334-380-2893.

University of South Florida, College of Education, Department of Adult and Vocational Education, Program in Business and Office Education, Tampa, FL 33620-9951. Awards MA. Accredited by NCATE. Part-time and evening/weekend programs available. Students: 1 (woman) full-time, 8 part-time (6 women); includes 4 minority (1 African American, 1 Asian American, 2 Hispanics). Average age 32. 4 applicants, 100% accepted. In 1997, 5 degrees awarded. *Entrance requirements:* GRE General Test (minimum combined score of 1000), minimum GPA of 3.5 in last 60 hours. Application deadline: 5/15 (10/15 for spring admission). Application fee: $20. Electronic applications accepted. *Tuition:* $142 per credit hour for state residents; $486 per credit hour for nonresidents. *Financial aid:* Federal Work-Study, institutionally sponsored loans available. Aid available to part-time students. Financial aid applicants required to submit FAFSA. *Faculty research:* Facilitative approaches to learning, teacher motivation, school reform. • Application contact: Janet Scaglione, Coordinator, 813-974-0038. Fax: 813-974-5423. E-mail: scaglione@tempest.coedu.usf.edu.

University of South Florida, College of Education, Department of Adult and Vocational Education, Program in Distributive and Marketing Education, Tampa, FL 33620-9951. Awards MA. Accredited by NCATE. Part-time and evening/weekend programs available. Students: 1 part-time (0 women). 0 applicants. *Entrance requirements:* GRE General Test (minimum combined score of 1000), minimum GPA of 3.5 in last 60 hours. Application deadline: 6/1 (10/15 for spring admission). Application fee: $20. Electronic applications accepted. *Tuition:* $142 per credit hour for state residents; $486 per credit hour for nonresidents. *Financial aid:* Federal Work-Study, institutionally sponsored loans available. Aid available to part-time students. Financial aid applicants required to submit FAFSA. *Faculty research:* Facilitative approaches to learning, teacher motivation, school reform. • Application contact: Janet Scaglione, Coordinator, 813-974-0038. Fax: 813-974-5423. E-mail: scaglione@tempest.coedu.usf.edu.

University of Toledo, College of Education and Allied Professions, Department of Curriculum and Instruction, Toledo, OH 43606-3398. Offerings include business education (M Ed). Accredited by NCATE. Department faculty: 27 full-time (9 women). *Application deadline:* 8/1 (priority date; rolling processing). *Application fee:* $30. *Tuition:* $5907 per year full-time, $246 per hour part-time for state residents; $11,835 per year full-time, $493 per hour part-time for nonresidents. • Dr. James R. Gress, Chair, 419-530-2468. Fax: 419-530-7719. E-mail: jgress@uoft02.utoledo.edu.

University of Wisconsin–Whitewater, College of Business and Economics, Department of Business Education, Whitewater, WI 53190-1790. Awards MS. Accredited by NCATE. Part-time and evening/weekend programs available. *Degree requirements:* Thesis or alternative required, foreign language not required. *Entrance requirements:* GMAT, interview. Application deadline: rolling. Application fee: $38.

Utah State University, College of Business, Department of Business Information Systems and Education, Logan, UT 84322. Offers programs in business education (MS), business information systems (MS, Ed D, PhD), marketing education (MS), training and development (MS). Part-time and evening/weekend programs available. Postbaccalaureate distance learning degree programs offered (no on-campus study). Faculty: 10 full-time (0 women). Students: 53 full-time (26 women), 12 part-time (4 women). Average age 30. 27 applicants, 67% accepted. In 1997, 28 master's awarded. Terminal master's awarded for partial completion of doctoral program. *Degree requirements:* For master's, computer language required, thesis optional, foreign language not required; for doctorate, computer language, dissertation required, foreign language not required. *Entrance requirements:* For master's, GMAT (score in 40th percentile or higher), TOEFL (minimum score 550), minimum GPA of 3.0; for doctorate, GRE General Test (score in 40th percentile or higher), TOEFL (minimum score 550), minimum GPA of 3.0. Application deadline: 6/15 (priority date; rolling processing; 10/15 for spring admission). Application fee: $40. *Expenses:* Tuition $1448 per year full-time, $624 per year part-time for state residents; $5082 per year full-time, $2192 per year part-time for nonresidents. Fees $421 per year full-time, $165 per year part-time. *Financial aid:* Fellowships, research assistantships, teaching assistantships, Federal Work-Study, and career-related internships or fieldwork available. Financial aid application deadline: 3/1. *Faculty research:* Oral and written communication, methods of teaching, CASE tools, object-oriented programming, decision support systems, reengineering. • Dr. Lloyd Bartholome, Head, 435-797-2341. E-mail: lbart@b202.usu.edu. Application contact: Dr. Thomas Hilton, Graduate Adviser, 435-797-2353. Fax: 435-797-2351. E-mail: hilton@cc.usu.edu.

Utah State University, College of Education, Doctoral Program in Education, Logan, UT 84322. Offerings include business information systems and education (Ed D, PhD). Program faculty: 65 full-time (17 women). *Degree requirements:* Dissertation required, foreign language not required. *Entrance requirements:* GRE General Test (score in 40th percentile or higher), TOEFL (minimum score 550), minimum GPA of 3.0. Application deadline: 6/15 (priority date; rolling processing; 10/15 for spring admission). Application fee: $40. *Expenses:* Tuition $1448 per year full-time, $624 per year part-time for state residents; $5082 per year full-time, $2192 per year part-time for nonresidents. Fees $421 per year full-time, $165 per year part-time. • Application contact: Louann Parkinson, Administrative Assistant, 435-797-1470. Fax: 435-797-3939. E-mail: luannp@coe.usu.edu.

Valdosta State University, College of Education, Department of Business and Vocational Education, Valdosta, GA 31698. Offers programs in adult and vocational education (Ed D), business education (M Ed, Ed S), vocational education (M Ed). Accredited by NCATE. Faculty: 9 full-time (2 women). Students: 16 full-time (11 women), 19 part-time (12 women); includes 1 minority (African American). 42 applicants, 95% accepted. In 1997, 4 master's awarded. *Entrance requirements:* For master's, GRE General Test (minimum combined score of 800); for doctorate, GRE General Test (minimum combined score of 1000); for Ed S, GRE General Test (minimum combined score of 900). Application deadline: 8/1 (rolling processing; 11/15 for spring admission). Application fee: $10. *Expenses:* Tuition $2472 per year full-time, $83 per semester hour part-time for state residents; $8472 per year full-time, $333 per semester hour part-time for nonresidents. Fees $236 per year full-time. • Donnie McGahee, Head, 912-333-5928.

Wayne State College, Division of Education, Program in Curriculum and Instruction, Wayne, NE 68787. Offerings include business education (MSE). Accredited by NCATE. *Degree requirements:* Comprehensive exam, research paper required, foreign language not required. *Entrance requirements:* GRE General Test. Application deadline: rolling. Application fee: $10. *Expenses:* Tuition $1788 per year full-time, $75 per credit hour part-time for state residents; $3576 per year full-time, $149 per credit hour part-time for nonresidents. Fees $360 per year full-time, $15 per credit hour part-time. • Dr. Diane Alexander, Head, Division of Education, 402-375-7389.

Western Kentucky University, College of Education, Department of Teacher Education, Program in Business Education, Bowling Green, KY 42101-3576. Awards MA Ed. Accredited by NCATE. Part-time and evening/weekend programs available. Faculty: 1 (woman) full-time. Students: 4 part-time (3 women). Average age 32. *Entrance requirements:* GRE General Test (minimum combined score of 1150 on three sections; average 1400), minimum GPA of 2.5. Application deadline: 8/1 (priority date; rolling processing; 12/1 for spring admission). Application fee: $20. *Tuition:* $2460 per year full-time, $133 per credit hour part-time for state residents; $6700 per year full-time, $369 per credit hour part-time for nonresidents. *Financial aid:* Federal Work-Study, institutionally sponsored loans available. Aid available to part-time students. Financial aid application deadline: 4/1; applicants required to submit FAFSA. • Dr. Jacqueline Schlieffer, Head, 502-745-3097.

Winona State University, Graduate Studies, College of Business, Department of Administrative Information Systems, Winona, MN 55987-5838. Offers program in business education (MS). Part-time programs available. Faculty: 4 full-time (2 women). Students: 5 part-time (4 women). 0 applicants. In 1997, 1 degree awarded. *Degree requirements:* Thesis or alternative required, foreign language not required. *Entrance requirements:* GRE General Test. Application deadline: 8/8 (priority date; rolling processing; 2/17 for spring admission). Application fee: $20. *Financial aid:* Assistantships available. • Dr. J. William Murphy, Chairperson, 507-457-5698. E-mail: bmurphy@vax2.winona.msus.edu.

Winthrop University, College of Education, Program in Business Education, Rock Hill, SC 29733. Awards MAT, MS. Accredited by NCATE. Part-time programs available. Students: 7 full-time (5 women), 11 part-time (10 women); includes 7 minority (all African Americans). Average age 33. In 1997, 18 degrees awarded. *Degree requirements:* Thesis optional, foreign language not required. *Entrance requirements:* GMAT, GRE General Test (minimum combined score of 800), or MAT (minimum score 40); NTE, minimum GPA of 3.0, sample of written work. Application deadline: 7/15 (priority date; rolling processing; 12/1 for spring admission). Application fee: $35. *Tuition:* $3928 per year full-time, $164 per credit hour part-time for state residents; $7060 per year full-time, $294 per credit hour part-time for nonresidents. *Financial aid:* Graduate assistantships, graduate scholarships, Federal Work-Study available. Aid available to part-time students. Financial aid application deadline: 2/1; applicants required to submit FAFSA. • Dr. Richard Ingram, Chairman, 803-323-2151. Fax: 803-323-2585. E-mail: ingramr@winthrop.edu. Application contact: Sharon Johnson, Director of Graduate Studies, 803-323-2204. Fax: 803-323-2292. E-mail: johnsons@winthrop.edu.

Wright State University, College of Education and Human Services, Department of Teacher Education, Programs in Business Education and Vocational Education, Dayton, OH 45435. Offerings in business education (MA, M Ed), vocational education (MA, M Ed). Accredited by NCATE. Students: 4 full-time (all women), 19 part-time (16 women); includes 1 minority (African American). 11 applicants, 73% accepted. In 1997, 6 degrees awarded. *Degree requirements:* Thesis required (for some programs), foreign language not required. *Entrance requirements:* GRE General Test, MAT, TOEFL (minimum score 550). Application fee: $25. *Tuition:* $5109 per year full-time, $161 per credit hour part-time for state residents; $9039 per year full-time, $282 per credit hour part-time for nonresidents. *Financial aid:* Available to part-time students. Financial aid applicants required to submit FAFSA. • Dr. Donna Courtney, Coordinator, 937-775-3598. Fax: 937-775-3301. Application contact: Gerald C. Malicki, Assistant Dean and Director of Graduate Admissions and Records, 937-775-2976. Fax: 937-775-2357. E-mail: wsugrad@wright.edu.

Computer Education

Allentown College of St. Francis de Sales, Graduate Division, Program in Education, Center Valley, PA 18034-9568. Offerings include computer education (M Ed), computer science (M Ed). Program faculty: 18 full-time (4 women), 25 part-time (6 women). *Degree requirements:* Capstone Course or Project required, foreign language not required. *Average time to degree:* master's–3 years part-time. *Entrance requirements:* Teaching certificate. Application deadline: 8/24 (priority date; rolling processing). Application fee: $35. *Tuition:* $285 per credit. • Dr. Irene Pompetti-Szul, Director, 610-282-1100 Ext. 1401. Fax: 610-282-2254.

Ashland University, College of Education, Graduate Studies in Teacher Education, Program in Curriculum and Instruction, Ashland, OH 44805-3702. Offerings include computer education (M Ed). Accredited by NCATE. Program faculty: 8 full-time (4 women), 24 part-time (9 women). *Degree requirements:* Practicum or thesis. *Entrance requirements:* GRE General Test or MAT, teaching certificate. Application deadline: rolling. Application fee: $15. *Tuition:* $275 per credit hour. • Carl Walley, Program Team Leader, 419-289-5355. E-mail: cwalley@ashland.edu. Application contact: Dr. Joe Bailey, Director, 419-289-5377. Fax: 419-289-5097. E-mail: jbailey@ashland.edu.

Augustana College, Department of Education, Program in Special Education, Sioux Falls, SD 57197. Offerings include computer applications in special education (MA). Accredited by NCATE. Program faculty: 6 full-time. *Degree requirements:* Comprehensive and oral exams required, foreign language and thesis not required. *Entrance requirements:* Appropriate bachelor's degree, minimum GPA of 3.0. Application deadline: 6/1 (priority date; rolling processing). Application fee: $50. *Tuition:* $14,726 per year full-time, $250 per credit hour part-time. • Application contact: Kay West, Secretary, 605-336-4126. Fax: 605-336-4450.

Directory: Computer Education

Beaver College, Department of Education, Glenside, PA 19038-3295. Offerings include computer education (M Ed, CAS), computer education 7–12 (MA Ed). *Application fee:* $35. *Expenses:* Tuition $6570 per year full-time, $365 per credit part-time. Fees $35 per year.

Bemidji State University, Division of Social and Natural Sciences, Field of Computer Science, Bemidji, MN 56601-2699. Awards MS Ed. Part-time programs available. Students: 1 (woman) full-time, 1 part-time (0 women). Average age 30. In 1997, 1 degree awarded. *Application deadline:* 5/1. *Application fee:* $20. *Expenses:* Tuition $128 per credit for state residents; $134 per credit (minimum) for nonresidents. Fees $517 per year full-time, $35 per credit (minimum) part-time. *Financial aid:* Teaching assistantships, Federal Work-Study, and career-related internships or fieldwork available. Aid available to part-time students. Financial aid application deadline: 5/1. • Dr. James L. Richards, Chair, 218-755-2840. E-mail: jlrich@vax1.bemidji.msus.edu.

California State University, Dominguez Hills, School of Education, Department of Graduate Education, Program in Computer-Based Education, Carson, CA 90747-0001. Awards MA, Certificate. *Entrance requirements:* For master's, minimum GPA of 2.75. Application deadline: 6/1. Application fee: $55. *Expenses:* Tuition $0 for state residents; $246 per unit for nonresidents. Fees $1896 per year full-time, $1230 per year part-time. • Application contact: Admissions Office, 310-243-3600.

California State University, Los Angeles, School of Education, Division of Educational Foundations and Interdivisional Studies, Major in Computer Education, Los Angeles, CA 90032-8530. Awards MA. Accredited by NCATE. Students: 8 full-time (6 women), 15 part-time (6 women); includes 11 minority (2 African Americans, 4 Asian Americans, 5 Hispanics), 2 international. In 1997, 6 degrees awarded. *Entrance requirements:* TOEFL (minimum score 550), minimum GPA of 2.75 in last 90 units, teaching certificate. Application deadline: 6/30 (rolling processing; 2/1 for spring admission). Application fee: $55. *Expenses:* Tuition $0 for state residents; $164 per unit for nonresidents. Fees $1763 per year full-time, $1097 per year part-time. *Financial aid:* 5 students received aid. Financial aid application deadline: 3/1. • Dr. Simeon Slovacek, Chair, Division of Educational Foundations and Interdivisional Studies, 213-343-4330.

California University of Pennsylvania, School of Science and Technology, Department of Mathematics and Computer Sciences, 250 University Avenue, California, PA 15419-1394. Offerings include computer science (M Ed). Department faculty: 9 part-time (2 women). *Degree requirements:* Comprehensive exam required, thesis optional, foreign language not required. *Entrance requirements:* TOEFL (minimum score 550), MAT (minimum score 35) or minimum GPA of 2.5, teaching certificate (M Ed). Application deadline: rolling. Application fee: $25. *Expenses:* Tuition $3468 per year full-time, $193 per credit part-time for state residents; $6236 per year full-time, $346 per credit part-time for nonresidents. Fees $886 per year full-time, $153 per semester (minimum) part-time. • Dr. Andrew Machusko, Chairperson, 724-938-4078.

Cardinal Stritch University, College of Arts and Sciences, Department of Educational Computing, Milwaukee, WI 53217-3985. Offers programs in computer science education (MS), educational computing (M Ed). Students: 211. *Application deadline:* 4/1 (priority date; rolling processing). *Application fee:* $20. *Expenses:* Tuition $338 per credit. Fees $25 per semester. *Financial aid:* Federal Work-Study available. Financial aid applicants required to submit FAFSA. • Dr. James Kasum, Chair, 414-410-4021. Application contact: Amy Knox, Graduate Admissions Officer, 414-410-4042.

Cleveland State University, College of Education, Department of Curriculum and Foundations, Cleveland, OH 44115-2440. Offerings include computer uses in education (M Ed). Department faculty: 14 full-time (9 women). *Entrance requirements:* GRE General Test or MAT (score in 50th percentile or higher). Application deadline: 9/1 (priority date; rolling processing). Application fee: $25. *Expenses:* Tuition $5252 per year full-time, $202 per credit hour part-time for state residents; $10,504 per year full-time, $404 per credit hour part-time for nonresidents. Fees $2.25 per credit hour (minimum). • Dr. David Adams, Interim Chairperson, 216-687-7128. Fax: 216-687-5370. E-mail: d.adams@csuohio.edu.

Concordia University, Program in Mathematics/Computer Science Education, River Forest, IL 60305-1499. Awards MA, CAS. Part-time and evening/weekend programs available. Faculty: 8 full-time (3 women), 4 part-time (1 woman). Students: 15 (9 women); includes 2 minority (1 African American, 1 Asian American), 3 international. In 1997, 3 master's awarded. *Degree requirements:* For master's, comprehensive exam required, thesis optional, foreign language not required; for CAS, thesis, final project required, foreign language not required. *Entrance requirements:* For master's, minimum GPA of 2.9; for CAS, master's degree. Application deadline: rolling. Application fee: $0. *Tuition:* $372 per semester hour. *Financial aid:* Research assistantships, institutionally sponsored loans available. Aid available to part-time students. *Faculty research:* Technology used in parochial high schools in teaching math. • Dr. Manfred Boos, Coordinator, 708-209-3088. Application contact: Mary Betancourt, Admissions Secretary, 708-209-4093. Fax: 708-209-3454. E-mail: crfdngrad@curf.edu.

Eastern Washington University, College of Science, Mathematics and Technology, Department of Computer Science, Cheney, WA 99004-2431. Awards M Ed, MS. Accredited by NCATE. Part-time programs available. Faculty: 10 full-time (2 women). Students: 10 full-time (2 women), 12 part-time (2 women); includes 1 minority (Asian American). 15 applicants, 80% accepted. In 1997, 4 degrees awarded. *Degree requirements:* Thesis or alternative, comprehensive oral exam. *Entrance requirements:* Minimum GPA of 3.0. Application deadline: 4/1 (priority date; rolling processing; 1/15 for spring admission). Application fee: $35. *Tuition:* $4200 per year full-time, $140 per credit part-time for state residents; $12,780 per year full-time, $415 per credit part-time for nonresidents. *Financial aid:* Research assistantships, teaching assistantships, Federal Work-Study, institutionally sponsored loans available. Financial aid application deadline: 2/1. • Dr. Ray Hamel, Chairman, 509-359-6260. Application contact: Dr. Steve Simmons, Adviser, 509-359-6064.

Florida Institute of Technology, College of Science and Liberal Arts, Department of Science Education, Melbourne, FL 32901-6975. Offerings include computer science education (MSE, PhD, Ed S). Terminal master's awarded for partial completion of doctoral program. Department faculty: 4 full-time (1 woman), 2 part-time (both women). *Degree requirements:* For master's, oral comprehensive exam required, thesis optional, foreign language not required; for Ed S, comprehensive exam required, foreign language and thesis not required. *Entrance requirements:* For master's and Ed S, minimum GPA of 3.0. Application deadline: rolling. Application fee: $50. *Tuition:* $550 per credit hour. • Dr. Robert H. Fronk, Head, 407-674-8126. Fax: 407-674-7598. E-mail: fronk@fit.edu. Application contact: Carolyn P. Farrior, Associate Dean of Graduate Admissions, 407-674-7118. Fax: 407-723-9468. E-mail: cfarrior@fit.edu.

Fontbonne College, Department of Mathematics and Computer Science, St. Louis, MO 63105-3098. Offers program in computer education (MS). Faculty: 1 (woman) full-time, 5 part-time (3 women). Students: 2 full-time (1 woman), 95 part-time (82 women); includes 24 minority (22 African Americans, 1 Asian American, 1 Native American), 3 international. Average age 42. In 1997, 21 degrees awarded. *Degree requirements:* Computer language required, thesis optional, foreign language not required. *Entrance requirements:* Minimum GPA of 3.0. Application deadline: 8/1 (priority date; rolling processing; 12/15 for spring admission). Application fee: $20. *Expenses:* Tuition $10,650 per year full-time, $346 per credit hour part-time. Fees $160 per year full-time, $7 per credit hour part-time. • Dr. Elizabeth Newton, Chairperson, 314-889-4508. Fax: 314-889-1401. E-mail: bnewton@fontbonne.edu. Application contact: Dr. Mary Abkemeier, Director, 314-889-1497. Fax: 314-889-1451. E-mail: mabkemei@fontbonne.edu.

Fort Hays State University, College of Arts and Sciences, Department of Mathematics and Computer Science, Hays, KS 67601-4099. Offerings include computer science (MAT). Department faculty: 9 full-time (1 woman). *Degree requirements:* Thesis or alternative required, foreign language not required. *Application deadline:* 7/1 (priority date; rolling processing). *Application fee:* $25 ($35 for international students). *Tuition:* $94 per credit hour for state residents; $249 per credit hour for nonresidents. • Dr. Ronald Sandstrom, Chair, 785-628-4240.

Gonzaga University, Graduate School, College of Arts and Sciences, Program in Mathematics and Computer Science, Spokane, WA 99258-0001. Awards MAT. *Degree requirements:* Comprehensive exam. *Entrance requirements:* GRE General Test or MAT, TOEFL (minimum score 550), minimum GPA of 3.0. Application deadline: 7/20 (priority date; rolling processing; 11/1 for spring admission). Application fee: $40. *Tuition:* $7380 per year (minimum) full-time, $410 per credit (minimum) part-time. *Financial aid:* Application deadline 3/1. • Dr. Robert L. Bryant, Chairperson. Application contact: Dr. Leonard Doohan, Dean of the Graduate School, 509-328-4220 Ext. 3546. Fax: 509-324-5399.

Gonzaga University, Graduate School, School of Education, Program in Computer Education, Spokane, WA 99258-0001. Awards MACE. Accredited by NCATE. Part-time programs available. Faculty: 2 full-time (1 woman), 2 part-time (1 woman). Students: 30 full-time (19 women); includes 13 international. Average age 38. In 1997, 1 degree awarded. *Degree requirements:* Computer language, comprehensive exam, project required, foreign language and thesis not required. *Entrance requirements:* GRE General Test or MAT, TOEFL (minimum score 550). Application deadline: 7/20 (priority date; rolling processing; 11/1 for spring admission). Application fee: $40. *Tuition:* $7380 per year (minimum) full-time, $410 per credit (minimum) part-time. *Financial aid:* Application deadline 3/1. • Dr. Angie Parker, Director, 509-328-4220 Ext. 3494.

Jacksonville University, College of Arts and Sciences, Division of Education, Program in Computer Education, 2800 University Boulevard North, Jacksonville, FL 32211-3394. Awards MAT. Part-time and evening/weekend programs available. *Degree requirements:* Computer language, comprehensive exam required, foreign language and thesis not required. *Entrance requirements:* GRE General Test (minimum combined score of 900), TOEFL (minimum score 500), minimum GPA of 3.0. Application deadline: 8/1 (priority date; rolling processing; 11/1 for spring admission). Application fee: $25.

Knowledge Systems Institute, Program in Computer and Information Sciences, Skokie, IL 60076. Offerings include education (MS). Institute faculty: 4 full-time (0 women), 23 part-time (3 women), 10 FTE. *Application fee:* $40. *Tuition:* $6600 per year full-time, $715 per course part-time. • Judy Pan, Executive Director, 847-679-3135. Fax: 847-679-3166. E-mail: judy@ksi.edu.

Lesley College, School of Education, Cambridge, MA 02138-2790. Offerings include computers in education (M Ed, CAGS). Postbaccalaureate distance learning degree programs offered (no on-campus study). School faculty: 36 full-time (31 women), 340 part-time (220 women). *Degree requirements:* Computer language required, foreign language and thesis not required. *Entrance requirements:* For master's, TOEFL (minimum score 550); for CAGS, interview, master's degree. Application deadline: rolling. Application fee: $45. *Tuition:* $425 per credit. • Dr. William L. Dandridge, Dean, 617-349-8375. Application contact: Graduate Admissions, 617-349-8300. Fax: 617-349-8366.

Long Island University, C.W. Post Campus, College of Liberal Arts and Sciences, Department of Computer Sciences, Brookville, NY 11548-1300. Offerings include computer science education (MS). Department faculty: 6 full-time (2 women), 6 part-time (0 women). *Degree requirements:* Computer language, thesis or alternative, comprehensive exam required, foreign language not required. *Entrance requirements:* Bachelor's degree in science, mathematics, or engineering. Application deadline: rolling. Application fee: $30. Electronic applications accepted. *Expenses:* Tuition $480 per credit. Fees $316 per year full-time, $71 per semester (minimum) part-time. • Dr. Susan Dorchak, Chair, 516-299-2293. E-mail: dorchak@homet.liunet.edu. Application contact: John Keane, Graduate Adviser, 516-299-2293.

Long Island University, C.W. Post Campus, School of Education, Department of Educational Technology, Brookville, NY 11548-1300. Offers program in computers in education (MS, CAS). Part-time and evening/weekend programs available. Faculty: 4 full-time (1 woman), 4 part-time (3 women). Students: 76 part-time. 16 applicants, 69% accepted. In 1997, 71 master's awarded. *Degree requirements:* For master's, computer language, research project required, foreign language and thesis not required; for CAS, computer language required, foreign language and thesis not required. *Entrance requirements:* For master's, interview; minimum GPA of 2.75 in major, 2.5 overall. Application deadline: rolling. Application fee: $30. Electronic applications accepted. *Expenses:* Tuition $480 per credit. Fees $316 per year full-time, $71 per semester (minimum) part-time. *Financial aid:* In 1997–98, 4 teaching assistantships were awarded; career-related internships or fieldwork also available. Aid available to part-time students. Financial aid application deadline: 5/15; applicants required to submit FAFSA. *Faculty research:* Desktop publishing, higher-order thinking skills, interactive learning environments. • Dr. Michael M. Byrne, Co-Chairperson, 516-299-2147. E-mail: edt_byrne@eagle.liunet.edu. Application contact: Christine Hoyler, Program Manager, 516-299-2147. Fax: 516-299-4167. E-mail: choyler@eagle.liunet.edu.

Marlboro College, Graduate Center, Program in Teaching with Internet Technologies, Brattleboro, VT 05302. Awards MAT. Evening/weekend programs available. Postbaccalaureate distance learning degree programs offered (minimal on-campus study). Faculty: 2 full-time (0 women), 4 part-time (1 woman). Students: 9. *Degree requirements:* Capstone Project. *Application deadline:* 3/12 (priority date; rolling processing). *Tuition:* $15,000 per year. *Financial aid:* Career-related internships or fieldwork available. Financial aid applicants required to submit FAFSA. • Application contact: Mary B. Greene, Director of Academic Programs, 802-258-9200. Fax: 802-258-9201. E-mail: mbgreene@gradcenter.marlboro.edu.

See in-depth description on page 1183.

Mississippi College, School of Education, Programs in Secondary Education, Program in Computer Science Education, Clinton, MS 39058. Awards M Ed. Accredited by NCATE. *Degree requirements:* Comprehensive exam required, foreign language and thesis not required. *Entrance requirements:* GRE or NTE, minimum GPA of 2.5, Class A Certificate. Application deadline: 8/15 (priority date; rolling processing). Application fee: $25 ($75 for international students). *Expenses:* Tuition $6624 per year full-time, $276 per hour part-time. Fees $230 per year full-time, $35 per semester (minimum) part-time. *Financial aid:* Application deadline 4/1. • Dr. Thomas Taylor, Dean, School of Education, 601-925-3402.

Morningside College, Department of Education, Program in Technology Based Learning, Sioux City, IA 51106-1751. Awards MAT. Accredited by NCATE. Part-time and evening/weekend programs available. Faculty: 8 (3 women). *Entrance requirements:* MAT, writing sample. Application deadline: rolling. Application fee: $15. *Tuition:* $245 per credit hour. *Financial aid:* Partial tuition waivers, institutionally sponsored loans available. Aid available to part-time students. • Dr. Mary Herring, Head, 712-274-5375.

Nazareth College of Rochester, Graduate Studies, Department of Education, Program in Computer Education, Rochester, NY 14618-3790. Awards MS Ed. Part-time and evening/weekend programs available. Faculty: 2 full-time (0 women), 1 part-time (0 women). Students: 42 part-time (25 women). 9 applicants, 100% accepted. In 1997, 14 degrees awarded. *Degree requirements:* Comprehensive exam required, foreign language and thesis not required. *Entrance requirements:* Minimum GPA of 2.7. Application deadline: 6/1 (11/1 for spring admission). Application fee: $40. *Expenses:* Tuition $436 per credit hour. Fees $20 per semester. • James Fenwick, Director, 716-389-2630. Application contact: Dr. Kay F. Marshman, Dean, 716-389-2815. Fax: 716-389-2452.

Northwest Missouri State University, College of Professional and Applied Studies, Program in Educational Uses of Computer, 800 University Drive, Maryville, MO 64468-6001. Awards MS Ed. Accredited by NCATE. Part-time programs available. Faculty: 9 full-time (3 women). Students: 17 part-time (16 women). 5 applicants, 100% accepted. In 1997, 2 degrees awarded.

Degree requirements: Comprehensive exam required, foreign language and thesis not required. *Entrance requirements:* GRE General Test, GRE Subject Test, TOEFL (minimum score 550), minimum GPA of 2.5, teaching certificate, writing sample. Application deadline: 7/1 (rolling processing); 12/1 for spring admission). Application fee: $0 ($50 for international students). *Expenses:* Tuition $113 per credit hour for state residents; $197 per credit hour for nonresidents. Fees $3 per credit hour. *Financial aid:* In 1997–98, 1 teaching assistantship averaging $585 per month was awarded. Financial aid application deadline: 3/1. • Dr. William Hinckley, Adviser, 816-562-1563. Application contact: Dr. Frances Shipley, Dean of Graduate School, 816-562-1145. E-mail: gradsch@acad.nwmissouri.edu.

Nova Southeastern University, Fischler Center for the Advancement of Education, Graduate Teacher Education Program, Fort Lauderdale, FL 33314-7721. Offerings include computer education (MS, Ed S), computer science education (MS, Ed S). *Degree requirements:* Thesis, practicum required, foreign language not required. *Entrance requirements:* For master's, teaching certificate; for Ed S, master's degree, teaching certificate. Application deadline: rolling. Application fee: $50. *Tuition:* $245 per credit hour (minimum). • Dr. Deo Nellis, Dean, 954-262-8601. E-mail: deo@fcae.nova.edu. Application contact: Dr. Mark Seldine, Director of Student Affairs, 954-262-8689. Fax: 954-262-3910. E-mail: seldines@fcae.nova.edu.

Nova Southeastern University, Fischler Center for the Advancement of Education, Programs in Higher Education, Fort Lauderdale, FL 33314-7721. Offerings include computing and information technology (Ed D). *Degree requirements:* Dissertation, practicum required, foreign language not required. *Entrance requirements:* Master's degree, work experience in field. Application deadline: rolling. Application fee: $50. *Tuition:* $8460 per year. • Dr. Ross E. Moreton, Dean, 954-262-8526. E-mail: moreton@fcae.nova.edu. Application contact: Dr. Delores Smiley, 800-986-3223 Ext. 8527. Fax: 954-262-3903. E-mail: smiley@fcae.nova.edu.

Ohio University, Graduate Studies, College of Education, School of Curriculum and Instruction, Athens, OH 45701-2979. Offerings include computers in education (M Ed). Accredited by NCATE. School faculty: 21 full-time (7 women), 16 part-time (11 women). *Application deadline:* rolling. *Application fee:* $30. *Tuition:* $5430 per year full-time, $216 per quarter hour part-time for state residents; $10,431 per year full-time, $423 per quarter hour part-time for nonresidents. • Dr. Ralph Martin, Director, 740-593-4422. Application contact: Dr. Bonnie Beach, Graduate Chair, 740-593-0523.

Oklahoma State University, College of Arts and Sciences, Department of Computer Science, Stillwater, OK 74078. Offerings include computer education (Ed D). Department faculty: 9 full-time (2 women). *Application deadline:* 7/1 (priority date). *Application fee:* $25. • Dr. Blaine Mayfield, Head, 405-744-5668. Fax: 405-774-9097.

Philadelphia College of Textiles and Science, School of Science and Health, Program in Instructional Technology, Philadelphia, PA 19144-5497. Awards MS, MBA/MS. Part-time and evening/weekend programs available. *Entrance requirements:* GRE or MAT, minimum GPA of 2.85. Application deadline: rolling. Application fee: $35. *Tuition:* $427 per credit hour. *Financial aid:* Research assistantships, graduate assistantships, residential assistantships, Federal Work-Study, and career-related internships or fieldwork available. Financial aid applicants required to submit FAFSA. • Dr. Terry Olivier, Director, 215-951-2872. Fax: 215-951-2615. E-mail: oliviert@phila.col.com. Application contact: Robert J. Reed, Director of Graduate Admissions, 215-951-2943. Fax: 215-951-2907. E-mail: gradadm@phila.col.edu.

Plymouth State College of the University System of New Hampshire, Department of Education, Program in Educational Computing, Plymouth, NH 03264-1595. Awards M Ed. Program being phased out; applicants no longer accepted. Part-time and evening/weekend programs available. Students: 1 full-time (0 women), 2 part-time (1 woman). Average age 49. In 1997, 2 degrees awarded. *Tuition:* $232 per credit for state residents; $254 per credit for nonresidents. *Financial aid:* Institutionally sponsored loans and career-related internships or fieldwork available. Aid available to part-time students. • Dr. Stephen Weissmann, Coordinator, 603-535-2449.

Rivier College, Graduate Education Department, Nashua, NH 03060-5086. Offerings include computers in education (MA). *Application deadline:* rolling. *Application fee:* $25.

Rosemont College, College of Graduate Studies, Program in Technology in Education, Rosemont, PA 19010-1699. Offerings include educational computing and technology literacy (CPS). Program faculty: 2 full-time (1 woman), 7 part-time (3 women). *Application deadline:* rolling. *Application fee:* $50. *Tuition:* $375 per credit. • Dr. Robert J. Siegfried, Director, 610-527-0200 Ext. 2344. E-mail: rsiegfried@rosemont.edu. Application contact: Stan Rostkowski, Enrollment Coordinator, 610-527-0200 Ext. 2187. Fax: 610-526-2964. E-mail: roscolgrad@rosemont.edu.

Rowan University, College of Education, Department of Elementary Education, Glassboro, NJ 08028-1701. Offerings include computers in education (Certificate). Accredited by NCATE. *Application deadline:* 11/1 (priority date; rolling processing; 4/1 for spring admission). *Application fee:* $50. *Tuition:* $5728 per year full-time, $258 per credit hour part-time for state residents; $8968 per year full-time, $393 per credit hour part-time for nonresidents. • Dr. Carl Calliari, Adviser, 609-256-4763.

Saint Martin's College, Graduate Programs, Department of Education, Lacey, WA 98503-7500. Offerings include computers in education (M Ed). Department faculty: 8 full-time (3 women), 5 part-time (2 women). *Application deadline:* 7/1 (priority date; rolling processing; 12/1 for spring admission). *Application fee:* $25. • Dr. Paul Nelson, Director, 360-438-4529. Application contact: Michelle Roman, Administrative Assistant, 360-438-4333.

Shenandoah University, School of Arts and Sciences, 1460 University Drive, Winchester, VA 22601-5195. Offerings include computer education (MSC). Postbaccalaureate distance learning degree programs offered (minimal on-campus study). School faculty: 7 full-time (2 women), 4 part-time (2 women). *Application deadline:* 7/1 (priority date; rolling processing). *Application fee:* $30. Electronic applications accepted. *Tuition:* $470 per credit. • Dr. Catherine Tisinger, Dean, 540-665-4587. Fax: 540-665-4644. E-mail: ctisinge@su.edu. Application contact: Michael Carpenter, Director of Admissions, 540-665-4581. Fax: 540-665-4627. E-mail: admit@su.edu.

Shippensburg University of Pennsylvania, College of Arts and Sciences, Department of Mathematics and Computer Science, Shippensburg, PA 17257-2299. Offerings include computer education (M Ed). Department faculty: 13 full-time (1 woman). *Application deadline:* rolling. *Application fee:* $25. Electronic applications accepted. *Expenses:* Tuition $3468 per year full-time, $193 per credit hour part-time for state residents; $6236 per year full-time, $346 per credit hour part-time for nonresidents. Fees $678 per year full-time, $108 per semester (minimum) part-time. • Dr. Fred Nordai, Chairperson, 717-532-1431.

Shippensburg University of Pennsylvania, College of Education and Human Services, Department of Teacher Education, Shippensburg, PA 17257-2299. Offerings include computer education (M Ed). Accredited by NCATE. Department faculty: 16 full-time (11 women), 10 part-time (7 women). *Application deadline:* rolling. *Application fee:* $25. Electronic applications accepted. *Expenses:* Tuition $3468 per year full-time, $193 per credit hour part-time for state residents; $6236 per year full-time, $346 per credit hour part-time for nonresidents. Fees $678 per year full-time, $108 per semester (minimum) part-time. • Dr. Audrey Sprenger, Chairperson, 717-532-1688.

State University of New York College at Buffalo, Faculty of Applied Science and Education, Program in Educational Computing, Buffalo, NY 14222-1095. Awards MS Ed. Accredited by NCATE. Part-time and evening/weekend programs available. Faculty: 3 full-time (0 women). Students: 11 full-time (8 women), 64 part-time (42 women); includes 4 minority (3 African Americans, 1 Hispanic), 1 international. Average age 31. 23 applicants, 100% accepted. In 1997, 15 degrees awarded. *Degree requirements:* Thesis, project required, foreign language not required. *Application deadline:* 5/1 (10/1 for spring admission). *Application fee:* $50. *Expenses:* Tuition $5100 per year full-time, $213 per credit hour part-time for state residents; $8416 per year full-time, $351 per credit hour part-time for nonresidents. Fees $195 per year full-time, $8.60 per credit hour part-time. *Financial aid:* Fellowships available. Financial aid application deadline: 3/1. • Dr. Anthony Nowakowski, Coordinator, 716-878-4923.

Teachers College, Columbia University, Graduate Faculty of Education, Department of Scientific Foundations, Program in Computing in Education, 525 West 120th Street, New York, NY 10027-6696. Awards MA. Part-time and evening/weekend programs available. Faculty: 5 full-time (1 woman), 13 part-time (0 women), 12.2 FTE. Students: 4 full-time (2 women), 56 part-time (41 women); includes 8 minority (6 African Americans, 2 Asian Americans), 2 international. Average age 36. 17 applicants, 71% accepted. In 1997, 30 degrees awarded. *Degree requirements:* Computer language required, foreign language and thesis not required. *Application deadline:* 5/15 (12/1 for spring admission). *Application fee:* $50. *Expenses:* Tuition $640 per credit. Fees $120 per semester. *Financial aid:* Full and partial tuition waivers, Federal Work-Study, institutionally sponsored loans, and career-related internships or fieldwork available. Aid available to part-time students. Financial aid application deadline: 2/1. *Faculty research:* Visual and interactive learning, global curriculum, cognition and learning. • Application contact: Barbara Reinhalter, Office of Admissions, 212-678-3710. Fax: 212-678-4171.

Thomas College, Programs in Business, Waterville, ME 04901-5097. Offerings include computer technology education (MS). Faculty: 13 full-time, 17 part-time. *Average time to degree:* master's–3 years full-time, 4.5 years part-time. *Application deadline:* rolling. *Application fee:* $40. *Tuition:* $450 per course. • Robert M. Whitcomb, Dean, Graduate and Continuing Education, Graduate School, 207-877-0102. Application contact: Dr. Nelson Madore, Graduate Adviser, 207-873-0771 Ext. 323. Fax: 207-877-0114.

Union College, Graduate and Continuing Studies, Programs in Education, Schenectady, NY 12308-2311. Offerings include mathematics/computer science (MS). *Application deadline:* 5/15. *Application fee:* $35. *Tuition:* $1155 per course. • Dr. Patrick Allen, Educational Studies Director, 518-388-6361.

University of Bridgeport, College of Graduate and Undergraduate Studies, School of Education and Human Resources, Division of Education, Program in Secondary Education, 380 University Avenue, Bridgeport, CT 06601. Offerings include computer specialist (MS, Diploma). Program faculty: 8 full-time (2 women), 57 part-time (26 women), 27 FTE. *Degree requirements:* For master's, computer language, final exam, final project, or thesis required, foreign language not required; for Diploma, thesis or alternative, final project required, foreign language not required. *Entrance requirements:* For master's, GRE General Test, MAT (score in 35th percentile or higher), minimum undergraduate QPA of 2.5; for Diploma, GRE General Test or MAT (score in 40th percentile or higher), minimum graduate QPA of 3.0. Application deadline: rolling. Application fee: $35 ($50 for international students). *Tuition:* $340 per credit. • Dr. Allen P. Cook, Associate Dean, Division of Education, 203-576-4206.

University of Central Oklahoma, College of Mathematics and Science, Department of Mathematics, Edmond, OK 73034-5209. Offerings include applied mathematical sciences (MS), with options in computer science, mathematics, mathematics/computer science teaching, statistics. Accredited by NCATE. *Degree requirements:* Computer language, thesis required, foreign language not required. *Application deadline:* 8/18 (priority date; rolling processing). *Application fee:* $15. *Tuition:* $76 per credit hour for state residents; $178 per credit hour for nonresidents.

University of Florida, College of Education, Department of Instruction and Curriculum, Gainesville, FL 32611. Offerings include computer education (MAE, M Ed, Ed D, PhD, Ed S). Accredited by NCATE. Department faculty: 42. *Degree requirements:* For master's, thesis optional, foreign language not required; for doctorate, variable foreign language requirement, dissertation. *Entrance requirements:* For master's and doctorate, GRE General Test (minimum combined score of 1000), minimum GPA of 3.0; for Ed S, GRE General Test. Application deadline: 6/5. Application fee: $20. *Tuition:* $138 per credit hour for state residents; $481 per credit hour for nonresidents. • Dr. Mary Grace Kantowski, Chair, 352-392-9191 Ext. 200. E-mail: mgk@coe.ufl.edu. Application contact: Dr. Ben Nelms, Graduate Coordinator, 352-392-9191 Ext. 225. Fax: 352-392-9193. E-mail: bfn@coe.ufl.edu.

University of Georgia, College of Education, Program in Computer-Based Education, Athens, GA 30602. Awards M Ed. Accredited by NCATE. Faculty: 10 full-time (2 women). Students: 10 full-time (6 women), 6 part-time (4 women); includes 2 minority (1 African American, 1 Hispanic), 3 international. 11 applicants, 45% accepted. In 1997, 10 degrees awarded. *Entrance requirements:* GRE General Test or MAT. Application deadline: 7/1 (priority date; 11/15 for spring admission). Application fee: $30. Electronic applications accepted. *Tuition:* $3290 per year full-time, $643 per semester (minimum) part-time for state residents; $11,300 per year full-time, $1645 per semester (minimum) part-time for nonresidents. *Financial aid:* Fellowships, research assistantships, teaching assistantships, assistantships available. • Dr. Lloyd P. Rieber, Graduate Coordinator, 706-542-3958. Fax: 706-542-4032. E-mail: lrieber@coe.uga.edu.

University of Michigan, School of Education, Programs in Educational Studies, Ann Arbor, MI 48109. Offerings include educational technology (AM, MS, PhD). *Degree requirements:* For master's, thesis required (for some programs), foreign language not required; for doctorate, dissertation, preliminary exam required, foreign language not required. *Entrance requirements:* GRE General Test (minimum combined score of 1800 on three sections), TOEFL (minimum score 600). Application deadline: 1/15 (priority date). Application fee: $55. Electronic applications accepted. • Dr. Ronald Marx, Chairperson, 734-763-9497. E-mail: ronmarx@umich.edu. Application contact: Karen Wixson, Associate Dean, 734-764-9470. Fax: 734-763-1229. E-mail: kwixson@umich.edu.

University of Northern Iowa, College of Natural Sciences, Department of Computer Science, Cedar Falls, IA 50614. Offerings include computer science education (MA). MA being phased out; applicants no longer accepted. *Application deadline:* 8/1 (priority date; rolling processing). *Application fee:* $20 ($30 for international students). *Expenses:* Tuition $3166 per year full-time, $176 per hour part-time for state residents; $7805 per year full-time, $176 per hour part-time for nonresidents. Fees $194 per year full-time, $12.50 per semester (minimum) part-time. • Dr. John McCormick, Head, 319-273-2618.

University of North Texas, College of Education, Department of Technology and Cognition, Program in Computer Education and Cognitive Systems, Denton, TX 76203-6737. Awards MS. Accredited by NCATE. *Entrance requirements:* GRE General Test. Application deadline: 7/17. Application fee: $25 ($50 for international students). *Tuition:* $2063 per year full-time, $815 per year part-time for state residents; $5897 per year full-time, $2100 per year part-time for nonresidents. *Financial aid:* Fellowships, research assistantships, teaching assistantships, Federal Work-Study, institutionally sponsored loans, and career-related internships or fieldwork available. Financial aid application deadline: 4/1. • Application contact: Terry Holcomb, Adviser, 940-565-2093.

Webster University, School of Education, Department of Multidisciplinary Studies, St. Louis, MO 63119-3194. Offerings include computer studies (MAT). Department faculty: 7 full-time (5 women). *Entrance requirements:* 2 years of work experience in education, interview, min GPA of 2.5. Application deadline: rolling. Application fee: $25 ($50 for international students). *Tuition:* $350 per credit hour. • Roy Tamashiro, Chair, 314-968-7098. Fax: 314-968-7118. E-mail: tamashro@webster.edu. Application contact: Beth Russell, Director of Graduate Admissions, 314-968-7089. Fax: 314-968-7166. E-mail: russelmb@webster.edu.

Wilkes University, Department of Education, Wilkes-Barre, PA 18766-0002. Offerings include educational computing (MS Ed). Department faculty: 6 full-time, 14 part-time. *Application deadline:* rolling. *Application fee:* $30. *Expenses:* Tuition $12,552 per year full-time, $523 per credit hour part-time. Fees $240 per year full-time, $10 per credit hour part-time. • Dr. Douglas Lynch, Chair, 717-408-4680.

Counselor Education

Abilene Christian University, College of Arts and Sciences, Department of Education, Program in Guidance Services, Abilene, TX 79699-9100. Awards M Ed. Part-time programs available. Faculty: 11 part-time (4 women). Students: 2 full-time (1 woman), 5 part-time (all women); includes 1 minority (African American). 4 applicants, 100% accepted. In 1997, 9 degrees awarded (100% found work related to degree). *Degree requirements:* Comprehensive exam required, foreign language and thesis not required. *Entrance requirements:* GRE General Test or MAT. Application deadline: 4/1 (priority date; rolling processing; 11/1 for spring admission). Application fee: $25 ($45 for international students). *Expenses:* Tuition $308 per credit hour. Fees $430 per year full-time, $85 per semester (minimum) part-time. *Financial aid:* Federal Work-Study available. Aid available to part-time students. Financial aid application deadline: 4/1. • Dr. Roger Gee, Graduate Adviser, 915-674-2122. Application contact: Dr. Carley Dodd, Graduate Dean, 915-674-2354. Fax: 915-674-6717. E-mail: gradinfo@nicanor.acu.edu.

Acadia University, Faculty of Professional Studies, School of Education, Program in Counseling, Wolfville, NS B0P 1X0, Canada. Awards M Ed. Part-time and evening/weekend programs available. Students: 18 full-time (15 women), 40 part-time. Average age 35. In 1997, 10 degrees awarded. *Degree requirements:* Thesis required, foreign language not required. *Entrance requirements:* Minimum B average in undergraduate course work, 2 years of teaching experience. Application deadline: 2/1. Application fee: $25. *Expenses:* Tuition $4095 per year for Canadian residents; $8190 per year for nonresidents. Fees $145 per year. *Financial aid:* Teaching assistantships available. Financial aid application deadline: 2/1. *Faculty research:* Self-concept theory, special need learners, school counseling. • Dr. Bryant Griffith, Director, School of Education, 902-585-1229. E-mail: bryant.griffith@acadiau.ca. Application contact: Sheila Langille, Secretary, 902-585-1229. Fax: 902-585-1071.

Adams State College, School of Education and Graduate Studies, Department of Counselor Education, Alamosa, CO 81102. Offers program in counseling (MA). Accredited by NCATE. Part-time programs available. In 1997, 24 degrees awarded. *Degree requirements:* Internship, qualifying exam required, foreign language and thesis not required. *Entrance requirements:* GRE General Test or MAT, minimum undergraduate GPA of 2.75. Application deadline: 5/15 (priority date; rolling processing; 10/15 for spring admission). Application fee: $25. *Tuition:* $2164 per year full-time, $111 per credit part-time for state residents; $7284 per year full-time, $377 per credit part-time for nonresidents. *Financial aid:* In 1997–98, 6 graduate assistantships (4 to first-year students) averaging $500 per month and totaling $24,000 were awarded; Federal Work-Study, institutionally sponsored loans, and career-related internships or fieldwork also available. Aid available to part-time students. Financial aid application deadline: 4/15; applicants required to submit FAFSA. • Dr. Don Basse, Head, 719-587-7626.

Alabama Agricultural and Mechanical University, School of Education, Department of Counseling and Special Education, Area in Psychology and Counseling, PO Box 1357, Normal, AL 35762-1357. Offerings include counseling and guidance (MS, Ed S). Accredited by NCATE. Faculty: 7 full-time (3 women), 1 part-time (0 women). *Degree requirements:* For master's, thesis or alternative, comprehensive exam required, foreign language not required. *Entrance requirements:* For master's, GRE General Test. Application deadline: 5/1. Application fee: $15 ($20 for international students). *Expenses:* Tuition $2782 per year full-time, $565 per semester (minimum) part-time for state residents; $5164 per year full-time, $1015 per semester (minimum) part-time for nonresidents. Fees $560 per year full-time, $390 per year part-time. • Dr. Annie Grace Robinson, Chair, Department of Counseling and Special Education, 205-851-5533.

Alabama State University, School of Graduate Studies, College of Education, Department of Instructional Support, Program in Guidance and Counseling, Montgomery, AL 36101-0271. Awards M Ed, MS, Ed S. Students: 31 full-time (22 women), 99 part-time (70 women); includes 99 minority (98 African Americans, 1 Hispanic). In 1997, 32 master's, 3 Ed Ss awarded. *Degree requirements:* For master's, comprehensive exam required, thesis optional; for Ed S, thesis. *Entrance requirements:* For master's, GRE General Test, MAT or NTE. Application deadline: 7/15 (rolling processing; 12/15 for spring admission). Application fee: $10. *Expenses:* Tuition $85 per credit hour for state residents; $170 per credit hour for nonresidents. Fees $486 per year. *Faculty research:* Enhancing self-concept, drug abuse education and training, comparison of group techniques, collaborative counseling. • Application contact: Dr. Fred Dauser, Dean of Graduate Studies, 334-229-4276. Fax: 334-229-4928.

Alcorn State University, School of Psychology and Education, Lorman, MS 39096-9402. Offerings include guidance and counseling (MS Ed). Accredited by NCATE. *Degree requirements:* Thesis optional, foreign language not required. *Application deadline:* 7/1 (priority date; rolling processing; 12/1 for spring admission). *Application fee:* $10. *Tuition:* $2470 per year full-time, $378 per semester (minimum) part-time for state residents; $5331 per year full-time, $855 per semester (minimum) part-time for nonresidents.

Alfred University, Graduate School, Division of Education, Alfred, NY 14802-1205. Offerings include counseling (MS Ed). Division faculty: 45 full-time (12 women). *Degree requirements:* Thesis required (for some programs), foreign language not required. *Entrance requirements:* TOEFL. Application deadline: rolling. Application fee: $50. *Expenses:* Tuition $20,376 per year full-time, $390 per credit hour (minimum) part-time. Fees $546 per year. • Dr. Katherine D. Wiesendanger, Chair, 607-871-2219. E-mail: fwiesendange@bigvax.alfred.edu. Application contact: Cathleen R. Johnson, Assistant Director of Admissions, 607-871-2141. Fax: 607-871-2198. E-mail: johnsonc@bigvax.alfred.edu.

Angelo State University, College of Professional Studies, Department of Education, Program in Guidance and Counseling, San Angelo, TX 76909. Awards M Ed. Part-time and evening/weekend programs available. Students: 27 part-time (22 women); includes 4 minority (1 African American, 3 Asian Americans). Average age 37. 16 applicants, 81% accepted. In 1997, 13 degrees awarded. *Degree requirements:* Comprehensive exam required, thesis optional, foreign language not required. *Entrance requirements:* GRE General Test, minimum GPA of 2.5. Application deadline: 8/7 (priority date; rolling processing; 1/2 for spring admission). Application fee: $25 ($50 for international students). *Expenses:* Tuition $1022 per year full-time, $36 per semester hour part-time for state residents; $7382 per year full-time, $246 per semester hour part-time for nonresidents. Fees $1140 per year full-time, $165 per semester (minimum) part-time. *Financial aid:* In 1997–98, 5 fellowships, 1 graduate assistantship were awarded; teaching assistantships, partial tuition waivers, Federal Work-Study, and career-related internships or fieldwork also available. Aid available to part-time students. Financial aid application deadline: 8/1. • Dr. James Hademenos, Head, Department of Education, 915-942-2052.

Appalachian State University, College of Education, Department of Human Development and Psychological Counseling, Boone, NC 28608. Offers programs in community counseling (MA), marriage and family therapy (MA), school counseling (MA, Ed S), student development (MA, Ed S). Accredited by NCATE. Part-time programs available. Faculty: 17 full-time (7 women), 5 part-time (4 women). Students: 108 full-time (78 women), 27 part-time (22 women); includes 11 minority (all African Americans). 145 applicants, 51% accepted. In 1997, 30 master's awarded. *Degree requirements:* For master's, thesis or alternative, comprehensive exams required, foreign language not required; for Ed S, comprehensive exams required, foreign language not required. *Entrance requirements:* GRE General Test. Application deadline: 2/1 (priority date; rolling processing). Application fee: $35. *Tuition:* $1811 per year full-time, $354 per semester (minimum) part-time for state residents; $9081 per year full-time, $2171 per semester (minimum) part-time for nonresidents. *Financial aid:* In 1997–98, 11 students received aid, including 3 research assistantships, 2 teaching assistantships, 3 assistantships; fellowships and career-related internships or fieldwork also available. Aid available to part-time students. *Faculty research:* Multicultural counseling, addictions counseling, play therapy, expressive arts, child and adolescent therapy, sexual abuse counseling. • Dr. Lee Baruth, Chairman, 704-262-2055.

Arizona State University, College of Education, Division of Psychology in Education, Academic Program in Counseling, Tempe, AZ 85287-0611. Awards MC, M Ed. *Degree requirements:* Thesis or alternative. *Entrance requirements:* GRE General Test or MAT. Application fee: $45. *Expenses:* Tuition $2088 per year full-time, $110 per hour part-time for state residents; $9040 per year full-time, $377 per hour part-time for nonresidents. Fees $72 per year full-time, $18 per semester (minimum) part-time. *Faculty research:* Counselor training, student development, gerontological counseling, ethics, marriage and family counseling. • Dr. William A. Cabianca, Coordinator, 602-965-2713.

Arkansas State University, College of Education, Department of Psychology and Counseling, State University, AR 72467. Offers programs in counselor education (MSE, Ed S), including elementary counselor education (MSE), secondary counselor education (MSE); rehabilitation counseling (MRC). Accredited by NCATE. Part-time programs available. Faculty: 13 full-time (5 women), 1 part-time (0 women). Students: 33 full-time (27 women), 81 part-time (71 women); includes 12 minority (11 African Americans, 1 Native American), 1 international. Average age 32. In 1997, 24 master's awarded. *Degree requirements:* For master's, thesis or alternative, comprehensive exam required, foreign language not required; for Ed S, 2 years of professional experience, written comprehensive exams required, foreign language and thesis not required. *Entrance requirements:* For master's, GRE General Test or MAT (MSE), appropriate bachelor's degree; for Ed S, GRE General Test or MAT, master's degree. Application deadline: 7/1 (priority date; rolling processing; 11/15 for spring admission). Application fee: $15 ($25 for international students). *Expenses:* Tuition $2760 per year full-time, $115 per credit hour part-time for state residents; $6936 per year full-time, $289 per credit hour part-time for nonresidents. Fees $506 per year full-time, $44 per semester (minimum) part-time. *Financial aid:* Teaching assistantships and career-related internships or fieldwork available. Aid available to part-time students. Financial aid application deadline: 7/1; applicants required to submit FAFSA. • Dr. Lynn Howerton, Chair, 870-972-3064. Fax: 870-972-3828. E-mail: howerton@kiowa.astate.edu.

Auburn University, College of Education, Department of Counseling and Counseling Psychology, Auburn University, AL 36849-0001. Offers programs in college student development (M Ed, MS, Ed D, PhD, Ed S), community agency counseling (M Ed, MS, Ed D, PhD, Ed S), counseling psychology (PhD), school counseling (M Ed, MS, Ed D, PhD, Ed S), school psychometry (M Ed, MS, Ed D, PhD, Ed S). Accredited by NCATE. One or more programs accredited by APA. Part-time programs available. Faculty: 10 full-time (5 women). Students: 52 full-time (38 women), 52 part-time (38 women); includes 17 minority (13 African Americans, 1 Asian American, 3 Hispanics), 3 international. 157 applicants, 14% accepted. In 1997, 17 master's, 8 doctorates awarded. *Degree requirements:* For master's, thesis (MS) required, foreign language not required; for doctorate, dissertation required, foreign language not required; for Ed S, thesis or alternative required, foreign language not required. *Entrance requirements:* For master's and Ed S, GRE General Test; for doctorate, GRE General Test (minimum score 400 on each section), GRE Subject Test. Application deadline: 6/15. Application fee: $25 ($50 for international students). *Expenses:* Tuition $2760 per year full-time, $76 per credit hour part-time for state residents; $8280 per year full-time, $228 per credit hour part-time for nonresidents. Fees $30 per year full-time, $160 per quarter part-time for state residents; $30 per year full-time, $480 per quarter part-time for nonresidents. *Financial aid:* Research assistantships, traineeships, Federal Work-Study available. Aid available to part-time students. Financial aid application deadline: 3/15. *Faculty research:* At-risk students, substance abuse, gender roles, AIDS, professional ethics. • Dr. Holly Stadler, Head, 334-844-5160. Application contact: Dr. John F. Pritchett, Dean of the Graduate School, 334-844-4700.

Auburn University Montgomery, School of Education, Department of Counselor Leadership and Special Education, Montgomery, AL 36124-4023. Offers programs in counseling (M Ed, Ed S), education administration (M Ed, Ed S), special education (M Ed, Ed S). Accredited by NCATE. Part-time and evening/weekend programs available. Students: 72 full-time (56 women), 61 part-time (55 women); includes 56 minority (53 African Americans, 3 Hispanics). Average age 34. In 1997, 16 master's, 12 Ed Ss awarded. *Degree requirements:* For master's, comprehensive exam required, foreign language and thesis not required; for Ed S, comprehensive exam required, foreign language not required. *Entrance requirements:* For master's, GRE General Test or MAT, certification, BS in teaching; for Ed S, GRE General Test or MAT, certification. Application deadline: 9/1 (priority date; rolling processing; 3/28 for spring admission). Application fee: $25. Electronic applications accepted. *Tuition:* $2664 per year full-time, $85 per quarter hour part-time for state residents; $7080 per year full-time, $255 per quarter hour part-time for nonresidents. *Financial aid:* In 1997–98, 1 teaching assistantship was awarded. • Dr. James Wright, Head, 334-244-3457.

Augusta State University, College of Education, Program in Counseling/Guidance, Augusta, GA 30904-2200. Awards M Ed, Ed S. Accredited by NCATE. Part-time and evening/weekend programs available. Faculty: 2 full-time (1 woman). Students: 30 full-time (27 women), 19 part-time (14 women); includes 12 minority (all African Americans). Average age 35. 10 applicants, 100% accepted. In 1997, 10 master's awarded. *Degree requirements:* For master's, comprehensive exam required, foreign language and thesis not required; for Ed S, thesis, comprehensive exam required, foreign language not required. *Entrance requirements:* For master's, GRE, MAT, minimum GPA of 2.5; for Ed S, GRE, MAT, minimum GPA of 3.25. Application deadline: 7/26 (priority date; rolling processing). Application fee: $10. *Tuition:* $2260 per year full-time, $83 per credit hour part-time for state residents; $8260 per year full-time, $333 per credit hour part-time for nonresidents. *Financial aid:* Graduate assistantships, Federal Work-Study, institutionally sponsored loans available. Aid available to part-time students. Financial aid application deadline: 4/15; applicants required to submit FAFSA. *Faculty research:* Counseling for AIDS patients, counseling for drug and alcohol abuse. • Dr. C. Jay Hertzog, Chair, 706-737-1497. E-mail: jhertzog@aug.edu. Application contact: Heather Eakin, Secretary to the Dean, 706-737-1499. Fax: 706-667-4706. E-mail: heakin@aug.edu.

Austin Peay State University, College of Arts and Sciences, Department of Psychology, Clarksville, TN 37044-0001. Offerings include guidance and counseling (MS). Accredited by NCATE. *Application deadline:* 7/31 (priority date; rolling processing; 12/4 for spring admission). *Application fee:* $15. *Expenses:* Tuition $2438 per year full-time, $123 per semester hour part-time for state residents; $7034 per year full-time, $324 per semester hour part-time for nonresidents. Fees $484 per year (minimum) full-time, $154 per semester (minimum) part-time. • Garland Blair, Chair, 931-648-7233. Fax: 931-648-6267. E-mail: blairg@apsu.edu.

Austin Peay State University, College of Education, Department of Education, Clarksville, TN 37044-0001. Offerings include counseling and guidance (Ed S). Accredited by NCATE. Ed S offered jointly with Tennessee State University. *Entrance requirements:* GRE General Test (minimum score 350 on verbal and quantitative sections), master's degree, minimum graduate GPA of 3.0. Application deadline: 7/31 (priority date; rolling processing; 12/4 for spring admission). Application fee: $15. *Expenses:* Tuition $2438 per year full-time, $123 per semester hour part-time for state residents; $7034 per year full-time, $324 per semester hour part-time for nonresidents. Fees $484 per year (minimum) full-time, $154 per semester (minimum) part-time. • J. Ronald Groseclose, Interim Chair, 931-648-7585. Fax: 931-648-5991. E-mail: grosecloseg@apsu.edu.

Baptist Bible College of Pennsylvania, Graduate School, Clarks Summit, PA 18411-1297. Offers programs in Christian school education (MS), counseling (MS). Faculty: 2 full-time, 12 part-time. Students: 45. *Application deadline:* rolling. *Application fee:* $25. *Expenses:* Tuition $214 per credit hour (minimum). Fees $16 per credit hour. • Dr. Hubert Hartzler, Director of Graduate Studies, 717-585-9226.

Barry University, School of Education, Program in Counseling, Miami Shores, FL 33161-6695. Awards MS, Ed S. Part-time and evening/weekend programs available. *Degree requirements:* For master's, written comprehensive exam required, foreign language and thesis not required. *Entrance requirements:* For master's, GRE General Test or MAT, minimum GPA of 3.0; for Ed S, GRE General Test, minimum GPA of 3.0. Application deadline: 5/1 (priority date; rolling processing). Application fee: $30. *Tuition:* $450 per credit (minimum). *Financial aid:* Application deadline 5/1. • Maureen Duffy, Director, 305-899-3701. Fax: 305-899-3630. E-mail: mduffy@aquinas.barry.edu. Application contact: Angela Scott, Enrollment Services, Assistant Dean, 305-899-3112. Fax: 305-899-3149. E-mail: ascott@jeanne.barry.edu.

Barry University, School of Education, Program in Guidance and Counseling, Miami Shores, FL 33161-6695. Awards MS, Ed S. Part-time and evening/weekend programs available. Faculty: 4 full-time (1 woman), 2 part-time (both women). Students: 5 full-time (4 women), 21 part-time (20 women); includes 14 minority (9 African Americans, 5 Hispanics). Average age 37. In 1997, 2 master's awarded. *Degree requirements:* For master's, scholarly paper, written comprehensive exam required, foreign language and thesis not required; for Ed S, written comprehensive exam required, foreign language and thesis not required. *Entrance requirements:* For master's, GRE General Test or MAT, minimum GPA of 3.0; for Ed S, GRE General Test, minimum GPA of 3.0. Application deadline: 5/1 (priority date; rolling processing). Application fee: $30. Electronic applications accepted. *Tuition:* $450 per credit (minimum). *Financial aid:* Partial tuition waivers available. Aid available to part-time students. Financial aid application deadline: 5/1; applicants required to submit FAFSA. • Dr. Maureen Duffy, Director, 305-899-3701. Fax: 305-899-3630. E-mail: mduffy@aquinas.barry.edu. Application contact: Angela Scott, Enrollment Services, Assistant Dean, 305-899-3112. Fax: 305-899-3149. E-mail: ascott@jeanne.barry.edu.

Barry University, School of Education, Program in Leadership and Education, Miami Shores, FL 33161-6695. Offerings include counseling (PhD). Program faculty: 1 full-time (0 women), 2 part-time (1 woman), 2 FTE. *Degree requirements:* Dissertation. *Entrance requirements:* GRE General Test, minimum GPA of 3.25. Application deadline: 5/1 (priority date; rolling processing). Application fee: $30. Electronic applications accepted. *Tuition:* $450 per credit (minimum). • Dr. Jack Dezek, Chair, 305-899-3700. Fax: 305-899-3630. E-mail: dezek@aquinas.barry.edu. Application contact: Angela Scott, Enrollment Services, Assistant Dean, 305-899-3112. Fax: 305-899-3149. E-mail: ascott@jeanne.barry.edu.

Barry University, School of Education, Program in Mental Health Counseling, Miami Shores, FL 33161-6695. Awards MS, Ed S. Part-time and evening/weekend programs available. Faculty: 4 full-time (1 woman), 2 part-time (both women). Students: 8 full-time (all women), 15 part-time (11 women); includes 8 minority (1 African American, 7 Hispanics). Average age 36. 16 applicants. In 1997, 13 master's, 1 Ed S awarded. *Degree requirements:* For master's, scholarly paper, written comprehensive exam required, foreign language and thesis not required; for Ed S, written comprehensive exam required, foreign language and thesis not required. *Entrance requirements:* For master's, GRE General Test or MAT, minimum GPA of 3.0; for Ed S, GRE General Test, minimum GPA of 3.0. Application deadline: 5/1 (priority date; rolling processing). Application fee: $30. Electronic applications accepted. *Tuition:* $450 per credit (minimum). *Financial aid:* Career-related internships or fieldwork available. Aid available to part-time students. Financial aid application deadline: 5/1; applicants required to submit FAFSA. • Dr. Maureen Duffy, Director, 305-899-3701. Fax: 305-899-3630. E-mail: mduffy@aquinas.barry.edu. Application contact: Angela Scott, Enrollment Services, Assistant Dean, 305-899-3112. Fax: 305-899-3149. E-mail: ascott@jeanne.barry.edu.

Boise State University, College of Education, Department of Counseling, Program in School Counseling, Boise, ID 83725-0399. Awards MA. Accredited by NCATE. Faculty: 6 full-time (4 women), 7 part-time (3 women). Students: 7 full-time (6 women), 40 part-time (32 women); includes 3 minority (2 African Americans, 1 Hispanic), 1 international. Average age 34. 16 applicants, 75% accepted. In 1997, 7 degrees awarded. *Application deadline:* 7/26 (priority date; rolling processing; 11/29 for spring admission). *Application fee:* $20 ($30 for international students). Electronic applications accepted. *Tuition:* $3020 per year full-time, $135 per credit part-time for state residents; $8900 per year full-time, $135 per credit part-time for nonresidents. *Financial aid:* Federal Work-Study, institutionally sponsored loans available. Aid available to part-time students. Financial aid application deadline: 3/1; applicants required to submit FAFSA. • Dr. Margaret Miller, Coordinator, 208-385-1209.

Boston University, School of Education, Department of Developmental Studies and Counseling, Program in Counseling, Boston, MA 02215. Awards Ed M, CAGS. Students: 30 full-time (28 women), 13 part-time (12 women); includes 3 minority (2 African Americans, 1 Asian American), 4 international. Average age 26. In 1997, 31 master's, 4 CAGSs awarded. *Degree requirements:* For CAGS, comprehensive exam required, foreign language and thesis not required. *Entrance requirements:* GRE General Test or MAT, TOEFL. Application deadline: 2/15 (priority date; rolling processing). Application fee: $50. *Expenses:* Tuition $22,830 per year full-time, $713 per credit part-time. Fees $218 per year full-time, $40 per semester part-time. *Financial aid:* Application deadline 3/30. • Dr. Mary Ni, Coordinator, 617-353-4655. E-mail: mni@bu.edu.

Bowie State University, Programs in Education, Program in Guidance and Counseling, 14000 Jericho Park Road, Bowie, MD 20715. Awards M Ed. Part-time and evening/weekend programs available. *Degree requirements:* Research paper, written comprehensive exam required, thesis optional. *Entrance requirements:* Teaching experience. Application deadline: 8/16 (priority date; rolling processing). Application fee: $30. *Expenses:* Tuition $169 per credit hour for state residents; $304 per credit hour for nonresidents. Fees $171 per year.

Bowling Green State University, College of Education and Allied Professions, Department of Educational Foundations and Inquiry, Bowling Green, OH 43403. Offers program in guidance and counseling (MA, M Ed). Accredited by NCATE. Faculty: 4 full-time (3 women). Students: 51 full-time (37 women), 46 part-time (37 women); includes 18 minority (13 African Americans, 1 Asian American, 3 Hispanics, 1 Native American), 2 international. 42 applicants, 74% accepted. In 1997, 44 degrees awarded. *Degree requirements:* Thesis or alternative required, foreign language not required. *Entrance requirements:* GRE General Test, TOEFL (minimum score 580). Application deadline: rolling. Application fee: $30. Electronic applications accepted. *Tuition:* $6070 per year full-time, $284 per credit hour part-time for state residents; $11,358 per year full-time, $536 per credit hour part-time for nonresidents. *Financial aid:* In 1997–98, 23 assistantships were awarded; career-related internships or fieldwork also available. Financial aid application deadline: 2/15; applicants required to submit FAFSA. *Faculty research:* Perfectionism, multicultural counseling, suicide, ethics and legal issues related to counseling, play therapy, counselor mental health. • Dr. Jane Wolfle, Chair, 419-372-7322. Application contact: Dr. Peterann Siehl, Graduate Coordinator, 419-372-7307.

Bradley University, College of Education and Health Sciences, Department of Counseling and Human Development, Peoria, IL 61625-0002. Offers programs in human development counseling (MA), including community agency counseling, school counseling; leadership in educational administration (MA); leadership in human services administration (MA). Accredited by NCATE. Part-time and evening/weekend programs available. *Degree requirements:* Comprehensive exams required, foreign language and thesis not required. *Entrance requirements:* MAT, TOEFL (minimum score 500), interview. Application deadline: 7/1 (priority date; rolling processing; 11/1 for spring admission). Application fee: $35. *Tuition:* $13,240 per year full-time, $359 per semester hour (minimum) part-time.

Brandon University, Faculty of Education, Brandon, MB R7A 6A9, Canada. Offerings include guidance and counseling (M Ed). Faculty: 27 full-time (3 women), 1 part-time (0 women). *Degree requirements:* Thesis. *Average time to degree:* master's–2 years full-time; other advanced degree–1 year full-time. *Entrance requirements:* TOEFL (minimum score 550), minimum GPA of 3.0, teaching certificate or equivalent. Application deadline: 3/1. Application fee: $30. *Expenses:* Tuition $421 per course (minimum). Fees $24.95 per year. • Dean, 204-728-9520. Application contact: Faye Douglas, Admissions Director, 204-727-7352. Fax: 204-725-2143. E-mail: douglas@brandonu.ca.

Bridgewater State College, School of Education, Department of Secondary Education and Professional Programs, Program in Counseling, Bridgewater, MA 02325-0001. Awards M Ed. Accredited by NCATE. Evening/weekend programs available. *Entrance requirements:* GRE General Test. Application deadline: 4/1 (10/1 for spring admission). Application fee: $25. *Expenses:* Tuition $1675 per year full-time, $70 per credit part-time for state residents; $6450 per year full-time, $269 per credit part-time for nonresidents. Fees $1588 per year full-time, $66 per credit hour part-time for state residents; $1588 per year full-time, $66 per credit part-time for nonresidents. *Financial aid:* Career-related internships or fieldwork available. • Application contact: Graduate School, 508-697-1300.

Brigham Young University, David O. McKay School of Education, Department of Counseling and Special Education, Provo, UT 84602-1001. Offers programs in counseling and school psychology (MS), counseling psychology (PhD), special education (MS). Faculty: 10 full-time (2 women), 12 part-time (7 women). Students: 73 full-time (29 women); includes 1 minority (Hispanic), 5 international. Average age 34. 106 applicants, 33% accepted. In 1997, 28 master's, 3 doctorates awarded. *Degree requirements:* For master's, written comprehensive exams required, thesis not required; for doctorate, dissertation, written comprehensive exams. *Entrance requirements:* For master's, GRE General Test, minimum GPA of 3.0 in last 60 hours; for doctorate, GRE General Test, minimum GPA of 3.4 in last 60 hours. Application deadline: 2/1. Application fee: $30. *Tuition:* $3200 per year full-time, $178 per credit hour part-time for state residents; $4800 per year full-time, $266 per credit hour part-time for nonresidents. *Financial aid:* In 1997–98, 38 students received aid, including 6 research assistantships (3 to first-year students) averaging $407 per month, 10 teaching assistantships (5 to first-year students) averaging $407 per month; partial tuition waivers, institutionally sponsored loans, and career-related internships or fieldwork also available. *Faculty research:* Learning, hardiness, values and mental health, distance education. • Dr. Ronald D. Bingham, Chair, 801-378-3857. E-mail: ron_bingham@byu.edu. Application contact: Diane Hancock, Secretary, 801-378-3859. E-mail: diane_hancock@byu.edu.

Brooklyn College of the City University of New York, School of Education, Program in Guidance and Counseling, 2900 Bedford Avenue, Brooklyn, NY 11210-2889. Awards MS Ed, CAS. Part-time programs available. Students: 46 full-time (36 women), 70 part-time (62 women); includes 65 minority (46 African Americans, 2 Asian Americans, 17 Hispanics), 1 international. In 1997, 54 master's, 34 CASs awarded. *Degree requirements:* For master's, comprehensive exam, internship required, foreign language and thesis not required. *Entrance requirements:* For master's, interview, previous course work in education and psychology, teaching certificate; for CAS, master's degree. Application deadline: 3/1 (11/1 for spring admission). Application fee: $40. *Expenses:* Tuition $4350 per year full-time, $185 per credit part-time for state residents; $7600 per year full-time, $320 per credit part-time for nonresidents. Fees $500 per year for state residents; $806 per year for nonresidents. *Financial aid:* Partial tuition waivers and career-related internships or fieldwork available. Financial aid application deadline: 5/1; applicants required to submit FAFSA. *Faculty research:* Urban school counseling, parent involvement, multicultural competence and counselor training. • Dr. Hollyce Giles, Head, 718-951-5938.

Bucknell University, College of Arts and Sciences, Department of Education, Specialization in Elementary and Secondary Counseling, Lewisburg, PA 17837. Awards MA, MS Ed. Faculty: 8 full-time. *Degree requirements:* Thesis or alternative required, foreign language not required. *Entrance requirements:* GRE General Test (minimum combined score of 1000), TOEFL (minimum score 550), minimum GPA of 2.8. Application deadline: 6/1 (priority date; rolling processing; 12/1 for spring admission). Application fee: $25. *Tuition:* $2410 per course. *Financial aid:* Assistantships available. Financial aid application deadline: 3/1. • Adviser, 717-524-1133.

Buena Vista University, School of Education, Storm Lake, IA 50588. Offerings include school guidance and counseling (MS Ed). Offered in summer only. Postbaccalaureate distance learning degree programs offered (minimal on-campus study). School faculty: 7 full-time (2 women). *Degree requirements:* Thesis, fieldwork/practicum required, foreign language not required. *Entrance requirements:* GRE, minimum undergraduate GPA of 2.75. Application fee: $0. • F. Kline Capps, Dean, 712-749-2275. E-mail: cappsk@bvu.edu. Application contact: Jon E. Hixon, Director of Graduate Studies, 712-749-2190. Fax: 712-749-2035. E-mail: hixon@bvu.edu.

Butler University, College of Education, Indianapolis, IN 46208-3485. Offerings include school counseling (MS, Ed S). Accredited by NCATE. College faculty: 10 full-time (3 women), 22 part-time (8 women), 22.5 FTE. *Degree requirements:* For Ed S, thesis required, foreign language not required. *Average time to degree:* master's–7 years part-time; other advanced degree–5 years part-time. *Entrance requirements:* For master's, GRE General Test, MAT (minimum score 40), interview. Application deadline: 8/15 (priority date; rolling processing). Application fee: $25. *Tuition:* $220 per credit hour. • Dr. Saundra Tracy, Dean, 317-940-9514. Fax: 317-940-6481. E-mail: stracy@butler.edu.

California Lutheran University, School of Education, Emphasis in Counseling and Guidance, Thousand Oaks, CA 91360-2787. Awards MS. Part-time programs available. Students: 22 full-time (18 women), 100 part-time (80 women). Average age 35. 36 applicants, 72% accepted. In 1997, 14 degrees awarded. *Degree requirements:* Thesis or comprehensive exam required, foreign language not required. *Entrance requirements:* GRE General Test, minimum GPA of 3.0. Application deadline: 8/1 (priority date; rolling processing; 12/1 for spring admission). Application fee: $50. *Tuition:* $335 per unit. • Dr. Joan Blacher, Head, 805-493-3420.

California Polytechnic State University, San Luis Obispo, Center for Teacher Education, Program in Counseling, San Luis Obispo, CA 93407. Offers education (MA). Part-time programs available. *Degree requirements:* Comprehensive exam required, thesis optional, foreign language not required. *Entrance requirements:* Minimum GPA of 3.0. Application deadline: 4/1 (12/15 for spring admission). Application fee: $55. *Expenses:* Tuition $0 for state residents; $164 per unit for nonresidents. Fees $2102 per year full-time, $1632 per year part-time. • Bob Levison, Coordinator, 805-756-1573.

California State University, Bakersfield, School of Education, Program in Counseling, 9001 Stockdale Highway, Bakersfield, CA 93311-1099. Awards MS. Accredited by NCATE. In 1997, 16 degrees awarded. *Degree requirements:* Thesis or alternative, culminating projects. *Application deadline:* rolling. *Application fee:* $55. *Expenses:* Tuition $0 for state residents; $246 per unit full-time, $164 per unit part-time for nonresidents. Fees $1584 per year full-time, $918 per year part-time. • Dr. Nils Carlson, Coordinator, 805-664-3137.

California State University, Bakersfield, School of Education, Program in Counseling and Personnel Services, 9001 Stockdale Highway, Bakersfield, CA 93311-1099. Awards MA. Accredited by NCATE. *Degree requirements:* Thesis or alternative, culminating projects. *Application deadline:* rolling. *Application fee:* $55. *Expenses:* Tuition $0 for state residents; $246 per unit full-time, $164 per unit part-time for nonresidents. Fees $1584 per year full-time, $918 per year part-time. • Dr. Nils Carlson, Coordinator, 805-664-3137.

California State University, Dominguez Hills, School of Education, Department of Graduate Education, Program in Counseling, Carson, CA 90747-0001. Awards MA. *Entrance requirements:* Minimum GPA of 2.75. Application deadline: 6/1. Application fee: $55. *Expenses:* Tuition $0 for state residents; $246 per unit for nonresidents. Fees $1896 per year full-time, $1230 per year part-time. • Application contact: Admissions Office, 310-243-3600.

California State University, Fresno, Division of Graduate Studies, School of Education and Human Development, Department of Counseling and Special Education, Program in Counseling and Student Services, 5241 North Maple Avenue, Fresno, CA 93740. Offers education (MA). Accredited by NCATE. Part-time and evening/weekend programs available. Faculty: 2 full-time (0 women). Students: 36 full-time (27 women), 29 part-time (17 women); includes 36 minority (1 African American, 10 Asian Americans, 25 Hispanics), 1 international. Average age 31. 39 applicants, 92% accepted. In 1997, 13 degrees awarded. *Degree requirements:* Thesis or alternative required, foreign language not required. *Average time to degree:* master's–3.5 years full-time. *Entrance requirements:* GRE General Test, TOEFL (minimum score 550), MAT,

Directory: Counselor Education

California State University, Fresno (continued)
minimum GPA of 2.75. Application deadline: 4/1 (priority date; rolling processing; 11/1 for spring admission). Application fee: $55. Electronic applications accepted. *Expenses:* Tuition $0 for state residents; $246 per unit for nonresidents. Fees $1872 per year full-time, $1206 per year part-time. *Financial aid:* In 1997–98, 2 fellowships totaling $6,750, 33 research awards, travel grants, scholarships totaling $44,370 were awarded; Federal Work-Study and career-related internships or fieldwork also available. Financial aid application deadline: 3/1; applicants required to submit FAFSA. • Albert Valencia, Graduate Program Coordinator, 209-278-0283. Fax: 209-278-0404.

California State University, Fullerton, School of Human Development and Community Service, Department of Counseling, PO Box 34080, Fullerton, CA 92834-9480. Awards MS. Accredited by NCATE. Part-time programs available. Faculty: 4 full-time (3 women), 14 part-time, 6.7 FTE. Students: 45 full-time (39 women), 151 part-time (129 women); includes 52 minority (5 African Americans, 14 Asian Americans, 33 Hispanics), 6 international. Average age 35. 55 applicants, 73% accepted. In 1997, 59 degrees awarded. *Degree requirements:* Comprehensive exam, project or thesis required, foreign language not required. *Entrance requirements:* GRE General Test, minimum GPA of 3.0 in behavioral science, 2.5 overall. Application fee: $55. *Expenses:* Tuition $0 for state residents; $246 per unit for nonresidents. Fees $1947 per year full-time, $1281 per year part-time. *Financial aid:* Teaching assistantships, state grants, Federal Work-Study, institutionally sponsored loans, and career-related internships or fieldwork available. Aid available to part-time students. Financial aid application deadline: 3/1. • Dr. Judith Ramirez, Head, 714-278-2254.

California State University, Hayward, School of Education, Department of Educational Psychology, Counseling Program, Hayward, CA 94542-3000. Awards MS. Accredited by NCATE. Faculty: 22 full-time (5 women). Students: 214 full-time (181 women), 45 part-time (34 women); includes 98 minority (37 African Americans, 29 Asian Americans, 28 Hispanics, 4 Native Americans), 2 international. 143 applicants, 71% accepted. In 1997, 99 degrees awarded. *Degree requirements:* Comprehensive exam, project, or thesis required, foreign language not required. *Entrance requirements:* GRE or MAT, interview, minimum GPA of 2.5 during previous 2 years. Application deadline: 4/19 (priority date; rolling processing; 1/5 for spring admission). Application fee: $55. *Expenses:* Tuition $0 for state residents; $164 per unit for nonresidents. Fees $1827 per year full-time, $1161 per year part-time. *Financial aid:* Federal Work-Study, institutionally sponsored loans, and career-related internships or fieldwork available. Aid available to part-time students. Financial aid application deadline: 3/1. • Dr. Jack Guthrie, Head, 510-885-3011. Application contact: Dr. Maria De Anda-Ramos, Executive Director, Admissions and Outreach, 510-885-2624.

California State University, Long Beach, College of Education, Department of Educational Psychology and Administration, Program in Guidance and Counseling, Long Beach, CA 90840-2201. Awards MS, Certificate. Students: 67 full-time (56 women), 104 part-time (72 women); includes 62 minority (17 African Americans, 16 Asian Americans, 29 Hispanics), 3 international. Average age 32. 110 applicants, 48% accepted. In 1997, 26 master's awarded. *Degree requirements:* For master's, comprehensive exam or thesis required, foreign language not required. *Entrance requirements:* For master's, GRE General Test, minimum GPA of 2.75. Application deadline: 8/1 (rolling processing; 12/1 for spring admission). Application fee: $55. *Expenses:* Tuition $0 for state residents; $246 per unit for nonresidents. Fees $1846 per year full-time, $1180 per year part-time. *Financial aid:* Application deadline 3/2. • Dr. Robert Berdan, Chair, Department of Educational Psychology and Administration, 562-985-4517. Fax: 562-985-4534. E-mail: rberdan@csulb.edu.

California State University, Los Angeles, School of Education, Division of Administration and Counseling, Major in Counseling, Los Angeles, CA 90032-8530. Offers programs in applied behavior analysis (MS), community college counseling (MS), rehabilitation counseling (MS), school counseling and school psychology (MS). Accredited by NCATE. Part-time and evening/weekend programs available. Students: 129 full-time (102 women), 137 part-time (92 women); includes 172 minority (36 African Americans, 24 Asian Americans, 112 Hispanics), 3 international. In 1997, 62 degrees awarded. *Degree requirements:* Comprehensive exam, project, or thesis required, foreign language not required. *Entrance requirements:* TOEFL (minimum score 550), interview, minimum GPA of 2.75 in last 90 units, teaching certificate. Application deadline: 6/30 (rolling processing; 2/1 for spring admission). Application fee: $55. *Expenses:* Tuition $0 for state residents; $164 per unit for nonresidents. Fees $1763 per year full-time, $1097 per year part-time. *Financial aid:* 63 students received aid; Federal Work-Study and career-related internships or fieldwork available. Aid available to part-time students. Financial aid application deadline: 3/1. • Dr. Raymond Hillis, Chair, Division of Administration and Counseling, 213-343-4250.

California State University, Northridge, College of Education, Department of Educational Leadership and Policy Studies, Program in Counseling and Guidance, Northridge, CA 91330. Offers counseling (MS); marriage, family and child counseling (MFCC). Accredited by NCATE. Part-time and evening/weekend programs available. Students: 236 full-time (193 women), 122 part-time (96 women); includes 106 minority (31 African Americans, 21 Asian Americans, 53 Hispanics, 1 Native American), 7 international. Average age 36. 102 applicants, 90% accepted. *Degree requirements:* For master's, comprehensive exam or thesis required, foreign language not required. *Entrance requirements:* For master's, TOEFL, GRE General Test, MAT, or minimum GPA of 3.0. Application deadline: 11/30. Application fee: $55. *Expenses:* Tuition $0 for state residents; $246 per unit for nonresidents. Fees $1970 per year full-time, $1304 per year part-time. *Financial aid:* Scholarships available. Financial aid application deadline: 3/1. • Application contact: Rie Rogers Mitchell, Graduate Coordinator.

California State University, Sacramento, School of Education, Department of Counseling and Guidance, Sacramento, CA 95819-6048. Offers programs in career counseling (MS), generic counseling (MS), guidance (MA), school counseling (MS), school psychology (MS). *Degree requirements:* Thesis or alternative, writing proficiency exam. *Entrance requirements:* TOEFL (minimum score 550), minimum GPA of 2.5. Application deadline: 4/15 (11/1 for spring admission). Application fee: $55. *Expenses:* Tuition $0 for state residents; $246 per unit for nonresidents. Fees $2012 per year full-time, $1346 per year part-time. *Financial aid:* Federal Work-Study and career-related internships or fieldwork available. Aid available to part-time students. Financial aid application deadline: 3/1. • Dr. Bernadette Halbrook, Chair, 916-278-6310. Application contact: Dr. Guy Deaner, Coordinator, 916-278-6663.

California State University, San Bernardino, Graduate Studies, School of Education, Program in Counselor Education, San Bernardino, CA 92407-2397. Offers counseling/guidance (MS), counselor education (MA). Part-time and evening/weekend programs available. Faculty: 6 full-time (3 women), 2 part-time (1 woman). Students: 83 full-time (53 women), 34 part-time (26 women); includes 54 minority (19 African Americans, 4 Asian Americans, 30 Hispanics, 1 Native American). 49 applicants, 96% accepted. In 1997, 15 degrees awarded. *Degree requirements:* Thesis or alternative required, foreign language not required. *Entrance requirements:* Minimum GPA of 3.0 in education. Application deadline: 8/31 (priority date). Application fee: $55. *Expenses:* Tuition $0 for state residents; $164 per unit for nonresidents. Fees $1922 per year full-time, $1256 per year part-time. *Financial aid:* Federal Work-Study and career-related internships or fieldwork available. Aid available to part-time students. • Dr. Kathryn C. Reilly, Chairman, 909-880-5672.

California State University, Stanislaus, School of Education, Department of Advanced Studies in Education, Program in School Counseling, Turlock, CA 95382. Awards MA Ed. Accredited by NCATE. Part-time programs available. Faculty: 2 full-time (both women). Students: 14 (11 women); includes 3 minority (1 Asian American, 2 Hispanics). 12 applicants, 83% accepted. In 1997, 3 degrees awarded. *Degree requirements:* Thesis or alternative required, foreign language not required. *Entrance requirements:* MAT. Application fee: $55. *Expenses:* Tuition $0 for state residents; $246 per unit for nonresidents. Fees $1779 per year full-time, $1113 per year part-time. *Financial aid:* Application deadline 3/2; applicants required to submit FAFSA. *Faculty research:* Death education and counseling, sex equity, substance abuse. • Dr. Nina Ribak-Rosenthal, Coordinator, 209-667-3364.

California University of Pennsylvania, School of Education, Department of Counselor Education and Services, 250 University Avenue, California, PA 15419-1394. Offers program in guidance and counseling (M Ed, MS). Accredited by NCATE. Part-time and evening/weekend programs available. Faculty: 3 full-time (1 woman), 3 part-time (1 woman). Students: 47 full-time (37 women), 48 part-time (37 women); includes 3 minority (2 African Americans, 1 Native American). 58 applicants, 86% accepted. In 1997, 52 degrees awarded. *Degree requirements:* Comprehensive exam required, thesis optional, foreign language not required. *Entrance requirements:* MAT (minimum score 45), TOEFL (minimum score 550), minimum GPA of 3.0. Application deadline: rolling. Application fee: $25. *Expenses:* Tuition $3468 per year full-time, $193 per credit part-time for state residents; $6236 per year full-time, $346 per credit part-time for nonresidents. Fees $886 per year full-time, $153 per semester (minimum) part-time. *Financial aid:* Graduate assistantships and career-related internships or fieldwork available. • Dr. William Parnell, Chair, 724-938-4123.

Campbell University, School of Education, Buies Creek, NC 27506. Offerings include community counseling (MA), school counseling (M Ed). One or more programs accredited by NCATE. School faculty: 8 full-time (6 women), 6 part-time (0 women). *Application deadline:* 8/1 (priority date; rolling processing; 1/2 for spring admission). *Application fee:* $25. *Tuition:* $168 per credit hour (minimum). • Dr. Margaret Giesbrecht, Dean, 910-893-1630. Fax: 910-893-1999. E-mail: giesbrec@mailcenter.campbell.edu. Application contact: James S. Farthing, Director of Graduate Admissions, 910-893-1200 Ext. 1318. Fax: 910-893-1288.

Canisius College, School of Education and Human Services, Department of Counselor Education, Buffalo, NY 14208-1098. Awards MS, CAS. Part-time and evening/weekend programs available. Faculty: 3 full-time (1 woman), 17 part-time (4 women). Students: 62 full-time (50 women), 134 part-time (100 women). 66 applicants, 91% accepted. *Degree requirements:* For master's, research project required, foreign language and thesis not required. *Entrance requirements:* For master's, California Psychological Inventory, GRE General Test, interview, minimum GPA of 2.5. Application deadline: 8/15 (priority date; rolling processing). Application fee: $20. *Expenses:* Tuition $415 per credit hour. Fees $15 per credit hour. *Financial aid:* Graduate assistantships, Federal Work-Study, institutionally sponsored loans, and career-related internships or fieldwork available. Aid available to part-time students. *Faculty research:* Counseling process, counseling the deaf, family counseling, high school admissions, elementary school counseling. • Dr. David L. Farrugia, Chairman, 716-888-2393. Application contact: Kevin Smith, Graduate Recruitment and Admissions, 716-888-2544. Fax: 716-888-3290.

Carson-Newman College, Graduate Program in Education, Jefferson City, TN 37760. Offerings include school counseling (M Ed). Accredited by NCATE. College faculty: 18 full-time (8 women), 7 part-time (5 women). *Application deadline:* 7/15 (priority date; rolling processing). *Application fee:* $25 ($50 for international students). *Expenses:* Tuition $190 per credit hour. Fees $10 per year. • Dr. Margaret A. Hypes, Chair, 423-471-3461. Application contact: Jane W. McGill, Graduate Admissions and Services Adviser, 423-471-3460. Fax: 423-471-3475.

Carthage College, Division of Teacher Education, Kenosha, WI 53140-1994. Offerings include classroom guidance and counseling (M Ed). College faculty: 6 full-time (4 women), 13 part-time (8 women). *Degree requirements:* Thesis optional, foreign language not required. *Average time to degree:* master's–5 years part-time. *Entrance requirements:* MAT, minimum B average. Application deadline: rolling. Application fee: $25. • Dr. Judith B. Schaumberg, Director of Graduate Programs, 414-551-5876. Fax: 414-551-5704.

The Catholic University of America, School of Arts and Sciences, Department of Education, Washington, DC 20064. Offerings include counselor education (MA). Accredited by NCATE. MA (English as a second language) new for fall 1998. Department faculty: 13 full-time (8 women), 2 part-time (both women), 14 FTE. *Degree requirements:* Comprehensive exam required, foreign language not required. *Entrance requirements:* GRE General Test, TOEFL. Application deadline: 8/1 (priority date; rolling processing; 12/1 for spring admission). Application fee: $50. *Expenses:* Tuition $17,325 per year full-time, $668 per credit hour part-time. Fees $680 per year full-time, $360 per year part-time. • Chair, 202-319-5800. Fax: 202-319-5815.

Central Connecticut State University, School of Education and Professional Studies, Department of Health and Human Service Professions, New Britain, CT 06050-4010. Offers program in counseling (MS). Part-time and evening/weekend programs available. Faculty: 9 full-time (6 women), 18 part-time (10 women), 14.2 FTE. Students: 85 full-time (69 women), 200 part-time (164 women); includes 26 minority (16 African Americans, 5 Asian Americans, 5 Hispanics), 4 international. Average age 34. 202 applicants, 73% accepted. In 1997, 33 degrees awarded. *Degree requirements:* Thesis or alternative, special project required, foreign language not required. *Entrance requirements:* TOEFL (minimum score 550), minimum GPA of 2.7. Application deadline: 6/1 (priority date; rolling processing; 12/1 for spring admission). Application fee: $40. *Expenses:* Tuition $4458 per year full-time, $175 per credit hour part-time for state residents; $9943 per year full-time, $175 per credit hour part-time for nonresidents. Fees $45 per semester. *Financial aid:* In 1997–98, 1 research assistantship (to a first-year student) was awarded; Federal Work-Study and career-related internships or fieldwork also available. Financial aid application deadline: 3/15; applicants required to submit FAFSA. *Faculty research:* Elementary/secondary school counseling, marriage/family therapy, rehabilitation counseling, counseling in higher educational settings. • Dr. Judith Hriceniak, Chair, 860-832-2145.

Central Michigan University, College of Education and Human Services, Department of Counseling and Special Education, Program in Counselor Education, Mount Pleasant, MI 48859. Offers counselor education (MA), guidance and counselor education (Ed S). Accredited by NCATE. Students: 46 full-time (32 women), 137 part-time (109 women); includes 10 minority (5 African Americans, 1 Asian American, 3 Hispanics, 1 Native American). Average age 35. In 1997, 64 master's awarded. *Degree requirements:* Thesis or alternative required, foreign language not required. *Entrance requirements:* For master's, MAT, teaching certificate. Application deadline: 2/1 (9/1 for spring admission). Application fee: $30. *Expenses:* Tuition $139 per credit hour (minimum) for state residents; $276 per credit hour (minimum) for nonresidents. Fees $260 per year full-time, $150 per semester part-time. *Financial aid:* Federal Work-Study and career-related internships or fieldwork available. Financial aid application deadline: 3/7. *Faculty research:* Stress, school counseling. • Dr. D. Terry Rawls, Chairperson, Department of Counseling and Special Education, 517-774-3205. Fax: 517-774-4374. E-mail: d.terry.rawls@cmich.edu.

Central Missouri State University, College of Education and Human Services, Department of Psychology and Counselor Education, Warrensburg, MO 64093. Offers programs in human services/guidance and counseling (Ed S), psychology (MS), school counseling (MS). One or more programs accredited by NCATE. Part-time programs available. Faculty: 15 full-time. Students: 28 full-time (22 women), 77 part-time (66 women). In 1997, 34 master's awarded. *Degree requirements:* For master's, comprehensive exam required, thesis not required; for Ed S, thesis. *Entrance requirements:* For master's, GRE General Test, GRE Subject Test, minimum GPA of 2.75, Missouri teaching certificate, 2 years of teaching experience (school counseling), previous course work in psychology; for Ed S, MS in counselor education or equivalent. Application deadline: 6/30 (priority date; rolling processing). Application fee: $25 ($50 for international students). *Tuition:* $3288 per year full-time, $137 per credit hour part-time for state residents; $5928 per year full-time, $274 per credit hour part-time for nonresidents. *Financial aid:* In 1997–98, 7 research assistantships, 3 teaching assistantships, 4 administrative and laboratory assistantships were awarded; Federal Work-Study also available. Aid available to part-time students. Financial aid application deadline: 3/1; applicants required to submit FAFSA. • Dr. Robert Ahlering, Interim Chair, 660-543-4185. Fax: 660-543-8505.

Central Washington University, College of the Sciences, Department of Psychology, Program in Guidance and Counseling, Ellensburg, WA 98926. Awards M Ed. Faculty: 24 full-time (7 women). Students: 1 (woman) full-time. 4 applicants, 25% accepted. In 1997, 1 degree awarded. *Degree requirements:* Thesis, internship required, foreign language not required. *Entrance requirements:* GRE General Test, minimum GPA of 3.0. Application deadline: 4/1 (priority date; rolling processing). Application fee: $35. *Expenses:* Tuition $4200 per year full-time, $140 per credit hour part-time for state residents; $12,780 per year full-time, $426 per credit hour part-time for nonresidents. Fees $240 per year. *Financial aid:* Research assistantships, Federal Work-Study, and career-related internships or fieldwork available. Financial aid application deadline: 2/15. • Application contact: Christie A. Fevergeon, Program Coordinator, Graduate Studies and Research, 509-963-3103. Fax: 509-963-1799. E-mail: masters@cwu.edu.

Chadron State College, Department of Education, Chadron, NE 69337. Offerings include counseling (MA Ed, Sp Ed). Accredited by NCATE. Sp Ed (counseling) admissions temporarily suspended. *Application deadline:* rolling. *Application fee:* $15. *Expenses:* Tuition $1788 per year full-time, $75 per credit hour part-time for state residents; $3588 per year full-time, $149 per credit hour part-time for nonresidents. Fees $388 per year full-time, $1232 per year part-time. • Dr. Pat Colgate, Dean, School of Graduate Studies, 308-432-6330. Fax: 308-432-6454. E-mail: pcolgate@csc1.csc.edu.

Chapman University, School of Education, Program in Counseling, Orange, CA 92866. Offers career counseling (MA), school counseling (MA). Evening/weekend programs available. Faculty: 10 full-time (8 women). Students: 7. *Degree requirements:* Comprehensive exam required, thesis not required. *Entrance requirements:* GRE General Test (minimum combined score of 900), MAT (minimum score 45), or PRAXIS. Application deadline: rolling. Application fee: $40. *Tuition:* $7020 per year full-time, $390 per credit part-time. *Financial aid:* Application deadline 3/1. • Dr. Michael Hass, Coordinator, 714-977-6781.

Chicago State University, College of Arts and Sciences, Department of Psychology, Chicago, IL 60628. Offers program in school guidance and counseling (MA). One or more programs accredited by NCATE. *Degree requirements:* Comprehensive exam required, thesis optional, foreign language not required. *Entrance requirements:* Minimum GPA of 2.75. Application deadline: 7/1 (11/10 for spring admission). *Tuition:* $2268 per year full-time, $95 per credit hour part-time for state residents; $6804 per year full-time, $284 per credit hour part-time for nonresidents.

The Citadel, The Military College of South Carolina, Department of Education, Program in Guidance and Counseling, Charleston, SC 29409. Awards M Ed. Accredited by NCATE. Faculty: 3 full-time (1 woman), 4 part-time (2 women). Students: 38 full-time (29 women), 126 part-time (99 women); includes 20 minority (18 African Americans, 1 Asian American, 1 Native American). In 1997, 48 degrees awarded. *Entrance requirements:* GRE, MAT, or 12 hours of graduate course work with a minimum GPA of 3.0. Application deadline: rolling. Application fee: $25. *Expenses:* Tuition $130 per credit hour for state residents; $260 per credit hour for nonresidents. Fees $30 per semester. • Dr. Robert Carter, Head, Department of Education, 803-953-5097.

City College of the City University of New York, Graduate School, School of Education, Department of School Services, Convent Avenue at 138th Street, New York, NY 10031-6977. Offerings include guidance and counseling (MS). *Degree requirements:* Thesis, research paper required, foreign language not required. *Entrance requirements:* TOEFL (minimum score 500), interview, minimum GPA of 3.0 in major, 2.5 overall. Application fee: $40. *Expenses:* Tuition $4350 per year full-time, $185 per credit part-time for state residents; $7600 per year full-time, $320 per credit part-time for nonresidents. Fees $41 per year. • Chair, 212-650-7980.

Clark Atlanta University, School of Education, Department of Counseling and Psychological Services, Atlanta, GA 30314. Offers programs in counseling (MA, PhD), education psychology (MA). Students: 83 full-time (67 women), 62 part-time (51 women); includes 142 minority (all African Americans), 2 international. In 1997, 59 master's, 3 doctorates awarded. *Degree requirements:* For master's, 1 foreign language (computer language can substitute), thesis; for doctorate, 2 foreign languages (computer language can substitute for one), dissertation. *Entrance requirements:* For master's, GRE General Test, minimum undergraduate GPA of 2.5; for doctorate, GRE General Test, minimum graduate GPA of 3.0. Application deadline: 4/1 (rolling processing; 11/1 for spring admission). Application fee: $30. *Expenses:* Tuition $9672 per year full-time, $403 per credit hour part-time. Fees $200 per year. *Financial aid:* Career-related internships or fieldwork available. Financial aid application deadline: 4/30. • Dr. Lloyd Williams, Interim Chairperson, 404-880-8516. Application contact: Michelle Clark-Davis, Graduate Program Assistant, 404-880-8709.

Clemson University, College of Health, Education, and Human Development, Department of Counseling and Educational Leadership, Program in Counseling and Guidance Services, Clemson, SC 29634. Awards M Ed. Accredited by NCATE. Students: 60 full-time (42 women), 252 part-time (188 women); includes 48 minority (46 African Americans, 2 Hispanics), 3 international. 154 applicants, 78% accepted. In 1997, 96 degrees awarded. *Entrance requirements:* TOEFL. Application deadline: 6/1. Application fee: $35. *Expenses:* Tuition $3154 per year full-time, $130 per credit hour part-time for state residents; $6452 per year full-time, $264 per credit hour part-time for nonresidents. Fees $190 per year. *Financial aid:* Application deadline 6/1. • Dr. Don F. Keller, Coordinator, 864-656-5107. Fax: 864-656-2652. E-mail: kdon@clemson.edu.

Cleveland State University, College of Education, Department of Counseling, Administration, Supervision and Adult Learning, Program in School and Professional Counseling, Cleveland, OH 44115-2440. Awards M Ed, Ed S. Students: 3 full-time (1 woman), 40 part-time (33 women); includes 9 minority (all African Americans). Average age 36. In 1997, 52 master's awarded. *Degree requirements:* For master's, comprehensive exam required, thesis optional, foreign language not required; for Ed S, comprehensive exam, internship required, thesis optional, foreign language not required. *Entrance requirements:* For master's, GRE General Test or MAT (score in 50th percentile or higher). Application deadline: 9/1 (priority date; rolling processing). Application fee: $25. *Expenses:* Tuition $5252 per year full-time, $202 per credit hour part-time for state residents; $10,504 per year full-time, $404 per credit hour part-time for nonresidents. Fees $2.25 per credit hour (minimum). *Financial aid:* Career-related internships or fieldwork available. *Faculty research:* Career development, counseling process, school guidance programming, ethics in counseling, human development. • Dr. Elizabeth Welfel, Coordinator, 216-687-4605.

The College of New Jersey, Graduate Division, School of Education, Department of Counseling and Personnel Services, Program in Community Counseling, Ewing, NJ 08628. Awards MA. Students: 10 full-time (9 women), 65 part-time (61 women); includes 8 minority (4 African Americans, 4 Hispanics), 2 international. In 1997, 28 degrees awarded. *Degree requirements:* Comprehensive exam required, foreign language and thesis not required. *Average time to degree:* master's–2 years full-time. *Entrance requirements:* GRE General Test, minimum GPA of 3.0 in field or 2.75 overall, interview. Application deadline: 4/15. Application fee: $50. *Expenses:* Tuition $6892 per year full-time, $287 per credit hour part-time for state residents; $9602 per year full-time, $402 per credit hour part-time for nonresidents. Fees $799 per year full-time, $33 per credit hour part-time. *Financial aid:* Application deadline 5/1; applicants required to submit FAFSA. • Dr. Roland Worthington, Coordinator, 609-771-2478. Fax: 609-637-5166.

The College of New Jersey, Graduate Division, School of Education, Department of Counseling and Personnel Services, Program in School Counseling, Ewing, NJ 08628. Awards MA. Accredited by NCATE. Students: 4 full-time (all women), 42 part-time (35 women); includes 6 minority (2 African Americans, 4 Hispanics). Average age 27. In 1997, 14 degrees awarded. *Degree requirements:* Comprehensive exam required, foreign language and thesis not required. *Average time to degree:* master's–2 years full-time. *Entrance requirements:* GRE General Test, minimum GPA of 3.0 in field or 2.75 overall, interview. Application deadline: 4/15. Application fee: $50. *Expenses:* Tuition $6892 per year full-time, $287 per credit hour part-time for state residents; $9602 per year full-time, $402 per credit hour part-time for nonresidents. Fees $799 per year full-time, $33 per credit hour part-time. *Financial aid:* Application deadline 5/1; applicants required to submit FAFSA. • Dr. MaryLou Ramsey, Coordinator, 609-771-3033. Fax: 609-637-5166.

The College of Saint Rose, School of Education, Educational Support Department, Program in Counseling, Albany, NY 12203-1419. Offers college student personnel (MS Ed), community counseling (MS Ed), school counseling (MS Ed). Part-time and evening/weekend programs available. Faculty: 2 full-time (1 woman), 3 part-time (1 woman). Students: 21 full-time (17 women), 53 part-time (44 women); includes 4 minority (1 African American, 2 Hispanics, 1 Native American). Average age 30. In 1997, 23 degrees awarded. *Degree requirements:* Thesis or alternative, comprehensive exam. *Entrance requirements:* Interview, minimum undergraduate GPA of 3.0. Application deadline: 7/15 (priority date; rolling processing; 12/1 for spring admission). Application fee: $30. *Expenses:* Tuition $338 per credit. Fees $60 per year. *Financial aid:* Research assistantships, partial tuition waivers, and career-related internships or fieldwork available. Aid available to part-time students. Financial aid application deadline: 3/1; applicants required to submit FAFSA. • Application contact: Graduate Office, 518-454-5136. Fax: 518-458-5479. E-mail: ace@rosnet.strose.edu.

College of Santa Fe, Department of Education, Program in At-Risk Youth, Santa Fe, NM 87505-7634. Offerings include community counseling (MA), school counseling (MA). Program faculty: 7 full-time (5 women), 14 part-time (10 women). *Entrance requirements:* Minimum GPA of 3.0. Application deadline: rolling. Application fee: $25. *Expenses:* Tuition $237 per credit hour. Fees $25 per year. • Dr. Barbara Reider, Chair, Department of Education, 800-246-2673. Fax: 505-473-6510.

College of the Southwest, School of Education and Professional Studies, Hobbs, NM 88240-9129. Offerings include educational counseling (MS). Postbaccalaureate distance learning degree programs offered. School faculty: 4 full-time (all women), 6 part-time (2 women). *Entrance requirements:* GRE General Test (minimum combined score of 1200). Application deadline: 3/1 (priority date; rolling processing; 10/1 for spring admission). Application fee: $50. *Expenses:* Tuition $150 per credit hour. Fees $140 per year. • Dr. Marilyn Smith, Dean, 505-392-6561.

College of William and Mary, School of Education, Program in Counseling, Williamsburg, VA 23187-8795. Awards M Ed, Ed D, PhD. Accredited by NCATE. Part-time and evening/weekend programs available. Faculty: 5 full-time (1 woman), 3 part-time (2 women). Students: 35 full-time (28 women), 40 part-time (31 women); includes 12 minority (5 African Americans, 5 Asian Americans, 2 Hispanics). Average age 38. 92 applicants, 47% accepted. In 1997, 36 master's, 6 doctorates awarded. *Degree requirements:* For doctorate, dissertation required, foreign language not required. *Entrance requirements:* For master's, GRE or MAT, minimum GPA of 2.5; for doctorate, GRE or MAT, minimum GPA of 3.5. Application deadline: 2/15. Application fee: $30. *Tuition:* $5262 per year full-time, $165 per semester hour part-time for state residents; $16,138 per year full-time, $500 per semester hour part-time for nonresidents. *Financial aid:* In 1997–98, 17 graduate assistantships (8 to first-year students) averaging $667 per month were awarded; fellowships, research assistantships, and career-related internships or fieldwork also available. Financial aid application deadline: 2/15. *Faculty research:* Sexuality, multicultural education, substance abuse, transpersonal psychology. • Dr. Roger Ries, Coordinator, 757-221-4300. E-mail: rrries@facstaff.wm.edu.

Columbus State University, College of Education, Department of Counseling and Clinical Programs, Columbus, GA 31907-5645. Offerings include school counseling (M Ed, Ed S). Accredited by NCATE. M Ed (reading), Ed S (special education) being phased out; applicants no longer accepted. *Degree requirements:* For Ed S, thesis or alternative required, foreign language not required. *Entrance requirements:* For Ed S, GRE General Test (minimum combined score of 900), MAT (minimum score 44). Application deadline: 7/10 (priority date; rolling processing; 10/23 for spring admission). Application fee: $20. *Tuition:* $1718 per year full-time, $151 per semester hour part-time for state residents; $6218 per year full-time, $401 per semester hour part-time for nonresidents. • Dr. Joyce Hickson, Chair, 706-568-2222. Fax: 706-569-3134. E-mail: hickson_joyce@colstate.edu. Application contact: Katie Thornton, Graduate Admissions, 706-568-2279. Fax: 706-568-2462. E-mail: thornton_katie@colstate.edu.

Concordia University, Program in School Guidance and Counseling, River Forest, IL 60305-1499. Awards MA, CAS. Accredited by NCATE. Part-time and evening/weekend programs available. Faculty: 11 full-time (4 women), 10 part-time (4 women). Students: 16 (14 women). In 1997, 7 master's awarded. *Degree requirements:* For master's, comprehensive exams required, thesis optional, foreign language not required; for CAS, thesis, final project required, foreign language not required. *Entrance requirements:* For master's, minimum GPA of 2.9; for CAS, master's degree. Application deadline: rolling. Application fee: $0. *Tuition:* $372 per semester hour. *Financial aid:* Research assistantships, institutionally sponsored loans available. Aid available to part-time students. *Faculty research:* Development of comprehensive school counseling education, training of school counselors for parochial schools. • Dr. Dale Septeowski, Coordinator, 708-209-3059. Application contact: Mary Betancourt, Admissions Secretary, 708-209-4093. Fax: 708-209-3454. E-mail: crfdngrad@curf.edu.

Concordia University Wisconsin, Division of Graduate Studies, Education Department, Program in Counseling, Mequon, WI 53097-2402. Awards MS Ed. Postbaccalaureate distance learning degree programs offered (minimal on-campus study). *Degree requirements:* Thesis or alternative, comprehensive exam. *Entrance requirements:* TOEFL (minimum score 550), minimum GPA of 3.0, teaching license. *Tuition:* $250 per credit. *Financial aid:* Career-related internships or fieldwork available. Financial aid application deadline: 8/1. • Dr. Jan Heinitz, Co-Director, 414-243-4222. E-mail: jheinitz@bach.cuw.edu. Application contact: Brooke Tireman, Graduate Admissions, 414-243-4248. Fax: 414-243-4428. E-mail: btireman@back.cuw.edu.

Creighton University, College of Arts and Sciences, Department of Education, Program in Guidance and Counseling, Omaha, NE 68178-0001. Awards MS. Part-time and evening/weekend programs available. Faculty: 4 full-time, 3 part-time. Students: 5 full-time (2 women), 28 part-time (21 women); includes 4 minority (2 African Americans, 1 Asian American, 1 Hispanic). In 1997, 18 degrees awarded. *Entrance requirements:* GRE General Test, TOEFL (minimum score 550). Application deadline: 3/1 (rolling processing). Application fee: $30. *Expenses:* Tuition $402 per credit hour. Fees $536 per year full-time, $28 per semester part-time. • Dr. Debra Ponec, Director, 402-280-2557. Application contact: Dr. Barbara J. Braden, Dean, Graduate School, 402-280-2870. Fax: 402-280-5762.

Dallas Baptist University, College of Humanities and Social Sciences, Counseling Program, Dallas, TX 75211-9299. Awards MA. Part-time and evening/weekend programs available. Faculty: 6 full-time (1 woman), 7 part-time (5 women). Students: 39 full-time (29 women), 89 part-time (66 women). Average age 37. 74 applicants, 80% accepted. In 1997, 35 degrees awarded. *Entrance requirements:* GRE General Test, TOEFL (minimum score 550). Application deadline: rolling. Application fee: $25. *Tuition:* $285 per hour. *Financial aid:* In 1997–98, 31 scholarships (5 to first-year students) totaling $42,688 were awarded; Federal Work-Study also available. Aid available to part-time students. Financial aid applicants required to submit FAFSA. *Faculty research:* Therapy effectiveness. • Dr. Mary Becerril, Director, 214-333-5273. Fax: 214-333-5323. Application contact: Travis Bundrick, Director of Graduate Programs, 214-333-5243. Fax: 214-333-5579. E-mail: graduate@dbu.edu.

Dallas Baptist University, Dorothy M. Bush College of Education, School Counseling Program, Dallas, TX 75211-9299. Awards M Ed. Students: 21 full-time (all women), 26 part-time (all women). Average age 37. 17 applicants, 65% accepted. In 1997, 7 degrees awarded. *Entrance requirements:* GRE General Test, TOEFL (minimum score 550). Application deadline: rolling. Application fee: $25. *Tuition:* $285 per hour. *Financial aid:* In 1997–98, 24 scholarships (11 to first-year students) totaling $27,530 were awarded. • Dr. Mike Rosato, Director, 214-333-5200. Fax: 214-333-5551. Application contact: Travis Bundrick, Director of Graduate Programs, 214-333-5243. Fax: 214-333-5579. E-mail: graduate@dbu.edu.

Directory: Counselor Education

Delta State University, School of Education, Division of Behavioral Sciences, Program in Guidance and Counseling, Cleveland, MS 38733-0001. Awards M Ed. Accredited by NCATE. Part-time and evening/weekend programs available. *Degree requirements:* Practicum required, thesis optional, foreign language not required. *Entrance requirements:* GRE General Test (minimum combined score of 800) or MAT (minimum score 34). Application deadline: 8/1 (priority date; rolling processing). Application fee: $0. *Tuition:* $2596 per year full-time, $121 per semester hour part-time for state residents; $5546 per year full-time, $285 per semester hour part-time for nonresidents. *Financial aid:* Research assistantships, Federal Work-Study, institutionally sponsored loans, and career-related internships or fieldwork available. Aid available to part-time students. Financial aid application deadline: 6/1. • Application contact: Dr. John Thornell, Dean of Graduate Studies and Continuing Education, 601-846-4310. Fax: 601-846-4016.

DePaul University, School of Education, Program in Human Services and Counseling, Chicago, IL 60604-2287. Offers agencies, family concerns, and higher education (MA, M Ed); elementary schools (MA, M Ed); human services management (MA, M Ed); secondary schools (MA, M Ed). Accredited by NCATE. Faculty: 3 full-time (1 woman). Students: 49 full-time (42 women), 52 part-time (42 women); includes 32 minority (22 African Americans, 3 Asian Americans, 6 Hispanics, 1 Native American), 3 international. Average age 32. 47 applicants, 83% accepted. In 1997, 16 degrees awarded. *Degree requirements:* Oral exam or thesis required, foreign language not required. *Entrance requirements:* Interview, minimum GPA of 2.75, work experience. Application deadline: rolling. Application fee: $25. *Expenses:* Tuition $320 per credit hour. Fees $30 per year. *Financial aid:* Career-related internships or fieldwork available. • Dr. Barbara Sizemore, Dean, School of Education, 312-325-7000 Ext. 1666. Fax: 312-325-7748. Application contact: Director of Graduate Admissions, 312-325-7000 Ext. 1666. E-mail: mmurphy@wppost.depaul.edu.

Doane College, Program in Counseling, Crete, NE 68333-2430. Awards MAC. *Degree requirements:* Thesis required, foreign language not required. *Entrance requirements:* Minimum GPA of 2.5. Application deadline: rolling. Application fee: $25. *Tuition:* $185 per credit hour. • Dr. Kenneth K. Berry, Dean, 402-466-4774. Fax: 402-466-4228. E-mail: kberry@doane.edu.

Drake University, School of Education, Department of Special Education, Counseling and Vocational Rehabilitation, Des Moines, IA 50311-4516. Offerings include counselor education (MSE, Ed D). Department faculty: 5 full-time (2 women), 10 part-time (6 women). *Degree requirements:* For doctorate, dissertation required, foreign language not required. *Entrance requirements:* For doctorate, GRE General Test (minimum combined score of 1000) or MAT (minimum score 43). Application deadline: rolling. Application fee: $25. *Tuition:* $16,000 per year full-time, $260 per hour (minimum) part-time. • Dr. Marion Panyan, Chair, 515-271-2143. Application contact: Ann J. Martin, Graduate Coordinator, 515-271-3871. Fax: 515-271-2831. E-mail: ajm@admin.drake.edu.

Duquesne University, School of Education, Department of Counseling, Psychology, and Special Education, Program in Counselor Education, Pittsburgh, PA 15282-0001. Awards MS Ed. Part-time programs available. Faculty: 6 full-time (2 women), 8 part-time (3 women). Students: 148. 39 applicants, 77% accepted. In 1997, 43 degrees awarded. *Average time to degree:* master's–2 years full-time, 3.5 years part-time. *Entrance requirements:* MAT. Application deadline: 8/1 (rolling processing; 12/1 for spring admission). Application fee: $40. *Expenses:* Tuition $481 per credit. Fees $39 per credit. • Dr. Nicholas J. Hanna, Coordinator, 412-396-6105. Fax: 412-396-5585.

East Carolina University, School of Education, Department of Counselor Education, Greenville, NC 27858-4353. Offers programs in adult education (MA Ed), counselor education (MA Ed, CAS). Accredited by NCATE. Part-time and evening/weekend programs available. Faculty: 5 full-time (1 woman). Students: 46 full-time (30 women), 75 part-time (56 women); includes 22 minority (21 African Americans, 1 Asian American). Average age 33. 95 applicants, 59% accepted. In 1997, 51 master's awarded. *Degree requirements:* For master's, comprehensive exams. *Entrance requirements:* For master's, GRE General Test or MAT, TOEFL, interview. Application deadline: 5/15 (priority date; rolling processing). Application fee: $40. *Tuition:* $1886 per year full-time, $472 per semester (minimum) part-time for state residents; $9156 per year full-time, $2289 per semester (minimum) part-time for nonresidents. *Financial aid:* Federal Work-Study available. Aid available to part-time students. Financial aid application deadline: 6/1. • Dr. John Schmidt, Chairperson, 252-328-6856. Fax: 252-328-4219. E-mail: edjschmi@ecuvm.cis.ecu.edu.

East Central University, Department of Human Resources, Ada, OK 74820-6899. Offerings include counseling (MSHR). Department faculty: 7 part-time (3 women). *Degree requirements:* Thesis optional, foreign language not required. *Entrance requirements:* GRE General Test, MAT, minimum GPA of 2.5. Application deadline: rolling. Application fee: $0 ($50 for international students). *Expenses:* Tuition $75 per semester hour for state residents; $177 per semester hour for nonresidents. Fees $39 per year full-time, $31 per year part-time. • Dr. Richard Baumgartner, Chairman, 405-332-8000.

Eastern College, Programs in Counseling, Program in Educational Counseling, St. Davids, PA 19087-3696. Offers school counseling (MA), school psychology (MS). Students: 14 full-time, 36 part-time. In 1997, 10 degrees awarded. *Degree requirements:* Internship required, foreign language and thesis not required. *Entrance requirements:* TOEFL, minimum GPA of 2.5. Application deadline: rolling. Application fee: $35. • Lynn Brandsma, Head, 610-341-1484. Application contact: Megan Miscioscia, Graduate Admissions Representative, 610-341-5972. Fax: 610-341-1466.

Eastern Illinois University, College of Education and Professional Studies, Department of Educational Psychology and Guidance, 600 Lincoln Avenue, Charleston, IL 61920-3099. Awards MS Ed, Ed S. Accredited by NCATE. Ed S being phased out; applicants no longer accepted. Part-time and evening/weekend programs available. Faculty: 8 full-time (2 women). Students: 78 full-time (53 women), 137 part-time (108 women); includes 26 minority (24 African Americans, 2 Hispanics). In 1997, 77 master's, 1 Ed S awarded. *Degree requirements:* For master's, comprehensive exam required, foreign language and thesis not required; for Ed S, thesis required, foreign language not required. *Entrance requirements:* For master's, GRE General Test or MAT. Application deadline: 7/31 (priority date; rolling processing). Application fee: $25. *Expenses:* Tuition $3459 per year full-time, $96 per semester hour part-time for state residents; $10,377 per year full-time, $288 per semester hour part-time for nonresidents. Fees $1566 per year full-time, $37 per semester hour part-time. *Financial aid:* In 1997–98, 4 research assistantships were awarded. • Dr. Lynda Kayser, Chairperson, 217-581-2400. Fax: 217-581-7417. E-mail: cflk2@eiu.edu.

Eastern Kentucky University, College of Education, Department of Administration, Counseling, and Educational Studies, Richmond, KY 40475-3101. Offers programs in administration and supervision (Ed S), community counseling (MA), elementary counseling (MA Ed), secondary counseling (MA Ed), student personnel counseling (MA, Ed S). Accredited by NCATE. Part-time programs available. Postbaccalaureate distance learning degree programs offered. Faculty: 17 full-time (5 women), 8 part-time (4 women), 19 FTE. Students: 242. In 1997, 79 master's awarded. *Degree requirements:* For Ed S, thesis, research project. *Entrance requirements:* GRE General Test, minimum GPA of 2.5. Application fee: $0. *Tuition:* $2390 per year full-time, $133 per credit hour part-time for state residents; $6630 per year full-time, $365 per credit hour part-time for nonresidents. *Financial aid:* In 1997–98, 2 research assistantships totaling $5,500, 10 scholarships were awarded; teaching assistantships, Federal Work-Study, and career-related internships or fieldwork also available. Aid available to part-time students. • Dr. Leonard Burns, Chair, 606-622-1124. E-mail: eadburns@acs.eku.edu.

Eastern Michigan University, College of Education, Department of Leadership and Counseling, Program in Guidance and Counseling, Ypsilanti, MI 48197. Offers advanced counseling (MA), community counseling (MA), guidance and counseling (MA, SPA). Accredited by NCATE. Evening/weekend programs available. In 1997, 51 master's, 1 SPA awarded. *Entrance requirements:* For master's, GRE General Test, TOEFL (minimum score 550). Application deadline: 5/15 (rolling processing; 3/15 for spring admission). Application fee: $30. *Expenses:* Tuition $2691 per year full-time, $150 per credit hour part-time for state residents; $6300 per year full-time, $350 per credit hour part-time for nonresidents. Fees $368 per year full-time, $88 per semester (minimum) part-time. *Financial aid:* Fellowships, teaching assistantships, and career-related internships or fieldwork available. Aid available to part-time students. Financial aid application deadline: 3/15; applicants required to submit FAFSA. • Dr. Sue Stichel, Head, 734-487-0255.

Eastern New Mexico University, College of Education and Technology, School of Education, Program in Counseling and Guidance, Portales, NM 88130. Awards M Ed. Students: 1 (woman) part-time; includes 1 minority (Hispanic). 0 applicants. In 1997, 1 degree awarded. *Degree requirements:* Thesis optional, foreign language not required. *Entrance requirements:* Minimum GPA of 2.5. Application deadline: rolling. Application fee: $10. *Tuition:* $1956 per year full-time, $82 per credit hour part-time for state residents; $6702 per year full-time, $280 per credit hour part-time for nonresidents. *Financial aid:* Application deadline 4/1. • Dr. Sherrie Bettenhausen, Graduate Coordinator, School of Education, 505-562-2603.

Eastern Washington University, College of Education and Human Development, Department of Applied Psychology, Program in School Counseling, Cheney, WA 99004-2431. Offers counseling psychology (MS), school counseling (MS). Accredited by NCATE. *Degree requirements:* Thesis or alternative, comprehensive exam. *Entrance requirements:* GRE General Test, minimum GPA of 3.0. Application deadline: 2/1 (rolling processing). Application fee: $35. *Tuition:* $4200 per year full-time, $140 per credit part-time for state residents; $12,780 per year full-time, $415 per credit part-time for nonresidents. *Financial aid:* Application deadline 2/1. • Dr. Cass Dykeman, Director, 509-359-4677.

East Tennessee State University, College of Education, Department of Human Development and Learning, Johnson City, TN 37614-0734. Offerings include counseling (MA, M Ed). Accredited by NCATE. Department faculty: 22 full-time (8 women). *Degree requirements:* Thesis (for some programs), comprehensive exam required, foreign language not required. *Entrance requirements:* GRE General Test, TOEFL (minimum score 550), minimum GPA of 3.0. Application deadline: 7/15 (priority date; rolling processing; 11/1 for spring admission). Application fee: $25 ($35 for international students). *Tuition:* $2944 per year full-time, $158 per credit hour part-time for state residents; $7770 per year full-time, $369 per credit hour part-time for nonresidents. • Dr. James Bitter, Chair, 423-439-4194. Fax: 423-439-5764. E-mail: bitterj@etsu-tn.edu.

Edinboro University of Pennsylvania, School of Education, Department of Counseling and Human Development, Program in Counseling, Edinboro, PA 16444. Offers counseling-elementary guidance (MA), counseling-rehabilitation (MA), counseling-secondary guidance (MA), counseling-student personnel services (MA). Evening/weekend programs available. Students: 38 full-time (32 women), 59 part-time (39 women); includes 5 minority (4 African Americans, 1 Asian American), 1 international. Average age 32. In 1997, 52 degrees awarded. *Degree requirements:* Thesis or alternative required, foreign language not required. *Entrance requirements:* GRE or MAT (score in 30th percentile or higher). Application deadline: rolling. Application fee: $25. *Expenses:* Tuition $3468 per year full-time, $193 per credit part-time for state residents; $6236 per year full-time, $346 per credit part-time for nonresidents. Fees $898 per year full-time, $50 per semester (minimum) part-time. *Financial aid:* In 1997–98, 19 assistantships were awarded; career-related internships or fieldwork also available. • Application contact: Dr. Philip Kerstetter, Dean of Graduate Studies, 814-732-2856. Fax: 814-732-2611. E-mail: kerstetter@edinboro.edu.

Emporia State University, School of Graduate Studies, The Teachers College, Division of Counselor Education and Rehabilitation Programs, Program in School Counseling, Emporia, KS 66801-5087. Offers elementary counseling (MS), general counseling (MS), school counseling (MS), secondary counseling (MS). Accredited by NCATE. Students: 29 full-time (24 women), 63 part-time (51 women); includes 2 minority (1 African American, 1 Hispanic), 3 international. 29 applicants, 62% accepted. In 1997, 52 degrees awarded. *Degree requirements:* Comprehensive exam or thesis required, foreign language not required. *Entrance requirements:* GRE General Test (minimum combined score of 850) or MAT (minimum score 40), TOEFL (minimum score 550), written exam. Application deadline: 8/15 (priority date; rolling processing). Application fee: $30 ($75 for international students). Electronic applications accepted. *Tuition:* $2300 per year full-time, $103 per credit hour part-time for state residents; $6012 per year full-time, $258 per credit hour part-time for nonresidents. *Financial aid:* Federal Work-Study, institutionally sponsored loans, and career-related internships or fieldwork available. Financial aid application deadline: 3/15; applicants required to submit FAFSA. • Dr. Edward R. Butler, Chair, Division of Counselor Education and Rehabilitation Programs, 316-341-5220. E-mail: butlered@emporia.edu.

Fairfield University, Graduate School of Education and Allied Professions, Department of Counselor Education, Fairfield, CT 06430-5195. Offers programs in community counseling (MA), counselor education (CAS), school counseling (MA), student affairs (MA). Part-time and evening/weekend programs available. Faculty: 3 full-time (2 women), 4 part-time (all women), 4 FTE. Students: 16 full-time (14 women), 70 part-time (60 women); includes 4 minority (2 African Americans, 1 Asian American, 1 Hispanic). Average age 30. 57 applicants, 56% accepted. In 1997, 16 master's, 1 CAS awarded. *Degree requirements:* For master's, thesis or alternative, comprehensive exams required, foreign language not required. *Entrance requirements:* For master's, PRAXIS I (CBT), TOEFL, minimum QPA of 2.67. Application deadline: 7/1 (11/1 for spring admission). Application fee: $40. *Expenses:* Tuition $350 per credit hour (minimum). Fees $20 per semester (minimum). *Financial aid:* Partial tuition waivers and career-related internships or fieldwork available. Aid available to part-time students. • Dr. Harold Hackney, Chair, 203-254-4000 Ext. 2396. Application contact: Karen Creecy, Assistant Dean, 203-254-4250. Fax: 203-254-4241. E-mail: klcreecy@fair1.fairfield.edu.

Fitchburg State College, Programs in Counseling, Fitchburg, MA 01420-2697. Offerings in adolescent and family therapy (Certificate), child protective services (Certificate), elementary school guidance counseling (MS), forensic case work (Certificate), mental health counseling (MS), school guidance counselor (Certificate), secondary school guidance counseling (MS). Accredited by NCATE. Part-time and evening/weekend programs available. *Degree requirements:* For master's, practicum required, foreign language and thesis not required. *Entrance requirements:* For master's, GRE General Test or MAT (minimum score 47), interview, previous course work in psychology; for Certificate, master's degree. Application deadline: rolling. Application fee: $10. *Expenses:* Tuition $147 per credit. Fees $55 per semester. *Financial aid:* Graduate assistantships, Federal Work-Study available. Aid available to part-time students. Financial aid application deadline: 3/30; applicants required to submit FAFSA. • Dr. Richard Spencer, Chair, 978-665-3349. Fax: 978-665-3658. E-mail: dgce@fsc.edu. Application contact: James DuPont, Director of Admissions, 978-665-3144. Fax: 978-665-4540. E-mail: admissions@fsc.edu.

Florida Agricultural and Mechanical University, Division of Graduate Studies, Research, and Continuing Education, College of Education, Department of Educational Leadership and Human Services, Tallahassee, FL 32307-3200. Offerings include guidance and counseling (M Ed, MS Ed). Accredited by NCATE. *Entrance requirements:* GRE General Test (minimum combined score of 1000), minimum GPA of 3.0. Application deadline: 5/13. Application fee: $20. *Expenses:* Tuition $140 per credit hour for state residents; $484 per credit hour for nonresidents. Fees $130 per year. • Dr. Ada Burnette, Chairperson, 850-599-3191. Fax: 850-561-2211.

Florida Atlantic University, College of Education, Department of Counselor Education, Boca Raton, FL 33431-0991. Awards M Ed, Ed S. Accredited by NCATE. Part-time programs available. Faculty: 7 full-time (3 women), 14 part-time (5 women). Students: 32 full-time (28 women), 113 part-time (103 women); includes 30 minority (13 African Americans, 17 Hispanics), 3 international. Average age 29. 87 applicants, 64% accepted. In 1997, 54 master's awarded. *Degree* *requirements:* For Ed S, departmental qualifying exam required, foreign language and thesis not required. *Entrance requirements:* For master's, GRE General Test, minimum GPA of 3.0 during previous 2 years; for Ed S, GRE General Test, GRE Subject Test, minimum graduate GPA of 3.25. Application deadline: rolling. Application fee: $20. *Expenses:* Tuition $2520 per year full-time, $140 per credit hour part-time for state residents; $8712 per year full-time, $484 per credit hour part-time for nonresidents. Fees $5 per year (minimum). *Financial aid:* Research assistantships, teaching assistantships, and career-related internships or fieldwork available. *Faculty research:* Brief therapy, psychological type, marriage and family counseling, international programs, integrated services. • Dr. William Nicoll, Chair, 561-297-3625.

Florida Gulf Coast University, College of Professional Studies, School of Education, Program in Counselor Education, Fort Myers, FL 33965-6565. Awards MA, M Ed. Part-time and evening/weekend programs available. Faculty: 3 full-time (2 women), 4 part-time (2 women), 4 FTE. Students: 4 full-time (all women), 80 part-time (70 women); includes 9 minority (4 African Americans, 5 Hispanics). Average age 38. 25 applicants, 80% accepted. *Degree requirements:* Thesis or alternative required, foreign language not required. *Entrance requirements:* GRE General Test (minimum combined score of 900), MAT (minimum score 40), minimum GPA of 3.0. Application deadline: 6/1 (priority date; rolling processing; 11/1 for spring admission). Application fee: $20. Electronic applications accepted. *Faculty research:* Sexuality, confidentiality, school counselor roles, distance learning, exceptional students. • Application contact: Mike Tyler, Coordinator, 941-590-7792. E-mail: jtyler@fgcu.edu.

Florida International University, College of Education, Department of Educational Psychology and Special Education, Program in Counselor Education, Miami, FL 33199. Awards MS. Accredited by NCATE. Part-time and evening/weekend programs available. Students: 28 full-time (27 women), 45 part-time (38 women); includes 50 minority (6 African Americans, 1 Asian American, 42 Hispanics, 1 Native American), 1 international. Average age 32. 34 applicants, 47% accepted. In 1997, 20 degrees awarded. *Degree requirements:* Internship required, foreign language and thesis not required. *Entrance requirements:* GRE General Test (minimum combined score of 1000) or minimum GPA of 3.0 in last 60 credits of baccalaureate. Application deadline: 4/1 (priority date; rolling processing; 10/1 for spring admission). Application fee: $20. *Expenses:* Tuition $138 per credit hour for state residents; $482 per credit hour for nonresidents. Fees $46 per semester. *Faculty research:* Cross-cultural counseling, psychotherapy assessment of culturally different cognitive and learning styles. • Dr. Wendy Cheyney, Chairperson, Department of Educational Psychology and Special Education, 305-348-2551. Fax: 305-348-4125.

Florida State University, College of Education, Department of Human Services and Studies, Program in Counseling and Human Systems, Tallahassee, FL 32306. Awards MS, Ed S. Faculty: 6 full-time (2 women), 4 part-time (1 woman). Students: 49 full-time (42 women), 5 part-time (4 women); includes 15 minority (9 African Americans, 4 Asian Americans, 2 Hispanics). 81 applicants, 47% accepted. In 1997, 33 master's awarded. *Degree requirements:* Comprehensive exam required, thesis optional. *Entrance requirements:* GRE General Test (minimum combined score of 1000), minimum GPA of 3.0. Application deadline: 7/1 (priority date; rolling processing; 11/1 for spring admission). Application fee: $20. *Tuition:* $139 per credit hour for state residents; $482 per credit hour for nonresidents. *Financial aid:* Fellowships, research assistantships, teaching assistantships, and career-related internships or fieldwork available. • Dr. Cheryl Beeler, Chair, Department of Human Services and Studies, 850-644-3854. E-mail: beeler@mail.coe.fsu.edu. Application contact: Admissions Secretary, 850-644-3854. Fax: 850-644-4335.

Fordham University, Graduate School of Education, Division of Psychological and Educational Services, New York, NY 10023. Offerings include counseling and personnel services (MSE, Adv C). One or more programs accredited by NCATE. Accredited by NCATE. *Application fee:* $50. • Dr. Giselle Esquivel, Chairman, 212-636-6460.

Fort Hays State University, College of Education, Department of Education, Administration and Counseling, Program in Counseling, Hays, KS 67601-4099. Awards MS. Accredited by NCATE. Part-time programs available. Faculty: 10 full-time (1 woman). Students: 15 full-time (14 women), 63 part-time (55 women); includes 6 minority (1 African American, 3 Hispanics, 2 Native Americans), 2 international. Average age 36. 21 applicants, 76% accepted. In 1997, 34 degrees awarded. *Degree requirements:* Thesis or alternative required, foreign language not required. *Entrance requirements:* GRE General Test, minimum undergraduate GPA of 3.0. Application deadline: 7/1 (priority date; rolling processing). Application fee: $25 ($35 for international students). *Tuition:* $94 per credit hour for state residents; $249 per credit hour for nonresidents. *Financial aid:* Research assistantships, teaching assistantships available. *Faculty research:* Career education, evaluation and plans, counseling the disabled, marriage and family parenting, underemployment and work in the family. • Dr. James L. Murphy, Chair, Department of Education, Administration and Counseling, 785-628-4283.

Fort Valley State University, Department of Counseling Psychology, Program in Guidance and Counseling, Fort Valley, GA 31030-3298. Awards MS, Ed S. One or more programs accredited by NCATE. Part-time programs available. Faculty: 2 full-time (1 woman), 3 part-time (0 women). Students: 32 full-time (22 women), 56 part-time (44 women); includes 63 minority (62 African Americans, 1 Asian American). In 1997, 4 master's awarded. *Degree requirements:* For master's, thesis optional, foreign language not required. *Entrance requirements:* For master's, GRE General Test (minimum combined score of 800) or MAT (minimum score 44); for Ed S, GRE General Test (minimum combined score of 900) or MAT (minimum score 48). Application deadline: 8/23. Application fee: $20. *Tuition:* $2486 per year full-time, $83 per semester hour part-time for state residents; $8486 per year full-time, $333 per semester hour part-time for nonresidents. *Financial aid:* Federal Work-Study available. Aid available to part-time students. Financial aid application deadline: 5/1; applicants required to submit FAFSA. • Dr. Linda Price, Head, Department of Counseling Psychology, 912-825-6237.

Freed–Hardeman University, Program in Counseling, 158 East Main Street, Henderson, TN 38340-2399. Awards MS. Part-time and evening/weekend programs available. Faculty: 5 full-time (0 women), 4 part-time (1 woman). Students: 16 full-time (11 women), 42 part-time (32 women); includes 16 minority (all African Americans). Average age 33. 21 applicants, 100% accepted. In 1997, 13 degrees awarded. *Degree requirements:* Practicum. *Entrance requirements:* GRE General Test (minimum combined score of 800) or MAT (minimum score 28). Application deadline: 8/1 (priority date; rolling processing; 12/1 for spring admission). Application fee: $25. *Tuition:* $159 per semester hour. *Financial aid:* Graduate assistantships, partial tuition waivers, Federal Work-Study, and career-related internships or fieldwork available. Aid available to part-time students. Financial aid application deadline: 8/1; applicants required to submit FAFSA. • Dr. Mike Cravens, Director, Graduate Studies in Counseling, 901-989-6666. Fax: 901-989-6065. E-mail: mcravens@fhu.edu.

Fresno Pacific University, Graduate School, Programs in Education, Division of Pupil Personnel, Program in School Counseling, Fresno, CA 93702-4709. Awards MA Ed. Faculty: 2 full-time (0 women), 8 part-time (1 woman). Students: 57 part-time (40 women). *Application deadline:* 7/31. *Application fee:* $75. *Tuition:* $250 per unit. • Diane Talbot, Head.

Frostburg State University, School of Education, Department of Educational Professions, Program in Guidance and Counseling, Frostburg, MD 21532-1099. Awards M Ed. Part-time and evening/weekend programs available. *Entrance requirements:* GRE or MAT. Application deadline: 7/15 (rolling processing). Application fee: $30.

Gallaudet University, School of Education and Human Services, Department of Counseling, Washington, DC 20002-3625. Offers programs in community counseling (MA), mental health counseling (MA), school counseling (MA). Accredited by NCATE. *Degree requirements:* Thesis optional, foreign language not required. *Entrance requirements:* GRE General Test or MAT. Application deadline: 2/15 (priority date; rolling processing). Application fee: $50. *Expenses:* Tuition $7064 per year full-time, $392 per credit part-time. Fees $50 (one-time charge). *Financial aid:* Federal Work-Study and career-related internships or fieldwork available. Financial aid application deadline: 8/1. • Dr. Roger Beach, Chair, 202-651-5515. Application contact: Deborah DeStefano, Director of Admissions, 202-651-5253. Fax: 202-651-5744. E-mail: adm_destefan@gallua.bitnet.

George Mason University, Graduate School of Education, Program in Counseling and Development, Fairfax, VA 22030-4444. Awards M Ed. Accredited by NCATE. Part-time and evening/weekend programs available. Faculty: 42 full-time (24 women), 65 part-time (51 women), 58.73 FTE. Students: 58 full-time (51 women), 136 part-time (110 women); includes 23 minority (9 African Americans, 4 Asian Americans, 10 Hispanics), 3 international. Average age 35. 114 applicants, 58% accepted. In 1997, 42 degrees awarded. *Degree requirements:* Computer language, thesis (for some programs) required, foreign language not required. *Entrance requirements:* Interview, minimum GPA of 3.0 in last 60 hours, 1 year of related work experience. Application deadline: 5/1 (11/1 for spring admission). Application fee: $30. Electronic applications accepted. *Tuition:* $4344 per year full-time, $181 per credit hour part-time for state residents; $12,504 per year full-time, $521 per credit hour part-time for nonresidents. *Financial aid:* Fellowships, research assistantships, teaching assistantships, and career-related internships or fieldwork available. Aid available to part-time students. Financial aid application deadline: 3/1; applicants required to submit FAFSA. • Dr. Mary Ann Dzaman, Coordinator, 703-993-2049. Fax: 703-993-2082.

The George Washington University, Graduate School of Education and Human Development, Department of Counseling, Human and Organizational Services, Program in Counseling, Washington, DC 20052. Awards Ed D, Ed S. Accredited by NCATE. Part-time and evening/weekend programs available. Faculty: 7 full-time (3 women), 5 part-time (2 women). Students: 12 full-time (8 women), 23 part-time (15 women); includes 10 minority (5 African Americans, 1 Asian American, 3 Hispanics, 1 Native American), 4 international. Average age 38. 26 applicants, 65% accepted. In 1997, 6 doctorates, 1 Ed S awarded. *Degree requirements:* For doctorate, dissertation, comprehensive exam required, foreign language not required; for Ed S, comprehensive exam required, thesis not required. *Entrance requirements:* For doctorate, GRE General Test or MAT, interview, minimum GPA of 3.3; for Ed S, GRE General Test or MAT, minimum GPA of 3.3. Application deadline: 3/1 (priority date; rolling processing; 10/1 for spring admission). Application fee: $50. *Expenses:* Tuition $680 per semester hour. Fees $35 per semester hour. *Financial aid:* Fellowships, research assistantships, partial tuition waivers, Federal Work-Study, and career-related internships or fieldwork available. Financial aid applicants required to submit FAFSA. *Faculty research:* Values in counseling, religion and counseling. • Dr. Eugene Kelly, Faculty Coordinator, 202-994-0829.

The George Washington University, Graduate School of Education and Human Development, Department of Counseling, Human and Organizational Services, Program in Counseling: School, Community and Rehabilitation, Washington, DC 20052. Awards MA Ed, Ed D. Accredited by NCATE. Faculty: 6 full-time (2 women). Students: 46 full-time (37 women), 51 part-time (42 women); includes 31 minority (21 African Americans, 4 Asian Americans, 6 Hispanics), 6 international. Average age 32. 95 applicants, 85% accepted. In 1997, 21 master's awarded. *Degree requirements:* For master's, comprehensive exam required, foreign language and thesis not required; for doctorate, dissertation, comprehensive exam required, foreign language not required. *Entrance requirements:* For master's, GRE General Test or MAT, minimum GPA of 2.75; for doctorate, GRE General Test or MAT, interview, minimum GPA of 3.3. Application deadline: 3/1 (priority date; rolling processing; 10/1 for spring admission). Application fee: $50. *Expenses:* Tuition $680 per semester hour. Fees $35 per semester hour. *Financial aid:* Fellowships, research assistantships, full and partial tuition waivers, Federal Work-Study, and career-related internships or fieldwork available. *Faculty research:* Adjustment to disability, head injury rehabilitation, cross-cultural counseling. • Dr. Donald Linkowski, Director, 202-994-7204. Fax: 202-994-3436.

Georgia Southern University, College of Education, Department of Leadership, Technology, and Human Development, Program in Counselor Education, Statesboro, GA 30460-8126. Awards M Ed, Ed S. Accredited by NCATE. Part-time and evening/weekend programs available. Students: 62 full-time (51 women), 76 part-time (63 women); includes 36 minority (32 African Americans, 2 Asian Americans, 1 Hispanic, 1 Native American), 1 international. Average age 31. 43 applicants, 60% accepted. In 1997, 60 master's, 10 Ed Ss awarded. *Degree requirements:* Exams required, foreign language and thesis not required. *Entrance requirements:* For master's, GRE General Test (minimum score 450 on each section) or MAT (minimum score 44), minimum GPA of 2.5; for Ed S, GRE General Test (minimum score 450 on each section) or MAT (minimum score 49), minimum graduate GPA of 3.25. Application deadline: 4/1 (priority date; rolling processing). Application fee: $0. Electronic applications accepted. *Tuition:* $2619 per year full-time, $287 per semester (minimum) part-time for state residents; $8619 per year full-time, $1037 per semester (minimum) part-time for nonresidents. *Financial aid:* Research assistantships, teaching assistantships, Federal Work-Study, and career-related internships or fieldwork available. Aid available to part-time students. Financial aid application deadline: 4/15. *Faculty research:* School counseling, test development, gender equity, career counseling. • Application contact: Dr. John R. Diebolt, Associate Graduate Dean, 912-681-5384. Fax: 912-681-0740. E-mail: gradschool@gsvms2.cc.gasou.edu.

Georgia State University, College of Education, Department of Counseling and Psychological Services, Program in Professional Counseling, Atlanta, GA 30303-3083. Offerings include counseling (PhD). One or more programs accredited by APA. Accredited by NCATE. *Degree requirements:* Dissertation, comprehensive exam. *Entrance requirements:* GRE General Test (minimum score 500 on each section) or MAT (minimum score 53), minimum GPA of 3.3. Application fee: $25. *Expenses:* Tuition $2673 per year full-time, $99 per semester hour part-time for state residents; $10,692 per year full-time, $396 per semester hour part-time for nonresidents. Fees $228 per year. • Dr. Richard Smith, Chairman, Department of Counseling and Psychological Services, 404-651-2550.

Georgia State University, College of Education, Department of Counseling and Psychological Services, Program in School Counseling, Atlanta, GA 30303-3083. Awards M Ed, Ed S. Accredited by NCATE. Students: 40 full-time (37 women), 33 part-time (30 women); includes 5 minority (all African Americans). Average age 32. 56 applicants, 43% accepted. In 1997, 31 master's, 7 Ed Ss awarded. *Degree requirements:* For master's, comprehensive exams. *Entrance requirements:* For master's, GRE General Test (minimum combined score of 800), minimum GPA of 2.5; for Ed S, GRE General Test (minimum combined score of 900), minimum graduate GPA of 3.25. Application deadline: 4/15. Application fee: $25. *Expenses:* Tuition $2673 per year full-time, $99 per semester hour part-time for state residents; $10,692 per year full-time, $396 per semester hour part-time for nonresidents. Fees $228 per year. *Financial aid:* Scholarships available. Financial aid application deadline: 4/1. *Faculty research:* Play therapy, inner city elementary counseling programming. • Dr. Richard Smith, Chairman, Department of Counseling and Psychological Services, 404-651-2550.

Governors State University, College of Education, Division of Psychology and Counseling, Program in Counseling, University Park, IL 60466. Awards MA. Part-time and evening/weekend programs available. Faculty: 6 full-time (2 women), 3 part-time (2 women). In 1997, 19 degrees awarded. *Degree requirements:* Practicum required, foreign language and thesis not required. *Entrance requirements:* Minimum GPA of 2.5 in last 60 hours or GPA of 2.25 and GRE General Test (minimum combined score of 1050). Application deadline: 7/15 (priority date; rolling processing; 11/10 for spring admission). Application fee: $0. *Expenses:* Tuition $1140 per trimester full-time, $95 per credit hour part-time for state residents; $3420 per trimester full-time, $285 per credit hour part-time for nonresidents. Fees $95 per trimester. *Financial aid:* Full and partial tuition waivers, Federal Work-Study, institutionally sponsored loans, and career-related internships or fieldwork available. Aid available to part-time students. Financial aid application deadline: 5/1. • Dr. Addison Woodward, Chairperson, Division of Psychology and Counseling, 708-534-4840.

Gwynedd–Mercy College, Graduate Education Programs, Gwynedd Valley, PA 19437-0901. Offerings include mental health counseling (MS), school counseling (MS). Faculty: 4 full-time (all women), 11 part-time (7 women). *Degree requirements:* Thesis, internship, practicum

Directory: Counselor Education

Gwynedd–Mercy College (continued)

required, foreign language not required. *Average time to degree:* master's–3 years part-time. *Entrance requirements:* GRE or MAT. Application deadline: rolling. Application fee: $25. *Expenses:* Tuition $299 per credit. Fees $50 per year. • Dr. Lorraine Cavaliere, Dean, 215-641-5549. Application contact: Maureen Coyle, Program Administrator, 215-641-5561. Fax: 215-542-4695.

Hampton University, Program in Counseling, Hampton, VA 23668. Offers college student development (MA), community agency counseling (MA). Accredited by NCATE. Part-time and evening/weekend programs available. Faculty: 4 full-time (2 women), 2 part-time (0 women). Students: 28 full-time (22 women), 22 part-time (18 women); includes 46 minority (45 African Americans, 1 Native American), 2 international. In 1997, 12 degrees awarded. *Degree requirements:* Thesis optional, foreign language not required. *Entrance requirements:* GRE General Test (minimum score 450 on verbal section). Application deadline: 6/1 (priority date; rolling processing; 11/1 for spring admission). Application fee: $25. *Expenses:* Tuition $9038 per year full-time, $220 per credit part-time. Fees $70 per year. *Financial aid:* Fellowships, research assistantships, teaching assistantships, scholarships, Federal Work-Study, institutionally sponsored loans, and career-related internships or fieldwork available. Aid available to part-time students. Financial aid application deadline: 5/1; applicants required to submit FAFSA. • Dr. Wanda Mitchell, Coordinator, 757-727-5300. Application contact: Erika Henderson, Director, Graduate Programs, 757-727-5454. Fax: 757-727-5084.

Hardin–Simmons University, Irvin School of Education, Department of Counseling and Human Development, Abilene, TX 79698-0001. Awards M Ed. Part-time programs available. Faculty: 4 full-time (1 woman). Students: 23 full-time (15 women), 24 part-time (22 women); includes 7 minority (1 African American, 6 Hispanics), 1 international. Average age 34. In 1997, 17 degrees awarded. *Application deadline:* (1/5 for spring admission). *Application fee:* $25. *Expenses:* Tuition $280 per semester hour. Fees $630 per year full-time. *Financial aid:* In 1997–98, 45 students received aid, including 7 fellowships (2 to first-year students) averaging $250 per month and totaling $7,000; full and partial tuition waivers, Federal Work-Study, and career-related internships or fieldwork also available. Aid available to part-time students. Financial aid application deadline: 3/15; applicants required to submit FAFSA. *Faculty research:* Logotherapy as a psychological intervention. • Dr. Robert Barnes, Head, 915-670-1451. Fax: 915-670-5859. Application contact: Dr. J. Paul Sorrels, Dean of Graduate Studies, 915-670-1298. Fax: 915-670-1564.

Heidelberg College, Graduate Programs, Program in Counseling, Tiffin, OH 44883-2462. Awards MA. Part-time and evening/weekend programs available. Faculty: 4 full-time (2 women), 11 part-time (6 women). Students: 19 full-time (16 women), 142 part-time (106 women). Average age 37. In 1997, 25 degrees awarded (100% found work related to degree). *Degree requirements:* Counseling practicum, internship required, foreign language and thesis not required. *Average time to degree:* master's–2.5 years full-time, 4 years part-time. *Entrance requirements:* GRE General Test (minimum combined score of 1000), TOEFL (minimum score 550), 12 hours in behavioral science or psychology. Application deadline: rolling. Application fee: $20. *Tuition:* $250 per semester hour. *Financial aid:* Available to part-time students. Financial aid application deadline: 4/15; applicants required to submit FAFSA. • Dr. Gary Lacy, Graduate Director, 419-448-2300. Fax: 419-448-2124. E-mail: glacy@nike.heidelberg.edu.

Henderson State University, School of Education, Department of Counselor Education, Arkadelphia, AR 71999-0001. Offers programs in community counseling (MS), elementary school counseling (MSE), secondary school counseling (MSE). Accredited by NCATE. Part-time programs available. Students: 7 full-time (4 women), 62 part-time (50 women); includes 6 minority (all African Americans). Average age 35. 69 applicants, 100% accepted. In 1997, 15 degrees awarded. *Entrance requirements:* GRE General Test or MAT, minimum GPA of 2.7, teacher certification. Application deadline: 7/31 (priority date; rolling processing). Application fee: $0. Electronic applications accepted. *Expenses:* Tuition $120 per credit hour for state residents; $240 per credit hour for nonresidents. Fees $105 per semester (minimum) full-time, $52 per semester (minimum) part-time. *Financial aid:* Federal Work-Study, institutionally sponsored loans available. Aid available to part-time students. Financial aid application deadline: 7/31. • Dr. Charles Weiner, Chairperson, 870-230-5163. Fax: 870-230-5455. E-mail: weiner@holly.hsu.edu.

Heritage College, Graduate Program in Education, Program in Counseling, Toppenish, WA 98948-9599. Awards M Ed. *Degree requirements:* Comprehensive exam required, thesis optional, foreign language not required. *Application deadline:* rolling. *Application fee:* $35 ($75 for international students). *Tuition:* $270 per credit. • Application contact: Dr. Margaret Blue, Director, 509-865-2244.

Hofstra University, School of Education and Allied Human Services, Department of Counseling, Research, Special Education and Rehabilitation, Program in Counseling, Hempstead, NY 11549. Awards MS Ed, CAS, PD. Accredited by NCATE. Part-time and evening/weekend programs available. Faculty: 2 full-time (both women), 10 part-time (5 women). Students: 1 (woman) full-time, 63 part-time (52 women); includes 3 minority (2 African Americans, 1 Hispanic). Average age 26. 52 applicants, 48% accepted. In 1997, 32 master's awarded. *Degree requirements:* For master's, comprehensive exam, departmental qualifying exam required, foreign language and thesis not required. *Entrance requirements:* For master's, GRE General Test, interview; for other advanced degree, GRE General Test (minimum combined score of 1000), interview, minimum GPA of 3.0. Application deadline: rolling. Application fee: $40 ($75 for international students). *Expenses:* Tuition $10,968 per year full-time, $457 per credit hour part-time. Fees $670 per year full-time, $112 per semester (minimum) part-time. *Financial aid:* In 1997–98, 15 financial aid awards totaling $13,000 were awarded; Federal Work-Study, institutionally sponsored loans, and career-related internships or fieldwork also available. Aid available to part-time students. Financial aid application deadline: 6/1. *Faculty research:* Multicultural counseling, counseling at-risk youth, crisis interventions in schools, counceling children in families with cancer, counselor accountability. Total annual research expenditures: $1000. • Dr. Laurie Johnson, Coordinator, 516-463-5754. Fax: 516-463-6503. E-mail: cprlzj@hofstra.edu. Application contact: Mary Beth Carey, Dean of Admissions, 516-463-6700. Fax: 516-560-7660. E-mail: hofstra@hofstra.edu.

Houston Baptist University, College of Education and Behavioral Sciences, Programs in Education, Houston, TX 77074-3298. Offerings include counselor education (M Ed). Faculty: 9 full-time (5 women), 4 part-time (3 women). *Degree requirements:* Comprehensive exam required, foreign language and thesis not required. *Entrance requirements:* GRE General Test (minimum combined score of 850), minimum GPA of 2.5, teaching certificate. Application deadline: 7/1 (priority date; rolling processing; 1/1 for spring admission). Application fee: $25 ($85 for international students). *Expenses:* Tuition $280 per semester hour. Fees $235 per quarter. • Dr. John Lutjemeier, Head, 281-649-3000 Ext. 2336. Application contact: Judy Ferguson, Program Assistant, 281-649-3241.

Howard University, School of Education, Department of Human Development and Psychoeducational Studies, Program in Guidance and Counseling and Counseling Psychology, 2400 Sixth Street, NW, Washington, DC 20059-0002. Offers counseling psychology (MA, M Ed, Ed D, PhD, CAGS), guidance and counseling (MA, M Ed, CAGS). Accredited by NCATE. MA offered through the Graduate School of Arts and Sciences. Part-time programs available. Faculty: 15. Students: 108. In 1997, 21 master's, 5 doctorates awarded. *Degree requirements:* For master's, thesis or alternative, comprehensive exam, expository writing exam required, foreign language not required; for doctorate, 1 foreign language, dissertation, comprehensive exam, expository writing exam, internship. *Average time to degree:* master's–2 years full-time, 4 years part-time. *Entrance requirements:* For master's, GRE General Test, minimum GPA of 2.7; for doctorate, GRE General Test, minimum GPA of 3.4; for CAGS, GRE General Test, minimum graduate GPA of 3.0. Application deadline: 4/1 (priority date; rolling processing; 11/1 for spring admission). Application fee: $45. *Expenses:* Tuition $10,200 per year full-time, $567 per credit hour part-time. Fees $405 per year. *Financial aid:* Fellowships, research assistantships, teaching assistantships, grants, scholarships, full and partial tuition waivers, Federal Work-Study, institutionally sponsored loans, and career-related internships or fieldwork available. Financial aid application deadline: 4/30. • Dr. Aaron B. Stills, Coordinator, 202-806-7350.

Hunter College of the City University of New York, Division of Education, Department of Educational Foundations and Counseling Programs, Programs in Guidance and Counseling, 695 Park Avenue, New York, NY 10021-5085. Awards MS Ed. Part-time and evening/weekend programs available. *Degree requirements:* Audio tapes and papers from fieldwork required, foreign language and thesis not required. *Entrance requirements:* TOEFL (minimum score 575), interview, minimum GPA of 2.7. Application deadline: 4/7 (rolling processing; 11/7 for spring admission). Application fee: $40. *Expenses:* Tuition $4350 per year full-time, $185 per credit part-time for state residents; $7600 per year full-time, $320 per credit part-time for nonresidents. Fees $26 per year.

Idaho State University, College of Health Professions, Department of Counseling, Pocatello, ID 83209. Offerings include counseling (M Coun, Ed S), with options in counseling (Ed S), mental health counseling (M Coun), school counseling (M Coun), student affairs and college counseling (M Coun); counselor education and counseling (Ed D). One or more programs accredited by NCATE. Department faculty: 6 full-time (1 woman), 10 part-time (6 women). *Degree requirements:* For doctorate and Ed S, thesis/dissertation required, foreign language not required. *Entrance requirements:* For master's, GRE General Test, MAT, minimum GPA of 2.75; for doctorate, GRE General Test, MAT, minimum graduate GPA of 3.0; for Ed S, GRE General Test, minimum graduate GPA of 3.0. Application deadline: 2/15 (priority date; rolling processing). Application fee: $55. *Tuition:* $3130 per year full-time, $136 per credit hour part-time for state residents; $9370 per year full-time, $226 per credit hour part-time for nonresidents. • Dr. Virginia Allen, Chair, 208-236-3156.

Illinois State University, College of Education, Department of Specialized Educational Development, Program in Guidance and Counseling, Normal, IL 61790-2200. Awards MA, MS, MS Ed. Accredited by NCATE. Students: 8 full-time (7 women), 19 part-time (15 women); includes 4 minority (3 African Americans, 1 Native American). 0 applicants. In 1997, 19 degrees awarded. *Degree requirements:* Practicum required, thesis not required. *Entrance requirements:* GRE General Test (minimum combined score of 900), minimum GPA of 3.0 in last 60 hours, undergraduate major in related area. Application deadline: rolling. Application fee: $0. *Expenses:* Tuition $2454 per year full-time, $102 per hour part-time for state residents; $7362 per year full-time, $307 per hour part-time for nonresidents. Fees $1048 per year full-time, $44 per hour part-time. *Financial aid:* Teaching assistantships, full tuition waivers available. Financial aid application deadline: 4/1. • Dr. Paula Smith, Chairperson, Department of Specialized Educational Development, 309-438-5419.

Immaculata College, Graduate Division, Programs in Psychology, Immaculata, PA 19345-0500. Offerings include counseling psychology (MA, Certificate), with options in school guidance counselor (Certificate), school psychologist (Certificate). *Application fee:* $25 ($200 for international students). *Expenses:* Tuition $345 per credit (minimum). Fees $60 per year. • Dr. Jed A. Yalof, Chair, 610-647-4400 Ext. 3503. Application contact: Office of Graduate Admission, 610-647-4400 Ext. 3211.

Indiana State University, School of Education, Department of Counseling, Terre Haute, IN 47809-1401. Offers programs in agency counseling (MA, MS); college student personnel (MA, MS, PhD), including college student personnel work (MA, MS), student personnel work in higher education (PhD); counseling psychology (PhD); counselor education (PhD); guidance (PhD, Ed S); higher education (MA, MS); marriage and family counseling (MA, MS); school counseling (M Ed). Accredited by NCATE. One or more programs accredited by APA. Part-time and evening/weekend programs available. Faculty: 14 full-time (3 women), 1 (woman) part-time. Students: 80 full-time (54 women), 49 part-time (34 women); includes 16 minority (11 African Americans, 1 Asian American, 3 Hispanics, 1 Native American), 3 international. Average age 31. 148 applicants, 32% accepted. In 1997, 29 master's, 10 doctorates awarded. *Degree requirements:* For doctorate, 2 foreign languages, computer language, dissertation. *Entrance requirements:* For master's, minimum undergraduate GPA of 2.5; for doctorate, GRE General Test (minimum score 500 on each section), master's degree, minimum undergraduate GPA of 3.5; for Ed S, GRE General Test (minimum combined score of 900), minimum graduate GPA of 3.25. Application deadline: 2/15 (rolling processing). Application fee: $20. *Tuition:* $143 per credit hour for state residents; $325 per credit hour for nonresidents. *Financial aid:* In 1997–98, 19 fellowships (1 to a first-year student), 22 research assistantships (8 to first-year students), 2 teaching assistantships were awarded; career-related internships or fieldwork also available. Financial aid application deadline: 3/1. *Faculty research:* Vocational development supervision. • Dr. William Osmon, Chairperson, 812-237-2868.

Indiana University Bloomington, School of Education, Department of Counseling and Educational Psychology, Program in Counseling Psychology, Bloomington, IN 47405. Offerings include counseling/counselor education (MS, Ed S). Accredited by NCATE. *Degree requirements:* For master's, thesis optional, foreign language not required; for Ed S, comprehensive exam or project required, foreign language and thesis not required. *Entrance requirements:* GRE General Test (minimum combined score of 1300 on three sections). Application deadline: 6/1. Application fee: $35. *Expenses:* Tuition $153 per credit hour for state residents; $446 per credit hour for nonresidents. Fees $343 per year. • Dr. Jack Cummings, Chairperson, Department of Counseling and Educational Psychology, 812-856-8300. Application contact: Brenda Helms, Administrative Assistant, 812-856-8300. Fax: 812-856-8333.

Indiana University of Pennsylvania, College of Education, Department of Counseling, Indiana, PA 15705-1087. Offers programs in community counseling (MA), counseling services (MA), counselor education (M Ed). Accredited by NCATE. Part-time and evening/weekend programs available. Students: 52 full-time (44 women), 66 part-time (48 women); includes 3 minority (all African Americans), 3 international. Average age 29. 42 applicants, 55% accepted. In 1997, 28 degrees awarded. *Degree requirements:* Thesis optional, foreign language not required. *Entrance requirements:* TOEFL (minimum score 500). Application deadline: 7/1 (priority date; rolling processing; 11/1 for spring admission). Application fee: $30. *Expenses:* Tuition $3468 per year full-time, $193 per credit part-time for state residents; $6236 per year full-time, $346 per credit part-time for nonresidents. Fees $313 per year (minimum) full-time, $84 per year part-time. *Financial aid:* Research assistantships, Federal Work-Study, and career-related internships or fieldwork available. Aid available to part-time students. Financial aid application deadline: 3/15. • Dr. Claire Dandeneau, Chairperson and Graduate Coordinator, 724-357-2306. E-mail: cdanden@grove.iup.edu.

Indiana University–Purdue University Fort Wayne, School of Education, Program in Counselor Education, Fort Wayne, IN 46805-1499. Awards MS Ed. Accredited by NCATE. Evening/weekend programs available. Faculty: 2 full-time (0 women), 4 part-time (2 women), 3 FTE. Students: 1 full-time (0 women), 67 part-time (52 women); includes 3 minority (all African Americans). Average age 36. 33 applicants, 91% accepted. In 1997, 19 degrees awarded (100% found work related to degree). *Entrance requirements:* Minimum GPA of 2.5. Application deadline: 8/1 (priority date; rolling processing; 12/1 for spring admission). Application fee: $30. *Expenses:* Tuition $2356 per year full-time, $131 per credit hour part-time for state residents; $5253 per year full-time, $292 per credit hour part-time for nonresidents. Fees $183 per year full-time, $10.15 per credit hour part-time. *Financial aid:* Application deadline 3/1. • Betty Steffy, Dean, School of Education, 219-481-6456. Fax: 219-481-6083.

Indiana University–Purdue University Indianapolis, School of Education, Department of Counseling and Counselor Education, Indianapolis, IN 46202-2896. Awards MS. Faculty: 4 full-time (1 woman), 5 part-time (2 women). Students: 13 full-time (9 women), 66 part-time (53 women); includes 7 minority (6 African Americans, 1 Hispanic), 1 international. Average age 34. In 1997, 25 degrees awarded. *Entrance requirements:* GRE General Test (minimum combined score of 1300; average 1500), minimum GPA of 3.0. Application deadline: 3/1 (priority date; 11/1 for spring admission). Application fee: $35. *Expenses:* Tuition $3602 per year full-time, $150 per credit hour part-time for state residents; $10,392 per year full-time,

$433 per credit hour part-time for nonresidents. Fees $100 per year (minimum) full-time, $40 per year (minimum) part-time. *Financial aid:* Federal Work-Study available. *Faculty research:* Counseling techniques, interactive video applications, family and marriage, school counseling. • Keith Morran, Coordinator, 317-274-6850. Application contact: Dr. O. Gilbert Brown, Assistant Dean for Education Student Services, 317-274-0649. Fax: 317-274-6864. E-mail: ogbrown@iupui.edu.

Indiana University South Bend, Division of Education, Department of Counseling and Human Services, South Bend, IN 46634-7111. Awards MS Ed. Accredited by NCATE. Part-time and evening/weekend programs available. Faculty: 4 full-time (1 woman), 6 part-time (2 women), 6 FTE. Students: 27 part-time (21 women); includes 6 minority (5 African Americans, 1 Asian American), 1 international. Average age 37. 48 applicants, 58% accepted. In 1997, 22 degrees awarded. *Degree requirements:* Thesis or alternative, exit project required, foreign language not required. *Entrance requirements:* TOEFL (minimum score 550). Application deadline: rolling. Application fee: $35 ($40 for international students). *Expenses:* Tuition $3024 per year full-time, $126 per credit hour part-time for state residents; $7320 per year full-time, $305 per credit hour part-time for nonresidents. Fees $222 per year full-time, $34 per semester (minimum) part-time. *Financial aid:* Federal Work-Study available. Financial aid application deadline: 3/1. *Faculty research:* Counselor education textbook. • Dr. J. Vincent Peterson, Director, 219-237-4403. Fax: 219-237-4590. E-mail: vpeterson@iusb.edu. Application contact: Graduate Director, 219-237-4183. Fax: 219-237-6549.

Indiana University Southeast, Division of Education, Program in Counselor Education, New Albany, IN 47150-6405. Awards MS Ed. Accredited by NCATE. Part-time programs available. Faculty: 2 full-time (both women), 3 part-time (2 women). Students: 32 part-time (25 women); includes 1 international. Average age 32. 22 applicants, 100% accepted. In 1997, 17 degrees awarded (100% found work related to degree). *Degree requirements:* Thesis or alternative, internship, practicum required, foreign language not required. *Entrance requirements:* Appropriate bachelor's degree, minimum GPA of 2.75. Application deadline: 6/1 (rolling processing). Application fee: $28. *Expenses:* Tuition $125 per credit hour (minimum) for state residents; $284 per credit hour (minimum) for nonresidents. Fees $33 per year full-time, $2.75 per credit hour part-time. *Financial aid:* Institutionally sponsored loans and career-related internships or fieldwork available. Aid available to part-time students. Financial aid application deadline: 3/1; applicants required to submit FAFSA. *Faculty research:* Group work with children, group work training. Total annual research expenditures: $5000. • Dr. Teesue H. Fields, Coordinator, 812-941-2658. Fax: 812-941-2667. E-mail: thfields@iusmail.indiana.edu.

Indiana Wesleyan University, Program in Counseling, Marion, IN 46953-4999. Awards MA. Faculty: 4 full-time (1 woman). In 1997, 2 degrees awarded. *Application fee:* $10. *Tuition:* $402 per hour. *Financial aid:* In 1997–98, 1 teaching assistantship was awarded. • Dr. Jerry Davis, Director of Graduate Counseling Studies, 765-677-2995.

Inter American University of Puerto Rico, Metropolitan Campus, Division of Education, Program in Guidance and Counseling, San Juan, PR 00919-1293. Awards MA. Students: 11 full-time (8 women), 82 part-time (64 women); includes 93 minority (all Hispanics). In 1997, 23 degrees awarded. *Degree requirements:* Comprehensive exam required, foreign language and thesis not required. *Entrance requirements:* GRE or PAEG, interview. Application deadline: 5/15 (priority date; rolling processing; 11/15 for spring admission). Application fee: $31. Electronic applications accepted. *Expenses:* Tuition $3272 per year full-time, $1740 per year part-time. Fees $328 per year full-time, $176 per year part-time. *Financial aid:* Federal Work-Study available. Aid available to part-time students. • Dr. Amalia Charneco, Director, Division of Education, 787-758-5652. Application contact: Jenny Maldonado, Administrative Assistant, 787-250-1912 Ext. 2393. Fax: 787-250-1197.

Inter American University of Puerto Rico, San Germán Campus, Department of Education, Program in Guidance and Counseling, San Germán, PR 00683-5008. Awards MA Ed. Part-time and evening/weekend programs available. Faculty: 8 full-time (1 woman), 13 part-time (7 women). In 1997, 30 degrees awarded. *Degree requirements:* Comprehensive exam required, foreign language and thesis not required. *Entrance requirements:* Minimum GPA of 3.0, GRE General Test, or PAEG. Application deadline: 4/30 (priority date; rolling processing; 11/15 for spring admission). Application fee: $31. *Expenses:* Tuition $150 per credit. Fees $177 per semester. *Financial aid:* Teaching assistantships available. • Application contact: Mildred Camacho, Admissions Director, 787-892-3090. Fax: 787-892-6350.

Iowa State University of Science and Technology, College of Education, Department of Educational Leadership and Policy Studies, Program in Counselor Education, Ames, IA 50011. Awards MS. *Degree requirements:* Thesis or alternative. *Entrance requirements:* TOEFL. Application fee: $20 ($30 for international students). *Expenses:* Tuition $3166 per year full-time, $176 per credit part-time for state residents; $9324 per year full-time, $518 per credit part-time for nonresidents. Fees $200 per year. • Dr. John M. Littrell, Coordinator, 515-294-5746. E-mail: jlittrel@iastate.edu.

Jackson State University, School of Education, Department of Counseling and Human Resource Education, Jackson, MS 39217. Offers programs in community and agency counseling (MS), including rehabilitation services; guidance and counseling (MS, MS Ed, Ed S). Accredited by NCATE. Part-time and evening/weekend programs available. Faculty: 5 full-time (2 women), 2 part-time (1 woman). Students: 60 full-time (49 women), 83 part-time (62 women); includes 137 minority (all African Americans). 63 applicants, 73% accepted. In 1997, 30 master's, 1 Ed S awarded. *Degree requirements:* For master's, thesis or alternative, comprehensive exam. *Entrance requirements:* For master's, GRE General Test (minimum combined score of 1000), TOEFL (minimum score 550). Application deadline: 3/1 (priority date; rolling processing; 10/1 for spring admission). Application fee: $20. *Tuition:* $2688 per year (minimum) full-time, $150 per semester hour part-time for state residents; $5546 per year (minimum) full-time, $309 per semester hour part-time for nonresidents. *Financial aid:* Federal Work-Study available. Financial aid application deadline: 3/1. • Dr. Walter Crockett, Chair, 601-968-2361. Fax: 601-968-2213. Application contact: Mae Robinson, Admissions Coordinator, 601-968-2455. Fax: 601-968-8246. E-mail: mrobinson@ccaix.jsums.edu.

Jacksonville State University, College of Education, Program in Guidance and Counseling, Jacksonville, AL 36265-9982. Awards MS. Accredited by NCATE. Faculty: 3 full-time (2 women). Students: 51 full-time (39 women), 122 part-time (95 women); includes 69 minority (67 African Americans, 2 Hispanics). In 1997, 45 degrees awarded. *Degree requirements:* Thesis optional. *Entrance requirements:* GRE General Test or MAT. Application deadline: rolling. Application fee: $20. *Expenses:* Tuition $2140 per year full-time, $107 per semester hour part-time for state residents; $4280 per year full-time, $214 per semester hour part-time for nonresidents. Fees $30 per semester. *Financial aid:* Available to part-time students. Financial aid application deadline: 4/1. • Application contact: College of Graduate Studies and Continuing Education, 205-782-5329.

John Brown University, Department of Counselor Education, Siloam Springs, AR 72761-2121. Offers programs in licensed professional counseling (MS), marriage and family therapy (MS), school counseling (MS). Part-time and evening/weekend programs available. Faculty: 1 full-time (0 women), 7 part-time (2 women), 2.16 FTE. Students: 21 full-time (15 women), 2 part-time (both women); includes 1 minority (Hispanic). Average age 32. In 1997, 15 degrees awarded (93% found work related to degree, 7% continued full-time study). *Average time to degree:* master's–2.5 years full-time. *Entrance requirements:* GRE General Test (minimum combined score of 900), MAT (minimum score 35), minimum GPA of 3.0. Application deadline: 8/15 (priority date; rolling processing). Application fee: $25. *Tuition:* $420 per credit hour. • Dr. James D. Worthington, Chair, 501-524-7147. Fax: 501-524-9548. E-mail: jdworthi@acc.jbu.edu. Application contact: Gil Pineira, Graduate Admissions Counselor, 501-524-7169. Fax: 501-524-4196. E-mail: gpineira@adm.jbu.edu.

John Carroll University, Program in Counseling and Human Services, University Heights, OH 44118-4581. Offers clinical counseling (Certificate), counseling (MA). Part-time and evening/weekend programs available. Faculty: 7 full-time (4 women), 18 part-time (10 women), 10 FTE. Students: 31 full-time (30 women), 120 part-time (100 women); includes 7 minority (6 African Americans, 1 Asian American). Average age 35. 52 applicants, 96% accepted. In 1997, 39 master's awarded. *Degree requirements:* For master's, comprehensive exam, internship, practicum required, foreign language and thesis not required. *Average time to degree:* master's–2 years full-time, 3.5 years part-time. *Entrance requirements:* For master's, MAT (average 52), minimum GPA of 2.75. Application deadline: 8/15 (priority date; rolling processing; 1/3 for spring admission). Application fee: $25 ($35 for international students). *Tuition:* $450 per credit. *Financial aid:* In 1997–98, 1 student received aid, including 1 assistantship (to a first-year student); institutionally sponsored loans and career-related internships or fieldwork also available. Financial aid application deadline: 3/1; applicants required to submit FAFSA. *Faculty research:* Child and adolescent development, HIV, clinical hypnosis, wellness, women's issues. • Dr. Christopher M. Faiver, Coordinator, 216-397-3001. E-mail: faiver@jcvaxa.jcu.edu.

John Carroll University, Department of Education and Allied Studies, Program in Guidance and Counseling, University Heights, OH 44118-4581. Awards MA, M Ed. Accredited by NCATE. Faculty: 4 full-time (2 women), 6 part-time (5 women). Students: 3 full-time (2 women), 40 part-time (32 women); includes 9 minority (all African Americans). In 1997, 19 degrees awarded. *Degree requirements:* Comprehensive exam, research essay or thesis required, foreign language not required. *Entrance requirements:* GRE General Test or MAT, minimum GPA of 2.75. Application deadline: 8/15 (priority date; rolling processing; 1/3 for spring admission). Application fee: $25 ($35 for international students). *Tuition:* $450 per credit. *Financial aid:* Partial tuition waivers available. Financial aid application deadline: 3/1; applicants required to submit FAFSA. • Dr. Christopher M. Faiver, Coordinator, 216-397-4331.

Johns Hopkins University, School of Continuing Studies, Division of Education, Department of Counseling and Human Services, Baltimore, MD 21218-2699. Offers programs in addictions counseling (Certificate), career counseling (Certificate), counseling (MS, Ed D, CAGS), counseling at-risk students (Certificate), organizations and counseling (Certificate). *Degree requirements:* For doctorate, dissertation, comprehensive exam required, foreign language not required. *Entrance requirements:* For master's, minimum GPA of 3.0, interview; for doctorate, MAT, interview, master's degree, minimum GPA of 3.25; for other advanced degree, master's or doctoral degree. Application fee: $50. • Mark Ginsberg, Chair, 410-516-7928.

Johnson State College, Graduate Program in Education, Program in Counseling, Johnson, VT 05656-9405. Awards MA. Part-time programs available. Faculty: 5 full-time (2 women), 5 part-time (4 women). Students: 38 full-time (28 women), 55 part-time (35 women). *Degree requirements:* Comprehensive exam required, foreign language and thesis not required. *Entrance requirements:* Interview. Application deadline: 4/1 (priority date; 11/1 for spring admission). Application fee: $30. *Expenses:* Tuition $164 per credit for state residents; $383 per credit for nonresidents. Fees $15.90 per credit. *Financial aid:* Federal Work-Study, institutionally sponsored loans, and career-related internships or fieldwork available. Financial aid application deadline: 3/1; applicants required to submit FAFSA. • Application contact: Catherine H. Higley, Administrative Assistant, 802-635-2356 Ext. 1244. Fax: 802-635-1248. E-mail: higleyc@badger.jsc.vsc.edu.

Kansas State University, College of Education, Department of Counseling and Educational Psychology, Manhattan, KS 66506. Offers programs in counselor education (Ed D, PhD), educational psychology (Ed D), school counseling (MS), student affairs in higher education (PhD), student personnel services (MS). Accredited by NCATE. Faculty: 8 full-time (1 woman), 3 part-time (1 woman), 8.9 FTE. Students: 16 full-time (11 women), 72 part-time (51 women); includes 3 minority (1 African American, 2 Hispanics), 3 international. 46 applicants, 57% accepted. *Degree requirements:* For master's, thesis or alternative required, foreign language not required; for doctorate, dissertation required, foreign language not required. *Entrance requirements:* For master's, GRE General Test (minimum combined score of 1000; average 1021), MAT (minimum score 40; average 48), minimum B average; for doctorate, GRE General Test (minimum combined score of 1000; average 1106), minimum B average. Application deadline: 3/1 (priority date; rolling processing; 8/1 for spring admission). Application fee: $0 ($25 for international students). Electronic applications accepted. *Tuition:* $2218 per year full-time, $401 per semester (minimum) part-time for state residents; $6336 per year full-time, $1087 per semester (minimum) part-time for nonresidents. *Financial aid:* In 1997–98, teaching assistantships averaging $850 per month were awarded; research assistantships also available. • Michael Dannells, Chair, 785-532-5541. Application contact: Paul Burden, Assistant Dean, 785-532-5595. Fax: 785-532-7304. E-mail: gradstudy@mail.educ.ksu.edu.

Kean University, School of Education, Department of Special Education and Individualized Services, Program in Counselor Education, Union, NJ 07083. Offers alcohol and drug abuse counseling (MA), business and industry counseling (MA, PMC), community/agency counseling (MA), school counseling (MA). Accredited by NCATE. PMC offered jointly with the Department of Psychology. Part-time programs available. Students: 17 full-time (13 women), 110 part-time (96 women); includes 14 minority (7 African Americans, 2 Asian Americans, 4 Hispanics, 1 Native American). Average age 34. In 1997, 33 master's awarded. *Degree requirements:* For master's, thesis, comprehensive exams required, foreign language not required. *Entrance requirements:* For master's, GRE General Test or MAT. Application deadline: 6/15 (11/15 for spring admission). Application fee: $35. *Tuition:* $5926 per year full-time, $248 per credit part-time for state residents; $7312 per year full-time, $304 per credit part-time for nonresidents. *Financial aid:* Graduate assistantships and career-related internships or fieldwork available. • Dr. Betty Dodd, Coordinator, 908-527-2264. Application contact: Joanne Morris, Director of Graduate Admissions, 908-527-2665. Fax: 908-527-2286. E-mail: grad_adm@turbo.kean.edu.

Keene State College, Program in Counseling and Consultation, Keene, NH 03435. Awards M Ed. Part-time and evening/weekend programs available. Students: 4 full-time (all women), 25 part-time (19 women). Average age 43. 13 applicants, 100% accepted. In 1997, 7 degrees awarded. *Degree requirements:* Project required, foreign language and thesis not required. *Entrance requirements:* Resume. Application deadline: 6/15 (rolling processing; 10/15 for spring admission). Application fee: $25 ($35 for international students). *Financial aid:* Research assistantships, Federal Work-Study, institutionally sponsored loans, and career-related internships or fieldwork available. Financial aid application deadline: 3/1; applicants required to submit FAFSA. • Dr. Karen Abrams, Coordinator, 603-358-2862. Application contact: Peter Tandy, Academic Counselor, 603-358-2332. Fax: 603-358-2257. E-mail: ptandy@keene.edu.

Kent State University, Graduate School of Education, Department of Adult, Counseling, Health and Vocational Education, Program in Community Counseling, Kent, OH 44242-0001. Offers community counseling (MA, M Ed), counseling (Ed S). Accredited by NCATE. Students: 94 full-time (73 women), 42 part-time (33 women); includes 11 minority (all African Americans), 2 international. In 1997, 28 master's awarded. *Degree requirements:* For master's, thesis (MA) required, foreign language not required. *Application deadline:* rolling. *Application fee:* $30. *Tuition:* $4752 per year full-time, $216 per credit hour part-time for state residents; $9213 per year full-time, $419 per credit hour part-time for nonresidents. *Financial aid:* Application deadline 4/1. • Dr. Ferguson B. Meadows Jr., Associate Professor, 330-672-2662. E-mail: fmeadows@emerald.educ.kent.edu. Application contact: Deborah Barber, Director, Office of Academic Services, 330-672-2862. Fax: 330-672-3549.

Kent State University, Graduate School of Education, Department of Adult, Counseling, Health and Vocational Education, Program in Counseling and Human Development Services, Kent, OH 44242-0001. Offers counseling (Ed S), counseling and human development services (PhD). Accredited by NCATE. Faculty: 10 full-time (5 women), 17 part-time (7 women). Students: 59 full-time (40 women), 48 part-time (30 women); includes 18 minority (16 African Americans, 1 Hispanic, 1 Native American), 3 international. In 1997, 15 doctorates awarded. *Degree requirements:* For doctorate, dissertation required, foreign language not required. *Entrance requirements:* For doctorate, GRE General Test (minimum score 550 on verbal section). Application deadline: rolling. Application fee: $30. *Tuition:* $4752 per year full-time,

Directory: Counselor Education

Kent State University (continued)
$216 per credit hour part-time for state residents; $9213 per year full-time, $419 per credit hour part-time for nonresidents. *Financial aid:* Application deadline 4/1. • Dr. John West, Coordinator, 330-672-2662. Application contact: Deborah Barber, Director, Office of Academic Services, 330-672-2862. Fax: 330-672-3549.

Kent State University, Graduate School of Education, Department of Adult, Counseling, Health and Vocational Education, Program in School Counseling, Kent, OH 44242-0001. Offers counseling (Ed S), school counseling (MA, M Ed). Accredited by NCATE. Students: 5 full-time (4 women), 45 part-time (35 women); includes 5 minority (3 African Americans, 1 Hispanic, 1 Native American). In 1997, 23 master's awarded. *Degree requirements:* For master's, thesis (MA) required, foreign language not required. *Application deadline:* rolling. *Application fee:* $30. *Tuition:* $4752 per year full-time, $216 per credit hour part-time for state residents; $9213 per year full-time, $419 per credit hour part-time for nonresidents. *Financial aid:* Application deadline 4/1. • Dr. Ferguson B. Meadows Jr., Associate Professor, 330-672-2662. E-mail: fmeadows@emerald.educ.kent.edu. Application contact: Deborah Barber, Director, Office of Academic Services, 330-672-2862. Fax: 330-672-3549.

Kutztown University of Pennsylvania, Graduate School, College of Education, Program in Guidance and Counseling, Kutztown, PA 19530. Offers counselor education (M Ed), including elementary counseling, secondary counseling. Accredited by NCATE. Part-time and evening/weekend programs available. Faculty: 7 full-time (4 women). Students: 12 full-time (10 women), 56 part-time (45 women); includes 1 African American, 1 Hispanic. Average age 33. In 1997, 10 degrees awarded. *Degree requirements:* Comprehensive exam required, thesis optional, foreign language not required. *Entrance requirements:* GRE General Test, TOEFL, TSE, interview. Application deadline: 3/1 (8/1 for spring admission). Application fee: $25. *Tuition:* $4111 per year full-time, $225 per credit hour part-time for state residents; $6879 per year full-time, $393 per credit hour part-time for nonresidents. *Financial aid:* Graduate assistantships, partial tuition waivers, Federal Work-Study, and career-related internships or fieldwork available. Financial aid application deadline: 3/15; applicants required to submit FAFSA. *Faculty research:* Family addictions, family roles. • Dr. Margaret A. Herrick, Chairperson, 610-683-4204.

Lamar University, College of Education and Human Development, Department of Educational Leadership, Program in Counseling and Development, Beaumont, TX 77710. Awards M Ed. Faculty: 2 full-time (1 woman), 1 (woman) part-time. Students: 60 full-time (46 women), 27 part-time (22 women); includes 10 minority (5 African Americans, 4 Hispanics, 1 Native American). Average age 40. In 1997, 20 degrees awarded. *Degree requirements:* Thesis optional, foreign language not required. *Average time to degree:* master's–2 years full-time, 3.5 years part-time. *Entrance requirements:* GRE General Test (minimum combined score of 900), TOEFL (minimum score 500), minimum GPA of 2.5. Application deadline: 8/1 (rolling processing; 12/1 for spring admission). Application fee: $0. *Expenses:* Tuition $1296 per year full-time, $360 per year part-time for state residents; $6432 per year full-time, $1608 per year part-time for nonresidents. Fees $238 per year full-time, $103 per year part-time. *Financial aid:* In 1997–98, 2 fellowships were awarded. Financial aid application deadline: 4/1. • Dr. Carolyn Crawford, Chair, Department of Educational Leadership, 409-880-8689.

La Sierra University, School of Education, Department of Educational Psychology and Counseling, Riverside, CA 92515-8247. Offers programs in counseling (MA), educational psychology (Ed S), school psychology (Ed S). Part-time and evening/weekend programs available. Faculty: 3 full-time (1 woman), 4 part-time (2 women), 4 FTE. Students: 27. Average age 35. In 1997, 4 master's, 4 Ed Ss awarded. *Degree requirements:* For master's, thesis optional, foreign language not required; for Ed S, practicum (educational psychology) required, foreign language and thesis not required. *Entrance requirements:* For master's, California Basic Educational Skills Test, NTE, minimum GPA of 3.0; for Ed S, minimum GPA of 3.3. Application deadline: rolling. Application fee: $30. *Financial aid:* Graduate assistantships, Federal Work-Study, institutionally sponsored loans, and career-related internships or fieldwork available. Aid available to part-time students. Financial aid application deadline: 2/10. *Faculty research:* Equivalent score scales, self perception. • Dr. Roger Handysides, Chair, 909-785-2267. Application contact: Myrna Costa-Casado, Director of Admissions, 909-785-2176. Fax: 909-785-2447. E-mail: mcosta@lasierra.edu.

Lehigh University, College of Education, Department of Education and Human Services, Program in Counseling Psychology, Bethlehem, PA 18015-3094. Offerings include counseling and human services (M Ed), school counseling (M Ed, Certificate). Program faculty: 4 full-time (2 women), 5 part-time (4 women). *Entrance requirements:* For master's, GRE General Test or MAT, TOEFL, minimum GPA of 2.75; for Certificate, TOEFL (minimum score 550). Application deadline: 2/1. Application fee: $40. Electronic applications accepted. *Expenses:* Tuition $470 per credit. Fees $12 per semester full-time, $6 per semester part-time. • Dr. April E. Metzler, Coordinator, 610-758-6093. Fax: 610-758-6223. E-mail: aem3@lehigh.edu.

Lehman College of the City University of New York, Division of Education, Department of Specialized Services in Education, Program in Guidance and Counseling, 250 Bedford Park Boulevard West, Bronx, NY 10468-1589. Awards MS Ed. Part-time and evening/weekend programs available. Faculty: 3 full-time (2 women). Students: 111 part-time (92 women). Average age 34. *Degree requirements:* Thesis. *Entrance requirements:* Minimum GPA of 2.7. Application deadline: 4/1 (priority date; rolling processing; 11/1 for spring admission). Application fee: $40. *Expenses:* Tuition $4350 per year full-time, $185 per credit part-time for state residents; $7600 per year full-time, $320 per credit part-time for nonresidents. Fees $120 per year full-time, $80 per year part-time. *Financial aid:* Full and partial tuition waivers, Federal Work-Study available. Aid available to part-time students. Financial aid application deadline: 5/15; applicants required to submit FAFSA. *Faculty research:* Crisis intervention, domestic violence, alcohol abuse, gender issues. • Faith Deveaux, Adviser, 718-960-8173.

Lenoir–Rhyne College, Division of Graduate Programs, Department of Education, Program in Guidance and Counseling, Hickory, NC 28601. Offers counselor education (MA, Ed S). Part-time and evening/weekend programs available. Students: 11 full-time (10 women), 70 part-time (61 women); includes 1 international. Average age 29. In 1997, 25 master's awarded. *Degree requirements:* For master's, internship required, thesis optional, foreign language not required; for Ed S, thesis, internship required, foreign language not required. *Entrance requirements:* For master's, GRE General Test (minimum score 450 on verbal section, 1350 combined), minimum GPA of 2.7; for Ed S, GRE General Test (minimum score 450 on verbal section, 900 combined), minimum GPA of 3.0. Application deadline: 8/1 (12/1 for spring admission). Application fee: $25. *Tuition:* $190 per credit hour. *Financial aid:* Career-related internships or fieldwork available. • Dr. Martha Rhyne-Winkler, Head, 828-328-7221. Application contact: Dr. Thomas W. Fauquet, Dean of Graduate Studies, 828-328-7275. Fax: 828-328-7368. E-mail: fauquet@lrc.edu.

Lincoln University, Graduate School, College of Arts and Sciences, Department of Education, Jefferson City, MO 65102. Offerings include guidance and counseling (M Ed), with options in agency, elementary, secondary. Accredited by NCATE. Department faculty: 2 full-time (0 women), 10 part-time (6 women). *Entrance requirements:* GRE General Test or MAT, minimum GPA of 2.75 in major, 2.5 overall. Application deadline: 7/25 (rolling processing; 12/15 for spring admission). Application fee: $17. *Expenses:* Tuition $117 per credit hour for state residents; $234 per credit hour for nonresidents. Fees $552 per year (minimum) for state residents; $1104 per year (minimum) for nonresidents. • Dr. Marilyn Hofmann, Acting Head, 573-681-5250.

Long Island University, Brooklyn Campus, School of Education, Department of Counseling and Development, Brooklyn, NY 11201-8423. Offers programs in alcoholism counseling (Certificate), counseling and development (MS Ed), family counseling (MS), gerontological counseling (Certificate). Part-time and evening/weekend programs available. Faculty: 4 full-time (1 woman), 7 part-time (3 women). Students: 114 full-time (94 women), 115 part-time (90 women); includes 157 minority (116 African Americans, 6 Asian Americans, 32 Hispanics, 3 Native Americans). 170 applicants, 92% accepted. In 1997, 76 master's awarded. *Degree requirements:* For master's, thesis optional, foreign language not required. *Application deadline:* rolling. *Application fee:* $30. Electronic applications accepted. *Expenses:* Tuition $480 per credit. Fees $415 per year full-time, $73 per semester (minimum) part-time. *Financial aid:* Career-related internships or fieldwork available. • Dr. Stanley Nass, Chair, 718-488-1069. Application contact: Bernard W. Sullivan, Associate Director of Admissions, 718-488-1011.

Long Island University, C.W. Post Campus, School of Education, Department of Counseling and Development, Brookville, NY 11548-1300. Offers programs in college student development counseling (MS), mental health counseling (MS), school counseling (MS). Part-time and evening/weekend programs available. Faculty: 9 full-time (4 women), 12 part-time (5 women). Students: 56 full-time, 200 part-time. 111 applicants, 58% accepted. In 1997, 114 degrees awarded. *Degree requirements:* Comprehensive exam or thesis required, foreign language not required. *Entrance requirements:* Interview; minimum GPA of 3.25 in major, 3.0 overall. Application deadline: 7/15 (rolling processing; 10/15 for spring admission). Application fee: $30. Electronic applications accepted. *Expenses:* Tuition $480 per credit. Fees $316 per year full-time, $71 per semester (minimum) part-time. *Financial aid:* In 1997–98, 8 research assistantships were awarded; career-related internships or fieldwork also available. Financial aid application deadline: 5/15; applicants required to submit FAFSA. *Faculty research:* Alcohol studies, hypnocounseling, women's issues, holistic counseling. • Dr. A. Scott McGowan, Chairperson, 516-299-2814. Application contact: Fran Riordan, Academic Counselor, 516-299-2183. Fax: 516-299-4167. E-mail: friordan@eagle.liunet.edu.

Longwood College, Department of Education, Farmville, VA 23909-1800. Offerings include community and college counseling (MS), guidance and counseling (MS). One or more programs accredited by NCATE. Department faculty: 34 part-time. *Degree requirements:* Thesis (for some programs), comprehensive exam. *Entrance requirements:* Minimum GPA of 2.5. Application deadline: 5/1 (priority date; rolling processing; 10/15 for spring admission). Application fee: $25. *Expenses:* Tuition $3048 per year full-time, $127 per credit hour part-time for state residents; $8160 per year full-time, $340 per credit hour part-time for nonresidents. Fees $920 per year full-time, $31 per credit hour part-time. • Dr. Frank Howe, Chair, 804-395-2324. Application contact: Admissions Office, 804-395-2060.

Loras College, Program in Counseling: Elementary and Secondary, Dubuque, IA 52004-0178. Awards MA. Faculty: 3. Students: 16. *Application deadline:* rolling. *Application fee:* $25. *Tuition:* $320 per credit. • Dr. James Allan, Chair, 319-588-7157. Application contact: Office of Admissions, 319-588-7236. Fax: 319-588-7964.

Louisiana State University and Agricultural and Mechanical College, College of Education, Department of Administrative and Foundational Services, Baton Rouge, LA 70803. Offerings include counseling (MA, M Ed, Ed S). Accredited by NCATE. Department faculty: 16 full-time (5 women), 1 part-time (0 women). *Degree requirements:* For Ed S, thesis optional, foreign language not required. *Entrance requirements:* For master's, GRE General Test (minimum combined score of 1000; average 1080), minimum GPA of 3.0. Application deadline: 1/25 (priority date; rolling processing). Application fee: $25. *Tuition:* $2736 per year full-time, $285 per semester (minimum) part-time for state residents; $6636 per year full-time, $460 per semester (minimum) part-time for nonresidents. • Barbara Fuhrmann, Chair, 504-388-6900. Application contact: Jim Fox, Graduate Adviser, 504-388-6933. Fax: 504-388-6918.

Louisiana Tech University, College of Education, Department of Behavioral Sciences, Ruston, LA 71272. Offerings include counseling (MA, Ed S). Accredited by NCATE. Department faculty: 14 full-time (4 women). *Degree requirements:* For master's, computer language, thesis or alternative required, foreign language not required. *Entrance requirements:* For master's, GRE General Test. Application deadline: 7/29 (2/3 for spring admission). Application fee: $20 ($30 for international students). *Tuition:* $2382 per year full-time, $223 per quarter (minimum) part-time for state residents; $5307 per year full-time, $223 per quarter (minimum) part-time for nonresidents. • Dr. JoAnn Dauzat, Acting Head, 318-257-4315.

Loyola College, College of Arts and Sciences, Department of Education, Program in Guidance and Counseling, Baltimore, MD 21210-2699. Awards MA, M Ed, CAS. Part-time and evening/weekend programs available. Students: 37 full-time (32 women), 166 part-time (135 women); includes 25 minority (21 African Americans, 1 Asian American, 3 Hispanics), 1 international. In 1997, 78 master's, 1 CAS awarded. *Entrance requirements:* For CAS, master's degree. Application deadline: 8/1 (rolling processing; 12/1 for spring admission). Application fee: $35. *Tuition:* $222 per credit (minimum). *Financial aid:* Career-related internships or fieldwork available. • Dr. Lee Richmond, Coordinator, 410-617-2667.

Loyola Marymount University, School of Education, Program in Counseling, Los Angeles, CA 90045-8350. Awards MA. Part-time and evening/weekend programs available. Faculty: 14 full-time (8 women), 25 part-time (20 women). Students: 62 full-time (53 women), 21 part-time (16 women); includes 35 minority (9 African Americans, 8 Asian Americans, 17 Hispanics, 1 Native American), 2 international. In 1997, 37 degrees awarded. *Degree requirements:* Comprehensive exam required, foreign language and thesis not required. *Entrance requirements:* GRE General Test, TOEFL (minimum score 550), interview. Application fee: $35. Electronic applications accepted. *Expenses:* Tuition $500 per unit. Fees $111 per year full-time, $28 per year part-time. *Financial aid:* In 1997–98, 65 students received aid, including 9 research assistantships totaling $8,965, 1 teaching assistantship totaling $2,640, 22 grants, scholarships (5 to first-year students) totaling $19,130. Aid available to part-time students. Financial aid application deadline: 3/2; applicants required to submit FAFSA. • Dr. Paul DeSena, Coordinator, 310-338-2863.

Loyola University Chicago, School of Education, Department of Counseling Psychology, Program in Community Counseling, 820 North Michigan Avenue, Chicago, IL 60611-2196. Awards MA, M Ed. MA offered through the Graduate School. Part-time programs available. Faculty: 10 full-time (5 women), 9 part-time (8 women). Students: 51 full-time (43 women), 30 part-time (21 women); includes 13 minority (3 African Americans, 3 Asian Americans, 6 Hispanics, 1 Native American). Average age 25. In 1997, 15 degrees awarded. *Degree requirements:* Thesis, comprehensive exam required, foreign language not required. *Average time to degree:* master's–2 years full-time, 4 years part-time. *Entrance requirements:* GRE General Test (minimum combined score of 1100; average 1200). Application deadline: 2/15 (9/15 for spring admission). Application fee: $35. *Tuition:* $467 per semester hour. *Financial aid:* In 1997–98, fellowships averaging $800 per month, research assistantships averaging $800 per month were awarded; Federal Work-Study and career-related internships or fieldwork also available. Financial aid application deadline: 2/1; applicants required to submit FAFSA. *Faculty research:* Career development, multicultural counseling, group counseling, counseling process, family therapy. • Dr. Manuel Silverman, Director, 847-853-3343. Fax: 847-853-3375. E-mail: msilvel@orion.it.luc.edu.

Loyola University Chicago, School of Education, Department of Counseling Psychology, Program in School Counseling, 820 North Michigan Avenue, Chicago, IL 60611-2196. Awards M Ed. Faculty: 10 full-time (5 women), 9 part-time (8 women). Students: 7 full-time (all women), 4 part-time (3 women); includes 2 minority (both Hispanics). Average age 25. In 1997, 4 degrees awarded. *Degree requirements:* Comprehensive exam required, foreign language and thesis not required. *Average time to degree:* master's–2 years full-time, 4 years part-time. *Entrance requirements:* GRE General Test (minimum combined score of 1100; average 1200). Application deadline: 2/15 (9/15 for spring admission). Application fee: $35. *Tuition:* $467 per semester hour. *Financial aid:* Federal Work-Study and career-related internships or fieldwork available. Financial aid application deadline: 2/1; applicants required to submit FAFSA. *Faculty research:* Career development, group counseling, family therapy, child and adolescent development, multicultural counseling. • Dr. Edward Quinnan, SJ, Director, 847-853-3337. Fax: 847-853-3875. E-mail: equinno@wpo.it.luc.edu.

Loyola University New Orleans, College of Arts and Sciences, Department of Education, Program in Counseling, New Orleans, LA 70118-6195. Awards MS. Part-time and evening/weekend programs available. Faculty: 3 full-time (1 woman), 5 part-time (4 women). Students: 12 full-time (11 women), 11 part-time (9 women); includes 6 minority (4 African Americans, 1 Asian American, 1 Hispanic), 1 international. Average age 32. 14 applicants, 79% accepted. In 1997, 12 degrees awarded. *Degree requirements:* Comprehensive exam required, foreign language and thesis not required. *Entrance requirements:* GRE, MAT (preferred), interview, sample of written work. Application deadline: 8/1 (priority date; rolling processing; 12/1 for spring admission). Application fee: $20. Electronic applications accepted. *Expenses:* Tuition $386 per credit hour. Fees $556 per year full-time, $164 per year part-time. *Financial aid:* 12 students received aid; research assistantships, partial tuition waivers, Federal Work-Study, and career-related internships or fieldwork available. Aid available to part-time students. Financial aid application deadline: 5/1; applicants required to submit FAFSA. *Faculty research:* Counseling theory, evaluation, computer-based counseling strategies. • Dr. Justin E. Levitov, Director, 504-865-3540. Fax: 504-865-3571. E-mail: levitov@loyno.edu.

Lynchburg College, School of Education and Human Development, Program in Counseling, Lynchburg, VA 24501-3199. Offers agency counseling (M Ed), school counseling (M Ed). *Entrance requirements:* Minimum GPA of 3.0 (undergraduate). Application fee: $20.

Lyndon State College, Graduate Programs in Education, Department of Psychology, Lyndonville, VT 05851. Offers program in teaching and counseling (M Ed). *Degree requirements:* Exam or major field project required, foreign language and thesis not required. *Entrance requirements:* GRE General Test or MAT. Application deadline: 2/28 (priority date; 10/31 for spring admission). *Expenses:* Tuition $3924 per year full-time, $164 per credit part-time for state residents; $9192 per year full-time, $383 per credit part-time for nonresidents. Fees $632 per year. • Application contact: Elaine L. Turner, Administrative Secretary, 802-626-6497. Fax: 802-626-9770. E-mail: turnere@king.lsc.vsc.edu.

Malone College, Graduate School, Program in Education, Canton, OH 44709-3897. Offerings include community counseling (MA), school counseling (MA). Program faculty: 10 full-time (6 women), 11 part-time (5 women), 12.68 FTE. *Degree requirements:* Research practicum required, foreign language and thesis not required. *Entrance requirements:* Minimum GPA of 3.0, teaching license. Application deadline: 9/6 (rolling processing; 1/2 for spring admission). Application fee: $20. *Tuition:* $300 per credit hour. • Dr. Marietta Daulton, Director, 330-471-8447. Fax: 330-471-8478. E-mail: mdaulton@malone.edu. Application contact: Dan Depasquale, Director of Graduate Student Services, 800-257-4723. Fax: 330-471-8343. E-mail: depasquale@malone.edu.

Manhattan College, School of Education, Program in Counseling, Riverdale, NY 10471. Awards MA, Diploma. Part-time and evening/weekend programs available. Faculty: 2 full-time (both women), 6 part-time (2 women). Students: 15 full-time (13 women), 38 part-time (29 women); includes 7 minority (6 African Americans, 1 Hispanic), 3 international. Average age 32. 39 applicants, 100% accepted. In 1997, 16 master's awarded (100% entered university research/teaching); 3 Diplomas awarded. *Degree requirements:* For master's, thesis, internship. *Entrance requirements:* For master's, minimum GPA of 3.0. Application deadline: 8/10 (priority date; rolling processing; 1/7 for spring admission). Application fee: $50. *Expenses:* Tuition $385 per credit. Fees $100 per year. *Financial aid:* In 1997–98, 19 scholarships were awarded. Financial aid application deadline: 2/1. *Faculty research:* Sports counseling. • Adviser, 718-862-7416. Application contact: William J. Bisset Jr., Dean of Admissions/Financial Aid, 718-862-7200. Fax: 718-863-8019. E-mail: admit@manhattan.edu.

Mankato State University, College of Education, Department of Counseling and Student Personnel, South Rd and Ellis Ave, PO Box 8400, Mankato, MN 56002-8400. Awards MS. Accredited by NCATE. Faculty: 6 full-time (5 women). Students: 103 full-time (77 women), 44 part-time (38 women); includes 4 minority (2 African Americans, 2 Hispanics), 1 international. Average age 30. 64 applicants, 66% accepted. In 1997, 35 degrees awarded. *Degree requirements:* Thesis or alternative, comprehensive exam. *Entrance requirements:* GRE General Test or MAT, minimum GPA of 3.0 during previous 2 years. Application deadline: 7/10 (priority date; rolling processing; 10/30 for spring admission). Application fee: $20. *Tuition:* $126 per credit (minimum) for state residents; $200 per credit for nonresidents. *Financial aid:* Teaching assistantships, Federal Work-Study, institutionally sponsored loans, and career-related internships or fieldwork available. Aid available to part-time students. Financial aid application deadline: 3/15; applicants required to submit FAFSA. • Dr. Joanne Brandt, Chairperson, 507-389-5654. Application contact: Joni Roberts, Admissions Coordinator, 507-389-2321. Fax: 507-389-5974. E-mail: grad@mankato.msus.edu.

Marshall University, Graduate School of Education and Professional Studies, Program in Counseling, South Charleston, WV 25303-1600. Awards MA, Ed S. Accredited by NCATE. Part-time and evening/weekend programs available. Faculty: 6 full-time (2 women), 15 part-time (5 women), 8.5 FTE. Students: 22 full-time (15 women), 253 part-time (198 women); includes 20 minority (19 African Americans, 1 Hispanic). Average age 38. In 1997, 80 master's, 1 Ed S awarded. *Degree requirements:* For master's, thesis, comprehensive or oral exam required, foreign language not required. *Entrance requirements:* For master's, GRE General Test, MAT, minimum undergraduate GPA of 2.5. Application deadline: 8/1 (priority date; rolling processing). Application fee: $0. *Tuition:* $2364 per year full-time, $132 per hour part-time for state residents; $6894 per year full-time, $383 per hour part-time for nonresidents. *Financial aid:* Full tuition waivers and career-related internships or fieldwork available. Aid available to part-time students. Financial aid applicants required to submit FAFSA. • Dr. James Ranson, Dean, Graduate School of Education and Professional Studies, 304-746-1998. Fax: 304-746-1942.

Marshall University, College of Education, Division of Human Development and Allied Technology, Program in Counseling, Huntington, WV 25755-2020. Awards MA. Accredited by NCATE. Evening/weekend programs available. Faculty: 6 (2 women). Students: 95 full-time (72 women), 49 part-time (40 women); includes 7 minority (6 African Americans, 1 Asian American), 1 international. In 1997, 33 degrees awarded. *Degree requirements:* Thesis optional, foreign language not required. *Entrance requirements:* GRE General Test (minimum combined score of 1200). *Tuition:* $2364 per year full-time, $132 per hour part-time for state residents; $6894 per year full-time, $383 per hour part-time for nonresidents. • Dr. Donald L. Hall, Chairman, 304-696-3355. Application contact: Dr. James Harless, Director of Admissions, 304-696-3160.

Marymount University, School of Education and Human Services, Program in Psychology, Arlington, VA 22207-4299. Offerings include school counseling (MA). Accredited by NCATE. *Degree requirements:* Thesis or alternative required, foreign language not required. *Entrance requirements:* GRE General Test or MAT, interview. Application deadline: rolling. Application fee: $35. *Expenses:* Tuition $465 per credit hour. Fees $120 per year full-time, $5 per credit hour part-time. • Dr. Wayne Lesko, Dean, School of Education and Human Services, 703-284-1624. Fax: 703-284-1631. E-mail: wayne.lesko@marymount.edu.

Marywood University, Graduate School of Arts and Sciences, Department of Counseling/Psychology, Program in Counselor Education-Elementary, Scranton, PA 18509-1598. Awards MS. Students: 6 full-time (all women), 3 part-time (1 woman). Average age 29. 6 applicants, 83% accepted. *Degree requirements:* Comprehensive exam, internship/practicum required, foreign language and thesis not required. *Entrance requirements:* GRE or MAT, TOEFL (minimum score 550; average 590). Application deadline: 7/15 (priority date; rolling processing; 12/1 for spring admission). Application fee: $20. *Expenses:* Tuition $449 per credit hour. Fees $530 per year full-time, $180 per year part-time. *Financial aid:* Research assistantships, scholarships/tuition reductions, partial tuition waivers, and career-related internships or fieldwork available. Aid available to part-time students. Financial aid application deadline: 2/15; applicants required to submit FAFSA. • Application contact: Deborah M. Flynn, Coordinator of Admissions, 717-340-6002. Fax: 717-961-4745. E-mail: gsas_adm@ac.marywood.edu.

Marywood University, Graduate School of Arts and Sciences, Department of Counseling/Psychology, Program in Counselor Education-Secondary, Scranton, PA 18509-1598. Awards MS. Students: 7 full-time (6 women), 21 part-time (14 women). Average age 30. 11 applicants, 91% accepted. *Degree requirements:* Comprehensive exam, internship/practicum required, foreign language and thesis not required. *Entrance requirements:* GRE or MAT, TOEFL (minimum score 550; average 590). Application deadline: 7/15 (priority date; rolling processing; 12/1 for spring admission). Application fee: $20. *Expenses:* Tuition $449 per credit hour. Fees $530 per year full-time, $180 per year part-time. *Financial aid:* Research assistantships, scholarships/tuition reductions, partial tuition waivers, and career-related internships or fieldwork available. Aid available to part-time students. Financial aid application deadline: 2/15; applicants required to submit FAFSA. • Application contact: Deborah M. Flynn, Coordinator of Admissions, 717-340-6002. Fax: 717-961-4745. E-mail: gsas_adm@ac.marywood.edu.

McNeese State University, College of Education, Department of Psychology, Program in Counseling and Guidance, Lake Charles, LA 70609-2495. Awards M Ed. Evening/weekend programs available. Faculty: 8 full-time (2 women). Students: 4 full-time (3 women), 24 part-time (23 women). In 1997, 6 degrees awarded. *Entrance requirements:* GRE General Test, teaching certificate, 3 years of teaching experience, 18 hours in professional education. Application deadline: 7/15 (priority date; rolling processing). Application fee: $10 ($25 for international students). *Tuition:* $2118 per year full-time, $344 per semester (minimum) part-time for state residents; $7308 per year full-time, $344 per semester (minimum) part-time for nonresidents. *Financial aid:* Application deadline 5/1. • Dr. Jess Feist, Head, Department of Psychology, 318-475-5457.

Michigan State University, College of Education, Department of Counseling, Educational Psychology and Special Education, East Lansing, MI 48824-1020. Offerings include counseling (MA), rehabilitation counseling and school counseling (PhD). Department faculty: 42 (14 women). *Degree requirements:* For doctorate, dissertation required, foreign language not required. *Entrance requirements:* For master's, GRE General Test (combined average 1500 on three sections); for doctorate, GRE General Test (combined average 1800 on three sections). Application deadline: rolling. Application fee: $30 ($40 for international students). *Expenses:* Tuition $4609 per year full-time, $223 per credit hour (minimum) part-time for state residents; $8704 per year full-time, $450 per credit hour (minimum) part-time for nonresidents. Fees $576 per year full-time, $476 per year part-time. • Dr. Richard Prawat, Chairperson, 517-353-6417. Application contact: Sharon Anderson, Graduate Secretary, 517-355-6683. Fax: 517-353-6393. E-mail: sharand@msu.edu.

Middle Tennessee State University, College of Education, Department of Psychology, Program in School Counseling, Murfreesboro, TN 37132. Awards M Ed, Ed S. Accredited by NCATE. Students: 22 full-time (20 women), 47 part-time (41 women); includes 6 minority (all African Americans). Average age 28. 39 applicants, 38% accepted. In 1997, 6 master's, 5 Ed Ss awarded. *Degree requirements:* Comprehensive exams required, foreign language and thesis not required. *Entrance requirements:* For master's, Cooperative English Test, MAT. Application deadline: 8/1 (priority date). Application fee: $5. *Expenses:* Tuition $2560 per year full-time, $129 per semester hour part-time for state residents; $7386 per year full-time, $340 per semester hour part-time for nonresidents. Fees $486 per year full-time, $17 per semester (minimum) part-time. *Financial aid:* Teaching assistantships available. Financial aid application deadline: 5/1. • Dr. Keith W. Carlson, Coordinator, 615-898-2007. Fax: 615-898-5027. E-mail: kcarlson@mtsu.edu.

Midwestern State University, Division of Education, Program in Guidance and Counseling, Wichita Falls, TX 76308-2096. Offers general counseling (MA), human resource development (MA), school counseling (M Ed). Part-time and evening/weekend programs available. Students: 80. Average age 35. In 1997, 33 degrees awarded. *Degree requirements:* Thesis required (for some programs), foreign language not required. *Entrance requirements:* GRE General Test, MAT (average 46), TOEFL (minimum score 550). Application deadline: 8/7 (12/15 for spring admission). Application fee: $0 ($50 for international students). *Expenses:* Tuition $44 per hour for state residents; $259 per hour for nonresidents. Fees $90 per year (minimum) full-time, $9 per semester (minimum) part-time. *Financial aid:* Teaching assistantships available. • Dr. Emerson Capps, Director, Division of Education, 940-397-4313.

Millersville University of Pennsylvania, School of Education, Department of Psychology, Program in Counselor Education, Millersville, PA 17551-0302. Awards M Ed. Accredited by NCATE. Part-time and evening/weekend programs available. Students: 6 full-time (4 women), 52 part-time (45 women); includes 3 minority (2 African Americans, 1 Hispanic). Average age 31. 36 applicants, 69% accepted. In 1997, 16 degrees awarded. *Degree requirements:* Departmental exam required, foreign language and thesis not required. *Entrance requirements:* GRE General Test (minimum score 475 on each of three sections), minimum undergraduate GPA of 2.75, interview. Application deadline: 5/1 (priority date; rolling processing). Application fee: $25. *Tuition:* $3468 per year full-time, $234 per credit part-time for state residents; $6236 per year full-time, $387 per credit part-time for nonresidents. *Financial aid:* In 1997–98, 14 graduate assistantships (7 to first-year students) averaging $445 per month and totaling $56,000 were awarded; Federal Work-Study, institutionally sponsored loans, and career-related internships or fieldwork also available. Aid available to part-time students. Financial aid application deadline: 5/1. *Faculty research:* Guidance program development, brief counseling. • Joyce Smedley, Coordinator, 717-872-3097. Application contact: Dr. Robert J. Labriola, Dean of Graduate Studies, 717-872-3030. Fax: 717-871-2022.

Mississippi College, School of Education, Programs in Guidance and Counseling, Clinton, MS 39058. Offerings in counseling psychology (MCP), guidance and counseling (M Ed, Ed S). Accredited by NCATE. Evening/weekend programs available. *Degree requirements:* For master's, comprehensive exam required, foreign language and thesis not required. *Entrance requirements:* For master's, GRE or NTE, minimum GPA of 2.5, Class A Certificate; for Ed S, NTE, minimum GPA of 3.0. Application deadline: 8/15 (priority date; rolling processing). Application fee: $25 ($75 for international students). *Expenses:* Tuition $6624 per year full-time, $276 per hour part-time. Fees $230 per year full-time, $35 per semester (minimum) part-time. *Financial aid:* Professional development scholarships and career-related internships or fieldwork available. Aid available to part-time students. Financial aid application deadline: 4/1. • Dr. Bill Wheeler, Head, 601-925-3842. Application contact: Graduate School Office, 601-925-3225.

Mississippi State University, College of Education, Department of Counselor Education and Educational Psychology, Mississippi State, MS 39762. Offers programs in counselor education (MS), including community counseling, counseling services, rehabilitation, school counseling, student development services; general education psychology (MS), including research and evaluation. Accredited by NCATE. Part-time programs available. Faculty: 17 full-time (7 women), 7 part-time (2 women). Students: 126 full-time (106 women), 85 part-time (70 women); includes 64 minority (63 African Americans, 1 Asian American), 1 international. Average age 33. 158 applicants, 93% accepted. In 1997, 83 degrees awarded. *Degree requirements:* Comprehensive oral or written exam required, thesis optional, foreign language not required. *Entrance requirements:* GRE, minimum QPA of 3.0 in last 2 years. Application deadline: 3/1. Application fee: $0 ($25 for international students). *Tuition:* $3017 per year full-time, $168 per credit hour part-time for state residents; $6119 per year full-time, $340 per credit hour part-time for nonresidents. *Financial aid:* In 1997–98, 2 research assistantships (both to first-year students), 8 teaching assistantships (all to first-year students) were awarded; Federal Work-Study, institutionally sponsored loans, and career-related internships or fieldwork also available. Aid available to part-time students. Financial aid application deadline: 3/1. *Faculty research:* Counselor evaluation, personal development and counselor effectiveness, counselor ethics, disabled work adjustment, substance abuse, school counselor supervison. • Dr. Tom Hosie, Head, 601-325-3426. Fax: 601-325-3263. E-mail: hosie@colled.msstate.edu.

Mississippi State University, College of Education, Program Under Dean of Education, Mississippi State, MS 39762. Offerings include counselor education (PhD). Accredited by NCATE. *Tuition:* $3017 per year full-time, $168 per credit hour part-time for state residents;

Directory: Counselor Education

Mississippi State University (continued)
$6119 per year full-time, $340 per credit hour part-time for nonresidents. • Dr. William H. Graves, Dean, College of Education, 601-325-3717. Fax: 601-325-8784. E-mail: whg1@ra.msstate.edu.

Montana State University–Billings, College of Education and Human Services, Department of Educational Foundation and Counseling, Option in School Counseling, Billings, MT 59101-9984. Awards M Ed. Accredited by NCATE. Part-time programs available. *Degree requirements:* Thesis or professional paper and/or field experience required, foreign language not required. *Entrance requirements:* GRE General Test (minimum combined score of 1350 on three sections) or MAT (minimum score 38), minimum GPA of 3.0 (undergraduate), 3.25 (graduate). Application deadline: 8/1 (priority date; rolling processing; 1/1 for spring admission). Application fee: $30. *Expenses:* Tuition $2253 per year full-time, $397 per semester (minimum) part-time for state residents; $5313 per year full-time, $907 per semester (minimum) part-time for nonresidents. Fees $378 per year full-time, $105 per semester (minimum) part-time.

Montana State University–Billings, College of Education and Human Services, Department of Special Education and Reading, Program in Special Education, Billings, MT 59101-9984. Offerings include community counseling (MS Sp Ed). Accredited by NCATE. *Degree requirements:* Thesis or professional paper and/or field experience required, foreign language not required. *Entrance requirements:* GRE General Test (minimum combined score of 1350 on three sections) or MAT (minimum score 38), minimum GPA of 3.0 (undergraduate), 3.25 (graduate). Application deadline: 8/1 (priority date; rolling processing; 1/1 for spring admission). Application fee: $30. *Expenses:* Tuition $2253 per year full-time, $397 per semester (minimum) part-time for state residents; $5313 per year full-time, $907 per semester (minimum) part-time for nonresidents. Fees $378 per year full-time, $105 per semester (minimum) part-time.

Montana State University–Northern, Option in Counseling and Development, Havre, MT 59501-7751. Awards M Ed. Evening/weekend programs available. Faculty: 5 full-time (3 women), 5 part-time (1 woman). Students: 40 full-time (24 women), 52 part-time (36 women); includes 8 minority (2 African Americans, 6 Native Americans). Average age 37. *Degree requirements:* Comprehensive and oral exams required, thesis optional, foreign language not required. *Entrance requirements:* GRE General Test, minimum GPA of 3.0. Application deadline: 9/20 (priority date; rolling processing). Application fee: $30. *Tuition:* $3090 per year full-time, $696 per semester (minimum) part-time for state residents; $8044 per year full-time, $1758 per semester (minimum) part-time for nonresidents. *Financial aid:* Teaching assistantships, Federal Work-Study, institutionally sponsored loans available. Aid available to part-time students. Financial aid application deadline: 4/1; applicants required to submit FAFSA. • Dr. Ben Johnson, Director of Education and Graduate Programs, Department of Education, 406-265-3738. Fax: 406-265-3570. E-mail: johnson@nmcl.nmclites.edu.

Montclair State University, College of Education and Human Services, Department of Counseling, Human Development, and Educational Leadership, Program in Counseling and Guidance, Upper Montclair, NJ 07043-1624. Awards MA. Accredited by NCATE. Part-time and evening/weekend programs available. Faculty: 12 full-time. Students: 79 full-time (66 women), 179 part-time (170 women); includes 39 minority (23 African Americans, 15 Hispanics, 1 Native American), 10 international. In 1997, 109 degrees awarded. *Degree requirements:* Thesis or alternative, comprehensive exam. *Entrance requirements:* GRE General Test or MAT, interview. Application deadline: 4/1 (rolling processing; 11/1 for spring admission). Application fee: $40. *Expenses:* Tuition $201 per credit for state residents; $257 per credit for nonresidents. Fees $22.05 per credit. *Financial aid:* Research assistantships available. Financial aid application deadline: 3/1; applicants required to submit FAFSA. • Dr. Arlene King, Chairperson, Department of Counseling, Human Development, and Educational Leadership, 973-655-5175.

Moorhead State University, Department of Education, Program in Counseling and Student Affairs, Moorhead, MN 56563-0002. Awards MS. Accredited by NCATE. Part-time and evening/weekend programs available. Faculty: 2 full-time (0 women), 4 part-time (2 women). Students: 13 full-time (11 women), 20 part-time (15 women); includes 1 minority (Native American). 13 applicants, 92% accepted. In 1997, 10 degrees awarded. *Degree requirements:* Final oral exam, internship, project or thesis, written comprehensive exam required, foreign language not required. *Entrance requirements:* GRE or MAT, TOEFL (minimum score 550), interview, minimum GPA of 3.0, sample of written work. Application deadline: 5/1 (priority date; rolling processing; 9/1 for spring admission). Application fee: $20 ($35 for international students). Electronic applications accepted. *Tuition:* $145 per credit hour for state residents; $220 per credit hour for nonresidents. *Financial aid:* In 1997–98, 5 administrative assistantships were awarded; Federal Work-Study and career-related internships or fieldwork also available. Financial aid application deadline: 7/15; applicants required to submit FAFSA. • William Packwood, Coordinator, 218-236-2044.

Morehead State University, College of Education and Behavioral Sciences, Department of Leadership and Secondary Education, Program in Guidance and Counseling, Morehead, KY 40351. Awards MA Ed, Ed S. Accredited by NCATE. Part-time and evening/weekend programs available. Faculty: 5 full-time (3 women), 3 part-time (2 women). Students: 10 full-time (5 women), 131 part-time (109 women); includes 1 minority (African American). Average age 25. 46 applicants, 100% accepted. In 1997, 40 master's awarded. *Degree requirements:* For master's, oral and/or written comprehensive exams required, foreign language and thesis not required; for Ed S, thesis, oral exam required, foreign language not required. *Entrance requirements:* For master's, GRE General Test (minimum combined score of 1050), minimum GPA of 2.5, teaching certificate, 2 years of work experience; for Ed S, GRE General Test (minimum combined score of 1200), interview, master's degree, minimum GPA of 3.5, work experience. Application deadline: 8/1 (priority date; rolling processing; 12/1 for spring admission). Application fee: $0. *Tuition:* $2470 per year full-time, $138 per semester hour part-time for state residents; $6710 per year full-time, $373 per semester hour part-time for nonresidents. *Financial aid:* Research assistantships, teaching assistantships, Federal Work-Study available. Financial aid application deadline: 4/1; applicants required to submit FAFSA. *Faculty research:* Child abuse and neglect, school-to-work transformation, computer use by school counselors, adult children of alcoholics. • Application contact: Betty Cowsert, Graduate Admissions Officer, 606-783-2039. Fax: 606-783-5061.

Murray State University, College of Education, Department of Educational Leadership and Counseling, Program in Community and Agency Counseling, Murray, KY 42071-0009. Awards Ed S. Accredited by NCATE. Part-time programs available. Students: 2 full-time (0 women), 4 part-time (3 women). 2 applicants, 100% accepted. In 1997, 2 degrees awarded. *Degree requirements:* Thesis required, foreign language not required. *Entrance requirements:* GRE General Test, TOEFL (minimum score 500). Application deadline: rolling. Application fee: $20. *Expenses:* Tuition $2500 per year full-time, $124 per hour part-time for state residents; $6740 per year full-time, $357 per hour part-time for nonresidents. Fees $360 per year full-time, $180 per year part-time. *Financial aid:* Research assistantships, teaching assistantships, Federal Work-Study available. Financial aid application deadline: 4/1. • Dr. Thomas Holcomb, Director, 502-762-2797. Fax: 502-762-3799.

Murray State University, College of Education, Department of Educational Leadership and Counseling, Programs in Guidance and Counseling, Murray, KY 42071-0009. Awards MA Ed, MS, Ed S. Accredited by NCATE. Part-time programs available. Students: 6 full-time (5 women), 115 part-time (100 women); includes 4 minority (all African Americans). 14 applicants, 100% accepted. In 1997, 15 master's awarded. *Degree requirements:* For master's, thesis required (for some programs), foreign language not required. *Entrance requirements:* For master's, GRE General Test or MAT, TOEFL (minimum score 500). Application deadline: rolling. Application fee: $20. *Expenses:* Tuition $2500 per year full-time, $124 per hour part-time for state residents; $6740 per year full-time, $357 per hour part-time for nonresidents. Fees $360 per year full-time, $180 per year part-time. *Financial aid:* Research assistantships, teaching assistantships, Federal Work-Study available. Financial aid application deadline: 4/1. • Dr. Thomas Holcomb, Director, 502-762-2797. Fax: 502-762-3799.

National University, School of Education and Human Services, Department of Special Education and Pupil Personnel Services, La Jolla, CA 92037-1011. Offerings include educational counseling (MS). *Entrance requirements:* Interview, minimum GPA of 2.5. Application deadline: rolling. Application fee: $60 ($100 for international students). *Tuition:* $7830 per year full-time, $870 per course part-time. • Dr. Judy Mantel, Chair, 619-642-8347. Application contact: Nancy Rohland, Director of Enrollment Management, 619-563-7100. Fax: 619-563-7393.

New Mexico Highlands University, School of Education, Las Vegas, NM 87701. Offerings include guidance and counseling (MA). School faculty: 32 full-time (14 women). *Degree requirements:* Thesis or alternative required, foreign language not required. *Entrance requirements:* Minimum undergraduate GPA of 3.0. Application deadline: 8/1 (priority date; rolling processing). Application fee: $15. *Expenses:* Tuition $1816 per year full-time, $227 per hour part-time for state residents; $7468 per year full-time, $227 per hour part-time for nonresidents. Fees $10 per year. • Dr. James Abreu, Dean, 505-454-3357. Application contact: Dr. Glen W. Davidson, Academic Vice President, 505-454-3311. Fax: 505-454-3558. E-mail: glendavidson@venus.nmhu.edu.

New Mexico State University, College of Education, Department of Counseling and Educational Psychology, Las Cruces, NM 88003-8001. Offers programs in counseling and guidance (MA, Ed S), counseling psychology (PhD). Accredited by NCATE. One or more programs accredited by APA. Part-time programs available. Faculty: 12 full-time (4 women), 1 (woman) part-time. Students: 56 full-time (43 women), 25 part-time (17 women); includes 26 minority (3 African Americans, 23 Hispanics), 1 international. Average age 35. 115 applicants, 9% accepted. In 1997, 21 master's, 4 doctorates awarded. *Degree requirements:* For master's, internship required, thesis optional, foreign language not required; for doctorate, dissertation, internship required, foreign language not required; for Ed S, thesis or alternative, internship required, foreign language not required. *Entrance requirements:* For master's, GRE General Test; for doctorate, GRE General Test, master's degree in counseling; for Ed S, GRE General Test, master's degree. Application deadline: 7/1 (priority date; rolling processing; 11/1 for spring admission). Application fee: $15 ($35 for international students). Electronic applications accepted. *Tuition:* $2514 per year full-time, $105 per credit hour part-time for state residents; $7848 per year full-time, $327 per credit hour part-time for nonresidents. *Financial aid:* Fellowships, teaching assistantships, Federal Work-Study, and career-related internships or fieldwork available. Aid available to part-time students. Financial aid application deadline: 3/1. *Faculty research:* Cultural diversity, family counseling, group counseling, supervision, professional issues. • Dr. Michael Waldo, Head, 505-646-2121. Fax: 505-646-8035. E-mail: cepdept@nmsu.edu.

New York University, School of Education, Department of Applied Psychology, Program in Counselor Education, New York, NY 10012-1019. Offers counseling and guidance (MA, PhD, CAS), including bilingual school counseling (MA); counseling psychology (PhD). One or more programs accredited by APA. Part-time and evening/weekend programs available. Faculty: 8 full-time, 8 part-time. Students: 103 full-time, 95 part-time. 278 applicants, 33% accepted. In 1997, 51 master's, 6 doctorates awarded. Terminal master's awarded for partial completion of doctoral program. *Degree requirements:* For master's, thesis required (for some programs), foreign language not required; for doctorate, dissertation. *Entrance requirements:* For master's and CAS, TOEFL; for doctorate, GRE General Test, TOEFL, interview. Application deadline: 2/1 (priority date; rolling processing; 12/1 for spring admission). Application fee: $40 ($60 for international students). *Financial aid:* In 1997–98, teaching assistantships averaging $850 per month were awarded; partial tuition waivers, Federal Work-Study, institutionally sponsored loans, and career-related internships or fieldwork also available. Aid available to part-time students. Financial aid application deadline: 3/1; applicants required to submit FAFSA. *Faculty research:* Cross-cultural counseling, thanatology, group dynamics, sex and race discrimination, substance abuse. • Samuel Juni, Co-Director, 212-998-5548. Application contact: Office of Graduate Admissions, 212-998-5030. Fax: 212-995-4328.

Niagara University, Graduate Division of Education, Concentration in Mental Health Counseling, Niagara University, NY 14109. Awards MS Ed. Faculty: 2 full-time (1 woman), 3 part-time (all women). Students: 11 full-time (9 women), 9 part-time (all women); includes 4 international. In 1997, 6 degrees awarded. *Entrance requirements:* GRE General Test or MAT. Application deadline: 8/1 (rolling processing). Application fee: $30. *Expenses:* Tuition $4950 per year full-time, $275 per credit hour part-time. Fees $25 per semester. *Financial aid:* Fellowships, Federal Work-Study, and career-related internships or fieldwork available. Financial aid application deadline: 3/15. • Dr. Deborah Erickson, Chairman, 716-286-8547. Application contact: Rev. Daniel F. O'Leary, OMI, Dean of Education, 716-286-8560.

Niagara University, Graduate Division of Education, Concentration in School Counseling, Niagara University, NY 14109. Awards MS Ed, PD. Accredited by NCATE. Part-time and evening/weekend programs available. Faculty: 2 full-time (1 woman), 3 part-time (all women). Students: 7 full-time (all women), 32 part-time (25 women); includes 3 minority (2 African Americans, 1 Asian American), 4 international. In 1997, 15 master's awarded. *Entrance requirements:* For master's, GRE General Test or MAT; for PD, GRE General Test, GRE Subject Test or MAT. Application deadline: 8/1 (rolling processing). Application fee: $30. *Expenses:* Tuition $4950 per year full-time, $275 per credit hour part-time. Fees $25 per semester. *Financial aid:* Federal Work-Study and career-related internships or fieldwork available. Financial aid application deadline: 3/15. • Dr. Paul J. Vermette, Chairman, 716-286-8550. Application contact: Rev. Daniel F. O'Leary, OMI, Dean of Education, 716-286-8560.

Nicholls State University, College of Education, Department of Psychology and Counselor Education, Thibodaux, LA 70310. Offers programs in counselor education (M Ed), psychological counseling (MA), school psychology (Ed S). Accredited by NCATE. Part-time and evening/weekend programs available. Faculty: 10 full-time (2 women). Students: 22 full-time (21 women), 50 part-time (41 women). In 1997, 17 master's awarded (100% found work related to degree); 2 Ed Ss awarded (100% found work related to degree). *Entrance requirements:* For master's, GRE General Test, GRE Subject Test. Application deadline: 6/17 (priority date; rolling processing; 11/15 for spring admission). Application fee: $10 ($60 for international students). *Tuition:* $2136 per year full-time, $283 per semester (minimum) part-time for state residents; $5376 per year full-time, $283 per semester (minimum) part-time for nonresidents. *Financial aid:* Research assistantships, teaching assistantships available. Financial aid application deadline: 6/17. • Dr. Earl Folse, Head, 504-448-4371.

North Carolina Agricultural and Technical State University, Graduate School, School of Education, Department of Human Development and Services, Greensboro, NC 27411. Offerings include guidance and counseling (MS). Accredited by NCATE. Department faculty: 7 full-time (3 women). *Degree requirements:* Thesis, comprehensive exam, qualifying exam required, foreign language not required. *Entrance requirements:* GRE General Test, minimum GPA of 3.0. Application deadline: 6/1 (priority date; rolling processing; 12/1 for spring admission). Application fee: $35. *Tuition:* $1662 per year full-time, $272 per semester (minimum) part-time for state residents; $8790 per year full-time, $2054 per semester (minimum) part-time for nonresidents. • Dr. Wyatt Kirk, Chairperson, 336-334-7916. Fax: 336-334-7280. E-mail: kirkw@aurora.ncat.edu.

North Carolina Central University, Division of Academic Affairs, School of Education, Programs in Counseling, Durham, NC 27707-3129. Offerings in agency counseling (MA), career counseling (MA), school counseling (MA). Accredited by NCATE. Part-time and evening/weekend programs available. Students: 15 full-time (13 women), 99 part-time (73 women); includes 76 minority (all African Americans). Average age 35. 52 applicants, 42% accepted. In 1997, 29 degrees awarded. *Degree requirements:* Thesis or alternative, comprehensive exam required, foreign language not required. *Entrance requirements:* Minimum GPA of 3.0 in major, 2.5 overall. Application deadline: 8/1. Application fee: $30. *Tuition:* $2027 per year full-time, $508 per semester (minimum) part-time for state residents; $9155 per year full-time, $2290 per semester (minimum) part-time for nonresidents. *Financial aid:* Fellowships, teaching assistantships, Federal Work-Study, institutionally sponsored loans, and career-related internships or fieldwork available. Aid available to part-time students. Financial aid application deadline: 5/1.

Faculty research: Becoming a leader, skill building in academia. • Dr. H. Donell Lewis, Director, 919-560-6479. Application contact: Dr. Cecelia Steppe-Jones, Associate Dean of Graduate Studies and Administration, 919-560-6478.

North Carolina State University, College of Education and Psychology, Department of Counselor Education, Raleigh, NC 27695. Awards M Ed, MS, Ed D, PhD, CAGS. Accredited by NCATE. Part-time programs available. Faculty: 9 full-time (1 woman), 8 part-time (4 women). Students: 53 full-time (42 women), 54 part-time (42 women); includes 27 minority (21 African Americans, 1 Asian American, 2 Hispanics, 3 Native Americans). Average age 34. 129 applicants, 40% accepted. In 1997, 18 master's, 2 doctorates awarded. *Degree requirements:* For master's, comprehensive exam required, foreign language and thesis not required; for doctorate and CAGS, thesis/dissertation, comprehensive exam required, foreign language not required. *Entrance requirements:* For master's and CAGS, GRE General Test or MAT, minimum GPA of 3.0 in major; for doctorate, GRE General Test or MAT, minimum GPA of 3.0, interview, sample of work. Application deadline: 2/1. Application fee: $45. *Tuition:* $2370 per year full-time, $517 per semester (minimum) part-time for state residents; $11,536 per year full-time, $2809 per semester (minimum) part-time for nonresidents. *Financial aid:* In 1997–98, 2 fellowships totaling $3,090, 2 research assistantships averaging $919 per month and totaling $8,268, 12 teaching assistantships (4 to first-year students) totaling $28,340, 6 minority grants were awarded; Federal Work-Study, institutionally sponsored loans, and career-related internships or fieldwork also available. Aid available to part-time students. *Faculty research:* Cognitive developmental applications to elementary, secondary, college, and adult populations. Total annual research expenditures: $785,196. • Dr. Stanley B. Baker, Director of Graduate Programs, 919-515-6360. Fax: 919-515-6891. E-mail: sbaker@poe.coe.ncsu.edu.

North Dakota State University, College of Human Development and Education, School of Education, Program in Counselor Education, Fargo, ND 58105. Awards MA, M Ed, MS. Accredited by NCATE. Faculty: 4 full-time (1 woman), 3 part-time (2 women). Students: 12 full-time (10 women), 27 part-time (23 women); includes 2 minority (both Native Americans). Average age 35. 30 applicants, 67% accepted. In 1997, 31 degrees awarded (100% found work related to degree). *Degree requirements:* Thesis or alternative required, foreign language not required. *Entrance requirements:* GRE, MAT, TOEFL (minimum score 525), interview. Application deadline: 2/15 (rolling processing). Application fee: $25. *Tuition:* $2572 per year full-time, $107 per credit part-time for state residents; $6868 per year full-time, $286 per credit part-time for nonresidents. *Financial aid:* Teaching assistantships, full tuition waivers, Federal Work-Study, institutionally sponsored loans, and career-related internships or fieldwork available. Financial aid application deadline: 4/15. *Faculty research:* Supervision, program assessment, multicultural issues. • Dr. Bob Nielsen, Coordinator, 701-231-7202.

Northeastern Illinois University, College of Education, Department of Counselor Education, Chicago, IL 60625-4699. Offers program in guidance and counseling (MA), including career development, community and family counseling, elementary school counseling, secondary school counseling. Part-time and evening/weekend programs available. Faculty: 9 full-time (4 women). Students: 21 full-time (19 women), 116 part-time (87 women); includes 25 minority (14 African Americans, 5 Asian Americans, 6 Hispanics). Average age 42. 45 applicants, 78% accepted. In 1997, 46 degrees awarded. *Degree requirements:* Thesis or alternative, comprehensive exam, internship, practicum required, foreign language not required. *Entrance requirements:* GRE, minimum GPA of 2.75, workshop. Application deadline: 3/18 (priority date; rolling processing; 9/30 for spring admission). Application fee: $0. *Expenses:* Tuition $2226 per year full-time, $93 per credit hour part-time for state residents; $6678 per year full-time, $278 per credit hour part-time for nonresidents. Fees $358 per year full-time, $14.90 per credit hour part-time. *Financial aid:* In 1997–98, 31 students received aid, including 5 research assistantships averaging $450 per month; full and partial tuition waivers, Federal Work-Study, institutionally sponsored loans, and career-related internships or fieldwork also available. Aid available to part-time students. *Faculty research:* Substance abuse and the brain, psychological factors of the visually impaired, reclaiming self through art, ego development. • Dr. Alice Murata, Chairperson, 773-794-2785. Application contact: Dr. Mohan K. Sood, Dean of Graduate College, 773-583-4050 Ext. 6143. Fax: 773-794-6670.

Northeastern State University, College of Behavioral and Social Sciences, Department of Psychology and Counseling, Program in School Counseling, Tahlequah, OK 74464-2399. Awards M Ed. Part-time and evening/weekend programs available. Faculty: 3 full-time (1 woman), 1 part-time (0 women). Students: 136 (122 women). In 1997, 46 degrees awarded. *Degree requirements:* Thesis or alternative required, foreign language not required. *Entrance requirements:* GRE General Test (minimum combined score of 900) or MAT (minimum score 33), minimum GPA of 2.5. Application deadline: 6/1 (priority date; rolling processing). Application fee: $0. *Expenses:* Tuition $74 per credit hour for state residents; $176 per credit hour for nonresidents. Fees $30 per year. *Financial aid:* Teaching assistantships, Federal Work-Study available. Financial aid application deadline: 3/1. • Dr. Bill Schiller, Head, Department of Psychology and Counseling, 918-456-5511 Ext. 3015.

Northeastern University, Bouvé College of Pharmacy and Health Sciences Graduate School, Department of Counseling Psychology, Rehabilitation, and Special Education, Program in Applied Educational Psychology, Boston, MA 02115-5096. Offerings include school counseling (MS). Program faculty: 5 full-time (3 women), 4 part-time (2 women). *Entrance requirements:* GRE General Test or MAT. Application deadline: rolling. Application fee: $50. *Expenses:* Tuition $440 per credit hour. Fees $55 per quarter full-time, $13.25 per quarter part-time. • Dr. Ena Vazquez-Nuttall, Program Director, 617-373-2708. Application contact: Bill Purnell, Director of Graduate Admissions, 617-373-2708. Fax: 617-373-4701. E-mail: w.purnell@nunet.neu.edu.

Northeastern University, Bouvé College of Pharmacy and Health Sciences Graduate School, Department of Counseling Psychology, Rehabilitation, and Special Education, Program in College Student Development and Counseling, Boston, MA 02115-5096. Awards MS. Part-time and evening/weekend programs available. Faculty: 1 (woman) full-time, 4 part-time (all women). Students: 24 full-time (15 women), 12 part-time (8 women). Average age 27. 32 applicants, 88% accepted. In 1997, 22 degrees awarded. *Entrance requirements:* GRE General Test or MAT. Application fee: $50. *Expenses:* Tuition $440 per credit hour. Fees $55 per quarter full-time, $13.25 per quarter part-time. *Financial aid:* Administrative assistantships, Federal Work-Study, and career-related internships or fieldwork available. Aid available to part-time students. Financial aid application deadline: 3/1. • Dr. Lawrence Litwack, Director, 617-373-2485. Application contact: Bill Purnell, Director of Graduate Admissions, 617-373-2708. Fax: 617-373-4701. E-mail: w.purnell@nunet.neu.edu.

Northeastern University, Bouvé College of Pharmacy and Health Sciences Graduate School, Department of Counseling Psychology, Rehabilitation, and Special Education, Program in Human Resource Counseling, Boston, MA 02115-5096. Awards MS. Part-time programs available. Faculty: 1 full-time (0 women), 2 part-time (1 woman). Students: 9 full-time (7 women), 8 part-time (5 women). Average age 30. 15 applicants, 87% accepted. In 1997, 15 degrees awarded. *Entrance requirements:* GRE General Test or MAT. Application deadline: rolling. Application fee: $50. *Expenses:* Tuition $440 per credit hour. Fees $55 per quarter full-time, $13.25 per quarter part-time. *Financial aid:* Administrative assistantships, Federal Work-Study, and career-related internships or fieldwork available. Aid available to part-time students. Financial aid application deadline: 3/1; applicants required to submit FAFSA. *Faculty research:* Philosophy of mind and science. • Dr. William Quill, Director, 617-373-3276. Application contact: Bill Purnell, Director of Graduate Admissions, 617-373-2708. Fax: 617-373-4701. E-mail: w.purnell@nunet.neu.edu.

Northeast Louisiana University, College of Education, Department of Educational Leadership and Counseling, Program in Counseling, Monroe, LA 71209-0001. Awards M Ed, Ed S. Accredited by NCATE. Part-time and evening/weekend programs available. *Degree requirements:* For master's, comprehensive exam required, foreign language and thesis not required; for Ed S, thesis, comprehensive exam required, foreign language not required. *Entrance requirements:* For master's, GRE General Test, minimum GPA of 2.8 in last 60 hours; for Ed S, GRE General Test. Application deadline: 6/1 (priority date; rolling processing; 11/1 for spring admission). Application fee: $15 ($25 for international students). *Tuition:* $2028 per year full-time, $240 per semester (minimum) part-time for state residents; $6852 per year full-time, $240 per semester (minimum) part-time for nonresidents.

Northern Arizona University, Center for Excellence in Education, Programs in Counseling, Flagstaff, AZ 86011. Awards MA, M Ed, Ed D. Part-time programs available. Students: 170 full-time (125 women), 335 part-time (255 women); includes 99 minority (25 African Americans, 4 Asian Americans, 63 Hispanics, 7 Native Americans), 4 international. Average age 34. 303 applicants, 56% accepted. In 1997, 161 master's, 5 doctorates awarded. *Degree requirements:* For master's, thesis optional, foreign language not required; for doctorate, computer language, dissertation required, foreign language not required. *Entrance requirements:* For master's, GRE General Test, minimum GPA of 3.0; for doctorate, GRE General Test, GRE Subject Test, minimum graduate GPA of 3.3. Application fee: $45. *Expenses:* Tuition $2088 per year full-time, $330 per semester (minimum) part-time for state residents; $8004 per year full-time, $1002 per semester (minimum) part-time for nonresidents. Fees $72 per year full-time, $18 per semester (minimum) part-time. *Financial aid:* Research assistantships, teaching assistantships, full and partial tuition waivers, Federal Work-Study, and career-related internships or fieldwork available. *Faculty research:* Early childhood assessment and development, cognitive psychology, multicultural issues, family functioning in abusive families, rehabilitation. • Dr. William Martin, Chair, 520-523-6757.

Northern Illinois University, College of Education, Department of Educational Psychology, Counseling, and Special Education, Program in Counseling, De Kalb, IL 60115-2854. Awards MS Ed, Ed D. Accredited by NCATE. Part-time and evening/weekend programs available. Faculty: 8 full-time (3 women), 1 (woman) part-time. Students: 37 full-time (29 women), 111 part-time (77 women); includes 12 minority (10 African Americans, 1 Asian American, 1 Hispanic), 1 international. Average age 35. 52 applicants, 54% accepted. In 1997, 34 master's, 5 doctorates awarded. *Degree requirements:* For master's, comprehensive exam required, thesis optional, foreign language not required; for doctorate, candidacy exam, dissertation defense required, foreign language not required. *Entrance requirements:* For master's, GRE General Test, TOEFL (minimum score 550), minimum GPA of 2.75; for doctorate, GRE General Test, TOEFL (minimum score 550), minimum GPA of 2.75 (undergraduate), 3.2 (graduate), interview, master's degree. Application deadline: 4/1 (priority date; rolling processing; 11/1 for spring admission). Application fee: $30. *Tuition:* $3984 per year full-time, $154 per credit hour part-time for state residents; $8160 per year full-time, $328 per credit hour part-time for nonresidents. *Financial aid:* Fellowships, research assistantships, teaching assistantships, staff assistantships, full tuition waivers, Federal Work-Study, and career-related internships or fieldwork available. Aid available to part-time students. • Dr. Rick Myer, Faculty Chair, 815-753-8431.

Northern State University, Division of Graduate Studies in Education, Program in Guidance and Counseling, Aberdeen, SD 57401-7198. Awards MS Ed. Accredited by NCATE. Offered jointly with Huron University, Jamestown College, and the University of Mary. Part-time and evening/weekend programs available. Faculty: 6 full-time (4 women). Students: 30 full-time (23 women), 6 part-time (4 women); includes 3 minority (1 Hispanic, 2 Native Americans). Average age 32. In 1997, 15 degrees awarded. *Degree requirements:* Thesis optional, foreign language not required. *Average time to degree:* master's–1.5 years full-time. *Entrance requirements:* Minimum GPA of 2.75. Application deadline: 8/15 (priority date; rolling processing; 12/15 for spring admission). Application fee: $15. *Expenses:* Tuition $1999 per year full-time, $83 per credit hour part-time for state residents; $6034 per year full-time, $251 per credit hour part-time for nonresidents. Fees $954 per year full-time, $40 per credit hour part-time. *Financial aid:* 24 students received aid; teaching assistantships, Federal Work-Study, institutionally sponsored loans, and career-related internships or fieldwork available. Aid available to part-time students. Financial aid application deadline: 3/1. • Dr. Paul Deputy, Head, 605-626-2415. Application contact: Dr. Sharon Tebben, Director of Graduate Studies, 605-626-2558. Fax: 605-626-2542.

Northwestern Oklahoma State University, School of Education, Psychology, and Health and Physical Education, Program in Guidance and Counseling K–12, Alva, OK 73717. Awards M Ed. Accredited by NCATE. Part-time programs available. Faculty: 7 full-time (4 women). Students: 2 full-time (1 woman), 32 part-time (24 women); includes 3 minority (2 African Americans, 1 Native American). Average age 32. 19 applicants, 100% accepted. In 1997, 7 degrees awarded (100% found work related to degree). *Entrance requirements:* GRE General Test (minimum combined score of 900) or MAT (minimum score 38), minimum GPA of 2.75. Application deadline: rolling. Application fee: $15. *Tuition:* $73 per semester hour for state residents; $175 per semester hour for nonresidents. *Financial aid:* Federal Work-Study available. Aid available to part-time students. Financial aid application deadline: 5/1. • Dr. Nancy Knous, Coordinator, 405-327-8443. Application contact: Dr. Ed Huckeby, Dean of Graduate School, 405-327-8410.

Northwestern State University of Louisiana, Division of Education, Program in Human Services, Natchitoches, LA 71497. Offerings include counseling and guidance (M Ed, Ed S). Accredited by NCATE. Program faculty: 3 full-time (2 women), 2 part-time (1 woman). *Application deadline:* 8/1 (priority date; rolling processing; 1/10 for spring admission). *Application fee:* $15 ($25 for international students). *Tuition:* $2147 per year full-time, $336 per semester (minimum) part-time for state residents; $6437 per year full-time, $336 per semester (minimum) part-time for nonresidents. • Dr. Hurst Hall, Head, 318-357-4169. Application contact: Dr. Tom Hanson, Dean, Graduate Studies and Research, 318-357-5851. Fax: 318-357-5019.

Northwest Missouri State University, College of Education and Human Services, Department of Psychology and Sociology, Program in Guidance and Counseling, 800 University Drive, Maryville, MO 64468-6001. Awards MS Ed. Accredited by NCATE. Faculty: 8 full-time (2 women). Students: 29 full-time (25 women), 2 part-time (both women). 6 applicants, 100% accepted. In 1997, 9 degrees awarded. *Degree requirements:* Thesis, comprehensive exam required, foreign language not required. *Entrance requirements:* GRE General Test (minimum combined score of 1500 on three sections), GRE Subject Test, TOEFL (minimum score 550), teaching certificate; 2 years of experience; minimum undergraduate GPA of 2.5, 3.0 in major; writing sample. Application deadline: 3/1 (rolling processing). Application fee: $0 ($50 for international students). *Expenses:* Tuition $113 per credit hour for state residents; $197 per credit hour for nonresidents. Fees $3 per credit hour. *Financial aid:* In 1997–98, 1 research assistantship averaging $585 per month was awarded. Financial aid application deadline: 3/1. • Dr. Kenneth Hill, Chairperson, 816-562-1852. Application contact: Dr. Frances Shipley, Dean of Graduate School, 816-562-1145. E-mail: gradsch@acad.nwmissouri.edu.

Northwest Nazarene College, Department of Graduate Studies, Graduate Program in Teacher Education, Nampa, ID 83686-5897. Offerings include school counseling (M Ed). Accredited by NCATE. Postbaccalaureate distance learning degree programs offered. Program faculty: 3 full-time (2 women), 13 part-time (3 women). *Degree requirements:* Action research project required, foreign language and thesis not required. *Application deadline:* 9/1 (rolling processing). *Application fee:* $25. • Dr. Dennis Cartwright, Chair, 208-467-8258. E-mail: ddcartwright@wiley.nnc.edu.

Notre Dame College, Education Division, Program in School Counseling, Manchester, NH 03104-2299. Awards M Ed. Faculty: 1 full-time (0 women), 6 part-time (4 women). Students: 19 full-time (17 women), 15 part-time (11 women). Average age 36. 18 applicants, 50% accepted. In 1997, 8 degrees awarded. *Degree requirements:* Comprehensive exams or thesis required, foreign language not required. *Entrance requirements:* GRE General Test or MAT. Application deadline: rolling. Application fee: $35. *Tuition:* $299 per credit. • Dr. Edward Mahoney, Director, 603-647-5500 Ext. 230.

Oakland University, School of Education and Human Services, Program in Counseling, Rochester, MI 48309-4401. Awards MA, Certificate. Accredited by NCATE. Part-time and evening/weekend programs available. Faculty: 9 full-time. Students: 133 full-time (115 women),

Directory: Counselor Education

Oakland University (continued)

199 part-time (166 women); includes 16 minority (10 African Americans, 4 Asian Americans, 1 Hispanic, 1 Native American), 8 international. Average age 34. 136 applicants, 77% accepted. In 1997, 88 master's awarded. *Entrance requirements:* For master's, minimum GPA of 3.0 for unconditional admission. Application deadline: 7/1 (3/1 for spring admission). Application fee: $30. *Expenses:* Tuition $3852 per year full-time, $214 per credit hour part-time for state residents; $8532 per year full-time, $474 per credit hour part-time for nonresidents. Fees $420 per year. *Financial aid:* Full tuition waivers, Federal Work-Study, institutionally sponsored loans, and career-related internships or fieldwork available. Financial aid application deadline: 3/1; applicants required to submit FAFSA. • Dr. Luellen Ramey, Director, 248-370-4185.

Ohio University, Graduate Studies, College of Education, School of Applied Behavioral Sciences and Educational Leadership, Program in Guidance and Counseling, Athens, OH 45701-2979. Awards M Ed, PhD. Accredited by NCATE. Part-time and evening/weekend programs available. Students: 71 full-time (48 women), 42 part-time (36 women); includes 3 minority (all African Americans), 5 international. 96 applicants, 61% accepted. Terminal master's awarded for partial completion of doctoral program. *Degree requirements:* For master's, thesis or alternative required, foreign language not required; for doctorate, dissertation. *Entrance requirements:* For master's, GRE General Test (minimum combined score of 1000) or MAT (minimum score 48); for doctorate, GRE General Test (minimum combined score of 1000), MAT (minimum score 45), minimum GPA of 3.0, work experience. Application deadline: rolling. Application fee: $30. *Tuition:* $5430 per year full-time, $216 per quarter hour part-time for state residents; $10,431 per year full-time, $423 per quarter hour part-time for nonresidents. *Financial aid:* In 1997–98, 17 students received aid, including 16 teaching assistantships (4 to first-year students), 7 assistantships (2 to first-year students); full tuition waivers, Federal Work-Study, institutionally sponsored loans also available. Financial aid application deadline: 3/15. • Application contact: Dr. Patricia Beamish, Graduate Chair, 740-593-4440.

Oklahoma State University, College of Education, Department of Applied Behavioral Studies, Program in Counseling and Student Personnel, Stillwater, OK 74078. Awards MS. *Application deadline:* 7/1 (priority date). *Application fee:* $25. *Financial aid:* Partial tuition waivers, Federal Work-Study, and career-related internships or fieldwork available. Aid available to part-time students. Financial aid application deadline: 3/1. • Dr. Dale Fuqua, Head, Department of Applied Behavioral Studies, 405-744-6040.

Old Dominion University, Darden College of Education, Department of Educational Leadership and Counseling, Program in Counseling, Norfolk, VA 23529. Offers community agency counseling (MS), counseling (CAS), school counseling (MS), student development counseling in higher education (MS). Accredited by NCATE. Part-time and evening/weekend programs available. Postbaccalaureate distance learning degree programs offered (minimal on-campus study). Students: 57 full-time (45 women), 118 part-time (107 women); includes 30 minority (23 African Americans, 6 Hispanics, 1 Native American), 5 international. Average age 34. In 1997, 42 master's, 3 CASs awarded. *Degree requirements:* Written comprehensive exam required, foreign language and thesis not required. *Entrance requirements:* For master's, GRE General Test or MAT; for CAS, GRE General Test or MAT, interview, minimum graduate GPA of 3.25. Application deadline: 6/1 (10/1 for spring admission). Application fee: $30. *Expenses:* Tuition $180 per credit hour for state residents; $477 per credit hour for nonresidents. Fees $140 per year full-time, $32 per semester part-time. *Financial aid:* In 1997–98, 47 students received aid, including 1 fellowship (to a first-year student) totaling $3,520, 7 research assistantships (4 to first-year students) totaling $25,782, 10 tuition grants (1 to a first-year student) totaling $10,016; teaching assistantships, partial tuition waivers, and career-related internships or fieldwork also available. Aid available to part-time students. Financial aid application deadline: 2/15; applicants required to submit FAFSA. *Faculty research:* Group counseling, loss and grief, marriage and family, substance abuse, counselor education. • Dr. Garrett McAuliffe, Director, 757-683-3225. Fax: 757-683-5756. E-mail: gmcaulif@odu.edu.

Oregon State University, Graduate School, College of Home Economics and Education, School of Education, Program in Counseling, Corvallis, OR 97331. Awards MS, PhD. Accredited by NCATE. Students: 40 full-time, 22 part-time; includes 5 minority (1 African American, 1 Asian American, 2 Hispanics, 1 Native American), 2 international. Average age 37. 31 applicants, 90% accepted. In 1997, 18 master's, 3 doctorates awarded. *Degree requirements:* For master's, thesis or alternative, minimum GPA of 3.0 required, foreign language not required; for doctorate, 1 foreign language, dissertation, minimum GPA of 3.0. *Entrance requirements:* For master's, TOEFL (minimum score 550), minimum GPA of 3.0 in last 90 hours; for doctorate, GRE or MAT, TOEFL (minimum score 550), master's degree, minimum GPA of 3.0 in last 90 hours, 2 years of teaching experience. Application deadline: 2/1 (rolling processing). Application fee: $50. *Tuition:* $6207 per year full-time, $810 per quarter (minimum) part-time for state residents; $10,551 per year full-time, $1293 per quarter (minimum) part-time for nonresidents. *Financial aid:* Teaching assistantships, Federal Work-Study, institutionally sponsored loans, and career-related internships or fieldwork available. Aid available to part-time students. Financial aid application deadline: 2/1. *Faculty research:* Counseling and guidance improvement in social services agencies, elementary and secondary schools. • Dr. Reese House, Director, 541-737-5975.

Our Lady of Holy Cross College, Program in Education, New Orleans, LA 70131-7399. Offerings include counseling (M Ed), with options in marriage and family counseling, school counseling. Program faculty: 5 full-time (2 women), 7 part-time (3 women). *Degree requirements:* Thesis required, foreign language not required. *Entrance requirements:* GRE General Test (minimum combined score of 800), minimum GPA of 2.7. Application deadline: 9/1. Application fee: $20. *Expenses:* Tuition $5760 per year full-time, $240 per semester hour part-time. Fees $167 per year. • Dr. Judith G. Miranti, Dean, 504-394-7744.

Our Lady of the Lake University of San Antonio, School of Education and Clinical Studies, Program in School Counseling, 411 Southwest 24th Street, San Antonio, TX 78207-4689. Awards MS. Part-time and evening/weekend programs available. Faculty: 1 (woman) full-time. Students: 4 part-time (3 women); includes 2 minority (both Hispanics). Average age 44. In 1997, 3 degrees awarded. *Degree requirements:* Computer language, comprehensive exam, practicum required, thesis optional, foreign language not required. *Entrance requirements:* GRE General Test or MAT. Application deadline: rolling. Application fee: $15. *Expenses:* Tuition $371 per credit hour. Fees $57 per semester full-time, $32 per semester part-time. *Financial aid:* Application deadline 4/15. • Dr. Nadene Peterson, Head, 210-434-6711 Ext. 301. Application contact: Debbie Hamilton, Director of Admissions, 210-434-6711 Ext. 314. Fax: 210-436-2314.

Palm Beach Atlantic College, School of Education and Behavioral Studies, Program in Counseling Psychology, West Palm Beach, FL 33416-4708. Offerings include school guidance counseling (MSCP). Program faculty: 2 full-time (0 women), 6 part-time (3 women). *Entrance requirements:* GRE General Test (combined average 1000), minimum GPA of 3.0 in last 60 hours. Application deadline: 7/15 (priority date; rolling processing; 11/15 for spring admission). Application fee: $35. *Tuition:* $280 per credit hour. • Dr. Joe Kloba, Director, 561-803-2367. Fax: 561-803-2186. E-mail: klobaj@pbac.edu. Application contact: Carolanne M. Brown, Director of Graduate Admissions, 800-281-3466. Fax: 561-803-2115. E-mail: grad@pbac.edu.

Pennsylvania State University University Park Campus, College of Education, Department of Counselor Education, Counseling Psychology and Rehabilitation Services, Program in Counselor Education, University Park, PA 16802-1503. Offers counselor education (D Ed), elementary counseling (M Ed, MS). Accredited by NCATE. Students: 71 full-time (50 women), 96 part-time (71 women). In 1997, 56 master's, 3 doctorates awarded. *Entrance requirements:* GRE General Test. Application fee: $40. *Expenses:* Tuition $6534 per year full-time, $276 per credit part-time for state residents; $13,460 per year full-time, $561 per credit part-time for nonresidents. Fees $252 per year (minimum) full-time, $43 per semester (minimum) part-time. • Dr. Donald B. Keat, Professor in Charge, 814-863-2415.

Pittsburg State University, School of Education, Department of Psychology and Counseling, Program in Counselor Education, Pittsburg, KS 66762-5880. Offers counseling (MS). Accredited by NCATE. Students: 3 full-time (2 women), 3 part-time (1 woman). *Degree requirements:* Thesis or alternative required, foreign language not required. *Entrance requirements:* GRE General Test, minimum GPA of 2.8. Application fee: $40. *Tuition:* $2418 per year full-time, $103 per credit hour part-time for state residents; $6130 per year full-time, $258 per credit hour part-time for nonresidents. *Financial aid:* Teaching assistantships, Federal Work-Study, and career-related internships or fieldwork available. • Dr. David Solly, Chairman, Department of Psychology and Counseling, 316-235-4523.

Plattsburgh State University of New York, Faculty of Professional Studies, Department of Counselor Education, Plattsburgh, NY 12901-2681. Offers programs in college/agency counseling (MS), including community counseling, student affairs practice; school counseling (CAS). Part-time programs available. Students: 48 full-time (30 women), 17 part-time (12 women); includes 9 minority (7 African Americans, 1 Hispanic, 1 Native American), 1 international. 40 applicants, 73% accepted. In 1997, 32 master's, 19 CASs awarded. *Degree requirements:* Comprehensive exam required, thesis optional, foreign language not required. *Entrance requirements:* For master's, GRE General Test or MAT, minimum GPA of 2.5. Application deadline: rolling. Application fee: $50. *Expenses:* Tuition $5100 per year full-time, $213 per credit hour part-time for state residents; $8416 per year full-time, $351 per credit hour part-time for nonresidents. Fees $395 per year full-time, $15.10 per credit hour part-time. *Financial aid:* In 1997–98, 41 students received aid, including 1 teaching assistantship (to a first-year student) averaging $420 per month and totaling $3,360; research assistantships, administrative assistantships, editorial assistantships, Federal Work-Study, and career-related internships or fieldwork also available. Aid available to part-time students. Financial aid application deadline: 4/15; applicants required to submit FAFSA. *Faculty research:* Campus violence, program accreditation, substance abuse, vocational assessment, group counseling, divorce. Total annual research expenditures: $15,880. • Dr. Donald Haight, Coordinator, 518-564-4178.

Plymouth State College of the University System of New Hampshire, Department of Education, Program in Guidance and Counseling, Plymouth, NH 03264-1595. Awards M Ed. Accredited by NCATE. Part-time and evening/weekend programs available. Students: 11 full-time (9 women), 22 part-time (17 women); includes 1 international. Average age 41. 14 applicants, 71% accepted. In 1997, 22 degrees awarded. *Entrance requirements:* GRE General Test (average 500 on each section) or MAT (minimum score 50), minimum GPA of 3.0. Application deadline: 9/1 (priority date; rolling processing). Application fee: $25 ($35 for international students). *Tuition:* $232 per credit for state residents; $254 per credit for nonresidents. *Financial aid:* Graduate assistantships, institutionally sponsored loans, and career-related internships or fieldwork available. Aid available to part-time students. Financial aid application deadline: 3/15; applicants required to submit FAFSA. • Dr. Gary Goodnough, Co-Adviser, 603-535-2821. Application contact: Maryann Szabadics, Administrative Assistant, 603-535-2636. Fax: 603-535-2572. E-mail: for.grad@psc.plymouth.edu.

Portland State University, School of Education, Department of Special Education and Counselor Education, Program in Counselor Education, Portland, OR 97207-0751. Awards MA, MS. Accredited by NCATE. Part-time and evening/weekend programs available. Faculty: 24 full-time (13 women), 1 part-time (0 women), 24.2 FTE. Students: 37 full-time (27 women), 59 part-time (38 women); includes 7 minority (2 African Americans, 4 Hispanics, 1 Native American), 1 international. Average age 38. 84 applicants, 57% accepted. *Degree requirements:* Variable foreign language requirement, thesis or alternative, written exam. *Entrance requirements:* California Basic Educational Skills Test, GRE General Test or MAT, TOEFL (minimum score 550), minimum GPA of 3.0 in upper-division course work or 2.75 overall. Application deadline: 2/1. Application fee: $50. *Tuition:* $6101 per year full-time, $689 per semester (minimum) part-time for state residents; $10,445 per year full-time, $689 per semester (minimum) part-time for nonresidents. *Financial aid:* Research assistantships, teaching assistantships, Federal Work-Study, institutionally sponsored loans, and career-related internships or fieldwork available. Aid available to part-time students. Financial aid application deadline: 3/1; applicants required to submit FAFSA. *Faculty research:* Suicide, careers, human growth and development, supervision, gangs. Total annual research expenditures: $3000. • Dr. Hanoch Livneh, Coordinator, 503-725-4632. E-mail: hanoch@ed.pdx.edu. Application contact: Amber Jones, Graduate Secretary, 503-725-4632. Fax: 503-725-5599. E-mail: amber@ed.pdx.edu.

Prairie View A&M University, College of Education, Department of School Services, Prairie View, TX 77446-0188. Offerings include counseling (MA, MS Ed). Accredited by NCATE. Department faculty: 8 full-time (1 woman). *Average time to degree:* master's–2.5 years full-time, 4 years part-time. *Application deadline:* 7/1 (priority date; rolling processing; 11/1 for spring admission). *Application fee:* $10. *Tuition:* $2202 per year full-time, $336 per semester (minimum) part-time for state residents; $6000 per year full-time, $963 per semester (minimum) part-time for nonresidents. • Dr. William H. Parker, Head, 409-857-2312. Fax: 409-857-2911.

Providence College, Department of Education, Program in Guidance and Counseling, Providence, RI 02918. Awards M Ed. Part-time and evening/weekend programs available. Faculty: 1 full-time (0 women), 7 part-time (1 woman). Students: 3 full-time (all women), 42 part-time (36 women); includes 1 minority (African American). Average age 32. 19 applicants, 95% accepted. In 1997, 35 degrees awarded (100% found work related to degree). *Degree requirements:* Comprehensive exam required, foreign language and thesis not required. *Entrance requirements:* GRE General Test (minimum combined score of 1000) or MAT (minimum score 45), TOEFL. Application deadline: 8/12 (priority date; rolling processing; 12/1 for spring admission). Application fee: $40. *Tuition:* $621 per course. *Financial aid:* In 1997–98, 4 graduate assistantships (all to first-year students) averaging $650 per month and totaling $31,200 were awarded; institutionally sponsored loans and career-related internships or fieldwork also available. Aid available to part-time students. Financial aid applicants required to submit FAFSA. • Dr. Thomas F. Flaherty, Dean, Graduate School, 401-865-2247. Fax: 401-865-2057.

Purdue University, School of Education, Department of Educational Studies, West Lafayette, IN 47907. Offerings include counseling and development (MS, MS Ed, PhD, Ed S). Accredited by NCATE. Department faculty: 26 full-time (13 women), 23 part-time (14 women). *Degree requirements:* For master's, thesis optional; for doctorate, dissertation, oral and written exams; for Ed S, oral presentation, project required, thesis not required. *Entrance requirements:* For master's, TOEFL (minimum score 550), minimum B average; for doctorate, GRE General Test (minimum score 500 on each section), TOEFL (minimum score 550); for Ed S, minimum B average. Application deadline: 2/1 (9/15 for spring admission). Application fee: $30. Electronic applications accepted. *Tuition:* $3500 per year full-time, $126 per credit hour part-time for state residents; $11,720 per year full-time, $387 per credit hour part-time for nonresidents. • Dr. D. H. Schunk, Head, 765-494-9170. Fax: 765-496-1228. E-mail: dschunk@purdue.edu. Application contact: Christine Larsen, Coordinator of Graduate Studies, 765-494-2345. Fax: 765-494-5832. E-mail: gradoffice@soe.purdue.edu.

Purdue University Calumet, School of Professional Studies, Department of Education, Program in Counseling and Personnel Services, Hammond, IN 46323-2094. Awards MS Ed. *Entrance requirements:* TOEFL. Application fee: $30.

Queens College of the City University of New York, Social Science Division, School of Education, Department of Educational and Community Programs, Program in Counselor Education, 65-30 Kissena Boulevard, Flushing, NY 11367-1597. Awards MS Ed. Part-time programs available. Students: 39 full-time (31 women), 66 part-time (55 women); includes 32 minority (11 African Americans, 5 Asian Americans, 15 Hispanics, 1 Native American), 1 international. 108 applicants, 65% accepted. In 1997, 31 degrees awarded. *Degree requirements:* Research project required, foreign language and thesis not required. *Entrance requirements:* TOEFL (minimum score 600), minimum GPA of 3.0. Application deadline: 4/1 (rolling processing; 11/1 for spring admission). Application fee: $40. *Expenses:* Tuition $4350 per year full-time, $185 per credit part-time for state residents; $7600 per year full-time, $320 per credit part-time for nonresidents. Fees $104 per year. *Financial aid:* Partial tuition waivers, Federal Work-Study, institutionally sponsored loans, and career-related internships or fieldwork available.

Aid available to part-time students. Financial aid application deadline: 4/1; applicants required to submit FAFSA. • Dr. Lester Schwartz, Coordinator and Graduate Adviser, 718-997-5240. Application contact: Mario Caruso, Director of Graduate Admissions, 718-997-5200. Fax: 718-997-5193. E-mail: graduate%queens.bitnet@cunyvm.cuny.edu.

Radford University, Graduate College, College of Education and Human Development, Department of Counselor Education, Radford, VA 24142. Awards MS. Accredited by NCATE. Part-time programs available. Postbaccalaureate distance learning degree programs offered (minimal on-campus study). Faculty: 7 full-time (3 women), 3 part-time (2 women), 7.3 FTE. Students: 50 full-time (34 women), 35 part-time (27 women); includes 9 minority (7 African Americans, 1 Asian American, 1 Hispanic). Average age 31. 61 applicants, 56% accepted. In 1997, 29 degrees awarded. *Degree requirements:* Comprehensive exam required, foreign language and thesis not required. *Entrance requirements:* GMAT, GRE General Test, MAT, or NTE; TOEFL (minimum score 550), minimum GPA of 2.7. Application deadline: 2/1 (priority date; rolling processing; 10/1 for spring admission). Application fee: $25. Electronic applications accepted. *Expenses:* Tuition $2302 per year full-time, $147 per credit hour part-time for state residents; $5672 per year full-time, $287 per credit hour part-time for nonresidents. Fees $1222 per year full-time. *Financial aid:* In 1997–98, 67 students received aid, including 12 fellowships totaling $57,150, 9 research assistantships totaling $34,450, 4 teaching assistantships totaling $27,156, scholarships/grants totaling $427,620; Federal Work-Study, institutionally sponsored loans, and career-related internships or fieldwork also available. Financial aid application deadline: 2/1; applicants required to submit FAFSA. • Dr. Donald Anderson, Chairperson, 540-831-6265. Fax: 540-831-6053. E-mail: danderso@runet.edu.

Regent University, Graduate School, School of Counseling and Human Services, Virginia Beach, VA 23464-9800. Awards MA, Psy D, MBA/MA, M Div/MA, M Ed/MA. Programs in counseling (MA), counseling psychology (Psy D). Part-time programs available. Faculty: 6 full-time (2 women), 3 part-time (all women), 8 FTE. Students: 114 full-time (94 women), 39 part-time (27 women); includes 35 minority (24 African Americans, 4 Asian Americans, 6 Hispanics, 1 Native American). Average age 34. 130 applicants, 54% accepted. In 1997, 50 master's awarded. *Degree requirements:* For master's, thesis or alternative, internship, practicum, written competency exam required, foreign language not required. *Average time to degree:* master's–2 years full-time, 3.5 years part-time. *Entrance requirements:* For master's, GRE General Test or MAT, minimum undergraduate GPA of 2.75. Application deadline: 6/1 (priority date; rolling processing). Application fee: $40. *Expenses:* Tuition $300 per credit hour (minimum). Fees $18 per semester. *Financial aid:* 71 students received aid; full and partial tuition waivers and career-related internships or fieldwork available. Financial aid application deadline: 5/1. *Faculty research:* Biblical hermeneutics, character formation, substance abuse, counseling techniques, dysfunctional human relationships. • Dr. Rosemarie Hughes, Dean, 757-226-4269. Fax: 757-226-4262. E-mail: rosehug@regent.edu. Application contact: Cindy Richman, Director of Admissions for Counseling, 757-226-4121. Fax: 757-226-4263. E-mail: counschool@regent.edu.

Rhode Island College, School of Graduate Studies, School of Education and Human Development, Department of Counseling and Educational Psychology, Program in Agency Counseling, Providence, RI 02908-1924. Awards MA. Accredited by NCATE. Faculty: 9 full-time (2 women), 8 part-time (5 women). Students: 10 full-time (8 women), 41 part-time (33 women); includes 2 minority (1 Asian American, 1 Hispanic). In 1997, 22 degrees awarded. *Entrance requirements:* GRE General Test or MAT. Application deadline: 4/1 (rolling processing). Application fee: $25. *Tuition:* $4064 per year full-time, $214 per credit part-time for state residents; $7658 per year full-time, $376 per credit part-time for nonresidents. *Financial aid:* Application deadline 4/1. • Dr. Murray H. Finley, Chair, Department of Counseling and Educational Psychology, 401-456-8023.

Rhode Island College, School of Graduate Studies, School of Education and Human Development, Department of Counseling and Educational Psychology, Program in Counselor Education, Providence, RI 02908-1924. Awards M Ed, CAGS. Accredited by NCATE. Faculty: 9 full-time (2 women), 8 part-time (5 women). Students: 2 full-time (0 women), 17 part-time (12 women); includes 1 minority (African American). In 1997, 4 master's, 2 CAGSs awarded. *Degree requirements:* For CAGS, thesis required, foreign language not required. *Entrance requirements:* For master's, GRE General Test or MAT. Application deadline: 4/1 (rolling processing). Application fee: $25. *Tuition:* $4064 per year full-time, $214 per credit part-time for state residents; $7658 per year full-time, $376 per credit part-time for nonresidents. *Financial aid:* Application deadline 4/1. • Dr. Murray H. Finley, Chair, Department of Counseling and Educational Psychology, 401-456-8023.

Rider University, School of Graduate Education and Human Services, Program in Counseling Services, Lawrenceville, NJ 08648-3001. Awards MA, Ed S. Accredited by NCATE. Part-time and evening/weekend programs available. Faculty: 7 full-time (3 women), 5 part-time (1 woman). Students: 9 full-time (6 women), 141 part-time (115 women). Average age 36. 49 applicants, 51% accepted. In 1997, 73 master's awarded. *Degree requirements:* For master's, comprehensive exams, research project required, foreign language and thesis not required. *Entrance requirements:* For master's, GRE or MAT, interview, minimum GPA of 2.5. Application deadline: 8/1 (priority date; rolling processing; 11/1 for spring admission). Application fee: $35. *Tuition:* $329 per credit hour. *Financial aid:* In 1997–98, 6 research assistantships were awarded; career-related internships or fieldwork also available. Aid available to part-time students. *Faculty research:* Integrating the use of computers in counseling, self-esteem, hope collaboration. • Dr. Emmanual Ahia, Adviser, 609-896-5339. Application contact: Dr. John Carpenter, Dean, Continuing Studies, 609-896-5036. Fax: 609-896-5261.

Rivier College, Graduate Education Department, Program in Counselor Education, Nashua, NH 03060-5086. Awards M Ed. Part-time and evening/weekend programs available. *Entrance requirements:* GRE General Test or MAT. Application deadline: rolling. Application fee: $25.

Rollins College, Program in Counseling, Winter Park, FL 32789-4499. Offers mental health counseling (MA), school counseling (MA). Part-time and evening/weekend programs available. Faculty: 4 full-time (3 women), 8 part-time (3 women), 8 FTE. Students: 37 full-time (30 women), 105 part-time (91 women); includes 7 minority (4 African Americans, 3 Hispanics), 2 international. Average age 30. 110 applicants, 59% accepted. In 1997, 38 degrees awarded. *Degree requirements:* Comprehensive exam required, foreign language and thesis not required. *Entrance requirements:* GRE General Test or MAT, interview. Application deadline: 4/15 (priority date). Application fee: $50. *Tuition:* $256 per hour. *Financial aid:* In 1997–98, 57 students received aid, including 2 teaching assistantships totaling $8,800. Financial aid application deadline: 3/23. • Dr. Allan Dye, Director, 407-646-2307. Application contact: Laura Pfister, Coordinator of Records and Registration, 407-646-2416. Fax: 407-646-1551.

Roosevelt University, College of Education, Chicago, IL 60605-1394. Offerings include guidance and counseling (MA). Accredited by NCATE. *Application deadline:* 6/1 (priority date; rolling processing). *Application fee:* $25 ($35 for international students). *Expenses:* Tuition $445 per credit hour. Fees $100 per year. • Dr. George Lowery, Dean, 312-341-3700. Application contact: Joanne Canyon-Heller, Coordinator of Graduate Admissions, 312-341-3612.

Rosemont College, College of Graduate Studies, Program in Counseling Psychology, Rosemont, PA 19010-1699. Offerings include school counseling (MA). Program faculty: 4 full-time (2 women), 5 part-time (2 women). *Degree requirements:* Thesis or alternative required, foreign language not required. *Entrance requirements:* GRE or MAT. Application deadline: rolling. Application fee: $50. *Tuition:* $425 per credit. • Edward Samulewicz, Director, 610-527-0200 Ext. 2359. Application contact: Stan Rostkowski, Enrollment Coordinator, 610-527-0200 Ext. 2187. Fax: 610-526-2964. E-mail: roscolgrad@rosemont.edu.

Sage Graduate School, Graduate School, Division of Education, Program in Guidance and Counseling, Troy, NY 12180-4115. Awards MS Ed, PMC. Part-time and evening/weekend programs available. Students: 32 full-time (29 women), 54 part-time (35 women). *Entrance requirements:* For master's, GRE General Test, minimum GPA of 2.75. Application deadline: 8/1 (rolling processing; 12/15 for spring admission). Application fee: $25. *Expenses:* Tuition $360 per credit hour. Fees $50 per semester. *Financial aid:* Research assistantships and career-related internships or fieldwork available. Aid available to part-time students. Financial aid application deadline: 7/1; applicants required to submit FAFSA. *Faculty research:* Roles and responsibilities of guidance personnel, projections of need for guidance counselors. • Dr. Robert R. Giammatteo, Coordinator, 518-244-2499. Fax: 518-244-2334. E-mail: giammr@sage.edu. Application contact: Melissa Robertson, Associate Director of Admissions, 518-244-6878. Fax: 518-244-6880. E-mail: sgsadm@sage.edu.

St. Bonaventure University, School of Education, Program in Counselor Education, St. Bonaventure, NY 14778-2284. Offers counseling education (Adv C), counseling education-agency (MS, MS Ed), counseling education-school (MS, MS Ed). Faculty: 4 full-time (0 women), 1 part-time (0 women). Students: 75 full-time (56 women), 42 part-time (25 women); includes 6 minority (3 African Americans, 2 Hispanics, 1 Native American). 59 applicants, 97% accepted. In 1997, 45 master's, 5 Adv Cs awarded. *Degree requirements:* For master's, written comprehensive exams required, thesis optional, foreign language not required. *Entrance requirements:* For master's, GRE, interview, writing sample. Application deadline: 8/1 (rolling processing). Application fee: $35. *Tuition:* $8100 per year full-time, $450 per credit hour part-time. *Financial aid:* In 1997–98, 7 students received aid, including 2 research assistantships (1 to a first-year student); career-related internships or fieldwork also available. Aid available to part-time students. *Faculty research:* Parent education, learning disabilities, stress management. • Dr. Alan Silliker, Director, 716-375-2368. Fax: 716-375-2360. E-mail: asilliker@sbu.edu.

St. Cloud State University, College of Education, Department of Applied Psychology, Program in Counseling, St. Cloud, MN 56301-4498. Offers community counseling (MS), rehabilitation counseling (MS), secondary school counseling (MS). Accredited by NCATE. Students: 53 full-time (44 women), 24 part-time (16 women). *Degree requirements:* Thesis or alternative required, foreign language not required. *Entrance requirements:* GRE General Test, minimum GPA of 2.75. Application deadline: 4/15. Application fee: $20 ($100 for international students). *Expenses:* Tuition $128 per credit for state residents; $203 per credit for nonresidents. Fees $16.32 per credit. *Financial aid:* In 1997–98, 16 graduate assistantships were awarded; Federal Work-Study and career-related internships or fieldwork also available. Financial aid application deadline: 3/1. • Dr. Niloufer Merchant, Coordinator, 320-255-3131. Application contact: Ann Anderson, Graduate Studies Office, 320-255-2113. Fax: 320-654-5371. E-mail: anna@grad.stcloud.msus.edu.

St. John's University, School of Education and Human Services, Division of Human Services and Counseling, Program in School Counseling/Bilingual School Counseling, Jamaica, NY 11439. Awards MS Ed. Part-time and evening/weekend programs available. Students: 17 full-time (11 women), 83 part-time (68 women); includes 39 minority (13 African Americans, 1 Asian American, 24 Hispanics, 1 Native American), 2 international. Average age 33. 61 applicants, 70% accepted. In 1997, 29 degrees awarded. *Degree requirements:* Internship, 2 practica required, foreign language and thesis not required. *Entrance requirements:* Interview, minimum GPA of 3.0, 18 credits in behavioral sciences. Application deadline: 6/1 (rolling processing; 10/1 for spring admission). Application fee: $40. *Expenses:* Tuition $525 per credit. Fees $150 per year. *Financial aid:* Administrative assistantships, Federal Work-Study, and career-related internships or fieldwork available. Aid available to part-time students. Financial aid application deadline: 3/1; applicants required to submit FAFSA. *Faculty research:* Counseling techniques, communication skills in counseling, learning styles and counseling, computers in counseling. • Dr. Shirley Griggs, Coordinator, 718-990-1558. Fax: 718-990-1614. Application contact: Shamus J. McGrenra, TOR, Associate Director, Graduate Admissions, 718-990-6107. Fax: 718-990-5736. E-mail: mcgrenrs@stjohns.edu.

Saint Joseph College, Field of Education and Counseling, Counseling Institute, Program in Counseling, West Hartford, CT 06117-2700. Awards MA, Certificate. Certificate admissions temporarily suspended. Students: 104 (89 women). Average age 27. In 1997, 28 master's, 2 Certificates awarded. *Degree requirements:* For master's, thesis or alternative required, foreign language not required. *Application deadline:* 8/29 (rolling processing). *Application fee:* $25. *Tuition:* $395 per credit. *Financial aid:* Application deadline 8/31. • Dr. Nancy Lund, Director, Counseling Institute, 860-232-4571 Ext. 343.

St. Lawrence University, Department of Education, Program in Counseling and Human Development, Canton, NY 13617-1455. Awards M Ed, CAS. Part-time and evening/weekend programs available. Faculty: 2 full-time (0 women), 6 part-time (2 women). Students: 10 full-time, 20 part-time. *Entrance requirements:* For master's, GRE General Test. Application deadline: rolling. Application fee: $0. *Expenses:* Tuition $460 per credit hour. Fees $35 per year. *Financial aid:* In 1997–98, 1 research assistantship (to a first-year student) totaling $10,000 was awarded. *Faculty research:* Defense mechanisms and mediation. • Dr. Arthur Clark, Coordinator, 315-229-5863.

Saint Louis University, Institute for Leadership and Public Service, Programs in Education, Department of Counseling and Family Therapy, St. Louis, MO 63103-2097. Offers programs in counseling and family therapy (PhD), human development counseling (MA), school counseling (MA). Accredited by NCATE. Faculty: 4 full-time (2 women), 7 part-time (3 women). *Degree requirements:* For master's, comprehensive oral exam required, foreign language and thesis not required; for doctorate, dissertation, preliminary oral and written exams. *Entrance requirements:* For master's, GRE General Test or MAT, interview; for doctorate, GRE General Test, interview. Application deadline: 2/1 (rolling processing; 11/1 for spring admission). Application fee: $40. *Tuition:* $542 per credit hour. *Financial aid:* Application deadline 4/1. *Faculty research:* Learning styles/personality differences, black males' counseling perspectives, adult-sibling relationships, clinical supervision, low-income clients. • Dr. John DiTiberio, Director, 314-977-2479. Application contact: Dr. Marcia Buresch, Assistant Dean of the Graduate School, 314-977-2240. Fax: 314-977-3943.

Saint Martin's College, Graduate Programs, Department of Education, Lacey, WA 98503-7500. Offerings include counseling and guidance (M Ed). Department faculty: 8 full-time (3 women), 5 part-time (2 women). *Application deadline:* 7/1 (priority date; rolling processing; 12/1 for spring admission). *Application fee:* $25. • Dr. Paul Nelson, Director, 360-438-4529. Application contact: Michelle Roman, Administrative Assistant, 360-438-4333.

Saint Mary's College of California, School of Education, Program in Counseling Leadership, Moraga, CA 94575. Awards MA. Part-time and evening/weekend programs available. Faculty: 3 full-time (1 woman), 6 part-time (5 women). Students: 21 full-time (18 women), 50 part-time (44 women); includes 12 minority (3 African Americans, 2 Asian Americans, 7 Hispanics), 2 international. Average age 35. 30 applicants, 90% accepted. In 1997, 17 degrees awarded (100% found work related to degree). *Degree requirements:* Thesis or alternative required, foreign language not required. *Entrance requirements:* Interview, minimum GPA of 3.0. Application deadline: rolling. Application fee: $50. *Tuition:* $1319 per course. *Financial aid:* Career-related internships or fieldwork available. Aid available to part-time students. Financial aid application deadline: 2/15. *Faculty research:* Counselor training effectiveness. • Colette Fleuridas, Director, 925-631-4489.

St. Thomas University, School of Graduate Studies, Department of Education, Program in Guidance and Counseling, Miami, FL 33054-6459. Awards MS, Certificate. Part-time and evening/weekend programs available. *Degree requirements:* For master's, comprehensive exam required, foreign language and thesis not required. *Average time to degree:* master's–2 years full-time. *Entrance requirements:* For master's, TOEFL (minimum score 550), interview, minimum GPA of 3.0 or GRE. Application deadline: 6/15 (priority date; rolling processing; 11/15 for spring admission). Application fee: $30. *Tuition:* $410 per credit.

Salem State College, Department of Education, Program in Guidance and Counseling, Salem, MA 01970-5353. Awards M Ed. Accredited by NCATE. *Entrance requirements:* GRE

Directory: Counselor Education

Salem State College (continued)
General Test. Application deadline: rolling. Application fee: $25. *Expenses:* Tuition $140 per credit hour for state residents; $230 per credit hour for nonresidents. Fees $20 per credit hour.

Sam Houston State University, College of Education and Applied Science, Department of Education and Applied Science, Department of Educational Leadership and Counseling, Counseling Program, Huntsville, TX 77341. Awards MA, M Ed. Accredited by NCATE. Part-time programs available. Students: 18 full-time (17 women), 105 part-time (85 women). Average age 30. In 1997, 53 degrees awarded. *Entrance requirements:* GRE General Test (minimum combined score of 800). Application fee: $15. *Tuition:* $1810 per year full-time, $297 per semester (minimum) part-time for state residents; $6922 per year full-time, $924 per semester (minimum) part-time for nonresidents. *Financial aid:* Federal Work-Study and career-related internships or fieldwork available. Aid available to part-time students. *Faculty research:* Family counseling, career counseling, business emergent counseling. • Dr. Genevieve Brown, Chair, Department of Educational Leadership and Counseling, 409-294-1144. Fax: 409-294-1102. E-mail: edu_gxb@shsu.edu.

San Diego State University, College of Education, Department of Counseling and School Psychology, San Diego, CA 92182. Awards MS. Accredited by NCATE. Evening/weekend programs available. Students: 100 full-time (66 women), 29 part-time (22 women); includes 71 minority (25 African Americans, 10 Asian Americans, 31 Hispanics, 5 Native Americans), 3 international. Average age 30. *Entrance requirements:* GRE General Test (minimum combined score of 950), TOEFL (minimum score 550), interview. Application deadline: 6/1 (priority date; rolling processing; 12/1 for spring admission). Application fee: $55. *Expenses:* Tuition $0 for state residents; $246 per unit for nonresidents. Fees $1932 per year full-time, $1266 per year part-time. *Financial aid:* Career-related internships or fieldwork available. *Faculty research:* Multicultural and cross-cultural counseling and training, AIDS counseling. Total annual research expenditures: $150,000. • Emery Cummins, Interim Chair, 619-594-6109. Fax: 619-594-7025. E-mail: emery.cummins@sdsu.edu. Application contact: Linda Terry, Graduate Adviser, 619-594-7455.

San Francisco State University, College of Health and Human Services, Department of Counseling, Program in Counseling, San Francisco, CA 94132-1722. Awards MS. Part-time programs available. *Degree requirements:* Culminating written description of internship required, foreign language and thesis not required. *Entrance requirements:* Minimum GPA of 2.5 in last 60 units. Application deadline: 2/15 (priority date; rolling processing). Application fee: $55. *Expenses:* Tuition $0 for state residents; $246 per unit for nonresidents. Fees $1982 per year full-time, $1316 per year part-time.

San Jose State University, College of Education, Program in Counseling, San Jose, CA 95192-0001. Awards MA. Accredited by NCATE. Evening/weekend programs available. Faculty: 6 full-time (1 woman), 2 part-time (1 woman). Students: 61 full-time (46 women), 65 part-time (47 women); includes 61 minority (12 African Americans, 16 Asian Americans, 33 Hispanics). Average age 36. 88 applicants, 83% accepted. In 1997, 32 degrees awarded. *Degree requirements:* Thesis or alternative required, foreign language not required. *Application deadline:* 6/1 (rolling processing). *Application fee:* $59. *Expenses:* Tuition $0 for state residents; $246 per unit for nonresidents. Fees $2017 per year full-time, $1351 per year part-time. *Financial aid:* Career-related internships or fieldwork available. • Dr. Gary Johnson, Director, 408-924-3634.

Santa Clara University, Division of Counseling Psychology and Education, Program in Counseling, Santa Clara, CA 95053-0001. Offers health psychology (MA), pastoral counseling (MA). Part-time and evening/weekend programs available. Students: 7 full-time (all women), 17 part-time (15 women); includes 2 minority (1 African American, 1 Asian American), 1 international. Average age 35. 5 applicants, 100% accepted. In 1997, 17 degrees awarded. *Degree requirements:* Comprehensive exam required, thesis optional, foreign language not required. *Entrance requirements:* GRE or MAT, TOEFL, minimum GPA of 3.0, 1 year of related experience. Application deadline: 5/1 (2/1 for spring admission). Application fee: $30. *Financial aid:* Fellowships, teaching assistantships, Federal Work-Study, and career-related internships or fieldwork available. Aid available to part-time students. Financial aid application deadline: 2/1. • Director, 408-554-4434. Application contact: Barbara F. Simmons, Assistant to the Dean, 408-554-4355. Fax: 408-554-2392.

Seattle Pacific University, School of Education, Program in School Counseling, Seattle, WA 98119-1997. Awards M Ed. Accredited by NCATE. Part-time programs available. Students: 8 full-time (all women), 33 part-time (23 women); includes 3 minority (1 African American, 1 Asian American, 1 Hispanic), 2 international. Average age 31. In 1997, 15 degrees awarded. *Average time to degree:* master's–3 years part-time. *Entrance requirements:* MAT (minimum score 35) or GRE General Test (minimum score 300 on verbal section, 350 on quantitative, 950 combined), minimum GPA of 3.0. Application deadline: 7/1 (priority date; rolling processing; 3/1 for spring admission). Application fee: $50. *Tuition:* $274 per credit. *Financial aid:* In 1997–98, 4 research assistantships were awarded. • Dr. Ginger MacDonald, Chair, 206-281-2707. Fax: 206-281-2756. E-mail: gmac@spu.edu.

Seattle University, School of Education, Division of Leadership and Service, Program in Counseling, Seattle, WA 98122. Awards MA. Accredited by NCATE. Part-time and evening/weekend programs available. Students: 8 full-time (7 women), 121 part-time (105 women); includes 9 minority (2 African Americans, 6 Asian Americans, 1 Hispanic), 1 international. Average age 33. 48 applicants, 42% accepted. In 1997, 23 degrees awarded. *Degree requirements:* Comprehensive exam required, foreign language and thesis not required. *Entrance requirements:* Interview; GRE, MAT, or minimum GPA of 3.0; related work experience. Application deadline: 3/1 (11/1 for spring admission). Application fee: $55. *Expenses:* Tuition $339 per credit hour (minimum). Fees $70 per year. • Dr. Jackie Leibsohn, Coordinator, 206-296-5750.

Seton Hall University, College of Education and Human Services, Department of Professional Psychology and Family Therapy, Programs in Counselor Preparation, South Orange, NJ 07079-2697. Awards MA. Part-time and evening/weekend programs available. *Degree requirements:* Comprehensive exam required, foreign language and thesis not required. *Entrance requirements:* GRE or MAT, interview. Application deadline: rolling. Application fee: $50. *Expenses:* Tuition $500 per credit. Fees $610 per year full-time, $185 per semester part-time. *Financial aid:* Application deadline 2/1. *Faculty research:* Vocational indecision, life skills, counseling process. • Dr. Delores Thompson, Director, 973-275-2742. E-mail: thompsde@shu.edu.

Shippensburg University of Pennsylvania, College of Education and Human Services, Department of Counseling, Shippensburg, PA 17257-2299. Offers programs in counseling (MS), guidance and counseling (M Ed). Accredited by NCATE. Faculty: 10 full-time (3 women), 2 part-time (1 woman). Students: 65 full-time (49 women), 81 part-time (59 women); includes 11 minority (7 African Americans, 1 Asian American, 3 Native Americans), 3 international. Average age 31. In 1997, 46 degrees awarded. *Degree requirements:* Thesis optional, foreign language not required. *Entrance requirements:* GRE General Test or minimum GPA of 2.5, interview. Application deadline: rolling. Application fee: $25. Electronic applications accepted. *Expenses:* Tuition $3468 per year full-time, $193 per credit hour part-time for state residents; $6236 per year full-time, $346 per credit hour part-time for nonresidents. Fees $678 per year full-time, $108 per semester (minimum) part-time. *Financial aid:* In 1997–98, 59 graduate assistantships were awarded. Financial aid application deadline: 3/1. • Dr. Thomas L. Hozman, Chairperson, 717-532-1668.

Siena Heights University, Program in Counselor Education, Adrian, MI 49221-1796. Offers agency counseling (MA), school counseling (MA). Part-time and evening/weekend programs available. *Degree requirements:* Computer language, thesis, presentation required, foreign language not required. *Average time to degree:* master's–2.5 years full-time, 4 years part-time. *Entrance requirements:* Minimum GPA of 3.0, interview. Application deadline: 7/1 (priority date; rolling processing; 12/1 for spring admission). Application fee: $25. *Faculty research:* Consultation, special education competencies of school counselors.

Simon Fraser University, Faculty of Education, Program in Guidance and Counselling, Burnaby, BC V5A 1S6, Canada. Awards MA, M Ed. *Degree requirements:* Thesis (for some programs), project or thesis required, foreign language not required. *Entrance requirements:* TOEFL (minimum score 570), TWE (minimum score 5), or International English Language Test (minimum score 7.5), minimum GPA of 3.0. Application fee: $55. *Expenses:* Tuition $768 per trimester. Fees $207 per year full-time, $61 per trimester part-time. • Application contact: Graduate Secretary, 604-291-4787. Fax: 604-291-3203.

Slippery Rock University of Pennsylvania, College of Education, Department of Counseling and Educational Psychology, Slippery Rock, PA 16057. Offers programs in counseling (MA), including child and youth counseling, gerontological counseling, student personnel, substance abuse counseling; counseling psychology (MA); elementary guidance (M Ed); secondary guidance (M Ed). Accredited by NCATE. Part-time and evening/weekend programs available. *Degree requirements:* Comprehensive exams required, thesis optional, foreign language not required. *Entrance requirements:* GRE, minimum GPA of 2.75. Application deadline: 7/1 (priority date; rolling processing; 11/1 for spring admission). Application fee: $25. *Tuition:* $4484 per year full-time, $247 per credit part-time for state residents; $7667 per year full-time, $423 per credit part-time for nonresidents.

Sonoma State University, School of Social Sciences, Department of Counseling, Rohnert Park, CA 94928-3609. Offers programs in counseling (MA); marriage, family, and child counseling (MA); pupil personnel services (MA). Part-time programs available. Faculty: 5 full-time (3 women), 4 part-time (3 women). Students: 58 full-time (44 women), 27 part-time (22 women); includes 22 minority (4 African Americans, 5 Asian Americans, 12 Hispanics, 1 Native American), 2 international. Average age 34. 129 applicants, 38% accepted. In 1997, 38 degrees awarded. *Degree requirements:* Internship required, foreign language and thesis not required. *Entrance requirements:* Minimum GPA of 3.0. Application deadline: 11/30. Application fee: $55. *Expenses:* Tuition $0 for state residents; $246 per unit for nonresidents. Fees $2130 per year full-time, $1464 per year part-time. *Financial aid:* Career-related internships or fieldwork available. Aid available to part-time students. Financial aid application deadline: 3/2. *Faculty research:* Self-esteem, relationship of emotion and health, at-risk youth, feminist issues, supervision strategies. • Dr. Skip Holmgren, Chair, 707-664-2544. E-mail: skip.holmgren@sonoma.edu.

South Carolina State University, School of Education, Department of Counselor Education and Psychological Foundations, 300 College Street Northeast, Orangeburg, SC 29117-0001. Offers programs in elementary counselor education (M Ed), secondary counselor education (M Ed). Accredited by NCATE. Part-time and evening/weekend programs available. Faculty: 5 full-time (2 women), 1 (woman) part-time. Students: 28 full-time (24 women), 24 part-time (18 women); includes 49 minority (all African Americans). Average age 25. In 1997, 29 degrees awarded. *Degree requirements:* Comprehensive exam required, foreign language and thesis not required. *Entrance requirements:* GRE General Test (minimum combined score of 800) or MAT (minimum score 35), NTE (minimum score 644 on general knowledge section, 645 on specialty skills), interview. Application deadline: 7/15 (priority date; rolling processing; 11/10 for spring admission). Application fee: $25. *Tuition:* $2974 per year full-time, $165 per credit hour part-time. *Financial aid:* Fellowships, research assistantships, institutionally sponsored loans, and career-related internships or fieldwork available. Financial aid application deadline: 6/1. *Faculty research:* Decision making, relaxation theory, learning styles, student recruitment, academic achievement. • Dr. Doris S. Cantey, Chairperson, 803-536-7147. Application contact: Dr. Gail Joyner-Fleming, Interim Associate Dean and Director, Graduate Teacher Education, 803-536-8824. Fax: 803-536-8492.

South Carolina State University, School of Education, Department of Teacher Education, 300 College Street Northeast, Orangeburg, SC 29117-0001. Offerings include secondary education (M Ed), with options in biology education, business education, counselor education, English education, home economics education, industrial education, mathematics education, science education, social studies education. Accredited by NCATE. Department faculty: 7 full-time (3 women), 2 part-time (1 woman). *Average time to degree:* master's–2 years full-time, 4 years part-time. *Application deadline:* 7/15 (priority date; rolling processing; 11/10 for spring admission). *Application fee:* $25. *Tuition:* $2974 per year full-time, $165 per credit hour part-time. • Dr. Jesse Kinard, Chairman, 803-536-8934. Application contact: Dr. Gail Joyner-Fleming, Interim Associate Dean and Director, Graduate Teacher Education, 803-536-8824. Fax: 803-536-8492.

South Dakota State University, College of Education and Counseling, Department of Counseling and Human Resource Development, Brookings, SD 57007. Awards MS. Accredited by NCATE. Faculty: 8 full-time (6 women). Students: 35 full-time (25 women), 83 part-time (59 women); includes 17 minority (6 African Americans, 2 Asian Americans, 1 Hispanic, 8 Native Americans), 1 international. 26 applicants, 100% accepted. In 1997, 59 degrees awarded. *Degree requirements:* Thesis, comprehensive and oral exams required, foreign language not required. *Entrance requirements:* TOEFL (minimum score 525), minimum GPA of 2.75. Application deadline: 5/1 (rolling processing; 10/1 for spring admission). Application fee: $15. *Expenses:* Tuition $82 per credit hour for state residents; $242 per credit hour for nonresidents. Fees $37 per credit hour. *Financial aid:* Research assistantships, teaching assistantships, administrative assistantships available. *Faculty research:* Rural mental health, family issues, psychopathology, domestic and sexual abuse. • Dr. Nona Wilson, Acting Head, 605-688-4190.

Southeastern Louisiana University, College of Education, Department of Counseling, Family Studies, and Educational Leadership, Hammond, LA 70402. Offers programs in counselor education (M Ed), educational administration (Ed S), school administration and supervision (M Ed). Accredited by NCATE. Ed S being phased out; applicants no longer accepted. Part-time programs available. Faculty: 7 full-time, 6 part-time. Students: 28 full-time (21 women), 122 part-time (100 women); includes 15 minority (12 African Americans, 3 Asian Americans). Average age 34. In 1997, 51 master's awarded. *Entrance requirements:* For master's, GRE. Application deadline: 7/15 (priority date; rolling processing; 12/15 for spring admission). Application fee: $10 ($25 for international students). Electronic applications accepted. *Expenses:* Tuition $2010 per year full-time, $287 per semester (minimum) part-time for state residents; $5232 per year full-time, $287 per semester (minimum) part-time for nonresidents. Fees $5 per year. *Financial aid:* Research assistantships, teaching assistantships, administrative assistantships, Federal Work-Study, and career-related internships or fieldwork available. Aid available to part-time students. Financial aid application deadline: 5/1; applicants required to submit FAFSA. *Faculty research:* Transformational leadership, contraceptive implants, women's issues, family resource centers, leadership for the twenty-first century. Total annual research expenditures: $60,000. • Dr. Peter Emerson, Head, 504-549-2309. E-mail: pemerson@selu.edu. Application contact: Dr. Sue Austin, Graduate Coordinator, 504-549-2181. Fax: 504-549-3758. E-mail: saustin@selu.edu.

Southeastern Oklahoma State University, School of Education, Durant, OK 74701-0609. Offerings include guidance and counseling (MBS), school counseling (M Ed). One or more programs accredited by NCATE. School faculty: 69 full-time (23 women), 3 part-time (0 women), 69.7 FTE. *Degree requirements:* Thesis optional, foreign language not required. *Entrance requirements:* GRE General Test (MBS), minimum GPA of 3.0 in last 60 hours or 2.75 overall. Application deadline: 8/1. *Tuition:* $76 per credit hour for state residents; $178 per credit hour for nonresidents. • Dr. Barbara Decker, Dean, 580-924-0121 Ext. 2251. Fax: 580-920-7473.

Southeast Missouri State University, Department of Educational Administration and Counseling, Program in Guidance and Counseling, Cape Girardeau, MO 63701-4799. Offers guidance and counseling (MA), psychological counseling (MA). Accredited by NCATE. Evening/weekend programs available. *Degree requirements:* Thesis or alternative required, foreign language not required. *Entrance requirements:* GRE General Test (score in 50th percentile or higher), minimum GPA of 3.0. Application deadline: 4/1 (priority date; rolling processing; 11/21 for spring admission). Application fee: $20 ($100 for international students). *Tuition:* $2034 per year full-time, $113 per credit hour part-time for state residents; $3672 per year full-time, $204 per credit hour part-time for nonresidents. *Financial aid:* Research assistantships and career-related internships or fieldwork available. • Ann Paryear, Head, 573-651-2137. Application contact: Office of Graduate Studies, 573-651-2192.

Southern Adventist University, School of Education, Collegedale, TN 37315-0370. Offerings include community counseling (MS). School faculty: 8 full-time (5 women), 7 part-time (1 woman). *Degree requirements:* Thesis (for some programs), written comprehensive exam required, foreign language not required. *Entrance requirements:* GRE. Application deadline: rolling. Application fee: $25. *Tuition:* $275 per credit hour. • Dr. Alberto dos Santos, Dean, 423-238-2779. Fax: 423-238-2468. E-mail: adossant@southern.edu.

Southern Arkansas University–Magnolia, Graduate Program in Education, Program in Agency Counseling and Guidance, Magnolia, AR 71753. Offers agency counseling (M Ed). Students: 8 full-time (5 women), 24 part-time (17 women); includes 13 minority (12 African Americans, 1 Hispanic). Average age 32. 11 applicants, 91% accepted. *Degree requirements:* Thesis or alternative, comprehensive exam required, foreign language not required. *Average time to degree:* master's–2 years full-time. *Entrance requirements:* GRE, minimum GPA of 2.5. Application deadline: 8/15. Application fee: $0. *Expenses:* Tuition $95 per hour for state residents; $138 per hour for nonresidents. Fees $2 per hour. *Financial aid:* Research assistantships, teaching assistantships, and career-related internships or fieldwork available. Financial aid application deadline: 8/15. • Dr. Danield L. Bernard, Dean, Graduate Studies, Graduate Program in Education, 870-235-4055. Fax: 870-235-5035. E-mail: dlbernard@mail.saumag.edu.

Southern Arkansas University–Magnolia, Graduate Program in Education, Program in Elementary Education, Magnolia, AR 71753. Offerings include elementary counseling (M Ed). Program faculty: 5 part-time. *Degree requirements:* Thesis or alternative, comprehensive exam required, foreign language not required. *Average time to degree:* master's–2 years full-time. *Entrance requirements:* GRE, minimum GPA of 2.5. Application deadline: 8/15 (rolling processing). Application fee: $0. *Expenses:* Tuition $95 per hour for state residents; $138 per hour for nonresidents. Fees $2 per hour. • Dr. Danield L. Bernard, Dean, Graduate Studies, Graduate Program in Education, 870-235-4055. Fax: 870-235-5035. E-mail: dlbernard@mail.saumag.edu.

Southern Arkansas University–Magnolia, Graduate Program in Education, Program in Secondary Education, Magnolia, AR 71753. Offerings include secondary counseling (M Ed). *Degree requirements:* Thesis or alternative, comprehensive exam required, foreign language not required. *Average time to degree:* master's–2 years full-time. *Entrance requirements:* GRE, minimum GPA of 2.5. Application deadline: 8/15. Application fee: $0. *Expenses:* Tuition $95 per hour for state residents; $138 per hour for nonresidents. Fees $2 per hour. • Dr. Danield L. Bernard, Dean, Graduate Studies, Graduate Program in Education, 870-235-4055. Fax: 870-235-5035. E-mail: dlbernard@mail.saumag.edu.

Southern Connecticut State University, School of Education, Department of Counseling and School Psychology, New Haven, CT 06515-1355. Offers programs in counseling (MS, Diploma), counseling and school psychology (Diploma), school psychology (MS). Faculty: 4 full-time, 11 part-time. Students: 69 full-time (54 women), 134 part-time (108 women); includes 14 minority (7 African Americans, 2 Asian Americans, 5 Hispanics). 184 applicants, 18% accepted. In 1997, 41 master's, 16 Diplomas awarded. *Degree requirements:* For master's, thesis or alternative required, foreign language not required. *Entrance requirements:* For master's, interview, previous course work in behavioral sciences; for Diploma, master's degree. Application deadline: 1/15 (10/15 for spring admission). Application fee: $40. *Expenses:* Tuition $2632 per year full-time, $188 per credit part-time for state residents; $7200 per year full-time, $188 per credit part-time for nonresidents. Fees $1806 per year full-time, $45 per semester part-time for state residents; $2703 per year full-time, $45 per semester part-time for nonresidents. *Financial aid:* Teaching assistantships and career-related internships or fieldwork available. • Dr. Michael Martin, Chair, 203-392-5912.

Southern Illinois University at Carbondale, College of Education, Department of Educational Psychology and Special Education, Program in Educational Psychology, Carbondale, IL 62901-6806. Offerings include counselor education (MS Ed, PhD). Accredited by NCATE. Program faculty: 18 full-time (5 women), 5 part-time (1 woman). *Degree requirements:* Thesis/dissertation required, foreign language not required. *Entrance requirements:* For master's, GRE General Test, TOEFL (minimum score 550), minimum GPA of 2.7; for doctorate, TOEFL (minimum score 550), minimum GPA of 3.25. Application deadline: 6/15 (priority date; rolling processing). Application fee: $20. *Expenses:* Tuition $2964 per year full-time, $99 per semester hour part-time for state residents; $8892 per year full-time, $270 per semester hour part-time for nonresidents. Fees $1034 per year full-time, $298 per semester (minimum) part-time. • Application contact: Laurie Viernum, Graduate Secretary, 618-536-7763. Fax: 618-453-7110.

Southern Oregon University, School of Social Science, Health and Physical Education, Department of Psychology, Ashland, OR 97520. Offerings include social science (MA, MS), with options in professional counseling, psychology. *Degree requirements:* Comprehensive exam (MA) required, thesis optional. *Entrance requirements:* GRE General Test, minimum GPA of 3.0. Application deadline: 2/1. Application fee: $50. *Tuition:* $5187 per year full-time, $586 per quarter (minimum) part-time for state residents; $9228 per year full-time, $586 per quarter (minimum) part-time for nonresidents. • Karen Salley, Chair, 541-552-6948.

Southern University and Agricultural and Mechanical College, College of Education, Department of Behavioral Studies and Educational Leadership, Baton Rouge, LA 70813. Offers programs in administration and supervision (M Ed), counselor education (MA), mental health counseling (MA). Accredited by NCATE. Faculty: 10 full-time (3 women). Students: 39 full-time (25 women), 139 part-time (97 women); includes 157 minority (all African Americans). Average age 30. 72 applicants, 79% accepted. In 1997, 59 degrees awarded. *Degree requirements:* Thesis optional. *Entrance requirements:* GMAT or GRE General Test, TOEFL. Application deadline: 6/1 (priority date; rolling processing; 11/1 for spring admission). Application fee: $5. *Tuition:* $2226 per year full-time, $267 per semester (minimum) part-time for state residents; $6262 per year full-time, $267 per semester (minimum) part-time for nonresidents. *Financial aid:* Application deadline 4/15. • Dr. Harry Albert, Chairman, 504-771-2890.

Southwestern College, Program in Counseling, Santa Fe, NM 87502-4788. Awards MA. Part-time and evening/weekend programs available. Faculty: 18 full-time (12 women), 7 part-time (6 women). Students: 43 full-time, 39 part-time; includes 3 minority (2 Hispanics, 1 Native American). Average age 41. 56 applicants, 89% accepted. In 1997, 25 degrees awarded. *Degree requirements:* Internship required, foreign language and thesis not required. *Application deadline:* 7/1 (priority date; rolling processing). *Application fee:* $50. *Tuition:* $10,500 per year full-time, $210 per quarter hour part-time. *Financial aid:* In 1997–98, 40 students received aid, including 8 scholarships (2 to first-year students); institutionally sponsored loans and career-related internships or fieldwork also available. Aid available to part-time students. Financial aid applicants required to submit FAFSA. • Dr. Susan Schmall, Chair, 505-471-5756. Application contact: Debra Thompson-Morris, Director of Admissions, 505-471-5756. Fax: 505-471-4071.

Southwestern Oklahoma State University, School of Education, Program in Agency Counseling, Weatherford, OK 73096-3098. Awards M Ed. Accredited by NCATE. M Ed distance learning degree program offered to Oklahoma residents only. Part-time and evening/weekend programs available. Postbaccalaureate distance learning degree programs offered (minimal on-campus study). Students: 17 full-time (15 women), 21 part-time (15 women); includes 5 minority (2 African Americans, 1 Hispanic, 2 Native Americans). 7 applicants, 100% accepted. In 1997, 9 degrees awarded. *Degree requirements:* Exam required, foreign language and thesis not required. *Entrance requirements:* GRE General Test, TOEFL (minimum score 550), minimum GPA of 2.5. Application deadline: rolling. Application fee: $15. *Expenses:* Tuition $60 per credit hour (minimum) for state residents; $147 per credit hour (minimum) for nonresidents. Fees $109 per year full-time, $24 per semester (minimum) part-time. *Financial aid:* Research assistantships, teaching assistantships, partial tuition waivers, Federal Work-Study, institutionally sponsored loans, and career-related internships or fieldwork available. Aid available to part-time students. Financial aid application deadline: 3/1; applicants required to submit FAFSA. • Dr. Greg Moss, Chair, School Service Programs, 580-774-3140. Application contact: Dolores Russell, Adviser, 580-774-3142.

Southwestern Oklahoma State University, School of Education, Program in School Counseling, Weatherford, OK 73096-3098. Awards M Ed. Accredited by NCATE. M Ed distance learning degree program offered to Oklahoma residents only. Part-time and evening/weekend programs available. Postbaccalaureate distance learning degree programs offered (minimal on-campus study). Students: 7 full-time (5 women), 42 part-time (32 women); includes 4 minority (2 African Americans, 2 Native Americans). 3 applicants, 100% accepted. In 1997, 18 degrees awarded. *Degree requirements:* Exam required, foreign language and thesis not required. *Entrance requirements:* GRE General Test, TOEFL (minimum score 550), minimum GPA of 2.5. Application deadline: rolling. Application fee: $15. *Expenses:* Tuition $60 per credit hour (minimum) for state residents; $147 per credit hour (minimum) for nonresidents. Fees $109 per year full-time, $24 per semester (minimum) part-time. *Financial aid:* Research assistantships, teaching assistantships, partial tuition waivers, Federal Work-Study, institutionally sponsored loans, and career-related internships or fieldwork available. Aid available to part-time students. Financial aid application deadline: 3/1; applicants required to submit FAFSA. • Dr. Greg Moss, Chair of School Service Programs, 580-774-3140.

Southwest Missouri State University, College of Education, Department of Guidance and Counseling, Springfield, MO 65804-0094. Awards MS. Part-time and evening/weekend programs available. Faculty: 3 full-time (0 women), 2 part-time (0 women). Students: 39 full-time (29 women), 238 part-time (195 women); includes 8 minority (1 African American, 2 Asian Americans, 1 Hispanic, 4 Native Americans), 2 international. Average age 33. In 1997, 57 degrees awarded. *Degree requirements:* Thesis or alternative, comprehensive exam required, foreign language not required. *Entrance requirements:* Minimum GPA of 2.75. Application deadline: 8/7 (priority date; rolling processing; 12/17 for spring admission). Application fee: $25. *Expenses:* Tuition $1980 per year full-time, $110 per credit hour part-time for state residents; $3960 per year full-time, $220 per credit hour part-time for nonresidents. Fees $274 per year full-time, $73 per semester part-time. *Financial aid:* In 1997–98, 1 graduate assistantship averaging $583 per month and totaling $5,250 was awarded; teaching assistantships also available. *Faculty research:* Self-esteem development, stress management, ethnic counseling prejudices. • Dr. Charles Bark e, Head, 417-836-5392. Fax: 417-836-6905. E-mail: crb024f@upgate.smsu.edu.

Southwest Texas State University, School of Education, Department of Educational Administration and Psychological Services, Program in Counseling and Guidance, San Marcos, TX 78666. Offers counseling and guidance (M Ed), professional counseling (MA). Part-time and evening/weekend programs available. Students: 42 full-time (39 women), 135 part-time (105 women); includes 16 minority (4 African Americans, 1 Asian American, 10 Hispanics, 1 Native American), 2 international. Average age 35. In 1997, 53 degrees awarded. *Degree requirements:* Thesis (for some programs), comprehensive exam required, foreign language not required. *Entrance requirements:* GRE General Test (minimum combined score of 900), TOEFL (minimum score 550), minimum GPA of 3.0 in last 60 hours. Application deadline: 7/15 (rolling processing; 11/15 for spring admission). Application fee: $25 ($50 for international students). *Expenses:* Tuition $648 per year full-time, $120 per semester (minimum) part-time for state residents; $4500 per year full-time, $750 per semester (minimum) part-time for nonresidents. Fees $1264 per year full-time, $314 per semester (minimum) part-time. *Financial aid:* Federal Work-Study, institutionally sponsored loans, and career-related internships or fieldwork available. Aid available to part-time students. Financial aid application deadline: 4/1; applicants required to submit FAFSA. *Faculty research:* Visiting teachers. • Dr. Michael Carns, Graduate Adviser, 512-245-2575. E-mail: mc17@swt.edu.

Spalding University, School of Education, Programs in Teacher Education and Administration, Louisville, KY 40203-2188. Offerings include guidance (MA). Accredited by NCATE. Faculty: 7 full-time (5 women), 5 part-time (4 women). *Application deadline:* 8/15 (priority date; rolling processing). *Application fee:* $30. *Expenses:* Tuition $350 per credit hour (minimum). Fees $48 per year full-time, $4 per credit hour part-time. • Application contact: Jeanne Anderson, Assistant to the Provost and Director of Graduate Office, 502-585-7105. Fax: 502-585-7158. E-mail: gradoffc@spalding6.win.net.

Springfield College, Program in Education, Springfield, MA 01109-3797. Offerings include counseling and secondary education (M Ed, MS). Program faculty: 7 full-time (4 women), 2 part-time (both women), 8 FTE. *Degree requirements:* Comprehensive exam required, foreign language and thesis not required. *Application deadline:* (12/1 for spring admission). *Application fee:* $40. *Expenses:* Tuition $474 per credit. Fees $25 per year. • Dr. Thomas L. Bernard, Director, 413-748-3251. Application contact: Donald J. Shaw Jr., Director of Graduate Admissions, 413-748-3225. Fax: 413-748-3694. E-mail: dshaw@spfldcol.edu.

Springfield College, Programs in Counseling and Psychological Services, Springfield, MA 01109-3797. Offerings include school guidance and counseling (M Ed, MS, CAS). Faculty: 9 full-time (5 women), 15 part-time (8 women), 13 FTE. *Degree requirements:* For master's, thesis (for some programs), comprehensive exam required, foreign language not required. *Entrance requirements:* Interview. Application deadline: 2/1 (priority date; rolling processing; 12/1 for spring admission). Application fee: $40. *Expenses:* Tuition $474 per credit. Fees $25 per year. • Dr. Barbara Mandell, Director, 413-748-3328. Application contact: Donald J. Shaw Jr., Director of Graduate Admissions, 413-748-3225. Fax: 413-748-3694. E-mail: dshaw@spfldcol.edu.

State University of New York at Albany, School of Education, Department of Counseling Psychology, Albany, NY 12222-0001. Offerings include school counselor (CAS). Department faculty: 10 full-time (4 women), 1 part-time (0 women). *Application fee:* $50. *Expenses:* Tuition $5100 per year full-time, $213 per credit hour part-time for state residents; $8416 per year full-time, $351 per credit hour part-time for nonresidents. Fees $705 per year full-time, $26.85 per credit hour part-time. • Dr. Monroe Bruch, Chair, 518-442-5040.

State University of New York at Buffalo, Graduate School, Graduate School of Education, Department of Counseling and Educational Psychology, Buffalo, NY 14260. Offers programs in counseling psychology (PhD), counselor education (PhD), educational psychology (MA, PhD), rehabilitation counseling (MS), school counseling (Ed M, Certificate), school psychology (MA). Part-time programs available. Faculty: 11 full-time (3 women), 3 part-time (all women). Students: 101 full-time (76 women), 85 part-time (59 women); includes 14 minority (7 African Americans, 1 Asian American, 5 Hispanics, 1 Native American), 7 international. Average age 25. 240 applicants, 23% accepted. In 1997, 43 master's, 17 doctorates awarded. Terminal master's awarded for partial completion of doctoral program. *Degree requirements:* For master's, thesis required (for some programs), foreign language not required; for doctorate, dissertation required, foreign language not required. *Average time to degree:* master's–2 years full-time, 3 years part-time; doctorate–7 years full-time, 10 years part-time. *Entrance requirements:* For master's, GRE General Test, TOEFL (minimum score 550), interview; for doctorate, GRE General Test (minimum combined score of 1100), TOEFL (minimum score 550), interview. Application deadline: 2/1 (priority date). Application fee: $50. *Tuition:* $5970 per year full-time, $288 per credit hour part-time for state residents; $9286 per year full-time, $426 per credit hour part-time for nonresidents. *Financial aid:* In 1997–98, 19 students received aid, including 5 fellowships (2 to first-year students), 12 graduate assistantships (5 to first-year students); research assistantships, teaching assistantships, Federal Work-Study, institutionally sponsored loans, and career-related internships or fieldwork also available. Financial aid application deadline: 2/1. *Faculty research:* Counseling process, vocational psychology, assessment, learning and development, grief counseling. • Dr. Thomas T. Frantz, Chairperson, 716-645-2485. Fax: 716-645-6616. E-mail: ttfranz@acsu.buffalo.edu.

Directory: Counselor Education

State University of New York College at Brockport, School of Professions, Department of Counselor Education, Brockport, NY 14420-2997. Awards MS Ed, CAS. Evening/weekend programs available. Faculty: 6 full-time (2 women), 3 part-time (1 woman), 7 FTE. Students: 31 full-time (23 women), 80 part-time (63 women); includes 13 minority (9 African Americans, 1 Asian American, 3 Hispanics). Average age 32. 94 applicants, 41% accepted. In 1997, 29 master's, 4 CASs awarded. *Degree requirements:* For master's, internship, project required, foreign language and thesis not required. *Entrance requirements:* For master's, interview. Application deadline: 4/15 (priority date; 11/15 for spring admission). Application fee: $50. *Expenses:* Tuition $5100 per year full-time, $213 per credit hour part-time for state residents; $8416 per year full-time, $351 per credit hour part-time for nonresidents. Fees $440 per year full-time, $22.60 per credit hour part-time. *Financial aid:* In 1997–98, 5 fellowships were awarded; Federal Work-Study and career-related internships or fieldwork also available. Aid available to part-time students. Financial aid application deadline: 4/1; applicants required to submit FAFSA. *Faculty research:* Community, college, and school counseling. • Dr. Joseph Kandor, Chairperson, 716-395-2258.

State University of New York College at Oneonta, Department of Education, Programs in Counseling, Oneonta, NY 13820-4015. Awards MS, MS Ed, CAS. Part-time and evening/weekend programs available. Students: 29 full-time (23 women), 47 part-time (37 women). In 1997, 45 master's, 11 CASs awarded. *Degree requirements:* For master's, comprehensive exam. *Entrance requirements:* For master's, GRE General Test. Application deadline: 4/15. Application fee: $50. *Expenses:* Tuition $5100 per year full-time, $213 per credit hour part-time for state residents; $8416 per year full-time, $351 per credit hour part-time for nonresidents. Fees $482 per year full-time, $6.85 per credit hour part-time. • Dr. Walter vom Saal, Coordinator, 607-436-3711.

State University of West Georgia, College of Education, Department of Counseling and Educational Psychology, Carrollton, GA 30118. Offers program in counseling and guidance (M Ed, Ed S). Accredited by NCATE. Part-time and evening/weekend programs available. Faculty: 12 full-time (6 women). Students: 108 full-time (92 women), 126 part-time (104 women); includes 40 minority (38 African Americans, 2 Hispanics). Average age 35. In 1997, 81 master's, 23 Ed Ss awarded. *Degree requirements:* For Ed S, research project required, foreign language and thesis not required. *Entrance requirements:* For master's, GRE General Test (minimum combined score of 800), minimum GPA of 2.5; for Ed S, GRE General Test (minimum combined score of 800), master's degree, minimum graduate GPA of 3.25. Application deadline: 8/30 (rolling processing). Application fee: $15. *Expenses:* Tuition $2428 per year full-time, $83 per semester hour part-time for state residents; $8428 per year full-time, $250 per semester hour part-time for nonresidents. Fees $428 per year. *Financial aid:* Research assistantships, assistantships, and career-related internships or fieldwork available. Aid available to part-time students. Financial aid applicants required to submit FAFSA. *Faculty research:* Academic and career development counseling. • Dr. Brent M. Snow, Chairman, 770-836-6554. Application contact: Dr. Jack O. Jenkins, Dean, Graduate School, 770-836-6419. Fax: 770-836-2301. E-mail: jjenkins@cob.as.westga.edu.

State University of West Georgia, College of Education, Program in School Home Services, Carrollton, GA 30118. Awards M Ed, Ed S. Accredited by NCATE. Faculty: 3 full-time (1 woman). Students: 0. In 1997, 3 master's awarded. *Degree requirements:* For Ed S, research project required, foreign language and thesis not required. *Entrance requirements:* For master's, GRE General Test (minimum combined score of 800), minimum GPA of 2.5; for Ed S, GRE General Test (minimum combined score of 800), master's degree, minimum graduate GPA of 3.25. Application deadline: 8/30 (rolling processing). Application fee: $15. *Expenses:* Tuition $2428 per year full-time, $83 per semester hour part-time for state residents; $8428 per year full-time, $250 per semester hour part-time for nonresidents. Fees $428 per year. • Dr. Brent Snow, Head, 770-836-6554. Application contact: Dr. Jack O. Jenkins, Dean, Graduate School, 770-836-6419. Fax: 770-836-2301. E-mail: jjenkins@cob.as.westga.edu.

Stephen F. Austin State University, College of Education, Department of Counseling and Special Education, Nacogdoches, TX 75962. Offers programs in counseling (MA), school psychology (MA), special education (M Ed), speech pathology (MS). Faculty: 13 full-time (2 women), 3 part-time (1 woman). Students: 60 full-time (51 women), 127 part-time (109 women); includes 14 minority (11 African Americans, 1 Asian American, 2 Hispanics). 71 applicants, 52% accepted. In 1997, 55 degrees awarded. *Degree requirements:* Comprehensive exam required, foreign language and thesis not required. *Entrance requirements:* GRE General Test (minimum combined score of 1000), minimum GPA of 2.8. Application deadline: 3/1 (10/1 for spring admission). Application fee: $0 ($25 for international students). *Tuition:* $1465 per year full-time, $263 per semester (minimum) part-time for state residents; $5299 per year full-time, $890 per semester (minimum) part-time for nonresidents. *Financial aid:* Research assistantships, teaching assistantships, Federal Work-Study, institutionally sponsored loans, and career-related internships or fieldwork available. Financial aid application deadline: 3/1. • Dr. Anna Bradfield, Chair, 409-468-2906.

Stephens College, School of Graduate and Continuing Education, Department of Elementary and Secondary Education, Program in Counseling, 1200 East Broadway, Columbia, MO 65215-0002. Awards M Ed. Part-time programs available. Faculty: 5 full-time (4 women). Students: 6 part-time (all women). *Degree requirements:* Thesis required, foreign language not required. *Entrance requirements:* GRE, TOEFL (minimum score 550), minimum GPA of 3.0 in last 60 hours. Application deadline: (4/1 for spring admission). Application fee: $25. *Tuition:* $690 per course. *Financial aid:* Available to part-time students. • Dr. Rosemary Barrow, Director, 573-442-2211 Ext. 130. Fax: 573-876-7223. Application contact: Dr. Joan T. Rines, Director of Graduate Programs, 800-388-7579. Fax: 573-876-7248. E-mail: grad@wc.stephens.edu.

Stetson University, College of Arts and Sciences, Department of Counselor Education, 421 North Woodland Boulevard, DeLand, FL 32720-3781. Offers programs in marriage and family therapy (MS), mental health counseling (MS). Evening/weekend programs available. Faculty: 2 full-time (1 woman), 6 part-time (5 women). Students: 19 full-time (13 women), 55 part-time (45 women); includes 6 minority (1 African American, 1 Asian American, 4 Hispanics), 1 international. Average age 35. 46 applicants, 89% accepted. In 1997, 12 degrees awarded. *Entrance requirements:* GRE General Test (minimum combined score of 1000). Application deadline: 3/1 (priority date; rolling processing; 11/1 for spring admission). Application fee: $25. *Tuition:* $370 per credit hour. • Dr. Mark Young, Chair, 904-822-8901. Application contact: Pat LeClaire, Office of Graduate Studies, 904-822-7075.

Suffolk University, College of Liberal Arts and Sciences, Department of Education and Human Services, Program in Counseling and Human Relations, Boston, MA 02108-2770. Awards M Ed, MS, CAGS, MPA/MS. Offerings include counseling and human relations (CAGS), human resource development (MS, CAGS), mental health counseling (MS), school counseling (M Ed). Part-time and evening/weekend programs available. Faculty: 10. *Entrance requirements:* For master's, GRE General Test (average 500 on each section) or MAT (average 50). Application deadline: 6/15 (priority date; rolling processing; 11/15 for spring admission). Application fee: $50. *Expenses:* Tuition $14,544 per year full-time, $1452 per course part-time. Fees $20 per year full-time, $10 per year part-time. *Financial aid:* Fellowships, Federal Work-Study, institutionally sponsored loans, and career-related internships or fieldwork available. Aid available to part-time students. Financial aid application deadline: 4/1; applicants required to submit FAFSA. *Faculty research:* Alumni follow-up. • Dr. R. Arthur Winters, Director, 617-573-8269. Fax: 617-722-9440. Application contact: Judy Reynolds, Acting Director of Graduate Admissions, 617-573-8302. Fax: 617-523-0116. E-mail: grad.admission@admin.suffolk.edu.

Sul Ross State University, Rio Grande College of Sul Ross State University, Alpine, TX 79832. Offerings include teacher education (M Ed), with options in bilingual education, counseling, educational diagnostics, elementary education, general education, reading, school administration, secondary education. College faculty: 16 full-time (2 women), 2 part-time (1 woman). *Application deadline:* rolling. *Application fee:* $0 ($50 for international students). *Expenses:* Tuition $864 per year full-time, $120 per semester (minimum) part-time for state residents; $5976 per year full-time, $747 per semester (minimum) part-time for nonresidents. Fees $754 per year full-time, $105 per semester (minimum) part-time. • Dr. Frank Abbott, Dean, 512-278-3339. Fax: 512-278-3330.

Sul Ross State University, Department of Teacher Education, Program in Counseling, Alpine, TX 79832. Awards M Ed. Part-time and evening/weekend programs available. Students: 55 full-time (38 women), 125 part-time (99 women); includes 87 minority (3 African Americans, 2 Asian Americans, 81 Hispanics, 1 Native American). Average age 37. In 1997, 78 degrees awarded. *Degree requirements:* Thesis optional, foreign language not required. *Entrance requirements:* GMAT (minimum score 400) or GRE General Test (minimum combined score of 850), minimum GPA of 2.5 in last 60 hours of undergraduate work. Application deadline: rolling. Application fee: $0 ($50 for international students). *Expenses:* Tuition $864 per year full-time, $120 per semester (minimum) part-time for state residents; $5976 per year full-time, $747 per semester (minimum) part-time for nonresidents. Fees $754 per year full-time, $105 per semester (minimum) part-time. *Financial aid:* Federal Work-Study, institutionally sponsored loans, and career-related internships or fieldwork available. Aid available to part-time students. Financial aid application deadline: 5/1; applicants required to submit FAFSA. *Faculty research:* Input variable effects on EXCET for graduate students. • Dr. Mary Ann Weinacht, Director, Department of Teacher Education, 915-837-8170. Fax: 915-837-8390.

Syracuse University, School of Education, Counseling and Human Services Program, Program in Counselor Education, Syracuse, NY 13244-0003. Awards MS, Ed D, PhD, CAS. Students: 43 full-time (32 women), 47 part-time (41 women); includes 10 minority (8 African Americans, 1 Asian American, 1 Hispanic), 5 international. 53 applicants, 87% accepted. In 1997, 28 master's, 2 doctorates awarded. *Degree requirements:* For master's, thesis or alternative required, foreign language not required; for doctorate and CAS, thesis/dissertation required, foreign language not required. *Entrance requirements:* GRE. Application fee: $40. *Tuition:* $13,320 per year full-time, $555 per credit hour part-time. *Financial aid:* Application deadline 3/1. • Dr. Alan Goldberg, Chair, Counseling and Human Services Program, 315-443-2266. Fax: 315-443-5732.

Tarleton State University, College of Education, Department of Education and Psychology, Program in Guidance and Counseling, Stephenville, TX 76402. Awards M Ed. Part-time programs available. Students: 16 full-time (7 women), 184 part-time (159 women); includes 15 minority (3 African Americans, 3 Asian Americans, 8 Hispanics, 1 Native American). 31 applicants, 97% accepted. In 1997, 41 degrees awarded. *Degree requirements:* Comprehensive exam required, foreign language and thesis not required. *Entrance requirements:* GRE General Test, minimum GPA of 2.9 during last 60 hours. Application deadline: 8/5 (priority date; rolling processing; 12/1 for spring admission). Application fee: $25 ($100 for international students). *Expenses:* Tuition $46 per hour for state residents; $249 per hour for nonresidents. Fees $49 per hour. *Financial aid:* Teaching assistantships, Federal Work-Study, institutionally sponsored loans, and career-related internships or fieldwork available. Aid available to part-time students. Financial aid application deadline: 5/1; applicants required to submit FAFSA. • Dr. Linda Duncan, Coordinator, 254-968-9816.

Temple University, College of Education, Department of Psychological Studies in Education, Program in Counseling Psychology, Philadelphia, PA 19122-6096. Offerings include counselor education (Ed M). Accredited by NCATE. Program faculty: 7 full-time (4 women). *Degree requirements:* Thesis or alternative required, foreign language not required. *Entrance requirements:* GRE General Test (minimum combined score of 1000) or MAT (minimum score 39), minimum GPA of 2.8. Application deadline: 2/15. Application fee: $40. *Expenses:* Tuition $323 per semester hour for state residents; $444 per semester hour for nonresidents. Fees $170 per year full-time, $28 per semester (minimum) part-time. • Dr. James Bolden, Coordinator, 215-204-7331.

Tennessee State University, College of Education, Department of Psychology, Nashville, TN 37209-1561. Offerings include counseling and guidance (MS), with options in counseling, elementary school counseling, organizational counseling, secondary school counseling. Accredited by NCATE. Department faculty: 13 full-time (6 women), 9 part-time (7 women), 14 FTE. *Degree requirements:* Comprehensive exam or thesis required, foreign language not required. *Entrance requirements:* GRE General Test (minimum combined score of 870). Application deadline: rolling. Application fee: $15. *Tuition:* $2962 per year full-time, $182 per credit hour part-time for state residents; $7788 per year full-time, $393 per credit hour part-time for nonresidents. • Dr. Helen Barrett, Head, 615-963-5139. Fax: 615-963-5140. E-mail: barrett@acad.tnstate.edu. Application contact: Dr. Clinton M. Lipsey, Dean of the Graduate School, 615-963-5901. Fax: 615-963-5963. E-mail: clipsey@picard.tnstate.edu.

Texas A&M International University, Division of Teacher Education and Psychology, 5201 University Boulevard, Laredo, TX 78041-1900. Offerings include guidance and counseling (MS Ed). *Degree requirements:* Thesis required (for some programs), foreign language not required. *Entrance requirements:* GRE General Test. Application deadline: 7/15 (priority date; rolling processing; 11/12 for spring admission). Application fee: $0.

Texas A&M University–Commerce, College of Education, Department of Counseling, Commerce, TX 75429-3011. Awards M Ed, MS, Ed D. Faculty: 10 full-time (4 women), 2 part-time (0 women). Students: 86 full-time (69 women), 228 part-time (180 women); includes 50 minority (37 African Americans, 4 Asian Americans, 8 Hispanics, 1 Native American), 6 international. In 1997, 67 master's, 5 doctorates awarded. Terminal master's awarded for partial completion of doctoral program. *Degree requirements:* For master's, thesis (for some programs), comprehensive exam; for doctorate, dissertation, departmental qualifying exam. *Entrance requirements:* GRE General Test. Application deadline: rolling. Application fee: $0 ($25 for international students). *Tuition:* $2382 per year full-time, $343 per semester (minimum) part-time for state residents; $7518 per year full-time, $343 per semester (minimum) part-time for nonresidents. *Financial aid:* Research assistantships, teaching assistantships, Federal Work-Study, institutionally sponsored loans available. • Dr. Richard E. Lampe, Head, 903-886-5637. Application contact: Pam Hammonds, Graduate Admissions Adviser, 903-886-5167. Fax: 903-886-5165.

Texas A&M University–Corpus Christi, College of Education, Program in Guidance and Counseling, Corpus Christi, TX 78412-5503. Awards MS. Part-time and evening/weekend programs available. Students: 38 full-time (29 women), 89 part-time (68 women); includes 64 minority (8 African Americans, 56 Hispanics). Average age 37. In 1997, 120 degrees awarded. *Entrance requirements:* GRE General Test. Application deadline: 7/15 (priority date; rolling processing; 11/15 for spring admission). Application fee: $10 ($30 for international students). *Expenses:* Tuition $648 per year full-time, $120 per semester (minimum) part-time for state residents; $4482 per year full-time, $747 per semester (minimum) part-time for nonresidents. Fees $1010 per year full-time, $205 per semester part-time. *Financial aid:* Federal Work-Study, institutionally sponsored loans, and career-related internships or fieldwork available. Aid available to part-time students. Financial aid application deadline: 3/15; applicants required to submit FAFSA. • Dr. Arturo Medina, Graduate Adviser, 512-994-2667. E-mail: adedu005@tamucc.edu. Application contact: Mary Margaret Dechant, Director of Admissions, 512-994-2624. Fax: 512-994-5887.

Texas A&M University–Kingsville, College of Education, Department of Education, Program in Guidance and Counseling, Kingsville, TX 78363. Awards MA, MS. MS offered jointly with the University of North Texas. Part-time and evening/weekend programs available. Faculty: 1 full-time, 4 part-time. *Degree requirements:* Comprehensive exam, mini-thesis required, foreign language not required. *Entrance requirements:* GRE General Test (minimum combined score of 1000), MAT (minimum score 34), minimum GPA of 3.0. Application deadline: 6/1 (rolling processing; 11/15 for spring admission). Application fee: $15 ($25 for international students). *Tuition:* $1822 per year full-time, $281 per semester (minimum) part-time for state residents; $6934 per year full-time, $908 per semester (minimum) part-time for nonresidents. *Financial* *aid:* Application deadline 5/15. *Faculty research:* Diagnostician requirements for certification, teaching methods for adult learner. • Dr. Travis Polk, Chair, Department of Education, 512-593-3204.

Texas Southern University, College of Education, Department of Counseling, Guidance, and Psychology, Houston, TX 77004-4584. Offers programs in counseling and guidance (MA); counseling, guidance, and psychology (MA, M Ed, Ed D). Faculty: 7 full-time (2 women), 1 part-time (0 women). Students: 53 full-time (38 women), 18 part-time (17 women). Average age 31. 155 applicants, 65% accepted. In 1997, 21 master's awarded (100% found work related to degree); 6 doctorates awarded. *Degree requirements:* For master's, 1 foreign language, comprehensive exam; for doctorate, dissertation, comprehensive exam required, foreign language not required. *Entrance requirements:* For master's, GRE General Test, TOEFL, minimum GPA of 2.5; for doctorate, GRE General Test or MAT, master's degree, minimum B+ average. Application deadline: 7/15 (priority date; rolling processing). Application fee: $35 ($75 for international students). *Financial aid:* Fellowships, teaching assistantships, Federal Work-Study, institutionally sponsored loans, and career-related internships or fieldwork available. Financial aid application deadline: 5/1. *Faculty research:* Clinical and urban psychology. • Dr. Delbert Garnes, Head, 713-313-7344.

Texas Tech University, Graduate School, College of Education, Division of Educational Psychology and Leadership, Lubbock, TX 79409. Offerings include counselor education (M Ed, Ed D, Certificate). Accredited by NCATE. Division faculty: 28 full-time (13 women), 3 part-time (1 woman), 29.29 FTE. *Degree requirements:* For master's, computer language required, thesis optional, foreign language not required; for doctorate, dissertation required, foreign language not required. *Entrance requirements:* For master's, GRE General Test (combined average 1034); for doctorate, GRE General Test. Application deadline: 4/15 (priority date; rolling processing; 11/1 for spring admission). Application fee: $25 ($50 for international students). Electronic applications accepted. *Expenses:* Tuition $864 per year full-time, $120 per semester (minimum) part-time for state residents; $5976 per year full-time, $747 per semester (minimum) part-time for nonresidents. Fees $2321 per year full-time, $302 per semester (minimum) part-time. • Dr. Loretta J. Bradley, Chair, 806-742-2393.

Texas Woman's University, College of Education and Human Ecology, Family Sciences Department, Program in Counseling and Development, Denton, TX 76204. Awards M Ed, MS. Part-time and evening/weekend programs available. Faculty: 4 full-time (3 women). Students: 18 full-time (17 women), 100 part-time (94 women); includes 21 minority (9 African Americans, 2 Asian Americans, 10 Hispanics). Average age 37. 19 applicants, 63% accepted. In 1997, 14 degrees awarded. *Degree requirements:* Thesis or professional paper required, foreign language not required. *Entrance requirements:* GRE General Test (minimum combined score of 850). Application deadline: 1/7 (8/31 for spring admission). Application fee: $25. *Financial aid:* 20 students received aid; institutionally sponsored loans and career-related internships or fieldwork available. Aid available to part-time students. Financial aid application deadline: 2/1. *Faculty research:* Empathy, marriage satisfaction after birth of first child, counseling the gifted, teenage suicide. • Dr. Jennifer Martin, Acting Chair, Family Sciences Department, 940-898-2685. Fax: 940-898-2676.

Trevecca Nazarene University, Division of Social and Behavioral Sciences, Major in Counseling, Nashville, TN 37210-2834. Awards MA. Part-time and evening/weekend programs available. Students: 75 full-time (60 women), 26 part-time (16 women); includes 12 minority (11 African Americans, 1 Hispanic), 1 international. In 1997, 37 degrees awarded. *Degree requirements:* Comprehensive exam, practicum required, foreign language and thesis not required. *Entrance requirements:* GRE General Test, MAT, minimum GPA of 2.7. Application deadline: 8/31 (rolling processing; 1/18 for spring admission). Application fee: $25. *Expenses:* Tuition $248 per hour. Fees $60 per year. *Financial aid:* Career-related internships or fieldwork available. Financial aid applicants required to submit FAFSA. • Dr. Peter Wilson, Director of Graduate Counseling Psychology Program, 615-248-1417. Fax: 615-248-7728.

Trinity College, School of Professional Studies, Programs in Education, Washington, DC 20017-1094. Offerings include guidance and counseling (MA). Faculty: 6 full-time (5 women), 18 part-time (13 women). *Application deadline:* rolling. *Application fee:* $35. *Tuition:* $460 per credit hour. • Sr. Rosemarie Bosler, Division Chair, 202-884-9557. Application contact: Karen Goodwin, Director of Graduate Admissions, 202-884-9400. Fax: 202-884-9229.

Troy State University, Graduate School, School of Education, Program in Counseling and Human Development, Troy, AL 36082. Awards MS. Accredited by NCATE. Part-time and evening/weekend programs available. Students: 63 full-time (45 women), 48 part-time (37 women); includes 37 minority (34 African Americans, 2 Hispanics, 1 Native American), 2 international. Average age 30. In 1997, 98 degrees awarded. *Degree requirements:* Thesis, comprehensive exam. *Entrance requirements:* Minimum GPA of 2.5. Application deadline: rolling. Application fee: $20. Electronic applications accepted. *Expenses:* Tuition $2040 per year full-time, $68 per hour part-time for state residents; $4200 per year full-time, $140 per hour part-time for nonresidents. Fees $240 per year full-time, $27 per quarter (minimum) part-time. • Dr. Pamela Manners, Chair, 334-670-3272. Fax: 334-670-3474. E-mail: pmanners@trojan.troyst.edu. Application contact: Teresa Rodgers, Director of Graduate Admissions, 334-670-3188. Fax: 334-670-3733. E-mail: trodgers@trojan.troyst.edu.

Troy State University, Graduate School, School of Education, Program in School Counseling, Troy, AL 36082. Offers counselor education (MS), guidance services (MS). Accredited by NCATE. Part-time and evening/weekend programs available. Students: 37 full-time (33 women), 57 part-time (52 women); includes 67 minority (all African Americans). Average age 30. In 1997, 7 degrees awarded. *Degree requirements:* Thesis, comprehensive exam. *Entrance requirements:* Minimum GPA of 2.5. Application deadline: rolling. Application fee: $20. Electronic applications accepted. *Expenses:* Tuition $2040 per year full-time, $68 per hour part-time for state residents; $4200 per year full-time, $140 per hour part-time for nonresidents. Fees $240 per year full-time, $27 per quarter (minimum) part-time. • Martha Hall, Chair, 334-448-5140. Fax: 334-448-5205. Application contact: Teresa Rodgers, Director of Graduate Admissions, 334-670-3188. Fax: 334-670-3733. E-mail: trodgers@trojan.troyst.edu.

Troy State University Dothan, School of Education, Dothan, AL 36304-0368. Offerings include counseling and psychology (MS), school counseling (MS Ed, Ed S). One or more programs accredited by NCATE. *Degree requirements:* For master's, written comprehensive exam required, thesis optional, foreign language not required. *Entrance requirements:* For master's, GRE General Test or MAT, minimum GPA of 2.5. Application fee: $20. *Expenses:* Tuition $68 per credit hour for state residents; $140 per credit hour for nonresidents. Fees $2 per credit hour. • Dr. Betty Anderson, Dean, 334-983-6556. Application contact: Reta Cordell, Director of Admissions and Records, 334-983-6556. Fax: 334-983-6322. E-mail: rcordell@tsud.edu.

Troy State University Montgomery, Division of Counseling, Education, and Psychology, Program in Counseling, PO Drawer 4419, Montgomery, AL 36103-4419. Offers counseling and human development (MS, Ed S). Part-time and evening/weekend programs available. In 1997, 29 master's, 2 Ed Ss awarded. *Degree requirements:* Thesis or alternative. *Entrance requirements:* For master's, GRE, MAT, or NTE; TOEFL; for Ed S, GRE General Test, MAT, or NTE; TOEFL. Application deadline: rolling. Application fee: $20. Electronic applications accepted. *Expenses:* Tuition $52 per quarter hour for state residents; $104 per quarter hour for nonresidents. Fees $30 per year. • Dr. John Patrick, Coordinator, 334-241-9593. E-mail: jpatrick@tsum.edu.

Tuskegee University, College of Liberal Arts and Education, Department of Counseling and Student Development, Program in Counseling and Student Development, Tuskegee, AL 36088. Awards M Ed, MS. Accredited by NCATE. Faculty: 1 (woman) full-time, 2 part-time (both women). Students: 11 full-time (7 women), 2 part-time (both women); includes 13 minority (all African Americans). Average age 24. In 1997, 8 degrees awarded. *Entrance requirements:* GRE General Test. Application deadline: 7/15 (rolling processing). Application fee: $25 ($35 for international students). *Financial aid:* Application deadline 4/15. • Dr. Fannie R. Cooley, Head, Department of Counseling and Student Development, 334-727-8135.

Tuskegee University, College of Liberal Arts and Education, Department of Counseling and Student Development, Program in School Counseling, Tuskegee, AL 36088. Awards M Ed, MS. Accredited by NCATE. Faculty: 1 (woman) full-time, 2 part-time (both women). Students: 0. *Entrance requirements:* GRE General Test. Application deadline: 7/15 (rolling processing). Application fee: $25 ($35 for international students). *Financial aid:* Application deadline 4/15. • Dr. Fannie R. Cooley, Head, Department of Counseling and Student Development, 334-727-8135.

Université de Moncton, Faculty of Education, Graduate Studies in Education, Moncton, NB E1A 3E9, Canada. Offerings include guidance (MA Ed, M Ed). Faculty: 25 full-time (12 women). *Degree requirements:* Proficiency in English and French. *Entrance requirements:* Minimum GPA of 3.0. Application deadline: 6/1 (rolling processing). Application fee: $30. • Léonard Goguen, Director, 506-858-4409. Fax: 506-858-4317. E-mail: goguenl@umoncton.ca. Application contact: Nicole Savoie, Conseillière à l'admission, 506-858-4115. Fax: 506-858-4544. E-mail: savoien@umoncton.ca.

Université de Sherbrooke, Faculty of Education, Program in Counseling, Sherbrooke, PQ J1K 2R1, Canada. Awards M Ed. Part-time and evening/weekend programs available. *Degree requirements:* Thesis. *Application deadline:* 6/1. *Application fee:* $15.

Université Laval, Faculty of Education, Department of Guidance and Counseling, Administration and Evaluation in Education, Program in Guidance and Counseling, Sainte-Foy, PQ G1K 7P4, Canada. Awards MA, PhD. Students: 212 full-time (173 women), 131 part-time (104 women). 193 applicants, 81% accepted. In 1997, 95 master's, 2 doctorates awarded. *Application deadline:* 3/1. *Application fee:* $30. *Expenses:* Tuition $1334 per year (minimum) full-time, $56 per credit (minimum) part-time for Canadian residents; $5966 per year (minimum) full-time, $249 per credit (minimum) part-time for nonresidents. Fees $150 per year full-time, $6.25 per credit part-time. *Faculty research:* Counseling psychology, psychological education, vocational guidance, growth and development. • Pauline Fahmy, Director, 418-656-2131 Ext. 2240. Fax: 418-656-2885. E-mail: pauline.fahmy@fse.ulaval.ca.

The University of Akron, College of Education, Department of Counseling and Special Education, Program in Community Counseling, Akron, OH 44325-0001. Awards MA, MS. Accredited by NCATE. Students: 39 full-time (34 women), 106 part-time (83 women); includes 19 minority (15 African Americans, 1 Asian American, 3 Hispanics). Average age 36. In 1997, 11 degrees awarded. *Degree requirements:* Written comprehensive exam required, foreign language not required. *Entrance requirements:* MAT (minimum score 35), minimum GPA of 2.75. Application deadline: 8/15 (rolling processing). Application fee: $25 ($50 for international students). *Expenses:* Tuition $178 per credit hour for state residents; $333 per credit hour for nonresidents. Fees $145 per year full-time, $32 per semester (minimum) part-time. • Patricia Parr, Coordinator, 330-972-8151. Application contact: Dr. Robert Eley, Director of Student Services, 330-972-7750. E-mail: reley@uakron.edu.

The University of Akron, College of Education, Department of Counseling and Special Education, Program in Elementary School Counseling, Akron, OH 44325-0001. Awards MA, MS. Accredited by NCATE. Students: 14 part-time (11 women); includes 1 minority (African American). Average age 35. In 1997, 3 degrees awarded. *Degree requirements:* Written comprehensive exam required, foreign language not required. *Entrance requirements:* MAT (minimum score 35), minimum GPA of 2.75. Application deadline: 8/15 (rolling processing). Application fee: $25 ($50 for international students). *Expenses:* Tuition $178 per credit hour for state residents; $333 per credit hour for nonresidents. Fees $145 per year full-time, $32 per semester (minimum) part-time. • Patricia Parr, Coordinator, 330-972-8151. Application contact: Dr. Robert Eley, Director of Student Services, 330-972-7750. E-mail: reley@uakron.edu.

The University of Akron, College of Education, Department of Counseling and Special Education, Program in Secondary School Counseling, Akron, OH 44325-0001. Awards MA, MS. Accredited by NCATE. Students: 1 (woman) full-time, 21 part-time (16 women); includes 1 minority (African American). Average age 34. In 1997, 2 degrees awarded. *Degree requirements:* Written comprehensive exam required, foreign language not required. *Entrance requirements:* MAT (minimum score 35), minimum GPA of 2.75. Application deadline: 8/15 (rolling processing). Application fee: $25 ($50 for international students). *Expenses:* Tuition $178 per credit hour for state residents; $333 per credit hour for nonresidents. Fees $145 per year full-time, $32 per semester (minimum) part-time. • Patricia Parr, Coordinator, 330-972-8151. Application contact: Dr. Robert Eley, Director of Student Services, 330-972-7750. E-mail: reley@uakron.edu.

The University of Alabama, College of Education, Area of Professional Studies, Program in Counselor Education, Tuscaloosa, AL 35487. Awards Ed D, PhD, Ed S. Accredited by NCATE. *Degree requirements:* For doctorate, 1 foreign language, computer language, dissertation. *Entrance requirements:* For doctorate, GRE General Test, MAT (score in 50th percentile or higher), or NTE (minimum score 658 on each core battery test), minimum GPA of 3.0. Application deadline: 7/6 (rolling processing). Application fee: $25. *Tuition:* $2684 per year full-time, $594 per semester (minimum) part-time for state residents; $7216 per year full-time, $1248 per semester (minimum) part-time for nonresidents. *Financial aid:* Application deadline 7/14. • Dr. R. Carl Westerfield, Head, Area of Professional Studies, 205-348-8362. Fax: 205-348-0867. E-mail: cwesterf@bamaed.ua.edu.

The University of Alabama at Birmingham, Graduate School, School of Education, Department of Human Studies, Program in Counseling, Birmingham, AL 35294. Offers agency counseling (MA), marriage and family counseling (MA), rehabilitation counseling (MA), school counseling (MA), school psychology (MA Ed). Accredited by NCATE. Students: 91 full-time (72 women), 95 part-time (76 women); includes 29 minority (22 African Americans, 3 Asian Americans, 4 Native Americans). 193 applicants, 96% accepted. In 1997, 64 degrees awarded. *Degree requirements:* Thesis optional, foreign language not required. *Entrance requirements:* GRE General Test, MAT, or NTE, minimum GPA of 3.0. Application deadline: rolling. Application fee: $30 ($60 for international students). Electronic applications accepted. *Expenses:* Tuition $99 per credit hour for state residents; $198 per credit hour for nonresidents. Fees $516 per year (minimum) full-time, $73 per quarter (minimum) part-time for state residents; $516 per year (minimum) full-time, $73 per unit (minimum) part-time for nonresidents. *Financial aid:* Career-related internships or fieldwork available. • Dr. David M. Macrina, Chairperson, Department of Human Studies, 205-934-2446.

University of Alaska Anchorage, College of Health, Education and Social Welfare, School of Education, Program in Counseling and Guidance, Anchorage, AK 99508-8060. Awards M Ed. Part-time programs available. Students: 15 full-time (13 women), 18 part-time (15 women); includes 3 minority (2 African Americans, 1 Hispanic). 21 applicants, 76% accepted. In 1997, 40 degrees awarded. *Entrance requirements:* GRE Subject Test, interview. Application deadline: 5/1 (rolling processing). Application fee: $45. *Expenses:* Tuition $2988 per year full-time, $1990 per year part-time for state residents; $5814 per year full-time, $3876 per year part-time for nonresidents. Fees $298 per year. *Financial aid:* Federal Work-Study and career-related internships or fieldwork available. Aid available to part-time students. Financial aid application deadline: 4/1. • Dr. Chris Jensen, Head, 907-786-4415. Fax: 907-786-4444. Application contact: Linda Berg Smith, Associate Vice Chancellor for Enrollment Services, 907-786-1529.

University of Alaska Fairbanks, Graduate School, School of Education, Fairbanks, AK 99775-7480. Offerings include guidance and counseling (M Ed). School faculty: 23 full-time (13 women), 2 part-time (both women). *Degree requirements:* Thesis or alternative, comprehensive exam required, foreign language not required. *Entrance requirements:* GRE General Test, TOEFL (minimum score 550). Application deadline: 4/1 (10/1 for spring admission). Application fee: $35. *Expenses:* Tuition $162 per credit for state residents; $316 per credit for nonresidents. Fees $520 per year full-time, $45 per semester (minimum) part-time. • Dr. Joe Kan, Director, 907-474-7341.

Directory: Counselor Education

University of Alberta, Faculty of Graduate Studies and Research, Department of Educational Psychology, Edmonton, AB T6G 2E1, Canada. Offerings include school counseling (M Ed). Department faculty: 36 full-time (11 women), 23 part-time (9 women), 41.75 FTE. *Application deadline:* 2/1 (priority date; rolling processing). *Application fee:* $60. *Expenses:* Tuition $390 per course for Canadian residents; $781 per course for nonresidents. Fees $500 per year full-time, $184 per year part-time. • Dr. L. L. Stewin, Chair, 403-492-2389. Fax: 403-492-1318. E-mail: len.stewin@ualberta.ca.

University of Arkansas, College of Education, Department of Educational Leadership, Counseling and Foundations, Program in Counseling Education, Fayetteville, AR 72701-1201. Awards MS, PhD, Ed S. Accredited by NCATE. Students: 50 full-time (39 women), 22 part-time (18 women); includes 13 minority (6 African Americans, 3 Hispanics, 4 Native Americans), 1 international. 33 applicants, 58% accepted. In 1997, 17 master's, 1 doctorate, 1 Ed S awarded. *Degree requirements:* For master's, thesis optional, foreign language not required; for doctorate, dissertation. *Entrance requirements:* For master's, GRE General Test or MAT. Application fee: $25 ($35 for international students). *Tuition:* $3144 per year full-time, $173 per credit hour part-time for state residents; $7140 per year full-time, $395 per credit hour part-time for nonresidents. *Financial aid:* Research assistantships, teaching assistantships, Federal Work-Study, and career-related internships or fieldwork available. Aid available to part-time students. Financial aid application deadline: 4/1; applicants required to submit FAFSA. • Dr. John Murry, Coordinator, 501-575-2207.

University of Arkansas at Little Rock, College of Education, Department of Educational Leadership, Program in Counselor Education, Little Rock, AR 72204-1099. Offers school counseling (M Ed). Part-time and evening/weekend programs available. Students: 3 full-time (all women), 28 part-time (25 women); includes 8 minority (all African Americans). Average age 35. 23 applicants, 83% accepted. In 1997, 12 degrees awarded. *Degree requirements:* Comprehensive exam, portfolio or thesis required, foreign language not required. *Entrance requirements:* GRE General Test (minimum combined score of 1000 on three sections), minimum GPA of 2.75, teaching certificate. Application deadline: rolling. Application fee: $25 ($30 for international students). *Expenses:* Tuition $2466 per year full-time, $137 per credit hour part-time for state residents; $5256 per year full-time, $292 per credit hour part-time for nonresidents. Fees $216 per year full-time, $36 per semester (minimum) part-time. *Financial aid:* Research assistantships, Federal Work-Study, institutionally sponsored loans, and career-related internships or fieldwork available. Aid available to part-time students. • Dr. Keith B. Runion, Adviser, 501-569-3267.

University of Central Arkansas, College of Education, Department of Counseling and Psychology, Program in Guidance and Counseling, Conway, AR 72035-0001. Offers counseling psychology (MS), elementary school counseling (MS), secondary school counseling (MS). Accredited by NCATE. Students: 13 full-time (10 women), 71 part-time (60 women); includes 12 minority (9 African Americans, 2 Asian Americans, 1 Native American), 1 international. 34 applicants, 94% accepted. In 1997, 23 degrees awarded. *Degree requirements:* Comprehensive exam required, thesis optional. *Entrance requirements:* GRE General Test, minimum GPA of 2.7. Application deadline: 3/1 (priority date; rolling processing; 10/1 for spring admission). Application fee: $15 ($40 for international students). *Expenses:* Tuition $161 per credit hour for state residents; $298 per credit hour for nonresidents. Fees $50 per year full-time, $30 per year part-time. *Financial aid:* In 1997–98, 8 assistantships were awarded; career-related internships or fieldwork also available. Financial aid application deadline: 2/15. • Dr. Terry Smith, Associate Professor, 501-450-3193. Fax: 501-450-5424. E-mail: terrys@mail.uca.edu.

University of Central Florida, College of Education, Department of Educational Services, Program in Counselor Education, Orlando, FL 32816. Awards MA, M Ed. Accredited by NCATE. Part-time and evening/weekend programs available. Students: 103 full-time (82 women), 39 part-time (32 women); includes 19 minority (9 African Americans, 2 Asian Americans, 7 Hispanics, 1 Native American). Average age 37. 62 applicants, 45% accepted. In 1997, 40 degrees awarded. *Degree requirements:* Thesis or alternative required, foreign language not required. *Entrance requirements:* GRE General Test (minimum combined score of 840). Application deadline: 2/1 (9/1 for spring admission). Application fee: $20. *Expenses:* Tuition $3288 per year full-time, $137 per credit hour part-time for state residents; $11,520 per year full-time, $480 per credit hour part-time for nonresidents. Fees $105 per year. *Financial aid:* Teaching assistantships, Federal Work-Study, institutionally sponsored loans, and career-related internships or fieldwork available. Aid available to part-time students. • Application contact: Dr. Andrew Creamer, Coordinator, 407-823-6044. E-mail: creamer@pegasus.cc.ucf.edu.

University of Central Oklahoma, College of Education, Department of Professional Teacher Education, Program in Guidance and Counseling, Edmond, OK 73034-5209. Awards M Ed. Accredited by NCATE. Part-time and evening/weekend programs available. *Entrance requirements:* GRE General Test. Application deadline: 8/18. Application fee: $15. *Tuition:* $76 per credit hour for state residents; $178 per credit hour for nonresidents.

University of Cincinnati, College of Education, Division of Human Services, Department of Counselor Education and School Psychology, Program in Counselor Education, Cincinnati, OH 45221. Offers counselor education (M Ed, Ed D, CAGS), rehabilitation counseling (MA, CAGS). Accredited by NCATE. Part-time programs available. Students: 53 full-time (41 women), 67 part-time (52 women); includes 16 minority (13 African Americans, 1 Asian American, 2 Native Americans), 3 international. 92 applicants, 41% accepted. In 1997, 35 master's, 8 doctorates awarded. *Degree requirements:* For master's, thesis or alternative required, foreign language not required; for doctorate, dissertation required, foreign language not required. *Average time to degree:* master's–3.3 years full-time; doctorate–6.7 years full-time. *Entrance requirements:* For master's, GRE General Test; for doctorate, GRE General Test, GRE Subject Test. Application deadline: 2/1. Application fee: $30. *Tuition:* $7228 per year full-time, $185 per credit hour part-time for state residents; $13,812 per year full-time, $352 per credit hour part-time for nonresidents. *Financial aid:* Fellowships, graduate assistantships, full tuition waivers available. Aid available to part-time students. Financial aid application deadline: 5/1. • Application contact: Ellen Cook, Graduate Program Director, 513-556-3343. Fax: 513-556-2483. E-mail: ellen.cook@uc.edu.

University of Colorado at Colorado Springs, School of Education, Colorado Springs, CO 80933-7150. Offerings include counseling and human services (MA). Accredited by NCATE. School faculty: 13 full-time (6 women). *Degree requirements:* Thesis or alternative, comprehensive exams, microcomputer proficiency required, foreign language not required. *Entrance requirements:* GRE General Test, MAT. Application deadline: rolling. Application fee: $40 ($50 for international students). *Expenses:* Tuition $2760 per year full-time, $115 per credit hour part-time for state residents; $9960 per year full-time, $415 per credit hour part-time for nonresidents. Fees $399 per year (minimum) full-time, $106 per year (minimum) part-time. • Dr. Greg R. Weisenstein, Dean, 719-262-4103. E-mail: gweisens@mail.uccs.edu. Application contact: Connie Wroten, Academic Adviser, 719-262-3268. Fax: 719-262-3554. E-mail: cwroten@mail.uccs.edu.

University of Colorado at Denver, School of Education, Program in Counseling Psychology and Counselor Education, Denver, CO 80217-3364. Awards MA. Accredited by NCATE. Part-time and evening/weekend programs available. Students: 94 full-time (77 women), 125 part-time (102 women); includes 32 minority (11 African Americans, 6 Asian Americans, 13 Hispanics, 2 Native Americans), 3 international. Average age 34. 120 applicants, 52% accepted. In 1997, 66 degrees awarded. *Degree requirements:* Thesis or alternative required, foreign language not required. *Entrance requirements:* GRE or MAT, minimum GPA of 2.75. Application deadline: 4/15 (rolling processing; 9/15 for spring admission). Application fee: $50 ($60 for international students). Electronic applications accepted. *Expenses:* Tuition $3530 per year full-time, $199 per semester hour part-time for state residents; $12,722 per year full-time, $764 per semester hour part-time for nonresidents. Fees $252 per year. *Financial aid:* Research assistantships, teaching assistantships, Federal Work-Study available. Financial aid application deadline: 3/1; applicants required to submit FAFSA. • Robert Smith, Area Coordinator, 303-556-2563. Application contact: Karen Smiddy, Administrative Assistant, 303-556-8367. Fax: 303-556-4479.

University of Dayton, School of Education, Department of Counselor Education and Human Services, Dayton, OH 45469-1611. Offers programs in college student personnel services (MS Ed), school counseling (MS Ed), school psychology (MS Ed), school social worker (MS Ed), social agency counseling (MS Ed). Accredited by NCATE. Part-time and evening/weekend programs available. Faculty: 8 full-time (1 woman), 5 part-time (4 women). Students: 90 full-time (70 women), 773 part-time (602 women); includes 96 minority (71 African Americans, 8 Asian Americans, 15 Hispanics, 2 Native Americans), 6 international. Average age 32. 147 applicants, 51% accepted. In 1997, 251 degrees awarded. *Degree requirements:* Exit exam required, thesis optional, foreign language not required. *Average time to degree:* master's–2 years full-time, 3.5 years part-time. *Entrance requirements:* GRE General Test (minimum score 430 on verbal section, 490 on analytical), minimum GPA of 2.75. Application deadline: 2/15 (priority date; rolling processing). Application fee: $30. *Financial aid:* In 1997–98, 4 research assistantships were awarded; Federal Work-Study, institutionally sponsored loans also available. • Dr. William Drury, Chairperson, 937-229-3644.

University of Delaware, College of Human Resources, Education and Public Policy, School of Education, Newark, DE 19716. Offerings include school counseling (M Ed). School faculty: 54 (24 women). *Application deadline:* 7/1 (rolling processing; 1/15 for spring admission). *Application fee:* $45. *Expenses:* Tuition $4250 per year full-time, $236 per credit hour part-time for state residents; $12,250 per year full-time, $681 per credit hour part-time for nonresidents. Fees $466 per year full-time, $15 per semester (minimum) part-time. • Dr. Robert Hampel, Director, 302-831-2573.

University of Detroit Mercy, College of Education and Human Services, Department of Education, Program in Counseling, Detroit, MI 48219-0900. Awards MA. Part-time and evening/weekend programs available. *Degree requirements:* Thesis or alternative. *Entrance requirements:* Minimum GPA of 2.75. Application deadline: 8/1. Application fee: $25.

University of Evansville, Graduate Programs, School of Education, Program in Counseling, Evansville, IN 47722-0002. Awards MA, MS Coun. Accredited by NCATE. MS Coun being phased out; applicants no longer accepted. Faculty: 4 full-time (2 women). Students: 1 (woman) full-time, 10 part-time (5 women); includes 3 minority (all African Americans). Average age 35. *Entrance requirements:* GRE. Application deadline: 7/1. Application fee: $20. *Expenses:* Tuition $395 per credit hour. Fees $30 per year. *Financial aid:* Research assistantships available. Financial aid application deadline: 7/1. • Dr. Davies Bellamy, Director, 812-479-2367.

University of Florida, College of Education, Department of Counselor Education, Gainesville, FL 32611. Offers programs in marriage and family counseling (M Ed, Ed D, PhD, Ed S), mental health counseling (M Ed, Ed D, PhD, Ed S), school counseling and guidance (M Ed, Ed D, Ed S), student counseling and guidance (PhD), student personnel services in higher education (M Ed, Ed D, PhD, Ed S). Accredited by NCATE. Part-time programs available. Faculty: 25. Students: 83 full-time (61 women), 117 part-time (85 women); includes 40 minority (12 African Americans, 10 Asian Americans, 18 Hispanics), 2 international. 166 applicants, 58% accepted. In 1997, 40 master's, 7 doctorates, 43 Ed Ss awarded. Terminal master's awarded for partial completion of doctoral program. *Degree requirements:* For doctorate, dissertation required, foreign language not required. *Entrance requirements:* For master's and doctorate, GRE General Test, minimum GPA of 3.0 (undergraduate), 3.5 (graduate); for Ed S, GRE General Test. Application deadline: 2/27 (priority date; rolling processing). Application fee: $20. *Tuition:* $138 per credit hour for state residents; $481 per credit hour for nonresidents. *Financial aid:* In 1997–98, 33 students received aid, including 15 fellowships averaging $686 per month, 3 research assistantships averaging $618 per month, 15 teaching assistantships averaging $540 per month; graduate assistantships and career-related internships or fieldwork also available. *Total annual research expenditures:* $50,000. • Dr. Harry Daniels, Chairman, 352-392-0731 Ext. 226. Application contact: Dr. Peter Sherrard, Graduate Coordinator, 352-392-0731 Ext. 234. Fax: 352-392-7159 Ext. 225. E-mail: psherrard@coe.ufl.edu.

University of Georgia, College of Education, Department of Counseling and Human Development Services, Athens, GA 30602. Offers programs in counseling and student personnel services (PhD), counseling psychology (PhD), education (MA), guidance and counseling (M Ed), rehabilitation counseling (M Ed), student personnel in higher education (M Ed). Accredited by NCATE. One or more programs accredited by APA. Faculty: 10 full-time (4 women). Students: 104 full-time, 39 part-time; includes 30 minority (23 African Americans, 4 Asian Americans, 2 Hispanics, 1 Native American), 1 international. 364 applicants, 13% accepted. In 1997, 54 master's, 14 doctorates awarded. *Degree requirements:* For master's, thesis (MA) required, foreign language not required; for doctorate, variable foreign language requirement, dissertation. *Entrance requirements:* For master's, GRE General Test or MAT; for doctorate, GRE General Test. Application deadline: 7/1 (priority date; 11/15 for spring admission). Application fee: $30. Electronic applications accepted. *Tuition:* $3290 per year full-time, $643 per semester (minimum) part-time for state residents; $11,300 per year full-time, $1645 per semester (minimum) part-time for nonresidents. *Financial aid:* Fellowships, research assistantships, teaching assistantships, assistantships available. • Dr. John C. Dagley Jr., Graduate Coordinator, 706-542-1813. Fax: 706-542-4130.

University of Great Falls, Graduate Studies Division, Programs in Education, Great Falls, MT 59405. Offerings include guidance and counseling (ME). Postbaccalaureate distance learning degree programs offered (minimal on-campus study). Faculty: 4 part-time (2 women). *Entrance requirements:* GRE General Test (minimum score 500 on each section; combined average 1000). Application deadline: 8/15 (priority date; rolling processing). Application fee: $35. *Expenses:* Tuition $327 per credit. Fees $150 per year full-time, $45 per semester (minimum) part-time. • Dr. Al Johnson, Dean, Graduate Studies Division, 406-791-5337. Fax: 406-791-5991. E-mail: ajohnson@ugf.edu.

University of Guam, College of Education, Program in Counseling, 303 University Drive, UOG Station, Mangilao, GU 96923. Awards MA. *Degree requirements:* Comprehensive oral and written exams, special project or thesis required, foreign language not required. *Entrance requirements:* GRE General Test. Application deadline: 5/31. Application fee: $31 ($56 for international students). *Faculty research:* Drugs in the local schools, standardized teaching procedures in the elementary school, how to address the dropout problems.

University of Hartford, College of Education, Nursing, and Health Professions, Program in Counseling, West Hartford, CT 06117-1599. Awards M Ed, MS, Certificate. Accredited by NCATE. Part-time and evening/weekend programs available. Faculty: 3 full-time (0 women), 1 (woman) part-time. Students: 5 full-time (4 women), 15 part-time (12 women). Average age 32. 14 applicants, 57% accepted. In 1997, 11 master's awarded. *Degree requirements:* Comprehensive exam required, foreign language and thesis not required. *Entrance requirements:* GRE General Test or MAT, interview. Application deadline: 5/15 (priority date; rolling processing; 12/15 for spring admission). Application fee: $40 ($55 for international students). Electronic applications accepted. *Financial aid:* Federal Work-Study available. Aid available to part-time students. Financial aid application deadline: 6/1; applicants required to submit FAFSA. • Dr. Joachim Pengel, Director, 860-768-4774. Application contact: Susan Garcia, Coordinator of Student Services, 860-768-5038. E-mail: gettoknow@mail.hartford.edu.

University of Hawaii at Manoa, College of Education, Department of Counselor Education, Honolulu, HI 96822. Awards M Ed. Part-time programs available. Faculty: 6 full-time (2 women). Students: 74 full-time (43 women), 31 part-time (19 women); includes 84 Asian Americans, 1 international. Average age 27. 43 applicants, 28% accepted. In 1997, 25 degrees awarded. *Degree requirements:* Thesis or alternative required, foreign language not required. *Average time to degree:* master's–2.5 years full-time, 4 years part-time. *Entrance requirements:* GRE General Test. Application deadline: 3/1 (9/1 for spring admission). Application fee: $0. *Tuition:* $4029 per year full-time, $214 per credit hour part-time for state residents; $9957 per year full-time, $461 per credit hour part-time for nonresidents. *Financial aid:* In 1997–98, 6 students received aid, including research assistantships averaging $512 per month and totaling $12,300; career-related internships or fieldwork also available. *Faculty research:* Multicultural counseling, self-esteem enhancement, homeless, group counseling, developing intervention. • Dr. Michael Omizo, Chairperson, 808-956-4388. Fax: 808-956-3814. E-mail: omizo@hawaii.edu.

University of Houston–Clear Lake, School of Education, Houston, TX 77058-1098. Offerings include counseling (MS). Accredited by NCATE. School faculty: 34 full-time (23 women), 17 part-time (12 women), 39 FTE. *Application deadline:* rolling. *Application fee:* $30 ($60 for international students). *Tuition:* $207 per credit hour for state residents; $336 per credit hour for nonresidents. • Dr. Dennis Spuck, Dean, 281-283-3501. Application contact: Dr. Doris L. Prater, Associate Dean, 281-283-3600.

University of Idaho, College of Graduate Studies, College of Education, Division of Adult, Counselor, and Technology Education, Program in Counseling and Human Services, Moscow, ID 83844-4140. Awards M Ed, MS, Ed D, PhD, CHSS. Accredited by NCATE. Ed D and PhD offered through the College of Education. Students: 38 full-time (29 women), 51 part-time (34 women); includes 6 minority (3 African Americans, 1 Hispanic, 2 Native Americans), 2 international. *Degree requirements:* For doctorate, dissertation. *Entrance requirements:* For master's, minimum GPA of 2.8; for doctorate, minimum undergraduate GPA of 2.8, 3.0 graduate. Application fee: $35 ($45 for international students). *Expenses:* Tuition $0 for state residents; $6000 per year full-time, $95 per credit part-time for nonresidents. Fees $2676 per year full-time, $134 per credit part-time. *Financial aid:* Teaching assistantships available. • Dr. Gerald Tuchscherer, Director, Division of Adult, Counselor, and Technology Education, 208-885-6556.

The University of Iowa, College of Education, Division of Counseling, Rehabilitation, and Student Development, Iowa City, IA 52242-1316. Offers programs in college student development (Ed S), counselor education (MA, PhD), rehabilitation counseling (MA, PhD). Faculty: 14 full-time, 1 part-time. Students: 66 full-time (48 women), 69 part-time (53 women); includes 21 minority (13 African Americans, 1 Asian American, 6 Hispanics, 1 Native American), 5 international. 104 applicants, 56% accepted. In 1997, 26 master's, 7 doctorates awarded. *Degree requirements:* For master's, exam required, foreign language not required; for doctorate, computer language, dissertation, comprehensive exams required, foreign language not required; for Ed S, computer language, exam required, foreign language not required. *Entrance requirements:* For master's and Ed S, GRE General Test, minimum GPA of 2.5; for doctorate, GRE General Test, minimum GPA of 3.0. Application fee: $30 ($50 for international students). *Expenses:* Tuition $3166 per year full-time, $176 per semester hour part-time for state residents; $10,202 per year full-time, $176 per semester hour part-time for nonresidents. Fees $202 per year full-time, $52 per year (minimum) part-time. *Financial aid:* In 1997–98, 13 fellowships (7 to first-year students), 18 research assistantships (7 to first-year students), 24 teaching assistantships (6 to first-year students) were awarded. Financial aid applicants required to submit FAFSA. • E. Richard Dustin, Chair, 319-335-5275.

University of La Verne, Department of Education, Program in School Counseling, La Verne, CA 91750-4443. Awards MS. *Entrance requirements:* TOEFL (minimum score 550), minimum GPA of 2.5. Application fee: $25. *Expenses:* Tuition $370 per unit (minimum). Fees $60 per year.

University of La Verne, Department of Education, Program in Special Emphasis (Classroom Guidance), La Verne, CA 91750-4443. Awards M Ed. *Entrance requirements:* TOEFL (minimum score 550), minimum GPA of 2.5. Application fee: $25. *Expenses:* Tuition $370 per unit (minimum). Fees $60 per year.

University of Louisville, School of Education, Department of Educational Psychology and Counseling, Louisville, KY 40292-0001. Offers programs in college student personnel services (M Ed), community counseling (M Ed), counseling and student personnel (Ed D), elementary school guidance (M Ed), guidance and personnel (Ed S), secondary school guidance (M Ed). Accredited by NCATE. Faculty: 11 full-time (2 women), 9 part-time (3 women), 14 FTE. Students: 110 full-time (80 women), 190 part-time (157 women); includes 58 minority (44 African Americans, 11 Asian Americans, 3 Hispanics), 2 international. Average age 34. In 1997, 59 master's, 4 doctorates, 1 Ed S awarded. *Degree requirements:* For doctorate, dissertation required, foreign language not required. *Entrance requirements:* GRE General Test. Application deadline: rolling. Application fee: $25. • Dr. Daya S. Sandhu, Chair, 502-852-6884.

University of Maine, College of Education and Human Development, Program in Counselor Education, Orono, ME 04469. Awards MAT, M Ed, MS, CAS. Accredited by NCATE. Part-time and evening/weekend programs available. *Degree requirements:* For master's, thesis or alternative required, foreign language not required. *Entrance requirements:* For master's, MAT, TOEFL (minimum score 550); for CAS, MAT, MA, M Ed, or MS. Application deadline: 2/1 (priority date; rolling processing; 10/15 for spring admission). Application fee: $50. *Expenses:* Tuition $194 per credit hour for state residents; $548 per credit hour for nonresidents. Fees $378 per year full-time, $33 per semester (minimum) part-time. *Financial aid:* Research assistantships, teaching assistantships, and career-related internships or fieldwork available. Financial aid application deadline: 3/1. • Application contact: Scott Delcourt, Director of the Graduate School, 207-581-3218. Fax: 207-581-3232. E-mail: graduate@maine.edu.

University of Manitoba, Faculty of Education, Department of Educational Psychology, Winnipeg, MB R3T 2N2, Canada. Offerings include counselor education (M Ed). *Degree requirements:* Thesis or alternative required, foreign language not required.

University of Maryland, College Park, College of Education, Department of Counseling and Personnel Services, College Park, MD 20742-5045. Offers programs in college student personnel (MA, M Ed), college student personnel administration (PhD), community counseling (CAGS), community/career counseling (MA, M Ed), counseling and personnel services (MA, M Ed, PhD), counseling psychology (PhD), counselor education (PhD), rehabilitation counseling (MA, M Ed), school counseling (MA, M Ed), school psychology (MA, M Ed, PhD). Accredited by NCATE. Faculty: 15 full-time (8 women), 2 part-time (both women). Students: 139 full-time (110 women), 80 part-time (62 women); includes 75 minority (51 African Americans, 13 Asian Americans, 10 Hispanics, 1 Native American), 2 international. 356 applicants, 24% accepted. In 1997, 94 master's, 8 doctorates awarded. *Degree requirements:* For master's, thesis or alternative required, foreign language not required; for doctorate, dissertation required, foreign language not required. *Entrance requirements:* For master's, GRE General Test or MAT, minimum GPA of 3.0; for doctorate, GRE General Test or MAT, minimum GPA of 3.5. Application deadline: rolling. Application fee: $50 ($70 for international students). *Expenses:* Tuition $272 per credit hour for state residents; $400 per credit hour for nonresidents. Fees $564 per year full-time, $342 per year part-time. *Financial aid:* In 1997–98, 19 fellowships, 10 teaching assistantships were awarded; research assistantships and career-related internships or fieldwork also available. • Dr. Paul Power, Chairman, 301-405-2858. Fax: 301-314-9278. Application contact: John Mollish, Director, Graduate Admissions and Records, 301-405-4198. Fax: 301-314-9305.

University of Maryland Eastern Shore, Department of Education, Program in Guidance and Counseling, Princess Anne, MD 21853-1299. Awards M Ed. Faculty: 3 full-time (all women), 6 part-time (3 women). Students: 15 full-time (7 women), 29 part-time (18 women); includes 21 minority (20 African Americans, 1 Hispanic), 3 international. Average age 35. 14 applicants, 100% accepted. In 1997, 22 degrees awarded (100% found work related to degree). *Degree requirements:* Comprehensive exams, practicum, seminar paper required, foreign language and thesis not required. *Average time to degree:* master's–2 years full-time, 3.5 years part-time. *Entrance requirements:* TOEFL (minimum score 550), interview, minimum GPA of 3.0. Application deadline: 6/1 (priority date; rolling processing; 11/1 for spring admission). Application fee: $30. *Expenses:* Tuition $143 per credit hour for state residents; $253 per credit hour for nonresidents. Fees $50 per year. *Financial aid:* In 1997–98, 3 students received aid, including 3 teaching assistantships; research assistantships, Federal Work-Study, and career-related internships or fieldwork also available. Aid available to part-time students. Financial aid application deadline: 3/1. *Faculty research:* Cross-cultural counseling, racial identity, racial socialization. • Dr. Rhonda Jeter, Coordinator, 410-651-6218. Fax: 410-651-7962. E-mail: rjeter@umes-bird.umd.edu.

University of Massachusetts Amherst, School of Education, Program in Education, Amherst, MA 01003-0001. Offerings include school psychology and school counseling (M Ed, Ed D, CAGS). Accredited by NCATE. *Degree requirements:* For doctorate, dissertation required, foreign language not required. *Entrance requirements:* For master's and doctorate, GRE General Test. Application deadline: 3/1 (rolling processing; 10/1 for spring admission). Application fee: $40. *Expenses:* Tuition $2640 per year full-time, $110 per credit part-time for state residents; $3690 per year (minimum) full-time, $165 per credit (minimum) part-time for nonresidents. Fees $2856 per year full-time, $422 per semester part-time for state residents; $3204 per year full-time, $480 per semester part-time for nonresidents. • John C. Carey, Director, 413-545-0236.

University of Massachusetts Boston, Graduate College of Education, Counseling and School Psychology Department, Program in Counseling, Boston, MA 02125-3393. Awards M Ed, CAGS. Students: 89 full-time (73 women), 124 part-time (94 women); includes 29 minority (17 African Americans, 4 Asian Americans, 6 Hispanics, 2 Native Americans), 4 international. 149 applicants, 54% accepted. In 1997, 57 master's, 4 CAGSs awarded. *Degree requirements:* Comprehensive exams required, foreign language and thesis not required. *Entrance requirements:* For master's, GRE General Test or MAT, minimum GPA of 2.75; for CAGS, minimum GPA of 2.75. Application deadline: 3/1 (priority date; 11/1 for spring admission). Application fee: $25 ($35 for international students). *Expenses:* Tuition $2640 per year full-time, $110 per credit part-time for state residents; $8930 per year full-time, $373 per credit part-time for nonresidents. Fees $2650 per year full-time, $420 per semester (minimum) part-time for state residents; $2736 per year full-time, $420 per semester (minimum) part-time for nonresidents. *Financial aid:* In 1997–98, 5 research assistantships (2 to first-year students) averaging $225 per month and totaling $10,700, 3 teaching assistantships averaging $225 per month and totaling $7,000 were awarded; administrative assistantships also available. Financial aid application deadline: 3/1; applicants required to submit FAFSA. • Dr. MaryAnna Ham, Director, 617-287-7617. Application contact: Lisa Lavely, Director of Graduate Admissions and Records, 617-287-6400. Fax: 617-287-6236.

The University of Memphis, College of Education, Department of Counseling, Educational Psychology and Research, Memphis, TN 38152. Offers programs in counseling and personnel services (MS, Ed D), including community agency counseling (MS), rehabilitation counseling (MS), school counseling (MS), student personnel services (MS); counseling psychology (PhD); educational psychology and research (MS, Ed D, PhD), including educational psychology (MS, Ed D), educational research (MS, Ed D). Accredited by NCATE. One or more programs accredited by APA. Faculty: 23 full-time (11 women), 17 part-time (8 women). Students: 95 full-time (76 women), 172 part-time (129 women); includes 56 minority (53 African Americans, 3 Asian Americans), 4 international. Average age 34. 153 applicants, 37% accepted. In 1997, 58 master's, 24 doctorates awarded. *Degree requirements:* For master's, thesis or alternative, comprehensive exam required, foreign language not required; for doctorate, dissertation, comprehensive exam required, foreign language not required. *Entrance requirements:* For master's, GRE General Test or MAT, minimum GPA of 2.5; for doctorate, GRE General Test. Application deadline: 8/1 (12/1 for spring admission). Application fee: $25 ($50 for international students). *Tuition:* $2862 per year full-time, $166 per credit hour part-time for state residents; $6696 per year full-time, $379 per credit hour part-time for nonresidents. *Financial aid:* In 1997–98, 5 research assistantships totaling $32,992, 10 teaching assistantships totaling $66,336 were awarded; career-related internships or fieldwork also available. *Faculty research:* Anger management, aging and disability, supervision, multicultural counseling. • Dr. Ronnie Priest, Chair and Coordinator of Graduate Studies, 901-678-2841.

University of Missouri–Kansas City, School of Education, Division of Counselor Education, Kansas City, MO 64110-2499. Offers programs in counseling and guidance (MA, Ed S), counseling psychology (PhD). Accredited by NCATE. One or more programs accredited by APA. Part-time and evening/weekend programs available. Students: 61 full-time (45 women), 100 part-time (74 women); includes 31 minority (18 African Americans, 7 Asian Americans, 5 Hispanics, 1 Native American), 2 international. Average age 32. In 1997, 36 master's, 11 doctorates, 1 Ed S awarded. *Degree requirements:* For master's, internship/thesis, practicum required, foreign language not required; for doctorate, dissertation, internship, practicum required, foreign language not required; for Ed S, practicum required, foreign language and thesis not required. *Average time to degree:* master's–3 years full-time, 7 years part-time; doctorate–5 years full-time, 7 years part-time. *Entrance requirements:* For master's, MAT, minimum GPA of 2.75; for doctorate, GRE, minimum GPA of 3.0; for Ed S, minimum GPA of 3.0. Application deadline: 3/1. Application fee: $25. *Expenses:* Tuition $182 per credit hour for state residents; $508 per credit hour for nonresidents. Fees $60 per year. *Financial aid:* In 1997–98, 1 research assistantship averaging $858 per month was awarded; teaching assistantships, full and partial tuition waivers, Federal Work-Study, institutionally sponsored loans, and career-related internships or fieldwork also available. Aid available to part-time students. *Faculty research:* Career development, counseling ethics, sport psychology, communication, counseling process. • Dr. Robert Paul, Chairperson, 816-235-2722.

University of Missouri–St. Louis, School of Education, Program in Counseling, St. Louis, MO 63121-4499. Awards M Ed. Accredited by NCATE. Faculty: 23 (8 women). Students: 52 full-time (39 women), 310 part-time (266 women); includes 81 minority (73 African Americans, 2 Asian Americans, 4 Hispanics, 2 Native Americans), 3 international. In 1997, 101 degrees awarded. *Degree requirements:* Thesis required, foreign language not required. *Application deadline:* 7/1 (priority date; rolling processing; 12/1 for spring admission). *Application fee:* $0. Electronic applications accepted. *Expenses:* Tuition $3903 per year full-time, $167 per credit hour part-time for state residents; $11,745 per year full-time, $489 per credit hour part-time for nonresidents. Fees $816 per year full-time, $34 per credit hour part-time. *Financial aid:* In 1997–98, 4 teaching assistantships averaging $833 per month were awarded. *Faculty research:* Vocational interests, self-concept, decision-making factors, developmental differences. • Dr. George Yard, Chair, 314-516-5782. Application contact: Graduate Admissions, 314-516-5458. Fax: 314-516-6759. E-mail: gradadm@umslvma.umsl.edu.

The University of Montana–Missoula, School of Education, Department of Professional Education, Program in Guidance and Counseling, Missoula, MT 59812-0002. Awards MA, M Ed, Ed D, Ed S. Accredited by NCATE. Students: 22 full-time (14 women); includes 3 minority (1 African American, 2 Asian Americans). Average age 31. 7 applicants, 57% accepted. In 1997, 5 master's awarded. *Degree requirements:* For doctorate, dissertation; for Ed S, thesis required, foreign language not required. *Entrance requirements:* For master's, GRE General Test (minimum score 450 on each section), minimum GPA of 3.0; for doctorate, GRE General Test (minimum score 500 on verbal section, 1100 combined), GRE Subject Test, minimum graduate GPA of 3.5; for Ed S, GRE General Test. Application deadline: 2/15 (priority date). Application fee: $30. *Tuition:* $2499 per year (minimum) full-time, $376 per semester (minimum) part-time for state residents; $6528 per year (minimum) full-time, $1048 per semester (minimum) part-time for nonresidents. *Financial aid:* In 1997–98, 1 teaching assistantship was awarded; Federal Work-Study and career-related internships or fieldwork also available. Financial aid application deadline: 3/1. • Dr. Rita Somers-Flanagan, Director, 406-243-5252.

University of Montevallo, College of Education, Program in Guidance and Counseling, Montevallo, AL 35115. Awards M Ed. Accredited by NCATE. Part-time and evening/weekend programs available. *Entrance requirements:* GRE General Test (minimum combined score of 850), MAT (minimum score 35), minimum undergraduate GPA of 2.75 in last 60 hours or 2.5 overall. Application deadline: 7/15 (11/15 for spring admission). Application fee: $10.

University of Nebraska at Kearney, College of Education, Department of Counseling and School Psychology, Kearney, NE 68849-0001. Offers programs in counseling (MS Ed, Ed S),

Directory: Counselor Education

University of Nebraska at Kearney (continued)

school psychology (Ed S). Accredited by NCATE. Part-time and evening/weekend programs available. Faculty: 6 full-time (2 women). Students: 46 full-time (42 women), 138 part-time (108 women); includes 4 minority (1 Asian American, 2 Hispanics, 1 Native American), 2 international. In 1997, 46 master's, 10 Ed Ss awarded. *Degree requirements:* For master's, thesis optional. *Entrance requirements:* For master's, GRE General Test, interview; for Ed S, GRE General Test. Application deadline: 8/1 (priority date; rolling processing; 12/15 for spring admission). Application fee: $35. *Expenses:* Tuition $1494 per year full-time, $83 per credit hour part-time for state residents; $2826 per year full-time, $157 per credit hour part-time for nonresidents. Fees $229 per year full-time, $11.25 per semester (minimum) part-time. *Financial aid:* In 1997–98, 3 research assistantships, 3 teaching assistantships were awarded; career-related internships or fieldwork also available. Aid available to part-time students. Financial aid application deadline: 3/1; applicants required to submit FAFSA. • Dr. Kent Estes, Chair, 308-865-8508.

University of Nebraska at Omaha, College of Education, Department of Counseling, Omaha, NE 68182. Offers programs in community counseling (MA, MS), counseling gerontology (MA, MS), school counseling-elementary (MA, MS), school counseling-secondary (MA, MS), student affairs practice in higher education (MA, MS). Accredited by NCATE. Part-time and evening/weekend programs available. Faculty: 5 full-time (1 woman), 1 part-time (0 women). Students: 37 full-time (29 women), 131 part-time (112 women); includes 18 minority (9 African Americans, 3 Asian Americans, 5 Hispanics, 1 Native American), 6 international. Average age 34. 61 applicants, 33% accepted. In 1997, 52 degrees awarded. *Degree requirements:* Thesis (for some programs), comprehensive exam required, foreign language not required. *Entrance requirements:* GRE General Test, MAT, or department test, interview, minimum GPA of 3.0. Application deadline: 3/1 (priority date; rolling processing; 10/1 for spring admission). Application fee: $35. *Expenses:* Tuition $1670 per year full-time, $94 per credit hour part-time for state residents; $4082 per year full-time, $227 per credit hour part-time for nonresidents. Fees $302 per year full-time, $108 per semester (minimum) part-time. *Financial aid:* In 1997–98, 60 students received aid, including 2 research assistantships; fellowships, full tuition waivers, Federal Work-Study, institutionally sponsored loans also available. Aid available to part-time students. Financial aid application deadline: 3/1; applicants required to submit FAFSA. • Dr. Joseph Davis, Chairperson, 402-554-2306.

University of Nevada, Reno, College of Education, Department of Counseling and Educational Psychology, Reno, NV 89557. Awards MA, M Ed, MS, Ed D, PhD, Ed S. Accredited by NCATE. Faculty: 13 (7 women). Students: 58 full-time (47 women), 79 part-time (58 women); includes 17 minority (6 African Americans, 3 Asian Americans, 6 Hispanics, 2 Native Americans). Average age 38. 54 applicants, 48% accepted. In 1997, 27 master's, 1 doctorate awarded. Terminal master's awarded for partial completion of doctoral program. *Degree requirements:* For master's, thesis optional, foreign language not required; for doctorate, dissertation required, foreign language not required. *Entrance requirements:* For master's, GRE, TOEFL (minimum score 500), minimum GPA of 2.75; for doctorate, GRE, TOEFL (minimum score 500), minimum GPA of 3.0. Application deadline: 2/15 (priority date; 9/15 for spring admission). Application fee: $40. *Expenses:* Tuition $0 for state residents; $5770 per year full-time, $200 per credit part-time for nonresidents. Fees $93 per credit. *Financial aid:* Research assistantships, teaching assistantships, grants, Federal Work-Study, institutionally sponsored loans available. Financial aid application deadline: 3/1. *Faculty research:* Marriage and family counseling, substance abuse attitudes of teachers, current supply of counseling educators, HIV-positive services for patients, family counseling for youth at risk. • Dr. Marlowe Smaby, Chair, 702-784-6637. E-mail: smaby@unr.edu.

University of New Brunswick, Faculty of Education, Division of Educational Foundations, Fredericton, NB E3B 5A3, Canada. Offerings include guidance and counseling (M Ed). *Degree requirements:* Thesis or alternative required, foreign language not required. *Entrance requirements:* TOEFL, TWE, minimum GPA of 3.0. Application deadline: 3/1 (priority date; rolling processing). Application fee: $25.

University of New Hampshire, College of Liberal Arts, Department of Education, Program in Counseling, Durham, NH 03824. Awards MA, M Ed. Accredited by NCATE. Part-time programs available. Students: 19 full-time (16 women), 52 part-time (36 women); includes 6 minority (4 African Americans, 1 Asian American, 1 Hispanic), 1 international. Average age 35. 51 applicants, 82% accepted. In 1997, 29 degrees awarded. *Degree requirements:* Thesis required (for some programs), foreign language not required. *Entrance requirements:* GRE General Test. Application deadline: 4/1 (priority date; rolling processing). Application fee: $50. *Expenses:* Tuition $5440 per year full-time, $302 per credit hour part-time for state residents; $8160 per year (minimum) full-time, $453 per credit hour (minimum) part-time for nonresidents. Fees $868 per year full-time, $15 per year part-time. *Financial aid:* In 1997–98, 4 teaching assistantships (2 to first-year students), 5 scholarships (1 to a first-year student) were awarded; research assistantships, full and partial tuition waivers, Federal Work-Study, and career-related internships or fieldwork also available. Aid available to part-time students. Financial aid application deadline: 2/15. *Faculty research:* Generic approach to counseling. • Dr. Angelo Boy, Coordinator, 603-862-3722. Application contact: Dr. Todd DeMitchell, Graduate Coordinator, 603-862-2317.

University of New Orleans, College of Education, Department of Educational Leadership, Counseling, and Foundations, Program in Counselor Education, New Orleans, LA 70148. Awards M Ed, PhD, Certificate. Accredited by NCATE. Evening/weekend programs available. Faculty: 4 full-time (3 women), 5 part-time (2 women). Students: 56 full-time (40 women), 77 part-time (63 women); includes 33 minority (29 African Americans, 2 Asian Americans, 2 Hispanics), 7 international. Average age 36. 22 applicants, 36% accepted. In 1997, 36 master's, 4 doctorates awarded. Terminal master's awarded for partial completion of doctoral program. *Degree requirements:* For master's, thesis required (for some programs), foreign language not required; for doctorate, variable foreign language requirement, dissertation. *Entrance requirements:* For master's, GRE General Test; for doctorate, GRE General Test (minimum combined score of 1000). Application deadline: 7/1 (priority date; rolling processing). Application fee: $20. *Expenses:* Tuition $2362 per year full-time, $373 per semester (minimum) part-time for state residents; $7888 per year full-time, $1423 per semester (minimum) part-time for nonresidents. Fees $170 per year full-time, $25 per semester (minimum) part-time. *Financial aid:* Fellowships, research assistantships, teaching assistantships, partial tuition waivers, and career-related internships or fieldwork available. • Application contact: Dr. Ted Remley, Graduate Coordinator, 504-280-7450. Fax: 504-280-6065. E-mail: tprel@uno.edu.

University of North Alabama, College of Education, Department of Secondary Education, Program in Counseling, Florence, AL 35632-0001. Offers counseling (MA Ed), non-school-based counseling (MA), non-school-based teaching (MA). Accredited by NCATE. Part-time and evening/weekend programs available. Faculty: 3 part-time (2 women). Students: 21 full-time (14 women), 54 part-time (39 women); includes 9 minority (all African Americans). Average age 33. In 1997, 23 degrees awarded. *Degree requirements:* Final written comprehensive exam required, foreign language and thesis not required. *Entrance requirements:* GRE, MAT, or NTE, minimum GPA of 2.5, Alabama Class B Certificate or equivalent, teaching experience. Application deadline: 7/1 (priority date; rolling processing; 12/1 for spring admission). Application fee: $25. *Expenses:* Tuition $2448 per year full-time, $102 per credit hour part-time for state residents; $4896 per year full-time, $204 per credit hour part-time for nonresidents. Fees $3 per semester. *Financial aid:* Federal Work-Study available. Aid available to part-time students. Financial aid application deadline: 4/1. • Application contact: Dr. Sue Wilson, Dean of Enrollment Management, 205-765-4316.

The University of North Carolina at Chapel Hill, School of Education, Program in School Counseling, Chapel Hill, NC 27599. Awards MA, M Ed. Accredited by NCATE. Students: 12 full-time (10 women). 70 applicants, 24% accepted. *Degree requirements:* Thesis (for some programs), comprehensive exam required, foreign language not required. *Entrance requirements:* GRE General Test (minimum combined score of 1000), minimum GPA of 3.0 during last 2 years of undergraduate course work. Application deadline: 1/1 (rolling processing). Application fee: $55. *Expenses:* Tuition $1428 per year full-time, $357 per semester (minimum) part-time for state residents; $10,414 per year full-time, $2604 per semester (minimum) part-time for nonresidents. Fees $782 per year full-time, $332 per semester (minimum) part-time. *Financial aid:* Federal Work-Study available. Aid available to part-time students. Financial aid application deadline: 1/1. *Faculty research:* Career counseling, development and assessment, multicultural counseling, measurement. • Dr. Duane Brown, Coordinator, 919-966-5266. Application contact: Janet Carroll, Registrar, 919-966-1346. Fax: 919-962-1533. E-mail: jscarrol@email.unc.edu.

University of North Carolina at Charlotte, College of Education, Charlotte, NC 28223-0001. Offerings include counseling and guidance (MA). Accredited by NCATE. College faculty: 61 full-time (31 women), 7 part-time (6 women), 62.75 FTE. *Application deadline:* 7/1. *Application fee:* $35. *Tuition:* $1786 per year full-time, $339 per semester (minimum) part-time for state residents; $8914 per year full-time, $2121 per semester (minimum) part-time for nonresidents. • Dr. John M. Nagle, Dean, 704-547-4707. Application contact: Kathy Barringer, Assistant Director of Graduate Admissions, 704-547-3366. Fax: 704-547-3279. E-mail: gradadm@email.uncc.edu.

University of North Carolina at Greensboro, School of Education, Department of Counseling and Educational Development, Greensboro, NC 27412-0001. Offers programs in gerontological counseling (PMC), guidance and counseling (MS, Ed D, PhD, MS/Ed S), marriage and family counseling (PMC), school counseling (PMC). Accredited by NCATE. Faculty: 8 full-time (2 women), 2 part-time. Students: 119 full-time (85 women), 9 part-time (8 women); includes 12 minority (6 African Americans, 4 Asian Americans, 1 Hispanic, 1 Native American), 2 international. 243 applicants, 31% accepted. In 1997, 20 master's, 11 doctorates, 17 PMCs awarded. *Degree requirements:* For master's, comprehensive exam, practicum, internship required, foreign language and thesis not required; for doctorate, dissertation, comprehensive exam required, foreign language not required. *Entrance requirements:* GRE General Test. Application deadline: 3/1. Application fee: $35. *Expenses:* Tuition $1842 per year full-time, $370 per semester (minimum) part-time for state residents; $10,296 per year full-time, $2484 per semester (minimum) part-time for nonresidents. Fees $806 per year full-time, $111 per semester (minimum) part-time. *Financial aid:* In 1997–98, 57 students received aid, including 10 fellowships totaling $33,000, 51 graduate assistantships totaling $263,000; research assistantships, teaching assistantships, and career-related internships or fieldwork also available. *Faculty research:* Gerontology, invitational theory, career development, marriage and family therapy, drug and alcohol abuse prevention. • Dr. Dianne Borders, Chairman, 336-334-3423.

University of North Carolina at Pembroke, Graduate Studies, Department of Psychology, Program in School Counseling, Pembroke, NC 28372-1510. Awards MA. Accredited by NCATE. Part-time and evening/weekend programs available. Faculty: 8 full-time (3 women), 2 part-time (both women). Students: 6 full-time (all women), 77 part-time (62 women); includes 29 minority (14 African Americans, 1 Asian American, 2 Hispanics, 12 Native Americans). In 1997, 12 degrees awarded. *Degree requirements:* Comprehensive exams required, thesis optional, foreign language not required. *Average time to degree:* master's–2 years full-time, 3.5 years part-time. *Entrance requirements:* GRE General Test or MAT, minimum GPA of 3.0 in major, 2.5 overall. Application deadline: rolling. Application fee: $25. *Tuition:* $1554 per year full-time, $610 per semester (minimum) part-time for state residents; $8824 per year full-time, $2122 per semester (minimum) part-time for nonresidents. *Financial aid:* In 1997–98, 1 graduate assistantship (to a first-year student) averaging $700 per month and totaling $5,600 was awarded; career-related internships or fieldwork also available. Financial aid application deadline: 4/15. • Dr. Ray Von Beatty, Coordinator, 910-521-6456. Application contact: Director of Graduate Studies, 910-521-6271. Fax: 910-521-6497.

University of North Carolina at Pembroke, Graduate Studies, Department of Psychology, Program in Service Agency Counseling, Pembroke, NC 28372-1510. Awards MA. Part-time and evening/weekend programs available. Faculty: 8 full-time (3 women), 1 (woman) part-time. Students: 1 (woman) full-time, 29 part-time (20 women); includes 9 minority (5 African Americans, 4 Native Americans). In 1997, 4 degrees awarded. *Degree requirements:* Comprehensive exams required, thesis optional, foreign language not required. *Entrance requirements:* GRE General Test or MAT, minimum GPA of 3.0 in major, 2.5 overall. Application deadline: rolling. Application fee: $25. *Tuition:* $1554 per year full-time, $610 per semester (minimum) part-time for state residents; $8824 per year full-time, $2122 per semester (minimum) part-time for nonresidents. *Financial aid:* Graduate assistantships and career-related internships or fieldwork available. Aid available to part-time students. Financial aid application deadline: 4/15. • Dr. Ray Von Beatty, Coordinator, 910-521-6456. Application contact: Director of Graduate Studies, 910-521-6271. Fax: 910-521-6497.

University of Northern Colorado, College of Education, Division of Professional Psychology, Program in Counselor Education and Counseling Psychology, Greeley, CO 80639. Offers agency counseling (MA), counseling psychology (Psy D), counselor education (Ed D), elementary school counseling (MA), secondary and postsecondary school counseling (MA). One or more programs accredited by NCATE. Part-time programs available. Faculty: 7 full-time (4 women). Students: 88 full-time (65 women), 27 part-time (23 women); includes 13 minority (3 African Americans, 1 Asian American, 8 Hispanics, 1 Native American), 4 international. Average age 36. 118 applicants, 61% accepted. In 1997, 58 master's, 10 doctorates awarded. *Degree requirements:* For master's, comprehensive exams; for doctorate, dissertation, comprehensive exams. *Entrance requirements:* For doctorate, GRE General Test. Application deadline: rolling. Application fee: $35. *Expenses:* Tuition $2327 per year full-time, $129 per credit hour part-time for state residents; $9578 per year full-time, $532 per credit hour part-time for nonresidents. Fees $752 per year full-time, $184 per semester (minimum) part-time. *Financial aid:* In 1997–98, 79 students received aid, including 21 fellowships (9 to first-year students) totaling $29,221, 1 teaching assistantship totaling $8,217, 9 graduate assistantships (4 to first-year students) totaling $66,463. Financial aid application deadline: 3/1. • Dr. Tracy Baldo, Coordinator, 970-351-2544.

University of Northern Iowa, College of Education, Department of Educational Leadership, Counseling, and Postsecondary Education, Program in Counseling, Cedar Falls, IA 50614. Offers counseling (MA, Ed D), school counseling (MA Ed). Part-time and evening/weekend programs available. Students: 22 full-time (20 women), 54 part-time (47 women); includes 3 minority (2 African Americans, 1 Asian American), 1 international. Average age 33. 32 applicants, 66% accepted. In 1997, 19 master's, 1 doctorate awarded. *Degree requirements:* Thesis/dissertation or alternative required, foreign language not required. *Entrance requirements:* For master's, minimum GPA of 3.5, 3 years of educational experience; for doctorate, minimum GPA of 3.2, 3 years of educational experience, master's degree. Application deadline: 8/1 (priority date; rolling processing). Application fee: $20 ($30 for international students). *Expenses:* Tuition $3166 per year full-time, $176 per hour part-time for state residents; $7805 per year full-time, $176 per hour part-time for nonresidents. Fees $194 per year full-time, $12.50 per semester (minimum) part-time. *Financial aid:* Full and partial tuition waivers, Federal Work-Study, and career-related internships or fieldwork available. Aid available to part-time students. Financial aid application deadline: 3/1. • Dr. Ann Vernon, Head, 319-273-2226.

University of North Florida, College of Education, Division of Educational Services and Research, Program in Counselor Education, Jacksonville, FL 32224-2645. Awards M Ed. Accredited by NCATE. Part-time and evening/weekend programs available. Faculty: 5 full-time (3 women). Students: 24 full-time (22 women), 52 part-time (48 women); includes 10 minority (9 African Americans, 1 Asian American), 1 international. Average age 36. 4 applicants, 50% accepted. In 1997, 30 degrees awarded. *Entrance requirements:* GRE General Test (minimum combined score of 1000), minimum GPA of 3.0. Application deadline: rolling. Application fee: $20. *Tuition:* $3388 per year full-time, $141 per credit hour part-time for state residents; $11,634 per year full-time, $485 per credit hour part-time for nonresidents. *Financial aid:* Federal Work-Study, institutionally sponsored loans, and career-related internships or fieldwork available. Financial aid application deadline: 4/1. *Faculty research:* Guidance for handicapped students, assessment, full-service schools, gender equity. • Judy Lombana, Director, 904-646-2838. Fax: 904-646-1025.

University of North Texas, College of Education, Department of Counseling, Development and Higher Education, Program in Counselor Education, Denton, TX 76203-6737. Offers counseling and student services (M Ed, MS, PhD), counselor education (MS). Accredited by NCATE. Evening/weekend programs available. *Degree requirements:* For master's, thesis optional, foreign language not required; for doctorate, dissertation. *Entrance requirements:* For master's, GRE General Test (minimum combined score of 1200 on three sections). Application deadline: 7/17. Application fee: $25 ($50 for international students). *Tuition:* $2063 per year full-time, $815 per year part-time for state residents; $5897 per year full-time, $2100 per year part-time for nonresidents. *Financial aid:* Teaching assistantships, Federal Work-Study, institutionally sponsored loans, and career-related internships or fieldwork available. Financial aid application deadline: 4/1. • Application contact: Jan Holden, Adviser, 940-565-2910.

University of Oklahoma, College of Education, Department of Educational Psychology, Program in Counseling Psychology, Norman, OK 73019-0390. Offerings include community counseling (M Ed). *Degree requirements:* Comprehensive exam required, foreign language and thesis not required. *Entrance requirements:* GRE General Test, TOEFL (minimum score 550), minimum GPA of 3.0, 12 hours of course work in education. Application fee: $25. *Expenses:* Tuition $1920 per year full-time, $80 per credit hour part-time for state residents; $6108 per year full-time, $255 per credit hour part-time for nonresidents. Fees $468 per year full-time, $12 per semester (minimum) part-time. • Dr. Raymond B. Miller, Chair, Department of Educational Psychology, 405-325-5974.

University of Phoenix, Graduate Programs, Counseling Programs, 4615 East Elwood St, PO Box 52069, Phoenix, AZ 85072-2069. Offerings in community counseling (MC); marriage, family, and child therapy (MC); mental health counseling (MC). Programs offered at campuses in Phoenix, Puerto Rico, Tucson, and Utah. Evening/weekend programs available. Students: 558 full-time (418 women); includes 216 minority (28 African Americans, 13 Asian Americans, 167 Hispanics, 8 Native Americans). Average age 34. In 1997, 55 degrees awarded. *Degree requirements:* Thesis or alternative required, foreign language not required. *Entrance requirements:* Comprehensive cognitive assessment (COCA). Application deadline: rolling. Application fee: $50. *Tuition:* $232 per credit hour. • Dr. Patrick Romine, Dean, 602-966-9577 Ext. 1074. Fax: 602-968-1159. Application contact: Campus Information Center, 602-966-9577.

University of Phoenix, Graduate Programs, Programs in Education, Specialization in Educational Counseling, 4615 East Elwood St, PO Box 52069, Phoenix, AZ 85072-2069. Awards MA Ed. Programs offered at campuses in Phoenix, Puerto Rico, Tucson, and Utah. *Degree requirements:* Thesis or alternative. *Entrance requirements:* Comprehensive cognitive assessment (COCA). Application deadline: rolling. Application fee: $50. *Tuition:* $197 per credit hour. • Application contact: Campus Information Center, 602-966-9577.

University of Pittsburgh, School of Education, Department of Psychology in Education, Program in Counseling, Pittsburgh, PA 15260. Offers school counseling (MA, M Ed). Part-time and evening/weekend programs available. 106 applicants, 86% accepted. *Degree requirements:* Thesis required, foreign language not required. *Average time to degree:* master's–2 years full-time, 4 years part-time. *Entrance requirements:* TOEFL (minimum score 650). Application deadline: 2/1. Application fee: $30 ($40 for international students). *Expenses:* Tuition $8018 per year full-time, $329 per credit part-time for state residents; $16,508 per year full-time, $680 per credit part-time for nonresidents. Fees $480 per year full-time, $180 per year part-time. *Financial aid:* Partial tuition waivers, Federal Work-Study, institutionally sponsored loans, and career-related internships or fieldwork available. Aid available to part-time students. Financial aid application deadline: 5/1; applicants required to submit FAFSA. • Application contact: Jackie Harden, Manager, 412-648-7060. Fax: 412-648-1899. E-mail: jackie@sched.fsl.pitt.edu.

University of Puerto Rico, Río Piedras, College of Education, Program in Guidance and Counseling, San Juan, PR 00931. Awards M Ed, Ed D. Part-time programs available. *Degree requirements:* Thesis/dissertation required, foreign language not required. *Entrance requirements:* For master's, PAEG, interview, minimum GPA of 3.0; for doctorate, GRE or PAEG, master's degree, minimum GPA of 3.0. Application deadline: 2/21. Application fee: $17.

University of Puget Sound, School of Education, Program in Education, Tacoma, WA 98416-0005. Offerings include counselor education (M Ed). Accredited by NCATE. Program faculty: 12 full-time (9 women), 3 part-time (all women), 12.83 FTE. *Average time to degree:* master's–2 years full-time. *Entrance requirements:* GRE General Test (score in 50th percentile or higher), minimum GPA of 3.0. Application deadline: 2/1. Application fee: $40. *Expenses:* Tuition $19,640 per year full-time, $2480 per course part-time. Fees $155 per year. • Dr. Carol Merz, Dean, School of Education, 253-756-3377.

University of Saint Francis, Department of Psychology and Counseling, Fort Wayne, IN 46808-3994. Offerings include school guidance and counseling (MS Ed). Department faculty: 2 full-time (1 woman), 5 part-time (3 women). *Average time to degree:* master's–2.5 years full-time, 4.5 years part-time. *Application deadline:* 7/1 (rolling processing; 11/1 for spring admission). *Application fee:* $20. *Expenses:* Tuition $350 per semester hour. Fees $390 per year full-time, $69 per semester (minimum) part-time. • Dr. Jacqueline Carl, Chair, 219-434-3208. E-mail: jcarl@sfc.edu. Application contact: Scott Flanagan, Director of Admissions, 219-434-3264. Fax: 219-434-3183. E-mail: sflanagan@sfc.edu.

University of San Diego, School of Education, Program in Counselor Education, San Diego, CA 92110-2492. Awards MA, M Ed. Part-time and evening/weekend programs available. Faculty: 3 full-time (1 woman), 9 part-time (7 women). Students: 54 full-time (47 women), 35 part-time (29 women); includes 35 minority (6 African Americans, 12 Asian Americans, 16 Hispanics, 1 Native American), 3 international. 91 applicants, 76% accepted. In 1997, 30 degrees awarded (100% found work related to degree). *Degree requirements:* Comprehensive exam required, foreign language and thesis not required. *Entrance requirements:* TOEFL (minimum score 580), TWE, minimum GPA of 2.75. Application deadline: 5/1 (priority date; rolling processing; 11/15 for spring admission). Application fee: $45. *Expenses:* Tuition $585 per unit (minimum). Fees $50 per year full-time, $30 per year part-time. *Financial aid:* Fellowships, assistantships, stipends, Federal Work-Study, institutionally sponsored loans, and career-related internships or fieldwork available. Aid available to part-time students. Financial aid application deadline: 5/1; applicants required to submit FAFSA. *Faculty research:* Counseling applications of microcomputers, human resources. • Dr. Ronn Johnson, Coordinator, 619-260-4600 Ext. 4702. Fax: 619-260-6835. Application contact: Mary Jane Tiernan, Director of Graduate Admissions, 619-260-4524. Fax: 619-260-4158. E-mail: grads@acusd.edu.

University of San Francisco, School of Education, Department of Counseling Psychology, San Francisco, CA 94117-1080. Offerings include counseling (MA), with options in educational counseling, life transitions counseling, marital and family therapy. Department faculty: 10 full-time (3 women), 41 part-time (21 women). *Application fee:* $40. *Tuition:* $658 per unit (minimum). • Dr. Larry Palmatier, Chair, 415-422-6868.

University of Sarasota, College of Behavioral Sciences, Program in Counseling, Sarasota, FL 34235-8246. Offers counseling psychology (Ed D), guidance counseling (MA), marriage and family counseling (MA), mental health counseling (MA). Part-time and evening/weekend programs available. Postbaccalaureate distance learning degree programs offered (minimal on-campus study). Faculty: 3 full-time (0 women), 4 part-time (1 woman). Students: 138 full-time (69 women), 268 part-time (134 women). Terminal master's awarded for partial completion of doctoral program. *Degree requirements:* For master's, thesis optional; for doctorate, dissertation, comprehensive exam required, foreign language not required. *Average time to degree:* master's–2 years full-time, 3 years part-time; doctorate–3 years full-time, 4 years part-time. *Entrance requirements:* For master's, TOEFL (minimum score 500); for doctorate, TOEFL (minimum score 550). Application deadline: rolling. Application fee: $50. *Financial aid:* Available to part-time students. Financial aid applicants required to submit FAFSA. • Dr. J. Maxwell Jackson, Director, 800-331-5995. Fax: 941-379-0464. E-mail: maxwell_jackson@embanet.com. Application contact: Kathy Ketterer, Admissions Representative, 800-331-5995. Fax: 941-371-8910. E-mail: kathy_ketterer@embanet.com.

University of Scranton, Department of Counseling and Human Services, Program in School Counseling, Scranton, PA 18510-4622. Awards MS. Accredited by NCATE. Part-time and evening/weekend programs available. Students: 19 full-time (13 women), 54 part-time (37 women); includes 1 international. Average age 29. 40 applicants, 90% accepted. In 1997, 11 degrees awarded. *Degree requirements:* Comprehensive exam required, foreign language and thesis not required. *Entrance requirements:* TOEFL (minimum score 575), minimum GPA of 2.75. Application deadline: 3/1 (11/1 for spring admission). Application fee: $35. *Expenses:* Tuition $465 per credit. Fees $25 per semester. *Financial aid:* Teaching assistantships, Federal Work-Study, and career-related internships or fieldwork available. Aid available to part-time students. Financial aid application deadline: 3/1. • Dr. Lee Ann M. Eschbach, Director, 717-941-6299. Fax: 717-941-4201. E-mail: eschbach@uofs.edu.

University of South Alabama, College of Education, Department of Behavioral Studies and Educational Technology, Mobile, AL 36688-0002. Offers programs in counseling (M Ed, MS, Ed S), educational media (M Ed, MS), instructional design (MS). Accredited by NCATE. Part-time programs available. Faculty: 14 full-time (5 women). Students: 137 full-time (110 women), 137 part-time (112 women); includes 53 minority (48 African Americans, 2 Asian Americans, 2 Hispanics, 1 Native American), 3 international. 103 applicants, 90% accepted. In 1997, 66 master's awarded. *Degree requirements:* For master's, comprehensive exam required, foreign language and thesis not required. *Entrance requirements:* For master's, GRE General Test (minimum combined score of 1000) or MAT (minimum score 37), minimum GPA of 3.0. Application deadline: 9/1 (priority date; rolling processing). Application fee: $25. *Financial aid:* In 1997–98, 5 research assistantships were awarded; career-related internships or fieldwork also available. Aid available to part-time students. Financial aid application deadline: 4/1. *Faculty research:* Agency counseling, rehabilitation counseling, school psychometry. • Dr. John Lane, Chairman, 334-380-2861.

University of South Carolina, Graduate School, College of Education, Department of Educational Psychology, Program in Counseling Education, Columbia, SC 29208. Awards PhD, Ed S. Accredited by NCATE. Faculty: 11 full-time (3 women), 2 part-time (0 women). Students: 47 full-time (37 women), 74 part-time (57 women); includes 34 minority (32 African Americans, 2 Hispanics), 2 international. Average age 37. In 1997, 5 doctorates, 24 Ed Ss awarded. *Degree requirements:* For doctorate, 1 foreign language (computer language can substitute), dissertation, comprehensive exam; for Ed S, thesis. *Entrance requirements:* For doctorate, GRE General Test, interview. Application deadline: 4/1 (priority date; rolling processing; 10/15 for spring admission). Application fee: $35. Electronic applications accepted. *Expenses:* Tuition $3894 per year full-time, $193 per credit hour part-time for state residents; $8114 per year full-time, $404 per credit hour part-time for nonresidents. Fees $125 per year full-time, $37 per semester (minimum) part-time. *Financial aid:* Research assistantships available. *Faculty research:* Multicultural counseling, children's fears, career development, family counseling. • Dr. Walter Bailey III, Coordinator, 803-777-3047. Application contact: Office of Intercollegiate Teacher Education and Student Affairs, 803-777-6732. Fax: 803-777-3068.

University of South Carolina, Graduate School, College of Education, Department of Educational Psychology, Program in Elementary School Counseling, Columbia, SC 29208. Awards MA, M Ed. Accredited by NCATE. Faculty: 3 full-time (1 woman), 2 part-time (0 women). Students: 29 full-time (26 women), 47 part-time (43 women); includes 21 minority (all African Americans), 1 international. Average age 29. In 1997, 33 degrees awarded. *Degree requirements:* Comprehensive exam required, foreign language not required. *Entrance requirements:* GRE, interview. Application deadline: 4/1 (rolling processing; 10/15 for spring admission). Application fee: $35. Electronic applications accepted. *Expenses:* Tuition $3894 per year full-time, $193 per credit hour part-time for state residents; $8114 per year full-time, $404 per credit hour part-time for nonresidents. Fees $125 per year full-time, $37 per semester (minimum) part-time. *Financial aid:* Research assistantships available. *Faculty research:* Childhood fears, counseling through play advocacy, career development. • Dr. Walter Bailey III, Coordinator, 803-777-3047. Application contact: Office of Intercollegiate Teacher Education and Student Affairs, 803-777-6732. Fax: 803-777-3068.

University of South Carolina, Graduate School, College of Education, Department of Educational Psychology, Program in Secondary School Counseling, Columbia, SC 29208. Awards MA, M Ed. Accredited by NCATE. Faculty: 5 full-time (2 women). Students: 41 full-time (30 women), 65 part-time (47 women); includes 29 minority (27 African Americans, 1 Asian American, 1 Hispanic), 1 international. Average age 34. In 1997, 32 degrees awarded. *Entrance requirements:* GRE, interview. Application deadline: 4/1 (rolling processing; 10/15 for spring admission). Application fee: $35. Electronic applications accepted. *Expenses:* Tuition $3894 per year full-time, $193 per credit hour part-time for state residents; $8114 per year full-time, $404 per credit hour part-time for nonresidents. Fees $125 per year full-time, $37 per semester (minimum) part-time. *Faculty research:* Multicultural counseling, family preservation, career development, ethics. Total annual research expenditures: $500,000. • Dr. Walter Bailey III, Coordinator, 803-777-3047. Application contact: Office of Intercollegiate Teacher Education and Student Affairs, 803-777-6732. Fax: 803-777-3068.

University of South Dakota, School of Education, Division of Counseling and Psychology in Education, Vermillion, SD 57069-2390. Awards MA, Ed D, Ed S. Accredited by NCATE. Part-time programs available. Faculty: 10 full-time (3 women), 3 part-time (1 woman). Students: 101 full-time (63 women), 27 part-time (19 women); includes 6 minority (2 Asian Americans, 1 Hispanic, 3 Native Americans), 3 international. 82 applicants, 68% accepted. In 1997, 39 master's, 8 doctorates awarded. *Degree requirements:* For doctorate, dissertation required, foreign language not required. *Entrance requirements:* For master's and doctorate, GRE General Test. Application deadline: rolling. Application fee: $15. *Expenses:* Tuition $1530 per year full-time, $85 per credit hour part-time for state residents; $4518 per year full-time, $251 per credit hour part-time for nonresidents. Fees $792 per year full-time, $44 per credit hour part-time. *Financial aid:* Teaching assistantships and career-related internships or fieldwork available. • Dr. Frank Main, Chair, 605-677-5250.

University of Southern Maine, College of Education and Human Development, Program in Counselor Education, Portland, ME 04104-9300. Awards MS, CAS. Part-time and evening/weekend programs available. Faculty: 7 full-time (2 women), 6 part-time (2 women). Students: 74 full-time (52 women), 43 part-time (28 women); includes 2 minority (1 Asian American, 1 Native American). 105 applicants, 41% accepted. In 1997, 24 master's awarded. *Degree requirements:* For master's, thesis or alternative, comprehensive exam required, foreign language not required; for CAS, thesis or alternative required, foreign language not required. *Entrance requirements:* For master's, GRE General Test (minimum combined score of 900), MAT (minimum score 40), TOEFL, interview. Application deadline: 2/1. Application fee: $25. *Expenses:* Tuition $178 per credit hour for state residents; $267 per credit hour (minimum) for nonresidents. Fees $282 per year full-time, $83 per semester (minimum) part-time. *Financial aid:* Research assistantships, scholarships, Federal Work-Study, institutionally sponsored loans, and career-related internships or fieldwork available. Aid available to part-time students. Financial aid application deadline: 3/1; applicants required to submit FAFSA. *Faculty research:* Counselor licensure. • Dr. C. E. VanZandt, Chair, Human Resource Development Department, 207-780-5316. Application contact: Teresa Belsan, Admissions and Academic Counselor, 207-780-5306. Fax: 207-780-5315. E-mail: belsan@usm.maine.edu.

University of South Florida, College of Education, Department of Psychological and Social Foundations of Education, Department of Counselor Education, Tampa, FL 33620-9951. Awards MA. Accredited by NCATE. Part-time and evening/weekend programs available. Students: 41 full-time (36 women), 173 part-time (141 women); includes 36 minority (16 African Americans, 3 Asian Americans, 17 Hispanics), 7 international. Average age 35. 74 applicants, 65% accepted. In 1997, 92 degrees awarded. *Entrance requirements:* GRE General Test (minimum combined score of 1000), minimum GPA of 3.5 in last 60 hours. Application deadline: 1/15 (9/1 for spring admission). Application fee: $20. Electronic applications accepted. *Tuition:* $142 per

Directory: Counselor Education

University of South Florida (continued)

credit hour for state residents; $486 per credit hour for nonresidents. *Financial aid:* Federal Work-Study, institutionally sponsored loans available. Aid available to part-time students. Financial aid applicants required to submit FAFSA. *Faculty research:* Encouragement of students, human sexuality, multicultural issues, Tourette's syndrome. • Application contact: Sue Street, Coordinator, 813-974-1262. Fax: 813-974-5814. E-mail: street@tempest.coedu.usf.edu.

University of Southwestern Louisiana, College of Education, Graduate Studies and Research in Education, Program in Guidance and Counseling, Lafayette, LA 70503. Awards M Ed. Accredited by NCATE. Faculty: 6 full-time (1 woman). Students: 2 full-time (both women), 23 part-time (21 women); includes 3 minority (2 African Americans, 1 Native American). 11 applicants, 82% accepted. In 1997, 6 degrees awarded. *Degree requirements:* Thesis or alternative required, foreign language not required. *Entrance requirements:* GRE General Test, teaching certificate. Application deadline: 8/15. Application fee: $5 ($15 for international students). *Tuition:* $2012 per year full-time, $300 per semester (minimum) part-time for state residents; $7244 per year full-time, $300 per semester (minimum) part-time for nonresidents. *Financial aid:* Fellowships, research assistantships, Federal Work-Study available. Financial aid application deadline: 5/1. • Dr. Daniel Jordan, Director, Graduate Studies and Research in Education, 318-482-6747.

University of Tennessee at Chattanooga, School of Education, Education Graduate Studies Division, Chattanooga, TN 37403-2598. Offerings include guidance and counseling (M Ed). Accredited by NCATE. Division faculty: 15 full-time (5 women), 7 part-time (3 women). *Degree requirements:* Comprehensive exams required, thesis optional, foreign language not required. *Entrance requirements:* GRE General Test or MAT, teaching certificate. Application deadline: rolling. Application fee: $25. *Tuition:* $2864 per year full-time, $160 per credit hour part-time for state residents; $6806 per year full-time, $379 per credit hour part-time for nonresidents. • Dr. Tom Bibler, Acting Head, 423-755-4211. Fax: 423-755-5380. E-mail: tom-bibler@utc.edu. Application contact: Dr. Deborah Arfken, Assistant Provost for Graduate Studies, 423-755-4667. Fax: 423-755-4478.

The University of Tennessee at Martin, School of Education, Program in Counseling, Martin, TN 38238-1000. Awards MS Ed. Accredited by NCATE. Students: 28 full-time (21 women), 49 part-time (40 women); includes 13 minority (all African Americans). 32 applicants, 88% accepted. In 1997, 6 degrees awarded. *Degree requirements:* Comprehensive exam required, foreign language and thesis not required. *Entrance requirements:* GRE General Test (minimum combined score of 650), MAT (minimum score 32), or NTE (minimum combined score of 1930), minimum GPA of 2.5. Application deadline: rolling. Application fee: $25 ($50 for international students). *Tuition:* $2962 per year full-time, $165 per semester hour part-time for state residents; $7788 per year full-time, $434 per semester hour part-time for nonresidents. *Financial aid:* Fellowships, research assistantships, teaching assistantships, graduate assistantships, partial tuition waivers available. Aid available to part-time students. Financial aid application deadline: 3/1. • Dr. Robbie Kendall-Melton, Coordinator, 901-587-7129. E-mail: rkendall@utm.edu.

University of Tennessee, Knoxville, College of Education, Program in Counseling, Knoxville, TN 37996. Offers community counseling (MS), rehabilitation counseling (MS), school counseling (MS). Accredited by NCATE. Part-time and evening/weekend programs available. Students: 41 full-time (31 women), 13 part-time (10 women); includes 2 minority (both African Americans), 1 international. 54 applicants, 50% accepted. In 1997, 22 degrees awarded. *Degree requirements:* Thesis optional, foreign language not required. *Entrance requirements:* GRE General Test, TOEFL (minimum score 550), minimum GPA of 2.7. Application deadline: 2/1 (priority date; rolling processing). Application fee: $35. Electronic applications accepted. *Tuition:* $3354 per year full-time, $181 per semester hour part-time for state residents; $8410 per year full-time, $462 per semester hour part-time for nonresidents. *Financial aid:* Application deadline 2/1. • Dr. Tom George, Associate Dean, 423-974-0907. Fax: 423-974-8718. E-mail: tgeorge1@utk.edu.

University of Tennessee, Knoxville, College of Education, Program in Education II, Knoxville, TN 37996. Offerings include school counseling (Ed S). *Degree requirements:* Thesis optional, foreign language not required. *Entrance requirements:* TOEFL (minimum score 550), GRE General Test, minimum GPA of 2.7. Application deadline: 2/1 (priority date; rolling processing). Application fee: $35. Electronic applications accepted. *Tuition:* $3354 per year full-time, $181 per semester hour part-time for state residents; $8410 per year full-time, $462 per semester hour part-time for nonresidents. • Dr. Tom George, Associate Dean, 423-974-0907. Fax: 423-974-8718. E-mail: tgeorge1@utk.edu.

The University of Texas at Brownsville, Graduate Studies, School of Education, Brownsville, TX 78520-4991. Offerings include counseling and guidance (M Ed). School faculty: 18 full-time (10 women). *Degree requirements:* Thesis optional, foreign language not required. *Entrance requirements:* GRE General Test, TOEFL (minimum score 550). Application deadline: 8/1 (priority date; rolling processing; 1/1 for spring admission). Application fee: $15. *Expenses:* Tuition $648 per year full-time, $120 per semester hour part-time for state residents; $4698 per year full-time, $783 per semester hour part-time for nonresidents. Fees $593 per year full-time, $109 per year part-time. • Dr. Sylvia C. Peña, Dean, 956-983-7219. Fax: 956-982-0293. E-mail: scpena@utb1.utb.edu.

The University of Texas of the Permian Basin, Graduate School, School of Education, Program in Counseling, Odessa, TX 79762-0001. Awards MA. *Degree requirements:* Thesis required, foreign language not required. *Entrance requirements:* GRE General Test (minimum combined score of 1200). *Expenses:* Tuition $1314 per year full-time, $73 per hour part-time for state residents; $4896 per year full-time, $272 per hour part-time for nonresidents. Fees $383 per year full-time, $111 per semester (minimum) part-time.

The University of Texas–Pan American, College of Education, Department of Educational Psychology, Edinburg, TX 78539-2999. Offerings include counseling and guidance (M Ed). *Application deadline:* 7/17 (11/16 for spring admission). *Application fee:* $0. *Tuition:* $2156 per year full-time, $283 per semester (minimum) part-time for state residents; $6788 per year full-time, $862 per semester (minimum) part-time for nonresidents.

University of the District of Columbia, College of Arts and Sciences, School of Science and Mathematics, Department of Psychology and Counseling, 4200 Connecticut Avenue, NW, Washington, DC 20008-1175. Offers program in counseling (MA). *Degree requirements:* Comprehensive exam, seminar paper required, thesis optional, foreign language not required. *Entrance requirements:* GRE General Test, writing proficiency exam. Application deadline: 6/14 (priority date; rolling processing; 11/15 for spring admission). Application fee: $20. *Expenses:* Tuition $3564 per year full-time, $198 per credit part-time for district residents; $5922 per year full-time, $329 per credit part-time for nonresidents. Fees $990 per year full-time, $55 per credit part-time.

University of the Pacific, School of Education, Department of Educational and Counseling Psychology, Stockton, CA 95211-0197. Offerings include counseling (MA). Accredited by NCATE. *Degree requirements:* Thesis required (for some programs), foreign language not required. *Entrance requirements:* GRE General Test, GRE Subject Test. Application deadline: 3/1 (priority date; rolling processing; 10/15 for spring admission). Application fee: $50. *Expenses:* Tuition $19,000 per year full-time, $594 per unit part-time. Fees $30 per year (minimum). • Dr. Mari Irvin, Chairperson, 209-946-2559. E-mail: mirvin@uop.edu.

University of Toledo, College of Education and Allied Professions, Department of Counselor and Human Services Education, Toledo, OH 43606-3398. Offers programs in counselor education (M Ed); guidance and counseling (Ed D, PhD, Ed S), including counselor education (Ed D, PhD), school psychology (Ed D, PhD, Ed S); school psychology (M Ed). Accredited by NCATE. Ed D admissions temporarily suspended. Faculty: 6 full-time (3 women). Students: 26 full-time (20 women), 128 part-time (101 women); includes 14 minority (11 African Americans, 2 Asian Americans, 1 Hispanic), 10 international. Average age 37. 79 applicants, 61% accepted. In 1997, 27 master's, 3 doctorates awarded. *Degree requirements:* For master's, seminar paper required, foreign language and thesis not required; for doctorate, dissertation, comprehensive exams required, foreign language not required; for Ed S, thesis optional, foreign language not required. *Entrance requirements:* For master's, GRE General Test (minimum combined score of 800), interview, minimum GPA of 3.0; for doctorate, GRE General Test (minimum combined score of 1040), interview; minimum GPA of 3.0 (undergraduate), 3.5 (graduate); for Ed S, GRE, minimum GPA of 3.0 (undergraduate), 3.5 (graduate). Application deadline: 6/15 (priority date; rolling processing). Application fee: $30. Electronic applications accepted. *Tuition:* $5907 per year full-time, $246 per hour part-time for state residents; $11,835 per year full-time, $493 per hour part-time for nonresidents. *Financial aid:* In 1997–98, 7 teaching assistantships were awarded; full tuition waivers, Federal Work-Study, institutionally sponsored loans, and career-related internships or fieldwork also available. Aid available to part-time students. Financial aid application deadline: 4/1. *Faculty research:* Training and supervision, ethics and standards, therapist development, multicultural issues, substance abuse screening. • Dr. Robert Wendt, Chair, 419-530-2013. Fax: 419-530-7719. E-mail: fac0122@uoft01.utoledo.edu. Application contact: Dr. Melanie Warnke, 419-530-4311. Fax: 419-530-2718. E-mail: mwarnke@utnet.utoledo.edu.

University of Vermont, College of Education and Social Services, Department of Integrated Professional Studies, Program in Counseling, Burlington, VT 05405-0160. Awards MS. Accredited by NCATE. Students: 55; includes 3 minority (1 African American, 1 Asian American, 1 Hispanic), 1 international. 37 applicants, 65% accepted. In 1997, 17 degrees awarded. *Degree requirements:* Thesis or alternative required, foreign language not required. *Entrance requirements:* GRE General Test, TOEFL (minimum score 550). Application deadline: 3/1. Application fee: $25. *Expenses:* Tuition $302 per credit for state residents; $755 per credit for nonresidents. Fees $434 per year full-time, $46 per semester (minimum) part-time. *Financial aid:* Fellowships, research assistantships, teaching assistantships available. Financial aid application deadline: 3/1. • Dr. J. Peterson, Coordinator, 802-656-3888.

University of Victoria, Faculty of Education, Department of Psychological Foundations, Victoria, BC V8W 2Y2, Canada. Offerings include counseling (MA, M Ed). Postbaccalaureate distance learning degree programs offered. Department faculty: 15 full-time (5 women). *Degree requirements:* Thesis (for some programs), comprehensive exam (M Ed) required, foreign language not required. *Average time to degree:* master's–2.3 years full-time; doctorate–4.0 years full-time. *Entrance requirements:* 2 years of work experience in relevant field, minimum B average. Application deadline: 4/30 (rolling processing). Application fee: $50. *Tuition:* $2080 per year full-time, $557 per semester part-time. • Dr. Walter Muir, Chair, 250-721-7799. Fax: 250-721-6190. Application contact: Sarah Baylow, Graduate Secretary, 250-721-7882. Fax: 250-721-7767. E-mail: sbaylow@uvic.ca.

University of Virginia, Curry School of Education, Department of Human Services, Program in Counselor Education, Charlottesville, VA 22903. Awards M Ed, Ed D, Ed S. Accredited by NCATE. Faculty: 36 full-time (12 women), 2 part-time (1 woman), 37 FTE. Students: 66 full-time (58 women), 17 part-time (11 women); includes 19 minority (9 African Americans, 7 Asian Americans, 3 Hispanics). Average age 27. 97 applicants, 39% accepted. In 1997, 40 master's, 1 doctorate, 1 Ed S awarded. *Degree requirements:* For doctorate, dissertation required, foreign language not required. *Entrance requirements:* GRE General Test. Application deadline: 3/1 (11/15 for spring admission). Application fee: $40. *Tuition:* $4876 per year full-time, $944 per semester (minimum) part-time for state residents; $15,824 per year full-time, $2748 per semester (minimum) part-time for nonresidents. • Application contact: Linda Berry, Student Enrollment Coordinator, 804-924-0738. E-mail: lrb8e@virginia.edu.

University of Washington, College of Education, Program in School Counseling and School Psychology, Seattle, WA 98195. Offers human development and cognition (M Ed, PhD), measurement and research (M Ed, PhD), school counseling (M Ed, PhD), school psychology (M Ed, PhD). One or more programs accredited by APA. *Degree requirements:* For master's, thesis optional, foreign language not required; for doctorate, dissertation. *Entrance requirements:* GRE General Test, TOEFL, minimum GPA of 3.0. Application fee: $45. *Tuition:* $5433 per year full-time, $775 per quarter (minimum) part-time for state residents; $13,479 per year full-time, $1925 per quarter (minimum) part-time for nonresidents. • Dr. Allen Glenn, Dean, College of Education, 206-543-5390. Fax: 206-685-1713. E-mail: aglenn@u.washington.edu. Application contact: Richard Neel, Associate Dean, 206-543-7833. Fax: 206-543-8439. E-mail: edinfo@u.washington.edu.

The University of West Alabama, College of Education, Department of Instructional Support, Program in Guidance and Counseling, Livingston, AL 35470. Offers continuing education (MSCE), guidance and counseling (M Ed). Accredited by NCATE. Part-time and evening/weekend programs available. *Average time to degree:* master's–1 year full-time, 2 years part-time. *Entrance requirements:* GRE General Test, MAT, minimum GPA of 2.75. Application deadline: 9/10 (priority date; rolling processing; 3/21 for spring admission). Application fee: $15. *Tuition:* $70 per quarter hour.

The University of Western Ontario, Social Sciences Division, Faculty of Education, Program in Counseling, London, ON N6A 5B8, Canada. Awards M Ed. Part-time programs available. Faculty: 3 full-time (1 woman). Students: 19 full-time (all women), 6 part-time (5 women). Average age 26. 79 applicants, 15% accepted. In 1997, 12 degrees awarded. *Average time to degree:* master's–2 years full-time, 3 years part-time. *Entrance requirements:* Minimum B average. Application deadline: 2/1. Application fee: $50. *Financial aid:* In 1997–98, 17 students received aid, including 14 teaching assistantships (5 to first-year students) averaging $650 per month; research assistantships and career-related internships or fieldwork also available. Financial aid application deadline: 4/1. *Faculty research:* Women's issues in counseling, causes for sexual harrasment in the workplace, counselor memory and confidence in clinical judgements. • Dr. S. Haggerty, Graduate Chair, 519-661-2099. E-mail: haggerty@edu.uwo.ca. Application contact: L. Kulak, Graduate Supervisor, 519-661-2099. Fax: 519-661-3833. E-mail: kulak@edu.uwo.ca.

University of Wisconsin–Madison, School of Education, Department of Counseling Psychology, Program in Counseling, Madison, WI 53706-1380. Awards MS. *Application fee:* $38. *Tuition:* $4928 per year full-time, $926 per semester (minimum) part-time for state residents; $15,190 per year full-time, $2849 per semester (minimum) part-time for nonresidents.

University of Wisconsin–Oshkosh, College of Education and Human Services, Department of Counselor Education, Oshkosh, WI 54901-8602. Offers program in counseling (MSE). Offered jointly with University of Wisconsin–Stevens Point. Part-time and evening/weekend programs available. Faculty: 7 full-time (3 women), 4 part-time (2 women). Students: 31 full-time (24 women), 112 part-time (88 women); includes 10 minority (3 African Americans, 3 Asian Americans, 3 Hispanics, 1 Native American), 3 international. 65 applicants, 58% accepted. In 1997, 50 degrees awarded (100% found work related to degree). *Degree requirements:* Thesis optional, foreign language not required. *Entrance requirements:* Interview, GRE General Test or minimum GPA of 3.0. Application deadline: 9/1 (priority date; 2/1 for spring admission). Application fee: $45. *Tuition:* $3638 per year full-time, $609 per semester (minimum) part-time for state residents; $11,282 per year full-time, $1884 per semester (minimum) part-time for nonresidents. *Financial aid:* Federal Work-Study, institutionally sponsored loans, and career-related internships or fieldwork available. Financial aid application deadline: 3/15. *Faculty research:* Gender issues, grief and loss, addictions, career development, close relationships. • Dr. Margaret Olson, Chair, 920-424-1475. E-mail: olsonmj@uwosh.edu.

University of Wisconsin–Platteville, College of Liberal Arts and Education, Department of Counselor Education, Platteville, WI 53818-3099. Awards MSE. Accredited by NCATE. Part-time programs available. Faculty: 4 full-time (1 woman), 7 part-time (2 women). Students: 36 full-time (32 women), 46 part-time (34 women); includes 1 minority (African American). 38 applicants, 63% accepted. In 1997, 31 degrees awarded. *Degree requirements:* Thesis or alternative, comprehensive exam required, foreign language not required. *Entrance requirements:* TOEFL (minimum score 500). Application deadline: 7/1 (priority date; rolling processing; 11/1 for spring admission). Application fee: $45. *Financial aid:* In 1997–98, 17 assistantships (7 to first-year students) were awarded; Federal Work-Study, institutionally sponsored loans, and career-related internships or fieldwork also available. Aid available to part-time students. • Dr. Nick Johansen, Chair, Graduate Administrative Committee, 608-342-1206. E-mail: johansen@uwplatt.edu.

University of Wisconsin–River Falls, College of Education and Graduate Studies, Department of Counseling and School Psychology, River Falls, WI 54022-5001. Offers programs in counseling (MSE), school psychology (MSE). Accredited by NCATE. Students: 111 (86 women). *Application deadline:* 2/1. *Application fee:* $45. *Financial aid:* Research assistantships, Federal Work-Study available. Financial aid application deadline: 3/1. • John LeCapitaine, Chair, 715-425-3889. E-mail: john.e.lecapitaine@uwrf.edu.

University of Wisconsin–Stevens Point, College of Professional Studies, School of Education, Program in Guidance and Counseling, Stevens Point, WI 54481-3897. Awards MSE. Offered jointly with the University of Wisconsin–Oshkosh. *Application deadline:* rolling. *Application fee:* $38. *Tuition:* $3702 per year full-time, $664 per semester (minimum) part-time for state residents; $11,346 per year full-time, $1938 per semester (minimum) part-time for nonresidents. *Financial aid:* Application deadline 5/1. • Dr. Leslie McClaine-Ruelle, Head, School of Education, 715-346-2040.

University of Wisconsin–Stout, College of Human Development, Program in Guidance and Counseling, Menomonie, WI 54751. Awards MS, Ed S. Part-time programs available. Students: 60 full-time (46 women), 62 part-time (44 women); includes 10 minority (2 African Americans, 5 Asian Americans, 3 Native Americans), 2 international. 40 applicants, 45% accepted. In 1997, 48 master's, 3 Ed Ss awarded. *Degree requirements:* Thesis required, foreign language not required. *Application deadline:* 2/1 (rolling processing; 10/1 for spring admission). *Application fee:* $45. *Tuition:* $3284 per year full-time, $183 per credit hour part-time for state residents; $7644 per year full-time, $425 per credit hour part-time for nonresidents. *Financial aid:* In 1997–98, 8 research assistantships, 1 teaching assistantship were awarded; full and partial tuition waivers, Federal Work-Study also available. Aid available to part-time students. Financial aid application deadline: 4/1; applicants required to submit FAFSA. • Dr. Ed Biggerstaff, Director of Education Specialist Program, 715-232-2687. Application contact: Graduate College, 715-232-2211.

University of Wisconsin–Superior, Department of Counselor Education, Superior, WI 54880-2873. Awards MSE. Part-time and evening/weekend programs available. Students: 85 (64 women). 18 applicants, 100% accepted. In 1997, 25 degrees awarded (100% found work related to degree). *Degree requirements:* Comprehensive exam, position paper required, foreign language and thesis not required. *Entrance requirements:* California Psychological Inventory, MAT, minimum GPA of 2.75. Application deadline: 4/1 (priority date; rolling processing). Application fee: $45. *Tuition:* $3628 per year full-time, $222 per credit hour part-time for state residents; $11,272 per year full-time, $647 per credit hour part-time for nonresidents. *Financial aid:* In 1997–98, 2 research assistantships (1 to a first-year student) averaging $850 per month and totaling $15,428 were awarded; partial tuition waivers, Federal Work-Study, and career-related internships or fieldwork also available. Aid available to part-time students. Financial aid application deadline: 5/1. *Faculty research:* Women and power, intrafamily dynamics. • Dr. James A. Holter, Chairperson, 715-394-8151.

University of Wisconsin–Whitewater, College of Education, Department of Counselor Education, Whitewater, WI 53190-1790. Awards MS. Accredited by NCATE. *Application deadline:* rolling. *Application fee:* $38.

Valdosta State University, College of Education, Department of Psychology, Counseling, and Guidance, Program in Guidance and Counseling, Valdosta, GA 31698. Awards M Ed, Ed S. Accredited by NCATE. Faculty: 9 full-time (0 women). Students: 33 full-time (29 women), 35 part-time (27 women); includes 3 minority (2 African Americans, 1 Hispanic), 1 international. 85 applicants, 49% accepted. In 1997, 27 master's awarded. *Degree requirements:* For master's, thesis or alternative. *Entrance requirements:* For master's, GRE General Test (minimum combined score of 1000); for Ed S, GRE General Test (minimum combined score of 900). Application deadline: 8/1 (rolling processing; 11/15 for spring admission). Application fee: $10. *Expenses:* Tuition $2472 per year full-time, $83 per semester hour part-time for state residents; $8472 per year full-time, $333 per semester hour part-time for nonresidents. Fees $236 per year full-time. • Dr. R. Bauer, Head, Department of Psychology, Counseling, and Guidance, 912-333-5930. E-mail: bbauer@grits.valdosta.peachnet.edu.

Vanderbilt University, Peabody College, Department of Human Resources, Nashville, TN 37240-1001. Offerings include human development counseling (M Ed). *Application deadline:* 3/1 (priority date; rolling processing). *Application fee:* $35. • Robert B. Innes, Acting Chair, 615-322-6881.

Villanova University, Graduate School of Liberal Arts and Sciences, Department of Education and Human Services, Program in Community Counseling, Villanova, PA 19085-1699. Offers counseling and human relations (MS). Students: 16 full-time (14 women), 32 part-time (26 women); includes 3 minority (2 African Americans, 1 Hispanic), 1 international. Average age 35. 36 applicants, 53% accepted. *Degree requirements:* Comprehensive exam required, foreign language and thesis not required. *Entrance requirements:* GRE or MAT, minimum GPA of 3.0. Application deadline: 8/1 (priority date; 12/1 for spring admission). Application fee: $40. *Expenses:* Tuition $400 per credit. Fees $60 per year. *Financial aid:* Application deadline 4/1. • Dr. Kenneth M. Davis, Coordinator, 610-519-4634.

Villanova University, Graduate School of Liberal Arts and Sciences, Department of Education and Human Services, Program in Elementary Guidance and Counseling, Villanova, PA 19085-1699. Offers counseling and human relations (MS). Part-time and evening/weekend programs available. Students: 5 full-time (all women), 16 part-time (15 women); includes 1 minority (African American). Average age 30. 8 applicants, 63% accepted. *Degree requirements:* Comprehensive exam required, foreign language and thesis not required. *Entrance requirements:* GRE or MAT, minimum GPA of 3.0. Application deadline: 8/1 (priority date; 12/1 for spring admission). Application fee: $40. *Expenses:* Tuition $400 per credit. Fees $60 per year. *Financial aid:* Federal Work-Study and career-related internships or fieldwork available. Financial aid application deadline: 4/1. • Coordinator, 610-519-4620.

Villanova University, Graduate School of Liberal Arts and Sciences, Department of Education and Human Services, Program in Secondary Guidance and Counseling, Villanova, PA 19085-1699. Offers counseling and human relations (MS). Students: 8 full-time (all women), 14 part-time (11 women); includes 3 minority (2 African Americans, 1 Hispanic), 1 international. Average age 33. 17 applicants, 35% accepted. *Degree requirements:* Comprehensive exam required, foreign language and thesis not required. *Entrance requirements:* GRE or MAT, minimum GPA of 3.0. Application deadline: 8/1 (priority date; 12/1 for spring admission). Application fee: $40. *Expenses:* Tuition $400 per credit. Fees $60 per year. *Financial aid:* Application deadline 4/1. • Dr. Kenneth M. Davis, Coordinator, 610-519-4634.

Virginia Commonwealth University, School of Education, Program in Counselor Education, Richmond, VA 23284-9005. Awards M Ed. Accredited by NCATE. Faculty: 4 full-time. Students: 39 full-time (32 women), 57 part-time (47 women); includes 25 minority (22 African Americans, 1 Asian American, 1 Hispanic, 1 Native American). Average age 30. 54 applicants, 74% accepted. In 1997, 45 degrees awarded. *Entrance requirements:* GRE General Test or MAT. Application deadline: 7/1 (11/15 for spring admission). Application fee: $30 ($0 for international students). *Tuition:* $4960 per year full-time, $257 per credit part-time for state residents; $12,652 per year full-time, $684 per credit part-time for nonresidents. *Financial aid:* Full and partial tuition waivers and career-related internships or fieldwork available. Aid available to part-time students. Financial aid application deadline: 3/1. • Dr. John Seyfarth, Division Head, 804-828-1332. Application contact: Dr. Michael D. Davis, Interim Director, Graduate Studies, 804-828-6530. Fax: 804-828-1323. E-mail: mddavis@vcu.edu.

Virginia State University, School of Liberal Arts and Education, Department of Educational Leadership and Community Services, Program in Guidance, 1 Hayden Drive, Petersburg, VA 23806-2096. Awards M Ed, MS. Accredited by NCATE. Faculty: 2 full-time (0 women). In 1997, 33 degrees awarded. *Application deadline:* 8/15 (rolling processing). *Application fee:* $25. *Tuition:* $3739 per year full-time, $133 per credit hour part-time for state residents; $9056 per year full-time, $364 per credit hour part-time for nonresidents. *Financial aid:* 5 students received aid. Financial aid application deadline: 5/1. • Dr. J. Cary Houseman, Coordinator, 804-524-5258. Application contact: Dr. Wayne F. Virag, Dean, Graduate Studies and Continuing Education, 804-524-5985. Fax: 804-524-5104. E-mail: wvirag@vsu.edu.

Wake Forest University, Department of Education, Winston-Salem, NC 27109. Offerings include guidance and counseling (MA Ed). Accredited by NCATE. Department faculty: 10 full-time (5 women), 3 part-time (2 women). *Degree requirements:* Thesis optional, foreign language not required. *Entrance requirements:* GRE General Test. Application deadline: 2/15. Application fee: $25. *Tuition:* $17,150 per year full-time, $550 per hour part-time. • Dr. Joseph O. Milner, Chairman, 336-759-5341. Application contact: Loraine Stewart, Certification Officer, 336-759-5990. Fax: 336-759-4591.

Walla Walla College, Department of Education and Psychology, Specialization in School Counseling, College Place, WA 99324-1198. Awards MA, M Ed. *Degree requirements:* Thesis required (for some programs), foreign language not required. *Entrance requirements:* GRE General Test, minimum GPA of 2.75, 3 years of certified teaching experience, Washington teaching certificate or equivalent. Application deadline: 4/1 (priority date; rolling processing). Application fee: $40. *Tuition:* $346 per quarter hour. *Financial aid:* Application deadline 4/1; applicants required to submit FAFSA. *Faculty research:* Admissions/retention, moral development, instructional psychology. • Application contact: Dr. Joe Galusha, Dean of Graduate Studies, 509-527-2421. Fax: 509-527-2253. E-mail: galujo@wwc.edu.

Walsh University, Graduate Studies, Program in Counseling and Human Development, North Canton, OH 44720-3396. Awards MA. Part-time and evening/weekend programs available. Faculty: 4 full-time (2 women), 4 part-time (2 women), 6 FTE. Students: 73 part-time. *Degree requirements:* Comprehensive exam, internship, practicum required, foreign language and thesis not required. *Average time to degree:* master's–4.5 years part-time. *Entrance requirements:* MAT (minimum score 40), interview, minimum GPA of 2.6, writing sample. Application deadline: 7/15 (priority date; rolling processing). Application fee: $25. *Expenses:* Tuition $363 per credit hour. Fees $10 per credit hour. *Financial aid:* Career-related internships or fieldwork available. *Faculty research:* Multicultural issues in counseling, gender issues in counseling, family issues. • Dr. Sandra I. Lopez-Baez, Director, 330-490-7231. E-mail: lopezbaez@alex.walsh.edu. Application contact: Brett Freshour, Dean of Enrollment Management, 330-490-7171. Fax: 330-490-7165.

Wayne State College, Division of Education, Program in Guidance and Counseling, Wayne, NE 68787. Offers counselor education (MSE). Accredited by NCATE. Students: 13 full-time (12 women), 172 part-time (130 women); includes 3 minority (1 Hispanic, 2 Native Americans). Average age 35. In 1997, 24 degrees awarded. *Degree requirements:* Comprehensive exam, research paper required, thesis optional, foreign language not required. *Entrance requirements:* GRE General Test, minimum GPA of 3.0. Application deadline: rolling. Application fee: $10. *Expenses:* Tuition $1788 per year full-time, $75 per credit hour part-time for state residents; $3576 per year full-time, $149 per credit hour part-time for nonresidents. Fees $360 per year full-time, $15 per credit hour part-time. *Financial aid:* Teaching assistantships and career-related internships or fieldwork available. Financial aid application deadline: 5/1; applicants required to submit FAFSA. *Faculty research:* Stress management, physiology of learning, alcohol and sexual behavior, at-risk and control, marriage and family. • Dr. Steven C. Dinsmore, Coordinator, 402-375-7386.

Wayne State University, College of Education, Division of Theoretical and Behavioral Foundations, Detroit, MI 48202. Offerings include counseling (MA, M Ed, Ed D, PhD, Ed S). Accredited by NCATE. PhD (history, philosophy, and sociology of education) admissions temporarily suspended. Division faculty: 90. *Degree requirements:* For doctorate, dissertation required, foreign language not required. *Entrance requirements:* For master's, GRE (school psychology); for doctorate, GRE (educational psychology), interview, minimum GPA of 3.0. Application deadline: 7/1. Application fee: $20 ($30 for international students). *Expenses:* Tuition $163 per credit hour for state residents; $355 per credit hour for nonresidents. Fees $498 per year full-time, $114 per semester (minimum) part-time. • Dr. JoAnne Holbert, Associate Dean, 313-577-0210.

West Chester University of Pennsylvania, School of Education, Department of Counselor, Secondary and Professional Education, West Chester, PA 19383. Offers programs in educational research (MS), school counseling (M Ed, MS), secondary education (M Ed). Accredited by NCATE. Faculty: 8 part-time. Students: 55 full-time (39 women), 154 part-time (127 women); includes 16 minority (11 African Americans, 5 Asian Americans), 2 international. Average age 33. 98 applicants, 71% accepted. In 1997, 69 degrees awarded. *Degree requirements:* Comprehensive exam required, foreign language and thesis not required. *Entrance requirements:* GRE or MAT. Application deadline: 4/15 (priority date; rolling processing; 10/15 for spring admission). Application fee: $25. *Expenses:* Tuition $3468 per year full-time, $193 per credit part-time for state residents; $6236 per year full-time, $346 per credit part-time for nonresidents. Fees $660 per year full-time, $38 per credit part-time. *Financial aid:* Research assistantships available. Aid available to part-time students. Financial aid application deadline: 2/15. • Dr. John Hynes, Chair, 610-436-2411. Application contact: Dr. Kimberlee Brown, Graduate Coordinator, School Counseling, 610-436-2950.

Western Carolina University, College of Education and Allied Professions, Department of Human Services, Program in Counseling, Cullowhee, NC 28723. Offers community counseling (MS), counseling (MA Ed), school counseling (MA Ed). Accredited by NCATE. Part-time and evening/weekend programs available. Students: 27 full-time (23 women), 40 part-time (31 women); includes 4 minority (2 African Americans, 2 Native Americans), 1 international. 70 applicants, 39% accepted. In 1997, 21 degrees awarded. *Degree requirements:* Comprehensive exam required, foreign language and thesis not required. *Entrance requirements:* GRE General Test. Application deadline: 1/1. Application fee: $35. *Tuition:* $1799 per year full-time, $144 per credit hour (minimum) part-time for state residents; $9069 per year full-time, $1053 per credit hour (minimum) part-time for nonresidents. *Financial aid:* In 1997–98, 15 students received aid, including 1 fellowship (to a first-year student) totaling $5,000, 8 research assistantships (1 to a first year student) totaling $31,462, 6 teaching assistantships (4 to first-year students) totaling $27,778; Federal Work-Study, institutionally sponsored loans also available. Financial aid application deadline: 3/15. • Application contact: Kathleen Owen, Assistant to the Dean, 828-227-7398. Fax: 828-227-6280.

Western Connecticut State University, School of Professional Studies, Department of Education and Educational Psychology, Program in Guidance and Counseling, Danbury, CT 06810-6885. Offers school counselor (MS). Part-time and evening/weekend programs available. Students: 4 full-time (3 women), 74 part-time (63 women); includes 6 minority (3 African Americans, 3 Hispanics). In 1997, 7 degrees awarded. *Degree requirements:* Thesis or research project required, foreign language not required. *Entrance requirements:* Minimum GPA of 2.67. Application deadline: 8/1 (priority date; rolling processing). Application fee: $40. *Expenses:* Tuition $4127 per year (minimum) full-time, $178 per credit hour part-time for state residents; $9581 per year (minimum) full-time, $178 per credit hour part-time for nonresidents. Fees $25 per year part-time. *Financial aid:* Fellowships, Federal Work-Study, and career-related internships or fieldwork available. Aid available to part-time students. Financial aid application deadline: 5/1. • Dr. Thomas Cordy, Chair, Department of Education and Educational Psychology, 203-837-8520.

Directory: Counselor Education

Western Illinois University, College of Education and Human Services, Department of Counselor Education and College Student Personnel, Program in Counselor Education, Macomb, IL 61455-1390. Offers counseling (MS Ed). Accredited by NCATE. Part-time programs available. Faculty: 16 full-time (4 women). Students: 24 full-time (22 women), 84 part-time (71 women); includes 10 minority (9 African Americans, 1 Hispanic). Average age 35. 28 applicants, 18% accepted. In 1997, 29 degrees awarded. *Degree requirements:* Thesis or alternative required, foreign language not required. *Entrance requirements:* Interview. Application deadline: rolling. Application fee: $0 ($25 for international students). *Expenses:* Tuition $2304 per year full-time, $96 per semester hour part-time for state residents; $6912 per year full-time, $288 per semester hour part-time for nonresidents. Fees $944 per year full-time, $33 per semester hour part-time. *Financial aid:* In 1997–98, 12 students received aid, including 12 research assistantships averaging $610 per month; full tuition waivers also available. Financial aid applicants required to submit FAFSA. • Dr. Jerry Oliver, Graduate Committee Chairperson, 309-298-1529. Application contact: Barbara Baily, Director of Graduate Studies, 309-298-1806. Fax: 309-298-2245. E-mail: barb_baily@ccmail.wiu.edu.

Western Kentucky University, College of Education, Department of Educational Leadership, Program in Guidance and Counseling, Bowling Green, KY 42101-3576. Awards MA Ed, Ed S. Accredited by NCATE. Part-time and evening/weekend programs available. Postbaccalaureate distance learning degree programs offered (minimal on-campus study). Faculty: 10 full-time (3 women), 1 part-time (0 women), 10.5 FTE. Students: 62 full-time (53 women), 264 part-time (212 women); includes 14 minority (12 African Americans, 1 Hispanic, 1 Native American). Average age 32. 84 applicants, 64% accepted. In 1997, 93 master's, 1 Ed S awarded. *Degree requirements:* For master's, thesis optional, foreign language not required; for Ed S, thesis, oral exam required, foreign language not required. *Entrance requirements:* For master's, GRE General Test (minimum combined score of 1150 on three sections; average 1319), minimum GPA of 2.5; for Ed S, GRE General Test (minimum combined score of 1250 on three sections), minimum GPA of 3.5. Application deadline: 8/1 (priority date; rolling processing; 12/1 for spring admission). Application fee: $20. *Tuition:* $2460 per year full-time, $133 per credit hour part-time for state residents; $6700 per year full-time, $369 per credit hour part-time for nonresidents. *Financial aid:* Service awards, Federal Work-Study, institutionally sponsored loans available. Financial aid application deadline: 4/1; applicants required to submit FAFSA. • Dr. Stephen B. Schnacke, Head, Department of Educational Leadership, 502-745-4997. Fax: 502-745-5445.

Western Maryland College, Department of Education, Program in Guidance and Counseling, Westminster, MD 21157-4390. Awards MS. Part-time and evening/weekend programs available. Faculty: 2 full-time (1 woman), 6 part-time (3 women). Students: 15 full-time (11 women), 235 part-time (206 women). In 1997, 39 degrees awarded. *Degree requirements:* Thesis optional, foreign language not required. *Entrance requirements:* GRE General Test, MAT, or NTE. Application deadline: rolling. Application fee: $35. *Expenses:* Tuition $210 per credit hour. Fees $30 per semester. *Financial aid:* Career-related internships or fieldwork available. Financial aid application deadline: 3/1. • Dr. Julia Orza, Coordinator, 410-857-2500. Application contact: Jeanette Witt, Coordinator of Graduate Records, 410-857-2513. Fax: 410-857-2515. E-mail: jwitt@wmdc.edu.

Western Michigan University, College of Education, Department of Counselor Education and Counseling Psychology, Kalamazoo, MI 49008. Offers programs in counseling psychology (PhD), counselor education (MA, Ed D, PhD), counselor education and counseling psychology (MA, PhD), counselor psychology (MA). Accredited by NCATE. One or more programs accredited by APA. Students: 128 full-time (90 women), 406 part-time (316 women); includes 40 minority (28 African Americans, 2 Asian Americans, 5 Hispanics, 5 Native Americans), 14 international. 226 applicants, 42% accepted. In 1997, 113 master's, 7 doctorates awarded. *Degree requirements:* For doctorate, dissertation, oral exams. *Entrance requirements:* For doctorate, GRE General Test. Application deadline: 1/15 (rolling processing). Application fee: $25. *Expenses:* Tuition $154 per credit hour for state residents; $372 per credit hour for nonresidents. Fees $602 per year full-time, $132 per semester part-time. *Financial aid:* Fellowships, research assistantships, teaching assistantships, Federal Work-Study available. Financial aid application deadline: 2/15; applicants required to submit FAFSA. • Dr. Joseph Morris, Chairperson, 616-387-5100. Application contact: Paula J. Boodt, Coordinator, Graduate Admissions and Recruitment, 616-387-2000. E-mail: paulaboodt@wmich.edu.

Western New Mexico University, School of Education, Silver City, NM 88062-0680. Offerings include counselor education (MA). School faculty: 16 full-time (9 women). *Application deadline:* rolling. *Application fee:* $10. *Tuition:* $1516 per year full-time, $55 per credit part-time for state residents; $5604 per year full-time, $55 per credit part-time for nonresidents. • Dr. Bonnie Maldonado, Dean, 505-538-6415.

Western Washington University, College of Arts and Sciences, Department of Psychology, Program in School Counseling, Bellingham, WA 98225-5996. Awards M Ed. Part-time programs available. Students: 11 full-time (8 women), 1 (woman) part-time. 21 applicants, 52% accepted. In 1997, 7 degrees awarded. *Degree requirements:* Comprehensive exam required, foreign language and thesis not required. *Entrance requirements:* GRE General Test, TOEFL (average 567), minimum GPA of 3.0 in last 60 semester hours or last 90 quarter hours. Application deadline: 2/1 (priority date). Application fee: $35. *Expenses:* Tuition $4200 per year full-time, $140 per credit part-time for state residents; $12,780 per year full-time, $426 per credit part-time for nonresidents. Fees $249 per year full-time, $83 per quarter part-time. *Financial aid:* Teaching assistantships, partial tuition waivers, Federal Work-Study, institutionally sponsored loans, and career-related internships or fieldwork available. Aid available to part-time students. Financial aid application deadline: 3/31. • Dr. Arleen Lewis, Adviser, 360-650-3523.

Westminster College, Programs in Education, Program in Guidance and Counseling, South Market Street, New Wilmington, PA 16172-0001. Awards M Ed, Certificate. Part-time and evening/weekend programs available. Students: 1 (woman) full-time, 53 part-time (33 women). In 1997, 8 master's awarded (100% found work related to degree). *Degree requirements:* For master's, computer language required, foreign language and thesis not required. *Average time to degree:* master's–1.5 years full-time, 2.5 years part-time. *Entrance requirements:* For master's, minimum GPA of 2.75. Application deadline: 8/30 (priority date; rolling processing; 1/15 for spring admission). Application fee: $20. *Expenses:* Tuition $1104 per course. Fees $30 per course. *Financial aid:* Grants and career-related internships or fieldwork available. • Dr. Samuel A. Farmerie, Graduate Director, Programs in Education, 724-946-7181. Fax: 724-946-7171. E-mail: farmersa@westminster.edu.

West Texas A&M University, College of Education and Social Sciences, Division of Education, Program in Counseling Education, Canyon, TX 79016-0001. Awards M Ed. Part-time and evening/weekend programs available. Students: 9 full-time (all women), 41 part-time (36 women); includes 1 international. 11 applicants, 45% accepted. In 1997, 12 degrees awarded. *Degree requirements:* Comprehensive exam required, foreign language and thesis not required. *Average time to degree:* master's–3 years full-time, 6 years part-time. *Entrance requirements:* GRE General Test (combined average 964). Application deadline: rolling. Application fee: $0 ($50 for international students). Electronic applications accepted. *Expenses:* Tuition $46 per semester hour for state residents; $259 per semester hour for nonresidents. Fees $156 per semester (minimum). *Financial aid:* Partial tuition waivers, Federal Work-Study, institutionally sponsored loans, and career-related internships or fieldwork available. Aid available to part-time students. Financial aid applicants required to submit CSS PROFILE or FAFSA. *Faculty research:* Reducing the somatoform patient's reliance on primary care through cognitive-relational group therapy. Total annual research expenditures: $4630. • Application contact: Dr. Janice Robinson, Graduate Adviser, 806-651-2612. Fax: 806-651-2601. E-mail: janice.robinson@wtamu.edu.

West Texas A&M University, College of Education and Social Sciences, Division of Education, Program in Professional Counseling, Canyon, TX 79016-0001. Awards M Ed. Part-time programs available. Students: 44 (34 women); includes 6 minority (1 African American, 4 Hispanics, 1 Native American). Average age 34. 11 applicants, 18% accepted. In 1997, 17 degrees awarded. *Degree requirements:* Comprehensive exam required, foreign language and thesis not required. *Average time to degree:* master's–3 years full-time, 6 years part-time. *Entrance requirements:* GRE General Test (combined average 964). Application fee: $0 ($50 for international students). Electronic applications accepted. *Expenses:* Tuition $46 per semester hour for state residents; $259 per semester hour for nonresidents. Fees $156 per semester (minimum). *Financial aid:* Partial tuition waivers, Federal Work-Study, institutionally sponsored loans, and career-related internships or fieldwork available. Aid available to part-time students. Financial aid applicants required to submit CSS PROFILE or FAFSA. • Application contact: Dr. Janice Robinson, Graduate Adviser, 806-651-2612. Fax: 806-651-2601. E-mail: janice.robinson@wtamu.edu.

Whitworth College, Graduate Studies in Education, Program in Guidance and Counseling, Spokane, WA 99251-0001. Offers school counselors (M Ed), social agency/church setting (M Ed). Accredited by NCATE. Part-time and evening/weekend programs available. *Degree requirements:* Comprehensive exams, internship, practicum, research project, or thesis required, foreign language not required. *Entrance requirements:* GRE General Test. Application deadline: 9/1 (priority date; rolling processing; 2/1 for spring admission). Application fee: $25. *Faculty research:* Church counseling service support.

Wichita State University, College of Education, Department of Administration, Counseling, Educational and School Psychology, Wichita, KS 67260. Offerings include counseling (M Ed). Accredited by NCATE. Department faculty: 15 full-time (7 women), 71 part-time (33 women). *Degree requirements:* Comprehensive exam required, thesis optional, foreign language not required. *Entrance requirements:* TOEFL (minimum score 550), minimum GPA of 2.75. Application deadline: 7/1 (priority date; rolling processing; 1/1 for spring admission). Application fee: $25 ($40 for international students). Electronic applications accepted. *Expenses:* Tuition $2303 per year full-time, $96 per credit hour part-time for state residents; $7691 per year full-time, $321 per credit hour part-time for nonresidents. Fees $490 per year full-time, $75 per semester (minimum) part-time. • Dr. Orpha Duell, Chairperson, 316-978-6299. Fax: 316-978-3102. E-mail: oduell@wsuhub.uc.twsu.edu.

William Paterson University of New Jersey, College of Education, Department of Special Education and Counseling Services, Program in Counseling Services, Wayne, NJ 07470-8420. Offers counseling (M Ed). Accredited by NCATE. Students: 5 full-time (4 women), 24 part-time (21 women); includes 1 minority (African American). Average age 37. 27 applicants, 26% accepted. In 1997, 9 degrees awarded. *Degree requirements:* Thesis, comprehensive exam, research design required, foreign language not required. *Entrance requirements:* GRE General Test (minimum combined score of 850), MAT (minimum score 42), minimum GPA of 2.75, teaching certificate. Application deadline: 4/1 (rolling processing; 10/15 for spring admission). Application fee: $35. *Expenses:* Tuition $230 per credit for state residents; $327 per credit for nonresidents. Fees $3.25 per credit. *Financial aid:* In 1997–98, 2 students received aid, including 1 graduate assistantship totaling $6,000; career-related internships or fieldwork also available. Aid available to part-time students. Financial aid application deadline: 4/1; applicants required to submit FAFSA. • Application contact: Office of Graduate Studies, 973-720-2237. Fax: 973-720-2035.

Wilmington College, Division of Education, New Castle, DE 19720-6491. Offerings include elementary and secondary school counseling (M Ed). *Application deadline:* rolling. *Application fee:* $25. *Expenses:* Tuition $4410 per year full-time, $735 per course part-time. Fees $50 per year. • Dr. Barbara Raetsch, Chair, 302-328-9401. Application contact: Michael Lee, Director of Admissions and Financial Aid, 302-328-9401 Ext. 102.

Winona State University, Graduate Studies, College of Education, Department of Counselor Education, Winona, MN 55987-5838. Awards MS. Accredited by NCATE. Part-time and evening/weekend programs available. Faculty: 5 full-time (3 women). Students: 18 full-time (14 women), 96 part-time (78 women); includes 2 international. 42 applicants, 88% accepted. In 1997, 25 degrees awarded. *Degree requirements:* Thesis or alternative required, foreign language not required. *Entrance requirements:* GRE General Test. Application deadline: 8/8 (priority date; rolling processing; 2/17 for spring admission). Application fee: $20. *Financial aid:* In 1997–98, 3 assistantships were awarded; Federal Work-Study and career-related internships or fieldwork also available. Aid available to part-time students. • Dr. Tim Hatfield, Chairperson, 507-457-5337. E-mail: thatfield@vax2.winona.msus.edu.

Winthrop University, College of Education, Program in Counseling and Development, Rock Hill, SC 29733. Offers agency counseling (M Ed), school counseling (M Ed). Accredited by NCATE. Part-time programs available. Students: 12 full-time (11 women), 38 part-time (32 women); includes 15 minority (14 African Americans, 1 Hispanic). Average age 33. In 1997, 33 degrees awarded. *Degree requirements:* Comprehensive exam required, foreign language and thesis not required. *Entrance requirements:* GRE General Test (minimum combined score of 800) or MAT (minimum score 40), South Carolina Class III teaching certificate. Application deadline: 7/15 (priority date; rolling processing; 12/1 for spring admission). Application fee: $35. *Tuition:* $3928 per year full-time, $164 per credit hour part-time for state residents; $7060 per year full-time, $294 per credit hour part-time for nonresidents. *Financial aid:* Graduate assistantships, graduate scholarships, Federal Work-Study, and career-related internships or fieldwork available. Aid available to part-time students. Financial aid application deadline: 2/1; applicants required to submit FAFSA. • Dr. George Reddick, Chairman, 803-323-2151. Fax: 803-323-4755. E-mail: reddickg@winthrop.edu. Application contact: Sharon Johnson, Director of Graduate Studies, 803-323-2204. Fax: 803-323-2292. E-mail: johnsons@winthrop.edu.

Wright State University, College of Education and Human Services, Department of Human Services, Programs in Counseling, Dayton, OH 45435. Offerings in counseling (MA, MS), including business and industrial, community counseling, exceptional children, gerontology, marriage and family, mental health, student affairs in higher education counseling; student personnel services (MA, M Ed), including school counseling. Accredited by NCATE. Students: 67 full-time (56 women), 63 part-time (50 women); includes 16 minority (13 African Americans, 2 Asian Americans, 1 Hispanic). Average age 36. 66 applicants, 50% accepted. In 1997, 43 degrees awarded. *Degree requirements:* Thesis (for some programs), comprehensive exam required, foreign language not required. *Entrance requirements:* GRE General Test, MAT, TOEFL (minimum score 550), interview. Application fee: $25. *Tuition:* $5109 per year full-time, $161 per credit hour part-time for state residents; $9039 per year full-time, $282 per credit hour part-time for nonresidents. *Financial aid:* In 1997–98, 5 graduate assistantships were awarded; full and partial tuition waivers also available. Aid available to part-time students. Financial aid applicants required to submit FAFSA. • Application contact: Gerald C. Malicki, Assistant Dean and Director of Graduate Admissions and Records, 937-775-2976. Fax: 937-775-2357. E-mail: wsugrad@wright.edu.

Xavier University, College of Social Sciences, Department of Education, Program in Agency and Community Counseling, Cincinnati, OH 45207-2111. Awards M Ed. Part-time and evening/weekend programs available. Faculty: 4 full-time (0 women), 4 part-time (2 women), 5 FTE. Students: 40 full-time (35 women), 83 part-time (72 women); includes 22 minority (21 African Americans, 1 Hispanic). Average age 33. 36 applicants, 83% accepted. In 1997, 52 degrees awarded. *Degree requirements:* Comprehensive exam or fieldwork, research project required, foreign language and thesis not required. *Entrance requirements:* MAT (minimum score 35), minimum GPA of 2.8. Application deadline: 8/15 (priority date; rolling processing). Application fee: $25. *Financial aid:* In 1997–98, 22 students received aid, including 22 scholarships (5 to first-year students). Aid available to part-time students. *Faculty research:* Reality therapy, career development. • Dr. Lon Kriner, Director, 513-745-3822. Fax: 513-745-2920. E-mail: kriner@admin.xu.edu. Application contact: Sheila Speth, Director of Graduate Services, 513-745-3360. Fax: 513-745-1048. E-mail: xugrad@admin.xu.edu.

Xavier University, College of Social Sciences, Department of Education, Program in School Counseling, Cincinnati, OH 45207-2111. Offers counseling (M Ed), school counseling (M Ed). Part-time and evening/weekend programs available. Faculty: 4 full-time (0 women), 4 part-time (2 women), 5 FTE. Students: 8 full-time (7 women), 84 part-time (75 women); includes 8 minority (7 African Americans, 1 Hispanic), 1 international. Average age 35. 23 applicants, 65% accepted. In 1997, 25 degrees awarded. *Degree requirements:* Comprehensive exam or fieldwork, research project required, foreign language and thesis not required. *Entrance requirements:* GRE or MAT (minimum score 35), minimum GPA of 2.8. Application deadline: 8/15 (priority date; rolling processing). Application fee: $25. *Financial aid:* In 1997–98, 19 students received aid, including 19 scholarships (4 to first-year students). Aid available to part-time students. • Dr. Lon Kriner, Director, 513-745-3822. Fax: 513-745-2920. E-mail: kriner@admin.xu.edu. Application contact: Sheila Speth, Director of Graduate Services, 513-745-3360. Fax: 513-745-1048. E-mail: xugrad@admin.xu.edu.

Xavier University of Louisiana, Programs in Education, New Orleans, LA 70125-1098. Offerings include guidance and counseling (MA). Accredited by NCATE. Faculty: 9 full-time (6 women), 12 part-time (5 women). *Average time to degree:* master's–3 years full-time, 7 years part-time. *Application deadline:* 7/1 (rolling processing; 12/1 for spring admission). *Application fee:* $30. *Tuition:* $200 per semester hour. • Dr. Rosalind Hale, Chair, Division of Education, 504-483-7536. Fax: 504-485-7909. Application contact: Marlene Robinson, Director of Graduate Admissions, 504-483-7487. Fax: 504-485-7921. E-mail: mrobinso@xula.edu.

Youngstown State University, College of Education, Department of Counseling, Youngstown, OH 44555-0002. Awards MS Ed. Accredited by NCATE. Part-time and evening/weekend programs available. Faculty: 9 full-time (5 women), 17 part-time (5 women). Students: 42 full-time (35 women), 121 part-time (94 women); includes 12 minority (8 African Americans, 1 Asian American, 3 Hispanics), 2 international. 27 applicants, 85% accepted. In 1997, 32 degrees awarded. *Degree requirements:* Comprehensive exam required, foreign language and thesis not required. *Entrance requirements:* MAT (minimum score 40), TOEFL (minimum score 550), interview, minimum GPA of 2.7. Application deadline: 8/15 (priority date; rolling processing; 2/15 for spring admission). Application fee: $30 ($75 for international students). *Expenses:* Tuition $90 per credit hour for state residents; $144 per credit hour (minimum) for nonresidents. Fees $528 per year full-time, $244 per year (minimum) part-time. *Financial aid:* In 1997–98, 34 students received aid, including 13 research assistantships averaging $666 per month and totaling $110,760, 2 teaching assistantships totaling $17,040, 19 scholarships totaling $17,114; Federal Work-Study, institutionally sponsored loans, and career-related internships or fieldwork also available. Aid available to part-time students. Financial aid application deadline: 3/1. *Faculty research:* Suicide, euthanasia, ethical issues, marriage and family. • Dr. James Rogers, Chair, 330-742-3257. Application contact: Dr. Peter J. Kasvinsky, Dean of Graduate Studies, 330-742-3091. Fax: 330-742-1580. E-mail: amgrad03@ysub.ysu.edu.

English Education

Adelphi University, School of Education, Program in Secondary Education, Garden City, NY 11530. Offerings include English (MA). *Application deadline:* rolling. *Application fee:* $50. *Expenses:* Tuition $16,000 per year full-time, $485 per credit part-time. Fees $500 per year full-time, $150 per semester part-time. • Director, 516-877-4090. Application contact: Jennifer Spiegel, Associate Director of Graduate Admissions, 516-877-3055.

Agnes Scott College, Secondary English Program, Decatur, GA 30030-3797. Awards MAT. Part-time programs available. Faculty: 6 full-time (3 women), 2 part-time (both women). Students: 14 full-time (13 women), 7 part-time (6 women); includes 3 minority (all African Americans). Average age 37. 32 applicants, 75% accepted. In 1997, 22 degrees awarded (100% found work related to degree). *Average time to degree:* master's–1 year full-time. *Entrance requirements:* Minimum GPA of 2.75, interview. Application deadline: 7/15 (priority date). Application fee: $35. *Expenses:* Tuition $7670 per year full-time, $320 per credit hour part-time. Fees $145 per year. *Financial aid:* 17 students received aid. Aid available to part-time students. Financial aid applicants required to submit FAFSA. • Ruth Bettandorff, Associate Dean of the College, 404-638-6228. Fax: 404-638-6083. E-mail: rbettandorff@asc.agnesscott.edu.

Alabama State University, School of Graduate Studies, College of Education, Department of Curriculum and Instruction, Program in Secondary Education, Montgomery, AL 36101-0271. Offerings include English education (M Ed). Program faculty: 2 full-time (1 woman). *Degree requirements:* Comprehensive exam required, thesis optional. *Entrance requirements:* GRE General Test, MAT or NTE. Application deadline: 7/15 (rolling processing; 12/15 for spring admission). Application fee: $10. *Expenses:* Tuition $85 per credit hour for state residents; $170 per credit hour for nonresidents. Fees $486 per year. • Dr. Linda Bradford, Coordinator, 334-229-4485. Fax: 334-229-4904. E-mail: lbradford@asunet.alasu.edu. Application contact: Dr. Fred Dauser, Dean of Graduate Studies, 334-229-4276. Fax: 334-229-4928.

Albany State University, School of Education, Program in English Education, Albany, GA 31705-2717. Awards M Ed. Accredited by NCATE. Students: 5. In 1997, 1 degree awarded. *Degree requirements:* Comprehensive exam. *Entrance requirements:* GRE General Test (minimum combined score of 800), MAT (minimum score 44) or NTE (minimum score 550). Application deadline: 9/1. Application fee: $10. *Financial aid:* Application deadline 4/1. • Dr. Velma Grant, Chair, 912-430-4883. Fax: 912-430-4296. E-mail: vfgrant@fld94.alsnet.peachnet.edu.

Alfred University, Graduate School, Division of Education, Alfred, NY 14802-1205. Offerings include secondary education (MS Ed), with options in biology education, chemistry education, earth science education, English education, mathematics education, physics education, social studies education. Division faculty: 45 full-time (12 women). *Degree requirements:* Thesis required (for some programs), foreign language not required. *Entrance requirements:* TOEFL. Application deadline: rolling. Application fee: $50. *Expenses:* Tuition $20,376 per year full-time, $390 per credit hour (minimum) part-time. Fees $546 per year. • Dr. Katherine D. Wiesendanger, Chair, 607-871-2219. E-mail: fwiesendange@bigvax.alfred.edu. Application contact: Cathleen R. Johnson, Assistant Director of Admissions, 607-871-2141. Fax: 607-871-2198. E-mail: johnsonc@bigvax.alfred.edu.

Allentown College of St. Francis de Sales, Graduate Division, Program in Education, Center Valley, PA 18034-9568. Offerings include English (M Ed). Program faculty: 18 full-time (4 women), 25 part-time (6 women). *Degree requirements:* Capstone Course or Project required, foreign language not required. *Average time to degree:* master's–3 years part-time. *Entrance requirements:* Teaching certificate. Application deadline: 8/24 (priority date; rolling processing). Application fee: $35. *Tuition:* $285 per credit. • Dr. Irene Pompetti-Szul, Director, 610-282-1100 Ext. 1401. Fax: 610-282-2254.

American International College, School of Continuing Education and Graduate Studies, School of Psychology and Education, Department of Education, Springfield, MA 01109-3189. Offerings include English (MAT). Department faculty: 5 full-time (3 women), 15 part-time (9 women). *Application fee:* $15 ($25 for international students). *Expenses:* Tuition $363 per credit hour. Fees $25 per semester. • C. Gerald Weaver, Dean, School of Psychology and Education, 413-747-6338.

Andrews University, School of Graduate Studies, College of Arts and Sciences, Department of English, Berrien Springs, MI 49104. Awards MA, MAT. Part-time programs available. Faculty: 10 full-time (4 women), 3 part-time (2 women). *Degree requirements:* 1 foreign language required, thesis optional. *Entrance requirements:* GRE Subject Test. Application deadline: 8/15 (rolling processing). Application fee: $30. *Expenses:* Tuition $290 per quarter hour (minimum). Fees $75 per quarter. *Financial aid:* Fellowships, research assistantships, teaching assistantships, Federal Work-Study, and career-related internships or fieldwork available. *Faculty research:* Christianity and literature, Victorian literature, social linguistics, rhetoric, American literature. • Dr. F. Estella Greig, Chairperson, 616-471-3298.

Andrews University, School of Graduate Studies, School of Education, Department of Teaching/Learning/Administration, Berrien Springs, MI 49104. Offerings include secondary education (MAT), with options in biology, education, English, English as a second language, French, history, physics. *Application deadline:* 8/15 (rolling processing). *Application fee:* $30. *Expenses:* Tuition $290 per quarter hour (minimum). Fees $75 per quarter. • Dr. William H. Green, Chair, 616-471-3465.

Arkansas State University, College of Arts and Sciences, Department of English and Philosophy, State University, AR 72467. Offerings include English education (MSE, SCCT). Accredited by NCATE. Department faculty: 22 full-time (5 women), 1 (woman) part-time. *Degree requirements:* For SCCT, comprehensive exam required, foreign language and thesis not required. *Entrance requirements:* For SCCT, GRE General Test or MAT, master's degree. Application deadline: 7/1 (priority date; rolling processing; 11/15 for spring admission). Application fee: $15 ($25 for international students). *Expenses:* Tuition $2760 per year full-time, $115 per credit hour part-time for state residents; $6936 per year full-time, $289 per credit hour part-time for nonresidents. Fees $506 per year full-time, $44 per semester (minimum) part-time. • Dr. Charles Carr, Chair, 870-972-3043. Fax: 870-972-2795. E-mail: crcarr@toltec.astate.edu.

Arkansas Tech University, School of Education, Department of Curriculum and Instruction, Russellville, AR 72801-2222. Offerings include English (M Ed). Accredited by NCATE. *Application deadline:* 3/1 (priority date; rolling processing; 10/1 for spring admission). *Application fee:* $0 ($30 for international students). *Expenses:* Tuition $98 per credit hour for state residents; $196 per credit hour for nonresidents. Fees $30 per semester. • Head, 501-968-0290. Fax: 501-964-0811.

Auburn University, College of Education, Department of Curriculum and Teaching, Auburn University, AL 36849-0001. Offerings include secondary education (M Ed, MS, PhD, Ed S), with options in English language arts, mathematics, science, social studies. Accredited by NCATE. Department faculty: 20 full-time (11 women). *Degree requirements:* For master's, thesis (MS) required, foreign language not required; for doctorate, dissertation required, foreign language not required; for Ed S, field project required, foreign language and thesis not required. *Entrance requirements:* For master's and Ed S, GRE General Test; for doctorate, GRE General Test (minimum score 450 on each section, 1000 combined). Application deadline: 9/1 (rolling processing; 3/1 for spring admission). Application fee: $25 ($50 for international students). *Expenses:* Tuition $2760 per year full-time, $76 per credit hour part-time for state residents; $8280 per year full-time, $228 per credit hour part-time for nonresidents. Fees $30 per year full-time, $160 per quarter part-time for state residents; $30 per year full-time, $480 per quarter part-time for nonresidents. • Dr. Andrew M. Weaver, Head, 334-844-4434. E-mail: weaveam@mail.auburn.edu. Application contact: Dr. John F. Pritchett, Dean of the Graduate School, 334-844-4700.

Beaver College, Department of Education, Glenside, PA 19038-3295. Offerings include English education (MA Ed), language arts (M Ed, CAS), written communication (MA Ed). *Application fee:* $35. *Expenses:* Tuition $6570 per year full-time, $365 per credit part-time. Fees $35 per year.

Belmont University, Graduate Studies in Education, Nashville, TN 37212-3757. Offerings include English (M Ed). Accredited by NCATE. Faculty: 31 full-time (16 women), 1 (woman) part-time. *Average time to degree:* master's–2 years full-time, 5 years part-time. *Application deadline:* 7/15 (priority date; rolling processing; 11/15 for spring admission). *Application fee:* $50. • Dr. Norma Stevens, Associate Dean, 615-460-6233. E-mail: stevensn@belmont.edu. Application contact: Lois Smith, Admissions Counselor, 615-460-5483. Fax: 615-385-5084. E-mail: smithl@belmont.edu.

Boston College, Graduate School of Education, Department of Teacher Education/Special Education and Curriculum and Instruction, Program in Secondary Education, Chestnut Hill, MA 02167-9991. Offerings include English (MAT). Accredited by NCATE. *Application deadline:* 3/15 (11/15 for spring admission). *Application fee:* $40. *Expenses:* Tuition $626 per semester hour. Fees $80 per year (minimum) full-time, $30 per semester part-time. • Application contact: Arline Riordan, Graduate Admissions Director, 617-552-4214. Fax: 617-552-0812. E-mail: riordana@bc.edu.

Boston University, School of Education, Department of Curriculum and Teaching, Program in English and Language Arts, Boston, MA 02215. Offers English and language arts (Ed M, Ed D, CAGS), English education (MAT). Students: 29 full-time (19 women), 4 part-time (3 women); includes 1 international. Average age 25. In 1997, 17 master's awarded. *Degree requirements:* For doctorate, dissertation, comprehensive exam required, foreign language not required; for CAGS, comprehensive exam required, foreign language and thesis not required. *Entrance requirements:* For master's and CAGS, GRE or MAT, TOEFL; for doctorate, GRE General Test or MAT, TOEFL. Application deadline: 2/15 (priority date; rolling processing). Application fee: $50. *Expenses:* Tuition $22,830 per year full-time, $713 per credit part-time. Fees $218 per year full-time, $40 per semester part-time. *Financial aid:* Application deadline 3/30. • Dr. Thomas E. Culliton Jr., Coordinator, 617-353-3223. E-mail: culliton@bu.edu.

Brooklyn College of the City University of New York, School of Education, Division of Secondary Education, 2900 Bedford Avenue, Brooklyn, NY 11210-2889. Offerings include English education (MA). *Application deadline:* 3/1 (11/1 for spring admission). *Application fee:* $40. *Expenses:* Tuition $4350 per year full-time, $185 per credit part-time for state residents; $7600 per year full-time, $320 per credit part-time for nonresidents. Fees $500 per year for state residents; $806 per year for nonresidents. • Dr. Peter Taubman, Coordinator, 718-951-5218. Fax: 718-951-4816. E-mail: ptaubman@brooklyn.cuny.edu.

Brown University, Department of Education, Providence, RI 02912. Offerings include secondary English (MAT). MAT (elementary education K–6) new for fall 1998. Department faculty: 4 full-time (2 women), 20 part-time (15 women). *Average time to degree:* master's–1 year full-time. *Entrance requirements:* GRE (score in 95th percentile or higher). Application deadline: 1/2 (priority date). Application fee: $60. *Expenses:* Tuition $23,616 per year. Fees $436 per year. • Lawrence Wakeford, Chairman, 401-863-2407. Application contact: Yvette Nachmias, Teacher Education Coordinator, 401-863-3364. Fax: 401-863-1276. E-mail: yvette_nachmias@brown.edu.

California Baptist College, Graduate Program in Education, Riverside, CA 92504-3206. Offerings include English education (MS Ed). Program faculty: 8 full-time (7 women), 4 part-time (2 women). *Application deadline:* rolling. *Application fee:* $40. *Expenses:* Tuition $275 per

Directory: English Education

California Baptist College (continued)
unit. Fees $100 per year. • Dr. Marsha Savage, Chair, 909-689-5771. Application contact: Gail Ronveaux, Director of Graduate Services, 909-343-4249. Fax: 909-351-1808. E-mail: gradser@cal.baptist.edu.

California State University, San Bernardino, Graduate Studies, School of Education, San Bernardino, CA 92407-2397. Offerings include history and English for secondary teachers (MA). School faculty: 77 full-time (38 women). *Application deadline:* 8/31 (priority date). *Application fee:* $55. *Expenses:* Tuition $0 for state residents; $164 per unit for nonresidents. Fees $1922 per year full-time, $1256 per year part-time. • Patricia Arlin, Dean, 909-880-3600. Fax: 909-880-7011.

Campbell University, School of Education, Buies Creek, NC 27506. Offerings include English education (M Ed). Accredited by NCATE. School faculty: 8 full-time (6 women), 6 part-time (0 women). *Application deadline:* 8/1 (priority date; rolling processing; 1/2 for spring admission). *Application fee:* $25. *Tuition:* $168 per credit hour (minimum). • Dr. Margaret Giesbrecht, Dean, 910-893-1630. Fax: 910-893-1999. E-mail: giesbrec@mailcenter.campbell.edu. Application contact: James S. Farthing, Director of Graduate Admissions, 910-893-1200 Ext. 1318. Fax: 910-893-1288.

Carthage College, Division of Teacher Education, Kenosha, WI 53140-1994. Offerings include language arts (M Ed). College faculty: 6 full-time (4 women), 13 part-time (8 women). *Degree requirements:* Thesis optional, foreign language not required. *Average time to degree:* master's–5 years part-time. *Entrance requirements:* MAT, minimum B average. Application deadline: rolling. Application fee: $25. • Dr. Judith B. Schaumberg, Director of Graduate Programs, 414-551-5876. Fax: 414-551-5704.

Catawba College, Program in Education, Salisbury, NC 28144-2488. Offerings include language arts (M Ed). Accredited by NCATE. Program faculty: 5 full-time (4 women), 2 part-time (both women). *Degree requirements:* Comprehensive written exams required, thesis not required. *Average time to degree:* master's–4 years part-time. *Entrance requirements:* NTE, PRAXIS. Application deadline: 8/1 (priority date; rolling processing). Application fee: $15. *Tuition:* $90 per semester hour. • Dr. Shirley Haworth, Chair, 704-637-4461. Fax: 704-637-4732.

Central Missouri State University, College of Arts and Sciences, Department of English and Philosophy, Warrensburg, MO 64093. Offerings include English education (MSE). Accredited by NCATE. Department faculty: 30 full-time. *Application deadline:* 6/30 (priority date; rolling processing). *Application fee:* $25 ($50 for international students). *Tuition:* $3288 per year full-time, $137 per credit hour part-time for state residents; $5928 per year full-time, $274 per credit hour part-time for nonresidents. • Dr. David Smith, Chair, 660-543-4425. Fax: 660-543-8544. E-mail: mxs51750@cmsu2.cmsu.edu.

Central Washington University, College of Arts and Humanities, Department of English, Ellensburg, WA 98926. Offerings include English language learning (MA). Department faculty: 21 full-time (7 women). *Degree requirements:* Thesis or alternative required, foreign language not required. *Entrance requirements:* GRE General Test, minimum GPA of 3.0, sample of written work. Application deadline: 4/1 (priority date; rolling processing; 1/1 for spring admission). Application fee: $35. *Expenses:* Tuition $4200 per year full-time, $140 per credit hour part-time for state residents; $12,780 per year full-time, $426 per credit hour part-time for nonresidents. Fees $240 per year. • Dr. Patricia Callaghan, Chair, 509-963-1546. Application contact: Christie A. Fevergeon, Program Coordinator, Graduate Studies and Research, 509-963-3103. Fax: 509-963-1799. E-mail: masters@cwu.edu.

Chadron State College, Department of Education, Chadron, NE 69337. Offerings include language and literature (MA Ed). Accredited by NCATE. *Application deadline:* rolling. *Application fee:* $15. *Expenses:* Tuition $1788 per year full-time, $75 per credit hour part-time for state residents; $3588 per year full-time, $149 per credit hour part-time for nonresidents. Fees $388 per year full-time, $1232 per year part-time. • Dr. Pat Colgate, Dean, School of Graduate Studies, 308-432-6330. Fax: 308-432-6454. E-mail: pcolgate@csc1.csc.edu.

Chapman University, School of Communication Arts, Program in English, Orange, CA 92866. Offerings include English education (MA), teaching literature and composition (MA). Program faculty: 22 full-time (12 women). *Degree requirements:* Comprehensive exam required, thesis not required. *Entrance requirements:* GRE General Test (minimum combined score of 900), MAT (minimum score 52). Application deadline: rolling. Application fee: $40. *Tuition:* $460 per credit. • Dr. Matthew Schneider, Coordinator, 714-997-6750.

Charleston Southern University, Programs in Education, Charleston, SC 29423-8087. Offerings include English (MAT). Faculty: 16 full-time (5 women), 5 part-time (3 women), 17.6 FTE. *Application deadline:* rolling. *Application fee:* $25. *Tuition:* $9821 per year full-time, $173 per hour (minimum) part-time. • Dr. Martha Watson, Director of Graduate Programs, 803-863-7555.

City College of the City University of New York, Graduate School, School of Education, Department of Secondary and Continuing Education, Convent Avenue at 138th Street, New York, NY 10031-6977. Offerings include English education (MA). *Degree requirements:* Thesis required, foreign language not required. *Entrance requirements:* TOEFL (minimum score 500). Application fee: $40. *Expenses:* Tuition $4350 per year full-time, $185 per credit part-time for state residents; $7600 per year full-time, $320 per credit part-time for nonresidents. Fees $41 per year. • Hope Hartman, Chair, 212-650-7954.

Clemson University, College of Health, Education, and Human Development, Department of Curriculum and Instruction, Program in Secondary Education, Clemson, SC 29634. Offerings include English (M Ed). Accredited by NCATE. *Entrance requirements:* TOEFL, teaching certificate. Application deadline: 6/1. Application fee: $35. *Expenses:* Tuition $3154 per year full-time, $130 per credit hour part-time for state residents; $6452 per year full-time, $264 per credit hour part-time for nonresidents. Fees $190 per year. • Dr. Robert Green, Chair, Department of Curriculum and Instruction, 864-656-5108. Fax: 864-656-1322. E-mail: rpgreen@clemson.edu.

College of Notre Dame, Department of Education, Emphasis in Secondary Education, Belmont, CA 94002-1997. Offerings include teaching English (MAT). Faculty: 5 full-time, 8 part-time. *Application deadline:* rolling. *Application fee:* $50 ($500 for international students). *Tuition:* $460 per unit. • Dr. Kim Tolley, Program Director, 650-508-3456.

College of Our Lady of the Elms, Department of Education, Chicopee, MA 01013-2839. Offerings include secondary education (MAT), with options in biology education, English education, Spanish education. Department faculty: 7 full-time (all women), 6 part-time (5 women). *Application deadline:* rolling. *Application fee:* $30. *Expenses:* Tuition $320 per credit. Fees $40 per year. • Sr. Kathleen M. Kirley, Dean of Continuing Education and Graduate Studies, 413-594-2761. Fax: 413-592-4871. Application contact: Dr. Mary Janeczek, Director, 413-594-2761.

Colorado State University, College of Liberal Arts, Department of English, Fort Collins, CO 80523-0015. Offerings include English as a second language (MA). Accredited by NCATE. Department faculty: 32 full-time (9 women), 8 part-time (4 women). *Application deadline:* 2/1 (priority date; rolling processing). *Application fee:* $30. Electronic applications accepted. *Expenses:* Tuition $2632 per year full-time, $109 per credit hour part-time for state residents; $10,216 per year full-time, $425 per credit hour part-time for nonresidents. Fees $708 per year full-time, $32 per semester (minimum) part-time. • Pattie Cowell, Chair, 970-491-6428. Application contact: Carol Cantrell, Coordinator, 970-491-6428. Fax: 970-491-5601. E-mail: tbarber@vines.colostate.edu.

Colorado State University, College of Liberal Arts, Department of Foreign Languages and Literatures, Fort Collins, CO 80523-0015. Offerings include French/TESL (MA), German/TESL (MA), Spanish/TESL (MA). MA (TESL) offered jointly with the Department of English. Department faculty: 20 full-time (11 women), 2 part-time (1 woman). *Degree requirements:* 2 foreign languages, thesis or paper. *Entrance requirements:* GRE General Test, TOEFL, minimum GPA of 3.0. Application deadline: 2/1 (priority date; rolling processing; 10/1 for spring admission). Application fee: $30. Electronic applications accepted. *Expenses:* Tuition $2632 per year full-time, $109 per credit hour part-time for state residents; $10,216 per year full-time, $425 per credit hour part-time for nonresidents. Fees $708 per year full-time, $32 per semester (minimum) part-time. • Sara Saz, Chair, 970-491-6155. E-mail: ssaz@vines.colostate.edu. Application contact: Irmgard Hunt, Graduate Coordinator, 970-491-5377. Fax: 970-491-2822. E-mail: ihunt@vines.colostate.edu.

Columbia College, Department of Educational Studies, 600 South Michigan Avenue, Chicago, IL 60605-1997. Offerings include English (MAT). *Application deadline:* 7/15 (rolling processing; 12/4 for spring admission). *Application fee:* $35. *Expenses:* Tuition $392 per credit hour. Fees $170 per year full-time, $150 per year part-time.

Columbus State University, College of Education, Department of Curriculum and Instruction, Columbus, GA 31907-5645. Offerings include secondary education (M Ed, Ed S), with options in biology (M Ed), English (M Ed, Ed S), general science (M Ed), history (M Ed), mathematics (M Ed, Ed S), political science (M Ed), science/biology (Ed S), social science (M Ed, Ed S). Accredited by NCATE. Ed S (mathematics) offered jointly with Georgia Southwestern University. M Ed (political science) being phased out; applicants no longer accepted. *Degree requirements:* For master's, exit exam required, foreign language and thesis not required; for Ed S, thesis or alternative required, foreign language not required. *Entrance requirements:* For master's, GRE General Test (minimum combined score of 800), MAT (minimum score 44); for Ed S, GRE General Test (minimum combined score of 900), MAT (minimum score 44). Application deadline: 7/10 (priority date; rolling processing; 10/23 for spring admission). Application fee: $20. *Tuition:* $1718 per year full-time, $151 per semester hour part-time for state residents; $6218 per year full-time, $401 per semester hour part-time for nonresidents. • Dr. David Shoemaker, Chair, 706-568-2255. Fax: 706-568-3134. E-mail: shoemaker_david@colstate.edu. Application contact: Katie Thornton, Graduate Admissions, 706-568-2279. Fax: 706-568-2462. E-mail: thornton_katie@colstate.edu.

Connecticut College, Department of English, New London, CT 06320-4196. Awards MA, MAT. Part-time programs available. *Degree requirements:* 1 foreign language, thesis. *Entrance requirements:* GRE General Test, GRE Subject Test. Application deadline: 2/2. Application fee: $35.

Delta State University, School of Arts and Sciences, Department of Languages and Literature, Cleveland, MS 38733-0001. Offers program in English education (M Ed). Part-time programs available. Faculty: 11 full-time (2 women). Students: 4 full-time (all women), 6 part-time (4 women); includes 1 minority (African American). Average age 34. 18 applicants, 94% accepted. In 1997, 1 degree awarded. *Degree requirements:* Thesis or alternative required, foreign language not required. *Entrance requirements:* GRE General Test (minimum combined score of 800) or MAT (minimum score 34). Application deadline: 8/1 (priority date; rolling processing). Application fee: $0. *Tuition:* $2596 per year full-time, $121 per semester hour part-time for state residents; $5546 per year full-time, $285 per semester hour part-time for nonresidents. *Financial aid:* Research assistantships, Federal Work-Study, institutionally sponsored loans, and career-related internships or fieldwork available. Aid available to part-time students. Financial aid application deadline: 6/1. • Dorothy Shawhan, Chairperson, 601-846-4016. E-mail: dshawhan@dsu.deltast.edu. Application contact: Dr. John Thornell, Dean of Graduate Studies and Continuing Education, 601-846-4310. Fax: 601-846-4016.

Eastern Kentucky University, College of Education, Department of Curriculum and Instruction, Program in Secondary and Higher Education, Richmond, KY 40475-3101. Offerings include English education (MA Ed). Accredited by NCATE. *Entrance requirements:* GRE General Test, minimum GPA of 2.5. Application fee: $0. *Tuition:* $2390 per year full-time, $133 per credit hour part-time for state residents; $6630 per year full-time, $365 per credit hour part-time for nonresidents. • Dr. Imogene Ramsey, Chair, Department of Curriculum and Instruction, 606-622-2154.

Edinboro University of Pennsylvania, School of Education, Department of Elementary Education, Program in Elementary Education, Edinboro, PA 16444. Offerings include language arts (M Ed). *Degree requirements:* Thesis or alternative required, foreign language not required. *Entrance requirements:* GRE or MAT (score in 30th percentile or higher). Application deadline: rolling. Application fee: $25. *Expenses:* Tuition $3468 per year full-time, $193 per credit part-time for state residents; $6236 per year full-time, $346 per credit part-time for nonresidents. Fees $898 per year full-time, $50 per semester (minimum) part-time. • Application contact: Dr. Philip Kerstetter, Dean of Graduate Studies, 814-732-2856. Fax: 814-732-2611. E-mail: kerstetter@edinboro.edu.

Fairleigh Dickinson University, Teaneck–Hackensack Campus, University College: Arts, Sciences, and Professional Studies, Peter Sammartino School of Education, Program in English Education, 1000 River Road, Teaneck, NJ 07666-1914. Awards MAT. Faculty: 11 full-time (8 women), 27 part-time (10 women). *Degree requirements:* Research project required, thesis not required. *Application deadline:* rolling. *Application fee:* $35. *Expenses:* Tuition $522 per credit. Fees $302 per year full-time, $138 per year part-time. *Faculty research:* Mathematics for students with learning disabilities, gender issues in education, social problem-solving and conflict resolution in the classroom, multicultural education in the elementary classroom, problems encountered by international students in college programs. • Dr. Eloise Forster, Interim Director, Peter Sammartino School of Education, 201-692-2834. Fax: 201-692-2603.

Fitchburg State College, Programs in Teaching English (Secondary Level), Fitchburg, MA 01420-2697. Awards MA, MAT. Accredited by NCATE. Part-time and evening/weekend programs available. *Entrance requirements:* GRE General Test or MAT (minimum score 47), interview. Application deadline: rolling. Application fee: $10. *Expenses:* Tuition $147 per credit. Fees $55 per semester. *Financial aid:* Graduate assistantships, Federal Work-Study available. Aid available to part-time students. Financial aid application deadline: 3/30; applicants required to submit FAFSA. • Dr. Marilyn McCaffrey, Chair, 978-665-3362. Fax: 978-665-3658. E-mail: dgce@fsc.edu. Application contact: James DuPont, Director of Admissions, 978-665-3144. Fax: 978-665-4540. E-mail: admissions@fsc.edu.

Florida International University, College of Education, Department of Subject Specializations, Program in English Education, Miami, FL 33199. Awards MS. Accredited by NCATE. Part-time and evening/weekend programs available. Students: 14 full-time (12 women), 23 part-time (19 women); includes 25 minority (10 African Americans, 1 Asian American, 14 Hispanics). Average age 31. 17 applicants, 76% accepted. In 1997, 12 degrees awarded. *Entrance requirements:* GRE General Test (minimum combined score of 1000) or minimum GPA of 3.0. Application deadline: 4/1 (priority date; rolling processing; 10/1 for spring admission). Application fee: $20. *Expenses:* Tuition $138 per credit hour for state residents; $482 per credit hour for nonresidents. Fees $46 per semester. *Faculty research:* Computer-assisted instruction, classroom teaching. • Dr. Dean Hauenstein, Chairperson, Department of Subject Specializations, 305-348-2005. Fax: 305-348-2086.

Florida State University, College of Education, Department of Curriculum and Instruction, Program in English Education, Tallahassee, FL 32306. Awards MS, PhD, Ed S. Part-time programs available. Faculty: 3 full-time (2 women). Students: 15 full-time (12 women), 9 part-time (4 women); includes 1 minority (African American). 27 applicants, 89% accepted. In 1997, 11 master's, 2 doctorates awarded. *Degree requirements:* For master's and Ed S, comprehensive exam required, thesis optional; for doctorate, dissertation, comprehensive exam. *Entrance requirements:* GRE General Test (minimum combined score of 1000), minimum GPA of 3.0. Application deadline: 7/1 (priority date; rolling processing; 11/1 for spring admission). Application fee: $20. *Tuition:* $139 per credit hour for state residents; $482 per credit hour for nonresidents. *Financial aid:* Fellowships, research assistantships, teaching assistantships available. • Dr. David Foulk, Chair, Department of Curriculum and Instruction, 850-644-6553. E-mail: foulk@mail.coe.fsu.edu. Application contact: Admissions Secretary, 850-644-6553. Fax: 850-644-1880.

Framingham State College, Graduate Programs, Department of English, Framingham, MA 01701-9101. Awards M Ed. Faculty: 3 full-time, 1 part-time. Students: 3 full-time, 4 part-time. *Tuition:* $4184 per year full-time, $523 per course part-time for state residents; $4848 per year full-time, $606 per course part-time for nonresidents. • Dr. Alan Feldman, Chairperson, 508-620-1220 Ext. 331. Application contact: Graduate Office, 508-626-4550.

Gardner–Webb University, Department of English, Boiling Springs, NC 28017. Offers program in English education (MA). Part-time and evening/weekend programs available. Faculty: 6 full-time (5 women). Students: 9 part-time (8 women). Average age 30. 2 applicants, 100% accepted. In 1997, 2 degrees awarded. *Degree requirements:* Comprehensive exam required, foreign language and thesis not required. *Entrance requirements:* GRE General Test (minimum combined score of 900), MAT (minimum score 35) or NTE, minimum GPA of 2.5. Application deadline: 8/1. Application fee: $25. *Tuition:* $178 per semester hour full-time, $220 per semester hour part-time. *Financial aid:* In 1997–98, 2 assistantships (1 to a first-year student) averaging $450 per month were awarded. • Dr. Gayle Price, Chair, 704-434-4414. Fax: 704-434-3921. E-mail: gprice@gardner-webb.edu.

Georgia Southern University, College of Education, Department of Middle Grades and Secondary Education, Program in English, Statesboro, GA 30460-8126. Awards M Ed, Ed S. Accredited by NCATE. Part-time and evening/weekend programs available. Students: 2 full-time (both women), 10 part-time (8 women); includes 1 minority (African American). Average age 31. 9 applicants, 56% accepted. In 1997, 6 master's, 1 Ed S awarded. *Degree requirements:* Exams required, foreign language and thesis not required. *Entrance requirements:* For master's, GRE General Test (minimum score 450 on each section) or MAT (minimum score 44), minimum GPA of 2.5; for Ed S, GRE General Test (minimum score 450 on each section) or MAT (minimum score 49), minimum graduate GPA of 3.25. Application deadline: 7/15 (priority date; rolling processing; 11/15 for spring admission). Application fee: $0. Electronic applications accepted. *Tuition:* $2619 per year full-time, $287 per semester (minimum) part-time for state residents; $8619 per year full-time, $1037 per semester (minimum) part-time for nonresidents. *Financial aid:* Application deadline 4/15. • Application contact: Dr. John R. Diebolt, Associate Graduate Dean, 912-681-5384. Fax: 912-681-0740. E-mail: gradschool@gsvms2.cc.gasou.edu.

Georgia State University, College of Education, Department of Middle, Secondary Education and Instructional Technology, Programs in Secondary Education, Atlanta, GA 30303-3083. Offerings include English education (M Ed, Ed S), language and literacy education (PhD). One or more programs accredited by NCATE. *Degree requirements:* For master's, comprehensive exam; for doctorate, dissertation, comprehensive exam; for Ed S, project/exam. *Entrance requirements:* For master's, GRE General Test (minimum combined score of 800) or MAT (minimum score 44), minimum GPA of 2.5; for doctorate, GRE General Test (minimum score 500 on verbal section, 500 on either quantitative or analytical sections) or MAT (minimum score 53), minimum GPA of 3.3; for Ed S, GRE General Test (minimum combined score of 900) or MAT (minimum score 48), minimum graduate GPA of 3.25. Application fee: $25. *Expenses:* Tuition $2673 per year full-time, $99 per semester hour part-time for state residents; $10,692 per year full-time, $396 per semester hour part-time for nonresidents. Fees $228 per year. • Dr. Beverly J. Armento, Chair, Department of Middle, Secondary Education and Instructional Technology, 404-651-2510.

Grand Valley State University, School of Education, Programs in General Education, Program in Secondary, Adult and Higher Education, Allendale, MI 49401-9403. Offerings include English (M Ed). Accredited by NCATE. *Degree requirements:* Thesis or alternative, applied research project. *Entrance requirements:* GRE General Test (minimum combined score of 1300) or minimum GPA of 3.0. Application deadline: rolling. Application fee: $20. • Application contact: Admissions Office, 616-895-2025. Fax: 616-895-3081.

Henderson State University, School of Education, Department of Secondary Education, Arkadelphia, AR 71999-0001. Offerings include English education (MSE). Accredited by NCATE. Postbaccalaureate distance learning degree programs offered (minimal on-campus study). *Degree requirements:* Thesis optional, foreign language not required. *Entrance requirements:* GRE General Test or MAT, minimum GPA of 2.7, teacher certification. Application deadline: 7/31 (priority date; rolling processing). Application fee: $15. Electronic applications accepted. *Expenses:* Tuition $120 per credit hour for state residents; $240 per credit hour for nonresidents. Fees $105 per semester (minimum) full-time, $52 per semester (minimum) part-time. • Dr. Charles Weiner, Chairperson, 870-230-5163. Fax: 870-230-5455. E-mail: weinerc@holly.hsu.edu.

Hofstra University, School of Education and Allied Human Services, Department of Curriculum and Teaching, Program in Teaching of Writing, Hempstead, NY 11549. Awards MA, CAS. Accredited by NCATE. Students: 15 full-time (all women), 2 part-time (both women); includes 1 minority (African American). Average age 34. 8 applicants, 75% accepted. In 1997, 12 master's awarded. *Degree requirements:* For master's, departmental qualifying exam. *Entrance requirements:* For CAS, minimum GPA of 2.5. Application deadline: rolling. Application fee: $40 ($75 for international students). *Expenses:* Tuition $10,968 per year full-time, $457 per credit hour part-time. Fees $670 per year full-time, $112 per semester (minimum) part-time. *Financial aid:* Application deadline 9/1. • Dr. Charol Shakeshaft, Director, 516-463-5762. Fax: 516-463-6503. E-mail: edacss@hofstra.edu. Application contact: Mary Beth Carey, Dean of Admissions, 516-463-6700. Fax: 516-560-7660. E-mail: hofstra@hofstra.edu.

Hunter College of the City University of New York, Division of Education, Secondary Education Curriculum, Concentration in English Education, 695 Park Avenue, New York, NY 10021-5085. Awards MA. Part-time programs available. *Entrance requirements:* TOEFL (minimum score 575). Application deadline: 4/28 (rolling processing; 11/21 for spring admission). Application fee: $35. *Expenses:* Tuition $4350 per year full-time, $185 per credit part-time for state residents; $7600 per year full-time, $320 per credit part-time for nonresidents. Fees $26 per year.

Indiana University Bloomington, College of Arts and Sciences, Department of English, Bloomington, IN 47405. Offerings include English education (MAT). Department faculty: 59 full-time (20 women). *Application deadline:* 1/15 (priority date; 9/1 for spring admission). *Application fee:* $35. *Expenses:* Tuition $153 per credit hour for state residents; $446 per credit hour for nonresidents. Fees $343 per year. • Kenneth R. Johnston, Chair, 812-855-8224. Application contact: Donna Stanger, Director of Graduate Studies, 812-855-1543. Fax: 812-855-9535.

Indiana University of Pennsylvania, College of Humanities and Social Sciences, Department of English, Program in Rhetoric and Linguistics, Indiana, PA 15705-1087. Offerings include teaching English (MAT). *Application deadline:* 7/1 (priority date; rolling processing; 11/1 for spring admission). *Application fee:* $30. *Expenses:* Tuition $3468 per year full-time, $193 per credit part-time for state residents; $6236 per year full-time, $346 per credit part-time for nonresidents. Fees $313 per year (minimum) full-time, $84 per year part-time. • Dr. Dan Tannacito, Graduate Coordinator, 724-357-7675. E-mail: djt@grove.iup.edu.

Iona College, School of Arts and Science, Program in Secondary School Subjects, 715 North Avenue, New Rochelle, NY 10801-1890. Offerings include English education (MS Ed, MST). Program faculty: 4 full-time (1 woman), 8 part-time (2 women). *Degree requirements:* Thesis or alternative required, foreign language not required. *Entrance requirements:* Minimum GPA of 2.5 (MST), New York teaching certificate (MS Ed). Application deadline: rolling. Application fee: $25. *Expenses:* Tuition $455 per credit hour. Fees $25 per semester. • Dr. Lucy Murphy, Chair, 914-633-2210. Fax: 914-633-2608. Application contact: Arlene Melillo, Director of Graduate Recruitment, 914-633-2328. Fax: 914-633-2023.

Jackson State University, School of Liberal Arts, Department of English and Modern Foreign Languages, Jackson, MS 39217. Offerings include teaching English (MAT). Department faculty: 11 full-time (10 women), 1 (woman) part-time. *Application deadline:* 3/1 (priority date; rolling processing; 10/1 for spring admission). *Application fee:* $20. *Tuition:* $2688 per year (minimum) full-time, $150 per semester hour part-time for state residents; $5546 per year (minimum) full-time, $309 per semester hour part-time for nonresidents. • Dr. Inez Morris, Chair, 601-968-2111. Fax: 601-974-5942. Application contact: Mae Robinson, Admissions Coordinator, 601-968-2455. Fax: 601-968-8246. E-mail: mrobinson@ccaix.jsums.edu.

Jacksonville University, College of Arts and Sciences, Division of Education, Program in English, 2800 University Boulevard North, Jacksonville, FL 32211-3394. Awards MAT. Part-time and evening/weekend programs available. *Degree requirements:* Comprehensive exam required, foreign language and thesis not required. *Entrance requirements:* GRE General Test (minimum combined score of 900), TOEFL (minimum score 500), minimum GPA of 3.0. Application deadline: 8/1 (priority date; rolling processing; 11/1 for spring admission). Application fee: $25.

Kutztown University of Pennsylvania, Graduate School, College of Education, Program in Secondary Education, Kutztown, PA 19530. Offerings include English (M Ed). Accredited by NCATE. Program faculty: 7 full-time (1 woman). *Degree requirements:* Comprehensive exam required, thesis optional, foreign language not required. *Entrance requirements:* GRE General Test, TOEFL, TSE. Application deadline: 3/1 (8/1 for spring admission). Application fee: $25. *Tuition:* $4111 per year full-time, $225 per credit hour part-time for state residents; $6879 per year full-time, $393 per credit hour part-time for nonresidents. • Kathleen Dolgos, Chairperson, 610-683-4259.

Lander University, School of Education, Greenwood, SC 29649-2099. Offerings include English (MAT). School faculty: 9 full-time (5 women). *Application deadline:* rolling. *Application fee:* $25. *Tuition:* $3700 per year full-time, $148 per semester hour part-time for state residents; $6326 per year full-time, $253 per semester hour part-time for nonresidents. • Dr. Phil Bennett, Dean, 864-388-8225.

Lehman College of the City University of New York, Division of Education, Department of Secondary, Adult and Business Education, Program in English Education, 250 Bedford Park Boulevard West, Bronx, NY 10468-1589. Awards MS Ed. Students: 3 full-time (2 women), 35 part-time (22 women). *Entrance requirements:* Minimum GPA of 3.0 in English, 2.8 overall; teaching certificate. Application deadline: 4/1 (rolling processing; 11/1 for spring admission). Application fee: $40. *Expenses:* Tuition $4350 per year full-time, $185 per credit part-time for state residents; $7600 per year full-time, $320 per credit part-time for nonresidents. Fees $120 per year full-time, $80 per year part-time. *Financial aid:* Full and partial tuition waivers, Federal Work-Study available. Aid available to part-time students. Financial aid application deadline: 5/15; applicants required to submit FAFSA. • Stanley Banks, Adviser, 718-960-8171.

Long Island University, Brooklyn Campus, Richard L. Conolly College of Liberal Arts and Sciences, Department of English, Brooklyn, NY 11201-8423. Offerings include teaching of writing (MA). Department faculty: 13 full-time, 1 part-time. *Degree requirements:* Thesis or alternative required, foreign language not required. *Application deadline:* rolling. *Application fee:* $30. Electronic applications accepted. *Expenses:* Tuition $480 per credit. Fees $415 per year full-time, $73 per semester (minimum) part-time. • Dr. Barbara Henning, Chair, 718-488-1050. Application contact: Bernard W. Sullivan, Associate Director of Admissions, 718-488-1011.

Long Island University, C.W. Post Campus, School of Education, Department of Curriculum and Instruction, Brookville, NY 11548-1300. Offerings include English education (MS). Department faculty: 10 full-time (5 women), 46 part-time (19 women). *Application deadline:* rolling. *Application fee:* $30. Electronic applications accepted. *Expenses:* Tuition $480 per credit. Fees $316 per year full-time, $71 per semester (minimum) part-time. • Dr. Anthony De Falco, Chairperson, 516-299-2372. Application contact: Camille Marziliano, Academic Counselor, 516-299-2123. Fax: 516-299-4167. E-mail: cmarzili@eagle.liunet.edu.

Longwood College, Department of Education, Farmville, VA 23909-1800. Offerings include curriculum and instruction specialist-elementary (MS), with options in English (MS), mild disabilities (MS), modern language (MS), physical education (MS), speech and drama (MS). Accredited by NCATE. Department faculty: 34 part-time. *Degree requirements:* Thesis (for some programs), comprehensive exam. *Entrance requirements:* Minimum GPA of 2.5. Application deadline: 5/1 (priority date; rolling processing; 10/15 for spring admission). Application fee: $25. *Expenses:* Tuition $3048 per year full-time, $127 per credit hour part-time for state residents; $8160 per year full-time, $340 per credit hour part-time for nonresidents. Fees $920 per year full-time, $31 per credit hour part-time. • Dr. Frank Howe, Chair, 804-395-2324. Application contact: Admissions Office, 804-395-2060.

Louisiana Tech University, College of Education, Department of Curriculum, Instruction and Leadership, Ruston, LA 71272. Offerings include secondary education (M Ed), with options in business education, English education, foreign language education, health and physical education, mathematics education, science education, social studies education, speech education. Accredited by NCATE. Department faculty: 16 full-time (11 women). *Application deadline:* 7/29 (2/3 for spring admission). *Application fee:* $20 ($30 for international students). *Tuition:* $2382 per year full-time, $223 per quarter (minimum) part-time for state residents; $5307 per year full-time, $223 per quarter (minimum) part-time for nonresidents. • Dr. Samuel V. Dauzat, Head, 318-257-4609.

Loyola Marymount University, School of Education, Program in Teaching, Los Angeles, CA 90045-8350. Offerings include English education (MAT). Program faculty: 14 full-time (8 women), 25 part-time (20 women). *Degree requirements:* Thesis or alternative, comprehensive exam required, foreign language not required. *Entrance requirements:* GRE General Test, TOEFL (minimum score 550), interview. Application fee: $35. Electronic applications accepted. *Expenses:* Tuition $500 per unit. Fees $111 per year full-time, $28 per year part-time. • Coordinator, 310-338-7307.

Lynchburg College, School of Education and Human Development, Lynchburg, VA 24501-3199. Offerings include English education (M Ed). M Ed (adapted physical education, physical education) admissions temporarily suspended. *Entrance requirements:* Minimum GPA of 3.0 (undergraduate). Application fee: $20.

Manhattanville College, School of Education, Program in Secondary Education, Purchase, NY 10577-2132. Offerings include English (MAT). *Degree requirements:* Thesis, comprehensive exam or research project required, foreign language not required. *Entrance requirements:* Minimum undergraduate GPA of 3.0. Application deadline: rolling. Application fee: $40. *Expenses:* Tuition $410 per credit (minimum). Fees $25 per semester. • Application contact: Carol Messar, Director of Admissions, 914-323-5142. Fax: 914-323-5493.

Mankato State University, College of Arts and Humanities, Department of English, South Rd and Ellis Ave, PO Box 8400, Mankato, MN 56002-8400. Offerings include teaching English (MS, MT). One or more programs accredited by NCATE. Department faculty: 24 full-time (12 women). *Application deadline:* 7/10 (priority date; rolling processing; 10/30 for spring admission). *Application fee:* $20. *Tuition:* $126 per credit (minimum) for state residents; $200 per credit for nonresidents. • Anne O'Meara, Chairperson, 507-389-2117. Application contact: Joni Roberts, Admissions Coordinator, 507-389-2321. Fax: 507-389-5974. E-mail: grad@mankato.msus.edu.

McNeese State University, College of Education, Department of Curriculum and Instruction, Program in Secondary Education, Lake Charles, LA 70609-2495. Offerings include English education (M Ed). Program faculty: 8 full-time (3 women). *Entrance requirements:* GRE General Test, teaching certificate. Application deadline: 7/15 (priority date; rolling processing). Application fee: $10 ($25 for international students). *Tuition:* $2118 per year full-time, $344 per

Directory: English Education

McNeese State University (continued)
semester (minimum) part-time for state residents; $7308 per year full-time, $344 per semester (minimum) part-time for nonresidents. • Dr. Everett Waddell Burge, Head, Department of Curriculum and Instruction, 318-475-5404.

Mercer University, School of Education, 1400 Coleman Avenue, Macon, GA 31207-0003. Offerings include English education (M Ed). School faculty: 11 full-time (5 women), 17 part-time (11 women). *Degree requirements:* Research project report required, foreign language and thesis not required. *Entrance requirements:* GRE, MAT, NTE, minimum GPA of 2.75. Application deadline: 8/1 (priority date; rolling processing; 12/1 for spring admission). Application fee: $25. *Tuition:* $180 per credit hour. • Dr. Anne Hathaway, Dean, 912-752-5397. Fax: 912-752-2280. E-mail: hathaway_ha@mercer.edu. Application contact: Dr. Louis Gallien, Chair, Department of Teacher Education, 912-752-2585. Fax: 912-752-2576. E-mail: gallien_lb@mercer.edu.

Miami University, College of Arts and Sciences, Department of English, Oxford, OH 45056. Offerings include English education (MAT). Accredited by NCATE. Department faculty: 60. *Application deadline:* 2/1 (rolling processing; 12/1 for spring admission). *Application fee:* $35. *Tuition:* $5932 per year full-time, $255 per credit hour part-time for state residents; $12,392 per year full-time, $524 per credit hour part-time for nonresidents. • Kerry Powell, Director of Graduate Study, 513-529-7530.

Michigan State University, College of Arts and Letters, Department of English, East Lansing, MI 48824-1020. Offerings include secondary school/community college teaching (MA). Department faculty: 51 (17 women). *Degree requirements:* Thesis (for some programs). *Entrance requirements:* GRE General Test, GRE Subject Test. Application deadline: 1/10 (priority date; rolling processing). Application fee: $30 ($40 for international students). *Expenses:* Tuition $4609 per year full-time, $223 per credit hour (minimum) part-time for state residents; $8704 per year full-time, $450 per credit hour (minimum) part-time for nonresidents. Fees $576 per year full-time, $476 per year part-time. • Dr. Patrick O'Donnell, Interim Chairperson, 517-355-7570. Application contact: Dr. Robert Uphaus, Associate Chairperson, Graduate Studies, 517-355-7570. Fax: 517-353-3755. E-mail: uphaus@pilot.msu.edu.

Millersville University of Pennsylvania, School of Humanities and Social Sciences, Department of English, Millersville, PA 17551-0302. Offerings include English education (M Ed). Accredited by NCATE. Department faculty: 24 full-time (13 women), 14 part-time (10 women). *Application deadline:* 5/1 (priority date; rolling processing). *Application fee:* $25. *Tuition:* $3468 per year full-time, $234 per credit part-time for state residents; $6236 per year full-time, $387 per credit part-time for nonresidents. • Dr. Robert Carballo, Coordinator, 717-872-3848. Fax: 717-871-2003. Application contact: Dr. Robert J. Labriola, Dean of Graduate Studies, 717-872-3030. Fax: 717-871-2022.

Mills College, Education Department, Oakland, CA 94613-1000. Offerings include education (MA), with options in curriculum and instruction, elementary education, English education, mathematics education, science education, secondary education, social sciences education, teaching. Department faculty: 8 full-time (6 women), 13 part-time (11 women), 11 FTE. *Degree requirements:* Comprehensive exam required, thesis not required. *Average time to degree:* master's–2 years full-time. *Entrance requirements:* TOEFL (minimum score 550). Application deadline: 2/1 (priority date; rolling processing; 11/1 for spring admission). Application fee: $50. Electronic applications accepted. *Expenses:* Tuition $10,600 per year full-time, $2560 per year part-time. Fees $468 per year. • Jane Bowyer, Chairperson, 510-430-2118. Fax: 510-430-3314. E-mail: grad-studies@mills.edu. Application contact: La Vonna S. Brown, Coordinator of Graduate Studies, 510-430-3309. Fax: 510-430-2159. E-mail: grad-studies@mills.edu.

Minot State University, Program in English, Minot, ND 58707-0002. Awards MAT. *Entrance requirements:* GRE General Test (minimum combined score of 1100 rquired) or minimum GPA of 3.0. Application fee: $25. *Tuition:* $2714 per year for state residents; $3235 per year (minimum) for nonresidents. *Financial aid:* Application deadline 4/1. • Dr. Thomas Van Gunden, Chairperson. Application contact: Tammy White, Administrative Secretary, 701-858-3250. Fax: 701-839-6933.

National–Louis University, National College of Education, McGaw Graduate School, Programs in Reading and Language, 2840 Sheridan Road, Evanston, IL 60201-1730. Offerings in language and literacy (M Ed, MS Ed, CAS), reading recovery (CAS), reading specialist (M Ed, MS Ed, CAS). Part-time and evening/weekend programs available. Students: 4 full-time (all women), 84 part-time (82 women); includes 2 minority (1 Asian American, 1 Hispanic). Average age 39. In 1997, 47 master's, 2 CASs awarded. *Degree requirements:* For master's, thesis required (for some programs), foreign language not required. *Entrance requirements:* For master's, MAT, minimum GPA of 3.0. Application deadline: rolling. Application fee: $25. *Tuition:* $411 per semester hour. *Financial aid:* Fellowships, research assistantships, and career-related internships or fieldwork available. Aid available to part-time students. Financial aid applicants required to submit FAFSA. • Dr. Camille Blachowicz, Coordinator, 847-475-1100 Ext. 2558. Application contact: Dr. David McCulloch, Vice President for University Services, 800-443-5522 Ext. 5127. Fax: 847-465-0593. E-mail: dmcc@wheeling1.nl.edu.

New York University, School of Education, Department of Teaching and Learning, Program in English Education, New York, NY 10012-1019. Awards MA, PhD, CAS. Part-time and evening/weekend programs available. Faculty: 4 full-time (1 woman), 13 part-time. Students: 52 full-time, 117 part-time. 115 applicants, 63% accepted. In 1997, 37 master's, 13 doctorates awarded. Terminal master's awarded for partial completion of doctoral program. *Degree requirements:* For master's, thesis required (for some programs), foreign language not required; for doctorate, dissertation. *Entrance requirements:* For master's, TOEFL; for doctorate, GRE General Test, TOEFL, interview; for CAS, TOEFL, master's degree. Application deadline: 2/1 (priority date; rolling processing; 12/1 for spring admission). Application fee: $40 ($60 for international students). *Financial aid:* Partial tuition waivers, Federal Work-Study, institutionally sponsored loans, and career-related internships or fieldwork available. Aid available to part-time students. Financial aid application deadline: 3/1; applicants required to submit FAFSA. *Faculty research:* Educational linguistics and language development, making meaning of literature, teaching of literature, sociolinguistics. • John Mayher, Director, 212-998-5233. Application contact: Office of Graduate Admissions, 212-998-5030. Fax: 212-995-4328.

North Carolina Agricultural and Technical State University, Graduate School, School of Education, Department of Curriculum and Instruction, Program in Intermediate Education, Greensboro, NC 27411. Offerings include English education (MS). Accredited by NCATE. *Degree requirements:* Thesis (for some programs), comprehensive exam, qualifying exam required, foreign language not required. *Entrance requirements:* GRE General Test, minimum GPA of 3.0. Application deadline: 6/1 (priority date; rolling processing; 12/1 for spring admission). Application fee: $35. *Tuition:* $1662 per year full-time, $272 per semester (minimum) part-time for state residents; $8790 per year full-time, $2054 per semester (minimum) part-time for nonresidents. • Dr. Dorothy Leflore, Interim Chairperson, Department of Curriculum and Instruction, 336-334-7848.

Northeastern Illinois University, College of Education, Department of Teacher Education, Chicago, IL 60625-4699. Offerings include instruction (MSI), with option in language arts; teaching (MAT), with option in language arts; teaching of language arts (M Ed). Department faculty: 29 full-time (19 women), 10 part-time (8 women). *Application deadline:* 3/18 (priority date; rolling processing; 9/30 for spring admission). *Application fee:* $0. *Expenses:* Tuition $2226 per year full-time, $93 per credit hour part-time for state residents; $6678 per year full-time, $278 per credit hour part-time for nonresidents. Fees $358 per year full-time, $14.90 per credit hour part-time. • Dr. Beverly Otto, Chairperson, 773-794-2751. Application contact: Dr. Mohan K. Sood, Dean of Graduate College, 773-583-4050 Ext. 6143. Fax: 773-794-6670.

Northeast Louisiana University, College of Education, Department of Curriculum and Instruction, Monroe, LA 71209-0001. Offerings include English education (M Ed). Accredited by NCATE. *Entrance requirements:* GRE General Test, minimum GPA of 2.5. Application fee: $15 ($25 for international students). *Tuition:* $2028 per year full-time, $240 per semester (minimum) part-time for state residents; $6852 per year full-time, $240 per semester (minimum) part-time for nonresidents.

Northern State University, Division of Graduate Studies in Education, Program in Teaching and Learning, Aberdeen, SD 57401-7198. Offerings include language and literacy (MS Ed). Accredited by NCATE. Offered jointly with Huron University, Jamestown College, and the University of Mary. Program faculty: 98 full-time (28 women). *Degree requirements:* Thesis required, foreign language not required. *Average time to degree:* master's–1.5 years full-time. *Entrance requirements:* Minimum GPA of 2.75. Application deadline: 8/15 (priority date; rolling processing; 12/15 for spring admission). Application fee: $15. *Expenses:* Tuition $1999 per year full-time, $83 per credit hour part-time for state residents; $6034 per year full-time, $251 per credit hour part-time for nonresidents. Fees $954 per year full-time, $40 per credit hour part-time. • Dr. Paul Deputy, Head, 605-626-2415. Application contact: Dr. Sharon Tebben, Director of Graduate Studies, 605-626-2558. Fax: 605-626-2542.

North Georgia College & State University, Graduate School, Program in Education, Dahlonega, GA 30597-1001. Offerings include secondary education (M Ed), with options in art education, biology education, chemistry education, English education, mathematics education, modern languages education, physical education, science education, social science education. Accredited by NCATE. Program faculty: 57 full-time (15 women), 7 part-time (4 women). *Degree requirements:* Comprehensive exam required, thesis optional, foreign language not required. *Entrance requirements:* GRE General Test (minimum combined score of 800) or MAT (minimum score 44), minimum GPA of 2.75. Application deadline: 9/1 (priority date; rolling processing). Application fee: $25. • Dr. Bob Michael, Dean, School of Education, 706-864-1533. Application contact: Mai-Lan Ledbetter, Coordinator of Graduate Admissions, 706-864-1543. Fax: 706-864-1668. E-mail: mledbetter@nugget.ngc.peachnet.edu.

Northwestern State University of Louisiana, Department of Language and Communication, Natchitoches, LA 71497. Offerings include English education (MA). Accredited by NCATE. Department faculty: 6 full-time (3 women). *Degree requirements:* 1 foreign language, thesis or alternative. *Entrance requirements:* GRE General Test (minimum combined score of 800), minimum undergraduate GPA of 2.5. Application deadline: 8/1 (priority date; rolling processing; 1/10 for spring admission). Application fee: $15 ($25 for international students). *Tuition:* $2147 per year full-time, $336 per semester (minimum) part-time for state residents; $6437 per year full-time, $336 per semester (minimum) part-time for nonresidents. • Dr. Gary Ross, Chairman, 318-357-6272. Application contact: Dr. Tom Hanson, Dean, Graduate Studies and Research, 318-357-5851. Fax: 318-357-5019.

Northwest Missouri State University, College of Arts and Sciences, Department of English, 800 University Drive, Maryville, MO 64468-6001. Offerings include teaching English (MS Ed). Department faculty: 16 full-time (5 women). *Application deadline:* rolling. *Application fee:* $0 ($50 for international students). *Expenses:* Tuition $113 per credit hour for state residents; $197 per credit hour for nonresidents. Fees $3 per credit hour. • Dr. Allen Schwab, Chairperson, 816-562-1265. Application contact: Dr. Frances Shipley, Dean of Graduate School, 816-562-1145. E-mail: gradsch@acad.nwmissouri.edu.

Nova Southeastern University, Fischler Center for the Advancement of Education, Graduate Teacher Education Program, Fort Lauderdale, FL 33314-7721. Offerings include English (MS, Ed S). *Degree requirements:* Thesis, practicum required, foreign language not required. *Entrance requirements:* For master's, teaching certificate; for Ed S, master's degree, teaching certificate. Application deadline: rolling. Application fee: $50. *Tuition:* $245 per credit hour (minimum). • Dr. Deo Nellis, Dean, 954-262-8601. E-mail: deo@fcae.nova.edu. Application contact: Dr. Mark Seldine, Director of Student Affairs, 954-262-8689. Fax: 954-262-3910. E-mail: seldines@fcae.nova.edu.

Occidental College, Department of Education, Program in Secondary Education, Los Angeles, CA 90041-3392. Offerings include English and comparative literary studies (MAT). Program faculty: 4 full-time (1 woman). *Degree requirements:* Internship required, foreign language and thesis not required. *Entrance requirements:* GRE General Test (minimum score 550 on each section or combined score of 1650 on three sections), TOEFL (minimum score 600), minimum GPA of 3.0. Application deadline: 3/1 (priority date; rolling processing; 10/1 for spring admission). Application fee: $40. *Expenses:* Tuition $21,256 per year full-time, $865 per unit part-time. Fees $314 per year. • Application contact: Susan Molik, Administrative Assistant, Graduate Office, 213-259-2921.

Oregon State University, Graduate School, College of Liberal Arts, Department of English, Program in Language Arts Education, Corvallis, OR 97331. Awards MAT. Accredited by NCATE. Faculty: Students: 6 full-time (all women). Average age 29. 20 applicants, 50% accepted. In 1997, 5 degrees awarded (100% found work related to degree). *Degree requirements:* 1 foreign language, thesis, minimum GPA of 3.0. *Entrance requirements:* GRE General Test, TOEFL (minimum score 550), NTE, California Basic Educational Skills Test, minimum GPA of 3.0 in last 90 hours. Application deadline: 1/15 (rolling processing). Application fee: $50. *Tuition:* $6207 per year full-time, $810 per quarter (minimum) part-time for state residents; $10,551 per year full-time, $1293 per quarter (minimum) part-time for nonresidents. *Financial aid:* In 1997–98, 2 students received aid, including 2 fellowships (both to first-year students); Federal Work-Study, institutionally sponsored loans, and career-related internships or fieldwork also available. Aid available to part-time students. Financial aid application deadline: 2/1. *Faculty research:* Literacy and composition, literacy and literature. Total annual research expenditures: $1500. • Dr. Anita Helle, Coordinator, 541-737-1630. E-mail: hellea@cla.orst.edu. Application contact: Lance Haddon, 541-737-5956.

Plattsburgh State University of New York, Faculty of Professional Studies, Center for Educational Studies and Services, Program in Secondary Education, Plattsburgh, NY 12901-2681. Offerings include English (MS Ed, MST). *Degree requirements:* Comprehensive exam or research project required, thesis optional. *Entrance requirements:* GRE General Test or MAT, minimum GPA of 2.5. Application deadline: rolling. Application fee: $50. *Expenses:* Tuition $5100 per year full-time, $213 per credit hour part-time for state residents; $8416 per year full-time, $351 per credit hour part-time for nonresidents. Fees $395 per year full-time, $15.10 per credit hour part-time. • Dr. Raymond Domenico, Director and Associate Dean, Center for Educational Studies and Services, 518-564-2122.

Purdue University, School of Education, Department of Curriculum and Instruction, West Lafayette, IN 47907. Offerings include language arts (MS Ed, PhD, Ed S). Accredited by NCATE. Department faculty: 34 full-time (15 women), 3 part-time (1 woman). *Degree requirements:* For master's, thesis optional; for doctorate, dissertation, oral and written exams; for Ed S, oral presentation, project required, thesis not required. *Entrance requirements:* For master's, TOEFL (minimum score 550), minimum B average; for doctorate, GRE General Test (minimum score 500 on each section), TOEFL (minimum score 550); for Ed S, minimum B average. Application deadline: 1/15 (priority date; 9/15 for spring admission). Application fee: $30. Electronic applications accepted. *Tuition:* $3500 per year full-time, $126 per credit hour part-time for state residents; $11,720 per year full-time, $387 per credit hour part-time for nonresidents. • Dr. J. L. Peters, Head, 765-494-9172. Fax: 765-496-1622. E-mail: peters@purdue.edu. Application contact: Christine Larsen, Coordinator of Graduate Studies, 765-494-2345. Fax: 765-494-5832. E-mail: gradoffice@soe.purdue.edu.

Queens College of the City University of New York, Social Science Division, School of Education, Department of Secondary Education, 65-30 Kissena Boulevard, Flushing, NY 11367-1597. Offerings include English (MS Ed, AC). *Degree requirements:* For master's, research project required, foreign language and thesis not required; for AC, thesis optional, foreign language not required. *Entrance requirements:* For master's, TOEFL (minimum score 600), minimum GPA of 3.0; for AC, TOEFL (minimum score 600). Application deadline: 4/1 (rolling processing; 11/1 for spring admission). Application fee: $40. *Expenses:* Tuition $4350 per year full-time, $185 per credit part-time for state residents; $7600 per year full-time, $320 per credit part-time for nonresidents. Fees $104 per year. • Dr. Philip Anderson, Chairperson, 718-997-5150. Application contact: Mario Caruso, Director of Graduate Admissions, 718-997-5200. Fax: 718-997-5193. E-mail: graduate%queens.bitnet@cunyvm.cuny.edu.

Quinnipiac College, School of Liberal Arts, Program in Secondary and Middle School Teaching, Hamden, CT 06518-1904. Offerings include English (MAT). Program faculty: 21 full-time (5 women), 16 part-time (9 women). *Degree requirements:* Thesis. *Average time to degree:* master's–1.5 years full-time, 3 years part-time. *Entrance requirements:* PRAXIS I, minimum GPA of 2.67. Application deadline: rolling. Application fee: $45. Electronic applications accepted. *Expenses:* Tuition $395 per credit hour. Fees $380 per year full-time. • Carol Orticari, Director, 203-281-8978. Fax: 203-281-8709. E-mail: orticari@quinnipiac.edu. Application contact: Scott Farber, Director of Graduate Admissions, 203-281-8795. Fax: 203-287-5238. E-mail: qcgradadmi@quinnipiac.edu.

Rockford College, Department of Education, Program in Secondary Education, Rockford, IL 61108-2393. Offerings include English (MAT). Program faculty: 15 full-time (2 women), 8 part-time (6 women), 17 FTE. *Degree requirements:* Thesis optional, foreign language not required. *Entrance requirements:* GRE General Test (minimum combined score of 1000). Application deadline: rolling. Application fee: $35. *Tuition:* $15,500 per year full-time, $400 per credit part-time. • Dr. Debra Dew, Head, 815-392-5202. Fax: 815-226-4119.

Rollins College, Program in Education, Winter Park, FL 32789-4499. Offerings include secondary education (MAT), with options in English, mathematics, music. Program faculty: 13 full-time (8 women), 11 part-time (4 women), 17 FTE. *Application deadline:* rolling. *Application fee:* $50. *Tuition:* $190 per hour. • Dr. Nancy McAleer, Director, 407-646-2305. Application contact: Laura Pfister, Coordinator of Records and Registration, 407-646-2416. Fax: 407-646-1551.

Rutgers, The State University of New Jersey, New Brunswick, Graduate School of Education, Department of Learning and Teaching, Program in English Education, New Brunswick, NJ 08903. Awards Ed M. Part-time programs available. Faculty: 2 full-time (1 woman). Students: 51; includes 8 minority (2 African Americans, 4 Asian Americans, 2 Hispanics). 58 applicants, 55% accepted. In 1997, 15 degrees awarded. *Degree requirements:* Comprehensive exam or paper required, thesis not required. *Entrance requirements:* GRE General Test. Application deadline: 3/1 (11/1 for spring admission). Application fee: $40. *Expenses:* Tuition $6492 per year full-time, $268 per credit part-time for state residents; $9520 per year full-time, $395 per credit part-time for nonresidents. Fees $208 per year (minimum). *Financial aid:* Application deadline 3/1. • Dr. Michael Smith, Coordinator, 732-932-7496 Ext. 120.

Salem State College, Department of Education, Salem, MA 01970-5353. Offerings include English (MAT). Accredited by NCATE. MAT (English as a second language) offered jointly with the Department of English. *Application deadline:* rolling. *Application fee:* $25. *Expenses:* Tuition $140 per credit hour for state residents; $230 per credit hour for nonresidents. Fees $20 per credit hour.

Salisbury State University, Department of Education, Salisbury, MD 21801-6837. Offerings include English (M Ed). Department faculty: 19 full-time (10 women), 2 part-time (1 woman). *Application deadline:* 8/1 (priority date; rolling processing; 1/1 for spring admission). *Application fee:* $30. *Expenses:* Tuition $158 per credit hour for state residents; $310 per credit hour for nonresidents. Fees $4 per credit hour. • Dr. Ellen Whitford, Chair, 410-543-6294. E-mail: evwhitford@ssu.edu. Application contact: Phyllis Meyer, Administrative Aide II, 410-543-6281. Fax: 410-548-2593. E-mail: phmeyer@ssu.edu.

San Francisco State University, College of Humanities, Department of English Language and Literature, San Francisco, CA 94132-1722. Offerings include teaching composition (Certificate). *Average time to degree:* master's–2 years full-time, 3.5 years part-time. *Application deadline:* rolling. *Application fee:* $55. *Expenses:* Tuition $0 for state residents; $246 per unit for nonresidents. Fees $1982 per year full-time, $1316 per year part-time.

Smith College, Department of Education and Child Study, Program in Secondary Education, Northampton, MA 01063. Offerings include English education (MAT). Program faculty: 6 full-time (3 women), 3 part-time (2 women). *Degree requirements:* 1 foreign language required, thesis not required. *Average time to degree:* master's–1 year full-time, 4 years part-time. *Entrance requirements:* GRE General Test or MAT. Application deadline: 4/15 (12/1 for spring admission). Application fee: $50. *Tuition:* $21,680 per year full-time, $2720 per course part-time. • Rosetta Cohen, Head, 413-585-3266. E-mail: rcohen@sophia.smith.edu.

South Carolina State University, School of Education, Department of Teacher Education, 300 College Street Northeast, Orangeburg, SC 29117-0001. Offerings include secondary education (M Ed), with options in biology education, business education, counselor education, English education, home economics education, industrial education, mathematics education, science education, social studies education. Accredited by NCATE. Department faculty: 7 full-time (3 women), 2 part-time (1 woman). *Average time to degree:* master's–2 years full-time, 4 years part-time. *Application deadline:* 7/15 (priority date; rolling processing; 11/10 for spring admission). *Application fee:* $25. *Tuition:* $2974 per year full-time, $165 per credit hour part-time. • Dr. Jesse Kinard, Chairman, 803-536-8934. Application contact: Dr. Gail Joyner-Fleming, Interim Associate Dean and Director, Graduate Teacher Education, 803-536-8824. Fax: 803-536-8492.

Southern Illinois University at Edwardsville, College of Arts and Sciences, Department of English Language and Literature, Program in Teaching of Writing, Edwardsville, IL 62026-0001. Awards MA. Students: 8 full-time (7 women), 1 (woman) part-time; includes 1 minority (African American). 4 applicants, 75% accepted. In 1997, 4 degrees awarded. *Degree requirements:* 1 foreign language, thesis or alternative, final exam. *Application deadline:* 7/24. *Application fee:* $25. *Expenses:* Tuition $1716 per year full-time, $95 per credit hour part-time for state residents; $5149 per year full-time, $286 per credit hour part-time for nonresidents. Fees $463 per year full-time, $433 per year part-time. *Financial aid:* In 1997–98, 4 teaching assistantships, 3 assistantships were awarded; fellowships, research assistantships, Federal Work-Study, institutionally sponsored loans also available. Aid available to part-time students. • Application contact: David Butler, Director, 618-692-2060.

Stanford University, School of Education, Teacher Education Program, Stanford, CA 94305-9991. Offerings include English education (AM). *Degree requirements:* Thesis required, foreign language not required. *Entrance requirements:* GRE General Test. Application deadline: 1/15. Application fee: $65 ($75 for international students). *Expenses:* Tuition $22,110 per year. Fees $156 per year. • Administrator, 650-723-4891. Application contact: Graduate Admissions Office, 650-723-2110.

State University of New York at Binghamton, School of Education and Human Development, Program in Secondary Education, Binghamton, NY 13902-6000. Offerings include English education (MAT, MS Ed, MST). *Entrance requirements:* GRE General Test, TOEFL. Application deadline: 4/15 (priority date; rolling processing; 11/1 for spring admission). Application fee: $50. Electronic applications accepted. *Expenses:* Tuition $5100 per year full-time, $213 per credit hour part-time for state residents; $8416 per year full-time, $351 per credit hour part-time for nonresidents. Fees $654 per year full-time, $75 per semester (minimum) part-time. • Dr. Wayne Ross, Coordinator, 607-777-2478.

State University of New York at Buffalo, Graduate School, Graduate School of Education, Department of Learning and Instruction, Buffalo, NY 14260. Offerings include secondary education (Ed M, Ed D, PhD), with options in English education (Ed D, PhD), foreign language education (Ed D, PhD), mathematics education (Ed D, PhD), science education (PhD). Terminal master's awarded for partial completion of doctoral program. Department faculty: 20 full-time (9 women), 7 part-time (2 women). *Degree requirements:* Dissertation, research analysis exam required, foreign language not required. *Entrance requirements:* GRE General Test, TOEFL (minimum score 600), interview. Application deadline: 2/1 (11/15 for spring admission). Application fee: $50. *Tuition:* $5970 per year full-time, $288 per credit hour part-time for state residents; $9286 per year full-time, $426 per credit hour part-time for nonresidents. • Dr. Michael Kibby, Chair, 716-645-2455. Application contact: Barbara Cracchiolo, Admissions Secretary, 716-645-2457. Fax: 716-645-3161.

State University of New York at Stony Brook, School of Professional Development and Continuing Studies, Stony Brook, NY 11794. Offerings include English-grade 7-12 (MAT). School faculty: 1 full-time, 101 part-time. *Application deadline:* 1/15. *Application fee:* $50. *Expenses:* Tuition $5100 per year full-time, $213 per credit hour part-time for state residents; $8416 per year full-time, $351 per credit hour part-time for nonresidents. Fees $529 per year full-time, $77 per semester (minimum) part-time. • Dr. Paul J. Edelson, Dean, 516-632-7052. E-mail: paul.edelson@sunysb.edu. Application contact: Sandra Romansky, Director of Admissions and Advisement, 516-632-7050. Fax: 516-632-9046. E-mail: sandra.romansky@sunysb.edu.

State University of New York College at Brockport, School of Professions, Department of Education and Human Development, Programs in Secondary Education, Brockport, NY 14420-2997. Offerings include English education (MS Ed). *Degree requirements:* Thesis or alternative required, foreign language not required. *Entrance requirements:* Minimum GPA of 3.0. Application deadline: 1/15 (priority date; 9/15 for spring admission). Application fee: $50. *Expenses:* Tuition $5100 per year full-time, $213 per credit hour part-time for state residents; $8416 per year full-time, $351 per credit hour part-time for nonresidents. Fees $440 per year full-time, $22.60 per credit hour part-time. • William Veenis, Chairperson, Department of Education and Human Development, 716-395-2205.

State University of New York College at Buffalo, Faculty of Arts and Humanities, Department of English, Buffalo, NY 14222-1095. Offerings include secondary education (MS Ed), with option in English. Department faculty: 16 full-time (4 women), 1 (woman) part-time. *Application deadline:* 5/1 (10/1 for spring admission). *Application fee:* $50. *Expenses:* Tuition $5100 per year full-time, $213 per credit hour part-time for state residents; $8416 per year full-time, $351 per credit hour part-time for nonresidents. Fees $195 per year full-time, $8.60 per credit hour part-time. • Dr. Craig Werner, Chairperson, 716-878-5416.

State University of New York College at Buffalo, Faculty of Applied Science and Education, Department of Elementary Education and Reading, Program in Elementary and Early Secondary Education, Buffalo, NY 14222-1095. Offerings include English education (MS Ed). Accredited by NCATE. *Degree requirements:* Thesis or project required, foreign language not required. *Entrance requirements:* Minimum GPA of 2.5 in last 60 hours, New York teaching certificate. Application deadline: 5/1 (10/1 for spring admission). Application fee: $50. *Expenses:* Tuition $5100 per year full-time, $213 per credit hour part-time for state residents; $8416 per year full-time, $351 per credit hour part-time for nonresidents. Fees $195 per year full-time, $8.60 per credit hour part-time. • Dr. Maria Ceprano, Chairperson, Department of Elementary Education and Reading, 716-878-5916.

State University of New York College at Cortland, Division of Professional Studies, Department of Education, Programs in Elementary Education, Cortland, NY 13045. Offerings include English education (MS Ed). *Degree requirements:* 1 foreign language, computer language, thesis (for some programs), comprehensive exams. *Entrance requirements:* Provisional certification. Application deadline: rolling. Application fee: $50. *Expenses:* Tuition $5100 per year full-time, $213 per credit hour part-time for state residents; $8416 per year full-time, $351 per credit hour part-time for nonresidents. Fees $644 per year full-time, $79 per semester (minimum) part-time. • Application contact: Jeanne M. Bechtel, Director of Admissions, 607-753-4711. Fax: 607-753-5998.

State University of New York College at Oneonta, Department of Education, Oneonta, NY 13820-4015. Offerings include elementary education (MS Ed), with options in early secondary English (N–9), early secondary math (N–9), early secondary social science (N–9), general science (N–9); secondary education (MS Ed), with options in biology education, chemistry education, earth science education, English education, home economics education, mathematics education, physics education, social science education. *Application deadline:* 4/15. *Application fee:* $50. *Expenses:* Tuition $5100 per year full-time, $213 per credit hour part-time for state residents; $8416 per year full-time, $351 per credit hour part-time for nonresidents. Fees $482 per year full-time, $6.85 per credit hour part-time. • Dr. Ronald Cromwell, Chair, 607-436-2538.

Syracuse University, School of Education, Department of Reading and Language Arts, Program in English Education, Syracuse, NY 13244-0003. Awards MS, Ed D, PhD, CAS. Students: 17 full-time (11 women), 11 part-time (9 women); includes 3 minority (2 African Americans, 1 Asian American), 1 international. 20 applicants, 60% accepted. In 1997, 14 master's, 1 doctorate awarded. *Degree requirements:* For master's, thesis or alternative; for doctorate and CAS, thesis/dissertation. *Entrance requirements:* GRE. Application fee: $40. *Tuition:* $13,320 per year full-time, $555 per credit hour part-time. *Financial aid:* Application deadline 3/1. • Dr. Susan Hynds, Chair, 315-443-4755.

Teachers College, Columbia University, Graduate Faculty of Education, Department of Arts and Humanities, Program in Teaching of English and English Education, 525 West 120th Street, New York, NY 10027-6696. Awards Ed M, MA, Ed D, PhD. Part-time and evening/weekend programs available. Faculty: 3 full-time (2 women), 18 part-time (9 women), 11 FTE. Students: 109 full-time (87 women), 97 part-time (77 women); includes 32 minority (18 African Americans, 7 Asian Americans, 7 Hispanics), 8 international. Average age 30. 216 applicants, 73% accepted. In 1997, 82 master's, 1 doctorate awarded. Terminal master's awarded for partial completion of doctoral program. *Degree requirements:* For doctorate, 2 foreign languages, dissertation. *Application deadline:* 5/15 (12/1 for spring admission). *Application fee:* $50. *Expenses:* Tuition $640 per credit. Fees $120 per semester. *Financial aid:* Fellowships, research assistantships, teaching assistantships, full and partial tuition waivers, Federal Work-Study, institutionally sponsored loans, and career-related internships or fieldwork available. Aid available to part-time students. Financial aid application deadline: 2/1. *Faculty research:* Teaching of writing and reading, language and curriculum, literacy and health, narrative and action research. Total annual research expenditures: $50,000. • Application contact: Amy Rotheim, Office of Admissions, 212-678-3710. Fax: 212-678-4171.

Texas A&M University–Commerce, College of Arts and Sciences, Department of Literature and Languages, Commerce, TX 75429-3011. Offerings include college teaching of English (Ed D). Terminal master's awarded for partial completion of doctoral program. Department faculty: 12 full-time (5 women), 1 part-time (0 women). *Degree requirements:* 1 foreign language (computer language can substitute), dissertation, departmental qualifying exam. *Entrance requirements:* GRE General Test. Application deadline: rolling. Application fee: $0 ($25 for international students). *Tuition:* $2382 per year full-time, $343 per semester (minimum) part-time for state residents; $7518 per year full-time, $343 per semester (minimum) part-time for nonresidents. • Dr. Gerald Duchovnay Jr., Head, 903-886-5260. Application contact: Pam Hammonds, Graduate Admissions Adviser, 903-886-5167. Fax: 903-886-5165.

Union College, Graduate and Continuing Studies, Programs in Education, Schenectady, NY 12308-2311. Offerings include English (MAT). *Application deadline:* 5/15. *Application fee:* $35. *Tuition:* $1155 per course. • Dr. Patrick Allen, Educational Studies Director, 518-388-6361.

University of Alaska Fairbanks, Graduate School, School of Education, Fairbanks, AK 99775-7480. Offerings include language and literature (M Ed). School faculty: 23 full-time (13 women), 2 part-time (both women). *Degree requirements:* Thesis or alternative, comprehensive exam required, foreign language not required. *Entrance requirements:* GRE General Test, TOEFL (minimum score 550). Application deadline: 4/1 (10/1 for spring admission). Application fee: $35. *Expenses:* Tuition $162 per credit for state residents; $316 per credit for nonresidents. Fees $520 per year full-time, $45 per semester (minimum) part-time. • Dr. Joe Kan, Director, 907-474-7341.

Directory: English Education

The University of Arizona, College of Humanities, Department of English, Tucson, AZ 85721. Offerings include rhetoric, composition and teaching of English (PhD). Terminal master's awarded for partial completion of doctoral program. *Degree requirements:* 1 foreign language, dissertation, preliminary and qualifying exams. *Entrance requirements:* GRE General Test, GRE Subject Test (literature), TOEFL, sample of written work. Application fee: $35. *Tuition:* $2162 per year full-time, $337 per semester (minimum) part-time for state residents; $6860 per year full-time, $1138 per semester (minimum) part-time for nonresidents.

University of Arkansas at Pine Bluff, Program in Education, Pine Bluff, AR 71601-2799. Offerings include secondary education (M Ed), with options in aquaculture, English, general science, mathematics, physical education, social studies. Accredited by NCATE. Program faculty: 51. *Entrance requirements:* GRE, minimum GPA of 2.75; NTE or Standard Arkansas Teaching Certificate. Application deadline: rolling. Application fee: $0. *Expenses:* Tuition $82 per credit hour for state residents; $192 per credit hour for nonresidents. Fees $25 per year. • Dr. Calvin Johnson, Dean, 870-543-8256.

University of British Columbia, Faculty of Education, Department of Language Education, Vancouver, BC V6T 1Z2, Canada. Offerings include English education (MA, M Ed, PhD). *Degree requirements:* For master's, thesis (MA) required, foreign language not required. *Entrance requirements:* For master's, TOEFL (minimum score 550), minimum B average in most recent 2 years of study with minimum of two courses at A standing. Application deadline: 2/28 (priority date; rolling processing; 8/1 for spring admission). Application fee: $60.

University of California, Berkeley, School of Education, Division of Education in Language, Literature, and Culture, Berkeley, CA 94720-1500. Offerings include English (Certificate). Division faculty: 10 full-time (5 women), 5 part-time (2 women). *Application deadline:* 12/15. *Application fee:* $40. *Expenses:* Tuition $0 for state residents; $9384 per year for nonresidents. Fees $4409 per year. • Robert B. Ruddell, Chair, 510-642-0746. Application contact: Admissions Office, 510-642-0841.

University of Central Florida, College of Education, Department of Instructional Programs, Program in English Language Education, Orlando, FL 32816. Awards MA, M Ed. Accredited by NCATE. Students: 15 full-time (13 women), 10 part-time (9 women); includes 7 minority (3 African Americans, 1 Asian American, 3 Hispanics). Average age 32. 16 applicants, 63% accepted. In 1997, 14 degrees awarded. *Degree requirements:* Thesis or alternative required, foreign language not required. *Entrance requirements:* GRE General Test (minimum combined score of 840). Application deadline: 7/15 (12/15 for spring admission). Application fee: $20. *Expenses:* Tuition $3288 per year full-time, $137 per credit hour part-time for state residents; $11,520 per year full-time, $480 per credit hour part-time for nonresidents. Fees $105 per year. • Application contact: Dr. Janet Allen, Coordinator, 407-823-6125. E-mail: allenj@pegasus.cc.ucf.edu.

University of Connecticut, School of Education, Field of English Education, Storrs, CT 06269. Awards MA, PhD. Accredited by NCATE. Faculty: 2. Students: 15 full-time (11 women), 1 (woman) part-time; includes 1 minority (Native American). Average age 26. 13 applicants, 100% accepted. In 1997, 14 master's awarded. Terminal master's awarded for partial completion of doctoral program. *Degree requirements:* For master's, thesis or alternative; for doctorate, dissertation. *Entrance requirements:* For doctorate, GRE General Test. Application deadline: 6/1 (priority date; rolling processing; 11/1 for spring admission). Application fee: $40 ($45 for international students). *Expenses:* Tuition $5272 per year full-time, $293 per credit part-time for state residents; $13,696 per year full-time, $761 per credit part-time for nonresidents. Fees $948 per year full-time, $640 per year part-time. *Financial aid:* In 1997–98, 5 research assistantships (2 to first-year students) totaling $22,444, 2 teaching assistantships (1 to a first-year student) totaling $9,619 were awarded. Financial aid application deadline: 2/15. • Thomas P. Weinland, Head, 860-486-2433.

University of Delaware, College of Arts and Science, Department of English, Newark, DE 19716. Offerings include English education (MA). Department faculty: 41 full-time (16 women). *Degree requirements:* 1 foreign language required, thesis optional. *Entrance requirements:* GRE General Test, GRE Subject Test. Application deadline: 3/1 (priority date; rolling processing; 12/1 for spring admission). Application fee: $45. *Expenses:* Tuition $4250 per year full-time, $236 per credit hour part-time for state residents; $12,250 per year full-time, $681 per credit hour part-time for nonresidents. Fees $466 per year full-time, $15 per semester (minimum) part-time. • Ann Ardis, Director of Graduate Studies in English, 302-831-2363. Fax: 302-831-1586. E-mail: dlyall@odin.udel.edu.

University of Florida, College of Education, Department of Instruction and Curriculum, Gainesville, FL 32611. Offerings include English education (MAE, M Ed, Ed D, PhD, Ed S). Accredited by NCATE. Department faculty: 42. *Degree requirements:* For master's, thesis optional, foreign language not required; for doctorate, variable foreign language requirement, dissertation. *Entrance requirements:* For master's and doctorate, GRE General Test (minimum combined score of 1000), minimum GPA of 3.0; for Ed S, GRE General Test. Application deadline: 6/5. Application fee: $20. *Tuition:* $138 per credit hour for state residents; $481 per credit hour for nonresidents. • Dr. Mary Grace Kantowski, Chair, 352-392-9191 Ext. 200. E-mail: mgk@coe.ufl.edu. Application contact: Dr. Ben Nelms, Graduate Coordinator, 352-392-9191 Ext. 225. Fax: 352-392-9193. E-mail: bfn@coe.ufl.edu.

University of Georgia, College of Education, Programs in Secondary Education, Athens, GA 30602. Offerings include English education (M Ed, Ed S). Accredited by NCATE. Faculty: 46 full-time (17 women). *Entrance requirements:* For Ed S, GRE General Test or MAT. Application deadline: 7/1 (priority date; 11/15 for spring admission). Application fee: $30. Electronic applications accepted. *Tuition:* $3290 per year full-time, $643 per semester (minimum) part-time for state residents; $11,300 per year full-time, $1645 per semester (minimum) part-time for nonresidents. • Dr. Russell H. Yeany, Dean, 706-542-3866. Fax: 706-542-0360.

University of Idaho, College of Graduate Studies, College of Letters and Science, Department of English, Program in English, Moscow, ID 83844-4140. Offerings include English education (MAT). Accredited by NCATE. *Application deadline:* 8/1 (12/15 for spring admission). *Application fee:* $35 ($45 for international students). *Expenses:* Tuition $0 for state residents; $6000 per year full-time, $95 per credit part-time for nonresidents. Fees $2676 per year full-time, $134 per credit part-time. • Dr. Douglas Q. Adams, Chair, Department of English, 208-885-6156.

University of Illinois at Chicago, College of Liberal Arts and Sciences, Department of English, Chicago, IL 60607-7128. Offerings include English (MA, PhD), with options in creative writing (MA, PhD), language, literacy and rhetoric (PhD), literature (MA, PhD), teaching of English (MA). Department faculty: 43 full-time (12 women). *Entrance requirements:* GRE General Test, GRE Subject Test, TOEFL. Application fee: $40 ($50 for international students). • Donald G. Marshall, Head, 312-413-2200. Application contact: Thomas Bestul, Director of Graduate Studies, 312-413-2240.

University of Indianapolis, School of Education, Indianapolis, IN 46227-3697. Offerings include secondary education (MA), with options in art education, education, English education, social studies education. Accredited by NCATE. *Average time to degree:* master's–5 years part-time. *Entrance requirements:* GRE Subject Test. Application deadline: rolling. Application fee: $30.

The University of Iowa, College of Liberal Arts, Department of English, Iowa City, IA 52242-1316. Offerings include pedagogy (PhD). Department faculty: 63 full-time, 8 part-time. *Degree requirements:* Dissertation, comprehensive exam. *Entrance requirements:* GRE General Test. Application fee: $30 ($50 for international students). *Expenses:* Tuition $3166 per year full-time, $176 per semester hour part-time for state residents; $10,202 per year full-time, $176 per semester hour part-time for nonresidents. Fees $202 per year full-time, $52 per year (minimum) part-time. • Adalaide Morris, Chair, 319-335-0454. Fax: 319-335-2535.

University of Michigan, Interdepartmental Program in English and Education, Ann Arbor, MI 48109. Awards PhD. Faculty: 7 full-time (4 women). Students: 21 full-time (15 women); includes 4 minority (1 African American, 1 Asian American, 2 Hispanics). Average age 31. 25 applicants, 16% accepted. In 1997, 1 degree awarded (100% entered university research/teaching). *Degree requirements:* 1 foreign language, dissertation, oral defense of dissertation, preliminary exam. *Entrance requirements:* GRE General Test, master's degree, teaching experience. Application deadline: 1/15 (rolling processing). Application fee: $55. *Financial aid:* 21 students received aid; fellowships, research assistantships, teaching assistantships available. Financial aid application deadline: 3/15. • Anne Ruggles Gere, Chair, 734-763-6643. E-mail: argere@umich.edu. Application contact: Michelle M. Thomas, Student Services Associate, 734-763-6643. Fax: 734-763-1229. E-mail: mmthomas@umich.edu.

University of Michigan, School of Education, Programs in Educational Studies, Ann Arbor, MI 48109. Offerings include English education (AM). *Application deadline:* 1/15 (priority date). *Application fee:* $55. Electronic applications accepted. • Dr. Ronald Marx, Chairperson, 734-763-9497. E-mail: ronmarx@umich.edu. Application contact: Karen Wixson, Associate Dean, 734-764-9470. Fax: 734-763-1229. E-mail: kwixson@umich.edu.

University of Minnesota, Twin Cities Campus, College of Education and Human Development, Department of Curriculum and Instruction, Minneapolis, MN 55455-0213. Offerings include English education (MA, M Ed). • Fred Finley, Chairman, 612-625-2545.

The University of Montana–Missoula, College of Arts and Sciences, Department of English, Program in English Education, Missoula, MT 59812-0002. Awards MA. *Entrance requirements:* GRE General Test, sample of written work. Application deadline: 2/1. Application fee: $30. *Tuition:* $2499 per year (minimum) full-time, $376 per semester (minimum) part-time for state residents; $6528 per year (minimum) full-time, $1048 per semester (minimum) part-time for nonresidents. *Financial aid:* Application deadline 2/1. • John Hunt, Director of Graduate Studies, 406-243-2928. Fax: 406-243-4076. E-mail: enbos@selway.umt.edu.

University of Nebraska at Kearney, College of Fine Arts and Humanities, Department of English, Kearney, NE 68849-0001. Offerings include English education (MA Ed). Accredited by NCATE. MA Ed being phased out; applicants no longer accepted. Department faculty: 13 full-time (6 women). *Application deadline:* 8/1 (priority date; rolling processing; 12/15 for spring admission). *Application fee:* $35. *Expenses:* Tuition $1494 per year full-time, $83 per credit hour part-time for state residents; $2826 per year full-time, $157 per credit hour part-time for nonresidents. Fees $229 per year full-time, $11.25 per semester (minimum) part-time. • Dr. Robert Luscher, Chair, 308-865-8299.

University of Nevada, Las Vegas, College of Education, Department of Instructional and Curricular Studies, Las Vegas, NV 89154-9900. Offerings include English/language arts (M Ed, MS), language and literacy education (M Ed, MS). One or more programs accredited by NCATE. Department faculty: 34 full-time (16 women). *Degree requirements:* Thesis (for some programs), oral or written comprehensive exam required, foreign language not required. *Entrance requirements:* Minimum GPA of 3.0. Application deadline: 2/15 (9/30 for spring admission). Application fee: $40 ($95 for international students). *Expenses:* Tuition $93 per credit for state residents; $93 per credit full-time, $190 per credit part-time for nonresidents. Fees $5570 per year full-time for nonresidents. • Dr. Jan McCarthy, Chair, 702-895-3241. Application contact: Graduate College Admissions Evaluator, 702-895-3320.

University of New Hampshire, College of Liberal Arts, Department of English, Durham, NH 03824. Offerings include English education (MST). Department faculty: 42 full-time. *Application deadline:* 2/15 (priority date; rolling processing). *Application fee:* $50. *Expenses:* Tuition $5440 per year full-time, $302 per credit hour part-time for state residents; $8160 per year (minimum) full-time, $453 per credit hour (minimum) part-time for nonresidents. Fees $868 per year full-time, $15 per year part-time. • Rachelle Lieber, Head, 603-862-3964. Application contact: Douglas Lanier, 603-862-3796.

The University of North Carolina at Chapel Hill, School of Education, Programs in Teacher Education, Program in Secondary Education, Chapel Hill, NC 27599. Offerings include English (MAT). Accredited by NCATE. *Degree requirements:* Comprehensive exam required, foreign language and thesis not required. *Entrance requirements:* GRE General Test (minimum combined score of 1000), minimum GPA of 3.0 during last 2 years of undergraduate course work. Application deadline: 1/1 (rolling processing). Application fee: $55. *Expenses:* Tuition $1428 per year full-time, $357 per semester (minimum) part-time for state residents; $10,414 per year full-time, $2604 per semester (minimum) part-time for nonresidents. Fees $782 per year full-time, $332 per semester (minimum) part-time. • Dr. Walter Pryzwansky, Director of Graduate Studies, 919-966-7000. Application contact: Janet Carroll, Registrar, 919-966-1346. Fax: 919-962-1533. E-mail: jscarrol@email.unc.edu.

University of North Carolina at Greensboro, College of Arts and Sciences, Department of English, Program in English, Greensboro, NC 27412-0001. Awards MA, M Ed, PhD. One or more programs accredited by NCATE. Students: 58 full-time (38 women), 27 part-time (16 women); includes 2 minority (both African Americans), 1 international. 97 applicants, 41% accepted. In 1997, 15 master's, 12 doctorates awarded. *Degree requirements:* For master's, thesis or alternative, comprehensive exam; for doctorate, variable foreign language requirement, dissertation, preliminary exam. *Entrance requirements:* For master's, GRE General Test, GRE Subject Test, minimum GPA of 3.0; for doctorate, GRE General Test, GRE Subject Test, critical writing sample, minimum GPA of 3.0. Application fee: $35. *Expenses:* Tuition $1842 per year full-time, $370 per semester (minimum) part-time for state residents; $10,296 per year full-time, $2484 per semester (minimum) part-time for nonresidents. Fees $806 per year full-time, $111 per semester (minimum) part-time. *Financial aid:* Fellowships, research assistantships, teaching assistantships available. • Dr. James Evans, Chairman, Department of English, 336-334-5311. Application contact: Director of Graduate Studies, 336-334-5221.

University of North Carolina at Pembroke, Graduate Studies, Department of Communicative Arts, Program in English Education, Pembroke, NC 28372-1510. Awards MA. Accredited by NCATE. Part-time and evening/weekend programs available. Faculty: 12 full-time (3 women). Students: 2 full-time (both women), 10 part-time (7 women); includes 2 minority (1 African American, 1 Native American). In 1997, 5 degrees awarded. *Degree requirements:* Comprehensive exam required, thesis optional, foreign language not required. *Average time to degree:* master's–1.5 years full-time, 2.5 years part-time. *Entrance requirements:* GRE, MAT, or NTE, minimum GPA of 3.0 in major or 2.5 overall. Application deadline: rolling. Application fee: $25. *Tuition:* $1554 per year full-time, $610 per semester (minimum) part-time for state residents; $8824 per year full-time, $2122 per semester (minimum) part-time for nonresidents. *Financial aid:* In 1997–98, 1 graduate assistantship (to a first-year student) averaging $700 per month and totaling $5,600 was awarded. Aid available to part-time students. Financial aid application deadline: 4/15. • Dr. Patricia D. Valenti, Coordinator, 910-521-6430. Application contact: Dean of Graduate Studies, 910-521-6271. Fax: 910-521-6497.

University of Oklahoma, College of Education, Department of Instructional Leadership and Academic Curriculum, Program in Instructional Leadership and Academic Curriculum, Norman, OK 73019-0390. Offerings include English education (M Ed, PhD). Accredited by NCATE. Program faculty: 19 full-time (12 women), 12 part-time (11 women). *Degree requirements:* For doctorate, variable foreign language requirement, dissertation. *Entrance requirements:* For master's, TOEFL (minimum score 550), 12 hours of course work in education; for doctorate, GRE General Test (minimum combined score of 1000), TOEFL (minimum score 500), master's degree, minimum graduate GPA of 3.0. Application deadline: 6/1 (priority date; rolling processing). Application fee: $25. *Expenses:* Tuition $1920 per year full-time, $80 per credit hour part-time for state residents; $6108 per year full-time, $255 per credit hour part-time for nonresidents. Fees $468 per year full-time, $12 per semester (minimum) part-time. • Dr. Bonnie Konopak, Chair, Department of Instructional Leadership and Academic Curriculum, 405-325-1498.

University of Pittsburgh, School of Education, Department of Instruction and Learning, Program in Secondary Education, Pittsburgh, PA 15260. Offerings include English/

communications education (MAT, M Ed, Ed D, PhD). *Degree requirements:* For doctorate, dissertation required, foreign language not required. *Average time to degree:* master's–2 years full-time, 4 years part-time; doctorate–4 years full-time, 6 years part-time. *Entrance requirements:* For doctorate, GRE General Test, TOEFL (minimum score 650). Application deadline: 2/1. Application fee: $30 ($40 for international students). *Expenses:* Tuition $8018 per year full-time, $329 per credit part-time for state residents; $16,508 per year full-time, $680 per credit part-time for nonresidents. Fees $480 per year full-time, $180 per year part-time. • Application contact: Jackie Harden, Manager, 412-648-7060. Fax: 412-648-1899. E-mail: jackie@sched.fsl.pitt.edu.

University of Puerto Rico, Río Piedras, College of Education, Program in Curriculum and Teaching, San Juan, PR 00931. Offerings include English education (M Ed). *Degree requirements:* Thesis required, foreign language not required. *Entrance requirements:* PAEG, minimum GPA of 3.0. Application deadline: 2/21. Application fee: $17.

University of South Carolina, Graduate School, College of Liberal Arts, Department of English, Columbia, SC 29208. Offerings include English education (MAT). Accredited by NCATE. MAT offered in cooperation with the College of Education. Department faculty: 51 full-time (17 women). *Application deadline:* 5/15 (priority date; rolling processing). *Application fee:* $35. Electronic applications accepted. *Expenses:* Tuition $3894 per year full-time, $193 per credit hour part-time for state residents; $8114 per year full-time, $404 per credit hour part-time for nonresidents. Fees $125 per year full-time, $37 per semester (minimum) part-time. • Dr. Robert Newman, Chair, 803-777-7120. Application contact: Steven Lynn, Director of Graduate Studies, 803-777-5063.

University of South Florida, College of Education, Department of Secondary Education, Program in English Education, Tampa, FL 33620-9951. Awards MA, M Ed, PhD, Ed S. Accredited by NCATE. Part-time and evening/weekend programs available. Students: 18 full-time (15 women), 50 part-time (34 women); includes 5 minority (3 African Americans, 1 Asian American, 1 Hispanic), 6 international. Average age 31. 21 applicants, 71% accepted. In 1997, 9 master's awarded. *Degree requirements:* For doctorate, dissertation, 2 tools of research in foreign language, statistics, and/or computers. *Entrance requirements:* For master's, GRE General Test (minimum combined score of 1000), minimum GPA of 3.5 in last 60 hours; for doctorate, GRE General Test (minimum combined score of 1000), minimum GPA of 3.0 (undergraduate) or 3.5 (graduate); for Ed S, GRE General Test (minimum combined score of 1000). Application deadline: 6/1 (10/15 for spring admission). Application fee: $20. Electronic applications accepted. *Tuition:* $142 per credit hour for state residents; $486 per credit hour for nonresidents. *Financial aid:* Federal Work-Study, institutionally sponsored loans available. Aid available to part-time students. Financial aid applicants required to submit FAFSA. • Application contact: Joan Kaywell, Coordinator, 813-974-3516. Fax: 813-974-3837. E-mail: kaywell@tempest.coedu.usf.edu.

University of Tennessee, Knoxville, College of Education, Program in Education II, Knoxville, TN 37996. Offerings include English education (MS, Ed D, Ed S). Accredited by NCATE. *Degree requirements:* For master's and Ed S, thesis optional, foreign language not required; for doctorate, dissertation required, foreign language not required. *Entrance requirements:* For master's, TOEFL (minimum score 550), minimum GPA of 2.7; for doctorate, GRE General Test, TOEFL (minimum score 550), minimum GPA of 2.7; for Ed S, TOEFL (minimum score 550), GRE General Test, minimum GPA of 2.7. Application deadline: 2/1 (priority date; rolling processing). Application fee: $35. Electronic applications accepted. *Tuition:* $3354 per year full-time, $181 per semester hour part-time for state residents; $8410 per year full-time, $462 per semester hour part-time for nonresidents. • Dr. Tom George, Associate Dean, 423-974-0907. Fax: 423-974-8718. E-mail: tgeorge1@utk.edu.

The University of Texas at Tyler, School of Education and Psychology, Department of Curriculum and Instruction, Tyler, TX 75799-0001. Offerings include elementary education (M Ed, Certificate), with options in biology, English, history, reading; secondary education (M Ed, Certificate), with options in biology, English, history, mathematics. Department faculty: 13 full-time (8 women). *Application fee:* $0 ($50 for international students). *Tuition:* $2144 per year full-time, $337 per semester (minimum) part-time for state residents; $7256 per year full-time, $964 per semester (minimum) part-time for nonresidents. • Dr. Bill Bruce, Chair, 903-566-7133. E-mail: wbruce@mail.uttyl.edu. Application contact: Martha D. Wheat, Director of Admissions and Student Records, 903-566-7201. Fax: 903-566-7068.

University of the District of Columbia, College of Arts and Sciences, School of Arts and Education, Division of Education, Program in English Composition and Rhetoric, 4200 Connecticut Avenue, NW, Washington, DC 20008-1175. Awards MA. *Degree requirements:* Comprehensive exam required, foreign language not required. *Entrance requirements:* Writing proficiency exam. Application deadline: 6/14 (priority date; rolling processing; 11/15 for spring admission). Application fee: $20. *Expenses:* Tuition $3564 per year full-time, $198 per credit part-time for district residents; $5922 per year full-time, $329 per credit part-time for nonresidents. Fees $990 per year full-time, $55 per credit part-time.

University of Vermont, College of Arts and Sciences, Department of English, Burlington, VT 05405-0160. Offerings include English education (MAT). Accredited by NCATE. *Application deadline:* 4/1 (priority date; rolling processing). *Application fee:* $25. *Expenses:* Tuition $302 per credit for state residents; $755 per credit for nonresidents. Fees $434 per year full-time, $46 per semester (minimum) part-time. • Dr. A. Broughton, Chairperson, 802-656-3056. Application contact: Dr. W. Stephany, Coordinator, 802-656-3056.

University of Victoria, Faculty of Education, Department of Communication and Social Foundations, Victoria, BC V8W 2Y2, Canada. Offerings include English language arts (MA, M Ed), language arts (PhD). Postbaccalaureate distance learning degree programs offered (minimal on-campus study). Department faculty: 17 full-time (9 women), 14 part-time (9 women). *Degree requirements:* For master's, thesis, project (M Ed) required, foreign language not required; for doctorate, dissertation required, foreign language not required. *Average time to degree:* master's–3.3 years full-time; doctorate–4.4 years full-time. *Entrance requirements:* For master's, minimum B average. Application deadline: 4/30 (rolling processing). Application fee: $50. *Tuition:* $2080 per year full-time, $557 per semester part-time. • Dr. G. Potter, Chair, 250-721-7802. Application contact: Sarah Baylow, Graduate Secretary, 250-721-7882. Fax: 250-721-7767. E-mail: sbaylow@uvic.ca.

The University of West Alabama, College of Education, Department of Foundations, Livingston, AL 35470. Offerings include secondary education (MAT, M Ed), with options in biology with certification (MAT), environmental science with certification (MAT), history with certification (MAT), language arts with certification (MAT), library media with certification (MAT), mathematics with certification (MAT). Accredited by NCATE. *Application deadline:* 9/10 (priority date; rolling processing; 3/24 for spring admission). *Application fee:* $15. *Tuition:* $70 per quarter hour.

The University of West Alabama, College of Liberal Arts, Department of English and Language Arts, Livingston, AL 35470. Offers program in language arts (MAT). Accredited by NCATE. *Tuition:* $70 per quarter hour.

University of Wisconsin–Eau Claire, College of Professional Studies, School of Education, Program in Secondary Education, Eau Claire, WI 54702-4004. Offerings include English (MAT, MST). *Application deadline:* 7/1 (rolling processing; 12/1 for spring admission). *Application fee:* $45. *Tuition:* $3651 per year full-time, $611 per semester (minimum) part-time for state residents; $11,295 per year full-time, $1886 per semester (minimum) part-time for nonresidents. • Stephen Kurth, Associate Dean, School of Education, 715-836-3671.

University of Wisconsin–Madison, School of Education, Department of Curriculum and Instruction, Madison, WI 53706-1380. Offerings include English education (MA). *Application fee:* $38. *Tuition:* $4928 per year full-time, $926 per semester (minimum) part-time for state residents; $15,190 per year full-time, $2849 per semester (minimum) part-time for nonresidents.

University of Wisconsin–River Falls, College of Arts and Science, Department of English, River Falls, WI 54022-5001. Offers program in language, literature, and communication education (MSE). One or more programs accredited by NCATE. Students: 15 (9 women). *Degree requirements:* Thesis required, foreign language not required. *Application deadline:* 3/1. *Application fee:* $45. *Financial aid:* Research assistantships available. Financial aid application deadline: 3/1. • Richard Beckham, Chair, 715-425-3537. Application contact: Graduate Admissions, 715-425-3843.

Vanderbilt University, Peabody College, Department of Teaching and Learning, Nashville, TN 37240-1001. Offerings include English education (M Ed, Ed D). Accredited by NCATE. *Entrance requirements:* GRE General Test, MAT. Application deadline: 3/1 (priority date; rolling processing). Application fee: $35. • Carolyn Evertson, Chair, 615-322-8100.

Washington State University, College of Liberal Arts, Department of English, Pullman, WA 99164-1610. Offerings include teaching of English (MA). Department faculty: 34 (17 women). *Degree requirements:* Variable foreign language requirement, thesis (for some programs), oral exam. *Average time to degree:* master's–2 years full-time; doctorate–5 years full-time. *Entrance requirements:* GRE General Test, minimum GPA of 3.0. Application deadline: 3/1 (priority date; rolling processing). Application fee: $35. *Tuition:* $5334 per year full-time, $267 per credit hour part-time for state residents; $13,380 per year full-time, $677 per credit hour part-time for nonresidents. • Dr. Sue McLeod, Chair, 509-335-2581. Application contact: Dr. Nick Kiesling, Director, Graduate Studies.

Wayne State College, Division of Humanities, Program in English Education, Wayne, NE 68787. Awards MSE. One or more programs accredited by NCATE. Students: 1 (woman) full-time, 7 part-time (all women); includes 1 minority (African American). Average age 28. In 1997, 3 degrees awarded. *Degree requirements:* Thesis or alternative, comprehensive exam, research paper required, foreign language not required. *Entrance requirements:* GRE General Test, minimum GPA of 2.7. Application deadline: rolling. Application fee: $10. *Expenses:* Tuition $1788 per year full-time, $75 per credit hour part-time for state residents; $3576 per year full-time, $149 per credit hour part-time for nonresidents. Fees $360 per year full-time, $15 per credit hour part-time. *Financial aid:* Teaching assistantships and career-related internships or fieldwork available. Financial aid application deadline: 5/1; applicants required to submit FAFSA. • Dr. Ed Battistella, Head, Division of Humanities, 402-375-7394.

Western Carolina University, College of Education and Allied Professions, Department of Administration, Curriculum and Instruction, Programs in Secondary Education, Cullowhee, NC 28723. Offerings include English (MAT). Accredited by NCATE. *Degree requirements:* Comprehensive exam required, foreign language and thesis not required. *Entrance requirements:* GRE General Test. Application deadline: rolling. Application fee: $35. *Tuition:* $1799 per year full-time, $144 per credit hour (minimum) part-time for state residents; $9069 per year full-time, $1053 per credit hour (minimum) part-time for nonresidents. • Application contact: Kathleen Owen, Assistant to the Dean, 828-227-7398. Fax: 828-227-7480.

Western Kentucky University, Potter College of Arts and Humanities, Department of English, Bowling Green, KY 42101-3576. Offerings include English (MA Ed). Accredited by NCATE. Department faculty: 24 full-time (13 women). *Application deadline:* 8/1 (priority date; rolling processing; 12/1 for spring admission). *Application fee:* $20. *Tuition:* $2460 per year full-time, $133 per credit hour part-time for state residents; $6700 per year full-time, $369 per credit hour part-time for nonresidents. • Dr. Mary Ellen Pitts, Head, 502-745-3043. Fax: 502-745-2533.

Wilkes University, Department of Education, Wilkes-Barre, PA 18766-0002. Offerings include secondary education (MS Ed), with options in biology, chemistry, English, history. Department faculty: 6 full-time, 14 part-time. *Application deadline:* rolling. *Application fee:* $30. *Expenses:* Tuition $12,552 per year full-time, $523 per credit hour part-time. Fees $240 per year full-time, $10 per credit hour part-time. • Dr. Douglas Lynch, Chair, 717-408-4680.

Worcester State College, Graduate Studies, Department of Language and Literature, Worcester, MA 01602-2597. Offers program in English (M Ed). Part-time and evening/weekend programs available. Students: 2 full-time (1 woman), 4 part-time (2 women). Average age 37. 3 applicants, 100% accepted. *Degree requirements:* Comprehensive exam required, foreign language and thesis not required. *Entrance requirements:* GRE General Test or MAT, 18 undergraduate credits in English, excluding composition. Application deadline: rolling. Application fee: $10 ($40 for international students). *Tuition:* $127 per credit hour. *Financial aid:* Career-related internships or fieldwork available. • Dr. Ruth Haber, Coordinator, 508-929-8706. Application contact: Andrea Wetmore, Graduate Admissions Counselor, 508-929-8120. E-mail: awetmore@worc.mass.edu.

Xavier University, College of Social Sciences, Department of Education, Cincinnati, OH 45207-2111. Offerings include English (M Ed). Department faculty: 32 full-time (14 women), 49 part-time (31 women), 44.25 FTE. *Application deadline:* rolling. *Application fee:* $25. • Dr. James Boothe, Chair, 513-745-2951. Fax: 513-745-1052. E-mail: boothe@admin.xu.edu. Application contact: Sheila Speth, Director of Graduate Services, 513-745-3360. Fax: 513-745-1048. E-mail: xugrad@admin.xu.edu.

Foreign Languages Education

Adelphi University, School of Education, Program in Secondary Education, Garden City, NY 11530. Offerings include Spanish (MA). *Application deadline:* rolling. *Application fee:* $50. *Expenses:* Tuition $16,000 per year full-time, $485 per credit part-time. Fees $500 per year full-time, $150 per semester part-time. • Director, 516-877-4090. Application contact: Jennifer Spiegel, Associate Director of Graduate Admissions, 516-877-3055.

American University in Cairo, Graduate Studies, School of Humanities and Social Sciences, Arabic Language Institute, Cairo, Egypt. Offers program in teaching Arabic as a foreign language (MA). *Entrance requirements:* English entrance exam and/or TOEFL. Application fee: $35.

Andrews University, School of Graduate Studies, College of Arts and Sciences, Department of Modern Languages, Berrien Springs, MI 49104. Awards MAT. *Application deadline:* rolling. *Application fee:* $30. *Expenses:* Tuition $290 per quarter hour (minimum). Fees $75 per quarter. • Dr. Michel Pichot, Chairman, 616-471-3180.

Andrews University, School of Graduate Studies, School of Education, Department of Teaching/Learning/Administration, Berrien Springs, MI 49104. Offerings include secondary education (MAT), with options in biology, education, English, English as a second language, French, history, physics. *Application deadline:* 8/15 (rolling processing). *Application fee:* $30. *Expenses:* Tuition $290 per quarter hour (minimum). Fees $75 per quarter. • Dr. William H. Green, Chair, 616-471-3465.

Auburn University, College of Education, Department of Curriculum and Teaching, Auburn University, AL 36849-0001. Offerings include foreign languages (M Ed, MS). Accredited by NCATE. Department faculty: 20 full-time (11 women). *Degree requirements:* Thesis (MS) required, foreign language not required. *Entrance requirements:* GRE General Test. Application deadline: 9/1 (rolling processing; 3/1 for spring admission). Application fee: $25 ($50 for international students). *Expenses:* Tuition $2760 per year full-time, $76 per credit hour part-time for state residents; $8280 per year full-time, $228 per credit hour part-time for nonresidents. Fees $30 per year full-time, $160 per quarter part time for state residents; $30 per year full-time, $480 per quarter part-time for nonresidents. • Dr. Andrew M. Weaver, Head, 334-844-4434. E-mail: weaveam@mail.auburn.edu. Application contact: Dr. John F. Pritchett, Dean of the Graduate School, 334-844-4700.

Boston College, Graduate School of Education, Department of Teacher Education/Special Education and Curriculum and Instruction, Program in Secondary Education, Chestnut Hill, MA 02167-9991. Offerings include Romance languages (MAT). Accredited by NCATE. *Application deadline:* 3/15 (11/15 for spring admission). *Application fee:* $40. *Expenses:* Tuition $626 per semester hour. Fees $80 per year (minimum) full-time, $30 per semester part-time. • Application contact: Arline Riordan, Graduate Admissions Director, 617-552-4214. Fax: 617-552-0812. E-mail: riordana@bc.edu.

Boston University, School of Education, Department of Developmental Studies and Counseling, Program in Modern Foreign Language Education, Boston, MA 02215. Awards MAT. Students: 5 full-time (all women), 1 (woman) part-time; includes 1 minority (Asian American). Average age 23. In 1997, 3 degrees awarded. *Degree requirements:* Thesis or alternative required, foreign language not required. *Entrance requirements:* GRE or MAT, TOEFL. Application deadline: 2/15 (priority date; rolling processing). Application fee: $50. *Expenses:* Tuition $22,830 per year full-time, $713 per credit part-time. Fees $218 per year full-time, $40 per semester part-time. *Financial aid:* Application deadline 3/30. • Dr. Yuan Feng, Coordinator, 619-353-5248. E-mail: feng@bu.edu.

Bowling Green State University, College of Arts and Sciences, Department of Romance Languages, Bowling Green, OH 43403. Offerings include French (MA, MAT), with options in French (MA), French education (MAT); Spanish (MA, MAT), with options in Spanish (MA), Spanish education (MAT). Department faculty: 12 full-time (4 women), 3 part-time (1 woman). *Application fee:* $30. Electronic applications accepted. *Tuition:* $6070 per year full-time, $284 per credit hour part-time for state residents; $11,358 per year full-time, $536 per credit hour part-time for nonresidents. • Dr. Henry Garrity, Chair, 419-372-2667.

Brigham Young University, College of Humanities, Department of Spanish and Portuguese, Provo, UT 84602-1001. Offerings include Spanish teaching (MA). Department faculty: 22 full-time (4 women). *Degree requirements:* 1 foreign language, thesis. *Average time to degree:* master's–2.5 years full-time, 5 years part-time. *Entrance requirements:* Minimum GPA of 3.5 in Spanish or Portuguese, 3.3 overall. Application deadline: 2/1. Application fee: $30. *Tuition:* $3200 per year full-time, $178 per credit hour part-time for state residents; $4800 per year full-time, $266 per credit hour part-time for nonresidents. • Dr. Christopher Lund, Chair, 801-378-2837. Fax: 801-378-8932. Application contact: Office of Graduate Studies, 801-378-4091.

Brooklyn College of the City University of New York, School of Education, Division of Secondary Education, 2900 Bedford Avenue, Brooklyn, NY 11210-2889. Offerings include French (MA), Spanish education (MA). *Application deadline:* 3/1 (11/1 for spring admission). *Application fee:* $40. *Expenses:* Tuition $4350 per year full-time, $185 per credit part-time for state residents; $7600 per year full-time, $320 per credit part-time for nonresidents. Fees $500 per year for state residents; $806 per year for nonresidents. • Dr. Peter Taubman, Coordinator, 718-951-5218. Fax: 718-951-4816. E-mail: ptaubman@brooklyn.cuny.edu.

College of Notre Dame, Department of Education, Emphasis in Secondary Education, Belmont, CA 94002-1997. Offerings include teaching French (MAT). Faculty: 5 full-time, 8 part-time. *Application deadline:* rolling. *Application fee:* $50 ($500 for international students). *Tuition:* $460 per unit. • Dr. Kim Tolley, Program Director, 650-508-3456.

College of Our Lady of the Elms, Department of Education, Chicopee, MA 01013-2839. Offerings include secondary education (MAT), with options in biology education, English education, Spanish education. Department faculty: 7 full-time (all women), 6 part-time (5 women). *Application deadline:* rolling. *Application fee:* $30. *Expenses:* Tuition $320 per credit. Fees $40 per year. • Sr. Kathleen M. Kirley, Dean of Continuing Education and Graduate Studies, 413-594-2761. Fax: 413-592-4871. Application contact: Dr. Mary Janeczek, Director, 413-594-2761.

Connecticut College, Department of French and Italian, New London, CT 06320-4196. Awards MA, MAT. Part-time programs available. *Degree requirements:* 1 foreign language, thesis or alternative. *Application deadline:* 2/2. *Application fee:* $35.

Connecticut College, Department of German, New London, CT 06320-4196. Awards MAT. Part-time programs available. *Entrance requirements:* MAT. Application deadline: 2/2. Application fee: $35.

Connecticut College, Department of Russian Studies, New London, CT 06320-4196. Awards MAT. Part-time programs available. *Entrance requirements:* MAT. Application deadline: 2/2. Application fee: $35.

Eastern Washington University, College of Letters and Social Sciences, Department of Modern Languages and Literatures, Cheney, WA 99004-2431. Offers program in French education (M Ed). Accredited by NCATE. Faculty: 8 full-time (3 women). Students: 1 (woman) full-time. 2 applicants, 100% accepted. In 1997, 1 degree awarded. *Degree requirements:* Comprehensive exam. *Entrance requirements:* Minimum GPA of 3.0. Application deadline: 4/1 (priority date; rolling processing; 1/15 for spring admission). Application fee: $35. *Tuition:* $4200 per year full-time, $140 per credit part-time for state residents; $12,780 per year full-time, $415 per credit part-time for nonresidents. *Financial aid:* Federal Work-Study, institutionally sponsored loans available. Financial aid application deadline: 2/1. • Dr. Wayne Kraft, Chairman, 509-359-2861. Application contact: Alys Seifert, Adviser, 509-359-6001.

Florida Atlantic University, College of Arts and Letters, Department of Languages and Linguistics, Boca Raton, FL 33431-0991. Offerings include teaching French (MAT), teaching German (MAT), teaching Spanish (MAT). Department faculty: 14 full-time. *Application deadline:* 6/1 (priority date; rolling processing; 11/1 for spring admission). *Application fee:* $15. *Expenses:* Tuition $2520 per year full-time, $140 per credit hour part-time for state residents; $8712 per year full-time, $484 per credit hour part-time for nonresidents. Fees $5 per year (minimum). • Dr. Ernest Weiser, Chair, 561-297-3860. Fax: 561-297-2752. E-mail: weiser@fau.edu.

Florida International University, College of Education, Department of Subject Specializations, Program in Modern Language Education, Miami, FL 33199. Awards MS. Accredited by NCATE. Part-time and evening/weekend programs available. Students: 5 full-time (2 women), 16 part-time (12 women); includes 19 minority (3 African Americans, 16 Hispanics). Average age 36. 6 applicants, 83% accepted. In 1997, 6 degrees awarded. *Entrance requirements:* GRE General Test (minimum combined score of 1000) or minimum GPA of 3.0. Application deadline: 4/1 (priority date; rolling processing; 10/1 for spring admission). Application fee: $20. *Expenses:* Tuition $138 per credit hour for state residents; $482 per credit hour for nonresidents. Fees $46 per semester. *Faculty research:* Language and business, teaching English to speakers of other languages (TESOL). • Dr. Dean Hauenstein, Chairperson, Department of Subject Specializations, 305-348-2005. Fax: 305-348-2086.

Georgia Southern University, College of Education, Department of Middle Grades and Secondary Education, Program in French, Statesboro, GA 30460-8126. Awards M Ed. Accredited by NCATE. Part-time and evening/weekend programs available. Students: 2 full-time (1 woman), 2 part-time (1 woman). 1 applicant, 100% accepted. In 1997, 1 degree awarded. *Degree requirements:* 1 foreign language, exams required, thesis not required. *Entrance requirements:* GRE General Test (minimum score 450 on each section) or MAT (minimum score 44), minimum GPA of 2.5. Application deadline: 7/15 (priority date; rolling processing; 11/15 for spring admission). Application fee: $0. Electronic applications accepted. *Tuition:* $2619 per year full-time, $287 per semester (minimum) part-time for state residents; $8619 per year full-time, $1037 per semester (minimum) part-time for nonresidents. *Financial aid:* Application deadline 4/15. • Application contact: Dr. John R. Diebolt, Associate Graduate Dean, 912-681-5384. Fax: 912-681-0740. E-mail: gradschool@gsvms2.cc.gasou.edu.

Georgia Southern University, College of Education, Department of Middle Grades and Secondary Education, Program in German, Statesboro, GA 30460-8126. Awards M Ed. Accredited by NCATE. Part-time and evening/weekend programs available. Students: 0. Average age 37. 0 applicants. *Degree requirements:* 1 foreign language, exams required, thesis not required. *Entrance requirements:* GRE General Test (minimum score 450 on each section) or MAT (minimum score 44), minimum GPA of 2.5. Application deadline: 7/15 (priority date; rolling processing; 11/15 for spring admission). Application fee: $0. Electronic applications accepted. *Tuition:* $2619 per year full-time, $287 per semester (minimum) part-time for state residents; $8619 per year full-time, $1037 per semester (minimum) part-time for nonresidents. *Financial aid:* Application deadline 4/15. • Application contact: Dr. John R. Diebolt, Associate Graduate Dean, 912-681-5384. Fax: 912-681-0740. E-mail: gradschool@gsvms2.cc.gasou.edu.

Georgia Southern University, College of Education, Department of Middle Grades and Secondary Education, Program in Spanish, Statesboro, GA 30460-8126. Awards M Ed. Accredited by NCATE. Part-time and evening/weekend programs available. Students: 1 (woman) full-time, 6 part-time (3 women). Average age 33. 4 applicants, 50% accepted. In 1997, 3 degrees awarded. *Degree requirements:* 1 foreign language, exams required, thesis not required. *Entrance requirements:* GRE General Test (minimum score 450 on each section) or MAT (minimum score 44), minimum GPA of 2.5. Application deadline: 7/15 (priority date; rolling processing; 11/15 for spring admission). Application fee: $0. Electronic applications accepted. *Tuition:* $2619 per year full-time, $287 per semester (minimum) part-time for state residents; $8619 per year full-time, $1037 per semester (minimum) part-time for nonresidents. *Financial aid:* Application deadline 4/15. • Application contact: Dr. John R. Diebolt, Associate Graduate Dean, 912-681-5384. Fax: 912-681-0740. E-mail: gradschool@gsvms2.cc.gasou.edu.

Hardin–Simmons University, Irvin School of Education, Department of Elementary and Secondary Education, Abilene, TX 79698-0001. Offerings include elementary education (M Ed), with options in psychology, reading, Spanish, speech; secondary education (M Ed), with options in psychology, reading, Spanish, speech. Department faculty: 6 full-time (3 women), 4 part-time (3 women). *Degree requirements:* Project required, foreign language and thesis not required. *Application deadline:* 8/15 (priority date; rolling processing; 1/5 for spring admission). *Application fee:* $25. *Expenses:* Tuition $280 per semester hour. Fees $630 per year full-time. • Dr. Bertie Kingore, Head, 915-670-1353. Fax: 915-670-5859. Application contact: Dr. J. Paul Sorrels, Dean of Graduate Studies, 915-670-1298. Fax: 915-670-1564.

Hunter College of the City University of New York, Division of Education, Secondary Education Curriculum, Concentration in French Education, 695 Park Avenue, New York, NY 10021-5085. Awards MA. *Degree requirements:* Comprehensive exam required, foreign language and thesis not required. *Entrance requirements:* TOEFL (minimum score 575). Application deadline: 4/28 (priority date; 11/21 for spring admission). Application fee: $40. *Expenses:* Tuition $4350 per year full-time, $185 per credit part-time for state residents; $7600 per year full-time, $320 per credit part-time for nonresidents. Fees $26 per year.

Hunter College of the City University of New York, Division of Education, Secondary Education Curriculum, Concentration in Italian Education, 695 Park Avenue, New York, NY 10021-5085. Awards MA. *Degree requirements:* Comprehensive exam required, foreign language and thesis not required. *Entrance requirements:* TOEFL (minimum score 575). Application deadline: 4/28 (rolling processing; 11/21 for spring admission). Application fee: $40. *Expenses:* Tuition $4350 per year full-time, $185 per credit part-time for state residents; $7600 per year full-time, $320 per credit part-time for nonresidents. Fees $26 per year.

Hunter College of the City University of New York, Division of Education, Secondary Education Curriculum, Concentration in Spanish Education, 695 Park Avenue, New York, NY 10021-5085. Awards MA. *Degree requirements:* Comprehensive exam required, foreign language and thesis not required. *Entrance requirements:* TOEFL (minimum score 575). Application deadline: 4/28 (rolling processing; 11/21 for spring admission). Application fee: $40. *Expenses:* Tuition $4350 per year full-time, $185 per credit part-time for state residents; $7600 per year full-time, $320 per credit part-time for nonresidents. Fees $26 per year.

Indiana University Bloomington, College of Arts and Sciences, Department of Germanic Studies, Bloomington, IN 47405. Offerings include teaching German (MAT). Department faculty: 11 full-time (3 women). *Average time to degree:* master's–2 years full-time, 4 years part-time. *Application deadline:* 1/15 (priority date; 9/1 for spring admission). *Application fee:* $35. *Expenses:* Tuition $153 per credit hour for state residents; $446 per credit hour for nonresidents. Fees $343 per year. • Terence Thayer, Director, 812-855-1553. Application contact: Cathrine Streeval, Graduate Secretary, 812-855-7947. E-mail: germanic@indiana.edu.

Indiana University Bloomington, College of Arts and Sciences, Department of Spanish and Portuguese, Bloomington, IN 47405. Offerings include teaching Spanish (MAT). Department faculty: 15 full-time (7 women). *Application deadline:* 1/15 (priority date; 9/1 for spring admission). *Application fee:* $35. *Expenses:* Tuition $153 per credit hour for state residents; $446 per credit hour for nonresidents. Fees $343 per year. • Darlene Sadlier, Chair, 812-855-8498. Application contact: Carol Glaze, 812-855-9194.

Indiana University Bloomington, College of Arts and Sciences, Department of French and Italian, Programs in French, Bloomington, IN 47405. Offerings include teaching French (MAT). *Application deadline:* 1/15 (priority date; 9/1 for spring admission). *Application fee:* $35. *Expenses:* Tuition $153 per credit hour for state residents; $446 per credit hour for nonresidents. Fees $343 per year. • Rosemary Lloyd, Chairman, Department of French and Italian, 812-855-1952. E-mail: rolloyd@ucs.indiana.edu. Application contact: Isabel Piedmont, Secretary, 812-855-1088. E-mail: fritdept@indiana.edu.

Indiana University–Purdue University Indianapolis, School of Education, Department of Language Education, Indianapolis, IN 46202-2896. Awards MS. Faculty: 4 full-time (3 women), 4 part-time (2 women). Students: 1 (woman) full-time, 14 part-time (11 women); includes 1 minority (Hispanic), 3 international. Average age 32. In 1997, 8 degrees awarded. *Degree requirements:* Thesis optional, foreign language not required. *Entrance requirements:* GRE General Test (minimum combined score of 1300), minimum GPA of 3.0. Application deadline: 3/1 (priority date; 11/1 for spring admission). Application fee: $35. *Expenses:* Tuition $3602 per year full-time, $150 per credit hour part-time for state residents; $10,392 per year full-time, $433 per credit hour part-time for nonresidents. Fees $100 per year (minimum) full-time, $40 per year (minimum) part-time. *Financial aid:* Federal Work-Study available. *Faculty research:* Emergent literacy, adult literacy, whole language. • Michael Cohen, Director, Teacher Education, 317-274-6814. Application contact: Dr. O. Gilbert Brown, Assistant Dean for Education Student Services, 317-274-0649. Fax: 317-274-6864. E-mail: ogbrown@iupui.edu.

Iona College, School of Arts and Science, Program in Secondary School Subjects, 715 North Avenue, New Rochelle, NY 10801-1890. Offerings include Spanish education (MS Ed, MST). Program faculty: 4 full-time (1 woman), 8 part-time (2 women). *Degree requirements:* Thesis or alternative required, foreign language not required. *Entrance requirements:* Minimum GPA of 2.5 (MST), New York teaching certificate (MS Ed). Application deadline: rolling. Application fee: $25. *Expenses:* Tuition $455 per credit hour. Fees $25 per semester. • Dr. Lucy Murphy, Chair, 914-633-2210. Fax: 914-633-2608. Application contact: Arlene Melillo, Director of Graduate Recruitment, 914-633-2328. Fax: 914-633-2023.

Jacksonville University, College of Arts and Sciences, Division of Education, Program in Foreign Language, 2800 University Boulevard North, Jacksonville, FL 32211-3394. Offers French (MAT), Spanish (MAT). Part-time and evening/weekend programs available. *Degree requirements:* Comprehensive exam required, foreign language and thesis not required. *Entrance requirements:* GRE General Test (minimum combined score of 900), TOEFL (minimum score 500), minimum GPA of 3.0. Application deadline: 8/1 (priority date; rolling processing; 11/1 for spring admission). Application fee: $25.

Long Island University, C.W. Post Campus, School of Education, Department of Curriculum and Instruction, Brookville, NY 11548-1300. Offerings include Spanish education (MS). Department faculty: 10 full-time (5 women), 46 part-time (19 women). *Application deadline:* rolling. *Application fee:* $30. Electronic applications accepted. *Expenses:* Tuition $480 per credit. Fees $316 per year full-time, $71 per semester (minimum) part-time. • Dr. Anthony De Falco, Chairperson, 516-299-2372. Application contact: Camille Marziliano, Academic Counselor, 516-299-2123. Fax: 516-299-4167. E-mail: cmarzili@eagle.liunet.edu.

Louisiana Tech University, College of Education, Department of Curriculum, Instruction and Leadership, Ruston, LA 71272. Offerings include secondary education (M Ed), with options in business education, English education, foreign language education, health and physical education, mathematics education, science education, social studies education, speech education. Accredited by NCATE. Department faculty: 16 full-time (11 women). *Application deadline:* 7/29 (2/3 for spring admission). *Application fee:* $20 ($30 for international students). *Tuition:* $2382 per year full-time, $223 per quarter (minimum) part-time for state residents; $5307 per year full-time, $223 per quarter (minimum) part-time for nonresidents. • Dr. Samuel V. Dauzat, Head, 318-257-4609.

Loyola Marymount University, School of Education, Program in Teaching, Los Angeles, CA 90045-8350. Offerings include Latin education (MAT). Program faculty: 14 full-time (8 women), 25 part-time (20 women). *Degree requirements:* Thesis or alternative, comprehensive exam required, foreign language not required. *Entrance requirements:* GRE General Test, TOEFL (minimum score 550), interview. Application fee: $35. Electronic applications accepted. *Expenses:* Tuition $500 per unit. Fees $111 per year full-time, $28 per year part-time. • Coordinator, 310-338-7307.

Manhattanville College, School of Education, Program in Secondary Education, Purchase, NY 10577-2132. Offerings include languages (MAT), with options in French, Spanish. *Degree requirements:* Thesis, comprehensive exam or research project required, foreign language not required. *Entrance requirements:* Minimum undergraduate GPA of 3.0. Application deadline: rolling. Application fee: $40. *Expenses:* Tuition $410 per credit (minimum). Fees $25 per semester. • Application contact: Carol Messar, Director of Admissions, 914-323-5142. Fax: 914-323-5493.

Marygrove College, Division of Education, Program in Modern Language Translation, Detroit, MI 48221-2599. Awards M Ed. Accredited by NCATE. *Degree requirements:* Research project required, foreign language and thesis not required. *Average time to degree:* master's–2.5 years full-time, 3 years part-time. *Entrance requirements:* MAT, 20 hours of French, Spanish, or equivalent; interview, minimum undergraduate GPA of 3.0; teaching certificate. Application deadline: 8/15 (rolling processing). Application fee: $25.

McGill University, Faculty of Graduate Studies and Research, Faculty of Education, Department of Second Language Education, Program in Teaching French as a Second Language, Montréal, PQ H3A 2T5, Canada. Awards M Ed. Part-time programs available. Faculty: 7 full-time (5 women). Students: 8 part-time (5 women). Average age 25. 10 applicants, 80% accepted. In 1997, 2 degrees awarded. *Degree requirements:* Monograph required, thesis not required. *Entrance requirements:* TOEFL (minimum score 550), mastery of spoken and written French, minimum GPA of 3.0. Application deadline: 3/1 (priority date; rolling processing). Application fee: $60. *Expenses:* Tuition $1668 per year for Canadian residents; $8268 per year for nonresidents. Fees $828 per year for Canadian residents; $1216 per year for nonresidents. *Financial aid:* Fellowships, teaching assistantships, full tuition waivers available. *Faculty research:* Language acquisition, second language teaching and learning, immersion programs, second language development, classroom-centered research in L2 learning. • Application contact: Joyce Gaul, Administrative Assistant, 514-398-6982. Fax: 514-398-5595. E-mail: gaul@education.mcgill.ca.

Michigan State University, College of Arts and Letters, Department of Romance and Classical Languages, East Lansing, MI 48824-1020. Offerings include French (MA), with options in French, French secondary school teaching; Spanish (MA), with options in Spanish, Spanish secondary school teaching. Department faculty: 25 full-time (8 women). *Degree requirements:* Departmental exam required, thesis not required. *Application deadline:* 1/15 (priority date; rolling processing). *Application fee:* $30 ($40 for international students). *Expenses:* Tuition $4609 per year full-time, $223 per credit hour (minimum) part-time for state residents; $8704 per year full-time, $450 per credit hour (minimum) part-time for nonresidents. Fees $576 per year full-time, $476 per year part-time. • Dr. Michael Koppisch, Chairperson, 517-355-8352. Fax: 517-432-3844. E-mail: koppisch@pilot.msu.edu.

Middle Tennessee State University, College of Liberal Arts, Department of Foreign Languages and Literatures, Murfreesboro, TN 37132. Awards MAT. Faculty: 7 full-time (5 women). Students: 10 full-time (5 women), 6 part-time (all women); includes 2 minority (1 Hispanic, 1 Native American), 1 international. Average age 31. 5 applicants, 80% accepted. In 1997, 5 degrees awarded. *Degree requirements:* Comprehensive exams. *Entrance requirements:* GRE. Application deadline: 8/1 (priority date). Application fee: $5. *Expenses:* Tuition $2560 per year full-time, $129 per semester hour part-time for state residents; $7386 per year full-time, $340 per semester hour part-time for nonresidents. Fees $486 per year full-time, $17 per semester (minimum) part-time. *Financial aid:* Institutionally sponsored loans and career-related internships or fieldwork available. Aid available to part-time students. Financial aid application deadline: 5/1; applicants required to submit FAFSA. • Dr. Judith Rusciolelli, Chair, 615-898-2981. Fax: 615-898-5826. E-mail: judithr@mtsu.edu.

Millersville University of Pennsylvania, School of Humanities and Social Sciences, Department of Foreign Languages, Millersville, PA 17551-0302. Offers programs in French (MA, M Ed), German (MA, M Ed), Spanish (MA, M Ed). One or more programs accredited by NCATE. Part-time programs available. Faculty: 14 full-time (8 women), 1 (woman) part-time. Students: 4 full-time (all women), 8 part-time (6 women). Average age 32. 15 applicants, 87% accepted. In 1997, 16 degrees awarded. *Degree requirements:* 1 foreign language, departmental exam required, thesis optional. *Entrance requirements:* GRE or MAT, 24 undergraduate credits in language of concentration, minimum undergraduate GPA of 2.75. Application deadline: 5/1 (priority date; rolling processing). Application fee: $25. *Tuition:* $3468 per year full-time, $234 per credit part-time for state residents; $6236 per year full-time, $387 per credit part-time for nonresidents. *Financial aid:* Federal Work-Study, institutionally sponsored loans available. Aid available to part-time students. Financial aid application deadline: 5/1. *Faculty research:* French architecture and literature, German literature, Spanish literature, classical studies. • Dr. Fred Oppenheimer, Coordinator, 717-872-3526. Fax: 717-871-2003. Application contact: Dr. Robert J. Labriola, Dean of Graduate Studies, 717-872-3030. Fax: 717-871-2022.

Monterey Institute of International Studies, Graduate School of Language and Educational Linguistics, Program in Teaching Foreign Language, 425 Van Buren Street, Monterey, CA 93940-2691. Awards MATFL. Faculty: 9 full-time (5 women), 2 part-time (1 woman). Students: 14 full-time (13 women), 33 part-time (21 women); includes 9 minority (1 African American, 4 Asian Americans, 4 Hispanics), 5 international. Average age 28. 30 applicants, 70% accepted. In 1997, 12 degrees awarded. *Degree requirements:* Portfolio and oral defense. *Average time to degree:* master's–1.5 years full-time, 3 years part-time. *Entrance requirements:* TOEFL (minimum score 600), bachelor's degree in an appropriate language, minimum GPA of 3.0. Application deadline: 8/1 (priority date; rolling processing; 12/1 for spring admission). Application fee: $50. *Expenses:* Tuition $18,200 per year full-time, $760 per semester hour part-time. Fees $45 per year. *Financial aid:* Application deadline 3/15; applicants required to submit FAFSA. • Dr. Jean Turner, Head, 408-647-3522. Fax: 408-647-6650. Application contact: Admissions Office, 408-647-4123. Fax: 408-647-6405. E-mail: admit@miis.edu.

New York University, School of Education, Department of Teaching and Learning, Program in Multilingual/Multicultural Studies, New York, NY 10012-1019. Offerings include foreign language education (MA, CAS). Program faculty: 3 full-time, 7 part-time. *Degree requirements:* For master's, thesis required (for some programs), foreign language not required. *Entrance requirements:* For master's, TOEFL; for CAS, TOEFL, master's degree. Application deadline: 2/1 (priority date; rolling processing; 12/1 for spring admission). Application fee: $40 ($60 for international students). • Harvey Nadler, Director, 212-998-5494. Application contact: Office of Graduate Admissions, 212-998-5030. Fax: 212-995-4328.

North Georgia College & State University, Graduate School, Program in Education, Dahlonega, GA 30597-1001. Offerings include secondary education (M Ed), with options in art education, biology education, chemistry education, English education, mathematics education, modern languages education, physical education, science education, social science education. Accredited by NCATE. Program faculty: 57 full-time (15 women), 7 part-time (4 women). *Degree requirements:* Comprehensive exam required, thesis optional, foreign language not required. *Entrance requirements:* GRE General Test (minimum combined score of 800) or MAT (minimum score 44), minimum GPA of 2.75. Application deadline: 9/1 (priority date; rolling processing). Application fee: $25. • Dr. Bob Michael, Dean, School of Education, 706-864-1533. Application contact: Mai-Lan Ledbetter, Coordinator of Graduate Admissions, 706-864-1543. Fax: 706-864-1668. E-mail: mledbetter@nugget.ngc.peachnet.edu.

Occidental College, Department of Education, Program in Secondary Education, Los Angeles, CA 90041-3392. Offerings include French (MAT), Spanish (MAT). Program faculty: 4 full-time (1 woman). *Degree requirements:* Internship required, foreign language and thesis not required. *Entrance requirements:* GRE General Test (minimum score 550 on each section or combined score of 1650 on three sections), TOEFL (minimum score 600), minimum GPA of 3.0. Application deadline: 3/1 (priority date; rolling processing; 10/1 for spring admission). Application fee: $40. *Expenses:* Tuition $21,256 per year full-time, $865 per unit part-time. Fees $314 per year. • Application contact: Susan Molik, Administrative Assistant, Graduate Office, 213-259-2921.

Plattsburgh State University of New York, Faculty of Professional Studies, Center for Educational Studies and Services, Program in Secondary Education, Plattsburgh, NY 12901-2681. Offerings include French (MST), Spanish (MST). *Application deadline:* rolling. *Application fee:* $50. *Expenses:* Tuition $5100 per year full-time, $213 per credit hour part-time for state residents; $8416 per year full-time, $351 per credit hour part-time for nonresidents. Fees $395 per year full-time, $15.10 per credit hour part-time. • Dr. Raymond Domenico, Director and Associate Dean, Center for Educational Studies and Services, 518-564-2122.

Purdue University, School of Education, Department of Curriculum and Instruction, West Lafayette, IN 47907. Offerings include foreign language education (MS Ed, PhD, Ed S). Accredited by NCATE. Department faculty: 34 full-time (15 women), 3 part-time (1 woman). *Degree requirements:* For master's, thesis optional; for doctorate, dissertation, oral and written exams; for Ed S, oral presentation, project required, thesis not required. *Entrance requirements:* For master's, TOEFL (minimum score 550), minimum B average; for doctorate, GRE General Test (minimum score 500 on each section), TOEFL (minimum score 550); for Ed S, minimum B average. Application deadline: 1/15 (priority date; 9/15 for spring admission). Application fee: $30. Electronic applications accepted. *Tuition:* $3500 per year full-time, $126 per credit hour part-time for state residents; $11,720 per year full-time, $387 per credit hour part-time for nonresidents. • Dr. J. L. Peters, Head, 765-494-9172. Fax: 765-496-1622. E-mail: peters@purdue.edu. Application contact: Christine Larsen, Coordinator of Graduate Studies, 765-494-2345. Fax: 765-494-5832. E-mail: gradoffice@soe.purdue.edu.

Purdue University, School of Liberal Arts, Department of Foreign Languages and Literatures, West Lafayette, IN 47907. Offerings include French (MA, MAT, PhD), with options in French (MA, PhD), French education (MAT); German (MA, MAT, PhD), with options in German (MA, PhD), German education (MAT); Spanish (MA, MAT, PhD), with options in Spanish (MA, PhD), Spanish education (MAT). One or more programs accredited by NCATE. Department faculty: 39 full-time, 27 part-time. *Average time to degree:* master's–2 years full-time; doctorate–5 years full-time. *Application deadline:* 7/15 (rolling processing; 10/15 for spring admission). *Application fee:* $30. Electronic applications accepted. *Tuition:* $3500 per year full-time, $126 per credit hour part-time for state residents; $11,720 per year full-time, $387 per credit hour part-time for nonresidents. • Dr. C. E. Keck, Head, 765-494-3834. E-mail: cekeck@purdue.edu. Application contact: Dr. A. J. Tamburri, Coordinator of Graduate Studies, 765-494-3839. E-mail: tamburri@purdue.edu.

Queens College of the City University of New York, Social Science Division, School of Education, Department of Secondary Education, 65-30 Kissena Boulevard, Flushing, NY 11367-1597. Offerings include French (MS Ed, AC), Italian (MS Ed, AC), Spanish (MS Ed, AC). *Degree requirements:* For master's, research project required, foreign language and thesis not required; for AC, thesis optional, foreign language not required. *Entrance requirements:* For master's, TOEFL (minimum score 600), minimum GPA of 3.0; for AC, TOEFL (minimum score 600). Application deadline: 4/1 (rolling processing; 11/1 for spring admission). Application fee: $40. *Expenses:* Tuition $4350 per year full-time, $185 per credit part-time for state residents; $7600 per year full-time, $320 per credit part-time for nonresidents. Fees $104 per year. • Dr. Philip Anderson, Chairperson, 718-997-5150. Application contact: Mario Caruso, Director of Graduate Admissions, 718-997-5200. Fax: 718-997-5193. E-mail: graduate%queens.bitnet@cunyvm.cuny.edu.

Quinnipiac College, School of Liberal Arts, Program in Secondary and Middle School Teaching, Hamden, CT 06518-1904. Offerings include French (MAT), Spanish (MAT). Program

Directory: Foreign Languages Education

Quinnipiac College (continued)

faculty: 21 full-time (5 women), 16 part-time (9 women). *Degree requirements:* Thesis. *Average time to degree:* master's–1.5 years full-time, 3 years part-time. *Entrance requirements:* PRAXIS I, minimum GPA of 2.67. Application deadline: rolling. Application fee: $45. Electronic applications accepted. *Expenses:* Tuition $395 per credit hour. Fees $380 per year full-time. • Carol Orticari, Director, 203-281-8978. Fax: 203-281-8709. E-mail: orticari@quinnipiac.edu. Application contact: Scott Farber, Director of Graduate Admissions, 203-281-8795. Fax: 203-287-5238. E-mail: qcgradadmi@quinnipiac.edu.

Rhode Island College, School of Graduate Studies, Faculty of Arts and Sciences, Department of Modern Languages, Providence, RI 02908-1924. Offerings include Spanish (MAT). Accredited by NCATE. Department faculty: 8 full-time (3 women). *Application deadline:* 4/1 (rolling processing). *Application fee:* $25. *Tuition:* $4064 per year full-time, $214 per credit part-time for state residents; $7658 per year full-time, $376 per credit part-time for nonresidents. • Dr. Olga Juzyn-Amestoy, Chair, 401-456-8029.

Rivier College, Department of Modern Languages, Nashua, NH 03060-5086. Awards MAT. Part-time and evening/weekend programs available. *Application deadline:* rolling. *Application fee:* $25.

Rutgers, The State University of New Jersey, New Brunswick, Program in French, New Brunswick, NJ 08903. Offerings include French studies (MAT). Program faculty: 18 full-time (10 women). *Application deadline:* 6/15. *Application fee:* $40. *Expenses:* Tuition $6492 per year full-time, $268 per credit part-time for state residents; $9520 per year full-time, $395 per credit part-time for nonresidents. Fees $208 per year (minimum). • Francois Cornilliat, Director, 732-932-3750. Fax: 732-932-8327. E-mail: frenchl@rci.rutgers.edu.

Rutgers, The State University of New Jersey, New Brunswick, Program in Italian, New Brunswick, NJ 08903. Offerings include language, literature and civilization (MAT). Program faculty: 5 full-time (1 woman). *Application deadline:* 7/1. *Application fee:* $40. *Expenses:* Tuition $6492 per year full-time, $268 per credit part-time for state residents; $9520 per year full-time, $395 per credit part-time for nonresidents. Fees $208 per year (minimum). • Dr. Laura S. White, Director, 732-932-7031.

Rutgers, The State University of New Jersey, New Brunswick, Graduate School of Education, Department of Learning and Teaching, Program in Language Education, New Brunswick, NJ 08903. Offers English as a second language education (Ed M, Ed D), language education (Ed M, Ed D, Ed S). Part-time programs available. Faculty: 3 full-time (2 women). Students: 71. 90 applicants, 39% accepted. In 1997, 28 master's, 1 doctorate awarded. Terminal master's awarded for partial completion of doctoral program. *Degree requirements:* For master's, comprehensive exam required, thesis not required; for doctorate, dissertation, concept paper and qualifying exam. *Average time to degree:* master's–1.5 years full-time, 3 years part-time; doctorate–4 years full-time, 7 years part-time. *Entrance requirements:* For master's, GRE General Test (minimum combined score of 1000; average 1100), TOEFL (minimum score 600), minimum GPA of 3.0; for doctorate and Ed S, GRE General Test (minimum combined score of 1100; average 1150), TOEFL (minimum score 600), minimum GPA of 3.5. Application deadline: 3/1 (11/1 for spring admission). Application fee: $40. *Expenses:* Tuition $6492 per year full-time, $268 per credit part-time for state residents; $9520 per year full-time, $395 per credit part-time for nonresidents. Fees $208 per year (minimum). *Financial aid:* 18 students received aid. Financial aid application deadline: 3/1. *Faculty research:* Linguistics, sociolinguistics, cross-cultural/international communication. • Dr. Eliane C. Condon, Coordinator, 732-932-7496 Ext. 123. Fax: 732-932-7552. E-mail: condon@rci.rutgers.edu.

School for International Training, Program in Teaching, Brattleboro, VT 05302-0676. Offerings include French (MAT), Spanish (MAT). Program faculty: 20 full-time (12 women), 4 part-time (3 women). *Degree requirements:* 1 foreign language, thesis, practice teaching. *Entrance requirements:* TOEFL (minimum score 550). Application deadline: rolling. Application fee: $45. *Expenses:* Tuition $18,000 per year (minimum). Fees $1283 per year (minimum). • Claire Stanley, Director, 802-257-7751 Ext.3300. Application contact: Fiona Cook, Admissions Counselor, 802-258-3270. Fax: 802-258-3500.

Smith College, Department of Education and Child Study, Program in Secondary Education, Northampton, MA 01063. Offerings include classics education (MAT), French education (MAT), Spanish education (MAT). Program faculty: 6 full-time (3 women), 3 part-time (2 women). *Degree requirements:* 1 foreign language required, thesis not required. *Average time to degree:* master's–1 year full-time, 4 years part-time. *Entrance requirements:* GRE General Test or MAT. Application deadline: 4/15 (12/1 for spring admission). Application fee: $50. *Tuition:* $21,680 per year full-time, $2720 per course part-time. • Rosetta Cohen, Head, 413-585-3266. E-mail: rcohen@sophia.smith.edu.

Southwest Texas State University, School of Liberal Arts, Department of Modern Languages, Program in Spanish, San Marcos, TX 78666. Offerings include Spanish education (MAT). Program faculty: 7 full-time (5 women). *Application deadline:* 7/15 (priority date; rolling processing; 11/15 for spring admission). *Application fee:* $25 ($50 for international students). *Expenses:* Tuition $648 per year full-time, $120 per semester (minimum) part-time for state residents; $4500 per year full-time, $750 per semester (minimum) part-time for nonresidents. Fees $1264 per year full-time, $314 per semester (minimum) part-time. • Dr. Catherine Jaffe, Graduate Adviser, 512-245-2360. Fax: 512-245-8298. E-mail: cj10@swt.edu.

Stanford University, School of Education, Teacher Education Program, Stanford, CA 94305-9991. Offerings include languages education (AM). *Degree requirements:* Thesis required, foreign language not required. *Entrance requirements:* GRE General Test. Application deadline: 1/15. Application fee: $65 ($75 for international students). *Expenses:* Tuition $22,110 per year. Fees $156 per year. • Administrator, 650-723-4891. Application contact: Graduate Admissions Office, 650-723-2110.

Stanford University, School of Humanities and Sciences, Department of French and Italian, Stanford, CA 94305-9991. Offerings include French education (MAT). Department faculty: 15 full-time (4 women). *Application deadline:* 1/1. *Application fee:* $65 ($75 for international students). *Expenses:* Tuition $22,110 per year. Fees $156 per year. • Ralph Hester, Chair, 650-723-3292. Fax: 650-723-0482. E-mail: rmhester@leland.stanford.edu. Application contact: Graduate Admissions Coordinator, 650-723-4186.

Stanford University, School of Humanities and Sciences, Department of Slavic Languages and Literatures, Stanford, CA 94305-9991. Offerings include Slavic languages and literatures (MAT, PhD). Terminal master's awarded for partial completion of doctoral program. Department faculty: 5 full-time (1 woman). *Degree requirements:* For doctorate, 3 foreign languages, dissertation. *Entrance requirements:* For doctorate, GRE General Test, TOEFL, language proficiency test. Application deadline: 1/1. Application fee: $65 ($75 for international students). *Expenses:* Tuition $22,110 per year. Fees $156 per year. • Gregory Freidin, Chair, 650-725-0006. Fax: 650-725-0011. E-mail: gfreidin@leland.stanford.edu. Application contact: Departmental Administrator, 650-723-4438.

State University of New York at Binghamton, School of Education and Human Development, Program in Secondary Education, Binghamton, NY 13902-6000. Offerings include French education (MAT, MST), Spanish education (MAT, MST). *Application deadline:* 4/15 (priority date; rolling processing; 11/1 for spring admission). *Application fee:* $50. Electronic applications accepted. *Expenses:* Tuition $5100 per year full-time, $213 per credit hour part-time for state residents; $8416 per year full-time, $351 per credit hour part-time for nonresidents. Fees $654 per year full-time, $75 per semester (minimum) part-time. • Dr. Wayne Ross, Coordinator, 607-777-2478.

State University of New York at Buffalo, Graduate School, Graduate School of Education, Department of Learning and Instruction, Buffalo, NY 14260. Offerings include secondary education (Ed M, Ed D, PhD), with options in English education (Ed D, PhD), foreign language education (Ed D, PhD), mathematics education (Ed D, PhD), science education (PhD). Terminal master's awarded for partial completion of doctoral program. Department faculty: 20 full-time (9 women), 7 part-time (2 women). *Degree requirements:* Dissertation, research analysis exam required, foreign language not required. *Entrance requirements:* GRE General Test, TOEFL (minimum score 600), interview. Application deadline: 2/1 (11/15 for spring admission). Application fee: $50. *Tuition:* $5970 per year full-time, $288 per credit hour part-time for state residents; $9286 per year full-time, $426 per credit hour part-time for nonresidents. • Dr. Michael Kibby, Chair, 716-645-2455. Application contact: Barbara Cracchiolo, Admissions Secretary, 716-645-2457. Fax: 716-645-3161.

State University of New York at Stony Brook, School of Professional Development and Continuing Studies, Stony Brook, NY 11794. Offerings include French-grade 7-12 (MAT), German-grade 7-12 (MAT), Italian-grade 7-12 (MAT), Russian-grade 7-12 (MAT). School faculty: 1 full-time, 101 part-time. *Application deadline:* 1/15. *Application fee:* $50. *Expenses:* Tuition $5100 per year full-time, $213 per credit hour part-time for state residents; $8416 per year full-time, $351 per credit hour part-time for nonresidents. Fees $529 per year full-time, $77 per semester (minimum) part-time. • Dr. Paul J. Edelson, Dean, 516-632-7052. E-mail: paul.edelson@sunysb.edu. Application contact: Sandra Romansky, Director of Admissions and Advisement, 516-632-7050. Fax: 516-632-9046. E-mail: sandra.romansky@sunysb.edu.

State University of New York College at Cortland, Division of Arts and Sciences, Program in Secondary Education, Cortland, NY 13045. Offerings include French (MS Ed). *Application deadline:* rolling. *Application fee:* $50. *Expenses:* Tuition $5100 per year full-time, $213 per credit hour part-time for state residents; $8416 per year full-time, $351 per credit hour part-time for nonresidents. Fees $644 per year full-time, $79 per semester (minimum) part-time. • Roger Sipher, Head, 607-753-2723. Application contact: Jeanne M. Bechtel, Director of Admissions, 607-753-4711. Fax: 607-753-5998.

State University of New York College at Cortland, Division of Professional Studies, Department of Education, Cortland, NY 13045. Offerings include secondary education (MS Ed), with options in biology, chemistry, earth science, French, mathematics, physics. *Application deadline:* rolling. *Application fee:* $50. *Expenses:* Tuition $5100 per year full-time, $213 per credit hour part-time for state residents; $8416 per year full-time, $351 per credit hour part-time for nonresidents. Fees $644 per year full-time, $79 per semester (minimum) part-time. • Mary Ware, Chair, 607-753-2705. Application contact: Jeanne M. Bechtel, Director of Admissions, 607-753-4711. Fax: 607-753-5998.

Teachers College, Columbia University, Graduate Faculty of Education, Department of Arts and Humanities, Program in Teaching of Spanish, 525 West 120th Street, New York, NY 10027-6696. Awards Ed M, MA, Ed D, Ed DCT, PhD. Part-time programs available. Faculty: 1 full-time (0 women), 1 part-time (0 women), 1.4 FTE. Students: 19 full-time (12 women), 27 part-time (20 women); includes 24 minority (2 African Americans, 2 Asian Americans, 20 Hispanics), 2 international. Average age 35. 25 applicants, 100% accepted. In 1997, 7 master's, 1 doctorate awarded. Terminal master's awarded for partial completion of doctoral program. *Degree requirements:* For doctorate, dissertation. *Application deadline:* 5/15 (12/1 for spring admission). *Application fee:* $50. *Expenses:* Tuition $640 per credit. Fees $120 per semester. *Financial aid:* Full and partial tuition waivers, Federal Work-Study, institutionally sponsored loans, and career-related internships or fieldwork available. Aid available to part-time students. Financial aid application deadline: 2/1. *Faculty research:* Content of teacher training, curriculum, applied linguistics in the teaching of Spanish, distance learning, poetry in Spanish. • Application contact: Amy Rotheim, Office of Admissions, 212-678-3710. Fax: 212-678-4171.

Union College, Graduate and Continuing Studies, Programs in Education, Schenectady, NY 12308-2311. Offerings include French (MAT), German (MAT), Latin (MAT), Spanish (MAT). *Application deadline:* 5/15. *Application fee:* $35. *Tuition:* $1155 per course. • Dr. Patrick Allen, Educational Studies Director, 518-388-6361.

University of Central Florida, College of Education, Department of Instructional Programs, Program in Foreign Language Education, Orlando, FL 32816. Awards MA, M Ed. Accredited by NCATE. Students: 0. *Degree requirements:* Thesis or alternative required, foreign language not required. *Entrance requirements:* GRE General Test (minimum combined score of 840). Application deadline: 7/15. Application fee: $20. *Expenses:* Tuition $3288 per year full-time, $137 per credit hour part-time for state residents; $11,520 per year full-time, $480 per credit hour part-time for nonresidents. Fees $105 per year. • Dr. John Armstrong, Interim Chair, Department of Instructional Programs, 407-823-2006.

University of Connecticut, School of Education, Field of Foreign Languages Education, Storrs, CT 06269. Awards MA, PhD. Accredited by NCATE. Faculty: 1. Students: 2 full-time (both women). Average age 22. 3 applicants, 67% accepted. Terminal master's awarded for partial completion of doctoral program. *Degree requirements:* For master's, thesis or alternative; for doctorate, dissertation. *Entrance requirements:* For doctorate, GRE General Test. Application deadline: 6/1 (priority date; rolling processing; 11/1 for spring admission). Application fee: $40 ($45 for international students). *Expenses:* Tuition $5272 per year full-time, $293 per credit part-time for state residents; $13,696 per year full-time, $761 per credit part-time for nonresidents. Fees $948 per year full-time, $640 per year part-time. *Financial aid:* Teaching assistantships available. Financial aid application deadline: 2/15. • Thomas P. Weinland, Head, 860-486-2433.

University of Delaware, College of Arts and Science, Department of Foreign Languages and Literatures, Newark, DE 19716. Offerings include foreign language pedagogy (MA). Department faculty: 26 full-time (11 women). *Degree requirements:* 2 foreign languages, thesis or alternative, comprehensive exam. *Average time to degree:* master's–2 years full-time. *Entrance requirements:* GRE General Test, TOEFL (minimum score 550). Application deadline: 3/1 (priority date; rolling processing; 11/1 for spring admission). Application fee: $45. Electronic applications accepted. *Expenses:* Tuition $4250 per year full-time, $236 per credit hour part-time for state residents; $12,250 per year full-time, $681 per credit hour part-time for nonresidents. Fees $466 per year full-time, $15 per semester (minimum) part-time. • Dr. Mary Donaldson-Evans, Chair, 302-831-2588. E-mail: maryde@brahms.udel.edu. Application contact: Lucille Short, Graduate Secretary, 302-831-4385. E-mail: lucille.short@mvs.udel.edu.

University of Florida, College of Education, Department of Instruction and Curriculum, Gainesville, FL 32611. Offerings include foreign language education (MAE, M Ed, Ed D, PhD, Ed S). Accredited by NCATE. Department faculty: 42. *Degree requirements:* For master's, thesis optional, foreign language not required; for doctorate, variable foreign language requirement, dissertation. *Entrance requirements:* For master's and doctorate, GRE General Test (minimum combined score of 1000), minimum GPA of 3.0; for Ed S, GRE General Test. Application deadline: 6/5. Application fee: $20. *Tuition:* $138 per credit hour for state residents; $481 per credit hour for nonresidents. • Dr. Mary Grace Kantowski, Chair, 352-392-9191 Ext. 200. E-mail: mgk@coe.ufl.edu. Application contact: Dr. Ben Nelms, Graduate Coordinator, 352-392-9191 Ext. 225. Fax: 352-392-9193. E-mail: bfn@coe.ufl.edu.

University of Georgia, College of Education, Programs in Secondary Education, Athens, GA 30602. Offerings include language education (M Ed, PhD, Ed S). Accredited by NCATE. Faculty: 46 full-time (17 women). *Entrance requirements:* For Ed S, GRE General Test or MAT. Application deadline: 7/1 (priority date; 11/15 for spring admission). Application fee: $30. Electronic applications accepted. *Tuition:* $3290 per year full-time, $643 per semester (minimum) part-time for state residents; $11,300 per year full-time, $1645 per semester (minimum) part-time for nonresidents. • Dr. Russell H. Yeany, Dean, 706-542-3866. Fax: 706-542-0360.

University of Hawaii at Manoa, College of Arts and Sciences, College of Language, Linguistics and Literature, Department of English as a Second Language, Honolulu, HI 96822. Offerings include second language acquisition (PhD). Department faculty: 13 full-time (4 women). *Degree requirements:* 2 foreign languages (computer language can substitute for one), dissertation, comprehensive exams. *Average time to degree:* master's–2 years full-time, 3.5 years part-time; doctorate–5 years full-time. *Entrance requirements:* GRE General Test, TOEFL (minimum score 600), MA, scholarly publications. Application deadline: rolling. Application fee: $25 ($50 for international students). *Tuition:* $4029 per year full-time, $214 per credit hour part-time for state residents; $9957 per year full-time, $461 per credit hour part-time for nonresidents. • Dr. Roderick A. Jacobs, Chairperson, 808-956-8610. E-mail: rjacobs@hawaii.edu. Application contact: Graduate Chair, 808-956-8610. Fax: 808-956-2802. E-mail: desl@hawaii.edu.

University of Idaho, College of Graduate Studies, College of Letters and Science, Department of Foreign Languages and Literatures, Moscow, ID 83844-4140. Offerings include French (MAT), Spanish (MAT). One or more programs accredited by NCATE. Department faculty: 10 full-time (0 women), 6 part-time (2 women), 11.16 FTE. *Entrance requirements:* Minimum GPA of 2.8. Application deadline: 8/1 (12/15 for spring admission). Application fee: $35 ($45 for international students). *Expenses:* Tuition $0 for state residents; $6000 per year full-time, $95 per credit part-time for nonresidents. Fees $2676 per year full-time, $134 per credit part-time. • Dr. James Reece, Chair, 208-885-6179.

University of Illinois at Urbana–Champaign, College of Liberal Arts and Sciences, Department of Spanish, Italian and Portuguese, Urbana, IL 61801. Offerings include Spanish (MAT). Department faculty: 22 full-time (7 women). *Application deadline:* rolling. *Application fee:* $40 ($50 for international students). • Ronald W. Sousa, Head, 217-244-3250.

University of Louisville, College of Arts and Sciences, Department of Classical and Modern Languages, Program in Foreign Language Education, Louisville, KY 40292-0001. Awards MA. One or more programs accredited by NCATE. Students: 4 part-time (2 women). Average age 31. In 1997, 1 degree awarded. *Entrance requirements:* GRE General Test. Application deadline: rolling. Application fee: $25. • Dr. Wendy Pfeffer, Chair, Department of Classical and Modern Languages, 502-852-6681.

University of Maine, College of Liberal Arts and Sciences, Department of Modern Languages and Classics, Orono, ME 04469. Offerings include German (MAT), Spanish (MAT). MAT (German, Spanish) admissions temporarily suspended. Department faculty: 12 full-time (6 women). *Application deadline:* 2/1 (priority date; rolling processing; 10/15 for spring admission). *Application fee:* $50. *Expenses:* Tuition $194 per credit hour for state residents; $548 per credit hour for nonresidents. Fees $378 per year full-time, $33 per semester (minimum) part-time. • Dr. Kristina Passman, Chair, 207-581-2073. Fax: 207-581-1832. Application contact: Scott Delcourt, Director of the Graduate School, 207-581-3218. Fax: 207-581-3232. E-mail: graduate@maine.edu.

University of Manitoba, Faculty of Education, Department of Curriculum: Humanities and Social Sciences, Winnipeg, MB R3T 2N2, Canada. Offerings include French as a second language (M Ed), modern languages (M Ed). *Degree requirements:* Thesis or alternative required, foreign language not required.

University of Massachusetts Amherst, College of Humanities and Fine Arts, Department of French and Italian, Amherst, MA 01003-0001. Offerings include Italian studies (MAT). Accredited by NCATE. Department faculty: 14 full-time (4 women). *Application deadline:* 3/1 (priority date; rolling processing; 10/1 for spring admission). *Application fee:* $40. *Expenses:* Tuition $2640 per year full-time, $110 per credit part-time for state residents; $3690 per year (minimum) full-time, $165 per credit (minimum) part-time for nonresidents. Fees $2856 per year full-time, $422 per semester part-time for state residents; $3204 per year full-time, $480 per semester part-time for nonresidents. • Dr. Dennis Porter, Director, 413-545-2314. E-mail: dporter@frital.umass.edu.

University of Michigan, College of Literature, Science, and the Arts, Department of Classical Studies, Ann Arbor, MI 48109. Offerings include teaching Latin (MAT). Department faculty: 16 full-time (6 women), 7 part-time (3 women), 19.5 FTE. *Application deadline:* 1/10. *Application fee:* $55. Electronic applications accepted. • Sharon C. Herbert, Chair, 734-764-0360. Fax: 734-763-4959. E-mail: classics@umich.edu.

University of Nebraska at Kearney, College of Fine Arts and Humanities, Department of Modern Languages, Kearney, NE 68849-0001. Offers programs in French (MA Ed), German (MA Ed), Spanish (MA Ed). Accredited by NCATE. Part-time and evening/weekend programs available. Faculty: 5 full-time (2 women). Students: 1 full-time (0 women), 2 part-time (both women). In 1997, 2 degrees awarded. *Degree requirements:* Thesis optional. *Entrance requirements:* GRE General Test. Application deadline: 8/1 (priority date; rolling processing; 12/15 for spring admission). Application fee: $35. *Expenses:* Tuition $1494 per year full-time, $83 per credit hour part-time for state residents; $2826 per year full-time, $157 per credit hour part-time for nonresidents. Fees $229 per year full-time, $11.25 per semester (minimum) part-time. *Financial aid:* In 1997–98, 2 teaching assistantships were awarded; research assistantships and career-related internships or fieldwork also available. Aid available to part-time students. Financial aid application deadline: 3/1; applicants required to submit FAFSA. • Dr. Anita Hart, Chair, 308-865-8536.

The University of North Carolina at Chapel Hill, School of Education, Programs in Teacher Education, Program in Secondary Education, Chapel Hill, NC 27599. Offerings include French (MAT), German (MAT), Japanese (MAT), Latin (MAT), Spanish (MAT). One or more programs accredited by NCATE. *Degree requirements:* Comprehensive exam required, foreign language and thesis not required. *Entrance requirements:* GRE General Test (minimum combined score of 1000), minimum GPA of 3.0 during last 2 years of undergraduate course work. Application deadline: 1/1 (rolling processing). Application fee: $55. *Expenses:* Tuition $1428 per year full-time, $357 per semester (minimum) part-time for state residents; $10,414 per year full-time, $2604 per semester (minimum) part-time for nonresidents. Fees $782 per year full-time, $332 per semester (minimum) part-time. • Dr. Walter Pryzwansky, Director of Graduate Studies, 919-966-7000. Application contact: Janet Carroll, Registrar, 919-966-1346. Fax: 919-962-1533. E-mail: jscarrol@email.unc.edu.

University of Pittsburgh, School of Education, Department of Instruction and Learning, Program in Secondary Education, Pittsburgh, PA 15260. Offerings include foreign languages education (MA, MAT, M Ed, Ed D, PhD). *Degree requirements:* For doctorate, dissertation required, foreign language not required. *Average time to degree:* master's–2 years full-time, 4 years part-time; doctorate–4 years full-time, 6 years part-time. *Entrance requirements:* For doctorate, GRE General Test, TOEFL (minimum score 650). Application deadline: 2/1. Application fee: $30 ($40 for international students). *Expenses:* Tuition $8018 per year full-time, $329 per credit part-time for state residents; $16,508 per year full-time, $680 per credit part-time for nonresidents. Fees $480 per year full-time, $180 per year part-time. • Application contact: Jackie Harden, Manager, 412-648-7060. Fax: 412-648-1899. E-mail: jackie@sched.fsl.pitt.edu.

University of Puerto Rico, Río Piedras, College of Education, Program in Curriculum and Teaching, San Juan, PR 00931. Offerings include Spanish education (M Ed). *Degree requirements:* Thesis required, foreign language not required. *Entrance requirements:* PAEG, minimum GPA of 3.0. Application deadline: 2/21. Application fee: $17.

University of South Carolina, Graduate School, College of Liberal Arts, Department of French and Classics, Columbia, SC 29208. Offerings include French education (IMA, MAT). Accredited by NCATE. IMA and MAT (French education) offered in cooperation with the College of Education. Department faculty: 12 full-time (6 women). *Application deadline:* 5/1 (priority date; rolling processing). *Application fee:* $35. Electronic applications accepted. *Expenses:* Tuition $3894 per year full-time, $193 per credit hour part-time for state residents; $8114 per year full-time, $404 per credit hour part-time for nonresidents. Fees $125 per year full-time, $37 per semester (minimum) part-time. • William F. Edmiston, Chair, 803-777-9734. Fax: 803-777-0454. E-mail: edmistonw@sc.edu.

University of South Carolina, Graduate School, College of Liberal Arts, Department of Germanic, Slavic and Oriental Languages, Columbia, SC 29208. Offerings include German education (IMA, MAT). Accredited by NCATE. IMA and MAT offered in cooperation with the College of Education. Department faculty: 7 full-time (2 women). *Application deadline:* 5/1 (priority date; rolling processing). *Application fee:* $35. Electronic applications accepted. *Expenses:* Tuition $3894 per year full-time, $193 per credit hour part-time for state residents; $8114 per year full-time, $404 per credit hour part-time for nonresidents. Fees $125 per year full-time, $37 per semester (minimum) part-time. • Dr. Margit Resch, Chair, 803-777-4882. E-mail: reschm@garnet.cla.sc.edu. Application contact: Dr. Wolfgang D. Elfe, Graduate Director, 803-777-2904. Fax: 803-777-0132. E-mail: elfew@garnet.cla.sc.edu.

University of Southern Mississippi, College of Liberal Arts, Department of Foreign Languages and Literatures, Hattiesburg, MS 39406-5167. Awards MATL. Faculty: 10 full-time (5 women). Students: 19 full-time (11 women), 49 part-time (41 women); includes 10 minority (1 African American, 2 Asian Americans, 7 Hispanics), 10 international. Average age 32. 28 applicants, 68% accepted. In 1997, 56 degrees awarded. *Entrance requirements:* GRE General Test. Application deadline: rolling. Application fee: $0 ($25 for international students). *Tuition:* $2870 per year full-time, $137 per credit hour part-time for state residents; $5972 per year full-time, $172 per credit hour part-time for nonresidents. *Financial aid:* Teaching assistantships available. Financial aid application deadline: 3/15. • Dr. Rafael Sanchez, Chair, 601-266-4964.

University of South Florida, College of Education, Department of Secondary Education, Program in Foreign Language Education, Tampa, FL 33620-9951. Awards MA, M Ed. Accredited by NCATE. Part-time and evening/weekend programs available. Students: 7 full-time (4 women), 14 part-time (9 women); includes 7 minority (1 African American, 6 Hispanics), 6 international. Average age 33. 5 applicants, 100% accepted. In 1997, 1 degree awarded. *Entrance requirements:* GRE General Test (minimum combined score of 1000), minimum GPA of 3.5 in last 60 hours. Application deadline: 6/1 (10/15 for spring admission). Application fee: $20. Electronic applications accepted. *Tuition:* $142 per credit hour for state residents; $486 per credit hour for nonresidents. *Financial aid:* Federal Work-Study, institutionally sponsored loans available. Aid available to part-time students. Financial aid applicants required to submit FAFSA. • Application contact: Carine Feyten, Coordinator, 813-974-3504. Fax: 813-974-3837. E-mail: feyten@tempest.coedu.usf.edu.

University of Tennessee, Knoxville, College of Education, Program in Education I, Knoxville, TN 37996. Offerings include English, foreign language and ESL education (PhD). Accredited by NCATE. *Degree requirements:* 1 foreign language (computer language can substitute), dissertation. *Entrance requirements:* GRE General Test, TOEFL (minimum score 550), minimum GPA of 2.7. Application deadline: 2/1 (priority date; rolling processing). Application fee: $35. Electronic applications accepted. *Tuition:* $3354 per year full-time, $181 per semester hour part-time for state residents; $8410 per year full-time, $462 per semester hour part-time for nonresidents. • Dr. Tom George, Associate Dean, 423-974-0907. Fax: 423-974-8718. E-mail: tgeorge1@utk.edu.

University of Tennessee, Knoxville, College of Education, Program in Education II, Knoxville, TN 37996. Offerings include foreign language/ESL education (MS, Ed D, Ed S). Accredited by NCATE. *Degree requirements:* For master's and Ed S, thesis optional, foreign language not required; for doctorate, dissertation required, foreign language not required. *Entrance requirements:* For master's, TOEFL (minimum score 550), minimum GPA of 2.7; for doctorate, GRE General Test, TOEFL (minimum score 550), minimum GPA of 2.7; for Ed S, TOEFL (minimum score 550), GRE General Test, minimum GPA of 2.7. Application deadline: 2/1 (priority date; rolling processing). Application fee: $35. Electronic applications accepted. *Tuition:* $3354 per year full-time, $181 per semester hour part-time for state residents; $8410 per year full-time, $462 per semester hour part-time for nonresidents. • Dr. Tom George, Associate Dean, 423-974-0907. Fax: 423-974-8718. E-mail: tgeorge1@utk.edu.

The University of Texas at Austin, Graduate School, College of Education, Program in Foreign Language Education, Austin, TX 78712. Awards MA, PhD. Students: 106 (72 women); includes 7 minority (5 Asian Americans, 2 Hispanics), 40 international. 93 applicants, 51% accepted. In 1997, 15 master's, 18 doctorates awarded. *Degree requirements:* 1 foreign language, thesis/dissertation. *Entrance requirements:* GRE General Test. Application deadline: 2/1 (rolling processing; 10/1 for spring admission). Application fee: $50 ($75 for international students). Electronic applications accepted. *Expenses:* Tuition $2592 per year full-time, $324 per semester (minimum) part-time for state residents; $7704 per year full-time, $963 per semester (minimum) part-time for nonresidents. Fees $778 per year full-time, $161 per semester (minimum) part-time. *Financial aid:* In 1997–98, 5 fellowships totaling $49,500 were awarded. Financial aid application deadline: 2/1. • Application contact: Elaine K. Horwitz, Graduate Adviser, 512-471-4078. Fax: 512-471-8460. E-mail: horwitz@mail.utexas.edu.

University of Utah, College of Humanities, Department of Languages and Literature, Program in Language Pedagogy, Salt Lake City, UT 84112-1107. Awards MAT. *Entrance requirements:* TOEFL. Application deadline: 7/1. Application fee: $30 ($50 for international students). *Tuition:* $2045 per year full-time, $562 per semester (minimum) part-time for state residents; $6129 per year full-time, $1607 per semester (minimum) part-time for nonresidents. • Carolyn R. Morrow, Chair, Department of Languages and Literature, 801-581-7561. E-mail: carolyn.morrow@m.cc.utah.edu.

University of Vermont, College of Arts and Sciences, Department of Classics, Burlington, VT 05405-0160. Offerings include Greek and Latin (MAT). *Application deadline:* 4/1 (priority date; rolling processing). *Application fee:* $25. *Expenses:* Tuition $302 per credit for state residents; $755 per credit for nonresidents. Fees $434 per year full-time, $46 per semester (minimum) part-time. • Dr. R. Rodgers, Chair, 802-656-3210.

University of Vermont, College of Arts and Sciences, Department of German and Russian, Burlington, VT 05405-0160. Offerings include German education (MAT). Accredited by NCATE. *Application deadline:* 4/1 (priority date; rolling processing). *Application fee:* $25. *Expenses:* Tuition $302 per credit for state residents; $755 per credit for nonresidents. Fees $434 per year full-time, $46 per semester (minimum) part-time. • Dr. W. Mieder, Chairperson, 802-656-3430. Application contact: Dr. D. Scrase, Coordinator, 802-656-3430.

University of Vermont, College of Arts and Sciences, Department of Romance Languages, Burlington, VT 05405-0160. Offerings include French education (MAT). Accredited by NCATE. *Application deadline:* 4/1 (priority date; rolling processing). *Application fee:* $25. *Expenses:* Tuition $302 per credit for state residents; $755 per credit for nonresidents. Fees $434 per year full-time, $46 per semester (minimum) part-time. • Dr. J. Weiger, Chairperson, 802-656-3196. Application contact: Dr. J. Whatley, Coordinator, 802-656-3196.

University of Virginia, Graduate School of Arts and Sciences, Department of Spanish, Italian, and Portuguese, Program in Spanish, Charlottesville, VA 22903. Offerings include teaching Spanish (MAT). Accredited by NCATE. Program faculty: 19 full-time (8 women), 1 (woman) part-time. *Application deadline:* 7/15 (rolling processing; 12/1 for spring admission). *Application fee:* $40. *Tuition:* $4870 per year full-time, $941 per semester (minimum) part-time for state residents; $15,818 per year full-time, $2745 per semester (minimum) part-time for nonresidents. • Application contact: Duane J. Osheim, Associate Dean, 804-924-7184.

University of Wisconsin–Madison, School of Education, Department of Curriculum and Instruction, Madison, WI 53706-1380. Offerings include French education (MA), German education (MA), Latin education (MA), Spanish education (MA). *Application fee:* $38. *Tuition:* $4928 per year full-time, $926 per semester (minimum) part-time for state residents; $15,190 per year full-time, $2849 per semester (minimum) part-time for nonresidents.

West Chester University of Pennsylvania, College of Arts and Sciences, Department of Foreign Languages, West Chester, PA 19383. Offerings include German (M Ed), Latin (M Ed). One or more programs accredited by NCATE. Department faculty: 3 part-time. *Application deadline:* 4/15 (priority date; rolling processing; 10/15 for spring admission). *Application fee:* $25. *Expenses:* Tuition $3468 per year full-time, $193 per credit part-time for state residents; $6236 per year full-time, $346 per credit part-time for nonresidents. Fees $660 per year

Directories: Foreign Languages Education; Health Education

West Chester University of Pennsylvania (continued)
full-time, $38 per credit part-time. • Dr. Jerome Williams, Chair, 610-436-2700. Application contact: Rebecca Pauly, Graduate Coordinator, 610-436-2382.

Western Kentucky University, Potter College of Arts and Humanities, Department of Modern Languages and Intercultural Studies, Bowling Green, KY 42101-3576. Offerings include French (MA Ed), German (MA Ed), Spanish (MA Ed). One or more programs accredited by NCATE. Department faculty: 12 full-time (6 women). *Application deadline:* 8/1 (priority date; rolling processing; 12/1 for spring admission). *Application fee:* $20. *Tuition:* $2460 per year full-time, $133 per credit hour part-time for state residents; $6700 per year full-time, $369 per credit hour part-time for nonresidents. • Dr. Thomas Baldwin, Head, 502-745-5900. Fax: 502-745-6859. E-mail: mlis@wku.edu.

Health Education

Adams State College, School of Education and Graduate Studies, Department of Health, Physical Education, and Recreation, Alamosa, CO 81102. Awards MA. Accredited by NCATE. Part-time programs available. In 1997, 11 degrees awarded. *Degree requirements:* Comprehensive exam required, foreign language and thesis not required. *Entrance requirements:* GRE General Test or MAT, minimum undergraduate GPA of 2.75. Application deadline: 5/15 (priority date; rolling processing; 10/15 for spring admission). Application fee: $25. *Tuition:* $2164 per year full-time, $111 per credit part-time for state residents; $7284 per year full-time, $377 per credit part-time for nonresidents. *Financial aid:* In 1997–98, 8 coaching assistantships (6 to first-year students) averaging $500 per month and totaling $32,000 were awarded; Federal Work-Study, institutionally sponsored loans, and career-related internships or fieldwork also available. Aid available to part-time students. Financial aid application deadline: 4/15; applicants required to submit FAFSA. • Dr. Jeff Geiser, Head, 719-587-7402.

Adelphi University, School of Education, Department of Health Studies, Garden City, NY 11530. Offers programs in community health education (MA, Certificate), school health education (MA). Part-time and evening/weekend programs available. Students: 1 (woman) full-time, 66 part-time (46 women); includes 7 minority (5 African Americans, 1 Asian American, 1 Hispanic). Average age 31. In 1997, 23 master's awarded. *Degree requirements:* For master's, internship required, foreign language and thesis not required. *Entrance requirements:* For master's, previous course work in behavioral science, health-related background. Application deadline: rolling. Application fee: $50. *Expenses:* Tuition $16,000 per year full-time, $485 per credit part-time. Fees $500 per year full-time, $150 per semester part-time. *Financial aid:* Teaching assistantships available. Financial aid application deadline: 3/1. *Faculty research:* Sexuality, thanatology, stress, aging, alcohol education. • Dr. Monica M. Homer, Chairperson, 516-877-4950.

Albany State University, School of Education, Program in Health and Physical Education, Albany, GA 31705-2717. Awards M Ed. Accredited by NCATE. Faculty: 4 part-time (0 women). Students: 14 full-time (4 women). Average age 30. 3 applicants, 100% accepted. In 1997, 3 degrees awarded. *Degree requirements:* Comprehensive exam. *Entrance requirements:* GRE General Test (minimum combined score of 800), MAT (minimum score 44) or NTE (minimum score 550 required. Application deadline: 9/1. Application fee: $10. *Financial aid:* Federal Work-Study and career-related internships or fieldwork available. Aid available to part-time students. Financial aid application deadline: 4/1. *Faculty research:* Strength training, sport psychology. • Dr. Wilburn Campbell, Chairman, 912-430-4762. Fax: 912-430-3020. E-mail: wilburnc@fld94.alsnet.peachnet.edu.

Alcorn State University, School of Psychology and Education, Lorman, MS 39096-9402. Offerings include secondary education (MS Ed), with option in health and physical education. Accredited by NCATE. *Degree requirements:* Thesis optional, foreign language not required. *Application deadline:* 7/1 (priority date; rolling processing; 12/1 for spring admission). *Application fee:* $10. *Tuition:* $2470 per year full-time, $378 per semester (minimum) part-time for state residents; $5331 per year full-time, $855 per semester (minimum) part-time for nonresidents.

Allegheny University of the Health Sciences, School of Health Professions, Department of Liberal Arts and Applied Sciences, Philadelphia, PA 19102-1192. Offers program in health care education technology (MS). *Degree requirements:* Comprehensive exam required, foreign language not required. *Entrance requirements:* GRE General Test, minimum GPA of 3.0. Application fee: $50. *Expenses:* Tuition $11,500 per year full-time, $640 per credit part-time. Fees $125 per year. *Financial aid:* Partial tuition waivers, Federal Work-Study, institutionally sponsored loans, and career-related internships or fieldwork available. Aid available to part-time students. Financial aid application deadline: 5/1; applicants required to submit FAFSA. • John Lewis, Chair, 215-762-7910.

Arkansas Tech University, School of Education, Department of Health and Physical Education, Russellville, AR 72801-2222. Awards M Ed, PhD. Accredited by NCATE. *Degree requirements:* For master's, action research project, comprehensive exam required, thesis optional. *Entrance requirements:* For master's, GRE General Test. Application deadline: rolling. Application fee: $0 ($30 for international students). *Expenses:* Tuition $98 per credit hour for state residents; $196 per credit hour for nonresidents. Fees $30 per semester. *Financial aid:* Application deadline 4/15. • Dr. Annette Holeyfield, Head, 501-968-0344.

Auburn University, College of Education, Department of Health and Human Performance, Auburn University, AL 36849-0001. Awards M Ed, MS, Ed D, PhD, Ed S. Accredited by NCATE. Part-time programs available. Faculty: 14 full-time (3 women). Students: 56 full-time (23 women), 31 part-time (11 women); includes 6 minority (3 African Americans, 3 Hispanics), 6 international. 84 applicants, 37% accepted. In 1997, 27 master's, 1 doctorate awarded. *Degree requirements:* For master's, thesis (MS) required, foreign language not required; for doctorate, dissertation required, foreign language not required; for Ed S, exam, field project required, foreign language and thesis not required. *Entrance requirements:* For master's, GRE General Test; for doctorate, GRE General Test (minimum score 400 on each section), interview, master's degree; for Ed S, GRE General Test, interview, master's degree. Application deadline: 9/1 (rolling processing; 3/1 for spring admission). Application fee: $25 ($50 for international students). *Expenses:* Tuition $2760 per year full-time, $76 per credit hour part-time for state residents; $8280 per year full-time, $228 per credit hour part-time for nonresidents. Fees $30 per year full-time, $160 per quarter part-time for state residents; $30 per year full-time, $480 per quarter part-time for nonresidents. *Financial aid:* Research assistantships, teaching assistantships, Federal Work-Study available. Aid available to part-time students. Financial aid application deadline: 3/15. *Faculty research:* Biomechanics, exercise physiology, motor skill learning, school health, curriculum development. • Dr. Dennis G. Wilson, Head, 334-844-4483. Application contact: Dr. John F. Pritchett, Dean of the Graduate School, 334-844-4700.

Austin Peay State University, Department of Health and Human Performance, Clarksville, TN 37044-0001. Awards MA Ed, MS. Part-time and evening/weekend programs available. Students: 31 full-time (19 women), 21 part-time (13 women); includes 11 minority (all African Americans), 1 international. In 1997, 17 degrees awarded. *Entrance requirements:* GRE General Test. Application deadline: 7/31 (priority date; rolling processing; 12/4 for spring admission). Application fee: $15. *Expenses:* Tuition $2438 per year full-time, $123 per semester hour part-time for state residents; $7034 per year full-time, $324 per semester hour part-time for nonresidents. Fees $484 per year (minimum) full-time, $154 per semester (minimum) part-time. *Financial aid:* Graduate assistantships, Federal Work-Study, institutionally sponsored loans, and career-related internships or fieldwork available. Aid available to part-time students. Financial aid application deadline: 4/1; applicants required to submit FAFSA. *Faculty research:* Aging, aging and physical activity. • Rebecca Glass, Chair, 931-648-6111. Fax: 931-648-7040. E-mail: glassr@apsu.edu.

Ball State University, College of Sciences and Humanities, Department of Physiology and Health Science, Program in Health Education, 2000 University Avenue, Muncie, IN 47306-1099. Awards MA, MAE. Accredited by NCATE. Students: 6 full-time (4 women), 7 part-time (all women). Average age 27. 18 applicants, 61% accepted. In 1997, 11 degrees awarded. *Application fee:* $15 ($25 for international students). *Expenses:* Tuition $3454 per year full-time, $518 per semester (minimum) part-time for state residents; $9316 per year full-time, $1221 per semester (minimum) part-time for nonresidents. Fees $242 per year full-time, $18 per semester (minimum) part-time. *Financial aid:* Teaching assistantships available. • Dale Hahn, Chairman, Department of Physiology and Health Science, 765-885-5961.

Baylor College of Dentistry, Program in Health Professions Education, Dallas, TX 75266-0677. Awards MS. Part-time programs available. Faculty: 17 full-time (5 women). Students: 2 full-time (1 woman), 1 part-time (0 women); includes 3 minority (1 African American, 2 Hispanics). Average age 35. 2 applicants, 50% accepted. *Degree requirements:* Thesis required, foreign language not required. *Entrance requirements:* GRE General Test, TOEFL, DDS or DMD. Application deadline: rolling. Application fee: $35. *Expenses:* Tuition $48 per quarter hour for state residents; $166 per quarter hour for nonresidents. Fees $24 per quarter hour. *Financial aid:* 2 students received aid; fellowships, research assistantships, teaching assistantships, institutionally sponsored loans available. Aid available to part-time students. Financial aid application deadline: 2/23; applicants required to submit FAFSA. *Faculty research:* Craniofacial biology, dematoglypics, alternative curricula, admissions criteria, competency-based program assessment. • Dr. Peter H. Cohen, Associate Dean, 214-828-8207. Fax: 214-828-9496. E-mail: pcohen@tambcd.edu. Application contact: Dr. Ernestine S. Brooks, Director, 214-828-8374. Fax: 214-828-8496.

Baylor University, School of Education, Department of Health, Human Performance and Recreation, Waco, TX 76798. Awards MS Ed. Accredited by NCATE. Part-time programs available. Faculty: 13 full-time (5 women), 3 part-time (1 woman). Students: 34 full-time (17 women), 18 part-time (6 women); includes 2 minority (1 African American, 1 Asian American), 2 international. 30 applicants, 87% accepted. In 1997, 20 degrees awarded. *Degree requirements:* Thesis optional, foreign language not required. *Average time to degree:* master's–2 years full-time, 2.5 years part-time. *Entrance requirements:* GRE General Test. Application deadline: 4/1 (priority date; rolling processing; 10/1 for spring admission). Application fee: $25. Electronic applications accepted. *Expenses:* Tuition $7392 per year full-time, $308 per semester hour part-time. Fees $1024 per year. *Financial aid:* In 1997–98, 35 students received aid, including 22 teaching assistantships averaging $800 per month; recreation supplements, partial tuition waivers, Federal Work-Study, institutionally sponsored loans, and career-related internships or fieldwork also available. *Faculty research:* Behavior change theory, pedagogy, nutrition and enzyme therapy, exercise testing, health planning, ethics. • Dr. Nancy Goodloe, Director of Graduate Studies, 254-710-3505. E-mail: nancy_goodloe@baylor.edu.

Beaver College, Department of Education, Program in Allied Health, Glenside, PA 19038-3295. Awards MA Ed, MHA, MSH Ed. Part-time and evening/weekend programs available. *Entrance requirements:* GMAT or GRE (MHA). Application deadline: rolling. Application fee: $35. *Expenses:* Tuition $6570 per year full-time, $365 per credit part-time. Fees $35 per year.

Boston University, School of Education, Department of Developmental Studies and Counseling, Program in Health Education, Boston, MA 02215. Awards Ed M, CAGS. Students: 2 full-time (1 woman), 6 part-time (5 women); includes 2 minority (both Asian Americans), 1 international. Average age 25. In 1997, 3 master's awarded. *Degree requirements:* For CAGS, comprehensive exam required, foreign language and thesis not required. *Entrance requirements:* GRE or MAT, TOEFL. Application deadline: 2/15 (priority date; rolling processing). Application fee: $50. *Expenses:* Tuition $22,830 per year full-time, $713 per credit part-time. Fees $218 per year full-time, $40 per semester part-time. *Financial aid:* Application deadline 3/30. *Faculty research:* Substance abuse, therapeutic recreation, motor development and performance, stress management. • Dr. Gerald Fain, Coordinator, 617-353-4478. E-mail: fain@bu.edu.

Brigham Young University, College of Physical Education, Department of Health Sciences, Provo, UT 84602-1001. Awards MS. Faculty: 9 full-time (0 women). Students: 10 full-time (5 women); includes 1 minority (Asian American). Average age 28. 11 applicants, 73% accepted. In 1997, 7 degrees awarded. *Degree requirements:* Thesis, oral exam required, foreign language not required. *Average time to degree:* master's–1.5 years full-time, 3 years part-time. *Entrance requirements:* GRE General Test (minimum combined score of 1400 on three sections), minimum GPA of 3.0 in last 60 hours. Application deadline: 2/1 (rolling processing). Application fee: $30. *Tuition:* $3200 per year full-time, $178 per credit hour part-time for state residents; $4800 per year full-time, $266 per credit hour part-time for nonresidents. *Financial aid:* In 1997–98, 10 students received aid, including 3 research assistantships (1 to a first-year student) totaling $7,800, 7 teaching assistantships (all to first-year students) totaling $47,600, 9 scholarships (3 to first-year students) totaling $5,400; fellowships, partial tuition waivers, institutionally sponsored loans, and career-related internships or fieldwork also available. Aid available to part-time students. Financial aid application deadline: 3/1. *Faculty research:* Alcohol and tobacco policy and education, mind-body health, worksite health promotion practices. • Dr. Keith J. Karren, Chair, 801-378-4428. Application contact: Dr. Joyce M. Harrison, Associate Dean, 801-378-4271. Fax: 801-378-6585. E-mail: harrisonj@byu.edu.

Brooklyn College of the City University of New York, Department of Health and Nutrition Science and Division of Secondary Education, Program in Health and Nutrition Sciences, 2900 Bedford Avenue, Brooklyn, NY 11210-2889. Awards MS Ed. Part-time programs available. Students: 4 full-time (all women), 85 part-time (69 women); includes 26 minority (19 African Americans, 4 Asian Americans, 2 Hispanics, 1 Native American), 3 international. In 1997, 23 degrees awarded. *Degree requirements:* Thesis or alternative required, foreign language not required. *Entrance requirements:* TOEFL (minimum score 500), 18 credits in health-related areas. Application deadline: 3/1 (11/1 for spring admission). Application fee: $40. *Expenses:* Tuition $4350 per year full-time, $185 per credit part-time for state residents; $7600 per year full-time, $320 per credit part-time for nonresidents. Fees $500 per year for state residents; $806 per year for nonresidents. *Financial aid:* Federal Work-Study available. Financial aid application deadline: 5/1; applicants required to submit FAFSA. *Faculty research:* Medical ethics, AIDS, history of public health, diet restriction, palliative care, risk reduction/disease prevention. • Dr. Erika Friedmann, Chairperson, Department of Health and Nutrition Science, 718-951-5026. E-mail: erikaf@brooklyn.cuny.edu. Application contact: Jerrold Mirotznik, Deputy Chairperson for Graduate Studies, 718-951-4197. Fax: 718-951-4670.

California State University, Long Beach, College of Health and Human Services, Department of Health Science, Long Beach, CA 90840-4902. Offers programs in community health education (MPH), health science (MS). Students: 25 full-time (21 women), 27 part-time (23 women); includes 26 minority (3 African Americans, 10 Asian Americans, 13 Hispanics), 1 international. Average age 31. 58 applicants, 40% accepted. In 1997, 11 degrees awarded. *Entrance requirements:* Minimum GPA of 3.0. Application deadline: 8/1 (rolling processing; 12/1 for spring admission). Application fee: $55. *Expenses:* Tuition $0 for state residents; $246 per unit for nonresidents. Fees $1846 per year full-time, $1180 per year part-time. *Financial aid:* Application deadline 3/2. • Dr. Robert Friis, Chair, 562-985-4057. E-mail: rfriis@csulb.edu. Application contact: Dr. Mohammed Forouzesh, Graduate Coordinator, 562-985-8072. Fax: 562-985-2384. E-mail: mforouze@csulb.edu.

California State University, Los Angeles, School of Health and Human Services, Department of Health and Nutritional Sciences, Major in Health Science, Los Angeles, CA 90032-8530. Awards MA. Students: 5 full-time (all women), 28 part-time (21 women); includes 19 minority (5 African Americans, 8 Asian Americans, 6 Hispanics). In 1997, 6 degrees awarded. *Degree requirements:* Comprehensive exam, project, or thesis required, foreign language not required. *Entrance requirements:* TOEFL (minimum score 550). Application deadline: 6/30 (rolling processing; 2/1 for spring admission). Application fee: $55. *Expenses:* Tuition $0 for state residents; $164 per unit for nonresidents. Fees $1763 per year full-time, $1097 per year part-time. *Financial aid:* 7 students received aid; Federal Work-Study and career-related internships or fieldwork available. Aid available to part-time students. Financial aid application deadline: 3/1. • Dr. Bob Miller, Acting Chair, Department of Health and Nutritional Sciences, 213-343-4740.

California State University, Northridge, College of Health and Human Development, Department of Health Sciences, Program in Health Education, Northridge, CA 91330. Awards MS. Students: 23 full-time (18 women), 25 part-time (24 women); includes 15 minority (3 African Americans, 4 Asian Americans, 7 Hispanics, 1 Native American). Average age 33. 39 applicants, 77% accepted. *Entrance requirements:* TOEFL, GRE General Test or minimum GPA of 3.0. Application deadline: 11/30. Application fee: $55. *Expenses:* Tuition $0 for state residents; $246 per unit for nonresidents. Fees $1970 per year full-time, $1304 per year part-time. *Financial aid:* Application deadline 3/1. • Dr. Miriam Cotler, Chair, Department of Health Sciences, 818-677-3101. Application contact: Dr. Roberta Madison, Graduate Coordinator, 818-677-2015 Ext. 3101.

Central Washington University, College of Education and Professional Studies, Department of Physical Education, Health Education and Leisure Services, Ellensburg, WA 98926. Offers program in health, physical education and recreation (MS). Accredited by NCATE. Part-time programs available. Faculty: 16 full-time (5 women). Students: 12 full-time (9 women), 4 part-time (2 women); includes 1 minority (Hispanic). 24 applicants, 50% accepted. In 1997, 7 degrees awarded. *Degree requirements:* Thesis or alternative required, foreign language not required. *Entrance requirements:* Minimum GPA of 3.0. Application deadline: 4/1 (priority date; rolling processing; 1/1 for spring admission). Application fee: $35. *Expenses:* Tuition $4200 per year full-time, $140 per credit hour part-time for state residents; $12,780 per year full-time, $426 per credit hour part-time for nonresidents. Fees $240 per year. *Financial aid:* In 1997–98, 10 teaching assistantships (7 to first-year students) averaging $1,108 per month and totaling $99,720 were awarded; research assistantships, Federal Work-Study also available. Financial aid application deadline: 2/15. • Dr. John Gregor, Chairman, 509-963-1911. Application contact: Christie A. Fevergeon, Program Coordinator, Graduate Studies and Research, 509-963-3103. Fax: 509-963-1799. E-mail: masters@cwu.edu.

The Citadel, The Military College of South Carolina, Department of Health and Physical Education, Charleston, SC 29409. Awards M Ed. Accredited by NCATE. Faculty: 3 full-time (0 women), 1 part-time (0 women). Students: 3 full-time (2 women), 24 part-time (7 women); includes 4 minority (all African Americans). In 1997, 2 degrees awarded. *Entrance requirements:* GRE, MAT, or 12 hours of graduate course work with a minimum GPA of 3.0. Application deadline: rolling. Application fee: $25. *Expenses:* Tuition $130 per credit hour for state residents; $260 per credit hour for nonresidents. Fees $30 per semester. • Dr. Gary Wilson, Head, 803-953-5060.

Cleveland State University, College of Education, Department of Health, Physical Education, Recreation and Dance, Cleveland, OH 44115-2440. Offers programs in community health (M Ed), exercise science (M Ed), health education (M Ed), human performance (M Ed), pedagogy (M Ed), recreation (M Ed), sport education (M Ed), sport management (M Ed), sport management/exercise science (M Ed). Part-time programs available. Faculty: 11 full-time (6 women). Students: 7 full-time (4 women), 10 part-time (3 women); includes 2 minority (both African Americans). Average age 26. 18 applicants, 61% accepted. In 1997, 31 degrees awarded. *Degree requirements:* Thesis optional, foreign language not required. *Entrance requirements:* GRE General Test or MAT (score in 50th percentile or higher), minimum undergraduate GPA of 2.75. Application deadline: 9/1 (priority date; rolling processing). Application fee: $25. *Expenses:* Tuition $5252 per year full-time, $202 per credit hour part-time for state residents; $10,504 per year full-time, $404 per credit hour part-time for nonresidents. Fees $2.25 per credit hour (minimum). *Financial aid:* In 1997–98, 4 teaching assistantships were awarded; career-related internships or fieldwork also available. Financial aid application deadline: 3/31. *Faculty research:* Mental imagery in motor learning, biomechanical analysis of motor skill, improvement of speed in running, instructional design. • Dr. Vincent Melograno, Chairman, 216-687-4878. Fax: 216-687-5410. E-mail: v.melograno@popmail.csuohio.edu.

College of Mount Saint Vincent, Program in Allied Health, Riverdale, NY 10471-1093. Offerings include allied health studies (MS), with options in addictions, child and family health, community health education, counseling, health care management, health care systems and policies. Program faculty: 1 (woman) full-time, 8 part-time (4 women), 3.6 FTE. *Degree requirements:* Thesis or alternative required, foreign language not required. *Average time to degree:* master's–2 years part-time. *Entrance requirements:* Sample of written work. Application deadline: 9/23 (priority date; rolling processing). Application fee: $50. • Dr. Rita Scher Dytell, Director, 718-405-3788. Fax: 718-405-3249.

The College of New Jersey, Graduate Division, School of Education, Department of Health and Physical Education, Program in Health Education, Ewing, NJ 08628. Offers health (MAT), physical education (M Ed). Accredited by NCATE. Students: 2 full-time (0 women), 17 part-time (16 women); includes 1 minority (African American). Average age 26. In 1997, 2 degrees awarded. *Degree requirements:* Comprehensive exam required, foreign language and thesis not required. *Average time to degree:* master's–2 years full-time. *Entrance requirements:* MAT, minimum GPA of 3.0 in field or 2.75 overall. Application deadline: 4/15 (10/15 for spring admission). Application fee: $50. *Expenses:* Tuition $6892 per year full-time, $287 per credit hour part-time for state residents; $9602 per year full-time, $402 per credit hour part-time for nonresidents. Fees $799 per year full-time, $33 per credit hour part-time. *Financial aid:* Graduate assistantships available. Financial aid application deadline: 5/1; applicants required to submit FAFSA. • Dr. Aristomen Chilakos, Coordinator, 609-771-3160. Fax: 609-637-5153.

The College of New Jersey, Graduate Division, School of Education, Department of Health and Physical Education, Programs in Health and Physical Education, Ewing, NJ 08628. Awards M Ed. Accredited by NCATE. Part-time and evening/weekend programs available. Students: 1 full-time (0 women), 17 part-time (9 women); includes 2 minority (1 Hispanic, 1 Native American). Average age 28. In 1997, 8 degrees awarded. *Degree requirements:* Comprehensive exam required, foreign language and thesis not required. *Average time to degree:* master's–2 years full-time. *Entrance requirements:* MAT, minimum GPA of 2.75 overall or 3.0 in field. Application deadline: 4/15 (10/15 for spring admission). Application fee: $50. *Expenses:* Tuition $6892 per year full-time, $287 per credit hour part-time for state residents; $9602 per year full-time, $402 per credit hour part-time for nonresidents. Fees $799 per year full-time, $33 per credit hour part-time. *Financial aid:* Graduate assistantships available. Financial aid application deadline: 5/1; applicants required to submit FAFSA. • Dr. Aristomen Chilakos, Coordinator, 609-771-3160. Fax: 609-637-5153.

Dalhousie University, Faculty of Health Professions, School of Health and Human Performance, Division of Health Education, Halifax, NS B3H 3J5, Canada. Awards MA. Part-time programs available. Faculty: 6 full-time (2 women), 1 (woman) part-time. Students: 10 full-time (9 women), 4 part-time (all women); includes 2 minority (both Asian Americans). 10 applicants, 30% accepted. In 1997, 7 degrees awarded (14% entered university research/teaching, 86% found other work related to degree). *Degree requirements:* Thesis required, foreign language not required. *Average time to degree:* master's–2 years full-time. *Entrance requirements:* TOEFL (minimum score 580). Application deadline: 6/1 (rolling processing). Application fee: $55. *Financial aid:* 4 students received aid; research assistantships, teaching assistantships, institutionally sponsored loans available. *Faculty research:* AIDS research, health knowledge of adolescents, evaluating health promotion, program evaluation. • Dr. C. Putnam, Associate Director, School of Health and Human Performance, 902-494-1167. Fax: 902-494-5120. E-mail: putnam@ac.dal.ca.

East Carolina University, School of Health and Human Performance, Department of Health Education, Greenville, NC 27858-4353. Awards MA, MA Ed. Accredited by NCATE. Faculty: 9 full-time (3 women). Students: 14 full-time (11 women), 19 part-time (16 women); includes 4 minority (all African Americans). Average age 30. 20 applicants, 85% accepted. In 1997, 13 degrees awarded. *Degree requirements:* Comprehensive exams required, thesis optional, foreign language not required. *Entrance requirements:* GRE General Test or MAT, TOEFL. Application deadline: 6/1 (priority date; rolling processing). Application fee: $40. *Tuition:* $1886 per year full-time, $472 per semester (minimum) part-time for state residents; $9156 per year full-time, $2289 per semester (minimum) part-time for nonresidents. *Financial aid:* Available to part-time students. Financial aid application deadline: 6/1. • Dr. Michael Felts, Coordinator of Graduate Studies, 252-328-4636. Fax: 252-328-6562. E-mail: feltsm@mail.ecu.edu.

Eastern College, Graduate Education Programs, Program in School Health Services, St. Davids, PA 19087-3696. Awards M Ed. Students: 8 full-time, 56 part-time. In 1997, 14 degrees awarded. *Entrance requirements:* TOEFL, minimum GPA of 2.5. Application deadline: rolling. Application fee: $35. *Financial aid:* Research assistantships, teaching assistantships available. • Application contact: Megan Miscioscia, Graduate Admissions Representative, 610-341-5972. Fax: 610-341-1466.

Eastern Kentucky University, College of Education, Department of Curriculum and Instruction, Program in Secondary and Higher Education, Richmond, KY 40475-3101. Offerings include allied health sciences education (MA Ed), school health education (MA Ed). One or more programs accredited by NCATE. *Entrance requirements:* GRE General Test, minimum GPA of 2.5. Application fee: $0. *Tuition:* $2390 per year full-time, $133 per credit hour part-time for state residents; $6630 per year full-time, $365 per credit hour part-time for nonresidents. • Dr. Imogene Ramsey, Chair, Department of Curriculum and Instruction, 606-622-2154.

East Stroudsburg University of Pennsylvania, School of Health Sciences and Human Performance, Department of Health, East Stroudsburg, PA 18301-2999. Offers programs in community health education (MPH), health education (MS). Part-time and evening/weekend programs available. *Degree requirements:* Comprehensive exam required, foreign language and thesis not required. *Entrance requirements:* Minimum GPA of 3.0 in major, 2.5 overall. Application deadline: 7/31 (priority date; rolling processing; 11/30 for spring admission). Application fee: $15 ($25 for international students). *Expenses:* Tuition $3468 per year full-time, $193 per credit part-time for state residents; $6236 per year full-time, $346 per credit part-time for nonresidents. Fees $700 per year full-time, $39 per credit part-time. *Faculty research:* HIV presention, wellness, international health issues.

East Stroudsburg University of Pennsylvania, School of Health Sciences and Human Performance, Department of Movement Studies and Exercise Science, East Stroudsburg, PA 18301-2999. Offers programs in cardiac rehabilitation and exercise science (MS); health and physical education (M Ed), including sports management; physical education (MS). Part-time and evening/weekend programs available. *Degree requirements:* Thesis (for some programs), comprehensive exam required, foreign language not required. *Application deadline:* 7/31 (priority date; rolling processing; 11/30 for spring admission). *Application fee:* $15 ($25 for international students). *Expenses:* Tuition $3468 per year full-time, $193 per credit part-time for state residents; $6236 per year full-time, $346 per credit part-time for nonresidents. Fees $700 per year full-time, $39 per credit part-time.

Edinboro University of Pennsylvania, School of Education, Department of Health and Physical Education, Edinboro, PA 16444. Awards Certificate. Students: 1 part-time (0 women). Average age 37. *Degree requirements:* Thesis required, foreign language not required. *Entrance requirements:* GRE or MAT (score in 30th percentile or higher). Application deadline: rolling. Application fee: $25. *Expenses:* Tuition $3468 per year full-time, $193 per credit part-time for state residents; $6236 per year full-time, $346 per credit part-time for nonresidents. Fees $898 per year full-time, $50 per semester (minimum) part-time. • Dr. Kenneth Felker, Chair, 814-732-2777. Application contact: Dr. Philip Kerstetter, Dean of Graduate Studies, 814-732-2856. Fax: 814-732-2611. E-mail: kerstetter@edinboro.edu.

Florida Agricultural and Mechanical University, Division of Graduate Studies, Research, and Continuing Education, College of Education, Department of Health, Physical Education, and Recreation, Tallahassee, FL 32307-3200. Awards M Ed, MS Ed. Accredited by NCATE. Part-time and evening/weekend programs available. Students: 12 (3 women); includes 10 minority (all African Americans). Average age 23. In 1997, 5 degrees awarded. *Degree requirements:* Thesis optional, foreign language not required. *Entrance requirements:* GRE General Test (minimum combined score of 1000), minimum GPA of 3.0. Application deadline: 5/13. Application fee: $20. *Expenses:* Tuition $140 per credit hour for state residents; $484 per credit hour for nonresidents. Fees $130 per year. *Financial aid:* Teaching assistantships, Federal Work-Study, institutionally sponsored loans available. *Faculty research:* Administration/curriculum, work behavior, psychology. • Dr. Barbara Thompson, Chairperson, 850-599-3135.

Florida International University, College of Education, Department of Health, Physical Education, and Recreation, Program in Health Education, Miami, FL 33199. Awards MS. Accredited by NCATE. Part-time and evening/weekend programs available. Students: 9 full-time (4 women), 11 part-time (5 women); includes 11 minority (1 Asian American, 10 Hispanics). Average age 27. 11 applicants, 91% accepted. In 1997, 6 degrees awarded. *Entrance requirements:* GRE General Test (minimum combined score of 1000) or minimum GPA of 3.0. Application deadline: 4/1 (priority date; rolling processing; 10/1 for spring admission). Application fee: $20. *Expenses:* Tuition $138 per credit hour for state residents; $482 per credit hour for nonresidents. Fees $46 per semester. • Dr. Robert Wolff, Chairperson, Department of Health, Physical Education, and Recreation, 305-348-3486. Fax: 305-348-3571. E-mail: wolffr@fiu.edu.

Florida International University, College of Education, Department of Subject Specializations, Program in Health Occupations Education, Miami, FL 33199. Awards MS. Accredited by NCATE. Part-time and evening/weekend programs available. Students: 0. 0 applicants. *Entrance requirements:* GRE General Test (minimum combined score of 1000) or minimum GPA of 3.0 in last 60 credits of baccalaureate, interview. Application deadline: 4/1 (priority date; rolling processing; 10/1 for spring admission). Application fee: $20. *Expenses:* Tuition $138 per credit hour for state residents; $482 per credit hour for nonresidents. Fees $46 per semester. *Financial aid:* Research assistantships available. *Faculty research:* Teacher education, preparation of teachers for the health field, integration of computers. • Dr. Dean Hauenstein, Chairperson, Department of Subject Specializations, 305-348-2005. Fax: 305-348-2086.

Florida State University, College of Human Sciences, Department of Nutrition, Food, and Movement Sciences, Tallahassee, FL 32306. Offerings include human science (MS), with options in clinical nutrition, food science, nutrition and sport, nutrition science, nutrition, education and health promotion. Department faculty: 13 full-time (9 women). *Degree requirements:* Thesis optional, foreign language not required. *Entrance requirements:* GRE General Test (minimum combined score of 1000), minimum GPA of 3.0. Application fee: $20. *Tuition:* $139 per credit hour for state residents; $482 per credit hour for nonresidents. • Dr. Robert Moffatt, Chair, 850-644-1828. E-mail: rmoffatt@mailer.fsu.edu. Application contact: Dr. Cathy Levenson, Graduate Coordinator, 850-644-4800. Fax: 850-644-0700.

Directory: Health Education

Florida State University, College of Education, Department of Curriculum and Instruction, Program in Health Education, Tallahassee, FL 32306. Awards MS. Part-time programs available. Faculty: 1 (woman) full-time, 1 part-time (0 women). Students: 4 full-time (all women), 2 part-time (1 woman); includes 2 minority (both African Americans). 12 applicants, 100% accepted. In 1997, 1 degree awarded. *Degree requirements:* Comprehensive exam required, thesis optional. *Entrance requirements:* GRE General Test (minimum combined score of 1000), minimum GPA of 3.0. Application deadline: 7/1 (priority date; rolling processing; 11/1 for spring admission). Application fee: $20. *Tuition:* $139 per credit hour for state residents; $482 per credit hour for nonresidents. *Financial aid:* Fellowships and career-related internships or fieldwork available. • Dr. David Foulk, Chair, Department of Curriculum and Instruction, 850-644-6553. E-mail: foulk@mail.coe.fsu.edu. Application contact: Admissions Secretary, 850-644-6553. Fax: 850-644-1880.

Fort Hays State University, College of Health and Life Sciences, Department of Health and Human Performance, Hays, KS 67601-4099. Offers program in health, physical education, and recreation (MS). Part-time programs available. Faculty: 4 full-time (0 women). Students: 22 full-time (7 women), 17 part-time (6 women); includes 1 minority (Hispanic). Average age 29. 17 applicants, 82% accepted. In 1997, 20 degrees awarded. *Entrance requirements:* GRE General Test or MAT. Application deadline: 7/1 (priority date; rolling processing). Application fee: $25 ($35 for international students). *Tuition:* $94 per credit hour for state residents; $249 per credit hour for nonresidents. *Financial aid:* Research assistantships, teaching assistantships available. *Faculty research:* Isoproterenol hydrochloride and exercise, dehydrogenase and high-density lipoprotein levels in athletics, venous blood parameters to adipose fat. • Dr. Don Fuertges, Chairman, 785-628-4352.

Frostburg State University, School of Education, Department of Educational Professions, Program in Health and Physical Education, Frostburg, MD 21532-1099. Awards M Ed. Part-time and evening/weekend programs available. *Application deadline:* 7/15 (rolling processing). *Application fee:* $30.

Furman University, Department of Health and Exercise Science, Greenville, SC 29613. Awards MA. Students: 19 full-time (11 women), 34 part-time (18 women). *Application deadline:* rolling. *Application fee:* $25. *Tuition:* $185 per credit hour. • Dr. William Pierce, Chairman.

Georgia College and State University, School of Health Sciences, Department of Health, Physical Education, and Recreation, Milledgeville, GA 31061. Offers program in health and physical education (M Ed, Ed S). One or more programs accredited by NCATE. Students: 32 full-time (20 women), 18 part-time (11 women); includes 4 minority (all African Americans), 4 international. Average age 32. In 1997, 12 master's, 2 Ed Ss awarded. *Degree requirements:* For master's, computer language required, foreign language and thesis not required; for Ed S, computer language, oral exam, research project required, foreign language and thesis not required. *Entrance requirements:* For master's, GRE General Test (minimum combined score of 800) or NTE (minimum score 550 on each core battery test), minimum GPA of 2.5, NT-4 certificate; for Ed S, GRE General Test (minimum combined score of 900) or NTE (minimum score 575 on each core battery test), master's degree, minimum graduate GPA of 3.25, NT-5 certificate, 2 years of teaching experience. Application deadline: 7/31 (priority date; rolling processing). Application fee: $10. *Financial aid:* Assistantships, Federal Work-Study, and career-related internships or fieldwork available. Aid available to part-time students. Financial aid application deadline: 4/15. • Dr. James Lidstone, Chair, 912-445-4072.

Georgia Southern University, College of Education, Department of Middle Grades and Secondary Education, Program in Health and Physical Education, Statesboro, GA 30460-8126. Awards M Ed, Ed S. One or more programs accredited by NCATE. Part-time programs available. Students: 4 full-time (1 woman), 8 part-time (4 women). Average age 30. 2 applicants, 50% accepted. In 1997, 6 master's awarded. *Degree requirements:* For master's, exams required, foreign language and thesis not required; for Ed S, exams required, thesis not required. *Entrance requirements:* For master's, GRE General Test (minimum score 450 on each section) or MAT (minimum score 44), minimum GPA of 2.5; for Ed S, GRE General Test (minimum score 450 on each section) or MAT (minimum score 49), minimum graduate GPA of 3.25. Application deadline: 7/15 (priority date; rolling processing; 11/15 for spring admission). Application fee: $0. Electronic applications accepted. *Tuition:* $2619 per year full-time, $287 per semester (minimum) part-time for state residents; $8619 per year full-time, $1037 per semester (minimum) part-time for nonresidents. *Financial aid:* Federal Work-Study and career-related internships or fieldwork available. Aid available to part-time students. Financial aid application deadline: 4/15. • Application contact: Dr. John R. Diebolt, Associate Graduate Dean, 912-681-5384. Fax: 912-681-0740. E-mail: gradschool@gsvms2.cc.gasou.edu.

Georgia Southwestern State University, School of Education, Americus, GA 31709-4693. Offerings include health and physical education (M Ed). Accredited by NCATE. *Entrance requirements:* GRE General Test (minimum score 400 on each section) or MAT (minimum score 44), minimum GPA of 2.5. Application deadline: 9/1 (rolling processing; 3/15 for spring admission). Application fee: $10. • Dr. Kurt Myers, Chair, 912-931-2145. Application contact: Chris Laney, Graduate Admissions Specialist, 912-931-2027. Fax: 912-931-2059. E-mail: claney@gsw1500.gsw.peachnet.edu.

Hofstra University, School of Education and Allied Human Services, Department of Health, Physical Education and Recreation, Program in Health Education, Hempstead, NY 11549. Awards MS Ed. Accredited by NCATE. Evening/weekend programs available. Faculty: 4 full-time (1 woman), 10 part-time (4 women). Students: 4 full-time (3 women), 52 part-time (32 women); includes 1 minority (Hispanic), 1 international. Average age 32. 25 applicants, 80% accepted. In 1997, 22 degrees awarded. *Degree requirements:* Departmental qualifying exam, final essay. *Entrance requirements:* Interview, minimum GPA of 2.75. Application deadline: rolling. Application fee: $40 ($75 for international students). *Expenses:* Tuition $10,968 per year full-time, $457 per credit hour part-time. Fees $670 per year full-time, $112 per semester (minimum) part-time. *Financial aid:* 1 student received aid; fellowships, research assistantships available. • Dr. Estelle Weinstein, Coordinator, 516-463-5817. Fax: 516-463-4810. E-mail: hprezw@hofstra.edu. Application contact: Mary Beth Carey, Dean of Admissions, 516-463-6700. Fax: 516-560-7660. E-mail: hofstra@hofstra.edu.

Howard University, Graduate School of Arts and Sciences, Department of Physical Education, Recreation, and Health Education, 2400 Sixth Street, NW, Washington, DC 20059-0002. Offers programs in exercise physiology (MS), recreation and leisure studies (MS), school and community health education (MS). Part-time programs available. Faculty: 8 full-time (4 women). Students: 19 full-time (10 women); includes 19 minority (all African Americans). In 1997, 3 degrees awarded. *Degree requirements:* Thesis, comprehensive exam. *Average time to degree:* master's–2 years full-time, 3 years part-time. *Entrance requirements:* GRE General Test, minimum GPA of 3.0. Application deadline: 4/1 (11/1 for spring admission). Application fee: $45. *Expenses:* Tuition $10,200 per year full-time, $567 per credit hour part-time. Fees $405 per year. *Financial aid:* Research assistantships, teaching assistantships, grants, institutionally sponsored loans, and career-related internships or fieldwork available. Financial aid application deadline: 4/1. *Faculty research:* Women's health, work and health, AIDS, men's health, hypertension, sports nutrition, social science, urban recreation, therapeutic recreation, commercial recreation. • Dr. Marshall Banks, Chair, 202-806-7142.

Illinois State University, College of Applied Science and Technology, Department of Health, Physical Education and Recreation, Normal, IL 61790-2200. Offers programs in health education (MA, MS), physical education (MA, MS). Faculty: 12 full-time (6 women). Students: 74 full-time (35 women), 38 part-time (18 women); includes 11 minority (6 African Americans, 1 Asian American, 4 Hispanics), 3 international. 64 applicants, 95% accepted. In 1997, 38 degrees awarded. *Degree requirements:* Thesis or alternative. *Entrance requirements:* GRE General Test (minimum combined score of 1000), minimum GPA of 2.6 in last 60 hours. Application deadline: rolling. Application fee: $0. *Expenses:* Tuition $2454 per year full-time, $102 per hour part-time for state residents; $7362 per year full-time, $307 per hour part-time for nonresidents. Fees $1048 per year full-time, $44 per hour part-time. *Financial aid:* In 1997–98, 1 teaching assistantship, 50 assistantships averaging $453 per month were awarded; research assistantships, full and partial tuition waivers, Federal Work-Study, and career-related internships or fieldwork also available. Financial aid application deadline: 4/1. *Total annual research expenditures:* $38,761. • Dr. Marlene Mawson, Chairperson, 309-438-8661.

Indiana State University, School of Health and Human Performance, Department of Health and Safety, Terre Haute, IN 47809-1401. Offers programs in health program and facility administration (MA, MS), occupational safety management (MA, MS), school health and safety (MA, MS). One or more programs accredited by NCATE. Faculty: 11 full-time (4 women). Students: 6 full-time (2 women), 27 part-time (6 women); includes 2 minority (both Hispanics). Average age 35. 16 applicants, 50% accepted. In 1997, 10 degrees awarded. *Application deadline:* rolling. *Application fee:* $20. *Tuition:* $143 per credit hour for state residents; $325 per credit hour for nonresidents. *Financial aid:* In 1997–98, 1 teaching assistantship (to a first-year student) was awarded; research assistantships, graduate assistantships, full tuition waivers also available. Financial aid application deadline: 3/1. • Dr. Portia Plummer, Chairperson, 812-237-3071. Application contact: Dr. Richard Spear, Graduate Adviser, 812-237-3107.

Indiana University Bloomington, School of Health, Physical Education and Recreation, Program in Applied Health Science, Bloomington, IN 47405. Offerings include public health education (HS Dir), school and college health education (HS Dir), school health education (MS). Program faculty: 14 full-time (6 women). *Degree requirements:* For HS Dir, thesis or alternative required, foreign language not required. *Entrance requirements:* For HS Dir, GRE. Application deadline: rolling. Application fee: $35. *Expenses:* Tuition $153 per credit hour for state residents; $446 per credit hour for nonresidents. Fees $343 per year. • James W. Crowe, Chair, 812-855-3627. Application contact: Mohammad Torabi, Graduate Coordinator, 812-855-4806. Fax: 812-855-3936.

Indiana University of Pennsylvania, College of Health and Human Services, Department of Health and Physical Education, Indiana, PA 15705-1087. Offers programs in aquatics administration and facilities management (MS), sport broadcast journalism (MS), sport management (MS), sports studies (MS). Part-time programs available. Students: 8 full-time (2 women), 5 part-time (1 woman); includes 2 minority (both African Americans). Average age 27. 12 applicants, 75% accepted. In 1997, 9 degrees awarded. *Degree requirements:* Thesis optional, foreign language not required. *Entrance requirements:* TOEFL (minimum score 500). Application deadline: 7/1 (priority date; rolling processing; 11/1 for spring admission). Application fee: $30. *Expenses:* Tuition $3468 per year full-time, $193 per credit part-time for state residents; $6236 per year full-time, $346 per credit part-time for nonresidents. Fees $313 per year (minimum) full-time, $84 per year part-time. *Financial aid:* Application deadline 3/15. • Dr. James Mill, Chairperson and Graduate Coordinator, 724-357-2770. E-mail: jimmill@grove.iup.edu.

Inter American University of Puerto Rico, Metropolitan Campus, Division of Education, Program in Health and Physical Education, San Juan, PR 00919-1293. Awards MA. Students: 13 part-time (4 women); includes 13 minority (all Hispanics). In 1997, 9 degrees awarded. *Degree requirements:* Comprehensive exam required, foreign language and thesis not required. *Entrance requirements:* GRE or PAEG, interview. Application deadline: 5/15 (priority date; rolling processing; 11/15 for spring admission). Application fee: $31. Electronic applications accepted. *Expenses:* Tuition $3272 per year full-time, $1740 per year part-time. Fees $328 per year full-time, $176 per year part-time. *Financial aid:* Federal Work-Study available. Aid available to part-time students. • Dr. Amalia Charneco, Director, Division of Education, 787-758-5652. Application contact: Jenny Maldonado, Administrative Assistant, 787-250-1912 Ext. 2393. Fax: 787-250-1197.

Iowa State University of Science and Technology, College of Education, Department of Health and Human Performance, Ames, IA 50011. Awards MS. Faculty: 18 full-time, 1 part-time. Students: 32 full-time (13 women), 29 part-time (15 women); includes 5 minority (2 African Americans, 3 Hispanics), 2 international. 65 applicants, 77% accepted. In 1997, 14 degrees awarded. *Degree requirements:* Thesis or alternative. *Entrance requirements:* GRE General Test, TOEFL. Application deadline: 3/1 (priority date). Application fee: $20 ($30 for international students). *Expenses:* Tuition $3166 per year full-time, $176 per credit part-time for state residents; $9324 per year full-time, $518 per credit part-time for nonresidents. Fees $200 per year. *Financial aid:* In 1997–98, 14 research assistantships (7 to first-year students), 18 teaching assistantships (4 to first-year students), 2 scholarships (1 to a first-year student) were awarded; fellowships and career-related internships or fieldwork also available. • Dr. Shirley Wood, Interim Chair, 515-294-6459. E-mail: sjwood@iastate.edu. Application contact: Richard Engelhorn, 515-294-8131. E-mail: hhpgrad@iastate.edu.

Jackson State University, School of Education, Department of Health, Physical Education and Recreation, Jackson, MS 39217. Awards MS Ed. Accredited by NCATE. Part-time and evening/weekend programs available. Faculty: 5 full-time (0 women). Students: 5 full-time (1 woman), 13 part-time (2 women); includes 17 minority (all African Americans). 6 applicants, 67% accepted. In 1997, 6 degrees awarded. *Degree requirements:* Thesis or alternative, comprehensive exam. *Entrance requirements:* GRE General Test (minimum combined score of 1000), TOEFL (minimum score 550). Application deadline: 3/1 (priority date; rolling processing; 10/1 for spring admission). Application fee: $20. *Tuition:* $2688 per year (minimum) full-time, $150 per semester hour part-time for state residents; $5546 per year (minimum) full-time, $309 per semester hour part-time for nonresidents. *Financial aid:* Application deadline 3/1. • Dr. Melvin Evans, Chair, 601-968-2373. Fax: 601-968-2374. Application contact: Mae Robinson, Admissions Coordinator, 601-968-2455. Fax: 601-968-8246. E-mail: mrobinson@ccaix.jsums.edu.

Jacksonville State University, College of Education, Program in Health and Physical Education, Jacksonville, AL 36265-9982. Awards MS Ed. Accredited by NCATE. Part-time and evening/weekend programs available. Faculty: 7 full-time (2 women). Students: 4 full-time (3 women), 32 part-time (10 women); includes 4 minority (all African Americans). In 1997, 23 degrees awarded. *Degree requirements:* Thesis optional. *Entrance requirements:* GRE General Test or MAT. Application deadline: rolling. Application fee: $20. *Expenses:* Tuition $2140 per year full-time, $107 per semester hour part-time for state residents; $4280 per year full-time, $214 per semester hour part-time for nonresidents. Fees $30 per semester. *Financial aid:* Available to part-time students. Financial aid application deadline: 4/1. • Application contact: College of Graduate Studies and Continuing Education, 205-782-5329.

James Madison University, College of Integrated Science and Technology, Department of Health Sciences, Harrisonburg, VA 22807. Awards MS, MS Ed. Part-time programs available. Faculty: 10 full-time (4 women). Students: 16 full-time (12 women), 12 part-time (8 women); includes 5 minority (2 African Americans, 2 Asian Americans, 1 Hispanic), 1 international. Average age 30. In 1997, 14 degrees awarded. *Degree requirements:* Thesis or alternative required, foreign language not required. *Entrance requirements:* GRE General Test. Application deadline: 7/1 (priority date; rolling processing). Application fee: $50. *Tuition:* $134 per credit hour for state residents; $404 per credit hour for nonresidents. *Financial aid:* In 1997–98, 1 teaching assistantship totaling $10,170, 9 assistantships totaling $77,760 were awarded; fellowships, Federal Work-Study also available. Financial aid application deadline: 2/15; applicants required to submit FAFSA. • Dr. Stephen H. Stewart, Head, 540-568-6510.

John F. Kennedy University, Graduate School for Holistic Studies, Program in Holistic Health Education, Orinda, CA 94563-2689. Awards MA. Part-time and evening/weekend programs available. Faculty: 2 full-time (both women), 47 part-time (29 women). Students: 13 full-time (8 women), 30 part-time (28 women); includes 5 minority (2 African Americans, 1 Asian American, 2 Hispanics). Average age 38. 14 applicants, 86% accepted. In 1997, 10 degrees awarded. *Degree requirements:* Thesis or alternative required, foreign language not required. *Entrance requirements:* TOEFL (minimum score 550), interview. Application deadline: 8/1 (priority date; 3/1 for spring admission). Application fee: $50. *Expenses:* Tuition $316 per unit. Fees $9 per quarter. *Financial aid:* Application deadline 3/2. • Marsha Hiller, Chair, 925-254-0105. Application contact: Ellena Bloedorn, Director of Admissions, 925-258-2213. Fax: 925-254-6964.

Kent State University, Graduate School of Education, Department of Adult, Counseling, Health and Vocational Education, Program in Health and Safety Education, Kent, OH 44242-0001. Offers health education (MA, M Ed). Accredited by NCATE. Faculty: 7 full-time (5 women), 10 part-time (6 women). Students: 5 full-time (all women), 19 part-time (18 women); includes 1 minority (African American). In 1997, 12 degrees awarded. *Degree requirements:* Thesis (MA) required, foreign language not required. *Entrance requirements:* Minimum GPA of 2.75. Application deadline: rolling. Application fee: $30. *Tuition:* $4752 per year full-time, $216 per credit hour part-time for state residents; $9213 per year full-time, $419 per credit hour part-time for nonresidents. *Financial aid:* Application deadline 4/1. • Dr. Jean Byrne, Coordinator, 330-672-7977. Application contact: Deborah Barber, Director, Office of Academic Services, 330-672-2862. Fax: 330-672-3549.

Lehman College of the City University of New York, Division of Natural and Social Sciences, Department of Health Services, Program in Health Education and Promotion, 250 Bedford Park Boulevard West, Bronx, NY 10468-1589. Awards MA. Part-time and evening/weekend programs available. Faculty: 2 full-time (1 woman). Students: 25 part-time (12 women). *Degree requirements:* Thesis or alternative. *Entrance requirements:* Minimum GPA of 2.7. Application deadline: 4/1 (priority date; rolling processing; 11/1 for spring admission). Application fee: $40. *Expenses:* Tuition $4350 per year full-time, $185 per credit part-time for state residents; $7600 per year full-time, $320 per credit part-time for nonresidents. Fees $120 per year full-time, $80 per year part-time. *Financial aid:* Full and partial tuition waivers, Federal Work-Study available. Aid available to part-time students. Financial aid application deadline: 5/15; applicants required to submit FAFSA. • Nicholas Galli, Adviser, 718-960-8775.

Lehman College of the City University of New York, Division of Natural and Social Sciences, Department of Health Services, Program in Health N–12 Teacher, 250 Bedford Park Boulevard West, Bronx, NY 10468-1589. Awards MS Ed. Faculty: 2 full-time (1 woman). Students: 29 part-time (24 women). *Degree requirements:* Thesis or alternative. *Application deadline:* 4/1 (priority date; rolling processing; 11/1 for spring admission). *Application fee:* $40. *Expenses:* Tuition $4350 per year full-time, $185 per credit part-time for state residents; $7600 per year full-time, $320 per credit part-time for nonresidents. Fees $120 per year full-time, $80 per year part-time. *Financial aid:* Full and partial tuition waivers, Federal Work-Study available. Aid available to part-time students. Financial aid application deadline: 5/15; applicants required to submit FAFSA. • Nicholas Galli, Adviser, 718-960-8775.

Lesley College, Graduate School of Arts and Social Sciences, Cambridge, MA 02138-2790. Offerings include intercultural relations (MA, CAGS), with options in development project administration (MA), individually designed (MA), intercultural conflict resolution (MA), intercultural health and human services (MA), intercultural training and consulting (MA), international education exchange (MA), international student advising (MA), managing culturally diverse human resources (MA), multicultural education (MA). Postbaccalaureate distance learning degree programs offered (minimal on-campus study). School faculty: 24 full-time (14 women), 344 part-time (225 women). *Application deadline:* rolling. *Application fee:* $45. *Tuition:* $425 per credit. • Dr. Martha B. McKenna, Dean, 617-349-8467. Application contact: Graduate Admissions, 617-349-8300. Fax: 617-349-8366.

Loma Linda University, School of Public Health, Programs in Health Promotion and Education, Loma Linda, CA 92350. Awards MPH, Dr PH. Students: 29 full-time (18 women), 115 part-time (87 women). 41 applicants, 85% accepted. In 1997, 64 master's awarded. *Degree requirements:* For doctorate, dissertation. *Entrance requirements:* For master's, Michigan English Language Assessment Battery (minimum score 92) or TOEFL (minimum score 600); for doctorate, GRE General Test (minimum combined score of 1500 on three sections). Application deadline: rolling. Application fee: $100. *Tuition:* $380 per unit. *Financial aid:* Application deadline 5/15. • Dr. Christine Neish, Chair, 909-824-4575. Fax: 909-824-4087. Application contact: Terri Tamayose, Director of Admissions and Academic Records, 909-824-4694. Fax: 909-824-8087. E-mail: ttamayose@sph.llu.edu.

Long Island University, Brooklyn Campus, School of Health Professions, Division of Sports Sciences, Brooklyn, NY 11201-8423. Offerings include health sciences (MS). Division faculty: 3 full-time (0 women), 9 part-time (1 woman). *Application deadline:* rolling. *Application fee:* $30. Electronic applications accepted. *Expenses:* Tuition $480 per credit. Fees $415 per year full-time, $73 per semester (minimum) part-time. • Dr. Milorad Stricevic, Associate Dean, 718-488-1026. Application contact: Bernard W. Sullivan, Associate Director of Admissions, 718-488-1011.

Louisiana Tech University, College of Education, Department of Curriculum, Instruction and Leadership, Ruston, LA 71272. Offerings include secondary education (M Ed), with options in business education, English education, foreign language education, health and physical education, mathematics education, science education, social studies education, speech education. Accredited by NCATE. Department faculty: 16 full-time (11 women). *Application deadline:* 7/29 (2/3 for spring admission). *Application fee:* $20 ($30 for international students). *Tuition:* $2382 per year full-time, $223 per quarter (minimum) part-time for state residents; $5307 per year full-time, $223 per quarter (minimum) part-time for nonresidents. • Dr. Samuel V. Dauzat, Head, 318-257-4609.

Louisiana Tech University, College of Education, Department of Health and Physical Education, Ruston, LA 71272. Awards MS. Accredited by NCATE. Part-time programs available. Faculty: 9 full-time (3 women). Students: 13 full-time (8 women), 2 part-time (1 woman); includes 1 minority (African American), 10 international. Average age 27. In 1997, 14 degrees awarded. *Degree requirements:* Computer language, thesis or alternative required, foreign language not required. *Entrance requirements:* GRE General Test. Application deadline: 7/29 (2/3 for spring admission). Application fee: $20 ($30 for international students). *Tuition:* $2382 per year full-time, $223 per quarter (minimum) part-time for state residents; $5307 per year full-time, $223 per quarter (minimum) part-time for nonresidents. *Financial aid:* Fellowships, research assistantships available. Financial aid application deadline: 2/1. • Dr. Billy Jack Talton, Head, 318-257-4432.

Mankato State University, College of Allied Health and Nursing, Department of Health Science, South Rd and Ellis Ave, PO Box 8400, Mankato, MN 56002-8400. Offers programs in community health (MS), health science (MS, MT). Faculty: 8 full-time (4 women). Students: 22 full-time (17 women), 32 part-time (27 women); includes 4 minority (1 African American, 1 Asian American, 2 Hispanics), 1 international. Average age 32. 18 applicants, 67% accepted. In 1997, 8 degrees awarded. *Degree requirements:* Thesis or alternative, comprehensive exam required, foreign language not required. *Entrance requirements:* GRE General Test, minimum GPA of 3.0 during previous 2 years. Application deadline: 7/10 (priority date; rolling processing; 10/30 for spring admission). Application fee: $20. *Tuition:* $126 per credit (minimum) for state residents; $200 per credit for nonresidents. *Financial aid:* Teaching assistantships, Federal Work-Study, and career-related internships or fieldwork available. Aid available to part-time students. Financial aid application deadline: 3/15; applicants required to submit FAFSA. *Faculty research:* Teaching methods, stress prophylaxis and management, effects of alcohol. • Dr. Harold Slobof, Chairperson, 507-389-1528. Application contact: Joni Roberts, Admissions Coordinator, 507-389-2321. Fax: 507-389-5974. E-mail: grad@mankato.msus.edu.

Marshall University, College of Education, Division of Health, Physical Education and Recreation, Program in Health and Physical Education, Huntington, WV 25755-2020. Offers athletic training (MS), health and physical education (MS). Accredited by NCATE. Faculty: 6 (1 woman). Students: 41 full-time (14 women), 8 part-time (2 women); includes 4 minority (all African Americans), 2 international. In 1997, 15 degrees awarded. *Degree requirements:* Thesis optional. *Entrance requirements:* GRE General Test (minimum combined score of 1200). *Tuition:* $2364 per year full-time, $132 per hour part-time for state residents; $6894 per year full-time, $383 per hour part-time for nonresidents. • Application contact: Dr. James Harless, Director of Admissions, 304-696-3160.

Marshall University, College of Education, Division of Human Development and Allied Technology, Program in Safety, Huntington, WV 25755-2020. Awards MS. Accredited by NCATE. Faculty: 3 (0 women). Students: 43 full-time (18 women), 32 part-time (4 women); includes 11 minority (all African Americans), 1 international. In 1997, 31 degrees awarded. *Degree requirements:* Thesis optional. *Entrance requirements:* GRE General Test (minimum combined score of 1200). *Tuition:* $2364 per year full-time, $132 per hour part-time for state residents; $6894 per year full-time, $383 per hour part-time for nonresidents. • Dr. Allan Stern, Coordinator, 304-696-3069. Application contact: Dr. James Harless, Director of Admissions, 304-696-3160.

McNeese State University, College of Education, Department of Health and Human Performance, Lake Charles, LA 70609-2495. Offers program in health and physical education (M Ed). Evening/weekend programs available. Faculty: 7 full-time (2 women). Students: 1 (woman) full-time, 3 part-time (2 women). In 1997, 9 degrees awarded. *Entrance requirements:* GRE General Test, teaching certificate, 18 hours in professional education. Application deadline: 7/15 (priority date; rolling processing). Application fee: $10 ($25 for international students). *Tuition:* $2118 per year full-time, $344 per semester (minimum) part-time for state residents; $7308 per year full-time, $344 per semester (minimum) part-time for nonresidents. *Financial aid:* Application deadline 5/1. • Dr. Hans Leis Jr., Head, 318-475-5374.

Medical University of South Carolina, College of Health Professions, Department of Rehabilitation Sciences, Program in Health Professions Education, Charleston, SC 29425-0002. Awards MS. Part-time and evening/weekend programs available. Faculty: 3 full-time (all women), 8 part-time (6 women), 7 FTE. In 1997, 3 degrees awarded (100% found work related to degree). *Degree requirements:* Thesis required, foreign language not required. *Average time to degree:* master's–1.5 years full-time, 3 years part-time. *Entrance requirements:* GRE General Test (minimum combined score of 800), MAT (minimum score 30), interview, minimum GPA of 3.0, professional health license. Application fee: $55. *Expenses:* Tuition $4072 per year full-time, $221 per semester hour part-time for state residents; $7064 per year full-time, $387 per semester hour part-time for nonresidents. Fees $150 per year (minimum). *Financial aid:* 2 students received aid; Federal Work-Study available. Aid available to part-time students. Financial aid application deadline: 4/1; applicants required to submit FAFSA. *Faculty research:* Teaching methods, research models, health education, nutrition education. Total annual research expenditures: $44,288. • Dr. Maralynne Mitcham, Director, 843-792-3784. Fax: 843-792-9710. E-mail: mitchamm@musc.edu. Application contact: Helen Pye, Student Services, 843-792-3784. Fax: 843-792-0710. E-mail: pyeh@musc.edu.

Middle Tennessee State University, College of Education, Department of Health, Physical Education, Recreation and Safety, Murfreesboro, TN 37132. Awards MS, DA. One or more programs accredited by NCATE. Faculty: 17 full-time (6 women). Students: 50 full-time (28 women), 70 part-time (39 women); includes 21 minority (17 African Americans, 1 Asian American, 3 Hispanics), 1 international. Average age 30. 80 applicants, 66% accepted. In 1997, 31 master's, 1 doctorate awarded. *Degree requirements:* For master's, comprehensive exams required, foreign language and thesis not required; for doctorate, dissertation, comprehensive exams required, foreign language not required. *Entrance requirements:* For master's, Cooperative English Test, MAT; for doctorate, GRE or MAT. Application deadline: 8/1 (priority date). Application fee: $5. *Expenses:* Tuition $2560 per year full-time, $129 per semester hour part-time for state residents; $7386 per year full-time, $340 per semester hour part-time for nonresidents. Fees $486 per year full-time, $17 per semester (minimum) part-time. *Financial aid:* Teaching assistantships, institutionally sponsored loans, and career-related internships or fieldwork available. Aid available to part-time students. Financial aid application deadline: 5/1; applicants required to submit FAFSA. • Dr. Martha Whaley, Chair, 615-898-2811. Fax: 615-898-5020. E-mail: mwhaley@mtsu.edu.

Mississippi State University, College of Education, Department of Physical Health, Education, Recreation, and Sports, Mississippi State, MS 39762. Offerings include physical education (MS), with options in exercise science, health education/health promotion, sport administration, teaching/coaching. Accredited by NCATE. Department faculty: 9 full-time (2 women), 1 part-time (0 women). *Degree requirements:* Comprehensive oral or written exam required, thesis optional, foreign language not required. *Entrance requirements:* Minimum QPA of 2.75 in last 2 years. Application deadline: 7/26 (priority date; rolling processing; 11/10 for spring admission). Application fee: $0 ($25 for international students). *Tuition:* $3017 per year full-time, $168 per credit hour part-time for state residents; $6119 per year full-time, $340 per credit hour part-time for nonresidents. • Dr. Robert Boling, Head, 601-325-2963. Fax: 601-325-4525. E-mail: rbb4@ra.msstate.edu.

Montclair State University, College of Education and Human Services, Department of Health Professions, Physical Education, Recreation, and Leisure Studies, Program in Health Education, Upper Montclair, NJ 07043-1624. Awards MA. Accredited by NCATE. Part-time and evening/weekend programs available. Faculty: 21 full-time. Students: 6 full-time (5 women), 55 part-time (50 women); includes 4 minority (3 African Americans, 1 Hispanic). In 1997, 12 degrees awarded. *Degree requirements:* Comprehensive exam. *Entrance requirements:* GRE General Test. Application deadline: 4/1 (rolling processing; 11/1 for spring admission). Application fee: $40. *Expenses:* Tuition $201 per credit for state residents; $257 per credit for nonresidents. Fees $22.05 per credit. *Financial aid:* Research assistantships available. Financial aid application deadline: 3/1; applicants required to submit FAFSA. • Dr. Reza Shahrokh, Adviser, 973-655-7115.

Morehead State University, College of Education and Behavioral Sciences, Department of Health, Physical Education and Recreation, Morehead, KY 40351. Offers programs in health, physical education and recreation (MA, Ed D); sports administration (MS). Accredited by NCATE. MS offered jointly with Eastern Kentucky University. Part-time and evening/weekend programs available. Faculty: 9 full-time (4 women), 6 part-time (3 women). Students: 15 full-time (7 women), 4 part-time (1 woman); includes 1 minority (African American), 1 international. Average age 25. 14 applicants, 100% accepted. In 1997, 17 master's awarded. *Degree requirements:* For master's, oral exam, written core exam required, thesis optional, foreign language not required. *Entrance requirements:* For master's, GRE General Test (minimum combined score of 1000), minimum GPA of 2.5; major/minor in health, physical education, or recreation. Application deadline: 8/1 (priority date; rolling processing; 12/1 for spring admission). Application fee: $0. *Tuition:* $2470 per year full-time, $138 per semester hour part-time for state residents; $6710 per year full-time, $373 per semester hour part-time for nonresidents. *Financial aid:* In 1997–98, 2 teaching assistantships (1 to a first-year student) averaging $471 per month and totaling $8,000 were awarded; research assistantships, Federal Work-Study also available. Financial aid application deadline: 4/1; applicants required to submit FAFSA. *Faculty research:* Child growth and performance, instructional strategies, outdoor leadership qualities, exercise science, athletic training. • Dr. Jack Sheltmire, Chair, 606-783-2180. Fax: 606-783-5058. E-mail: j.sheltmire@morehead-st.edu. Application contact: Betty Cowsert, Graduate Admissions Officer, 606-783-2039. Fax: 606-783-5061.

Mount Mary College, Graduate Programs, Program in Dietetics, Milwaukee, WI 53222-4597. Offerings include nutrition education (MS). Program faculty: 1 (woman) full-time, 6 part-time (4 women), 4 FTE. *Degree requirements:* Thesis. *Average time to degree:* master's–4 years part-time. *Entrance requirements:* TOEFL (minimum score 550), minimum GPA of 2.75, completion of ADA and DPD requirements. Application deadline: 8/15 (priority date). Application fee: $35. *Tuition:* $370 per credit hour. • Dr. Lisa Stark, Director, 414-258-4810 Ext. 398.

New Jersey City University, School of Professional Studies and Education, Department of Health Sciences, Jersey City, NJ 07305-1957. Offerings include community health education (MS). *Degree requirements:* Thesis or alternative, internship required, foreign language not required. *Entrance requirements:* GRE, TOEFL or MAT. Application deadline: 8/1 (priority date; rolling processing; 12/1 for spring admission). Application fee: $0.

New York University, School of Education, Department of Health Studies, Program in Health Education, New York, NY 10012-1019. Offers administrators and supervisors of health educa-

Directory: Health Education

New York University (continued)

tion (CAS), including human sexuality education, school and college health education; community health education (MPH, Ed D, PhD), including alcohol studies (MPH), international community health education (MPH, Ed D, PhD); human sexuality education (MA, Ed D, PhD); school and college health education (MA, Ed D, PhD). Part-time and evening/weekend programs available. Faculty: 6 full-time (3 women), 7 part-time. Students: 51 full-time, 63 part-time. 114 applicants, 57% accepted. In 1997, 28 master's, 4 doctorates awarded. Terminal master's awarded for partial completion of doctoral program. *Degree requirements:* For master's, thesis required (for some programs), foreign language not required; for doctorate, dissertation. *Entrance requirements:* For master's, TOEFL; for doctorate, GRE General Test, TOEFL, interview; for CAS, TOEFL, master's degree. Application deadline: 2/1 (priority date; rolling processing; 12/1 for spring admission). Application fee: $40 ($60 for international students). *Financial aid:* Partial tuition waivers, Federal Work-Study, institutionally sponsored loans, and career-related internships or fieldwork available. Aid available to part-time students. Financial aid application deadline: 3/1; applicants required to submit FAFSA. *Faculty research:* Poverty and prevention of chronic and infectious diseases, poverty and public health, women's health, sex education for children, health and ethnicity. • Sally Guttmacher, Director, 212-998-5786. Application contact: Office of Graduate Admissions, 212-998-5030. Fax: 212-995-4328.

See in-depth description on page 757.

North Carolina Agricultural and Technical State University, Graduate School, School of Education, Department of Health and Physical Education, Greensboro, NC 27411. Awards MS. Accredited by NCATE. Part-time and evening/weekend programs available. Faculty: 6 full-time (1 woman). Students: 6 full-time (2 women), 14 part-time (8 women); includes 8 minority (all African Americans). Average age 32. 16 applicants, 56% accepted. In 1997, 5 degrees awarded. *Degree requirements:* Thesis or alternative, comprehensive exam, qualifying exam required, foreign language not required. *Entrance requirements:* GRE General Test, minimum GPA of 3.0. Application deadline: 6/1 (priority date; rolling processing; 12/1 for spring admission). Application fee: $35. *Tuition:* $1662 per year full-time, $272 per semester (minimum) part-time for state residents; $8790 per year full-time, $2054 per semester (minimum) part-time for nonresidents. *Financial aid:* Research assistantships, teaching assistantships, graduate assistantships available. Financial aid application deadline: 6/1. • Dr. Deborah Callaway, Chairperson, 336-334-7719. Fax: 336-334-7258.

Northeast Louisiana University, College of Education, Department of Health and Human Performance, Monroe, LA 71209-0001. Awards M Ed. Accredited by NCATE. Part-time and evening/weekend programs available. *Degree requirements:* Thesis optional, foreign language not required. *Entrance requirements:* GRE General Test. Application deadline: 6/1 (priority date; rolling processing; 11/1 for spring admission). Application fee: $15 ($25 for international students). *Tuition:* $2028 per year full-time, $240 per semester (minimum) part-time for state residents; $6852 per year full-time, $240 per semester (minimum) part-time for nonresidents. *Faculty research:* Cardiovascular disease risk factors; exercise and immunological system; attitude, exercise, and the aged.

Northern Arizona University, College of Health Professions, Department of Health, Physical Education, Exercise Science, and Nutrition, Program in Public Health, Flagstaff, AZ 86011. Offerings include health education and health promotion (MPH). Offered jointly with University of Arizona. *Degree requirements:* Thesis or alternative required, foreign language not required. *Entrance requirements:* GRE General Test, minimum GPA of 3.0. Application fee: $45. *Expenses:* Tuition $2088 per year full-time, $330 per semester (minimum) part-time for state residents; $8004 per year full-time, $1002 per semester (minimum) part-time for nonresidents. Fees $72 per year full-time, $18 per semester (minimum) part-time. • Dr. John P. Sciacca, Director, 520-523-4122.

Northern State University, Division of Graduate Studies in Education, Program in Teaching and Learning, Aberdeen, SD 57401-7198. Offerings include health, physical education, and coaching (MS Ed). Accredited by NCATE. Offered jointly with Huron University, Jamestown College, and the University of Mary. Program faculty: 98 full-time (28 women). *Degree requirements:* Thesis required, foreign language not required. *Average time to degree:* master's–1.5 years full-time. *Entrance requirements:* Minimum GPA of 2.75. Application deadline: 8/15 (priority date; rolling processing; 12/15 for spring admission). Application fee: $15. *Expenses:* Tuition $1999 per year full-time, $83 per credit hour part-time for state residents; $6034 per year full-time, $251 per credit hour part-time for nonresidents. Fees $954 per year full-time, $40 per credit hour part-time. • Dr. Paul Deputy, Head, 605-626-2415. Application contact: Dr. Sharon Tebben, Director of Graduate Studies, 605-626-2558. Fax: 605-626-2542.

Northwest Missouri State University, College of Education and Human Services, Department of Health, Physical Education, Recreation and Dance, 800 University Drive, Maryville, MO 64468-6001. Offers program in health and physical education (MS Ed). Accredited by NCATE. Part-time programs available. Faculty: 13 full-time (4 women). Students: 24 full-time (6 women), 12 part-time (2 women); includes 1 minority (African American). 21 applicants, 100% accepted. In 1997, 21 degrees awarded. *Degree requirements:* Comprehensive exam required, foreign language and thesis not required. *Entrance requirements:* GRE General Test (minimum combined score of 700), TOEFL (minimum score 550), minimum undergraduate GPA of 2.75, teaching certificate, writing sample. Application deadline: rolling. Application fee: $0 ($50 for international students). *Expenses:* Tuition $113 per credit hour for state residents; $197 per credit hour for nonresidents. Fees $3 per credit hour. *Financial aid:* In 1997–98, 11 research assistantships averaging $585 per month, 16 teaching assistantships averaging $585 per month, 4 administrative assistantships averaging $585 per month were awarded. Financial aid application deadline: 3/1. • Dr. Terry Barmann, Program Director, 816-562-1706. Application contact: Dr. Frances Shipley, Dean of Graduate School, 816-562-1145. E-mail: gradsch@acad.nwmissouri.edu.

Nova Southeastern University, Fischler Center for the Advancement of Education, Programs in Higher Education, Fort Lauderdale, FL 33314-7721. Offerings include health care education (Ed D). *Degree requirements:* Dissertation, practicum required, foreign language not required. *Entrance requirements:* Master's degree, work experience in field. Application deadline: rolling. Application fee: $50. *Tuition:* $8460 per year. • Dr. Ross E. Moreton, Dean, 954-262-8526. E-mail: moreton@fcae.nova.edu. Application contact: Dr. Delores Smiley, 800-986-3223 Ext. 8527. Fax: 954-262-3903. E-mail: smiley@fcae.nova.edu.

The Ohio State University, College of Education, School of Physical Activity and Educational Services, Program in Health, Physical Education, and Recreation, Columbus, OH 43210. Awards MA, M Ed, PhD. Accredited by NCATE. Part-time programs available. Faculty: 44. Students: 114 full-time (56 women), 38 part-time (26 women); includes 27 minority (18 African Americans, 6 Asian Americans, 2 Hispanics, 1 Native American), 20 international. 241 applicants, 34% accepted. In 1997, 46 master's, 11 doctorates awarded. *Degree requirements:* For master's, thesis optional, foreign language not required; for doctorate, dissertation required, foreign language not required. *Entrance requirements:* GRE. Application deadline: 8/15 (rolling processing). Application fee: $30 ($40 for international students). *Tuition:* $5472 per year full-time, $554 per quarter (minimum) part-time for state residents; $14,172 per year full-time, $1424 per quarter (minimum) part-time for nonresidents. *Financial aid:* Fellowships, research assistantships, teaching assistantships, administrative assistantships, Federal Work-Study, institutionally sponsored loans available. Aid available to part-time students. • Dr. W. Michael Sherman, Director, School of Physical Activity and Educational Services, 614-292-5679. Fax: 614-688-4613. E-mail: sherman.4@osu.edu.

Oklahoma State University, College of Education, School of Health, Physical Education, and Leisure, Stillwater, OK 74078. Offers programs in health (MS, Ed D), leisure sciences (MS, Ed D), physical education (MS, Ed D), physical education and leisure sciences (Ed D). Faculty: 13 full-time (5 women). Students: 29 full-time (17 women), 45 part-time (26 women); includes 6 minority (3 African Americans, 2 Hispanics, 1 Native American), 2 international. Average age 32. In 1997, 9 master's, 1 doctorate awarded. *Degree requirements:* For doctorate, dissertation. *Entrance requirements:* TOEFL (minimum score 550). Application deadline: 7/1 (priority date). Application fee: $25. *Financial aid:* In 1997–98, 10 students received aid, including 10 teaching assistantships (2 to first-year students) averaging $1,008 per month and totaling $90,750; partial tuition waivers, Federal Work-Study, and career-related internships or fieldwork also available. Aid available to part-time students. Financial aid application deadline: 3/1. • Dr. Lowell Caneday, Director, 405-744-5493.

Oregon State University, Graduate School, College of Health and Human Performance, Department of Public Health, Program in Health Education, Corvallis, OR 97331. Awards MAIS, MAT, MS. Students: 0. 9 applicants, 100% accepted. *Degree requirements:* Minimum GPA of 3.0 required, foreign language not required. *Entrance requirements:* NTE, California Basic Educational Skills Test, TOEFL (minimum score 550), minimum GPA of 3.0 in last 90 hours. Application deadline: 3/1 (rolling processing). Application fee: $50. *Tuition:* $6207 per year full-time, $810 per quarter (minimum) part-time for state residents; $10,551 per year full-time, $1293 per quarter (minimum) part-time for nonresidents. *Financial aid:* Fellowships, Federal Work-Study, institutionally sponsored loans, and career-related internships or fieldwork available. Aid available to part-time students. Financial aid application deadline: 2/1. • Dr. Margaret M. Smith, Coordinator, 541-737-2686.

Pennsylvania State University Harrisburg Campus of the Capital College, Division of Behavioral Sciences and Education, Program in Health Education, Middletown, PA 17057-4898. Awards M Ed. Evening/weekend programs available. Students: 4 full-time (all women), 122 part-time (99 women). Average age 33. In 1997, 29 degrees awarded. *Degree requirements:* Thesis or alternative required, foreign language not required. *Entrance requirements:* GRE General Test, minimum GPA of 2.5. Application deadline: 7/26. Application fee: $40. *Expenses:* Tuition $6534 per year full-time, $276 per credit part-time for state residents; $12,516 per year full-time, $523 per credit part-time for nonresidents. Fees $232 per year (minimum) full-time, $40 per semester (minimum) part-time. *Financial aid:* Career-related internships or fieldwork available. • Dr. Samuel Monismith, Coordinator, 717-948-6505.

Plymouth State College of the University System of New Hampshire, Department of Education, Program in Health Education, Plymouth, NH 03264-1595. Awards M Ed. Part-time and evening/weekend programs available. Students: 1 (woman) full-time, 6 part-time (all women). Average age 40. 2 applicants, 0% accepted. In 1997, 11 degrees awarded. *Entrance requirements:* GRE General Test (average 500 on each section) or MAT (minimum score 50), minimum GPA of 3.0. Application deadline: 9/1 (priority date; rolling processing). Application fee: $25 ($35 for international students). *Tuition:* $232 per credit for state residents; $254 per credit for nonresidents. *Financial aid:* Graduate assistantships, institutionally sponsored loans, and career-related internships or fieldwork available. Aid available to part-time students. Financial aid application deadline: 3/15; applicants required to submit FAFSA. • Dr. Nancy Strapko, Adviser, 603-535-2508. Application contact: Maryann Szabadics, Administrative Assistant, 603-535-2636. Fax: 603-535-2572. E-mail: for.grad@psc.plymouth.edu.

Portland State University, College of Urban and Public Affairs, School of Community Health, Division of Health Education, Portland, OR 97207-0751. Offerings include health education (MA, MS), health education and health promotion (MPH). One or more programs accredited by NCATE. MPH offered jointly with Oregon Health Sciences University and Oregon State University. Division faculty: 8 full-time (5 women), 25 part-time (17 women), 10 FTE. *Application deadline:* 4/1 (11/1 for spring admission). *Application fee:* $50. *Tuition:* $6101 per year full-time, $689 per semester (minimum) part-time for state residents; $10,445 per year full-time, $689 per semester (minimum) part-time for nonresidents. • Application contact: Elizabeth Bull, 503-725-4401. Fax: 503-725-5100. E-mail: eliz@upa.pdx.edu.

Prairie View A&M University, College of Education, Department of Health and Human Performance, Prairie View, TX 77446-0188. Offers programs in health education (MA Ed, MS Ed), physical education (MA Ed, MS Ed). Accredited by NCATE. Faculty: 2 full-time (1 woman). Students: 6 full-time (1 woman), 3 part-time (2 women); includes 9 minority (8 African Americans, 1 Hispanic). Average age 31. In 1997, 7 degrees awarded (100% found work related to degree). *Degree requirements:* Thesis optional, foreign language not required. *Average time to degree:* master's–2.5 years full-time, 4 years part-time. *Entrance requirements:* GRE General Test. Application deadline: 7/1 (priority date; rolling processing; 11/1 for spring admission). Application fee: $10. *Tuition:* $2202 per year full-time, $336 per semester (minimum) part-time for state residents; $6000 per year full-time, $963 per semester (minimum) part-time for nonresidents. *Financial aid:* Career-related internships or fieldwork available. Financial aid application deadline: 6/31. • Dr. Mary V. White, Head, 409-857-4210. Fax: 409-857-2911.

Rhode Island College, School of Graduate Studies, School of Education and Human Development, Department of Health and Physical Education, Providence, RI 02908-1924. Offers program in health education (M Ed). Accredited by NCATE. Evening/weekend programs available. Faculty: 5 full-time (2 women), 2 part-time (1 woman). Students: 6 full-time (all women), 66 part-time (62 women). In 1997, 21 degrees awarded. *Entrance requirements:* GRE General Test or MAT. Application deadline: 4/1 (rolling processing). Application fee: $25. *Tuition:* $4064 per year full-time, $214 per credit part-time for state residents; $7658 per year full-time, $376 per credit part-time for nonresidents. *Financial aid:* Application deadline 4/1. • Dr. Kenneth I. Ainley, Chair, 401-456-8046.

Rowan University, College of Education, Department of Health and Exercise Science, Glassboro, NJ 08028-1701. Offers programs in administration and supervision in health and physical education or athletics (MA), health and exercise science (Certificate). Accredited by NCATE. Part-time and evening/weekend programs available. Students: 20 (18 women); includes 1 minority (African American). 24 applicants, 88% accepted. *Application deadline:* 11/1 (priority date; rolling processing; 4/1 for spring admission). *Application fee:* $50. *Tuition:* $5728 per year full-time, $258 per credit hour part-time for state residents; $8968 per year full-time, $393 per credit hour part-time for nonresidents. • Dr. James Burd, Adviser, 609-256-4783.

Sage Graduate School, Graduate School, Division of Psychology, Troy, NY 12180-4115. Offerings include community psychology (MA), with options in chemical dependency, child care and children's services, community counseling, community health educator, general psychology, visual art therapy. Division faculty: 2 full-time (1 woman), 2 part-time (both women). *Degree requirements:* Thesis or alternative required, foreign language not required. *Entrance requirements:* GRE General Test, minimum GPA of 2.75. Application deadline: 8/1 (rolling processing; 12/15 for spring admission). Application fee: $25. *Expenses:* Tuition $360 per credit hour. Fees $50 per semester. • Dr. Patricia O'Connor, Director, 518-244-2221. Fax: 518-244-4545. E-mail: occonp@sage.edu. Application contact: Melissa Robertson, Associate Director of Admissions, 518-244-6878. Fax: 518-244-6880. E-mail: sgsadm@sage.edu.

Sage Graduate School, Graduate School, Division of Education, Program in Health Education, Troy, NY 12180-4115. Offers community health (MS), nutrition and dietetics (MS), school health (MS). Part-time and evening/weekend programs available. *Degree requirements:* Thesis optional, foreign language not required. *Entrance requirements:* Minimum GPA of 2.75. Application deadline: 8/1 (rolling processing; 12/15 for spring admission). Application fee: $25. *Expenses:* Tuition $360 per credit hour. Fees $50 per semester. *Financial aid:* Research assistantships and career-related internships or fieldwork available. Aid available to part-time students. Financial aid application deadline: 7/1; applicants required to submit FAFSA. *Faculty research:* Policy development in health education and health care. • Dr. John J. Pelizza, Adviser, 518-244-2051. Fax: 218-244-2334. Application contact: Melissa Robertson, Associate Director of Admissions, 518-244-6878. Fax: 518-244-6880. E-mail: sgsadm@sage.edu.

Sage Graduate School, Graduate School, Division of Management Studies, Program in Health Services Administration, Troy, NY 12180-4115. Offerings include health education (MS). Program faculty: 1 full-time (0 women), 4 part-time (1 woman). *Entrance requirements:* Minimum GPA of 2.75. Application deadline: 8/1 (rolling processing; 12/15 for spring admission). Application fee: $25. *Expenses:* Tuition $360 per credit hour. Fees $50 per semester. • Application contact: Melissa Robertson, Associate Director of Admissions, 518-244-6878. Fax: 518-244-6880. E-mail: sgsadm@sage.edu.

Saint Joseph's University, Department of Health Services, Program in Health Education, Philadelphia, PA 19131-1395. Awards MS. Evening/weekend programs available. Students: 119 (110 women). In 1997, 41 degrees awarded. *Entrance requirements:* TOEFL, GRE General Test, MAT, or minimum undergraduate GPA of 2.5. Application deadline: 7/15. Application fee: $30. *Tuition:* $470 per credit hour. *Financial aid:* Fellowships and career-related internships or fieldwork available. • Dr. Laura Frank, Director, 610-660-1580.

Saint Mary's College of California, School of Liberal Arts, Program in Health, Physical Education, and Recreation, Moraga, CA 94575. Awards MA. Part-time programs available. Faculty: 6 part-time (1 woman). Students: 71 full-time (18 women), 15 part-time (5 women); includes 15 minority (8 African Americans, 3 Asian Americans, 4 Hispanics). Average age 26. 65 applicants, 45% accepted. In 1997, 18 degrees awarded. *Degree requirements:* Comprehensive exams or thesis required, foreign language not required. *Average time to degree:* master's–3 years full-time. *Entrance requirements:* Minimum GPA of 2.75, BA in physical education, field experience. Application deadline: 8/1 (priority date; rolling processing; 12/15 for spring admission). Application fee: $20. *Tuition:* $1319 per course. *Financial aid:* In 1997–98, 6 teaching assistantships were awarded; fellowships, institutionally sponsored loans, and career-related internships or fieldwork also available. Aid available to part-time students. Financial aid applicants required to submit FAFSA. *Faculty research:* Administrative aspects of physical education and athletics. • Dr. Craig Johnson, Chair, 925-631-4377. Fax: 925-376-0829.

Sam Houston State University, College of Education and Applied Science, Division of Health and Kinesiology, Program in Health Education, Huntsville, TX 77341. Awards MA. Accredited by NCATE. Part-time and evening/weekend programs available. Students: 4 full-time (2 women), 7 part-time (6 women); includes 1 minority (Hispanic), 1 international. Average age 30. In 1997, 4 degrees awarded. *Degree requirements:* Internship required, foreign language and thesis not required. *Entrance requirements:* GRE General Test (minimum combined score of 800), MAT. Application fee: $15. *Tuition:* $1810 per year full-time, $297 per semester (minimum) part-time for state residents; $6922 per year full-time, $924 per semester (minimum) part-time for nonresidents. *Financial aid:* Federal Work-Study, institutionally sponsored loans, and career-related internships or fieldwork available. *Faculty research:* Alcohol abuse, prenatal health, nutrition. • Dr. William Hyman, Coordinator, 409-294-1211.

San Francisco State University, College of Health and Human Services, Department of Health Education, San Francisco, CA 94132-1722. Offers program in health science (MS). Part-time programs available. *Degree requirements:* Culminating project required, foreign language not required. *Average time to degree:* master's–3.5 years part-time. *Entrance requirements:* Minimum GPA of 2.5 in last 60 units. Application deadline: 11/30 (priority date; rolling processing). Application fee: $55. *Expenses:* Tuition $0 for state residents; $246 per unit for nonresidents. Fees $1982 per year full-time, $1316 per year part-time. *Faculty research:* Health behavior, gerontology, homelessness, community health.

South Dakota State University, College of Arts and Science, Department of Health, Physical Education and Recreation, Brookings, SD 57007. Awards MS. Faculty: 3 full-time (1 woman). Students: 13 full-time (5 women), 12 part-time (2 women); includes 1 minority (African American). 19 applicants, 100% accepted. In 1997, 9 degrees awarded. *Degree requirements:* Thesis, oral and written exams required, foreign language not required. *Average time to degree:* master's–2 years full-time, 4 years part-time. *Entrance requirements:* GRE, TOEFL (minimum score 525). Application deadline: 10/15 (priority date; rolling processing; 3/15 for spring admission). Application fee: $15. *Expenses:* Tuition $82 per credit hour for state residents; $242 per credit hour for nonresidents. Fees $37 per credit hour. *Financial aid:* In 1997–98, 7 teaching assistantships (6 to first-year students), 1 administrative assistantship (to a first-year student) were awarded; Federal Work-Study and career-related internships or fieldwork also available. *Faculty research:* Reaction time in the elderly wellness center facilities and programming, effective teaching behaviors in physical education, assessment of human fitness. • Dr. Patty Hacker, Acting Head, 605-688-5625. Fax: 605-688-5999.

Southeastern Louisiana University, College of Education, Department of Kinesiology and Health Studies, Hammond, LA 70402. Offers programs in health studies (MA), kinesiology (MA). Accredited by NCATE. Part-time programs available. Faculty: 11 full-time, 2 part-time. Students: 3 full-time (1 woman), 10 part-time (8 women); includes 1 international. Average age 30. In 1997, 12 degrees awarded. *Degree requirements:* Thesis optional, foreign language not required. *Entrance requirements:* GRE General Test (minimum combined score of 800), minimum GPA of 2.5, 30 hours of physical education. Application deadline: 7/15 (priority date; rolling processing; 12/15 for spring admission). Application fee: $10 ($25 for international students). Electronic applications accepted. *Expenses:* Tuition $2010 per year full-time, $287 per semester (minimum) part-time for state residents; $5232 per year full-time, $287 per semester (minimum) part-time for nonresidents. Fees $5 per year. *Financial aid:* Research assistantships, teaching assistantships, Federal Work-Study, and career-related internships or fieldwork available. Aid available to part-time students. Financial aid application deadline: 5/1; applicants required to submit FAFSA. *Faculty research:* Endocrine response/adaption to exercise, hemispheric function and the teaching of motor skills, teacher knowledge and elementary physical education analysis of HARE self-esteem scale with elementary students. Total annual research expenditures: $12,000. • Dr. Parris R. Watts, Head, 504-549-2129. Fax: 504-549-5119. E-mail: pwatts@selu.edu.

Southern Arkansas University–Magnolia, Graduate Program in Education, Program in Secondary Education, Magnolia, AR 71753. Offerings include health, kinesiology and recreation (M Ed). *Degree requirements:* Thesis or alternative, comprehensive exam required, foreign language not required. *Average time to degree:* master's–2 years full-time. *Entrance requirements:* GRE, minimum GPA of 2.5. Application deadline: 8/15. Application fee: $0. *Expenses:* Tuition $95 per hour for state residents; $138 per hour for nonresidents. Fees $2 per hour. • Dr. Danield L. Bernard, Dean, Graduate Studies, Graduate Program in Education, 870-235-4055. Fax: 870-235-5035. E-mail: dlbernard@mail.saumag.edu.

Southern Connecticut State University, School of Education, Department of School Health Education, New Haven, CT 06515-1355. Offers program in health science (MS Ed). Faculty: 2 full-time. Students: 7 full-time (4 women), 69 part-time (41 women); includes 1 minority (African American). 58 applicants, 24% accepted. In 1997, 31 degrees awarded. *Entrance requirements:* Interview. Application deadline: 7/15 (priority date; rolling processing). Application fee: $40. *Expenses:* Tuition $2632 per year full-time, $188 per credit part-time for state residents; $7200 per year full-time, $188 per credit part-time for nonresidents. Fees $1806 per year full-time, $45 per semester part-time for state residents; $2703 per year full-time, $45 per semester part-time for nonresidents. • Dr. Jerry Ainsworth, Coordinator, 203-392-6909.

Southern Illinois University at Carbondale, College of Education, Department of Health Education and Recreation, Program in Health Education, Carbondale, IL 62901-6806. Awards MS Ed, PhD. Accredited by NCATE. Part-time programs available. Faculty: 7 full-time (5 women). Students: 21 full-time (14 women), 8 part-time (4 women); includes 4 minority (all African Americans), 1 international. Average age 30. 9 applicants, 44% accepted. In 1997, 11 master's, 5 doctorates awarded. *Degree requirements:* Thesis/dissertation required, foreign language not required. *Entrance requirements:* For master's, MAT, TOEFL (minimum score 550), minimum GPA of 2.7; for doctorate, MAT, TOEFL (minimum score 550), minimum GPA of 3.25. Application deadline: 2/15 (9/15 for spring admission). Application fee: $20. *Expenses:* Tuition $2964 per year full-time, $99 per semester hour part-time for state residents; $8892 per year full-time, $270 per semester hour part-time for nonresidents. Fees $1034 per year full-time, $298 per semester (minimum) part-time. *Financial aid:* In 1997–98, 1 fellowship, 10 teaching assistantships (5 to first-year students) averaging $1,000 per month were awarded; research assistantships, full tuition waivers, Federal Work-Study, institutionally sponsored loans, and career-related internships or fieldwork also available. Aid available to part-time students. *Faculty research:* Sexuality education, research design, injury control, program evaluation. • Application contact: Phyllis McCowen, Administrative Assistant, 618-453-2582. Fax: 618-453-1829. E-mail: mccowen@siu.edu.

Southern Illinois University at Edwardsville, School of Education, Department of Health, Recreation, and Physical Education, Edwardsville, IL 62026-0001. Awards MS Ed. Accredited by NCATE. Part-time programs available. Students: 37 full-time (12 women), 19 part-time (7 women); includes 4 minority (2 African Americans, 1 Asian American, 1 Hispanic), 4 international. 35 applicants, 80% accepted. In 1997, 10 degrees awarded. *Degree requirements:* Thesis or alternative, final exam required, foreign language not required. *Application deadline:* 7/24. *Application fee:* $25. *Expenses:* Tuition $1716 per year full-time, $95 per credit hour part-time for state residents; $5149 per year full-time, $286 per credit hour part-time for nonresidents. Fees $463 per year full-time, $433 per year part-time. *Financial aid:* In 1997–98, 6 teaching assistantships, 13 assistantships were awarded; fellowships, research assistantships, Federal Work-Study, institutionally sponsored loans also available. Aid available to part-time students. • Dr. John Baker, Chairperson, 618-692-3028. Application contact: Kay Covington, Graduate Program Director, 618-692-3226.

Southwestern Oklahoma State University, School of Education, Program in Health, Physical Education and Recreation, Weatherford, OK 73096-3098. Awards M Ed. Accredited by NCATE. M Ed distance learning degree program offered to Oklahoma residents only. Part-time programs available. Postbaccalaureate distance learning degree programs offered. Students: 3 full-time (2 women), 1 part-time (0 women); includes 2 minority (1 African American, 1 Asian American). 1 applicant, 100% accepted. In 1997, 1 degree awarded. *Degree requirements:* Exam required, foreign language and thesis not required. *Entrance requirements:* GRE General Test, TOEFL (minimum score 550), minimum GPA of 2.5. Application deadline: rolling. Application fee: $15. *Expenses:* Tuition $60 per credit hour (minimum) for state residents; $147 per credit hour (minimum) for nonresidents. Fees $109 per year full-time, $24 per semester (minimum) part-time. *Financial aid:* Research assistantships, teaching assistantships, partial tuition waivers, Federal Work-Study, institutionally sponsored loans, and career-related internships or fieldwork available. Aid available to part-time students. Financial aid application deadline: 3/1; applicants required to submit FAFSA. • Dr. Ken Rose, Chair, 580-774-3254.

Southwest Texas State University, School of Education, Department of Health, Physical Education, and Recreation, Program in Health and Physical Education, San Marcos, TX 78666. Awards MA. Part-time and evening/weekend programs available. Students: 0. *Degree requirements:* Thesis, comprehensive exam required, foreign language not required. *Entrance requirements:* GRE General Test (minimum combined score of 900), TOEFL (minimum score 550), minimum GPA of 2.75 in last 60 hours. Application deadline: 7/15 (priority date; rolling processing; 11/15 for spring admission). Application fee: $25 ($50 for international students). *Expenses:* Tuition $648 per year full-time, $120 per semester (minimum) part-time for state residents; $4500 per year full-time, $750 per semester (minimum) part-time for nonresidents. Fees $1264 per year full-time, $314 per semester (minimum) part-time. *Financial aid:* Teaching assistantships, Federal Work-Study, institutionally sponsored loans, and career-related internships or fieldwork available. Financial aid application deadline: 4/1; applicants required to submit FAFSA. *Faculty research:* HIV/AIDS, youth fitness, leisure behavior, leisure program services and management evaluation. • Dr. Robert Patton, Graduate Adviser, 512-245-2938. Fax: 512-245-8678. E-mail: rp03@swt.edu.

Southwest Texas State University, School of Education, Department of Health, Physical Education, and Recreation, Program in Health Education, San Marcos, TX 78666. Awards M Ed. Part-time and evening/weekend programs available. Students: 5 full-time (all women), 13 part-time (10 women); includes 3 minority (all Hispanics), 1 international. Average age 28. In 1997, 3 degrees awarded. *Degree requirements:* Comprehensive exam required, foreign language and thesis not required. *Entrance requirements:* GRE General Test (minimum combined score of 900), TOEFL (minimum score 550), minimum GPA of 2.75 in last 60 hours. Application deadline: 7/15 (priority date; rolling processing; 11/15 for spring admission). Application fee: $25 ($50 for international students). *Expenses:* Tuition $648 per year full-time, $120 per semester (minimum) part-time for state residents; $4500 per year full-time, $750 per semester (minimum) part-time for nonresidents. Fees $1264 per year full-time, $314 per semester (minimum) part-time. *Financial aid:* Teaching assistantships, Federal Work-Study, institutionally sponsored loans, and career-related internships or fieldwork available. Aid available to part-time students. Financial aid application deadline: 4/1; applicants required to submit FAFSA. *Faculty research:* AIDS education, employee wellness, isometric strength evaluation. • Dr. Robert Patton, Graduate Adviser, 512-245-2938. Fax: 512-245-8678. E-mail: rp03@swt.edu.

Springfield College, Programs in Health Science, Springfield, MA 01109-3797. Offerings in health fitness (M Ed, MPE, MS), sports injury prevention and management (M Ed, MPE, MS). Part-time programs available. Faculty: 5 full-time (2 women), 6 part-time (1 woman), 7 FTE. Students: 9 full-time, 7 part-time; includes 2 international. Average age 26. 15 applicants, 80% accepted. In 1997, 8 degrees awarded. *Degree requirements:* Thesis (for some programs), comprehensive exam required, foreign language not required. *Application deadline:* (12/1 for spring admission). *Application fee:* $40. *Expenses:* Tuition $474 per credit. Fees $25 per year. *Financial aid:* In 1997–98, 3 teaching assistantships (all to first-year students) were awarded; fellowships, full and partial tuition waivers, Federal Work-Study, and career-related internships or fieldwork also available. Financial aid application deadline: 3/1. • Charles J. Redmond, Director, 413-748-3231. Application contact: Donald J. Shaw Jr., Director of Graduate Admissions, 413-748-3225. Fax: 413-748-3694. E-mail: dshaw@spfldcol.edu.

State University of New York College at Brockport, School of Professions, Department of Health Science, Brockport, NY 14420-2997. Awards MS Ed. Part-time and evening/weekend programs available. Faculty: 10 full-time (4 women), 5 part-time (2 women), 11.2 FTE. Students: 6 full-time (4 women), 31 part-time (26 women). Average age 34. 30 applicants, 73% accepted. In 1997, 6 degrees awarded. *Degree requirements:* Thesis or alternative required, foreign language not required. *Entrance requirements:* Health science graduate, writing competency, minimum GPA of 3.0. Application deadline: 4/1 (11/1 for spring admission). Application fee: $50. *Expenses:* Tuition $5100 per year full-time, $213 per credit hour part-time for state residents; $8416 per year full-time, $351 per credit hour part-time for nonresidents. Fees $440 per year full-time, $22.60 per credit hour part-time. *Financial aid:* Federal Work-Study and career-related internships or fieldwork available. Aid available to part-time students. Financial aid application deadline: 4/1; applicants required to submit FAFSA. *Faculty research:* Stress management, alcohol and drug prevention educaton, sexuality, health care delivery system, nutrition. • Dr. Eileen Daniel, Chairperson, 716-395-5481. Application contact: Dr. Patti Follansbee, Director, Health Science Graduate Admissions, 716-395-5483. Fax: 716-395-5246.

State University of New York College at Cortland, Division of Professional Studies, Department of Health Education, Cortland, NY 13045. Awards MS Ed. Part-time and evening/weekend programs available. In 1997, 33 degrees awarded. *Application deadline:* rolling. *Application fee:* $50. *Expenses:* Tuition $5100 per year full-time, $213 per credit hour part-time for state residents; $8416 per year full-time, $351 per credit hour part-time for nonresidents. Fees $644 per year full-time, $79 per semester (minimum) part-time. *Financial aid:* Partial tuition waivers, Federal Work-Study, and career-related internships or fieldwork available. Aid available to part-time students. Financial aid applicants required to submit CSS PROFILE or FAFSA. • Dr. Joseph Governali, Chair, 607-753-4225. Application contact: Jeanne M. Bechtel, Director of Admissions, 607-753-4711. Fax: 607-753-5998.

Stephen F. Austin State University, College of Education, Department of Kinesiology and Health Science, Nacogdoches, TX 75962. Offers programs in health education (M Ed), physical education (M Ed). Accredited by NCATE. Faculty: 9 full-time (4 women), 1 part-time (0 women). Students: 9 full-time (2 women), 9 part-time (7 women); includes 4 minority (3 African Americans, 1 Hispanic). 12 applicants, 75% accepted. In 1997, 16 degrees awarded. *Degree requirements:* Comprehensive exam required, foreign language and thesis not required. *Entrance*

Directory: Health Education

Stephen F. Austin State University (continued)

requirements: GRE General Test (minimum combined score of 1000). Application deadline: 8/1 (priority date; rolling processing; 12/15 for spring admission). Application fee: $0 ($25 for international students). *Tuition:* $1465 per year full-time, $263 per semester (minimum) part-time for state residents; $5299 per year full-time, $890 per semester (minimum) part-time for nonresidents. *Financial aid:* Teaching assistantships available. Financial aid application deadline: 3/1. • Dr. Mel Finkenberg, Chair, 409-468-3503.

Syracuse University, School of Education, Health and Physical Education Program, Syracuse, NY 13244-0003. Offers health and physical education (MS, CAS), including exercise science. Faculty: 5 full-time (2 women), 3 part-time (1 woman). Students: 35 full-time (18 women), 13 part-time (9 women); includes 5 minority (2 African Americans, 1 Asian American, 2 Hispanics), 1 international. 32 applicants, 84% accepted. In 1997, 11 master's awarded. *Degree requirements:* For master's, thesis or alternative; for CAS, thesis. *Entrance requirements:* GRE. Application deadline: rolling. Application fee: $40. *Tuition:* $13,320 per year full-time, $555 per credit hour part-time. *Financial aid:* Fellowships, research assistantships, teaching assistantships, administrative assistantships, Federal Work-Study, and career-related internships or fieldwork available. Aid available to part-time students. Financial aid application deadline: 3/1. *Faculty research:* Bone density, obesity in females, cardiovascular functioning, attitudes toward physical eduation, sports management and psychology. • Dr. Jay Graves, Chair, 315-443-9696.

Tarleton State University, College of Education, Department of Health and Physical Education, Stephenville, TX 76402. Awards M Ed, Certificate. Part-time and evening/weekend programs available. Faculty: 4 full-time (0 women). Students: 21 full-time (7 women), 26 part-time (9 women); includes 5 minority (3 African Americans, 2 Hispanics). In 1997, 15 master's awarded. *Degree requirements:* For master's, comprehensive exam required, foreign language and thesis not required. *Entrance requirements:* For master's, GRE General Test, minimum GPA of 2.9 during last 60 hours. Application deadline: 8/5 (priority date; rolling processing; 12/1 for spring admission). Application fee: $25 ($100 for international students). *Expenses:* Tuition $46 per hour for state residents; $249 per hour for nonresidents. Fees $49 per hour. *Financial aid:* Teaching assistantships, Federal Work-Study, institutionally sponsored loans, and career-related internships or fieldwork available. Aid available to part-time students. Financial aid application deadline: 5/1; applicants required to submit FAFSA. • Dr. Ron Newsome, Head, 254-968-9186.

Teachers College, Columbia University, Graduate Faculty of Education, Department of Health and Behavior Studies, Program in Health Education, 525 West 120th Street, New York, NY 10027-6696. Awards MA, MS, Ed D. Part-time and evening/weekend programs available. Faculty: 3 full-time (0 women), 5 part-time (4 women), 4.8 FTE. Students: 22 full-time (18 women), 62 part-time (50 women); includes 26 minority (15 African Americans, 5 Asian Americans, 6 Hispanics), 4 international. Average age 36. 28 applicants, 93% accepted. In 1997, 12 master's, 3 doctorates awarded. Terminal master's awarded for partial completion of doctoral program. *Degree requirements:* For master's, integrative project required, thesis optional, foreign language not required; for doctorate, dissertation required, foreign language not required. *Entrance requirements:* For doctorate, GRE or MAT. Application deadline: 5/15 (12/1 for spring admission). Application fee: $50. *Expenses:* Tuition $640 per credit. Fees $120 per semester. *Financial aid:* Fellowships, research assistantships available. Financial aid application deadline: 2/1. *Faculty research:* Health education program planning and evaluation, educational interventions in patient care, community health promotion and disease prevention, chemical dependency and addiction. Total annual research expenditures: $400,000. • Application contact: Ursula Felton, Office of Admissions, 212-678-3710. Fax: 212-678-4171.

Teachers College, Columbia University, Graduate Faculty of Education, Department of Health and Behavior Studies, Program in Nutrition and Education, 525 West 120th Street, New York, NY 10027-6696. Offers nutrition education (Ed M, MS, Ed D); nutrition education and public health nutrition (Ed M, MS, Ed D), including community nutrition education (Ed M), nutrition and public health (MS, Ed D), nutrition education (MS, Ed D). Part-time and evening/weekend programs available. Faculty: 2 full-time (both women), 5 part-time (4 women), 4.4 FTE. Students: 6 full-time (all women), 66 part-time (60 women); includes 13 minority (5 African Americans, 5 Asian Americans, 3 Hispanics), 7 international. Average age 36. 22 applicants, 86% accepted. In 1997, 13 master's, 1 doctorate awarded. Terminal master's awarded for partial completion of doctoral program. *Degree requirements:* For master's, integrative project required, thesis optional, foreign language not required; for doctorate, dissertation required, foreign language not required. *Entrance requirements:* For master's, GRE General Test or MAT, previous course work in science; for doctorate, GRE General Test, sample of written work, previous course work in science. Application deadline: 5/15 (12/1 for spring admission). Application fee: $50. *Expenses:* Tuition $640 per credit. Fees $120 per semester. *Financial aid:* Fellowships, research assistantships, full and partial tuition waivers, Federal Work-Study, institutionally sponsored loans, and career-related internships or fieldwork available. Aid available to part-time students. Financial aid application deadline: 2/1. *Faculty research:* Psychosocial determinants of eating behavior, food supply and environmental education, development and evaluation of nutrition education. • Application contact: Ursula Felton, Office of Admissions, 212-678-3710. Fax: 212-678-4171.

Temple University, School of Social Administration, Department of Health Studies, Program in Health Studies, Philadelphia, PA 19122-6096. Offers health studies (PhD), school health education (Ed M), therapeutic recreation (Ed M). Part-time and evening/weekend programs available. Faculty: 11 full-time (8 women). Students: 45 (38 women); includes 9 minority (7 African Americans, 2 Hispanics). 32 applicants, 56% accepted. In 1997, 4 master's, 6 doctorates awarded. Terminal master's awarded for partial completion of doctoral program. *Degree requirements:* For doctorate, dissertation required, foreign language not required. *Entrance requirements:* For doctorate, minimum undergraduate GPA of 2.8, 3.0 during last 2 years. Application deadline: 2/1 (10/15 for spring admission). Application fee: $40. *Expenses:* Tuition $323 per semester hour for state residents; $444 per semester hour for nonresidents. Fees $170 per year full-time, $28 per semester (minimum) part-time. • Application contact: Dr. Sheryl B. Ruzek, Graduate Coordinator, 215-204-5110. Fax: 215-204-1455.

See in-depth description on page 1517.

Tennessee State University, College of Education, Department of Health, Physical Education and Recreation, Nashville, TN 37209-1561. Awards MA Ed. Accredited by NCATE. Part-time and evening/weekend programs available. Faculty: 6 full-time (2 women). Students: 5 full-time (1 woman), 3 part-time (1 woman); includes 8 minority (all African Americans). Average age 28. 15 applicants, 80% accepted. In 1997, 6 degrees awarded. *Degree requirements:* Thesis required, foreign language not required. *Average time to degree:* master's–1.5 years full-time, 2 years part-time. *Entrance requirements:* GRE General Test or MAT, minimum GPA of 2.5. Application deadline: rolling. Application fee: $15. *Tuition:* $2962 per year full-time, $182 per credit hour part-time for state residents; $7788 per year full-time, $393 per credit hour part-time for nonresidents. *Financial aid:* In 1997–98, 2 teaching assistantships (1 to a first-year student) averaging $550 per month and totaling $7,500 were awarded; fellowships also available. Aid available to part-time students. Financial aid application deadline: 5/1. *Faculty research:* Speed and strength, agility assessment, physical fitness testing, athletes' attitudes toward school. • Dr. Kim Freeland, Head, 615-963-7486. Fax: 615-963-5594. Application contact: Dr. Clinton M. Lipsey, Dean of the Graduate School, 615-963-5901. Fax: 615-963-5963. E-mail: clipsey@picard.tnstate.edu.

Tennessee Technological University, College of Education, Department of Health and Physical Education, Cookeville, TN 38505. Awards MA. Accredited by NCATE. Part-time programs available. Faculty: 7 full-time (0 women). Students: 11 full-time (3 women), 4 part-time (0 women); includes 1 minority (African American). Average age 27. 6 applicants, 100% accepted. In 1997, 13 degrees awarded. *Entrance requirements:* MAT, TOEFL (minimum score 525). Application deadline: 3/1 (priority date; 8/1 for spring admission). Application fee: $25 ($30 for international students). *Tuition:* $2960 per year full-time, $147 per semester hour part-time for state residents; $7786 per year full-time, $358 per semester hour part-time for nonresidents. *Financial aid:* In 1997–98, 13 students received aid, including 2 research assistantships, 11 teaching assistantships (7 to first-year students); fellowships and career-related internships or fieldwork also available. Financial aid application deadline: 4/1. • Dr. Bower L. Johnston, Interim Chairperson, 615-372-3467. Fax: 615-372-6319. E-mail: bjohnston@tntech.edu. Application contact: Dr. Rebecca F. Quattlebaum, Dean of the Graduate School, 615-372-3233. Fax: 615-372-3497. E-mail: rquattlebaum@tntech.edu.

Texas A&M University, College of Education, Department of Health and Kinesiology, Program in Health Education, College Station, TX 77843. Awards M Ed, MS, PhD. Accredited by NCATE. Students: 20 full-time (10 women), 6 part-time (5 women); includes 1 minority (African American). Average age 28. 17 applicants, 24% accepted. In 1997, 4 doctorates awarded. *Degree requirements:* For master's, thesis required (for some programs), foreign language not required; for doctorate, dissertation required, foreign language not required. *Entrance requirements:* GRE General Test, TOEFL. Application deadline: rolling. Application fee: $35 ($75 for international students). *Financial aid:* In 1997–98, 1 fellowship averaging $1,000 per month, 6 teaching assistantships averaging $675 per month and totaling $36,500 were awarded; research assistantships, institutionally sponsored loans, and career-related internships or fieldwork also available. Financial aid application deadline: 4/15. *Faculty research:* Health promotion, HIV/AIDS education, multicultural issues, barriers to care, at-risk/disadvantaged youth. • Application contact: Susan Lanier, Graduate Secretary, 409-845-4530. Fax: 409-847-8987.

Texas A&M University–Commerce, College of Education, Department of Health and Physical Education, Commerce, TX 75429-3011. Awards M Ed, MS. Faculty: 7 full-time (3 women), 2 part-time (1 woman). Students: 18 full-time (5 women), 25 part-time (10 women); includes 6 minority (3 African Americans, 2 Hispanics, 1 Native American). In 1997, 20 degrees awarded. *Degree requirements:* Thesis (for some programs), comprehensive exam required, foreign language not required. *Entrance requirements:* GRE General Test. Application deadline: rolling. Application fee: $0 ($25 for international students). *Tuition:* $2382 per year full-time, $343 per semester (minimum) part-time for state residents; $7518 per year full-time, $343 per semester (minimum) part-time for nonresidents. *Financial aid:* Research assistantships, teaching assistantships, Federal Work-Study, institutionally sponsored loans available. • Dr. Margaret Harbison, Head, 903-886-5549. Application contact: Pam Hammonds, Graduate Admissions Adviser, 903-886-5167. Fax: 903-886-5165.

Texas A&M University–Kingsville, College of Education, Department of Health and Kinesiology, Kingsville, TX 78363. Awards MA, MS. Part-time programs available. Faculty: 6 part-time (3 women). Students: 6 full-time (3 women), 15 part-time (6 women); includes 12 minority (all Hispanics). Average age 24. *Degree requirements:* Thesis or alternative, comprehensive exam required, foreign language not required. *Entrance requirements:* GRE General Test (minimum combined score of 1000), minimum GPA of 3.0. Application deadline: 6/1 (rolling processing; 11/15 for spring admission). Application fee: $15 ($25 for international students). *Tuition:* $1822 per year full-time, $281 per semester (minimum) part-time for state residents; $6934 per year full-time, $908 per semester (minimum) part-time for nonresidents. *Financial aid:* Teaching assistantships, partial tuition waivers, Federal Work-Study, institutionally sponsored loans available. Financial aid application deadline: 5/15. *Faculty research:* Body composition, electromyography. • Randy Hughes, Chairman, 512-593-2301.

Texas Southern University, College of Education, Department of Health, Physical Education and Recreation, Houston, TX 77004-4584. Offers programs in health education (MS), physical education (MS). Part-time and evening/weekend programs available. Faculty: 3 full-time (1 woman). Students: 5 full-time (4 women), 8 part-time (2 women); includes 2 international. Average age 26. 12 applicants, 50% accepted. In 1997, 1 degree awarded. *Degree requirements:* Comprehensive exam required, thesis optional, foreign language not required. *Entrance requirements:* GRE General Test, TOEFL, minimum GPA of 2.5. Application deadline: 7/15 (priority date; rolling processing). Application fee: $35 ($75 for international students). • Dr. T. Robinson, Head, 713-313-7087.

Texas Woman's University, College of Health Sciences, Department of Health Studies, Denton, TX 76204. Offers programs in health education (Ed D, PhD), health studies (MS). Part-time and evening/weekend programs available. Faculty: 6 full-time (3 women), 3 part-time (2 women). Students: 15 full-time (14 women), 61 part-time (58 women); includes 7 minority (6 African Americans, 1 Hispanic). Average age 38. 24 applicants, 79% accepted. In 1997, 8 master's awarded; 5 doctorates awarded (100% entered university research/teaching). *Degree requirements:* For master's, thesis optional, foreign language not required; for doctorate, dissertation, qualifying exam required, foreign language not required. *Average time to degree:* master's–2.1 years full-time, 3.5 years part-time; doctorate–3 years full-time, 5 years part-time. *Entrance requirements:* For master's, GRE General Test (minimum combined score of 850) or MAT (minimum score 50), minimum GPA of 3.0; for doctorate, GRE General Test (minimum combined score of 950), MAT (minimum score 55), minimum GPA of 3.0. Application deadline: 4/1 (priority date; rolling processing; 10/1 for spring admission). Application fee: $25. *Financial aid:* In 1997–98, 9 students received aid, including 1 research assistantship (to a first-year student) averaging $776 per month and totaling $3,873, 7 teaching assistantships (6 to first-year students) averaging $827 per month and totaling $58,774; partial tuition waivers, Federal Work-Study, institutionally sponsored loans, and career-related internships or fieldwork also available. Aid available to part-time students. Financial aid application deadline: 4/1. *Faculty research:* Health promotion, stress management, development of healthy lifestyles, health behavior, women's health. • Dr. Susan Ward, Interim Chair, 940-898-2860. Application contact: Dr. Judith A. Baker, Coordinator, Graduate Studies, 940-898-2842. Fax: 940-898-3198.

Tulane University, School of Public Health and Tropical Medicine, Department of Community Health Sciences, Program in Health Communication/Education, New Orleans, LA 70118-5669. Awards MPH. Students: 50 full-time (39 women), 11 part-time (8 women); includes 21 minority (15 African Americans, 5 Asian Americans, 1 Hispanic), 13 international. Average age 28. *Degree requirements:* 1 foreign language required, thesis not required. *Entrance requirements:* GRE General Test (minimum combined score of 1000; average 1100), TOEFL (minimum score 525). Application deadline: 4/15 (priority date; rolling processing; 10/15 for spring admission). Application fee: $40. *Financial aid:* Application deadline 2/1. • Dr. Judith LaRosa, Chair, 504-584-3539. Fax: 504-584-3540.

Union College, Department of Health and Physical Education, Barbourville, KY 40906-1499. Offers program in health (MA Ed). *Degree requirements:* Thesis optional, foreign language not required. *Entrance requirements:* GRE General Test, NTE. Application deadline: rolling. Application fee: $15. *Tuition:* $220 per hour. • Dr. Larry Inkster, Head, 606-546-4151.

The University of Alabama, College of Education, Area of Professional Studies, Program in Health Education, Tuscaloosa, AL 35487. Awards MA, Ed S. Accredited by NCATE. *Entrance requirements:* For master's, GRE General Test, MAT (score in 50th percentile or higher), or NTE (minimum score 658 on each core battery test), minimum GPA of 3.0; for Ed S, minimum GPA of 3.0 during previous 2 years. Application deadline: 7/6 (rolling processing). Application fee: $25. *Tuition:* $2684 per year full-time, $594 per semester (minimum) part-time for state residents; $7216 per year full-time, $1248 per semester (minimum) part-time for nonresidents. *Financial aid:* Application deadline 7/14. • Dr. R. Carl Westerfield, Head, Area of Professional Studies, 205-348-8362. Fax: 205-348-0867. E-mail: cwesterf@bamaed.ua.edu.

The University of Alabama, College of Education, Area of Professional Studies, Program in Health Education and Promotion, Tuscaloosa, AL 35487. Awards MA, PhD. Accredited by NCATE. PhD offered jointly with the University of Alabama at Birmingham. *Degree requirements:* For doctorate, 1 foreign language, computer language, dissertation. *Average time to degree:* doctorate–3 years full-time, 6 years part-time. *Entrance requirements:* GRE General Test, MAT (score in 50th percentile or higher), or NTE (minimum score 658 on each core battery test), minimum GPA of 3.0. Application deadline: 7/6 (rolling processing). Application fee: $25. *Financial aid:* Fellowships, research assistantships, teaching assistantships, Federal Work-Study, institutionally sponsored loans, and career-related internships or fieldwork available. Financial aid application deadline: 7/14. • Dr. James Eddy, Head, 205-348-2956. Fax: 205-348-7568. E-mail: jeddy@bamaed.ua.edu.

The University of Alabama at Birmingham, Graduate School, School of Education, Department of Curriculum and Instruction, Program in Allied Health-Education, Birmingham, AL 35294. Awards MA Ed, Ed S. Accredited by NCATE. Students: 2 full-time (both women), 3 part-time (2 women); includes 1 minority (Asian American). 1 applicant, 100% accepted. In 1997, 2 master's awarded. *Degree requirements:* For master's, thesis optional; for Ed S, comprehensive exam. *Entrance requirements:* For master's, GRE General Test, MAT, or NTE, minimum GPA of 3.0. Application deadline: rolling. Application fee: $30 ($60 for international students). Electronic applications accepted. *Expenses:* Tuition $99 per credit hour for state residents; $198 per credit hour for nonresidents. Fees $516 per year (minimum) full-time, $73 per quarter (minimum) part-time for state residents; $516 per year (minimum) full-time, $73 per unit (minimum) part-time for nonresidents. • Dr. Joseph C. Burns, Chair, Department of Curriculum and Instruction, 205-934-5371.

The University of Alabama at Birmingham, Graduate School, School of Education, Department of Human Studies, Program in Health Education, Birmingham, AL 35294. Awards MA Ed, Ed S. Accredited by NCATE. Students: 15 full-time (11 women), 6 part-time (4 women); includes 6 minority (4 African Americans, 2 Asian Americans). 35 applicants, 100% accepted. In 1997, 3 master's awarded. *Degree requirements:* For master's, thesis optional, foreign language not required; for Ed S, comprehensive exam. *Entrance requirements:* For master's, GRE General Test, MAT, or NTE, minimum GPA of 3.0. Application deadline: rolling. Application fee: $30 ($60 for international students). Electronic applications accepted. *Expenses:* Tuition $99 per credit hour for state residents; $198 per credit hour for nonresidents. Fees $516 per year (minimum) full-time, $73 per quarter (minimum) part-time for state residents; $516 per year (minimum) full-time, $73 per unit (minimum) part-time for nonresidents. • Dr. David M. Macrina, Chairperson, Department of Human Studies, 205-934-2446.

The University of Alabama at Birmingham, Graduate School, School of Education, Department of Human Studies, Program in Health Education/Health Promotion, Birmingham, AL 35294. Awards PhD, Ed S. Accredited by NCATE. Offered jointly with The University of Alabama–Tuscaloosa. Students: 10 full-time (7 women), 5 part-time (4 women); includes 6 minority (5 African Americans, 1 Asian American). 26 applicants, 92% accepted. In 1997, 4 doctorates awarded. *Degree requirements:* For doctorate, dissertation; for Ed S, comprehensive exam. *Application fee:* $30 ($55 for international students). Electronic applications accepted. *Expenses:* Tuition $99 per credit hour for state residents; $198 per credit hour for nonresidents. Fees $516 per year (minimum) full-time, $73 per quarter (minimum) part-time for state residents; $516 per year (minimum) full-time, $73 per unit (minimum) part-time for nonresidents. • Dr. David M. Macrina, Chairperson, Department of Human Studies, 205-934-2446.

The University of Arizona, School of Health Related Professions, Program in Health Education, Tucson, AZ 85721. Awards M Ed. Part-time programs available. *Entrance requirements:* TOEFL (minimum score 550), minimum GPA of 2.5. Application deadline: 8/1 (rolling processing). Application fee: $35. *Tuition:* $2162 per year full-time, $337 per semester (minimum) part-time for state residents; $6860 per year full-time, $1138 per semester (minimum) part-time for nonresidents. *Faculty research:* Traffic accident prevention by perceptual education and behavior modification, curriculum and programs for grades K–12, nonteaching option programs with emphasis on community service.

University of Arkansas, College of Education, Department of Health Science, Kinesiology, Recreation and Dance, Program in Health Science, Fayetteville, AR 72701-1201. Awards MS, PhD. Accredited by NCATE. Students: 26 full-time (18 women), 6 part-time (3 women); includes 3 minority (2 African Americans, 1 Asian American), 1 international. 16 applicants, 75% accepted. In 1997, 31 master's, 3 doctorates awarded. *Degree requirements:* For doctorate, dissertation. *Application fee:* $25 ($35 for international students). *Tuition:* $3144 per year full-time, $173 per credit hour part-time for state residents; $7140 per year full-time, $395 per credit hour part-time for nonresidents. *Financial aid:* Research assistantships, teaching assistantships, Federal Work-Study, and career-related internships or fieldwork available. Aid available to part-time students. Financial aid application deadline: 4/1; applicants required to submit FAFSA. • Dr. Dean Gorman, Coordinator, 501-575-2890.

University of California, Berkeley, School of Public Health, Master Internationalist Program, Berkeley, CA 94720-1500. Offerings include community health education (MPH). MA (community health education) admissions temporarily suspended. *Entrance requirements:* GRE General Test, minimum GPA of 3.0. Application deadline: 1/12 (rolling processing). Application fee: $40. *Expenses:* Tuition $0 for state residents; $9384 per year for nonresidents. Fees $4409 per year. • Application contact: Sharon Harper, Student Affairs Officer, 510-642-4706. Fax: 510-643-5676. E-mail: sharper@socrates.berkeley.edu.

University of Central Arkansas, College of Health and Applied Sciences, Department of Health Sciences, Conway, AR 72035-0001. Awards MS. Faculty: 7 full-time (5 women). Students: 6 full-time (5 women), 7 part-time (5 women); includes 3 minority (all African Americans). 4 applicants, 75% accepted. *Degree requirements:* Comprehensive exam required, thesis optional. *Entrance requirements:* GRE General Test, minimum GPA of 2.7. Application deadline: 3/1 (priority date; rolling processing; 10/1 for spring admission). Application fee: $15 ($40 for international students). *Expenses:* Tuition $161 per credit hour for state residents; $298 per credit hour for nonresidents. Fees $50 per year full-time, $30 per year part-time. *Financial aid:* In 1997–98, 2 assistantships were awarded; Federal Work-Study also available. Financial aid application deadline: 2/15. • Emogene Fox, Chairperson, 501-450-3194. Fax: 501-450-5515. E-mail: emogenef@mail.uca.edu.

University of Central Oklahoma, College of Education, Department of Occupational and Technical Education, Program in Professional Health Occupations, Edmond, OK 73034-5209. Awards M Ed. Accredited by NCATE. Part-time and evening/weekend programs available. *Entrance requirements:* GRE General Test. Application deadline: 8/18. Application fee: $15. *Tuition:* $76 per credit hour for state residents; $178 per credit hour for nonresidents.

University of Cincinnati, College of Education, Division of Human Services, Department of Health Promotion, Cincinnati, OH 45221. Offers programs in community health (M Ed), health promotion and education (M Ed). Accredited by NCATE. Part-time programs available. Students: 14 full-time (12 women), 32 part-time (28 women); includes 6 minority (4 African Americans, 2 Asian Americans), 1 international. 38 applicants, 34% accepted. In 1997, 9 degrees awarded. *Degree requirements:* Thesis or alternative required, foreign language not required. *Average time to degree:* master's–2.9 years full-time. *Entrance requirements:* GRE General Test. Application deadline: 2/1. Application fee: $30. *Tuition:* $7228 per year full-time, $185 per credit hour part-time for state residents; $13,812 per year full-time, $352 per credit hour part-time for nonresidents. *Financial aid:* Fellowships, graduate assistantships, full tuition waivers available. Aid available to part-time students. Financial aid application deadline: 5/1. • Application contact: Bradley Wilson, Graduate Program Director, 513-556-3862. Fax: 513-556-2483. E-mail: bradley.wilson@uc.edu.

University of Colorado at Denver, College of Liberal Arts and Sciences, Program in Health and Behavioral Science, Denver, CO 80217-3364. Awards PhD. Part-time and evening/weekend programs available. Faculty: 2 full-time (1 woman). Students: 3 full-time (1 woman), 19 part-time (13 women); includes 2 minority (1 Asian American, 1 Hispanic). Average age 43. 9 applicants, 89% accepted. *Degree requirements:* 1 foreign language, dissertation. *Entrance requirements:* GRE. Application deadline: 7/22 (rolling processing; 11/1 for spring admission). Application fee: $50 ($60 for international students). *Expenses:* Tuition $2996 per year full-time, $181 per semester hour part-time for state residents; $11,954 per year full-time, $717 per semester hour part-time for nonresidents. Fees $252 per year. *Financial aid:* Federal Work-Study and career-related internships or fieldwork available. Financial aid application deadline: 3/1; applicants required to submit FAFSA. • Craig Janes, Director, 303-556-4300.

University of Detroit Mercy, College of Health Professions, Program in Health Care Education, Detroit, MI 48219-0900. Awards MS. *Degree requirements:* Thesis or alternative. *Entrance requirements:* GRE General Test (minimum combined score of 1200), minimum GPA of 3.0. Application fee: $25. *Faculty research:* Curriculum structure, merging health facilities, education for health and diversity.

University of Florida, College of Health and Human Performance, Department of Health Science Education, Gainesville, FL 32611. Awards MHSE, MS, MSHSE, PhD. One or more programs accredited by NCATE. Part-time programs available. Faculty: 8. Students: 12 full-time (10 women), 8 part-time (all women); includes 2 minority (both Hispanics). 18 applicants, 67% accepted. In 1997, 4 master's awarded. Terminal master's awarded for partial completion of doctoral program. *Degree requirements:* For master's, thesis (for some programs); for doctorate, dissertation. *Entrance requirements:* GRE General Test, minimum GPA of 3.0. Application deadline: 6/5 (priority date; rolling processing). Application fee: $20. *Tuition:* $138 per credit hour for state residents; $481 per credit hour for nonresidents. *Financial aid:* In 1997–98, 8 students received aid, including 1 fellowship averaging $760 per month, 7 teaching assistantships averaging $450 per month; research assistantships, institutionally sponsored loans, and career-related internships or fieldwork also available. *Faculty research:* Adolescent health, human sexuality and HIV/AIDS, substance use, worksite health promotion, nutrition. • W. William Chen Jr., Chair, 352-392-0583. Application contact: Dr. Steve Dorman, Graduate Coordinator, 352-392-0583. Fax: 352-392-3186. E-mail: sdorman@hhp.ufl.edu.

University of Georgia, College of Education, School of Health and Human Performance, Department of Health Promotion and Behavior, Athens, GA 30602. Offers programs in education (MA), health promotion and behavior (PhD), health promotion and behavior and safety education (M Ed), safety education (Ed S). One or more programs accredited by NCATE. Faculty: 5 full-time (1 woman). Students: 30 full-time, 9 part-time (all women); includes 4 minority (all African Americans), 3 international. 44 applicants, 43% accepted. In 1997, 13 master's awarded. *Degree requirements:* For master's, thesis (MA) required, foreign language not required; for doctorate, dissertation required, foreign language not required. *Entrance requirements:* For master's and Ed S, GRE General Test or MAT; for doctorate, GRE General Test. Application deadline: 7/1 (priority date; 11/15 for spring admission). Application fee: $30. Electronic applications accepted. *Tuition:* $3290 per year full-time, $643 per semester (minimum) part-time for state residents; $11,300 per year full-time, $1645 per semester (minimum) part-time for nonresidents. *Financial aid:* Fellowships, research assistantships, teaching assistantships, assistantships available. • Dr. Mark G. Wilson, Graduate Coordinator, 706-542-3313. Fax: 706-542-4956.

University of Hawaii at Manoa, College of Health Sciences and Social Welfare, School of Public Health, Program in Community Health Development and Education, Honolulu, HI 96822. Awards MPH, MS. Part-time programs available. Faculty: 2 full-time (1 woman), 1 (woman) part-time, 2.85 FTE. Students: 25 full-time (19 women), 9 part-time (5 women); includes 19 minority (2 African Americans, 15 Asian Americans, 2 Hispanics). 48 applicants, 40% accepted. In 1997, 17 degrees awarded. *Degree requirements:* Thesis (for some programs). *Average time to degree:* master's–1.2 years full-time, 3 years part-time. *Application deadline:* 3/1 (9/1 for spring admission). *Application fee:* $25 ($50 for international students). *Tuition:* $4029 per year full-time, $214 per credit hour part-time for state residents; $9957 per year full-time, $461 per credit hour part-time for nonresidents. *Financial aid:* Career-related internships or fieldwork available. *Faculty research:* Gerontology, community-based health professional education. • Dr. Jerome Grossman, Head, 808-956-5769. Application contact: Nancy Kilonsky, Assistant Dean, 808-956-8267.

University of Houston, College of Education, Department of Health and Human Performance, 4800 Calhoun, Houston, TX 77204-2163. Offers programs in allied health (M Ed, Ed D), exercise science (MS), health education (M Ed), physical education (M Ed, Ed D). One or more programs accredited by NCATE. Ed D (allied health) offered jointly with Baylor College of Medicine. Part-time and evening/weekend programs available. Faculty: 10 full-time (3 women), 9 part-time (5 women). Students: 48 full-time (27 women), 61 part-time (42 women); includes 33 minority (17 African Americans, 4 Asian Americans, 11 Hispanics, 1 Native American), 8 international. Average age 35. In 1997, 21 master's, 2 doctorates awarded. *Degree requirements:* For master's, comprehensive exam or thesis required, foreign language not required; for doctorate, dissertation, comprehensive exam required, foreign language not required. *Entrance requirements:* For master's, GRE General Test or MAT; for doctorate, GRE General Test, interview. Application deadline: 7/3. Application fee: $35 ($75 for international students). *Expenses:* Tuition $1152 per year full-time, $120 per semester (minimum) part-time for state residents; $4482 per year full-time, $249 per credit hour part-time for nonresidents. Fees $977 per year full-time, $119 per semester (minimum) part-time. *Financial aid:* In 1997–98, 26 teaching assistantships averaging $700 per month were awarded; research assistantships, Federal Work-Study, and career-related internships or fieldwork also available. *Faculty research:* Motor development, physical fitness, comprehensive school health, leadership, sports law. • Dr. Dennis Smith, Chairperson, 713-743-9853. Fax: 713-743-9860.

University of Illinois at Chicago, College of Medicine and Graduate College, Graduate Programs in Medicine, Department of Medical Education, Chicago, IL 60607-7128. Awards MHPE. Part-time programs available. Faculty: 14 full-time (4 women). Students: 5 full-time (1 woman), 23 part-time (15 women); includes 1 minority (Hispanic), 16 international. Average age 35. 19 applicants, 63% accepted. In 1997, 3 degrees awarded. *Degree requirements:* Thesis required, foreign language not required. *Entrance requirements:* GRE General Test, TOEFL (minimum score 550). Application deadline: 6/15. Application fee: $40 ($50 for international students). *Financial aid:* Research assistantships available. • Les Sandlow, Acting Director, 312-996-3590. Application contact: Emile Wijnans, Coordinator of Educational Programs, 312-996-4666.

University of Kansas, School of Education, Department of Health, Sport, and Exercise Sciences, Lawrence, KS 66045. Offers programs in health education (MS Ed), physical education (MS Ed, Ed D, PhD). Accredited by NCATE. Faculty: 10 full-time. Students: 64 full-time (28 women), 141 part-time (72 women); includes 10 minority (4 African Americans, 2 Asian Americans, 1 Hispanic, 3 Native Americans), 7 international. In 1997, 54 master's, 7 doctorates awarded. *Degree requirements:* For doctorate, variable foreign language requirement, dissertation. *Entrance requirements:* For master's, minimum GPA of 3.0; for doctorate, GRE General Test (minimum combined score of 1000), minimum graduate GPA of 3.5. Application deadline: 7/1. Application fee: $25. *Expenses:* Tuition $2400 per year full-time, $100 per credit hour part-time for state residents; $7890 per year full-time, $329 per credit hour part-time for nonresidents. Fees $428 per year full-time, $31 per credit hour part-time. *Financial aid:* Fellowships, research assistantships, teaching assistantships available. • Joseph Donnelly, Chair, 785-864-3371. Application contact: Dr. James D. LaPoint, Graduate Coordinator, 785-864-0785. Fax: 785-864-3343. E-mail: jdl@falcon.cc.ukans.edu.

University of Manitoba, Faculty of Education, Department of Curriculum: Mathematics and Natural Sciences, Winnipeg, MB R3T 2N2, Canada. Offerings include health education (M Ed). *Degree requirements:* Thesis or alternative required, foreign language not required.

University of Maryland, Baltimore County, Graduate School, Department of Emergency Health Services, Baltimore, MD 21250-5398. Offerings include education (MS). *Entrance requirements:* GRE General Test, minimum GPA of 3.0. Application deadline: 7/1. Application fee: $40. *Expenses:* Tuition $260 per credit hour for state residents; $468 per credit hour for nonresidents. Fees $39 per credit hour.

University of Maryland, College Park, College of Health and Human Performance, Department of Health Education, College Park, MD 20742-5045. Awards MA, Ed D, PhD. Faculty: 23 full-time (10 women), 4 part-time (3 women). Students: 19 full-time (15 women), 58 part-time

Directory: Health Education

University of Maryland, College Park (continued)
(52 women); includes 17 minority (12 African Americans, 3 Asian Americans, 1 Hispanic, 1 Native American). 63 applicants, 27% accepted. In 1997, 7 master's, 6 doctorates awarded. *Degree requirements:* For master's, thesis or alternative required, foreign language not required; for doctorate, dissertation required, foreign language not required. *Entrance requirements:* For master's, GRE General Test, minimum GPA of 3.0; for doctorate, GRE General Test, minimum GPA of 3.3. Application deadline: (1/15 for spring admission). Application fee: $50 ($70 for international students). *Expenses:* Tuition $272 per credit hour for state residents; $400 per credit hour for nonresidents. Fees $564 per year full-time, $342 per year part-time. *Financial aid:* In 1997–98, 2 fellowships, 3 research assistantships, 10 teaching assistantships were awarded; career-related internships or fieldwork also available. *Faculty research:* Safety education, health behavior, controlling stress and tension. • Dr. Laura Wilson, Acting Chair, 301-405-2467. Fax: 301-314-9167. Application contact: John Mollish, Director, Graduate Admissions and Records, 301-405-4198. Fax: 301-314-9305.

University of Medicine and Dentistry of New Jersey, School of Health Related Professions, Newark, NJ 07107-3001. Offerings include health professions education (MA). MS, PhD (biomedical informatics) offered jointly with New Jersey Institute of Technology; MS, PhD (health science), MS (physician assistant), MA offered jointly with Seton Hall University; MPT offered jointly with Rutgers, The State University of New Jersey, Camden. School faculty: 44 full-time (36 women), 15 part-time (10 women), 51.55 FTE. *Application deadline:* rolling. *Application fee:* $35. • Dr. David M. Gibson, Dean, 973-972-4276. Application contact: Dr. Laura Nelson, Associate Dean of Academic and Student Services, 973-972-5453. Fax: 973-972-7028. E-mail: shrp.adm@umdnj.edu.

See in-depth description on page 1267.

University of Michigan–Flint, School of Health Professions and Studies, Program in Health Education, Flint, MI 48502-1950. Awards MS. Part-time and evening/weekend programs available. Faculty: 1 (woman) full-time, 3 part-time (all women), 1.75 FTE. Students: 6 full-time (4 women), 23 part-time (20 women); includes 5 minority (3 African Americans, 2 Asian Americans). Average age 38. 20 applicants, 90% accepted. *Degree requirements:* Thesis required, foreign language not required. *Entrance requirements:* GRE, minimum GPA of 2.8. Application deadline: 7/15 (rolling processing; 3/15 for spring admission). Application fee: $50. *Financial aid:* Fellowships and career-related internships or fieldwork available. Aid available to part-time students. Financial aid application deadline: 4/1. • Dr. Suzanne M. Selig, Director, 810-762-3172. Fax: 810-762-3003. E-mail: sselig@umich.edu. Application contact: Office of Graduate Programs, 810-762-3171.

The University of Montana–Missoula, School of Education, Department of Health and Human Performance, Missoula, MT 59812-0002. Awards MS. Accredited by NCATE. Part-time programs available. Faculty: 10 full-time (3 women). Students: 18 full-time (16 women). Average age 30. 28 applicants, 61% accepted. In 1997, 8 degrees awarded. *Degree requirements:* Thesis or alternative required, foreign language not required. *Average time to degree:* master's–2 years full-time. *Entrance requirements:* GRE General Test (minimum score 450 on each section), minimum GPA of 3.0. Application deadline: 3/15. Application fee: $30. *Tuition:* $2499 per year (minimum) full-time, $376 per semester (minimum) part-time for state residents; $6528 per year (minimum) full-time, $1048 per semester (minimum) part-time for nonresidents. *Financial aid:* In 1997–98, 4 students received aid, including 4 teaching assistantships; Federal Work-Study also available. Financial aid application deadline: 3/1. *Faculty research:* Exercise physiology, performance psychology, nutrition, pre-employment physical screening, program evaluation, ethics. • Dr. Sharon Uhlig, Chair, 406-243-4211.

University of Montevallo, College of Education, Department of Health, Physical Education, and Recreation, Montevallo, AL 35115. Awards M Ed, Ed S. Accredited by NCATE. Part-time and evening/weekend programs available. *Entrance requirements:* For master's, GRE General Test (minimum combined score of 850), MAT (minimum score 35), minimum undergraduate GPA of 2.75 in last 60 hours or 2.5 overall. Application deadline: 7/15 (11/15 for spring admission). Application fee: $10.

University of Nebraska at Omaha, College of Education, School of Health, Physical Education and Recreation, Omaha, NE 68182. Awards MA, MS. Part-time programs available. Faculty: 9 full-time (1 woman). Students: 28 full-time (14 women), 111 part-time (76 women); includes 5 minority (all African Americans), 6 international. Average age 34. 75 applicants, 81% accepted. In 1997, 27 degrees awarded. *Degree requirements:* Thesis (for some programs), comprehensive exam required, foreign language not required. *Entrance requirements:* Minimum GPA of 3.0. Application deadline: 7/1 (priority date; rolling processing; 12/1 for spring admission). Application fee: $35. *Expenses:* Tuition $1670 per year full-time, $94 per credit hour part-time for state residents; $4082 per year full-time, $227 per credit hour part-time for nonresidents. Fees $302 per year full-time, $108 per semester (minimum) part-time. *Financial aid:* In 1997–98, 67 students received aid, including 8 research assistantships; fellowships, full tuition waivers, Federal Work-Study, institutionally sponsored loans also available. Aid available to part-time students. Financial aid application deadline: 3/1; applicants required to submit FAFSA. • Dr. Dan Blanke, Director, 402-554-2670.

University of Nebraska–Lincoln, Teachers College, School of Health and Human Performance, Lincoln, NE 68588. Offers program in health, physical education, and recreation (M Ed, MPE). Accredited by NCATE. Faculty: 12 full-time (2 women). Students: 21 full-time (8 women), 14 part-time (10 women); includes 1 minority (Asian American), 6 international. Average age 29. 27 applicants, 74% accepted. In 1997, 19 degrees awarded. *Degree requirements:* Thesis required (for some programs), foreign language not required. *Entrance requirements:* GRE General Test or MAT, TOEFL (minimum score 500). Application deadline: 3/1 (priority date; rolling processing). Application fee: $35. Electronic applications accepted. *Expenses:* Tuition $110 per credit hour for state residents; $270 per credit hour for nonresidents. Fees $480 per year full-time, $110 per semester part-time. *Financial aid:* In 1997–98, 1 fellowship totaling $700, 11 research assistantships totaling $74,250 were awarded; teaching assistantships, Federal Work-Study also available. Aid available to part-time students. Financial aid application deadline: 2/15. *Faculty research:* Exercise science, health behaviors, fitness, teacher effectiveness. Total annual research expenditures: $18,167. • William Murphy, Chair, 402-472-3882. E-mail: wmurphy@unlinfo.unl.edu.

University of New Mexico, College of Education, Program in Health Education, Albuquerque, NM 87131-2039. Awards MS. Accredited by NCATE. Part-time and evening/weekend programs available. Students: 7 full-time (6 women), 27 part-time (22 women); includes 9 minority (1 African American, 6 Hispanics, 2 Native Americans). Average age 37. 9 applicants, 89% accepted. In 1997, 20 degrees awarded. *Application deadline:* 5/1 (11/1 for spring admission). *Application fee:* $25. *Expenses:* Tuition $2442 per year full-time, $103 per credit hour part-time for state residents; $8691 per year full-time, $103 per credit hour (minimum) part-time for nonresidents. Fees $32 per year. *Financial aid:* In 1997–98, 5 teaching assistantships averaging $888 per month and totaling $44,400 were awarded; fellowships, research assistantships, partial tuition waivers, Federal Work-Study, institutionally sponsored loans, and career-related internships or fieldwork also available. *Faculty research:* Alcohol and families, health behaviors and sexuality, multicultural health behavior, health promotion policy, school-based prevention. • Bill Kane, Graduate Coordinator, 505-277-0337. E-mail: kane@unm.edu. Application contact: Angie Rudy, Administrative Assistant, 505-277-0337. Fax: 505-277-8427. E-mail: arudy@unm.edu.

University of New Mexico, College of Education, Program in Health, Physical Education and Recreation, Albuquerque, NM 87131-2039. Awards Ed D, PhD. Accredited by NCATE. Part-time programs available. Faculty: 15 full-time (7 women), 14 part-time (4 women), 18.55 FTE. Students: 56 full-time (30 women), 53 part-time (29 women); includes 23 minority (5 African Americans, 2 Asian Americans, 11 Hispanics, 5 Native Americans), 18 international. Average age 39. 33 applicants, 67% accepted. In 1997, 21 doctorates awarded. Terminal master's awarded for partial completion of doctoral program. *Degree requirements:* For doctorate, dissertation required, foreign language not required. *Application fee:* $25. *Expenses:* Tuition $2442 per year full-time, $103 per credit hour part-time for state residents; $8691 per year full-time, $103 per credit hour (minimum) part-time for nonresidents. Fees $32 per year. *Financial aid:* In 1997–98, 17 students received aid, including 3 research assistantships (1 to a first-year student) averaging $770 per month and totaling $23,100, 14 teaching assistantships (6 to first-year students) averaging $770 per month and totaling $107,800; fellowships, Federal Work-Study, institutionally sponsored loans, and career-related internships or fieldwork also available. Aid available to part-time students. *Faculty research:* Physical education pedagogy, sports psychology, sports administration, cardic rehabilitation, sports physiology, physical fitness assessment, exercise prescription. Total annual research expenditures: $17,132. • Dr. Mary Jo Campbell, Graduate Coordinator, 505-277-5151. Application contact: Sally Renfro, Division Administrator, 505-277-5151. Fax: 505-277-6227.

University of New Orleans, College of Education, Department of Health and Physical Education, New Orleans, LA 70148. Offers programs in adapted physical education (MA); exercise physiology (MA); gerontology (Certificate); health and physical education (Certificate); physical education (M Ed); science, pedagogy and coaching sport management (MA). Accredited by NCATE. Evening/weekend programs available. Faculty: 9 full-time (5 women). Students: 31 full-time (14 women), 40 part-time (24 women); includes 15 minority (14 African Americans, 1 Hispanic), 18 international. Average age 32. 27 applicants, 100% accepted. In 1997, 52 master's awarded. *Entrance requirements:* For master's, GRE General Test. Application deadline: 7/1 (priority date; rolling processing). Application fee: $20. *Expenses:* Tuition $2362 per year full-time, $373 per semester (minimum) part-time for state residents; $7888 per year full-time, $1423 per semester (minimum) part-time for nonresidents. Fees $170 per year full-time, $25 per semester (minimum) part-time. *Financial aid:* Teaching assistantships, grants, partial tuition waivers available. *Faculty research:* Motor control, health science, biomechanics. Total annual research expenditures: $71,902. • Dr. Robert Eason, Chairperson, 504-280-6420. E-mail: blehp@uno.edu. Application contact: Dr. Mark Loftin, Graduate Coordinator, 504-280-6417. Fax: 504-280-6018. E-mail: mxlhp@uno.edu.

The University of North Carolina at Chapel Hill, School of Public Health, Department of Health Behavior and Health Education, Chapel Hill, NC 27599. Awards MPH, Dr PH, PhD. Faculty: 13 full-time (8 women), 58 part-time (34 women). Students: 92 full-time (76 women), 15 part-time (13 women); includes 24 minority (9 African Americans, 11 Asian Americans, 4 Hispanics), 7 international. Average age 29. 246 applicants, 43% accepted. In 1997, 39 master's, 2 doctorates awarded. *Degree requirements:* For master's, thesis, major paper, comprehensive exam required, foreign language not required; for doctorate, dissertation, comprehensive exam required, foreign language not required. *Average time to degree:* master's–2 years full-time; doctorate–4 years full-time. *Entrance requirements:* GRE General Test (minimum combined score of 1000), minimum GPA of 3.0. Application deadline: 1/1 (rolling processing). Application fee: $55. *Expenses:* Tuition $2008 per year full-time, $502 per semester (minimum) part-time for state residents; $10,414 per year full-time, $2604 per semester (minimum) part-time for nonresidents. Fees $782 per year full-time, $332 per semester (minimum) part-time. *Financial aid:* In 1997–98, 4 fellowships (2 to first-year students), 15 research assistantships (8 to first-year students), 2 teaching assistantships were awarded; graduate assistantships, Federal Work-Study, institutionally sponsored loans, and career-related internships or fieldwork also available. Financial aid application deadline: 1/1; applicants required to submit FAFSA. *Faculty research:* Cancer prevention and control, aging health promotion and disease prevention, adolescent health, nutrition intervention. • Dr. JoAnne L. Earp, Chair, 919-966-3918. E-mail: jearp@sph.unc.edu. Application contact: Linda W. Cook, Registrar, 919-966-5771. Fax: 919-966-2921. E-mail: lcook@sph.unc.edu.

See in-depth description on page 1539.

University of North Carolina at Charlotte, College of Nursing and Health Professions, Department of Health Promotion and Kinesiology, Charlotte, NC 28223-0001. Offers program in health education (M Ed). Faculty: 5 full-time (3 women). Students: 11 full-time (10 women), 34 part-time (27 women); includes 10 minority (all African Americans). Average age 32. 20 applicants, 60% accepted. In 1997, 12 degrees awarded. *Entrance requirements:* GRE General Test or MAT, minimum GPA of 3.0 during previous 2 years, 2.75 overall. Application deadline: 7/1. Application fee: $35. *Tuition:* $1786 per year full-time, $339 per semester (minimum) part-time for state residents; $8914 per year full-time, $2121 per semester (minimum) part-time for nonresidents. *Financial aid:* In 1997–98, 2 teaching assistantships averaging $825 per month and totaling $13,200 were awarded. Financial aid application deadline: 4/1. • Dr. J. Timothy Lightfoot, Chair, 704-547-4695. Application contact: Kathy Barringer, Assistant Director of Graduate Admissions, 704-547-3366. Fax: 704-547-3279. E-mail: gradadm@email.uncc.edu.

University of Northern Iowa, College of Education, School of Health, Physical Education, and Leisure Services, Program in Health Education, Cedar Falls, IA 50614. Awards MA. Part-time and evening/weekend programs available. Students: 9 full-time (8 women), 18 part-time (15 women). Average age 33. 8 applicants, 100% accepted. In 1997, 7 degrees awarded. *Degree requirements:* Thesis or alternative required, foreign language not required. *Entrance requirements:* Minimum GPA of 3.5, 3 years of educational experience. Application deadline: 8/1 (priority date; rolling processing). Application fee: $20 ($30 for international students). *Expenses:* Tuition $3166 per year full-time, $176 per hour part-time for state residents; $7805 per year full-time, $176 per hour part-time for nonresidents. Fees $194 per year full-time, $12.50 per semester (minimum) part-time. *Financial aid:* Full and partial tuition waivers, Federal Work-Study, and career-related internships or fieldwork available. Aid available to part-time students. Financial aid application deadline: 3/1. • Dr. Sharon Huddleston, Head, 319-273-2730.

University of Pittsburgh, School of Education, Department of Health, Physical, and Recreation Education, Pittsburgh, PA 15260. Offerings include movement science (MHPE, MS, PhD), with options in developmental movement (MS, PhD), exercise physiology (MS, PhD), health promotion and education (MHPE), sports medicine (MS, PhD). MHPE offered jointly with the Graduate School of Public Health. Department faculty: 10 full-time (6 women). *Average time to degree:* master's–2 years full-time, 4 years part-time; doctorate–4 years full-time, 6 years part-time. *Application deadline:* 2/1. *Application fee:* $30 ($40 for international students). *Expenses:* Tuition $8018 per year full-time, $329 per credit part-time for state residents; $16,508 per year full-time, $680 per credit part-time for nonresidents. Fees $480 per year full-time, $180 per year part-time. • Dr. Louis A. Pingel, Associate Dean, 412-648-1775. E-mail: pingel1+@pitt.edu. Application contact: Jackie Harden, Manager, 412-648-7060. Fax: 412-648-1899. E-mail: jackie@sched.fsl.pitt.edu.

University of Puerto Rico, Medical Sciences Campus, Graduate School of Public Health, Department of Social Sciences, Program in Health Education, San Juan, PR 00936-5067. Awards MPHE. Part-time programs available. Students: 46 (40 women). 35 applicants, 94% accepted. In 1997, 6 degrees awarded. *Degree requirements:* Thesis required, foreign language not required. *Entrance requirements:* GRE, previous course work in education, social sciences, algebra, and natural sciences. Application deadline: 3/3. Application fee: $15. *Financial aid:* Research assistantships, teaching assistantships, Federal Work-Study, institutionally sponsored loans, and career-related internships or fieldwork available. Financial aid application deadline: 4/30. • Dr. Maria del C. Ortiz, Coordinator, 787-758-2525 Ext. 1417. Application contact: Mayra E. Santiago-Vargas, Counselor, 787-756-5244. Fax: 787-759-6719.

University of Rhode Island, College of Human Science and Services, Department of Physical Education, Health and Recreation, Kingston, RI 02881. Offers programs in health (MS), physical education (MS), recreation (MS). One or more programs accredited by NCATE. *Entrance requirements:* MAT or GRE. Application deadline: 4/15 (priority date; rolling processing; 11/15 for spring admission). Application fee: $35. *Expenses:* Tuition $3446 per year full-time, $191 per credit part-time for state residents; $9850 per year full-time, $547 per credit part-time for nonresidents. Fees $1276 per year full-time, $135 per semester (minimum) part-time.

University of South Alabama, College of Education, Department of Health, Physical Education and Leisure Services, Mobile, AL 36688-0002. Offers programs in exercise technology (MS), health education (M Ed), leisure services (MS), physical education (M Ed), therapeutic recreation (MS). One or more programs accredited by NCATE. Part-time programs available. Faculty: 10 full-time (2 women). Students: 28 full-time (17 women), 17 part-time (11 women); includes 7 minority (6 African Americans, 1 Hispanic), 2 international. 22 applicants, 91% accepted. In 1997, 17 degrees awarded. *Degree requirements:* Comprehensive exam required, foreign language and thesis not required. *Entrance requirements:* GRE General Test (minimum combined score of 1000) or MAT (minimum score 37). Application deadline: 9/1 (priority date; rolling processing). Application fee: $25. *Financial aid:* In 1997–98, 10 teaching assistantships were awarded; career-related internships or fieldwork also available. Aid available to part-time students. Financial aid application deadline: 4/1. • Dr. Frederick Scaffidi, Chairman, 334-460-7131.

University of South Carolina, Graduate School, School of Public Health, Department of Health Promotion and Education, Columbia, SC 29208. Offers programs in alcohol and drug studies (Certificate), health education administration (Ed D), health promotion and education (MAT, MPH, MS, MSPH, Dr PH, PhD), school health education (Certificate). MAT and Ed D offered in cooperation with the College of Education. Faculty: 11 full-time (3 women). Students: 86 full-time (73 women), 55 part-time (52 women); includes 24 minority (22 African Americans, 1 Asian American, 1 Hispanic), 12 international. Average age 32. 99 applicants, 64% accepted. In 1997, 46 master's, 10 doctorates, 10 Certificates awarded. *Degree requirements:* For master's, thesis or alternative, practicum (MPH), project (MS) required, foreign language not required; for doctorate, dissertation. *Entrance requirements:* For master's and doctorate, GRE General Test. Application deadline: rolling. Application fee: $35. Electronic applications accepted. *Expenses:* Tuition $4480 per year full-time, $220 per credit hour part-time for state residents; $9338 per year full-time, $457 per credit hour part-time for nonresidents. Fees $125 per year full-time, $37 per semester (minimum) part-time. *Financial aid:* Research assistantships, teaching assistantships, traineeships, and career-related internships or fieldwork available. *Faculty research:* Implementation and evaluation of health behavior change programs, nutrition behavior, work site health promotion, AIDS education. • Dr. Donna L. Richter, Chair, 803-777-6558. Application contact: Dr. Murray Vincent, Graduate Director, 803-777-7096. Fax: 803-777-4783.

University of South Carolina, Departments of Instruction and Teacher Education and Health Promotion and Education, Program in Health Education Administration, Columbia, SC 29208. Awards Ed D. Accredited by NCATE. Faculty: 11 full-time (3 women). Students: 3 full-time (2 women), 3 part-time (2 women); includes 1 minority (African American), 1 international. Average age 38. 4 applicants, 25% accepted. *Degree requirements:* 1 foreign language, dissertation, comprehensive exam. *Entrance requirements:* GRE General Test (minimum combined score of 1000) or MAT. Application deadline: rolling. Application fee: $35. Electronic applications accepted. *Expenses:* Tuition $3894 per year full-time, $193 per credit hour part-time for state residents; $8114 per year full-time, $404 per credit hour part-time for nonresidents. Fees $125 per year full-time, $37 per semester (minimum) part-time. *Financial aid:* In 1997–98, research assistantships averaging $555 per month and totaling $5,000, teaching assistantships averaging $555 per month and totaling $5,000 were awarded; fellowships, partial tuition waivers, Federal Work-Study, institutionally sponsored loans also available. *Faculty research:* Behavioral and social science applied to public health problems. • Dr. John R. Ureda, Chair, 803-777-6558. Application contact: Dr. Murray Vincent, Graduate Director, 803-777-5152. Fax: 803-777-4783.

University of South Dakota, School of Education, Division of Health, Physical Education and Recreation, Vermillion, SD 57069-2390. Awards MA. Accredited by NCATE. Part-time programs available. Faculty: 5 full-time (2 women), 1 (woman) part-time. Students: 20 full-time (6 women), 7 part-time (2 women). 20 applicants, 45% accepted. In 1997, 9 degrees awarded. *Degree requirements:* Thesis required (for some programs), foreign language not required. *Entrance requirements:* GRE General Test, MAT. Application deadline: rolling. Application fee: $15. *Expenses:* Tuition $1530 per year full-time, $85 per credit hour part-time for state residents; $4518 per year full-time, $251 per credit hour part-time for nonresidents. Fees $792 per year full-time, $44 per credit hour part-time. *Financial aid:* Teaching assistantships available. • Dr. Gale Weidow, Chair, 605-677-5336.

University of Southern Mississippi, College of Health and Human Sciences, Center for Community Health, Hattiesburg, MS 39406-5167. Offerings include health education (MPH). Center faculty: 6 full-time (3 women), 1 (woman) part-time. *Degree requirements:* Comprehensive exam required, foreign language and thesis not required. *Entrance requirements:* GRE General Test, minimum GPA of 2.75. Application deadline: 8/9 (priority date; rolling processing). Application fee: $0 ($25 for international students). *Tuition:* $2870 per year full-time, $137 per credit hour part-time for state residents; $5972 per year full-time, $172 per credit hour part-time for nonresidents. • Dr. Agnes Hinton, Interim Director, 601-266-5437.

University of Tennessee, Knoxville, College of Human Ecology, Department of Health and Safety Sciences, Program in Health Education, Knoxville, TN 37996. Awards Ed D. Accredited by NCATE. Program being phased out; applicants no longer accepted. Students: 6 part-time (3 women). In 1997, 2 degrees awarded. *Tuition:* $3354 per year full-time, $181 per semester hour part-time for state residents; $8410 per year full-time, $462 per semester hour part-time for nonresidents. • Dr. Bill Wallace, Graduate Representative, 423-974-5041.

University of Tennessee, Knoxville, College of Human Ecology, Department of Health and Safety Sciences, Program in Health Promotion and Health Education, Knoxville, TN 37996. Awards MS. Part-time programs available. Students: 3 full-time (2 women), 11 part-time (9 women); includes 2 minority (both African Americans), 1 international. 7 applicants, 71% accepted. In 1997, 8 degrees awarded. *Degree requirements:* Thesis optional, foreign language not required. *Entrance requirements:* TOEFL (minimum score 550), minimum GPA of 2.7. Application deadline: 2/1 (priority date; rolling processing). Application fee: $35. Electronic applications accepted. *Tuition:* $3354 per year full-time, $181 per semester hour part-time for state residents; $8410 per year full-time, $462 per semester hour part-time for nonresidents. *Financial aid:* Application deadline 2/1. • Dr. Jack Ellison, Graduate Representative, 423-974-5041.

See in-depth description on page 1185.

University of Tennessee, Knoxville, College of Human Ecology, Department of Health and Safety Sciences, Program in Safety Education and Service, Knoxville, TN 37996. Awards MS. Accredited by NCATE. Part-time programs available. Students: 1 (woman) full-time, 30 part-time (9 women); includes 1 minority (African American). 12 applicants, 58% accepted. In 1997, 8 degrees awarded. *Degree requirements:* Thesis optional, foreign language not required. *Entrance requirements:* TOEFL (minimum score 550), minimum GPA of 2.7. Application deadline: 2/1 (priority date; rolling processing). Application fee: $35. Electronic applications accepted. *Tuition:* $3354 per year full-time, $181 per semester hour part-time for state residents; $8410 per year full-time, $462 per semester hour part-time for nonresidents. • Dr. Susan Smith, Graduate Representative, 423-974-5041. E-mail: smsmith@utk.edu.

See in-depth description on page 1185.

The University of Texas at Austin, Graduate School, College of Education, Department of Kinesiology and Health Education, Austin, TX 78712. Offers programs in health education (MA, M Ed, Ed D, PhD), kinesiology (MA, M Ed, Ed D, PhD). Part-time programs available. Faculty: 19 full-time (9 women). Students: 97 full-time (55 women), 29 part-time (19 women); includes 23 minority (8 African Americans, 1 Asian American, 12 Hispanics, 2 Native Americans), 12 international. 135 applicants, 51% accepted. In 1997, 40 master's, 3 doctorates awarded. Terminal master's awarded for partial completion of doctoral program. *Degree requirements:* For master's, thesis (for some programs); for doctorate, dissertation. *Entrance requirements:* GRE General Test (minimum combined score of 1000; average 1100). Application deadline: 2/1 (priority date; rolling processing; 5/1 for spring admission). Application fee: $50 ($75 for international students). Electronic applications accepted. *Expenses:* Tuition $2592 per year full-time, $324 per semester (minimum) part-time for state residents; $7704 per year full-time, $963 per semester (minimum) part-time for nonresidents. Fees $778 per year full-time, $161 per semester (minimum) part-time. *Financial aid:* In 1997–98, 2 fellowships, 20 research assistantships, 30 teaching assistantships were awarded; Federal Work-Study and career-related internships or fieldwork also available. Financial aid application deadline: 2/1; applicants required to submit FAFSA. *Faculty research:* Health promotion, human performance, exercise biochemistry, motor behavior, sports administration. • Dr. Dorothy Lovett, Chairperson, 512-471-1273. E-mail: dot.lovett@utxvm.cc.utexas.edu. Application contact: Ann M. Scarborough, Graduate Adviser, 512-471-1273. Fax: 512-471-8914. E-mail: a.scarborough@utexas.edu.

The University of Texas at Tyler, School of Education and Psychology, Department of Health and Kinesiology, Tyler, TX 75799-0001. Offers programs in allied health/interdisciplinary studies (MS), clinical exercise physiology (MS), health and kinesiology (M Ed), kinesiology (MS), kinesiology/interdisciplinary studies (MS). Part-time programs available. Faculty: 4 full-time (2 women), 6 part-time (3 women). In 1997, 10 degrees awarded. *Degree requirements:* Thesis (for some programs), comprehensive exam required, foreign language not required. *Application fee:* $0 ($50 for international students). *Tuition:* $2144 per year full-time, $337 per semester (minimum) part-time for state residents; $7256 per year full-time, $964 per semester (minimum) part-time for nonresidents. *Financial aid:* Laboratory technicianships available. Financial aid application deadline: 7/1. *Faculty research:* Osteoporosis, muscle soreness, economy of locomotion, adoption of rehabilitation programs. • Dr. James Schwane, Chairperson, 903-566-7031. Fax: 903-566-7065. E-mail: jschwane@mail.uttyl.edu. Application contact: Martha D. Wheat, Director of Admissions and Student Records, 903-566-7201. Fax: 903-566-7068.

The University of Texas Medical Branch at Galveston, Graduate School of Biomedical Sciences, Program in Allied Health Sciences, Galveston, TX 77555. Offerings include health education and promotion (MS). Program faculty: 15 full-time (4 women). *Degree requirements:* Thesis or alternative required, foreign language not required. *Entrance requirements:* GRE General Test (minimum combined score of 1100). Application deadline: 8/15 (rolling processing). Application fee: $25 ($50 for international students). *Expenses:* Tuition $36 per credit hour for state residents; $249 per credit hour for nonresidents. Fees $146 per year full-time, $124 per semester (minimum) part-time. • Dr. David Chiriboga, Director, 409-772-3038. Fax: 409-747-1610. E-mail: dchiribo@utmb.edu.

University of Toledo, College of Education and Allied Professions, Department of Health Promotion and Human Performance, Toledo, OH 43606-3398. Offerings include health education (M Ed, Ed D, PhD). Accredited by NCATE. Department faculty: 17 full-time (5 women). *Degree requirements:* For doctorate, dissertation, comprehensive exams required, foreign language not required. *Entrance requirements:* For doctorate, GRE, minimum GPA of 2.7 (undergraduate), 3.0 (graduate). Application deadline: 8/1 (priority date; rolling processing). Application fee: $30. Electronic applications accepted. *Tuition:* $5907 per year full-time, $246 per hour part-time for state residents; $11,835 per year full-time, $493 per hour part-time for nonresidents. • Dr. Carol Plimpton, Chair, 419-530-2747. Fax: 419-530-4759. E-mail: cplimpt@utnet.utoledo.edu.

University of Utah, College of Health, Department of Health Promotion and Education, Salt Lake City, UT 84112-1107. Awards M Phil, MS, Ed D, PhD. Part-time programs available. Faculty: 6 full-time (3 women), 15 part-time (11 women). Students: 19 full-time (10 women), 14 part-time (9 women); includes 1 minority (Asian American). Average age 34. In 1997, 2 master's, 3 doctorates awarded. Terminal master's awarded for partial completion of doctoral program. *Degree requirements:* Thesis/dissertation or alternative, comprehensive exam, field experience required, foreign language not required. *Entrance requirements:* For master's, GRE General Test (minimum combined score of 1000), TOEFL (minimum score 500), minimum GPA of 3.0; for doctorate, GRE General Test (minimum combined score of 1000) or MAT (minimum score 51), TOEFL (minimum score 500), minimum GPA of 3.2, 2 years of teaching experience, writing sample. Application deadline: 7/1. Application fee: $30 ($50 for international students). *Tuition:* $2045 per year full-time, $562 per semester (minimum) part-time for state residents; $6129 per year full-time, $1607 per semester (minimum) part-time for nonresidents. *Financial aid:* In 1997–98, 4 teaching assistantships were awarded; Federal Work-Study, institutionally sponsored loans, and career-related internships or fieldwork also available. Financial aid application deadline: 3/28. *Faculty research:* Health behavior and counseling, health service administration, evaluation of health programs. • Iona R. Grosshans, Chair, 801-581-8095. Application contact: Eric Trunnell, Director of Graduate Studies, 801-581-4462.

University of Virginia, Curry School of Education, Department of Human Services, Program in Health and Physical Education, Charlottesville, VA 22903. Awards M Ed, Ed D. Accredited by NCATE. Faculty: 36 full-time (12 women), 2 part-time (1 woman), 37 FTE. Students: 42 full-time (23 women), 5 part-time (all women); includes 5 minority (3 African Americans, 2 Hispanics). Average age 27. 109 applicants, 31% accepted. In 1997, 39 master's, 4 doctorates awarded. *Degree requirements:* For doctorate, dissertation required, foreign language not required. *Entrance requirements:* GRE General Test. Application deadline: 3/1 (11/15 for spring admission). Application fee: $40. *Tuition:* $4876 per year full-time, $944 per semester (minimum) part-time for state residents; $15,824 per year full-time, $2748 per semester (minimum) part-time for nonresidents. • Application contact: Linda Berry, Student Enrollment Coordinator, 804-924-0738. E-mail: lrb8e@virginia.edu.

University of Waterloo, Faculty of Applied Health Sciences, Department of Health Studies and Gerontology, Waterloo, ON N2L 3G1, Canada. Offers programs in health behavior (M Sc), health studies (PhD). Part-time programs available. Faculty: 12 full-time (8 women), 10 part-time (4 women). Students: 15 full-time (11 women), 5 part-time (all women). 34 applicants, 21% accepted. In 1997, 4 master's, 6 doctorates awarded. *Degree requirements:* Computer language, thesis/dissertation required, foreign language not required. *Average time to degree:* master's–2 years full-time, 5 years part-time; doctorate–3 years full-time, 4 years part-time. *Entrance requirements:* For master's, TOEFL (minimum score 550), honors degree, minimum B average; for doctorate, GRE, TOEFL (minimum score 550), master's degree. Application deadline: 2/1. Application fee: $50. *Tuition:* $3220 per year. *Financial aid:* In 1997–98, 2 fellowships (both to first-year students), 3 research assistantships (2 to first-year students), 11 teaching assistantships (9 to first-year students) averaging $1,238 per month were awarded; scholarships and career-related internships or fieldwork also available. *Faculty research:* Health behavior modification, smoking, obesity, nutrition. • Dr. P. E. Wainwright, Chair, 519-888-4567 Ext. 3924. Application contact: Dr. M. Stones, Associate Chair, Graduate Studies, 519-888-4567 Ext. 5685. Fax: 519-746-2510. E-mail: mjstones@healthy.uwaterloo.ca.

University of West Florida, College of Arts and Social Sciences, Department of Health, Leisure, and Sports, Pensacola, FL 32514-5750. Offers programs in health (MS); health, leisure, and sports (MS); physical education (MS). Part-time and evening/weekend programs available. Students: 23 full-time (17 women), 31 part-time (25 women); includes 7 minority (5 African Americans, 1 Asian American, 1 Native American), 1 international. Average age 35. 25 applicants, 100% accepted. In 1997, 20 degrees awarded. *Degree requirements:* Thesis or alternative. *Entrance requirements:* GRE General Test (minimum combined score of 1000), minimum GPA of 3.0. Application deadline: 7/1 (rolling processing; 11/1 for spring admission). Application fee: $20. *Tuition:* $131 per credit hour (minimum) for state residents; $436 per credit hour (minimum) for nonresidents. *Financial aid:* Teaching assistantships available. • Dr. C. B. Williamson, Chairperson, 850-474-2592.

University of Wisconsin–La Crosse, College of Health, Physical Education and Recreation, Department of Health Education, La Crosse, WI 54601-3742. Offerings include school health (MS). Accredited by NCATE. Department faculty: 8 full-time (2 women). *Application fee:* $38. *Tuition:* $3737 per year full-time, $208 per credit part-time for state residents; $11,921 per year full-time, $633 per credit part-time for nonresidents. • Dr. Gary D. Gilmore, Director, Community and Health Education, 608-785-8163. E-mail: gilmore@mail.uwlax.edu. Application contact: Tim Lewis, Director of Admissions, 608-785-8939. Fax: 608-785-6695. E-mail: admissions@mail.uwlax.edu.

Directories: Health Education; Home Economics Education

University of Wyoming, College of Health Sciences, Department of Physical and Health Education, Laramie, WY 82071. Awards MS. Accredited by NCATE. Part-time programs available. Faculty: 8 full-time (3 women). Students: 11 full-time (7 women), 13 part-time (5 women). Average age 26. 21 applicants, 43% accepted. In 1997, 13 degrees awarded (38% found work related to degree, 62% continued full-time study). *Degree requirements:* Thesis optional, foreign language not required. *Average time to degree:* master's–2 years full-time, 4 years part-time. *Entrance requirements:* GRE General Test (minimum combined score of 900), minimum GPA of 3.0. Application deadline: 6/1 (priority date; rolling processing; 11/1 for spring admission). Application fee: $40. *Expenses:* Tuition $2430 per year full-time, $135 per credit hour part-time for state residents; $7518 per year full-time, $418 per credit hour part-time for nonresidents. Fees $386 per year full-time, $9.25 per credit hour part-time. *Financial aid:* In 1997–98, 18 students received aid, including 7 graduate assistantships (4 to first-year students) averaging $470 per month; career-related internships or fieldwork also available. Financial aid application deadline: 3/1. *Faculty research:* Teacher effectiveness, effects of exercising on heart function, physiological responses of overtraining, psychological benefits of physical activity, instruction assessment and supervision of effective teaching in physical education, physical activity of children. Total annual research expenditures: $25,000. • Dr. Paul Thomas, Associate Dean, 307-766-5285. Application contact: Dr. Mark Byra, Graduate Coordinator, 307-766-5227. Fax: 307-766-4098. E-mail: byra@uwyo.edu.

Utah State University, College of Education, Department of Health, Physical Education and Recreation, Logan, UT 84322. Offers programs in health education (MS), physical education (M Ed, MS). Accredited by NCATE. Faculty: 12 full-time (5 women). Students: 46 full-time (17 women), 14 part-time (7 women). Average age 34. 21 applicants, 76% accepted. In 1997, 12 degrees awarded. *Entrance requirements:* GRE General Test (score in 40th percentile or higher) or MAT, TOEFL (minimum score 550), minimum GPA of 3.0. Application deadline: 6/15 (priority date; rolling processing; 10/15 for spring admission). Application fee: $40. *Expenses:* Tuition $1448 per year full-time, $624 per year part-time for state residents; $5082 per year full-time, $2192 per year part-time for nonresidents. Fees $421 per year full-time, $165 per year part-time. *Financial aid:* Teaching assistantships, full tuition waivers, Federal Work-Study, institutionally sponsored loans, and career-related internships or fieldwork available. Financial aid application deadline: 2/10. *Faculty research:* Sport psychology intervention, motor learning biomechanics, pedagogy, physiology. • Dr. Art Jones, Head, 435-797-1499. E-mail: ajonz@fsl.ed.usu.edu. Application contact: Dr. Richard Gordin, Graduate Program Chair, 435-797-1506. Fax: 435-797-3759. E-mail: gordin@cc.usu.edu.

Valdosta State University, College of Education, Department of Health and Physical Education, Valdosta, GA 31698. Awards M Ed. Accredited by NCATE. Faculty: 3 full-time (0 women). Students: 13 full-time (4 women), 4 part-time (0 women); includes 1 minority (Asian American), 1 international. 10 applicants, 70% accepted. In 1997, 12 degrees awarded. *Entrance requirements:* GRE General Test (minimum combined score of 800). Application deadline: 8/1 (rolling processing). Application fee: $10. *Expenses:* Tuition $2472 per year full-time, $83 per semester hour part-time for state residents; $8472 per year full-time, $333 per semester hour part-time for nonresidents. Fees $236 per year full-time. *Financial aid:* Teaching assistantships available. • Dr. Stan Andrews, Head, 912-333-7161. E-mail: sandrews@grits.valdosta.peachnet.edu. Application contact: Coordinator, 912-333-7161. Fax: 912-333-5972.

Vanderbilt University, Peabody College, Department of Human Resources, Nashville, TN 37240-1001. Offerings include health promotion education (M Ed). Accredited by NCATE. *Application deadline:* 3/1 (priority date; rolling processing). *Application fee:* $35. • Robert B. Innes, Acting Chair, 615-322-6881.

Virginia Polytechnic Institute and State University, College of Human Resources and Education, Department of Teaching and Learning, Blacksburg, VA 24061. Offerings include health and physical education (MS Ed). Accredited by NCATE. *Application deadline:* 12/1 (priority date; rolling processing). *Application fee:* $25. *Tuition:* $4927 per year full-time, $792 per semester (minimum) part-time for state residents; $7537 per year full-time, $1227 per semester (minimum) part-time for nonresidents. • Dr. John Burton, Head, 540-231-5347. E-mail: teach@vt.edu.

Wayne State College, Division of Education, Program in Curriculum and Instruction, Wayne, NE 68787. Offerings include health and physical education/health (MSE), health and physical education/pedagogy (MSE). One or more programs accredited by NCATE. *Degree requirements:* Comprehensive exam, research paper required, foreign language not required. *Entrance requirements:* GRE General Test. Application deadline: rolling. Application fee: $10. *Expenses:* Tuition $1788 per year full-time, $75 per credit hour part-time for state residents; $3576 per year full-time, $149 per credit hour part-time for nonresidents. Fees $360 per year full-time, $15 per credit hour part-time. • Dr. Diane Alexander, Head, Division of Education, 402-375-7389.

Wayne State University, College of Education, Division of Health and Physical Education, Detroit, MI 48202. Offers programs in health education (M Ed), physical education (M Ed), recreation and park services (MA), sports administration (MA). Accredited by NCATE. Faculty: 34. Students: 30 full-time (14 women), 144 part-time (73 women). 79 applicants, 75% accepted. In 1997, 48 degrees awarded. *Degree requirements:* Thesis required (for some programs), foreign language not required. *Entrance requirements:* GRE General Test. Application deadline: 7/1. Application fee: $20 ($30 for international students). *Expenses:* Tuition $163 per credit hour for state residents; $355 per credit hour for nonresidents. Fees $498 per year full-time, $114 per semester (minimum) part-time. *Financial aid:* In 1997–98, 5 teaching assistantships (2 to first-year students) averaging $800 per month and totaling $40,000 were awarded; career-related internships or fieldwork also available. *Faculty research:* Fitness in urban children, motor development of crack babies, effects of caffeine on metabolism/exercise, body composition of elite youth sports participants, systematic observation of teaching. • Dr. Sarah Erbaugh, Assistant Dean, 313-577-4265. Application contact: John Wirth, Graduate Program Coordinator, 313-577-5896. Fax: 313-577-5999.

West Chester University of Pennsylvania, School of Health Sciences, Department of Health, West Chester, PA 19383. Awards M Ed, MS. One or more programs accredited by NCATE. Faculty: 5 part-time. Students: 7 full-time (6 women), 33 part-time (24 women); includes 6 minority (5 African Americans, 1 Asian American). Average age 33. 34 applicants, 59% accepted. In 1997, 15 degrees awarded. *Degree requirements:* Thesis (for some programs), comprehensive exam required, foreign language not required. *Entrance requirements:* GRE. Application deadline: 4/15 (priority date; rolling processing; 10/15 for spring admission). Application fee: $25. *Expenses:* Tuition $3468 per year full-time, $193 per credit part-time for state residents; $6236 per year full-time, $346 per credit part-time for nonresidents. Fees $660 per year full-time, $38 per credit part-time. *Financial aid:* In 1997–98, 3 research assistantships were awarded. Financial aid application deadline: 2/15. • Dr. Sheila Patterson, Chair, 610-436-2931. Application contact: Dr. Gopal Sankaran, Graduate Coordinator, 610-436-2250.

Western Illinois University, College of Education and Human Services, Department of Health Education and Promotion, Macomb, IL 61455-1390. Awards MS. Accredited by NCATE. Part-time programs available. Faculty: 13 full-time (3 women). Students: 15 full-time (12 women), 27 part-time (21 women); includes 5 minority (4 African Americans, 1 Asian American), 5 international. Average age 36. 21 applicants, 81% accepted. In 1997, 14 degrees awarded. *Degree requirements:* Thesis or alternative required, foreign language not required. *Entrance requirements:* Minimum GPA of 2.75. Application deadline: rolling. Application fee: $0 ($25 for international students). *Expenses:* Tuition $2304 per year full-time, $96 per semester hour part-time for state residents; $6912 per year full-time, $288 per semester hour part-time for nonresidents. Fees $944 per year full-time, $33 per semester hour part-time. *Financial aid:* In 1997–98, 10 students received aid, including 10 research assistantships averaging $610 per month; full tuition waivers also available. Financial aid applicants required to submit FAFSA. *Faculty research:* Alcohol-impaired DUI program, rural health, lead poisoning prevention, fire safety. • Dr. B. Nicholas DiGrino, Interim Chairperson, 309-298-1076. Application contact: Barbara Baily, Director of Graduate Studies, 309-298-1806. Fax: 309-298-2245. E-mail: barb_baily@ccmail.wiu.edu.

Western Kentucky University, Ogden College of Science, Technology, and Health, Department of Public Health, Bowling Green, KY 42101-3576. Offerings include health education (MA Ed), public health education (MS). Department faculty: 11 full-time (4 women). *Degree requirements:* Variable foreign language requirement, thesis or alternative. *Entrance requirements:* GRE General Test. Application deadline: 8/1 (priority date; rolling processing; 12/1 for spring admission). Application fee: $20. *Tuition:* $2460 per year full-time, $133 per credit hour part-time for state residents; $6700 per year full-time, $369 per credit hour part-time for nonresidents. • Dr. J. David Dunn, Head, 502-745-4797. Fax: 502-745-4437. E-mail: david.dunn@wku.edu.

Western University of Health Sciences, School of Allied Health Professions, Program in Health Professions Education, Pomona, CA 91766-1854. Awards MS. Students: 13. *Application deadline:* rolling. *Application fee:* $45. *Tuition:* $175 per unit. • Application contact: Susan M. Hanson, Director of Admissions, 909-469-5335.

Worcester State College, Graduate Studies, Department of Education, Program in Health Education, Worcester, MA 01602-2597. Awards M Ed. Part-time and evening/weekend programs available. Students: 2 full-time (0 women), 24 part-time (19 women). Average age 39. 5 applicants, 100% accepted. In 1997, 9 degrees awarded. *Degree requirements:* Comprehensive exam. *Entrance requirements:* GRE General Test or MAT. Application deadline: rolling. Application fee: $10 ($40 for international students). *Tuition:* $127 per credit hour. *Financial aid:* Career-related internships or fieldwork available. • Dr. Michael Burke, Coordinator, 508-929-8643. Application contact: Andrea Wetmore, Graduate Admissions Counselor, 508-929-8120. E-mail: awetmore@worc.mass.edu.

Wright State University, College of Education and Human Services, Department of Health, Physical Education, and Recreation, Dayton, OH 45435. Awards MA, M Ed. Accredited by NCATE. Students: 3 full-time (2 women), 2 part-time (1 woman). Average age 30. 2 applicants, 50% accepted. *Degree requirements:* Thesis (for some programs), comprehensive exam required, foreign language not required. *Entrance requirements:* GRE General Test, MAT, TOEFL (minimum score 550). Application fee: $25. *Tuition:* $5109 per year full-time, $161 per credit hour part-time for state residents; $9039 per year full-time, $282 per credit hour part-time for nonresidents. *Financial aid:* Available to part-time students. Financial aid applicants required to submit FAFSA. *Faculty research:* Motor learning, motor development, exercise physiology, adapted physical education. • Dr. G. William Gayle, Chair, 937-775-3223. Fax: 937-775-3301. Application contact: Gerald C. Malicki, Assistant Dean and Director of Graduate Admissions and Records, 937-775-2976. Fax: 937-775-2357. E-mail: wsugrad@wright.edu.

Home Economics Education

Brooklyn College of the City University of New York, School of Education, Division of Secondary Education, 2900 Bedford Avenue, Brooklyn, NY 11210-2889. Offerings include home economics education (MS Ed). *Application deadline:* 3/1 (11/1 for spring admission). *Application fee:* $40. *Expenses:* Tuition $4350 per year full-time, $185 per credit part-time for state residents; $7600 per year full-time, $320 per credit part-time for nonresidents. Fees $500 per year for state residents; $806 per year for nonresidents. • Dr. Peter Taubman, Coordinator, 718-951-5218. Fax: 718-951-4816. E-mail: ptaubman@brooklyn.cuny.edu.

Central Washington University, College of Education and Professional Studies, Department of Family and Consumer Sciences, Ellensburg, WA 98926. Offerings include family and consumer sciences education (MS). Accredited by NCATE. Department faculty: 8 full-time (6 women). *Degree requirements:* Thesis or alternative required, foreign language not required. *Entrance requirements:* GRE General Test (nutrition), minimum GPA of 3.0. Application deadline: 4/1 (priority date; rolling processing; 1/1 for spring admission). Application fee: $35. *Expenses:* Tuition $4200 per year full-time, $140 per credit hour part-time for state residents; $12,780 per year full-time, $426 per credit hour part-time for nonresidents. Fees $240 per year. • Dr. Jan Bowers, Chair, 509-963-2766. Application contact: Christie A. Fevergeon, Program Coordinator, Graduate Studies and Research, 509-963-3103. Fax: 509-963-1799. E-mail: masters@cwu.edu.

Eastern Kentucky University, College of Education, Department of Curriculum and Instruction, Program in Secondary and Higher Education, Richmond, KY 40475-3101. Offerings include home economics education (MA Ed). Accredited by NCATE. *Entrance requirements:* GRE General Test, minimum GPA of 2.5. Application fee: $0. *Tuition:* $2390 per year full-time, $133 per credit hour part-time for state residents; $6630 per year full-time, $365 per credit hour part-time for nonresidents. • Dr. Imogene Ramsey, Chair, Department of Curriculum and Instruction, 606-622-2154.

Florida International University, College of Education, Department of Subject Specializations, Program in Home Economics Education, Miami, FL 33199. Offers non-school based home economics education (MS), vocational home economics education (MS). Accredited by NCATE. Part-time and evening/weekend programs available. Students: 4 part-time (all women); includes 1 minority (African American). Average age 34. 1 applicant, 100% accepted. In 1997, 4 degrees awarded. *Entrance requirements:* GRE General Test (minimum combined score of 1000) or minimum GPA of 3.0 in last 60 credits of baccalaureate, interview. Application deadline: 4/1 (priority date; rolling processing; 10/1 for spring admission). Application fee: $20. *Expenses:* Tuition $138 per credit hour for state residents; $482 per credit hour for nonresidents. Fees $46 per semester. *Financial aid:* Research assistantships available. *Faculty research:* Certification needs, curriculum improvement in home economics, teacher competence, effectiveness of program. • Dr. Dean Hauenstein, Chairperson, Department of Subject Specializations, 305-348-2005. Fax: 305-348-2086.

Framingham State College, Graduate Programs, Department of Family and Consumer Sciences, Program in Family and Consumer Sciences Education, Framingham, MA 01701-9101. Awards M Ed. Students: 2 full-time, 3 part-time. *Tuition:* $4184 per year full-time, $523 per course part-time for state residents; $4848 per year full-time, $606 per course part-time for nonresidents. • Dr. Patricia Plummer, Adviser, 508-626-4703. Application contact: Graduate Office, 508-626-4550.

Idaho State University, College of Education, Division II, Pocatello, ID 83209. Offerings include family and consumer sciences (M Ed). Accredited by NCATE. Postbaccalaureate distance learning degree programs offered (no on-campus study). Division faculty: 11 full-time (2 women). *Average time to degree:* master's–2 years full-time, 4 years part-time; other advanced degree–1 year full-time, 2 years part-time. *Application deadline:* 7/1 (priority date; rolling processing; 12/1 for spring admission). *Application fee:* $30. *Tuition:* $3130 per year full-time, $136 per credit hour part-time for state residents; $9370 per year full-time, $226 per credit hour part-time for nonresidents. • Dr. T. C. Mattocks, Director. E-mail: matttheo@isu.edu. Application contact: Dr. Stephanie Salzman, Director, Office of Standards and Assessment, 208-236-3114. Fax: 208-236-4697. E-mail: salzstep@isu.edu.

Iowa State University of Science and Technology, College of Family and Consumer Sciences, Department of Family and Consumer Sciences Education and Studies, Ames, IA 50011. Awards M Ed, MS, PhD. Faculty: 10 full-time, 2 part-time. Students: 11 full-time (10 women), 5 part-time (4 women); includes 1 minority (African American), 5 international. 9 applicants, 78% accepted. In 1997, 6 master's, 4 doctorates awarded. *Degree requirements:* For master's, thesis (for some programs); for doctorate, dissertation. *Entrance requirements:* GRE General Test, TOEFL. Application deadline: 1/15 (priority date; 9/15 for spring admission). Application fee: $20 ($30 for international students). *Expenses:* Tuition $3166 per year full-time, $176 per credit part-time for state residents; $9324 per year full-time, $518 per credit part-time for nonresidents. Fees $200 per year. *Financial aid:* In 1997–98, 7 research assistantships (1 to a first-year student), 2 teaching assistantships (1 to a first-year student), 1 scholarship were awarded. • Dr. Rosalie Amos, Chair, 515-294-6444. E-mail: ramos@iastate.edu. Application contact: Cheryl Hausafus, 515-294-5307. E-mail: fceds@iastate.edu.

Louisiana State University and Agricultural and Mechanical College, College of Agriculture, School of Vocational Education, Baton Rouge, LA 70803. Offerings include vocational home economics education (MS). Accredited by NCATE. School faculty: 11 full-time (3 women). *Degree requirements:* Thesis required (for some programs), foreign language not required. *Entrance requirements:* GRE General Test (minimum combined score of 1000), minimum GPA of 3.0. Application deadline: 1/25 (priority date; rolling processing). Application fee: $25. *Tuition:* $2736 per year full-time, $285 per semester (minimum) part-time for state residents; $6636 per year full-time, $460 per semester (minimum) part-time for nonresidents. • Dr. Michael F. Burnett, Director, 504-388-5748.

Michigan State University, College of Human Ecology, Department of Family and Child Ecology, East Lansing, MI 48824-1020. Offerings include home economics education (MA). Postbaccalaureate distance learning degree programs offered. Department faculty: 23 (14 women). *Application deadline:* rolling. *Application fee:* $30 ($40 for international students). *Expenses:* Tuition $4609 per year full-time, $223 per credit hour (minimum) part-time for state residents; $8704 per year full-time, $450 per credit hour (minimum) part-time for nonresidents. Fees $576 per year full-time, $476 per year part-time. • Dr. Marjorie Kostelnik, Chairperson, 517-355-7680.

Montclair State University, College of Education and Human Services, Department of Human Ecology, Upper Montclair, NJ 07043-1624. Offerings include home economics education (MA). Accredited by NCATE. Department faculty: 20 full-time. *Degree requirements:* Thesis or alternative, comprehensive exam. *Application deadline:* 4/1 (rolling processing; 11/1 for spring admission). *Application fee:* $40. *Expenses:* Tuition $201 per credit for state residents; $257 per credit for nonresidents. Fees $22.05 per credit. • Dr. Elaine Flint, Chairperson, 973-655-4171. Application contact: Dr. Karen Todd, Adviser, 973-655-4171.

North Dakota State University, College of Human Development and Education, School of Education, Program in Family and Consumer Sciences Education, Fargo, ND 58105. Awards M Ed, MS. Accredited by NCATE. Part-time programs available. Faculty: 1 (woman) full-time. Students: 2 part-time (both women). Average age 40. 1 applicant, 100% accepted. *Degree requirements:* Thesis or alternative required, foreign language not required. *Entrance requirements:* MAT, TOEFL (minimum score 525). Application deadline: rolling. Application fee: $25. *Tuition:* $2572 per year full-time, $107 per credit part-time for state residents; $6868 per year full-time, $286 per credit part-time for nonresidents. *Financial aid:* Teaching assistantships, institutionally sponsored loans, and career-related internships or fieldwork available. Financial aid application deadline: 4/15. *Faculty research:* Needs of beginning teachers, learning styles and achievement, school-level variables and curriculum change. • Application contact: Dr. Diane H. Jackman, Assistant Professor, 701-231-7102. Fax: 701-231-9685. E-mail: jackman@plains.nodak.edu.

Northwestern State University of Louisiana, Division of Education, Program in Home Economics Education, Natchitoches, LA 71497. Awards M Ed. Accredited by NCATE. Faculty: 2 full-time (both women), 1 (woman) part-time. Students: 0. *Degree requirements:* Thesis or alternative required, foreign language not required. *Entrance requirements:* GRE General Test (minimum combined score of 800), GRE Subject Test, minimum undergraduate GPA of 2.5. Application deadline: 8/1 (priority date; rolling processing; 1/10 for spring admission). Application fee: $15 ($25 for international students). *Tuition:* $2147 per year full-time, $336 per semester (minimum) part-time for state residents; $6437 per year full-time, $336 per semester (minimum) part-time for nonresidents. *Financial aid:* Application deadline 7/15. • Dr. Virginia Crossno, Chair, 318-357-5587. Application contact: Dr. Tom Hanson, Dean, Graduate Studies and Research, 318-357-5851. Fax: 318-357-5019.

The Ohio State University, College of Human Ecology, Department of Human Development and Family Science, Program in Family and Consumer Sciences Education, Columbus, OH 43210. Awards MS, PhD. Faculty: 7. Students: 11 full-time (all women), 11 part-time (all women); includes 2 minority (both African Americans), 3 international. 9 applicants, 33% accepted. In 1997, 4 master's awarded. *Degree requirements:* For master's, thesis optional, foreign language not required; for doctorate, dissertation required, foreign language not required. *Entrance requirements:* GRE General Test. Application deadline: 8/15 (rolling processing). Application fee: $30 ($40 for international students). *Tuition:* $5472 per year full-time, $554 per quarter (minimum) part-time for state residents; $14,172 per year full-time, $1424 per quarter (minimum) part-time for nonresidents. *Financial aid:* Fellowships, research assistantships, teaching assistantships, Federal Work-Study, institutionally sponsored loans available. Aid available to part-time students. • Albert J. Davis, Chairperson, 614-292-7705. Fax: 614-292-4365. E-mail: davis.7@osu.edu.

Oregon State University, Graduate School, College of Home Economics and Education, School of Education, Program in Home Economics Education, Corvallis, OR 97331. Awards MAT, MS. Accredited by NCATE. Part-time programs available. Students: 0. Average age 30. 5 applicants, 100% accepted. *Degree requirements:* Thesis (for some programs), minimum GPA of 3.0 required, foreign language not required. *Entrance requirements:* NTE, California Basic Educational Skills Test, TOEFL (minimum score 550), minimum GPA of 3.0 in last 90 hours. Application deadline: 1/15. Application fee: $50. *Tuition:* $6207 per year full-time, $810 per quarter (minimum) part-time for state residents; $10,551 per year full-time, $1293 per quarter (minimum) part-time for nonresidents. *Financial aid:* Fellowships, Federal Work-Study, institutionally sponsored loans, and career-related internships or fieldwork available. Aid available to part-time students. Financial aid application deadline: 2/1. *Faculty research:* Economy of time and methods. • Dr. Chris L. Southers, Director, 541-737-1080.

Purdue University, School of Education, Department of Curriculum and Instruction, West Lafayette, IN 47907. Offerings include consumer and family sciences and extension education (MS Ed, PhD, Ed S). Accredited by NCATE. Department faculty: 34 full-time (15 women), 3 part-time (1 woman). *Degree requirements:* For master's, thesis optional; for doctorate, dissertation, oral and written exams; for Ed S, oral presentation, project required, thesis not required. *Entrance requirements:* For master's, TOEFL (minimum score 550), minimum B average; for doctorate, GRE General Test (minimum score 500 on each section), TOEFL (minimum score 550); for Ed S, minimum B average. Application deadline: 1/15 (priority date; 9/15 for spring admission). Application fee: $30. Electronic applications accepted. *Tuition:* $3500 per year full-time, $126 per credit hour part-time for state residents; $11,720 per year full-time, $387 per credit hour part-time for nonresidents. • Dr. J. L. Peters, Head, 765-494-9172. Fax: 765-496-1622. E-mail: peters@purdue.edu. Application contact: Christine Larsen, Coordinator of Graduate Studies, 765-494-2345. Fax: 765-494-5832. E-mail: gradoffice@soe.purdue.edu.

Queens College of the City University of New York, Mathematics and Natural Sciences Division, Department of Family, Nutrition and Exercise Sciences, Program in Home Economics, 65-30 Kissena Boulevard, Flushing, NY 11367-1597. Awards MS Ed. Degree awarded through the School of Education. Part-time and evening/weekend programs available. Students: 29 part-time (all women); includes 5 minority (3 African Americans, 2 Asian Americans). 26 applicants, 96% accepted. In 1997, 12 degrees awarded. *Degree requirements:* Thesis, research project required, foreign language not required. *Entrance requirements:* TOEFL (minimum score 600), minimum GPA of 3.0. Application deadline: 4/1 (rolling processing; 11/1 for spring admission). Application fee: $40. *Expenses:* Tuition $4350 per year full-time, $185 per credit part-time for state residents; $7600 per year full-time, $320 per credit part-time for nonresidents. Fees $104 per year. *Financial aid:* Partial tuition waivers, Federal Work-Study, institutionally sponsored loans, and career-related internships or fieldwork available. Aid available to part-time students. Financial aid application deadline: 4/1; applicants required to submit FAFSA. • Dr. Lakshmi Malroutu, Graduate Adviser, 718-997-4150. Application contact: Mario Caruso, Director of Graduate Admissions, 718-997-5200. Fax: 718-997-5193. E-mail: graduate%queens.bitnet@cunyvm.cuny.edu.

South Carolina State University, School of Education, Department of Teacher Education, 300 College Street Northeast, Orangeburg, SC 29117-0001. Offerings include secondary education (M Ed), with options in biology education, business education, counselor education, English education, home economics education, industrial education, mathematics education, science education, social studies education. Accredited by NCATE. Department faculty: 7 full-time (3 women), 2 part-time (1 woman). *Average time to degree:* master's–2 years full-time, 4 years part-time. *Application deadline:* 7/15 (priority date; rolling processing; 11/10 for spring admission). *Application fee:* $25. *Tuition:* $2974 per year full-time, $165 per credit hour part-time. • Dr. Jesse Kinard, Chairman, 803-536-8934. Application contact: Dr. Gail Joyner-Fleming, Interim Associate Dean and Director, Graduate Teacher Education, 803-536-8824. Fax: 803-536-8492.

State University of New York College at Oneonta, Department of Education, Program in Secondary Education, Oneonta, NY 13820-4015. Offerings include home economics education (MS Ed). *Entrance requirements:* GRE General Test. Application deadline: 4/15. Application fee: $50. *Expenses:* Tuition $5100 per year full-time, $213 per credit hour part-time for state residents; $8416 per year full-time, $351 per credit hour part-time for nonresidents. Fees $482 per year full-time, $6.85 per credit hour part-time. • Dr. John Clow, Coordinator, 607-436-3275.

Texas Southern University, College of Arts and Sciences, Department of Home Economics, Houston, TX 77004-4584. Offerings include home economics education (MA, MS), with options in child development (MS), foods and nutrition (MS), home economics education (MS). Department faculty: 4 full-time (3 women), 1 (woman) part-time. *Degree requirements:* Thesis (for some programs), comprehensive exam required, foreign language not required. *Average time to degree:* master's–2 years full-time, 3 years part-time. *Entrance requirements:* GRE General Test, TOEFL, minimum GPA of 2.5. Application deadline: 7/15 (priority date; rolling processing). Application fee: $35 ($75 for international students). • Dr. Oddis Turner, Chairman, 713-313-7699. Fax: 713-313-7228.

Texas Tech University, Graduate School, College of Human Sciences, Department of Education, Nutrition, and Restaurant/Hotel Management, Program in Family and Consumer Sciences Education, Lubbock, TX 79409. Awards MS, PhD. Part-time programs available. Faculty: 4 full-time (all women), 2 part-time (both women), 4.5 FTE. Students: 4 full-time (all women), 7 part-time (5 women). Average age 30. 4 applicants, 25% accepted. In 1997, 1 master's awarded (100% found work related to degree); 4 doctorates awarded (100% found work related to degree). Terminal master's awarded for partial completion of doctoral program. *Degree requirements:* For master's, thesis optional, foreign language not required; for doctorate, dissertation required, foreign language not required. *Average time to degree:* master's–1.5 years full-time; doctorate–6 years part-time. *Entrance requirements:* For master's, GRE General Test (minimum combined score of 850); for doctorate, GRE General Test (minimum combined score of 1000). Application deadline: 4/15 (priority date; rolling processing). Application fee: $25 ($50 for international students). *Expenses:* Tuition $864 per year full-time, $120 per semester (minimum) part-time for state residents; $5976 per year full-time, $747 per semester (minimum) part-time for nonresidents. Fees $2321 per year full-time, $302 per semester (minimum) part-time. *Financial aid:* In 1997–98, 1 teaching assistantship averaging $850 per month and totaling $8,000 was awarded; fellowships, research assistantships, Federal Work-Study, institutionally sponsored loans, and career-related internships or fieldwork also available. Aid available to part-time students. Financial aid application deadline: 2/1. *Faculty research:* Work and family interaction, intergenerational initiatives, gender equity, curriculum, supervision, national standards. Total annual research expenditures: $5000. • Dr. Virginia Felstehausen, Graduate Adviser, 806-742-3068. Fax: 806-742-3042. E-mail: gfelste@hs.ttu.edu.

The University of Arizona, College of Agriculture, School of Family and Consumer Resources, Tucson, AZ 85721. Offerings include home economics education (MHE Ed). *Application fee:* $35. *Tuition:* $2162 per year full-time, $337 per semester (minimum) part-time for state residents; $6860 per year full-time, $1138 per semester (minimum) part-time for nonresidents.

University of British Columbia, Faculty of Education, Department of Curriculum Studies, Vancouver, BC V6T 1Z2, Canada. Offerings include home economics education (MA, M Ed, PhD). *Degree requirements:* For master's, thesis (MA) required, foreign language not required; for doctorate, dissertation required, foreign language not required. *Entrance requirements:* TOEFL (minimum score 550). Application deadline: 3/1 (12/1 for spring admission). Application fee: $60.

University of Georgia, College of Education, Department of Occupational Studies, Athens, GA 30602. Offerings include home economics education (M Ed). Accredited by NCATE. Department faculty: 12 full-time (4 women). *Degree requirements:* Thesis required (for some programs), foreign language not required. *Entrance requirements:* GRE General Test, MAT. Application deadline: 7/1 (priority date; 11/15 for spring admission). Application fee: $30. Electronic applications accepted. *Tuition:* $3290 per year full-time, $643 per semester (minimum) part-time for state residents; $11,300 per year full-time, $1645 per semester (minimum) part-time for nonresidents. • Dr. Robert C. Wicklein, Graduate Coordinator, 706-542-3132. Fax: 706-542-1765.

University of Manitoba, Faculty of Education, Department of Curriculum: Mathematics and Natural Sciences, Winnipeg, MB R3T 2N2, Canada. Offerings include home economics education (M Ed). *Degree requirements:* Thesis or alternative required, foreign language not required.

University of Montevallo, College of Arts and Sciences, Department of Home Economics, Montevallo, AL 35115. Awards MAT. Accredited by NCATE. *Entrance requirements:* GRE General Test (minimum combined score of 850), MAT (minimum score 35), minimum undergraduate GPA of 2.75 in last 60 hours or 2.5 overall. Application deadline: 7/15 (11/15 for spring admission). Application fee: $10.

University of North Carolina at Greensboro, School of Human Environmental Sciences, Department of Human Development and Family Studies, Greensboro, NC 27412-0001. Offerings include home economics education (M Ed, MS, PhD). Accredited by NCATE. Department faculty: 15 full-time (10 women), 6 part-time. *Degree requirements:* For master's, 1 foreign language; for doctorate, 1 foreign language, dissertation. *Entrance requirements:* GRE General Test. Application deadline: 3/15. Application fee: $35. • Dr. David Demo, Chair, 336-334-5315.

Directories: Home Economics Education; Mathematics Education

University of Puerto Rico, Río Piedras, College of Education, Program in Home Economics, San Juan, PR 00931. Awards M Ed. Part-time programs available. *Degree requirements:* Thesis required, foreign language not required. *Entrance requirements:* PAEG, minimum GPA of 3.0. Application deadline: 2/21. Application fee: $17.

University of Rhode Island, College of Human Science and Services, Department of Education, Kingston, RI 02881. Offerings include home economics education (MS). Accredited by NCATE. *Application deadline:* 4/15 (priority date; rolling processing; 11/15 for spring admission). *Application fee:* $35. *Expenses:* Tuition $3446 per year full-time, $191 per credit part-time for state residents; $9850 per year full-time, $547 per credit part-time for nonresidents. Fees $1276 per year full-time, $135 per semester (minimum) part-time.

Western Carolina University, College of Applied Science, Department of Human Environmental Sciences, Cullowhee, NC 28723. Offerings include family and consumer sciences (MAT, MS). Accredited by NCATE. MS being phased out; applicants no longer accepted. Department faculty: 5 (4 women). *Degree requirements:* Comprehensive exam required, thesis optional, foreign language not required. *Entrance requirements:* GRE General Test. Application deadline: rolling. Application fee: $35. *Tuition:* $1799 per year full-time, $144 per credit hour (minimum) part-time for state residents; $9069 per year full-time, $1053 per credit hour (minimum) part-time for nonresidents. • Davia M. Allen, Head, 828-227-7272. Application contact: Kathleen Owen, Assistant to the Dean, 828-227-7398. Fax: 828-227-7480.

Western Carolina University, College of Education and Allied Professions, Department of Administration, Curriculum and Instruction, Programs in Secondary Education, Cullowhee, NC 28723. Offerings include family and consumer sciences (MAT). Accredited by NCATE. *Degree requirements:* Comprehensive exam required, foreign language and thesis not required. *Entrance requirements:* GRE General Test. Application deadline: rolling. Application fee: $35. *Tuition:* $1799 per year full-time, $144 per credit hour (minimum) part-time for state residents; $9069 per year full-time, $1053 per credit hour (minimum) part-time for nonresidents. • Application contact: Kathleen Owen, Assistant to the Dean, 828-227-7398. Fax: 828-227-7480.

Western Kentucky University, College of Education, Department of Consumer and Family Sciences, Bowling Green, KY 42101-3576. Offerings include home economics education (MA Ed). Accredited by NCATE. Admissions temporarily suspended. Department faculty: 3 full-time (all women). *Tuition:* $2460 per year full-time, $133 per credit hour part-time for state residents; $6700 per year full-time, $369 per credit hour part-time for nonresidents. • Dr. Louella Fong, Interim Head, 502-745-4352. Fax: 502-745-2084.

Western Michigan University, College of Education, Department of Family and Consumer Sciences, Program in Family and Consumer Sciences, Kalamazoo, MI 49008. Awards MA. Accredited by NCATE. Students: 33 part-time (32 women); includes 5 minority (4 African Americans, 1 Hispanic), 1 international. 23 applicants, 91% accepted. In 1997, 4 degrees awarded. *Application deadline:* 2/15 (priority date; rolling processing). *Application fee:* $25. *Expenses:* Tuition $154 per credit hour for state residents; $372 per credit hour for nonresidents. Fees $602 per year full-time, $132 per semester part-time. *Financial aid:* Fellowships, research assistantships, teaching assistantships, Federal Work-Study, and career-related internships or fieldwork available. Financial aid application deadline: 2/15; applicants required to submit FAFSA. *Faculty research:* Use of computers in custom designing of personal patterns for the handicapped. • Application contact: Paula J. Boodt, Coordinator, Graduate Admissions and Recruitment, 616-387-2000. E-mail: paulaboodt@wmich.edu.

Winthrop University, College of Education, Program in Family and Consumer Sciences, Rock Hill, SC 29733. Awards MS. Accredited by NCATE. Part-time programs available. Students: 1 (woman) full-time, 1 (woman) part-time. Average age 33. In 1997, 2 degrees awarded. *Degree requirements:* Thesis optional, foreign language not required. *Entrance requirements:* GRE General Test (minimum combined score of 800), MAT (minimum score 40), or NTE, minimum GPA of 3.0, sample of written work. Application deadline: 7/15 (priority date; rolling processing; 12/1 for spring admission). Application fee: $35. *Tuition:* $3928 per year full-time, $164 per credit hour part-time for state residents; $7060 per year full-time, $294 per credit hour part-time for nonresidents. *Financial aid:* Graduate assistantships, graduate scholarships, Federal Work-Study, and career-related internships or fieldwork available. Aid available to part-time students. Financial aid application deadline: 2/1; applicants required to submit FAFSA. • Dr. Richard Ingram, Chairman, 803-323-2151. Fax: 803-323-2585. E-mail: ingramr@winthrop.edu. Application contact: Sharon Johnson, Director of Graduate Studies, 803-323-2204. Fax: 803-323-2292. E-mail: johnsons@winthrop.edu.

Mathematics Education

Adelphi University, School of Education, Program in Secondary Education, Garden City, NY 11530. Offerings include mathematics (MA). *Application deadline:* rolling. *Application fee:* $50. *Expenses:* Tuition $16,000 per year full-time, $485 per credit part-time. Fees $500 per year full-time, $150 per semester part-time. • Director, 516-877-4090. Application contact: Jennifer Spiegel, Associate Director of Graduate Admissions, 516-877-3055.

Alabama State University, School of Graduate Studies, College of Education, Department of Curriculum and Instruction, Program in Secondary Education, Montgomery, AL 36101-0271. Offerings include mathematics education (M Ed). Program faculty: 2 full-time (1 woman). *Degree requirements:* Comprehensive exam required, thesis optional. *Entrance requirements:* GRE General Test, MAT or NTE. Application deadline: 7/15 (rolling processing; 12/15 for spring admission). Application fee: $10. *Expenses:* Tuition $85 per credit hour for state residents; $170 per credit hour for nonresidents. Fees $486 per year. • Dr. Linda Bradford, Coordinator, 334-229-4485. Fax: 334-229-4904. E-mail: lbradford@asunet.alasu.edu. Application contact: Dr. Fred Dauser, Dean of Graduate Studies, 334-229-4276. Fax: 334-229-4928.

Albany State University, School of Education, Program in Mathematics Education, Albany, GA 31705-2717. Awards M Ed. Accredited by NCATE. Faculty: 5. Students: 5. In 1997, 5 degrees awarded. *Degree requirements:* Comprehensive exam. *Entrance requirements:* GRE General Test (minimum combined score of 800), MAT (minimum score 44) or NTE (minimum score 550). Application deadline: 9/1. Application fee: $10. *Financial aid:* Application deadline 4/1. • Connie Leggett, Chair, 912-430-4886. Fax: 912-430-7895. E-mail: cleggett@fld94.alsnet.peachnet.edu.

Alfred University, Graduate School, Division of Education, Alfred, NY 14802-1205. Offerings include secondary education (MS Ed), with options in biology education, chemistry education, earth science education, English education, mathematics education, physics education, social studies education. Division faculty: 45 full-time (12 women). *Degree requirements:* Thesis required (for some programs), foreign language not required. *Entrance requirements:* TOEFL. Application deadline: rolling. Application fee: $50. *Expenses:* Tuition $20,376 per year full-time, $390 per credit hour (minimum) part-time. Fees $546 per year. • Dr. Katherine D. Wiesendanger, Chair, 607-871-2219. E-mail: fwiesendange@bigvax.alfred.edu. Application contact: Cathleen R. Johnson, Assistant Director of Admissions, 607-871-2141. Fax: 607-871-2198. E-mail: johnsonc@bigvax.alfred.edu.

Allentown College of St. Francis de Sales, Graduate Division, Program in Education, Center Valley, PA 18034-9568. Offerings include mathematics (M Ed). Program faculty: 18 full-time (4 women), 25 part-time (6 women). *Degree requirements:* Capstone Course or Project required, foreign language not required. *Average time to degree:* master's–3 years part-time. *Entrance requirements:* Teaching certificate. Application deadline: 8/24 (priority date; rolling processing). Application fee: $35. *Tuition:* $285 per credit. • Dr. Irene Pompetti-Szul, Director, 610-282-1100 Ext. 1401. Fax: 610-282-2254.

American International College, School of Continuing Education and Graduate Studies, School of Psychology and Education, Department of Education, Springfield, MA 01109-3189. Offerings include mathematics (MAT). Department faculty: 5 full-time (3 women), 15 part-time (9 women). *Application fee:* $15 ($25 for international students). *Expenses:* Tuition $363 per credit hour. Fees $25 per semester. • C. Gerald Weaver, Dean, School of Psychology and Education, 413-747-6338.

American University, Department of Mathematics and Statistics and School of Education, Program in Mathematics Education, Washington, DC 20016-8001. Awards PhD. Part-time and evening/weekend programs available. Faculty: 25 full-time (10 women), 2 part-time (0 women). Students: 3 full-time (1 woman), 14 part-time (9 women); includes 4 minority (all African Americans), 2 international. 11 applicants, 82% accepted. In 1997, 2 degrees awarded. *Degree requirements:* 2 foreign languages (computer language can substitute for one), dissertation, comprehensive exam. *Entrance requirements:* Master's degree in education or mathematics. Application deadline: 2/1 (10/1 for spring admission). Application fee: $50. *Expenses:* Tuition $687 per credit hour. Fees $180 per year full-time, $110 per year part-time. *Financial aid:* Fellowships, teaching assistantships available. Financial aid application deadline: 2/1. • Dr. Virginia Stallings, Chair, Department of Mathematics and Statistics, 202-885-3120. Fax: 202-885-3155.

Arkansas Tech University, School of Education, Department of Curriculum and Instruction, Russellville, AR 72801-2222. Offerings include mathematics (M Ed). Accredited by NCATE. *Application deadline:* 3/1 (priority date; rolling processing; 10/1 for spring admission). *Application fee:* $0 ($30 for international students). *Expenses:* Tuition $98 per credit hour for state residents; $196 per credit hour for nonresidents. Fees $30 per semester. • Head, 501-968-0290. Fax: 501-964-0811.

Auburn University, College of Education, Department of Curriculum and Teaching, Auburn University, AL 36849-0001. Offerings include secondary education (M Ed, MS, PhD, Ed S), with options in English language arts, mathematics, science, social studies. Accredited by NCATE. Department faculty: 20 full-time (11 women). *Degree requirements:* For master's, thesis (MS) required, foreign language not required; for doctorate, dissertation required, foreign language not required; for Ed S, field project required, foreign language and thesis not required. *Entrance requirements:* For master's and Ed S, GRE General Test; for doctorate, GRE General Test (minimum score 450 on each section, 1000 combined). Application deadline: 9/1 (rolling processing; 3/1 for spring admission). Application fee: $25 ($50 for international students). *Expenses:* Tuition $2760 per year full-time, $76 per credit hour part-time for state residents; $8280 per year full-time, $228 per credit hour part-time for nonresidents. Fees $30 per year full-time, $160 per quarter part-time for state residents; $30 per year full-time, $480 per quarter part-time for nonresidents. • Dr. Andrew M. Weaver, Head, 334-844-4434. E-mail: weaveam@mail.auburn.edu. Application contact: Dr. John F. Pritchett, Dean of the Graduate School, 334-844-4700.

Ball State University, College of Sciences and Humanities, Department of Mathematical Sciences, Program in Mathematics, 2000 University Avenue, Muncie, IN 47306-1099. Offerings include mathematics education (MAE). Accredited by NCATE. *Application fee:* $15 ($25 for international students). *Expenses:* Tuition $3454 per year full-time, $518 per semester (minimum) part-time for state residents; $9316 per year full-time, $1221 per semester (minimum) part-time for nonresidents. Fees $242 per year full-time, $18 per semester (minimum) part-time. • Charles Parish, Director, 765-285-8645.

Bank Street College of Education, Program in Educational Leadership, 610 West 112th Street, New York, NY 10025-1120. Offerings include leadership in mathematics education (MS Ed). MS Ed (supervision and administration in the visual arts) offered jointly with Parsons School of Design, New School of Social Research. *Application deadline:* 3/1 (priority date; rolling processing; 11/1 for spring admission). *Application fee:* $50. *Tuition:* $560 per credit. • Dr. Frank Pignatelli, Chairperson, 212-875-4710. Application contact: Ann Morgan, Director of Admissions, 212-875-4404. Fax: 212-875-4678. E-mail: amorgan@bnkst.edu.

Beaver College, Department of Education, Glenside, PA 19038-3295. Offerings include mathematics education (MA Ed, M Ed, CAS). *Application fee:* $35. *Expenses:* Tuition $6570 per year full-time, $365 per credit part-time. Fees $35 per year.

Bemidji State University, Division of Social and Natural Sciences, Field of Mathematics, Bemidji, MN 56601-2699. Awards MS Ed. Accredited by NCATE. Part-time programs available. Students: 1 full-time (0 women), 1 part-time (0 women). Average age 24. In 1997, 5 degrees awarded. *Application deadline:* 5/1. *Application fee:* $20. *Expenses:* Tuition $128 per credit for state residents; $134 per credit (minimum) for nonresidents. Fees $517 per year full-time, $35 per credit (minimum) part-time. *Financial aid:* Teaching assistantships, Federal Work-Study, and career-related internships or fieldwork available. Aid available to part-time students. Financial aid application deadline: 5/1. • Dr. James L. Richards, Chair, 218-755-2840. E-mail: jlrich@vax1.bemidji.msus.edu.

Boise State University, College of Education, Programs in Teacher Education, Program in Mathematics Education, Boise, ID 83725-0399. Awards MS. Accredited by NCATE. Part-time programs available. Faculty: 27 full-time (4 women). Students: 0. 0 applicants. *Degree requirements:* Thesis optional. *Application deadline:* 7/26 (priority date; rolling processing; 11/29 for spring admission). *Application fee:* $20 ($30 for international students). Electronic applications accepted. *Tuition:* $3020 per year full-time, $135 per credit part-time for state residents; $8900 per year full-time, $135 per credit part-time for nonresidents. *Financial aid:* Federal Work-Study, institutionally sponsored loans, and career-related internships or fieldwork available. Aid available to part-time students. Financial aid application deadline: 3/1. • Dr. Steve Grantham, Chair, Department of Mathematics, 208-385-1172. Fax: 208-385-1356.

Boston College, Graduate School of Education, Department of Teacher Education/Special Education and Curriculum and Instruction, Program in Secondary Education, Chestnut Hill, MA 02167-9991. Offerings include mathematics (MST). Accredited by NCATE. *Application deadline:* 3/15 (11/15 for spring admission). *Application fee:* $40. *Expenses:* Tuition $626 per semester hour. Fees $80 per year (minimum) full-time, $30 per semester part-time. • Application contact: Arline Riordan, Graduate Admissions Director, 617-552-4214. Fax: 617-552-0812. E-mail: riordana@bc.edu.

Boston University, School of Education, Department of Curriculum and Teaching, Program in Mathematics Education, Boston, MA 02215. Awards Ed M, MAT, Ed D, CAGS. Students: 10 full-time (9 women), 5 part-time (all women); includes 1 minority (Hispanic). Average age 27. In 1997, 9 master's, 1 doctorate, 1 CAGS awarded. *Degree requirements:* For doctorate, dissertation, comprehensive exam required, foreign language not required; for CAGS, comprehensive exam required, foreign language and thesis not required. *Entrance requirements:* For master's and CAGS, GRE or MAT, TOEFL; for doctorate, GRE General Test or MAT, TOEFL. Application deadline: 2/15 (priority date; rolling processing). Application fee: $50. *Expenses:* Tuition $22,830 per year full-time, $713 per credit part-time. Fees $218 per year full-time, $40 per semester part-time. *Financial aid:* Application deadline 3/30. *Faculty research:* Learning theory, impact of computers, problem solving. • Dr. Carol Findell, Coordinator, 617-353-4226. E-mail: cfindell@bu.edu.

Bowling Green State University, College of Arts and Sciences, Department of Mathematics and Statistics, Bowling Green, OH 43403. Offerings include mathematics supervision (Ed S). Department faculty: 22 full-time (1 woman), 7 part-time (0 women). *Degree requirements:* Internship required, foreign language and thesis not required. *Application deadline:* 8/7. *Application fee:* $30. Electronic applications accepted. *Tuition:* $6070 per year full-time, $284 per credit hour part-time for state residents; $11,358 per year full-time, $536 per credit hour part-time for nonresidents. • Dr. John Hayden, Chair, 419-372-2636. Application contact: Dr. Neal Carothers, Graduate Coordinator, 419-372-8317.

Bowling Green State University, College of Education and Allied Professions, Department of Educational Administration and Supervision, Bowling Green, OH 43403. Offerings include math supervision (Ed S). Accredited by NCATE. Department faculty: 5 full-time (2 women), 5 part-time (2 women). *Degree requirements:* Field experience or internship required, foreign language and thesis not required. *Entrance requirements:* GRE General Test. Application deadline: rolling. Application fee: $30. *Tuition:* $6070 per year full-time, $284 per credit hour part-time for state residents; $11,358 per year full-time, $536 per credit hour part-time for nonresidents. • Dr. Eugene Sanders, Chair, 419-372-7377.

Bridgewater State College, School of Arts and Sciences, Department of Mathematics and Computer Science, Bridgewater, MA 02325-0001. Offerings include mathematics (MAT). Accredited by NCATE. *Application deadline:* 4/1 (10/1 for spring admission). *Application fee:* $25. *Expenses:* Tuition $1675 per year full-time, $70 per credit part-time for state residents; $6450 per year full-time, $269 per credit part-time for nonresidents. Fees $1588 per year full-time, $66 per credit hour part-time for state residents; $1588 per year full-time, $66 per credit part-time for nonresidents. • Application contact: Graduate School, 508-697-1300.

Brooklyn College of the City University of New York, Department of Mathematics, 2900 Bedford Avenue, Brooklyn, NY 11210-2889. Offerings include secondary mathematics education (MA). Department faculty: 21 full-time, 17 part-time, 29.5 FTE. *Degree requirements:* Thesis or alternative, comprehensive exam (mathematics) required, foreign language not required. *Entrance requirements:* TOEFL (minimum score 500), minimum GPA of 3.0. Application deadline: 3/1 (11/1 for spring admission). Application fee: $40. *Expenses:* Tuition $4350 per year full-time, $185 per credit part-time for state residents; $7600 per year full-time, $320 per credit part-time for nonresidents. Fees $500 per year for state residents; $806 per year for nonresidents. • Dr. George Shapiro, Chairperson, 718-951-5246. Application contact: Dr. Kishore Marathe, Graduate Deputy, 718-951-5832. E-mail: kbm@bklyn.edu.

Brooklyn College of the City University of New York, School of Education, Division of Secondary Education, 2900 Bedford Avenue, Brooklyn, NY 11210-2889. Offerings include mathematics education (MA). *Application deadline:* 3/1 (11/1 for spring admission). *Application fee:* $40. *Expenses:* Tuition $4350 per year full-time, $185 per credit part-time for state residents; $7600 per year full-time, $320 per credit part-time for nonresidents. Fees $500 per year for state residents; $806 per year for nonresidents. • Dr. Peter Taubman, Coordinator, 718-951-5218. Fax: 718-951-4816. E-mail: ptaubman@brooklyn.cuny.edu.

Brooklyn College of the City University of New York, School of Education, Division of Elementary School Education, Program in Elementary Mathematics Education, 2900 Bedford Avenue, Brooklyn, NY 11210-2889. Awards MS Ed. Part-time and evening/weekend programs available. Students: 1 full-time (0 women), 60 part-time (50 women); includes 22 minority (17 African Americans, 2 Asian Americans, 3 Hispanics). 40 applicants, 95% accepted. In 1997, 23 degrees awarded. *Average time to degree:* master's–2.5 years part-time. *Entrance requirements:* TOEFL (minimum score 500), interview, previous course work in education, writing sample. Application deadline: 3/1 (11/1 for spring admission). Application fee: $40. *Expenses:* Tuition $4350 per year full-time, $185 per credit part-time for state residents; $7600 per year full-time, $320 per credit part-time for nonresidents. Fees $500 per year for state residents; $806 per year for nonresidents. *Financial aid:* Institutionally sponsored loans available. Aid available to part-time students. Financial aid application deadline: 5/1; applicants required to submit FAFSA. *Faculty research:* Geometric thinking, mastery of basic facts, problem-solving strategies. • Dr. David Fuys, Adviser, 718-951-5937. Fax: 718-951-4816. E-mail: djfbc@cunyvm.cuny.edu.

California State University, Fullerton, School of Natural Science and Mathematics, Department of Mathematics, PO Box 34080, Fullerton, CA 92834-9480. Offerings include mathematics for secondary school teachers (MA). Department faculty: 24 full-time (3 women), 39 part-time, 37.7 FTE. *Degree requirements:* Comprehensive exam or project required, foreign language not required. *Entrance requirements:* Minimum GPA of 2.5 in last 60 units, major in mathematics or related field. Application fee: $55. *Expenses:* Tuition $0 for state residents; $246 per unit for nonresidents. Fees $1947 per year full-time, $1281 per year part-time. • Dr. James Friel, Chair, 714-278-3631.

California University of Pennsylvania, School of Science and Technology, Department of Mathematics and Computer Sciences, 250 University Avenue, California, PA 15419-1394. Offerings include mathematics (M Ed). Department faculty: 9 part-time (2 women). *Degree requirements:* Comprehensive exam required, thesis optional, foreign language not required. *Entrance requirements:* TOEFL (minimum score 550), MAT (minimum score 35) or minimum GPA of 2.5, teaching certificate (M Ed). Application deadline: rolling. Application fee: $25. *Expenses:* Tuition $3468 per year full-time, $193 per credit part-time for state residents; $6236 per year full-time, $346 per credit part-time for nonresidents. Fees $886 per year full-time, $153 per semester (minimum) part-time. • Dr. Andrew Machusko, Chairperson, 724-938-4078.

Campbell University, School of Education, Buies Creek, NC 27506. Offerings include mathematics education (M Ed). Accredited by NCATE. School faculty: 8 full-time (6 women), 6 part-time (0 women). *Application deadline:* 8/1 (priority date; rolling processing; 1/2 for spring admission). *Application fee:* $25. *Tuition:* $168 per credit hour (minimum). • Dr. Margaret Giesbrecht, Dean, 910-893-1630. Fax: 910-893-1999. E-mail: giesbrec@mailcenter.campbell.edu. Application contact: James S. Farthing, Director of Graduate Admissions, 910-893-1200 Ext. 1318. Fax: 910-893-1288.

Catawba College, Program in Education, Salisbury, NC 28144-2488. Offerings include mathematics (M Ed). Accredited by NCATE. Program faculty: 5 full-time (4 women), 2 part-time (both women). *Degree requirements:* Comprehensive written exams required, thesis not required. *Average time to degree:* master's–4 years part-time. *Entrance requirements:* NTE, PRAXIS. Application deadline: 8/1 (priority date; rolling processing). Application fee: $15. *Tuition:* $90 per semester hour. • Dr. Shirley Haworth, Chair, 704-637-4461. Fax: 704-637-4732.

Central Missouri State University, College of Arts and Sciences, Department of Mathematics and Computer Sciences, Warrensburg, MO 64093. Offerings include mathematics education (MSE). Accredited by NCATE. Department faculty: 23 full-time. *Application deadline:* 6/30 (priority date; rolling processing). *Application fee:* $25 ($50 for international students). *Tuition:* $3288 per year full-time, $137 per credit hour part-time for state residents; $5928 per year full-time, $274 per credit hour part-time for nonresidents. • Dr. Edward W. Davenport, Chair, 660-543-4931. Fax: 660-543-8006. E-mail: ewd4931@cmsu2.cmsu.edu.

Christopher Newport University, Graduate Studies, Department of Education, 1 University Place, Newport News, VA 23606-2998. Offerings include teaching mathematics (MAT), with options in elementary mathematics education, high school teaching, middle school teaching. Department faculty: 25 full-time (12 women), 1 part-time (0 women). *Degree requirements:* Thesis or alternative, comprehensive exam required, foreign language not required. *Average time to degree:* master's–3.5 years part-time. *Entrance requirements:* GRE, minimum GPA of 3.0. Application deadline: 8/1 (priority date; rolling processing; 12/15 for spring admission). Application fee: $40. *Expenses:* Tuition $3474 per year full-time, $145 per credit hour part-time for state residents; $8424 per year full-time, $351 per credit hour part-time for nonresidents. Fees $40 per year. • Dr. Marsha Sprague, Coordinator, 757-594-7973. Fax: 757-594-7862. E-mail: msprague@cnu.edu. Application contact: Graduate Admissions, 800-333-4268. Fax: 757-594-7333. E-mail: admit@cnu.edu.

The Citadel, The Military College of South Carolina, Department of Mathematics and Computer Science, Charleston, SC 29409. Offers program in mathematics education (MAE). One or more programs accredited by NCATE. Faculty: 3 full-time (1 woman). Students: 7 part-time (5 women). In 1997, 3 degrees awarded. *Entrance requirements:* GRE, MAT. Application deadline: rolling. Application fee: $25. *Expenses:* Tuition $130 per credit hour for state residents; $260 per credit hour for nonresidents. Fees $30 per semester. • Dr. Stephen Comer, Head, 803-953-5048.

City College of the City University of New York, Graduate School, School of Education, Department of Secondary and Continuing Education, Convent Avenue at 138th Street, New York, NY 10031-6977. Offerings include mathematics education (MA). *Degree requirements:* Thesis required, foreign language not required. *Entrance requirements:* TOEFL (minimum score 500). Application fee: $40. *Expenses:* Tuition $4350 per year full-time, $185 per credit part-time for state residents; $7600 per year full-time, $320 per credit part-time for nonresidents. Fees $41 per year. • Hope Hartman, Chair, 212-650-7954.

Claremont Graduate University, Department of Education, Claremont, CA 91711-6163. Offerings include mathematics education (MA). PhD offered jointly with San Diego State University; MA (mathematics education) offered jointly with the Department of Mathematics. Department faculty: 13 full-time (6 women), 13 part-time (10 women). *Degree requirements:* Thesis or alternative. *Entrance requirements:* GRE General Test. Application deadline: 2/15 (priority date; rolling processing). Application fee: $40. Electronic applications accepted. *Expenses:* Tuition $20,250 per year full-time, $913 per unit part-time. Fees $130 per year. • David Drew, Chair, 909-621-8075. Application contact: Ethel Rogers, Associate Director, 909-621-8317. Fax: 909-621-8734. E-mail: educ@cgu.edu.

Claremont Graduate University, Department of Mathematics, Claremont, CA 91711-6163. Offerings include mathematics education (MA). PhD (engineering mathematics) offered jointly with California State University, Long Beach. MA (mathematics education) offered jointly with the Department of Education. MS (financial engineering) offered jointly with the Peter F. Drucker Graduate Management Center. Department faculty: 5 full-time (0 women), 2 part-time (0 women). *Application deadline:* 2/15 (priority date; rolling processing). *Application fee:* $40. Electronic applications accepted. *Expenses:* Tuition $20,250 per year full-time, $913 per unit part-time. Fees $130 per year. • Robert Williamson, Chair, 909-621-8080. Application contact: Mary Solberg, Program Secretary, 909-621-8080. Fax: 909-621-8390. E-mail: math@cgu.edu.

Clarion University of Pennsylvania, College of Arts and Sciences, Department of Mathematics, Clarion, PA 16214. Awards M Ed. Students: 0. 0 applicants. *Entrance requirements:* Minimum QPA of 2.75. Application deadline: 8/1 (priority date; rolling processing). Application fee: $25. *Expenses:* Tuition $3468 per year full-time, $193 per credit hour part-time for state residents; $6236 per year full-time, $346 per credit hour part-time for nonresidents. Fees $921 per year full-time, $90 per credit hour part-time for state residents; $921 per year full-time, $89 per credit hour part-time for nonresidents. *Financial aid:* Research assistantships available. Aid available to part-time students. Financial aid application deadline: 5/1. • Dr. Benjamin Freed, Chairman, 814-226-2592.

Clemson University, College of Health, Education, and Human Development, Department of Curriculum and Instruction, Program in Secondary Education, Clemson, SC 29634. Offerings include mathematics (M Ed). Accredited by NCATE. *Entrance requirements:* TOEFL, teaching certificate. Application deadline: 6/1. Application fee: $35. *Expenses:* Tuition $3154 per year full-time, $130 per credit hour part-time for state residents; $6452 per year full-time, $264 per credit hour part-time for nonresidents. Fees $190 per year. • Dr. Robert Green, Chair, Department of Curriculum and Instruction, 864-656-5108. Fax: 864-656-1322. E-mail: rpgreen@clemson.edu.

The Colorado College, Department of Education, Program in Secondary Education, Colorado Springs, CO 80903-3294. Offerings include mathematics teaching (MAT). Program faculty: 2 full-time (1 woman), 3 part-time (2 women). *Degree requirements:* Thesis, internship required, foreign language not required. *Entrance requirements:* GRE Subject Test (score in 50th percentile or higher), Program for Licensing Assessments for Colorado Educators Basic Skills Test. Application deadline: 3/1. Application fee: $40. • Paul J. Kuerbis, Director, 719-389-6726. Application contact: Marsha Unruh, Educational Services Coordinator, 719-389-6472. Fax: 719-389-6473.

Columbus State University, College of Education, Department of Curriculum and Instruction, Columbus, GA 31907-5645. Offerings include secondary education (M Ed, Ed S), with options in biology (M Ed), English (M Ed, Ed S), general science (M Ed), history (M Ed), mathematics (M Ed, Ed S), political science (M Ed), science/biology (Ed S), social science (M Ed, Ed S). Accredited by NCATE. Ed S (mathematics) offered jointly with Georgia Southwestern University. M Ed (political science) being phased out; applicants no longer accepted. *Degree requirements:* For master's, exit exam required, foreign language and thesis not required; for Ed S, thesis or alternative required, foreign language not required. *Entrance requirements:* For master's, GRE General Test (minimum combined score of 800), MAT (minimum score 44); for Ed S, GRE General Test (minimum combined score of 900), MAT (minimum score 44). Application deadline: 7/10 (priority date; rolling processing; 10/23 for spring admission). Application fee: $20. *Tuition:* $1718 per year full-time, $151 per semester hour part-time for state residents; $6218 per year full-time, $401 per semester hour part-time for nonresidents. • Dr. David Shoemaker, Chair, 706-568-2255. Fax: 706-568-3134. E-mail: shoemaker_david@colstate.edu. Application contact: Katie Thornton, Graduate Admissions, 706-568-2279. Fax: 706-568-2462. E-mail: thornton_katie@colstate.edu.

Concordia University, Program in Mathematics/Computer Science Education, River Forest, IL 60305-1499. Awards MA, CAS. Part-time and evening/weekend programs available. Faculty: 8 full-time (3 women), 4 part-time (1 woman). Students: 15 (9 women); includes 2 minority (1 African American, 1 Asian American), 3 international. In 1997, 3 master's awarded. *Degree requirements:* For master's, comprehensive exam required, thesis optional, foreign language not required; for CAS, thesis, final project required, foreign language not required. *Entrance requirements:* For master's, minimum GPA of 2.9; for CAS, master's degree. Application deadline: rolling. Application fee: $0. *Tuition:* $372 per semester hour. *Financial aid:* Research assistantships, institutionally sponsored loans available. Aid available to part-time students. *Faculty research:* Technology used in parochial high schools in teaching math. • Dr. Manfred Boos, Coordinator, 708-209-3088. Application contact: Mary Betancourt, Admissions Secretary, 708-209-4093. Fax: 708-209-3454. E-mail: crfdngrad@curf.edu.

Concordia University, Faculty of Arts and Science, Department of Mathematics and Statistics, Montréal, PQ H3G 1M8, Canada. Offerings include teaching of mathematics (MTM, Diploma). *Entrance requirements:* For Diploma, Quebec teaching certificate. Application deadline: 4/1. Application fee: $30. *Expenses:* Tuition $56 per credit (minimum) for Canadian residents; $249 per credit (minimum) for nonresidents. Fees $158 per year full-time, $117 per year (minimum) part-time. • Dr. J. Hillel, Chair, 514-848-3234. Application contact: Dr. Ronald Stern, Director, 514-848-3250. Fax: 514-848-2831.

Connecticut College, Department of Mathematics, New London, CT 06320-4196. Awards MAT. Part-time programs available. *Entrance requirements:* MAT. Application deadline: 2/2. Application fee: $35.

Directory: Mathematics Education

Cornell University, Graduate Fields of Agriculture and Life Sciences, Field of Education, Ithaca, NY 14853-0001. Offerings include mathematics (MAT, MS). Faculty: 26 full-time. *Application deadline:* 5/1. *Application fee:* $65. Electronic applications accepted. • Director of Graduate Studies, 607-255-4278. Application contact: Graduate Field Assistant, 607-255-4278. E-mail: edgrfld@cornell.edu.

Delta State University, School of Arts and Sciences, Department of Mathematics, Cleveland, MS 38733-0001. Offers program in mathematics education (M Ed). Part-time programs available. Faculty: 3 full-time (1 woman), 1 (woman) part-time, 3.75 FTE. Students: 3 part-time (all women). Average age 34. 0 applicants. In 1997, 2 degrees awarded. *Degree requirements:* Thesis or alternative required, foreign language not required. *Entrance requirements:* GRE General Test (minimum combined score of 800) or MAT (minimum score 34). Application deadline: 8/1 (priority date; rolling processing). Application fee: $0. *Tuition:* $2596 per year full-time, $121 per semester hour part-time for state residents; $5546 per year full-time, $285 per semester hour part-time for nonresidents. *Financial aid:* Institutionally sponsored loans and career-related internships or fieldwork available. Aid available to part-time students. Financial aid application deadline: 6/1. • Dr. Rose Strahan, Chairperson, 601-846-4505. Fax: 601-846-4498. E-mail: rstrahan@dsu.deltast.edu. Application contact: Dr. John Thornell, Dean of Graduate Studies and Continuing Education, 601-846-4310. Fax: 601-846-4016.

DePaul University, College of Liberal Arts and Sciences, Department of Mathematical Sciences, Program in Mathematics Education, Chicago, IL 60604-2287. Awards MA. Students: 35 full-time (31 women), 27 part-time (18 women); includes 10 minority (7 African Americans, 3 Asian Americans). Average age 33. 24 applicants, 100% accepted. In 1997, 19 degrees awarded. *Degree requirements:* Computer language required, foreign language and thesis not required. *Application deadline:* rolling. *Application fee:* $25. *Expenses:* Tuition $320 per credit hour. Fees $30 per year. *Financial aid:* Full and partial tuition waivers available. • Dr. Jerry Goldman, Director, 312-362-8254.

Eastern Connecticut State University, School of Education and Professional Studies/ Graduate Division, Program in Mathematics Education, Willimantic, CT 06226-2295. Awards MS. Faculty: 1 full-time (0 women), 2 part-time (both women). Students: 0. *Degree requirements:* Comprehensive exam or thesis required, foreign language not required. *Entrance requirements:* Minimum GPA of 2.7. Application fee: $40. *Expenses:* Tuition $2632 per year full-time, $175 per credit hour part-time for state residents; $7220 per year full-time, $175 per credit hour part-time for nonresidents. Fees $1851 per year full-time, $20 per semester part-time for state residents; $2748 per year full-time, $20 per semester part-time for nonresidents. *Financial aid:* Application deadline 3/15. • Hari Koirala, Coordinator, 860-465-4556. E-mail: koiralah@ecsu.ctstateu.edu. Application contact: Edith Mavor, Graduate Division Director, 860-465-4543. E-mail: mavor@ecsuc.ctstateu.edu.

Eastern Illinois University, College of Sciences, Department of Mathematics, 600 Lincoln Avenue, Charleston, IL 61920-3099. Offerings include mathematics education (MA). Department faculty: 30 full-time (6 women). *Entrance requirements:* GRE General Test. Application deadline: 7/31 (priority date; rolling processing). Application fee: $25. *Expenses:* Tuition $3459 per year full-time, $96 per semester hour part-time for state residents; $10,377 per year full-time, $288 per semester hour part-time for nonresidents. Fees $1566 per year full-time, $37 per semester hour part-time. • Dr. Claire E. Krukenberg, Chair, 217-581-2028. E-mail: cfcek@eiu.edu. Application contact: Dr. Duane Broline, Coordinator, 217-581-3217. Fax: 217-581-6284.

Eastern Kentucky University, College of Education, Department of Curriculum and Instruction, Program in Secondary and Higher Education, Richmond, KY 40475-3101. Offerings include mathematical sciences education (MA Ed). Accredited by NCATE. *Entrance requirements:* GRE General Test, minimum GPA of 2.5. Application fee: $0. *Tuition:* $2390 per year full-time, $133 per credit hour part-time for state residents; $6630 per year full-time, $365 per credit hour part-time for nonresidents. • Dr. Imogene Ramsey, Chair, Department of Curriculum and Instruction, 606-622-2154.

Eastern Washington University, College of Science, Mathematics and Technology, Department of Mathematics, Cheney, WA 99004-2431. Awards M Ed, MS. Accredited by NCATE. Part-time programs available. Faculty: 16 full-time (3 women). Students: 5 full-time (2 women), 6 part-time (2 women). 5 applicants, 20% accepted. In 1997, 4 degrees awarded. *Degree requirements:* Thesis (for some programs), comprehensive oral exam. *Entrance requirements:* GRE General Test, departmental qualifying exam, minimum GPA of 3.0. Application deadline: 4/1 (priority date; rolling processing; 1/15 for spring admission). Application fee: $35. *Tuition:* $4200 per year full-time, $140 per credit part-time for state residents; $12,780 per year full-time, $415 per credit part-time for nonresidents. *Financial aid:* Teaching assistantships, Federal Work-Study, institutionally sponsored loans available. Financial aid application deadline: 2/1. • Dr. Sherry Renga, Chair, 509-359-6225. Application contact: Dr. Yves Nievergelt, Adviser, 509-359-2219.

Edinboro University of Pennsylvania, School of Education, Department of Elementary Education, Program in Elementary Education, Edinboro, PA 16444. Offerings include mathematics (M Ed). *Degree requirements:* Thesis or alternative required, foreign language not required. *Entrance requirements:* GRE or MAT (score in 30th percentile or higher). Application deadline: rolling. Application fee: $25. *Expenses:* Tuition $3468 per year full-time, $193 per credit part-time for state residents; $6236 per year full-time, $346 per credit part-time for nonresidents. Fees $898 per year full-time, $50 per semester (minimum) part-time. • Application contact: Dr. Philip Kerstetter, Dean of Graduate Studies, 814-732-2856. Fax: 814-732-2611. E-mail: kerstetter@edinboro.edu.

Fairleigh Dickinson University, Teaneck–Hackensack Campus, University College: Arts, Sciences, and Professional Studies, Peter Sammartino School of Education, Program in Mathematics Education, 1000 River Road, Teaneck, NJ 07666-1914. Awards MAT. Faculty: 11 full-time (8 women), 27 part-time (10 women). *Degree requirements:* Research project required, thesis not required. *Application deadline:* rolling. *Application fee:* $35. *Expenses:* Tuition $522 per credit. Fees $302 per year full-time, $138 per year part-time. *Faculty research:* Mathematics for students with learning disabilities, gender issues in education, social problem-solving and conflict resolution in the classroom, multicultural education in the elementary classroom, problems encountered by international students in college programs. • Dr. Eloise Forster, Interim Director, Peter Sammartino School of Education, 201-692-2834. Fax: 201-692-2603.

Fayetteville State University, Programs in Educational Leadership and Secondary Education, 1200 Murchison Road, Fayetteville, NC 28301-4298. Offerings include mathematics (MAT). Accredited by NCATE. *Application deadline:* 8/1 (rolling processing; 12/15 for spring admission). *Application fee:* $20. *Tuition:* $1498 per year full-time, $327 per semester (minimum) part-time for state residents; $8768 per year full-time, $2144 per semester (minimum) part-time for nonresidents.

Fitchburg State College, Programs in Teaching Mathematics (Secondary Level), Fitchburg, MA 01420-2697. Awards MAT. Accredited by NCATE. Program new for fall 1998. Part-time and evening/weekend programs available. *Entrance requirements:* GRE General Test or MAT. Application deadline: rolling. Application fee: $10. *Expenses:* Tuition $147 per credit. Fees $55 per semester. *Financial aid:* Graduate assistantships, Federal Work-Study available. Aid available to part-time students. Financial aid application deadline: 3/30; applicants required to submit FAFSA. • Dr. Gerald Higdon, Chair, 978-665-3271. Fax: 978-665-3658. E-mail: dgce@fsc.edu. Application contact: James DuPont, Director of Admissions, 978-665-3144. Fax: 978-665-4540. E-mail: admissions@fsc.edu.

Florida Institute of Technology, College of Science and Liberal Arts, Department of Science Education, Melbourne, FL 32901-6975. Offerings include mathematics education (MSE, PhD, Ed S). Terminal master's awarded for partial completion of doctoral program. Department faculty: 4 full-time (1 woman), 2 part-time (both women). *Degree requirements:* For master's, oral comprehensive exam required, thesis optional, foreign language not required; for Ed S, comprehensive exam required, foreign language and thesis not required. *Entrance requirements:* For master's and Ed S, minimum GPA of 3.0. Application deadline: rolling. Application fee: $50. *Tuition:* $550 per credit hour. • Dr. Robert H. Fronk, Head, 407-674-8126. Fax: 407-674-7598. E-mail: fronk@fit.edu. Application contact: Carolyn P. Farrior, Associate Dean of Graduate Admissions, 407-674-7118. Fax: 407-723-9468. E-mail: cfarrior@fit.edu.

Florida International University, College of Education, Department of Subject Specializations, Program in Mathematics Education, Miami, FL 33199. Awards MS. Accredited by NCATE. Part-time and evening/weekend programs available. Students: 2 full-time (0 women), 8 part-time (6 women); includes 6 minority (1 African American, 5 Hispanics), 1 international. Average age 20. 7 applicants, 29% accepted. In 1997, 8 degrees awarded. *Entrance requirements:* GRE General Test (minimum combined score of 1000) or minimum GPA of 3.0. Application deadline: 4/1 (priority date; rolling processing; 10/1 for spring admission). Application fee: $20. *Expenses:* Tuition $138 per credit hour for state residents; $482 per credit hour for nonresidents. Fees $46 per semester. *Faculty research:* Problem solving, heuristics, microcomputers. • Dr. Dean Hauenstein, Chairperson, Department of Subject Specializations, 305-348-2005. Fax: 305-348-2086.

Florida State University, College of Education, Department of Curriculum and Instruction, Program in Mathematics Education, Tallahassee, FL 32306. Awards MS, PhD, Ed S. Part-time programs available. Postbaccalaureate distance learning degree programs offered. Faculty: 4 full-time (1 woman), 1 (woman) part-time. Students: 21 full-time (10 women), 68 part-time (56 women); includes 45 minority (23 African Americans, 8 Asian Americans, 13 Hispanics, 1 Native American). 31 applicants, 100% accepted. In 1997, 11 master's, 3 doctorates awarded. *Degree requirements:* For master's and Ed S, comprehensive exam required, thesis optional; for doctorate, dissertation, comprehensive exam. *Entrance requirements:* GRE General Test (minimum combined score of 1000), minimum GPA of 3.0. Application deadline: 7/1 (priority date; rolling processing; 11/1 for spring admission). Application fee: $20. *Tuition:* $139 per credit hour for state residents; $482 per credit hour for nonresidents. *Financial aid:* Fellowships, research assistantships, teaching assistantships, and career-related internships or fieldwork available. • Dr. David Foulk, Chair, Department of Curriculum and Instruction, 850-644-6553. E-mail: foulk@mail.coe.fsu.edu. Application contact: Admissions Secretary, 850-644-6553. Fax: 850-644-1880.

Fort Hays State University, College of Arts and Sciences, Department of Mathematics and Computer Science, Hays, KS 67601-4099. Offerings include mathematics (MAT). Accredited by NCATE. Department faculty: 9 full-time (1 woman). *Degree requirements:* Thesis or alternative required, foreign language not required. *Application deadline:* 7/1 (priority date; rolling processing). *Application fee:* $25 ($35 for international students). *Tuition:* $94 per credit hour for state residents, $249 per credit hour for nonresidents. • Dr. Ronald Sandstrom, Chair, 785-628-4240.

Framingham State College, Graduate Programs, Program in Mathematics, Framingham, MA 01701-9101. Awards M Ed. Faculty: 3 full-time. Students: 3 full-time, 5 part-time. In 1997, 2 degrees awarded. *Entrance requirements:* GRE General Test, minimum GPA of 3.0. *Tuition:* $4184 per year full-time, $523 per course part-time for state residents; $4848 per year full-time, $606 per course part-time for nonresidents. • Dr. Walter Czarnec, Chair, 508-626-4500. Application contact: Graduate Office, 508-626-4550.

Fresno Pacific University, Graduate School, Programs in Education, Division of Mathematics/ Science/Computer Education, Program in Integrated Mathematics/Science Education, Fresno, CA 93702-4709. Awards MA Ed. Faculty: 2 full-time (1 woman), 4 part-time (3 women). Students: 2 full-time (1 woman), 113 part-time (74 women). *Degree requirements:* Thesis or alternative required, foreign language not required. *Application deadline:* 7/31 (rolling processing). *Application fee:* $75. *Tuition:* $250 per unit. • Dave Young, Director, 209-453-2244. Fax: 209-453-2001.

Fresno Pacific University, Graduate School, Programs in Education, Division of Mathematics/ Science/Computer Education, Program in Mathematics Education, Fresno, CA 93702-4709. Offers middle school mathematics (MA Ed), secondary school mathematics (MA Ed). Faculty: 2 full-time (0 women), 4 part-time (0 women). Students: 32 part-time (11 women). *Degree requirements:* Thesis or alternative required, foreign language not required. *Application deadline:* 7/31 (rolling processing). *Application fee:* $75. *Tuition:* $250 per unit. • Dr. Richard Thiessen, Head, Division of Mathematics/Science/Computer Education, 209-453-2209. Fax: 209-453-2001.

Georgia Southern University, College of Education, Department of Middle Grades and Secondary Education, Program in Mathematics, Statesboro, GA 30460-8126. Awards M Ed, Ed S. Accredited by NCATE. Part-time and evening/weekend programs available. Students: 5 full-time (all women), 11 part-time (10 women); includes 3 minority (all African Americans). Average age 34. 11 applicants, 27% accepted. In 1997, 8 master's, 2 Ed Ss awarded. *Degree requirements:* Exams required, foreign language and thesis not required. *Entrance requirements:* For master's, GRE General Test (minimum score 450 on each section) or MAT (minimum score 44), minimum GPA of 2.5; for Ed S, GRE General Test (minimum score 450 on each section) or MAT (minimum score 49), minimum graduate GPA of 3.25. Application deadline: 7/15 (priority date; rolling processing; 11/15 for spring admission). Application fee: $0. Electronic applications accepted. *Tuition:* $2619 per year full-time, $287 per semester (minimum) part-time for state residents; $8619 per year full-time, $1037 per semester (minimum) part-time for nonresidents. *Financial aid:* Application deadline 4/15. • Application contact: Dr. John R. Diebolt, Associate Graduate Dean, 912-681-5384. Fax: 912-681-0740. E-mail: gradschool@gsvms2.cc.gasou.edu.

Georgia State University, College of Education, Department of Middle, Secondary Education and Instructional Technology, Programs in Secondary Education, Atlanta, GA 30303-3083. Offerings include mathematics education (M Ed, PhD, Ed S). Accredited by NCATE. *Degree requirements:* For master's, comprehensive exam; for doctorate, dissertation, comprehensive exam; for Ed S, project/exam. *Entrance requirements:* For master's, GRE General Test (minimum combined score of 800) or MAT (minimum score 44), minimum GPA of 2.5; for doctorate, GRE General Test (minimum score 500 on verbal section, 500 on either quantitative or analytical sections) or MAT (minimum score 53), minimum GPA of 3.3; for Ed S, GRE General Test (minimum combined score of 900) or MAT (minimum score 48), minimum graduate GPA of 3.25. Application fee: $25. *Expenses:* Tuition $2673 per year full-time, $99 per semester hour part-time for state residents; $10,692 per year full-time, $396 per semester hour part-time for nonresidents. Fees $228 per year. • Dr. Beverly J. Armento, Chair, Department of Middle, Secondary Education and Instructional Technology, 404-651-2510.

Grand Valley State University, School of Education, Programs in General Education, Program in Secondary, Adult and Higher Education, Allendale, MI 49401-9403. Offerings include mathematics (M Ed). Accredited by NCATE. *Degree requirements:* Thesis or alternative, applied research project. *Entrance requirements:* GRE General Test (minimum combined score of 1300) or minimum GPA of 3.0. Application deadline: rolling. Application fee: $20. • Application contact: Admissions Office, 616-895-2025. Fax: 616-895-3081.

Harvard University, Graduate School of Education, Area of Learning and Teaching, Cambridge, MA 02138. Offerings include mid-career mathematics and science (teaching certification) (Ed M, CAS). Faculty: 7 full-time (5 women), 16 part-time (8 women), 10.3 FTE. *Average time to degree:* master's–1 year full-time, 2.1 years part-time; doctorate–6.3 years full-time, 9 years part-time; other advanced degree–1 year full-time, 2 years part-time. *Entrance requirements:* GRE General Test, TOEFL (minimum score 600), TWE (minimum score 5.0). Application deadline: 1/2. Application fee: $60. • Robert Kegan, Chair, 617-496-2974. Fax: 617-495-7843. Application contact: Roland Hence, Director of Admissions, 617-495-3414. Fax: 617-496-3577. E-mail: gseadmissions@harvard.edu.

Henderson State University, School of Education, Department of Secondary Education, Arkadelphia, AR 71999-0001. Offerings include mathematics education (MSE). Accredited by

NCATE. Postbaccalaureate distance learning degree programs offered (minimal on-campus study). *Degree requirements:* Thesis optional, foreign language not required. *Entrance requirements:* GRE General Test or MAT, minimum GPA of 2.7, teacher certification. Application deadline: 7/31 (priority date; rolling processing). Application fee: $15. Electronic applications accepted. *Expenses:* Tuition $120 per credit hour for state residents; $240 per credit hour for nonresidents. Fees $105 per semester (minimum) full-time, $52 per semester (minimum) part-time. • Dr. Charles Weiner, Chairperson, 870-230-5163. Fax: 870-230-5455. E-mail: weinerc@holly.hsu.edu.

Hofstra University, School of Education and Allied Human Services, Department of Curriculum and Teaching, Program in Mathematics, Science, and Technology in Elementary Education, Hempstead, NY 11549. Awards MA. Accredited by NCATE. Part-time and evening/weekend programs available. Faculty: 8 full-time (6 women). Students: 21 full-time (all women), 2 part-time (both women); includes 1 minority (Hispanic). Average age 27. 0 applicants. In 1997, 7 degrees awarded. *Degree requirements:* 1 foreign language, thesis, departmental qualifying exam. *Application deadline:* rolling. *Application fee:* $40 ($75 for international students). *Expenses:* Tuition $10,968 per year full-time, $457 per credit hour part-time. Fees $670 per year full-time, $112 per semester (minimum) part-time. *Financial aid:* In 1997–98, 3 research assistantships averaging $260 per month were awarded; Federal Work-Study, institutionally sponsored loans, and career-related internships or fieldwork also available. Financial aid application deadline: 9/1; applicants required to submit FAFSA. *Faculty research:* Integrating math, science and technology; creating gender equitable learning environments; technology design for elementary education. Total annual research expenditures: $10,000. • Janice Koch, Co-Coordinator, 516-463-5777. Application contact: Mary Beth Carey, Dean of Admissions, 516-463-6700. Fax: 516-560-7660. E-mail: hofstra@hofstra.edu.

Hood College, Department of Education, Frederick, MD 21701-8575. Offerings include curriculum and instruction (MS), with options in early childhood education, elementary education, elementary school science and mathematics, reading, secondary education, special education. *Entrance requirements:* Minimum GPA of 2.5. Application deadline: rolling. Application fee: $30. *Tuition:* $285 per credit. • Dr. Patricia Bartlett, Chairperson, 301-696-3471. E-mail: bartlett@nimue.hood.edu. Application contact: Hood College Graduate School, 301-696-3600. Fax: 301-696-3597. E-mail: postmaster@nimue.hood.edu.

Hunter College of the City University of New York, Division of Education, Secondary Education Curriculum, Concentration in Mathematics Education, 695 Park Avenue, New York, NY 10021-5085. Awards MA. *Degree requirements:* Comprehensive exam required, foreign language and thesis not required. *Entrance requirements:* TOEFL (minimum score 575). Application deadline: 4/7 (rolling processing; 11/7 for spring admission). Application fee: $40. *Expenses:* Tuition $4350 per year full-time, $185 per credit part-time for state residents; $7600 per year full-time, $320 per credit part-time for nonresidents. Fees $26 per year.

Illinois State University, College of Arts and Sciences, Department of Mathematics, Program in Mathematics Education, Normal, IL 61790-2200. Awards PhD. Students: 6 full-time (3 women), 19 part-time (13 women); includes 4 minority (all African Americans), 1 international. 17 applicants, 94% accepted. In 1997, 3 degrees awarded. *Degree requirements:* Variable foreign language requirement, dissertation, 2 terms of residency, oral comprehensive exam. *Entrance requirements:* GRE General Test. Application deadline: rolling. Application fee: $0. *Expenses:* Tuition $2454 per year full-time, $102 per hour part-time for state residents; $7362 per year full-time, $307 per hour part-time for nonresidents. Fees $1048 per year full-time, $44 per hour part-time. *Financial aid:* Application deadline 4/1. • Dr. Lotus Hershberger, Chairperson, Department of Mathematics, 309-438-8781.

Indiana University Bloomington, College of Arts and Sciences, Department of Mathematics, Bloomington, IN 47405. Offerings include mathematics education (MAT). Department faculty: 46 full-time (1 woman). *Application deadline:* 1/15 (priority date; 9/1 for spring admission). *Application fee:* $35. *Expenses:* Tuition $153 per credit hour for state residents; $446 per credit hour for nonresidents. Fees $343 per year. • Robert Glassey, Chair, 812-855-3171. E-mail: glassey@ucs.indiana.edu. Application contact: Misty Cummings, Graduate Secretary, 812-855-2645. Fax: 812-855-0046. E-mail: gradmath@ucs.indiana.edu.

Indiana University of Pennsylvania, College of Natural Sciences and Mathematics, Department of Mathematics, Program in Elementary and Middle School Mathematics Education, Indiana, PA 15705-1087. Awards M Ed. Accredited by NCATE. Students: 3 full-time (all women), 11 part-time (9 women); includes 1 international. Average age 29. 4 applicants, 100% accepted. In 1997, 9 degrees awarded. *Degree requirements:* Thesis optional, foreign language not required. *Entrance requirements:* TOEFL (minimum score 500). Application deadline: 7/1 (priority date; rolling processing; 11/1 for spring admission). Application fee: $30. *Expenses:* Tuition $3468 per year full-time, $193 per credit part-time for state residents; $6236 per year full-time, $346 per credit part-time for nonresidents. Fees $313 per year (minimum) full-time, $84 per year part-time. *Financial aid:* Research assistantships, Federal Work-Study available. Aid available to part-time students. Financial aid application deadline: 3/15. • Dr. Lawrence M. Feldman, Graduate Coordinator, 724-357-4767. E-mail: lmfeldman@grove.iup.edu.

Indiana University of Pennsylvania, College of Natural Sciences and Mathematics, Department of Mathematics, Program in Mathematics Education, Indiana, PA 15705-1087. Awards M Ed. Accredited by NCATE. Part-time programs available. Students: 5 part-time (0 women). Average age 28. 2 applicants, 50% accepted. In 1997, 3 degrees awarded. *Degree requirements:* Thesis optional, foreign language not required. *Entrance requirements:* TOEFL (minimum score 500). Application deadline: 7/1 (priority date; rolling processing; 11/1 for spring admission). Application fee: $30. *Expenses:* Tuition $3468 per year full-time, $193 per credit part-time for state residents; $6236 per year full-time, $346 per credit part-time for nonresidents. Fees $313 per year (minimum) full-time, $84 per year part-time. *Financial aid:* Research assistantships, Federal Work-Study, and career-related internships or fieldwork available. Aid available to part-time students. Financial aid application deadline: 3/15. • Dr. Joseph Angelo, Graduate Coordinator, 724-357-2283. E-mail: jangelo@grove.iup.edu.

Iona College, School of Arts and Science, Program in Secondary School Subjects, 715 North Avenue, New Rochelle, NY 10801-1890. Offerings include mathematics education (MS Ed, MST). Program faculty: 4 full-time (1 woman), 8 part-time (2 women). *Degree requirements:* Thesis or alternative required, foreign language not required. *Entrance requirements:* Minimum GPA of 2.5 (MST), New York teaching certificate (MS Ed). Application deadline: rolling. Application fee: $25. *Expenses:* Tuition $455 per credit hour. Fees $25 per semester. • Dr. Lucy Murphy, Chair, 914-633-2210. Fax: 914-633-2608. Application contact: Arlene Melillo, Director of Graduate Recruitment, 914-633-2328. Fax: 914-633-2023.

Iowa State University of Science and Technology, College of Liberal Arts and Sciences, Department of Mathematics, Ames, IA 50011. Offerings include school mathematics (MSM). Department faculty: 50 full-time. *Application deadline:* 2/1 (priority date; 10/15 for spring admission). *Application fee:* $20 ($30 for international students). *Expenses:* Tuition $3166 per year full-time, $176 per credit part-time for state residents; $9324 per year full-time, $518 per credit part-time for nonresidents. Fees $200 per year. • Dr. Max D. Gunzburger, Chair, 515-294-1752. E-mail: gunzburg@iastate.edu.

Jacksonville University, College of Arts and Sciences, Division of Education, Program in Mathematics, 2800 University Boulevard North, Jacksonville, FL 32211-3394. Awards MAT. Part-time and evening/weekend programs available. *Degree requirements:* Comprehensive exam required, foreign language and thesis not required. *Entrance requirements:* GRE General Test (minimum combined score of 900), TOEFL (minimum score 500). Application deadline: 8/1 (priority date; rolling processing; 11/1 for spring admission). Application fee: $25.

Kean University, School of Natural Sciences, Mathematics, and Nursing, Department of Mathematics, Union, NJ 07083. Offers program in mathematics education (MA). One or more programs accredited by NCATE. Part-time and evening/weekend programs available. Students: 5 full-time (1 woman), 14 part-time (8 women); includes 4 minority (3 African Americans, 1 Asian American). Average age 39. In 1997, 6 degrees awarded. *Degree requirements:* Thesis or alternative required, foreign language not required. *Entrance requirements:* GRE General Test. Application deadline: 6/15 (11/15 for spring admission). Application fee: $35. *Tuition:* $5926 per year full-time, $248 per credit part-time for state residents; $7312 per year full-time, $304 per credit part-time for nonresidents. *Financial aid:* Graduate assistantships available. • Dr. Francine Abeles, Coordinator, 908-527-2104. Application contact: Joanne Morris, Director of Graduate Admissions, 908-527-2665. Fax: 908-527-2286. E-mail: grad_adm@turbo.kean.edu.

Kean University, School of Education, Department of Instruction, Curriculum and Administration, Instruction and Curriculum Program, Union, NJ 07083. Offerings include mathematics/science/computer education (MA). Accredited by NCATE. *Degree requirements:* Thesis, comprehensive exams required, foreign language not required. *Entrance requirements:* GRE General Test or MAT. Application deadline: 6/15 (rolling processing; 11/15 for spring admission). Application fee: $35. *Tuition:* $5926 per year full-time, $248 per credit part-time for state residents; $7312 per year full-time, $304 per credit part-time for nonresidents. • Dr. Janet Prince, Coordinator, 908-527-2525. Application contact: Joanne Morris, Director of Graduate Admissions, 908-527-2665. Fax: 908-527-2286. E-mail: grad_adm@turbo.kean.edu.

Kutztown University of Pennsylvania, Graduate School, College of Education, Program in Secondary Education, Kutztown, PA 19530. Offerings include mathematics (M Ed). Accredited by NCATE. Program faculty: 7 full-time (1 woman). *Degree requirements:* Comprehensive exam required, thesis optional, foreign language not required. *Entrance requirements:* GRE General Test, TOEFL, TSE. Application deadline: 3/1 (8/1 for spring admission). Application fee: $25. *Tuition:* $4111 per year full-time, $225 per credit hour part-time for state residents; $6879 per year full-time, $393 per credit hour part-time for nonresidents. • Kathleen Dolgos, Chairperson, 610-683-4259.

Lehman College of the City University of New York, Division of Education, Department of Secondary, Adult and Business Education, Program in Mathematics 7–12, 250 Bedford Park Boulevard West, Bronx, NY 10468-1589. Awards MS Ed. Part-time and evening/weekend programs available. Students: 39 part-time (13 women). *Degree requirements:* Comprehensive exam or thesis. *Entrance requirements:* 18 credits in mathematics, 12 credits in education. Application deadline: 4/1 (rolling processing; 11/1 for spring admission). Application fee: $40. *Expenses:* Tuition $4350 per year full-time, $185 per credit part-time for state residents; $7600 per year full-time, $320 per credit part-time for nonresidents. Fees $120 per year full-time, $80 per year part-time. *Financial aid:* Full and partial tuition waivers, Federal Work-Study available. Aid available to part-time students. Financial aid application deadline: 5/15; applicants required to submit FAFSA. *Faculty research:* Mathematical problem solving, Piagetian cognitive theory. • Stanley F. Taback, Adviser, 718-960-8171.

Long Island University, Brooklyn Campus, School of Education, Department of Education, Program in Secondary Education, Brooklyn, NY 11201-8423. Offers mathematics education (MS Ed). Part-time and evening/weekend programs available. 17 applicants, 82% accepted. In 1997, 7 degrees awarded. *Degree requirements:* Thesis optional, foreign language not required. *Application deadline:* rolling. *Application fee:* $30. Electronic applications accepted. *Expenses:* Tuition $480 per credit. Fees $415 per year full-time, $73 per semester (minimum) part-time. • Application contact: Bernard W. Sullivan, Associate Director of Admissions, 718-488-1011.

Long Island University, C.W. Post Campus, College of Liberal Arts and Sciences, Department of Mathematics, Brookville, NY 11548-1300. Offerings include mathematics for secondary school teachers (MS). Department faculty: 15 full-time (4 women). *Degree requirements:* Thesis or alternative, oral presentation required, foreign language not required. *Application deadline:* rolling. *Application fee:* $30. Electronic applications accepted. *Expenses:* Tuition $480 per credit. Fees $316 per year full-time, $71 per semester (minimum) part-time. • Dr. Neo Cleopa, Chairman, 516-299-2448. Fax: 516-299-4140. E-mail: ncleopa@eagle.liunet.edu. Application contact: Dr. Shahla Ahdout, Graduate Adviser, 516-299-2448.

Long Island University, C.W. Post Campus, School of Education, Department of Curriculum and Instruction, Brookville, NY 11548-1300. Offerings include mathematics education (MS). Department faculty: 10 full-time (5 women), 46 part-time (19 women). *Application deadline:* rolling. *Application fee:* $30. Electronic applications accepted. *Expenses:* Tuition $480 per credit. Fees $316 per year full-time, $71 per semester (minimum) part-time. • Dr. Anthony De Falco, Chairperson, 516-299-2372. Application contact: Camille Marziliano, Academic Counselor, 516-299-2123. Fax: 516-299-4167. E-mail: cmarzili@eagle.liunet.edu.

Louisiana Tech University, College of Education, Department of Curriculum, Instruction and Leadership, Ruston, LA 71272. Offerings include secondary education (M Ed), with options in business education, English education, foreign language education, health and physical education, mathematics education, science education, social studies education, speech education. Accredited by NCATE. Department faculty: 16 full-time (11 women). *Application deadline:* 7/29 (2/3 for spring admission). *Application fee:* $20 ($30 for international students). *Tuition:* $2382 per year full-time, $223 per quarter (minimum) part-time for state residents; $5307 per year full-time, $223 per quarter (minimum) part-time for nonresidents. • Dr. Samuel V. Dauzat, Head, 318-257-4609.

Loyola Marymount University, School of Education, Program in Teaching, Los Angeles, CA 90045-8350. Offerings include mathematics education (MAT). Program faculty: 14 full-time (8 women), 25 part-time (20 women). *Degree requirements:* Thesis or alternative, comprehensive exam required, foreign language not required. *Entrance requirements:* GRE General Test, TOEFL (minimum score 550), interview. Application fee: $35. Electronic applications accepted. *Expenses:* Tuition $500 per unit. Fees $111 per year full-time, $28 per year part-time. • Coordinator, 310-338-7307.

Manhattanville College, School of Education, Program in Secondary Education, Purchase, NY 10577-2132. Offerings include mathematics (MAT). *Degree requirements:* Thesis, comprehensive exam or research project required, foreign language not required. *Entrance requirements:* Minimum undergraduate GPA of 3.0. Application deadline: rolling. Application fee: $40. *Expenses:* Tuition $410 per credit (minimum). Fees $25 per semester. • Application contact: Carol Messar, Director of Admissions, 914-323-5142. Fax: 914-323-5493.

Mankato State University, College of Science, Engineering and Technology, Department of Mathematics and Statistics, South Rd and Ellis Ave, PO Box 8400, Mankato, MN 56002-8400. Offerings include teaching mathematics (MT). Department faculty: 13 full-time (3 women). *Application deadline:* 7/10 (priority date; rolling processing; 10/30 for spring admission). *Application fee:* $20. *Tuition:* $126 per credit (minimum) for state residents; $200 per credit for nonresidents. • Mary Ann Lee, Chairperson, 507-389-1453. Application contact: Joni Roberts, Admissions Coordinator, 507-389-2321. Fax: 507-389-5974. E-mail: grad@mankato.msus.edu.

Marquette University, College of Arts and Sciences, Department of Mathematics, Statistics, and Computer Science, Milwaukee, WI 53201-1881. Offerings include mathematics education (MS). Department faculty: 24 full-time (3 women). *Degree requirements:* Thesis or alternative, comprehensive exam required, foreign language not required. *Entrance requirements:* TOEFL (minimum score 550). Application fee: $40. *Tuition:* $490 per credit. • Dr. Douglas Harris, Chairman, 414-288-7573. Fax: 414-288-1578. Application contact: Dr. Karl Byleen, Director of Graduate Studies, 414-288-6343.

McNeese State University, College of Education, Department of Curriculum and Instruction, Program in Secondary Education, Lake Charles, LA 70609-2495. Offerings include mathematics education (M Ed). Program faculty: 8 full-time (3 women). *Entrance requirements:* GRE General Test, teaching certificate. Application deadline: 7/15 (priority date; rolling processing). Application fee: $10 ($25 for international students). *Tuition:* $2118 per year full-time, $344 per semester (minimum) part-time for state residents; $7308 per year full-time, $344 per semester

Directory: Mathematics Education

McNeese State University (continued)
(minimum) part-time for nonresidents. • Dr. Everett Waddell Burge, Head, Department of Curriculum and Instruction, 318-475-5404.

Mercer University, School of Education, 1400 Coleman Avenue, Macon, GA 31207-0003. Offerings include mathematics education (M Ed). School faculty: 11 full-time (5 women), 17 part-time (11 women). *Degree requirements:* Research project report required, foreign language and thesis not required. *Entrance requirements:* GRE, MAT, NTE, minimum GPA of 2.75. Application deadline: 8/1 (priority date; rolling processing; 12/1 for spring admission). Application fee: $25. *Tuition:* $180 per credit hour. • Dr. Anne Hathaway, Dean, 912-752-5397. Fax: 912-752-2280. E-mail: hathaway_ha@mercer.edu. Application contact: Dr. Louis Gallien, Chair, Department of Teacher Education, 912-752-2585. Fax: 912-752-2576. E-mail: gallien_lb@mercer.edu.

Michigan State University, College of Natural Science, Department of Mathematics, East Lansing, MI 48824-1020. Offerings include mathematics (MAT, MS, PhD), mathematics education (PhD). Terminal master's awarded for partial completion of doctoral program. Department faculty: 65 (9 women). *Degree requirements:* For master's, certifying exam required, foreign language and thesis not required; for doctorate, 1 foreign language, dissertation, exams, seminar. *Application deadline:* rolling. *Application fee:* $30 ($40 for international students). *Expenses:* Tuition $4609 per year full-time, $223 per credit hour (minimum) part-time for state residents; $8704 per year full-time, $450 per credit hour (minimum) part-time for nonresidents. Fees $576 per year full-time, $476 per year part-time. • Dr. Peter Lappan, Chairperson, 517-355-9681.

Middle Tennessee State University, College of Basic and Applied Sciences, Department of Mathematics, Murfreesboro, TN 37132. Offerings include mathematics education (MST). Department faculty: 22 full-time (4 women). *Application deadline:* 8/1 (priority date). *Application fee:* $5. *Expenses:* Tuition $2560 per year full-time, $129 per semester hour part-time for state residents; $7386 per year full-time, $340 per semester hour part-time for nonresidents. Fees $486 per year full-time, $17 per semester (minimum) part-time. • Dr. E. Ray Phillips, Chair, 615-898-2669. Fax: 615-898-5422 Ext. EPHI. E-mail: aphillip@mtsu.edu.

Millersville University of Pennsylvania, School of Science and Mathematics, Department of Mathematics, Millersville, PA 17551-0302. Offers program in mathematics (M Ed). Accredited by NCATE. Part-time and evening/weekend programs available. Faculty: 19 full-time (4 women), 2 part-time (both women). Students: 5 full-time (3 women), 14 part-time (8 women); includes 1 international. Average age 32. 14 applicants, 93% accepted. In 1997, 10 degrees awarded. *Degree requirements:* Departmental exam required, thesis optional, foreign language not required. *Entrance requirements:* GRE or MAT, minimum undergraduate GPA of 2.75, bachelor's degree in mathematics. Application deadline: 5/1 (priority date; rolling processing). Application fee: $25. *Tuition:* $3468 per year full-time, $234 per credit part-time for state residents; $6236 per year full-time, $387 per credit part-time for nonresidents. *Financial aid:* Graduate assistantships, Federal Work-Study, institutionally sponsored loans available. Aid available to part-time students. Financial aid application deadline: 5/1. *Faculty research:* Algebraic topology, real analysis, applied mathematics, mathematical modeling. • Dr. Bernard Schroeder, Coordinator, 717-872-3009. Fax: 717-872-3985. Application contact: Dr. Robert J. Labriola, Dean of Graduate Studies, 717-872-3030. Fax: 717-871-2022.

Mills College, Education Department, Oakland, CA 94613-1000. Offerings include education (MA), with options in curriculum and instruction, elementary education, English education, mathematics education, science education, secondary education, social sciences education, teaching. Department faculty: 8 full-time (6 women), 13 part-time (11 women), 11 FTE. *Degree requirements:* Comprehensive exam required, thesis not required. *Average time to degree:* master's–2 years full-time. *Entrance requirements:* TOEFL (minimum score 550). Application deadline: 2/1 (priority date; rolling processing; 11/1 for spring admission). Application fee: $50. Electronic applications accepted. *Expenses:* Tuition $10,600 per year full-time, $2560 per year part-time. Fees $468 per year. • Jane Bowyer, Chairperson, 510-430-2118. Fax: 510-430-3314. E-mail: grad-studies@mills.edu. Application contact: La Vonna S. Brown, Coordinator of Graduate Studies, 510-430-3309. Fax: 510-430-2159. E-mail: grad-studies@mills.edu.

Minot State University, Program in Mathematics and Computer Science, Minot, ND 58707-0002. Offers mathematics (MAT). Faculty: 4 full-time (0 women). Students: 2 part-time (both women). 2 applicants, 100% accepted. In 1997, 10 degrees awarded. *Degree requirements:* Thesis required, foreign language not required. *Entrance requirements:* Minimum GPA of 3.0 or GRE General (minimum combined score of 1100), undergraduate major in math, teacher certification. Application deadline: rolling. Application fee: $25. *Tuition:* $2714 per year for state residents; $3235 per year (minimum) for nonresidents. *Financial aid:* 2 students received aid; research assistantships, teaching assistantships, institutionally sponsored loans, and career-related internships or fieldwork available. Aid available to part-time students. Financial aid application deadline: 4/1. *Faculty research:* Mathematics education. • Dr. Robert L. Holmen, Chairperson, 701-858-3073. E-mail: holmen@warple.cs.misu.nodak.edu. Application contact: Tammy White, Administrative Secretary, 701-858-3250. Fax: 701-839-6933.

Mississippi College, School of Education, Programs in Secondary Education, Program in Mathematics Education, Clinton, MS 39058. Awards M Ed. Accredited by NCATE. *Degree requirements:* Comprehensive exam required, foreign language and thesis not required. *Entrance requirements:* GRE or NTE, minimum GPA of 2.5, Class A Certificate. Application deadline: 8/15 (priority date; rolling processing). Application fee: $25 ($75 for international students). *Expenses:* Tuition $6624 per year full-time, $276 per hour part-time. Fees $230 per year full-time, $35 per semester (minimum) part-time. *Financial aid:* Professional development scholarships and career-related internships or fieldwork available. Aid available to part-time students. Financial aid application deadline: 4/1. • Dr. Thomas Leavelle, Head, 601-925-3463.

Montclair State University, College of Science and Mathematics, Department of Mathematics and Computer Science, Programs in Mathematics, Concentration in Mathematics Education, Upper Montclair, NJ 07043-1624. Awards MS. Accredited by NCATE. Part-time and evening/weekend programs available. Faculty: 39 full-time. *Degree requirements:* Written comprehensive exam required, foreign language and thesis not required. *Entrance requirements:* GRE General Test, minimum GPA of 2.67. Application deadline: 4/1 (rolling processing; 11/1 for spring admission). Application fee: $40. *Expenses:* Tuition $201 per credit for state residents; $257 per credit for nonresidents. Fees $22.05 per credit. *Financial aid:* Available to part-time students. Financial aid application deadline: 3/1; applicants required to submit FAFSA. • Application contact: Dr. Helen Roberts, Adviser, 973-655-7262.

National–Louis University, National College of Education, McGaw Graduate School, Program in Mathematics Education, 2840 Sheridan Road, Evanston, IL 60201-1730. Awards M Ed, MS Ed, CAS. Part-time and evening/weekend programs available. Students: 1 (woman) full-time, 17 part-time (16 women); includes 2 minority (both Asian Americans). Average age 34. In 1997, 7 master's awarded. *Degree requirements:* For master's, thesis required (for some programs), foreign language not required. *Entrance requirements:* For master's, MAT, minimum GPA of 3.0. Application deadline: rolling. Application fee: $25. *Tuition:* $411 per semester hour. *Financial aid:* Fellowships available. Aid available to part-time students. Financial aid applicants required to submit FAFSA. • Dr. Arthur Hyde, Coordinator, 847-475-1100 Ext. 4520. Application contact: Dr. David McCulloch, Vice President for University Services, 800-443-5522 Ext. 5127. Fax: 847-465-0593. E-mail: dmcc@wheeling1.nl.edu.

New Jersey City University, School of Arts and Sciences, Department of Mathematics, Jersey City, NJ 07305-1957. Offers program in mathematics education (MA). Evening/weekend programs available. *Degree requirements:* Comprehensive exam required, thesis optional, foreign language not required. *Entrance requirements:* GRE General Test or MAT, TOEFL. Application deadline: 8/1 (priority date; rolling processing; 12/1 for spring admission). Application fee: $0.

New York University, School of Education, Department of Teaching and Learning, Program in Mathematics Education, New York, NY 10012-1019. Awards MA, PhD. Part-time and evening/weekend programs available. Faculty: 2 full-time (1 woman), 3 part-time. Students: 12 full-time, 34 part-time. 50 applicants, 56% accepted. In 1997, 15 master's awarded. *Degree requirements:* For master's, thesis required (for some programs), foreign language not required; for doctorate, dissertation. *Entrance requirements:* For master's, TOEFL; for doctorate, GRE General Test, TOEFL, interview. Application deadline: 2/1 (priority date; rolling processing; 12/1 for spring admission). Application fee: $40 ($60 for international students). *Financial aid:* Partial tuition waivers, Federal Work-Study, institutionally sponsored loans, and career-related internships or fieldwork available. Aid available to part-time students. Financial aid application deadline: 3/1; applicants required to submit FAFSA. *Faculty research:* Mathematics anxiety, women and mathematics learning disabilities, technology in teaching of mathematics, mathematical modeling. • Kenneth Goldberg, Director, 212-998-5200. Application contact: Office of Graduate Admissions, 212-998-5030. Fax: 212-995-4328.

North Carolina Agricultural and Technical State University, Graduate School, College of Arts and Sciences, Department of Mathematics, Greensboro, NC 27411. Offers program in mathematics education (MS), including applied mathematics, mathematics, secondary education. One or more programs accredited by NCATE. Part-time and evening/weekend programs available. Faculty: 6 full-time (1 woman). Students: 13 full-time (6 women), 6 part-time (5 women); includes 16 minority (all African Americans). Average age 30. 9 applicants, 67% accepted. In 1997, 4 degrees awarded. *Degree requirements:* Thesis or alternative, comprehensive exam, qualifying exam required, foreign language not required. *Entrance requirements:* GRE General Test, minimum GPA of 3.0. Application deadline: 6/1 (priority date; rolling processing; 12/1 for spring admission). Application fee: $35. *Tuition:* $1662 per year full-time, $272 per semester (minimum) part-time for state residents; $8790 per year full-time, $2054 per semester (minimum) part-time for nonresidents. *Financial aid:* Research assistantships, teaching assistantships available. Financial aid application deadline: 6/1. • Dr. Wilbur Smith, Chairperson, 336-334-7822. E-mail: smithw@aurora.ncat.edu.

North Carolina State University, College of Education and Psychology, Department of Mathematics, Science, and Technology Education, Program in Mathematics Education, Raleigh, NC 27695. Awards M Ed, MS, PhD. Accredited by NCATE. Part-time programs available. Faculty: 19 full-time (5 women), 9 part-time (2 women). Students: 11 full-time (10 women), 17 part-time (10 women); includes 10 minority (7 African Americans, 2 Asian Americans, 1 Hispanic). Average age 36. 10 applicants, 70% accepted. In 1997, 4 master's, 4 doctorates awarded. *Degree requirements:* For master's, thesis (for some programs), oral exam required, foreign language not required; for doctorate, 1 foreign language, dissertation, oral and written exams. *Entrance requirements:* For master's, GRE General Test or MAT, minimum GPA of 3.0; for doctorate, GRE General Test or MAT, minimum GPA of 3.0, interview. Application deadline: 4/15 (priority date; rolling processing; 11/15 for spring admission). Application fee: $45. *Tuition:* $2370 per year full-time, $517 per semester (minimum) part-time for state residents; $11,536 per year full-time, $2809 per semester (minimum) part-time for nonresidents. *Financial aid:* Fellowships, research assistantships, teaching assistantships, Federal Work-Study, institutionally sponsored loans, and career-related internships or fieldwork available. • Dr. Willam M. Waters Jr., Director of Graduate Programs, 919-515-6906. E-mail: waters@poe.coe.ncsu.edu. Application contact: Linda Trogdon, Graduate Secretary, 919-515-1740. Fax: 919-515-1063. E-mail: trogdon@poe.coe.ncsu.edu.

Northeastern Illinois University, College of Arts and Sciences, Department of Mathematics, Programs in Mathematics, Chicago, IL 60625-4699. Offerings include mathematics for elementary school teachers (MA). Faculty: 14 full-time (5 women), 14 part-time (6 women). *Application deadline:* 3/18 (priority date; rolling processing; 9/30 for spring admission). *Application fee:* $0. *Expenses:* Tuition $2226 per year full-time, $93 per credit hour part-time for state residents; $6678 per year full-time, $278 per credit hour part-time for nonresidents. Fees $358 per year full-time, $14.90 per credit hour part-time. • Dr. Paul O'Hara, Coordinator, 773-794-2566. Application contact: Dr. Mohan K. Sood, Dean of Graduate College, 773-583-4050 Ext. 6143. Fax: 773-794-6670.

Northern Michigan University, College of Arts and Sciences, Glenn T. Seaborg Center, Marquette, MI 49855-5301. Offers programs in mathematics education (MS), science education (MS). Offered during summer only. Students: 24 part-time (12 women). In 1997, 1 degree awarded. *Entrance requirements:* Minimum GPA of 2.7 in major. Application deadline: 7/1 (priority date; rolling processing; 11/1 for spring admission). Application fee: $25. *Expenses:* Tuition $135 per credit hour for state residents; $215 per credit hour for nonresidents. Fees $183 per year full-time, $94 per year (minimum) part-time. *Financial aid:* Application deadline 3/1. • Dr. Peggy House, Head, 906-227-2002.

North Georgia College & State University, Graduate School, Program in Education, Dahlonega, GA 30597-1001. Offerings include secondary education (M Ed), with options in art education, biology education, chemistry education, English education, mathematics education, modern languages education, physical education, science education, social science education. Accredited by NCATE. Program faculty: 57 full-time (15 women), 7 part-time (4 women). *Degree requirements:* Comprehensive exam required, thesis optional, foreign language not required. *Entrance requirements:* GRE General Test (minimum combined score of 800) or MAT (minimum score 44), minimum GPA of 2.75. Application deadline: 9/1 (priority date; rolling processing). Application fee: $25. • Dr. Bob Michael, Dean, School of Education, 706-864-1533. Application contact: Mai-Lan Ledbetter, Coordinator of Graduate Admissions, 706-864-1543. Fax: 706-864-1668. E-mail: mledbetter@nugget.ngc.peachnet.edu.

Northwestern State University of Louisiana, Division of Education, Natchitoches, LA 71497. Offerings include mathematics education (M Ed). Accredited by NCATE. Division faculty: 10 full-time (7 women), 4 part-time (2 women). *Application deadline:* 8/1 (priority date; rolling processing; 1/10 for spring admission). *Application fee:* $15 ($25 for international students). *Tuition:* $2147 per year full-time, $336 per semester (minimum) part-time for state residents; $6437 per year full-time, $336 per semester (minimum) part-time for nonresidents. • Dr. Sue Weaver, Chair, 318-357-5195. Application contact: Dr. Tom Hanson, Dean, Graduate Studies and Research, 318-357-5851. Fax: 318-357-5019.

Northwest Missouri State University, College of Arts and Sciences, Department of Mathematics and Statistics, 800 University Drive, Maryville, MO 64468-6001. Offers program in mathematics education (MS Ed). Part-time programs available. Faculty: 12 full-time (3 women). Students: 3 part-time (2 women). 0 applicants. In 1997, 1 degree awarded. *Degree requirements:* Comprehensive exam required, foreign language and thesis not required. *Entrance requirements:* GRE General Test (minimum combined score of 700), TOEFL (minimum score 550), minimum undergraduate GPA of 2.5, writing sample. Application deadline: rolling. Application fee: $0 ($50 for international students). *Expenses:* Tuition $113 per credit hour for state residents; $197 per credit hour for nonresidents. Fees $3 per credit hour. *Financial aid:* In 1997–98, 3 teaching assistantships averaging $585 per month were awarded. Financial aid application deadline: 3/1. • Dr. Dennis Malm, Chairperson, 816-562-1807. Application contact: Dr. Frances Shipley, Dean of Graduate School, 816-562-1145. E-mail: gradsch@acad.nwmissouri.edu.

Nova Southeastern University, Fischler Center for the Advancement of Education, Graduate Teacher Education Program, Fort Lauderdale, FL 33314-7721. Offerings include mathematics (MS, Ed S). *Degree requirements:* Thesis, practicum required, foreign language not required. *Entrance requirements:* For master's, teaching certificate; for Ed S, master's degree, teaching certificate. Application deadline: rolling. Application fee: $50. *Tuition:* $245 per credit hour (minimum). • Dr. Deo Nellis, Dean, 954-262-8601. E-mail: deo@fcae.nova.edu. Application contact: Dr. Mark Seldine, Director of Student Affairs, 954-262-8689. Fax: 954-262-3910. E-mail: seldines@fcae.nova.edu.

Occidental College, Department of Education, Program in Secondary Education, Los Angeles, CA 90041-3392. Offerings include mathematics (MAT). Program faculty: 4 full-time (1 woman). *Degree requirements:* Internship required, foreign language and thesis not required. *Entrance* *requirements:* GRE General Test (minimum score 550 on each section or combined score of 1650 on three sections), TOEFL (minimum score 600), minimum GPA of 3.0. Application deadline: 3/1 (priority date; rolling processing; 10/1 for spring admission). Application fee: $40. *Expenses:* Tuition $21,256 per year full-time, $865 per unit part-time. Fees $314 per year. • Application contact: Susan Molik, Administrative Assistant, Graduate Office, 213-259-2921.

Ohio University, Graduate Studies, College of Education, School of Curriculum and Instruction, Athens, OH 45701-2979. Offerings include mathematics education (M Ed, PhD). Accredited by NCATE. Terminal master's awarded for partial completion of doctoral program. School faculty: 21 full-time (7 women), 16 part-time (11 women). *Degree requirements:* For doctorate, dissertation. *Entrance requirements:* For doctorate, GRE General Test, MAT, minimum GPA of 3.0, work experience. Application deadline: rolling. Application fee: $30. *Tuition:* $5430 per year full-time, $216 per quarter hour part-time for state residents; $10,431 per year full-time, $423 per quarter hour part-time for nonresidents. • Dr. Ralph Martin, Director, 740-593-4422. Application contact: Dr. Bonnie Beach, Graduate Chair, 740-593-0523.

Oregon State University, Graduate School, College of Science, Department of Science and Mathematics Education, Program in Advanced Mathematics Education, Corvallis, OR 97331. Awards MAT. Accredited by NCATE. Students: 6 full-time (3 women), 9 part-time; includes 1 Native American. *Degree requirements:* Minimum GPA of 3.0. *Entrance requirements:* TOEFL (minimum score 550), minimum GPA of 3.0 in last 90 hours. Application fee: $50. *Tuition:* $6207 per year full-time, $810 per quarter (minimum) part-time for state residents; $10,551 per year full-time, $1293 per quarter (minimum) part-time for nonresidents. *Financial aid:* Application deadline 2/1. • Dr. Margaret L. Niess, Chair, Department of Science and Mathematics Education, 541-737-1818. Fax: 541-737-1817. E-mail: niessm@ucs.orst.edu.

Oregon State University, Graduate School, College of Science, Department of Science and Mathematics Education, Program in Mathematics Education, Corvallis, OR 97331. Awards MA, MAT, MS, PhD. Accredited by NCATE. Faculty: 2 full-time (both women), 1 (woman) part-time. Students: 6 full-time (3 women), 9 part-time (5 women); includes 1 minority (Asian American), 1 international. Average age 34. In 1997, 14 master's, 1 doctorate awarded. *Degree requirements:* For master's, variable foreign language requirement, minimum GPA of 3.0 required, thesis not required; for doctorate, 1 foreign language, dissertation, minimum GPA of 3.0. *Entrance requirements:* For master's, TOEFL (minimum score 550), minimum GPA of 3.0 in last 90 hours; for doctorate, GRE or MAT, TOEFL (minimum score 550), minimum GPA of 3.0 in last 90 hours. Application deadline: 3/1 (rolling processing). Application fee: $50. *Tuition:* $6207 per year full-time, $810 per quarter (minimum) part-time for state residents; $10,551 per year full-time, $1293 per quarter (minimum) part-time for nonresidents. *Financial aid:* Teaching assistantships, Federal Work-Study, institutionally sponsored loans available. Aid available to part-time students. Financial aid application deadline: 2/1. *Faculty research:* Teacher action when focused on standards, teacher belief, integration of technology. • Dr. Margaret L. Niess, Chair, Department of Science and Mathematics Education, 541-737-1818. Fax: 541-737-1817. E-mail: niessm@ucs.orst.edu.

Plattsburgh State University of New York, Faculty of Professional Studies, Center for Educational Studies and Services, Program in Secondary Education, Plattsburgh, NY 12901-2681. Offerings include mathematics (MST). *Application deadline:* rolling. *Application fee:* $50. *Expenses:* Tuition $5100 per year full-time, $213 per credit hour part-time for state residents; $8416 per year full-time, $351 per credit hour part-time for nonresidents. Fees $395 per year full-time, $15.10 per credit hour part-time. • Dr. Raymond Domenico, Director and Associate Dean, Center for Educational Studies and Services, 518-564-2122.

Plymouth State College of the University System of New Hampshire, Department of Education, Program in Mathematics Education, Plymouth, NH 03264-1595. Awards M Ed. Part-time and evening/weekend programs available. Students: 2 full-time (both women), 3 part-time (0 women). Average age 26. 2 applicants, 100% accepted. In 1997, 3 degrees awarded. *Degree requirements:* Comprehensive exam required, thesis optional, foreign language not required. *Entrance requirements:* GRE General Test or MAT (minimum score 50), minimum GPA of 3.0. Application deadline: 9/1 (priority date; rolling processing). Application fee: $25 ($35 for international students). *Tuition:* $232 per credit for state residents; $254 per credit for nonresidents. *Financial aid:* Institutionally sponsored loans and career-related internships or fieldwork available. Aid available to part-time students. Financial aid application deadline: 3/15; applicants required to submit FAFSA. • Dr. Richard Evans, Adviser, 603-535-2487. Application contact: Maryann Szabadics, Administrative Assistant, 603-535-2636. Fax: 603-535-2572. E-mail: for.grad@psc.plymouth.edu.

Portland State University, College of Liberal Arts and Sciences, Department of Mathematical Sciences, Portland, OR 97207-0751. Offerings include mathematics education (PhD). PhD (mathematical sciences) offered in conjunction with the Systems Science Program. PhD (mathematics education) new for fall 1998. Department faculty: 26 full-time (8 women), 7 part-time (4 women), 27 FTE. *Degree requirements:* 2 foreign languages, dissertation, exams. *Entrance requirements:* GRE General Test. Application deadline: 4/1 (rolling processing; 11/1 for spring admission). Application fee: $50. *Tuition:* $6101 per year full-time, $689 per semester (minimum) part-time for state residents; $10,445 per year full-time, $689 per semester (minimum) part-time for nonresidents. • Dr. Eugene Enneking, Head, 503-725-3621. Application contact: J. Erdman, 503-725-3621. Fax: 503-725-3661.

Providence College, Department of Mathematics, Providence, RI 02918. Awards MAT. Part-time and evening/weekend programs available. Faculty: 3 full-time (0 women). Students: 2 full-time (both women), 15 part-time (12 women). Average age 39. 12 applicants, 67% accepted. In 1997, 9 degrees awarded (100% entered university research/teaching). *Entrance requirements:* TOEFL. Application deadline: 8/12 (priority date; rolling processing; 12/1 for spring admission). Application fee: $40. *Tuition:* $621 per course. *Financial aid:* Graduate assistantships, institutionally sponsored loans available. Aid available to part-time students. Financial aid applicants required to submit FAFSA. *Faculty research:* Mathematics education, history of mathematics, differential equations. • Dr. Clement DeMayo, Director, 401-865-2633.

Purdue University, School of Education, Department of Curriculum and Instruction, West Lafayette, IN 47907. Offerings include math/science education (Ed S), mathematics/science education (MS Ed, PhD). One or more programs accredited by NCATE. Department faculty: 34 full-time (15 women), 3 part-time (1 woman). *Degree requirements:* For master's, thesis optional; for doctorate, dissertation, oral and written exams; for Ed S, oral presentation, project required, thesis not required. *Entrance requirements:* For master's, TOEFL (minimum score 550), minimum B average; for doctorate, GRE General Test (minimum score 500 on each section), TOEFL (minimum score 550); for Ed S, minimum B average. Application deadline: 1/15 (priority date; 9/15 for spring admission). Application fee: $30. Electronic applications accepted. *Tuition:* $3500 per year full-time, $126 per credit hour part-time for state residents; $11,720 per year full-time, $387 per credit hour part-time for nonresidents. • Dr. J. L. Peters, Head, 765-494-9172. Fax: 765-496-1622. E-mail: peters@purdue.edu. Application contact: Christine Larsen, Coordinator of Graduate Studies, 765-494-2345. Fax: 765-494-5832. E-mail: gradoffice@soe.purdue.edu.

Queens College of the City University of New York, Social Science Division, School of Education, Department of Secondary Education, 65-30 Kissena Boulevard, Flushing, NY 11367-1597. Offerings include mathematics (MS Ed, AC). *Degree requirements:* For master's, research project required, foreign language and thesis not required; for AC, thesis optional, foreign language not required. *Entrance requirements:* For master's, TOEFL (minimum score 600), minimum GPA of 3.0; for AC, TOEFL (minimum score 600). Application deadline: 4/1 (rolling processing; 11/1 for spring admission). Application fee: $40. *Expenses:* Tuition $4350 per year full-time, $185 per credit part-time for state residents; $7600 per year full-time, $320 per credit part-time for nonresidents. Fees $104 per year. • Dr. Philip Anderson, Chairperson, 718-997-5150. Application contact: Mario Caruso, Director of Graduate Admissions, 718-997-5200. Fax: 718-997-5193. E-mail: graduate%queens.bitnet@cunyvm.cuny.edu.

Quinnipiac College, School of Liberal Arts, Program in Secondary and Middle School Teaching, Hamden, CT 06518-1904. Offerings include mathematics (MAT). Program faculty: 21 full-time (5 women), 16 part-time (9 women). *Degree requirements:* Thesis. *Average time to degree:* master's–1.5 years full-time, 3 years part-time. *Entrance requirements:* PRAXIS I, minimum GPA of 2.67. Application deadline: rolling. Application fee: $45. Electronic applications accepted. *Expenses:* Tuition $395 per credit hour. Fees $380 per year full-time. • Carol Orticari, Director, 203-281-8978. Fax: 203-281-8709. E-mail: orticari@quinnipiac.edu. Application contact: Scott Farber, Director of Graduate Admissions, 203-281-8795. Fax: 203-287-5238. E-mail: qcgradadmi@quinnipiac.edu.

Rollins College, Program in Education, Winter Park, FL 32789-4499. Offerings include secondary education (MAT), with options in English, mathematics, music. Program faculty: 13 full-time (8 women), 11 part-time (4 women), 17 FTE. *Application deadline:* rolling. *Application fee:* $50. *Tuition:* $190 per hour. • Dr. Nancy McAleer, Director, 407-646-2305. Application contact: Laura Pfister, Coordinator of Records and Registration, 407-646-2416. Fax: 407-646-1551.

Rowan University, College of Education, Department of Elementary Education, Glassboro, NJ 08028-1701. Offerings include elementary mathematics achievement (Certificate). Accredited by NCATE. *Application deadline:* 11/1 (priority date; rolling processing; 4/1 for spring admission). *Application fee:* $50. *Tuition:* $5728 per year full-time, $258 per credit hour part-time for state residents; $8968 per year full-time, $393 per credit hour part-time for nonresidents. • Dr. Carl Calliari, Adviser, 609-256-4763.

Rowan University, College of Education, Department of Secondary Education-Education Foundations, Program in Subject Matter Teaching, Program in Mathematics Education, Glassboro, NJ 08028-1701. Awards MA. Accredited by NCATE. Part-time and evening/weekend programs available. Students: 5 (4 women); includes 1 minority (African American). 4 applicants, 25% accepted. In 1997, 3 degrees awarded. *Degree requirements:* Thesis, comprehensive exams required, foreign language not required. *Entrance requirements:* GRE General Test, minimum GPA of 2.8. Application deadline: 11/1 (priority date; rolling processing; 4/1 for spring admission). Application fee: $50. *Tuition:* $5728 per year full-time, $258 per credit hour part-time for state residents; $8968 per year full-time, $393 per credit hour part-time for nonresidents. *Financial aid:* Assistantships, Federal Work-Study available. • Dr. Ron Czochor, Adviser, 609-256-4500 Ext. 3872.

Rutgers, The State University of New Jersey, New Brunswick, Graduate School of Education, Department of Learning and Teaching, Program in Mathematics Education, New Brunswick, NJ 08903. Awards Ed M, Ed D, Ed S. Part-time programs available. Faculty: 3 full-time (1 woman). Students: 59; includes 10 minority (5 African Americans, 3 Asian Americans, 2 Hispanics). 41 applicants, 76% accepted. In 1997, 22 master's, 2 doctorates awarded. Terminal master's awarded for partial completion of doctoral program. *Degree requirements:* For master's, comprehensive exam required, thesis not required; for doctorate, dissertation, qualifying exam. *Entrance requirements:* GRE General Test. Application deadline: 3/1 (11/1 for spring admission). Application fee: $40. *Expenses:* Tuition $6492 per year full-time, $268 per credit-part-time for state residents; $9520 per year full-time, $395 per credit part-time for nonresidents. Fees $208 per year (minimum). *Financial aid:* Fellowships, teaching assistantships, and career-related internships or fieldwork available. Financial aid application deadline: 3/1. • Warren Crown, Coordinator, 732-932-7496 Ext. 102. Fax: 732-932-7552. E-mail: wcrown@rci.rutgers.edu.

St. John Fisher College, School of Adult and Graduate Education, Mathematics/Science/Technology Education Program, Rochester, NY 14618-3597. Awards MS. Faculty: 1 (woman) full-time. Students: 0. *Degree requirements:* Computer language required, thesis not required. *Application deadline:* 8/1 (priority date; rolling processing; 1/1 for spring admission). *Application fee:* $30. *Tuition:* $13,500 per year full-time, $375 per credit hour part-time. • Dr. Carol Freeman, Graduate Director, 716-385-8132. E-mail: freeman@sjfc.edu. Application contact: Steven T. Hoskins, Director, Graduate Admissions, 716-385-8161. Fax: 716-385-8344. E-mail: hoskins@sjfc.edu.

Saint Joseph's University, Department of Education, Program in Mathematics Education, Philadelphia, PA 19131-1395. Awards MS. Students: 7 (4 women). *Degree requirements:* Computer language required, foreign language and thesis not required. *Entrance requirements:* TOEFL. Application deadline: 7/15. Application fee: $30. *Tuition:* $510 per credit hour. *Financial aid:* Fellowships available. • Dr. Mary DeKonty Applegate, Director, Department of Education, 610-660-1583.

Salem State College, Department of Education, Salem, MA 01970-5353. Offerings include mathematics (MAT). Accredited by NCATE. MAT (English as a second language) offered jointly with the Department of English. *Application deadline:* rolling. *Application fee:* $25. *Expenses:* Tuition $140 per credit hour for state residents; $230 per credit hour for nonresidents. Fees $20 per credit hour.

Salisbury State University, Department of Education, Salisbury, MD 21801-6837. Offerings include mathematics (M Ed). Department faculty: 19 full-time (10 women), 2 part-time (1 woman). *Application deadline:* 8/1 (priority date; rolling processing; 1/1 for spring admission). *Application fee:* $30. *Expenses:* Tuition $158 per credit hour for state residents; $310 per credit hour for nonresidents. Fees $4 per credit hour. • Dr. Ellen Whitford, Chair, 410-543-6294. E-mail: evwhitford@ssu.edu. Application contact: Phyllis Meyer, Administrative Aide II, 410-543-6281. Fax: 410-548-2593. E-mail: phmeyer@ssu.edu.

San Diego State University, College of Sciences, Department of Mathematical Sciences, San Diego, CA 92182. Offerings include mathematics and science education (PhD). PhD offered jointly with the University of California, San Diego. *Degree requirements:* Dissertation. *Application deadline:* 6/1 (priority date; rolling processing; 12/1 for spring admission). *Application fee:* $55. *Expenses:* Tuition $0 for state residents; $246 per unit for nonresidents. Fees $1932 per year full-time, $1266 per year part-time. • John D. Elwin, Chair, 619-594-6191. E-mail: elwin@saturn.sdsu.edu. Application contact: Edgar J. Howard, Graduate Coordinator, 619-594-5971. Fax: 619-594-6746. E-mail: ehoward@saturn.sdsu.edu.

San Francisco State University, College of Education, Department of Elementary Education, Program in Mathematics Education, San Francisco, CA 94132-1722. Awards MA. Accredited by NCATE. Part-time programs available. *Degree requirements:* Thesis or alternative. *Entrance requirements:* Minimum GPA of 2.5 in last 60 units. Application deadline: 11/30 (priority date; rolling processing). Application fee: $55. *Expenses:* Tuition $0 for state residents; $246 per unit for nonresidents. Fees $1982 per year full-time, $1316 per year part-time.

Shippensburg University of Pennsylvania, College of Arts and Sciences, Department of Mathematics and Computer Science, Shippensburg, PA 17257-2299. Offerings include mathematics (M Ed, MS). Department faculty: 13 full-time (1 woman). *Entrance requirements:* GRE General Test or minimum GPA of 2.5. Application deadline: rolling. Application fee: $25. Electronic applications accepted. *Expenses:* Tuition $3468 per year full-time, $193 per credit hour part-time for state residents; $6236 per year full-time, $346 per credit hour part-time for nonresidents. Fees $678 per year full-time, $108 per semester (minimum) part-time. • Dr. Fred Nordai, Chairperson, 717-532-1431.

Slippery Rock University of Pennsylvania, College of Education, Department of Secondary Education/Foundations of Education, Slippery Rock, PA 16057. Offers program in secondary education in math/science (M Ed). Accredited by NCATE. *Degree requirements:* Comprehensive exams. *Entrance requirements:* GRE, minimum GPA of 2.75. Application deadline: 7/1 (priority date; rolling processing; 11/1 for spring admission). Application fee: $25. *Tuition:* $4484 per year full-time, $247 per credit part-time for state residents; $7667 per year full-time, $423 per credit part-time for nonresidents.

Smith College, Department of Education and Child Study, Program in Secondary Education, Northampton, MA 01063. Offerings include mathematics education (MAT). Program faculty: 6 full-time (3 women), 3 part-time (2 women). *Degree requirements:* 1 foreign language required,

Directory: Mathematics Education

Smith College (continued)

thesis not required. *Average time to degree:* master's–1 year full-time, 4 years part-time. *Entrance requirements:* GRE General Test or MAT. Application deadline: 4/15 (12/1 for spring admission). Application fee: $50. *Tuition:* $21,680 per year full-time, $2720 per course part-time. • Rosetta Cohen, Head, 413-585-3266. E-mail: rcohen@sophia.smith.edu.

South Carolina State University, School of Education, Department of Teacher Education, 300 College Street Northeast, Orangeburg, SC 29117-0001. Offerings include mathematics (MAT); secondary education (M Ed), with options in biology education, business education, counselor education, English education, home economics education, industrial education, mathematics education, science education, social studies education. One or more programs accredited by NCATE. Department faculty: 7 full-time (3 women), 2 part-time (1 woman). *Degree requirements:* Departmental qualifying exam required, thesis optional. *Average time to degree:* master's–2 years full-time, 4 years part-time. *Entrance requirements:* GRE General Test (minimum combined score of 850) or MAT (minimum score 35), NTE (minimum score 650 on each core battery test), interview, teaching certificate. Application deadline: 7/15 (priority date; rolling processing; 11/10 for spring admission). Application fee: $25. *Tuition:* $2974 per year full-time, $165 per credit hour part-time. • Dr. Jesse Kinard, Chairman, 803-536-8934. Application contact: Dr. Gail Joyner-Fleming, Interim Associate Dean and Director, Graduate Teacher Education, 803-536-8824. Fax: 803-536-8492.

Southern Arkansas University–Magnolia, Graduate Program in Education, Program in Secondary Education, Magnolia, AR 71753. Offerings include mathematics and general science education (M Ed). *Degree requirements:* Thesis or alternative, comprehensive exam required, foreign language not required. *Average time to degree:* master's–2 years full-time. *Entrance requirements:* GRE, minimum GPA of 2.5. Application deadline: 8/15. Application fee: $0. *Expenses:* Tuition $95 per hour for state residents; $138 per hour for nonresidents. Fees $2 per hour. • Dr. Danield L. Bernard, Dean, Graduate Studies, Graduate Program in Education, 870-235-4055. Fax: 870-235-5035. E-mail: dlbernard@mail.saumag.edu.

Southern Connecticut State University, School of Arts and Sciences, Department of Mathematics, New Haven, CT 06515-1355. Awards MS Ed. Faculty: 10 full-time. Students: 10 full-time (2 women), 29 part-time (16 women); includes 1 minority (African American). 51 applicants, 14% accepted. In 1997, 5 degrees awarded. *Degree requirements:* Thesis or alternative. *Entrance requirements:* Interview. Application deadline: 7/15 (priority date; rolling processing). Application fee: $40. *Expenses:* Tuition $2632 per year full-time, $188 per credit part-time for state residents; $7200 per year full-time, $188 per credit part-time for nonresidents. Fees $1806 per year full-time, $45 per semester part-time for state residents; $2703 per year full-time, $45 per semester part-time for nonresidents. • Dr. Leo Kuczynski, Chair, 203-392-5586.

Stanford University, School of Education, Teacher Education Program, Stanford, CA 94305-9991. Offerings include mathematics education (AM). *Degree requirements:* Thesis required, foreign language not required. *Entrance requirements:* GRE General Test. Application deadline: 1/15. Application fee: $65 ($75 for international students). *Expenses:* Tuition $22,110 per year. Fees $156 per year. • Administrator, 650-723-4891. Application contact: Graduate Admissions Office, 650-723-2110.

State University of New York at Albany, College of Arts and Sciences, Department of Mathematics and Statistics, Albany, NY 12222-0001. Offerings include secondary teaching (MA). Department faculty: 29 full-time (2 women), 1 part-time (0 women). *Application fee:* $50. *Expenses:* Tuition $5100 per year full-time, $213 per credit hour part-time for state residents; $8416 per year full-time, $351 per credit hour part-time for nonresidents. Fees $705 per year full-time, $26.85 per credit hour part-time. • Timothy Lance, Chair, 518-442-4602.

State University of New York at Binghamton, School of Education and Human Development, Program in Secondary Education, Binghamton, NY 13902-6000. Offerings include mathematical sciences education (MAT, MS Ed, MST). *Entrance requirements:* GRE General Test, TOEFL. Application deadline: 4/15 (priority date; rolling processing; 11/1 for spring admission). Application fee: $50. Electronic applications accepted. *Expenses:* Tuition $5100 per year full-time, $213 per credit hour part-time for state residents; $8416 per year full-time, $351 per credit hour part-time for nonresidents. Fees $654 per year full-time, $75 per semester (minimum) part-time. • Dr. Wayne Ross, Coordinator, 607-777-2478.

State University of New York at Buffalo, Graduate School, Graduate School of Education, Department of Learning and Instruction, Buffalo, NY 14260. Offerings include secondary education (Ed M, Ed D, PhD), with options in English education (Ed D, PhD), foreign language education (Ed D, PhD), mathematics education (Ed D, PhD), science education (PhD). Terminal master's awarded for partial completion of doctoral program. Department faculty: 20 full-time (9 women), 7 part-time (2 women). *Degree requirements:* Dissertation, research analysis exam required, foreign language not required. *Entrance requirements:* GRE General Test, TOEFL (minimum score 600), interview. Application deadline: 2/1 (11/15 for spring admission). Application fee: $50. *Tuition:* $5970 per year full-time, $288 per credit hour part-time for state residents; $9286 per year full-time, $426 per credit hour part-time for nonresidents. • Dr. Michael Kibby, Chair, 716-645-2455. Application contact: Barbara Cracchiolo, Admissions Secretary, 716-645-2457. Fax: 716-645-3161.

State University of New York College at Brockport, School of Professions, Department of Education and Human Development, Programs in Secondary Education, Brockport, NY 14420-2997. Offerings include mathematics education (MS Ed). *Degree requirements:* Thesis or alternative required, foreign language not required. *Entrance requirements:* Minimum GPA of 3.0. Application deadline: 1/15 (priority date; 9/15 for spring admission). Application fee: $50. *Expenses:* Tuition $5100 per year full-time, $213 per credit hour part-time for state residents; $8416 per year full-time, $351 per credit hour part-time for nonresidents. Fees $440 per year full-time, $22.60 per credit hour part-time. • William Veenis, Chairperson, Department of Education and Human Development, 716-395-2205.

State University of New York College at Buffalo, Faculty of Natural and Social Sciences, Department of Mathematics, Buffalo, NY 14222-1095. Offers program in mathematics education (MS Ed). Accredited by NCATE. Part-time and evening/weekend programs available. Faculty: 10 full-time (3 women). Students: 15 part-time (7 women). Average age 29. 5 applicants, 80% accepted. In 1997, 5 degrees awarded. *Degree requirements:* Thesis or alternative required, foreign language not required. *Entrance requirements:* Minimum GPA of 2.5 in last 60 hours, 18 undergraduate hours in upper-level mathematics. Application deadline: 5/1 (10/1 for spring admission). Application fee: $50. *Expenses:* Tuition $5100 per year full-time, $213 per credit hour part-time for state residents; $8416 per year full-time, $351 per credit hour part-time for nonresidents. Fees $195 per year full-time, $8.60 per credit hour part-time. *Financial aid:* Fellowships, Federal Work-Study available. Aid available to part-time students. Financial aid application deadline: 3/1. • Dr. Robert Frascatore, Interim Chairperson, 716-878-5621.

State University of New York College at Buffalo, Faculty of Applied Science and Education, Department of Elementary Education and Reading, Program in Elementary and Early Secondary Education, Buffalo, NY 14222-1095. Offerings include mathematics education (MS Ed). Accredited by NCATE. *Degree requirements:* Thesis or project required, foreign language not required. *Entrance requirements:* Minimum GPA of 2.5 in last 60 hours, New York teaching certificate. Application deadline: 5/1 (10/1 for spring admission). Application fee: $50. *Expenses:* Tuition $5100 per year full-time, $213 per credit hour part-time for state residents; $8416 per year full-time, $351 per credit hour part-time for nonresidents. Fees $195 per year full-time, $8.60 per credit hour part-time. • Dr. Maria Ceprano, Chairperson, Department of Elementary Education and Reading, 716-878-5916.

State University of New York College at Cortland, Division of Arts and Sciences, Program in Secondary Education, Cortland, NY 13045. Offerings include mathematics (MAT, MS Ed). *Degree requirements:* 1 foreign language, thesis (for some programs), comprehensive exam. *Application deadline:* rolling. *Application fee:* $50. *Expenses:* Tuition $5100 per year full-time, $213 per credit hour part-time for state residents; $8416 per year full-time, $351 per credit hour part-time for nonresidents. Fees $644 per year full-time, $79 per semester (minimum) part-time. • Roger Sipher, Head, 607-753-2723. Application contact: Jeanne M. Bechtel, Director of Admissions, 607-753-4711. Fax: 607-753-5998.

State University of New York College at Cortland, Division of Professional Studies, Department of Education, Cortland, NY 13045. Offerings include elementary education (MS Ed), with options in English education, general science education, mathematics education, social studies education; secondary education (MS Ed), with options in biology, chemistry, earth science, French, mathematics, physics. *Application deadline:* rolling. *Application fee:* $50. *Expenses:* Tuition $5100 per year full-time, $213 per credit hour part-time for state residents; $8416 per year full-time, $351 per credit hour part-time for nonresidents. Fees $644 per year full-time, $79 per semester (minimum) part-time. • Mary Ware, Chair, 607-753-2705. Application contact: Jeanne M. Bechtel, Director of Admissions, 607-753-4711. Fax: 607-753-5998.

State University of New York College at Oneonta, Department of Education, Oneonta, NY 13820-4015. Offerings include elementary education (MS Ed), with options in early secondary English (N–9), early secondary math (N–9), early secondary social science (N–9), general science (N–9); secondary education (MS Ed), with options in biology education, chemistry education, earth science education, English education, home economics education, mathematics education, physics education, social science education. *Application deadline:* 4/15. *Application fee:* $50. *Expenses:* Tuition $5100 per year full-time, $213 per credit hour part-time for state residents; $8416 per year full-time, $351 per credit hour part-time for nonresidents. Fees $482 per year full-time, $6.85 per credit hour part-time. • Dr. Ronald Cromwell, Chair, 607-436-2538.

Stephen F. Austin State University, College of Sciences and Mathematics, Department of Mathematics and Statistics, Nacogdoches, TX 75962. Offerings include mathematics education (MS). Department faculty: 14 full-time (1 woman). *Degree requirements:* Comprehensive exam required, thesis optional, foreign language not required. *Entrance requirements:* GRE General Test, minimum GPA of 2.8 in last 60 hours, 2.5 overall. Application deadline: 8/1 (priority date; rolling processing; 12/15 for spring admission). Application fee: $0 ($25 for international students). *Tuition:* $1465 per year full-time, $263 per semester (minimum) part-time for state residents; $5299 per year full-time, $890 per semester (minimum) part-time for nonresidents. • Dr. Jasper Adams, Chair, 409-468-3805.

Syracuse University, College of Arts and Sciences, Department of Mathematics, Syracuse, NY 13244-0003. Offerings include mathematics education (MS, PhD). Terminal master's awarded for partial completion of doctoral program. Department faculty: 35. *Degree requirements:* For doctorate, 2 foreign languages, dissertation, qualifying exam. *Entrance requirements:* GRE General Test, GRE Subject Test, TOEFL. Application deadline: rolling. Application fee: $40. *Tuition:* $13,320 per year full-time, $555 per credit hour part-time. • Douglas Anderson, Chair, 315-443-1472. Application contact: Mark Watkins, Graduate Program Director, 315-443-1471.

Syracuse University, School of Education, Teaching and Leadership Programs, Program in Mathematics Education, Syracuse, NY 13244-0003. Awards MS, Ed D, PhD, CAS. Students: 17 full-time (11 women), 4 part-time (all women); includes 2 minority (1 African American, 1 Asian American), 3 international. 14 applicants, 79% accepted. In 1997, 12 master's, 1 doctorate awarded. *Degree requirements:* For master's, thesis or alternative; for doctorate and CAS, thesis/dissertation. *Entrance requirements:* GRE. Application fee: $40. *Tuition:* $13,320 per year full-time, $555 per credit hour part-time. *Financial aid:* Application deadline 3/1. • Dr. Howard Johnson, Chair, 315-443-1483.

Teachers College, Columbia University, Graduate Faculty of Education, Department of Scientific Foundations, Program in Mathematics Education, 525 West 120th Street, New York, NY 10027-6696. Awards Ed M, MA, MS, Ed D, Ed DCT, PhD. Faculty: 2 full-time (1 woman), 3 part-time (1 woman), 3 FTE. Students: 33 full-time (20 women), 87 part-time (40 women); includes 46 minority (24 African Americans, 14 Asian Americans, 7 Hispanics, 1 Native American), 8 international. Average age 36. 71 applicants, 59% accepted. In 1997, 22 master's, 8 doctorates awarded. *Degree requirements:* For doctorate, dissertation. *Entrance requirements:* For master's, undergraduate major or minor in mathematics; for doctorate, MA in mathematics or mathematics education. Application deadline: 5/15 (12/1 for spring admission). Application fee: $50. *Expenses:* Tuition $640 per credit. Fees $120 per semester. *Financial aid:* Full and partial tuition waivers, Federal Work-Study, institutionally sponsored loans, and career-related internships or fieldwork available. Aid available to part-time students. Financial aid application deadline: 2/1. *Faculty research:* Problem solving, curriculum development, international education, history of mathematics. • Application contact: Barbara Reinhalter, Office of Admissions, 212-678-3710. Fax: 212-678-4171.

Temple University, College of Education, Department of Curriculum, Instruction, and Technology in Education, Philadelphia, PA 19122-6096. Offerings include math/science education (Ed D), mathematics/science education (Ed M). One or more programs accredited by NCATE. Terminal master's awarded for partial completion of doctoral program. Department faculty: 33 full-time (14 women). *Degree requirements:* For doctorate, dissertation required, foreign language not required. *Entrance requirements:* For doctorate, GRE General Test (minimum combined score of 1000) or MAT (minimum score 39). Application deadline: 2/15 (10/1 for spring admission). Application fee: $40. *Expenses:* Tuition $323 per semester hour for state residents; $444 per semester hour for nonresidents. Fees $170 per year full-time, $28 per semester (minimum) part-time. • Dr. Raymond Lolla, Chair, 215-204-6387. Fax: 215-204-1414.

Texas A&M University, College of Education, Department of Educational Curriculum and Instruction, Unit in Math/Science, College Station, TX 77843. Awards M Ed, MS, Ed D, PhD. Accredited by NCATE. *Degree requirements:* For doctorate, dissertation required, foreign language not required. *Entrance requirements:* GRE General Test, TOEFL. Application fee: $35 ($75 for international students). *Financial aid:* Fellowships, research assistantships, teaching assistantships available. • Charles Lamb, Coordinator, 409-845-8395.

Union College, Graduate and Continuing Studies, Programs in Education, Schenectady, NY 12308-2311. Offerings include mathematics (MAT), mathematics/computer science (MS). *Application deadline:* 5/15. *Application fee:* $35. *Tuition:* $1155 per course. • Dr. Patrick Allen, Educational Studies Director, 518-388-6361.

University of Alaska Fairbanks, Graduate School, College of Science, Engineering and Mathematics, Department of Mathematical Sciences, Fairbanks, AK 99775-7480. Offerings include mathematics (MAT, MS, PhD). Terminal master's awarded for partial completion of doctoral program. Department faculty: 23 full-time (3 women), 1 part-time (0 women). *Degree requirements:* For master's, comprehensive exam, project required, foreign language not required; for doctorate, 1 foreign language (computer language can substitute), dissertation, comprehensive exam. *Entrance requirements:* GRE General Test, GRE Subject Test, TOEFL (minimum score 550). Application deadline: 8/1 (priority date). Application fee: $35. *Expenses:* Tuition $162 per credit for state residents; $316 per credit for nonresidents. Fees $520 per year full-time, $45 per semester (minimum) part-time. • Dr. Clifton Lando, Head, 907-474-7332.

University of Arkansas, J. William Fulbright College of Arts and Sciences, Department of Mathematical Sciences, Program in Secondary Mathematics, Fayetteville, AR 72701-1201. Awards MA. Accredited by NCATE. Students: 0. 2 applicants, 100% accepted. *Degree requirements:* Written exam required, foreign language not required. *Application fee:* $25 ($35 for international students). *Tuition:* $3144 per year full-time, $173 per credit hour part-time for state residents; $7140 per year full-time, $395 per credit hour part-time for nonresidents. *Financial aid:* Teaching assistantships, Federal Work-Study, and career-related internships or fieldwork available. Aid available to part-time students. Financial aid application deadline: 4/1; applicants required to submit FAFSA. • Dr. Itrel Monroe, Chairman of Studies, 501-575-3351.

University of Arkansas at Pine Bluff, Program in Education, Pine Bluff, AR 71601-2799. Offerings include secondary education (M Ed), with options in aquaculture, English, general science, mathematics, physical education, social studies. Accredited by NCATE. Program faculty: 51. *Entrance requirements:* GRE, minimum GPA of 2.75; NTE or Standard Arkansas Teaching Certificate. Application deadline: rolling. Application fee: $0. *Expenses:* Tuition $82 per credit hour for state residents; $192 per credit hour for nonresidents. Fees $25 per year. • Dr. Calvin Johnson, Dean, 870-543-8256.

University of British Columbia, Faculty of Education, Department of Curriculum Studies, Vancouver, BC V6T 1Z2, Canada. Offerings include math education (MA, M Ed, PhD). *Degree requirements:* For master's, thesis (MA) required, foreign language not required; for doctorate, dissertation required, foreign language not required. *Entrance requirements:* TOEFL (minimum score 550). Application deadline: 3/1 (12/1 for spring admission). Application fee: $60.

University of California, Berkeley, School of Education, Division of Cognition and Development, Group in Science and Mathematics Education, Berkeley, CA 94720-1500. Awards PhD. *Application deadline:* 12/15. *Expenses:* Tuition $0 for state residents; $9384 per year for nonresidents. Fees $4409 per year. *Financial aid:* Application deadline 12/15. • Barbara White, Chair. Application contact: Kate Capps, Graduate Assistant/Admissions, 510-642-4206. Fax: 510-642-3769. E-mail: kate@socrates.berkeley.edu.

University of California, Berkeley, School of Education, Division of Cognition and Development, Program in Education in Mathematics, Science, and Technology, Berkeley, CA 94720-1500. Awards MA, PhD. *Application deadline:* 12/15. *Expenses:* Tuition $0 for state residents; $9384 per year for nonresidents. Fees $4409 per year. *Financial aid:* Application deadline 12/15. • Application contact: Kate Capps, Program Assistant, 510-642-4206. E-mail: gse_info@uclink.berkeley.edu.

University of California, Berkeley, School of Education, Division of Cognition and Development, Science and Mathematics Education Program, Berkeley, CA 94720-1500. Offers education/single subject teaching: mathematics (MA), education/single subject teaching: science (MA). *Expenses:* Tuition $0 for state residents; $9384 per year for nonresidents. Fees $4409 per year. • Daniel Zimmerlin, Academic Coordinator.

University of Central Florida, College of Education, Department of Instructional Programs, Program in Mathematics Education, Orlando, FL 32816. Awards MA, M Ed. Accredited by NCATE. Students: 17 full-time (10 women), 18 part-time (15 women); includes 7 minority (5 African Americans, 1 Asian American, 1 Hispanic). Average age 34. 8 applicants, 88% accepted. In 1997, 4 degrees awarded. *Degree requirements:* Thesis or alternative required, foreign language not required. *Entrance requirements:* GRE General Test (minimum combined score of 840). Application deadline: 7/15 (12/15 for spring admission). Application fee: $20. *Expenses:* Tuition $3288 per year full-time, $137 per credit hour part-time for state residents; $11,520 per year full-time, $480 per credit hour part-time for nonresidents. Fees $105 per year. • Application contact: Dr. Douglas Brumbaugh, Coordinator, 407-823-2045. E-mail: brumbad@pegasus.cc.ucf.edu.

University of Central Oklahoma, College of Mathematics and Science, Department of Mathematics, Edmond, OK 73034-5209. Offerings include applied mathematical sciences (MS), with options in computer science, mathematics, mathematics/computer science teaching, statistics. Accredited by NCATE. *Degree requirements:* Computer language, thesis required, foreign language not required. *Application deadline:* 8/18 (priority date; rolling processing). *Application fee:* $15. *Tuition:* $76 per credit hour for state residents; $178 per credit hour for nonresidents.

University of Cincinnati, McMicken College of Arts and Sciences, Department of Mathematics, Cincinnati, OH 45221. Offerings include mathematics education (MAT). Accredited by NCATE. Department faculty: 40 full-time. *Average time to degree:* master's–3.9 years full-time; doctorate–5.8 years full-time. *Application deadline:* 2/1. *Application fee:* $30. *Tuition:* $7228 per year full-time, $185 per credit hour part-time for state residents; $13,812 per year full-time, $352 per credit hour part-time for nonresidents. • James Osterburg, Head, 513-556-4054. E-mail: james.osterburg@uc.edu. Application contact: Diego Murio, Graduate Program Director, 513-556-4088. Fax: 513-556-3417. E-mail: diego.murio@uc.edu.

University of Connecticut, School of Education, Field of Mathematics Education, Storrs, CT 06269. Awards MA, PhD. Accredited by NCATE. Faculty: 1. Students: 4 full-time (3 women), 1 part-time (0 women); includes 1 minority (Hispanic). Average age 24. 8 applicants, 100% accepted. In 1997, 7 master's awarded. Terminal master's awarded for partial completion of doctoral program. *Degree requirements:* For doctorate, dissertation. *Entrance requirements:* For doctorate, GRE General Test. Application deadline: 6/1 (priority date; rolling processing; 11/1 for spring admission). Application fee: $40 ($45 for international students). *Expenses:* Tuition $5272 per year full-time, $293 per credit part-time for state residents; $13,696 per year full-time, $761 per credit part-time for nonresidents. Fees $948 per year full-time, $640 per year part-time. *Financial aid:* In 1997–98, 2 research assistantships (both to first-year students) totaling $9,619, 1 teaching assistantship (to a first-year student) totaling $3,206 were awarded; fellowships also available. Financial aid application deadline: 2/15. • Thomas P. Weinland, Head, 860-486-2433.

University of Detroit Mercy, College of Engineering and Science, Department of Mathematics and Computer Science, Detroit, MI 48219-0900. Offerings include elementary mathematics education (MATM), junior high mathematics education (MATM), secondary mathematics education (MATM). *Application deadline:* 8/1 (priority date; rolling processing). *Application fee:* $25 ($35 for international students).

University of Florida, College of Education, Department of Instruction and Curriculum, Gainesville, FL 32611. Offerings include mathematics education (MAE, M Ed, Ed D, PhD, Ed S). Accredited by NCATE. Department faculty: 42. *Degree requirements:* For master's, thesis optional, foreign language not required; for doctorate, variable foreign language requirement, dissertation. *Entrance requirements:* For master's and doctorate, GRE General Test (minimum combined score of 1000), minimum GPA of 3.0; for Ed S, GRE General Test. Application deadline: 6/5. Application fee: $20. *Tuition:* $138 per credit hour for state residents; $481 per credit hour for nonresidents. • Dr. Mary Grace Kantowski, Chair, 352-392-9191 Ext. 200. E-mail: mgk@coe.ufl.edu. Application contact: Dr. Ben Nelms, Graduate Coordinator, 352-392-9191 Ext. 225. Fax: 352-392-9193. E-mail: bfn@coe.ufl.edu.

University of Florida, College of Liberal Arts and Sciences, Department of Mathematics, Gainesville, FL 32611. Offerings include mathematics teaching (MAT, MST). Accredited by NCATE. Department faculty: 58. *Application deadline:* 6/5 (priority date; rolling processing). *Application fee:* $20. Electronic applications accepted. *Tuition:* $138 per credit hour for state residents; $481 per credit hour for nonresidents. • Dr. Joseph Glover, Chairman, 352-392-0281. Application contact: Dr. Bernard Mair, Graduate Coordinator, 352-392-0281. Fax: 352-392-8357. E-mail: bam@math.ufl.edu.

University of Georgia, College of Education, Programs in Secondary Education, Athens, GA 30602. Offerings include mathematics education (M Ed, Ed D, PhD, Ed S). Accredited by NCATE. Faculty: 46 full-time (17 women). *Degree requirements:* For doctorate, dissertation required, foreign language not required. *Entrance requirements:* For doctorate, GRE General Test; for Ed S, GRE General Test or MAT. Application deadline: 7/1 (priority date; 11/15 for spring admission). Application fee: $30. Electronic applications accepted. *Tuition:* $3290 per year full-time, $643 per semester (minimum) part-time for state residents; $11,300 per year full-time, $1645 per semester (minimum) part-time for nonresidents. • Dr. Russell H. Yeany, Dean, 706-542-3866. Fax: 706-542-0360.

University of Houston, College of Education, Department of Curriculum and Instruction, 4800 Calhoun, Houston, TX 77204-2163. Offerings include mathematics education (M Ed). Accredited by NCATE. Department faculty: 37 full-time (19 women), 10 part-time (7 women). *Degree requirements:* Comprehensive exam or thesis required, foreign language not required. *Entrance requirements:* GRE General Test or MAT. Application deadline: 7/3 (priority date; rolling processing). Application fee: $35 ($75 for international students). *Expenses:* Tuition $1152 per year full-time, $120 per semester (minimum) part-time for state residents; $4482 per year full-time, $249 per credit hour part-time for nonresidents. Fees $977 per year full-time, $119 per semester (minimum) part-time. • Wilford Weber, Chair, 713-743-4970. Fax: 713-743-9870. E-mail: wweber@uh.edu.

University of Idaho, College of Graduate Studies, College of Letters and Science, Department of Mathematics and Statistics, Program in Mathematics, Moscow, ID 83844-4140. Offerings include mathematics education (MAT). Accredited by NCATE. Program faculty: 24 full-time (6 women), 3 part-time (1 woman), 25.25 FTE. *Application deadline:* 8/1 (12/15 for spring admission). *Application fee:* $35 ($45 for international students). *Expenses:* Tuition $0 for state residents; $6000 per year full-time, $95 per credit part-time for nonresidents. Fees $2676 per year full-time, $134 per credit part-time. • Dr. Erol Barbut, Chair, Department of Mathematics and Statistics, 208-885-6742.

University of Illinois at Chicago, College of Liberal Arts and Sciences, Department of Mathematics, Statistics, and Computer Science, Program in Teaching of Mathematics, Chicago, IL 60607-7128. Awards MST. Students: 12 full-time (8 women), 23 part-time (13 women); includes 7 minority (2 African Americans, 1 Asian American, 4 Hispanics). Average age 35. 14 applicants, 86% accepted. In 1997, 24 degrees awarded. *Degree requirements:* Comprehensive exam required, foreign language and thesis not required. *Entrance requirements:* GRE General Test, TOEFL (minimum score 550), minimum GPA of 3.75 on a 5.0 scale. Application deadline: 7/3 (11/8 for spring admission). Application fee: $40 ($50 for international students). *Financial aid:* In 1997–98, 1 research assistantship, 4 teaching assistantships were awarded; fellowships also available. • Application contact: David Radford, Director of Graduate Studies, 312-996-3041.

University of Illinois at Urbana–Champaign, College of Liberal Arts and Sciences, Department of Mathematics, Urbana, IL 61801. Offerings include teaching of mathematics (MS). Department faculty: 81 full-time (6 women). *Entrance requirements:* Minimum GPA of 4.0 on a 5.0 scale. Application deadline: rolling. Application fee: $40 ($50 for international students). • Philippe Tondeur, Chair, 217-333-3352.

University of Manitoba, Faculty of Education, Department of Curriculum: Mathematics and Natural Sciences, Winnipeg, MB R3T 2N2, Canada. Offerings include mathematics education (M Ed). *Degree requirements:* Thesis or alternative required, foreign language not required.

University of Massachusetts Lowell, College of Education, Program in Math and Science Education, 1 University Avenue, Lowell, MA 01854-2881. Awards Ed D. Accredited by NCATE. Students: 2 full-time (1 woman), 26 part-time (13 women); includes 2 minority (1 Asian American, 1 Hispanic). In 1997, 2 degrees awarded. *Degree requirements:* Dissertation. *Entrance requirements:* GRE General Test. Application deadline: 4/1 (priority date; rolling processing; 10/1 for spring admission). Application fee: $20 ($35 for international students). *Tuition:* $4867 per year full-time, $618 per semester (minimum) part-time for state residents; $10,276 per year full-time, $1294 per semester (minimum) part-time for nonresidents. *Financial aid:* Application deadline 4/1. • Dr. Brenda Jochums, Coordinator, 978-934-4620.

University of Michigan, School of Education, Programs in Educational Studies, Ann Arbor, MI 48109. Offerings include mathematics education (AM, MS, PhD). *Degree requirements:* For master's, thesis required (for some programs), foreign language not required; for doctorate, dissertation, preliminary exam required, foreign language not required. *Entrance requirements:* GRE General Test (minimum combined score of 1800 on three sections), TOEFL (minimum score 600). Application deadline: 1/15 (priority date). Application fee: $55. Electronic applications accepted. • Dr. Ronald Marx, Chairperson, 734-763-9497. E-mail: ronmarx@umich.edu. Application contact: Karen Wixson, Associate Dean, 734-764-9470. Fax: 734-763-1229. E-mail: kwixson@umich.edu.

University of Minnesota, Twin Cities Campus, College of Education and Human Development, Department of Curriculum and Instruction, Minneapolis, MN 55455-0213. Offerings include mathematics education (MA, M Ed, PhD). • Fred Finley, Chairman, 612-625-2545.

University of Missouri–Rolla, College of Arts and Sciences, Department of Mathematics and Statistics, Program in Mathematics, Rolla, MO 65409-0910. Offerings include mathematics education (MST). *Degree requirements:* Thesis or alternative required, foreign language not required. *Entrance requirements:* GRE General Test, GRE Subject Test. Application deadline: 7/1 (rolling processing). Application fee: $20. Electronic applications accepted. *Expenses:* Tuition $3902 per year full-time, $163 per credit hour part-time for state residents; $11,738 per year full-time, $489 per credit hour part-time for nonresidents. Fees $610 per year (minimum) full-time, $146 per year (minimum) part-time. • Application contact: Dr. Leon Hall, Director of Graduate Studies, 573-341-4911. Fax: 573-341-4741. E-mail: lmhall@umr.edu.

The University of Montana–Missoula, College of Arts and Sciences, Department of Mathematical Sciences, Missoula, MT 59812-0002. Offerings include mathematics (MAT), mathematics education (PhD). Terminal master's awarded for partial completion of doctoral program. Department faculty: 20 full-time (3 women). *Degree requirements:* For doctorate, 1 foreign language, dissertation. *Entrance requirements:* For doctorate, GRE General Test. Application deadline: 3/1 (priority date). Application fee: $30. *Tuition:* $2499 per year (minimum) full-time, $376 per semester (minimum) part-time for state residents; $6528 per year (minimum) full-time, $1048 per semester (minimum) part-time for nonresidents. • Dr. Gloria Hewitt, Chair, 406-243-5311.

University of Nebraska at Kearney, College of Natural and Social Sciences, Department of Mathematics and Statistics, Kearney, NE 68849-0001. Offers program in mathematics education (MS Ed). One or more programs accredited by NCATE. Part-time and evening/weekend programs available. Faculty: 6 full-time (1 woman). Students: 5 part-time (2 women). In 1997, 2 degrees awarded. *Degree requirements:* Thesis optional. *Entrance requirements:* GRE General Test. Application deadline: 8/1 (priority date; rolling processing; 12/15 for spring admission). Application fee: $35. *Expenses:* Tuition $1494 per year full-time, $83 per credit hour part-time for state residents; $2826 per year full-time, $157 per credit hour part-time for nonresidents. Fees $229 per year full-time, $11.25 per semester (minimum) part-time. *Financial aid:* Research assistantships, teaching assistantships, and career-related internships or fieldwork available. Aid available to part-time students. Financial aid application deadline: 3/1; applicants required to submit FAFSA. • Dr. Randall Heckman, Chair, 308-865-8531.

University of Nevada, Las Vegas, College of Education, Department of Instructional and Curricular Studies, Las Vegas, NV 89154-9900. Offerings include mathematics education (M Ed, MS). Accredited by NCATE. Department faculty: 34 full-time (16 women). *Degree requirements:* Thesis (for some programs), oral or written comprehensive exam required, foreign language not required. *Entrance requirements:* Minimum GPA of 3.0. Application deadline: 2/15 (9/30 for spring admission). Application fee: $40 ($95 for international students). *Expenses:* Tuition $93 per credit for state residents; $93 per credit full-time, $190 per credit part-time for nonresidents. Fees $5570 per year full-time for nonresidents. • Dr. Jan McCarthy, Chair, 702-895-3241. Application contact: Graduate College Admissions Evaluator, 702-895-3320.

University of Nevada, Reno, College of Arts and Science, Department of Mathematics, Reno, NV 89557. Offerings include teaching mathematics (MATM). Department faculty: 17 full-time (1 woman). *Application deadline:* 3/1 (priority date; rolling processing). *Application fee:* $40. *Expenses:* Tuition $0 for state residents; $5770 per year full-time, $200 per credit part-time for nonresidents. Fees $93 per credit. • Dr. Jerry Johnson, Chair, 702-784-6773. Application contact: Dr. Sitadri Bagchi, Graduate Director, 702-784-6775. E-mail: bagchi@math.unr.edu.

University of New Hampshire, College of Engineering and Physical Sciences, Department of Mathematics, Durham, NH 03824. Offerings include mathematics education (PhD). Terminal

Directory: Mathematics Education

University of New Hampshire (continued)

master's awarded for partial completion of doctoral program. Department faculty: 24 full-time. *Degree requirements:* 2 foreign languages (computer language can substitute for one), dissertation. *Application deadline:* 4/1 (priority date; rolling processing). *Application fee:* $50. *Expenses:* Tuition $5440 per year full-time, $302 per credit hour part-time for state residents; $8160 per year (minimum) full-time, $453 per credit hour (minimum) part-time for nonresidents. Fees $868 per year full-time, $15 per year part-time. • Dr. Kenneth I. Appel, Chairperson, 603-862-2673. Application contact: Dr. Edward K. Hinson, Graduate Coordinator, 603-862-2688. E-mail: ekh@christa.unh.edu.

The University of North Carolina at Chapel Hill, School of Education, Programs in Teacher Education, Program in Secondary Education, Chapel Hill, NC 27599. Offerings include mathematics (MAT). Accredited by NCATE. *Degree requirements:* Comprehensive exam required, foreign language and thesis not required. *Entrance requirements:* GRE General Test (minimum combined score of 1000), minimum GPA of 3.0 during last 2 years of undergraduate course work. Application deadline: 1/1 (rolling processing). Application fee: $55. *Expenses:* Tuition $1428 per year full-time, $357 per semester (minimum) part-time for state residents; $10,414 per year full-time, $2604 per semester (minimum) part-time for nonresidents. Fees $782 per year full-time, $332 per semester (minimum) part-time. • Dr. Walter Pryzwansky, Director of Graduate Studies, 919-966-7000. Application contact: Janet Carroll, Registrar, 919-966-1346. Fax: 919-962-1533. E-mail: jscarrol@email.unc.edu.

University of North Carolina at Charlotte, College of Arts and Sciences, Department of Mathematics, Charlotte, NC 28223-0001. Offerings include mathematics education (MA). Accredited by NCATE. Department faculty: 38 full-time (5 women). *Application deadline:* 7/1. *Application fee:* $35. *Tuition:* $1786 per year full-time, $339 per semester (minimum) part-time for state residents; $8914 per year full-time, $2121 per semester (minimum) part-time for nonresidents. • Dr. Ram C. Tiwari, Chair, 704-547-4551. Application contact: Kathy Barringer, Assistant Director of Graduate Admissions, 704-547-3366. Fax: 704-547-3279. E-mail: gradadm@email.uncc.edu.

University of North Carolina at Pembroke, Graduate Studies, Department of Mathematics and Computer Science, Program in Mathematics Education, Pembroke, NC 28372-1510. Awards MA Ed. Accredited by NCATE. Part-time and evening/weekend programs available. Faculty: 9 full-time (0 women). Students: 9 part-time (3 women); includes 6 minority (all Native Americans). In 1997, 2 degrees awarded. *Degree requirements:* Comprehensive exam required, thesis optional, foreign language not required. *Average time to degree:* master's–2 years full-time, 3 years part-time. *Entrance requirements:* GRE General Test or MAT, bachelor's degree in mathematics or mathematics education, minimum GPA of 3.0 in major, 2.5 overall. Application deadline: rolling. Application fee: $25. *Tuition:* $1554 per year full-time, $610 per semester (minimum) part-time for state residents; $8824 per year full-time, $2122 per semester (minimum) part-time for nonresidents. *Financial aid:* Graduate assistantships available. Aid available to part-time students. Financial aid application deadline: 4/15. • Dr. Gilbert Sampson, Coordinator, 910-521-6244. Application contact: Director of Graduate Studies, 910-521-6271. Fax: 910-521-6497.

University of Northern Colorado, College of Arts and Sciences, Department of Mathematics, Greeley, CO 80639. Offerings include educational mathematics (MA, PhD). One or more programs accredited by NCATE. Department faculty: 14 full-time (2 women). *Degree requirements:* For master's, thesis or alternative, comprehensive exams; for doctorate, dissertation, comprehensive exams. *Entrance requirements:* GRE General Test. Application deadline: rolling. Application fee: $35. *Expenses:* Tuition $2327 per year full-time, $129 per credit hour part-time for state residents; $9578 per year full-time, $532 per credit hour part-time for nonresidents. Fees $752 per year full-time, $184 per semester (minimum) part-time. • Dr. Richard Grassl, Chairperson, 970-351-2820.

University of Northern Iowa, College of Natural Sciences, Department of Mathematics, Cedar Falls, IA 50614. Offerings include mathematics for elementary and middle school (MA). Department faculty: 14 full-time (3 women). *Degree requirements:* Thesis or alternative required, foreign language not required. *Application deadline:* 8/1 (priority date; rolling processing). *Application fee:* $20 ($30 for international students). *Expenses:* Tuition $3166 per year full-time, $176 per hour part-time for state residents; $7805 per year full-time, $176 per hour part-time for nonresidents. Fees $194 per year full-time, $12.50 per semester (minimum) part-time. • Dr. Joel Haack, Head, 319-273-2631.

University of North Florida, College of Education, Department of Elementary and Secondary Education, Program in Mathematics Education, Jacksonville, FL 32224-2645. Awards M Ed. Accredited by NCATE. Part-time and evening/weekend programs available. Faculty: 2 full-time (both women). Students: 1 (woman) part-time. 0 applicants. *Entrance requirements:* GRE General Test (minimum combined score of 1000), minimum GPA of 3.0. Application deadline: rolling. Application fee: $20. *Tuition:* $3388 per year full-time, $141 per credit hour part-time for state residents; $11,634 per year full-time, $485 per credit hour part-time for nonresidents. • Dr. Dennis Holt, Chairperson, Department of Elementary and Secondary Education, 904-646-2610.

University of Oklahoma, College of Education, Department of Instructional Leadership and Academic Curriculum, Program in Instructional Leadership and Academic Curriculum, Norman, OK 73019-0390. Offerings include math education (M Ed, PhD). Accredited by NCATE. Program faculty: 19 full-time (12 women), 12 part-time (11 women). *Degree requirements:* For doctorate, variable foreign language requirement, dissertation. *Entrance requirements:* For master's, TOEFL (minimum score 550), 12 hours of course work in education; for doctorate, GRE General Test (minimum combined score of 1000), TOEFL (minimum score 500), master's degree, minimum graduate GPA of 3.0. Application deadline: 6/1 (priority date; rolling processing). Application fee: $25. *Expenses:* Tuition $1920 per year full-time, $80 per credit hour part-time for state residents; $6108 per year full-time, $255 per credit hour part-time for nonresidents. Fees $468 per year full-time, $12 per semester (minimum) part-time. • Dr. Bonnie Konopak, Chair, Department of Instructional Leadership and Academic Curriculum, 405-325-1498.

University of Pittsburgh, School of Education, Department of Instruction and Learning, Program in Secondary Education, Pittsburgh, PA 15260. Offerings include mathematics education (MAT, M Ed, Ed D). *Average time to degree:* master's–2 years full-time, 4 years part-time; doctorate–4 years full-time, 6 years part-time. *Application deadline:* 2/1. *Application fee:* $30 ($40 for international students). *Expenses:* Tuition $8018 per year full-time, $329 per credit part-time for state residents; $16,508 per year full-time, $680 per credit part-time for nonresidents. Fees $480 per year full-time, $180 per year part-time. • Application contact: Jackie Harden, Manager, 412-648-7060. Fax: 412-648-1899. E-mail: jackie@sched.fsl.pitt.edu.

University of Puerto Rico, Río Piedras, College of Education, Program in Curriculum and Teaching, San Juan, PR 00931. Offerings include mathematics education (M Ed). *Degree requirements:* Thesis required, foreign language not required. *Entrance requirements:* PAEG, minimum GPA of 3.0. Application deadline: 2/21. Application fee: $17.

University of Rio Grande, Graduate School, Rio Grande, OH 45674. Offerings include classroom teaching (M Ed), with options in fine arts, learning disabilities, mathematics, reading education. School faculty: 9 full-time (3 women), 6 part-time (2 women). *Degree requirements:* Final research project, portfolio required, foreign language and thesis not required. *Entrance requirements:* Minimum GPA of 2.7 in major, 2.5 overall. Application deadline: rolling. Application fee: $20. • Dr. Greg Miller, Coordinator, 740-245-7364. Application contact: Dr. Mark Abell, Director of Administration, 740-245-5353.

University of South Carolina, Graduate School, College of Science and Mathematics, Department of Mathematics, Columbia, SC 29208. Offerings include mathematics education (MAT, M Math). Accredited by NCATE. MAT offered in cooperation with the College of Education. Department faculty: 32 full-time (1 woman). *Application deadline:* 7/1 (priority date; rolling processing). *Application fee:* $35. Electronic applications accepted. *Expenses:* Tuition $3894 per year full-time, $193 per credit hour part-time for state residents; $8114 per year full-time, $404 per credit hour part-time for nonresidents. Fees $125 per year full-time, $37 per semester (minimum) part-time. • Dr. R. M. Stephenson Jr., Chair, 803-777-4224. E-mail: chairman@milo.math.scarolina.edu. Application contact: Dr. Anton R. Schep, Graduate Director, 803-777-4226. Fax: 803-777-3783. E-mail: graddir@milo.math.scarolina.edu.

University of South Florida, College of Education, Department of Secondary Education, Program in Mathematics Education, Tampa, FL 33620-9951. Awards MA, M Ed, PhD, Ed S. Accredited by NCATE. Part-time and evening/weekend programs available. Students: 7 full-time (5 women), 36 part-time (21 women); includes 5 minority (1 African American, 2 Asian Americans, 2 Hispanics), 3 international. Average age 37. 7 applicants, 57% accepted. In 1997, 10 master's awarded. *Degree requirements:* For doctorate, dissertation, 2 tools of research in foreign language, statistics, and/or computers. *Entrance requirements:* For master's, GRE General Test (minimum combined score of 1000), minimum GPA of 3.5 in last 60 hours; for doctorate, GRE General Test (minimum combined score of 1000), minimum GPA of 3.0 (undergraduate) or 3.5 (graduate); for Ed S, GRE General Test (minimum combined score of 1000). Application deadline: 6/1 (10/15 for spring admission). Application fee: $20. Electronic applications accepted. *Tuition:* $142 per credit hour for state residents; $486 per credit hour for nonresidents. *Financial aid:* Federal Work-Study, institutionally sponsored loans available. Aid available to part-time students. Financial aid applicants required to submit FAFSA. • Application contact: Richard Austin, Coordinator, 813-974-2852. Fax: 813-974-3837. E-mail: austin@tempest.coedu.usf.edu.

University of Tennessee, Knoxville, College of Education, Program in Education I, Knoxville, TN 37996. Offerings include math science and social studies education (PhD). Accredited by NCATE. *Degree requirements:* 1 foreign language (computer language can substitute), dissertation. *Entrance requirements:* GRE General Test, TOEFL (minimum score 550), minimum GPA of 2.7. Application deadline: 2/1 (priority date; rolling processing). Application fee: $35. Electronic applications accepted. *Tuition:* $3354 per year full-time, $181 per semester hour part-time for state residents; $8410 per year full-time, $462 per semester hour part-time for nonresidents. • Dr. Tom George, Associate Dean, 423-974-0907. Fax: 423-974-8718. E-mail: tgeorge1@utk.edu.

University of Tennessee, Knoxville, College of Education, Program in Education II, Knoxville, TN 37996. Offerings include mathematics education (MS, Ed D, Ed S). Accredited by NCATE. *Degree requirements:* For master's and Ed S, thesis optional, foreign language not required; for doctorate, dissertation required, foreign language not required. *Entrance requirements:* For master's, TOEFL (minimum score 550), minimum GPA of 2.7; for doctorate, GRE General Test, TOEFL (minimum score 550), minimum GPA of 2.7; for Ed S, TOEFL (minimum score 550), GRE General Test, minimum GPA of 2.7. Application deadline: 2/1 (priority date; rolling processing). Application fee: $35. Electronic applications accepted. *Tuition:* $3354 per year full-time, $181 per semester hour part-time for state residents; $8410 per year full-time, $462 per semester hour part-time for nonresidents. • Dr. Tom George, Associate Dean, 423-974-0907. Fax: 423-974-8718. E-mail: tgeorge1@utk.edu.

The University of Texas at Austin, Graduate School, College of Education, Programs in Science/Mathematics Education, Program in Mathematics Education, Austin, TX 78712. Awards MA, M Ed, PhD. Students: 17 full-time (12 women), 23 part-time (17 women); includes 9 international. 22 applicants, 64% accepted. *Entrance requirements:* GRE General Test. Application deadline: 4/1 (priority date; rolling processing; 10/1 for spring admission). Application fee: $50 ($75 for international students). Electronic applications accepted. *Expenses:* Tuition $2592 per year full-time, $324 per semester (minimum) part-time for state residents; $7704 per year full-time, $963 per semester (minimum) part-time for nonresidents. Fees $778 per year full-time, $161 per semester (minimum) part-time. *Financial aid:* Application deadline 2/1. • Application contact: Graduate Coordinator, 512-471-3747. Fax: 512-471-8460.

The University of Texas at Dallas, School of Natural Sciences and Mathematics, Program in Mathematics and Science Education, Richardson, TX 75083-0688. Offers mathematics education (MAT), science education (MAT). Part-time and evening/weekend programs available. Faculty: 3 full-time (1 woman). Students: 3 full-time (2 women), 19 part-time (18 women); includes 3 minority (2 African Americans, 1 Hispanic). Average age 39. 9 applicants, 89% accepted. In 1997, 3 degrees awarded. *Degree requirements:* Computer language, minimum GPA of 3.0 required, foreign language and thesis not required. *Entrance requirements:* GRE General Test (minimum combined score of 1000), TOEFL (minimum score 550), minimum GPA of 3.0 in upper-level course work in field. Application deadline: 7/15 (rolling processing; 11/15 for spring admission). Application fee: $25 ($75 for international students). *Financial aid:* 2 students received aid; research assistantships, teaching assistantships, Federal Work-Study available. Aid available to part-time students. Financial aid application deadline: 11/1. *Faculty research:* Techniques for training teachers, philosophic definitions of science held by working scientists, science teachers, science students. • Dr. Frederick Fifer, Head, 972-883-2496. Fax: 972-883-6371. E-mail: ffifer@utdallas.edu.

The University of Texas at Dallas, School of Natural Sciences and Mathematics, Programs in Mathematical Sciences, Richardson, TX 75083-0688. Offerings include mathematics (MAT). Faculty: 17 full-time (1 woman), 12 part-time (2 women). *Application deadline:* 7/15 (rolling processing; 11/15 for spring admission). *Application fee:* $25 ($75 for international students). • Dr. John Wiorkowski, Associate Provost and Program Head, 972-883-2161. Fax: 972-883-6622. E-mail: wiorkow@utdallas.edu.

The University of Texas at San Antonio, College of Sciences and Engineering, Division of Mathematics and Statistics, San Antonio, TX 78249-0617. Offerings include mathematics (MS), with options in mathematics education, statistics. Division faculty: 21 full-time (6 women), 32 part-time (11 women). *Degree requirements:* Computer language, comprehensive exam required, foreign language and thesis not required. *Entrance requirements:* GRE General Test, TOEFL, minimum GPA of 3.0. Application deadline: 7/1 (rolling processing). Application fee: $20. *Expenses:* Tuition $2476 per year full-time, $309 per semester (minimum) part-time for state residents; $7584 per year full-time, $948 per semester (minimum) part-time for nonresidents. Fees $361 per year full-time, $133 per semester (minimum) part-time. • Dr. Lawrence Williams, Interim Director, 210-458-4451.

The University of Texas at Tyler, School of Education and Psychology, Department of Curriculum and Instruction, Program in Secondary Education, Tyler, TX 75799-0001. Offerings include mathematics (M Ed, Certificate). *Degree requirements:* For master's, comprehensive and departmental qualifying exams required, foreign language not required. *Entrance requirements:* For master's, GRE General Test. Application fee: $0 ($50 for international students). *Tuition:* $2144 per year full-time, $337 per semester (minimum) part-time for state residents; $7256 per year full-time, $964 per semester (minimum) part-time for nonresidents. • Application contact: Martha D. Wheat, Director of Admissions and Student Records, 903-566-7201. Fax: 903-566-7068.

University of Tulsa, College of Arts and Sciences, School of Education, Program in Math/Science Education, Tulsa, OK 74104-3189. Awards MSMSE. Accredited by NCATE. Part-time programs available. Students: 1 (woman) full-time, 5 part-time (all women). Average age 41. 4 applicants, 100% accepted. In 1997, 12 degrees awarded. *Entrance requirements:* GRE General Test (minimum combined score of 1000), TOEFL (minimum score 575), minimum GPA of 3.0. Application deadline: rolling. Application fee: $30. Electronic applications accepted. *Expenses:* Tuition $480 per credit hour. Fees $2 per credit hour. *Financial aid:* In 1997–98, 1 student received aid, including 1 teaching assistantship totaling $15,840; fellowships, research assistantships, partial tuition waivers, Federal Work-Study also available. Aid available to part-time students. Financial aid application deadline: 2/1; applicants required to submit FAFSA. • Dr. Eileen W. Kelble, Adviser, 918-631-2720. Fax: 918-631-2133.

University of Vermont, College of Engineering and Mathematics, Department of Mathematics and Statistics, Program in Mathematics, Burlington, VT 05405-0160. Offerings include mathematics education (MAT, MST). Accredited by NCATE. *Application deadline:* 4/1 (priority date; rolling processing). *Application fee:* $25. *Expenses:* Tuition $302 per credit for state residents; $755 per credit for nonresidents. Fees $434 per year full-time, $46 per semester (minimum) part-time. • Dr. R. Wright, Coordinator, 802-656-2940.

University of Victoria, Faculty of Education, Department of Social and Natural Sciences, Victoria, BC V8W 2Y2, Canada. Offerings include curriculum and instruction (MA), with options in mathematics, science, social studies; mathematics education (M Ed). Postbaccalaureate distance learning degree programs offered (minimal on-campus study). Department faculty: 13 full-time (4 women). *Degree requirements:* Thesis (for some programs), project (M Ed) required, foreign language not required. *Average time to degree:* master's–3.3 years full-time. *Entrance requirements:* Minimum B average. Application deadline: 4/30 (rolling processing). Application fee: $50. *Tuition:* $2080 per year full-time, $557 per semester part-time. • Dr. G. Snively, Chair, 250-721-7769. E-mail: gsnivley@uvic.ca. Application contact: Sarah Baylow, Graduate Secretary, 250-721-7882. Fax: 250-721-7767. E-mail: sbaylow@uvic.ca.

The University of West Alabama, College of Education, Department of Foundations, Livingston, AL 35470. Offerings include secondary education (MAT, M Ed), with options in biology with certification (MAT), environmental science with certification (MAT), history with certification (MAT), language arts with certification (MAT), library media with certification (MAT), mathematics with certification (MAT). Accredited by NCATE. *Application deadline:* 9/10 (priority date; rolling processing; 3/24 for spring admission). *Application fee:* $15. *Tuition:* $70 per quarter hour.

The University of West Alabama, College of Natural Sciences and Mathematics, Department of Mathematics, Livingston, AL 35470. Awards MAT. Accredited by NCATE. *Tuition:* $70 per quarter hour.

University of West Florida, College of Science and Technology, Department of Mathematics and Statistics, Pensacola, FL 32514-5750. Offerings include mathematics education (MAT). Accredited by NCATE. *Application deadline:* 7/19. *Application fee:* $20. *Tuition:* $131 per credit hour (minimum) for state residents; $436 per credit hour (minimum) for nonresidents. • Dr. Rohan Hemasinha, Chairperson, 850-474-2276.

University of Wisconsin–Eau Claire, College of Professional Studies, School of Education, Program in Secondary Education, Eau Claire, WI 54702-4004. Offerings include mathematics (MAT, MST). *Application deadline:* 7/1 (rolling processing; 12/1 for spring admission). *Application fee:* $45. *Tuition:* $3651 per year full-time, $611 per semester (minimum) part-time for state residents; $11,295 per year full-time, $1886 per semester (minimum) part-time for nonresidents. • Stephen Kurth, Associate Dean, School of Education, 715-836-3671.

University of Wisconsin–Madison, School of Education, Department of Curriculum and Instruction, Program in Education and Mathematics, Madison, WI 53706-1380. Awards MA. *Application fee:* $38. *Tuition:* $4928 per year full-time, $926 per semester (minimum) part-time for state residents; $15,190 per year full-time, $2849 per semester (minimum) part-time for nonresidents.

University of Wisconsin–Oshkosh, College of Letters and Science, Department of Mathematics, Oshkosh, WI 54901-8602. Offers program in mathematics education (MS). Part-time programs available. Faculty: 15 full-time (3 women). Students: 1 full-time (0 women), 11 part-time (6 women); includes 1 minority (Asian American). Average age 38. 0 applicants. In 1997, 9 degrees awarded. *Degree requirements:* Comprehensive exam required, thesis optional, foreign language not required. *Entrance requirements:* 30 undergraduate credits in mathematics. Application deadline: rolling. Application fee: $45. *Tuition:* $3638 per year full-time, $609 per semester (minimum) part-time for state residents; $11,282 per year full-time, $1884 per semester (minimum) part-time for nonresidents. *Financial aid:* Application deadline 3/15. *Faculty research:* Problem solving, number theory, discrete mathematics, statistics. • Dr. Patrick C. Collier, Chair, 920-424-1333. Application contact: Dr. John Koker, Coordinator, 920-424-1058. E-mail: koker@uwosh.edu.

University of Wisconsin–River Falls, College of Arts and Science, Program in Science and Mathematics, River Falls, WI 54022-5001. Offers mathematics education (MSE), science education (MSE). One or more programs accredited by NCATE. Students: 23 (9 women). *Degree requirements:* Thesis (for some programs). *Application deadline:* 3/1. *Application fee:* $45. *Financial aid:* Research assistantships available. Financial aid application deadline: 3/1. • Don Leake, Coordinator, 715-425-3326. E-mail: don.leake@uwrf.edu. Application contact: Graduate Admissions, 715-425-3843.

Vanderbilt University, Peabody College, Department of Teaching and Learning, Nashville, TN 37240-1001. Offerings include mathematics education (M Ed, Ed D). Accredited by NCATE. *Entrance requirements:* GRE General Test, MAT. Application deadline: 3/1 (priority date; rolling processing). Application fee: $35. • Carolyn Evertson, Chair, 615-322-8100.

Villanova University, Graduate School of Liberal Arts and Sciences, Department of Mathematical Sciences, Program in Teaching of Mathematics, Villanova, PA 19085-1699. Awards MATM. Students: 3 part-time (2 women). Average age 28. 2 applicants, 100% accepted. In 1997, 1 degree awarded. *Entrance requirements:* Minimum GPA of 3.0. Application deadline: 8/1 (priority date; 12/1 for spring admission). Application fee: $40. *Expenses:* Tuition $400 per credit. Fees $60 per year. *Financial aid:* Federal Work-Study available. Financial aid application deadline: 4/1. • Dr. David J. Sprows, Director, 610-519-4850.

Virginia Commonwealth University, School of Education, Program in Mathematics Education, Richmond, VA 23284-9005. Awards M Ed. Accredited by NCATE. Program being phased out; applicants no longer accepted. Students: 2 part-time (both women). Average age 38. In 1997, 4 degrees awarded. *Tuition:* $4960 per year full-time, $257 per credit part-time for state residents; $12,652 per year full-time, $684 per credit part-time for nonresidents. • Dr. Alan M. McLeod, Division Head, 804-828-1305. Fax: 804-828-1323. E-mail: ammcleod@vcu.edu.

Virginia State University, School of Agriculture, Science and Technology, Department of Mathematics, 1 Hayden Drive, Petersburg, VA 23806-2096. Offerings include mathematics education (M Ed). Accredited by NCATE. Department faculty: 5 full-time (2 women). *Application deadline:* 8/15 (rolling processing). *Application fee:* $25. *Tuition:* $3739 per year full-time, $133 per credit hour part-time for state residents; $9056 per year full-time, $364 per credit hour part-time for nonresidents. • Dr. George W. Wimbush, Chair, 804-524-5920. Application contact: Dr. Wayne F. Virag, Dean, Graduate Studies and Continuing Education, 804-524-5985. Fax: 804-524-5104. E-mail: wvirag@vsu.edu.

Washington University in St. Louis, Graduate School of Arts and Sciences, Department of Mathematics, St. Louis, MO 63130-4899. Offerings include mathematics education (MAT). Accredited by NCATE. *Application deadline:* 1/15 (priority date; rolling processing). *Application fee:* $35. *Tuition:* $22,200 per year full-time, $925 per credit hour part-time. • Dr. Edward Wilson, Chairman, 314-935-6760.

Wayne State College, Division of Math and Science, Wayne, NE 68787. Awards MSE. One or more programs accredited by NCATE. Faculty: 16 part-time (3 women). Students: 9 part-time (4 women); includes 1 minority (African American). Average age 32. In 1997, 5 degrees awarded. *Degree requirements:* Comprehensive exam, research paper. *Entrance requirements:* GRE General Test. Application deadline: rolling. Application fee: $10. *Expenses:* Tuition $1788 per year full-time, $75 per credit hour part-time for state residents; $3576 per year full-time, $149 per credit hour part-time for nonresidents. Fees $360 per year full-time, $15 per credit hour part-time. *Financial aid:* In 1997–98, 2 teaching assistantships were awarded. Financial aid application deadline: 5/1; applicants required to submit FAFSA. • Dr. J. S. Johar, Head, 402-375-7329.

Wayne State College, Division of Education, Program in Curriculum and Instruction, Wayne, NE 68787. Offerings include mathematics education (MSE). Accredited by NCATE. *Degree requirements:* Comprehensive exam, research paper required, foreign language not required. *Entrance requirements:* GRE General Test. Application deadline: rolling. Application fee: $10. *Expenses:* Tuition $1788 per year full-time, $75 per credit hour part-time for state residents; $3576 per year full-time, $149 per credit hour part-time for nonresidents. Fees $360 per year full-time, $15 per credit hour part-time. • Dr. Diane Alexander, Head, Division of Education, 402-375-7389.

Webster University, School of Education, Department of Multidisciplinary Studies, St. Louis, MO 63119-3194. Offerings include mathematics education (MAT). Department faculty: 7 full-time (5 women). *Entrance requirements:* 2 years of work experience in education, interview, min GPA of 2.5. Application deadline: rolling. Application fee: $25 ($50 for international students). *Tuition:* $350 per credit hour. • Roy Tamashiro, Chair, 314-968-7098. Fax: 314-968-7118. E-mail: tamashro@webster.edu. Application contact: Beth Russell, Director of Graduate Admissions, 314-968-7089. Fax: 314-968-7166. E-mail: russelmb@webster.edu.

Wesleyan College, Department of Education, Program in Middle-Level Mathematics and Middle-Level Science Education, Macon, GA 31210-4462. Awards MA. Offered during summer only. Part-time programs available. Faculty: 10 full-time (4 women), 3 part-time (2 women). Students: 7 full-time (all women). Average age 32. 12 applicants, 75% accepted. *Degree requirements:* Practicum, professional portfolio required, thesis optional, foreign language not required. *Average time to degree:* master's–3 years full-time, 6 years part-time. *Entrance requirements:* TOEFL (minimum score 550), interview, teaching certificate. Application deadline: rolling. Application fee: $25. *Tuition:* $150 per semester hour. *Financial aid:* Federal Work-Study available. Financial aid application deadline: 4/15; applicants required to submit FAFSA. *Faculty research:* Instructional technology, cognitive development, verbal classroom interactions. • Application contact: Dr. Patricia R. Hardeman, Assistant Dean and Registrar, 912-477-1110. Fax: 912-757-4030.

Western Carolina University, College of Education and Allied Professions, Department of Administration, Curriculum and Instruction, Programs in Secondary Education, Cullowhee, NC 28723. Offerings include mathematics (MAT). Accredited by NCATE. *Degree requirements:* Comprehensive exam required, foreign language and thesis not required. *Entrance requirements:* GRE General Test. Application deadline: rolling. Application fee: $35. *Tuition:* $1799 per year full-time, $144 per credit hour (minimum) part-time for state residents; $9069 per year full-time, $1053 per credit hour (minimum) part-time for nonresidents. • Application contact: Kathleen Owen, Assistant to the Dean, 828-227-7398. Fax: 828-227-7480.

Western Kentucky University, Ogden College of Science, Technology, and Health, Department of Physics and Astronomy, Bowling Green, KY 42101-3576. Offerings include mathematics and science (MA Ed). Department faculty: 6 full-time (0 women). *Degree requirements:* Thesis. *Entrance requirements:* GRE General Test (minimum combined score of 1150 on three sections), minimum GPA of 2.5. Application deadline: 8/1 (priority date; rolling processing; 12/1 for spring admission). Application fee: $20. *Tuition:* $2460 per year full-time, $133 per credit hour part-time for state residents; $6700 per year full-time, $369 per credit hour part-time for nonresidents. • Dr. Charles McGruder, Head, 502-745-4357.

Western Michigan University, College of Arts and Sciences, Department of Mathematics and Statistics, Programs in Mathematics, Kalamazoo, MI 49008. Offerings include mathematics education (MA, PhD). One or more programs accredited by NCATE. *Degree requirements:* For master's, oral exams required, thesis not required; for doctorate, 1 foreign language, dissertation, oral exams. *Entrance requirements:* For doctorate, GRE General Test. Application deadline: 2/15 (priority date; rolling processing). Application fee: $25. *Expenses:* Tuition $154 per credit hour for state residents; $372 per credit hour for nonresidents. Fees $602 per year full-time, $132 per semester part-time. • Application contact: Paula J. Boodt, Coordinator, Graduate Admissions and Recruitment, 616-387-2000. E-mail: paulaboodt@wmich.edu.

Western Oregon University, School of Education, Department of Secondary Education, Monmouth, OR 97361. Offerings include mathematics (MAT, MS Ed). Accredited by NCATE. Department faculty: 83 full-time (28 women), 26 part-time (11 women), 92.81 FTE. *Degree requirements:* Written exam required, thesis optional, foreign language not required. *Average time to degree:* master's–1 year full-time, 4 years part-time. *Entrance requirements:* GRE General (average 450 on each section) or MAT (minimum score 30), minimum GPA of 3.0, teaching license. Application deadline: rolling. Application fee: $50. • Dr. George Cabrera, Chair, 503-838-8471. Fax: 503-838-8228. E-mail: cabrerg@wou.edu. Application contact: Alison Marshall, Director of Admissions, 503-838-8211. Fax: 503-838-8067. E-mail: marshaa@wou.edu.

Wheeling Jesuit University, Department of Mathematics, Wheeling, WV 26003-6295. Offers programs in mathematics education (MS), science education (MS). Admissions temporarily suspended. Students: 0. *Degree requirements:* Thesis optional, foreign language not required. *Tuition:* $360 per credit hour.

Wilkes University, Department of Mathematics, Wilkes-Barre, PA 18766-0002. Awards MS, MS Ed. Faculty: 10 full-time. Students: 2 part-time (0 women). *Degree requirements:* Thesis or alternative required, foreign language not required. *Entrance requirements:* GRE. Application deadline: rolling. Application fee: $30. *Expenses:* Tuition $12,552 per year full-time, $523 per credit hour part-time. Fees $240 per year full-time, $10 per credit hour part-time. *Financial aid:* Application deadline 2/28; applicants required to submit FAFSA. • Dr. Louise Berard, Chair, 717-408-4830.

Xavier University, College of Social Sciences, Department of Education, Cincinnati, OH 45207-2111. Offerings include mathematics (M Ed). Department faculty: 32 full-time (14 women), 49 part-time (31 women), 44.25 FTE. *Application deadline:* rolling. *Application fee:* $25. • Dr. James Boothe, Chair, 513-745-2951. Fax: 513-745-1052. E-mail: boothe@admin.xu.edu. Application contact: Sheila Speth, Director of Graduate Services, 513-745-3360. Fax: 513-745-1048. E-mail: xugrad@admin.xu.edu.

Music Education

Adelphi University, School of Education, Program in Secondary Education, Garden City, NY 11530. Offerings include music (MA). *Application deadline:* rolling. *Application fee:* $50. *Expenses:* Tuition $16,000 per year full-time, $485 per credit part-time. Fees $500 per year full-time, $150 per semester part-time. • Director, 516-877-4090. Application contact: Jennifer Spiegel, Associate Director of Graduate Admissions, 516-877-3055.

Alabama Agricultural and Mechanical University, School of Education, Department of Curriculum and Instruction, Area in Music Education, PO Box 1357, Normal, AL 35762-1357. Offers programs in music (MS), music education (M Ed). Accredited by NCATE. Part-time and evening/weekend programs available. Faculty: 2 full-time (0 women). *Degree requirements:* Comprehensive exam required, foreign language not required. *Entrance requirements:* GRE General Test. Application deadline: 5/1. Application fee: $15 ($20 for international students). *Expenses:* Tuition $2782 per year full-time, $565 per semester (minimum) part-time for state residents; $5164 per year full-time, $1015 per semester (minimum) part-time for nonresidents. Fees $560 per year full-time, $390 per year part-time. *Financial aid:* Fellowships and career-related internships or fieldwork available. Financial aid application deadline: 4/1. *Faculty research:* Jazz and black music, Alabama folk music. • Dr. Earnest Dees, Chair, Department of Curriculum and Instruction, 205-851-5520. Fax: 205-851-5526.

Alabama State University, School of Graduate Studies, School of Music, Montgomery, AL 36101-0271. Offerings include music education (MME). School faculty: 4 full-time (0 women). *Application deadline:* 7/15 (rolling processing; 12/15 for spring admission). *Application fee:* $10. *Expenses:* Tuition $85 per credit hour for state residents; $170 per credit hour for nonresidents. Fees $486 per year. • Dr. Horace B. Lamar, Dean, 334-229-4341. Fax: 334-229-4901. Application contact: Dr. Fred Dauser, Dean of Graduate Students, 334-229-4276. Fax: 334-229-4928.

Albany State University, School of Education, Program in Music Education, Albany, GA 31705-2717. Awards M Ed. Accredited by NCATE. Part-time programs available. Faculty: 3 part-time (0 women). Students: 0. 0 applicants. *Degree requirements:* Comprehensive exam, teaching demonstration. *Entrance requirements:* GRE General Test (minimum combined score of 800), MAT (minimum score 44) or NTE (minimum score 550 required, minimum GPA of 2.5, previous course work in music history and theory. Application deadline: 9/1. Application fee: $10. *Financial aid:* Federal Work-Study and career-related internships or fieldwork available. Aid available to part-time students. Financial aid application deadline: 4/1. • Dr. Leroy Bynum, Interim Chairman, 912-430-4849. Fax: 912-430-4296. E-mail: lbynum@fld94.alsnet.peachnet.edu.

Angelo State University, College of Liberal and Fine Arts, Department of Art and Music, San Angelo, TX 76909. Awards MME. Faculty: 2 full-time (0 women). Students: 0. 0 applicants. *Degree requirements:* Comprehensive exam required, foreign language not required. *Entrance requirements:* GRE General Test, minimum GPA of 2.5. Application deadline: 8/7 (priority date; rolling processing; 1/2 for spring admission). Application fee: $0 ($50 for international students). *Expenses:* Tuition $1022 per year full-time, $36 per semester hour part-time for state residents; $7382 per year full-time, $246 per semester hour part-time for nonresidents. Fees $1140 per year full-time, $165 per semester (minimum) part-time. *Financial aid:* Fellowships available. Financial aid application deadline: 8/1. • Dr. Koste Belcheff, Head, 915-942-2085.

Appalachian State University, School of Music, Program in Music Education, Boone, NC 28608. Awards MM. Accredited by NCATE. Member of NASM. Faculty: 21 full-time (2 women). Students: 12 full-time (6 women), 1 (woman) part-time; includes 2 international. 12 applicants, 67% accepted. In 1997, 3 degrees awarded. *Degree requirements:* Thesis or alternative, comprehensive exams required, foreign language not required. *Entrance requirements:* GRE General Test. Application deadline: 7/31 (priority date). Application fee: $35. *Tuition:* $1811 per year full-time, $354 per semester (minimum) part-time for state residents; $9081 per year full-time, $2171 per semester (minimum) part-time for nonresidents. *Financial aid:* In 1997–98, 1 fellowship was awarded; research assistantships, teaching assistantships, assistantships, and career-related internships or fieldwork also available. • Dr. William Harbinson, Graduate Adviser, 704-262-6446.

Arkansas State University, College of Fine Arts, Department of Music, State University, AR 72467. Offerings include music education (MME, SCCT). Accredited by NCATE. One or more programs accredited by NASM. Department faculty: 13 full-time (2 women). *Degree requirements:* For SCCT, comprehensive exam required, foreign language and thesis not required. *Entrance requirements:* For SCCT, GRE General Test or MAT, master's degree. Application deadline: 7/1 (priority date; rolling processing; 11/15 for spring admission). Application fee: $15 ($25 for international students). *Expenses:* Tuition $2760 per year full-time, $115 per credit hour part-time for state residents; $6936 per year full-time, $289 per credit hour part-time for nonresidents. Fees $506 per year full-time, $44 per semester (minimum) part-time. • Dr. William Holmes, Chair, 870-972-2094. Fax: 870-972-3932. E-mail: wholmes@aztec.astate.edu.

Auburn University, College of Education, Department of Curriculum and Teaching, Auburn University, AL 36849-0001. Offerings include music education (M Ed, MS, PhD, Ed S). Accredited by NCATE. One or more programs accredited by NASM. Department faculty: 20 full-time (11 women). *Degree requirements:* For master's, thesis (MS) required, foreign language not required; for doctorate, dissertation required, foreign language not required; for Ed S, field project required, foreign language and thesis not required. *Entrance requirements:* For master's and Ed S, GRE General Test; for doctorate, GRE General Test (minimum score 450 on each section, 1000 combined). Application deadline: 9/1 (rolling processing; 3/1 for spring admission). Application fee: $25 ($50 for international students). *Expenses:* Tuition $2760 per year full-time, $76 per credit hour part-time for state residents; $8280 per year full-time, $228 per credit hour part-time for nonresidents. Fees $30 per year full-time, $160 per quarter part-time for state residents; $30 per year full-time, $480 per quarter part-time for nonresidents. • Dr. Andrew M. Weaver, Head, 334-844-4434. E-mail: weaveam@mail.auburn.edu. Application contact: Dr. John F. Pritchett, Dean of the Graduate School, 334-844-4700.

Austin Peay State University, College of Arts and Sciences, Department of Music, Clarksville, TN 37044-0001. Offerings include music education (M Mu). Member of NASM. Department faculty: 13 full-time (4 women). *Degree requirements:* Thesis optional, foreign language not required. *Average time to degree:* master's–2 years full-time, 4 years part-time. *Entrance requirements:* GRE General Test, GRE Subject Test, audition. Application deadline: 7/31 (priority date; rolling processing; 12/4 for spring admission). Application fee: $15. *Expenses:* Tuition $2438 per year full-time, $123 per semester hour part-time for state residents; $7034 per year full-time, $324 per semester hour part-time for nonresidents. Fees $484 per year (minimum) full-time, $154 per semester (minimum) part-time. • Solie Fott, Chair, 931-648-7818. E-mail: fotts@apsu.edu. Application contact: Sharon Mabry, Director of Graduate Program, 931-648-7818. Fax: 931-648-5992. E-mail: mabrys@apsu.edu.

Azusa Pacific University, School of Music, Azusa, CA 91702-7000. Offerings include education (M Mus). Postbaccalaureate distance learning degree programs offered (no on-campus study). School faculty: 5 full-time, 1 part-time. *Degree requirements:* Recital/thesis required, foreign language and thesis not required. *Application fee:* $45 ($65 for international students). *Expenses:* Tuition $350 per unit. Fees $57 per year. • Dr. Don Neufeld, Professor, 626-812-3020. Application contact: Graduate Admissions, 626-815-5470. Fax: 626-815-3867.

Ball State University, College of Fine Arts, School of Music, 2000 University Avenue, Muncie, IN 47306-1099. Offers program in music education (MA, MM, DA). Member of NASM. One or more programs accredited by NCATE. Faculty: 42. Students: 26 full-time (14 women), 62 part-time (28 women); includes 2 minority (both African Americans), 19 international. Average age 28. 36 applicants, 64% accepted. In 1997, 12 master's, 8 doctorates awarded. *Degree requirements:* For doctorate, dissertation required, foreign language not required. *Entrance requirements:* For doctorate, GRE General Test (minimum combined score of 1000), minimum graduate GPA of 3.2. Application fee: $15 ($25 for international students). *Expenses:* Tuition $3454 per year full-time, $518 per semester (minimum) part-time for state residents; $9316 per year full-time, $1221 per semester (minimum) part-time for nonresidents. Fees $242 per year full-time, $18 per semester (minimum) part-time. *Financial aid:* Teaching assistantships available. • Dr. Robert Kvam, Director, 765-285-5400.

Baylor University, School of Music, Waco, TX 76798. Offerings include music education (MM). Member of NASM. *Degree requirements:* Variable foreign language requirement, thesis (for some programs). *Entrance requirements:* GRE General Test. Application deadline: 8/1 (rolling processing; 12/1 for spring admission). Application fee: $25. *Expenses:* Tuition $7392 per year full-time, $308 per semester hour part-time. Fees $1024 per year. • Dr. Harry Elzinga, Director of Graduate Studies, 254-710-1161.

Beaver College, Department of Education, Glenside, PA 19038-3295. Offerings include music education (MA Ed). *Application fee:* $35. *Expenses:* Tuition $6570 per year full-time, $365 per credit part-time. Fees $35 per year.

Belmont University, Graduate Studies in Education, Nashville, TN 37212-3757. Offerings include music education (MME). Member of NASM. Accredited by NCATE. Faculty: 31 full-time (16 women), 1 (woman) part-time. *Average time to degree:* master's–2 years full-time, 5 years part-time. *Application deadline:* 7/15 (priority date; rolling processing; 11/15 for spring admission). *Application fee:* $50. • Dr. Norma Stevens, Associate Dean, 615-460-6233. E-mail: stevensn@belmont.edu. Application contact: Lois Smith, Admissions Counselor, 615-460-5483. Fax: 615-385-5084. E-mail: smithl@belmont.edu.

Boise State University, College of Arts and Sciences, Department of Music, Program in Music Education, Boise, ID 83725-0399. Awards MM. Member of NASM. Accredited by NCATE. Part-time programs available. Faculty: 16 full-time (2 women), 1 (woman) part-time. Students: 5 full-time (3 women), 4 part-time (3 women); includes 1 international. Average age 35. 6 applicants, 100% accepted. *Degree requirements:* Thesis or alternative. *Entrance requirements:* Performance demonstration. Application deadline: 7/26 (priority date; rolling processing; 11/29 for spring admission). Application fee: $20 ($30 for international students). Electronic applications accepted. *Tuition:* $3020 per year full-time, $135 per credit part-time for state residents; $8900 per year full-time, $135 per credit part-time for nonresidents. *Financial aid:* Graduate assistantships, Federal Work-Study, institutionally sponsored loans, and career-related internships or fieldwork available. Aid available to part-time students. Financial aid application deadline: 3/1. • Dr. Jeanne Belfy, Coordinator, 208-385-1216.

Boise State University, College of Arts and Sciences, Department of Music, Program in Pedagogy, Boise, ID 83725-0399. Awards MM. Accredited by NCATE. Part-time programs available. Faculty: 16 full-time (2 women), 1 (woman) part-time. Students: 7 full-time (3 women), 1 (woman) part-time; includes 1 minority (Hispanic), 1 international. Average age 35. 3 applicants, 100% accepted. In 1997, 2 degrees awarded. *Degree requirements:* Thesis or alternative. *Entrance requirements:* Minimum GPA of 2.75, performance demonstration. Application deadline: 7/26 (priority date; rolling processing; 11/29 for spring admission). Application fee: $20 ($30 for international students). Electronic applications accepted. *Tuition:* $3020 per year full-time, $135 per credit part-time for state residents; $8900 per year full-time, $135 per credit part-time for nonresidents. *Financial aid:* Federal Work-Study, institutionally sponsored loans, and career-related internships or fieldwork available. Aid available to part-time students. Financial aid application deadline: 3/1. • Dr. Jeanne Belfy, Coordinator, 208-385-1216.

Boston Conservatory, Music Division, Department of Music Education, Boston, MA 02215. Awards MM. Member of NASM. *Degree requirements:* Thesis (for some programs), comprehensive oral exam, thesis or recital. *Average time to degree:* master's–2 years full-time. *Entrance requirements:* Audition, interview. Application deadline: 3/1 (priority date; 12/1 for spring admission). Application fee: $60.

Boston University, Graduate School of Arts and Sciences, Department of Music, Boston, MA 02215. Offerings include music education (MA). Member of NASM. Department faculty: 14 full-time (2 women). *Degree requirements:* 2 foreign languages, comprehensive exam or thesis. *Average time to degree:* master's–3 years full-time; doctorate–5 years full-time. *Entrance requirements:* GRE General Test, GRE Subject Test, TOEFL (minimum score 600), musical composition or research paper. Application deadline: 3/15 (rolling processing; 10/15 for spring admission). Application fee: $50. *Expenses:* Tuition $22,830 per year full-time, $713 per credit part-time. Fees $218 per year full-time, $40 per semester part-time. • John J. Daverio, Chairman, 617-353-3354. E-mail: daverio@bu.edu.

Boston University, School for the Arts, Division of Music, Program in Music Education, Boston, MA 02215. Awards Mus M, Mus AD. Member of NASM. Students: 26 full-time (18 women); includes 1 minority (African American), 9 international. Average age 33. In 1997, 3 master's awarded. *Degree requirements:* For master's, thesis; for doctorate, 2 foreign languages, dissertation. *Entrance requirements:* For master's, TOEFL (minimum score 550). Application deadline: 3/1 (priority date; rolling processing). Application fee: $50. *Expenses:* Tuition $22,830 per year full-time, $713 per credit part-time. Fees $218 per year full-time, $40 per semester part-time. *Financial aid:* Fellowships, teaching assistantships available. Financial aid application deadline: 3/1. • Gerald Weale, Chair, 617-353-6888. Application contact: Patricia Mitro, Assistant Dean for Enrollment Services, 617-353-3350.

Bowling Green State University, College of Musical Arts, Bowling Green, OH 43403. Offerings include music education (MM). Member of NASM. College faculty: 48 full-time (16 women), 8 part-time (2 women). *Degree requirements:* Thesis or alternative, recitals required, foreign language not required. *Entrance requirements:* GRE General Test, TOEFL (minimum score 550), audition, interview, diagnostic placement exams in music history and theory. Application deadline: 4/1. Application fee: $30. Electronic applications accepted. *Tuition:* $6070 per year full-time, $284 per credit hour part-time for state residents; $11,358 per year full-time, $536 per credit hour part-time for nonresidents. • Dr. H. Lee Riggins, Dean, 419-372-2181. Application contact: Dr. Richard Kennell, Graduate Coordinator, 419-372-2182.

Brandon University, School of Music, Brandon, MB R7A 6A9, Canada. Offerings include music education (M Mus). School faculty: 9 full-time (2 women). *Degree requirements:* Thesis or alternative required, foreign language not required. *Entrance requirements:* B Mus. Application deadline: 3/1 (priority date; rolling processing). Application fee: $30. *Expenses:* Tuition $421 per course (minimum). Fees $24.95 per year. • Dr. T. Patrick Carrabré, Acting Dean. Application contact: Robert Richardson, Graduate Chair, 204-727-7343. Fax: 204-728-6839. E-mail: richardsonr@brandonu.ca.

Brigham Young University, College of Fine Arts and Communications, School of Music, Provo, UT 84602-1001. Offerings include music education (MA, MM). Member of NASM. School faculty: 39 full-time (7 women), 11 part-time (5 women). *Degree requirements:* Variable foreign language requirement, thesis (for some programs). *Average time to degree:* master's–2 years full-time, 3 years part-time. *Entrance requirements:* GRE Subject Test (MA), minimum GPA of 3.0 in last 60 hours. Application deadline: 2/1 (priority date). Application fee: $30. *Tuition:* $3200 per year full-time, $178 per credit hour part-time for state residents; $4800 per year full-time, $266 per credit hour part-time for nonresidents. • Dr. David M. Randall, Director, 801-378-6304. Application contact: Dr. Thomas L. Durham, Graduate Coordinator, 801-378-3226. Fax: 801-378-5973.

Brooklyn College of the City University of New York, Conservatory of Music, 2900 Bedford Avenue, Brooklyn, NY 11210-2889. Offerings include music education (MA). Conservatory faculty: 15 full-time, 27 part-time, 28.5 FTE. *Application deadline:* 3/1 (11/1 for spring admission).

Application fee: $40. *Expenses:* Tuition $4350 per year full-time, $185 per credit part-time for state residents; $7600 per year full-time, $320 per credit part-time for nonresidents. Fees $500 per year for state residents; $806 per year for nonresidents. • Dr. Nancy Hager, Chairperson, 718-951-5286. E-mail: nhager@brooklyn.cuny.edu. Application contact: Dr. Bruce MacIntyre, Graduate Deputy Chairperson, 718-921-5954. Fax: 718-951-4502. E-mail: brucem@brooklyn.cuny.edu.

Brooklyn College of the City University of New York, School of Education, Division of Elementary School Education, 2900 Bedford Avenue, Brooklyn, NY 11210-2889. Offerings include music education (MS Ed). *Average time to degree:* master's–1.5 years full-time, 3 years part-time. *Entrance requirements:* TOEFL (minimum score 500), interview, previous course work in education, writing sample. Application deadline: 3/1 (rolling processing; 11/1 for spring admission). Application fee: $40. *Expenses:* Tuition $4350 per year full-time, $185 per credit part-time for state residents; $7600 per year full-time, $320 per credit part-time for nonresidents. Fees $500 per year for state residents; $806 per year for nonresidents. • Dr. Milga Morales, Coordinator, 718-951-5933.

Brooklyn College of the City University of New York, School of Education, Division of Secondary Education, 2900 Bedford Avenue, Brooklyn, NY 11210-2889. Offerings include music (MS Ed). *Application deadline:* 3/1 (11/1 for spring admission). *Application fee:* $40. *Expenses:* Tuition $4350 per year full-time, $185 per credit part-time for state residents; $7600 per year full-time, $320 per credit part-time for nonresidents. Fees $500 per year for state residents; $806 per year for nonresidents. • Dr. Peter Taubman, Coordinator, 718-951-5218. Fax: 718-951-4816. E-mail: ptaubman@brooklyn.cuny.edu.

Butler University, Jordan College of Fine Arts, Department of Music, Indianapolis, IN 46208-3485. Offerings include music education (MM). Member of NASM. Accredited by NCATE. Department faculty: 19 full-time (1 woman), 18 part-time (9 women), 20.9 FTE. *Degree requirements:* Thesis required (for some programs), foreign language not required. *Average time to degree:* master's–2 years full-time, 6 years part-time. *Entrance requirements:* GRE General Test, GRE Subject Test, audition, interview. Application deadline: 8/15 (priority date; rolling processing). Application fee: $25. *Tuition:* $220 per credit hour. • Dr. Michael Bolin, Chairman, 317-940-9988. Fax: 317-940-9658.

California State University, Fresno, Division of Graduate Studies, School of Arts and Humanities, Department of Music, 5241 North Maple Avenue, Fresno, CA 93740. Offerings include music education (MA). Department faculty: 13 full-time (5 women). *Degree requirements:* Thesis or alternative required, foreign language not required. *Average time to degree:* master's–3.5 years full-time. *Entrance requirements:* GRE General Test, TOEFL (minimum score 550), diagnostic exam, minimum GPA of 3.0. Application deadline: 8/1 (priority date; rolling processing; 12/1 for spring admission). Application fee: $55. Electronic applications accepted. *Expenses:* Tuition $0 for state residents; $246 per unit for nonresidents. Fees $1872 per year full-time, $1206 per year part-time. • Dr. Jack Fortner, Chair, 209-278-2654. E-mail: jack_fortner@csufresno.edu. Application contact: Dr. Teresa Beaman, Graduate Adviser, 209-278-2654. Fax: 209-278-6800. E-mail: teresa_beaman@csufresno.edu.

California State University, Fullerton, School of the Arts, Department of Music, PO Box 34080, Fullerton, CA 92834-9480. Offerings include music education (MA). Member of NASM. Department faculty: 19 full-time (3 women), 35 part-time, 27 FTE. *Application fee:* $55. *Expenses:* Tuition $0 for state residents; $246 per unit for nonresidents. Fees $1947 per year full-time, $1281 per year part-time. • Dr. Gordon Paine, Chair, 714-278-3511. Application contact: Dr. Mitch Fennell, Adviser, 714-278-3511.

California State University, Los Angeles, School of Arts and Letters, Department of Music, Los Angeles, CA 90032-8530. Offerings include music education (MA). Department faculty: 22 full-time, 33 part-time. *Application deadline:* 6/30 (rolling processing; 2/1 for spring admission). *Application fee:* $55. *Expenses:* Tuition $0 for state residents; $164 per unit for nonresidents. Fees $1763 per year full-time, $1097 per year part-time. • Dr. David Caffey, Chair, 213-343-4060.

California State University, Northridge, College of the Arts, Media, and Communications, Department of Music, Northridge, CA 91330. Offerings include music education (MA). Member of NASM. Department faculty: 23 full-time, 56 part-time. *Application deadline:* 11/30. *Application fee:* $55. *Expenses:* Tuition $0 for state residents; $246 per unit for nonresidents. Fees $1970 per year full-time, $1304 per year part-time. • Jerry D. Leudders, Chair, 818-677-3184. Application contact: Dr. Gerald Lawson, Graduate Coordinator, 818-677-3181.

Campbellsville University, Division of Education, Program in Music Education, Campbellsville, KY 42718-2799. Awards MA Ed. Faculty: 7. Students: 10. *Application deadline:* rolling. *Application fee:* $0. *Tuition:* $7800 per year. • Robert Gaddis, Head, 502-789-5269.

Case Western Reserve University, Department of Music, Program in Music Education, Cleveland, OH 44106. Awards MA, PhD. Member of NASM. Faculty: 3 full-time (0 women). Students: 4 full-time (2 women), 10 part-time (7 women). Average age 30. 6 applicants, 100% accepted. In 1997, 1 master's, 2 doctorates awarded. *Degree requirements:* For master's, thesis required (for some programs), foreign language not required; for doctorate, computer language, dissertation. *Entrance requirements:* TOEFL (minimum score 550), audition. Application fee: $25. *Tuition:* $18,400 per year full-time, $767 per credit hour part-time. *Financial aid:* In 1997–98, 14 teaching assistantships (6 to first-year students) were awarded; fellowships, full tuition waivers, and career-related internships or fieldwork also available. *Faculty research:* Psychology of music, creative thinking, computer applications, educational psychology. • Gary M. Ciepluch, Director, 216-368-2361. Fax: 216-368-6557.

The Catholic University of America, The Benjamin T. Rome School of Music, Program in Music Education, Washington, DC 20064. Awards MM, DMA. Member of NASM. Accredited by NCATE. Part-time programs available. Students: 2 full-time (both women), 6 part-time (4 women); includes 2 minority (1 African American, 1 Hispanic), 1 international. Average age 42. 2 applicants, 50% accepted. In 1997, 1 master's, 1 doctorate awarded. *Degree requirements:* For master's, thesis or alternative, comprehensive exam required, foreign language not required; for doctorate, dissertation, comprehensive exams required, foreign language not required. *Entrance requirements:* For master's, theory placement test, audition; for doctorate, school qualifying exams, audition. Application deadline: 8/1 (priority date; rolling processing; 12/1 for spring admission). Application fee: $50. *Expenses:* Tuition $17,325 per year full-time, $668 per credit hour part-time. Fees $680 per year full-time, $360 per year part-time. *Financial aid:* Full and partial tuition waivers, Federal Work-Study, institutionally sponsored loans, and career-related internships or fieldwork available. Aid available to part-time students. Financial aid application deadline: 2/1; applicants required to submit FAFSA. • Dr. Elaine R. Walter, Dean, The Benjamin T. Rome School of Music, 202-319-5417. Application contact: Paul G. Taylor, Assistant Dean, 202-319-5414.

The Catholic University of America, The Benjamin T. Rome School of Music, Program in Piano, Washington, DC 20064. Offerings include piano pedagogy (MM, DMA). Member of NASM. *Degree requirements:* For master's, variable foreign language requirement, thesis (for some programs), recital; for doctorate, variable foreign language requirement, lecture-recital, recitals required, dissertation not required. *Entrance requirements:* For master's, theory placement test, audition or recital; for doctorate, school qualifying exams, recital. Application deadline: 8/1 (priority date; rolling processing; 12/1 for spring admission). Application fee: $50. *Expenses:* Tuition $17,325 per year full-time, $668 per credit hour part-time. Fees $680 per year full-time, $360 per year part-time. • Dr. Elaine R. Walter, Dean, The Benjamin T. Rome School of Music, 202-319-5417. Application contact: Paul G. Taylor, Assistant Dean, 202-319-5414.

The Catholic University of America, The Benjamin T. Rome School of Music, Program in Voice, Washington, DC 20064. Offerings include vocal pedagogy (MM), voice pedagogy and performance (DMA). Member of NASM. *Degree requirements:* For master's, 3 foreign languages, thesis (for some programs), recital; for doctorate, 3 foreign languages, dissertation, comprehensive exams, recitals. *Entrance requirements:* For master's, theory placement test, audition or recital; for doctorate, school qualifying exams, recital. Application deadline: 8/1 (priority date; rolling processing; 12/1 for spring admission). Application fee: $50. *Expenses:* Tuition $17,325 per year full-time, $668 per credit hour part-time. Fees $680 per year full-time, $360 per year part-time. • Dr. Elaine R. Walter, Dean, The Benjamin T. Rome School of Music, 202-319-5417. Application contact: Paul G. Taylor, Assistant Dean, 202-319-5414.

Central Connecticut State University, School of Arts and Sciences, Department of Music, New Britain, CT 06050-4010. Offers program in music education (MS). Part-time and evening/weekend programs available. Faculty: 7 full-time (4 women), 19 part-time (8 women), 12.2 FTE. Students: 8 full-time (4 women), 22 part-time (17 women); includes 1 minority (Native American). Average age 36. 31 applicants, 94% accepted. In 1997, 5 degrees awarded. *Degree requirements:* Thesis or alternative, comprehensive exam or special project required, foreign language not required. *Entrance requirements:* TOEFL (minimum score 550), audition, minimum GPA of 2.7. Application deadline: 6/1 (priority date; rolling processing; 12/1 for spring admission). Application fee: $40. *Expenses:* Tuition $4458 per year full-time, $175 per credit hour part-time for state residents; $9943 per year full-time, $175 per credit hour part-time for nonresidents. Fees $45 per semester. *Financial aid:* In 1997–98, 1 teaching assistantship was awarded; Federal Work-Study also available. Financial aid application deadline: 3/15; applicants required to submit FAFSA. *Faculty research:* Applied music. • Dr. Linda Laurent, Chair, 860-832-2900.

Central Michigan University, College of Communication and Fine Arts, School of Music, Program in Music Education and Supervision, Mount Pleasant, MI 48859. Awards MM. Member of NASM. Accredited by NCATE. Students: 2 full-time (both women), 7 part-time (4 women). Average age 33. In 1997, 4 degrees awarded. *Degree requirements:* Thesis or alternative required, foreign language not required. *Entrance requirements:* Audition, interview, minimum GPA of 2.7. Application deadline: 3/1 (priority date; rolling processing). Application fee: $30. *Expenses:* Tuition $139 per credit hour (minimum) for state residents; $276 per credit hour (minimum) for nonresidents. Fees $260 per year full-time, $150 per semester part-time. *Financial aid:* Federal Work-Study available. Financial aid application deadline: 3/7. • Dr. Edward Kvet, Chairperson, School of Music, 517-774-3281. Fax: 517-774-3766. E-mail: 32dysxd@cmich.edu.

Claremont Graduate University, Department of Music, Claremont, CA 91711-6163. Offerings include music education (MA). Department faculty: 3 full-time (1 woman), 1 part-time (0 women). *Degree requirements:* 1 foreign language, thesis (for some programs), oral and written qualifying exams, recitals. *Entrance requirements:* GRE General Test, auditions, compositions, or papers. Application deadline: 2/15 (priority date; rolling processing). Application fee: $40. Electronic applications accepted. *Expenses:* Tuition $20,250 per year full-time, $913 per unit part-time. Fees $130 per year. • Frank Traficante, Chair, 909-621-8081. Application contact: Mary Bennett, Administrative Assistant, 909-621-8081. Fax: 909-621-8390. E-mail: music@cgu.edu.

Cleveland State University, College of Arts and Sciences, Department of Music, Cleveland, OH 44115-2440. Offerings include education and performance (MM). Member of NASM. Department faculty: 13 full-time (4 women). *Degree requirements:* Thesis or recital. *Entrance requirements:* Minimum undergraduate GPA of 3.0. Application deadline: 9/1 (priority date; rolling processing). Application fee: $25. *Expenses:* Tuition $5252 per year full-time, $202 per credit hour part-time for state residents; $10,504 per year full-time, $404 per credit hour part-time for nonresidents. Fees $2.25 per credit hour (minimum). • Dr. Howard Meeker, Chairperson, 216-687-2301. Fax: 216-687-9279. Application contact: Dr. Judith Eckelmeyer, Program Director, 216-687-2035.

College of Notre Dame, Department of Music, Belmont, CA 94002-1997. Offerings include pedagogy (MM). Member of NASM. Department faculty: 4 full-time, 5 part-time. *Degree requirements:* Exams. *Entrance requirements:* TOEFL (minimum score 550), audition, appropriate bachelor's degree, minimum GPA of 2.5. Application deadline: rolling. Application fee: $50 ($500 for international students). *Tuition:* $460 per unit. • Dr. Birgitte Moyer, Program Director, 650-508-3597.

College of Notre Dame, Department of Education, Emphasis in Secondary Education, Belmont, CA 94002-1997. Offerings include teaching music (MAT). One or more programs accredited by NASM. Faculty: 5 full-time, 8 part-time. *Application deadline:* rolling. *Application fee:* $50 ($500 for international students). *Tuition:* $460 per unit. • Dr. Kim Tolley, Program Director, 650-508-3456.

The College of Saint Rose, School of Arts and Humanities, Music Department, Program in Music Education, Albany, NY 12203-1419. Awards MS Ed. Faculty: 8 full-time (4 women), 1 (woman) part-time. Students: 5 full-time (4 women), 37 part-time (22 women); includes 2 minority (1 Asian American, 1 Hispanic). Average age 31. In 1997, 10 degrees awarded. *Degree requirements:* Thesis or alternative, final performance. *Entrance requirements:* Audition, minimum undergraduate GPA of 3.0. Application deadline: 7/15 (priority date; rolling processing; 12/1 for spring admission). Application fee: $30. *Expenses:* Tuition $338 per credit. Fees $60 per year. *Financial aid:* Research assistantships, partial tuition waivers, and career-related internships or fieldwork available. Aid available to part-time students. Financial aid application deadline: 3/1; applicants required to submit FAFSA. • Application contact: Graduate Office, 518-454-5136. Fax: 518-458-5479. E-mail: ace@rosnet.strose.edu.

Colorado State University, College of Liberal Arts, Department of Music, Fort Collins, CO 80523-0015. Offerings include music education (MM). Member of NASM. Department faculty: 21 full-time (3 women), 6 part-time (all women). *Degree requirements:* Thesis (for some programs), 2 recitals, project. *Entrance requirements:* GRE General Test, GRE Subject Test, TOEFL, minimum GPA of 3.0. Application deadline: 2/1 (priority date; rolling processing). Application fee: $30. Electronic applications accepted. *Expenses:* Tuition $2632 per year full-time, $109 per credit hour part-time for state residents; $10,216 per year full-time, $425 per credit hour part-time for nonresidents. Fees $708 per year full-time, $32 per semester (minimum) part-time. • William E. Runyan, Chairman, 970-491-5533. E-mail: wrunyan@vines.colostate.edu. Application contact: Michael Thaut, Director, 970-491-5529. Fax: 970-491-7541. E-mail: mthaut@vines.colostate.edu.

Columbus State University, College of Arts and Letters, Programs in Music, Columbus, GA 31907-5645. Offerings in music education (MM), piano pedagogy (MM). Member of NASM. One or more programs accredited by NCATE. Part-time and evening/weekend programs available. Faculty: 15 full-time, 12 part-time. Students: 6 full-time (4 women), 2 part-time (1 woman); includes 3 minority (all Hispanics), 3 international. Average age 36. 3 applicants, 100% accepted. In 1997, 2 degrees awarded (100% found work related to degree). *Degree requirements:* Exit exam required, foreign language and thesis not required. *Average time to degree:* master's–2 years full-time, 4 years part-time. *Entrance requirements:* GRE General Test (minimum combined score of 800), MAT (minimum score 44), audition. Application deadline: 7/10 (priority date; rolling processing; 10/23 for spring admission). Application fee: $20. *Tuition:* $1718 per year full-time, $151 per semester hour part-time for state residents; $6218 per year full-time, $401 per semester hour part-time for nonresidents. *Financial aid:* In 1997–98, 8 research assistantships (4 to first-year students) were awarded; teaching assistantships, full tuition waivers, Federal Work-Study, institutionally sponsored loans, and career-related internships or fieldwork also available. Aid available to part-time students. Financial aid application deadline: 7/15; applicants required to submit FAFSA. • L. Rexford Whiddon, Associate Professor, Music, 706-568-2049. E-mail: whiddon_rexford@colstate.edu. Application contact: Katie Thornton, Graduate Admissions, 706-568-2279. Fax: 706-568-2462. E-mail: thornton_katie@colstate.edu.

Connecticut College, Department of Music, New London, CT 06320-4196. Awards MA, MAT. Part-time programs available. *Degree requirements:* 1 foreign language, thesis. *Entrance*

Directory: Music Education

Connecticut College (continued)

requirements: MAT, audition. Application deadline: 2/2. Application fee: $35. *Faculty research:* Applied music, composition, history, theory.

Converse College, School of Music, Spartanburg, SC 29302-0006. Offerings include music education (MM), piano pedagogy (MM). Member of NASM. School faculty: 18 full-time (5 women), 2 part-time (both women). *Degree requirements:* Variable foreign language requirement, recitals. *Average time to degree:* master's–2 years full-time, 3 years part-time. *Entrance requirements:* GRE General Test or NTE, audition. Application deadline: rolling. Application fee: $35. *Tuition:* $185 per credit. • Dr. Jack Bowman, Dean, 864-596-9021. E-mail: jack.bowman@converse.edu. Application contact: Alice Eanes, Assistant to the Dean, 864-596-9166. Fax: 864-596-9167. E-mail: alice.eanes@converse.edu.

Delta State University, School of Arts and Sciences, Department of Music, Cleveland, MS 38733-0001. Offers program in music education (MM Ed). Member of NASM. Accredited by NCATE. Part-time programs available. Faculty: 13 full-time (4 women). Students: 2 full-time (1 woman), 2 part-time (1 woman). Average age 33. 1 applicant, 100% accepted. In 1997, 1 degree awarded. *Degree requirements:* Thesis or alternative required, foreign language not required. *Entrance requirements:* GRE General Test (minimum combined score of 800) or MAT (minimum score 34), audition. Application deadline: 8/1 (priority date; rolling processing). Application fee: $0. *Tuition:* $2596 per year full-time, $121 per semester hour part-time for state residents; $5546 per year full-time, $285 per semester hour part-time for nonresidents. *Financial aid:* Research assistantships, Federal Work-Study, institutionally sponsored loans, and career-related internships or fieldwork available. Aid available to part-time students. Financial aid application deadline: 6/1. • Dr. Doug Wheeler, Chairperson, 601-846-4615. E-mail: dwheeler@dsu.deltast.edu. Application contact: Dr. John Thornell, Dean of Graduate Studies and Continuing Education, 601-846-4310. Fax: 601-846-4016.

DePaul University, School of Music, Program in Music Education, Chicago, IL 60604-2287. Awards MM. Member of NASM. Part-time programs available. Students: 4 part-time (2 women). Average age 36. 2 applicants, 100% accepted. In 1997, 1 degree awarded. *Degree requirements:* Final project, written comprehensive exam required, foreign language and thesis not required. *Entrance requirements:* Minimum GPA of 3.0, bachelor's degree in music or related field, interview. Application deadline: rolling. Application fee: $25. *Expenses:* Tuition $393 per credit hour. Fees $30 per year. *Financial aid:* Fellowships, full tuition waivers, Federal Work-Study available. Financial aid application deadline: 4/30. *Faculty research:* Instrumental teaching methods, curriculum assessment. • Judy Bundra, Chair, 312-325-7000 Ext. 1037. Application contact: Ross Beacraft, Coordinator of Admissions, 773-325-7444. Fax: 773-325-7429.

Drake University, College of Arts and Sciences, School of Fine Arts, Department of Music, Program in Music Education, Des Moines, IA 50311-4516. Awards MME. Member of NASM. Part-time programs available. Faculty: 3 full-time (0 women). Students: 7 part-time (3 women). Average age 35. 8 applicants, 100% accepted. In 1997, 1 degree awarded (100% continued full-time study). *Degree requirements:* Thesis or alternative required, foreign language not required. *Average time to degree:* master's–2 years full-time, 4 years part-time. *Entrance requirements:* GRE General Test (minimum combined score of 1000) or MAT (minimum score 36), audition, sample of written work. Application deadline: rolling. Application fee: $25. *Tuition:* $16,000 per year full-time, $260 per hour (minimum) part-time. *Financial aid:* 7 students received aid; partial tuition waivers available. Financial aid application deadline: 3/15. *Faculty research:* Choral music education, instrumental music education, elementary education, secondary education. • Dr. William Dougherty, Chairperson, Department of Music, 515-271-3975. Fax: 515-271-2558. Application contact: Dr. David Harris, 515-271-3104.

Duquesne University, School of Music, Pittsburgh, PA 15282-0001. Offerings include music education (MM). Member of NASM. School faculty: 25 full-time (7 women), 68 part-time (25 women). *Degree requirements:* Thesis (for some programs), recital (performance majors). *Entrance requirements:* GRE, audition (MM). Application deadline: 8/1 (priority date; rolling processing; 12/1 for spring admission). Application fee: $45. *Expenses:* Tuition $560 per credit. Fees $39 per credit. • Dr. Robert Shankovich, Graduate Chair, 412-396-6676. E-mail: shankovi@duq2.cc.duq.edu. Application contact: Sally K. Coletti, 412-396-5064. Fax: 412-396-5479.

East Carolina University, School of Music, Greenville, NC 27858-4353. Offerings include music education (MM). Member of NASM. School faculty: 23 full-time (4 women). *Degree requirements:* Comprehensive exams required, thesis optional, foreign language not required. *Entrance requirements:* GRE General Test or MAT, TOEFL. Application deadline: 6/1 (priority date; rolling processing). Application fee: $40. *Tuition:* $1886 per year full-time, $472 per semester (minimum) part-time for state residents; $9156 per year full-time, $2289 per semester (minimum) part-time for nonresidents. • Dr. Rodney Schmidt, Director of Graduate Studies, 252-328-6282. Fax: 252-328-6258. E-mail: schmidtr@mail.ecu.edu. Application contact: Dr. Paul D. Tschetter, Associate Dean, 252-328-6012. Fax: 252-328-6071. E-mail: grad@mail.ecu.edu.

Eastern Kentucky University, College of Education, Department of Curriculum and Instruction, Richmond, KY 40475-3101. Offerings include music education (MA Ed). Accredited by NCATE. Member of NASM. *Entrance requirements:* GRE General Test, minimum GPA of 2.5. Application fee: $0. *Tuition:* $2390 per year full-time, $133 per credit hour part-time for state residents; $6630 per year full-time, $365 per credit hour part-time for nonresidents. • Dr. Imogene Ramsey, Chair, 606-622-2154.

Eastern Nazarene College, Graduate Studies, Division of Education, Quincy, MA 02170-2999. Offerings include music education (M Ed, Certificate). M Ed and Certificate also available through weekend program for administration, special needs, and reading only. Division faculty: 9 full-time (5 women), 11 part-time (5 women). *Entrance requirements:* For master's, TOEFL (minimum score 500). Application deadline: rolling. Application fee: $35. *Expenses:* Tuition $350 per credit. Fees $125 per semester full-time, $15 per semester part-time. • Dr. Lorne Ranstrom, Chair, 617-745-3528. Application contact: Cleo P. Cakridas, Graduate Enrollment Counselor, 617-745-3870. Fax: 617-745-3907. E-mail: cakridac@enc.edu.

Eastern Washington University, College of Letters and Social Sciences, Department of Music, Cheney, WA 99004-2431. Offerings include music education (MA). Accredited by NCATE. Department faculty: 13 full-time (2 women). *Degree requirements:* Thesis or alternative, comprehensive oral exam required, foreign language not required. *Entrance requirements:* GRE General Test, GRE Subject Test, minimum GPA of 3.0. Application deadline: 4/1 (priority date; rolling processing; 1/15 for spring admission). Application fee: $35. *Tuition:* $4200 per year full-time, $140 per credit part-time for state residents; $12,780 per year full-time, $415 per credit part-time for nonresidents. • Dr. Lynn Brinkmeyer, Chair, 509-359-2241. Application contact: Dr. David Rostkoski, Graduate Director, 509-359-6119.

East Tennessee State University, College of Arts and Sciences, Department of Music, Johnson City, TN 37614-0734. Awards M Mu Ed. Member of NASM. Part-time and evening/weekend programs available. Faculty: 13 full-time (3 women). Students: 5 full-time (1 woman), 7 part-time (5 women). Average age 34. 2 applicants, 0% accepted. In 1997, 2 degrees awarded. *Degree requirements:* Thesis required, foreign language not required. *Entrance requirements:* GRE General Test, TOEFL (minimum score 550). Application deadline: 7/15 (priority date; rolling processing; 11/1 for spring admission). Application fee: $25 ($35 for international students). *Tuition:* $2944 per year full-time, $158 per credit hour part-time for state residents; $7770 per year full-time, $369 per credit hour part-time for nonresidents. *Financial aid:* Fellowships, research assistantships available. Financial aid application deadline: 3/1. *Faculty research:* Music performance. • Dr. James Stafford, Chair, 423-439-6948. Application contact: Dr. Benjamin Caton, Graduate Coordinator, 423-439-4270. Fax: 423-439-7088.

Emporia State University, School of Graduate Studies, College of Liberal Arts and Sciences, Division of Music, Emporia, KS 66801-5087. Offerings include music education (MM), with options in instrumental, vocal. Member of NASM. Division faculty: 12 full-time (6 women), 4 part-time (2 women). *Degree requirements:* Comprehensive exam or thesis required, foreign language not required. *Entrance requirements:* TOEFL (minimum score 550), written exam, audition. Application deadline: 8/15 (priority date; rolling processing). Application fee: $30 ($75 for international students). Electronic applications accepted. *Tuition:* $2300 per year full-time, $103 per credit hour part-time for state residents; $6012 per year full-time, $258 per credit hour part-time for nonresidents. • Dr. Marie C. Miller, Chair, 316-341-5431. E-mail: millerma@emporia.edu. Application contact: Dr. Penelope Speedie, Graduate Adviser, 316-341-5438. E-mail: speediep@emporia.edu.

Five Towns College, Department of Music, Dix Hills, NY 11746-6055. Offerings include music education (MM). College faculty: 9 full-time (2 women), 14 part-time (4 women), 11.33 FTE. *Degree requirements:* Exams, major composition or Capstone Project, recital required, foreign language and thesis not required. *Entrance requirements:* English essay exam, audition, bachelor's degree in music or music education, minimum GPA of 2.75, 36 hours of course work in performance. Application deadline: rolling. Application fee: $50. • Dr. Bruce Purrington, Chair, 516-424-7000. Application contact: Christina Kuhl, Admissions Coordinator, 516-424-7000. Fax: 516-424-7006.

Florida International University, College of Arts and Sciences, School of Music, Program in Music Education, Miami, FL 33199. Awards MS. Part-time and evening/weekend programs available. *Entrance requirements:* GRE General Test (minimum combined score of 1000) or minimum GPA of 3.0. Application deadline: 4/1 (priority date; rolling processing; 10/1 for spring admission). Application fee: $20. *Expenses:* Tuition $138 per credit hour for state residents; $482 per credit hour for nonresidents. Fees $46 per semester. *Faculty research:* Psychology of music teaching, classroom methodology, biofeedback. • Fredrick Kaufman, Director, School of Music, 305-348-2896. Fax: 305-348-4073. E-mail: kaufmanf@scvrms.fiu.edu.

Florida State University, School of Music, Program in Music Education, Tallahassee, FL 32306. Awards MM Ed, Ed D, PhD. Member of NASM. Faculty: 72 full-time, 8 part-time. Students: 62 full-time (18 women); includes 12 minority (5 African Americans, 1 Asian American, 6 Hispanics), 2 international. Average age 23. In 1997, 11 master's awarded; 5 doctorates awarded (100% entered university research/teaching). *Degree requirements:* For master's, departmental qualifying exam required, thesis optional, foreign language not required; for doctorate, dissertation, departmental qualifying exam required, foreign language not required. *Average time to degree:* master's–2 years full-time; doctorate–6 years full-time. *Entrance requirements:* Minimum GPA of 3.0 or GRE General Test. Application deadline: 7/18 (rolling processing; 11/15 for spring admission). Application fee: $20. *Tuition:* $139 per credit hour for state residents, $482 per credit hour for nonresidents. *Financial aid:* In 1997–98, 24 teaching assistantships (7 to first-year students) were awarded; fellowships, research assistantships, Federal Work-Study, and career-related internships or fieldwork also available. Aid available to part-time students. Financial aid application deadline: 3/20; applicants required to submit FAFSA. • Application contact: Dr. John J. Deal, Director, Graduate Studies, 850-644-5848. Fax: 850-644-2033. E-mail: deal_j@otto.cmr.fsu.edu.

George Mason University, College of Arts and Sciences, Department of Music, Fairfax, VA 22030-4444. Offerings include music education (MA). Member of NASM. Accredited by NCATE. Department faculty: 12 full-time (3 women), 10 part-time (5 women), 14.4 FTE. *Degree requirements:* Thesis (for some programs). *Entrance requirements:* Music teaching certificate. Application deadline: 5/1 (11/1 for spring admission). Application fee: $30. Electronic applications accepted. *Tuition:* $4344 per year full-time, $181 per credit hour part-time for state residents; $12,504 per year full-time, $521 per credit hour part-time for nonresidents. • Dr. Joseph Shirk, Chairman, 703-993-1380. Fax: 703-993-1394.

Georgia Southern University, College of Education, Department of Middle Grades and Secondary Education, Program in Music, Statesboro, GA 30460-8126. Awards M Ed, Ed S. Accredited by NCATE. Member of NASM. Part-time and evening/weekend programs available. Students: 3 full-time (1 woman), 3 part-time (2 women); includes 2 minority (both African Americans). Average age 35. 1 applicant, 100% accepted. In 1997, 4 master's, 5 Ed Ss awarded. *Degree requirements:* Exams required, foreign language and thesis not required. *Entrance requirements:* For master's, GRE General Test (minimum score 450 on each section) or MAT (minimum score 44), minimum GPA of 2.5; for Ed S, GRE General Test (minimum score 450 on each section) or MAT (minimum score 49), minimum graduate GPA of 3.25. Application deadline: 7/15 (priority date; rolling processing; 11/15 for spring admission). Application fee: $0. Electronic applications accepted. *Tuition:* $2619 per year full-time, $287 per semester (minimum) part-time for state residents; $8619 per year full-time, $1037 per semester (minimum) part-time for nonresidents. *Financial aid:* Federal Work-Study and career-related internships or fieldwork available. Aid available to part-time students. Financial aid application deadline: 4/15. • Application contact: Dr. John R. Diebolt, Associate Graduate Dean, 912-681-5384. Fax: 912-681-0740. E-mail: gradschool@gsvms2.cc.gasou.edu.

Georgia State University, College of Arts and Sciences, School of Music, Atlanta, GA 30303-3083. Offerings include music education (M Mu), piano pedagogy (M Mu). Member of NASM. School faculty: 26 full-time (6 women), 6 part-time (2 women). *Degree requirements:* 1 foreign language (computer language can substitute), recital. *Entrance requirements:* GRE General Test or MAT (music education), TOEFL (minimum score 550), minimum GPA of 3.0, audition. Application fee: $25. *Expenses:* Tuition $2673 per year full-time, $99 per semester hour part-time for state residents; $10,692 per year full-time, $396 per semester hour part-time for nonresidents. Fees $228 per year. • Dr. John Haberlen, Director, 404-651-3676. E-mail: dasjbh@langate.gsu.edu. Application contact: Dr. James Lyke, Director of Graduate Studies, 404-651-3676. Fax: 404-651-1583. E-mail: musjbl@panther.gsu.edu.

Georgia State University, College of Education, Department of Middle, Secondary Education and Instructional Technology, Programs in Secondary Education, Atlanta, GA 30303-3083. Offerings include music education (Ed S). Accredited by NCATE. Member of NASM. *Degree requirements:* Project/exam. *Entrance requirements:* GRE General Test (minimum combined score of 900) or MAT (minimum score 48), minimum graduate GPA of 3.25. Application fee: $25. *Expenses:* Tuition $2673 per year full-time, $99 per semester hour part-time for state residents; $10,692 per year full-time, $396 per semester hour part-time for nonresidents. Fees $228 per year. • Dr. Beverly J. Armento, Chair, Department of Middle, Secondary Education and Instructional Technology, 404-651-2510.

Hardin–Simmons University, School of Music, Abilene, TX 79698-0001. Offerings include music education (MM). Member of NASM. School faculty: 7 full-time (2 women). *Degree requirements:* 1 foreign language, thesis (for some programs). *Application deadline:* 8/15 (priority date; rolling processing; 1/5 for spring admission). *Application fee:* $25. *Expenses:* Tuition $280 per semester hour. Fees $630 per year full-time. • Dr. Loyd Hawthorne, Dean, 915-670-1426. Fax: 915-670-5873. Application contact: Dr. J. Paul Sorrels, Dean of Graduate Studies, 915-670-1298. Fax: 915-670-1564.

Hofstra University, School of Education and Allied Human Services, Department of Curriculum and Teaching, Hempstead, NY 11549. Offerings include elementary and early childhood education (MA, MS Ed), with options in art education (MA, MS Ed), early childhood education (MA), elementary education (MA, MS Ed), music education (MA, MS Ed); secondary education (MA, MS Ed), with options in art education (MA), music education (MA), secondary education (MA, MS Ed). One or more programs accredited by NCATE. Department faculty: 24 full-time (20 women), 77 part-time (45 women). *Degree requirements:* Departmental qualifying exam. *Application deadline:* rolling. *Application fee:* $40 ($75 for international students). *Expenses:* Tuition $10,968 per year full-time, $457 per credit hour part-time. Fees $670 per year full-time, $112 per semester (minimum) part-time. • Dr. Doris Fromberg, Chairperson, 516-463-5749. Fax: 516-463-6503. E-mail: catdpf@hofstra.edu. Application contact: Mary Beth Carey, Dean of Admissions, 516-463-6700. Fax: 516-560-7660. E-mail: hofstra@hofstra.edu.

Holy Names College, Department of Music, 3500 Mountain Boulevard, Oakland, CA 94619-1699. Offerings include Kodály music education (Certificate); music education with a Kodály emphasis (MM); piano pedagogy (MM); piano pedagogy with Suzuki emphasis (Certificate). Department faculty: 6 full-time (3 women), 7 part-time (5 women). *Degree requirements:* For master's, comprehensive exam, recital required, thesis not required. *Average time to degree:* master's–1 year full-time, 2 years part-time; other advanced degree–2 years part-time. *Entrance requirements:* For master's, TOEFL (minimum score 550), minimum undergraduate GPA of 2.6 overall, 3.0 in major. Application deadline: 8/1 (rolling processing; 12/1 for spring admission). Application fee: $35. *Tuition:* $7650 per year full-time, $425 per unit part-time. • Betty Woo, Program Co-Director, 510-436-1330. Application contact: Graduate Admissions Office, 800-430-1321. Fax: 510-436-1317. E-mail: garner@admin.hnc.edu.

Howard University, Division of Fine Arts, Department of Music, Program in Music Education, 2400 Sixth Street, NW, Washington, DC 20059-0002. Awards MM Ed. Member of NASM. Part-time programs available. *Degree requirements:* 1 foreign language, thesis or alternative, departmental qualifying exam, recital, comprehensive exam. *Entrance requirements:* Minimum GPA of 2.9, bachelor's degree in music or music education. Application deadline: 4/1. Application fee: $45. *Expenses:* Tuition $10,200 per year full-time, $567 per credit hour part-time. Fees $405 per year. *Financial aid:* Fellowships, research assistantships, teaching assistantships, grants, institutionally sponsored loans available. Financial aid application deadline: 4/1. • Dr. George Winfield, Chair, Department of Music, 202-806-7082.

Hunter College of the City University of New York, Division of Education, Program in Music Education, 695 Park Avenue, New York, NY 10021-5085. Awards MA. *Degree requirements:* Comprehensive exam required, foreign language not required. *Entrance requirements:* TOEFL. Application deadline: 4/1 (11/7 for spring admission). Application fee: $40. *Expenses:* Tuition $4350 per year full-time, $185 per credit part-time for state residents; $7600 per year full-time, $320 per credit part-time for nonresidents. Fees $26 per year.

Indiana State University, College of Arts and Sciences, Department of Music, Terre Haute, IN 47809-1401. Offerings include music education (MA, MME, MS). One or more programs accredited by NCATE and NASM. Department faculty: 19 full-time (5 women). *Application deadline:* rolling. *Application fee:* $20. *Tuition:* $143 per credit hour for state residents; $325 per credit hour for nonresidents. • Dr. James O'Donnell, Chairperson, 812-237-2768.

Indiana University of Pennsylvania, College of Fine Arts, Department of Music, Indiana, PA 15705-1087. Offerings include music education (MA). Member of NASM. *Degree requirements:* Thesis optional, foreign language not required. *Entrance requirements:* TOEFL (minimum score 500). Application deadline: 7/1 (priority date; rolling processing; 11/1 for spring admission). Application fee: $30. *Expenses:* Tuition $3468 per year full-time, $193 per credit part-time for state residents; $6236 per year full-time, $346 per credit part-time for nonresidents. Fees $313 per year (minimum) full-time, $84 per year part-time. • John Scandrett, Chairperson, 724-357-2390. E-mail: jscandt@grove.iup.edu. Application contact: Dr. Calvin Weber, Graduate Coordinator, 724-357-5644.

Indiana University South Bend, Division of Arts, South Bend, IN 46634-7111. Offerings include music in secondary education (MS Ed). Division faculty: 8 full-time (1 woman), 7 part-time (2 women), 10 FTE. *Application deadline:* 7/1 (priority date; rolling processing; 11/1 for spring admission). *Application fee:* $35 ($40 for international students). *Expenses:* Tuition $3024 per year full-time, $126 per credit hour part-time for state residents; $7320 per year full-time, $305 per credit hour part-time for nonresidents. Fees $222 per year full-time, $34 per semester (minimum) part-time. • Dr. Robert W. Demaree Jr., Dean, 219-237-4170. Fax: 219-237-4317. E-mail: rdemaree@iusb.edu. Application contact: Graduate Director, 219-237-4183. Fax: 219-237-6549.

Ithaca College, School of Music, Program in Music and Music Education, Ithaca, NY 14850-7020. Offers composition (MM); conducting (MM); music education (MM, MS); music theory (MM); performance (MM); strings, woodwinds, or brasses (MM); Suzuki pedagogy (MM). Member of NASM. Part-time programs available. Faculty: 49 full-time (17 women), 5 part-time (2 women), 50.9 FTE. Students: 34 full-time (12 women), 4 part-time (3 women); includes 3 minority (1 African American, 1 Asian American, 1 Hispanic), 3 international. Average age 26. 57 applicants, 72% accepted. In 1997, 21 degrees awarded. *Degree requirements:* Thesis (for some programs), comprehensive exams required, foreign language not required. *Entrance requirements:* TOEFL (minimum score 550), audition. Application deadline: 3/1 (priority date; rolling processing; 12/1 for spring admission). Application fee: $30. *Tuition:* $552 per credit hour. *Financial aid:* In 1997–98, 34 students received aid, including 1 fellowship totaling $9,624, 29 graduate assistantships (12 to first-year students) totaling $255,258; career-related internships or fieldwork also available. Financial aid application deadline: 3/1; applicants required to submit FAFSA. *Faculty research:* Music history. • Dr. Gregory Woodward, Chair, 607-274-3688.

Jackson State University, School of Liberal Arts, Department of Music, Jackson, MS 39217. Offers program in music education (MM Ed). Member of NASM. Part-time and evening/weekend programs available. Faculty: 9 full-time (4 women). Students: 3 full-time (0 women), 2 part-time (1 woman); includes 5 minority (all African Americans). 6 applicants, 83% accepted. In 1997, 1 degree awarded. *Degree requirements:* Thesis or alternative, comprehensive exam. *Entrance requirements:* GRE General Test (minimum combined score of 1000), TOEFL (minimum score 550). Application deadline: 3/1 (priority date; rolling processing; 10/1 for spring admission). Application fee: $20. *Tuition:* $2688 per year (minimum) full-time, $150 per semester hour part-time for state residents; $5546 per year (minimum) full-time, $309 per semester hour part-time for nonresidents. *Financial aid:* Application deadline 3/1. • Dr. Jimmie James, Chair, 601-968-2141. Fax: 601-968-2568. Application contact: Mae Robinson, Admissions Coordinator, 601-968-2455. Fax: 601-968-8246. E-mail: mrobinson@ccaix.jsums.edu.

Jacksonville State University, College of Education, Program in Music Education, Jacksonville, AL 36265-9982. Awards MM Ed. Accredited by NCATE. Faculty: 10 full-time (2 women). Students: 3 full-time (0 women), 11 part-time (5 women); includes 1 minority (African American). In 1997, 4 degrees awarded. *Degree requirements:* Thesis optional. *Entrance requirements:* GRE General Test or MAT. Application deadline: rolling. Application fee: $20. *Expenses:* Tuition $2140 per year full-time, $107 per semester hour part-time for state residents; $4280 per year full-time, $214 per semester hour part-time for nonresidents. Fees $30 per semester. *Financial aid:* Application deadline 4/1. • Application contact: College of Graduate Studies and Continuing Education, 205-782-5329.

Jacksonville University, College of Arts and Sciences, Division of Education, Program in Music, 2800 University Boulevard North, Jacksonville, FL 32211-3394. Awards MAT. Part-time and evening/weekend programs available. *Degree requirements:* Comprehensive exam required, foreign language and thesis not required. *Entrance requirements:* GRE General Test (minimum combined score of 900), TOEFL (minimum score 500), minimum GPA of 3.0. Application deadline: 8/1 (priority date; rolling processing; 11/1 for spring admission). Application fee: $25.

James Madison University, College of Arts and Letters, School of Music, Harrisonburg, VA 22807. Offerings include music education (MM). Member of NASM. Accredited by NCATE. School faculty: 13 full-time (3 women). *Entrance requirements:* Audition. Application deadline: 7/1 (priority date; rolling processing). Application fee: $50. *Tuition:* $134 per credit hour for state residents; $404 per credit hour for nonresidents. • Dr. Mellasenah Y. Morris, Director, 540-568-6197.

Kent State University, College of Fine and Professional Arts, Hugh A. Glauser School of Music, Kent, OH 44242-0001. Offerings include music education (MM, PhD), piano pedagogy (MM). Member of NASM. School faculty: 42 full-time. *Degree requirements:* For doctorate, variable foreign language requirement, dissertation. *Entrance requirements:* For doctorate, master's thesis or scholarly paper, minimum GPA of 3.0. Application deadline: 7/12 (rolling processing; 11/29 for spring admission). Application fee: $30. *Tuition:* $4752 per year full-time, $216 per credit hour part-time for state residents; $9213 per year full-time, $419 per credit hour part-time for nonresidents. • Dr. John M. Lee, Director, 330-672-2172. Fax: 330-672-7837.

Lamar University, College of Fine Arts and Communication, Department of Music, Theatre, and Dance, Program in Music Education, Beaumont, TX 77710. Awards MM Ed. Member of NASM. Faculty: 11 full-time (2 women). Students: 2 part-time (1 woman). Average age 25. In 1997, 3 degrees awarded (100% found work related to degree). *Entrance requirements:* GRE General Test (minimum score 450 on each section), TOEFL (minimum score 500). Application deadline: 8/1 (rolling processing; 12/1 for spring admission). Application fee: $0. *Expenses:* Tuition $1072 per year full-time, $748 per year part-time for state residents; $4924 per year full-time, $3316 per year part-time for nonresidents. Fees $458 per year full-time, $332 per year part-time. *Financial aid:* Teaching assistantships available. Financial aid application deadline: 4/1. • Dr. Barry Johnson, Interim Chair, Department of Music, Theatre, and Dance, 409-880-8144. Fax: 409-880-8143.

Lewis & Clark College, Department of Education, Program in Music Education, Portland, OR 97219-7899. Awards MAT. *Degree requirements:* Thesis or alternative required, foreign language not required. *Entrance requirements:* California Basic Educational Skills Test (preservice), GRE General Test or MAT; NTE, minimum GPA of 2.75. Application deadline: 1/15. Application fee: $45.

Long Island University, C.W. Post Campus, School of Education, Department of Curriculum and Instruction, Brookville, NY 11548-1300. Offerings include music education (MS). Department faculty: 10 full-time (5 women), 46 part-time (19 women). *Application deadline:* rolling. *Application fee:* $30. Electronic applications accepted. *Expenses:* Tuition $480 per credit. Fees $316 per year full-time, $71 per semester (minimum) part-time. • Dr. Anthony De Falco, Chairperson, 516-299-2372. Application contact: Camille Marziliano, Academic Counselor, 516-299-2123. Fax: 516-299-4167. E-mail: cmarzili@eagle.liunet.edu.

Long Island University, C.W. Post Campus, School of Visual and Performing Arts, Department of Music, Brookville, NY 11548-1300. Offerings include music education (MS). Department faculty: 6 full-time (2 women), 25 part-time (12 women). *Average time to degree:* master's–2 years full-time, 4 years part-time. *Application deadline:* rolling. *Application fee:* $30. Electronic applications accepted. *Expenses:* Tuition $480 per credit. Fees $316 per year full-time, $71 per semester (minimum) part-time. • Alexander Dashnaw, Chairman, 516-299-2474. Application contact: John Meschi, Adviser, 516-299-2105. E-mail: jmeschi@eagle.liu.edu.

Louisiana State University and Agricultural and Mechanical College, School of Music, Baton Rouge, LA 70803. Offerings include music education (PhD). Member of NASM. Accredited by NCATE. Terminal master's awarded for partial completion of doctoral program. School faculty: 42 full-time (13 women), 1 part-time (0 women). *Application deadline:* 3/15 (priority date; rolling processing). *Application fee:* $25. *Tuition:* $2736 per year full-time, $285 per semester (minimum) part-time for state residents; $6636 per year full-time, $460 per semester (minimum) part-time for nonresidents. • Dr. Ronald Ross, Dean, 504-388-3261. Fax: 504-388-2562. E-mail: rross@lsuvm.sncc.lsu.edu. Application contact: Dr. Kathleen Rountree, Graduate Adviser, 504-388-3261.

Manhattanville College, School of Education, Program in Music Education, Purchase, NY 10577-2132. Awards MAT. *Degree requirements:* Thesis, comprehensive exam or research project required, foreign language not required. *Entrance requirements:* Minimum undergraduate GPA of 3.0. Application deadline: rolling. Application fee: $40. *Expenses:* Tuition $410 per credit (minimum). Fees $25 per semester. • Application contact: Carol Messar, Director of Admissions, 914-323-5142. Fax: 914-323-5493.

Mansfield University of Pennsylvania, Department of Music, Mansfield, PA 16933. Offers program in music education (MM). Member of NASM. Part-time and evening/weekend programs available. Faculty: 17 part-time (3 women). Students: 3 full-time (all women), 8 part-time (4 women). Average age 27. 1 applicant, 100% accepted. In 1997, 3 degrees awarded. *Entrance requirements:* GRE, NTE, or minimum GPA of 3.0. Application deadline: rolling. Application fee: $25. *Expenses:* Tuition $3468 per year full-time, $193 per credit part-time for state residents; $6236 per year full-time, $346 per credit part-time for nonresidents. Fees $236 per year full-time, $18.25 per semester (minimum) part-time for state residents; $266 per year full-time, $18.25 per semester (minimum) part-time for nonresidents. *Financial aid:* In 1997–98, 1 graduate assistantship (to a first-year student) was awarded; career-related internships or fieldwork also available. Financial aid application deadline: 5/1; applicants required to submit FAFSA. • Dr. Joseph Murphy, Chairperson, 717-662-4734.

Marywood University, Graduate School of Arts and Sciences, Music Department, Program in Music Education, Scranton, PA 18509-1598. Awards MA. Accredited by NCATE. Students: 4 part-time (3 women). Average age 38. 1 applicant, 100% accepted. *Degree requirements:* Thesis or alternative, comprehensive exam required, foreign language not required. *Entrance requirements:* GRE Subject Test, TOEFL (minimum score 550; average 590), audition. Application deadline: 7/15 (priority date; rolling processing; 12/1 for spring admission). Application fee: $20. *Expenses:* Tuition $449 per credit hour. Fees $530 per year full-time, $180 per year part-time. *Financial aid:* Research assistantships, scholarships/tuition reductions, partial tuition waivers, and career-related internships or fieldwork available. Aid available to part-time students. Financial aid application deadline: 2/15; applicants required to submit FAFSA. • Application contact: Deborah M. Flynn, Coordinator of Admissions, 717-340-6002. Fax: 717-961-4745. E-mail: gsas_adm@ac.marywood.edu.

McGill University, Faculty of Graduate Studies and Research, Faculty of Music, Montréal, PQ H3A 2T5, Canada. Offerings include music education (MA, PhD). Faculty: 45 full-time (5 women), 30 part-time (2 women). *Application deadline:* 1/15 (priority date; rolling processing). *Application fee:* $60. *Expenses:* Tuition $1668 per year for Canadian residents; $8268 per year for nonresidents. Fees $828 per year for Canadian residents; $1216 per year for nonresidents. • R. Lawton, Dean, 514-398-4538. E-mail: lawton@music.mcgill.ca. Application contact: Veronica Slobodian, Admissions Officer, 514-398-4546. Fax: 514-398-8061. E-mail: vslobod@music.mcgill.ca.

McNeese State University, College of Liberal Arts, Department of Music, Program in Music Education, Lake Charles, LA 70609-2495. Awards MM Ed. Evening/weekend programs available. Faculty: 15 full-time (4 women). Students: 2 full-time (1 woman), 1 (woman) part-time. *Entrance requirements:* GRE General Test. Application deadline: 7/15 (priority date; rolling processing). Application fee: $10 ($25 for international students). *Tuition:* $2118 per year full-time, $344 per semester (minimum) part-time for state residents; $7308 per year full-time, $344 per semester (minimum) part-time for nonresidents. *Financial aid:* Teaching assistantships available. • Michele Martin, Head, Department of Music, 318-475-5028.

Miami University, School of Fine Arts, Department of Music, Program in Music Education, Oxford, OH 45056. Awards MM. Member of NASM. Faculty: 26. Students: 8 full-time (4 women), 2 part-time (1 woman); includes 1 minority (African American). 12 applicants, 75% accepted. In 1997, 2 degrees awarded. *Degree requirements:* Final and oral exams, recital required, foreign language and thesis not required. *Entrance requirements:* Audition, minimum undergraduate GPA of 3.0 during previous 2 years or 3.0 overall. Application deadline: 3/1 (priority date; rolling processing). Application fee: $35. *Tuition:* $5932 per year full-time, $255 per credit hour part-time for state residents; $12,392 per year full-time, $524 per credit hour part-time for nonresidents. *Financial aid:* Research assistantships, teaching assistantships, full tuition waivers, Federal Work-Study available. Financial aid application deadline: 3/1. • Dr. William Albin, Director of Graduate Study, Department of Music, 513-529-3094.

Michigan State University, College of Arts and Letters, School of Music, East Lansing, MI 48824-1020. Offerings include music education (M Mus, PhD). Member of NASM. School faculty: 47 full-time (11 women). *Application deadline:* rolling. *Application fee:* $30 ($40 for

Directory: Music Education

Michigan State University (continued)

international students). *Expenses:* Tuition $4609 per year full-time, $223 per credit hour (minimum) part-time for state residents; $8704 per year full-time, $450 per credit hour (minimum) part-time for nonresidents. Fees $576 per year full-time, $476 per year part-time. • Dr. James Forger, Director, 517-355-4583. E-mail: forger@pilot.msu.edu. Application contact: Dorothy Bartholic, Admissions Coordinator, 517-355-2140. Fax: 517-432-2880. E-mail: barthol3@pilot.msu.edu.

Minot State University, Program in Humanities and Social Science, Minot, ND 58707-0002. Offers music education (MME). One or more programs accredited by NASM. Program offered during summer only. Faculty: 6 full-time (1 woman). Students: 1 (woman) part-time. 7 applicants, 100% accepted. *Degree requirements:* Thesis or alternative required, foreign language not required. *Entrance requirements:* Music exam, GRE General Test (minimum combined score of 1100 rquired) or minimum GPA of 3.0. Application deadline: rolling. Application fee: $25. *Tuition:* $2714 per year for state residents; $3235 per year (minimum) for nonresidents. *Financial aid:* Research assistantships, teaching assistantships, institutionally sponsored loans, and career-related internships or fieldwork available. Aid available to part-time students. Financial aid application deadline: 4/1. • Bob Larson, Chairperson, 701-858-3185. Application contact: Tammy White, Administrative Secretary, 701-858-3250. Fax: 701-839-6933.

Mississippi College, College of Arts and Sciences, Department of Music, Program in Music Education, Clinton, MS 39058. Awards MM. Member of NASM. Accredited by NCATE. Part-time and evening/weekend programs available. *Degree requirements:* Comprehensive exam, recital required, foreign language not required. *Entrance requirements:* GRE, minimum GPA of 2.5. Application deadline: 8/15 (priority date; rolling processing). Application fee: $25 ($75 for international students). *Expenses:* Tuition $6624 per year full-time, $276 per hour part-time. Fees $230 per year full-time, $35 per semester (minimum) part-time. *Financial aid:* Professional development scholarships available. Aid available to part-time students. Financial aid application deadline: 4/1. • Dr. Richard Joiner, Head, Department of Music, 601-925-3441.

Mississippi State University, College of Education, Department of Music Education, Mississippi State, MS 39762. Offers programs in church music education (MM Ed), instrumental (MM Ed), keyboard (MM Ed), piano pedagogy (MM Ed), voice (MM Ed). Accredited by NCATE. Program being phased out; applicants no longer accepted. Part-time programs available. Faculty: 14 full-time (5 women). Students: 1 part-time (0 women). Average age 30. *Degree requirements:* Comprehensive oral or written exam, recital, research project required, foreign language and thesis not required. *Tuition:* $3017 per year full-time, $168 per credit hour part-time for state residents; $6119 per year full-time, $340 per credit hour part-time for nonresidents. *Financial aid:* Research assistantships, teaching assistantships, Federal Work-Study available. Aid available to part-time students. *Faculty research:* Administration practices, undergraduate teacher education. • Dr. Randi L'Hommedieu, Head, 601-325-3070. Fax: 601-325-8784.

Montclair State University, School of the Arts, Department of Music, Upper Montclair, NJ 07043-1624. Offerings include music education (MA). Member of NASM. Accredited by NCATE. Department faculty: 17 full-time. *Degree requirements:* Compositions, comprehensive exam, or recitals required, foreign language and thesis not required. *Entrance requirements:* GRE General Test, audition. Application deadline: 4/1 (rolling processing; 11/1 for spring admission). Application fee: $40. *Expenses:* Tuition $201 per credit for state residents; $257 per credit for nonresidents. Fees $22.05 per credit. • Dr. Robert Stephens, Acting Chairperson, 973-655-7212. Application contact: Dr. Ting Ho, Adviser, 973-655-7221.

Moorhead State University, Department of Music, Moorhead, MN 56563-0002. Offerings include music education (MS). Member of NASM. Department faculty: 7 full-time (2 women), 3 part-time (2 women). *Degree requirements:* Thesis, final oral exam, project or recital, written comprehensive exam required, foreign language not required. *Entrance requirements:* TOEFL (minimum score 550), bachelor's degree in music or equivalent, minimum GPA of 3.0. Application deadline: 5/1 (priority date; rolling processing; 9/1 for spring admission). Application fee: $20 ($35 for international students). Electronic applications accepted. *Tuition:* $145 per credit hour for state residents; $220 per credit hour for nonresidents. • Dr. Ruth Dahlke, Chairperson, 218-236-2103.

Morehead State University, Caudill College of Humanities, Department of Music, Program in Music Education, Morehead, KY 40351. Awards MM. Member of NASM. Part-time and evening/weekend programs available. Faculty: 8 full-time (1 woman). Students: 3 full-time (0 women), 1 (woman) part-time; includes 1 minority (African American). Average age 25. 2 applicants, 100% accepted. In 1997, 2 degrees awarded. *Degree requirements:* Oral and written exams required, thesis optional, foreign language not required. *Entrance requirements:* Departmental exams, GRE General Test (minimum combined score of 1200 on three sections), minimum GPA of 3.0 in music, 2.5 overall. Application deadline: 8/1 (priority date; rolling processing; 12/1 for spring admission). Application fee: $0. *Tuition:* $2470 per year full-time, $138 per semester hour part-time for state residents; $6710 per year full-time, $373 per semester hour part-time for nonresidents. *Financial aid:* In 1997–98, teaching assistantships averaging $471 per month and totaling $20,000 were awarded; research assistantships, Federal Work-Study also available. Financial aid application deadline: 4/1; applicants required to submit FAFSA. *Faculty research:* Computer-assisted instruction in music, musical instrument digital interface (MIDI) applications. • Application contact: Betty Cowsert, Graduate Admissions Officer, 606-783-2039. Fax: 606-783-5061.

Murray State University, College of Fine Arts and Communications, Department of Music, Program in Music Education, Murray, KY 42071-0009. Awards MME. Member of NASM. Accredited by NCATE. Part-time programs available. Faculty: 10 full-time (1 woman). Students: 2 full-time (both women), 8 part-time (6 women); includes 1 international. 4 applicants, 100% accepted. In 1997, 6 degrees awarded. *Entrance requirements:* GRE General Test or MAT, TOEFL (minimum score 500). Application deadline: rolling. Application fee: $20. *Expenses:* Tuition $2500 per year full-time, $124 per hour part-time for state residents; $6740 per year full-time, $357 per hour part-time for nonresidents. Fees $360 per year full-time, $180 per year part-time. *Financial aid:* Research assistantships, teaching assistantships, Federal Work-Study available. Financial aid application deadline: 4/1. • Application contact: Dr. Pam Wurgler, Graduate Coordinator, 502-762-6452. Fax: 502-762-3965.

Nazareth College of Rochester, Graduate Studies, Department of Music, Program in Music Education, Rochester, NY 14618-3790. Awards MS Ed. Part-time and evening/weekend programs available. Faculty: 3 full-time (0 women), 2 part-time (1 woman). Students: 1 full-time (0 women), 8 part-time (7 women). 2 applicants, 50% accepted. In 1997, 3 degrees awarded. *Degree requirements:* Comprehensive exam required, foreign language and thesis not required. *Entrance requirements:* Audition, minimum GPA of 2.7. Application fee: $40. *Expenses:* Tuition $436 per credit hour. Fees $20 per semester. • Dr. Ross Miller, Director, 716-389-2697. Application contact: Dr. Kay F. Marshman, Dean, 716-389-2815. Fax: 716-389-2452.

New Jersey City University, School of Arts and Sciences, Department of Music, Jersey City, NJ 07305-1957. Offers program in music education (MA). Member of NASM. Evening/weekend programs available. *Degree requirements:* Recital required, thesis optional, foreign language not required. *Entrance requirements:* GRE General Test or MAT, TOEFL. Application deadline: 8/1 (priority date; rolling processing; 12/1 for spring admission). Application fee: $0.

New York University, School of Education, Department of Music and Performing Arts Professions, Program in Music Education, New York, NY 10012-1019. Awards MA, Ed D, PhD, CAS. Member of NASM. Part-time and evening/weekend programs available. Faculty: 11 full-time, 3 part-time. Students: 12 full-time, 21 part-time. 28 applicants, 43% accepted. In 1997, 6 master's, 3 doctorates awarded. Terminal master's awarded for partial completion of doctoral program. *Degree requirements:* For master's, thesis required (for some programs), foreign language not required; for doctorate, dissertation. *Entrance requirements:* For master's, TOEFL; for doctorate, GRE General Test, TOEFL, interview; for CAS, TOEFL, master's degree. Application deadline: 2/1 (priority date; rolling processing; 12/1 for spring admission). Application fee: $40 ($60 for international students). *Financial aid:* Partial tuition waivers, Federal Work-Study, institutionally sponsored loans, and career-related internships or fieldwork available. Aid available to part-time students. Financial aid application deadline: 3/1; applicants required to submit FAFSA. • Sylvia Gholson, Director, 212-998-5769. Application contact: Office of Graduate Admissions, 212-998-5030. Fax: 212-995-4328.

Norfolk State University, School of Arts and Letters, Department of Music, 2401 Corprew Avenue, Norfolk, VA 23504-3907. Offerings include music education (MM). Member of NASM. One or more programs accredited by NCATE. Department faculty: 21 full-time, 3 part-time. *Degree requirements:* Thesis or alternative required, foreign language not required. *Entrance requirements:* Minimum GPA of 2.7. Application deadline: 8/1. Application fee: $30. *Tuition:* $3718 per year full-time, $198 per credit hour part-time for state residents; $7668 per year full-time, $404 per credit hour part-time for nonresidents. • Dr. Dexter Allgood, Head, 757-683-8544. Application contact: Dr. Allan Shaffer, Coordinator, 757-683-9522.

Northwestern University, School of Music, Department of Music Academic Studies and Composition, Evanston, IL 60208. Offerings include music education (MM, PhD). Member of NASM. PhD admissions and degree offered through The Graduate School. Department faculty: 27 full-time (6 women), 2 part-time (both women). *Entrance requirements:* For master's, portfolio or research papers. Application fee: $40. *Tuition:* $20,430 per year full-time, $2272 per course part-time. • Richard Green, Associate Dean, 847-491-5558. E-mail: rgreen@nwu.edu. Application contact: Heather A. Landes, Director of Music Admission, 847-491-3141. Fax: 847-491-5260. E-mail: hlandes@nwu.edu.

Northwest Missouri State University, College of Arts and Sciences, Department of Music, 800 University Drive, Maryville, MO 64468-6001. Offers program in teaching music (MS Ed). Part-time programs available. Faculty: 12 full-time (2 women). Students: 3 full-time (2 women), 5 part-time (all women). 3 applicants, 100% accepted. In 1997, 2 degrees awarded. *Degree requirements:* Comprehensive exam required, foreign language and thesis not required. *Entrance requirements:* GRE General Test (minimum combined score of 700), TOEFL (minimum score 550), minimum undergraduate GPA of 2.5, writing sample. Application deadline: rolling. Application fee: $0 ($50 for international students). *Expenses:* Tuition $113 per credit hour for state residents; $197 per credit hour for nonresidents. Fees $3 per credit hour. *Financial aid:* In 1997–98, 3 research assistantships averaging $585 per month were awarded. Financial aid application deadline: 3/1. • Steven Brown, Chairperson, 816-562-1315. Application contact: Dr. Frances Shipley, Dean of Graduate School, 816-562-1145. E-mail: gradsch@acad.nwmissouri.edu.

Occidental College, Department of Education, Program in Secondary Education, Los Angeles, CA 90041-3392. Offerings include music (MAT). Program faculty: 4 full-time (1 woman). *Degree requirements:* Internship required, foreign language and thesis not required. *Entrance requirements:* GRE General Test (minimum score 550 on each section or combined score of 1650 on three sections), TOEFL (minimum score 600), minimum GPA of 3.0. Application deadline: 3/1 (priority date; rolling processing; 10/1 for spring admission). Application fee: $40. *Expenses:* Tuition $21,256 per year full-time, $865 per unit part-time. Fees $314 per year. • Application contact: Susan Molik, Administrative Assistant, Graduate Office, 213-259-2921.

Oregon State University, Graduate School, College of Liberal Arts, Department of Music, Corvallis, OR 97331. Offers program in music education (MAT). Accredited by NCATE. Faculty: Students: 0. Average age 23. 0 applicants. *Degree requirements:* Thesis, minimum GPA of 3.0. *Average time to degree:* master's–1 year full-time. *Entrance requirements:* GRE General Test, NTE, California Basic Educational Skills Test, TOEFL (minimum score 550), minimum GPA of 3.0 in last 90 hours. Application deadline: 3/1 (rolling processing). Application fee: $50. *Tuition:* $6207 per year full-time, $810 per quarter (minimum) part-time for state residents; $10,551 per year full-time, $1293 per quarter (minimum) part-time for nonresidents. *Financial aid:* Federal Work-Study, institutionally sponsored loans, and career-related internships or fieldwork available. Financial aid application deadline: 2/1. • Dr. Marian Carlson, Chair, 541-737-4061. Application contact: Dr. Tina Scott, MAT Coordinator, 541-737-5603.

Pennsylvania State University University Park Campus, College of Arts and Architecture, School of Music and Music Education, Program in Music Education, University Park, PA 16802-1503. Awards M Ed, PhD. Member of NASM. Accredited by NCATE. Students: 9 full-time (4 women), 12 part-time (4 women). *Entrance requirements:* GRE General Test. Application fee: $40. *Expenses:* Tuition $6534 per year full-time, $276 per credit part-time for state residents; $13,460 per year full-time, $561 per credit part-time for nonresidents. Fees $252 per year (minimum) full-time, $43 per semester (minimum) part-time. • Dr. Dale Monson, Head, 814-865-0431.

Pittsburg State University, College of Arts and Sciences, Department of Music, Pittsburg, KS 66762-5880. Offerings include instrumental music education (MM), vocal music education (MM). Member of NASM. Department faculty: 6 full-time (2 women). *Degree requirements:* Thesis or alternative required, foreign language not required. *Application fee:* $40. *Tuition:* $2418 per year full-time, $103 per credit hour part-time for state residents; $6130 per year full-time, $258 per credit hour part-time for nonresidents. • Dr. Keith Ward, Chairman, 316-235-4466.

Portland State University, School of Fine and Performing Arts, Department of Music, Portland, OR 97207-0751. Offerings include music education (MAT, MST). Accredited by NCATE. Department faculty: 22 full-time (6 women), 2 part-time (1 woman), 23 FTE. *Application deadline:* 4/1 (priority date; rolling processing; 2/1 for spring admission). *Application fee:* $50. *Tuition:* $6101 per year full-time, $689 per semester (minimum) part-time for state residents; $10,445 per year full-time, $689 per semester (minimum) part-time for nonresidents. • Dr. T. Stanley Stanford, Head, 503-725-3011. E-mail: stan@fph.lh.pdx.edu. Application contact: Dr. Marilyn Shotola, Graduate Coordinator, 503-725-3011. Fax: 503-725-8215. E-mail: marilyn@fpa.lh.pdx.edu.

Queens College of the City University of New York, Social Science Division, School of Education, Department of Secondary Education, 65-30 Kissena Boulevard, Flushing, NY 11367-1597. Offerings include music (MS Ed, AC). *Degree requirements:* For master's, research project required, foreign language and thesis not required; for AC, thesis optional, foreign language not required. *Entrance requirements:* For master's, TOEFL (minimum score 600), minimum GPA of 3.0; for AC, TOEFL (minimum score 600). Application deadline: 4/1 (rolling processing; 11/1 for spring admission). Application fee: $40. *Expenses:* Tuition $4350 per year full-time, $185 per credit part-time for state residents; $7600 per year full-time, $320 per credit part-time for nonresidents. Fees $104 per year. • Dr. Philip Anderson, Chairperson, 718-997-5150. Application contact: Mario Caruso, Director of Graduate Admissions, 718-997-5200. Fax: 718-997-5193. E-mail: graduate%queens.bitnet@cunyvm.cuny.edu.

Radford University, Graduate College, College of Visual and Performing Arts, Department of Music, Radford, VA 24142. Offerings include music education (MS). Member of NASM. Postbaccalaureate distance learning degree programs offered (minimal on-campus study). Department faculty: 14 full-time (4 women). *Application deadline:* 2/1 (priority date; rolling processing; 10/1 for spring admission). *Application fee:* $25. Electronic applications accepted. *Expenses:* Tuition $2302 per year full-time, $147 per credit hour part-time for state residents; $5672 per year full-time, $287 per credit hour part-time for nonresidents. Fees $1222 per year full-time. • Dr. Eugene C. Fellin, Chairperson, 540-831-5177. Fax: 540-831-6313. E-mail: efellin@runet.edu.

Rhode Island College, School of Graduate Studies, Faculty of Arts and Sciences, Department of Music, Providence, RI 02908-1924. Offerings include music education (MAT). Member of NASM. Accredited by NCATE. Department faculty: 11 full-time (2 women), 4 part-time (2 women). *Application deadline:* 4/1 (rolling processing). *Application fee:* $25. *Tuition:* $4064 per year full-time, $214 per credit part-time for state residents; $7658 per year full-time, $376 per credit part-time for nonresidents. • Dr. Robert W. Elam, Chair, 401-456-8244.

Rollins College, Program in Education, Winter Park, FL 32789-4499. Offerings include secondary education (MAT), with options in English, mathematics, music. Program faculty: 13 full-time (8 women), 11 part-time (4 women), 17 FTE. *Application deadline:* rolling. *Application fee:* $50. *Tuition:* $190 per hour. • Dr. Nancy McAleer, Director, 407-646-2305. Application contact: Laura Pfister, Coordinator of Records and Registration, 407-646-2416. Fax: 407-646-1551.

Roosevelt University, College of the Performing Arts, Chicago Musical College, Chicago, IL 60605-1394. Offerings include music education (MM Ed), piano pedagogy (Diploma). Member of NASM. One or more programs accredited by NCATE. *Application deadline:* 6/1 (priority date; rolling processing). *Application fee:* $25 ($35 for international students). *Expenses:* Tuition $445 per credit hour. Fees $100 per year. • Application contact: Joanne Canyon-Heller, Coordinator of Graduate Admissions, 312-341-3612.

Rowan University, College of Education, Department of Secondary Education-Education Foundations, Program in Subject Matter Teaching, Program in Music Education, Glassboro, NJ 08028-1701. Awards MA. Member of NASM. Part-time and evening/weekend programs available. Students: 9 (7 women). 2 applicants, 50% accepted. In 1997, 1 degree awarded. *Degree requirements:* Thesis, comprehensive exams required, foreign language not required. *Entrance requirements:* GRE General Test (minimum combined score of 800), minimum GPA of 2.8. Application deadline: 11/1 (priority date; rolling processing; 4/1 for spring admission). Application fee: $50. *Tuition:* $5728 per year full-time, $258 per credit hour part-time for state residents; $8968 per year full-time, $393 per credit hour part-time for nonresidents. *Financial aid:* Federal Work-Study available. • Dr. Lili Levinowitz, Adviser, 609-256-4500 Ext. 3716.

St. Cloud State University, College of Fine Arts and Humanities, Department of Music, St. Cloud, MN 56301-4498. Offerings include music education (MM). Member of NASM. Department faculty: 17 full-time (8 women). *Degree requirements:* Thesis or alternative required, foreign language not required. *Entrance requirements:* GRE General Test, minimum GPA of 2.75. Application fee: $20 ($100 for international students). *Expenses:* Tuition $128 per credit for state residents; $203 per credit for nonresidents. Fees $16.32 per credit. • Dr. Bruce Wood, Chairperson, 320-255-3223. Application contact: Ann Anderson, Graduate Studies Office, 320-255-2113. Fax: 320-654-5371. E-mail: anna@grad.stcloud.msus.edu.

Salisbury State University, Department of Education, Salisbury, MD 21801-6837. Offerings include music (M Ed). Department faculty: 19 full-time (10 women), 2 part-time (1 woman). *Application deadline:* 8/1 (priority date; rolling processing; 1/1 for spring admission). *Application fee:* $30. *Expenses:* Tuition $158 per credit hour for state residents; $310 per credit hour for nonresidents. Fees $4 per credit hour. • Dr. Ellen Whitford, Chair, 410-543-6294. E-mail: evwhitford@ssu.edu. Application contact: Phyllis Meyer, Administrative Aide II, 410-543-6281. Fax: 410-548-2593. E-mail: phmeyer@ssu.edu.

Samford University, School of Education, Program in Elementary Education, Birmingham, AL 35229-0002. Offerings include music education (MS Ed). Accredited by NCATE. *Entrance requirements:* GRE or MAT, minimum GPA of 2.75. Application deadline: rolling. Application fee: $25. *Tuition:* $344 per credit hour. • Dr. David Little, Coordinator, 205-870-2371. Application contact: Dr. Alyce Golowash, Counselor, 205-870-2121.

Sam Houston State University, College of Arts and Sciences, Department of Music, Huntsville, TX 77341. Offerings include Kodály pedagogy (MM); music education (M Ed). Member of NASM. One or more programs accredited by NCATE. *Application deadline:* 8/1 (priority date; rolling processing). *Application fee:* $15. *Tuition:* $1810 per year full-time, $297 per semester (minimum) part-time for state residents; $6922 per year full-time, $924 per semester (minimum) part-time for nonresidents. • Dr. Rodney M. Cannon, Chair, 409-294-1360. E-mail: mus_rmc@shsu.edu. Application contact: Dr. Alan Strong, Assistant Chair, 409-294-1375. Fax: 409-294-3765. E-mail: mus_ads@shsu.edu.

Shenandoah University, Shenandoah Conservatory, 1460 University Drive, Winchester, VA 22601-5195. Offerings include music education (MME, DMA). Member of NASM. Terminal master's awarded for partial completion of doctoral program. Conservatory faculty: 32 full-time (15 women), 13 part-time (5 women). *Degree requirements:* For doctorate, dissertation or teaching project required, foreign language not required. *Entrance requirements:* For doctorate, 2 years of teaching experience, sample of written work, videotaped interview. Application deadline: 7/1 (priority date; rolling processing). Application fee: $30. Electronic applications accepted. *Tuition:* $470 per credit. • Dr. Charlotte A. Collins, Dean, 540-665-4600. Fax: 540-665-5402. E-mail: ccollins@su.edu. Application contact: Michael Carpenter, Director of Admissions, 540-665-4581. Fax: 540-665-4627. E-mail: admit@su.edu.

Smith College, Department of Education and Child Study, Program in Secondary Education, Northampton, MA 01063. Offerings include music education (MAT). Program faculty: 6 full-time (3 women), 3 part-time (2 women). *Degree requirements:* 1 foreign language required, thesis not required. *Average time to degree:* master's–1 year full-time, 4 years part-time. *Entrance requirements:* GRE General Test or MAT. Application deadline: 4/15 (12/1 for spring admission). Application fee: $50. *Tuition:* $21,680 per year full-time, $2720 per course part-time. • Rosetta Cohen, Head, 413-585-3266. E-mail: rcohen@sophia.smith.edu.

Southeast Missouri State University, Department of Music, Cape Girardeau, MO 63701-4799. Offers program in music education (MME). Member of NASM. One or more programs accredited by NCATE. *Degree requirements:* Thesis or alternative required, foreign language not required. *Entrance requirements:* Audition, minimum GPA of 3.0. Application deadline: 4/1 (priority date; rolling processing; 11/21 for spring admission). Application fee: $20 ($100 for international students). *Tuition:* $2034 per year full-time, $113 per credit hour part-time for state residents; $3672 per year full-time, $204 per credit hour part-time for nonresidents. • Dr. Robert Fruehwald, Chairperson, 573-651-2141. Application contact: Office of Graduate Studies, 573-651-2192.

Southern Illinois University at Carbondale, College of Liberal Arts, School of Music, Carbondale, IL 62901-6806. Offerings include music education (MM), piano pedagogy (MM). Member of NASM. School faculty: 25 full-time (5 women). *Degree requirements:* 1 foreign language, thesis or alternative. *Entrance requirements:* TOEFL (minimum score 550), audition, minimum GPA of 2.7. Application deadline: rolling. Application fee: $0. *Expenses:* Tuition $2964 per year full-time, $99 per semester hour part-time for state residents; $8892 per year full-time, $270 per semester hour part-time for nonresidents. Fees $1034 per year full-time, $298 per semester (minimum) part-time. • Robert Weiss, Director, 618-536-7505. Application contact: Frank Stemper, Graduate Coordinator, 618-536-7505.

Southwest Texas State University, School of Fine Arts and Communication, Department of Music, Program in Music Education, San Marcos, TX 78666. Awards MM. Member of NASM. Part-time programs available. Students: 8 part-time (6 women); includes 3 minority (all Hispanics). Average age 32. In 1997, 5 degrees awarded. *Degree requirements:* Comprehensive exam required, foreign language and thesis not required. *Entrance requirements:* GRE General Test (minimum combined score of 900), TOEFL (minimum score 550), minimum GPA of 2.75 in last 60 hours. Application deadline: 7/15 (priority date; rolling processing; 11/15 for spring admission). Application fee: $25 ($50 for international students). *Expenses:* Tuition $648 per year full-time, $120 per semester (minimum) part-time for state residents; $4500 per year full-time, $750 per semester (minimum) part-time for nonresidents. Fees $1264 per year full-time, $314 per semester (minimum) part-time. *Financial aid:* Teaching assistantships, scholarships, Federal Work-Study, institutionally sponsored loans, and career-related internships or fieldwork available. Aid available to part-time students. Financial aid application deadline: 4/1; applicants required to submit FAFSA. • Dr. Russell Riepe, Graduate Adviser, 512-245-3375. Fax: 512-245-8181. E-mail: rr14@swt.edu.

State University of New York at Buffalo, Graduate School, Faculty of Arts and Letters, Department of Music, Buffalo, NY 14260. Offerings include music education (MA, MM, CAS). Member of NASM. Department faculty: 22 full-time (7 women), 22 part-time (8 women). *Degree requirements:* For master's, variable foreign language requirement, thesis (for some programs), comprehensive exam, recitals (MM). *Entrance requirements:* For master's, GRE General Test, MAT (music education), TOEFL (minimum score 550), audition (MM). Application deadline: 2/1 (priority date; rolling processing; 12/1 for spring admission). Application fee: $35. *Tuition:* $5970 per year full-time, $288 per credit hour part-time for state residents; $9286 per year full-time, $426 per credit hour part-time for nonresidents. • David Felder, Chairperson, 716-645-2764. Application contact: Michael P. Burke, Director of Student Programs, 716-645-2758.

State University of New York at New Paltz, Faculty of Fine and Performing Arts, Department of Music, New Paltz, NY 12561-2499. Offerings include piano pedagogy (MA, MFA). *Degree requirements:* Thesis required, foreign language not required. *Entrance requirements:* Minimum GPA of 3.0. Application deadline: 3/15 (priority date; rolling processing). Application fee: $50. *Expenses:* Tuition $5100 per year full-time, $213 per credit hour part-time for state residents; $8416 per year full-time, $351 per credit hour part-time for nonresidents. Fees $493 per year full-time, $48 per semester (minimum) part-time. • Dr. Lee Pritchard, Chair, 914-257-2700.

State University of New York College at Fredonia, School of Music, Program in Music Education, Fredonia, NY 14063. Awards MM. Member of NASM. Part-time and evening/weekend programs available. Faculty: 2 full-time (1 woman). Students: 3 full-time (2 women), 14 part-time (8 women). 17 applicants, 100% accepted. In 1997, 8 degrees awarded. *Degree requirements:* Thesis required, foreign language not required. *Application deadline:* 7/5. *Application fee:* $50. *Expenses:* Tuition $5100 per year full-time, $213 per credit hour part-time for state residents; $8416 per year full-time, $351 per credit hour part-time for nonresidents. Fees $725 per year full-time, $30 per credit hour part-time. *Financial aid:* Research assistantships, teaching assistantships, full and partial tuition waivers available. Aid available to part-time students. Financial aid application deadline: 3/15. • Dr. Peter Schoenbach, Director, School of Music, 716-673-3151.

State University of New York College at Potsdam, Crane School of Music, Potsdam, NY 13676. Offerings include music education (MM). Member of NASM. School faculty: 12 full-time (4 women), 1 part-time (0 women). *Degree requirements:* Variable foreign language requirement, thesis. *Entrance requirements:* Audition, minimum GPA of 3.0. Application deadline: rolling. Application fee: $50. *Expenses:* Tuition $5100 per year full-time, $213 per credit hour part-time for state residents; $8416 per year full-time, $351 per credit hour part-time for nonresidents. Fees $315 per year full-time, $12.50 per credit hour part-time. • Dr. James Stoltie, Dean, 315-267-2415. Fax: 315-267-2413. E-mail: stoltijm@potsdam.edu. Application contact: Dr. William Amoriell, Dean of Education and Graduate Studies, 315-267-2515. Fax: 315-267-4802.

State University of West Georgia, College of Arts and Sciences, Department of Music, Program in Music Education, Carrollton, GA 30118. Awards MM. Member of NASM. Accredited by NCATE. Part-time programs available. Faculty: 9 full-time (2 women), 2 part-time (0 women). Students: 1 full-time (0 women), 9 part-time (4 women); includes 2 minority (both African Americans). Average age 32. In 1997, 3 degrees awarded (100% found work related to degree). *Degree requirements:* Comprehensive exam, departmental qualifying exam required, foreign language and thesis not required. *Entrance requirements:* GRE General Test (minimum combined score of 800) or MAT (minimum score 44), minimum GPA of 2.5. Application deadline: 8/30 (rolling processing). Application fee: $15. *Expenses:* Tuition $2428 per year full-time, $83 per semester hour part-time for state residents; $8428 per year full-time, $250 per semester hour part-time for nonresidents. Fees $428 per year. *Financial aid:* Assistantships and career-related internships or fieldwork available. Aid available to part-time students. Financial aid applicants required to submit FAFSA. • Application contact: Dr. Jack O. Jenkins, Dean, Graduate School, 770-836-6419. Fax: 770-836-2301. E-mail: jjenkins@cob.as.westga.edu.

Syracuse University, School of Education, Teaching and Leadership Programs, Program in Music Education, Syracuse, NY 13244-0003. Awards M Mu, MS. Member of NASM. Students: 8 full-time (4 women), 8 part-time (6 women); includes 1 minority (Native American), 1 international. 8 applicants, 100% accepted. In 1997, 5 degrees awarded. *Degree requirements:* Thesis or alternative. *Entrance requirements:* GRE. Application fee: $40. *Tuition:* $13,320 per year full-time, $555 per credit hour part-time. *Financial aid:* Application deadline 3/1. • Dr. Ruth Brittin, Chair, 315-443-5896.

Teachers College, Columbia University, Graduate Faculty of Education, Department of Arts and Humanities, Program in Music and Music Education, 525 West 120th Street, New York, NY 10027-6696. Awards Ed M, MA, Ed D, Ed DCT. Part-time programs available. Faculty: 3 full-time (2 women), 4 part-time (2 women), 4.4 FTE. Students: 37 full-time (24 women), 82 part-time (57 women); includes 25 minority (6 African Americans, 15 Asian Americans, 4 Hispanics), 24 international. Average age 35. 41 applicants, 83% accepted. In 1997, 18 master's, 9 doctorates awarded. Terminal master's awarded for partial completion of doctoral program. *Degree requirements:* For master's, thesis, project required, foreign language not required; for doctorate, variable foreign language requirement, dissertation. *Entrance requirements:* Diagnostic exam. Application deadline: 5/15. Application fee: $50. *Expenses:* Tuition $640 per credit. Fees $120 per semester. *Financial aid:* Fellowships, research assistantships, teaching assistantships, full and partial tuition waivers, Federal Work-Study, institutionally sponsored loans, and career-related internships or fieldwork available. Aid available to part-time students. Financial aid application deadline: 2/1. *Faculty research:* Artistry, creativity, and proficiency in production and performance; educational theory and practice; piano pedagogy; research strategies in music pedagogy. • Application contact: Amy Rotheim, Office of Admissions, 212-678-3710. Fax: 212-678-4171.

Temple University, Esther Boyer College of Music, Program in Music Education, Philadelphia, PA 19122-6096. Offers music education (MM, PhD), music therapy (MMT). Member of NASM. Evening/weekend programs available. Faculty: 6 full-time (3 women). Students: 42 (23 women); includes 10 minority (5 African Americans, 4 Asian Americans, 1 Hispanic), 11 international. 35 applicants, 51% accepted. In 1997, 3 master's, 2 doctorates awarded. *Degree requirements:* Thesis/dissertation, compositions, recitals required, foreign language not required. *Entrance requirements:* For master's, audition (MMT); for doctorate, GRE General Test (minimum combined score of 1000) or MAT. Application deadline: 8/15 (rolling processing; 12/15 for spring admission). Application fee: $40. *Expenses:* Tuition $323 per semester hour for state residents; $444 per semester hour for nonresidents. Fees $170 per year full-time, $28 per semester (minimum) part-time. *Financial aid:* Fellowships, teaching assistantships, Federal Work-Study, and career-related internships or fieldwork available. Financial aid application deadline: 3/1. *Faculty research:* Music learning theory, guided imagery in music, computer learning theory. • Dr. Roger Dean, Department Chair, 215-204-8310. Application contact: Linda White, Director of Music Admissions, 215-204-8598. Fax: 215-204-4957.

Tennessee State University, College of Arts and Sciences, Department of Music, Nashville, TN 37209-1561. Offers program in music education (MS). Member of NASM. Faculty: 4 full-time (2 women). Students: 2 full-time (1 woman), 4 part-time (2 women); includes 5 minority (all African Americans). Average age 33. 8 applicants, 75% accepted. In 1997, 2 degrees awarded. *Average time to degree:* master's–2 years full-time, 3.5 years part-time. *Entrance requirements:* MAT (minimum score 25). Application deadline: rolling. Application fee: $15. *Tuition:* $2962 per year full-time, $182 per credit hour part-time for state residents; $7788 per year full-time, $393 per credit hour part-time for nonresidents. *Financial aid:* In 1997–98, 2 assistantships (both to first-year students) averaging $600 per month and totaling $7,200 were awarded. Aid available to part-time students. Financial aid application deadline: 5/1. • Dr. Ralph Simpson, Head, 615-963-5341.

Texas A&M University–Commerce, College of Arts and Sciences, Department of Music, Commerce, TX 75429-3011. Offerings include music education (MM, MS). Member of NASM. Department faculty: 8 full-time (1 woman), 1 part-time (0 women). *Degree requirements:* Thesis (for some programs), comprehensive exam. *Entrance requirements:* GRE General Test. Application deadline: rolling. Application fee: $0 ($25 for international students). *Tuition:*

Directory: Music Education

Texas A&M University–Commerce (continued)
$2382 per year full-time, $343 per semester (minimum) part-time for state residents; $7518 per year full-time, $343 per semester (minimum) part-time for nonresidents. • Dr. James W. Deaton, Head, 903-886-5303. Application contact: Pam Hammonds, Graduate Admissions Adviser, 903-886-5167. Fax: 903-886-5165.

Texas A&M University–Kingsville, College of Arts and Sciences, Department of Music, Kingsville, TX 78363. Offers program in music education (MM). Member of NASM. Faculty: 4 full-time. Students: 2 part-time (0 women). Average age 36. In 1997, 1 degree awarded. *Degree requirements:* Thesis or alternative, comprehensive exam required, foreign language not required. *Entrance requirements:* GRE General Test (minimum combined score of 800), TOEFL (minimum score 500), minimum GPA of 3.0. Application deadline: 6/1 (rolling processing; 11/15 for spring admission). Application fee: $15 ($25 for international students). *Tuition:* $1822 per year full-time, $281 per semester (minimum) part-time for state residents; $6934 per year full-time, $908 per semester (minimum) part-time for nonresidents. *Financial aid:* Fellowships available. Financial aid application deadline: 5/15. • Dr. Robert Scott, Graduate Coordinator, 512-593-2804.

Texas Christian University, College of Fine Arts and Communication, Department of Music, Fort Worth, TX 76129-0002. Offerings include music education (MM Ed). Member of NASM. *Application deadline:* 3/1 (rolling processing; 12/1 for spring admission). *Application fee:* $0. *Expenses:* Tuition $10,350 per year full-time, $345 per credit hour part-time. Fees $1240 per year full-time, $50 per credit hour part-time. • Dr. Kenneth D. Raessler, Chairperson, 817-257-7602.

Texas Tech University, Graduate School, College of Arts and Sciences, School of Music, Lubbock, TX 79409. Offerings include music education (MME). Member of NASM. School faculty: 36 full-time (10 women), 2 part-time (1 woman), 37.24 FTE. *Application deadline:* 4/15 (priority date; rolling processing; 11/1 for spring admission). *Application fee:* $25 ($50 for international students). Electronic applications accepted. *Expenses:* Tuition $864 per year full-time, $120 per semester (minimum) part-time for state residents; $5976 per year full-time, $747 per semester (minimum) part-time for nonresidents. Fees $1961 per year full-time, $257 per semester (minimum) part-time. • Dr. Wayne A. Bailey, Chairperson, 806-742-2270. Fax: 806-742-2294.

Texas Tech University, Graduate School, College of Education, Division of Curriculum and Instruction, Lubbock, TX 79409. Offerings include music education (Certificate). Accredited by NCATE. Division faculty: 23 full-time (12 women). *Application deadline:* 4/15 (priority date; rolling processing; 11/1 for spring admission). *Application fee:* $25 ($50 for international students). Electronic applications accepted. *Expenses:* Tuition $864 per year full-time, $120 per semester (minimum) part-time for state residents; $5976 per year full-time, $747 per semester (minimum) part-time for nonresidents. Fees $2321 per year full-time, $302 per semester (minimum) part-time. • Dr. William E. Sparkman, Chair, 805-742-2371.

Texas Woman's University, College of Arts and Sciences, Department of Performing Arts, Program in Music, Denton, TX 76204. Offerings include music education (MA), music pedagogy (MA). Member of NASM. Program faculty: 13 full-time (7 women), 5 part-time (2 women), 14 FTE. *Degree requirements:* Project recital required, thesis optional, foreign language not required. *Average time to degree:* master's–2 years full-time, 4 years part-time. *Entrance requirements:* Audition, minimum GPA of 3.0. Application deadline: 7/10. Application fee: $25. • Dr. Richard Rodean, Chair, Department of Performing Arts, 940-898-2500.

Towson University, Program in Music Education, Towson, MD 21252-0001. Offers Dalcroze (Certificate); Kodály (Certificate); music education (MS); Orff (Certificate). Member of NASM. Part-time and evening/weekend programs available. Faculty: 12 full-time (2 women). Students: 1 (woman) full-time, 34 part-time (24 women); includes 2 minority (1 African American, 1 Native American), 1 international. In 1997, 6 master's awarded. *Degree requirements:* For master's, exam required, thesis optional. *Application deadline:* 3/1 (priority date; rolling processing; 10/1 for spring admission). *Application fee:* $40. *Expenses:* Tuition $187 per credit hour for state residents; $364 per credit hour for nonresidents. Fees $40 per credit hour. *Financial aid:* Assistantships, Federal Work-Study available. Financial aid application deadline: 4/1; applicants required to submit FAFSA. • Dr. Michael Jothen, Director, 410-830-2257. Fax: 410-830-3434. E-mail: mjothen@towson.edu. Application contact: Fran Musotto, Office Manager, 410-830-2501. Fax: 410-830-4675. E-mail: fmusotto@towson.edu.

Union College, Department of Education, Program in Music Education, Barbourville, KY 40906-1499. Awards MA Ed. *Degree requirements:* Thesis optional, foreign language not required. *Entrance requirements:* GRE General Test, NTE. Application deadline: rolling. Application fee: $15. *Tuition:* $220 per hour. • Dr. William E. Bernhardt, Dean of Graduate Academic Affairs, Graduate Programs, 606-546-1210. Fax: 606-546-2217.

The University of Akron, College of Fine and Applied Arts, School of Music, Program in Music Education, Akron, OH 44325-0001. Awards MM. Accredited by NCATE. Students: 12 full-time (7 women), 16 part-time (15 women); includes 2 minority (both Hispanics). Average age 34. *Degree requirements:* Thesis required (for some programs), foreign language not required. *Entrance requirements:* Minimum GPA of 2.75, interview, audition. Application deadline: 3/31 (rolling processing). Application fee: $25 ($50 for international students). *Expenses:* Tuition $178 per credit hour for state residents; $333 per credit hour for nonresidents. Fees $145 per year full-time, $32 per semester (minimum) part-time. *Financial aid:* Application deadline 3/1. • Application contact: Dr. Ralph Turek, Coordinator of Graduate Studies, 330-972-5761.

The University of Alabama, College of Arts and Sciences, School of Music, Tuscaloosa, AL 35487. Offerings include music education (Ed D, Ed S). Accredited by NCATE. Ed D and Ed S offered jointly with the College of Education. School faculty: 29 full-time (7 women). *Average time to degree:* master's–2 years full-time; doctorate–3.5 years full-time. *Application deadline:* 7/6 (priority date; rolling processing). *Application fee:* $25. *Tuition:* $2684 per year full-time, $594 per semester (minimum) part-time for state residents; $7216 per year full-time, $1248 per semester (minimum) part-time for nonresidents. • Dr. Richard Diehl, Acting Chair, 205-348-7110. Fax: 205-348-1473.

The University of Alabama, College of Education, Area of Teacher Education, Tuscaloosa, AL 35487. Offerings include music education (MA, Ed D). Member of NASM. Accredited by NCATE. Faculty: 32 full-time (18 women), 8 part-time (4 women). *Entrance requirements:* For master's, GRE General Test, MAT (score in 50th percentile or higher), or NTE (minimum score 658 on each core battery test), minimum GPA of 3.0. Application deadline: 7/6 (priority date; rolling processing). Application fee: $25. *Tuition:* $2684 per year full-time, $594 per semester (minimum) part-time for state residents; $7216 per year full-time, $1248 per semester (minimum) part-time for nonresidents. • Dr. Lea McGee, Head, 205-348-1196. Fax: 205-348-9863. E-mail: lmcgee@bamaed.ua.edu.

The University of Alabama at Birmingham, Graduate School, School of Education, Department of Curriculum and Instruction, Birmingham, AL 35294. Offerings include music education (MA Ed). Accredited by NCATE. *Degree requirements:* Thesis optional. *Entrance requirements:* GRE General Test, MAT, or NTE, minimum GPA of 3.0. Application deadline: rolling. Application fee: $30 ($60 for international students). Electronic applications accepted. *Expenses:* Tuition $99 per credit hour for state residents; $198 per credit hour for nonresidents. Fees $516 per year (minimum) full-time, $73 per quarter (minimum) part-time for state residents; $516 per year (minimum) full-time, $73 per unit (minimum) part-time for nonresidents. • Dr. Joseph C. Burns, Chair, 205-934-5371.

University of Alaska Fairbanks, Graduate School, College of Liberal Arts, Department of Music, Fairbanks, AK 99775-7480. Offerings include music (MAT), music education (MA). Member of NASM. Department faculty: 10 full-time (4 women), 7 part-time (5 women). *Application deadline:* 8/1. *Application fee:* $35. *Expenses:* Tuition $162 per credit for state residents; $316 per credit for nonresidents. Fees $520 per year full-time, $45 per semester (minimum) part-time. • Dr. Madeline Schatz, Head, 907-474-7555.

The University of Arizona, College of Fine Arts, School of Music and Dance, Tucson, AZ 85721. Offerings include music education (MM, PhD). *Degree requirements:* For master's, thesis required (for some programs), foreign language not required. *Entrance requirements:* For master's, TOEFL (minimum score 550), minimum GPA of 3.0. Application deadline: 3/1 (rolling processing). Application fee: $35. *Tuition:* $2162 per year full-time, $337 per semester (minimum) part-time for state residents; $6860 per year full-time, $1138 per semester (minimum) part-time for nonresidents.

University of Arkansas, J. William Fulbright College of Arts and Sciences, Department of Music, Program in Music, Fayetteville, AR 72701-1201. Offerings include music education (MM). Accredited by NCATE. *Entrance requirements:* GRE General Test. Application fee: $25 ($35 for international students). *Tuition:* $3144 per year full-time, $173 per credit hour part-time for state residents; $7140 per year full-time, $395 per credit hour part-time for nonresidents. • Stephen Gates, Head, 501-575-5764.

University of British Columbia, Faculty of Education, Department of Curriculum Studies, Vancouver, BC V6T 1Z2, Canada. Offerings include music education (MA, M Ed, PhD). *Degree requirements:* For master's, thesis (MA) required, foreign language not required; for doctorate, dissertation required, foreign language not required. *Entrance requirements:* TOEFL (minimum score 550). Application deadline: 3/1 (12/1 for spring admission). Application fee: $60.

University of Central Arkansas, College of Fine Arts and Communication, Department of Music, Conway, AR 72035-0001. Offerings include music education (MM). Member of NASM. Department faculty: 19 full-time (7 women), 6 part-time (4 women), 21 FTE. *Degree requirements:* Comprehensive exam required, thesis optional. *Entrance requirements:* GRE General Test, minimum GPA of 2.7. Application deadline: 3/1 (priority date; rolling processing; 10/1 for spring admission). Application fee: $15 ($40 for international students). *Expenses:* Tuition $161 per credit hour for state residents; $298 per credit hour for nonresidents. Fees $50 per year full-time, $30 per year part-time. • Dr. Anne Patterson, Interim Chairperson, 501-450-3293. Fax: 501-450-5773. E-mail: annep@mail.uca.edu.

University of Central Florida, College of Education, Department of Instructional Programs, Program in Music Education, Orlando, FL 32816. Awards MA, M Ed. Member of NASM. Accredited by NCATE. Part-time and evening/weekend programs available. Students: 4 full-time (2 women), 7 part-time (3 women); includes 2 minority (1 African American, 1 Hispanic). Average age 35. 6 applicants, 33% accepted. In 1997, 4 degrees awarded. *Degree requirements:* Thesis or alternative required, foreign language not required. *Entrance requirements:* GRE General Test (minimum combined score of 840). Application deadline: 7/15 (12/15 for spring admission). Application fee: $20. *Expenses:* Tuition $3288 per year full-time, $137 per credit hour part-time for state residents; $11,520 per year full-time, $480 per credit hour part-time for nonresidents. Fees $105 per year. *Financial aid:* Teaching assistantships, Federal Work-Study, institutionally sponsored loans, and career-related internships or fieldwork available. Aid available to part-time students. • Application contact: Dr. Carol Scott-Kassner, Coordinator, 407-823-6493.

University of Central Oklahoma, College of Liberal Arts, Department of Music, Edmond, OK 73034-5209. Offerings include music education (MM). Accredited by NCATE. *Application deadline:* 8/18. *Application fee:* $15. *Tuition:* $76 per credit hour for state residents; $178 per credit hour for nonresidents.

University of Cincinnati, College-Conservatory of Music, Program in Music Education, Cincinnati, OH 45221. Awards MM, DME. Member of NASM. Accredited by NCATE. Faculty: 4 full-time. Students: 5 full-time (4 women), 9 part-time (2 women); includes 1 minority (Asian American), 2 international. 10 applicants, 40% accepted. In 1997, 2 master's, 1 doctorate awarded. *Degree requirements:* For master's, paper or thesis required, foreign language not required; for doctorate, 1 foreign language, dissertation. *Average time to degree:* master's–8.3 years full-time; doctorate–4.3 years full-time. *Entrance requirements:* For master's, GRE General Test, GRE Subject Test, interview; for doctorate, GRE General Test, GRE Subject Test, 3 years of teaching experience, interview. Application deadline: 2/1 (rolling processing). Application fee: $30. *Tuition:* $7228 per year full-time, $185 per credit hour part-time for state residents; $13,812 per year full-time, $352 per credit hour part-time for nonresidents. *Financial aid:* Fellowships, research assistantships, teaching assistantships, graduate assistantships, full tuition waivers, Federal Work-Study available. Financial aid application deadline: 2/1. *Faculty research:* Choral, orchestral, and wind conducting; Kodaly; Orff-Schulwerk; jazz studies; string education. • Application contact: Paul R. Hillner, Assistant Dean for Admissions and Student Services, 513-556-5462. Fax: 513-556-1028. E-mail: paul.hillner@uc.edu.

University of Colorado at Boulder, College of Music, Boulder, CO 80309. Offerings include music education (M Mus Ed, PhD), pedagogy (M Mus, D Mus A). Member of NASM. Terminal master's awarded for partial completion of doctoral program. College faculty: 50 full-time (14 women). *Application deadline:* 3/1 (priority date; rolling processing). *Application fee:* $40 ($60 for international students). *Expenses:* Tuition $3170 per year full-time, $531 per semester (minimum) part-time for state residents; $14,652 per year full-time, $2442 per semester (minimum) part-time for nonresidents. Fees $667 per year full-time, $130 per semester (minimum) part-time. • Daniel P. Sher, Dean, 303-492-7505. E-mail: daniel.sher@colorado.edu. Application contact: Margaret Kneebone, Assistant to Dean, Graduate Studies, 303-492-2207. Fax: 303-492-5619. E-mail: gradmusc@colorado.edu.

University of Connecticut, School of Fine Arts, Field of Music, Storrs, CT 06269. Offerings include music education (M Mus, PhD). Member of NASM. Terminal master's awarded for partial completion of doctoral program. Faculty: 17. *Application fee:* $40 ($45 for international students). *Expenses:* Tuition $5272 per year full-time, $293 per credit part-time for state residents; $13,696 per year full-time, $761 per credit part-time for nonresidents. Fees $948 per year full-time, $640 per year part-time. • W. Richard Bass Jr., Acting Head, 860-486-3728.

University of Denver, Graduate Studies, Faculty of Arts and Humanities/Social Sciences, Lamont School of Music, Denver, CO 80208. Offerings include music education (MA). Member of NASM. School faculty: 23 full-time (4 women). *Degree requirements:* Thesis (for some programs), recital or project, 1 year of foreign language (2 years for performance and music history and literature). *Entrance requirements:* GRE General Test, music history and theory qualifying exams, TOEFL (minimum score 550). Application deadline: rolling. Application fee: $40 ($45 for international students). *Expenses:* Tuition $18,216 per year full-time, $506 per credit hour part-time. Fees $159 per year. • Joseph Docksey, Director, 303-871-6400. Application contact: Dr. Ann Culver, Graduate Adviser, 303-871-6988.

University of Florida, College of Fine Arts, School of Music, Gainesville, FL 32611. Offerings include music education (MM, PhD). Member of NASM. Accredited by NCATE. School faculty: 28. *Degree requirements:* For master's, variable foreign language requirement, thesis; for doctorate, dissertation. *Entrance requirements:* Audition, GRE General Test or minimum GPA of 3.0. Application deadline: 6/5 (priority date; rolling processing). Application fee: $20. *Tuition:* $138 per credit hour for state residents; $481 per credit hour for nonresidents. • Dr. Giacomo Oliva, Chair, 352-392-0223. E-mail: jackoli@nervm.nerdc.ufl.edu. Application contact: Dr. David Kushner, Graduate Coordinator, 352-392-0223 Ext. 216. Fax: 352-392-0461. E-mail: dzk7777@nervm.nerdc.ufl.edu.

University of Georgia, College of Education, Program in Music Education, Athens, GA 30602. Awards MM Ed, Ed D, Ed S. Member of NASM. Accredited by NCATE. Faculty: 33 full-time (8 women). Students: 14 full-time, 11 part-time; includes 1 minority (Asian American). 15 applicants, 67% accepted. In 1997, 4 master's awarded. *Degree requirements:* For doctorate, dissertation required, foreign language not required. *Entrance requirements:* For master's, GRE General

Test, MAT; for doctorate, GRE General Test; for Ed S, GRE General Test or MAT. Application deadline: 7/1 (priority date; 11/15 for spring admission). Application fee: $30. Electronic applications accepted. *Tuition:* $3290 per year full-time, $643 per semester (minimum) part-time for state residents; $11,300 per year full-time, $1645 per semester (minimum) part-time for nonresidents. *Financial aid:* Fellowships, research assistantships, teaching assistantships, assistantships available. • Dr. Donald R. Lowe, Graduate Coordinator, 706-542-2743. Fax: 706-542-2773.

University of Hartford, Hartt School of Music, West Hartford, CT 06117-1599. Offerings include applied music (MM, DMA, Diploma), with options in accompanying (MM), pedagogy (MM), performance (MM); music education (MM, DMA), with options in conducting (MM), early childhood education (MM), pedagogy (MM), performance (MM), research (MM). Member of NASM. One or more programs accredited by NCATE. School faculty: 36 full-time (4 women), 35 part-time (9 women). *Degree requirements:* Variable foreign language requirement, thesis/dissertation (for some programs). *Entrance requirements:* For master's, TOEFL, audition; for doctorate, placement exam, TOEFL, audition, interview, research paper. Application deadline: 4/1 (priority date; rolling processing). Application fee: $40 ($55 for international students). Electronic applications accepted. *Expenses:* Tuition $5720 per year (minimum) full-time, $260 per credit hour (minimum) part-time. Fees $60 per year. • Dr. Malcolm Morrison, Interim Dean, 860-768-4468. Application contact: Dr. Adriene Maslin, Assistant Dean, 860-768-5389. Fax: 860-768-4441. E-mail: maslin@mail.hartford.edu.

University of Houston, College of Humanities, Fine Arts and Communication, Moores School of Music, 4800 Calhoun, Houston, TX 77204-2163. Offerings include music education (MM, DMA). Member of NASM. Accredited by NCATE. School faculty: 40 full-time (8 women), 12 part-time (4 women). *Degree requirements:* For master's, variable foreign language requirement, thesis (for some programs), departmental comprehensive exam, recital; for doctorate, 1 foreign language, dissertation, departmental qualifying exam, recitals. *Entrance requirements:* For master's, GRE General Test, audition; for doctorate, GRE General Test, GRE Subject Test, audition. Application deadline: 7/1 (priority date; rolling processing). Application fee: $0 ($75 for international students). *Expenses:* Tuition $1152 per year full-time, $120 per semester (minimum) part-time for state residents; $4482 per year full-time, $249 per credit hour part-time for nonresidents. Fees $977 per year full-time, $119 per semester (minimum) part-time. • David Tomatz, Director, 713-743-3009. Application contact: David A. White, Director of Graduate Studies, 713-743-3151. Fax: 713-743-3166.

The University of Iowa, College of Education, Division of Secondary Education, Iowa City, IA 52242-1316. Offerings include music education (MA, MAT, PhD). Member of NASM. Division faculty: 21 full-time. *Degree requirements:* For master's, exam required, foreign language not required; for doctorate, computer language, dissertation, comprehensive exams required, foreign language not required. *Entrance requirements:* For master's, minimum GPA of 2.5; for doctorate, minimum GPA of 3.0. Application fee: $30 ($50 for international students). *Expenses:* Tuition $3166 per year full-time, $176 per semester hour part-time for state residents; $10,202 per year full-time, $176 per semester hour part-time for nonresidents. Fees $202 per year full-time, $52 per year (minimum) part-time. • William Nibbelink, Chair, 319-335-5324. Fax: 319-335-5608.

University of Kansas, School of Fine Arts, Department of Music and Dance, Lawrence, KS 66045. Offerings include music education (MME, PhD). Member of NASM. Department faculty: 47 full-time. *Application deadline:* 3/1 (priority date; rolling processing). *Application fee:* $25. *Expenses:* Tuition $2400 per year full-time, $100 per credit hour part-time for state residents; $7890 per year full-time, $329 per credit hour part-time for nonresidents. Fees $428 per year full-time, $31 per credit hour part-time. • Stephen Anderson, Chairperson, 785-864-3436. Application contact: Carole Ross, Associate Dean, 785-864-3421. Fax: 785-864-5387.

University of Louisville, School of Music, Program in Music Education, Louisville, KY 40292-0001. Awards MME. Part-time programs available. Students: 6 full-time (4 women), 10 part-time (5 women); includes 1 minority (African American). Average age 30. In 1997, 4 degrees awarded. *Entrance requirements:* GRE General Test. Application deadline: rolling. Application fee: $25. • Dr. Herbert L. Koerselman, Dean, School of Music, 502-852-6907.

University of Louisville, School of Education, Department of Secondary Education, Program in Music Education, Louisville, KY 40292-0001. Awards MAT. Accredited by NCATE. Students: 4 full-time (3 women); includes 1 minority (Asian American). Average age 26. *Entrance requirements:* GRE General Test. Application deadline: rolling. Application fee: $25. • Dr. Allan E. Dittmer, Chair, Department of Secondary Education, 502-852-6591.

University of Manitoba, Faculty of Education, Department of Curriculum: Humanities and Social Sciences, Winnipeg, MB R3T 2N2, Canada. Offerings include music education (M Ed). *Degree requirements:* Thesis or alternative required, foreign language not required.

University of Maryland, College Park, College of Arts and Humanities, School of Music, College Park, MD 20742-5045. Awards M Ed, MM, M Mus, DMA, Ed D, PhD. Member of NASM. One or more programs accredited by NCATE. M Ed and Ed D offered in cooperation with the College of Education. Faculty: 44 full-time (11 women), 38 part-time (15 women). Students: 112 full-time (67 women), 128 part-time (65 women); includes 45 minority (11 African Americans, 28 Asian Americans, 6 Hispanics), 61 international. 196 applicants, 47% accepted. In 1997, 28 master's, 19 doctorates awarded. *Degree requirements:* For master's, variable foreign language requirement, thesis, public performance; for doctorate, variable foreign language requirement, dissertation. *Entrance requirements:* For master's, GRE General Test, GRE Subject Test, minimum GPA of 3.0, auditions; for doctorate, GRE General Test, GRE Subject Test. Application deadline: rolling. Application fee: $50 ($70 for international students). *Expenses:* Tuition $272 per credit hour for state residents; $400 per credit hour for nonresidents. Fees $564 per year full-time, $342 per year part-time. *Financial aid:* In 1997–98, 9 fellowships, 69 teaching assistantships were awarded; research assistantships also available. *Faculty research:* Ethnomusicology; music history, performance, and theory; conducting; composition. • Dr. Christopher Kendall, Director, 301-405-5553. Fax: 301-314-9504. Application contact: John Mollish, Director, Graduate Admissions and Records, 301-405-4198. Fax: 301-314-9305.

University of Massachusetts Lowell, College of Music, Department of Music Education, 1 University Avenue, Lowell, MA 01854-2881. Awards MM. Member of NASM. Accredited by NCATE. Part-time programs available. Faculty: 3 full-time (2 women). Students: 9 part-time (6 women); includes 2 minority (both Hispanics). 12 applicants, 42% accepted. *Degree requirements:* 1 foreign language, thesis. *Entrance requirements:* MAT, audition. Application deadline: 4/1 (priority date; rolling processing; 10/1 for spring admission). Application fee: $20 ($35 for international students). *Tuition:* $4867 per year full-time, $618 per semester (minimum) part-time for state residents; $10,276 per year full-time, $1294 per semester (minimum) part-time for nonresidents. *Financial aid:* Fellowships, teaching assistantships available. Financial aid application deadline: 4/1. • Gerald Lloyd, Dean, College of Music, 978-934-3856. Application contact: Anthony Mele, Coordinator, 978-934-3877. E-mail: anthony_mele@woods.uml.edu.

The University of Memphis, College of Communication and Fine Arts, Department of Music, Memphis, TN 38152. Offerings include music education (M Mu, DMA), piano pedagogy (M Mu), Suzuki pedagogy-piano (M Mu). Member of NASM. Terminal master's awarded for partial completion of doctoral program. Department faculty: 28 full-time (6 women). *Degree requirements:* For master's, thesis or alternative, comprehensive exam. *Entrance requirements:* For master's, GRE General Test or MAT, proficiency exam, audition. Application deadline: 8/1 (rolling processing; 12/1 for spring admission). Application fee: $25 ($50 for international students). *Tuition:* $2862 per year full-time, $166 per credit hour part-time for state residents; $6696 per year full-time, $379 per credit hour part-time for nonresidents. • Dr. B. Glenn Chandler, Chairman, 901-678-3764. Application contact: Dr. John David Peterson, Coordinator of Graduate Studies, 901-678-3769.

University of Miami, School of Music, Department of Music Education and Music Therapy, Coral Gables, FL 33124. Offers programs in music education (MM, PhD, Ed S), music therapy (MM). Member of NASM. Accredited by NCATE. *Degree requirements:* For master's, thesis; for doctorate, dissertation, 2 research tools; for Ed S, thesis, research project. *Entrance requirements:* For master's and doctorate, GRE General Test, TOEFL (minimum score 550). Application deadline: 3/15 (priority date; rolling processing). Application fee: $35. *Expenses:* Tuition $815 per credit hour. Fees $174 per year. *Financial aid:* Application deadline 3/1. • Joyce Jordan, Chair, 305-284-6252.

University of Michigan, School of Music, Program in Music Education, Ann Arbor, MI 48109. Awards PhD. Member of NASM. Offered through the Horace H. Rackham School of Graduate Studies. Students: 6 full-time (2 women). 8 applicants, 50% accepted. *Degree requirements:* Oral and preliminary exams. *Application deadline:* 2/1. *Application fee:* $55. *Financial aid:* Teaching assistantships available. Financial aid application deadline: 2/1. • Paul C. Boylan, Dean, School of Music, 734-764-0590. Application contact: Laura J. Strozeski, Senior Admissions Counselor, 734-764-0593. Fax: 734-763-5097. E-mail: music.admissions@umich.edu.

University of Minnesota, Duluth, Graduate School, School of Fine Arts, Department of Music, Duluth, MN 55812-2496. Offers program in music education (MM). Member of NASM. Part-time programs available. Faculty: 10 full-time (2 women). Students: 1 full-time (0 women), 15 part-time (11 women). Average age 24. 2 applicants, 100% accepted. In 1997, 1 degree awarded (100% found work related to degree). *Degree requirements:* Thesis required (for some programs), foreign language not required. *Entrance requirements:* Audition, minimum GPA of 3.0, sample of written work, interview. Application deadline: 7/15 (rolling processing; 1/15 for spring admission). Application fee: $40 ($50 for international students). *Expenses:* Tuition $5130 per year full-time, $299 per credit part-time for state residents; $10,074 per year full-time, $536 per credit part-time for nonresidents. Fees $612 per year full-time, $76 per quarter part-time. *Financial aid:* In 1997–98, 4 students received aid, including 4 teaching assistantships (2 to first-year students); fellowships, Federal Work-Study, institutionally sponsored loans also available. *Faculty research:* Band composition, psychoacoustics, music aesthetics, learning theory. Total annual research expenditures: $2000. • Dr. Judith Kritzmire, Director of Graduate Studies, 218-726-8260.

University of Missouri–Kansas City, Conservatory of Music, Program in Music Education, Kansas City, MO 64110-2499. Offers choral music education (MME), elementary music education (MME), instrumental music education (MME), music education (PhD). Member of NASM. One or more programs accredited by NCATE. PhD offered through the School of Graduate Studies. Part-time programs available. Students: 4 full-time (2 women), 13 part-time (10 women); includes 1 minority (African American), 1 international. Average age 36. In 1997, 2 master's awarded. *Degree requirements:* Thesis/dissertation required, foreign language not required. *Entrance requirements:* For master's, GRE, minimum GPA of 3.0 in major; for doctorate, minimum graduate GPA of 3.5. Application fee: $25. *Expenses:* Tuition $182 per credit hour for state residents; $508 per credit hour for nonresidents. Fees $60 per year. *Financial aid:* In 1997–98, 2 fellowships averaging $666 per month and totaling $12,000 were awarded; partial tuition waivers, Federal Work-Study, institutionally sponsored loans, and career-related internships or fieldwork also available. Aid available to part-time students. *Faculty research:* Affective response, multicultural pedagogy, music preception, aural skills, real time music assessment. • Dr. Terry L. Applebaum, Dean, Conservatory of Music, 816-235-2731. Fax: 816-235-5265. E-mail: tapplebaum@cctr.umkc.edu. Application contact: James Elswick, Coordinator for Admissions, 816-235-2932. Fax: 816-235-5264. E-mail: cadmissions@cctr.umkc.edu.

University of Missouri–St. Louis, College of Arts and Sciences, Program in Music Education, St. Louis, MO 63121-4499. Awards MME. Member of NASM. Part-time and evening/weekend programs available. Faculty: 11 (2 women). Students: 13 part-time (11 women); includes 2 minority (both African Americans). *Entrance requirements:* Departmental test. Application deadline: 7/1 (priority date; rolling processing; 12/1 for spring admission). Application fee: $0. Electronic applications accepted. *Expenses:* Tuition $3903 per year full-time, $167 per credit hour part-time for state residents; $11,745 per year full-time, $489 per credit hour part-time for nonresidents. Fees $816 per year full-time, $34 per credit hour part-time. *Faculty research:* Musicology. • Dr. Fred Willman, Director of Graduate Studies, 314-516-5980. Fax: 314-516-6593. E-mail: sfwillm@umslvma.umsl.edu. Application contact: Graduate Admissions, 314-516-5458. Fax: 314-516-6759. E-mail: gradadm@umslvma.umsl.edu.

The University of Montana–Missoula, School of Fine Arts, Department of Music, Program in Music Education, Missoula, MT 59812-0002. Awards MME. Member of NASM. Students: 2 full-time (0 women). Average age 31. 1 applicant, 100% accepted. In 1997, 3 degrees awarded. *Degree requirements:* 1 foreign language, thesis or alternative. *Entrance requirements:* GRE General Test, GRE Subject Test, portfolio. Application deadline: 8/1 (12/1 for spring admission). Application fee: $30. *Tuition:* $2499 per year (minimum) full-time, $376 per semester (minimum) part-time for state residents; $6528 per year (minimum) full-time, $1048 per semester (minimum) part-time for nonresidents. *Financial aid:* Federal Work-Study available. Financial aid application deadline: 3/1. • Dr. Thomas Cook, Chair, Department of Music, 406-243-4481.

University of Nebraska at Kearney, College of Fine Arts and Humanities, Department of Music, Kearney, NE 68849-0001. Offers program in music education (MA Ed). Member of NASM. Accredited by NCATE. Part-time and evening/weekend programs available. Faculty: 3 full-time (0 women). Students: 1 part-time (0 women). In 1997, 2 degrees awarded. *Degree requirements:* Thesis optional. *Entrance requirements:* GRE General Test. Application deadline: 8/1 (priority date; rolling processing; 12/15 for spring admission). Application fee: $35. *Expenses:* Tuition $1494 per year full-time, $83 per credit hour part-time for state residents; $2826 per year full-time, $157 per credit hour part-time for nonresidents. Fees $229 per year full-time, $11.25 per semester (minimum) part-time. *Financial aid:* In 1997–98, 1 teaching assistantship was awarded; research assistantships and career-related internships or fieldwork also available. Aid available to part-time students. Financial aid application deadline: 3/1; applicants required to submit FAFSA. • Dr. Ronald Crocker, Chair, 308-865-8618.

University of Nevada, Las Vegas, College of Fine Arts, Department of Music, Las Vegas, NV 89154-9900. Offerings include music education (MM). Member of NASM. Accredited by NCATE. Department faculty: 11 full-time (3 women). *Degree requirements:* Oral and/or written comprehensive exam required, thesis optional, foreign language not required. *Entrance requirements:* Minimum GPA of 3.0. Application deadline: 6/15 (11/15 for spring admission). Application fee: $40 ($95 for international students). *Expenses:* Tuition $93 per credit for state residents; $93 per credit full-time, $190 per credit part-time for nonresidents. Fees $5570 per year full-time for nonresidents. • Paul Kreider, Chair, 702-895-3332. Application contact: Graduate College Admissions Evaluator, 702-895-3320.

University of New Hampshire, College of Liberal Arts, Department of Music, Durham, NH 03824. Offerings include music education (MS). Member of NASM. Department faculty: 17 full-time. *Application deadline:* 4/1 (priority date; rolling processing). *Application fee:* $50. *Expenses:* Tuition $5440 per year full-time, $302 per credit hour part-time for state residents; $8160 per year (minimum) full-time, $453 per credit hour (minimum) part-time for nonresidents. Fees $868 per year full-time, $15 per year part-time. • Peggy Vagts, Chairperson, 603-862-3254. Application contact: Dr. Robert Stibler, Graduate Coordinator, 603-862-2404.

The University of North Carolina at Chapel Hill, School of Education, Programs in Teacher Education, Program in Secondary Education, Chapel Hill, NC 27599. Offerings include music (MAT). Accredited by NCATE. *Degree requirements:* Comprehensive exam required, foreign language and thesis not required. *Entrance requirements:* GRE General Test (minimum combined score of 1000), minimum GPA of 3.0 during last 2 years of undergraduate course work. Application deadline: 1/1 (rolling processing). Application fee: $55. *Expenses:* Tuition $1428 per year full-time, $357 per semester (minimum) part-time for state residents; $10,414 per year full-time, $2604 per semester (minimum) part-time for nonresidents. Fees $782 per year full-time, $332 per semester (minimum) part-time. • Dr. Walter Pryzwansky, Director of

Directory: Music Education

The University of North Carolina at Chapel Hill (continued)
Graduate Studies, 919-966-7000. Application contact: Janet Carroll, Registrar, 919-966-1346. Fax: 919-962-1533. E-mail: jscarrol@email.unc.edu.

University of North Carolina at Greensboro, School of Music, Greensboro, NC 27412-0001. Offerings include education (MM), music education (PhD). Member of NASM. One or more programs accredited by NCATE. School faculty: 38 full-time (9 women), 10 part-time (4 women). *Degree requirements:* For master's, variable foreign language requirement, thesis (for some programs), recital. *Entrance requirements:* For master's, GRE General Test, NTE (professional knowledge score for education), audition. Application deadline: 3/1. Application fee: $35. *Expenses:* Tuition $1842 per year full-time, $370 per semester (minimum) part-time for state residents; $10,296 per year full-time, $2484 per semester (minimum) part-time for nonresidents. Fees $806 per year full-time, $111 per semester (minimum) part-time. • Arthur Tollefson, Dean, 336-334-5560.

University of North Dakota, College of Fine Arts, Department of Music, Grand Forks, ND 58202. Offerings include music education (M Mus). Member of NASM. Department faculty: 9 full-time (4 women). *Degree requirements:* Thesis or alternative required, foreign language not required. *Entrance requirements:* TOEFL (minimum score 550), minimum GPA of 3.0. Application deadline: 3/1 (priority date; rolling processing). Application fee: $20. • Dr. E. John Miller, Chairperson, 701-777-2644. Fax: 701-777-3320. E-mail: johmille@badlands.nodak.edu.

University of Northern Colorado, College of Performing and Visual Arts, School of Music, Greeley, CO 80639. Awards MM, MME, DA. Member of NASM. One or more programs accredited by NCATE. Faculty: 27 full-time (6 women), 2 part-time (0 women). Students: 71 full-time (27 women), 3 part-time (0 women); includes 6 minority (2 Asian Americans, 3 Hispanics, 1 Native American), 5 international. Average age 33. 56 applicants, 73% accepted. In 1997, 20 master's, 8 doctorates awarded. *Degree requirements:* For master's, thesis or alternative, comprehensive exams; for doctorate, dissertation, comprehensive exams. *Entrance requirements:* For master's, audition; for doctorate, GRE General Test, audition. Application deadline: rolling. Application fee: $35. *Expenses:* Tuition $2327 per year full-time, $129 per credit hour part-time for state residents; $9578 per year full-time, $532 per credit hour part-time for nonresidents. Fees $752 per year full-time, $184 per semester (minimum) part-time. *Financial aid:* In 1997–98, 63 students received aid, including 12 fellowships (5 to first-year students) totaling $15,650, 23 teaching assistantships (8 to first-year students) totaling $95,217, 13 graduate assistantships (4 to first-year students) totaling $42,994. Financial aid application deadline: 3/1. • Dr. Rob Hollquist, Interim Director, 970-351-2194.

University of Northern Iowa, College of Humanities and Fine Arts, School of Music, Program in Music Education, Cedar Falls, IA 50614. Awards MM. Member of NASM. Part-time and evening/weekend programs available. Students: 16 full-time (10 women), 18 part-time (12 women); includes 8 international. Average age 33. 20 applicants, 65% accepted. In 1997, 7 degrees awarded. *Degree requirements:* Thesis or alternative required, foreign language not required. *Entrance requirements:* GRE. Application deadline: 8/1 (priority date; rolling processing). Application fee: $20 ($30 for international students). *Expenses:* Tuition $3166 per year full-time, $176 per hour part-time for state residents; $7805 per year full-time, $176 per hour part-time for nonresidents. Fees $194 per year full-time, $12.50 per semester (minimum) part-time. *Financial aid:* Full and partial tuition waivers, Federal Work-Study, and career-related internships or fieldwork available. Aid available to part-time students. Financial aid application deadline: 3/1. • Patricia W. Hughes, Head, 319-273-6865.

University of North Florida, College of Education, Department of Elementary and Secondary Education, Program in Music Education, Jacksonville, FL 32224-2645. Awards M Ed. Accredited by NCATE. Part-time and evening/weekend programs available. Faculty: 2 full-time (1 woman). Students: 1 part-time (0 women). Average age 38. 0 applicants. *Entrance requirements:* GRE General Test (minimum combined score of 1000), minimum GPA of 3.0. Application deadline: rolling. Application fee: $20. *Tuition:* $3388 per year full-time, $141 per credit hour part-time for state residents; $11,634 per year full-time, $485 per credit hour part-time for nonresidents. *Financial aid:* Career-related internships or fieldwork available. *Faculty research:* Performance measurement system. • Dr. Dennis Holt, Chairperson, Department of Elementary and Secondary Education, 904-646-2610.

University of North Texas, College of Music, Denton, TX 76203-6737. Offerings include music education (MM, MME, PhD). Member of NASM. Terminal master's awarded for partial completion of doctoral program. College faculty: 88 full-time (21 women), 9 part-time (5 women). *Application deadline:* 7/17. *Application fee:* $25 ($50 for international students). *Tuition:* $2063 per year full-time, $815 per year part-time for state residents; $5897 per year full-time, $2100 per year part-time for nonresidents. • Dr. David L. Shrader, Dean, 940-565-2791. Application contact: Dr. Edward Baird, Graduate Director, 940-565-3733. Fax: 940-565-2002.

University of Oklahoma, College of Fine Arts, School of Music, Norman, OK 73019-0390. Offerings include music education (M Mus Ed, PhD). Member of NASM. School faculty: 49 full-time (8 women), 9 part-time (3 women). *Application deadline:* 6/1 (priority date; rolling processing). *Application fee:* $25. *Expenses:* Tuition $1920 per year full-time, $80 per credit hour part-time for state residents; $6108 per year full-time, $255 per credit hour part-time for nonresidents. Fees $468 per year full-time, $12 per semester (minimum) part-time. • Dr. Allan Ross, Interim Director, 405-325-2081. Application contact: Roger Rideout, Graduate Coordinator, 405-325-2081.

University of Oregon, Graduate School, School of Music, Program in Music Education, Eugene, OR 97403. Awards M Mus, DMA, PhD. Member of NASM. Part-time programs available. Faculty: 35 full-time (10 women), 4 part-time (1 woman), 36.74 FTE. Students: 22 full-time (13 women), 3 part-time (2 women); includes 3 minority (1 African American, 1 Asian American, 1 Native American), 4 international. 10 applicants, 70% accepted. In 1997, 5 master's, 1 doctorate awarded. Terminal master's awarded for partial completion of doctoral program. *Degree requirements:* For master's, variable foreign language requirement, thesis (for some programs); for doctorate, 1 foreign language, dissertation, comprehensive exam. *Entrance requirements:* For master's, TOEFL (minimum score 575); for doctorate, GRE General Test, GRE Subject Test, MAT, TOEFL (minimum score 600). Application deadline: 7/1. Application fee: $50. *Tuition:* $6429 per year full-time, $873 per quarter (minimum) part-time for state residents; $10,857 per year full-time, $1360 per quarter (minimum) part-time for nonresidents. *Financial aid:* In 1997–98, 6 teaching assistantships (2 to first-year students) were awarded; Federal Work-Study and career-related internships or fieldwork also available. Financial aid application deadline: 3/1. *Faculty research:* Psalms of DeLasso, stress and muscular tension in stringed instrument performance, piano music of Stravinsky, learning aptitudes in elementary music. • David Doerksen, Head, 541-346-5664. Application contact: Jill Michelle Cosart, Graduate Secretary, 541-346-5664.

University of Portland, College of Arts and Sciences, Department of Performing and Fine Arts, Program in Music, Portland, OR 97203-5798. Offerings include music education (MM Ed). Program faculty: 4 full-time (0 women). *Application deadline:* 8/1 (priority date; rolling processing; 12/1 for spring admission). *Application fee:* $40. *Tuition:* $515 per semester hour. • Dr. Kenneth Kleszynski, Director, 503-283-7294. E-mail: kkleszyn@up.edu.

University of Rochester, Eastman School of Music, Rochester, NY 14604. Offerings include education (MA, PhD), music education (MM, DMA). Member of NASM. School faculty: 80 full-time. *Degree requirements:* For master's, variable foreign language requirement, thesis (for some programs). *Entrance requirements:* For master's, GRE. Application deadline: 2/1. Application fee: $50. • James Undercofler, Director, 716-274-1010. Application contact: Charles Krusenstjerna, Director of Admissions, 716-274-1060.

University of St. Thomas, Graduate School of Arts and Sciences, Department of Music Education, St. Paul, MN 55105-1096. Awards MA. Member of NASM. Part-time programs available. Faculty: 2 full-time (both women), 36 part-time (18 women). Students: 50 part-time (42 women); includes 2 minority (1 African American, 1 Hispanic), 2 international. Average age 32. 7 applicants, 100% accepted. In 1997, 11 degrees awarded. *Degree requirements:* Thesis, 2 teaching videotape assessments required, foreign language not required. *Entrance requirements:* Teaching videotape, performance audition. Application deadline: 7/1 (priority date; rolling processing; 4/1 for spring admission). Application fee: $30. *Tuition:* $349 per credit hour. *Financial aid:* In 1997–98, 6 research assistantships totaling $1,992 were awarded; fellowships, teaching assistantships, institutionally sponsored loans, and career-related internships or fieldwork also available. Aid available to part-time students. Financial aid application deadline: 4/1. *Faculty research:* Assessment of Orff-Schulwerk, Kodaly-based classroom music programs. Total annual research expenditures: $2324. • Jane Frazee, Director, 800-328-6819. Application contact: Jane Stendahl, Administrative Assistant, 800-328-6819.

University of South Alabama, College of Education, Department of Curriculum and Instruction, Mobile, AL 36688-0002. Offerings include art/music education (M Ed). Accredited by NCATE. Department faculty: 13 full-time (6 women). *Degree requirements:* Comprehensive exams required, foreign language and thesis not required. *Entrance requirements:* GRE General Test (minimum combined score of 1000) or MAT (minimum score 37), minimum GPA of 3.0. Application deadline: 9/1 (priority date; rolling processing). Application fee: $25. • Dr. Walter S. Hopkins, Chairman, 334-380-2893.

University of South Carolina, Graduate School, School of Music, Program in Music Education, Columbia, SC 29208. Awards MM Ed, PhD. Member of NASM. Accredited by NCATE. Faculty: 39 full-time (7 women), 4 part-time. Students: 10 full-time (6 women), 11 part-time (6 women); includes 3 minority (all African Americans), 1 international. Average age 34. In 1997, 4 master's, 2 doctorates awarded. Terminal master's awarded for partial completion of doctoral program. *Degree requirements:* For master's, recital or thesis required, foreign language not required; for doctorate, 1 foreign language, dissertation. *Entrance requirements:* GRE General Test or MAT, music diagnostic exam. Application deadline: 7/1 (rolling processing; 11/1 for spring admission). Application fee: $35. Electronic applications accepted. *Expenses:* Tuition $3894 per year full-time, $193 per credit hour part-time for state residents; $8114 per year full-time, $404 per credit hour part-time for nonresidents. Fees $125 per year full-time, $37 per semester (minimum) part-time. *Financial aid:* In 1997–98, 3 teaching assistantships (2 to first-year students) were awarded. • Application contact: Dr. William H. Bates, Graduate Director, 803-777-1901. Fax: 803-777-6508. E-mail: gradmus@mozart.sc.edu.

University of Southern California, Graduate School, School of Music, Program in Music Education, Los Angeles, CA 90089. Awards MM, MM Ed, DMA. Member of NASM. Students: 29 full-time (18 women), 19 part-time (12 women); includes 20 minority (6 African Americans, 13 Asian Americans, 1 Hispanic), 10 international. Average age 38. 32 applicants, 66% accepted. In 1997, 9 master's, 3 doctorates awarded. *Degree requirements:* For doctorate, dissertation. *Application deadline:* 7/1 (priority date; 12/1 for spring admission). *Application fee:* $55. *Expenses:* Tuition $16,944 per year full-time, $706 per unit part-time. Fees $414 per year full-time, $32 per year part-time. *Financial aid:* In 1997–98, 6 fellowships, 7 teaching assistantships, 1 scholarship were awarded; research assistantships, Federal Work-Study, institutionally sponsored loans also available. Aid available to part-time students. Financial aid application deadline: 2/15; applicants required to submit FAFSA. • Jay Zorn, Chair.

University of Southern Mississippi, College of the Arts, School of Music, Hattiesburg, MS 39406-5167. Offerings include music education (MME, DME, PhD). Member of NASM. Terminal master's awarded for partial completion of doctoral program. School faculty: 35 full-time (7 women), 1 (woman) part-time. *Application deadline:* 8/9 (priority date; rolling processing; 12/13 for spring admission). *Application fee:* $0 ($25 for international students). *Tuition:* $2870 per year full-time, $137 per credit hour part-time for state residents; $5972 per year full-time, $172 per credit hour part-time for nonresidents. • Dr. Peter Ciurczak, Director, 601-266-5363. Application contact: Rebecca Britain, Coordinator, Graduate Studies, 601-266-5369.

University of South Florida, College of Education, Department of Music Education, Tampa, FL 33620-9951. Awards MA, PhD. Member of NASM. Accredited by NCATE. Offered in cooperation with the Department of Music. Part-time and evening/weekend programs available. Students: 6 part-time (all women). Average age 35. 1 applicant, 100% accepted. In 1997, 5 master's, 1 doctorate awarded. *Degree requirements:* For doctorate, dissertation, 2 tools of research in foreign language, statistics, and/or computers. *Entrance requirements:* For master's, GRE General Test (minimum combined score of 1000), minimum GPA of 3.5 in last 60 hours; for doctorate, GRE General Test (minimum combined score of 1000), minimum GPA of 3.0 (undergraduate) or 3.5 (graduate). Application deadline: 6/1 (10/15 for spring admission). Application fee: $20. Electronic applications accepted. *Tuition:* $142 per credit hour for state residents; $486 per credit hour for nonresidents. *Financial aid:* Federal Work-Study, institutionally sponsored loans available. Aid available to part-time students. Financial aid applicants required to submit FAFSA. • Christopher Doane, Director, School of Music, 813-974-2311. E-mail: doane@satie.arts.usf.edu. Application contact: Jack Heller, Coordinator, 813-974-2311. Fax: 813-974-2091. E-mail: heller@satie.arts.usf.edu.

University of South Florida, College of Fine Arts, School of Music, Tampa, FL 33620-9951. Offerings include music education (MA, PhD). Member of NASM. Accredited by NCATE. School faculty: 26 full-time (6 women), 12 part-time (5 women). *Degree requirements:* For doctorate, dissertation. *Average time to degree:* master's–1 year full-time, 3 years part-time. *Application deadline:* 6/5 (priority date; 10/23 for spring admission). *Application fee:* $20. *Tuition:* $142 per credit hour for state residents; $486 per credit hour for nonresidents. • Christopher Doane, Director, 813-974-2311. E-mail: doane@arts.usf.edu. Application contact: Don Owen, Director of Graduate Studies, 813-974-2311.

University of Southwestern Louisiana, College of the Arts, School of Music, Lafayette, LA 70503. Offerings include music (MM), with options in conducting, pedagogy, vocal and instrumental performance. Member of NASM. School faculty: 16 full-time (4 women). *Entrance requirements:* GRE General Test, minimum GPA of 2.75. Application deadline: 8/15. Application fee: $5 ($15 for international students). *Tuition:* $2012 per year full-time, $300 per semester (minimum) part-time for state residents; $7244 per year full-time, $300 per semester (minimum) part-time for nonresidents. • Dr. A. C. Himes, Head, 318-482-6016. Application contact: Dr. Andrea Loewy, Graduate Coordinator, 318-482-5214.

University of Tennessee, Knoxville, College of Arts and Sciences, Department of Music, Knoxville, TN 37996. Offerings include music education (MM), piano pedagogy and literature (MM), string pedagogy (MM). One or more programs accredited by NCATE. Member of NASM. Department faculty: 38 full-time (10 women), 2 part-time (1 woman). *Degree requirements:* Thesis required (for some programs), foreign language not required. *Entrance requirements:* TOEFL (minimum score 550), audition, minimum GPA of 2.7. Application deadline: 2/1 (priority date; rolling processing). Application fee: $35. Electronic applications accepted. *Tuition:* $3354 per year full-time, $181 per semester hour part-time for state residents; $8410 per year full-time, $462 per semester hour part-time for nonresidents. • Dolly Davis, Head, 423-974-3241. Fax: 423-974-1941. E-mail: dcdavis@utk.edu. Application contact: Dr. John Brock, Graduate Representative, 423-974-7539. E-mail: johnbrock@utk.edu.

The University of Texas at El Paso, College of Liberal Arts, Department of Music, 500 West University Avenue, El Paso, TX 79968-0001. Offerings include music education (MM). Member of NASM. *Degree requirements:* Thesis required, foreign language not required. *Entrance requirements:* Departmental exam, TOEFL (minimum score 550 reqired). Application deadline: 7/1 (priority date; rolling processing; 11/1 for spring admission). Application fee: $15 ($65 for international students). Electronic applications accepted. *Tuition:* $1559 per year full-time, $230 per credit hour part-time for state residents; $5393 per year full-time, $405 per credit hour part-time for nonresidents.

University of the Arts, Philadelphia College of Performing Arts, School of Music, Department of Music Education, 320 South Broad Street, Philadelphia, PA 19102-4944. Awards MAT.

Directory: Music Education

Member of NASM. *Degree requirements:* Thesis, project, performance, comprehensive exams. *Entrance requirements:* TOEFL (minimum score 500), audition. Application deadline: 3/1 (12/15 for spring admission).

University of Toledo, College of Arts and Sciences, Department of Music, Toledo, OH 43606-3398. Offerings include music education (MM). Member of NASM. Department faculty: 8 full-time (4 women). *Entrance requirements:* Audition (performance), minimum A average in student teaching or teaching experience (music education). Application fee: $30. Electronic applications accepted. *Tuition:* $5907 per year full-time, $246 per hour part-time for state residents; $11,835 per year full-time, $493 per hour part-time for nonresidents. • Dr. Robert DeYarman, Co-Chairperson, 419-530-5062. E-mail: rdeyarm@uoft02.utoledo.edu.

University of Tulsa, College of Arts and Sciences, School of Music, Tulsa, OK 74104-3189. Offerings include music education (MME). Member of NASM. Accredited by NCATE. School faculty: 14 full-time (5 women). *Application deadline:* rolling. *Application fee:* $30. Electronic applications accepted. *Expenses:* Tuition $480 per credit hour. Fees $2 per credit hour. • Dr. Francis J. Ryan, Chairperson, 918-631-2805. Application contact: Dr. Joseph L. Rivers, Adviser, 918-631-2234. Fax: 918-631-3589.

University of Victoria, Faculty of Education, Department of Arts in Education, Victoria, BC V8W 2Y2, Canada. Offers programs in art education (M Ed), music education (MA, M Ed). Part-time programs available. Faculty: 7 full-time (3 women), 4 part-time (2 women). Students: 14 full-time (11 women), 15 part-time (all women); includes 2 international. Average age 39. 3 applicants, 33% accepted. In 1997, 3 degrees awarded. *Degree requirements:* Thesis (for some programs), project (M Ed). *Average time to degree:* master's–3.1 years full-time. *Entrance requirements:* Minimum B average. Application deadline: 5/31 (priority date; rolling processing). Application fee: $50. *Tuition:* $2080 per year full-time, $557 per semester part-time. *Financial aid:* In 1997–98, 3 students received aid, including 1 fellowship (to a first-year student); teaching assistantships, institutionally sponsored loans also available. Financial aid application deadline: 2/15. *Faculty research:* Multicultural and first nations art, multimedia performance artistry, gender issues in art education, critical thinking, reflective practice. • Dr. B. Hanley, Chair, 250-721-7836. Fax: 250-721-6589. E-mail: bhanley@uvic.ca. Application contact: Sarah Baylow, Graduate Secretary, 250-721-7882. Fax: 250-721-7767. E-mail: sbaylow@uvic.ca.

University of Washington, College of Arts and Sciences, School of Music, Concentration in Music Education, Seattle, WA 98195. Awards MA, PhD. Member of NASM. Faculty: 3 full-time (1 woman). Students: 4 full-time (3 women), 7 part-time (5 women). 4 applicants, 100% accepted. In 1997, 6 master's awarded (100% found work related to degree); 3 doctorates awarded (100% found work related to degree). *Degree requirements:* For doctorate, dissertation required, foreign language not required. *Entrance requirements:* For master's, GRE General Test, GRE Subject Test, TOEFL (minimum score 500), minimum GPA of 3.0; for doctorate, GRE General Test, GRE Subject Test, TOEFL (minimum score 500), minimum GPA of 3.0, sample of scholarly writing, videotape of teaching. Application deadline: 5/15 (priority date; rolling processing; 2/1 for spring admission). Application fee: $45. *Tuition:* $5433 per year full-time, $775 per quarter (minimum) part-time for state residents; $13,479 per year full-time, $1925 per quarter (minimum) part-time for nonresidents. *Financial aid:* In 1997–98, 6 students received aid, including 1 fellowship, 3 teaching assistantships (2 to first-year students), 3 scholarships (1 to a first-year student); Federal Work-Study also available. Financial aid application deadline: 3/1. *Faculty research:* Multiethnic issues in music instruction, affective responses to music. • Patricia Campbell, Head, 206-543-4768. E-mail: westphal@u.washington.edu. Application contact: Elizabeth Westphal, Director of Advising, 206-543-2726. Fax: 206-616-6879. E-mail: westphal@u.washington.edu.

University of Wisconsin–Madison, School of Education, Department of Curriculum and Instruction, Madison, WI 53706-1380. Offerings include music education (MS). Member of NASM. *Application fee:* $38. *Tuition:* $4928 per year full-time, $926 per semester (minimum) part-time for state residents; $15,190 per year full-time, $2849 per semester (minimum) part-time for nonresidents.

University of Wisconsin–Madison, College of Letters and Science, School of Music, Program in Music Education, Madison, WI 53706-1380. Offers curriculum and instruction (PhD), music education (MM). Member of NASM. Faculty: 4 full-time (2 women). *Degree requirements:* For doctorate, dissertation. *Application fee:* $45. *Tuition:* $4928 per year full-time, $926 per semester (minimum) part-time for state residents; $15,190 per year full-time, $2849 per semester (minimum) part-time for nonresidents. • Application contact: John C. Stowe, Director of Graduate Studies, 608-263 -5016. Fax: 608-262-8876. E-mail: jcstowe@facstaff.wisc.edu.

University of Wisconsin–Stevens Point, College of Fine Arts and Communication, Department of Music, Stevens Point, WI 54481-3897. Awards MM Ed. Member of NASM. Part-time programs available. Faculty: 21 (5 women). Students: 1 full-time (0 women), 3 part-time (all women). In 1997, 4 degrees awarded. *Degree requirements:* Thesis or alternative required, foreign language not required. *Entrance requirements:* Teaching certificate. Application deadline: rolling. Application fee: $38. *Tuition:* $3702 per year full-time, $664 per semester (minimum) part-time for state residents; $11,346 per year full-time, $1938 per semester (minimum) part-time for nonresidents. *Financial aid:* Graduate assistantships, Federal Work-Study, institutionally sponsored loans, and career-related internships or fieldwork available. Aid available to part-time students. Financial aid application deadline: 5/1; applicants required to submit FAFSA. • David Hastings, Chair, 715-346-3107. Fax: 715-346-2718.

University of Wyoming, College of Arts and Sciences, Department of Music, Laramie, WY 82071. Offerings include music education (MA). Member of NASM. Department faculty: 10 (2 women). *Application deadline:* 3/1 (priority date). *Application fee:* $40. *Expenses:* Tuition $2430 per year full-time, $135 per credit hour part-time for state residents; $7518 per year full-time, $418 per credit hour part-time for nonresidents. Fees $386 per year full-time, $9.25 per credit hour part-time. • Gary Smart, Head, 307-766-5242. Fax: 307-766-5326. E-mail: gls@uwyo.edu.

Valdosta State University, Colleges of Education and Fine Arts, Department of Music, Valdosta, GA 31698. Offers program in music education (MME). Member of NASM. One or more programs accredited by NCATE. Part-time programs available. Faculty: 5 full-time (0 women). Students: 9 full-time (4 women), 4 part-time (2 women); includes 3 minority (all African Americans). 7 applicants, 86% accepted. In 1997, 1 degree awarded. *Entrance requirements:* GRE General Test (minimum combined score of 800). Application deadline: 8/1 (rolling processing; 11/15 for spring admission). Application fee: $10. *Expenses:* Tuition $2472 per year full-time, $83 per semester hour part-time for state residents; $8472 per year full-time, $333 per semester hour part-time for nonresidents. Fees $236 per year full-time. • Dr. C. Tayloe Harding, Head, 912-333-5804. Fax: 912-245-3799. E-mail: tharding@grits.valdosta.peachnet.edu.

VanderCook College of Music, Program in Music Education, Chicago, IL 60616-3886. Awards MM Ed. Member of NASM. Offered during summer only. Part-time programs available. Faculty: 10 full-time, 24 part-time. Students: 115 full-time; includes 11 minority (7 African Americans, 4 Hispanics). Average age 31. *Degree requirements:* Oral comprehensive exam required, thesis optional, foreign language not required. *Entrance requirements:* Minimum GPA of 3.0. Application deadline: rolling. Application fee: $25. *Financial aid:* Application deadline 5/1. *Faculty research:* Pedagogy in elementary music. • Ruth Rhodes, Dean, 312-225-6288. Application contact: George Pierard, Director of Admissions, 312-225-6288. Fax: 312-225-5211. E-mail: vcmusic@mcs.com.

Virginia Commonwealth University, School of the Arts, Department of Music, Richmond, VA 23284-9005. Offerings include education (MM). Member of NASM. Department faculty: 19 full-time (5 women). *Degree requirements:* Departmental qualifying exam, recital. *Entrance requirements:* GRE Subject Test, audition. Application deadline: 7/1 (12/1 for spring admission). Application fee: $30 ($0 for international students). *Tuition:* $4960 per year full-time, $257 per credit part-time for state residents; $12,652 per year full-time, $684 per credit part-time for nonresidents. • Dr. David Cordle, Chair, 804-828-8008. Fax: 804-828-6469. E-mail: dcordle@saturn.vcu.edu.

Wayne State College, Division of Education, Program in Curriculum and Instruction, Wayne, NE 68787. Offerings include music education (MSE). Accredited by NCATE. *Degree requirements:* Comprehensive exam, research paper required, foreign language not required. *Entrance requirements:* GRE General Test. Application deadline: rolling. Application fee: $10. *Expenses:* Tuition $1788 per year full-time, $75 per credit hour part-time for state residents; $3576 per year full-time, $149 per credit hour part-time for nonresidents. Fees $360 per year full-time, $15 per credit hour part-time. • Dr. Diane Alexander, Head, Division of Education, 402-375-7389.

Wayne State University, College of Fine, Performing and Communication Arts, Department of Music, Detroit, MI 48202. Offerings include music education (MM). Member of NASM. Department faculty: 18. *Application deadline:* 4/1. *Application fee:* $20 ($30 for international students). *Expenses:* Tuition $163 per credit hour for state residents; $355 per credit hour for nonresidents. Fees $498 per year full-time, $114 per semester (minimum) part-time. • Dr. Dennis Tini, Chairman, 313-577-1795. Application contact: Mary Wischusen, Graduate Committee Chair, 313-577-2612.

Webster University, College of Fine Arts, Department of Music, St. Louis, MO 63119-3194. Offerings include music education (MM). Member of NASM. Department faculty: 3 full-time (1 woman). *Application deadline:* rolling. *Application fee:* $25 ($50 for international students). *Tuition:* $350 per credit hour. • Michael Parkinson, Chair, 314-968-7033. Fax: 314-963-6048. E-mail: parkinmi@webster.edu. Application contact: Beth Russell, Director of Graduate Admissions, 314-968-7089. Fax: 314-968-7166. E-mail: russellmb@webster.edu.

West Chester University of Pennsylvania, School of Music, Department of Keyboard Music, West Chester, PA 19383. Offerings include piano pedagogy (MM). Member of NASM. Department faculty: 10. *Degree requirements:* Comprehensive exam, recital required, thesis optional, foreign language not required. *Entrance requirements:* GRE General Test, audition. Application deadline: 4/15 (priority date; rolling processing; 10/15 for spring admission). Application fee: $25. *Expenses:* Tuition $3468 per year full-time, $193 per credit part-time for state residents; $6236 per year full-time, $346 per credit part-time for nonresidents. Fees $660 per year full-time, $38 per credit part-time. • Shirley Aliferis, Chair, 610-436-2262.

West Chester University of Pennsylvania, School of Music, Department of Music Education, West Chester, PA 19383. Awards MM. Member of NASM. Accredited by NCATE. Faculty: 3. Students: 3 full-time (2 women), 19 part-time (13 women); includes 1 minority (African American), 1 international. Average age 30. 10 applicants, 40% accepted. In 1997, 9 degrees awarded. *Degree requirements:* Comprehensive exam, recital required, thesis optional, foreign language not required. *Entrance requirements:* GRE General Test, audition. Application deadline: 4/15 (priority date; rolling processing; 10/15 for spring admission). Application fee: $25. *Expenses:* Tuition $3468 per year full-time, $193 per credit part-time for state residents; $6236 per year full-time, $346 per credit part-time for nonresidents. Fees $660 per year full-time, $38 per credit part-time. *Financial aid:* In 1997–98, 1 research assistantship was awarded. Aid available to part-time students. Financial aid application deadline: 2/15. • Dr. Carol Belmain, Chair, 610-436-3027.

Western Connecticut State University, School of Professional Studies, Department of Education and Educational Psychology, Program in Music Education, Danbury, CT 06810-6885. Awards MS. Part-time and evening/weekend programs available. Students: 25 part-time (15 women). *Degree requirements:* Thesis or research project required, foreign language not required. *Entrance requirements:* Minimum GPA of 2.67. Application deadline: 8/1 (priority date; rolling processing). Application fee: $40. *Expenses:* Tuition $4127 per year (minimum) full-time, $178 per credit hour part-time for state residents; $9581 per year (minimum) full-time, $178 per credit hour part-time for nonresidents. Fees $25 per year part-time. *Financial aid:* Fellowships, Federal Work-Study, and career-related internships or fieldwork available. Aid available to part-time students. Financial aid application deadline: 5/1. • Dr. Lawrence Huntley, Chair, 203-837-8351.

Western Kentucky University, Potter College of Arts and Humanities, Department of Music, Bowling Green, KY 42101-3576. Awards MA Ed. Member of NASM. Accredited by NCATE. Part-time programs available. Faculty: 9 full-time (3 women). Students: 2 full-time (1 woman), 9 part-time (5 women). Average age 31. 4 applicants, 75% accepted. In 1997, 3 degrees awarded. *Degree requirements:* Written exam required, thesis not required. *Entrance requirements:* GRE General Test (minimum combined score of 1150 on three sections; average 1580), minimum GPA of 3.0. Application deadline: 8/1 (priority date; rolling processing; 12/1 for spring admission). Application fee: $20. *Tuition:* $2460 per year full-time, $133 per credit hour part-time for state residents; $6700 per year full-time, $369 per credit hour part-time for nonresidents. *Financial aid:* In 1997–98, 4 service awards (3 to first-year students) averaging $444 per month and totaling $16,000 were awarded; research assistantships, Federal Work-Study, institutionally sponsored loans also available. Aid available to part-time students. Financial aid application deadline: 4/1; applicants required to submit FAFSA. • Dr. John Duff, Head, 502-745-3751. Fax: 502-745-6855.

Wichita State University, College of Fine Arts, School of Music, Wichita, KS 67260. Offerings include music education (MME). Member of NASM. School faculty: 44 full-time (17 women), 11 part-time (5 women). *Application deadline:* 7/1 (priority date; rolling processing; 1/1 for spring admission). *Application fee:* $25 ($40 for international students). Electronic applications accepted. *Expenses:* Tuition $2303 per year full-time, $96 per credit hour part-time for state residents; $7691 per year full-time, $321 per credit hour part-time for nonresidents. Fees $490 per year full-time, $75 per semester (minimum) part-time. • Dr. William Thompson, Chair, 316-978-3500. E-mail: thomson@twsuvm.uc.twsu.edu. Application contact: Tom Fowler, Graduate Coordinator, 316-978-3103. E-mail: tfowler@twsuvm.uc.twsu.edu.

Winthrop University, School of Visual and Performing Arts, Department of Music, Rock Hill, SC 29733. Offerings include music education (MME). Accredited by NCATE. Member of NASM. Department faculty: 11 full-time (2 women). *Application deadline:* 7/15 (priority date; rolling processing; 12/1 for spring admission). *Application fee:* $35. *Tuition:* $3928 per year full-time, $164 per credit hour part-time for state residents; $7060 per year full-time, $294 per credit hour part-time for nonresidents. • Donald Rogers, Interim Chairman, 803-323-2255. Fax: 803-323-2343. E-mail: rogersd@winthrop.edu. Application contact: Sharon Johnson, Director of Graduate Studies, 803-323-2204. Fax: 803-323-2292. E-mail: johnsons@winthrop.edu.

Wright State University, College of Liberal Arts, Department of Music, Dayton, OH 45435. Offers program in music education (M Mus). Member of NASM. Part-time programs available. Students: 12 full-time (9 women), 5 part-time (3 women); includes 3 minority (2 African Americans, 1 Asian American). Average age 29. 9 applicants, 89% accepted. In 1997, 3 degrees awarded. *Degree requirements:* Thesis or alternative, oral exam required, foreign language not required. *Entrance requirements:* Theory placement test, TOEFL (minimum score 550), BA in music. Application fee: $25. *Tuition:* $5109 per year full-time, $161 per credit hour part-time for state residents; $9039 per year full-time, $282 per credit hour part-time for nonresidents. *Financial aid:* In 1997–98, 4 teaching assistantships were awarded; fellowships, research assistantships, graduate assistantships also available. Aid available to part-time students. Financial aid applicants required to submit FAFSA. *Faculty research:* General music, current needs, role of teacher, expectations in music education. • Dr. Sharon Nelson, Interim Chair, 937-775-2346. Fax: 937-775-3786.

Xavier University, College of Social Sciences, Department of Education, Cincinnati, OH 45207-2111. Offerings include music (M Ed). Department faculty: 32 full-time (14 women), 49 part-time (31 women), 44.25 FTE. *Application deadline:* rolling. *Application fee:* $25. • Dr. James Boothe, Chair, 513-745-2951. Fax: 513-745-1052. E-mail: boothe@admin.xu.edu.

Directories: Music Education; Reading Education

Xavier University (continued)
Application contact: Sheila Speth, Director of Graduate Services, 513-745-3360. Fax: 513-745-1048. E-mail: xugrad@admin.xu.edu.

Youngstown State University, College of Fine and Performing Arts, School of Music, Youngstown, OH 44555-0002. Offerings include music education (MM). Member of NASM. School faculty: 32 full-time (15 women), 11 part-time (6 women). *Degree requirements:* 1 foreign language, final qualifying exam required, thesis optional. *Entrance requirements:* TOEFL (minimum score 550), audition, GRE General Test or minimum GPA of 2.7. Application deadline: 8/15 (priority date; rolling processing; 2/15 for spring admission). Application fee: $30 ($75 for international students). *Expenses:* Tuition $90 per credit hour for state residents; $144 per credit hour (minimum) for nonresidents. Fees $528 per year full-time, $244 per year (minimum) part-time. • Joseph Edwards, Director, 330-742-3636. Application contact: Dr. Peter J. Kasvinsky, Dean of Graduate Studies, 330-742-3091. Fax: 330-742-1580. E-mail: amgrad03@ysub.ysu.edu.

Reading Education

Abilene Christian University, College of Arts and Sciences, Department of Education, Reading Specialist Program, Abilene, TX 79699-9100. Awards M Ed. Part-time programs available. Faculty: 11 part-time (4 women). Students: 1 (woman) full-time, 3 part-time (all women); includes 1 minority (Native American). 5 applicants, 80% accepted. In 1997, 2 degrees awarded. *Degree requirements:* Comprehensive exam required, foreign language and thesis not required. *Entrance requirements:* GRE General Test or MAT. Application deadline: 4/1 (priority date; rolling processing; 11/1 for spring admission). Application fee: $25 ($45 for international students). *Expenses:* Tuition $308 per credit hour. Fees $430 per year full-time, $85 per semester (minimum) part-time. *Financial aid:* Federal Work-Study available. Aid available to part-time students. Financial aid application deadline: 4/1. • Dr. Roger Gee, Graduate Adviser, 915-674-2122. Application contact: Dr. Carley Dodd, Graduate Dean, 915-674-2354. Fax: 915-674-6717. E-mail: gradinfo@nicanor.acu.edu.

Adelphi University, School of Education, Program in Reading, Garden City, NY 11530. Awards MS, PD. Part-time and evening/weekend programs available. Students: 20 full-time (18 women), 162 part-time (127 women); includes 16 minority (11 African Americans, 5 Hispanics). Average age 33. In 1997, 81 master's, 2 PDs awarded. *Application deadline:* rolling. *Application fee:* $50. *Expenses:* Tuition $16,000 per year full-time, $485 per credit part-time. Fees $500 per year full-time, $150 per semester part-time. *Financial aid:* Research assistantships, teaching assistantships, assistantships available. Financial aid application deadline: 3/1. *Faculty research:* Decoding, adult literacy, whole language. • Dr. Gerald Glass, Director, 516-877-4410.

Albany State University, School of Education, Program in Reading Education, Albany, GA 31705-2717. Awards M Ed. Accredited by NCATE. Faculty: 1 (woman) full-time. Students: 1 (woman) full-time, 2 part-time (both women). *Degree requirements:* Comprehensive exam. *Entrance requirements:* GRE General Test (minimum combined score of 800), MAT (minimum score 44) or NTE (minimum score 550 required, minimum GPA of 2.5. Application deadline: 9/1. Application fee: $10. *Financial aid:* Application deadline 4/1. • Dr. Claude Perkins, Dean, School of Education, 912-430-4715. Fax: 912-430-4993. E-mail: cperkins@fld94.alsnet.peachnet.edu.

Alfred University, Graduate School, Division of Education, Alfred, NY 14802-1205. Offerings include reading (MS Ed). Division faculty: 45 full-time (12 women). *Degree requirements:* Thesis required (for some programs), foreign language not required. *Entrance requirements:* TOEFL. Application deadline: rolling. Application fee: $50. *Expenses:* Tuition $20,376 per year full-time, $390 per credit hour (minimum) part-time. Fees $546 per year. • Dr. Katherine D. Wiesendanger, Chair, 607-871-2219. E-mail: fwiesendange@bigvax.alfred.edu. Application contact: Cathleen R. Johnson, Assistant Director of Admissions, 607-871-2141. Fax: 607-871-2198. E-mail: johnsonc@bigvax.alfred.edu.

American International College, School of Continuing Education and Graduate Studies, School of Psychology and Education, Department of Education, Springfield, MA 01109-3189. Offerings include reading (M Ed, CAGS). Department faculty: 5 full-time (3 women), 15 part-time (9 women). *Degree requirements:* For CAGS, practicum required, foreign language not required. *Application fee:* $15 ($25 for international students). *Expenses:* Tuition $363 per credit hour. Fees $25 per semester. • C. Gerald Weaver, Dean, School of Psychology and Education, 413-747-6338.

Andrews University, School of Graduate Studies, School of Education, Department of Teaching/Learning/Administration, Program in Reading, Berrien Springs, MI 49104. Awards MA. *Degree requirements:* Thesis optional, foreign language not required. *Entrance requirements:* GRE Subject Test. Application deadline: 8/15 (rolling processing). Application fee: $30. *Expenses:* Tuition $290 per quarter hour (minimum). Fees $75 per quarter. *Financial aid:* Fellowships, research assistantships, teaching assistantships, partial tuition waivers, Federal Work-Study, institutionally sponsored loans, and career-related internships or fieldwork available. Aid available to part-time students. • Dr. William H. Green, Chair, Department of Teaching/Learning/Administration, 616-471-3465.

Angelo State University, College of Professional Studies, Department of Education, Program in Reading Specialist, San Angelo, TX 76909. Awards M Ed. Part-time and evening/weekend programs available. Students: 2 full-time (1 woman), 5 part-time (4 women). Average age 40. 6 applicants, 100% accepted. In 1997, 4 degrees awarded. *Degree requirements:* Comprehensive exam required, thesis optional, foreign language not required. *Entrance requirements:* GRE General Test, minimum GPA of 2.5. Application deadline: 8/7 (priority date; rolling processing; 1/2 for spring admission). Application fee: $25 ($50 for international students). *Expenses:* Tuition $1022 per year full-time, $36 per semester hour part-time for state residents; $7382 per year full-time, $246 per semester hour part-time for nonresidents. Fees $1140 per year full-time, $165 per semester (minimum) part-time. *Financial aid:* In 1997–98, 4 fellowships were awarded; teaching assistantships, graduate assistantships, partial tuition waivers, Federal Work-Study, and career-related internships or fieldwork also available. Aid available to part-time students. Financial aid application deadline: 8/1. • Dr. James Hademenos, Head, Department of Education, 915-942-2052.

Appalachian State University, College of Education, Department of Language, Reading and Exceptionalities, Boone, NC 28608. Offers programs in reading education (MA, Ed S), special education (MA), speech pathology and audiology (MA). Accredited by NCATE. Faculty: 25 full-time (12 women), 13 part-time (11 women). Students: 109 full-time (104 women), 30 part-time (27 women); includes 4 minority (1 African American, 2 Hispanics, 1 Native American). 272 applicants, 28% accepted. In 1997, 47 master's awarded. *Degree requirements:* For master's, thesis or alternative, comprehensive exams required, foreign language not required; for Ed S, comprehensive exam required, foreign language not required. *Average time to degree:* master's–2 years full-time, 4 years part-time. *Entrance requirements:* GRE General Test. Application deadline: 7/31 (priority date). Application fee: $35. *Tuition:* $1811 per year full-time, $354 per semester (minimum) part-time for state residents; $9081 per year full-time, $2171 per semester (minimum) part-time for nonresidents. *Financial aid:* In 1997–98, 1 teaching assistantship, 23 assistantships were awarded; fellowships, research assistantships also available. Aid available to part-time students. • Dr. Tim Harris, Chairperson, 704-262-2182.

Arkansas State University, College of Education, Department of Elementary Education, State University, AR 72467. Offerings include reading (MSE, SCCT). Accredited by NCATE. Department faculty: 10 full-time (8 women). *Degree requirements:* For SCCT, comprehensive exam required, thesis not required. *Entrance requirements:* For SCCT, GRE General Test or MAT, master's degree. Application deadline: 7/1 (priority date; rolling processing; 11/15 for spring admission). Application fee: $15 ($25 for international students). *Expenses:* Tuition $2760 per year full-time, $115 per credit hour part-time for state residents; $6936 per year full-time, $289 per credit hour part-time for nonresidents. Fees $506 per year full-time, $44 per semester (minimum) part-time. • Dr. Roberta Daniels, Interim Chair, 870-972-3059. Fax: 870-972-3828. E-mail: rdaniels@kiowa.astate.edu.

Ashland University, College of Education, Graduate Studies in Teacher Education, Program in Reading, Ashland, OH 44805-3702. Awards M Ed. Accredited by NCATE. Part-time and evening/weekend programs available. Faculty: 4 full-time (3 women), 2 part-time (both women). In 1997, 23 degrees awarded. *Degree requirements:* Practicum. *Entrance requirements:* GRE General Test or MAT, teaching certificate. Application deadline: rolling. Application fee: $15. *Tuition:* $275 per credit hour. • Jim Rycik, Program Team Leader, 419-289-5359. Application contact: Dr. Joe Bailey, Director, 419-289-5377. Fax: 419-289-5097. E-mail: jbailey@ashland.edu.

Auburn University, College of Education, Department of Curriculum and Teaching, Auburn University, AL 36849-0001. Offerings include reading education (PhD, Ed S). Accredited by NCATE. Department faculty: 20 full-time (11 women). *Degree requirements:* For doctorate, dissertation required, foreign language not required; for Ed S, field project required, foreign language and thesis not required. *Entrance requirements:* For doctorate, GRE General Test (minimum score 450 on each section, 1000 combined); for Ed S, GRE General Test. Application deadline: 9/1 (rolling processing; 3/1 for spring admission). Application fee: $25 ($50 for international students). *Expenses:* Tuition $2760 per year full-time, $76 per credit hour part-time for state residents; $8280 per year full-time, $228 per credit hour part-time for nonresidents. Fees $30 per year full-time, $160 per quarter part-time for state residents; $30 per year full-time, $480 per quarter part-time for nonresidents. • Dr. Andrew M. Weaver, Head, 334-844-4434. E-mail: weaveam@mail.auburn.edu. Application contact: Dr. John F. Pritchett, Dean of the Graduate School, 334-844-4700.

Auburn University Montgomery, School of Education, Department of Early Childhood, Elementary, and Reading Education, Montgomery, AL 36124-4023. Offers programs in early childhood education (M Ed, Ed S), elementary education (M Ed, Ed S), reading education (M Ed, Ed S). Accredited by NCATE. Part-time and evening/weekend programs available. Students: 71 full-time (65 women), 58 part-time (49 women); includes 46 minority (45 African Americans, 1 Hispanic), 1 international. Average age 32. In 1997, 77 master's, 3 Ed Ss awarded. *Degree requirements:* Comprehensive exam required, foreign language and thesis not required. *Entrance requirements:* For master's, GRE General Test or MAT, certification, BS in teaching; for Ed S, GRE General Test or MAT, certification. Application deadline: 9/1 (priority date; rolling processing; 3/28 for spring admission). Application fee: $25. Electronic applications accepted. *Tuition:* $2664 per year full-time, $85 per quarter hour part-time for state residents; $7080 per year full-time, $255 per quarter hour part-time for nonresidents. *Financial aid:* In 1997–98, 3 teaching assistantships were awarded; career-related internships or fieldwork also available. • Dr. Janet Warren, Head, 334-244-3422.

Austin Peay State University, College of Education, Department of Education, Clarksville, TN 37044-0001. Offerings include reading (MA Ed). Accredited by NCATE. *Application deadline:* 7/31 (priority date; rolling processing; 12/4 for spring admission). *Application fee:* $15. *Expenses:* Tuition $2438 per year full-time, $123 per semester hour part-time for state residents; $7034 per year full-time, $324 per semester hour part-time for nonresidents. Fees $484 per year (minimum) full-time, $154 per semester (minimum) part-time. • J. Ronald Groseclose, Interim Chair, 931-648-7585. Fax: 931-648-5991. E-mail: groseclosеg@apsu.edu.

Averett College, Division of Education, Program in Reading, Danville, VA 24541-3692. Awards M Ed. Part-time and evening/weekend programs available. Faculty: 4 full-time (3 women). Students: 9 part-time (8 women). Average age 30. 1 applicant, 100% accepted. In 1997, 7 degrees awarded (100% found work related to degree). *Degree requirements:* Comprehensive exam required, foreign language not required. *Entrance requirements:* GRE, MAT, or PRAXIS (test scores should be no older than 5 years), minimum GPA of 3.0 in previous 2 years, teaching certificate. Application deadline: 8/1 (priority date; rolling processing; 4/15 for spring admission). Application fee: $25. *Tuition:* $225 per credit hour. • Dr. Elizabeth Compton, Academic Vice President, Division of Education, 804-791-5656. Fax: 804-791-0658.

Baldwin-Wallace College, Division of Education, Specialization in Reading, Berea, OH 44017-2088. Awards MA Ed. Accredited by NCATE. Part-time and evening/weekend programs available. *Entrance requirements:* Bachelor's degree in field, MAT or minimum GPA of 2.75. Application fee: $15. *Financial aid:* Career-related internships or fieldwork available. • Dr. Patrick F. Cosiano, Chairman, Division of Education, 440-826-2168. Fax: 440-826-3779. E-mail: pcosiano@bw.edu. Application contact: Dr. Jane F. Cavanaugh, Director of Continuing Education, 440-826-2222. Fax: 440-826-3640. E-mail: admission@bw.edu.

Ball State University, Teachers College, Department of Elementary Education, Program in Reading Education, 2000 University Avenue, Muncie, IN 47306-1099. Awards MAE, Ed D. Accredited by NCATE. Students: 0. 2 applicants, 50% accepted. *Degree requirements:* For doctorate, dissertation required, foreign language not required. *Entrance requirements:* For doctorate, GRE General Test (minimum combined score of 1000), minimum graduate GPA of 3.2. Application fee: $15 ($25 for international students). *Expenses:* Tuition $3454 per year full-time, $518 per semester (minimum) part-time for state residents; $9316 per year full-time, $1221 per semester (minimum) part-time for nonresidents. Fees $242 per year full-time, $18 per semester (minimum) part-time. • James Stroud, Head, 765-285-8560.

Bank Street College of Education, Program in Early Childhood and Elementary Teacher Education, 610 West 112th Street, New York, NY 10025-1120. Offerings include reading/literacy (MS Ed). MSW/MS Ed (infant and parent development) offered jointly with Hunter College of the City University of New York. *Degree requirements:* 1 foreign language, thesis. *Entrance requirements:* TOEFL (minimum score 550). Application deadline: 3/1 (priority date; rolling processing; 11/1 for spring admission). Application fee: $50. *Tuition:* $560 per credit. • Linda Levine, Chairperson, 212-875-4480. Application contact: Ann Morgan, Director of Admissions, 212-875-4404. Fax: 212-875-4678. E-mail: amorgan@bnkst.edu.

Barry University, School of Education, Program in Reading, Miami Shores, FL 33161-6695. Awards MS, Ed S. Part-time and evening/weekend programs available. Faculty: 1 (woman) full-time, 2 part-time (both women). Students: 4 full-time (3 women), 25 part-time (23 women); includes 17 minority (14 African Americans, 3 Hispanics), 1 international. Average age 36. In 1997, 13 master's, 2 Ed Ss awarded. *Degree requirements:* For master's, practicum, written comprehensive exam required, foreign language and thesis not required; for Ed S, practicum required, foreign language and thesis not required. *Entrance requirements:* For master's, GRE General Test or MAT, minimum GPA of 3.0, previous course work in children's literature; for Ed S, GRE General Test, minimum GPA of 3.0. Application deadline: 5/1 (priority date; rolling processing). Application fee: $30. Electronic applications accepted. *Tuition:* $450 per credit (minimum). *Financial aid:* Partial tuition waivers and career-related internships or fieldwork available. Aid available to part-time students. Financial aid application deadline: 5/1; applicants required to submit FAFSA. • Dr. Ann Murphy, Director, 305-899-3700. Fax: 305-899-3630. E-mail: carneal@aquinas.barry.edu. Application contact: Angela Scott, Enrollment Services, Assistant Dean, 305-899-3112. Fax: 305-899-3149. E-mail: ascott@jeanne.barry.edu.

Beaver College, Department of Education, Glenside, PA 19038-3295. Offerings include reading (M Ed, CAS). *Application fee:* $35. *Expenses:* Tuition $6570 per year full-time, $365 per credit part-time. Fees $35 per year.

Berry College, Graduate Programs in Education, Program in Reading, Mount Berry, GA 30149-0159. Awards M Ed. Accredited by NCATE. Part-time programs available. Faculty: 1 (woman) part-time.5 FTE. Students: 2 part-time (both women). Average age 30. 0 applicants. In 1997, 2 degrees awarded (100% found work related to degree). *Degree requirements:* Oral exams required, thesis optional, foreign language not required. *Average time to degree:* master's–2 years full-time, 3 years part-time. *Entrance requirements:* GRE General Test, MAT, or NTE, minimum GPA of 2.5. Application deadline: 7/29 (rolling processing; 12/16 for spring admission). Application fee: $25 ($30 for international students). *Tuition:* $146 per semester hour. *Financial aid:* Assistantships available. Financial aid application deadline: 4/1; applicants required to submit FAFSA. *Faculty research:* Reading remediation, literacy education. Total annual research expenditures: $25,000. • Application contact: George Gaddie, Dean of Admissions, 706-236-2215. Fax: 706-290-2178.

Bloomsburg University of Pennsylvania, School of Graduate Studies, College of Professional Studies, School of Education, Department of Curriculum and Foundations, Program in Reading, Bloomsburg, PA 17815-1905. Awards M Ed. Accredited by NCATE. Faculty: 2 full-time (1 woman). Students: 12 full-time (all women), 48 part-time (42 women); includes 1 minority (African American), 1 international. Average age 29. 24 applicants, 100% accepted. In 1997, 45 degrees awarded. *Entrance requirements:* Minimum QPA of 2.5. Application deadline: rolling. Application fee: $25. *Expenses:* Tuition $3468 per year full-time, $193 per credit part-time for state residents; $6236 per year full-time, $346 per credit part-time for nonresidents. Fees $748 per year full-time, $166 per semester (minimum) part-time. *Faculty research:* Diagnosis, remediation, parental involvement, language arts, child literacy. • Dr. Edward Poostay, Coordinator, 717-389-4092.

Boise State University, College of Education, Programs in Teacher Education, Program in Reading, Boise, ID 83725-0399. Awards MA. Accredited by NCATE. Part-time programs available. Faculty: 8 full-time (4 women). Students: 8 full-time (6 women), 67 part-time (66 women); includes 1 minority (Hispanic), 1 international. Average age 40. 10 applicants, 100% accepted. In 1997, 19 degrees awarded. *Degree requirements:* Thesis optional. *Application deadline:* 7/26 (priority date; rolling processing; 11/29 for spring admission). *Application fee:* $20 ($30 for international students). Electronic applications accepted. *Tuition:* $3020 per year full-time, $135 per credit part-time for state residents; $8900 per year full-time, $135 per credit part-time for nonresidents. *Financial aid:* Graduate assistantships, Federal Work-Study, institutionally sponsored loans, and career-related internships or fieldwork available. Aid available to part-time students. Financial aid application deadline: 3/1. • Dr. Roger Stewart, Coordinator, Programs in Teacher Education, 208-385-1731. Fax: 208-385-4365.

Boston College, Graduate School of Education, Department of Teacher Education/Special Education and Curriculum and Instruction, Reading Specialist Program, Chestnut Hill, MA 02167-9991. Awards M Ed, CAES. Accredited by NCATE. Students: 15 full-time (14 women), 17 part-time (all women); includes 1 international. 34 applicants, 76% accepted. In 1997, 7 master's awarded. *Degree requirements:* Comprehensive exam required, thesis not required. *Entrance requirements:* For master's, GRE General Test; for CAES, GRE General Test or MAT. Application deadline: 3/15 (11/15 for spring admission). Application fee: $40. *Expenses:* Tuition $626 per semester hour. Fees $80 per year (minimum) full-time, $30 per semester part-time. *Financial aid:* Fellowships, research assistantships, teaching assistantships, administrative assistantships, merit scholarships, Federal Work-Study, and career-related internships or fieldwork available. Aid available to part-time students. *Faculty research:* Reading instruction, educational publishing, children's literature, teaching writing, literacy. • Application contact: Arline Riordan, Graduate Admissions Director, 617-552-4214. Fax: 617-552-0812. E-mail: riordana@bc.edu.

Boston University, School of Education, Department of Curriculum and Teaching, Program in Reading, Boston, MA 02215. Awards Ed M, Ed D, CAGS. Students: 7 full-time (6 women), 2 part-time (both women). Average age 24. In 1997, 4 master's awarded. *Degree requirements:* For doctorate, dissertation, comprehensive exam required, foreign language not required; for CAGS, comprehensive exam required, foreign language and thesis not required. *Entrance requirements:* For master's and CAGS, GRE or MAT, TOEFL; for doctorate, GRE General Test or MAT, TOEFL. Application deadline: 2/15 (priority date; rolling processing). Application fee: $50. *Expenses:* Tuition $22,830 per year full-time, $713 per credit part-time. Fees $218 per year full-time, $40 per semester part-time. *Financial aid:* Application deadline 3/30. *Faculty research:* Reading diagnosis (disabilities), professional preparation. • Dr. Thomas E. Culliton Jr., Coordinator, 617-353-3223. E-mail: culliton@bu.edu.

Bowie State University, Programs in Education, Program in Reading Education, 14000 Jericho Park Road, Bowie, MD 20715. Awards M Ed. Part-time and evening/weekend programs available. *Degree requirements:* Research paper, written comprehensive exam required, thesis optional. *Entrance requirements:* Minimum GPA of 2.5, teaching certificate, teaching experience. Application deadline: 8/16 (priority date; rolling processing). Application fee: $30. *Expenses:* Tuition $169 per credit hour for state residents; $304 per credit hour for nonresidents. Fees $171 per year. *Faculty research:* Literacy education, multicultural education.

Bowling Green State University, College of Education and Allied Professions, Department of Educational Curriculum and Instruction, Program in Reading, Bowling Green, OH 43403. Awards M Ed, Ed S. Accredited by NCATE. Part-time programs available. Faculty: 4 full-time (3 women), 3 part-time (2 women). Students: 12 full-time (11 women), 23 part-time (22 women); includes 6 minority (2 African Americans, 4 Hispanics), 1 international. 13 applicants, 85% accepted. In 1997, 12 master's, 1 Ed S awarded. *Degree requirements:* For master's, thesis or alternative required, foreign language not required; for Ed S, practicum or field experience required, foreign language and thesis not required. *Entrance requirements:* For master's, GRE General Test, TOEFL (minimum score 550); for Ed S, GRE General Test, TOEFL (minimum score 600). Application deadline: rolling. Application fee: $30. *Tuition:* $6070 per year full-time, $284 per credit hour part-time for state residents; $11,358 per year full-time, $536 per credit hour part-time for nonresidents. *Financial aid:* Federal Work-Study, institutionally sponsored loans, and career-related internships or fieldwork available. Financial aid application deadline: 2/15; applicants required to submit FAFSA. *Faculty research:* Children's literature, attention deficit disorder/reading correlations, content area reading, reading instruction, reading/writing connection. • Application contact: Dr. Cindy Gillespie, Graduate Coordinator, 419-372-7341.

Bridgewater State College, School of Education, Department of Elementary and Early Childhood Education, Program in Reading, Bridgewater, MA 02325-0001. Awards M Ed. Accredited by NCATE. Evening/weekend programs available. *Entrance requirements:* GRE General Test, 1 year of teaching experience. Application deadline: 4/1 (10/1 for spring admission). Application fee: $25. *Expenses:* Tuition $1675 per year full-time, $70 per credit part-time for state residents; $6450 per year full-time, $269 per credit part-time for nonresidents. Fees $1588 per year full-time, $66 per credit hour part-time for state residents; $1588 per year full-time, $66 per credit part-time for nonresidents. *Financial aid:* Career-related internships or fieldwork available. • Application contact: Graduate School, 508-697-1300.

Brigham Young University, David O. McKay School of Education, Department of Teacher Education, Provo, UT 84602-1001. Offerings include reading (Ed D). Accredited by NCATE. Department faculty: 15 full-time (1 woman). *Degree requirements:* Dissertation. *Average time to degree:* master's–2 years full-time, 3 years part-time. *Entrance requirements:* GRE General Test (minimum combined score of 1000), valid teaching credential, minimum 3 years of teaching experience, minimum GPA of 3.5 in last 60 hours. Application deadline: 2/15 (rolling processing). Application fee: $30. *Tuition:* $3200 per year full-time, $178 per credit hour part-time for state residents; $4800 per year full-time, $266 per credit hour part-time for nonresidents. • Dr. M. Winston Egan, Chair, 801-378-4077. E-mail: winn_egan@byu.edu. Application contact: Eual E. Monroe, Graduate Coordinator, 801-378-4843. Fax: 801-378-3570. E-mail: eula_monroe@byu.edu.

Brooklyn College of the City University of New York, School of Education, Program in Reading and Language Arts, 2900 Bedford Avenue, Brooklyn, NY 11210-2889. Awards MS Ed. Part-time and evening/weekend programs available. Students: 9 full-time (all women), 193 part-time (182 women); includes 80 minority (68 African Americans, 3 Asian Americans, 9 Hispanics), 1 international. Average age 30. 80 applicants, 75% accepted. In 1997, 48 degrees awarded (10% entered university research/teaching, 90% found other work related to degree). *Degree requirements:* Practicum required, foreign language and thesis not required. *Average time to degree:* master's–2.5 years part-time. *Entrance requirements:* TOEFL (minimum score 500), interview, minimum GPA of 2.85, previous course work in education and psychology, teaching certificate. Application deadline: 3/1 (11/1 for spring admission). Application fee: $40. *Expenses:* Tuition $4350 per year full-time, $185 per credit part-time for state residents; $7600 per year full-time, $320 per credit part-time for nonresidents. Fees $500 per year for state residents; $806 per year for nonresidents. *Financial aid:* Career-related internships or fieldwork available. Financial aid application deadline: 5/1; applicants required to submit FAFSA. *Faculty research:* Inclusion, reader response. • Dr. Margaret Waters, Head, 718-951-5950.

Bucknell University, College of Arts and Sciences, Department of Education, Specialization in Reading, Lewisburg, PA 17837. Awards MA, MS Ed. *Degree requirements:* Thesis or alternative required, foreign language not required. *Entrance requirements:* GRE General Test (minimum combined score of 1000), TOEFL (minimum score 550), minimum GPA of 2.8. Application deadline: 6/1 (priority date; rolling processing; 12/1 for spring admission). Application fee: $25. *Tuition:* $2410 per course. *Financial aid:* Assistantships available. Financial aid application deadline: 3/1. • Dr. Robert Midkiff, Head, Department of Education, 717-524-1133.

Butler University, College of Education, Indianapolis, IN 46208-3485. Offerings include reading (MS). Accredited by NCATE. College faculty: 10 full-time (3 women), 22 part-time (8 women), 22.5 FTE. *Average time to degree:* master's–7 years part-time; other advanced degree–5 years part-time. *Entrance requirements:* GRE General Test, MAT (minimum score 40), interview. Application deadline: 8/15 (priority date; rolling processing). Application fee: $25. *Tuition:* $220 per credit hour. • Dr. Saundra Tracy, Dean, 317-940-9514. Fax: 317-940-6481. E-mail: stracy@butler.edu.

California Baptist College, Graduate Program in Education, Riverside, CA 92504-3206. Offerings include reading (MS Ed). Program faculty: 8 full-time (7 women), 4 part-time (2 women). *Application deadline:* rolling. *Application fee:* $40. *Expenses:* Tuition $275 per unit. Fees $100 per year. • Dr. Marsha Savage, Chair, 909-689-5771. Application contact: Gail Ronveaux, Director of Graduate Services, 909-343-4249. Fax: 909-351-1808. E-mail: gradser@cal.baptist.edu.

California Lutheran University, School of Education, Emphasis in Curriculum and Instruction, Thousand Oaks, CA 91360-2787. Offers program in reading education (MA). Part-time programs available. Students: 4 full-time (2 women), 84 part-time (75 women). 23 applicants, 65% accepted. In 1997, 12 degrees awarded. *Degree requirements:* Thesis or comprehensive exam required, foreign language not required. *Entrance requirements:* GRE General Test, minimum GPA of 3.0. Application deadline: 8/1 (priority date; rolling processing; 12/1 for spring admission). Application fee: $50. *Tuition:* $335 per unit. • Dr. Mildred Murray-Ward, Head, 805-493-3420.

California Polytechnic State University, San Luis Obispo, Center for Teacher Education, Program in Reading, San Luis Obispo, CA 93407. Awards MA. Part-time programs available. In 1997, 6 degrees awarded. *Degree requirements:* Comprehensive exam required, thesis optional, foreign language not required. *Entrance requirements:* Minimum GPA of 3.0. Application deadline: 4/1 (priority date; rolling processing; 12/15 for spring admission). Application fee: $55. *Expenses:* Tuition $0 for state residents; $164 per unit for nonresidents. Fees $2102 per year full-time, $1632 per year part-time. *Financial aid:* Federal Work-Study, institutionally sponsored loans, and career-related internships or fieldwork available. • Howard Drucker, Coordinator, 805-756-1575.

California State University, Bakersfield, School of Education, Program in Reading Education, 9001 Stockdale Highway, Bakersfield, CA 93311-1099. Awards MA. Accredited by NCATE. *Degree requirements:* Thesis or alternative, culminating projects. *Application deadline:* rolling. *Application fee:* $55. *Expenses:* Tuition $0 for state residents; $246 per unit full-time, $164 per unit part-time for nonresidents. Fees $1584 per year full-time, $918 per year part-time. • Dr. Lon Kellenberger, Interim Dean, School of Education, 805-664-2219. Application contact: Dr. Dianne Turner, Graduate Coordinator, 805-664-2422. Fax: 805-664-2063.

California State University, Chico, College of Communication and Education, School of Education, Department of Professional Studies in Education, Chico, CA 95929-0722. Offerings include education (MA), with options in linguistically and culturally diverse learners, reading and language arts, special education. *Application deadline:* 4/1 (rolling processing). *Application fee:* $55. *Expenses:* Tuition $0 for state residents; $246 per unit for nonresidents. Fees $2108 per year full-time, $1442 per year part-time. • Dr. James Richmond, Chair, 530-898-5398.

California State University, Fresno, Division of Graduate Studies, School of Education and Human Development, Department of Literacy and Early Education, 5241 North Maple Avenue, Fresno, CA 93740. Offers program in education (MA), including early childhood education, reading/language arts. Accredited by NCATE. Part-time and evening/weekend programs available. Faculty: 6 full-time (4 women). Students: 12 full-time (11 women), 77 part-time (73 women); includes 24 minority (1 African American, 4 Asian Americans, 17 Hispanics, 2 Native Americans), 1 international. Average age 31. 18 applicants, 89% accepted. In 1997, 28 degrees awarded. *Degree requirements:* Thesis or alternative. *Average time to degree:* master's–3.5 years full-time. *Entrance requirements:* GRE General Test, TOEFL (minimum score 550), MAT, minimum GPA of 2.75. Application deadline: 4/1 (priority date; rolling processing; 11/1 for spring admission). Application fee: $55. Electronic applications accepted. *Expenses:* Tuition $0 for state residents; $246 per unit for nonresidents. Fees $1872 per year full-time, $1206 per year part-time. *Financial aid:* In 1997–98, 3 research awards, travel grants, scholarships totaling $2,065 were awarded; fellowships, research assistantships, Federal Work-Study, and career-related internships or fieldwork also available. Financial aid application deadline: 3/1; applicants required to submit FAFSA. *Faculty research:* Reading recovery, monitoring/tutoring programs. • Jacques Benninga, Chair, 209-278-0250. Fax: 209-278-0404.

California State University, Fullerton, School of Human Development and Community Service, Program in Reading, PO Box 34080, Fullerton, CA 92834-9480. Awards MS. Accredited by NCATE. Part-time programs available. Faculty: 8 part-time, 3 FTE. Students: 2 full-time (both women), 96 part-time (89 women); includes 24 minority (1 African American, 6 Asian Americans, 17 Hispanics). Average age 38. 48 applicants, 94% accepted. In 1997, 19 degrees awarded. *Degree requirements:* Comprehensive exam, project or thesis required, foreign language not required. *Entrance requirements:* Minimum GPA of 2.5. Application fee: $55. *Expenses:* Tuition $0 for state residents; $246 per unit for nonresidents. Fees $1947 per year full-time, $1281 per

Directory: Reading Education

California State University, Fullerton (continued)
year part-time. *Financial aid:* State grants, Federal Work-Study, institutionally sponsored loans, and career-related internships or fieldwork available. Aid available to part-time students. Financial aid application deadline: 3/1. *Faculty research:* Partnership programs for under-represented students. • Dr. Ashley Bishop, Coordinator, 714-278-3356.

California State University, Los Angeles, School of Education, Division of Curriculum and Instruction, Major in Reading, Los Angeles, CA 90032-8530. Awards MA. Accredited by NCATE. Part-time and evening/weekend programs available. Students: 20 full-time (all women), 63 part-time (57 women); includes 53 minority (4 African Americans, 15 Asian Americans, 34 Hispanics), 1 international. In 1997, 19 degrees awarded. *Degree requirements:* Comprehensive exam, project, or thesis required, foreign language not required. *Entrance requirements:* TOEFL (minimum score 550), minimum GPA of 2.75 in last 90 units, teaching certificate. Application deadline: 6/30 (rolling processing; 2/1 for spring admission). Application fee: $55. *Expenses:* Tuition $0 for state residents; $164 per unit for nonresidents. Fees $1763 per year full-time, $1097 per year part-time. *Financial aid:* 3 students received aid; Federal Work-Study available. Aid available to part-time students. Financial aid application deadline: 3/1. • Dr. Judith Washburn, Chair, Division of Curriculum and Instruction, 213-343-4350.

California State University, Sacramento, School of Education, Department of Teacher Education, Program in Reading Education, Sacramento, CA 95819-6048. Awards MA. Part-time programs available. *Degree requirements:* Thesis or alternative, writing proficiency exam. *Entrance requirements:* TOEFL (minimum score 550), minimum GPA of 3.0, teaching credentials. Application deadline: 4/15 (11/1 for spring admission). Application fee: $55. *Expenses:* Tuition $0 for state residents; $246 per unit for nonresidents. Fees $2012 per year full-time, $1346 per year part-time. *Financial aid:* Federal Work-Study and career-related internships or fieldwork available. Aid available to part-time students. Financial aid application deadline: 3/1. • Dr. Ed Arnsdorf, Chair, Department of Teacher Education, 916-278-6155. Application contact: Dr. Robert Edwards, Graduate Coordinator, 916-278-5559.

California State University, San Bernardino, Graduate Studies, School of Education, Program in Reading, San Bernardino, CA 92407-2397. Awards MA. Part-time and evening/weekend programs available. Faculty: 3 full-time (2 women), 1 (woman) part-time. Students: 86 full-time (58 women), 121 part-time (90 women); includes 55 minority (11 African Americans, 3 Asian Americans, 41 Hispanics), 6 international. 88 applicants, 98% accepted. In 1997, 169 degrees awarded. *Degree requirements:* Thesis or alternative required, foreign language not required. *Entrance requirements:* Minimum GPA of 3.0 in education. Application deadline: 8/31 (priority date). Application fee: $55. *Expenses:* Tuition $0 for state residents; $164 per unit for nonresidents. Fees $1922 per year full-time, $1256 per year part-time. *Financial aid:* Federal Work-Study and career-related internships or fieldwork available. Aid available to part-time students. • Todd Jennings, Chairman, 909-880-5655.

California State University, Stanislaus, School of Education, Department of Teacher Education, Program in Curriculum and Instruction, Concentration in Reading Education, Turlock, CA 95382. Awards MA Ed. Accredited by NCATE. Part-time programs available. Students: 3 (all women). In 1997, 3 degrees awarded. *Degree requirements:* Thesis required, foreign language not required. *Entrance requirements:* MAT. Application fee: $55. *Expenses:* Tuition $0 for state residents; $246 per unit for nonresidents. Fees $1779 per year full-time, $1113 per year part-time. *Financial aid:* Application deadline 3/2; applicants required to submit FAFSA. *Faculty research:* Metacognition, Sohema theory, computers and reading. • Dr. Janet Towell, Coordinator, 209-667-3357.

California University of Pennsylvania, School of Education, Department of Elementary Education, Reading Specialist and Reading Supervision Programs, 250 University Avenue, California, PA 15419-1394. Offering in reading specialist (M Ed). Accredited by NCATE. Part-time and evening/weekend programs available. Faculty: 5 part-time (2 women). Students: 13 full-time (12 women), 45 part-time (42 women). 26 applicants, 92% accepted. In 1997, 23 degrees awarded. *Degree requirements:* Comprehensive exam, practicum required, thesis optional, foreign language not required. *Entrance requirements:* MAT (minimum score 35), TOEFL (minimum score 600), minimum GPA of 3.0, teaching certificate. Application deadline: rolling. Application fee: $25. *Expenses:* Tuition $3468 per year full-time, $193 per credit part-time for state residents; $6236 per year full-time, $346 per credit part-time for nonresidents. Fees $886 per year full-time, $153 per semester (minimum) part-time. *Financial aid:* Graduate assistantships available. • Dr. Diane Nettles, Coordinator, 724-938-4135.

Calvin College, Graduate Programs in Education, Grand Rapids, MI 49546-4388. Offerings include reading (M Ed). Accredited by NCATE. M Ed (reading, school administration) admissions temporarily suspended. Faculty: 1 (woman) full-time, 15 part-time (6 women). *Degree requirements:* Thesis required, foreign language not required. *Entrance requirements:* GRE General Test, TOEFL, teaching certificate. Application deadline: 8/15 (priority date; rolling processing; 1/15 for spring admission). Application fee: $0. Electronic applications accepted. *Tuition:* $250 per semester hour. • Dr. Robert S. Fortner, Director of Graduate Studies, 616-957-8533. Fax: 616-957-8551. E-mail: forr@calvin.edu.

Canisius College, School of Education and Human Services, Program in Reading, Buffalo, NY 14208-1098. Awards MS Ed. Offered jointly with Medaille College. Part-time and evening/weekend programs available. Faculty: 2 full-time (1 woman), 5 part-time (4 women). Students: 11 full-time (9 women), 51 part-time (45 women). 42 applicants, 95% accepted. *Degree requirements:* Research project required, foreign language and thesis not required. *Entrance requirements:* GRE General Test, minimum GPA of 2.5. Application deadline: 8/15 (priority date; rolling processing). Application fee: $20. *Expenses:* Tuition $415 per credit hour. Fees $15 per credit hour. *Financial aid:* Graduate assistantships, Federal Work-Study, institutionally sponsored loans, and career-related internships or fieldwork available. Aid available to part-time students. • Dr. Sharon Kulhanek, Director, 716-888-2390. Application contact: Kevin Smith, Graduate Recruitment and Admissions, 716-888-2544. Fax: 716-888-3290.

Cardinal Stritch University, College of Education, Department of Reading/Language Arts, Milwaukee, WI 53217-3985. Awards MA. Accredited by NCATE. Students: 144. *Application deadline:* 4/1 (priority date; rolling processing). *Application fee:* $20. *Expenses:* Tuition $338 per credit. Fees $25 per semester. *Financial aid:* Federal Work-Study available. Financial aid applicants required to submit FAFSA. • Dr. JoAnne Caldwell, Chair, 414-410-4484. Application contact: Amy Knox, Graduate Admissions Officer, 414-410-4042.

Carthage College, Division of Teacher Education, Kenosha, WI 53140-1994. Offerings include reading (M Ed, Certificate). College faculty: 6 full-time (4 women), 13 part-time (8 women). *Degree requirements:* For master's, thesis optional, foreign language not required. *Average time to degree:* master's–5 years part-time. *Entrance requirements:* For master's, MAT, minimum B average. Application deadline: rolling. Application fee: $25. • Dr. Judith B. Schaumberg, Director of Graduate Programs, 414-551-5876. Fax: 414-551-5704.

Castleton State College, Department of Education, Program in Language Arts and Reading, Castleton, VT 05735. Awards MA Ed, CAGS. Part-time and evening/weekend programs available. Faculty: 9 full-time (5 women), 7 part-time (4 women). *Degree requirements:* For master's, thesis or written exams required, foreign language not required; for CAGS, written exams, publishable paper required, foreign language and thesis not required. *Entrance requirements:* For master's, GRE General Test (minimum combined score of 1000), MAT (minimum score 50), interview, minimum undergraduate GPA of 3.0; for CAGS, educational research, master's degree, minimum undergraduate GPA of 3.0. Application deadline: 7/1 (10/1 for spring admission). Application fee: $30. *Expenses:* Tuition $3924 per year full-time, $164 per credit part-time for state residents; $9192 per year full-time, $383 per credit part-time for nonresidents. Fees $902 per year full-time, $26 per credit part-time. *Financial aid:* Federal Work-Study and career-related internships or fieldwork available. • Application contact: Mary Frucelli, Graduate Assistant, 802-468-1441. Fax: 802-468-5237.

Central Connecticut State University, School of Education and Professional Studies, Department of Reading, New Britain, CT 06050-4010. Awards MS, Sixth Year Certificate. Part-time and evening/weekend programs available. Faculty: 6 full-time (4 women), 11 part-time (9 women), 9 FTE. Students: 6 full-time (all women), 162 part-time (158 women); includes 4 minority (1 African American, 1 Asian American, 2 Hispanics). Average age 33. 67 applicants, 87% accepted. In 1997, 40 master's, 3 Sixth Year Certificates awarded. *Degree requirements:* For master's, thesis or alternative, comprehensive exam required, foreign language not required; for Sixth Year Certificate, qualifying exam required, foreign language and thesis not required. *Entrance requirements:* For master's, TOEFL (minimum score 550), minimum GPA of 2.7. Application deadline: 6/1 (priority date; rolling processing; 12/1 for spring admission). Application fee: $40. *Expenses:* Tuition $4458 per year full-time, $175 per credit hour part-time for state residents; $9943 per year full-time, $175 per credit hour part-time for nonresidents. Fees $45 per semester. *Financial aid:* In 1997–98, 1 research assistantship (to a first-year student) was awarded; Federal Work-Study also available. Financial aid application deadline: 3/15; applicants required to submit FAFSA. *Faculty research:* Developmental, clinical, and administrative aspects of reading and language arts instruction. • Dr. Barry Davies, Chair, 860-832-2175.

Central Missouri State University, College of Education and Human Services, Department of Curriculum and Instruction, Warrensburg, MO 64093. Offerings include reading (MSE). Accredited by NCATE. Department faculty: 20 full-time. *Degree requirements:* Comprehensive exam or thesis. *Entrance requirements:* GRE General Test, minimum GPA of 2.75, teaching certificate. Application deadline: 6/30 (priority date; rolling processing). Application fee: $25 ($50 for international students). *Tuition:* $3288 per year full-time, $137 per credit hour part-time for state residents; $5928 per year full-time, $274 per credit hour part-time for nonresidents. • Dr. Ted Garten, Chair, 660-543-4235. Fax: 660-543-4167.

Central State University, Program in Education, Wilberforce, OH 45384. Offerings include literacy (M Ed). Program faculty: 3 full-time. *Tuition:* $120 per credit hour for state residents; $206 per credit hour for nonresidents. • Constance Robinson, Coordinator, 937-376-6536.

Central Washington University, College of Education and Professional Studies, Department of Teacher Education, Program in Reading Education, Ellensburg, WA 98926. Awards M Ed. Part-time programs available. Faculty: 21 full-time (10 women). Students: 1 (woman) full-time, 9 part-time (all women); includes 1 minority (Hispanic). 5 applicants, 100% accepted. In 1997, 8 degrees awarded. *Degree requirements:* Thesis or alternative required, foreign language not required. *Entrance requirements:* Minimum GPA of 3.0. Application deadline: 4/1 (priority date; rolling processing; 1/1 for spring admission). Application fee: $35. *Expenses:* Tuition $4200 per year full-time, $140 per credit hour part-time for state residents; $12,780 per year full-time, $426 per credit hour part-time for nonresidents. Fees $240 per year. *Financial aid:* Research assistantships, teaching assistantships, Federal Work-Study available. Financial aid application deadline: 2/15. • Application contact: Christie A. Fevergeon, Program Coordinator, Graduate Studies and Research, 509-963-3103. Fax: 509-963-1799. E-mail: masters@cwu.edu.

Chapman University, School of Education, Concentration in Reading Education, Orange, CA 92866. Awards MA. Faculty: 10 full-time (8 women). Students: 2. *Degree requirements:* Comprehensive exam required, thesis not required. *Entrance requirements:* GRE General Test (minimum combined score of 900), MAT (minimum score 45), or PRAXIS. Application deadline: rolling. Application fee: $40. *Tuition:* $7020 per year full-time, $390 per credit part-time. *Financial aid:* Application deadline 3/1. • Dr. Dolores Gaunty-Porter, Coordinator, 714-997-6781.

Chicago State University, College of Education, Department of Reading, Chicago, IL 60628. Offers program in teaching of reading (MS Ed). Accredited by NCATE. *Degree requirements:* Thesis required, foreign language not required. *Entrance requirements:* Minimum GPA of 2.75. Application deadline: 7/1 (11/10 for spring admission). *Tuition:* $2268 per year full-time, $95 per credit hour part-time for state residents; $6804 per year full-time, $284 per credit hour part-time for nonresidents.

Christopher Newport University, Graduate Studies, Department of Education, 1 University Place, Newport News, VA 23606-2998. Offerings include teaching language arts (MAT), with options in elementary language arts education, high school language arts education, middle school teaching. Department faculty: 25 full-time (12 women), 1 part-time (0 women). *Degree requirements:* Thesis or alternative, comprehensive exam required, foreign language not required. *Average time to degree:* master's–3.5 years part-time. *Entrance requirements:* GRE, minimum GPA of 3.0. Application deadline: 8/1 (priority date; rolling processing; 12/15 for spring admission). Application fee: $40. *Expenses:* Tuition $3474 per year full-time, $145 per credit hour part-time for state residents; $8424 per year full-time, $351 per credit hour part-time for nonresidents. Fees $40 per year. • Dr. Marsha Sprague, Coordinator, 757-594-7973. Fax: 757-594-7862. E-mail: msprague@cnu.edu. Application contact: Graduate Admissions, 800-333-4268. Fax: 757-594-7333. E-mail: admit@cnu.edu.

The Citadel, The Military College of South Carolina, Department of Education, Program in Reading, Charleston, SC 29409. Awards M Ed. Accredited by NCATE. Faculty: 1 full-time (0 women), 1 (woman) part-time. Students: 1 (woman) full-time, 14 part-time (all women); includes 2 minority (both African Americans). 0 applicants. In 1997, 14 degrees awarded. *Entrance requirements:* GRE, MAT, or 12 hours of graduate course work with a minimum GPA of 3.0. Application deadline: rolling. Application fee: $25. *Expenses:* Tuition $130 per credit hour for state residents; $260 per credit hour for nonresidents. Fees $30 per semester. • Dr. Robert Carter, Head, Department of Education, 803-953-5097.

City College of the City University of New York, Graduate School, School of Education, Department of Elementary Education, Programs in Reading, Convent Avenue at 138th Street, New York, NY 10031-6977. Awards MS, AC. Students: 2 full-time (both women), 52 part-time (5 women). In 1997, 21 master's awarded. *Degree requirements:* For master's, thesis required, foreign language not required. *Entrance requirements:* For master's, TOEFL (minimum score 500). Application fee: $40. *Expenses:* Tuition $4350 per year full-time, $185 per credit part-time for state residents; $7600 per year full-time, $320 per credit part-time for nonresidents. Fees $41 per year. *Financial aid:* Career-related internships or fieldwork available. • Oliver Patterson, Head, 212-650-6256.

City College of the City University of New York, Graduate School, College of Liberal Arts and Science, Division of the Humanities and Arts, Department of English, Program in Language and Literacy, Convent Avenue at 138th Street, New York, NY 10031-6977. Awards MA. Students: 3 full-time (all women), 17 part-time (12 women). In 1997, 10 degrees awarded. *Degree requirements:* 1 foreign language, thesis, comprehensive exam. *Entrance requirements:* TOEFL (minimum score 500), minimum GPA of 3.0. Application fee: $40. *Expenses:* Tuition $4350 per year full-time, $185 per credit part-time for state residents; $7600 per year full-time, $320 per credit part-time for nonresidents. Fees $41 per year. • Fred Reynolds, Graduate Adviser, 212-650-8095.

Claremont Graduate University, Department of Education, Claremont, CA 91711-6163. Offerings include reading and language development (MA, PhD). PhD offered jointly with San Diego State University; MA (mathematics education) offered jointly with the Department of Mathematics. Terminal master's awarded for partial completion of doctoral program. Department faculty: 13 full-time (6 women), 13 part-time (10 women). *Degree requirements:* For master's, thesis or alternative; for doctorate, dissertation. *Entrance requirements:* GRE General Test. Application deadline: 2/15 (priority date; rolling processing). Application fee: $40. Electronic applications accepted. *Expenses:* Tuition $20,250 per year full-time, $913 per unit part-time. Fees $130 per year. • David Drew, Chair, 909-621-8075. Application contact: Ethel Rogers, Associate Director, 909-621-8317. Fax: 909-621-8734. E-mail: educ@cgu.edu.

Clarion University of Pennsylvania, College of Education and Human Services, Department of Education, Program in Reading, Clarion, PA 16214. Awards M Ed. Accredited by NCATE. Part-time programs available. Students: 4 full-time (3 women), 23 part-time (22 women). 23 applicants, 57% accepted. In 1997, 14 degrees awarded. *Degree requirements:* Thesis or alternative required, foreign language not required. *Entrance requirements:* Minimum QPA of 2.75. Application deadline: 8/1 (priority date; rolling processing). Application fee: $25. *Expenses:* Tuition $3468 per year full-time, $193 per credit hour part-time for state residents; $6236 per year full-time, $346 per credit hour part-time for nonresidents. Fees $921 per year full-time, $90 per credit hour part-time for state residents; $921 per year full-time, $89 per credit hour part-time for nonresidents. *Financial aid:* In 1997–98, 3 research assistantships (2 to first-year students) averaging $533 per month were awarded. Aid available to part-time students. Financial aid application deadline: 5/1. • Application contact: Dr. Gail Grejda, Graduate Coordinator, 814-226-2058.

Clarke College, Program in Education, Dubuque, IA 52001-3198. Offerings include reading: elementary (MA). Accredited by NCATE. Program faculty: 8 part-time (4 women). *Degree requirements:* Comprehensive exam, minimum GPA of 3.25 required, thesis optional, foreign language not required. *Average time to degree:* master's–4 years part-time. *Entrance requirements:* GRE General Test or MAT, minimum GPA of 2.75. Application deadline: rolling. Application fee: $25. Electronic applications accepted. *Expenses:* Tuition $12,688 per year full-time, $315 per credit hour part-time. Fees $240 per year. • Dr. Margaret Feldner, Chair, 319-588-6397. E-mail: mfeldner@clarke.edu. Application contact: Admissions Office, 800-383-2345. Fax: 319-588-6789. E-mail: graduate@clarke.edu.

Clemson University, College of Health, Education, and Human Development, Department of Curriculum and Instruction, Program in Reading, Clemson, SC 29634. Awards M Ed. Accredited by NCATE. Students: 1 (woman) full-time, 31 part-time (30 women); includes 8 minority (7 African Americans, 1 Native American). 12 applicants, 83% accepted. In 1997, 9 degrees awarded. *Entrance requirements:* TOEFL, teaching certificate. Application deadline: 6/1. Application fee: $35. *Expenses:* Tuition $3154 per year full-time, $130 per credit hour part-time for state residents; $6452 per year full-time, $264 per credit hour part-time for nonresidents. Fees $190 per year. *Financial aid:* Application deadline 6/1. *Faculty research:* Literature, writing, reading recovery across the curriculum. • Dr. Robert Green, Chair, Department of Curriculum and Instruction, 864-656-5108. Fax: 864-656-1322. E-mail: rpgreen@clemson.edu.

Cleveland State University, College of Education, Department of Specialized Instructional Programs, Cleveland, OH 44115-2440. Offerings include curriculum and instruction (M Ed), with options in bilingual education, early childhood education, early childhood/special education, education of emerging adolescents, elementary education, English as a second language, learning disabilities, Montessori education, multihandicapped, reading, secondary education. Department faculty: 18 full-time (12 women). *Entrance requirements:* GRE General Test or MAT (score in 50th percentile or higher). Application deadline: 9/1 (priority date; rolling processing). Application fee: $25. *Expenses:* Tuition $5252 per year full-time, $202 per credit hour part-time for state residents; $10,504 per year full-time, $404 per credit hour part-time for nonresidents. Fees $2.25 per credit hour (minimum). • Dr. Jane Zaharias, Chairperson, 216-687-4585. Fax: 216-687-5379. E-mail: j.zaharias@csuohio.edu.

College of Mount St. Joseph, Education Department, Program in Reading, Cincinnati, OH 45233-1670. Awards MA Ed. Part-time and evening/weekend programs available. Faculty: 3 full-time, 3 part-time. *Degree requirements:* Comprehensive exam required, foreign language and thesis not required. *Entrance requirements:* GRE General Test (minimum combined score of 825), minimum GPA of 2.7. Application deadline: rolling. Application fee: $0. *Tuition:* $320 per credit hour. *Financial aid:* Application deadline 6/1. • Application contact: Jean Abrams, Graduate Secretary, 513-244-4812.

The College of New Jersey, Graduate Division, School of Education, Department of Language and Communication Sciences, Program in Developmental Reading, Ewing, NJ 08628. Awards M Ed. Accredited by NCATE. Students: 24 part-time (22 women); includes 2 minority (1 Hispanic, 1 Native American), 2 international. Average age 26. In 1997, 9 degrees awarded. *Degree requirements:* Comprehensive exam required, foreign language and thesis not required. *Entrance requirements:* GRE General Test, minimum GPA of 3.0 in field or 2.75 overall. Application deadline: 4/15 (10/15 for spring admission). Application fee: $50. *Expenses:* Tuition $6892 per year full-time, $287 per credit hour part-time for state residents; $9602 per year full-time, $402 per credit hour part-time for nonresidents. Fees $799 per year full-time, $33 per credit hour part-time. *Financial aid:* Application deadline 5/1. • Dr. Susan Blair-Larsen, Graduate Coordinator, 609-771-2217.

College of New Rochelle, Division of Education, Program in Reading/Adult Communication Skills, New Rochelle, NY 10805-2308. Awards MS Ed. Part-time and evening/weekend programs available. Faculty: 2 full-time (both women), 3 part-time (all women), 3 FTE. Students: 2 full-time (both women), 89 part-time (87 women); includes 7 minority (5 African Americans, 1 Asian American, 1 Hispanic). 14 applicants, 79% accepted. In 1997, 42 degrees awarded. *Degree requirements:* Practicum required, foreign language not required. *Average time to degree:* master's–1.5 years full-time, 3 years part-time. *Entrance requirements:* Interview; minimum GPA of 3.0 in field, 2.7 overall. Application deadline: 8/1 (priority date; rolling processing). Application fee: $35. *Tuition:* $329 per credit. *Financial aid:* In 1997–98, 8 students received aid, including 2 scholarships totaling $1,896; research assistantships also available. • Dr. Melanie Hannigan, Division Head, Division of Education, 914-654-5330.

College of Our Lady of the Elms, Department of Education, Chicopee, MA 01013-2839. Offerings include reading (MAT). Department faculty: 7 full-time (all women), 6 part-time (5 women). *Application deadline:* rolling. *Application fee:* $30. *Expenses:* Tuition $320 per credit. Fees $40 per year. • Sr. Kathleen M. Kirley, Dean of Continuing Education and Graduate Studies, 413-594-2761. Fax: 413-592-4871. Application contact: Dr. Mary Janeczek, Director, 413-594-2761.

College of St. Joseph, Division of Education, Program in Reading, Rutland, VT 05701-3899. Awards M Ed. Students: 1 (woman) full-time, 22 part-time (all women). *Degree requirements:* Comprehensive exams required, foreign language and thesis not required. *Entrance requirements:* GRE General Test (combined average 1100), interview. Application deadline: rolling. Application fee: $25. *Tuition:* $7950 per year full-time, $220 per credit part-time. *Financial aid:* Application deadline 3/1. • Application contact: Steve Soba, Director of Admissions, 802-773-5900 Ext. 206. Fax: 802-773-5900 Ext. 258. E-mail: suite9@aol.com.

The College of Saint Rose, School of Education, Reading/Special Education Department, Program in Reading, Albany, NY 12203-1419. Awards MS Ed. Part-time and evening/weekend programs available. Faculty: 3 full-time (all women), 3 part-time (2 women). Students: 7 full-time (6 women), 61 part-time (53 women); includes 3 minority (2 African Americans, 1 Asian American). Average age 31. In 1997, 26 degrees awarded. *Degree requirements:* Thesis or alternative, comprehensive exam required, foreign language not required. *Entrance requirements:* Minimum undergraduate GPA of 3.0. Application deadline: 7/15 (priority date; rolling processing; 12/1 for spring admission). Application fee: $30. *Expenses:* Tuition $338 per credit. Fees $60 per year. *Financial aid:* Research assistantships, partial tuition waivers, and career-related internships or fieldwork available. Aid available to part-time students. Financial aid application deadline: 3/1; applicants required to submit FAFSA. • Dr. Kathleen Lyon, Head, 518-454-5257. Application contact: Graduate Office, 518-454-5136. Fax: 518-458-5479. E-mail: ace@rosnet.strose.edu.

Columbus State University, College of Education, Department of Counseling and Clinical Programs, Columbus, GA 31907-5645. Offerings include reading (M Ed, Ed S). Accredited by NCATE. M Ed (reading), Ed S (special education) being phased out; applicants no longer accepted. *Degree requirements:* For Ed S, thesis or alternative required, foreign language not required. *Entrance requirements:* For Ed S, GRE General Test (minimum combined score of 900), MAT (minimum score 44). Application deadline: 7/10 (priority date; rolling processing; 10/23 for spring admission). Application fee: $20. *Tuition:* $1718 per year full-time, $151 per semester hour part-time for state residents; $6218 per year full-time, $401 per semester hour part-time for nonresidents. • Dr. Joyce Hickson, Chair, 706-568-2222. Fax: 706-569-3134. E-mail: hickson_joyce@colstate.edu. Application contact: Katie Thornton, Graduate Admissions, 706-568-2279. Fax: 706-568-2462. E-mail: thornton_katie@colstate.edu.

Concordia University, Program in Reading Instruction, River Forest, IL 60305-1499. Awards MA, CAS. Part-time and evening/weekend programs available. Faculty: 9 full-time (4 women), 8 part-time (4 women). Students: 18 (all women). In 1997, 9 master's awarded. *Degree requirements:* For master's, comprehensive exams required, thesis optional, foreign language not required; for CAS, thesis, final project required, foreign language not required. *Entrance requirements:* For master's, minimum GPA of 2.9; for CAS, master's degree. Application deadline: rolling. Application fee: $0. *Tuition:* $372 per semester hour. *Financial aid:* Research assistantships, institutionally sponsored loans available. Aid available to part-time students. *Faculty research:* Early literacy, classroom management and organization in reading, minority students and reading. • Dr. Timothy Krenzke, Coordinator, 708-209-3081. Application contact: Mary Betancourt, Admissions Secretary, 708-209-4093. Fax: 708-209-3454. E-mail: crfdngrad@curf.edu.

Concordia University, Graduate Programs in Education, Program in Reading Education, Seward, NE 68434-1599. Awards M Ed. Accredited by NCATE. Part-time programs available. Faculty: 8 full-time (3 women), 3 part-time (all women). Students: 1 (woman) full-time, 13 part-time (all women). 1 applicant, 100% accepted. *Degree requirements:* Thesis or alternative required, foreign language not required. *Entrance requirements:* 0RE, MAT, or NTE, minimum GPA of 3.0, BS in education or equivalent. Application deadline: 8/1 (priority date; rolling processing; 12/1 for spring admission). Application fee: $15. *Tuition:* $127 per hour. *Financial aid:* Federal Work-Study, institutionally sponsored loans available. Aid available to part-time students. Financial aid applicants required to submit FAFSA. • Dr. Priscilla Lawin, Coordinator, 402-643-7227.

Concordia University Wisconsin, Division of Graduate Studies, Education Department, Program in Reading, Mequon, WI 53097-2402. Awards MS Ed. Part-time and evening/weekend programs available. Postbaccalaureate distance learning degree programs offered (minimal on-campus study). *Degree requirements:* Thesis or alternative, comprehensive exam. *Entrance requirements:* TOEFL (minimum score 550), minimum GPA of 3.0, teaching license. *Tuition:* $250 per credit. *Financial aid:* Application deadline 8/1. • Dr. Marsha Konz, Director, 414-243-4253. E-mail: mkonz@bach.cuw.edu. Application contact: Brooke Tireman, Graduate Admissions, 414-243-4248. Fax: 414-243-4428. E-mail: btireman@back.cuw.edu.

Cumberland College, Reading Specialist Program, 6178 College Station Drive, Williamsburg, KY 40769-1372. Awards MA Ed. Evening/weekend programs available. Faculty: 4 full-time (2 women), 5 part-time (2 women). *Degree requirements:* Comprehensive exam required, foreign language and thesis not required. *Entrance requirements:* GRE or NTE, Kentucky teaching certificate. Application deadline: 8/26 (rolling processing). Application fee: $25. *Tuition:* $175 per credit. • Application contact: Erica Harris, Admissions Office, 606-539-4241.

Curry College, Graduate Program in Education, Milton, MA 02186-9984. Offerings include reading (M Ed, Certificate). Certificate (learning disabilities across the lifespan, adult education) new for fall 1998. College faculty: 10. *Degree requirements:* For master's, research project required, foreign language and thesis not required. *Application deadline:* 8/1 (priority date; 1/1 for spring admission). *Application fee:* $50. Electronic applications accepted. *Tuition:* $325 per credit. • Dr. Jane Utley Adelizzi, Director, 617-333-2130. Fax: 617-333-9722. E-mail: jutleyad@curry.edu.

Dallas Baptist University, Dorothy M. Bush College of Education, Education Program, Dallas, TX 75211-9299. Offerings include elementary reading education (M Ed), reading specialist (M Ed). Program faculty: 15 full-time (4 women), 5 part-time (3 women). *Entrance requirements:* GRE General Test, TOEFL (minimum score 550). Application deadline: rolling. Application fee: $25. *Tuition:* $285 per hour. • Dr. Bill Gilbert, Director, 214-333-5404. Fax: 214-333-5551. Application contact: Travis Bundrick, Director of Graduate Programs, 214-333-5243. Fax: 214-333-5579. E-mail: graduate@dbu.edu.

DePaul University, School of Education, Program in Reading and Learning Disabilities, Chicago, IL 60604-2287. Offers adolescent learning disabilities (MA, M Ed), bilingual multicultural learning disabilities (MA, M Ed), reading and learning disabilities (MA, M Ed). Accredited by NCATE. Faculty: 3 full-time (all women), 2 part-time (both women). Students: 34 full-time (32 women), 46 part-time (42 women); includes 13 minority (7 African Americans, 6 Hispanics), 1 international. Average age 29. 34 applicants, 85% accepted. In 1997, 19 degrees awarded. *Degree requirements:* Oral exam or thesis required, foreign language not required. *Entrance requirements:* Interview, minimum GPA of 2.75, work experience. Application deadline: rolling. Application fee: $25. *Expenses:* Tuition $320 per credit hour. Fees $30 per year. *Financial aid:* Teaching assistantships and career-related internships or fieldwork available. *Faculty research:* Reading specialist theory, behavior disorders. • Dr. Barbara Sizemore, Dean, School of Education, 312-325-7000 Ext. 1666. Fax: 312-325-7748. Application contact: Director of Graduate Admissions, 312-325-7000 Ext. 1666. E-mail: mmurphy@wppost.depaul.edu.

Dowling College, Program in Reading, Oakdale, NY 11769-1999. Awards MS Ed. Part-time and evening/weekend programs available. Faculty: 3 full-time (2 women), 5 part-time (all women). Students: 1 (woman) full-time, 264 part-time (241 women); includes 8 minority (1 African American, 1 Asian American, 5 Hispanics, 1 Native American). Average age 32. In 1997, 75 degrees awarded. *Degree requirements:* Comprehensive exam required, foreign language and thesis not required. *Entrance requirements:* Provisional teaching certificate. Application deadline: 9/1 (priority date; rolling processing). Application fee: $0. *Financial aid:* General graduate assistantships, Federal Work-Study, and career-related internships or fieldwork available. Aid available to part-time students. Financial aid application deadline: 4/30. • Dr. George Cauuto, Discipline Coordinator, 516-244-3308. Fax: 516-589-6644. Application contact: Kate Rowe, Director of Admissions, 516-244-3030. Fax: 516-563-3827. E-mail: rowek@dowling.edu.

Dowling College, Program in Reading/Special Education, Oakdale, NY 11769-1999. Awards MS Ed. Part-time and evening/weekend programs available. Students: 3 full-time (all women), 185 part-time (172 women); includes 17 minority (7 African Americans, 1 Asian American, 9 Hispanics). Average age 32. In 1997, 55 degrees awarded. *Degree requirements:* Comprehensive exam required, foreign language and thesis not required. *Entrance requirements:* Provisional teaching certificate. Application deadline: 9/1 (priority date; rolling processing). Application fee: $0. *Financial aid:* General graduate assistantships available. Financial aid application deadline: 4/30. • Application contact: Kate Rowe, Director of Admissions, 516-244-3030. Fax: 516-563-3827. E-mail: rowek@dowling.edu.

Duquesne University, School of Education, Department of Elementary, Secondary, and Reading Education, Program in Reading and Language Arts, Pittsburgh, PA 15282-0001. Awards MS Ed. Part-time programs available. Faculty: 2 full-time (0 women), 3 part-time (2 women). Students: 80. 30 applicants, 63% accepted. In 1997, 30 degrees awarded. *Average time to degree:* master's–1.5 years full-time, 2.5 years part-time. *Entrance requirements:* MAT. Application deadline: 8/1 (rolling processing; 12/1 for spring admission). Application fee: $40. *Expenses:* Tuition $481 per credit. Fees $39 per credit. • Application contact: Dr. Joseph T. Brennan, Coordinator, 412-396-6089. Fax: 412-396-5585.

East Carolina University, School of Education, Department of Elementary Education, Greenville, NC 27858-4353. Offerings include reading education (MA Ed). Accredited by NCATE. Department faculty: 8 full-time (5 women). *Degree requirements:* Comprehensive exams required, thesis optional. *Entrance requirements:* GRE General Test or MAT, TOEFL. Application deadline: 6/1 (priority date; rolling processing). Application fee: $40. *Tuition:* $1886 per year full-time, $472 per semester (minimum) part-time for state residents; $9156 per year full-time, $2289 per semester (minimum) part-time for nonresidents. • Dr. Parmalee Hawk, Acting Chair, 252-328-6271. Fax: 252-328-4219. E-mail: hawkp@mail.ecu.edu.

Directory: Reading Education

Eastern Connecticut State University, School of Education and Professional Studies/ Graduate Division, Program in Reading and Language Arts, Willimantic, CT 06226-2295. Awards MS. Faculty: 2 full-time (1 woman), 1 (woman) part-time. Students: 41 part-time (all women). Average age 34. 25 applicants, 100% accepted. In 1997, 19 degrees awarded. *Degree requirements:* Comprehensive exam or thesis required, foreign language not required. *Entrance requirements:* Minimum GPA of 2.7, teaching certificate. Application fee: $40. *Expenses:* Tuition $2632 per year full-time, $175 per credit hour part-time for state residents; $7220 per year full-time, $175 per credit hour part-time for nonresidents. Fees $1851 per year full-time, $20 per semester part-time for state residents; $2748 per year full-time, $20 per semester part-time for nonresidents. *Financial aid:* Career-related internships or fieldwork available. Aid available to part-time students. Financial aid application deadline: 3/15. • Dr. Shirley Ernst, Adviser, 860-465-4533. Application contact: Edith Mavor, Graduate Division Director, 860-465-4543. E-mail: mavor@ecsuc.ctstateu.edu.

Eastern Kentucky University, College of Education, Department of Curriculum and Instruction, Program in Secondary and Higher Education, Richmond, KY 40475-3101. Offerings include reading (MA Ed). Accredited by NCATE. *Entrance requirements:* GRE General Test, minimum GPA of 2.5. Application fee: $0. *Tuition:* $2390 per year full-time, $133 per credit hour part-time for state residents; $6630 per year full-time, $365 per credit hour part-time for nonresidents. • Dr. Imogene Ramsey, Chair, Department of Curriculum and Instruction, 606-622-2154.

Eastern Michigan University, College of Education, Department of Teacher Education, Program in Reading, Ypsilanti, MI 48197. Awards MA. Accredited by NCATE. Evening/weekend programs available. In 1997, 55 degrees awarded. *Entrance requirements:* GRE, TOEFL (minimum score 500). Application deadline: 5/15 (rolling processing; 3/15 for spring admission). Application fee: $30. *Expenses:* Tuition $2691 per year full-time, $150 per credit hour part-time for state residents; $6300 per year full-time, $350 per credit hour part-time for nonresidents. Fees $368 per year full-time, $88 per semester (minimum) part-time. *Financial aid:* Fellowships, teaching assistantships available. Aid available to part-time students. Financial aid application deadline: 3/15; applicants required to submit FAFSA. • Dr. Jane Gordon, Coordinator, 734-487-3185.

Eastern Nazarene College, Graduate Studies, Division of Education, Quincy, MA 02170-2999. Offerings include teacher of reading (M Ed, Certificate). M Ed and Certificate also available through weekend program for administration, special needs, and reading only. Division faculty: 9 full-time (5 women), 11 part-time (5 women). *Entrance requirements:* For master's, TOEFL (minimum score 500). Application deadline: rolling. Application fee: $35. *Expenses:* Tuition $350 per credit. Fees $125 per semester full-time, $15 per semester part-time. • Dr. Lorne Ranstrom, Chair, 617-745-3528. Application contact: Cleo P. Cakridas, Graduate Enrollment Counselor, 617-745-3870. Fax: 617-745-3907. E-mail: cakridac@enc.edu.

Eastern Washington University, College of Education and Human Development, Department of Education, Program in Literacy Specialist, Cheney, WA 99004-2431. Awards M Ed. Accredited by NCATE. *Degree requirements:* Comprehensive exam required, thesis not required. *Entrance requirements:* Minimum GPA of 3.0. Application deadline: 4/1 (priority date; rolling processing; 1/15 for spring admission). Application fee: $35. *Tuition:* $4200 per year full-time, $140 per credit part-time for state residents; $12,780 per year full-time, $415 per credit part-time for nonresidents. *Financial aid:* Application deadline 2/1. • Dr. Marcia Grace, Adviser, 509-359-7045.

East Stroudsburg University of Pennsylvania, School of Professional Studies, Department of Reading, East Stroudsburg, PA 18301-2999. Awards M Ed. Part-time and evening/weekend programs available. *Degree requirements:* Comprehensive exam required, foreign language and thesis not required. *Application deadline:* 7/31 (priority date; rolling processing; 11/30 for spring admission). *Application fee:* $15 ($25 for international students). *Expenses:* Tuition $3468 per year full-time, $193 per credit part-time for state residents; $6236 per year full-time, $346 per credit part-time for nonresidents. Fees $700 per year full-time, $39 per credit part-time. *Faculty research:* Portfolio assessment, reading assessment.

East Tennessee State University, College of Education, Department of Curriculum and Instruction, Johnson City, TN 37614-0734. Offerings include reading (MA, M Ed), story arts (MA, M Ed). One or more programs accredited by NCATE. Department faculty: 17 full-time (8 women). *Application deadline:* 7/15 (priority date; rolling processing; 12/1 for spring admission). *Application fee:* $25 ($35 for international students). *Tuition:* $2944 per year full-time, $158 per credit hour part-time for state residents; $7770 per year full-time, $369 per credit hour part-time for nonresidents. • Dr. Jack Rhoton, Chair, 423-439-4426. Fax: 423-439-8362.

Edinboro University of Pennsylvania, School of Education, Department of Elementary Education, Program in Reading, Edinboro, PA 16444. Awards M Ed, Certificate. Evening/ weekend programs available. Faculty: 16 full-time (10 women). Students: 10 full-time (9 women), 39 part-time (35 women). Average age 32. In 1997, 10 master's, 2 Certificates awarded. *Degree requirements:* For master's, thesis or alternative required, foreign language not required. *Entrance requirements:* For master's, GRE or MAT (score in 30th percentile or higher). Application deadline: rolling. Application fee: $25. *Expenses:* Tuition $3468 per year full-time, $193 per credit part-time for state residents; $6236 per year full-time, $346 per credit part-time for nonresidents. Fees $898 per year full-time, $50 per semester (minimum) part-time. *Financial aid:* In 1997–98, 7 assistantships were awarded; career-related internships or fieldwork also available. • Dr. Rosemary Treloar, Head, 814-732-2951. E-mail: rtreloar@edinboro.edu. Application contact: Dr. Philip Kerstetter, Dean of Graduate Studies, 814-732-2856. Fax: 814-732-2611. E-mail: kerstetter@edinboro.edu.

Elmira College, Graduate Programs in Education, Program in Reading, Elmira, NY 14901. Awards MS Ed. Part-time and evening/weekend programs available. Faculty: 3 full-time (all women), 12 part-time (5 women). Students: 35. *Degree requirements:* Thesis or alternative required, foreign language not required. *Application fee:* $35. *Tuition:* $344 per credit hour. *Financial aid:* Career-related internships or fieldwork available. Aid available to part-time students. • Dr. Linda Pratt, Director of Graduate and Reading Programs, 607-735-1912. Application contact: Judith B. Clack, Dean for Graduate Studies, 607-735-1825.

Emporia State University, School of Graduate Studies, The Teachers College, Division of Early Childhood/Elementary Teacher Education, Program in Curriculum and Instruction, Emporia, KS 66801-5087. Offerings include reading, elementary/secondary (MS). Accredited by NCATE. *Degree requirements:* Comprehensive exam or thesis required, foreign language not required. *Entrance requirements:* GRE General Test or MAT, TOEFL (minimum score 550), written exam. Application deadline: 8/15 (priority date; rolling processing). Application fee: $30 ($75 for international students). Electronic applications accepted. *Tuition:* $2300 per year full-time, $103 per credit hour part-time for state residents; $6012 per year full-time, $258 per credit hour part-time for nonresidents. • Dr. Eileen Hogan, Chair, Division of Early Childhood/ Elementary Teacher Education, 316-341-5751. E-mail: hoganeil@emporia.edu.

Endicott College, School of Continuing Education and Graduate Studies, Program in Reading and Literacy, Beverly, MA 01915-2096. Awards M Ed. Part-time and evening/weekend programs available. Postbaccalaureate distance learning degree programs offered (minimal on-campus study). Faculty: 7 part-time (5 women). Students: 14 full-time (all women). Average age 35. 6 applicants, 100% accepted. *Degree requirements:* Written comprehensive exams required, foreign language and thesis not required. *Entrance requirements:* MAT (minimum score 50). Application deadline: rolling. Application fee: $50. Electronic applications accepted. *Tuition:* $585 per course. *Financial aid:* Federal Work-Study, institutionally sponsored loans, and career-related internships or fieldwork available. • Dr. Paul J. Tortolani, Dean, School of Continuing Education and Graduate Studies, 978-232-2199. Fax: 978-232-3000. E-mail: ptortola@endicott.edu.

Florida Atlantic University, College of Education, Department of Teacher Education, Program in Reading Education, Boca Raton, FL 33431-0991. Awards M Ed. Accredited by NCATE. Admissions temporarily suspended. Faculty: 3 full-time (2 women). Students: 0. In 1997, 1 degree awarded. *Expenses:* Tuition $2520 per year full-time, $140 per credit hour part-time for state residents; $8712 per year full-time, $484 per credit hour part-time for nonresidents. Fees $5 per year (minimum). • Dr. Peter Messmore, Coordinator, 561-367-3588.

Florida International University, College of Education, Department of Elementary Education, Program in Reading Education, Miami, FL 33199. Awards MS. Accredited by NCATE. Part-time and evening/weekend programs available. Students: 2 full-time (both women), 53 part-time (all women); includes 40 minority (4 African Americans, 1 Asian American, 35 Hispanics). Average age 28. 30 applicants, 43% accepted. In 1997, 44 degrees awarded. *Degree requirements:* Thesis optional, foreign language not required. *Entrance requirements:* GRE General Test (minimum combined score of 1000) or minimum GPA of 3.25. Application deadline: 4/1 (priority date; rolling processing; 10/1 for spring admission). Application fee: $20. *Expenses:* Tuition $138 per credit hour for state residents; $482 per credit hour for nonresidents. Fees $46 per semester. *Faculty research:* Understanding reading comprehension, improving reading instruction, racial issues in reading and learning. • Dr. George O'Brien, Chairperson, Department of Elementary Education, 305-348-2561. E-mail: obrieng@fiu.edu.

Florida State University, College of Education, Department of Educational Theory and Practice, Program in Reading Education/Language Arts, Tallahassee, FL 32306. Awards MS, Ed D, PhD, Ed S. Part-time programs available. Faculty: 5 full-time (4 women). Students: 8 full-time (7 women), 15 part-time (14 women); includes 6 minority (5 African Americans, 1 Hispanic). 12 applicants, 75% accepted. In 1997, 5 master's, 2 doctorates awarded. *Degree requirements:* For master's and Ed S, comprehensive exams required, thesis optional; for doctorate, dissertation, comprehensive exams. *Entrance requirements:* GRE General Test (minimum combined score of 1000), minimum GPA of 3.0. Application deadline: 7/1 (priority date; rolling processing; 11/1 for spring admission). Application fee: $20. *Tuition:* $139 per credit hour for state residents; $482 per credit hour for nonresidents. *Financial aid:* Fellowships, research assistantships, teaching assistantships, and career-related internships or fieldwork available. • Dr. Charles Wolfgang, Chair, Department of Educational Theory and Practice, 850-644-5458. E-mail: wolfgang@mail.coe.fsu.edu. Application contact: Admissions Secretary, 850-644-5458. Fax: 850-644-7736.

Fordham University, Graduate School of Education, Division of Curriculum and Teaching, New York, NY 10023. Offerings include reading education (MSE, Adv C). Accredited by NCATE. *Degree requirements:* For Adv C, thesis required, foreign language not required. *Application fee:* $50. • Dr. Angela Carrasquillo, Chairperson, 212-636-6427.

Framingham State College, Graduate Programs, Department of Education, Program in Literacy and Language, Framingham, MA 01701-9101. Awards M Ed. Part-time and evening/ weekend programs available. Faculty: 3 part-time. Students: 53 part-time. In 1997, 5 degrees awarded. *Entrance requirements:* MAT. *Tuition:* $4184 per year full-time, $523 per course part-time for state residents; $4848 per year full-time, $606 per course part-time for nonresidents. • Diane Lowe, Director, 508-620-1441. Application contact: Graduate Office, 508-626-4550.

Fresno Pacific University, Graduate School, Programs in Education, Division of Language, Literacy, and Culture, Program in Language Development, Fresno, CA 93702-4709. Awards MA Ed. Faculty: 4 full-time (3 women), 6 part-time (4 women). Students: 6 full-time (5 women), 54 part-time (46 women). *Degree requirements:* Thesis or alternative. *Application deadline:* 7/31. *Application fee:* $75. *Tuition:* $250 per unit. • Dr. David Freeman, Director, 209-453-2201. Fax: 209-453-2001.

Fresno Pacific University, Graduate School, Programs in Education, Division of Language, Literacy, and Culture, Program in Reading, Fresno, CA 93702-4709. Offers reading/English as a second language (MA Ed), reading/language arts (MA Ed). Faculty: 4 full-time (3 women), 6 part-time (4 women). Students: 57 part-time (50 women). *Degree requirements:* Thesis or alternative. *Application deadline:* 7/31. *Application fee:* $75. *Tuition:* $250 per unit. • Jean Fennacy, Head, Division of Language, Literacy, and Culture, 209-453-2203. Fax: 209-453-2001.

Frostburg State University, School of Education, Department of Educational Professions, Program in Reading, Frostburg, MD 21532-1099. Awards M Ed. *Application deadline:* 7/15 (rolling processing). *Application fee:* $30.

Furman University, Department of Education, Greenville, SC 29613. Offerings include reading (MA Ed). *Degree requirements:* Comprehensive written exam. *Application deadline:* rolling. *Application fee:* $25. *Tuition:* $185 per credit hour. • Dr. Hazel W. Harris, Director, 864-294-2213.

Gannon University, School of Graduate Studies, College of Humanities, Business, and Education, School of Education, Program in Reading, Erie, PA 16541. Awards M Ed, Certificate. Part-time and evening/weekend programs available. Students: 1 part-time (0 women). Average age 44. 3 applicants, 100% accepted. *Degree requirements:* For master's, thesis, comprehensive exam. *Entrance requirements:* For master's, GRE General Test or MAT, NTE (reading), interview, teaching certificate. Application deadline: rolling. Application fee: $25. *Expenses:* Tuition $405 per credit. Fees $200 per year full-time, $8 per credit part-time. *Financial aid:* Application deadline 3/1; applicants required to submit FAFSA. • Roberta Barilla, Director, 814-871-5451. Application contact: Beth Nemenz, Director of Admissions, 814-871-7240. Fax: 814-871-5803. E-mail: admissions@gannon.edu.

George Mason University, Graduate School of Education, Program in Reading, Fairfax, VA 22030-4444. Awards M Ed. Accredited by NCATE. Part-time and evening/weekend programs available. Faculty: 42 full-time (24 women), 65 part-time (51 women), 58.73 FTE. Students: 1 (woman) full-time, 15 part-time (all women). Average age 31. 12 applicants, 92% accepted. In 1997, 10 degrees awarded. *Degree requirements:* Computer language required, foreign language not required. *Entrance requirements:* NTE, minimum GPA of 3.0 in last 60 hours. Application deadline: 5/1 (11/1 for spring admission). Application fee: $30. Electronic applications accepted. *Tuition:* $4344 per year full-time, $181 per credit hour part-time for state residents; $12,504 per year full-time, $521 per credit hour part-time for nonresidents. *Financial aid:* Career-related internships or fieldwork available. Aid available to part-time students. Financial aid application deadline: 3/1; applicants required to submit FAFSA. • Dr. Mary Ann Dzama, Coordinator, 703-993-4648. Fax: 703-993-2013.

Georgian Court College, Program in Education, Lakewood, NJ 08701-2697. Offerings include reading specialization (MA). *Application deadline:* 8/25 (rolling processing; 1/15 for spring admission). *Application fee:* $30. *Tuition:* $350 per credit. • Application contact: Renee Loew, Director of Graduate Admissions and Records, 732-367-1717. Fax: 732-364-4516.

Georgia Southern University, College of Education, Department of Early Childhood Education and Reading, Program in Reading Specialist, Statesboro, GA 30460-8126. Awards M Ed, Ed S. Accredited by NCATE. Part-time and evening/weekend programs available. Students: 6 full-time (all women), 10 part-time (all women). Average age 36. 6 applicants, 50% accepted. In 1997, 3 master's, 5 Ed Ss awarded. *Degree requirements:* For master's, comprehensive written exams required, foreign language and thesis not required; for Ed S, oral exams required, foreign language and thesis not required. *Entrance requirements:* For master's, GRE General Test (minimum score 450 on each section) or MAT (minimum score 44), minimum GPA of 2.5; for Ed S, GRE General Test (minimum score 450 on each section) or MAT (minimum score 49), minimum graduate GPA of 3.25. Application deadline: 7/15 (priority date; rolling processing; 11/15 for spring admission). Application fee: $0. Electronic applications accepted. *Tuition:* $2619 per year full-time, $287 per semester (minimum) part-time for state residents; $8619 per year full-time, $1037 per semester (minimum) part-time for nonresidents. *Financial aid:* Research assistantships, Federal Work-Study, and career-related internships or fieldwork available. Aid available to part-time students. Financial aid application deadline: 4/15.

Faculty research: Multiculturalism, bibliotherapy, technology, strategies for literacy development, application of reading skills in content areas. • Application contact: Dr. John R. Diebolt, Associate Graduate Dean, 912-681-5384. Fax: 912-681-0740. E-mail: gradschool@gsvms2.cc.gasou.edu.

Georgia Southwestern State University, School of Education, Americus, GA 31709-4693. Offerings include reading (M Ed). Accredited by NCATE. *Entrance requirements:* GRE General Test (minimum score 400 on each section) or MAT (minimum score 44), minimum GPA of 2.5. Application deadline: 9/1 (rolling processing; 3/15 for spring admission). Application fee: $10. • Dr. Kurt Myers, Chair, 912-931-2145. Application contact: Chris Laney, Graduate Admissions Specialist, 912-931-2027. Fax: 912-931-2059. E-mail: claney@gsw1500.gsw.peachnet.edu.

Georgia State University, College of Education, Department of Middle, Secondary Education and Instructional Technology, Program in Reading Instruction, Atlanta, GA 30303-3083. Awards M Ed, Ed S. Accredited by NCATE. Part-time and evening/weekend programs available. Students: 17 full-time (16 women), 29 part-time (all women); includes 6 minority (all African Americans). Average age 35. 17 applicants, 100% accepted. In 1997, 15 master's, 2 Ed Ss awarded. *Degree requirements:* For master's, comprehensive exams; for Ed S, project/exam. *Entrance requirements:* For master's, GRE General Test (minimum combined score of 800) or MAT (minimum score 44), minimum GPA of 2.5; for Ed S, GRE General Test (minimum combined score of 900) or MAT (minimum score 48), minimum graduate GPA of 3.25. Application deadline: 7/15 (1/15 for spring admission). Application fee: $25. *Expenses:* Tuition $2673 per year full-time, $99 per semester hour part-time for state residents; $10,692 per year full-time, $396 per semester hour part-time for nonresidents. Fees $228 per year. *Financial aid:* Federal Work-Study, institutionally sponsored loans, and career-related internships or fieldwork available. *Faculty research:* Language development, attribution theory, linguistics. • Dr. Beverly J. Armento, Chair, Department of Middle, Secondary Education and Instructional Technology, 404-651-2510.

Grand Canyon University, College of Education, Phoenix, AZ 85017-3030. Offerings include reading education (MA). College faculty: 8 full-time (5 women), 2 part-time (1 woman). *Application deadline:* rolling. *Application fee:* $25. • Dr. Betz Fredrick, Director, 602-589-2472.

Grand Valley State University, School of Education, Program in Reading Education, Allendale, MI 49401-9403. Offers reading/language arts (M Ed). Accredited by NCATE. Part-time and evening/weekend programs available. Faculty: 4 full-time (2 women), 2 part-time (both women). Students: 1 (woman) full-time, 55 part-time (53 women); includes 2 minority (1 Hispanic, 1 Native American), 1 international. Average age 34. 45 applicants, 98% accepted. In 1997, 28 degrees awarded (100% found work related to degree). *Degree requirements:* Thesis or alternative, applied research project. *Entrance requirements:* GRE General Test (minimum combined score of 1300) or minimum GPA of 3.0. Application deadline: rolling. Application fee: $20. *Financial aid:* Research assistantships, Federal Work-Study, and career-related internships or fieldwork available. *Faculty research:* Diagnostic reading, elementary methods, multilingual reading methods, adult literacy, gender. • Dr. Donald Pottorff, Coordinator, 616-771-6650. Application contact: Admissions Office, 616-895-2025. Fax: 616-895-3081.

Gwynedd–Mercy College, Graduate Education Programs, Gwynedd Valley, PA 19437-0901. Offerings include reading (MS). Faculty: 4 full-time (all women), 11 part-time (7 women). *Degree requirements:* Thesis, internship, practicum required, foreign language not required. *Average time to degree:* master's–3 years part-time. *Entrance requirements:* GRE or MAT. Application deadline: rolling. Application fee: $25. *Expenses:* Tuition $299 per credit. Fees $50 per year. • Dr. Lorraine Cavaliere, Dean, 215-641-5549. Application contact: Maureen Coyle, Program Administrator, 215-641-5561. Fax: 215-542-4695.

Hardin–Simmons University, Irvin School of Education, Department of Elementary and Secondary Education, Reading Specialist Program, Abilene, TX 79698-0001. Awards M Ed. Part-time programs available. Faculty: 3 full-time (all women). Students: 7 part-time (all women). Average age 42. In 1997, 1 degree awarded. *Degree requirements:* Project required, foreign language and thesis not required. *Application deadline:* 8/15 (priority date; rolling processing; 1/5 for spring admission). *Application fee:* $25. *Expenses:* Tuition $280 per semester hour. Fees $630 per year full-time. *Financial aid:* In 1997–98, 2 fellowships averaging $188 per month and totaling $1,500 were awarded; full and partial tuition waivers, Federal Work-Study, and career-related internships or fieldwork also available. Aid available to part-time students. Financial aid application deadline: 3/15; applicants required to submit FAFSA. *Faculty research:* Metacognition, questioning strategies, meaning construction. • Application contact: Dr. J. Paul Sorrels, Dean of Graduate Studies, 915-670-1298. Fax: 915-670-1564.

Harvard University, Graduate School of Education, Area of Human Development and Psychology, Cambridge, MA 02138. Offerings include language and literacy (Ed M, Ed D, CAS). Terminal master's awarded for partial completion of doctoral program. Faculty: 13 full-time (7 women), 33 part-time (12 women), 22.9 FTE. *Degree requirements:* For doctorate, dissertation required, foreign language not required. *Average time to degree:* master's–1.1 years full-time, 2 years part-time; doctorate–6 years full-time, 7.8 years part-time; other advanced degree–1 year full-time, 3 years part-time. *Entrance requirements:* GRE General Test, TOEFL (minimum score 600), TWE (minimum score 5.0). Application deadline: 1/2. Application fee: $60. • Catherine Snow, Chair, 617-495-3563. Application contact: Roland Hence, Director of Admissions, 617-495-3414. Fax: 617-496-3577. E-mail: gseadmissions@harvard.edu.

Hofstra University, School of Education and Allied Human Services, Department of Reading, Hempstead, NY 11549. Awards MA, MS Ed, Ed D, PhD, CAS, PD. Accredited by NCATE. Evening/weekend programs available. Faculty: 5 full-time (4 women), 7 part-time (4 women). Students: 1 (woman) full-time, 143 part-time (136 women); includes 8 minority (3 African Americans, 2 Asian Americans, 3 Hispanics), 1 international. Average age 33. 85 applicants, 41% accepted. In 1997, 33 master's awarded. Terminal master's awarded for partial completion of doctoral program. *Degree requirements:* For master's, departmental qualifying exam required, thesis not required; for doctorate, dissertation, comprehensive exam. *Entrance requirements:* For master's, MAT, NTE, interview; for doctorate, GRE General Test, MAT, interview; for other advanced degree, GRE General Test, MAT, minimum GPA of 2.9. Application deadline: rolling. Application fee: $40 ($75 for international students). *Expenses:* Tuition $10,968 per year full-time, $457 per credit hour part-time. Fees $670 per year full-time, $112 per semester (minimum) part-time. *Financial aid:* Fellowships, teaching assistantships, and career-related internships or fieldwork available. Aid available to part-time students. Financial aid applicants required to submit FAFSA. *Faculty research:* Psycholinguistics, comprehension and cognition. Total annual research expenditures: $10,460. • Dr. Charol Shakeshaft, Chairperson, 516-463-5372. E-mail: edacss@hofstra.edu. Application contact: Mary Beth Carey, Dean of Admissions, 516-463-6700. Fax: 516-560-7660. E-mail: hofstra@hofstra.edu.

Holy Family College, Graduate Studies, Program in Education, Philadelphia, PA 19114-2094. Offerings include reading specialist (M Ed). Program faculty: 11 full-time (6 women), 22 part-time (10 women), 16.5 FTE. *Average time to degree:* master's–3.5 years part-time. *Entrance requirements:* GRE or MAT, interview. Application deadline: 4/30 (priority date; rolling processing; 11/15 for spring admission). Application fee: $25. *Expenses:* Tuition $320 per credit hour. Fees $65 per semester. • Leonard Soroka, Chair, 215-637-7700 Ext. 3565. Fax: 215-824-2438. Application contact: Joseph Canaday, Graduate Coordinator, 215-637-7203. Fax: 215-637-1478. E-mail: jcanaday@hfc.edu.

Hood College, Department of Education, Frederick, MD 21701-8575. Offerings include curriculum and instruction (MS), with options in early childhood education, elementary education, elementary school science and mathematics, reading, secondary education, special education. *Entrance requirements:* Minimum GPA of 2.5. Application deadline: rolling. Application fee: $30. *Tuition:* $285 per credit. • Dr. Patricia Bartlett, Chairperson, 301-696-3471. E-mail: bartlett@nimue.hood.edu. Application contact: Hood College Graduate School, 301-696-3600. Fax: 301-696-3597. E-mail: postmaster@nimue.hood.edu.

Houston Baptist University, College of Education and Behavioral Sciences, Programs in Education, Houston, TX 77074-3298. Offerings include reading education (M Ed). Faculty: 9 full-time (5 women), 4 part-time (3 women). *Degree requirements:* Comprehensive exam required, foreign language and thesis not required. *Entrance requirements:* GRE General Test (minimum combined score of 850), minimum GPA of 2.5, teaching certificate. Application deadline: 7/1 (priority date; rolling processing; 1/1 for spring admission). Application fee: $25 ($85 for international students). *Expenses:* Tuition $280 per semester hour. Fees $235 per quarter. • Dr. John Lutjemeier, Head, 281-649-3000 Ext. 2336. Application contact: Judy Ferguson, Program Assistant, 281-649-3241.

Howard University, School of Education, Department of Curriculum and Instruction, Program in Reading, 2400 Sixth Street, NW, Washington, DC 20059-0002. Awards MA, MAT, M Ed, CAGS. Accredited by NCATE. MA offered through the Graduate School of Arts and Sciences. Part-time programs available. Faculty: 1 (woman) full-time, 1 (woman) part-time. Students: 6. *Degree requirements:* For master's, thesis (for some programs), comprehensive exam, expository writing exam, internships, practicum required, foreign language not required; for CAGS, thesis or alternative required, foreign language not required. *Entrance requirements:* For master's, GRE General Test, minimum GPA of 2.7; for CAGS, GRE General Test. Application deadline: 4/1 (priority date; rolling processing; 11/1 for spring admission). Application fee: $45. *Expenses:* Tuition $10,200 per year full-time, $567 per credit hour part-time. Fees $405 per year. *Financial aid:* Fellowships, research assistantships, teaching assistantships, grants, scholarships, full and partial tuition waivers, Federal Work-Study, institutionally sponsored loans, and career-related internships or fieldwork available. Financial aid application deadline: 4/1. • Dr. Dolores P. Dickerson, Coordinator, 202-806-7348. Fax: 202-806-7018. E-mail: dpdickerson@fac.howard.edu.

Hunter College of the City University of New York, Division of Education, Department of Curriculum and Teaching, 695 Park Avenue, New York, NY 10021-5085. Offerings include corrective reading (K–12) (MS Ed). *Application deadline:* /1 (rolling processing). *Application fee:* $40. *Expenses:* Tuition $4350 per year full-time, $185 per credit part-time for state residents; $7600 per year full-time, $320 per credit part-time for nonresidents. Fees $26 per year.

Idaho State University, College of Education, Division I, Pocatello, ID 83209. Offerings include literacy (M Ed). Accredited by NCATE. Postbaccalaureate distance learning degree programs offered (no on-campus study). Division faculty: 19 full-time (8 women), 4 part-time (0 women). *Degree requirements:* Oral exam, written exam required, thesis optional, foreign language not required. *Average time to degree:* master's–2 years full-time, 4 years part-time; other advanced degree–1 year full-time, 2 years part-time. *Entrance requirements:* GRE General Test (score in 35th percentile or higher on one section) or MAT (minimum score 48), minimum undergraduate GPA of 3.0. Application deadline: 7/1 (priority date; rolling processing; 12/1 for spring admission). Application fee: $30. *Tuition:* $3130 per year full-time, $136 per credit hour part-time for state residents; $9370 per year full-time, $226 per credit hour part-time for nonresidents. • Dr. Peter Denner, Director, 208-236-4230. E-mail: dennpete@isu.edu. Application contact: Dr. Stephanie Salzman, Director, Office of Standards and Assessment, 208-236-3114. Fax: 208-236-4697. E-mail: salzstep@isu.edu.

Illinois State University, College of Education, Department of Specialized Educational Development, Program in Reading Education, Normal, IL 61790-2200. Awards MS Ed. Accredited by NCATE. Students: 5 full-time (all women), 114 part-time (113 women); includes 3 minority (all African Americans). 9 applicants, 100% accepted. In 1997, 44 degrees awarded. *Degree requirements:* Practicum required, thesis not required. *Entrance requirements:* GRE General Test (minimum combined score of 900), minimum GPA of 3.0 in last 60 hours, previous course work in reading. Application deadline: rolling. Application fee: $0. *Expenses:* Tuition $2454 per year full-time, $102 per hour part-time for state residents; $7362 per year full-time, $307 per hour part-time for nonresidents. Fees $1048 per year full-time, $44 per hour part-time. *Financial aid:* Full tuition waivers available. Financial aid application deadline: 4/1. • Dr. Paula Smith, Chairperson, Department of Specialized Educational Development, 309-438-5419.

Indiana State University, School of Education, Department of Elementary and Early Childhood Education, Terre Haute, IN 47809-1401. Offerings include reading education (M Ed, PhD, Ed S). Accredited by NCATE. Department faculty: 13 full-time (10 women). *Degree requirements:* For doctorate, 2 foreign languages, computer language, dissertation. *Entrance requirements:* For master's, minimum undergraduate GPA of 2.5; for doctorate, GRE General Test (minimum score 500 on each section), minimum undergraduate GPA of 3.5; for Ed S, GRE General Test (minimum combined score of 900), minimum graduate GPA of 3.25. Application deadline: rolling. Application fee: $20. *Tuition:* $143 per credit hour for state residents; $325 per credit hour for nonresidents. • Dr. Sandra DeCosta, Chairperson, 812-237-2852.

Indiana University Bloomington, School of Education, Department of Language Education, Bloomington, IN 47405. Awards MS, Ed D, PhD, Ed S. Accredited by NCATE. PhD offered through the University Graduate School. Part-time and evening/weekend programs available. Faculty: 7 full-time (4 women). Students: 32 full-time (23 women), 67 part-time (52 women); includes 1 African American, 3 Asian Americans, 1 Hispanic, 34 international. In 1997, 15 master's, 12 doctorates awarded. Terminal master's awarded for partial completion of doctoral program. *Degree requirements:* For doctorate, dissertation, internship required, foreign language not required; for Ed S, comprehensive exam or project required, foreign language not required. *Entrance requirements:* For master's, GRE General Test; for doctorate, GRE General Test (minimum combined score of 1500 on three sections); for Ed S, GRE General Test (minimum combined score of 1300 on three sections). Application deadline: 6/1. Application fee: $35. *Expenses:* Tuition $153 per credit hour for state residents; $446 per credit hour for nonresidents. Fees $343 per year. *Financial aid:* Fellowships, research assistantships, teaching assistantships, full and partial tuition waivers, Federal Work-Study, institutionally sponsored loans, and career-related internships or fieldwork available. Aid available to part-time students. *Faculty research:* Relationship of reading, writing, and speaking; job related literacy; assessment; sociolinguistics. • Dr. Larry Mikulecky, Chair, 812-856-8260. Fax: 812-856-8287. Application contact: Sue Sanford, Office Manager, 812-856-8260. E-mail: langed@indiana.edu.

Indiana University of Pennsylvania, College of Education, Department of Professional Studies in Education, Program in Literacy, Indiana, PA 15705-1087. Awards M Ed, Certificate. Accredited by NCATE. Part-time programs available. Students: 2 full-time (both women), 20 part-time (17 women); includes 1 international. Average age 29. 14 applicants, 93% accepted. In 1997, 20 master's awarded. *Degree requirements:* For master's, thesis optional, foreign language not required. *Entrance requirements:* For master's, TOEFL (minimum score 500); for Certificate, GRE General Test, GRE Subject Test, TOEFL (minimum score 500). Application deadline: 7/1 (priority date; rolling processing; 11/1 for spring admission). Application fee: $30. *Expenses:* Tuition $3468 per year full-time, $193 per credit part-time for state residents; $6236 per year full-time, $346 per credit part-time for nonresidents. Fees $313 per year (minimum) full-time, $84 per year part-time. *Financial aid:* Research assistantships, Federal Work-Study, and career-related internships or fieldwork available. Aid available to part-time students. Financial aid application deadline: 3/15. • Dr. Nedra Nastase, Graduate Coordinator, 724-357-7796. E-mail: nnastase@grove.iup.edu.

Jacksonville University, College of Arts and Sciences, Division of Education, Program in Reading, 2800 University Boulevard North, Jacksonville, FL 32211-3394. Awards MAT. Part-time and evening/weekend programs available. *Degree requirements:* Comprehensive exam required, foreign language and thesis not required. *Entrance requirements:* GRE General Test (minimum combined score of 900), TOEFL (minimum score 500), minimum GPA of 3.0. Application deadline: 8/1 (priority date; rolling processing; 11/1 for spring admission). Application fee: $25.

James Madison University, College of Education and Psychology, School of Education, Program in Reading Education, Harrisonburg, VA 22807. Awards M Ed. Accredited by NCATE.

Directory: Reading Education

James Madison University (continued)
Program being phased out; applicants no longer accepted. Part-time programs available. Students: 3 part-time (all women). Average age 30. In 1997, 13 degrees awarded. *Tuition:* $134 per credit hour for state residents; $404 per credit hour for nonresidents. *Financial aid:* Fellowships, teaching assistantships, assistantships, Federal Work-Study available. Financial aid applicants required to submit FAFSA. • Dr. Arlene Carter-Pounds, Coordinator, 540-568-6255.

Johns Hopkins University, School of Continuing Studies, Division of Education, Department of Teacher Development and Leadership, Baltimore, MD 21218-2699. Offerings include reading (MS, Certificate). *Application fee:* $50. • Rochelle Ingram, Chair, 410-516-4957.

Johnson State College, Graduate Program in Education, Program in Reading Education, Johnson, VT 05656-9405. Awards MA Ed. Students: 4 part-time (all women). *Degree requirements:* Thesis or alternative, comprehensive exam required, foreign language not required. *Entrance requirements:* Interview. Application deadline: 7/15 (priority date; rolling processing; 11/1 for spring admission). Application fee: $30. *Expenses:* Tuition $164 per credit for state residents; $383 per credit for nonresidents. Fees $15.90 per credit. *Financial aid:* Federal Work-Study, institutionally sponsored loans, and career-related internships or fieldwork available. Aid available to part-time students. Financial aid application deadline: 3/1; applicants required to submit FAFSA. • Application contact: Catherine H. Higley, Administrative Assistant, 802-635-2356 Ext. 1244. Fax: 802-635-1248. E-mail: higleyc@badger.jsc.vsc.edu.

Kean University, School of Education, Department of Communication Sciences, Union, NJ 07083. Offers programs in reading specialization (MA), teaching of reading (Certificate). Accredited by NCATE. Part-time programs available. Students: 2 full-time (both women), 59 part-time (56 women); includes 1 minority (African American). Average age 34. In 1997, 14 master's awarded. *Degree requirements:* For master's, thesis, comprehensive exams required, foreign language not required. *Entrance requirements:* For master's, GRE General Test or MAT; for Certificate, GRE General Test. Application deadline: 6/15 (11/15 for spring admission). Application fee: $35. *Tuition:* $5926 per year full-time, $248 per credit part-time for state residents; $7312 per year full-time, $304 per credit part-time for nonresidents. *Financial aid:* Graduate assistantships and career-related internships or fieldwork available. • Richard Walter, Coordinator, 908-527-2649. Application contact: Joanne Morris, Director of Graduate Admissions, 908-527-2665. Fax: 908-527-2286. E-mail: grad_adm@turbo.kean.edu.

Kent State University, Graduate School of Education, Department of Teaching, Leadership, and Curriculum Studies, Program in Reading, Kent, OH 44242-0001. Awards MA, M Ed. Accredited by NCATE. Faculty: 7 full-time (5 women), 5 part-time (4 women). Students: 1 (woman) full-time, 34 part-time (32 women); includes 1 minority (African American). In 1997, 22 degrees awarded. *Degree requirements:* Thesis (MA) required, foreign language not required. *Application deadline:* rolling. *Application fee:* $30. *Tuition:* $4752 per year full-time, $216 per credit hour part-time for state residents; $9213 per year full-time, $419 per credit hour part-time for nonresidents. *Financial aid:* Application deadline 4/1. • Dr. Nancy Padak, Coordinator, 330-672-2836. Application contact: Deborah Barber, Director, Office of Academic Services, 330-672-2862. Fax: 330-672-3549.

King's College, College of Arts and Sciences, Wilkes-Barre, PA 18711-0801. Offerings include reading (M Ed). Postbaccalaureate distance learning degree programs offered (minimal on-campus study). College faculty: 2 full-time (both women), 1 (woman) part-time. *Degree requirements:* Thesis required, foreign language not required. *Average time to degree:* master's–2.5 years part-time. *Entrance requirements:* GRE. Application deadline: 7/31 (priority date; rolling processing; 12/1 for spring admission). Application fee: $35. *Tuition:* $460 per credit. • Dr. William A. Shergalis, Dean, 717-208-5901. E-mail: washerga@rs01.kings.edu. Application contact: Dr. Elizabeth S. Lott, Director of Graduate Programs, 717-208-5991. Fax: 717-825-9049. E-mail: eslott@rs02.kings.edu.

Kutztown University of Pennsylvania, Graduate School, College of Education, Program in Reading, Kutztown, PA 19530. Awards M Ed. Accredited by NCATE. Part-time and evening/weekend programs available. Faculty: 15 full-time (8 women). Students: 65 part-time (60 women); includes 1 African American. Average age 33. In 1997, 18 degrees awarded. *Degree requirements:* Comprehensive project required, foreign language and thesis not required. *Entrance requirements:* GRE General Test, TOEFL, TSE. Application deadline: 3/1 (8/1 for spring admission). Application fee: $25. *Tuition:* $4111 per year full-time, $225 per credit hour part-time for state residents; $6879 per year full-time, $393 per credit hour part-time for nonresidents. *Financial aid:* Graduate assistantships, partial tuition waivers, Federal Work-Study, and career-related internships or fieldwork available. Financial aid application deadline: 3/15; applicants required to submit FAFSA. • Dr. Beth Herbine, Coordinator, 610-683-4271.

Lake Erie College, Division of Education, Painesville, OH 44077-3389. Offerings include reading (MS Ed). Division faculty: 4 full-time (2 women), 2 part-time (0 women). *Degree requirements:* Thesis, applied research project, comprehensive exam required, foreign language not required. *Entrance requirements:* GRE General Test (minimum score 440 on verbal section, 500 on quantitative) or minimum GPA of 2.75. Application deadline: 8/1 (priority date; rolling processing; 12/15 for spring admission). Application fee: $20 ($50 for international students). *Expenses:* Tuition $294 per credit hour. Fees $20 per credit hour. • Dr. Carol Ramsay, Associate Dean of Teacher Education and Certification, 440-639-4749. Application contact: Director of Admissions, 440-639-7879. Fax: 440-352-3533.

Lehman College of the City University of New York, Division of Education, Department of Specialized Services in Education, Program in Reading Teacher, 250 Bedford Park Boulevard West, Bronx, NY 10468-1589. Awards MS Ed. Evening/weekend programs available. Faculty: 1 full-time (0 women), 5 part-time (4 women). Students: 53 part-time (47 women). *Entrance requirements:* Interview, minimum GPA of 2.7. Application deadline: 4/1 (priority date; rolling processing; 11/1 for spring admission). Application fee: $40. *Expenses:* Tuition $4350 per year full-time, $185 per credit part-time for state residents; $7600 per year full-time, $320 per credit part-time for nonresidents. Fees $120 per year full-time, $80 per year part-time. *Financial aid:* Full and partial tuition waivers, Federal Work-Study available. Aid available to part-time students. Financial aid application deadline: 5/15; applicants required to submit FAFSA. *Faculty research:* Emergent literacy, language-based classrooms, primary and secondary social contexts of language and literacy, innovative in-service education models, adult literacy. • Gaoyin Qian, Adviser, 718-960-8173.

Lenoir–Rhyne College, Division of Graduate Programs, Department of Education, Program in Reading, Hickory, NC 28601. Awards MA. Students: 1 (woman) part-time. *Degree requirements:* Thesis optional, foreign language not required. *Entrance requirements:* GRE General Test (minimum score 450 on verbal section, 1350 combined), minimum GPA of 2.7. Application deadline: 8/1 (12/1 for spring admission). Application fee: $25. *Tuition:* $190 per credit hour. • Application contact: Dr. Thomas W. Fauquet, Dean of Graduate Studies, 828-328-7275. Fax: 828-328-7368. E-mail: fauquet@lrc.edu.

Lesley College, School of Education, Cambridge, MA 02138-2790. Offerings include reading (M Ed, CAGS). Postbaccalaureate distance learning degree programs offered (no on-campus study). School faculty: 36 full-time (31 women), 340 part-time (220 women). *Degree requirements:* Computer language required, foreign language and thesis not required. *Entrance requirements:* For master's, TOEFL (minimum score 550); for CAGS, interview, master's degree. Application deadline: rolling. Application fee: $45. *Tuition:* $425 per credit. • Dr. William L. Dandridge, Dean, 617-349-8375. Application contact: Graduate Admissions, 617-349-8300. Fax: 617-349-8366.

Liberty University, School of Education, 1971 University Road, Lynchburg, VA 24502. Offerings include reading (M Ed). School faculty: 3 full-time (1 woman), 4 part-time (2 women). *Degree requirements:* Thesis optional, foreign language not required. *Entrance requirements:* GRE General Test (minimum combined score of 900). Application deadline: 8/15 (priority date; rolling processing). Application fee: $35. *Tuition:* $280 per credit hour. • Dr. Pauline Donaldson, Dean, 804-582-2314. Application contact: Bill Wegert, Coordinator of Graduate Admissions, 804-582-2175.

Long Island University, Brooklyn Campus, School of Education, Department of Education, Program in Reading, Brooklyn, NY 11201-8423. Awards MS Ed. Part-time and evening/weekend programs available. 15 applicants, 87% accepted. In 1997, 6 degrees awarded. *Degree requirements:* Thesis optional, foreign language not required. *Application deadline:* rolling. *Application fee:* $30. Electronic applications accepted. *Expenses:* Tuition $480 per credit. Fees $415 per year full-time, $73 per semester (minimum) part-time. • Application contact: Bernard W. Sullivan, Associate Director of Admissions, 718-488-1011.

Long Island University, C.W. Post Campus, School of Education, Department of Special Education and Reading, Brookville, NY 11548-1300. Offers programs in reading (MS), special education (MS). Part-time and evening/weekend programs available. Faculty: 11 full-time (4 women), 14 part-time (4 women). Students: 3 full-time, 362 part-time. 135 applicants, 91% accepted. In 1997, 215 degrees awarded. *Degree requirements:* Research project, comprehensive exam or thesis required, foreign language not required. *Entrance requirements:* Writing proficiency test, interview. Application deadline: rolling. Application fee: $30. Electronic applications accepted. *Expenses:* Tuition $480 per credit. Fees $316 per year full-time, $71 per semester (minimum) part-time. *Financial aid:* In 1997–98, 5 research assistantships were awarded; career-related internships or fieldwork also available. Aid available to part-time students. Financial aid application deadline: 5/15; applicants required to submit FAFSA. *Faculty research:* Autism, mainstreaming, robotics and microcomputers in special education, transition from school to work. • Dr. Alvin Kravitz, Chairperson, 516-299-2245. Application contact: Linda D'Agostino, Academic Counselor, 516-299-2199. Fax: 516-299-4167.

Long Island University, Southampton College, Education Division, Program in Reading, Southampton, NY 11968-9822. Awards MS Ed. Faculty: 1 full-time (0 women), 1 (woman) part-time. *Degree requirements:* Computer language, thesis. *Entrance requirements:* MAT. Application deadline: 4/15 (priority date; 11/30 for spring admission). Application fee: $30. • Dr. R. Lawrence McCann, Director, Education Division, 516-287-8211 Ext. 211.

Longwood College, Department of Education, Farmville, VA 23909-1800. Offerings include reading specialist (MS). Accredited by NCATE. Department faculty: 34 part-time. *Degree requirements:* Thesis (for some programs), comprehensive exam. *Entrance requirements:* Minimum GPA of 2.5. Application deadline: 5/1 (priority date; rolling processing; 10/15 for spring admission). Application fee: $25. *Expenses:* Tuition $3048 per year full-time, $127 per credit hour part-time for state residents; $8160 per year full-time, $340 per credit hour part-time for nonresidents. Fees $920 per year full-time, $31 per credit hour part-time. • Dr. Frank Howe, Chair, 804-395-2324. Application contact: Admissions Office, 804-395-2060.

Louisiana Tech University, College of Education, Department of Curriculum, Instruction and Leadership, Ruston, LA 71272. Offerings include reading (Ed S). Accredited by NCATE. Department faculty: 16 full-time (11 women). *Application deadline:* 7/29 (2/3 for spring admission). *Application fee:* $20 ($30 for international students). *Tuition:* $2382 per year full-time, $223 per quarter (minimum) part-time for state residents; $5307 per year full-time, $223 per quarter (minimum) part-time for nonresidents. • Dr. Samuel V. Dauzat, Head, 318-257-4609.

Loyola College, College of Arts and Sciences, Department of Education, Program in Reading, Baltimore, MD 21210-2699. Awards MA, M Ed, CAS. Part-time and evening/weekend programs available. Students: 3 full-time (all women), 149 part-time (147 women); includes 5 minority (4 African Americans, 1 Hispanic). In 1997, 34 master's awarded. *Entrance requirements:* For CAS, master's degree. Application deadline: 8/1 (rolling processing; 12/1 for spring admission). Application fee: $35. *Tuition:* $222 per credit (minimum). *Financial aid:* Career-related internships or fieldwork available. • Donald Hofler, Director, 410-617-2455.

Loyola Marymount University, School of Education, Program in Literacy and Language, Los Angeles, CA 90045-8350. Awards M Ed. Faculty: 14 full-time (8 women), 25 part-time (20 women). Students: 12 full-time (11 women); includes 8 minority (1 African American, 1 Asian American, 6 Hispanics). *Degree requirements:* Thesis or alternative, comprehensive exam required, foreign language not required. *Entrance requirements:* GRE General Test, TOEFL (minimum score 550), interview. Application fee: $35. Electronic applications accepted. *Expenses:* Tuition $500 per unit. Fees $111 per year full-time, $28 per year part-time. *Financial aid:* Federal Work-Study available. Aid available to part-time students. Financial aid application deadline: 3/2; applicants required to submit FAFSA. • Dr. Candace Poindexter, Coordinator, 310-338-7314.

Loyola Marymount University, School of Education, Program in Reading/Language Arts, Los Angeles, CA 90045-8350. Awards M Ed. Part-time and evening/weekend programs available. Faculty: 14 full-time (8 women), 25 part-time (20 women). Students: 7 full-time (all women), 2 part-time (both women); includes 2 minority (both Hispanics). In 1997, 5 degrees awarded. *Degree requirements:* Comprehensive exam required, foreign language and thesis not required. *Entrance requirements:* GRE General Test, TOEFL (minimum score 550), interview. Application fee: $35. Electronic applications accepted. *Expenses:* Tuition $500 per unit. Fees $111 per year full-time, $28 per year part-time. *Financial aid:* In 1997–98, 4 grants, scholarships totaling $5,100 were awarded; Federal Work-Study also available. Aid available to part-time students. Financial aid application deadline: 3/2; applicants required to submit FAFSA. • Dr. Candace Poindexter, Coordinator, 310-338-7314.

Loyola University New Orleans, College of Arts and Sciences, Department of Education, Program in Reading Education, New Orleans, LA 70118-6195. Awards MS. Part-time and evening/weekend programs available. Faculty: 2 full-time (both women), 3 part-time (all women). Students: 5 part-time (all women). Average age 27. 8 applicants, 0% accepted. In 1997, 1 degree awarded. *Degree requirements:* Comprehensive exam required, foreign language and thesis not required. *Entrance requirements:* GRE, MAT (preferred), interview, sample of written work. Application deadline: 8/1 (priority date; rolling processing; 12/1 for spring admission). Application fee: $20. Electronic applications accepted. *Expenses:* Tuition $247 per credit hour. Fees $556 per year full-time, $164 per year part-time. *Financial aid:* Research assistantships, partial tuition waivers, Federal Work-Study, and career-related internships or fieldwork available. Aid available to part-time students. Financial aid application deadline: 5/1; applicants required to submit FAFSA. *Faculty research:* Remediation, special education. • Dr. Margaret Dermody, Director, 504-865-3540. Fax: 504-865-3571.

Lynchburg College, School of Education and Human Development, Program in Reading, Lynchburg, VA 24501-3199. Awards M Ed. *Entrance requirements:* Minimum GPA of 3.0 (undergraduate). Application fee: $20.

Lyndon State College, Graduate Programs in Education, Department of Education, Lyndonville, VT 05851. Offerings include reading specialist (M Ed). *Degree requirements:* Exam or major field project required, foreign language and thesis not required. *Entrance requirements:* GRE General Test or MAT. Application deadline: 2/28 (priority date; 10/31 for spring admission). Application fee: $30. *Expenses:* Tuition $3924 per year full-time, $164 per credit part-time for state residents; $9192 per year full-time, $383 per credit part-time for nonresidents. Fees $632 per year. • Application contact: Elaine L. Turner, Administrative Secretary, 802-626-6497. Fax: 802-626-9770. E-mail: turnere@king.lsc.vsc.edu.

Madonna University, Programs in Education, Livonia, MI 48150-1173. Offerings include literacy education (MAT). Accredited by NCATE. Faculty: 7 full-time (4 women), 3 part-time (2 women). *Application deadline:* 8/1 (priority date; rolling processing). *Application fee:* $0. *Expenses:* Tuition $260 per credit hour (minimum). Fees $50 per semester. • Dr. Robert Kimball, Chair, Education Department, 734-432-5652. E-mail: kimball@smtp.munet.edu. Application contact: Sandra Kellums, Coordinator of Graduate Admissions, 734-432-5666. Fax: 734-432-5393. E-mail: kellums@smtp.munet.edu.

Directory: Reading Education

Malone College, Graduate School, Program in Education, Canton, OH 44709-3897. Offerings include reading (MA). Program faculty: 10 full-time (6 women), 11 part-time (5 women), 12.68 FTE. *Degree requirements:* Research practicum required, foreign language and thesis not required. *Entrance requirements:* Minimum GPA of 3.0, teaching license. Application deadline: 9/6 (rolling processing; 1/2 for spring admission). Application fee: $20. *Tuition:* $300 per credit hour. • Dr. Marietta Daulton, Director, 330-471-8447. Fax: 330-471-8478. E-mail: mdaulton@malone.edu. Application contact: Dan Depasquale, Director of Graduate Student Services, 800-257-4723. Fax: 330-471-8343. E-mail: depasquale@malone.edu.

Manhattanville College, School of Education, Program in Reading and Writing, Purchase, NY 10577-2132. Awards MPS. *Degree requirements:* Thesis, comprehensive exam or research project required, foreign language not required. *Entrance requirements:* Minimum undergraduate GPA of 3.0. Application deadline: rolling. Application fee: $40. *Expenses:* Tuition $410 per credit (minimum). Fees $25 per semester. • Application contact: Carol Messar, Director of Admissions, 914-323-5142. Fax: 914-323-5493.

Manhattanville College, School of Education, Program in Special Education, Purchase, NY 10577-2132. Offerings include special education and reading (MPS). *Application deadline:* rolling. *Application fee:* $40. *Expenses:* Tuition $410 per credit (minimum). Fees $25 per semester. • Dr. Rebecca Rich, Coordinator, 914-323-5143. Application contact: Carol Messar, Director of Admissions, 914-323-5142. Fax: 914-323-5493.

Mankato State University, College of Education, Department of Curriculum and Instruction, Reading Consultant Program, South Rd and Ellis Ave, PO Box 8400, Mankato, MN 56002-8400. Awards MS. Accredited by NCATE. Part-time programs available. Students: 3 full-time (all women), 1 (woman) part-time. Average age 32. 0 applicants. *Degree requirements:* Thesis or alternative, comprehensive exam required, foreign language not required. *Entrance requirements:* GRE General Test or MAT, minimum GPA of 3.0 during previous 2 years. Application deadline: 7/10 (priority date; rolling processing; 10/30 for spring admission). Application fee: $20. *Tuition:* $126 per credit (minimum) for state residents; $200 per credit for nonresidents. *Financial aid:* Teaching assistantships, Federal Work-Study, and career-related internships or fieldwork available. Aid available to part-time students. Financial aid application deadline: 3/15; applicants required to submit FAFSA. • Dr. Howard Schroeder, Coordinator, 507-389-5713. Application contact: Joni Roberts, Admissions Coordinator, 507-389-2321. Fax: 507-389-5974. E-mail: grad@mankato.msus.edu.

Marshall University, Graduate School of Education and Professional Studies, Program in Reading Education, South Charleston, WV 25303-1600. Awards MA, Ed S. Accredited by NCATE. Part-time and evening/weekend programs available. Faculty: 4 full-time (2 women), 4 part-time (all women), 5.1 FTE. Students: 10 full-time (all women), 141 part-time (134 women); includes 5 minority (4 African Americans, 1 Asian American). Average age 38. In 1997, 20 master's awarded. *Degree requirements:* For master's, comprehensive or oral exam, final project required, foreign language and thesis not required; for Ed S, research project required, foreign language and thesis not required. *Entrance requirements:* For master's, GRE General Test, minimum undergraduate GPA of 2.5; for Ed S, master's degree in reading, minimum GPA of 3.0. Application deadline: 8/1 (priority date; rolling processing). Application fee: $0. *Tuition:* $2364 per year full-time, $132 per hour part-time for state residents; $6894 per year full-time, $383 per hour part-time for nonresidents. *Financial aid:* Full tuition waivers available. Aid available to part-time students. Financial aid applicants required to submit FAFSA. • Dr. James Ranson, Dean, Graduate School of Education and Professional Studies, 304-746-1998. Fax: 304-746-1942.

Marshall University, College of Education, Division of Teacher Education, Program in Reading Education, Huntington, WV 25755-2020. Awards MA. Accredited by NCATE. Evening/weekend programs available. Faculty: 1 (woman). Students: 8 full-time (7 women), 37 part-time (all women). In 1997, 7 degrees awarded. *Degree requirements:* Thesis optional. *Entrance requirements:* GRE General Test (minimum combined score of 1200). *Tuition:* $2364 per year full-time, $132 per hour part-time for state residents; $6894 per year full-time, $383 per hour part-time for nonresidents. • Dr. Susan Ferrell, Coordinator, 304-696-2893. Application contact: Dr. James Harless, Director of Admissions, 304-696-3160.

Marycrest International University, Division of Education, Davenport, IA 52804-4096. Offerings include reading specialist (MA). Division faculty: 4 full-time (all women), 3 part-time (0 women), 4.8 FTE. *Average time to degree:* master's–2.5 years part-time. *Application deadline:* 4/15 (priority date; rolling processing; 12/1 for spring admission). *Application fee:* $25. *Expenses:* Tuition of $198 per credit hour for students holding a valid teaching certificate (for MA in education and reading specialist only); $413 per credit hour for other degree programs. • Dr. Michelle Schiffgens, Chair, 319-326-9241. Fax: 319-326-9250.

Marygrove College, Division of Education, Program in Reading Education, Detroit, MI 48221-2599. Awards M Ed. Accredited by NCATE. Part-time and evening/weekend programs available. *Degree requirements:* Practicum, research project required, foreign language and thesis not required. *Average time to degree:* master's–2 years full-time, 3 years part-time. *Entrance requirements:* MAT, interview, minimum undergraduate GPA of 3.0, teaching certificate. Application deadline: 8/15 (rolling processing). Application fee: $25.

Marywood University, Graduate School of Arts and Sciences, Department of Education, Program in Reading Education, Scranton, PA 18509-1598. Awards MS. Accredited by NCATE. Part-time and evening/weekend programs available. Students: 20 part-time (all women). Average age 30. 4 applicants, 100% accepted. In 1997, 14 degrees awarded. *Degree requirements:* Thesis or alternative, internship/practicum required, foreign language not required. *Entrance requirements:* GRE or MAT, TOEFL (minimum score 550; average 590). Application deadline: 7/15 (priority date; rolling processing; 12/1 for spring admission). Application fee: $20. *Expenses:* Tuition $449 per credit hour. Fees $530 per year full-time, $180 per year part-time. *Financial aid:* Research assistantships, scholarships/tuition reductions, partial tuition waivers, and career-related internships or fieldwork available. Aid available to part-time students. Financial aid application deadline: 2/15; applicants required to submit FAFSA. *Faculty research:* Design of school reading programs, whole language. • Dr. Nancy Nagy, Director, 717-348-6211 Ext. 2407. Application contact: Deborah M. Flynn, Coordinator of Admissions, 717-340-6002. Fax: 717-961-4745.

Massachusetts College of Liberal Arts, Graduate Program in Education, North Adams, MA 01247-4100. Offerings include reading (M Ed). Program faculty: 8 full-time (5 women), 4 part-time (2 women). *Degree requirements:* Thesis required, foreign language not required. *Average time to degree:* master's–3 years part-time. *Entrance requirements:* Writing sample. Application deadline: rolling. Application fee: $0. *Expenses:* Tuition $130 per credit. Fees $15 per credit. • Dr. Susanne Chandler, Chair, 413-662-5381.

McGill University, Faculty of Graduate Studies and Research, Faculty of Education, Department of Educational Studies, Montréal, PQ H3A 2T5, Canada. Offerings include curriculum and instruction (M Ed), with options in curriculum studies, literacy studies. Department faculty: 24 full-time (10 women), 1 part-time. *Application deadline:* 3/1 (priority date; rolling processing; 3/1 for spring admission). *Application fee:* $60. *Expenses:* Tuition $1668 per year for Canadian residents; $8268 per year for nonresidents. Fees $828 per year for Canadian residents; $1216 per year for nonresidents. • Dr. Lynn Butler-Kisber, Director of Graduate Studies, 514-398-4531. E-mail: lbk@cel.lan.mcgill.ca. Application contact: Tina Shiavone, Graduate Program Coordinator, 514-398-4531. Fax: 514-398-7436.

McNeese State University, College of Education, Department of Curriculum and Instruction, Program in Reading Education, Lake Charles, LA 70609-2495. Awards M Ed. Evening/weekend programs available. Faculty: 8 full-time (3 women). Students: 0. *Entrance requirements:* GRE General Test, teaching certificate. Application deadline: 7/15 (priority date; rolling processing). Application fee: $10 ($25 for international students). *Tuition:* $2118 per year full-time, $344 per semester (minimum) part-time for state residents; $7308 per year full-time, $344 per semester (minimum) part-time for nonresidents. *Financial aid:* Application deadline 5/1. • Dr. Everett Waddell Burge, Head, Department of Curriculum and Instruction, 318-475-5404.

Mercer University, School of Education, 1400 Coleman Avenue, Macon, GA 31207-0003. Offerings include reading specialist (M Ed). School faculty: 11 full-time (5 women), 17 part-time (11 women). *Degree requirements:* Research project report required, foreign language and thesis not required. *Entrance requirements:* GRE, MAT, NTE, minimum GPA of 2.75. Application deadline: 8/1 (priority date; rolling processing; 12/1 for spring admission). Application fee: $25. *Tuition:* $180 per credit hour. • Dr. Anne Hathaway, Dean, 912-752-5397. Fax: 912-752-2280. E-mail: hathaway_ha@mercer.edu. Application contact: Dr. Louis Gallien, Chair, Department of Teacher Education, 912-752-2585. Fax: 912-752-2576. E-mail: gallien_lb@mercer.edu.

Miami University, School of Education and Allied Professions, Department of Teacher Education, Program in Reading Education, Oxford, OH 45056. Awards M Ed, MS. Accredited by NCATE. Part-time programs available. Students: 1 (woman) full-time, 7 part-time (all women). 10 applicants, 90% accepted. In 1997, 4 degrees awarded. *Degree requirements:* Final exam required, foreign language and thesis not required. *Entrance requirements:* MAT, minimum undergraduate GPA of 3.0 during previous 2 years or 2.75 overall. Application deadline: 3/1 (priority date; rolling processing; 12/15 for spring admission). Application fee: $35. *Tuition:* $5932 per year full-time, $255 per credit hour part-time for state residents; $12,392 per year full-time, $524 per credit hour part-time for nonresidents. *Financial aid:* Research assistantships, teaching assistantships, full tuition waivers, Federal Work-Study, and career-related internships or fieldwork available. Financial aid application deadline: 3/1. *Faculty research:* Teacher effectiveness. • Dr. Robert Shearer, Director of Graduate Study, 513-529-5708.

Michigan State University, College of Education, Program in Literacy Instruction, East Lansing, MI 48824-1020. Awards MA. Faculty: 8 (4 women). Students: 44 (41 women); includes 3 minority (2 African Americans, 1 Asian American). In 1997, 18 degrees awarded. *Application deadline:* rolling. *Application fee:* $30 ($40 for international students). *Expenses:* Tuition $4609 per year full-time, $223 per credit hour (minimum) part-time for state residents; $8704 per year full-time, $450 per credit hour (minimum) part-time for nonresidents. Fees $576 per year full-time, $476 per year part-time. *Faculty research:* Language culture and literacy education, writing, integrating the language arts, assessment, teacher research. • Dr. Taffy Raphael, Coordinator, 517-355-1786.

Middle Tennessee State University, College of Education, Department of Elementary and Special Education, Major in Reading, Murfreesboro, TN 37132. Awards M Ed. Accredited by NCATE. Students: 1 (woman) full-time, 17 part-time (all women); includes 1 minority (African American). Average age 33. 10 applicants, 80% accepted. In 1997, 17 degrees awarded. *Degree requirements:* Comprehensive exams required, foreign language and thesis not required. *Entrance requirements:* Cooperative English Test, MAT. Application deadline: 8/1 (priority date). Application fee: $5. *Expenses:* Tuition $2560 per year full-time, $129 per semester hour part-time for state residents; $7386 per year full-time, $340 per semester hour part-time for nonresidents. Fees $486 per year full-time, $17 per semester (minimum) part-time. *Financial aid:* Teaching assistantships available. Financial aid application deadline: 5/1. • Dr. Charles Babb, Chair, Department of Elementary and Special Education, 615-898-2680. Fax: 615-898-5309. E-mail: cwbabb@mtsu.edu.

Midwestern State University, Division of Education, Program in Reading Education, Wichita Falls, TX 76308-2096. Awards M Ed. Part-time and evening/weekend programs available. Students: 6. Average age 35. *Entrance requirements:* GRE General Test, MAT (average 46), TOEFL (minimum score 550). Application deadline: 8/7 (12/15 for spring admission). Application fee: $0 ($50 for international students). *Expenses:* Tuition $44 per hour for state residents; $259 per hour for nonresidents. Fees $90 per year (minimum) full-time, $9 per semester (minimum) part-time. • Dr. Emerson Capps, Director, Division of Education, 940-397-4313.

Millersville University of Pennsylvania, School of Education, Department of Elementary and Early Childhood Education, Program in Reading/Language Arts Education, Millersville, PA 17551-0302. Awards M Ed. Accredited by NCATE. Students: 5 full-time (all women), 46 part-time (45 women); includes 1 minority (Hispanic), 1 international. Average age 30. 23 applicants, 91% accepted. In 1997, 30 degrees awarded. *Degree requirements:* Thesis optional, foreign language not required. *Entrance requirements:* MAT (minimum score 35) or GRE General Test (minimum score 450 on each section), minimum undergraduate GPA of 2.75, Pennsylvania Instructional Certificate. Application deadline: 5/1 (priority date; rolling processing). Application fee: $25. *Tuition:* $3468 per year full-time, $234 per credit part-time for state residents; $6236 per year full-time, $387 per credit part-time for nonresidents. *Financial aid:* In 1997–98, 3 graduate assistantships (all to first-year students) averaging $445 per month and totaling $12,000 were awarded; Federal Work-Study, institutionally sponsored loans, and career-related internships or fieldwork also available. Aid available to part-time students. Financial aid application deadline: 5/1. *Faculty research:* Reading disabilities, racism and sexism, fairy tales. • Dr. Mary Anne Gray-Schlegel, Coordinator, 717-872-3394. Fax: 717-872-3856. Application contact: Dr. Robert J. Labriola, Dean of Graduate Studies, 717-872-3030. Fax: 717-871-2022.

Monmouth University, School of Education, West Long Branch, NJ 07764-1898. Offerings include reading specialist (MS Ed, Certificate). Certificate (learning disabilities-teacher consultant, reading specialist, supervision) new for fall 1998. School faculty: 9 full-time (7 women), 14 part-time (9 women). *Application deadline:* 8/1 (priority date; rolling processing; 12/1 for spring admission). *Application fee:* $35. *Expenses:* Tuition $459 per credit. Fees $274 per semester full-time, $137 per semester part-time. • Dr. Bernice Willis, Dean, 732-571-7518. Fax: 732-263-5277. Application contact: Office of Graduate Admissions, 732-571-3452. Fax: 732-571-5123.

Montana State University–Billings, College of Education and Human Services, Department of Special Education and Reading, Option in Reading, Billings, MT 59101-9984. Awards M Ed. Accredited by NCATE. Part-time programs available. *Degree requirements:* Thesis or professional paper and/or field experience required, foreign language not required. *Entrance requirements:* GRE General Test (minimum combined score of 1350 on three sections) or MAT (minimum score 38), minimum GPA of 3.0 (undergraduate), 3.25 (graduate). Application deadline: 8/1 (priority date; rolling processing; 1/1 for spring admission). Application fee: $30. *Expenses:* Tuition $2253 per year full-time, $397 per semester (minimum) part-time for state residents; $5313 per year full-time, $907 per semester (minimum) part-time for nonresidents. Fees $378 per year full-time, $105 per semester (minimum) part-time.

Montclair State University, College of Education and Human Services, Department of Reading and Educational Media, Program in Reading, Upper Montclair, NJ 07043-1624. Awards MA. Accredited by NCATE. Part-time and evening/weekend programs available. Faculty: 6 full-time. Students: 2 full-time (both women), 68 part-time (66 women); includes 4 minority (3 African Americans, 1 Hispanic). In 1997, 8 degrees awarded. *Degree requirements:* Clinical experience, comprehensive exam, portfolio required, thesis not required. *Entrance requirements:* GRE General Test. Application deadline: 4/1 (rolling processing; 11/1 for spring admission). Application fee: $40. *Expenses:* Tuition $201 per credit for state residents; $257 per credit for nonresidents. Fees $22.05 per credit. *Financial aid:* Research assistantships available. Financial aid application deadline: 3/1; applicants required to submit FAFSA. • Dr. Diana Joy Stone, Chairperson, Department of Reading and Educational Media, 973-655-5183.

Moorhead State University, Department of Education, Program in Reading, Moorhead, MN 56563-0002. Awards MS. Accredited by NCATE. Part-time and evening/weekend programs available. Faculty: 5 full-time (all women). Students: 3 part-time (2 women). 0 applicants. In 1997, 1 degree awarded. *Degree requirements:* Final oral exam, project or thesis, written comprehensive exam required, foreign language not required. *Entrance requirements:* MAT, TOEFL (minimum score 550), minimum GPA of 2.75, 2 years of teaching experience. Applica-

Directory: Reading Education

Moorhead State University (continued)
tion deadline: 5/1 (priority date; rolling processing; 9/1 for spring admission). Application fee: $20 ($35 for international students). Electronic applications accepted. *Tuition:* $145 per credit hour for state residents; $220 per credit hour for nonresidents. *Financial aid:* Administrative assistantships, Federal Work-Study, and career-related internships or fieldwork available. Financial aid application deadline: 7/15; applicants required to submit FAFSA. • Dr. Roberta Shreve, Chairperson, 218-236-2022.

Morehead State University, College of Education and Behavioral Sciences, Department of Elementary, Reading, and Special Education, Program in Elementary Education, Morehead, KY 40351. Offerings include reading (MA Ed). Accredited by NCATE. Program faculty: 15 full-time (8 women), 1 part-time (0 women). *Degree requirements:* Written comprehensive exams required, foreign language and thesis not required. *Entrance requirements:* GRE General Test (minimum combined score of 1200), minimum GPA of 2.75, teaching certificate. Application deadline: 8/1 (priority date; rolling processing; 12/1 for spring admission). Application fee: $0. *Tuition:* $2470 per year full-time, $138 per semester hour part-time for state residents; $6710 per year full-time, $373 per semester hour part-time for nonresidents. • Application contact: Betty Cowsert, Graduate Admissions Officer, 606-783-2039. Fax: 606-783-5061.

Morningside College, Department of Education, Program in Reading Specialist, Sioux City, IA 51106-1751. Awards MAT. Accredited by NCATE. Part-time and evening/weekend programs available. Faculty: 12 full-time (5 women), 3 part-time (all women). *Entrance requirements:* MAT, writing sample. Application deadline: rolling. Application fee: $15. *Tuition:* $245 per credit hour. *Financial aid:* Partial tuition waivers, institutionally sponsored loans available. • Dr. Glenna Tevis, Director, Graduate Division, 712-274-5375.

Mount Saint Vincent University, Department of Education, Program in Literacy Education, Halifax, NS B3M 2J6, Canada. Awards MA, MA Ed, MA(R), M Ed. Part-time and evening/weekend programs available. Faculty: 6 full-time (3 women), 7 part-time (4 women). Students: 7 full-time (6 women), 72 part-time (61 women). Average age 36. 146 applicants, 92% accepted. In 1997, 102 degrees awarded. *Degree requirements:* Thesis. *Entrance requirements:* Minimum B average, 1 year of teaching experience, bachelor's degree in related field. Application deadline: 3/1 (priority date; rolling processing; 3/1 for spring admission). Application fee: $40. *Expenses:* Tuition $1024 per course. Fees $25 per course. *Financial aid:* In 1997–98, 1 fellowship (to a first-year student) totaling $500 was awarded. Financial aid application deadline: 5/1. *Faculty research:* Writing processes and instruction, assessment and evaluation of literacy education, critical literacy, early literacy development, gender and literacy. • Dr. Allan Neilsen, Head, 902-457-6181. Fax: 902-457-4911. E-mail: allan.neilsen@msvu.ca.

Murray State University, College of Education, Department of Reading Education, Murray, KY 42071-0009. Awards MA Ed. Accredited by NCATE. Faculty: 1 (woman) full-time. Students: 78 part-time (77 women); includes 1 minority (Asian American). 6 applicants, 100% accepted. In 1997, 23 degrees awarded. *Entrance requirements:* TOEFL (minimum score 500). Application deadline: rolling. Application fee: $20. *Expenses:* Tuition $2500 per year full-time, $124 per hour part-time for state residents; $6740 per year full-time, $357 per hour part-time for nonresidents. Fees $360 per year full-time, $180 per year part-time. *Financial aid:* Research assistantships, teaching assistantships available. Financial aid application deadline: 4/1. • Dr. Chuck Hulick, Director, 502-762-2496. Fax: 502-762-2540.

Murray State University, College of Education, Department of Special Education, Murray, KY 42071-0009. Offerings include reading education (MA Ed). Accredited by NCATE. Department faculty: 11 full-time (9 women). *Application deadline:* rolling. *Application fee:* $20. *Expenses:* Tuition $2500 per year full-time, $124 per hour part-time for state residents; $6740 per year full-time, $357 per hour part-time for nonresidents. Fees $360 per year full-time, $180 per year part-time. • Dr. Elizabeth Blodgett, Chairman, 502-762-6810. Fax: 502-762-6803.

National-Louis University, National College of Education, McGaw Graduate School, Programs in Reading and Language, 2840 Sheridan Road, Evanston, IL 60201-1730. Offerings in language and literacy (M Ed, MS Ed, CAS), reading recovery (CAS), reading specialist (M Ed, MS Ed, CAS). Part-time and evening/weekend programs available. Students: 4 full-time (all women), 84 part-time (82 women); includes 2 minority (1 Asian American, 1 Hispanic). Average age 39. In 1997, 47 master's, 2 CASs awarded. *Degree requirements:* For master's, thesis required (for some programs), foreign language not required. *Entrance requirements:* For master's, MAT, minimum GPA of 3.0. Application deadline: rolling. Application fee: $25. *Tuition:* $411 per semester hour. *Financial aid:* Fellowships, research assistantships, and career-related internships or fieldwork available. Aid available to part-time students. Financial aid applicants required to submit FAFSA. • Dr. Camille Blachowicz, Coordinator, 847-475-1100 Ext. 2558. Application contact: Dr. David McCulloch, Vice President for University Services, 800-443-5522 Ext. 5127. Fax: 847-465-0593. E-mail: dmcc@wheeling1.nl.edu.

National-Louis University, National College of Education, McGaw Graduate School, Doctoral Programs in Education, Program in Reading and Language, 2840 Sheridan Road, Evanston, IL 60201-1730. Awards Ed D. Part-time and evening/weekend programs available. Students: 2 full-time (both women), 26 part-time (23 women); includes 4 minority (1 African American, 3 Asian Americans). Average age 45. In 1997, 4 degrees awarded. *Degree requirements:* Dissertation, comprehensive exams, internship required, foreign language not required. *Entrance requirements:* GRE General Test, minimum GPA of 3.25. Application deadline: 12/15. Application fee: $25. *Tuition:* $411 per semester hour. *Financial aid:* Fellowships, research assistantships, teaching assistantships, institutionally sponsored loans available. Aid available to part-time students. Financial aid application deadline: 4/15; applicants required to submit FAFSA. • Dr. Peter Fisher, Coordinator, 708-475-1100 Ext. 2379. Application contact: Dr. David McCulloch, Vice President for University Services, 800-443-5522 Ext. 5127. Fax: 847-465-0593. E-mail: dmcc@wheeling1.nl.edu.

Nazareth College of Rochester, Graduate Studies, Department of Education, Program in Reading, Rochester, NY 14618-3790. Awards MS Ed. Part-time and evening/weekend programs available. Faculty: 2 full-time (1 woman), 9 part-time (8 women). Students: 10 full-time (all women), 110 part-time (106 women); includes 2 minority (1 African American, 1 Hispanic). 41 applicants, 100% accepted. In 1997, 46 degrees awarded. *Degree requirements:* Comprehensive exam required, foreign language and thesis not required. *Entrance requirements:* Minimum GPA of 2.7. Application deadline: 6/1 (11/1 for spring admission). Application fee: $40. *Expenses:* Tuition $436 per credit hour. Fees $20 per semester. • Dr. Kenneth Weiss, Director, 716-389-2590. Application contact: Dr. Kay F. Marshman, Dean, 716-389-2815. Fax: 716-389-2452.

New Jersey City University, School of Professional Studies and Education, Department of Literary Education, Jersey City, NJ 07305-1957. Awards MA. Evening/weekend programs available. *Degree requirements:* Comprehensive exam required, foreign language and thesis not required. *Entrance requirements:* GRE General Test, TOEFL or MAT. Application deadline: 8/1 (priority date; rolling processing; 12/1 for spring admission). Application fee: $0. *Faculty research:* Reading clinic.

New Mexico State University, College of Education, Department of Curriculum and Instruction, Las Cruces, NM 88003-8001. Offerings include reading (Ed S). Accredited by NCATE. Department faculty: 20 full-time (12 women). *Application deadline:* 7/1 (priority date; rolling processing; 11/1 for spring admission). *Application fee:* $15 ($35 for international students). *Tuition:* $2514 per year full-time, $105 per credit hour part-time for state residents; $7848 per year full-time, $327 per credit hour part-time for nonresidents. • Dr. Jeanette Martin, Head, 505-646-4820. Fax: 505-646-5436. E-mail: jeamarti@nmsu.edu.

New York University, School of Education, Department of Applied Psychology, Program in Applied Psychology, New York, NY 10012-1019. Offerings include psychological foundations of reading (MA, PhD), with options in learning disabilities and reading (MA), supervisors of reading (MA), teachers of reading (MA). Terminal master's awarded for partial completion of doctoral program. Program faculty: 12 full-time, 14 part-time. *Degree requirements:* For master's, thesis required (for some programs), foreign language not required. *Entrance requirements:* For master's, TOEFL. Application deadline: 2/1 (priority date; rolling processing; 12/1 for spring admission). Application fee: $40 ($60 for international students). • Catherine Tamis-Lemonda, Director, 212-998-5399. Application contact: Office of Graduate Admissions, 212-998-5030. Fax: 212-995-4328.

North Carolina Agricultural and Technical State University, Graduate School, School of Education, Department of Curriculum and Instruction, Program in Reading, Greensboro, NC 27411. Awards MS. Accredited by NCATE. Part-time and evening/weekend programs available. Students: 2 full-time (1 woman), 17 part-time (all women); includes 6 minority (all African Americans). 14 applicants, 93% accepted. In 1997, 8 degrees awarded. *Degree requirements:* Thesis or alternative, comprehensive exam, qualifying exam required, foreign language not required. *Entrance requirements:* GRE General Test, minimum GPA of 3.0. Application deadline: 6/1 (priority date; rolling processing; 12/1 for spring admission). Application fee: $35. *Tuition:* $1662 per year full-time, $272 per semester (minimum) part-time for state residents; $8790 per year full-time, $2054 per semester (minimum) part-time for nonresidents. *Financial aid:* Fellowships available. Financial aid application deadline: 6/1. • Dr. Dorothy Leflore, Interim Chairperson, Department of Curriculum and Instruction, 336-334-7848.

Northeastern Illinois University, College of Education, Department of Teacher Education, Program in Reading, Chicago, IL 60625-4699. Awards MA. Part-time and evening/weekend programs available. Faculty: 8 full-time (6 women), 1 (woman) part-time. Students: 3 full-time (all women), 101 part-time (96 women); includes 13 minority (7 African Americans, 2 Asian Americans, 4 Hispanics). Average age 33. 37 applicants, 78% accepted. In 1997, 23 degrees awarded. *Degree requirements:* Comprehensive exam required, thesis optional, foreign language not required. *Entrance requirements:* Course in psychology or tests and measurements, minimum GPA of 2.75. Application deadline: 3/18 (priority date; rolling processing; 9/30 for spring admission). Application fee: $0. *Expenses:* Tuition $2226 per year full-time, $93 per credit hour part-time for state residents; $6678 per year full-time, $278 per credit hour part-time for nonresidents. Fees $358 per year full-time, $14.90 per credit hour part-time. *Financial aid:* In 1997–98, 40 students received aid, including 2 research assistantships averaging $450 per month; full and partial tuition waivers, Federal Work-Study, institutionally sponsored loans, and career-related internships or fieldwork also available. Aid available to part-time students. Financial aid applicants required to submit FAFSA. *Faculty research:* Early literacy, reading disabilities, cognitive processes, multicultural and linguistic diversity, use of literature in the classroom. • Dr. Ahmed Fareed, Coordinator, 773-794-2969. Application contact: Dr. Mohan K. Sood, Dean of Graduate College, 773-583-4050 Ext. 6143. Fax: 773-794-6670.

Northeastern State University, College of Education, Department of Curriculum and Instruction, Program in Reading, Tahlequah, OK 74464-2399. Awards M Ed. Part-time and evening/weekend programs available. Faculty: 5 part-time (1 woman). Students: 67 (64 women); includes 1 international. In 1997, 19 degrees awarded. *Degree requirements:* Thesis or alternative required, foreign language not required. *Entrance requirements:* GRE General Test (minimum combined score of 900) or MAT (minimum score 35), minimum GPA of 2.5. Application deadline: 6/1 (priority date; rolling processing). Application fee: $0. *Expenses:* Tuition $74 per credit hour for state residents; $176 per credit hour for nonresidents. Fees $30 per year. *Financial aid:* Teaching assistantships, Federal Work-Study available. Financial aid application deadline: 3/1. • Dr. Karen Gunter, Coordinator, 918-456-5511 Ext. 3771.

Northeastern University, Graduate School of Arts and Sciences, Department of Education, Boston, MA 02115-5096. Offerings include reading (M Ed). Department faculty: 11 full-time (3 women), 3 part-time (2 women). *Average time to degree:* master's–3 years full-time, 5 years part-time. *Entrance requirements:* GRE General Test or MAT. Application deadline: 7/15 (rolling processing; 2/1 for spring admission). Application fee: $50. *Expenses:* Tuition $440 per credit hour. Fees $55 per quarter full-time, $13.25 per quarter part-time. • Dr. James W. Fraser, Acting Chair, 617-373-3302. Application contact: Dr. Mervin Lynch, Director of Graduate Admissions, 617-373-3302. Fax: 617-373-5261.

Northeast Louisiana University, College of Education, Department of Curriculum and Instruction, Program in Reading, Monroe, LA 71209-0001. Awards M Ed. Accredited by NCATE. *Entrance requirements:* GRE General Test, minimum GPA of 2.5. Application deadline: 6/1 (priority date; rolling processing; 11/1 for spring admission). Application fee: $15 ($25 for international students). *Tuition:* $2028 per year full-time, $240 per semester (minimum) part-time for state residents; $6852 per year full-time, $240 per semester (minimum) part-time for nonresidents.

Northern Arizona University, Center for Excellence in Education, Program in Reading and Learning Disabilities, Flagstaff, AZ 86011. Awards M Ed. Students: 1 (woman) full-time, 4 part-time (all women). Average age 29. 3 applicants, 33% accepted. In 1997, 1 degree awarded. *Degree requirements:* Thesis optional, foreign language not required. *Entrance requirements:* GRE General Test or minimum GPA of 3.0. Application deadline: 3/15 (priority date; rolling processing). Application fee: $45. *Expenses:* Tuition $2088 per year full-time, $330 per semester (minimum) part-time for state residents; $8004 per year full-time, $1002 per semester (minimum) part-time for nonresidents. Fees $72 per year full-time, $18 per semester (minimum) part-time. *Financial aid:* Full and partial tuition waivers, Federal Work-Study, and career-related internships or fieldwork available. *Faculty research:* Mild to moderate disabilities. • Dr. Malathi Sandhu, Interim Chair, 520-523-5342.

Northern Illinois University, College of Education, Department of Curriculum and Instruction, Program in Reading, De Kalb, IL 60115-2854. Awards MS Ed, Ed D. Accredited by NCATE. Part-time and evening/weekend programs available. Faculty: 7 full-time (4 women). Students: 2 full-time (both women), 76 part-time (74 women); includes 3 minority (1 African American, 1 Asian American, 1 Hispanic). Average age 34. 26 applicants, 81% accepted. In 1997, 50 master's, 2 doctorates awarded. *Degree requirements:* For master's, comprehensive exam required, thesis optional, foreign language not required; for doctorate, candidacy exam, dissertation defense required, foreign language not required. *Entrance requirements:* For master's, GRE General Test or MAT, TOEFL (minimum score 550), minimum GPA of 2.75; for doctorate, GRE General Test or MAT, TOEFL (minimum score 550), minimum GPA of 2.75 (undergraduate), 3.2 (graduate). Application deadline: 6/1 (rolling processing; 11/1 for spring admission). Application fee: $30. *Tuition:* $3984 per year full-time, $154 per credit hour part-time for state residents; $8160 per year full-time, $328 per credit hour part-time for nonresidents. *Financial aid:* Fellowships, research assistantships, teaching assistantships, staff assistantships, full tuition waivers, Federal Work-Study, and career-related internships or fieldwork available. Aid available to part-time students. • Dr. Norman Stahl, Chair, Department of Curriculum and Instruction, 815-753-9032.

Northern State University, Division of Graduate Studies in Education, Program in Teaching and Learning, Aberdeen, SD 57401-7198. Offerings include language and literacy (MS Ed). Accredited by NCATE. Offered jointly with Huron University, Jamestown College, and the University of Mary. Program faculty: 98 full-time (28 women). *Degree requirements:* Thesis required, foreign language not required. *Average time to degree:* master's–1.5 years full-time. *Entrance requirements:* Minimum GPA of 2.75. Application deadline: 8/15 (priority date; rolling processing; 12/15 for spring admission). Application fee: $15. *Expenses:* Tuition $1999 per year full-time, $83 per credit hour part-time for state residents; $6034 per year full-time, $251 per credit hour part-time for nonresidents. Fees $954 per year full-time, $40 per credit hour part-time. • Dr. Paul Deputy, Head, 605-626-2415. Application contact: Dr. Sharon Tebben, Director of Graduate Studies, 605-626-2558. Fax: 605-626-2542.

Northwestern Oklahoma State University, School of Education, Psychology, and Health and Physical Education, Reading Specialist Program, Alva, OK 73717. Awards M Ed. Accredited by NCATE. Part-time programs available. Faculty: 2 full-time (1 woman). Students: 1 (woman) full-time, 3 part-time (all women); includes 1 minority (Hispanic). 2 applicants, 100% accepted. In 1997, 1 degree awarded. *Entrance requirements:* GRE General Test (minimum combined score of 900) or MAT (minimum score 38), minimum GPA of 2.75. Application fee: $15. *Tuition:*

$73 per semester hour for state residents; $175 per semester hour for nonresidents. *Financial aid:* Application deadline 5/1. • Dr. Eugene Geist, Coordinator, 405-327-8451. Application contact: Dr. Ed Huckeby, Dean of Graduate School, 405-327-8410.

Northwestern State University of Louisiana, Division of Education, Emphasis in Reading, Natchitoches, LA 71497. Awards M Ed, Ed S. Accredited by NCATE. Faculty: 2 full-time (1 woman), 2 part-time (1 woman). Students: 2 part-time (both women); includes 1 minority (African American). Average age 37. *Entrance requirements:* For master's, GRE General Test (minimum combined score of 800), GRE Subject Test, minimum undergraduate GPA of 2.5. Application deadline: 8/1 (priority date; rolling processing; 1/10 for spring admission). Application fee: $15 ($25 for international students). *Tuition:* $2147 per year full-time, $336 per semester (minimum) part-time for state residents; $6437 per year full-time, $336 per semester (minimum) part-time for nonresidents. *Financial aid:* Career-related internships or fieldwork available. Financial aid application deadline: 7/15. • Application contact: Dr. Tom Hanson, Dean, Graduate Studies and Research, 318-357-5851. Fax: 318-357-5019.

Northwest Missouri State University, College of Education and Human Services, Department of Curriculum and Instruction, Program in Reading Education, 800 University Drive, Maryville, MO 64468-6001. Awards MS Ed. Accredited by NCATE. Part-time programs available. Faculty: 14 full-time (12 women). Students: 39 part-time (all women); includes 2 minority (1 African American, 1 Hispanic). 3 applicants, 100% accepted. In 1997, 16 degrees awarded. *Degree requirements:* Comprehensive exam required, foreign language and thesis not required. *Entrance requirements:* GRE General Test (minimum combined score of 700), TOEFL (minimum score 550), minimum undergraduate GPA of 2.5, teaching certificate, writing sample. Application deadline: rolling. Application fee: $0 ($50 for international students). *Expenses:* Tuition $113 per credit hour for state residents; $197 per credit hour for nonresidents. Fees $3 per credit hour. *Financial aid:* In 1997–98, 5 teaching assistantships averaging $585 per month, 1 administrative assistantship averaging $585 per month were awarded. Financial aid application deadline: 3/1. • Dr. Betty Bush, Director, 816-562-1359. Application contact: Dr. Frances Shipley, Dean of Graduate School, 816-562-1145. E-mail: gradsch@acad.nwmissouri.edu.

Notre Dame College, Education Division, Program in Advanced Reading, Manchester, NH 03104-2299. Awards M Ed. Part-time programs available. Faculty: 1 (woman) full-time, 2 part-time (both women). Students: 13 part-time (all women). Average age 38. 5 applicants, 80% accepted. In 1997, 5 degrees awarded. *Degree requirements:* Comprehensive exams, portfolio, or thesis required, foreign language not required. *Entrance requirements:* GRE General Test or MAT, teaching certificate. Application deadline: rolling. Application fee: $35. *Tuition:* $299 per credit. *Financial aid:* Fellowships, assistantships available. • Dr. Malvena Baxter, Director, 603-669-4298.

Nova Southeastern University, Fischler Center for the Advancement of Education, Graduate Teacher Education Program, Fort Lauderdale, FL 33314-7721. Offerings include reading (MS, Ed S). *Degree requirements:* Thesis, practicum required, foreign language not required. *Entrance requirements:* For master's, teaching certificate; for Ed S, master's degree, teaching certificate. Application deadline: rolling. Application fee: $50. *Tuition:* $245 per credit hour (minimum). • Dr. Deo Nellis, Dean, 954-262-8601. E-mail: deo@fcae.nova.edu. Application contact: Dr. Mark Seldine, Director of Student Affairs, 954-262-8689. Fax: 954-262-3910. E-mail: seldines@fcae.nova.edu.

Oakland University, School of Education and Human Services, Program in Reading, Rochester, MI 48309-4401. Awards MAT, PhD, Certificate. Accredited by NCATE. Faculty: 14 full-time. Students: 55 full-time (51 women), 333 part-time (318 women); includes 23 minority (17 African Americans, 2 Asian Americans, 3 Hispanics, 1 Native American), 11 international. Average age 37. 118 applicants, 85% accepted. In 1997, 104 master's, 9 doctorates awarded. *Degree requirements:* For doctorate, dissertation. *Entrance requirements:* For master's, minimum GPA of 3.0 for unconditional admission. Application deadline: 7/15 (3/15 for spring admission). Application fee: $30. *Expenses:* Tuition $3852 per year full-time, $214 per credit hour part-time for state residents, $8532 per year full-time, $474 per credit hour part-time for nonresidents. Fees $420 per year. *Financial aid:* Full tuition waivers, Federal Work-Study, institutionally sponsored loans, and career-related internships or fieldwork available. Financial aid application deadline: 3/1; applicants required to submit FAFSA. • Dr. Robert Schwartz, Chair, 248-370-3065.

Ohio University, Graduate Studies, College of Education, School of Curriculum and Instruction, Program in Reading, Athens, OH 45701-2979. Awards M Ed, PhD. Accredited by NCATE. Part-time and evening/weekend programs available. Students: 7 full-time (3 women), 6 part-time (5 women); includes 9 international. 10 applicants, 70% accepted. Terminal master's awarded for partial completion of doctoral program. *Degree requirements:* For master's, thesis or alternative required, foreign language not required; for doctorate, dissertation, comprehensive exams. *Entrance requirements:* For master's, GRE General Test or MAT; for doctorate, GRE General Test, MAT, minimum GPA of 3.0, work experience. Application deadline: rolling. Application fee: $30. *Tuition:* $5430 per year full-time, $216 per quarter hour part-time for state residents; $10,431 per year full-time, $423 per quarter hour part-time for nonresidents. *Financial aid:* In 1997–98, 2 teaching assistantships, 2 assistantships were awarded; full tuition waivers, Federal Work-Study, institutionally sponsored loans also available. Financial aid application deadline: 3/15. • Application contact: Dr. Bonnie Beach, Graduate Chair, 740-593-0523.

Old Dominion University, Darden College of Education, Department of Educational Curriculum and Instruction, Program in Reading, Norfolk, VA 23529. Awards MS. Accredited by NCATE. Part-time and evening/weekend programs available. Students: 1 (woman) full-time, 49 part-time (48 women); includes 10 minority (9 African Americans, 1 Hispanic). Average age 36. In 1997, 26 degrees awarded. *Degree requirements:* Comprehensive exam required, thesis optional, foreign language not required. *Entrance requirements:* GRE General Test, MAT, minimum GPA of 3.0 in major, 2.5 overall; teaching certificate. Application deadline: 7/1 (rolling processing). Application fee: $30. *Expenses:* Tuition $180 per credit hour for state residents; $477 per credit hour for nonresidents. Fees $140 per year full-time, $32 per semester part-time. *Financial aid:* In 1997–98, 11 students received aid, including 2 research assistantships totaling $10,220, 9 tuition grants totaling $3,566; teaching assistantships, Federal Work-Study, institutionally sponsored loans, and career-related internships or fieldwork also available. Aid available to part-time students. Financial aid application deadline: 2/15; applicants required to submit FAFSA. *Faculty research:* Metacognition and reading, eye movement studies and reading, reading in content areas. • Dr. Raymond F. Morgan, Director, 757-683-5103. Fax: 757-683-5862. E-mail: rmorgan@odu.edu.

Our Lady of Holy Cross College, Program in Education, New Orleans, LA 70131-7399. Offerings include curriculum and instruction (M Ed), with option in reading. Program faculty: 5 full-time (2 women), 7 part-time (3 women). *Degree requirements:* Thesis required, foreign language not required. *Entrance requirements:* GRE General Test (minimum combined score of 800), minimum GPA of 2.7. Application deadline: 9/1. Application fee: $20. *Expenses:* Tuition $5760 per year full-time, $240 per semester hour part-time. Fees $167 per year. • Dr. Judith G. Miranti, Dean, 504-394-7744.

Pacific Lutheran University, School of Education, Program in Literacy Education, Tacoma, WA 98447. Offers classroom language and literacy focus (MA), language and literacy (MA), school library media (MA). Accredited by NCATE. Part-time and evening/weekend programs available. Faculty: 6 full-time (5 women). Students: 8 part-time (7 women); includes 1 minority (Asian American). Average age 33. 6 applicants, 100% accepted. In 1997, 4 degrees awarded. *Degree requirements:* Comprehensive exam, research project or thesis required, foreign language not required. *Entrance requirements:* GRE General Test or MAT, TOEFL (minimum score 550), interview. Application deadline: rolling. Application fee: $35. *Tuition:* $490 per semester hour. *Financial aid:* Fellowships, research assistantships, scholarships, Federal Work-Study available. Financial aid application deadline: 3/1. • Dr. Leon Reisberg, Graduate Director, 253-535-7272. Application contact: Marjo Burdick, Office of Admissions, 253-535-7151. Fax: 253-535-8320. E-mail: admissions@plu.edu.

Pennsylvania State University University Park Campus, College of Education, Department of Curriculum and Instruction, University Park, PA 16802-1503. Offerings include language arts and reading (M Ed, MS, D Ed, PhD). Accredited by NCATE. *Degree requirements:* For doctorate, dissertation. *Entrance requirements:* GRE General Test or MAT. Application fee: $40. *Expenses:* Tuition $6534 per year full-time, $276 per credit part-time for state residents; $13,460 per year full-time, $561 per credit part-time for nonresidents. Fees $252 per year (minimum) full-time, $43 per semester (minimum) part-time. • Dr. Peter A. Rubb, Head, 814-865-5433.

Pittsburg State University, School of Education, Department of Curriculum and Instruction, Pittsburg, KS 66762-5880. Offerings include elementary reading (Ed S). Accredited by NCATE. *Application fee:* $40. *Tuition:* $2418 per year full-time, $103 per credit hour part-time for state residents; $6130 per year full-time, $258 per credit hour part-time for nonresidents. • Dr. Sandra Greer, Chairperson, 316-235-4496.

Pittsburg State University, School of Education, Department of Special Services and Leadership Studies, Program in Secondary Education, Pittsburg, KS 66762-5880. Offerings include secondary reading (Ed S). Accredited by NCATE. *Application fee:* $40. *Tuition:* $2418 per year full-time, $103 per credit hour part-time for state residents; $6130 per year full-time, $258 per credit hour part-time for nonresidents. • Dr. Steve Scott, Chairman, Department of Special Services and Leadership Studies, 316-235-4487.

Plattsburgh State University of New York, Faculty of Professional Studies, Center for Educational Studies and Services, Program in Reading, Plattsburgh, NY 12901-2681. Awards MS. Students: 5 full-time (all women), 13 part-time (11 women). 10 applicants, 90% accepted. In 1997, 12 degrees awarded. *Degree requirements:* Comprehensive exam or research project required, thesis optional. *Entrance requirements:* GRE General Test or MAT, minimum GPA of 2.5. Application deadline: rolling. Application fee: $50. *Expenses:* Tuition $5100 per year full-time, $213 per credit hour part-time for state residents; $8416 per year full-time, $351 per credit hour part-time for nonresidents. Fees $395 per year full-time, $15.10 per credit hour part-time. *Financial aid:* 9 students received aid; Federal Work-Study available. Aid available to part-time students. Financial aid application deadline: 4/15; applicants required to submit FAFSA. • Dr. Raymond Domenico, Director and Associate Dean, Center for Educational Studies and Services, 518-564-2122.

Plymouth State College of the University System of New Hampshire, Department of Education, Program in Reading Specialist, Plymouth, NH 03264-1595. Awards M Ed. Part-time and evening/weekend programs available. Students: 8 part-time (all women). Average age 35. 5 applicants, 80% accepted. In 1997, 3 degrees awarded. *Entrance requirements:* GRE General Test or MAT (minimum score 50), minimum GPA of 3.0. Application deadline: 9/1 (priority date; rolling processing). Application fee: $25 ($35 for international students). *Tuition:* $232 per credit for state residents; $254 per credit for nonresidents. *Financial aid:* Graduate assistantships, institutionally sponsored loans, and career-related internships or fieldwork available. Aid available to part-time students. Financial aid application deadline: 3/15; applicants required to submit FAFSA. • Dr. Dennise Bartelo, Adviser, 603-535-2286. Application contact: Maryann Szabadics, Administrative Assistant, 603-535-2636. Fax: 603-535-2572. E-mail: for.grad@psc.plymouth.edu.

Portland State University, School of Education, Department of Curriculum and Instruction, Program in Reading, Portland, OR 97207-0751. Awards MA, MS. Accredited by NCATE. Part-time programs available. Faculty: 16 full-time (9 women), 6 part-time (4 women), 17 FTE. Students: 0. 0 applicants. *Degree requirements:* Variable foreign language requirement, special project or thesis, written exam. *Entrance requirements:* California Basic Educational Skills Test, TOEFL (minimum score 550), minimum GPA of 3.0 in upper-division course work or 2.75 overall. Application deadline: 4/1 (rolling processing; 11/1 for spring admission). Application fee: $50. *Tuition:* $6101 per year full-time, $689 per semester (minimum) part-time for state residents; $10,445 per year full-time, $689 per semester (minimum) part-time for nonresidents. *Financial aid:* Research assistantships, teaching assistantships, Federal Work-Study, institutionally sponsored loans, and career-related internships or fieldwork available. Aid available to part-time students. Financial aid application deadline: 3/1; applicants required to submit FAFSA. *Faculty research:* Whole language, spelling, informal reading inventories, teacher preparation for pre-service reading, early detection of reading difficulties. • Application contact: Sandra Wilde, Associate Professor, 503-725-4681. Fax: 503-725-8475. E-mail: sandra@ed.pdx.edu.

Purdue University, School of Education, Department of Curriculum and Instruction, West Lafayette, IN 47907. Offerings include literacy (MS Ed, PhD, Ed S). Accredited by NCATE. Department faculty: 34 full-time (15 women), 3 part-time (1 woman). *Degree requirements:* For master's, thesis optional; for doctorate, dissertation, oral and written exams; for Ed S, oral presentation, project required, thesis not required. *Entrance requirements:* For master's, TOEFL (minimum score 550), minimum B average; for doctorate, GRE General Test (minimum score 500 on each section), TOEFL (minimum score 550); for Ed S, minimum B average. Application deadline: 1/15 (priority date; 9/15 for spring admission). Application fee: $30. Electronic applications accepted. *Tuition:* $3500 per year full-time, $126 per credit hour part-time for state residents; $11,720 per year full-time, $387 per credit hour part-time for nonresidents. • Dr. J. L. Peters, Head, 765-494-9172. Fax: 765-496-1622. E-mail: peters@purdue.edu. Application contact: Christine Larsen, Coordinator of Graduate Studies, 765-494-2345. Fax: 765-494-5832. E-mail: gradoffice@soe.purdue.edu.

Queens College of the City University of New York, Social Science Division, School of Education, Department of Educational and Community Programs, Program in Reading, 65-30 Kissena Boulevard, Flushing, NY 11367-1597. Awards MS Ed. Part-time programs available. Students: 89 part-time (87 women); includes 5 minority (3 African Americans, 1 Hispanic, 1 Native American). 98 applicants, 68% accepted. In 1997, 39 degrees awarded. *Degree requirements:* Research project required, foreign language and thesis not required. *Entrance requirements:* TOEFL (minimum score 600), minimum GPA of 3.0. Application deadline: 4/1 (rolling processing; 11/1 for spring admission). Application fee: $40. *Expenses:* Tuition $4350 per year full-time, $185 per credit part-time for state residents; $7600 per year full-time, $320 per credit part-time for nonresidents. Fees $104 per year. *Financial aid:* Partial tuition waivers, Federal Work-Study, institutionally sponsored loans, and career-related internships or fieldwork available. Aid available to part-time students. Financial aid application deadline: 4/1; applicants required to submit FAFSA. • Dr. Howard Margolis, Graduate Adviser, 718-997-5240. Application contact: Mario Caruso, Director of Graduate Admissions, 718-997-5200. Fax: 718-997-5193. E-mail: graduate%queens.bitnet@cunyvm.cuny.edu.

Radford University, Graduate College, College of Education and Human Development, Department of Educational Studies, Program in Reading, Radford, VA 24142. Awards MS. Accredited by NCATE. Part-time programs available. Postbaccalaureate distance learning degree programs offered (minimal on-campus study). Students: 2 full-time (both women), 29 part-time (28 women); includes 2 minority (both African Americans). Average age 36. 18 applicants, 94% accepted. In 1997, 7 degrees awarded. *Degree requirements:* Comprehensive exam required, foreign language and thesis not required. *Entrance requirements:* GMAT, GRE General Test, MAT, or NTE; TOEFL (minimum score 550), minimum GPA of 2.7. Application deadline: 2/1 (priority date; rolling processing; 10/1 for spring admission). Application fee: $25. Electronic applications accepted. *Expenses:* Tuition $2302 per year full-time, $147 per credit hour part-time for state residents; $5672 per year full-time, $287 per credit hour part-time for nonresidents. Fees $1222 per year full-time. *Financial aid:* In 1997–98, 1 research assistantship totaling $3,100, 13 scholarships/grants totaling $8,258 were awarded; fellowships, teaching assistantships, Federal Work-Study, institutionally sponsored loans, and career-related internships or fieldwork also available. Financial aid application deadline: 2/1; applicants required to submit FAFSA. • Dr. Anita L. Corey, Director, 540-831-5806. Fax: 540-831-6053. E-mail: acorey@runet.edu.

Rhode Island College, School of Graduate Studies, School of Education and Human Development, Department of Elementary Education, Program in Reading Education, Providence, RI

Directory: Reading Education

Rhode Island College (continued)

02908-1924. Awards M Ed, CAGS. Accredited by NCATE. Evening/weekend programs available. Faculty: 19 full-time (9 women), 9 part-time (7 women). Students: 51 part-time (50 women); includes 1 minority (Asian American). In 1997, 12 master's awarded. *Degree requirements:* For CAGS, thesis required, foreign language not required. *Entrance requirements:* For master's, GRE General Test or MAT. Application deadline: 4/1 (rolling processing). Application fee: $25. *Tuition:* $4064 per year full-time, $214 per credit part-time for state residents; $7658 per year full-time, $376 per credit part-time for nonresidents. *Financial aid:* Application deadline 4/1. • Dr. Patricia Cordeiro, Chair, Department of Elementary Education, 401-456-8016.

Rider University, School of Graduate Education and Human Services, Program in Reading/Language Arts, Lawrenceville, NJ 08648-3001. Awards MA. Accredited by NCATE. Part-time and evening/weekend programs available. Faculty: 1 (woman) full-time, 5 part-time (all women). Students: 3 full-time, 43 part-time. Average age 32. 9 applicants, 89% accepted. In 1997, 14 degrees awarded. *Degree requirements:* Comprehensive exams, research project required, foreign language and thesis not required. *Entrance requirements:* Interview, minimum GPA of 2.5. Application deadline: 8/15 (priority date; rolling processing; 12/15 for spring admission). Application fee: $35. *Tuition:* $329 per credit hour. *Financial aid:* Career-related internships or fieldwork available. Aid available to part-time students. *Faculty research:* Ethnography in the reading/language arts process. • Dr. Susan Glazer, Adviser, 609-896-5316. Application contact: Dr. John Carpenter, Dean, Continuing Studies, 609-896-5036. Fax: 609-896-5261.

Rivier College, Graduate Education Department, Program in Reading, Nashua, NH 03060-5086. Awards M Ed. Part-time and evening/weekend programs available. *Entrance requirements:* GRE General Test or MAT. Application deadline: rolling. Application fee: $25.

Rockford College, Department of Education, Program in Remedial Reading, Rockford, IL 61108-2393. Awards MAT. Part-time and evening/weekend programs available. Faculty: 3 full-time (1 woman), 6 part-time (all women), 4 FTE. Students: 20 part-time (18 women); includes 1 minority (African American). Average age 35. 3 applicants, 100% accepted. In 1997, 4 degrees awarded. *Degree requirements:* Thesis optional, foreign language not required. *Entrance requirements:* GRE General Test (minimum combined score of 1000). Application deadline: rolling. Application fee: $35. *Tuition:* $15,500 per year full-time, $400 per credit part-time. • Dr. Lou Ferroli, Head, 815-226-4182.

Roosevelt University, College of Education, Chicago, IL 60605-1394. Offerings include reading education (MA). Accredited by NCATE. *Application deadline:* 6/1 (priority date; rolling processing). *Application fee:* $25 ($35 for international students). *Expenses:* Tuition $445 per credit hour. Fees $100 per year. • Dr. George Lowery, Dean, 312-341-3700. Application contact: Joanne Canyon-Heller, Coordinator of Graduate Admissions, 312-341-3612.

Rowan University, College of Education, Department of Reading Education, Glassboro, NJ 08028-1701. Awards MA. Accredited by NCATE. Part-time and evening/weekend programs available. Students: 55 (54 women); includes 3 minority (2 African Americans, 1 Asian American). 20 applicants, 65% accepted. In 1997, 14 degrees awarded. *Degree requirements:* Thesis, comprehensive exams required, foreign language not required. *Entrance requirements:* GRE General Test (minimum combined score of 800), GRE Subject Test, interview, minimum GPA of 2.8. Application deadline: 11/1 (priority date; rolling processing; 4/1 for spring admission). Application fee: $50. *Tuition:* $5728 per year full-time, $258 per credit hour part-time for state residents; $8968 per year full-time, $393 per credit hour part-time for nonresidents. *Financial aid:* Federal Work-Study and career-related internships or fieldwork available. • Dr. Nick DiObilda, Adviser, 609-256-4772.

Rutgers, The State University of New Jersey, New Brunswick, Graduate School of Education, Department of Learning and Teaching, Program in Literacy Education, New Brunswick, NJ 08903. Awards Ed M, Ed D, Ed S. Part-time programs available. Faculty: 5 full-time (4 women), 2 part-time (both women). Students: 21 full-time (16 women), 32 part-time (26 women). 59 applicants, 71% accepted. In 1997, 4 master's awarded. Terminal master's awarded for partial completion of doctoral program. *Degree requirements:* For master's, comprehensive exam required, thesis not required; for doctorate, dissertation, qualifying exam. *Entrance requirements:* For master's, GRE General Test (minimum combined score of 1000), minimum undergraduate GPA of 3.0; for doctorate, GRE General Test (minimum combined score of 1100), minimum graduate GPA of 3.5, certification and 2 years of teaching experience; for Ed S, GRE General Test. Application deadline: 3/1 (11/1 for spring admission). Application fee: $40. *Expenses:* Tuition $6492 per year full-time, $268 per credit part-time for state residents; $9520 per year full-time, $395 per credit part-time for nonresidents. Fees $208 per year (minimum). *Financial aid:* In 1997–98, 2 teaching assistantships were awarded. Financial aid application deadline: 3/1. *Faculty research:* Early childhood literacy development, discourse analysis-adult literacy. • Dr. Michael Smith, Coordinator, 732-932-7496 Ext. 120.

Sage Graduate School, Graduate School, Division of Education, Program in Reading, Troy, NY 12180-4115. Awards MS Ed. Part-time and evening/weekend programs available. *Entrance requirements:* Minimum GPA of 2.75. Application deadline: 8/1 (rolling processing; 12/15 for spring admission). Application fee: $25. *Expenses:* Tuition $360 per credit hour. Fees $50 per semester. *Financial aid:* Research assistantships and career-related internships or fieldwork available. Aid available to part-time students. Financial aid application deadline: 7/1; applicants required to submit FAFSA. *Faculty research:* Literacy development in at-risk children. • Dr. Peter McDermott, Adviser, 518-244-2493. Fax: 518-244-2334. E-mail: mcderp@sage.edu. Application contact: Melissa Robertson, Associate Director of Admissions, 518-244-6878. Fax: 518-244-6880. E-mail: sgsadm@sage.edu.

Sage Graduate School, Graduate School, Division of Education, Program in Reading/Special Education, Troy, NY 12180-4115. Awards MS Ed. Part-time and evening/weekend programs available. *Entrance requirements:* Minimum GPA of 2.75. Application deadline: 8/1 (rolling processing; 12/15 for spring admission). Application fee: $25. *Expenses:* Tuition $360 per credit hour. Fees $50 per semester. *Financial aid:* Research assistantships and career-related internships or fieldwork available. Aid available to part-time students. Financial aid application deadline: 7/1; applicants required to submit FAFSA. *Faculty research:* Commonalities in the roles of reading specialists and resource/consultant teachers. • Dr. Connell Frazer, Adviser, 518-244-2403. Fax: 518-244-2334. E-mail: frazec@sage.edu. Application contact: Melissa Robertson, Associate Director of Admissions, 518-244-6878. Fax: 518-244-6880. E-mail: sgsadm@sage.edu.

Saginaw Valley State University, College of Education, Program in Reading, University Center, MI 48710. Awards MAT. Accredited by NCATE. Part-time and evening/weekend programs available. Faculty: 12 full-time (9 women). Students: 69 part-time (60 women); includes 2 minority (both African Americans). In 1997, 11 degrees awarded. *Entrance requirements:* Minimum GPA of 3.0, teaching certificate. Application deadline: rolling. Application fee: $25. *Expenses:* Tuition $159 per credit hour for state residents; $311 per credit hour for nonresidents. Fees $8.70 per credit hour. • Application contact: Dr. Elaine Stephens, Coordinator, 517-790-4317. E-mail: stephens@tardis.svsu.edu.

St. Bonaventure University, School of Education, Program in Reading, St. Bonaventure, NY 14778-2284. Awards MS Ed. Part-time and evening/weekend programs available. Faculty: 2 full-time (0 women), 2 part-time (both women). Students: 45 full-time (41 women), 23 part-time (3 women); includes 2 minority (both African Americans). Average age 24. *Degree requirements:* Comprehensive exam required, thesis optional, foreign language not required. *Average time to degree:* master's–2 years full-time, 3 years part-time. *Entrance requirements:* TOEFL (minimum score 600). Application deadline: 8/1 (rolling processing). Application fee: $35. *Tuition:* $8100 per year full-time, $450 per credit hour part-time. *Financial aid:* Research assistantships and career-related internships or fieldwork available. *Faculty research:* Children's literary tastes, reading diagnosis. • Dr. Joe Zimmer, Director, 716-375-2388.

St. Cloud State University, College of Education, Department of Teacher Development, Program in Reading, St. Cloud, MN 56301-4498. Awards MS. Accredited by NCATE. Faculty: 2 full-time (1 woman). Students: 1 (woman) part-time. *Degree requirements:* Thesis or alternative, foreign language not required. *Entrance requirements:* GRE General Test, minimum GPA of 2.75. Application fee: $20 ($100 for international students). *Expenses:* Tuition $128 per credit for state residents; $203 per credit for nonresidents. Fees $16.32 per credit. *Financial aid:* Graduate assistantships, Federal Work-Study available. Financial aid application deadline: 3/1. • Application contact: Ann Anderson, Graduate Studies Office, 320-255-2113. Fax: 320-654-5371. E-mail: anna@grad.stcloud.msus.edu.

St. John's University, School of Education and Human Services, Division of Human Services and Counseling, Reading Specialist Program, Jamaica, NY 11439. Awards MS Ed, PD. Part-time and evening/weekend programs available. Students: 18 full-time (all women), 162 part-time (158 women); includes 12 minority (5 African Americans, 1 Asian American, 3 Hispanics, 3 Native Americans). Average age 30. 83 applicants, 90% accepted. In 1997, 67 master's awarded. *Entrance requirements:* For master's, minimum GPA of 3.0, New York teaching certificate; for PD, minimum GPA of 3.0, MS Ed, New York teaching certificate. Application deadline: 6/1 (rolling processing; 10/1 for spring admission). Application fee: $40. *Expenses:* Tuition $525 per credit. Fees $150 per year. *Financial aid:* Administrative assistantships, Federal Work-Study, and career-related internships or fieldwork available. Aid available to part-time students. Financial aid application deadline: 3/1; applicants required to submit FAFSA. *Faculty research:* Visual fluency and reading proficiency, sementric mapping and literacy proficiency, beginning literacy, literature approaches to literacy. • Dr. Paul Wielan, Coordinator, 718-990-1564. Application contact: Shamus J. McGrenra, TOR, Associate Director, Graduate Admissions, 718-990-6107. Fax: 718-990-5736. E-mail: mcgrenrs@stjohns.edu.

Saint Joseph's University, Department of Education, Program in Reading, Philadelphia, PA 19131-1395. Awards MS. Evening/weekend programs available. Students: 191 (161 women). In 1997, 29 degrees awarded. *Entrance requirements:* TOEFL. Application deadline: 7/15. Application fee: $30. *Tuition:* $510 per credit hour. *Financial aid:* Fellowships available. • Dr. Mary DeKonty Applegate, Director, Department of Education, 610-660-1583.

Saint Martin's College, Graduate Programs, Department of Education, Lacey, WA 98503-7500. Offerings include reading (M Ed). Department faculty: 8 full-time (3 women), 5 part-time (2 women). *Application deadline:* 7/1 (priority date; rolling processing; 12/1 for spring admission). *Application fee:* $25. • Dr. Paul Nelson, Director, 360-438-4529. Application contact: Michelle Roman, Administrative Assistant, 360-438-4333.

Saint Mary's College of California, School of Education, Program in Reading Leadership, Moraga, CA 94575. Awards MA. Part-time and evening/weekend programs available. Faculty: Students: 31 part-time (all women). Average age 38. 0 applicants. In 1997, 1 degree awarded. *Degree requirements:* Thesis or alternative required, foreign language not required. *Entrance requirements:* Interview, minimum GPA of 3.0. Application deadline: rolling. Application fee: $50. *Tuition:* $1319 per course. *Financial aid:* Career-related internships or fieldwork available. Aid available to part-time students. Financial aid application deadline: 2/15. • Candy Boyd, Director, 925-631-4700.

St. Mary's University of San Antonio, Department of Education, San Antonio, TX 78228-8507. Offerings include reading (MA). *Entrance requirements:* GRE General Test. Application deadline: 8/1. Application fee: $15. *Expenses:* Tuition $383 per credit hour (minimum). Fees $217 per year full-time, $58 per semester part-time.

Saint Michael's College, Program in Education, Colchester, VT 05439. Offerings include reading (M Ed). Program faculty: 5 full-time (4 women), 70 part-time (54 women). *Degree requirements:* Computer language, thesis required, foreign language not required. *Entrance requirements:* Minimum GPA of 2.8. Application deadline: rolling. Application fee: $25. • Dr. Aostre Johnson, Director, 802-654-2436. Fax: 802-654-2664.

Saint Peter's College, Graduate Programs in Education, Reading Specialist Program, 2641 Kennedy Boulevard, Jersey City, NJ 07306-5997. Awards MA. Part-time and evening/weekend programs available. Faculty: 2 full-time (0 women), 3 part-time (2 women). Students: 1 full-time (0 women), 9 part-time (all women); includes 2 minority (1 African American, 1 Hispanic). Average age 25. In 1997, 4 degrees awarded. *Degree requirements:* Departmental qualifying exam required, foreign language and thesis not required. *Entrance requirements:* GRE or MAT (minimum score 40). Application deadline: 8/1 (priority date; rolling processing). Application fee: $20. *Tuition:* $516 per credit. *Financial aid:* Career-related internships or fieldwork available. Aid available to part-time students. Financial aid application deadline: 7/1. • Dr. Joseph McLaughlin, Director, Graduate Programs in Education, 201-915-9254. Fax: 201-915-9074. Application contact: Nancy P. Campbell, Associate Vice President for Enrollment, 201-915-9213. Fax: 201-432-5860. E-mail: admissions@spcvxa.spc.edu.

St. Thomas Aquinas College, Division of Teacher Education, Program in Reading, Sparkill, NY 10976. Awards MS Ed. Faculty: 6 full-time (4 women), 6 part-time (3 women). *Degree requirements:* Comprehensive professional portfolio required, thesis not required. *Entrance requirements:* New York State Qualifying Exam, GRE General Test or minimum GPA of 3.0, teaching certificate. Application deadline: 7/31 (priority date; rolling processing; 12/1 for spring admission). Application fee: $35. Electronic applications accepted. *Expenses:* Tuition $390 per credit. Fees $10 per year. *Financial aid:* In 1997–98, 2 assistantships (both to first-year students) were awarded; partial tuition waivers also available. Financial aid application deadline: 2/15. *Faculty research:* Literacy: reading and writing connections, technology infused instruction. • Application contact: Joseph L. Chillo, Executive Director of Enrollment Services, 914-398-4100. Fax: 914-398-4224. E-mail: joestacenroll@rockland.net.

Saint Xavier University, School of Education, Chicago, IL 60655-3105. Offerings include reading (MA). School faculty: 16 full-time (12 women), 3 part-time (1 woman). *Degree requirements:* Thesis or project required, thesis optional. *Entrance requirements:* MAT, minimum GPA of 3.0. Application deadline: 8/15 (priority date; rolling processing). Application fee: $35. *Expenses:* Tuition $435 per hour. Fees $50 per year. • Dr. Beverly Gulley, Dean, 773-298-3221. Fax: 773-779-9061. E-mail: gulley@sxu.edu. Application contact: Sr. Evelyn McKenna, Vice President of Enrollment Management, 773-298-3050. Fax: 773-298-3076. E-mail: mckenna@sxu.edu.

Salem College, Department of Education, PO Box 10548, Winston-Salem, NC 27108-0548. Offerings include language and literacy (M Ed). Accredited by NCATE. College faculty: 10 full-time (7 women), 2 part-time (both women). *Average time to degree:* master's–1.5 years full-time, 3 years part-time. *Application deadline:* rolling. *Application fee:* $35. *Tuition:* $195 per hour. • Dr. Robin L. Smith, Director of Graduate Studies, 336-721-2656. Fax: 336-721-2683. E-mail: smith@salem.edu.

Salem State College, Department of Education, Program in Reading, Salem, MA 01970-5353. Awards M Ed. Accredited by NCATE. *Entrance requirements:* GRE General Test. Application deadline: rolling. Application fee: $25. *Expenses:* Tuition $140 per credit hour for state residents; $230 per credit hour for nonresidents. Fees $20 per credit hour.

Salisbury State University, Department of Education, Concentration in Reading Education, Salisbury, MD 21801-6837. Awards M Ed. *Application deadline:* 8/1 (rolling processing; 1/1 for spring admission). *Application fee:* $30. *Expenses:* Tuition $158 per credit hour for state residents; $310 per credit hour for nonresidents. Fees $4 per credit hour. • Dr. Ellen Whitford, Chair, Department of Education, 410-543-6294. E-mail: evwhitford@ssu.edu. Application contact: Phyllis Meyer, Administrative Aide II, 410-543-6281. Fax: 410-548-2593. E-mail: phmeyer@ssu.edu.

Sam Houston State University, College of Education and Applied Science, Department of Language, Literacy, and Special Populations, Reading Program, Huntsville, TX 77341. Awards M Ed. Accredited by NCATE. Part-time and evening/weekend programs available. Students: 1

(woman) full-time, 22 part-time (21 women); includes 2 minority (1 African American, 1 Hispanic). In 1997, 7 degrees awarded. *Entrance requirements:* GRE General Test (minimum combined score of 800), minimum GPA of 2.5. Application deadline: 9/1. Application fee: $15. *Tuition:* $1810 per year full-time, $297 per semester (minimum) part-time for state residents; $6922 per year full-time, $924 per semester (minimum) part-time for nonresidents. *Financial aid:* Teaching assistantships available. *Faculty research:* Reading-writing relationships, literacy assessment, special needs assessment, teacher research, integrated language arts. • Dr. Hollis Lowery-Moore, Chair, Department of Language, Literacy, and Special Populations, 409-294-1595. Fax: 409-294-1131. E-mail: edu_lap@shsu.edu.

San Diego State University, College of Education, School of Teacher Education, Program in Reading Education, San Diego, CA 92182. Awards MA. Accredited by NCATE. Part-time programs available. Students: 8 full-time (all women), 30 part-time (29 women); includes 6 minority (1 Asian American, 5 Hispanics), 1 international. Average age 29. *Average time to degree:* master's–3 years part-time. *Entrance requirements:* GRE General Test (minimum combined score of 950), TOEFL (minimum score 550). Application deadline: 6/1 (priority date; rolling processing; 12/1 for spring admission). Application fee: $55. *Expenses:* Tuition $0 for state residents; $246 per unit for nonresidents. Fees $1932 per year full-time, $1266 per year part-time. *Faculty research:* Literacy, writing, reading/writing connection, class size reduction in reading, bookclubs, evaluation instruments in reading/language arts. • Debra Bayles, Graduate Coordinator, 619-594-6131. Fax: 619-594-7828.

San Francisco State University, College of Humanities, Department of English Language and Literature, San Francisco, CA 94132-1722. Offerings include teaching post-secondary reading (Certificate). *Average time to degree:* master's–2 years full-time, 3.5 years part-time. *Application deadline:* rolling. *Application fee:* $55. *Expenses:* Tuition $0 for state residents; $246 per unit for nonresidents. Fees $1982 per year full-time, $1316 per year part-time.

Seattle Pacific University, School of Education, Program in Curriculum and Instruction, Seattle, WA 98119-1997. Offerings include reading/language arts education (M Ed). Accredited by NCATE. Program faculty: 8 full-time (1 woman), 8 part-time (5 women). *Average time to degree:* master's–3 years part-time. *Entrance requirements:* MAT (minimum score 35) or GRE General Test (minimum score 300 on verbal section, 350 on quantitative, 950 combined), minimum GPA of 3.0. Application deadline: 7/1 (priority date; rolling processing; 3/1 for spring admission). Application fee: $35. *Tuition:* $274 per credit. • Patricia Hammill, Chair, 206-281-2380. Fax: 206-281-2756.

Shippensburg University of Pennsylvania, College of Education and Human Services, Department of Teacher Education, Shippensburg, PA 17257-2299. Offerings include reading (M Ed). Accredited by NCATE. Department faculty: 16 full-time (11 women), 10 part-time (7 women). *Application deadline:* rolling. *Application fee:* $25. Electronic applications accepted. *Expenses:* Tuition $3468 per year full-time, $193 per credit hour part-time for state residents; $6236 per year full-time, $346 per credit hour part-time for nonresidents. Fees $678 per year full-time, $108 per semester (minimum) part-time. • Dr. Audrey Sprenger, Chairperson, 717-532-1688.

Siena Heights University, Program in Teacher Education, Adrian, MI 49221-1796. Offerings include elementary education (MA), with option in elementary education/reading; secondary education (MA), with option in secondary education/reading. *Degree requirements:* Computer language, thesis, presentation required, foreign language not required. *Entrance requirements:* Minimum GPA of 3.0, interview. Application deadline: 7/1 (priority date; rolling processing; 12/1 for spring admission). Application fee: $25.

Slippery Rock University of Pennsylvania, College of Education, Department of Elementary Education and Early Childhood, Program in Reading, Slippery Rock, PA 16057. Awards M Ed. Accredited by NCATE. Part-time and evening/weekend programs available. *Degree requirements:* Comprehensive exams required, thesis optional. *Entrance requirements:* GRE, minimum GPA of 2.75. Application deadline: 7/1 (priority date; rolling processing; 11/1 for spring admission). Application fee: $25. *Tuition:* $4484 per year full-time, $247 per credit part-time for state residents; $7667 per year full-time, $423 per credit part-time for nonresidents.

Sonoma State University, School of Education, Program in Reading, Rohnert Park, CA 94928-3609. Awards MA. Part-time and evening/weekend programs available. Students: 1 (woman) full-time, 21 part-time (20 women); includes 2 minority (both Hispanics). Average age 39. 5 applicants, 100% accepted. In 1997, 4 degrees awarded. *Degree requirements:* Thesis or alternative required, foreign language not required. *Entrance requirements:* GRE General Test, minimum GPA of 2.5. Application fee: $55. *Expenses:* Tuition $0 for state residents; $246 per unit for nonresidents. Fees $2130 per year full-time, $1464 per year part-time. *Financial aid:* Application deadline 3/2. • Dr. Marty Ruddell, Advocate, 707-664-2556. E-mail: martha.ruddell@sonoma.edu.

Southeastern Louisiana University, College of Education, Department of Teacher Education, Hammond, LA 70402. Offerings include reading (M Ed). Accredited by NCATE. Department faculty: 22 full-time, 14 part-time. *Entrance requirements:* GRE, teaching certificate. Application deadline: 7/15 (priority date; rolling processing; 12/15 for spring admission). Application fee: $10 ($25 for international students). Electronic applications accepted. *Expenses:* Tuition $2010 per year full-time, $287 per semester (minimum) part-time for state residents; $5232 per year full-time, $287 per semester (minimum) part-time for nonresidents. Fees $5 per year. • Dr. Martha Head, Head, 504-549-2221. E-mail: mhead@selu.edu. Application contact: Dr. Jeanne Burns, Graduate Coordinator, 504-549-2221. Fax: 504-549-5009. E-mail: jburns@selu.edu.

Southern Arkansas University–Magnolia, Graduate Program in Education, Program in Elementary Education, Magnolia, AR 71753. Offerings include reading education (M Ed). Program faculty: 5 part-time. *Degree requirements:* Thesis or alternative, comprehensive exam required, foreign language not required. *Average time to degree:* master's–2 years full-time. *Entrance requirements:* GRE, minimum GPA of 2.5. Application deadline: 8/15 (rolling processing). Application fee: $0. *Expenses:* Tuition $95 per hour for state residents; $138 per hour for nonresidents. Fees $2 per hour. • Dr. Danield L. Bernard, Dean, Graduate Studies, Graduate Program in Education, 870-235-4055. Fax: 870-235-5035. E-mail: dlbernard@mail.saumag.edu.

Southern Connecticut State University, School of Education, Department of Reading, New Haven, CT 06515-1355. Awards MS Ed, Diploma. Faculty: 3 full-time, 1 part-time. Students: 1 (woman) full-time, 105 part-time (100 women); includes 8 minority (3 African Americans, 4 Hispanics, 1 Native American). 77 applicants, 29% accepted. In 1997, 30 master's, 1 Diploma awarded. *Degree requirements:* For master's, thesis or alternative required, foreign language not required. *Entrance requirements:* For master's, interview, teaching certificate; for Diploma, master's degree. Application deadline: 7/15 (priority date; rolling processing). Application fee: $40. *Expenses:* Tuition $2632 per year full-time, $188 per credit part-time for state residents; $7200 per year full-time, $188 per credit part-time for nonresidents. Fees $1806 per year full-time, $45 per semester part-time for state residents; $2703 per year full-time, $45 per semester part-time for nonresidents. • Dr. Irving Newman, Chairman, 203-392-6407.

Southern Oregon University, School of Social Science, Health and Physical Education, Department of Education, Ashland, OR 97520. Offerings include elementary education (MA Ed, MS Ed), with options in classroom teacher, early childhood, handicapped learner, reading, supervision; secondary education (MA Ed, MS Ed), with options in classroom teacher, handicapped learner, reading, supervision. *Application deadline:* 2/1. *Application fee:* $50. *Tuition:* $5187 per year full-time, $586 per quarter (minimum) part-time for state residents; $9228 per year full-time, $586 per quarter (minimum) part-time for nonresidents. • Dr. Mary-Curtis Gramley, Associate Dean of Education, 541-552-6918.

Southwest Missouri State University, College of Education, Department of Reading and Special Education, Springfield, MO 65804-0094. Awards MS Ed. Part-time and evening/weekend programs available. Faculty: 7 full-time (5 women). Students: 7 full-time (all women), 81 part-time (75 women); includes 2 minority (1 African American, 1 Native American), 2 international. In 1997, 28 degrees awarded. *Degree requirements:* Thesis or alternative, comprehensive exam required, foreign language not required. *Entrance requirements:* Minimum GPA of 2.75, teaching certificate. Application deadline: 8/7 (priority date; rolling processing; 12/17 for spring admission). Application fee: $25. *Expenses:* Tuition $1980 per year full-time, $110 per credit hour part-time for state residents; $3960 per year full-time, $220 per credit hour part-time for nonresidents. Fees $274 per year full-time, $73 per semester part-time. • Dr. Christopher Craig, Head, 417-836-6769. Fax: 417-836-4884. E-mail: cjc886@wpgate.smsu.edu.

Southwest Texas State University, School of Education, Department of Curriculum and Instruction, Program in Reading Education, San Marcos, TX 78666. Awards M Ed. Part-time and evening/weekend programs available. Students: 2 full-time (both women), 28 part-time (27 women); includes 4 minority (3 African Americans, 1 Hispanic), 1 international. Average age 34. In 1997, 7 degrees awarded. *Degree requirements:* Comprehensive exam required, thesis optional, foreign language not required. *Entrance requirements:* GRE General Test (minimum combined score of 900), TOEFL (minimum score 550), minimum GPA of 2.75 in last 60 hours, teaching experience. Application deadline: 7/15 (priority date; rolling processing; 11/15 for spring admission). Application fee: $25 ($50 for international students). *Expenses:* Tuition $648 per year full-time, $120 per semester (minimum) part-time for state residents; $4500 per year full-time, $750 per semester (minimum) part-time for nonresidents. Fees $1264 per year full-time, $314 per semester (minimum) part-time. *Financial aid:* Federal Work-Study, institutionally sponsored loans, and career-related internships or fieldwork available. Aid available to part-time students. Financial aid application deadline: 4/1; applicants required to submit FAFSA. *Faculty research:* Reading comprehension, computer-assisted instruction. • Dr. Marguerite Gillis, Graduate Adviser, 512-245-2157. E-mail: mg06@swt.edu. Application contact: Dr. J. Michael Willoughby, Dean of the Graduate School, 512-245-2581. Fax: 512-245-8365. E-mail: jw02@swt.edu.

Spalding University, School of Education, Programs in Teacher Education and Administration, Louisville, KY 40203-2188. Offerings include reading specialist (MA). Accredited by NCATE. Faculty: 7 full-time (5 women), 5 part-time (4 women). *Application deadline:* 8/15 (priority date; rolling processing). *Application fee:* $30. *Expenses:* Tuition $350 per credit hour (minimum). Fees $48 per year full-time, $4 per credit hour part-time. • Application contact: Jeanne Anderson, Assistant to the Provost and Director of Graduate Office, 502-585-7105. Fax: 502-585-7158. E-mail: gradoffc@spalding6.win.net.

Spring Hill College, Graduate Programs, Program in Education, Mobile, AL 36608-1791. Offerings include teaching of reading (MS Ed). Program faculty: 5 full-time (3 women), 5 part-time (1 woman). *Average time to degree:* master's–2 years part-time. *Application deadline:* rolling. *Application fee:* $25. • Dr. B. C. Algero, Chair, 334-380-3477.

State University of New York at Albany, School of Education, Department of Reading, Albany, NY 12222-0001. Awards MS, Ed D, CAS. Evening/weekend programs available. Faculty: 7 full-time (3 women), 2 part-time (both women). Students: 37 full-time (31 women), 184 part-time (163 women); includes 10 minority (6 African Americans, 1 Asian American, 3 Hispanics), 3 international. 59 applicants, 95% accepted. In 1997, 103 master's, 4 doctorates awarded. *Degree requirements:* For doctorate, 1 foreign language, dissertation. *Entrance requirements:* For doctorate, GRE General Test. Application fee: $50. *Expenses:* Tuition $5100 per year full-time, $213 per credit hour part-time for state residents; $8416 per year full-time, $351 per credit hour part-time for nonresidents. Fees $705 per year full-time, $26.85 per credit hour part-time. *Financial aid:* Fellowships available. • Richard Allington, Chair, 518-442-5100.

State University of New York at Binghamton, School of Education and Human Development, Program in Reading Education, Binghamton, NY 13902-6000. Awards MS Ed. Part-time and evening/weekend programs available. Students: 2 full-time (both women), 28 part-time (26 women); includes 1 minority (Hispanic). Average age 29. 7 applicants, 71% accepted. In 1997, 17 degrees awarded. *Entrance requirements:* GRE General Test, TOEFL. Application deadline: 4/15 (priority date; rolling processing; 11/1 for spring admission). Application fee: $50. Electronic applications accepted. *Expenses:* Tuition $5100 per year full-time, $213 per credit hour part-time for state residents; $8416 per year full-time, $351 per credit hour part-time for nonresidents. Fees $654 per year full-time, $75 per semester (minimum) part-time. *Financial aid:* In 1997–98, 1 graduate assistantship averaging $680 per month and totaling $6,800 was awarded; research assistantships, Federal Work-Study, institutionally sponsored loans, and career-related internships or fieldwork also available. Aid available to part-time students. Financial aid application deadline: 2/15. • Dr. Karen M. Bromley, Coordinator, 607-777-2301.

State University of New York at Buffalo, Graduate School, Graduate School of Education, Department of Learning and Instruction, Buffalo, NY 14260. Offerings include reading education (Ed M, Ed D, PhD). Terminal master's awarded for partial completion of doctoral program. Department faculty: 20 full-time (9 women), 7 part-time (2 women). *Degree requirements:* For master's, comprehensive exam required, foreign language and thesis not required; for doctorate, dissertation, research analysis exam required, foreign language not required. *Entrance requirements:* For master's, GRE General Test, TOEFL (minimum score 590); for doctorate, GRE General Test, TOEFL (minimum score 600), interview. Application deadline: 2/1 (11/15 for spring admission). Application fee: $50. *Tuition:* $5970 per year full-time, $288 per credit hour part-time for state residents; $9286 per year full-time, $426 per credit hour part-time for nonresidents. • Dr. Michael Kibby, Chair, 716-645-2455. Application contact: Barbara Cracchiolo, Admissions Secretary, 716-645-2457. Fax: 716-645-3161.

State University of New York at New Paltz, Faculty of Education, Department of Elementary Education, New Paltz, NY 12561-2499. Offerings include reading (MS Ed). *Application deadline:* 3/15 (priority date; rolling processing). *Application fee:* $50. *Expenses:* Tuition $5100 per year full-time, $213 per credit hour part-time for state residents; $8416 per year full-time, $351 per credit hour part-time for nonresidents. Fees $493 per year full-time, $48 per semester (minimum) part-time. • Dr. Rose Rudnitski, Chair, 914-257-2860.

State University of New York at Oswego, School of Education, Department of Curriculum and Instruction, Oswego, NY 13126. Offerings include reading education (MS Ed). MS Ed (special education) offered jointly with the State University of New York College at Geneseo. Department faculty: 17 full-time, 5 part-time. *Application deadline:* 7/1. *Application fee:* $50. *Expenses:* Tuition $5100 per year full-time, $213 per credit hour part-time for state residents; $8416 per year full-time, $351 per credit hour part-time for nonresidents. Fees $135 per year (minimum). • Dr. Frank Bickel, Chairman, 315-341-4052. Application contact: Dr. Terrance Lindenberg, Coordinator, Graduate Education, 315-341-4052.

State University of New York College at Brockport, School of Professions, Department of Education and Human Development, Program in Reading, Brockport, NY 14420-2997. Awards MS Ed. Part-time and evening/weekend programs available. Students: 1 full-time (0 women), 47 part-time (45 women); includes 2 minority (both African Americans). Average age 31. 19 applicants, 58% accepted. In 1997, 19 degrees awarded. *Degree requirements:* Thesis or alternative required, foreign language not required. *Entrance requirements:* Minimum GPA of 3.0. Application deadline: 1/15 (priority date; 9/15 for spring admission). Application fee: $50. *Expenses:* Tuition $5100 per year full-time, $213 per credit hour part-time for state residents; $8416 per year full-time, $351 per credit hour part-time for nonresidents. Fees $440 per year full-time, $22.60 per credit hour part-time. *Financial aid:* Federal Work-Study and career-related internships or fieldwork available. Aid available to part-time students. Financial aid application deadline: 4/1; applicants required to submit FAFSA. *Faculty research:* Reading readiness, language acquisition, reading methodology. • William Veenis, Chairperson, Department of Education and Human Development, 716-395-2205.

Directory: Reading Education

State University of New York College at Buffalo, Faculty of Applied Science and Education, Department of Elementary Education and Reading, Program in Reading, Buffalo, NY 14222-1095. Awards MPS, MS Ed. Accredited by NCATE. Part-time and evening/weekend programs available. Students: 1 (woman) full-time, 66 part-time (62 women). Average age 30. 18 applicants, 61% accepted. In 1997, 18 degrees awarded. *Degree requirements:* Project required, foreign language and thesis not required. *Entrance requirements:* Minimum GPA of 3.0 in last 60 hours. Application deadline: 5/1 (10/1 for spring admission). Application fee: $50. *Expenses:* Tuition $5100 per year full-time, $213 per credit hour part-time for state residents; $8416 per year full-time, $351 per credit hour part-time for nonresidents. Fees $195 per year full-time, $8.60 per credit hour part-time. *Financial aid:* Fellowships, Federal Work-Study available. Aid available to part-time students. Financial aid application deadline: 3/1. • Dr. Rosemary Lonberger, Coordinator, 716-878-5916.

State University of New York College at Cortland, Division of Professional Studies, Department of Education, Program in Reading, Cortland, NY 13045. Awards MS Ed. Part-time and evening/weekend programs available. In 1997, 167 degrees awarded. *Degree requirements:* 1 foreign language, thesis (for some programs), comprehensive exam. *Application deadline:* rolling. *Application fee:* $50. *Expenses:* Tuition $5100 per year full-time, $213 per credit hour part-time for state residents; $8416 per year full-time, $351 per credit hour part-time for nonresidents. Fees $644 per year full-time, $79 per semester (minimum) part-time. *Financial aid:* Partial tuition waivers, Federal Work-Study, and career-related internships or fieldwork available. Aid available to part-time students. Financial aid applicants required to submit CSS PROFILE or FAFSA. • Application contact: Jeanne M. Bechtel, Director of Admissions, 607-753-4711. Fax: 607-753-5998.

State University of New York College at Fredonia, Department of Education, Program in Reading, Fredonia, NY 14063. Awards MS Ed. Part-time and evening/weekend programs available. Students: 13 part-time (all women). 0 applicants. In 1997, 32 degrees awarded. *Degree requirements:* Thesis or alternative required, foreign language not required. *Application deadline:* 7/5. *Application fee:* $50. *Expenses:* Tuition $5100 per year full-time, $213 per credit hour part-time for state residents; $8416 per year full-time, $351 per credit hour part-time for nonresidents. Fees $725 per year full-time, $30 per credit hour part-time. *Financial aid:* Research assistantships, teaching assistantships, full and partial tuition waivers, and career-related internships or fieldwork available. Aid available to part-time students. Financial aid application deadline: 3/15. • Dr. Julius Adams, Chair, Department of Education, 716-673-3311.

State University of New York College at Geneseo, School of Education, Program in Reading, Geneseo, NY 14454-1401. Awards MPS, MS Ed. Part-time and evening/weekend programs available. Faculty: 4 full-time (3 women). Students: 4 full-time (all women), 38 part-time (34 women). Average age 24. 56 applicants, 71% accepted. In 1997, 24 degrees awarded. *Degree requirements:* Thesis optional, foreign language not required. *Entrance requirements:* GRE General Test. Application deadline: 6/1 (priority date; 10/1 for spring admission). Application fee: $35. *Expenses:* Tuition $5100 per year full-time, $213 per credit hour part-time for state residents; $8416 per year full-time, $351 per credit hour part-time for nonresidents. Fees $375 per year full-time, $15.35 per credit hour part-time. *Financial aid:* 3 students received aid; Federal Work-Study, institutionally sponsored loans, and career-related internships or fieldwork available. Financial aid application deadline: 4/1; applicants required to submit FAFSA. • Dr. Gary DeBolt, Head, School of Education, 716-245-5558. Fax: 716-245-5220. E-mail: debolt@uno.cc.geneseo.edu.

State University of New York College at Oneonta, Department of Education, Program in Reading, Oneonta, NY 13820-4015. Awards MS Ed. Part-time and evening/weekend programs available. Students: 6 full-time (all women), 51 part-time (40 women); includes 1 minority (Hispanic). In 1997, 38 degrees awarded. *Entrance requirements:* GRE General Test. Application deadline: 4/15. Application fee: $50. *Expenses:* Tuition $5100 per year full-time, $213 per credit hour part-time for state residents; $8416 per year full-time, $351 per credit hour part-time for nonresidents. Fees $482 per year full-time, $6.85 per credit hour part-time. • Dr. Ronald Cromwell, Chair, Department of Education, 607-436-2538.

State University of New York College at Potsdam, School of Education, Program in Reading Education, Potsdam, NY 13676. Awards MS Ed. Part-time programs available. Faculty: 4 full-time (0 women), 1 (woman) part-time. Students: 73; includes 1 minority (Native American). *Degree requirements:* Culminating experience required, thesis optional, foreign language not required. *Entrance requirements:* New York State Teachers Certification Exam Liberal Arts and Science Test (minimum score 220), New York State Teachers Certification Exam Assesment of Teaching Skills-Writing (minimum score 220), minimum GPA of 2.75 in last 60 hours. Application deadline: 4/1 (priority date; 10/15 for spring admission). Application fee: $50. *Expenses:* Tuition $5100 per year full-time, $213 per credit hour part-time for state residents; $8416 per year full-time, $351 per credit hour part-time for nonresidents. Fees $315 per year full-time, $12.50 per credit hour part-time. *Financial aid:* Fellowships, teaching assistantships, Federal Work-Study, and career-related internships or fieldwork available. Aid available to part-time students. Financial aid application deadline: 3/1. • Charles Mlynarczyk, Chairperson, Teacher Education Department, 315-267-2535. E-mail: mlynarhc@potsdam.edu. Application contact: Dr. William Amoriell, Dean of Education and Graduate Studies, 315-267-2515. Fax: 315-267-4802.

State University of West Georgia, College of Education, Department of Early Childhood Education and Reading, Program in Reading, Carrollton, GA 30118. Awards M Ed, Ed S. Accredited by NCATE. Part-time and evening/weekend programs available. Faculty: 4 full-time (1 woman). Students: 3 part-time (all women). Average age 45. In 1997, 2 master's, 2 Ed Ss awarded. *Degree requirements:* For Ed S, research project required, foreign language and thesis not required. *Entrance requirements:* For master's, GRE General Test (minimum combined score of 800), minimum GPA of 2.5; for Ed S, GRE General Test (minimum combined score of 800), master's degree, minimum graduate GPA of 3.25. Application deadline: 8/30 (rolling processing). Application fee: $15. *Expenses:* Tuition $2428 per year full-time, $83 per semester hour part-time for state residents; $8428 per year full-time, $250 per semester hour part-time for nonresidents. Fees $428 per year. *Financial aid:* Assistantships and career-related internships or fieldwork available. Aid available to part-time students. Financial aid applicants required to submit FAFSA. • Application contact: Dr. Jack O. Jenkins, Dean, Graduate School, 770-836-6419. Fax: 770-836-2301. E-mail: jjenkins@cob.as.westga.edu.

Sul Ross State University, Rio Grande College of Sul Ross State University, Alpine, TX 79832. Offerings include teacher education (M Ed), with options in bilingual education, counseling, educational diagnostics, elementary education, general education, reading, school administration, secondary education. College faculty: 16 full-time (2 women), 2 part-time (1 woman). *Application deadline:* rolling. *Application fee:* $0 ($50 for international students). *Expenses:* Tuition $864 per year full-time, $120 per semester (minimum) part-time for state residents; $5976 per year full-time, $747 per semester (minimum) part-time for nonresidents. Fees $754 per year full-time, $105 per semester (minimum) part-time. • Dr. Frank Abbott, Dean, 512-278-3339. Fax: 512-278-3330.

Sul Ross State University, Department of Teacher Education, Program in Reading Specialist, Alpine, TX 79832. Awards M Ed. Part-time and evening/weekend programs available. Students: 7 full-time (6 women), 22 part-time (19 women); includes 6 minority (all Hispanics). Average age 38. In 1997, 6 degrees awarded. *Degree requirements:* Thesis optional, foreign language not required. *Entrance requirements:* GMAT (minimum score 400) or GRE General Test (minimum combined score of 850), minimum GPA of 2.5 in last 60 hours of undergraduate work. Application deadline: rolling. Application fee: $0 ($50 for international students). *Expenses:* Tuition $864 per year full-time, $120 per semester (minimum) part-time for state residents; $5976 per year full-time, $747 per semester (minimum) part-time for nonresidents. Fees $754 per year full-time, $105 per semester (minimum) part-time. *Financial aid:* Federal Work-Study, institutionally sponsored loans, and career-related internships or fieldwork available. Aid available to part-time students. Financial aid application deadline: 5/1; applicants required to submit FAFSA. • Dr. Mary Ann Weinacht, Director, Department of Teacher Education, 915-837-8170. Fax: 915-837-8390.

Syracuse University, School of Education, Department of Reading and Language Arts, Program in Reading and Language Arts, Syracuse, NY 13244-0003. Awards MS, Ed D, PhD, CAS. Faculty: 5 full-time (3 women). Students: 14 full-time (11 women), 16 part-time (14 women); includes 3 minority (all African Americans), 1 international. 17 applicants, 82% accepted. In 1997, 24 master's, 2 doctorates awarded. *Degree requirements:* For master's, thesis or alternative required, foreign language not required; for doctorate and CAS, thesis/dissertation required, foreign language not required. *Entrance requirements:* GRE. Application deadline: rolling. Application fee: $40. *Tuition:* $13,320 per year full-time, $555 per credit hour part-time. *Financial aid:* Fellowships, research assistantships, teaching assistantships, administrative assistantships, Federal Work-Study, and career-related internships or fieldwork available. Aid available to part-time students. Financial aid application deadline: 3/1. *Faculty research:* Literacy, knowledge modeling, assessment, teaching of literature, writing. • Dr. Peter Mosenthal, Chair, Department of Reading and Language Arts, 315-443-4757. Fax: 315-443-5732.

Tarleton State University, College of Education, Department of Education and Psychology, Stephenville, TX 76402. Offerings include reading (Certificate). Postbaccalaureate distance learning degree programs offered. Department faculty: 28 full-time (9 women). *Application deadline:* 8/5 (priority date; rolling processing; 12/1 for spring admission). *Application fee:* $25 ($100 for international students). *Expenses:* Tuition $46 per hour for state residents; $249 per hour for nonresidents. Fees $49 per hour. • Dr. Bob Newby, Head, 254-968-9091.

Teachers College, Columbia University, Graduate Faculty of Education, Program in Reading/Learning Disability, 525 West 120th Street, New York, NY 10027-6696. Awards Ed M. Students: 3 full-time (all women), 6 part-time (5 women); includes 1 minority (Hispanic), 1 international. Average age 31. 7 applicants, 86% accepted. In 1997, 4 degrees awarded. *Application deadline:* 5/15. *Application fee:* $50. *Expenses:* Tuition $640 per credit. Fees $120 per semester. *Financial aid:* Partial tuition waivers, Federal Work-Study, institutionally sponsored loans, and career-related internships or fieldwork available. Aid available to part-time students. Financial aid application deadline: 2/1. *Faculty research:* Reading and spelling disorders, workplace literacy, reading and writing among children and adults. • Arthur Levine, President, Graduate Faculty of Education, 212-678-3050. Application contact: John Fisher, Executive Director of Admissions and Financial Aid, 212-678-3710. Fax: 212-678-4171.

Teachers College, Columbia University, Graduate Faculty of Education, Department of Health and Behavior Studies, Program in Reading Specialist, 525 West 120th Street, New York, NY 10027-6696. Awards MA. Faculty: 1 (woman) full-time, 7 part-time (4 women), 3.2 FTE. Students: 6 full-time (5 women), 36 part-time (35 women); includes 4 minority (1 African American, 2 Asian Americans, 1 Hispanic), 1 international. Average age 29. 24 applicants, 67% accepted. In 1997, 8 degrees awarded. *Application deadline:* 5/15. *Application fee:* $50. *Expenses:* Tuition $640 per credit. Fees $120 per semester. *Financial aid:* Application deadline 2/1. • Application contact: Ursula Felton, Office of Admissions, 212-678-3710. Fax: 212-678-4171.

Temple University, College of Education, Department of Curriculum, Instruction, and Technology in Education, Philadelphia, PA 19122-6096. Offerings include reading and language education (Ed M, MS, Ed D). Accredited by NCATE. Terminal master's awarded for partial completion of doctoral program. Department faculty: 33 full-time (14 women). *Degree requirements:* For master's, thesis or alternative required, foreign language not required; for doctorate, dissertation required, foreign language not required. *Entrance requirements:* For master's, GRE General Test (minimum combined score of 1000) or MAT (minimum score 39), minimum GPA of 2.8; for doctorate, GRE General Test (minimum combined score of 1000) or MAT (minimum score 39). Application deadline: 2/15 (10/1 for spring admission). Application fee: $40. *Expenses:* Tuition $323 per semester hour for state residents; $444 per semester hour for nonresidents. Fees $170 per year full-time, $28 per semester (minimum) part-time. • Dr. Raymond Lolla, Chair, 215-204-6387. Fax: 215-204-1414.

Tennessee State University, College of Education, Department of Teaching and Learning, Program in Secondary Education, Nashville, TN 37209-1561. Offerings include reading (M Ed). Accredited by NCATE. *Application deadline:* rolling. *Application fee:* $15. *Tuition:* $2962 per year full-time, $182 per credit hour part-time for state residents; $7788 per year full-time, $393 per credit hour part-time for nonresidents. • Application contact: Dr. Clinton M. Lipsey, Dean of the Graduate School, 615-963-5901. Fax: 615-963-5963. E-mail: clipsey@picard.tnstate.edu.

Tennessee Technological University, College of Education, Department of Curriculum and Instruction, Program in Reading, Cookeville, TN 38505. Awards MA, Ed S. Accredited by NCATE. Part-time and evening/weekend programs available. Faculty: 2 full-time (both women). Students: 1 (woman) full-time, 10 part-time (all women). Average age 27. 5 applicants, 80% accepted. In 1997, 3 master's awarded. *Degree requirements:* For Ed S, thesis or alternative required, foreign language not required. *Entrance requirements:* For master's, MAT, TOEFL (minimum score 525); for Ed S, MAT, NTE. Application deadline: 3/1 (priority date; 8/1 for spring admission). Application fee: $25 ($30 for international students). *Tuition:* $2960 per year full-time, $147 per semester hour part-time for state residents; $7786 per year full-time, $358 per semester hour part-time for nonresidents. *Financial aid:* In 1997–98, 1 student received aid, including 1 research assistantship (to a first-year student); fellowships, teaching assistantships, and career-related internships or fieldwork also available. Financial aid application deadline: 4/1. • Application contact: Dr. Rebecca F. Quattlebaum, Dean of the Graduate School, 615-372-3233. Fax: 615-372-3497. E-mail: rquattlebaum@tntech.edu.

Texas A&M International University, Division of Teacher Education and Psychology, 5201 University Boulevard, Laredo, TX 78041-1900. Offerings include reading (MS Ed). *Degree requirements:* Thesis required (for some programs), foreign language not required. *Entrance requirements:* GRE General Test. Application deadline: 7/15 (priority date; rolling processing; 11/12 for spring admission). Application fee: $0.

Texas A&M University, College of Education, Department of Educational Curriculum and Instruction, Unit in Reading, College Station, TX 77843. Awards M Ed, MS, Ed D, PhD. Accredited by NCATE. *Degree requirements:* For doctorate, dissertation required, foreign language not required. *Entrance requirements:* GRE General Test, TOEFL. Application fee: $35 ($75 for international students). *Financial aid:* Fellowships, research assistantships, teaching assistantships, and career-related internships or fieldwork available. • John Stansell, Coordinator, 409-845-8189.

Texas A&M University–Commerce, College of Education, Department of Elementary Education, Commerce, TX 75429-3011. Offerings include reading (MA, M Ed, MS). MA, M Ed, and MS (early childhood education) offered jointly with Texas Woman's University and the University of North Texas. Department faculty: 15 full-time (6 women), 4 part-time (2 women). *Degree requirements:* Thesis (for some programs), comprehensive exam. *Entrance requirements:* GRE General Test. Application deadline: rolling. Application fee: $0 ($25 for international students). *Tuition:* $2382 per year full-time, $343 per semester (minimum) part-time for state residents; $7518 per year full-time, $343 per semester (minimum) part-time for nonresidents. • Dr. Wayne Linek, Head, 903-886-5537. Application contact: Pam Hammonds, Graduate Admissions Adviser, 903-886-5167. Fax: 903-886-5165.

Texas A&M University–Kingsville, College of Education, Department of Education, Program in Reading Specialization, Kingsville, TX 78363. Awards MS. Part-time and evening/weekend programs available. Faculty: 3 full-time. *Degree requirements:* Comprehensive exam, mini-thesis required, foreign language not required. *Entrance requirements:* GRE General Test (minimum combined score of 1000), MAT (minimum score 34), minimum GPA of 3.0. Application deadline: 6/1 (rolling processing; 11/15 for spring admission). Application fee: $15 ($25 for international students). *Tuition:* $1822 per year full-time, $281 per semester (minimum) part-time for state residents; $6934 per year full-time, $908 per semester (minimum) part-time for nonresidents. *Financial aid:* Application deadline 5/15. *Faculty research:* Reading programs for preparing the handicapped, reading methods in elementary education, literature-based reading instruction. • Dr. Sue Mohrman, Director, 512-593-3203.

Texas Southern University, College of Education, Area of Curriculum and Instruction, Houston, TX 77004-4584. Offerings include reading education (M Ed). Faculty: 15 full-time (7 women), 4 part-time (all women). *Degree requirements:* Comprehensive exam required, foreign language not required. *Entrance requirements:* GRE General Test, TOEFL, minimum GPA of 2.5. Application deadline: 7/15 (priority date; rolling processing). Application fee: $35 ($75 for international students). • Dr. Claudette Ligon, Chairperson, 713-313-7775.

Texas Tech University, Graduate School, College of Education, Division of Curriculum and Instruction, Lubbock, TX 79409. Offerings include reading education (M Ed, Ed D). Accredited by NCATE. Division faculty: 23 full-time (12 women). *Degree requirements:* For master's, computer language required, thesis optional, foreign language not required; for doctorate, dissertation required, foreign language not required. *Entrance requirements:* For master's, GRE General Test (combined average 992); for doctorate, GRE General Test. Application deadline: 4/15 (priority date; rolling processing; 11/1 for spring admission). Application fee: $25 ($50 for international students). Electronic applications accepted. *Expenses:* Tuition $864 per year full-time, $120 per semester (minimum) part-time for state residents; $5976 per year full-time, $747 per semester (minimum) part-time for nonresidents. Fees $2321 per year full-time, $302 per semester (minimum) part-time. • Dr. William E. Sparkman, Chair, 805-742-2371.

Texas Tech University, Graduate School, College of Education, Division of Educational Psychology and Leadership, Lubbock, TX 79409. Offerings include reading specialist (Certificate). Accredited by NCATE. Division faculty: 28 full-time (13 women), 3 part-time (1 woman), 29.29 FTE. *Application deadline:* 4/15 (priority date; rolling processing; 11/1 for spring admission). *Application fee:* $25 ($50 for international students). Electronic applications accepted. *Expenses:* Tuition $864 per year full-time, $120 per semester (minimum) part-time for state residents; $5976 per year full-time, $747 per semester (minimum) part-time for nonresidents. Fees $2321 per year full-time, $302 per semester (minimum) part-time. • Dr. Loretta J. Bradley, Chair, 806-742-2393.

Texas Woman's University, College of Education and Human Ecology, Department of Reading and Bilingual Education, Program in Reading, Denton, TX 76204. Awards MA, M Ed, MS, Ed D, PhD. Part-time programs available. Faculty: 6 full-time (all women), 30 part-time (all women). Students: 42 full-time (41 women), 522 part-time (463 women); includes 176 minority (106 African Americans, 6 Asian Americans, 61 Hispanics, 3 Native Americans), 1 international. Average age 37. In 1997, 11 master's, 1 doctorate awarded. Terminal master's awarded for partial completion of doctoral program. *Degree requirements:* Thesis/dissertation required, foreign language not required. *Entrance requirements:* For master's, GRE General Test (minimum combined score of 750), minimum GPA of 3.0; for doctorate, GRE General Test (minimum combined score of 1000), minimum graduate GPA of 3.0. Application fee: $25. *Financial aid:* In 1997–98, 10 students received aid, including 2 research assistantships (both to first-year students), 1 teaching assistantship (to a first-year student); fellowships, Federal Work-Study, institutionally sponsored loans, and career-related internships or fieldwork also available. Aid available to part-time students. Financial aid application deadline: 4/1. *Faculty research:* Early literacy, content area reading, reading interests, written discourse. • Rodolfo Rodriguez, Chair, Department of Reading and Bilingual Education, 940-898-2227. Fax: 940-898-2224. E-mail: d_rodriguez@twu.edu.

Towson University, Program in Reading Education, Towson, MD 21252-0001. Awards M Ed, Spec. M Ed offered jointly with Morgan State University. Part-time and evening/weekend programs available. Faculty: 3 full-time (1 woman). Students: 4 full-time (all women), 101 part-time (all women); includes 8 minority (7 African Americans, 1 Asian American). In 1997, 26 master's awarded. *Degree requirements:* For master's, exam required, foreign language and thesis not required. *Application deadline:* 3/1 (priority date; rolling processing; 10/1 for spring admission). *Application fee:* $40. *Expenses:* Tuition $187 per credit hour for state residents; $364 per credit hour for nonresidents. Fees $40 per credit hour. *Financial aid:* Assistantships available. Financial aid application deadline: 4/1; applicants required to submit FAFSA. *Faculty research:* Teacher training. • Dr. Karen Blair, Director, 410-830-2348. Fax: 410-830-3434. E-mail: kblair@towson.edu. Application contact: Fran Musotto, Office Manager, 410-830-2501. Fax: 410-830-4675. E-mail: fmusotto@towson.edu.

Trinity College, School of Professional Studies, Programs in Education, Washington, DC 20017-1094. Offerings include curriculum and instruction (M Ed), with options in literacy, urban learner. Faculty: 6 full-time (5 women), 18 part-time (13 women). *Application deadline:* rolling. *Application fee:* $35. *Tuition:* $460 per credit hour. • Sr. Rosemarie Bosler, Division Chair, 202-884-9557. Application contact: Karen Goodwin, Director of Graduate Admissions, 202-884-9400. Fax: 202-884-9229.

Union College, Department of Education, Reading Specialist Program, Barbourville, KY 40906-1499. Awards MA Ed. *Degree requirements:* Thesis optional, foreign language not required. *Entrance requirements:* GRE General Test, NTE. Application deadline: rolling. Application fee: $15. *Tuition:* $220 per hour. • Dr. Frieda Kalb, Assistant Professor of Education, 606-546-1263. Fax: 606-546-1217.

The University of Arizona, College of Education, Department of Language, Reading, and Culture, Tucson, AZ 85721. Offers programs in bilingual education (M Ed); bilingual/multicultural education (MA); language, reading and culture (MA, Ed D, PhD, Ed S); reading (MA, M Ed, Ed D, PhD, Ed S). *Degree requirements:* For master's, thesis (MA) required, foreign language not required; for doctorate, dissertation required, foreign language not required. *Entrance requirements:* For master's, TOEFL (minimum score 550); for doctorate, GRE, TOEFL (minimum score 550); for Ed S, TOEFL (minimun score of 550). Application deadline: 4/15 (rolling processing). Application fee: $35. *Tuition:* $2162 per year full-time, $337 per semester (minimum) part-time for state residents; $6860 per year full-time, $1138 per semester (minimum) part-time for nonresidents. *Faculty research:* Bilingual/bicultural literacy, influence of original and adapted texts on readers, readability, bilingual reading.

University of Arkansas at Little Rock, College of Education, Department of Teacher Education, Program in Elementary Education, Little Rock, AR 72204-1099. Offerings include reading (M Ed, Ed S). Accredited by NCATE. *Degree requirements:* For master's, thesis or alternative, Arkansas Department of Education certification, comprehensive exam required, foreign language not required; for Ed S, comprehensive exams, oral defense of thesis required, foreign language not required. *Entrance requirements:* For master's, minimum GPA of 2.75, teaching certificate; for Ed S, GRE General Test (minimum combined score of 1350 on three sections) or MAT (minimum score 40), Arkansas teaching certificate, interview, M Ed, minimum GPA of 3.3. Application deadline: rolling. Application fee: $25 ($30 for international students). *Expenses:* Tuition $2466 per year full-time, $137 per credit hour part-time for state residents; $5256 per year full-time, $292 per credit hour part-time for nonresidents. Fees $216 per year full-time, $36 per semester (minimum) part-time. • Dr. Jamie Foster, Adviser, 501-569-3124.

University of Bridgeport, College of Graduate and Undergraduate Studies, School of Education and Human Resources, Division of Education, Program in Secondary Education, 380 University Avenue, Bridgeport, CT 06601. Offerings include reading specialist (MS, Diploma). Program faculty: 8 full-time (2 women), 57 part-time (26 women), 27 FTE. *Degree requirements:* For master's, computer language, final exam, final project, or thesis required, foreign language not required; for Diploma, thesis or alternative, final project required, foreign language not required. *Entrance requirements:* For master's, GRE General Test, MAT (score in 35th percentile or higher), minimum undergraduate QPA of 2.5; for Diploma, GRE General Test or MAT (score in 40th percentile or higher), minimum graduate QPA of 3.0. Application deadline: rolling. Application fee: $35 ($50 for international students). *Tuition:* $340 per credit. • Dr. Allen P. Cook, Associate Dean, Division of Education, 203-576-4206.

University of British Columbia, Faculty of Education, Department of Language Education, Vancouver, BC V6T 1Z2, Canada. Offers programs in English education (MA, M Ed, PhD), library education (MA, M Ed, PhD), modern language education (MA, M Ed, PhD), reading education (MA, M Ed, Ed D, PhD), teaching English as a second language (MA, M Ed, PhD). Part-time and evening/weekend programs available. *Degree requirements:* For master's, thesis (MA) required, foreign language not required; for doctorate, dissertation required, foreign language not required. *Entrance requirements:* TOEFL (minimum score 550), minimum B average in most recent 2 years of study with minimum of two courses at A standing. Application deadline: 2/28 (priority date; rolling processing; 8/1 for spring admission). Application fee: $60. *Faculty research:* Language and literacy development, second language acquisition, Asia Pacific language curriculum, children's literature, whole language instruction.

University of California, Berkeley, School of Education, Division of Education in Language, Literature, and Culture, Berkeley, CA 94720-1500. Offers programs in advanced reading and language leadership (MA), including reading/reading and language arts; English (Certificate); language, literacy, and culture (MA, Ed D, PhD), including athletes and academic achievement (MA), language, literacy, and culture (MA). Faculty: 10 full-time (5 women), 5 part-time (2 women). *Degree requirements:* For master's, exam or thesis required, foreign language not required; for doctorate, dissertation, oral qualifying exam (PhD) required, foreign language not required. *Entrance requirements:* For master's and doctorate, GRE General Test, minimum GPA of 3.0 during last 2 years of undergraduate course work. Application deadline: 12/15. Application fee: $40. *Expenses:* Tuition $0 for state residents; $9384 per year for nonresidents. Fees $4409 per year. *Financial aid:* Fellowships, research assistantships, teaching assistantships available. Financial aid application deadline: 12/15. *Faculty research:* Literature, English education, reading education, second language teaching and learning, teacher education. • Robert B. Ruddell, Chair, 510-642-0746. Application contact: Admissions Office, 510-642-0841.

University of Central Arkansas, College of Education, Department of Childhood and Special Education, Program in Reading Education, Conway, AR 72035-0001. Awards MSE. Accredited by NCATE. Students: 4 full-time (all women), 20 part-time (all women); includes 1 minority (African American). 5 applicants, 100% accepted. In 1997, 18 degrees awarded. *Degree requirements:* Comprehensive exam required, thesis optional. *Entrance requirements:* GRE General Test, minimum GPA of 2.7. Application deadline: rolling. Application fee: $15 ($40 for international students). *Expenses:* Tuition $161 per credit hour for state residents; $298 per credit hour for nonresidents. Fees $50 per year full-time, $30 per year part-time. *Financial aid:* Federal Work-Study available. Financial aid application deadline: 2/15. • Mary Mosley, Coordinator, 501-450-5461. Fax: 501-450-5358. E-mail: marym@mail.uca.edu.

University of Central Florida, College of Education, Department of Instructional Programs, Program in Reading, Orlando, FL 32816. Awards M Ed. Accredited by NCATE. Part-time and evening/weekend programs available. Students: 7 full-time (all women), 10 part-time (all women); includes 3 minority (2 African Americans, 1 Hispanic), 1 international. Average age 31. 14 applicants, 36% accepted. In 1997, 6 degrees awarded. *Degree requirements:* Thesis or alternative required, foreign language not required. *Entrance requirements:* GRE General Test (minimum combined score of 840). Application deadline: 7/15 (12/15 for spring admission). Application fee: $20. *Expenses:* Tuition $3288 per year full-time, $137 per credit hour part-time for state residents; $11,520 per year full-time, $480 per credit hour part-time for nonresidents. Fees $105 per year. *Financial aid:* Teaching assistantships, Federal Work-Study, institutionally sponsored loans, and career-related internships or fieldwork available. Aid available to part-time students. • Application contact: Dr. Rosie Joels, Coordinator, 407-823-2008. E-mail: ajoels@pegasus.cc.ucf.edu.

University of Central Oklahoma, College of Education, Department of Curriculum and Instruction, Program in Reading, Edmond, OK 73034-5209. Awards M Ed. Accredited by NCATE. Part-time and evening/weekend programs available. *Entrance requirements:* GRE General Test. Application deadline: 8/18. Application fee: $15. *Tuition:* $76 per credit hour for state residents; $178 per credit hour for nonresidents.

University of Cincinnati, College of Education, Division of Teacher Education, Department of Curriculum and Instruction, Program in Reading/Literacy, Cincinnati, OH 45221. Awards M Ed, Ed D. Accredited by NCATE. Part-time programs available. Students: 35; includes 2 minority (1 African American, 1 Asian American), 6 international. 1 applicant, 0% accepted. In 1997, 14 master's, 3 doctorates awarded. *Degree requirements:* For doctorate, dissertation required, foreign language not required. *Average time to degree:* master's–3.5 years full-time; doctorate–7.1 years full-time. *Entrance requirements:* For master's, GRE General Test. Application deadline: 2/1. Application fee: $30. *Tuition:* $7228 per year full-time, $185 per credit hour part-time for state residents; $13,812 per year full-time, $352 per credit hour part-time for nonresidents. *Financial aid:* Fellowships, graduate assistantships, full tuition waivers available. Aid available to part-time students. Financial aid application deadline: 5/1. • Application contact: Dr. Glenn Markle, Graduate Program Director, 513-556-3582. Fax: 513-556-2483. E-mail: glenn.markle@uc.edu.

University of Connecticut, School of Education, Field of Reading Education, Storrs, CT 06269. Awards MA, PhD. Accredited by NCATE. Faculty: 3. Students: 5 part-time (all women). Average age 33. 2 applicants, 100% accepted. In 1997, 1 master's awarded. Terminal master's awarded for partial completion of doctoral program. *Degree requirements:* For master's, thesis or alternative; for doctorate, dissertation. *Entrance requirements:* For doctorate, GRE General Test. Application deadline: 6/1 (priority date; rolling processing; 11/1 for spring admission). Application fee: $40 ($45 for international students). *Expenses:* Tuition $5272 per year full-time, $293 per credit part-time for state residents; $13,696 per year full-time, $761 per credit part-time for nonresidents. Fees $948 per year full-time, $640 per year part-time. *Financial aid:* Fellowships, teaching assistantships available. Financial aid application deadline: 2/15. • Thomas P. Weinland, Head, 860-486-2433.

University of Florida, College of Education, Department of Instruction and Curriculum, Gainesville, FL 32611. Offerings include reading and language arts (MAE, M Ed, Ed D, PhD, Ed S). Accredited by NCATE. Department faculty: 42. *Degree requirements:* For master's, thesis optional, foreign language not required; for doctorate, variable foreign language requirement, dissertation. *Entrance requirements:* For master's and doctorate, GRE General Test (minimum combined score of 1000), minimum GPA of 3.0; for Ed S, GRE General Test. Application deadline: 6/5. Application fee: $20. *Tuition:* $138 per credit hour for state residents; $481 per credit hour for nonresidents. • Dr. Mary Grace Kantowski, Chair, 352-392-9191 Ext. 200. E-mail: mgk@coe.ufl.edu. Application contact: Dr. Ben Nelms, Graduate Coordinator, 352-392-9191 Ext. 225. Fax: 352-392-9193. E-mail: bfn@coe.ufl.edu.

University of Georgia, College of Education, Department of Reading Education, Athens, GA 30602. Awards MA, M Ed, Ed D, PhD, Ed S. Accredited by NCATE. Faculty: 11 full-time (8 women). Students: 18 full-time (15 women), 29 part-time; includes 1 minority (Asian American). 22 applicants, 73% accepted. In 1997, 6 master's, 1 doctorate, 2 Ed Ss awarded. *Degree requirements:* For master's, thesis (MA) required, foreign language not required; for doctorate, variable foreign language requirement, dissertation. *Entrance requirements:* For master's and Ed S, GRE General Test or MAT; for doctorate, GRE General Test. Application deadline: 7/1 (priority date; 11/15 for spring admission). Application fee: $30. Electronic applications accepted. *Tuition:* $3290 per year full-time, $643 per semester (minimum) part-time for state residents; $11,300 per year full-time, $1645 per semester (minimum) part-time for nonresidents. *Financial aid:* Fellowships, research assistantships, teaching assistantships, assistantships available. • Dr. Linda Labbo, Graduate Coordinator, 706-542-0193. Fax: 706-542-4623. E-mail: llabbo@coe.uga.edu.

University of Guam, College of Education, Program in Language and Literacy, 303 University Drive, UOG Station, Mangilao, GU 96923. Awards M Ed. *Degree requirements:* Comprehensive oral and written exams, special project or thesis required, foreign language not required.

Directory: Reading Education

University of Guam (continued)
Entrance requirements: GRE General Test. Application deadline: 5/31. Application fee: $31 ($56 for international students).

University of Houston, College of Education, Department of Curriculum and Instruction, 4800 Calhoun, Houston, TX 77204-2163. Offerings include reading and language arts education (M Ed). Accredited by NCATE. Department faculty: 37 full-time (19 women), 10 part-time (7 women). *Degree requirements:* Comprehensive exam or thesis required, foreign language not required. *Entrance requirements:* GRE General Test or MAT. Application deadline: 7/3 (priority date; rolling processing). Application fee: $35 ($75 for international students). *Expenses:* Tuition $1152 per year full-time, $120 per semester (minimum) part-time for state residents; $4482 per year full-time, $249 per credit hour part-time for nonresidents. Fees $977 per year full-time, $119 per semester (minimum) part-time. • Wilford Weber, Chair, 713-743-4970. Fax: 713-743-9870. E-mail: wweber@uh.edu.

University of Houston–Clear Lake, School of Education, Houston, TX 77058-1098. Offerings include reading (MS). Accredited by NCATE. School faculty: 34 full-time (23 women), 17 part-time (12 women), 39 FTE. *Application deadline:* rolling. *Application fee:* $30 ($60 for international students). *Tuition:* $207 per credit hour for state residents; $336 per credit hour for nonresidents. • Dr. Dennis Spuck, Dean, 281-283-3501. Application contact: Dr. Doris L. Prater, Associate Dean, 281-283-3600.

University of Illinois at Chicago, College of Education, Department of Curriculum and Instruction, Chicago, IL 60607-7128. Offerings include instructional leadership (M Ed), with options in elementary education, reading, secondary education. Department faculty: 28 full-time (13 women), 1 part-time (0 women). *Entrance requirements:* TOEFL (minimum score 550), minimum GPA of 3.75 on a 5.0 scale. Application deadline: 2/15. Application fee: $40 ($50 for international students). • Dr. John Smart, Area Chair, 312-996-4526. Application contact: Victoria Hare, Director of Graduate Studies, 312-996-4520.

University of Kansas, School of Education, Department of Teaching and Leadership, Program in Reading, Lawrence, KS 66045. Awards MS Ed, Ed D, PhD, Ed S. Accredited by NCATE. *Degree requirements:* For doctorate, variable foreign language requirement, dissertation. *Entrance requirements:* For master's and Ed S, minimum GPA of 3.0; for doctorate, GRE General Test, minimum graduate GPA of 3.5. Application deadline: 7/1. Application fee: $25. *Expenses:* Tuition $2400 per year full-time, $100 per credit hour part-time for state residents; $7890 per year full-time, $329 per credit hour part-time for nonresidents. Fees $428 per year full-time, $31 per credit hour part-time. • Marc Mahlios, Chair, Department of Teaching and Leadership, 785-864-4435.

University of La Verne, Department of Education, Program in Reading, La Verne, CA 91750-4443. Awards M Ed. *Entrance requirements:* TOEFL (minimum score 550), minimum GPA of 2.5. Application fee: $25. *Expenses:* Tuition $370 per unit (minimum). Fees $60 per year.

University of Louisville, School of Education, Department of Early and Middle Childhood Education, Program in Reading Education, Louisville, KY 40292-0001. Awards M Ed. Accredited by NCATE. Students: 3 full-time (all women), 44 part-time (43 women); includes 3 minority (all African Americans). Average age 34. In 1997, 9 degrees awarded. *Entrance requirements:* GRE General Test. Application deadline: rolling. Application fee: $25. • Dr. Diane W. Kyle, Chair, Department of Early and Middle Childhood Education, 502-852-6431.

University of Maine, College of Education and Human Development, Program in Literacy Education, Orono, ME 04469. Awards MAT, M Ed, MS, Ed D, CAS. Accredited by NCATE. Part-time and evening/weekend programs available. *Degree requirements:* For master's, thesis or alternative; for doctorate, dissertation. *Entrance requirements:* For master's, MAT, TOEFL (minimum score 550); for doctorate, GRE General Test, TOEFL (minimum score 550), MA, M Ed, or MS; for CAS, MAT, MA, M Ed, or MS. Application deadline: 2/1 (priority date; rolling processing; 10/15 for spring admission). Application fee: $50. *Expenses:* Tuition $194 per credit hour for state residents; $548 per credit hour for nonresidents. Fees $378 per year full-time, $33 per semester (minimum) part-time. *Financial aid:* Teaching assistantships and career-related internships or fieldwork available. Aid available to part-time students. Financial aid application deadline: 3/1. • Application contact: Scott Delcourt, Director of the Graduate School, 207-581-3218. Fax: 207-581-3232. E-mail: graduate@maine.edu.

University of Manitoba, Faculty of Education, Department of Curriculum: Humanities and Social Sciences, Winnipeg, MB R3T 2N2, Canada. Offerings include reading (M Ed). *Degree requirements:* Thesis or alternative required, foreign language not required.

University of Mary Hardin–Baylor, School of Education, Belton, TX 76513. Offerings include reading education (M Ed). School faculty: 6 full-time (2 women). *Average time to degree:* master's–2 years full-time, 3.5 years part-time. *Entrance requirements:* GRE General Test (minimum combined score of 850), minimum GPA of 2.5. Application deadline: 8/1 (priority date; rolling processing; 1/10 for spring admission). Application fee: $35 ($135 for international students). *Expenses:* Tuition $270 per semester hour. Fees $15 per semester hour. • Dr. Clarence E. Ham, Dean, 254-295-4573. Fax: 254-933-4480. E-mail: ham@tenet.edu.

University of Maryland, College Park, College of Education, Department of Curriculum and Instruction, College Park, MD 20742-5045. Offerings include reading (MA, M Ed, PhD, CAGS). Accredited by NCATE. Postbaccalaureate distance learning degree programs offered. Department faculty: 29 full-time (14 women), 11 part-time (8 women). *Entrance requirements:* For master's, GRE General Test or MAT, minimum GPA of 3.0. Application deadline: rolling. Application fee: $50 ($70 for international students). *Expenses:* Tuition $272 per credit hour for state residents; $400 per credit hour for nonresidents. Fees $564 per year full-time, $342 per year part-time. • Dr. Martin Johnson, Chairman, 301-405-3117. Fax: 301-314-9278. Application contact: John Mollish, Director, Graduate Admissions and Records, 301-405-4198. Fax: 301-314-9305.

University of Massachusetts Amherst, School of Education, Program in Education, Amherst, MA 01003-0001. Offerings include reading and writing (M Ed, Ed D, CAGS). Accredited by NCATE. *Degree requirements:* For doctorate, dissertation required, foreign language not required. *Entrance requirements:* For master's and doctorate, GRE General Test. Application deadline: 3/1 (rolling processing; 10/1 for spring admission). Application fee: $40. *Expenses:* Tuition $2640 per year full-time, $110 per credit part-time for state residents; $3690 per year (minimum) full-time, $165 per credit (minimum) part-time for nonresidents. Fees $2856 per year full-time, $422 per semester part-time for state residents; $3204 per year full-time, $480 per semester part-time for nonresidents. • John C. Carey, Director, 413-545-0236.

University of Massachusetts Lowell, College of Education, Program in Language Arts and Literacy, 1 University Avenue, Lowell, MA 01854-2881. Awards Ed D. Accredited by NCATE. Students: 2 full-time (1 woman), 24 part-time (19 women); includes 4 minority (1 African American, 3 Hispanics). In 1997, 8 degrees awarded. *Degree requirements:* Dissertation. *Entrance requirements:* GRE General Test. Application deadline: 4/1 (priority date; rolling processing; 10/1 for spring admission). Application fee: $20 ($35 for international students). *Tuition:* $4867 per year full-time, $618 per semester (minimum) part-time for state residents; $10,276 per year full-time, $1294 per semester (minimum) part-time for nonresidents. *Financial aid:* Research assistantships, teaching assistantships, Federal Work-Study, institutionally sponsored loans, and career-related internships or fieldwork available. Aid available to part-time students. Financial aid application deadline: 4/1. • Dr. Brenda Jochums, Coordinator, 978-934-4620.

University of Massachusetts Lowell, College of Education, Program in Reading and Language, 1 University Avenue, Lowell, MA 01854-2881. Awards M Ed, Ed D, CAGS. Accredited by NCATE. Part-time and evening/weekend programs available. In 1997, 11 master's, 8 doctorates awarded. Terminal master's awarded for partial completion of doctoral program. *Degree requirements:* For master's, thesis required (for some programs), foreign language not required; for doctorate, dissertation. *Entrance requirements:* For master's, MAT; for doctorate, GRE General Test. Application deadline: 4/1 (priority date; rolling processing; 10/1 for spring admission). Application fee: $20 ($35 for international students). *Tuition:* $4867 per year full-time, $618 per semester (minimum) part-time for state residents; $10,276 per year full-time, $1294 per semester (minimum) part-time for nonresidents. *Financial aid:* Career-related internships or fieldwork available. Financial aid application deadline: 4/1. *Faculty research:* Reading comprehension, adult literacy, assessment and evaluation, whole language. • Dr. Brenda Jochums, Coordinator, 978-934-4620.

The University of Memphis, College of Education, Department of Instruction and Curriculum Leadership, Memphis, TN 38152. Offerings include reading (MS, Ed D). Accredited by NCATE. Terminal master's awarded for partial completion of doctoral program. Department faculty: 34 full-time (17 women), 22 part-time (13 women). *Degree requirements:* For doctorate, dissertation, comprehensive exam required, foreign language not required. *Entrance requirements:* For doctorate, GRE General Test, GRE Subject Test, 2 years of teaching experience. Application deadline: 8/1 (12/1 for spring admission). Application fee: $25 ($50 for international students). *Tuition:* $2862 per year full-time, $166 per credit hour part-time for state residents; $6696 per year full-time, $379 per credit hour part-time for nonresidents. • Dr. Dennie Smith, Interim Chair, 901-678-2771. Application contact: Dr. Carole L. Bond, Coordinator of Graduate Studies, 901-678-3490.

University of Miami, School of Education, Department of Teaching and Learning, Program in Special Education and Reading, Coral Gables, FL 33124. Awards MS Ed, PhD, Ed S. Accredited by NCATE. Faculty: 8 full-time (5 women), 1 (woman) part-time. Students: 17 full-time (13 women), 18 part-time (17 women); includes 14 minority (5 African Americans, 3 Asian Americans, 6 Hispanics), 3 international. Average age 32. 14 applicants, 57% accepted. In 1997, 11 master's, 2 Ed Ss awarded. *Degree requirements:* For doctorate, dissertation required, foreign language not required; for Ed S, thesis optional, foreign language not required. *Entrance requirements:* For master's, GRE General Test (minimum combined score of 1000), TOEFL (minimum score 550); for doctorate, GRE General Test, GRE Subject Test, TOEFL (minimum score 550); for Ed S, GRE General Test, TOEFL (minimum score 550). Application deadline: rolling. Application fee: $35. *Expenses:* Tuition $815 per credit hour. Fees $174 per year. *Financial aid:* In 1997–98, 6 graduate assistantships were awarded. Financial aid application deadline: 3/1. *Faculty research:* Inclusion, behavior disorders, learning disabilities, literacy. • Dr. Marjorie Montague, Coordinator, 305-284-2902. Fax: 305-284-3003. E-mail: mmontagu@umiami.ir.miami.edu.

University of Michigan, School of Education, Programs in Educational Studies, Ann Arbor, MI 48109. Offerings include literacy education (AM, PhD). *Degree requirements:* For doctorate, dissertation, preliminary exam required, foreign language not required. *Entrance requirements:* For doctorate, GRE General Test (minimum combined score of 1800 on three sections), TOEFL (minimum score 600). Application deadline: 1/15 (priority date). Application fee: $55. Electronic applications accepted. • Dr. Ronald Marx, Chairperson, 734-763-9497. E-mail: ronmarx@umich.edu. Application contact: Karen Wixson, Associate Dean, 734-764-9470. Fax: 734-763-1229. E-mail: kwixson@umich.edu.

University of Minnesota, Twin Cities Campus, College of Education and Human Development, Department of Curriculum and Instruction, Minneapolis, MN 55455-0213. Offerings include literacy (MA), remedial and reading supervisor endorsement (MA). • Fred Finley, Chairman, 612-625-2545.

University of Missouri–Kansas City, School of Education, Division of Language and Literacy, Kansas City, MO 64110-2499. Awards MA, Ed S. Accredited by NCATE. Part-time and evening/weekend programs available. Students: 3 full-time (2 women), 46 part-time (42 women); includes 11 minority (8 African Americans, 1 Asian American, 2 Hispanics), 1 international. Average age 36. In 1997, 10 master's, 4 Ed Ss awarded. *Degree requirements:* Final exam required, foreign language and thesis not required. *Average time to degree:* master's–2 years full-time, 4 years part-time; other advanced degree–2 years full-time, 4 years part-time. *Entrance requirements:* For master's, minimum GPA of 2.75; for Ed S, minimum GPA of 3.0. Application deadline: 7/1 (priority date; rolling processing; 12/1 for spring admission). Application fee: $25. *Expenses:* Tuition $182 per credit hour for state residents; $508 per credit hour for nonresidents. Fees $60 per year. *Financial aid:* In 1997–98, 3 research assistantships averaging $858 per month were awarded; teaching assistantships, full and partial tuition waivers, Federal Work-Study, institutionally sponsored loans also available. Aid available to part-time students. *Faculty research:* Degrees of reading power, metacognition, semantic mapping, schema theory, creative process. • Dr. Warren Wheelock, Chairperson, 816-235-1545.

University of Nebraska at Kearney, College of Education, Department of Elementary/Early Childhood Education, Kearney, NE 68849-0001. Offerings include reading education (MA Ed). Accredited by NCATE. Department faculty: 4 full-time (1 woman). *Degree requirements:* Thesis optional. *Entrance requirements:* GRE General Test. Application deadline: 8/1 (priority date; rolling processing; 12/15 for spring admission). Application fee: $35. *Expenses:* Tuition $1494 per year full-time, $83 per credit hour part-time for state residents; $2826 per year full-time, $157 per credit hour part-time for nonresidents. Fees $229 per year full-time, $11.25 per semester (minimum) part-time. • Dr. Ed Walker, Chair, 308-865-8513.

University of Nebraska at Omaha, College of Education, Department of Teacher Education, Program in Reading Education, Omaha, NE 68182. Awards MA, MS. Accredited by NCATE. Part-time and evening/weekend programs available. Faculty: 2 full-time (1 woman), 1 part-time (0 women). Students: 5 full-time (4 women), 51 part-time (47 women). Average age 34. 13 applicants, 69% accepted. In 1997, 20 degrees awarded. *Degree requirements:* Comprehensive exam required, foreign language not required. *Entrance requirements:* GRE General Test (minimum combined score of 840) or MAT (minimum score 35), minimum GPA of 3.0. Application deadline: 7/1 (priority date; rolling processing; 12/1 for spring admission). Application fee: $35. *Expenses:* Tuition $1670 per year full-time, $94 per credit hour part-time for state residents; $4082 per year full-time, $227 per credit hour part-time for nonresidents. Fees $302 per year full-time, $108 per semester (minimum) part-time. *Financial aid:* 7 students received aid; fellowships, teaching assistantships, full tuition waivers, Federal Work-Study, institutionally sponsored loans available. Aid available to part-time students. Financial aid application deadline: 3/1. • Dr. Carol V. Lloyd, Adviser, 402-554-3471.

University of New Hampshire, College of Liberal Arts, Department of Education, Program in Reading, Durham, NH 03824. Offers reading (M Ed), reading and writing instruction (PhD). Accredited by NCATE. Part-time programs available. Students: 16 full-time (12 women), 18 part-time (all women); includes 2 minority (1 African American, 1 Hispanic), 2 international. Average age 41. 14 applicants, 43% accepted. In 1997, 7 master's, 1 doctorate awarded. *Degree requirements:* For master's, thesis or alternative required, foreign language not required; for doctorate, dissertation required, foreign language not required. *Entrance requirements:* For master's, GRE General Test; for doctorate, GRE General Test, sample of written work. Application deadline: rolling. Application fee: $50. *Expenses:* Tuition $5440 per year full-time, $302 per credit hour part-time for state residents; $8160 per year (minimum) full-time, $453 per credit hour (minimum) part-time for nonresidents. Fees $868 per year full-time, $15 per year part-time. *Financial aid:* In 1997–98, 1 research assistantship, 7 teaching assistantships (2 to first-year students), 4 scholarships were awarded; fellowships, full and partial tuition waivers, Federal Work-Study, and career-related internships or fieldwork also available. Aid available to part-time students. Financial aid application deadline: 2/15. *Faculty research:* Reading foundations; clinical components; consultant, supervisory, and research skills. • Dr. John Carney, Coordinator, 603-862-2373. Application contact: Dr. Todd DeMitchell, Graduate Coordinator, 603-862-2317.

University of North Alabama, College of Education, Department of Elementary Education, Program in Reading Specialization, Florence, AL 35632-0001. Awards MA Ed. Accredited by NCATE. Part-time and evening/weekend programs available. Students: 0. *Degree requirements:*

Final written comprehensive exam required, foreign language and thesis not required. *Entrance requirements:* GRE, MAT, or NTE, minimum GPA of 2.5, Alabama Class B Certificate or equivalent, teaching experience. Application deadline: 7/1 (priority date; rolling processing; 12/1 for spring admission). Application fee: $25. *Expenses:* Tuition $2448 per year full-time, $102 per credit hour part-time for state residents; $4896 per year full-time, $204 per credit hour part-time for nonresidents. Fees $3 per semester. *Financial aid:* Federal Work-Study available. Aid available to part-time students. Financial aid application deadline: 4/1. • Application contact: Dr. Sue Wilson, Dean of Enrollment Management, 205-765-4316.

The University of North Carolina at Chapel Hill, School of Education, Doctoral Program in Education, Chapel Hill, NC 27599. Offerings include early childhood, family, and literacy studies (PhD). Accredited by NCATE. Program new for fall 1998. *Degree requirements:* Dissertation, comprehensive exams required, foreign language not required. *Entrance requirements:* GRE General Test (minimum combined score of 1000), minimum GPA of 3.0 during last 2 years of undergraduate course work. Application deadline: 1/1 (priority date). *Expenses:* Tuition $1428 per year full-time, $357 per semester (minimum) part-time for state residents; $10,414 per year full-time, $2604 per semester (minimum) part-time for nonresidents. Fees $782 per year full-time, $332 per semester (minimum) part-time. • Dr. Walter Pryzwansky, Director of Graduate Studies, 919-966-7000. Application contact: Janet Carroll, Registrar, 919-966-1346. Fax: 919-962-1533. E-mail: jscarrol@email.unc.edu.

University of North Carolina at Charlotte, College of Education, Charlotte, NC 28223-0001. Offerings include reading education (M Ed). Accredited by NCATE. College faculty: 61 full-time (31 women), 7 part-time (6 women), 62.75 FTE. *Application deadline:* 7/1. *Application fee:* $35. *Tuition:* $1786 per year full-time, $339 per semester (minimum) part-time for state residents; $8914 per year full-time, $2121 per semester (minimum) part-time for nonresidents. • Dr. John M. Nagle, Dean, 704-547-4707. Application contact: Kathy Barringer, Assistant Director of Graduate Admissions, 704-547-3366. Fax: 704-547-3279. E-mail: gradadm@email.uncc.edu.

University of North Carolina at Pembroke, Graduate Studies, Department of Education, Program in Reading Education, Pembroke, NC 28372-1510. Awards MA Ed. Accredited by NCATE. Part-time and evening/weekend programs available. Faculty: 7 full-time (2 women). Students: 0. *Degree requirements:* Comprehensive exams required, thesis optional, foreign language not required. *Average time to degree:* master's–2 years full-time, 3 years part-time. *Entrance requirements:* GRE General Test or MAT, minimum GPA of 3.0 in major, 2.5 overall. Application deadline: rolling. Application fee: $25. *Tuition:* $1554 per year full-time, $610 per semester (minimum) part-time for state residents; $8824 per year full-time, $2122 per semester (minimum) part-time for nonresidents. *Financial aid:* Graduate assistantships and career-related internships or fieldwork available. Aid available to part-time students. Financial aid application deadline: 4/15. • Dr. Donald Little, Coordinator, 910-521-6221. Application contact: Director of Graduate Studies, 910-521-6271. Fax: 910-521-6497.

University of North Carolina at Wilmington, School of Education, Department of Curricular Studies, Program in Reading Education, Wilmington, NC 28403-3201. Awards M Ed. Accredited by NCATE. Part-time and evening/weekend programs available. Students: 9 full-time (7 women), 20 part-time (19 women); includes 1 minority (African American). Average age 38. 23 applicants, 52% accepted. In 1997, 19 degrees awarded. *Degree requirements:* Comprehensive exams required, foreign language and thesis not required. *Entrance requirements:* GRE General Test, MAT, minimum B average in upper-division undergraduate course work. Application deadline: 7/1 (rolling processing). Application fee: $35. *Tuition:* $1748 per year full-time, $270 per semester (minimum) part-time for state residents; $8882 per year full-time, $2058 per semester (minimum) part-time for nonresidents. *Financial aid:* Assistantships available. Financial aid application deadline: 3/15. • Application contact: Neil F. Hadley, Dean, Graduate School, 910-962-4117.

University of North Dakota, College of Education and Human Development, Program in Reading Education, Grand Forks, ND 58202. Awards M Ed, MS. Accredited by NCATE. Part-time programs available. Postbaccalaureate distance learning degree programs offered (minimal on-campus study). Faculty: 4 full-time (3 women). Students: 7 full-time (all women), 10 part-time (all women). 2 applicants, 100% accepted. *Degree requirements:* Thesis or alternative. *Entrance requirements:* TOEFL (minimum score 550), minimum GPA of 3.0. Application deadline: 3/1 (priority date; rolling processing). Application fee: $20. *Financial aid:* In 1997–98, 1 student received aid, including 1 fellowship totaling $2,400; research assistantships, teaching assistantships, full and partial tuition waivers, Federal Work-Study, institutionally sponsored loans, and career-related internships or fieldwork also available. Financial aid application deadline: 3/15. *Faculty research:* Whole language, multicultural education, child-focused learning, experiential science, cooperative learning. • Dr. Deanna Strackbein, Chair, 701-777-2861. Fax: 701-777-4393. E-mail: strackbe@badlands.nodak.edu.

University of Northern Colorado, College of Education, School for the Study of Teaching and Teacher Education, Program in Reading Education, Greeley, CO 80639. Awards MA. Accredited by NCATE. Part-time programs available. Faculty: 5 full-time (3 women). Students: 25 full-time (24 women), 22 part-time (all women); includes 4 minority (all Hispanics), 2 international. Average age 38. 7 applicants, 57% accepted. In 1997, 9 degrees awarded. *Degree requirements:* Thesis or alternative, comprehensive exams. *Entrance requirements:* GRE General Test. Application deadline: rolling. Application fee: $35. *Expenses:* Tuition $2327 per year full-time, $129 per credit hour part-time for state residents; $9578 per year full-time, $532 per credit hour part-time for nonresidents. Fees $752 per year full-time, $184 per semester (minimum) part-time. *Financial aid:* In 1997–98, 11 students received aid, including 1 fellowship (to a first-year student) totaling $3,000, 1 teaching assistantship totaling $7,200; graduate assistantships also available. Financial aid application deadline: 3/1. • Dr. Karen Crabtree, Coordinator, 970-351-2145.

University of Northern Iowa, College of Education, Department of Curriculum and Instruction, Program in Reading, Cedar Falls, IA 50614. Awards MA Ed. Part-time and evening/weekend programs available. Students: 5 full-time (3 women), 22 part-time (all women); includes 1 minority (African American), 1 international. Average age 33. 44 applicants, 100% accepted. In 1997, 13 degrees awarded. *Degree requirements:* Thesis or alternative required, foreign language not required. *Entrance requirements:* Minimum GPA of 3.5, 3 years of educational experience. Application deadline: 8/1 (priority date; rolling processing). Application fee: $20 ($30 for international students). *Expenses:* Tuition $3166 per year full-time, $176 per hour part-time for state residents; $7805 per year full-time, $176 per hour part-time for nonresidents. Fees $194 per year full-time, $12.50 per semester (minimum) part-time. *Financial aid:* Full and partial tuition waivers, Federal Work-Study, and career-related internships or fieldwork available. Aid available to part-time students. Financial aid application deadline: 3/1. • Dr. Ned Ratekin, Head, 319-273-2724.

University of North Texas, College of Education, Department of Teacher Education and Administration, Program in Reading, Denton, TX 76203-6737. Awards M Ed, MS, Ed D, PhD. Accredited by NCATE. Ed D and PhD offered jointly with Texas Woman's University. *Degree requirements:* For doctorate, dissertation. *Entrance requirements:* For master's, GRE General Test (minimum score 350 on each section, 800 combined); for doctorate, GRE General Test (minimum score 400 on each section, 1000 combined). Application deadline: 7/17. Application fee: $25 ($50 for international students). *Tuition:* $2063 per year full-time, $815 per year part-time for state residents; $5897 per year full-time, $2100 per year part-time for nonresidents. *Financial aid:* Fellowships, research assistantships, teaching assistantships, Federal Work-Study, institutionally sponsored loans, and career-related internships or fieldwork available. Financial aid application deadline: 4/1. • Application contact: Madge Craig, Co-Adviser, 940-565-2920.

University of Oklahoma, College of Education, Department of Instructional Leadership and Academic Curriculum, Program in Instructional Leadership and Academic Curriculum, Norman, OK 73019-0390. Offerings include reading education (M Ed, PhD). Accredited by NCATE. Program faculty: 19 full-time (12 women), 12 part-time (11 women). *Degree requirements:* For doctorate, variable foreign language requirement, dissertation. *Entrance requirements:* For master's, TOEFL (minimum score 550), 12 hours of course work in education; for doctorate, GRE General Test (minimum combined score of 1000), TOEFL (minimum score 500), master's degree, minimum graduate GPA of 3.0. Application deadline: 6/1 (priority date; rolling processing). Application fee: $25. *Expenses:* Tuition $1920 per year full-time, $80 per credit hour part-time for state residents; $6108 per year full-time, $255 per credit hour part-time for nonresidents. Fees $468 per year full-time, $12 per semester (minimum) part-time. • Dr. Bonnie Konopak, Chair, Department of Instructional Leadership and Academic Curriculum, 405-325-1498.

University of Pennsylvania, Graduate School of Education, Division of Language in Education, Program in Reading, Writing, and Literacy, Philadelphia, PA 19104. Awards MS Ed, Ed D, PhD. Part-time programs available. Faculty: 4 full-time (3 women). Students: 91. In 1997, 15 master's, 11 doctorates awarded. *Degree requirements:* For master's, comprehensive exam required, foreign language and thesis not required; for doctorate, 1 foreign language, dissertation, preliminary exam. *Entrance requirements:* GRE General Test or MAT, TOEFL (minimum score 550). Application fee: $65. Electronic applications accepted. *Expenses:* Tuition $22,716 per year full-time, $2876 per course part-time. Fees $1484 per year full-time, $181 per course part-time. *Financial aid:* Fellowships, Federal Work-Study, institutionally sponsored loans, and career-related internships or fieldwork available. Financial aid application deadline: 1/2; applicants required to submit FAFSA. *Faculty research:* Reading and writing relationships, classroom teachers as researchers, comprehension processes. • Dr. Susan Lytle, Director, 215-898-4800. Application contact: Keith Watanabe, Coordinator, 215-898-3245. Fax: 215-573-2109.

University of Pittsburgh, School of Education, Department of Instruction and Learning, Program in Secondary Education, Pittsburgh, PA 15260. Offerings include reading education (M Ed, Ed D, PhD). *Degree requirements:* For doctorate, dissertation required, foreign language not required. *Average time to degree:* master's–2 years full-time, 4 years part-time; doctorate–4 years full-time, 6 years part-time. *Entrance requirements:* For doctorate, GRE General Test, TOEFL (minimum score 650). Application deadline: 2/1. Application fee: $30 ($40 for international students). *Expenses:* Tuition $8018 per year full-time, $329 per credit part-time for state residents; $16,508 per year full-time, $680 per credit part-time for nonresidents. Fees $480 per year full-time, $180 per year part-time. • Application contact: Jackie Harden, Manager, 412-648-7060. Fax: 412-648-1899. E-mail: jackie@sched.fsl.pitt.edu.

University of Puget Sound, School of Education, Program in Education, Tacoma, WA 98416-0005. Offerings include improvement of instruction (M Ed), with options in elementary education, reading, secondary education. Accredited by NCATE. Program faculty: 12 full-time (9 women), 3 part-time (all women), 12.83 FTE. *Average time to degree:* master's–2 years full-time. *Entrance requirements:* GRE General Test (score in 50th percentile or higher), minimum GPA of 3.0. Application deadline: 2/1. Application fee: $40. *Expenses:* Tuition $19,640 per year full-time, $2480 per course part-time. Fees $155 per year. • Dr. Carol Merz, Dean, School of Education, 253-756-3377.

University of Rhode Island, College of Human Science and Services, Department of Education, Program in Reading, Kingston, RI 02881. Awards MA. Accredited by NCATE. *Entrance requirements:* MAT or GRE, TOEFL (minimum score 600). Application deadline: 4/15 (priority date; rolling processing; 11/15 for spring admission). Application fee: $35. *Expenses:* Tuition $3446 per year full-time, $191 per credit part-time for state residents; $9850 per year full-time, $547 per credit part-time for nonresidents. Fees $1276 per year full-time, $135 per semester (minimum) part-time.

University of Richmond, Department of Education, Reading Specialization Program, University of Richmond, VA 23173. Awards M Ed. Part-time and evening/weekend programs available. Faculty: 3 full-time (all women), 2 part-time (both women). *Degree requirements:* Comprehensive exam required, foreign language and thesis not required. *Entrance requirements:* GRE General Test, PRAXIS I, teaching certificate. Application deadline: 5/15 (priority date; 12/1 for spring admission). Application fee: $30. *Tuition:* $18,695 per year full-time, $320 per credit hour part-time. *Financial aid:* Research assistantships, tuition awards, partial tuition waivers, Federal Work-Study, institutionally sponsored loans, and career-related internships or fieldwork available. Financial aid application deadline: 3/15. • Dr. Mavis Brown, Coordinator, Department of Education, 804-289-8429.

University of Rio Grande, Graduate School, Rio Grande, OH 45674. Offerings include classroom teaching (M Ed), with options in fine arts, learning disabilities, mathematics, reading education. School faculty: 9 full-time (3 women), 6 part-time (2 women). *Degree requirements:* Final research project, portfolio required, foreign language and thesis not required. *Entrance requirements:* Minimum GPA of 2.7 in major, 2.5 overall. Application deadline: rolling. Application fee: $20. • Dr. Greg Miller, Coordinator, 740-245-7364. Application contact: Dr. Mark Abell, Director of Administration, 740-245-5353.

University of Saint Francis, Department of Education, Fort Wayne, IN 46808-3994. Offerings include reading (MS Ed). Accredited by NCATE. Department faculty: 4 full-time, 9 part-time. *Entrance requirements:* MAT (average 40), minimum GPA of 2.5. Application deadline: 7/1 (priority date; rolling processing; 11/1 for spring admission). Application fee: $20. *Expenses:* Tuition $350 per semester hour. Fees $390 per year full-time, $69 per semester (minimum) part-time. • Dr. Nancy Clements, Chair, 219-434-3271. E-mail: nclements@sfc.edu. Application contact: Scott Flanagan, Director of Admissions, 219-434-3264. Fax: 219-434-3183. E-mail: sflanagan@sfc.edu.

University of Scranton, Department of Education, Program in Reading, Scranton, PA 18510-4622. Awards MS. Accredited by NCATE. Part-time and evening/weekend programs available. Students: 3 full-time (all women), 16 part-time (15 women). Average age 31. 9 applicants, 100% accepted. In 1997, 4 degrees awarded. *Degree requirements:* Comprehensive exam required, foreign language and thesis not required. *Entrance requirements:* TOEFL (minimum score 500), minimum GPA of 2.75. Application deadline: rolling. Application fee: $35. *Expenses:* Tuition $465 per credit. Fees $25 per semester. *Financial aid:* Teaching assistantships, teaching fellowships, Federal Work-Study, and career-related internships or fieldwork available. Aid available to part-time students. Financial aid application deadline: 3/1. • Dr. R. Jeffrey Cantrell, Director, 717-941-6282. Fax: 717-941-7401. E-mail: cantrellr1@uofs.edu.

University of Sioux Falls, Program in Education, Sioux Falls, SD 57105-1699. Offerings include reading (M Ed). Accredited by NCATE. Summer admission only. Program faculty: 5 full-time (4 women), 7 part-time (4 women). *Entrance requirements:* Minimum GPA of 3.0, 1 year of teaching experience. Application deadline: rolling. Application fee: $25. *Tuition:* $195 per credit hour. • Dr. Donna Goldammer, Chair, 605-331-6713. Application contact: Dr. Nancy Johnson, Director of Graduate Studies, 605-331-6710. Fax: 605-331-6615. E-mail: nancy.johnson@thecoo.edu.

University of South Alabama, College of Education, Department of Curriculum and Instruction, Mobile, AL 36688-0002. Offerings include reading (M Ed). Accredited by NCATE. Department faculty: 13 full-time (6 women). *Degree requirements:* Comprehensive exams required, foreign language and thesis not required. *Entrance requirements:* GRE General Test (minimum combined score of 1000) or MAT (minimum score 37), minimum GPA of 3.0. Application deadline: 9/1 (priority date; rolling processing). Application fee: $25. • Dr. Walter S. Hopkins, Chairman, 334-380-2893.

University of South Carolina, Graduate School, College of Education, Department of Instruction and Teacher Education, Program in Reading Education, Columbia, SC 29208. Awards MA, M Ed, PhD. Accredited by NCATE. Faculty: 4 full-time (2 women). Students: 4 full-time (all women), 21 part-time (20 women); includes 4 minority (3 African Americans, 1 Asian American), 1 international. Average age 38. In 1997, 11 master's, 1 doctorate awarded. *Degree requirements:* For master's, thesis required (for some programs), foreign language not required; for doctorate, 1 foreign language (computer language can substitute), dissertation, comprehensive exam. *Entrance requirements:* For master's, GRE General Test or MAT, teaching certificate;

Directory: Reading Education

University of South Carolina (continued)
for doctorate, GRE General Test. Application deadline: rolling. Application fee: $35. Electronic applications accepted. *Expenses:* Tuition $3894 per year full-time, $193 per credit hour part-time for state residents; $8114 per year full-time, $404 per credit hour part-time for nonresidents. Fees $125 per year full-time, $37 per semester (minimum) part-time. *Financial aid:* Research assistantships, teaching assistantships available. *Faculty research:* Remedial and compensatory education, metacognition and learning. • Dr. Michael Rowls, Coordinator, 803-777-2233. Application contact: Office of Intercollegiate Teacher Education and Student Affairs, 803-777-6732. Fax: 803-777-3068.

University of Southern California, Graduate School, School of Education, Department of Curriculum and Instruction, Los Angeles, CA 90089. Offerings include language, literacy, and learning (PhD). *Application deadline:* 7/1 (priority date; 11/1 for spring admission). *Application fee:* $55. *Expenses:* Tuition $16,944 per year full-time, $706 per unit part-time. Fees $414 per year full-time, $32 per year part-time. • Dr. Edgar Williams, Chair.

University of Southern Maine, College of Education and Human Development, Program in Literacy Education, Portland, ME 04104-9300. Awards MS Ed, CAS. Accredited by NCATE. Part-time and evening/weekend programs available. Faculty: 3 full-time (1 woman), 5 part-time (4 women). Students: 3 full-time (2 women), 44 part-time (40 women). 32 applicants, 91% accepted. In 1997, 34 master's awarded. *Degree requirements:* For master's, thesis or alternative, comprehensive exam required, foreign language not required; for CAS, thesis or alternative required, foreign language not required. *Entrance requirements:* For master's, GRE General Test (minimum combined score of 900), MAT (minimum score 40), TOEFL. Application deadline: 2/1 (9/15 for spring admission). Application fee: $25. *Expenses:* Tuition $178 per credit hour for state residents; $267 per credit hour (minimum) for nonresidents. Fees $282 per year full-time, $83 per semester (minimum) part-time. *Financial aid:* Research assistantships, scholarships, Federal Work-Study, institutionally sponsored loans, and career-related internships or fieldwork available. Aid available to part-time students. Financial aid application deadline: 3/1; applicants required to submit FAFSA. • Dr. Margo Wood, Chair, Professional Education Department, 207-780-5400. Application contact: Teresa Belsan, Admissions and Academic Counselor, 207-780-5306. Fax: 207-780-5315. E-mail: belsan@usm.maine.edu.

University of Southern Mississippi, College of Education and Psychology, Department of Curriculum and Instruction, Hattiesburg, MS 39406-5167. Offerings include reading (M Ed, MS, Ed S). Department faculty: 11 full-time (7 women), 1 part-time (0 women). *Degree requirements:* For master's, thesis or alternative required, foreign language not required; for Ed S, thesis required, foreign language not required. *Entrance requirements:* For master's, GRE General Test, minimum GPA of 2.75; for Ed S, GRE General Test, minimum GPA of 3.25. Application deadline: 8/9 (priority date; rolling processing). Application fee: $0 ($25 for international students). *Tuition:* $2870 per year full-time, $137 per credit hour part-time for state residents; $5972 per year full-time, $172 per credit hour part-time for nonresidents. • Dr. Carolyn Reeves-Kazelskis, Acting Chair, 601-266-4547. Fax: 601-266-4175.

University of South Florida, College of Education, Department of Childhood/Language Arts/Reading Education, Program in Reading Education, Tampa, FL 33620-9951. Awards MA, PhD, Ed S. Accredited by NCATE. Part-time and evening/weekend programs available. Students: 8 full-time (all women), 33 part-time (31 women); includes 4 minority (1 African American, 1 Asian American, 2 Hispanics), 1 international. Average age 39. 10 applicants, 80% accepted. In 1997, 9 master's, 3 doctorates awarded. *Degree requirements:* For doctorate, dissertation, 2 tools of research in foreign language, statistics, and/or computers. *Entrance requirements:* For master's, GRE General Test (minimum combined score of 1000), minimum GPA of 3.5 in last 60 hours; for doctorate, GRE General Test (minimum combined score of 1000), minimum GPA of 3.0 (undergraduate) or 3.5 (graduate); for Ed S, GRE General Test (minimum combined score of 1000). Application deadline: 6/1 (10/15 for spring admission). Application fee: $20. Electronic applications accepted. *Tuition:* $142 per credit hour for state residents; $486 per credit hour for nonresidents. *Financial aid:* Fellowships, research assistantships, Federal Work-Study, institutionally sponsored loans available. Aid available to part-time students. Financial aid applicants required to submit FAFSA. *Faculty research:* Literacy-phonemic awareness, word recognition and spelling, at-risk vocabulary, critical literacy, early intervention. • Application contact: Mary Alice Barksdale-Ladd, Coordinator, 813-974-1065. Fax: 813-974-0938. E-mail: barksdal@tempest.coedu.usf.edu.

University of Tennessee at Chattanooga, School of Education, Education Graduate Studies Division, Chattanooga, TN 37403-2598. Offerings include reading (M Ed). Accredited by NCATE. Division faculty: 15 full-time (5 women), 7 part-time (3 women). *Degree requirements:* Comprehensive exams required, thesis optional, foreign language not required. *Entrance requirements:* GRE General Test or MAT, teaching certificate. Application deadline: rolling. Application fee: $25. *Tuition:* $2864 per year full-time, $160 per credit hour part-time for state residents; $6806 per year full-time, $379 per credit hour part-time for nonresidents. • Dr. Tom Bibler, Acting Head, 423-755-4211. Fax: 423-755-5380. E-mail: tom-bibler@utc.edu. Application contact: Dr. Deborah Arfken, Assistant Provost for Graduate Studies, 423-755-4667. Fax: 423-755-4478.

University of Tennessee, Knoxville, College of Education, Program in Education I, Knoxville, TN 37996. Offerings include literacy studies (PhD). Accredited by NCATE. *Degree requirements:* 1 foreign language (computer language can substitute), dissertation. *Entrance requirements:* GRE General Test, TOEFL (minimum score 550), minimum GPA of 2.7. Application deadline: 2/1 (priority date; rolling processing). Application fee: $35. Electronic applications accepted. *Tuition:* $3354 per year full-time, $181 per semester hour part-time for state residents; $8410 per year full-time, $462 per semester hour part-time for nonresidents. • Dr. Tom George, Associate Dean, 423-974-0907. Fax: 423-974-8718. E-mail: tgeorge1@utk.edu.

University of Tennessee, Knoxville, College of Education, Program in Education II, Knoxville, TN 37996. Offerings include reading education (MS, Ed D, Ed S). Accredited by NCATE. *Degree requirements:* For master's and Ed S, thesis optional, foreign language not required; for doctorate, dissertation required, foreign language not required. *Entrance requirements:* For master's, TOEFL (minimum score 550), minimum GPA of 2.7; for doctorate, GRE General Test, TOEFL (minimum score 550), minimum GPA of 2.7; for Ed S, TOEFL (minimum score 550), GRE General Test, minimum GPA of 2.7. Application deadline: 2/1 (priority date; rolling processing). Application fee: $35. Electronic applications accepted. *Tuition:* $3354 per year full-time, $181 per semester hour part-time for state residents; $8410 per year full-time, $462 per semester hour part-time for nonresidents. • Dr. Tom George, Associate Dean, 423-974-0907. Fax: 423-974-8718. E-mail: tgeorge1@utk.edu.

The University of Texas at Brownsville, Graduate Studies, School of Education, Brownsville, TX 78520-4991. Offerings include reading (M Ed). School faculty: 18 full-time (10 women). *Degree requirements:* Thesis optional, foreign language not required. *Entrance requirements:* GRE General Test, TOEFL (minimum score 550). Application deadline: 8/1 (priority date; rolling processing; 1/1 for spring admission). Application fee: $15. *Expenses:* Tuition $648 per year full-time, $120 per semester hour part-time for state residents; $4698 per year full-time, $783 per semester hour part-time for nonresidents. Fees $593 per year full-time, $109 per year part-time. • Dr. Sylvia C. Peña, Dean, 956-983-7219. Fax: 956-982-0293. E-mail: scpena@utb1.utb.edu.

The University of Texas at Tyler, School of Education and Psychology, Department of Curriculum and Instruction, Program in Elementary Education, Tyler, TX 75799-0001. Offerings include reading (M Ed, Certificate). *Degree requirements:* For master's, comprehensive and departmental qualifying exams required, foreign language not required. *Entrance requirements:* For master's, GRE General Test. Application fee: $0 ($50 for international students). *Tuition:* $2144 per year full-time, $337 per semester (minimum) part-time for state residents; $7256 per year full-time, $964 per semester (minimum) part-time for nonresidents. • Application contact: Martha D. Wheat, Director of Admissions and Student Records, 903-566-7201. Fax: 903-566-7068.

The University of Texas at Tyler, School of Education and Psychology, Department of Special Services, Program in Reading, Tyler, TX 75799-0001. Awards MA, M Ed, Certificate. Part-time programs available. Faculty: 5 full-time (4 women). Students: 20 part-time (19 women). Average age 32. 25 applicants, 100% accepted. In 1997, 10 master's awarded. *Degree requirements:* For master's, comprehensive exam and/or thesis required, foreign language not required. *Average time to degree:* master's–3 years full-time. *Entrance requirements:* For master's, GRE General Test (minimum combined score of 1200), previous course work in reading. Application fee: $0 ($50 for international students). *Tuition:* $2144 per year full-time, $337 per semester (minimum) part-time for state residents; $7256 per year full-time, $964 per semester (minimum) part-time for nonresidents. *Financial aid:* Application deadline 7/1. *Faculty research:* Early literacy, literacy training, reading recovery, comic media in the classroom. • Dr. Gary Wright, Head, 903-566-7055. Application contact: Martha D. Wheat, Director of Admissions and Student Records, 903-566-7201. Fax: 903-566-7068.

The University of Texas of the Permian Basin, Graduate School, School of Education, Program in Reading, Odessa, TX 79762-0001. Awards MA. *Degree requirements:* Thesis required, foreign language not required. *Entrance requirements:* GRE General Test (minimum combined score of 1200). *Expenses:* Tuition $1314 per year full-time, $73 per hour part-time for state residents; $4896 per year full-time, $272 per hour part-time for nonresidents. Fees $383 per year full-time, $111 per semester (minimum) part-time.

The University of Texas–Pan American, College of Education, Department of Curriculum and Instruction: Elementary and Secondary, Edinburg, TX 78539-2999. Offerings include reading (M Ed). *Degree requirements:* Thesis optional. *Entrance requirements:* GRE General Test. Application deadline: 7/17 (11/16 for spring admission). Application fee: $0. *Tuition:* $2156 per year full-time, $283 per semester (minimum) part-time for state residents; $6788 per year full-time, $862 per semester (minimum) part-time for nonresidents.

University of the Incarnate Word, School of Graduate Studies, College of Professional Studies, Programs in Education, Program in Reading, San Antonio, TX 78209-6397. Offers reading (MA, M Ed), reading specialist (MA, M Ed). Evening/weekend programs available. *Entrance requirements:* GRE, MAT, TOEFL (minimum score 550). Application deadline: 8/15 (priority date; rolling processing; 12/31 for spring admission). Application fee: $20. *Expenses:* Tuition $350 per semester hour. Fees $180 per year full-time, $111 per semester (minimum) part-time. *Faculty research:* Adult literacy. • Application contact: Brian F. Dalton, Dean of Enrollment Services, 210-829-6005. Fax: 210-829-3921.

University of Vermont, College of Education and Social Services, Department of Education, Program in Reading and Language Arts, Burlington, VT 05405-0160. Awards M Ed. Accredited by NCATE. Students: 2. 1 applicant, 100% accepted. In 1997, 1 degree awarded. *Degree requirements:* Thesis or alternative required, foreign language not required. *Entrance requirements:* GRE General Test, TOEFL (minimum score 550). Application deadline: 4/1 (priority date; rolling processing). Application fee: $25. *Expenses:* Tuition $302 per credit for state residents; $755 per credit for nonresidents. Fees $434 per year full-time, $46 per semester (minimum) part-time. *Financial aid:* Teaching assistantships and career-related internships or fieldwork available. Financial aid application deadline: 3/1. • Dr. R. Agne, Coordinator, 802-656-3356.

University of West Florida, College of Education, Division of Teacher Education, Program in Reading, Pensacola, FL 32514-5750. Awards M Ed. Accredited by NCATE. Part-time and evening/weekend programs available. Students: 1 (woman) full-time, 2 part-time (both women); includes 1 minority (African American). Average age 38. In 1997, 2 degrees awarded. *Degree requirements:* Thesis or alternative required, foreign language not required. *Entrance requirements:* GRE General Test (minimum combined score of 1000) or minimum GPA of 3.0. Application deadline: 7/1 (rolling processing; 11/1 for spring admission). Application fee: $20. *Tuition:* $131 per credit hour (minimum) for state residents; $436 per credit hour (minimum) for nonresidents. *Financial aid:* Fellowships and career-related internships or fieldwork available. *Faculty research:* Diagnostic/prescriptive teaching, college reading improvement programs, adolescent/adult literacy. • Dr. William Evans, Chairperson, Division of Teacher Education, 850-474-2891.

University of Wisconsin–Eau Claire, College of Professional Studies, School of Education, Program in Reading, Eau Claire, WI 54702-4004. Awards MST. Students: 22 part-time (all women). In 1997, 3 degrees awarded. *Degree requirements:* Oral and written comprehensive exams required, thesis optional, foreign language not required. *Application deadline:* 7/1 (rolling processing; 12/1 for spring admission). *Application fee:* $35. *Tuition:* $3651 per year full-time, $611 per semester (minimum) part-time for state residents; $11,295 per year full-time, $1886 per semester (minimum) part-time for nonresidents. *Financial aid:* Federal Work-Study available. Financial aid application deadline: 3/1. • Stephen Kurth, Associate Dean, School of Education, 715-836-3671.

University of Wisconsin–La Crosse, School of Education, Program in Reading, La Crosse, WI 54601-3742. Awards MS Ed. Accredited by NCATE. Part-time programs available. Students: 1 (woman) full-time, 8 part-time (all women). Average age 35. 13 applicants, 100% accepted. In 1997, 9 degrees awarded (100% found work related to degree). *Degree requirements:* Comprehensive exam or thesis required, foreign language not required. *Entrance requirements:* Minimum GPA of 2.85. Application deadline: rolling. Application fee: $38. *Tuition:* $3737 per year full-time, $208 per credit part-time for state residents; $11,921 per year full-time, $633 per credit part-time for nonresidents. *Financial aid:* In 1997–98, 2 students received aid, including 2 assistantships (both to first-year students) averaging $546 per month and totaling $9,828; Federal Work-Study also available. Financial aid application deadline: 3/15; applicants required to submit FAFSA. *Faculty research:* Study skills, assessment, diagnosis, early intervention, middle school education. • Dr. Jane Greenewald, Coordinator, 608-785-8135. Application contact: Tim Lewis, Director of Admissions, 608-785-8939. Fax: 608-785-6695. E-mail: admissions@mail.uwlax.edu.

University of Wisconsin–Milwaukee, School of Education, Department of Curriculum and Instruction, Milwaukee, WI 53201-0413. Offerings include reading education (MS). Offered jointly with University of Wisconsin–Green Bay. Department faculty: 28 full-time (17 women). *Degree requirements:* Thesis or alternative required, foreign language not required. *Application deadline:* 1/1 (priority date; rolling processing; 9/1 for spring admission). *Application fee:* $45 ($75 for international students). *Tuition:* $4996 per year full-time, $1030 per semester (minimum) part-time for state residents; $15,216 per year full-time, $2947 per semester (minimum) part-time for nonresidents. • Linda Post, Chair, 414-229-4884.

University of Wisconsin–Oshkosh, College of Education and Human Services, Department of Reading Education, Oshkosh, WI 54901-8602. Awards MSE. Accredited by NCATE. Offered jointly with University of Wisconsin–Green Bay. Part-time and evening/weekend programs available. Faculty: 5 full-time (4 women), 1 (woman) part-time. Students: 80 part-time (75 women); includes 3 minority (1 Hispanic, 2 Native Americans). Average age 35. 7 applicants, 100% accepted. In 1997, 15 degrees awarded (100% found work related to degree). *Degree requirements:* Thesis or comprehensive exams required, foreign language not required. *Entrance requirements:* Teaching certificate. Application deadline: rolling. Application fee: $45. *Tuition:* $3638 per year full-time, $609 per semester (minimum) part-time for state residents; $11,282 per year full-time, $1884 per semester (minimum) part-time for nonresidents. *Financial aid:* Federal Work-Study, institutionally sponsored loans, and career-related internships or fieldwork available. Financial aid application deadline: 3/15. *Faculty research:* Writing and reading, assessment, learner-centered instruction, multicultural literature, family literacy. • Dr. Judy C. Lambert, Chair, 920-424-2478. Fax: 920-424-0858. E-mail: lambert@uwosh.edu.

University of Wisconsin–River Falls, College of Education and Graduate Studies, Department of Teacher Education, Program in Reading, River Falls, WI 54022-5001. Awards MSE.

Accredited by NCATE. *Degree requirements:* Written comprehensive exam required, foreign language and thesis not required. *Application deadline:* 3/1. *Application fee:* $45. *Financial aid:* Federal Work-Study and career-related internships or fieldwork available. Financial aid application deadline: 3/1. • Kathleen Daly, Director, 715-425-3774.

University of Wisconsin–Stevens Point, College of Professional Studies, School of Education, Program in Education—General/Reading, Stevens Point, WI 54481-3897. Awards MSE. Students: 1 (woman) full-time, 49 part-time (40 women). In 1997, 74 degrees awarded. *Application deadline:* rolling. *Application fee:* $38. *Tuition:* $3702 per year full-time, $664 per semester (minimum) part-time for state residents; $11,346 per year full-time, $1938 per semester (minimum) part-time for nonresidents. *Financial aid:* Graduate assistantships available. Financial aid application deadline: 5/1; applicants required to submit FAFSA. • Dr. Leslie McClaine-Ruelle, Head, School of Education, 715-346-2040.

University of Wisconsin–Superior, Department of Teacher Education, Program in Teaching Reading, Superior, WI 54880-2873. Awards MSE. Part-time and evening/weekend programs available. Students: 11 (10 women). 2 applicants, 50% accepted. In 1997, 7 degrees awarded (100% found work related to degree). *Degree requirements:* Thesis or alternative, comprehensive exam, research project required, foreign language not required. *Entrance requirements:* Minimum GPA of 2.75, teaching certificate. Application deadline: 4/1 (priority date; rolling processing). Application fee: $45. *Tuition:* $3628 per year full-time, $222 per credit hour part-time for state residents; $11,272 per year full-time, $647 per credit hour part-time for nonresidents. *Financial aid:* Partial tuition waivers, Federal Work-Study, and career-related internships or fieldwork available. Aid available to part-time students. Financial aid application deadline: 5/1. • Dr. Walter Prentice, Coordinator, 715-394-8155. E-mail: wprentic@staff.uwsuper.edu.

University of Wisconsin–Whitewater, College of Education, Department of Curriculum and Instruction, Program in Reading, Whitewater, WI 53190-1790. Awards MS Ed. Accredited by NCATE. Part-time and evening/weekend programs available. *Degree requirements:* Thesis or alternative required, foreign language not required. *Entrance requirements:* Wisconsin teaching certificate. Application deadline: rolling. Application fee: $38.

Valdosta State University, College of Education, Department of Early Childhood and Reading Education, Valdosta, GA 31698. Offerings include reading (M Ed, Ed S). Accredited by NCATE. Department faculty: 11 full-time (9 women). *Entrance requirements:* For master's, GRE General Test (minimum combined score of 800); for Ed S, GRE General Test (minimum combined score of 900). Application deadline: 8/1 (rolling processing; 11/15 for spring admission). Application fee: $10. *Expenses:* Tuition $2472 per year full-time, $83 per semester hour part-time for state residents; $8472 per year full-time, $333 per semester hour part-time for nonresidents. Fees $236 per year full-time. • Dr. Brenda Dixey, Head, 912-333-5929. Fax: 912-333-7167. E-mail: bdixey@grits.valdosta.peachnet.edu.

Vanderbilt University, Peabody College, Department of Teaching and Learning, Nashville, TN 37240-1001. Offerings include reading education (M Ed, Ed D). Accredited by NCATE. *Entrance requirements:* GRE General Test, MAT. Application deadline: 3/1 (priority date; rolling processing). Application fee: $35. • Carolyn Evertson, Chair, 615-322-8100.

Virginia Commonwealth University, School of Education, Program in Reading, Richmond, VA 23284-9005. Awards M Ed. Accredited by NCATE. Faculty: 5 full-time (4 women). Students: 2 full-time (both women), 14 part-time (13 women). Average age 34. 18 applicants, 78% accepted. In 1997, 7 degrees awarded. *Entrance requirements:* GRE General Test or MAT. Application deadline: 7/1 (rolling processing; 11/15 for spring admission). Application fee: $30 ($0 for international students). *Tuition:* $4960 per year full-time, $257 per credit part-time for state residents; $12,652 per year full-time, $684 per credit part-time for nonresidents. *Financial aid:* Partial tuition waivers, Federal Work-Study, institutionally sponsored loans available. Financial aid application deadline: 3/1. • Dr. Alan M. McLeod, Division Head, 804-828-1305. Application contact: Dr. Michael D. Davis, Interim Director, Graduate Studies, 804-828-6530. Fax: 804-828-1323. E-mail: mddavis@vcu.edu.

Walla Walla College, Department of Education and Psychology, Specialization in Literacy Instruction, College Place, WA 99324-1198. Awards MA, M Ed. *Degree requirements:* Thesis required (for some programs), foreign language not required. *Entrance requirements:* GRE General Test, minimum GPA of 2.75. Application deadline: 4/1 (priority date; rolling processing). Application fee: $40. *Tuition:* $346 per quarter hour. *Financial aid:* Application deadline 4/1; applicants required to submit FAFSA. • Application contact: Dr. Joe Galusha, Dean of Graduate Studies, 509-527-2421. Fax: 509-527-2253. E-mail: galujo@wwc.edu.

Washburn University of Topeka, College of Arts and Sciences, Department of Education, Program in Reading, Topeka, KS 66621. Awards M Ed. Accredited by NCATE. Part-time programs available. Faculty: 2 full-time, 4 part-time. Students: 15 part-time (all women). Average age 29. In 1997, 1 degree awarded (100% found work related to degree). *Degree requirements:* Thesis or alternative, comprehensive exam required, foreign language not required. *Entrance requirements:* GRE General Test, minimum GPA of 3.0 during previous 2 years. Application deadline: 5/1. Application fee: $0. *Financial aid:* Application deadline 3/15. • Dr. David Van Cleaf, Chairperson, Department of Education, 785-231-1010 Ext. 1430.

Wayne State University, College of Education, Division of Teacher Education, Detroit, MI 48202. Offerings include reading (Ed S), reading education (Ed D). One or more programs accredited by NCATE. Division faculty: 53. *Application deadline:* 7/1. *Application fee:* $20 ($30 for international students). *Expenses:* Tuition $163 per credit hour for state residents; $355 per credit hour for nonresidents. Fees $498 per year full-time, $114 per semester (minimum) part-time. • Dr. Sharon Elliott, Assistant Dean, 313-577-0902.

West Chester University of Pennsylvania, School of Education, Department of Childhood Studies and Reading, West Chester, PA 19383. Offers programs in elementary education (M Ed), reading (M Ed). Accredited by NCATE. Faculty: 10 part-time. Students: 10 full-time (9 women), 129 part-time (122 women); includes 2 minority (1 African American, 1 Hispanic). Average age 33. 95 applicants, 77% accepted. In 1997, 61 degrees awarded. *Degree requirements:* Comprehensive exam required, thesis optional, foreign language not required. *Entrance requirements:* GRE or MAT, instructional certificate, minimum GPA of 3.0. Application deadline: 4/15 (priority date; rolling processing; 10/15 for spring admission). Application fee: $25. *Expenses:* Tuition $3468 per year full-time, $193 per credit part-time for state residents; $6236 per year full-time, $346 per credit part-time for nonresidents. Fees $660 per year full-time, $38 per credit part-time. *Financial aid:* In 1997–98, 2 research assistantships were awarded. Aid available to part-time students. Financial aid application deadline: 2/15. • Mary Ann Maggitti, Chair, 610-436-2944. Application contact: Dr. Dave Brown, Graduate Coordinator, 610-436-3225.

Western Carolina University, College of Education and Allied Professions, Department of Administration, Curriculum and Instruction, Programs in Secondary Education, Cullowhee, NC 28723. Offerings include reading (MAT). Accredited by NCATE. *Degree requirements:* Comprehensive exam required, foreign language and thesis not required. *Entrance requirements:* GRE General Test. Application deadline: rolling. Application fee: $35. *Tuition:* $1799 per year full-time, $144 per credit hour (minimum) part-time for state residents; $9069 per year full-time, $1053 per credit hour (minimum) part-time for nonresidents. • Application contact: Kathleen Owen, Assistant to the Dean, 828-227-7398. Fax: 828-227-7480.

Western Carolina University, College of Education and Allied Professions, Department of Elementary and Middle Grades Education, Program in Reading Education, Cullowhee, NC 28723. Awards MAT. Accredited by NCATE. Part-time and evening/weekend programs available. Students: 2 part-time (both women). 0 applicants. *Degree requirements:* Comprehensive exam required, foreign language and thesis not required. *Entrance requirements:* GRE General Test. Application deadline: rolling. Application fee: $35. *Tuition:* $1799 per year full-time, $144 per credit hour (minimum) part-time for state residents; $9069 per year full-time, $1053 per credit hour (minimum) part-time for nonresidents. *Financial aid:* Fellowships, research assistantships, teaching assistantships, Federal Work-Study, institutionally sponsored loans available. Financial aid application deadline: 3/15. • Application contact: Kathleen Owen, Assistant to the Dean, 828-227-7398. Fax: 828-227-7480.

Western Connecticut State University, School of Professional Studies, Department of Education and Educational Psychology, Program in Reading Education, Danbury, CT 06810-6885. Offers reading (MS). Part-time and evening/weekend programs available. Students: 67 part-time (63 women); includes 1 minority (Asian American). In 1997, 34 degrees awarded. *Degree requirements:* Thesis or research project required, foreign language not required. *Entrance requirements:* Minimum GPA of 2.67. Application deadline: 8/1 (priority date; rolling processing). Application fee: $40. *Expenses:* Tuition $4127 per year (minimum) full-time, $178 per credit hour part-time for state residents; $9581 per year (minimum) full-time, $178 per credit hour part-time for nonresidents. Fees $25 per year part-time. *Financial aid:* Federal Work-Study and career-related internships or fieldwork available. Aid available to part-time students. Financial aid application deadline: 5/1. • Dr. Darla Shaw, Coordinator, 203-837-8412.

Western Illinois University, College of Education and Human Services, Department of Elementary Education and Reading, Program in Reading, Macomb, IL 61455-1390. Awards MS Ed. Accredited by NCATE. Part-time programs available. Faculty: 7 full-time (5 women). Students: 3 full-time (2 women), 82 part-time (80 women); includes 3 minority (1 African American, 2 Hispanics). Average age 36. 3 applicants, 67% accepted. In 1997, 30 degrees awarded. *Degree requirements:* Thesis or alternative required, foreign language not required. *Application deadline:* rolling. *Application fee:* $0 ($25 for international students). *Expenses:* Tuition $2304 per year full-time, $96 per semester hour part-time for state residents; $6912 per year full-time, $288 per semester hour part-time for nonresidents. Fees $944 per year full-time, $33 per semester hour part-time. *Financial aid:* In 1997–98, 3 students received aid, including 3 research assistantships averaging $610 per month; full tuition waivers also available. Financial aid applicants required to submit FAFSA. • Dr. Linda Thistlethwaite, Graduate Committee Chairperson, 309-298-1961. Application contact: Barbara Baily, Director of Graduate Studies, 309-298-1806. Fax: 309-298-2245. E-mail: barb_baily@ccmail.wiu.edu.

Western Kentucky University, College of Education, Department of Teacher Education, Program in Reading, Bowling Green, KY 42101-3576. Awards MA Ed. Accredited by NCATE. Part-time and evening/weekend programs available. Faculty: 4 full-time (3 women). Students: 2 full-time (both women), 42 part-time (all women). Average age 31. 3 applicants, 67% accepted. In 1997, 1 degree awarded. *Entrance requirements:* GRE General Test (minimum combined score of 1150 on three sections; average 1140), minimum GPA of 2.5. Application deadline: 8/1 (priority date; rolling processing; 12/1 for spring admission). Application fee: $20. *Tuition:* $2460 per year full-time, $133 per credit hour part-time for state residents; $6700 per year full-time, $369 per credit hour part-time for nonresidents. *Financial aid:* Federal Work-Study, institutionally sponsored loans available. Aid available to part-time students. Financial aid application deadline: 4/1; applicants required to submit FAFSA. • Dr. Ann Ruff, Head, 502-745-4452.

Western Maryland College, Department of Education, Program in Reading Education, Westminster, MD 21157-4390. Awards MS. Part-time and evening/weekend programs available. Faculty: 1 (woman) full-time, 3 part-time (all women). Students: 3 full-time (all women), 73 part-time (71 women). In 1997, 15 degrees awarded. *Degree requirements:* Thesis optional, foreign language not required. *Entrance requirements:* GRE General Test, MAT, or NTE. Application deadline: rolling. Application fee: $35. *Expenses:* Tuition $210 per credit hour. Fees $30 per semester. *Financial aid:* Application deadline 3/1. • Dr. Joan Develin Coley, Coordinator, 410-857-2501. Application contact: Jeanette Witt, Coordinator of Graduate Records, 410-857-2513. Fax: 410-857-2515. E-mail: jwitt@wmdc.edu.

Western Michigan University, College of Education, Department of Education and Professional Development, Program in Reading, Kalamazoo, MI 49008. Awards MA. Accredited by NCATE. Students: 1 (woman) full-time, 128 part-time (122 women); includes 4 minority (3 African Americans, 1 Asian American). 76 applicants, 33% accepted. In 1997, 63 degrees awarded. *Application deadline:* 2/15 (priority date; rolling processing). *Application fee:* $25. *Expenses:* Tuition $154 per credit hour for state residents; $372 per credit hour for nonresidents. Fees $602 per year full-time, $132 per semester part-time. *Financial aid:* Fellowships, research assistantships, teaching assistantships, Federal Work-Study available. Financial aid application deadline: 2/15; applicants required to submit FAFSA. • Application contact: Paula J. Boodt, Coordinator, Graduate Admissions and Recruitment, 616-387-2000. E-mail: paulaboodt@wmich.edu.

Western New Mexico University, School of Education, Silver City, NM 88062-0680. Offerings include reading (MAT). School faculty: 16 full-time (9 women). *Application deadline:* rolling. *Application fee:* $10. *Tuition:* $1516 per year full-time, $55 per credit part-time for state residents; $5604 per year full-time, $55 per credit part-time for nonresidents. • Dr. Bonnie Maldonado, Dean, 505-538-6415.

Western Oregon University, School of Education, Program in Reading Education, Monmouth, OR 97361. Awards MS Ed. Accredited by NCATE. Faculty: 2 full-time (1 woman). Students: 0. *Entrance requirements:* GRE General Test (average 450 on each section) or MAT (minimum score 30), minimum GPA of 3.0, teaching license. Application deadline: rolling. Application fee: $50. *Financial aid:* Research assistantships, teaching assistantships, full and partial tuition waivers, and career-related internships or fieldwork available. Financial aid application deadline: 3/1; applicants required to submit FAFSA. • Dr. Susan Dauer, Director, 503-838-8471. Fax: 503-838-8228. E-mail: dauers@wou.edu. Application contact: Alison Marshall, Director of Admissions, 503-838-8211. Fax: 503-838-8067. E-mail: marshaa@wou.edu.

Western Washington University, Woodring College of Education, Program in Reading, Bellingham, WA 98225-5996. Awards M Ed. Accredited by NCATE. Part-time programs available. Students: 0. 0 applicants. In 1997, 1 degree awarded. *Degree requirements:* Comprehensive exams required, thesis optional, foreign language not required. *Entrance requirements:* GRE General Test, TOEFL, minimum GPA of 3.0 in last 60 semester hours or last 90 quarter hours. Application deadline: 6/1 (rolling processing; 2/1 for spring admission). Application fee: $35. *Expenses:* Tuition $4200 per year full-time, $140 per credit part-time for state residents; $12,780 per year full-time, $426 per credit part-time for nonresidents. Fees $249 per year full-time, $83 per quarter part-time. *Financial aid:* Teaching assistantships, partial tuition waivers, Federal Work-Study, institutionally sponsored loans, and career-related internships or fieldwork available. Aid available to part-time students. Financial aid application deadline: 3/31. *Faculty research:* Language acquisition and reading, integrating reading and writing, teaching of comprehension. • Dr. Phil Riner, Graduate Adviser, 360-650-3416.

Westfield State College, Department of Education, Program in Reading, Westfield, MA 01086. Awards M Ed. *Degree requirements:* Comprehensive exam, practicum required, foreign language and thesis not required. *Entrance requirements:* GRE General Test or MAT, minimum undergraduate GPA of 2.7. Application deadline: rolling. Application fee: $30. *Expenses:* Tuition $145 per credit for state residents; $155 per credit for nonresidents. Fees $90 per semester. *Financial aid:* Application deadline 4/1. • Application contact: Marcia Davio, Graduate Records Clerk, 413-572-8024.

Westminster College, Programs in Education, Program in Reading, South Market Street, New Wilmington, PA 16172-0001. Awards M Ed, Certificate. Part-time and evening/weekend programs available. Students: 16 part-time (all women). In 1997, 6 master's awarded (100% found work related to degree). *Average time to degree:* master's–1.5 years full-time, 2.5 years part-time. *Entrance requirements:* For master's, minimum GPA of 2.75. Application deadline: 8/30 (priority date; rolling processing; 1/15 for spring admission). Application fee: $20. *Expenses:* Tuition $1104 per course. Fees $30 per course. *Financial aid:* Grants and career-related internships or fieldwork available. • Dr. Charlene Klassen-Endrizzi, Coordinator, 724-946-7183.

Directories: Reading Education; Religious Education

West Texas A&M University, College of Education and Social Sciences, Division of Education, Program in Reading, Canyon, TX 79016-0001. Awards M Ed. Part-time and evening/weekend programs available. Students: 2 part-time (both women). Average age 34. 0 applicants. *Degree requirements:* Comprehensive exam required, foreign language and thesis not required. *Entrance requirements:* GRE General Test (combined average 964). Application deadline: rolling. Application fee: $0 ($50 for international students). Electronic applications accepted. *Expenses:* Tuition $46 per semester hour for state residents; $259 per semester hour for nonresidents. Fees $156 per semester (minimum). *Financial aid:* Federal Work-Study, institutionally sponsored loans available. Aid available to part-time students. Financial aid applicants required to submit FAFSA. • Application contact: Dr. Barbara Tyler, Graduate Adviser, 806-651-2618. Fax: 806-651-2601. E-mail: barbara.tyler@wtamu.edu.

West Virginia University, College of Human Resources and Education, Department of Educational Theory and Practice, Program in Reading, Morgantown, WV 26506. Offers reading (MA). Accredited by NCATE. Part-time programs available. Students: 15 full-time (all women), 66 part-time (65 women); includes 2 minority (1 African American, 1 Asian American). Average age 31. 16 applicants, 100% accepted. In 1997, 22 degrees awarded (100% found work related to degree). *Degree requirements:* Content exams required, thesis optional, foreign language not required. *Average time to degree:* master's–3 years full-time, 8 years part-time. *Entrance requirements:* TOEFL (minimum score 550), minimum GPA of 2.75. Application deadline: rolling. Application fee: $45. *Tuition:* $2820 per year full-time, $149 per credit hour part-time for state residents; $8104 per year full-time, $443 per credit hour part-time for nonresidents. *Financial aid:* In 1997–98, 3 teaching assistantships (1 to a first-year student), 1 graduate administrative assistantship (to a first-year student) were awarded; full and partial tuition waivers, Federal Work-Study, institutionally sponsored loans also available. Financial aid application deadline: 2/1; applicants required to submit FAFSA. *Faculty research:* Teacher education, current practices, protocol research, metacognitive studies. • Dr. Steven Rinehart, Coordinator, 304-293-4442. Fax: 304-293-7388. Application contact: Risa Moore, Administrative Secretary, 304-293-4769. Fax: 304-293-3802.

Wheelock College, Graduate School, Program in Language and Literacy Education, Boston, MA 02215. Awards MS, CAGS. Accredited by NCATE. Students: 1 (woman) full-time, 12 part-time (11 women). *Degree requirements:* For CAGS, thesis. *Entrance requirements:* For CAGS, interview. Application deadline: rolling. Application fee: $35 ($40 for international students). Electronic applications accepted. *Tuition:* $525 per credit. *Financial aid:* Graduate assistantships, grants, Federal Work-Study, institutionally sponsored loans, and career-related internships or fieldwork available. Aid available to part-time students. Financial aid application deadline: 4/1; applicants required to submit FAFSA. *Faculty research:* Symbolic learning, emergent literacy. • Dr. Susan Harris-Sharples, Coordinator, 617-734-5200 Ext. 226. E-mail: sharrissharples@wheelock.edu. Application contact: Martha Sheehan, Director of Graduate Admissions, 617-734-5200 Ext. 212. Fax: 617-232-7127. E-mail: msheehan@wheelock.edu.

Whitworth College, Graduate Studies in Education, Program in Reading, Spokane, WA 99251-0001. Awards MAT. Accredited by NCATE. Part-time and evening/weekend programs available. *Degree requirements:* Comprehensive exams, internship, practicum, research project, or thesis required, foreign language not required. *Entrance requirements:* GRE General Test. Application deadline: 9/1 (priority date; rolling processing; 2/1 for spring admission). Application fee: $25.

William Paterson University of New Jersey, College of Education, Department of Curriculum and Instruction, Program in Reading, Wayne, NJ 07470-8420. Awards M Ed. Accredited by NCATE. Students: 21 part-time (all women); includes 1 minority (Asian American). Average age 32. 7 applicants, 43% accepted. In 1997, 14 degrees awarded. *Degree requirements:* Comprehensive exam, research design required, foreign language and thesis not required. *Entrance requirements:* GRE General Test (minimum combined score of 850), MAT (minimum score 42), minimum GPA of 2.75, teaching certificate. Application deadline: 4/1 (rolling processing; 10/15 for spring admission). Application fee: $35. *Expenses:* Tuition $230 per credit for state residents; $327 per credit for nonresidents. Fees $3.25 per credit. *Financial aid:* 1 student received aid; fellowships, graduate assistantships, and career-related internships or fieldwork available. Aid available to part-time students. Financial aid application deadline: 4/1; applicants required to submit FAFSA. *Faculty research:* Reading improvement, urban education. • Dr. Dorothy Feola, Coordinator, Graduate Program, 973-720-2577. Application contact: Office of Graduate Studies, 973-720-2237. Fax: 973-720-2035.

Winthrop University, College of Education, Program in Reading Education, Rock Hill, SC 29733. Awards M Ed. Accredited by NCATE. Part-time programs available. Students: 2 full-time (both women), 19 part-time (all women); includes 4 minority (all African Americans). Average age 33. In 1997, 9 degrees awarded. *Entrance requirements:* GRE General Test or NTE, South Carolina Class III teaching certificate, 1 year of teaching experience. Application deadline: 7/15 (priority date; rolling processing; 12/1 for spring admission). Application fee: $35. *Tuition:* $3928 per year full-time, $164 per credit hour part-time for state residents; $7060 per year full-time, $294 per credit hour part-time for nonresidents. *Financial aid:* Graduate assistantships, graduate scholarships, Federal Work-Study, and career-related internships or fieldwork available. Aid available to part-time students. Financial aid application deadline: 2/1; applicants required to submit FAFSA. • Dr. Richard Ingram, Chairman, 803-323-2151. Fax: 803-323-2585. E-mail: ingramr@winthrop.edu. Application contact: Sharon Johnson, Director of Graduate Studies, 803-323-2204. Fax: 803-323-2292. E-mail: johnsons@winthrop.edu.

Worcester State College, Graduate Studies, Department of Education, Program in Reading, Worcester, MA 01602-2597. Awards M Ed, Certificate. In 1997, 10 master's awarded. *Degree requirements:* For master's, comprehensive exam. *Entrance requirements:* For master's, GRE General Test or MAT. Application fee: $10 ($40 for international students). *Tuition:* $127 per credit hour. • Dr. Elaine Tateronis, Graduate Coordinator, 508-929-8823. Application contact: Andrea Wetmore, Graduate Admissions Counselor, 508-929-8120. E-mail: awetmore@worc.mass.edu.

Xavier University, College of Social Sciences, Department of Education, Program in Reading Specialist, Cincinnati, OH 45207-2111. Awards M Ed. Part-time and evening/weekend programs available. Faculty: 2 full-time (both women), 7 part-time (6 women), 3.75 FTE. Students: 1 (woman) full-time, 20 part-time (18 women); includes 2 minority (both African Americans). Average age 37. 10 applicants, 100% accepted. In 1997, 8 degrees awarded (100% found work related to degree). *Degree requirements:* Comprehensive exam, research project required, foreign language and thesis not required. *Entrance requirements:* GRE or MAT (minimum score 35), minimum GPA of 2.8. Application deadline: 8/15 (priority date; rolling processing). Application fee: $25. *Financial aid:* In 1997–98, 10 students received aid, including 10 scholarships (4 to first-year students). Aid available to part-time students. *Faculty research:* Emergent reading, Mische analysis, analysis of reader response to children's literature in the U.S. and Canada. • Dr. Leslie Prosak-Beres, Director, 513-745-3652. Fax: 513-745-1052. E-mail: prosak@xavier.xu.edu. Application contact: Sheila Speth, Director of Graduate Services, 513-745-3360. Fax: 513-745-1048. E-mail: xugrad@admin.xu.edu.

Youngstown State University, College of Education, Department of Teacher Education, Program in Early and Middle Childhood Education, Youngstown, OH 44555-0002. Offerings include teaching—secondary reading (MS Ed). Accredited by NCATE. Program faculty: 9 full-time (6 women), 8 part-time (all women). *Degree requirements:* Comprehensive exam required, foreign language and thesis not required. *Entrance requirements:* TOEFL (minimum score 550), GRE, MAT, or teaching certificate; minimum GPA of 2.5. Application deadline: 8/15 (priority date; rolling processing; 2/15 for spring admission). Application fee: $30 ($75 for international students). *Expenses:* Tuition $90 per credit hour for state residents; $144 per credit hour (minimum) for nonresidents. Fees $528 per year full-time, $244 per year (minimum) part-time. • Application contact: Dr. Peter J. Kasvinsky, Dean of Graduate Studies, 330-742-3091. Fax: 330-742-1580. E-mail: amgrad03@ysub.ysu.edu.

Religious Education

Abilene Christian University, College of Biblical and Family Studies, Department of Graduate Biblical Studies, Abilene, TX 79699-9100. Offerings include Christian education (MS). Department faculty: 1 full-time (0 women), 27 part-time (2 women). *Application deadline:* 4/1 (priority date; rolling processing; 11/1 for spring admission). *Application fee:* $25 ($45 for international students). *Expenses:* Tuition $308 per credit hour. Fees $430 per year full-time, $85 per semester (minimum) part-time. • Dr. James Thompson, Chairman, 915-674-3781. Application contact: Dr. Carley Dodd, Graduate Dean, 915-674-2354. Fax: 915-674-6717. E-mail: gradinfo@nicanor.acu.edu.

American Bible College and Seminary, Graduate and Professional Programs, Program in Christian Education, Bethany, OK 73008-0099. Awards MA. Part-time and evening/weekend programs available. Postbaccalaureate distance learning degree programs offered (no on-campus study). *Degree requirements:* Thesis. *Application deadline:* rolling. *Application fee:* $50. *Tuition:* $125 per credit hour. *Financial aid:* Application deadline 5/5. • Dr. Mark Mann, Director, 405-495-2526. Application contact: Perry Kepford, Admissions, 405-495-2526. Fax: 405-495-2521. E-mail: ubss@cris.com.

Andover Newton Theological School, Newton Centre, MA 02159-2243. Offerings include religious education (MA). Postbaccalaureate distance learning degree programs offered (minimal on-campus study). School faculty: 23 full-time (8 women), 68 part-time (25 women). *Application deadline:* 8/1 (priority date; rolling processing; 12/1 for spring admission). *Application fee:* $15. *Expenses:* Tuition $324 per credit hour. Fees $280 per year. • Dr. Benjamin Griffin, President, 617-964-1100. Application contact: Elaine M. Lapomardo, Director of Enrollment, 800-964-2687 Ext. 272. Fax: 617-965-9756.

Andrews University, School of Graduate Studies, School of Education, Department of Teaching/Learning/Administration, Program in Religious Education, Berrien Springs, MI 49104. Awards MA, Ed D, PhD, Ed S. Part-time programs available. Terminal master's awarded for partial completion of doctoral program. *Degree requirements:* For doctorate, dissertation. *Entrance requirements:* For master's, GRE Subject Test. Application deadline: 8/31 (rolling processing). Application fee: $30. *Expenses:* Tuition $290 per quarter hour (minimum). Fees $75 per quarter. *Financial aid:* Fellowships, research assistantships, teaching assistantships, and career-related internships or fieldwork available. Financial aid application deadline: 6/1. *Faculty research:* Marriage and family, spiritual gifts and temperament. • Dr. William H. Green, Chair, Department of Teaching/Learning/Administration, 616-471-3465.

Asbury Theological Seminary, School of Theology, 204 North Lexington Avenue, Wilmore, KY 40390-1199. Offerings include Christian education (MA). MA/MSW and M Div/MSW offered jointly with the University of Kentucky. School faculty: 29 full-time (4 women), 40 part-time (7 women), 41 FTE. *Degree requirements:* Thesis optional, foreign language not required. *Entrance requirements:* English language exam or TOEFL (minimum score 550). Application deadline: 5/1 (priority date; rolling processing; 12/1 for spring admission). Application fee: $25. *Expenses:* Tuition $270 per credit hour. Fees $150 per year full-time, $45 per semester part-time. • Dr. Kenneth C. Kinghorn, Dean, 606-858-2214. Fax: 606-858-2371. E-mail: ken_kinghorn@ats.wilmore.ky.us. Application contact: W. Thomas Pope, Director of Admissions, 606-858-2250. Fax: 606-858-2287. E-mail: admissions_office@ats.wilmore.ky.us.

Ashland University, Theological Seminary, Ashland, OH 44805-3702. Offerings include Christian education (MACE). Seminary faculty: 19 full-time (2 women), 39 part-time (8 women). *Application deadline:* 8/8 (rolling processing). *Application fee:* $30. *Tuition:* $5976 per year full-time, $166 per credit hour part-time. • Dr. Frederick J. Finks, President, 419-289-5160. Application contact: Mario Guerreiro, Director of Admissions, 419-289-5704. Fax: 419-289-5969.

Assumption College, Department of Theology, Program in Religious Education, 500 Salisbury Street, PO Box 15005, Worcester, MA 01615-0005. Awards MA. Part-time and evening/weekend programs available. *Degree requirements:* Oral and written comprehensive exams, practicum. *Entrance requirements:* TOEFL. Application deadline: rolling. Application fee: $20. *Expenses:* Tuition $297 per credit hour. Fees $10 per semester.

Baptist Bible College of Pennsylvania, Graduate School, Clarks Summit, PA 18411-1297. Offers programs in Christian school education (MS), counseling (MS). Faculty: 2 full-time, 12 part-time. Students: 45. *Application deadline:* rolling. *Application fee:* $25. *Expenses:* Tuition $214 per credit hour (minimum). Fees $16 per credit hour. • Dr. Hubert Hartzler, Director of Graduate Studies, 717-585-9226.

Bethel Theological Seminary, St. Paul, MN 55112-6998. Offerings include Christian education (M Div, MACE). Postbaccalaureate distance learning degree programs offered (minimal on-campus study). Seminary faculty: 20 full-time (1 woman), 28 part-time (5 women), 26.13 FTE. *Degree requirements:* For first professional, 1 foreign language required, thesis not required. *Application deadline:* 8/1 (priority date; rolling processing). *Application fee:* $20. *Expenses:* Tuition $170 per credit hour. Fees $15 per year. • Dr. Leland Eliason, Executive Vice President and Dean, 612-638-6182. Application contact: Morris Anderson, Director of Admissions, 612-638-6288. Fax: 612-638-6002.

Biola University, Talbot School of Theology, La Mirada, CA 90639-0001. Offerings include Christian education (MACE), education (Ed D). School faculty: 37 full-time (3 women), 22 part-time (2 women). *Average time to degree:* doctorate–5 years full-time, 7 years part-time; first professional–3 years full-time, 5 years part-time. *Application deadline:* 8/1 (rolling processing; 1/1 for spring admission). *Application fee:* $35. *Expenses:* Tuition $9810 per year full-time, $327 per unit part-time. Fees $40 per year full-time. • Dr. Dennis Dirks, Dean, 562-903-4816. Fax: 562-903-4748. Application contact: Roy Allinson, Director of Graduate Admissions, 562-903-4752. Fax: 562-903-4709. E-mail: admissions@biola.edu.

Boston College, Graduate School of Arts and Sciences, Institute of Religious Education and Pastoral Ministry, Chestnut Hill, MA 02167-9991. Awards MA, PhD, MA/MA, MA/MSW. Programs in leadership/church management (MA); pastoral ministry (MA), including Hispanic ministry, liturgy, pastoral counseling, spirituality; religious education (MA, PhD); social justice/social ministry (MA). MA/MA offered jointly with the Program in Counseling Psychology. Part-time programs available. Faculty: 6 full-time (2 women), 10 part-time (5 women). Students: 23 full-time (15 women), 69 part-time (55 women); includes 5 minority (1 African American, 2 Asian Americans, 2 Hispanics), 10 international. 85 applicants, 69% accepted. In 1997, 48 master's, 3 doctorates awarded. Terminal master's awarded for partial completion of doctoral program. *Degree requirements:* For doctorate, 1 foreign language, dissertation. *Entrance* *requirements:* For doctorate, GRE. Application deadline: 3/1 (priority date). Application fee: $40. *Expenses:* Tuition $626 per semester hour. Fees $80 per year (minimum) full-time, $30 per semester part-time. *Financial aid:* Fellowships, full and partial tuition waivers, Federal Work-Study, and career-related internships or fieldwork available. Aid available to part-time students. Financial aid application deadline: 3/15; applicants required to submit FAFSA. *Faculty research:* Philosophy and practice of religious education, pastoral psychology, liturgical and spiritual theology, spiritual formation for the practice of ministry. • Dr. Claire Lowery, Chairperson, 617-552-8440. E-mail: claire.lowery@bc.edu. Application contact: Dr. Harold Horell, Assistant Director, Academic Affairs, 617-552-8440. E-mail: horell@bc.edu.

Boston College, Graduate School of Education, Department of Teacher Education/Special Education and Curriculum and Instruction, Program in Secondary Education, Religious Education Specialization, Chestnut Hill, MA 02167-9991. Awards M Ed. Accredited by NCATE. Students: 13 full-time (5 women), 16 part-time (6 women); includes 1 minority (Hispanic), 5 international. 16 applicants, 75% accepted. In 1997, 19 degrees awarded. *Degree requirements:* Comprehensive exam required, thesis not required. *Entrance requirements:* GRE General Test. Application deadline: 3/15 (11/15 for spring admission). Application fee: $40. *Expenses:* Tuition $626 per semester hour. Fees $80 per year (minimum) full-time, $30 per semester part-time. *Financial aid:* Research assistantships available. • Application contact: Arline Riordan, Graduate Admissions Director, 617-552-4214. Fax: 617-552-0812. E-mail: riordana@bc.edu.

Calvin Theological Seminary, Grand Rapids, MI 49546-4387. Offerings include educational ministry (MA). Seminary faculty: 16 full-time (0 women), 14 part-time (0 women), 18 FTE. *Application deadline:* 3/1 (priority date; rolling processing). *Application fee:* $25. *Tuition:* $120 per quarter hour (minimum). • Dr. James A. De Jong, President, 616-957-6086. Application contact: John Vander Lugt, Registrar, 616-957-6027. Fax: 616-957-8621.

Campbell University, Divinity School, Buies Creek, NC 27506. Offerings include Christian education (MA). School faculty: 3 full-time (0 women), 10 part-time (3 women). *Entrance requirements:* Minimum GPA of 2.5. Application deadline: 7/15 (rolling processing; 12/1 for spring admission). Application fee: $20. *Tuition:* $168 per credit hour (minimum). • Dr. Michael Cogdill, Dean, 910-893-1830. E-mail: cogdill@mailcenter.campbell.edu. Application contact: Clella A. Lee, Director of Admissions, 910-893-1200 Ext. 1677. Fax: 910-893-1835. E-mail: lee@mailcenter.campbell.edu.

Canadian Theological Seminary, Regina, SK S4T 0H8, Canada. Offerings include religious education (MRE). Postbaccalaureate distance learning degree programs offered (minimal on-campus study). Seminary faculty: 10 full-time (2 women), 10 part-time (2 women). *Average time to degree:* master's–2 years full-time, 4 years part-time; doctorate–6 years part-time; first professional–3 years full-time, 5 years part-time; other advanced degree–1 year full-time, 2 years part-time. *Application deadline:* 8/31 (priority date; rolling processing). *Application fee:* $30. Electronic applications accepted. *Expenses:* Tuition $4320 per year full-time, $140 per credit hour part-time. Fees $652 per year full-time, $16 per credit hour part-time. • Dr. Raymond Downey, Acting Dean, 306-545-1515. Application contact: Sharon Ralph, Recruitment Officer, 306-545-1515. Fax: 306-545-0210. E-mail: sralph@cbccts.sk.ca.

Cardinal Stritch University, College of Education, Department of Education, Milwaukee, WI 53217-3985. Offerings include Catholic urban educator (ME). Accredited by NCATE. ME (Catholic urban educator) offered in collaboration with the Archdiocese of Milwaukee. *Application deadline:* 4/1 (priority date; rolling processing). *Application fee:* $20. *Expenses:* Tuition $338 per credit. Fees $25 per semester. • Dr. Nancy Blair, Chair, 414-410-4367. Application contact: Amy Knox, Graduate Admissions Officer, 414-410-4042.

The Catholic University of America, School of Religious Studies, Department of Religion and Religious Education, Program in Religious Education, Washington, DC 20064. Awards MA, MRE, PhD. Faculty: 16 full-time (4 women), 2 part-time (0 women), 17 FTE. Students: 29 full-time (9 women), 48 part-time (25 women); includes 9 minority (1 African American, 4 Asian Americans, 4 Hispanics), 14 international. Average age 37. 7 applicants, 86% accepted. In 1997, 8 master's, 6 doctorates awarded. *Degree requirements:* For master's, 1 foreign language, comprehensive exam required, thesis optional; for doctorate, 2 foreign languages (computer language can substitute for one), dissertation, comprehensive exam. *Entrance requirements:* GRE General Test, MAT. Application deadline: 8/1 (priority date; rolling processing; 12/1 for spring admission). Application fee: $50. *Expenses:* Tuition $17,325 per year full-time, $668 per credit hour part-time. Fees $680 per year full-time, $360 per year part-time. *Financial aid:* In 1997–98, 2 research assistantships averaging $250 per month and totaling $2,000, 10 teaching assistantships averaging $1,300 per month and totaling $105,000 were awarded; full and partial tuition waivers, Federal Work-Study, institutionally sponsored loans, and career-related internships or fieldwork also available. Aid available to part-time students. Financial aid application deadline: 2/1. *Faculty research:* Method in theology and religious study hermenutics, liturgy, Catholic theological tradition, interreligion dialogue. • Dr. Stephen Happel, Chair, Department of Religion and Religious Education, 202-319-5700. Fax: 202-319-5704. E-mail: happel@cua.edu.

Chicago Theological Seminary, Chicago, IL 60637-1507. Offerings include clinical pastoral education (D Min). Seminary faculty: 9 full-time (2 women), 11 part-time (2 women). *Application deadline:* 5/1 (2/1 for spring admission). *Application fee:* $50. • Dr. William Myers, Dean, 773-752-5757 Ext. 224. Application contact: Veronica O'Neill Morrison, Admissions, Recruitment and Financial Planning, 773-752-5757 Ext. 221. Fax: 773-752-5925.

Christian Theological Seminary, Programs in Theology, Indianapolis, IN 46208-3301. Offerings include Christian education (MA). Faculty: 19 full-time (5 women), 29 part-time (7 women), 25 FTE. *Application deadline:* 4/1 (priority date; rolling processing; 12/1 for spring admission). *Application fee:* $30. Electronic applications accepted. *Tuition:* $225 per credit hour. • Dr. Clark Williamson, Director of Admissions, 317-931-2300. Fax: 317-923-1961.

Cincinnati Bible College and Seminary, 2700 Glenway Avenue, Cincinnati, OH 45204-1799. Offerings include religious education (MRE). Seminary faculty: 6 full-time (0 women), 12 part-time (3 women). *Application deadline:* 8/10 (priority date; rolling processing; 12/10 for spring admission). *Application fee:* $35. *Expenses:* Tuition $185 per hour. Fees $25 per semester (minimum). • Dr. William C. Weber, Dean, 513-244-8192. E-mail: bill.weber@cincybible.edu. Application contact: Shan Caldwell, Graduate Admissions Director, 513-244-8145. Fax: 513-244-8434. E-mail: shan.caldwell@cincybible.edu.

College of Notre Dame, Department of Education, Emphasis in Secondary Education, Belmont, CA 94002-1997. Offerings include teaching religious studies (MAT). Faculty: 5 full-time, 8 part-time. *Application deadline:* rolling. *Application fee:* $50 ($500 for international students). *Tuition:* $460 per unit. • Dr. Kim Tolley, Program Director, 650-508-3456.

Columbia International University, Columbia Biblical Seminary and Graduate School of Missions, Columbia, SC 29230-3122. Offerings include Christian education (M Div, MACE), education (PhD), international theological education (MA). MACE offered jointly with Erskine Theological Seminary; PhD offered jointly with the University of South Carolina. Seminary faculty: 36 full-time (3 women), 38 part-time (1 woman). *Degree requirements:* For M Div, 1 foreign language, internship required, thesis not required. *Application deadline:* rolling. *Application fee:* $25. *Expenses:* Tuition $7410 per year full-time, $285 per semester hour part-time. Fees $150 per year. • Dr. Ken B. Mulholland, Dean, 803-754-4100. E-mail: kenm@ciu.edu. Application contact: Brian O'Donnell, Director of Admissions, 803-754-4100. Fax: 803-786-4209. E-mail: bodonell@ciu.edu.

Concordia University, Graduate Programs in Education, Program in Parish Education, Seward, NE 68434-1599. Awards MPE. Accredited by NCATE. Part-time and evening/weekend programs available. Faculty: 6 full-time (1 woman). Students: 10 full-time (7 women), 35 part-time (14 women); includes 1 minority (Asian American), 2 international. 9 applicants, 100% accepted. In 1997, 2 degrees awarded (100% found work related to degree). *Degree requirements:* Thesis or alternative required, foreign language not required. *Entrance requirements:* GRE, MAT, or NTE, minimum GPA of 3.0, BS in education or equivalent. Application deadline: 8/1 (priority date; rolling processing; 12/1 for spring admission). Application fee: $15. *Tuition:* $127 per hour. *Financial aid:* Federal Work-Study, institutionally sponsored loans available. Aid available to part-time students. Financial aid applicants required to submit FAFSA. • Coordinator, 402-643-7377.

Dallas Theological Seminary, Dallas, TX 75204-6499. Offerings include Christian education (MA, D Min). MA (biblical exegesis and linguistics) offered jointly with the Summer Institute of Linguistics. Extension branches located in Chattanooga (TN), Houston (TX), Philadelphia (PA), San Antonio (TX), and the Tampa Bay area (FL). Seminary faculty: 60 full-time, 25 part-time. *Average time to degree:* master's–3 years full-time, 4.5 years part-time; other advanced degree–1 year full-time, 2 years part-time. *Application deadline:* 7/1 (priority date; rolling processing; 11/15 for spring admission). *Application fee:* $30. *Expenses:* Tuition $220 per credit hour. Fees $170 per year full-time, $40 per semester (minimum) part-time. • Dr. Mark L. Bailey, Academic Dean and Vice President for Academic Affairs, 214-841-3676. Fax: 214-841-3565. Application contact: Eugene W. Pond, Director of Admissions, 800-992-0998. Fax: 214-841-3664. E-mail: admissions@dts.edu.

Fordham University, Graduate School of Religion and Religious Education, New York, NY 10458. Awards MA, MS, PD. Part-time programs available. Faculty: 6 full-time (2 women), 7 part-time (3 women). Students: 80 full-time (38 women), 38 part-time (18 women); includes 4 minority (2 African Americans, 2 Hispanics), 48 international. Average age 40. 36 applicants, 100% accepted. In 1997, 40 master's, 5 PDs awarded. *Degree requirements:* For master's, thesis. *Application deadline:* 8/28 (rolling processing). *Application fee:* $55. *Financial aid:* In 1997–98, 100 students received aid, including 3 assistantships (all to first-year students); full and partial tuition waivers, Federal Work-Study also available. Aid available to part-time students. *Faculty research:* Spirituality and spiritual direction, pastoral care and counseling, adult family and community, young adults, social ministry, peace and justice. • Rev. Vincent M. Novak, SJ, Dean, 718-817-4800.

George Fox University, Western Evangelical Seminary, Newberg, OR 97132-2697. Offerings include Christian education (MA). Seminary faculty: 14 full-time (3 women), 1 (woman) part-time. *Degree requirements:* Variable foreign language requirement, internship required, thesis optional. *Application deadline:* 7/1 (rolling processing; 12/1 for spring admission). *Application fee:* $30. • Dr. Tom Johnson, Academic Dean, 503-538-8383. Application contact: Todd M. McCollum, Director of Enrollment Services, 503-598-4309. Fax: 503-598-4338.

Golden Gate Baptist Theological Seminary, Mill Valley, CA 94941-3197. Offerings include Christian education (MACE). Seminary faculty: 25 full-time (2 women), 18 part-time (8 women), 29 FTE. *Average time to degree:* master's–2 years full-time, 3 years part-time; doctorate–3 years full-time; first professional–3 years full-time, 5 years part-time. *Application deadline:* 7/15 (rolling processing; 12/27 for spring admission). *Application fee:* $25. • Dr. Rodrick Durst, Dean of Academic Affairs, 415-380-1508. Fax: 415-383-0723. Application contact: Director of Admissions, 415-380-1600. Fax: 415-380-1602.

Gordon-Conwell Theological Seminary, South Hamilton, MA 01982-2395. Offerings include Christian education (MACE). Seminary faculty: 27 full-time (2 women), 24 part-time (3 women). *Application deadline:* rolling. *Application fee:* $25. *Tuition:* $8600 per year full-time, $940 per course part-time. • Kenneth Swetland, Academic Dean, 978-468-7111 Ext. 331. Application contact: Tim Myrick, Director of Admissions, 800-428-7329. Fax: 978-468-6691. E-mail: adminfo@gcts.edu.

Grace University, Graduate Studies, Omaha, NE 68108. Offerings include educational ministries (MA). MA (educational ministries) new for fall 1998. Faculty: 7 full-time (1 woman), 5 part-time (2 women). *Entrance requirements:* Minimum undergraduate GPA of 3.0. Application deadline: 8/15 (priority date; rolling processing; 1/1 for spring admission). Application fee: $50. Electronic applications accepted. *Tuition:* $295 per credit hour. • Dr. Ronald L. Rushing, Chair, Program of Biblical Studies, 402-449-2842. E-mail: academics@graceu.edu. Application contact: Debi Mitchell, Graduate Admissions Counselor, 402-449-2817. Fax: 402-341-9587. E-mail: admissions@graceu.edu.

Graduate Theological Union, Graduate Programs, Berkeley, CA 94709-1212. Offerings include religious education (MA). PhD (Jewish studies, Near Eastern religions) offered jointly with the University of California, Berkeley; MA/M Div offered jointly with individual denominations. Faculty: 80 (19 women). *Degree requirements:* 1 foreign language, thesis. *Average time to degree:* master's–2 years full-time; doctorate–6 years full-time. *Entrance requirements:* GRE General Test (minimum score 550 on verbal section), TOEFL (minimum score 550). Application fee: $30. *Tuition:* $13,400 per year. • Dr. Margaret R. Miles, Dean, 510-649-2440. Application contact: A. K. Anderson, Director of Admissions, 800-826-4488. Fax: 510-649-1730. E-mail: gtuadm@gtu.edu.

Grand Rapids Baptist Seminary, Graduate Programs, Grand Rapids, MI 49525-5897. Offerings include Christian education (M Div, MA, MRE), education/management (D Min), religious education (MRE). Postbaccalaureate distance learning degree programs offered (minimal on-campus study). Seminary faculty: 9 full-time (0 women), 6 part-time (0 women). *Degree requirements:* For doctorate, 2 foreign languages, dissertation (for some programs), oral exam. *Application deadline:* 8/15 (rolling processing). *Application fee:* $25. *Expenses:* Tuition $245 per credit hour. Fees $244 per year. • James M. Grier, Dean, 616-222-1422. Application contact: John F. VerBerkmoes, Director of Admissions, 616-222-1422 Ext. 1255. Fax: 616-222-1414.

Gratz College, Program in Jewish Education, Old York Road and Melrose Avenue, Melrose Park, PA 19027. Awards MA, Certificate, MA/Certificate, MA/MA. Part-time and evening/weekend programs available. Faculty: 8 full-time (3 women), 11 part-time (7 women). *Degree requirements:* For master's, 1 foreign language, internship required, thesis not required. *Entrance requirements:* For master's, interview. Application deadline: rolling. Application fee: $50. *Tuition:* $8500 per year full-time, $395 per credit part-time. *Financial aid:* Fellowships and career-related internships or fieldwork available. Aid available to part-time students. Financial aid application deadline: 4/1. • Dr. Saul Wachs, Coordinator, 215-635-7300. Application contact: Evelyn Klein, Director of Admissions, 215-635-7300. Fax: 215-635-7320. E-mail: gratzinfo@aol.com.

Hebrew College, Shoolman Graduate School of Education, 43 Hawes Street, Brookline, MA 02146-5495. Awards MJ Ed. Part-time and evening/weekend programs available. Faculty: 20. Students: 9 full-time, 10 part-time; includes 2 international. Average age 37. In 1997, 4 degrees awarded. *Degree requirements:* 1 foreign language. *Average time to degree:* master's–2.5 years full-time. *Entrance requirements:* GRE General Test, interview. Application deadline: 4/15 (priority date; rolling processing; 11/30 for spring admission). Application fee: $45. *Expenses:* Tuition $395 per credit. Fees $90 per year. *Financial aid:* Partial tuition waivers and career-related internships or fieldwork available. Aid available to part-time students. Financial aid application deadline: 4/15. • Harvey Shapiro, Director, 617-278-4942. E-mail: hshapiro@lynx.neu.edu. Application contact: Norma Frankel, Registrar, 617-278-4947. Fax: 617-264-9264. E-mail: nfrankel@lynx.neu.edu.

Hebrew Union College–Jewish Institute of Religion, Rhea Hirsch School of Education, Los Angeles, CA 90007-3796. Awards MAJE, PhD, MAJCS/MAJE. Faculty: 3 full-time (2 women), 6 part-time (1 woman). Students: 9 full-time (8 women). Average age 27. In 1997, 12 master's awarded (90% found work related to degree, 10% continued full-time study). Terminal master's awarded for partial completion of doctoral program. *Degree requirements:* For master's, 1 foreign language, Hebrew; for doctorate, 1 foreign language, dissertation. *Average time to degree:* master's–3 years full-time; doctorate–5 years part-time. *Entrance requirements:* GRE General Test. Application deadline: 3/15. Application fee: $55. *Expenses:* Tuition $7500 per year full-time, $315 per unit part-time. Fees $296 per year full-time. *Financial aid:* Institutionally sponsored loans and career-related internships or fieldwork available. Financial aid applicants

Directory: Religious Education

Hebrew Union College–Jewish Institute of Religion (continued)
required to submit FAFSA. • Sara Lee, Director, 213-749-3424. Application contact: Rabbi Sheldon Marder, Associate Dean, 213-749-3424. Fax: 213-747-6128. E-mail: marder@mizar.usc.edu.

Hebrew Union College–Jewish Institute of Religion, School of Education, New York, NY 10012-1186. Awards MAJS, MARE. Part-time programs available. *Degree requirements:* 1 foreign language, thesis. *Entrance requirements:* GRE, minimum 1 year of college-level Hebrew. Application fee: $35.

Huntington College, Graduate School of Christian Ministries, Huntington, IN 46750-1299. Offerings include educational ministry (MA). School faculty: 2 full-time (0 women), 5 part-time (1 woman). *Degree requirements:* Thesis or alternative. *Average time to degree:* master's–2 years full-time. *Application deadline:* rolling. *Application fee:* $15. *Expenses:* Tuition $215 per credit hour. Fees $5 per course (minimum). • Dr. David D. Rahn, Associate Dean for the Graduate School, 219-359-4039. E-mail: drahn@huntington.edu. Application contact: Graduate Admissions Department, 219-359-4036. Fax: 219-358-3700. E-mail: gscm@huntington.edu.

Jewish Theological Seminary of America, William Davidson Graduate School of Jewish Education, 3080 Broadway, New York, NY 10027-4649. Awards MA, Ed D, PhD. Offered in conjunction with Rabbinical School; H. L. Miller Cantorial School and College of Jewish Music; Teacher's College, Columbia University; and Union Theological Seminary. Faculty: 8 full-time (2 women), 7 part-time (2 women). Students: 48 full-time (33 women), 33 part-time (27 women); includes 8 international. Average age 31. *Application deadline:* 2/15 (priority date; rolling processing). *Application fee:* $50. *Tuition:* $11,800 per year full-time, $511 per credit part-time. *Financial aid:* Fellowships and career-related internships or fieldwork available. Financial aid application deadline: 3/1. • Dr. Aryeh Davidson, Dean, 212-678-8030. Fax: 212-749-9085.

Jewish University of America, Program in Jewish Education, Skokie, IL 60077-3248. Awards MJ Ed, DJ Ed. *Degree requirements:* For master's, thesis optional, foreign language not required; for doctorate, 1 foreign language, dissertation. *Entrance requirements:* Interview. Application deadline: rolling. Application fee: $10. *Tuition:* $140 per credit. • Rabbi Leonard Matanky, Chairman, 773-539-8312. Application contact: Dr. Steven Greenspan, Associate Dean, 773-539-8312. Fax: 847-933-1089.

La Sierra University, School of Religion, Riverside, CA 92515-8247. Offerings include religious education (MA). School faculty: 7 full-time (1 woman), 5 part-time (1 woman), 8.7 FTE. *Degree requirements:* 1 foreign language, thesis or alternative. *Entrance requirements:* GRE General Test (minimum combined score of 1000), minimum GPA of 3.0. Application deadline: 8/1 (rolling processing). Application fee: $30. • Dr. John Jones, Dean, 909-785-2041. Fax: 909-785-2199. E-mail: jjones@polaris.lasierra.edu. Application contact: Myrna Costa-Casado, Director of Admissions, 909-785-2176. Fax: 909-785-2447. E-mail: mcosta@lasierra.edu.

Louisville Presbyterian Theological Seminary, Louisville, KY 40205-1798. Offerings include Christian education (MA). Seminary faculty: 19 full-time (7 women), 33 part-time (12 women). *Application deadline:* 6/1 (priority date; rolling processing; 11/15 for spring admission). *Application fee:* $30. *Expenses:* Tuition $6210 per year full-time, $230 per credit hour part-time. Fees $245 per year. • Dr. W. Eugene March, Dean, 502-895-3411. Application contact: James A. Hubert, Director of Admissions, 502-895-3411. Fax: 502-895-1096.

Loyola University Chicago, Graduate School, Institute of Pastoral Studies, Program in Religious Education, 820 North Michigan Avenue, Chicago, IL 60611-2196. Awards M Rel Ed. Part-time and evening/weekend programs available. Faculty: 11 full-time (4 women), 39 part-time (12 women). Students: 12 full-time (7 women), 11 part-time (8 women); includes 3 minority (1 Asian American, 2 Hispanics), 3 international. Average age 35. 14 applicants, 86% accepted. In 1997, 11 degrees awarded (9% entered university research/teaching, 82% found other work related to degree, 9% continued full-time study). *Average time to degree:* master's–2.5 years full-time, 4 years part-time. *Application deadline:* 8/1 (priority date; rolling processing; 12/1 for spring admission). *Application fee:* $35. *Tuition:* $467 per semester hour. *Financial aid:* In 1997–98, 20 students received aid, including 11 fellowships; grants, Federal Work-Study, and career-related internships or fieldwork also available. Aid available to part-time students. Financial aid application deadline: 3/1; applicants required to submit FAFSA. *Faculty research:* Systematic theology, liturgical theology, scripture, narrative theology, pedagogy. • Peter Gilmour, Graduate Director, 773-508-6016. E-mail: pgilmou@wpo.it.luc.edu. Application contact: Mimi Newton, Admissions Secretary, 773-508-2326. Fax: 773-508-2319. E-mail: mnewton@luc.edu.

Luther Rice Bible College and Seminary, Graduate Programs, Lithonia, GA 30038-2418. Offerings include Christian education (M Div, MRE). Postbaccalaureate distance learning degree programs offered (no on-campus study). Seminary faculty: 7 full-time (0 women), 9 part-time (2 women). *Application deadline:* rolling. *Application fee:* $50. *Tuition:* $318 per course. • Dr. James Kinnebrew, Dean, 770-484-1204. Application contact: Dr. Dennis Dieringer, Director of Admissions and Records, 770-484-1204. Fax: 770-484-1155.

Meadville/Lombard Theological School, Chicago, IL 60637-1602. Offerings include religious education (MA). School faculty: 6 full-time (3 women), 1 part-time (0 women). *Application deadline:* 4/15 (priority date; rolling processing). *Application fee:* $45. *Expenses:* Tuition $9900 per year full-time, $1100 per credit part-time. Fees $450 per year. • William R. Murry, President and Academic Dean, 773-256-3000 Ext. 224. Application contact: Kerry Smith, Admissions Officer, 773-256-3000 Ext. 237. Fax: 773-256-3006. E-mail: ksmith@meadville.edu.

Michigan Theological Seminary, Graduate Programs, Plymouth, MI 48170. Offerings include Christian education (MA). Seminary faculty: 6 full-time (0 women), 4 part-time (0 women). *Degree requirements:* 1 foreign language, thesis. *Average time to degree:* master's–3 years full-time. *Application deadline:* 9/1 (priority date; rolling processing; 1/1 for spring admission). *Application fee:* $25. *Expenses:* Tuition $155 per credit hour. Fees $50 per semester. • David L. Masterson, Academic Dean, 313-207-9581. Application contact: Kris Udd, Registrar/Admissions, 313-207-9581. Fax: 313-207-9582.

Midwestern Baptist Theological Seminary, Kansas City, MO 64118-4697. Offerings include Christian education (MACE). Seminary faculty: 20 full-time, 22 part-time. *Application deadline:* 7/19 (rolling processing). *Application fee:* $25. *Expenses:* Tuition $65 per credit hour (minimum). Fees $100 per year. • Dr. James Cogdill Sr., Academic Dean, 816-453-4600. Application contact: Office of Student Enlistment, 800-944-6287. E-mail: admissions@mbts.edu.

Nazarene Theological Seminary, Kansas City, MO 64131-1263. Offerings include religious education (MRE). Seminary faculty: 19 full-time (1 woman), 13 part-time (1 woman). *Average time to degree:* master's–3 years full-time, 5 years part-time; doctorate–4 years full-time, 6 years part-time; first professional–4 years full-time, 6 years part-time. *Application deadline:* 8/1 (priority date; rolling processing; 12/1 for spring admission). *Application fee:* $20. Electronic applications accepted. *Expenses:* Tuition $220 per credit hour. Fees $100 per year. • Dr. Edwin Robinson, Dean, 816-333-6255 Ext. 220. E-mail: ehrobinson@nts.edu. Application contact: Susan Middendorf, Director of Enrollment Services, 816-333-6255 Ext. 233. Fax: 816-333-6271. E-mail: smmiddendorf@nts.edu.

Newman Theological College, Religious Education Program, Edmonton, AB T6V 1H3, Canada. Awards MRE, GDRE. Part-time programs available. Postbaccalaureate distance learning degree programs offered (no on-campus study). Faculty: 1 (woman) full-time, 1 part-time (0 women), 1.2 FTE. Students: 12 full-time (9 women), 15 part-time (9 women). Average age 38. 9 applicants, 100% accepted. In 1997, 2 master's awarded (100% found work related to degree); 16 GDREs awarded (100% found work related to degree). *Degree requirements:* Thesis or alternative required, foreign language not required. *Average time to degree:* master's–1 year full-time, 3 years part-time; other advanced degree–1 year full-time, 2 years part-time. *Entrance requirements:* For master's, GDRE, 2 years of successful teaching experience; for GDRE, bachelor's degree in education, teaching certificate. Application deadline: 8/25 (priority date; 12/22 for spring admission). Application fee: $25. *Financial aid:* In 1997–98, 1 student received aid, including 1 tuition bursary totaling $945. Aid available to part-time students. Financial aid application deadline: 5/31. • Sr. Teresita Kambeitz OSU, Director, 403-447-2993. Application contact: Rose Marie Fowler, Registrar, 403-447-2993. Fax: 403-447-2685. E-mail: registrar@newman.edu.

New Orleans Baptist Theological Seminary, Division of Christian Education Ministries, New Orleans, LA 70126-4858. Offers program in Christian education (M Div, MACE, DEM, D Min, PhD). Evening/weekend programs available. Faculty: 7 full-time (2 women). *Degree requirements:* For M Div, project report required, foreign language and thesis not required; for doctorate, dissertation required, foreign language not required. *Entrance requirements:* For doctorate, GRE General Test (minimum combined score of 1500 on three sections). Application deadline: 8/1 (priority date; rolling processing). Application fee: $25. *Tuition:* $125 per hour. *Financial aid:* Institutionally sponsored loans available. Aid available to part-time students. • Dr. Janine Bozman, Chairman, 504-282-4455. Application contact: Dr. Paul E. Gregoire Jr., Director of Admissions and Registrar, 504-282-4455. Fax: 504-286-3591.

North Park Theological Seminary, Program in Religious Education, Chicago, IL 60625-4895. Awards MACE. Part-time programs available. Faculty: 17 full-time (4 women), 13 part-time (3 women), 19 FTE. Students: 5 full-time (4 women), 3 part-time (2 women); includes 1 minority (African American), 4 international. Average age 33. 9 applicants, 44% accepted. In 1997, 4 degrees awarded (100% found work related to degree). *Entrance requirements:* TOEFL (minimum score 550), minimum GPA of 2.5. Application deadline: 8/1 (priority date; rolling processing; 3/1 for spring admission). Application fee: $25. *Tuition:* $7300 per year full-time, $365 per credit hour part-time. *Financial aid:* Career-related internships or fieldwork available. Financial aid application deadline: 9/7; applicants required to submit FAFSA. • Dr. Paul Bramer, Acting Head, 773-244-6245. Application contact: Mark Washington, Associate Director, 800-964-0101. Fax: 773-244-6244. E-mail: semadmissions@northpark.edu.

Nyack College, Alliance Theological Seminary, Nyack, NY 10960-3698. Offerings include Christian education (M Div). *Degree requirements:* 2 foreign languages, internship required, thesis not required. *Entrance requirements:* Proficiency in New Testament Greek. Application deadline: rolling. Application fee: $20.

Oklahoma City University, School of Religion and Church Vocations, Oklahoma City, OK 73106-1402. Offerings include religious education (M Rel). School faculty: 4 full-time (2 women), 3 part-time (1 woman). *Application deadline:* 8/20 (priority date; rolling processing; 1/9 for spring admission). *Application fee:* $35 ($55 for international students). *Expenses:* Tuition $318 per hour. Fees $124 per year. • Dr. Donald Emler, Dean, 405-521-5284. E-mail: dgemler@frodo.okcu.edu. Application contact: Laura L. Rahhal, Director of Graduate Admissions, 800-633-7242 Ext. 2. Fax: 405-521-5356. E-mail: lrahhal1@frodo.okcu.edu.

Oral Roberts University, School of Education, Tulsa, OK 74171-0001. Offerings include Christian school teaching (MA Ed). Postbaccalaureate distance learning degree programs offered (minimal on-campus study). School faculty: 7 full-time (2 women), 13 part-time (3 women). *Degree requirements:* Thesis (for some programs), comprehensive exam. *Average time to degree:* master's–1.5 years full-time, 3 years part-time. *Entrance requirements:* GRE General Test (minimum combined score of 1000) or MAT, minimum GPA of 3.0. Application deadline: rolling. Application fee: $35. • Dr. David Hand, Dean, 918-495-7084. Fax: 918-495-6050. Application contact: David H. Fulmer III, Coordinator of Graduate Admissions, 918-495-6058. Fax: 918-495-7214. E-mail: dhfulmer@oru.edu.

Oral Roberts University, School of Theology, Tulsa, OK 74171-0001. Offerings include Christian education (MA). School faculty: 18 full-time (2 women), 7 part-time (3 women). *Degree requirements:* Thesis (for some programs), practicum/internship. *Average time to degree:* master's–2 years full-time, 3 years part-time; doctorate–3 years full-time, 4 years part-time; first professional–3 years full-time, 4 years part-time. *Entrance requirements:* GRE General Test (minimum combined score of 900), MAT (minimum score 40), TOEFL (minimum score 550), minimum GPA of 2.5. Application deadline: rolling. Application fee: $35. • Dr. Jerry W. Horner, Dean, 918-495-6096. Fax: 918-495-6259. Application contact: David H. Fulmer III, Coordinator of Graduate Admissions, 918-495-6238. Fax: 918-495-7214. E-mail: dhfulmer@oru.edu.

Pfeiffer University, Program in Religion, Philosophy, and Christian Education, Charlotte, NC 28209. Awards MACE. Part-time and evening/weekend programs available. Faculty: 3 full-time (0 women), 1 part-time (0 women), 4 FTE. Students: 39. *Average time to degree:* master's–2 years full-time, 5 years part-time. *Entrance requirements:* Minimum GPA of 2.75. Application deadline: 8/21 (priority date; rolling processing). Application fee: $50. *Tuition:* $245 per hour (minimum). • Kay Kilbourne, Coordinator, 704-463-1360.

Providence College, Department of Religious Studies, Providence, RI 02918. Offerings include religious education (MA). MA (religious education) admissions temporarily suspended. Department faculty: 6 full-time (0 women), 2 part-time (0 women). *Degree requirements:* Greek and Hebrew (biblical studies) required, thesis not required. *Entrance requirements:* TOEFL. Application deadline: 8/12 (priority date; rolling processing; 12/1 for spring admission). Application fee: $40. *Tuition:* $621 per course. • Rev. Robert J. Hennessey, OP, Director, 401-865-2274.

Providence College and Theological Seminary, Theological Seminary, Otterburne, MB R0A 1G0, Canada. Offerings include Christian education (MA). Seminary faculty: 13 full-time (4 women), 8 part-time (2 women), 17 FTE. *Degree requirements:* Variable foreign language requirement, thesis (for some programs). *Average time to degree:* master's–2 years full-time; first professional–3 years full-time. *Application deadline:* 8/25 (priority date; rolling processing). *Application fee:* $25. • Dr. David L. Smith, Vice President of Seminary Academics, 204-433-7488. E-mail: dsmith@providence.mb.ca. Application contact: Dewey Thiele, Director of Enrollment Management, 204-433-7488. Fax: 204-433-7158. E-mail: dthiele@providence.mb.ca.

Reformed Theological Seminary, Jackson, MS 39209-3099. Offerings include Christian education (M Div, MA). Seminary faculty: 17 full-time (0 women), 17 part-time (4 women). *Degree requirements:* For M Div, 2 foreign languages, thesis (for some programs). *Entrance requirements:* For M Div, TOEFL (minimum score 550), minimum GPA of 2.6. Application deadline: rolling. Application fee: $20. *Expenses:* Tuition $5460 per year full-time, $220 per semester hour part-time. Fees $70 per year. • Dr. Allen Curry, Dean, 601-922-4988. Application contact: Brian Gault, Director of Admissions, 601-922-4988 Ext. 286. Fax: 601-922-1153.

Saint Meinrad School of Theology, Program in Theological Studies, Saint Meinrad, IN 47577. Offerings include religious education (MRE). MRE being phased out; applicants no longer accepted. Program faculty: 16 full-time (1 woman), 5 part-time (1 woman), 18 FTE. *Average time to degree:* master's–2 years full-time. *Application deadline:* 6/1 (priority date; rolling processing). *Application fee:* $0. *Tuition:* $10,450 per year full-time, $224 per credit part-time. • Sr. Shirley Ann Warner, OSU, Acting Associate Dean of Lay Students, 812-357-6209. Fax: 812-357-6816. Application contact: Rev. Amador Garza, Associate Director of Enrollment, 812-357-6971. Fax: 812-357-6977.

Saint Vincent Seminary, School of Theology, Latrobe, PA 15650-2690. Offerings include religious education (MRE). School faculty: 6 full-time (1 woman), 24 part-time (3 women), 10.8 FTE. *Average time to degree:* master's–2 years full-time, 5 years part-time; first professional–3 years full-time. *Application deadline:* 8/15 (priority date; rolling processing). *Application fee:* $25. *Expenses:* Tuition $368 per credit. Fees $50 per year. • Sr. Cecilia Murphy, RSM, Academic Dean, 724-539-9761. Fax: 724-532-5052.

St. Vladimir's Orthodox Theological Seminary, Graduate School of Theology, Crestwood, NY 10707-1699. Offerings include religious education (MA). MA (general theological studies),

M Div offered jointly with St. Nersess Seminary. Seminary faculty: 9 full-time (1 woman), 7 part-time (1 woman). *Average time to degree:* master's–2 years full-time; doctorate–3 years full-time; first professional–3 years full-time. *Application deadline:* 8/1 (priority date; rolling processing). *Application fee:* $50. *Expenses:* Tuition $4200 per year full-time, $235 per credit part-time. Fees $200 per year. • Rev. Thomas Hopko, Dean, 914-961-8313. Application contact: Ann Sanchez, Student Affairs Administrator, 914-961-8313 Ext. 323. Fax: 914-961-4507. E-mail: aks@svots.edu.

Southeastern Baptist Theological Seminary, Wake Forest, NC 27588-1889. Offerings include Christian education (M Div, MACE). Seminary faculty: 47 full-time (0 women). *Degree requirements:* For M Div, supervised ministry required, foreign language and thesis not required. *Application deadline:* 7/15 (priority date; rolling processing; 12/15 for spring admission). *Application fee:* $25. *Expenses:* Tuition $75 per semester hour (minimum). Fees $60 per semester. • Dr. L. Russ Bush, Dean of the Faculty, 919-556-3101. Application contact: Anthony Allen, Admissions Director, 919-556-3101. Fax: 919-556-0998.

Southern Baptist Theological Seminary, School of Christian Education and Leadership, Louisville, KY 40280-0004. Awards M Div, MACE, Ed D, PhD. EdD new for fall 1998. Part-time programs available. Postbaccalaureate distance learning degree programs offered (minimal on-campus study). Faculty: 6 full-time (1 woman), 5 part-time (2 women). In 1997, 26 M Divs, 38 master's, 1 doctorate awarded. *Degree requirements:* For M Div, 2 foreign languages required, thesis not required; for doctorate, dissertation required, foreign language not required. *Entrance requirements:* For doctorate, GRE General Test (minimum score 500 on each section), MAT (minimum score 55), TOEFL (minimum score 550), TSW, TWE, interview, M Div or MACE, field essay. Application deadline: 8/1 (priority date; rolling processing; 1/2 for spring admission). Application fee: $35. *Expenses:* Tuition $105 per credit hour (minimum). Fees $25 per semester. *Financial aid:* In 1997–98, 1 research assistantship averaging $160 per month and totaling $1,300, 18 teaching assistantships averaging $160 per month and totaling $11,700 were awarded; partial tuition waivers, institutionally sponsored loans, and career-related internships or fieldwork also available. Financial aid application deadline: 4/1. *Faculty research:* Gerontology, creative teaching methods, faith development in children, faith development in youth, transformational learning. • Dr. Dennis E. Williams, Dean, 800-626-5525 Ext. 4813. Application contact: Robert Cheong, Director of Admissions, 800-626-5525.

Southwestern Baptist Theological Seminary, School of Educational Ministries, Fort Worth, TX 76122-0000. Awards MACCM, MA Comm, MAMFC, MARE, PhD, M Div/MA Comm, M Div/MARE. Part-time and evening/weekend programs available. Faculty: 23 full-time, 21 part-time, 34.9 FTE. Students: 1,001. Average age 32. 376 applicants, 84% accepted. In 1997, 259 master's, 11 doctorates awarded. *Entrance requirements:* For doctorate, master's degree. Application deadline: 7/15 (rolling processing; 12/1 for spring admission). Application fee: $35. *Expenses:* Tuition $70 per hour (minimum). Fees $500 per year (minimum). *Financial aid:* Fellowships, research assistantships, teaching assistantships, institutionally sponsored loans, and career-related internships or fieldwork available. Aid available to part-time students. • Daryl Eldridge, Dean, 817-923-1921 Ext. 2140. Application contact: Judy Morris, Director of Admissions, 817-923-1921 Ext. 2600. Fax: 817-923-1921 Ext. 2342.

Spertus Institute of Jewish Studies, Judaica Studies Graduate Programs Institute of Advanced Judaica, Programs in Jewish Education, 618 South Michigan Avenue, Chicago, IL 60605-1901. Awards MAJ Ed. Part-time and evening/weekend programs available. Faculty: 1 full-time (0 women), 9 part-time (2 women). Students: 1 (woman) part-time. 0 applicants. *Degree requirements:* 1 foreign language, thesis. *Average time to degree:* master's–1.5 years full-time, 2.5 years part-time. *Entrance requirements:* BAJS. Application deadline: rolling. Application fee: $50. *Expenses:* Tuition $8000 per year full-time, $165 per quarter hour part-time. Fees $75 per year. *Financial aid:* 1 student received aid; scholarships available. Financial aid applicants required to submit FAFSA. • Application contact: Lisa Burnstein, Director of Student Services, 312-922-9012. Fax: 312-922-6406. E-mail: college@spertus.edu.

Stanford University, School of Education, Special Programs in Education, Stanford, CA 94305-9991. Offerings include Jewish education (PhD). *Degree requirements:* Dissertation required, foreign language not required. *Entrance requirements:* GRE General Test. Application deadline: 1/2. Application fee: $65 ($75 for international students). *Expenses:* Tuition $22,110 per year. Fees $156 per year. • Application contact: Graduate Admissions Office, 650-723-4794.

Teachers College, Columbia University, Graduate Faculty of Education, Department of Arts and Humanities, Program in Religion and Education, 525 West 120th Street, New York, NY 10027-6696. Awards Ed M, MA, Ed D. Faculty: 1 full-time (0 women). Students: 7 full-time (3 women), 24 part-time (10 women); includes 7 minority (4 African Americans, 2 Asian Americans, 1 Hispanic), 3 international. Average age 41. 11 applicants, 82% accepted. In 1997, 1 doctorate awarded. *Degree requirements:* For doctorate, dissertation. *Application deadline:* 5/15 (12/1 for spring admission). *Application fee:* $50. *Expenses:* Tuition $640 per credit. Fees $120 per semester. *Financial aid:* Full and partial tuition waivers, Federal Work-Study, institutionally sponsored loans, and career-related internships or fieldwork available. Aid available to part-time students. Financial aid application deadline: 2/1. *Faculty research:* Epistemology; science and education; Waldorf education; epistemological, cultural, and spiritual foundations of education. • Application contact: Amy Rotheim, Office of Admissions, 212-678-3710. Fax: 212-678-4171.

Toccoa Falls College, Graduate Studies, Toccoa Falls, GA 30598-1000. Offers programs in Christian education (MA), intercultural studies (MA), pastoral ministries (MA). Part-time programs available. Faculty: 14 part-time (0 women). Students: 3 full-time (2 women), 42 part-time (10 women); includes 7 minority (4 African Americans, 1 Asian American, 1 Hispanic, 1 Native American). In 1997, 3 degrees awarded. *Average time to degree:* master's–2 years part-time. *Application fee:* $25. *Tuition:* $315 per hour. *Financial aid:* Available to part-time students. • Dr. Kenneth O. Gangel, Executive Director, 706-886-6831. E-mail: kgangel@toccoafalls.edu. Application contact: Allen M. Bañez, Coordinator, 706-886-6831 Ext. 5423. Fax: 706-282-6003. E-mail: gradstud@toccoafalls.edu.

Trinity International University, Trinity Evangelical Divinity School, Deerfield, IL 60015-1284. Offerings include Christian education (MA), educational studies (PhD). *Tuition:* $9230 per year full-time, $462 per hour part-time. • Dr. W. Bingham Hunter, Dean, 847-317-8002. Fax: 847-317-8014. Application contact: Ken Botton, Director of Admissions, 800-345-8337. Fax: 847-317-8097. E-mail: kbotton@tiu.edu.

Union Theological Seminary and Presbyterian School of Christian Education, School of Christian Education, Richmond, VA 23227-4597. Awards MA, Ed D, Ed S, M Div/MA, MSW/MA. MSW/MA offered jointly with Virginia Commonwealth University. Part-time and evening/weekend programs available. Postbaccalaureate distance learning degree programs offered (minimal on-campus study). Faculty: 9 full-time (5 women), 4 part-time (2 women). Students: 94 full-time (63 women), 14 part-time (11 women); includes 21 minority (15 African Americans, 5 Asian Americans, 1 Hispanic), 17 international. Average age 34. 60 applicants, 85% accepted. In 1997, 41 master's awarded. *Degree requirements:* For master's, oral and written exams required, foreign language and thesis not required; for doctorate, dissertation, oral and written comprehensive exams required, foreign language not required; for Ed S, comprehensive exams, research project required, foreign language and thesis not required. *Entrance requirements:* For master's and Ed S, TOEFL, TWE; for doctorate, GRE General Test, TOEFL, TWE. Application deadline: 8/1 (rolling processing; 1/15 for spring admission). Application fee: $45. *Tuition:* $600 per course. *Financial aid:* 67 students received aid; teaching assistantships, institutionally sponsored loans, and career-related internships or fieldwork available. Financial aid application deadline: 8/1; applicants required to submit FAFSA. • Dr. James Brashler, Dean of Faculty, 804-254-8047. Application contact: James W. Dale, Director of Admissions, 804-355-0671. Fax: 804-355-3919. E-mail: admissn@utsva.edu.

University of Portland, School of Education, Department of Foundations, Program in Religious Education, Portland, OR 97203-5798. Awards MA, M Ed. *Degree requirements:* Thesis optional, foreign language not required. *Entrance requirements:* GRE General Test (MA), GRE General Test or MAT (M Ed), TOEFL (minimum score 550), minimum GPA of 3.0, teaching certificate. Application deadline: 8/1 (priority date; rolling processing; 12/1 for spring admission). Application fee: $40. *Tuition:* $515 per semester hour. *Financial aid:* Federal Work-Study available. Financial aid application deadline: 3/15. • Dr. Dann Danner, Director, 503-283-7369. E-mail: danner@up.edu.

University of St. Thomas, St. Paul Seminary School of Divinity, Program in Theology/Pastoral Studies, St. Paul, MN 55105-1096. Offerings include religious education (MA). *Degree requirements:* 1 foreign language, thesis, comprehensive exams. *Average time to degree:* master's–2.5 years full-time. *Entrance requirements:* MAT (score in 50th percentile or higher), minimum undergraduate GPA of 3.0. Application deadline: rolling. Application fee: $30. *Expenses:* Tuition $378 per credit hour. Fees $20 per semester. • Rev. Phil Rask, Rector, 612-962-5052. E-mail: pjrask@stthomas.edu. Application contact: Rev. Donald Bowers, Vice Rector/Admission Chair, 612-962-5068. Fax: 612-962-5790.

University of San Diego, College of Arts and Sciences, Program in Practical Theology, San Diego, CA 92110-2492. Offerings include religious education (MA). Program faculty: 14 full-time (6 women). *Degree requirements:* Comprehensive exam, field supervision required, foreign language and thesis not required. *Entrance requirements:* GRE, TOEFL (minimum score 580), TWE (minimum score 4.5), 12 units in religion or theology or equivalent, minimum GPA of 3.0. Application deadline: 5/1 (priority date; rolling processing; 11/15 for spring admission). Application fee: $45. *Expenses:* Tuition $585 per unit (minimum). Fees $50 per year full-time, $30 per year part-time. • Rev. Ronald Pachence, Director, 619-260-4784. Fax: 619-260-2260. E-mail: pachence@acusd.edu. Application contact: Mary Jane Tiernan, Director of Graduate Admissions, 619-260-4524. Fax: 619-260-4158. E-mail: grads@acusd.edu.

University of San Francisco, College of Arts and Sciences, Department of Theology and Pastoral Studies, San Francisco, CA 94117-1080. Offerings include religious education (Certificate). Certificate being phased out; applicants no longer accepted. Department faculty: 8 full-time (1 woman), 5 part-time (0 women). *Application deadline:* 5/15 (priority date; rolling processing). *Application fee:* $40 ($50 for international students). *Tuition:* $658 per unit (minimum). • Rev. Paul Bernadicou SJ, Chair, 415-422-6601.

Western Seminary, Program in Church Education, Portland, OR 97215-3367. Awards M Div, MA. Faculty: 3 full-time (1 woman), 3 part-time (0 women). Students: 6. 2 applicants, 100% accepted. In 1997, 8 master's awarded. *Degree requirements:* For M Div, 2 foreign languages; for master's, thesis or alternative required, foreign language not required. *Application deadline:* 8/1 (priority date; rolling processing). *Application fee:* $40. *Financial aid:* In 1997–98, 1 fellowship was awarded; career-related internships or fieldwork also available. Aid available to part-time students. • Dr. Robert Radcliffe, Director, 503-233-8561. Application contact: Dr. Robert W. Wiggins, Registrar/Vice President of Student Services, 503-233-8561. Fax: 503-239-4216.

Western Seminary, Program in Educational Ministry, Portland, OR 97215-3367. Awards MA. *Application deadline:* 8/1 (priority date; rolling processing). *Application fee:* $40. • Application contact: Dr. Robert W. Wiggins, Registrar/Vice President of Student Services, 503-233-8561. Fax: 503-239-4216.

Wheaton College, Department of Educational Ministries, Program in Educational Ministries, Wheaton, IL 60187-5593. Awards MA. *Degree requirements:* Thesis or alternative required, foreign language not required. *Entrance requirements:* GRE General Test (minimum combined score of 1000; average 1150). Application deadline: 3/1 (priority date; rolling processing; 10/15 for spring admission). Application fee: $20. *Tuition:* $365 per credit hour (minimum).

Winebrenner Theological Seminary, Professional Studies, Findlay, OH 45839-0478. Offerings include Christian education (M Div, MA). Seminary faculty: 6 full-time (2 women), 8 part-time (1 woman), 8 FTE. *Degree requirements:* For M Div, 1 foreign language, internship required, thesis not required. *Average time to degree:* master's–2 years full-time, 3 years part-time; first professional–3 years full-time, 6 years part-time. *Application deadline:* 8/31 (priority date; rolling processing). *Application fee:* $25. *Expenses:* Tuition $6280 per year full-time, $290 per semester hour part-time. Fees $24 per year full-time, $12 per year part-time. • Dale R. Brougher, Academic Dean, 419-422-4824. Application contact: Jenifer J. Cobb, Admissions Counselor, 419-422-4824. Fax: 419-422-3999.

Xavier University, College of Social Sciences, Department of Education, Cincinnati, OH 45207-2111. Offerings include theology (M Ed). Department faculty: 32 full-time (14 women), 49 part-time (31 women), 44.25 FTE. *Application deadline:* rolling. *Application fee:* $25. • Dr. James Boothe, Chair, 513-745-2951. Fax: 513-745-1052. E-mail: boothe@admin.xu.edu. Application contact: Sheila Speth, Director of Graduate Services, 513-745-3360. Fax: 513-745-1048. E-mail: xugrad@admin.xu.edu.

Yeshiva University, Azrieli Graduate School of Jewish Education and Administration, New York, NY 10033-3201. Awards MS, Ed D, Specialist. Part-time and evening/weekend programs available. Faculty: 1 full-time (0 women), 18 part-time (4 women). Students: 146 part-time (59 women); includes 8 international. Average age 25. 58 applicants, 83% accepted. In 1997, 27 master's, 1 doctorate, 1 Specialist awarded. Terminal master's awarded for partial completion of doctoral program. *Degree requirements:* For master's, 1 foreign language, student teaching, comprehensive exam or thesis required, thesis optional; for doctorate, 1 foreign language, dissertation, certifying and comprehensive exams, internship; for Specialist, 1 foreign language, certifying and comprehensive exams, internship required, thesis not required. *Entrance requirements:* For master's, GRE General Test (minimum score 500 on each section; average 630), BA in Jewish studies or equivalent; for doctorate, GRE General Test (minimum score 500 on each section), master's degree in Jewish education, 2 years of teaching experience; for Specialist, GRE General Test, master's degree in Jewish education, 2 years of teaching experience. Application deadline: rolling. Application fee: $35. *Expenses:* Tuition $475 per credit. Fees $100 per year. *Financial aid:* In 1997–98, 118 students received aid, including 23 fellowships (all to first-year students), 95 scholarships (35 to first-year students); partial tuition waivers, institutionally sponsored loans also available. Aid available to part-time students. Financial aid application deadline: 4/1. *Faculty research:* Jewish elementary and secondary curriculum development, administration and supervision, effects of day school education on adult attitudes and behavior, adult Jewish education. • Dr. Yitzchak Handel, Director, 212-340-7705. Fax: 212-340-7787.

Science Education

Adelphi University, School of Education, Program in Secondary Education, Garden City, NY 11530. Offerings include biology (MA), chemistry (MA), physics (MA). *Application deadline:* rolling. *Application fee:* $50. *Expenses:* Tuition $16,000 per year full-time, $485 per credit part-time. Fees $500 per year full-time, $150 per semester part-time. • Director, 516-877-4090. Application contact: Jennifer Spiegel, Associate Director of Graduate Admissions, 516-877-3055.

Alabama State University, School of Graduate Studies, College of Arts and Sciences, Department of Biology, Montgomery, AL 36101-0271. Offerings include biology education (Ed S). Department faculty: 2 full-time (0 women). *Degree requirements:* Thesis. *Application deadline:* 7/15 (rolling processing; 12/15 for spring admission). *Application fee:* $10. *Expenses:* Tuition $85 per credit hour for state residents; $170 per credit hour for nonresidents. Fees $486 per year. • Dr. Shiva P. Singh, Acting Chair, 334-229-4467. Fax: 334-229-1007. Application contact: Dr. Fred Dauser, Dean of Graduate Studies, 334-229-4276. Fax: 334-229-4928.

Alabama State University, School of Graduate Studies, College of Education, Department of Curriculum and Instruction, Program in Secondary Education, Montgomery, AL 36101-0271. Offerings include biology education (M Ed). Program faculty: 2 full-time (1 woman). *Degree requirements:* Comprehensive exam required, thesis optional. *Entrance requirements:* GRE General Test, MAT or NTE. Application deadline: 7/15 (rolling processing; 12/15 for spring admission). Application fee: $10. *Expenses:* Tuition $85 per credit hour for state residents; $170 per credit hour for nonresidents. Fees $486 per year. • Dr. Linda Bradford, Coordinator, 334-229-4485. Fax: 334-229-4904. E-mail: lbradford@asunet.alasu.edu. Application contact: Dr. Fred Dauser, Dean of Graduate Studies, 334-229-4276. Fax: 334-229-4928.

Albany State University, School of Education, Program in Science Education, Albany, GA 31705-2717. Awards M Ed. Accredited by NCATE. *Degree requirements:* Comprehensive exam. *Entrance requirements:* GRE General Test (minimum combined score of 800), MAT (minimum score 44) or NTE (minimum score 550). Application deadline: 9/1. Application fee: $10. *Financial aid:* Application deadline 4/1. • Dr. Claude Perkins, Dean, School of Education, 912-430-4715. Fax: 912-430-4993. E-mail: cperkins@fld94.alsnet.peachnet.edu.

Alfred University, Graduate School, Division of Education, Alfred, NY 14802-1205. Offerings include secondary education (MS Ed), with options in biology education, chemistry education, earth science education, English education, mathematics education, physics education, social studies education. Division faculty: 45 full-time (12 women). *Degree requirements:* Thesis required (for some programs), foreign language not required. *Entrance requirements:* TOEFL. Application deadline: rolling. Application fee: $50. *Expenses:* Tuition $20,376 per year full-time, $390 per credit hour (minimum) part-time. Fees $546 per year. • Dr. Katherine D. Wiesendanger, Chair, 607-871-2219. E-mail: fwiesendange@bigvax.alfred.edu. Application contact: Cathleen R. Johnson, Assistant Director of Admissions, 607-871-2141. Fax: 607-871-2198. E-mail: johnsonc@bigvax.alfred.edu.

Allentown College of St. Francis de Sales, Graduate Division, Program in Education, Center Valley, PA 18034-9568. Offerings include biology (M Ed), chemistry (M Ed). Program faculty: 18 full-time (4 women), 25 part-time (6 women). *Degree requirements:* Capstone Course or Project required, foreign language not required. *Average time to degree:* master's–3 years part-time. *Entrance requirements:* Teaching certificate. Application deadline: 8/24 (priority date; rolling processing). Application fee: $35. *Tuition:* $285 per credit. • Dr. Irene Pompetti-Szul, Director, 610-282-1100 Ext. 1401. Fax: 610-282-2254.

Andrews University, School of Graduate Studies, College of Arts and Sciences, Department of Biology, Berrien Springs, MI 49104. Awards MAT, MS. Faculty: 7 full-time (0 women). *Degree requirements:* Thesis, comprehensive exam. *Entrance requirements:* GRE Subject Test. Application deadline: 8/15 (rolling processing). Application fee: $30. *Expenses:* Tuition $290 per quarter hour (minimum). Fees $75 per quarter. *Financial aid:* Fellowships, research assistantships, teaching assistantships, Federal Work-Study, institutionally sponsored loans, and career-related internships or fieldwork available. Financial aid application deadline: 3/15. • Dr. John F. Stout, Chairman, 616-471-3243.

Andrews University, School of Graduate Studies, School of Education, Department of Teaching/Learning/Administration, Berrien Springs, MI 49104. Offerings include secondary education (MAT), with options in biology, education, English, English as a second language, French, history, physics. *Application deadline:* 8/15 (rolling processing). *Application fee:* $30. *Expenses:* Tuition $290 per quarter hour (minimum). Fees $75 per quarter. • Dr. William H. Green, Chair, 616-471-3465.

Antioch New England Graduate School, Graduate School, Department of Education, Program in Elementary Education/Early Childhood Education, Program in Science and Environmental Education, 40 Avon Street, Keene, NH 03431-3516. Awards M Ed. Faculty: 7 full-time (2 women), 12 part-time (11 women). Students: 15 full-time (11 women). Average age 32. In 1997, 10 degrees awarded. *Degree requirements:* Internship required, foreign language and thesis not required. *Entrance requirements:* Previous course work and work experience in education. Application deadline: 8/1 (rolling processing). Application fee: $40. *Expenses:* Tuition $12,700 per year full-time, $330 per credit part-time. Fees $165 per year. *Financial aid:* Federal Work-Study and career-related internships or fieldwork available. Financial aid applicants required to submit FAFSA. *Faculty research:* Developmentally appropriate environmental education, map-making, ecological literacy, The Chase Collection. • Application contact: Diane K. Hewitt, Co-Director of Admissions, 603-357-6265 Ext. 286. Fax: 603-357-0718. E-mail: dhewitt@antiochne.edu.

Arkansas State University, College of Arts and Sciences, Department of Biological Sciences, State University, AR 72467. Offerings include biology education (MSE, SCCT). Accredited by NCATE. Department faculty: 18 full-time (3 women). *Degree requirements:* For SCCT, comprehensive exam required, thesis not required. *Entrance requirements:* For SCCT, GRE General Test or MAT, master's degree. Application deadline: 7/1 (priority date; rolling processing; 11/15 for spring admission). Application fee: $15 ($25 for international students). *Expenses:* Tuition $2760 per year full-time, $115 per credit hour part-time for state residents; $6936 per year full-time, $289 per credit hour part-time for nonresidents. Fees $506 per year full-time, $44 per semester (minimum) part-time. • Dr. Lynita Cooksey, Acting Chair, 870-972-3082. Fax: 870-972-2638. E-mail: lcooksey@navajo.astate.edu.

Arkansas State University, College of Arts and Sciences, Department of Chemistry, Biochemistry, and Physics, State University, AR 72467. Offerings include chemistry education (MSE, SCCT). Accredited by NCATE. Department faculty: 9 full-time (0 women). *Degree requirements:* For SCCT, comprehensive exam required, foreign language and thesis not required. *Entrance requirements:* For SCCT, GRE General Test or MAT, master's degree. Application deadline: 7/1 (priority date; rolling processing; 11/15 for spring admission). Application fee: $15 ($25 for international students). *Expenses:* Tuition $2760 per year full-time, $115 per credit hour part-time for state residents; $6936 per year full-time, $289 per credit hour part-time for nonresidents. Fees $506 per year full-time, $44 per semester (minimum) part-time. • Dr. Paul Nave, Chairman, 870-972-3086. Fax: 870-972-3827. E-mail: pnave@navajo.astate.edu.

Auburn University, College of Education, Department of Curriculum and Teaching, Auburn University, AL 36849-0001. Offerings include secondary education (M Ed, MS, PhD, Ed S), with options in English language arts, mathematics, science, social studies. Accredited by NCATE. Department faculty: 20 full-time (11 women). *Degree requirements:* For master's, thesis (MS) required, foreign language not required; for doctorate, dissertation required, foreign language not required; for Ed S, field project required, foreign language and thesis not required. *Entrance requirements:* For master's and Ed S, GRE General Test; for doctorate, GRE General Test (minimum score 450 on each section, 1000 combined). Application deadline: 9/1 (rolling processing; 3/1 for spring admission). Application fee: $25 ($50 for international students). *Expenses:* Tuition $2760 per year full-time, $76 per credit hour part-time for state residents; $8280 per year full-time, $228 per credit hour part-time for nonresidents. Fees $30 per year full-time, $160 per quarter part-time for state residents; $30 per year full-time, $480 per quarter part-time for nonresidents. • Dr. Andrew M. Weaver, Head, 334-844-4434. E-mail: weaveam@mail.auburn.edu. Application contact: Dr. John F. Pritchett, Dean of the Graduate School, 334-844-4700.

Ball State University, College of Sciences and Humanities, Department of Biology, 2000 University Avenue, Muncie, IN 47306-1099. Offerings include biology education (Ed D). Accredited by NCATE. Department faculty: 21. *Degree requirements:* Dissertation required, foreign language not required. *Entrance requirements:* GRE General Test (minimum combined score of 1000), minimum graduate GPA of 3.2. Application fee: $15 ($25 for international students). *Expenses:* Tuition $3454 per year full-time, $518 per semester (minimum) part-time for state residents; $9316 per year full-time, $1221 per semester (minimum) part-time for nonresidents. Fees $242 per year full-time, $18 per semester (minimum) part-time. • Dr. Carl E. Warnes, Chairman, 765-285-8820.

Beaver College, Department of Education, Glenside, PA 19038-3295. Offerings include biology education (MA Ed), chemistry education (MA Ed), environmental education (MA Ed, CAS), science education (M Ed, CAS). *Application fee:* $35. *Expenses:* Tuition $6570 per year full-time, $365 per credit part-time. Fees $35 per year.

Bemidji State University, Division of Social and Natural Sciences, Field of Science, Bemidji, MN 56601-2699. Awards MS Ed. Accredited by NCATE. Part-time programs available. Students: 1 part-time (0 women). Average age 29. In 1997, 1 degree awarded. *Application deadline:* 5/1. *Application fee:* $20. *Expenses:* Tuition $128 per credit for state residents; $134 per credit (minimum) for nonresidents. Fees $517 per year full-time, $35 per credit (minimum) part-time. *Financial aid:* Federal Work-Study and career-related internships or fieldwork available. Financial aid application deadline: 5/1. • Dr. John Truedson, Coordinator, 218-755-2796. E-mail: truedson@vax1.bemidji.msus.edu.

Bloomsburg University of Pennsylvania, School of Graduate Studies, College of Arts and Sciences, Department of Biological and Allied Health Sciences, Program in Biology Education, Bloomsburg, PA 17815-1905. Awards M Ed. Accredited by NCATE. Students: 1 part-time (0 women). Average age 38. *Degree requirements:* Thesis or alternative required, foreign language not required. *Entrance requirements:* GRE General Test, GRE Subject Test, teaching certificate, minimum QPA of 2.5. Application deadline: rolling. Application fee: $25. *Expenses:* Tuition $3468 per year full-time, $193 per credit part-time for state residents; $6236 per year full-time, $346 per credit part-time for nonresidents. Fees $748 per year full-time, $166 per semester (minimum) part-time. • Dr. Margaret Till, Coordinator, 717-389-4780. Fax: 717-389-3028. E-mail: till@bloomu.edu.

Boise State University, College of Education, Programs in Teacher Education, Program in Earth Science Education, Boise, ID 83725-0399. Awards MS. Accredited by NCATE. Part-time programs available. Students: 1 (woman) full-time, 4 part-time (3 women). Average age 38. 0 applicants. In 1997, 1 degree awarded. *Degree requirements:* Thesis optional. *Application deadline:* 7/26 (priority date; rolling processing; 11/29 for spring admission). *Application fee:* $20 ($30 for international students). Electronic applications accepted. *Tuition:* $3020 per year full-time, $135 per credit part-time for state residents; $8900 per year full-time, $135 per credit part-time for nonresidents. *Financial aid:* Graduate assistantships, Federal Work-Study, institutionally sponsored loans, and career-related internships or fieldwork available. Aid available to part-time students. Financial aid application deadline: 3/1. • Dr. Charles J. Waag, Coordinator, 208-385-1631. Application contact: Dr. Roger Stewart, Coordinator, 208-385-1731. Fax: 208-385-4365.

Boston College, Graduate School of Education, Department of Teacher Education/Special Education and Curriculum and Instruction, Program in Secondary Education, Chestnut Hill, MA 02167-9991. Offerings include biology (MST), chemistry (MST), geology (MST), physics (MST). One or more programs accredited by NCATE. *Application deadline:* 3/15 (11/15 for spring admission). *Application fee:* $40. *Expenses:* Tuition $626 per semester hour. Fees $80 per year (minimum) full-time, $30 per semester part-time. • Application contact: Arline Riordan, Graduate Admissions Director, 617-552-4214. Fax: 617-552-0812. E-mail: riordana@bc.edu.

Boston University, School of Education, Department of Curriculum and Teaching, Program in Science Education, Boston, MA 02215. Awards Ed M, MAT, Ed D, CAGS. Students: 9 full-time (7 women), 3 part-time (all women); includes 1 international. Average age 24. In 1997, 3 master's awarded. *Degree requirements:* For doctorate, dissertation, comprehensive exam required, foreign language not required; for CAGS, comprehensive exam required, foreign language and thesis not required. *Entrance requirements:* For master's and CAGS, GRE or MAT, TOEFL; for doctorate, GRE General Test or MAT, TOEFL. Application deadline: 2/15 (priority date; rolling processing). Application fee: $50. *Expenses:* Tuition $22,830 per year full-time, $713 per credit part-time. Fees $218 per year full-time, $40 per semester part-time. *Financial aid:* Application deadline 3/30. *Faculty research:* Teacher training, leadership. • Dr. Stephan Ellenwood, Coordinator, 617-353-3238. E-mail: ellenwoo@bu.edu.

Bowling Green State University, College of Arts and Sciences, Department of Biological Sciences, Bowling Green, OH 43403. Offerings include biological sciences (MAT, MS, PhD). Department faculty: 26 full-time (8 women). *Degree requirements:* For master's, thesis or alternative required, foreign language not required; for doctorate, dissertation required, foreign language not required. *Entrance requirements:* GRE General Test, GRE Subject Test, TOEFL (minimum score 590). Application fee: $30. *Tuition:* $6070 per year full-time, $284 per credit hour part-time for state residents; $11,358 per year full-time, $536 per credit hour part-time for nonresidents. • Dr. George Bullerjahn, Chair, 419-372-2332. Application contact: Dr. Stan Smith, Graduate Coordinator, 419-372-2332.

Bowling Green State University, College of Arts and Sciences, Department of Chemistry, Bowling Green, OH 43403. Offerings include chemistry (MAT, MS). Department faculty: 14 full-time (1 woman). *Degree requirements:* Thesis or alternative required, foreign language not required. *Entrance requirements:* GRE General Test, TOEFL (minimum score 600). Application deadline: 12/15 (priority date; rolling processing). Application fee: $30. *Tuition:* $6070 per year full-time, $284 per credit hour part-time for state residents; $11,358 per year full-time, $536 per credit hour part-time for nonresidents. • Dr. Michael Rodgers, Chair, 419-372-2031. Application contact: Dr. Tom Kinstle, Graduate Coordinator, 419-372-2658.

Bowling Green State University, College of Arts and Sciences, Department of Physics and Astronomy, Bowling Green, OH 43403. Offerings include physics (MAT, MS), physics and astronomy (MAT). Department faculty: 8 full-time (0 women). *Degree requirements:* Thesis or alternative required, foreign language not required. *Entrance requirements:* GRE General Test, TOEFL (minimum score 550). Application deadline: 8/15. Application fee: $30. Electronic applications accepted. *Tuition:* $6070 per year full-time, $284 per credit hour part-time for state residents; $11,358 per year full-time, $536 per credit hour part-time for nonresidents. • Dr. Robert I. Boughton, Chair, 419-372-2421. Application contact: Dr. Lewis Fulcher, Graduate Coordinator, 419-372-2635.

Bridgewater State College, School of Arts and Sciences, Department of Earth Sciences and Geography, Bridgewater, MA 02325-0001. Offers programs in earth sciences (MAT), geography (MAT). Accredited by NCATE. *Entrance requirements:* GRE General Test. Application deadline: 4/1 (10/1 for spring admission). Application fee: $25. *Expenses:* Tuition $1675 per year full-time, $70 per credit part-time for state residents; $6450 per year full-time, $269 per credit part-time for nonresidents. Fees $1588 per year full-time, $66 per credit hour part-time for state residents; $1588 per year full-time, $66 per credit part-time for nonresidents. • Application contact: Graduate School, 508-697-1300.

Bridgewater State College, School of Arts and Sciences, Department of Physics, Bridgewater, MA 02325-0001. Awards MAT. One or more programs accredited by NCATE. *Entrance requirements:* GRE General Test. Application deadline: 4/1 (10/1 for spring admission). Application fee: $25. *Expenses:* Tuition $1675 per year full-time, $70 per credit part-time for state residents; $6450 per year full-time, $269 per credit part-time for nonresidents. Fees $1588 per year full-time, $66 per credit hour part-time for state residents; $1588 per year full-time, $66 per credit part-time for nonresidents. • Application contact: Graduate School, 508-697-1300.

Bridgewater State College, School of Arts and Sciences, Program in Physical Sciences, Bridgewater, MA 02325-0001. Awards MAT. Accredited by NCATE. *Entrance requirements:* GRE General Test. Application deadline: 4/1 (10/1 for spring admission). Application fee: $25. *Expenses:* Tuition $1675 per year full-time, $70 per credit part-time for state residents; $6450 per year full-time, $269 per credit part-time for nonresidents. Fees $1588 per year full-time, $66 per credit hour part-time for state residents; $1588 per year full-time, $66 per credit part-time for nonresidents. • Application contact: Graduate School, 508-697-1300.

Brigham Young University, College of Biological and Agricultural Sciences, Department of Botany and Range Science, Provo, UT 84602-1001. Offerings include biological science education (MS). *Degree requirements:* Thesis. *Entrance requirements:* GRE General Test (minimum combined score of 1100), minimum GPA of 3.2 during previous 2 years. Application deadline: 2/1 (rolling processing). Application fee: $30. *Tuition:* $3200 per year full-time, $178 per credit hour part-time for state residents; $4800 per year full-time, $266 per credit hour part-time for nonresidents.

Brigham Young University, College of Biological and Agricultural Sciences, Department of Zoology, Provo, UT 84602-1001. Offerings include biological science education (MS). *Degree requirements:* Thesis required, foreign language not required. *Average time to degree:* master's–2.5 years full-time; doctorate–5 years full-time. *Entrance requirements:* GRE General Test (minimum combined score of 1600 on three sections), minimum GPA of 3.0 during previous 2 years. Application deadline: 2/1 (priority date). Application fee: $30. Electronic applications accepted. *Tuition:* $3200 per year full-time, $178 per credit hour part-time for state residents; $4800 per year full-time, $266 per credit hour part-time for nonresidents.

Brooklyn College of the City University of New York, School of Education, Division of Secondary Education, 2900 Bedford Avenue, Brooklyn, NY 11210-2889. Offerings include biology education (MA), chemistry education (MA), general science education (MA), physics education (MA). *Application deadline:* 3/1 (11/1 for spring admission). *Application fee:* $40. *Expenses:* Tuition $4350 per year full-time, $185 per credit part-time for state residents; $7600 per year full-time, $320 per credit part-time for nonresidents. Fees $500 per year for state residents; $806 per year for nonresidents. • Dr. Peter Taubman, Coordinator, 718-951-5218. Fax: 718-951-4816. E-mail: ptaubman@brooklyn.cuny.edu.

Brooklyn College of the City University of New York, School of Education, Division of Elementary School Education, Program in Science and Environmental Education, 2900 Bedford Avenue, Brooklyn, NY 11210-2889. Awards MS Ed. Part-time and evening/weekend programs available. Students: 1 full-time (0 women), 38 part-time (33 women); includes 11 minority (9 African Americans, 1 Asian American, 1 Hispanic). Average age 25. In 1997, 27 degrees awarded. *Degree requirements:* Comprehensive exam required, thesis not required. *Average time to degree:* master's–2 years part-time. *Entrance requirements:* TOEFL (minimum score 500), interview, previous course work in education, writing sample. Application deadline: 3/1 (11/1 for spring admission). Application fee: $40. *Expenses:* Tuition $4350 per year full-time, $185 per credit part-time for state residents; $7600 per year full-time, $320 per credit part-time for nonresidents. Fees $500 per year for state residents; $806 per year for nonresidents. *Financial aid:* Institutionally sponsored loans and career-related internships or fieldwork available. Financial aid application deadline: 5/1; applicants required to submit FAFSA. *Faculty research:* Urban science education, school change. • Dr. Paul Jablon, Adviser, 718-951-5061. Fax: 718-951-3115. E-mail: pcjbc@cunyvm.cuny.edu.

Brown University, Department of Education, Providence, RI 02912. Offerings include secondary biology (MAT). MAT (elementary education K–6) new for fall 1998. Department faculty: 4 full-time (2 women), 20 part-time (15 women). *Average time to degree:* master's–1 year full-time. *Entrance requirements:* GRE (score in 95th percentile or higher). Application deadline: 1/2 (priority date). Application fee: $60. *Expenses:* Tuition $23,616 per year. Fees $436 per year. • Lawrence Wakeford, Chairman, 401-863-2407. Application contact: Yvette Nachmias, Teacher Education Coordinator, 401-863-3364. Fax: 401-863-1276. E-mail: yvette_nachmias@brown.edu.

California State University, Fullerton, School of Natural Science and Mathematics, Program in Science Education, PO Box 34080, Fullerton, CA 92834-9480. Offers teaching science (MA). Part-time programs available. Faculty: 1 (woman) full-time, 7 part-time, 2 FTE. Students: 1 full-time (0 women), 13 part-time (7 women); includes 1 minority (Hispanic). Average age 41. 3 applicants, 67% accepted. In 1997, 17 degrees awarded. *Degree requirements:* Project or thesis. *Entrance requirements:* Diagnostic exam, minimum GPA of 2.5 in last 60 units, teaching credential, bachelor's degree in science. Application fee: $55. *Expenses:* Tuition $0 for state residents; $246 per unit for nonresidents. Fees $1947 per year full-time, $1281 per year part-time. *Financial aid:* State grants, Federal Work-Study, institutionally sponsored loans available. Aid available to part-time students. Financial aid application deadline: 3/1. *Faculty research:* Earth and space science education. • Dr. Eric Streitberger, Coordinator, 714-278-3877. Application contact: Dr. Gaylen Carlson, Adviser, 714-278-3942.

California State University, San Bernardino, Graduate Studies, School of Education, San Bernardino, CA 92407-2397. Offerings include environmental education (MA). School faculty: 77 full-time (38 women). *Application deadline:* 8/31 (priority date). *Application fee:* $55. *Expenses:* Tuition $0 for state residents; $164 per unit for nonresidents. Fees $1922 per year full-time, $1256 per year part-time. • Patricia Arlin, Dean, 909-880-3600. Fax: 909-880-7011.

California University of Pennsylvania, School of Science and Technology, Department of Biological and Environmental Sciences, 250 University Avenue, California, PA 15419-1394. Offerings include biology (M Ed, MS). Department faculty: 5 part-time (0 women). *Degree requirements:* Thesis, comprehensive exam required, foreign language not required. *Entrance requirements:* GRE General Test, TOEFL (minimum score 550), minimum GPA of 2.5, teaching certificate. Application deadline: rolling. Application fee: $25. *Expenses:* Tuition $3468 per year full-time, $193 per credit part-time for state residents; $6236 per year full-time, $346 per credit part-time for nonresidents. Fees $886 per year full-time, $153 per semester (minimum) part-time. • Dr. Barry Hunter, Chairman, 724-938-4200.

Carthage College, Division of Teacher Education, Kenosha, WI 53140-1994. Offerings include natural sciences (M Ed). College faculty: 6 full-time (4 women), 13 part-time (8 women). *Degree requirements:* Thesis optional, foreign language not required. *Average time to degree:* master's–5 years part-time. *Entrance requirements:* MAT, minimum B average. Application deadline: rolling. Application fee: $25. • Dr. Judith B. Schaumberg, Director of Graduate Programs, 414-551-5876. Fax: 414-551-5704.

Central Michigan University, College of Science and Technology, Department of Chemistry, Mount Pleasant, MI 48859. Offerings include teaching chemistry (MA). Accredited by NCATE. Department faculty: 25 full-time (2 women). *Application fee:* $30. *Expenses:* Tuition $139 per credit hour (minimum) for state residents; $276 per credit hour (minimum) for nonresidents. Fees $260 per year full-time, $150 per semester part-time. • Dr. John Lorand, Chairperson, 517-774-3981. Fax: 517-774-7106. E-mail: savfpij@cmich.edu.

Charleston Southern University, Programs in Education, Charleston, SC 29423-8087. Offerings include science (MAT). Faculty: 16 full-time (5 women), 5 part-time (3 women), 17.6 FTE. *Application deadline:* rolling. *Application fee:* $25. *Tuition:* $9821 per year full-time, $173 per hour (minimum) part-time. • Dr. Martha Watson, Director of Graduate Programs, 803-863-7555.

Christopher Newport University, Graduate Studies, Department of Education, 1 University Place, Newport News, VA 23606-2998. Offerings include teaching science (MAT), with options in elementary science education, middle school teaching. Department faculty: 25 full-time (12 women), 1 part-time (0 women). *Degree requirements:* Thesis or alternative, comprehensive exam required, foreign language not required. *Average time to degree:* master's–3.5 years part-time. *Entrance requirements:* GRE, minimum GPA of 3.0. Application deadline: 8/1 (priority date; rolling processing; 12/15 for spring admission). Application fee: $40. *Expenses:* Tuition $3474 per year full-time, $145 per credit hour part-time for state residents; $8424 per year full-time, $351 per credit hour part-time for nonresidents. Fees $40 per year. • Dr. Marsha Sprague, Coordinator, 757-594-7973. Fax: 757-594-7862. E-mail: msprague@cnu.edu. Application contact: Graduate Admissions, 800-333-4268. Fax: 757-594-7333. E-mail: admit@cnu.edu.

The Citadel, The Military College of South Carolina, Department of Biology, Charleston, SC 29409. Offers program in biology education (MAE). One or more programs accredited by NCATE. Part-time programs available. Faculty: 3 full-time (0 women). Students: 2 full-time (both women), 17 part-time (11 women); includes 1 minority (African American). In 1997, 6 degrees awarded. *Entrance requirements:* GRE, MAT, or 12 hours of graduate course work with a minimum GPA of 3.0. Application deadline: rolling. Application fee: $25. *Expenses:* Tuition $130 per credit hour for state residents; $260 per credit hour for nonresidents. Fees $30 per semester. • Dr. Robert Baldwin, Head, 803-953-7875.

City College of the City University of New York, Graduate School, School of Education, Department of Secondary and Continuing Education, Program in Environmental Education, Convent Avenue at 138th Street, New York, NY 10031-6977. Awards MA. Students: 2 full-time (0 women), 27 part-time (15 women). In 1997, 16 degrees awarded. *Degree requirements:* Thesis required, foreign language not required. *Entrance requirements:* TOEFL (minimum score 500). Application fee: $40. *Expenses:* Tuition $4350 per year full-time, $185 per credit part-time for state residents; $7600 per year full-time, $320 per credit part-time for nonresidents. Fees $41 per year. *Financial aid:* Application deadline 5/1. • Chairman, 212-650-7953.

City College of the City University of New York, Graduate School, School of Education, Department of Secondary and Continuing Education, Program in Secondary Science Education, Convent Avenue at 138th Street, New York, NY 10031-6977. Awards MA. Students: 4 full-time (3 women), 26 part-time (10 women). In 1997, 12 degrees awarded. *Degree requirements:* Thesis required, foreign language not required. *Entrance requirements:* TOEFL (minimum score 500). Application fee: $40. *Expenses:* Tuition $4350 per year full-time, $185 per credit part-time for state residents; $7600 per year full-time, $320 per credit part-time for nonresidents. Fees $41 per year. *Financial aid:* Application deadline 5/1. • Chairman, 212-650-7953.

Clarion University of Pennsylvania, College of Arts and Sciences, Department of Biology, Program in Science Education, Clarion, PA 16214. Awards M Ed. Faculty: 20 full-time (2 women). Students: 6 full-time (4 women), 9 part-time (6 women); includes 1 minority (African American). 12 applicants, 75% accepted. In 1997, 14 degrees awarded. *Degree requirements:* Thesis or alternative required, foreign language not required. *Entrance requirements:* GRE General Test, minimum QPA of 2.75. Application deadline: 8/1 (priority date; rolling processing). Application fee: $25. *Expenses:* Tuition $3468 per year full-time, $193 per credit hour part-time for state residents; $6236 per year full-time, $346 per credit hour part-time for nonresidents. Fees $921 per year full-time, $90 per credit hour part-time for state residents; $921 per year full-time, $89 per credit hour part-time for nonresidents. *Financial aid:* In 1997–98, 3 research assistantships (2 to first-year students) averaging $533 per month were awarded. Financial aid application deadline: 5/1. • Application contact: Dr. Ed Zielinski, Graduate Coordinator, 814-226-2559.

Clark Atlanta University, School of Arts and Sciences, Department of Chemistry, Atlanta, GA 30314. Offerings include science education (DA). *Application deadline:* 4/1 (rolling processing; 11/1 for spring admission). *Application fee:* $40. *Expenses:* Tuition $9672 per year full-time, $403 per credit hour part-time. Fees $200 per year. • Dr. Reynold Verrett, Chairperson, 404-880-8154. Application contact: Michelle Clark-Davis, Graduate Program Assistant, 404-880-8709.

Clemson University, College of Health, Education, and Human Development, Department of Curriculum and Instruction, Program in Secondary Education, Clemson, SC 29634. Offerings include natural sciences (M Ed). Accredited by NCATE. *Entrance requirements:* TOEFL, teaching certificate. Application deadline: 6/1. Application fee: $35. *Expenses:* Tuition $3154 per year full-time, $130 per credit hour part-time for state residents; $6452 per year full-time, $264 per credit hour part-time for nonresidents. Fees $190 per year. • Dr. Robert Green, Chair, Department of Curriculum and Instruction, 864-656-5108. Fax: 864-656-1322. E-mail: rpgreen@clemson.edu.

College of Notre Dame, Department of Education, Emphasis in Secondary Education, Belmont, CA 94002-1997. Offerings include teaching biology (MAT). Faculty: 5 full-time, 8 part-time. *Application deadline:* rolling. *Application fee:* $50 ($500 for international students). *Tuition:* $460 per unit. • Dr. Kim Tolley, Program Director, 650-508-3456.

College of Our Lady of the Elms, Department of Education, Chicopee, MA 01013-2839. Offerings include secondary education (MAT), with options in biology education, English education, Spanish education. Department faculty: 7 full-time (all women), 6 part-time (5 women). *Application deadline:* rolling. *Application fee:* $30. *Expenses:* Tuition $320 per credit. Fees $40 per year. • Sr. Kathleen M. Kirley, Dean of Continuing Education and Graduate Studies, 413-594-2761. Fax: 413-592-4871. Application contact: Dr. Mary Janeczek, Director, 413-594-2761.

The Colorado College, Department of Education, Program in Secondary Education, Colorado Springs, CO 80903-3294. Offerings include science teaching (MAT). Program faculty: 2 full-time (1 woman), 3 part-time (2 women). *Degree requirements:* Thesis, internship required, foreign language not required. *Entrance requirements:* GRE Subject Test (score in 50th percentile or higher), Program for Licensing Assessments for Colorado Educators Basic Skills Test. Application deadline: 3/1. Application fee: $40. • Paul J. Kuerbis, Director, 719-389-6726. Application contact: Marsha Unruh, Educational Services Coordinator, 719-389-6472. Fax: 719-389-6473.

Columbus State University, College of Education, Department of Curriculum and Instruction, Columbus, GA 31907-5645. Offerings include secondary education (M Ed, Ed S), with options in biology (M Ed), English (M Ed, Ed S), general science (M Ed), history (M Ed), mathematics (M Ed, Ed S), political science (M Ed), science/biology (Ed S), social science (M Ed, Ed S). Accredited by NCATE. Ed S (mathematics) offered jointly with Georgia Southwestern University. M Ed (political science) being phased out; applicants no longer accepted. *Degree requirements:* For master's, exit exam required, foreign language and thesis not required; for Ed S, thesis or alternative required, foreign language not required. *Entrance requirements:* For master's, GRE General Test (minimum combined score of 800), MAT (minimum score 44); for Ed S, GRE General Test (minimum combined score of 900), MAT (minimum score 44). Application deadline: 7/10 (priority date; rolling processing; 10/23 for spring admission). Application fee: $20. *Tuition:* $1718 per year full-time, $151 per semester hour part-time for state residents; $6218 per year full-time, $401 per semester hour part-time for nonresidents. • Dr. David Shoemaker, Chair, 706-568-2255. Fax: 706-568-3134. E-mail: shoemaker_david@colstate.edu. Application contact: Katie Thornton, Graduate Admissions, 706-568-2279. Fax: 706-568-2462. E-mail: thornton_katie@colstate.edu.

Directory: Science Education

Connecticut College, Department of Botany, New London, CT 06320-4196. Awards MA, MAT. Part-time programs available. *Degree requirements:* Thesis required, foreign language not required. *Entrance requirements:* GRE or MAT. Application deadline: 2/2. Application fee: $35. *Faculty research:* Tidal marsh ecology, upland vegetation dynamics, plant development, halophyte physiology.

Connecticut College, Department of Chemistry, New London, CT 06320-4196. Awards MAT. Part-time programs available. *Entrance requirements:* MAT. Application deadline: 2/2. Application fee: $35.

Connecticut College, Department of Physics, New London, CT 06320-4196. Awards MAT. Part-time programs available. *Entrance requirements:* MAT. Application deadline: 2/2. Application fee: $35.

Cornell University, Graduate Fields of Agriculture and Life Sciences, Field of Education, Ithaca, NY 14853-0001. Offerings include biology (MAT), chemistry (MAT), earth science (MAT), physics (MAT). Faculty: 26 full-time. *Application deadline:* 5/1. *Application fee:* $65. Electronic applications accepted. • Director of Graduate Studies, 607-255-4278. Application contact: Graduate Field Assistant, 607-255-4278. E-mail: edgrfld@cornell.edu.

Delaware State University, Department of Biology, Dover, DE 19901-2277. Offerings include biology education (MS). *Degree requirements:* Thesis required (for some programs), foreign language not required. *Entrance requirements:* GRE, minimum GPA of 3.0 in major, 2.75 overall. Application deadline: 6/30 (priority date; rolling processing). Application fee: $10.

Delaware State University, Department of Physics, Dover, DE 19901-2277. Offerings include physics teaching (MS). *Entrance requirements:* Minimum GPA of 2.75 overall, 3.0 in major. Application deadline: 6/30. Application fee: $10.

Delaware State University, Department of Education, Program in Science Education, Dover, DE 19901-2277. Awards MA. Part-time and evening/weekend programs available. *Degree requirements:* Comprehensive exam required, thesis optional, foreign language not required. *Entrance requirements:* GRE General Test, minimum GPA of 3.0 in major, 2.75 overall. Application deadline: 6/30 (priority date; rolling processing). Application fee: $10. *Faculty research:* Imagery and conceptual change.

DePaul University, College of Liberal Arts and Sciences, Department of Physics, Program in Teaching of Physics, Chicago, IL 60604-2287. Awards MS. Faculty: 7 full-time (0 women), 2 part-time (0 women). Students: 0. *Degree requirements:* Thesis, oral exams required, foreign language not required. *Entrance requirements:* Minimum GPA of 2.7. Application deadline: 6/15 (priority date; rolling processing; 9/1 for spring admission). Application fee: $25. *Expenses:* Tuition $320 per credit hour. Fees $30 per year. *Faculty research:* Experimental physics, optics, solid-state physics, computational physics, atomic physics. • Dr. Anthony F. Behof, Chairman, Department of Physics, 773-325-7330. E-mail: abehof@wppost.depaul.edu. Application contact: Department Office, 773-325-7330. Fax: 773-325-7334. E-mail: cgoedde@condor.depaul.edu.

East Carolina University, School of Education, Department of Science Education, Greenville, NC 27858-4353. Awards MA, MA Ed. Accredited by NCATE. Part-time programs available. Faculty: 2 full-time (1 woman). Students: 11 full-time (5 women), 6 part-time (all women); includes 1 minority (African American). Average age 27. 9 applicants, 100% accepted. In 1997, 4 degrees awarded. *Degree requirements:* Comprehensive exams required, thesis optional, foreign language not required. *Entrance requirements:* GRE General Test or MAT, TOEFL. Application deadline: 6/1 (priority date; rolling processing). Application fee: $0. *Tuition:* $1886 per year full-time, $472 per semester (minimum) part-time for state residents; $9156 per year full-time, $2289 per semester (minimum) part-time for nonresidents. *Financial aid:* Federal Work-Study available. Financial aid application deadline: 6/1. • Dr. Frank Crawley, Chairperson, 252-328-6736. Fax: 252-328-6218. E-mail: crawleyf@mail.ecu.edu. Application contact: Dr. Paul D. Tschetter, Associate Dean, 252-328-6012. Fax: 252-328-6071. E-mail: grad@mail.ecu.edu.

Eastern Connecticut State University, School of Education and Professional Studies/Graduate Division, Program in Science Education, Willimantic, CT 06226-2295. Awards MS. Faculty: 1 (woman) full-time. Students: 8 part-time (6 women). Average age 35. In 1997, 4 degrees awarded. *Degree requirements:* Comprehensive exam or thesis required, foreign language not required. *Entrance requirements:* Minimum GPA of 2.7, teaching certificate. Application fee: $40. *Expenses:* Tuition $2632 per year full-time, $175 per credit hour part-time for state residents; $7220 per year full-time, $175 per credit hour part-time for nonresidents. Fees $1851 per year full-time, $20 per semester part-time for state residents; $2748 per year full-time, $20 per semester part-time for nonresidents. *Financial aid:* Application deadline 3/15. • Jacqueline K. Bowman, Adviser, 860-465-4532. E-mail: bowmanj@scsu.ctstateu.edu. Application contact: Edith Mavor, Graduate Division Director, 860-465-4543. E-mail: mavor@ecsuc.ctstateu.edu.

Eastern Kentucky University, College of Education, Department of Curriculum and Instruction, Program in Secondary and Higher Education, Richmond, KY 40475-3101. Offerings include biological sciences education (MA Ed), chemistry education (MA Ed), earth science education (MA Ed), general science education (MA Ed), physics education (MA Ed). One or more programs accredited by NCATE. *Entrance requirements:* GRE General Test, minimum GPA of 2.5. Application fee: $0. *Tuition:* $2390 per year full-time, $133 per credit hour part-time for state residents; $6630 per year full-time, $365 per credit hour part-time for nonresidents. • Dr. Imogene Ramsey, Chair, Department of Curriculum and Instruction, 606-622-2154.

Eastern Michigan University, College of Arts and Sciences, Department of Physics and Astronomy, Program in Physics Education, Ypsilanti, MI 48197. Awards MS. In 1997, 3 degrees awarded. *Entrance requirements:* TOEFL (minimum score 500). Application deadline: 5/15 (rolling processing; 3/15 for spring admission). Application fee: $30. *Expenses:* Tuition $2691 per year full-time, $150 per credit hour part-time for state residents; $6300 per year full-time, $350 per credit hour part-time for nonresidents. Fees $368 per year full-time, $88 per semester (minimum) part-time. *Financial aid:* Application deadline 3/15. • Dr. Daniel Trochet, Coordinator, 734-487-4144.

Eastern Washington University, College of Education and Human Development, Department of Education, Program in Science Education, Cheney, WA 99004-2431. Awards M Ed. Accredited by NCATE. *Degree requirements:* Thesis or alternative, comprehensive exam. *Entrance requirements:* Minimum GPA of 3.0. Application deadline: 4/1 (priority date; rolling processing; 1/15 for spring admission). Application fee: $35. *Tuition:* $4200 per year full-time, $140 per credit part-time for state residents; $12,780 per year full-time, $415 per credit part-time for nonresidents. *Financial aid:* Application deadline 2/1. • Dr. Jerry Logan, Adviser, 509-359-6192.

East Stroudsburg University of Pennsylvania, School of Arts and Sciences, Department of Biology, East Stroudsburg, PA 18301-2999. Offerings include biology (M Ed, MS). *Degree requirements:* Thesis or alternative, comprehensive exam required, foreign language not required. *Entrance requirements:* Undergraduate major in life sciences, previous course work in organic chemistry. Application deadline: 7/31 (rolling processing; 11/30 for spring admission). Application fee: $15 ($25 for international students). *Expenses:* Tuition $3468 per year full-time, $193 per credit part-time for state residents; $6236 per year full-time, $346 per credit part-time for nonresidents. Fees $700 per year full-time, $39 per credit part-time.

East Stroudsburg University of Pennsylvania, School of Arts and Sciences, Program in General Science, East Stroudsburg, PA 18301-2999. Offerings include general science (M Ed, MS). *Degree requirements:* Thesis (for some programs), comprehensive exam. *Application deadline:* 7/31 (priority date; rolling processing; 11/30 for spring admission). *Application fee:* $15 ($25 for international students). *Expenses:* Tuition $3468 per year full-time, $193 per credit part-time for state residents; $6236 per year full-time, $346 per credit part-time for nonresidents. Fees $700 per year full-time, $39 per credit part-time.

Edinboro University of Pennsylvania, School of Education, Department of Elementary Education, Program in Elementary Education, Edinboro, PA 16444. Offerings include science (M Ed). *Degree requirements:* Thesis or alternative required, foreign language not required. *Entrance requirements:* GRE or MAT (score in 30th percentile or higher). Application deadline: rolling. Application fee: $25. *Expenses:* Tuition $3468 per year full-time, $193 per credit part-time for state residents; $6236 per year full-time, $346 per credit part-time for nonresidents. Fees $898 per year full-time, $50 per semester (minimum) part-time. • Application contact: Dr. Philip Kerstetter, Dean of Graduate Studies, 814-732-2856. Fax: 814-732-2611. E-mail: kerstetter@edinboro.edu.

Fairleigh Dickinson University, Teaneck–Hackensack Campus, University College: Arts, Sciences, and Professional Studies, Peter Sammartino School of Education, Program in Biological Science Education, 1000 River Road, Teaneck, NJ 07666-1914. Awards MAT. Faculty: 11 full-time (8 women), 27 part-time (10 women). *Degree requirements:* Research project required, thesis not required. *Application deadline:* rolling. *Application fee:* $35. *Expenses:* Tuition $522 per credit. Fees $302 per year full-time, $138 per year part-time. *Faculty research:* Mathematics for students with learning disabilities, gender issues in education, social problem-solving and conflict resolution in the classroom, multicultural education in the elementary classroom, problems encountered by international students in college programs. • Dr. Eloise Forster, Interim Director, Peter Sammartino School of Education, 201-692-2834. Fax: 201-692-2603.

Fairleigh Dickinson University, Teaneck–Hackensack Campus, University College: Arts, Sciences, and Professional Studies, Peter Sammartino School of Education, Program in Physical Science Education, 1000 River Road, Teaneck, NJ 07666-1914. Offers physical education (MAT), science education (MAT). Faculty: 11 full-time (8 women), 27 part-time (10 women). *Degree requirements:* Research project required, thesis not required. *Application deadline:* rolling. *Application fee:* $35. *Expenses:* Tuition $522 per credit. Fees $302 per year full-time, $138 per year part-time. *Faculty research:* Mathematics for students with learning disabilities, gender issues in education, social problem-solving and conflict resolution in the classroom, multicultural education in the elementary classroom, problems encountered by international students in college programs. • Dr. Eloise Forster, Interim Director, Peter Sammartino School of Education, 201-692-2834. Fax: 201-692-2603.

Fayetteville State University, Programs in Educational Leadership and Secondary Education, 1200 Murchison Road, Fayetteville, NC 28301-4298. Offerings include biology (MAT). Accredited by NCATE. *Application deadline:* 8/1 (rolling processing; 12/15 for spring admission). *Application fee:* $20. *Tuition:* $1498 per year full-time, $327 per semester (minimum) part-time for state residents; $8768 per year full-time, $2144 per semester (minimum) part-time for nonresidents.

Fitchburg State College, Program in Science Education, Fitchburg, MA 01420-2697. Awards M Ed. Accredited by NCATE. Part-time and evening/weekend programs available. *Entrance requirements:* GRE General Test or MAT (minimum score 47), interview, teaching certification. Application deadline: rolling. Application fee: $10. *Expenses:* Tuition $147 per credit. Fees $55 per semester. *Financial aid:* Graduate assistantships, Federal Work-Study available. Aid available to part-time students. Financial aid application deadline: 3/30; applicants required to submit FAFSA. • Dr. George Babich, Chair, 978-665-3245. Fax: 978-665-3658. E-mail: dgce@fsc.edu. Application contact: James DuPont, Director of Admissions, 978-665-3144. Fax: 978-665-4540. E-mail: admissions@fsc.edu.

Fitchburg State College, Program in Teaching Biology (Secondary Level), Fitchburg, MA 01420-2697. Awards MA, MAT. Accredited by NCATE. Part-time and evening/weekend programs available. *Entrance requirements:* GRE General Test or MAT (minimum score 47), interview. Application deadline: rolling. Application fee: $10. *Expenses:* Tuition $147 per credit. Fees $55 per semester. *Financial aid:* Graduate assistantships, Federal Work-Study available. Aid available to part-time students. Financial aid application deadline: 3/30; applicants required to submit FAFSA. • Dr. George Babich, Chair, 978-665-3245. Fax: 978-665-3658. E-mail: dgce@fsc.edu. Application contact: James DuPont, Director of Admissions, 978-665-3144. Fax: 978-665-4540. E-mail: admissions@fsc.edu.

Fitchburg State College, Program in Teaching Earth Science (Secondary Level), Fitchburg, MA 01420-2697. Awards MAT. Accredited by NCATE. Part-time and evening/weekend programs available. *Average time to degree:* master's–2.5 years part-time. *Entrance requirements:* GRE General Test or MAT, interview. Application deadline: rolling. Application fee: $10. *Expenses:* Tuition $147 per credit. Fees $55 per semester. *Financial aid:* Graduate assistantships, Federal Work-Study available. Aid available to part-time students. Financial aid application deadline: 3/30; applicants required to submit FAFSA. • Dr. Robert Champlin, Chair, 978-665-3381. Fax: 978-665-3658. E-mail: dgce@fsc.edu. Application contact: James DuPont, Director of Admissions, 978-665-3144. Fax: 978-665-4540. E-mail: admissions@fsc.edu.

Florida Institute of Technology, College of Science and Liberal Arts, Department of Science Education, Melbourne, FL 32901-6975. Offers programs in biology education (PhD, Ed S), chemistry education (PhD, Ed S), computer science education (MSE, PhD, Ed S), environmental education (MSE), environmental science education (PhD, Ed S), general science education (MSE, PhD, Ed S), mathematics education (MSE, PhD, Ed S), physics education (MSE, Ed S), science education (Ed D, PhD). Part-time programs available. Faculty: 4 full-time (1 woman), 2 part-time (both women). Students: 12 full-time (11 women), 28 part-time (17 women); includes 3 minority (2 African Americans, 1 Asian American), 7 international. Average age 36. 44 applicants, 84% accepted. In 1997, 15 master's awarded; 6 doctorates awarded (100% entered university research/teaching). Terminal master's awarded for partial completion of doctoral program. *Degree requirements:* For master's, oral comprehensive exam required, thesis optional, foreign language not required; for doctorate, dissertation, oral defense of dissertation required, foreign language not required; for Ed S, comprehensive exam required, foreign language and thesis not required. *Entrance requirements:* For master's and Ed S, minimum GPA of 3.0; for doctorate, minimum GPA of 3.2. Application deadline: rolling. Application fee: $50. *Tuition:* $550 per credit hour. *Financial aid:* In 1997–98, 2 research assistantships (1 to a first-year student) averaging $829 per month and totaling $6,630, 1 teaching assistantship averaging $808 per month and totaling $3,230, 5 tuition remissions (2 to first-year students) averaging $1,333 per month and totaling $23,985 were awarded; career-related internships or fieldwork also available. Aid available to part-time students. Financial aid application deadline: 3/1; applicants required to submit FAFSA. *Faculty research:* Measurement and evaluation, science/math education, computers in education, educational technology, environmental education. Total annual research expenditures: $575,385. • Dr. Robert H. Fronk, Head, 407-674-8126. Fax: 407-674-7598. E-mail: fronk@fit.edu. Application contact: Carolyn P. Farrior, Associate Dean of Graduate Admissions, 407-674-7118. Fax: 407-723-9468. E-mail: cfarrior@fit.edu.

Florida International University, College of Education, Department of Subject Specializations, Program in Science Education, Miami, FL 33199. Awards MS. Accredited by NCATE. Part-time and evening/weekend programs available. Students: 7 full-time (2 women), 17 part-time (11 women); includes 10 minority (2 African Americans, 8 Hispanics). Average age 36. 13 applicants, 46% accepted. In 1997, 8 degrees awarded. *Entrance requirements:* GRE General Test (minimum combined score of 1000) or minimum GPA of 3.0. Application deadline: 4/1 (priority date; rolling processing; 10/1 for spring admission). Application fee: $20. *Expenses:* Tuition $138 per credit hour for state residents; $482 per credit hour for nonresidents. Fees $46 per semester. *Faculty research:* Science processes, attitudes, bilingual science education, computers in science education. • Dr. Dean Hauenstein, Chairperson, Department of Subject Specializations, 305-348-2005. Fax: 305-348-2086.

Florida State University, College of Education, Department of Curriculum and Instruction, Program in Science Education, Tallahassee, FL 32306. Awards MS, PhD, Ed S. Part-time programs available. Postbaccalaureate distance learning degree programs offered. Faculty: 3 full-time (1 woman). Students: 20 full-time (14 women), 23 part-time (15 women); includes 9 minority (8 African Americans, 1 Hispanic). 27 applicants, 96% accepted. In 1997, 3 master's, 3 doctorates awarded. *Degree requirements:* For master's and Ed S, comprehensive exam required, thesis optional; for doctorate, dissertation, comprehensive exam. *Entrance requirements:* GRE General Test (minimum combined score of 1000), minimum GPA of 3.0. Application deadline: 7/1 (priority date; rolling processing; 11/1 for spring admission). Application fee: $20. *Tuition:* $139 per credit hour for state residents; $482 per credit hour for nonresidents. *Financial aid:* Fellowships, research assistantships, teaching assistantships, and career-related internships or fieldwork available. • Dr. David Foulk, Chair, Department of Curriculum and Instruction, 850-644-6553. E-mail: foulk@mail.coe.fsu.edu. Application contact: Admissions Secretary, 850-644-6553. Fax: 850-644-1880.

Fresno Pacific University, Graduate School, Programs in Education, Division of Mathematics/Science/Computer Education, Program in Integrated Mathematics/Science Education, Fresno, CA 93702-4709. Awards MA Ed. Faculty: 2 full-time (1 woman), 4 part-time (3 women). Students: 2 full-time (1 woman), 113 part-time (74 women). *Degree requirements:* Thesis or alternative required, foreign language not required. *Application deadline:* 7/31 (rolling processing). *Application fee:* $75. *Tuition:* $250 per unit. • Dave Young, Director, 209-453-2244. Fax: 209-453-2001.

Fresno Pacific University, Graduate School, Programs in Education, Division of Mathematics/Science/Computer Education, Program in Science Education, Fresno, CA 93702-4709. Awards MA Ed. Faculty: 1 full-time (0 women), 2 part-time (0 women). Students: 18 part-time (9 women). *Degree requirements:* Thesis or alternative required, foreign language not required. *Application deadline:* 7/31 (rolling processing). *Application fee:* $75. *Tuition:* $250 per unit. • Dr. Ben VanWagner, Director, 209-453-2278. Fax: 209-453-2001.

Frostburg State University, School of Education, Department of Educational Professions, Program in Biology Education, Frostburg, MD 21532-1099. Awards M Ed. *Application deadline:* 7/15 (rolling processing). *Application fee:* $30.

Gannon University, School of Graduate Studies, College of Sciences, Engineering, and Health Sciences, School of Sciences and Engineering, Program in Natural Sciences/Environmental Education, Erie, PA 16541. Awards M Ed, Certificate. Part-time and evening/weekend programs available. Students: 4 full-time (2 women), 10 part-time (2 women); includes 1 minority (Asian American). Average age 34. 2 applicants, 100% accepted. In 1997, 2 master's awarded. *Degree requirements:* For master's, thesis, comprehensive exam. *Entrance requirements:* For master's, GRE Subject Test. Application deadline: rolling. Application fee: $25. *Expenses:* Tuition $405 per credit. Fees $200 per year full-time, $8 per credit part-time. *Financial aid:* Career-related internships or fieldwork available. Aid available to part-time students. Financial aid application deadline: 3/1; applicants required to submit FAFSA. • Dr. Kenneth Andersen, Director, 814-871-7633. Application contact: Beth Nemenz, Director of Admissions, 814-871-7240. Fax: 814-871-5803. E-mail: admissions@gannon.edu.

Georgia Southern University, College of Education, Department of Middle Grades and Secondary Education, Program in Science, Statesboro, GA 30460-8126. Awards M Ed, Ed S. Accredited by NCATE. Part-time and evening/weekend programs available. Students: 7 full-time (5 women), 9 part-time (4 women); includes 1 minority (African American). Average age 36. 10 applicants, 30% accepted. In 1997, 7 master's, 3 Ed Ss awarded. *Degree requirements:* Exams required, foreign language and thesis not required. *Entrance requirements:* For master's, GRE General Test (minimum score 450 on each section) or MAT (minimum score 44), minimum GPA of 2.5; for Ed S, GRE General Test (minimum score 450 on each section) or MAT (minimum score 49), minimum graduate GPA of 3.25. Application deadline: 7/15 (priority date; rolling processing; 11/15 for spring admission). Application fee: $0. Electronic applications accepted. *Tuition:* $2619 per year full-time, $287 per semester (minimum) part-time for state residents; $8619 per year full-time, $1037 per semester (minimum) part-time for nonresidents. *Financial aid:* Application deadline 4/15. • Application contact: Dr. John R. Diebolt, Associate Graduate Dean, 912-681-5384. Fax: 912-681-0740. E-mail: gradschool@gsvms2.cc.gasou.edu.

Georgia State University, College of Education, Department of Middle, Secondary Education and Instructional Technology, Programs in Secondary Education, Atlanta, GA 30303-3083. Offerings include science education (M Ed, PhD, Ed S). Accredited by NCATE. *Degree requirements:* For master's, comprehensive exam; for doctorate, dissertation, comprehensive exam; for Ed S, project/exam. *Entrance requirements:* For master's, GRE General Test (minimum combined score of 800) or MAT (minimum score 44), minimum GPA of 2.5; for doctorate, GRE General Test (minimum score 500 on verbal section, 500 on either quantitative or analytical sections) or MAT (minimum score 53), minimum GPA of 3.3; for Ed S, GRE General Test (minimum combined score of 900) or MAT (minimum score 48), minimum graduate GPA of 3.25. Application fee: $25. *Expenses:* Tuition $2673 per year full-time, $99 per semester hour part-time for state residents; $10,692 per year full-time, $396 per semester hour part-time for nonresidents. Fees $228 per year. • Dr. Beverly J. Armento, Chair, Department of Middle, Secondary Education and Instructional Technology, 404-651-2510.

Grambling State University, College of Science and Technology, Grambling, LA 71245. Offers program in natural sciences (MAT). Part-time and evening/weekend programs available. Students: 17 full-time (9 women), 4 part-time (1 woman); includes 20 minority (all African Americans), 1 international. Average age 28. 5 applicants, 100% accepted. In 1997, 4 degrees awarded (75% entered university research/teaching, 25% found other work related to degree). *Degree requirements:* Computer language required, foreign language and thesis not required. *Average time to degree:* master's–3 years full-time, 5 years part-time. *Entrance requirements:* GRE General Test (combined average 1167). Application deadline: rolling. Application fee: $15. *Tuition:* $1960 per year full-time, $297 per semester (minimum) part-time for state residents; $7110 per year full-time, $297 per semester (minimum) part-time for nonresidents. *Financial aid:* In 1997–98, 12 students received aid, including 10 teaching assistantships (5 to first-year students) averaging $500 per month and totaling $42,750; Federal Work-Study, institutionally sponsored loans also available. Financial aid application deadline: 5/31. *Faculty research:* Energy, human chromosomes, hypertension, advanced distributed simulation, polymer synthesis. • Dr. Emma Hill, Dean, 318-274-2414. Fax: 318-274-6041.

Grand Valley State University, School of Education, Programs in General Education, Program in Secondary, Adult and Higher Education, Allendale, MI 49401-9403. Offerings include biology (M Ed), physics (M Ed). One or more programs accredited by NCATE. *Degree requirements:* Thesis or alternative, applied research project. *Entrance requirements:* GRE General Test (minimum combined score of 1300) or minimum GPA of 3.0. Application deadline: rolling. Application fee: $20. • Application contact: Admissions Office, 616-895-2025. Fax: 616-895-3081.

Harvard University, Graduate School of Education, Area of Learning and Teaching, Cambridge, MA 02138. Offerings include mid-career mathematics and science (teaching certification) (Ed M, CAS). Faculty: 7 full-time (5 women), 16 part-time (8 women), 10.3 FTE. *Average time to degree:* master's–1 year full-time, 2.1 years part-time; doctorate–6.3 years full-time, 9 years part-time; other advanced degree–1 year full-time, 2 years part-time. *Entrance requirements:* GRE General Test, TOEFL (minimum score 600), TWE (minimum score 5.0). Application deadline: 1/2. Application fee: $60. • Robert Kegan, Chair, 617-496-2974. Fax: 617-495-7843. Application contact: Roland Hence, Director of Admissions, 617-495-3414. Fax: 617-496-3577. E-mail: gseadmissions@harvard.edu.

Henderson State University, School of Education, Department of Secondary Education, Arkadelphia, AR 71999-0001. Offerings include biology education (MSE). Postbaccalaureate distance learning degree programs offered (minimal on-campus study). *Degree requirements:* Thesis optional, foreign language not required. *Entrance requirements:* GRE General Test or MAT, minimum GPA of 2.7, teacher certification. Application deadline: 7/31 (priority date; rolling processing). Application fee: $15. Electronic applications accepted. *Expenses:* Tuition $120 per credit hour for state residents; $240 per credit hour for nonresidents. Fees $105 per semester (minimum) full-time, $52 per semester (minimum) part-time. • Dr. Charles Weiner, Chairperson, 870-230-5163. Fax: 870-230-5455. E-mail: weinerc@holly.hsu.edu.

Hofstra University, School of Education and Allied Human Services, Department of Curriculum and Teaching, Program in Mathematics, Science, and Technology in Elementary Education, Hempstead, NY 11549. Awards MA. Accredited by NCATE. Part-time and evening/weekend programs available. Faculty: 8 full-time (6 women). Students: 21 full-time (all women), 2 part-time (both women); includes 1 minority (Hispanic). Average age 27. 0 applicants. In 1997, 7 degrees awarded. *Degree requirements:* 1 foreign language, thesis, departmental qualifying exam. *Application deadline:* rolling. *Application fee:* $40 ($75 for international students). *Expenses:* Tuition $10,968 per year full-time, $457 per credit hour part-time. Fees $670 per year full-time, $112 per semester (minimum) part-time. *Financial aid:* In 1997–98, 3 research assistantships averaging $260 per month were awarded; Federal Work-Study, institutionally sponsored loans, and career-related internships or fieldwork also available. Financial aid application deadline: 9/1; applicants required to submit FAFSA. *Faculty research:* Integrating math, science and technology; creating gender equitable learning environments; technology design for elementary education. Total annual research expenditures: $10,000. • Janice Koch, Co-Coordinator, 516-463-5777. Application contact: Mary Beth Carey, Dean of Admissions, 516-463-6700. Fax: 516-560-7660. E-mail: hofstra@hofstra.edu.

Hood College, Department of Education, Frederick, MD 21701-8575. Offerings include curriculum and instruction (MS), with options in early childhood education, elementary education, elementary school science and mathematics, reading, secondary education, special education. *Entrance requirements:* Minimum GPA of 2.5. Application deadline: rolling. Application fee: $30. *Tuition:* $285 per credit. • Dr. Patricia Bartlett, Chairperson, 301-696-3471. E-mail: bartlett@nimue.hood.edu. Application contact: Hood College Graduate School, 301-696-3600. Fax: 301-696-3597. E-mail: postmaster@nimue.hood.edu.

Hunter College of the City University of New York, Division of Education, Secondary Education Curriculum, Concentration in Biology and General Science Education, 695 Park Avenue, New York, NY 10021-5085. Awards MA. *Degree requirements:* Comprehensive exam required, foreign language not required. *Entrance requirements:* TOEFL (minimum score 575). Application deadline: rolling. Application fee: $40. *Expenses:* Tuition $4350 per year full-time, $185 per credit part-time for state residents; $7600 per year full-time, $320 per credit part-time for nonresidents. Fees $26 per year.

ICR Graduate School, Graduate Programs, Santee, CA 92071. Offerings include science education (MS). Faculty: 7 full-time (0 women), 8 part-time (0 women), 10.2 FTE. *Degree requirements:* Thesis required (for some programs), foreign language not required. *Average time to degree:* master's–3 years full-time, 5 years part-time. *Application deadline:* rolling. *Application fee:* $30. *Tuition:* $150 per unit. • Kenneth B. Cumming, Dean, 619-448-0900. Application contact: Dr. Jack Kriege, Registrar, 619-448-0900. Fax: 619-448-3469.

Indiana State University, College of Arts and Sciences, Department of Science Education, Terre Haute, IN 47809-1401. Awards MA, MS. Accredited by NCATE. Faculty: 3 full-time (1 woman). Students: 1 full-time (0 women), 2 part-time (both women). Average age 29. 1 applicant, 100% accepted. In 1997, 2 degrees awarded. *Application deadline:* rolling. *Application fee:* $20. *Tuition:* $143 per credit hour for state residents; $325 per credit hour for nonresidents. *Financial aid:* Teaching assistantships available. Financial aid application deadline: 3/1. • Dr. Charlotte Boener, Chairperson, 812-237-3311.

Indiana University Bloomington, College of Arts and Sciences, Department of Biology, Bloomington, IN 47405. Offerings include biology education (MAT). Department faculty: 20 full-time (5 women). *Application deadline:* 1/15 (priority date; 9/1 for spring admission). *Application fee:* $35. *Expenses:* Tuition $153 per credit hour for state residents; $446 per credit hour for nonresidents. Fees $343 per year. • Dr. Jeffrey D. Palmer, Chair, 812-855-6283. Application contact: Gretchen Clearwater, Administrative Assistant for Graduate Affairs, 812-855-1861. E-mail: gclearwa@ucs.indiana.edu.

Indiana University of Pennsylvania, College of Education, Department of Professional Studies in Education, Indiana, PA 15705-1087. Offerings include elementary science (M Ed). Accredited by NCATE. *Degree requirements:* Thesis optional, foreign language not required. *Entrance requirements:* TOEFL (minimum score 500). Application deadline: 7/1 (priority date; rolling processing; 11/1 for spring admission). Application fee: $30. *Expenses:* Tuition $3468 per year full-time, $193 per credit part-time for state residents; $6236 per year full-time, $346 per credit part-time for nonresidents. Fees $313 per year (minimum) full-time, $84 per year part-time. • Dr. Edwina Vold, Chairperson, 724-357-2400. E-mail: ebvold@grove.iup.edu. Application contact: Dr. Gail Gerlach, Assistant Chair, 724-357-2400. E-mail: ggerlach@grove.iup.edu.

Instituto Tecnológico y de Estudios Superiores de Monterrey, Program in Natural and Social Sciences, Monterrey, Nuevo León 64849, Mexico. Offerings include education (MA). *Application deadline:* 4/30 (priority date).

Inter American University of Puerto Rico, Metropolitan Campus, Division of Education, Program in Teaching of Science, San Juan, PR 00919-1293. Awards MA Ed. *Degree requirements:* Comprehensive exam. *Entrance requirements:* GRE or PAEG, interview. Application deadline: 5/15 (priority date; rolling processing; 11/15 for spring admission). Application fee: $31. Electronic applications accepted. *Expenses:* Tuition $3272 per year full-time, $1740 per year part-time. Fees $328 per year full-time, $176 per year part-time. • Application contact: Jenny Maldonado, Administrative Assistant, 787-250-1912 Ext. 2393. Fax: 787-250-1197.

Inter American University of Puerto Rico, San Germán Campus, Department of Education, Program in Science Education, San Germán, PR 00683-5008. Awards MA. Part-time and evening/weekend programs available. Faculty: 8 full-time (1 woman), 13 part-time (7 women). In 1997, 9 degrees awarded. *Degree requirements:* Comprehensive exam required, foreign language and thesis not required. *Entrance requirements:* Minimum GPA of 3.0, GRE General Test, or PAEG. Application deadline: 4/30 (priority date; rolling processing; 11/15 for spring admission). Application fee: $31. *Expenses:* Tuition $150 per credit. Fees $177 per semester. *Financial aid:* Teaching assistantships available. • Application contact: Mildred Camacho, Admissions Director, 787-892-3090. Fax: 787-892-6350.

Iona College, School of Arts and Science, Program in Elementary School Science, 715 North Avenue, New Rochelle, NY 10801-1890. Awards MS Ed. Part-time and evening/weekend programs available. Faculty: 2 full-time (1 woman), 6 part-time (3 women). Students: 11 part-time (9 women). Average age 24. In 1997, 10 degrees awarded. *Entrance requirements:* New York teaching certificate. Application deadline: rolling. Application fee: $25. *Expenses:* Tuition $455 per credit hour. Fees $25 per semester. *Financial aid:* Graduate assistantships, partial tuition waivers available. Aid available to part-time students. *Faculty research:* Reading/writing assessment, multicultural education, administration, technology and education. • Dr. Lucy Murphy, Chair, 914-633-2210. Fax: 914-633-2608. Application contact: Arlene Melillo, Director of Graduate Recruitment, 914-633-2328. Fax: 914-633-2023.

Iona College, School of Arts and Science, Program in Secondary School Subjects, 715 North Avenue, New Rochelle, NY 10801-1890. Offerings include biology education (MS Ed, MST). Program faculty: 4 full-time (1 woman), 8 part-time (2 women). *Degree requirements:* Thesis or alternative required, foreign language not required. *Entrance requirements:* Minimum GPA of 2.5 (MST), New York teaching certificate (MS Ed). Application deadline: rolling. Application fee: $25. *Expenses:* Tuition $455 per credit hour. Fees $25 per semester. • Dr. Lucy Murphy, Chair, 914-633-2210. Fax: 914-633-2608. Application contact: Arlene Melillo, Director of Graduate Recruitment, 914-633-2328. Fax: 914-633-2023.

Directory: Science Education

Jackson State University, School of Science and Technology, Department of Biology, Jackson, MS 39217. Offerings include biology education (MST). Department faculty: 9 full-time (1 woman), 2 part-time (1 woman). *Application deadline:* 3/1 (priority date; rolling processing; 10/1 for spring admission). *Application fee:* $20. *Tuition:* $2688 per year (minimum) full-time, $150 per semester hour part-time for state residents; $5546 per year (minimum) full-time, $309 per semester hour part-time for nonresidents. • Dr. Mark Hardy, Acting Chair, 601-968-2586. Fax: 601-974-5853. E-mail: mhardy@ccaix.jsums.edu. Application contact: Mae Robinson, Admissions Coordinator, 601-968-2455. Fax: 601-968-8246. E-mail: mrobinson@ccaix.jsums.edu.

Jackson State University, School of Science and Technology, Department of Physics, Atmospheric Sciences, and General Science, Jackson, MS 39217. Offers program in science education (MST). Part-time and evening/weekend programs available. Faculty: 2 full-time (0 women). Students: 2 part-time (0 women); includes 1 minority (African American). 5 applicants, 60% accepted. In 1997, 4 degrees awarded. *Degree requirements:* Comprehensive exam. *Entrance requirements:* GRE General Test (minimum combined score of 1000), TOEFL (minimum score 550). Application deadline: 3/1 (priority date; rolling processing; 10/1 for spring admission). Application fee: $20. *Tuition:* $2688 per year (minimum) full-time, $150 per semester hour part-time for state residents; $5546 per year (minimum) full-time, $309 per semester hour part-time for nonresidents. *Financial aid:* Application deadline 3/1. • Dr. Kunal Ghosh, Chair, 601-968-7012. Fax: 601-973-3630. E-mail: kghosh@ccaix.jsums.edu. Application contact: Mae Robinson, Admissions Coordinator, 601-968-2455. Fax: 601-968-8246. E-mail: mrobinson@ccaix.jsums.edu.

Kean University, School of Education, Department of Instruction, Curriculum and Administration, Instruction and Curriculum Program, Union, NJ 07083. Offerings include earth science (MA), mathematics/science/computer education (MA). One or more programs accredited by NCATE. *Degree requirements:* Thesis, comprehensive exams required, foreign language not required. *Entrance requirements:* GRE General Test or MAT. Application deadline: 6/15 (rolling processing; 11/15 for spring admission). Application fee: $35. *Tuition:* $5926 per year full-time, $248 per credit part-time for state residents; $7312 per year full-time, $304 per credit part-time for nonresidents. • Dr. Janet Prince, Coordinator, 908-527-2525. Application contact: Joanne Morris, Director of Graduate Admissions, 908-527-2665. Fax: 908-527-2286. E-mail: grad_adm@turbo.kean.edu.

Kutztown University of Pennsylvania, Graduate School, College of Education, Program in Secondary Education, Kutztown, PA 19530. Offerings include biology (M Ed). Accredited by NCATE. Program faculty: 7 full-time (1 woman). *Degree requirements:* Comprehensive exam required, thesis optional, foreign language not required. *Entrance requirements:* GRE General Test, TOEFL, TSE. Application deadline: 3/1 (8/1 for spring admission). Application fee: $25. *Tuition:* $4111 per year full-time, $225 per credit hour part-time for state residents; $6879 per year full-time, $393 per credit hour part-time for nonresidents. • Kathleen Dolgos, Chairperson, 610-683-4259.

Lander University, School of Education, Greenwood, SC 29649-2099. Offerings include science (MAT). School faculty: 9 full-time (5 women). *Application deadline:* rolling. *Application fee:* $25. *Tuition:* $3700 per year full-time, $148 per semester hour part-time for state residents; $6326 per year full-time, $253 per semester hour part-time for nonresidents. • Dr. Phil Bennett, Dean, 864-388-8225.

La Roche College, Program in Science Education, Pittsburgh, PA 15237-5898. Awards MS. Admissions temporarily suspended. Part-time and evening/weekend programs available. Faculty: 1 full-time (0 women), 2 part-time (0 women). Students: 1 (woman) part-time. Average age 47. *Tuition:* $385 per credit. • Roland Gagne, Director, Graduate Studies, 412-536-1260. Fax: 412-536-1283.

Lawrence Technological University, College of Arts and Sciences, 21000 West Ten Mile Road, Southfield, MI 48075-1058. Offers program in science education (MSE). Part-time and evening/weekend programs available. Faculty: 2 full-time (1 woman), 2 part-time (0 women), 3 FTE. Students: 15 part-time (12 women); includes 2 minority (1 African American, 1 Hispanic). Average age 36. 15 applicants, 67% accepted. *Application deadline:* 8/1 (priority date; rolling processing; 1/1 for spring admission). *Application fee:* $50. Electronic applications accepted. *Expenses:* Tuition $11,400 per year full-time, $380 per credit hour part-time. Fees $100 per year. • Dr. James Rodgers, Dean, 248-204-3500. E-mail: scidean@ltu.edu. Application contact: Paul Kinder, Director of Admissions, 248-204-3160. Fax: 248-204-3188. E-mail: admissions@ltu.edu.

Lehman College of the City University of New York, Division of Education, Department of Secondary, Adult and Business Education, Program in Science Education, 250 Bedford Park Boulevard West, Bronx, NY 10468-1589. Awards MS Ed. Students: 2 full-time (both women), 31 part-time (16 women). *Application deadline:* 4/1 (rolling processing; 11/1 for spring admission). *Application fee:* $40. *Expenses:* Tuition $4350 per year full-time, $185 per credit part-time for state residents; $7600 per year full-time, $320 per credit part-time for nonresidents. Fees $120 per year full-time, $80 per year part-time. *Financial aid:* Full and partial tuition waivers, Federal Work-Study available. Aid available to part-time students. Financial aid application deadline: 5/15; applicants required to submit FAFSA. • Ronald Ellis, Adviser, 718-960-8171.

Long Island University, C.W. Post Campus, School of Education, Department of Curriculum and Instruction, Brookville, NY 11548-1300. Offerings include biology education (MS), earth science (MS). Department faculty: 10 full-time (5 women), 46 part-time (19 women). *Application deadline:* rolling. *Application fee:* $30. Electronic applications accepted. *Expenses:* Tuition $480 per credit. Fees $316 per year full-time, $71 per semester (minimum) part-time. • Dr. Anthony De Falco, Chairperson, 516-299-2372. Application contact: Camille Marziliano, Academic Counselor, 516-299-2123. Fax: 516-299-4167. E-mail: cmarzili@eagle.liunet.edu.

Louisiana State University in Shreveport, College of Sciences, Shreveport, LA 71115-2399. Offerings include teaching (MST). College faculty: 22 full-time (4 women). *Average time to degree:* master's–2.5 years part-time. *Application deadline:* 8/5 (priority date; rolling processing; 12/15 for spring admission). *Application fee:* $10. • Dr. Alfred McKinney, Dean, 318-797-5231.

Louisiana Tech University, College of Education, Department of Curriculum, Instruction and Leadership, Ruston, LA 71272. Offerings include secondary education (M Ed), with options in business education, English education, foreign language education, health and physical education, mathematics education, science education, social studies education, speech education. Accredited by NCATE. Department faculty: 16 full-time (11 women). *Application deadline:* 7/29 (2/3 for spring admission). *Application fee:* $20 ($30 for international students). *Tuition:* $2382 per year full-time, $223 per quarter (minimum) part-time for state residents; $5307 per year full-time, $223 per quarter (minimum) part-time for nonresidents. • Dr. Samuel V. Dauzat, Head, 318-257-4609.

Loyola Marymount University, School of Education, Program in Teaching, Los Angeles, CA 90045-8350. Offerings include biology education (MAT). Program faculty: 14 full-time (8 women), 25 part-time (20 women). *Degree requirements:* Thesis or alternative, comprehensive exam required, foreign language not required. *Entrance requirements:* GRE General Test, TOEFL (minimum score 550), interview. Application fee: $35. Electronic applications accepted. *Expenses:* Tuition $500 per unit. Fees $111 per year full-time, $28 per year part-time. • Coordinator, 310-338-7307.

Lyndon State College, Graduate Programs in Education, Department of Natural Sciences, Lyndonville, VT 05851. Offers program in science education (MST). Part-time programs available. Faculty: 4 full-time (0 women), 2 part-time (both women). Average age 35. 1 applicant, 100% accepted. In 1997, 1 degree awarded (100% found work related to degree). *Degree requirements:* Exam or major field project required, foreign language and thesis not required. *Average time to degree:* master's–5 years part-time. *Entrance requirements:* GRE General Test or MAT, teaching certificate or 1 year of teaching experience. Application deadline: 2/28 (priority date; 10/31 for spring admission). Application fee: $30. *Expenses:* Tuition $3924 per year full-time, $164 per credit part-time for state residents; $9192 per year full-time, $383 per credit part-time for nonresidents. Fees $632 per year. *Faculty research:* Fern genetics, comparative butterfly research. • Dr. Metin Yersel, Chair. E-mail: yerselm@queen.lsc.vsc.edu. Application contact: Elaine L. Turner, Administrative Secretary, 802-626-6497. Fax: 802-626-9770. E-mail: turnere@king.lsc.vsc.edu.

Manhattanville College, School of Education, Program in Secondary Education, Purchase, NY 10577-2132. Offerings include science (MAT), with options in biology, chemistry. *Degree requirements:* Thesis, comprehensive exam or research project required, foreign language not required. *Entrance requirements:* Minimum undergraduate GPA of 3.0. Application deadline: rolling. Application fee: $40. *Expenses:* Tuition $410 per credit (minimum). Fees $25 per semester. • Application contact: Carol Messar, Director of Admissions, 914-323-5142. Fax: 914-323-5493.

Maryville University of Saint Louis, School of Education, St. Louis, MO 63141-7299. Offerings include environmental education (MA). Accredited by NCATE. School faculty: 9 full-time (7 women), 15 part-time (9 women). *Degree requirements:* Thesis, project required, foreign language not required. *Average time to degree:* master's–2 years full-time, 4 years part-time. *Entrance requirements:* Minimum GPA of 3.0. Application deadline: rolling. Application fee: $20. Electronic applications accepted. *Expenses:* Tuition $11,480 per year full-time, $345 per credit hour part-time. Fees $120 per year full-time, $60 per year part-time. • Dr. Kathe Rasch, Dean, 314-529-9466. Fax: 314-529-9921. E-mail: krasch@maryville.edu.

McNeese State University, College of Education, Department of Curriculum and Instruction, Program in Secondary Education, Lake Charles, LA 70609-2495. Offerings include biology education (M Ed). Program faculty: 8 full-time (3 women). *Entrance requirements:* GRE General Test, teaching certificate. Application deadline: 7/15 (priority date; rolling processing). Application fee: $10 ($25 for international students). *Tuition:* $2118 per year full-time, $344 per semester (minimum) part-time for state residents; $7308 per year full-time, $344 per semester (minimum) part-time for nonresidents. • Dr. Everett Waddell Burge, Head, Department of Curriculum and Instruction, 318-475-5404.

Mercer University, School of Education, 1400 Coleman Avenue, Macon, GA 31207-0003. Offerings include science education (M Ed). School faculty: 11 full-time (5 women), 17 part-time (11 women). *Degree requirements:* Research project report required, foreign language and thesis not required. *Entrance requirements:* GRE, MAT, NTE, minimum GPA of 2.75. Application deadline: 8/1 (priority date; rolling processing; 12/1 for spring admission). Application fee: $25. *Tuition:* $180 per credit hour. • Dr. Anne Hathaway, Dean, 912-752-5397. Fax: 912-752-2280. E-mail: hathaway_ha@mercer.edu. Application contact: Dr. Louis Gallien, Chair, Department of Teacher Education, 912-752-2585. Fax: 912-752-2576. E-mail: gallien_lb@mercer.edu.

Michigan State University, College of Natural Science, Department of Chemistry, East Lansing, MI 48824-1020. Offerings include chemistry (MAT). Department faculty: 34 full-time (3 women). *Application deadline:* rolling. *Application fee:* $30 ($40 for international students). *Expenses:* Tuition $4609 per year full-time, $223 per credit hour (minimum) part-time for state residents; $8704 per year full-time, $450 per credit hour (minimum) part-time for nonresidents. Fees $576 per year full-time, $476 per year part-time. • Dr. Gerald Babcock, Chairperson, 517-355-9715 Ext. 346. Application contact: Dr. Richard Schwendeman, Associate Chair, Graduate Program, 517-355-9715 Ext. 344. Fax: 517-353-1793. E-mail: grad@arnou.cem.msu.edu.

Michigan State University, College of Natural Science, Department of Physics and Astronomy, East Lansing, MI 48824-1020. Offerings include physics (MAT, MS, PhD). Terminal master's awarded for partial completion of doctoral program. Department faculty: 56 (3 women). *Degree requirements:* For master's, thesis or alternative required, foreign language not required; for doctorate, dissertation required, foreign language not required. *Application deadline:* 3/15 (rolling processing). *Application fee:* $30 ($40 for international students). *Expenses:* Tuition $4609 per year full-time, $223 per credit hour (minimum) part-time for state residents; $8704 per year full-time, $450 per credit hour (minimum) part-time for nonresidents. Fees $576 per year full-time, $476 per year part-time. • Dr. Raymond Brock, Chairperson, 517-353-8662.

Middle Tennessee State University, College of Basic and Applied Sciences, Department of Aerospace, Murfreesboro, TN 37132. Offerings include aerospace education (M Ed). Accredited by NCATE. Department faculty: 3 full-time (0 women), 2 part-time (0 women). *Application deadline:* 8/1 (priority date). *Application fee:* $5. *Expenses:* Tuition $2560 per year full-time, $129 per semester hour part-time for state residents; $7386 per year full-time, $340 per semester hour part-time for nonresidents. Fees $486 per year full-time, $17 per semester (minimum) part-time. • Ronald J. Ferrara, Chair, 615-898-3515. E-mail: rferrara@frank.mtsu.edu.

Mills College, Education Department, Oakland, CA 94613-1000. Offerings include education (MA), with options in curriculum and instruction, elementary education, English education, mathematics education, science education, secondary education, social sciences education, teaching. Department faculty: 8 full-time (6 women), 13 part-time (11 women), 11 FTE. *Degree requirements:* Comprehensive exam required, thesis not required. *Average time to degree:* master's–2 years full-time. *Entrance requirements:* TOEFL (minimum score 550). Application deadline: 2/1 (priority date; rolling processing; 11/1 for spring admission). Application fee: $50. Electronic applications accepted. *Expenses:* Tuition $10,600 per year full-time, $2560 per year part-time. Fees $468 per year. • Jane Bowyer, Chairperson, 510-430-2118. Fax: 510-430-3314. E-mail: grad-studies@mills.edu. Application contact: La Vonna S. Brown, Coordinator of Graduate Studies, 510-430-3309. Fax: 510-430-2159. E-mail: grad-studies@mills.edu.

Minot State University, Program in Biological and Agricultural Sciences, Minot, ND 58707-0002. Offers science (MAT). Faculty: 9 full-time (2 women). Students: 0. In 1997, 3 degrees awarded. *Degree requirements:* Thesis required, foreign language not required. *Entrance requirements:* Minimum GPA of 3.0 or GRE General Test (minimum combined score of 1100), secondary teaching certificate. Application deadline: rolling. Application fee: $25. *Tuition:* $2714 per year for state residents; $3235 per year (minimum) for nonresidents. *Financial aid:* Research assistantships, teaching assistantships, institutionally sponsored loans, and career-related internships or fieldwork available. Financial aid application deadline: 4/1. • Dr. Randolph Rodewald, Chairperson, 701-858-3066. Fax: 701-858-3163. E-mail: rodewald@warple.cs.misu.nodak.edu. Application contact: Tammy White, Administrative Secretary, 701-858-3250. Fax: 701-839-6933.

Mississippi College, School of Education, Programs in Secondary Education, Program in Biology Education, Clinton, MS 39058. Awards M Ed. Accredited by NCATE. *Degree requirements:* Comprehensive exam required, foreign language and thesis not required. *Entrance requirements:* GRE or NTE, minimum GPA of 2.5, Class A Certificate. Application deadline: 8/15 (priority date; rolling processing). Application fee: $25 ($75 for international students). *Expenses:* Tuition $6624 per year full-time, $276 per hour part-time. Fees $230 per year full-time, $35 per semester (minimum) part-time. *Financial aid:* Application deadline 4/1. • Dr. Thomas Taylor, Dean, School of Education, 601-925-3402.

Mississippi College, School of Education, Programs in Secondary Education, Program in Sciences Education, Clinton, MS 39058. Awards M Ed. Accredited by NCATE. *Degree requirements:* Comprehensive exam required, foreign language and thesis not required. *Entrance requirements:* GRE or NTE, minimum GPA of 2.5, Class A Certificate. Application deadline: 8/15 (priority date; rolling processing). Application fee: $25 ($75 for international students). *Expenses:* Tuition $6624 per year full-time, $276 per hour part-time. Fees $230 per year full-time, $35 per semester (minimum) part-time. *Financial aid:* Application deadline 4/1. • Dr. Thomas Taylor, Dean, School of Education, 601-925-3402.

Montana State University–Northern, Option in General Science, Havre, MT 59501-7751. Awards M Ed. Students: 8 full-time (3 women), 10 part-time (4 women); includes 1 minority (Native American). Average age 38. *Degree requirements:* Comprehensive and oral exams required, thesis optional, foreign language not required. *Entrance requirements:* GRE General Test, minimum GPA of 3.0. Application deadline: 9/20 (priority date; rolling processing). Application fee: $30. *Tuition:* $3090 per year full-time, $696 per semester (minimum) part-time for state residents; $8044 per year full-time, $1758 per semester (minimum) part-time for nonresidents. *Financial aid:* Teaching assistantships, Federal Work-Study, institutionally sponsored loans available. Aid available to part-time students. Financial aid application deadline: 4/1. • Dr. Ben Johnson, Director of Education and Graduate Programs, Department of Education, 406-265-3738. Fax: 406-265-3570. E-mail: johnson@nmcl.nmclites.edu.

Montclair State University, College of Science and Mathematics, Department of Earth and Environmental Studies, Upper Montclair, NJ 07043-1624. Offerings include environmental studies (MS), with options in environmental education, environmental health, environmental management, environmental science. Department faculty: 11 full-time. *Degree requirements:* Comprehensive exam required, foreign language not required. *Entrance requirements:* GRE General Test. Application deadline: 4/1 (rolling processing; 11/1 for spring admission). Application fee: $40. *Expenses:* Tuition $201 per credit for state residents; $257 per credit for nonresidents. Fees $22.05 per credit. • Dr. Jonathan Lincoln, Chairperson, 973-655-4448.

National–Louis University, National College of Education, McGaw Graduate School, Program in Science Education, 2840 Sheridan Road, Evanston, IL 60201-1730. Awards M Ed, MS Ed, CAS. Part-time and evening/weekend programs available. Students: 1 (woman) full-time, 21 part-time (20 women); includes 5 minority (all African Americans). Average age 37. In 1997, 6 master's, 1 CAS awarded. *Degree requirements:* For master's, thesis required (for some programs), foreign language not required. *Entrance requirements:* For master's, MAT, minimum GPA of 3.0. Application deadline: rolling. Application fee: $25. *Tuition:* $411 per semester hour. *Financial aid:* Fellowships available. Aid available to part-time students. Financial aid applicants required to submit FAFSA. • Dr. Vito Dipinto, Coordinator, 847-475-1100 Ext. 2559. Application contact: Dr. David McCulloch, Vice President for University Services, 800-443-5522 Ext. 5127. Fax: 847-465-0593. E-mail: dmcc@wheeling1.nl.edu.

New Mexico Institute of Mining and Technology, Program in Science Teaching, Socorro, NM 87801. Awards MST. Faculty: 9 full-time (1 woman). Students: 14. 28 applicants, 64% accepted. In 1997, 7 degrees awarded. *Degree requirements:* Thesis optional, foreign language not required. *Entrance requirements:* GRE General Test, TOEFL (minimum score 540). Application deadline: 3/1 (priority date; rolling processing; 6/1 for spring admission). Application fee: $16. *Expenses:* Tuition $1612 per year full-time, $90 per hour part-time for state residents; $6646 per year full-time, $369 per hour part-time for nonresidents. Fees $911 per year. *Financial aid:* Federal Work-Study, institutionally sponsored loans available. Financial aid application deadline: 3/1; applicants required to submit CSS PROFILE or FAFSA. *Faculty research:* Teaching secondary school science and/or mathematics. • Dr. Vannetta Perry, Coordinator, 505-835-5678. Fax: 505-835-5274. E-mail: science@nmt.edu. Application contact: Dr. David Johnson, Dean of Graduate Studies, 505-835-5513. Fax: 505-835-5476. E-mail: djohnson@nmt.edu.

New York University, School of Education, Department of Culture and Communication, Program in Environmental Conservation Education, New York, NY 10012-1019. Awards MA. Part-time and evening/weekend programs available. Faculty: 2 full-time (0 women), 1 part-time. Students: 6 full-time, 17 part-time. 13 applicants, 92% accepted. In 1997, 9 degrees awarded. *Degree requirements:* Thesis required (for some programs), foreign language not required. *Entrance requirements:* TOEFL. Application deadline: 2/1 (priority date; rolling processing; 12/1 for spring admission). Application fee: $40 ($60 for international students). *Financial aid:* Partial tuition waivers, Federal Work-Study, institutionally sponsored loans, and career-related internships or fieldwork available. Aid available to part-time students. Financial aid application deadline: 3/1; applicants required to submit FAFSA. • Dr. Thomas Colwell, Co-Director, 212-998-5637. Application contact: Office of Graduate Admissions, 212-998-5030. Fax: 212-995-4328.

New York University, School of Education, Department of Teaching and Learning, Program in Science Education, New York, NY 10012-1019. Awards MA. Part-time and evening/weekend programs available. Faculty: 3 full-time (1 woman). Students: 8 full-time, 16 part-time. 27 applicants, 70% accepted. In 1997, 12 degrees awarded. *Degree requirements:* Thesis required (for some programs), foreign language not required. *Entrance requirements:* TOEFL. Application deadline: 2/1 (priority date; rolling processing; 12/1 for spring admission). Application fee: $40 ($60 for international students). *Financial aid:* Partial tuition waivers, Federal Work-Study, institutionally sponsored loans, and career-related internships or fieldwork available. Aid available to part-time students. Financial aid application deadline: 3/1; applicants required to submit FAFSA. *Faculty research:* Science curriculum development, gender and ethnicity, technology use. • Pamela Fraser-Abder, Director, 212-998-5200. Application contact: Office of Graduate Admissions, 212-998-5030. Fax: 212-995-4328.

Niagara University, Graduate Division of Education, Niagara University, NY 14109. Offerings include biology (MAT). Accredited by NCATE. Division faculty: 10 full-time (2 women), 18 part-time (8 women). *Application deadline:* 8/1 (rolling processing). *Application fee:* $30. *Expenses:* Tuition $4950 per year full-time, $275 per credit hour part-time. Fees $25 per semester. • Rev. Daniel F. O'Leary, OMI, Dean, 716-286-8560.

North Carolina Agricultural and Technical State University, Graduate School, School of Education, Department of Curriculum and Instruction, Program in Intermediate Education, Greensboro, NC 27411. Offerings include biology education (MS), chemistry education (MS). One or more programs accredited by NCATE. *Degree requirements:* Thesis (for some programs), comprehensive exam, qualifying exam required, foreign language not required. *Entrance requirements:* GRE General Test, minimum GPA of 3.0. Application deadline: 6/1 (priority date; rolling processing; 12/1 for spring admission). Application fee: $35. *Tuition:* $1662 per year full-time, $272 per semester (minimum) part-time for state residents; $8790 per year full-time, $2054 per semester (minimum) part-time for nonresidents. • Dr. Dorothy Leflore, Interim Chairperson, Department of Curriculum and Instruction, 336-334-7848.

North Carolina State University, College of Education and Psychology, Department of Mathematics, Science, and Technology Education, Program in Science Education, Raleigh, NC 27695. Awards M Ed, MS, PhD. Accredited by NCATE. Part-time programs available. Faculty: 11 full-time (5 women), 3 part-time (1 woman). Students: 9 full-time (7 women), 20 part-time (15 women); includes 3 minority (2 African Americans, 1 Hispanic). Average age 36. 12 applicants, 50% accepted. In 1997, 4 master's awarded. *Degree requirements:* For master's, thesis (for some programs), oral exam required, foreign language not required; for doctorate, 1 foreign language, dissertation, oral and written exams. *Entrance requirements:* For master's, GRE General Test or MAT, minimum GPA of 3.0; for doctorate, GRE General Test or MAT, minimum GPA of 3.0, interview. Application deadline: 4/15 (priority date; rolling processing; 11/15 for spring admission). Application fee: $45. *Tuition:* $2370 per year full-time, $517 per semester (minimum) part-time for state residents; $11,536 per year full-time, $2809 per semester (minimum) part-time for nonresidents. *Financial aid:* Fellowships, research assistantships, teaching assistantships, Federal Work-Study, institutionally sponsored loans, and career-related internships or fieldwork available. *Faculty research:* Leadership, creative problem solving, student evaluation, planning of change, technological problem solving. • Dr. Susan L. Westbrook, Director of Graduate Programs, 919-515-4053. E-mail: westbrk@poe.coe.ncsu.edu. Application contact: Linda Trogdon, Graduate Secretary, 919-515-1740. Fax: 919-515-1063. E-mail: trogdon@poe.coe.ncsu.edu.

Northeastern University, Graduate School of Arts and Sciences, Department of Biology, Boston, MA 02115-5096. Offerings include biology education (MAT). Department faculty: 23 full-time (7 women), 4 part-time (2 women). *Application deadline:* 2/1 (priority date). *Application fee:* $50. *Expenses:* Tuition $440 per credit hour. Fees $55 per quarter full-time, $13.25 per quarter part-time. • Dr. Edward Jarroll, Chairman, 617-373-2260. Application contact: Florence Lewis, Graduate Secretary, 617-373-2262. Fax: 617-373-3724. E-mail: f.lewis@nunet.neu.edu.

Northeastern University, Graduate School of Arts and Sciences, Department of Chemistry, Boston, MA 02115-5096. Offerings include chemistry (MAT, MS, PhD). Terminal master's awarded for partial completion of doctoral program. Department faculty: 19 full-time (3 women), 1 part-time (0 women), 20 FTE. *Degree requirements:* For master's, thesis (for some programs); for doctorate, dissertation, qualifying exam in specialty area required, foreign language not required. *Average time to degree:* master's–2 years full-time; doctorate–5 years full-time. *Entrance requirements:* TOEFL (minimum score 580). Application deadline: 4/15 (rolling processing). Application fee: $50. *Expenses:* Tuition $440 per credit hour. Fees $55 per quarter full-time, $13.25 per quarter part-time. • Dr. John Roebber, Executive Officer, 617-373-2383. Fax: 617-373-8795. E-mail: chemistry-grad-info@neu.edu. Application contact: Dr. David A. Forsyth, Chair, Graduate Admissions Committee, 617-373-2822.

Northern Arizona University, College of Arts and Sciences, Department of Biological Sciences, Flagstaff, AZ 86011. Offerings include biology education (MAT). Department faculty: 40 full-time (10 women), 21 part-time (7 women). *Application deadline:* 2/15. *Application fee:* $45. *Expenses:* Tuition $2088 per year full-time, $330 per semester (minimum) part-time for state residents; $8004 per year full-time, $1002 per semester (minimum) part-time for nonresidents. Fees $72 per year full-time, $18 per semester (minimum) part-time. • Dr. William Gaud, Chairman, 520-523-2381.

Northern Arizona University, College of Arts and Sciences, Department of Physics and Astronomy, Flagstaff, AZ 86011. Offers program in physical science (MAT). Part-time programs available. Faculty: 14 full-time (2 women), 11 part-time (5 women). Students: 4 full-time (2 women), 3 part-time (2 women); includes 1 minority (Asian American). 1 applicant, 100% accepted. In 1997, 2 degrees awarded. *Application deadline:* 3/15 (priority date; rolling processing). *Application fee:* $45. *Expenses:* Tuition $2088 per year full-time, $330 per semester (minimum) part-time for state residents; $8004 per year full-time, $1002 per semester (minimum) part-time for nonresidents. Fees $72 per year full-time, $18 per semester (minimum) part-time. *Financial aid:* Federal Work-Study available. • Dr. Barry Lutz, Chair, 520-523-9117. Application contact: Dr. Dan MacIsaac, Graduate Coordinator, 520-523-5921.

Northern Michigan University, College of Arts and Sciences, Glenn T. Seaborg Center, Marquette, MI 49855-5301. Offers programs in mathematics education (MS), science education (MS). Offered during summer only. Students: 24 part-time (12 women). In 1997, 1 degree awarded. *Entrance requirements:* Minimum GPA of 2.7 in major. Application deadline: 7/1 (priority date; rolling processing; 11/1 for spring admission). Application fee: $25. *Expenses:* Tuition $135 per credit hour for state residents; $215 per credit hour for nonresidents. Fees $183 per year full-time, $94 per year (minimum) part-time. *Financial aid:* Application deadline 3/1. • Dr. Peggy House, Head, 906-227-2002.

North Georgia College & State University, Graduate School, Program in Education, Dahlonega, GA 30597-1001. Offerings include secondary education (M Ed), with options in art education, biology education, chemistry education, English education, mathematics education, modern languages education, physical education, science education, social science education. Accredited by NCATE. Program faculty: 57 full-time (15 women), 7 part-time (4 women). *Degree requirements:* Comprehensive exam required, thesis optional, foreign language not required. *Entrance requirements:* GRE General Test (minimum combined score of 800) or MAT (minimum score 44), minimum GPA of 2.75. Application deadline: 9/1 (priority date; rolling processing). Application fee: $25. • Dr. Bob Michael, Dean, School of Education, 706-864-1533. Application contact: Mai-Lan Ledbetter, Coordinator of Graduate Admissions, 706-864-1543. Fax: 706-864-1668. E-mail: mledbetter@nugget.ngc.peachnet.edu.

Northwestern State University of Louisiana, Division of Education, Natchitoches, LA 71497. Offerings include science education (M Ed). Accredited by NCATE. Division faculty: 10 full-time (7 women), 4 part-time (2 women). *Application deadline:* 8/1 (priority date; rolling processing; 1/10 for spring admission). *Application fee:* $15 ($25 for international students). *Tuition:* $2147 per year full-time, $336 per semester (minimum) part-time for state residents; $6437 per year full-time, $336 per semester (minimum) part-time for nonresidents. • Dr. Sue Weaver, Chair, 318-357-5195. Application contact: Dr. Tom Hanson, Dean, Graduate Studies and Research, 318-357-5851. Fax: 318-357-5019.

Northwest Missouri State University, College of Education and Human Services, Program in Science Education, 800 University Drive, Maryville, MO 64468-6001. Awards MS Ed. Accredited by NCATE. Part-time programs available. Faculty: 8 full-time (2 women). Students: 1 (woman) full-time, 4 part-time (2 women). 2 applicants, 100% accepted. In 1997, 1 degree awarded. *Degree requirements:* Comprehensive exam required, thesis optional, foreign language not required. *Entrance requirements:* GRE General Test (minimum combined score of 700), TOEFL (minimum score 550), minimum GPA of 2.75 in major, 2.5 overall; teaching certificate; writing sample. Application deadline: rolling. Application fee: $0 ($50 for international students). *Expenses:* Tuition $113 per credit hour for state residents; $197 per credit hour for nonresidents. Fees $3 per credit hour. *Financial aid:* In 1997–98, 3 research assistantships averaging $585 per month were awarded; teaching assistantships also available. Financial aid application deadline: 3/1. • Dr. Edward Farquhar, Chairperson, 816-562-1209. Application contact: Dr. Frances Shipley, Dean of Graduate School, 816-562-1145. E-mail: gradsch@acad.nwmissouri.edu.

Nova Southeastern University, Fischler Center for the Advancement of Education, Graduate Teacher Education Program, Fort Lauderdale, FL 33314-7721. Offerings include science (MS, Ed S). *Degree requirements:* Thesis, practicum required, foreign language not required. *Entrance requirements:* For master's, teaching certificate; for Ed S, master's degree, teaching certificate. Application deadline: rolling. Application fee: $50. *Tuition:* $245 per credit hour (minimum). • Dr. Deo Nellis, Dean, 954-262-8601. E-mail: deo@fcae.nova.edu. Application contact: Dr. Mark Seldine, Director of Student Affairs, 954-262-8689. Fax: 954-262-3910. E-mail: seldines@fcae.nova.edu.

Occidental College, Department of Education, Program in Secondary Education, Los Angeles, CA 90041-3392. Offerings include life science (MAT), physical science (MAT). Program faculty: 4 full-time (1 woman). *Degree requirements:* Internship required, foreign language and thesis not required. *Entrance requirements:* GRE General Test (minimum score 550 on each section or combined score of 1650 on three sections), TOEFL (minimum score 600), minimum GPA of 3.0. Application deadline: 3/1 (priority date; rolling processing; 10/1 for spring admission). Application fee: $40. *Expenses:* Tuition $21,256 per year full-time, $865 per unit part-time. Fees $314 per year. • Application contact: Susan Molik, Administrative Assistant, Graduate Office, 213-259-2921.

Oregon State University, Graduate School, College of Science, Department of Science and Mathematics Education, Program in Biology Education, Corvallis, OR 97331. Awards MAT. Accredited by NCATE. Students: 0. Average age 36. *Degree requirements:* Minimum GPA of 3.0. *Entrance requirements:* TOEFL (minimum score 550), minimum GPA of 3.0 in last 90 hours. Application deadline: 1/15. Application fee: $50. *Tuition:* $6207 per year full-time, $810 per quarter (minimum) part-time for state residents; $10,551 per year full-time, $1293 per quarter (minimum) part-time for nonresidents. • Dr. Norm Lederman, Associate Professor, 541-737-4031. Fax: 541-737-1817. E-mail: lederman@ucs.orst.edu.

Oregon State University, Graduate School, College of Science, Department of Science and Mathematics Education, Program in Chemistry Education, Corvallis, OR 97331. Awards MAT. Accredited by NCATE. Students: 0. *Degree requirements:* Minimum GPA of 3.0. *Entrance requirements:* TOEFL (minimum score 550), minimum GPA of 3.0 in last 90 hours. Application deadline: 1/15. Application fee: $50. *Tuition:* $6207 per year full-time, $810 per quarter (minimum) part-time for state residents; $10,551 per year full-time, $1293 per quarter (minimum)

Directory: Science Education

Oregon State University (continued)

part-time for nonresidents. • Dr. Larry Flick, Assistant Professor, 541-737-4031. Fax: 541-737-1817. E-mail: flickl@ucs.orst.edu.

Oregon State University, Graduate School, College of Science, Department of Science and Mathematics Education, Program in Integrated Science Education, Corvallis, OR 97331. Awards MAT. Accredited by NCATE. Students: 7 full-time (2 women), 17 part-time; includes 1 Hispanic. In 1997, 20 degrees awarded. *Degree requirements:* Minimum GPA of 3.0. *Entrance requirements:* TOEFL (minimum score 550), minimum GPA of 3.0 in last 90 hours. Application deadline: 3/1. Application fee: $50. *Tuition:* $6207 per year full-time, $810 per quarter (minimum) part-time for state residents; $10,551 per year full-time, $1293 per quarter (minimum) part-time for nonresidents. *Financial aid:* Application deadline 2/1. • Dr. Margaret L. Niess, Chair, Department of Science and Mathematics Education, 541-737-1818. Fax: 541-737-1817. E-mail: niessm@ucs.orst.edu.

Oregon State University, Graduate School, College of Science, Department of Science and Mathematics Education, Program in Physics Education, Corvallis, OR 97331. Awards MAT. Accredited by NCATE. Part-time programs available. Students: 0. Average age 28. *Degree requirements:* Thesis (for some programs), minimum GPA of 3.0 required, foreign language not required. *Entrance requirements:* TOEFL (minimum score 550), minimum GPA of 3.0 in last 90 hours. Application deadline: 1/15. Application fee: $50. *Tuition:* $6207 per year full-time, $810 per quarter (minimum) part-time for state residents; $10,551 per year full-time, $1293 per quarter (minimum) part-time for nonresidents. *Financial aid:* Application deadline 2/1. • Dr. Larry Flick, Assistant Professor, 541-737-4031. Fax: 541-737-1817. E-mail: flickl@ucs.orst.edu.

Oregon State University, Graduate School, College of Science, Department of Science and Mathematics Education, Program in Science Education, Corvallis, OR 97331. Awards MA, MAT, MS, PhD. Accredited by NCATE. Students: 0. Average age 34. *Degree requirements:* For master's, minimum GPA of 3.0 required, thesis not required; for doctorate, dissertation, minimum GPA of 3.0. *Entrance requirements:* For master's, TOEFL (minimum score 550), minimum GPA of 3.0 in last 90 hours; for doctorate, GRE or MAT, TOEFL (minimum score 550), minimum GPA of 3.0 in last 90 hours. Application deadline: 3/1. Application fee: $50. *Tuition:* $6207 per year full-time, $810 per quarter (minimum) part-time for state residents; $10,551 per year full-time, $1293 per quarter (minimum) part-time for nonresidents. *Financial aid:* Teaching assistantships, Federal Work-Study, institutionally sponsored loans available. Financial aid application deadline: 2/1. *Faculty research:* Teacher thought processes, pedagogical content knowledge and teacher preparation. • Dr. Norman G. Lederman, Associate Professor, 541-737-4031. Fax: 541-737-1817. E-mail: lederman@ucs.orst.edu.

Pennsylvania State University University Park Campus, College of Education, Department of Curriculum and Instruction, University Park, PA 16802-1503. Offerings include science education (M Ed, MS, D Ed, PhD). Accredited by NCATE. *Degree requirements:* For doctorate, dissertation. *Entrance requirements:* GRE General Test or MAT. Application fee: $40. *Expenses:* Tuition $6534 per year full-time, $276 per credit part-time for state residents; $13,460 per year full-time, $561 per credit part-time for nonresidents. Fees $252 per year (minimum) full-time, $43 per semester (minimum) part-time. • Dr. Peter A. Rubb, Head, 814-865-5433.

Plattsburgh State University of New York, Faculty of Professional Studies, Center for Educational Studies and Services, Program in Secondary Education, Plattsburgh, NY 12901-2681. Offerings include biology (MST), earth sciences (MST), physics (MST). *Application deadline:* rolling. *Application fee:* $50. *Expenses:* Tuition $5100 per year full-time, $213 per credit hour part-time for state residents; $8416 per year full-time, $351 per credit hour part-time for nonresidents. Fees $395 per year full-time, $15.10 per credit hour part-time. • Dr. Raymond Domenico, Director and Associate Dean, Center for Educational Studies and Services, 518-564-2122.

Plymouth State College of the University System of New Hampshire, Department of Education, Program in Environmental Science Education, Plymouth, NH 03264-1595. Awards M Ed. Part-time and evening/weekend programs available. Students: 0. 2 applicants, 0% accepted. In 1997, 8 degrees awarded. *Entrance requirements:* GRE General Test (average 500 on each section) or MAT (minimum score 50), minimum GPA of 3.0. Application deadline: 9/1 (priority date; rolling processing). Application fee: $25 ($35 for international students). *Tuition:* $232 per credit for state residents; $254 per credit for nonresidents. *Financial aid:* Graduate assistantships, institutionally sponsored loans, and career-related internships or fieldwork available. Aid available to part-time students. Financial aid application deadline: 3/15; applicants required to submit FAFSA. • Dr. Richard Fralick, Adviser, 603-535-2226. Application contact: Maryann Szabadics, Administrative Assistant, 603-535-2636. Fax: 603-535-2572. E-mail: for.grad@psc.plymouth.edu.

Portland State University, College of Liberal Arts and Sciences, Department of Geology, Portland, OR 97207-0751. Offerings include science/geology (MAT, MST). Department faculty: 7 full-time (0 women), 1 part-time (0 women). *Application deadline:* 4/1 (priority date; rolling processing). *Application fee:* $50. *Tuition:* $6101 per year full-time, $689 per semester (minimum) part-time for state residents; $10,445 per year full-time, $689 per semester (minimum) part-time for nonresidents. • Dr. Ansel Johnson, Head, 503-725-3022. Fax: 503-725-3025. E-mail: ansel@ch1.ch.pdx.edu.

Portland State University, College of Liberal Arts and Sciences, Interdisciplinary Programs in General Science, General Social Science, and General Arts and Letters, Portland, OR 97207-0751. Offerings in general arts and letters education (MAT, MST), general science education (MAT, MST), general social science education (MAT, MST). Part-time and evening/weekend programs available. Faculty: 263 full-time (97 women), 84 part-time (51 women), 278 FTE. Students: 12 full-time (7 women), 11 part-time (5 women); includes 1 international. Average age 32. 17 applicants, 59% accepted. In 1997, 6 degrees awarded. *Degree requirements:* Variable foreign language requirement, written exam. *Entrance requirements:* TOEFL (minimum score 550), minimum GPA of 3.0 in upper-division course work or 2.75 overall. Application deadline: 4/1. Application fee: $50. *Tuition:* $6101 per year full-time, $689 per semester (minimum) part-time for state residents; $10,445 per year full-time, $689 per semester (minimum) part-time for nonresidents. *Financial aid:* Federal Work-Study, institutionally sponsored loans available. Aid available to part-time students. Financial aid application deadline: 3/1; applicants required to submit FAFSA. • Robert Mercer, Senior Academic Adviser, 503-725-3822.

Prescott College, Graduate Programs, Program in Environmental Studies, Prescott, AZ 86301-2990. Offerings include environmental education (MA). MA (environmental education) offered jointly with Teton Science School. Postbaccalaureate distance learning degree programs offered (minimal on-campus study). *Degree requirements:* Thesis, fieldwork or internship, practicum required, foreign language not required. *Application deadline:* 6/1 (11/1 for spring admission). *Application fee:* $40. *Tuition:* $9000 per year. • Joel Barnes, Head, 520-445-8048. Application contact: Joan Clingan, Graduate Director, 520-776-5130. Fax: 520-776-5137. E-mail: mapmail@northlink.com.

Purdue University, School of Education, Department of Curriculum and Instruction, West Lafayette, IN 47907. Offerings include math/science education (Ed S), mathematics/science education (MS Ed, PhD). One or more programs accredited by NCATE. Department faculty: 34 full-time (15 women), 3 part-time (1 woman). *Degree requirements:* For master's, thesis optional; for doctorate, dissertation, oral and written exams; for Ed S, oral presentation, project required, thesis not required. *Entrance requirements:* For master's, TOEFL (minimum score 550), minimum B average; for doctorate, GRE General Test (minimum score 500 on each section), TOEFL (minimum score 550); for Ed S, minimum B average. Application deadline: 1/15 (priority date; 9/15 for spring admission). Application fee: $30. Electronic applications accepted. *Tuition:* $3500 per year full-time, $126 per credit hour part-time for state residents; $11,720 per year full-time, $387 per credit hour part-time for nonresidents. • Dr. J. L. Peters, Head, 765-494-9172. Fax: 765-496-1622. E-mail: peters@purdue.edu. Application contact: Christine Larsen, Coordinator of Graduate Studies, 765-494-2345. Fax: 765-494-5832. E-mail: gradoffice@soe.purdue.edu.

Purdue University, School of Science, Department of Chemistry, West Lafayette, IN 47907. Offerings include chemical education (MS, PhD). One or more programs accredited by NCATE. Terminal master's awarded for partial completion of doctoral program. Department faculty: 46 full-time, 1 part-time. *Degree requirements:* Thesis/dissertation required, foreign language not required. *Entrance requirements:* TOEFL (minimum score 550). Application fee: $30. Electronic applications accepted. *Tuition:* $3500 per year full-time, $126 per credit hour part-time for state residents; $11,720 per year full-time, $387 per credit hour part-time for nonresidents. • Dr. R. A. Walton, Head, 765-494-5203. Application contact: R. E. Wild, Chairman, Graduate Admissions, 765-494-5200. E-mail: wild@chem.purdue.edu.

Queens College of the City University of New York, Social Science Division, School of Education, Department of Secondary Education, 65-30 Kissena Boulevard, Flushing, NY 11367-1597. Offerings include biology (MS Ed, AC), chemistry (MS Ed, AC), earth sciences (MS Ed, AC), physics (MS Ed, AC). *Degree requirements:* For master's, research project required, foreign language and thesis not required; for AC, thesis optional, foreign language not required. *Entrance requirements:* For master's, TOEFL (minimum score 600), minimum GPA of 3.0; for AC, TOEFL (minimum score 600). Application deadline: 4/1 (rolling processing; 11/1 for spring admission). Application fee: $40. *Expenses:* Tuition $4350 per year full-time, $185 per credit part-time for state residents; $7600 per year full-time, $320 per credit part-time for nonresidents. Fees $104 per year. • Dr. Philip Anderson, Chairperson, 718-997-5150. Application contact: Mario Caruso, Director of Graduate Admissions, 718-997-5200. Fax: 718-997-5193. E-mail: graduate%queens.bitnet@cunyvm.cuny.edu.

Quinnipiac College, School of Liberal Arts, Program in Secondary and Middle School Teaching, Hamden, CT 06518-1904. Offerings include biology (MAT), chemistry (MAT), physics (MAT). Program faculty: 21 full-time (5 women), 16 part-time (9 women). *Degree requirements:* Thesis. *Average time to degree:* master's–1.5 years full-time, 3 years part-time. *Entrance requirements:* PRAXIS I, minimum GPA of 2.67. Application deadline: rolling. Application fee: $45. Electronic applications accepted. *Expenses:* Tuition $395 per credit hour. Fees $380 per year full-time. • Carol Orticari, Director, 203-281-8978. Fax: 203-281-8709. E-mail: orticari@quinnipiac.edu. Application contact: Scott Farber, Director of Graduate Admissions, 203-281-8795. Fax: 203-287-5238. E-mail: qcgradadmi@quinnipiac.edu.

Rhode Island College, School of Graduate Studies, Faculty of Arts and Sciences, Department of Physical Science, Providence, RI 02908-1924. Offers programs in general science (MAT), physical science (MAT). Faculty: 13 full-time (2 women), 2 part-time (1 woman). Students: 3 full-time (2 women), 2 part-time (both women). In 1997, 6 degrees awarded. *Application deadline:* 4/1 (rolling processing). *Application fee:* $25. *Tuition:* $4064 per year full-time, $214 per credit part-time for state residents; $7658 per year full-time, $376 per credit part-time for nonresidents. *Financial aid:* Application deadline 4/1. • Dr. David Greene, Chair, 401-456-8049.

Rowan University, School of Liberal Arts and Sciences, Department of Life Sciences, Glassboro, NJ 08028-1701. Offers program in environmental education (MA). Part-time and evening/weekend programs available. Students: 7 (3 women). 3 applicants, 100% accepted. In 1997, 6 degrees awarded. *Degree requirements:* Thesis, comprehensive exam. *Entrance requirements:* GRE General Test (minimum combined score of 950), interview, minimum GPA of 2.8. Application deadline: 11/1 (priority date; rolling processing; 4/1 for spring admission). Application fee: $50. *Tuition:* $5728 per year full-time, $258 per credit hour part-time for state residents; $8968 per year full-time, $393 per credit hour part-time for nonresidents. *Financial aid:* Federal Work-Study and career-related internships or fieldwork available. *Faculty research:* Pinelands ecology. • Dr. Elizabeth Moore, Chair, 609-256-4834. Application contact: Gary Patterson, Adviser, 609-256-4500 Ext. 3587.

Rowan University, College of Education, Department of Secondary Education-Education Foundations, Program in Subject Matter Teaching, Program in Science Education, Glassboro, NJ 08028-1701. Offers biological science education (MA), physical science education (MA). Accredited by NCATE. Students: 3 (all women). 0 applicants. In 1997, 1 degree awarded. *Degree requirements:* Thesis, comprehensive exams required, foreign language not required. *Entrance requirements:* GRE General Test (minimum combined score of 800), minimum GPA of 2.8. Application deadline: 11/1 (priority date; rolling processing; 4/1 for spring admission). Application fee: $50. *Tuition:* $5728 per year full-time, $258 per credit hour part-time for state residents; $8968 per year full-time, $393 per credit hour part-time for nonresidents. *Financial aid:* Federal Work-Study available. • Dr. Robert Newland, Adviser, 609-256-4856.

Rutgers, The State University of New Jersey, New Brunswick, Program in Chemistry, New Brunswick, NJ 08903. Offerings include chemistry education (MST). Program faculty: 44 full-time (9 women), 4 part-time (2 women). *Average time to degree:* master's–3 years full-time, 5 years part-time; doctorate–5 years full-time, 8 years part-time. *Application deadline:* 7/1 (priority date; rolling processing; 11/1 for spring admission). *Application fee:* $40. *Expenses:* Tuition $6492 per year full-time, $268 per credit part-time for state residents; $9520 per year full-time, $395 per credit part-time for nonresidents. Fees $208 per year (minimum). • Dr. Martha A. Cotter, Director, 732-445-2259. Fax: 732-445-5312. E-mail: gradexec@rutchem.rutgers.edu.

Rutgers, The State University of New Jersey, New Brunswick, Graduate School of Education, Department of Learning and Teaching, Program in Science Education, New Brunswick, NJ 08903. Awards Ed M, Ed D, Ed S. Part-time programs available. Faculty: 2 full-time (1 woman). Students: 48; includes 5 minority (1 African American, 4 Asian Americans). 34 applicants, 65% accepted. In 1997, 5 master's awarded. Terminal master's awarded for partial completion of doctoral program. *Degree requirements:* For master's, comprehensive exam required, thesis not required; for doctorate, dissertation, qualifying exam. *Entrance requirements:* For master's, GRE General Test (minimum combined score of 1000); for doctorate, GRE General Test (minimum combined score of 1100); for Ed S, GRE General Test. Application deadline: 3/1 (11/1 for spring admission). Application fee: $40. *Expenses:* Tuition $6492 per year full-time, $268 per credit part-time for state residents; $9520 per year full-time, $395 per credit part-time for nonresidents. Fees $208 per year (minimum). *Financial aid:* Application deadline 3/1. • George Pallrand, Coordinator, 732-932-7496 Ext. 101.

Saginaw Valley State University, College of Education, Program in Natural Science Teaching, University Center, MI 48710. Awards MAT. Accredited by NCATE. Program new for fall 1998. *Entrance requirements:* Minimum GPA of 3.0, teaching certificate. Application deadline: rolling. Application fee: $25. *Expenses:* Tuition $159 per credit hour for state residents; $311 per credit hour for nonresidents. Fees $8.70 per credit hour. • Dr. Ken Wahl, Interim Dean, College of Education, 517-790-5648. Application contact: Jean Chipman, Certification Officer, 517-790-4057.

St. John Fisher College, School of Adult and Graduate Education, Mathematics/Science/Technology Education Program, Rochester, NY 14618-3597. Awards MS. Faculty: 1 (woman) full-time. Students: 0. *Degree requirements:* Computer language required, thesis not required. *Application deadline:* 8/1 (priority date; rolling processing; 1/1 for spring admission). *Application fee:* $30. *Tuition:* $13,500 per year full-time, $375 per credit hour part-time. • Dr. Carol Freeman, Graduate Director, 716-385-8132. E-mail: freeman@sjfc.edu. Application contact: Steven T. Hoskins, Director, Graduate Admissions, 716-385-8161. Fax: 716-385-8344. E-mail: hoskins@sjfc.edu.

Saint Joseph College, Field of Natural Sciences, Department of General Science and Science Education, West Hartford, CT 06117-2700. Offers programs in general science (MS), science education (MS). Faculty: 2 full-time (1 woman), 2 part-time (1 woman). Students: 14 (10 women). *Degree requirements:* Thesis or alternative required, foreign language not required. *Application deadline:* 8/29 (rolling processing). *Application fee:* $25. *Tuition:* $395 per credit.

Financial aid: Application deadline 8/31. • Dr. Harold T. McKone, Chair, 860-232-4571 Ext. 241. Fax: 860-233-5695.

Saint Joseph's University, Department of Education, Program in Chemistry Education, Philadelphia, PA 19131-1395. Awards MS. Students: 1 (woman). *Degree requirements:* Computer language required, foreign language and thesis not required. *Entrance requirements:* TOEFL. Application deadline: 7/15. Application fee: $30. *Tuition:* $510 per credit hour. *Financial aid:* Fellowships available. • Dr. Mary DeKonty Applegate, Director, Department of Education, 610-660-1583.

Salem State College, Department of Education, Salem, MA 01970-5353. Offerings include chemistry (MAT). Accredited by NCATE. MAT (English as a second language) offered jointly with the Department of English. *Application deadline:* rolling. *Application fee:* $25. *Expenses:* Tuition $140 per credit hour for state residents; $230 per credit hour for nonresidents. Fees $20 per credit hour.

Salisbury State University, Department of Education, Salisbury, MD 21801-6837. Offerings include science (M Ed). Department faculty: 19 full-time (10 women), 2 part-time (1 woman). *Application deadline:* 8/1 (priority date; rolling processing; 1/1 for spring admission). *Application fee:* $30. *Expenses:* Tuition $158 per credit hour for state residents; $310 per credit hour for nonresidents. Fees $4 per credit hour. • Dr. Ellen Whitford, Chair, 410-543-6294. E-mail: evwhitford@ssu.edu. Application contact: Phyllis Meyer, Administrative Aide II, 410-543-6281. Fax: 410-548-2593. E-mail: phmeyer@ssu.edu.

San Diego State University, College of Sciences, Department of Mathematical Sciences, San Diego, CA 92182. Offerings include mathematics and science education (PhD). PhD offered jointly with the University of California, San Diego. *Degree requirements:* Dissertation. *Application deadline:* 6/1 (priority date; rolling processing; 12/1 for spring admission). *Application fee:* $55. *Expenses:* Tuition $0 for state residents; $246 per unit for nonresidents. Fees $1932 per year full-time, $1266 per year part-time. • John D. Elwin, Chair, 619-594-6191. E-mail: elwin@saturn.sdsu.edu. Application contact: Edgar J. Howard, Graduate Coordinator, 619-594-5971. Fax: 619-594-6746. E-mail: ehoward@saturn.sdsu.edu.

Slippery Rock University of Pennsylvania, College of Education, Department of Secondary Education/Foundations of Education, Slippery Rock, PA 16057. Offers program in secondary education in math/science (M Ed). Accredited by NCATE. *Degree requirements:* Comprehensive exams. *Entrance requirements:* GRE, minimum GPA of 2.75. Application deadline: 7/1 (priority date; rolling processing; 11/1 for spring admission). Application fee: $25. *Tuition:* $4484 per year full-time, $247 per credit part-time for state residents; $7667 per year full-time, $423 per credit part-time for nonresidents.

Smith College, Department of Education and Child Study, Program in Secondary Education, Northampton, MA 01063. Offerings include biological sciences education (MAT), chemistry education (MAT), physics education (MAT). Program faculty: 6 full-time (3 women), 3 part-time (2 women). *Degree requirements:* 1 foreign language required, thesis not required. *Average time to degree:* master's–1 year full-time, 4 years part-time. *Entrance requirements:* GRE General Test or MAT. Application deadline: 4/15 (12/1 for spring admission). Application fee: $50. *Tuition:* $21,680 per year full-time, $2720 per course part-time. • Rosetta Cohen, Head, 413-585-3266. E-mail: rcohen@sophia.smith.edu.

South Carolina State University, School of Education, Department of Teacher Education, 300 College Street Northeast, Orangeburg, SC 29117-0001. Offerings include engineering (MAT); general science (MAT); secondary education (M Ed), with options in biology education, business education, counselor education, English education, home economics education, industrial education, mathematics education, science education, social studies education. One or more programs accredited by NCATE. Department faculty: 7 full-time (3 women), 2 part-time (1 woman). *Degree requirements:* Departmental qualifying exam required, thesis optional. *Average time to degree:* master's–2 years full-time, 4 years part-time. *Entrance requirements:* GRE General Test (minimum combined score of 850) or MAT (minimum score 35), NTE (minimum score 650 on each core battery test), interview, teaching certificate. Application deadline: 7/15 (priority date; rolling processing; 11/10 for spring admission). Application fee: $25. *Tuition:* $2974 per year full-time, $165 per credit hour part-time. • Dr. Jesse Kinard, Chairman, 803-536-8934. Application contact: Dr. Gail Joyner-Fleming, Interim Associate Dean and Director, Graduate Teacher Education, 803-536-8824. Fax: 803-536-8492.

Southeast Missouri State University, Department of Sciences, Cape Girardeau, MO 63701-4799. Offers program in science education (MNS). Program new for fall 1998. *Application deadline:* (11/21 for spring admission). *Application fee:* $20 ($100 for international students). *Tuition:* $2034 per year full-time, $113 per credit hour part-time for state residents; $3672 per year full-time, $204 per credit hour part-time for nonresidents. • Dr. Earnest Kern, Coordinator, 573-651-2516. Application contact: Office of Graduate Studies, 573-651-2192.

Southern Arkansas University–Magnolia, Graduate Program in Education, Program in Secondary Education, Magnolia, AR 71753. Offerings include mathematics and general science education (M Ed). *Degree requirements:* Thesis or alternative, comprehensive exam required, foreign language not required. *Average time to degree:* master's–2 years full-time. *Entrance requirements:* GRE, minimum GPA of 2.5. Application deadline: 8/15. Application fee: $0. *Expenses:* Tuition $95 per hour for state residents; $138 per hour for nonresidents. Fees $2 per hour. • Dr. Danield L. Bernard, Dean, Graduate Studies, Graduate Program in Education, 870-235-4055. Fax: 870-235-5035. E-mail: dlbernard@mail.saumag.edu.

Southern Connecticut State University, School of Arts and Sciences, Department of Chemistry, New Haven, CT 06515-1355. Offerings include chemistry education (MS Ed). Department faculty: 5 full-time. *Application deadline:* 7/15. *Application fee:* $40. *Expenses:* Tuition $2632 per year full-time, $188 per credit part-time for state residents; $7200 per year full-time, $188 per credit part-time for nonresidents. Fees $1806 per year full-time, $45 per semester part-time for state residents; $2703 per year full-time, $45 per semester part-time for nonresidents. • Dr. James Barrante, Chairman, 203-392-6267.

Southern Connecticut State University, School of Education, Program in Environmental Education/Science Education, New Haven, CT 06515-1355. Offers environmental education (MS), science education (MS, Diploma). Faculty: 2 full-time. Students: 11 full-time (7 women), 100 part-time (72 women); includes 7 minority (2 African Americans, 5 Hispanics). 75 applicants, 37% accepted. In 1997, 93 master's awarded. *Degree requirements:* For master's, thesis or alternative. *Entrance requirements:* For master's, interview; for Diploma, master's degree. Application deadline: 7/15 (priority date; rolling processing). Application fee: $40. *Expenses:* Tuition $2632 per year full-time, $188 per credit part-time for state residents; $7200 per year full-time, $188 per credit part-time for nonresidents. Fees $1806 per year full-time, $45 per semester part-time for state residents; $2703 per year full-time, $45 per semester part-time for nonresidents. • Dr. Susan Hageman, Graduate Coordinator, 203-392-6600.

Southern Oregon University, School of Sciences, Ashland, OR 97520. Offerings include environmental education (MA, MS). *Degree requirements:* Comprehensive exam (MA) required, thesis optional. *Entrance requirements:* GRE General Test, minimum GPA of 3.0. Application deadline: rolling. Application fee: $50. *Tuition:* $5187 per year full-time, $586 per quarter (minimum) part-time for state residents; $9228 per year full-time, $586 per quarter (minimum) part-time for nonresidents. • Dr. Joseph Graf, Dean, 541-552-6474.

Southwest Missouri State University, College of Natural and Applied Sciences, Department of Biology, Springfield, MO 65804-0094. Offerings include biology education (MS). Department faculty: 19 full-time (2 women), 1 part-time (0 women). *Degree requirements:* Thesis or alternative, oral and written comprehensive exams required, foreign language not required. *Average time to degree:* master's–2.5 years full-time, 5 years part-time. *Entrance requirements:* Minimum GPA of 2.75. Application deadline: 6/1 (priority date; rolling processing; 12/1 for spring admission). Application fee: $25. *Expenses:* Tuition $1980 per year full-time, $110 per credit hour part-time for state residents; $3960 per year full-time, $220 per credit hour part-time for nonresidents. Fees $274 per year full-time, $73 per semester part-time. • Dr. Robert Wilkinson, Head, 417-836-5126. E-mail: rfw144f@wpgate.smsu.edu. Application contact: Dr. Thomas Tomasi, Graduate Adviser, 417-836-5126. Fax: 417-836-6934. E-mail: tet962f@vma.smsu.edu.

Stanford University, School of Education, Teacher Education Program, Stanford, CA 94305-9991. Offerings include science education (AM). *Degree requirements:* Thesis required, foreign language not required. *Entrance requirements:* GRE General Test. Application deadline: 1/15. Application fee: $65 ($75 for international students). *Expenses:* Tuition $22,110 per year. Fees $156 per year. • Administrator, 650-723-4891. Application contact: Graduate Admissions Office, 650-723-2110.

State University of New York at Binghamton, School of Education and Human Development, Program in Secondary Education, Binghamton, NY 13902-6000. Offerings include biology education (MAT, MS Ed, MST), earth science education (MAT, MS Ed, MST), physics (MAT, MS Ed, MST). *Entrance requirements:* GRE General Test, TOEFL. Application deadline: 4/15 (priority date; rolling processing; 11/1 for spring admission). Application fee: $50. Electronic applications accepted. *Expenses:* Tuition $5100 per year full-time, $213 per credit hour part-time for state residents; $8416 per year full-time, $351 per credit hour part-time for nonresidents. Fees $654 per year full-time, $75 per semester (minimum) part-time. • Dr. Wayne Ross, Coordinator, 607-777-2478.

State University of New York at Buffalo, Graduate School, Graduate School of Education, Department of Learning and Instruction, Buffalo, NY 14260. Offerings include secondary education (Ed M, Ed D, PhD), with options in English education (Ed D, PhD), foreign language education (Ed D, PhD), mathematics education (Ed D, PhD), science education (PhD). Terminal master's awarded for partial completion of doctoral program. Department faculty: 20 full-time (9 women), 7 part-time (2 women). *Application deadline:* 2/1 (11/15 for spring admission). *Application fee:* $50. *Tuition:* $5970 per year full-time, $288 per credit hour part-time for state residents; $9286 per year full-time, $426 per credit hour part-time for nonresidents. • Dr. Michael Kibby, Chair, 716-645-2455. Application contact: Barbara Cracchiolo, Admissions Secretary, 716-645-2457. Fax: 716-645-3161.

State University of New York at New Paltz, Faculty of Education, Department of Elementary Education, New Paltz, NY 12561-2499. Offerings include environmental education (MS Ed). *Application deadline:* 3/15 (priority date; rolling processing). *Application fee:* $50. *Expenses:* Tuition $5100 per year full-time, $213 per credit hour part-time for state residents; $8416 per year full-time, $351 per credit hour part-time for nonresidents. Fees $493 per year full-time, $48 per semester (minimum) part-time. • Dr. Rose Rudnitski, Chair, 914-257-2860.

State University of New York at Stony Brook, School of Professional Development and Continuing Studies, Stony Brook, NY 11794. Offerings include chemistry-grade 7-12 (MAT), earth science-grade 7-12 (MAT), physics-grade 7-12 (MAT). School faculty: 1 full-time, 101 part-time. *Application deadline:* 1/15. *Application fee:* $50. *Expenses:* Tuition $5100 per year full-time, $213 per credit hour part-time for state residents; $8416 per year full-time, $351 per credit hour part-time for nonresidents. Fees $529 per year full-time, $77 per semester (minimum) part-time. • Dr. Paul J. Edelson, Dean, 516-632-7052. E-mail: paul.edelson@sunysb.edu. Application contact: Sandra Romansky, Director of Admissions and Advisement, 516-632-7050. Fax: 516-632-9046. E-mail: sandra.romansky@sunysb.edu.

State University of New York College at Brockport, School of Professions, Department of Education and Human Development, Programs in Secondary Education, Brockport, NY 14420-2997. Offerings include biology education (MS Ed), chemistry education (MS Ed), earth science education (MS Ed), physics education (MS Ed). *Degree requirements:* Thesis or alternative required, foreign language not required. *Entrance requirements:* Minimum GPA of 3.0. Application deadline: 1/15 (priority date; 9/15 for spring admission). Application fee: $50. *Expenses:* Tuition $5100 per year full-time, $213 per credit hour part-time for state residents; $8416 per year full-time, $351 per credit hour part-time for nonresidents. Fees $440 per year full-time, $22.60 per credit hour part-time. • William Veenis, Chairperson, Department of Education and Human Development, 716-395-2205.

State University of New York College at Buffalo, Faculty of Natural and Social Sciences, Department of Biology, Buffalo, NY 14222-1095. Offerings include secondary education (MS Ed), with option in biology. One or more programs accredited by NCATE. Department faculty: 14 full-time (1 woman), 1 part-time (0 women). *Application deadline:* 5/1 (10/1 for spring admission). *Application fee:* $50. *Expenses:* Tuition $5100 per year full-time, $213 per credit hour part-time for state residents; $8416 per year full-time, $351 per credit hour part-time for nonresidents. Fees $195 per year full-time, $8.60 per credit hour part-time. • Dr. Javier Penalosa, Chairperson, 716-878-5203.

State University of New York College at Buffalo, Faculty of Natural and Social Sciences, Department of Chemistry, Buffalo, NY 14222-1095. Offerings include secondary education (MS Ed), with option in chemistry. One or more programs accredited by NCATE. Department faculty: 7 full-time (2 women). *Application deadline:* 5/1 (10/1 for spring admission). *Application fee:* $50. *Expenses:* Tuition $5100 per year full-time, $213 per credit hour part-time for state residents; $8416 per year full-time, $351 per credit hour part-time for nonresidents. Fees $195 per year full-time, $8.60 per credit hour part-time. • Dr. Gregory Ebert, Chairperson, 716-878-5204.

State University of New York College at Buffalo, Faculty of Natural and Social Sciences, Department of Earth Science and Science Education, Buffalo, NY 14222-1095. Offers program in secondary education (MS Ed), including geoscience, science. One or more programs accredited by NCATE. Part-time and evening/weekend programs available. Faculty: 11 full-time (1 woman). Students: 1 full-time (0 women), 36 part-time (21 women); includes 2 minority (both African Americans). Average age 31. 2 applicants, 100% accepted. In 1997, 8 degrees awarded. *Degree requirements:* Thesis or alternative, project required, foreign language not required. *Entrance requirements:* 36 undergraduate hours in mathematics and science. Application deadline: 5/1 (10/1 for spring admission). Application fee: $50. *Expenses:* Tuition $5100 per year full-time, $213 per credit hour part-time for state residents; $8416 per year full-time, $351 per credit hour part-time for nonresidents. Fees $195 per year full-time, $8.60 per credit hour part-time. *Financial aid:* In 1997–98, 1 assistantship was awarded; fellowships also available. Financial aid application deadline: 3/1. • Dr. Jill Singer, Chairperson, 716-878-6731.

State University of New York College at Buffalo, Faculty of Applied Science and Education, Department of Elementary Education and Reading, Program in Elementary and Early Secondary Education, Buffalo, NY 14222-1095. Offerings include general science education (MS Ed). Accredited by NCATE. *Degree requirements:* Thesis or project required, foreign language not required. *Entrance requirements:* Minimum GPA of 2.5 in last 60 hours, New York teaching certificate. Application deadline: 5/1 (10/1 for spring admission). Application fee: $50. *Expenses:* Tuition $5100 per year full-time, $213 per credit hour part-time for state residents; $8416 per year full-time, $351 per credit hour part-time for nonresidents. Fees $195 per year full-time, $8.60 per credit hour part-time. • Dr. Maria Ceprano, Chairperson, Department of Elementary Education and Reading, 716-878-5916.

State University of New York College at Cortland, Division of Arts and Sciences, Program in Secondary Education, Cortland, NY 13045. Offerings include biology (MAT, MS Ed), chemistry (MAT, MS Ed), earth science (MAT, MS Ed), physics (MAT, MS Ed). *Degree requirements:* 1 foreign language, thesis (for some programs), comprehensive exam. *Application deadline:* rolling. *Application fee:* $50. *Expenses:* Tuition $5100 per year full-time, $213 per credit hour part-time for state residents; $8416 per year full-time, $351 per credit hour part-time for nonresidents. Fees $644 per year full-time, $79 per semester (minimum) part-time. • Roger Sipher, Head, 607-753-2723. Application contact: Jeanne M. Bechtel, Director of Admissions, 607-753-4711. Fax: 607-753-5998.

Directory: Science Education

State University of New York College at Cortland, Division of Professional Studies, Department of Education, Cortland, NY 13045. Offerings include elementary education (MS Ed), with options in English education, general science education, mathematics education, social studies education; secondary education (MS Ed), with options in biology, chemistry, earth science, French, mathematics, physics. *Application deadline:* rolling. *Application fee:* $50. *Expenses:* Tuition $5100 per year full-time, $213 per credit hour part-time for state residents; $8416 per year full-time, $351 per credit hour part-time for nonresidents. Fees $644 per year full-time, $79 per semester (minimum) part-time. • Mary Ware, Chair, 607-753-2705. Application contact: Jeanne M. Bechtel, Director of Admissions, 607-753-4711. Fax: 607-753-5998.

State University of New York College at Oneonta, Department of Education, Oneonta, NY 13820-4015. Offerings include elementary education (MS Ed), with options in early secondary English (N–9), early secondary math (N–9), early secondary social science (N–9), general science (N–9); secondary education (MS Ed), with options in biology education, chemistry education, earth science education, English education, home economics education, mathematics education, physics education, social science education. *Application deadline:* 4/15. *Application fee:* $50. *Expenses:* Tuition $5100 per year full-time, $213 per credit hour part-time for state residents; $8416 per year full-time, $351 per credit hour part-time for nonresidents. Fees $482 per year full-time, $6.85 per credit hour part-time. • Dr. Ronald Cromwell, Chair, 607-436-2538.

Syracuse University, School of Education, Teaching and Leadership Programs, Program in Science Education, Syracuse, NY 13244-0003. Awards MS, Ed D, PhD, CAS. Students: 17 full-time (4 women), 6 part-time (4 women); includes 1 minority (Asian American), 2 international. 17 applicants, 82% accepted. In 1997, 4 master's, 2 doctorates awarded. *Degree requirements:* For master's, thesis or alternative; for doctorate and CAS, thesis/dissertation. *Entrance requirements:* GRE. Application fee: $40. *Tuition:* $13,320 per year full-time, $555 per credit hour part-time. *Financial aid:* Application deadline 3/1. • Dr. Marvin Druger, Chair, 315-443-2586.

Teachers College, Columbia University, Graduate Faculty of Education, Department of Scientific Foundations, Programs in Science Education, 525 West 120th Street, New York, NY 10027-6696. Awards Ed M, MA, MS, Ed D, Ed DCT, PhD. Part-time and evening/weekend programs available. Faculty: 3 full-time (1 woman), 1 part-time (0 women), 3.2 FTE. Students: 25 full-time (18 women), 70 part-time (33 women); includes 31 minority (12 African Americans, 8 Asian Americans, 10 Hispanics, 1 Native American), 3 international. Average age 37. 73 applicants, 66% accepted. In 1997, 28 master's, 4 doctorates awarded. Terminal master's awarded for partial completion of doctoral program. *Degree requirements:* For master's, culminating paper required, foreign language not required; for doctorate, dissertation. *Entrance requirements:* 24 credits in science. Application deadline: 5/15 (12/1 for spring admission). Application fee: $50. *Expenses:* Tuition $640 per credit. Fees $120 per semester. *Financial aid:* Fellowships, full and partial tuition waivers, Federal Work-Study, institutionally sponsored loans, and career-related internships or fieldwork available. Aid available to part-time students. Financial aid application deadline: 2/1. *Faculty research:* Cell biology and physiological ecology of protozoa, teaching and learning of pre-college and college sciences, homelessness. Total annual research expenditures: $100,000. • Application contact: Barbara Reinhalter, Office of Admissions, 212-678-3710. Fax: 212-678-4171.

Temple University, College of Education, Department of Curriculum, Instruction, and Technology in Education, Philadelphia, PA 19122-6096. Offerings include math/science education (Ed D), mathematics/science education (Ed M). One or more programs accredited by NCATE. Terminal master's awarded for partial completion of doctoral program. Department faculty: 33 full-time (14 women). *Degree requirements:* For doctorate, dissertation required, foreign language not required. *Entrance requirements:* For doctorate, GRE General Test (minimum combined score of 1000) or MAT (minimum score 39). Application deadline: 2/15 (10/1 for spring admission). Application fee: $40. *Expenses:* Tuition $323 per semester hour for state residents; $444 per semester hour for nonresidents. Fees $170 per year full-time, $28 per semester (minimum) part-time. • Dr. Raymond Lolla, Chair, 215-204-6387. Fax: 215-204-1414.

Texas A&M University, College of Education, Department of Educational Curriculum and Instruction, Unit in Math/Science, College Station, TX 77843. Awards M Ed, MS, Ed D, PhD. Accredited by NCATE. *Degree requirements:* For doctorate, dissertation required, foreign language not required. *Entrance requirements:* GRE General Test, TOEFL. Application fee: $35 ($75 for international students). *Financial aid:* Fellowships, research assistantships, teaching assistantships available. • Charles Lamb, Coordinator, 409-845-8395.

Texas Woman's University, College of Arts and Sciences, Department of Biology, Denton, TX 76204. Offerings include biology teaching (MS). Department faculty: 11 full-time (4 women), 2 part-time (1 woman), 12 FTE. *Degree requirements:* Thesis required (for some programs), foreign language not required. *Average time to degree:* master's–2.5 years full-time, 4 years part-time; doctorate–5 years full-time, 8 years part-time. *Entrance requirements:* GRE General Test (minimum combined score of 800), minimum GPA of 3.0. Application deadline: 4/1 (priority date; rolling processing; 8/1 for spring admission). Application fee: $25. • Dr. Fritz Schwalm, Chair, 940-898-2351. Fax: 940-898-2382. E-mail: d_schwalm@venus.twu.edu.

Tuskegee University, College of Liberal Arts and Education, Department of Curriculum, Instruction and Administration, Program in General Science Education, Tuskegee, AL 36088. Awards M Ed, MS. Accredited by NCATE. Faculty: 2 full-time (both women), 4 part-time (1 woman). Students: 0. *Entrance requirements:* GRE General Test. Application deadline: 7/15 (rolling processing). Application fee: $25 ($35 for international students). *Financial aid:* Application deadline 4/15. • H. Frank Leftwich, Acting Head, Department of Curriculum, Instruction and Administration, 334-727-8599.

Union College, Graduate and Continuing Studies, Programs in Education, Schenectady, NY 12308-2311. Offerings include biology (MAT), chemistry (MAT), earth science (MAT), general science (MAT), natural sciences (MS), physical sciences (MS), physics (MAT). *Application deadline:* 5/15. *Application fee:* $35. *Tuition:* $1155 per course. • Dr. Patrick Allen, Educational Studies Director, 518-388-6361.

Universidad Metropolitana, Graduate Programs in Education, Program in Environmental Education, Río Piedras, PR 00928-1150. Awards MA. *Application deadline:* rolling. *Application fee:* $0. • Dr. Ana Delgado, Dean, Graduate Programs in Education, 787-766-1717 Ext. 6409.

Université du Québec à Montréal, Program in Education, Montréal, PQ H3C 3P8, Canada. Offerings include education of the environmental sciences (Diploma). PhD offered jointly with the Université du Québec à Chicoutimi, the Université du Québec à Hull, the Université du Québec à Rimouski, the Université du Québec à Trois-Rivières, and the Université du Québec en Abitibi-Témiscamingue; Diploma new for fall 1997. *Entrance requirements:* Appropriate bachelor's degree or equivalent and proficiency in French. Application deadline: 2/15. Application fee: $50.

University of Alaska Fairbanks, Graduate School, College of Science, Engineering and Mathematics, Department of Geology and Geophysics, Fairbanks, AK 99775-7480. Offerings include geoscience (MAT). Department faculty: 21 full-time (3 women). *Application deadline:* 3/1. *Application fee:* $35. *Expenses:* Tuition $162 per credit for state residents; $316 per credit for nonresidents. Fees $520 per year full-time, $45 per semester (minimum) part-time. • Dr. Paul Layer, Head, 907-474-7565. Application contact: Doug Christensen, Adviser, 907-474-7426.

University of Alaska Fairbanks, Graduate School, College of Science, Engineering and Mathematics, Department of Biology and Wildlife, Program in Biological Sciences, Fairbanks, AK 99775-7480. Offerings include biology (MAT, MS, PhD). Program faculty: 24 full-time (2 women), 2 part-time (0 women). *Degree requirements:* For master's, thesis, comprehensive exam required, foreign language not required; for doctorate, 1 foreign language (computer language can substitute), dissertation, comprehensive exam. *Entrance requirements:* GRE General Test, GRE Subject Test, TOEFL (minimum score 550). Application deadline: 8/1 (rolling processing). Application fee: $35. *Expenses:* Tuition $162 per credit for state residents; $316 per credit for nonresidents. Fees $520 per year full-time, $45 per semester (minimum) part-time. • Dr. Ed Murphy, Head, Department of Biology and Wildlife, 907-474-7661.

University of Arkansas at Pine Bluff, Program in Education, Pine Bluff, AR 71601-2799. Offerings include secondary education (M Ed), with options in aquaculture, English, general science, mathematics, physical education, social studies. Accredited by NCATE. Program faculty: 51. *Entrance requirements:* GRE, minimum GPA of 2.75; NTE or Standard Arkansas Teaching Certificate. Application deadline: rolling. Application fee: $0. *Expenses:* Tuition $82 per credit hour for state residents; $192 per credit hour for nonresidents. Fees $25 per year. • Dr. Calvin Johnson, Dean, 870-543-8256.

University of British Columbia, Faculty of Education, Department of Curriculum Studies, Vancouver, BC V6T 1Z2, Canada. Offerings include science education (MA, M Ed, PhD). *Degree requirements:* For master's, thesis (MA) required, foreign language not required; for doctorate, dissertation required, foreign language not required. *Entrance requirements:* TOEFL (minimum score 550). Application deadline: 3/1 (12/1 for spring admission). Application fee: $60.

University of California, Berkeley, School of Education, Division of Cognition and Development, Group in Science and Mathematics Education, Berkeley, CA 94720-1500. Awards PhD. *Application deadline:* 12/15. *Expenses:* Tuition $0 for state residents; $9384 per year for nonresidents. Fees $4409 per year. *Financial aid:* Application deadline 12/15. • Barbara White, Chair. Application contact: Kate Capps, Graduate Assistant/Admissions, 510-642-4206. Fax: 510-642-3769. E-mail: kate@socrates.berkeley.edu.

University of California, Berkeley, School of Education, Division of Cognition and Development, Program in Education in Mathematics, Science, and Technology, Berkeley, CA 94720-1500. Awards MA, PhD. *Application deadline:* 12/15. *Expenses:* Tuition $0 for state residents; $9384 per year for nonresidents. Fees $4409 per year. *Financial aid:* Application deadline 12/15. • Application contact: Kate Capps, Program Assistant, 510-642-4206. E-mail: gse_info@uclink.berkeley.edu.

University of California, Berkeley, School of Education, Division of Cognition and Development, Science and Mathematics Education Program, Berkeley, CA 94720-1500. Offers education/single subject teaching: mathematics (MA), education/single subject teaching: science (MA). *Expenses:* Tuition $0 for state residents; $9384 per year for nonresidents. Fees $4409 per year. • Daniel Zimmerlin, Academic Coordinator.

University of California, Los Angeles, College of Letters and Science, Department of Physics and Astronomy, Program in Physics, Los Angeles, CA 90095. Offerings include physics education (MAT). MAT admits only applicants whose objective is PhD. Program faculty: 75. *Degree requirements:* Comprehensive exam or thesis required, foreign language not required. *Entrance requirements:* GRE General Test, GRE Subject Test, minimum GPA of 3.0. Application deadline: 12/15. Application fee: $40. Electronic applications accepted. *Expenses:* Tuition $0 for state residents; $9384 per year for nonresidents. Fees $4551 per year. • Application contact: Departmental Office, 310-825-2307. E-mail: plucky@physics.ucla.edu.

University of Central Florida, College of Education, Department of Instructional Programs, Program in Science Education, Orlando, FL 32816. Awards MA, M Ed. Accredited by NCATE. Students: 11 full-time (7 women), 16 part-time (11 women); includes 1 minority (African American). Average age 35. 7 applicants, 57% accepted. In 1997, 6 degrees awarded. *Degree requirements:* Thesis or alternative required, foreign language not required. *Entrance requirements:* GRE General Test (minimum combined score of 840). Application deadline: 7/15 (12/15 for spring admission). Application fee: $20. *Expenses:* Tuition $3288 per year full-time, $137 per credit hour part-time for state residents; $11,520 per year full-time, $480 per credit hour part-time for nonresidents. Fees $105 per year. • Application contact: Dr. Judith Johnson, Coordinator, 407-823-2950. E-mail: jajohnso@pegasus.cc.ucf.edu.

University of Connecticut, School of Education, Field of Science Education, Storrs, CT 06269. Awards MA, PhD. Accredited by NCATE. Faculty: 1. Students: 12 full-time (7 women), 5 part-time (2 women); includes 2 minority (1 Asian American, 1 Hispanic). Average age 31. 7 applicants, 100% accepted. In 1997, 5 master's awarded. Terminal master's awarded for partial completion of doctoral program. *Degree requirements:* For master's, thesis or alternative; for doctorate, dissertation. *Entrance requirements:* For doctorate, GRE General Test. Application deadline: 6/1 (priority date; rolling processing; 11/1 for spring admission). Application fee: $40 ($45 for international students). *Expenses:* Tuition $5272 per year full-time, $293 per credit part-time for state residents; $13,696 per year full-time, $761 per credit part-time for nonresidents. Fees $948 per year full-time, $640 per year part-time. *Financial aid:* In 1997–98, 1 research assistantship (to a first-year student) totaling $6,413 was awarded; fellowships, teaching assistantships also available. Financial aid application deadline: 2/15. • Thomas P. Weinland, Head, 860-486-2433.

University of Florida, College of Education, Department of Instruction and Curriculum, Gainesville, FL 32611. Offerings include science education (MAE, M Ed, Ed D, PhD, Ed S). Accredited by NCATE. Department faculty: 42. *Degree requirements:* For master's, thesis optional, foreign language not required; for doctorate, variable foreign language requirement, dissertation. *Entrance requirements:* For master's and doctorate, GRE General Test (minimum combined score of 1000), minimum GPA of 3.0; for Ed S, GRE General Test. Application deadline: 6/5. Application fee: $20. *Tuition:* $138 per credit hour for state residents; $481 per credit hour for nonresidents. • Dr. Mary Grace Kantowski, Chair, 352-392-9191 Ext. 200. E-mail: mgk@coe.ufl.edu. Application contact: Dr. Ben Nelms, Graduate Coordinator, 352-392-9191 Ext. 225. Fax: 352-392-9193. E-mail: bfn@coe.ufl.edu.

University of Florida, Colleges of Liberal Arts and Sciences and Agriculture, Department of Botany, Gainesville, FL 32611-2009. Offerings include botany education (MST). Department faculty: 22. *Application deadline:* 6/5 (priority date; rolling processing). *Application fee:* $20. *Tuition:* $138 per credit hour for state residents; $481 per credit hour for nonresidents. • Dr. David A. Jones, Chair, 352-392-1175. E-mail: djones@botany.ufl.edu. Application contact: Dr. Alice Harmon, Graduate Coordinator, 352-392-3217. Fax: 352-392-3993. E-mail: harmon@botany.ufl.edu.

University of Florida, College of Liberal Arts and Sciences, Department of Geology, Gainesville, FL 32611. Offerings include geology education (MST). Department faculty: 15 full-time (2 women), 11 part-time (3 women). *Application deadline:* 6/5 (priority date; rolling processing). *Application fee:* $20. Electronic applications accepted. *Tuition:* $138 per credit hour for state residents; $481 per credit hour for nonresidents. • Dr. Paul Mueller, Chair, 352-392-2231. E-mail: mueller@geology.ufl.edu. Application contact: Dr. Michael R. Perfit, Graduate Coordinator, 352-392-2128. Fax: 352-392-9294. E-mail: perfit@geology.ufl.edu.

University of Florida, College of Liberal Arts and Sciences, Department of Physics, Gainesville, FL 32611. Offerings include physics education (MST). Accredited by NCATE. Department faculty: 55 full-time. *Application deadline:* 6/5 (priority date; rolling processing). *Application fee:* $20. *Tuition:* $138 per credit hour for state residents; $481 per credit hour for nonresidents. • Dr. Neil Sullivan Jr., Chair, 352-392-0521. Fax: 352-392-0524. E-mail: sullivan@phys.ufl.edu. Application contact: Dr. John Yelton, Graduate Coordinator, 352-392-8475. Fax: 352-392-6694. E-mail: yelton@phys.ufl.edu.

University of Georgia, College of Education, Programs in Secondary Education, Athens, GA 30602. Offerings include science education (M Ed, Ed D, PhD, Ed S). Accredited by NCATE. Faculty: 46 full-time (17 women). *Degree requirements:* For doctorate, dissertation required, foreign language not required. *Entrance requirements:* For doctorate, GRE General Test; for Ed S, GRE General Test or MAT. Application deadline: 7/1 (priority date; 11/15 for spring admission). Application fee: $30. Electronic applications accepted. *Tuition:* $3290 per year full-time, $643 per semester (minimum) part-time for state residents; $11,300 per year full-time, $1645 per semester (minimum) part-time for nonresidents. • Dr. Russell H. Yeany, Dean, 706-542-3866. Fax: 706-542-0360.

University of Houston, College of Education, Department of Curriculum and Instruction, 4800 Calhoun, Houston, TX 77204-2163. Offerings include science education (M Ed). Accredited by NCATE. Department faculty: 37 full-time (19 women), 10 part-time (7 women). *Degree requirements:* Comprehensive exam or thesis required, foreign language not required. *Entrance requirements:* GRE General Test or MAT. Application deadline: 7/3 (priority date; rolling processing). Application fee: $35 ($75 for international students). *Expenses:* Tuition $1152 per year full-time, $120 per semester (minimum) part-time for state residents; $4482 per year full-time, $249 per credit hour part-time for nonresidents. Fees $977 per year full-time, $119 per semester (minimum) part-time. • Wilford Weber, Chair, 713-743-4970. Fax: 713-743-9870. E-mail: wweber@uh.edu.

University of Idaho, College of Graduate Studies, College of Letters and Science, Department of Chemistry, Moscow, ID 83844-4140. Offerings include chemistry education (MAT). Accredited by NCATE. Department faculty: 18 full-time (3 women), 1 part-time (0 women), 18.5 FTE. *Application deadline:* 8/1 (12/15 for spring admission). *Application fee:* $35 ($45 for international students). *Expenses:* Tuition $0 for state residents; $6000 per year full-time, $95 per credit part-time for nonresidents. Fees $2676 per year full-time, $134 per credit part-time. • Dr. Chien M. Wai, Head, 208-885-6552.

University of Idaho, College of Graduate Studies, College of Letters and Science, Department of Physics, Moscow, ID 83844-4140. Offerings include physics education (MAT). Accredited by NCATE. Department faculty: 10 full-time (1 woman). *Application deadline:* 8/1 (12/15 for spring admission). *Application fee:* $35 ($45 for international students). *Expenses:* Tuition $0 for state residents; $6000 per year full-time, $95 per credit part-time for nonresidents. Fees $2676 per year full-time, $134 per credit part-time. • Dr. Henry Willmes, Chair, 208-885-6380.

The University of Iowa, College of Liberal Arts, Program in Science Education, Iowa City, IA 52242-1316. Awards MS, PhD. Faculty: 11 full-time. Students: 50 full-time (26 women), 40 part-time (20 women); includes 6 minority (3 African Americans, 1 Asian American, 1 Hispanic, 1 Native American), 7 international. 27 applicants, 78% accepted. In 1997, 24 master's, 10 doctorates awarded. *Degree requirements:* For master's, thesis optional; for doctorate, dissertation, comprehensive exam. *Entrance requirements:* GRE General Test. Application fee: $30 ($50 for international students). *Expenses:* Tuition $3166 per year full-time, $176 per semester hour part-time for state residents; $10,202 per year full-time, $176 per semester hour part-time for nonresidents. Fees $202 per year full-time, $52 per year (minimum) part-time. *Financial aid:* In 1997–98, 1 fellowship, 8 research assistantships (3 to first-year students), 11 teaching assistantships (3 to first-year students) were awarded. Financial aid applicants required to submit FAFSA. • Robert Yager, Coordinator, 319-335-1173. Fax: 319-335-1188.

University of Maine, College of Education and Human Development, Program in Science Education, Orono, ME 04469. Awards M Ed, MS, CAS. Accredited by NCATE. Part-time and evening/weekend programs available. *Degree requirements:* For master's, thesis or alternative. *Entrance requirements:* For master's, TOEFL (minimum score 550); for CAS, MA, M Ed, or MS. Application deadline: 2/1 (priority date; rolling processing; 10/15 for spring admission). Application fee: $50. *Expenses:* Tuition $194 per credit hour for state residents; $548 per credit hour for nonresidents. Fees $378 per year full-time, $33 per semester (minimum) part-time. *Financial aid:* Application deadline 3/1. • Application contact: Scott Delcourt, Director of the Graduate School, 207-581-3218. Fax: 207-581-3232. E-mail: graduate@maine.edu.

University of Manitoba, Faculty of Education, Department of Curriculum: Mathematics and Natural Sciences, Winnipeg, MB R3T 2N2, Canada. Offerings include science education (M Ed). *Degree requirements:* Thesis or alternative required, foreign language not required.

University of Maryland, College Park, College of Agriculture and Natural Resources, Department of Agricultural and Extension Education, College Park, MD 20742-5045. Offerings include environmental education (MS, PhD, AGSC). Program being phased out; applicants no longer accepted. Department faculty: 1 (0 women). *Degree requirements:* For doctorate, dissertation. *Expenses:* Tuition $272 per credit hour for state residents; $400 per credit hour for nonresidents. Fees $564 per year full-time, $342 per year part-time. • Ronald Seibel, Director, Applied Agriculture, 301-405-4685. Fax: 301-314-9300. E-mail: grschool@deans.umd.edu.

University of Massachusetts Lowell, College of Education, Program in Math and Science Education, 1 University Avenue, Lowell, MA 01854-2881. Awards Ed D. Accredited by NCATE. Students: 2 full-time (1 woman), 26 part-time (13 women); includes 2 minority (1 Asian American, 1 Hispanic). In 1997, 2 degrees awarded. *Degree requirements:* Dissertation. *Entrance requirements:* GRE General Test. Application deadline: 4/1 (priority date; rolling processing; 10/1 for spring admission). Application fee: $20 ($35 for international students). *Tuition:* $4867 per year full-time, $618 per semester (minimum) part-time for state residents; $10,276 per year full-time, $1294 per semester (minimum) part-time for nonresidents. *Financial aid:* Application deadline 4/1. • Dr. Brenda Jochums, Coordinator, 978-934-4620.

University of Michigan, School of Education, Programs in Educational Studies, Ann Arbor, MI 48109. Offerings include science education (AM, MS, PhD). *Degree requirements:* For master's, thesis required (for some programs), foreign language not required; for doctorate, dissertation, preliminary exam required, foreign language not required. *Entrance requirements:* GRE General Test (minimum combined score of 1800 on three sections), TOEFL (minimum score 600). Application deadline: 1/15 (priority date). Application fee: $55. Electronic applications accepted. • Dr. Ronald Marx, Chairperson, 734-763-9497. E-mail: ronmarx@umich.edu. Application contact: Karen Wixson, Associate Dean, 734-764-9470. Fax: 734-763-1229. E-mail: kwixson@umich.edu.

University of Minnesota, Twin Cities Campus, College of Education and Human Development, Department of Curriculum and Instruction, Minneapolis, MN 55455-0213. Offerings include science education (MA, M Ed, PhD). • Fred Finley, Chairman, 612-625-2545.

University of Missouri–Rolla, College of Arts and Sciences, Department of Chemistry, Rolla, MO 65409-0910. Offerings include chemistry education (MST). Department faculty: 18 full-time (2 women), 2 part-time (0 women). *Application deadline:* 7/1 (rolling processing). *Application fee:* $20. Electronic applications accepted. *Expenses:* Tuition $3902 per year full-time, $163 per credit hour part-time for state residents; $11,738 per year full-time, $489 per credit hour part-time for nonresidents. Fees $610 per year (minimum) full-time, $146 per year (minimum) part-time. • Dr. Harvest L. Collier, Interim Chairman, 573-341-4420. Fax: 573-341-6033. E-mail: hcollier@umr.edu.

The University of Montana–Missoula, College of Arts and Sciences, Department of Chemistry, Missoula, MT 59812-0002. Offerings include chemistry teaching (MST). Department faculty: 14 full-time (3 women), 1 part-time (0 women). *Application deadline:* 2/1 (priority date; rolling processing; 10/15 for spring admission). *Application fee:* $30. *Tuition:* $2499 per year (minimum) full-time, $376 per semester (minimum) part-time for state residents; $6528 per year (minimum) full-time, $1048 per semester (minimum) part-time for nonresidents. • Dr. Garon C. Smith, Chair, 406-243-4022. Fax: 406-243-4227.

The University of Montana–Missoula, Division of Biological Sciences, Program in Teaching Biological Sciences, Missoula, MT 59812-0002. Awards MST. Faculty: 19 full-time (2 women), 10 part-time (3 women). Students: 1 (woman) full-time. 1 applicant, 100% accepted. In 1997, 2 degrees awarded. *Entrance requirements:* GRE General Test. Application deadline: 2/1. Application fee: $30. *Tuition:* $2499 per year (minimum) full-time, $376 per semester (minimum) part-time for state residents; $6528 per year (minimum) full-time, $1048 per semester (minimum) part-time for nonresidents. *Financial aid:* Application deadline 3/1. • Application contact: Janean Clark, Graduate Programs Secretary, 406-243-5222. Fax: 406-243-4184. E-mail: jmclark@selway.umt.edu.

University of Nebraska at Kearney, College of Natural and Social Sciences, Department of Biology, Kearney, NE 68849-0001. Offerings include biology education (MS Ed), science/mathematics teaching (MS Ed). MS Ed being phased out; applicants no longer accepted. Department faculty: 8 full-time (2 women). *Application deadline:* 8/1 (priority date; rolling processing; 12/15 for spring admission). *Application fee:* $35. *Expenses:* Tuition $1494 per year full-time, $83 per credit hour part-time for state residents; $2826 per year full-time, $157 per credit hour part-time for nonresidents. Fees $229 per year full-time, $11.25 per semester (minimum) part-time. • Dr. Charles Bicak, Chair, 308-865-8548.

University of New Orleans, College of Sciences, Department of Science Teaching, New Orleans, LA 70148. Awards MA. One or more programs accredited by NCATE. Students: 13 part-time (6 women); includes 1 international. Average age 35. 4 applicants, 100% accepted. In 1997, 2 degrees awarded. *Application deadline:* 7/1 (priority date; rolling processing). *Application fee:* $20. *Expenses:* Tuition $2362 per year full-time, $373 per semester (minimum) part-time for state residents; $7888 per year full-time, $1423 per semester (minimum) part-time for nonresidents. Fees $170 per year full-time, $25 per semester (minimum) part-time. • Dr. Larry Hargis, Graduate Coordinator, 504-280-6726. E-mail: dlhel@uno.edu.

The University of North Carolina at Chapel Hill, School of Education, Programs in Teacher Education, Program in Secondary Education, Chapel Hill, NC 27599. Offerings include science (MAT). Accredited by NCATE. *Degree requirements:* Comprehensive exam required, foreign language and thesis not required. *Entrance requirements:* GRE General Test (minimum combined score of 1000), minimum GPA of 3.0 during last 2 years of undergraduate course work. Application deadline: 1/1 (rolling processing). Application fee: $55. *Expenses:* Tuition $1428 per year full-time, $357 per semester (minimum) part-time for state residents; $10,414 per year full-time, $2604 per semester (minimum) part-time for nonresidents. Fees $782 per year full-time, $332 per semester (minimum) part-time. • Dr. Walter Pryzwansky, Director of Graduate Studies, 919-966-7000. Application contact: Janet Carroll, Registrar, 919-966-1346. Fax: 919-962-1533. E-mail: jscarrol@email.unc.edu.

University of Northern Colorado, College of Arts and Sciences, Department of Biological Sciences, Greeley, CO 80639. Offerings include biological education (PhD). Department faculty: 7 full-time (3 women). *Degree requirements:* Dissertation, comprehensive exams. *Entrance requirements:* GRE General Test. Application deadline: rolling. Application fee: $35. *Expenses:* Tuition $2327 per year full-time, $129 per credit hour part-time for state residents; $9578 per year full-time, $532 per credit hour part-time for nonresidents. Fees $752 per year full-time, $184 per semester (minimum) part-time. • Dr. Curt Peterson, Chairperson, 970-351-2921.

University of Northern Colorado, College of Arts and Sciences, Department of Chemistry, Greeley, CO 80639. Offerings include chemical education (MA, PhD). One or more programs accredited by NCATE. Department faculty: 9 full-time (1 woman). *Degree requirements:* For master's, thesis or alternative, comprehensive exams; for doctorate, dissertation, comprehensive exams. *Entrance requirements:* For doctorate, GRE General Test. Application deadline: rolling. Application fee: $35. *Expenses:* Tuition $2327 per year full-time, $129 per credit hour part-time for state residents; $9578 per year full-time, $532 per credit hour part-time for nonresidents. Fees $752 per year full-time, $184 per semester (minimum) part-time. • Dr. David Pringle, Chairperson, 970-351-2559.

University of Northern Iowa, College of Natural Sciences, Department of Physics, Cedar Falls, IA 50614. Offers program in science education (MA), including physics education. Students: 1 (woman) full-time. 1 applicant, 0% accepted. In 1997, 2 degrees awarded. *Degree requirements:* Thesis or alternative required, foreign language not required. *Application deadline:* 8/1 (priority date; rolling processing). *Application fee:* $20 ($30 for international students). *Expenses:* Tuition $3166 per year full-time, $176 per hour part-time for state residents; $7805 per year full-time, $176 per hour part-time for nonresidents. Fees $194 per year full-time, $12.50 per semester (minimum) part-time. *Financial aid:* Application deadline 3/1. • Dr. Hilliard K. Macomber, Acting Head, 319-273-2420.

University of Northern Iowa, College of Natural Sciences, Interdisciplinary Program in Science Education, Cedar Falls, IA 50614. Awards MA, SP. Students: 4 full-time (2 women), 7 part-time (3 women); includes 3 international. Average age 33. 3 applicants, 100% accepted. In 1997, 10 master's awarded. *Degree requirements:* For master's, thesis or alternative required, foreign language not required. *Application deadline:* 8/1 (priority date; rolling processing). *Application fee:* $20 ($30 for international students). *Expenses:* Tuition $3166 per year full-time, $176 per hour part-time for state residents; $7805 per year full-time, $176 per hour part-time for nonresidents. Fees $194 per year full-time, $12.50 per semester (minimum) part-time. *Financial aid:* Application deadline 3/1. • Dr. Tim Cooney, Head, 319-273-2380.

University of North Florida, College of Education, Department of Elementary and Secondary Education, Program in Science Education, Jacksonville, FL 32224-2645. Awards M Ed. Accredited by NCATE. Part-time and evening/weekend programs available. Faculty: 2 full-time (1 woman). Students: 1 part-time (0 women). Average age 40. 0 applicants. *Entrance requirements:* GRE General Test (minimum combined score of 1000), minimum GPA of 3.0. Application deadline: rolling. Application fee: $20. *Tuition:* $3388 per year full-time, $141 per credit hour part-time for state residents; $11,634 per year full-time, $485 per credit hour part-time for nonresidents. *Faculty research:* Memory and learning, effective schools. • Dr. Dennis Holt, Chairperson, Department of Elementary and Secondary Education, 904-646-2610.

University of Oklahoma, College of Education, Department of Instructional Leadership and Academic Curriculum, Program in Instructional Leadership and Academic Curriculum, Norman, OK 73019-0390. Offerings include science education (M Ed, PhD). Accredited by NCATE. Program faculty: 19 full-time (12 women), 12 part-time (11 women). *Degree requirements:* For doctorate, variable foreign language requirement, dissertation. *Entrance requirements:* For master's, TOEFL (minimum score 550), 12 hours of course work in education; for doctorate, GRE General Test (minimum combined score of 1000), TOEFL (minimum score 500), master's degree, minimum graduate GPA of 3.0. Application deadline: 6/1 (priority date; rolling processing). Application fee: $25. *Expenses:* Tuition $1920 per year full-time, $80 per credit hour part-time for state residents; $6108 per year full-time, $255 per credit hour part-time for nonresidents. Fees $468 per year full-time, $12 per semester (minimum) part-time. • Dr. Bonnie Konopak, Chair, Department of Instructional Leadership and Academic Curriculum, 405-325-1498.

University of Pittsburgh, School of Education, Department of Instruction and Learning, Program in Secondary Education, Pittsburgh, PA 15260. Offerings include science education (MAT, M Ed, MS, Ed D, PhD). *Degree requirements:* For doctorate, dissertation required, foreign language not required. *Average time to degree:* master's–2 years full-time, 4 years part-time; doctorate–4 years full-time, 6 years part-time. *Entrance requirements:* For doctorate, GRE General Test, TOEFL (minimum score 650). Application deadline: 2/1. Application fee: $30 ($40 for international students). *Expenses:* Tuition $8018 per year full-time, $329 per credit part-time for state residents; $16,508 per year full-time, $680 per credit part-time for nonresidents. Fees $480 per year full-time, $180 per year part-time. • Application contact: Jackie Harden, Manager, 412-648-7060. Fax: 412-648-1899. E-mail: jackie@sched.fsl.pitt.edu.

University of Puerto Rico, Río Piedras, College of Education, Program in Curriculum and Teaching, San Juan, PR 00931. Offerings include biology education (M Ed), chemistry education (M Ed), physics education (M Ed). *Degree requirements:* Thesis required, foreign language not required. *Entrance requirements:* PAEG, minimum GPA of 3.0. Application deadline: 2/21. Application fee: $17.

University of South Alabama, College of Education, Department of Curriculum and Instruction, Mobile, AL 36688-0002. Offerings include natural science education (M Ed), science education (M Ed). One or more programs accredited by NCATE. Department faculty: 13 full-time (6 women). *Degree requirements:* Comprehensive exams required, foreign language

Directory: Science Education

University of South Alabama (continued)

and thesis not required. *Entrance requirements:* GRE General Test (minimum combined score of 1000) or MAT (minimum score 37), minimum GPA of 3.0. Application deadline: 9/1 (priority date; rolling processing). Application fee: $25. • Dr. Walter S. Hopkins, Chairman, 334-380-2893.

University of South Carolina, Graduate School, College of Liberal Arts, Department of Geography, Columbia, SC 29208. Offerings include geography education (IMA, MAT). Accredited by NCATE. IMA and MAT offered in cooperation with the College of Education. Department faculty: 19 full-time (3 women), 3 part-time (0 women). *Application deadline:* 4/1 (rolling processing; 11/1 for spring admission). *Application fee:* $35. Electronic applications accepted. *Expenses:* Tuition $3894 per year full-time, $193 per credit hour part-time for state residents; $8114 per year full-time, $404 per credit hour part-time for nonresidents. Fees $125 per year full-time, $37 per semester (minimum) part-time. • Dr. Susan L. Cutter, Chair, 803-777-5236. Fax: 807-777-4972. E-mail: scutter@garnet.cla.sc.edu. Application contact: Dr. Lisle Mitchell, Director of Graduate Studies, 803-777-5234. Fax: 803-777-4972. E-mail: mitchell@garnet.cla.sc.edu.

University of South Carolina, Graduate School, College of Science and Mathematics, Department of Biological Sciences, Columbia, SC 29208. Offerings include biology education (IMA, MAT). Accredited by NCATE. IMA and MAT offered in cooperation with the College of Education. Department faculty: 43 full-time (6 women). *Application deadline:* 2/15 (priority date). *Application fee:* $35. Electronic applications accepted. *Expenses:* Tuition $3894 per year full-time, $193 per credit hour part-time for state residents; $8114 per year full-time, $404 per credit hour part-time for nonresidents. Fees $125 per year full-time, $37 per semester (minimum) part-time. • Dr. Franklin Berger, Chair, 803-777-4141. Application contact: Dr. Franklyn F. Bolander, Director of Graduate Studies, 803-777-2755. Fax: 803-777-4002. E-mail: bolander@sc.edu.

University of Southern Mississippi, College of Science and Technology, Center for Science Education, Hattiesburg, MS 39406-5167. Awards M Ed, MS, Ed D, PhD. Faculty: 5 part-time (0 women). Students: 8 full-time (4 women), 17 part-time (12 women); includes 2 minority (both Asian Americans), 2 international. Average age 43. 9 applicants, 56% accepted. In 1997, 8 master's, 5 doctorates awarded. *Degree requirements:* For master's, thesis or alternative; for doctorate, 2 foreign languages (computer language can substitute for one), dissertation. *Entrance requirements:* For master's, GRE General Test, minimum GPA of 2.5; for doctorate, GRE General Test, minimum GPA of 3.5. Application deadline: 8/9 (priority date; rolling processing). Application fee: $0 ($25 for international students). *Tuition:* $2870 per year full-time, $137 per credit hour part-time for state residents; $5972 per year full-time, $172 per credit hour part-time for nonresidents. *Financial aid:* Fellowships, teaching assistantships, Federal Work-Study available. Financial aid application deadline: 3/15. • Dr. Don Cotten, Director, 601-266-4739.

University of South Florida, College of Education, Department of Secondary Education, Program in Science Education, Tampa, FL 33620-9951. Awards MA, M Ed, PhD, Ed S. Accredited by NCATE. Part-time and evening/weekend programs available. Students: 3 full-time (all women), 20 part-time (14 women); includes 1 minority (African American), 3 international. Average age 33. 12 applicants, 58% accepted. In 1997, 6 master's, 1 doctorate awarded. *Degree requirements:* For doctorate, dissertation, 2 tools of research in foreign language, statistics, and/or computers. *Entrance requirements:* For master's, GRE General Test (minimum combined score of 1000), minimum GPA of 3.5 in last 60 hours; for doctorate, GRE General Test (minimum combined score of 1000), minimum GPA of 3.0 (undergraduate) or 3.5 (graduate), for Ed S, GRE General Test (minimum combined score of 1000). Application deadline: 6/1 (10/15 for spring admission). Application fee: $20. Electronic applications accepted. *Tuition:* $142 per credit hour for state residents; $486 per credit hour for nonresidents. *Financial aid:* Federal Work-Study, institutionally sponsored loans available. Aid available to part-time students. Financial aid applicants required to submit FAFSA. • Application contact: Fred Prince, Coordinator, 813-974-2816. Fax: 813-974-3837. E-mail: prince@tempest.coedu.usf.edu.

University of Tennessee, Knoxville, College of Education, Program in Education I, Knoxville, TN 37996. Offerings include math science and social studies education (PhD). Accredited by NCATE. *Degree requirements:* 1 foreign language (computer language can substitute), dissertation. *Entrance requirements:* GRE General Test, TOEFL (minimum score 550), minimum GPA of 2.7. Application deadline: 2/1 (priority date; rolling processing). Application fee: $35. Electronic applications accepted. *Tuition:* $3354 per year full-time, $181 per semester hour part-time for state residents; $8410 per year full-time, $462 per semester hour part-time for nonresidents. • Dr. Tom George, Associate Dean, 423-974-0907. Fax: 423-974-8718. E-mail: tgeorge1@utk.edu.

University of Tennessee, Knoxville, College of Education, Program in Education II, Knoxville, TN 37996. Offerings include science education (MS, Ed D, Ed S). Accredited by NCATE. *Degree requirements:* For master's and Ed S, thesis optional, foreign language not required; for doctorate, dissertation required, foreign language not required. *Entrance requirements:* For master's, TOEFL (minimum score 550), minimum GPA of 2.7; for doctorate, GRE General Test, TOEFL (minimum score 550), minimum GPA of 2.7; for Ed S, TOEFL (minimum score 550), GRE General Test, minimum GPA of 2.7. Application deadline: 2/1 (priority date; rolling processing). Application fee: $35. Electronic applications accepted. *Tuition:* $3354 per year full-time, $181 per semester hour part-time for state residents; $8410 per year full-time, $462 per semester hour part-time for nonresidents. • Dr. Tom George, Associate Dean, 423-974-0907. Fax: 423-974-8718. E-mail: tgeorge1@utk.edu.

The University of Texas at Austin, Graduate School, College of Education, Programs in Science/Mathematics Education, Program in Science Education, Austin, TX 78712. Awards MA, M Ed, PhD. Students: 76 (46 women); includes 6 minority (3 African Americans, 3 Hispanics), 14 international. 23 applicants, 83% accepted. *Entrance requirements:* GRE General Test. Application fee: $50 ($75 for international students). *Expenses:* Tuition $2592 per year full-time, $324 per semester (minimum) part-time for state residents; $7704 per year full-time, $963 per semester (minimum) part-time for nonresidents. Fees $778 per year full-time, $161 per semester (minimum) part-time. *Financial aid:* Application deadline 2/1. • Application contact: Lowell J. Bethel, Graduate Adviser.

The University of Texas at Dallas, School of Natural Sciences and Mathematics, Program in Mathematics and Science Education, Richardson, TX 75083-0688. Offers mathematics education (MAT), science education (MAT). Part-time and evening/weekend programs available. Faculty: 3 full-time (1 woman). Students: 3 full-time (2 women), 19 part-time (18 women); includes 3 minority (2 African Americans, 1 Hispanic). Average age 39. 9 applicants, 89% accepted. In 1997, 3 degrees awarded. *Degree requirements:* Computer language, minimum GPA of 3.0 required, foreign language and thesis not required. *Entrance requirements:* GRE General Test (minimum combined score of 1000), TOEFL (minimum score 550), minimum GPA of 3.0 in upper-level course work in field. Application deadline: 7/15 (rolling processing; 11/15 for spring admission). Application fee: $25 ($75 for international students). *Financial aid:* 2 students received aid; research assistantships, teaching assistantships, Federal Work-Study available. Aid available to part-time students. Financial aid application deadline: 11/1. *Faculty research:* Techniques for training teachers, philosophic definitions of science held by working scientists, science teachers, science students. • Dr. Frederick Fifer, Head, 972-883-2496. Fax: 972-883-6371. E-mail: ffifer@utdallas.edu.

The University of Texas at Tyler, School of Education and Psychology, Department of Curriculum and Instruction, Tyler, TX 75799-0001. Offerings include elementary education (M Ed, Certificate), with options in biology, English, history, reading; secondary education (M Ed, Certificate), with options in biology, English, history, mathematics. Department faculty: 13 full-time (8 women). *Application fee:* $0 ($50 for international students). *Tuition:* $2144 per year full-time, $337 per semester (minimum) part-time for state residents; $7256 per year full-time, $964 per semester (minimum) part-time for nonresidents. • Dr. Bill Bruce, Chair, 903-566-7133. E-mail: wbruce@mail.uttyl.edu. Application contact: Martha D. Wheat, Director of Admissions and Student Records, 903-566-7201. Fax: 903-566-7068.

University of the Sciences in Philadelphia, Program in Science Teaching, Philadelphia, PA 19104-4495. Awards MS. Program new for fall 1998. *Entrance requirements:* GRE General Test, TOEFL. Application deadline: 5/1 (rolling processing; 10/1 for spring admission). Application fee: $30. • Dr. Lois Peck, Director, 215-596-8922.

University of Tulsa, College of Arts and Sciences, School of Education, Program in Math/Science Education, Tulsa, OK 74104-3189. Awards MSMSE. Accredited by NCATE. Part-time programs available. Students: 1 (woman) full-time, 5 part-time (all women). Average age 41. 4 applicants, 100% accepted. In 1997, 12 degrees awarded. *Entrance requirements:* GRE General Test (minimum combined score of 1000), TOEFL (minimum score 575), minimum GPA of 3.0. Application deadline: rolling. Application fee: $30. Electronic applications accepted. *Expenses:* Tuition $480 per credit hour. Fees $2 per credit hour. *Financial aid:* In 1997–98, 1 student received aid, including 1 teaching assistantship totaling $15,840; fellowships, research assistantships, partial tuition waivers, Federal Work-Study also available. Aid available to part-time students. Financial aid application deadline: 2/1; applicants required to submit FAFSA. • Dr. Eileen W. Kelble, Adviser, 918-631-2720. Fax: 918-631-2133.

University of Utah, College of Science, Department of Chemistry, Salt Lake City, UT 84112-1107. Offerings include science teacher education (MS). Department faculty: 30 full-time (2 women), 27 part-time (2 women). *Application deadline:* 7/1. *Application fee:* $30 ($50 for international students). *Tuition:* $2045 per year full-time, $562 per semester (minimum) part-time for state residents; $6129 per year full-time, $1607 per semester (minimum) part-time for nonresidents. • C. Dale Poulter, Chair, 801-581-6685. Fax: 801-581-4391. Application contact: Charles A. Wight, Director of Graduate Studies, 801-581-8796.

University of Vermont, College of Agriculture and Life Sciences, Department of Botany, Burlington, VT 05405-0160. Offerings include biology (MST), botany (MAT, MS, PhD). One or more programs accredited by NCATE. *Degree requirements:* For doctorate, 1 foreign language, dissertation. *Entrance requirements:* For doctorate, GRE General Test, GRE Subject Test, TOEFL (minimum score 550). Application deadline: 2/15. Application fee: $25. *Expenses:* Tuition $302 per credit for state residents; $755 per credit for nonresidents. Fees $434 per year full-time, $46 per semester (minimum) part-time. • Dr. D. Barrington, Interim Chairperson, 802-656-2930. Application contact: Dr. C. Paris, Coordinator, 802-656-2930.

University of Vermont, College of Arts and Sciences, Department of Biology, Burlington, VT 05405-0160. Offerings include biology education (MAT, MST). Accredited by NCATE. Department faculty: 17. *Application deadline:* 4/1 (priority date; rolling processing). *Application fee:* $25. *Expenses:* Tuition $302 per credit for state residents; $755 per credit for nonresidents. Fees $434 per year full-time, $46 per semester (minimum) part-time. • Dr. Judith Van Houten, Chairperson, 802-656-2922. Application contact: N. Gotelli, Coordinator, 802-656-2922.

University of Vermont, College of Arts and Sciences, Department of Chemistry, Burlington, VT 05405-0160. Offerings include chemistry education (MAT). Accredited by NCATE. *Application deadline:* 4/1 (priority date; rolling processing). *Application fee:* $25. *Expenses:* Tuition $302 per credit for state residents; $755 per credit for nonresidents. Fees $434 per year full-time, $46 per semester (minimum) part-time. • Dr. C. H. Bushweller, Chairperson, 802-656-2594. Application contact: Dr. W. Geiger, Coordinator, 802-656-2594.

University of Vermont, College of Arts and Sciences, Department of Geology, Burlington, VT 05405-0122. Offerings include geology education (MAT, MST). *Application deadline:* 4/1 (priority date; rolling processing). *Application fee:* $25. *Expenses:* Tuition $302 per credit for state residents; $755 per credit for nonresidents. Fees $434 per year full-time, $46 per semester (minimum) part-time. • Dr. B. Doolan, Acting Chairperson, 802-656-3396. Application contact: Dr. P. Bierman, Coordinator, 802-656-3396.

University of Vermont, College of Arts and Sciences, Department of Physics, Burlington, VT 05405-0160. Offerings include physical sciences (MST), physics (MAT, MS). *Application deadline:* 4/1 (priority date; rolling processing). *Application fee:* $25. *Expenses:* Tuition $302 per credit for state residents; $755 per credit for nonresidents. Fees $434 per year full-time, $46 per semester (minimum) part-time. • Dr. David Smith, Chairperson, 802-656-2644. Application contact: R. Dentenbeck, Coordinator, 802-656-2644.

University of Victoria, Faculty of Education, Department of Social and Natural Sciences, Victoria, BC V8W 2Y2, Canada. Offerings include curriculum and instruction (MA), with options in mathematics, science, social studies; science education (M Ed). Postbaccalaureate distance learning degree programs offered (minimal on-campus study). Department faculty: 13 full-time (4 women). *Degree requirements:* Thesis (for some programs), project (M Ed) required, foreign language not required. *Average time to degree:* master's–3.3 years full-time. *Entrance requirements:* Minimum B average. Application deadline: 4/30 (rolling processing). Application fee: $50. *Tuition:* $2080 per year full-time, $557 per semester part-time. • Dr. G. Snively, Chair, 250-721-7769. E-mail: gsnivley@uvic.ca. Application contact: Sarah Baylow, Graduate Secretary, 250-721-7882. Fax: 250-721-7767. E-mail: sbaylow@uvic.ca.

University of Virginia, Graduate School of Arts and Sciences, Department of Biology, Charlottesville, VA 22903. Offerings include biology education (MAT). Accredited by NCATE. Department faculty: 39 full-time (8 women), 3 part-time (0 women), 40 FTE. *Application fee:* $40. *Tuition:* $4870 per year full-time, $941 per semester (minimum) part-time for state residents; $15,818 per year full-time, $2745 per semester (minimum) part-time for nonresidents. • W. Otto Friesen, Chairman, 804-924-7118. Application contact: Duane J. Osheim, Associate Dean, 804-924-7184.

University of Virginia, Graduate School of Arts and Sciences, Department of Chemistry, Charlottesville, VA 22903. Offerings include chemistry education (MAT). Accredited by NCATE. Department faculty: 27 full-time (2 women), 1 (woman) part-time. *Application deadline:* 7/15 (rolling processing; 12/1 for spring admission). *Application fee:* $40. *Tuition:* $4870 per year full-time, $941 per semester (minimum) part-time for state residents; $15,818 per year full-time, $2745 per semester (minimum) part-time for nonresidents. • Timothy L. MacDonald, Chairman, 804-924-3344. Application contact: Duane J. Osheim, Associate Dean, 804-924-7184.

The University of West Alabama, College of Education, Department of Foundations, Livingston, AL 35470. Offerings include secondary education (MAT, M Ed), with options in biology with certification (MAT), environmental science with certification (MAT), history with certification (MAT), language arts with certification (MAT), library media with certification (MAT), mathematics with certification (MAT). Accredited by NCATE. *Application deadline:* 9/10 (priority date; rolling processing; 3/24 for spring admission). *Application fee:* $15. *Tuition:* $70 per quarter hour.

The University of West Alabama, College of Natural Sciences and Mathematics, Department of Biological Sciences, Livingston, AL 35470. Awards MAT. Accredited by NCATE. *Tuition:* $70 per quarter hour.

The University of West Alabama, College of Natural Sciences and Mathematics, Department of Environmental Science, Livingston, AL 35470. Awards MAT. *Tuition:* $70 per quarter hour.

University of West Florida, College of Science and Technology, Department of Biology, Program in General Biology, Pensacola, FL 32514-5750. Offerings include biology education (MST). Accredited by NCATE. *Application deadline:* 7/1 (rolling processing; 11/1 for spring admission). *Application fee:* $20. *Tuition:* $131 per credit hour (minimum) for state residents; $436 per credit hour (minimum) for nonresidents. • Dr. J. Riehm, Chairperson, Department of Biology, 850-474-2748.

University of Wisconsin–Eau Claire, College of Professional Studies, School of Education, Program in Secondary Education, Eau Claire, WI 54702-4004. Offerings include biology (MAT, MST). *Application deadline:* 7/1 (rolling processing; 12/1 for spring admission). *Application fee:* $45. *Tuition:* $3651 per year full-time, $611 per semester (minimum) part-time for state residents; $11,295 per year full-time, $1886 per semester (minimum) part-time for nonresidents. • Stephen Kurth, Associate Dean, School of Education, 715-836-3671.

University of Wisconsin–Madison, School of Education, Department of Curriculum and Instruction, Program in Science Education, Madison, WI 53706-1380. Awards MS. *Application fee:* $38. *Tuition:* $4928 per year full-time, $926 per semester (minimum) part-time for state residents; $15,190 per year full-time, $2849 per semester (minimum) part-time for nonresidents.

University of Wisconsin–Oshkosh, College of Letters and Science, Department of Physics and Astronomy, Oshkosh, WI 54901-8602. Offerings include physics (MS), with options in instrumentation, physics education. Department faculty: 6 full-time (1 woman). *Degree requirements:* Thesis required, foreign language not required. *Entrance requirements:* Minimum GPA of 2.75, BS in physics or related field. Application deadline: rolling. Application fee: $45. *Tuition:* $3638 per year full-time, $609 per semester (minimum) part-time for state residents; $11,282 per year full-time, $1884 per semester (minimum) part-time for nonresidents. • Dr. Merlin Passow, Chair, 920-424-7108. Application contact: Dr. Sandra Gade, Coordinator, 920-424-7103. E-mail: gade@uwosh.edu.

University of Wisconsin–River Falls, College of Arts and Science, Program in Science and Mathematics, River Falls, WI 54022-5001. Offers mathematics education (MSE), science education (MSE). One or more programs accredited by NCATE. Students: 23 (9 women). *Degree requirements:* Thesis (for some programs). *Application deadline:* 3/1. *Application fee:* $45. *Financial aid:* Research assistantships available. Financial aid application deadline: 3/1. • Don Leake, Coordinator, 715-425-3326. E-mail: don.leake@uwrf.edu. Application contact: Graduate Admissions, 715-425-3843.

University of Wyoming, College of Arts and Sciences, Natural Science Program, Laramie, WY 82071. Awards MS, MST. Faculty: 1 full-time (0 women). Students: 4 full-time (3 women), 4 part-time (3 women). 14 applicants, 50% accepted. In 1997, 3 degrees awarded. *Entrance requirements:* GRE General Test, minimum GPA of 3.0. Application deadline: 6/1 (priority date; rolling processing). Application fee: $40. *Expenses:* Tuition $2430 per year full-time, $135 per credit hour part-time for state residents; $7518 per year full-time, $418 per credit hour part-time for nonresidents. Fees $386 per year full-time, $9.25 per credit hour part-time. *Financial aid:* In 1997–98, 1 teaching assistantship (to a first-year student) was awarded; Federal Work-Study, institutionally sponsored loans also available. Financial aid application deadline: 3/1; applicants required to submit FAFSA. • Ronald Canterna, Head, 307-766-6381.

Vanderbilt University, Peabody College, Department of Teaching and Learning, Nashville, TN 37240-1001. Offerings include science education (M Ed, Ed D). Accredited by NCATE. *Entrance requirements:* GRE General Test, MAT. Application deadline: 3/1 (priority date; rolling processing). Application fee: $35. • Carolyn Evertson, Chair, 615-322-8100.

Wayne State College, Division of Math and Science, Wayne, NE 68787. Awards MSE. One or more programs accredited by NCATE. Faculty: 16 part-time (3 women). Students: 9 part-time (4 women); includes 1 minority (African American). Average age 32. In 1997, 5 degrees awarded. *Degree requirements:* Comprehensive exam, research paper. *Entrance requirements:* GRE General Test. Application deadline: rolling. Application fee: $10. *Expenses:* Tuition $1788 per year full-time, $75 per credit hour part-time for state residents; $3576 per year full-time, $149 per credit hour part-time for nonresidents. Fees $360 per year full-time, $15 per credit hour part-time. *Financial aid:* In 1997–98, 2 teaching assistantships were awarded. Financial aid application deadline: 5/1; applicants required to submit FAFSA. • Dr. J. S. Johar, Head, 402-375-7329.

Wayne State College, Division of Education, Program in Curriculum and Instruction, Wayne, NE 68787. Offerings include science education (MSE). Accredited by NCATE. *Degree requirements:* Comprehensive exam, research paper required, foreign language not required. *Entrance requirements:* GRE General Test. Application deadline: rolling. Application fee: $10. *Expenses:* Tuition $1788 per year full-time, $75 per credit hour part-time for state residents; $3576 per year full-time, $149 per credit hour part-time for nonresidents. Fees $360 per year full-time, $15 per credit hour part-time. • Dr. Diane Alexander, Head, Division of Education, 402-375-7389.

Wayne State University, College of Education, Division of Teacher Education, Detroit, MI 48202. Offerings include science (Ed S). Accredited by NCATE. Division faculty: 53. *Application deadline:* 7/1. *Application fee:* $20 ($30 for international students). *Expenses:* Tuition $163 per credit hour for state residents; $355 per credit hour for nonresidents. Fees $498 per year full-time, $114 per semester (minimum) part-time. • Dr. Sharon Elliott, Assistant Dean, 313-577-0902.

Webster University, School of Education, Department of Multidisciplinary Studies, St. Louis, MO 63119-3194. Offerings include science education (MAT). Department faculty: 7 full-time (5 women). *Entrance requirements:* 2 years of work experience in education, interview, min GPA of 2.5. Application deadline: rolling. Application fee: $25 ($50 for international students). *Tuition:* $350 per credit hour. • Roy Tamashiro, Chair, 314-968-7098. Fax: 314-968-7118. E-mail: tamashro@webster.edu. Application contact: Beth Russell, Director of Graduate Admissions, 314-968-7089. Fax: 314-968-7166. E-mail: russelmb@webster.edu.

Wesleyan College, Department of Education, Program in Middle-Level Mathematics and Middle-Level Science Education, Macon, GA 31210-4462. Awards MA. Offered during summer only. Part-time programs available. Faculty: 10 full-time (4 women), 3 part-time (2 women). Students: 7 full-time (all women). Average age 32. 12 applicants, 75% accepted. *Degree requirements:* Practicum, professional portfolio required, thesis optional, foreign language not required. *Average time to degree:* master's–3 years full-time, 6 years part-time. *Entrance requirements:* TOEFL (minimum score 550), interview, teaching certificate. Application deadline: rolling. Application fee: $25. *Tuition:* $150 per semester hour. *Financial aid:* Federal Work-Study available. Financial aid application deadline: 4/15; applicants required to submit FAFSA. *Faculty research:* Instructional technology, cognitive development, verbal classroom interactions. • Application contact: Dr. Patricia R. Hardeman, Assistant Dean and Registrar, 912-477-1110. Fax: 912-757-4030.

Western Carolina University, College of Education and Allied Professions, Department of Administration, Curriculum and Instruction, Programs in Secondary Education, Cullowhee, NC 28723. Offerings include biology (MAT), chemistry (MAT). One or more programs accredited by NCATE. *Degree requirements:* Comprehensive exam required, foreign language and thesis not required. *Entrance requirements:* GRE General Test. Application deadline: rolling. Application fee: $35. *Tuition:* $1799 per year full-time, $144 per credit hour (minimum) part-time for state residents; $9069 per year full-time, $1053 per credit hour (minimum) part-time for nonresidents. • Application contact: Kathleen Owen, Assistant to the Dean, 828-227-7398. Fax: 828-227-7480.

Western Kentucky University, Ogden College of Science, Technology, and Health, Department of Biology, Bowling Green, KY 42101-3576. Offerings include biology (MA Ed, MS). One or more programs accredited by NCATE. Department faculty: 18 full-time (3 women). *Degree requirements:* Thesis (for some programs), research tool required, foreign language not required. *Average time to degree:* master's–2 years full-time. *Entrance requirements:* GRE General Test. Application deadline: 8/1 (priority date; rolling processing; 12/1 for spring admission). Application fee: $20. *Tuition:* $2460 per year full-time, $133 per credit hour part-time for state residents; $6700 per year full-time, $369 per credit hour part-time for nonresidents. • Blaine Ferrell, Acting Head, 502-745-3696. Fax: 502-745-6856.

Western Kentucky University, Ogden College of Science, Technology, and Health, Department of Chemistry, Bowling Green, KY 42101-3576. Offerings include chemistry (MA Ed, MS). One or more programs accredited by NCATE. Department faculty: 16 full-time (0 women). *Degree requirements:* 1 foreign language (computer language can substitute), thesis. *Average time to degree:* master's–2 years full-time, 3 years part-time. *Entrance requirements:* GRE General Test (minimum combined score of 1150 on three sections; average 1425), previous course work in chemistry (MS). Application deadline: 8/1 (priority date; rolling processing; 12/1 for spring admission). Application fee: $20. *Tuition:* $2460 per year full-time, $133 per credit hour part-time for state residents; $6700 per year full-time, $369 per credit hour part-time for nonresidents. • Dr. Lowell Shank, Head, 502-745-4986. E-mail: lowell.shank@wku.edu. Application contact: Wei-Ping Pan, Professor, 502-745-5322. Fax: 502-745-5361. E-mail: wei-ping.pan@wku.edu.

Western Kentucky University, Ogden College of Science, Technology, and Health, Department of Physics and Astronomy, Bowling Green, KY 42101-3576. Offers programs in mathematics and science (MA Ed), science (MA Ed). Part-time programs available. Faculty: 6 full-time (0 women). Students: 0. 0 applicants. *Degree requirements:* Thesis. *Entrance requirements:* GRE General Test (minimum combined score of 1150 on three sections), minimum GPA of 2.5. Application deadline: 8/1 (priority date; rolling processing; 12/1 for spring admission). Application fee: $20. *Tuition:* $2460 per year full-time, $133 per credit hour part-time for state residents; $6700 per year full-time, $369 per credit hour part-time for nonresidents. *Financial aid:* Federal Work-Study, institutionally sponsored loans available. Aid available to part-time students. Financial aid application deadline: 4/1; applicants required to submit FAFSA. *Faculty research:* Biophysics and nuclear physics. • Dr. Charles McGruder, Head, 502-745-4357.

Western Michigan University, College of Arts and Sciences, Program in Science Education, Kalamazoo, MI 49008. Awards MA, PhD. Students: 8 full-time (3 women), 34 part-time (21 women); includes 3 minority (2 African Americans, 1 Asian American), 1 international. 10 applicants, 40% accepted. In 1997, 7 master's, 4 doctorates awarded. *Degree requirements:* For doctorate, dissertation, oral and written exams. *Entrance requirements:* For doctorate, GRE General Test. Application deadline: 2/15 (priority date; rolling processing). Application fee: $25. *Expenses:* Tuition $154 per credit hour for state residents; $372 per credit hour for nonresidents. Fees $602 per year full-time, $132 per semester part-time. *Financial aid:* Fellowships, research assistantships, teaching assistantships, Federal Work-Study available. Financial aid application deadline: 2/15; applicants required to submit FAFSA. • Dr. Robert Poel, Director, 616-387-5398. Application contact: Paula J. Boodt, Coordinator, Graduate Admissions and Recruitment, 616-387-2000. E-mail: paulaboodt@wmich.edu.

Western Oregon University, School of Education, Department of Secondary Education, Monmouth, OR 97361. Offerings include science (MAT, MS Ed). Accredited by NCATE. Department faculty: 83 full-time (28 women), 26 part-time (11 women), 92.81 FTE. *Degree requirements:* Written exam required, thesis optional, foreign language not required. *Average time to degree:* master's–1 year full-time, 4 years part-time. *Entrance requirements:* GRE General (average 450 on each section) or MAT (minimum score 30), minimum GPA of 3.0, teaching license. Application deadline: rolling. Application fee: $50. • Dr. George Cabrera, Chair, 503-838-8471. Fax: 503-838-8228. E-mail: cabrerg@wou.edu. Application contact: Alison Marshall, Director of Admissions, 503-838-8211. Fax: 503-838-8067. E-mail: marshaa@wou.edu.

Western Washington University, College of Arts and Sciences, Program in Science Education, Bellingham, WA 98225-5996. Awards M Ed. Part-time programs available. Students: 7 full-time (4 women), 8 part-time (6 women). 6 applicants, 100% accepted. In 1997, 13 degrees awarded. *Degree requirements:* Comprehensive exam required, thesis optional, foreign language not required. *Entrance requirements:* GRE General Test, TOEFL (average 567), minimum GPA of 3.0 in last 60 semester hours or last 90 quarter hours. Application deadline: 6/1 (rolling processing; 2/1 for spring admission). Application fee: $35. *Expenses:* Tuition $4200 per year full-time, $140 per credit part-time for state residents; $12,780 per year full-time, $426 per credit part-time for nonresidents. Fees $249 per year full-time, $83 per quarter part-time. *Financial aid:* Application deadline 3/31. • Dr. John Miller, Coordinator, 360-650-3167.

Wheeling Jesuit University, Department of Mathematics, Wheeling, WV 26003-6295. Offers programs in mathematics education (MS), science education (MS). Admissions temporarily suspended. Students: 0. *Degree requirements:* Thesis optional, foreign language not required. *Tuition:* $360 per credit hour.

Wilkes University, Department of Education, Wilkes-Barre, PA 18766-0002. Offerings include secondary education (MS Ed), with options in biology, chemistry, English, history. Department faculty: 6 full-time, 14 part-time. *Application deadline:* rolling. *Application fee:* $30. *Expenses:* Tuition $12,552 per year full-time, $523 per credit hour part-time. Fees $240 per year full-time, $10 per credit hour part-time. • Dr. Douglas Lynch, Chair, 717-408-4680.

Wilkes University, Department of Physics, Wilkes-Barre, PA 18766-0002. Awards MS, MS Ed. Faculty: 3 full-time. Students: 1 full-time (0 women), 1 (woman) part-time. In 1997, 2 degrees awarded. *Degree requirements:* Thesis or alternative required, foreign language not required. *Entrance requirements:* GRE. Application deadline: rolling. Application fee: $30. *Expenses:* Tuition $12,552 per year full-time, $523 per credit hour part-time. Fees $240 per year full-time, $10 per credit hour part-time. *Financial aid:* Application deadline 2/28; applicants required to submit FAFSA. • Dr. Roger Maxwell, Chairman, 717-408-4822.

Wright State University, College of Science and Mathematics, Department of Geological Sciences, Program in Earth Science Education, Dayton, OH 45435. Awards MST. Students: 3 full-time (2 women), 4 part-time (3 women). 4 applicants, 100% accepted. In 1997, 1 degree awarded. *Degree requirements:* Computer language required, thesis optional, foreign language not required. *Entrance requirements:* GRE General Test, TOEFL (minimum score 550). Application fee: $25. *Tuition:* $5109 per year full-time, $161 per credit hour part-time for state residents; $9039 per year full-time, $282 per credit hour part-time for nonresidents. *Financial aid:* Fellowships, research assistantships, teaching assistantships available. Aid available to part-time students. Financial aid application deadline: 3/1; applicants required to submit FAFSA. *Faculty research:* Pedagogy. • Dr. Benjamin Richard, Coordinator, 937-775-3455. Application contact: Deborah Cowles, Assistant to Chair, 937-775-3455. Fax: 937-775-3301.

Wright State University, College of Science and Mathematics, Department of Physics, Program in Physics Education, Dayton, OH 45435. Awards MST. Part-time and evening/weekend programs available. Students: 1 full-time (0 women), 2 part-time (both women). Average age 35. 2 applicants, 100% accepted. *Degree requirements:* Thesis optional, foreign language not required. *Entrance requirements:* TOEFL (minimum score 550). Application deadline: 3/1 (priority date; rolling processing). Application fee: $25. *Tuition:* $5109 per year full-time, $161 per credit hour part-time for state residents; $9039 per year full-time, $282 per credit hour part-time for nonresidents. *Financial aid:* Fellowships, research assistantships, teaching assistantships, full and partial tuition waivers, Federal Work-Study, institutionally sponsored loans available. Aid available to part-time students. Financial aid application deadline: 3/1; applicants required to submit FAFSA. *Faculty research:* Pedagogy. • Dr. Gust Bambakidis, Chair, Department of Physics, 937-775-2954. Fax: 937-775-3301.

Social Sciences Education

Adelphi University, School of Education, Program in Secondary Education, Garden City, NY 11530. Offerings include social studies (MA). *Application deadline:* rolling. *Application fee:* $50. *Expenses:* Tuition $16,000 per year full-time, $485 per credit part-time. Fees $500 per year full-time, $150 per semester part-time. • Director, 516-877-4090. Application contact: Jennifer Spiegel, Associate Director of Graduate Admissions, 516-877-3055.

Alabama State University, School of Graduate Studies, College of Education, Department of Curriculum and Instruction, Program in Secondary Education, Montgomery, AL 36101-0271. Offerings include history education (M Ed). Program faculty: 2 full-time (1 woman). *Degree requirements:* Comprehensive exam required, thesis optional. *Entrance requirements:* GRE General Test, MAT or NTE. Application deadline: 7/15 (rolling processing; 12/15 for spring admission). Application fee: $10. *Expenses:* Tuition $85 per credit hour for state residents; $170 per credit hour for nonresidents. Fees $486 per year. • Dr. Linda Bradford, Coordinator, 334-229-4485. Fax: 334-229-4904. E-mail: lbradford@asunet.alasu.edu. Application contact: Dr. Fred Dauser, Dean of Graduate Studies, 334-229-4276. Fax: 334-229-4928.

Alfred University, Graduate School, Division of Education, Alfred, NY 14802-1205. Offerings include secondary education (MS Ed), with options in biology education, chemistry education, earth science education, English education, mathematics education, physics education, social studies education. Division faculty: 45 full-time (12 women). *Degree requirements:* Thesis required (for some programs), foreign language not required. *Entrance requirements:* TOEFL. Application deadline: rolling. Application fee: $50. *Expenses:* Tuition $20,376 per year full-time, $390 per credit hour (minimum) part-time. Fees $546 per year. • Dr. Katherine D. Wiesendanger, Chair, 607-871-2219. E-mail: fwiesendange@bigvax.alfred.edu. Application contact: Cathleen R. Johnson, Assistant Director of Admissions, 607-871-2141. Fax: 607-871-2198. E-mail: johnsonc@bigvax.alfred.edu.

American International College, School of Continuing Education and Graduate Studies, School of Psychology and Education, Department of Education, Springfield, MA 01109-3189. Offerings include history (MAT). Department faculty: 5 full-time (3 women), 15 part-time (9 women). *Application fee:* $15 ($25 for international students). *Expenses:* Tuition $363 per credit hour. Fees $25 per semester. • C. Gerald Weaver, Dean, School of Psychology and Education, 413-747-6338.

Andrews University, School of Graduate Studies, College of Arts and Sciences, Department of History, Berrien Springs, MI 49104. Awards MA, MAT. Part-time programs available. Faculty: 4 full-time (0 women), 2 part-time (0 women). *Degree requirements:* Variable foreign language requirement, thesis optional. *Entrance requirements:* GRE Subject Test. Application deadline: 7/1 (rolling processing). Application fee: $30. *Expenses:* Tuition $290 per quarter hour (minimum). Fees $75 per quarter. *Financial aid:* Fellowships, graduate assistantships, Federal Work-Study, institutionally sponsored loans available. Financial aid application deadline: 6/1. *Faculty research:* American intellectual history, Civil War, American church history, modern German history. • Dr. Gary G. Land, Chairman, 616-471-3292.

Andrews University, School of Graduate Studies, School of Education, Department of Teaching/Learning/Administration, Berrien Springs, MI 49104. Offerings include secondary education (MAT), with options in biology, education, English, English as a second language, French, history, physics. *Application deadline:* 8/15 (rolling processing). *Application fee:* $30. *Expenses:* Tuition $290 per quarter hour (minimum). Fees $75 per quarter. • Dr. William H. Green, Chair, 616-471-3465.

Arkansas Tech University, School of Education, Department of Curriculum and Instruction, Russellville, AR 72801-2222. Offerings include social studies (M Ed). Accredited by NCATE. *Application deadline:* 3/1 (priority date; rolling processing; 10/1 for spring admission). *Application fee:* $0 ($30 for international students). *Expenses:* Tuition $98 per credit hour for state residents; $196 per credit hour for nonresidents. Fees $30 per semester. • Head, 501-968-0290. Fax: 501-964-0811.

Auburn University, College of Education, Department of Curriculum and Teaching, Auburn University, AL 36849-0001. Offerings include secondary education (M Ed, MS, PhD, Ed S), with options in English language arts, mathematics, science, social studies. Accredited by NCATE. Department faculty: 20 full-time (11 women). *Degree requirements:* For master's, thesis (MS) required, foreign language not required; for doctorate, dissertation required, foreign language not required; for Ed S, field project required, foreign language and thesis not required. *Entrance requirements:* For master's and Ed S, GRE General Test; for doctorate, GRE General Test (minimum score 450 on each section, 1000 combined). Application deadline: 9/1 (rolling processing; 3/1 for spring admission). Application fee: $25 ($50 for international students). *Expenses:* Tuition $2760 per year full-time, $76 per credit hour part-time for state residents; $8280 per year full-time, $228 per credit hour part-time for nonresidents. Fees $30 per year full-time, $160 per quarter part-time for state residents; $30 per year full-time, $480 per quarter part-time for nonresidents. • Dr. Andrew M. Weaver, Head, 334-844-4434. E-mail: weaveam@mail.auburn.edu. Application contact: Dr. John F. Pritchett, Dean of the Graduate School, 334-844-4700.

Beaver College, Department of Education, Glenside, PA 19038-3295. Offerings include history education (MA Ed). *Application fee:* $35. *Expenses:* Tuition $6570 per year full-time, $365 per credit part-time. Fees $35 per year.

Boston College, Graduate School of Education, Department of Teacher Education/Special Education and Curriculum and Instruction, Program in Secondary Education, Chestnut Hill, MA 02167-9991. Offerings include history (MAT), Latin and classics (MAT). One or more programs accredited by NCATE. *Application deadline:* 3/15 (11/15 for spring admission). *Application fee:* $40. *Expenses:* Tuition $626 per semester hour. Fees $80 per year (minimum) full-time, $30 per semester part-time. • Application contact: Arline Riordan, Graduate Admissions Director, 617-552-4214. Fax: 617-552-0812. E-mail: riordana@bc.edu.

Boston University, School of Education, Department of Curriculum and Teaching, Program in Social Studies Education, Boston, MA 02215. Awards Ed M, MAT, Ed D, CAGS. Students: 8 full-time (5 women), 5 part-time (2 women). Average age 27. In 1997, 4 master's awarded. *Degree requirements:* For doctorate, dissertation, comprehensive exam required, foreign language not required; for CAGS, comprehensive exam required, foreign language and thesis not required. *Entrance requirements:* For master's and CAGS, GRE or MAT, TOEFL; for doctorate, GRE General Test or MAT, TOEFL. Application deadline: 2/15 (priority date; rolling processing). Application fee: $50. *Expenses:* Tuition $22,830 per year full-time, $713 per credit part-time. Fees $218 per year full-time, $40 per semester part-time. *Financial aid:* Application deadline 3/30. *Faculty research:* Law-focused and intercultural education. • Dr. Stephan Ellenwood, Coordinator, 617-353-3238. E-mail: ellenwoo@bu.edu.

Brooklyn College of the City University of New York, School of Education, Division of Elementary School Education, 2900 Bedford Avenue, Brooklyn, NY 11210-2889. Offerings include humanities education (MS Ed), social science (MS Ed). *Average time to degree:* master's–1.5 years full-time, 3 years part-time. *Entrance requirements:* TOEFL (minimum score 500), interview, previous course work in education, writing sample. Application deadline: 3/1 (rolling processing; 11/1 for spring admission). Application fee: $40. *Expenses:* Tuition $4350 per year full-time, $185 per credit part-time for state residents; $7600 per year full-time, $320 per credit part-time for nonresidents. Fees $500 per year for state residents; $806 per year for nonresidents. • Dr. Milga Morales, Coordinator, 718-951-5933.

Brooklyn College of the City University of New York, School of Education, Division of Secondary Education, 2900 Bedford Avenue, Brooklyn, NY 11210-2889. Offerings include social studies education (MA), speech (MA). *Application deadline:* 3/1 (11/1 for spring admission). *Application fee:* $40. *Expenses:* Tuition $4350 per year full-time, $185 per credit part-time for state residents; $7600 per year full-time, $320 per credit part-time for nonresidents. Fees $500 per year for state residents; $806 per year for nonresidents. • Dr. Peter Taubman, Coordinator, 718-951-5218. Fax: 718-951-4816. E-mail: ptaubman@brooklyn.cuny.edu.

Brown University, Department of Education, Providence, RI 02912. Offerings include secondary social studies (MAT). MAT (elementary education K–6) new for fall 1998. Department faculty: 4 full-time (2 women), 20 part-time (15 women). *Average time to degree:* master's–1 year full-time. *Entrance requirements:* GRE (score in 95th percentile or higher). Application deadline: 1/2 (priority date). Application fee: $60. *Expenses:* Tuition $23,616 per year. Fees $436 per year. • Lawrence Wakeford, Chairman, 401-863-2407. Application contact: Yvette Nachmias, Teacher Education Coordinator, 401-863-3364. Fax: 401-863-1276. E-mail: yvette_nachmias@brown.edu.

California State University, San Bernardino, Graduate Studies, School of Education, San Bernardino, CA 92407-2397. Offerings include history and English for secondary teachers (MA). School faculty: 77 full-time (38 women). *Application deadline:* 8/31 (priority date). *Application fee:* $55. *Expenses:* Tuition $0 for state residents; $164 per unit for nonresidents. Fees $1922 per year full-time, $1256 per year part-time. • Patricia Arlin, Dean, 909-880-3600. Fax: 909-880-7011.

California State University, Stanislaus, College of Arts, Letters, and Sciences, Department of History, Turlock, CA 95382. Offerings include secondary school history teaching (MA). *Degree requirements:* 1 foreign language, thesis. *Entrance requirements:* GRE General Test, GRE Subject Test, minimum undergraduate GPA of 3.0. Application fee: $55. *Expenses:* Tuition $0 for state residents; $246 per unit for nonresidents. Fees $1779 per year full-time, $1113 per year part-time. • Dr. Austin Ahanotu, Chair, 209-667-3238. Application contact: Dr. Nancy J. Taniguchi, Graduate Coordinator, 209-667-3522.

Campbell University, School of Education, Buies Creek, NC 27506. Offerings include social science education (M Ed). Accredited by NCATE. School faculty: 8 full-time (6 women), 6 part-time (0 women). *Application deadline:* 8/1 (priority date; rolling processing; 1/2 for spring admission). *Application fee:* $25. *Tuition:* $168 per credit hour (minimum). • Dr. Margaret Giesbrecht, Dean, 910-893-1630. Fax: 910-893-1999. E-mail: giesbrec@mailcenter.campbell.edu. Application contact: James S. Farthing, Director of Graduate Admissions, 910-893-1200 Ext. 1318. Fax: 910-893-1288.

Carthage College, Division of Teacher Education, Kenosha, WI 53140-1994. Offerings include social sciences (M Ed). College faculty: 6 full-time (4 women), 13 part-time (8 women). *Degree requirements:* Thesis optional, foreign language not required. *Average time to degree:* master's–5 years part-time. *Entrance requirements:* MAT, minimum B average. Application deadline: rolling. Application fee: $25. • Dr. Judith B. Schaumberg, Director of Graduate Programs, 414-551-5876. Fax: 414-551-5704.

Central Missouri State University, College of Arts and Sciences, Department of History, Warrensburg, MO 64093. Offerings include social studies (MSE). Accredited by NCATE. Department faculty: 9 full-time. *Application deadline:* 6/30 (priority date; rolling processing). *Application fee:* $25 ($50 for international students). *Tuition:* $3288 per year full-time, $137 per credit hour part-time for state residents; $5928 per year full-time, $274 per credit hour part-time for nonresidents. • Dr. David Rice, Chair, 660-543-4404.

Chadron State College, Department of Education, Chadron, NE 69337. Offerings include history (MA Ed). Accredited by NCATE. *Application deadline:* rolling. *Application fee:* $15. *Expenses:* Tuition $1788 per year full-time, $75 per credit hour part-time for state residents; $3588 per year full-time, $149 per credit hour part-time for nonresidents. Fees $388 per year full-time, $1232 per year part-time. • Dr. Pat Colgate, Dean, School of Graduate Studies, 308-432-6330. Fax: 308-432-6454. E-mail: pcolgate@csc1.csc.edu.

Chaminade University of Honolulu, Program in Education, Honolulu, HI 96816-1578. Offerings include social science via peace education (M Ed). Program faculty: 8 full-time (6 women), 28 part-time (23 women). *Degree requirements:* Thesis required, foreign language not required. *Average time to degree:* master's–2 years full-time, 2.5 years part-time. *Entrance requirements:* TOEFL (minimum score 550), minimum GPA of 2.75. Application deadline: 9/15 (priority date; rolling processing; 3/1 for spring admission). Application fee: $50. • Bryan Man, Director, 808-735-4850. Fax: 808-739-4607. E-mail: bman@chaminade.edu.

Charleston Southern University, Programs in Education, Charleston, SC 29423-8087. Offerings include social studies (MAT). Faculty: 16 full-time (5 women), 5 part-time (3 women), 17.6 FTE. *Application deadline:* rolling. *Application fee:* $25. *Tuition:* $9821 per year full-time, $173 per hour (minimum) part-time. • Dr. Martha Watson, Director of Graduate Programs, 803-863-7555.

The Citadel, The Military College of South Carolina, Department of Political Science, Charleston, SC 29409. Offers program in social studies education (MAE). Faculty: 2 full-time (1 woman), 1 part-time (0 women). Students: 2 full-time (0 women), 12 part-time (1 woman). In 1997, 2 degrees awarded. *Entrance requirements:* GRE, MAT. Application deadline: rolling. Application fee: $25. *Expenses:* Tuition $130 per credit hour for state residents; $260 per credit hour for nonresidents. Fees $30 per semester. • Dr. Milton Boykin, Head, 803-953-5072.

City College of the City University of New York, Graduate School, School of Education, Department of Secondary and Continuing Education, Convent Avenue at 138th Street, New York, NY 10031-6977. Offerings include social studies education (MA). *Degree requirements:* Thesis required, foreign language not required. *Entrance requirements:* TOEFL (minimum score 500). Application fee: $40. *Expenses:* Tuition $4350 per year full-time, $185 per credit part-time for state residents; $7600 per year full-time, $320 per credit part-time for nonresidents. Fees $41 per year. • Hope Hartman, Chair, 212-650-7954.

Claremont Graduate University, Graduate Humanities Center, Department of Philosophy, Claremont, CA 91711-6163. Offerings include philosophy and education (MA, PhD). Department faculty: 3 full-time (1 woman), 1 part-time (0 women). *Degree requirements:* For master's, 1 foreign language, thesis; for doctorate, 2 foreign languages, dissertation. *Entrance requirements:* GRE General Test. Application deadline: 2/15 (priority date; rolling processing). Application fee: $40. *Expenses:* Tuition $20,250 per year full-time, $913 per unit part-time. Fees $130 per year. • Jack Vickers, Chair, 909-621-8082. Application contact: Delores Abdella, Program Secretary, 909-621-8082. Fax: 909-621-8905. E-mail: phil@cgu.edu.

Clemson University, College of Health, Education, and Human Development, Department of Curriculum and Instruction, Program in Secondary Education, Clemson, SC 29634. Offerings include history and government (M Ed). Accredited by NCATE. *Entrance requirements:* TOEFL, teaching certificate. Application deadline: 6/1. Application fee: $35. *Expenses:* Tuition $3154 per year full-time, $130 per credit hour part-time for state residents; $6452 per year full-time, $264 per credit hour part-time for nonresidents. Fees $190 per year. • Dr. Robert Green, Chair, Department of Curriculum and Instruction, 864-656-5108. Fax: 864-656-1322. E-mail: rpgreen@clemson.edu.

College of Notre Dame, Department of Education, Emphasis in Secondary Education, Belmont, CA 94002-1997. Offerings include teaching social sciences (MAT). Faculty: 5 full-time, 8 part-time. *Application deadline:* rolling. *Application fee:* $50 ($500 for international students). *Tuition:* $460 per unit. • Dr. Kim Tolley, Program Director, 650-508-3456.

Columbus State University, College of Education, Department of Curriculum and Instruction, Columbus, GA 31907-5645. Offerings include secondary education (M Ed, Ed S), with options in biology (M Ed), English (M Ed, Ed S), general science (M Ed), history (M Ed), mathematics (M Ed, Ed S), political science (M Ed), science/biology (Ed S), social science (M Ed, Ed S).

Accredited by NCATE. Ed S (mathematics) offered jointly with Georgia Southwestern University. M Ed (political science) being phased out; applicants no longer accepted. *Degree requirements:* For master's, exit exam required, foreign language and thesis not required; for Ed S, thesis or alternative required, foreign language not required. *Entrance requirements:* For master's, GRE General Test (minimum combined score of 800), MAT (minimum score 44); for Ed S, GRE General Test (minimum combined score of 900), MAT (minimum score 44). Application deadline: 7/10 (priority date; rolling processing; 10/23 for spring admission). Application fee: $20. *Tuition:* $1718 per year full-time, $151 per semester hour part-time for state residents; $6218 per year full-time, $401 per semester hour part-time for nonresidents. • Dr. David Shoemaker, Chair, 706-568-2255. Fax: 706-568-3134. E-mail: shoemaker_david@colstate.edu. Application contact: Katie Thornton, Graduate Admissions, 706-568-2279. Fax: 706-568-2462. E-mail: thornton_katie@colstate.edu.

Delta State University, School of Arts and Sciences, Department of History, Cleveland, MS 38733-0001. Offers program in history education (M Ed). Part-time programs available. Faculty: 5 full-time (1 woman). Students: 5 full-time (1 woman), 6 part-time (1 woman); includes 3 minority (2 African Americans, 1 Hispanic). Average age 29. 7 applicants, 86% accepted. In 1997, 2 degrees awarded. *Degree requirements:* Thesis or alternative required, foreign language not required. *Entrance requirements:* GRE General Test (minimum combined score of 800) or MAT (minimum score 34). Application deadline: 8/1 (priority date; rolling processing). Application fee: $0. *Tuition:* $2596 per year full-time, $121 per semester hour part-time for state residents; $5546 per year full-time, $285 per semester hour part-time for nonresidents. *Financial aid:* Research assistantships, Federal Work-Study, institutionally sponsored loans, and career-related internships or fieldwork available. Aid available to part-time students. Financial aid application deadline: 6/1. • Dr. Allen Dennis, Chairperson, 601-846-4171. E-mail: adennis@dsu.deltast.edu. Application contact: Dr. John Thornell, Dean of Graduate Studies and Continuing Education, 601-846-4310. Fax: 601-846-4016.

Delta State University, School of Arts and Sciences, Department of Social Sciences, Program in Social Science Education, Cleveland, MS 38733-0001. Awards M Ed. Part-time programs available. *Degree requirements:* Thesis or alternative required, foreign language not required. *Entrance requirements:* GRE General Test (minimum combined score of 800) or MAT (minimum score 34). Application deadline: 8/1 (priority date; rolling processing). Application fee: $0. *Tuition:* $2596 per year full-time, $121 per semester hour part-time for state residents; $5546 per year full-time, $285 per semester hour part-time for nonresidents. *Financial aid:* Research assistantships, Federal Work-Study, institutionally sponsored loans, and career-related internships or fieldwork available. Aid available to part-time students. Financial aid application deadline: 6/1. • Application contact: Dr. John Thornell, Dean of Graduate Studies and Continuing Education, 601-846-4310. Fax: 601-846-4016.

DePaul University, School of Education, Program in Curriculum Development, Chicago, IL 60604-2287. Offerings include economic education (MA, M Ed), liberal studies (MA, M Ed). One or more programs accredited by NCATE. *Degree requirements:* Oral exam or thesis required, foreign language not required. *Entrance requirements:* Interview, minimum GPA of 2.75, work experience. Application deadline: rolling. Application fee: $25. *Expenses:* Tuition $320 per credit hour. Fees $30 per year. • Dr. Barbara Sizemore, Dean, School of Education, 312-325-7000 Ext. 1666. Fax: 312-325-7748. Application contact: Director of Graduate Admissions, 312-325-7000 Ext. 1666. E-mail: mmurphy@wppost.depaul.edu.

East Carolina University, College of Arts and Sciences, Department of History, Greenville, NC 27858-4353. Offerings include social studies (MA Ed). Accredited by NCATE. Department faculty: 22 full-time (3 women). *Application deadline:* 6/1 (priority date; rolling processing; 10/15 for spring admission). *Application fee:* $40. *Tuition:* $1886 per year full-time, $472 per semester (minimum) part-time for state residents; $9156 per year full-time, $2289 per semester (minimum) part-time for nonresidents. • Dr. Roger Biles, Chairperson, 252-328-6155. Fax: 252-328-6774. E-mail: bilesr@mail.ecu.edu. Application contact: Dr. Paul D. Tschetter, Associate Dean, 252-328-6012. Fax: 252-328-6071. E-mail: grad@mail.ecu.edu.

Eastern Kentucky University, College of Education, Department of Curriculum and Instruction, Program in Secondary and Higher Education, Richmond, KY 40475-3101. Offerings include geography education (MA Ed), history education (MA Ed), political science education (MA Ed), psychology education (MA Ed), sociology education (MA Ed). One or more programs accredited by NCATE. *Entrance requirements:* GRE General Test, minimum GPA of 2.5. Application fee: $0. *Tuition:* $2390 per year full-time, $133 per credit hour part-time for state residents; $6630 per year full-time, $365 per credit hour part-time for nonresidents. • Dr. Imogene Ramsey, Chair, Department of Curriculum and Instruction, 606-622-2154.

Eastern Washington University, College of Education and Human Development, Department of Education, Program in Social Science Education, Cheney, WA 99004-2431. Awards M Ed. Accredited by NCATE. *Degree requirements:* Comprehensive exam required, thesis not required. *Entrance requirements:* Minimum GPA of 3.0. Application deadline: 4/1 (priority date; rolling processing; 1/15 for spring admission). Application fee: $35. *Tuition:* $4200 per year full-time, $140 per credit part-time for state residents; $12,780 per year full-time, $415 per credit part-time for nonresidents. *Financial aid:* Application deadline 2/1. • Dr. Rita Seedorf, Adviser, 509-359-7029.

Edinboro University of Pennsylvania, School of Education, Department of Elementary Education, Program in Elementary Education, Edinboro, PA 16444. Offerings include social studies (M Ed). *Degree requirements:* Thesis or alternative required, foreign language not required. *Entrance requirements:* GRE or MAT (score in 30th percentile or higher). Application deadline: rolling. Application fee: $25. *Expenses:* Tuition $3468 per year full-time, $193 per credit part-time for state residents; $6236 per year full-time, $346 per credit part-time for nonresidents. Fees $898 per year full-time, $50 per semester (minimum) part-time. • Application contact: Dr. Philip Kerstetter, Dean of Graduate Studies, 814-732-2856. Fax: 814-732-2611. E-mail: kerstetter@edinboro.edu.

Emporia State University, School of Graduate Studies, College of Liberal Arts and Sciences, Division of Social Sciences, Program in Social Sciences, Emporia, KS 66801-5087. Offers American history (MAT), anthropology (MAT), economics (MAT), geography (MAT), political science (MAT), social studies education (MAT), sociology (MAT), world history (MAT). Accredited by NCATE. Students: 2 full-time (0 women), 4 part-time (2 women). 2 applicants, 100% accepted. In 1997, 9 degrees awarded. *Degree requirements:* Comprehensive exam or thesis required, foreign language not required. *Entrance requirements:* TOEFL (minimum score 550). Application deadline: 8/15 (priority date; rolling processing). Application fee: $30 ($75 for international students). Electronic applications accepted. *Tuition:* $2300 per year full-time, $103 per credit hour part-time for state residents; $6012 per year full-time, $258 per credit hour part-time for nonresidents. *Financial aid:* Federal Work-Study, institutionally sponsored loans available. Financial aid application deadline: 3/15; applicants required to submit FAFSA. • Application contact: Dr. Sam Dicks, Associate Chair, 316-341-5579. E-mail: dickssam@emporia.edu.

Fairleigh Dickinson University, Teaneck–Hackensack Campus, University College: Arts, Sciences, and Professional Studies, Peter Sammartino School of Education, Program in Social Studies Education, 1000 River Road, Teaneck, NJ 07666-1914. Awards MAT. Faculty: 11 full-time (8 women), 27 part-time (10 women). *Degree requirements:* Research project required, thesis not required. *Application deadline:* rolling. *Application fee:* $35. *Expenses:* Tuition $522 per credit. Fees $302 per year full-time, $138 per year part-time. *Faculty research:* Mathematics for students with learning disabilities, gender issues in education, social problem-solving and conflict resolution in the classroom, multicultural education in the elementary classroom, problems encountered by international students in college programs. • Dr. Eloise Forster, Interim Director, Peter Sammartino School of Education, 201-692-2834. Fax: 201-692-2603.

Fayetteville State University, Programs in Educational Leadership and Secondary Education, 1200 Murchison Road, Fayetteville, NC 28301-4298. Offerings include history (MAT), political science (MAT), sociology (MAT). One or more programs accredited by NCATE. *Application deadline:* 8/1 (rolling processing; 12/15 for spring admission). *Application fee:* $20. *Tuition:* $1498 per year full-time, $327 per semester (minimum) part-time for state residents; $8768 per year full-time, $2144 per semester (minimum) part-time for nonresidents.

Fitchburg State College, Program in Teaching History (Secondary Level), Fitchburg, MA 01420-2697. Awards MA, MAT. Accredited by NCATE. Part-time and evening/weekend programs available. *Entrance requirements:* GRE General Test or MAT (minimum score 47), interview. Application deadline: rolling. Application fee: $10. *Expenses:* Tuition $147 per credit. Fees $55 per semester. *Financial aid:* Graduate assistantships, Federal Work-Study available. Aid available to part-time students. Financial aid application deadline: 3/30; applicants required to submit FAFSA. • Dr. Susan Williams, Chair, 978-665-3085. Fax: 978-665-3658. E-mail: dgce@fsc.edu. Application contact: James DuPont, Director of Admissions, 978-665-3144. Fax: 978-665-4540. E-mail: admissions@fsc.edu.

Florida International University, College of Education, Department of Subject Specializations, Program in Social Studies Education, Miami, FL 33199. Awards MS. Accredited by NCATE. Part-time and evening/weekend programs available. Students: 17 full-time (10 women), 20 part-time (12 women); includes 27 minority (5 African Americans, 1 Asian American, 21 Hispanics). Average age 31. 13 applicants, 85% accepted. In 1997, 13 degrees awarded. *Entrance requirements:* GRE General Test (minimum combined score of 1000) or minimum GPA of 3.0. Application deadline: 4/1 (priority date; rolling processing; 10/1 for spring admission). Application fee: $20. *Expenses:* Tuition $138 per credit hour for state residents; $482 per credit hour for nonresidents. Fees $46 per semester. *Faculty research:* Pedagogical knowledge base for teaching social studies, global education. • Dr. Dean Hauenstein, Chairperson, Department of Subject Specializations, 305-348-2005. Fax: 305-348-2086.

Florida State University, College of Education, Department of Educational Theory and Practice, Program in Social Science Education, Tallahassee, FL 32306. Awards MS, Ed D, PhD, Ed S. Part-time programs available. Faculty: 2 full-time (0 women). Students: 17 full-time (10 women), 9 part-time (3 women); includes 9 minority (5 African Americans, 3 Hispanics, 1 Native American). 18 applicants, 100% accepted. In 1997, 32 master's, 7 doctorates awarded. *Degree requirements:* For master's and Ed S, comprehensive exam required, thesis optional; for doctorate, dissertation, comprehensive exams. *Entrance requirements:* GRE General Test (minimum combined score of 1000), minimum GPA of 3.0. Application deadline: 7/1 (priority date; rolling processing; 11/1 for spring admission). Application fee: $20. *Tuition:* $139 per credit hour for state residents; $482 per credit hour for nonresidents. *Financial aid:* Fellowships, research assistantships, teaching assistantships, and career-related internships or fieldwork available. • Dr. Charles Wolfgang, Chair, Department of Educational Theory and Practice, 850-644-5458. E-mail: wolfgang@mail.coe.fsu.edu. Application contact: Admissions Secretary, 850-644-5458. Fax: 850-644-7736.

Framingham State College, Graduate Programs, Program in History, Framingham, MA 01701-9101. Awards M Ed. Faculty: 2 full-time, 2 part-time. Students: 1 full-time, 4 part-time. In 1997, 2 degrees awarded. *Tuition:* $4184 per year full-time, $523 per course part-time for state residents; $4848 per year full-time, $606 per course part-time for nonresidents. • Dr. Brad Nutting, Chairperson, 508-626-4500. Application contact: Graduate Office, 508-626-4550.

Furman University, Department of Education, Greenville, SC 29613. Offerings include social studies (MA Ed). *Degree requirements:* Comprehensive written exam. *Application deadline:* rolling. *Application fee:* $25. *Tuition:* $185 per credit hour. • Dr. Hazel W. Harris, Director, 864-294-2213.

Georgia Southern University, College of Education, Department of Middle Grades and Secondary Education, Program in Social Science, Statesboro, GA 30460-8126. Awards M Ed, Ed S. Accredited by NCATE. Part-time and evening/weekend programs available. Students: 12 full-time (6 women), 11 part-time (7 women); includes 1 minority (African American). Average age 35. 9 applicants, 56% accepted. In 1997, 8 master's, 2 Ed Ss awarded. *Degree requirements:* Exams required, foreign language and thesis not required. *Entrance requirements:* For master's, GRE General Test (minimum score 450 on each section) or MAT (minimum score 44), minimum GPA of 2.5; for Ed S, GRE General Test (minimum score 450 on each section) or MAT (minimum score 49), minimum graduate GPA of 3.25. Application deadline: 7/15 (priority date; rolling processing; 11/15 for spring admission). Application fee: $0. Electronic applications accepted. *Tuition:* $2619 per year full-time, $287 per semester (minimum) part-time for state residents; $8619 per year full-time, $1037 per semester (minimum) part-time for nonresidents. *Financial aid:* Application deadline 4/15. • Application contact: Dr. John R. Diebolt, Associate Graduate Dean, 912-681-5384. Fax: 912-681-0740. E-mail: gradschool@gsvms2.cc.gasou.edu.

Georgia State University, College of Education, Department of Middle, Secondary Education and Instructional Technology, Programs in Secondary Education, Atlanta, GA 30303-3083. Offerings include social science education (Ed S), social studies education (M Ed, PhD). One or more programs accredited by NCATE. *Degree requirements:* For master's, comprehensive exam; for doctorate, dissertation, comprehensive exam; for Ed S, project/exam. *Entrance requirements:* For master's, GRE General Test (minimum combined score of 800) or MAT (minimum score 44), minimum GPA of 2.5; for doctorate, GRE General Test (minimum score 500 on verbal section, 500 on either quantitative or analytical sections) or MAT (minimum score 53), minimum GPA of 3.3; for Ed S, GRE General Test (minimum combined score of 900) or MAT (minimum score 48), minimum graduate GPA of 3.25. Application fee: $25. *Expenses:* Tuition $2673 per year full-time, $99 per semester hour part-time for state residents; $10,692 per year full-time, $396 per semester hour part-time for nonresidents. Fees $228 per year. • Dr. Beverly J. Armento, Chair, Department of Middle, Secondary Education and Instructional Technology, 404-651-2510.

Gonzaga University, Graduate School, College of Arts and Sciences, Program in History, Spokane, WA 99258-0001. Awards MAT. *Degree requirements:* Comprehensive exam. *Entrance requirements:* GRE General Test or MAT, TOEFL (minimum score 550), minimum GPA of 3.0. Application deadline: 7/20 (priority date; rolling processing; 11/1 for spring admission). Application fee: $40. *Tuition:* $7380 per year (minimum) full-time, $410 per credit (minimum) part-time. *Financial aid:* Application deadline 3/1. • Dr. Stephen E. Balzarini, Chairperson. Application contact: Dr. Leonard Doohan, Dean of the Graduate School, 509-328-4220 Ext. 3546. Fax: 509-324-5399.

Grambling State University, College of Liberal Arts, Program in Social Sciences, Grambling, LA 71245. Awards MAT. Part-time and evening/weekend programs available. Faculty: 1 full-time (0 women), 3 part-time (2 women), 2.3 FTE. Students: 28 full-time (24 women), 15 part-time (13 women); includes 43 minority (all African Americans). Average age 30. 8 applicants, 100% accepted. In 1997, 12 degrees awarded. *Degree requirements:* Thesis optional, foreign language not required. *Entrance requirements:* GRE. Application deadline: rolling. Application fee: $15. *Tuition:* $1960 per year full-time, $297 per semester (minimum) part-time for state residents; $7110 per year full-time, $297 per semester (minimum) part-time for nonresidents. *Financial aid:* Application deadline 5/31. • Mildred Gallot, Coordinator, 318-274-2738. Fax: 318-274-3260.

Grand Valley State University, School of Education, Programs in General Education, Program in Secondary, Adult and Higher Education, Allendale, MI 49401-9403. Offerings include history (M Ed). Accredited by NCATE. *Degree requirements:* Thesis or alternative, applied research project. *Entrance requirements:* GRE General Test (minimum combined score of 1300) or minimum GPA of 3.0. Application deadline: rolling. Application fee: $20. • Application contact: Admissions Office, 616-895-2025. Fax: 616-895-3081.

Hardin–Simmons University, Irvin School of Education, Department of Elementary and Secondary Education, Abilene, TX 79698-0001. Offerings include elementary education (M Ed),

Directory: Social Sciences Education

Hardin–Simmons University (continued)
with options in psychology, reading, Spanish, speech; secondary education (M Ed), with options in psychology, reading, Spanish, speech. Department faculty: 6 full-time (3 women), 4 part-time (3 women). *Degree requirements:* Project required, foreign language and thesis not required. *Application deadline:* 8/15 (priority date; rolling processing; 1/5 for spring admission). *Application fee:* $25. *Expenses:* Tuition $280 per semester hour. Fees $630 per year full-time. • Dr. Bertie Kingore, Head, 915-670-1353. Fax: 915-670-5859. Application contact: Dr. J. Paul Sorrels, Dean of Graduate Studies, 915-670-1298. Fax: 915-670-1564.

Henderson State University, School of Education, Department of Secondary Education, Arkadelphia, AR 71999-0001. Offerings include social sciences education (MSE). Accredited by NCATE. Postbaccalaureate distance learning degree programs offered (minimal on-campus study). *Degree requirements:* Thesis optional, foreign language not required. *Entrance requirements:* GRE General Test or MAT, minimum GPA of 2.7, teacher certification. Application deadline: 7/31 (priority date; rolling processing). Application fee: $15. Electronic applications accepted. *Expenses:* Tuition $120 per credit hour for state residents; $240 per credit hour for nonresidents. Fees $105 per semester (minimum) full-time, $52 per semester (minimum) part-time. • Dr. Charles Weiner, Chairperson, 870-230-5163. Fax: 870-230-5455. E-mail: weinerc@holly.hsu.edu.

Hunter College of the City University of New York, Division of Education, Secondary Education Curriculum, Concentration in Social Studies Education, 695 Park Avenue, New York, NY 10021-5085. Awards MA. *Degree requirements:* Comprehensive exam required, foreign language and thesis not required. *Entrance requirements:* TOEFL (minimum score 575). Application deadline: 4/7 (rolling processing; 11/7 for spring admission). Application fee: $40. *Expenses:* Tuition $4350 per year full-time, $185 per credit part-time for state residents; $7600 per year full-time, $320 per credit part-time for nonresidents. Fees $26 per year.

Indiana University Bloomington, School of Education, Department of Curriculum and Instruction, Bloomington, IN 47405. Offerings include social studies education (MS). Accredited by NCATE. Department faculty: 23 full-time (9 women). *Entrance requirements:* GRE General Test (minimum combined score of 1300 on three sections). Application deadline: 3/1 (priority date; rolling processing). Application fee: $35. *Expenses:* Tuition $153 per credit hour for state residents; $446 per credit hour for nonresidents. Fees $343 per year. • Peter Kloosterman, Chairperson, 812-856-8100. Application contact: Sara White, 812-856-8100.

Iona College, School of Arts and Science, Program in Secondary School Subjects, 715 North Avenue, New Rochelle, NY 10801-1890. Offerings include social studies education (MS Ed, MST). Program faculty: 4 full-time (1 woman), 8 part-time (2 women). *Degree requirements:* Thesis or alternative required, foreign language not required. *Entrance requirements:* Minimum GPA of 2.5 (MST), New York teaching certificate (MS Ed). Application deadline: rolling. Application fee: $25. *Expenses:* Tuition $455 per credit hour. Fees $25 per semester. • Dr. Lucy Murphy, Chair, 914-633-2210. Fax: 914-633-2608. Application contact: Arlene Melillo, Director of Graduate Recruitment, 914-633-2328. Fax: 914-633-2023.

Kutztown University of Pennsylvania, Graduate School, College of Education, Program in Secondary Education, Kutztown, PA 19530. Offerings include social studies (M Ed). Accredited by NCATE. Program faculty: 7 full-time (1 woman). *Degree requirements:* Comprehensive exam required, thesis optional, foreign language not required. *Entrance requirements:* GRE General Test, TOEFL, TSE. Application deadline: 3/1 (8/1 for spring admission). Application fee: $25. *Tuition:* $4111 per year full-time, $225 per credit hour part-time for state residents; $6879 per year full-time, $393 per credit hour part-time for nonresidents. • Kathleen Dolgos, Chairperson, 610-683-4259.

Lehman College of the City University of New York, Division of Education, Department of Secondary, Adult and Business Education, Program in Social Studies 7–12, 250 Bedford Park Boulevard West, Bronx, NY 10468-1589. Awards MA. Students: 6 full-time (3 women), 36 part-time (12 women). *Entrance requirements:* Minimum GPA of 3.0 in social sciences, 2.7 overall. Application deadline: 4/1 (rolling processing; 11/1 for spring admission). Application fee: $40. *Expenses:* Tuition $4350 per year full-time, $185 per credit part-time for state residents; $7600 per year full-time, $320 per credit part-time for nonresidents. Fees $120 per year full-time, $80 per year part-time. *Financial aid:* Full and partial tuition waivers, Federal Work-Study available. Aid available to part-time students. Financial aid application deadline: 5/15; applicants required to submit FAFSA. • Russell Bradshaw, Adviser, 718-960-8171.

Long Island University, C.W. Post Campus, School of Education, Department of Curriculum and Instruction, Brookville, NY 11548-1300. Offerings include history education (MS). Department faculty: 10 full-time (5 women), 46 part-time (19 women). *Application deadline:* rolling. *Application fee:* $30. Electronic applications accepted. *Expenses:* Tuition $480 per credit. Fees $316 per year full-time, $71 per semester (minimum) part-time. • Dr. Anthony De Falco, Chairperson, 516-299-2372. Application contact: Camille Marziliano, Academic Counselor, 516-299-2123. Fax: 516-299-4167. E-mail: cmarzili@eagle.liunet.edu.

Longwood College, Department of Education, Farmville, VA 23909-1800. Offerings include curriculum and instruction specialist-elementary (MS), with options in English (MS), mild disabilities (MS), modern language (MS), physical education (MS), speech and drama (MS). Accredited by NCATE. Department faculty: 34 part-time. *Degree requirements:* Thesis (for some programs), comprehensive exam. *Entrance requirements:* Minimum GPA of 2.5. Application deadline: 5/1 (priority date; rolling processing; 10/15 for spring admission). Application fee: $25. *Expenses:* Tuition $3048 per year full-time, $127 per credit hour part-time for state residents; $8160 per year full-time, $340 per credit hour part-time for nonresidents. Fees $920 per year full-time, $31 per credit hour part-time. • Dr. Frank Howe, Chair, 804-395-2324. Application contact: Admissions Office, 804-395-2060.

Louisiana Tech University, College of Education, Department of Curriculum, Instruction and Leadership, Ruston, LA 71272. Offerings include secondary education (M Ed), with options in business education, English education, foreign language education, health and physical education, mathematics education, science education, social studies education, speech education. Accredited by NCATE. Department faculty: 16 full-time (11 women). *Application deadline:* 7/29 (2/3 for spring admission). *Application fee:* $20 ($30 for international students). *Tuition:* $2382 per year full-time, $223 per quarter (minimum) part-time for state residents; $5307 per year full-time, $223 per quarter (minimum) part-time for nonresidents. • Dr. Samuel V. Dauzat, Head, 318-257-4609.

Loyola Marymount University, School of Education, Program in Teaching, Los Angeles, CA 90045-8350. Offerings include communications education (MAT), history education (MAT), social studies education (MAT). Program faculty: 14 full-time (8 women), 25 part-time (20 women). *Degree requirements:* Thesis or alternative, comprehensive exam required, foreign language not required. *Entrance requirements:* GRE General Test, TOEFL (minimum score 550), interview. Application fee: $35. Electronic applications accepted. *Expenses:* Tuition $500 per unit. Fees $111 per year full-time, $28 per year part-time. • Coordinator, 310-338-7307.

Manhattanville College, School of Education, Program in Secondary Education, Purchase, NY 10577-2132. Offerings include social studies (MAT). *Degree requirements:* Thesis, comprehensive exam or research project required, foreign language not required. *Entrance requirements:* Minimum undergraduate GPA of 3.0. Application deadline: rolling. Application fee: $40. *Expenses:* Tuition $410 per credit (minimum). Fees $25 per semester. • Application contact: Carol Messar, Director of Admissions, 914-323-5142. Fax: 914-323-5493.

Mankato State University, College of Social and Behavioral Sciences, Department of History, South Rd and Ellis Ave, PO Box 8400, Mankato, MN 56002-8400. Offerings include social studies (MS), teaching history (MS, MT). Department faculty: 10 full-time (3 women). *Application deadline:* 7/10 (priority date; rolling processing; 10/30 for spring admission). *Application fee:* $20. *Tuition:* $126 per credit (minimum) for state residents; $200 per credit for nonresidents. • Dr. Erwin Grieshaber, Chairperson, 507-389-1618. Application contact: Joni Roberts, Admissions Coordinator, 507-389-2321. Fax: 507-389-5974. E-mail: grad@mankato.msus.edu.

Marshall University, College of Education, Division of Educational Leadership, Program in Social Studies, Huntington, WV 25755-2020. Awards MA. Accredited by NCATE. Program being phased out; applicants no longer accepted. Students: 3 part-time (1 woman). *Degree requirements:* Thesis optional, foreign language not required. *Tuition:* $2364 per year full-time, $132 per hour part-time for state residents; $6894 per year full-time, $383 per hour part-time for nonresidents. • Dr. Frank S. Riddel, Coordinator, 304-696-6610.

McNeese State University, College of Education, Department of Curriculum and Instruction, Program in Secondary Education, Lake Charles, LA 70609-2495. Offerings include social science education (M Ed), speech education (M Ed). Program faculty: 8 full-time (3 women). *Entrance requirements:* GRE General Test, teaching certificate. Application deadline: 7/15 (priority date; rolling processing). Application fee: $10 ($25 for international students). *Tuition:* $2118 per year full-time, $344 per semester (minimum) part-time for state residents; $7308 per year full-time, $344 per semester (minimum) part-time for nonresidents. • Dr. Everett Waddell Burge, Head, Department of Curriculum and Instruction, 318-475-5404.

Mercer University, School of Education, 1400 Coleman Avenue, Macon, GA 31207-0003. Offerings include social sciences education (M Ed). School faculty: 11 full-time (5 women), 17 part-time (11 women). *Degree requirements:* Research project report required, foreign language and thesis not required. *Entrance requirements:* GRE, MAT, NTE, minimum GPA of 2.75. Application deadline: 8/1 (priority date; rolling processing; 12/1 for spring admission). Application fee: $25. *Tuition:* $180 per credit hour. • Dr. Anne Hathaway, Dean, 912-752-5397. Fax: 912-752-2280. E-mail: hathaway_ha@mercer.edu. Application contact: Dr. Louis Gallien, Chair, Department of Teacher Education, 912-752-2585. Fax: 912-752-2576. E-mail: gallien_lb@mercer.edu.

Michigan State University, College of Arts and Letters, Department of History, East Lansing, MI 48824-1020. Offerings include history-secondary school teaching (MA). Department faculty: 45 full-time (16 women). *Degree requirements:* 1 foreign language, thesis or alternative. *Entrance requirements:* GRE General Test, minimum GPA of 3.25 in history. Application deadline: 1/1. Application fee: $30 ($40 for international students). Electronic applications accepted. *Expenses:* Tuition $4609 per year full-time, $223 per credit hour (minimum) part-time for state residents; $8704 per year full-time, $450 per credit hour (minimum) part-time for nonresidents. Fees $576 per year full-time, $476 per year part-time. • Dr. Henry Silverman, Chairperson, 517-355-7500. Application contact: Lewis Siegelbaum, Graduate Director, 517-355-7500. Fax: 517-353-5599.

Mills College, Education Department, Oakland, CA 94613-1000. Offerings include education (MA), with options in curriculum and instruction, elementary education, English education, mathematics education, science education, secondary education, social sciences education, teaching. Department faculty: 8 full-time (6 women), 13 part-time (11 women), 11 FTE. *Degree requirements:* Comprehensive exam required, thesis not required. *Average time to degree:* master's–2 years full-time. *Entrance requirements:* TOEFL (minimum score 550). Application deadline: 2/1 (priority date; rolling processing; 11/1 for spring admission). Application fee: $50. Electronic applications accepted. *Expenses:* Tuition $10,600 per year full-time, $2560 per year part-time. Fees $468 per year. • Jane Bowyer, Chairperson, 510-430-2118. Fax: 510-430-3314. E-mail: grad-studies@mills.edu. Application contact: La Vonna S. Brown, Coordinator of Graduate Studies, 510-430-3309. Fax: 510-430-2159. E-mail: grad-studies@mills.edu.

Montclair State University, College of Education and Human Services, Department of Curriculum and Teaching, Program in Teaching, Upper Montclair, NJ 07043-1624. Offers teaching middle school philosophy (MAT). Accredited by NCATE. Faculty: 15 full-time. Students: 101 full-time (74 women), 131 part-time (101 women); includes 3 minority (2 African Americans, 1 Hispanic). In 1997, 71 degrees awarded. *Degree requirements:* Comprehensive exam, field experience. *Entrance requirements:* GRE General Test, minimum GPA of 2.67. Application deadline: 3/1 (rolling processing; 10/1 for spring admission). Application fee: $40. *Expenses:* Tuition $201 per credit for state residents; $257 per credit for nonresidents. Fees $22.05 per credit. *Financial aid:* Application deadline 3/1; applicants required to submit FAFSA. • Dr. Catherine Becker, Adviser, 973-655-5187.

New York University, School of Education, Department of Culture and Communication, Program in Studies in Arts and Humanities Education, New York, NY 10012-1019. Awards MA, PhD. Part-time and evening/weekend programs available. Faculty: 3 full-time (1 woman). Students: 8 full-time, 20 part-time. 27 applicants, 37% accepted. In 1997, 4 master's, 1 doctorate awarded. Terminal master's awarded for partial completion of doctoral program. *Degree requirements:* For master's, thesis required (for some programs), foreign language not required; for doctorate, dissertation. *Entrance requirements:* For master's, TOEFL; for doctorate, GRE General Test, TOEFL, interview. Application deadline: 2/1 (priority date; rolling processing; 12/1 for spring admission). Application fee: $40 ($60 for international students). *Financial aid:* Partial tuition waivers, Federal Work-Study, institutionally sponsored loans available. Aid available to part-time students. Financial aid application deadline: 3/1; applicants required to submit FAFSA. *Faculty research:* Interrelationships between film and literature; literary rhetoric, stylistics, and the creative process; relationships among culture, aesthetic response, and learning. • Carl P. Schmidt, Director, 212-998-5245. Application contact: Office of Graduate Admissions, 212-998-5030. Fax: 212-995-4328.

New York University, School of Education, Department of Teaching and Learning, Program in International and Social Studies Education, New York, NY 10012-1019. Offers international education (MA, PhD), including Asian studies (MA); social studies (MA). Part-time and evening/weekend programs available. Faculty: 2 full-time (0 women), 4 part-time. Students: 31 full-time, 47 part-time. 99 applicants, 68% accepted. In 1997, 26 master's awarded. Terminal master's awarded for partial completion of doctoral program. *Degree requirements:* For master's, thesis required (for some programs), foreign language not required; for doctorate, dissertation. *Entrance requirements:* For master's, TOEFL; for doctorate, GRE General Test, TOEFL, interview. Application deadline: 2/1 (priority date; rolling processing; 12/1 for spring admission). Application fee: $40 ($60 for international students). *Financial aid:* Partial tuition waivers, Federal Work-Study, institutionally sponsored loans, and career-related internships or fieldwork available. Aid available to part-time students. Financial aid application deadline: 3/1; applicants required to submit FAFSA. • Dr. Donald J. Johnson, Director, 212-998-5498. Application contact: Office of Graduate Admissions, 212-998-5030. Fax: 212-995-4328.

North Carolina Agricultural and Technical State University, Graduate School, College of Arts and Sciences, Department of History and Social Science Education, Greensboro, NC 27411. Offers programs in history education (MS), social science education (MS). One or more programs accredited by NCATE. Students: 12 full-time (5 women), 17 part-time (7 women); includes 18 minority (all African Americans). Average age 30. In 1997, 3 degrees awarded. *Degree requirements:* Comprehensive exam, qualifying exam required, foreign language not required. *Entrance requirements:* GRE General Test. Application deadline: 6/1 (priority date; rolling processing; 12/1 for spring admission). Application fee: $35. *Tuition:* $1662 per year full-time, $272 per semester (minimum) part-time for state residents; $8790 per year full-time, $2054 per semester (minimum) part-time for nonresidents. *Financial aid:* Application deadline 6/1. • Dr. Peter Meyers, Chairperson, 336-334-7831. E-mail: peterm@ncat.edu.

North Carolina Agricultural and Technical State University, Graduate School, School of Education, Department of Curriculum and Instruction, Program in Intermediate Education, Greensboro, NC 27411. Offerings include history education (MS), social science education (MS). One or more programs accredited by NCATE. *Degree requirements:* Thesis (for some programs), comprehensive exam, qualifying exam required, foreign language not required. *Entrance requirements:* GRE General Test, minimum GPA of 3.0. Application deadline: 6/1 (priority date; rolling processing; 12/1 for spring admission). Application fee: $35. *Tuition:* $1662 per year full-time, $272 per semester (minimum) part-time for state residents; $8790 per year full-time, $2054 per semester (minimum) part-time for nonresidents. • Dr. Dorothy Leflore, Interim Chairperson, Department of Curriculum and Instruction, 336-334-7848.

North Georgia College & State University, Graduate School, Program in Education, Dahlonega, GA 30597-1001. Offerings include secondary education (M Ed), with options in art education, biology education, chemistry education, English education, mathematics education, modern languages education, physical education, science education, social science education. Accredited by NCATE. Program faculty: 57 full-time (15 women), 7 part-time (4 women). *Degree requirements:* Comprehensive exam required, thesis optional, foreign language not required. *Entrance requirements:* GRE General Test (minimum combined score of 800) or MAT (minimum score 44), minimum GPA of 2.75. Application deadline: 9/1 (priority date; rolling processing). Application fee: $25. • Dr. Bob Michael, Dean, School of Education, 706-864-1533. Application contact: Mai-Lan Ledbetter, Coordinator of Graduate Admissions, 706-864-1543. Fax: 706-864-1668. E-mail: mledbetter@nugget.ngc.peachnet.edu.

Northwestern State University of Louisiana, Department of Social Sciences, Natchitoches, LA 71497. Offerings include social sciences education (M Ed). Accredited by NCATE. Department faculty: 6 full-time (2 women). *Application deadline:* 8/1 (priority date; rolling processing; 1/10 for spring admission). *Application fee:* $15 ($25 for international students). *Tuition:* $2147 per year full-time, $336 per semester (minimum) part-time for state residents; $6437 per year full-time, $336 per semester (minimum) part-time for nonresidents. • Dr. Kahleen Byrd, Chair, 318-357-6195. Application contact: Dr. Tom Hanson, Dean, Graduate Studies and Research, 318-357-5851. Fax: 318-357-5019.

Northwest Missouri State University, College of Arts and Sciences, Department of History and Humanities, 800 University Drive, Maryville, MO 64468-6001. Offerings include teaching history (MS Ed). Department faculty: 8 full-time (1 woman). *Application deadline:* rolling. *Application fee:* $0 ($50 for international students). *Expenses:* Tuition $113 per credit hour for state residents; $197 per credit hour for nonresidents. Fees $3 per credit hour. • Thomas Carneal, Chairperson, 816-562-1289. Application contact: Dr. Frances Shipley, Dean of Graduate School, 816-562-1145. E-mail: gradsch@acad.nwmissouri.edu.

Nova Southeastern University, Fischler Center for the Advancement of Education, Graduate Teacher Education Program, Fort Lauderdale, FL 33314-7721. Offerings include social studies (MS, Ed S). *Degree requirements:* Thesis, practicum required, foreign language not required. *Entrance requirements:* For master's, teaching certificate; for Ed S, master's degree, teaching certificate. Application deadline: rolling. Application fee: $50. *Tuition:* $245 per credit hour (minimum). • Dr. Deo Nellis, Dean, 954-262-8601. E-mail: deo@fcae.nova.edu. Application contact: Dr. Mark Seldine, Director of Student Affairs, 954-262-8689. Fax: 954-262-3910. E-mail: seldines@fcae.nova.edu.

Occidental College, Department of Education, Program in Secondary Education, Los Angeles, CA 90041-3392. Offerings include history (MAT). Program faculty: 4 full-time (1 woman). *Degree requirements:* Internship required, foreign language and thesis not required. *Entrance requirements:* GRE General Test (minimum score 550 on each section or combined score of 1650 on three sections), TOEFL (minimum score 600), minimum GPA of 3.0. Application deadline: 3/1 (priority date; rolling processing; 10/1 for spring admission). Application fee: $40. *Expenses:* Tuition $21,256 per year full-time, $865 per unit part-time. Fees $314 per year. • Application contact: Susan Molik, Administrative Assistant, Graduate Office, 213-259-2921.

Ohio University, Graduate Studies, College of Education, School of Curriculum and Instruction, Athens, OH 45701-2979. Offerings include economic education (MA, PhD), social sciences (PhD). One or more programs accredited by NCATE. Terminal master's awarded for partial completion of doctoral program. School faculty: 21 full-time (7 women), 16 part-time (11 women). *Degree requirements:* For doctorate, dissertation. *Entrance requirements:* For doctorate, GRE General Test, MAT, minimum GPA of 3.0, work experience. Application deadline: rolling. Application fee: $30. *Tuition:* $5430 per year full-time, $216 per quarter hour part-time for state residents; $10,431 per year full-time, $423 per quarter hour part-time for nonresidents. • Dr. Ralph Martin, Director, 740-593-4422. Application contact: Dr. Bonnie Beach, Graduate Chair, 740-593-0523.

Pennsylvania State University University Park Campus, College of Education, Department of Curriculum and Instruction, University Park, PA 16802-1503. Offerings include social studies education (MS, D Ed, PhD). Accredited by NCATE. *Degree requirements:* For doctorate, dissertation. *Entrance requirements:* For doctorate, GRE General Test or MAT. Application fee: $40. *Expenses:* Tuition $6534 per year full-time, $276 per credit part-time for state residents; $13,460 per year full-time, $561 per credit part-time for nonresidents. Fees $252 per year (minimum) full-time, $43 per semester (minimum) part-time. • Dr. Peter A. Rubb, Head, 814-865-5433.

Plattsburgh State University of New York, Faculty of Professional Studies, Center for Educational Studies and Services, Program in Secondary Education, Plattsburgh, NY 12901-2681. Offerings include social studies (MS Ed, MST). *Degree requirements:* Comprehensive exam or research project required, thesis optional. *Entrance requirements:* GRE General Test or MAT, minimum GPA of 2.5. Application deadline: rolling. Application fee: $50. *Expenses:* Tuition $5100 per year full-time, $213 per credit hour part-time for state residents; $8416 per year full-time, $351 per credit hour part-time for nonresidents. Fees $395 per year full-time, $15.10 per credit hour part-time. • Dr. Raymond Domenico, Director and Associate Dean, Center for Educational Studies and Services, 518-564-2122.

Plymouth State College of the University System of New Hampshire, Department of Education, Program in Heritage Studies, Plymouth, NH 03264-1595. Awards M Ed. Part-time and evening/weekend programs available. Students: 3 full-time (1 woman), 1 part-time (0 women). Average age 35. 2 applicants, 100% accepted. In 1997, 3 degrees awarded. *Entrance requirements:* GRE General Test (average 500 on each section) or MAT (minimum score 50), minimum GPA of 3.0. Application deadline: 9/1 (priority date; rolling processing). Application fee: $25 ($35 for international students). *Tuition:* $232 per credit for state residents; $254 per credit for nonresidents. *Financial aid:* Graduate assistantships, institutionally sponsored loans, and career-related internships or fieldwork available. Aid available to part-time students. Financial aid application deadline: 3/15; applicants required to submit FAFSA. • Dr. Katherine Donahue, Adviser, 603-535-2424. Application contact: Maryann Szabadics, Administrative Assistant, 603-535-2636. Fax: 603-535-2572. E-mail: for.grad@psc.plymouth.edu.

Portland State University, College of Liberal Arts and Sciences, Interdisciplinary Programs in General Science, General Social Science, and General Arts and Letters, Portland, OR 97207-0751. Offerings in general arts and letters education (MAT, MST), general science education (MAT, MST), general social science education (MAT, MST). Part-time and evening/weekend programs available. Faculty: 263 full-time (97 women), 84 part-time (51 women), 278 FTE. Students: 12 full-time (7 women), 11 part-time (5 women); includes 1 international. Average age 32. 17 applicants, 59% accepted. In 1997, 6 degrees awarded. *Degree requirements:* Variable foreign language requirement, written exam. *Entrance requirements:* TOEFL (minimum score 550), minimum GPA of 3.0 in upper-division course work or 2.75 overall. Application deadline: 4/1. Application fee: $50. *Tuition:* $6101 per year full-time, $689 per semester (minimum) part-time for state residents; $10,445 per year full-time, $689 per semester (minimum) part-time for nonresidents. *Financial aid:* Federal Work-Study, institutionally sponsored loans available. Aid available to part-time students. Financial aid application deadline: 3/1; applicants required to submit FAFSA. • Robert Mercer, Senior Academic Adviser, 503-725-3822.

Princeton University, Department of History, Princeton, NJ 08544-1019. Offerings include community college history teaching (PhD). Department faculty: 44 full-time (16 women). *Degree requirements:* Variable foreign language requirement, dissertation. *Average time to degree:* doctorate–6.2 years full-time. *Entrance requirements:* GRE General Test, sample of written work. Application deadline: 1/4. Application fee: $55 ($60 for international students). *Tuition:* $24,330 per year. • Director of Graduate Studies, 609-258-5529. Application contact: Director of Graduate Admissions, 609-258-3034.

Purdue University, School of Education, Department of Curriculum and Instruction, West Lafayette, IN 47907. Offerings include social studies (MS Ed, PhD), social studies education (Ed S). One or more programs accredited by NCATE. Department faculty: 34 full-time (15 women), 3 part-time (1 woman). *Degree requirements:* For master's, thesis optional; for doctorate, dissertation, oral and written exams; for Ed S, oral presentation, project required, thesis not required. *Entrance requirements:* For master's, TOEFL (minimum score 550), minimum B average; for doctorate, GRE General Test (minimum score 500 on each section), TOEFL (minimum score 550); for Ed S, minimum B average. Application deadline: 1/15 (priority date; 9/15 for spring admission). Application fee: $30. Electronic applications accepted. *Tuition:* $3500 per year full-time, $126 per credit hour part-time for state residents; $11,720 per year full-time, $387 per credit hour part-time for nonresidents. • Dr. J. L. Peters, Head, 765-494-9172. Fax: 765-496-1622. E-mail: peters@purdue.edu. Application contact: Christine Larsen, Coordinator of Graduate Studies, 765-494-2345. Fax: 765-494-5832. E-mail: gradoffice@soe.purdue.edu.

Queens College of the City University of New York, Social Science Division, School of Education, Department of Secondary Education, 65-30 Kissena Boulevard, Flushing, NY 11367-1597. Offerings include social studies (MS Ed, AC). *Degree requirements:* For master's, research project required, foreign language and thesis not required; for AC, thesis optional, foreign language not required. *Entrance requirements:* For master's, TOEFL (minimum score 600), minimum GPA of 3.0; for AC, TOEFL (minimum score 600). Application deadline: 4/1 (rolling processing; 11/1 for spring admission). Application fee: $40. *Expenses:* Tuition $4350 per year full-time, $185 per credit part-time for state residents; $7600 per year full-time, $320 per credit part-time for nonresidents. Fees $104 per year. • Dr. Philip Anderson, Chairperson, 718-997-5150. Application contact: Mario Caruso, Director of Graduate Admissions, 718-997-5200. Fax: 718-997-5193. E-mail: graduate%queens.bitnet@cunyvm.cuny.edu.

Quinnipiac College, School of Liberal Arts, Program in Secondary and Middle School Teaching, Hamden, CT 06518-1904. Offerings include history/social studies (MAT). Program faculty: 21 full-time (5 women), 16 part-time (9 women). *Degree requirements:* Thesis. *Average time to degree:* master's–1.5 years full-time, 3 years part-time. *Entrance requirements:* PRAXIS I, minimum GPA of 2.67. Application deadline: rolling. Application fee: $45. Electronic applications accepted. *Expenses:* Tuition $395 per credit hour. Fees $380 per year full-time. • Carol Orticari, Director, 203-281-8978. Fax: 203-281-8709. E-mail: orticari@quinnipiac.edu. Application contact: Scott Farber, Director of Graduate Admissions, 203-281-8795. Fax: 203-287-5238. E-mail: qcgradadmi@quinnipiac.edu.

Rockford College, Department of Education, Program in Secondary Education, Rockford, IL 61108-2393. Offerings include history (MAT), political science (MAT), social sciences (MAT). Program faculty: 15 full-time (2 women), 8 part-time (6 women), 17 FTE. *Degree requirements:* Thesis optional, foreign language not required. *Entrance requirements:* GRE General Test (minimum combined score of 1000). Application deadline: rolling. Application fee: $35. *Tuition:* $15,500 per year full-time, $400 per credit part-time. • Dr. Debra Dew, Head, 815-392-5202. Fax: 815-226-4119.

Rutgers, The State University of New Jersey, New Brunswick, Graduate School of Education, Department of Educational Theory, Policy and Administration, Program in Social Studies Education, New Brunswick, NJ 08903. Awards Ed M, Ed D, Ed S. Part-time and evening/weekend programs available. Faculty: 2 full-time. Students: 7 full-time, 44 part-time. Average age 28. 15 applicants, 80% accepted. In 1997, 6 master's awarded (100% found work related to degree). Terminal master's awarded for partial completion of doctoral program. *Degree requirements:* For master's, comprehensive exam required, thesis not required; for doctorate and Ed S, thesis/dissertation, qualifying exam. *Entrance requirements:* GRE General Test. Application deadline: 3/1 (11/1 for spring admission). Application fee: $40. *Expenses:* Tuition $6492 per year full-time, $268 per credit part-time for state residents; $9520 per year full-time, $395 per credit part-time for nonresidents. Fees $208 per year (minimum). *Financial aid:* In 1997–98, 10 students received aid, including 10 teaching assistantships; Federal Work-Study, institutionally sponsored loans, and career-related internships or fieldwork also available. Financial aid application deadline: 3/1. *Faculty research:* Academic freedom, equal educational opportunity, social studies curricula. • Kenneth Carlson, Coordinator, 732-932-7496 Ext. 232. Fax: 732-932-6803. Application contact: Dr. Donald J. Taylor, Director of Graduate Admissions, 732-932-7711. Fax: 732-932-8231. E-mail: kdc@rci.rutgers.edu.

Salem State College, Department of Education, Salem, MA 01970-5353. Offerings include geography (MAT), history (MAT). One or more programs accredited by NCATE. MAT (English as a second language) offered jointly with the Department of English. *Application deadline:* rolling. *Application fee:* $25. *Expenses:* Tuition $140 per credit hour for state residents; $230 per credit hour for nonresidents. Fees $20 per credit hour.

Salisbury State University, Department of Education, Salisbury, MD 21801-6837. Offerings include geography (M Ed), history (M Ed), psychology (M Ed). Department faculty: 19 full-time (10 women), 2 part-time (1 woman). *Application deadline:* 8/1 (priority date; rolling processing; 1/1 for spring admission). *Application fee:* $30. *Expenses:* Tuition $158 per credit hour for state residents; $310 per credit hour for nonresidents. Fees $4 per credit hour. • Dr. Ellen Whitford, Chair, 410-543-6294. E-mail: evwhitford@ssu.edu. Application contact: Phyllis Meyer, Administrative Aide II, 410-543-6281. Fax: 410-548-2593. E-mail: phmeyer@ssu.edu.

Smith College, Department of Education and Child Study, Program in Secondary Education, Northampton, MA 01063. Offerings include history education (MAT). Program faculty: 6 full-time (3 women), 3 part-time (2 women). *Degree requirements:* 1 foreign language required, thesis not required. *Average time to degree:* master's–1 year full-time, 4 years part-time. *Entrance requirements:* GRE General Test or MAT. Application deadline: 4/15 (12/1 for spring admission). Application fee: $50. *Tuition:* $21,680 per year full-time, $2720 per course part-time. • Rosetta Cohen, Head, 413-585-3266. E-mail: rcohen@sophia.smith.edu.

South Carolina State University, School of Education, Department of Teacher Education, 300 College Street Northeast, Orangeburg, SC 29117-0001. Offerings include secondary education (M Ed), with options in biology education, business education, counselor education, English education, home economics education, industrial education, mathematics education, science education, social studies education. Accredited by NCATE. Department faculty: 7 full-time (3 women), 2 part-time (1 woman). *Average time to degree:* master's–2 years full-time, 4 years part-time. *Application deadline:* 7/15 (priority date; rolling processing; 11/10 for spring admission). *Application fee:* $25. *Tuition:* $2974 per year full-time, $165 per credit hour part-time. • Dr. Jesse Kinard, Chairman, 803-536-8934. Application contact: Dr. Gail Joyner-Fleming, Interim Associate Dean and Director, Graduate Teacher Education, 803-536-8824. Fax: 803-536-8492.

Southwest Texas State University, School of Liberal Arts, Department of Geography and Planning, Program in Geography, San Marcos, TX 78666. Offerings include geography education (PhD). *Degree requirements:* Dissertation required, foreign language not required. *Entrance requirements:* GRE General Test (minimum combined score of 1100), TOEFL (minimum score 550), minimum GPA of 3.5, master's degree in geography. Application deadline: 7/15 (priority date; rolling processing; 11/15 for spring admission). Application fee: $25 ($50 for international students). *Expenses:* Tuition $648 per year full-time, $120 per semester (minimum) part-time for state residents; $4500 per year full-time, $750 per semester (minimum) part-time for nonresidents. Fees $1264 per year full-time, $314 per semester (minimum) part-time. • Dr. Fred Shelley, Graduate Adviser, 512-245-2170. Fax: 512-245-8353. E-mail: fs03@swt.edu.

Southwest Texas State University, School of Liberal Arts, Department of Political Science, Program in Political Science, San Marcos, TX 78666. Offerings include political science education (M Ed). *Application deadline:* 7/15 (priority date; rolling processing; 11/15 for spring admission). *Application fee:* $25 ($50 for international students). *Expenses:* Tuition $648 per year full-time, $120 per semester (minimum) part-time for state residents; $4500 per year full-time, $750 per semester (minimum) part-time for nonresidents. Fees $1264 per year

Directory: Social Sciences Education

Southwest Texas State University (continued)
full-time, $314 per semester (minimum) part-time. • Dr. Robert Gorman, Graduate Adviser, 512-245-2143. Fax: 512-245-7815. E-mail: rg06@swt.edu.

Stanford University, School of Education, Program in Social Sciences in Educational Practice, Stanford, CA 94305-9991. Offerings include social science in education (AM), with option in gender studies; interdisciplinary; social sciences in education (PhD). *Entrance requirements:* For master's, GRE General Test. Application deadline: 1/2. Application fee: $65 ($75 for international students). *Expenses:* Tuition $22,110 per year. Fees $156 per year. • Application contact: Graduate Admissions Office, 650-723-4794.

Stanford University, School of Education, Teacher Education Program, Stanford, CA 94305-9991. Offerings include social studies education (AM). *Degree requirements:* Thesis required, foreign language not required. *Entrance requirements:* GRE General Test. Application deadline: 1/15. Application fee: $65 ($75 for international students). *Expenses:* Tuition $22,110 per year. Fees $156 per year. • Administrator, 650-723-4891. Application contact: Graduate Admissions Office, 650-723-2110.

State University of New York at Binghamton, School of Education and Human Development, Program in Secondary Education, Binghamton, NY 13902-6000. Offerings include social studies (MAT, MS Ed, MST). *Entrance requirements:* GRE General Test, TOEFL. Application deadline: 4/15 (priority date; rolling processing; 11/1 for spring admission). Application fee: $50. Electronic applications accepted. *Expenses:* Tuition $5100 per year full-time, $213 per credit hour part-time for state residents; $8416 per year full-time, $351 per credit hour part-time for nonresidents. Fees $654 per year full-time, $75 per semester (minimum) part-time. • Dr. Wayne Ross, Coordinator, 607-777-2478.

State University of New York at Stony Brook, School of Professional Development and Continuing Studies, Stony Brook, NY 11794. Offerings include social studies (MAT). School faculty: 1 full-time, 101 part-time. *Application deadline:* 1/15. *Application fee:* $50. *Expenses:* Tuition $5100 per year full-time, $213 per credit hour part-time for state residents; $8416 per year full-time, $351 per credit hour part-time for nonresidents. Fees $529 per year full-time, $77 per semester (minimum) part-time. • Dr. Paul J. Edelson, Dean, 516-632-7052. E-mail: paul.edelson@sunysb.edu. Application contact: Sandra Romansky, Director of Admissions and Advisement, 516-632-7050. Fax: 516-632-9046. E-mail: sandra.romansky@sunysb.edu.

State University of New York College at Brockport, School of Professions, Department of Education and Human Development, Programs in Secondary Education, Brockport, NY 14420-2997. Offerings include social studies education (MS Ed). *Degree requirements:* Thesis or alternative required, foreign language not required. *Entrance requirements:* Minimum GPA of 3.0. Application deadline: 1/15 (priority date; 9/15 for spring admission). Application fee: $50. *Expenses:* Tuition $5100 per year full-time, $213 per credit hour part-time for state residents; $8416 per year full-time, $351 per credit hour part-time for nonresidents. Fees $440 per year full-time, $22.60 per credit hour part-time. • William Veenis, Chairperson, Department of Education and Human Development, 716-395-2205.

State University of New York College at Buffalo, Faculty of Natural and Social Sciences, Department of History and Social Studies, Buffalo, NY 14222-1095. Offerings include secondary education (MS Ed), with option in social studies. Department faculty: 12 full-time (2 women). *Application deadline:* 5/1 (10/1 for spring admission). *Application fee:* $50. *Expenses:* Tuition $5100 per year full-time, $213 per credit hour part-time for state residents; $8416 per year full-time, $351 per credit hour part-time for nonresidents. Fees $195 per year full-time, $8.60 per credit hour part-time. • Dr. E. O. Smith, Chairperson, 716-878-5412.

State University of New York College at Buffalo, Faculty of Applied Science and Education, Department of Elementary Education and Reading, Program in Elementary and Early Secondary Education, Buffalo, NY 14222-1095. Offerings include social studies education (MS Ed). Accredited by NCATE. *Degree requirements:* Thesis or project required, foreign language not required. *Entrance requirements:* Minimum GPA of 2.5 in last 60 hours, New York teaching certificate. Application deadline: 5/1 (10/1 for spring admission). Application fee: $50. *Expenses:* Tuition $5100 per year full-time, $213 per credit hour part-time for state residents; $8416 per year full-time, $351 per credit hour part-time for nonresidents. Fees $195 per year full-time, $8.60 per credit hour part-time. • Dr. Maria Ceprano, Chairperson, Department of Elementary Education and Reading, 716-878-5916.

State University of New York College at Cortland, Division of Arts and Sciences, Program in Secondary Education, Cortland, NY 13045. Offerings include social studies (MS Ed). *Application deadline:* rolling. *Application fee:* $50. *Expenses:* Tuition $5100 per year full-time, $213 per credit hour part-time for state residents; $8416 per year full-time, $351 per credit hour part-time for nonresidents. Fees $644 per year full-time, $79 per semester (minimum) part-time. • Roger Sipher, Head, 607-753-2723. Application contact: Jeanne M. Bechtel, Director of Admissions, 607-753-4711. Fax: 607-753-5998.

State University of New York College at Cortland, Division of Professional Studies, Department of Education, Programs in Elementary Education, Cortland, NY 13045. Offerings include social studies education (MS Ed). *Degree requirements:* 1 foreign language, computer language, thesis (for some programs), comprehensive exams. *Entrance requirements:* Provisional certification. Application deadline: rolling. Application fee: $50. *Expenses:* Tuition $5100 per year full-time, $213 per credit hour part-time for state residents; $8416 per year full-time, $351 per credit hour part-time for nonresidents. Fees $644 per year full-time, $79 per semester (minimum) part-time. • Application contact: Jeanne M. Bechtel, Director of Admissions, 607-753-4711. Fax: 607-753-5998.

State University of New York College at Oneonta, Department of Education, Oneonta, NY 13820-4015. Offerings include elementary education (MS Ed), with options in early secondary English (N–9), early secondary math (N–9), early secondary social science (N–9), general science (N–9); secondary education (MS Ed), with options in biology education, chemistry education, earth science education, English education, home economics education, mathematics education, physics education, social science education. *Application deadline:* 4/15. *Application fee:* $50. *Expenses:* Tuition $5100 per year full-time, $213 per credit hour part-time for state residents; $8416 per year full-time, $351 per credit hour part-time for nonresidents. Fees $482 per year full-time, $6.85 per credit hour part-time. • Dr. Ronald Cromwell, Chair, 607-436-2538.

Syracuse University, School of Education, Teaching and Leadership Programs, Program in Social Studies Education, Syracuse, NY 13244-0003. Awards MS, CAS. Students: 7 full-time (1 woman), 6 part-time (3 women); includes 2 minority (both African Americans). 10 applicants, 80% accepted. In 1997, 7 master's awarded. *Degree requirements:* For master's, thesis or alternative; for CAS, thesis. *Entrance requirements:* GRE. Application fee: $40. *Tuition:* $13,320 per year full-time, $555 per credit hour part-time. *Financial aid:* Application deadline 3/1. • Dr. John Briggs, Chair, 315-443-9077.

Teachers College, Columbia University, Graduate Faculty of Education, Department of Arts and Humanities, Program in History and Education, 525 West 120th Street, New York, NY 10027-6696. Awards Ed M, MA, Ed D, PhD. Faculty: 1 full-time (0 women). Students: 5 full-time (3 women), 19 part-time (8 women); includes 7 minority (5 African Americans, 1 Asian American, 1 Hispanic), 1 international. Average age 35. 27 applicants, 52% accepted. In 1997, 2 master's, 6 doctorates awarded. *Degree requirements:* For doctorate, dissertation. *Entrance requirements:* For master's, sample of historical writing (Ed M); for doctorate, sample of historical writing. Application deadline: 5/15 (12/1 for spring admission). Application fee: $50. *Expenses:* Tuition $640 per credit. Fees $120 per semester. *Financial aid:* Full and partial tuition waivers, Federal Work-Study, institutionally sponsored loans, and career-related internships or fieldwork available. Aid available to part-time students. Financial aid application deadline: 2/1. *Faculty research:* History of American education. • Application contact: Amy Rotheim, Office of Admissions, 212-678-3710. Fax: 212-678-4171.

Teachers College, Columbia University, Graduate Faculty of Education, Department of Arts and Humanities, Program in Social Studies Education, 525 West 120th Street, New York, NY 10027-6696. Awards Ed M, MA, Ed D, PhD. Part-time and evening/weekend programs available. Faculty: 2 full-time (1 woman), 4 part-time (2 women), 4.6 FTE. Students: 36 full-time (19 women), 47 part-time (28 women); includes 13 minority (7 African Americans, 4 Asian Americans, 2 Hispanics), 1 international. Average age 29. 110 applicants, 75% accepted. In 1997, 49 master's awarded. Terminal master's awarded for partial completion of doctoral program. *Degree requirements:* For doctorate, dissertation required, foreign language not required. *Application deadline:* 5/15. *Application fee:* $50. *Expenses:* Tuition $640 per credit. Fees $120 per semester. *Financial aid:* Fellowships, research assistantships, teaching assistantships, full and partial tuition waivers, Federal Work-Study, institutionally sponsored loans, and career-related internships or fieldwork available. Aid available to part-time students. Financial aid application deadline: 2/1. *Faculty research:* History of social studies education, social studies curriculum and teaching, women's history, gender and diversity issues in the classroom. • Application contact: Amy Rotheim, Office of Admissions, 212-678-3710. Fax: 212-678-4171.

Texas A&M University–Commerce, College of Arts and Sciences, Department of History, Commerce, TX 75429-3011. Offerings include social sciences (M Ed, MS). Department faculty: 6 full-time (1 woman), 1 part-time (0 women). *Application deadline:* rolling. *Application fee:* $0 ($25 for international students). *Tuition:* $2382 per year full-time, $343 per semester (minimum) part-time for state residents; $7518 per year full-time, $343 per semester (minimum) part-time for nonresidents. • Dr. Harry Wade, Head, 903-886-5226. Application contact: Pam Hammonds, Graduate Admissions Adviser, 903-886-5167. Fax: 903-886-5165.

Union College, Graduate and Continuing Studies, Programs in Education, Schenectady, NY 12308-2311. Offerings include social studies (MAT). *Application deadline:* 5/15. *Application fee:* $35. *Tuition:* $1155 per course. • Dr. Patrick Allen, Educational Studies Director, 518-388-6361.

University of Arkansas at Pine Bluff, Program in Education, Pine Bluff, AR 71601-2799. Offerings include secondary education (M Ed), with options in aquaculture, English, general science, mathematics, physical education, social studies. Accredited by NCATE. Program faculty: 51. *Entrance requirements:* GRE, minimum GPA of 2.75; NTE or Standard Arkansas Teaching Certificate. Application deadline: rolling. Application fee: $0. *Expenses:* Tuition $82 per credit hour for state residents; $192 per credit hour for nonresidents. Fees $25 per year. • Dr. Calvin Johnson, Dean, 870-543-8256.

University of British Columbia, Faculty of Education, Department of Curriculum Studies, Vancouver, BC V6T 1Z2, Canada. Offerings include social studies education (MA, M Ed, PhD). *Degree requirements:* For master's, thesis (MA) required, foreign language not required; for doctorate, dissertation required, foreign language not required. *Entrance requirements:* TOEFL (minimum score 550). Application deadline: 3/1 (12/1 for spring admission). Application fee: $60.

University of Central Florida, College of Education, Department of Instructional Programs, Program in Social Science Education, Orlando, FL 32816. Awards MA, M Ed. Accredited by NCATE. Students: 8 full-time (3 women), 4 part-time (1 woman); includes 3 minority (2 African Americans, 1 Hispanic). Average age 29. 7 applicants, 43% accepted. In 1997, 6 degrees awarded. *Degree requirements:* Thesis or alternative required, foreign language not required. *Entrance requirements:* GRE General Test (minimum combined score of 840). Application deadline: 7/15 (12/15 for spring admission). Application fee: $20. *Expenses:* Tuition $3288 per year full-time, $137 per credit hour part-time for state residents; $11,520 per year full-time, $480 per credit hour part-time for nonresidents. Fees $105 per year. • Application contact: Dr. Jeff Cornett, Coordinator, 407-823-0215. E-mail: cornett@pegasus.cc.ucf.edu.

University of Connecticut, School of Education, Field of History and Social Science Education, Storrs, CT 06269. Awards MA, PhD. Accredited by NCATE. Faculty: 2. Students: 11 full-time (5 women), 1 part-time (0 women); includes 1 international. Average age 24. 12 applicants, 100% accepted. In 1997, 10 master's awarded. Terminal master's awarded for partial completion of doctoral program. *Degree requirements:* For master's, thesis or alternative; for doctorate, dissertation. *Entrance requirements:* For doctorate, GRE General Test. Application deadline: 6/1 (priority date; rolling processing; 11/1 for spring admission). Application fee: $40 ($45 for international students). *Expenses:* Tuition $5272 per year full-time, $293 per credit part-time for state residents; $13,696 per year full-time, $761 per credit part-time for nonresidents. Fees $948 per year full-time, $640 per year part-time. *Financial aid:* In 1997–98, 2 research assistantships (1 to a first-year student) totaling $6,413, 2 teaching assistantships totaling $12,825 were awarded; fellowships also available. Financial aid application deadline: 2/15. • Thomas P. Weinland, Head, 860-486-2433.

University of Denver, Graduate Studies, Faculty of Arts and Humanities/Social Sciences, Department of Sociology, Denver, CO 80208. Offerings include education (MA). Department faculty: 9 full-time (4 women). *Application deadline:* rolling. *Application fee:* $40 ($45 for international students). *Expenses:* Tuition $18,216 per year full-time, $506 per credit hour part-time. Fees $159 per year. • Dr. Nancy Reichman, Chairperson, 303-871-2061.

University of Florida, College of Education, Department of Instruction and Curriculum, Gainesville, FL 32611. Offerings include economics education (MAE, M Ed, Ed D, PhD, Ed S), social studies education (MAE, M Ed, Ed D, PhD, Ed S). One or more programs accredited by NCATE. Department faculty: 42. *Degree requirements:* For master's, thesis optional, foreign language not required; for doctorate, variable foreign language requirement, dissertation. *Entrance requirements:* For master's and doctorate, GRE General Test (minimum combined score of 1000), minimum GPA of 3.0; for Ed S, GRE General Test. Application deadline: 6/5. Application fee: $20. *Tuition:* $138 per credit hour for state residents; $481 per credit hour for nonresidents. • Dr. Mary Grace Kantowski, Chair, 352-392-9191 Ext. 200. E-mail: mgk@coe.ufl.edu. Application contact: Dr. Ben Nelms, Graduate Coordinator, 352-392-9191 Ext. 225. Fax: 352-392-9193. E-mail: bfn@coe.ufl.edu.

University of Georgia, College of Education, Programs in Secondary Education, Athens, GA 30602. Offerings include social science education (PhD), social sciences education (M Ed, Ed D, Ed S). One or more programs accredited by NCATE. Faculty: 46 full-time (17 women). *Entrance requirements:* For Ed S, GRE General Test or MAT. Application deadline: 7/1 (priority date; 11/15 for spring admission). Application fee: $30. Electronic applications accepted. *Tuition:* $3290 per year full-time, $643 per semester (minimum) part-time for state residents; $11,300 per year full-time, $1645 per semester (minimum) part-time for nonresidents. • Dr. Russell H. Yeany, Dean, 706-542-3866. Fax: 706-542-0360.

University of Houston, College of Education, Department of Curriculum and Instruction, 4800 Calhoun, Houston, TX 77204-2163. Offerings include social studies education (M Ed). Accredited by NCATE. Department faculty: 37 full-time (19 women), 10 part-time (7 women). *Degree requirements:* Comprehensive exam or thesis required, foreign language not required. *Entrance requirements:* GRE General Test or MAT. Application deadline: 7/3 (priority date; rolling processing). Application fee: $35 ($75 for international students). *Expenses:* Tuition $1152 per year full-time, $120 per semester (minimum) part-time for state residents; $4482 per year full-time, $249 per credit hour part-time for nonresidents. Fees $977 per year full-time, $119 per semester (minimum) part-time. • Wilford Weber, Chair, 713-743-4970. Fax: 713-743-9870. E-mail: wweber@uh.edu.

University of Idaho, College of Graduate Studies, College of Letters and Science, Department of History, Moscow, ID 83844-4140. Offerings include history education (MAT). Accredited by NCATE. Department faculty: 10 full-time (4 women), 3 part-time (1 woman), 11.2 FTE. *Application deadline:* 8/1 (12/15 for spring admission). *Application fee:* $35 ($45 for international students). *Expenses:* Tuition $0 for state residents; $6000 per year full-time, $95 per credit part-time for nonresidents. Fees $2676 per year full-time, $134 per credit part-time. • Dr. Richard B. Spence, Chair, 208-885-6253.

University of Indianapolis, School of Education, Indianapolis, IN 46227-3697. Offerings include secondary education (MA), with options in art education, education, English education, social studies education. Accredited by NCATE. *Average time to degree:* master's–5 years part-time. *Entrance requirements:* GRE Subject Test. Application deadline: rolling. Application fee: $30.

University of Maine, College of Education and Human Development, Program in Social Studies Education, Orono, ME 04469. Awards MAT, M Ed, MS, CAS. Accredited by NCATE. Part-time and evening/weekend programs available. *Degree requirements:* For master's, thesis or alternative. *Entrance requirements:* For master's, TOEFL (minimum score 550); for CAS, MA, M Ed, or MS. Application deadline: 2/1 (priority date; rolling processing; 10/15 for spring admission). Application fee: $50. *Expenses:* Tuition $194 per credit hour for state residents; $548 per credit hour for nonresidents. Fees $378 per year full-time, $33 per semester (minimum) part-time. *Financial aid:* Application deadline 3/1. • Application contact: Scott Delcourt, Director of the Graduate School, 207-581-3218. Fax: 207-581-3232. E-mail: graduate@maine.edu.

University of Manitoba, Faculty of Education, Department of Curriculum: Humanities and Social Sciences, Winnipeg, MB R3T 2N2, Canada. Offerings include social studies education (M Ed). *Degree requirements:* Thesis or alternative required, foreign language not required.

University of Michigan, School of Education, Programs in Educational Studies, Ann Arbor, MI 48109. Offerings include social studies education (AM). *Application deadline:* 1/15 (priority date). *Application fee:* $55. Electronic applications accepted. • Dr. Ronald Marx, Chairperson, 734-763-9497. E-mail: ronmarx@umich.edu. Application contact: Karen Wixson, Associate Dean, 734-764-9470. Fax: 734-763-1229. E-mail: kwixson@umich.edu.

University of Minnesota, Twin Cities Campus, College of Education and Human Development, Department of Curriculum and Instruction, Minneapolis, MN 55455-0213. Offerings include social studies education (MA, M Ed, PhD). • Fred Finley, Chairman, 612-625-2545.

University of Nebraska at Kearney, College of Natural and Social Sciences, Department of History, Kearney, NE 68849-0001. Offerings include history education (MA Ed). MA Ed being phased out; applicants no longer accepted. Department faculty: 9 full-time (2 women). *Application deadline:* 8/1 (priority date; rolling processing; 12/15 for spring admission). *Application fee:* $35. *Expenses:* Tuition $1494 per year full-time, $83 per credit hour part-time for state residents; $2826 per year full-time, $157 per credit hour part-time for nonresidents. Fees $229 per year full-time, $11.25 per semester (minimum) part-time. • Dr. James German, Chair, 308-865-8509.

The University of North Carolina at Chapel Hill, School of Education, Programs in Teacher Education, Program in Secondary Education, Chapel Hill, NC 27599. Offerings include social studies/social science (MAT). Accredited by NCATE. *Degree requirements:* Comprehensive exam required, foreign language and thesis not required. *Entrance requirements:* GRE General Test (minimum combined score of 1000), minimum GPA of 3.0 during last 2 years of undergraduate course work. Application deadline: 1/1 (rolling processing). Application fee: $55. *Expenses:* Tuition $1428 per year full-time, $357 per semester (minimum) part-time for state residents; $10,414 per year full-time, $2604 per semester (minimum) part-time for nonresidents. Fees $782 per year full-time, $332 per semester (minimum) part-time. • Dr. Walter Pryzwansky, Director of Graduate Studies, 919-966-7000. Application contact: Janet Carroll, Registrar, 919-966-1346. Fax: 919-962-1533. E-mail: jscarrol@email.unc.edu.

University of Oklahoma, College of Education, Department of Instructional Leadership and Academic Curriculum, Program in Instructional Leadership and Academic Curriculum, Norman, OK 73019-0390. Offerings include social studies education (M Ed, PhD). Accredited by NCATE. Program faculty: 19 full-time (12 women), 12 part-time (11 women). *Degree requirements:* For doctorate, variable foreign language requirement, dissertation. *Entrance requirements:* For master's, TOEFL (minimum score 550), 12 hours of course work in education; for doctorate, GRE General Test (minimum combined score of 1000), TOEFL (minimum score 500), master's degree, minimum graduate GPA of 3.0. Application deadline: 6/1 (priority date; rolling processing). Application fee: $25. *Expenses:* Tuition $1920 per year full-time, $80 per credit hour part-time for state residents; $6108 per year full-time, $255 per credit hour part-time for nonresidents. Fees $468 per year full-time, $12 per semester (minimum) part-time. • Dr. Bonnie Konopak, Chair, Department of Instructional Leadership and Academic Curriculum, 405-325-1498.

University of Pittsburgh, School of Education, Department of Instruction and Learning, Program in Secondary Education, Pittsburgh, PA 15260. Offerings include social studies education (MAT, M Ed, Ed D, PhD). *Degree requirements:* For doctorate, dissertation required, foreign language not required. *Average time to degree:* master's–2 years full-time, 4 years part-time; doctorate–4 years full-time, 6 years part-time. *Entrance requirements:* For doctorate, GRE General Test, TOEFL (minimum score 650). Application deadline: 2/1. Application fee: $30 ($40 for international students). *Expenses:* Tuition $8018 per year full-time, $329 per credit part-time for state residents; $16,508 per year full-time, $680 per credit part-time for nonresidents. Fees $480 per year full-time, $180 per year part-time. • Application contact: Jackie Harden, Manager, 412-648-7060. Fax: 412-648-1899. E-mail: jackie@sched.fsl.pitt.edu.

University of Puerto Rico, Río Piedras, College of Education, Program in Curriculum and Teaching, San Juan, PR 00931. Offerings include history education (M Ed). *Degree requirements:* Thesis required, foreign language not required. *Entrance requirements:* PAEG, minimum GPA of 3.0. Application deadline: 2/21. Application fee: $17.

University of South Carolina, Graduate School, College of Liberal Arts, Department of History, Columbia, SC 29208. Offerings include history education (IMA, MAT). Accredited by NCATE. IMA and MAT offered in cooperation with the College of Education. Department faculty: 30 full-time (4 women), 6 part-time (0 women). *Application deadline:* 2/15. *Application fee:* $35. Electronic applications accepted. *Expenses:* Tuition $3894 per year full-time, $193 per credit hour part-time for state residents; $8114 per year full-time, $404 per credit hour part-time for nonresidents. Fees $125 per year full-time, $37 per semester (minimum) part-time. • Peter Becker, Chair, 803-777-5195. Application contact: Walter B. Edgar, Director of Graduate Studies, 803-777-2340. Fax: 803-777-4494.

University of South Florida, College of Education, Department of Secondary Education, Program in Social Science Education, Tampa, FL 33620-9951. Awards MA, M Ed. Accredited by NCATE. Part-time and evening/weekend programs available. Students: 12 full-time (4 women), 24 part-time (11 women); includes 4 minority (2 African Americans, 2 Hispanics). Average age 32. 11 applicants, 100% accepted. In 1997, 6 degrees awarded. *Entrance requirements:* GRE General Test (minimum combined score of 1000), minimum GPA of 3.5 in last 60 hours. Application deadline: 6/1 (10/15 for spring admission). Application fee: $20. Electronic applications accepted. *Tuition:* $142 per credit hour for state residents; $486 per credit hour for nonresidents. *Financial aid:* Federal Work-Study, institutionally sponsored loans available. Aid available to part-time students. Financial aid applicants required to submit FAFSA. • Application contact: James Duplass, Coordinator, 813-974-4895. Fax: 813-974-3837. E-mail: duplass@tempest.coedu.usf.edu.

University of Tennessee, Knoxville, College of Education, Program in Education II, Knoxville, TN 37996. Offerings include social sciences education (MS, Ed D, Ed S). Accredited by NCATE. *Degree requirements:* For master's and Ed S, thesis optional, foreign language not required; for doctorate, dissertation required, foreign language not required. *Entrance requirements:* For master's, TOEFL (minimum score 550), minimum GPA of 2.7; for doctorate, GRE General Test, TOEFL (minimum score 550), minimum GPA of 2.7; for Ed S, TOEFL (minimum score 550), GRE General Test, minimum GPA of 2.7. Application deadline: 2/1 (priority date; rolling processing). Application fee: $35. Electronic applications accepted. *Tuition:* $3354 per year full-time, $181 per semester hour part-time for state residents; $8410 per year full-time, $462 per semester hour part-time for nonresidents. • Dr. Tom George, Associate Dean, 423-974-0907. Fax: 423-974-8718. E-mail: tgeorge1@utk.edu.

The University of Texas at Tyler, School of Education and Psychology, Department of Curriculum and Instruction, Tyler, TX 75799-0001. Offerings include elementary education (M Ed, Certificate), with options in biology, English, history, reading; secondary education (M Ed, Certificate), with options in biology, English, history, mathematics. Department faculty: 13 full-time (8 women). *Application fee:* $0 ($50 for international students). *Tuition:* $2144 per year full-time, $337 per semester (minimum) part-time for state residents; $7256 per year full-time, $964 per semester (minimum) part-time for nonresidents. • Dr. Bill Bruce, Chair, 903-566-7133. E-mail: wbruce@mail.uttyl.edu. Application contact: Martha D. Wheat, Director of Admissions and Student Records, 903-566-7201. Fax: 903-566-7068.

University of Vermont, College of Arts and Sciences, Department of History, Burlington, VT 05405-0160. Offerings include history education (MAT). *Application deadline:* 4/1 (priority date; rolling processing). *Application fee:* $25. *Expenses:* Tuition $302 per credit for state residents; $755 per credit for nonresidents. Fees $434 per year full-time, $46 per semester (minimum) part-time. • Dr. P. Hutton, Chairperson, 802-656-3180. Application contact: M. True, Coordinator, 802-656-3180.

University of Victoria, Faculty of Education, Department of Social and Natural Sciences, Victoria, BC V8W 2Y2, Canada. Offerings include curriculum and instruction (MA), with options in mathematics, science, social studies; social studies education (M Ed). Postbaccalaureate distance learning degree programs offered (minimal on-campus study). Department faculty: 13 full-time (4 women). *Degree requirements:* Thesis (for some programs), project (M Ed) required, foreign language not required. *Average time to degree:* master's–3.3 years full-time. *Entrance requirements:* Minimum B average. Application deadline: 4/30 (rolling processing). Application fee: $50. *Tuition:* $2080 per year full-time, $557 per semester part-time. • Dr. G. Snively, Chair, 250-721-7769. E-mail: gsnivley@uvic.ca. Application contact: Sarah Baylow, Graduate Secretary, 250-721-7882. Fax: 250-721-7767. E-mail: sbaylow@uvic.ca.

The University of West Alabama, College of Education, Department of Foundations, Livingston, AL 35470. Offerings include secondary education (MAT, M Ed), with options in biology with certification (MAT), environmental science with certification (MAT), history with certification (MAT), language arts with certification (MAT), library media with certification (MAT), mathematics with certification (MAT). Accredited by NCATE. *Application deadline:* 9/10 (priority date; rolling processing; 3/24 for spring admission). *Application fee:* $15. *Tuition:* $70 per quarter hour.

The University of West Alabama, College of Liberal Arts, Department of History and Social Sciences, Livingston, AL 35470. Offers programs in history (MAT), social science (MAT). Accredited by NCATE. *Tuition:* $70 per quarter hour.

University of Wisconsin–Eau Claire, College of Professional Studies, School of Education, Program in Secondary Education, Eau Claire, WI 54702-4004. Offerings include history (MAT, MST). *Application deadline:* 7/1 (rolling processing; 12/1 for spring admission). *Application fee:* $45. *Tuition:* $3651 per year full-time, $611 per semester (minimum) part-time for state residents; $11,295 per year full-time, $1886 per semester (minimum) part-time for nonresidents. • Stephen Kurth, Associate Dean, School of Education, 715-836-3671.

University of Wisconsin–Madison, School of Education, Department of Curriculum and Instruction, Madison, WI 53706-1380. Offerings include geography education (MS). *Application fee:* $38. *Tuition:* $4928 per year full-time, $926 per semester (minimum) part-time for state residents; $15,190 per year full-time, $2849 per semester (minimum) part-time for nonresidents.

University of Wisconsin–River Falls, College of Arts and Science, Department of History, River Falls, WI 54022-5001. Offers program in social science education (MSE). Students: 21 (11 women). *Degree requirements:* Thesis required (for some programs), foreign language not required. *Application deadline:* 3/1. *Application fee:* $45. *Financial aid:* Federal Work-Study available. Financial aid application deadline: 3/1. • Kurt Leichtle, Chair, 715-425-3164. Application contact: Graduate Admissions, 715-425-3843.

Vanderbilt University, Peabody College, Department of Teaching and Learning, Nashville, TN 37240-1001. Offerings include social studies education (M Ed, Ed D). Accredited by NCATE. *Entrance requirements:* GRE General Test, MAT. Application deadline: 3/1 (priority date; rolling processing). Application fee: $35. • Carolyn Evertson, Chair, 615-322-8100.

Wayne State College, Division of Social Sciences, Wayne, NE 68787. Offers programs in history (MSE), social science (MSE). Accredited by NCATE. Faculty: 12 part-time (5 women). Students: 1 (woman) full-time, 3 part-time (2 women). Average age 39. In 1997, 1 degree awarded. *Degree requirements:* Comprehensive exam, research paper required, thesis optional, foreign language not required. *Entrance requirements:* GRE General Test (score in 40th percentile or higher on verbal section) or minimum GPA of 3.0. Application deadline: rolling. Application fee: $10. *Expenses:* Tuition $1788 per year full-time, $75 per credit hour part-time for state residents; $3576 per year full-time, $149 per credit hour part-time for nonresidents. Fees $360 per year full-time, $15 per credit hour part-time. *Financial aid:* In 1997–98, 2 teaching assistantships (both to first-year students) were awarded; career-related internships or fieldwork also available. Financial aid application deadline: 5/1; applicants required to submit FAFSA. *Faculty research:* Rural poverty, early national history, American military and diplomatic history, American cultural and intellectual history, medieval France. • Dr. Jean Karlen, Head, 402-375-7292.

Wayne State University, College of Education, Division of Teacher Education, Detroit, MI 48202. Offerings include social studies (Ed S). Accredited by NCATE. Division faculty: 53. *Application deadline:* 7/1. *Application fee:* $20 ($30 for international students). *Expenses:* Tuition $163 per credit hour for state residents; $355 per credit hour for nonresidents. Fees $498 per year full-time, $114 per semester (minimum) part-time. • Dr. Sharon Elliott, Assistant Dean, 313-577-0902.

Webster University, School of Education, Department of Multidisciplinary Studies, St. Louis, MO 63119-3194. Offerings include social science education (MAT). Department faculty: 7 full-time (5 women). *Entrance requirements:* 2 years of work experience in education, interview, min GPA of 2.5. Application deadline: rolling. Application fee: $25 ($50 for international students). *Tuition:* $350 per credit hour. • Roy Tamashiro, Chair, 314-968-7098. Fax: 314-968-7118. E-mail: tamashro@webster.edu. Application contact: Beth Russell, Director of Graduate Admissions, 314-968-7089. Fax: 314-968-7166. E-mail: russelmb@webster.edu.

Western Carolina University, College of Arts and Sciences, Department of History, Cullowhee, NC 28723. Offerings include social sciences (MAT). Accredited by NCATE. Department faculty: 20 (4 women). *Application deadline:* rolling. *Application fee:* $35. *Tuition:* $1799 per year full-time, $144 per credit hour (minimum) part-time for state residents; $9069 per year full-time, $1053 per credit hour (minimum) part-time for nonresidents. • Curtis Wood, Head, 828-227-7243. Application contact: Kathleen Owen, Assistant to the Dean, 828-227-7398. Fax: 828-227-7480.

Western Carolina University, College of Education and Allied Professions, Department of Administration, Curriculum and Instruction, Programs in Secondary Education, Cullowhee, NC 28723. Offerings include social sciences (MAT). Accredited by NCATE. *Degree requirements:* Comprehensive exam required, foreign language and thesis not required. *Entrance requirements:* GRE General Test. Application deadline: rolling. Application fee: $35. *Tuition:* $1799 per year full-time, $144 per credit hour (minimum) part-time for state residents; $9069 per year full-time, $1053 per credit hour (minimum) part-time for nonresidents. • Application contact: Kathleen Owen, Assistant to the Dean, 828-227-7398. Fax: 828-227-7480.

Directories: Social Sciences Education; Vocational and Technical Education

Western Kentucky University, Potter College of Arts and Humanities, Department of Communication and Broadcasting, Bowling Green, KY 42101-3576. Offerings include communication education (MA Ed). Department faculty: 11 full-time (5 women), 1 part-time (0 women), 11.5 FTE. *Application deadline:* 8/1 (priority date; rolling processing; 12/1 for spring admission). *Application fee:* $20. *Tuition:* $2460 per year full-time, $133 per credit hour part-time for state residents; $6700 per year full-time, $369 per credit hour part-time for nonresidents. • Dr. Larry Winn, Head, 502-745-5134. Fax: 502-745-3295.

Western Oregon University, School of Education, Department of Secondary Education, Monmouth, OR 97361. Offerings include social science (MAT, MS Ed). Accredited by NCATE. Department faculty: 83 full-time (28 women), 26 part-time (11 women), 92.81 FTE. *Degree requirements:* Written exam required, thesis optional, foreign language not required. *Average time to degree:* master's–1 year full-time, 4 years part-time. *Entrance requirements:* GRE General (average 450 on each section) or MAT (minimum score 30), minimum GPA of 3.0, teaching license. Application deadline: rolling. Application fee: $50. • Dr. George Cabrera, Chair, 503-838-8471. Fax: 503-838-8228. E-mail: cabrerg@wou.edu. Application contact: Alison Marshall, Director of Admissions, 503-838-8211. Fax: 503-838-8067. E-mail: marshaa@wou.edu.

Wilkes University, Department of Education, Wilkes-Barre, PA 18766-0002. Offerings include secondary education (MS Ed), with options in biology, chemistry, English, history. Department faculty: 6 full-time, 14 part-time. *Application deadline:* rolling. *Application fee:* $30. *Expenses:* Tuition $12,552 per year full-time, $523 per credit hour part-time. Fees $240 per year full-time, $10 per credit hour part-time. • Dr. Douglas Lynch, Chair, 717-408-4680.

Worcester State College, Graduate Studies, Department of History and Political Science, Worcester, MA 01602-2597. Offers program in history (M Ed). Part-time and evening/weekend programs available. Faculty: 3 part-time (0 women). Students: 2 full-time (0 women), 11 part-time (4 women). Average age 40. 5 applicants, 40% accepted. In 1997, 3 degrees awarded. *Degree requirements:* Comprehensive exam. *Entrance requirements:* GRE General Test or MAT, 18 undergraduate credits in history, including U.S. history and Western civilizations. Application deadline: rolling. Application fee: $10 ($40 for international students). *Tuition:* $127 per credit hour. *Financial aid:* Career-related internships or fieldwork available. *Faculty research:* Labor history, Middle East politics, American-Russian relations, American–East Asian relations. • Dr. Emmett Shea, Coordinator, 508-929-8692. Application contact: Andrea Wetmore, Graduate Admissions Counselor, 508-929-8120. E-mail: awetmore@worc.mass.edu.

Vocational and Technical Education

Alabama Agricultural and Mechanical University, School of Engineering and Technology, Area in Industrial Technology, PO Box 1357, Normal, AL 35762-1357. Offers programs in industry and education (MS), trade and industrial education (M Ed). Accredited by NCATE. M Ed offered jointly with the School of Education. Part-time and evening/weekend programs available. Faculty: 4 full-time (0 women). Students: 1 full-time (0 women), 16 part-time (all women); includes 5 African Americans, 1 international. In 1997, 4 degrees awarded. *Degree requirements:* Comprehensive exam required, thesis optional, foreign language not required. *Entrance requirements:* GRE General Test. Application deadline: 5/1. Application fee: $15 ($20 for international students). *Expenses:* Tuition $2782 per year full-time, $565 per semester (minimum) part-time for state residents; $5164 per year full-time, $1015 per semester (minimum) part-time for nonresidents. Fees $560 per year full-time, $390 per year part-time. *Financial aid:* Fellowships and career-related internships or fieldwork available. Financial aid application deadline: 4/1. *Faculty research:* Ionized gases, hypersonic flow, phenomenology, robotic systems development. • Dr. Arthur Bond, Dean, School of Engineering and Technology, 205-851-5560.

Alcorn State University, School of Psychology and Education, Lorman, MS 39096-9402. Offerings include industrial education (MS Ed). Accredited by NCATE. *Degree requirements:* Thesis optional, foreign language not required. *Application deadline:* 7/1 (priority date; rolling processing; 12/1 for spring admission). *Application fee:* $10. *Tuition:* $2470 per year full-time, $378 per semester (minimum) part-time for state residents; $5331 per year full-time, $855 per semester (minimum) part-time for nonresidents.

Appalachian State University, College of Fine and Applied Arts, Department of Technology, Boone, NC 28608. Offers programs in industrial education (MA), industrial technology (MA). Faculty: 12 full-time (3 women), 1 part-time (0 women). Students: 13 full-time (3 women), 3 part-time (1 woman); includes 1 minority (African American), 3 international. Average age 23. 6 applicants, 50% accepted. In 1997, 8 degrees awarded. *Degree requirements:* Comprehensive exam required, foreign language and thesis not required. *Average time to degree:* master's–2 years full-time, 3 years part-time. *Entrance requirements:* GRE General Test. Application deadline: 7/31 (priority date; rolling processing; 1/7 for spring admission). Application fee: $35. *Tuition:* $1811 per year full-time, $354 per semester (minimum) part-time for state residents; $9081 per year full-time, $2171 per semester (minimum) part-time for nonresidents. *Financial aid:* In 1997–98, 4 research assistantships, 3 teaching assistantships, 1 assistantship were awarded; fellowships, Federal Work-Study, institutionally sponsored loans, and career-related internships or fieldwork also available. Aid available to part-time students. Financial aid application deadline: 3/2. • Dr. Mark Estepp, Chair, 704-262-6351. Application contact: Dr. Brenda Wey, Coordinator, 704-262-3110.

Auburn University, College of Education, Department of Vocational and Adult Education, Auburn University, AL 36849-0001. Awards M Ed, MS, Ed D, Ed S. Accredited by NCATE. Part-time programs available. Faculty: 7 full-time (4 women). Students: 27 full-time (14 women), 59 part-time (36 women); includes 17 minority (16 African Americans, 1 Hispanic). 28 applicants, 43% accepted. In 1997, 24 master's, 2 doctorates awarded. *Degree requirements:* For master's, thesis (MS) required, foreign language not required; for doctorate, dissertation required, foreign language not required; for Ed S, research project required, foreign language and thesis not required. *Entrance requirements:* For master's and Ed S, GRE General Test; for doctorate, GRE General Test (minimum score 400 on each section), 3 years of experience. Application deadline: 9/1 (rolling processing; 3/1 for spring admission). Application fee: $25 ($50 for international students). *Expenses:* Tuition $2760 per year full-time, $76 per credit hour part-time for state residents; $8280 per year full-time, $228 per credit hour part-time for nonresidents. Fees $30 per year full-time, $160 per quarter part-time for state residents; $30 per year full-time, $480 per quarter part-time for nonresidents. *Financial aid:* Research assistantships, teaching assistantships, Federal Work-Study available. Aid available to part-time students. Financial aid application deadline: 3/15. *Faculty research:* Agriculture education, business education, home economics education, industrial arts education. • Dr. Bonnie J. White, Interim Head, 334-844-3800. Application contact: Dr. John F. Pritchett, Dean of the Graduate School, 334-844-4700.

Ball State University, College of Applied Science and Technology, Department of Industry and Technology, 2000 University Avenue, Muncie, IN 47306-1099. Awards MA, MAE. One or more programs accredited by NCATE. Faculty: 13. Students: 9 full-time (0 women), 6 part-time (0 women). Average age 27. 19 applicants, 84% accepted. In 1997, 8 degrees awarded. *Application fee:* $15 ($25 for international students). *Expenses:* Tuition $3454 per year full-time, $518 per semester (minimum) part-time for state residents; $9316 per year full-time, $1221 per semester (minimum) part-time for nonresidents. Fees $242 per year full-time, $18 per semester (minimum) part-time. *Financial aid:* Teaching assistantships available. • Dr. Jack Wescott, Chairperson, 765-285-5641.

Bemidji State University, Division of Professional Studies, Field of Industrial Education, Bemidji, MN 56601-2699. Awards MS Ed. Accredited by NCATE. Part-time programs available. Students: 1 (woman) full-time, 5 part-time (0 women). Average age 38. In 1997, 1 degree awarded. *Degree requirements:* Thesis required, foreign language not required. *Application deadline:* 5/1. *Application fee:* $20. *Expenses:* Tuition $128 per credit for state residents; $134 per credit (minimum) for nonresidents. Fees $517 per year full-time, $35 per credit (minimum) part-time. *Financial aid:* Teaching assistantships, Federal Work-Study, and career-related internships or fieldwork available. Aid available to part-time students. Financial aid application deadline: 5/1. • Dr. Wallace Peck, Chair, 218-755-3790. E-mail: wpeck@vax1.bemidji.msus.edu.

Bowling Green State University, College of Technology, Program in Career and Technology Education, Bowling Green, OH 43403. Awards M Ed. Part-time and evening/weekend programs available. Students: 15 full-time (9 women), 16 part-time (4 women); includes 6 minority (4 African Americans, 1 Hispanic, 1 Native American), 1 international. 11 applicants, 100% accepted. In 1997, 17 degrees awarded. *Degree requirements:* Thesis or alternative required, foreign language not required. *Entrance requirements:* GRE General Test, TOEFL (minimum score 550). Application fee: $30. *Tuition:* $6070 per year full-time, $284 per credit hour part-time for state residents; $11,358 per year full-time, $536 per credit hour part-time for nonresidents. *Financial aid:* Full and partial tuition waivers, Federal Work-Study, and career-related internships or fieldwork available. Financial aid application deadline: 2/15; applicants required to submit FAFSA. *Faculty research:* Curriculum in technology education. • Dr. Larry Hatch, Chair, 419-372-2437. Application contact: Dr. Ernie Savage, Graduate Coordinator, 419-372-7613.

Bowling Green State University, College of Education and Allied Professions, Department of Educational Curriculum and Instruction, Program in Classroom Technology, Bowling Green, OH 43403. Awards M Ed. Accredited by NCATE. Part-time programs available. Students: 31 part-time (27 women). 4 applicants, 50% accepted. *Degree requirements:* Thesis or alternative required, foreign language not required. *Entrance requirements:* GRE General Test, TOEFL. Application fee: $30. *Tuition:* $6070 per year full-time, $284 per credit hour part-time for state residents; $11,358 per year full-time, $536 per credit hour part-time for nonresidents. *Financial aid:* Institutionally sponsored loans and career-related internships or fieldwork available. Financial aid application deadline: 2/15; applicants required to submit FAFSA. • Application contact: Dr. Nancy Brownell, Graduate Coordinator, 419-372-7392.

Brigham Young University, College of Engineering and Technology, Department of Technology Education and Construction Management, Provo, UT 84602-1001. Awards MS. Part-time programs available. Faculty: 7 full-time (0 women). Students: 1 full-time (0 women), 28 part-time (3 women); includes 2 minority (both Native Americans). Average age 35. 8 applicants, 50% accepted. In 1997, 5 degrees awarded. *Degree requirements:* Thesis (for some programs), field project required, foreign language not required. *Average time to degree:* master's–4 years part-time. *Entrance requirements:* Minimum GPA of 3.0 in last 60 hours. Application deadline: 2/15 (priority date; rolling processing). Application fee: $30. *Tuition:* $3200 per year full-time, $178 per credit hour part-time for state residents; $4800 per year full-time, $266 per credit hour part-time for nonresidents. *Financial aid:* 21 students received aid; teaching assistantships, partial tuition waivers, institutionally sponsored loans available. Aid available to part-time students. Financial aid application deadline: 6/15. *Faculty research:* High-technology curriculum development, educational lasers, development of teaching aids to implement technolomanagement. • Dr. Garth A. Hill, Chair, 801-378-2021. Application contact: Ronald Gonzales, Graduate Coordinator, 801-378-6490. Fax: 801-378-7519. E-mail: ron_gonzales@byu.edu.

California Baptist College, Graduate Program in Education, Riverside, CA 92504-3206. Offerings include educational technology (MS Ed). Program faculty: 8 full-time (7 women), 4 part-time (2 women). *Application deadline:* rolling. *Application fee:* $40. *Expenses:* Tuition $275 per unit. Fees $100 per year. • Dr. Marsha Savage, Chair, 909-689-5771. Application contact: Gail Ronveaux, Director of Graduate Services, 909-343-4249. Fax: 909-351-1808. E-mail: gradser@cal.baptist.edu.

California State University, Long Beach, College of Health and Human Services, Department of Occupational Studies, Long Beach, CA 90840-5601. Awards MA. Part-time and evening/weekend programs available. Faculty: 5 full-time (1 woman). Students: 3 full-time (2 women), 52 part-time (35 women); includes 28 minority (21 Asian Americans, 6 Hispanics, 1 Native American), 1 international. Average age 42. 19 applicants, 63% accepted. In 1997, 11 degrees awarded. *Degree requirements:* Comprehensive exam or thesis required, foreign language not required. *Application deadline:* 8/1 (rolling processing; 12/1 for spring admission). *Application fee:* $55. *Expenses:* Tuition $0 for state residents; $246 per unit for nonresidents. Fees $1846 per year full-time, $1180 per year part-time. *Financial aid:* Application deadline 3/2. *Faculty research:* Special needs, leadership, training and development. • Dr. Paul Bott, Chair, 562-985-5633. E-mail: pbott@csulb.edu. Application contact: Dr. Leonard Albright, Graduate Coordinator, 562-985-8103. Fax: 562-985-8815. E-mail: lalbrigh@csulb.edu.

California State University, Los Angeles, School of Engineering and Technology, Department of Technology, Major in Vocational Education, Los Angeles, CA 90032-8530. Awards MA. Program being phased out; applicants no longer accepted. Students: 1 part-time (0 women). *Degree requirements:* Computer language, project or thesis required, foreign language not required. *Expenses:* Tuition $0 for state residents; $164 per unit for nonresidents. Fees $1763 per year full-time, $1097 per year part-time. *Financial aid:* 1 student received aid. • Dr. Jim Heideman, Head, 213-343-4573.

California State University, San Bernardino, Graduate Studies, School of Education, Program in Vocational Education, San Bernardino, CA 92407-2397. Awards MA. Part-time and evening/weekend programs available. Faculty: 3 full-time (0 women), 2 part-time (0 women). Students: 22 full-time (17 women), 35 part-time (30 women); includes 17 minority (2 African Americans, 3 Asian Americans, 12 Hispanics), 11 international. 30 applicants, 97% accepted. *Degree requirements:* Thesis required, foreign language not required. *Entrance requirements:* Minimum GPA of 3.0 in education, vocational teaching credential. Application deadline: 8/31 (priority date). Application fee: $55. *Expenses:* Tuition $0 for state residents; $164 per unit for nonresidents. Fees $1922 per year full-time, $1256 per year part-time. *Financial aid:* Federal Work-Study and career-related internships or fieldwork available. Aid available to part-time students. • Coordinator, Designated Subjects, 909-880-5637.

California University of Pennsylvania, School of Education, Department of Technology Education, 250 University Avenue, California, PA 15419-1394. Awards M Ed. Accredited by NCATE. Part-time and evening/weekend programs available. Faculty: 3 part-time (0 women). Students: 2 full-time (0 women), 12 part-time (0 women). 6 applicants, 100% accepted. In 1997, 4 degrees awarded. *Degree requirements:* Comprehensive exam required, thesis optional, foreign language not required. *Entrance requirements:* MAT (minimum score 35), TOEFL (minimum score 550), minimum GPA of 2.5, teaching experience in industrial arts. Application deadline: rolling. Application fee: $25. *Expenses:* Tuition $3468 per year full-time, $193 per credit part-time for state residents; $6236 per year full-time, $346 per credit part-time for nonresidents. Fees $886 per year full-time, $153 per semester (minimum) part-time. *Financial aid:* Graduate assistantships available. • Dr. Stanley Komacek, Coordinator, 724-938-4085.

Central Connecticut State University, School of Technology, Department of Technology Education, New Britain, CT 06050-4010. Awards MS. Part-time and evening/weekend programs available. Faculty: 6 full-time (0 women), 7 part-time (4 women), 8.5 FTE. Students: 8 full-time (1 woman), 34 part-time (5 women); includes 2 minority (1 African American, 1 Hispanic), 1 international. Average age 38. 26 applicants, 73% accepted. In 1997, 9 degrees awarded. *Degree requirements:* Thesis or alternative, comprehensive exam or special project required, foreign language not required. *Entrance requirements:* TOEFL (minimum score 550), minimum GPA of 2.7. Application deadline: 6/1 (priority date; rolling processing; 12/1 for spring admission). Application fee: $40. *Expenses:* Tuition $4458 per year full-time, $175 per credit hour part-time for state residents; $9943 per year full-time, $175 per credit hour part-time for nonresidents. Fees $45 per semester. *Financial aid:* Federal Work-Study available. Financial aid application deadline: 3/15; applicants required to submit FAFSA. *Faculty research:* Instruction, curriculum development, administration, occupational training. • Dr. W. Tad Foster, Chair, 860-832-1850.

Central Michigan University, College of Science and Technology, Department of Industrial and Engineering Technology, Mount Pleasant, MI 48859. Offers programs in industrial education (MA), industrial education administration (MAV Ed), industrial management and technology (MA). MAV Ed being phased out; applicants no longer accepted. Faculty: 16 full-time (3 women). Students: 7 full-time (2 women), 9 part-time (2 women); includes 8 international. Average age 28. In 1997, 9 degrees awarded. *Entrance requirements:* 2 years of teaching experience, undergraduate major/minor in industrial engineering or related field. Application deadline: 3/1 (priority date; rolling processing). Application fee: $30. *Expenses:* Tuition $139 per credit hour (minimum) for state residents; $276 per credit hour (minimum) for nonresidents. Fees $260 per year full-time, $150 per semester part-time. *Financial aid:* In 1997–98, 4 teaching assistantships (3 to first-year students) were awarded; fellowships, research assistantships, Federal Work-Study, and career-related internships or fieldwork also available. Financial aid application deadline: 3/7. *Faculty research:* Computer applications, manufacturing process control, automation, industrial activities. • Dr. Larry Fryda, Chairperson, 517-774-3033. Fax: 517-774-4700. E-mail: 3z3iihn@cmich.edu.

Central Missouri State University, College of Applied Sciences and Technology, Program in Industrial Arts and Technology, Warrensburg, MO 64093. Offers human services/industrial arts and technology (Ed S); industrial, vocational, and technical education (MS); K–12 education/industrial arts and technology (MSE). One or more programs accredited by NCATE. Part-time programs available. Students: 7 full-time (3 women), 20 part-time (4 women). In 1997, 11 master's, 1 Ed S awarded. *Degree requirements:* For master's, comprehensive exam (MS), comprehensive exam or thesis (MSE); for Ed S, thesis, comprehensive exam. *Entrance requirements:* For master's, GRE General Test (MSE), minimum GPA of 2.5 (MS); minimum GPA of 2.75, teaching certificate (MSE); for Ed S, GRE General Test, minimum graduate GPA of 3.25, teaching certificate. Application deadline: 6/30 (priority date; rolling processing). Application fee: $25 ($50 for international students). *Tuition:* $3288 per year full-time, $137 per credit hour part-time for state residents; $5928 per year full-time, $274 per credit hour part-time for nonresidents. *Financial aid:* In 1997–98, 1 research assistantship, 2 teaching assistantships, 2 administrative and laboratory assistantships were awarded; Federal Work-Study also available. Aid available to part-time students. Financial aid application deadline: 3/1; applicants required to submit FAFSA. • Dr. William Downs, Chair, 660-543-4727. Fax: 660-543-8031. E-mail: wad4452@cmsu2.cmsu.edu.

Chicago State University, College of Education, Department of Occupational Education, Chicago, IL 60628. Awards MS Ed. *Degree requirements:* Thesis optional, foreign language not required. *Entrance requirements:* Minimum GPA of 2.75. Application deadline: 7/1 (11/10 for spring admission). *Tuition:* $2268 per year full-time, $95 per credit hour part-time for state residents; $6804 per year full-time, $284 per credit hour part-time for nonresidents.

City College of the City University of New York, Graduate School, School of Education, Department of Secondary and Continuing Education, Convent Avenue at 138th Street, New York, NY 10031-6977. Offerings include technology education (MA). *Degree requirements:* Thesis required, foreign language not required. *Entrance requirements:* TOEFL (minimum score 500). Application fee: $40. *Expenses:* Tuition $4350 per year full-time, $185 per credit part-time for state residents; $7600 per year full-time, $320 per credit part-time for nonresidents. Fees $41 per year. • Hope Hartman, Chair, 212-650-7954.

City College of the City University of New York, Graduate School, School of Education, Department of Technology Education, Convent Avenue at 138th Street, New York, NY 10031-6977. Awards MS Ed. Students: 12 part-time (2 women). In 1997, 18 degrees awarded. *Degree requirements:* Research paper required, foreign language and thesis not required. *Entrance requirements:* TOEFL (minimum score 500), minimum B average in undergraduate course work. Application fee: $40. *Expenses:* Tuition $4350 per year full-time, $185 per credit part-time for state residents; $7600 per year full-time, $320 per credit part-time for nonresidents. Fees $41 per year. *Financial aid:* Fellowships, research assistantships, partial tuition waivers, Federal Work-Study available. Financial aid application deadline: 5/1. • Chairman, 212-650-7139.

Clemson University, College of Health, Education, and Human Development, Department of Technology and Human Resource Development, Program in Industrial Education, Clemson, SC 29634. Awards M In Ed. Accredited by NCATE. Students: 20 full-time (9 women), 17 part-time (5 women); includes 3 minority (all African Americans), 1 international. 18 applicants, 67% accepted. In 1997, 18 degrees awarded. *Entrance requirements:* TOEFL, teaching certificate. Application deadline: 6/1. Application fee: $35. *Expenses:* Tuition $3154 per year full-time, $130 per credit hour part-time for state residents; $6452 per year full-time, $264 per credit hour part-time for nonresidents. Fees $190 per year. • Dr. Gerald Lovedahl, Chair, Department of Technology and Human Resource Development, 864-656-3447. Fax: 864-656-4808. E-mail: march21@clemson.edu.

Clemson University, College of Health, Education, and Human Development, Department of Technology and Human Resource Development, Program in Vocational/Technical Education, Clemson, SC 29634. Awards Ed D. Accredited by NCATE. Part-time programs available. Students: 3 full-time (1 woman), 15 part-time (8 women); includes 1 minority (Hispanic), 1 international. 7 applicants, 29% accepted. In 1997, 10 degrees awarded. *Degree requirements:* Dissertation. *Entrance requirements:* GRE General Test (minimum combined score of 1450 on three sections), TOEFL. Application deadline: 6/1 (11/1 for spring admission). Application fee: $35. *Expenses:* Tuition $3154 per year full-time, $130 per credit hour part-time for state residents; $6452 per year full-time, $264 per credit hour part-time for nonresidents. Fees $190 per year. • Dr. Gerald Lovedahl, Chair, Department of Technology and Human Resource Development, 864-656-3447. Fax: 864-656-4808. E-mail: march21@clemson.edu.

Colorado State University, College of Applied Human Sciences, Department of Manufacturing Technology and Construction Management, Fort Collins, CO 80523-0015. Offerings include industrial sciences and technology education (MS). Department faculty: 16 full-time (1 woman), 4 part-time (1 woman). *Degree requirements:* Computer language, thesis (for some programs) required, foreign language not required. *Entrance requirements:* GRE General Test, TOEFL. Application deadline: 2/1 (priority date; rolling processing). Application fee: $30. Electronic applications accepted. *Expenses:* Tuition $2632 per year full-time, $109 per credit hour part-time for state residents; $10,216 per year full-time, $425 per credit hour part-time for nonresidents. Fees $708 per year full-time, $32 per semester (minimum) part-time. • Larry Grosse, Head, 970-491-7958. Application contact: Linda Burrous, Department Secretary, 970-491-7355. Fax: 970-491-2473. E-mail: burrous@cahs.colostate.edu.

Colorado State University, College of Applied Human Sciences, School of Education, Fort Collins, CO 80523-0015. Offers programs in student affairs (MS), vocational education (M Ed, PhD). Accredited by NCATE. Faculty: 35 full-time (14 women), 8 part-time (all women). Students: 104 full-time (70 women), 232 part-time (155 women); includes 44 minority (14 African Americans, 9 Asian Americans, 18 Hispanics, 3 Native Americans), 7 international. Average age 38. 254 applicants, 56% accepted. In 1997, 62 master's, 25 doctorates awarded. *Degree requirements:* Thesis/dissertation optional, foreign language not required. *Entrance requirements:* GRE General Test, TOEFL. Application deadline: 2/1 (priority date; rolling processing). Application fee: $30. Electronic applications accepted. *Expenses:* Tuition $2632 per year full-time, $109 per credit hour part-time for state residents; $10,216 per year full-time, $425 per credit hour part-time for nonresidents. Fees $708 per year full-time, $32 per semester (minimum) part-time. *Financial aid:* In 1997–98, 4 fellowships, 49 research assistantships, 5 teaching assistantships were awarded; traineeships, Federal Work-Study, institutionally sponsored loans, and career-related internships or fieldwork also available. Financial aid application deadline: 4/5. *Faculty research:* Integration of academic and vocational education; high-risk youth; diversity/gender issues; empowerment of individual, family, and community. • Dr. Rick Ginsberg, Interim Director, 970-491-6317. E-mail: love@condor.cahs.colostate.edu. Application contact: Gene Gloeckner, Director of Graduate Programs, 970-491-1963. Fax: 970-491-1317. E-mail: cobb@condor.cahs.colostate.edu.

Drake University, School of Education, Department of Special Education, Counseling and Vocational Rehabilitation, Program in Vocational Rehabilitation, Des Moines, IA 50311-4516. Awards MS. Faculty: 2 full-time (0 women), 2 part-time (1 woman). Students: 2 full-time (both women), 30 part-time (24 women). 26 applicants, 77% accepted. In 1997, 15 degrees awarded. *Entrance requirements:* GRE General Test (minimum combined score of 1000) or MAT (minimum score 36). Application deadline: rolling. Application fee: $25. *Tuition:* $16,000 per year full-time, $260 per hour (minimum) part-time. *Financial aid:* Career-related internships or fieldwork available. Aid available to part-time students. • Dr. Robert Stensrud, Head, 515-271-3061. Application contact: Ann J. Martin, Graduate Coordinator, 515-271-3871. Fax: 515-271-2831.

East Carolina University, School of Education, Department of Business, Vocational, and Technical Education, Greenville, NC 27858-4353. Offers program in vocational education (MS). Accredited by NCATE. Faculty: 5 full-time (2 women). Students: 6 full-time (3 women), 19 part-time (17 women); includes 6 minority (all African Americans). Average age 33. 10 applicants, 80% accepted. In 1997, 13 degrees awarded. *Degree requirements:* Comprehensive exams. *Application deadline:* 6/1 (priority date; rolling processing). *Application fee:* $40. *Tuition:* $1886 per year full-time, $472 per semester (minimum) part-time for state residents; $9156 per year full-time, $2289 per semester (minimum) part-time for nonresidents. *Financial aid:* Federal Work-Study available. Aid available to part-time students. Financial aid application deadline: 6/1. • Dr. Vivian Arnold, Director of Graduate Studies, 252-328-6983. Fax: 252-328-6525. E-mail: arnoldv@mail.ecu.edu. Application contact: Dr. Paul D. Tschetter, Associate Dean, 252-328-6012. Fax: 252-328-6071. E-mail: grad@mail.ecu.edu.

Eastern Kentucky University, College of Applied Arts and Technology, Department of Technology, Program in Industrial Education, Richmond, KY 40475-3101. Offers industrial training (MS), technology education (MS), vocational administration (MS). Accredited by NCATE. Part-time programs available. Students: 14. In 1997, 5 degrees awarded. *Entrance requirements:* GRE General Test (minimum combined score of 1000), minimum GPA of 2.5. Application fee: $0. *Tuition:* $2390 per year full-time, $133 per credit hour part-time for state residents; $6630 per year full-time, $365 per credit hour part-time for nonresidents. *Financial aid:* Research assistantships, teaching assistantships, Federal Work-Study available. Aid available to part-time students. • Clyde O. Craft, Chair, Department of Technology, 606-622-3232.

Eastern Kentucky University, College of Education, Department of Curriculum and Instruction, Program in Secondary and Higher Education, Richmond, KY 40475-3101. Offerings include industrial education (MA Ed). Accredited by NCATE. *Entrance requirements:* GRE General Test, minimum GPA of 2.5. Application fee: $0. *Tuition:* $2390 per year full-time, $133 per credit hour part-time for state residents; $6630 per year full-time, $365 per credit hour part-time for nonresidents. • Dr. Imogene Ramsey, Chair, Department of Curriculum and Instruction, 606-622-2154.

Eastern Michigan University, College of Technology, Department of Business and Technology Education, Program in Technology Education, Ypsilanti, MI 48197. Awards MA. Accredited by NCATE. Evening/weekend programs available. In 1997, 6 degrees awarded. *Degree requirements:* Thesis optional, foreign language not required. *Entrance requirements:* GRE General Test, TOEFL (minimum score 500). Application deadline: 5/15 (rolling processing; 3/15 for spring admission). Application fee: $30. *Expenses:* Tuition $2691 per year full-time, $150 per credit hour part-time for state residents; $6300 per year full-time, $350 per credit hour part-time for nonresidents. Fees $368 per year full-time, $88 per semester (minimum) part-time. *Financial aid:* Fellowships, teaching assistantships available. Aid available to part-time students. Financial aid application deadline: 3/15; applicants required to submit FAFSA. • Dr. Earl Meyer, Coordinator, 734-487-4330.

Eastern Washington University, College of Business Administration, Department of Management Information Systems, Cheney, WA 99004-2431. Offerings include vocational administration (M Ed). Admissions temporarily suspended. *Degree requirements:* Comprehensive exam required, thesis optional, foreign language not required. *Tuition:* $4200 per year full-time, $140 per credit part-time for state residents; $12,780 per year full-time, $415 per credit part-time for nonresidents. • Dr. John Zurenko, Chair, 509-358-2285.

Eastern Washington University, College of Science, Mathematics and Technology, Department of Technology, Cheney, WA 99004-2431. Awards M Ed. One or more programs accredited by NCATE. Faculty: 8 full-time (0 women). Students: 2 full-time (1 woman), 1 (woman) part-time. 3 applicants, 33% accepted. *Degree requirements:* Comprehensive oral exam required, thesis optional. *Entrance requirements:* Minimum GPA of 3.0. Application deadline: 4/1 (priority date; rolling processing; 1/15 for spring admission). Application fee: $35. *Tuition:* $4200 per year full-time, $140 per credit part-time for state residents; $12,780 per year full-time, $415 per credit part-time for nonresidents. *Financial aid:* Teaching assistantships available. Financial aid application deadline: 2/1. • Dr. Jim Ruch, Chair, 509-359-2436.

Ferris State University, College of Education, Center for Occupational Education, Big Rapids, MI 49307-2742. Awards MS. Part-time and evening/weekend programs available. Faculty: 2 full-time (1 woman), 4 part-time (0 women), 3.25 FTE. Students: 2 full-time (0 women), 64 part-time (39 women); includes 3 minority (2 African Americans, 1 Hispanic). Average age 35. 17 applicants, 100% accepted. In 1997, 21 degrees awarded. *Degree requirements:* Thesis, research paper. *Average time to degree:* master's–1 year full-time, 3 years part-time. *Entrance requirements:* Minimum GPA of 3.0, 2 years of work experience. Application deadline: 8/31 (priority date; rolling processing). Application fee: $20. *Expenses:* Tuition $220 per credit hour for state residents; $450 per credit hour for nonresidents. Fees $100 per year. *Financial aid:* Full and partial tuition waivers and career-related internships or fieldwork available. Aid available to part-time students. • Dr. Karen L. Norman, Coordinator, 616-592-5025. E-mail: karen_l_norman@ferris.edu. Application contact: Helen Bacon, Administrative Assistant, 616-592-3652. Fax: 616-592-3792. E-mail: hbacon@music.ferris.edu.

Fitchburg State College, Program in Occupational Education, Fitchburg, MA 01420-2697. Awards M Ed. Accredited by NCATE. Part-time and evening/weekend programs available. *Entrance requirements:* GRE General Test or MAT (minimum score 47), interview, industrial arts teaching certificate. Application deadline: rolling. Application fee: $10. *Expenses:* Tuition $147 per credit. Fees $55 per semester. *Financial aid:* Graduate assistantships, Federal Work-Study available. Aid available to part-time students. Financial aid application deadline: 3/30; applicants required to submit FAFSA. • Dr. Lloyd Harte, Chair, 978-665-3047. Fax: 978-665-3658. E-mail: dgce@fsc.edu. Application contact: James DuPont, Director of Admissions, 978-665-3144. Fax: 978-665-4540. E-mail: admissions@fsc.edu.

Directory: Vocational and Technical Education

Fitchburg State College, Program in Technology Education, Fitchburg, MA 01420-2697. Awards M Ed. Accredited by NCATE. Part-time and evening/weekend programs available. *Entrance requirements:* GRE General Test or MAT (minimum score 47). Application deadline: rolling. Application fee: $10. *Expenses:* Tuition $147 per credit. Fees $55 per semester. *Financial aid:* Graduate assistantships, Federal Work-Study available. Aid available to part-time students. Financial aid application deadline: 3/30; applicants required to submit FAFSA. • Dr. Stanley Bucholc, Chair, 978-665-3256. Fax: 978-665-3658. E-mail: dgce@fsc.edu. Application contact: James DuPont, Director of Admissions, 978-665-3144. Fax: 978-665-4540. E-mail: admissions@fsc.edu.

Florida Agricultural and Mechanical University, Division of Graduate Studies, Research, and Continuing Education, College of Education, Department of Industrial Arts and Vocational Education, Tallahassee, FL 32307-3200. Offers programs in business education (MBE), industrial education (M Ed, MS Ed). Accredited by NCATE. Students: 8 (5 women); includes 6 minority (all African Americans). *Entrance requirements:* GRE General Test (minimum combined score of 1000), minimum GPA of 3.0. Application deadline: 5/13. Application fee: $20. *Expenses:* Tuition $140 per credit hour for state residents; $484 per credit hour for nonresidents. Fees $130 per year. • Dr. Jerrlyne Jackson, Chairperson, 850-599-3061.

Florida International University, College of Education, Department of Subject Specializations, Program in Technical Education, Miami, FL 33199. Awards MS. Accredited by NCATE. Part-time and evening/weekend programs available. Students: 3 part-time (0 women); includes 1 minority (African American). Average age 42. 4 applicants, 50% accepted. *Entrance requirements:* GRE General Test (minimum combined score of 1000) or minimum GPA of 3.0 in last 60 credits of baccalaureate, interview. Application deadline: 4/1 (priority date; rolling processing; 10/1 for spring admission). Application fee: $20. *Expenses:* Tuition $138 per credit hour for state residents; $482 per credit hour for nonresidents. Fees $46 per semester. *Financial aid:* Research assistantships, Federal Work-Study, institutionally sponsored loans available. • Dr. Dean Hauenstein, Chairperson, Department of Subject Specializations, 305-348-2005. Fax: 305-348-2086.

Florida International University, College of Education, Department of Subject Specializations, Program in Vocational Industrial Education, Miami, FL 33199. Awards MS. Accredited by NCATE. Part-time and evening/weekend programs available. Students: 1 full-time (0 women), 1 part-time (0 women); includes 2 minority (both Hispanics). Average age 32. 1 applicant, 0% accepted. *Entrance requirements:* GRE General Test (minimum combined score of 1000) or minimum GPA of 3.0 in last 60 credits of baccalaureate, interview. Application deadline: 4/1 (priority date; rolling processing; 10/1 for spring admission). Application fee: $20. *Expenses:* Tuition $138 per credit hour for state residents; $482 per credit hour for nonresidents. Fees $46 per semester. *Financial aid:* Research assistantships available. *Faculty research:* Administration and supervision. • Dr. Dean Hauenstein, Chairperson, Department of Subject Specializations, 305-348-2005. Fax: 305-348-2086.

Florida State University, College of Education, Department of Educational Leadership, Program in Comprehensive Vocational Education, Tallahassee, FL 32306. Awards PhD, Ed S. Part-time and evening/weekend programs available. Faculty: 1 full-time (0 women), 2 part-time (0 women). Students: 6 full-time (4 women), 10 part-time (3 women); includes 6 minority (4 African Americans, 2 Asian Americans). 6 applicants, 100% accepted. In 1997, 1 doctorate, 1 Ed S awarded. Terminal master's awarded for partial completion of doctoral program. *Degree requirements:* For doctorate, dissertation, comprehensive exam; for Ed S, comprehensive exam required, thesis optional. *Entrance requirements:* For doctorate and Ed S, GRE General Test (minimum combined score of 1000), minimum graduate GPA of 3.0. Application deadline: 7/1 (priority date; rolling processing; 11/1 for spring admission). Application fee: $20. *Tuition:* $139 per credit hour for state residents; $482 per credit hour for nonresidents. *Financial aid:* Fellowships, research assistantships, and career-related internships or fieldwork available. • Dr. Hollie Thomas, Head, Department of Educational Leadership, 850-644-6777. E-mail: thomas@mail.coe.fsu.edu. Application contact: Admissions Secretary, 850-644-6777. Fax: 850-644-1258.

Georgia Southern University, College of Education, Department of Leadership, Technology, and Human Development, Program in Adult and Vocational Education, Statesboro, GA 30460-8126. Awards M Ed. Accredited by NCATE. Part-time and evening/weekend programs available. Students: 7 full-time (4 women), 9 part-time (7 women); includes 2 minority (both African Americans). Average age 40. 4 applicants, 100% accepted. In 1997, 11 degrees awarded. *Degree requirements:* Exams required, foreign language and thesis not required. *Entrance requirements:* GRE General Test (minimum score 450 on each section) or MAT (minimum score 44), minimum GPA of 2.5. Application deadline: 7/15 (priority date; rolling processing; 11/15 for spring admission). Application fee: $0. Electronic applications accepted. *Tuition:* $2619 per year full-time, $287 per semester (minimum) part-time for state residents; $8619 per year full-time, $1037 per semester (minimum) part-time for nonresidents. *Financial aid:* Research assistantships, teaching assistantships, Federal Work-Study, and career-related internships or fieldwork available. Aid available to part-time students. Financial aid application deadline: 4/15. • Dr. Catherine Hansman, Coordinator, 912-681-0032. Fax: 912-486-7104. E-mail: chansman@gsvm2.cc.gasou.edu. Application contact: Dr. John R. Diebolt, Associate Graduate Dean, 912-681-5384. Fax: 912-681-0740. E-mail: gradschool@gsvms2.cc.gasou.edu.

Georgia Southern University, College of Education, Department of Middle Grades and Secondary Education, Program in Technology Education, Statesboro, GA 30460-8126. Awards M Ed, Ed S. Part-time and evening/weekend programs available. Students: 10 full-time (3 women), 6 part-time (2 women); includes 1 minority (African American). Average age 40. 4 applicants, 75% accepted. In 1997, 6 master's, 2 Ed Ss awarded. *Degree requirements:* Exams required, foreign language and thesis not required. *Entrance requirements:* For master's, GRE General Test (minimum score 450 on each section) or MAT (minimum score 44), minimum GPA of 2.5; for Ed S, GRE General Test (minimum score 450 on each section) or MAT (minimum score 49), minimum graduate GPA of 3.25. Application deadline: 7/15 (priority date; rolling processing; 11/15 for spring admission). Application fee: $0. Electronic applications accepted. *Tuition:* $2619 per year full-time, $287 per semester (minimum) part-time for state residents; $8619 per year full-time, $1037 per semester (minimum) part-time for nonresidents. *Financial aid:* Application deadline 4/15. • Dr. Ronnie Sheppard, Chair, 912-681-5203. Fax: 912-681-5093. Application contact: Dr. John R. Diebolt, Associate Graduate Dean, 912-681-5384. Fax: 912-681-0740. E-mail: gradschool@gsvms2.cc.gasou.edu.

Georgia State University, College of Education, Department of Educational Policy Studies, Program in Vocational Education, Atlanta, GA 30303-3083. Offers vocational education (M Ed, Ed S), vocational leadership (PhD). Accredited by NCATE. Program being phased out; applicants no longer accepted. Students: 7 part-time (4 women). Average age 49. In 1997, 1 master's, 4 doctorates awarded. *Degree requirements:* For master's and Ed S, comprehensive exam; for doctorate, dissertation, comprehensive exam. *Expenses:* Tuition $2673 per year full-time, $99 per semester hour part-time for state residents; $10,692 per year full-time, $396 per semester hour part-time for nonresidents. Fees $228 per year. *Financial aid:* Research assistantships available. *Faculty research:* Vocational and technical education and leadership, administrative performance. • Dr. H. Parker Blount, Chair, Department of Educational Policy Studies, 404-651-2582.

Georgia State University, College of Education, Department of Middle, Secondary Education and Instructional Technology, Programs in Secondary Education, Atlanta, GA 30303-3083. Offerings include vocational education (M Ed). Accredited by NCATE. *Degree requirements:* Comprehensive exam. *Entrance requirements:* GRE General Test (minimum combined score of 800) or MAT (minimum score 44), minimum GPA of 2.5. Application fee: $25. *Expenses:* Tuition $2673 per year full-time, $99 per semester hour part-time for state residents; $10,692 per year full-time, $396 per semester hour part-time for nonresidents. Fees $228 per year. • Dr. Beverly J. Armento, Chair, Department of Middle, Secondary Education and Instructional Technology, 404-651-2510.

Idaho State University, College of Education, Division II, Pocatello, ID 83209. Offerings include occupational training management (M Ed). Accredited by NCATE. Postbaccalaureate distance learning degree programs offered (no on-campus study). Division faculty: 11 full-time (2 women). *Average time to degree:* master's–2 years full-time, 4 years part-time; other advanced degree–1 year full-time, 2 years part-time. *Application deadline:* 7/1 (priority date; rolling processing; 12/1 for spring admission). *Application fee:* $30. *Tuition:* $3130 per year full-time, $136 per credit hour part-time for state residents; $9370 per year full-time, $226 per credit hour part-time for nonresidents. • Dr. T. C. Mattocks, Director. E-mail: matttheo@isu.edu. Application contact: Dr. Stephanie Salzman, Director, Office of Standards and Assessment, 208-236-3114. Fax: 208-236-4697. E-mail: salzstep@isu.edu.

Indiana State University, School of Education, Department of Curriculum and Instruction and Media Technology, Terre Haute, IN 47809-1401. Offerings include industrial arts education (PhD). Accredited by NCATE. Department faculty: 16 full-time (4 women). *Degree requirements:* 2 foreign languages, computer language, dissertation. *Entrance requirements:* GRE General Test (minimum score 500 on each section). Application deadline: rolling. Application fee: $20. *Tuition:* $143 per credit hour for state residents; $325 per credit hour for nonresidents. • Dr. Jerry A. Summers, Chairperson, 812-237-2960. Application contact: Dr. Robert Williams, Graduate Adviser, 812-237-2952.

Indiana State University, School of Technology, Department of Industrial Technology Education, Terre Haute, IN 47809-1401. Offers programs in curriculum and instruction (PhD), human resource development (MS), technology education (MA, MS), vocational technical education (MA, MS). One or more programs accredited by NCATE. PhD offered through the Department of Curriculum and Instruction and Media Technology. Faculty: 8 full-time (1 woman). Students: 31 full-time (15 women), 76 part-time (38 women); includes 16 minority (14 African Americans, 1 Asian American, 1 Native American), 10 international. Average age 35. 42 applicants, 76% accepted. In 1997, 34 master's awarded. *Degree requirements:* For doctorate, computer language, dissertation required, foreign language not required. *Entrance requirements:* For master's, TOEFL (minimum score 550), bachelor's degree in industrial technology or related field, minimum undergraduate GPA of 2.5; for doctorate, GRE General Test. Application deadline: rolling. Application fee: $20. *Tuition:* $143 per credit hour for state residents; $325 per credit hour for nonresidents. *Financial aid:* In 1997–98, 2 fellowships (1 to a first-year student), 1 research assistantship (to a first-year student), 1 teaching assistantship were awarded; institutionally sponsored loans also available. Financial aid application deadline: 3/1. • Dr. Anthony Gilberti, Chairperson, 812-237-2640.

Inter American University of Puerto Rico, Metropolitan Campus, Division of Education, Program in Occupational Education, San Juan, PR 00919-1293. Awards MA. *Degree requirements:* Comprehensive exam. *Entrance requirements:* GRE or PAEG, interview. Application deadline: 5/15 (priority date; rolling processing; 11/15 for spring admission). Application fee: $31. Electronic applications accepted. *Expenses:* Tuition $3272 per year full-time, $1740 per year part-time. Fees $328 per year full-time, $176 per year part-time. • Application contact: Jenny Maldonado, Administrative Assistant, 787-250-1912 Ext. 2393. Fax: 787-250-1197.

Inter American University of Puerto Rico, Metropolitan Campus, Division of Education, Program in Vocational Evaluation, San Juan, PR 00919-1293. Awards MA. *Degree requirements:* Comprehensive exam. *Entrance requirements:* GRE or PAEG, interview. Application deadline: 5/15 (priority date; rolling processing; 11/15 for spring admission). Application fee: $31. Electronic applications accepted. *Expenses:* Tuition $3272 per year full-time, $1740 per year part-time. Fees $328 per year full-time, $176 per year part-time. • Application contact: Jenny Maldonado, Administrative Assistant, 787-250-1912 Ext. 2393. Fax: 787-250-1197.

Iowa State University of Science and Technology, College of Education, Department of Educational Leadership and Policy Studies, Ames, IA 50011. Offerings include vocational education (MS). Department faculty: 22 full-time, 3 part-time. *Application fee:* $20 ($30 for international students). *Expenses:* Tuition $3166 per year full-time, $176 per credit part-time for state residents; $9324 per year full-time, $518 per credit part-time for nonresidents. Fees $200 per year. • Daniel Robinson, Interim Chair, 515-294-1241. E-mail: edldrshp@iastate.edu.

Iowa State University of Science and Technology, College of Education, Department of Industrial Education and Technology, Ames, IA 50011. Awards MS, PhD. Faculty: 9 full-time. Students: 13 full-time (7 women), 29 part-time (5 women); includes 12 minority (7 African Americans, 2 Asian Americans, 3 Hispanics), 12 international. 16 applicants, 75% accepted. In 1997, 6 master's, 4 doctorates awarded. *Degree requirements:* For master's, thesis or alternative; for doctorate, dissertation. *Entrance requirements:* For master's, TOEFL; for doctorate, GRE General Test, TOEFL. Application deadline: 4/1 (priority date; 10/1 for spring admission). Application fee: $20 ($30 for international students). *Expenses:* Tuition $3166 per year full-time, $176 per credit part-time for state residents; $9324 per year full-time, $518 per credit part-time for nonresidents. Fees $200 per year. *Financial aid:* In 1997–98, 6 research assistantships (1 to a first-year student), 8 teaching assistantships (4 to first-year students), 3 scholarships (1 to a first-year student) were awarded; fellowships also available. *Faculty research:* Industrial technology, technology education, training and development, technical education. • Dr. Roger A. Smith, Interim Chair, 515-294-8528. E-mail: indtech@iastate.edu.

Jackson State University, School of Science and Technology, Department of Technology and Industrial Arts, Jackson, MS 39217. Offers programs in hazardous materials management (MS), industrial arts education (MS Ed). Part-time and evening/weekend programs available. Faculty: 3 full-time (0 women). Students: 10 full-time (6 women), 9 part-time (3 women); includes 17 minority (all African Americans). 12 applicants, 75% accepted. In 1997, 9 degrees awarded. *Degree requirements:* Thesis or alternative, comprehensive exam. *Entrance requirements:* GRE General Test (minimum combined score of 1000), TOEFL (minimum score 550). Application deadline: 3/1 (priority date; rolling processing; 10/1 for spring admission). Application fee: $20. *Tuition:* $2688 per year (minimum) full-time, $150 per semester hour part-time for state residents; $5546 per year (minimum) full-time, $309 per semester hour part-time for nonresidents. *Financial aid:* Federal Work-Study available. Financial aid application deadline: 3/1. • Dr. Sonny Bolls, Chair, 601-968-2466. Fax: 601-968-2344. Application contact: Mae Robinson, Admissions Coordinator, 601-968-2455. Fax: 601-968-8246. E-mail: mrobinson@ccaix.jsums.edu.

James Madison University, College of Education and Psychology, School of Education, Program in Adult Education/Human Resource Development, Harrisonburg, VA 22807. Offers vocational education (MS Ed). Accredited by NCATE. Part-time and evening/weekend programs available. Students: 5 full-time (4 women), 12 part-time (10 women). Average age 30. In 1997, 12 degrees awarded. *Entrance requirements:* GRE General Test. Application deadline: 7/1 (priority date; rolling processing). Application fee: $50. *Tuition:* $134 per credit hour for state residents; $404 per credit hour for nonresidents. *Financial aid:* In 1997–98, 2 assistantships totaling $17,280 were awarded; fellowships, teaching assistantships also available. Financial aid application deadline: 2/15; applicants required to submit FAFSA. • Dr. Diane Foucar-Szocki, Coordinator, 540-568-6927.

Kent State University, Graduate School of Education, Department of Adult, Counseling, Health and Vocational Education, Program in Vocational and Technical Education, Kent, OH 44242-0001. Offers vocational education (MA, M Ed). Faculty: 1 full-time (0 women), 8 part-time (3 women). Students: 4 full-time (0 women), 13 part-time (4 women). In 1997, 5 degrees awarded. *Degree requirements:* Thesis (MA) required, foreign language not required. *Application deadline:* rolling. *Application fee:* $30. *Tuition:* $4752 per year full-time, $216 per credit hour part-time for state residents; $9213 per year full-time, $419 per credit hour part-time for nonresidents. *Financial aid:* Application deadline 4/1. • Dr. Patrick O'Connor, Coordinator, 330-672-2656. Application contact: Deborah Barber, Director, Office of Academic Services, 330-672-2862. Fax: 330-672-3549.

Louisiana State University and Agricultural and Mechanical College, College of Agriculture, School of Vocational Education, Baton Rouge, LA 70803. Offers programs in comprehensive vocational education (MS, PhD), extension and international education (MS, PhD), industrial education (MS), vocational agriculture education (MS, PhD), vocational business education (MS), vocational home economics education (MS). Accredited by NCATE. Part-time programs available. Faculty: 11 full-time (3 women). Students: 22 full-time (13 women), 93 part-time (55 women); includes 11 minority (10 African Americans, 1 Hispanic), 3 international. Average age 40. 38 applicants, 66% accepted. In 1997, 17 master's, 7 doctorates awarded. Terminal master's awarded for partial completion of doctoral program. *Degree requirements:* For master's, thesis required (for some programs), foreign language not required; for doctorate, dissertation required, foreign language not required. *Entrance requirements:* GRE General Test (minimum combined score of 1000), minimum GPA of 3.0. Application deadline: 1/25 (priority date; rolling processing). Application fee: $25. *Tuition:* $2736 per year full-time, $285 per semester (minimum) part-time for state residents; $6636 per year full-time, $460 per semester (minimum) part-time for nonresidents. *Financial aid:* In 1997–98, 27 students received aid, including 3 fellowships (1 to a first-year student), 8 research assistantships (2 to first-year students); teaching assistantships, service assistantships, institutionally sponsored loans, and career-related internships or fieldwork also available. Financial aid application deadline: 3/1. *Faculty research:* Adult education, history and philosophy of vocational education, curriculum and instruction, career decision making. • Dr. Michael F. Burnett, Director, 504-388-5748.

Mankato State University, College of Education, Department of Business and Technology Education, South Rd and Ellis Ave, PO Box 8400, Mankato, MN 56002-8400. Offers programs in business education (MS, MT), technology education (MS, MT). Accredited by NCATE. Faculty: 1 full-time (0 women). Students: 3 part-time (0 women). Average age 45. 0 applicants. In 1997, 1 degree awarded. *Degree requirements:* Thesis or alternative, comprehensive exam required, foreign language not required. *Entrance requirements:* GRE General Test, minimum GPA of 3.0 during previous 2 years. Application deadline: 7/10 (priority date; rolling processing; 10/30 for spring admission). Application fee: $20. *Tuition:* $126 per credit (minimum) for state residents; $200 per credit for nonresidents. *Financial aid:* Teaching assistantships, Federal Work-Study, and career-related internships or fieldwork available. Aid available to part-time students. Financial aid application deadline: 3/15; applicants required to submit FAFSA. *Faculty research:* Longitudinal studies of business communications. • Dr. Janet Adams, Chairperson, 507-389-6116. Application contact: Joni Roberts, Admissions Coordinator, 507-389-2321. Fax: 507-389-5974. E-mail: grad@mankato.msus.edu.

Marshall University, College of Education, Division of Human Development and Allied Technology, Program in Adult and Technical Education, Huntington, WV 25755-2020. Awards MS. Accredited by NCATE. Evening/weekend programs available. Faculty: 4 (2 women). Students: 16 full-time (11 women), 71 part-time (52 women); includes 5 minority (all African Americans), 3 international. In 1997, 19 degrees awarded. *Degree requirements:* Thesis optional. *Entrance requirements:* GRE General Test (minimum combined score of 1200). *Tuition:* $2364 per year full-time, $132 per hour part-time for state residents; $6894 per year full-time, $383 per hour part-time for nonresidents. • Dr. Laura Wyant, Director, 304-696-3073. Application contact: Dr. James Harless, Director of Admissions, 304-696-3160.

Middle Tennessee State University, College of Basic and Applied Sciences, Department of Engineering Technology and Industrial Studies, Murfreesboro, TN 37132. Awards MS, MVTE. Part-time programs available. Faculty: 12 full-time (1 woman), 3 part-time (0 women). Students: 12 full-time (6 women), 34 part-time (13 women); includes 4 minority (all African Americans), 5 international. Average age 37. 20 applicants, 50% accepted. In 1997, 11 degrees awarded. *Degree requirements:* 1 foreign language, comprehensive exams required, thesis not required. *Entrance requirements:* Cooperative English Test, MAT. Application deadline: 8/1 (priority date). Application fee: $5. *Expenses:* Tuition $2560 per year full-time, $129 per semester hour part-time for state residents; $7386 per year full-time, $340 per semester hour part-time for nonresidents. Fees $486 per year full-time, $17 per semester (minimum) part-time. *Financial aid:* Teaching assistantships, institutionally sponsored loans available. Aid available to part-time students. Financial aid application deadline: 5/1; applicants required to submit FAFSA. • Dr. James H. Lorenz, Interim Chair, 615-898-2776. Fax: 615-898-5697.

Millersville University of Pennsylvania, School of Education, Department of Industry and Technology, Millersville, PA 17551-0302. Offers program in industrial arts/technology education (M Ed). Accredited by NCATE. Part-time and evening/weekend programs available. Faculty: 19 full-time (0 women). Students: 9 full-time (1 woman), 24 part-time (4 women); includes 1 minority (African American), 1 international. Average age 31. 4 applicants, 75% accepted. In 1997, 1 degree awarded. *Degree requirements:* Departmental exam required, thesis optional, foreign language not required. *Entrance requirements:* MAT (minimum score 35), GRE General Test (minimum score 500 on each section), minimum undergraduate GPA of 2.75, teaching certificate in industrial arts. Application deadline: 5/1 (priority date; rolling processing). Application fee: $25. *Tuition:* $3468 per year full-time, $234 per credit part-time for state residents; $6236 per year full-time, $387 per credit part-time for nonresidents. *Financial aid:* In 1997–98, 3 graduate assistantships (all to first-year students) averaging $445 per month and totaling $12,000 were awarded; Federal Work-Study, institutionally sponsored loans, and career-related internships or fieldwork also available. Aid available to part-time students. Financial aid application deadline: 5/1. *Faculty research:* Human-powered submarine, oil additives, technology education, futurology and impacts on technology, engineering in school and work. Total annual research expenditures: $23,000. • Dr. Joseph M. McCade, Coordinator, 717-872-3883. Fax: 717-872-3856. Application contact: Dr. Robert J. Labriola, Dean of Graduate Studies, 717-872-3030. Fax: 717-871-2022.

Mississippi State University, College of Education, Department of Technology and Education, Mississippi State, MS 39762. Offers programs in instructional technology (MSIT); technology (MS), including business education, industrial technology, instructional technology, vocational education. Accredited by NCATE. Part-time programs available. Faculty: 12 full-time (5 women), 3 part-time (0 women), 13 FTE. Students: 16 full-time (12 women), 42 part-time (40 women); includes 13 minority (all African Americans), 2 international. Average age 31. 62 applicants, 89% accepted. In 1997, 32 degrees awarded. *Degree requirements:* Comprehensive oral or written exam required, thesis optional, foreign language not required. *Entrance requirements:* Minimum QPA of 2.75 in last 2 years. Application deadline: 7/26 (priority date; rolling processing; 11/10 for spring admission). Application fee: $0 ($25 for international students). Electronic applications accepted. *Tuition:* $3017 per year full-time, $168 per credit hour part-time for state residents; $6119 per year full-time, $340 per credit hour part-time for nonresidents. *Financial aid:* In 1997–98, 9 students received aid, including 2 teaching assistantships (both to first-year students) averaging $640 per month and totaling $11,000, 7 service assistantships (2 to first-year students) averaging $640 per month and totaling $38,500; research assistantships, Federal Work-Study also available. Aid available to part-time students. Financial aid application deadline: 4/1. *Faculty research:* Computer technology, nontraditional students, interactive video. • Dr. John F. Perry Jr., Interim Head, 601-325-2281. Fax: 601-325-7599. E-mail: jfp1@ra.msstate.edu.

Montana State University–Northern, Option in Vocational Education, Havre, MT 59501-7751. Awards M Ed. Faculty: 2 full-time (1 woman). Students: 5 full-time (3 women), 10 part-time (5 women). Average age 44. *Degree requirements:* Comprehensive and oral exams required, thesis optional, foreign language not required. *Entrance requirements:* GRE General Test, minimum GPA of 3.0. Application deadline: 9/20 (priority date; rolling processing). Application fee: $30. *Tuition:* $3090 per year full-time, $696 per semester (minimum) part-time for state residents; $8044 per year full-time, $1758 per semester (minimum) part-time for nonresidents. *Financial aid:* Teaching assistantships, Federal Work-Study, institutionally sponsored loans available. Aid available to part-time students. Financial aid application deadline: 4/1; applicants required to submit FAFSA. • Dr. Ben Johnson, Director of Education and Graduate Programs, Department of Education, 406-265-3738. Fax: 406-265-3570. E-mail: johnson@nmcl.nmclites.edu.

Montclair State University, College of Education and Human Services, Department of Curriculum and Teaching, Program in Technology, Upper Montclair, NJ 07043-1624. Offers industrial technology and education (MA). Accredited by NCATE. Part-time and evening/weekend programs available. Faculty: 15 full-time. Students: 7 full-time (0 women), 10 part-time (1 woman); includes 2 minority (1 African American, 1 Hispanic). In 1997, 4 degrees awarded. *Degree requirements:* Thesis or alternative, comprehensive exam, field experience required, foreign language not required. *Entrance requirements:* GRE General Test, appropriate bachelor's degree, minimum GPA of 2.67. Application deadline: 4/1 (rolling processing; 11/1 for spring admission). Application fee: $40. *Expenses:* Tuition $201 per credit for state residents; $257 per credit for nonresidents. Fees $22.05 per credit. *Financial aid:* Application deadline 3/1; applicants required to submit FAFSA. • Dr. Winfield Parsons, Head, 973-655-7350. Application contact: Dr. Vincent Walencik, Adviser, 973-655-4161.

Morehead State University, College of Science and Technology, Program in Vocational Education, Morehead, KY 40351. Awards MS, Ed D. One or more programs accredited by NCATE. Ed D offered jointly with the University of Kentucky. Part-time and evening/weekend programs available. Faculty: 8 full-time (3 women). Students: 1 full-time (0 women), 20 part-time (7 women). Average age 25. 3 applicants, 100% accepted. In 1997, 6 master's awarded. *Degree requirements:* For master's, oral and/or written final exam required, foreign language and thesis not required. *Entrance requirements:* For master's, GRE General Test (minimum combined score of 900), minimum GPA of 3.0 in major, 2.5 overall. Application deadline: 8/1 (priority date; rolling processing; 12/1 for spring admission). Application fee: $0. *Tuition:* $2470 per year full-time, $138 per semester hour part-time for state residents; $6710 per year full-time, $373 per semester hour part-time for nonresidents. *Financial aid:* In 1997–98, 4 teaching assistantships (1 to a first-year student) averaging $471 per month and totaling $16,000 were awarded; research assistantships, Federal Work-Study also available. Financial aid application deadline: 4/1; applicants required to submit FAFSA. *Faculty research:* Robotics, herbicide safeners and forage grass species, computer-animated learning modules. • Application contact: Betty Cowsert, Graduate Admissions Officer, 606-783-2039. Fax: 606-783-5061.

Murray State University, College of Industry and Technology, Program in Industrial and Technical Education, Murray, KY 42071-0009. Awards MA Ed, MS. Accredited by NCATE. Part-time programs available. Faculty: 6 full-time (0 women). Students: 3 full-time (1 woman), 20 part-time (10 women); includes 1 minority (African American), 1 international. 2 applicants, 100% accepted. In 1997, 5 degrees awarded. *Degree requirements:* Thesis required (for some programs), foreign language not required. *Entrance requirements:* GRE General Test, TOEFL (minimum score 500). Application deadline: rolling. Application fee: $20. *Expenses:* Tuition $2500 per year full-time, $124 per hour part-time for state residents; $6740 per year full-time, $357 per hour part-time for nonresidents. Fees $360 per year full-time, $180 per year part-time. *Financial aid:* Research assistantships, teaching assistantships, Federal Work-Study available. Financial aid application deadline: 4/1. • Dr. Paul McNeary, Director, 502-762-6905. Fax: 502-762-6919.

North Carolina Agricultural and Technical State University, Graduate School, School of Technology, Department of Graphic Communication Systems and Technological Education, Greensboro, NC 27411. Offers programs in industrial arts education (MS), technology education (MS), vocational-industrial education (MS). One or more programs accredited by NCATE. Part-time and evening/weekend programs available. Faculty: 4 full-time (2 women), 2 part-time (0 women). Students: 3 full-time (2 women), 32 part-time (17 women); includes 19 minority (17 African Americans, 1 Hispanic, 1 Native American), 1 international. Average age 34. 27 applicants, 85% accepted. In 1997, 14 degrees awarded. *Degree requirements:* Thesis or alternative, comprehensive exam, qualifying exam required, foreign language not required. *Entrance requirements:* GRE General Test, minimum GPA of 3.0. Application deadline: 6/1 (priority date; rolling processing; 12/1 for spring admission). Application fee: $35. *Tuition:* $1662 per year full-time, $272 per semester (minimum) part-time for state residents; $8790 per year full-time, $2054 per semester (minimum) part-time for nonresidents. *Financial aid:* Research assistantships, teaching assistantships available. Financial aid application deadline: 6/1. • Dr. Frazer Barnette, Chairperson, 336-334-7550. Fax: 336-334-7577. E-mail: barnette@aurora.ncat.edu.

North Carolina State University, College of Education and Psychology, Department of Mathematics, Science, and Technology Education, Program in Occupational Education, Raleigh, NC 27695. Offers agricultural education (M Ed, MS, CAGS), health occupations education (M Ed, MS), occupational education (M Ed, MS, Ed D, CAGS), technology education (M Ed, MS), training and development (MS). Accredited by NCATE. Part-time programs available. Faculty: 1 full-time (0 women), 7 part-time (0 women). Students: 11 full-time (6 women), 26 part-time (19 women); includes 10 minority (8 African Americans, 1 Hispanic, 1 Native American), 1 international. Average age 43. 13 applicants, 92% accepted. In 1997, 1 master's, 1 doctorate awarded. *Degree requirements:* For master's, oral exam required, foreign language not required; for doctorate, dissertation, oral and written exams required, foreign language not required. *Entrance requirements:* For master's and doctorate, GRE General Test or MAT, minimum GPA of 3.0 in major; for CAGS, GRE General Test, MAT, minimum GPA of 3.0 in major. Application deadline: 4/15 (priority date; rolling processing; 11/15 for spring admission). Application fee: $45. *Tuition:* $2370 per year full-time, $517 per semester (minimum) part-time for state residents; $11,536 per year full-time, $2809 per semester (minimum) part-time for nonresidents. *Financial aid:* Fellowships, research assistantships, teaching assistantships, and career-related internships or fieldwork available. Financial aid application deadline: 6/1. *Faculty research:* Job satisfaction among allied health professionals, effective teaching and instructional methodology, video teaching and student achievement, learning styles and marketing education, teacher behavior and tech prep initiatives. Total annual research expenditures: $28,228. • Dr. Robert E. Wenig, Director of Graduate Programs, 919-515-1742. Fax: 919-515-6892. E-mail: wenig@poe.coe.ncsu.edu. Application contact: Linda Trogdon, Graduate Secretary, 919-515-1740. Fax: 919-515-7634. E-mail: trogdon@poe.coe.ncsu.edu.

Northern Arizona University, Center for Excellence in Education, Program in Vocational Education, Flagstaff, AZ 86011. Awards MVE. Students: 1 (woman) full-time, 19 part-time (12 women); includes 6 minority (3 Hispanics, 3 Native Americans). Average age 38. 7 applicants, 0% accepted. In 1997, 13 degrees awarded. *Degree requirements:* Departmental qualifying exam, final oral exam/project required, foreign language and thesis not required. *Application deadline:* 3/15 (priority date; rolling processing). *Application fee:* $45. *Expenses:* Tuition $2088 per year full-time, $330 per semester (minimum) part-time for state residents; $8004 per year full-time, $1002 per semester (minimum) part-time for nonresidents. Fees $72 per year full-time, $18 per semester (minimum) part-time. *Financial aid:* Partial tuition waivers, Federal Work-Study available. • Dr. Michael Roberts, Coordinator, 520-523-9408.

Northwest Missouri State University, College of Professional and Applied Studies, Program in Teaching Vocational Business, 800 University Drive, Maryville, MO 64468-6001. Awards MS Ed. Part-time programs available. Faculty: 2 full-time (1 woman), 7 part-time (all women). Students: 1 (woman) full-time, 3 part-time (all women). 0 applicants. In 1997, 3 degrees awarded. *Degree requirements:* Comprehensive exam required, foreign language and thesis not required. *Entrance requirements:* GRE General Test (minimum combined score of 700), TOEFL (minimum score 550), minimum GPA of 2.5, teaching certificate, writing sample. Application deadline: 7/1 (rolling processing; 12/1 for spring admission). Application fee: $0 ($50 for international students). *Expenses:* Tuition $113 per credit hour for state residents; $197 per credit hour for nonresidents. Fees $3 per credit hour. *Financial aid:* 2 students received aid; teaching assistantships available. Financial aid application deadline: 3/1. • Dr. Nancy Zeliff, Instructor, Computer Science and Information Systems, 816-562-1292. Application contact: Dr. Frances Shipley, Dean of Graduate School, 816-562-1145. E-mail: gradsch@acad.nwmissouri.edu.

Nova Southeastern University, Fischler Center for the Advancement of Education, Programs in Higher Education, Fort Lauderdale, FL 33314-7721. Offerings include vocational, occupational and technical education (Ed D). *Degree requirements:* Dissertation, practicum required, foreign language not required. *Entrance requirements:* Master's degree, work experience in field.

Directory: Vocational and Technical Education

Nova Southeastern University (continued)

Application deadline: rolling. Application fee: $50. *Tuition:* $8460 per year. • Dr. Ross E. Moreton, Dean, 954-262-8526. E-mail: moreton@fcae.nova.edu. Application contact: Dr. Delores Smiley, 800-986-3223 Ext. 8527. Fax: 954-262-3903. E-mail: smiley@fcae.nova.edu.

The Ohio State University, College of Food, Agricultural, and Environmental Sciences, Department of Agricultural Education, Comprehensive Program in Vocational Education, Columbus, OH 43210. Awards PhD. Faculty: 9. Students: 3 part-time (1 woman); includes 1 minority (African American), 1 international. 1 applicant, 0% accepted. In 1997, 4 degrees awarded. *Degree requirements:* Dissertation required, foreign language not required. *Entrance requirements:* Interview, minimum graduate GPA of 3.5. Application deadline: 8/15 (rolling processing). Application fee: $30 ($40 for international students). *Tuition:* $5472 per year full-time, $554 per quarter (minimum) part-time for state residents; $14,172 per year full-time, $1424 per quarter (minimum) part-time for nonresidents. *Financial aid:* Fellowships, Federal Work-Study, institutionally sponsored loans available. Aid available to part-time students. • Larry E. Miller, Graduate Studies Committee Chair, 614-292-4624. Fax: 614-292-7007. E-mail: miller.103@osu.edu.

Oklahoma State University, College of Education, Department of Occupational and Adult Education, Stillwater, OK 74078. Offers programs in technical education (MS, Ed D, Ed S), trade and industrial education (MS, Ed D, Ed S). Faculty: 9 full-time (2 women). Students: 26 full-time (12 women), 193 part-time (103 women); includes 40 minority (21 African Americans, 7 Asian Americans, 3 Hispanics, 9 Native Americans), 8 international. Average age 41. In 1997, 24 master's, 17 doctorates awarded. *Degree requirements:* For master's, thesis or alternative; for doctorate, dissertation. *Entrance requirements:* For master's, TOEFL (minimum score 550); for doctorate, GRE General Test or MAT, TOEFL (minimum score 550). Application deadline: 7/1 (priority date). Application fee: $25. *Financial aid:* In 1997–98, 6 students received aid, including 6 research assistantships (2 to first-year students) averaging $1,033 per month and totaling $55,800; partial tuition waivers, Federal Work-Study, and career-related internships or fieldwork also available. Aid available to part-time students. Financial aid application deadline: 3/1. • Melvin D. Miller, Head, 405-744-6275.

Old Dominion University, Darden College of Education, Department of Occupational and Technical Studies, Program in Industrial Education, Norfolk, VA 23529. Awards MS Ed. Accredited by NCATE. Part-time and evening/weekend programs available. Students: 15 full-time (2 women), 14 part-time (1 woman); includes 8 minority (7 African Americans, 1 Native American). Average age 43. 29 applicants, 90% accepted. In 1997, 3 degrees awarded. *Degree requirements:* Thesis, comprehensive exams required, foreign language not required. *Entrance requirements:* GRE General Test (minimum combined score of 900), BS in field; minimum GPA of 3.0 in major, 2.5 overall. Application deadline: 7/1 (rolling processing; 12/1 for spring admission). Application fee: $30. *Expenses:* Tuition $180 per credit hour for state residents; $477 per credit hour for nonresidents. Fees $140 per year full-time, $32 per semester part-time. *Financial aid:* In 1997–98, 8 students received aid, including 1 fellowship totaling $3,000, 2 teaching assistantships totaling $10,656, 3 tuition grants totaling $9,108; research assistantships, partial tuition waivers, and career-related internships or fieldwork also available. Aid available to part-time students. Financial aid application deadline: 2/15; applicants required to submit FAFSA. *Faculty research:* Technology education, training, curriculum. • Dr. John M. Ritz, Chair, Department of Occupational and Technical Studies, 757-683-4305. Fax: 757-683-5227. E-mail: jritz@odu.edu.

Oregon State University, Graduate School, College of Home Economics and Education, School of Education, Program in Professional Technical Education, Corvallis, OR 97331. Awards MAT. Accredited by NCATE. Part-time programs available. Students: 6 full-time. Average age 28. 1 applicant, 100% accepted. In 1997, 9 degrees awarded. *Degree requirements:* Thesis (for some programs), minimum GPA of 3.0 required, foreign language not required. *Entrance requirements:* NTE, California Basic Educational Skills Test, TOEFL (minimum score 550), minimum GPA of 3.0 in last 90 hours. Application deadline: 3/1 (rolling processing). Application fee: $50. *Tuition:* $6207 per year full-time, $810 per quarter (minimum) part-time for state residents; $10,551 per year full-time, $1293 per quarter (minimum) part-time for nonresidents. *Financial aid:* Research assistantships, teaching assistantships, Federal Work-Study, institutionally sponsored loans, and career-related internships or fieldwork available. Aid available to part-time students. Financial aid application deadline: 2/1. • Dr. Sam Stern, Coordinator, 541-737-6392.

Pennsylvania State University University Park Campus, College of Education, Department of Adult Education, Instructional Systems, and Workforce Education and Development, Program in Workforce Education and Development, University Park, PA 16802-1503. Awards M Ed, MS, D Ed, PhD. Accredited by NCATE. Students: 58 full-time (27 women), 44 part-time (22 women). *Application fee:* $40. *Expenses:* Tuition $6534 per year full-time, $276 per credit part-time for state residents; $13,460 per year full-time, $561 per credit part-time for nonresidents. Fees $252 per year (minimum) full-time, $43 per semester (minimum) part-time. • Dr. Edgar I. Farmer, Professor in Charge, 814-863-3858.

Pittsburg State University, School of Technology, Department of Technical Education, Pittsburg, KS 66762-5880. Offers programs in human resource development (MS), industrial education (Ed S), technical education (MS), technical teacher education (MS), trade and technical education (Ed S). One or more programs accredited by NCATE. Faculty: 6 full-time (0 women). Students: 86 full-time (36 women), 76 part-time (39 women); includes 6 minority (2 African Americans, 2 Asian Americans, 2 Native Americans), 62 international. In 1997, 97 master's awarded. *Degree requirements:* For master's, thesis or alternative required, foreign language not required. *Application fee:* $40. *Tuition:* $2418 per year full-time, $103 per credit hour part-time for state residents; $6130 per year full-time, $258 per credit hour part-time for nonresidents. *Financial aid:* Teaching assistantships, Federal Work-Study, and career-related internships or fieldwork available. • Dr. Mark Johnson, Chairperson, 316-235-4631.

Purdue University, School of Education, Department of Curriculum and Instruction, West Lafayette, IN 47907. Offerings include vocational/industrial education (MS Ed, PhD, Ed S), vocational/technical education (MS Ed, PhD, Ed S). One or more programs accredited by NCATE. Department faculty: 34 full-time (15 women), 3 part-time (1 woman). *Degree requirements:* For master's, thesis optional; for doctorate, dissertation, oral and written exams; for Ed S, oral presentation, project required, thesis not required. *Entrance requirements:* For master's, TOEFL (minimum score 550), minimum B average; for doctorate, GRE General Test (minimum score 500 on each section), TOEFL (minimum score 550); for Ed S, minimum B average. Application deadline: 1/15 (priority date; 9/15 for spring admission). Application fee: $30. Electronic applications accepted. *Tuition:* $3500 per year full-time, $126 per credit hour part-time for state residents; $11,720 per year full-time, $387 per credit hour part-time for nonresidents. • Dr. J. L. Peters, Head, 765-494-9172. Fax: 765-496-1622. E-mail: peters@purdue.edu. Application contact: Christine Larsen, Coordinator of Graduate Studies, 765-494-2345. Fax: 765-494-5832. E-mail: gradoffice@soe.purdue.edu.

Purdue University, School of Technology, Department of Industrial Technology, West Lafayette, IN 47907. Awards MS. Faculty: 77 full-time (13 women). Students: 82 full-time (25 women), 10 part-time (3 women); includes 12 minority (8 African Americans, 1 Asian American, 1 Hispanic, 2 Native Americans), 4 international. Average age 29. 39 applicants, 85% accepted. In 1997, 32 degrees awarded. *Degree requirements:* Oral exam required, thesis not required. *Average time to degree:* master's–2 years full-time. *Entrance requirements:* GRE General Test, TOEFL (minimum score 550), minimum GPA of 3.0. Application deadline: 5/1 (priority date; rolling processing). Application fee: $30. Electronic applications accepted. *Tuition:* $3500 per year full-time, $126 per credit hour part-time for state residents; $11,720 per year full-time, $387 per credit hour part-time for nonresidents. *Financial aid:* In 1997–98, 37 teaching assistantships (24 to first-year students) were awarded; fellowships also available. Aid available to part-time students. Financial aid applicants required to submit FAFSA. • Dr. D. R. Depew, Head, 765-494-1101. Application contact: Jude Wood, Graduate Secretary, 765-494-1101.

Rhode Island College, School of Graduate Studies, School of Education and Human Development, Department of Educational Studies, Program in Technology Education, Providence, RI 02908-1924. Awards M Ed. Accredited by NCATE. Evening/weekend programs available. Faculty: 8 full-time (2 women). Students: 5 part-time (1 woman). In 1997, 2 degrees awarded. *Degree requirements:* Comprehensive exam required, thesis not required. *Entrance requirements:* GRE General Test or MAT. Application deadline: 4/1 (rolling processing). Application fee: $25. *Tuition:* $4064 per year full-time, $214 per credit part-time for state residents; $7658 per year full-time, $376 per credit part-time for nonresidents. *Financial aid:* Application deadline 4/1. • Dr. James McCrystal, Head, 401-456-8018.

Rutgers, The State University of New Jersey, New Brunswick, Graduate School of Education, Department of Educational Theory, Policy and Administration, Program in Vocational-Technical Education, New Brunswick, NJ 08903. Awards Ed M, Ed D, Ed S. Faculty: 2 full-time (1 woman). Students: 20 part-time; includes 1 minority (African American). In 1997, 2 master's, 3 doctorates awarded. *Degree requirements:* For doctorate, dissertation. *Entrance requirements:* GRE General Test. Application deadline: 3/1 (priority date; rolling processing; 11/1 for spring admission). Application fee: $40. Electronic applications accepted. *Expenses:* Tuition $6492 per year full-time, $268 per credit part-time for state residents; $9520 per year full-time, $395 per credit part-time for nonresidents. Fees $208 per year (minimum). *Financial aid:* Federal Work-Study, institutionally sponsored loans, and career-related internships or fieldwork available. Financial aid application deadline: 3/1. *Faculty research:* School-to-work transition, evaluation in vocational education, policy analysis in vocational education. • Annell L. Simcoe, Coordinator, 732-932-7496 Ext. 134. Fax: 732-932-8206.

Sam Houston State University, College of Education and Applied Science, Department of Technology, Huntsville, TX 77341. Offers programs in industrial education (MA, M Ed), industrial technology (MA). One or more programs accredited by NCATE. Part-time programs available. Students: 2 full-time (0 women), 26 part-time (10 women); includes 13 minority (12 Asian Americans, 1 Hispanic), 2 international. Average age 30. In 1997, 6 degrees awarded (100% found work related to degree). *Degree requirements:* Thesis (for some programs). *Entrance requirements:* GRE General Test (minimum combined score of 800). Application deadline: 8/1 (priority date; rolling processing; 12/1 for spring admission). Application fee: $15. *Tuition:* $1810 per year full-time, $297 per semester (minimum) part-time for state residents; $6922 per year full-time, $924 per semester (minimum) part-time for nonresidents. *Financial aid:* Research assistantships, teaching assistantships, Federal Work-Study, institutionally sponsored loans available. Financial aid application deadline: 2/28; applicants required to submit FAFSA. • Dr. Thomas D. Higgins, Chair, 409-294-1204. Fax: 409-294-1193. E-mail: ith_tdh@shsu.edu.

Sam Houston State University, College of Education and Applied Science, Department of Agricultural Sciences and Vocational Education, Program in Vocational Education, Huntsville, TX 77341. Awards M Ed, MS. Accredited by NCATE. Part-time and evening/weekend programs available. Students: 1 part-time (0 women). *Degree requirements:* Thesis optional, foreign language not required. *Entrance requirements:* GRE General Test (minimum combined score of 800), minimum GPA of 2.5. Application deadline: 5/1. Application fee: $15. *Tuition:* $1810 per year full-time, $297 per semester (minimum) part-time for state residents; $6922 per year full-time, $924 per semester (minimum) part-time for nonresidents. *Financial aid:* Career-related internships or fieldwork available. Financial aid application deadline: 5/1. • Dr. Herbert Schumann, Coordinator, 409-294-1186. Fax: 409-294-1232. E-mail: agr_hbs@shsu.edu.

South Carolina State University, School of Education, Department of Teacher Education, 300 College Street Northeast, Orangeburg, SC 29117-0001. Offerings include secondary education (M Ed), with options in biology education, business education, counselor education, English education, home economics education, industrial education, mathematics education, science education, social studies education. Accredited by NCATE. Department faculty: 7 full-time (3 women), 2 part-time (1 woman). *Average time to degree:* master's–2 years full-time, 4 years part-time. *Application deadline:* 7/15 (priority date; rolling processing; 11/10 for spring admission). *Application fee:* $25. *Tuition:* $2974 per year full-time, $165 per credit hour part-time. • Dr. Jesse Kinard, Chairman, 803-536-8934. Application contact: Dr. Gail Joyner-Fleming, Interim Associate Dean and Director, Graduate Teacher Education, 803-536-8824. Fax: 803-536-8492.

Southern Illinois University at Carbondale, College of Education, Department of Workforce Education and Development, Carbondale, IL 62901-6806. Awards MS Ed, PhD. Accredited by NCATE. Part-time programs available. Faculty: 15 full-time (6 women), 3 part-time (2 women). Students: 133 full-time (84 women), 64 part-time (40 women); includes 40 minority (29 African Americans, 5 Asian Americans, 4 Hispanics, 2 Native Americans), 20 international. Average age 32. 77 applicants, 65% accepted. In 1997, 58 master's, 6 doctorates awarded. *Degree requirements:* For master's, thesis required, foreign language not required; for doctorate, dissertation. *Entrance requirements:* For master's, TOEFL (minimum score 550), minimum GPA of 2.7; for doctorate, GRE General Test, TOEFL (minimum score 550), minimum GPA of 3.25. Application deadline: rolling. Application fee: $20. *Expenses:* Tuition $2964 per year full-time, $99 per semester hour part-time for state residents; $8892 per year full-time, $270 per semester hour part-time for nonresidents. Fees $1034 per year full-time, $298 per semester (minimum) part-time. *Financial aid:* In 1997–98, 25 students received aid, including 4 research assistantships, 10 teaching assistantships, 8 administrative assistantships; fellowships, full tuition waivers, Federal Work-Study, institutionally sponsored loans, and career-related internships or fieldwork also available. Aid available to part-time students. *Faculty research:* Career education, technical training, curriculum development, competency-based instruction, impact of technology on workplace and workforce. • Dr. A. R. Putnam, Chairperson, 618-453-3321. E-mail: bputnam@siu.edu. Application contact: Dr. Marcia Anderson, Coordinator, 618-453-3321. Fax: 618-453-1909. E-mail: mandersn@siu.edu.

Southwest Texas State University, School of Education, Department of Educational Administration and Psychological Services, Program in Management of Vocational/Technical Education, San Marcos, TX 78666. Awards M Ed. Part-time and evening/weekend programs available. Students: 1 part-time (0 women). Average age 48. In 1997, 2 degrees awarded. *Degree requirements:* Comprehensive exam required, foreign language and thesis not required. *Entrance requirements:* GRE General Test (minimum combined score of 900), TOEFL (minimum score 550), minimum GPA of 2.75 in last 60 hours. Application deadline: 7/15 (rolling processing; 11/15 for spring admission). Application fee: $25 ($50 for international students). *Expenses:* Tuition $648 per year full-time, $120 per semester (minimum) part-time for state residents; $4500 per year full-time, $750 per semester (minimum) part-time for nonresidents. Fees $1264 per year full-time, $314 per semester (minimum) part-time. *Financial aid:* Federal Work-Study, institutionally sponsored loans, and career-related internships or fieldwork available. Aid available to part-time students. Financial aid application deadline: 4/1; applicants required to submit FAFSA. *Faculty research:* Vocational teaching, counseling, coordinating, and supervising. • Dr. William H. Kurtz, Graduate Adviser, 512-245-3755. E-mail: wk01@swt.edu.

State University of New York at Oswego, School of Education, Department of Technology, Oswego, NY 13126. Awards MS Ed. Part-time programs available. Faculty: 3 full-time. Students: 3 full-time (0 women), 18 part-time (2 women). Average age 25. 23 applicants, 96% accepted. In 1997, 31 degrees awarded (100% found work related to degree). *Degree requirements:* Departmental exam required, thesis optional, foreign language not required. *Entrance requirements:* Provisional teaching certificate in industrial arts. Application deadline: 7/1. Application fee: $50. *Expenses:* Tuition $5100 per year full-time, $213 per credit hour part-time for state residents; $8416 per year full-time, $351 per credit hour part-time for nonresidents. Fees $135 per year (minimum). *Financial aid:* In 1997–98, 1 teaching assistantship (to a first-year student) was awarded; partial tuition waivers, Federal Work-Study, institutionally sponsored loans also available. *Faculty research:* Curriculum development, microcomputer applications. • Dr. Linda Markert, Chair, 315-341-3011.

State University of New York at Oswego, School of Education, Department of Vocational-Technical Education, Oswego, NY 13126. Awards MS Ed. Faculty: 5 full-time, 4 part-time. Students: 7 full-time (2 women), 44 part-time (30 women); includes 2 minority (1 African

American, 1 Hispanic). Average age 40. 33 applicants, 100% accepted. In 1997, 28 degrees awarded. *Degree requirements:* Thesis or alternative required, foreign language not required. *Application deadline:* 7/1. *Application fee:* $50. *Expenses:* Tuition $5100 per year full-time, $213 per credit hour part-time for state residents; $8416 per year full-time, $351 per credit hour part-time for nonresidents. Fees $135 per year (minimum). *Financial aid:* Partial tuition waivers, Federal Work-Study, institutionally sponsored loans, and career-related internships or fieldwork available. • Dr. John Boronkay, Chair, 315-341-2214.

State University of New York College at Buffalo, Faculty of Applied Science and Education, Department of Educational Foundations, Program in Vocational Technical Education, Buffalo, NY 14222-1095. Awards MS Ed. Accredited by NCATE. Part-time and evening/weekend programs available. Students: 8 full-time (3 women), 42 part-time (13 women); includes 3 minority (all African Americans). Average age 38. 14 applicants, 100% accepted. In 1997, 15 degrees awarded. *Degree requirements:* Thesis or project required, foreign language not required. *Entrance requirements:* Minimum GPA of 2.5 in last 60 hours, New York teaching certificate. Application deadline: 5/1 (10/1 for spring admission). Application fee: $50. *Expenses:* Tuition $5100 per year full-time, $213 per credit hour part-time for state residents; $8416 per year full-time, $351 per credit hour part-time for nonresidents. Fees $195 per year full-time, $8.60 per credit hour part-time. *Financial aid:* Fellowships, assistantships available. Financial aid application deadline: 3/1. • Dr. John Popovich, Coordinator, 716-878-4717.

State University of New York College at Buffalo, Faculty of Applied Science and Education, Department of Technology, Program in Technology Education, Buffalo, NY 14222-1095. Awards MS Ed. Accredited by NCATE. Students: 1 (woman) full-time, 7 part-time (0 women); includes 1 minority (African American). Average age 31. 2 applicants, 100% accepted. In 1997, 6 degrees awarded. *Degree requirements:* Thesis or project required, foreign language not required. *Entrance requirements:* Minimum GPA of 2.5 in last 60 hours, New York teaching certificate. Application deadline: 5/1 (10/1 for spring admission). Application fee: $50. *Expenses:* Tuition $5100 per year full-time, $213 per credit hour part-time for state residents; $8416 per year full-time, $351 per credit hour part-time for nonresidents. Fees $195 per year full-time, $8.60 per credit hour part-time. *Financial aid:* Fellowships available. Financial aid application deadline: 3/1. • Richard Butz, Coordinator, 716-878-4717.

Sul Ross State University, Department of Industrial Technology, Alpine, TX 79832. Offers program in industrial arts (M Ed). Part-time programs available. Faculty: 2 full-time (0 women). Students: 1 full-time (0 women), 1 part-time (0 women); includes 1 minority (African American). Average age 29. *Entrance requirements:* GMAT (minimum score 400) or GRE General Test (minimum combined score of 850), minimum GPA of 2.5 in last 60 hours of undergraduate work. Application deadline: rolling. Application fee: $0 ($50 for international students). *Expenses:* Tuition $864 per year full-time, $120 per semester (minimum) part-time for state residents; $5976 per year full-time, $747 per semester (minimum) part-time for nonresidents. Fees $754 per year full-time, $105 per semester (minimum) part-time. *Financial aid:* Federal Work-Study, institutionally sponsored loans available. Aid available to part-time students. Financial aid application deadline: 5/1; applicants required to submit FAFSA. • Dr. Dan Vrudny, Chair, 915-837-8137. Fax: 915-837-8046.

Temple University, College of Education, Department of Curriculum, Instruction, and Technology in Education, Philadelphia, PA 19122-6096. Offerings include vocational education (Ed M, MS). Accredited by NCATE. Department faculty: 33 full-time (14 women). *Degree requirements:* Thesis or alternative required, foreign language not required. *Entrance requirements:* GRE General Test (minimum combined score of 1000) or MAT (minimum score 39), minimum GPA of 2.8. Application deadline: 2/15 (10/1 for spring admission). Application fee: $40. *Expenses:* Tuition $323 per semester hour for state residents; $444 per semester hour for nonresidents. Fees $170 per year full-time, $28 per semester (minimum) part-time. • Dr. Raymond Lolla, Chair, 215-204-6387. Fax: 215-204-1414.

Texas A&M University, College of Education, Department of Educational Human Resource Development, College Station, TX 77843. Offerings include industrial education (M Ed, MS, Ed D, PhD). Accredited by NCATE. Department faculty: 14 full-time (5 women). *Degree requirements:* For doctorate, dissertation required, foreign language not required. *Entrance requirements:* GRE General Test, TOEFL. Application fee: $35 ($75 for international students). • Lloyd Korhonan, Head, 409-845-3016. E-mail: lloyd@summa.tamu.edu. Application contact: Anne Koppa, Graduate Admissions Supervisor, 409-862-4154. Fax: 409-845-0409. E-mail: cak5866@zeys.tamu.edu.

Texas A&M University, College of Education, Department of Educational Psychology, College Station, TX 77843. Offerings include vocational education (Ed D, PhD); vocational education/school counseling (M Ed), with option in gifted and talented education. One or more programs accredited by NCATE. Department faculty: 26 full-time (10 women), 2 part-time (both women), 26.9 FTE. *Degree requirements:* For doctorate, dissertation. *Entrance requirements:* For doctorate, GRE General Test, TOEFL. Application deadline: 2/1. Application fee: $35 ($75 for international students). • Douglas J. Palmer, Head, 409-845-1831. Fax: 409-862-1256. Application contact: Graduate Adviser, 409-845-1833.

Texas A&M University–Commerce, College of Education, Department of Secondary and Higher Education, Commerce, TX 75429-3011. Offerings include vocational/technical education (MA, M Ed, MS). Department faculty: 10 full-time (3 women), 2 part-time (1 woman). *Degree requirements:* Thesis (for some programs), comprehensive exam. *Entrance requirements:* GRE General Test. Application deadline: rolling. Application fee: $0 ($25 for international students). *Tuition:* $2382 per year full-time, $343 per semester (minimum) part-time for state residents; $7518 per year full-time, $343 per semester (minimum) part-time for nonresidents. • Dr. Robert Munday, Head, 903-886-5607. Application contact: Pam Hammonds, Graduate Admissions Adviser, 903-886-5167. Fax: 903-886-5165.

Texas A&M University–Corpus Christi, College of Education, Program in Occupational Education, Corpus Christi, TX 78412-5503. Awards MS. Part-time and evening/weekend programs available. Faculty: 2 full-time, 3 part-time. Students: 2 full-time (both women), 18 part-time (11 women); includes 12 minority (all Hispanics). Average age 43. In 1997, 27 degrees awarded. *Entrance requirements:* GRE General Test. Application deadline: 7/15 (priority date; rolling processing; 11/15 for spring admission). Application fee: $10 ($30 for international students). *Expenses:* Tuition $648 per year full-time, $120 per semester (minimum) part-time for state residents; $4482 per year full-time, $747 per semester (minimum) part-time for nonresidents. Fees $1010 per year full-time, $205 per semester part-time. *Financial aid:* Federal Work-Study, institutionally sponsored loans available. Aid available to part-time students. Financial aid application deadline: 3/15; applicants required to submit FAFSA. • Dr. Arturo Medina, Graduate Adviser, 512-994-2667. E-mail: adedu005@tamucc.edu. Application contact: Mary Margaret Dechant, Director of Admissions, 512-994-2624. Fax: 512-994-5887.

Texas Woman's University, College of Education and Human Ecology, Department of Educational Leadership, Program in Vocational-Technical Education, Denton, TX 76204. Awards MA, M Ed, MS, Ed D, PhD. Program being phased out; applicants no longer accepted. Faculty: 1 (woman) part-time.125 FTE. Students: 1 (woman) part-time. *Degree requirements:* For master's, thesis or professional paper required, foreign language not required; for doctorate, dissertation. *Average time to degree:* doctorate–6 years part-time. *Application fee:* $25. • Dr. Howard L. Stone, Chair, Department of Educational Leadership, 940-898-2241. Fax: 940-898-2224. E-mail: d_stone@twu.edu.

Tuskegee University, College of Liberal Arts and Education, Department of Curriculum, Instruction and Administration, Program in Extension and Technical Education, Tuskegee, AL 36088. Awards M Ed, MS. Accredited by NCATE. Faculty: 2 full-time (both women), 4 part-time (1 woman). Students: 0. *Entrance requirements:* GRE General Test. Application deadline: 7/15 (rolling processing). Application fee: $25 ($35 for international students). *Financial aid:* Application deadline 4/15. • H. Frank Leftwich, Acting Head, Department of Curriculum, Instruction and Administration, 334-727-8599.

The University of Akron, College of Education, Department of Curricular and Instructional Studies, Program in Technical Education, Akron, OH 44325-0001. Offers technical education administration (MSTE), technical education guidance (MSTE), technical education instructional technology (MSTE), technical education supervision (MSTE), technical education teaching (MSTE), technical education training (MSTE). Accredited by NCATE. Students: 7 full-time (4 women), 44 part-time (33 women); includes 7 minority (5 African Americans, 1 Hispanic, 1 Native American). Average age 39. In 1997, 14 degrees awarded. *Degree requirements:* Thesis or alternative, written comprehensive exam required, foreign language not required. *Entrance requirements:* MAT, minimum GPA of 2.75. Application deadline: 8/15 (rolling processing). Application fee: $25 ($50 for international students). *Expenses:* Tuition $178 per credit hour for state residents; $333 per credit hour for nonresidents. Fees $145 per year full-time, $32 per semester (minimum) part-time. *Financial aid:* Fellowships, research assistantships, teaching assistantships, administrative assistantships, Federal Work-Study available. • Dr. Susan Olson, Coordinator, 330-972-7118. E-mail: solson@uakron.edu. Application contact: Dr. Robert Eley, Director of Student Services, 330-972-7750. E-mail: reley@uakron.edu.

University of Alaska Anchorage, Community and Technical College, Program in Vocational Education, Anchorage, AK 99508-8060. Awards MS. Part-time programs available. Students: 6 full-time (2 women), 8 part-time (5 women); includes 1 minority (Hispanic). 8 applicants, 100% accepted. In 1997, 5 degrees awarded. *Degree requirements:* Computer language, thesis or alternative required, foreign language not required. *Entrance requirements:* GRE General Test, 1 year of occupational experience, AA or AAS in vocational area. Application deadline: rolling. *Expenses:* Tuition $2988 per year full-time, $1990 per year part-time for state residents; $5814 per year full-time, $3876 per year part-time for nonresidents. Fees $298 per year. *Financial aid:* Application deadline 4/1. • Application contact: Linda Berg Smith, Associate Vice Chancellor for Enrollment Services, 907-786-1529.

University of Arkansas, College of Education, Department of Vocational and Adult Education, Program in Vocational Education, Fayetteville, AR 72701-1201. Awards MAT, M Ed, Ed D, Ed S. Accredited by NCATE. Students: 20 full-time (14 women), 8 part-time (3 women); includes 2 minority (1 African American, 1 Native American), 1 international. 13 applicants, 77% accepted. In 1997, 8 master's, 5 doctorates awarded. *Degree requirements:* For master's, thesis optional, foreign language not required; for doctorate, dissertation. *Application fee:* $25 ($35 for international students). *Tuition:* $3144 per year full-time, $173 per credit hour part-time for state residents; $7140 per year full-time, $395 per credit hour part-time for nonresidents. *Financial aid:* Research assistantships, teaching assistantships, Federal Work-Study, and career-related internships or fieldwork available. Aid available to part-time students. Financial aid application deadline: 4/1; applicants required to submit FAFSA. • Dr. B. R. Lyle, Coordinator, 501-575-4759.

University of British Columbia, Faculty of Education, Department of Curriculum Studies, Vancouver, BC V6T 1Z2, Canada. Offerings include technical studies education (MA, M Ed, PhD). *Degree requirements:* For master's, thesis (MA) required, foreign language not required; for doctorate, dissertation required, foreign language not required. *Entrance requirements:* TOEFL (minimum score 550). Application deadline: 3/1 (12/1 for spring admission). Application fee: $60.

University of Central Florida, College of Education, Department of Instructional Programs, Program in Vocational Education, Orlando, FL 32816. Awards MA, M Ed. Accredited by NCATE. Part-time and evening/weekend programs available. Students: 7 full-time (3 women), 6 part-time (2 women); includes 2 minority (both African Americans). Average age 40. 7 applicants, 71% accepted. In 1997, 3 degrees awarded. *Degree requirements:* Thesis or alternative required, foreign language not required. *Entrance requirements:* GRE General Test (minimum combined score of 840). Application deadline: 7/15 (12/15 for spring admission). Application fee: $20. *Expenses:* Tuition $3288 per year full-time, $137 per credit hour part-time for state residents; $11,520 per year full-time, $480 per credit hour part-time for nonresidents. Fees $105 per year. *Financial aid:* Teaching assistantships, Federal Work-Study, institutionally sponsored loans, and career-related internships or fieldwork available. Aid available to part-time students. • Application contact: Dr. Larry Hudson, Coordinator, 407-823-2848.

University of Connecticut, School of Education, Field of Adult and Vocational Education, Storrs, CT 06269. Awards MA, PhD. Accredited by NCATE. Faculty: 5. Students: 6 full-time (5 women), 36 part-time (24 women); includes 1 minority (African American), 3 international. Average age 43. 10 applicants, 60% accepted. In 1997, 2 master's, 7 doctorates awarded. Terminal master's awarded for partial completion of doctoral program. *Degree requirements:* For master's, thesis or alternative required, foreign language not required; for doctorate, dissertation. *Entrance requirements:* GRE General Test. Application deadline: 6/1 (priority date; rolling processing; 11/1 for spring admission). Application fee: $40 ($45 for international students). *Expenses:* Tuition $5272 per year full-time, $293 per credit part-time for state residents; $13,696 per year full-time, $761 per credit part-time for nonresidents. Fees $948 per year full-time, $640 per year part-time. *Financial aid:* In 1997–98, 3 fellowships totaling $3,185, 2 research assistantships totaling $27,000, 3 teaching assistantships totaling $27,750 were awarded. • Patrick B. Mullarney, Head, 860-486-6278.

University of Georgia, College of Education, Department of Occupational Studies, Athens, GA 30602. Offers programs in agricultural education (M Ed), business education (M Ed), home economics education (M Ed), marketing education (M Ed), occupational studies (M Ed, Ed D, Ed S), technological studies (M Ed). Accredited by NCATE. Faculty: 12 full-time (4 women). Students: 58 full-time, 98 part-time (52 women); includes 17 minority (11 African Americans, 1 Asian American, 1 Hispanic, 4 Native Americans), 2 international. 77 applicants, 75% accepted. In 1997, 40 master's, 7 doctorates, 7 Ed Ss awarded. *Degree requirements:* For master's, thesis required (for some programs), foreign language not required; for doctorate, dissertation required, foreign language not required. *Entrance requirements:* For master's, GRE General Test, MAT; for doctorate, GRE General Test; for Ed S, GRE General Test or MAT. Application deadline: 7/1 (priority date; 11/15 for spring admission). Application fee: $30. Electronic applications accepted. *Tuition:* $3290 per year full-time, $643 per semester (minimum) part-time for state residents; $11,300 per year full-time, $1645 per semester (minimum) part-time for nonresidents. *Financial aid:* Fellowships, research assistantships, teaching assistantships, assistantships available. • Dr. Robert C. Wicklein, Graduate Coordinator, 706-542-3132. Fax: 706-542-1765.

University of Idaho, College of Graduate Studies, College of Education, Division of Adult, Counselor, and Technology Education, Program in Industrial Technology Education, Moscow, ID 83844-4140. Awards M Ed, MS, Ed D, PhD. Accredited by NCATE. Ed D and PhD offered through the College of Education. Students: 3 full-time (0 women), 21 part-time (5 women); includes 1 international. *Degree requirements:* For doctorate, dissertation. *Entrance requirements:* For master's, minimum GPA of 2.8; for doctorate, minimum undergraduate GPA of 2.8, 3.0 graduate. Application deadline: 8/1 (12/15 for spring admission). Application fee: $35 ($45 for international students). *Expenses:* Tuition $0 for state residents; $6000 per year full-time, $95 per credit part-time for nonresidents. Fees $2676 per year full-time, $134 per credit part-time. *Financial aid:* Application deadline 2/15. • Dr. Gerald Tuchscherer, Director, Division of Adult, Counselor, and Technology Education, 208-885-6556.

University of Idaho, College of Graduate Studies, College of Education, Division of Adult, Counselor, and Technology Education, Program in Vocational Education, Moscow, ID 83844-4140. Awards M Ed, MS, Ed D, PhD, V Ed S. Accredited by NCATE. Ed D and PhD offered through the College of Education. Students: 3 full-time (1 woman), 46 part-time (26 women); includes 2 minority (1 Asian American, 1 Native American). *Degree requirements:* For doctorate, dissertation. *Entrance requirements:* For master's, minimum GPA of 2.8; for doctorate, minimum undergraduate GPA of 2.8, 3.0 graduate. Application deadline: 8/1 (12/15 for spring admission). Application fee: $35 ($45 for international students). *Expenses:* Tuition $0 for state residents; $6000 per year full-time, $95 per credit part-time for nonresidents. Fees $2676 per year full-time, $134 per credit part-time. *Financial aid:* Application deadline 2/15. • Dr. Gerald Tuchscherer, Director, Division of Adult, Counselor, and Technology Education, 208-885-6556.

Directory: Vocational and Technical Education

University of Illinois at Urbana–Champaign, College of Education, Department of Vocational and Technical Education, Urbana, IL 61801. Awards AM, Ed M, MS, Ed D, PhD, AC. Faculty: 7 full-time (3 women), 7 part-time (4 women). Students: 76 full-time (44 women); includes 6 minority (all African Americans), 14 international. 40 applicants, 65% accepted. In 1997, 29 master's, 13 doctorates awarded. *Degree requirements:* For master's, thesis (for some programs); for doctorate, dissertation. *Application deadline:* rolling. *Application fee:* $40 ($50 for international students). *Financial aid:* In 1997–98, 1 fellowship, 21 research assistantships, 1 teaching assistantship were awarded; full and partial tuition waivers and career-related internships or fieldwork also available. Financial aid application deadline: 2/15. • Tim L. Wentling, Head, 217-333-0807.

University of Kentucky, Graduate School Programs from the College of Education, Program in Vocational Education, Lexington, KY 40506-0032. Awards MA Ed U, MS Ed U, MSVE, Ed D, Ed S. Accredited by NCATE. Faculty: 4 full-time (1 woman), 1 part-time (0 women). Students: 24 full-time (6 women), 24 part-time (9 women); includes 1 minority (African American), 1 international. 18 applicants, 100% accepted. In 1997, 18 master's, 3 doctorates awarded. Terminal master's awarded for partial completion of doctoral program. *Degree requirements:* For master's, comprehensive exam required, thesis optional, foreign language not required; for doctorate, dissertation, comprehensive exam required, foreign language not required. *Entrance requirements:* For master's, GRE General Test, minimum undergraduate GPA of 2.5; for doctorate, GRE General Test, minimum graduate GPA of 3.0. Application deadline: 7/19 (rolling processing). Application fee: $30 ($35 for international students). *Financial aid:* In 1997–98, 3 teaching assistantships were awarded; fellowships, research assistantships, Federal Work-Study, institutionally sponsored loans, and career-related internships or fieldwork also available. Aid available to part-time students. • Dr. Charles Byers, Director of Graduate Studies, 606-257-8796. Application contact: Dr. Constance L. Wood, Associate Dean, 606-257-4613. Fax: 606-323-1928.

University of Louisville, School of Education, Department of Occupational and Career Education, Louisville, KY 40292-0001. Awards M Ed. Accredited by NCATE. Faculty: 5 full-time (1 woman), 4 part-time (1 woman), 6 FTE. Students: 18 full-time (10 women), 90 part-time (55 women); includes 16 minority (13 African Americans, 1 Asian American, 2 Hispanics). Average age 36. In 1997, 60 degrees awarded. *Entrance requirements:* GRE General Test. Application deadline: rolling. Application fee: $25. • Dr. Richard K. Crosby, Chair, 502-852-6667.

University of Manitoba, Faculty of Education, Department of Curriculum: Mathematics and Natural Sciences, Winnipeg, MB R3T 2N2, Canada. Offerings include industrial/vocational/business education (M Ed). *Degree requirements:* Thesis or alternative required, foreign language not required.

University of Maryland, College Park, College of Education, Department of Industrial, Technological, and Occupational Education, College Park, MD 20742-5045. Offers programs in business education (MA, M Ed, Ed D, PhD, CAGS); industrial, technological, and occupational education (MA, M Ed, Ed D, PhD, CAGS). Accredited by NCATE. Program being phased out; applicants no longer accepted. Students: 2 full-time (1 woman), 9 part-time (3 women); includes 5 minority (3 African Americans, 2 Asian Americans). In 1997, 2 master's, 1 doctorate awarded. *Degree requirements:* For doctorate, dissertation. *Application deadline:* rolling. *Expenses:* Tuition $272 per credit hour for state residents; $400 per credit hour for nonresidents. Fees $564 per year full-time, $342 per year part-time. *Financial aid:* Fellowships, teaching assistantships, and career-related internships or fieldwork available. • Dr. Willis Hawley, Dean, College of Education, 301-405-2334. Fax: 301-314-9890. Application contact: John Mollish, Director, Graduate Admissions and Records, 301-405-4198. Fax: 301-314-9305.

University of Minnesota, Twin Cities Campus, College of Education and Human Development, Department of Work, Community, and Family Education, Program in Industrial Education, Minneapolis, MN 55455-0213. Offers vocational education (M Ed). • David Pucel, Coordinator, 612-624-3004.

University of Missouri–Columbia, College of Education, Department of Practical Arts and Vocational Technical Education, Columbia, MO 65211. Awards M Ed, Ed D, PhD, Ed S. Part-time programs available. Faculty: 13 full-time (1 woman). Students: 32 full-time (16 women), 53 part-time (23 women); includes 8 minority (7 African Americans, 1 Asian American), 19 international. In 1997, 30 master's, 14 doctorates awarded. *Degree requirements:* For doctorate, dissertation. *Entrance requirements:* GRE General Test, minimum GPA of 3.0. Application deadline: rolling. Application fee: $25 ($50 for international students). *Expenses:* Tuition $3240 per year full-time, $180 per credit hour part-time for state residents; $9108 per year full-time, $506 per credit hour part-time for nonresidents. Fees $55 per year full-time. *Financial aid:* Career-related internships or fieldwork available. *Faculty research:* Vocational administration, leadership development, sex equity. • Dr. Bob Stewart, Director of Graduate Studies, 573-882-9689.

University of Nebraska–Lincoln, Teachers College, Department of Vocational and Adult Education, Lincoln, NE 68588. Awards MA, M Ed. Accredited by NCATE. Faculty: 7 full-time (2 women). Students: 6 full-time (2 women), 25 part-time (21 women); includes 1 international. Average age 35. 7 applicants, 43% accepted. In 1997, 19 degrees awarded. *Degree requirements:* Thesis optional. *Entrance requirements:* TOEFL (minimum score 500). Application deadline: 3/1 (priority date; rolling processing). Application fee: $35. Electronic applications accepted. *Expenses:* Tuition $110 per credit hour for state residents; $270 per credit hour for nonresidents. Fees $480 per year full-time, $110 per semester part-time. *Financial aid:* In 1997–98, 5 research assistantships totaling $27,661, 3 teaching assistantships totaling $16,250 were awarded; fellowships, Federal Work-Study also available. Aid available to part-time students. Financial aid application deadline: 2/15. *Faculty research:* Leadership, technology, adult learning, curriculum and instruction, human resource development. • Dr. Steven Eggland, Graduate Committee Chair, 402-472-2552.

University of Nevada, Las Vegas, College of Education, Department of Instructional and Curricular Studies, Las Vegas, NV 89154-9900. Offerings include vocational education (M Ed, MS). Accredited by NCATE. Department faculty: 34 full-time (16 women). *Degree requirements:* Thesis (for some programs), oral or written comprehensive exam required, foreign language not required. *Entrance requirements:* Minimum GPA of 3.0. Application deadline: 2/15 (9/30 for spring admission). Application fee: $40 ($95 for international students). *Expenses:* Tuition $93 per credit for state residents; $93 per credit full-time, $190 per credit part-time for nonresidents. Fees $5570 per year full-time for nonresidents. • Dr. Jan McCarthy, Chair, 702-895-3241. Application contact: Graduate College Admissions Evaluator, 702-895-3320.

University of New Brunswick, Faculty of Education, Division of Vocational Education, Fredericton, NB E3B 5A3, Canada. Offers programs in adult education (M Ed), vocational education (M Ed). Part-time programs available. *Entrance requirements:* TOEFL, TWE, minimum GPA of 3.0. Application deadline: 3/1 (priority date; rolling processing). Application fee: $25.

University of New Hampshire, College of Life Sciences and Agriculture, Program in Adult and Occupational Education, Durham, NH 03824. Awards MAOE. Part-time programs available. Faculty: 4 full-time. Students: 6 full-time (5 women), 17 part-time (16 women); includes 1 minority (Hispanic). Average age 40. 7 applicants, 100% accepted. In 1997, 6 degrees awarded. *Degree requirements:* Thesis or alternative required, foreign language not required. *Entrance requirements:* GRE General Test or MAT. Application deadline: 7/1 (priority date; rolling processing). Application fee: $50. *Expenses:* Tuition $5440 per year full-time, $302 per credit hour part-time for state residents; $8160 per year (minimum) full-time, $453 per credit hour (minimum) part-time for nonresidents. Fees $868 per year full-time, $15 per year part-time. *Financial aid:* In 1997–98, 1 teaching assistantship, 5 scholarships (1 to a first-year student) were awarded; fellowships, research assistantships, full and partial tuition waivers, Federal Work-Study, and career-related internships or fieldwork also available. Aid available to part-time students. Financial aid application deadline: 2/15. • Dr. Bruce E. Lindsay, Chairperson, 603-862-3923. Application contact: David Howell, Graduate Coordinator, 603-862-1760.

University of North Dakota, College of Business and Public Administration, Department of Business and Vocational Education, Grand Forks, ND 58202. Offers programs in business education (MS), vocational education (MS). Part-time programs available. Faculty: 4 full-time (1 woman). Students: 3 full-time (1 woman), 2 part-time (1 woman). 1 applicant, 100% accepted. In 1997, 8 degrees awarded. *Degree requirements:* Thesis or alternative required, foreign language not required. *Entrance requirements:* TOEFL (minimum score 550), minimum GPA of 3.0. Application deadline: 3/1 (priority date; rolling processing). Application fee: $20. *Financial aid:* In 1997–98, 5 teaching assistantships totaling $36,250, 1 assistantship totaling $3,625 were awarded; fellowships, research assistantships, full and partial tuition waivers, Federal Work-Study, institutionally sponsored loans also available. Financial aid application deadline: 3/15. • Dr. James Navara, Chairperson, 701-777-2517. Fax: 701-777-5099. E-mail: navara@badlands.nodak.edu.

University of Northern Iowa, College of Natural Sciences, Department of Industrial Technology, Cedar Falls, IA 50614. Awards MA, DIT. Faculty: 13 full-time (0 women). Students: 13 full-time (1 woman), 16 part-time (2 women); includes 1 minority (Asian American), 9 international. Average age 33. 20 applicants, 90% accepted. In 1997, 7 master's, 6 doctorates awarded. *Degree requirements:* For master's, thesis or alternative required, foreign language not required; for doctorate, dissertation. *Entrance requirements:* For master's, GRE. Application deadline: 8/1 (priority date; rolling processing). Application fee: $20 ($30 for international students). *Expenses:* Tuition $3166 per year full-time, $176 per hour part-time for state residents; $7805 per year full-time, $176 per hour part-time for nonresidents. Fees $194 per year full-time, $12.50 per semester (minimum) part-time. *Financial aid:* Teaching assistantships, scholarships, full and partial tuition waivers, Federal Work-Study, and career-related internships or fieldwork available. Aid available to part-time students. Financial aid application deadline: 3/1. • Dr. Mohammed Fahmy, Head, 319-273-2561.

University of North Texas, College of Education, Department of Technology and Cognition, Program in Applied Technology and Training Development, Denton, TX 76203-6737. Offers applied technology and training development (M Ed, MS, Ed D, PhD), vocational counselor (Certificate). Accredited by NCATE. *Degree requirements:* For doctorate, 1 foreign language (computer language can substitute), dissertation, internship. *Entrance requirements:* For master's, GRE General Test; for doctorate, GRE General Test, admissions exam. Application deadline: 7/17. Application fee: $25 ($50 for international students). *Tuition:* $2063 per year full-time, $815 per year part-time for state residents; $5897 per year full-time, $2100 per year part-time for nonresidents. *Financial aid:* Fellowships, research assistantships, teaching assistantships, Federal Work-Study, institutionally sponsored loans, and career-related internships or fieldwork available. Financial aid application deadline: 4/1. • Application contact: Jerry Wircenski, Adviser, 940-565-2093.

University of Regina, Faculty of Graduate Studies and Research, Faculty of Education, Department of Adult Vocational/Technical Education, Regina, SK S4S 0A2, Canada. Awards MVT Ed, Diploma. Students: 33 part-time. Average age 35. 4 applicants, 25% accepted. In 1997, 1 master's, 1 Diploma awarded. *Degree requirements:* For master's, practicum, project, or thesis required, thesis optional, foreign language not required. *Entrance requirements:* For master's, TOEFL (minimum score 580), bachelor's degree in education, 2 years of teaching experience. Application deadline: 3/15 (12/15 for spring admission). Application fee: $0. *Tuition:* $196 per credit for Canadian residents; $383 per credit for nonresidents. *Financial aid:* Fellowships, research assistantships, teaching assistantships available. Financial aid application deadline: 6/15. *Faculty research:* Program and instruction. • Dr. Kevin Quinlan, Director, 306-585-4607. E-mail: kevin.quinlan@uregina.ca. Application contact: Dr. M. Taylor, Chair, Graduate Programs, 306-585-4606. Fax: 306-585-4880. E-mail: marlene.taylor@uregina.ca.

University of South Carolina, Graduate School, College of Education, Department of Instruction and Teacher Education, Community and Occupational Programs in Education, Columbia, SC 29208. Awards MA, M Ed. Accredited by NCATE. Part-time and evening/weekend programs available. Faculty: 3 full-time (1 woman). Students: 13 full-time (8 women), 97 part-time (67 women); includes 26 minority (all African Americans), 1 international. Average age 38. In 1997, 21 degrees awarded. *Degree requirements:* Thesis (for some programs). *Entrance requirements:* GRE General Test (minimum combined score of 800) or MAT (minimum score 35). Application deadline: rolling. Application fee: $35. Electronic applications accepted. *Expenses:* Tuition $3894 per year full-time, $193 per credit hour part-time for state residents; $8114 per year full-time, $404 per credit hour part-time for nonresidents. Fees $125 per year full-time, $37 per semester (minimum) part-time. *Faculty research:* Adult education/lifelong learning, rural education. • Dr. Jack Lyday, Coordinator, 803-777-7748. Fax: 803-777-3193. Application contact: Office of Intercollegiate Teacher Education and Student Affairs, 803-777-6732. Fax: 803-777-3068.

University of Southern Maine, College of Education and Human Development, Program in Industrial/Technology Education, Portland, ME 04104-9300. Awards MS Ed. Accredited by NCATE. Part-time and evening/weekend programs available. Faculty: 1 part-time (0 women). Students: 2 full-time (0 women), 3 part-time (0 women). 0 applicants. *Degree requirements:* Thesis or alternative, practicum required, foreign language not required. *Entrance requirements:* GRE General Test (minimum combined score of 900), MAT (minimum score 40), TOEFL. Application deadline: 2/1. Application fee: $25. *Expenses:* Tuition $178 per credit hour for state residents; $267 per credit hour (minimum) for nonresidents. Fees $282 per year full-time, $83 per semester (minimum) part-time. *Financial aid:* Federal Work-Study, institutionally sponsored loans, and career-related internships or fieldwork available. Financial aid application deadline: 3/1; applicants required to submit FAFSA. • Dr. Robert Nannay, Coordinator, Technology Education, 207-780-5450. Application contact: Teresa Belsan, Admissions and Academic Counselor, 207-780-5306. Fax: 207-780-5315. E-mail: belsan@usm.maine.edu.

University of Southern Mississippi, College of Education and Psychology, Department of Technology Education, Hattiesburg, MS 39406-5167. Offers programs in business technology education (MS), technical occupational education (MS). Part-time programs available. Faculty: 5 full-time (1 woman). Students: 3 full-time (2 women), 34 part-time (26 women); includes 2 minority (both African Americans), 1 international. Average age 39. 16 applicants, 81% accepted. In 1997, 27 degrees awarded. *Entrance requirements:* GRE General Test, minimum GPA of 2.75. Application deadline: 8/9 (priority date; rolling processing). Application fee: $0 ($25 for international students). *Tuition:* $2870 per year full-time, $137 per credit hour part-time for state residents; $5972 per year full-time, $172 per credit hour part-time for nonresidents. *Financial aid:* Application deadline 3/15. • Dr. William B. Burns, Chairman, 601-266-4446.

University of South Florida, College of Education, Department of Adult and Vocational Education, Program in Industrial Technical Education, Tampa, FL 33620-9951. Awards MA. Accredited by NCATE. Part-time and evening/weekend programs available. Students: 13 part-time (4 women); includes 1 minority (Hispanic). Average age 45. 1 applicant, 0% accepted. In 1997, 9 degrees awarded. *Entrance requirements:* GRE General Test (minimum combined score of 1000), minimum GPA of 3.5 in last 60 hours, related work experience. Application deadline: 6/1 (10/15 for spring admission). Application fee: $20. Electronic applications accepted. *Tuition:* $142 per credit hour for state residents; $486 per credit hour for nonresidents. *Financial aid:* Federal Work-Study, institutionally sponsored loans available. Aid available to part-time students. Financial aid applicants required to submit FAFSA. *Faculty research:* Technological literacy, workplace literacy, work attitudes, curricular reform. • Application contact: Charles Gagel, Coordinator, 813-974-0040. Fax: 813-974-5423. E-mail: gagel@tempest.coedu.usf.edu.

University of South Florida, College of Education, Department of Adult and Vocational Education, Program in Vocational Education, Tampa, FL 33620-9951. Awards Ed D, PhD, Ed S. Accredited by NCATE. Part-time and evening/weekend programs available. Students: 7 full-time (2 women), 14 part-time (8 women); includes 1 minority (Hispanic). Average age 47.

4 applicants, 50% accepted. *Degree requirements:* For doctorate, dissertation, 2 tools of research in foreign language, statistics, and/or computers. *Entrance requirements:* For doctorate, GRE General Test (minimum combined score of 1000), minimum GPA of 3.0 (undergraduate) or 3.5 (graduate); for Ed S, GRE General Test (minimum combined score of 1000), minimum GPA of 3.0 in last 60 hours. Application deadline: 6/1 (10/15 for spring admission). Application fee: $20. Electronic applications accepted. *Tuition:* $142 per credit hour for state residents; $486 per credit hour for nonresidents. *Financial aid:* Federal Work-Study, institutionally sponsored loans available. Aid available to part-time students. Financial aid applicants required to submit FAFSA. *Faculty research:* School reform, integration of vocational and academic education. • Application contact: William E. Blank, Coordinator, 813-974-3455. Fax: 813-974-5423. E-mail: blank@tempest.coedu.usf.edu.

The University of Texas at Tyler, School of Education and Psychology, Department of Technology, Tyler, TX 75799-0001. Awards MS. Faculty: 7 full-time (0 women). In 1997, 26 degrees awarded. *Degree requirements:* Comprehensive exam required, foreign language and thesis not required. *Entrance requirements:* GRE General Test. Application fee: $0 ($50 for international students). *Tuition:* $2144 per year full-time, $337 per semester (minimum) part-time for state residents; $7256 per year full-time, $964 per semester (minimum) part-time for nonresidents. *Financial aid:* Application deadline 7/1. *Faculty research:* At-risk students, training and development, economic development, teaching methods. • Dr. Clayton Allen, Chairperson, 903-566-7310. Application contact: Martha D. Wheat, Director of Admissions and Student Records, 903-566-7201. Fax: 903-566-7068.

University of Toledo, College of Education and Allied Professions, Department of Educational Leadership, Program in Vocational Education, Toledo, OH 43606-3398. Awards M Ed. Accredited by NCATE. Students: 20 part-time (11 women); includes 1 minority (Hispanic), 2 international. In 1997, 4 degrees awarded. *Degree requirements:* Thesis or alternative, comprehensive exam required, foreign language not required. *Entrance requirements:* Minimum GPA of 2.7. Application deadline: 8/15 (priority date; rolling processing). Application fee: $30. Electronic applications accepted. *Tuition:* $5907 per year full-time, $246 per hour part-time for state residents; $11,835 per year full-time, $493 per hour part-time for nonresidents. *Financial aid:* Application deadline 4/1. • Dr. Daniel Merritt, Interim Chair, Department of Educational Leadership, 419-530-2461. Fax: 419-530-7719.

University of Vermont, College of Agriculture and Life Sciences, Department of Nutritional Sciences, Burlington, VT 05405-0160. Offerings include occupational and practical arts (MAT). Department faculty: 8 full-time (5 women), 3 part-time (2 women). *Application deadline:* 4/1 (priority date; rolling processing; 11/15 for spring admission). *Application fee:* $25. *Expenses:* Tuition $302 per credit for state residents; $755 per credit for nonresidents. Fees $434 per year full-time, $46 per semester (minimum) part-time. • Dr. R. S. Tyzbir, Director, 802-656-3374. Fax: 802-656-0407.

University of West Florida, College of Education, Division of Teacher Education, Program in Vocational Education, Pensacola, FL 32514-5750. Awards M Ed. Accredited by NCATE. Part-time and evening/weekend programs available. Students: 1 full-time (0 women), 1 (woman) part-time; includes 1 international. Average age 32. 0 applicants. In 1997, 1 degree awarded. *Entrance requirements:* GRE General Test (minimum combined score of 1000) or minimum GPA of 3.0. Application deadline: 7/1 (rolling processing; 11/1 for spring admission). Application fee: $20. *Tuition:* $131 per credit hour (minimum) for state residents; $436 per credit hour (minimum) for nonresidents. *Financial aid:* Fellowships and career-related internships or fieldwork available. *Faculty research:* Dropout prevention, technology/educational enhancement. • Dr. William Evans, Chairperson, Division of Teacher Education, 850-474-2891.

University of Wisconsin–Madison, Schools of Education and Human Ecology and College of Agricultural and Life Sciences, Department of Continuing and Vocational Education, Madison, WI 53706-1380. Awards MS, PhD. *Degree requirements:* For doctorate, dissertation. *Application fee:* $38. *Tuition:* $4928 per year full-time, $926 per semester (minimum) part-time for state residents; $15,190 per year full-time, $2849 per semester (minimum) part-time for nonresidents.

University of Wisconsin–Platteville, College of Liberal Arts and Education, School of Education, Platteville, WI 53818-3099. Offerings include vocational and technical education (MSE). Accredited by NCATE. School faculty: 8 part-time (3 women). *Degree requirements:* Thesis or alternative, comprehensive exam required, foreign language not required. *Entrance requirements:* TOEFL (minimum score 500). Application deadline: 7/1 (priority date; rolling processing; 11/1 for spring admission). Application fee: $45. • Dr. Sally Standiford, Director, 608-342-1131. Fax: 608-342-1133. E-mail: standiford@uwplatt.edu.

University of Wisconsin–Stout, College of Technology, Engineering, and Management, Program in Industrial and Vocational Education, Menomonie, WI 54751. Offers industrial and vocational education (Ed S), vocational education (MS). Part-time programs available. Students: 5 full-time (3 women), 24 part-time (10 women); includes 3 minority (1 Asian American, 1 Hispanic, 1 Native American), 3 international. 8 applicants, 88% accepted. In 1997, 12 master's, 5 Ed Ss awarded. *Degree requirements:* Thesis required, foreign language not required. *Application deadline:* rolling. *Application fee:* $45. *Tuition:* $3284 per year full-time, $183 per credit hour part-time for state residents; $7644 per year full-time, $425 per credit hour part-time for nonresidents. *Financial aid:* In 1997–98, 1 research assistantship was awarded; teaching assistantships, full and partial tuition waivers, Federal Work-Study also available. Aid available to part-time students. Financial aid application deadline: 4/1; applicants required to submit FAFSA. • Dr. Orville Nelson, Director, 715-232-1362.

University of Wisconsin–Stout, College of Technology, Engineering, and Management, Program in Industrial/Technology Education, Menomonie, WI 54751. Awards MS. Part-time programs available. Students: 6 full-time (1 woman), 10 part-time (1 woman). 10 applicants, 90% accepted. In 1997, 7 degrees awarded. *Degree requirements:* Thesis required, foreign language not required. *Application deadline:* rolling. *Application fee:* $45. *Tuition:* $3284 per year full-time, $183 per credit hour part-time for state residents; $7644 per year full-time, $425 per credit hour part-time for nonresidents. *Financial aid:* Research assistantships, teaching assistantships, full and partial tuition waivers, Federal Work-Study available. Aid available to part-time students. Financial aid application deadline: 4/1; applicants required to submit FAFSA. • Dr. Leonard Sterry, Director, 715-232-1367.

Utah State University, College of Engineering, Department of Industrial Technology and Education, Logan, UT 84322. Offers program in industrial technology (MS). Part-time and evening/weekend programs available. Faculty: 8 full-time (0 women), 2 part-time (0 women). Students: 5 full-time (0 women), 7 part-time (1 woman). Average age 31. 4 applicants, 0% accepted. In 1997, 3 degrees awarded (100% found work related to degree). *Degree requirements:* Thesis optional, foreign language not required. *Entrance requirements:* GRE General Test (score in 40th percentile or higher), TOEFL (minimum score 550), minimum GPA of 3.0 in last 30 hours. Application deadline: 6/15 (priority date; rolling processing; 10/15 for spring admission). Application fee: $40. *Expenses:* Tuition $1448 per year full-time, $624 per year part-time for state residents; $5082 per year full-time, $2192 per year part-time for nonresidents. Fees $421 per year full-time, $165 per year part-time. *Financial aid:* Fellowships, research assistantships, teaching assistantships, partial tuition waivers, institutionally sponsored loans, and career-related internships or fieldwork available. *Faculty research:* Computer-aided design drafting, technology and the public school, materials, electronics, aviation. • Maurice G. Thomas, Head, 435-797-1795. Fax: 435-797-2567.

Valdosta State University, College of Education, Department of Business and Vocational Education, Valdosta, GA 31698. Offers programs in adult and vocational education (Ed D), business education (M Ed, Ed S), vocational education (M Ed). Accredited by NCATE. Faculty: 9 full-time (2 women). Students: 16 full-time (11 women), 19 part-time (12 women); includes 1 minority (African American). 42 applicants, 95% accepted. In 1997, 4 master's awarded. *Entrance requirements:* For master's, GRE General Test (minimum combined score of 800); for doctorate, GRE General Test (minimum combined score of 1000); for Ed S, GRE General Test (minimum combined score of 900). Application deadline: 8/1 (rolling processing; 11/15 for spring admission). Application fee: $10. *Expenses:* Tuition $2472 per year full-time, $83 per semester hour part-time for state residents; $8472 per year full-time, $333 per semester hour part-time for nonresidents. Fees $236 per year full-time. • Donnie McGahee, Head, 912-333-5928.

Virginia Polytechnic Institute and State University, College of Human Resources and Education, Department of Teaching and Learning, Blacksburg, VA 24061. Offerings include vocational-technical education (MS Ed, Ed D, PhD, CAGS). Accredited by NCATE. *Degree requirements:* For doctorate, dissertation. *Entrance requirements:* For doctorate, GRE, TOEFL; for CAGS, TOEFL. Application deadline: 12/1 (priority date; rolling processing). Application fee: $25. *Tuition:* $4927 per year full-time, $792 per semester (minimum) part-time for state residents; $7537 per year full-time, $1227 per semester (minimum) part-time for nonresidents. • Dr. John Burton, Head, 540-231-5347. E-mail: teach@vt.edu.

Virginia State University, School of Agriculture, Science and Technology, Program in Vocational Technical Education, 1 Hayden Drive, Petersburg, VA 23806-2096. Awards M Ed, MS, CAGS. Faculty: 7 full-time (2 women). In 1997, 15 master's awarded. *Application deadline:* 8/15 (rolling processing). *Application fee:* $25. *Tuition:* $3739 per year full-time, $133 per credit hour part-time for state residents; $9056 per year full-time, $364 per credit hour part-time for nonresidents. *Financial aid:* 3 students received aid. Financial aid application deadline: 5/1. • Dr. Marlene Simpson, Coordinator, 804-524-5771. Application contact: Dr. Wayne F. Virag, Dean, Graduate Studies and Continuing Education, 804-524-5985. Fax: 804-524-5104. E-mail: wvirag@vsu.edu.

Wayne State College, Division of Education, Program in Curriculum and Instruction, Wayne, NE 68787. Offerings include industrial technology education (MSE). Accredited by NCATE. *Degree requirements:* Comprehensive exam, research paper required, foreign language not required. *Entrance requirements:* GRE General Test. Application deadline: rolling. Application fee: $10. *Expenses:* Tuition $1788 per year full-time, $75 per credit hour part-time for state residents; $3576 per year full-time, $149 per credit hour part-time for nonresidents. Fees $360 per year full-time, $15 per credit hour part-time. • Dr. Diane Alexander, Head, Division of Education, 402-375-7389.

Western Michigan University, College of Education, Department of Family and Consumer Sciences, Program in Career and Technical Education, Kalamazoo, MI 49008. Awards MA. Accredited by NCATE. Students: 1 (woman) full-time, 33 part-time (14 women); includes 1 minority (African American), 2 international. In 1997, 13 degrees awarded. *Application deadline:* 2/15 (priority date; rolling processing). *Application fee:* $25. *Expenses:* Tuition $154 per credit hour for state residents; $372 per credit hour for nonresidents. Fees $602 per year full-time, $132 per semester part-time. *Financial aid:* Application deadline 2/15. • Application contact: Paula J. Boodt, Coordinator, Graduate Admissions and Recruitment, 616-387-2000. E-mail: paulaboodt@wmich.edu.

Westfield State College, Department of Education, Program in Occupational Education, Westfield, MA 01086. Awards M Ed. *Degree requirements:* Comprehensive exam, practicum required, foreign language and thesis not required. *Entrance requirements:* GRE General Test or MAT, minimum undergraduate GPA of 2.7. Application deadline: rolling. Application fee: $30. *Expenses:* Tuition $145 per credit for state residents; $155 per credit for nonresidents. Fees $90 per semester. *Financial aid:* Application deadline 4/1. • Application contact: Marcia Davio, Graduate Records Clerk, 413-572-8024.

West Virginia University, College of Human Resources and Education, Department of Advanced Educational Studies, Morgantown, WV 26506. Offerings include technology education (MA, Ed D), with options in education (Ed D), technology education (MA). Accredited by NCATE. *Degree requirements:* For doctorate, dissertation required, foreign language not required. *Entrance requirements:* TOEFL (minimum score 550). Application deadline: rolling. Application fee: $45. *Tuition:* $2820 per year full-time, $149 per credit hour part-time for state residents; $8104 per year full-time, $443 per credit hour part-time for nonresidents. • Dr. David L. McCrory, Chair, 304-283-3803 Ext. 1706. Fax: 304-293-2279. E-mail: dmccrory@wvu.edu.

West Virginia University, College of Human Resources and Education, Program in Technology Education, Morgantown, WV 26506. Offers education (Ed D), technology education (MA). Accredited by NCATE. Students: 12 full-time (7 women), 11 part-time (4 women); includes 3 minority (all African Americans), 1 international. Average age 37. 11 applicants, 82% accepted. In 1997, 2 master's awarded (100% continued full-time study); 2 doctorates awarded (50% entered university research/teaching, 50% found other work related to degree). *Degree requirements:* Thesis/dissertation required, foreign language not required. *Entrance requirements:* For master's, GRE General Test (minimum combined score of 1000) or MAT (minimum score 50), TOEFL (minimum score 550), minimum GPA of 2.5; for doctorate, GRE General Test or MAT, TOEFL (minimum score 550), interview. Application deadline: rolling. Application fee: $45. *Tuition:* $2820 per year full-time, $149 per credit hour part-time for state residents; $8104 per year full-time, $443 per credit hour part-time for nonresidents. *Financial aid:* In 1997–98, 11 research assistantships (1 to a first-year student) averaging $1,021 per month and totaling $134,772, 1 teaching assistantship averaging $612 per month and totaling $7,344 were awarded; full and partial tuition waivers, Federal Work-Study, institutionally sponsored loans, and career-related internships or fieldwork also available. Financial aid application deadline: 2/1; applicants required to submit FAFSA. *Faculty research:* Appropriate technology, alternative energy, computer applications for education and training, telecommunication, professional development. Total annual research expenditures: $100,000. • Dr. William L. Deaton, Dean, College of Human Resources and Education, 304-293-5703. E-mail: wdeaton@wvu.edu. Application contact: Dr. Anne Nardi, Coordinator, Graduate Studies, 304-293-5703. Fax: 304-293-7565. E-mail: anardi@wvu.edu.

Wright State University, College of Education and Human Services, Department of Teacher Education, Programs in Business Education and Vocational Education, Dayton, OH 45435. Offerings in business education (MA, M Ed), vocational education (MA, M Ed). Accredited by NCATE. Students: 4 full-time (all women), 19 part-time (16 women); includes 1 minority (African American). 11 applicants, 73% accepted. In 1997, 6 degrees awarded. *Degree requirements:* Thesis required (for some programs), foreign language not required. *Entrance requirements:* GRE General Test, MAT, TOEFL (minimum score 550). Application fee: $25. *Tuition:* $5109 per year full-time, $161 per credit hour part-time for state residents; $9039 per year full-time, $282 per credit hour part-time for nonresidents. *Financial aid:* Available to part-time students. Financial aid applicants required to submit FAFSA. • Dr. Donna Courtney, Coordinator, 937-775-3598. Fax: 937-775-3301. Application contact: Gerald C. Malicki, Assistant Dean and Director of Graduate Admissions and Records, 937-775-2976. Fax: 937-775-2357. E-mail: wsugrad@wright.edu.

Cross-Discipline Announcements

Texas A&M University, College of Science, Department of Mathematics, College Station, TX 77843.

Mathematics Teaching Option is a nonthesis degree plan aimed primarily at students who wish to be high school or two-year- college teachers. Students must complete a core of regular and specialized graduate mathematics courses as well as supporting course work in education and statistical methods. See in-depth description in Book 4, section 7.

Walden University, Graduate Programs, Program in Human Services, 155 Fifth Avenue South, Minneapolis, MN 55401.

The distance learning doctoral program (PhD) in human services offers a specialization in social work and counseling. Concentration areas in social work include advanced clinical practice and human services administration. Concentration areas in counseling include substance abuse, career, community mental health, marriage and family, multicultural, rehabilitation, school, and vocational counseling. Applicants must have completed a master's degree in social work, counseling, or a related field. For more information, see Book 1 of this series.

MARLBORO COLLEGE

The Graduate Center
Master of Science in Internet Strategy Management
Master of Arts in Teaching with Internet Technologies

Programs of Study

The mission of the Graduate Center of Marlboro College is to train individuals to lead the Internet and online strategies of corporate, nonprofit, and educational institutions. The Graduate Center offers a Master of Science (M.S.) in Internet strategy management and a Master of Arts in Teaching (M.A.T.) with Internet technologies.

The Graduate Center's programs are designed for working professionals who are balancing work, family, and education; classes meet every other weekend and on line. Faculty members are practicing professionals on the cutting edge of their respective areas of expertise in the field. Programs are concluded within one calendar year, or three trimesters. The programs integrate practical, hands-on skills and operational training with the interdisciplinary and conceptual understanding necessary to cope with an ever-changing landscape of tools and technologies, positioning graduates as strategic leaders within the new economy. Graduates are immediately marketable as a result of their experience with cutting-edge technologies, real-world practice, collaborative team-based training, and interaction with an unparalleled network of professionals during and after their participation in the program.

The Master of Science in Internet Strategy Management (I.S.M.) program prepares students to lead the overall development and management of an organization's Internet and Intranet strategy; offers comprehensive training, which incorporates technical, design, marketing, theoretical, and strategic issues; and employs state-of-the-art technological and business practices. Successful completion of the degree requires the preparation of a capstone project.

The Master of Arts in Teaching with Internet Technologies program prepares primarily K–12 teachers and administrators to lead a school's effort to use the Internet and other new media technologies in pedagogically sound ways. Students address the myriad issues facing schools (many of which are creating and using electronic learning spaces), including the design and development of those spaces, pedagogy, and policy regarding training, support, access, and matching technology to need.

The Graduate Center is fully accredited by the New England Association of Schools and Colleges.

Research Facilities

The Graduate Center is a state-of-the-art facility that includes laboratories with the most advanced technological tools available. These include high-end graphics-manipulation programs; specialty and task-specific computer systems, including workstations dedicated to digital image processing; and servers set up solely for educational and experimental use. All workstations are connected to a 100 Base-T Ethernet-based LAN, which is supported by both UNIX and NT servers. The Graduate Center has a dedicated T1 connection to the Internet that enables fast, unrestricted access. Library resources include both on-site and off-site access to several databases, including an online library catalog; InfoTrac, a full-text magazine index; and UnCover, an index to more than 17,000 magazines. There are also two computer science databases (Microcomputer Abstracts and Computer Science Abstracts) and extensive links to other resources.

Financial Aid

The Graduate Center of Marlboro College participates in such federal assistance programs as the Federal Direct Stafford Loan and the Federal Perkins Loan. The Office of Financial Aid assists students with information, resources, and processing.

Cost of Study

Tuition is $5000 per trimester, or $15,000 to complete the 30-credit program.

Living and Housing Costs

The majority of Graduate Center students travel considerable distances to attend the on-site classes every other Friday and Saturday, requiring overnight accommodations every other Friday night. The Graduate Center has no residence facilities; however, it does have arrangements for discounts with a variety of area establishments for its students. There are many dining facilities nearby.

Student Group

The Graduate Center currently has about 100 students, with no more than 15 in each class. The roughly even number of men and women range in age from 22 to 70. In the I.S.M. program, students come from diverse professional backgrounds and are often characterized by a strong entrepreneurial spirit. The M.A.T. program is composed primarily of K–12 teachers, librarians, and media specialists.

Location

The Graduate Center is centrally located in Brattleboro, Vermont, minutes from Interstate 91, and is easily accessible throughout the greater New England region. The Graduate Center is 2 hours from Boston, 80 minutes from Hartford, and less than 4 hours from New York City. Nearby natural resources include some of the finest skiing, hiking, mountain biking, and canoeing in the East, with many cultural opportunities also available.

The College

Marlboro College, founded in 1946, is ranked among the top Liberal Arts I colleges, as classified by the Carnegie Foundation. Its tenets include a commitment to interdisciplinary study, intellectual rigor, and clear thinking. Termed "one of the small jewels of American education" by Harvard economist John Kenneth Galbraith, Marlboro was recently awarded a major grant by the MacArthur Foundation for its innovation in education. Marlboro College is accredited by the New England Association of Schools and Colleges.

Applying

Applications are accepted on a rolling admissions basis. Applicants must have completed an undergraduate degree. The requirements for admission are a complete application, a letter of intent, two official transcripts of all credits earned from accredited undergraduate and graduate schools, two letters of reference, and an interview with the Director of Academic Programs. There is no admission fee.

Correspondence and Information

Director of Academic Programs
The Graduate Center of Marlboro College
28 Vernon Street, Suite #5
Brattleboro, Vermont 05302
Telephone: 802-258-9200
800-258-5665 (toll-free)
Fax: 802-258-9201
E-mail: gradcenter@marlboro.edu
World Wide Web: http://www.gradcenter.marlboro.edu

Marlboro College

THE FACULTY AND THEIR RESEARCH

All Graduate Center faculty members are practicing professionals at the cutting edge of their respective fields.

Mark Field, B.F.A, Massachusetts. Senior Designer/Art Director for Polese Clancy, leading provider of interactive multimedia service.
Mark Francillon, M.A., Ph.D. candidate, Chicago. Director of Computing at Marlboro College and digital integration technology specialist.
David Kahle, M.Ed., Harvard. Education technologist in the uses of Internet-based technologies and computer-mediated communications for learning and teaching.
Michael Knapp, Ph.D., Yale. Researcher and statistician in data warehousing, query tools, Internet-based research, and geographic information systems.
Laura Lee, B.S., Rutgers. Internet Strategy Manager for Polaroid Commeration's Commercial Imaging Group.
David Rose, M.Ed., Harvard. Graduate studies in cognitive science and artificial intelligence, Oberlin College and Massachusetts Institute of Technology Media Lab in Interactive Cinema. Founder and President of the Interactive Factory, a multimedia design company.
Lois Wasoff, J.D., NYU. Legal counsel for Houghton Mifflin Company and member of the president's commission to rewrite national electronic media legislation.
James Kenneth Woodell, M.Ed., Harvard. Professional development expert for Tom Snyder Productions.

UNIVERSITY OF TENNESSEE, KNOXVILLE

College of Human Ecology
Department of Health and Safety Sciences

Programs of Study

The Department of Health and Safety Sciences (HSS) offers Master of Science (M.S.) degrees, with majors in health promotion and health education and in safety education and service. Other graduate degrees offered include the Master of Public Health (M.P.H.) degree with a major in public health and the Doctor of Philosophy (Ph.D.) degree in human ecology with a concentration in community health.

The M.S. degree programs require completion of 30 semester hours of credit, with both thesis and nonthesis options available. Students in the safety education and service program may elect an internship experience in private industry or with a nonprofit organization and, electing the nonthesis option, may emphasize technology, management, or education and training.

The M.P.H. program, accredited by the Council on Education for Public Health, offers professional preparation in three concentrations of study: community health education, gerontology, and health planning/administration. The M.P.H. is a nonthesis program, requiring 38 semester hours of credit, including at least nine weeks of field practice in an affiliated health agency or organization. Minors in gerontology and statistics are also available. A dual degree (M.S./M.P.H.) is available for students in public health nutrition.

The Ph.D. degree with a major in human ecology represents the highest achievement in health education scholarship and research. The doctoral program is designed to produce health education and community health scholars capable of conducting significant research as well as communicating skillfully through teaching, professional presentation, and publication. Degree requirements include course work in research, natural or behavioral sciences, statistics, health education, and other relevant areas and the completion of a doctoral dissertation.

Research Facilities

The 350,000-square-foot John C. Hodges Library is the largest library in Tennessee. More than 2 million volumes and more than 18,000 periodicals and other serial titles support research and instruction. As a designated depository for U.S. government publications, Hodges Library receives about 90 percent of the written materials offered by the federal government. The online catalog is accessible via computer terminals in the library or off-site. Access to many computerized databases, including a CD-ROM collection, is available.

The Knoxville/Oak Ridge area is of sufficient size to offer numerous community resources for research, teaching/learning, and community-based service. Within a 20-mile radius, governmental organizations, nonprofit organizations, proprietary health organizations, business and industrial organizations, and various independent projects engage in coordinated activities with the University.

Financial Aid

Research and teaching assistantships are provided for 10 graduate students in HSS, with approximately four assistantships available for entering students each year. Stipends for half-time assistantships range from $7000 to $9235, depending on the source of the assistantship. In addition, assistantships provide waiver of maintenance fees and tuition for fall, spring, and summer terms.

Cost of Study

All fees, except a $140 per-semester program and services fee and a $100 per-semester technology fee, are waived for full-time students awarded a graduate assistantship. For those not supported by an assistantship, full-time fees were $1571 per semester for in-state students and $3912 per semester for out-of-state students in 1997–98.

Living and Housing Costs

University apartments are available for both single and married graduate students with or without families. Privately owned apartments, renting within a wide price range, are also available in the campus area.

Student Group

Approximately 145 students are enrolled in graduate programs within the department. Of these, about 65 percent are women and 3 percent are international students. Working students represent about 60 percent of the total enrollment. On average each year, 50 HSS students earn a graduate degree. Some students enter the programs directly following undergraduate studies, but many students have prior employment or other academic experience.

Student Outcomes

Rewarding careers are available in the health and safety industries. Doctoral graduates accept academic and research appointments in universities or health-related settings. Master's-level graduates are employed by wellness, health, and fitness centers; public health and other governmental agencies; mental health facilities, hospitals, and other health-care organizations; private industry; and nonprofit agencies.

Location

The University is located along the Tennessee River in the foothills of the Smoky Mountains, approximately 30 minutes from the Great Smoky Mountains National Park. The Knoxville metropolitan area has a population of about 600,000. The scenic East Tennessee area offers an exceptionally high quality of life, a mild climate year-round, low-cost housing, a variety of cultural events and recreational activities, and easy access to major cities in the Southeast and on the Atlantic seaboard.

The University

The University of Tennessee, founded in 1794, is a comprehensive state research university with a strong commitment to graduate research and training. The University has several campuses across the state. The main campus, the agricultural campus, the school of veterinary medicine, and a graduate medical campus are in Knoxville, and the medical school is in Memphis. The total enrollment is approximately 26,000 students, about 25 percent of whom are graduate students.

Applying

Application packets should be requested from the department. For most programs, a graduate application, three recommendations (five for doctoral degree applicants), and statements regarding educational and career goals are required. GRE scores are required for the Ph.D. program only. For the M.P.H. degree program, deadlines for completed applications are February 1 and April 1, respectively, for summer and fall admissions. For the M.S. degree program in health promotion and health education, the dates are February 1, April 1, and October 1. TOEFL scores are required of students whose primary language is not English.

Correspondence and Information

Dr. Charles B. Hamilton
Department of Health and Safety Sciences
University of Tennessee, Knoxville
1914 Andy Holt Avenue
Knoxville, Tennessee 37996-2710
Telephone: 423-974-5041
Fax: 423-974-6439

University of Tennessee, Knoxville

THE FACULTY AND THEIR RESEARCH

Barbara P. Clarke, Adjunct Assistant Professor; Ph.D., Virginia Tech. Adolescent health, women's wellness, later life health promotion, coalition building/management.

Jack S. Ellison, Assistant Professor; Ed.D., Tennessee; Certified Health Education Specialist and Certified Crisis Intervention Specialist. Alcohol and other drug use and abuse, mental health, suicide and crisis intervention, epidemiology.

Eugene C. Fitzhugh, Assistant Professor; Ph.D., Alabama at Birmingham; Certified Health Education Specialist. Adolescent tobacco control and prevention targeted at understudied populations, worksite health promotion, secondary data analysis of national public health databases, with a focus on health promotion and health education.

June D. Gorski, Professor; Dr.P.H., UCLA; Certified Health Education Specialist. Health education/health promotion for preventive services, interventions affecting individuals and communities, women's and adolescents' health.

Charles B. Hamilton, Professor and Department Head; Dr.P.H., Oklahoma. Primary health care access, health policy, environmental health issues, interdisciplinary health teams.

Betsy Haughton, Adjunct Associate Professor; Ed.D., Columbia; Registered Dietitian. Public health nutrition practice for maternal and child health, continuing education interventions, food and nutrition policy.

Robert H. Kirk, Professor; H.S.D., Indiana. Health and safety.

Tyler A. Kress, Adjunct Assistant Professor; Ph.D., Tennessee. Reduction of cumulative trauma injuries such as carpal tunnel syndrome, product design, sports biomechanics, vehicle safety, injury causation analyses for various types of industrial and consumer accidents and injuries (both acute and cumulative).

James J. Neutens, Adjunct Professor; Ph.D., Illinois; Certified Health Education Specialist. Research methods and design, sexuality education and counseling, medical education.

Robert J. Pursley, Associate Professor; Ph.D., Iowa. Adolescent health; health risk appraisal of children, adolescents, mid-life adults, and elder Americans; microcomputer applications related to public health departments and health-care facilities.

Susan M. Smith, Assistant Professor; Ed.D., Tennessee. Emergency response and evacuation needs of high-risk populations, injury and accident reporting and evaluation tools, health and safety risk reduction in the school, home, and workplace.

Bill C. Wallace, Professor; Ed.D., Northern Colorado; Certified Health Education Specialist. Gerontology and health education.

Paula C. Zemel, Associate Professor; Ph.D., Wayne State; Registered Dietitian. Public health nutrition, maternal-child health, technology-based and continuing nutrition education.

Academic and Professional Programs in the Health-Related Professions

This part of Book 6 consists of five sections covering the health-related professions. Each section has a table of contents (listing the program directories, announcements, and in-depth descriptions); program directories, which consist of brief profiles of programs in the relevant fields (and that include 50-word or 100-word announcements following the profiles, if programs have chosen to include them); Cross-Discipline Announcements, if any programs have chosen to submit such entries; and in-depth descriptions, which are more individualized statements included, if programs have chosen to submit them.

Section 26
Allied Health

This section contains directories of institutions offering graduate work in allied health, clinical laboratory sciences, communication disorders, dental hygiene, emergency medical services, medical technology, occupational therapy, physical therapy, physician assistant studies, and rehabilitation sciences, followed by in-depth entries submitted by institutions that chose to prepare detailed program descriptions. Additional information about programs listed in the directories but not augmented by an in-depth entry may be obtained by writing directly to the dean of a graduate school or chair of a department at the address given in the directory.

For programs offering related work, see also in this book Administration, Instruction, and Theory (Education Psychology); Dentistry and Dental Sciences; Health Services; Public Health; Special Focus (Education of the Multiply Handicapped); Social Work; and Subject Areas (Counselor Education); in Book 2, Art and Art History (Art Therapy), Home Economics and Family Studies (Gerontology), Performing Arts (Therapies), and Psychology and Counseling; in Book 3, Anatomy, Biophysics, Microbiological Sciences, Pathology, and Physiology; in Book 4, Physics (Acoustics); and in Book 5, Bioengineering, Biomedical Engineering, and Biotechnology; and Energy and Power Engineering (Nuclear Engineering).

CONTENTS

Program Directories

Announcements

Cross-Discipline Announcements

In-Depth Descriptions

See also:

Allied Health—General

Alabama State University, School of Graduate Studies, College of Arts and Sciences, Department of Allied Health Science, Montgomery, AL 36101-0271. Offers program in physical therapy (MS). *Application deadline:* 7/15 (rolling processing; 12/15 for spring admission). *Application fee:* $10. *Expenses:* Tuition $85 per credit hour for state residents; $170 per credit hour for nonresidents. Fees $486 per year. • Dr. Claudelle Carruthers, Associate Dean, 334-229-4707.

Alderson–Broaddus College, Medical Science Department, Philippi, WV 26416. Offers programs in medical science (MS), including emergency medical care, rural primary care; physician assistant (MS), including emergency medicine, rural primary care. Postbaccalaureate distance learning degree programs offered (minimal on-campus study). Faculty: 17 part-time (0 women). Students: 48 full-time (16 women); includes 6 minority (5 African Americans, 1 Hispanic). Average age 35. 48 applicants, 60% accepted. In 1997, 21 degrees awarded (0% entered university research/teaching, 0% found other work related to degree, 10% continued full-time study). *Degree requirements:* Thesis, 2 years of clinical experience required, foreign language not required. *Average time to degree:* master's–2 years full-time. *Entrance requirements:* National Commission on Certification of Physician Assistants certification or bachelor's degree in related field, full-time clinical employment. Application deadline: 6/1 (priority date; rolling processing). Application fee: $35. *Tuition:* $420 per credit hour. *Financial aid:* Institutionally sponsored loans and career-related internships or fieldwork available. Aid available to part-time students. Financial aid application deadline: 6/1. • Dr. Sharon Boni, Chairperson, 304-457-6284. Fax: 304-457-6239. Application contact: Dick Mercer, Director, Master's Degree Program, 304-457-6356. Fax: 304-457-6308. E-mail: mercer@ab.edu.

Allegheny University of the Health Sciences, School of Health Professions, Philadelphia, PA 19102-1192. Awards MA, MEMS, MFT, MGCOD, MGPGP, MPT, MS, PhD, JD/PhD. Part-time and evening/weekend programs available. Faculty: 108 full-time (60 women), 100 part-time (58 women). Students: 443 full-time (345 women), 67 part-time (54 women); includes 53 minority (25 African Americans, 19 Asian Americans, 9 Hispanics), 16 international. Average age 28. 950 applicants, 33% accepted. In 1997, 125 master's, 14 doctorates awarded. Terminal master's awarded for partial completion of doctoral program. *Degree requirements:* For master's, comprehensive exam required, foreign language not required; for doctorate, dissertation, qualifying exam required, foreign language not required. *Entrance requirements:* For doctorate, GRE General Test. Application fee: $50. *Expenses:* Tuition $11,500 per year full-time, $640 per credit part-time. Fees $125 per year. *Financial aid:* Fellowships, research assistantships, teaching assistantships, partial tuition waivers, Federal Work-Study, institutionally sponsored loans, and career-related internships or fieldwork available. Aid available to part-time students. Financial aid application deadline: 5/1; applicants required to submit FAFSA. • Dr. Will Green, Dean. Application contact: Paula Greenberg, Director of Admissions and Recruitment, 215-762-8288. Fax: 215-762-6194.

See in-depth description on page 1231.

Andrews University, School of Graduate Studies, College of Arts and Sciences, Allied Health Department, Berrien Springs, MI 49104. Awards MSMT. Faculty: 4 full-time (2 women). *Application deadline:* 8/15 (rolling processing). *Application fee:* $30. *Expenses:* Tuition $290 per quarter hour (minimum). Fees $75 per quarter. • Marcia A. Kilsby, Chair, 616-471-9891.

Baylor University, Academy of Health Sciences, Fort Sam Houston, TX 78234. Awards MHA, MPT. Students: 124 full-time (34 women); includes 12 minority (3 African Americans, 3 Asian Americans, 6 Hispanics). In 1997, 77 degrees awarded (100% found work related to degree). *Entrance requirements:* GRE General Test (minimum combined score of 1000). Application deadline: rolling. Application fee: $25. *Expenses:* Program is fully funded by the Department of the Army. Applicants are only accepted from the federal sector. • Col. T. R. Byrne, Dean, 210-221-5187.

Boston University, Sargent College of Health and Rehabilitation Sciences, Boston, MA 02215. Awards MS, MSOT, MSPT, D Sc, CAGS. Part-time and evening/weekend programs available. Faculty: 50 full-time (33 women), 50 part-time (35 women), 70 FTE. Students: 567 full-time (458 women), 76 part-time (59 women); includes 51 minority (7 African Americans, 37 Asian Americans, 6 Hispanics, 1 Native American), 23 international. Average age 27. 1,246 applicants, 33% accepted. In 1997, 249 master's, 7 doctorates, 6 CAGSs awarded. *Degree requirements:* For doctorate, dissertation required, foreign language not required. *Entrance requirements:* For master's, GRE General Test; for doctorate, GRE General Test (minimum combined score of 1000), master's degree. Application fee: $50. *Expenses:* Tuition $22,830 per year full-time, $713 per credit part-time. Fees $218 per year full-time, $40 per semester part-time. *Financial aid:* Fellowships, research assistantships, teaching assistantships, scholarships, Federal Work-Study, institutionally sponsored loans, and career-related internships or fieldwork available. Aid available to part-time students. Financial aid application deadline: 4/15. *Faculty research:* Outcome measurement, gerontology, memory, hearing loss. Total annual research expenditures: $2.5 million. • Dr. Alan M. Jette, Dean, 617-353-2704. Application contact: Susan Hussan, Senior Admissions Coordinator, 617-353-2713. Fax: 617-353-7500.

See in-depth description on page 1235.

Chatham College, School of Graduate Studies, Programs in Health Sciences, Pittsburgh, PA 15232-2826. Offerings in counseling psychology (MS), including community counseling, industrial/organizational, lifespan development; occupational therapy (MOT); physical therapy (MPT); physician assistant studies (MPAS). Part-time and evening/weekend programs available. Faculty: 19 full-time (16 women). Students: 244 full-time (187 women); includes 10 minority (4 African Americans, 5 Asian Americans, 1 Hispanic). 318 applicants, 60% accepted. In 1997, 97 degrees awarded (100% found work related to degree). *Degree requirements:* Clinical experience. *Average time to degree:* master's–2 years full-time. *Application fee:* $45. Electronic applications accepted. *Expenses:* Tuition $23,688 per year full-time, $395 per credit part-time. Fees $312 per year. *Financial aid:* Career-related internships or fieldwork available. Aid available to part-time students. Financial aid applicants required to submit FAFSA. • Dr. Sue Bemis, Assistant Dean and Director of Graduate Health Sciences, 412-365-1409. Fax: 412-365-1213. E-mail: bemis@chatham.edu. Application contact: Heidi Hemming, Graduate Admissions, 412-365-1290. Fax: 412-365-1609. E-mail: admissions@chatham.edu.

College of Mount Saint Vincent, Program in Allied Health, Riverdale, NY 10471-1093. Offers allied health studies (MS), including addictions, child and family health, community health education, counseling, health care management, health care systems and policies; counseling (Certificate); health care management (Certificate); health care systems and policies (Certificate). Part-time and evening/weekend programs available. Faculty: 1 (woman) full-time, 8 part-time (4 women), 3.6 FTE. Students: 15 full-time (12 women), 25 part-time (19 women); includes 22 minority (12 African Americans, 2 Asian Americans, 8 Hispanics), 1 international. Average age 31. *Degree requirements:* For master's, thesis or alternative required, foreign language not required. *Average time to degree:* master's–2 years part-time. *Entrance requirements:* For master's, sample of written work. Application deadline: 9/23 (priority date; rolling processing). Application fee: $50. *Financial aid:* Career-related internships or fieldwork available. Financial aid applicants required to submit FAFSA. *Faculty research:* Work and family stress, siblings, women's health issues. • Dr. Rita Scher Dytell, Director, 718-405-3788. Fax: 718-405-3249.

Creighton University, School of Pharmacy and Allied Health Professions, Omaha, NE 68178-0001. Awards Pharm D, DPT, OTD. Postbaccalaureate distance learning degree programs offered (no on-campus study). Faculty: 66 full-time (37 women), 5 part-time (2 women). Students: 550 full-time (341 women); includes 121 minority (15 African Americans, 88 Asian Americans, 17 Hispanics, 1 Native American), 20 international. Average age 26. 1,242 applicants, 13% accepted. In 1997, 80 Pharm Ds, 59 doctorates awarded. *Average time to degree:* doctorate–3 years full-time; first professional–6 years full-time. *Application fee:* $50. *Expenses:* Tuition $6772 per year. Fees $268 per year. *Financial aid:* Federal Work-Study, institutionally sponsored loans, and career-related internships or fieldwork available. Aid available to part-time students. Financial aid applicants required to submit CSS PROFILE or FAFSA. *Faculty research:* Drug synthesis, molecular mechanisms of toxicity, pharmaceutics, health care systems, biomechanics, ethics. • Dr. Sidney J. Stohs, Dean, 402-280-2950. Fax: 402-280-5738. E-mail: stohs@creighton.edu. Application contact: John J. Flemming, Director of Admissions, 402-280-2662. Fax: 402-280-5739. E-mail: spahp_admin8@creighton.edu.

Duquesne University, John G. Rangos, Sr. School of Health Sciences, Pittsburgh, PA 15282-0001. Awards MHMS, MOT, MPA, MPT, MSLP, MBA/MSHMS. Programs in health management systems (MHMS), occupational therapy (MOT), physical therapy (MPT), physician assistant (MPA), speech-language pathology (MSLP). Faculty: 30 full-time (17 women), 12 part-time (6 women), 34.8 FTE. Students: 233 full-time (164 women), 29 part-time (18 women); includes 16 minority (3 African Americans, 8 Asian Americans, 5 Hispanics), 1 international. Average age 25. 368 applicants, 7% accepted. In 1997, 119 degrees awarded. *Degree requirements:* Computer language required, foreign language and thesis not required. *Average time to degree:* master's–2 years full-time. *Application deadline:* 12/1 (priority date). *Application fee:* $45. Electronic applications accepted. *Expenses:* Tuition $510 per credit. Fees $39 per credit. *Financial aid:* Federal Work-Study available. *Faculty research:* Family dynamics, reproduction, biomechanics, infant play behavior, mental health, muscle tissue, components of skilled motor performance. Total annual research expenditures: $27,792. • Dr. Jerome L. Martin, Dean, 412-396-6012. E-mail: martin2@duq2.cc.duq.edu. Application contact: Deborah L. Durica, Director of Student and Alumni Services, 412-396-6652. Fax: 412-396-5554. E-mail: durica@duq2.cc.duq.edu.

East Carolina University, School of Allied Health Sciences, Greenville, NC 27858-4353. Awards MPT, MS, MSEH, MSSL, PhD. Part-time and evening/weekend programs available. Faculty: 19 full-time (4 women). Students: 227 full-time (176 women), 47 part-time (36 women); includes 16 minority (11 African Americans, 4 Asian Americans, 1 Native American), 1 international. Average age 28. 607 applicants, 30% accepted. In 1997, 55 master's awarded. *Degree requirements:* For master's, comprehensive exams. *Entrance requirements:* For master's, TOEFL. Application fee: $40. *Tuition:* $1886 per year full-time, $472 per semester (minimum) part-time for state residents; $9156 per year full-time, $2289 per semester (minimum) part-time for nonresidents. *Financial aid:* Research assistantships, teaching assistantships, grants, Federal Work-Study, and career-related internships or fieldwork available. Aid available to part-time students. Financial aid application deadline: 6/1; applicants required to submit FAFSA. • Dr. Harold Jones, Dean, 252-328-6961. E-mail: jonesh@mail.ecu.edu. Application contact: Dr. Paul D. Tschetter, Associate Dean, 252-328-6012. Fax: 252-328-6071. E-mail: grad@mail.ecu.edu.

Eastern Kentucky University, College of Allied Health and Nursing, Richmond, KY 40475-3101. Awards MS, MSN. Part-time programs available. Students: 122. In 1997, 25 degrees awarded. *Entrance requirements:* GRE General Test. Application fee: $0. *Tuition:* $2390 per year full-time, $133 per credit hour part-time for state residents; $6630 per year full-time, $365 per credit hour part-time for nonresidents. *Financial aid:* Institutionally sponsored loans and career-related internships or fieldwork available. Financial aid applicants required to submit CSS PROFILE. • Dr. David Gale, Dean, 606-622-1523.

East Tennessee State University, College of Public and Allied Health, Johnson City, TN 37614-0734. Awards MPH, MS, MSEH. Part-time and evening/weekend programs available. Faculty: 23 full-time (7 women). Students: 68 full-time (54 women), 55 part-time (32 women); includes 9 minority (6 African Americans, 2 Asian Americans, 1 Native American), 3 international. Average age 29. 223 applicants, 33% accepted. In 1997, 54 degrees awarded. *Degree requirements:* Comprehensive exam required, foreign language not required. *Entrance requirements:* TOEFL (minimum score 550). Application fee: $25 ($35 for international students). *Tuition:* $2944 per year full-time, $158 per credit hour part-time for state residents; $7770 per year full-time, $369 per credit hour part-time for nonresidents. *Financial aid:* In 1997–98, 11 research assistantships (6 to first-year students), 4 teaching assistantships, 12 assistantships, grants (6 to first-year students) were awarded; fellowships, full tuition waivers, Federal Work-Study, institutionally sponsored loans, and career-related internships or fieldwork also available. Aid available to part-time students. • Dr. Wilsie Bishop, Dean, 423-439-4243. Fax: 423-439-5238.

Emory University, School of Medicine, Programs in Allied Health Professions, Atlanta, GA 30322-1100. Offerings in anesthesiology/patient monitoring systems (MM Sc), including anesthesiology/patient monitoring systems, critical care medicine; ophthalmic technology (MM Sc); physical therapy (MM Sc, MPT); physician assistant (MM Sc); radiation oncology physics (MM Sc). Faculty: 17 full-time (13 women), 13 part-time (4 women). Students: 332 full-time (188 women), 1 (woman) part-time; includes 38 minority (12 African Americans, 21 Asian Americans, 5 Hispanics), 2 international. Average age 26. 1,289 applicants, 12% accepted. In 1997, 119 degrees awarded. *Financial aid:* Federal Work-Study, institutionally sponsored loans available. Aid available to part-time students. Financial aid application deadline: 3/15; applicants required to submit CSS PROFILE or FAFSA. • Dr. Jonas A. Shulman, Executive Associate Dean, 404-727-5655. Application contact: Sybil T. Bridges, Office of Allied Health, 404-727-5682. Fax: 404-727-0045. E-mail: sbridges@rwwhsc.medadm.emory.edu.

Finch University of Health Sciences/The Chicago Medical School, School of Related Health Sciences, North Chicago, IL 60064-3095. Awards MS. Part-time and evening/weekend programs available. Postbaccalaureate distance learning degree programs offered (minimal on-campus study). Faculty: 23 full-time (16 women), 24 part-time (12 women). Students: 129 full-time (97 women), 134 part-time (114 women); includes 22 minority (7 African Americans, 4 Asian Americans, 10 Hispanics, 1 Native American), 1 international. In 1997, 61 degrees awarded. *Application deadline:* rolling. *Tuition:* $403 per credit hour. *Financial aid:* Teaching assistantships, partial tuition waivers, institutionally sponsored loans, and career-related internships or fieldwork available. Aid available to part-time students. Financial aid applicants required to submit FAFSA. • Dr. Cynthia Adams, Dean, 847-578-3304. Fax: 847-578-3015. E-mail: adamsc@mis.finchcms.edu.

See in-depth description on page 1237.

Florida Atlantic University, College of Education, Department of Health Sciences, Boca Raton, FL 33431-0991. Offers programs in communication disorders (M Ed), exercise science/wellness (MS), physical therapy (MS). Faculty: 13 full-time (7 women), 4 part-time (all women). Students: 27 full-time (19 women), 53 part-time (40 women); includes 18 minority (7 African Americans, 11 Hispanics). Average age 30. 250 applicants, 20% accepted. In 1997, 28 degrees awarded. *Entrance requirements:* GRE General Test. Application deadline: rolling. Application fee: $20. *Expenses:* Tuition $2520 per year full-time, $140 per credit hour part-time for state residents; $8712 per year full-time, $484 per credit hour part-time for nonresidents. Fees $5 per year (minimum). *Financial aid:* Career-related internships or fieldwork available. • Dr. Simon Ogamdi, Chairperson, 954-236-1264.

Florida Gulf Coast University, College of Health Professions, Fort Myers, FL 33965-6565. Awards MS. Part-time and evening/weekend programs available. Postbaccalaureate distance learning degree programs offered. Students: 31 full-time (21 women), 5 part-time (4 women); includes 4 minority (3 Asian Americans, 1 Hispanic). 90 applicants, 46% accepted. *Application fee:* $20. Electronic applications accepted. *Financial aid:* Federal Work-Study, institutionally sponsored loans, and career-related internships or fieldwork available. • James Blagg, Dean, 941-590-7451. E-mail: jblagg@fgcu.edu.

Georgia Southern University, College of Health and Professional Studies, Statesboro, GA 30460-8126. Awards MS, MSN, Certificate. Part-time and evening/weekend programs available. Faculty: 35 full-time (20 women). Students: 96 full-time (66 women), 16 part-time (12 women);

includes 13 minority (7 African Americans, 2 Asian Americans, 3 Hispanics, 1 Native American), 3 international. Average age 35. 80 applicants, 46% accepted. In 1997, 66 master's awarded. *Entrance requirements:* For master's, GRE General Test (minimum score 450 on each section). Application deadline: 7/15 (priority date; rolling processing; 11/15 for spring admission). Application fee: $0. Electronic applications accepted. *Tuition:* $2619 per year full-time, $287 per semester (minimum) part-time for state residents; $8619 per year full-time, $1037 per semester (minimum) part-time for nonresidents. *Financial aid:* In 1997–98, 3 teaching assistantships totaling $14,490, 23 assistantships were awarded; research assistantships, Federal Work-Study, and career-related internships or fieldwork also available. Aid available to part-time students. Financial aid application deadline: 4/15. *Faculty research:* Hope and humor in the chronically and terminally ill, rural nursing and underserved populations, social influence in exercise and sport, nutrition and ergogenic acids. • Dr. Frederick Whitt, Dean, 912-681-5322. Fax: 912-681-5349. E-mail: fwhitt@gsvms2.cc.gasou.edu. Application contact: Dr. John R. Diebolt, Associate Graduate Dean, 912-681-5384. Fax: 912-681-0740. E-mail: gradschool@gsvms2.cc.gasou.edu.

Georgia State University, College of Health and Human Sciences, Atlanta, GA 30303-3083. Awards MS, PhD. Part-time and evening/weekend programs available. Faculty: 76 full-time (55 women), 8 part-time (all women). Students: 145 full-time (127 women), 207 part-time (189 women). Average age 33. 217 applicants, 54% accepted. In 1997, 122 master's, 9 doctorates awarded. *Degree requirements:* For doctorate, dissertation required, foreign language not required. *Entrance requirements:* For doctorate, GRE General Test. Application fee: $25. *Expenses:* Tuition $2673 per year full-time, $99 per semester hour part-time for state residents; $10,692 per year full-time, $396 per semester hour part-time for nonresidents. Fees $228 per year. *Financial aid:* Fellowships, research assistantships, teaching assistantships, minority scholarships, minority fellowships, Federal Work-Study, institutionally sponsored loans available. Aid available to part-time students. Financial aid application deadline: 4/15; applicants required to submit FAFSA. • Dr. Sherry K. Gaines, Dean, 404-651-3030. Application contact: Office of Academic Assistance, 404-651-3064. Fax: 404-651-4871.

Governors State University, College of Health Professions, Division of Nursing and Health Science, University Park, IL 60466. Awards MHS, MOT, MPT, MSN. Part-time and evening/weekend programs available. In 1997, 39 degrees awarded. *Degree requirements:* Thesis or alternative required, foreign language not required. *Application fee:* $0. *Expenses:* Tuition $1140 per trimester full-time, $95 per credit hour part-time for state residents; $3420 per trimester full-time, $285 per credit hour part-time for nonresidents. Fees $95 per trimester. *Financial aid:* Research assistantships, scholarships, full and partial tuition waivers, Federal Work-Study, institutionally sponsored loans, and career-related internships or fieldwork available. Aid available to part-time students. Financial aid application deadline: 5/1. • Dr. Connie Edwards, Chairperson, 708-534-4040.

Grand Valley State University, Science and Mathematics Division, School of Health Sciences, Allendale, MI 49401-9403. Awards MHS, MS. Part-time programs available. Faculty: 33 full-time (18 women), 165 part-time (83 women). Students: 216 full-time (154 women), 14 part-time (4 women); includes 8 minority (1 African American, 3 Asian Americans, 1 Hispanic, 3 Native Americans), 3 international. Average age 28. In 1997, 40 degrees awarded. *Application fee:* $20. Electronic applications accepted. *Financial aid:* Research assistantships, Federal Work-Study, institutionally sponsored loans, and career-related internships or fieldwork available. *Faculty research:* Skeletal muscle structure, blood platelets, thrombospondin activity, FES exercise for quadriplegics. • Dr. Jane Toot, Acting Director, 616-895-3318. Application contact: Dr. Therese Bacon-Baquely, Graduate Adviser, 616-895-3442.

Idaho State University, College of Health Professions, Pocatello, ID 83209. Awards M Coun, MHE, MOT, MPH, MPT, MS, Ed D, Certificate, Ed S. Part-time programs available. Faculty: 48 full-time (21 women), 25 part-time (11 women). Students: 240 full-time (166 women), 82 part-time (72 women); includes 9 minority (2 African Americans, 3 Asian Americans, 3 Hispanics, 1 Native American), 3 international. Average age 33. In 1997, 105 master's, 4 doctorates, 1 other advanced degree awarded. *Degree requirements:* For doctorate, dissertation required, foreign language not required. *Entrance requirements:* For master's and other advanced degree, GRE General Test; for doctorate, GRE General Test, MAT. *Tuition:* $3130 per year full-time, $136 per credit hour part-time for state residents; $9370 per year full-time, $226 per credit hour part-time for nonresidents. *Financial aid:* Fellowships, teaching assistantships, scholarships, traineeships, full and partial tuition waivers, Federal Work-Study, institutionally sponsored loans, and career-related internships or fieldwork available. Aid available to part-time students. • Dr. Linda Hatzenbuehler, Dean, 208-236-3287. Fax: 208-236-4000.

Ithaca College, School of Health Sciences and Human Performance, Ithaca, NY 14850-7020. Awards MS. Part-time and evening/weekend programs available. Faculty: 25 full-time (10 women). Students: 167 full-time (130 women), 3 part-time (all women); includes 6 minority (1 Asian American, 5 Hispanics), 5 international. Average age 24. 177 applicants, 46% accepted. In 1997, 114 degrees awarded. *Degree requirements:* Thesis optional, foreign language not required. *Entrance requirements:* TOEFL (minimum score 550). *Tuition:* $552 per credit hour. *Financial aid:* In 1997–98, 138 students received aid, including 38 graduate assistantships (19 to first-year students) totaling $301,044; career-related internships or fieldwork also available. Financial aid applicants required to submit CSS PROFILE or FAFSA. • Dr. Richard Miller, Dean, 607-274-3100. Fax: 607-244-1137.

Kirksville College of Osteopathic Medicine, Arizona School of Health Sciences, PO Box 11037, Phoenix, AZ 85061-1037. Offers programs in occupational therapy (MS), physical therapy (MS), physician assistant (MS), sports health care (MS). Faculty: 30 full-time (18 women), 14 part-time (8 women). Students: 343 full-time (215 women); includes 26 minority (2 African Americans, 13 Asian Americans, 8 Hispanics, 3 Native Americans). Average age 29. 702 applicants, 20% accepted. In 1997, 41 degrees awarded (100% found work related to degree). *Degree requirements:* Thesis required, foreign language not required. *Average time to degree:* master's–2 years full-time. *Entrance requirements:* GRE General Test (combined average 1639 on three sections), MCAT (average 25 for physician assistant). Application deadline: 2/1 (rolling processing). Application fee: $50. *Tuition:* $15,990 per year. *Financial aid:* 302 students received aid; Federal Work-Study and career-related internships or fieldwork available. Financial aid application deadline: 6/1; applicants required to submit FAFSA. • Dr. James Dearing, Associate Dean, 602-841-4077. Fax: 602-841-4092. Application contact: Stephanie Seyer, Assistant Director of Admissions, 660-626-2237. Fax: 660-626-2815.

Loma Linda University, School of Allied Health Professions, Loma Linda, CA 92350. Awards MPT, DPT. Faculty: 17 full-time (8 women), 14 part-time (9 women). Students: 92 full-time (41 women), 16 part-time (11 women); includes 34 minority (4 African Americans, 17 Asian Americans, 13 Hispanics). 485 applicants, 46% accepted. In 1997, 105 master's awarded. *Application deadline:* rolling. *Application fee:* $50. *Tuition:* $380 per unit. • Dr. Joyce Hopp, Dean, 909-824-4545. Application contact: Helen Greenwood, Director, Admissions and Records, 909-824-4599. Fax: 909-824-4809. E-mail: hgreenwood@sahp.llu.edu.

Long Island University, C.W. Post Campus, School of Health Professions, Brookville, NY 11548-1300. Awards MS, Certificate. Part-time and evening/weekend programs available. Faculty: 12 full-time (8 women), 19 part-time (11 women). Students: 29 full-time (25 women), 96 part-time (69 women). Average age 30. 163 applicants, 56% accepted. In 1997, 29 master's, 20 Certificates awarded. *Degree requirements:* For master's, computer language, thesis required, foreign language not required. *Average time to degree:* master's–2 years full-time, 4 years part-time. *Entrance requirements:* For master's, TOEFL (minimum score 500). Application deadline: rolling. Application fee: $30. Electronic applications accepted. *Expenses:* Tuition $480 per credit. Fees $316 per year full-time, $71 per semester (minimum) part-time. *Financial aid:* In 1997–98, 45 students received aid, including 4 fellowships totaling $12,120, 6 teaching assistantships (3 to first-year students) averaging $300 per month and totaling $15,000; assistantships, partial tuition waivers, Federal Work-Study, institutionally sponsored loans, and career-related internships or fieldwork also available. Aid available to part-time students. Financial aid application deadline: 5/15; applicants required to submit FAFSA. • Stephen Gross, Dean, 516-299-2485. E-mail: smgross@hornet.liunet.edu. Application contact: Robin Steadman, Graduate Adviser, 516-299-2337.

Louisiana State University Medical Center, School of Allied Health Professions, Program in Health Science, 433 Bolivar Street, New Orleans, LA 70112-2223. Offers clinical concepts (MHS), education (MHS), management administration (MHS). Part-time and evening/weekend programs available. Students: 45 part-time (29 women); includes 4 minority (2 African Americans, 2 Hispanics). In 1997, 5 degrees awarded. *Degree requirements:* Thesis optional. *Average time to degree:* master's–4 years part-time. *Entrance requirements:* GRE General Test (minimum combined score of 1500 on three sections), minimum GPA of 2.5. Application deadline: 6/15 (11/15 for spring admission). Application fee: $50. *Expenses:* Tuition $2878 per year full-time, $421 per semester (minimum) part-time for state residents; $6003 per year full-time, $838 per semester (minimum) part-time for nonresidents. Fees $350 per year full-time, $90 per semester (minimum) part-time. • Dr. A. Carter Lewis, Associate Dean of Graduate Studies, 504-568-4243. Application contact: Joan Schuman, Office of Student Affairs, 504-568-4254. Fax: 504-568-4949. E-mail: alhpjbs@lsumc.edu.

Mankato State University, College of Allied Health and Nursing, South Rd and Ellis Ave, PO Box 8400, Mankato, MN 56002-8400. Awards MA, MS, MSN, MT, SP. Part-time programs available. Faculty: 46 full-time (31 women), 1 (woman) part-time. Students: 165 full-time (110 women), 84 part-time (64 women); includes 22 minority (15 African Americans, 3 Asian Americans, 3 Hispanics, 1 Native American), 6 international. Average age 33. 168 applicants, 65% accepted. In 1997, 68 master's awarded. *Degree requirements:* For master's, comprehensive exam; for SP, thesis required, foreign language not required. *Entrance requirements:* For master's, minimum GPA of 3.0 during previous 2 years; for SP, GRE General Test, minimum GPA of 3.0. Application deadline: 7/10 (priority date; rolling processing; 10/30 for spring admission). Application fee: $20. *Tuition:* $126 per credit (minimum) for state residents; $200 per credit for nonresidents. *Financial aid:* Research assistantships, teaching assistantships, Federal Work-Study, institutionally sponsored loans, and career-related internships or fieldwork available. Aid available to part-time students. Financial aid application deadline: 3/15; applicants required to submit FAFSA. • Dr. Cheryl Samuels, Dean, 507-389-6315. Application contact: Joni Roberts, Admissions Coordinator, 507-389-2321. Fax: 507-389-5974. E-mail: grad@mankato.msus.edu.

Marymount University, School of Health Professions, Arlington, VA 22207-4299. Awards MS, MSN. Part-time and evening/weekend programs available. Students: 159. In 1997, 40 degrees awarded. *Application deadline:* rolling. *Application fee:* $35. *Expenses:* Tuition $465 per credit hour. Fees $120 per year full-time, $5 per credit hour part-time. *Financial aid:* Research assistantships and career-related internships or fieldwork available. Aid available to part-time students. Financial aid applicants required to submit FAFSA. • Dr. Catherine Connelly, Dean, 703-284-1580. Fax: 703-284-3819. E-mail: catherine.connelly@marymount.edu.

Medical College of Georgia, Program in Allied Health Sciences, Augusta, GA 30912-1500. Offers allied health sciences (MS), health information management (MHE). Faculty: 8 full-time (6 women). Students: 2 part-time (1 woman). Average age 43. 1 applicant, 0% accepted. *Entrance requirements:* GRE General Test (minimum combined score of 1000), TOEFL (minimum score 600). Application deadline: 6/30 (priority date; rolling processing). Application fee: $0. *Expenses:* Tuition $2670 per year full-time, $111 per credit part-time for state residents; $10,680 per year full-time, $445 per credit part-time for nonresidents. Fees $286 per year. *Financial aid:* Federal Work-Study, institutionally sponsored loans available. Financial aid application deadline: 5/1. • Dr. Nancy D. Prendergast, Associate Dean, 706-721-2621. E-mail: nprender@mail.mcg.edu. Application contact: Dr. Gary C. Bond, Associate Dean, 706-721-3278. Fax: 706-721-6829. E-mail: gradstud@mail.mcg.edu.

Medical College of Ohio, School of Allied Health, Toledo, OH 43699-0008. Awards MOT, MS, MSBS, Certificate. Part-time programs available. In 1997, 34 degrees awarded. *Degree requirements:* Scholarly project required, foreign language not required. *Entrance requirements:* GRE General Test, minimum undergraduate GPA of 3.0. Application fee: $30. *Financial aid:* Scholarships, Federal Work-Study, institutionally sponsored loans available. Financial aid applicants required to submit FAFSA. • Dr. Christopher Bork, Dean, 419-383-4234. E-mail: mcogradschool@mco.edu. Application contact: Theresa Langenderfer, Secretary, 419-383-4160. Fax: 419-383-6140. E-mail: mcogradschool@mco.edu.

Medical University of South Carolina, College of Health Professions, Charleston, SC 29425-0002. Awards MHA, MHS, MS, MSR, DHA, Certificate, MHA/MHS. Part-time and evening/weekend programs available. Postbaccalaureate distance learning degree programs offered (minimal on-campus study). Faculty: 46 full-time (25 women), 15 part-time (8 women), 53 FTE. Students: 202 full-time (130 women), 69 part-time (43 women); includes 24 minority (17 African Americans, 4 Asian Americans, 3 Hispanics), 5 international. Average age 32. 176 applicants, 81% accepted. In 1997, 117 master's awarded. *Entrance requirements:* For master's, GRE General Test, interview, minimum GPA of 2.75. Application fee: $55. *Expenses:* Tuition $4072 per year full-time, $221 per semester hour part-time for state residents; $7064 per year full-time, $387 per semester hour part-time for nonresidents. Fees $150 per year (minimum). *Financial aid:* In 1997–98, 260 students received aid, including 1 fellowship, 7 research assistantships (all to first-year students), 2 graduate assistantships (both to first-year students); teaching assistantships, Federal Work-Study, institutionally sponsored loans, and career-related internships or fieldwork also available. Aid available to part-time students. Financial aid application deadline: 4/1; applicants required to submit FAFSA. *Total annual research expenditures:* $398,263. • Dr. Valerie T. West, Interim Dean, 843-792-3328. E-mail: westvt@musc.edu. Application contact: Jerry L. Blackwell, Associate Dean, 843-792-3326. Fax: 843-792-3322. E-mail: blackwjl@musc.edu.

MGH Institute of Health Professions, 101 Merrimac Street, Boston, MA 02114-4719. Awards MS, MSN, Certificate. Part-time and evening/weekend programs available. Faculty: 43 full-time (35 women), 15 part-time (10 women), 48.05 FTE. Students: 269 full-time (232 women), 146 part-time (120 women); includes 26 minority (4 African Americans, 16 Asian Americans, 3 Hispanics, 3 Native Americans), 31 international. Average age 38. 591 applicants, 38% accepted. In 1997, 148 master's awarded (100% found work related to degree). *Entrance requirements:* For master's, GRE General Test. Application fee: $50. *Expenses:* Tuition $20,320 per year full-time, $530 per credit part-time. Fees $300 per year. *Financial aid:* In 1997–98, 253 students received aid, including 35 assistantships, traineeships (4 to first-year students); full and partial tuition waivers and career-related internships or fieldwork also available. Aid available to part-time students. Financial aid application deadline: 3/6; applicants required to submit FAFSA. *Faculty research:* Long-term care, pain mechanisms, communication disorders, patient self-care, disability in the elderly, dyslexia, communication disorders. • Ann W. Caldwell, Interim President, 617-726-8002. Fax: 617-726-3716. E-mail: caldwell.ann@mgh.harvard.edu. Application contact: Office of Student Affairs, 617-726-3140. Fax: 617-726-8010.

Midwestern University, College of Allied Health Professions, Downers Grove, IL 60515-1235. Offers programs in occupational therapy (MOT), physical therapy (MPT), physician assistant studies (MS). Faculty: 21 full-time (16 women), 40 part-time (16 women). Students: 198 full-time (154 women), 44 part-time (28 women); includes 24 minority (2 African Americans, 16 Asian Americans, 5 Hispanics, 1 Native American). Average age 26. *Application deadline:* rolling. *Application fee:* $30. *Financial aid:* Federal Work-Study, institutionally sponsored loans available. • Dr. Stephen Kopp, Dean, 630-515-6388. Application contact: Julie Rosenthall, Director of Admissions, 800-458-6253. Fax: 630-971-6086. E-mail: mwuinfo@mwu.edu.

Northern Arizona University, College of Health Professions, Flagstaff, AZ 86011. Awards MA, MPH, MPT, MS, MSN. Part-time programs available. Faculty: 36 full-time (19 women), 2 part-time (both women). Students: 189 full-time (129 women), 24 part-time (21 women); includes 18 minority (3 Asian Americans, 13 Hispanics, 2 Native Americans), 4 international. 318 applicants, 32% accepted. In 1997, 68 degrees awarded. *Entrance requirements:* Minimum GPA of 3.0. Application fee: $45. *Expenses:* Tuition $2088 per year full-time, $330 per semester (minimum) part-time for state residents; $8004 per year full-time, $1002 per semester

Directory: Allied Health—General

Northern Arizona University (continued)
(minimum) part-time for nonresidents. Fees $72 per year full-time, $18 per semester (minimum) part-time. *Financial aid:* In 1997–98, 3 research assistantships, 28 teaching assistantships, 1 assistantship were awarded; fellowships, full and partial tuition waivers, Federal Work-Study, institutionally sponsored loans, and career-related internships or fieldwork also available. • Dr. Susan Peterson-Mansfield, Interim Dean, 520-523-4331.

Northern Michigan University, College of Nursing and Allied Health Science, Marquette, MI 49855-5301. Awards MA, MSN. Part-time and evening/weekend programs available. Faculty: 12 full-time (8 women), 1 part-time (0 women). Students: 38 full-time (33 women), 50 part-time (all women); includes 2 minority (both Native Americans). 20 applicants, 100% accepted. In 1997, 25 degrees awarded. *Degree requirements:* Thesis or alternative required, foreign language not required. *Entrance requirements:* GRE General Test, minimum GPA of 3.0. Application deadline: (11/1 for spring admission). Application fee: $25. *Expenses:* Tuition $135 per credit hour for state residents; $215 per credit hour for nonresidents. Fees $183 per year full-time, $94 per year (minimum) part-time. *Financial aid:* In 1997–98, 11 graduate assistantships averaging $770 per month were awarded; Federal Work-Study, institutionally sponsored loans, and career-related internships or fieldwork also available. Aid available to part-time students. Financial aid application deadline: 3/1. • Betty J. Hill, Dean, 906-227-2830.

Nova Southeastern University, Health Professions Division, College of Allied Health, Fort Lauderdale, FL 33314-7721. Awards MOT, MPT, Dr OT. Students: 465 full-time (315 women), 6 part-time (all women); includes 89 minority (14 African Americans, 20 Asian Americans, 54 Hispanics, 1 Native American), 1 international. In 1997, 97 master's awarded. *Degree requirements:* For doctorate, dissertation. *Entrance requirements:* For doctorate, GRE General Test (minimum combined score of 1000). Application fee: $50. *Expenses:* Tuition $15,500 per year for state residents; $17,500 per year for nonresidents. Fees $100 per year. *Financial aid:* Teaching assistantships, graduate assistantships, institutionally sponsored loans available. • Dr. Raul Cuadrado, Director, 954-262-1203. Application contact: Carla Straus, Admissions Counselor, 954-262-1100.

Oakland University, School of Health Sciences, Rochester, MI 48309-4401. Awards MPT, MS. Faculty: 9 full-time. Students: 68 full-time (50 women), 60 part-time (38 women); includes 7 minority (2 African Americans, 3 Asian Americans, 2 Hispanics), 9 international. 37 applicants, 81% accepted. In 1997, 61 degrees awarded. *Entrance requirements:* Minimum GPA of 3.0 for unconditional admission. Application deadline: 7/15 (3/15 for spring admission). Application fee: $30. *Expenses:* Tuition $3852 per year full-time, $214 per credit hour part-time for state residents; $8532 per year full-time, $474 per credit hour part-time for nonresidents. Fees $420 per year. *Financial aid:* Fellowships, full tuition waivers, Federal Work-Study, institutionally sponsored loans available. Financial aid application deadline: 3/1; applicants required to submit FAFSA. • Dr. Ronald E. Olson, Dean, 248-370-3562.

The Ohio State University, College of Medicine and Public Health and Graduate School, Graduate Programs in the Basic Medical Sciences, School of Allied Medical Professions, Columbus, OH 43210. Offers program in allied medicine (MS). Part-time programs available. Faculty: 29 full-time (19 women), 13 part-time (4 women). Students: 16 full-time (10 women), 79 part-time (72 women); includes 4 minority (1 African American, 2 Asian Americans, 1 Hispanic), 6 international. Average age 31. 24 applicants, 88% accepted. In 1997, 23 degrees awarded. *Degree requirements:* Thesis or alternative required, foreign language not required. *Entrance requirements:* GRE General Test. Application deadline: 8/15 (rolling processing; 3/1 for spring admission). Application fee: $30 ($40 for international students). *Tuition:* $5472 per year full-time, $554 per quarter (minimum) part-time for state residents; $14,172 per year full-time, $1424 per quarter (minimum) part-time for nonresidents. *Financial aid:* In 1997–98, 10 students received aid, including 1 research assistantship averaging $840 per month, 7 teaching assistantships (2 to first-year students) averaging $840 per month, 2 administrative assistantships, traineeships (both to first-year students) averaging $840 per month; fellowships, Federal Work-Study, institutionally sponsored loans also available. Aid available to part-time students. *Faculty research:* Geriatrics, quality assurance, nutrition, interdisciplinary health care. • Dr. Stephen L. Wilson, Director, 614-292-5645. Application contact: Jill Clutter, Program Coordinator, 614-292-9579. Fax: 614-292-0210. E-mail: clutter.1@osu.edu.

Old Dominion University, College of Health Sciences, Norfolk, VA 23529. Awards MPH, MS, MSN, PhD, Certificate. Part-time programs available. Postbaccalaureate distance learning degree programs offered (no on-campus study). Faculty: 24 full-time (21 women), 18 part-time (11 women), 30 FTE. Students: 277 full-time (206 women), 108 part-time (88 women); includes 56 minority (35 African Americans, 15 Asian Americans, 1 Hispanic, 5 Native Americans), 21 international. Average age 34. In 1997, 175 master's, 1 doctorate awarded. *Degree requirements:* For doctorate, dissertation, comprehensive exams required, foreign language not required. *Entrance requirements:* For doctorate, GMAT (minimum score 500), GRE General Test (minimum combined score of 1100), MAT, minimum GPA of 3.0. Application deadline: rolling. Application fee: $30. Electronic applications accepted. *Expenses:* Tuition $180 per credit hour for state residents; $477 per credit hour for nonresidents. Fees $140 per year full-time, $32 per semester part-time. *Financial aid:* In 1997–98, 181 students received aid, including 2 fellowships (1 to a first-year student) totaling $3,000, 18 research assistantships (5 to first-year students) totaling $140,364, 58 tuition grants (13 to first-year students) totaling $447,450; teaching assistantships, partial tuition waivers, and career-related internships or fieldwork also available. Aid available to part-time students. Financial aid application deadline: 2/15; applicants required to submit FAFSA. *Faculty research:* Health promotion and wellness, health care ethics, health policy. Total annual research expenditures: $196,135. • Dr. Lindsay L. Rettie, Dean, 757-683-4960. Fax: 757-683-5674. E-mail: lrettie@odu.edu.

Quinnipiac College, School of Health Sciences, Hamden, CT 06518-1904. Awards MHS, MS, MSN, MSPT. Part-time and evening/weekend programs available. Faculty: 34 full-time (10 women), 15 part-time (6 women). Students: 133 full-time (81 women), 67 part-time (50 women); includes 23 minority (2 African Americans, 14 Asian Americans, 7 Hispanics). Average age 28. 885 applicants, 13% accepted. In 1997, 55 degrees awarded. *Degree requirements:* Thesis optional. *Average time to degree:* master's–2 years full-time, 4 years part-time. *Application deadline:* rolling. *Application fee:* $45. Electronic applications accepted. *Expenses:* Tuition $395 per credit hour. Fees $380 per year full-time. *Financial aid:* Research assistantships, partial tuition waivers, and career-related internships or fieldwork available. Aid available to part-time students. Financial aid applicants required to submit FAFSA. • Joseph Woods, Dean, 203-281-8674. Fax: 203-281-8706. Application contact: Scott Farber, Director of Graduate Admissions, 203-281-8795. Fax: 203-287-5238. E-mail: qcgradadmi@quinnipiac.edu.

Regis University, School for Healthcare Professions, Denver, CO 80221-1099. Awards MSN, MSPT. Students: 102 full-time (85 women); includes 23 minority (12 African Americans, 2 Asian Americans, 7 Hispanics, 2 Native Americans), 1 international. *Tuition:* $250 per semester hour. *Financial aid:* Nursing internships, Federal Work-Study, and career-related internships or fieldwork available. *Faculty research:* Normal and pathological balance and gait research, normal/pathological upper limb motor control/biomechanics, exercise energy/metabolism research, optical treatment protocols for therapeutic modalities. • Dr. Patricia Ladewig, Academic Dean, 303-458-4174. Application contact: Assistant to the Dean, 303-458-4174. Fax: 303-964-5533. E-mail: aschulz@regis.edu.

Saint Louis University, School of Allied Health Professions, St. Louis, MO 63104. Awards MS, MSPT, MS(R)PT, MPH/MS. Faculty: 11 full-time (8 women), 8 part-time (7 women). Students: 24 full-time (22 women), 43 part-time (38 women); includes 6 minority (3 African Americans, 2 Asian Americans, 1 Hispanic), 7 international. 33 applicants, 76% accepted. In 1997, 7 degrees awarded. *Degree requirements:* Comprehensive oral exam required, foreign language not required. *Entrance requirements:* GRE General Test. Application deadline: 7/1 (rolling processing; 11/1 for spring admission). Application fee: $40. *Tuition:* $542 per credit hour. *Financial aid:* In 1997–98, 4 teaching assistantships were awarded; career-related internships or fieldwork also available. Financial aid application deadline: 4/1. • Dr. Frances Horvath, Dean, 314-577-8501. Application contact: Dr. Marcia Buresch, Assistant Dean of the Graduate School, 314-977-2240. Fax: 314-977-3943.

Seton Hall University, School of Graduate Medical Education, Program in Health Sciences, South Orange, NJ 07079-2697. Awards MS, PhD. Offered jointly with the University of Medicine and Dentistry of New Jersey. *Degree requirements:* For master's, practicum, research project; for doctorate, dissertation, qualifying exam. *Entrance requirements:* TOEFL (minimum score 550), interview, minimum GPA of 3.0. Application deadline: 7/1. *Expenses:* Tuition $500 per credit. Fees $610 per year full-time, $185 per semester part-time. • Application contact: Office of Graduate Medical Education, 973-761-7145. Fax: 973-275-2370. E-mail: gradmeded@shu.edu.

Slippery Rock University of Pennsylvania, College of Human Service Professions, Department of Allied Health, Slippery Rock, PA 16057. Awards MS. Program being phased out; applicants no longer accepted. Part-time and evening/weekend programs available. *Degree requirements:* Thesis. *Tuition:* $4484 per year full-time, $247 per credit part-time for state residents; $7667 per year full-time, $423 per credit part-time for nonresidents. *Faculty research:* Teacher cognition, athletes' nutrition analysis, assessment in management.

Southwest Texas State University, School of Health Professions, San Marcos, TX 78666. Awards MA, MSCDIS, MSHP, MSPT, MSW. Part-time and evening/weekend programs available. Faculty: 33 full-time (18 women), 5 part-time (2 women). Students: 165 full-time (122 women), 134 part-time (92 women); includes 52 minority (10 African Americans, 11 Asian Americans, 30 Hispanics, 1 Native American), 4 international. Average age 30. In 1997, 92 degrees awarded. *Degree requirements:* Comprehensive exam required, foreign language not required. *Entrance requirements:* GRE General Test, TOEFL (minimum score 550). Application deadline: rolling. *Expenses:* Tuition $648 per year full-time, $120 per semester (minimum) part-time for state residents; $4500 per year full-time, $750 per semester (minimum) part-time for nonresidents. Fees $1264 per year full-time, $314 per semester (minimum) part-time. *Financial aid:* Fellowships, research assistantships, teaching assistantships, Federal Work-Study, institutionally sponsored loans, and career-related internships or fieldwork available. Aid available to part-time students. Financial aid application deadline: 4/1; applicants required to submit FAFSA. • Dr. Rumaldo Z. Juarez, Dean, 512-245-3300. Fax: 512-245-3791. E-mail: rj05@swt.edu. Application contact: Dr. J. Michael Willoughby, Dean of the Graduate School, 512-245-2581. Fax: 512-245-8365. E-mail: jw02@swt.edu.

State University of New York at Buffalo, Graduate School, School of Health Related Professions, Buffalo, NY 14260. Awards MS, PhD. Part-time and evening/weekend programs available. Faculty: 28 full-time (14 women), 5 part-time (2 women). Students: 41 full-time (27 women), 38 part-time (32 women); includes 5 minority (1 African American, 4 Asian Americans), 24 international. Average age 28. In 1997, 22 master's awarded. Terminal master's awarded for partial completion of doctoral program. *Degree requirements:* For doctorate, dissertation, comprehensive exam required, foreign language not required. *Entrance requirements:* For master's, TOEFL (minimum score 550); for doctorate, GRE General Test, TOEFL (minimum score 550). Application fee: $35. *Tuition:* $5970 per year full-time, $288 per credit hour part-time for state residents; $9286 per year full-time, $426 per credit hour part-time for nonresidents. *Financial aid:* Fellowships, research assistantships, teaching assistantships, graduate assistantships, full and partial tuition waivers, Federal Work-Study, institutionally sponsored loans, and career-related internships or fieldwork available. *Faculty research:* Biomechanics, nutrition and cancer, rehabilitation, erythrocyte differentiation, assistive technology, exercise science. Total annual research expenditures: $3.51 million. • Dr. Barry S. Eckert, Dean, 716-829-3434. Fax: 716-829-2034.

State University of New York Health Science Center at Syracuse, College of Health Related Professions, Syracuse, NY 13210-2334. Awards MPS, MS. Faculty: 6 full-time (4 women), 4 part-time (3 women), 7.5 FTE. Students: 32 full-time (15 women), 1 (woman) part-time; includes 5 minority (1 African American, 2 Asian Americans, 2 Hispanics). 297 applicants, 11% accepted. *Application deadline:* rolling. *Expenses:* Tuition $5100 per year full-time, $213 per credit hour part-time for state residents; $8416 per year full-time, $351 per credit hour part-time for nonresidents. Fees $405 per year full-time, $108 per semester (minimum) part-time. *Financial aid:* 26 students received aid; Federal Work-Study, institutionally sponsored loans available. Aid available to part-time students. Financial aid applicants required to submit FAFSA. • Dr. Hugh W. Bonner, Dean. Application contact: Jennifer Welch, Director of Admissions, 315-464-4570. Fax: 315-464-8867. E-mail: welchj@vax.cs.hscsyr.edu.

Temple University, Health Sciences Center and Graduate School, College of Allied Health Professions, Philadelphia, PA 19140. Awards MA, MPT, MS, MSN, PhD. Part-time and evening/weekend programs available. Faculty: 39 full-time (30 women). Students: 426 (336 women). 858 applicants, 29% accepted. In 1997, 116 master's, 4 doctorates awarded. *Degree requirements:* For doctorate, dissertation. *Application fee:* $40. *Expenses:* Tuition $323 per semester hour for state residents; $444 per semester hour for nonresidents. Fees $170 per year full-time, $28 per semester (minimum) part-time. *Financial aid:* Fellowships, research assistantships, teaching assistantships, traineeships, partial tuition waivers, Federal Work-Study, institutionally sponsored loans, and career-related internships or fieldwork available. Aid available to part-time students. *Faculty research:* Early intervention, abuse, balance dysfunction, development across life span, administration, clinical expertise. Total annual research expenditures: $145,000. • Amy Hecht, Dean, 215-707-4800.

See in-depth description on page 1263.

Tennessee State University, School of Allied Health Professions, Nashville, TN 37209-1561. Awards M Ed. Part-time and evening/weekend programs available. Faculty: 10 full-time (7 women), 4 part-time (3 women). Students: 63 full-time (60 women), 2 part-time (both women); includes 32 minority (26 African Americans, 5 Asian Americans, 1 Hispanic), 4 international. Average age 25. 232 applicants, 87% accepted. In 1997, 27 degrees awarded. *Average time to degree:* master's–2 years full-time, 4 years part-time. *Entrance requirements:* GRE General Test (minimum combined score of 870), MAT (minimum score 30), minimum GPA of 3.5. Application deadline: rolling. Application fee: $15. Electronic applications accepted. *Tuition:* $2962 per year full-time, $182 per credit hour part-time for state residents; $7788 per year full-time, $393 per credit hour part-time for nonresidents. *Financial aid:* In 1997–98, fellowships averaging $800 per month, 9 research assistantships averaging $800 per month, 4 scholarships averaging $600 per month were awarded. Financial aid application deadline: 3/15. *Faculty research:* Community problems of the elderly; language disorders in children; aphasia; sickle cell disturbances; regional and foreign dialects; oral, tactile, and auditory perception. Total annual research expenditures: $100,775. • Dr. Andrew Bond, Dean, 615-963-5927. Fax: 615-963-5926. Application contact: Dr. Harold R. Mitchell, Head, Department of Speech Pathology and Audiology, 615-963-7009. Fax: 615-963-7119.

Texas Tech University Health Sciences Center, School of Allied Health, Lubbock, TX 79430-0002. Offers programs in communication disorders (MS), physical therapy (MPT). Faculty: 21 full-time (9 women), 2 part-time (1 woman). Students: 229 full-time (148 women); includes 19 minority (2 African Americans, 15 Hispanics, 2 Native Americans). Average age 22. 311 applicants, 27% accepted. In 1997, 79 degrees awarded (100% found work related to degree). *Average time to degree:* master's–2 years full-time. *Application fee:* $30. *Expenses:* Tuition $36 per credit hour for state residents; $249 per credit hour for nonresidents. Fees $1348 per year full-time for state residents; $1349 per year full-time for nonresidents. *Financial aid:* Fellowships, research assistantships, teaching assistantships, full tuition waivers, and career-related internships or fieldwork available. Financial aid application deadline: 9/1. • Dr. Hal S. Larsen, Interim Dean, 806-743-3247. E-mail: alhhsl@ttuhsc.edu. Application contact: Rob Shive, Assistant Dean, Admissions and Student Affairs, 806-743-3220. Fax: 806-743-3249. E-mail: sahras@ttuhsc.edu.

Announcement: The Health Sciences Center works as a partner with Texas Tech University to provide high-quality education and clinical instruction for those who wish to achieve the baccalaureate and master's degrees in the health professions. Together, Texas Tech University and Texas Tech University Health Sciences Center, a premier center of higher education in Texas, serve the citizens of west Texas.

Towson University, Program in Health Sciences, Towson, MD 21252-0001. Offers allied health professions (MS). Part-time and evening/weekend programs available. Faculty: 9 full-time (7 women). Students: 10 full-time (all women), 106 part-time (91 women); includes 22 minority (21 African Americans, 1 Hispanic), 2 international. In 1997, 28 degrees awarded. *Degree requirements:* Thesis optional, foreign language not required. *Entrance requirements:* Previous course work in health sciences. Application deadline: 3/1 (priority date; rolling processing; 10/1 for spring admission). Application fee: $40. *Expenses:* Tuition $187 per credit hour for state residents; $364 per credit hour for nonresidents. Fees $40 per credit hour. *Financial aid:* Assistantships, Federal Work-Study available. Financial aid application deadline: 4/1; applicants required to submit FAFSA. *Faculty research:* Issues of the aging, drug and alcohol use prevention, health education, health policy, adolescent/student health. • Dr. Susan Radius, Director, 410-830-4216. Fax: 410-830-3434. E-mail: sradius@towson.edu. Application contact: Fran Musotto, Office Manager, 410-830-2501. Fax: 410-830-4675. E-mail: fmusotto@towson.edu.

The University of Alabama at Birmingham, Graduate School, School of Health Related Professions, Birmingham, AL 35294. Awards MNA, MS, MSCLS, MSHA, PhD, Certificate. Students: 357 full-time (211 women), 58 part-time (31 women); includes 53 minority (26 African Americans, 17 Asian Americans, 7 Hispanics, 3 Native Americans). 317 applicants, 86% accepted. In 1997, 122 master's, 6 doctorates, 20 Certificates awarded. *Degree requirements:* For doctorate, dissertation. *Application deadline:* rolling. *Application fee:* $30 ($60 for international students). Electronic applications accepted. *Expenses:* Tuition $129 per credit hour for state residents; $258 per credit hour for nonresidents. Fees $627 per year (minimum) full-time, $110 per quarter (minimum) part-time. *Financial aid:* Fellowships, research assistantships, teaching assistantships, assistantships, Federal Work-Study, institutionally sponsored loans, and career-related internships or fieldwork available. Aid available to part-time students. • Dr. Charles L. Joiner, Dean, 205-934-5149.

University of Connecticut, School of Allied Health Professions, Storrs, CT 06269. Awards MS. Faculty: 15. Students: 16 full-time (12 women), 21 part-time (17 women); includes 5 international. Average age 33. 18 applicants, 78% accepted. In 1997, 13 degrees awarded. *Entrance requirements:* GRE General Test. Application deadline: 6/1 (priority date; rolling processing; 11/1 for spring admission). Application fee: $40 ($45 for international students). *Expenses:* Tuition $5272 per year full-time, $293 per credit part-time for state residents; $13,696 per year full-time, $761 per credit part-time for nonresidents. Fees $948 per year full-time, $640 per year part-time. *Financial aid:* In 1997–98, 7 research assistantships (3 to first-year students) totaling $64,125, 7 teaching assistantships (2 to first-year students) totaling $73,744 were awarded; fellowships also available. Financial aid application deadline: 2/15. • Joseph W. Smey, Dean, 860-486-4734. Application contact: Pouran Faghri, Chairperson, 860-486-0018.

University of Detroit Mercy, College of Health Professions, Detroit, MI 48219-0900. Awards MS. *Entrance requirements:* GRE General Test (minimum combined score of 1200), minimum GPA of 3.0. Application fee: $25. *Faculty research:* Research design, respiratory physiology, AIDS prevention, adolescent health, community, low income health education.

University of Florida, College of Health Professions, Gainesville, FL 32611. Awards MHA, MHS, MPT, Au D, PhD, MBA/MHA. Part-time programs available. Faculty: 65. Students: 130 full-time (89 women), 68 part-time (43 women); includes 11 African Americans, 13 Asian Americans, 17 Hispanics, 8 international. 283 applicants, 18% accepted. In 1997, 76 master's, 12 doctorates awarded. *Degree requirements:* For doctorate, dissertation required, foreign language not required. *Entrance requirements:* For master's, GRE General Test; for doctorate, GRE General Test, minimum GPA of 3.0. Application deadline: rolling. Application fee: $20. *Tuition:* $138 per credit hour for state residents; $481 per credit hour for nonresidents. *Financial aid:* In 1997–98, 64 students received aid, including 12 fellowships averaging $808 per month, 20 research assistantships averaging $600 per month, 3 teaching assistantships averaging $750 per month, 29 graduate assistantships averaging $604 per month; Federal Work-Study, institutionally sponsored loans, and career-related internships or fieldwork also available. Aid available to part-time students. • Dr. Robert Frank, Dean, 352-392-2631. E-mail: robert-frank@ufl.edu. Application contact: Dr. Stephanie Hanson, Associate Dean, 352-846-2379. Fax: 352-392-6529. E-mail: shanson@hp.ufl.edu.

University of Illinois at Chicago, College of Associated Health Professions, Chicago, IL 60607-7128. Awards MAMS, MS, PhD. Part-time programs available. Faculty: 43 full-time (26 women), 8 part-time (5 women). Students: 71 full-time (52 women), 105 part-time (73 women); includes 26 minority (4 African Americans, 12 Asian Americans, 9 Hispanics, 1 Native American), 19 international. Average age 31. 192 applicants, 47% accepted. In 1997, 52 master's awarded. *Degree requirements:* For doctorate, dissertation. *Entrance requirements:* For master's, GRE General Test, TOEFL (minimum score 550), minimum GPA of 3.75 on a 5.0 scale. Application fee: $40 ($50 for international students). *Financial aid:* Fellowships, research assistantships, teaching assistantships, traineeships, full and partial tuition waivers, Federal Work-Study, institutionally sponsored loans, and career-related internships or fieldwork available. *Faculty research:* Care of the elderly, nutritional status for various diseases, immunohematology, computer-aided graphics. • Leopold Selker, Dean, 312-996-6697.

University of Kansas, School of Allied Health, Kansas City, KS 66160. Awards MA, MS, PhD. Part-time programs available. Faculty: 39 full-time (27 women), 10 part-time (all women). Students: 187 full-time (136 women), 51 part-time (45 women); includes 14 minority (2 African Americans, 4 Asian Americans, 4 Hispanics, 4 Native Americans), 2 international. Average age 29. 482 applicants, 26% accepted. In 1997, 83 master's awarded. Terminal master's awarded for partial completion of doctoral program. *Degree requirements:* For master's, thesis required, foreign language not required; for doctorate, dissertation, comprehensive oral exam. *Entrance requirements:* For master's, TOEFL (minimum score 570); for doctorate, GRE, TOEFL (minimum score 570). Application fee: $25. *Expenses:* Tuition $2400 per year full-time, $100 per credit hour part-time for state residents; $7890 per year full-time, $329 per credit hour part-time for nonresidents. Fees $428 per year full-time, $31 per credit hour part-time. *Financial aid:* 156 students received aid; fellowships, research assistantships, teaching assistantships, traineeships, Federal Work-Study, institutionally sponsored loans, and career-related internships or fieldwork available. Aid available to part-time students. Financial aid application deadline: 4/3; applicants required to submit FAFSA. • Dr. Karen Miller, Dean, 913-588-5235. Application contact: Moffett Ferguson, Student Affairs Coordinator, 913-588-5235. Fax: 913-588-5254. E-mail: mfergus@kumc.edu.

University of Kentucky, Graduate School Programs from the College of Allied Health, Lexington, KY 40506-0032. Awards MSCD, MSCNU, MSHP, MSPT, MSRMP. Part-time programs available. Faculty: 20 full-time (8 women), 1 part-time (0 women). Students: 185 full-time (134 women), 15 part-time (12 women); includes 7 minority (5 African Americans, 1 Asian American, 1 Hispanic), 3 international. 118 applicants, 75% accepted. In 1997, 93 degrees awarded. *Degree requirements:* Comprehensive exam required, foreign language not required. *Entrance requirements:* GRE General Test, minimum undergraduate GPA of 2.5. Application deadline: 7/19 (rolling processing). Application fee: $30 ($35 for international students). *Financial aid:* In 1997–98, 7 fellowships, 1 research assistantship were awarded; teaching assistantships, Federal Work-Study, institutionally sponsored loans, and career-related internships or fieldwork also available. Aid available to part-time students. • Dr. Thomas Robinson, Dean, 606-233-6003. Application contact: Dr. Constance L. Wood, Associate Dean, 606-257-4613. Fax: 606-323-1928.

University of Louisville, School of Allied Health Sciences, Louisville, KY 40292-0001. Awards MA. Faculty: 21 full-time (17 women), 6 part-time (4 women), 23 FTE. Students: 36 full-time (33 women), 1 (woman) part-time; includes 3 minority (2 African Americans, 1 Hispanic). Average age 28. In 1997, 12 degrees awarded. *Entrance requirements:* GRE General Test. Application deadline: rolling. Application fee: $25. • Alfred Thompson, Interim Dean, 502-852-5299.

University of Massachusetts Lowell, College of Health Professions, 1 University Avenue, Lowell, MA 01854-2881. Awards MS, PhD. Part-time programs available. Faculty: 36 full-time (27 women). Students: 150 full-time (107 women), 179 part-time (148 women); includes 13 minority (4 African Americans, 7 Asian Americans, 2 Hispanics), 8 international. 453 applicants, 34% accepted. In 1997, 98 master's awarded. *Degree requirements:* For master's, thesis optional, foreign language not required; for doctorate, dissertation. *Entrance requirements:* GRE General Test. Application deadline: rolling. Application fee: $20 ($35 for international students). *Tuition:* $4867 per year full-time, $618 per semester (minimum) part-time for state residents; $10,276 per year full-time, $1294 per semester (minimum) part-time for nonresidents. *Financial aid:* In 1997–98, 28 fellowships, 49 teaching assistantships were awarded; Federal Work-Study, institutionally sponsored loans, and career-related internships or fieldwork also available. Aid available to part-time students. • Dr. Janice Stecchi, Dean, 978-934-4510.

University of Medicine and Dentistry of New Jersey, School of Health Related Professions, Newark, NJ 07107-3001. Offers programs in biomedical informatics (MS, PhD), clinical nutrition (MS), dietetic internship (Certificate), health care informatics (Certificate), health professions education (MA), health science (MS), health sciences (PhD), nurse midwifery (Certificate), physical therapy (MPT, MS), physician assistant (MS), psychiatric rehabilitation (MS). MS, PhD (biomedical informatics) offered jointly with New Jersey Institute of Technology; MS, PhD (health science), MS (physician assistant), MA offered jointly with Seton Hall University; MPT offered jointly with Rutgers, The State University of New Jersey, Camden. Part-time programs available. Faculty: 44 full-time (36 women), 15 part-time (10 women), 51.55 FTE. Students: 378 full-time (272 women), 143 part-time (97 women). 1,260 applicants, 27% accepted. In 1997, 67 master's, 34 Certificates awarded. *Degree requirements:* For master's, thesis required (for some programs), foreign language not required. *Entrance requirements:* For master's, GRE; for Certificate, RN license (nurse midwifery). Application deadline: rolling. Application fee: $35. *Financial aid:* Fellowships, research assistantships, teaching assistantships, Federal Work-Study, institutionally sponsored loans available. Financial aid application deadline: 5/1. *Faculty research:* Clinical outcomes. • Dr. David M. Gibson, Dean, 973-972-4276. Application contact: Dr. Laura Nelson, Associate Dean of Academic and Student Services, 973-972-5453. Fax: 973-972-7028. E-mail: shrp.adm@umdnj.edu.

See in-depth description on page 1267.

University of Nebraska Medical Center, School of Allied Health Professions, Omaha, NE 68198-0001. Awards MPA, MPT.

The University of North Carolina at Chapel Hill, School of Medicine and Graduate School, Graduate Programs in Medicine, Department of Medical Allied Health Professions, Chapel Hill, NC 27599. Offers programs in occupational science (MS); physical therapy (MPT, MS), including human movement science (MS), physical therapy (MPT); rehabilitation psychology and counseling (MS); speech and hearing sciences (MS). Faculty: 37 full-time, 19 part-time. Students: 243; includes 39 minority (18 African Americans, 7 Asian Americans, 11 Hispanics, 3 Native Americans), 3 international. 902 applicants, 18% accepted. In 1997, 96 degrees awarded. *Degree requirements:* Comprehensive exam. *Entrance requirements:* GRE General Test, minimum GPA of 3.0. *Expenses:* Tuition $1428 per year for state residents; $10,414 per year for nonresidents. Fees $782 per year. *Financial aid:* In 1997–98, 33 fellowships (15 to first-year students), 8 research assistantships, 3 graduate assistantships (2 to first-year students) were awarded; teaching assistantships, Federal Work-Study, institutionally sponsored loans, and career-related internships or fieldwork also available. Financial aid applicants required to submit FAFSA. • Dr. David Yoder, Chairman, 919-966-9040. Fax: 919-966-3678. E-mail: dyoder@css.unc.edu.

University of North Florida, College of Health, Jacksonville, FL 32224-2645. Offers programs in addictions counseling (MS), advanced practice nursing (MSN), aging studies (Certificate), employee health services (MS), health administration (MHA), health care administration (MS), human ecology and nutrition (MS), human performance (MS). MSN new for fall 1998. Faculty: 14 full-time (9 women). Students: 39 full-time (31 women), 105 part-time (79 women); includes 28 minority (13 African Americans, 9 Asian Americans, 5 Hispanics, 1 Native American), 1 international. Average age 33. 32 applicants, 97% accepted. In 1997, 26 master's awarded. *Entrance requirements:* For master's, GMAT (MHA), GRE General Test (MS), minimum GPA of 3.0. Application deadline: rolling. Application fee: $20. *Tuition:* $3388 per year full-time, $141 per credit hour part-time for state residents; $11,634 per year full-time, $485 per credit hour part-time for nonresidents. *Financial aid:* Research assistantships and career-related internships or fieldwork available. *Faculty research:* Adolescent substance abuse. • Dr. Joan Farrell, Dean, 904-646-2840.

University of Oklahoma Health Sciences Center, College of Allied Health, Oklahoma City, OK 73190. Awards MS, PhD, Certificate. Part-time programs available. Faculty: 38 full-time (21 women), 22 part-time (15 women). Students: 92 full-time (79 women), 32 part-time (25 women); includes 10 minority (1 African American, 1 Asian American, 8 Native Americans), 4 international. Average age 23. 153 applicants, 44% accepted. In 1997, 46 master's awarded. Terminal master's awarded for partial completion of doctoral program. *Degree requirements:* For master's, comprehensive exam required, thesis optional, foreign language not required; for doctorate, 1 foreign language, computer language, dissertation, oral and written comprehensive exam. *Entrance requirements:* For master's and doctorate, GRE General Test, TOEFL (minimum score 550). Application deadline: 7/1 (priority date; 12/1 for spring admission). Application fee: $25 ($50 for international students). *Financial aid:* Fellowships, traineeships, Federal Work-Study, institutionally sponsored loans, and career-related internships or fieldwork available. Aid available to part-time students. • Dr. Carole Sullivan, Dean.

University of Puerto Rico, Medical Sciences Campus, College of Health Related Professions, San Juan, PR 00936-5067. Awards MS. Part-time programs available. *Degree requirements:* 1 foreign language. *Average time to degree:* master's–2 years full-time, 4 years part-time. *Entrance requirements:* PAEG (minimum score 295; average 521), interview. Application deadline: 2/15 (priority date; rolling processing). Application fee: $15. *Faculty research:* Infantile autism, aphasia, language problems, toxicology, immuno-hematology.

University of South Alabama, College of Allied Health Professions, Mobile, AL 36688-0002. Awards MHS, MS, PhD. Faculty: 8 full-time (2 women). Students: 101 full-time (65 women), 18 part-time (15 women); includes 10 minority (4 African Americans, 3 Asian Americans, 2 Hispanics, 1 Native American). 116 applicants, 27% accepted. In 1997, 18 master's, 1 doctorate awarded. *Degree requirements:* For master's, externship required, thesis optional, foreign language not required; for doctorate, dissertation, clinical internship required, foreign language not required. *Entrance requirements:* For master's, GRE General Test (minimum combined score of 1000). Application deadline: 9/1 (priority date; rolling processing). Application fee: $25. *Financial aid:* In 1997–98, 7 fellowships, 1 research assistantship were awarded; career-related internships or fieldwork also available. Aid available to part-time students. Financial aid application deadline: 4/1. • Dr. Patsy Covey, Dean, 334-380-2785. Application contact: Dr. Stephen Hood, Director of Graduate Studies, 334-380-2600.

University of South Dakota, School of Medicine and Graduate School, Graduate Programs in Health Sciences, Vermillion, SD 57069-2390. Offerings in occupational therapy (MS), physical therapy (MS). Faculty: 8 full-time (5 women), 5 part-time (all women). Students: 129 full-time (100 women). Average age 25. 331 applicants, 16% accepted. In 1997, 52 degrees awarded (100% found work related to degree). *Average time to degree:* master's–2.2 years full-time. *Entrance requirements:* GRE General Test, GRE Subject Test. Application fee: $15. *Financial aid:* Career-related internships or fieldwork available. • Dr. Frank Brady, Dean, 605-677-6572. Fax: 605-677-6569. Application contact: Dr. Charles N. Kaufman, Dean of the Graduate School, 605-677-6498.

Directories: Allied Health—General; Clinical Laboratory Sciences

University of Southern California, Graduate School, School of Health Affairs, Los Angeles, CA 90089. Awards MA, MS, DPT, PhD, Certificate, MBA/MS. Students: 468 full-time (343 women), 59 part-time (45 women); includes 163 minority (10 African Americans, 128 Asian Americans, 23 Hispanics, 2 Native Americans), 13 international. Average age 33. 465 applicants, 39% accepted. In 1997, 79 master's, 11 doctorates awarded. *Degree requirements:* For doctorate, dissertation. *Entrance requirements:* For master's and doctorate, GRE General Test. Application fee: $55. *Expenses:* Tuition $16,944 per year full-time, $706 per unit part-time. Fees $414 per year full-time, $32 per year part-time. *Financial aid:* In 1997–98, 73 fellowships, 3 research assistantships, 36 teaching assistantships, 18 scholarships were awarded; Federal Work-Study, institutionally sponsored loans also available. Aid available to part-time students. Financial aid application deadline: 2/15; applicants required to submit FAFSA. • Joseph P. Van Der Meulen, Vice President, 213-342-2077.

University of Tennessee, Memphis, College of Allied Health Sciences, Memphis, TN 38163-0002. Awards MSPT. *Degree requirements:* Thesis.

The University of Texas at El Paso, College of Nursing and Health Science, Department of Health Sciences, 500 West University Avenue, El Paso, TX 79968-0001. Awards MS. *Entrance requirements:* GRE General Test, TOEFL (minimum score 550), course work in statistics. Application deadline: 7/1 (priority date; rolling processing; 11/1 for spring admission). Application fee: $15 ($65 for international students). *Tuition:* $2063 per year full-time, $284 per credit hour part-time for state residents; $5753 per year full-time, $425 per credit hour part-time for nonresidents.

The University of Texas Medical Branch at Galveston, School of Allied Health Sciences, Galveston, TX 77555. Awards MPT. Faculty: 9 full-time (7 women). Students: 120 full-time (105 women); includes 18 minority (1 African American, 7 Asian Americans, 10 Hispanics). Average age 25. 275 applicants, 13% accepted. In 1997, 40 degrees awarded (100% found work related to degree). *Degree requirements:* Thesis or alternative required, foreign language not required. *Average time to degree:* master's–2.5 years full-time. *Entrance requirements:* Health Occupations Aptitude Examination, experience in field, minimum GPA of 3.0. Application deadline: 11/1. Application fee: $30. *Expenses:* Tuition $36 per credit hour for state residents; $249 per credit hour for nonresidents. Fees $146 per year full-time, $124 per semester (minimum) part-time. *Financial aid:* 70 students received aid; Federal Work-Study, institutionally sponsored loans, and career-related internships or fieldwork available. *Faculty research:* Clinical education, educational outcomes, movement analysis, biomechanics, cardiorespiratory fitness. Total annual research expenditures: $120,000. • Dr. Charles Christiansen, Dean, 409-772-3001. Application contact: Richard Lewis, Registrar, 409-772-1215. Fax: 409-772-5056.

The University of Texas Medical Branch at Galveston, Graduate School of Biomedical Sciences, Program in Allied Health Sciences, Galveston, TX 77555. Offers clinical gerontology (MS), health education and promotion (MS). Part-time programs available. Faculty: 15 full-time (4 women). Students: 9 full-time (6 women), 9 part-time (6 women); includes 10 minority (3 African Americans, 1 Asian American, 5 Hispanics, 1 Native American), 1 international. Average age 33. 10 applicants, 70% accepted. In 1997, 4 degrees awarded (50% found work related to degree, 50% continued full-time study). *Degree requirements:* Thesis or alternative required, foreign language not required. *Entrance requirements:* GRE General Test (minimum combined score of 1100). Application deadline: 8/15 (rolling processing). Application fee: $25 ($50 for international students). *Expenses:* Tuition $36 per credit hour for state residents; $249 per credit hour for nonresidents. Fees $146 per year full-time, $124 per semester (minimum) part-time. *Financial aid:* In 1997–98, 5 research assistantships were awarded; Federal Work-Study, institutionally sponsored loans, and career-related internships or fieldwork also available. Aid available to part-time students. Financial aid applicants required to submit FAFSA. *Faculty research:* Health promotion and disease prevention, health and social problems of the aged, health promotion and the aged, minority health. • Dr. David Chiriboga, Director, 409-772-3038. Fax: 409-747-1610. E-mail: dchiribo@utmb.edu.

University of Vermont, School of Allied Health Sciences, Burlington, VT 05405-0160. Awards MS. Part-time programs available. Students: 11. 9 applicants, 33% accepted. In 1997, 1 degree awarded. *Degree requirements:* Thesis required, foreign language not required. *Entrance requirements:* GRE General Test, TOEFL (minimum score 550). Application deadline: 4/1 (priority date; rolling processing). Application fee: $25. *Expenses:* Tuition $302 per credit for state residents; $755 per credit for nonresidents. Fees $434 per year full-time, $46 per semester (minimum) part-time. *Financial aid:* Fellowships, research assistantships, teaching assistantships, Federal Work-Study available. Financial aid application deadline: 3/1. • Dr. L. McCrorey, Dean, 802-656-3811.

University of Wisconsin–Eau Claire, College of Professional Studies, School of Human Sciences and Services, Division of Allied Health Professions, Eau Claire, WI 54702-4004. Offers program in environmental and public health (MS). Students: 16 full-time (8 women), 5 part-time (1 woman); includes 3 minority (2 African Americans, 1 Asian American). In 1997, 11 degrees awarded. *Degree requirements:* Thesis, oral and written exams required, foreign language not required. *Application deadline:* 3/1 (rolling processing). *Application fee:* $45. *Tuition:* $3651 per year full-time, $611 per semester (minimum) part-time for state residents; $11,295 per year full-time, $1886 per semester (minimum) part-time for nonresidents. *Financial aid:* Federal Work-Study available. Financial aid application deadline: 3/1. • Dr. Dale Taylor, Director, 715-836-2628.

University of Wisconsin–Milwaukee, School of Allied Health Professions, Milwaukee, WI 53201-0413. Awards MS. Part-time programs available. Faculty: 40 full-time (24 women). Students: 53 full-time (47 women), 48 part-time (38 women); includes 8 minority (3 African Americans, 4 Asian Americans, 1 Native American), 3 international. 115 applicants, 46% accepted. In 1997, 18 degrees awarded. *Application deadline:* 1/1 (priority date; rolling processing; 9/1 for spring admission). *Application fee:* $45 ($75 for international students). *Tuition:* $4996 per year full-time, $1030 per semester (minimum) part-time for state residents; $15,216 per year full-time, $2947 per semester (minimum) part-time for nonresidents. *Financial aid:* In 1997–98, 1 research assistantship, 8 teaching assistantships were awarded; fellowships, project assistantships, Federal Work-Study, and career-related internships or fieldwork also available. Aid available to part-time students. Financial aid application deadline: 4/15. • Fred Pairent, Dean, 414-229-4712.

Virginia Commonwealth University, School of Allied Health Professions, Richmond, VA 23284-9005. Awards MHA, MS, MSHA, MSNA, MSOT, PhD, CAS, CPC, JD/MHA. PhD (health related sciences) new for fall 1998. Part-time programs available. Faculty: 73 (30 women). Students: 524. Terminal master's awarded for partial completion of doctoral program. *Application fee:* $30 ($0 for international students). *Tuition:* $4960 per year full-time, $257 per credit part-time for state residents; $12,652 per year full-time, $684 per credit part-time for nonresidents. *Financial aid:* Fellowships, research assistantships, teaching assistantships, full and partial tuition waivers, and career-related internships or fieldwork available. • Dr. Cecil B. Drain, Interim Dean, 804-828-7247. E-mail: cdrain@gems.vcu.edu. Application contact: Dr. Delores Clement, Associate Dean, 804-828-7247. Fax: 804-828-8656. E-mail: dgclemen@vcu.edu.

Washington University in St. Louis, School of Medicine, Graduate Programs in Medicine, St. Louis, MO 63130-4899. Awards MA, MHA, MHS, MSOT, MSPT, PhD, JD/MHA, MBA/MHA, MD/PhD, MD/MHA, MHA/MHRM, MHA/MIM, MHA/MSW. Offerings include health administration (MHA), occupational therapy (MA, MSOT), physical therapy (MHS, MSPT, PhD). Students: 512 full-time, 9 part-time; includes 56 minority (11 African Americans, 38 Asian Americans, 5 Hispanics, 2 Native Americans), 5 international. In 1997, 209 master's awarded. *Degree requirements:* For doctorate, dissertation required, foreign language not required. *Financial aid:* Fellowships, research assistantships, Federal Work-Study, institutionally sponsored loans, and career-related internships or fieldwork available. Aid available to part-time students. Financial aid applicants required to submit FAFSA. • Dr. William A. Peck, Dean, School of Medicine, 314-362-6827. Application contact: Dr. W. Edwin Dodson, Associate Dean, 314-362-6848. Fax: 314-362-4658. E-mail: wumscoa@msnotes.wustl.edu.

Wayne State University, College of Pharmacy and Allied Health Professions, Faculty of Allied Health Professions, Detroit, MI 48202. Awards MS, MSPT. Part-time and evening/weekend programs available. Faculty: 7 full-time (4 women), 22 part-time (5 women), 9 FTE. Students: 84 full-time (52 women), 45 part-time (27 women); includes 7 minority (4 African Americans, 3 Asian Americans), 10 international. Average age 30. 81 applicants, 73% accepted. In 1997, 38 degrees awarded. *Degree requirements:* Thesis optional, foreign language not required. *Application fee:* $20 ($30 for international students). *Expenses:* Tuition $163 per credit hour for state residents; $355 per credit hour for nonresidents. Fees $498 per year full-time, $114 per semester (minimum) part-time. *Financial aid:* Teaching assistantships, scholarships, and career-related internships or fieldwork available. Aid available to part-time students. • Dr. George C. Fuller, Dean, College of Pharmacy and Allied Health Professions, 313-577-1574. Application contact: Dr. Jan Nagwekan, Interim Graduate Officer, 313-577-0820. Fax: 313-577-5589.

Western University of Health Sciences, School of Allied Health Professions, Pomona, CA 91766-1854. Awards MPT, MS, Certificate. Faculty: 66. Students: 233. • Dr. Gary Gugelchuk, Dean, 909-469-5378. Application contact: Susan M. Hanson, Director of Admissions, 909-469-5335.

Wichita State University, College of Health Professions, Wichita, KS 67260. Awards MPH, MPT, MSN, MSN/MBA. Part-time programs available. Faculty: 24 full-time (18 women), 1 part-time (0 women). Students: 110 full-time (81 women), 233 part-time (202 women); includes 22 minority (9 African Americans, 6 Asian Americans, 2 Hispanics, 5 Native Americans), 9 international. Average age 39. 282 applicants, 27% accepted. In 1997, 69 degrees awarded. *Entrance requirements:* GRE, TOEFL. Application deadline: rolling. Application fee: $25 ($40 for international students). Electronic applications accepted. *Expenses:* Tuition $2303 per year full-time, $96 per credit hour part-time for state residents; $7691 per year full-time, $321 per credit hour part-time for nonresidents. Fees $490 per year full-time, $75 per semester (minimum) part-time. *Financial aid:* In 1997–98, 5 research assistantships averaging $849 per month and totaling $20,120, 9 teaching assistantships averaging $564 per month and totaling $33,294, 2 graduate assistantships averaging $417 per month and totaling $7,500 were awarded; full and partial tuition waivers, Federal Work-Study, institutionally sponsored loans, and career-related internships or fieldwork also available. Aid available to part-time students. Financial aid application deadline: 4/1; applicants required to submit FAFSA. • Dr. Michael C. Vincent, Acting Dean, Graduate School, 316-978-3095. E-mail: vincent@twsuvm.uc.twsu.edu. Application contact: Margaret E. Wood, Assistant to the Dean, 316-978-3095. Fax: 316-978-3253. E-mail: mewood@twsuvm.uc.twsu.edu.

Clinical Laboratory Sciences

California State University, Dominguez Hills, School of Health, Department of Clinical Sciences, Carson, CA 90747-0001. Awards MS, Certificate. Accredited by NAACLS. Faculty: 8 full-time (5 women), 7 part-time (2 women). Students: 15 full-time (7 women), 23 part-time (16 women); includes 17 minority (3 African Americans, 12 Asian Americans, 2 Hispanics), 6 international. Average age 32. 25 applicants, 48% accepted. In 1997, 12 master's awarded. *Entrance requirements:* For master's, TOEFL (minimum score 550), minimum GPA of 2.5. Application deadline: 6/1. Application fee: $55. *Expenses:* Tuition $0 for state residents; $246 per unit for nonresidents. Fees $1896 per year full-time, $1230 per year part-time. • Dr. Kathleen McEnerney, Chair, 310-243-3748.

The Catholic University of America, School of Arts and Sciences, Department of Biology, Program in Clinical Laboratory Science, Washington, DC 20064. Awards MS, PhD. Part-time programs available. Students: 2 part-time (1 woman); includes 2 international. Average age 31. 0 applicants. In 1997, 3 master's awarded. *Degree requirements:* For master's, thesis or alternative, comprehensive exam required, foreign language not required; for doctorate, dissertation, comprehensive exam required, foreign language not required. *Entrance requirements:* For master's, GRE General Test, GRE Subject Test, Medical Technology Registry Exam, TOEFL, professional certification; for doctorate, GRE General Test, GRE Subject Test, professional certification. Application deadline: 8/1 (priority date; rolling processing; 12/1 for spring admission). Application fee: $50. *Expenses:* Tuition $17,325 per year full-time, $668 per credit hour part-time. Fees $680 per year full-time, $360 per year part-time. *Financial aid:* Teaching assistantships, full and partial tuition waivers, institutionally sponsored loans, and career-related internships or fieldwork available. Aid available to part-time students. Financial aid application deadline: 2/1. *Faculty research:* Clinical and pathogenic microbiology, toxicology and therapeutic drug monitoring, clinical chemistry, clinical immunology, molecular pathology. • Dr. Barbara J. Howard, Director, 202-319-5270. Fax: 202-319-5721.

Duke University, School of Medicine, Clinical Research Program, Durham, NC 27708-0586. Awards MHS. Students: 14 part-time (6 women). In 1997, 5 degrees awarded. *Entrance requirements:* GRE. *Tuition:* $425 per credit. *Financial aid:* Application deadline 5/1. • Dr. Bill Wilkinson, Director, 919-681-4560. Fax: 919-681-4569.

Finch University of Health Sciences/The Chicago Medical School, School of Related Health Sciences, Department of Clinical Laboratory Science, North Chicago, IL 60064-3095. Awards MS. Accredited by NAACLS. Part-time programs available. Faculty: 3 full-time (all women), 1 (woman) part-time. Students: 14 part-time (9 women); includes 1 international. Average age 32. 6 applicants, 83% accepted. In 1997, 7 degrees awarded (86% found work related to degree, 14% continued full-time study). *Degree requirements:* Computer language, thesis required, foreign language not required. *Average time to degree:* master's–2 years part-time. *Entrance requirements:* TOEFL, minimum GPA of 2.8 in science, 2.5 overall; certified medical technologist. Application deadline: 7/1 (priority date; rolling processing; 2/1 for spring admission). Application fee: $30. *Tuition:* $403 per credit hour. *Financial aid:* Partial tuition waivers, institutionally sponsored loans available. Aid available to part-time students. Financial aid application deadline: 2/1. *Faculty research:* Clinical microbiology, hematology, and chemistry. • Janet M. DeRobertis, Chair, 847-578-3303. Fax: 847-578-3015.

See in-depth description on page 1237.

Indiana State University, College of Arts and Sciences, Department of Life Sciences, Terre Haute, IN 47809-1401. Offerings include clinical laboratory sciences (MS). Department faculty: 28 full-time (5 women), 1 part-time (0 women). *Application deadline:* rolling. *Application fee:* $20. *Tuition:* $143 per credit hour for state residents; $325 per credit hour for nonresidents. • Dr. Charles Amlaner, Chairperson, 812-237-2400.

Johns Hopkins University, School of Hygiene and Public Health, Program in Clinical Investigation, Baltimore, MD 21205. Awards Sc M, PhD. Sc M new for fall 1998. Students: 26 (17 women); includes 5 minority (1 African American, 4 Asian Americans), 1 international. 9 applicants, 100% accepted. In 1997, 2 doctorates awarded. *Degree requirements:* Thesis/dissertation required, foreign language not required. *Entrance requirements:* For doctorate, GRE General Test. Application deadline: 2/1 (rolling processing). Application fee: $60. *Financial aid:* Application deadline 4/15. • Dr. N. Franklin Adkinson Jr., Director, 410-550-2051. Fax: 410-550-2055. Application contact: Linda R. Myers, Director of Admissions, 410-955-3543. Fax: 410-955-0464. E-mail: lmyers@jhsph.edu.

Long Island University, C.W. Post Campus, School of Health Professions, Department of Health Sciences, Program in Clinical Laboratory Management, Brookville, NY 11548-1300. Awards MS. Part-time programs available. Faculty: 4 full-time (1 woman), 9 part-time (5 women), 6 FTE. Students: 8 part-time (7 women). In 1997, 1 degree awarded (100% found work related to degree). *Degree requirements:* Computer language, thesis required, foreign language not required. *Average time to degree:* master's–2 years full-time, 4 years part-time. *Entrance requirements:* TOEFL (minimum score 500), minimum GPA of 2.75 in major. Application deadline: rolling. Application fee: $30. Electronic applications accepted. *Expenses:* Tuition $480 per credit. Fees $316 per year full-time, $71 per semester (minimum) part-time. *Financial aid:* In 1997–98, 2 students received aid, including 1 fellowship totaling $3,000, 1 assistantship averaging $300 per month and totaling $1,200; Federal Work-Study, institutionally sponsored loans also available. Aid available to part-time students. Financial aid application deadline: 5/15. • Dr. Ronald R. Modesto, Co-Chair, 516-299-2762. E-mail: rmodesto@eagle.liunet.edu. Application contact: Robin Steadman, Graduate Adviser, 516-299-2337.

Medical University of South Carolina, College of Health Professions, Department of Medical Laboratory Science, Program in Clinical Laboratory Science, Charleston, SC 29425-0002. Offers cytotechnology (MS). Accredited by NAACLS. Part-time programs available. Faculty: 8 full-time (6 women). *Degree requirements:* Research project. *Entrance requirements:* GRE General Test (minimum combined score of 1000), minimum GPA of 3.0. Application fee: $55. *Expenses:* Tuition $4072 per year full-time, $221 per semester hour part-time for state residents; $7064 per year full-time, $387 per semester hour part-time for nonresidents. Fees $150 per year (minimum). *Financial aid:* 4 students received aid; Federal Work-Study available. Aid available to part-time students. Financial aid application deadline: 4/1; applicants required to submit FAFSA. *Faculty research:* Uterine cancer. • Janice M. Hundley, Chair, Department of Medical Laboratory Science, 843-792-3169. Fax: 843-792-3383. E-mail: hundleyj@musc.edu.

Michigan State University, College of Natural Science, Medical Technology Program, East Lansing, MI 48824-1020. Offerings include clinical laboratory science (MS). Program faculty: 4 (0 women). *Application deadline:* rolling. *Application fee:* $30 ($40 for international students). *Expenses:* Tuition $4609 per year full-time, $223 per credit hour (minimum) part-time for state residents; $8704 per year full-time, $450 per credit hour (minimum) part-time for nonresidents. Fees $576 per year full-time, $476 per year part-time. • Dr. Douglas Estry, Director, 517-353-7800.

Quinnipiac College, School of Health Sciences, Program for Pathologists' Assistant, Hamden, CT 06518-1904. Awards MHS. Faculty: 5 full-time (0 women), 1 part-time (0 women). Students: 27 full-time (14 women); includes 3 minority (1 Asian American, 2 Hispanics). Average age 26. 77 applicants, 19% accepted. In 1997, 13 degrees awarded (100% found work related to degree). *Degree requirements:* Residency required, thesis optional. *Average time to degree:* master's–2 years full-time. *Entrance requirements:* Interview, BS in biomedical science, minimum GPA of 2.8. Application deadline: 2/15. Application fee: $45. *Expenses:* Tuition $395 per credit hour. Fees $380 per year full-time. *Financial aid:* Career-related internships or fieldwork available. Aid available to part-time students. Financial aid application deadline: 3/1; applicants required to submit FAFSA. • Dr. Kenneth Kaloustian, Director, 203-281-8676. Fax: 203-281-8706. E-mail: kaloustian@quinnipiac.edu. Application contact: Scott Farber, Director of Graduate Admissions, 203-281-8795. Fax: 203-287-5238. E-mail: qcgradadmi@quinnipiac.edu.

See in-depth description on page 1253.

Quinnipiac College, School of Health Sciences, Programs in Medical Laboratory Sciences, Hamden, CT 06518-1904. Offerings in biomedical sciences (MHS), laboratory management (MHS), microbiology (MHS). Part-time and evening/weekend programs available. Faculty: 8 full-time (1 woman), 3 part-time (0 women). Students: 3 full-time (all women), 28 part-time (21 women); includes 3 minority (2 Asian Americans, 1 Hispanic). Average age 28. 17 applicants, 76% accepted. In 1997, 8 degrees awarded (100% found work related to degree). *Degree requirements:* Comprehensive exam required, thesis optional. *Average time to degree:* master's–2 years full-time, 4 years part-time. *Entrance requirements:* Minimum GPA of 2.5. Application deadline: rolling. Application fee: $45. Electronic applications accepted. *Expenses:* Tuition $395 per credit hour. Fees $380 per year full-time. *Financial aid:* Career-related internships or fieldwork available. Aid available to part-time students. Financial aid applicants required to submit FAFSA. *Faculty research:* Microbial physiology, fermentation technology. • Dr. Kenneth Kaloustian, Director, 203-281-8676. Fax: 203-281-8706. E-mail: kaloustian@quinnipiac.edu. Application contact: Scott Farber, Director of Graduate Admissions, 203-281-8795. Fax: 203-287-5238. E-mail: qcgradadmi@quinnipiac.edu.

See in-depth description on page 1251.

San Francisco State University, College of Science, Center for Biomedical Laboratory Science, San Francisco, CA 94132-1722. Awards MS. Part-time programs available. *Degree requirements:* Thesis required, foreign language not required. *Entrance requirements:* TOEFL, minimum GPA of 2.5 in last 60 units. Application deadline: 11/30 (priority date; rolling processing). Application fee: $55. *Expenses:* Tuition $0 for state residents; $246 per unit for nonresidents. Fees $1982 per year full-time, $1316 per year part-time. *Faculty research:* Immunology, hematology, microbiology, clinical chemistry, virology.

State University of New York at Buffalo, Graduate School, School of Health Related Professions, Department of Clinical Laboratory Science, Buffalo, NY 14260. Awards MS. Part-time programs available. Faculty: 7 full-time (4 women), 1 (woman) part-time. Students: 14 full-time (7 women), 6 part-time (4 women); includes 2 minority (both Asian Americans), 8 international. Average age 27. 15 applicants, 60% accepted. In 1997, 9 degrees awarded. *Degree requirements:* Thesis or alternative, project required, foreign language not required. *Entrance requirements:* GRE General Test (minimum combined score of 1500), TOEFL (minimum score 550). Application deadline: rolling. Application fee: $35. *Tuition:* $5970 per year full-time, $288 per credit hour part-time for state residents; $9286 per year full-time, $426 per credit hour part-time for nonresidents. *Financial aid:* In 1997–98, 7 students received aid, including 2 research assistantships totaling $8,100, 3 teaching assistantships (all to first-year students) totaling $40,431; full and partial tuition waivers, Federal Work-Study, institutionally sponsored loans, and career-related internships or fieldwork also available. Financial aid application deadline: 5/1. *Faculty research:* Endocrine-immune interaction, tumor immunology, molecular biology, oxidative stress, cell differentiation. • Dr. Stephen T. Koury, Director of Graduate Studies, 716-829-3630 Ext. 107. Fax: 716-829-3601. E-mail: stvkoury@acsu.buffalo.edu.

Universidad de las Américas–Puebla, Division of Graduate Studies, School of Sciences, Program in Clinical Analysis, Cholula 72820, Mexico. Awards MS. Part-time and evening/weekend programs available. Faculty: 4 full-time (2 women), 10 part-time (2 women). Students: 5 full-time (3 women); includes 5 minority (all Hispanics). Average age 27. *Degree requirements:* 1 foreign language, thesis. *Average time to degree:* master's–2.5 years full-time, 3.5 years part-time. *Application deadline:* 7/18 (rolling processing). *Application fee:* $0. *Expenses:* Tuition $5400 per year full-time, $113 per year part-time. Fees $361 per year. *Financial aid:* 5 students received aid; research assistantships available. Aid available to part-time students. Financial aid application deadline: 5/15. *Faculty research:* Clinical techniques, clinical research. Total annual research expenditures: $33,000. • José Luis Sánchez, Coordinator, 22-29-20-67. Fax: 22-29-20-66. E-mail: jluis@mail.udlap.mx. Application contact: Jorge Varela, Dean of Admissions Office, 22-29-20-17. Fax: 22-29-20-18. E-mail: admision@mail.udlap.mx.

Université de Sherbrooke, Faculty of Medicine, Graduate Programs in Medicine, Program in Clinical Science, Sherbrooke, PQ J1K 2R1, Canada. Awards M Sc, PhD. Part-time programs available. *Degree requirements:* Thesis/dissertation. *Application fee:* $30.

The University of Alabama at Birmingham, Graduate School, School of Health Related Professions, Program in Clinical Laboratory Sciences, Birmingham, AL 35294. Awards MSCLS. Students: 6 full-time (5 women), 5 part-time (2 women); includes 1 minority (Asian American). 19 applicants, 53% accepted. In 1997, 3 degrees awarded. *Entrance requirements:* GRE General Test (minimum score 500 on each section), interview. Application fee: $30 ($60 for international students). Electronic applications accepted. *Expenses:* Tuition $129 per credit hour for state residents; $258 per credit hour for nonresidents. Fees $627 per year (minimum) full-time, $110 per quarter (minimum) part-time. *Faculty research:* Computer enhanced instruction, antiphospholipid antibodies, alternate site testing, technology assessment. • Virginia Randolph, Director, 205-934-4863. Fax: 205-975-7302. E-mail: randolpv@admin.shrp.uab.edu.

University of Colorado Health Sciences Center, Programs in Biological and Medical Sciences, Program in Clinical Science, Denver, CO 80262. Awards PhD. *Degree requirements:* Dissertation required, foreign language not required. *Entrance requirements:* GRE General Test, minimum GPA of 2.75. Application deadline: 1/31. Application fee: $30. *Financial aid:* Fellowships, research assistantships, teaching assistantships, Federal Work-Study, institutionally sponsored loans available. Aid available to part-time students. Financial aid application deadline: 3/15. • Dr. James Crapo, Director, 303-398-1436.

University of Illinois at Chicago, College of Associated Health Professions, Program in Medical Laboratory Sciences, Chicago, IL 60607-7128. Awards MS. Part-time programs available. Faculty: 2 full-time (both women). Students: 5 full-time (3 women), 11 part-time (7 women); includes 3 minority (all Asian Americans), 3 international. 11 applicants, 64% accepted. In 1997, 2 degrees awarded. *Degree requirements:* Thesis required, foreign language not required. *Entrance requirements:* GRE General Test, TOEFL (minimum score 550), minimum GPA of 3.75 on a 5.0 scale, medical technologist certification. Application deadline: 7/3 (11/8 for spring admission). Application fee: $40 ($50 for international students). *Financial aid:* In 1997–98, 1 research assistantship was awarded; fellowships, teaching assistantships, full and partial tuition waivers, institutionally sponsored loans also available. *Faculty research:* Platelet metabolism, macrophage function, human pathogenic organism metabolism, transfusion therapy. • June Wencel-Drake, Coordinator, 312-996-6746.

University of Massachusetts Lowell, College of Health Professions, Department of Clinical Laboratory Studies, 1 University Avenue, Lowell, MA 01854-2881. Awards MS. Part-time programs available. Faculty: 9 full-time (4 women). Students: 7 full-time (3 women), 12 part-time (9 women); includes 2 minority (both Asian Americans), 3 international. Average age 27. 7 applicants, 57% accepted. In 1997, 5 degrees awarded. *Degree requirements:* Thesis optional, foreign language not required. *Average time to degree:* master's–2 years full-time, 4 years part-time. *Entrance requirements:* GRE General Test. Application deadline: 4/1 (priority date; rolling processing; 10/1 for spring admission). Application fee: $20 ($35 for international students). *Tuition:* $4867 per year full-time, $618 per semester (minimum) part-time for state residents; $10,276 per year full-time, $1294 per semester (minimum) part-time for nonresidents. *Financial aid:* In 1997–98, 3 teaching assistantships were awarded; Federal Work-Study, institutionally sponsored loans also available. Aid available to part-time students. Financial aid application deadline: 4/1. *Faculty research:* Cardiovascular disease, lipoprotein metabolism, micronutrient evaluation, alcohol metabolism, mycobacterial drug resistance. • Dr. Eugene Rogers, Chair, 978-934-4403. E-mail: eugene_rogers@woods.uml.edu.

University of Minnesota, Twin Cities Campus, Medical School and Graduate School, Graduate Programs in Medicine, Department of Laboratory Medicine and Pathology, Program in Clinical Laboratory Sciences, Minneapolis, MN 55455-0213. Awards MS. Accredited by NAACLS. Part-time programs available. *Degree requirements:* Thesis required, foreign language not required. *Average time to degree:* master's–2 years full-time. *Entrance requirements:* GRE General Test. Application deadline: 1/15 (priority date; rolling processing; 12/15 for spring admission). Application fee: $40 ($50 for international students). *Faculty research:* Bacterial translocation, B cell development, molecular diagnostics, cardiovascular risk factors, extracellular matrix proteins.

Announcement: The MS degree is a multidisciplinary program designed to prepare the medical technology and basic science undergraduate for a career in research and teaching in a specialized area of laboratory medicine. Students can concentrate in clinical chemistry, hematology, immunology, genetics, or microbiology. Teaching experience is also available. The faculty brings together research teams from the University of Minnesota as well as from area hospitals. The great variety of faculty research gives graduate students an extraordinarily broad range of choices for thesis research, including immunology, immunopathology, cancer biology, cancer cytogenetics, molecular genetics, cell biology, and microbiology. Research assistantships are available.

University of Mississippi Medical Center, Program in Clinical Health Sciences, Jackson, MS 39216-4505. Awards MS, PhD. Part-time programs available. Faculty: 22 full-time (11 women). Students: 37 part-time (33 women); includes 5 minority (all African Americans). 25 applicants, 60% accepted. In 1997, 1 master's awarded. Terminal master's awarded for partial completion of doctoral program. *Degree requirements:* For master's, computer language required, thesis optional, foreign language not required; for doctorate, computer language, dissertation required, foreign language not required. *Average time to degree:* master's–2 years part-time. *Entrance requirements:* GRE, 1 year of clinical experience. Application deadline: 4/1. Application fee: $10. *Expenses:* Tuition $2196 per year full-time, $122 per hour part-time for state residents; $3470 per year full-time, $193 per hour part-time for nonresidents. Fees $176 per year. *Financial aid:* Federal Work-Study, institutionally sponsored loans available. Aid available to part-time students. Financial aid application deadline: 4/1. *Faculty research:* Clinical outcomes assessment via qualitative measures; health information systems; experimental laboratory evaluation of materials, drugs, hormones, and techniques used in clinical practice. Total annual research expenditures: $141,944. • Dr. Ben H. Douglas, Assistant Vice Chancellor, 601-984-1195. Application contact: Dr. Billy M. Bishop, Director, Student Services and Records, 601-984-1080. Fax: 601-984-1079. E-mail: bmb@fiona.umsmed.edu.

University of Pittsburgh, School of Health and Rehabilitation Sciences, Interdisciplinary Program in Health and Rehabilitation Sciences, Pittsburgh, PA 15260. Offerings include clinical laboratory sciences (MS). *Entrance requirements:* GRE General Test, TOEFL, minimum QPA of 3.0. Application deadline: rolling. Application fee: $30 ($40 for international students). *Expenses:* Tuition $9402 per year full-time, $388 per credit part-time for state residents; $19,372 per year full-time, $799 per credit part-time for nonresidents. Fees $480 per year full-time, $180 per year part-time. • Dr. George Carvell, Associate Dean of Graduate Studies, 412-647-1296. E-mail: shrsadmit+@pitt.edu. Application contact: Shameem Gangjee, Director of Admissions, 412-647-1258. Fax: 412-647-1255. E-mail: shrsadmit+@pitt.edu.

See in-depth description on page 1351.

University of Puerto Rico, Medical Sciences Campus, College of Health Related Professions, Department of Collaborative Medical Programs, Program in Clinical Laboratory Science, San Juan, PR 00936-5067. Awards MS. Part-time programs available. *Degree requirements:* 1 foreign language, computer language, thesis or alternative. *Entrance requirements:* PAEG (minimum score 414; average 568), interview. Application deadline: 2/15 (priority date; rolling processing). Application fee: $15. *Faculty research:* Toxicology, virology, biochemistry, immunohematology, PCR.

University of Rhode Island, College of Continuing Education, Program in Clinical Laboratory Sciences, Kingston, RI 02881. Awards MS. *Entrance requirements:* GRE. Application deadline: 4/15 (priority date; rolling processing). Application fee: $35. *Expenses:* Tuition $3446 per year

University of Rhode Island (continued)
full-time, $191 per credit part-time for state residents; $9850 per year full-time, $547 per credit part-time for nonresidents. Fees $226 per year full-time, $51 per semester (minimum) part-time.

University of Washington, School of Medicine and Graduate School, Graduate Programs in Medicine, Department of Laboratory Medicine, Seattle, WA 98195. Awards MS. Part-time programs available. Faculty: 26 full-time (5 women). Students: 4 full-time (3 women), 6 part-time (4 women); includes 3 minority (all Asian Americans). Average age 34. In 1997, 4 degrees awarded. *Degree requirements:* Thesis required, foreign language not required. *Average time to degree:* master's–2 years full-time, 4.5 years part-time. *Entrance requirements:* GRE General Test, medical technology certification or specialist in an area of laboratory medicine. Application fee: $45. • Vidmantas A. Raisys, Graduate Program Coordinator, 206-548-6131.

University of Wisconsin–Milwaukee, School of Allied Health Professions, Program in Clinical Laboratory Science, Milwaukee, WI 53201-0413. Awards MS. Part-time programs available. Faculty: 19 full-time (8 women). Students: 5 full-time (4 women), 14 part-time (11 women); includes 6 minority (3 African Americans, 3 Asian Americans), 3 international. 18 applicants, 72% accepted. In 1997, 1 degree awarded. *Entrance requirements:* GRE General Test. Application deadline: 1/1 (priority date; rolling processing; 9/1 for spring admission). Application fee: $45 ($75 for international students). *Tuition:* $4996 per year full-time, $1030 per semester (minimum) part-time for state residents; $15,216 per year full-time, $2947 per semester (minimum) part-time for nonresidents. *Financial aid:* In 1997–98, 4 teaching assistantships were awarded; fellowships, research assistantships, project assistantships, and career-related internships or fieldwork also available. Aid available to part-time students. Financial aid application deadline: 4/15. • Randall Lambrecht, Representative, 414-229-2645.

Virginia Commonwealth University, School of Allied Health Professions, Department of Clinical Laboratory Sciences, Richmond, VA 23284-9005. Awards MS. Faculty: 6 (4 women). Students: 10 full-time (5 women), 3 part-time (all women); includes 4 minority (1 African American, 1 Asian American, 1 Hispanic, 1 Native American), 4 international. Average age 26. 14 applicants, 71% accepted. In 1997, 3 degrees awarded. *Degree requirements:* 1 foreign language, thesis. *Entrance requirements:* GRE General Test, current medical technologist certification. Application deadline: 7/1. Application fee: $30 ($0 for international students). *Tuition:* $4960 per year full-time, $257 per credit part-time for state residents; $12,652 per year full-time, $684 per credit part-time for nonresidents. *Faculty research:* Educational outcomes assessment, virtual instrumentation development, cost-effective treatment of bacteremia using third generation cephalosporins. • Barbara Lindsey, Chair, 804-828-9469. E-mail: blindsey@vcu.edu. Application contact: Terence C. Karselis, Assistant Chair, 804-828-9469. Fax: 804-828-1911. E-mail: tckarsel@vcu.edu.

Wayne State University, College of Pharmacy and Allied Health Professions, Faculty of Allied Health Professions, Department of Clinical Laboratory Sciences, Detroit, MI 48202. Offers program in medical technology (MS). Faculty: 4 full-time (3 women), 1 (woman) part-time. Students: 0. 1 applicant, 0% accepted. *Degree requirements:* Thesis optional, foreign language not required. *Application fee:* $20 ($30 for international students). *Expenses:* Tuition $163 per credit hour for state residents; $355 per credit hour for nonresidents. Fees $498 per year full-time, $114 per semester (minimum) part-time. *Financial aid:* Scholarships available. • Gerald W. Aldridge, Acting Administrative Director, 313-577-1384.

Communication Disorders

Adelphi University, School of Education, Programs in Speech Pathology and Audiology and Education of the Deaf, Garden City, NY 11530. Offerings in communicative disorders (MS, DA), education of the speech and hearing handicapped (MS). Accredited by ASHA. Part-time programs available. Students: 59 full-time (all women), 99 part-time (97 women); includes 11 minority (6 African Americans, 2 Asian Americans, 3 Hispanics), 2 international. Average age 29. In 1997, 52 master's awarded. *Degree requirements:* For master's, comprehensive exam required, foreign language and thesis not required; for doctorate, 1 foreign language, dissertation. *Entrance requirements:* For master's, GRE General Test. Application deadline: 4/15. Application fee: $50. *Expenses:* Tuition $16,000 per year full-time, $485 per credit part-time. Fees $500 per year full-time, $150 per semester part-time. *Financial aid:* Assistantships available. Financial aid application deadline: 3/1. *Faculty research:* Recovery of language in aphasia, stuttering in children, clinical supervisory process. • Dr. Elaine Sands, Chairperson, 516-877-4770.

Alabama Agricultural and Mechanical University, School of Education, Department of Counseling and Special Education, Area in Speech Pathology, PO Box 1357, Normal, AL 35762-1357. Awards M Ed, MS. Part-time programs available. Faculty: 3 full-time (all women). *Degree requirements:* Comprehensive exam required, foreign language and thesis not required. *Entrance requirements:* GRE General Test, minimum GPA of 2.5. Application deadline: 5/1 (priority date; rolling processing). Application fee: $15 ($20 for international students). *Expenses:* Tuition $2782 per year full-time, $565 per semester (minimum) part-time for state residents; $5164 per year full-time, $1015 per semester (minimum) part-time for nonresidents. Fees $560 per year full-time, $390 per year part-time. *Financial aid:* Fellowships, research assistantships, and career-related internships or fieldwork available. Aid available to part-time students. Financial aid application deadline: 4/1. *Faculty research:* Alternative methods of teaching speech and language to handicapped individuals. • Dr. Annie Grace Robinson, Chair, Department of Counseling and Special Education, 205-851-5533.

Appalachian State University, College of Education, Department of Language, Reading and Exceptionalities, Boone, NC 28608. Offerings include speech pathology and audiology (MA). Department faculty: 25 full-time (12 women), 13 part-time (11 women). *Degree requirements:* Thesis or alternative, comprehensive exams required, foreign language not required. *Average time to degree:* master's–2 years full-time, 4 years part-time. *Entrance requirements:* GRE General Test. Application deadline: 7/31 (priority date). Application fee: $35. *Tuition:* $1811 per year full-time, $354 per semester (minimum) part-time for state residents; $9081 per year full-time, $2171 per semester (minimum) part-time for nonresidents. • Dr. Tim Harris, Chairperson, 704-262-2182.

Arizona State University, Interdisciplinary Program in Speech and Hearing Science, Tempe, AZ 85287. Awards PhD. *Application fee:* $45. *Expenses:* Tuition $2088 per year full-time, $110 per hour part-time for state residents; $9040 per year full-time, $377 per hour part-time for nonresidents. Fees $72 per year full-time, $18 per semester (minimum) part-time. • Dr. Sydney Bacon, Director, 602-965-8227.

Arizona State University, College of Liberal Arts and Sciences, Department of Speech and Hearing Science, Tempe, AZ 85287. Offers program in communication disorders (MS). One or more programs accredited by ASHA. Faculty: 29 full-time (21 women). Students: 88 full-time (81 women), 16 part-time (14 women); includes 13 minority (3 African Americans, 9 Hispanics, 1 Native American), 7 international. Average age 28. 209 applicants, 32% accepted. In 1997, 25 degrees awarded. *Degree requirements:* Thesis or alternative, oral and written exams. *Entrance requirements:* GRE. Application fee: $45. *Expenses:* Tuition $2088 per year full-time, $110 per hour part-time for state residents; $9040 per year full-time, $377 per hour part-time for nonresidents. Fees $72 per year full-time, $18 per semester (minimum) part-time. *Faculty research:* Speech perception in normal and hearing-impaired populations, voice disorders, child and adult aural rehabilitation. • Dr. M. Jeanne Wilcox, Chair, 602-965-2374. Application contact: Graduate Secretary, 602-965-9396.

Arkansas State University, College of Nursing and Health Professions, Program in Communication Disorders, State University, AR 72467. Awards MCD. Accredited by ASHA. Part-time programs available. Faculty: 6 full-time (2 women). Students: 35 full-time (all women), 1 (woman) part-time; includes 1 minority (African American). Average age 27. In 1997, 20 degrees awarded. *Degree requirements:* Thesis or alternative, comprehensive exam. *Entrance requirements:* GRE General Test, appropriate bachelor's degree, resume, writing sample. Application deadline: 7/1 (priority date; rolling processing; 11/15 for spring admission). Application fee: $15 ($25 for international students). *Expenses:* Tuition $2760 per year full-time, $115 per credit hour part-time for state residents; $6936 per year full-time, $289 per credit hour part-time for nonresidents. Fees $506 per year full-time, $44 per semester (minimum) part-time. *Financial aid:* Application deadline 7/1. • Dr. D. Mike McDaniel, Director, 870-972-3106. Fax: 870-972-2040. E-mail: dmcdan@crow.astate.edu.

Auburn University, College of Liberal Arts, Department of Communication Disorders, Auburn University, AL 36849-0001. Offers programs in audiology (MCD, MS), speech pathology (MCD, MS). One or more programs accredited by ASHA. Part-time programs available. Faculty: 7 full-time (2 women). Students: 44 full-time (43 women), 12 part-time (all women); includes 1 minority (African American), 1 international. 151 applicants, 17% accepted. In 1997, 35 degrees awarded. *Degree requirements:* Comprehensive exam (MCD), thesis (MS) required, foreign language not required. *Entrance requirements:* GRE General Test. Application deadline: 9/1 (rolling processing; 3/1 for spring admission). Application fee: $25 ($50 for international students). *Expenses:* Tuition $2760 per year full-time, $76 per credit hour part-time for state residents; $8280 per year full-time, $228 per credit hour part-time for nonresidents. Fees $30 per year full-time, $160 per quarter part-time for state residents; $30 per year full-time, $480 per quarter part-time for nonresidents. *Financial aid:* Research assistantships, teaching assistantships, Federal Work-Study available. Aid available to part-time students. Financial aid application deadline: 3/15. • Dr. Michael Moran, Chair, 334-844-9600. Application contact: Dr. John F. Pritchett, Dean of the Graduate School, 334-844-4700.

Ball State University, College of Sciences and Humanities, Department of Speech Pathology and Audiology, 2000 University Avenue, Muncie, IN 47306-1099. Awards MA, Au D. Accredited by ASHA. Faculty: 6. Students: 47 full-time (46 women), 19 part-time (18 women); includes 2 minority (1 African American, 1 Native American), 1 international. Average age 24. In 1997, 35 master's awarded. *Degree requirements:* For other advanced degree, thesis required, foreign language not required. *Entrance requirements:* For other advanced degree, GRE General Test. Application fee: $15 ($25 for international students). *Expenses:* Tuition $3454 per year full-time, $518 per semester (minimum) part-time for state residents; $9316 per year full-time, $1221 per semester (minimum) part-time for nonresidents. Fees $242 per year full-time, $18 per semester (minimum) part-time. *Financial aid:* Research assistantships and career-related internships or fieldwork available. *Faculty research:* Adult neurological disorders, stuttering, tinnitus masking, brain stem responses. • Dr. Gary Lindell, Chairman, 765-285-8162.

Baylor College of Medicine, Division of Audiology and Bioacoustics, Houston, TX 77030-3498. Awards PhD, MD/PhD. Candidate for accreditation by ASHA. Faculty: 6 full-time (2 women). Students: 1 full-time (0 women). Average age 40. 2 applicants, 0% accepted. Terminal master's awarded for partial completion of doctoral program. *Degree requirements:* For doctorate, dissertation, comprehensive exams required, foreign language not required. *Entrance requirements:* For doctorate, GRE General Test (score in 70th percentile or higher on three sections; average 80th percentile), GRE Subject Test (strongly recommended), TOEFL, minimum GPA of 3.0. Application deadline: 2/1 (priority date). Application fee: $30. Electronic applications accepted. *Expenses:* Tuition $8200 per year. Fees $175 per year (minimum). *Financial aid:* Research assistantships, full tuition waivers, Federal Work-Study, institutionally sponsored loans, and career-related internships or fieldwork available. Financial aid application deadline: 4/16. *Faculty research:* Audiology correlates of central auditory disorders, evoked potentials from brain stem auditory pathways, techniques for evaluation of hearing aid performance. • Dr. William E. Brownell, Director, 713-798-5916. Application contact: Gloria Levin, Graduate Program Administrator, 713-798-5916. Fax: 713-796-9438. E-mail: glevin@bcm.tmc.edu.

Baylor University, College of Arts and Sciences, Department of Communication Sciences and Disorders, Waco, TX 76798. Awards MA, MSCSD. One or more programs accredited by ASHA. Faculty: 9 full-time (6 women), 1 (woman) part-time, 9.5 FTE. Students: 59 full-time (55 women), 3 part-time (all women); includes 7 minority (4 African Americans, 3 Hispanics), 2 international. 35% of applicants accepted. In 1997, 33 degrees awarded. *Entrance requirements:* GRE General Test. Application deadline: rolling. Application fee: $25. *Expenses:* Tuition $7392 per year full-time, $308 per semester hour part-time. Fees $1024 per year. *Financial aid:* In 1997–98, 25 students received aid, including 20 fellowships (all to first-year students); partial tuition waivers, Federal Work-Study, institutionally sponsored loans also available. Financial aid application deadline: 5/1. *Faculty research:* Nasality, language impairment, stuttering, Spanish speech perception. • Dr. Jeffrey Cokely, Director of Graduate Studies, 254-710-2567.

Bloomsburg University of Pennsylvania, School of Graduate Studies, College of Professional Studies, School of Education, Department of Communication Disorders and Special Education, Program in Communication Disorders/Education of Deaf/Hard of Hearing, Bloomsburg, PA 17815-1905. Awards MS. Faculty: 3 full-time (1 woman). Students: 9 full-time (8 women), 1 (woman) part-time; includes 1 international. Average age 25. 9 applicants, 100% accepted. In 1997, 10 degrees awarded. *Entrance requirements:* GRE General Test or NTE, minimum QPA of 2.5. Application deadline: 3/15. Application fee: $25. *Expenses:* Tuition $3468 per year full-time, $193 per credit part-time for state residents; $6236 per year full-time, $346 per credit part-time for nonresidents. Fees $748 per year full-time, $166 per semester (minimum) part-time. *Faculty research:* Teaching sign language and speech reading through videodisc technology, oral communication skills, sign language. • Dr. Samuel Slike, Coordinator, 717-389-4436. Fax: 717-389-3980. E-mail: slike@planetx.bloomu.edu.

Bloomsburg University of Pennsylvania, School of Graduate Studies, College of Professional Studies, School of Health Sciences, Department of Special Education and Communication Disorders, Program in Communication Disorders/Audiology, Bloomsburg, PA 17815-1905. Awards MS. Faculty: 3 full-time (1 woman). Students: 9 full-time (7 women), 10 part-time (all women); includes 3 international. Average age 24. 9 applicants, 100% accepted. In 1997, 9 degrees awarded. *Degree requirements:* Thesis or alternative required, foreign language not required. *Entrance requirements:* GRE General Test, minimum QPA of 2.5. Application deadline: 3/15. Application fee: $25. *Expenses:* Tuition $3468 per year full-time, $193 per credit part-time for state residents; $6236 per year full-time, $346 per credit part-time for nonresidents. Fees $748 per year full-time, $166 per semester (minimum) part-time. *Faculty research:* Electrophysiological, industrial, and clinical audiology; hearing aid education. • Dr. G. Donald Miller, Coordinator, 717-389-4436. Fax: 717-389-3980. E-mail: gdmiller@planetx.bloomu.edu.

Bloomsburg University of Pennsylvania, School of Graduate Studies, College of Professional Studies, School of Health Sciences, Department of Special Education and Communication Disorders, Program in Communication Disorders/Speech Pathology, Bloomsburg, PA 17815-1905. Awards MS. Faculty: 4 full-time (2 women). Students: 33 full-time (all women), 1 (woman) part-time; includes 1 minority (Hispanic). Average age 23. 20 applicants, 100% accepted. In 1997, 17 degrees awarded. *Entrance requirements:* GRE General Test, minimum QPA of 2.8. Application deadline: 3/15. Application fee: $25. *Expenses:* Tuition $3468 per year full-time, $193 per credit part-time for state residents; $6236 per year full-time, $346 per credit part-time for nonresidents. Fees $748 per year full-time, $166 per semester (minimum) part-time. *Faculty research:* Language disorders in children, augmentative communication, neurogenic disorders of speech and language, stuttering, speech science. • Dr. G. Donald Miller, Coordinator, 717-389-4436. Fax: 717-389-3980. E-mail: gdmiller@planetx.bloomu.edu.

Boston University, Sargent College of Health and Rehabilitation Sciences, Department of Communication Disorders, Boston, MA 02215. Offers programs in audiology (D Sc), speech-language pathology (MS, D Sc, CAGS). One or more programs accredited by ASHA. Part-time programs available. Faculty: 9 full-time (3 women), 10 part-time (9 women). Students: 75 full-time (71 women), 6 part-time (all women); includes 1 minority (Asian American), 7 international. Average age 25. 327 applicants, 41% accepted. In 1997, 28 master's, 3 doctorates awarded. *Degree requirements:* For doctorate, computer language, dissertation required, foreign language not required. *Entrance requirements:* For master's, GRE General Test (minimum combined score of 1000); for doctorate, GRE General Test (minimum combined score of 1000), master's degree; for CAGS, GRE General Test, master's degree, clinical competency certificate. Application deadline: 3/1 (priority date; rolling processing; 10/1 for spring admission). Application fee: $50. *Expenses:* Tuition $22,830 per year full-time, $713 per credit part-time. Fees $218 per year full-time, $40 per semester part-time. *Financial aid:* In 1997–98, 6 fellowships, 5 research assistantships (3 to first-year students), 5 teaching assistantships (1 to a first-year student) were awarded; scholarships, Federal Work-Study, institutionally sponsored loans, and career-related internships or fieldwork also available. Financial aid application deadline: 4/15. *Faculty research:* Articulation/phonology, fluency, voice and speech science, perception of complex sounds. • Dr. Gerald Kidd Jr., Chairman, 617-353-3188.

See in-depth description on page 1235.

Bowling Green State University, College of Health and Human Services, Department of Communication Disorders, Bowling Green, OH 43403. Awards MS, PhD. One or more programs accredited by ASHA. Faculty: 2 full-time (0 women), 4 part-time (1 woman). Students: 41 full-time (39 women), 2 part-time (1 woman); includes 1 minority (Asian American), 1 international. 170 applicants, 15% accepted. In 1997, 17 master's awarded. *Degree requirements:* For master's, thesis or alternative; for doctorate, dissertation, foreign language or research tool course work. *Entrance requirements:* For master's, GRE General Test, TOEFL (minimum score 550), minimum GPA of 3.0; for doctorate, GRE General Test, TOEFL (minimum score 600), minimum GPA of 3.0. Application deadline: 3/15. Application fee: $30. *Tuition:* $6070 per year full-time, $284 per credit hour part-time for state residents; $11,358 per year full-time, $536 per credit hour part-time for nonresidents. *Financial aid:* In 1997–98, 42 assistantships were awarded; Federal Work-Study, institutionally sponsored loans, and career-related internships or fieldwork also available. Financial aid application deadline: 2/15; applicants required to submit FAFSA. *Faculty research:* Rehabilitation and mental disorders, forensic rehabilitation, rehabilitation and substance abuse, private rehabilitation and disability management, adjustment to disability. • Dr. Linda Petrosino, Chair, 419-372-2515. Application contact: Dr. Larry Small, Graduate Coordinator, 419-372-7182.

Brigham Young University, David O. McKay School of Education, Department of Audiology and Speech-Language Pathology, Provo, UT 84602-1001. Offers programs in audiology (MS), speech-language pathology (MS). Accredited by ASHA. Faculty: 7 full-time (2 women). Students: 36 full-time (31 women), 11 part-time (9 women); includes 2 minority (1 Asian American, 1 Hispanic), 1 international. Average age 24. 42 applicants, 45% accepted. In 1997, 16 degrees awarded. *Degree requirements:* Thesis, PRAXIS (75th percentile) required, foreign language not required. *Average time to degree:* master's–2 years full-time. *Entrance requirements:* GRE General Test (minimum combined score of 1600 on three sections), minimum GPA of 3.0. Application deadline: 2/1 (2/1 for spring admission). Application fee: $30. *Tuition:* $3200 per year full-time, $178 per credit hour part-time for state residents; $4800 per year full-time, $266 per credit hour part-time for nonresidents. *Financial aid:* In 1997–98, 35 students received aid, including 14 fellowships (6 to first-year students) averaging $153 per month and totaling $17,096, 11 research assistantships (7 to first-year students) averaging $236 per month and totaling $20,788, 16 teaching assistantships (9 to first-year students) averaging $210 per month and totaling $26,864, scholarships totaling $1,200; partial tuition waivers, institutionally sponsored loans also available. Aid available to part-time students. *Faculty research:* Child language, auditory physiology, computerized language analysis, digital hearing aids. Total annual research expenditures: $80,000. • Dr. David L. McPherson, Chair, 801-378-6458. Fax: 801-378-3962. E-mail: david_mcpherson@byu.edu.

Brooklyn College of the City University of New York, Department of Speech, Program in Speech-Language Pathology and Audiology, 2900 Bedford Avenue, Brooklyn, NY 11210-2889. Offers audiology (MS), pathology (MS), speech and hearing science (MS). Accredited by ASHA. Students: 16 full-time (all women), 108 part-time (103 women); includes 3 minority (1 African American, 2 Hispanics). Average age 28. 250 applicants, 14% accepted. In 1997, 31 degrees awarded (90% found work related to degree, 10% continued full-time study). *Degree requirements:* Comprehensive exam, NTE, practicum required, foreign language and thesis not required. *Entrance requirements:* NTE, TOEFL (minimum score 500), 24-31 credits in speech, minimum GPA of 3.0. Application deadline: 3/1 (11/1 for spring admission). Application fee: $40. *Expenses:* Tuition $4350 per year full-time, $185 per credit part-time for state residents; $7600 per year full-time, $320 per credit part-time for nonresidents. Fees $500 per year for state residents; $806 per year for nonresidents. *Financial aid:* Full and partial tuition waivers available. Financial aid application deadline: 5/1; applicants required to submit FAFSA. *Faculty research:* Language and learning disorders, aphasia, auditory disorders, voice and fluency disorders. • Application contact: Dr. Gail Gurland, Graduate Deputy, 718-951-5186.

California State University, Chico, College of Communication and Education, Department of Communication Arts and Sciences, Program in Speech Pathology and Audiology, Chico, CA 95929-0722. Awards MA. Accredited by ASHA. Students: 46 full-time (45 women); includes 5 minority (1 Asian American, 4 Hispanics), 1 international. Average age 32. In 1997, 22 degrees awarded. *Degree requirements:* Thesis or alternative, oral exam required, foreign language not required. *Entrance requirements:* GRE General Test or MAT. Application deadline: 4/1 (rolling processing). Application fee: $55. *Expenses:* Tuition $0 for state residents; $246 per unit for nonresidents. Fees $2108 per year full-time, $1442 per year part-time. *Financial aid:* Teaching assistantships and career-related internships or fieldwork available. • Dr. Patrick McCaffrey, Graduate Coordinator, 530-898-6394.

California State University, Fresno, Division of Graduate Studies, School of Health and Social Work, Department of Communicative Disorders, 5241 North Maple Avenue, Fresno, CA 93740. Offers program in communicative disorders (MA), including education of the deaf, speech/language pathology. One or more programs accredited by ASHA. Part-time programs available. Faculty: 12 full-time (6 women). Students: 51 full-time (49 women), 4 part-time (3 women); includes 6 minority (2 African Americans, 4 Hispanics), 2 international. Average age 31. 24 applicants, 63% accepted. In 1997, 18 degrees awarded. *Degree requirements:* Thesis or alternative required, foreign language not required. *Average time to degree:* master's–3.5 years full-time. *Entrance requirements:* GRE General Test, TOEFL (minimum score 550), minimum GPA of 3.0. Application deadline: 2/1 (priority date; rolling processing; 10/1 for spring admission). Application fee: $55. Electronic applications accepted. *Expenses:* Tuition $0 for state residents; $246 per unit for nonresidents. Fees $1872 per year full-time, $1206 per year part-time. *Financial aid:* In 1997–98, 1 teaching assistantship totaling $2,088, 50 scholarships totaling $67,564 were awarded; fellowships, research assistantships, Federal Work-Study, and career-related internships or fieldwork also available. Financial aid application deadline: 3/1; applicants required to submit FAFSA. *Faculty research:* Disabilities education, technology, writing skills at multiple levels, stuttering treatment. • Dr. Stuart Ritterman, Chair, 209-278-2423. E-mail: stuart_ritterman@csufresno.edu. Application contact: Steven Wadsworth, Graduate Coordinator, 209-278-4218. Fax: 209-278-5187. E-mail: steven_wadsworth@csufresno.edu.

California State University, Fullerton, School of Communications, Department of Speech Communication, PO Box 34080, Fullerton, CA 92834-9480. Offerings include communicative disorders (MA). Department faculty: 21 full-time (8 women), 27 part-time, 31 FTE. *Degree requirements:* Thesis or alternative, comprehensive exam required, foreign language not required. *Entrance requirements:* Minimum GPA of 3.0 in major. Application fee: $55. *Expenses:* Tuition $0 for state residents; $246 per unit for nonresidents. Fees $1947 per year full-time, $1281 per year part-time. • Dr. Robert Emry, Chair, 714-278-3617. Application contact: Dr. William Gudykunst, Adviser, 714-278-3617.

California State University, Fullerton, School of Humanities and Social Sciences, Program in Linguistics, PO Box 34080, Fullerton, CA 92834-9480. Offerings include disorders of communication (MA). *Degree requirements:* 1 foreign language, thesis or alternative, comprehensive exam, project. *Entrance requirements:* Minimum GPA of 3.0, undergraduate major in linguistics or related field. Application fee: $55. *Expenses:* Tuition $0 for state residents; $246 per unit for nonresidents. Fees $1947 per year full-time, $1281 per year part-time. • Dr. Angela Della Volpe, Coordinator, 714-278-2441. Application contact: Dr. Franz Muller-Gotama, Adviser, 714-278-2441.

California State University, Hayward, School of Arts, Letters, and Social Sciences, Department of Communicative Sciences and Disorders, Hayward, CA 94542-3000. Offers program in speech pathology (MS). One or more programs accredited by ASHA. Part-time programs available. Faculty: 4 full-time (2 women). Students: 65 full-time (61 women), 27 part-time (23 women); includes 11 minority (6 Asian Americans, 5 Hispanics), 4 international. 86 applicants, 31% accepted. In 1997, 12 degrees awarded. *Degree requirements:* Comprehensive exam, internship or thesis required, foreign language not required. *Entrance requirements:* Minimum GPA of 3.0 in last 2 years. Application deadline: 4/19 (priority date; rolling processing; 1/5 for spring admission). Application fee: $55. *Expenses:* Tuition $0 for state residents; $164 per unit for nonresidents. Fees $1827 per year full-time, $1161 per year part-time. *Financial aid:* Federal Work-Study, institutionally sponsored loans, and career-related internships or fieldwork available. Aid available to part-time students. Financial aid application deadline: 3/1. • Dr. Robert Veder, Chair, 510-885-3233. Application contact: Dr. Maria De Anda-Ramos, Executive Director, Admissions and Outreach, 510-885-2624.

California State University, Long Beach, College of Health and Human Services, Department of Communicative Disorders, Long Beach, CA 90840-2501. Offers programs in audiology (MA), speech pathology (MA). One or more programs accredited by ASHA. Part-time programs available. Students: 51 full-time (47 women), 32 part-time (28 women); includes 24 minority (1 African American, 14 Asian Americans, 7 Hispanics, 2 Native Americans), 1 international. Average age 30. 139 applicants, 33% accepted. In 1997, 18 degrees awarded. *Degree requirements:* Comprehensive exam or thesis required, foreign language not required. *Entrance requirements:* Minimum GPA of 3.0. Application deadline: 8/1 (rolling processing; 12/1 for spring admission). Application fee: $55. *Expenses:* Tuition $0 for state residents; $246 per unit for nonresidents. Fees $1846 per year full-time, $1180 per year part-time. *Financial aid:* Application deadline 3/2. • Dr. Lynn Snyder Jr., Chair, 562-985-4594. E-mail: lsnyder@csulb.edu. Application contact: Dr. Randall Beattie, Graduate Adviser, 562-985-5281. Fax: 562-985-4584. E-mail: beattier@csulb.edu.

California State University, Los Angeles, School of Health and Human Services, Department of Communicative Disorders, Major in Communicative Disorders, Los Angeles, CA 90032-8530. Awards MA. Students: 10 full-time (8 women), 19 part-time (18 women); includes 11 minority (2 African Americans, 1 Asian American, 8 Hispanics), 2 international. *Degree requirements:* Comprehensive exam required, foreign language and thesis not required. *Entrance requirements:* TOEFL (minimum score 550), undergraduate major in communication disorders or related area, minimum GPA of 2.75 in last 90 units. Application deadline: 6/30 (rolling processing; 2/1 for spring admission). Application fee: $55. *Expenses:* Tuition $0 for state residents; $164 per unit for nonresidents. Fees $1763 per year full-time, $1097 per year part-time. *Financial aid:* Application deadline 3/1. • Dr. Miles Peterson, Chair, Department of Communicative Disorders, 213-343-4690.

California State University, Los Angeles, School of Health and Human Services, Department of Communicative Disorders, Major in Hearing Clinic, Los Angeles, CA 90032-8530. Awards MA. Students: 4 full-time (3 women), 13 part-time (9 women); includes 8 minority (1 African American, 4 Asian Americans, 3 Hispanics), 1 international. In 1997, 4 degrees awarded. *Degree requirements:* Comprehensive exam required, foreign language and thesis not required. *Entrance requirements:* GRE, TOEFL (minimum score 550), undergraduate major in communication disorders or related area, minimum GPA of 2.75 in last 90 units. Application deadline: 6/30 (rolling processing; 2/1 for spring admission). Application fee: $55. *Expenses:* Tuition $0 for state residents; $164 per unit for nonresidents. Fees $1763 per year full-time, $1097 per year part-time. *Financial aid:* Application deadline 3/1. • Dr. May E. Chin, Director, 213-343-4698.

California State University, Los Angeles, School of Health and Human Services, Department of Communicative Disorders, Major in Speech Clinic, Los Angeles, CA 90032-8530. Awards MA. Students: 16 full-time (13 women), 41 part-time (38 women); includes 14 minority (6 Asian Americans, 8 Hispanics), 2 international. In 1997, 9 degrees awarded. *Degree requirements:* Comprehensive exam required, foreign language and thesis not required. *Entrance requirements:* TOEFL (minimum score 550), undergraduate major in communication disorders or related area, minimum GPA of 2.75 in last 90 units. Application deadline: 6/30 (rolling processing; 2/1 for spring admission). Application fee: $55. *Expenses:* Tuition $0 for state residents; $164 per unit for nonresidents. Fees $1763 per year full-time, $1097 per year part-time. *Financial aid:* Application deadline 3/1. *Faculty research:* Language acquisition, language disorders, multicultural issues. • Lisa O'Connor, Director, 213-343-4692.

California State University, Northridge, College of Health and Human Development, Department of Communicative Disorders and Sciences, Northridge, CA 91330. Awards MA. One or more programs accredited by ASHA. Faculty: 6 full-time, 17 part-time. Students: 67 full-time (63 women), 17 part-time (16 women); includes 15 minority (2 African Americans, 6 Asian Americans, 6 Hispanics, 1 Native American), 2 international. Average age 31. 43 applicants, 72% accepted. *Entrance requirements:* TOEFL, GRE or minimum GPA of 3.5. Application deadline: 11/30. Application fee: $55. *Expenses:* Tuition $0 for state residents; $246 per unit for nonresidents. Fees $1970 per year full-time, $1304 per year part-time. *Financial aid:* Application deadline 3/1. *Faculty research:* Infant stimulation, early intervention program. • Dr. J. Stephen Sinclair, Chair, 818-677-2852. Application contact: Dr. Elaine P. Hannah, Graduate Coordinator, 818-677-2852 Ext. 2822.

California State University, Sacramento, School of Health and Human Services, Department of Speech Pathology and Audiology, Sacramento, CA 95819-6048. Offers programs in audiology (MS), speech pathology (MS). One or more programs accredited by ASHA. *Degree requirements:* Thesis, writing proficiency exam required, foreign language not required. *Entrance requirements:* GRE General Test (minimum combined score of 900), TOEFL (minimum score 560), appropriate bachelor's degree, minimum GPA of 3.0 during previous 2 years. Application deadline: 4/15 (11/1 for spring admission). Application fee: $55. *Expenses:* Tuition $0 for state residents; $246 per unit for nonresidents. Fees $2012 per year full-time, $1346 per year part-time. *Financial aid:* Federal Work-Study and career-related internships or fieldwork available. Aid available to part-time students. Financial aid application deadline: 3/1. • Dr. Colette Coleman, Chair, 916-278-6679.

California University of Pennsylvania, School of Education, Department of Communication Disorders, 250 University Avenue, California, PA 15419-1394. Awards MS. One or more

Directory: Communication Disorders

California University of Pennsylvania (continued)
programs accredited by ASHA. Part-time and evening/weekend programs available. Faculty: 6 part-time (2 women). Students: 46 full-time (all women), 5 part-time (all women); includes 1 minority (African American). 88 applicants, 32% accepted. In 1997, 21 degrees awarded. *Degree requirements:* Comprehensive exam required, thesis optional, foreign language not required. *Entrance requirements:* GRE General Test, TOEFL (minimum score 550), minimum GPA of 3.0. Application deadline: 2/15 (priority date). Application fee: $25. *Expenses:* Tuition $3468 per year full-time, $193 per credit part-time for state residents; $6236 per year full-time, $346 per credit part-time for nonresidents. Fees $886 per year full-time, $153 per semester (minimum) part-time. *Financial aid:* Graduate assistantships available. • Albert Yates, Head, 724-938-4175.

Case Western Reserve University, Department of Communication Sciences, Cleveland, OH 44106. Offers programs in gerontology (Certificate), speech-language pathology (MA, PhD). One or more programs accredited by ASHA. Faculty: 5 full-time (3 women), 4 part-time (3 women). Students: 25 full-time (24 women), 15 part-time (all women); includes 1 minority (African American), 4 international. Average age 23. 90 applicants, 20% accepted. In 1997, 12 master's awarded (100% found work related to degree); 1 doctorate awarded. Terminal master's awarded for partial completion of doctoral program. *Degree requirements:* For master's, comprehensive exam required, thesis optional; for doctorate, dissertation. *Average time to degree:* master's–2 years full-time. *Entrance requirements:* For master's and doctorate, GRE General Test, TOEFL (minimum score 550). Application deadline: 3/1. Application fee: $25. *Tuition:* $18,400 per year full-time, $767 per credit hour part-time. *Financial aid:* In 1997–98, 19 students received aid, including 16 graduate assistantships/alumni scholarships (7 to first-year students); research assistantships, partial tuition waivers, Federal Work-Study, and career-related internships or fieldwork also available. Financial aid application deadline: 3/1; applicants required to submit FAFSA. *Faculty research:* Traumatic brain injury, phonological disorders, child language disorders, communication problems in the aged and Alzheimer's patients, cleft palate, voice disorders. • Kathy Chapman, Chair, 216-368-2556. Application contact: Dorothy Bandi, Assistant, 216-368-2470. Fax: 216-368-6078. E-mail: cosigrad@po.cwru.edu.

Central Michigan University, College of Health Professions, Department of Communications Disorders, Program in Audiology, Mount Pleasant, MI 48859. Awards Au D. Accredited by ASHA. Students: 24 full-time (all women), 6 part-time (5 women); includes 1 minority (African American), 1 international. Average age 24. *Degree requirements:* Dissertation or alternative required, foreign language not required. *Entrance requirements:* GRE, TOEFL (minimum score 600), interview. Application deadline: 3/1. Application fee: $30. *Expenses:* Tuition $139 per credit hour (minimum) for state residents; $276 per credit hour (minimum) for nonresidents. Fees $260 per year full-time, $150 per semester part-time. *Financial aid:* In 1997–98, 16 research assistantships (9 to first-year students) were awarded; Federal Work-Study and career-related internships or fieldwork also available. Financial aid application deadline: 3/7. • Gerald Church, Coordinator, 517-774-7301. Fax: 517-774-2799. E-mail: 3c4i5hr@cmich.edu.

Central Michigan University, College of Health Professions, Department of Communications Disorders, Program in Speech and Language Pathology, Mount Pleasant, MI 48859. Awards MA. Accredited by ASHA. Students: 40 full-time (37 women), 6 part-time (4 women); includes 2 Asian Americans, 1 Hispanic, 1 Native American, 1 international. Average age 27. *Degree requirements:* Thesis or alternative required, foreign language not required. *Entrance requirements:* Minimum GPA of 2.7 in last 60 hours. Application deadline: 3/1. Application fee: $30. *Expenses:* Tuition $169 per credit hour for state residents; $306 per credit hour for nonresidents. Fees $260 per year full-time, $150 per semester part-time. *Financial aid:* In 1997–98, 1 fellowship (to a first-year student), 19 teaching assistantships were awarded; Federal Work-Study and career-related internships or fieldwork also available. Financial aid application deadline: 3/7. *Faculty research:* Nonvocal persons, speech audiometry, phonological disorders. • Dr. Renny Tatchell, Chairperson, Department of Communications Disorders, 517-774-3472. Fax: 517-774-2799. E-mail: 3c7zcym@cmich.edu.

Central Missouri State University, College of Education and Human Services, Department of Communication Disorders, Warrensburg, MO 64093. Awards MS. One or more programs accredited by ASHA. Part-time programs available. Faculty: 10 full-time. Students: 50 full-time (47 women), 13 part-time (11 women). In 1997, 39 degrees awarded. *Degree requirements:* Project, research paper, or thesis. *Entrance requirements:* GRE, minimum GPA of 3.0. Application deadline: 6/30 (priority date; rolling processing). Application fee: $25 ($50 for international students). *Tuition:* $3288 per year full-time, $137 per credit hour part-time for state residents; $5928 per year full-time, $274 per credit hour part-time for nonresidents. *Financial aid:* In 1997–98, 1 teaching assistantship, 16 administrative and laboratory assistantships were awarded; Federal Work-Study also available. Aid available to part-time students. Financial aid application deadline: 3/1; applicants required to submit FAFSA. • Dr. Don Tibbits, Chair, 660-543-4993. Fax: 660-543-8234.

Clarion University of Pennsylvania, College of Education and Human Services, Department of Communication Sciences and Disorders, Clarion, PA 16214. Awards MS. One or more programs accredited by ASHA. Part-time programs available. Faculty: 9 full-time (7 women). Students: 54 full-time (50 women), 8 part-time (6 women); includes 1 minority (Asian American), 2 international. 162 applicants, 26% accepted. In 1997, 21 degrees awarded. *Degree requirements:* Thesis or alternative required, foreign language not required. *Entrance requirements:* GRE, minimum QPA of 3.0. Application deadline: 3/1. Application fee: $25. *Expenses:* Tuition $3468 per year full-time, $193 per credit hour part-time for state residents; $6236 per year full-time, $346 per credit hour part-time for nonresidents. Fees $921 per year full-time, $90 per credit hour part-time for state residents; $921 per year full-time, $89 per credit hour part-time for nonresidents. *Financial aid:* In 1997–98, 16 research assistantships (6 to first-year students) averaging $267 per month were awarded; career-related internships or fieldwork also available. Aid available to part-time students. Financial aid application deadline: 5/1. • Dr. Dennis Hetrick, Chairman, 814-226-2581. Application contact: Dr. Janis Jarecki-Liu, Graduate Coordinator, 814-226-2445.

Cleveland State University, College of Arts and Sciences, Department of Speech and Hearing, Cleveland, OH 44115-2440. Awards MA. One or more programs accredited by ASHA. Part-time programs available. Faculty: 3 full-time (0 women). Students: 33 full-time (32 women), 20 part-time (all women); includes 2 minority (both African Americans). Average age 27. 134 applicants, 25% accepted. In 1997, 39 degrees awarded. *Degree requirements:* Comprehensive exam required, thesis optional, foreign language not required. *Application deadline:* 8/1 (priority date; rolling processing; 12/1 for spring admission). *Application fee:* $25. *Expenses:* Tuition $5252 per year full-time, $202 per credit hour part-time for state residents; $10,504 per year full-time, $404 per credit hour part-time for nonresidents. Fees $2.25 per credit hour (minimum). *Financial aid:* In 1997–98, 15 administrative assistantships (3 to first-year students) were awarded; research assistantships, teaching assistantships, Federal Work-Study, and career-related internships or fieldwork also available. Financial aid application deadline: 4/1. *Faculty research:* Brain stem audiometry, hearing aids, variant dialects, applications of microcomputers, voice disorders. • Dr. Benjamin Wallace, Interim Chairperson, 216-687-6986. E-mail: b.wallace@csuohio.edu. Application contact: Jeanne Evers, Administrative Assistant to the Chairperson, 216-687-3807.

The College of New Jersey, Graduate Division, School of Education, Department of Language and Communication Sciences, Audiology Program, Ewing, NJ 08628. Awards MA. Accredited by ASHA. Part-time and evening/weekend programs available. Students: 12 full-time (10 women), 2 part-time (1 woman); includes 1 minority (African American). Average age 25. In 1997, 10 degrees awarded. *Degree requirements:* Clinical practicum, comprehensive exam required, foreign language and thesis not required. *Average time to degree:* master's–2 years full-time. *Entrance requirements:* GRE General Test, minimum GPA of 3.0 in field or 2.75 overall. Application deadline: 3/15. Application fee: $50. *Expenses:* Tuition $6892 per year full-time, $287 per credit hour part-time for state residents; $9602 per year full-time, $402 per credit hour part-time for nonresidents. Fees $799 per year full-time, $33 per credit hour part-time. *Financial aid:* Application deadline 5/1; applicants required to submit FAFSA. • Dr. William O. Jones, Chair, Department of Language and Communication Sciences, 609-771-2322.

The College of New Jersey, Graduate Division, School of Education, Department of Language and Communication Sciences, Speech Pathology Program, Ewing, NJ 08628. Awards MA. Accredited by ASHA. Part-time and evening/weekend programs available. Students: 26 full-time (all women), 28 part-time (all women); includes 9 minority (3 African Americans, 1 Asian American, 5 Hispanics). In 1997, 10 degrees awarded. *Degree requirements:* Clinical practicum, comprehensive exam required, foreign language and thesis not required. *Average time to degree:* master's–2 years full-time. *Entrance requirements:* GRE General Test, minimum GPA of 3.0 in field or 2.75 overall, bachelor's degree in speech pathology. Application deadline: 3/15. Application fee: $50. *Expenses:* Tuition $6892 per year full-time, $287 per credit hour part-time for state residents; $9602 per year full-time, $402 per credit hour part-time for nonresidents. Fees $799 per year full-time, $33 per credit hour part-time. *Financial aid:* Graduate assistantships available. Financial aid application deadline: 5/1; applicants required to submit FAFSA. • Dr. Elisa Matthes, Coordinator, 609-771-2322.

The College of Saint Rose, School of Education, Communication Disorders Department, Albany, NY 12203-1419. Awards MS Ed. One or more programs accredited by ASHA. Part-time and evening/weekend programs available. Faculty: 9 full-time (6 women), 7 part-time (6 women). Students: 50 full-time (all women), 78 part-time (73 women); includes 2 minority (1 African American, 1 Asian American). Average age 31. In 1997, 62 degrees awarded. *Degree requirements:* Thesis or alternative, comprehensive exam required, foreign language not required. *Entrance requirements:* Minimum undergraduate GPA of 3.0. Application deadline: 3/15 (priority date; rolling processing; 10/1 for spring admission). Application fee: $30. *Expenses:* Tuition $338 per credit. Fees $60 per year. *Financial aid:* Research assistantships and career-related internships or fieldwork available. Financial aid application deadline: 3/1. • Dr. Kathleen Whitmire, Head, 518-454-5116. Application contact: Graduate Office, 518-454-5136. Fax: 518-458-5479. E-mail: ace@rosnet.strose.edu.

Dalhousie University, Faculty of Health Professions, School of Human Communication Disorders, Halifax, NS B3H 3J5, Canada. Awards M Sc. Faculty: 9 full-time (6 women), 4 part-time (2 women), 10 FTE. Students: 82 full-time (75 women). 280 applicants, 14% accepted. In 1997, 25 degrees awarded. *Degree requirements:* Thesis required, foreign language not required. *Average time to degree:* master's–3 years full-time. *Entrance requirements:* TOEFL (minimum score 580). Application deadline: 3/1 (rolling processing). Application fee: $55. *Financial aid:* In 1997–98, 30 students received aid, including 3 fellowships (2 to first-year students) totaling $40,000, 9 research assistantships (3 to first-year students) totaling $13,500, 10 teaching assistantships (7 to first-year students) totaling $7,000; career-related internships or fieldwork also available. Financial aid application deadline: 3/1. *Faculty research:* Audiology, hearing aids, speech and voice disorders, language development and disorders, treatment efficacy. • Dr. J. Armson, Director, 902-494-7052. E-mail: j.armson@dal.ca. Application contact: Pat MacLeod, Administrative Assistant, 902-494-2506. Fax: 902-494-5151. E-mail: pat.macleod@dal.ca.

Duquesne University, John G. Rangos, Sr. School of Health Sciences, Pittsburgh, PA 15282-0001. Offerings include speech-language pathology (MSLP). School faculty: 30 full-time (17 women), 12 part-time (6 women), 34.8 FTE. *Average time to degree:* master's–2 years full-time. *Application deadline:* 12/1 (priority date). *Application fee:* $45. Electronic applications accepted. *Expenses:* Tuition $510 per credit. Fees $39 per credit. • Dr. Jerome L. Martin, Dean, 412-396-6012. E-mail: martin2@duq2.cc.duq.edu. Application contact: Deborah L. Durica, Director of Student and Alumni Services, 412-396-6652. Fax: 412-396-5554. E-mail: durica@duq2.cc.duq.edu.

East Carolina University, School of Allied Health Sciences, Department of Communication Sciences and Disorders, Greenville, NC 27858-4353. Awards MSSL, PhD. One or more programs accredited by ASHA. Part-time and evening/weekend programs available. Faculty: 7 full-time (1 woman). Students: 79 full-time (72 women), 14 part-time (13 women); includes 2 minority (1 African American, 1 Asian American). Average age 26. 249 applicants, 33% accepted. In 1997, 30 master's awarded. *Degree requirements:* For master's, thesis or alternative, comprehensive exams required, foreign language not required. *Entrance requirements:* For master's, GRE General Test, TOEFL. Application deadline: 4/1. Application fee: $40. *Tuition:* $1886 per year full-time, $472 per semester (minimum) part-time for state residents; $9156 per year full-time, $2289 per semester (minimum) part-time for nonresidents. *Financial aid:* Research assistantships, teaching assistantships, Federal Work-Study available. Aid available to part-time students. Financial aid application deadline: 6/1. • Dr. Gregg Givens, Director of Graduate Studies, 252-328-4404. Fax: 252-328-4470. E-mail: givensg@mail.ecu.edu. Application contact: Dr. Paul D. Tschetter, Associate Dean, 252-328-6012. Fax: 252-328-6071. E-mail: grad@mail.ecu.edu.

Eastern Illinois University, College of Sciences, Department of Communication Disorders and Sciences, 600 Lincoln Avenue, Charleston, IL 61920-3099. Awards MS. One or more programs accredited by ASHA. Faculty: 10 full-time (6 women). Students: 40 full-time (36 women), 6 part-time (all women); includes 1 minority (Hispanic). In 1997, 23 degrees awarded. *Degree requirements:* Comprehensive exam required, foreign language and thesis not required. *Application deadline:* 7/31 (priority date; rolling processing). *Application fee:* $25. *Expenses:* Tuition $3459 per year full-time, $96 per semester hour part-time for state residents; $10,377 per year full-time, $288 per semester hour part-time for nonresidents. Fees $1566 per year full-time, $37 per semester hour part-time. *Financial aid:* In 1997–98, 9 research assistantships were awarded. • Dr. Robert A. Augustine, Chairperson, 217-581-2712. E-mail: cfrma@eiu.edu. Application contact: Frank Goldacker, Coordinator, 217-581-2712. Fax: 217-581-7105. E-mail: cffeg@eiu.edu.

Eastern Kentucky University, College of Education, Department of Communication Disorders, Richmond, KY 40475-3101. Awards MA Ed. One or more programs accredited by ASHA. Faculty: 28. In 1997, 11 degrees awarded. *Entrance requirements:* GRE General Test, minimum GPA of 2.5. Application fee: $0. *Tuition:* $2390 per year full-time, $133 per credit hour part-time for state residents; $6630 per year full-time, $365 per credit hour part-time for nonresidents. • Dr. Martin Diebold, Chair, 602-622-4442.

Eastern Michigan University, College of Education, Department of Special Education, Program in Speech and Language Pathology, Ypsilanti, MI 48197. Awards MA. Accredited by ASHA. Evening/weekend programs available. *Entrance requirements:* GRE General Test, TOEFL (minimum score 570). Application deadline: 5/15 (rolling processing; 3/15 for spring admission). Application fee: $30. *Expenses:* Tuition $2691 per year full-time, $150 per credit hour part-time for state residents; $6300 per year full-time, $350 per credit hour part-time for nonresidents. Fees $368 per year full-time, $88 per semester (minimum) part-time. *Financial aid:* Fellowships, teaching assistantships available. Aid available to part-time students. Financial aid application deadline: 3/15; applicants required to submit FAFSA. • Dr. Ken Schatz, Adviser, 734-487-4413.

Eastern New Mexico University, College of Liberal Arts and Sciences, Department of Communicative Arts and Sciences, Program in Speech Pathology and Audiology, Portales, NM 88130. Awards MS. Accredited by ASHA. Part-time programs available. *Degree requirements:* Comprehensive exam required, thesis optional, foreign language not required. *Entrance requirements:* Minimum GPA of 2.5. Application deadline: rolling. Application fee: $10. *Tuition:* $1956 per year full-time, $82 per credit hour part-time for state residents; $6702 per year full-time, $280 per credit hour part-time for nonresidents. *Financial aid:* Fellowships, research assistantships, teaching assistantships, Federal Work-Study available. Aid available to part-time students. Financial aid application deadline: 4/1. • Dr. Lee Scanlon, Graduate Coordinator, Department of Communicative Arts and Sciences, 505-562-2114.

Eastern Washington University, College of Science, Mathematics and Technology, Department of Communication Disorders, Cheney, WA 99004-2431. Awards MS. One or more programs accredited by ASHA. Faculty: 7 full-time (4 women). Students: 25 full-time (23 women), 5 part-time (all women); includes 1 minority (African American). 71 applicants, 24% accepted. In 1997, 8 degrees awarded. *Degree requirements:* Thesis or alternative, comprehensive exam required, foreign language not required. *Entrance requirements:* GRE General Test, minimum GPA of 3.0. Application deadline: 3/1 (rolling processing). Application fee: $60. *Tuition:* $4200 per year full-time, $140 per credit part-time for state residents; $12,780 per year full-time, $415 per credit part-time for nonresidents. *Financial aid:* Research assistantships, teaching assistantships, Federal Work-Study, institutionally sponsored loans available. Financial aid application deadline: 2/1. • Dr. Sanford Gerber, Chairman, 509-359-6622. Application contact: Dr. David Haugen, Director, 509-359-6622.

East Stroudsburg University of Pennsylvania, School of Health Sciences and Human Performance, Department of Speech Pathology and Audiology, East Stroudsburg, PA 18301-2999. Awards MS. Candidate for accreditation by ASHA. Part-time and evening/weekend programs available. *Degree requirements:* Comprehensive exam required, foreign language not required. *Application deadline:* 7/31 (priority date; rolling processing; 11/30 for spring admission). *Application fee:* $15 ($25 for international students). *Expenses:* Tuition $3468 per year full-time, $193 per credit part-time for state residents; $6236 per year full-time, $346 per credit part-time for nonresidents. Fees $700 per year full-time, $39 per credit part-time. *Faculty research:* Computer assisted classroom instruction.

East Tennessee State University, College of Public and Allied Health, Department of Communicative Disorders, Johnson City, TN 37614-0734. Awards MS. One or more programs accredited by ASHA. Part-time and evening/weekend programs available. Faculty: 9 full-time (7 women). Students: 37 full-time (33 women), 7 part-time (all women); includes 1 minority (African American). Average age 26. 179 applicants, 26% accepted. In 1997, 23 degrees awarded. *Degree requirements:* Thesis or alternative, comprehensive exam required, foreign language not required. *Entrance requirements:* GRE General Test, TOEFL (minimum score 550), minimum GPA of 3.0. Application deadline: 2/15. Application fee: $25 ($35 for international students). *Tuition:* $2944 per year full-time, $158 per credit hour part-time for state residents; $7770 per year full-time, $369 per credit hour part-time for nonresidents. *Financial aid:* In 1997–98, 3 research assistantships (1 to a first-year student) were awarded; teaching assistantships, Federal Work-Study, institutionally sponsored loans, and career-related internships or fieldwork also available. *Faculty research:* Treatment efficacy, hearing aid trials, language development of cleft palate children, phonological processes, neurogenic disorders. Total annual research expenditures: $200,000. • Dr. Marshall Grube, Chair, 423-439-4272.

Edinboro University of Pennsylvania, School of Liberal Arts, Department of Speech Communications, Program in Speech-Language Pathology, Edinboro, PA 16444. Awards MA. Accredited by ASHA. Faculty: 3 full-time (0 women). Students: 36 full-time (33 women), 2 part-time (both women); includes 1 minority (African American), 1 international. Average age 29. In 1997, 15 degrees awarded. *Degree requirements:* Thesis optional, foreign language not required. *Entrance requirements:* GRE or MAT (score in 30th percentile or higher). Application deadline: rolling. Application fee: $25. *Expenses:* Tuition $3468 per year full-time, $193 per credit part-time for state residents; $6236 per year full-time, $346 per credit part-time for nonresidents. Fees $898 per year full-time, $50 per semester (minimum) part-time. *Financial aid:* In 1997–98, 14 assistantships were awarded. • Dr. Roy Shinn, Head, 814-732-2730. Fax: 814-732-2629. E-mail: shinn@edinboro.edu. Application contact: Dr. Philip Kerstetter, Dean of Graduate Studies, 814-732-2856. Fax: 814-732-2611. E-mail: kerstetter@edinboro.edu.

Emerson College, School of Communication Sciences and Disorders, Program in Communication Disorders, Boston, MA 02116-1511. Offers speech-language pathology (MS, PhD). One or more programs accredited by ASHA. Faculty: 11 full-time (4 women), 5 part-time (all women). Students: 73 full-time (71 women), 35 part-time (33 women); includes 3 minority (all African Americans), 1 international. Average age 25. 427 applicants, 26% accepted. *Degree requirements:* For master's, thesis or alternative, comprehensive exam; for doctorate, computer language. *Entrance requirements:* GRE General Test, minimum GPA of 3.0. Application deadline: 7/1 (rolling processing). Application fee: $45 ($75 for international students). *Expenses:* Tuition $566 per credit. Fees $30 per semester (minimum). *Financial aid:* Career-related internships or fieldwork available. Financial aid application deadline: 2/15; applicants required to submit CSS PROFILE. • Dr. Cynthia Bartlett, Graduate Coordinator, 617-824-8732. Application contact: Lynn Terrell, Director of Graduate Admissions, 617-824-8610. Fax: 617-824-8614. E-mail: gradapp@emerson.edu.

Florida Atlantic University, College of Education, Department of Health Sciences, Program in Communication Disorders, Boca Raton, FL 33431-0991. Awards M Ed. One or more programs accredited by ASHA. Faculty: 4 full-time (3 women), 4 part-time (all women). Students: 15 full-time (11 women), 35 part-time (30 women); includes 14 minority (6 African Americans, 8 Hispanics). Average age 30. 96 applicants, 25% accepted. In 1997, 24 degrees awarded. *Degree requirements:* Thesis optional, foreign language not required. *Entrance requirements:* GRE General Test (minimum combined score of 1000 required(, minimum GPA of 3.0 in last 60 hours of BA or 3.5 in graduate degree. Application deadline: 4/1. Application fee: $20. *Expenses:* Tuition $2520 per year full-time, $140 per credit hour part-time for state residents; $8712 per year full-time, $484 per credit hour part-time for nonresidents. Fees $5 per year (minimum). *Financial aid:* Career-related internships or fieldwork available. *Faculty research:* Fluency disorders, auditory processing, child language, adult language and cognition, multicultural speech and language issues. • Dr. Deena Wener, Coordinator, 561-297-2258.

Florida State University, College of Communication, Department of Communication Disorders, Tallahassee, FL 32306. Offers program in speech pathology (Adv M, MS, PhD). One or more programs accredited by ASHA. Part-time programs available. Faculty: 12 full-time (9 women), 3 part-time (all women). Students: 65 full-time (59 women), 27 part-time (25 women); includes 13 minority (7 African Americans, 2 Asian Americans, 3 Hispanics, 1 Native American). 217 applicants, 28% accepted. In 1997, 35 master's awarded (100% found work related to degree); 1 doctorate awarded (100% found work related to degree). *Degree requirements:* For master's, thesis optional, foreign language not required; for doctorate, dissertation required, foreign language not required. *Entrance requirements:* For master's, GRE General Test (minimum combined score of 1000) or minimum GPA of 3.0; for doctorate, GRE General Test (minimum combined score of 1000), minimum GPA of 3.0 (undergraduate), 3.5 (graduate). Application deadline: 2/1. Application fee: $20. *Tuition:* $139 per credit hour for state residents; $482 per credit hour for nonresidents. *Financial aid:* In 1997–98, 24 students received aid, including 12 research assistantships (6 to first-year students), 13 teaching assistantships (10 to first-year students); fellowships, institutionally sponsored loans, and career-related internships or fieldwork also available. *Faculty research:* Autism, gerontology, stuttering, speech disorders, early identification of language disorders. • Dr. Howard Goldstein, Chairperson, 850-644-2238. E-mail: hgoldste@garnet.acns.fsu.edu. Application contact: Secretary, 850-644-2253. Fax: 850-644-8994. E-mail: pwinne@mailer.fsu.edu.

Fontbonne College, Department of Communication Disorders, St. Louis, MO 63105-3098. Awards MS. One or more programs accredited by ASHA. Faculty: 5 full-time (all women), 2 part-time (1 woman). Students: 27 full-time (all women), 23 part-time (all women); includes 2 international. Average age 28. In 1997, 33 degrees awarded. *Degree requirements:* Thesis required, foreign language not required. *Entrance requirements:* Minimum GPA of 3.0. Application deadline: 8/1 (priority date; rolling processing; 12/15 for spring admission). Application fee: $20. *Expenses:* Tuition $378 per credit hour. Fees $160 per year full-time, $7 per credit hour part-time. • Janie Von Wolfseck, Chairperson, 314-889-1407. Fax: 314-889-1451. E-mail: jvonwolf@fontbonne.edu.

Fort Hays State University, College of Health and Life Sciences, Department of Communication Disorders, Hays, KS 67601-4099. Offers program in speech-language pathology (MS). One or more programs accredited by ASHA. Part-time programs available. Faculty: 4 full-time (2 women). Students: 32 full-time (29 women), 1 (woman) part-time; includes 2 minority (both Hispanics). Average age 28. 47 applicants, 36% accepted. In 1997, 14 degrees awarded. *Entrance requirements:* GRE General Test. Application deadline: 7/1 (priority date; rolling processing). Application fee: $25 ($35 for international students). *Tuition:* $94 per credit hour for state residents; $249 per credit hour for nonresidents. *Financial aid:* Research assistantships, teaching assistantships available. *Faculty research:* Aural rehabilitation, phonological and articulatory skill, middle ear diseases, output capability of stereo cassette units, language development. • Dr. Marcia Bannister, Chair, 785-628-5366.

Gallaudet University, School of Communication, Department of Audiology and Speech Language Pathology, Washington, DC 20002-3625. Offers programs in audiology (MS, Au D), speech and language pathology (MS). One or more programs accredited by ASHA. MS (audiology) being phased out; applicants no longer accepted. Au D new for fall 1998. *Degree requirements:* For master's, thesis optional; for doctorate, computer language, dissertation. *Entrance requirements:* For master's, GRE General Test or MAT; for doctorate, GRE General Test or MAT, interview. Application deadline: 2/15 (priority date; rolling processing). Application fee: $50. *Expenses:* Tuition $7064 per year full-time, $392 per credit part-time. Fees $50 (one-time charge). *Financial aid:* Application deadline 8/1. *Faculty research:* Aural rehabilitation, speech production. • Dr. James J. Mahshie, Chair, 202-651-5329. Application contact: Deborah DeStefano, Director of Admissions, 202-651-5253. Fax: 202-651-5744. E-mail: adm_destefan@gallua.bitnet.

The George Washington University, Columbian School of Arts and Sciences, Department of Speech and Hearing, Washington, DC 20052. Offers program in speech pathology and audiology (MA). One or more programs accredited by ASHA. Faculty: 6 full-time (3 women), 4 part-time (all women), 7 FTE. Students: 44 full-time (43 women), 14 part-time (all women); includes 6 minority (5 African Americans, 1 Hispanic), 2 international. Average age 26. 182 applicants, 34% accepted. In 1997, 24 degrees awarded. *Degree requirements:* Thesis or alternative, comprehensive exam required, foreign language not required. *Entrance requirements:* GRE General Test, interview, minimum GPA of 3.0. Application deadline: 5/1. Application fee: $50. *Expenses:* Tuition $680 per semester hour. Fees $35 per semester hour. *Financial aid:* In 1997–98, 6 fellowships totaling $107,400, 6 teaching assistantships totaling $14,400 were awarded; Federal Work-Study and career-related internships or fieldwork also available. Financial aid application deadline: 2/1. • Dr. Vernon Larson, Chair, 202-994-7362.

Georgia State University, College of Education, Department of Educational Psychology and Special Education, Program in Communication Disorders, Atlanta, GA 30303-3083. Awards M Ed. Accredited by ASHA. Students: 37 full-time (36 women), 14 part-time (all women); includes 6 minority (all African Americans). Average age 26. 201 applicants, 9% accepted. In 1997, 15 degrees awarded. *Degree requirements:* Comprehensive exams. *Entrance requirements:* GRE General Test (minimum combined score of 885), minimum GPA of 3.0. Application deadline: 2/15. Application fee: $25. *Expenses:* Tuition $2673 per year full-time, $99 per semester hour part-time for state residents; $10,692 per year full-time, $396 per semester hour part-time for nonresidents. Fees $228 per year. *Financial aid:* Research assistantships available. *Faculty research:* Language development, minority students. • Dr. Ron P. Colarusso, Chair, Department of Educational Psychology and Special Education, 404-651-2310.

Georgia State University, College of Education, Department of Educational Psychology and Special Education, Program in Education of the Hearing Impaired, Atlanta, GA 30303-3083. Awards M Ed. Students: 10 full-time (9 women), 7 part-time (all women); includes 2 minority (both African Americans). Average age 27. 11 applicants, 91% accepted. In 1997, 10 degrees awarded. *Degree requirements:* Comprehensive exams. *Entrance requirements:* GRE General Test (minimum combined score of 800) or MAT (minimum score 44), minimum GPA of 2.5. Application deadline: 7/15 (1/15 for spring admission). Application fee: $25. *Expenses:* Tuition $2673 per year full-time, $99 per semester hour part-time for state residents; $10,692 per year full-time, $396 per semester hour part-time for nonresidents. Fees $228 per year. *Faculty research:* Language acquisition in deaf children. • Dr. Ron P. Colarusso, Chair, Department of Educational Psychology and Special Education, 404-651-2310.

Governors State University, College of Health Professions, Division of Nursing and Health Science, Program in Communication Disorders, University Park, IL 60466. Awards MHS. Accredited by ASHA. Part-time and evening/weekend programs available. Faculty: 5 full-time (2 women), 15 part-time (12 women). In 1997, 17 degrees awarded. *Degree requirements:* Thesis or alternative, comprehensive exam, practicum required, foreign language not required. *Entrance requirements:* Minimum GPA of 3.3. Application deadline: 3/1 (priority date; rolling processing). Application fee: $0. *Expenses:* Tuition $1140 per trimester full-time, $95 per credit hour part-time for state residents; $3420 per trimester full-time, $285 per credit hour part-time for nonresidents. Fees $95 per trimester. *Financial aid:* Research assistantships, scholarships, full and partial tuition waivers, Federal Work-Study, institutionally sponsored loans, and career-related internships or fieldwork available. Aid available to part-time students. Financial aid application deadline: 5/1. *Faculty research:* Speech perception of hearing-impaired, effects of binaural listening, communication assessment of infants, voice characteristics of head-neck cancer patients. • Dr. Sandra Mayfield, Chairperson, 708-534-4590.

Graduate School and University Center of the City University of New York, Program in Speech and Hearing Sciences, New York, NY 10036-8099. Awards PhD. Faculty: 19 full-time (3 women). Students: 64 full-time (56 women), 1 part-time (0 women); includes 5 minority (4 African Americans, 1 Asian American), 11 international. Average age 38. 16 applicants, 44% accepted. In 1997, 4 doctorates awarded. Terminal master's awarded for partial completion of doctoral program. *Degree requirements:* For doctorate, 1 foreign language, dissertation. *Application deadline:* 3/1. *Application fee:* $40. *Expenses:* Tuition $4350 per year full-time, $185 per credit (minimum) part-time for state residents; $7600 per year full-time, $320 per credit (minimum) part-time for nonresidents. Fees $69 per year. *Financial aid:* In 1997–98, 33 students received aid, including 33 fellowships (4 to first-year students); research assistantships, teaching assistantships, full and partial tuition waivers, Federal Work-Study, institutionally sponsored loans, and career-related internships or fieldwork also available. Financial aid application deadline: 2/1; applicants required to submit FAFSA. • Dr. Irving Hochberg, Executive Officer, 212-642-2352.

Hampton University, Program in Communicative Sciences and Disorders, Hampton, VA 23668. Awards MA. One or more programs accredited by ASHA. Part-time and evening/weekend programs available. Faculty: 5 full-time (4 women), 1 (woman) part-time. Students: 30 full-time (29 women), 28 part-time (25 women); includes 32 minority (31 African Americans, 1 Asian American), 1 international. In 1997, 10 degrees awarded. *Entrance requirements:* GRE General Test (minimum score 450 on verbal section). Application deadline: 6/1 (priority date; rolling processing; 11/1 for spring admission). Application fee: $25. *Expenses:* Tuition $9038 per year full-time, $220 per credit part-time. Fees $70 per year. *Financial aid:* Fellowships, research assistantships, teaching assistantships, scholarships, Federal Work-Study, institutionally sponsored loans, and career-related internships or fieldwork available. Aid available to part-time students. Financial aid application deadline: 5/1; applicants required to submit FAFSA. *Faculty research:* Language development, language pathology. • Dr. Robert M. Screen, Chairman, 757-727-5436. Application contact: Erika Henderson, Director, Graduate Programs, 757-727-5454. Fax: 757-727-5084.

Announcement: The program in communicative sciences and disorders offers graduate training in the specialization of speech-language pathology. Accredited by the American Speech-Language-Hearing Association, the program prepares students to provide speech and language services to children and adults with a variety of communication disorders. Students receive the opportunity for diverse clinical experience in hospital, clinical, and school settings.

Harvard University, Medical School and Graduate School of Arts and Sciences, Division of Health Sciences and Technology, Speech and Hearing Sciences Program, Cambridge, MA 02138. Awards PhD, Sc D. Offered jointly with Massachusetts Institute of Technology. Faculty: 54 full-time (8 women). Students: 40 full-time (11 women); includes 3 minority (all Asian

Directory: Communication Disorders

Harvard University (continued)

Americans), 2 international. Average age 25. 28 applicants, 25% accepted. *Degree requirements:* Dissertation required, foreign language not required. *Entrance requirements:* Bachelor's degree in engineering or science. Application deadline: 1/15 (priority date; rolling processing). Application fee: $55. *Expenses:* Tuition $32,065 per year. Fees $645 per year. *Financial aid:* In 1997–98, 40 students received aid, including fellowships averaging $1,380 per month, 10 research assistantships averaging $1,475 per month, 3 teaching assistantships averaging $1,520 per month and totaling $55,165; institutionally sponsored loans also available. • Dr. Louis D. Braida, Director, 617-646-1253. E-mail: braida@cbgrle.mit.edu. Application contact: Dr. Joseph S. Perkell, 617-253-3223. E-mail: perkell@speech.mit.edu.

See in-depth description on page 1239.

Hofstra University, College of Liberal Arts and Sciences, Division of Humanities, Department of Speech Language-Hearing Sciences, Hempstead, NY 11549. Offers programs in audiology (MA), speech-language pathology (MA). One or more programs accredited by ASHA. Part-time programs available. Faculty: 8 full-time (4 women), 9 part-time (7 women). Students: 21 full-time (20 women), 99 part-time (91 women); includes 2 minority (1 African American, 1 Hispanic). Average age 26. 271 applicants, 28% accepted. In 1997, 29 degrees awarded. *Degree requirements:* Comprehensive exam. *Entrance requirements:* GRE General Test, minimum GPA of 3.0. Application deadline: rolling. Application fee: $40 ($75 for international students). *Expenses:* Tuition $10,968 per year full-time, $457 per credit hour part-time. Fees $670 per year full-time, $112 per semester (minimum) part-time. *Financial aid:* In 1997–98, 3 research assistantships, 13 scholarships (5 to first-year students) totaling $40,000 were awarded; Federal Work-Study and career-related internships or fieldwork also available. Aid available to part-time students. Financial aid application deadline: 3/1. *Faculty research:* Normal/disordered speech production, language, and language-learning disabilities; adult neurogenic disorders; audiology/perception; discourse relationship between language and brain; language development. • Dr. Ellen Parker, Director, 516-463-5508. Fax: 516-463-5260. Application contact: Mary Beth Carey, Dean of Admissions, 516-463-6700. Fax: 516-560-7660. E-mail: hofstra@hofstra.edu.

Howard University, School of Communications, Department of Communication Sciences and Disorders, 2400 Sixth Street, NW, Washington, DC 20059-0002. Offers programs in audiology (MS), communication sciences and disorders (PhD), speech pathology (MS). One or more programs accredited by ASHA. Offered through the Graduate School of Arts and Sciences. Faculty: 8 full-time (6 women), 3 part-time (2 women), 8.89 FTE. Students: 64 full-time (58 women), 16 part-time (14 women); includes 67 minority (65 African Americans, 1 Asian American, 1 Native American), 8 international. *Degree requirements:* For master's, thesis or alternative required, foreign language not required; for doctorate, 1 foreign language (computer language can substitute), dissertation, comprehensive exam. *Entrance requirements:* GRE General Test, minimum GPA of 3.0. Application deadline: 4/1 (11/1 for spring admission). Application fee: $45. *Expenses:* Tuition $10,200 per year full-time, $567 per credit hour part-time. Fees $405 per year. *Financial aid:* Grants, scholarships, full and partial tuition waivers, Federal Work-Study available. *Faculty research:* Multiculturalism, augmentative communication, adult neurological disorders, child language disorders. • Dr. Noma Anderson, Chair, 202-806-6990.

Hunter College of the City University of New York, School of Health Sciences, Communication Sciences Program, New York, NY 10010. Offers audiology (MS), speech language pathology (MS), teacher of speech and hearing handicapped (MS). One or more programs accredited by ASHA. Part-time programs available. Faculty: 8 full-time (all women), 8 part-time (7 women). Students: 15 full-time (13 women), 38 part-time (35 women); includes 9 minority (2 African Americans, 3 Asian Americans, 4 Hispanics). Average age 29. In 1997, 16 degrees awarded. *Degree requirements:* NTE, research project required, foreign language not required. *Average time to degree:* master's–2 years full-time, 5 years part-time. *Entrance requirements:* GRE General Test, TOEFL (minimum score 550). Application deadline: 3/7. Application fee: $40. *Expenses:* Tuition $4350 per year full-time, $185 per credit part-time for state residents; $7600 per year full-time, $320 per credit part-time for nonresidents. Fees $26 per year. *Financial aid:* In 1997–98, 20 students received aid, including 3 fellowships averaging $1,000 per month and totaling $24,000, 6 research assistantships (2 to first-year students) averaging $1,000 per month and totaling $60,000; full and partial tuition waivers, Federal Work-Study, institutionally sponsored loans, and career-related internships or fieldwork also available. Financial aid application deadline: 3/1. *Faculty research:* Aging and communication disorders, fluency, speech science, diagnostic audiology, amplification, language learning disorders. Total annual research expenditures: $600,000. • Dr. Dana Waltzman, Director, 212-481-4467. Application contact: Audrey Berman, Associate Director for Graduate Admissions, 212-772-4490.

Idaho State University, College of Health Professions, Department of Speech Pathology and Audiology, Pocatello, ID 83209. Offers programs in audiology (MS), deaf education (MS), speech language pathology (MS). One or more programs accredited by ASHA. Part-time programs available. Faculty: 15 full-time (8 women), 5 part-time (3 women). Students: 72 full-time (69 women), 15 part-time (14 women); includes 2 minority (1 Asian American, 1 Hispanic), 2 international. Average age 30. 150 applicants, 13% accepted. In 1997, 26 degrees awarded. *Degree requirements:* Thesis optional, foreign language not required. *Entrance requirements:* GRE General Test, minimum GPA of 3.0. Application deadline: 2/1 (priority date). Application fee: $30. *Tuition:* $3130 per year full-time, $136 per credit hour part-time for state residents; $9370 per year full-time, $226 per credit hour part-time for nonresidents. *Financial aid:* Teaching assistantships, scholarships, institutionally sponsored loans, and career-related internships or fieldwork available. Financial aid application deadline: 3/15. *Faculty research:* Clinical efficacy, voice disorders, closed head injury, phonology, assistive technology. • Dr. David Sorensen, Chairman, 208-236-3495. Fax: 208-236-4571. Application contact: Dr. Thayne Smedley, Director of Graduate Studies, 208-236-2190.

Illinois State University, College of Arts and Sciences, Department of Speech Pathology and Audiology, Normal, IL 61790-2200. Awards MA, MS. Accredited by ASHA. Faculty: 9 full-time (2 women). Students: 62 full-time (61 women), 21 part-time (20 women); includes 5 minority (4 African Americans, 1 Hispanic). 167 applicants, 28% accepted. In 1997, 38 degrees awarded. *Degree requirements:* Thesis or alternative, 1 term of residency, 2 practica. *Entrance requirements:* GRE General Test, minimum GPA of 3.0 in last 60 hours. Application deadline: rolling. Application fee: $0. *Expenses:* Tuition $2454 per year full-time, $102 per hour part-time for state residents; $7362 per year full-time, $307 per hour part-time for nonresidents. Fees $1048 per year full-time, $44 per hour part-time. *Financial aid:* In 1997–98, 7 assistantships averaging $481 per month were awarded; research assistantships, teaching assistantships, full tuition waivers also available. Financial aid application deadline: 4/1. • Dr. Clarence Bowman, Chairperson, 309-438-8643.

Indiana State University, School of Education, Department of Communication Disorders and Special Education, Terre Haute, IN 47809-1401. Offers programs in director of special education (M Ed), gifted/talented education (MA, MS, Ed S), special education (MA, MS, PhD), speech pathology and audiology (MA, MS). Part-time and evening/weekend programs available. Faculty: 14 full-time (8 women). Students: 28 full-time (all women), 9 part-time (7 women); includes 1 international. Average age 31. 52 applicants, 21% accepted. In 1997, 14 master's awarded. Terminal master's awarded for partial completion of doctoral program. *Degree requirements:* For doctorate, 2 foreign languages, computer language, dissertation; for Ed S, computer language, thesis. *Entrance requirements:* For master's, minimum undergraduate GPA of 2.5; for doctorate, GRE General Test (minimum score 500 on each section), minimum undergraduate GPA of 3.5; for Ed S, GRE General Test (minimum combined score of 900), minimum graduate GPA of 3.25. Application deadline: rolling. Application fee: $20. *Tuition:* $143 per credit hour for state residents; $325 per credit hour for nonresidents. *Financial aid:* In 1997–98, 6 research assistantships (5 to first-year students) were awarded; fellowships, teaching assistantships, institutionally sponsored loans also available. Aid available to part-time students. Financial aid application deadline: 3/1. *Faculty research:* Vocational/transitional programs, social adjustment, consultation with regular education, microcomputers, stuttering. • Dr. Raymond Quist, Chairperson, 812-237-3585.

Indiana University Bloomington, College of Arts and Sciences, Department of Speech and Hearing Sciences, Bloomington, IN 47405. Awards MA, MAT, PhD. One or more programs accredited by ASHA. PhD offered through the University Graduate School. Faculty: 14 full-time (9 women), 1 part-time (0 women). Students: 68 full-time (62 women), 31 part-time (24 women); includes 5 minority (1 African American, 2 Asian Americans, 2 Hispanics), 4 international. In 1997, 40 master's, 1 doctorate awarded. Terminal master's awarded for partial completion of doctoral program. *Degree requirements:* For master's, variable foreign language requirement, thesis (for some programs); for doctorate, 1 foreign language (computer language can substitute), dissertation. *Entrance requirements:* For master's, GRE General Test (minimum combined score of 1000); for doctorate, GRE General Test. Application deadline: 1/15 (priority date; 9/1 for spring admission). Application fee: $35. *Expenses:* Tuition $153 per credit hour for state residents; $446 per credit hour for nonresidents. Fees $343 per year. *Financial aid:* Fellowships, research assistantships, teaching assistantships, Federal Work-Study, institutionally sponsored loans available. Financial aid application deadline: 2/1. *Faculty research:* Speech training, deafness, voice supervision, linguistic analysis, speech reading. • Larry Humes, Chairperson, 812-855-4156. Fax: 812-855-4156. Application contact: Mark Shemanski, Graduate Secretary, 812-855-4202. E-mail: sphsdept@indiana.edu.

Indiana University of Pennsylvania, College of Education, Department of Special Education and Clinical Services, Program in Speech-Language Pathology, Indiana, PA 15705-1087. Awards MS. Accredited by ASHA. Students: 36 full-time (31 women), 2 part-time (both women); includes 1 minority (African American). Average age 25. 94 applicants, 20% accepted. In 1997, 17 degrees awarded. *Degree requirements:* Thesis optional, foreign language not required. *Entrance requirements:* TOEFL (minimum score 500). Application deadline: 7/1 (priority date; rolling processing; 11/1 for spring admission). Application fee: $30. *Expenses:* Tuition $3468 per year full-time, $193 per credit part-time for state residents; $6236 per year full-time, $346 per credit part-time for nonresidents. Fees $313 per year (minimum) full-time, $84 per year part-time. *Financial aid:* Research assistantships, Federal Work-Study, and career-related internships or fieldwork available. Aid available to part-time students. Financial aid application deadline: 3/15. • Dr. David Stein, Graduate Coordinator, 724-357-2454. E-mail: dwstein@grove.iup.edu.

Ithaca College, School of Health Sciences and Human Performance, Program in Speech-Language, Pathology, and Audiology, Ithaca, NY 14850-7020. Offers audiology (MS), speech pathology (MS), teacher of the speech and hearing handicapped (MS). Accredited by ASHA. Faculty: 6 full-time (2 women). Students: 50 full-time (48 women), 1 (woman) part-time; includes 1 minority (Hispanic), 5 international. Average age 26. 146 applicants, 35% accepted. In 1997, 30 degrees awarded (100% found work related to degree). *Degree requirements:* Thesis optional, foreign language not required. *Entrance requirements:* GRE General Test, TOEFL (minimum score 550), minimum GPA of 3.0. Application deadline: 3/1 (priority date; rolling processing). Application fee: $30. *Tuition:* $552 per credit hour. *Financial aid:* In 1997–98, 44 students received aid, including 23 graduate assistantships (9 to first-year students) totaling $153,732; career-related internships or fieldwork also available. Financial aid application deadline: 3/1; applicants required to submit FAFSA. *Faculty research:* Fluency, articulation, computer applications, child language, speech reception and noise. • Dr. Carol Crichley, Chairperson, 607-274-3101.

Jackson State University, School of Allied Health, Jackson, MS 39217. Offers program in communicative disorders (MS). Program new for fall 1998. *Degree requirements:* Comprehensive exam. *Entrance requirements:* GRE General Test (minimum combined score of 1000), TOEFL (minimum score 550). Application deadline: 3/1 (10/1 for spring admission). Application fee: $20. *Tuition:* $2688 per year (minimum) full-time, $150 per semester hour part-time for state residents; $5546 per year (minimum) full-time, $309 per semester hour part-time for nonresidents. *Financial aid:* Application deadline 3/1. • Dr. Zenobia Bagli, Dean, 601-982-6717. Application contact: Mae Robinson, Admissions Coordinator, 601-968-2455. Fax: 601-968-8246. E-mail: mrobinson@ccaix.jsums.edu.

James Madison University, College of Integrated Science and Technology, Department of Communication Sciences and Disorders, Program in Hearing Disorders, Harrisonburg, VA 22807. Awards M Ed. One or more programs accredited by ASHA. Part-time programs available. Students: 21 full-time (17 women), 1 (woman) part-time. Average age 30. In 1997, 5 degrees awarded. *Degree requirements:* Thesis required, foreign language not required. *Entrance requirements:* GRE General Test. Application deadline: 7/1 (priority date; rolling processing). Application fee: $50. *Tuition:* $134 per credit hour for state residents; $404 per credit hour for nonresidents. *Financial aid:* In 1997–98, 1 teaching assistantship totaling $10,170, 7 assistantships totaling $60,480 were awarded; fellowships, Federal Work-Study also available. Financial aid application deadline: 2/15; applicants required to submit FAFSA. • Dr. Nicholas Bankson, Head, Department of Communication Sciences and Disorders, 540-568-6440.

James Madison University, College of Integrated Science and Technology, Department of Communication Sciences and Disorders, Program in Speech Pathology, Harrisonburg, VA 22807. Awards MS. Accredited by ASHA. Part-time programs available. Students: 58 full-time (56 women), 15 part-time (all women); includes 6 minority (1 African American, 4 Hispanics, 1 Native American). Average age 30. In 1997, 32 degrees awarded. *Degree requirements:* Thesis required, foreign language not required. *Entrance requirements:* GRE General Test. Application deadline: 7/1 (priority date; rolling processing). Application fee: $50. *Tuition:* $134 per credit hour for state residents; $404 per credit hour for nonresidents. *Financial aid:* In 1997–98, 1 teaching assistantship totaling $8,640, 13 assistantships totaling $111,812 were awarded; fellowships, Federal Work-Study also available. Financial aid application deadline: 2/15; applicants required to submit FAFSA. • Dr. Nicholas Bankson, Head, Department of Communication Sciences and Disorders, 540-568-6440.

Kean University, School of Education, Department of Special Education and Individualized Services, Program in Speech Pathology, Union, NJ 07083. Awards MA. Accredited by ASHA. Part-time programs available. Students: 47 full-time (46 women), 45 part-time (43 women); includes 10 minority (5 African Americans, 2 Asian Americans, 3 Hispanics). Average age 30. In 1997, 54 degrees awarded. *Degree requirements:* Thesis, comprehensive exams required, foreign language not required. *Entrance requirements:* GRE General Test. Application deadline: 6/15 (11/15 for spring admission). Application fee: $35. *Tuition:* $5926 per year full-time, $248 per credit part-time for state residents; $7312 per year full-time, $304 per credit part-time for nonresidents. *Financial aid:* Graduate assistantships and career-related internships or fieldwork available. • Dr. Martin Shulman, Coordinator, 908-527-2217. Application contact: Joanne Morris, Director of Graduate Admissions, 908-527-2665. Fax: 908-527-2286. E-mail: grad_adm@turbo.kean.edu.

Kent State University, College of Fine and Professional Arts, School of Speech Pathology and Audiology, Kent, OH 44242-0001. Awards MA, PhD. Accredited by ASHA. Faculty: 13 full-time. Students: 104 full-time (93 women), 8 part-time (6 women); includes 7 international. 107 applicants, 56% accepted. In 1997, 56 master's, 2 doctorates awarded. *Degree requirements:* For master's, thesis optional, foreign language not required; for doctorate, dissertation required, foreign language not required. *Entrance requirements:* For master's, GRE General Test, minimum GPA of 2.75; for doctorate, GRE General Test, minimum GPA of 3.0. Application deadline: 7/12 (rolling processing; 11/29 for spring admission). Application fee: $30. *Tuition:* $4752 per year full-time, $216 per credit hour part-time for state residents; $9213 per year full-time, $419 per credit hour part-time for nonresidents. *Financial aid:* Fellowships, research assistantships, teaching assistantships, grants, full tuition waivers, Federal Work-Study, and career-related internships or fieldwork available. Financial aid application deadline: 3/1. • Dr. Peter B. Mueller, Director, 330-672-2672. Fax: 330-672-2643.

Lamar University, College of Fine Arts and Communication, Department of Communication Disorders, Program in Speech Language Pathology and Audiology, Beaumont, TX 77710.

Awards MS. Accredited by ASHA. Part-time and evening/weekend programs available. Faculty: 8 full-time (4 women). Students: 26 full-time (24 women), 6 part-time (3 women); includes 7 minority (2 Asian Americans, 5 Hispanics), 2 international. Average age 23. In 1997, 14 degrees awarded (100% found work related to degree). *Degree requirements:* Thesis optional, foreign language not required. *Average time to degree:* master's–2.5 years full-time. *Entrance requirements:* GRE General Test (minimum combined score of 950), TOEFL (minimum score 550), minimum GPA of 2.5, Performance IQ score of 115 required for deaf students. Application deadline: 8/1 (rolling processing; 12/1 for spring admission). Application fee: $0. *Expenses:* Tuition $1072 per year full-time, $748 per year part-time for state residents; $4924 per year full-time, $3316 per year part-time for nonresidents. Fees $458 per year full-time, $332 per year part-time. *Financial aid:* In 1997–98, 22 students received aid, including 4 fellowships totaling $4,000; research assistantships also available. Financial aid application deadline: 4/1. *Faculty research:* Voice, BSER, central audiology process, sign language. • Dr. Gabriel A. Martin, Chair, Department of Communication Disorders, 409-880-8175. Fax: 409-880-2265.

Laurentian University, Programme de Maîtrise en Orthophonie, Sudbury, ON P3E 2C6, Canada. Awards M Sc S. Open only to French-speaking students. Faculty: 1 (woman) full-time, 8 part-time (7 women). Students: 19 full-time (18 women), 1 (woman) part-time. 26 applicants, 46% accepted. In 1997, 1 degree awarded. *Application deadline:* 2/6. *Application fee:* $50. *Expenses:* Tuition $4977 per year full-time, $830 per course part-time for Canadian residents; $9072 per year full-time, $3024 per course part-time for nonresidents. Fees $194 per year full-time, $15 per year part-time. *Financial aid:* In 1997–98, 5 fellowships (all to first-year students) averaging $500 per month and totaling $7,500, 16 teaching assistantships (11 to first-year students) averaging $812 per month and totaling $84,500, scholarships totaling $16,859 were awarded. • Prof. Marine Blondeau, Coordonnatrice, 705-675-1151 Ext. 3437. Fax: 705-675-4858. Application contact: Office of Admissions, 705-675-1151 Ext. 3917. Fax: 705-675-4843.

Lehman College of the City University of New York, Department of Speech and Theater, 250 Bedford Park Boulevard West, Bronx, NY 10468-1589. Offers program in speech-language pathology and audiology (MA). One or more programs accredited by ASHA. Part-time and evening/weekend programs available. Faculty: 8 full-time (3 women), 3 part-time (all women). Students: 25 full-time (23 women), 81 part-time (75 women). *Degree requirements:* Thesis or alternative. *Application deadline:* 4/1 (rolling processing; 11/1 for spring admission). *Application fee:* $40. *Expenses:* Tuition $4350 per year full-time, $185 per credit part-time for state residents; $7600 per year full-time, $320 per credit part-time for nonresidents. Fees $120 per year full-time, $80 per year part-time. *Financial aid:* Partial tuition waivers, Federal Work-Study, and career-related internships or fieldwork available. Aid available to part-time students. Financial aid application deadline: 5/15; applicants required to submit FAFSA. • Martin R. Gitterman, Chairperson, 718-960-8134. Application contact: Barbara Weinstein, Adviser, 718-960-8138.

Lewis & Clark College, Department of Special Education—Hearing Impaired, Portland, OR 97219-7899. Awards M Ed. Part-time programs available. *Entrance requirements:* GRE General Test or MAT, interview. Application deadline: rolling. Application fee: $45. *Faculty research:* Language development, learning disabilities, parent support, sign communication, international perspectives.

Loma Linda University, Graduate School, Department of Speech-Language Pathology and Audiology, Loma Linda, CA 92350. Awards MS. One or more programs accredited by ASHA. Part-time programs available. *Degree requirements:* Thesis or alternative required, foreign language not required. *Entrance requirements:* GRE General Test (minimum combined score of 1500). Application deadline: 8/31 (rolling processing). Application fee: $40. *Tuition:* $380 per unit. *Financial aid:* Partial tuition waivers, Federal Work-Study available. Aid available to part-time students. • Dr. Jean Lowry, Coordinator, 909-824-4998.

Long Island University, Brooklyn Campus, Richard L. Conolly College of Liberal Arts and Sciences, Department of Speech, Brooklyn, NY 11201-8423. Offers program in speech-language pathology (MA). Candidate for accreditation by ASHA. Faculty: 6 full-time, 3 part-time. Students: 38 full-time (32 women), 49 part-time (43 women); includes 23 minority (10 African Americans, 1 Asian American, 12 Hispanics). 68 applicants, 35% accepted. *Application deadline:* rolling. *Application fee:* $30. Electronic applications accepted. *Expenses:* Tuition $480 per credit. Fees $415 per year full-time, $73 per semester (minimum) part-time. *Financial aid:* In 1997–98, 16 students received aid, including 6 research assistantships, 10 scholarships, assistantships. Financial aid application deadline: 8/1; applicants required to submit FAFSA. • Dr. Barbara Parisi, Chair, 718-488-1252. Application contact: Bernard W. Sullivan, Associate Director of Admissions, 718-488-1011.

Long Island University, C.W. Post Campus, School of Education, Speech and Hearing Program, Brookville, NY 11548-1300. Offers speech-language pathology (MA). One or more programs accredited by ASHA. Part-time and evening/weekend programs available. Faculty: 5 full-time (3 women), 3 part-time (all women). Students: 14 full-time, 52 part-time. 251 applicants, 12% accepted. In 1997, 23 degrees awarded. *Degree requirements:* Comprehensive exam or thesis required, foreign language not required. *Entrance requirements:* Minimum GPA of 3.0. Application deadline: 3/1. Application fee: $30. Electronic applications accepted. *Expenses:* Tuition $480 per credit. Fees $316 per year full-time, $71 per semester (minimum) part-time. *Financial aid:* In 1997–98, 5 research assistantships were awarded; career-related internships or fieldwork also available. Aid available to part-time students. Financial aid application deadline: 5/15; applicants required to submit FAFSA. • Dr. Dianne Slavin, Chairperson, 516-299-2436. E-mail: dslavin@titan.liunet.edu. Application contact: Diane Gimpel, Academic Adviser, 516-299-2995. Fax: 516-299-3151.

Louisiana State University and Agricultural and Mechanical College, College of Arts and Sciences, Department of Communication Sciences and Disorders, Baton Rouge, LA 70803. Awards MA, PhD. One or more programs accredited by ASHA. Faculty: 8 full-time (3 women), 3 part-time (2 women). Students: 50 full-time (43 women), 14 part-time (12 women); includes 2 minority (1 African American, 1 Hispanic), 1 international. Average age 30. 66 applicants, 56% accepted. In 1997, 33 master's awarded (100% found work related to degree). *Degree requirements:* For doctorate, dissertation. *Entrance requirements:* GRE General Test (minimum score 400 on each section, 1000 combined), minimum GPA of 3.0. Application deadline: 1/25 (priority date). Application fee: $25. *Tuition:* $2736 per year full-time, $285 per semester (minimum) part-time for state residents; $6636 per year full-time, $460 per semester (minimum) part-time for nonresidents. *Financial aid:* In 1997–98, 2 fellowships, 4 research assistantships, 5 teaching assistantships (2 to first-year students), 2 service assistantships were awarded; Federal Work-Study, institutionally sponsored loans also available. Financial aid application deadline: 4/1. *Faculty research:* Mechanisms of normal/disordered verbal communication, treatment/diagnosis of disordered communication. • Dr. M. Jane Collins, Chair, 504-388-2545. Application contact: John K. Cullen Jr., Graduate Committee Associate, 504-388-2545. Fax: 504-388-2995.

Louisiana State University Medical Center, School of Allied Health Professions, Program in Communication Disorders, 433 Bolivar Street, New Orleans, LA 70112-2223. Offers audiology (MCD), speech pathology (MCD). One or more programs accredited by ASHA. Faculty: 16 full-time (11 women). Students: 45 full-time (40 women), 4 part-time (all women). Average age 24. 104 applicants, 34% accepted. In 1997, 24 degrees awarded (100% found work related to degree). *Degree requirements:* Comprehensive exam required, foreign language and thesis not required. *Average time to degree:* master's–2 years full-time, 3 years part-time. *Entrance requirements:* GRE General Test (combined average 1034). Application deadline: 3/2. Application fee: $50. *Expenses:* Tuition $2878 per year full-time, $421 per semester (minimum) part-time for state residents; $6003 per year full-time, $838 per semester (minimum) part-time for nonresidents. Fees $350 per year full-time, $90 per semester (minimum) part-time. *Financial aid:* In 1997–98, 15 students received aid, including 6 work assistantships (3 to first-year students) averaging $240 per month. *Faculty research:* Hearing aids, electrophysiology, dysphagia, augmentative communication, phonology. Total annual research expenditures: $132,200. • Dr. Thomas Powell, Acting Department Head, 504-568-4345. Fax: 504-568-4352. E-mail: tpowel@lsumc.edu. Application contact: Joan Schuman, Office of Student Affairs, 504-568-4254. Fax: 504-568-4949. E-mail: alhpjbs@lsumc.edu.

Louisiana Tech University, College of Liberal Arts, Department of Speech, Ruston, LA 71272. Offerings include speech pathology and audiology (MA). Accredited by ASHA. Department faculty: 6 full-time (3 women). *Degree requirements:* Thesis or alternative required, foreign language not required. *Average time to degree:* master's–2 years full-time. *Entrance requirements:* GRE General Test. Application deadline: 7/29 (2/3 for spring admission). Application fee: $20 ($30 for international students). *Tuition:* $2382 per year full-time, $223 per quarter (minimum) part-time for state residents; $5307 per year full-time, $223 per quarter (minimum) part-time for nonresidents. • Guy Leake, Head, 318-257-4764. Application contact: Dr. Clarice Dans, Coordinator, 318-257-4764. Fax: 318-257-3935.

Loyola College, College of Arts and Sciences, Department of Speech Pathology and Audiology, Baltimore, MD 21210-2699. Awards MS, CAS. One or more programs accredited by ASHA. Evening/weekend programs available. Faculty: 4 full-time (all women), 13 part-time (12 women), 8 FTE. Students: 55 full-time (all women); includes 1 minority (Hispanic). 173 applicants, 36% accepted. In 1997, 35 master's awarded. *Entrance requirements:* For CAS, master's degree. Application deadline: 2/1 (rolling processing). Application fee: $35. *Tuition:* $11,000 per year. *Financial aid:* Research assistantships available. • Dr. Libby Kumin, Chair, 410-617-2242.

Mankato State University, College of Allied Health and Nursing, Department of Communication Disorders, South Rd and Ellis Ave, PO Box 8400, Mankato, MN 56002-8400. Awards MS. One or more programs accredited by ASHA. Part-time programs available. Faculty: 6 full-time (3 women), 1 (woman) part-time. Students: 21 full-time (18 women), 15 part-time (all women); includes 2 international. Average age 31. 45 applicants, 53% accepted. In 1997, 6 degrees awarded. *Degree requirements:* Thesis or alternative, comprehensive exam required, foreign language not required. *Entrance requirements:* GRE General Test, minimum GPA of 3.0 during previous 2 years. Application deadline: 7/10 (priority date; rolling processing; 10/30 for spring admission). Application fee: $20. *Tuition:* $126 per credit (minimum) for state residents; $200 per credit for nonresidents. *Financial aid:* Research assistantships, teaching assistantships, Federal Work-Study, institutionally sponsored loans, and career-related internships or fieldwork available. Aid available to part-time students. Financial aid application deadline: 3/15. *Faculty research:* Internet/technology issues related to speech-language pathology. • Dr. Patricia Hargrove, Chairperson, 507-389-1415. Application contact: Joni Roberts, Admissions Coordinator, 507-389-2321. Fax: 507-389-5974. E-mail: grad@mankato.msus.edu.

Marquette University, College of Communication, Program in Speech-Language Pathology, Milwaukee, WI 53201-1881. Awards MS. One or more programs accredited by ASHA. Faculty: 13 full-time (8 women), 1 (woman) part-time. Students: 45 full-time (44 women), 6 part-time (all women). Average age 25. 114 applicants, 40% accepted. In 1997, 26 degrees awarded. *Degree requirements:* Thesis, comprehensive exam required, foreign language not required. *Entrance requirements:* GRE General Test, TOEFL (minimum score 550). Application fee: $40. *Tuition:* $490 per credit. *Financial aid:* Research assistantships, teaching assistantships, full and partial tuition waivers, Federal Work-Study, institutionally sponsored loans, and career-related internships or fieldwork available. Aid available to part-time students. Financial aid application deadline: 2/15. *Faculty research:* Language processing in the brain, vocal aging, early language development, birth-to-three intervention, computer applications. Total annual research expenditures: $1200. • Dr. Edward W. Korabic, Chairman, 414-288-3428. Fax: 414-288-3980.

Marshall University, College of Liberal Arts, Department of Communication Disorders, Huntington, WV 25755-2020. Awards MA. One or more programs accredited by ASHA. Faculty: 7 (6 women). Students: 49 full-time (47 women), 23 part-time (21 women); includes 1 minority (Hispanic). In 1997, 27 degrees awarded. *Degree requirements:* Thesis optional, foreign language not required. *Entrance requirements:* GRE General Test (minimum combined score of 1200). *Tuition:* $2364 per year full-time, $132 per hour part-time for state residents; $6894 per year full-time, $383 per hour part-time for nonresidents. *Financial aid:* Fellowships available. • Kathryn Chezik, Chairperson, 304-696-3640. Application contact: Dr. James Harless, Director of Admissions, 304-696-3160.

Marywood University, Graduate School of Arts and Sciences, Department of Communication Sciences and Disorders, Scranton, PA 18509-1598. Offers program in speech language pathology (MS). Program new for fall 1998. *Entrance requirements:* TOEFL (minimum score 550; average 590). Application deadline: 7/15 (priority date; rolling processing; 12/1 for spring admission). Application fee: $20. *Expenses:* Tuition $449 per credit hour. Fees $530 per year full-time, $180 per year part-time. • Dr. Janet Bisset, Chairperson, 717-348-6211 Ext. 2314. Application contact: Deborah M. Flynn, Coordinator of Admissions, 717-340-6002. Fax: 717-961-4745. E-mail: gsas_adm@ac.marywood.edu.

Massachusetts Institute of Technology, Whitaker College of Health Sciences and Technology, Division of Health Sciences and Technology, Speech and Hearing Sciences Program, Cambridge, MA 02139-4307. Awards PhD, Sc D. Offered jointly with Harvard University. Faculty: 57 full-time (7 women). Students: 40 full-time (11 women); includes 3 minority (all Asian Americans), 2 international. Average age 25. 28 applicants, 25% accepted. *Degree requirements:* Dissertation required, foreign language not required. *Entrance requirements:* BS in engineering or science, previous course work in differential equations. Application deadline: 1/15 (priority date; rolling processing). Application fee: $55. *Expenses:* Tuition $32,065 per year. Fees $645 per year. *Financial aid:* In 1997–98, 40 students received aid, including fellowships averaging $1,380 per month, 10 research assistantships averaging $1,475 per month, 3 teaching assistantships averaging $1,520 per month and totaling $55,165; institutionally sponsored loans also available. Financial aid application deadline: 1/15. • Dr. Louis D. Braida, Director, 617-646-1253. E-mail: braida@cbgrle.mit.edu. Application contact: Dr. Joseph S. Perkell, 617-253-3223. E-mail: perkell@speech.mit.edu.

See in-depth description on page 1239.

McGill University, Faculty of Graduate Studies and Research, Faculty of Medicine, School of Communication Sciences and Disorders, Montréal, PQ H3A 2T5, Canada. Awards M Sc, M Sc A, PhD. Faculty: 9 full-time (8 women), 11 part-time (6 women). Students: 57 full-time (51 women); includes 3 international. Average age 23. 247 applicants, 17% accepted. In 1997, 23 master's awarded. *Degree requirements:* For master's, thesis (for some programs); for doctorate, dissertation. *Entrance requirements:* For master's, TOEFL (minimum score 550), minimum GPA of 3.0; for doctorate, TOEFL (minimum score 550). Application deadline: 2/15 (rolling processing). Application fee: $60. *Expenses:* Tuition $1668 per year for Canadian residents; $8268 per year for nonresidents. Fees $828 per year for Canadian residents; $1216 per year for nonresidents. *Financial aid:* Fellowships, research assistantships, institutionally sponsored loans, and career-related internships or fieldwork available. *Faculty research:* Auditory development, developmental language disorders, speech perception, reading development, language and aging. • Rachel Mayberry, Director, 514-398-4137. Application contact: André Yves Gagnon, Admissions Office, 514-398-4137.

Medical University of South Carolina, College of Health Professions, Department of Rehabilitation Sciences, Program in Communication Sciences and Disorders, Charleston, SC 29425-0002. Awards MSR. Candidate for accreditation by ASHA. Faculty: 2 full-time (both women), 2 part-time (both women), 3 FTE. *Degree requirements:* Thesis or alternative, research project required, foreign language not required. *Entrance requirements:* GRE General Test, interview, minimum GPA of 2.8. Application fee: $55. *Expenses:* Tuition $4072 per year full-time, $221 per semester hour part-time for state residents; $7064 per year full-time, $387 per semester hour part-time for nonresidents. Fees $150 per year (minimum). *Financial aid:* 11 students received aid; Federal Work-Study available. Aid available to part-time students. Financial aid application deadline: 4/1; applicants required to submit FAFSA. *Faculty research:* Sociolinguistic

Directory: Communication Disorders

Medical University of South Carolina (continued)

issues in Alzheimer's dementia, language development in student HIV/AIDS. Total annual research expenditures: $1785. • Application contact: Susan Johnson, Student Services, 843-792-2961. Fax: 843-792-0710. E-mail: johnsoss@musc.edu.

MGH Institute of Health Professions, Program in Communication Sciences and Disorders, 101 Merrimac Street, Boston, MA 02114-4719. Offers speech-language pathology (MS). One or more programs accredited by ASHA. Part-time programs available. Faculty: 7 full-time (4 women), 3 part-time (1 woman), 7.75 FTE. Students: 54 full-time (51 women), 9 part-time (7 women); includes 3 minority (2 Asian Americans, 1 Hispanic), 3 international. Average age 28. 136 applicants, 51% accepted. In 1997, 31 degrees awarded (100% found work related to degree). *Degree requirements:* Thesis or alternative, research proposal required, foreign language not required. *Average time to degree:* master's–2.5 years full-time. *Entrance requirements:* GRE General Test. Application deadline: 1/23. Application fee: $50. *Expenses:* Tuition $20,320 per year full-time, $530 per credit part-time. Fees $300 per year. *Financial aid:* In 1997–98, 52 students received aid, including 4 assistantships (2 to first-year students); full and partial tuition waivers and career-related internships or fieldwork also available. Aid available to part-time students. Financial aid application deadline: 3/6; applicants required to submit FAFSA. *Faculty research:* Children's language disorders, reading, speech disorders, voice disorders, augmentative communication. • Dr. Robert Hillman, Director, 617-726-8019. Fax: 617-726-8022. Application contact: Office of Student Affairs, 617-726-3140. Fax: 617-726-8010. E-mail: rhillman@epl.meei.harvard.edu.

See in-depth description on page 1435.

Miami University, College of Arts and Sciences, Department of Communication, Program in Speech Pathology and Audiology, Oxford, OH 45056. Awards MA, MS. Accredited by ASHA. Part-time programs available. Faculty: 16. Students: 36 full-time (32 women), 9 part-time (8 women); includes 3 minority (all African Americans), 1 international. 74 applicants, 61% accepted. In 1997, 20 degrees awarded. *Degree requirements:* Final exam required, thesis not required. *Entrance requirements:* Minimum undergraduate GPA of 3.0 during previous 2 years or 2.75 overall. Application deadline: 3/1. Application fee: $35. *Tuition:* $5932 per year full-time, $255 per credit hour part-time for state residents; $12,392 per year full-time, $524 per credit hour part-time for nonresidents. *Financial aid:* Fellowships, research assistantships, teaching assistantships, Federal Work-Study, and career-related internships or fieldwork available. Financial aid application deadline: 3/1. • Dr. Fofi Constantinidou, Director of Graduate Study, 513-529-7472.

Michigan State University, College of Communication Arts and Sciences, Department of Audiology and Speech Sciences, East Lansing, MI 48824-1020. Offers programs in audiology and speech sciences (MA, PhD), audiology and speech sciences-urban studies (PhD). One or more programs accredited by ASHA. Part-time programs available. Faculty: 10 (3 women). Students: 79 (72 women); includes 5 minority (4 African Americans, 1 Asian American), 2 international. In 1997, 23 master's, 1 doctorate awarded. *Degree requirements:* For master's, comprehensive exam or thesis required, foreign language not required; for doctorate, dissertation required, foreign language not required. *Entrance requirements:* For master's, minimum GPA of 3.0; for doctorate, GRE General Test, minimum GPA of 3.0. Application deadline: 2/15 (rolling processing). Application fee: $30 ($40 for international students). *Expenses:* Tuition $4609 per year full-time, $223 per credit hour (minimum) part-time for state residents; $8704 per year full-time, $450 per credit hour (minimum) part-time for nonresidents. Fees $576 per year full-time, $476 per year part-time. *Financial aid:* In 1997–98, 1 research assistantship (to a first-year student) averaging $550 per month, 4 teaching assistantships (3 to first-year students) averaging $550 per month were awarded; fellowships, Federal Work-Study, institutionally sponsored loans, and career-related internships or fieldwork also available. Aid available to part-time students. *Faculty research:* Childhood language, psychoacoustics, hearing aids, speech and voice disorders. • Dr. Jerry Punch, Chairperson, 517-353-7175. Application contact: Dr. Peter R. LaPine, Director of Graduate Studies and Admissions, 517-353-8780.

Minot State University, Program in Communication Disorders, Minot, ND 58707-0002. Offers audiology (MS), speech-language pathology (MS). One or more programs accredited by ASHA. Faculty: 14 full-time (10 women), 2 part-time (both women). Students: 32 full-time (27 women), 36 part-time (33 women). In 1997, 33 degrees awarded. *Degree requirements:* Thesis or alternative required, foreign language not required. *Entrance requirements:* GRE General Test (minimum combined score of 1100 rquired) or minimum GPA of 3.0. Application deadline: 2/15 (priority date). Application fee: $25. *Tuition:* $2714 per year for state residents; $3235 per year (minimum) for nonresidents. *Financial aid:* 8 students received aid; research assistantships, teaching assistantships, tuition waivers, institutionally sponsored loans, and career-related internships or fieldwork available. Aid available to part-time students. Financial aid application deadline: 2/5. *Faculty research:* Native American and early childhood language process, cross-categorical clinical emphasis. • Dr. David K. Williams, Chairperson, 701-858-3031. E-mail: williamd@warple.cs.misu.nodak.edu. Application contact: Tammy White, Administrative Secretary, 701-858-3250. Fax: 701-839-6933.

Mississippi University for Women, Division of Education and Human Sciences, Columbus, MS 39701-9998. Offerings include speech/language pathology (MS). Candidate for accreditation by ASHA. Division faculty: 13 full-time (11 women). *Application deadline:* 4/1 (priority date; rolling processing). *Application fee:* $0 ($25 for international students). *Tuition:* $2556 per year full-time, $142 per hour part-time for state residents; $5546 per year full-time, $308 per hour part-time for nonresidents. • Dr. Suzanne Bean, Head, 601-329-7175. Fax: 601-329-8515. E-mail: sbean@muw.edu.

Montclair State University, College of Humanities and Social Sciences, Department of Communication Sciences and Disorders, Upper Montclair, NJ 07043-1624. Offers programs in early childhood special education (MA), learning disabilities (MA), speech/language pathology (MA). One or more programs accredited by ASHA. Part-time and evening/weekend programs available. Faculty: 9 full-time. Students: 41 full-time (40 women), 122 part-time (118 women); includes 7 minority (3 African Americans, 2 Asian Americans, 2 Hispanics). In 1997, 55 degrees awarded. *Degree requirements:* Comprehensive exam or fieldwork/project required, foreign language and thesis not required. *Entrance requirements:* GRE General Test. Application deadline: 4/1 (rolling processing; 11/1 for spring admission). Application fee: $40. *Expenses:* Tuition $201 per credit for state residents; $257 per credit for nonresidents. Fees $22.05 per credit. *Financial aid:* Research assistantships available. Financial aid application deadline: 3/1; applicants required to submit FAFSA. • Dr. Warren Heiss, Chairperson, 973-655-4232.

Moorhead State University, Department of Speech/Language/Hearing Sciences, Moorhead, MN 56563-0002. Offers program in speech pathology and audiology (MS). One or more programs accredited by ASHA. Faculty: 5 full-time (1 woman), 2 part-time (1 woman). Students: 24 full-time (23 women), 2 part-time (both women); includes 4 international. 100 applicants, 12% accepted. In 1997, 6 degrees awarded. *Degree requirements:* Final oral exam, project or thesis, written comprehensive exam required, foreign language not required. *Entrance requirements:* GRE General Test, TOEFL (minimum score 550), minimum GPA of 2.75, undergraduate major in speech/language/hearing sciences. Application deadline: 2/1. Application fee: $20 ($35 for international students). Electronic applications accepted. *Tuition:* $145 per credit hour for state residents; $220 per credit hour for nonresidents. *Financial aid:* In 1997–98, 8 administrative assistantships were awarded; Federal Work-Study and career-related internships or fieldwork also available. Financial aid application deadline: 7/15; applicants required to submit FAFSA. • Dr. Arne Teigland, Chairperson, 218-236-2287. Application contact: Dr. Louis DeMaio, Coordinator, 218-236-4643.

Murray State University, College of Education, Department of Special Education, Program in Communication Disorders, Murray, KY 42071-0009. Awards MS. One or more programs accredited by ASHA. Part-time programs available. Faculty: 4 full-time (3 women). Students: 43 full-time (41 women), 6 part-time (5 women); includes 1 minority (African American). 123 applicants, 17% accepted. In 1997, 21 degrees awarded. *Entrance requirements:* GRE General Test or MAT, TOEFL (minimum score 500). Application deadline: rolling. Application fee: $20. *Expenses:* Tuition $2500 per year full-time, $124 per hour part-time for state residents; $6740 per year full-time, $357 per hour part-time for nonresidents. Fees $360 per year full-time, $180 per year part-time. *Financial aid:* Research assistantships, teaching assistantships, Federal Work-Study available. Financial aid application deadline: 4/1. • Dr. Creighton Miller, Director, 502-762-6822. Fax: 502-762-6803.

Nazareth College of Rochester, Graduate Studies, Department of Speech-Language Pathology, Program in Speech Pathology, Rochester, NY 14618-3790. Awards MS. Accredited by ASHA. Part-time programs available. Postbaccalaureate distance learning degree programs offered. Faculty: 7 full-time (5 women), 5 part-time (3 women). Students: 19 full-time (all women), 38 part-time (35 women); includes 2 minority (1 African American, 1 Asian American). 108 applicants, 27% accepted. In 1997, 23 degrees awarded. *Degree requirements:* Comprehensive exam required, foreign language and thesis not required. *Entrance requirements:* GRE General Test, minimum GPA of 2.7. Application deadline: 2/1 (10/1 for spring admission). Application fee: $40. *Expenses:* Tuition $436 per credit hour. Fees $20 per semester. • Application contact: Dr. Kay F. Marshman, Dean, 716-389-2815. Fax: 716-389-2452.

New Mexico State University, College of Education, Department of Special Education/Communication Disorders, Las Cruces, NM 88003-8001. Awards MA. Part-time programs available. Faculty: 12 full-time (7 women). 111 applicants, 30% accepted. In 1997, 164 degrees awarded. *Degree requirements:* Thesis or alternative. *Entrance requirements:* GRE General Test or MAT. Application deadline: 3/1 (priority date; rolling processing). Application fee: $15 ($35 for international students). Electronic applications accepted. *Tuition:* $2514 per year full-time, $105 per credit hour part-time for state residents; $7848 per year full-time, $327 per credit hour part-time for nonresidents. *Financial aid:* Research assistantships, teaching assistantships, Federal Work-Study, and career-related internships or fieldwork available. Aid available to part-time students. Financial aid application deadline: 3/1. *Faculty research:* Multicultural special education, multicultural communication disorders, mild handicaps, augmentative and alternative communication, transdisciplinary training. • Dr. Gerard Giordano, Head, 505-646-2402. Fax: 505-646-7712. E-mail: ggiordan@nmsu.edu.

New York University, School of Education, Department of Speech-Language Pathology and Audiology, New York, NY 10012-1019. Awards MA, PhD. Accredited by ASHA. Part-time and evening/weekend programs available. Faculty: 7 full-time (6 women), 14 part-time. Students: 88 full-time, 54 part-time. 413 applicants, 14% accepted. In 1997, 46 master's, 1 doctorate awarded. Terminal master's awarded for partial completion of doctoral program. *Degree requirements:* For master's, thesis required (for some programs), foreign language not required; for doctorate, dissertation. *Entrance requirements:* For master's, TOEFL; for doctorate, GRE General Test, TOEFL, interview. Application deadline: 2/1 (priority date; rolling processing; 12/1 for spring admission). Application fee: $40 ($60 for international students). *Financial aid:* Partial tuition waivers, Federal Work-Study, institutionally sponsored loans, and career-related internships or fieldwork available. Aid available to part-time students. Financial aid application deadline: 3/1; applicants required to submit FAFSA. *Faculty research:* Child language acquisition and disorders, neuromotor disorders, stuttering theory and therapy, cleft palate, aphasia. • Phyllis Tureen, Chairperson, 212-998-5265. Fax: 212-995-4356. Application contact: Office of Graduate Admissions, 212-998-5030. Fax: 212-995-4328.

North Carolina Central University, Division of Academic Affairs, School of Education, Program in Speech Pathology and Audiology, Durham, NC 27707-3129. Awards M Ed. Accredited by ASHA. Part-time and evening/weekend programs available. Students: 51 full-time (49 women), 11 part-time (9 women); includes 39 minority (36 African Americans, 2 Hispanics, 1 Native American). Average age 29. 98 applicants, 29% accepted. In 1997, 30 degrees awarded. *Degree requirements:* Computer language, thesis or alternative, comprehensive exam required, foreign language not required. *Entrance requirements:* Minimum GPA of 3.0 in major, 2.5 overall. Application deadline: 8/1. Application fee: $30. *Tuition:* $2027 per year full-time, $508 per semester (minimum) part-time for state residents; $9155 per year full-time, $2290 per semester (minimum) part-time for nonresidents. *Financial aid:* Fellowships, teaching assistantships, Federal Work-Study, institutionally sponsored loans, and career-related internships or fieldwork available. Aid available to part-time students. Financial aid application deadline: 5/1. *Faculty research:* Vocational programs for special needs learners. • Dr. H. Donell Lewis, Director, 919-560-6479. Application contact: Dr. Cecelia Steppe-Jones, Associate Dean of Graduate Studies and Administration, 919-560-6478.

Northeastern University, Bouvé College of Pharmacy and Health Sciences Graduate School, Department of Speech-Language Pathology and Audiology, Boston, MA 02115-5096. Offers programs in audiology (MS), speech-language pathology (MS). Accredited by ASHA. Faculty: 7 full-time (4 women), 7 part-time (4 women). Students: 75 full-time (70 women), 4 part-time (3 women). Average age 27. 409 applicants, 29% accepted. In 1997, 39 degrees awarded. *Degree requirements:* Comprehensive exam required, thesis optional, foreign language not required. *Entrance requirements:* GRE General Test or MAT. Application deadline: 2/15. Application fee: $50. *Expenses:* Tuition $440 per credit hour. Fees $55 per quarter full-time, $13.25 per quarter part-time. *Financial aid:* Fellowships, research assistantships, teaching assistantships, administrative assistantships, Federal Work-Study, and career-related internships or fieldwork available. Aid available to part-time students. Financial aid application deadline: 3/1; applicants required to submit FAFSA. *Faculty research:* Psychoacoustics, applied and theoretical aspects of aphasia, developmentally delayed children, hearing impairments. Total annual research expenditures: $200,000. • Dr. Kevin Kearns, Chairperson, 617-373-3698. Application contact: Bill Purnell, Director of Graduate Admissions, 617-373-2708. Fax: 617-373-4701. E-mail: w.purnell@nunet.neu.edu.

See in-depth description on page 1245.

Northeast Louisiana University, College of Liberal Arts, School of Communication, Department of Communicative Disorders, Monroe, LA 71209-0001. Awards MA. One or more programs accredited by ASHA. *Degree requirements:* Research course required, thesis optional, foreign language not required. *Entrance requirements:* GRE General Test (minimum combined score of 880), minimum GPA of 2.5 or GRE General Test (minimum combined score of 900). Application deadline: 3/1 (priority date; 10/1 for spring admission). Application fee: $15 ($25 for international students). *Tuition:* $2028 per year full-time, $240 per semester (minimum) part-time for state residents; $6852 per year full-time, $240 per semester (minimum) part-time for nonresidents. *Faculty research:* Child language, stuttering, multicultural issues, ethics.

Northern Arizona University, College of Health Professions, Department of Speech Pathology, Flagstaff, AZ 86011. Awards MS. One or more programs accredited by ASHA. Part-time programs available. Faculty: 9 full-time (5 women). Students: 40 full-time (39 women), 12 part-time (all women); includes 3 minority (2 Hispanics, 1 Native American), 2 international. Average age 25. 134 applicants, 28% accepted. In 1997, 11 degrees awarded. *Degree requirements:* Thesis optional, foreign language not required. *Entrance requirements:* GRE General Test, minimum GPA of 3.0. Application deadline: 1/31 (priority date). Application fee: $45. *Expenses:* Tuition $2088 per year full-time, $330 per semester (minimum) part-time for state residents; $8004 per year full-time, $1002 per semester (minimum) part-time for nonresidents. Fees $72 per year full-time, $18 per semester (minimum) part-time. *Financial aid:* In 1997–98, 15 teaching assistantships totaling $17,000 were awarded; traineeships, full and partial tuition waivers, Federal Work-Study, and career-related internships or fieldwork also available. Financial aid application deadline: 4/15. *Faculty research:* Meta-analysis of language, alaryngeal speech, aphasia. • Wayne Secord, Chair, 520-523-7443. Application contact: Dennis Tanner, Graduate Coordinator, 520-523-2969.

Northern Illinois University, College of Health and Human Sciences, Department of Communicative Disorders, De Kalb, IL 60115-2854. Awards MA. One or more programs accredited by ASHA. Faculty: 13 full-time (9 women), 1 part-time (0 women). Students: 99 full-time (94 women), 25 part-time (23 women); includes 9 minority (3 African Americans, 4 Asian Americans, 2 Hispanics), 1 international. Average age 27. 271 applicants, 25% accepted. In 1997, 46 degrees awarded. *Degree requirements:* Comprehensive exam required, thesis optional, foreign language not required. *Entrance requirements:* GRE General Test, TOEFL (minimum score 550), minimum undergraduate GPA of 3.0. Application deadline: 2/1 (priority date; rolling processing; 9/1 for spring admission). Application fee: $30. *Tuition:* $3984 per year full-time, $154 per credit hour part-time for state residents; $8160 per year full-time, $328 per credit hour part-time for nonresidents. *Financial aid:* In 1997–98, 42 research assistantships were awarded; fellowships, teaching assistantships, staff assistantships, full tuition waivers, Federal Work-Study, and career-related internships or fieldwork also available. Aid available to part-time students. • Dr. Earl Seaver, Chair, 815-753-1484.

Northern Michigan University, College of Nursing and Allied Health Science, Department of Communication Disorders, Marquette, MI 49855-5301. Awards MA. One or more programs accredited by ASHA. Part-time programs available. Faculty: 5 full-time (2 women). Students: 27 full-time (24 women), 2 part-time (both women); includes 1 minority (Native American). 27 applicants, 15% accepted. In 1997, 8 degrees awarded. *Degree requirements:* Thesis or alternative required, foreign language not required. *Entrance requirements:* GRE General Test, minimum GPA of 3.0. Application deadline: 7/1 (priority date; rolling processing; 11/1 for spring admission). Application fee: $25. *Expenses:* Tuition $135 per credit hour for state residents; $215 per credit hour for nonresidents. Fees $183 per year full-time, $94 per year (minimum) part-time. *Financial aid:* In 1997–98, 9 graduate assistantships averaging $770 per month were awarded; Federal Work-Study, institutionally sponsored loans, and career-related internships or fieldwork also available. Aid available to part-time students. Financial aid application deadline: 3/1. *Faculty research:* Auditory adaptation, learning disabilities. • Dr. Roger Towne, Interim Head, 906-227-2125.

Northwestern University, School of Speech, Department of Communication Sciences and Disorders, Program in Audiology and Hearing Sciences, Evanston, IL 60208. Awards MA, PhD. Admissions and degrees offered through The Graduate School. Students: 24 full-time (22 women); includes 1 minority (Asian American), 5 international. 44 applicants, 70% accepted. In 1997, 6 master's awarded. *Degree requirements:* For master's, seminar paper required, foreign language and thesis not required; for doctorate, dissertation, pre-dissertation research project, qualifying exam required, foreign language not required. *Entrance requirements:* GRE General Test, minimum GPA of 3.0. Application deadline: 8/30. Application fee: $50 ($55 for international students). *Tuition:* $20,430 per year full-time, $2424 per course part-time. *Financial aid:* In 1997–98, 1 fellowship (to a first-year student) averaging $1,256 per month, 1 research assistantship (to a first-year student) averaging $1,592 per month, 2 teaching assistantships averaging $1,296 per month were awarded; traineeships, Federal Work-Study, institutionally sponsored loans, and career-related internships or fieldwork also available. Financial aid application deadline: 1/15; applicants required to submit FAFSA. *Faculty research:* Auditory physiology, psychoacoustics, auditory evoked potentials, amplification, audiologic assessment and rehabilitation, speech perception, hearing loss and aging. • Dr. Mario A. Ruggero, Director, 847-491-3164. E-mail: mruggero@nwu.edu. Application contact: Luanne McMillen, Admission Contact, 847-491-3164. Fax: 847-491-2523. E-mail: l-mcmillen@nwu.edu.

See in-depth description on page 1247.

Northwestern University, School of Speech, Department of Communication Sciences and Disorders, Program in Speech and Language Pathology, Evanston, IL 60208. Awards MA, PhD. Accredited by ASHA. Admissions and degrees offered through The Graduate School. Students: 112 full-time (108 women), 4 part-time (all women); includes 15 minority (8 African Americans, 6 Asian Americans, 1 Hispanic), 8 international. 258 applicants, 48% accepted. In 1997, 47 master's, 3 doctorates awarded. *Degree requirements:* For master's, research paper, seminar required, thesis optional, foreign language not required; for doctorate, dissertation, pre-dissertation research project required, foreign language not required. *Entrance requirements:* GRE General Test (minimum combined score of 1000; average 1150), minimum GPA of 3.2, average 3.5. Application deadline: 8/30. Application fee: $50 ($55 for international students). *Tuition:* $20,430 per year full-time, $2424 per course part-time. *Financial aid:* In 1997–98, 63 students received aid, including 1 fellowship (to a first-year student) averaging $1,256 per month, 4 research assistantships (1 to a first-year student) averaging $1,592 per month, 5 teaching assistantships (1 to a first-year student) averaging $1,296 per month; Federal Work-Study, institutionally sponsored loans, and career-related internships or fieldwork also available. Financial aid application deadline: 1/15; applicants required to submit FAFSA. *Faculty research:* Voice science, language development, acquired neurogenic speech and language, swallowing physiology, acoustics of speech. Total annual research expenditures: $1.5 million. • Dr. Bruce L. Smith, Director, 847-491-5073. E-mail: b-smith2@nwu.edu. Application contact: Cindy Coy, Admission Contact, 847-491-5073. Fax: 847-467-2776. E-mail: ccoy@nwu.edu.

See in-depth description on page 1249.

Northwestern University, School of Speech, Department of Communication Sciences and Disorders, Program in Speech and Language Pathology and Learning Disabilities, Evanston, IL 60208. Awards MA. Accredited by ASHA. Admissions and degree offered through The Graduate School. Students: 4 full-time (all women); includes 1 international. 15 applicants, 47% accepted. *Degree requirements:* Seminar paper required, foreign language not required. *Entrance requirements:* GRE General Test. Application deadline: 8/30. Application fee: $50 ($55 for international students). *Tuition:* $20,430 per year full-time, $2424 per course part-time. *Financial aid:* Partial tuition scholarships, institutionally sponsored loans available. Financial aid application deadline: 1/15; applicants required to submit FAFSA. *Faculty research:* Language and cognitive development, phonological and reading development. • Dr. Bruce L. Smith, Director, 847-491-5073. E-mail: b-smith2@nwu.edu. Application contact: Cindy Coy, Admission Contact, 847-491-5073. Fax: 847-467-2776. E-mail: ccoy@nwu.edu.

Nova Southeastern University, Fischler Center for the Advancement of Education, Program in Speech-Language Pathology, Fort Lauderdale, FL 33314-7721. Offers audiology (Au D), speech-language pathology (MS, SLPD). Accredited by ASHA. Part-time and evening/weekend programs available. Students: 47 full-time (45 women), 322 part-time (307 women); includes 13 African Americans, 5 Asian Americans, 35 Hispanics, 9 international. In 1997, 55 master's awarded. *Degree requirements:* For master's, practicum required, foreign language and thesis not required. *Entrance requirements:* For master's, interview, minimum GPA of 3.0. Application deadline: rolling. Application fee: $50. *Tuition:* $620 per credit hour. *Financial aid:* Federal Work-Study and career-related internships or fieldwork available. Aid available to part-time students. • Dr. Barry A. Freeman, Dean, 954-262-7717. E-mail: freeman@fcae.nova.edu. Application contact: Elaine Bloom, Director, Student Services, 800-986-3223 Ext. 7712. Fax: 954-262-3940. E-mail: bloome@fcae.nova.edu.

The Ohio State University, College of Social and Behavioral Sciences, Department of Speech and Hearing Science, Columbus, OH 43210. Awards MA, PhD. One or more programs accredited by ASHA. Faculty: 14. Students: 82 full-time (71 women), 9 part-time (all women); includes 7 minority (6 African Americans, 1 Hispanic), 5 international. 213 applicants, 46% accepted. In 1997, 38 master's awarded (2% entered university research/teaching); 1 doctorate awarded. *Degree requirements:* For master's, thesis optional; for doctorate, dissertation. *Entrance requirements:* GRE General Test. Application deadline: 8/15 (rolling processing). Application fee: $30 ($40 for international students). *Tuition:* $5472 per year full-time, $554 per quarter (minimum) part-time for state residents; $14,172 per year full-time, $1424 per quarter (minimum) part-time for nonresidents. *Financial aid:* Fellowships, research assistantships, teaching assistantships, Federal Work-Study, institutionally sponsored loans available. Aid available to part-time students. • Robert A. Fox, Chairman, 614-292-8207. Fax: 614-292-7504. E-mail: fox.2@osu.edu.

Ohio University, Graduate Studies, College of Health and Human Services, School of Hearing and Speech Sciences, Athens, OH 45701-2979. Offers program in speech pathology and audiology (MA, PhD). One or more programs accredited by ASHA. Faculty: 9 full-time (3 women). Students: 54 full-time (51 women), 2 part-time (both women); includes 1 minority (African American), 1 international. Average age 25. 179 applicants, 12% accepted. In 1997, 24 master's, 1 doctorate awarded. *Degree requirements:* For master's, thesis optional, foreign language not required; for doctorate, dissertation required, foreign language not required. *Entrance requirements:* GRE or MAT, TOEFL. Application deadline: 3/1 (priority date; rolling processing). Application fee: $30. *Tuition:* $5430 per year full-time, $216 per quarter hour part-time for state residents; $10,431 per year full-time, $423 per quarter hour part-time for nonresidents. *Financial aid:* In 1997–98, 53 students received aid, including 43 research assistantships, 10 scholarships; full tuition waivers, Federal Work-Study, institutionally sponsored loans, and career-related internships or fieldwork also available. Financial aid application deadline: 3/1. *Faculty research:* Speech production, computer applications, phonological processing, bilingualism, language disorders. • Dr. Norman Garber, Director, 740-593-1407. E-mail: garber1@ohiou.edu. Application contact: Dr. Helen Ezell, Graduate Coordinator, 740-593-1417. Fax: 740-593-0287. E-mail: ezell1@ohiou.edu.

Oklahoma State University, College of Arts and Sciences, Department of Communications Sciences and Disorders, Stillwater, OK 74078. Awards MA. One or more programs accredited by ASHA. Faculty: 9 full-time (8 women), 1 part-time (0 women), 9.75 FTE. Students: 32 full-time (30 women), 7 part-time (all women); includes 2 minority (1 African American, 1 Native American). Average age 25. In 1997, 27 degrees awarded. *Entrance requirements:* TOEFL (minimum score 550). Application deadline: 7/1 (priority date). Application fee: $25. *Financial aid:* In 1997–98, 11 students received aid, including 11 teaching assistantships (4 to first-year students) totaling $54,450; partial tuition waivers, Federal Work-Study, and career-related internships or fieldwork also available. Aid available to part-time students. Financial aid application deadline: 3/1. *Faculty research:* Speech communications. • Dr. Arthur Pentz Jr., Head, 405-744-6021.

Old Dominion University, Darden College of Education, Department of Early Childhood, Speech-Language Pathology, and Special Education, Program in Speech Pathology and Audiology, Norfolk, VA 23529. Awards MS Ed. One or more programs accredited by ASHA. Part-time programs available. Students: 37 full-time (all women), 24 part-time (23 women); includes 7 minority (4 African Americans, 2 Asian Americans, 1 Hispanic). Average age 29. 187 applicants, 14% accepted. In 1997, 24 degrees awarded (100% found work related to degree). *Degree requirements:* Thesis, comprehensive and written exams, practica required, foreign language not required. *Entrance requirements:* GRE General Test (minimum combined score of 1200), minimum GPA of 3.0 in major, 2.75 overall. Application deadline: 3/14 (rolling processing; 10/14 for spring admission). Application fee: $30. Electronic applications accepted. *Expenses:* Tuition $180 per credit hour for state residents; $477 per credit hour for nonresidents. Fees $140 per year full-time, $32 per semester part-time. *Financial aid:* In 1997–98, 30 students received aid, including 8 fellowships (1 to a first-year student) totaling $24,080, 3 research assistantships (2 to first-year students) totaling $24,166, 3 tuition grants (1 to a first-year student) totaling $8,346; partial tuition waivers and career-related internships or fieldwork also available. Aid available to part-time students. Financial aid application deadline: 2/15; applicants required to submit CSS PROFILE or FAFSA. *Faculty research:* Childhood language disorders, phonological disorders, stuttering, social dialects, aphasia. • Dr. Nicholas G. Bountress, Director, 757-683-4117. Fax: 757-683-5593.

Our Lady of the Lake University of San Antonio, School of Education and Clinical Studies, Program in Communication and Learning Disorders, 411 Southwest 24th Street, San Antonio, TX 78207-4689. Awards MA. One or more programs accredited by ASHA. Part-time and evening/weekend programs available. Faculty: 9 full-time (7 women), 1 (woman) part-time. Students: 9 full-time (8 women), 36 part-time (33 women); includes 20 minority (19 Hispanics, 1 Native American). Average age 30. In 1997, 16 degrees awarded. *Degree requirements:* Computer language, comprehensive clinical practicum, comprehensive exam required, thesis optional, foreign language not required. *Entrance requirements:* GRE General Test or MAT, interview. Application deadline: 3/15. Application fee: $15. *Expenses:* Tuition $371 per credit hour. Fees $57 per semester full-time, $32 per semester part-time. *Financial aid:* Research assistantships, teaching assistantships, and career-related internships or fieldwork available. Aid available to part-time students. Financial aid application deadline: 3/15. *Faculty research:* Multicultural issues, neurogenic disorders, neural networks, equivalence learning. • Dr. Anthony Salvatore, Head, 210-434-6711 Ext. 410. E-mail: salva@lake.ollusa.edu. Application contact: Debbie Hamilton, Director of Admissions, 210-434-6711 Ext. 314. Fax: 210-436-2314.

Pennsylvania State University University Park Campus, College of Health and Human Development, Department of Communication Disorders, University Park, PA 16802-1503. Awards M Ed, MS, PhD. One or more programs accredited by ASHA. Students: 60 full-time (54 women), 2 part-time (1 woman). In 1997, 21 master's awarded. *Entrance requirements:* GRE General Test. Application fee: $40. *Expenses:* Tuition $6534 per year full-time, $276 per credit part-time for state residents; $13,460 per year full-time, $561 per credit part-time for nonresidents. Fees $252 per year (minimum) full-time, $43 per semester (minimum) part-time. • Dr. Gordon W. Blood, Head, 814-865-3177.

See in-depth description on page 1317.

Plattsburgh State University of New York, Faculty of Professional Studies, Department of Communication Disorders, Plattsburgh, NY 12901-2681. Offers program in speech-language pathology (MA). One or more programs accredited by ASHA. Part-time programs available. Students: 38 full-time (all women), 9 part-time (8 women); includes 1 minority (Hispanic), 5 international. 44 applicants, 32% accepted. In 1997, 18 degrees awarded. *Degree requirements:* NTE required, thesis optional, foreign language not required. *Entrance requirements:* GRE General Test, minimum GPA of 3.0. Application deadline: rolling. Application fee: $50. *Expenses:* Tuition $5100 per year full-time, $213 per credit hour part-time for state residents; $8416 per year full-time, $351 per credit hour part-time for nonresidents. Fees $395 per year full-time, $15.10 per credit hour part-time. *Financial aid:* 23 students received aid; Federal Work-Study and career-related internships or fieldwork available. Aid available to part-time students. Financial aid application deadline: 4/15; applicants required to submit FAFSA. *Faculty research:* Ototoxins and noise effects on hearing, language impairment in Alzheimer's disease, attitudes on stuttering, diagnostic audiology. Total annual research expenditures: $451,800. • Dr. Robert Davis, Chair, 518-564-2170. Fax: 518-564-4069. E-mail: davisri@splava.cc.plattsburgh.edu. Application contact: Dr. R. Wacker, Associate Professor, 518-564-2170.

Portland State University, College of Liberal Arts and Sciences, Department of Speech Communication, Program in Speech and Hearing Sciences, Portland, OR 97207-0751. Awards MA, MS. One or more programs accredited by ASHA. Faculty: 15 full-time (8 women), 20 part-time (16 women), 18 FTE. Students: 49 full-time (41 women), 11 part-time (all women); includes 5 minority (4 Asian Americans, 1 Hispanic), 2 international. Average age 29. 150 applicants, 17% accepted. In 1997, 25 degrees awarded. *Degree requirements:* Variable foreign language requirement, thesis or alternative, oral exam. *Entrance requirements:* TOEFL (minimum score 550), minimum GPA of 3.0 in upper-division course work or 2.75 overall. Application deadline: 1/1. Application fee: $50. *Tuition:* $6101 per year full-time, $689 per semester (minimum) part-time for state residents; $10,445 per year full-time, $689 per semester (minimum) part-time for nonresidents. *Financial aid:* Research assistantships, teaching assistantships, Federal Work-Study, institutionally sponsored loans, and career-related internships or fieldwork available. Aid available to part-time students. Financial aid application deadline: 3/1; applicants required to submit FAFSA. *Faculty research:* Adolescents with clefts, spectral analysis of stuttering, communication in late talkers, speech intelligibility, brainstem response in fitting hearing aids. • Dr. Doug Martin, Acting Director, 503-725-3533. Fax: 503-725-5385.

Purdue University, School of Liberal Arts, Department of Audiology and Speech Science, West Lafayette, IN 47907. Offers programs in audiology (MS, PhD), linguistics (MS, PhD), speech and hearing science (MS, PhD), speech-language pathology (MS, PhD). Accredited by ASHA. Faculty: 17 full-time (11 women), 4 part-time (1 woman), 18.5 FTE. Students: 78 full-time (71 women), 5 part-time (all women); includes 5 minority (2 African Americans, 1 Asian American, 2 Hispanics), 7 international. Average age 24. 234 applicants, 58% accepted. In 1997, 19 master's awarded (100% found work related to degree); 3 doctorates awarded (100% entered university research/teaching). *Degree requirements:* For master's, thesis optional,

Directory: Communication Disorders

Purdue University (continued)

foreign language not required; for doctorate, dissertation required, foreign language not required. *Average time to degree:* master's–2 years full-time; doctorate–4.5 years full-time. *Entrance requirements:* GRE, TOEFL (minimum score 600). Application deadline: 1/15. Application fee: $30. Electronic applications accepted. *Tuition:* $3500 per year full-time, $126 per credit hour part-time for state residents; $11,720 per year full-time, $387 per credit hour part-time for nonresidents. *Financial aid:* In 1997–98, 16 fellowships (3 to first-year students) averaging $930 per month, 27 research assistantships (10 to first-year students) averaging $1,094 per month, 36 teaching assistantships (11 to first-year students) averaging $821 per month were awarded; grants and career-related internships or fieldwork also available. Aid available to part-time students. Financial aid application deadline: 2/1; applicants required to submit FAFSA. *Faculty research:* Psychoacoustics, speech perception, speech physiology, stuttering, child language. Total annual research expenditures: $1.183 million. • Dr. Anne Smith, Head, 765-494-3788. Application contact: Susan Schneidt, Graduate Secretary, 765-494-3786. Fax: 765-494-0771. E-mail: sschneid@purdue.edu.

Announcement: Master's, doctoral, postdoctoral programs in speech-language pathology, audiology, speech and hearing sciences, and linguistics. Course work, clinical experiences, and research opportunities in all areas of communication disorders. Strong emphasis on normal processes of speech, language, and hearing as well. Areas of specialization include auditory psychophysics, aural rehabilitation, language development, child language disorders, voice disorders, stuttering and other fluency disorders, neurogenic speech and language disorders, developmental disabilities, hearing aid technology, linguistics of American Sign Language, neuroscience, augmentative and alternative communication, phonology and phonological disorders, speech physiology, as well as treatment efficacy. Fellowships and teaching, research, and administrative assistantships available. Purdue is an Equal Access/ Equal Opportunity university.

Queens College of the City University of New York, Arts Division, Department of Communication Arts and Sciences, Program in Speech Pathology, 65-30 Kissena Boulevard, Flushing, NY 11367-1597. Awards MA. Accredited by ASHA. Students: 29 full-time (all women). 164 applicants, 9% accepted. In 1997, 17 degrees awarded. *Degree requirements:* Clinical internships required, thesis optional, foreign language not required. *Entrance requirements:* GRE General Test (minimum combined score of 1000), TOEFL (minimum score 650), minimum GPA of 3.0. Application deadline: 4/1 (rolling processing; 11/1 for spring admission). Application fee: $40. *Expenses:* Tuition $4350 per year full-time, $185 per credit part-time for state residents; $7600 per year full-time, $320 per credit part-time for nonresidents. Fees $104 per year. *Financial aid:* Partial tuition waivers, Federal Work-Study, institutionally sponsored loans, and career-related internships or fieldwork available. Aid available to part-time students. Financial aid application deadline: 4/1; applicants required to submit FAFSA. • Robert L. Rosenbaum, Graduate Adviser, 718-520-7359. Application contact: Mario Caruso, Director of Graduate Admissions, 718-997-5200. Fax: 718-997-5193. E-mail: graduate%queens.bitnet@cunyvm.cuny.edu.

Radford University, Graduate College, College of Nursing and Health Services, Department of Communication Science and Disorders, Radford, VA 24142. Awards MA, MS. One or more programs accredited by ASHA. Part-time programs available. Postbaccalaureate distance learning degree programs offered (minimal on-campus study). Faculty: 7 full-time (5 women), 1 (woman) part-time, 7.2 FTE. Students: 41 full-time (38 women), 25 part-time (all women); includes 3 minority (2 African Americans, 1 Asian American). Average age 26. 186 applicants, 17% accepted. In 1997, 27 degrees awarded. *Degree requirements:* Thesis or alternative, comprehensive exam required, foreign language not required. *Entrance requirements:* GMAT, GRE General Test, MAT, or NTE; TOEFL (minimum score 550), minimum GPA of 2.7. Application deadline: 2/1 (priority date; rolling processing; 10/1 for spring admission). Application fee: $25. Electronic applications accepted. *Expenses:* Tuition $2302 per year full-time, $147 per credit hour part-time for state residents; $5672 per year full-time, $287 per credit hour part-time for nonresidents. Fees $1222 per year full-time. *Financial aid:* In 1997–98, 57 students received aid, including 14 fellowships totaling $47,275, 9 research assistantships totaling $25,110, scholarships/grants totaling $331,987; teaching assistantships, Federal Work-Study, institutionally sponsored loans, and career-related internships or fieldwork also available. Financial aid application deadline: 2/1; applicants required to submit FAFSA. • Dr. John M. Pettit, Chairperson, 540-831-5204. Fax: 540-831-6314. E-mail: jpettit@runet.edu.

Rush University, College of Health Sciences, Department of Communication Disorders and Sciences, Chicago, IL 60612-3832. Offers programs in audiology (MS), speech-language pathology (MS). One or more programs accredited by ASHA. Part-time programs available. Faculty: 14 full-time (12 women), 7 part-time (1 woman). Students: 23 full-time (20 women); includes 1 minority (Hispanic). Average age 24. 125 applicants, 24% accepted. In 1997, 13 degrees awarded (100% found work related to degree). *Degree requirements:* Thesis optional, foreign language not required. *Entrance requirements:* GRE General Test (minimum combined score of 950), minimum GPA of 3.0. Application deadline: 2/15 (priority date). Application fee: $40. *Tuition:* $8200 per year full-time, $370 per credit hour part-time. *Financial aid:* In 1997–98, 10 stipends, tuition scholarships were awarded; Federal Work-Study, institutionally sponsored loans, and career-related internships or fieldwork also available. Aid available to part-time students. Financial aid application deadline: 4/15. *Faculty research:* Voice analysis, aural rehabilitation, adult neurology, infant hearing, motor speech. Total annual research expenditures: $6000. • Dr. Dianne H. Meyer, Chairperson, 312-942-5332. Fax: 312-243-8280. Application contact: Donna Kayman, Assistant Director, College Admissions Services, 312-942-7100. Fax: 312-942-2219.

See in-depth description on page 1261.

St. Cloud State University, College of Fine Arts and Humanities, Department of Communication Disorders, St. Cloud, MN 56301-4498. Awards MS. One or more programs accredited by ASHA. Faculty: 5 full-time (4 women). Students: 25 full-time (24 women), 22 part-time (19 women). In 1997, 11 degrees awarded. *Degree requirements:* Thesis or alternative required, foreign language not required. *Entrance requirements:* GRE General Test, minimum GPA of 2.75. Application deadline: 1/15. Application fee: $20 ($100 for international students). *Expenses:* Tuition $128 per credit for state residents; $203 per credit for nonresidents. Fees $16.32 per credit. *Financial aid:* In 1997–98, 17 graduate assistantships were awarded; Federal Work-Study also available. Financial aid application deadline: 3/1. • Dr. Gerald LaVoi, Chairperson, 320-255-2092. Application contact: Ann Anderson, Graduate Studies Office, 320-255-2113. Fax: 320-654-5371. E-mail: anna@grad.stcloud.msus.edu.

St. John's University, Graduate School of Arts and Sciences, Department of Speech Pathology and Audiology, Jamaica, NY 11439. Awards MA. Accredited by ASHA. Evening/weekend programs available. Faculty: 14 full-time (8 women), 17 part-time (7 women). Students: 56 full-time (51 women), 56 part-time (47 women); includes 12 minority (5 African Americans, 7 Hispanics). Average age 30. 349 applicants, 8% accepted. In 1997, 48 degrees awarded. *Degree requirements:* Thesis optional. *Entrance requirements:* Minimum GPA of 3.0. Application deadline: 3/1 (rolling processing; 10/1 for spring admission). Application fee: $40. *Expenses:* Tuition $600 per credit. Fees $150 per year. *Financial aid:* In 1997–98, 4 research assistantships (2 to first-year students) averaging $667 per month were awarded; graduate assistantships, Federal Work-Study, and career-related internships or fieldwork also available. Aid available to part-time students. Financial aid application deadline: 3/1; applicants required to submit FAFSA. *Faculty research:* Experimental phonetics, coarticulation, language skills of the deaf and hearing-impaired, child language development, English as a second language. • Dr. Barbara Horn, Chair, 718-990-6452. Application contact: Shamus J. McGrenra, TOR, Associate Director, Graduate Admissions, 718-990-6107. Fax: 718-990-5736. E-mail: mcgrenrs@stjohns.edu.

Saint Louis University, Institute for Leadership and Public Service, Department of Communication Disorders, St. Louis, MO 63103-2097. Awards MA. One or more programs accredited by ASHA. Faculty: 12 full-time (8 women), 16 part-time (12 women). Students: 39 full-time (37 women); includes 8 minority (all African Americans). 94 applicants, 14% accepted. In 1997, 26 degrees awarded. *Degree requirements:* Comprehensive oral and written exams required, foreign language and thesis not required. *Entrance requirements:* GRE General Test. Application deadline: 2/1 (priority date). Application fee: $40. *Tuition:* $542 per credit hour. *Financial aid:* In 1997–98, 1 fellowship, 35 assistantships, traineeships were awarded; partial tuition waivers, Federal Work-Study, and career-related internships or fieldwork also available. Financial aid application deadline: 4/1. *Faculty research:* Voice disorders, multicultural issues, child language, phonology, hearing conservation. • Dr. Lynda Campbell, Chairperson, 314-977-2948. Fax: 314-977-3360. Application contact: Dr. Marcia Buresch, Assistant Dean of the Graduate School, 314-977-2240. Fax: 314-977-3943.

Saint Xavier University, School of Arts and Sciences, Department of Speech-Language Pathology, Chicago, IL 60655-3105. Awards MS. Candidate for accreditation by ASHA. Faculty: 6 full-time (4 women), 2 part-time (both women). Students: 46 full-time. In 1997, 14 degrees awarded. *Entrance requirements:* GRE General Test, minimum GPA of 3.0, prerequisite undergraduate course work in speech. Application deadline: 3/1. Application fee: $35. *Expenses:* Tuition $460 per hour. Fees $50 per year. *Financial aid:* Career-related internships or fieldwork available. Aid available to part-time students. Financial aid applicants required to submit FAFSA. • Dr. Michael Flahive, Graduate Director, 773-298-3566. Fax: 773-779-9061. E-mail: flahive@sxu.edu.

San Diego State University, College of Health and Human Services, Department of Communicative Disorders, San Diego, CA 92182. Offers programs in communicative disorders (MA), language and communicative disorders (PhD). One or more programs accredited by ASHA. PhD offered jointly with the University of California, San Diego. Part-time programs available. Students: 101 full-time (92 women), 30 part-time (29 women); includes 33 minority (3 African Americans, 6 Asian Americans, 23 Hispanics, 1 Native American), 6 international. Average age 29. 242 applicants, 20% accepted. In 1997, 36 master's awarded. *Degree requirements:* For doctorate, dissertation required, foreign language not required. *Entrance requirements:* For master's, GRE General Test, TOEFL (minimum score 550); for doctorate, GRE General Test. Application deadline: 2/15. Application fee: $55. *Expenses:* Tuition $0 for state residents; $246 per unit for nonresidents. Fees $1932 per year full-time, $1266 per year part-time. *Financial aid:* Fellowships, research assistantships, teaching assistantships, and career-related internships or fieldwork available. *Faculty research:* Brain/behavior relationships in language development, grammatical processing and language disorders, interdisciplinary training of bilingual speech pathologists. Total annual research expenditures: $660,000. • Steve Kramer, Chair, 619-594-6140. E-mail: skramer@mail.sdsu.edu. Application contact: Elizabeth Allen, Graduate Coordinator, 619-594-6354. Fax: 619-594-7109. E-mail: eallen@mail.sdsu.edu.

San Francisco State University, College of Education, Department of Special Education, Program in Communicative Disorders, San Francisco, CA 94132-1722. Awards MS. One or more programs accredited by ASHA. Part-time programs available. *Entrance requirements:* Minimum GPA of 2.5 in last 60 units. Application deadline: 11/30 (priority date; rolling processing). Application fee: $55. *Expenses:* Tuition $0 for state residents; $246 per unit for nonresidents. Fees $1982 per year full-time, $1316 per year part-time.

San Jose State University, College of Education, Program in Communication Disorders and Sciences, San Jose, CA 95192-0001. Offers audiology (MA), speech pathology (MA). One or more programs accredited by ASHA. Evening/weekend programs available. Faculty: 3 full-time (1 woman), 1 part-time (0 women). Students: 83 full-time (81 women), 13 part-time (12 women); includes 31 minority (5 African Americans, 12 Asian Americans, 13 Hispanics, 1 Native American), 6 international. Average age 30. 87 applicants, 68% accepted. In 1997, 39 degrees awarded. *Entrance requirements:* MAT. Application deadline: 6/1 (rolling processing). Application fee: $59. *Expenses:* Tuition $0 for state residents; $246 per unit for nonresidents. Fees $2017 per year full-time, $1351 per year part-time. *Financial aid:* Career-related internships or fieldwork available. • Gloria Weddington, Director, 408-924-3688.

San Jose State University, College of Education, Program in Sensory and Severe Disabilities, San Jose, CA 95192-0001. Offerings include education for the hearing impaired (MA). Program faculty: 3 full-time (1 woman), 2 part-time (0 women). *Degree requirements:* Thesis or alternative required, foreign language not required. *Entrance requirements:* GRE General Test. Application deadline: 6/1 (rolling processing). Application fee: $59. *Expenses:* Tuition $0 for state residents; $246 per unit for nonresidents. Fees $2017 per year full-time, $1351 per year part-time. • Sharon Sacks, Coordinator, 408-924-3695.

Seton Hall University, School of Graduate Medical Education, Program in Speech-Language Pathology, South Orange, NJ 07079-2697. Awards MS. Program new for fall 1998. *Entrance requirements:* GRE, clinical experience; bachelor's degree in speech-language pathology, speech and hearing sciences, or communication disorders; minimum GPA of 3.0. *Expenses:* Tuition $500 per credit. Fees $610 per year full-time, $185 per semester part-time. • Application contact: Office of Graduate Medical Education, 973-761-7145. Fax: 973-275-2370. E-mail: gradmeded@shu.edu.

South Carolina State University, School of Applied Professional Sciences, Department of Speech Pathology and Audiology, 300 College Street Northeast, Orangeburg, SC 29117-0001. Offers program in speech/language pathology (MA). Accredited by ASHA. Part-time and evening/weekend programs available. Faculty: 11 full-time (10 women), 3 part-time (1 woman). Students: 35 full-time (32 women), 41 part-time (all women). Average age 31. 52 applicants, 48% accepted. In 1997, 29 degrees awarded (100% found work related to degree). *Degree requirements:* Departmental qualifying exam required, thesis optional, foreign language not required. *Entrance requirements:* GRE or NTE, minimum GPA of 3.0. Application deadline: 7/10 (11/10 for spring admission). Application fee: $25. *Tuition:* $2974 per year full-time, $165 per credit hour part-time. *Financial aid:* Federal Work-Study, institutionally sponsored loans, and career-related internships or fieldwork available. Financial aid application deadline: 6/1. • Dr. Harriette Gregg, Chairperson, 803-536-8074. Fax: 803-533-3627.

South Carolina State University, School of Education, Department of Teacher Education, 300 College Street Northeast, Orangeburg, SC 29117-0001. Offerings include speech pathology (MAT). Department faculty: 7 full-time (3 women), 2 part-time (1 woman). *Average time to degree:* master's–2 years full-time, 4 years part-time. *Application deadline:* 7/15 (priority date; rolling processing; 11/10 for spring admission). *Application fee:* $25. *Tuition:* $2974 per year full-time, $165 per credit hour part-time. • Dr. Jesse Kinard, Chairman, 803-536-8934. Application contact: Dr. Gail Joyner-Fleming, Interim Associate Dean and Director, Graduate Teacher Education, 803-536-8824. Fax: 803-536-8492.

Southeast Missouri State University, Department of Communication Disorders, Cape Girardeau, MO 63701-4799. Awards MA. One or more programs accredited by ASHA. *Degree requirements:* Thesis or alternative required, foreign language not required. *Entrance requirements:* Minimum undergraduate GPA of 3.0. Application deadline: 1/31 (priority date; rolling processing; 11/21 for spring admission). Application fee: $20 ($100 for international students). *Tuition:* $2034 per year full-time, $113 per credit hour part-time for state residents; $3672 per year full-time, $204 per credit hour part-time for nonresidents. *Financial aid:* Teaching assistantships available. • Dr. Sakina Drummond, Chairperson, 573-651-2488. Application contact: Office of Graduate Studies, 573-651-2192.

Southern Connecticut State University, School of Professional Studies, Department of Communication Disorders, New Haven, CT 06515-1355. Offers program in speech pathology and audiology (MS). One or more programs accredited by ASHA. Part-time programs available. Faculty: 7 full-time, 6 part-time. Students: 106 full-time (99 women), 46 part-time (44 women); includes 11 minority (5 African Americans, 6 Hispanics). 350 applicants, 14% accepted. In 1997, 46 degrees awarded. *Degree requirements:* Clinical experience required, foreign language not required. *Entrance requirements:* GRE, interview, minimum QPA of 3.0. Application deadline:

3/1. Application fee: $40. *Expenses:* Tuition $2632 per year full-time, $188 per credit part-time for state residents; $7200 per year full-time, $188 per credit part-time for nonresidents. Fees $1806 per year full-time, $45 per semester part-time for state residents; $2703 per year full-time, $45 per semester part-time for nonresidents. *Financial aid:* Career-related internships or fieldwork available. • Dr. Marianne Kennedy, Chair, 203-392-5955. Application contact: Dr. Frank Sansone, Graduate Coordinator, 203-392-5955.

Southern Illinois University at Carbondale, College of Education, Rehabilitation Institute, Department of Communication Disorders and Sciences, Carbondale, IL 62901-6806. Awards MS. One or more programs accredited by ASHA. Faculty: 8 full-time (4 women). Students: 39 full-time (35 women), 1 (woman) part-time; includes 2 minority (1 African American, 1 Hispanic). Average age 29. 147 applicants, 12% accepted. In 1997, 21 degrees awarded. *Degree requirements:* Thesis required, foreign language not required. *Entrance requirements:* GRE, TOEFL (minimum score 550), minimum GPA of 3.0. Application deadline: 2/1. Application fee: $20. *Expenses:* Tuition $2964 per year full-time, $99 per semester hour part-time for state residents; $8892 per year full-time, $270 per semester hour part-time for nonresidents. Fees $1034 per year full-time, $298 per semester (minimum) part-time. *Financial aid:* In 1997–98, 9 students received aid, including 1 fellowship, 7 research assistantships; clinical assistantships, full tuition waivers, Federal Work-Study, institutionally sponsored loans, and career-related internships or fieldwork also available. *Faculty research:* Neurolinguistics, language processing, child language, fluency, phonology. • Dr. Gary Austin, Chairperson, 618-536-7704. Application contact: Secretary, 618-536-7704.

Southern Illinois University at Edwardsville, School of Education, Department of Speech Pathology and Audiology, Edwardsville, IL 62026-0001. Offers program in speech pathology (MS). Accredited by ASHA. Part-time programs available. Students: 40 full-time (39 women), 11 part-time (all women); includes 2 minority (1 African American, 1 Asian American). 103 applicants, 17% accepted. In 1997, 27 degrees awarded. *Degree requirements:* Thesis or alternative, final exam required, foreign language not required. *Application deadline:* 7/24. *Application fee:* $25. *Expenses:* Tuition $1716 per year full-time, $95 per credit hour part-time for state residents; $5149 per year full-time, $286 per credit hour part-time for nonresidents. Fees $463 per year full-time, $433 per year part-time. *Financial aid:* In 1997–98, 3 fellowships, 19 assistantships were awarded; research assistantships, teaching assistantships, Federal Work-Study, institutionally sponsored loans also available. Aid available to part-time students. • Dr. Nikki Murdick, Chair, 618-692-3662.

Southwest Missouri State University, College of Health and Human Services, Department of Communication Disorders, Springfield, MO 65804-0094. Awards MS. One or more programs accredited by ASHA. Faculty: 6 full-time (3 women). Students: 63 full-time (all women), 8 part-time (all women); includes 1 minority (Native American), 1 international. Average age 24. In 1997, 32 degrees awarded. *Degree requirements:* Thesis or alternative, comprehensive exam required, foreign language not required. *Average time to degree:* master's–2 years full-time. *Entrance requirements:* GRE General Test (minimum score 450 on each section), minimum GPA of 3.0. Application deadline: 2/1 (priority date). Application fee: $25. *Expenses:* Tuition $1980 per year full-time, $110 per credit hour part-time for state residents; $3960 per year full-time, $220 per credit hour part-time for nonresidents. Fees $274 per year full-time, $73 per semester part-time. *Financial aid:* In 1997–98, 8 graduate assistantships averaging $583 per month and totaling $42,000 were awarded; fellowships, research assistantships, teaching assistantships, Federal Work-Study, and career-related internships or fieldwork also available. Aid available to part-time students. *Faculty research:* Speech-language pathology, audiology, the hearing-impaired and deaf. • Dr. Neil DiSarno, Head, 417-836-5368. Fax: 417-836-7662. E-mail: njd579f@wpgate.smsu.edu.

Southwest Texas State University, School of Health Professions, Department of Communication Disorders, San Marcos, TX 78666. Awards MA, MSCDIS. One or more programs accredited by ASHA. Part-time programs available. Faculty: 6 full-time (3 women), 1 (woman) part-time. Students: 28 full-time (25 women); includes 4 minority (1 African American, 1 Asian American, 2 Hispanics). Average age 27. In 1997, 14 degrees awarded. *Degree requirements:* Thesis (for some programs), comprehensive exam, practicum required, foreign language not required. *Entrance requirements:* GRE General Test (minimum combined score of 900), TOEFL (minimum score 550), minimum GPA of 3.0 in communications disorders, 2.75 in last 60 hours. Application deadline: 4/15. Application fee: $25 ($50 for international students). *Expenses:* Tuition $648 per year full-time, $120 per semester (minimum) part-time for state residents; $4500 per year full-time, $750 per semester (minimum) part-time for nonresidents. Fees $1264 per year full-time, $314 per semester (minimum) part-time. *Financial aid:* In 1997–98, 2 fellowships (both to first-year students), 2 research assistantships (1 to a first-year student) averaging $360 per month and totaling $3,240, 2 scholarships were awarded; Federal Work-Study, institutionally sponsored loans, and career-related internships or fieldwork also available. Aid available to part-time students. Financial aid application deadline: 4/1; applicants required to submit FAFSA. *Faculty research:* Stuttering, aphasia, neurogenic disorders, child language, autism. • Dr. A. Richard Mallard III, Chair, 512-245-2330. Fax: 512-245-8244. E-mail: am02@swt.edu.

State University of New York at Buffalo, Graduate School, Faculty of Social Sciences, Department of Communicative Disorders, Buffalo, NY 14260. Offers programs in communicative disorders and sciences (PhD), speech-language pathology and audiology (MA). One or more programs accredited by ASHA. Faculty: 14 full-time (8 women), 5 part-time (3 women). Students: 69 full-time (62 women), 8 part-time (6 women); includes 2 minority (1 African American, 1 Hispanic), 11 international. Average age 24. 138 applicants, 22% accepted. In 1997, 36 master's awarded (100% found work related to degree); 1 doctorate awarded (100% entered university research/teaching). *Degree requirements:* For master's, thesis or alternative, exam required, foreign language not required; for doctorate, dissertation, exams required, foreign language not required. *Entrance requirements:* For master's, GRE General Test (minimum combined score of 1500), TOEFL (minimum score 550), minimum GPA of 3.0; for doctorate, GRE General Test (minimum combined score of 1500), TOEFL (minimum score 550). Application deadline: 3/1 (10/1 for spring admission). Application fee: $35. *Tuition:* $5970 per year full-time, $288 per credit hour part-time for state residents; $9286 per year full-time, $426 per credit hour part-time for nonresidents. *Financial aid:* In 1997–98, 21 students received aid, including 5 research assistantships (2 to first-year students) averaging $768 per month, 8 teaching assistantships (3 to first-year students) averaging $768 per month, 8 graduate assistantships (3 to first-year students) averaging $768 per month; fellowships, Federal Work-Study, institutionally sponsored loans, and career-related internships or fieldwork also available. Financial aid application deadline: 2/1. *Faculty research:* Hearing and speech science, central auditory evaluation, child and adult language disorders, augmentative communication, cochlear implants. Total annual research expenditures: $1 million. • Dr. Judith Duchan, Chairperson, 716-645-3400 Ext. 110. Application contact: Admissions Coordinator, 716-645-3400 Ext. 105. Fax: 716-645-2216.

State University of New York at New Paltz, Faculty of Liberal Arts and Sciences, Department of Communications, New Paltz, NY 12561-2499. Offers program in communication disorders (MS Ed). One or more programs accredited by ASHA. Students: 22 full-time (17 women), 28 part-time (25 women); includes 1 minority (Hispanic). In 1997, 22 degrees awarded. *Degree requirements:* Thesis, comprehensive exam. *Entrance requirements:* GRE General Test, minimum GPA of 3.0. Application deadline: 3/15 (priority date; rolling processing). Application fee: $50. *Expenses:* Tuition $5100 per year full-time, $213 per credit hour part-time for state residents; $8416 per year full-time, $351 per credit hour part-time for nonresidents. Fees $493 per year full-time, $48 per semester (minimum) part-time. *Financial aid:* Research assistantships, teaching assistantships, Federal Work-Study, institutionally sponsored loans, and career-related internships or fieldwork available. • Dr. Rob Miraldi, Chairman, 914-257-3460.

State University of New York College at Buffalo, Faculty of Applied Science and Education, Department of Speech Language Pathology, Buffalo, NY 14222-1095. Awards MS Ed. Accredited by ASHA. Part-time programs available. Faculty: 7 full-time (6 women). Students: 34 full-time (30 women), 11 part-time (all women); includes 2 minority (1 Asian American, 1 Hispanic). Average age 28. 79 applicants, 16% accepted. In 1997, 21 degrees awarded. *Degree requirements:* Thesis or alternative, project required, foreign language not required. *Entrance requirements:* Minimum GPA of 3.0 in last 60 hours, 24 hours in communication disorders. Application deadline: 3/1 (10/1 for spring admission). Application fee: $50. *Expenses:* Tuition $5100 per year full-time, $213 per credit hour part-time for state residents; $8416 per year full-time, $351 per credit hour part-time for nonresidents. Fees $195 per year full-time, $8.60 per credit hour part-time. *Financial aid:* Fellowships, assistantships, Federal Work-Study, and career-related internships or fieldwork available. Aid available to part-time students. Financial aid application deadline: 3/1. • Dr. Nan Lund, Chairperson, 716-878-5502.

State University of New York College at Fredonia, Department of Speech Pathology and Audiology, Fredonia, NY 14063. Awards MS. Accredited by ASHA. Part-time and evening/weekend programs available. Faculty: 6 full-time (3 women), 4 part-time (3 women). Students: 26 full-time (24 women), 7 part-time (all women); includes 3 international. 128 applicants, 26% accepted. In 1997, 28 degrees awarded. *Degree requirements:* Thesis or alternative, clinical practice required, foreign language not required. *Application deadline:* 7/5. *Application fee:* $50. *Expenses:* Tuition $5100 per year full-time, $213 per credit hour part-time for state residents; $8416 per year full-time, $351 per credit hour part-time for nonresidents. Fees $725 per year full-time, $30 per credit hour part-time. *Financial aid:* In 1997–98, 7 teaching assistantships were awarded; research assistantships, full and partial tuition waivers, and career-related internships or fieldwork also available. Aid available to part-time students. Financial aid application deadline: 4/1; applicants required to submit FAFSA. *Faculty research:* Voice problems of singers and actors, geriatric speech and language problems. • Dr. Dennis M. Perez, Chair, 716-673-3203.

State University of New York College at Geneseo, Department of Communicative Disorders and Sciences, Geneseo, NY 14454-1401. Awards MA. One or more programs accredited by ASHA. Faculty: 7 full-time (3 women), 12 part-time (9 women), 11 FTE. Students: 29 full-time (all women); includes 2 minority (1 Asian American, 1 Hispanic). Average age 24. 94 applicants, 41% accepted. In 1997, 20 degrees awarded. *Degree requirements:* Thesis optional, foreign language not required. *Entrance requirements:* GRE General Test. Application deadline: 2/1 (rolling processing). Application fee: $35. *Expenses:* Tuition $5100 per year full-time, $213 per credit hour part-time for state residents; $8416 per year full-time, $351 per credit hour part-time for nonresidents. Fees $375 per year full-time, $15.35 per credit hour part-time. *Financial aid:* In 1997–98, 2 students received aid, including 2 fellowships (both to first-year students); research assistantships, teaching assistantships, Federal Work-Study, institutionally sponsored loans, and career-related internships or fieldwork also available. Financial aid application deadline: 4/1; applicants required to submit FAFSA. *Faculty research:* Stuttering in young children. Total annual research expenditures: $6330. • Dr. Linda House, Chairperson, 716-245-5328. Fax: 716-245-5434. E-mail: house@uno.cc.geneseo.edu.

Stephen F. Austin State University, College of Education, Department of Counseling and Special Education, Nacogdoches, TX 75962. Offerings include speech pathology (MS). Accredited by ASHA. Department faculty: 13 full-time (2 women), 3 part-time (1 woman). *Application deadline:* 3/1 (10/1 for spring admission). *Application fee:* $0 ($25 for international students). *Tuition:* $1465 per year full-time, $263 per semester (minimum) part-time for state residents; $5299 per year full-time, $890 per semester (minimum) part-time for nonresidents. • Dr. Anna Bradfield, Chair, 409-468-2906.

Syracuse University, School of Education, Communication Sciences and Disorders Program, Syracuse, NY 13244-0003. Offers audiology and speech pathology (MS, PhD). One or more programs accredited by ASHA. Faculty: 6 full-time (3 women). Students: 66 full-time (62 women), 33 part-time (31 women); includes 6 minority (2 African Americans, 3 Asian Americans, 1 Hispanic), 6 international. 146 applicants, 59% accepted. In 1997, 31 master's awarded. *Degree requirements:* For master's, thesis or alternative required, foreign language not required; for doctorate, dissertation required, foreign language not required. *Entrance requirements:* GRE. Application deadline: rolling. Application fee: $40. *Tuition:* $13,320 per year full-time, $555 per credit hour part-time. *Financial aid:* Fellowships, research assistantships, teaching assistantships, administrative assistantships, Federal Work-Study, and career-related internships or fieldwork available. Aid available to part-time students. Financial aid application deadline: 3/1. *Faculty research:* Stuttering, disordered phonology in young children, disability prevention, language comprehension, psychoacoustics. • Dr. Corinne Smith, Interim Chair, 315-443-9645.

Teachers College, Columbia University, Graduate Faculty of Education, Department of Biobehavioral Studies, Program in Audiology, 525 West 120th Street, New York, NY 10027-6696. Awards Ed M, MS, Ed D, PhD. Faculty: 4 full-time (3 women), 10 part-time (8 women), 9.4 FTE. Students: 1 (woman) part-time. Average age 46. 2 applicants, 0% accepted. In 1997, 1 master's awarded. *Degree requirements:* For doctorate, computer language, dissertation required, foreign language not required. *Application deadline:* 2/1 (priority date). *Application fee:* $50. *Expenses:* Tuition $640 per credit. Fees $120 per semester. *Financial aid:* Fellowships, teaching assistantships, full and partial tuition waivers, Federal Work-Study, institutionally sponsored loans, and career-related internships or fieldwork available. Aid available to part-time students. Financial aid application deadline: 2/1. *Faculty research:* Clinical psychoacoustics. • Application contact: Victor Singletary, Office of Admissions, 212-678-3710. Fax: 212-678-4171.

Teachers College, Columbia University, Graduate Faculty of Education, Department of Biobehavioral Studies, Program in Speech-Language Pathology, 525 West 120th Street, New York, NY 10027-6696. Awards Ed M, MS, Ed D, PhD. Faculty: 4 full-time (3 women), 10 part-time (8 women), 9.4 FTE. Students: 60 full-time (57 women), 60 part-time (57 women); includes 22 minority (9 African Americans, 7 Asian Americans, 6 Hispanics), 4 international. Average age 28. 263 applicants, 29% accepted. In 1997, 42 master's, 1 doctorate awarded. Terminal master's awarded for partial completion of doctoral program. *Degree requirements:* For master's, computer language required, foreign language not required; for doctorate, computer language, dissertation required, foreign language not required. *Application deadline:* 2/1 (priority date). *Application fee:* $50. *Expenses:* Tuition $640 per credit. Fees $120 per semester. *Financial aid:* Fellowships, teaching assistantships, full and partial tuition waivers, Federal Work-Study, institutionally sponsored loans, and career-related internships or fieldwork available. Aid available to part-time students. Financial aid application deadline: 2/1. *Faculty research:* Neuropathology of speech, stuttering, language disorders in children and adults, motor speech. • Application contact: Victor Singletary, Office of Admissions, 212-678-3710. Fax: 212-678-4171.

Teachers College, Columbia University, Graduate Faculty of Education, Department of Health and Behavior Studies, Program in Hearing Impairment, 525 West 120th Street, New York, NY 10027-6696. Awards MA, Ed D. Faculty: 1 full-time (0 women), 4 part-time (3 women), 3.1 FTE. Students: 5 full-time (4 women), 42 part-time (33 women); includes 11 minority (3 African Americans, 3 Asian Americans, 5 Hispanics), 1 international. Average age 31. 32 applicants, 75% accepted. In 1997, 14 master's awarded. *Degree requirements:* For doctorate, dissertation. *Application deadline:* 5/15 (12/1 for spring admission). *Application fee:* $50. *Expenses:* Tuition $640 per credit. Fees $120 per semester. *Financial aid:* Fellowships, full and partial tuition waivers, Federal Work-Study, institutionally sponsored loans, and career-related internships or fieldwork available. Aid available to part-time students. Financial aid application deadline: 2/1. *Faculty research:* Language development, reading/writing, cognitive abilities, text analysis, auditory streaming, teaching the deaf and hard of hearing. • Application contact: Ursula Felton, Office of Admissions, 212-678-3710. Fax: 212-678-4171.

Temple University, Health Sciences Center and Graduate School, College of Allied Health Professions, Department of Communication Sciences, Philadelphia, PA 19122-6096. Offerings include speech-language-hearing (MA). Accredited by ASHA. Department faculty: 16 full-time (9 women). *Entrance requirements:* GRE General Test (minimum combined score of 1000), minimum GPA of 3.0 during previous 2 years, 2.8 overall. Application deadline: 3/1 (11/1 for spring admission). Application fee: $40. *Expenses:* Tuition $323 per semester hour for state

Directory: Communication Disorders

Temple University (continued)

residents; $444 per semester hour for nonresidents. Fees $170 per year full-time, $28 per semester (minimum) part-time. • Dr. Aquiles Iglesias, Chair, 215-204-1871. Application contact: Dr. Lori Russell, Graduate Chair, 215-204-1876.

Texas A&M University–Kingsville, College of Arts and Sciences, Department of Communication, Kingsville, TX 78363. Offers program in communication sciences and disorders (MS). Candidate for accreditation by ASHA. Students: 21 full-time (all women), 1 (woman) part-time; includes 13 minority (1 African American, 12 Hispanics), 1 international. *Degree requirements:* Thesis or alternative, comprehensive exam required, foreign language not required. *Entrance requirements:* GRE General Test, TOEFL (minimum score 500). Application deadline: 6/1 (rolling processing; 11/15 for spring admission). Application fee: $15 ($25 for international students). *Tuition:* $1822 per year full-time, $281 per semester (minimum) part-time for state residents; $6934 per year full-time, $908 per semester (minimum) part-time for nonresidents. *Financial aid:* Application deadline 5/15. • Dr. V. A. Smith, Coordinator, 512-593-3401.

Texas Christian University, College of Fine Arts and Communication, Department of Communication Sciences and Disorders, Fort Worth, TX 76129-0002. Offers program in speech-language pathology (MS). One or more programs accredited by ASHA. Part-time and evening/weekend programs available. Students: 22 (20 women); includes 3 minority (all Hispanics), 1 international. 141 applicants, 14% accepted. In 1997, 12 degrees awarded. *Degree requirements:* Comprehensive exam required, foreign language not required. *Entrance requirements:* GRE General Test (minimum combined score of 1000), TOEFL (minimum score 550). Application deadline: 3/1 (rolling processing; 12/1 for spring admission). Application fee: $0. *Expenses:* Tuition $10,350 per year full-time, $345 per credit hour part-time. Fees $1240 per year full-time, $50 per credit hour part-time. *Financial aid:* Graduate assistantships available. Financial aid application deadline: 3/1. • Dr. Jennifer B. Watson, Chairperson, 817-257-7621.

Texas Tech University Health Sciences Center, School of Allied Health, Program in Communication Disorders, Lubbock, TX 79430-0002. Awards MS. One or more programs accredited by ASHA. Faculty: 9 full-time (5 women). Students: 36 full-time (34 women); includes 2 minority (both Hispanics). Average age 22. 67 applicants, 28% accepted. In 1997, 15 degrees awarded (100% found work related to degree). *Degree requirements:* Thesis or alternative required, foreign language not required. *Entrance requirements:* GRE General Test (minimum combined score of 1000). Application deadline: 3/1 (rolling processing). Application fee: $30. *Expenses:* Tuition $36 per credit hour for state residents; $249 per credit hour for nonresidents. Fees $1348 per year full-time for state residents; $1349 per year full-time for nonresidents. *Financial aid:* In 1997–98, 15 students received aid, including 2 fellowships (1 to a first-year student) averaging $1,000 per month, 6 research assistantships (4 to first-year students) averaging $3,000 per month, 5 teaching assistantships averaging $800 per month; career-related internships or fieldwork also available. Financial aid application deadline: 9/1; applicants required to submit FAFSA. *Faculty research:* Craniofacial anomalies, evoked potentials, neurolinguistics, language simulations, vocal fold burns. Total annual research expenditures: $150,000. • Dr. Raymond Linville, Chairperson, 806-742-3907. Fax: 806-742-0907. E-mail: pdrnl@ttacs.ttu.edu. Application contact: Rob Shive, Assistant Dean, Admissions and Student Affairs, 806-743-3220. Fax: 806-743-3249. E-mail: sahras@ttuhsc.edu.

Texas Woman's University, College of Health Sciences, Department of Communication Sciences and Disorders, Denton, TX 76204. Offers programs in education of the hearing impaired (MS), speech-language pathology (MS). One or more programs accredited by ASHA. Part-time programs available. Postbaccalaureate distance learning degree programs offered. Faculty: 13 full-time (11 women), 6 part-time (4 women), 14 FTE. Students: 87 full-time (85 women), 127 part-time (121 women); includes 23 minority (4 African Americans, 1 Asian American, 18 Hispanics). Average age 31. 225 applicants, 11% accepted. In 1997, 31 degrees awarded. *Degree requirements:* Thesis required, foreign language not required. *Average time to degree:* master's–2 years full-time, 3 years part-time. *Entrance requirements:* GRE General Test (minimum combined score of 700), minimum GPA of 3.0. Application deadline: 2/1 (priority date). Application fee: $25. *Financial aid:* In 1997–98, 32 students received aid, including 2 teaching assistantships (1 to a first-year student) averaging $352 per month and totaling $6,024, 30 scholarships (19 to first-year students) totaling $13,224; partial tuition waivers, Federal Work-Study, institutionally sponsored loans, and career-related internships or fieldwork also available. Aid available to part-time students. Financial aid application deadline: 2/1. *Faculty research:* Cerebral blood flow for language tasks, auditory physiology at brain stem and mid-brain level, affective development of clinicians. • Dr. Alfred H. White, Chair, 940-898-2025. Fax: 940-898-2070.

Towson University, Program in Communication Sciences and Disorders, Towson, MD 21252-0001. Offers speech-language pathology and audiology (MS). One or more programs accredited by ASHA. Evening/weekend programs available. Faculty: 9 full-time (7 women), 2 part-time (both women). Students: 58 full-time (53 women), 11 part-time (10 women); includes 6 minority (3 African Americans, 3 Asian Americans). In 1997, 33 degrees awarded. *Degree requirements:* Exam required, foreign language and thesis not required. *Entrance requirements:* Minimum GPA of 3.0 in major. Application deadline: 2/1. Application fee: $40. *Expenses:* Tuition $187 per credit hour for state residents; $364 per credit hour for nonresidents. Fees $40 per credit hour. *Financial aid:* Assistantships, Federal Work-Study available. Financial aid application deadline: 4/1; applicants required to submit FAFSA. *Faculty research:* Oral-literate issues, narratives, localization in noise, cross-language assessment, temporal processing of speech. • Dr. Julie Ries, Director, 410-830-3105. Fax: 410-830-4131. E-mail: jries@towson.edu. Application contact: Fran Musotto, Office Manager, 410-830-2501. Fax: 410-830-4675. E-mail: fmusotto@towson.edu.

Truman State University, Division of Human Potential and Performance, Program in Communication Disorders, Kirksville, MO 63501-4221. Awards MA. One or more programs accredited by ASHA. *Degree requirements:* Comprehensive exams required, thesis optional, foreign language not required. *Entrance requirements:* GRE General Test, minimum GPA of 3.0. Application deadline: 6/15 (priority date; rolling processing; 11/1 for spring admission). Application fee: $0 ($25 for international students). *Tuition:* $2718 per year full-time, $151 per credit part-time for state residents; $4824 per year full-time, $268 per credit part-time for nonresidents.

Université de Montréal, Faculties of Medicine and Graduate Studies, Graduate Programs in Medicine, Department of Audiology and Speech Pathology, Montréal, PQ H3C 3J7, Canada. Offers program in speech-language pathology and audiology (MOA). Faculty: 15 full-time (9 women), 2 part-time (1 woman). Students: 109 full-time (105 women). 49 applicants, 94% accepted. In 1997, 38 degrees awarded. *Degree requirements:* Thesis. *Entrance requirements:* B Sc in speech-language pathology and audiology, proficiency in French, knowledge of English. Application deadline: 2/1. Application fee: $30. *Faculty research:* Aphasia in adults, dysarthria, speech and hearing-impaired children, noise-induced hearing impairment, computerized audiometry. • Jean-Pierre Gagné, Director, 514-343-7458. Application contact: Bernadette Ska, Graduate Director, 514-343-2485.

The University of Akron, College of Fine and Applied Arts, School of Speech-Language Pathology and Audiology, Program in Audiology, Akron, OH 44325-0001. Awards MA. Accredited by ASHA. Students: 21 full-time (15 women); includes 1 minority (African American). Average age 25. In 1997, 32 degrees awarded. *Degree requirements:* Thesis or alternative required, foreign language not required. *Entrance requirements:* GRE, minimum GPA of 3.0. Application deadline: 3/1 (rolling processing). Application fee: $25 ($50 for international students). *Expenses:* Tuition $178 per credit hour for state residents; $333 per credit hour for nonresidents. Fees $145 per year full-time, $32 per semester (minimum) part-time. *Financial aid:* Application deadline 3/1. • Application contact: Dr. Kenneth T. Siloac, Graduate Coordinator, 330-972-8185.

The University of Akron, College of Fine and Applied Arts, School of Speech-Language Pathology and Audiology, Program in Speech-Language Pathology, Akron, OH 44325-0001. Awards MA. Accredited by ASHA. Students: 31 full-time (all women), 6 part-time (all women); includes 3 minority (2 African Americans, 1 Asian American). Average age 28. In 1997, 32 degrees awarded. *Degree requirements:* Thesis or alternative required, foreign language not required. *Entrance requirements:* GRE, minimum GPA of 3.0. Application deadline: 3/1 (rolling processing). Application fee: $25 ($50 for international students). *Expenses:* Tuition $178 per credit hour for state residents; $333 per credit hour for nonresidents. Fees $145 per year full-time, $32 per semester (minimum) part-time. *Financial aid:* Application deadline 3/1. • Application contact: Dr. Kenneth T. Siloac, Graduate Coordinator, 330-972-8185.

The University of Alabama, College of Arts and Sciences, Department of Communicative Disorders, Tuscaloosa, AL 35487. Offers programs in audiology (MS), speech-language pathology (MS). Accredited by ASHA. Faculty: 3 full-time (2 women), 3 part-time (2 women). Students: 33 full-time (32 women), 1 (woman) part-time. Average age 23. 145 applicants, 12% accepted. In 1997, 23 degrees awarded (100% found work related to degree). *Degree requirements:* Thesis optional, foreign language not required. *Average time to degree:* master's–1 year full-time, 1.5 years part-time. *Entrance requirements:* GRE or MAT. Application deadline: 3/15 (priority date; rolling processing; 1/15 for spring admission). Application fee: $25. *Tuition:* $2684 per year full-time, $594 per semester (minimum) part-time for state residents; $7216 per year full-time, $1248 per semester (minimum) part-time for nonresidents. *Financial aid:* In 1997–98, 20 students received aid, including 10 teaching assistantships (7 to first-year students); Federal Work-Study, institutionally sponsored loans, and career-related internships or fieldwork also available. Financial aid application deadline: 7/14. *Faculty research:* Aphasia, aging, hearing loss, child language, literacy. • Dr. Gerald L. Culton, Chairperson, 205-348-7131.

University of Alberta, Faculty of Graduate Studies and Research, Department of Speech Pathology and Audiology, Edmonton, AB T6G 2E1, Canada. Offers program in speech-language pathology (M Sc, MSLP). Faculty: 7 full-time (5 women), 2 part-time (both women), 8 FTE. Students: 61 full-time (59 women), 17 part-time (all women). Average age 26. 175 applicants, 17% accepted. In 1997, 36 degrees awarded (95% found work related to degree, 5% continued full-time study). *Degree requirements:* Thesis (for some programs), clinical practicum (MSLP) required, foreign language not required. *Entrance requirements:* GRE, TOEFL or TSE, minimum GPA of 6.5 on a 9.0 scale. Application deadline: 2/15. Application fee: $60. *Expenses:* Tuition $390 per course for Canadian residents; $781 per course for nonresidents. Fees $500 per year full-time, $184 per year part-time. *Financial aid:* In 1997–98, 9 scholarships, tuition scholarships (4 to first-year students) were awarded; research assistantships, teaching assistantships, institutionally sponsored loans, and career-related internships or fieldwork also available. *Faculty research:* Clinical education, hearing conservation, motor speech disorders, child language, voice resonance. • Dr. P. Schneider, Chair, 403-492-5980. E-mail: phyllis.schneider@ualberta.ca. Application contact: Anita Moore, Administrative Assistant, Graduate Studies, 403-492-0840. Fax: 403-492-1626. E-mail: anita.moore@ualberta.ca.

The University of Arizona, College of Science, Department of Speech and Hearing Sciences, Tucson, AZ 85721. Awards MS, PhD. One or more programs accredited by ASHA. *Degree requirements:* For master's, thesis optional, foreign language not required; for doctorate, dissertation required, foreign language not required. *Entrance requirements:* GRE General Test, TOEFL (minimum score 550), minimum GPA of 3.0. Application deadline: 2/1 (rolling processing). Application fee: $35. *Tuition:* $2162 per year full-time, $337 per semester (minimum) part-time for state residents; $6860 per year full-time, $1138 per semester (minimum) part-time for nonresidents. *Faculty research:* Alzheimer's disease, speech motor control, auditory-evoked potentials, analyzing pathological speech.

University of Arkansas, College of Education, Department of Rehabilitation Education and Research, Program in Communication Disorders, Fayetteville, AR 72701-1201. Awards MS. Accredited by ASHA. Students: 25 full-time (22 women); includes 1 minority (Asian American). 34 applicants, 76% accepted. In 1997, 9 degrees awarded. *Degree requirements:* 8 week externship required, thesis optional, foreign language not required. *Application fee:* $25 ($35 for international students). *Tuition:* $3144 per year full-time, $173 per credit hour part-time for state residents; $7140 per year full-time, $395 per credit hour part-time for nonresidents. *Financial aid:* Research assistantships, teaching assistantships, Federal Work-Study, and career-related internships or fieldwork available. Aid available to part-time students. Financial aid application deadline: 4/1; applicants required to submit FAFSA. • Coordinator, 501-575-4917.

University of Arkansas for Medical Sciences, Graduate School, Program in Communicative Disorders, 4301 West Markham, Little Rock, AR 72205-7199. Awards MS. Offered jointly with the University of Arkansas at Little Rock. Part-time programs available. Faculty: 20 full-time (11 women). Students: 49 full-time (44 women), 5 part-time (4 women); includes 4 minority (2 African Americans, 2 Asian Americans), 1 international. In 1997, 23 degrees awarded. *Degree requirements:* Thesis or alternative required, foreign language not required. *Entrance requirements:* GRE General Test. Application fee: $0. *Tuition:* $3060 per year full-time, $153 per credit hour part-time for state residents; $6560 per year full-time, $328 per credit hour part-time for nonresidents. *Financial aid:* In 1997–98, 29 research assistantships were awarded. Aid available to part-time students. • Dr. J. Hope Keiser, Chair, 501-569-3155.

University of British Columbia, Faculties of Medicine and Graduate Studies, Graduate Programs in Medicine, School of Audiology and Speech Sciences, Vancouver, BC V6T 1W5, Canada. Awards M Sc, PhD. *Degree requirements:* For master's, thesis or alternative, externship; for doctorate, dissertation. *Average time to degree:* master's–2 years full-time. *Entrance requirements:* For master's, bachelor's degree with minimum B+ average over last 2 years; for doctorate, honors bachelor's and master's degree. Application deadline: 3/31 (rolling processing). Application fee: $50. *Faculty research:* Language development, aural rehabilitation, auditory electrophysiology, experimental phonetics, discourse, linguistic aphasiology.

University of California, San Diego, Interdisciplinary Program in Language and Communicative Disorders, 9500 Gilman Drive, La Jolla, CA 92093-5003. Awards PhD. Offered jointly with San Diego State University. Students: 6 (all women). *Expenses:* Tuition $0 for state residents; $9384 per year full-time, $4692 per year part-time for nonresidents. Fees $4887 per year full-time, $3344 per year part-time. • Elizabeth Bates, Chair. Application contact: Graduate Coordinator, 619-534-1148.

University of California, Santa Barbara, College of Letters and Science, Division of Math, Life and Physical Science, Department of Speech and Hearing Sciences, Santa Barbara, CA 93106. Awards MA, PhD. Admissions temporarily suspended. In 1997, 1 doctorate awarded. *Degree requirements:* Variable foreign language requirement, thesis/dissertation. *Expenses:* Tuition $0 for state residents; $9384 per year for nonresidents. Fees $4930 per year. • David Chapman, Acting Chair, 805-893-7064.

University of Central Arkansas, College of Health and Applied Sciences, Department of Speech-Language Pathology, Conway, AR 72035-0001. Awards MS. One or more programs accredited by ASHA. Faculty: 8 full-time (7 women), 2 part-time (both women), 8.66 FTE. Students: 71 full-time (68 women), 11 part-time (10 women); includes 3 minority (all African Americans). 95 applicants, 38% accepted. In 1997, 36 degrees awarded. *Degree requirements:* Comprehensive exams, portfolio. *Entrance requirements:* GRE General Test, NTE, minimum GPA of 2.7. Application deadline: 3/1 (priority date; rolling processing; 10/1 for spring admission). Application fee: $15 ($40 for international students). *Expenses:* Tuition $161 per credit hour for state residents; $298 per credit hour for nonresidents. Fees $150 per year. *Financial aid:* In 1997–98, 3 assistantships were awarded. Financial aid application deadline: 2/15. • Jim Thurman, Interim Chairperson, 501-450-3176. E-mail: jimt@mail.uca.edu. Application contact: Sharon Ross, Graduate Adviser, 501-450-5489. Fax: 501-450-5474. E-mail: sharonr@mail.uca.edu.

University of Central Florida, College of Health and Public Affairs, Department of Communicative Disorders, Orlando, FL 32816. Awards MA. One or more programs accredited by ASHA. Part-time and evening/weekend programs available. Faculty: 12. Students: 233 full-time (206 women), 19 part-time (18 women); includes 38 minority (21 African Americans, 3 Asian Americans, 12 Hispanics, 2 Native Americans), 3 international. Average age 31. 176 applicants, 22% accepted. In 1997, 69 degrees awarded. *Degree requirements:* Thesis or alternative required, foreign language not required. *Entrance requirements:* GRE General Test. Application deadline: 6/15 (rolling processing; 11/1 for spring admission). Application fee: $20. *Expenses:* Tuition $3288 per year full-time, $137 per credit hour part-time for state residents; $11,520 per year full-time, $480 per credit hour part-time for nonresidents. Fees $105 per year. *Financial aid:* Teaching assistantships, Federal Work-Study, institutionally sponsored loans, and career-related internships or fieldwork available. Aid available to part-time students. • Dr. Chad Nye, Chair, 407-384-2106. Application contact: Jane Sorrels, Coordinator, 407-384-4798.

University of Central Oklahoma, College of Education, Department of Curriculum and Instruction, Program in Speech-Language Pathology, Edmond, OK 73034-5209. Awards M Ed. Accredited by ASHA. Part-time and evening/weekend programs available. *Entrance requirements:* GRE General Test. Application deadline: 8/18. Application fee: $15. *Tuition:* $76 per credit hour for state residents; $178 per credit hour for nonresidents.

University of Cincinnati, Center for Health Related Programs, Department of Communication Sciences and Disorders, Cincinnati, OH 45221. Awards MA, PhD. One or more programs accredited by ASHA. Faculty: 8 full-time. Students: 79 full-time (72 women), 21 part-time (18 women); includes 9 minority (3 African Americans, 5 Asian Americans, 1 Hispanic), 2 international. 197 applicants, 18% accepted. In 1997, 70 master's, 2 doctorates awarded. *Degree requirements:* For master's, thesis optional, foreign language not required; for doctorate, dissertation required, foreign language not required. *Average time to degree:* master's–2.4 years full-time; doctorate–3.3 years full-time. *Entrance requirements:* For master's, GRE General Test, minimum GPA of 3.0; for doctorate, GRE General Test. Application deadline: 2/1. Application fee: $30. *Tuition:* $7228 per year full-time, $185 per credit hour part-time for state residents; $13,812 per year full-time, $352 per credit hour part-time for nonresidents. *Financial aid:* Fellowships, graduate assistantships, full tuition waivers, and career-related internships or fieldwork available. Aid available to part-time students. Financial aid application deadline: 5/1. • Dr. Nancy Creaghead, Head, 513-556-4480. E-mail: nancy.creaghead@uc.edu. Application contact: Linda Lee, Graduate Program Director, 513-556-4491. Fax: 513-556-5505.

University of Colorado at Boulder, College of Arts and Sciences, Department of Speech, Language and Hearing Science, Boulder, CO 80309. Offers programs in audiology (MA, PhD), speech-language pathology (MA, PhD). One or more programs accredited by ASHA. Faculty: 8 full-time (5 women). Students: 72 full-time (66 women), 1 (woman) part-time; includes 8 minority (2 Asian Americans, 6 Hispanics). Average age 27. 264 applicants, 30% accepted. In 1997, 29 master's, 4 doctorates awarded. Terminal master's awarded for partial completion of doctoral program. *Degree requirements:* For master's, thesis or alternative, comprehensive exam required, foreign language not required; for doctorate, 1 foreign language, dissertation. *Entrance requirements:* For master's, GRE General Test, minimum undergraduate GPA of 3.25; for doctorate, GRE General Test. Application deadline: 3/1 (priority date; rolling processing). Application fee: $40 ($60 for international students). *Expenses:* Tuition $3170 per year full-time, $531 per semester (minimum) part-time for state residents; $14,652 per year full-time, $2442 per semester (minimum) part-time for nonresidents. Fees $667 per year full-time, $130 per semester (minimum) part-time. *Financial aid:* Fellowships, research assistantships, teaching assistantships, full tuition waivers available. Financial aid application deadline: 2/1. *Total annual research expenditures:* $2 million. • Christine Yoshinaga-Itano, Chair, 303-492-3065. E-mail: christie.yoshi@colorado.edu. Application contact: Cynthia Ocken, Graduate Secretary, 303-492-6445. Fax: 303-492-3274 Ext. 4. E-mail: ocken@colorado.edu.

University of Connecticut, College of Liberal Arts and Sciences, Department of Communication Sciences, Program in Speech, Language, and Hearing, Storrs, CT 06269. Awards MA, PhD. Accredited by ASHA. Faculty: 10. Students: 50 full-time (44 women), 4 part-time (3 women); includes 3 minority (2 Hispanics, 1 Native American), 3 international. Average age 27. 187 applicants, 34% accepted. In 1997, 21 master's, 1 doctorate awarded. Terminal master's awarded for partial completion of doctoral program. *Degree requirements:* For master's, thesis optional; for doctorate, dissertation. *Entrance requirements:* GRE General Test. Application deadline: 4/1 (priority date; rolling processing; 11/1 for spring admission). Application fee: $40 ($45 for international students). *Expenses:* Tuition $5272 per year full-time, $293 per credit part-time for state residents; $13,696 per year full-time, $761 per credit part-time for nonresidents. Fees $948 per year full-time, $640 per year part-time. *Financial aid:* In 1997–98, 5 fellowships totaling $24,000, 3 research assistantships totaling $22,172, 18 teaching assistantships (6 to first-year students) totaling $143,211 were awarded. Financial aid application deadline: 2/15. • Application contact: Harvey R. Gilbert, Chairperson, 860-486-2628.

University of Florida, Colleges of Health Professions and Liberal Arts and Sciences, Program in Audiology, Gainesville, FL 32611. Awards Au D. Accredited by ASHA. Program new for fall 1998. *Entrance requirements:* GRE General Test (minimum combined score of 1000), minimum GPA of 3.0. Application fee: $20. *Tuition:* $138 per credit hour for state residents; $481 per credit hour for nonresidents. • Application contact: Dr. Scott Griffths, Graduate Coordinator, 352-392-2041. E-mail: sgriff@cpd.ufl.edu.

University of Florida, College of Liberal Arts and Sciences, Department of Communication Processes and Disorders, Gainesville, FL 32611. Offers program in communication sciences and disorders (MA, PhD). One or more programs accredited by ASHA. Faculty: 29. Students: 48 full-time (39 women), 13 part-time (11 women); includes 5 minority (2 African Americans, 2 Hispanics, 1 Native American), 3 international. 192 applicants, 28% accepted. In 1997, 25 master's, 3 doctorates awarded. *Degree requirements:* For master's, variable foreign language requirement, thesis optional; for doctorate, variable foreign language requirement, dissertation. *Entrance requirements:* GRE General Test, minimum GPA of 3.0. Application deadline: 6/5 (priority date; rolling processing). Application fee: $20. *Tuition:* $138 per credit hour for state residents; $481 per credit hour for nonresidents. *Financial aid:* In 1997–98, 21 students received aid, including 4 fellowships averaging $1,092 per month, 7 research assistantships averaging $496 per month, 6 teaching assistantships averaging $346 per month, 4 graduate assistantships averaging $328 per month; career-related internships or fieldwork also available. *Faculty research:* Phonetic science, cochlear implant, dyslexia, auditory development, voice. • Dr. William S. Brown Jr., Chairman, 352-392-2034. E-mail: sbrown@clas.ufl.edu. Application contact: Dr. Scott Griffths, Graduate Coordinator, 352-392-0241. Fax: 352-846-0243. E-mail: sgriff@cpd.ufl.edu.

University of Georgia, College of Education, Department of Communication Sciences and Disorders, Athens, GA 30602. Awards MA, M Ed, PhD, Ed S. One or more programs accredited by ASHA. Faculty: 8 full-time (6 women). Students: 87 full-time, 17 part-time (all women); includes 7 minority (6 African Americans, 1 Hispanic), 5 international. 300 applicants, 22% accepted. In 1997, 34 master's awarded. *Degree requirements:* For master's, thesis (MA) required, foreign language not required; for doctorate, 1 foreign language (computer language can substitute), dissertation. *Entrance requirements:* GRE General Test. Application deadline: 7/1 (priority date; 11/15 for spring admission). Application fee: $30. Electronic applications accepted. *Tuition:* $3290 per year full-time, $643 per semester (minimum) part-time for state residents; $11,300 per year full-time, $1645 per semester (minimum) part-time for nonresidents. *Financial aid:* Fellowships, research assistantships, teaching assistantships, assistantships available. • Dr. Robert J. Nozza, Graduate Coordinator, 706-542-4606. Fax: 706-542-5877. E-mail: bnozza@sage.coe.uga.edu.

University of Hawaii at Manoa, John A. Burns School of Medicine and Graduate Division, Graduate Programs in Biomedical Sciences, Department of Speech Pathology and Audiology, Honolulu, HI 96816. Awards MS. Accredited by ASHA. Faculty: 4 full-time (2 women), 5 part-time (4 women), 6.25 FTE. Students: 41 full-time (40 women), 3 part-time (all women); includes 19 minority (16 Asian Americans, 3 Hispanics), 4 international. Average age 26. 54 applicants, 50% accepted. In 1997, 14 degrees awarded (100% found work related to degree). *Degree requirements:* Thesis or alternative required, foreign language not required. *Average time to degree:* master's–2 years full-time. *Entrance requirements:* GRE, minimum GPA of 3.0. Application deadline: 3/1 (9/1 for spring admission). Application fee: $25 ($50 for international students). *Tuition:* $4029 per year full-time, $214 per credit hour part-time for state residents; $9957 per year full-time, $461 per credit hour part-time for nonresidents. *Financial aid:* In 1997–98, 10 students received aid, including 1 teaching assistantship; full and partial tuition waivers, Federal Work-Study, institutionally sponsored loans, and career-related internships or fieldwork also available. Aid available to part-time students. *Faculty research:* Emerging language (child phonology and special populations), central auditory function, developmental phonology, processing in the aging. • Dr. James T. Yates, Chairperson, 808-956-8279. Fax: 808-956-5482. E-mail: jyates@hawaii.edu.

University of Houston, College of Humanities, Fine Arts and Communication, School of Communication, Program in Communication Disorders, 4800 Calhoun, Houston, TX 77204-2163. Offers audiology (MA), communication sciences research (MA), medical speech pathology (MA). One or more programs accredited by ASHA. Part-time programs available. Faculty: 6 full-time (5 women), 2 part-time (1 woman). Students: 43 full-time (42 women), 29 part-time (all women); includes 5 minority (3 African Americans, 1 Asian American, 1 Hispanic). Average age 30. In 1997, 23 degrees awarded (100% found work related to degree). *Entrance requirements:* GRE General Test (minimum score 450 on each section), minimum GPA of 3.0 in last 60 hours and communication disorders course work. Application deadline: 7/3 (priority date; rolling processing). Application fee: $25 ($75 for international students). *Expenses:* Tuition $1152 per year full-time, $120 per semester (minimum) part-time for state residents; $4482 per year full-time, $249 per credit hour part-time for nonresidents. Fees $977 per year full-time, $119 per semester (minimum) part-time. *Financial aid:* Institutionally sponsored loans and career-related internships or fieldwork available. Financial aid application deadline: 7/15. *Faculty research:* Stuttering, voice disorders, language disorders, phonological processing. • Lynn Bliss, Director of Graduate Studies, 713-743-2896. Application contact: Regina Mays, Graduate Coordinator, 713-743-2897. Fax: 713-743-2926.

University of Illinois at Urbana–Champaign, College of Applied Life Studies, Department of Speech and Hearing Science, Urbana, IL 61801. Awards AM, MS, PhD. One or more programs accredited by ASHA. Faculty: 12 full-time (8 women). Students: 60 full-time (54 women); includes 9 minority (4 African Americans, 5 Asian Americans), 4 international. 199 applicants, 17% accepted. In 1997, 18 master's, 3 doctorates awarded. *Degree requirements:* For doctorate, dissertation required, foreign language not required. *Entrance requirements:* For master's, GRE General Test, minimum GPA of 4.0 on a 5.0 scale. Application deadline: rolling. Application fee: $40 ($50 for international students). *Financial aid:* In 1997–98, 2 research assistantships were awarded; fellowships, teaching assistantships, full and partial tuition waivers also available. Financial aid application deadline: 2/15. • Peter J. Alfonso, Head, 217-244-2537.

The University of Iowa, College of Liberal Arts, Department of Speech Pathology and Audiology, Program in Professional Speech Pathology and Audiology, Iowa City, IA 52242-1316. Awards MA. Accredited by ASHA. Students: 52 full-time (44 women); includes 2 minority (1 Hispanic, 1 Native American), 3 international. 224 applicants, 34% accepted. In 1997, 26 degrees awarded. *Degree requirements:* Thesis optional. *Application fee:* $30 ($50 for international students). *Expenses:* Tuition $3166 per year full-time, $176 per semester hour part-time for state residents; $10,202 per year full-time, $176 per semester hour part-time for nonresidents. Fees $202 per year full-time, $52 per year (minimum) part-time. *Financial aid:* In 1997–98, 8 fellowships (2 to first-year students), 5 research assistantships (2 to first-year students), 7 teaching assistantships (3 to first-year students) were awarded. Financial aid applicants required to submit FAFSA. • Richard R. Hurtig, Chair, Department of Speech Pathology and Audiology, 319-335-8718. Fax: 319-335-8851.

The University of Iowa, College of Liberal Arts, Department of Speech Pathology and Audiology, Program in Speech and Hearing Science, Iowa City, IA 52242-1316. Awards PhD. In 1997, 3 degrees awarded. *Degree requirements:* Dissertation, comprehensive exam. *Application fee:* $30 ($50 for international students). *Expenses:* Tuition $3166 per year full-time, $176 per semester hour part-time for state residents; $10,202 per year full-time, $176 per semester hour part-time for nonresidents. Fees $202 per year full-time, $52 per year (minimum) part-time. *Financial aid:* Fellowships, research assistantships, teaching assistantships available. Financial aid applicants required to submit FAFSA. • Richard R. Hurtig, Chair, Department of Speech Pathology and Audiology, 319-335-8718. Fax: 319-335-8851.

University of Kansas, College of Liberal Arts and Sciences, Department of Speech-Language-Hearing: Sciences and Disorders, Lawrence, KS 66045. Awards MA, PhD. Accredited by ASHA. Offered jointly with the Department of Hearing and Speech at the Kansas City campus. Faculty: 9 full-time. Students: 37 full-time (34 women), 3 part-time (2 women); includes 2 minority (both Native Americans), 3 international. 165 applicants, 18% accepted. In 1997, 22 master's, 2 doctorates awarded. *Degree requirements:* For master's, thesis or alternative required, foreign language not required; for doctorate, dissertation required, foreign language not required. *Entrance requirements:* GRE General Test (minimum combined score of 1600 on three sections), TOEFL. Application deadline: 2/15 (10/15 for spring admission). Application fee: $25. *Expenses:* Tuition $2400 per year full-time, $100 per credit hour part-time for state residents; $7890 per year full-time, $329 per credit hour part-time for nonresidents. Fees $428 per year full-time, $31 per credit hour part-time. *Financial aid:* In 1997–98, 20 students received aid, including 10 research assistantships (4 to first-year students), 3 teaching assistantships averaging $800 per month; fellowships, Federal Work-Study, institutionally sponsored loans, and career-related internships or fieldwork also available. Aid available to part-time students. Financial aid application deadline: 3/1; applicants required to submit FAFSA. *Faculty research:* Reading disorders, language acquisition, auditory electrophysiology, genetics of language, phonological development. • John Michel, Chair, 785-864-0630. Fax: 785-864-3974. Application contact: Hugh Catts, Graduate Director.

University of Kansas, School of Allied Health, Department of Hearing and Speech, Kansas City, KS 66160. Offers programs in audiology (MA, PhD), education of the deaf (MS), speech and hearing science (PhD), speech-language pathology (MA, PhD). Offered jointly with the Department of Speech-Language-Hearing: Sciences and Disorders at the Lawrence campus. Part-time programs available. Faculty: 11 full-time (7 women), 3 part-time (all women). Students: 38 full-time (all women), 16 part-time (13 women); includes 4 minority (2 Hispanics, 2 Native Americans). Average age 28. 190 applicants, 24% accepted. In 1997, 11 master's awarded. Terminal master's awarded for partial completion of doctoral program. *Degree requirements:* For master's, thesis, comprehensive exam required, foreign language not required; for doctorate, dissertation, comprehensive oral exam. *Entrance requirements:* For master's, GRE General Test (MS), TOEFL (minimum score 570); for doctorate, GRE, TOEFL (minimum score 570). Application deadline: 2/15 (priority date; rolling processing; 10/1 for spring admission). Application fee: $25. *Expenses:* Tuition $2400 per year full-time, $100 per credit hour part-time for state residents; $7890 per year full-time, $329 per credit hour part-time for nonresidents. Fees $428 per year full-time, $31 per credit hour part-time. *Financial aid:* 11 students received aid; research assistantships, teaching assistantships, Federal Work-Study, institutionally sponsored loans, and career-related internships or fieldwork available. Aid available to part-time students. Financial aid application deadline: 4/3; applicants required to submit FAFSA. • Dr. John A. Ferraro, Chairman, 913-588-5937. E-mail: jferraro@kumc.edu. Application contact: Diane Wright, Secretary, 913-588-5730. Fax: 913-588-5923. E-mail: dswright@kumc.edu.

University of Kentucky, Graduate School Programs from the College of Allied Health, Program in Communication Disorders, Lexington, KY 40506-0032. Awards MSCD. One or more programs accredited by ASHA. Faculty: 4 full-time (all women). Students: 43 full-time (42 women), 1 (woman) part-time; includes 2 minority (both African Americans). 25 applicants, 16% accepted. In 1997, 13 degrees awarded. *Degree requirements:* Comprehensive exam required, foreign language not required. *Entrance requirements:* GRE General Test, minimum undergraduate GPA of 2.5. Application deadline: 7/19 (rolling processing). Application fee: $30 ($35 for international students). *Financial aid:* In 1997–98, 1 fellowship was awarded. *Faculty research:* Swallowing disorders, infant speech development, child language intervention, augmentative communication. • Dr. Judith L. Page, Director of Graduate Studies, 606-257-

Directory: Communication Disorders

University of Kentucky (continued)
7922. Fax: 606-258-1928. E-mail: jlpage01@pop.uky.edu. Application contact: Dr. Constance L. Wood, Associate Dean, 606-257-4613. Fax: 606-323-1928.

University of Louisville, School of Medicine and Graduate School, Graduate Programs in Medicine, Department of Communicative Disorders, Louisville, KY 40292-0001. Awards MS. One or more programs accredited by ASHA. Students: 46 full-time (41 women), 5 part-time (all women). Average age 27. In 1997, 25 degrees awarded. *Degree requirements:* Oral and written comprehensive exams required, thesis optional, foreign language not required. *Entrance requirements:* GRE General Test, minimum GPA of 3.0. Application deadline: 1/15. Application fee: $15. *Financial aid:* Research assistantships, scholarships, institutionally sponsored loans, and career-related internships or fieldwork available. Financial aid application deadline: 4/30. *Faculty research:* Organic voice disorders, childhood language development, amplification systems, cochlear implantations. • Dr. David Cunningham, Director, 502-852-5274.

University of Maine, College of Liberal Arts and Sciences, Department of Communication Disorders, Orono, ME 04469. Awards MA. One or more programs accredited by ASHA. Faculty: 7 full-time (3 women), 3 part-time (2 women). Students: 20 full-time (all women), 2 part-time (both women); includes 1 minority (African American). Average age 28. 30 applicants, 67% accepted. *Entrance requirements:* GRE General Test, TOEFL (minimum score 550). Application deadline: 2/1 (priority date; rolling processing; 10/15 for spring admission). Application fee: $50. *Expenses:* Tuition $194 per credit hour for state residents; $548 per credit hour for nonresidents. Fees $378 per year full-time, $33 per semester (minimum) part-time. *Financial aid:* In 1997–98, 8 fellowships (5 to first-year students) were awarded; research assistantships, teaching assistantships, Federal Work-Study, institutionally sponsored loans, and career-related internships or fieldwork also available. Aid available to part-time students. Financial aid application deadline: 3/1. *Faculty research:* Interpersonal communication between supervisor and supervisees, clinicians and clients; language and voice impairments; children's pragmatics. • Dr. Kimbrough Oller, Chair, 207-581-2006. Fax: 207-581-1953. Application contact: Scott Delcourt, Director of the Graduate School, 207-581-3218. Fax: 207-581-3232. E-mail: graduate@maine.edu.

University of Maryland, College Park, College of Behavioral and Social Sciences, Department of Hearing and Speech Sciences, College Park, MD 20742-5045. Offers programs in audiology (MA, PhD), language pathology (MA, PhD), speech (MA, PhD). One or more programs accredited by ASHA. Faculty: 12 full-time (10 women), 10 part-time (7 women). Students: 46 full-time (43 women), 19 part-time (18 women). 226 applicants, 35% accepted. In 1997, 18 master's, 3 doctorates awarded. *Degree requirements:* For master's, thesis or alternative required, foreign language not required; for doctorate, variable foreign language requirement, dissertation. *Entrance requirements:* For master's, GRE General Test, minimum GPA of 3.5; for doctorate, GRE General Test. Application deadline: rolling. Application fee: $50 ($70 for international students). *Expenses:* Tuition $272 per credit hour for state residents; $400 per credit hour for nonresidents. Fees $564 per year full-time, $342 per year part-time. *Financial aid:* In 1997–98, 5 fellowships, 19 teaching assistantships were awarded; research assistantships and career-related internships or fieldwork also available. *Faculty research:* Acoustic and physiological phonetics, psychoacoustics, speech perception, neuropsychology. • Dr. Nan B. Ratner, Chair, 301-405-4217. Fax: 301-314-2023. E-mail: grschool@deans.umd.edu. Application contact: John Mollish, Director, Graduate Admissions and Records, 301-405-4198. Fax: 301-314-9305.

University of Massachusetts Amherst, School of Public Health and Health Sciences, Department of Communication Disorders, Amherst, MA 01003-0001. Awards MA, PhD. One or more programs accredited by ASHA. Part-time programs available. Faculty: 10 full-time (5 women). Students: 53 full-time (51 women), 10 part-time (all women); includes 6 minority (4 African Americans, 2 Hispanics), 2 international. Average age 29. 282 applicants, 26% accepted. In 1997, 23 master's awarded. *Degree requirements:* For master's, thesis optional, foreign language not required; for doctorate, dissertation required, foreign language not required. *Entrance requirements:* GRE General Test. Application deadline: 3/1 (priority date; rolling processing; 10/1 for spring admission). Application fee: $40. *Expenses:* Tuition $2640 per year full-time, $110 per credit part-time for state residents; $3690 per year (minimum) full-time, $165 per credit (minimum) part-time for nonresidents. Fees $2856 per year full-time, $422 per semester part-time for state residents; $3204 per year full-time, $480 per semester part-time for nonresidents. *Financial aid:* In 1997–98, 20 fellowships, 17 research assistantships, 3 teaching assistantships were awarded; Federal Work-Study also available. Aid available to part-time students. Financial aid application deadline: 3/1. • Dr. Harry Seymour, Director, 413-545-0131. Fax: 413-545-1264. E-mail: hseymour@comdis.umass.edu.

The University of Memphis, Division of Audiology and Speech Pathology, Memphis, TN 38152. Awards MA, PhD. Accredited by ASHA. Part-time programs available. Faculty: 11 full-time (3 women), 12 part-time (6 women). Students: 75 full-time (67 women), 8 part-time (7 women); includes 12 minority (11 African Americans, 1 Asian American), 1 international. Average age 28. 287 applicants, 29% accepted. In 1997, 38 master's, 1 doctorate awarded. Terminal master's awarded for partial completion of doctoral program. *Degree requirements:* For master's, thesis or alternative, comprehensive exam; for doctorate, dissertation, qualifying exam. *Entrance requirements:* For master's, GRE General Test (minimum combined score of 900) or MAT (minimum score 40), minimum GPA of 3.0; for doctorate, GRE General Test (minimum combined score of 1000), minimum GPA of 3.5. Application deadline: 8/1 (12/1 for spring admission). Application fee: $25 ($50 for international students). *Tuition:* $2862 per year full-time, $166 per credit hour part-time for state residents; $6696 per year full-time, $379 per credit hour part-time for nonresidents. *Financial aid:* In 1997–98, 37 research assistantships totaling $121,078 were awarded. *Faculty research:* Sickle cell disease, hearing aid characteristic selection, AIDS research, stroke recovery research, vowel misarticulation in children. • Dr. Maurice Mendel, Dean, 901-678-5800. Application contact: Dr. David J. Wark, Coordinator of Graduate Studies, 901-678-5800.

University of Minnesota, Duluth, Graduate School, College of Education and Human Service Professions, Program in Communication Disorders, Duluth, MN 55812-2496. Awards MA. One or more programs accredited by ASHA. Part-time programs available. Faculty: 6 full-time (3 women), 5 part-time (all women). Students: 28 full-time (all women); includes 2 international. Average age 24. 70 applicants, 54% accepted. In 1997, 15 degrees awarded (93% found work related to degree, 7% continued full-time study). *Degree requirements:* Written and oral exams required, foreign language and thesis not required. *Average time to degree:* master's–2 years full-time, 4 years part-time. *Entrance requirements:* Minimum GPA of 3.0. Application deadline: 2/15. Application fee: $40 ($50 for international students). *Expenses:* Tuition $5130 per year full-time, $299 per credit part-time for state residents; $10,074 per year full-time, $536 per credit part-time for nonresidents. Fees $612 per year full-time, $76 per quarter part-time. *Financial aid:* In 1997–98, 25 students received aid, including 25 fellowships (11 to first-year students) totaling $4,200; full and partial tuition waivers, Federal Work-Study, institutionally sponsored loans, and career-related internships or fieldwork also available. Financial aid application deadline: 2/15. *Faculty research:* Clinical supervision, gender and family communication patterns, augmentative communication, speech understanding, hearing aids. Total annual research expenditures: $1000. • Dr. Faith Loven, Director of Graduate Studies, 218-726-8204. Fax: 218-726-7073. E-mail: floven@d.umn.edu.

University of Minnesota, Twin Cities Campus, College of Liberal Arts, Department of Communication Disorders, Minneapolis, MN 55455-0213. Awards MA, PhD. One or more programs accredited by ASHA. Faculty: 17 full-time (10 women), 10 part-time (3 women), 18 FTE. Students: 91 full-time (80 women); includes 2 minority (1 Asian American, 1 Hispanic), 7 international. 219 applicants, 37% accepted. In 1997, 34 master's awarded (100% found work related to degree); 2 doctorates awarded (100% entered university research/teaching). *Degree requirements:* For master's, 360 client contact hours required, thesis not required; for doctorate, dissertation. *Average time to degree:* master's–2.5 years full-time; doctorate–4.5 years full-time. *Entrance requirements:* GRE General Test (combined average 1725 on three sections), TOEFL. Application deadline: 2/1. Application fee: $40 ($50 for international students). *Financial aid:* In 1997–98, 32 students received aid, including 1 fellowship averaging $1,300 per month, 19 research assistantships (4 to first-year students) averaging $600 per month, 10 teaching assistantships (4 to first-year students) averaging $500 per month, 2 traineeships averaging $500 per month and totaling $8,000; Federal Work-Study, institutionally sponsored loans, and career-related internships or fieldwork also available. Financial aid application deadline: 2/1; applicants required to submit CSS PROFILE. *Faculty research:* Hearing aids, motor speech disorders, language acquisition, augmentative communication systems, phonological development. • Charles Speaks, Chairman, 612-624-3322. E-mail: speak001@maroon.tc.umn.edu. Application contact: Joe Reichle, Director of Graduate Studies, 612-624-3322. Fax: 612-624-7586. E-mail: reich00@maroon.tc.umn.edu.

University of Mississippi, Graduate School, College of Liberal Arts, Department of Communicative Disorders, University, MS 38677-9702. Awards MS. One or more programs accredited by ASHA. Faculty: 5 full-time (3 women). Students: 47 full-time (45 women); includes 3 minority (all African Americans). In 1997, 25 degrees awarded. *Entrance requirements:* GRE General Test, TOEFL, minimum GPA of 3.0. Application deadline: 8/1 (rolling processing). Application fee: $0 ($25 for international students). *Financial aid:* Application deadline 3/1. • Dr. Thomas Crowe, Chairman, 601-232-5131.

University of Missouri–Columbia, School of Medicine, School of Health Related Professions, Program in Communication Science and Disorders, Columbia, MO 65211. Awards MHS. One or more programs accredited by ASHA. Faculty: 33 full-time (23 women), 2 part-time (both women). Students: 22 full-time (20 women), 2 part-time (both women); includes 1 international. In 1997, 11 degrees awarded. *Entrance requirements:* GRE General Test, minimum GPA of 3.0. Application deadline: 3/1 (priority date; rolling processing). Application fee: $25 ($50 for international students). *Expenses:* Tuition $14,036 per year for state residents; $28,224 per year for nonresidents. Fees $682 per year. • Dr. Martha Parnell, Director of Graduate Studies, 573-882-4278.

University of Montevallo, College of Arts and Sciences, Department of Speech Pathology and Audiology, Montevallo, AL 35115. Awards MS. Accredited by ASHA. Part-time programs available. *Entrance requirements:* GRE General Test (minimum combined score of 850), minimum GPA of 3.0. Application deadline: 7/15 (11/15 for spring admission). Application fee: $10.

University of Nebraska at Kearney, College of Education, Department of Special Education and Communication Disorders, Kearney, NE 68849-0001. Offers programs in early childhood special education (MA Ed), education of behaviorally disordered (MA Ed), education of the gifted and talented (MA Ed), mild/moderate handicapped (MA Ed), special education (MA Ed), specific learning disabilities (MA Ed), speech pathology (MS Ed). Part-time and evening/weekend programs available. Faculty: 5 full-time (4 women). Students: 30 full-time (28 women), 25 part-time (24 women); includes 2 minority (1 Asian American, 1 Hispanic), 2 international. In 1997, 21 degrees awarded. *Degree requirements:* Thesis optional. *Entrance requirements:* GRE General Test. Application deadline: 8/1 (priority date; rolling processing; 12/15 for spring admission). Application fee: $35. *Expenses:* Tuition $1494 per year full-time, $83 per credit hour part-time for state residents; $2826 per year full-time, $157 per credit hour part-time for nonresidents. Fees $229 per year full-time, $11.25 per semester (minimum) part-time. *Financial aid:* In 1997–98, 2 research assistantships, 3 teaching assistantships were awarded; career-related internships or fieldwork also available. Aid available to part-time students. Financial aid application deadline: 3/1; applicants required to submit FAFSA. • Dr. Lillian Larson, Chair, 308-865-8314.

University of Nebraska at Omaha, College of Education, Department of Special Education and Communication Disorders, Omaha, NE 68182. Offers programs in behavioral disorders (MS), mental retardation (MA), resource teaching and learning disabilities (MS), speech-language pathology (MA, MS), teaching the hearing impaired (MS), teaching the mentally retarded (MS). Part-time and evening/weekend programs available. Faculty: 10 full-time (2 women). Students: 5 full-time (all women), 48 part-time (47 women); includes 1 minority (African American). Average age 34. 17 applicants, 47% accepted. In 1997, 28 degrees awarded. *Degree requirements:* Thesis (for some programs), comprehensive exam required, foreign language not required. *Entrance requirements:* GRE General Test or MAT, minimum GPA of 3.0. Application deadline: 2/1 (priority date; rolling processing; 9/1 for spring admission). Application fee: $35. *Expenses:* Tuition $1670 per year full-time, $94 per credit hour part-time for state residents; $4082 per year full-time, $227 per credit hour part-time for nonresidents. Fees $302 per year full-time, $108 per semester (minimum) part-time. *Financial aid:* 17 students received aid; fellowships, research assistantships, full tuition waivers, Federal Work-Study, institutionally sponsored loans, and career-related internships or fieldwork available. Aid available to part-time students. Financial aid application deadline: 3/1. • Dr. John Christensen, Chairperson, 402-554-2203. Application contact: Dr. John Hill, Adviser, 402-554-2203.

University of Nebraska–Lincoln, Teachers College, Department of Special Education and Communication Disorders, Program in Speech-Language Pathology and Audiology, Lincoln, NE 68588. Awards MS. Accredited by ASHA. Students: 65 full-time (61 women), 10 part-time (all women); includes 1 minority (Asian American). Average age 26. 104 applicants, 38% accepted. In 1997, 32 degrees awarded. *Degree requirements:* Thesis optional. *Entrance requirements:* GRE General Test, TOEFL (minimum score 500). Application deadline: 2/15 (10/15 for spring admission). Application fee: $35. Electronic applications accepted. *Expenses:* Tuition $110 per credit hour for state residents; $270 per credit hour for nonresidents. Fees $480 per year full-time, $110 per semester part-time. *Financial aid:* In 1997–98, 14 fellowships totaling $28,650 were awarded; research assistantships, teaching assistantships, Federal Work-Study also available. Aid available to part-time students. Financial aid application deadline: 2/15. • Dr. Stanley Vasa, Graduate Committee Chair, 402-472-5494. E-mail: svasa@unl.edu.

University of Nevada, Reno, School of Medicine and Graduate School, Graduate Programs in Medicine, Department of Speech Pathology and Audiology, Reno, NV 89557. Offers programs in speech pathology (PhD), speech pathology and audiology (MS). One or more programs accredited by ASHA. Faculty: 6 (4 women). Students: 43 full-time (39 women); includes 4 minority (2 Asian Americans, 2 Hispanics). Average age 28. 111 applicants, 22% accepted. In 1997, 18 master's, 1 doctorate awarded. *Degree requirements:* For master's, thesis optional, foreign language not required; for doctorate, dissertation required, foreign language not required. *Entrance requirements:* For master's, GRE General Test, TOEFL (minimum score 500), minimum GPA of 2.75; for doctorate, GRE General Test, TOEFL (minimum score 500), minimum GPA of 3.0. Application deadline: 3/1 (priority date; rolling processing). Application fee: $40. *Financial aid:* Fellowships, research assistantships available. Financial aid application deadline: 3/1. *Faculty research:* Language impairment in children, voice disorders, stuttering. • Dr. Thomas L. Watterson, Chair, 702-784-4887. Application contact: Dr. Kerry Lewis, Director of Graduate Studies, 702-784-4887. E-mail: klewis@med.unr.edu.

University of New Hampshire, School of Health and Human Services, Department of Communication Disorders, Durham, NH 03824. Awards MS, MST. One or more programs accredited by ASHA. Part-time programs available. Faculty: 5 full-time. Students: 40 full-time (37 women), 9 part-time (all women); includes 1 minority (Asian American). Average age 35. 150 applicants, 27% accepted. In 1997, 21 degrees awarded. *Degree requirements:* Thesis or alternative required, foreign language not required. *Entrance requirements:* GRE General Test or MAT. Application deadline: 4/1 (priority date; rolling processing). Application fee: $50. *Expenses:* Tuition $5440 per year full-time, $302 per credit hour part-time for state residents; $8160 per year (minimum) full-time, $453 per credit hour (minimum) part-time for nonresidents. Fees $868 per year full-time, $15 per year part-time. *Financial aid:* In 1997–98, 2 fellowships, 7 teaching assistantships (all to first-year students), 3 scholarships (2 to first-year students) were awarded; full and partial tuition waivers, Federal Work-Study, and career-related internships or fieldwork also available. Aid available to part-time students. Financial aid application deadline: 2/15. *Faculty research:* Speech pathology. • Dr. Stephen Calculator, Chairperson, 603-862-3836.

University of New Mexico, College of Arts and Sciences, Department of Communicative Disorders, Albuquerque, NM 87131-2039. Awards MS. One or more programs accredited by ASHA. Faculty: 6 full-time (4 women), 7 part-time (6 women), 7.87 FTE. Students: 71 full-time (66 women), 11 part-time (all women); includes 10 minority (1 African American, 9 Hispanics), 1 international. Average age 32. 114 applicants, 33% accepted. In 1997, 31 degrees awarded. *Degree requirements:* Comprehensive exams required, foreign language and thesis not required. *Entrance requirements:* GRE General Test, minimum GPA of 3.2 during previous 2 years. Application fee: $25. *Expenses:* Tuition $2442 per year full-time, $103 per credit hour part-time for state residents; $8691 per year full-time, $103 per credit hour (minimum) part-time for nonresidents. Fees $32 per year. *Financial aid:* Fellowships and career-related internships or fieldwork available. *Faculty research:* Central auditory processing, children's language analysis, nonoral communication. Total annual research expenditures: $1582. • Dr. Linda L. Riensche, Chair, 505-277-4453. Fax: 505-277-0968.

The University of North Carolina at Chapel Hill, School of Medicine and Graduate School, Graduate Programs in Medicine, Department of Medical Allied Health Professions, Division of Speech and Hearing Sciences, Chapel Hill, NC 27599. Awards MS. One or more programs accredited by ASHA. Faculty: 10 full-time (5 women), 19 part-time (12 women). Students: 69 full-time (65 women); includes 15 minority (7 African Americans, 2 Asian Americans, 4 Hispanics, 2 Native Americans). Average age 27. 292 applicants, 24% accepted. In 1997, 33 degrees awarded. *Degree requirements:* Variable foreign language requirement, comprehensive exam required, thesis not required. *Entrance requirements:* GRE General Test (minimum combined score of 1000; average 1100), minimum GPA of 3.0. Application deadline: 1/31. Application fee: $65. Electronic applications accepted. *Expenses:* Tuition $1428 per year for state residents; $10,414 per year for nonresidents. Fees $782 per year. *Financial aid:* In 1997–98, 28 students received aid, including 5 fellowships (all to first-year students), 8 research assistantships totaling $8,000; teaching assistantships, graduate assistantships, fellow traineeships, Federal Work-Study, and career-related internships or fieldwork also available. Financial aid application deadline: 1/31. *Faculty research:* Adult audiologic rehabilitation; hearing aids; language development and disorders in infants, toddlers, and preschoolers; audiology and psychoacoustics; speech perception; literary development in the hearing impaired. Total annual research expenditures: $381,462. • Dr. Jackson Roush, Director, 919-966-9467. E-mail: jroush@css.unc.edu. Application contact: Dr. Elizabeth Crais, Admission Director, 919-966-9458. Fax: 919-966-0100. E-mail: bcrais@css.unc.edu.

University of North Carolina at Greensboro, School of Health and Human Performance, Department of Communication Science and Disorders, Programs in Speech Pathology and Audiology, Greensboro, NC 27412-0001. Awards MA. Accredited by ASHA. Faculty: 8 full-time (7 women). Students: 65 full-time (61 women); includes 2 minority (1 African American, 1 Native American). 228 applicants, 24% accepted. In 1997, 27 degrees awarded. *Degree requirements:* Thesis or alternative required, foreign language not required. *Entrance requirements:* GRE General Test. Application deadline: 2/15. Application fee: $35. *Expenses:* Tuition $1842 per year full-time, $370 per semester (minimum) part-time for state residents; $10,296 per year full-time, $2484 per semester (minimum) part-time for nonresidents. Fees $806 per year full-time, $111 per semester (minimum) part-time. *Financial aid:* Fellowships, research assistantships available. *Faculty research:* Signing systems, communication and aging, psychoacoustics, deaf culture. • Dr. Jacqueline Cimorelli, Head, Department of Communication Science and Disorders, 336-334-5184.

University of North Dakota, College of Arts and Sciences, Department of Communication Disorders, Grand Forks, ND 58202. Offers program in speech-language pathology (MS). One or more programs accredited by ASHA. Part-time programs available. Faculty: 5 full-time (1 woman). Students: 34 full-time (33 women), 4 part-time (all women). 61 applicants, 33% accepted. In 1997, 16 degrees awarded. *Degree requirements:* Thesis or alternative. *Entrance requirements:* GRE General Test, TOEFL (minimum score 550), minimum GPA of 3.0. Application deadline: 2/15. Application fee: $20. *Financial aid:* In 1997–98, 12 students received aid, including 6 fellowships totaling $14,400, 3 teaching assistantships totaling $5,436, 2 assistantships totaling $7,170; research assistantships, full and partial tuition waivers, Federal Work-Study, institutionally sponsored loans also available. Financial aid application deadline: 3/15. • Dr. Wayne Swisher, Chairperson, 701-777-3232. Fax: 701-777-3650. E-mail: swisher@badlands.nodak.edu.

University of Northern Colorado, College of Health and Human Sciences, Department of Communication Disorders, Greeley, CO 80639. Awards MA. One or more programs accredited by ASHA. Faculty: 8 full-time (4 women), 1 (woman) part-time. Students: 79 full-time (75 women), 35 part-time (34 women); includes 9 minority (1 African American, 3 Asian Americans, 5 Hispanics), 1 international. Average age 29. 203 applicants, 55% accepted. In 1997, 29 degrees awarded. *Degree requirements:* Thesis or alternative, comprehensive exams. *Entrance requirements:* GRE General Test. Application deadline: rolling. Application fee: $35. *Expenses:* Tuition $2327 per year full-time, $129 per credit hour part-time for state residents; $9578 per year full-time, $532 per credit hour part-time for nonresidents. Fees $752 per year full-time, $184 per semester (minimum) part-time. *Financial aid:* In 1997–98, 69 students received aid, including 5 fellowships (all to first-year students) totaling $6,200, 3 graduate assistantships (2 to first-year students) totaling $10,965; teaching assistantships also available. Financial aid application deadline: 3/1. • Dr. Katie Bright, Chairperson, 970-351-2734.

University of Northern Iowa, College of Humanities and Fine Arts, Department of Communicative Disorders, Cedar Falls, IA 50614. Offers programs in audiology (MA), speech pathology (MA). One or more programs accredited by ASHA. Part-time and evening/weekend programs available. Faculty: 9 full-time (3 women). Students: 39 full-time (35 women), 2 part-time (both women); includes 1 minority (African American). Average age 33. 79 applicants, 43% accepted. In 1997, 29 degrees awarded. *Entrance requirements:* GRE. Application deadline: 8/1 (priority date; rolling processing). Application fee: $20 ($30 for international students). *Expenses:* Tuition $3166 per year full-time, $176 per hour part-time for state residents; $7805 per year full-time, $176 per hour part-time for nonresidents. Fees $194 per year full-time, $12.50 per semester (minimum) part-time. *Financial aid:* Scholarships, full and partial tuition waivers, Federal Work-Study, and career-related internships or fieldwork available. Financial aid application deadline: 3/1. • Dr. Ken Bleile, Head, 319-273-2496.

University of North Texas, College of Arts and Sciences, Department of Speech and Hearing Sciences, Denton, TX 76203-6737. Offers program in speech-language pathology/audiology (MA, MS). One or more programs accredited by ASHA. Part-time programs available. Faculty: 9 full-time (7 women), 9 part-time (7 women), 10 FTE. Students: 56 full-time (42 women), 6 part-time (all women); includes 5 minority (3 Asian Americans, 2 Hispanics), 2 international. Average age 26. In 1997, 39 degrees awarded (100% found work related to degree). *Degree requirements:* Comprehensive exam, internship required, thesis optional, foreign language not required. *Entrance requirements:* GRE General Test (minimum score 400 on verbal section, 900 combined), minimum GPA of 3.0 in major, 2.8 overall; 15 hours in communication disorders. Application deadline: 7/17. Application fee: $25 ($50 for international students). *Tuition:* $2063 per year full-time, $815 per year part-time for state residents; $5897 per year full-time, $2100 per year part-time for nonresidents. *Financial aid:* Fellowships, research assistantships, teaching assistantships, clinical assistantships, Federal Work-Study, institutionally sponsored loans, and career-related internships or fieldwork available. Financial aid application deadline: 3/15. *Faculty research:* Communication disorders in aging, voice disorders, language development, speech perception, brain mapping. Total annual research expenditures: $90,000. • Dr. Ray Daniloff, Chair, 940-565-2262. Fax: 940-565-4058. E-mail: daniloff@cas.unt.edu.

University of Oklahoma Health Sciences Center, College of Allied Health, Department of Communication Sciences and Disorders, Oklahoma City, OK 73190. Offers programs in audiology (MS, PhD), communication sciences and disorders (Certificate), education of the deaf (MS), speech-language pathology (MS, PhD). One or more programs accredited by ASHA. Part-time programs available. Faculty: 19 full-time (12 women), 13 part-time (11 women). Students: 80 full-time (72 women), 15 part-time (12 women); includes 7 minority (1 African American, 1 Asian American, 5 Native Americans), 3 international. Average age 23. 131 applicants, 44% accepted. In 1997, 38 master's awarded. Terminal master's awarded for partial completion of doctoral program. *Degree requirements:* For master's, comprehensive exam required, thesis optional, foreign language not required; for doctorate, 1 foreign language, computer language, dissertation, oral and written comprehensive exam. *Entrance requirements:* For master's and doctorate, GRE General Test, TOEFL (minimum score 550). Application deadline: 7/1 (rolling processing; 12/1 for spring admission). Application fee: $25 ($50 for international students). *Financial aid:* Fellowships, traineeships, Federal Work-Study, institutionally sponsored loans, and career-related internships or fieldwork available. Aid available to part-time students. *Faculty research:* Event-related potentials, cleft palate, fluency disorders, language disorders, hearing and speech science. • Application contact: Dr. Ann Owens, Graduate Liaison, 405-271-4214. Fax: 405-271-1153. E-mail: ann-owens@uokhsc.edu.

University of Oregon, Graduate School, College of Education, Department of Applied Behavior and Communication Sciences, Program in Communication Disorders and Sciences, Eugene, OR 97403. Awards MA, M Ed, MS, D Ed, PhD. One or more programs accredited by ASHA. Students: 42 full-time (39 women), 8 part-time (all women); includes 2 minority (both Asian Americans). 88 applicants, 32% accepted. In 1997, 15 master's awarded (100% found work related to degree); 1 doctorate awarded. *Degree requirements:* For master's, thesis or alternative, exam, paper, or project required, foreign language not required; for doctorate, computer language, dissertation, comprehensive exam required, foreign language not required. *Entrance requirements:* GRE General Test, TOEFL (minimum score 600). Application deadline: 2/15. Application fee: $50. *Tuition:* $6429 per year full-time, $873 per quarter (minimum) part-time for state residents; $10,857 per year full-time, $1360 per quarter (minimum) part-time for nonresidents. *Financial aid:* In 1997–98, 5 teaching assistantships were awarded; fellowships, research assistantships, Federal Work-Study, institutionally sponsored loans, and career-related internships or fieldwork also available. *Faculty research:* Language, phonology, stuttering, early intervention. • Marilyn Nippold, Director, 541-346-5501. Application contact: Susan Hair, Graduate Secretary, 541-346-2457.

University of Ottawa, Faculty of Health Sciences, Audiology and Speech-Language Pathology Program, Ottawa, ON K1N 6N5, Canada. Awards M Sc. Offered jointly with Laurentian University. Part-time and evening/weekend programs available. Faculty: 2 full-time. Students: 42 full-time (39 women), 2 part-time (both women). Average age 27. In 1997, 16 degrees awarded. *Degree requirements:* Practicum required, foreign language and thesis not required. *Entrance requirements:* Honors degree or equivalent, minimum B average. Application fee: $60. *Expenses:* Tuition $4677 per year for Canadian residents; $9900 per year for nonresidents. Fees $230 per year. *Financial aid:* Fellowships, research assistantships, teaching assistantships, Federal Work-Study available. • Patricia Roberts, Director, 613-562-5800 Ext. 4861. Application contact: Karen Littlejohn, Academic Assistant, 613-562-5800 Ext. 3072. Fax: 613-562-5256.

University of Pittsburgh, School of Health and Rehabilitation Sciences, Department of Communication Science and Disorders, Pittsburgh, PA 15260. Awards MA, MS, PhD. One or more programs accredited by ASHA. Faculty: 11 full-time (9 women), 3 part-time (2 women). Students: 29 full-time (25 women), 8 part-time (7 women); includes 4 minority (2 African Americans, 2 Asian Americans), 2 international. 166 applicants, 40% accepted. In 1997, 16 master's, 3 doctorates awarded. *Degree requirements:* For master's, thesis required (for some programs), foreign language not required; for doctorate, dissertation required, foreign language not required. *Average time to degree:* master's–2 years full-time; doctorate–5 years full-time. *Entrance requirements:* GRE General Test, TOEFL. Application deadline: 3/20 (rolling processing). Application fee: $30 ($40 for international students). *Expenses:* Tuition $9402 per year full-time, $388 per credit part-time for state residents; $19,372 per year full-time, $799 per credit part-time for nonresidents. Fees $480 per year full-time, $180 per year part-time. *Financial aid:* In 1997–98, 29 students received aid, including 10 research assistantships (1 to a first-year student) averaging $1,200 per month, 4 teaching assistantships (2 to first-year students) averaging $1,300 per month, 15 traineeships (7 to first-year students) totaling $229,797; Federal Work-Study, institutionally sponsored loans, and career-related internships or fieldwork also available. *Faculty research:* Pediatric and geriatric neurogenic speech and language, pediatric hearing disorders, hearing aids, language development, speech motor control. Total annual research expenditures: $248,933. • Malcolm McNeil, Chairman, 412-647-1346. E-mail: mcneil+@pitt.edu. Application contact: Sally Samuels, Admissions Secretary, 412-647-1344. Fax: 412-647-1370. E-mail: samuels+@pitt.edu.

See in-depth description on page 1351.

University of Puerto Rico, Medical Sciences Campus, College of Health Related Professions, Department of Communicative Disorders, Program in Audiology, San Juan, PR 00936-5067. Awards MS. *Degree requirements:* 1 foreign language required, thesis not required. *Average time to degree:* master's–2 years full-time. *Entrance requirements:* PAEG (minimum score 295; average 521), interview. Application deadline: 2/15 (priority date; rolling processing). Application fee: $15. *Faculty research:* Hearing.

University of Puerto Rico, Medical Sciences Campus, College of Health Related Professions, Department of Communicative Disorders, Program in Speech-Language Pathology, San Juan, PR 00936-5067. Awards MS. *Degree requirements:* 1 foreign language, thesis or alternative. *Average time to degree:* master's–2 years full-time. *Entrance requirements:* PAEG (minimum score 295; average 521), interview. Application deadline: 2/15 (priority date; rolling processing). Application fee: $15. *Faculty research:* Aphasia, autism, language.

University of Redlands, Department of Communicative Disorders, PO Box 3080, Redlands, CA 92373-0999. Awards MS. One or more programs accredited by ASHA. Part-time programs available. Faculty: 7 full-time (3 women). Students: 42 full-time (36 women), 13 part-time (all women); includes 6 minority (1 African American, 3 Asian Americans, 2 Hispanics). Average age 26. 71 applicants, 34% accepted. In 1997, 30 degrees awarded. *Entrance requirements:* GMAT or GRE, TOEFL (minimum score 500), minimum GPA of 3.0. Application deadline: 9/1 (rolling processing). Application fee: $40. Electronic applications accepted. *Expenses:* Tuition $382 per unit. Fees $158 per year. *Financial aid:* Assistantships and career-related internships or fieldwork available. Financial aid application deadline: 9/1. • Dr. Chris Walker, Chairman, 909-793-2121 Ext. 4061.

University of Rhode Island, College of Human Science and Services, Department of Communicative Disorders, Kingston, RI 02881. Awards MA, MS. One or more programs accredited by ASHA. *Entrance requirements:* MAT or GRE. Application deadline: 4/15 (priority date; rolling processing; 11/15 for spring admission). Application fee: $35. *Expenses:* Tuition $3446 per year full-time, $191 per credit part-time for state residents; $9850 per year full-time, $547 per credit part-time for nonresidents. Fees $1276 per year full-time, $135 per semester (minimum) part-time.

University of South Alabama, College of Allied Health Professions, Department of Speech Pathology and Audiology, Mobile, AL 36688-0002. Offers programs in communication sciences and disorders (PhD), speech and hearing sciences (MS). Accredited by ASHA. Faculty: 8 full-time (2 women). Students: 35 full-time (30 women), 16 part-time (13 women); includes 3 minority (2 African Americans, 1 Hispanic). 116 applicants, 27% accepted. In 1997, 18 master's, 1 doctorate awarded. *Degree requirements:* For master's, externship required, thesis optional, foreign language not required; for doctorate, dissertation, clinical internship required, foreign language not required. *Entrance requirements:* For master's, GRE General Test (minimum combined score of 1000). Application deadline: 9/1 (priority date; rolling processing). Application fee: $25. *Financial aid:* In 1997–98, 7 fellowships, 1 research assistantship were awarded; career-related internships or fieldwork also available. Aid available to part-time students. Financial aid application deadline: 4/1. *Faculty research:* Computer applications to speech and hearing science, telecommunications and clinical research in articulation and languages. • Dr. Stephen Hood, Chairperson and Director of Graduate Studies, 334-380-2600.

Directory: Communication Disorders

University of South Carolina, Graduate School, School of Public Health, Department of Speech Language Pathology and Audiology, Columbia, SC 29208. Awards MCD, MSP, PhD. One or more programs accredited by ASHA. Faculty: 13 full-time (9 women), 1 (woman) part-time. Students: 83 full-time (80 women), 68 part-time (65 women); includes 23 minority (21 African Americans, 1 Asian American, 1 Hispanic). Average age 30. 148 applicants, 27% accepted. In 1997, 38 master's, 2 doctorates awarded. *Degree requirements:* For master's, thesis required, foreign language not required; for doctorate, dissertation. *Entrance requirements:* For master's, GRE, minimum GPA of 3.0; for doctorate, GRE, master's degree in audiology or speech pathology. Application deadline: rolling. Application fee: $35. Electronic applications accepted. *Expenses:* Tuition $4480 per year full-time, $220 per credit hour part-time for state residents; $9338 per year full-time, $457 per credit hour part-time for nonresidents. Fees $125 per year full-time, $37 per semester (minimum) part-time. *Financial aid:* Research assistantships and career-related internships or fieldwork available. *Faculty research:* Noise-induced hearing loss, recurrent laryngeal nerve regeneration, cleft palate, child language-phonology, epidemiology of craniofacial anomalies. • Dr. William A. Cooper Jr., Chair, 803-777-4822. Application contact: Dr. Hiram L. McDade, Graduate Director, 803-777-3080. Fax: 803-777-3081.

University of South Dakota, College of Arts and Sciences, Department of Communication Disorders, Vermillion, SD 57069-2390. Offers programs in audiology (MA), speech-language pathology (MA). One or more programs accredited by ASHA. Faculty: 5 full-time (1 woman), 1 part-time (0 women). Students: 51 full-time (47 women), 1 (woman) part-time; includes 1 Asian American, 1 international. 93 applicants, 26% accepted. In 1997, 12 degrees awarded. *Degree requirements:* Oral and written comprehensive exams required, foreign language and thesis not required. *Entrance requirements:* GRE, minimum GPA of 3.0. Application fee: $15. *Expenses:* Tuition $1530 per year full-time, $85 per credit hour part-time for state residents; $4518 per year full-time, $251 per credit hour part-time for nonresidents. Fees $792 per year full-time, $44 per credit hour part-time. *Financial aid:* Fellowships, research assistantships, teaching assistantships, clinical assistantships, Federal Work-Study, and career-related internships or fieldwork available. Aid available to part-time students. Financial aid application deadline: 5/1. *Faculty research:* Craniofacial anomalies, central auditory processing, phonological disorders. • Dr. Dean Lockwood, Chair, 605-677-5474.

University of Southern Mississippi, College of Liberal Arts, Department of Speech and Hearing Sciences, Hattiesburg, MS 39406-5167. Awards MA, MS, PhD. One or more programs accredited by ASHA. Faculty: 7 full-time (3 women), 1 (woman) part-time. Students: 46 full-time (44 women), 1 (woman) part-time. Average age 26. 97 applicants, 10% accepted. In 1997, 27 master's awarded. *Degree requirements:* For master's, variable foreign language requirement, thesis or alternative; for doctorate, 2 foreign languages (computer language can substitute for one), dissertation. *Entrance requirements:* For master's, GRE General Test, minimum GPA of 2.75; for doctorate, GRE General Test, minimum GPA of 3.5. Application deadline: 8/9 (priority date; rolling processing). Application fee: $0 ($25 for international students). *Tuition:* $2870 per year full-time, $137 per credit hour part-time for state residents; $5972 per year full-time, $172 per credit hour part-time for nonresidents. *Financial aid:* Research assistantships, teaching assistantships, full tuition waivers, Federal Work-Study, institutionally sponsored loans, and career-related internships or fieldwork available. Financial aid application deadline: 3/15. *Faculty research:* Voice disorders, auditory-evoked responses, acoustic analysis of speech, child language, parent-child interaction. • Dr. Stephen E. Oshrin, Chairman, 601-266-5216.

University of South Florida, College of Arts and Sciences, Department of Communication Sciences and Disorders, Program in Audiology, Tampa, FL 33620-9951. Awards MS. Accredited by ASHA. Part-time and evening/weekend programs available. Postbaccalaureate distance learning degree programs offered (minimal on-campus study). Students: 14 full-time (11 women), 5 part-time (4 women); includes 7 minority (5 African Americans, 2 Hispanics). Average age 25. 42 applicants, 31% accepted. In 1997, 11 degrees awarded. *Degree requirements:* Thesis optional. *Entrance requirements:* GRE General Test (minimum combined score of 1000), minimum GPA of 3.0 in last 60 hours. Application deadline: 6/1 (10/15 for spring admission). Application fee: $20. Electronic applications accepted. *Tuition:* $142 per credit hour for state residents; $486 per credit hour for nonresidents. *Financial aid:* 2 students received aid; Federal Work-Study, institutionally sponsored loans available. Aid available to part-time students. Financial aid applicants required to submit FAFSA. • Application contact: Peggy Ott, Office Manager, 813-974-9780. Fax: 813-974-0822.

University of South Florida, College of Arts and Sciences, Department of Communication Sciences and Disorders, Program in Aural Rehabilitation, Tampa, FL 33620-9951. Awards MS. One or more programs accredited by ASHA. Part-time and evening/weekend programs available. Postbaccalaureate distance learning degree programs offered (minimal on-campus study). Students: 2 full-time (both women), 1 (woman) part-time. Average age 34. 0 applicants. In 1997, 2 degrees awarded. *Degree requirements:* Thesis optional. *Entrance requirements:* GRE General Test (minimum combined score of 1000), minimum GPA of 3.0 in last 60 hours. Application deadline: 6/1 (10/15 for spring admission). Application fee: $20. Electronic applications accepted. *Tuition:* $142 per credit hour for state residents; $486 per credit hour for nonresidents. *Financial aid:* Federal Work-Study, institutionally sponsored loans available. Aid available to part-time students. Financial aid applicants required to submit FAFSA. • Application contact: Peggy Ott, Office Manager, 813-974-9780. Fax: 813-974-0822.

University of South Florida, College of Arts and Sciences, Department of Communication Sciences and Disorders, Program in Speech Pathology, Tampa, FL 33620-9951. Awards MS. Accredited by ASHA. Part-time and evening/weekend programs available. Postbaccalaureate distance learning degree programs offered (minimal on-campus study). Students: 84 full-time (80 women), 73 part-time (62 women); includes 35 minority (8 African Americans, 2 Asian Americans, 25 Hispanics), 1 international. Average age 31. 358 applicants, 20% accepted. In 1997, 39 degrees awarded. *Degree requirements:* Thesis optional. *Entrance requirements:* GRE General Test (minimum combined score of 1000), minimum GPA of 3.0 in last 60 hours. Application deadline: 2/1. Application fee: $20. *Tuition:* $142 per credit hour for state residents; $486 per credit hour for nonresidents. *Financial aid:* In 1997–98, 4 fellowships averaging $640 per month and totaling $23,000, 2 research assistantships averaging $500 per month and totaling $9,600, 3 teaching assistantships averaging $500 per month and totaling $9,100 were awarded; Federal Work-Study, institutionally sponsored loans also available. Aid available to part-time students. Financial aid applicants required to submit FAFSA. • Application contact: Peggy Ott, Office Manager, 813-974-9780. Fax: 813-974-0822.

University of Southwestern Louisiana, College of Liberal Arts, Department of Communicative Disorders, Lafayette, LA 70503. Awards MS. One or more programs accredited by ASHA. Faculty: 8 full-time (4 women). Students: 53 full-time (52 women), 3 part-time (2 women); includes 6 minority (3 African Americans, 1 Asian American, 1 Hispanic, 1 Native American), 2 international. 120 applicants, 34% accepted. In 1997, 24 degrees awarded. *Degree requirements:* Thesis or alternative required, foreign language not required. *Entrance requirements:* GRE General Test, minimum GPA of 2.75. Application deadline: 8/15. Application fee: $5 ($15 for international students). *Tuition:* $2012 per year full-time, $300 per semester (minimum) part-time for state residents; $7244 per year full-time, $300 per semester (minimum) part-time for nonresidents. *Financial aid:* Fellowships, research assistantships, teaching assistantships, Federal Work-Study available. Financial aid application deadline: 5/1. • Dr. John W. Oller Jr., Head, 318-482-6721. Application contact: Dr. Nancye Roussel, Graduate Coordinator, 318-482-6727.

University of Tennessee, Knoxville, College of Education, Program in Education II, Knoxville, TN 37996. Offerings include education of deaf and hard of hearing (MS). *Degree requirements:* Thesis optional, foreign language not required. *Entrance requirements:* TOEFL (minimum score 550), minimum GPA of 2.7. Application deadline: 2/1 (priority date; rolling processing). Application fee: $35. Electronic applications accepted. *Tuition:* $3354 per year full-time, $181 per semester hour part-time for state residents; $8410 per year full-time, $462 per semester hour part-time for nonresidents. • Dr. Tom George, Associate Dean, 423-974-0907. Fax: 423-974-8718. E-mail: tgeorge1@utk.edu.

University of Tennessee, Knoxville, College of Arts and Sciences, Department of Audiology and Speech Pathology, Program in Audiology, Knoxville, TN 37996. Awards MA. Accredited by ASHA. Students: 25 full-time (23 women); includes 3 minority (1 African American, 2 Asian Americans), 1 international. 44 applicants, 73% accepted. In 1997, 11 degrees awarded. *Degree requirements:* Thesis or alternative required, foreign language not required. *Entrance requirements:* GRE General Test, TOEFL (minimum score 550), minimum GPA of 2.7. Application deadline: 2/1 (priority date; rolling processing). Application fee: $35. Electronic applications accepted. *Tuition:* $3354 per year full-time, $181 per semester hour part-time for state residents; $8410 per year full-time, $462 per semester hour part-time for nonresidents. *Financial aid:* Application deadline 2/1. • Dr. Patrick J. Carney, Head, Department of Audiology and Speech Pathology, 423-974-5019. Fax: 423-974-1539. E-mail: jcarney@utk.edu.

University of Tennessee, Knoxville, College of Arts and Sciences, Department of Audiology and Speech Pathology, Program in Speech and Hearing Science, Knoxville, TN 37996. Offers audiology (PhD), hearing science (PhD), speech and language pathology (PhD), speech and language science (PhD). Students: 7 full-time (5 women), 3 part-time (1 woman); includes 1 minority (African American). 4 applicants, 25% accepted. In 1997, 2 degrees awarded. *Degree requirements:* Dissertation required, foreign language not required. *Entrance requirements:* GRE General Test, TOEFL (minimum score 550), minimum GPA of 2.7. Application deadline: 2/1 (priority date; rolling processing). Application fee: $35. Electronic applications accepted. *Tuition:* $3354 per year full-time, $181 per semester hour part-time for state residents; $8410 per year full-time, $462 per semester hour part-time for nonresidents. *Financial aid:* Application deadline 2/1. • Dr. Patrick J. Carney, Head, Department of Audiology and Speech Pathology, 423-974-5019. Fax: 423-974-1539. E-mail: jcarney@utk.edu.

University of Tennessee, Knoxville, College of Arts and Sciences, Department of Audiology and Speech Pathology, Program in Speech Pathology, Knoxville, TN 37996. Awards MA. Accredited by ASHA. Students: 101 full-time (96 women), 51 part-time (50 women); includes 16 minority (15 African Americans, 1 Native American), 2 international. 316 applicants, 29% accepted. In 1997, 49 degrees awarded. *Degree requirements:* Thesis or alternative required, foreign language not required. *Entrance requirements:* GRE General Test, TOEFL (minimum score 550), minimum GPA of 2.7. Application deadline: 2/1 (priority date; rolling processing). Application fee: $35. Electronic applications accepted. *Tuition:* $3354 per year full-time, $181 per semester hour part-time for state residents; $8410 per year full-time, $462 per semester hour part-time for nonresidents. *Financial aid:* Application deadline 2/1. • Dr. Patrick J. Carney, Head, Department of Audiology and Speech Pathology, 423-974-5019. Fax: 423-974-1539. E-mail: jcarney@utk.edu.

The University of Texas at Austin, Graduate School, College of Communication, Department of Communication Sciences and Disorders, Austin, TX 78712. Awards MA, PhD. One or more programs accredited by ASHA. Students: 117 (111 women). 173 applicants, 39% accepted. In 1997, 37 master's, 2 doctorates awarded. *Entrance requirements:* GRE General Test. Application fee: $50 ($75 for international students). *Expenses:* Tuition $2592 per year full-time, $324 per semester (minimum) part-time for state residents; $7704 per year full-time, $963 per semester (minimum) part-time for nonresidents. Fees $778 per year full-time, $161 per semester (minimum) part-time. *Financial aid:* Application deadline 2/1. • Rodge Dalston, Chair. Application contact: Mark Bernstein, Graduate Adviser.

The University of Texas at Dallas, School of Human Development, Program in Communications Disorders, Richardson, TX 75083-0688. Awards MS. One or more programs accredited by ASHA. Part-time and evening/weekend programs available. Faculty: 19 full-time (13 women). Students: 136 full-time (131 women), 8 part-time (all women); includes 9 minority (1 African American, 2 Asian Americans, 6 Hispanics). Average age 27. 199 applicants, 33% accepted. In 1997, 74 degrees awarded. *Degree requirements:* Minimum GPA of 3.0 required, thesis optional, foreign language not required. *Entrance requirements:* GRE General Test (minimum combined score of 1000), TOEFL (minimum score 550), minimum GPA of 3.0. Application deadline: 7/15 (rolling processing; 11/15 for spring admission). Application fee: $25 ($75 for international students). *Financial aid:* 15 students received aid; fellowships, research assistantships, teaching assistantships, Federal Work-Study available. Aid available to part-time students. Financial aid application deadline: 11/1. *Faculty research:* Brain mapping, evoked potentials, speech production, child language, aphasia. • Dr. Robert D. Stillman, Head, 972-883-3060. Fax: 972-883-3022. E-mail: stillman@utdallas.edu.

The University of Texas at El Paso, College of Nursing and Health Science, Program in Speech Language Pathology, 500 West University Avenue, El Paso, TX 79968-0001. Awards MS. Accredited by ASHA. Part-time and evening/weekend programs available. *Degree requirements:* 250 clock hours of supervised practicum, comprehensive exams required, foreign language and thesis not required. *Entrance requirements:* GRE General Test, TOEFL (minimum score 550), minimum GPA of 3.0 in undergraduate major, course work in statistics. Application deadline: 7/1 (priority date; rolling processing; 11/1 for spring admission). Application fee: $15 ($65 for international students). Electronic applications accepted. *Tuition:* $2063 per year full-time, $284 per credit hour part-time for state residents; $5753 per year full-time, $425 per credit hour part-time for nonresidents. *Faculty research:* Cleft palate, bilingual language disorders, clinical supervision, hearing loss.

The University of Texas–Pan American, College of Health and Human Services, Department of Communication Disorders, Edinburg, TX 78539-2999. Awards MA. One or more programs accredited by ASHA. Part-time programs available. *Degree requirements:* Thesis optional, foreign language not required. *Average time to degree:* master's–2 years full-time, 3.5 years part-time. *Entrance requirements:* GRE General Test (minimum combined score of 750; average 850), minimum GPA of 3.0 in major. Application deadline: 4/1 (rolling processing). Application fee: $20. *Tuition:* $2156 per year full-time, $283 per semester (minimum) part-time for state residents; $6788 per year full-time, $862 per semester (minimum) part-time for nonresidents. *Faculty research:* Bilingual/bicultural language development/disorders, elementary-age language disorders, supervision.

University of the District of Columbia, College of Arts and Sciences, School of Arts and Education, Division of Education, Program in Speech and Language Pathology, 4200 Connecticut Avenue, NW, Washington, DC 20008-1175. Awards MS. One or more programs accredited by ASHA. Part-time programs available. *Degree requirements:* Comprehensive exam required, thesis optional, foreign language not required. *Entrance requirements:* GRE General Test, writing proficiency exam. Application deadline: 6/14 (priority date; rolling processing; 11/15 for spring admission). Application fee: $20. *Expenses:* Tuition $3564 per year full-time, $198 per credit part-time for district residents; $5922 per year full-time, $329 per credit part-time for nonresidents. Fees $990 per year full-time, $55 per credit part-time. *Faculty research:* Child language, dialect variation, English as a second language.

University of the Pacific, Department of Communicative Disorders, Stockton, CA 95211-0197. Awards MA. One or more programs accredited by ASHA. Faculty: 4 full-time (1 woman), 3 part-time (all women). Students: 50 full-time (46 women), 3 part-time (all women). In 1997, 20 degrees awarded. *Entrance requirements:* GRE General Test. Application deadline: 2/1. Application fee: $50. *Expenses:* Tuition $19,000 per year full-time, $594 per unit part-time. Fees $30 per year (minimum). *Financial aid:* Institutionally sponsored loans available. Aid available to part-time students. Financial aid application deadline: 2/1. • Robert Hanyak, Chairman, 209-946-2381. E-mail: rhanyak@uop.edu.

University of Toledo, College of Education and Allied Professions, Department of Special Education Services, Toledo, OH 43606-3398. Offerings include speech-language pathology (M Ed). Accredited by ASHA. Department faculty: 9 full-time (5 women). *Degree requirements:* Thesis, comprehensive exam required, foreign language not required. *Entrance requirements:* Minimum GPA of 2.7. Application deadline: 8/1 (priority date; rolling processing). Application fee: $30. *Tuition:* $5907 per year full-time, $246 per hour part-time for state residents; $11,835 per year full-time, $493 per hour part-time for nonresidents. • Dr. Martha Carroll, Chair, 419-530-2055. E-mail: mcarrol@utnet.utoledo.edu.

University of Toronto, School of Graduate Studies, Life Sciences Division, Department of Speech-Language Pathology, Toronto, ON M5S 1A1, Canada. Awards MH Sc, M Sc, PhD. Part-time programs available. Faculty: 27. Students: 42 full-time (39 women), 4 part-time (all women). 153 applicants, 21% accepted. In 1997, 18 master's awarded. *Degree requirements:* For master's, thesis (for some programs); for doctorate, dissertation. *Application fee:* $75. *Expenses:* Tuition $4070 per year for Canadian residents; $7870 per year for nonresidents. Fees $628 per year. • Dr. P. A. Square, Chair, 416-978-8330. Application contact: Secretary, 416-978-1794. Fax: 416-978-1596. E-mail: speech.path@utoronto.ca.

University of Tulsa, College of Arts and Sciences, Program in Speech-Language Pathology, Tulsa, OK 74104-3189. Awards MA. Accredited by ASHA. Part-time programs available. Faculty: 5 full-time (2 women). Students: 38 full-time (all women), 1 (woman) part-time; includes 5 minority (1 Asian American, 1 Hispanic, 3 Native Americans). Average age 28. 68 applicants, 37% accepted. In 1997, 14 degrees awarded. *Degree requirements:* Thesis optional, foreign language not required. *Entrance requirements:* GRE General Test (minimum combined score of 800), TOEFL (minimum score 575). Application deadline: 2/1 (priority date; rolling processing). Application fee: $30. Electronic applications accepted. *Expenses:* Tuition $480 per credit hour. Fees $2 per credit hour. *Financial aid:* In 1997–98, 15 students received aid, including 4 fellowships (all to first-year students) totaling $57,120, 11 teaching assistantships (6 to first-year students) totaling $111,793; research assistantships, partial tuition waivers, Federal Work-Study also available. Aid available to part-time students. Financial aid application deadline: 2/1; applicants required to submit FAFSA. *Faculty research:* Speech-language pathology in handicapped preschool children, stuttering, hearing aid use, aphasia, language development. • Dr. James E. Green, Chairperson, 918-631-2919. Application contact: Dr. John M. Christensen, Adviser, 918-631-2903. Fax: 918-631-3668.

University of Utah, College of Health, Department of Communication Disorders, Salt Lake City, UT 84112-1107. Offers programs in audiology (MA, MS), speech-language pathology (MA, MS), speech-language pathology and audiology (M Phil, PhD). One or more programs accredited by ASHA. Faculty: 5 full-time (2 women), 49 part-time (33 women). Students: 33 full-time (30 women), 16 part-time (13 women); includes 2 minority (1 Asian American, 1 Native American), 2 international. Average age 29. In 1997, 31 master's, 1 doctorate awarded. *Degree requirements:* For master's, 1 foreign language, thesis or alternative, written exam; for doctorate, 1 foreign language (computer language can substitute), dissertation, written and oral exams. *Entrance requirements:* GRE, TOEFL (minimum score 500), minimum GPA of 3.0. Application deadline: 2/1. Application fee: $30 ($50 for international students). *Tuition:* $2045 per year full-time, $562 per semester (minimum) part-time for state residents; $6129 per year full-time, $1607 per semester (minimum) part-time for nonresidents. *Financial aid:* In 1997–98, 2 teaching assistantships were awarded; fellowships and career-related internships or fieldwork also available. *Faculty research:* Anatomy, vestibular disorders, rehabilitation, research audiology, motor speech disorders. • Dr. Mary Louise Willbrand, Chairman, 801-585-6151.

University of Virginia, Curry School of Education, Department of Human Services, Program in Communication Disorders, Charlottesville, VA 22903. Awards M Ed. One or more programs accredited by ASHA. Faculty: 36 full-time (12 women), 2 part-time (1 woman), 37 FTE. Students: 51 full-time (49 women), 3 part-time (all women). Average age 26. 184 applicants, 35% accepted. In 1997, 31 degrees awarded. *Entrance requirements:* GRE General Test. Application deadline: 3/1 (11/15 for spring admission). Application fee: $40. *Tuition:* $4876 per year full-time, $944 per semester (minimum) part-time for state residents; $15,824 per year full-time, $2748 per semester (minimum) part-time for nonresidents. • Application contact: Linda Berry, Student Enrollment Coordinator, 804-924-0738. E-mail: lrb8e@virginia.edu.

University of Washington, College of Arts and Sciences, Department of Speech and Hearing Sciences, Seattle, WA 98195. Awards MS, PhD. One or more programs accredited by ASHA. Faculty: 19 full-time (11 women), 13 part-time (7 women). Students: 78 full-time (69 women); includes 12 minority (2 African Americans, 8 Asian Americans, 2 Hispanics), 6 international. 181 applicants, 18% accepted. In 1997, 27 master's awarded; 1 doctorate awarded (100% entered university research/teaching). *Degree requirements:* For master's, thesis required (for some programs), foreign language not required; for doctorate, dissertation required, foreign language not required. *Entrance requirements:* For master's, GRE, TOEFL, minimum GPA of 3.0; for doctorate, GRE, TOEFL (minimum score 500), minimum GPA of 3.0. Application deadline: 2/3 (rolling processing). Application fee: $45. *Tuition:* $5433 per year full-time, $775 per quarter (minimum) part-time for state residents; $13,479 per year full-time, $1925 per quarter (minimum) part-time for nonresidents. *Financial aid:* In 1997–98, 33 students received aid, including 5 fellowships (1 to a first-year student), 11 research assistantships (3 to first-year students), 18 teaching assistantships (4 to first-year students), 7 traineeships (1 to a first-year student); Federal Work-Study, institutionally sponsored loans, and career-related internships or fieldwork also available. Financial aid application deadline: 3/1. *Faculty research:* Treatment of communication disorders across the life span, speech physiology, auditory perception, behavioral and physiologic audiology. Total annual research expenditures: $1.22 million. • Patricia K. Kuhl, Chair, 206-543-7974. Fax: 206-543-1093. E-mail: pkkuhl@u.washington.edu. Application contact: Melissa M. Johnson, Academic Services Director, 206-685-7402. E-mail: sphscadv@u.washington.edu.

The University of Western Ontario, Biosciences Division, School of Communicative Disorders, London, ON N6A 5B8, Canada. Offers programs in audiology (M Cl Sc, M Sc), speech-language pathology (M Cl Sc, M Sc). Faculty: 21 full-time (10 women), 8 part-time (all women). Students: 90 full-time (80 women). 370 applicants, 24% accepted. In 1997, 44 degrees awarded. *Degree requirements:* Supervised clinical practicum. *Entrance requirements:* GRE, minimum B average during last 2 years. Application deadline: 2/15. Application fee: $40. *Financial aid:* Application deadline 4/1. • Dr. J. L. Stouffer, Director, 519-661-2001. Application contact: Dr. J. B. Orange, Graduate Chair, 519-661-2001.

University of Wisconsin–Eau Claire, College of Professional Studies, School of Human Sciences and Services, Program in Communicative Disorders, Eau Claire, WI 54702-4004. Awards MS. One or more programs accredited by ASHA. Students: 29 full-time (27 women), 2 part-time (both women); includes 3 international. In 1997, 12 degrees awarded. *Degree requirements:* Written comprehensive exam required, thesis optional, foreign language not required. *Application deadline:* 3/1 (rolling processing). *Application fee:* $45. *Tuition:* $3651 per year full-time, $611 per semester (minimum) part-time for state residents; $11,295 per year full-time, $1886 per semester (minimum) part-time for nonresidents. *Financial aid:* Federal Work-Study and career-related internships or fieldwork available. Financial aid application deadline: 3/1. • Sylvia Steiner, Director, 715-836-4186.

University of Wisconsin–Madison, College of Letters and Science, Department of Communicative Disorders, Madison, WI 53706-1380. Awards MS, PhD. One or more programs accredited by ASHA. Students: 109 full-time (100 women), 19 part-time (16 women); includes 1 African American, 6 Asian Americans, 1 Hispanic, 7 international. Average age 25. 500 applicants, 50% accepted. In 1997, 44 master's awarded (100% found work related to degree); 6 doctorates awarded (100% entered university research/teaching). *Degree requirements:* For doctorate, dissertation. *Entrance requirements:* GRE. Application deadline: 2/1. Application fee: $45. *Tuition:* $4928 per year full-time, $926 per semester (minimum) part-time for state residents; $15,190 per year full-time, $2849 per semester (minimum) part-time for nonresidents. *Financial aid:* In 1997–98, 28 students received aid, including 2 fellowships, 12 research assistantships; project assistantships, traineeships, full and partial tuition waivers, Federal Work-Study, and career-related internships or fieldwork also available. *Faculty research:* Language disorders in children and adults, disorders of speech production, intelligibility, fluency, hearing impairment, deafness. Total annual research expenditures: $2.8 million. • Jon Miller, Chair, 608-262-6461. Application contact: Jackie Ballwey, Student Secretary, 608-262-6464. Fax: 608-262-6466. E-mail: jfballwe@facstaff.wisc.edu.

University of Wisconsin–Milwaukee, School of Allied Health Professions, Program in Communication Sciences and Disorders, Milwaukee, WI 53201-0413. Awards MS. One or more programs accredited by ASHA. Part-time programs available. Faculty: 6 full-time (5 women). Students: 43 full-time (40 women), 9 part-time (8 women); includes 2 minority (1 Asian American, 1 Native American). 87 applicants, 39% accepted. In 1997, 14 degrees awarded. *Degree requirements:* Thesis or alternative required, foreign language not required. *Application deadline:* 1/1 (priority date; rolling processing; 9/1 for spring admission). *Application fee:* $45 ($75 for international students). *Tuition:* $4996 per year full-time, $1030 per semester (minimum) part-time for state residents; $15,216 per year full-time, $2947 per semester (minimum) part-time for nonresidents. *Financial aid:* Fellowships, research assistantships, teaching assistantships, project assistantships, and career-related internships or fieldwork available. Aid available to part-time students. Financial aid application deadline: 4/15. • Paula Rhyner, Chair, 414-229-4263.

University of Wisconsin–Oshkosh, College of Letters and Science, Department of Communication, Oshkosh, WI 54901-8602. Offers program in speech and hearing science (MS), including audiology, speech pathology. One or more programs accredited by ASHA. Faculty: 7 full-time (4 women), 1 (woman) part-time. Students: 28 full-time (25 women), 9 part-time (7 women); includes 1 minority (Asian American). Average age 26. 57 applicants, 74% accepted. In 1997, 23 degrees awarded. *Degree requirements:* Thesis or alternative, 1 year residency required, foreign language not required. *Entrance requirements:* GRE General Test (combined average 1500 on three sections), minimum GPA of 3.0, BS in communication disorders. Application deadline: 1/1 (8/1 for spring admission). Application fee: $45. *Tuition:* $3638 per year full-time, $609 per semester (minimum) part-time for state residents; $11,282 per year full-time, $1884 per semester (minimum) part-time for nonresidents. *Financial aid:* Full and partial tuition waivers, Federal Work-Study, institutionally sponsored loans, and career-related internships or fieldwork available. Financial aid application deadline: 3/15. *Faculty research:* Infant-toddler assessment and intervention. • Dr. Anthony Palmeri, Chair, 920-424-4422. Application contact: Dr. Jack Kile, Coordinator, 920-424-4416. Fax: 920-424-0883. E-mail: kile@uwosh.edu.

University of Wisconsin–River Falls, College of Education and Graduate Studies, Department of Communicative Disorders, River Falls, WI 54022-5001. Awards MS. One or more programs accredited by ASHA. Students: 30 (26 women). *Degree requirements:* Comprehensive exam required, foreign language and thesis not required. *Application deadline:* 2/1. *Application fee:* $45. *Financial aid:* Research assistantships, Federal Work-Study available. Financial aid application deadline: 3/1. • Paul Hayden, Chair, 715-425-3830. Application contact: Graduate Admissions, 715-425-3843.

University of Wisconsin–Stevens Point, College of Professional Studies, School of Communicative Disorders, Stevens Point, WI 54481-3897. Awards MS. One or more programs accredited by ASHA. Faculty: 8 (3 women). Students: 68 full-time (66 women), 3 part-time (all women). In 1997, 33 degrees awarded. *Degree requirements:* Thesis optional, foreign language not required. *Average time to degree:* master's–2 years full-time. *Application deadline:* 2/15 (rolling processing; 10/15 for spring admission). *Application fee:* $38. *Tuition:* $3702 per year full-time, $664 per semester (minimum) part-time for state residents; $11,346 per year full-time, $1938 per semester (minimum) part-time for nonresidents. *Financial aid:* Research assistantships, teaching assistantships, graduate assistantships, Federal Work-Study available. Financial aid application deadline: 5/1; applicants required to submit FAFSA. • Dr. Dennis Nash, Head, 715-346-3920. Fax: 715-346-3751.

University of Wisconsin–Whitewater, College of Arts and Communications, Program in Communicative Disorders, Whitewater, WI 53190-1790. Awards MS. One or more programs accredited by ASHA. Part-time and evening/weekend programs available. *Degree requirements:* Thesis or alternative required, foreign language not required. *Application deadline:* rolling. *Application fee:* $38.

University of Wyoming, College of Health Sciences, Department of Speech Pathology and Audiology, Program in Audiology, Laramie, WY 82071. Awards MS. Accredited by ASHA. Faculty: 2 full-time (0 women). Students: 10 full-time (9 women), 2 part-time (1 woman). 13 applicants, 31% accepted. In 1997, 6 degrees awarded. *Average time to degree:* master's–2 years full-time. *Entrance requirements:* GRE General Test (minimum combined score of 900), minimum GPA of 3.0. Application deadline: 2/15 (priority date; rolling processing; 11/15 for spring admission). Application fee: $40. *Expenses:* Tuition $2430 per year full-time, $135 per credit hour part-time for state residents; $7518 per year full-time, $418 per credit hour part-time for nonresidents. Fees $386 per year full-time, $9.25 per credit hour part-time. *Financial aid:* In 1997–98, 2 research assistantships (both to first-year students) averaging $470 per month and totaling $8,451, 2 scholarships (both to first-year students) totaling $8,000 were awarded. Financial aid application deadline: 3/1. *Faculty research:* Audiometric techniques with infants, applications of insert earphones. Total annual research expenditures: $5000. • Dr. Janis Jelinek, Chair, Department of Speech Pathology and Audiology, 307-766-6427. Fax: 307-766-6829. E-mail: jelinek@uwyo.edu.

University of Wyoming, College of Health Sciences, Department of Speech Pathology and Audiology, Program in Speech-Language Pathology, Laramie, WY 82071. Awards MS. Accredited by ASHA. Postbaccalaureate distance learning degree programs offered (minimal on-campus study). Faculty: 5 full-time (all women). Students: 26 full-time (23 women), 18 part-time (17 women); includes 1 minority (Hispanic), 1 international. Average age 24. 114 applicants, 21% accepted. In 1997, 20 degrees awarded. *Average time to degree:* master's–2 years full-time. *Entrance requirements:* GRE General Test (minimum combined score of 900), minimum GPA of 3.0. Application deadline: 2/15 (priority date; rolling processing; 11/15 for spring admission). Application fee: $40. *Expenses:* Tuition $2430 per year full-time, $135 per credit hour part-time for state residents; $7518 per year full-time, $418 per credit hour part-time for nonresidents. Fees $386 per year full-time, $9.25 per credit hour part-time. *Financial aid:* In 1997–98, 6 research assistantships (all to first-year students) averaging $470 per month and totaling $25,358, 1 scholarship (to a first-year student) totaling $4,000 were awarded. Financial aid application deadline: 3/1. *Faculty research:* Intervention approaches for school age children with language disorders, multiple sclerosis, voice, effect of aging on voicing durations. Total annual research expenditures: $5000. • Dr. Janis Jelinek, Chair, Department of Speech Pathology and Audiology, 307-766-6427. Fax: 307-766-6829. E-mail: jelinek@uwyo.edu.

Utah State University, College of Education, Department of Communicative Disorders and Deaf Education, Logan, UT 84322. Offers programs in communicative disorders (MA, M Ed, MS), educational audiology (Ed S). One or more programs accredited by ASHA. Evening/weekend programs available. Faculty: 14 full-time (8 women), 11 part-time (all women). Students: 72 full-time (62 women), 10 part-time (all women). Average age 28. 92 applicants, 38% accepted. In 1997, 43 master's, 2 Ed Ss awarded. *Degree requirements:* For master's, thesis optional, foreign language not required; for Ed S, thesis or alternative required, foreign language not required. *Entrance requirements:* For master's, GRE General Test (score in 40th percentile or higher), TOEFL (minimum score 550), minimum GPA of 3.0; for Ed S, GRE General Test (score in 40th percentile or higher), GRE Subject Test, TOEFL (minimum score 550), minimum GPA of 3.25. Application deadline: 2/15 (10/15 for spring admission). Application fee: $40. *Expenses:* Tuition $1448 per year full-time, $624 per year part-time for state residents; $5082 per year full-time, $2192 per year part-time for nonresidents. Fees $421 per year full-time, $165 per year part-time. *Financial aid:* Fellowships, research assistantships, teaching assistantships, stipends, full and partial tuition waivers, Federal Work-Study, institutionally sponsored loans, and career-related internships or fieldwork available. Aid available to part-time students. Financial aid application deadline: 2/1. *Faculty research:* Parent-infant intervention with hearing-impaired infants, voice disorders, language development and disorders, oto-accoustic emissions, deaf or hard-of-hearing infants. • Dr. Thomas Johnson, Head, 435-797-1375. Fax: 435-797-3924.

Valdosta State University, College of Education, Department of Special Education, Valdosta, GA 31698. Offerings include speech-language pathology (M Ed). Accredited by ASHA. Depart-

Directory: Communication Disorders

Valdosta State University (continued)
ment faculty: 14 full-time (6 women). *Entrance requirements:* GRE General Test (minimum combined score of 800). Application deadline: 8/1 (rolling processing; 11/15 for spring admission). Application fee: $10. *Expenses:* Tuition $2472 per year full-time, $83 per semester hour part-time for state residents; $8472 per year full-time, $333 per semester hour part-time for nonresidents. Fees $236 per year full-time. • Dr. Phillip Gunter, Head, 912-333-5932. E-mail: pgunter@grits.valdosta.peachnet.edu.

Vanderbilt University, Graduate School, Department of Hearing and Speech Sciences, Nashville, TN 37240-1001. Awards MS, PhD. One or more programs accredited by ASHA. Faculty: 13 full-time (5 women), 2 part-time (0 women). Students: 58 full-time (49 women); includes 3 minority (all African Americans), 1 international. Average age 28. 145 applicants, 39% accepted. In 1997, 19 master's awarded (100% found work related to degree); 8 doctorates awarded (100% entered university research/teaching). *Degree requirements:* For master's, thesis optional, foreign language not required; for doctorate, dissertation, final and qualifying exams required, foreign language not required. *Average time to degree:* master's–2 years full-time; doctorate–5 years full-time. *Entrance requirements:* GRE General Test. Application deadline: 1/15. Application fee: $40. *Expenses:* Tuition $16,452 per year full-time, $914 per semester hour part-time. Fees $236 per year. *Financial aid:* In 1997–98, fellowships averaging $800 per month, research assistantships averaging $800 per month were awarded; full and partial tuition waivers, institutionally sponsored loans, and career-related internships or fieldwork also available. Financial aid application deadline: 1/15. *Faculty research:* Audiology, speech-language pathology, child language. • Fred H. Bess, Chairman, 615-320-5353. E-mail: bessxxfh@ctrvax.vanderbilt.edu. Application contact: Edward G. Conture, Director of Graduate Studies, 615-340-8272. Fax: 615-343-7705. E-mail: edward.g.conture@vanderbilt.edu.

Washington State University, College of Liberal Arts, Department of Speech and Hearing Sciences, Pullman, WA 99164-1610. Awards MA. One or more programs accredited by ASHA. Offered at Spokane campus only. Faculty: 8 full-time (7 women), 8 part-time (7 women). Students: 1 full-time (0 women), 7 part-time (6 women); includes 3 minority (1 Hispanic, 2 Native Americans). Average age 29. 122 applicants, 16% accepted. In 1997, 26 degrees awarded (100% found work related to degree). *Degree requirements:* Thesis required, foreign language not required. *Average time to degree:* master's–2 years full-time. *Entrance requirements:* GRE General Test, minimum GPA of 3.0. Application deadline: 2/1 (priority date; rolling processing; 9/1 for spring admission). Application fee: $35. Electronic applications accepted. *Tuition:* $5334 per year full-time, $267 per credit hour part-time for state residents; $13,380 per year full-time, $677 per credit hour part-time for nonresidents. *Financial aid:* Fellowships, research assistantships, teaching assistantships, graduate assistantships, partial tuition waivers, Federal Work-Study, institutionally sponsored loans, and career-related internships or fieldwork available. Financial aid application deadline: 4/1; applicants required to submit FAFSA. *Faculty research:* Speech therapy, communication disorders. Total annual research expenditures: $21,783. • Dr. Jeanne Johnson, Chair, 509-335-4525. Fax: 509-335-8357.

Washington University in St. Louis, Graduate School of Arts and Sciences, Department of Speech and Hearing, St. Louis, MO 63130-4899. Offers programs in audiology (MS), communication sciences (MA, PhD), speech and hearing (MS). One or more programs accredited by ASHA. Faculty: 23 full-time (16 women), 7 part-time (4 women). Students: 28 full-time (23 women), 4 part-time (3 women); includes 2 minority (1 African American, 1 Asian American), 4 international. Average age 25. 63 applicants, 35% accepted. In 1997, 16 master's awarded. *Entrance requirements:* For master's, GRE General Test, minimum B average in undergraduate course work; for doctorate, GRE General Test. Application deadline: 3/15 (priority date; rolling processing). Application fee: $35. *Tuition:* $960 per credit hour. *Financial aid:* 27 students received aid; fellowships, full tuition waivers, institutionally sponsored loans, and career-related internships or fieldwork available. Financial aid applicants required to submit FAFSA. *Faculty research:* Auditory physiology, sensory aids, noise, speech perception. • Dr. William W. Clark, Chairman, 314-977-0251.

Announcement: The Department of Speech and Hearing will offer tuition scholarships to qualified students accepted into the master's programs for the 1998–99 academic year. Education students receive 2 full semesters of practicum experience at a school for hearing-impaired children. Audiology students receive practicum experience in a variety of clinical, school, hospital, and other settings.

See in-depth description on page 1273.

Wayne State University, College of Science, Department of Audiology and Speech Language Pathology, Detroit, MI 48202. Awards MA, MS, PhD. One or more programs accredited by ASHA. PhD admissions temporarily suspended. Faculty: 26. Students: 62 full-time (56 women), 1 (woman) part-time. 114 applicants, 30% accepted. In 1997, 35 master's, 1 doctorate awarded. *Degree requirements:* For doctorate, dissertation. *Entrance requirements:* GRE. Application deadline: 7/1. Application fee: $20 ($30 for international students). *Expenses:* Tuition $163 per credit hour for state residents; $355 per credit hour for nonresidents. Fees $498 per year full-time, $114 per semester (minimum) part-time. *Financial aid:* 4 students received aid; fellowships, teaching assistantships, and career-related internships or fieldwork available. Aid available to part-time students. Financial aid application deadline: 2/1. *Faculty research:* Language disorders, phonology, pragmatics, hearing conservation, edinography. • Dr. Patricia Siple, Acting Chairperson, 313-577-3339.

West Chester University of Pennsylvania, School of Health Sciences, Department of Communicative Disorders, West Chester, PA 19383. Awards MA. One or more programs accredited by ASHA. Faculty: 4 part-time. Students: 27 full-time (all women), 28 part-time (all women); includes 3 minority (1 Asian American, 1 Hispanic, 1 Native American). Average age 30. 146 applicants, 31% accepted. In 1997, 14 degrees awarded. *Degree requirements:* Comprehensive exam required, foreign language and thesis not required. *Entrance requirements:* MAT. Application deadline: 4/15 (priority date; rolling processing; 10/15 for spring admission). Application fee: $25. *Expenses:* Tuition $3468 per year full-time, $193 per credit part-time for state residents; $6236 per year full-time, $346 per credit part-time for nonresidents. Fees $660 per year full-time, $38 per credit part-time. *Financial aid:* In 1997–98, 1 research assistantship was awarded. Aid available to part-time students. Financial aid application deadline: 2/15. • Dr. Joseph Stigora, Chair, 610-436-3447.

Western Carolina University, College of Education and Allied Professions, Department of Human Services, Program in Communication Disorders, Cullowhee, NC 28723. Awards MS. One or more programs accredited by ASHA. Part-time and evening/weekend programs available. Students: 46 full-time (45 women), 1 (woman) part-time. 151 applicants, 31% accepted. In 1997, 17 degrees awarded. *Degree requirements:* Comprehensive exam required, thesis optional, foreign language not required. *Entrance requirements:* GRE General Test. Application deadline: 3/21. Application fee: $35. *Tuition:* $1799 per year full-time, $144 per credit hour (minimum) part-time for state residents; $9069 per year full-time, $1053 per credit hour (minimum) part-time for nonresidents. *Financial aid:* In 1997–98, 34 students received aid, including 34 research assistantships (17 to first-year students) totaling $90,783; fellowships, teaching assistantships, Federal Work-Study, institutionally sponsored loans also available. Financial aid application deadline: 3/15. • Application contact: Kathleen Owen, Assistant to the Dean, 828-227-7398. Fax: 828-227-7480.

Western Illinois University, College of Fine Arts and Communication, Department of Communication Arts and Sciences, Program in Communication Sciences and Disorders, Macomb, IL 61455-1390. Awards MS. One or more programs accredited by ASHA. Part-time programs available. Faculty: 6 full-time (3 women). Students: 41 full-time (37 women); includes 5 minority (all African Americans), 1 international. Average age 26. 95 applicants, 28% accepted. In 1997, 25 degrees awarded. *Degree requirements:* Thesis or alternative required, foreign language not required. *Entrance requirements:* Minimum GPA of 3.0. Application deadline: rolling. Application fee: $0 ($25 for international students). *Expenses:* Tuition $2304 per year full-time, $96 per semester hour part-time for state residents; $6912 per year full-time, $288 per semester hour part-time for nonresidents. Fees $944 per year full-time, $33 per semester hour part-time. *Financial aid:* In 1997–98, 17 students received aid, including 17 research assistantships averaging $610 per month; full tuition waivers also available. Financial aid applicants required to submit FAFSA. • Dr. Robert Quesal, Graduate Committee Chairperson, 309-298-1955. Application contact: Barbara Baily, Director of Graduate Studies, 309-298-1806. Fax: 309-298-2245. E-mail: barb_baily@ccmail.wiu.edu.

Western Kentucky University, College of Education, Department of Teacher Education, Program in Communication Disorders, Bowling Green, KY 42101-3576. Awards MS. One or more programs accredited by ASHA. Part-time and evening/weekend programs available. Faculty: 4 full-time (1 woman), 1 (woman) part-time. Students: 18 full-time (17 women). Average age 25. 124 applicants, 15% accepted. In 1997, 18 degrees awarded. *Degree requirements:* Variable foreign language requirement, written exam required, thesis not required. *Entrance requirements:* GRE General Test (minimum combined score of 1200 on three sections; average 1331), minimum GPA of 3.2. Application deadline: 8/1 (priority date; rolling processing; 2/15 for spring admission). Application fee: $20. *Tuition:* $2460 per year full-time, $133 per credit hour part-time for state residents; $6700 per year full-time, $369 per credit hour part-time for nonresidents. *Financial aid:* Teaching assistantships, Federal Work-Study, institutionally sponsored loans, and career-related internships or fieldwork available. Aid available to part-time students. Financial aid application deadline: 4/1; applicants required to submit FAFSA. • Dr. Stanley Cooke, Head, 502-745-4303.

Western Michigan University, College of Health and Human Services, Department of Speech Pathology and Audiology, Kalamazoo, MI 49008. Offers programs in audiology (MA), speech pathology (MA). Accredited by ASHA. Students: 62 full-time (58 women), 5 part-time (all women); includes 1 minority (African American), 3 international. 174 applicants, 38% accepted. In 1997, 33 degrees awarded. *Entrance requirements:* GRE General Test. Application deadline: 3/15 (priority date; rolling processing). Application fee: $25. *Expenses:* Tuition $154 per credit hour for state residents; $372 per credit hour for nonresidents. Fees $602 per year full-time, $132 per semester part-time. *Financial aid:* Fellowships, research assistantships, teaching assistantships, Federal Work-Study available. Financial aid application deadline: 2/15; applicants required to submit FAFSA. • Dr. John Hanley, Chairperson, 616-387-8049. Application contact: Paula J. Boodt, Coordinator, Graduate Admissions and Recruitment, 616-387-2000. E-mail: paulaboodt@wmich.edu.

Western Washington University, College of Arts and Sciences, Department of Speech Pathology and Audiology, Bellingham, WA 98225-5996. Awards MA. Accredited by ASHA. Part-time programs available. Faculty: 5 (2 women). Students: 50 full-time (44 women), 8 part-time (7 women). 134 applicants, 36% accepted. In 1997, 30 degrees awarded. *Degree requirements:* Comprehensive exam required, thesis optional, foreign language not required. *Entrance requirements:* GRE General Test, TOEFL (average 567), minimum GPA of 3.0 in last 60 semester hours or last 90 quarter hours. Application deadline: 2/1. Application fee: $35. *Expenses:* Tuition $4200 per year full-time, $140 per credit part-time for state residents; $12,780 per year full-time, $426 per credit part-time for nonresidents. Fees $249 per year full-time, $83 per quarter part-time. *Financial aid:* Teaching assistantships, partial tuition waivers, Federal Work-Study, institutionally sponsored loans, and career-related internships or fieldwork available. Aid available to part-time students. Financial aid application deadline: 3/31. • Dr. Michael Seilo, Chairperson, 360-650-3885. Application contact: Dr. Lina Zeine, Graduate Adviser, 360-650-3178.

West Virginia University, College of Human Resources and Education, Department of Speech Pathology and Audiology, Morgantown, WV 26506. Awards MS. Accredited by ASHA. Faculty: 13 full-time (8 women), 1 part-time (0 women). Students: 57 full-time (all women), 17 part-time (16 women); includes 2 minority (1 Asian American, 1 Hispanic). Average age 24. 120 applicants, 44% accepted. In 1997, 22 degrees awarded (100% found work related to degree). *Degree requirements:* PRAXIS required, foreign language and thesis not required. *Average time to degree:* master's–2 years full-time. *Entrance requirements:* GRE General Test (combined average 1000), TOEFL (minimum score 550), minimum GPA of 3.0. Application deadline: 3/1. Application fee: $45. *Tuition:* $2820 per year full-time, $149 per credit hour part-time for state residents; $8104 per year full-time, $443 per credit hour part-time for nonresidents. *Financial aid:* In 1997–98, 12 research assistantships (9 to first-year students), 2 teaching assistantships (both to first-year students) were awarded; full and partial tuition waivers, Federal Work-Study, institutionally sponsored loans, and career-related internships or fieldwork also available. Financial aid application deadline: 3/1; applicants required to submit FAFSA. *Faculty research:* Speech perception, hearing aids, language disorders in children, infant language development, auditory skills. • Dr. Conrad Lundeen, Chair, 304-293-4241. Fax: 304-293-7565.

Wichita State University, College of Education, Department of Communicative Disorders and Sciences, Wichita, KS 67260. Offers programs in communications sciences (MA, PhD). One or more programs accredited by ASHA. Faculty: 9 full-time (5 women), 16 part-time (8 women). Students: 82 full-time (77 women), 19 part-time (17 women); includes 5 minority (1 African American, 2 Asian Americans, 2 Native Americans), 14 international. Average age 31. 119 applicants, 26% accepted. In 1997, 33 master's, 3 doctorates awarded. *Degree requirements:* For master's, comprehensive exam required, thesis not required; for doctorate, 1 foreign language, dissertation. *Entrance requirements:* For master's, GRE General Test, TOEFL (minimum score 550), minimum GPA of 2.75; for doctorate, GRE General Test, TOEFL (minimum score 550), appropriate master's degree. Application deadline: 7/1 (priority date; rolling processing; 1/1 for spring admission). Application fee: $25 ($40 for international students). *Expenses:* Tuition $2303 per year full-time, $96 per credit hour part-time for state residents; $7691 per year full-time, $321 per credit hour part-time for nonresidents. Fees $490 per year full-time, $75 per semester (minimum) part-time. *Financial aid:* In 1997–98, 1 fellowship averaging $1,200 per month and totaling $6,000, 6 research assistantships averaging $598 per month and totaling $17,195, 20 teaching assistantships averaging $740 per month and totaling $101,325, 7 graduate assistantships averaging $530 per month and totaling $27,120 were awarded; Federal Work-Study, institutionally sponsored loans, and career-related internships or fieldwork also available. Financial aid application deadline: 4/1; applicants required to submit FAFSA. • Dr. Wesley L. Faires, Chairperson, 316-978-3240. E-mail: faires@wsuhub.uc.twsu.edu. Application contact: Dr. Rosalind Scudder, Graduate Coordinator, 316-978-3240. Fax: 316-978-3302. E-mail: scudder@wsuhub.uc.twsu.edu.

William Paterson University of New Jersey, College of Science and Health, Department of Communication Disorders, Wayne, NJ 07470-8420. Offers program in speech pathology (MS). One or more programs accredited by ASHA. Part-time and evening/weekend programs available. Faculty: 5 full-time (2 women), 8 part-time (7 women). Students: 69 full-time (64 women), 25 part-time (23 women); includes 4 minority (1 African American, 1 Asian American, 2 Hispanics). Average age 28. 212 applicants, 32% accepted. In 1997, 14 degrees awarded. *Degree requirements:* 250 hours of clinical experience, comprehensive exam required, thesis optional, foreign language not required. *Entrance requirements:* GRE General Test (minimum score 450 on verbal section), MAT (minimum score 35), minimum GPA of 2.75. Application deadline: 3/15 (priority date). Application fee: $35. *Expenses:* Tuition $230 per credit for state residents; $327 per credit for nonresidents. Fees $3.25 per credit. *Financial aid:* In 1997–98, 42 students received aid, including 5 graduate assistantships totaling $30,000; career-related internships or fieldwork also available. Aid available to part-time students. Financial aid application deadline: 4/1; applicants required to submit FAFSA. *Faculty research:* Language development, methodological studies, language disorders, phonological disorders, speech and hearing science. • Dr. Jennifer Ryan Hsu, Graduate Coordinator, 973-720-2208. Application contact: Office of Graduate Studies, 973-720-2237. Fax: 973-720-2035.

Worcester State College, Graduate Studies, Program in Speech-Language Pathology, Worcester, MA 01602-2597. Awards MS. Accredited by ASHA. Part-time and evening/weekend programs available. Students: 31 full-time (30 women), 46 part-time (43 women).

Average age 32. 207 applicants, 13% accepted. In 1997, 19 degrees awarded. *Degree requirements:* Comprehensive exam required, thesis optional. *Entrance requirements:* GRE General Test or MAT, 15 credits in human communication process. Application deadline: 3/15. Application fee: $10 ($40 for international students). *Tuition:* $295 per credit hour. *Financial aid:* Career-related internships or fieldwork available. *Faculty research:* Hearing threshold norms, language learning disabilities. • Dr. Susan Rezen, Coordinator, 508-929-8551. Application contact: Andrea Wetmore, Graduate Admissions Counselor, 508-929-8120. E-mail: awetmore@worc.mass.edu.

Dental Hygiene

Baylor College of Dentistry, Department of Dental Hygiene, Dallas, TX 75266-0677. Awards MS. Part-time programs available. Students: 3 full-time (all women). *Degree requirements:* Thesis required, foreign language not required. *Entrance requirements:* GRE General Test, TOEFL. Application deadline: 1/15 (priority date; rolling processing). Application fee: $35. *Expenses:* Tuition $48 per quarter hour for state residents; $166 per quarter hour for nonresidents. Fees $24 per quarter hour. *Financial aid:* Fellowships, research assistantships, teaching assistantships, institutionally sponsored loans available. Aid available to part-time students. Financial aid application deadline: 2/23; applicants required to submit FAFSA. *Faculty research:* Assessment of outcomes, dental materials, educational research. • Marylou Gutmann, Director, 214-828-8406. Fax: 214-828-8196. E-mail: mgutmann@tambcd.edu.

Boston University, Henry M. Goldman School of Dental Medicine, Graduate Programs in Dentistry, Boston, MA 02215. Offerings include dental public health (MS, MSD, D Sc D, CAGS). Faculty: 83 full-time (23 women), 214 part-time (26 women). *Degree requirements:* For master's, thesis; for CAGS, thesis (for some programs). *Average time to degree:* master's–1 year full-time; doctorate–2 years full-time; other advanced degree–2.5 years full-time. *Entrance requirements:* For CAGS, dental degree. Application fee: $50. *Expenses:* Tuition $22,830 per year full-time, $713 per credit part-time. Fees $218 per year full-time, $40 per semester part-time. • Application contact: Postdoctoral Admissions, 617-638-4708.

See in-depth description on page 1709.

Dalhousie University, Faculties of Graduate Studies and Dentistry, Graduate Programs in Dentistry, Halifax, NS B3H 1W2, Canada. Offerings include dental hygiene (Diploma). *Application fee:* $55. • Dr. Peter J. Ricketts, Dean, Faculty of Graduate Studies, 902-494-2485. E-mail: graduate.studies@dal.ca. Application contact: Barbara Maynard, Admissions and Programme Officer, 902-494-2485. Fax: 902-494-8797. E-mail: graduate.studies@dal.ca.

Medical College of Georgia, Department of Associated Dental Sciences, Augusta, GA 30912-1500. Offers program in dental hygiene (MHE, MS). Part-time programs available. Faculty: 1 (woman) full-time. Students: 0. 0 applicants. *Entrance requirements:* GRE General Test (minimum combined score of 1000), TOEFL (minimum score 600). Application deadline: 6/30 (priority date; rolling processing; 1/15 for spring admission). Application fee: $0. *Expenses:* Tuition $2670 per year full-time, $111 per credit part-time for state residents; $10,680 per year full-time, $445 per credit part-time for nonresidents. Fees $286 per year. *Financial aid:* Teaching assistantships available. Financial aid application deadline: 5/1. • Gail P. Winkley, Chair, 706-721-2938. E-mail: gwinkley@mail.mcg.edu. Application contact: Dr. Gary C. Bond, Associate Dean, 706-721-3278. Fax: 706-721-6829. E-mail: gradstud@mail.mcg.edu.

Old Dominion University, College of Health Sciences, School of Dental Hygiene and Dental Assisting, Norfolk, VA 23529. Offers program in dental hygiene (MS). Part-time programs available. Faculty: 3 full-time (all women). Students: 4 full-time (all women), 3 part-time (all women); includes 2 international. Average age 32. 9 applicants, 44% accepted. In 1997, 4 degrees awarded. *Degree requirements:* Oral comprehensive exam required, thesis optional, foreign language not required. *Entrance requirements:* Dental Hygiene Board Exam, BS or certificate in dental hygiene or related area, minimum GPA of 2.5. Application deadline: 7/1 (rolling processing; 12/1 for spring admission). Application fee: $30. Electronic applications accepted. *Expenses:* Tuition $180 per credit hour for state residents; $477 per credit hour for nonresidents. Fees $140 per year full-time, $32 per semester part-time. *Financial aid:* In 1997–98, 3 students received aid, including 2 research assistantships (1 to a first-year student) totaling $16,416; teaching assistantships, tuition grants, partial tuition waivers, and career-related internships or fieldwork also available. Aid available to part-time students. Financial aid application deadline: 2/15; applicants required to submit CSS PROFILE or FAFSA. *Faculty research:* Clinical dental hygiene practice, dental hygiene client health behaviors, dental hygiene education interventions. Total annual research expenditures: $1162. • Deanne Shuman, Chair, 757-683-4310. Fax: 757-683-5239. E-mail: dshuman@odu.edu. Application contact: Michele L. Darby, Graduate Program Director, 757-683-4310. Fax: 757-683-5329. E-mail: mdarby@odu.edu.

University of Alberta, Faculty of Medicine and Oral Health Sciences, Department of Oral Health Sciences, Program in Dental Hygiene, Edmonton, AB T6G 2E1, Canada. Awards Certificate. *Degree requirements:* Thesis required, foreign language not required. *Entrance requirements:* DDS. • Prof. Jan Pimlott, Director, 403-492-4479. Application contact: Eleanor Mclaffaac, Administrative Assistant, 403-492-1319.

University of Maryland, Baltimore, Graduate School, Graduate Programs in Dentistry, Department of Dental Hygiene, Baltimore, MD 21201-1627. Awards MS. Faculty: 3 (all women). Students: 6 part-time (all women); includes 1 minority (African American). Average age 23. 1 applicant, 0% accepted. In 1997, 1 degree awarded. *Degree requirements:* Thesis or alternative required, foreign language not required. *Entrance requirements:* GRE General Test, TOEFL, minimum GPA of 3.0. Application deadline: 7/1. Application fee: $42. *Financial aid:* Fellowships available. Aid available to part-time students. Financial aid application deadline: 2/15. *Faculty research:* Dental hygiene education, health care management, health system theory and policy development, hospital dental hygiene, clinical practice. • Linda DeVore, Chairperson, 410-706-7773. Application contact: Dr. M. Elaine Parker, Graduate Program Director, 410-706-7773.

University of Missouri–Kansas City, School of Dentistry, Graduate Programs in Dentistry, Program in Dental Hygiene Education, Kansas City, MO 64110-2499. Awards MS. Students: 3 full-time (all women), 4 part-time (all women); includes 1 minority (Native American), 1 international. Average age 34. In 1997, 1 degree awarded. *Degree requirements:* Thesis required, foreign language not required. *Application deadline:* 10/1 (2/1 for spring admission). *Application fee:* $25. *Expenses:* Tuition $182 per credit hour for state residents; $508 per credit hour for nonresidents. Fees $60 per year. *Financial aid:* Research assistantships, full and partial tuition waivers, Federal Work-Study, institutionally sponsored loans, and career-related internships or fieldwork available. Aid available to part-time students. Financial aid application deadline: 3/15. *Faculty research:* Product efficacy, periodontal therapy, educational perceptions, dental fears, psychomotor skills. Total annual research expenditures: $112,030. • Maxine Tishk, Director, 816-235-2050. Fax: 816-235-2157.

The University of North Carolina at Chapel Hill, School of Dentistry and Graduate School, Graduate Programs in Dentistry, Chapel Hill, NC 27599. Offerings include dental hygiene education (MS). Faculty: 82 full-time (15 women). *Degree requirements:* Thesis required, foreign language not required. *Average time to degree:* master's–3 years full-time. *Entrance requirements:* Dental degree. Application deadline: 10/1. Application fee: $55. Electronic applications accepted. *Expenses:* Tuition $2502 per year full-time, $626 per semester (minimum) part-time for state residents; $12,764 per year full-time, $3191 per semester (minimum) part-time for nonresidents. Fees $1041 per year full-time, $461 per semester (minimum) part-time. • Dr. Ronald Hunt, Associate Dean for Academic Affairs, 919-966-4451. Fax: 919-966-7007. Application contact: Kim Miller, Admissions Office, School of Dentistry, 919-966-4451.

See in-depth description on page 1711.

Emergency Medical Services

Alderson–Broaddus College, Medical Science Department, Philippi, WV 26416. Offerings include medical science (MS), with options in emergency medical care, rural primary care; physician assistant (MS), with options in emergency medicine, rural primary care. Postbaccalaureate distance learning degree programs offered (minimal on-campus study). Department faculty: 17 part-time (0 women). *Degree requirements:* Thesis, 2 years of clinical experience required, foreign language not required. *Average time to degree:* master's–2 years full-time. *Entrance requirements:* National Commission on Certification of Physician Assistants certification or bachelor's degree in related field, full-time clinical employment. Application deadline: 6/1 (priority date; rolling processing; 12/1 for spring admission). Application fee: $35. *Tuition:* $420 per credit hour. • Dr. Sharon Boni, Chairperson, 304-457-6284. Fax: 304-457-6239. Application contact: Dick Mercer, Director, Master's Degree Program, 304-457-6356. Fax: 304-457-6308. E-mail: mercer@ab.edu.

Allegheny University of the Health Sciences, School of Health Professions, Department of Primary Care Education and Community Service, Emergency Medical Service Program, Philadelphia, PA 19102-1192. Awards MEMS. Part-time and evening/weekend programs available. Faculty: 1 (woman) full-time, 3 part-time (0 women). Students: 1 (woman) full-time, 2 part-time (both women). Average age 31. 7 applicants, 57% accepted. In 1997, 1 degree awarded. *Degree requirements:* Comprehensive exam required, foreign language and thesis not required. *Entrance requirements:* GRE General Test (minimum combined score of 1410 on three sections), minimum GPA of 2.75. Application deadline: 6/1 (rolling processing). Application fee: $50. *Expenses:* Tuition $400 per credit. Fees $125 per year. *Financial aid:* Federal Work-Study, institutionally sponsored loans, and career-related internships or fieldwork available. Aid available to part-time students. Financial aid application deadline: 5/1; applicants required to submit FAFSA. • Jean Will, Director, 215-762-8447.

New York Medical College, Graduate School of Health Sciences, Programs in International and Public Health, Valhalla, NY 10595-1691. Offerings include emergency medical services (MPH, MS). *Degree requirements:* Computer language required, foreign language not required. *Entrance requirements:* TOEFL. Application deadline: 7/20 (priority date; rolling processing; 12/1 for spring admission). Application fee: $35 ($60 for international students). *Tuition:* $415 per credit. • Dr. Cathey Falvo, Director, 914-594-4250.

Université de Montréal, Faculties of Medicine and Graduate Studies, Graduate Programs in Medicine, Program in Specialized Studies, Montréal, PQ H3C 3J7, Canada. Offerings include family medicine and emergency (DES). Program faculty: 204 full-time (32 women), 36 part-time (1 woman). *Application deadline:* 10/1. *Application fee:* $30. • Dr. Jean-Paul Perreault, Vice Dean, 514-343-7798.

Medical Technology

California State University, Long Beach, College of Natural Sciences, Department of Biological Sciences, Program in Microbiology, Long Beach, CA 90840-3702. Offerings include medical technology (MPH). Program faculty: 11 full-time. *Application deadline:* 8/1 (rolling processing; 12/1 for spring admission). *Application fee:* $55. *Expenses:* Tuition $0 for state residents; $246 per unit for nonresidents. Fees $1846 per year full-time, $1180 per year part-time. • Dr. Laura Kingsford, Acting Chair, Department of Biological Sciences, 562-985-4807. E-mail: lkingsfo@csulb.edu. Application contact: Dr. Charles Collins, Graduate Coordinator, 562-985-8503. Fax: 562-985-8878. E-mail: ccollins@csulb.edu.

Eastern Washington University, College of Science, Mathematics and Technology, Department of Biology, Program in Medical Technology, Cheney, WA 99004-2431. Awards MS. Faculty: 15 full-time (4 women), 1 (woman) part-time. *Degree requirements:* Thesis, comprehensive oral exam required, foreign language not required. *Entrance requirements:*

Directory: Medical Technology

Eastern Washington University (continued)
GRE General Test, minimum GPA of 3.0. Application deadline: 4/1 (priority date; rolling processing; 1/15 for spring admission). Application fee: $35. *Tuition:* $4200 per year full-time, $140 per credit part-time for state residents; $12,780 per year full-time, $415 per credit part-time for nonresidents. *Financial aid:* Application deadline 2/1. • Dr. Haideh Lightfoot, Director, 509-359-2339. Application contact: Dr. Ross Black, Graduate Adviser, 509-359-2339.

Florida International University, College of Health, Department of Medical Laboratory Sciences, Miami, FL 33199. Awards MS. Part-time programs available. Faculty: 6 full-time (4 women), 1 part-time (0 women), 6.5 FTE. Students: 3 full-time (2 women), 10 part-time (7 women); includes 7 minority (3 African Americans, 3 Asian Americans, 1 Hispanic), 3 international. Average age 31. 5 applicants, 0% accepted. In 1997, 2 degrees awarded. *Degree requirements:* Thesis optional, foreign language not required. *Entrance requirements:* GRE General Test (minimum combined score of 1000), minimum GPA of 3.0. Application deadline: 4/1 (priority date; rolling processing; 10/1 for spring admission). Application fee: $20. *Expenses:* Tuition $138 per credit hour for state residents; $482 per credit hour for nonresidents. Fees $46 per semester. *Financial aid:* Fellowships, research assistantships, teaching assistantships, Federal Work-Study, institutionally sponsored loans, and career-related internships or fieldwork available. • Dr. J. A. Lineback, Chairperson, 305-348-2870. Fax: 305-348-1997. E-mail: lineback@servms.fiu.edu.

Georgia State University, College of Health and Human Sciences, Program in Medical Technology, Atlanta, GA 30303-3083. Offers immunohematology (MS), laboratory management (MS). Program being phased out; applicants no longer accepted. Part-time and evening/weekend programs available. Faculty: 4 full-time (all women). Students: 6 part-time (3 women). Average age 33. In 1997, 4 degrees awarded. *Degree requirements:* Project required, thesis optional, foreign language not required. *Expenses:* Tuition $2673 per year full-time, $99 per semester hour part-time for state residents; $10,692 per year full-time, $396 per semester hour part-time for nonresidents. Fees $228 per year. *Financial aid:* Fellowships, research assistantships, teaching assistantships, Federal Work-Study, institutionally sponsored loans available. Aid available to part-time students. Financial aid applicants required to submit FAFSA. *Total annual research expenditures:* $23,915. • Dr. Stephanie Summers, Graduate Coordinator, 404-651-3034.

Inter American University of Puerto Rico, Metropolitan Campus, Division of Science and Technology, Program in Medical Technology, San Juan, PR 00919-1293. Awards MS. Part-time programs available. Faculty: 1 full-time (0 women), 7 part-time (3 women), 2.75 FTE. Students: 48 part-time (37 women); includes 48 minority (all Hispanics). 23 applicants, 96% accepted. In 1997, 5 degrees awarded. *Degree requirements:* Comprehensive exams required, foreign language and thesis not required. *Average time to degree:* master's–3 years part-time. *Entrance requirements:* BS in medical technology, minimum GPA of 2.5. Application deadline: 5/15 (priority date; rolling processing; 11/15 for spring admission). Application fee: $31. Electronic applications accepted. *Expenses:* Tuition $3272 per year full-time, $1740 per year part-time. Fees $328 per year full-time, $176 per year part-time. *Financial aid:* Federal Work-Study, institutionally sponsored loans available. • Livier González, Director, 787-250-8019. Fax: 787-250-8736.

Inter American University of Puerto Rico, San Germán Campus, Department of Medical Technology, San Germán, PR 00683-5008. Awards Certificate. Part-time and evening/weekend programs available. Faculty: 3 full-time (all women), 3 part-time (all women). Students: 34 full-time (30 women); includes 3 international. Average age 24. In 1997, 43 degrees awarded. *Entrance requirements:* ASPA, minimum GPA of 2.5. Application deadline: 4/30 (priority date; rolling processing; 11/15 for spring admission). Application fee: $31. *Expenses:* Tuition $150 per credit. Fees $177 per semester. • Ludai Rodriguez, Chair, 787-834-6070. Application contact: Mildred Camacho, Admissions Director, 787-892-3090. Fax: 787-892-6350.

Medical College of Georgia, Department of Medical Technology, Augusta, GA 30912-1500. Awards MHE, MS. Part-time programs available. Faculty: 4 full-time (3 women). Students: 4 full-time (0 women), 2 part-time (both women); includes 1 minority (Asian American). Average age 33. 2 applicants, 50% accepted. In 1997, 2 degrees awarded. *Average time to degree:* master's–3 years full-time, 5 years part-time. *Entrance requirements:* GRE General Test (minimum combined score of 1000), TOEFL (minimum score 600). Application deadline: 6/30 (priority date; rolling processing). Application fee: $0. *Expenses:* Tuition $2670 per year full-time, $111 per credit part-time for state residents; $10,680 per year full-time, $445 per credit part-time for nonresidents. Fees $286 per year. *Financial aid:* Federal Work-Study, institutionally sponsored loans available. Financial aid application deadline: 5/1. • Dr. Julia R. Crowley, Chair, 706-721-3046. E-mail: jcrowley@mail.mcg.edu. Application contact: Dr. Gary C. Bond, Associate Dean, 706-721-3278. Fax: 706-721-6829. E-mail: gradstud@mail.mcg.edu.

Medical University of South Carolina, College of Health Professions, Department of Medical Laboratory Science, Program in Medical Technology, Charleston, SC 29425-0002. Awards MS. Part-time programs available. Faculty: 8 full-time (6 women). *Degree requirements:* Research project. *Entrance requirements:* GRE General Test (minimum combined score of 1000), minimum GPA of 3.0. Application fee: $55. *Expenses:* Tuition $4072 per year full-time, $221 per semester hour part-time for state residents; $7064 per year full-time, $387 per semester hour part-time for nonresidents. Fees $150 per year (minimum). *Financial aid:* 9 students received aid; Federal Work-Study available. Aid available to part-time students. Financial aid application deadline: 4/1; applicants required to submit FAFSA. *Faculty research:* Immunotoxicology, urine analysis testing, bacteriology. Total annual research expenditures: $50,000. • Janice M. Hundley, Chair, Department of Medical Laboratory Science, 843-792-3169. Fax: 843-792-3383. E-mail: hundleyj@musc.edu.

Michigan State University, College of Natural Science, Medical Technology Program, East Lansing, MI 48824-1020. Offers clinical laboratory science (MS). Faculty: 4 (0 women). Students: 7 (4 women); includes 2 minority (1 African American, 1 Asian American), 1 international. In 1997, 4 degrees awarded. *Application deadline:* rolling. *Application fee:* $30 ($40 for international students). *Expenses:* Tuition $4609 per year full-time, $223 per credit hour (minimum) part-time for state residents; $8704 per year full-time, $450 per credit hour (minimum) part-time for nonresidents. Fees $576 per year full-time, $476 per year part-time. *Financial aid:* Teaching assistantships available. • Dr. Douglas Estry, Director, 517-353-7800.

Northeastern University, Bouvé College of Pharmacy and Health Sciences Graduate School, Program in Medical Laboratory Science, Boston, MA 02115-5096. Awards MS. Part-time and evening/weekend programs available. Faculty: 6 full-time (2 women), 12 part-time (5 women). Students: 10 full-time (5 women), 5 part-time (2 women). Average age 32. 23 applicants, 70% accepted. In 1997, 2 degrees awarded. *Degree requirements:* Comprehensive exam or thesis required, foreign language not required. *Entrance requirements:* Minimum GPA of 3.0, bachelor's degree in science. Application deadline: rolling. Application fee: $50. *Expenses:* Tuition $440 per credit hour. Fees $55 per quarter full-time, $13.25 per quarter part-time. *Financial aid:* In 1997–98, 1 teaching assistantship was awarded; Federal Work-Study also available. Aid available to part-time students. Financial aid application deadline: 3/1; applicants required to submit FAFSA. • Barbara Martin, Director, 617-373-4194. Application contact: Bill Purnell, Director of Graduate Admissions, 617-373-2708. Fax: 617-373-4701. E-mail: w.purnell@nunet.neu.edu.

Announcement: MS and PhD programs are administered through the biomedical sciences degree program. Students take a common core of courses in biomedical sciences and specialize in 1 area of medical laboratory science. Specialization-course sequences are offered in clinical/bioanalytical chemistry, hematology, immunology/immunohematology, and microbiology/cell biology. Management and health policy electives are available. MS students have thesis or comprehensive exam options. PhD and/or MS research projects currently available in bioanalytical chemistry, cancer cell biology, hematology, immunohematology, and immunology. Some teaching and research assistantships granted. Opportunities to qualify for medical technology board exams are available to students lacking certification credentials (required of MS students).

See in-depth description on page 1797.

Northeastern University, Bouvé College of Pharmacy and Health Sciences Graduate School, Programs in Biomedical Sciences, Boston, MA 02115-5096. Offerings include medical laboratory science (PhD). Terminal master's awarded for partial completion of doctoral program. Faculty: 14 full-time (1 woman), 14 part-time (5 women). *Degree requirements:* Dissertation, qualifying exam required, foreign language not required. *Entrance requirements:* GRE General Test, TOEFL. Application deadline: 2/15. Application fee: $50. *Expenses:* Tuition $440 per credit hour. Fees $55 per quarter full-time, $13.25 per quarter part-time. • Dr. Medhi Boroujerdi, Associate Dean, 617-373-3380. Fax: 617-266-6756. Application contact: Bill Purnell, Director of Graduate Admissions, 617-373-2708. Fax: 617-373-4701. E-mail: w.purnell@nunet.neu.edu.

Old Dominion University, College of Health Sciences, School of Medical Laboratory Sciences and Environmental Health, Norfolk, VA 23529. Awards MS. Program being phased out; applicants no longer accepted. Part-time programs available. Faculty: 7 full-time (3 women). Students: 3 part-time (all women); includes 1 minority (African American). Average age 40. In 1997, 2 degrees awarded. *Degree requirements:* Thesis required, foreign language not required. *Entrance requirements:* BS in medical technology or related area; minimum GPA of 3.0 in major, 2.5 overall; professional certification. *Expenses:* Tuition $180 per credit hour for state residents; $477 per credit hour for nonresidents. Fees $140 per year full-time, $32 per semester part-time. *Financial aid:* Research assistantships, teaching assistantships, tuition grants available. Financial aid applicants required to submit FAFSA. *Faculty research:* Instructional methods, student recruitment, retention effects of environmental pollution on marine life, sports physiology, breast cancer criteria. Total annual research expenditures: $3600. • Dr. C. Thomas Somma, Chair, 757-683-3589. E-mail: tsomma@odu.edu.

St. John's University, College of Pharmacy and Allied Health Professions, Graduate Programs in Pharmacy, Program in Medical Technology, Jamaica, NY 11439. Awards MS. Part-time and evening/weekend programs available. Students: 2 full-time (0 women), 3 part-time (all women); includes 3 minority (1 African American, 1 Asian American, 1 Hispanic), 1 international. Average age 26. 15 applicants, 40% accepted. *Degree requirements:* Comprehensive exam required, thesis optional, foreign language not required. *Entrance requirements:* Bachelor's degree in medical technology or equivalent, minimum GPA of 3.0. Application deadline: 6/1 (priority date; rolling processing; 10/1 for spring admission). Application fee: $40. *Expenses:* Tuition $675 per credit. Fees $150 per year. *Financial aid:* Teaching assistantships, Federal Work-Study, and career-related internships or fieldwork available. Aid available to part-time students. Financial aid application deadline: 3/1; applicants required to submit FAFSA. *Faculty research:* Administration, clinical management. • Dr. S. William Zito, Chair, 718-990-6678. Application contact: Shamus J. McGrenra, TOR, Associate Director, Graduate Admissions, 718-990-6107. Fax: 718-990-5736. E-mail: mcgrenrs@stjohns.edu.

Salve Regina University, Programs in Biomedical Technology/Management, Newport, RI 02840-4192. Awards MS. Part-time and evening/weekend programs available. Faculty: 1 (woman) full-time. Students: 5 full-time (all women), 3 part-time (all women). Average age 30. 8 applicants, 63% accepted. In 1997, 4 degrees awarded. *Average time to degree:* master's–2 years full-time, 3 years part-time. *Entrance requirements:* GMAT, GRE General Test, or MAT. Application deadline: rolling. Application fee: $35. *Expenses:* Tuition $275 per credit hour. Fees $70 per year. *Financial aid:* Federal Work-Study and career-related internships or fieldwork available. Aid available to part-time students. Financial aid application deadline: 3/1. • Dr. Mary Louise Greeley, Coordinator, 401-847-6650 Ext. 3105. Fax: 401-847-0372. Application contact: Laura E. McPhie, Dean of Enrollment Services, 401-847-6650 Ext. 2908. Fax: 401-848-2823. E-mail: sruadmis@salve.edu.

State University of New York Health Science Center at Syracuse, College of Health Related Professions, Program in Medical Technology, Syracuse, NY 13210-2334. Awards MS. Faculty: 1 (woman) part-time.25 FTE. Students: 1 (woman) part-time. Average age 27. 1 applicant, 0% accepted. *Degree requirements:* Thesis required, foreign language not required. *Entrance requirements:* GRE General Test, GRE Subject Test (minimum score 600), TOEFL (minimum score 550), TSE. Application deadline: 4/1 (priority date; rolling processing). Application fee: $40. *Expenses:* Tuition $5100 per year full-time, $213 per credit hour part-time for state residents; $8416 per year full-time, $351 per credit hour part-time for nonresidents. Fees $405 per year full-time, $108 per semester (minimum) part-time. *Financial aid:* Federal Work-Study, institutionally sponsored loans available. Aid available to part-time students. Financial aid application deadline: 4/15. • Dr. Betty Ann Forbes, Director, 315-464-4525. Application contact: Jennifer Welch, Director of Admissions, 315-464-4570. Fax: 315-464-8867. E-mail: welchj@vax.cs.hscsyr.edu.

Université de Montréal, Faculties of Medicine and Graduate Studies, Graduate Programs in Medicine, Program in Specialized Studies, Montréal, PQ H3C 3J7, Canada. Offerings include nuclear medicine (DES). Program faculty: 204 full-time (32 women), 36 part-time (1 woman). *Application deadline:* 10/1. *Application fee:* $30. • Dr. Jean-Paul Perreault, Vice Dean, 514-343-7798.

University of Alberta, Faculties of Medicine and Oral Health Sciences and Graduate Studies and Research, Graduate Programs in Medicine, Department of Laboratory Medicine and Pathology, Program in Medical Laboratory Science, Edmonton, AB T6G 2R7, Canada. Awards MLS, M Sc, PhD. Faculty: 11 full-time (3 women). Students: 6. 100 applicants, 20% accepted. In 1997, 2 master's awarded (50% entered university research/teaching, 50% continued full-time study). Terminal master's awarded for partial completion of doctoral program. *Degree requirements:* Thesis/dissertation required, foreign language not required. *Average time to degree:* master's–3 years full-time, 5 years part-time. *Application deadline:* rolling. *Application fee:* $60. *Financial aid:* Research assistantships available. *Total annual research expenditures:* $700,000. • Dr. Fiona Bamforth, Acting Director, 403-492-6601.

University of Guelph, Ontario Veterinary College and Faculty of Graduate Studies, Graduate Programs in Veterinary Sciences, Department of Clinical Studies, Guelph, ON N1G 2W1, Canada. Offerings include anesthesiology (M Sc, DV Sc), radiology (M Sc, DV Sc). Department faculty: 22 full-time (6 women), 3 part-time (1 woman). *Degree requirements:* Thesis/dissertation. *Average time to degree:* doctorate–3 years full-time; other advanced degree–1.5 years full-time. *Application deadline:* 2/1 (rolling processing). *Application fee:* $60. *Expenses:* Tuition $4725 per year full-time, $3165 per year part-time for Canadian residents; $6999 per year for nonresidents. Fees $612 per year full-time, $38 per year (minimum) part-time for Canadian residents; $612 per year for nonresidents. • Dr. S. Kruth, Chair, 519-823-8800 Ext. 4012. Application contact: Dr. M. Hurtig, Graduate Coordinator, 519-823-8800 Ext. 4028. Fax: 519-767-0311. E-mail: mhurtig@ovcnet.uoguelph.ca.

University of Maryland, Baltimore, Graduate School, Department of Medical and Research Technology, Baltimore, MD 21201. Awards MS. Part-time programs available. Faculty: 8 full-time. Students: 3 full-time (2 women), 17 part-time (13 women); includes 3 minority (all Asian Americans), 3 international. 20 applicants, 40% accepted. In 1997, 6 degrees awarded. *Degree requirements:* Thesis or management project. *Entrance requirements:* GRE General Test, TOEFL (minimum score 550), minimum GPA of 3.0. Application deadline: 5/1. Application fee: $42. *Expenses:* Tuition $253 per credit hour for state residents; $454 per credit hour for nonresidents. Fees $317 per year. *Financial aid:* Fellowships, research assistantships available. Financial aid application deadline: 3/1. *Faculty research:* Clinical microbiology, immunology, immunohematology, hematology, clinical chemistry, molecular biology. • Dr. Denise M. Harmening, Chair. Application contact: Dr. Ivana Vucenik, Graduate Co-Director, 410-706-7663.

Announcement: The Department of Medical and Research Technology offers 2 tracks: biomedical science (research track, thesis required) and laboratory management (management track, nonthesis option). In the biomedical science track, the student acquires advanced training in 1 of the following areas: clinical chemistry, hematology, immunohematology, immunology, microbiology, or molecular biology. The laboratory management track develops skills in laboratory administration. The program is designed for medical technologists and students with undergraduate life science degrees. The program is flexible and can be tailored and arranged to fit individual interests and backgrounds.

University of North Dakota, School of Medicine and Graduate School, Graduate Programs in Medicine, Department of Clinical Laboratory Science, Grand Forks, ND 58202. Awards MS. Postbaccalaureate distance learning degree programs offered (minimal on-campus study). Faculty: 3 full-time (1 woman). Students: 11 part-time (8 women). 2 applicants, 100% accepted. In 1997, 5 degrees awarded. *Degree requirements:* Thesis or alternative required, foreign language not required. *Entrance requirements:* TOEFL (minimum score 550), minimum GPA of 3.0. Application deadline: 3/1 (priority date; rolling processing). Application fee: $20. *Financial aid:* In 1997–98, 1 student received aid, including 1 teaching assistantship totaling $9,381; fellowships, full and partial tuition waivers, Federal Work-Study, institutionally sponsored loans also available. • Dr. Wayne Bruce, Director, 701-777-2561. Fax: 701-777-3108. E-mail: wbruce@mail.med.und.nodak.edu.

University of Southern Mississippi, College of Science and Technology, Department of Medical Technology, Hattiesburg, MS 39406-5167. Awards MS. Part-time programs available. Faculty: 5 full-time (all women). Students: 9 full-time (6 women); includes 2 African Americans, 3 Asian Americans, 3 international. Average age 29. 7 applicants, 57% accepted. In 1997, 4 degrees awarded. *Degree requirements:* Thesis optional, foreign language not required. *Entrance requirements:* GRE General Test, minimum GPA of 2.75. Application deadline: 8/9 (priority date; rolling processing). Application fee: $0 ($25 for international students). *Tuition:* $2870 per year full-time, $137 per credit hour part-time for state residents; $5972 per year full-time, $172 per credit hour part-time for nonresidents. *Financial aid:* Teaching assistantships, Federal Work-Study available. Financial aid application deadline: 3/15. • Dr. Jane Hudson, Chair, 601-266-4908.

University of the Sacred Heart, Graduate Programs, Department of Natural Sciences, Program in Medical Technology, San Juan, PR 00914-0383. Awards Certificate. Faculty: 3 full-time (all women). Students: 27 full-time (23 women), 1 (woman) part-time. 20 applicants, 100% accepted. In 1997, 31 degrees awarded. *Entrance requirements:* Allied Health Professions Admissions Test, interview. Application deadline: 5/15. Application fee: $25. *Expenses:* Tuition $150 per credit. Fees $240 per credit. • Sara Acosta de Malave, Coordinator, 787-728-1515 Ext. 4297. Fax: 787-728-1515 Ext. 4287. E-mail: c_padial@uscac1.usc.clu.edu. Application contact: Dr. Blanca Villamil, Acting Director, Admissions Office, 787-728-1515 Ext. 3237. Fax: 787-728-2066. E-mail: b_villami@uscsi.usc.clu.edu.

University of Utah, School of Medicine and Graduate School, Graduate Programs in Medicine, Program in Medical Laboratory Science, Salt Lake City, UT 84112-1107. Awards MS. Part-time programs available. Faculty: 16 full-time (6 women). Students: 4 full-time (1 woman), 13 part-time (6 women); includes 3 minority (all Asian Americans), 4 international. Average age 30. 12 applicants, 42% accepted. In 1997, 4 degrees awarded (100% entered university research/teaching). *Degree requirements:* Thesis, preliminary and comprehensive exams, research project required, foreign language not required. *Average time to degree:* master's–2 years full-time, 3 years part-time. *Entrance requirements:* Minimum GPA of 3.0 during last 2 years of undergraduate course work, BS in medical laboratory science or related field. Application deadline: 4/1 (priority date; rolling processing). Application fee: $40. *Tuition:* $2045 per year full-time, $562 per semester (minimum) part-time for state residents; $6129 per year full-time, $1607 per semester (minimum) part-time for nonresidents. *Financial aid:* 4 students received aid; research assistantships, teaching assistantships available. Aid available to part-time students. Financial aid application deadline: 11/30. *Faculty research:* Clinical chemistry, hematology, diagnostic microbiology, immunohematology, cell biology, immunology. • Dr. Joseph A. Knight, Co-Director, 801-581-4516. Application contact: JoAnn P. Fenn, Co-Director, 801-581-3971. Fax: 801-581-4517. E-mail: jfenn@medschool.med.utah.edu.

University of Vermont, School of Allied Health Sciences, Department of Biomedical Technologies, Burlington, VT 05405-0160. Awards MS. Part-time programs available. Students: 3. 3 applicants, 33% accepted. *Degree requirements:* Thesis required, foreign language not required. *Entrance requirements:* GRE General Test, TOEFL (minimum score 550). Application deadline: 4/1 (priority date; rolling processing). Application fee: $25. *Expenses:* Tuition $302 per credit for state residents; $755 per credit for nonresidents. Fees $434 per year full-time, $46 per semester (minimum) part-time. *Financial aid:* Fellowships, teaching assistantships, Federal Work-Study available. Financial aid application deadline: 3/1. *Faculty research:* Clinical science, laboratory administration. • Dr. A. Huot, Interim Chairperson, 802-656-3811.

Wayne State University, College of Pharmacy and Allied Health Professions, Faculty of Allied Health Professions, Department of Clinical Laboratory Sciences, Detroit, MI 48202. Offerings include medical technology (MS). Department faculty: 4 full-time (3 women), 1 (woman) part-time. *Degree requirements:* Thesis optional, foreign language not required. *Application fee:* $20 ($30 for international students). *Expenses:* Tuition $163 per credit hour for state residents; $355 per credit hour for nonresidents. Fees $498 per year full-time, $114 per semester (minimum) part-time. • Gerald W. Aldridge, Acting Administrative Director, 313-577-1384.

West Virginia University, School of Medicine, Graduate Programs in Basic Health Sciences, Medical Technology Program, Morgantown, WV 26506. Awards MS. Part-time programs available. Students: 1 (woman) full-time, 4 part-time (2 women); includes 1 minority (Asian American). Average age 31. 2 applicants, 100% accepted. *Degree requirements:* Thesis, problem study, written exam required, foreign language not required. *Average time to degree:* master's–2 years full-time, 3 years part-time. *Entrance requirements:* GRE, TOEFL (minimum score 550), minimum GPA of 2.5, interview. Application deadline: rolling. Application fee: $45. *Financial aid:* In 1997–98, 1 teaching assistantship (to a first-year student) averaging $1,055 per month and totaling $12,636 was awarded; Federal Work-Study, institutionally sponsored loans also available. Financial aid application deadline: 2/1; applicants required to submit FAFSA. *Faculty research:* Management, lipids, coagulation, blood bank, molecular pathology, hematology. • Dr. Jean Holter, Director, 304-293-2069.

Occupational Therapy

Belmont University, Program in Occupational Therapy, Nashville, TN 37212-3757. Awards MS. Faculty: 8 full-time (5 women), 1 (woman) part-time, 9 FTE. Students: 44 full-time (40 women); includes 1 minority (African American). Average age 24. 49 applicants, 65% accepted. *Degree requirements:* Thesis. *Entrance requirements:* GRE General Test (minimum combined score of 1000; average 1250), 50-100 volunteer hours. Application deadline: 2/1. Application fee: $50. *Tuition:* $560 per credit hour. *Financial aid:* Career-related internships or fieldwork available. *Faculty research:* Occupational therapy, pediatrics, gerontology, rehabilitation, applied functional anatomy. • Dr. Scott D. McPhee, Chair, 615-460-6700. Fax: 615-460-6475. E-mail: mcphees@belmont.edu.

Boston University, Sargent College of Health and Rehabilitation Sciences, Department of Occupational Therapy, Boston, MA 02215. Awards MS, MSOT, D Sc, CAGS. One or more programs accredited by AOTA. Part-time programs available. Faculty: 11 full-time (all women), 3 part-time (0 women). Students: 129 full-time (116 women), 12 part-time (all women); includes 7 minority (5 Asian Americans, 2 Hispanics), 6 international. Average age 27. 279 applicants, 36% accepted. In 1997, 59 master's awarded. *Degree requirements:* For master's, internships (MSOT), thesis (MS) required, foreign language not required; for doctorate, computer language, dissertation required, foreign language not required. *Entrance requirements:* For master's, GRE General Test (minimum combined score of 1000); for doctorate, GRE General Test (minimum combined score of 1000), MAT, master's degree. Application deadline: 3/1 (priority date; rolling processing). Application fee: $50. *Expenses:* Tuition $22,830 per year full-time, $713 per credit part-time. Fees $218 per year full-time, $40 per semester part-time. *Financial aid:* In 1997–98, 4 fellowships (2 to first-year students), 8 teaching assistantships were awarded; scholarships, Federal Work-Study, institutionally sponsored loans, and career-related internships or fieldwork also available. Financial aid application deadline: 4/15. *Faculty research:* Motor development, sensory integration, therapeutic intervention in perceptual and motor dysfunction. • Dr. Wendy J. Coster, Chair, 617-353-2727.

See in-depth description on page 1235.

Chatham College, School of Graduate Studies, Programs in Health Sciences, Program in Occupational Therapy, Pittsburgh, PA 15232-2826. Awards MOT. Accredited by AOTA. Faculty: 5 full-time (all women). Students: 86 full-time (73 women); includes 3 minority (2 Asian Americans, 1 Hispanic). 89 applicants, 74% accepted. In 1997, 43 degrees awarded (100% found work related to degree). *Degree requirements:* Clinical experience. *Average time to degree:* master's–2 years full-time. *Application deadline:* 1/15. *Application fee:* $45. Electronic applications accepted. *Expenses:* Tuition $23,688 per year full-time, $395 per credit part-time. Fees $312 per year. *Financial aid:* 80 students received aid; career-related internships or fieldwork available. Aid available to part-time students. Financial aid applicants required to submit FAFSA. • Dr. Eileen Henry, Director, 412-365-1143. Fax: 412-365-1213. E-mail: henry@chatham.edu. Application contact: Heidi Hemming, Graduate Admissions, 412-365-1290. Fax: 412-365-1609. E-mail: admissions@chatham.edu.

Announcement: Chatham College's MOT program prepares graduates as entry-level occupational therapists. Curriculum includes critical thinking, occupational therapy knowledge, professional development, and research. Students perform several fieldwork placements throughout the 2-year program in a variety of settings. One unique placement involves a setting in which occupational therapy is not present; students decide if therapy is beneficial and establish parameters for service. Admissions criteria include a baccalaureate degree, prerequisite course work, overall and prerequisite QPA of 3.0 or higher, interview and writing sample, evidence of OT volunteer experience, and evidence of community service. E-mail at admissions@chatham.edu or visit the Web site at http://www.chatham.edu

College Misericordia, Division of Health Sciences, Program in Occupational Therapy, Dallas, PA 18612-1098. Awards MSOT. Accredited by AOTA. Faculty: 10. Students: 249 full-time (219 women), 74 part-time (57 women). 206 applicants, 53% accepted. In 1997, 80 degrees awarded. *Application fee:* $15. • Christine Hischman, Director, 717-674-6481. Application contact: Barbara Leggat, Continuing Education Specialist, 800-852-7675. Fax: 717-675-2441.

College of St. Catherine, Graduate Program, Program in Occupational Therapy, St. Paul, MN 55105-1789. Awards MA. Accredited by AOTA. Part-time and evening/weekend programs available. Faculty: 16 (15 women). Students: 67 full-time (65 women), 7 part-time (all women); includes 2 minority (1 Asian American, 1 Native American). Average age 30. 150 applicants, 29% accepted. In 1997, 26 degrees awarded. *Degree requirements:* Thesis required, foreign language not required. *Entrance requirements:* GRE, Michigan English Language Assessment Battery (minimum score 90) or TOEFL (minimum score 600), minimum GPA of 3.0. Application deadline: 5/1 (priority date; rolling processing). Application fee: $25. *Expenses:* Tuition $460 per credit hour. Fees $20 per trimester. *Financial aid:* 65 students received aid; institutionally sponsored loans and career-related internships or fieldwork available. Aid available to part-time students. Financial aid application deadline: 4/1; applicants required to submit FAFSA. • Dr. Louise C. Fawcett, Director, 612-690-6606. Application contact: Office of Admission, 612-690-6505.

College of St. Scholastica, Program in Occupational Therapy, Duluth, MN 55811-4199. Awards MA. Accredited by AOTA. Faculty: 4 full-time (3 women), 2 part-time (both women). Students: 39 full-time (36 women), 30 part-time (25 women); includes 1 minority (Native American). Average age 27. 53 applicants, 57% accepted. In 1997, 23 degrees awarded. *Degree requirements:* Thesis. *Entrance requirements:* Minimum GPA of 2.7. Application deadline: 1/15. Application fee: $50. *Tuition:* $7968 per year full-time, $332 per credit part-time. *Financial aid:* 61 students received aid. Aid available to part-time students. Financial aid applicants required to submit FAFSA. • Dr. Thomas H. Dillon, Chair, 218-723-6698. Application contact: Debra Bekkering, Graduate Administrative Assistant, 218-723-6285. Fax: 218-723-6796. E-mail: dbekkeri@ess.edu.

Colorado State University, College of Applied Human Sciences, Department of Occupational Therapy, Fort Collins, CO 80523-0015. Awards MS. Accredited by AOTA. Part-time programs available. Faculty: 11 full-time (9 women), 6 part-time (all women), 14 FTE. Students: 39 full-time (34 women), 40 part-time (35 women); includes 5 minority (2 African Americans, 2 Asian Americans, 1 Hispanic). Average age 31. 197 applicants, 21% accepted. In 1997, 19 degrees awarded. *Degree requirements:* Thesis required (for some programs), foreign language not required. *Entrance requirements:* GRE General Test (minimum score 550). Application deadline: 12/1. Application fee: $30. Electronic applications accepted. *Expenses:* Tuition $2632 per year full-time, $109 per credit hour part-time for state residents; $10,216 per year full-time, $425 per credit hour part-time for nonresidents. Fees $708 per year full-time, $32 per semester (minimum) part-time. *Financial aid:* In 1997–98, 1 fellowship, 4 teaching assistantships (1 to a first-year student) averaging $921 per month and totaling $33,156 were awarded; research assistantships, traineeships, scholarships, Federal Work-Study, and career-related internships or fieldwork also available. Aid available to part-time students. Financial aid application deadline: 4/30. *Faculty research:* Program effectiveness technology, productive community living, assessment of play, motor and process skills. Total annual research expenditures: $913,000. • Jodiea Redditti Hanzlik, Head, 970-491-7804. E-mail: hanzlik@cahs.colostate.edu. Application contact: Wanda Mayberry, Graduate Coordinator, 970-491-4887. Fax: 970-491-6290. E-mail: mayberry@cahs.colostate.edu.

Columbia University, College of Physicians and Surgeons, Programs in Occupational Therapy, New York, NY 10032. Awards MS, MPH/MS. Offerings include occupational therapy (professional) (MS), occupational therapy administration or education (post-professional) (MS). Accredited by AOTA. Faculty: 6 full-time (all women), 8 part-time (5 women). Students: 87 full-time (78 women), 12 part-time (11 women); includes 10 minority (1 African American, 4 Asian Americans, 5 Hispanics), 2 international. Average age 27. 258 applicants, 24% accepted. In 1997, 43 degrees awarded (100% found work related to degree). *Degree requirements:*

Directory: Occupational Therapy

Columbia University (continued)

Project, 6 months of fieldwork required, foreign language not required. *Entrance requirements:* TOEFL (minimum score 600), undergraduate course work in biology, psychology, social sciences, humanities, English composition, physics. Application deadline: 12/31. Application fee: $70. *Tuition:* $19,980 per year full-time, $666 per credit part-time. *Financial aid:* In 1997–98, 80 students received aid, including 32 scholarships (20 to first-year students); Federal Work-Study, institutionally sponsored loans, and career-related internships or fieldwork also available. Financial aid application deadline: 4/15; applicants required to submit FAFSA. *Faculty research:* AIDS, community mental health, developmental tasks of late life, hand injuries, health care delivery systems, infant play. Total annual research expenditures: $30,000. • Dr. Cynthia Hughes Harris, Director, 212-305-3781. Fax: 212-305-4569. E-mail: chh14@columbia.edu.

Announcement: Comprehensive curriculum prepares self-directed graduates who possess problem-solving abilities and a capacity to develop specialty skills. Students receive strong foundation in major treatment areas and are fully prepared for work with all age groups in a vast array of institutional, community, and private-practice settings. University offers the nation's only joint MS/MPH degree program in occupational therapy and public health. Provides closely linked academic and clinical education. Faculty-student teams carry out collaborative research. Renowned University medical center offers exposure to distinguished health-care specialists. Diversity of excellent clinical facilities available for field experience.

Concordia University Wisconsin, Division of Graduate Studies, Program in Occupational Therapy, Mequon, WI 53097-2402. Awards MOT. Accredited by AOTA. Students: 5. *Degree requirements:* Thesis or alternative, comprehensive exam. *Entrance requirements:* TOEFL (minimum score 550). Application fee: $25 ($125 for international students). *Tuition:* $250 per credit. *Financial aid:* Application deadline 8/1. • Suzanne Floyd, Director, 414-243-4278. Application contact: Brooke Tireman, Graduate Admissions, 414-243-4248. Fax: 414-243-4428. E-mail: btireman@back.cuw.edu.

Creighton University, School of Pharmacy and Allied Health Professions, Program in Occupational Therapy, Omaha, NE 68178-0001. Awards OTD. Faculty: 10 full-time (9 women), 1 (woman) part-time. Students: 21 full-time (16 women); includes 2 minority (1 Hispanic, 1 Native American). Average age 29. 17 applicants, 71% accepted. In 1997, 8 degrees awarded. *Entrance requirements:* BS in occupational therapy. Application deadline: 3/15 (priority date). Application fee: $50. *Expenses:* Tuition $6772 per year. Fees $268 per year. *Financial aid:* Institutionally sponsored loans and career-related internships or fieldwork available. Financial aid applicants required to submit CSS PROFILE or FAFSA. *Faculty research:* Ethics, health care systems. • Claudia G. Peyton, Chair, 402-280-1856. Fax: 402-280-5692. Application contact: John J. Flemming, Director of Admissions, 402-280-2662. Fax: 402-280-5739. E-mail: spahp_admin8@creighton.edu.

Dominican College of Blauvelt, Department of Occupational Therapy, Orangeburg, NY 10962-1210. Awards MS. Students: 0. *Application deadline:* rolling. *Application fee:* $50. *Expenses:* Tuition $400 per credit hour. Fees $155 per year. • Rita Cottrell, Head, 914-359-7800.

Duquesne University, John G. Rangos, Sr. School of Health Sciences, Pittsburgh, PA 15282-0001. Offerings include occupational therapy (MOT). Accredited by AOTA. School faculty: 30 full-time (17 women), 12 part-time (6 women), 34.8 FTE. *Average time to degree:* master's–2 years full-time. *Application deadline:* 12/1 (priority date). *Application fee:* $45. Electronic applications accepted. *Expenses:* Tuition $510 per credit. Fees $39 per credit. • Dr. Jerome L. Martin, Dean, 412-396-6012. E-mail: martin2@duq2.cc.duq.edu. Application contact: Deborah L. Durica, Director of Student and Alumni Services, 412-396-6652. Fax: 412-396-5554. E-mail: durica@duq2.cc.duq.edu.

East Carolina University, School of Allied Health Sciences, Department of Occupational Therapy, Greenville, NC 27858-4353. Awards MS. Students: 2 part-time (both women). Average age 31. 2 applicants, 100% accepted. *Degree requirements:* Comprehensive exams required, foreign language and thesis not required. *Entrance requirements:* GRE, TOEFL. Application deadline: 6/1. Application fee: $0. *Tuition:* $1886 per year full-time, $472 per semester (minimum) part-time for state residents; $9156 per year full-time, $2289 per semester (minimum) part-time for nonresidents. *Financial aid:* Federal Work-Study and career-related internships or fieldwork available. Financial aid application deadline: 6/1; applicants required to submit FAFSA. • Dr. Anne Dickerson, Chairperson, 252-328-4441. Fax: 252-328-4770. E-mail: dickersona@mail.ecu.edu. Application contact: Dr. Paul D. Tschetter, Associate Dean, 252-328-6012. Fax: 252-328-6071. E-mail: grad@mail.ecu.edu.

Eastern Kentucky University, College of Allied Health and Nursing, Department of Occupational Therapy, Richmond, KY 40475-3101. Awards MS. Part-time programs available. Faculty: 14 full-time (12 women). Students: 22 full-time (19 women), 37 part-time (30 women); includes 2 minority (1 African American, 1 Hispanic). Average age 25. 61 applicants, 26% accepted. In 1997, 9 degrees awarded. *Degree requirements:* Thesis optional. *Entrance requirements:* GRE General Test, minimum GPA of 3.0. Application deadline: 6/1. Application fee: $0. *Tuition:* $2390 per year full-time, $133 per credit hour part-time for state residents; $6630 per year full-time, $365 per credit hour part-time for nonresidents. *Financial aid:* In 1997–98, 1 graduate assistantship was awarded; institutionally sponsored loans and career-related internships or fieldwork also available. Financial aid applicants required to submit CSS PROFILE. *Faculty research:* Rehabilitation, pediatrics, leadership issues. • Linda Martin, Chair, 606-622-3300. Fax: 606-622-1130. Application contact: Shirley O'Brien, Graduate Coordinator, 606-622-3300. Fax: 606-622-1140. E-mail: otsobrie@acs.eku.edu.

Eastern Michigan University, College of Health and Human Services, Department of Associated Health Professions, Ypsilanti, MI 48197. Offers program in occupational therapy (MOT, MS). One or more programs accredited by AOTA. Faculty: 14 full-time (8 women). 10 applicants, 70% accepted. In 1997, 2 degrees awarded. *Degree requirements:* Thesis required, foreign language not required. *Entrance requirements:* TOEFL (minimum score 500), occupational therapy certification. Application deadline: 5/15 (rolling processing; 3/15 for spring admission). Application fee: $30. *Expenses:* Tuition $2691 per year full-time, $150 per credit hour part-time for state residents; $6300 per year full-time, $350 per credit hour part-time for nonresidents. Fees $368 per year full-time, $88 per semester (minimum) part-time. *Financial aid:* Fellowships, teaching assistantships available. Aid available to part-time students. Financial aid application deadline: 3/15; applicants required to submit FAFSA. • Dr. Ruth Ann Hansen, Department Head, 734-487-3230.

Florida International University, College of Health, Department of Occupational Therapy, Miami, FL 33199. Awards MS. Part-time programs available. Faculty: 7 full-time (6 women), 1 (woman) part-time, 7.38 FTE. Students: 47 full-time (38 women), 23 part-time (18 women); includes 18 minority (5 African Americans, 4 Asian Americans, 9 Hispanics), 1 international. Average age 30. 24 applicants, 50% accepted. In 1997, 11 degrees awarded. *Degree requirements:* Thesis required, foreign language not required. *Entrance requirements:* GRE General Test (minimum combined score of 1000), minimum GPA of 3.0. Application deadline: 4/1 (priority date; rolling processing; 10/1 for spring admission). Application fee: $20. *Expenses:* Tuition $138 per credit hour for state residents; $482 per credit hour for nonresidents. Fees $46 per semester. *Financial aid:* Fellowships, research assistantships, teaching assistantships, Federal Work-Study, institutionally sponsored loans, and career-related internships or fieldwork available. • Dr. Pamela K. Shaffner, Chairperson, 305-348-2263. Fax: 305-348-1240. E-mail: shaffner@servax.fiu.edu.

Governors State University, College of Health Professions, Division of Nursing and Health Science, Program in Occupational Therapy, University Park, IL 60466. Awards MOT. Accredited by AOTA. *Degree requirements:* Thesis or alternative required, foreign language not required. *Entrance requirements:* Minimum GPA of 3.0 in field, 2.75 overall. Application deadline: 4/30 (priority date). Application fee: $0. *Expenses:* Tuition $1140 per trimester full-time, $95 per credit hour part-time for state residents; $3420 per trimester full-time, $285 per credit hour part-time for nonresidents. Fees $95 per trimester. *Financial aid:* Application deadline 5/1. • Beth Cada, Coordinator, 708-534-5000 Ext. 5489.

Grand Valley State University, Science and Mathematics Division, School of Health Sciences, Occupational Therapy Program, Allendale, MI 49401-9403. Awards MS. Accredited by AOTA. Faculty: 3 full-time (all women), 13 part-time (12 women), 5 FTE. Students: 16 full-time (13 women). Average age 30. In 1997, 1 degree awarded. *Degree requirements:* Thesis or alternative, fieldwork required, foreign language not required. *Entrance requirements:* Interview, sample of written work. Application fee: $20. *Faculty research:* Continuing education, teaching/learning methods. • Cynthia Grapczynski, Director, 616-895-3356. Fax: 616-895-3350. E-mail: grapczyc@gvsu.edu.

Idaho State University, College of Health Professions, Department of Physical and Occupational Therapy, Program in Occupational Therapy, Pocatello, ID 83209. Awards MOT. Program new for fall 1998. *Entrance requirements:* GRE General Test. *Tuition:* $3130 per year full-time, $136 per credit hour part-time for state residents; $9370 per year full-time, $226 per credit hour part-time for nonresidents. • Greg Wintz, Director, 208-236-4095.

Ithaca College, School of Health Sciences and Human Performance, Program in Occupational Therapy, Ithaca, NY 14850-7020. Awards MS. Students must enter the program as freshmen. Students: 0. *Degree requirements:* Clinical fieldwork, comprehensive exams required, thesis optional, foreign language not required. *Entrance requirements:* TOEFL (minimum score 550). Application deadline: 3/1 (priority date; rolling processing). Application fee: $40. *Tuition:* $552 per credit hour. *Financial aid:* Career-related internships or fieldwork available. Financial aid application deadline: 3/1; applicants required to submit FAFSA. • Dr. Catherine Gordon, Chairperson, 607-274-1975. Fax: 607-274-1968.

Kirksville College of Osteopathic Medicine, Arizona School of Health Sciences, PO Box 11037, Phoenix, AZ 85061-1037. Offerings include occupational therapy (MS). Accredited by AOTA. School faculty: 30 full-time (18 women), 14 part-time (8 women). *Degree requirements:* Thesis required, foreign language not required. *Average time to degree:* master's–2 years full-time. *Entrance requirements:* GRE General Test (combined average 1639 on three sections), MCAT (average 25 for physician assistant). Application deadline: 2/1 (rolling processing). Application fee: $50. *Tuition:* $15,990 per year. • Dr. James Dearing, Associate Dean, 602-841-4077. Fax: 602-841-4092. Application contact: Stephanie Seyer, Assistant Director of Admissions, 660-626-2237. Fax: 660-626-2815.

Medical College of Georgia, Department of Occupational Therapy, Augusta, GA 30912-1500. Awards MHE. Part-time programs available. Faculty: 4 full-time (all women). Students: 4 part-time (all women). Average age 40. 4 applicants, 75% accepted. In 1997, 1 degree awarded. *Entrance requirements:* GRE General Test (minimum combined score of 1000), TOEFL (minimum score 600). Application deadline: 6/30 (priority date; rolling processing). Application fee: $0. *Expenses:* Tuition $2670 per year full-time, $111 per credit part-time for state residents; $10,680 per year full-time, $445 per credit part-time for nonresidents. Fees $286 per year. *Financial aid:* Federal Work-Study, institutionally sponsored loans available. Financial aid application deadline: 5/1. • Dr. Nancy D. Prendergast, Acting Chair, 706-721-2621. Fax: 706-721-7312. E-mail: nprender@mail.mcg.edu. Application contact: Dr. Gary C. Bond, Associate Dean, 706-721-3278. Fax: 706-721-6829. E-mail: gradstud@mail.mcg.edu.

Medical College of Ohio, School of Allied Health, Concentration in Occupational Therapy, Toledo, OH 43699-0008. Awards MOT. Accredited by AOTA. Faculty: 6 full-time, 4 part-time. Average age 28. 66 applicants, 45% accepted. In 1997, 22 degrees awarded. *Degree requirements:* Scholarly project required, foreign language not required. *Entrance requirements:* GRE General Test, interview, minimum undergraduate GPA of 3.0, observations. Application deadline: 4/1 (rolling processing). Application fee: $30. *Financial aid:* Scholarships, Federal Work-Study, institutionally sponsored loans available. Financial aid applicants required to submit FAFSA. *Faculty research:* Therapeutic occupation, pediatric neuroscience, grief/loss. • Dr. Julie Thomas, Chair, 419-383-4429. E-mail: mcogradschool@mco.edu. Application contact: Theresa Langenderfer, Secretary, 419-383-4160. Fax: 419-383-6140. E-mail: mcogradschool@mco.edu.

Medical University of South Carolina, College of Health Professions, Department of Rehabilitation Sciences, Program in Occupational Therapy, Charleston, SC 29425-0002. Awards MHS, MSR. Faculty: 6 full-time (5 women), 1 (woman) part-time, 6.5 FTE. Students: 69 full-time (55 women); includes 4 minority (3 African Americans, 1 Asian American). Average age 28. 205 applicants, 18% accepted. In 1997, 3 degrees awarded (100% found work related to degree). *Degree requirements:* Thesis or alternative, research project required, foreign language not required. *Average time to degree:* master's–3 years full-time. *Entrance requirements:* GRE General Test, interview, minimum GPA of 2.8. Application deadline: 12/1 (rolling processing). Application fee: $55. *Expenses:* Tuition $4072 per year full-time, $221 per semester hour part-time for state residents; $7064 per year full-time, $387 per semester hour part-time for nonresidents. Fees $150 per year (minimum). *Financial aid:* In 1997–98, 30 students received aid, including 1 graduate assistantship (to a first-year student); Federal Work-Study also available. Aid available to part-time students. Financial aid application deadline: 4/1; applicants required to submit FAFSA. *Faculty research:* Distance education, efficacy of occupational therapy intervention, interdisciplinary teams, quality of life. • Dr. James A. Morrow, Chair, 843-792-2961. E-mail: morrowj@musc.edu. Application contact: Susan Johnson, Student Services, 843-792-2961. Fax: 843-792-0710. E-mail: johnsoss@musc.edu.

Mercy College, Program in Occupational Therapy, Dobbs Ferry, NY 10522-1189. Awards MS. Accredited by AOTA. Evening/weekend programs available. Students: 42 full-time (35 women). *Degree requirements:* Thesis, fieldwork. *Entrance requirements:* TOEFL, minimum GPA of 3.0. Application deadline: 2/1. Application fee: $60 ($400 for international students). *Tuition:* $427 per credit. *Financial aid:* Federal Work-Study, institutionally sponsored loans, and career-related internships or fieldwork available. Financial aid applicants required to submit FAFSA. *Faculty research:* Occupational therapy intervention, outcomes and assessment. • Joan Toglia, Director, 914-674-9331 Ext. 600. Fax: 914-674-9457. Application contact: Admissions Office, 800-MERCY-NY. Fax: 914-674-7382. E-mail: admission@merlin.mercynet.edu.

Midwestern University, College of Allied Health Professions, Program in Occupational Therapy, Downers Grove, IL 60515-1235. Awards MOT. Accredited by AOTA. Students: 60 full-time (55 women); includes 6 minority (1 African American, 4 Asian Americans, 1 Hispanic). *Application deadline:* rolling. *Application fee:* $30. *Expenses:* Tuition $15,252 per year for state residents; $17,644 per year for nonresidents. Fees $280 per year. • Tomas Laster, Director. Application contact: Julie Rosenthall, Director of Admissions, 800-458-6253. Fax: 630-971-6086. E-mail: mwuinfo@mwu.edu.

Announcement: Midwestern University is committed to educating the health-care team of the next century. The University administers the Chicago College of Osteopathic Medicine, the Chicago College of Pharmacy, the College of Allied Health Professions, the Arizona College of Osteopathic Medicine, and the College of Pharmacy–Glendale. The University operates campuses in Downers Grove, Illinois, and in Glendale, Arizona. The Occupational Therapy Program offers the Master of Occupational Therapy (MOT) degree. Focusing on holistic health care, the program includes collaborative learning between OT and PT students. The 30-month curriculum includes 23 weeks of full-time clinical experience under the supervision of licensed occupational therapists in various settings. Contact the Office of Admissions, Midwestern University, 555 31st Street, Downers Grove, IL 60515; 800-458-6253; e-mail: admiss@midwestern.edu; WWW: http://www.midwestern.edu

Milligan College, Program in Occupational Therapy, Milligan College, TN 37682. Awards MOT. Program new for fall 1998. *Entrance requirements:* Bachelor's degree in science. Application deadline: rolling. Application fee: $30. *Tuition:* $385 per hour. • Dan Poss, Director, 800-262-8337.

Mount Mary College, Graduate Programs, Program in Occupational Therapy, Milwaukee, WI 53222-4597. Awards MS. Part-time and evening/weekend programs available. Faculty: 1 (woman) full-time, 3 part-time (all women), 1.5 FTE. Students: 12 part-time (all women). 3 applicants, 100% accepted. *Degree requirements:* Thesis or alternative, professional development portfolio required, foreign language not required. *Entrance requirements:* TOEFL (minimum score 550), minimum GPA of 2.75, occupational therapy license, 1 year of work experience. Application deadline: 10/15 (priority date; 3/15 for spring admission). Application fee: $35. *Tuition:* $370 per credit hour. *Financial aid:* Career-related internships or fieldwork available. Aid available to part-time students. Financial aid application deadline: 5/1. *Faculty research:* Clinical reasoning, occupational science, sensory integration. • Dr. Jane Olson, Director, 414-258-4810 Ext. 348. E-mail: affeldtj@mmc.edu.

New York University, School of Education, Department of Occupational Therapy, New York, NY 10012-1019. Awards MA, PhD. One or more programs accredited by AOTA. Part-time and evening/weekend programs available. Faculty: 10 full-time (9 women), 45 part-time. Students: 174 full-time, 109 part-time. 460 applicants, 25% accepted. In 1997, 102 master's awarded. Terminal master's awarded for partial completion of doctoral program. *Degree requirements:* For master's, thesis (for some programs), project required, foreign language not required; for doctorate, dissertation. *Entrance requirements:* For master's, TOEFL; for doctorate, GRE General Test, TOEFL, interview. Application deadline: 2/1 (priority date; rolling processing; 12/1 for spring admission). Application fee: $40 ($60 for international students). *Financial aid:* In 1997–98, fellowships averaging $850 per month, research assistantships averaging $850 per month, teaching assistantships averaging $850 per month were awarded; traineeships, partial tuition waivers, Federal Work-Study, institutionally sponsored loans, and career-related internships or fieldwork also available. Aid available to part-time students. Financial aid application deadline: 3/1; applicants required to submit FAFSA. *Faculty research:* Pediatrics, assistive rehabilitation technology, adaptive computer technology for children with disabilities. • Deborah R. Labovitz, Chairperson, 212-998-5825. Fax: 212-995-4044. Application contact: Office of Graduate Admissions, 212-998-5030. Fax: 212-995-4328.

See in-depth description on page 1243.

Nova Southeastern University, Health Professions Division, College of Allied Health, Program in Occupational Therapy, Fort Lauderdale, FL 33314-7721. Awards MOT, Dr OT. One or more programs accredited by AOTA. Students: 184 full-time (157 women), 6 part-time (all women); includes 37 minority (6 African Americans, 7 Asian Americans, 23 Hispanics, 1 Native American), 1 international. In 1997, 39 master's awarded. *Degree requirements:* For doctorate, dissertation. *Average time to degree:* master's–2.5 years full-time; doctorate–2 years full-time, 4 years part-time. *Entrance requirements:* GRE General Test (minimum combined score of 1000). Application fee: $50. *Expenses:* Tuition $15,500 per year for state residents; $17,500 per year for nonresidents. Fees $100 per year. *Financial aid:* Teaching assistantships, graduate assistantships, institutionally sponsored loans available. • Dr. Reba L. Anderson, Director, 954-423-1242. Fax: 954-916-2290. E-mail: reba@hpd.acast.nova.edu. Application contact: Monica Roca, Admissions Counselor, 954-723-1110.

Pacific University, School of Occupational Therapy, Forest Grove, OR 97116-1797. Awards MOT. Faculty: 4 full-time (3 women), 4 part-time (3 women). Students: 45 full-time (37 women), 1 (woman) part-time; includes 3 minority (2 Asian Americans, 1 Native American), 1 international. Average age 29. 140 applicants, 17% accepted. *Degree requirements:* Research project. *Application deadline:* 12/9. *Application fee:* $45. *Financial aid:* Federal Work-Study and career-related internships or fieldwork available. Aid available to part-time students. Financial aid applicants required to submit FAFSA. *Faculty research:* Americans with Disabilities Act, sensory integration, nontraditional settings for fieldwork placement. • Molly McEwen, Director, 503-359-2789. Application contact: Darcey Gardner, Admissions Counselor, 503-359-2900. Fax: 503-359-2975. E-mail: admissions@pacificu.edu.

Philadelphia College of Textiles and Science, School of Science and Health, Program in Occupational Therapy, Philadelphia, PA 19144-5497. Awards MS. Part-time and evening/weekend programs available. *Degree requirements:* Practicum required, foreign language and thesis not required. *Entrance requirements:* GRE or MAT, minimum GPA of 2.85. Application deadline: rolling. Application fee: $35. *Tuition:* $448 per credit hour. *Financial aid:* Research assistantships, graduate assistantships, residential assistantships, Federal Work-Study, and career-related internships or fieldwork available. Financial aid applicants required to submit FAFSA. • Ellen Kolodner, Director, 215-951-6853. Fax: 215-951-2615. E-mail: kolodnere@phila.col.edu.

Rockhurst College, College of Arts and Sciences, Division of Natural, Applied and Quantitative Sciences, Program in Occupational Therapy Education, Kansas City, MO 64110-2561. Awards MOT. Accredited by AOTA. Part-time programs available. Faculty: 5 full-time (all women), 3 part-time (all women). Students: 92 full-time (78 women), 3 part-time (all women); includes 1 minority (Hispanic). Average age 27. 175 applicants, 21% accepted. In 1997, 38 degrees awarded. *Degree requirements:* Computer language required, foreign language and thesis not required. *Average time to degree:* master's–3 years full-time. *Entrance requirements:* Interview, minimum GPA of 3.0. Application deadline: 1/15. Application fee: $20. Electronic applications accepted. *Expenses:* Tuition $335 per semester hour. Fees $15 per year. *Financial aid:* In 1997–98, 82 students received aid, including 5 research assistantships, 10 teaching assistantships, 5 administrative assistantships; institutionally sponsored loans and career-related internships or fieldwork also available. Financial aid application deadline: 4/1; applicants required to submit FAFSA. *Faculty research:* Behavioral state in children with handicaps, women, independent living skills for homeless women, cortical visual impairment in children with multiple handicaps. • Dr. Jane P. Rues, Chair, 816-501-4635. E-mail: rues@rvax1.rockhurst.edu. Application contact: Mary B. Lewis, 816-501-4635. Fax: 816-501-4643.

Rush University, College of Health Sciences, Department of Occupational Therapy, Chicago, IL 60612-3832. Awards MS. Accredited by AOTA. Faculty: 3 full-time (all women), 16 part-time (13 women). Students: 51 full-time (44 women), 19 part-time (16 women); includes 6 minority (3 African Americans, 2 Asian Americans, 1 Hispanic). Average age 31. 174 applicants, 14% accepted. In 1997, 24 degrees awarded (100% found work related to degree). *Degree requirements:* Thesis required, foreign language not required. *Average time to degree:* master's–2 years full-time, 3 years part-time. *Entrance requirements:* GRE General Test (minimum combined score of 1500 on three sections). Application deadline: 11/1. Application fee: $40. *Tuition:* $8270 per year full-time, $370 per credit hour part-time. *Financial aid:* 56 students received aid; Federal Work-Study, institutionally sponsored loans, and career-related internships or fieldwork available. Aid available to part-time students. Financial aid application deadline: 4/15; applicants required to submit FAFSA. *Faculty research:* Investigation of occupations, occupational therapy theories and their application to target populations and healthcare settings. • Karin J. Opacich, Acting Co-Chair, 312-942-7138. Fax: 312-942-6989. Application contact: Hicela Castruita, Director, College Admissions Services, 312-942-7100. Fax: 312-942-2219.

See in-depth description on page 1259.

Saint Francis College, Occupational Therapy Program, Loretto, PA 15940-0600. Awards MOT. Program new for fall 1998. • Donald Walkovich, Chair, 814-472-3899. Application contact: Frank Crouse, Assistant Director of Admissions, 814-472-3110. Fax: 814-472-3335. E-mail: fcrouse@sfcpa.edu.

Samuel Merritt College, Department of Occupational Therapy, Oakland, CA 94609-3108. Awards MOT. Accredited by AOTA. Faculty: 6 full-time (3 women), 7 part-time (4 women), 8.07 FTE. Students: 122 full-time (100 women), 1 part-time (0 women); includes 31 minority (2 African Americans, 24 Asian Americans, 5 Hispanics). Average age 30. 120 applicants, 55% accepted. In 1997, 37 degrees awarded. *Average time to degree:* master's–2.2 years full-time. *Entrance requirements:* GRE General Test (minimum combined score of 1500 on three sections, 450 on verbal), TOEFL (minimum score 600), minimum GPA of 2.6 in science, 2.8 overall; volunteer or professional occupational therapy experience; interview. Application deadline: 2/15 (priority date). Application fee: $50. *Expenses:* Tuition $627 per unit. Fees $25 per year. *Financial aid:* In 1997–98, 80 students received aid, including scholarships totaling $10,000; Federal Work-Study and career-related internships or fieldwork also available. Aid available to part-time students. Financial aid application deadline: 3/2; applicants required to submit FAFSA. *Total annual research expenditures:* $4200. • Guy McCormack, Chair, 510-869-8923. Fax: 510-869-6282. Application contact: John Garten-Schuman, Director of Admissions, 510-869-6576. Fax: 510-869-6525.

San Jose State University, College of Applied Arts and Sciences, Department of Occupational Therapy, San Jose, CA 95192-0001. Awards MS. Accredited by AOTA. Faculty: 9 full-time (3 women), 3 part-time (1 woman). Students: 28 full-time (26 women), 3 part-time (all women); includes 5 minority (1 African American, 2 Asian Americans, 2 Hispanics), 1 international. Average age 31. 149 applicants, 15% accepted. In 1997, 26 degrees awarded. *Degree requirements:* Thesis or alternative. *Entrance requirements:* GRE, minimum GPA of 3.0. Application deadline: 6/1 (rolling processing). Application fee: $59. *Expenses:* Tuition $0 for state residents; $246 per unit for nonresidents. Fees $2017 per year full-time, $1351 per year part-time. *Financial aid:* In 1997–98, 3 teaching assistantships were awarded; Federal Work-Study, institutionally sponsored loans, and career-related internships or fieldwork also available. *Faculty research:* Generic occupational therapy, psychosocial rehabilitation, physical rehabilitation, organizational development, occupational performance. • Dr. Kay Schwartz, Chair, 408-924-3070.

Seton Hall University, School of Graduate Medical Education, Program in Occupational Therapy, South Orange, NJ 07079-2697. Awards MS. *Entrance requirements:* GRE, TOEFL, health care experience, minimum GPA of 3.0. *Expenses:* Tuition $500 per credit. Fees $610 per year full-time, $185 per semester part-time. • Application contact: Office of Graduate Medical Education, 973-761-7145. Fax: 973-275-2370. E-mail: gradmeded@shu.edu.

Shenandoah University, Department of Occupational Therapy, 1460 University Drive, Winchester, VA 22601-5195. Awards MS. Accredited by AOTA. Faculty: 6 full-time (all women), 3 part-time (all women). Students: 114 full-time (103 women), 2 part-time (both women); includes 8 minority (1 African American, 6 Hispanics, 1 Native American), 1 international. Average age 26. 169 applicants, 71% accepted. In 1997, 37 degrees awarded. *Degree requirements:* Thesis required, foreign language not required. *Entrance requirements:* GRE, fieldwork experience. Application deadline: 3/1. Application fee: $30. Electronic applications accepted. *Tuition:* $15,600 per year. *Faculty research:* Study of human occupations across different contexts, human structures related to human function, school-based occupational therapy practices. • Dr. Gretchen Stone, Chair, 540-665-5543. Fax: 540-665-5564. E-mail: gstone@su.edu. Application contact: Michael Carpenter, Director of Admissions, 540-665-4581. Fax: 540-665-4627. E-mail: admit@su.edu.

Springfield College, Program in Occupational Therapy, Springfield, MA 01109-3797. Awards M Ed, MS, CAS. One or more programs accredited by AOTA. Part-time programs available. Faculty: 5 full-time (all women), 4 part-time (all women), 6 FTE. Students: 76 full-time (67 women), 8 part-time (all women). Average age 30. 244 applicants, 32% accepted. In 1997, 34 master's, 2 CASs awarded. *Degree requirements:* For master's, comprehensive exam required, foreign language and thesis not required. *Entrance requirements:* For master's, interview. Application deadline: 1/1. Application fee: $40. *Expenses:* Tuition $474 per credit. Fees $25 per year. *Financial aid:* In 1997–98, 2 teaching assistantships (1 to a first-year student) were awarded; full and partial tuition waivers, Federal Work-Study, and career-related internships or fieldwork also available. Financial aid application deadline: 3/1. • Katherine Post, Director, 413-748-3581. Application contact: Donald J. Shaw Jr., Director of Graduate Admissions, 413-748-3225. Fax: 413-748-3694. E-mail: dshaw@spfldcol.edu.

State University of New York at Buffalo, Graduate School, School of Health Related Professions, Department of Occupational Therapy, Buffalo, NY 14260. Awards MS, PhD. Part-time and evening/weekend programs available. Faculty: 10 full-time (6 women), 3 part-time (1 woman). Students: 3 full-time (1 woman), 8 part-time (all women); includes 1 minority (African American), 4 international. Average age 30. 7 applicants, 43% accepted. In 1997, 6 master's awarded. Terminal master's awarded for partial completion of doctoral program. *Degree requirements:* For master's, thesis required, foreign language not required; for doctorate, dissertation, comprehensive exam required, foreign language not required. *Entrance requirements:* For master's, GRE General Test, TOEFL (minimum score 550), BS in occupational therapy; for doctorate, GRE General Test, TOEFL (minimum score 550). Application deadline: 6/1. Application fee: $35. *Tuition:* $5970 per year full-time, $288 per credit hour part-time for state residents; $9286 per year full-time, $426 per credit hour part-time for nonresidents. *Financial aid:* In 1997–98, 3 research assistantships (1 to a first-year student) totaling $12,000, 9 teaching assistantships (5 to first-year students) totaling $7,500 were awarded; fellowships, graduate assistantships, full and partial tuition waivers, Federal Work-Study, institutionally sponsored loans, and career-related internships or fieldwork also available. Financial aid application deadline: 4/15. *Faculty research:* Pediatrics, developmental disabilities, assistive technology, aging, motor control. • Dr. William J. Gavin, Director of Graduate Studies, 716-829-3141. Fax: 716-829-3217. E-mail: gavin@shaman.socsci.buffalo.edu.

Temple University, Health Sciences Center and Graduate School, College of Allied Health Professions, Department of Occupational Therapy, Philadelphia, PA 19140. Awards MS. Part-time and evening/weekend programs available. Faculty: 8 full-time (7 women). Students: 113 (94 women); includes 11 minority (8 African Americans, 1 Asian American, 2 Hispanics), 1 international. 188 applicants, 24% accepted. In 1997, 16 degrees awarded. *Degree requirements:* Thesis required, foreign language not required. *Entrance requirements:* GRE General Test or MAT (score in 50th percentile or higher), minimum GPA of 2.8, interview. Application deadline: 1/31. Application fee: $40. *Expenses:* Tuition $323 per semester hour for state residents; $444 per semester hour for nonresidents. Fees $170 per year full-time, $28 per semester (minimum) part-time. *Financial aid:* Research assistantships, teaching assistantships, Federal Work-Study, institutionally sponsored loans, and career-related internships or fieldwork available. *Faculty research:* Early intervention, pediatrics, gerontology, administration, assistive technology. Total annual research expenditures: $110,000. • Judith Perinchief, Chair, 215-707-4813. Fax: 215-707-7656.

See in-depth description on page 1263.

Texas Woman's University, School of Occupational Therapy, Denton, TX 76204. Awards MA, MOT, PhD. One or more programs accredited by AOTA. Part-time and evening/weekend programs available. Faculty: 26 full-time (24 women), 12 part-time (10 women), 29 FTE. Students: 276 full-time (230 women), 62 part-time (54 women); includes 29 minority (4 African Americans, 11 Asian Americans, 12 Hispanics, 2 Native Americans), 11 international. Average age 31. 250 applicants, 30% accepted. In 1997, 117 master's awarded (100% found work related to degree). *Degree requirements:* Thesis/dissertation required, foreign language not required. *Average time to degree:* master's–2.3 years full-time, 4 years part-time. *Entrance requirements:* For master's, GRE General Test (minimum combined score of 850), minimum GPA of 3.0; for doctorate, GRE General Test (minimum combined score of 1000), minimum GPA of 3.2. Application deadline: 1/15 (7/15 for spring admission). Application fee: $25. *Financial aid:* In 1997–98, 15 research assistantships averaging $745 per month and totaling $40,063, 2 teaching assistantships averaging $846 per month and totaling $7,614 were awarded; clinical assistantships, Federal Work-Study, institutionally sponsored loans, and career-related internships or fieldwork also available. Aid available to part-time students. Financial aid application deadline: 4/1. *Faculty research:* Adaption to community, nontraditional students, theory development, gerontology, community assessment. • Dr. Janette Schkade, Dean, 940-898-2802. E-mail: a_schkade@twu.edu. Application contact: Dr. Sally Schultz, Coordinator of Graduate Education, 940-898-2813. Fax: 940-898-2806.

Thomas Jefferson University, Program in Occupational Therapy, Philadelphia, PA 19107. Awards MS. Faculty: 4 full-time (3 women), 3 part-time (all women). Students: 47 full-time (39 women), 31 part-time (25 women); includes 7 minority (4 African Americans, 3 Asian Americans).

Directory: Occupational Therapy

Thomas Jefferson University (continued)
124 applicants, 40% accepted. In 1997, 23 degrees awarded. *Degree requirements:* Thesis or alternative required, foreign language not required. *Entrance requirements:* GRE or MAT. Application deadline: 2/1. Application fee: $30. *Tuition:* $18,100 per year full-time, $625 per credit part-time. *Financial aid:* Fellowships, research assistantships, Federal Work-Study, institutionally sponsored loans available. Aid available to part-time students. Financial aid application deadline: 5/1; applicants required to submit FAFSA. *Faculty research:* Therapist/patient interaction, skill development and empowerment of persons with illness and/or disabilities, stress management, gerontology. • Dr. Janice P. Burke, Graduate Director, 215-503-9606. Fax: 215-923-2475. E-mail: burkel@jeflin.tju.edu. Application contact: Jessie F. Pervall, Director of Admissions, 215-503-4400. Fax: 215-503-3433. E-mail: cgs-info@mail.tju.edu.

Touro College, Barry Z. Levine School of Health Sciences, Occupational Therapy Program, Dix Hills, NY 11746. Awards MS. Accredited by AOTA. Faculty: 14 full-time. Students: 36. *Entrance requirements:* Interview, minimum GPA of 2.8. Application fee: $40. • Dr. Anthony Hollander, Director, 516-673-3200. Application contact: Office of Admissions, 516-673-3200.

Towson University, Program in Occupational Therapy, Towson, MD 21252-0001. Awards MS. Accredited by AOTA. Part-time and evening/weekend programs available. Faculty: 6 full-time (all women), 2 part-time (both women). Students: 68 full-time (64 women), 28 part-time (26 women); includes 9 minority (5 African Americans, 1 Asian American, 3 Hispanics). In 1997, 21 degrees awarded. *Degree requirements:* Exam required, thesis optional. *Entrance requirements:* GRE General Test (minimum combined score of 800). Application deadline: 3/1 (rolling processing; 10/1 for spring admission). Application fee: $40. *Expenses:* Tuition $187 per credit hour for state residents; $364 per credit hour for nonresidents. Fees $40 per credit hour. *Financial aid:* Assistantships, Federal Work-Study available. Financial aid application deadline: 4/1; applicants required to submit FAFSA. *Faculty research:* Issues of the aging, training caregivers, hand function in children. • Dr. Regena G. Stevens-Ratchford, Director, 410-830-2381. Fax: 410-830-2322. E-mail: rstevensratchford@towson.edu. Application contact: Fran Musotto, Office Manager, 410-830-2501. Fax: 410-830-4675. E-mail: fmusotto@towson.edu.

Tufts University, Division of Graduate and Continuing Studies and Research, Graduate School of Arts and Sciences, Department of Occupational Therapy, Medford, MA 02155. Awards MA, MS. Accredited by AOTA. Faculty: 7 full-time, 6 part-time. Students: 128 (113 women); includes 10 minority (2 African Americans, 6 Asian Americans, 2 Hispanics), 1 international. 392 applicants, 26% accepted. In 1997, 81 degrees awarded. *Degree requirements:* Thesis required (for some programs), foreign language not required. *Entrance requirements:* GRE General Test, TOEFL (minimum score 550). Application deadline: 2/15 (rolling processing). Application fee: $50. *Expenses:* Tuition $17,879 per year. Fees $1200 per year. *Financial aid:* Teaching assistantships, scholarships, partial tuition waivers, Federal Work-Study, and career-related internships or fieldwork available. Aid available to part-time students. Financial aid application deadline: 2/15; applicants required to submit FAFSA. • Sharon Schwartzberg, Chair, 617-627-3720.

Tufts University, Division of Graduate and Continuing Studies and Research, Professional and Continuing Studies, Advanced Professional Study in Occupational Therapy Program, Medford, MA 02155. Awards Certificate. Part-time and evening/weekend programs available. Students: 0. 0 applicants. *Average time to degree:* other advanced degree–1 year part-time. *Application deadline:* 8/15 (priority date; 12/12 for spring admission). *Application fee:* $40. *Tuition:* $1100 per course. *Financial aid:* Career-related internships or fieldwork available. Aid available to part-time students. Financial aid application deadline: 5/1; applicants required to submit FAFSA. • Application contact: Liz Regan, Program Administrator, 617-627-3562. Fax: 617-627-3017. E-mail: pcs@infonet.tufts.edu.

The University of Alabama at Birmingham, Graduate School, School of Health Related Professions, Program in Occupational Therapy, Birmingham, AL 35294. Awards MS. Students: 29 full-time (23 women), 2 part-time (both women); includes 1 minority (Asian American). 17 applicants, 88% accepted. In 1997, 5 degrees awarded. *Degree requirements:* Thesis or alternative required, foreign language not required. *Entrance requirements:* GRE General Test (minimum score 500 on each section), minimum GPA of 3.0 in last 60 hours. Application deadline: rolling. Application fee: $30 ($60 for international students). Electronic applications accepted. *Expenses:* Tuition $129 per credit hour for state residents; $258 per credit hour for nonresidents. Fees $627 per year (minimum) full-time, $110 per quarter (minimum) part-time. *Faculty research:* Social relationships with disabled people, family unit, community health programs, psychosocial aspects, alternative therapies. • Caroline F. Amari, Director, 205-934-3568. Fax: 205-975-7302.

University of Alberta, Faculty of Graduate Studies and Research, Department of Occupational Therapy, Edmonton, AB T6G 2E1, Canada. Awards M Sc. Part-time programs available. Faculty: 8 full-time (6 women). Students: 3 full-time (all women), 7 part-time (all women). Average age 28. 2 applicants, 100% accepted. In 1997, 7 degrees awarded (100% found work related to degree). *Degree requirements:* Thesis required (for some programs), foreign language not required. *Entrance requirements:* TOEFL or TSE, bachelor's degree in occupational therapy, minimum GPA of 6.9 on a 9.0 scale. Application deadline: 4/1 (priority date; rolling processing; 10/15 for spring admission). Application fee: $60. *Expenses:* Tuition $390 per course for Canadian residents; $781 per course for nonresidents. Fees $500 per year full-time, $184 per year part-time. *Financial aid:* In 1997–98, 2 research assistantships, 1 teaching assistantship, 3 scholarships, tuition scholarships (1 to a first-year student) were awarded; institutionally sponsored loans and career-related internships or fieldwork also available. *Faculty research:* Work evaluation, pediatrics, geriatrics, program evaluation, community-based rehabilitation. • M. Miyazaki, Acting Chair, 403-492-0399. E-mail: masako.miyazaki@ualberta.ca. Application contact: Vicki Ross, Administrative Assistant, Graduate Studies, 403-492-1595. Fax: 403-492-1626. E-mail: vicki.ross@ualberta.ca.

University of Central Arkansas, College of Health and Applied Sciences, Department of Occupational Therapy, Conway, AR 72035-0001. Awards MS. Faculty: 2 full-time (both women), 1 (woman) part-time, 2.25 FTE. Students: 7 part-time (6 women); includes 1 minority (Asian American). 2 applicants, 100% accepted. In 1997, 2 degrees awarded. *Degree requirements:* Thesis optional. *Entrance requirements:* GRE General Test, minimum GPA of 2.7. Application deadline: 3/1 (priority date; rolling processing; 10/1 for spring admission). Application fee: $15 ($40 for international students). *Expenses:* Tuition $161 per credit hour for state residents; $298 per credit hour for nonresidents. Fees $150 per year. *Financial aid:* Application deadline 2/15. • Dr. Linda Shalik, Chair, 501-450-3192. Fax: 501-450-5503. E-mail: lindas@mail.uca.edu.

University of Florida, College of Health Professions, Department of Occupational Therapy, Gainesville, FL 32611. Awards MHS. Accredited by AOTA. Faculty: 4. Students: 28 full-time (21 women), 4 part-time (3 women); includes 7 minority (1 African American, 3 Asian Americans, 3 Hispanics). Average age 28. 39 applicants, 33% accepted. In 1997, 11 degrees awarded. *Degree requirements:* Research project required, thesis not required. *Entrance requirements:* GRE General Test (minimum combined score of 1000), minimum GPA of 3.0. Application deadline: 2/15 (10/15 for spring admission). Application fee: $20. *Tuition:* $138 per credit hour for state residents; $481 per credit hour for nonresidents. *Financial aid:* In 1997–98, 8 students received aid, including 8 graduate assistantships averaging $670 per month; fellowships, research assistantships, teaching assistantships, institutionally sponsored loans, and career-related internships or fieldwork also available. Aid available to part-time students. *Faculty research:* Occupational therapy related to ergonomics, body image, pediatrics, HIV, and hand therapy. Total annual research expenditures: $4998. • Dr. Kay F. Walker, Chairperson, 352-392-2617. Fax: 352-846-1042. E-mail: kwalker@hp.ufl.edu. Application contact: Dr. Julia VanDeusen, Graduate Coordinator, 352-392-2617. Fax: 352-846-1019. E-mail: jvandeusen@hp.ufl.edu.

University of Illinois at Chicago, College of Associated Health Professions, Program in Occupational Therapy, Chicago, IL 60607-7128. Awards MS. Accredited by AOTA. Part-time programs available. Faculty: 5 full-time (3 women). Students: 26 full-time (23 women), 7 part-time (all women); includes 3 minority (1 Asian American, 2 Hispanics), 2 international. Average age 31. 16 applicants, 63% accepted. In 1997, 6 degrees awarded. *Degree requirements:* Thesis required, foreign language not required. *Entrance requirements:* GRE General Test, TOEFL (minimum score 550), minimum GPA of 3.75 on a 5.0 scale, previous course work in statistics. Application deadline: 7/3 (11/8 for spring admission). Application fee: $40 ($50 for international students). *Financial aid:* In 1997–98, 2 research assistantships, 1 traineeship were awarded; fellowships, teaching assistantships, Federal Work-Study, and career-related internships or fieldwork also available. *Faculty research:* Sensory integration, perception, play, treatment efficacy, instrument development. • Dr. Gary Kielhofner, Head, 312-996-6901.

University of Indianapolis, Department of Occupational Therapy, Indianapolis, IN 46227-3697. Awards MS. Accredited by AOTA. Part-time and evening/weekend programs available. *Degree requirements:* Thesis required, foreign language not required. *Average time to degree:* master's–2.5 years full-time, 4 years part-time. *Entrance requirements:* GRE General Test. Application deadline: 1/2. Application fee: $50.

University of Kansas, School of Allied Health, Department of Occupational Therapy, Kansas City, KS 66160. Awards MS. Part-time programs available. Faculty: 6 full-time (5 women), 4 part-time (all women). Students: 6 part-time (all women). Average age 31. 5 applicants, 40% accepted. In 1997, 7 degrees awarded. *Degree requirements:* Thesis required, foreign language not required. *Entrance requirements:* GRE General Test, TOEFL (minimum score 570), bachelor's degree in occupational therapy, occupational therapist certificate, 1 year of occupational therapy experience. Application deadline: 4/1. Application fee: $25. *Expenses:* Tuition $2400 per year full-time, $100 per credit hour part-time for state residents; $7890 per year full-time, $329 per credit hour part-time for nonresidents. Fees $428 per year full-time, $31 per credit hour part-time. *Financial aid:* Research assistantships, traineeships, Federal Work-Study, institutionally sponsored loans, and career-related internships or fieldwork available. Aid available to part-time students. Financial aid application deadline: 4/3; applicants required to submit FAFSA. • Dr. Winifred W. Dunn, Chair, 913-588-7195. Application contact: Dr. Joan McDowd, Graduate Director, 913-588-7195. Fax: 913-588-4568. E-mail: jmcdowd@kumc.edu.

University of New Hampshire, School of Health and Human Services, Department of Occupational Therapy, Durham, NH 03824. Awards MS. Accredited by AOTA. Faculty: 8 full-time. Students: 34 part-time (33 women). Average age 36. 11 applicants, 100% accepted. In 1997, 5 degrees awarded. *Degree requirements:* Thesis or alternative required, foreign language not required. *Entrance requirements:* GRE General Test. Application deadline: 4/1. Application fee: $50. *Expenses:* Tuition $5440 per year full-time, $302 per credit hour part-time for state residents; $8160 per year (minimum) full-time, $453 per credit hour (minimum) part-time for nonresidents. Fees $868 per year full-time, $15 per year part-time. *Financial aid:* In 1997–98, 1 fellowship (to a first-year student) was awarded. Financial aid application deadline: 2/15. • Dr. Alice Seidel, Chairperson, 603-862-3422. Application contact: Lou Ann Griswold, Graduate Coordinator, 603-862-3438.

The University of North Carolina at Chapel Hill, School of Medicine and Graduate School, Graduate Programs in Medicine, Department of Medical Allied Health Professions, Division of Occupational Science, Chapel Hill, NC 27599. Awards MS. Accredited by AOTA. Faculty: 6 full-time (all women). Students: 46 full-time (40 women); includes 2 minority (both Asian Americans). Average age 32. 191 applicants, 13% accepted. In 1997, 19 degrees awarded. *Degree requirements:* Collaborative research project, comprehensive exam required, thesis optional, foreign language not required. *Average time to degree:* master's–2 years full-time. *Entrance requirements:* GRE General Test (combined average 1147). Application fee: $55. Electronic applications accepted. *Expenses:* Tuition $1428 per year for state residents; $10,414 per year for nonresidents. Fees $782 per year. *Financial aid:* 35 students received aid; graduate assistantships and career-related internships or fieldwork available. Financial aid application deadline: 3/1; applicants required to submit FAFSA. *Faculty research:* Parents and infants in co-occupations, psychosocial dysfunction, predictors of autism, factors influencing the occupation of primates, administration and leadership. Total annual research expenditures: $33,923. • Dr. Ruth Humphry, Director, 919-966-2451. E-mail: rhumphry@css.unc.edu. Application contact: Carol L. Perry, Coordinator, 919-966-2451. Fax: 919-966-9007. E-mail: cperry@css.unc.edu.

University of Pittsburgh, School of Health and Rehabilitation Sciences, Interdisciplinary Program in Health and Rehabilitation Sciences, Pittsburgh, PA 15260. Offerings include occupational therapy (MS). *Entrance requirements:* GRE General Test, TOEFL, minimum QPA of 3.0. Application deadline: rolling. Application fee: $30 ($40 for international students). *Expenses:* Tuition $9402 per year full-time, $388 per credit part-time for state residents; $19,372 per year full-time, $799 per credit part-time for nonresidents. Fees $480 per year full-time, $180 per year part-time. • Dr. George Carvell, Associate Dean of Graduate Studies, 412-647-1296. E-mail: shrsadmit+@pitt.edu. Application contact: Shameem Gangjee, Director of Admissions, 412-647-1258. Fax: 412-647-1255. E-mail: shrsadmit+@pitt.edu.

See in-depth description on page 1351.

University of Puget Sound, School of Occupational and Physical Therapy, Program in Occupational Therapy, Tacoma, WA 98416-0005. Awards MOT. Accredited by AOTA. Faculty: 7 full-time (4 women), 6 part-time (4 women), 7.76 FTE. Students: 39 full-time (33 women), 2 part-time (both women); includes 7 minority (5 Asian Americans, 2 Hispanics), 1 international. Average age 31. 156 applicants, 10% accepted. In 1997, 17 degrees awarded. *Degree requirements:* Thesis or alternative, publishable paper. *Entrance requirements:* GRE General Test, minimum GPA of 3.0. Application deadline: 2/1. Application fee: $40. *Expenses:* Tuition $19,640 per year full-time, $2480 per course part-time. Fees $155 per year. *Financial aid:* In 1997–98, 1 research assistantship, 3 teaching assistantships were awarded; Federal Work-Study and career-related internships or fieldwork also available. • Kathy Stewart, Chair, 253-756-1327. Application contact: George Mills, Director of Admissions, 253-756-3211.

University of St. Augustine for Health Sciences, Graduate Programs, Division of First Professional Education, St. Augustine, FL 32084. Awards MOT, MPT. Faculty: 13 full-time (7 women), 5 part-time (3 women). Students: 264 full-time (145 women), 2 part-time (0 women); includes 24 minority (5 African Americans, 10 Asian Americans, 9 Hispanics), 2 international. Average age 27. 284 applicants, 19% accepted. In 1997, 98 degrees awarded (100% found work related to degree). *Average time to degree:* master's–2 years full-time. *Entrance requirements:* GRE General Test (minimum combined score of 1000), minimum GPA of 3.0. Application deadline: 2/1 (priority date; 7/15 for spring admission). Application fee: $50. • Raymond M. Patterson, Director, 904-823-0013. Application contact: Julie T. Cook, Admissions Coordinator/Registrar, 904-810-0330. Fax: 904-826-4193.

University of South Dakota, School of Medicine and Graduate School, Graduate Programs in Health Sciences, Department of Occupational Therapy, Vermillion, SD 57069-2390. Awards MS. Accredited by AOTA. Faculty: 3 full-time (2 women), 2 part-time (both women). Students: 78 full-time (67 women). Average age 25. 106 applicants, 25% accepted. In 1997, 26 degrees awarded (100% found work related to degree). *Average time to degree:* master's–2.5 years full-time. *Entrance requirements:* GRE General Test, GRE Subject Test. Application deadline: 2/1. Application fee: $15. *Financial aid:* Career-related internships or fieldwork available. • Denise Rotert, Interim Chairperson, 605-677-6241. Application contact: Dr. Charles N. Kaufman, Dean of the Graduate School, 605-677-6498.

University of Southern California, Graduate School, School of Health Affairs, Department of Occupational Therapy, Program in Occupational Science, Los Angeles, CA 90089. Awards PhD. Students: 15 full-time (13 women), 12 part-time (11 women); includes 4 minority (2 African Americans, 1 Asian American, 1 Hispanic), 4 international. Average age 41. 6 applicants,

67% accepted. In 1997, 2 degrees awarded. *Degree requirements:* Dissertation. *Entrance requirements:* GRE General Test. Application deadline: 2/1 (priority date). Application fee: $55. *Expenses:* Tuition $16,944 per year full-time, $706 per unit part-time. Fees $414 per year full-time, $32 per year part-time. *Financial aid:* In 1997–98, 5 fellowships, 4 teaching assistantships, 6 scholarships were awarded; research assistantships, Federal Work-Study, institutionally sponsored loans also available. Aid available to part-time students. Financial aid application deadline: 2/15; applicants required to submit FAFSA. • Dr. Florence Clark, Chair, Department of Occupational Therapy, 323-442-2850.

University of Southern California, Graduate School, School of Health Affairs, Department of Occupational Therapy, Program in Occupational Therapy, Los Angeles, CA 90089. Awards MA. Accredited by AOTA. Students: 158 full-time (135 women), 8 part-time (5 women); includes 54 minority (2 African Americans, 50 Asian Americans, 2 Hispanics), 14 international. Average age 27. 31 applicants, 48% accepted. In 1997, 60 degrees awarded. *Degree requirements:* Thesis (for some programs). *Entrance requirements:* GRE General Test. Application deadline: 3/31 (priority date; rolling processing). Application fee: $55. *Expenses:* Tuition $16,944 per year full-time, $706 per unit part-time. Fees $414 per year full-time, $32 per year part-time. *Financial aid:* In 1997–98, 12 fellowships, 4 teaching assistantships, 10 scholarships were awarded; research assistantships, Federal Work-Study, institutionally sponsored loans also available. Aid available to part-time students. Financial aid application deadline: 2/15; applicants required to submit FAFSA. • Dr. Florence Clark, Chair, Department of Occupational Therapy, 323-442-2850.

University of Washington, School of Medicine and Graduate School, Graduate Programs in Medicine, Department of Rehabilitation Medicine, Program in Occupational Therapy, Seattle, WA 98195. Awards MS. Part-time programs available. Faculty: 4 full-time (3 women), 3 part-time (2 women), 4.6 FTE. Average age 32. 0 applicants. *Degree requirements:* Thesis required, foreign language not required. *Average time to degree:* master's–2 years full-time. *Entrance requirements:* GRE General Test (minimum score 500 on each section), professional degree in occupational therapy. Application deadline: 3/1 (priority date). *Financial aid:* Traineeships and career-related internships or fieldwork available. *Faculty research:* Pediatrics, technology, pain, mental health, physical disabilities. • Application contact: Jean L. Deitz, Graduate Coordinator, 206-685-7412. Fax: 206-685-3244. E-mail: ot@u.washington.edu.

The University of Western Ontario, Biosciences Division, School of Occupational Therapy, London, ON N6A 5B8, Canada. Awards M Sc. Part-time programs available. Postbaccalaureate distance learning degree programs offered (minimal on-campus study). Faculty: 8 full-time (all women). Students: 6 full-time (5 women), 8 part-time (all women). Average age 35. 9 applicants, 78% accepted. In 1997, 6 degrees awarded (16% entered university research/teaching, 68% found other work related to degree, 16% continued full-time study). *Degree requirements:* Thesis required, foreign language not required. *Average time to degree:* master's–1.3 years full-time, 1.9 years part-time. *Entrance requirements:* Canadian BA degree in occupational therapy or equivalent, minimum B+ average in last 2 years. Application deadline: 2/15 (priority date; rolling processing). *Financial aid:* In 1997–98, 5 students received aid, including 5 teaching assistantships (all to first-year students) averaging $1,000 per month and totaling $40,000, special university scholarships averaging $250 per month and totaling $16,000. Financial aid application deadline: 4/1. *Faculty research:* Human occupation, clumsy children, biomechanics, learning disabilities, ergonomics, mental health services. Total annual research expenditures: $192,587. • Dr. H. J. Polatajko, Director, 519-661-2124. E-mail: hpolataj@julian.uwo.ca. Application contact: Dr. S. Spaulding, Chair, Graduate Program, 519-661-2175 Ext. 8956. Fax: 519-661-3894. E-mail: sspauldi@julian.uwo.ca.

University of Wisconsin–Milwaukee, School of Allied Health Professions, Program in Occupational Therapy, Milwaukee, WI 53201-0413. Awards MS. Faculty: 7 full-time (5 women). Students: 10 part-time (all women). *Degree requirements:* Thesis or alternative. *Application deadline:* 1/1 (priority date; rolling processing; 9/1 for spring admission). *Application fee:* $45 ($75 for international students). *Tuition:* $4996 per year full-time, $1030 per semester (minimum) part-time for state residents; $15,216 per year full-time, $2947 per semester (minimum) part-time for nonresidents. *Financial aid:* In 1997–98, 1 research assistantship was awarded; fellowships, teaching assistantships, project assistantships also available. Aid available to part-time students. Financial aid application deadline: 4/15. • Judith Falconer, Director, 414-229-4713.

Virginia Commonwealth University, School of Allied Health Professions, Department of Occupational Therapy, Richmond, VA 23284-9005. Awards MS, MSOT. One or more programs accredited by AOTA. Faculty: 8 full-time. Students: 37 full-time (29 women); includes 1 minority (Asian American). Average age 27. 256 applicants, 13% accepted. In 1997, 19 degrees awarded. *Degree requirements:* Fieldwork. *Entrance requirements:* GRE General Test, supplemental application for MSOT. Application deadline: 2/1. Application fee: $30 ($0 for international students). *Tuition:* $4960 per year full-time, $257 per credit part-time for state residents; $12,652 per year full-time, $684 per credit part-time for nonresidents. *Faculty research:* Children with complex care needs, instrument development, carpal tunnel syndrome, development of oral-motor feeding programs, school system practice. • Dr. Shelly J. Lane, Chair, 804-828-2219. Fax: 804-828-0782. E-mail: sjlane@vcu.edu.

Washington University in St. Louis, School of Medicine, Graduate Programs in Medicine, Program in Occupational Therapy, St. Louis, MO 63108-2292. Awards MA, MSOT. Accredited by AOTA. Faculty: 21 full-time, 10 part-time, 28.45 FTE. Students: 213 full-time; includes 17 minority (4 African Americans, 10 Asian Americans, 2 Hispanics, 1 Native American). Average age 26. 240 applicants, 42% accepted. In 1997, 103 degrees awarded. *Average time to degree:* master's–2.5 years full-time, 3.5 years part-time. *Entrance requirements:* GRE General Test (combined average 1500 on three sections), minimum GPA of 3.0. Application deadline: 2/15. Application fee: $50. *Tuition:* $19,500 per year full-time, $650 per credit hour part-time. *Financial aid:* Fellowships, minority and need-based scholarships, cost stabilization programs available. Aid available to part-time students. Financial aid applicants required to submit FAFSA. *Faculty research:* Quality of life, cognitive assessment, child-parent interaction, work performance, disability technology. Total annual research expenditures: $400,000. • Dr. Carolyn Baum, Director, 314-286-1600. E-mail: wuotinfo@ot-link.wustl.edu. Application contact: Rhonda Corsey-Pratt, Coordinator, Recruitment and Public Relations, 314-286-1600. Fax: 314-286-1601. E-mail: wuotinfo@ot-lint.wustl.edu.

See in-depth description on page 1271.

Wayne State University, College of Pharmacy and Allied Health Professions, Faculty of Allied Health Professions, Department of Occupational Therapy, Detroit, MI 48202. Awards MS. Part-time programs available. Faculty: 5 full-time (all women), 1 (woman) part-time, 10.5 FTE. Students: 1 (woman) full-time, 9 part-time (8 women); includes 4 minority (2 African Americans, 2 Asian Americans), 1 international. Average age 35. 3 applicants, 67% accepted. In 1997, 3 degrees awarded. *Degree requirements:* Thesis optional, foreign language not required. *Application deadline:* 7/1 (rolling processing; 3/15 for spring admission). *Application fee:* $20 ($30 for international students). *Expenses:* Tuition $163 per credit hour for state residents; $355 per credit hour for nonresidents. Fees $498 per year full-time, $114 per semester (minimum) part-time. *Financial aid:* Teaching assistantships, scholarships, and career-related internships or fieldwork available. Aid available to part-time students. *Faculty research:* Gerontic occupational therapy, program evaluation, sensory integration, developmental disabilities. • Susan Esdaile, Chairperson, 313-577-1435.

Western Michigan University, College of Health and Human Services, Department of Occupational Therapy, Kalamazoo, MI 49008. Awards MS. Accredited by AOTA. Students: 49 full-time (41 women), 27 part-time (17 women); includes 8 minority (1 African American, 7 Asian Americans), 3 international. 180 applicants, 14% accepted. In 1997, 25 degrees awarded. *Entrance requirements:* GRE General Test. Application deadline: 3/15 (priority date; rolling processing). Application fee: $25. *Expenses:* Tuition $154 per credit hour for state residents; $372 per credit hour for nonresidents. Fees $602 per year full-time, $132 per semester part-time. *Financial aid:* Fellowships, research assistantships, teaching assistantships, Federal Work-Study available. Financial aid application deadline: 2/15; applicants required to submit FAFSA. • Dr. Susan Meyers, Chairperson, 616-387-3850. Application contact: Paula J. Boodt, Coordinator, Graduate Admissions and Recruitment, 616-387-2000. E-mail: paulaboodt@wmich.edu.

West Virginia University, School of Medicine, Graduate Programs in Human Performance and Applied Exercise Science, Program in Occupational Therapy, Morgantown, WV 26506. Awards MOT. Students enter program as undergraduates. *Degree requirements:* Clinical rotation. *Application deadline:* 3/1. *Application fee:* $45. *Tuition:* $9204 per year for state residents; $22,704 per year for nonresidents. • Reg Urbanowski, Chair, 304-293-8828. Fax: 304-293-7105. Application contact: Dr. Randy McCombie, Assistant Professor.

Worcester State College, Graduate Studies, Department of Occupational Therapy, Worcester, MA 01602-2597. Awards MS. *Degree requirements:* Comprehensive exam. *Entrance requirements:* GRE General Test or MAT, minimum undergraduate GPA of 3.2. Application deadline: 4/20. Application fee: $10 ($40 for international students). *Tuition:* $395 per credit hour. • Dr. Donna Joss, Chair, 508-929-8119. Application contact: Andrea Wetmore, Graduate Admissions Counselor, 508-929-8120. E-mail: awetmore@worc.mass.edu.

Xavier University, College of Social Sciences, Department of Occupational Therapy, Cincinnati, OH 45207-2111. Awards Certificate. Faculty: 4 full-time (all women), 2 part-time (1 woman), 4.5 FTE. Students: 25 full-time (22 women), 12 part-time (10 women); includes 1 minority (African American). Average age 32. 35 applicants, 49% accepted. In 1997, 11 degrees awarded. *Entrance requirements:* GRE, minimum GPA of 3.0. Application deadline: 2/1. Application fee: $25. *Tuition:* $475 per credit hour. *Financial aid:* In 1997–98, 3 students received aid, including 3 scholarships (2 to first-year students); career-related internships or fieldwork also available. Aid available to part-time students. • Jo Anne Estes, Interim Chair, 513-745-3150. Fax: 513-745-3261. E-mail: estesj@admin.xu.edu. Application contact: Sheila Speth, Director of Graduate Services, 513-745-3360. Fax: 513-745-1048. E-mail: xugrad@admin.xu.edu.

Physical Therapy

Alabama State University, School of Graduate Studies, College of Arts and Sciences, Department of Allied Health Science, Program in Physical Therapy, Montgomery, AL 36101-0271. Awards MS. Program new for fall 1998. *Application deadline:* 7/15 (rolling processing; 12/15 for spring admission). *Application fee:* $10. *Expenses:* Tuition $85 per credit hour for state residents; $170 per credit hour for nonresidents. Fees $486 per year. • Dr. Claudelle Carruthers, Associate Dean, Department of Allied Health Science, 334-229-4707.

Allegheny University of the Health Sciences, School of Health Professions, Department of Physical Therapy, Program in Movement Science in Physical Therapy, Philadelphia, PA 19102-1192. Awards MS, PhD. One or more programs accredited by APTA. Students: 1 (woman) full-time, 1 (woman) part-time; includes 1 international. Terminal master's awarded for partial completion of doctoral program. *Degree requirements:* For master's, thesis, comprehensive exam required, foreign language not required. *Entrance requirements:* For master's, GRE General Test, minimum GPA of 3.0. Application deadline: 6/1 (rolling processing). Application fee: $50. *Expenses:* Tuition $11,500 per year full-time, $640 per credit part-time. Fees $125 per year. *Financial aid:* Federal Work-Study, institutionally sponsored loans, and career-related internships or fieldwork available. Aid available to part-time students. Financial aid application deadline: 5/1; applicants required to submit FAFSA. • Robert Palisano, Director, 215-762-1006. E-mail: palisano@auhs.edu.

Allegheny University of the Health Sciences, School of Health Professions, Department of Physical Therapy, Program in Orthopedic Physical Therapy, Philadelphia, PA 19102-1192. Awards MS, PhD. One or more programs accredited by APTA. Part-time programs available. Faculty: 13 full-time (7 women), 14 part-time (11 women). Students: 4 full-time (3 women), 9 part-time (5 women); includes 1 minority (Asian American), 3 international. Average age 32. 13 applicants, 31% accepted. In 1997, 4 master's awarded. Terminal master's awarded for partial completion of doctoral program. *Degree requirements:* For master's, thesis, comprehensive exam required, foreign language not required; for doctorate, dissertation, qualifying exam required, foreign language not required. *Entrance requirements:* For master's, GRE General Test (minimum combined score of 1410 on three sections), physical therapist license, 2 years of experience, minimum GPA of 2.5; for doctorate, GRE General Test (minimum combined score of 1650 on three sections), physical therapist license, 2 years of experience, minimum GPA of 3.0. Application deadline: 6/1 (rolling processing). Application fee: $50. *Expenses:* Tuition $11,500 per year full-time, $640 per credit part-time. Fees $125 per year. *Financial aid:* Teaching assistantships, partial tuition waivers, institutionally sponsored loans, and career-related internships or fieldwork available. Aid available to part-time students. Financial aid application deadline: 5/1; applicants required to submit FAFSA. *Faculty research:* Posture analysis, muscle performance, functional anatomy, efficacy of clinical treatment approaches, developmental assessment. • Dr. Neal Pratt, Director, 215-762-4364.

See in-depth description on page 1233.

Allegheny University of the Health Sciences, School of Health Professions, Department of Physical Therapy, Program in Pediatric Physical Therapy, Philadelphia, PA 19102-1192. Awards MS, PhD. One or more programs accredited by APTA. Part-time programs available. Faculty: 13 full-time (7 women), 14 part-time (11 women). Students: 6 full-time (5 women), 9 part-time (8 women); includes 3 international. Average age 34. 11 applicants, 73% accepted. In 1997, 1 master's, 3 doctorates awarded. Terminal master's awarded for partial completion of doctoral program. *Degree requirements:* For master's, computer language, thesis, comprehensive exam required, foreign language not required; for doctorate, computer language, dissertation, qualifying exam required, foreign language not required. *Entrance requirements:* For master's, GRE General Test (minimum combined score of 1410 on three sections), physical therapist license, 2 years of experience, minimum GPA of 2.5; for doctorate, GRE General Test (minimum combined score of 1650 on three sections), physical therapist license, 2 years of experience, minimum GPA of 2.75. Application deadline: 6/1 (rolling processing). Application fee: $50. *Expenses:* Tuition $11,500 per year full-time, $640 per credit part-time. Fees $125 per year. *Financial aid:* Research assistantships, teaching assistantships, Federal Work-Study, institutionally sponsored loans, and career-related internships or fieldwork available. Aid available to part-time students. Financial aid application deadline: 5/1; applicants required to submit FAFSA.

Directory: Physical Therapy

Allegheny University of the Health Sciences (continued)

Faculty research: Pediatric gait dysfunction, cerebral palsy, measurement outcome, early intervention service delivery. • Dr. Susan Effgen, Director, 215-762-1758.

See in-depth description on page 1233.

Allegheny University of the Health Sciences, School of Health Professions, Department of Physical Therapy, Program in Physical Therapy, Philadelphia, PA 19102-1192. Awards MPT. Accredited by APTA. Faculty: 13 full-time (7 women), 14 part-time (11 women). Students: 165 full-time (114 women), 1 (woman) part-time; includes 13 minority (4 African Americans, 7 Asian Americans, 2 Hispanics). Average age 25. 510 applicants, 29% accepted. In 1997, 73 degrees awarded. *Degree requirements:* Complete research proposal, comprehensive exam required, foreign language and thesis not required. *Average time to degree:* master's–2 years full-time. *Entrance requirements:* GRE General Test (minimum combined score of 1500 on three sections), minimum GPA of 3.0. Application deadline: 12/15 (rolling processing). Application fee: $50. *Expenses:* Tuition $17,680 per year. Fees $338 per year. *Financial aid:* Teaching assistantships, rehabilitation training grants, Federal Work-Study, institutionally sponsored loans, and career-related internships or fieldwork available. Aid available to part-time students. Financial aid application deadline: 5/1; applicants required to submit FAFSA. *Faculty research:* Isokinetics, gait dysfunction, neuromuscular facilitation, early intervention pediatrics. • Dr. Risa Granick, Executive Director, 215-762-1750.

Announcement: The Department offers entry-level (MPT), a DPT extension program, and advanced master's (MS, MHS) and doctoral (PhD) education. A challenging and rewarding environment supports the attainment of competencies necessary for practice, teaching, and clinical research. A dynamic, multidisciplinary faculty fosters the knowledge and skills essential for careers in the health-care system and academe.

See in-depth description on page 1233.

American International College, School of Continuing Education and Graduate Studies, Program in Physical Therapy, Springfield, MA 01109-3189. Awards MPT. *Entrance requirements:* Minimum GPA of 3.0, sample of written work. Application fee: $15 ($25 for international students). *Expenses:* Tuition $363 per credit hour. Fees $25 per semester. *Financial aid:* Career-related internships or fieldwork available. Aid available to part-time students. • Edward Swanson, Director, 413-747-6412. Application contact: Peter Miller, Director of Admissions, 413-747-6201.

Andrews University, School of Graduate Studies, College of Arts and Sciences, Department of Physical Therapy, Master of Science Program in Physical Therapy, Berrien Springs, MI 49104. Awards MSPT. Accredited by APTA. Faculty: 10 full-time (5 women), 18 part-time (5 women). Students: 124 full-time (74 women); includes 34 minority (8 African Americans, 16 Asian Americans, 10 Hispanics), 20 international. Average age 23. 201 applicants, 36% accepted. In 1997, 36 degrees awarded (100% found work related to degree). *Degree requirements:* Research project, oral presentation, publishable paper required, foreign language and thesis not required. *Average time to degree:* master's–3 years full-time. *Entrance requirements:* GRE General Test, 2 years of college. Application deadline: 11/30. Application fee: $80. *Financial aid:* Federal Work-Study, institutionally sponsored loans available. Financial aid application deadline: 3/1; applicants required to submit FAFSA. *Faculty research:* Gait training on children with cerebral palsy, reliability of submaximal O&I2 consumption on children with MR, breeding success of marine birds. Total annual research expenditures: $2225. • Wayne L. Perry, Director, 616-471-2878. E-mail: perryw@andrews.edu. Application contact: MaryJane Rasnic, Director of Admissions, 800-827-2878. Fax: 616-471-2866. E-mail: pt-info@andrews.edu.

Andrews University, School of Graduate Studies, College of Arts and Sciences, Department of Physical Therapy, Master's Program in Physical Therapy, Dayton, Ohio 45469. Awards MPT. Accredited by APTA. Faculty: 8 full-time (3 women), 22 part-time (15 women). Students: 104 full-time (62 women); includes 7 minority (1 African American, 3 Asian Americans, 2 Hispanics, 1 Native American), 5 international. Average age 27. 468 applicants, 25% accepted. In 1997, 38 degrees awarded. *Degree requirements:* Research proposal. *Average time to degree:* master's–2 years full-time. *Entrance requirements:* GRE General Test, bachelor's degree with minimum GPA of 2.75. Application deadline: 11/30. Application fee: $80. *Financial aid:* 104 students received aid; Federal Work-Study, institutionally sponsored loans available. Financial aid application deadline: 3/1; applicants required to submit FAFSA. *Faculty research:* Effects of exercise on multiple sclerosis patients. Total annual research expenditures: $13,000. • Dr. Daryl Stuart, Director, 937-298-2878. Fax: 937-298-9500. E-mail: stuart@andrews.edu. Application contact: MaryJane Rasnic, Director of Admissions, 800-827-2878. Fax: 616-471-2866. E-mail: pt-info@andrews.edu.

Armstrong Atlantic State University, School of Graduate Studies, Program in Physical Therapy, Savannah, GA 31419-1997. Awards MSPT. Accredited by APTA. Faculty: 6. *Expenses:* Tuition $83 per quarter hour for state residents; $250 per quarter hour for nonresidents. Fees $145 per quarter hour for state residents; $228 per quarter hour for nonresidents. • Dr. David Lake, Department Head, 912-921-2327.

Azusa Pacific University, College of Liberal Arts and Sciences, Department of Physical Therapy, Azusa, CA 91702-7000. Awards MPT. Faculty: 3 full-time (1 woman). Students: 62 full-time. Average age 24. 40 applicants, 63% accepted. *Entrance requirements:* GRE General Test. Application deadline: 6/15 (rolling processing). Application fee: $45 ($65 for international students). *Expenses:* Tuition $380 per unit. Fees $57 per year. *Financial aid:* Career-related internships or fieldwork available. *Faculty research:* FES and spinal cord injury, electromyogram and muscle pathology, thermal regulation and body composition. • Dr. Michael Laymon, Chair, 626-815-6000 Ext. 5020.

Baylor University, Academy of Health Sciences, Program in Physical Therapy, Fort Sam Houston, TX 78234. Awards MPT. Accredited by APTA. Offered jointly with the U.S. Army. Students: 19 full-time (7 women). In 1997, 24 degrees awarded (100% found work related to degree). *Degree requirements:* Comprehensive oral exam, research paper required, foreign language and thesis not required. *Entrance requirements:* GRE General Test (minimum combined score of 1000). Application deadline: 2/1 (rolling processing). Application fee: $25. *Faculty research:* Effect of electrical stimulation on normal and immobilized muscle, effects of inversion traction. • Lt. Col. Michael A. Smutok, Director, 210-221-5187.

Beaver College, Department of Physical Therapy, Glenside, PA 19038-3295. Awards MSPT. Accredited by APTA. *Entrance requirements:* GRE, TOEFL. Application deadline: 1/31. Application fee: $45. *Expenses:* Tuition $18,970 per year. Fees $850 per year.

Belmont University, Program in Physical Therapy, Nashville, TN 37212-3757. Awards MPT. Faculty: 8 full-time (4 women), 33 part-time (17 women), 12 FTE. Students: 32 full-time (17 women); includes 2 minority (1 Asian American, 1 Native American). 70 applicants, 46% accepted. *Entrance requirements:* GRE General Test (minimum combined score of 1000; average 1070). Application deadline: 2/1. Application fee: $50. *Tuition:* $560 per credit hour. *Faculty research:* Clinical outcomes, assessment of curriculum, clinical electrophysiology, cardiopulmonary physical therapy, orthopedics, manual therapy. • Dr. David G. Greathouse, Chair, 615-963-4195. E-mail: greathouse@pcmail.belmont.edu. Application contact: Lucy Baltimore, Program Assistant, 615-963-4195. Fax: 615-963-4405. E-mail: baltimorel@pcmail.belmont.edu.

Boston University, Sargent College of Health and Rehabilitation Sciences, Department of Physical Therapy, Boston, MA 02215. Offers programs in applied kinesiology (D Sc), physical therapy (MS, MSPT). One or more programs accredited by APTA. Faculty: 14 full-time (11 women), 5 part-time (1 woman). Students: 280 full-time (206 women), 7 part-time (4 women); includes 31 minority (3 African Americans, 26 Asian Americans, 2 Hispanics), 1 international. Average age 25. 700 applicants, 13% accepted. In 1997, 123 master's awarded. *Degree requirements:* For master's, thesis (MS) required, foreign language not required; for doctorate, computer language, dissertation required, foreign language not required. *Entrance requirements:* For master's, GRE General Test (minimum combined score of 1000; average 1350); for doctorate, GRE General Test (minimum combined score of 1000; average 1350), master's degree. Application deadline: 2/1 (rolling processing). Application fee: $50. *Expenses:* Tuition $22,830 per year full-time, $713 per credit part-time. Fees $218 per year full-time, $40 per semester part-time. *Financial aid:* In 1997–98, 10 teaching assistantships were awarded; scholarships, Federal Work-Study, institutionally sponsored loans, and career-related internships or fieldwork also available. Financial aid application deadline: 4/15. *Faculty research:* EMG, gait, infant assessment, motor control, orthopedics. • Dr. Catherine Certo, Chairman, 617-353-2720.

See in-depth description on page 1235.

California State University, Fresno, Division of Graduate Studies, School of Health and Social Work, Department of Physical Therapy, 5241 North Maple Avenue, Fresno, CA 93740. Awards MPT. Accredited by APTA. Faculty: 10 full-time (5 women). Students: 91 full-time (63 women); includes 24 minority (1 African American, 12 Asian Americans, 8 Hispanics, 3 Native Americans). Average age 31. 30 applicants, 97% accepted. In 1997, 33 degrees awarded. *Average time to degree:* master's–3.5 years full-time. *Entrance requirements:* GRE General Test, TOEFL (minimum score 550), minimum GPA of 3.0. Application deadline: 10/31 (priority date; rolling processing). Application fee: $55. Electronic applications accepted. *Expenses:* Tuition $0 for state residents; $246 per unit for nonresidents. Fees $1872 per year full-time, $1206 per year part-time. *Financial aid:* In 1997–98, 1 fellowship totaling $4,500, graduate assistantships, scholarships totaling $119,114 was awarded; research assistantships also available. Financial aid application deadline: 3/1; applicants required to submit FAFSA. *Faculty research:* Dance, occupational health, ethics. • Darlene Stewart, Chair, 209-278-2625. Fax: 209-278-4437. E-mail: darlene_stewart@csufresno.edu. Application contact: Dr. Janet Duttarer, Graduate Coordinator, 209-278-2476. E-mail: janet_duttarer@csufresno.edu.

California State University, Northridge, College of Health and Human Development, Department of Health Sciences, Program in Physical Therapy, Northridge, CA 91330. Awards MS. Students: 43 full-time (28 women), 9 part-time (7 women); includes 10 minority (7 Asian Americans, 3 Hispanics). Average age 28. 39 applicants, 77% accepted. *Expenses:* Tuition $0 for state residents; $246 per unit for nonresidents. Fees $1970 per year full-time, $1304 per year part-time. • Dr. Donna Redman-Bentley, Adviser, 818-677-2340.

Carroll College, Program in Physical Therapy, Waukesha, WI 53186-5593. Awards MPT. Faculty: 14 (9 women). Students: 55 (31 women). *Application deadline:* 1/15. *Application fee:* $25. • Dr. Jane F. Hopp, Director, 414-524-7294. Application contact: Tina Wood, Coordinator of Admissions, 414-524-7640.

Central Michigan University, College of Health Professions, Department of Health Promotion and Rehabilitation, Mount Pleasant, MI 48859. Offerings include physical therapy (MS). Accredited by APTA. Department faculty: 41 full-time (13 women). *Application deadline:* 2/15. *Application fee:* $30. *Expenses:* Tuition $139 per credit hour (minimum) for state residents; $276 per credit hour (minimum) for nonresidents. Fees $260 per year full-time, $150 per semester part-time. • Dr. Herman Triezenberg, Chairperson, 517-774-3541. E-mail: 320ss5j@cmich.edu.

Chapman University, School of Physical Therapy, Orange, CA 92866. Awards MPT. Accredited by APTA. Faculty: 9 full-time (8 women). Students: 80. *Degree requirements:* Internship. *Application deadline:* 12/10 (priority date; rolling processing). *Application fee:* $80. *Tuition:* $515 per credit. *Financial aid:* Application deadline 3/1. • Marcia Greenberg, Director, 714-744-7820. Application contact: Dr. Janna Herman, Coordinator, 714-744-7623.

Chatham College, School of Graduate Studies, Programs in Health Sciences, Program in Physical Therapy, Pittsburgh, PA 15232-2826. Awards MPT. Accredited by APTA. Faculty: 6 full-time (all women). Students: 87 full-time (58 women); includes 3 minority (1 African American, 2 Asian Americans). 145 applicants, 59% accepted. In 1997, 42 degrees awarded (100% found work related to degree). *Degree requirements:* Clinical experience. *Average time to degree:* master's–2 years full-time. *Application deadline:* 1/15. *Application fee:* $45. Electronic applications accepted. *Expenses:* Tuition $23,688 per year full-time, $395 per credit part-time. Fees $312 per year. *Financial aid:* 79 students received aid; career-related internships or fieldwork available. Aid available to part-time students. Financial aid applicants required to submit FAFSA. • Application contact: Heidi Hemming, Graduate Admissions, 412-365-1290. Fax: 412-365-1609. E-mail: admissions@chatham.edu.

Announcement: Chatham College's MPT program produces physical therapists who practice independently, serve their community, educate future physical therapists, and promote the profession. This 2-year program incorporates 3 clinical experiences. The curriculum includes a service project that assists disadvantaged, underserved, or cross-cultural populations. Student groups travel to Haiti to provide service at the Hospital Albert Schweitzer. Primary teaching method is problem-based learning. Admissions criteria include a baccalaureate degree, prerequisite course work, overall and prerequisite QPA of 3.0 or higher, interview and writing sample, health-care volunteer experience, and community service. E-mail at admissions@chatham.edu or visit the Web site at http://www.chatham.edu

Clarke College, Physical Therapy Program, Dubuque, IA 52001-3198. Awards MSPT. Accredited by APTA. Freshman-entry master's degree program; entry to the MSPT is determined after junior year of the BS program. Faculty: 5 full-time (1 woman), 6 part-time (3 women). Students: 29 full-time (19 women). Average age 22. *Application fee:* $20. Electronic applications accepted. *Expenses:* Tuition $12,688 per year full-time, $315 per credit hour part-time. Fees $240 per year. *Financial aid:* 4 students received aid; career-related internships or fieldwork available. Aid available to part-time students. Financial aid applicants required to submit FAFSA. • Dr. Clyde Killian, Chair, 319-588-6382. E-mail: ckillian@clarke.edu. Application contact: Admissions Office, 800-383-2345. Fax: 319-588-6789. E-mail: admissions@clarke.edu.

College Misericordia, Division of Health Sciences, Program in Physical Therapy, Dallas, PA 18612-1098. Awards MSPT. Accredited by APTA. Faculty: 5 full-time (3 women), 4 part-time (3 women). Students: 267 full-time (176 women). 465 applicants, 33% accepted. In 1997, 47 degrees awarded. *Degree requirements:* Thesis optional, foreign language not required. *Average time to degree:* master's–5 years full-time. *Entrance requirements:* GRE General Test (minimum combined score of 1000; average 1100) or MAT. Application deadline: 12/15 (priority date; rolling processing). Application fee: $15. *Financial aid:* Teaching assistantships, partial tuition waivers, Federal Work-Study, and career-related internships or fieldwork available. *Faculty research:* Wound care, computer-assisted instruction, instruction in applied physiology, isokinetics, prosthetics, orthotics. • Dr. Catherine Perry Wilkinson, Director, 717-674-6465. Application contact: Barbara Leggat, Continuing Education Specialist, 800-852-7675. Fax: 717-675-2441.

College of St. Catherine, Graduate Program, Program in Physical Therapy, 601 25th Avenue South, Minneapolis, MN 55454. Awards MPT. Accredited by APTA. Offered at Minneapolis campus only. Faculty: 13 (10 women). Students: 90 full-time (74 women); includes 3 minority (all Hispanics), 1 international. Average age 25. 271 applicants, 17% accepted. In 1997, 30 degrees awarded. *Degree requirements:* Research project required, foreign language and thesis not required. *Entrance requirements:* MAT, Michigan English Language Assessment Battery (minimum score 90) or TOEFL (minimum score 600), minimum GPA of 3.0. Application deadline: 3/1. Application fee: $30. *Expenses:* Tuition $480 per credit hour. Fees $60 per year. *Financial aid:* 77 students received aid; institutionally sponsored loans available. Financial aid application deadline: 4/1; applicants required to submit FAFSA. • Debra Sellheim, Director, 612-690-7825. Application contact: Office of Admission, 612-690-7800.

College of St. Scholastica, Program in Physical Therapy, Duluth, MN 55811-4199. Awards MA. Accredited by APTA. Faculty: 7 full-time (3 women), 2 part-time (1 woman). Students: 68 full-time (44 women), 10 part-time (8 women); includes 2 minority (both Asian Americans), 2 international. Average age 28. 117 applicants, 31% accepted. In 1997, 34 degrees awarded (100% found work related to degree). *Degree requirements:* Thesis. *Entrance requirements:* Minimum GPA of 2.7. Application deadline: 3/1. Application fee: $50. *Tuition:* $7968 per year full-time, $332 per credit part-time. *Financial aid:* 71 students received aid. Aid available to part-time students. Financial aid applicants required to submit FAFSA. *Faculty research:* Gait and posture evaluation, low back pain and functional outcome, incidence of injury among golfers. • Sandra Marden-Lokken, Chair, 218-723-6090. Application contact: Debra Bekkering, Graduate Administrative Assistant, 218-723-6285. Fax: 218-723-6796. E-mail: dbekkeri@ess.edu.

Columbia University, College of Physicians and Surgeons, Program in Physical Therapy, New York, NY 10032. Awards MS. Accredited by APTA. Faculty: 8 full-time (6 women), 32 part-time (21 women). Students: 96 full-time (66 women); includes 20 minority (4 African Americans, 13 Asian Americans, 3 Hispanics). Average age 27. 565 applicants, 11% accepted. In 1997, 44 degrees awarded (100% found work related to degree). *Degree requirements:* Thesis, fieldwork required, foreign language not required. *Average time to degree:* master's–2 years full-time. *Entrance requirements:* GRE General Test, TOEFL (minimum score 550), previous undergraduate course work in physical and social sciences, work experience. Application deadline: 1/31 (rolling processing). Application fee: $80. *Tuition:* $21,312 per year. *Financial aid:* In 1997–98, 77 students received aid, including 28 scholarships (21 to first-year students); Federal Work-Study, institutionally sponsored loans, and career-related internships or fieldwork also available. Financial aid application deadline: 4/15; applicants required to submit FAFSA. *Faculty research:* Motor control, motion analysis, muscular dystrophy, back assessment. • Joan E. Edelstein, Director, 212-305-3781. Fax: 212-305-4569.

Announcement: Columbia offers an entry-level Master of Science physical therapy program. The goal of the curriculum is to prepare graduates who are self-directed generalists with clinical problem-solving skills. Graduates are prepared to develop specialty skills, contribute to the leadership and growth of physical therapy, and advance the quality of health care through clinical research and collaboration with other professionals. The Master of Science degree is awarded upon completion of academic study, research, and clinical internships. Students complete an independent faculty-directed research project culminating in a master's thesis. The program is located within a large world-renowned medical center, which enables interaction with outstanding health-care specialists. Excellent clinical facilities throughout the United States are available for field experience.

Concordia University Wisconsin, Division of Graduate Studies, Program in Physical Therapy, Mequon, WI 53097-2402. Awards MPT, MSPT. Accredited by APTA. Faculty: 5 (2 women). Students: 69 part-time (40 women). *Degree requirements:* Thesis or alternative, comprehensive exam. *Entrance requirements:* TOEFL (minimum score 550). Application deadline: 3/1. Application fee: $50 ($125 for international students). *Tuition:* $250 per credit. *Financial aid:* Application deadline 8/1. • Dr. Teresa Steffen, Director, 414-243-4280.

Creighton University, School of Pharmacy and Allied Health Professions, Program in Physical Therapy, Omaha, NE 68178-0001. Awards DPT. Accredited by APTA. Faculty: 14 full-time (9 women), 4 part-time (1 woman). Students: 158 full-time (94 women); includes 12 minority (4 African Americans, 4 Asian Americans, 4 Hispanics), 1 international. Average age 27. 422 applicants, 13% accepted. In 1997, 51 degrees awarded. *Application deadline:* 1/1. *Application fee:* $50. *Expenses:* Tuition $6772 per year. Fees $268 per year. • Dr. A. Joseph Threlkeld, Chair, 402-280-4581. Fax: 402-280-5692. E-mail: jthrel@creighton.edu. Application contact: John J. Flemming, Director of Admissions, 402-280-2662. Fax: 402-280-5739. E-mail: spahp_admin8@creighton.edu.

Daemen College, Program in Physical Therapy, Amherst, NY 14226-3592. Awards MS. Part-time and evening/weekend programs available. Faculty: 6 full-time (3 women), 1 (woman) part-time. Students: 3 full-time (all women), 17 part-time (11 women). Average age 31. 10 applicants, 80% accepted. In 1997, 5 degrees awarded. *Degree requirements:* Thesis or alternative required, foreign language not required. *Entrance requirements:* Physical therapy license and current state registration. Application deadline: 3/1 (priority date; rolling processing; 10/1 for spring admission). Application fee: $25. *Expenses:* Tuition $430 per credit. Fees $13 per credit. *Financial aid:* In 1997–98, 4 students received aid, including 4 graduate tuition assistantships totaling $6,448. Aid available to part-time students. Financial aid application deadline: 2/15; applicants required to submit FAFSA. *Faculty research:* Prevention and wellness in elderly, electrical stimulation in wound care, balance in elderly. • Dr. Joan Gunther, Director, 716-839-8411. E-mail: jgunther@daemen.edu. Application contact: Deborah Fargo, Associate Director of Admissions, 716-839-8225. Fax: 716-839-8516. E-mail: dfargo@daemen.edu.

Duke University, Graduate School, Department of Physical Therapy, Durham, NC 27708-0586. Awards MS. Accredited by APTA. Faculty: 10 full-time, 5 part-time. Students: 60 full-time (37 women); includes 5 minority (1 African American, 4 Asian Americans), 4 international. 394 applicants, 12% accepted. In 1997, 28 degrees awarded. *Entrance requirements:* GRE General Test. Application deadline: 12/31. Application fee: $75. *Financial aid:* 53 students received aid; scholarships, institutionally sponsored loans available. Financial aid application deadline: 12/31; applicants required to submit FAFSA. • Dr. Janet Gwyer, Director of Graduate Studies, 919-381-4380.

Duquesne University, John G. Rangos, Sr. School of Health Sciences, Pittsburgh, PA 15282-0001. Offerings include physical therapy (MPT). One or more programs accredited by APTA. School faculty: 30 full-time (17 women), 12 part-time (6 women), 34.8 FTE. *Average time to degree:* master's–2 years full-time. *Application deadline:* 12/1 (priority date). *Application fee:* $45. Electronic applications accepted. *Expenses:* Tuition $510 per credit. Fees $39 per credit. • Dr. Jerome L. Martin, Dean, 412-396-6012. E-mail: martin2@duq2.cc.duq.edu. Application contact: Deborah L. Durica, Director of Student and Alumni Services, 412-396-6652. Fax: 412-396-5554. E-mail: durica@duq2.cc.duq.edu.

D'Youville College, Division of Physical Therapy, Buffalo, NY 14201-1084. Awards MS. Accredited by APTA. Program new for spring 1999. *Application deadline:* rolling. *Application fee:* $25. *Expenses:* Tuition $357 per credit hour. Fees $350 per year. • Dr. Penelope Klein, Chair, 716-881-7044. E-mail: kleinpj@dyc.edu. Application contact: Joseph Syracuse, Graduate Admissions Director, 716-881-7676. Fax: 716-881-7790.

East Carolina University, School of Allied Health Sciences, Department of Physical Therapy, Greenville, NC 27858-4353. Awards MPT. Accredited by APTA. Faculty: 3 full-time (2 women). Students: 94 full-time (70 women); includes 3 minority (2 Asian Americans, 1 Native American). Average age 26. 308 applicants, 24% accepted. *Degree requirements:* Comprehensive exams required, foreign language and thesis not required. *Entrance requirements:* GRE General Test, TOEFL. Application deadline: 1/15. Application fee: $40. *Tuition:* $1886 per year full-time, $472 per semester (minimum) part-time for state residents; $9156 per year full-time, $2289 per semester (minimum) part-time for nonresidents. *Financial aid:* Application deadline 6/1. • Dr. Bruce Albright, Chair, 252-328-4450. E-mail: moyee@mail.ecu.edu. Application contact: Mary Templeton, Director of Graduate Studies, 252-328-4450. Fax: 252-328-4470. E-mail: grad@mail.ecu.edu.

Eastern Washington University, College of Science, Mathematics and Technology, Program in Physical Therapy, Cheney, WA 99004-2431. Awards MPT. Accredited by APTA. Faculty: 6 full-time (3 women). Students: 86 full-time (45 women). 124 applicants, 29% accepted. *Degree requirements:* Comprehensive exam. *Entrance requirements:* GRE General Test, minimum GPA of 3.0. Application fee: $75. *Tuition:* $4200 per year full-time, $140 per credit part-time for state residents; $12,780 per year full-time, $415 per credit part-time for nonresidents. *Financial aid:* Application deadline 2/1. • Prof. Walter Erikson, Chair, 509-458-6435. Application contact: Prof. Meryl Gersh, Adviser, 509-623-4304.

Elon College, Program in Physical Therapy, Elon College, NC 27244. Awards MPT. Faculty: 8. Students: 48 full-time (25 women); includes 4 minority (1 African American, 1 Asian American, 1 Hispanic, 1 Native American). Average age 25. 150 applicants, 37% accepted. *Degree requirements:* Computer language required, foreign language and thesis not required. *Entrance requirements:* GRE. Application deadline: (5/31 for spring admission). Application fee: $50. *Tuition:* $15,370 per year. *Financial aid:* Application deadline 10/1; applicants required to submit FAFSA. • Dr. Elizabeth A. Rogers, Director, 336-538-8470. Fax: 336-538-8476. E-mail: rogers@numen.elon.edu. Application contact: Alice N. Essen, Director of Graduate Admissions, 800-334-8448. Fax: 336-538-3986. E-mail: essen@numen.elon.edu.

Emory University, School of Medicine, Programs in Allied Health Professions, Program in Physical Therapy, Atlanta, GA 30322-1100. Awards MM Sc, MPT. One or more programs accredited by APTA. Faculty: 5 full-time (all women), 4 part-time (2 women). Students: 100 full-time (74 women), 1 (woman) part-time; includes 5 minority (all Asian Americans). Average age 25. 396 applicants, 16% accepted. In 1997, 34 degrees awarded (100% found work related to degree). *Entrance requirements:* GRE General Test (minimum combined score of 1500 on three sections). Application fee: $55. *Financial aid:* Federal Work-Study, institutionally sponsored loans available. Aid available to part-time students. Financial aid application deadline: 3/15; applicants required to submit CSS PROFILE or FAFSA. • Dr. P. A. Catlin, Director, 404-712-5683.

Finch University of Health Sciences/The Chicago Medical School, School of Related Health Sciences, Department of Physical Therapy, North Chicago, IL 60064-3095. Awards MS. Part-time programs available. Faculty: 9 full-time (5 women), 4 part-time (all women). Students: 14 part-time (6 women). Average age 30. 10 applicants, 10% accepted. In 1997, 10 degrees awarded (100% found work related to degree). *Degree requirements:* Computer language, thesis required, foreign language not required. *Average time to degree:* master's–2 years part-time. *Entrance requirements:* Minimum GPA of 2.8, physical therapy license. Application deadline: 6/1 (priority date; rolling processing). Application fee: $25. *Tuition:* $403 per credit hour. *Financial aid:* Partial tuition waivers, institutionally sponsored loans available. Aid available to part-time students. Financial aid application deadline: 2/1. *Faculty research:* Faculty research productivity, measurement, recruitment and retention, orthopedic dysfunction, spinal misfunction. • Dr. Judith Stoecker, Director, 847-578-8694. Fax: 847-578-8816.

See in-depth description on page 1237.

Florida Atlantic University, College of Education, Department of Health Sciences, Program in Physical Therapy, Boca Raton, FL 33431-0991. Awards MS. Faculty: 3 full-time (1 woman). *Entrance requirements:* GRE General Test. Application deadline: rolling. Application fee: $20. *Expenses:* Tuition $2520 per year full-time, $140 per credit hour part-time for state residents; $8712 per year full-time, $484 per credit hour part-time for nonresidents. Fees $5 per year (minimum). • Dr. Sandy Burhart, Coordinator, 954-236-1008.

Florida Gulf Coast University, College of Health Professions, Department of Physical Therapy, Fort Myers, FL 33965-6565. Awards MS. Part-time programs available. Postbaccalaureate distance learning degree programs offered (minimal on-campus study). Faculty: 6 full-time (4 women), 2 part-time (1 woman), 7 FTE. Students: 31 full-time (21 women); includes 4 minority (3 Asian Americans, 1 Hispanic). Average age 27. 80 applicants, 45% accepted. *Degree requirements:* Thesis or alternative required, foreign language not required. *Entrance requirements:* GRE General Test (minimum combined score of 1000), GMAT (minimum score 500), or MAT (minimum score 45). Application fee: $20. Electronic applications accepted. *Financial aid:* Federal Work-Study, institutionally sponsored loans, and career-related internships or fieldwork available. *Faculty research:* Physical therapy practice and education. • Ellen K. Williamson, Chair, 941-590-7530. Fax: 941-590-7474. E-mail: ekwill@fgcu.edu.

Florida International University, College of Health, Department of Physical Therapy, Miami, FL 33199. Awards MS. Accredited by APTA. Part-time programs available. Faculty: 8 full-time (5 women). Students: 2 part-time (1 woman); includes 1 minority (Hispanic). Average age 40. 6 applicants, 0% accepted. In 1997, 1 degree awarded. *Degree requirements:* Thesis required, foreign language not required. *Entrance requirements:* GRE General Test (minimum combined score of 1000), minimum GPA of 3.0, physical therapy license. Application deadline: 4/1 (priority date; rolling processing; 10/1 for spring admission). Application fee: $20. *Expenses:* Tuition $138 per credit hour for state residents; $482 per credit hour for nonresidents. Fees $46 per semester. *Faculty research:* Isokinetic test results and gait abnormalities after knee arthroscopy. • Colleen Rose-St. Prix, Chairperson, 305-348-3831. Fax: 305-348-1240. E-mail: stprix@servms.fiu.edu.

Gannon University, School of Graduate Studies, College of Sciences, Engineering, and Health Sciences, School of Health Sciences, Program in Physical Therapy, Erie, PA 16541. Awards MPT. Accredited by APTA. Students: 73 full-time (46 women); includes 4 minority (2 Asian Americans, 2 Hispanics). Average age 24. 100 applicants, 47% accepted. In 1997, 32 degrees awarded. *Degree requirements:* Thesis, research project. *Entrance requirements:* TOEFL, interview, minimum GPA of 3.0 in prerequisite course work. Application deadline: 10/15. Application fee: $50. *Expenses:* Tuition $21,735 per year full-time, $765 per credit part-time. Fees $200 per year full-time, $8 per credit part-time. *Financial aid:* Available to part-time students. Financial aid application deadline: 3/1; applicants required to submit FAFSA. • Dr. Helen M. LaFuria, Interim Director, 814-871-5639. Application contact: Beth Nemenz, Director of Admissions, 814-871-7240. Fax: 814-871-5803. E-mail: admissions@gannon.edu.

Georgia State University, College of Health and Human Sciences, Department of Cardiopulmonary Care Sciences, Atlanta, GA 30303-3083. Offerings include respiratory care (MS). Department faculty: 8 full-time (2 women). *Degree requirements:* Thesis required, foreign language not required. *Entrance requirements:* GRE General Test (minimum combined score of 900) or MAT (minimum score 45), RRT (CRTT) license. Application deadline: 5/15 (10/1 for spring admission). Application fee: $25. *Expenses:* Tuition $2673 per year full-time, $99 per semester hour part-time for state residents; $10,692 per year full-time, $396 per semester hour part-time for nonresidents. Fees $228 per year. • Dr. Joseph Rau, Chair, 404-651-3037. Application contact: Leigh Walling, Academic Adviser, 404-651-3064. Fax: 404-651-4871.

Georgia State University, College of Health and Human Sciences, Department of Physical Therapy, Atlanta, GA 30303-3083. Offers program in orthopedics (MS). Accredited by APTA. Part-time and evening/weekend programs available. Faculty: 9 full-time (6 women), 3 part-time (all women). Students: 4 full-time (1 woman), 9 part-time (5 women); includes 4 minority (2 African Americans, 2 Asian Americans), 3 international. Average age 32. 5 applicants, 100% accepted. In 1997, 2 degrees awarded. *Degree requirements:* Thesis required, foreign language not required. *Entrance requirements:* GRE General Test (minimum combined score of 1000) or MAT (minimum score 50). Application deadline: 5/15 (rolling processing; 10/1 for spring admission). Application fee: $25. *Expenses:* Tuition $2673 per year full-time, $99 per semester hour part-time for state residents; $10,692 per year full-time, $396 per semester hour part-time for nonresidents. Fees $228 per year. *Financial aid:* Fellowships, research assistantships, teaching assistantships, minority scholarships, Federal Work-Study, institutionally sponsored loans available. Aid available to part-time students. Financial aid application deadline: 4/15; applicants required to submit FAFSA. • Dr. Elizabeth Higbie, Graduate Coordinator, 404-651-3091. Application contact: Valerie Hardy, Academic Adviser, 404-651-3064. Fax: 404-651-4871.

Governors State University, College of Health Professions, Division of Nursing and Health Science, Program in Physical Therapy, University Park, IL 60466. Awards MPT. *Degree requirements:* Thesis or alternative required, foreign language not required. *Entrance requirements:* Minimum GPA of 3.0 in field, 2.75 overall. Application deadline: 1/31 (priority date). Application fee: $0. *Expenses:* Tuition $1140 per trimester full-time, $95 per credit hour part-time for state residents; $3420 per trimester full-time, $285 per credit hour part-time for nonresidents. Fees $95 per trimester. *Financial aid:* Application deadline 5/1. • Ann Vendrely,

Directory: Physical Therapy

Governors State University (continued)

Co-Coordinator, 708-534-5000 Ext. 7291. Application contact: Dr. Phyllis Klingensmith, Co-Coordinator, 708-534-5000 Ext. 4538.

Grand Valley State University, Science and Mathematics Division, School of Health Sciences, Department of Physical Therapy, Allendale, MI 49401-9403. Awards MS. Accredited by APTA. Faculty: 8 full-time (5 women), 8 part-time (7 women). Students: 142 full-time (102 women), 1 part-time (0 women); includes 4 minority (1 African American, 1 Asian American, 1 Hispanic, 1 Native American), 3 international. Average age 26. 300 applicants, 20% accepted. In 1997, 39 degrees awarded. *Degree requirements:* Thesis optional, foreign language not required. *Average time to degree:* master's–3 years full-time. *Entrance requirements:* Minimum GPA of 3.0, 50 hours of volunteer work. Application deadline: 1/15. Application fee: $20. *Financial aid:* Federal Work-Study, institutionally sponsored loans, and career-related internships or fieldwork available. Financial aid application deadline: 2/15. *Faculty research:* Motor control, motion analysis, gait analysis, geriatrics. • Dr. John Peck, Director, 616-895-3356. Application contact: Cindy Zehner, Secretary, 616-895-3356.

Hardin–Simmons University, Department of Physical Therapy, Abilene, TX 79698-0001. Awards MPT. Accredited by APTA. Faculty: 8 full-time (3 women), 2 part-time (0 women). Students: 34 full-time (17 women); includes 6 minority (1 Asian American, 4 Hispanics, 1 Native American). Average age 31. In 1997, 12 degrees awarded. *Entrance requirements:* Minimum GPA of 3.0 in last 60 hours and for prerequisite courses. Application deadline: 6/15 (rolling processing; 6/15 for spring admission). Application fee: $25. *Expenses:* Tuition $20,250 per year. Fees $945 per year. *Financial aid:* Full and partial tuition waivers, Federal Work-Study, and career-related internships or fieldwork available. Aid available to part-time students. Financial aid application deadline: 3/1; applicants required to submit FAFSA. *Faculty research:* Electromyography, geriatric physical therapy, pain control with non-invasive methods. • Dr. William Russel Gould, Head, 915-670-5860. Fax: 915-670-5868.

Husson College, Program in Physical Therapy, Bangor, ME 04401-2999. Awards MSPT. Freshman-entry master's degree program. Part-time and evening/weekend programs available. Faculty: 7. *Degree requirements:* Thesis optional, foreign language not required. *Application deadline:* 2/15. *Application fee:* $25. *Tuition:* $545 per course. • Dr. Sandra Curwin, Director, 207-941-7070.

Idaho State University, College of Health Professions, Department of Physical and Occupational Therapy, Program in Physical Therapy, Pocatello, ID 83209. Awards MPT. Accredited by APTA. Faculty: 6 full-time (4 women), 1 (woman) part-time. Students: 48 full-time (24 women); includes 2 minority (1 Asian American, 1 Hispanic). Average age 28. 221 applicants, 11% accepted. In 1997, 22 degrees awarded (100% found work related to degree). *Degree requirements:* Thesis optional, foreign language not required. *Entrance requirements:* GRE General Test. Application deadline: 12/15 (priority date). Application fee: $55. *Financial aid:* In 1997–98, 36 students received aid, including 7 scholarships (3 to first-year students); full tuition waivers, Federal Work-Study, institutionally sponsored loans, and career-related internships or fieldwork also available. Aid available to part-time students. *Faculty research:* Cardiovascular/pulmonary balance, neural plasticity, orthopedics, geriatrics, hypertension. Total annual research expenditures: $38,000. • Dr. Alexander Urfer, Chairperson, Department of Physical and Occupational Therapy, 208-236-4095.

Ithaca College, School of Health Sciences and Human Performance, Program in Physical Therapy, Ithaca, NY 14850-7020. Awards MS. Accredited by APTA. Students must enter the program as freshmen. Faculty: 5 full-time (3 women). Students: 95 full-time (72 women); includes 5 minority (1 Asian American, 4 Hispanics). Average age 22. In 1997, 74 degrees awarded. *Degree requirements:* Clinical fieldwork, comprehensive exams required, thesis optional, foreign language not required. *Entrance requirements:* TOEFL (minimum score 550). Application deadline: 11/1. Application fee: $40. *Tuition:* $552 per credit hour. *Financial aid:* 72 students received aid; career-related internships or fieldwork available. Financial aid application deadline: 1/15; applicants required to submit CSS PROFILE or FAFSA. *Faculty research:* Impairments and functions in older adults, rehabilitation of patellofemoral pain syndrome, service delivery models in physical and occupational therapy, motor control/learning and neural plasticity, home health physical therapy. • Katherine Beissner, Chairperson, 607-274-3342.

Kirksville College of Osteopathic Medicine, Arizona School of Health Sciences, PO Box 11037, Phoenix, AZ 85061-1037. Offerings include physical therapy (MS). School faculty: 30 full-time (18 women), 14 part-time (8 women). *Degree requirements:* Thesis required, foreign language not required. *Average time to degree:* master's–2 years full-time. *Entrance requirements:* GRE General Test (combined average 1639 on three sections), MCAT (average 25 for physician assistant). Application deadline: 2/1 (rolling processing). Application fee: $50. *Tuition:* $15,990 per year. • Dr. James Dearing, Associate Dean, 602-841-4077. Fax: 602-841-4092. Application contact: Stephanie Seyer, Assistant Director of Admissions, 660-626-2237. Fax: 660-626-2815.

Loma Linda University, School of Allied Health Professions, Loma Linda, CA 92350. Awards MPT, DPT. Accredited by APTA. Faculty: 17 full-time (8 women), 14 part-time (9 women). Students: 92 full-time (41 women), 16 part-time (11 women); includes 34 minority (4 African Americans, 17 Asian Americans, 13 Hispanics). 485 applicants, 46% accepted. In 1997, 105 master's awarded. *Application deadline:* rolling. *Application fee:* $50. *Tuition:* $380 per unit. • Dr. Joyce Hopp, Dean, 909-824-4545. Application contact: Helen Greenwood, Director, Admissions and Records, 909-824-4599. Fax: 909-824-4809. E-mail: hgreenwood@sahp.llu.edu.

Long Island University, Brooklyn Campus, School of Health Professions, Division of Physical Therapy, Brooklyn, NY 11201-8423. Awards MS. Accredited by APTA. Part-time and evening/weekend programs available. Faculty: 6 full-time (3 women), 14 part-time. Students: 38 full-time (28 women), 27 part-time (21 women); includes 17 minority (2 African Americans, 9 Asian Americans, 6 Hispanics). 49 applicants, 78% accepted. In 1997, 38 degrees awarded. *Application deadline:* rolling. *Application fee:* $30. Electronic applications accepted. *Expenses:* Tuition $480 per credit. Fees $415 per year full-time, $73 per semester (minimum) part-time. *Financial aid:* In 1997–98, 5 students received aid, including 5 assistantships. • Dr. William Mark Susman, Associate Dean, 718-488-1063. Application contact: Bernard W. Sullivan, Associate Director of Admissions, 718-488-1011.

Louisiana State University Medical Center, School of Allied Health Professions, Program in Physical Therapy, 433 Bolivar Street, New Orleans, LA 70112-2223. Awards MPT. Accredited by APTA. Faculty: 9 full-time (5 women), 6 part-time (5 women), 11 FTE. Students: 127 full-time (75 women); includes 10 minority (4 African Americans, 4 Asian Americans, 2 Native Americans). Average age 26. 204 applicants, 31% accepted. *Degree requirements:* Computer language required, foreign language and thesis not required. *Entrance requirements:* GRE General Test (combined average 1652 on three sections). Application deadline: 11/15. Application fee: $50. *Expenses:* Tuition $2878 per year full-time, $421 per semester (minimum) part-time for state residents; $6003 per year full-time, $838 per semester (minimum) part-time for nonresidents. Fees $350 per year full-time, $90 per semester (minimum) part-time. *Faculty research:* Wound healing, spinal cord injury, pain management, geriatrics. Total annual research expenditures: $80,000. • Dr. Elizabeth L. Weiss, Acting Head, 504-568-4288. Fax: 504-568-6552. E-mail: eweiss@lsumc.edu. Application contact: Joan Schuman, Office of Student Affairs, 504-568-4254. Fax: 504-568-4249. E-mail: alhpjbs@lsumc.edu.

Marquette University, Department of Physical Therapy, Milwaukee, WI 53201-1881. Awards MPT. Accredited by APTA. *Entrance requirements:* TOEFL (minimum score 550). Application fee: $40. *Tuition:* $490 per credit. *Financial aid:* Application deadline 2/15. • Dr. Lawrence G. Pan, Director, 414-288-5759. Fax: 414-288-5987.

Marymount University, School of Health Professions, Program in Physical Therapy, Arlington, VA 22207-4299. Awards MS. Faculty: 5 full-time (all women), 4 part-time (2 women). Students: 75 full-time. *Degree requirements:* Thesis optional, foreign language not required. *Entrance requirements:* GRE, 40 hours of clinical or work experience in physical therapy. Application deadline: 2/5. Application fee: $35. *Expenses:* Tuition $465 per credit hour. Fees $120 per year full-time, $5 per credit hour part-time. *Financial aid:* Career-related internships or fieldwork available. Aid available to part-time students. Financial aid applicants required to submit FAFSA. • Dr. Rita Wong, Chairperson, 703-284-5980. Fax: 703-284-3836. E-mail: rita.wong@marymount.edu.

Mayo School of Health-Related Sciences, Program in Physical Therapy, Rochester, MN 55905. Awards MPT. Accredited by APTA. Faculty: 4 full-time (0 women), 2 part-time (both women). Students: 103 full-time. *Degree requirements:* Comprehensive exam required, foreign language and thesis not required. *Entrance requirements:* GRE General Test, minimum GPA of 3.0. Application deadline: 2/1. Application fee: $50. • Dr. John P. Cummings, Director, 507-284-8487. Application contact: Rosalie Fountain, Secretary, 507-284-2054.

Medical College of Georgia, Department of Physical Therapy, Augusta, GA 30912-1500. Awards MHE, MPT, MS. One or more programs accredited by APTA. Postbaccalaureate distance learning degree programs offered (no on-campus study). Faculty: 3 full-time (2 women). Students: 100 full-time (73 women), 2 part-time (both women); includes 7 minority (3 African Americans, 4 Asian Americans). Average age 26. 136 applicants, 63% accepted. In 1997, 2 degrees awarded. *Degree requirements:* Thesis or alternative. *Entrance requirements:* GRE General Test (minimum combined score of 1000), TOEFL (minimum score 600). Application deadline: 6/30 (priority date; rolling processing). Application fee: $0. *Expenses:* Tuition $2670 per year full-time, $111 per credit part-time for state residents; $10,680 per year full-time, $445 per credit part-time for nonresidents. Fees $286 per year. *Financial aid:* Federal Work-Study, institutionally sponsored loans available. Financial aid application deadline: 5/1. • Dr. Jan F. Perry, Chair, 706-721-2141. E-mail: jperry@mail.mcg.edu. Application contact: Dr. Gary C. Bond, Associate Dean, 706-721-3278. Fax: 706-721-6829. E-mail: gradstud@mail.mcg.edu.

Medical University of South Carolina, College of Health Professions, Department of Rehabilitation Sciences, Program in Physical Therapy, Charleston, SC 29425-0002. Awards MHS, MSR. Accredited by APTA. Postbaccalaureate distance learning degree programs offered (minimal on-campus study). Faculty: 13 full-time (8 women), 1 (woman) part-time, 13.5 FTE. Students: 92 full-time (51 women), 1 part-time (0 women); includes 8 minority (all African Americans). Average age 28. 393 applicants, 18% accepted. In 1997, 19 degrees awarded (100% found work related to degree). *Degree requirements:* Thesis or alternative, research project required, foreign language not required. *Average time to degree:* master's–3 years full-time. *Entrance requirements:* GRE General Test, interview, minimum GPA of 2.8. Application deadline: 11/1. Application fee: $55. *Expenses:* Tuition $4072 per year full-time, $221 per semester hour part-time for state residents; $7064 per year full-time, $387 per semester hour part-time for nonresidents. Fees $150 per year (minimum). *Financial aid:* Federal Work-Study and career-related internships or fieldwork available. Aid available to part-time students. Financial aid application deadline: 4/1; applicants required to submit FAFSA. *Faculty research:* Efficacy of physical therapy intervention. Total annual research expenditures: $274. • Dr. James A. Morrow, Chair, 843-792-2961. E-mail: morrowj@musc.edu. Application contact: Susan Johnson, Student Services, 843-792-2961. Fax: 843-792-0710. E-mail: johnsoss@musc.edu.

Mercy College, Program in Physical Therapy, Dobbs Ferry, NY 10522-1189. Awards MS. Accredited by APTA. Evening/weekend programs available. Students: 83 full-time (53 women). *Degree requirements:* Thesis or alternative. *Entrance requirements:* Minimum GPA of 3.0 in final 30 credits, industry science prerequisites. Application deadline: 2/1. Application fee: $60. *Tuition:* $427 per credit. *Financial aid:* Teaching assistantships available. *Faculty research:* Functional outcomes, wound management, cardiopulmonary rehabilitation, academic predictors of success. • Claudia B. Fenderson, Director, 914-674-9331 Ext. 650. Fax: 914-674-9457. Application contact: Admissions Office, 800-MERCY-NY. Fax: 914-674-7382. E-mail: admission@merlin.mercynet.edu.

MGH Institute of Health Professions, Post-Professional Program in Physical Therapy, 101 Merrimac Street, Boston, MA 02114-4719. Awards MS. Part-time and evening/weekend programs available. Faculty: 1 (woman) full-time, 12 part-time (7 women), 5 FTE. Students: 7 full-time (4 women), 74 part-time (64 women); includes 2 minority (1 Asian American, 1 Hispanic), 27 international. Average age 31. 28 applicants, 50% accepted. In 1997, 20 degrees awarded (100% found work related to degree). *Degree requirements:* Thesis, clinical preceptorship required, foreign language not required. *Average time to degree:* master's–2 years full-time, 3.5 years part-time. *Entrance requirements:* GRE General Test, graduate of an approved program in physical therapy, 2 years of work experience as a physical therapist. Application deadline: 3/1 (11/1 for spring admission). Application fee: $50. *Expenses:* Tuition $20,320 per year full-time, $530 per credit part-time. Fees $300 per year. *Financial aid:* 1 student received aid; assistantships, full and partial tuition waivers, and career-related internships or fieldwork available. Aid available to part-time students. Financial aid application deadline: 3/6; applicants required to submit FAFSA. *Faculty research:* Disability in the elderly; gait, balance and posture; cardiac rehabilitation; relationship of impairment to disability; effect of muscle strengthening in the elderly. • Bette Ann Harris, Director, 617-726-8009. Fax: 617-726-8022. E-mail: harris.bette@mgh.harvard.edu. Application contact: Office of Student Affairs, 617-726-3140. Fax: 617-726-8010.

See in-depth description on page 1435.

MGH Institute of Health Professions, Professional Program in Physical Therapy, 101 Merrimac Street, Boston, MA 02114-4719. Awards MS. Accredited by APTA. Faculty: 5 full-time (all women), 4 part-time (all women), 7.35 FTE. Students: 63 full-time (45 women), 15 part-time (8 women); includes 5 minority (3 Asian Americans, 2 Native Americans), 1 international. Average age 29. 246 applicants, 21% accepted. In 1997, 18 degrees awarded. *Degree requirements:* Thesis or alternative, research project required, foreign language not required. *Average time to degree:* master's–2 years full-time. *Entrance requirements:* GRE General Test. Application deadline: 1/24. Application fee: $50. *Expenses:* Tuition $20,320 per year full-time, $530 per credit part-time. Fees $300 per year. *Financial aid:* In 1997–98, 59 students received aid, including 4 assistantships (2 to first-year students); full and partial tuition waivers and career-related internships or fieldwork also available. Financial aid application deadline: 3/6; applicants required to submit FAFSA. *Faculty research:* Disability in the elderly; gait, balance, and posture; cardiac rehabilitation: relationship of impairment to disability. • Dr. Leslie G. Portney, Director, 617-724-4841. Fax: 617-726-8022. E-mail: portney.leslie@mgh.harvard.edu. Application contact: Office of Student Affairs, 617-726-3140. Fax: 617-726-8010.

See in-depth description on page 1435.

Midwestern University, College of Allied Health Professions, Program in Physical Therapy, Downers Grove, IL 60515-1235. Awards MPT. Students: 131 full-time (85 women); includes 11 minority (1 African American, 8 Asian Americans, 2 Hispanics). *Application deadline:* rolling. *Application fee:* $30. *Expenses:* Tuition $16,148 per year for state residents; $18,492 per year for nonresidents. Fees $280 per year. • Application contact: Julie Rosenthall, Director of Admissions, 800-458-6253. Fax: 630-971-6086. E-mail: mwuinfo@mwu.edu.

Announcement: Midwestern University is committed to educating the health-care team of the next century. The University administers the Chicago College of Osteopathic Medicine, the Chicago College of Pharmacy, the College of Allied Health Professions, the Arizona College of Osteopathic Medicine, and the College of Pharmacy–Glendale. The University operates campuses in Downers Grove, Illinois, and in Glendale, Arizona. The Physical Therapy Program offers the Master of Physical Therapy (MPT) degree. The 30-month program includes classroom interaction—often with students in other programs, such as occupational therapy, providing students with valuable perspectives—and 23 weeks of full-time clinical experience under the supervision of licensed physical therapists in diverse hospital and clinical settings. Contact the

Office of Admissions, Midwestern University, 555 31st Street, Downers Grove, IL 60515; 800-458-6253; e-mail: admiss@midwestern.edu; WWW: http://www.midwestern.edu

Mount St. Mary's College, Department of Physical Therapy, Los Angeles, CA 90049-1597. Awards MPT. Accredited by APTA. *Entrance requirements:* GRE General Test, TOEFL, minimum GPA of 3.0. Application fee: $75.

Neumann College, Program in Physical Therapy, Aston, PA 19014-1298. Awards MS. Evening/weekend programs available. Faculty: 3 full-time (all women), 12 part-time (5 women). Students: 42 part-time (25 women); includes 4 minority (1 African American, 1 Asian American, 2 Hispanics). *Entrance requirements:* TOEFL. Application deadline: 12/1. Application fee: $50. *Tuition:* $530 per credit. *Financial aid:* Available to part-time students. Financial aid application deadline: 3/15; applicants required to submit FAFSA. • Robert Cullen, Program Director, 610-558-5233. Fax: 610-459-1370. E-mail: cullenr@smtpgate.neumann.edu. Application contact: Denise Ewing, Admissions Counselor, 610-558-5531. Fax: 610-558-5652. E-mail: nuecoladm@hslc.org.

New York Medical College, Graduate School of Health Sciences, Program in Physical Therapy, Valhalla, NY 10595-1691. Awards MS. Accredited by APTA. Faculty: 6 full-time (3 women), 23 part-time (14 women). Students: 73 full-time (44 women); includes 7 minority (3 Asian Americans, 3 Hispanics, 1 Native American), 2 international. Average age 27. 133 applicants, 44% accepted. *Degree requirements:* Computer language required, foreign language not required. *Entrance requirements:* GRE, TOEFL. Application deadline: 1/15. Application fee: $35 ($60 for international students). *Tuition:* $17,000 per year. *Financial aid:* Application deadline 4/30; applicants required to submit FAFSA. *Faculty research:* Neurobehavioral studies, biomechanical analysis at shoulder and knee, prediction of falls in elderly. • Dr. James Gordon, Director, 914-594-4915. Application contact: Admissions Office, 914-594-4510.

See in-depth description on page 1241.

New York University, School of Education, Department of Physical Therapy, New York, NY 10012-1019. Offers programs in pathokinesiology (MA), pediatrics (MA), physical therapy (DPS, PhD). One or more programs accredited by APTA. Part-time and evening/weekend programs available. Faculty: 8 full-time (6 women), 11 part-time. Students: 4 full-time, 50 part-time. 42 applicants, 57% accepted. In 1997, 23 master's, 2 doctorates awarded. Terminal master's awarded for partial completion of doctoral program. *Degree requirements:* For master's, thesis required (for some programs), foreign language not required; for doctorate, dissertation. *Entrance requirements:* For master's, TOEFL, physical therapy certificate; for doctorate, GRE General Test, TOEFL, interview, physical therapy certificate. Application deadline: 2/1 (priority date; rolling processing; 12/1 for spring admission). Application fee: $40 ($60 for international students). *Financial aid:* Partial tuition waivers, Federal Work-Study, institutionally sponsored loans, and career-related internships or fieldwork available. Aid available to part-time students. Financial aid application deadline: 3/1; applicants required to submit FAFSA. *Faculty research:* Developmental disabilities, movement analysis, exercise physiology, orthopedics. • Wen K. Ling, Chairperson, 212-998-9408. Fax: 212-995-4190. Application contact: Office of Graduate Admissions, 212-998-5030. Fax: 212-995-4328.

Northern Arizona University, College of Health Professions, Department of Physical Therapy, Flagstaff, AZ 86011. Awards MPT. Accredited by APTA. Faculty: 8 full-time (3 women). Students: 120 full-time (68 women); includes 10 minority (3 Asian Americans, 6 Hispanics, 1 Native American). Average age 25. 141 applicants, 30% accepted. In 1997, 40 degrees awarded. *Entrance requirements:* Minimum GPA of 3.0. Application deadline: 1/31 (priority date; rolling processing). Application fee: $45. *Expenses:* Tuition $2088 per year full-time, $330 per semester (minimum) part-time for state residents; $8004 per year full-time, $1002 per semester (minimum) part-time for nonresidents. Fees $72 per year full-time, $18 per semester (minimum) part-time. *Financial aid:* In 1997–98, 1 research assistantship was awarded. • Dr. Carl DeRosa, Chairperson, 520-523-4092.

North Georgia College & State University, Graduate School, Program in Physical Therapy, Dahlonega, GA 30597-1001. Awards MS. Accredited by APTA. Faculty: 7 full-time (5 women), 7 part-time (5 women). Students: 67 full-time (39 women); includes 8 minority (6 African Americans, 1 Asian American, 1 Hispanic). Average age 24. 195 applicants, 12% accepted. In 1997, 22 degrees awarded. *Degree requirements:* Computer language, thesis required, foreign language not required. *Entrance requirements:* GRE General Test (minimum combined score of 800), minimum GPA of 2.75. Application deadline: 12/1. Application fee: $90. *Financial aid:* Application deadline 5/1. *Faculty research:* Ergonomics, spinal mobility measurements, electrophysiology, orthopedic physical therapy. • Dr. Robert Laird, Chair, 706-864-1422. E-mail: rlaird@nugget.ngc.peachnet.edu.

Northwestern University, Medical School, Programs in Physical Therapy, 303 East Chicago Avenue, Chicago, IL 60611-3008. Awards MPT. Accredited by APTA. *Entrance requirements:* GRE General Test. Application deadline: 8/30 (rolling processing). *Faculty research:* Posture and balance, neuromuscular control, infant development, clinical decision making, functional states.

Nova Southeastern University, Health Professions Division, College of Allied Health, Program in Physical Therapy, Fort Lauderdale, FL 33314-7721. Awards MPT. Accredited by APTA. Students: 281 full-time (158 women); includes 52 minority (8 African Americans, 13 Asian Americans, 31 Hispanics). Average age 26. In 1997, 58 degrees awarded. *Degree requirements:* Thesis required, foreign language not required. *Average time to degree:* master's–2 years full-time. *Entrance requirements:* Allied Health Professions Admissions Test. Application deadline: 2/1 (rolling processing). Application fee: $50. *Tuition:* $17,000 per year for state residents; $19,500 per year for nonresidents. • Catherine Page, Director, 954-262-1266. Application contact: Monica Roca, Admissions Counselor, 954-723-1110.

Oakland University, School of Health Sciences, Program in Physical Therapy, Rochester, MI 48309-4401. Awards MPT, MS. Accredited by APTA. Faculty: 6 full-time. Students: 50 full-time (40 women), 28 part-time (16 women); includes 3 minority (1 African American, 1 Asian American, 1 Hispanic), 9 international. Average age 29. 10 applicants, 90% accepted. In 1997, 46 degrees awarded. *Entrance requirements:* Acceptance in the 2-year preparatory post-bacculaureate program, minimum GPA of 3.0 for unconditional admission. Application deadline: 7/15 (3/15 for spring admission). Application fee: $30. *Expenses:* Tuition $3852 per year full-time, $214 per credit hour part-time for state residents; $8532 per year full-time, $474 per credit hour part-time for nonresidents. Fees $420 per year. *Financial aid:* Full tuition waivers, Federal Work-Study, institutionally sponsored loans available. Financial aid application deadline: 3/1; applicants required to submit FAFSA. • Dr. Beth Marcoux, Director, 248-370-4041.

Ohio University, Graduate Studies, College of Health and Human Services, School of Physical Therapy, Athens, OH 45701-2979. Awards MPT. Accredited by APTA. Faculty: 6 full-time (3 women). Students: 77 full-time (56 women), 10 part-time (8 women). 150 applicants, 23% accepted. *Application fee:* $30. *Tuition:* $5430 per year full-time, $216 per quarter hour part-time for state residents; $10,431 per year full-time, $423 per quarter hour part-time for nonresidents. *Financial aid:* 2 students received aid; Federal Work-Study, institutionally sponsored loans available. Financial aid application deadline: 3/15. *Faculty research:* Muscle biomechanics, nerve regeneration, morphometrics, ethnography, postural control. • Dr. Averell S. Overby, Interim Director, 740-593-1225. Fax: 740-593-0292. Application contact: Rhonda Gibson, Secretary, 740-593-1224.

Old Dominion University, College of Health Sciences, School of Community Health Professions and Physical Therapy, Norfolk, VA 23529. Offerings include physical therapy (MS). One or more programs accredited by APTA. School faculty: 9 full-time (7 women), 5 part-time (3 women), 10.7 FTE. *Application deadline:* 2/15 (rolling processing). *Application fee:* $30. *Expenses:* Tuition $180 per credit hour for state residents; $477 per credit hour for nonresidents. Fees $140 per year full-time, $32 per semester part-time. • Dr. George Maihafer, Chair, 757-683-4520. E-mail: gmaihafer@odu.edu.

Pacific University, School of Physical Therapy, Forest Grove, OR 97116-1797. Awards MSHS, MSPT. Accredited by APTA. Faculty: 9 full-time (5 women), 6 part-time (5 women), 10.29 FTE. Students: 107 full-time (75 women); includes 10 minority (1 African American, 6 Asian Americans, 2 Hispanics, 1 Native American), 1 international. Average age 27. 495 applicants, 13% accepted. In 1997, 36 degrees awarded (100% found work related to degree). *Degree requirements:* Thesis required, foreign language not required. *Application deadline:* 12/4. *Application fee:* $55. *Financial aid:* Federal Work-Study and career-related internships or fieldwork available. Financial aid applicants required to submit FAFSA. *Faculty research:* Balance disorders, stroke treatment, motor control in children, geriatrics, treatment outcomes. • Dr. Daiva Banaitis, Director, 503-359-2846. Application contact: Darcey Gardner, Admissions Counselor, 503-359-2900. Fax: 503-359-2975. E-mail: admissions@pacificu.edu.

Quinnipiac College, School of Health Sciences, Program in Physical Therapy, Hamden, CT 06518-1904. Offers advanced clinical practice (MSPT), orthopedic physical therapy (MSPT). Accredited by APTA. Part-time and evening/weekend programs available. Faculty: 7 full-time (3 women), 9 part-time (4 women). Students: 6 full-time (2 women), 71 part-time (50 women); includes 15 minority (4 African Americans, 9 Asian Americans, 2 Hispanics). Average age 30. 19 applicants, 100% accepted. In 1997, 15 degrees awarded. *Degree requirements:* Comprehensive exams required, thesis optional. *Average time to degree:* master's–2 years full-time, 4 years part-time. *Entrance requirements:* Minimum GPA of 2.5, physical therapist license. Application deadline: 8/1 (priority date; rolling processing). Application fee: $45. Electronic applications accepted. *Expenses:* Tuition $395 per credit hour. Fees $380 per year full-time. *Financial aid:* Available to part-time students. Financial aid applicants required to submit FAFSA. • Russell Woodman, Director, 203-281-8684. Fax: 203-281-8706. E-mail: woodman@quinnipiac.edu. Application contact: Scott Farber, Director of Graduate Admissions, 203-281-8795. Fax: 203-287-5238. E-mail: qcgradadmi@quinnipiac.edu.

See in-depth description on page 1255.

Regis University, School for Healthcare Professions, Program in Physical Therapy, Denver, CO 80221-1099. Awards MSPT. Accredited by APTA. Offered at Northwest Denver Campus. Faculty: 9 full-time (3 women), 12 part-time (6 women). Students: 50 full-time (35 women). Average age 26. 300 applicants, 18% accepted. In 1997, 49 degrees awarded. *Degree requirements:* Computer language required, foreign language and thesis not required. *Average time to degree:* master's–2 years full-time. *Entrance requirements:* GRE General Test (combined average 1650 on three sections). Application fee: $75. *Expenses:* Tuition $15,334 per year. Fees $210 per year. *Financial aid:* Federal Work-Study available. • Dr. Barbara Tschoepe, Director, 303-458-4340. Application contact: Kim Frisch, Admissions Counselor, 303-458-4340. Fax: 303-964-5474.

The Richard Stockton College of New Jersey, Graduate Programs, Program in Physical Therapy, Pomona, NJ 08240-9988. Awards MPT. Accredited by APTA. Faculty: 6 full-time (5 women). Students: 20 full-time (10 women). Average age 27. 278 applicants, 9% accepted. *Degree requirements:* Clinical rotation, project. *Application deadline:* 1/8 (priority date; rolling processing). *Application fee:* $35. *Financial aid:* 16 students received aid; Federal Work-Study and career-related internships or fieldwork available. Aid available to part-time students. Financial aid application deadline: 3/1; applicants required to submit FAFSA. *Faculty research:* Spinal flexibility in the well elderly, use of traditional Chinese medicine concepts in physical therapy. • Bess Kathrins, Head, 609-652-4638. Application contact: Steve Phillips, Assistant Director of Admissions, 609-652-4261. Fax: 609-748-5541. E-mail: iaprod624@pollux.stockton.edu.

Rockhurst College, College of Arts and Sciences, Division of Natural, Applied and Quantitative Sciences, Program in Physical Therapy Education, Kansas City, MO 64110-2561. Awards MPT. Accredited by APTA. Faculty: 5 full-time (3 women), 7 part-time (5 women). Students: 88 full-time (62 women); includes 8 minority (5 African Americans, 2 Hispanics, 1 Native American). Average age 27. 250 applicants, 16% accepted. In 1997, 38 degrees awarded. *Entrance requirements:* Interview, minimum GPA of 3.0. Application deadline: 1/2. Application fee: $20. Electronic applications accepted. *Expenses:* Tuition $335 per semester hour. Fees $15 per year. *Financial aid:* In 1997–98, 76 students received aid, including 5 research assistantships, 10 teaching assistantships, 5 administrative assistantships; institutionally sponsored loans and career-related internships or fieldwork also available. Financial aid application deadline: 4/1; applicants required to submit FAFSA. *Faculty research:* Clinical decision making, effects of exercise on cardiovascular status, kinematic studies of motor performance in premature infants, geriatrics, infant pull to stand. • Ellen Spake, Chair, 816-501-4059. E-mail: spake@vax1.rockhurst.edu. Application contact: Stephanie Pruitt, 816-501-4059. Fax: 816-501-4169. E-mail: pruitt@vax1.rockhurst.edu.

Rutgers, The State University of New Jersey, Camden, Program in Physical Therapy, Camden, NJ 08102-1401. Awards MPT. Accredited by APTA. Offered jointly with the University of Medicine and Dentistry of New Jersey. Faculty: 4 full-time (all women), 6 part-time (3 women), 7.5 FTE. Students: 44 full-time (26 women); includes 7 minority (1 African American, 2 Asian Americans, 4 Hispanics). Average age 26. 297 applicants, 17% accepted. In 1997, 19 degrees awarded (100% found work related to degree). *Degree requirements:* Comprehensive exam, internships, major project required, foreign language and thesis not required. *Average time to degree:* master's–2 years full-time. *Entrance requirements:* GRE General Test (minimum score 500 on each section), physical therapy experience. Application deadline: 12/15. Application fee: $40. *Expenses:* Tuition $6492 per year full-time, $268 per credit part-time for state residents; $9520 per year full-time, $395 per credit part-time for nonresidents. Fees $891 per year full-time, $160 per semester (minimum) part-time. *Financial aid:* 35 students received aid; Federal Work-Study, institutionally sponsored loans, and career-related internships or fieldwork available. Aid available to part-time students. Financial aid application deadline: 3/15; applicants required to submit FAFSA. *Faculty research:* Clinical education, migrant workers, balance in the elderly, sports and orthopedics, cumulative trauma-upper extremity. • Dr. Marie Koval Nardone, Acting Director, 609-964-2690. Fax: 609-964-8304. E-mail: mnardone@umdnj.edu. Application contact: Pat Lubbe, 609-225-6104.

Sacred Heart University, College of Education and Health Professions, Faculty of Physical Therapy, 5151 Park Avenue, Fairfield, CT 06432-1000. Awards MSPT. Faculty: 7 full-time (4 women), 10 part-time (6 women). Students: 77 full-time (49 women); includes 7 minority (2 African Americans, 3 Asian Americans, 1 Hispanic, 1 Native American). 96 applicants, 59% accepted. *Application deadline:* 2/1 (rolling processing). *Application fee:* $40 ($100 for international students). *Expenses:* Tuition $365 per credit. Fees $78 per semester. • Dr. Michael Emery, Director, 203-365-7573. Application contact: Elizabeth Nugent, Graduate Admissions Counselor, 203-371-7880. Fax: 203-365-4732. E-mail: gradstudies@sacredheart.edu.

St. Ambrose University, College of Human Services, Physical Therapy Department, Davenport, IA 52803-2898. Awards MPT. Accredited by APTA. *Degree requirements:* Board exams required, foreign language and thesis not required. *Average time to degree:* master's–3 years full-time. *Entrance requirements:* GRE General Test (combined average 1700 on three sections), minimum undergraduate GPA of 2.8. Application deadline: 1/1 (priority date). Application fee: $25. *Faculty research:* Human motor control, orthopedic physical therapy, cardiopulmonary physical therapy, kinesiology/biomechanics.

Saint Francis College, Physical Therapy Program, Loretto, PA 15940-0600. Awards MPT. Program new for fall 1998. • Dr. Edward Pisarski, Chair, 814-472-3123.

Saint Louis University, School of Allied Health Professions, Program in Physical Therapy, St. Louis, MO 63104. Awards MSPT, MS(R)PT. Accredited by APTA. MS(R)PT being phased out; applicants no longer accepted. students enter MSPT program as freshmen. Faculty: 5 full-time (4 women), 4 part-time (3 women). Students: 1 (woman) full-time, 7 part-time (5 women); includes 1 minority (African American), 3 international. 4 applicants, 25% accepted. In 1997, 1

Directory: Physical Therapy

Saint Louis University (continued)

degree awarded. *Degree requirements:* Thesis, comprehensive oral exam required, foreign language not required. *Entrance requirements:* GRE General Test, physical therapy license. Application deadline: 7/1 (rolling processing; 11/1 for spring admission). Application fee: $40. *Tuition:* $542 per credit hour. *Financial aid:* In 1997–98, 1 teaching assistantship was awarded; career-related internships or fieldwork also available. Financial aid application deadline: 4/1. *Faculty research:* Pediatric physical therapy, geriatric physical therapy, spinal-cord injury, brain injury. • Dr. William Siler, Director, 314-577-8505. Application contact: Dr. Marcia Buresch, Assistant Dean of the Graduate School, 314-977-2240. Fax: 314-977-3943.

Samuel Merritt College, Department of Physical Therapy, Oakland, CA 94609-3108. Awards MPT, MSPT. Accredited by APTA. Faculty: 8 full-time (6 women), 12 part-time (9 women), 11.82 FTE. Students: 123 full-time (87 women), 14 part-time (6 women); includes 35 minority (27 Asian Americans, 8 Hispanics). Average age 31. 352 applicants, 23% accepted. In 1997, 32 degrees awarded. *Average time to degree:* master's–2.5 years full-time, 4.2 years part-time. *Entrance requirements:* GRE General Test (minimum combined score of 1500 on three sections required, 450 on verbal), TOEFL (minimum score 600), minimum GPA of 2.6 in science, 2.8 overall in last 60 hours; related work experience; interview. Application deadline: 1/2. Application fee: $50. *Expenses:* Tuition $605 per unit (minimum). Fees $25 per year. *Financial aid:* In 1997–98, 102 students received aid, including scholarships totaling $10,000; Federal Work-Study and career-related internships or fieldwork also available. Financial aid application deadline: 3/2; applicants required to submit FAFSA. *Faculty research:* Human movement, motor control. Total annual research expenditures: $6350. • Dr. Martha Jewell, Chairperson, 510-869-6241. Fax: 510-869-6282. Application contact: John Garten-Schumann, Director of Admissions, 510-869-6576. Fax: 510-869-6525.

San Francisco State University, College of Health and Human Services, Program in Physical Therapy, San Francisco, CA 94132-1722. Awards MPT. Accredited by APTA. Offered jointly with the University of California, San Francisco. *Degree requirements:* Comprehensive exam. *Average time to degree:* master's–2.3 years full-time. *Entrance requirements:* GRE, minimum GPA of 3.0, 150 hours of work experience. Application deadline: 11/15. Application fee: $55. *Expenses:* Tuition $0 for state residents; $246 per unit for nonresidents. Fees $1982 per year full-time, $1316 per year part-time. *Faculty research:* Balance disorders, movement disorders, gait, psychological issues in disability, cardiopulmonary disorders.

Shenandoah University, Department of Physical Therapy, 1460 University Drive, Winchester, VA 22601-5195. Awards MPT. Accredited by APTA. Faculty: 7 full-time (4 women), 1 (woman) part-time. Students: 116 full-time (69 women); includes 4 minority (3 Asian Americans, 1 Native American), 1 international. Average age 26. 444 applicants, 56% accepted. In 1997, 38 degrees awarded. *Degree requirements:* Design project, group research project required, foreign language and thesis not required. *Entrance requirements:* GRE. Application deadline: 2/1. Application fee: $30. Electronic applications accepted. *Tuition:* $15,600 per year. *Faculty research:* Movement analysis, life span development. • Dr. Camilla Wilson, Chair, 540-665-5520. Fax: 540-665-5530. E-mail: cwilson@su.edu. Application contact: Michael Carpenter, Director of Admissions, 540-665-4581. Fax: 540-665-4627. E-mail: admit@su.edu.

Simmons College, Graduate School for Health Studies, Program in Physical Therapy, Boston, MA 02115. Awards MS. Accredited by APTA. Faculty: 6 full-time (5 women), 10 part-time (all women). Students: 119 full-time (92 women); includes 4 minority (3 African Americans, 1 Hispanic). Average age 25. 514 applicants, 18% accepted. In 1997, 38 degrees awarded. *Entrance requirements:* GRE, TOEFL (minimum score 550). Application deadline: 2/1. Application fee: $50. *Expenses:* Tuition $587 per credit hour. Fees $20 per year. *Financial aid:* Federal Work-Study, institutionally sponsored loans available. Aid available to part-time students. Financial aid application deadline: 3/1; applicants required to submit FAFSA. *Faculty research:* Cardiopulmonary rehabilitation, manual physical therapy techniques, early child development of motor skills. • Diane Jette, Director, 617-521-2635. E-mail: djette@simmons.edu. Application contact: Christine Keuleyan, Admission Coordinator, 617-521-2650. Fax: 617-521-3137. E-mail: keuleyan@simmons.edu.

See in-depth description on page 1329.

Slippery Rock University of Pennsylvania, College of Human Service Professions, School of Physical Therapy, Slippery Rock, PA 16057. Awards DPT. Accredited by APTA. *Degree requirements:* Clinical residency. *Entrance requirements:* GRE, minimum GPA of 2.75. Application deadline: 7/1 (priority date; rolling processing; 11/1 for spring admission). Application fee: $35. *Tuition:* $4484 per year full-time, $247 per credit part-time for state residents; $7667 per year full-time, $423 per credit part-time for nonresidents.

Southwest Baptist University, School of Graduate Studies, Department of Physical Therapy, 1600 University Avenue, Bolivar, MO 65613-2597. Awards MSPT. Program admits applicants in the spring only. Faculty: 5 full-time (4 women), 8 part-time (2 women). Students: 40 full-time (17 women); includes 2 minority (both Asian Americans), 2 international. Average age 28. 95 applicants, 42% accepted. *Entrance requirements:* GRE General Test, interviews, minimum GPA of 2.75. Application deadline: (4/1 for spring admission). Application fee: $25. *Expenses:* Tuition $17,000 per year. Fees $300 per year. *Financial aid:* 40 students received aid. *Faculty research:* Pediatrics, balance disorders, senile dementia, clinical education, tissue dynamics. • Dr. Dorothy Hash, Chair, 417-326-1672. E-mail: dhash@sbuniv.edu. Application contact: Angela Carr, Office Manager, 417-326-1672. Fax: 417-326-1658. E-mail: pt@sbuniv.edu.

Southwest Texas State University, School of Health Professions, Department of Physical Therapy, San Marcos, TX 78666. Awards MSPT. Accredited by APTA. Applicants accepted in summer only. Faculty: 7 full-time (6 women), 1 (woman) part-time. Students: 35 full-time (24 women), 35 part-time (25 women); includes 10 minority (1 African American, 3 Asian Americans, 6 Hispanics), 1 international. Average age 28. In 1997, 31 degrees awarded. *Degree requirements:* Comprehensive exam required, thesis optional, foreign language not required. *Entrance requirements:* GRE General Test (minimum combined score of 1000), TOEFL (minimum score 550), minimum GPA of 3.0 in last 60 hours. Application deadline: 7/15 (priority date; 11/15 for spring admission). Application fee: $45 ($70 for international students). *Expenses:* Tuition $648 per year full-time, $120 per semester (minimum) part-time for state residents; $4500 per year full-time, $750 per semester (minimum) part-time for nonresidents. Fees $1264 per year full-time, $314 per semester (minimum) part-time. *Financial aid:* Federal Work-Study, institutionally sponsored loans, and career-related internships or fieldwork available. Aid available to part-time students. Financial aid application deadline: 4/1; applicants required to submit FAFSA. *Faculty research:* Exercise, gait training, wellness. • Dr. Barbara L. Sanders, Chair, 512-245-8351. Fax: 512-245-8352. E-mail: bs04@swt.edu.

Springfield College, Program in Physical Therapy, Springfield, MA 01109-3797. Awards MS. Accredited by APTA. Faculty: 7 full-time (5 women), 14 part-time (11 women), 11 FTE. Students: 69 full-time (57 women), 2 part-time (both women). Average age 23. 229 applicants, 23% accepted. In 1997, 48 degrees awarded. *Degree requirements:* Comprehensive exam, research project required, foreign language and thesis not required. *Entrance requirements:* Interview, minimum GPA of 3.0. Application deadline: 12/1. Application fee: $40. *Expenses:* Tuition $474 per credit. Fees $25 per year. *Financial aid:* In 1997–98, 2 teaching assistantships (both to first-year students) were awarded; fellowships, full and partial tuition waivers, Federal Work-Study, and career-related internships or fieldwork also available. Financial aid application deadline: 3/1. • Linda Tsoumas, Director, 413-748-3369. Application contact: Donald J. Shaw Jr., Director of Graduate Admissions, 413-748-3225. Fax: 413-748-3694. E-mail: dshaw@spfldcol.edu.

State University of New York Health Science Center at Syracuse, College of Health Related Professions, Department of Physical Therapy, Syracuse, NY 13210-2334. Awards MPS. Accredited by APTA. Faculty: 6 full-time (4 women), 3 part-time (2 women), 7.25 FTE. Students: 32 full-time (15 women); includes 5 minority (1 African American, 2 Asian Americans, 2 Hispanics). 296 applicants, 11% accepted. *Application deadline:* rolling. *Application fee:* $30. *Expenses:* Tuition $5100 per year full-time, $213 per credit hour part-time for state residents; $8416 per year full-time, $351 per credit hour part-time for nonresidents. Fees $405 per year full-time, $108 per semester (minimum) part-time. *Financial aid:* 26 students received aid; Federal Work-Study available. Aid available to part-time students. Financial aid application deadline: 4/1; applicants required to submit FAFSA. • Dr. Pamela Gramet, Interim Chair, 315-464-5101. Application contact: Jennifer Welch, Director of Admissions, 315-464-4570. Fax: 315-464-8867. E-mail: welchj@vax.cs.hscsyr.edu.

Temple University, Health Sciences Center and Graduate School, College of Allied Health Professions, Department of Physical Therapy, Philadelphia, PA 19140. Awards MPT, MS, PhD. One or more programs accredited by APTA. PhD new for fall 1998. Part-time and evening/weekend programs available. Faculty: 8 full-time (all women). Students: 143 (96 women); includes 33 minority (15 African Americans, 10 Asian Americans, 6 Hispanics, 2 Native Americans), 1 international. 408 applicants, 22% accepted. In 1997, 53 master's awarded. *Degree requirements:* For master's, research paper or thesis required, foreign language not required; for doctorate, dissertation. *Entrance requirements:* For master's, GRE General Test, interview. Application deadline: 12/15. Application fee: $40. *Expenses:* Tuition $323 per semester hour for state residents; $444 per semester hour for nonresidents. Fees $170 per year full-time, $28 per semester (minimum) part-time. *Financial aid:* Fellowships, research assistantships, institutionally sponsored loans, and career-related internships or fieldwork available. Aid available to part-time students. *Faculty research:* Balance dysfunction, biomechanics, development, qualitative research, developmental neuroscience, health services. • Dr. Laurita Hack, Chair, 215-707-8177. Fax: 215-707-7500.

See in-depth description on page 1263.

Texas Tech University Health Sciences Center, School of Allied Health, Program in Physical Therapy, Lubbock, TX 79430-0002. Awards MPT. Accredited by APTA. Faculty: 12 full-time (4 women), 2 part-time (1 woman). Students: 193 full-time (114 women); includes 17 minority (2 African Americans, 13 Hispanics, 2 Native Americans). Average age 23. 244 applicants, 27% accepted. In 1997, 64 degrees awarded (100% found work related to degree). *Average time to degree:* master's–3 years full-time. *Application deadline:* 1/15. *Application fee:* $30. *Expenses:* Tuition $36 per credit hour for state residents; $249 per credit hour for nonresidents. Fees $1348 per year full-time for state residents; $1349 per year full-time for nonresidents. *Financial aid:* Career-related internships or fieldwork available. Financial aid application deadline: 9/1; applicants required to submit FAFSA. *Faculty research:* Closed chain proprioception; effects of unloading; retrospective studies including ACL, kippotherapy, orthopedic/sports medicine injuries. • Dr. H. H. Merrifield, Chair, 806-743-3220. Application contact: Rob Shive, Assistant Dean, Admissions and Student Affairs, 806-743-3220. Fax: 806-743-3249. E-mail: sahras@ttuhsc.edu.

Texas Woman's University, School of Physical Therapy, Denton, TX 76204. Awards MS, PhD. One or more programs accredited by APTA. Part-time and evening/weekend programs available. Faculty: 19 full-time (16 women), 10 part-time (9 women). Students: 176 full-time (128 women), 143 part-time (107 women); includes 49 minority (6 African Americans, 25 Asian Americans, 18 Hispanics), 4 international. Average age 30. 315 applicants, 29% accepted. In 1997, 87 master's awarded (100% found work related to degree); 3 doctorates awarded. *Degree requirements:* For master's, thesis required, foreign language not required; for doctorate, 1 foreign language, computer language, dissertation. *Entrance requirements:* For master's, GRE General Test, minimum GPA of 3.0; for doctorate, GRE General Test, MAT, minimum GPA of 3.0. Application deadline: 10/1. Application fee: $25. *Financial aid:* Research assistantships, teaching assistantships, Federal Work-Study, institutionally sponsored loans, and career-related internships or fieldwork available. Aid available to part-time students. Financial aid application deadline: 4/1. *Faculty research:* Cardiopulmonary studies, neuromuscular studies. • Dr. Carolyn Rozier, Dean, 940-898-2460.

Thomas Jefferson University, Program in Physical Therapy, Philadelphia, PA 19107. Awards MS. Accredited by APTA. Faculty: 4 full-time (2 women). Students: 44 full-time (27 women); includes 1 minority (Hispanic). 44 applicants, 100% accepted. In 1997, 44 degrees awarded. *Degree requirements:* Thesis or alternative required, foreign language not required. *Entrance requirements:* Minimum GPA of 3.0 in major. Application fee: $30. *Tuition:* $18,100 per year full-time, $625 per credit part-time. *Financial aid:* Fellowships, Federal Work-Study, institutionally sponsored loans available. Aid available to part-time students. Financial aid application deadline: 5/1; applicants required to submit FAFSA. *Faculty research:* Gait and motion analysis, motor control and learning, single motor unit discharge in human muscle, musculoskeletal injuries, toddler motor skill level. • Dr. Roger M. Nelson, Graduate Director, 215-503-8961. Fax: 215-923-2475. E-mail: nelsonr@jeflin.tju.edu. Application contact: Jessie F. Pervall, Director of Admissions, 215-503-4400. Fax: 215-503-3433. E-mail: cgs-info@mail.tju.edu.

Touro College, Barry Z. Levine School of Health Sciences, Physical Therapy Program, Dix Hills, NY 11746. Awards MS. Accredited by APTA. Faculty: 20 full-time, 10 part-time. Students: 95. *Degree requirements:* Thesis, community service project. *Entrance requirements:* Interview, minimum GPA of 2.8, 100 hours of physical therapy work experience. Application fee: $40. • Jill Auster-Liebhaber, Director, 516-673-3200. Application contact: Office of Admissions, 516-673-3200.

The University of Alabama at Birmingham, Graduate School, School of Health Related Professions, Program in Physical Therapy, Birmingham, AL 35294. Awards MS. Accredited by APTA. Students: 98 full-time (66 women), 1 (woman) part-time; includes 10 minority (3 African Americans, 3 Asian Americans, 3 Hispanics, 1 Native American). 78 applicants, 100% accepted. In 1997, 42 degrees awarded. *Degree requirements:* Thesis optional. *Entrance requirements:* GRE General Test (minimum score 500 on each section, 1000 combined) or MAT (minimum score 50), minimum GPA of 3.0 in last 60 hours. Application fee: $30 ($60 for international students). Electronic applications accepted. *Expenses:* Tuition $129 per credit hour for state residents; $258 per credit hour for nonresidents. Fees $627 per year (minimum) full-time, $110 per quarter (minimum) part-time. *Financial aid:* In 1997–98, 22 students received aid, including 2 fellowships averaging $1,000 per month, 15 research assistantships averaging $900 per month; Federal Work-Study, institutionally sponsored loans, and career-related internships or fieldwork also available. *Faculty research:* Geriatrics, exercise physiology, aquatic therapy, industrial rehabilitation, outcome measurement. • Dr. Marilyn Gossman, Director, 205-934-3566.

University of Alberta, Faculty of Graduate Studies and Research, Department of Physical Therapy, Edmonton, AB T6G 2E1, Canada. Awards M Sc. Faculty: 8 full-time (5 women), 2 part-time (0 women), 8.75 FTE. Students: 4 full-time (all women), 5 part-time (all women). Average age 28. 6 applicants, 67% accepted. In 1997, 1 degree awarded (100% found work related to degree). *Degree requirements:* Thesis required, foreign language not required. *Entrance requirements:* TOEFL or TSE, bachelor's degree in physical therapy, minimum GPA of 6.5 on a 9.0 scale. Application deadline: 2/1 (priority date; rolling processing). Application fee: $60. *Expenses:* Tuition $390 per course for Canadian residents; $781 per course for nonresidents. Fees $500 per year full-time, $184 per year part-time. *Financial aid:* In 1997–98, 4 scholarships, tuition scholarships (1 to a first-year student) were awarded; research assistantships, teaching assistantships also available. *Faculty research:* Spinal disorders, musculoskeletal disorders, ergonomics, sports therapy, motor development. • Dr. M. Chrite-Battié, Chair, 403-492-5984. E-mail: mc.battie@ualberta.ca. Application contact: Anita Moore, Administrative Assistant, Graduate Studies, 403-492-0840. Fax: 403-492-1626. E-mail: anita.moore@ualberta.ca.

University of California, San Francisco, Program in Physical Therapy, San Francisco, CA 94143. Awards MPT. Accredited by APTA. Offered jointly with San Francisco State University. Faculty: 4 full-time (3 women), 1 (woman) part-time. In 1997, 31 degrees awarded. *Entrance requirements:* GRE General Test. Application fee: $40. *Expenses:* Tuition $0 for state residents; $9384 per year for nonresidents. Fees $4488 per year. *Financial aid:* Institutionally sponsored loans available. Financial aid application deadline: 1/10. • Dr. Nancy Byl, Director, 415-476-3146. Application contact: Lillie Wong, Program Assistant, 415-476-3147.

University of Central Arkansas, College of Health and Applied Sciences, Department of Physical Therapy, Conway, AR 72035-0001. Awards MS, PhD. Accredited by APTA. PhD new for fall 1998. Faculty: 5 full-time (2 women), 9 part-time (3 women), 11 FTE. Students: 174 full-time (97 women), 2 part-time (both women); includes 5 minority (1 Asian American, 2 Hispanics, 2 Native Americans), 1 international. 204 applicants, 46% accepted. In 1997, 71 master's awarded. *Degree requirements:* For master's, thesis optional. *Entrance requirements:* For master's, Allied Health Professions Admissions Test, minimum GPA of 2.7. Application deadline: 3/1 (priority date; rolling processing; 10/1 for spring admission). Application fee: $15 ($40 for international students). *Expenses:* Tuition $161 per credit hour for state residents; $298 per credit hour for nonresidents. Fees $150 per year. *Financial aid:* In 1997–98, 2 assistantships were awarded. Financial aid application deadline: 2/15. • Dr. Venita Lovelace-Chandler, Chairperson, 501-450-3611. E-mail: venital@mail.uca.edu.

University of Colorado Health Sciences Center, Program in Physical Therapy, Denver, CO 80262. Awards MS. Accredited by APTA. Students: 116 full-time (81 women), 5 part-time (4 women); includes 15 minority (2 African Americans, 7 Asian Americans, 5 Hispanics, 1 Native American). Average age 28. 414 applicants, 27% accepted. In 1997, 61 degrees awarded. *Entrance requirements:* GRE General Test, minimum GPA of 2.75. Application deadline: 1/2. Application fee: $30. • Dr. Carolyn B. Heriza, Director, 303-372-9144. Application contact: Cheryl Gilmer, Secretary, 303-372-9144.

University of Delaware, College of Arts and Science, Program in Physical Therapy, Newark, DE 19716. Awards MPT. Accredited by APTA. Faculty: 9 full-time (3 women), 20 part-time (10 women). Students: 70 full-time (46 women); includes 6 minority (4 African Americans, 2 Hispanics). Average age 25. 550 applicants, 7% accepted. In 1997, 38 degrees awarded. *Degree requirements:* Thesis optional, foreign language not required. *Average time to degree:* master's–2 years full-time. *Entrance requirements:* GRE General Test. Application deadline: 1/15. Application fee: $45. *Expenses:* Tuition $4250 per year full-time, $236 per credit hour part-time for state residents; $12,250 per year full-time, $681 per credit hour part-time for nonresidents. Fees $466 per year full-time, $15 per semester (minimum) part-time. *Financial aid:* In 1997–98, 4 fellowships (1 to a first-year student) averaging $1,300 per month and totaling $46,800 were awarded; Federal Work-Study and career-related internships or fieldwork also available. Financial aid application deadline: 1/15. *Faculty research:* Movement sciences, electrophysiology, applied physiology, health care of the elderly. • Paul Mettler, Chairman, 302-831-8910. E-mail: pmettler@brahms.udel.edu. Application contact: Patricia Simpson, Administrative Assistant, 302-831-8910. Fax: 302-831-4234. E-mail: patricia.simpson@mvs.udel.edu.

University of Florida, College of Health Professions, Department of Physical Therapy, Gainesville, FL 32611. Awards MHS, MPT. One or more programs accredited by APTA. Part-time programs available. Faculty: 8. Students: 2 full-time (both women), 14 part-time (9 women); includes 4 minority (all Asian Americans), 5 international. 13 applicants, 62% accepted. In 1997, 6 degrees awarded. *Entrance requirements:* GRE General Test, minimum GPA of 3.0. Application deadline: 6/5 (priority date; rolling processing). Application fee: $20. *Tuition:* $138 per credit hour for state residents; $481 per credit hour for nonresidents. *Financial aid:* In 1997–98, 1 student received aid, including 1 teaching assistantship averaging $1,382 per month; fellowships, research assistantships, and career-related internships or fieldwork also available. *Faculty research:* Exercise physiology, motor control, rehabilitation, geriatrics. • Carl G. Kukulka, Chair, 352-395-0085. Fax: 352-395-0731. E-mail: ckukulka@hp.ufl.edu. Application contact: Dr. Denis Brunt, Graduate Coordinator, 352-395-0085.

University of Illinois at Chicago, College of Associated Health Professions, Physical Therapy Program, Chicago, IL 60607-7128. Awards MS. Faculty: 5 full-time (3 women), 1 (woman) part-time. Students: 1 (woman) full-time, 4 part-time (3 women); includes 1 international. Average age 34. 9 applicants, 22% accepted. In 1997, 1 degree awarded. *Degree requirements:* Thesis required, foreign language not required. *Entrance requirements:* GRE General Test, TOEFL (minimum score 550), minimum GPA of 3.75 on a 5.0 scale. Application fee: $40 ($50 for international students). *Financial aid:* In 1997–98, 1 tuition service fee waiver was awarded; fellowships, research assistantships, teaching assistantships also available. • Jules Rothstein, Head, 312-996-2546.

University of Indianapolis, Krannert School of Physical Therapy, Indianapolis, IN 46227-3697. Awards MHS, MS. One or more programs accredited by APTA. Part-time and evening/weekend programs available. *Average time to degree:* master's–2.5 years full-time, 4 years part-time. *Entrance requirements:* GRE General Test. Application deadline: 12/1. Application fee: $50. *Faculty research:* Patella positioning, reaction time, allocation of physical therapy resources.

The University of Iowa, College of Medicine and Graduate College, Graduate Programs in Medicine, Program in Physical Therapy, Iowa City, IA 52242-1316. Awards MA, MPT, PhD. One or more programs accredited by APTA. Faculty: 4 full-time (0 women), 1 part-time (0 women), 4.65 FTE. Students: 81 full-time (55 women), 7 part-time (3 women); includes 2 minority (1 Asian American, 1 Hispanic), 4 international. Average age 24. 368 applicants, 10% accepted. In 1997, 39 master's awarded (95% found work related to degree, 5% continued full-time study); 1 doctorate awarded (100% entered university research/teaching). *Degree requirements:* Thesis/dissertation required, foreign language not required. *Average time to degree:* master's–2.5 years full-time, 3 years part-time; doctorate–4 years full-time. *Entrance requirements:* For master's, GRE, TOEFL (minimum score 600), bachelor's degree or certificate in physical therapy. Application deadline: 2/1. Application fee: $20. *Expenses:* Tuition $3166 per year full-time for state residents; $10,202 per year full-time for nonresidents. Fees $150 per year full-time. *Financial aid:* In 1997–98, 8 students received aid, including 2 research assistantships averaging $1,420 per month and totaling $22,706, 2 teaching assistantships (1 to a first-year student) averaging $1,420 per month and totaling $25,567; Federal Work-Study, institutionally sponsored loans also available. Aid available to part-time students. Financial aid application deadline: 1/1. *Faculty research:* Muscle fatigue, motor control, pain mechanisms, body composition, sports medicine, occupational safety. Total annual research expenditures: $48,079. • Dr. David H. Nielsen, Director, 319-335-9791. Fax: 319-335-9707. E-mail: david-nielsen@uiowa.edu.

University of Kansas, School of Allied Health, Department of Physical Therapy, Kansas City, KS 66160. Awards MS. Accredited by APTA. Part-time programs available. Faculty: 11 full-time (8 women), 2 part-time (both women). Students: 80 full-time (61 women), 1 (woman) part-time; includes 2 minority (both Asian Americans). Average age 27. 167 applicants, 26% accepted. In 1997, 34 degrees awarded. *Degree requirements:* Thesis, comprehensive exams required, foreign language not required. *Entrance requirements:* GRE General Test, TOEFL (minimum score 570), minimum GPA of 3.0. Application deadline: 11/1. Application fee: $25. *Expenses:* Tuition $2400 per year full-time, $100 per credit hour part-time for state residents; $7890 per year full-time, $329 per credit hour part-time for nonresidents. Fees $428 per year full-time, $31 per credit hour part-time. *Financial aid:* Federal Work-Study, institutionally sponsored loans, and career-related internships or fieldwork available. Aid available to part-time students. Financial aid application deadline: 4/3; applicants required to submit FAFSA. • Dr. Chukuka Enwemeka, Chairman, 913-588-6799. E-mail: enwemeka@kumc.edu. Application contact: Stephania Bell, Admissions Chairperson, 913-588-6799. Fax: 913-588-4568. E-mail: sbell2@kumc.edu.

University of Kentucky, Graduate School Programs from the College of Allied Health, Program in Physical Therapy, Lexington, KY 40506-0032. Awards MSPT. Accredited by APTA. Faculty: 5 full-time (1 woman). Students: 126 full-time (84 women), 4 part-time (2 women); includes 4 minority (2 African Americans, 1 Asian American, 1 Hispanic). 69 applicants, 94% accepted. In 1997, 64 degrees awarded. *Degree requirements:* Thesis, comprehensive exam required, foreign language not required. *Entrance requirements:* GRE General Test (minimum combined score of 1000 on three sections), minimum undergraduate GPA of 2.5, U.S. physical therapist license. Application deadline: 7/19 (rolling processing). Application fee: $30 ($35 for international students). *Financial aid:* In 1997–98, 2 fellowships were awarded; research assistantships, teaching assistantships also available. *Faculty research:* Orthopedics, biomechanics, electrophysiological stimulation, neural plasticity, brain damage and mechanism. Total annual research expenditures: $35,000. • Dr. Arthur J. Nitz, Director of Graduate Studies, 606-233-5274. Application contact: Dr. Constance L. Wood, Associate Dean, 606-257-4613. Fax: 606-323-1928.

University of Mary, Program in Physical Therapy, 7500 University Drive, Bismarck, ND 58504-9652. Awards MPT. Applications must be requested in writing. Faculty: 4 full-time (1 woman), 46 part-time (15 women). Students: 59 full-time (34 women); includes 1 minority (Native American). 77 applicants, 39% accepted. In 1997, 22 degrees awarded. *Degree requirements:* Directed study and professional paper required, foreign language and thesis not required. *Average time to degree:* master's–2.5 years full-time. *Entrance requirements:* Minimum GPA of 3.0 in core requirements. Application deadline: 4/1. Application fee: $25. *Financial aid:* Teaching assistantships and career-related internships or fieldwork available. • Michael Parker, Chairperson, 701-255-7500. Fax: 701-255-7687.

University of Maryland Eastern Shore, Department of Physical Therapy, Princess Anne, MD 21853-1299. Awards MPT. Accredited by APTA. Faculty: 5 full-time (3 women), 9 part-time (6 women). Students: 74 full-time (46 women); includes 22 minority (14 African Americans, 5 Asian Americans, 3 Hispanics), 1 international. Average age 22. 285 applicants, 11% accepted. In 1997, 11 degrees awarded (100% found work related to degree). *Degree requirements:* Clinical practicum, research project required, foreign language and thesis not required. *Average time to degree:* master's–3 years full-time. *Entrance requirements:* GRE, TOEFL (minimum score 550), interview, minimum GPA of 3.0. Application deadline: 2/1. Application fee: $30. *Expenses:* Tuition $143 per credit hour for state residents; $253 per credit hour for nonresidents. Fees $50 per year. *Financial aid:* In 1997–98, 2 students received aid, including 2 teaching assistantships; Federal Work-Study and career-related internships or fieldwork also available. Aid available to part-time students. Financial aid application deadline: 3/1. • Dr. Raymond Blakely, Chair, 410-651-6360. Fax: 410-651-6259. E-mail: rblakely@umes-bird.umd.edu.

University of Massachusetts Lowell, College of Health Professions, Department of Physical Therapy, 1 University Avenue, Lowell, MA 01854-2881. Awards MS. Accredited by APTA. Students: 100 full-time (65 women), 51 part-time (33 women); includes 5 minority (1 African American, 3 Asian Americans, 1 Hispanic). 300 applicants, 18% accepted. In 1997, 34 degrees awarded. *Degree requirements:* Thesis optional, foreign language not required. *Entrance requirements:* GRE General Test (minimum combined score of 1300). Application deadline: 2/15. Application fee: $20 ($35 for international students). *Tuition:* $4867 per year full-time, $618 per semester (minimum) part-time for state residents; $10,276 per year full-time, $1294 per semester (minimum) part-time for nonresidents. *Financial aid:* In 1997–98, 5 teaching assistantships were awarded; fellowships also available. Financial aid application deadline: 2/15. *Faculty research:* Orthopedics, pediatrics, electrophysiology, cardiopulmonary, neurology. • Dr. Joseph Dorsey, Chair, 978-934-4464. E-mail: joseph_dorsey@woods.uml.edu.

University of Medicine and Dentistry of New Jersey, School of Health Related Professions, Newark, NJ 07107-3001. Offerings include physical therapy (MPT, MS). One or more programs accredited by APTA. MS, PhD (biomedical informatics) offered jointly with New Jersey Institute of Technology; MS, PhD (health science), MS (physician assistant), MA offered jointly with Seton Hall University; MPT offered jointly with Rutgers, The State University of New Jersey, Camden. School faculty: 44 full-time (36 women), 15 part-time (10 women), 51.55 FTE. *Application deadline:* rolling. *Application fee:* $35. • Dr. David M. Gibson, Dean, 973-972-4276. Application contact: Dr. Laura Nelson, Associate Dean of Academic and Student Services, 973-972-5453. Fax: 973-972-7028. E-mail: shrp.adm@umdnj.edu.

See in-depth description on page 1267.

University of Miami, School of Medicine and Graduate School, Graduate Programs in Medicine, Physical Therapy Program, Coral Gables, FL 33124. Awards MSPT, PhD. One or more programs accredited by APTA. Faculty: 18 full-time (10 women), 3 part-time (2 women), 20 FTE. Students: 165 full-time (113 women), 1 (woman) part-time; includes 17 minority (3 African Americans, 5 Asian Americans, 7 Hispanics, 2 Native Americans). Average age 26. 450 applicants, 22% accepted. In 1997, 58 master's awarded. *Degree requirements:* For master's, thesis or alternative required, foreign language not required; for doctorate, dissertation required, foreign language not required. *Entrance requirements:* For master's, GRE General Test (minimum combined score of 1500 on three sections), TOEFL (minimum score 550), interview, 100 hours of experience; for doctorate, GRE General Test (minimum combined score of 1500 on three sections; average 1800), TOEFL. Application deadline: 11/15 (rolling processing). Application fee: $35. *Expenses:* Tuition $815 per credit hour. Fees $174 per year. *Financial aid:* In 1997–98, 140 students received aid, including 20 research assistantships (4 to first-year students), 24 teaching assistantships (2 to first-year students); Federal Work-Study, institutionally sponsored loans, and career-related internships or fieldwork also available. Financial aid application deadline: 3/1. *Faculty research:* Electrotherapy, SCI and immune system, backpain evaluation, gait analysis of amputees, balance, motor control. • Dr. Sherrill Hayes, Director, 305-284-4535. Application contact: Vivian Montti, Admissions Coordinator, 305-284-4535.

University of Michigan–Flint, School of Health Professions and Studies, Program in Physical Therapy, Flint, MI 48502-1950. Awards MPT. Accredited by APTA. Part-time programs available. Faculty: 8 full-time (5 women). Students: 37 full-time (29 women), 2 part-time (1 woman); includes 5 minority (1 African American, 4 Asian Americans). 208 applicants, 19% accepted. In 1997, 35 degrees awarded (100% found work related to degree). *Average time to degree:* master's–3 years full-time. *Application deadline:* 2/1. *Application fee:* $30. *Financial aid:* Federal Work-Study and career-related internships or fieldwork available. Aid available to part-time students. Financial aid application deadline: 4/1. *Faculty research:* Cumulative trauma disorders, motor control biomechanics, wound healing, oncology rehabilitation. • Dr. Paulette Cebulski, Director, 810-762-3373. Application contact: Mary Davis, Senior Admissions Counselor, 810-762-3300.

University of Minnesota, Twin Cities Campus, Medical School and Graduate School, Graduate Programs in Medicine, Department of Physical Medicine and Rehabilitation, Minneapolis, MN 55455-0213. Awards MS, PhD.

University of Minnesota, Twin Cities Campus, Medical School and Graduate School, Graduate Programs in Medicine, Program in Physical Therapy, Minneapolis, MN 55455-0213. Awards MS. Accredited by APTA. *Entrance requirements:* GRE, TOEFL (minimum score 550).

University of Missouri–Columbia, School of Medicine, School of Health Related Professions, Program in Physical Therapy, Columbia, MO 65211. Awards MPT. Accredited by APTA. Program new for fall 1998. *Expenses:* Tuition $14,036 per year for state residents; $28,224 per year for nonresidents. Fees $682 per year. • Dr. Marilyn Sanford, Director of Graduate Studies, 573-882-7103.

University of Mobile, Graduate Programs, School of Physical Therapy, Mobile, AL 36663-0220. Awards MSPT. Accredited by APTA. Faculty: 7 full-time (6 women), 7 part-time (6 women), 11 FTE. Students: 71 full-time (35 women); includes 2 minority (both African Americans), 1 international. Average age 28. *Degree requirements:* Comprehensive exam. *Entrance requirements:* GRE General Test (minimum combined score of 1500 on three sections), TOEFL (minimum score 550). Application deadline: 8/3 (priority date; rolling processing; 1/15 for spring admission). Application fee: $75. *Tuition:* $160 per semester hour. *Financial aid:* Application deadline 8/1. • Dr. Geneva R. Johnson, Dean, 334-431-3941.

The University of Montana–Missoula, School of Pharmacy and Allied Health Sciences, Program in Physical Therapy, Missoula, MT 59812-0002. Awards MS. Accredited by APTA. *Degree requirements:* Oral defense of thesis required, foreign language not required. *Entrance*

Directory: Physical Therapy

The University of Montana–Missoula (continued)

requirements: GRE General Test. Application deadline: 9/1 (rolling processing). Application fee: $30. *Tuition:* $2499 per year (minimum) full-time, $376 per semester (minimum) part-time for state residents; $6528 per year (minimum) full-time, $1048 per semester (minimum) part-time for nonresidents. *Financial aid:* Application deadline 2/15. • Dr. Ann K. Williams, Chairperson, 406-243-4753.

University of Nebraska Medical Center, School of Allied Health Professions, Division of Physical Therapy Education, Omaha, NE 68198-0001. Awards MPT. Accredited by APTA. *Faculty research:* Isokinetics, gait patterns, pediatrics, compliance of patients with home programs, biomechanics—norms versus hemiplegics.

The University of North Carolina at Chapel Hill, School of Medicine and Graduate School, Graduate Programs in Medicine, Department of Medical Allied Health Professions, Division of Physical Therapy, Program in Physical Therapy, Chapel Hill, NC 27599. Awards MPT. Accredited by APTA. Faculty: 16 full-time (13 women). Students: 80 full-time (59 women); includes 15 minority (5 African Americans, 2 Asian Americans, 7 Hispanics, 1 Native American). 366 applicants, 11% accepted. In 1997, 28 degrees awarded. *Entrance requirements:* GRE General Test (minimum combined score of 1000), minimum GPA of 3.0. Application deadline: 11/1. Application fee: $55. *Expenses:* Tuition $1428 per year for state residents; $10,414 per year for nonresidents. Fees $782 per year. *Financial aid:* Federal Work-Study, institutionally sponsored loans available. *Faculty research:* Motor development/motor control, sports, and orthopedic injuries, movement in older adults, postural control, functional assessment. • Dr. Darlene K. Sekerak, Director, Division of Physical Therapy, 919-966-4708. E-mail: dsekerak@css.unc.edu.

University of North Dakota, School of Medicine and Graduate School, Graduate Programs in Medicine, Department of Physical Therapy, Grand Forks, ND 58202. Awards MPT. Accredited by APTA. Faculty: 4 full-time (3 women). Students: 50 full-time (32 women). 50 applicants, 100% accepted. In 1997, 47 degrees awarded. *Degree requirements:* Thesis or alternative. *Entrance requirements:* GRE, TOEFL (minimum score 550), minimum GPA of 3.0, successful completion of pre-physical therapy program. Application deadline: 2/15 (priority date; rolling processing). Application fee: $20. *Financial aid:* In 1997–98, 1 student received aid, including 1 fellowship totaling $1,000; research assistantships, teaching assistantships also available. • Dr. Tom Mohr, Chairperson, 701-777-2831. Fax: 701-777-4199. E-mail: tommohr@mail.med.und.nodak.edu.

University of Osteopathic Medicine and Health Sciences, College of Health Sciences, Des Moines, IA 50312-4104. Offerings include physical therapy (MS). Accredited by APTA. College faculty: 21. *Entrance requirements:* Minimum GPA of 3.0. Application deadline: 12/31 (rolling processing). Application fee: $35. *Expenses:* Tuition $265 per credit hour. Fees $75 per year. • Dr. Susan Cigelman, Interim Dean, 515-271-1634. Application contact: Dr. Dennis L. Bates, Director of Admissions, 515-271-1450. Fax: 515-271-1578.

University of Pittsburgh, School of Health and Rehabilitation Sciences, Department of Physical Therapy, Pittsburgh, PA 15260. Awards MPT. Accredited by APTA. Students: 86 full-time (53 women), 2 part-time (both women); includes 5 minority (4 African Americans, 1 Asian American). 548 applicants, 12% accepted. In 1997, 38 degrees awarded. *Application fee:* $50. *Expenses:* Tuition $9402 per year full-time, $388 per credit part-time for state residents; $19,372 per year full-time, $799 per credit part-time for nonresidents. Fees $480 per year full-time, $180 per year part-time. *Financial aid:* In 1997–98, 1 teaching assistantship averaging $1,286 per month, 1 assistantship averaging $1,049 per month were awarded; Federal Work-Study, institutionally sponsored loans, and career-related internships or fieldwork also available. Aid available to part-time students. Financial aid applicants required to submit FAFSA. *Faculty research:* Biomechanics, neuromuscular system, sports medicine, movement analysis, validity/outcomes of clinical procedures. Total annual research expenditures: $480,272. • Dr. Anthony Delitto, Chairman, 412-647-1223. Fax: 412-647-1222. E-mail: delitto+@pitt.edu. Application contact: Shameem Gangjee, Director of Admissions, 412-647-1258. Fax: 412-647-1255. E-mail: shrsadmit+@pitt.edu.

See in-depth description on page 1351.

University of Pittsburgh, School of Health and Rehabilitation Sciences, Interdisciplinary Program in Health and Rehabilitation Sciences, Pittsburgh, PA 15260. Offerings include physical therapy (MS). Accredited by APTA. *Entrance requirements:* GRE General Test, TOEFL, minimum QPA of 3.0. Application deadline: rolling. Application fee: $30 ($40 for international students). *Expenses:* Tuition $9402 per year full-time, $388 per credit part-time for state residents; $19,372 per year full-time, $799 per credit part-time for nonresidents. Fees $480 per year full-time, $180 per year part-time. • Dr. George Carvell, Associate Dean of Graduate Studies, 412-647-1296. E-mail: shrsadmit+@pitt.edu. Application contact: Shameem Gangjee, Director of Admissions, 412-647-1258. Fax: 412-647-1255. E-mail: shrsadmit+@pitt.edu.

See in-depth description on page 1351.

University of Puget Sound, School of Occupational and Physical Therapy, Program in Physical Therapy, Tacoma, WA 98416-0005. Awards MPT. Accredited by APTA. Faculty: 6 full-time (4 women), 17 part-time (11 women), 8.45 FTE. Students: 88 full-time (58 women), 1 (woman) part-time; includes 17 minority (1 African American, 12 Asian Americans, 4 Hispanics). Average age 27. 311 applicants, 10% accepted. In 1997, 31 degrees awarded. *Degree requirements:* Thesis or alternative, publishable paper. *Entrance requirements:* GRE General Test, minimum GPA of 3.0. Application deadline: 2/1. Application fee: $40. *Expenses:* Tuition $19,640 per year full-time, $2480 per course part-time. Fees $155 per year. *Financial aid:* Federal Work-Study and career-related internships or fieldwork available. • Kathleen Hummel-Berry, Director, 253-756-3531. Application contact: George Mills, Director of Admissions, 253-756-3211.

University of Rhode Island, College of Human Science and Services, Department of Physical Therapy, Kingston, RI 02881. Awards MS. Accredited by APTA. *Entrance requirements:* MAT or GRE. Application deadline: 4/15 (priority date; rolling processing; 11/15 for spring admission). Application fee: $35. *Expenses:* Tuition $3446 per year full-time, $191 per credit part-time for state residents; $9850 per year full-time, $547 per credit part-time for nonresidents. Fees $1276 per year full-time, $135 per semester (minimum) part-time.

University of St. Augustine for Health Sciences, Graduate Programs, Division of Distance Education, St. Augustine, FL 32084. Awards M Sc PT. Part-time programs available. Postbaccalaureate distance learning degree programs offered (minimal on-campus study). Faculty: 22 part-time (5 women). Students: 284 part-time (124 women); includes 32 minority (6 African Americans, 19 Asian Americans, 6 Hispanics, 1 Native American), 17 international. 129 applicants, 100% accepted. In 1997, 1 degree awarded. *Average time to degree:* master's–5 years part-time. *Entrance requirements:* GRE General Test (minimum combined score of 1000), BS in physical therapy or equivalent. Application fee: $50. *Financial aid:* In 1997–98, 4 students received aid, including 1 teaching assistantship; career-related internships or fieldwork also available. Aid available to part-time students. *Faculty research:* Orthopaedic, end-feel exam, medical profile of physical therapy patients, efficacy of outcomes of physical therapy. • Patricia King Baker, Director, 904-826-0084 Ext. 208. E-mail: tkbaker@aug.com. Application contact: Barbara Bower, Administrative Assistant, 904-826-0084 Ext. 210. Fax: 904-826-0085.

University of St. Augustine for Health Sciences, Graduate Programs, Division of Doctoral Studies, St. Augustine, FL 32084. Awards DPT. Part-time programs available. Postbaccalaureate distance learning degree programs offered (minimal on-campus study). Students: 60 part-time (20 women); includes 7 minority (2 African Americans, 4 Asian Americans, 1 Hispanic), 1 international. 16 applicants, 94% accepted. In 1997, 1 degree awarded (100% found work related to degree). *Average time to degree:* doctorate–4 years part-time. *Entrance requirements:* GRE General Test (minimum combined score of 900), master's degree in related field. Application deadline: 10/1. Application fee: $300. *Financial aid:* In 1997–98, 1 teaching assistantship was awarded; partial tuition waivers and career-related internships or fieldwork also available. Aid available to part-time students. • Dr. Richard Jensen, Director, 904-826-0084. Fax: 904-826-0085.

University of St. Augustine for Health Sciences, Graduate Programs, Division of First Professional Education, St. Augustine, FL 32084. Awards MOT, MPT. One or more programs accredited by APTA. Faculty: 13 full-time (7 women), 5 part-time (3 women). Students: 264 full-time (145 women), 2 part-time (0 women); includes 24 minority (5 African Americans, 10 Asian Americans, 9 Hispanics), 2 international. Average age 27. 284 applicants, 19% accepted. In 1997, 98 degrees awarded (100% found work related to degree). *Average time to degree:* master's–2 years full-time. *Entrance requirements:* GRE General Test (minimum combined score of 1000), minimum GPA of 3.0. Application deadline: 2/1 (priority date; 7/15 for spring admission). Application fee: $50. • Raymond M. Patterson, Director, 904-823-0013. Application contact: Julie T. Cook, Admissions Coordinator/Registrar, 904-810-0330. Fax: 904-826-4193.

University of South Dakota, School of Medicine and Graduate School, Graduate Programs in Health Sciences, Department of Physical Therapy, Vermillion, SD 57069-2390. Awards MS. Accredited by APTA. Faculty: 5 full-time (3 women), 3 part-time (all women). Students: 51 full-time (33 women). Average age 24. 225 applicants, 12% accepted. In 1997, 26 degrees awarded (100% found work related to degree). *Average time to degree:* master's–2 years full-time. *Entrance requirements:* GRE General Test, GRE Subject Test. Application deadline: 1/1. Application fee: $15. *Financial aid:* Career-related internships or fieldwork available. • Lana Svien-Senne, Chairperson, 605-677-6241. Application contact: Dr. Charles N. Kaufman, Dean of the Graduate School, 605-677-6498.

University of Southern California, Graduate School, School of Health Affairs, Department of Biokinesiology and Physical Therapy, Program in Physical Therapy, Los Angeles, CA 90089. Awards MS, DPT. One or more programs accredited by APTA. Students: 247 full-time (151 women), 10 part-time (4 women); includes 84 minority (3 African Americans, 67 Asian Americans, 12 Hispanics, 2 Native Americans), 3 international. Average age 27. 373 applicants, 35% accepted. In 1997, 1 master's, 9 doctorates awarded. *Degree requirements:* For doctorate, dissertation required, foreign language not required. *Entrance requirements:* GRE General Test. Application deadline: 12/15 (priority date). Application fee: $55. *Financial aid:* In 1997–98, 26 fellowships, 7 teaching assistantships, 16 scholarships were awarded; research assistantships, Federal Work-Study, institutionally sponsored loans also available. Aid available to part-time students. Financial aid application deadline: 2/15; applicants required to submit FAFSA. • Dr. Sandra Howell, Interim Chair, Department of Biokinesiology and Physical Therapy, 213-342-2900.

University of Tennessee at Chattanooga, School of Human Services, Program in Physical Therapy, Chattanooga, TN 37403-2598. Awards MSPT. Accredited by APTA. Program new for fall 1998. *Degree requirements:* Qualifying exams required, foreign language and thesis not required. *Application deadline:* rolling. *Application fee:* $25. *Tuition:* $2864 per year full-time, $160 per credit hour part-time for state residents; $6806 per year full-time, $379 per credit hour part-time for nonresidents. *Financial aid:* Application deadline 4/1. • Dr. Galan Janeksela, Dean, School of Human Services, 423-755-4133. Fax: 423-755-4132. E-mail: galan-janeksela@utc.edu. Application contact: Dr. Deborah Arfken, Assistant Provost for Graduate Studies, 423-755-4667. Fax: 423-755-4478. E-mail: darfken@utcvm.utc.edu.

University of Tennessee, Memphis, College of Allied Health Sciences, Memphis, TN 38163-0002. Awards MSPT. Accredited by APTA. *Degree requirements:* Thesis.

The University of Texas Medical Branch at Galveston, School of Allied Health Sciences, Department of Physical Therapy, Galveston, TX 77555. Awards MPT. Accredited by APTA. Faculty: 9 full-time (7 women). Students: 120 full-time (105 women); includes 18 minority (1 African American, 7 Asian Americans, 10 Hispanics). Average age 25. 275 applicants, 13% accepted. In 1997, 40 degrees awarded (100% found work related to degree). *Degree requirements:* Thesis or alternative required, foreign language not required. *Average time to degree:* master's–2.5 years full-time. *Entrance requirements:* Health Occupations Aptitude Examination, experience in field, minimum GPA of 3.0. Application deadline: 11/1. Application fee: $30. *Expenses:* Tuition $36 per credit hour for state residents; $249 per credit hour for nonresidents. Fees $146 per year full-time, $124 per semester (minimum) part-time. *Financial aid:* 70 students received aid; Federal Work-Study, institutionally sponsored loans, and career-related internships or fieldwork available. *Faculty research:* Clinical education, educational outcomes, movement analysis, biomechanics, cardiorespiratory fitness. Total annual research expenditures: $120,000. • Kurt Mossberg, Chair, 409-772-3068. Fax: 409-772-1613. E-mail: kmossberg@utmb.edu. Application contact: Richard Lewis, Registrar, 409-772-1215. Fax: 409-772-5056.

University of the Pacific, Department of Physical Therapy, Stockton, CA 95211-0197. Awards MS. Accredited by APTA. Faculty: 4 full-time (3 women), 4 part-time (1 woman). Students: 64 full-time (36 women), 1 part-time (0 women); includes 8 minority (6 Asian Americans, 2 Hispanics), 1 international. Average age 25. 623 applicants, 5% accepted. In 1997, 32 degrees awarded (100% found work related to degree). *Entrance requirements:* GRE General Test, TOEFL, minimum GPA of 3.0. Application deadline: 1/4. Application fee: $50. *Expenses:* Tuition $19,000 per year full-time, $594 per unit part-time. Fees $30 per year (minimum). *Financial aid:* Federal Work-Study available. Financial aid application deadline: 3/1. • Carolyn Hultgren, Chair, 209-946-3159. Fax: 209-946-2410.

University of the Sciences in Philadelphia, Program in Physical Therapy, Philadelphia, PA 19104-4495. Awards MS. Program being phased out; applicants no longer accepted. Part-time and evening/weekend programs available. Faculty: 4 full-time (3 women). Students: 9 part-time (6 women). Average age 33. In 1997, 2 degrees awarded. *Degree requirements:* Thesis optional, foreign language not required. *Faculty research:* Orthopedic and neurologic physical therapy, motor control and orthotic evaluation, effects of electrical stimulation on wound healing. • Dr. Barbara Bourbon, Director, 215-596-8599. E-mail: b.bourbo@pcps.edu.

University of Utah, College of Health, Department of Physical Therapy, Salt Lake City, UT 84112-1107. Awards MPT. Accredited by APTA. Faculty: 4 full-time (2 women), 33 part-time (14 women). Students: 96 full-time (55 women); includes 5 minority (1 African American, 3 Asian Americans, 1 Hispanic), 1 international. Average age 27. *Entrance requirements:* TOEFL (minimum score 500). Application fee: $30 ($50 for international students). *Tuition:* $2045 per year full-time, $562 per semester (minimum) part-time for state residents; $6129 per year full-time, $1607 per semester (minimum) part-time for nonresidents. • Carolee E. Moncur, Co-Director, 801-581-8681. E-mail: cmoncur@phth.health.utah.edu.

University of Vermont, School of Allied Health Sciences, Department of Physical Therapy, Burlington, VT 05405-0160. Awards MS. Students: 8. 6 applicants, 33% accepted. In 1997, 1 degree awarded. *Degree requirements:* Thesis required, foreign language not required. *Entrance requirements:* GRE General Test, TOEFL (minimum score 550), physical therapist license. Application deadline: 4/1 (priority date; rolling processing; 11/15 for spring admission). Application fee: $25. *Expenses:* Tuition $302 per credit for state residents; $755 per credit for nonresidents. Fees $434 per year full-time, $46 per semester (minimum) part-time. *Financial aid:* Fellowships, research assistantships, teaching assistantships, Federal Work-Study available. Financial aid application deadline: 3/1. • Dr. Jean Held, Coordinator, 802-656-2659.

University of Washington, School of Medicine and Graduate School, Graduate Programs in Medicine, Department of Rehabilitation Medicine, Program in Physical Therapy, Seattle, WA 98195. Awards MPT, MS. Faculty: 5 full-time (3 women). Students: 0. Average age 32. 0 applicants. In 1997, 7 degrees awarded (100% found work related to degree). *Degree requirements:* Thesis required (for some programs), foreign language not required. *Average time to degree:* master's–1 year full-time, 4 years part-time. *Entrance requirements:* GRE General Test (minimum score 500 on each section), professional degree in physical thearpy. Application deadline: 3/15 (priority date). Application fee: $45. *Financial aid:* Traineeships and career-related internships or fieldwork available. *Faculty research:* Pediatrics. • Application contact: Coordinator, 206-685-7408. Fax: 206-685-3244. E-mail: gleep@u.washington.edu.

The University of Western Ontario, Biosciences Division, Department of Physical Therapy, London, ON N6A 5B8, Canada. Awards M Sc. *Financial aid:* Application deadline 4/1. • Dr. J. Kramer, Chair, 519-661-3360.

University of Wisconsin–La Crosse, College of Science and Allied Health, Department of Physical Therapy, La Crosse, WI 54601-3742. Awards MSPT. Accredited by APTA. Faculty: 8 full-time (4 women), 2 part-time (both women), 9.5 FTE. Students: 61 full-time (48 women); includes 1 international. Average age 26. 145 applicants, 22% accepted. *Degree requirements:* Thesis optional, foreign language not required. *Entrance requirements:* Minimum GPA of 3.2. Application deadline: 11/1. Application fee: $38. *Tuition:* $3737 per year full-time, $208 per credit part-time for state residents; $11,921 per year full-time, $633 per credit part-time for nonresidents. *Financial aid:* In 1997–98, 3 students received aid, including 1 research assistantship (to a first-year student) averaging $827 per month and totaling $7,444; Federal Work-Study and career-related internships or fieldwork also available. Financial aid application deadline: 6/30; applicants required to submit FAFSA. *Faculty research:* Exercise protocols with orthopedic patients, effects of exercise on chronic diseases and the disabled, effects of exercise on the elderly. • Dr. Karen Palmer-McLean, Coordinator, 608-785-8459. E-mail: mclean@mail.uwlax.edu. Application contact: Dennis Fater, Chair of Admissions Committee, 608-785-8471. Fax: 608-785-8460. E-mail: fater@mail.uwlax.edu.

Virginia Commonwealth University, School of Allied Health Professions, Department of Physical Therapy, Richmond, VA 23284-9005. Offerings include advanced physical therapy (MS), anatomy and physical therapy (PhD), entry-level physical therapy (MS), physiology and physical therapy (PhD). Department faculty: 11 full-time, 1 part-time. *Degree requirements:* For master's, thesis required, foreign language not required. *Entrance requirements:* GRE General Test. Application deadline: 2/1 (priority date). Application fee: $30 ($0 for international students). *Tuition:* $4960 per year full-time, $257 per credit part-time for state residents; $12,652 per year full-time, $684 per credit part-time for nonresidents. • Dr. Robert L. Lamb, Chair, 804-828-0234. Fax: 804-828-8111. E-mail: rllamb@vcu.edu.

Virginia Commonwealth University, Departments of Physical Therapy and Anatomy, Program in Anatomy and Physical Therapy, Richmond, VA 23284-9005. Awards PhD. *Entrance requirements:* GRE General Test. Application deadline: 5/1. Application fee: $30 ($0 for international students). *Tuition:* $4960 per year full-time, $257 per credit part-time for state residents; $12,652 per year full-time, $684 per credit part-time for nonresidents. • Application contact: Dr. Sheryl Finucane, 804-828-0234.

Walsh University, Graduate Studies, Program in Physical Therapy, North Canton, OH 44720-3396. Awards M Sc. Faculty: 4 full-time (3 women). Students: 26 full-time. *Degree requirements:* Practicum required, foreign language and thesis not required. *Entrance requirements:* Previous course work in anatomy, physiology, chemistry, and statistics. Application fee: $25. *Expenses:* Tuition $363 per credit hour. Fees $10 per credit hour. • Dr. Janis Daly, Director, 330-490-7362. Application contact: Brett Freshour, Dean of Enrollment Management, 330-490-7171. Fax: 330-490-7165.

Washington University in St. Louis, School of Medicine, Graduate Programs in Medicine, Program in Physical Therapy, St. Louis, MO 63130-4899. Awards MHS, MSPT, PhD. One or more programs accredited by APTA. Students: 237 full-time (190 women), 4 part-time (3 women); includes 19 minority (2 African Americans, 15 Asian Americans, 1 Hispanic, 1 Native American), 2 international. Average age 24. 536 applicants, 23% accepted. In 1997, 78 master's awarded. *Degree requirements:* For doctorate, dissertation required, foreign language not required. *Average time to degree:* master's–2.5 years full-time, 3.5 years part-time. *Entrance requirements:* For master's, GRE (MSPT), clinical experience; for doctorate, GRE, sample of written work. Application deadline: 1/31 (rolling processing). Application fee: $75. *Tuition:* $20,230 per year. *Financial aid:* 192 students received aid; Federal Work-Study, institutionally sponsored loans available. Aid available to part-time students. Financial aid applicants required to submit CSS PROFILE or FAFSA. *Faculty research:* Movement and movement dysfunction. • Dr. Susan S. Deusinger, Director, 314-286-1400. Application contact: Linda Murry, Coordinator of Admissions and Student Affairs, 314-286-1400.

Wayne State University, College of Pharmacy and Allied Health Professions, Faculty of Allied Health Professions, Department of Physical Therapy, Detroit, MI 48202. Awards MSPT. One or more programs accredited by APTA. Students: 62 full-time (39 women). 50 applicants, 78% accepted. *Expenses:* Tuition $163 per credit hour for state residents; $355 per credit hour for nonresidents. Fees $498 per year full-time, $114 per semester (minimum) part-time. • Louis Amundsen, Chairperson, 313-577-1432.

Western Carolina University, College of Applied Science, Department of Physical Therapy, Cullowhee, NC 28723. Awards MPT. Students: 31 full-time (20 women); includes 1 minority (Asian American). 142 applicants, 46% accepted. *Degree requirements:* Comprehensive exam required, foreign language and thesis not required. *Entrance requirements:* GRE General Test. Application deadline: 2/1 (rolling processing). Application fee: $35. *Tuition:* $1799 per year full-time, $144 per credit hour (minimum) part-time for state residents; $9069 per year full-time, $1053 per credit hour (minimum) part-time for nonresidents. *Financial aid:* In 1997–98, 1 student received aid, including 1 fellowship (to a first-year student) totaling $5,000. Financial aid application deadline: 3/15. • Dr. Katherine L. White, Head, 828-227-7070. Application contact: Kathleen Owen, Assistant to the Dean, 828-227-7398. Fax: 828-227-7480.

Western University of Health Sciences, School of Allied Health Professions, Program in Physical Therapy, Pomona, CA 91766-1854. Awards MPT. Accredited by APTA. Students: 104. *Application deadline:* 5/31. *Application fee:* $60. *Tuition:* $22,240 per year. • Application contact: Susan M. Hanson, Director of Admissions, 909-469-5335.

West Virginia University, School of Medicine, Graduate Programs in Human Performance and Applied Exercise Science, Program in Physical Therapy, Morgantown, WV 26506. Awards MPT. Accredited by APTA. Students enter program as undergraduates. *Degree requirements:* Clinical rotation. *Application deadline:* 2/15. *Application fee:* $45. *Tuition:* $9204 per year for state residents; $22,704 per year for nonresidents. • Dr. Mary Beth Mandich, Chair, 304-293-3610. Fax: 304-293-7105. E-mail: mmandich@wvuhsc1.hsc.wvu.edu.

Wheeling Jesuit University, Department of Physical Therapy, Wheeling, WV 26003-6295. Awards MSPT. Faculty: 14 (9 women). Students: 57 full-time (41 women); includes 2 minority (1 Asian American, 1 Hispanic). Average age 26. *Degree requirements:* 1 foreign language required, thesis not required. *Entrance requirements:* Minimum GPA of 3.0 in previous course work. Application deadline: 5/1 (9/1 for spring admission). Application fee: $25. *Faculty research:* Pediatrics. • Mary Jo Wisniewski, Director, 304-243-2432. Fax: 304-243-2500. Application contact: Carol Carroll, Graduate Secretary, 304-243-2344. Fax: 304-243-4441.

Wichita State University, College of Health Professions, School of Health Sciences, Department of Physical Therapy, Wichita, KS 67260. Awards MPT. Accredited by APTA. Faculty: 1 (woman) full-time. Students: 62 full-time (43 women), 2 part-time (1 woman); includes 5 minority (2 African Americans, 1 Asian American, 2 Native Americans), 3 international. Average age 27. 217 applicants, 15% accepted. In 1997, 32 degrees awarded. *Entrance requirements:* GRE, TOEFL (minimum score 550), minimum GPA of 3.0. Application deadline: 1/31 (9/30 for spring admission). Application fee: $25 ($40 for international students). Electronic applications accepted. *Expenses:* Tuition $2303 per year full-time, $96 per credit hour part-time for state residents; $7691 per year full-time, $321 per credit hour part-time for nonresidents. Fees $490 per year full-time, $75 per semester (minimum) part-time. *Financial aid:* In 1997–98, 5 teaching assistantships (2 to first-year students) averaging $453 per month and totaling $14,500, 2 graduate assistantships averaging $417 per month and totaling $7,500 were awarded; research assistantships, Federal Work-Study, institutionally sponsored loans, and career-related internships or fieldwork also available. Financial aid application deadline: 4/1; applicants required to submit FAFSA. • Linda Black, Interim Chair, 316-978-3604. E-mail: black@chp.twsu.edu. Application contact: Catherine Freeman, Secretary, 316-978-5770. Fax: 316-978-3025. E-mail: freeman@chp.twsu.edu.

Widener University, School of Human Service Professions, Institute for Physical Therapy Education, Chester, PA 19013-5792. Awards MS. Accredited by APTA. Faculty: 8 full-time (5 women), 17 part-time (4 women). Students: 116 full-time (69 women), 1 part-time (0 women); includes 1 minority (Native American). Average age 27. In 1997, 18 degrees awarded. *Average time to degree:* master's–3 years full-time. *Entrance requirements:* GRE. Application deadline: 1/30. Application fee: $40. *Tuition:* $16,500 per year full-time, $550 per credit hour part-time. *Financial aid:* Teaching assistantships, Federal Work-Study, institutionally sponsored loans available. *Faculty research:* Social support and recovery of function, movement dysfunction, circulation. • Dr. Stephen C. Wilhite, Acting Associate Dean and Director, 610-499-1275. Application contact: Carol Greenhalgh, Admissions Coordinator, 610-499-4272.

Worcester State College, Graduate Studies, Department of Physical Therapy, Worcester, MA 01602-2597. Awards MS. Program new for spring 1999. *Degree requirements:* Comprehensive exam. *Entrance requirements:* GRE General Test or MAT. Application fee: $10 ($40 for international students). *Tuition:* $395 per credit hour. • Michael Vaillancourt, Coordinator, 508-929-8869. Application contact: Andrea Wetmore, Graduate Admissions Counselor, 508-929-8120. E-mail: awetmore@worc.mass.edu.

Physician Assistant Studies

Alderson–Broaddus College, Medical Science Department, Philippi, WV 26416. Offerings include physician assistant (MS), with options in emergency medicine, rural primary care. Postbaccalaureate distance learning degree programs offered (minimal on-campus study). Department faculty: 17 part-time (0 women). *Degree requirements:* Thesis, 2 years of clinical experience required, foreign language not required. *Average time to degree:* master's–2 years full-time. *Entrance requirements:* National Commission on Certification of Physician Assistants certification or bachelor's degree in related field, full-time clinical employment. Application deadline: 6/1 (priority date; rolling processing). Application fee: $35. *Tuition:* $420 per credit hour. • Dr. Sharon Boni, Chairperson, 304-457-6284. Fax: 304-457-6239. Application contact: Dick Mercer, Director, Master's Degree Program, 304-457-6356. Fax: 304-457-6308. E-mail: mercer@ab.edu.

Allentown College of St. Francis de Sales, Graduate Division, Program in Physician Assistant Studies, Center Valley, PA 18034-9568. Awards MSPAS. Faculty: 5 full-time (4 women), 3 part-time (1 woman), 6 FTE. Students: 25 full-time (14 women). Average age 30. 100 applicants, 25% accepted. *Entrance requirements:* GRE General Test, healthcare experience. Application deadline: 1/15 (priority date; rolling processing). Application fee: $35. *Tuition:* $12,350 per year. *Faculty research:* Antibiotic usage, intestinal cystitis, postpartum depression. • Christine Bruce, Director, 610-282-1100 Ext. 1474. E-mail: chb0@email.allencol.edu. Application contact: Pamela Wertman, Administrative Assistant, 610-282-1100 Ext. 1415. Fax: 610-282-1893. E-mail: plw0@email.allencol.edu.

Barry University, School of Graduate Medical Sciences, Physician Assistant Program, Miami Shores, FL 33161-6695. Awards MCMS. Students: 31 full-time (24 women); includes 5 minority (2 African Americans, 2 Asian Americans, 1 Hispanic). Average age 31. 61 applicants, 51% accepted. *Application deadline:* 6/1 (rolling processing). *Application fee:* $95. Electronic applications accepted. *Tuition:* $16,800 per year full-time, $575 per credit part-time. • Application contact: Alex Collins, Director of Graduate Medical Sciences, 305-899-3130. Fax: 305-899-3253. E-mail: collins@jeanne.barry.edu.

Baylor College of Medicine, Medical School, Physician Assistant Program, Houston, TX 77030-3498. Awards MS. Students: 92 full-time (74 women); includes 16 minority (3 African Americans, 7 Asian Americans, 6 Hispanics). Average age 29. 620 applicants, 6% accepted. In 1997, 28 degrees awarded. *Degree requirements:* Thesis required, foreign language not required. *Average time to degree:* master's–2.5 years full-time. *Entrance requirements:* GRE General Test (minimum combined score of 1000), minimum GPA of 3.0. Application deadline: 1/1 (rolling processing). Application fee: $30. *Expenses:* Tuition $8200 per year. Fees $502 per year (minimum). *Financial aid:* 70 students received aid; Federal Work-Study, institutionally sponsored loans, and career-related internships or fieldwork available. Financial aid application deadline: 5/8; applicants required to submit FAFSA. • Albert Simon, Director, 713-798-4619. Fax: 713-798-6128. E-mail: asimon@bcm.tmc.edu. Application contact: Dr. L. Leighton Hill, Assistant Dean, 713-798-4842.

Beaver College, Program in Physician Assistant Studies, Glenside, PA 19038-3295. Awards MSPAS. *Entrance requirements:* GRE General Test or MCAT, TOEFL. *Expenses:* Tuition $19,800 per year. Fees $90 per year.

Central Michigan University, College of Health Professions, Department of Health Promotion and Rehabilitation, Mount Pleasant, MI 48859. Offerings include physician assistant (MS). Department faculty: 41 full-time (13 women). *Application deadline:* 2/15. *Application fee:* $30. *Expenses:* Tuition $139 per credit hour (minimum) for state residents; $276 per credit hour (minimum) for nonresidents. Fees $260 per year full-time, $150 per semester part-time. • Dr. Herman Triezenberg, Chairperson, 517-774-3541. E-mail: 320ss5j@cmich.edu.

Chatham College, School of Graduate Studies, Programs in Health Sciences, Program in Physician Assistant Studies, Pittsburgh, PA 15232-2826. Awards MPAS. Faculty: 8 full-time (5 women). Students: 71 full-time (56 women); includes 4 minority (3 African Americans, 1 Asian American). 84 applicants, 46% accepted. In 1997, 12 degrees awarded (100% found work related to degree). *Degree requirements:* Clinical experience. *Average time to degree:* master's–2 years full-time. *Application deadline:* 1/15. *Application fee:* $45. Electronic applications accepted. *Expenses:* Tuition $23,688 per year full-time, $395 per credit part-time. Fees $312 per year. *Financial aid:* 69 students received aid; career-related internships or fieldwork available. Aid available to part-time students. Financial aid applicants required to submit FAFSA. • Dr. Linda Allison, Director, 412-365-1412. Fax: 412-365-1213. E-mail: allison@chatham.edu. Application contact: Heidi Hemming, Graduate Admissions, 412-365-1290. Fax: 412-365-1609. E-mail: admissions@chatham.edu.

Announcement: Chatham College's MPAS program is a 2-year endeavor that emphasizes basic medicine and clinical methods. Teaching format is 100% problem-based learning, which involves tackling problems using clinical reasoning and research strategies under faculty

Directory: Physician Assistant Studies

Chatham College (continued)
supervision. Students are provided with excellent problem-solving skills needed for the required 10 clinical field placements. Students complete an intensive research project. Admissions requirements include a baccalaureate degree, prerequisite course work, overall and prerequisite QPA of 3.0 or higher, interview and writing sample, evidence of health-care volunteer experience, evidence of community service, and PA shadowing. E-mail at admissions@chatham.edu or visit the Web site at http://www.chatham.edu

---

Duke University, School of Medicine, Physician Assistant Program, Durham, NC 27708-0586. Awards MHS. Students: 86 full-time (67 women); includes 18 minority (6 African Americans, 5 Asian Americans, 5 Hispanics, 2 Native Americans). Average age 28. 574 applicants, 8% accepted. In 1997, 64 degrees awarded. *Entrance requirements:* GRE, minimum C average, 11 undergraduate hours in biology, 8 undergraduate hours in chemistry, minimum 6 months or 1000 hours of health care experience (preferably hands-on patient contact). Application deadline: 11/1 (rolling processing). Application fee: $55. *Expenses:* Tuition $19,710 per year. Fees $3707 per year. *Financial aid:* 76 students received aid; institutionally sponsored loans available. Financial aid application deadline: 5/1; applicants required to submit FAFSA. • Dr. Reginald D. Carter, Director, 919-681-3156. Fax: 919-681-3371.

Duquesne University, John G. Rangos, Sr. School of Health Sciences, Pittsburgh, PA 15282-0001. Offerings include physician assistant (MPA). School faculty: 30 full-time (17 women), 12 part-time (6 women), 34.8 FTE. *Average time to degree:* master's–2 years full-time. *Application deadline:* 12/1 (priority date). *Application fee:* $45. Electronic applications accepted. *Expenses:* Tuition $510 per credit. Fees $39 per credit. • Dr. Jerome L. Martin, Dean, 412-396-6012. E-mail: martin2@duq2.cc.duq.edu. Application contact: Deborah L. Durica, Director of Student and Alumni Services, 412-396-6652. Fax: 412-396-5554. E-mail: durica@duq2.cc.duq.edu.

Emory University, School of Medicine, Programs in Allied Health Professions, Program for Physician Assistant, Atlanta, GA 30322-1100. Awards MM Sc. Faculty: 7 full-time (5 women), 2 part-time (1 woman). Students: 149 full-time (84 women); includes 14 minority (7 African Americans, 3 Asian Americans, 4 Hispanics), 1 international. Average age 25. 781 applicants, 7% accepted. In 1997, 48 degrees awarded (100% found work related to degree). *Entrance requirements:* GRE General Test (minimum combined score of 1500 on three sections). Application deadline: 12/15. Application fee: $50. *Financial aid:* Federal Work-Study, institutionally sponsored loans available. Aid available to part-time students. Financial aid application deadline: 3/15; applicants required to submit CSS PROFILE or FAFSA. • Virginia Joslin, Director, 404-727-7827. E-mail: vjoslin@pa.emory.edu.

Finch University of Health Sciences/The Chicago Medical School, School of Related Health Sciences, Department of Physician Assistant, North Chicago, IL 60064-3095. Awards MS. Postbaccalaureate distance learning degree programs offered (minimal on-campus study). Faculty: 6 full-time (3 women), 8 part-time (3 women), 8.5 FTE. Students: 129 full-time (97 women). Average age 26. 143 applicants, 33% accepted. In 1997, 30 degrees awarded (100% found work related to degree). *Degree requirements:* Thesis required, foreign language not required. *Average time to degree:* master's–2 years full-time. *Entrance requirements:* Critical Thinking Exam (minimum score 47; average 68), GRE. Application deadline: 12/31 (rolling processing). Application fee: $25. *Tuition:* $403 per credit hour. *Faculty research:* Problem-based learning, testing in interview for future success, learning by case review via computer. • Patrick T. Knott, Chairman, 847-578-3312. E-mail: knottp@mis.finchcms.edu. Application contact: Allison Schlarbaum, Administrative Secretary, 847-578-3312. Fax: 847-578-8690. E-mail: schlarba@mis.finchcms.edu.

See in-depth description on page 1237.

Grand Valley State University, Science and Mathematics Division, School of Health Sciences, Physician Assistant Studies Program, Allendale, MI 49401-9403. Awards MS. Faculty: 3 full-time (0 women), 37 part-time (11 women). Students: 50 full-time (36 women); includes 3 minority (1 Asian American, 2 Native Americans). Average age 29. 125 applicants, 19% accepted. *Degree requirements:* Project required, foreign language and thesis not required. *Application fee:* $20. Electronic applications accepted. *Faculty research:* Clinical outcomes, geriatric medicine, dialysis, depression. • Dr. Frank Ward, Director, 616-895-2735. E-mail: wardf@gvsu.edu. Application contact: Carol Rappley, Secretary, 616-895-3356. Fax: 616-895-3350.

Kirksville College of Osteopathic Medicine, Arizona School of Health Sciences, PO Box 11037, Phoenix, AZ 85061-1037. Offerings include physician assistant (MS). School faculty: 30 full-time (18 women), 14 part-time (8 women). *Degree requirements:* Thesis required, foreign language not required. *Average time to degree:* master's–2 years full-time. *Entrance requirements:* GRE General Test (combined average 1639 on three sections), MCAT (average 25 for physician assistant). Application deadline: 2/1 (rolling processing). Application fee: $50. *Tuition:* $15,990 per year. • Dr. James Dearing, Associate Dean, 602-841-4077. Fax: 602-841-4092. Application contact: Stephanie Seyer, Assistant Director of Admissions, 660-626-2237. Fax: 660-626-2815.

Lock Haven University of Pennsylvania, Office of Graduate Studies, Department of Health Science, Lock Haven, PA 17745-2390. Offers program in physician assistant in rural primary care (MHS). Faculty: 4 full-time (1 woman), 3 part-time (0 women). Students: 51 full-time (32 women); includes 2 minority (1 African American, 1 Native American). Average age 24. 74 applicants, 36% accepted. *Application fee:* $25. Electronic applications accepted. *Expenses:* Tuition $3468 per year full-time, $193 per credit hour part-time for state residents; $6236 per year full-time, $346 per credit hour part-time for nonresidents. Fees $604 per year full-time, $46 per credit hour part-time for state residents; $604 per year full-time, $59 per credit hour part-time for nonresidents. *Financial aid:* Application deadline 8/1. • John Schroeder, Director, 717-893-2027. Application contact: Office of Admissions, 717-893-2027. Fax: 717-893-2201. E-mail: admissions@eagle.lhup.edu.

Marquette University, Department of Physician Assistant Studies, Milwaukee, WI 53201-1881. Awards MS. Students enter the program as undergraduates. *Entrance requirements:* TOEFL (minimum score 550). Application fee: $40. *Tuition:* $490 per credit. *Financial aid:* Application deadline 2/15. • Timothy Gengembre, Chair, 414-288-5688. Fax: 414-288-7951.

Medical College of Ohio, School of Allied Health, Physician Assistant Studies Program, Toledo, OH 43699-0008. Awards MSBS. Faculty: 3 full-time (2 women), 3 part-time (1 woman). Students: 12 (9 women). Average age 28. 70 applicants, 30% accepted. *Degree requirements:* Scholarly project required, foreign language and thesis not required. *Entrance requirements:* GRE, interview, minimum undergraduate GPA of 3.0, writing sample. Application deadline: 3/15. Application fee: $30. *Financial aid:* Scholarships, Federal Work-Study, institutionally sponsored loans available. Financial aid applicants required to submit FAFSA. • Anthony A. Miller, Director, 419-383-5408. E-mail: mcogradschool@mco.edu. Application contact: Theresa Langenderfer, Secretary, 419-383-4160. Fax: 419-383-6140. E-mail: mcogradschool@mco.edu.

Midwestern University, College of Allied Health Professions, Program in Physician Assistant Studies, Downers Grove, IL 60515-1235. Awards MS. Students: 51 full-time (42 women); includes 7 minority (4 Asian Americans, 2 Hispanics, 1 Native American). *Application deadline:* rolling. *Application fee:* $30. *Expenses:* Tuition $16,184 per year for state residents; $17,836 per year for nonresidents. Fees $280 per year. • Dr. Donald Sefcik, Acting Director, 630-515-6034. Application contact: Julie Rosenthall, Director of Admissions, 800-458-6253. Fax: 630-971-6086. E-mail: mwuinfo@mwu.edu.

Announcement: Midwestern University is committed to educating the health-care team of the next century. The University administers the Chicago College of Osteopathic Medicine, the Chicago College of Pharmacy, the College of Allied Health Professions, the Arizona College of Osteopathic Medicine, and the College of Pharmacy–Glendale. The University operates campuses in Downers Grove, Illinois, and in Glendale, Arizona. The Physician Assistant Program offers Bachelor of Medical Science (BMS) and Master of Medical Science (MMS) in physician assistant studies degrees at both the Downers Grove and Glendale campuses. Students may choose to complete the 24-month bachelor's track or the 27-month master's track. The program also offers a master's completion track for licensed PAs who already have a bachelor's degree. In addition to comprehensive basic science and clinical experiences, many PA students become involved in community service projects, further enhancing their perspectives on the PA's role in health care. Contact the Office of Admissions, Midwestern University, 555 31st Street, Downers Grove, IL 60515; 800-458-6253; e-mail: admiss@midwestern.edu; WWW: http://www.midwestern.edu

---

Northeastern University, Bouvé College of Pharmacy and Health Sciences Graduate School, Programs in Health Professions, Physician Assistant Program, Boston, MA 02115-5096. Awards MHP. Faculty: 4 full-time (3 women), 100 part-time (50 women). Students: 53 full-time (32 women), 2 part-time (both women). 536 applicants, 7% accepted. In 1997, 27 degrees awarded. *Degree requirements:* Comprehensive exam required, foreign language not required. *Entrance requirements:* Prior admission to Physician Assistant Certificate Program, minimum GPA of 3.0, bachelor's degree in science. Application fee: $50. *Expenses:* Tuition $440 per credit hour. Fees $55 per quarter full-time, $13.25 per quarter part-time. *Financial aid:* Available to part-time students. Financial aid application deadline: 3/1; applicants required to submit FAFSA. • Suzanne B. Greenberg, Director, 617-373-3195.

See in-depth description on page 1797.

Pacific University, School of Physician Assistant Studies, Forest Grove, OR 97116-1797. Awards MS. Students: 16 full-time (8 women). Average age 29. 77 applicants, 25% accepted. *Application deadline:* 10/30. *Application fee:* $55. • Christine Legler, Director, 503-359-2898. Application contact: Karen Dunston, Admissions Counselor, 503-359-2900. Fax: 503-359-2975. E-mail: admissions@pacific.edu.

Philadelphia College of Osteopathic Medicine, Physician Assistant Program, Philadelphia, PA 19131. Offers health sciences (MS). Program new for fall 1998. *Application deadline:* 1/15. *Application fee:* $50. *Tuition:* $21,925 per year. • Dr. Kenneth R. Harbert, Chair, 215-871-6772. Application contact: Carol A. Fox, Associate Dean for Admission and Enrollment Management, 215-871-6700. Fax: 215-871-6719.

Quinnipiac College, School of Health Sciences, Program for Pathologists' Assistant, Hamden, CT 06518-1904. Awards MHS. Faculty: 5 full-time (0 women), 1 part-time (0 women). Students: 27 full-time (14 women); includes 3 minority (1 Asian American, 2 Hispanics). Average age 26. 77 applicants, 19% accepted. In 1997, 13 degrees awarded (100% found work related to degree). *Degree requirements:* Residency required, thesis optional. *Average time to degree:* master's–2 years full-time. *Entrance requirements:* Interview, BS in biomedical science, minimum GPA of 2.8. Application deadline: 2/15. Application fee: $45. *Expenses:* Tuition $395 per credit hour. Fees $380 per year full-time. *Financial aid:* Career-related internships or fieldwork available. Aid available to part-time students. Financial aid application deadline: 3/1; applicants required to submit FAFSA. • Dr. Kenneth Kaloustian, Director, 203-281-8676. Fax: 203-281-8706. E-mail: kaloustian@quinnipiac.edu. Application contact: Scott Farber, Director of Graduate Admissions, 203-281-8795. Fax: 203-287-5238. E-mail: qcgradadmi@quinnipiac.edu.

See in-depth description on page 1253.

Quinnipiac College, School of Health Sciences, Program for Physician Assistant, Hamden, CT 06518-1904. Awards MHS. Faculty: 14 full-time (3 women), 3 part-time (2 women). Students: 64 full-time (41 women); includes 2 minority (1 African American, 1 Asian American). Average age 29. 758 applicants, 6% accepted. In 1997, 19 degrees awarded. *Degree requirements:* Comprehensive exam required, thesis optional. *Average time to degree:* master's–2 years full-time. *Entrance requirements:* Minimum GPA of 3.0; previous course work in the biological, physical, and behavioral sciences. Application deadline: 12/1. Application fee: $45. *Expenses:* Tuition $395 per credit hour. Fees $380 per year full-time. *Financial aid:* Career-related internships or fieldwork available. Financial aid applicants required to submit FAFSA. • Dana Sayre-Stanhope, Director, 203-281-8704. Fax: 203-281-8706. E-mail: dsayer@quinnipiac.edu. Application contact: Scott Farber, Director of Graduate Admissions, 203-281-8795. Fax: 203-287-5238. E-mail: qcgradadmi@quinnipiac.edu.

See in-depth description on page 1257.

Saint Francis College, Physician Assistant Program, Loretto, PA 15940-0600. Awards MPAS. Program new for fall 1998. Faculty: 7 full-time (all women), 5 part-time (0 women). *Entrance requirements:* Basic science test, interview. Application deadline: 11/15. Application fee: $35. • Albert Simon, Chair, 814-472-3130. Application contact: Frank Crouse, Assistant Director of Admissions, 814-472-3110. Fax: 814-472-3335. E-mail: fcrouse@sfcpa.edu.

Seton Hall University, School of Graduate Medical Education, Physician Assistant Program, South Orange, NJ 07079-2697. Awards MS. Offered jointly with the University of Medicine and Dentistry of New Jersey. *Entrance requirements:* GRE, TOEFL, health care experience, interview, minimum GPA of 3.0. *Expenses:* Tuition $500 per credit. Fees $610 per year full-time, $185 per semester part-time. • Application contact: Office of Graduate Medical Education, 973-761-7145. Fax: 973-275-2370. E-mail: gradmeded@shu.edu.

Trevecca Nazarene University, Division of Natural and Applied Sciences, Nashville, TN 37210-2834. Offers program in physician assistant (MS). Students: 33. *Degree requirements:* Qualifying exam required, foreign language and thesis not required. *Entrance requirements:* MAT (minimum score 30), health care experience. Application deadline: 12/1. Application fee: $45. *Expenses:* Tuition $230 per hour. Fees $60 per year. • Dr. Mike Movedock, Dean, 615-248-1225. E-mail: mmovedock@trevecca.edu. Application contact: Judy Spross, Admissions Coordinator, 615-248-1783. E-mail: jspross@trevecca.edu.

University of Colorado Health Sciences Center, Child Health Associate/Physician Assistant Program, Denver, CO 80262. Awards MS. Students: 31 full-time (28 women), 21 part-time (16 women); includes 5 minority (2 Asian Americans, 1 Hispanic, 2 Native Americans). Average age 29. 356 applicants, 10% accepted. In 1997, 3 degrees awarded. *Entrance requirements:* GRE General Test, minimum GPA of 2.75. Application fee: $30. *Financial aid:* Federal Work-Study, institutionally sponsored loans, and career-related internships or fieldwork available. Aid available to part-time students. Financial aid application deadline: 3/15. • Dr. Gerald B. Merenstein, Director, 303-315-7963.

University of Detroit Mercy, College of Health Professions, Physician Assistant Program, Detroit, MI 48219-0900. Awards MS. *Degree requirements:* Thesis or alternative required, foreign language not required. *Entrance requirements:* GRE General Test (minimum combined score of 1200), minimum GPA of 3.0. Application fee: $25. *Faculty research:* Substance abuse prevention, international health care, public health.

See in-depth description on page 1265.

University of Florida, College of Medicine, Program in Physician Assistant Studies, Gainesville, FL 32611. Awards MPAS, Pharm D/MPAS. Students: 115. *Entrance requirements:* GRE General Test (minimum combined score of 1000; average 1217), TOEFL (minimum score 550), minimum GPA of 3.0. Application deadline: 12/1. Application fee: $20. *Tuition:* $10,447 per year for state residents; $28,098 per year for nonresidents. • Wayne D. Bottom, Director, 352-395-7955.

The University of Iowa, College of Medicine and Graduate College, Graduate Programs in Medicine, Program in Physician Assistant, Iowa City, IA 52242-1316. Awards MPAS. Faculty: 3 full-time (1 woman), 1 part-time (0 women), 3.8 FTE. Students: 47 full-time (30 women); includes 3 minority (all Asian Americans). Average age 25. 289 applicants, 9% accepted. In 1997, 22 degrees awarded (100% found work related to degree). *Degree requirements:*

Comprehensive clinical exam required, foreign language and thesis not required. *Average time to degree:* master's–2 years full-time. *Entrance requirements:* GRE General Test (minimum combined score of 1000; average 1818), health care/research experience. Application deadline: (12/1 for spring admission). Application fee: $30. *Expenses:* Tuition $3166 per year full-time, $176 per semester hour part-time for state residents; $10,202 per year full-time, $176 per semester hour part-time for nonresidents. Fees $202 per year. *Financial aid:* In 1997–98, 42 students received aid, including 5 scholarships averaging $191 per month and totaling $11,485; institutionally sponsored loans also available. Aid available to part-time students. Financial aid application deadline: 3/1; applicants required to submit FAFSA. • Dr. David P. Asprey, Interim Director, 319-335-8922. Fax: 319-335-8923. E-mail: david-asprey@uiowa.edu.

University of Medicine and Dentistry of New Jersey, School of Health Related Professions, Newark, NJ 07107-3001. Offerings include physician assistant (MS). MS, PhD (biomedical informatics) offered jointly with New Jersey Institute of Technology; MS, PhD (health science), MS (physician assistant), MA offered jointly with Seton Hall University; MPT offered jointly with Rutgers, The State University of New Jersey, Camden. School faculty: 44 full-time (36 women), 15 part-time (10 women), 51.55 FTE. *Application deadline:* rolling. *Application fee:* $35. • Dr. David M. Gibson, Dean, 973-972-4276. Application contact: Dr. Laura Nelson, Associate Dean of Academic and Student Services, 973-972-5453. Fax: 973-972-7028. E-mail: shrp.adm@umdnj.edu.

See in-depth description on page 1267.

University of Nebraska Medical Center, School of Allied Health Professions, Division of Physician Assistant Education, Omaha, NE 68198-0001. Awards MPA.

University of New England, College of Health Professions, Program in Physician Assistant, Biddeford, ME 04005-9526. Awards MPA. Faculty: 2 full-time (1 woman), 98 part-time (39 women). Students: 56 full-time (32 women); includes 1 minority (Asian American). Average age 33. 307 applicants, 13% accepted. *Entrance requirements:* GRE General Test (minimum combined score of 1500 on three sections; average 1650). Application deadline: 1/15. Application fee: $40. *Expenses:* Tuition $17,250 per year. Fees $230 per year. *Financial aid:* Federal Work-Study available. Aid available to part-time students. Financial aid application deadline: 5/1; applicants required to submit FAFSA. • Carl Toney, Director, 207-283-0171 Ext. 2812. Fax: 207-282-6379. Application contact: Patricia T. Cribby, Dean of Admissions and Enrollment Management, 207-283-0171 Ext. 2297. Fax: 207-286-3678. E-mail: jshea@mailbox.une.edu.

University of South Alabama, College of Allied Health Professions, Department of Physician Assistant Studies, Mobile, AL 36688-0002. Awards MHS. Faculty: 5 full-time (1 woman). Students: 66 full-time (35 women), 2 part-time (both women); includes 7 minority (2 African Americans, 3 Asian Americans, 1 Hispanic, 1 Native American). 0 applicants. *Degree requirements:* Externship required, thesis optional, foreign language not required. *Entrance requirements:* GRE General Test (minimum combined score of 1000). Application deadline: 9/1 (priority date; rolling processing). Application fee: $25. *Financial aid:* Application deadline 4/1. • Dr. George L. White Jr., Chair, 334-434-3641. Fax: 334-434-3646.

Wayne State University, College of Pharmacy and Allied Health Professions, Department of Physician Assistant Studies, Detroit, MI 48202. Awards MS. Faculty: 8. Students: 64 full-time (51 women), 5 part-time (3 women). 3 applicants, 0% accepted. *Entrance requirements:* GRE General Test (combined average 1640 on three sections), TOEFL (minimum score 600), minimum GPA of 3.0, previous course work in science, 500 hours of work experience in health services). Application deadline: 10/1. Application fee: $0. *Expenses:* Tuition $163 per credit hour for state residents; $355 per credit hour for nonresidents. Fees $498 per year full-time, $114 per semester (minimum) part-time. *Financial aid:* Career-related internships or fieldwork available. Financial aid applicants required to submit FAFSA. *Faculty research:* Medical treatment outcomes, learning and performance evaluation. • Dr. Henry Wormser, Director, 313-577-1368. Application contact: Judith Kunkle, Academic Services Officer and Admissions Coordinator, 313-577-2320. Fax: 313-577-5589. E-mail: jkunkle@cms.cc.wayne.edu.

Western University of Health Sciences, School of Allied Health Professions, Program in Physician Assistant Studies, Pomona, CA 91766-1854. Awards Certificate. Students: 120. *Application deadline:* 12/31. *Application fee:* $45. *Tuition:* $21,500 per year. • Application contact: Susan M. Hanson, Director of Admissions, 909-469-5335.

Yale University, School of Medicine, Physician Associate Program, New Haven, CT 06510. Awards Certificate. Faculty: 3 full-time (all women), 16 part-time (4 women), 8 FTE. Students: 65 full-time (43 women); includes 10 minority (2 African Americans, 5 Asian Americans, 2 Hispanics, 1 Native American). Average age 28. 519 applicants, 8% accepted. In 1997, 30 degrees awarded. *Degree requirements:* Thesis required, foreign language not required. *Average time to degree:* other advanced degree–2 years full-time. *Entrance requirements:* GRE General Test (combined average on three sections 1500), TSE (average 55), TOEFL (average 550), experience in patient care. Application deadline: 8/4. Application fee: $35. *Financial aid:* 61 students received aid; institutionally sponsored loans and career-related internships or fieldwork available. Financial aid application deadline: 5/1; applicants required to submit FAFSA. • Elaine E. Grant, Assistant Dean, 203-785-2860. Application contact: Department Secretary, 203-785-4252. Fax: 203-785-3601.

Rehabilitation Sciences

East Carolina University, School of Allied Health Sciences, Rehabilitation Studies Program, Greenville, NC 27858-4353. Awards MS. Part-time and evening/weekend programs available. Faculty: 5 full-time (0 women). Students: 42 full-time (31 women), 28 part-time (20 women); includes 9 minority (8 African Americans, 1 Asian American). Average age 34. 36 applicants, 53% accepted. In 1997, 21 degrees awarded. *Degree requirements:* Thesis or alternative, comprehensive exams, internship. *Entrance requirements:* GRE General Test or MAT, TOEFL. Application deadline: 6/1 (priority date; rolling processing). Application fee: $40. *Tuition:* $1886 per year full-time, $472 per semester (minimum) part-time for state residents; $9156 per year full-time, $2289 per semester (minimum) part-time for nonresidents. *Financial aid:* Research assistantships, teaching assistantships, grants, Federal Work-Study available. Aid available to part-time students. Financial aid application deadline: 6/1. • Dr. Paul Alston, Chairperson, 252-328-4452. Fax: 252-328-4470. E-mail: alstonp@mail.ecu.edu. Application contact: Dr. Paul D. Tschetter, Associate Dean, 252-328-6012. Fax: 252-328-6071. E-mail: grad@mail.ecu.edu.

East Stroudsburg University of Pennsylvania, School of Health Sciences and Human Performance, Department of Movement Studies and Exercise Science, East Stroudsburg, PA 18301-2999. Offerings include cardiac rehabilitation and exercise science (MS). *Application deadline:* 7/31 (priority date; rolling processing; 11/30 for spring admission). *Application fee:* $15 ($25 for international students). *Expenses:* Tuition $3468 per year full-time, $193 per credit part-time for state residents; $6236 per year full-time, $346 per credit part-time for nonresidents. Fees $700 per year full-time, $39 per credit part-time.

McGill University, Faculty of Graduate Studies and Research, Faculty of Medicine, School of Physical and Occupational Therapy, Montréal, PQ H3A 2T5, Canada. Offers program in rehabilitation science (M Sc, M Sc A, PhD). Faculty: 13 full-time (12 women), 3 part-time (0 women). Students: 41 full-time (32 women); includes 1 international. Average age 31. 27 applicants, 63% accepted. In 1997, 5 master's, 2 doctorates awarded. Terminal master's awarded for partial completion of doctoral program. *Degree requirements:* Thesis/dissertation required, foreign language not required. *Average time to degree:* master's–3 years full-time; doctorate–6 years full-time. *Entrance requirements:* For master's, GRE General Test, TOEFL (minimum score 600), B Sc in related discipline, minimum GPA of 3.0; for doctorate, TOEFL (minimum score 600), M Sc in related discipline. Application deadline: 2/15 (priority date; rolling processing). Application fee: $60. *Expenses:* Tuition $1668 per year for Canadian residents; $8268 per year for nonresidents. Fees $828 per year for Canadian residents; $1216 per year for nonresidents. *Financial aid:* In 1997–98, 19 teaching assistantships were awarded; fellowships, research assistantships, full tuition waivers, institutionally sponsored loans also available. Financial aid application deadline: 10/1. *Faculty research:* Exercise and aging, biomechanics, spinal cord injury, spasticity, health outcome measures. • Annette Majnemer, Associate Director, 514-398-4515. E-mail: annette@physocc.lan.mcgill.ca. Application contact: J. Gauthier, Coordinator, 514-398-4504. Fax: 514-398-6360. E-mail: jackie@physocc.lan.mcgill.ca.

Medical University of South Carolina, College of Health Professions, Department of Rehabilitation Sciences, Charleston, SC 29425-0002. Offers programs in communication sciences and disorders (MSR), health professions education (MS), occupational therapy (MHS, MSR), physical therapy (MHS, MSR). Part-time and evening/weekend programs available. Postbaccalaureate distance learning degree programs offered. Faculty: 22 full-time (15 women), 10 part-time (6 women), 27 FTE. *Entrance requirements:* GRE General Test, interview, minimum GPA of 2.8. Application fee: $55. *Expenses:* Tuition $4072 per year full-time, $221 per semester hour part-time for state residents; $7064 per year full-time, $387 per semester hour part-time for nonresidents. Fees $150 per year (minimum). *Financial aid:* Graduate assistantships, Federal Work-Study, institutionally sponsored loans, and career-related internships or fieldwork available. Aid available to part-time students. *Faculty research:* Cue reactivity, efficacy of physical therapy intervention and occupational therapy intervention, distance education, quality of life, interdisciplinary teams, teaching methods, language development in students, HIV/AIDS. Total annual research expenditures: $229,590. • Dr. James A. Morrow, Chair, 843-792-2961. E-mail: morrowj@musc.edu. Application contact: Susan Johnson, Student Services, 843-792-2961. Fax: 843-792-0710. E-mail: johnsoss@musc.edu.

Northeastern Illinois University, College of Arts and Sciences, Department of Biology, Program in Exercise Science and Cardiac Rehabilitation, Chicago, IL 60625-4699. Awards MS. Part-time and evening/weekend programs available. Faculty: 3 full-time (1 woman), 1 part-time (0 women). Students: 11 full-time (7 women), 49 part-time (40 women); includes 5 minority (4 Asian Americans, 1 Hispanic), 3 international. Average age 35. 44 applicants, 100% accepted. In 1997, 20 degrees awarded. *Degree requirements:* Internship required, thesis optional, foreign language not required. *Entrance requirements:* 21 hours of undergraduate course work in sciences, previous field experience, minimum GPA of 2.75. Application deadline: 3/18 (priority date; rolling processing; 9/30 for spring admission). Application fee: $0. *Expenses:* Tuition $2226 per year full-time, $93 per credit hour part-time for state residents; $6678 per year full-time, $278 per credit hour part-time for nonresidents. Fees $358 per year full-time, $14.90 per credit hour part-time. *Financial aid:* In 1997–98, 18 students received aid, including 8 research assistantships averaging $450 per month; full and partial tuition waivers, Federal Work-Study, institutionally sponsored loans, and career-related internships or fieldwork also available. Aid available to part-time students. *Faculty research:* Behavioral medicine, health care cost containment, clinical cardiology, industrial medicine, muscle inflammation. • Dr. George Lesmes, Coordinator, 773-792-2888. Application contact: Dr. Mohan K. Sood, Dean of Graduate College, 773-583-4050 Ext. 6143. Fax: 773-794-6670.

Pennsylvania College of Optometry, Department of Vision Impairment, 8360 Old York Road, Elkins Park, PA 19027. Offerings include low vision rehabilitation (MS), orientation and mobility therapy (MS). Department faculty: 5 full-time (all women), 10 part-time (8 women). *Average time to degree:* master's–1 year full-time, 2.5 years part-time. *Application deadline:* 6/16 (rolling processing). *Application fee:* $50. • Dr. Kathleen M. Huebner, Assistant Dean, 215-276-6093. Fax: 215-276-6292. E-mail: kathyh@pco.edu. Application contact: Diane Wormsley, Recruitment Committee Chair, 215-780-1366. Fax: 215-780-1357. E-mail: lwormsley@pco.edu.

Queen's University at Kingston, Faculty of Medicine and School of Graduate Studies and Research, Graduate Programs in Medicine, Department of Rehabilitation Therapy, Kingston, ON K7L 3N6, Canada. Awards M Sc. Part-time programs available. Students: 19 full-time (17 women), 6 part-time (4 women). In 1997, 15 degrees awarded. *Degree requirements:* Thesis required, foreign language not required. *Entrance requirements:* TOEFL (minimum score 550). Application deadline: rolling. Application fee: $60. *Tuition:* $3803 per year (minimum) full-time, $1901 per year (minimum) part-time for Canadian residents; $7330 per year (minimum) for nonresidents. *Financial aid:* Fellowships, research assistantships, teaching assistantships, partial tuition waivers available. Aid available to part-time students. Financial aid application deadline: 3/1. • S. Olney, Director, 613-545-6102. Application contact: B. Brouwer, Graduate Coordinator, 613-545-6087.

State University of New York at Buffalo, Graduate School, School of Health Related Professions, Department of Rehabilitation Science at Roswell Park, Buffalo, NY 14260. Awards PhD. Program new for fall 1998. *Degree requirements:* Dissertation, comprehensive exam required, foreign language not required. *Entrance requirements:* GRE General Test, TOEFL (minimum score 550). Application fee: $35. *Tuition:* $5970 per year full-time, $288 per credit hour part-time for state residents; $9286 per year full-time, $426 per credit hour part-time for nonresidents. • Dr. Barry S. Eckert, Dean, School of Health Related Professions, 716-829-3434. Fax: 716-829-2034.

University of Alberta, Faculty of Graduate Studies and Research, Faculty of Rehabilitation Medicine, Edmonton, AB T6G 2E1, Canada. Awards PhD. PhD offered jointly with the Departments of Occupational Therapy, Physical Therapy, and Speech Pathology and Audiology. Faculty: 21 full-time (13 women), 3 part-time (0 women), 22.5 FTE. Students: 10 full-time (8 women), 3 part-time (all women); includes 3 international. Average age 32. 5 applicants, 80% accepted. *Degree requirements:* Dissertation required, foreign language not required. *Entrance requirements:* GRE, TOEFL or TSE, minimum GPA of 6.5 on a 9.0 scale. Application deadline: rolling. Application fee: $60. *Expenses:* Tuition $390 per course for Canadian residents; $781 per course for nonresidents. Fees $500 per year full-time, $184 per year part-time. *Financial aid:* In 1997–98, 3 fellowships (1 to a first-year student), 7 research assistantships (2 to first-year students), 5 teaching assistantships (1 to a first-year student), 6 scholarships, tuition scholarships were awarded; institutionally sponsored loans also available. *Faculty research:* Musculoskeletal disorders, neuromotor control, exercise physiology, motor speech disorders, assistive technologies. • A. Rochet, Associate Dean, Graduate Studies and Research, 403-492-9674. Application contact: Anita Moore, Administrative Assistant, Graduate Studies, 403-492-0840. Fax: 403-492-1626. E-mail: anita.moore@ualberta.ca.

University of British Columbia, Faculties of Medicine and Graduate Studies, Graduate Programs in Medicine, School of Rehabilitation Sciences, Vancouver, BC V6T 1W5, Canada.

Directory: Rehabilitation Sciences; Cross-Discipline Announcements

University of British Columbia (continued)

Awards M Sc. Part-time programs available. *Degree requirements:* Thesis required, foreign language not required. *Entrance requirements:* 1 year of experience in rehabilitation field. Application deadline: 1/5. Application fee: $50. *Faculty research:* Chronic illness and disability, neuromotor assessment, functional assessment in joint disease, cardiopulmonary rehabilitation.

University of Delaware, College of Health and Nursing Sciences, Department of Health and Exercise Scien ces, Newark, DE 19716. Offerings include cardiac rehabilitation (MS). Department faculty: 12 full-time (3 women). *Average time to degree:* master's–2.5 years full-time, 4.5 years part-time. *Application deadline:* 7/1 (priority date; rolling processing; 12/1 for spring admission). *Application fee:* $45. *Expenses:* Tuition $4250 per year full-time, $236 per credit hour part-time for state residents; $12,250 per year full-time, $681 per credit hour part-time for nonresidents. Fees $466 per year full-time, $15 per semester (minimum) part-time. • Application contact: Gail E. Manogue, Administrative Assistant, 302-831-8370.

University of Florida, College of Health Professions, Program in Rehabilitation Sciences, Gainesville, FL 32611. Awards PhD. Program new for fall 1998. *Degree requirements:* Dissertation required, foreign language not required. *Entrance requirements:* GRE General Test, minimum GPA of 3.0. Application fee: $20. *Tuition:* $138 per credit hour for state residents; $481 per credit hour for nonresidents. • Application contact: Dr. Denis Brunt, Graduate Coordinator, 352-395-0085. E-mail: dbrunt@hp.ufl.edu.

University of Illinois at Urbana–Champaign, College of Applied Life Studies, Department of Community Health, Division of Rehabilitation Education Services, Urbana, IL 61801. Offers program in rehabilitation (MS). Faculty: 5 full-time (2 women). Students: 33 full-time (28 women); includes 10 minority (6 African Americans, 1 Asian American, 3 Hispanics), 1 international. 28 applicants, 89% accepted. In 1997, 23 degrees awarded. *Degree requirements:* 600 clock hours of fieldwork required, foreign language and thesis not required. *Entrance requirements:* GRE General Test, minimum GPA of 4.0 on a 5.0 scale during last 60 hours. Application deadline: 4/15 (priority date; rolling processing). Application fee: $40 ($50 for international students). *Financial aid:* In 1997–98, 4 fellowships, 16 research assistantships were awarded; teaching assistantships, full tuition waivers, Federal Work-Study, institutionally sponsored loans, and career-related internships or fieldwork also available. Financial aid application deadline: 2/15. *Faculty research:* Transitions of severely disabled to work in independent living, psychosocial aspects of disabling conditions, multiculturalism. • Bradley N. Hedrick, Interim Director, 217-333-3789.

University of Manitoba, Faculties of Medicine and Graduate Studies, Graduate Programs in Medicine, School of Medical Rehabilitation, Winnipeg, MB R3T 2N2, Canada. Offers program in rehabilitation (M Sc). Part-time programs available. *Application fee:* $50. *Faculty research:* Understanding of human dynamics, motor control and neurological dysfunction, exercise physiology, functional motion of the upper extremity and effects of musculoskeletal disorders.

University of Minnesota, Twin Cities Campus, Medical School and Graduate School, Graduate Programs in Medicine, Department of Physical Medicine and Rehabilitation, Minneapolis, MN 55455-0213. Awards MS, PhD.

University of North Texas, School of Community Service, Center for Rehabilitation Studies, Denton, TX 76203-6737. Offers programs in rehabilitation counseling (MS), rehabilitation studies (MS), vocational evaluation (MS), work adjustment services (MS). Part-time programs available. Faculty: 9 full-time (5 women). Students: 15 full-time (8 women), 17 part-time (10 women); includes 7 minority (2 African Americans, 3 Hispanics, 2 Native Americans), 1 international. Average age 29. In 1997, 13 degrees awarded (100% found work related to degree). *Degree requirements:* Thesis optional, foreign language not required. *Entrance requirements:* GRE General Test (minimum combined score of 800), minimum GPA of 3.0 during last 60 hours, 2.8 overall. Application deadline: 7/17 (rolling processing; 12/1 for spring admission). Application fee: $25 ($50 for international students). *Tuition:* $2063 per year full-time, $815 per year part-time for state residents; $5897 per year full-time, $2100 per year part-time for nonresidents. *Financial aid:* Scholarships, Federal Work-Study, institutionally sponsored loans, and career-related internships or fieldwork available. Financial aid application deadline: 4/1. *Faculty research:* Biofeedback, job placement and development, adjustment services for handicapped. Total annual research expenditures: $55,000. • Thomas L. Evenson, Chair, 940-565-2488. Application contact: Eugenia Bodenhamer, Graduate Coordinator, 940-565-3467. Fax: 940-565-3960.

University of Oklahoma Health Sciences Center, College of Allied Health, Department of Rehabilitation Sciences, Oklahoma City, OK 73190. Awards MS. Faculty: 13 full-time (6 women), 9 part-time (4 women). Students: 5 full-time (1 woman), 11 part-time (8 women); includes 1 minority (Native American), 1 international. 16 applicants, 44% accepted. In 1997, 3 degrees awarded. *Degree requirements:* Comprehensive exam required, thesis optional, foreign language not required. *Entrance requirements:* GRE General Test, TOEFL (minimum score 550). Application deadline: 7/1 (12/1 for spring admission). Application fee: $25 ($50 for international students). • Dr. Martha Ferretti, Chair, 405-271-2131. Application contact: Dr. Mark Anderson, Graduate Liaison, 405-271-2131.

University of Pittsburgh, School of Health and Rehabilitation Sciences, Department of Rehabilitation Science and Technology, Pittsburgh, PA 15260. Offers programs in health and rehabilitation sciences (MS), rehabilitation engineering (Certificate), rehabilitation sciences (PhD), rehabilitation technology (Certificate). Faculty: 9 full-time (2 women). Students: 10 full-time (8 women), 11 part-time (4 women); includes 1 minority (Asian American), 4 international. *Entrance requirements:* For master's and doctorate, GRE General Test, TOEFL. Application fee: $30 ($40 for international students). *Expenses:* Tuition $9402 per year full-time, $388 per credit part-time for state residents; $19,372 per year full-time, $799 per credit part-time for nonresidents. Fees $480 per year full-time, $180 per year part-time. *Financial aid:* Federal Work-Study, institutionally sponsored loans available. • Application contact: Shameem Gangjee, Director of Admissions, 412-647-1258. Fax: 412-647-1255. E-mail: shrsadmit+@pitt.edu.

See in-depth descriptions on pages 1269 and 1351.

University of Pittsburgh, School of Health and Rehabilitation Sciences, Interdisciplinary Program in Health and Rehabilitation Sciences, Pittsburgh, PA 15260. Offers clinical laboratory sciences (MS), health care supervision and management (MS), health information systems (MS), occupational therapy (MS), physical therapy (MS), rehabilitation science (PhD), rehabilitation science and technology (MS), rehabilitation technology (Certificate), rehabilitation technology service delivery (Certificate). Part-time and evening/weekend programs available. Students: 23 full-time (16 women), 83 part-time (55 women); includes 10 minority (6 African Americans, 2 Asian Americans, 2 Hispanics), 7 international. 74 applicants, 85% accepted. In 1997, 28 master's awarded. *Degree requirements:* For doctorate, dissertation required, foreign language not required. *Entrance requirements:* For master's, GRE General Test, TOEFL, minimum QPA of 3.0; for doctorate, GRE General Test, TOEFL. Application deadline: rolling. Application fee: $30 ($40 for international students). *Expenses:* Tuition $9402 per year full-time, $388 per credit part-time for state residents; $19,372 per year full-time, $799 per credit part-time for nonresidents. Fees $480 per year full-time, $180 per year part-time. *Financial aid:* In 1997–98, 7 research assistantships (4 to first-year students) averaging $1,200 per month, 1 teaching assistantship (to a first-year student) averaging $1,286 per month, 3 assistantships averaging $1,049 per month were awarded; Federal Work-Study, institutionally sponsored loans also available. Aid available to part-time students. Financial aid applicants required to submit FAFSA. *Faculty research:* Assistive technology, seating and wheeled mobility, cellular neurophysiology, low back syndrome, augmentative communication. Total annual research expenditures: $1.941 million. • Dr. George Carvell, Associate Dean of Graduate Studies, 412-647-1296. E-mail: shrsadmit+@pitt.edu. Application contact: Shameem Gangjee, Director of Admissions, 412-647-1258. Fax: 412-647-1255. E-mail: shrsadmit+@pitt.edu.

See in-depth description on page 1351.

University of Toronto, School of Graduate Studies, Life Sciences Division, Department of Rehabilitation Science, Toronto, ON M5S 1A1, Canada. Awards M Sc. Faculty: 16. Students: 9 full-time (all women), 16 part-time (all women). 45 applicants, 42% accepted. *Degree requirements:* Thesis. *Application fee:* $75. *Expenses:* Tuition $4070 per year for Canadian residents; $7870 per year for nonresidents. Fees $628 per year. • M. Verrier, Acting Chair, 416-978-2769. Application contact: Secretary, 416-978-0300. Fax: 416-978-4363. E-mail: rehab.science@utoronto.ca.

University of Washington, School of Medicine and Graduate School, Graduate Programs in Medicine, Department of Rehabilitation Medicine, Program in Rehabilitation Medicine, Seattle, WA 98195. Awards MS. Program open only to physicians currently enrolled in the Residency Training Program in Physical Medicine and Rehabilitation at the University of Washington. Faculty: 27 part-time (8 women).05 FTE. Students: 3 part-time (1 woman); includes 3 minority (all Asian Americans). Average age 30. 3 applicants, 100% accepted. In 1997, 1 degree awarded. *Degree requirements:* Thesis required (for some programs), foreign language not required. *Average time to degree:* master's–3 years part-time. *Entrance requirements:* MD. Application fee: $45. • Application contact: Arissa Peterson, Coordinator, 206-685-0936. Fax: 206-685-3244. E-mail: arissa@u.washington.edu.

University of Wisconsin–La Crosse, College of Health, Physical Education and Recreation, Department of Exercise and Sport Science, Program in Adult Fitness/Cardiac Rehabilitation, La Crosse, WI 54601-3742. Awards MS. Faculty: 3 full-time (1 woman), 14 part-time (4 women), 4.5 FTE. Students: 13 full-time (5 women), 1 (woman) part-time; includes 1 minority (Asian American). Average age 24. 58 applicants, 26% accepted. In 1997, 15 degrees awarded (93% found work related to degree). *Degree requirements:* Thesis required, foreign language not required. *Entrance requirements:* Minimum GPA of 3.0. Application deadline: 2/1. Application fee: $38. *Tuition:* $3737 per year full-time, $208 per credit part-time for state residents; $11,921 per year full-time, $633 per credit part-time for nonresidents. *Financial aid:* In 1997–98, 9 students received aid, including 4 teaching assistantships (all to first-year students) averaging $546 per month and totaling $19,656; Federal Work-Study, institutionally sponsored loans, and career-related internships or fieldwork also available. Financial aid application deadline: 3/15; applicants required to submit FAFSA. *Faculty research:* Cardiovascular physiology, ECG, wellness, risk factors. • Dr. John Porcari, Coordinator, 608-785-8684. E-mail: porcari@mail.uwlax.edu. Application contact: Tim Lewis, Director of Admissions, 608-785-8939. Fax: 608-785-6695. E-mail: admissions@mail.uwlax.edu.

University of Wisconsin–Madison, School of Education, Department of Kinesiology, Therapeutic Science Program, Madison, WI 53706-1380. Awards MS. *Entrance requirements:* GRE General Test. Application fee: $38. *Tuition:* $4928 per year full-time, $926 per semester (minimum) part-time for state residents; $15,190 per year full-time, $2849 per semester (minimum) part-time for nonresidents.

Wayne State University, School of Medicine, Department of Rehabilitation Sciences, Detroit, MI 48202. Awards MS. Students: 2 full-time (1 woman). 0 applicants. *Entrance requirements:* MD or DO. *Expenses:* Tuition $10,739 per year for state residents; $21,812 per year for nonresidents. Fees $360 per year. *Faculty research:* Traumatic brain injury, biomechanics, spinal cord injury, spasticity, pediatric rehabilitation. • Dr. Bruce M. Gans, Chairman, Department of Physical Medicine and Rehabilitation, 313-345-9731. Fax: 313-993-0808. Application contact: James Novak, Education Director, 313-345-9852.

Cross-Discipline Announcements

Columbia University, Fu Foundation School of Engineering and Applied Science, Department of Applied Physics, New York, NY 10027.

Medical physics program leading to the MS degree is offered in collaboration with faculty members from the Columbia College of Physicians and Surgeons. Curriculum is designed to educate students for professional careers in medical physics and provide preparation toward certification by the American Board of Medical Physics. See in-depth description, Book 4, Physics section.

Florida International University, College of Health, Department of Dietetics and Nutrition, Miami, FL 33199.

The Department of Dietetics and Nutrition at Florida International University (FIU) offers a dynamic program leading to an MS or PhD in dietetics and nutrition. The program offers study in a multicultural environment and provides collaboration with community health sites and local clinical facilities. See in-depth description under Nutrition in Volume 3.

Los Angeles College of Chiropractic, Professional Program, 16200 E Amber Valley Dr, Box 1166, Whittier, CA 90604-4051.

Los Angeles College of Chiropractic is a dynamic research and learning center. A 3-year revision of the entire curriculum, focusing on 20 comprehensive chiropractic competencies, is now completed and in effect. From the beginning, students address clinical applications of all subjects and skills. An intensive 10-term program prepares them to become primary health-care providers, skilled in diagnosis and care of the human body through utilization of chiropractic principles and procedures. For further details, students should request the special brochure on the ADVANTAGE program of chiropractic education.

Northwestern College of Chiropractic, Professional Program, Bloomington, MN 55431-1599.

Northwestern College of Chiropractic is a regionally and professionally accredited institution offering the Doctor of Chiropractic degree. The 10-trimester curriculum emphasizes physical diagnosis and treatment, prevention, sports health, physical rehabilitation, and neuromusculoskeletal problems. The College maintains 1 student clinic and 4 public clinics within the Twin Cities metro area.

ALLEGHENY UNIVERSITY OF THE HEALTH SCIENCES

School of Health Professions Graduate Programs

Programs of Study

The School of Health Professions of Allegheny University of the Health Sciences (AUHS), formerly the Medical College of Pennsylvania (MCP) and Hahnemann University, offers an integrated program of formal course work, teaching experience, and investigative research in various professional programs in health-related fields. Doctor of Philosophy degrees are offered in advanced physician assistant studies, clinical psychology, couple and family therapy, and physical therapy. Master's degree programs are offered in clinical psychology, creative arts in therapy, emergency medical services, family therapy, group counseling and organizational dynamics, health care education technology, physical therapy (entry-level), and advanced physical therapy (specializations in movement science, orthopedic, pediatric, or hand/upper quadrant). The University and Villanova University Law School offer an integrated program in law and psychology leading to a Juris Doctor degree from Villanova and a Ph.D. in clinical psychology from AUHS. The University also offers a postbaccalaureate certificate program in gerontology.

Research Facilities

For clinical research, students have ready access to the University's comprehensive system of health care, including tertiary-care hospitals, a specialty children's hospital, community hospitals, a large number of practice sites, and active community outreach programs. The libraries and supporting services provide specialized facilities for a variety of research projects, and microcomputer facilities and online search capabilities are available to all students. The University's location in Philadelphia also provides students with access to other excellent libraries.

Financial Aid

Tuition scholarships may be available to qualified students in each of the School of Health Professions' graduate programs. Traineeships and teaching or research assistantships may be available to qualified doctoral students. All University students may apply for financial assistance through the Office of University Student Financial Affairs.

Cost of Study

Tuition and fees in 1997–98 were as follows: application fee, $50 (nonrefundable); tuition per semester, $5530 (some programs charge a higher tuition), with a $100 to $250 nonrefundable deposit, depending on the program; tuition per credit hour for nonmatriculating and part-time matriculating students, $615 (some programs charge a higher rate); and student activity fee, $30 per semester.

All students must maintain adequate medical insurance. Particulars relating to tuition, fees, or financial aid are subject to change.

Living and Housing Costs

Stiles Alumni Hall, a sixteen-story apartment building located on the Center City Campus, has 195 apartment-type units. The estimated cost for room and board is $7200 to $9200 per academic year. Other rooming and apartment facilities are located within easy commuting distance of the Center City Campus and within walking distance of the East Falls Campus.

Student Group

Approximately 556 graduate students are enrolled in the School of Health Professions, 64 percent in master's programs and 28 percent in doctoral programs. In addition, 8 percent are nonmatriculated students. Approximately 78 percent are women.

Location

Students are primarily located at the University's Center City Campus in Philadelphia, with easy access to all central Philadelphia attractions. Students can partake of the many historic, cultural, scientific, sports, entertainment, and dining advantages of the city, many of which are within walking distance. The University is convenient to and accessible by bus, rail, and subway lines. New York City, Atlantic City and other New Jersey shore points, the Pocono Mountains, and Washington, D.C., are but a few of the recreational areas within a 1- to 4-hour commute of the University.

The University

AUHS is an academic health center that includes more than 3,200 students in the MCP♦Hahnemann School of Medicine, the School of Health Professions, the School of Nursing, and the School of Public Health and grants degrees from the associate through the doctorate in more than forty programs. The University, with campuses in Philadelphia and Pittsburgh and more than 4,000 faculty members, was formed through the 1993 consolidation of the Medical College of Pennsylvania and Hahnemann University and was given its present name in June 1996.

Applying

Applicants must hold a baccalaureate degree from an accredited institution and present evidence of the ability to pursue graduate work, as exemplified by high scholarship achievement, high aptitude scores, and strong recommendations. The specific requirements of individual programs vary. The academic year usually begins in August. Each program sets its own application deadlines. Students should contact the University Office of Admissions and Recruitment for details.

Correspondence and Information

University Office of Admissions and Recruitment
Allegheny University of the Health Sciences
Broad & Vine, Mail Stop 472
Philadelphia, Pennsylvania 19102-1192
Telephone: 215-762-8288
Fax: 215-762-6194
World Wide Web: http://www.auhs.edu

Allegheny University of the Health Sciences

DIRECTORS OF GRADUATE PROGRAMS

Advanced Physician Assistant Studies Patrick C. Auth, Instructor, Department of Primary Care Education and Community Services, and Program Director; M.S., PA–C.

Clinical Psychology Ralph M. Turner, Professor, Department of Clinical and Health Psychology, and Program Director, Ph.D. Degree Program; Ph.D. Patrick W. McGuffin, Assistant Professor and Program Director, Master's Degree Program; Ph.D.

Couple and Family Therapy Marlene F. Watson, Associate Professor, Department of Mental Health Sciences, and Program Director; Ph.D.

Creative Arts in Therapy Ronald E. Hays, Assistant Professor, Department of Mental Health Sciences, and Program Director; M.S.

Emergency Medical Services Jean B. Will, Associate Professor, Department of Primary Care Education and Community Services, and Program Director; M.S.N.; RN, EMT-P.

Family Therapy Marlene F. Watson, Associate Professor, Department of Mental Health Sciences, and Program Director; Ph.D.

Gerontology Hugh Rosen, Professor and Chair, Department of Mental Health Sciences, and Program Director; D.S.W.

Group Counseling and Organizational Dynamics Fabian Ulitsky, Assistant Professor, Department of Mental Health Sciences, and Program Director; M.Ed.

Health Care Education Technology John S. Lewis, Associate Professor and Chair, Department of Liberal Arts and Applied Sciences, and Program Director; Ed.D.

Law-Psychology Kirk S. Heilbrun, Professor, Clinical and Health Psychology, and Program Director; Ph.D.

Physical Therapy Risa Granick, Associate Professor and Chair, Department of Physical Therapy, and M.P.T. Program Director; Ed.D., M.P.A. Neal E. Pratt, Professor, Orthopedic P.T., and Hand/Upper Quadrant P.T. Program Director; Ph.D. Susan K. Effgen, Professor and Pediatric P.T. Program Director; Ph.D. Robert Palisano, Associate Professor and Movement Science Program Director; Ph.D.

Allegheny University of the Health Sciences is not affiliated with Allegheny College, the liberal arts college in Meadville, Pennsylvania.

ALLEGHENY UNIVERSITY OF THE HEALTH SCIENCES

Department of Physical Therapy
Programs in Physical Therapy

Programs of Study

The Department of Physical Therapy offers both entry-level education for career preparation as a physical therapist and advanced master and doctoral education for practicing physical therapists seeking specialization in orthopedics, hand/upper quadrant rehabilitation, pediatrics, or movement science.

The entry-level program is a postbaccalaureate twenty-three-month curriculum integrating didactics and twenty-six weeks of full-time clinical education. The M.P.T. degree is awarded. A new doctoral extension program (DPT) to the M.P.T. curriculum will be initiated fall 1999. The M.P.T. curriculum follows a problem-solving, student self-directed learning approach emphasizing critical thinking for differential diagnosis and outcome assessment. Opportunities exist to work with faculty members and M.S./Ph.D. students on collaborative research projects. Students graduate with entry-level and advanced competencies due to elective courses and clinical affiliation options. The new DPT extension program will allow the M.P.T. student to continue for an additional seventeen months of more specialized practice consisting of twelve months of didactic and research related course work and a five-month clinical residency program. The advanced M.S. program provides practicing clinicians with specialized knowledge and skills in one of four specialty areas: orthopedics, hand/upper quadrant rehabilitation, pediatrics, or movement science. The curriculum comprises 38 semester credits and a thesis. A new Master of Health Science (M.H.S.) degree is now available for students who want advanced master's education but are not interested in writing a thesis. This nonthesis option requires some statistical courses and a case study to fulfill the requirements for graduation. Students can complete both the M.S. or M.H.S. on a part-time basis. The Ph.D. program prepares individuals for leadership, teaching, and research roles in the profession. A minimum of 96 credits beyond the baccalaureate or 60 credits beyond the master's degree is required, including qualifying comprehensive examinations and a dissertation.

Research Facilities

The Department of Physical Therapy has a new biomechanics/movement science laboratory with state-of-the-art equipment under the direction of a biomedical engineer. The libraries and other supporting services of the University as well as the vast array of affiliating clinical sites provide for a multiplicity of research projects. Microcomputer facilities and online search capabilities are available to all students.

Financial Aid

Scholarships are not available for M.P.T. students. The Office of Financial Aid works with students to obtain the funds needed to pursue their education from subsidized and unsubsidized federal loan programs and work-study. Many private organizations and foundations provide scholarship support for entry-level study. There is no departmental funding available for M.S. students. The majority of students complete this program on a part-time basis while maintaining employment as practicing physical therapists. Doctoral students, however, are eligible for full tuition and a stipend of $15,000 per year.

Cost of Study

The University tuition rate is set annually. Tuition expenses in 1997–98 were $17,000, with $1800 in fees for the M.P.T. program. Tuition for the new DPT Extension Program will be $17,000, plus $50 to remain matriculated during the clinical residency. Tuition for the M.S., M.H.S., and Ph.D. programs was $11,060 ($5530 per semester) or $615 per credit.

Living and Housing Costs

Allegheny University of the Health Sciences maintains a sixteen-story apartment building on campus. The Office of Student Services provides assistance to students in securing off-campus housing. The cost of living in Philadelphia is near the median for large East Coast cities and is estimated at $10,000 for apartment rental with utilities (twelve-month lease) and food.

Student Group

Class size for the M.P.T. program is 80, with approximately 37 percent men and 63 percent women. The DPT extension program will matriculate 15–20 students. Approximately 60 students are enrolled in the M.S. program and 16 in the Ph.D. program. Students in all programs consider the accessibility of faculty members as one of the department's strengths. The University has a total of 3,100 students in its Schools of Medicine, Health Professions, Public Health, and Nursing.

Student Outcomes

M.P.T. graduates plan, provide, and supervise patient care in hospitals, outpatient clinics, rehabilitation centers, home-care agencies, pediatric facilities, public schools, extended-care facilities, private practice, industry, and voluntary health agencies. M.S. graduates stay within the health-care system and assume greater responsibility in consultation activities with other health-care providers. Many are involved in clinical research and part-time teaching endeavors. Ph.D. graduates accept positions in academe.

Location

The Department of Physical Therapy, Programs in Physical Therapy, is part of the graduate division of the School of Health Professions, located on the University's Center-City Campus in Philadelphia. This urban setting gives students easy access to historic, cultural, scientific, sports, entertainment, and dining advantages of the city. New York City; Washington, D.C.; the Pocono Mountains; and New Jersey beaches are within easy commuting distances.

The University

Allegheny University of the Health Sciences is the academic anchor of Allegheny Health, Education and Research Foundation, a statewide health-care system. As a private nonprofit academic health center, the University is dedicated to teaching, healing the sick, and conserving health. The University is accredited by the Middle States Association of Colleges and Schools. The Department of Physical Therapy holds maximum accreditation status for its M.P.T. program from the Commission on Accreditation in Physical Therapy Education, American Physical Therapy Association. Only entry-level programs are accredited by the Commission; hence, the DPT extension program and M.S., M.H.S., and Ph.D. programs do not require professional accreditation status. The department's setting within a major academic health-care center affords students the opportunity to develop an understanding of the roles, responsibilities, and interrelationships of all members of the scientific and health-care communities within a rapidly changing health-care environment.

Applying

The M.P.T. program commences in July of each year. Applications are available August 15. The deadline for applying is December 15. Admission into the DPT extension program is done jointly with the M.P.T. program application. Admission is a selective process. The prospective applicant must hold a B.S. or B.A. degree; meet certain basic science, psychology, and statistic prerequisites; and submit Graduate Record Examinations (GRE) scores. A strong academic record as evidenced by a student's overall and science grade point averages, breadth of science background, and consistency of academic performance is important. A firm and clear motivation to physical therapy needs to be demonstrated by work or volunteer experiences, activities, and interests. Personal qualities such as maturity and effective interpersonal relationships as ascertained from letters of reference and the personal interview are highly regarded.

The M.S., M.H.S., and Ph.D. programs have admission deadlines of December 15 and June 1 for spring and fall matriculation, respectively. Applicants must be graduates of an accredited physical therapy program and be licensed to practice. Two years of clinical experience in the specialized area to be studied is recommended. Evaluation of the ability to do advanced graduate work is based on previous academic performance, Graduate Record Examinations (GRE) scores, curriculum vitae indicating professional activities, and a personal interview. International applicants must have their credentials evaluated by a Pennsylvania State Board of Physical Therapy Examiners–approved credentialing service and need to submit TOEFL scores. International applicants should allow additional time for processing application materials.

Other specific requirements of individual programs may vary, and applicants should consult program-specific information booklets available from the Department of Physical Therapy.

Correspondence and Information

Department of Physical Therapy
Programs in Physical Therapy, Mail Stop 502
Allegheny University of the Health Sciences
Broad and Vine Streets
Philadelphia, Pennsylvania 19102-1192
Telephone: 215-762-4974
Fax: 215-762-3886
World Wide Web: http://www.mcphu.edu

Allegheny University of the Health Sciences

FACULTY AND AREAS OF RESEARCH

DIRECTORS OF GRADUATE PROGRAMS

Entry-Level Master's Degree Program in Physical Therapy and Doctoral Extension Program: Kristin von Nieda, Assistant Professor; M.Ed., Temple; PT.

Doctoral Extension Program: Risa Granick, Associate Professor; Ed.D., Nova; PT.

M.S. and Ph.D. Programs in Orthopedics and Hand/Upper Quadrant Rehabilitation: Neal Pratt, Professor; Ph.D., Temple; PT.

M.S. and Ph.D. Programs in Pediatrics: Susan Effgen, Professor; Ph.D., Georgia State; PT.

M.S. and Ph.D. Programs in Movement Science: Robert Palisano, Professor; Sc.D., Boston University; PT.

There are 18 full-time faculty members, including 16 physical therapists, an exercise physiologist, and biomedical engineer, augmented by 9 part-time physical therapist clinical specialists and 5 adjunct faculty members in the basic sciences, medical sciences, and ethics. Research interests of faculty members vary by discipline. Two faculty members have received the Lindbach Award for Teaching Excellence; 3 faculty members are recognized clinical specialists by the American Physical Therapy Association in orthopedics, pediatrics, and neurology; 1 faculty member is a certified hand therapist by the American Hand Society; and 4 faculty members are authors of prominent texts.

SELECTED RESEARCH INTERESTS

Department research is divided into three primary areas: processes of motor skill acquisition with motor disability, musculoskeletal pathology, and educational pedagogy.

Educational Research: distance learning and integration of computerized techniques into educational programs, faculty development, curriculum development, cost-benefit analysis studies of education, problem-based learning evaluation.

Motor Learning/Control: motor learning in children with neurological disability, control of postural stability in children, development of motor coordination in children, application of motor learning principles to patients with CNS dysfunction, motor behavior in Parkinson's disease, development of assessment tools to evaluate postural control in children, measurements of intervention outcomes, occurrence of motor behaviors in children with developmental disabilities in early intervention settings.

Orthopedic rehabilitation: consequences of carpal tunnel release; patient classification of distal radius fractures; neuromuscular control of joint stability; muscle performance testing; shoulder biomechanics, kinematics, arthroplasty; clinical outcomes of spine-related disorders; spinal biomechanics; scapular kinematics.

Allegheny University of the Health Sciences is not affiliated with Allegheny College, the liberal arts college in Meadville, Pennsylvania.

BOSTON UNIVERSITY

Sargent College of Health and Rehabilitation Sciences

Programs of Study

Boston University Sargent College of Health and Rehabilitation Sciences offers basic and advanced professional degree programs in applied anatomy and physiology, applied kinesiology, nutrition, occupational therapy, physical therapy, speech-language pathology, audiology, and rehabilitation counseling. The basic Master of Science programs are designed for students with a variety of backgrounds who wish to acquire professional knowledge, research, and clinical skills. These programs lead to eligibility for professional certification or registration and entry-level practice. The advanced Master of Science, Certificate of Advanced Graduate Study, and Doctor of Science programs are designed for professionals who seek to develop expertise in a particular practice or to prepare for careers in teaching, research, or administration.

The Department of Communication Disorders offers a Master of Science program that prepares graduates for certification in speech-language pathology. The advanced programs include Certificate of Advanced Graduate Study (C.A.G.S.) and Doctor of Science degree programs in speech-language pathology or audiology. Students in the doctoral program in audiology may select a research track or a clinical track.

The Department of Health Sciences offers master's programs in applied anatomy and physiology and in nutrition. The department offers a doctoral program in applied anatomy and physiology that is designed to prepare professionals for careers in university teaching and research, cardiopulmonary research, institutes for environmental health, and corporate and industrial settings. The nutrition program offers opportunities to concentrate on health promotion, sports nutrition, clinical nutrition, and administration/private practice. An accredited AP4 internship program is also offered.

The master's program of the Department of Occupational Therapy for students with baccalaureate degrees in other disciplines prepares them to become registered occupational therapists. The advanced master's program, the Certificate of Advanced Graduate Study (C.A.G.S.) program, and the Doctor of Science program in therapeutic studies prepare experienced therapists to take on leadership positions in research, clinical practice, and academic and clinical education and administration.

The Department of Physical Therapy offers a master's program for graduates with baccalaureate degrees in other disciplines who wish to become physical therapists. The advanced master's program and the Doctor of Science degree in applied kinesiology prepare experienced therapists for leadership positions.

The Department of Rehabilitation Counseling's Master of Science program, offering specializations in psychiatric rehabilitation, industrial rehabilitation, and vocational evaluation, prepares students to become certified rehabilitation counselors. An off-campus Master of Science program is offered with a specialization in psychiatric rehabilitation. The Certificate of Advanced Graduate Study and the Doctor of Science programs prepare experienced rehabilitation counselors to assume leadership positions in the profession.

Research Facilities

Graduate students assist in serving clients and conduct research at the Sargent Clinic at Boston University, which offers speech-language pathology, audiology, vocational rehabilitation, and physical and occupational therapy services, and at the Fitness Evaluation Center, which offers cardiovascular fitness testing and nutritional counseling. Professional work experience can also be fulfilled through college affiliations with more than 550 hospitals, rehabilitation centers, schools, community health agencies, and research laboratories throughout the United States. The College's Center for Psychiatric Rehabilitation studies and develops training and treatment programs used nationwide. The College has specialized laboratories in biomechanics, neuroanatomy, gross anatomy, biochemistry, exercise physiology, human performance engineering, psychomotor learning, and communication sciences. Students also have the opportunity to be involved in research activities in health-care facilities in the Boston area.

Financial Aid

Financial assistance is supplemental to the student's or family's financial resources. Whenever possible, financial need is met through a combination of sources that may include federal or state loans, partial tuition scholarships, teaching and research assistantships or fellowships, federal or state traineeships, and Federal Work-Study Program awards.

Cost of Study

Full-time tuition for 1998–99 is $22,830; the George Sherman Union fee is $142; the health fee is $76. Part-time tuition is $713 per credit, and the registration fee is $40 per semester. Clinical affiliation fees are $1426 in the last year of study for occupational therapy majors and $713 per year for the last two years of study for physical therapy majors. Full-time students must purchase the University student health insurance plan unless they can demonstrate coverage under a qualifying medical insurance plan. Part-time students are also eligible to purchase medical insurance.

Living and Housing Costs

Boston University offers limited on-campus housing to full-time graduate students. Most graduate students live in apartments in the surrounding Boston area. Estimated living expenses (rent and food) for the academic year are $8385 for a single student and $10,000 for a married student living off campus.

Student Group

Sargent College enrolls about 400 graduate students. Seventy-five percent are full-time students. Two percent of the students are foreign nationals.

Location

The largest city in New England, Boston is rich in tradition and is one of the world's most respected centers for education, electronic and computer technology, research, and medicine. The extensive Boston medical community offers students a multitude of hospitals, research laboratories, medical centers, clinics, and health-care agencies in which they may gain research and professional experience.

The University and The College

Boston University is a private, independent, coeducational university located 1 mile from downtown Boston. Composed of fifteen schools and colleges, the University offers a wide range of specialized programs and degrees while allowing students to cross-register for courses in nearly all of the schools. Founded in 1881, Sargent College is one of the oldest and most respected schools of health sciences in the country.

Applying

Applicants must submit a Sargent College graduate application form with three letters of reference and results of the General Test of the Graduate Record Examinations. Students should contact the College for specific course prerequisites for each program.

Correspondence and Information

Graduate Admissions Office
Boston University
Sargent College of Health and Rehabilitation Sciences
Room 207
Boston, Massachusetts 02215

Telephone: 617-353-2713
E-mail: sargrad@bu.edu
World Wide Web: http://www.bu.edu/SARGENT

Boston University

THE FACULTY AND THEIR RESEARCH

Elsa Abele, Clinical Assistant Professor of Communication Disorders; M.S., Boston University. Adolescent language disorders.
William A. Anthony, Professor of Rehabilitation Counseling and Director, Center for Psychiatric Rehabilitation; Ph.D., SUNY at Buffalo. Psychiatric rehabilitation.
Helen Barbas, Associate Professor of Health Sciences; Ph.D., McGill. Anatomic organization of the prefrontal cortex in primates.
Theresa Ellis Brothers, Clinical Assistant Professor of Physical Therapy; M.S., Springfield. Muscle strength and functional status of persons with amyotrophic lateral sclerosis and Parkinson's disease.
Sara Brown, Clinical Assistant Professor of Physical Therapy and Director, Athletic Training Program; M.S., Arizona. Sports-related injuries.
Rebecca Butcher, Clinical Assistant Professor of Physical Therapy; M.S., Boston University. Neurology, analysis of gain in the stroke patient.
Lawrence Cahalin, Clinical Associate Professor of Physical Therapy; M.S., Iowa. Therapeutic intervention of end-state heart and lung disease.
Sharon A. Cermak, Professor of Occupational Therapy; Ed.D., Boston University. Sensory integration, developmental dyspraxia.
Wendy Coster, Associate Professor and Chairman of Occupational Therapy; Ph.D., Harvard. Therapist-child interaction during sensory integration treatment, psychosocial function in children with traumatic brain injury or developmental disorders.
Diane Dalton, Clinical Assistant Professor of Physical Therapy; M.S.P.T., Columbia. Orthopedics.
Karen Danley, Research Assistant Professor of Rehabilitation Counseling; Ph.D., Wayne State. Psychiatric rehabilitation career development and supported work.
Arthur Dell Orto, Professor and Chairman of Rehabilitation Counseling; Ph.D., Michigan State. Impact of illness on the family.
Margaret Denny, Assistant Professor of Communication Disorders; Ph.D., Purdue. Sensorimotor control of respiration for speech, physiological correlates of stuttering.
Linda W. Duncombe, Clinical Associate Professor of Occupational Therapy; M.S., Boston University. Mental health.
Roberta P. Durschlag, Assistant Professor of Health Sciences; Ph.D., Illinois at Urbana-Champaign. Protein nutrition, skeletal-muscle metabolism, obesity and energy balance.
Marianne Farkas, Research Associate Professor of Rehabilitation Counseling; Sc.D., Boston University. Psychiatric rehabilitation.
Linda Fetters, Associate Professor of Physical Therapy; Ph.D., Brandeis. Motor control in normal and atypical infants.
Roger A. Fielding, Clinical Assistant Professor of Health Sciences; Ph.D., Tufts. Exercise, aging, and protein metabolism.
Madeleine Foord, Clinical Associate Professor of Physical Therapy; M.S., Duke. Clinical education.
Elizabeth A. Gavett, Clinical Associate Professor of Communication Disorders; M.A., Pittsburgh. Fluency.
Lisa Giallonardo, Clinical Professor of Physical Therapy; M.S., Massachusetts General Hospital Institute of Health Professions. Foot and ankle dysfunction.
Stephen Haley, Associate Professor of Physical Therapy and Associate Dean; Ph.D., Washington (Seattle). Pediatric rehabilitation, outcome measurement and health services.
Pauline Hamel, Clinical Associate Professor of Physical Therapy; M.S., Northeastern. Geriatrics.
Joan Hargrave, Clinical Associate Professor of Communication Disorders; M.S., McGill. Voice disorders, clinical writing.
Kenneth Holt, Associate Professor of Physical Therapy; Ph.D., Massachusetts. Contribution of biomechanics, biophysics, and metabolism to the efficiency of human locomotion.
Norman C. Hursh, Associate Professor of Rehabilitation Counseling; Sc.D., Boston University. Vocational evaluation.
Karen Jacobs, Clinical Associate Professor of Occupational Therapy; Ed.D., Massachusetts Lowell. Work practice, marketing, ergonomics, technology and work.
Alan M. Jette, Professor of Physical Therapy and Dean; Ph.D., Michigan. Measurement, epidemiology, and prevention of disability among older adults.
Susan Kandarian, Associate Professor of Health Sciences; Ph.D., Michigan. Skeletal-muscle physiology, exercise physiology.
Ellen Cohen Kaplan, Clinical Instructor of Occupational Therapy; M.S., Johns Hopkins. Psychosocial theory and practice, wellness.
Gerald D. Kidd, Associate Professor and Chairman of Communication Disorders; Ph.D., Purdue. Perception of complex sounds, high-frequency audiometry, computer applications.
Joann Kluzik, Clinical Assistant Professor of Physical Therapy; M.S., Boston University. Pediatrics.
John Leard, Clinical Associate Professor of Physical Therapy; Ed.D., West Virginia. Sports medicine and orthopedics.
Steven F. Lewis, Associate Professor of Health Sciences; Ph.D., Stanford. Pathophysiology of exercise performance in disorders of muscle energy metabolism, cardiovascular regulation, muscle fatigue.
Melanie Matthies, Assistant Professor of Communication Disorders; Ph.D., Illinois. Perception of speech by persons with normal hearing and with hearing loss.
Deane McCraith, Clinical Associate Professor of Occupational Therapy; M.S., Boston University. Psychosocial intervention, systemic marriage and family therapy, substance and sexual abuse.
Paula McDonald, Clinical Assistant Professor of Health Sciences and Physical Therapy; M.S., Boston University. Gross anatomy, neuroanatomy.
Michelle Mentis, Associate Professor of Communication Disorders; Ph.D., California, Santa Barbara. Child language disorders, aphasia, closed head injury.
Patricia Nemec, Clinical Associate Professor of Rehabilitation Counseling; Psy.D., Massachusetts School of Professional Psychology. Issues in psychiatric rehabilitation.
Diane Parris, Clinical Assistant Professor of Communication Disorders; M.S., Boston University. Head trauma, aphasia and fluency disorders.
Nancy L. Peatman, Clinical Associate Professor of Physical Therapy; M.Ed., Fitchburg State. Clinical education.
Jean Peteet, Clinical Assistant Professor of Physical Therapy; M.P.H., Boston University. Management of health care and home care.
Carolyn Robinson, Clinical Assistant Professor of Occupational Therapy; M.A., Columbia. Motor learning of individuals with neurological insults.
Elliot Saltzman, Associate Professor of Physical Therapy; Ph.D., Minnesota. Dynamics of sensorimotor coordination in skilled activities of the limbs and speech articulators.
Judith L. Schotland, Assistant Professor of Health Sciences; Ph.D., Northwestern. Role of spinal neural networks in the organization of movements.
Gary S. Skrinar, Professor and Chairman of Health Sciences; Ph.D., Pittsburgh. Chronic exercise performance.
Julie Starr, Clinical Assistant Professor of Physical Therapy; M.S., Boston University. Adult and pediatric cardiopulmonary physical therapy.
Shari Thurer, Associate Professor of Rehabilitation Counseling; Sc.D., Boston University. Psychosocial aspects of disability.
Linda Tickle-Degnen, Assistant Professor of Occupational Therapy; Ph.D., Harvard. Nonverbal communication and the development of rapport.
Catherine A. Trombly, Professor of Occupational Therapy; Sc.D., Boston University. Adult physical dysfunction, motor control.
Carole Tucker, Assistant Professor of Physical Therapy; Ph.D., SUNY at Buffalo. Biomechanic electromyographic analysis of human movement.
Wayne Tyrrell, Clinical Associate Professor of Rehabilitation Counseling; Sc.D., Boston University. Developmental disabilities.
Elsie R. Vergara, Associate Professor of Occupational Therapy; Sc.D., Boston University. Neonatal intervention.
Gloria Waters, Professor of Communication Disorders; Ph.D., Concordia. Sentence comprehension, localization of language functions, differences in working memory capacity and language comprehension.
Mary-Margaret Windsor, Clinical Assistant Professor of Occupational Therapy; Sc.D., Boston University. Handwriting and sensory integration theory.

FINCH UNIVERSITY OF HEALTH SCIENCES / THE CHICAGO MEDICAL SCHOOL

School of Related Health Sciences

Programs of Study

Finch University of Health Sciences together with the Chicago Medical School offers basic and advanced degree programs in clinical laboratory sciences, health-care risk management, physician assistant studies, nutrition and clinical dietetics, and physical therapy. The basic Master of Science programs are designed for students with a variety of backgrounds who wish to acquire professional knowledge, research, and clinical skills. The advanced Master of Science degrees are designed for professionals who seek expertise in a particular practice or to prepare for careers in administration, teaching, or research.

The Department of Clinical Laboratory Sciences offers a Master of Science program to those individuals who have completed the baccalaureate degree and are seeking to further their knowledge base. The Department of Healthcare Risk Management Master of Science degree prepares future leaders of the profession with advanced knowledge and research skills to effectively manage the risk exposures of health-care entities. Students complete course work at home with campus residency required for two to three days at the end of each quarter. This program offers both two- and three-year educational pathways for completing the degree.

The Physician Assistant Department offers a Master of Science program for practicing PA's. This program is designed for working PA's who have a bachelor's degree and would like to enhance their education and professional careers by obtaining a Master of Science degree. The campus residency requirement for this long-distance learning program is one day for each course in which the student is enrolled per quarter. The Master of Science in Nutrition and Clinical Dietetics is a distance-learning program in which students complete course work at home and attend campus residency from one to three days on five occasions during program enrollment.

The Department of Physical Therapy offers an advanced Master of Science degree for practicing Physical Therapists. The students attend classes one day a week for two years in order to receive their master's degree. Graduate students are able to enroll in such courses in fields specializing in orthopedics, neurology, and administration and education.

Research Facilities

The School of Related Health Sciences uses its wet laboratories, clinics, hospital, and faculty research laboratories on campus.

Financial Aid

Financial assistance is supplemental to the student's or family's financial resources. To meet the cost of attending the School of Related Health Sciences, students, spouses, and parents are expected to provide financial support to the extent they are able. When family resources are insufficient to meet college costs, students are encouraged to seek assistance from the financial aid department. Financial aid is available in the form of scholarships, Federal Stafford Student Loan, Unsubsidized Federal Stafford Loan, Federal Perkins Loan, Excel, PLUS, and AHELP (Allied Health Education Loan) through the financial aid department. Students frequently are subsidized through their employers.

Cost of Study

Tuition for the graduate programs is $356 to $384 per credit hour, depending on the department. The University Health Insurance fee is required for full-time students. Proof of satisfactory hospitalization coverage is required. If not available, the student must make application for such coverage through the University Blue Cross/Blue Shield plan. Fees vary according to the amount of coverage. The average cost for single coverage per quarter is $159.33. Part-time students are also eligible to purchase medical insurance.

Living and Housing Costs

Finch University of Health Sciences does not offer on-campus housing. A list of housing and costs is provided for students as they are accepted. Most graduate students live in apartments in the surrounding area.

Student Group

The School of Related Health Sciences enrolls about 300 students.

Student Outcomes

The majority of the graduate students at Finch University are already employed in their respective fields. The students who are not, have an employment return of 100 percent once their degrees are received. Graduates have found employment in the areas of education and research and in hospitals and clinics.

Location

The School of Related Health Sciences is housed at the North Chicago Veterans Administration Medical Center, North Chicago, Illinois. This location is convenient to a variety of clinical facilities in both Lake and Cook Counties. Because of its proximity to major highways, the school is within easy access of metropolitan Chicago and Milwaukee.

The University and the School

Finch University is a private, independent university centrally located between Chicago and Milwaukee. The School of Related Health Sciences offers a multitude of hospitals, research laboratories, clinics, and health-care agencies in which students may gain research and professional experience.

Applying

Applicants must submit a graduate application that includes the application form, two letters of reference, and their most current transcripts. The TOEFL is required of all international applicants from countries in which English is not the native language. The application fee is $25. Student should contact the department chair for specific course prerequisites for each program.

Correspondence and Information

Admissions Office
Finch University of Health Sciences/The Chicago Medical School
3333 Green Bay Road
North Chicago, Illinois 60064
Telephone: 847-578-3209

Finch University of Health Sciences/The Chicago Medical School

THE FACULTY

Cynthia Adams, Dean and Professor, Leadership Skills; Ed.D., Wayne State, 1973; M.T.
Saralyn Byker, Instructor; M.S., Finch, 1996; PA-C.
Doris Cheung, Instructor; B.S., Illinois, 1991.
Elizabeth Coulson, Associate Professor, Ethics and Public Policy; M.B.A., Keller Graduate School of Management; PT.
James Dayhuff, Assistant Professor, Orthopedic Manual Therapy; M.S., Wisconsin–Madison, 1980.
Janet DeRobertis, Associate Professor and Chair, Clinical Microbiology/Immunology; M.S., M.T. (ASCP), Finch/Chicago Medical, 1985.
Donald Frosch, Academic Coordinator and Instructor; B.A., Wisconsin–Madison, 1983; PA-C. Clinical skills for primary care practitioners.
Donna Frownfelter, Assistant Professor, Cardiopulmonary; M.A., Northwestern, 1969; PT, CCS, RT.
Roberta Henderson, Assistant Professor, Clinical Electrophysiology; M.S., National, 1988.
Cathy Kapica, Assistant Professor, Nutrition and Clinical Dietetics; Ph.D., Illinois, 1984.
Patrick Knott, Assistant Professor; M.S., Finch, 1996.
Cynthia Krstansky, Assistant Professor, Medical Surgical Nursing; M.S., Northern Illinois, 1975; RN.
Dawn LaBarbera, Assistant Professor; M.S., Finch, 1994.
George Anthony Latham, Assistant Professor and Director of Post Professional Studies; Ed.D., Northern Illinois, 1998. Leadership skills.
Barbara Miller, Assistant Professor and Clinical Coordinator, Occupational Medicine; M.S., Northern Illinois, 1989. PA-C.
Albert Peterson, Associate Professor, Exercise Physiology; Ed.D., Arkansas, 1980.
Lillian Mundt, Assistant Professor, Hematology; M.H.S., M.T. (ASCP), S.H., Governor's State, 1982.
Wendy Rheault, Professor (Measurement and Statistics), Associate Dean, and Interim Chair; Ph.D., Chicago, 1989; PT.
Kathleen Ruroede, Assistant Professor and Chair, Healthcare Risk Management Program; Ph.D., Loyola, 1998; RN. Health-care risk management, statistics and research design.
Sandra Salloway, Associate Professor and Chair, Community Health Nursing Program; N.D., Northern Illinois, 1981; RN. Community health nursing, geriatric nursing.
Dale Schuit, Associate Professor and Chair, Kinesiology; Ph.D., Illinois, 1988; PT.
Melanie Shuran, Professor and Chair, Nutrition; Ph.D., Illinois at Urbana-Champaign, 1988; RD.
Judith Stoecker, Director of Post Professional Studies and Associate Professor, Public Policy Analysis; Ph.D., Illinois, 1990; PT.
Susan Tappert, Assistant Professor, Therapeutic Modalities; M.S., Finch/Chicago Medical, 1993; PT.
Rosanne Thomas, Assistant Professor, Neurology; M.S., Finch/Chicago Medical, 1996; PT.

HARVARD UNIVERSITY / MASSACHUSETTS INSTITUTE OF TECHNOLOGY

Division of Health Sciences and Technology
Speech and Hearing Sciences Program

Program of Study

A four-plus-year curriculum leads to a Ph.D in speech and hearing sciences awarded by Massachusetts Institute of Technology (MIT). This doctoral program is designed to develop research scientists who can apply the concepts and methods of the physical and biological sciences to basic and clinical problems in speech and hearing through innovative research. To meet this goal, the program combines a rigorous course curriculum in quantitative methods for studying speech and hearing with broad exposure to issues, including exposure to clinical diagnosis and treatment. The interdisciplinary nature of the program is illustrated by the diversity of interests of its faculty of about 50, which is drawn from about ten different departments at Harvard and MIT.

The first two to three years are devoted principally to course work in the anatomical, acoustical, physiological, perceptual, and cognitive basics and to clinical approaches to speech and hearing problems. Early introduction of key concepts in acoustics, anatomy, and physiology provides a solid base from which to pursue individual research interests. Students work with research advisers to develop a thorough understanding of basic concepts and tools in their fields of concentration. While students have considerable flexibility in changing their areas of concentration as their educational horizons expand, on admission to the program students should indicate their interests. Throughout the program, special attention is paid to teaching scientific values and discussing issues of integrity and scholarly practice.

Students must master core material in the field of speech and hearing that spans many traditional disciplines. Mastery of this core material is tested in the written part of the General Examination. Students must also plan a concentration, a program of course work and research in a focus area such as physiology and neuroscience, perception, signal and system analysis, or speech and language. The focus area forms the basis for the oral portion of the General Examination.

Active participation in research begins as early as the summer following the first year. By the end of the second year, students should have identified an area of professional interest. A research project is then chosen that will form the basis of a Ph.D. thesis and will also demonstrate the ability to do original research. Thesis research can be done at MIT, Harvard, or at one of the teaching hospitals.

Research Facilities

The resources available for research training include laboratories at MIT, Harvard University (including Harvard Medical School), and Harvard-affiliated hospitals. Students have free access to the libraries and other educational and recreational resources of both universities.

Financial Aid

The Division of Health Sciences and Technology (HST), primarily through an NIH training grant, provides full support for the students enrolled in this program provided they are citizens or permanent residents of the U.S. This includes a stipend of approximately $17,100 per year. This support continues through four years of study, after which support comes from the research laboratories where students conduct their Ph.D. research.

Cost of Study

For students who are not U.S. citizens or permanent residents, tuition for this program is approximately $32,750 per year. Applicants who fall into this category have to guarantee to the Institute that provisions have been made for their support if they wish to be considered.

Living and Housing Costs

For students who are not U.S. citizens or permanent residents, living expenses, including room, meals, and miscellaneous expenses, average $1400 per month for single students and slightly more for married students. Single graduate students at MIT may live in Ashdown House or Tang Hall. Married graduate students at MIT may live at Westgate or Eastgate. Many graduate students live in apartments and houses in the surrounding communities.

Student Group

The Speech and Hearing Sciences Program has admitted 51 students in its first seven classes.

Student Outcomes

The breadth of the program qualifies its graduates for a wide range of careers in basic and applied research in industry, universities, hospitals, or government laboratories concerned with biological and man-made communications systems. Specific areas include: (a) basic research on the neural, physiological, and perceptual processes that underlie communication by speech and hearing, (b) speech recognition systems that couple acoustic input to computer systems, (c) analysis of central nervous system behavior to determine neural abnormalities in people with speech-processing disorders, (d) development of measures of environments (e.g., conference room, airport terminal, open spaces, etc.) that provide specifications for effective voice communication, and (e) design of speech production and hearing prostheses to alleviate pathological conditions.

Location

Harvard and MIT are located in Cambridge, just across the Charles River from Boston.

The Institutions and The Division

Harvard is the oldest college in the United States, founded in 1636. MIT, founded in 1861 as a private, endowed institution committed to the extension of knowledge through teaching and research, has grown to be one of the foremost research universities in the world.

The HST Division, established in 1977, formalized a major collaborative effort in the health sciences that began in 1970. This effort, designed to focus science and technology on human needs, draws on the complementary strengths of the two institutions.

Applying

Applicants must have a baccalaureate degree in engineering or science. Recommended mathematical preparation includes at least one undergraduate subject in differential equations and one course in biology. While GRE scores are desirable, they are not required. Students apply through MIT, utilizing the standard graduate school application. Students do not apply to a specific department, but rather to the Division of HST, and should indicate on the application that the interdisciplinary program is HST/Speech and Hearing Sciences. The application deadline for September admissions is January 15 and should be directed to Office of Admissions, Room 3-103, Massachusetts Institute of Technology, Cambridge, Massachusetts 02139.

Correspondence and Information

Dr. Martha L. Gray
Co-Director, Division of HST
Room E25-519
Massachusetts Institute of Technology
Cambridge, Massachusetts 02139
Telephone: 617-258-8974
World Wide Web: http://web7.MIT.EDU/HSTSHS/WWW

Dr. Louis D. Braida
Program Director
Room 36-747
Massachusetts Institute of Technology
Cambridge, Massachusetts 02139
Telephone: 617-253-2575

Harvard University/Massachusetts Institute of Technology

THE FACULTY AND THEIR RESEARCH

Research facilities include sites at MIT, the Harvard Medical School, and several of the Harvard-affiliated teaching hospitals. Collaborative work with other local universities is possible by special arrangement. The key to the abbreviations in each faculty member's entry is BU: Boston University; HMS: Harvard Medical School; HU: Harvard University; MEEI: Massachusetts Eye and Ear Infirmary; MGH: Massachusetts General Hospital; and MIT: Massachusetts Institute of Technology.

Joe C. Adams, Ph.D.; HMS, MEEI. Auditory neuroanatomy.
Corine A. Bickley, Ph.D.; MIT. Speech communication.
Frederick R. Bieber, Ph.D.; HMS, Brigham and Women's Hospital. Congenital auditory pathology.
Louis D. Braida, Ph.D.; MIT. Auditory psychophysics, aids for the deaf.
M. Christian Brown, Ph.D.; HMS, MEEI. Auditory physiology.
David N. Caplan, M.D., Ph.D.; HMS, MGH. Neurological bases of language.
H. Steven Colburn, Ph.D.; BU. Binaural auditory psychophysics.
David P. Corey, Ph.D.; HMS, MGH. Cell and molecular biology of the ear.
Suzanne Corkin, Ph.D.; MIT, MGH. Brain and cognitive functions.
Bertrand Delgutte, Ph.D.; MIT, MEEI. Auditory physiology and perception.
Nathaniel I. Durlach, Ph.D.; MIT. Man-machine interactions.
Donald K. Eddington, Ph.D.; MIT, MEEI. Cochlear implants.
Dennis M. Freeman, Ph.D.; MIT. Auditory mechanisms in the ear.
Lawrence S. Frishkopf, Ph.D.; MIT. Sensory systems.
Barbara C. Fullerton, Ph.D.; HMS, MEEI. Auditory neuroanatomy.
John J. Guinan, Ph.D.; MEEI. Cochlear physiology and auditory reflexes.
Robert D. Hall, Ph.D.; MEEI. Animal models for cochlear implants.
Christopher H. Halpin, Ph.D.; HMS, MEEI. Audiology.
Marc D. Hauser, Ph.D.; HU. Neuroetiology of primate communication.
Gerald B. Healy, M.D.; HMS, Children's Hospital. Pediatric otolaryngology.
Barbara S. Herrmann, Ph.D.; HMS, MEEI. Evoked responses in audiology.
Robert E. Hillman, Ph.D.; HMS, MEEI. Voice testing.
Parvis Janfaza, M.D.; HMS, MEEI. Anatomy of head and neck structures.
Samuel J. Keyser, Ph.D.; MIT. Linguistics.
Nelson Y. S. Kiang, Ph.D.; MIT, HMS, MEEI, MGH. Auditory physiology, otology, and laryngology.
James B. Kobler, Ph.D.; HMS, MEEI. Neuroscience of speaking and swallowing.
Harlan Lane, Ph.D.; Northeastern University, MEEI. Psychology of deafness.
Robert A. Levine, M.D.; HMS, MEEI. Auditory neurology.
M. Charles Liberman, Ph.D.; HMS, MEEI. Auditory physiology.
Michael J. McKenna, M.D.; HMS, MEEI. Otolaryngology.
Jennifer R. Melcher, Ph.D.; MEEI. Cellular generators of the brainstem auditory evoked potential.
Saumil N. Merchant, M.D.; HMS, MEEI. Otology.
William W. Montgomery, M.D.; HMS, MEEI. Otolaryngology.
Cynthia Morton, Ph.D.; HMS, Brigham and Women's Hospital. Cytogenetics.
Edmund A. Mroz, Ph.D.; HMS, MEEI. Auditory neurochemistry.
Joseph B. Nadol Jr., M.D.; HMS, MEEI. Otology and laryngology.
William T. Peake, Sc.D.; MIT. Physiological acoustics.
Joseph S. Perkell, D.M.D., Ph.D.; MIT. Speech production.
Kenneth Pote, Ph.D.; HMS, Children's Hospital. Developmental biology of the ear.
Charlotte M. Reed, Ph.D.; MIT. Auditory psychophysics, aids for the deaf.
Bruce R. Rosen, M.D., Ph.D.; HMS, MGH. Magnetic resonance imaging.
John J. Rosowski, Ph.D.; HMS, MEEI. Comparative audition.
Gerald E. Schneider, Ph.D.; MIT. Neural development and plasticity.
William F. Sewell, Ph.D.; HMS, MEEI. Auditory neuropharmacology.
Howard C. Shane, Ph.D.; HMS, Children's Hospital. Assistive devices for the multihandicapped.
Stefanie Shattuck-Hufnagel, Ph.D.; MIT. Speech and language.
Kenneth N. Stevens, Sc.D.; MIT. Speech and language communication.
Aaron Thornton, Ph.D.; HMS, MEEI. Audiology.
Conrad Wall, Ph.D.; MEEI. Human vestibular function, human visual-vestibular sensory interactions.
Reiner Wilhelms-Tricarico, Ph.D.; MIT. Physiological modeling of speech production.
Patrick M. Zurek, Ph.D.; MIT. Auditory psychophysics.

NEW YORK MEDICAL COLLEGE

Graduate School of Health Sciences Program in Physical Therapy

Program of Study

The program in physical therapy is a master's degree (M.S.) program providing entry-level professional education in physical therapy. The program is designed to foster the development of physical therapists who are competent and caring, with the ability to practice in a variety of settings. The program prepares students to adapt to changes in the health-care system. By emphasizing a strong foundation in the basic sciences, the program prepares students to be independent learners capable of critical thinking and analysis. A major feature is a problem-based format for the courses in the clinical science of physical therapy. During the last two academic semesters, learning takes place primarily in small tutorial groups and through structured laboratory experiences. The problem-based approach provides an opportunity for students to take responsibility for their learning and to integrate basic and clinical science, clinical skills, and critical analysis. In addition, students spend a total of 24 weeks of full-time clinical education in different settings, where they learn clinical skills under the direct supervision of practicing physical therapists. The program admits full-time students only for an intensive two-year program, including summers.

The physical therapy program is accredited by the Commission on Accreditation in Physical Therapy Education (CAPTE).

Research Facilities

Research facilities include the Alumni Computer Laboratory and the Medical Sciences Library, which maintains a collection of more than 169,000 bound volumes and 2,100 journal titles. Online, CD-ROM, and networked databases include MEDLINE, PsychLIT, HealthPLAN, Reference Update, PDR, Entrez, and Grateful Med. A full array of reference and information services is provided. Included are individual consultations for assistance with research and group classes on the effective use of resources and databases.

The physical therapy program also has a well-equipped physical therapy laboratory for teaching and research. It uses the laboratories of the medical school's Department of Cell Biology and Anatomy for instruction in anatomy and histology.

Financial Aid

Financial aid is available. Students are encouraged to talk to staff members in Student Financial Planning who can help them to determine their needs and to apply for appropriate aid packages.

Cost of Study

For 1998–99, the tuition is $17,000. Annual fees total $270. Health insurance purchased through the College is separate.

Living and Housing Costs

On-campus housing is available on a limited basis for single and married students. The 1998–99 housing charges for single students range from $390 to $650 per month. Charges for unfurnished apartments vary based on size and location. Assistance in obtaining off-campus housing is available from the Office of Student Housing.

Student Group

The physical therapy program is a full-time program requiring two years of study. It is designed to accommodate about 48 students in each class.

Location

New York Medical College is located on a 565-acre campus shared with Westchester County Medical Center in Valhalla, New York. Its suburban site in the center of Westchester County is approximately 20 miles north of New York City. There are ample educational, recreational, and cultural opportunities available locally and in the New York metropolitan area.

The College

Founded in 1860, New York Medical College has a strong history of involvement in medical and health education and in training, research, and professional and community service. It is chartered as a health sciences university by the Regents of the State of New York and is a member of the Middle States Association of Colleges and Secondary Schools. The mission of New York Medical College is carried out through three schools: the Medical School; the Graduate School of Basic Medical Sciences, which originated in 1963; and the Graduate School of Health Science, which began in 1981.

Applying

Application packages and information about prerequisites are available from the Office of Admissions of the Graduate School of Health Sciences. A nonrefundable fee of $75 must accompany each application. Scores on the Graduate Record Examinations (GRE) are required. Applicants whose native language is not English are required to obtain a minimum TOEFL score of 600. Admission decisions are made without regard to race, color, national origin, religion, sex, or handicap.

Correspondence and Information

Ms. Dale M. Sweeney
Director of Admission and Recruitment
Graduate School of Health Sciences
Learning Center
New York Medical College
Valhalla, New York 10595
Telephone: 914-594-4510
Fax: 914-594-4292
E-mail: gshs_admissions@nymc.edu

New York Medical College

FACULTY

James E. Gordon, Program Director; Ed.D.; PT.
Catherine Culliton, M.P.A.; PT. Physical therapy.
Anna B. Drakontides, Ph.D. Cell biology and anatomy.
Carol Du Bois, M.S.; PT. Physical therapy.
Julie Fineman, M.A.; PT. Physical therapy.
Michael Gallucci, M.S.; PT. Physical therapy.
Gail B. Harris, M.S.; PT. Physical therapy.
Clifton B. Hertzberg, Ph.D. Cell biology and anatomy.
Jack Joe, M.S.; PT. Physical therapy.
Kevin J. McQuade, M.P.H., Ph.D.; PT. Physical therapy.
Lisa Muratori, B.S.; PT. Physical therapy.
Matthew A. Pravetz, O.F.M., M.Div., Ph.D. Cell biology and anatomy.
Lori Quinn, Ed.D.; PT. Physical therapy.
Sheila McGuane Reed, M.S.; PT. Physical therapy.
Sansor C. Sharma, Ph.D. Cell biology and anatomy.
Alfonso Solimene, Ph.D. Cell biology and anatomy.
Carl Thompson, Ph.D. Physiology.
Nancy Wood, M.S.; PT. Physical therapy.

NEW YORK UNIVERSITY

School of Education
Department of Occupational Therapy

Programs of Study

New York University's occupational therapy programs are ranked among the top such programs in the nation. NYU has one of two programs nationwide that award the Ph.D. in occupational therapy.

One M.A. program provides professional education and emphasizes a holistic approach to occupational therapy. The program is open to applicants who are not registered occupational therapists and who wish to become certified. Students must complete at least 76 points of course work over 2½ to 3 years. Four postprofessional concentrations in occupational therapy are designed for certified occupational therapists: an M.A. program focuses on the generic foundation of occupational therapy, with individually designed specialty areas that include physical disabilities, AIDS, and rehabilitation, using assistive technology; an M.A. program in occupational therapy for developmental disabilities/pediatrics; an M.A. program in occupational therapy in mental health; and a Ph.D. program in occupational therapy. The postprofessional M.A. programs require 36 points of course work, the Ph.D. program 62 points and a dissertation. A 36-point program in ergonomics and biomechanics offers the master's degree to individuals in allied health, engineering, and medicine.

Research Facilities

The NYU library system holds more than 3 million volumes. The occupational therapy classroom/laboratory areas contain the latest rehabilitation technology equipment. The NYU Medical Center, preeminent for innovative health care, teaching, and research, provides occupational therapy students with clinical experience and the opportunity to participate in joint research projects. More than 350 other health-related and education institutes in the area provide students with learning experiences. A complete laboratory for biomechanics and kinesiology research is located nearby, run in cooperation with the Orthopaedic Institute of the Hospital for Joint Diseases and the Occupational and Industrial Orthopedic Center (OIOC).

Financial Aid

Various University, state, and federal grants, loans, and stipends are available. For professional-level students, two graduate assistantships provide approximately $15,000 of stipend and tuition remission per year in 1998–99. A loanship program, in which students receive tuition assistance from clinical facilities in exchange for work commitment after graduation; work-study positions in University offices; and lists of smaller scholarships and grant opportunities are available. For postprofessional master's and doctoral students, teaching fellowships and additional research assistantships provide approximately $22,000 of tuition remission and stipend per year in 1998–99. In the developmental disabilities and mental health concentrations, students can earn full-time salaries averaging $38,000 per year for 3½–4 days of work per week, with 1–1½ days of educational release time, at jobs linked to the departmental programs.

Cost of Study

Graduate tuition cost was $610 per point in 1997–98. A health services fee of approximately $400 per year is required of full-time students, unless other health coverage exists.

Living and Housing Costs

Residential facilities for full-time graduate students comprise a variety of apartment-style accommodations. The contract period is for the entire year; rates vary from $5500 to $8500 per year, payable in thirds. Some unfurnished commercial apartments, leased by the University, are also available. Applications for graduate housing are distributed to new students. Information about residence-hall housing is available from the University Housing Office, 8 Washington Place. Students should contact the Off-Campus Housing Office, 4 Washington Square Village (telephone: 212-998-4620), for information regarding sublets, rentals, and other housing accommodations.

Student Group

There are an estimated 300 students enrolled in the department; approximately 10 percent attend part-time in the professional program, approximately 80 percent attend part-time in the postprofessional program, about 90 percent are women, and 14 percent are international. Students come from more than half of the fifty states and twenty other countries; more than 75 percent receive financial aid. Employment in occupational therapy in the New York metropolitan area and elsewhere is extremely high, due to the enormous demand for occupational therapists in schools, health-care facilities, and private practice.

Location

The University's main center is located at Washington Square in Greenwich Village. The University is an integral part of the metropolitan community, where major hospitals, national health organizations, and community clinics provide innumerable opportunities for fieldwork and clinical experience.

The University and The School

New York University is a private university in the public service. Founded in 1831, NYU is the nation's largest private university and one of only twenty-six institutions that have achieved membership in the Association of American Universities. The National Science Foundation has ranked NYU among the top four universities, judged by the number of leading intellectuals on the faculty. Its fourteen schools, colleges, and divisions have achieved international distinction in the liberal arts and sciences, law, medicine, business, the fine arts, and the performing arts. The School of Education is one of the oldest and largest schools in the nation devoted to the human services professions. More than 270 different areas of concentration are offered in almost fifty professional degree programs. Graduate programs are interprofessional, transcending customary and traditional fields of study. With a student-faculty ratio of 6:1, the School offers the benefits of both a medium-sized college and a major research university.

Applying

Entry for all programs is in the fall semester only; applications should be submitted by March 1. Applicants should submit the application form, official transcripts of all degrees and advanced course work, two letters of recommendation, and an autobiographical sketch. Applicants to the postprofessional programs should submit learning objectives. GRE scores are required for Ph.D. applicants only. Applicants whose native language is not English must submit TOEFL scores.

Correspondence and Information

For departmental information:

Paulette Bell (professional), Admissions Director
or
Jane Miller (postprofessional), Admissions Director
Department of Occupational Therapy
School of Education
New York University
35 West 4th Street, 11th floor
New York, New York 10012-1172

Telephone: 212-998-5825
Fax: 212-995-4044
E-mail: occupational.therapy@nyu.edu
World Wide Web: http://www.nyu.edu/education/ot/

For application forms:

Office of Graduate Admissions
School of Education
Pless Hall, Room 200
New York University
82 Washington Square East
New York, New York 10003-6644

Telephone: 212-998-5030
Fax: 212-995-4328
World Wide Web: http://www.nyu.edu/education

New York University

THE FACULTY AND THEIR RESEARCH

Deborah R. Labovitz, Professor and Department Chair; Ph.D., Pennsylvania, 1979; OTR/L. International occupational therapy; sociology of medicine, professions, and women. United States member, Editorial Board, *Occupational Therapy International.*

Marie-Louise F. Blount, Clinical Associate Professor and Director of Professional Programs; A.M., Boston University, 1964; OTR. Occupational therapy education. Co-editor, *Occupational Therapy in Mental Health.*

Karen A. Buckley, Clinical Assistant Professor; M.A., NYU, 1977; OT/L. Physical dysfunction, neurobehavioral treatment, neurodevelopmental treatment, neurological disorders, rehabilitation, augmentative communication.

Mary V. Donohue, Clinical Associate Professor; Ph.D., NYU, 1985; OTR/L. Occupational therapy in mental health, research methods, activity group process. Co-editor, *Occupational Therapy in Mental Health.*

Jim Hinojosa, Associate Professor and Director, Postprofessional Graduate Programs; Ph.D., NYU, 1989; OT. Pediatric occupational therapy practice. History, theory, and philosophy of the profession. Director, American Occupational Therapy Foundation; Author, *Frames of Reference for Pediatric Occupational Therapy* and *Evolution of Clients: Obtaining and Interpreting Data.*

Paula McCreedy, Clinical Assistant Professor and Fieldwork Coordinator; M.Ed., New Orleans, 1981; OT/L. Psychosocial practice.

Anne C. Mosey, Professor; Ph.D., NYU, 1968; OTR/L. Theory and philosophy of the profession. Eleanor Clarke Slagle Lectureship, The American Occupational Therapy Association, 1986; Author, *Applied Scientific Inquiry in the Health Professions: An Epistemological Orientation.*

Anita Perr, Clinical Assistant Professor; M.A., NYU, 1984; OT. Clinical rehabilitation, with specialty in assistive technology; NDT certified.

Sally E. Poole, Clinical Assistant Professor; M.A., NYU, 1975; OTR, CHT. Kinesiology, physical dysfunction, splinting, clinical conditions, hand rehabilitation.

Joyce Sabari, Associate Professor; Ph.D., NYU, 1992; OT. Adult neurorehabilitation, with emphasis on strokes. Author of textbook chapters and journal articles about occupational therapy approaches to stroke rehabilitation.

POSTPROFESSIONAL PART-TIME FACULTY

Adjunct Associate Professors and Training Specialists: Beverly Bain, Ed.D.; OTR. Gary Bedell, Ph.D.; OT.

Adjunct Associate Professors: Judy Grossman, Dr.P.H.; OTR. Margareta Nordin, Med.Dr.Sci.; RPT.

Adjunct Assistant Professor: Sherri Weiser-Horowitz, Ph.D.

Instructors: Nachman Halpern, M.A. Herman Sabath, M.A. Ali Sheikhzadeh, M.A.

PROFESSIONAL PART-TIME FACULTY

Adjunct Associate Professor: Anita Simons, M.S.; OTR/L.

Instructors: Katherine Barnicle, M.S.; OTR/L. Debra Beal, M.A.; OTR/L. Paulette Bell, M.A.; OTR/L. Serena Berger, M.A.; OTR/L. Cheryl Butler, M.A.; OTR/L. Isabel Cadenas, Ph.D. Maureen Cavanaugh, M.S.; OTR/L. Cheryl Colangelo, M.S.; OTR/L. Kerry Darrow, B.S.; OTR/L. Lisa Davis, M.A.; OTR/L. Hannah Diamond, M.A.; OTR/L. Judith Dicker-Friedman, M.A.; OTR/L. Malinda Dunn, M.S.; OTR/L. Nora Goldberg, M.A.; OTR/L. David Goldsheyder, M.A. Gloria Graham, M.A.; OTR/L. Doreen Torres Gray, M.A.; OTR/L. Susan Greene, M.A.; OTR/L. Lisa Gordon, M.A.; OTR/L. Prudence Heisler, M.A.; OTR/L. Sol Ittah, M.S.; OTR/L. Lauren Joachim, M.A.; OTR/L. Janine Kahan, M.A.; OTR/L. Virginia Kim, M.S.; OTR/L. Nancy Finkelstein Kline, Ph.D., OTR/L. Laurie Knis, M.A.; OTR/L. Antonia Leonard, M.B.A.; OTR/L. Rita Levey, M.A.; OTR/L. Ai-Lian Lim, M.A.; OTR/L. Colleen McCaul, B.A.; OTR/L. George McDermott, B.S.; OTR/L. Jane Miller, M.A.; OTR/L. Bernadette Mineo, M.A.; OTR/L. Phyllis Mirenberg, M.S.; OTR/L. Nancy Nichols, M.A.; OTR/L. Marilyn Rosee, B.A.; OTR/L. Abbey Brod Rosen, B.S.; OTR/L. Theresa Roth, M.A.; OTR/L. Susan Scanga, M.A.; OTR/L. Sarah Schoen, M.A.; OTR/L. Margery Szczepanski, M.A.; OTR/L. Jeffrey Tomlinson, M.S.W.; OTR/L. Sheri Wadler, M.S.; OTR/L. Suzanne White, M.A.; OTR/L. Diana Chen Wong, B.S.; OTR/L.

NORTHEASTERN UNIVERSITY

Bouvé College of Pharmacy and Health Sciences
Department of Speech-Language Pathology and Audiology

Programs of Study

Graduates of the College's speech-language pathology and audiology programs are employed nationally and internationally in hospital, clinical, rehabilitative, and educational facilities providing a full range of diagnostic and treatment services to individuals with communication disorders. Master of Science degrees are offered in both audiology and speech-language pathology. The programs are accredited by the American Speech-Language-Hearing Association.

The speech-language pathology and audiology programs require extensive clinical training and are full-time programs. Students who enter the programs with an undergraduate degree in speech-language pathology, audiology, or communication disorders typically complete their programs in two years. Prerequisite undergraduate courses are available for nonbackground students.

The College also offers the following graduate programs: Doctor of Philosophy (Ph.D.) in biomedical science, with specializations in medical laboratory science, medicinal chemistry, pharmaceutics, pharmacology, and toxicology and an interdisciplinary program in biomedical science; Doctor of Philosophy (Ph.D.) in counseling psychology and school psychology; and Certificate of Advanced Graduate Study (C.A.G.S.) in counseling psychology, school psychology, and rehabilitation counseling. The Master of Science degree is offered in applied behavior analysis, applied educational psychology with specialties in school counseling and school psychology, college student development and counseling, counseling psychology, clinical exercise physiology, general biomedical science, human resource counseling, medical laboratory science, medicinal chemistry, perfusion technology, pharmacology, and rehabilitation counseling. The Master of Health Professions (M.H.P.) is offered with the following options: general, health policy, physician assistant, and regulatory toxicology. The Master of Science in Education (M.S.Ed.) is offered in special needs and intensive special needs.

Research Facilities

The Department of Speech-Language Pathology and Audiology maintains laboratory facilities that provide students and faculty with the space and equipment needed to complete research projects. These facilities have state-of-the-art signal generation equipment with computer-assisted data management and analysis.

Research topics currently under investigation include the development and evaluation of treatment efficacy and generalization in aphasia and related disorders, issues in child language and phonology, computer-based interventions for developmental communication problems for foreign accent reduction, and augmentative communication.

The Division of Academic Computing provides access to computing resources. A high-speed data network links users and facilities on the central campus and on three satellite campuses. The campus network is also connected via the global Internet to computing resources around the world. Students have access to DEC VAX systems, public access microcomputer labs (PC and Macintosh), a computer and conferencing system, a multimedia lab, and specialized computing equipment.

University libraries contain more than 808,000 volumes, 1.8 million microforms, 170,000 government documents, 8,900 serial subscriptions, and 16,000 audio, video, and software titles. A central library contains technologically sophisticated services, including online catalog and circulation systems, a gateway to external networked information resources, and a network of CD-ROM optical disc databases. Students have access to major research collections through the Boston Library Consortium.

Financial Aid

Northeastern awards need-based aid through the Federal Perkins Loan, Federal Work-Study, and Federal Stafford Loan programs and also offers minority fellowships and Martin Luther King Jr. Scholarships. The Bouvé College also offers a limited number of teaching, research, and administrative assistantships that include tuition remission and a stipend typically ranging between $9750 and $12,075 and require a maximum of 20 hours of work per week. Also available are tuition assistantships that provide partial or full tuition remission and require a maximum of 10 hours of work per week.

Cost of Study

The cost of tuition for the 1998–99 academic year in the graduate school of Bouvé College of Pharmacy and Health Sciences is $440 per quarter hour of credit. Where applicable, special tuition charges are made for thesis, dissertation, teaching, practicums, or fieldwork. A booklet listing all fees and tuition costs is available upon request from the address below.

Living and Housing Costs

For 1998–99, quarterly on-campus room rates for a single bedroom range from $1340 to $1715. A single efficiency apartment is $2040 to $2325. A shared bedroom in an apartment ranges from $1630 to $1775 per quarter. While there are several board options available, graduate students typically pay approximately $1085 per quarter for ten meals per week. Off-campus living accommodations also exist in the vicinity of the University.

Student Group

In fall 1997, 19,691 undergraduate and 4,634 graduate students were enrolled at Northeastern University. Bouvé College of Pharmacy and Health Sciences had 677 students, 474 of whom attended full-time.

Location

Boston, the capital of Massachusetts, offers many academic, cultural, and recreational opportunities. In addition to the abundant resources available within Northeastern University, students have access to the resources of the other educational and cultural institutions of the greater Boston area. The city is home to people of every intellectual, political, economic, racial, ethnic, and religious background. Boston is a mixture of Colonial tradition and modern technology. It is a place where the past is appreciated, the present enjoyed, and the future anticipated.

The University

Founded in 1898, Northeastern is a privately endowed nonsectarian institution of higher learning and one of the largest private universities in the country. Northeastern has seven undergraduate colleges, nine graduate and professional schools, two part-time undergraduate divisions, a number of continuing and special education programs and institutes, several suburban campuses, and an extensive research division.

Applying

The application deadline for the M.S. programs in speech-language pathology and audiology is February 15. The following are required with the application: official transcripts for all college and university work, three references, a personal statement or essay, GRE (aptitude test only) or Miller Analogies Test (MAT) scores, and a $50 application fee. TOEFL scores (minimum score of 600) are required of those applicants whose native language is not English.

Correspondence and Information

William Purnell, Director of Graduate Admissions
Bouvé College of Pharmacy and Health Sciences
203 Mugar Life Science Building
Northeastern University
Boston, Massachusetts 02115

Telephone: 617-373-2708
E-mail: w.purnell@nunet.neu.edu

Northeastern University

THE FACULTY AND THEIR RESEARCH

Kevin Kearns, Associate Professor and Chairperson, Department of Speech-Language Pathology and Audiology; Ph.D., Kansas, 1979. Associate editor for the *Am. J. Speech-Language Pathology,* and editorial consultant to *JSHR, JSHD,* and *Aphasiology*. More than thirty publications in *ASHA* journals and *Clinical Aphasiology* and numerous invited presentations. Scholarly and research interests include the investigation of clinical aspects of neurogenic communication disorders and examination of issues relating to treatment efficacy and generalization. Recognized for contributions to the field by being elected as a Fellow of the American Speech-Language-Hearing Association.

Helen Anis, Clinical Specialist, Speech-Language Pathology; M.A., Connecticut, 1971; M.P.A., Northeastern, 1986. Speech and language problems in children and administration in areas of program development, evaluation, and quality assurance. Taught courses in articulation disorders and clinical practice in the Department of Speech-Language Pathology and Audiology. Member of the Massachusetts Speech-Language-Hearing Association (MASHA). Served on the Governmental Affairs Committee and as a regional representative. Member of the American Speech-Language-Hearing Association and the Council of Supervisors in Speech-Language Pathology and Audiology.

Jane Doyle, Clinical Supervisor; M.S., James Madison. Augmentative communication and assistive technology and American sign language.

Linda Ferrier, Associate Professor, Speech-Language Pathology; Ph.D., Boston University, 1986. Use of computer technology for the communicatively impaired. With Harriet Fell, of the College of Computer Science, developed the Baby Babble Blanket (BBB), a communication system for severely physically impaired infants and children. Awarded funding by the Federal Department of Education to finish the development and field-testing of this device. Another software project is the development of Macintosh programs for accent reduction for nonnative speakers of English. Two programs are now complete and are published by Trinity Software. Another research interest is in voice recognition technology for use as a writing system for individuals with cerebral palsy. Funding from United Cerebral Palsy Foundation with Howard Shane, of Children's Hospital in Boston, to evaluate the use of the DragonDictate[a], a voice recognition system, with individuals with dysarthria. Developing an Early Vocalization Analyzer (EVA), an automatic system for the recognition and analysis of infant vocalizations (with Fell).

Mary Florentine, Professor; Ph.D., Northeastern, 1978. Recently honored as the Northeastern University Matthews Distinguished Professor. Guest professor at the Acoustics Laboratory of the Technical University of Denmark. Research on auditory processing in normal and impaired listeners, the ability of nonnative listeners to understand speech in noise, cross-cultural attitudes toward noise, and hearing loss prevention through education. The National Institutes of Health funded a grant (with Professor Soren Buus) to study normal and hearing-impaired temporal processing of complex sounds. Currently, awarded a grant on intensity discrimination and masking in normal and impaired hearing is in its 12th year of continuous funding from the National Institutes of Health. A Fellow of the American Academy of Audiology and the Acoustical Society of America. This recognition was given for contributions to the study of the effects of hearing impairment on auditory processing.

Denise J. Frankoff, Clinical Specialist; M.A., Northeastern. Neurogenic communication disorders and assistive technology.

Arlene Greenstein, Professor, Associate Dean, and Director of Special Programs at University College; Ph.D., Wisconsin–Madison.

Mary Beth Lannon, Clinical Specialist, Audiology; Ed.D., Northeastern, 1991. Expanding Head Start screenings and evaluating infants and toddlers from the Parent Child Center in Dorchester and the Crispus Attucks Child Center in Roxbury. Director of the Infant Hearing Screening Program at St. Elizabeth's Medical Center as well as the audiologist for the Waltham Public School System. Works with military retirees at the Brighton Marine Health Center.

Gregory Lof, Assistant Professor; Ph.D., Wisconsin, 1994. Articulation/phonological development and disorders; published articles pertaining to this topic and dysphagia. Research focuses on the efficacy of phonological treatment and assessment and theoretical underpinnings of speech-sound stimulability.

Marjorie North, Clinical Supervisor; M.A., Adelphi. Private practice, public speaking training.

Christine Rankovic, Senior Research Scientist, Ph.D., Minnesota, 1989. NIH-sponsored research explores the application of a model of speech reception known as Articulation Theory to guide the selection and design of hearing aids that aim to reduce background noise problems. Experiments involve collecting percent-correct scores on nonsense syllable lists under noisy conditions that are signal processed to maximize speech reception according to the model, and comparing these results to performance under listener-preferred conditions. These studies will serve as the basis for developing procedures for fitting and assessing hearing aids in the audiology clinic and for the development of algorithms to control hearing aids that modify their frequency response to minimize background noise effects.

Robert Redden, Associate Professor, Audiology; Ed.D., Boston University, 1973. Fitting programmable hearing aids, private practice audiology.

NORTHWESTERN UNIVERSITY

Graduate Program in Audiology and Hearing Sciences

Program of Study

The Graduate Program in Audiology and Hearing Sciences prepares students for careers as clinical audiologists, university professors, and hearing scientists. Areas of specialization range from the study of animal auditory physiology to normal human hearing to evaluation and rehabilitation of individuals with impaired hearing.

The M.A. program may be completed in a five-quarter sequence. The Ph.D. program requires a minimum of three years of full-time study. Students with degrees in other fields may take slightly longer to complete the M.A. or Ph.D. degree requirements.

Master's degree students complete all academic and clinical practicum requirements necessary for the Certificate of Clinical Competence in Audiology awarded by the American Speech-Language-Hearing Association. They may also begin to acquire basic knowledge and skills necessary for a career in auditory research. To complete M.A. degree requirements, most students elect to take a comprehensive exam, although they have the opportunity to write and defend a master's thesis instead.

The Ph.D. degree is a research degree, sufficiently robust and varied to meet the interests and needs of either basic or clinical researchers. For the past forty years, the majority of doctoral students have prepared for university teaching careers. Most have had strong clinical audiology backgrounds, and their dissertations have reflected this orientation. Recently, however, doctoral students have been attracted not only from the field of clinical audiology but also from related disciplines. They are emphasizing development of research knowledge and skills in auditory physiology, psychoacoustics, and speech perception, in addition to the traditional areas within clinical audiology.

Each Ph.D. student's plan of study is tailored to the individual's experience, interest, and career goal. Students may take courses not only within the program but also in other programs and departments, such as bioengineering, computer science, linguistics, medicine, physiology, and psychology.

Research Facilities

Research conducted in the program's Hugh Knowles Center strives to further knowledge of the physiological and psychological bases of audition, to determine the differences between normal and abnormal auditory systems, and to develop better ways of evaluating the auditory system as well as to create procedures for improving communication for persons with hearing impairment.

Facilities on the Evanston and Chicago campuses include seven fully equipped test suites, an anechoic chamber, and a reverberation chamber. The hearing clinics have established working relationships with various centers, clinics, schools, laboratories, and physicians' offices in the metropolitan Chicago area. Thus, students are provided with an opportunity for clinical practicum experience not only on the University's Evanston and Chicago campuses but also at more than twenty-five off-campus facilities.

Financial Aid

A limited number of department fellowships are offered to applicants at the premaster's and predoctoral levels. In addition, doctoral students may apply for aid directly to the Graduate School.

Cost of Study

Tuition and fees in 1998–99 are $7747 per quarter. After the student is admitted to Ph.D. candidacy, these costs are reduced to $3207 per quarter.

Living and Housing Costs

The University has a limited number of living units for single and married students on the Chicago and Evanston campuses. University housing rates range from $502 to $875 per month. Many students find satisfactory accommodations in private homes and in apartments near the campuses; rents vary widely.

Student Group

About 10 master's and 3 doctoral students begin the graduate program each year. A small number of undergraduate students and postdoctoral fellows add to the student community in the audiology and hearing sciences program. They all relate closely to students in speech and language pathology and learning disabilities, the other programs within the Department of Communication Sciences and Disorders. There are approximately 13,000 full-time students enrolled on the two campuses of the University; approximately 40 percent of them are in graduate and professional programs.

Location

The main campus of the University is located in Evanston on the shore of Lake Michigan. The Chicago campus, about 12 miles south of Evanston, is also on the lakeshore near the center of the business district, one of Chicago's most attractive areas. An immense variety of cultural, social, and recreational activities are to be found on and near both campuses. The Chicago metropolitan area is the home of many great institutions of higher learning as well as the John Crerar Library. Northwestern Memorial Hospital, a complex of modern health-care and research facilities, is located on the Chicago campus.

The University

Northwestern University, one of the nation's largest private universities, was founded in 1851. The College of Arts and Sciences; the Technological Institute; the Schools of Education and Social Policy, Journalism, Music, and Speech; and the Graduate School of Management are located on the Evanston campus. The Medical and Dental Schools and the School of Law are located on the Chicago campus. During the past decade, there has been a continuing expansion of facilities and programs, much of it in science and medicine. This growth will continue during the next ten years and is supported by a vigorous program of financial contributions.

Applying

Applications are solicited from highly qualified students who generally have backgrounds in one of the following areas: speech and hearing, psychology, or science. Entering students are expected to have a high degree of interest in the various facets of hearing.

The program normally admits students in the spring to begin in the fall quarter. Although there is no deadline for the receipt of applications, students are urged to apply early. Scores on the General Test of the Graduate Record Examinations are required. Application forms may be obtained from the Northwestern University Graduate School, Evanston, Illinois 60208.

Correspondence and Information

Mario A. Ruggero, Head
Graduate Program in Audiology
and Hearing Sciences
Frances Searle Building
Northwestern University
2299 North Campus Drive
Evanston, Illinois 60208-3550
Telephone: 847-491-3164
Fax: 847-491-2523
E-mail: l-mcmillen@nwu.edu

Northwestern University

THE DEPARTMENT FACULTY AND THEIR RESEARCH

Margaret Aylesworth, M.A., Northwestern. Cerebral palsy, alternative systems of communication.
Elaine Brown-Grant (Emerita), M.A., Northwestern. Clinical supervision.
Gerald Canter (Emeritus), Ph.D., Northwestern. Neurology of speech and language.
Joanne Carlisle, Ph.D., Connecticut. Reading and written language.
Mary Ann Cheatham, Ph.D., Northwestern. Physiology of the cochlea.
Peter Dallos, Ph.D., Northwestern. Biophysics and physiology of the cochlea.
Hilda Fisher (Emerita), Ph.D., LSU. Vocal physiology and pathologies.
Kimberly Fisher, Ph.D., Oklahoma. Voice disorders, motor speech disorders.
Dean C. Garstecki, Chairman; Ph.D., Illinois at Urbana-Champaign. Hearing loss and aging.
Hugo H. Gregory (Emeritus), Ph.D., Northwestern. Speech fluency and stuttering.
Doris J. Johnson, Ph.D., Northwestern. Relationship between auditory disorders and higher levels of learning.
Dawn B. Koch, Ph.D., Northwestern. Speech processing and cochlea implantation.
Nina Kraus, Ph.D., Northwestern. Evoked potentials.
Charles R. Larson, Ph.D., Washington (Seattle). Motor speech control.
Jerilyn Ann Logemann, Ph.D., Northwestern. Structural anomalies of the vocal tract, dysphagia.
Karla McGregor, Ph.D., Purdue. Child language disorders.
Mario A. Ruggero, Ph.D., Chicago. Biophysics and physiology of the cochlea.
David Rutherford, Ph.D., Northwestern. Speech perception and production, word retrieval skills.
Jonathan Siegel, Ph.D., Washington (St. Louis). Biophysics and physiology of the cochlea.
Bruce Smith, Ph.D., Texas at Austin. Phonological and phonetic development.
Laszlo Stein, Ph.D., Northwestern. Pediatric audiology.
C. Addison Stone, Ph.D., Chicago. Cognitive development in normal and exceptional populations, language-learning disabilities.
Tom W. Tillman (Emeritus), Ph.D., Northwestern. Speech intelligibility testing.
Cynthia Thompson, Ph.D., Kansas. Neurological disorders of language and cognition.
Donna Whitlon, Ph.D., Wisconsin–Madison. Development of the cochlea and its innervation.
Laura Ann Wilber, Ph.D., Northwestern. Pediatric audiology, audiologic instrumentation.
Beverly Wright, Ph.D., Texas at Austin. Psychoacoustics.
Yi Xu, Ph.D., Connecticut. Speech acoustics, speech perception.
Steven Zecker, Ph.D., Wayne State. Lexical coding and reading disorders, attention deficits.

Lecturers and Clinical Faculty

Margaret Beeman, Ph.D., Northwestern. Bilingualism, early literacy.
Frances Block, M.A., Northwestern. Supervision, language disorders in older children.
Janet Bornhoeft, M.A., Northwestern. Supervision, learning disabilities.
Pamela Fiebig, M.A., Northwestern. Audiologic assessment and rehabilitation of adults and children.
Diane Hill, M.A., Northwestern. Stuttering problems in preschool children, differential evaluation and treatment.
Cathy Lazarus, Ph.D., Northwestern. Swallowing disorders, speech problems after treatment of head and neck cancer.
Monica Maso, M.A., Wisconsin. Habilitation/rehabilitation of children with impaired hearing.
Susan Mulhern, M.A., Northwestern. Articulation and language problems in children.
Barbara Nathanson, M.S., Illinois. Developmental delay, pediatric neurological disorders, preschool speech and language disorders.
Ann Oehring, M.A., Northwestern. Adult neurological disorders of speech and language.
Melinda Rice, B.A., Northwestern. Educational intervention, reading comprehension.
Jane Rosenberg, Ph.D., Northwestern. Educational programs in learning disabilities.
Amy Soifer, M.A., Northwestern. Swallowing, speech and language disorders.
Carrie Stangl, M.S., Wisconsin. Dysphagia, speech, language disorders after neurologic injury.
Sharon Veis, M.A., Northwestern. Swallowing disorders, language disorders after neurosurgery.

Adjunct Faculty

Martha Burns, Ph.D., Northwestern. Aphasia and adult neurological disorders.
David Hanson, M.D., Washington (Seattle). Physiology and objective measurement of laryngeal function and dysfunction.
Michael McCanna, Ph.D., DePaul. Behavior therapy, assessment of behavior disorders and learning disabilities, children's social skill development, parenting skills.
Harold Pelzer, M.D., Northwestern. Treatment for head and neck cancer.

NORTHWESTERN UNIVERSITY

Graduate Programs in Speech and Language Pathology

Programs of Study

The graduate programs lead to the M.A. or the Ph.D. degree and provide opportunity for postdoctoral study. Students are prepared for careers as teacher-investigators in colleges and universities, full-time researchers in laboratories, and clinicians in schools, hospitals, rehabilitation centers, and community clinics. The programs provide a broad range of basic science courses and specialized offerings covering the evaluation and treatment of problems of articulation, language, fluency, voice, swallowing, and neurophysiological and structural disorders affecting speech and language. There is access to cases handled by university clinics and many affiliated hospitals, clinics, and schools. Research interests include speech physiology and acoustics, child language, phonology, stuttering, vocal pathologies, neurological speech and language disorders of adults, swallowing, cerebral palsy, craniofacial disorders, and clinical supervision.

The M.A. program takes from six to ten quarters, depending on previous undergraduate background and on whether a specialization or general M.A. degree is pursued. The Ph.D. usually takes three years of full-time study for a student entering the program with an M.A. in the field. Toward the end of the second year, students who meet the requirements are admitted to candidacy and present a dissertation plan. Ordinarily, one full year should be planned for completing the dissertation.

The M.A. degree serves either as professional preparation for clinical certification by the American Speech-Language-Hearing Association or as background for graduate study leading to the Ph.D. Doctoral programs are tailored to individual interests and provide a comprehensive education in specific areas. Formal academic work includes courses and seminars in speech and language pathology, other areas of communicative disorders, and related fields, including linguistics, psychology, neurology, physiology, biomedical engineering, and computer science. Independent study and research are encouraged, and study groups and seminars of interest to students and faculty are available. Courses, laboratory work, and field activities offer opportunities to learn research methods and use scientific instruments. Doctoral students also have opportunities for supervised research, teaching, and clinical study.

Research Facilities

The Speech Acoustics Laboratory is composed of two components: the Speech Signal Laboratory and the Speech Perception Laboratory. Speech analysis, synthesis, and processing tasks are conducted in the Speech Signal Laboratory. The Speech Perception Laboratory is used to perform experiments that reveal the connections between the acoustics of speech, the perception of speech, and the production of speech. The Speech Physiology Laboratory is equipped to monitor and record electromyographic signals from speech muscles, electroencephalographic signals from the brain, and activity from single neurons within the brain. Available transducers allow for recording of speech articulators and laryngeal system activity.

The child-language lab, the stuttering research lab, and the adult aphasia lab each contain audiotape and videotape recording facilities as well as a variety of computers for data analysis.

The Human Voice Laboratory is equipped with instruments that make noninvasive physiologic and acoustic recordings possible. Facilities for audiotape playback and online visual monitoring of acoustic and physiologic signals provide means for perceptual and biofeedback studies of speech signals. The laboratory is also equipped to assess the effects of different sensory stimuli on the voice during speaking and singing.

The swallowing physiology laboratories are equipped for digital analyses of videofluoroscopic, manometric, and endoscopic studies of swallow.

Financial Aid

University fellowships and scholarships are available through the Graduate School. Aid available at the departmental or program level includes teaching and research assistantships and traineeships from the Rehabilitation Services Administration. Individual faculty members also have research grants that provide opportunities for assistance to students.

Cost of Study

Tuition and fees in 1998–99 are $7747 per quarter. These costs are reduced to $3207 per quarter for Ph.D. students admitted to candidacy.

Living and Housing Costs

The University has a limited number of living units for single and married students on the Chicago and Evanston campuses. University housing rates are $502 to $875 per month. Many students find satisfactory accommodations in private homes and in apartments in the vicinities of the campuses; rents vary widely.

Student Group

There are an average of 90 M.A. and 20 Ph.D. students in the program. Speech and language pathology and speech science majors relate closely to students in audiology and hearing science and in learning disabilities, two other programs in the Department of Communication Sciences and Disorders.

Location

The University's main campus is located in Evanston on the shore of Lake Michigan. The Chicago campus, about 12 miles south, is also on the lakeshore near the center of the business district. An immense variety of cultural, social, and recreational activities are to be found on and near both campuses.

The University

Northwestern University, one of the nation's largest private universities, was founded in 1851. The School of Speech; the College of Arts and Sciences; the Technological Institute; the Schools of Education, Journalism, and Music; and the Graduate School of Management are located on the Evanston campus. The Medical and Dental Schools and the School of Law are located on the Chicago campus.

Applying

Applications for admission must be made on forms obtainable from the Graduate School. Prospective students should apply to the Graduate School, forwarding GRE scores, letters of recommendation, and official transcripts. An informal statement describing the applicant's background, professional interests, and career goals should be included in the application as well.

Correspondence and Information

Bruce Smith, Ph.D.
Professor and Head
Speech and Language Pathology
Department of Communication Sciences
and Disorders
2299 North Campus Drive
Evanston, Illinois 60208-3570
Telephone: 847-491-5073
E-mail: bsmith@casbah.acns.nwu.edu

Admissions
Graduate School
Northwestern University
Evanston, Illinois 60208
Telephone: 847-491-7265

Northwestern University

THE DEPARTMENT FACULTY AND THEIR RESEARCH

Margaret Aylesworth, M.A., Northwestern. Cerebral palsy, alternative systems of communication.
Elaine Brown-Grant (Emerita), M.A., Northwestern. Clinical supervision.
Gerald Canter (Emeritus), Ph.D., Northwestern. Neurology of speech and language.
Joanne Carlisle, Ph.D., Connecticut. Reading and written language.
Mary Ann Cheatham, Ph.D., Northwestern. Physiology of the cochlea.
Peter Dallos, Ph.D., Northwestern. Biophysics and physiology of the cochlea.
Hilda Fisher (Emerita), Ph.D., LSU. Vocal physiology and pathologies.
Kimberly Fisher, Ph.D., Oklahoma. Voice disorders, motor speech disorders.
Dean C. Garstecki, Chairman; Ph.D., Illinois at Urbana-Champaign. Hearing loss and aging.
Hugo H. Gregory (Emeritus), Ph.D., Northwestern. Speech fluency and stuttering.
Doris J. Johnson, Ph.D., Northwestern. Relationship between auditory disorders and higher levels of learning.
Dawn B. Koch, Ph.D., Northwestern. Speech processing and cochlea implantation.
Nina Kraus, Ph.D., Northwestern. Evoked potentials.
Charles R. Larson, Ph.D., Washington (Seattle). Motor speech control.
Jerilyn Ann Logemann, Ph.D., Northwestern. Structural anomalies of the vocal tract, dysphagia.
Karla McGregor, Ph.D., Purdue. Child language disorders.
Mario A. Ruggero, Ph.D., Chicago. Biophysics and physiology of the cochlea.
David Rutherford, Ph.D., Northwestern. Speech perception and production, word retrieval skills.
Jonathan Siegel, Ph.D., Washington (St. Louis). Biophysics and physiology of the cochlea.
Bruce Smith, Ph.D., Texas at Austin. Phonological and phonetic development.
Laszlo Stein, Ph.D., Northwestern. Pediatric audiology.
C. Addison Stone, Ph.D., Chicago. Cognitive development in normal and exceptional populations, language-learning disabilities.
Tom W. Tillman (Emeritus), Ph.D., Northwestern. Speech intelligibility testing.
Cynthia Thompson, Ph.D., Kansas. Neurological disorders of language and cognition.
Donna Whitlon, Ph.D., Wisconsin–Madison. Development of the cochlea and its innervation.
Laura Ann Wilber, Ph.D., Northwestern. Pediatric audiology, audiologic instrumentation.
Beverly Wright, Ph.D., Texas at Austin. Psychoacoustics.
Yi Xu, Ph.D., Connecticut. Speech acoustics, speech perception.
Steven Zecker, Ph.D., Wayne State. Lexical coding and reading disorders, attention deficits.

Lecturers and Clinical Faculty
Margaret Beeman, Ph.D., Northwestern. Bilingualism, early literacy.
Frances Block, M.A., Northwestern. Supervision, language disorders in older children.
Janet Bornhoeft, M.A., Northwestern. Supervision, learning disabilities.
Pamela Fiebig, M.A., Northwestern. Audiologic assessment and rehabilitation of adults and children.
Diane Hill, M.A., Northwestern. Stuttering problems in preschool children, differential evaluation and treatment.
Cathy Lazarus, Ph.D., Northwestern. Swallowing disorders, speech problems after treatment of head and neck cancer.
Monica Maso, M.A., Wisconsin. Habilitation/rehabilitation of children with impaired hearing.
Susan Mulhern, M.A., Northwestern. Articulation and language problems in children.
Barbara Nathanson, M.S., Illinois. Developmental delay, pediatric neurological disorders, preschool speech and language disorders.
Ann Oehring, M.A., Northwestern. Adult neurological disorders of speech and language.
Melinda Rice, B.A., Northwestern. Educational intervention, reading comprehension.
Jane Rosenberg, Ph.D., Northwestern. Educational programs in learning disabilities.
Amy Soifer, M.A., Northwestern. Swallowing, speech and language disorders.
Carrie Stangl, M.S., Wisconsin. Dysphagia, speech, language disorders after neurologic injury.
Sharon Veis, M.A., Northwestern. Swallowing disorders, language disorders after neurosurgery.

Adjunct Faculty
Martha Burns, Ph.D., Northwestern. Aphasia and adult neurological disorders.
David Hanson, M.D., Washington (Seattle). Physiology and objective measurement of laryngeal function and dysfunction.
Michael McCanna, Ph.D., DePaul. Behavior therapy, assessment of behavior disorders and learning disabilities, children's social skill development, parenting skills.
Harold Pelzer, M.D., Northwestern. Treatment for head and neck cancer.

QUINNIPIAC COLLEGE

Medical Laboratory Sciences / Biomedical Sciences Program

Programs of Study

The Medical Laboratory Sciences/Biomedical Sciences Program offered through the School of Health Sciences at Quinnipiac College confers a Master of Health Science (M.H.S.) degree. The program provides students with the cutting-edge skills they need to manage the complex operations being carried out today in hospitals and research facilities. Today's laboratory professionals are called on more and more to solve problems in the laboratory, not just to carry out standard tests and procedures. In response to these changing needs in the workplace and to recent advances in biotechnology, the program focuses on the skills students need to perform more effectively in a number of diverse settings, including laboratories in hospitals, clinics, and medical diagnostic settings; pharmaceutical companies; and industrial and nonprofit research institutions. In addition to gaining up-to-date knowledge of the latest advances in biomedical, biotechnological, and laboratory science, students are guided in the principles and methods of scientific research.

Students choose to concentrate their work in one of three specialty areas: biomedical sciences, microbiology (biotechnology), or laboratory management. All students must choose between a thesis option and a nonthesis option. Thesis students complete 8 credits of research with a faculty member. Nonthesis students take additional courses as well as a comprehensive examination.

The faculty includes full-time professors as well as visiting professors and managers and researchers from corporations and clinics. The College's close ties with nearby major research and clinical facilities ensure that all degree candidates, even those not currently employed in a laboratory setting, gain valuable hands-on experience.

To accommodate students at various points in their professional development, Quinnipiac accepts candidates to this program on a part-time or full-time basis. Full-time students can complete the program in twenty-four months; most part-time students can complete the program in three years.

Research Facilities

Students in the Medical Laboratory Sciences/Biomedical Sciences Program spend much of their time in Echlin Health Sciences Center on campus. Echlin Center houses classrooms designed for clinical practice in the health sciences and extensive computer and robotics equipment as well as lecture halls and seminar rooms. Research and laboratory facilities are located primarily in Tator Hall.

Financial Aid

Several avenues are available to help both full- and part-time students fund their education. Students may be eligible for Federal Stafford Student Loans or for private commercial loans. In some cases, working professionals studying on a part-time basis may receive support through an employee assistance program, because the skills acquired through this curriculum are directly applicable to the work setting.

Cost of Study

In 1998–99, the tuition rate is $395 per credit hour. Part-time students pay a $20 registration fee each semester. Full-time students are charged a student fee of $185 per semester. The College offers a variety of payment plans, including deferred payment and installment programs, and coordinates employer reimbursement programs.

Living and Housing Costs

On-campus housing is available during the summer. Privately owned housing is available near the campus. For more information concerning off-campus housing, interested students should contact the Office of Residential Life at 203-281-8666.

Student Group

Full- and part-time students are enrolled in this program. Some are recent graduates of baccalaureate programs who majored in biological or health sciences, and some are working laboratory professionals and mid-level managers. There are some international students.

Student Outcomes

Approximately 75 percent of the graduates of this program assume or return to jobs in research facilities and corporations. The other 25 percent move on to positions in clinical diagnostic settings.

Location

Quinnipiac is located on a beautiful campus in Hamden, Connecticut, a suburb of New Haven. It is 30 minutes from Hartford, 1½ hours from New York City, and 2 hours from Boston.

The College

Quinnipiac enrolls 3,310 full-time undergraduates and approximately 1,300 graduate students. The College comprises the Schools of Health Sciences, Business, Law, and Liberal Arts and the College for Adults. A dean, reporting to the Provost/Vice President for Academic Affairs, heads each of these units, and a distinguished faculty of 170 full-time members and nearly 100 adjunct members provides instruction for the programs of the College.

Applying

Anyone who holds a baccalaureate degree in the biological, medical, or health sciences is eligible to apply for admission. A detailed autobiography of personal, professional, and educational achievements; two letters of reference; and copies of any relevant professional licenses or certificates must be submitted with the application forms. Applications are accepted on a rolling basis for admission in the spring, fall, or summer. The program is selective, but there is no entering class limit.

Correspondence and Information

Office of Graduate Admissions
Quinnipiac College
275 Mount Carmel Avenue
Hamden, Connecticut 06518
Telephone: 203-281-8672
800-462-1944 (toll-free)
Fax: 203-287-5238
E-mail: qcgradadmi@quinnipiac.edu

Quinnipiac College

THE FACULTY AND THEIR RESEARCH

Full-time Faculty

Richard Bernard, Ph.D., Michigan State. Embryology.
Thomas Brady, Ph.D., Connecticut. Clinical pathology.
Deborah Clark, Ph.D., Cornell. Biochemistry.
Ronald Dulac, Ph.D., Connecticut. Hematology.
Dwight Gordon, Ph.D., North Carolina State. Food and dairy bacteriology.
Charlotte Hammond, Ph.D., Connecticut. Molecular biology.
Kenneth Kaloustian, Ph.D., New Hampshire. Physiology and endocrinology.
Dennis Opheim, Ph.D., Minnesota. Molecular genetics.
Dennis Richardson, Ph.D., Nebraska–Lincoln. Parasitology.

Adjunct Faculty

Kenneth Carley, Dr.Ph., Alabama. Epidemiology.
Edward McDonough, M.D., New York Medical College. Forensic pathology.
Thomas Tinghitella, Ph.D., Notre Dame. Microbiology.
Gregory Tsongalis, Ph.D., University of Medicine and Dentistry of New Jersey. Molecular pathology.
David Valone, Ph.D., Chicago. History of sciences.

QUINNIPIAC COLLEGE

Pathologists' Assistant Program

Programs of Study

One of only three master's-level programs in the United States, Quinnipiac's Master of Health Science (M.H.S.) degree program in pathologists' assistant studies prepares candidates for a career that is in great demand across the country. Working in hospital laboratories, clinical laboratories, and medical research centers, pathologists' assistants are today required to carry out more and more increasingly sophisticated procedures, examinations, and determinations. Quinnipiac's commitment to combining intensive course work with rigorous supervised clinical training ensures that its graduates are trained in the latest methods and technology and that they are thoroughly prepared for the demanding positions open to qualified pathologists' assistants today.

The Pathologists' Assistant Program has received a full five-year approval, the highest status possible, from the American Association of Pathologists' Assistants. The program is also accredited by the National Accrediting Agency for Clinical Laboratory Sciences (NAACLS). Quinnipiac College is a sustaining member of the American Association of Pathologists' Assistants.

The full-time, six-semester curriculum begins early in June with the summer session and runs for a full two years. The first three semesters are devoted almost exclusively to course work, including basic and advanced anatomy and physiology, histology, pathology, and pathogenic microbiology. First-year students also attend weekly conferences at the West Haven Veterans Administration Medical Center (WHVAMC), which helps orient them to a hospital lab setting and sets the stage for the intensive clinical training of the second year. Students must attain a grade point average of 3.0 before they are permitted to enter the clinical year. Due to a cooperative partnership between Quinnipiac and leading area hospitals, second-year students rotate individually or in groups through a series of diverse clinical settings.

Through this program students gain a thorough knowledge of the scientific principles and facts essential to the practice of pathology; an understanding of the function of organs, tissues, and cells and how disease alters normal structure and function; experience in the operation and services of the anatomic pathology laboratory; the knowledge and skills needed to manage the surgical cutting room and autopsy suite; valuable, practical, hospital-based training; and experience in integrating biomedical knowledge with clinical techniques and procedures.

After completing all the requirements of the program, candidates receive an M.H.S. degree and are eligible to take the certification examination of the American Association of Pathologists' Assistants. Quinnipiac graduates historically have had the highest passing rate on this exam.

Research Facilities

Students in the Pathologists' Assistant Program spend much of their time in Echlin Health Sciences Center on campus. Echlin Center houses classrooms designed for clinical practice in the health sciences and extensive computer and robotics equipment as well as lecture halls and seminar rooms.

Financial Aid

Several avenues are available to help both full- and part-time students fund their education. Students may be eligible for Federal Stafford Student Loans or for private commercial loans.

Cost of Study

In 1998–99, the tuition rate is $395 per credit hour ($200 per credit hour during clinical residencies for pathologists' assistant students). Tuition for the M.H.S. program for pathologists' assistants is approximately $28,000. Full-time students are charged a student fee of $185 per semester. The College offers a variety of payment plans, including deferred payment and installment programs, and coordinates employer reimbursement programs.

Living and Housing Costs

On-campus housing is available during the summer. Privately owned housing is available near the campus. For more information concerning off-campus housing, interested students should contact the Office of Residential Life at 203-281-8666.

Student Group

This program enrolls 16 students per year.

Student Outcomes

Graduates of the program go on to work as pathologists' assistants in a variety of hospital and clinical settings. Some have used their degrees as a basis for advanced work in medicine or research.

Location

Quinnipiac is located on a beautiful campus in Hamden, Connecticut, a suburb of New Haven. It is 30 minutes from Hartford, 1½ hours from New York City, and 2 hours from Boston.

The College

Quinnipiac enrolls 3,310 full-time undergraduates and approximately 1,300 graduate students. The College comprises the Schools of Health Sciences, Business, Law, and Liberal Arts and the College for Adults. A dean, reporting to the Provost/Vice President for Academic Affairs, heads each of these units, and a distinguished faculty of 170 full-time members and nearly 100 adjunct members provides instruction for the programs of the College.

Applying

Yearly admission to this full-time program is selective and competitive. Students with baccalaureate degrees in the biological, medical, or health sciences are eligible to apply. A detailed autobiography of personal, professional, and educational achievements as well as two letters of reference and a copy of any relevant professional license or certificate must be submitted with the application.

Students are admitted to the program on a yearly basis for studies that begin in the summer. The application deadline is January 15. Interviews are conducted until March, and the class cycle begins the first week in June.

Correspondence and Information

Office of Graduate Admissions
Quinnipiac College
275 Mount Carmel Avenue
Hamden, Connecticut 06518
Telephone: 203-281-8672
800-462-1944 (toll-free)
Fax: 203-287-5238
E-mail: qcgradadmi@quinnipiac.edu

Quinnipiac College

THE FACULTY AND THEIR RESEARCH

Full-time Faculty

Richard Bernard, Ph.D., Michigan State. Embryology.
Thomas Brady, Ph.D., Connecticut. Clinical pathology.
Bruce Carpenter, M.S., Bridgeport. Biomedical photography and technology.
Gerald Conlogue, M.H.S., Quinnipiac. Epidemiology/public health.
Ronald Dulac, Ph.D., Connecticut. Hematology.
Dwight Gordon, Ph.D., North Carolina State. Food and dairy bacteriology.
William Hennessey, B.S., Montclair State; RT, (R)(M). Radiology.
Kenneth Kaloustian, Ph.D., New Hampshire. Physiology and endocrinology.
Edward Tantorski, M.P.H., Yale. Physical therapy.
Ralph Tolli, M.T.-S.M., (ASCP), S.M. (AMM), LIU, C.W. Post. Pathogenic microbiologist.

Adjunct Faculty

Steven Bilodeau, M.H.S., Quinnipiac; PA. Pathologists' assistant.
Leo Kelly, M.H.S., Quinnipiac; PA. Pathologists' assistant.
Edward McDonough, M.D., New York Medical College. Forensic pathology.
Erika Sembler, M.H.S., Quinnipiac; PA. Pathologists' assistant.

QUINNIPIAC COLLEGE

QUINNIPIAC COLLEGE

Physical Therapy Program

Programs of Study

Designed to enhance the knowledge and clinical skills of registered physical therapists, the Master of Science (M.S.) degree program for physical therapy at Quinnipiac College offers a sequence of classroom courses and internship rotations that prepare students for advanced positions in a variety of clinical settings as practicing therapists, educators, or administrators. The first graduate-level program for physical therapists to be licensed and accredited by the state of Connecticut and one of only sixteen in the United States to provide specialized training in orthopedics, Quinnipiac's program prepares candidates for eventual certification by the American Physical Therapy Association (APTA) as clinical specialists or orthopedics competency specialists.

Committed to ensuring that the graduates of the program emerge as better skilled, more talented, and more discerning clinicians, Quinnipiac's physical therapy faculty has designed a program with a very strong clinical base. Most of the faculty members are active in clinical practice as therapists, physicians, or dentists or in other health professions, and, due to the College's strong network of affiliations with clinics in the area, students are guaranteed opportunities to put into practice what they learn in the classroom.

The program of study is made up of a common core of 20 credit hours, a series of courses in one of the two areas of clinical concentration (12–14 credits), and electives (9 credits). The required core courses include orthopedics, differential diagnosis, biostatistics, the psychophysiology of pain, and directed research.

For their clinical concentration, students can choose either orthopedics or advanced clinical practice (a third track in neurorehabilitation is currently under development). Students who opt for the orthopedics track focus on such problems as postsurgical soft tissue restoration, mechanical derangements of the spine, bursitis, capsulitis, tendinitis, and muscular and ligamentous sprains. During a required clinical residency, students work with adjunct faculty members in clinics that have substantial orthopedic caseloads. Several of the courses in the program are based on the highly regarded work of such master clinicians as James Cyriax, M.D.; Brian Mulligan, PT; and Mariono Rocobado, PT. Students choosing to pursue the advanced clinical practice track receive a thorough grounding in a variety of areas regularly encountered in general practice. Particularly valuable to candidates who are either working or hope to work in hospital or family practice settings, this concentration provides the knowledge and expertise needed in such areas as wound care, orthopedics, cardiopulmonary rehabilitation, and neurology. Students in this track can also put together a customized group of electives in health management, sports medicine, or education. This track is especially useful for experienced clinicians who want to go on to more advanced administrative jobs as clinical mentors, supervisors, or program directors.

After completing their required course work, students select four elective courses within their concentration that best coincide with their backgrounds and professional goals. The open elective system allows students to choose courses from a variety of areas, such as health services administration, offered through the Quinnipiac College School of Business; education; or sports medicine. Students either concentrate their electives in one area or design a customized elective program in consultation with the program director. Students may also take fewer electives in order to free up time to work with a faculty member on an independent thesis project. At the conclusion of the program, either a comprehensive examination or submission of a graduate thesis is required. Part-time students usually take about three years to complete the program; full-time students can finish in about two years.

Research Facilities

Students in the physical therapy program spend much of their time in Echlin Health Sciences Center. Echlin Center houses classrooms designed for clinical practice in the health sciences and extensive computer and robotics equipment as well as lecture halls and seminar rooms.

Financial Aid

Several avenues are available to help both full- and part-time students fund their education. Students may be eligible for Federal Stafford Student Loans. Graduate assistantships are available on a limited basis to both full- and part-time students.

Cost of Study

In 1998–99, the tuition rate is $395 per credit hour. Part-time students pay a $20 registration fee each semester. Full-time students are charged a student fee of $185 each semester. The College offers a variety of payment plans, including deferred payment and installment programs, and coordinates employer reimbursement programs.

Living and Housing Costs

On-campus housing is available during the summer. Privately owned housing is available near the campus. For more information concerning off-campus housing, interested students should contact the Office of Residential Life at 203-281-8666.

Student Group

There are 77 students enrolled in the program. Known for the strength of its offerings, the program attracts candidates from across the country and from abroad. Since the program is restricted to practicing, licensed therapists, most candidates, approximately 85 percent, complete the program on a part-time basis, working during the day and taking classes in the evening.

Location

Quinnipiac is located on a beautiful campus in Hamden, Connecticut, a suburb of New Haven. It is 30 minutes from Hartford, 1½ hours from New York City, and 2 hours from Boston.

The College

Quinnipiac enrolls 3,310 full-time undergraduates and approximately 1,300 graduate students. The College comprises the Schools of Health Sciences, Business, Law, and Liberal Arts and the College for Adults. A dean, reporting to the Provost/Vice President for Academic Affairs, heads each of these units, and a distinguished faculty of 170 full-time members and nearly 100 adjunct members provides instruction.

Applying

Applicants to the M.S. program in physical therapy must be registered and licensed physical therapists. The admissions process is initiated by submission of an application, two letters of reference, an up-to-date resume, a copy of the candidate's physical therapist license, and official transcripts from all colleges attended. Clinical experience is taken into consideration. The admissions process for this program is rolling. Students may begin their studies in the fall, spring, or summer.

Correspondence and Information

Office of Graduate Admissions
Quinnipiac College
275 Mount Carmel Avenue
Hamden, Connecticut 06518

Telephone: 203-281-8672
Fax: 203-287-5238
E-mail: qcgradadmi@quinnipiac.edu

Quinnipiac College

THE FACULTY AND THEIR RESEARCH

Full-time Faculty

Richard Albro, Sixth Year, Southern Connecticut State. Biomechanics.
Ronald Beckett, Ph.D., Connecticut. Pulmonary and cardiac rehabilitation.
Michelle Broggi, M.S., Connecticut. Neurological rehabilitation.
Denise Cameron, M.S., Springfield. Orthopedic physical therapy.
Maureen Helgren, Ph.D., Allegheny University of the Health Sciences. Anatomy and neurobiology.
Christine Kasinskas, M.S., Southern Connecticut State. Cardiopulmonary rehabilitation.
Donald Kowalsky, M.S., Long Island University. Prosthetics, orthotics, spinal cord injury, board-certified pedorthist.
Dianna Piazza, Ed.D., Nova. Differential diagnosis.
Stanley Rothman, Ph.D., Wisconsin. Functional analysis, biostatistics.
Roseanna Tufano, M.F.T., Southern Connecticut State. Family therapy.
Russell Woodman, M.S., CUNY, Lehman. Orthopedic physical therapy.
Kathleen Zettergren, M.S., Boston University. Neurologic physical therapy.

Adjunct Faculty

Ronda Agostinucci, B.S., Quinnipiac. Physical therapy.
Steven Bessette, B.S., Quinnipiac. Physical therapy.
Katherine Biggs, B.S., Sage. Acute care, wound management.
David Brown, M.H.S., Quinnipiac. Orthopedic physical therapy.
John Cline, Ph.D., Toledo. Psychology.
Janet Dobos, B.S., Connecticut. Neurorehabilitation physical therapy.
Martin Gavin, D.P.M., Pennsylvania College of Podiatric Medicine. Podiatric medicine and surgery.
Frank T. Hacker Jr., B.S., Connecticut. Sports medicine and athletic training.
John Knecht, M.A., North Carolina. Sports medicine.
Ed Koziatek, M.S., Quinnipiac. Ulcerations of the foot.
John M. Letzia, J.D., Georgetown. Health-care and corporate counseling.
David Mikos, D.C., Bridgeport. Spinal mobilizations.
Stephen Moran, B.S., Quinnipiac. Manual physical therapy.
Roberta Nole, B.S., Connecticut. Board-certified pedorthist.
Julie Paolino, B.S., Quinnipiac. Physical therapy.
Edward Tantorski Jr., M.S., Springfield. Orthopedics.

QUINNIPIAC COLLEGE

Physician Assistant Program

Programs of Study

Quinnipiac College's graduate Physician Assistant Program is a full-time, twenty-seven month program that confers the M.H.S. degree to its graduates. Its goals include providing the comprehensive clinical and didactic training necessary to develop highly skilled, versatile physician assistants capable of providing high-quality health care in a variety of clinical settings. In addition to receiving rigorous clinical training, students are prepared to critically evaluate medical literature, policies, and systems, which enhances their leadership and management potential in a variety of community and professional settings.

The Physician Assistant Program is made up of three components. The first is an intensive three-semester didactic phase that covers basic medical and clinical sciences. Diagnostic methodologies are emphasized in classroom, laboratory, and clinical settings. During the first year, students are also introduced to the clinical aspects of their training by being paired with a graduate physician assistant or physician one day a week. This enables students to begin applying the skills and knowledge acquired in the classroom to the actual care of patients early in the program. Advancement to the clinical (second) phase of this program is contingent upon completion of the first year's course work with no less than a 3.0 grade point average.

The second component of the program involves twelve months of intense clinical preparation emphasizing, but not limited to, primary care. Clinical rotations during this phase include family medicine/primary care, internal medicine, pediatrics, psychiatry, obstetrics/gynecology, general surgery, and emergency medicine. Elective rotations in surgical subspecialty areas (i.e., cardiothoracic surgery, orthopedic surgery, and neurosurgery), geriatrics, rehabilitation medicine, preventative medicine, and infectious diseases are also available. All rotations require at least 32 hours a week; some require night calls and/or weekend duty.

The third component of the program is an advanced didactic phase, conducted in the summer session. It is made up of courses in ethics, epidemiology, human sexuality, and biostatistics; a graduate seminar; and a comprehensive examination.

Research Facilities

The students spend most of their time at the physician assistant program site, which is located in one of the College's off-campus facilities in Hamden (approximately a 3-minute drive from the main campus). Technical skills and physical examination techniques are taught in the state-of-the-art Clinical Skills lab and physician assistant exam rooms located on the main campus.

Financial Aid

Several avenues are available to help both full- and part-time students fund their education. Students may be eligible for Federal Stafford Student Loans or for private commercial loans.

Cost of Study

In 1998–99, the tuition rate is $395 per credit hour ($200 per credit hour during clinical residencies for physician assistant students). Tuition for the M.H.S. program for physician assistants is approximately $34,000. Full-time students are charged a student fee of $185 per semester. The College offers a variety of payment plans, including deferred payment and installment programs, and coordinates employer reimbursement programs.

Living and Housing Costs

On-campus housing is available during the summer. Privately owned housing is available near the campus. For more information concerning off-campus housing, interested students should contact the Office of Residential Life at 203-281-8666.

Student Group

The program attracts students from Connecticut, New England, and across the United States as well as some other countries. The percentage of women is 65 percent, consistent with the national average for physician assistant programs. The class has a maximum capacity of 50 students each year.

Location

Quinnipiac is located on a beautiful campus in Hamden, Connecticut, a suburb of New Haven. It is 30 minutes from Hartford, 1½ hours from New York City, and 2 hours from Boston.

The College

Quinnipiac enrolls 3,310 full-time undergraduates and approximately 1,300 graduate students. The College comprises the Schools of Health Sciences, Business, Law, and Liberal Arts and the College for Adults. A dean, reporting to the Provost/Vice President for Academic Affairs, heads each of these units, and a distinguished faculty of 170 full-time members and nearly 100 adjunct members provides instruction for the programs of the College.

Applying

Admission to the program is highly competitive. Applicants must, at the minimum, possess a baccalaureate degree from a regionally accredited or nationally recognized institution; 16 semester hours of biology, including 3 credits of microbiology and 6–8 credits of anatomy and physiology, with labs; 8 semester credits of chemistry, including 3–4 credits of organic chemistry and/or biochemistry, with labs; 3 semester credits of college-level mathematics; a cumulative QPA of 3.0; two letters of reference; and direct patient-care experience. Very strong applicants who lack direct patient-care experience but who have been successful in a human-services work environment are still considered, though clinical experience with patients is preferred. Personal interviews, required for admission, are scheduled for the most qualified applicants.

This program begins in the summer only. The application deadline is December 1. The average entering class size is 50.

Correspondence and Information

Office of Graduate Admissions
Quinnipiac College
275 Mount Carmel Avenue
Hamden, Connecticut 06518
Telephone: 203-281-8672
800-462-1944 (toll-free)
Fax: 203-287-5238
E-mail: qcgradadmi@quinnipiac.edu

Quinnipiac College

THE FACULTY AND THEIR RESEARCH

Full-time Faculty

Irwin Beitch, Ph.D., Virginia. Histology.
Thomas Brady, Ph.D., Connecticut. Clinical pathology.
Gerald Conlogue, M.H.S., Quinnipiac. Radiology.
Michelle Geremia, Ph.D., University of Medicine and Dentistry of New Jersey. Physiology.
Dwight Gordon, Ph.D., North Carolina State. Food/dairy bacteriology.
George Hillegas III, M.P.H., Berkeley; PA-C. Occupational medicine.
Kenneth Kaloustian, Ph.D., New Hampshire. Physiology and endocrinology.
William Kohlhepp, M.H.A., Quinnipiac; PA-C. Occupational medicine.
Cynthia Booth Lord, M.H.S., Quinnipiac; PA-C. Family medicine.
Michael Nabel, Ph.D., NYU. Biostatistics.
Stanley Rothman, Ph.D., Wisconsin. Mathematics.
Ralph Tolli, M.T.-S.M., (ASCP), S.M. (AMM), Post College. Pathogenic microbiologist.

Adjunct Faculty

Robert Ackroyd, M.H.S., Quinnipiac. Pathology.
Lisa Barratt, M.S., Saint Joseph (Connecticut); PA. Surgery.
Kenneth Carley, Dr.Ph., Alabama. Epidemiology.
Bernie Clark, M.D., George Washington. Cardiology.
Karen D'Avanzo, Ph.D., LIU, Brooklyn. Behavioral medicine.
Jill Fitzgerald, Pharm.D., North Carolina. Pharmacology.
Peter Juergensen, PA, Yale. Endocrinology.
Cynthia Kukoski, Pharm.D., Massachusetts College of Pharmacy. Pharmacology.
Judy Nunes, PA, Yale. Neurology.
Brian Peck, M.D., Virginia Commonwealth. Rheumatology.
John Pike, PA, Fairfax. Surgery.
Ronald Robbins, M.D., Universidad del Noreste. Primary care.
Sharon Sawitzke, Ph.D., CUNY, Hunter. Anatomy and embryology.
Michael Therrien, M.D., Connecticut. Cardiology.
Laura Troidle, PA, Yale. Internal medicine.
Elizabeth Udeh, Pharm.D., Texas Southern. Pharmacology.
Richard S. K. Young, M.P.H., M.D., Yale. Pediatrics.

RUSH UNIVERSITY

College of Health Sciences
Graduate Program in Occupational Therapy

Program of Study

The Department of Occupational Therapy offers a program leading to the Master of Science degree. The program provides the student with excellent preparation for making contributions to the field of occupational therapy. It is designed for individuals who have a bachelor's degree in another field and are seeking to become an occupational therapist.

The faculty emphasizes an educational approach that builds upon students' previous experiences and interweaves didactic instruction with clinical instruction and opportunities for clinical practice. This maximizes the student's ability to integrate the content and to understand the rationale underlying the instruction they receive. Concurrent sequencing of instruction in theory and clinical experience enable the student to draw on either or both learning environments according to which best facilitates the learning process. The early and continuous collaboration between the theoretical and the clinical learning environments encourages the development of a collegiality between faculty and students that in turn fosters the student's personal and intellectual growth. Students are provided with a variety of individualized learning options and experiences within the academic sequence.

Students enrolled in the department are required to conduct a graduate-level research project. Students' research is as varied as their interests. Some students opt to participate in experimental projects, either individually or in conjunction with faculty.

Research Facilities

Facilities for research in occupational therapy include the Rush-Presbyterian–St. Luke's Medical Center inpatient, outpatient, and home care units. Research opportunities in these settings encompass acute and chronic psychiatry, pediatrics, adult physical dysfunction, geriatrics, work hardening, and chemical dependence programs.

Financial Aid

Financial need is met through student and family resources, as well as loans and employment. A limited amount of scholarship assistance is available. The Student Financial Aid Office provides assistance for all admitted students in need, so that Rush University can be a viable choice for all who desire to attend.

Cost of Study

The tuition for 1997–98 was $3975 per quarter for 12 or more quarter hours for the Program in Occupational Therapy.

Living and Housing Costs

The student living on campus spends about $1020 per month for rent, food, transportation, and personal expenses. The student living off campus has expenses of $1300 per month. In addition, the estimated cost of books and supplies is $220 quarterly.

Student Group

Rush University enrolls about 500 graduate students. Fifty percent are full-time students; 5 percent are international students. Approximately 25 occupational therapy students are admitted each academic year.

Location

Rush University is located at Rush-Presbyterian–St. Luke's Medical Center on Chicago's Near West Side. Facilities on campus include the Presbyterian–St. Luke's Hospital, the Marshall Field outpatient mental health facility, a cancer center, research buildings, academic buildings, professional office buildings, apartment buildings, the Laurance Armour Day School, and the Johnston R. Bowman Health Center for the Elderly. The Medical Center, the University of Illinois at Chicago Health Sciences Center, Cook County Hospital, and Westside Veterans Administration Hospital constitute one of the largest medical center complexes in the world. Easily accessible are the Loop (downtown Chicago) and the western suburbs, both 15 minutes away. Lake Michigan, sports, and numerous cultural activities are available in the exciting Chicago area.

The University and The College

Rush University comprises the College of Nursing, the College of Health Sciences, the Graduate College, and Rush Medical College. Because the University believes that education of health professionals is best achieved in an institution committed to both education and service, all faculty members are practitioner-teachers. Rush University is part of a cooperative health-care delivery system that serves approximately 1.5 million people through its resources and those of affiliated health-care and academic institutions. Basic research and clinical investigation are an integral responsibility of each practitioner-teacher; consequently, research in both traditional disciplines and multidisciplinary fields is emphasized.

Rush University College of Health Sciences was established in 1975. Its present elements are the Departments of Clinical Nutrition, Communicative Disorders and Sciences, Health Systems Management, Medical Physics, Medical Technology, Occupational Therapy, and Religion and Health.

Applying

Each applicant must provide the admissions office with the following: a completed application, a $40 application fee, three recommendations, official transcripts of all undergraduate and graduate work, and results of the General Test of the Graduate Record Examinations or the Miller Analogies Test.

Correspondence and Information

College Admissions Services
Rush University
Armour Academic Center
600 South Paulina Street, Suite 440
Chicago, Illinois 60612

Rush University

THE FACULTY AND THEIR RESEARCH

Ralph Adams, Instructor; M.S., Rush. Chronic psychiatric dysfunction, occupational therapy history and philosophy, chemical dependency, spirituality, non-traditional practice and program development.
Lindsey Barnes, Instructor; B.S., SUNY at Buffalo. Adult and geriatric rehabilitation, multiple sclerosis.
Catherine Brady, Instructor; M.S., National-Louis. Management and supervision, working parents.
Kimberly Bryze, Assistant Professor; M.S., Illinois. Functional assessment, developmental disabilities, sensory integration, school-based practice, autism, pediatrics.
Marilyn Bubula, Lecturer; B.S., Western Michigan. Acute care and swallowing evaluation, cardiac care.
Kimberly Cambron-Levine, Instructor; B.S., Texas Woman's. Psychosocial assessment and evaluation.
Ronda Freemantle, Lecturer; B.S., Illinois. Psychosocial and vocational interventions.
Joyce Lane, Assistant Professor; M.Ed., Howard. Allied health minority recruitment and retention, policy analysis.
Janet Lisak, Instructor; M.O.T., Texas Woman's. Upper extremity, rehabilitation, home safety, gerontology.
Karin Opacich, Associate Professor; M.H.P.E., Illinois. Childhood occupation, infant feeding dysfunction, health professions education, accreditation, health care ethics, HIV and women.
Paula Silerzio, Instructor; M.O.T., Western Michigan. Mental health; child, adolescent, and adult chemical dependency; outpatient services and clinical education.

RUSH UNIVERSITY

College of Health Sciences
Graduate Programs in Speech-Language Pathology and Audiology

Programs of Study

The Department of Communication Disorders and Sciences offers programs leading to the Master of Science degree in audiology and in speech-language pathology. Each degree program is accredited by the Council on Academic Accreditation of the American Speech-Language-Hearing Association. Each program comprises seven quarters of academic and clinical studies, with an optional thesis. These programs are designed to provide professional education for speech-language pathologists and audiologists planning to practice in medical settings. Students learn from highly qualified teacher-practitioners, who are skilled scientists and clinicians. Supervised practicums are available in a variety of settings.

These programs are unique in that students learn in an environment where the link between academics and patient care is emphasized and modeled. Faculty members have dual roles as academicians and professional practitioners, thereby helping students to bridge the gap between classroom instruction and clinical service delivery. Course work is sequenced so that the study of basic sciences precedes the study of disorders and treatment; professional course work precedes or occurs concurrently with clinical practicum. Students are provided with a variety of individualized learning options and experiences within diversified work settings.

Research Facilities

The Department of Communication Disorders and Sciences has a speech physiology laboratory and extensive hearing science instrumentation. All aspects of ongoing research are supported by state-of-the-art instrumentation. Most of the projects result in direct application to the clinical process.

Financial Aid

Financial need is met through student and family resources, as well as loans and employment. A limited amount of scholarship assistance is available. The Student Financial Aid Office provides assistance for all admitted students in need, so that Rush University can be a viable choice for all who desire to attend.

Cost of Study

The tuition for 1997–98 was $3940 per quarter for full-time students.

Living and Housing Costs

The student living on campus spent about $1020 per month for rent, food, transportation, and personal expenses in 1997–98. The student living off campus had expenses of $1300 per month. In addition, the estimated cost of books and supplies was $220 quarterly.

Student Group

During 1997–98, Communication Disorders and Sciences enrolled 11 speech-language pathology and 6 audiology students.

Location

Rush University is located at Rush-Presbyterian–St. Luke's Medical Center on Chicago's Near West Side. Facilities on campus include the Presbyterian–St. Luke's Hospital, the Marshall Field outpatient mental health facility, a cancer center, research buildings, academic buildings, professional office buildings, apartment buildings, the Laurance Armour Day School, and the Johnston R. Bowman Health Center for the Elderly. The Medical Center, the University of Illinois at Chicago Health Sciences Center, Cook County Hospital, and Westside Veterans Administration Hospital constitute one of the largest medical center complexes in the world. Easily accessible are the Loop (downtown Chicago) and the western suburbs, both 15 minutes away. Lake Michigan, sports, and numerous cultural activities are available in the exciting Chicago area.

The University and The College

Rush University comprises the College of Nursing, the College of Health Sciences, the Graduate College, and Rush Medical College. Because the University believes that education of health professionals is best achieved in an institution committed to both education and service, all faculty members are practitioner-teachers. Rush University is part of a cooperative health-care delivery system that serves approximately 1.5 million people through its resources and those of affiliated health-care and academic institutions. Basic research and clinical investigation are an integral responsibility of each practitioner-teacher; consequently, research in both traditional disciplines and multidisciplinary fields is emphasized.

Rush University College of Health Sciences was established in 1975. Its present elements are the Departments of Clinical Nutrition, Communication Disorders and Sciences, Health and Human Values, Health Systems Management, Medical Physics, Medical Technology, Occupational Therapy, and Religion.

Applying

Each applicant must provide the admissions office with the following: a completed application, a $40 application fee, three recommendations, official transcripts of all undergraduate and graduate work, and results of the General Test of the Graduate Record Examinations.

Correspondence and Information

College Admissions Services
Rush University
600 South Paulina, Suite 440
Chicago, Illinois 60612
Telephone: 312-942-5099 (voice)
312-942-6080 (TTY)
Fax: 312-942-2219

Rush University

THE FACULTY AND THEIR RESEARCH

Dianne H. Meyer, Chairperson; Ph.D., Northwestern. Neonatal hearing assessment, auditory evoked responses.

Amy E. Archer, Lecturer; M.Aud., South Carolina. Clinical audiology, amplification.
Kimberley Austin, Instructor; M.A., Northwestern. Clinical audiology, neonatal hearing, cochlear implants.
Julia B. Bowman, Instructor; M.A., Tennessee. Head and neck cancer, dysphagia.
Amy M. Broxterman, M.S., Rush. Cognitive disorders, dysphagia, rehabilitation.
Wilene Chang, M.S., Arizona. Clinical audiology.
Nancy M. Gibbons, M.A., Northwestern. Cognitive disorders, dysphagia, rehabilitation.
Gail B. Kempster, Associate Professor; Ph.D., Northwestern. Voice, alaryngeal speech, swallowing.
David A. Klodd, Associate Professor; Ph.D., Bowling Green State. Amplification, electronystagmography, auditory evoked potentials, facial nerve disorders, industrial audiology, forensic audiology.
Patricia McCarthy, Professor; Ph.D., Denver. Rehabilitative audiology.
Richard Peach, Associate Professor; Ph.D., Northwestern. Neurogenic communication disorders.
Patricia VanSlyke, Instructor; Ph.D., Illinois at Chicago. Pediatric speech and language.
Qi Emily Wang, Assistant Professor; Ph.D., Connecticut. Motor movement disorders, dysfluency, voice.

TEMPLE UNIVERSITY

College of Allied Health Professions

Programs of Study

Temple University College of Allied Health Professions (CAHP) offers programs in communication sciences, health information management, nursing, occupational therapy, and physical therapy. Graduates are qualified to take the appropriate licensure or certification examinations in their respective fields. Entry-level and advanced professional degree programs are offered in communication sciences, nursing, occupational therapy, and physical therapy. Advanced master's and doctoral programs offer certified or licensed health professionals the opportunity to augment and extend their basic preparation by acquiring in-depth knowledge and expertise in specialty areas and developing education and management skills necessary for leadership roles in their professions. Communication sciences offers a Ph.D. program with concentration areas of linguistics, language pathology, speech science, speech pathology, hearing science, and audiology and Master of Arts degrees in applied communication or linguistics. The master's program of the Department of Nursing prepares experienced nurses to be either nurse practitioners or clinical nurse specialists. Temple's graduate nurse practitioner track prepares nurses to be adult-health primary-care nurses and is open to baccalaureate-prepared nurses and to clinical nurse specialists who have already earned a master's degree in nursing. The clinical nurse specialist track prepares graduates for roles in one of five specialty areas: acute adult care, maternal/infant health, psychiatric/mental health nursing, nurse anesthetist studies, or gerontological nursing. The master's program of the Department of Occupational Therapy prepares students with baccalaureate degrees in other disciplines to become registered occupational therapists. The advanced master's program prepares experienced occupational therapists to take on leadership positions in research, clinical practice, and academic and clinical education and administration. The Master of Physical Therapy (M.P.T.) program of the Department of Physical Therapy is a three-year entry-level degree program that prepares physical therapists to meet the needs of their patients and clients in an increasingly diverse society. The advanced Master of Science (M.S.) program prepares experienced physical therapists for leadership positions in clinical practice and academic and clinical education and administration. The Ph.D. in physical therapy prepares researchers and academicians for the discipline.

Research Facilities

Graduate students have the opportunity to be involved in research activities in health-care facilities in the Philadelphia area in general and within faculty research projects specifically. The Department of Physical Therapy has a motion analysis laboratory and a qualitative research analysis lab. The Department of Nursing recently established a Nursing Center, which also houses a Balance Center, in North Philadelphia. The Department of Communication Sciences maintains a clinic in speech and audiology.

Financial Aid

Financial assistance is supplemental to the student's or family's financial resources. Graduate students are eligible to apply for both University fellowships and CAHP teaching/research graduate assistantships. University fellowships are competitive across the University, while the graduate assistantships are within CAHP only.

Cost of Study

In-state tuition for 1997–98 was $308 per credit hour. Out-of-state tuition for 1997–98 was $435 per credit hour. Each program has specific course fees in addition to University-wide student fees.

Living and Housing Costs

There is on-campus student housing on Temple's main campus. Students also live in apartments and houses in the area.

Student Group

CAHP enrolls more than 500 graduate students. A great percentage of these students are enrolled full-time in the entry-level master's programs in physical therapy and occupational therapy.

Location

Philadelphia is rich in tradition and is one of the world's most respected centers for education, health care, and the arts. Located in North Philadelphia, Temple University's Health Sciences Center is 2 miles north of the main University campus and is convenient to Center City Philadelphia by public transportation.

The University and The College

Temple University is a state-related public university located about 2 miles from Center City Philadelphia. Composed of fourteen schools and colleges, the University offers a wide range of specialized programs and degrees. The College of Allied Health Professions was established in 1966 at Temple University's Health Sciences Center to meet a critical national need for increasing numbers of educated, highly skilled health-care professionals. Over thirty years, the College has become one of the leading centers of comprehensive health-care education in the nation, with three undergraduate programs and four graduate programs.

All CAHP programs share library, classroom, and computer learning facilities and other scholarly services with the Schools of Dentistry, Medicine, and Pharmacy. Its location on the Health Sciences Campus provides a rich experience for students as they interact with other health-care professionals from these schools in classes as well as socially.

Applying

Applicants must submit a graduate application form with three letters of reference, a personal statement, and results of the General Test of the Graduate Record Examinations. The Miller Analogies Test is also accepted for the programs in nursing and occupational therapy. An interview may be required. Students should contact the College for specific course prerequisites for each program. Applications for the entry-level program in physical therapy are due by December 15 and for occupational therapy by January 31. Applications for advanced master's and certificate programs are accepted at any time.

Correspondence and Information

College of Allied Health Professions
Temple University
3307 North Broad Street
Philadelphia, Pennsylvania 19140
Telephone: 215-707-4800
Fax: 215-707-7819
E-mail: http://www.temple.edu/CAHP

Temple University

THE FACULTY

Administration

Peter H. Doukas, Ph.D., Acting Dean.
Carole J. Simon, M.S., Acting Assistant Dean.
Vickie L. Sierchio, M.S., Director of Administration and Student Services.

Department of Communication Sciences

Doris Fallon-Snyder, M.A.; CCC/SLP-A. Diagnostic and rehabilitative audiology, child language.
Joseph Folger, Ph.D., Wisconsin. Conflict processes/intervention, small-group decision making, interpersonal communication.
Brian A. Goldstein, Ph.D., Temple; CCC/SLP.
Thomas F. Gordon, Ph.D., Michigan State. Communication theory, cognition and communication, psychophysiology of communication, research methods.
Aquiles Iglesias, Ph.D., Iowa; CCC/SLP. Speech and language services in multicultural populations.
Tricia S. Jones, Ph.D., Ohio State. Conflict processes, development of conflict competence in children, emotions and conflict escalation.
Camillia Keach, Ph.D., Massachusetts. Theoretical linguistics, sentence structure.
Elizabeth Kennedy, Ph.D., CUNY; CCC/A. Diagnostics and rehabilitative audiology, hearing aids, signal processing.
Rena A. Krakow, Ph.D., Yale. Speech motor control, speech acoustics and perception.
Joan H. Lovrinic, Ph.D., Pittsburgh; CCC/A. Normal and disordered hearing.
Barbara Mastriano, Ph.D., Temple; CCC/SLP. Adult neurological disorders, communication and aging, child language disorders.
Brian McHugh, Ph.D., UCLA. Phonology.
Gary Milsark, Ph.D., MIT. Linguistics, psycholinguistics, language acquisition.
Anita Pomerantz, Ph.D., California, Irvine. Language and social interaction, ethnographic fieldwork, communication and cultural difference.
Lorraine H. Russell, Ph.D., CUNY; CCC/SLP. Disorders articulation, developmental apraxis, early intervention.
Eleanor Saffron, Ph.D., Berkeley. Adult neurological disorders.
C. Woodruff Starkweather, Ph.D., Southern Illinois; CCC/SLP. Stuttering, learning theory.

Department of Health Information Management

Laurinda B. Harman, Ph.D., Fielding Institute; RRA. Social, ethical, legal, and health information management implications of collecting and disseminating genetic information.
Margaret M. Foley, M.B.A., Temple; RRA. Implementation of the International Classification of Disease, 10th Revision.
Karen McBride, B.S., Temple; RRA. Clinical affiliations.
Joan G. Liebler, M.P.A./M.A., Temple; RRA. Management theory and practice; documentation in nonacute care; ethical considerations in end-of-life decision making.

Department of Nursing

Nancy L. Rothman, Interim Chair; Ed.D., Temple; RN. Testing community-based prevention/intervention strategies.
Diane C. Adler, Ph.D., Pennsylvania; RN. Experience and caring needs of mechanically ventilated patients, methods of communicating with and for mechanically ventilated patients.
Lyn D. Boas, M.S., Villanova; RN.
Carol E. Dakin, Ph.D., Pennsylvania; RN. Teaching effectiveness, measurement, and documentation; stress management in students.
Janis Davidson, Ph.D., Boston College; CFNP. Quality of life of males with hypertension.
Susan B. Dickey, Ph.D., Pennsylvania; RNC. Ethicolegal aspects of adolescent health care, informed consent, adolescent capacity to make informed decisions.
Harriet W. Ferguson, Ed.D., Columbia Teachers College; RNC. Maternal attachment in adolescent women.
Susan P. Gauthier, Ph.D., Temple; RN. Genetic basis of disease, especially asthma; biology of gender and reproduction.
Elaine L. Gross, M.S.N., Villanova; RN. Developmental disabilties, medication administration training for unlicensed personnel.
Barbara Hughes, M.S.N., Pennsylvania; RN. Critical thinking; predictors of success in RN and B.S.N. students.
Anne-Marie Kiehne, M.S.N., Villanova; RN. Role of intercessory prayer in the maintenance and restoration of health.
Rita J. Lourie, M.S.N., Texas; RN. Disease prevention and health care to the underserved, especially lead poisoning and breastfeeding.
Kathleen Mahoney, M.S.N., NYU; CRBP. Perception of health of partner in spouses with chronic illness.
Maria L. Morsi, M.S., Drexel; RD.
Allen J. Orsi, Ph.D., Pennsylvania; RN. Experiences of couples living with life-threatening illness: patients and caregivers.
Dolores S. Patrinos, M.A., NYU; RN. Crises related to family/developmental issues.
Jane B. Pond, M.S.N., Pennsylvania; CRNP. Application of nursing theory to advance practice nursing.
Bonita Silverman, M.S., Thomas Jefferson; MT.
Jean H. Woods, Ph.D., Temple; RNCS. Child and adolescent growth, development, and sexuality; lifespan development psychology issues.
Dolores M. Zygmont, Ph.D., Temple; RN. Development of professional expertise in critical care nurses using the Triarchic Theory of Human Intelligence.

Department of Occupational Therapy

Judith Perinchief, Chair; M.S., Temple; OTR/L. Assistive technology applications/collaborations with consumers, professional behavior competencies as clinical performance predictors.
Ruth S. Farber, Ph.D., Temple; OTR. Career development of women across the family life cycle, family-centered care and parenting with a disability.
Marian Gillard, M.S., Temple; OTR/L. Outcomes research for rehabilitation population, association of life satisfaction and meaningful occupational performance, active learning.
Moya Kinnealey, Ph.D., Temple; OTR/L. Sensory integration, clinical descriptions and outcome studies in both children and adults.
Kristie P. Koenig, M.S., Temple; OTR/L. Sensory processing deficits in children and their effect on adaptability and temperament, predictors of student success transitioning from classroom to clinic.
Linda L. Levy, M.A., Temple; OTR/L. Gerontology, geriatrics psychological adaptation and aging, cognitive capacity related to functional outcome, falling, clinical reasoning.
Rosalyn S. Lipsitt, M.H.L., Boston Hebrew College; OTR/L. Interventions for Alzheimer's caregivers, OT education, multicultural issues in OT education and OT clinical practice.
C. Tom North, M.B.A., Temple; OTR/L. Stability of self-efficacy in clinical depression.
Donna Weiss, Ph.D., Temple; OTR/L. Group process, teaching/learning environments, clinical reasoning, faculty development.

Department of Physical Therapy

Laurita M. Hack, Chair; M.B.A., Ph.D., Pennsylvania; PT. Health services.
Mary F. Barbe, Ph.D., Wake Forest. Plasticity in the central nervous system during development and after injury.
Ann E. Barr, Ph.D., NYU; PT. Identification of risk factors, prevention and management of work-related musculoskeletal disorders.
Ronita L. Cromwell, Ph.D., Illinois at Urbana–Champaign. Examination of upper-body balance during locomotion and issues regarding head stability.
Carol G. Dichter, Ph.D., Hahnemann; PT. Improving motor function of children with Down Syndrome.
Janice L. Franklin, M.S., Temple; PT. Delivery of clinical education in various clinical settings, influences on clinical education related to a facility's organizational structure.
Roberta A. Newton, Ph.D., Virginia Commonwealth; PT. Prediction of falls in older adults, balance abilities in select populations.
Kim A. Nixon-Cave, M.S., Temple; PT.
Patricia O. Reger, M.S., Temple; PT. Orthopedic physical therapy.
Katherine F. Shepard, Ph.D., Stanford; PT. Expertise in clinical practice, qualitative strategies for health professions research.
Ann F. VanSant, Ph.D., Wisconsin–Madison; PT. Lifespan motor development in functional motor tasks.

UNIVERSITY OF DETROIT MERCY

College of Health Professions
Physician Assistant Program

Program of Study

The Master of Science degree in the physician assistant field is available as a two- or three-year course of study. It is dedicated to educating clinically competent medical professionals who assist the primary-care physician with medical and patient care responsibilities within the health-care system.

The first portion of the program is devoted to didactic education in the medical sciences and related educational experiences that address the medical and psychosocial needs of patients. Classes are sequenced and scheduled based on a twelve-month calendar. During the second portion, students acquire clinical experience through a broad range of mandatory and elective clinical rotations, including rural and urban clinical settings. These clinical rotations span fifty-one weeks and culminate in a preceptorship in primary care.

A three-year course of study is available. This program tract is designed for health professionals and others who wish to earn a master's degree while continuing employment or other obligations during the didactic phase.

The Master of Science degree is conferred at the completion of the program requirements, which include successful completion of a research project and a comprehensive examination. Graduates are eligible to sit for the national certifying examination administered by the National Commission on Certification of Physician Assistants (NCCPA).

The Physician Assistant Program is fully accredited by the Commission on Accreditation of Allied Health Education Programs (CAAHEP), holds membership in the Association of Physician Assistant Programs (APAP), and is host to a student chapter of the American Academy of Physician Assistants (AAPA).

Research Facilities

Five libraries provide research services for the University community. They include McNichols campus library and library media center, Outer Drive campus library, Outer Drive learning resource center, Kresge law library, and the School of Dentistry library.

More than 500,000 volumes; 3,100 literary, scientific, and professional journals; 20,000 audiovisual materials; and a collection of over 89,000 U.S. federal and state government documents make up the libraries' collections. The University libraries are members of DALNET, an automated network of thirteen major Detroit-area libraries. In addition, the libraries have access to more than 24 million records in the collections of the more than 16,000 member libraries of the Online Computer Library Center (OCLC), an international computer network.

Librarians also provide specialized computer literature search services. The databases contain citations to journal articles, dissertations, patents, technical meetings, and papers and books covering current research in all the academic disciplines. The newest service is WILS, which includes nine on-line services in art, business, social sciences, science and technology, humanities, and general information that can be searched directly by users.

In addition to the resources of the University, Grace Hospital, a part of the Detroit Medical Center, is the host educational site. Located 2 miles from the University, it provides a wealth of clinical resources as a major teaching center with a commitment to serving inner-city residents of Detroit.

Financial Aid

When applying for financial aid, the student must consider all educational expenses including basic living costs, medical insurance, books and medical equipment, malpractice insurance, professional dues, and transportation. A fact book of physician assistant student financial aid is published by the American Academy of Physician Assistants (telephone: 703-836-2272). In addition, the Financial Aid Office and the Physician Assistant Program keep information on various grants, loans, and other assistance available to physician assistant students. The Financial Aid Office at the University of Detroit Mercy can be reached at 313-993-6120.

Cost of Study

The total projected tuition for the two- or three-year education program in 1998–99 is $30,870. In addition, books and equipment can be expected to be $1500; insurance (liability and health insurance) is projected to be $998 for the entire program; fees, including the National Boards Examination, all registration fees, and graduation fees will be $1005; and travel costs for mileage and parking will be at least $1665 for the entire program. Educational expenses must also include the cost of a preadmission physical exam, which is $473.

Living and Housing Costs

Housing is available in University residence halls. Double-occupancy rates begin at $1260 per semester. Limited housing for married students is available starting at $2590 per semester. A variety of meal plans are available from $570 to $1180 per semester.

Student Group

The University of Detroit Mercy enrollment is consistent with physician assistant student enrollment trends across the country. In 1996, 80 percent of UDM physician assistant students were women, and 10 percent were persons of color. The mean age of all students in physician assistant programs in 1996 was 30.1 years; this is consistent with the UDM population. The majority of UDM students are seeking a midcareer change for advancement in the health-care field. A survey of UDM graduates reveals that the majority of graduates finds two or more opportunities for employment upon graduation. Graduates more often select family/general medicine as their choice of practice.

Location

UDM's Detroit location in southeastern Michigan places it amidst a corporate and educational community that rivals any other in the world for size and importance. Metropolitan Airport provides easy access from almost anywhere in the United States, and daily international flights offer links with major centers around the globe. From the Midwest, interstate highways allow reasonable driving from cities such as Buffalo, Chicago, Cincinnati, Milwaukee, and Pittsburgh.

The College of Health Professions offers courses at UDM's West Outer Drive campus in a residential area of northwest Detroit. The campus and the Detroit area offer a wide variety of cultural and recreational activities, including concerts and theatrical performance of national reputation plus museums, libraries, and four professional sports teams. Canada is just a few minutes away.

The University and The Program

The University of Detroit Mercy is an independent Catholic institution of higher learning that exists primarily for teaching, learning, and research. Its mission includes compassionate service to people in need, the service of faith, the promotion of justice, and a commitment to high-quality education. UDM is the largest private university in Michigan, operated under the sponsorship of the Society of Jesus and the Religious Sisters of Mercy.

The Physician Assistant Program, which began in 1972, tangibly addresses the University's mission by educating health-care professionals to serve in areas with limited access to health providers and services.

Applying

The admission deadline is February 15. Requirements for admission include a bachelor's degree from an accredited college or university; submission of all official college or university transcripts from previous academic work; submission of official GRE scores; successful completion of the following prerequisite courses within six years of admission: developmental psychology, medical ethics, advanced physiology, microbiology, graduate statistics, and nutrition; evidence of problem-solving ability and communication skills, particularly demonstrated by written responses to the program's admission questionnaire; twenty-four months of health-care/helping experience with increasing levels of responsibility and leadership; and a personal interview by invitation of the admission committee.

Correspondence and Information

Physician Assistant Program, Box 130-OD
University of Detroit Mercy
8200 West Outer Drive
P.O. Box 19900
Detroit, Michigan 48219-0900
Telephone: 313-993-6177
E-mail: admissions@udmercy.edu
healthprofessions@udmercy.edu

University of Detroit Mercy

THE FACULTY AND THEIR RESEARCH

Judith Daoust, Assistant Professor; M.S., Detroit Mercy, 1993. Certified Physician Assistant.
Kathleen Dobbs, Assistant Professor; M.S., Detroit Mercy, 1996; Certified Physician Assistant.
Wil Rapier, Assistant Professor; Ph.D., Iowa State, 1994. Certified Physician Assistant.
Suzanne Warnimont, Associate Professor; M.P.H., Michigan, 1990; Certified Physician Assistant.

UNIVERSITY OF MEDICINE AND DENTISTRY OF NEW JERSEY

School of Health Related Professions
Graduate Programs in Biomedical Informatics, Clinical Nutrition, Health Professions Education, Health Sciences, Physical Therapy, Physician Assistant Studies, and Psychiatric Rehabilitation

Programs of Study

UMDNJ–School of Health Related Professions (SHRP) offers entry-level and postprofessional master's degree programs. The entry-level programs provide students with professional knowledge, research, and clinical skills and lead to eligibility for professional certification and entry-level practice. The postprofessional programs are designed for health-care professionals who seek to develop expertise in a particular practice or to prepare for careers in teaching, research, and administration.

The Department of Health Informatics at UMDNJ-SHRP and New Jersey Institute of Technology (NJIT) jointly offer a Ph.D. degree in biomedical informatics, an M.S. degree in biomedical informatics, and an M.S.N. in nursing informatics with the UMDNJ-School of Nursing. In addition, the department also offers a postbaccalaureate-level certificate in health-care informatics. Biomedical informatics is an important emerging discipline in which health-care professionals apply computer and information sciences to manage all health-care activities and solve complex health problems. The University has designed the curriculum to meet the manpower needs of health-care organizations, health sciences research and education institutions, and the pharmaceutical industry. Students can pursue in-depth study in one of the following specialization tracks: biotechnology/bioinformatics, clinical decision support systems, hospital/health-care decision support systems, health sciences multimedia systems, and nursing informatics. Full- or part-time study is available.

The Doctor of Philosophy in health sciences is a 75-credit (minimum) program jointly offered with Seton Hall University. The following three tracks are available: movement science, for practicing physical therapists and occupational therapists; health professions leadership, for practicing health care professionals; and nutrition.

The Master of Science in clinical nutrition is a challenging graduate program designed for registered dietitians (RD). The program's goal is to provide RDs with the cognitive and scientific skills needed for advanced-level clinical practice (including cross-training), leadership, and research. This 30-credit full- or part-time program requires subspecialty practice and a thesis.

The Master of Arts in health professions education is a 36-credit program jointly offered with Seton Hall University. The program combines a theoretical base in health professions education with interdisciplinary education in instructional design and technology or organizational change.

The Master of Science in health sciences is a 39-credit program jointly offered with Seton Hall University. Two tracks are available, one in movement science, for practicing physical therapists and occupational therapists, and the other in health profession leadership for practicing health professionals.

The Department of Developmental and Rehabilitative Sciences offers two entry-level programs designed to prepare students to become physical therapists: an entry-level Master of Physical Therapy degree program, jointly sponsored with Rutgers University at the UMDNJ Stratford campus, and an entry-level Master of Science in Physical Therapy degree program, sponsored collaboratively with Seton Hall University and Kean College of New Jersey at the UMDNJ Newark Campus.

The Master of Science in physician assistant studies is offered jointly with Seton Hall University. The 106-credit three-year entry-level program is designed to prepare graduates to practice, with the supervision of a physician, in a variety of health-care settings, such as hospitals, long-term-care facilities, and private practitioners' offices. A Master of Science program for physician assistants is sponsored in collaboration with Rutgers University and offered on the Piscataway Campus of UMDNJ in central New Jersey. This three-year entry-level program prepares graduates to practice medicine with the supervision of a licensed physician. The first 1½ years of the curriculum consist of basic science and clinical science courses. The spring semester of the second year and the entire third year involve clinical experiences conducted in hospitals, clinics, and private office practices. A part-time daytime curriculum is also offered.

The Master of Science in psychiatric rehabilitation provides a curriculum for both entry-level and experienced psychiatric rehabilitation professionals. Courses in the treatment and rehabilitation of persons with serious mental illness, as well as research supervision, organization, and administration, are included in this 36-credit program. Full- or part-time study is available, with classes scheduled in the evening at both the Scotch Plains and Stratford Campuses.

Research Facilities

UMDNJ participates in New Jersey's health-care system and maintains affiliations with more than 100 health-care facilities throughout the state. Students utilize the UMDNJ–University Hospital; UMDNJ Community Mental Health facilities, located in Newark and Piscataway; and the affiliates for clinical training.

UMDNJ–SHRP is in the process of planning new classrooms and laboratories with state-of-the-art equipment. Plans include a series of simulated laboratories designed to train students to the optimum level in their field of expertise.

Students at UMDNJ–SHRP use the George F. Smith Library of the Health Sciences. The library receives more than 2,300 journals and houses in excess of 138,000 bound periodicals and monographs. Students also use the UMDNJ–SHRP Satellite Computer Based Instructional Laboratory and the Video Conferencing/Distance Learning Laboratory.

Financial Aid

Information about financial aid is available from the Financial Aid Office (telephone: 973-972-4376).

Cost of Study

The cost of graduate tuition varies by program and depends upon the academic affiliation of the program. Tuition for out-of-state residents is one third more than that of in-state residents. In 1997–98, the in-state UMDNJ rate was $249.50 per credit.

Living and Housing Costs

University housing is not available; however, furnished and unfurnished apartments are available throughout the area.

Student Group

UMDNJ attracts students primarily from the eastern United States as well as international students. The total graduate enrollment is in excess of 230 students.

Location

The Newark campus is located approximately 10 miles from New York City and within easy access of the Garden State Parkway and the New Jersey Turnpike. The School is convenient to New York City's cultural life and the many recreational beach areas of the New Jersey shoreline. Courses in the Master of Science programs in clinical nutrition and psychiatric rehabilitation and the M.A. in health professions education are offered via distance learning from the Newark and Scotch Plains Campuses to the Stratford Campus.

The University

UMDNJ is a state institution under the administration of a Board of Trustees appointed by the governor. It includes New Jersey Medical School, New Jersey Dental School, the Graduate School of Biomedical Sciences, the School of Nursing, the School of Health Related Professions, Robert Wood Johnson Medical School, and the School of Osteopathic Medicine. UMDNJ–SHRP has an enrollment of 916 full- and part-time students in undergraduate and graduate programs. The sites of programs differ, with programs in Camden, Blackwood, Piscataway, Scotch Plains, Newark, and Stratford.

Applying

Graduate admission requirements vary by program. In general, a bachelor's degree or its equivalent, with at least a B average in academic work, is required. Selection is made on the basis of previous academic work, letters of recommendation, and, in some programs, the Graduate Record Examinations. TOEFL scores are required of students from countries in which English is not the native language.

Correspondence and Information

UMDNJ–School of Health Related Professions
Office of Academic and Student Services
Martland Building, Room 101
65 Bergen Street
Newark, New Jersey 07107-3001
Telephone: 973-972-5454
E-mail: shrpadm@umdnj.edu

University of Medicine and Dentistry of New Jersey

THE FACULTY

Biomedical Informatics
Gregory Erianne, Clinical Assistant Professor; M.S., UMDNJ-Graduate School of Biomedical Sciences.
Syed Haque, Associate Professor; Ph.D., Michigan State.
Judith Redling, Clinical Assistant Professor; Ph.D., Rutgers.
Steven Shemlon, Clinical Assistant Professor; Ph.D., Rutgers.
Ching-Song D. Wei, Assistant Professor; Ph.D., NJIT.

Clinical Nutrition
David August, Clinical Associate Professor; M.D., Yale.
Jane Barracato, Clinical Instructor; M.S., UMDNJ-SHRP.
John Bogden, Clinical Professor, Ph.D., Seton Hall.
Karen Buzby, RD, Cornell.
Thomas Cavalieri, Clinical Associate Professor; D.O., Oklahoma College of Osteopathic Medicine and Surgery.
Elaine Diegmann, Professor, N.D., Case Western Reserve.
Edward T. Kelley II, Assistant Professor; Ed.M., Rutgers.
Julie O'Sullivan Maillet, Professor; Ph.D., NYU.
Marian Passannante, Adjunct Associate Professor; Ph.D., Johns Hopkins.
Thomas Reilly, Assistant Professor; Ph.D., Case Western Reserve.
Riva Touger-Decker, Assistant Professor; Ph.D., NYU.
Richard Vogel, Clinical Professor, D.M.D., UMDNJ-Dental School.
Bridget Wardley, Clinical Assistant Professor; M.S., NYU.

Health Professions Education
Louellen Lusk, Associate Professor of Clinical Dental Hygiene; Ed.D., Columbia.
John Martin, Professor; Ed.D., Penn State.
Ann W. Tucker, Associate Professor; D.Ed., Penn State

Physical Therapy–South Jersey
Patricia Adams, Assistant Professor of Clinical Physical Therapy; M.P.T., UMDNJ and Rutgers.
Dennise Krencicki, Assistant Professor; M.A., Columbia.
Patricia McGinnis, Clinical Assistant Professor; B.S., Delaware.
Marie Nardone, Associate Professor of Clinical Physical Therapy; M.S., Duke.
Mary Ellen O'Neill, Clinical Assistant Professor; M.S., Hahnemann.
Lesley Rogan, Assistant Professor of Clinical Physical Therapy; M.Ed., Cleveland State.
Jeffrey Snyder, Clinical Assistant Professor; M.A., NYU.
Donna Ziarkowski-Herb, Clinical Associate Professor; M.P.T., UMDNJ and Rutgers.

Physical Therapy–North Jersey
Lawrence Ambrose, Clinical Associate Professor; M.D., UMDNJ-Medical School.
Ellen Zambo Anderson, Assistant Professor of Clinical Therapy; M.A., Columbia.
Phyllis Bowlby, Clinical Assistant Professor; B.S., Pennsylvania.
Mark Campolo, Assistant Professor of Clinical Therapy; M.A., Adelphi.
Irene DeMasi, Clinical Assistant Professor; M.A., NYU.
Judith Deutsch, Assistant Professor; Ph.D., NYU.
Gary Drillings, Clinical Assistant Professor; M.D., SUNY Upstate Medical Center.
Patricia Fay, Assistant Professor of Clinical Physical Therapy; M.P.H., CUNY, Hunter.
Marda Herz, Clinical Assistant Professor; M.S., LIU.
Sandra Kaplan, Associate Professor of Clinical Physical Therapy; Ph.D., NYU.
Michael Katz, Clinical Associate Professor; B.S., Johns Hopkins.
Nancy Kirsch, Clinical Assistant Professor; M.A., Montclair State.
Gale Lavinder, Assistant Professor of Clinical Physical Therapy; M.A., Columbia.
William Mahalchick, Clinical Instructor; B.S., SUNY Downstate Medical Center.
Alma Merians, Associate Professor; Ph.D., NYU.
Mary Jane Myslinski, Assistant Professor of Clinical Therapy; Ed.D., Columbia.
Oscar Reicher, Clinical Assistant Professor; M.D., Pittsburgh.
Barbara Reiss, Associate Professor of Clinical Physical Therapy; M.S., Columbia.
Ellen Ross, Associate Professor of Clinical Physical Therapy; Ph.D., NYU.
Joel Stern, Clinical Instructor; M.S., Columbia.

Physician Assistant-North Jersey
Ellen Adducci, Assistant Professor of Clinical Primary Care; M.M.S., Emory.
Carol Biscardi, Assistant Professor; M.S., St. John's (New York).
Gary Bouchard, Clinical Assistant Professor; Ed.M., Rutgers.
Charlene Kostuk, Instructor; B.S., Alderson Broaddus; PA-C.
Joseph Thornton, Clinical Assistant Professor; M.P.H., UMDNJ and Rutgers.

Physician Assistant-South Jersey
Ruth Fixelle, Professor of Clinical Physician Assistant; Ed.M., Rutgers.
Claire O'Connell, Associate Professor; M.P.H., UMDNJ and Rutgers.
David Paulk, Assistant Professor; M.S., West Virginia.
Jill Reichman, Associate Professor of Clinical Physician Assistant; M.P.H., UMDNJ and Rutgers.
Carol Sadley, Clinical Assistant Professor; Ed.M., Rutgers.
Mark Spiegel, Clinical Assistant Professor; B.S., La Verne.
Robert Spierer, Clinical Associate Professor; M.D., Yeshiva (Einstein).
Lisa Van Heest, Clinical Assistant Professor; M.P.A., LIU.

Psychiatric Rehabilitation
Nora Barrett, Clinical Assistant Professor; M.S.W., NYU.
Joseph Birkmann, Assistant Professor; M.S.W., Columbia; M.P.A., CUNY, Baruch.
Linda Chalakani, Assistant Professor; M.S., Boston University.
Kenneth Gill, Associate Professor of Clinical Psychosocial Rehabilitation; Ph.D., Columbia.
William Green, Clinical Instructor; M.S., Boston University.
Sheree Neese-Todd, Assistant Professor of Clinical Psychosocial Rehabilitation; M.A., Rutgers.
Carlos Pratt, Clinical Professor; Ph.D., Hofstra.
Melissa Roberts, Clinical Assistant Professor; M.A., Kean.
Francis Ulrich, Clinical Assistant Professor; M.A., Duquesne; M.H.A., Pittsburgh.

UNIVERSITY OF PITTSBURGH

School of Health and Rehabilitation Sciences
Department of Rehabilitation Science and Technology

Programs of Study

The Department of Rehabilitation Science and Technology offers a Master of Science degree in rehabilitation science. Master's and doctoral degrees are available through the School of Health and Rehabilitation Sciences or the School of Engineering. A Certificate in Rehabilitation Engineering is available to qualified candidates who wish to pursue an advanced engineering degree with some specialization in rehabilitation. Similarly, students with rehabilitation or health sciences training (such as physical therapy, occupational therapy, or speech therapy) can pursue an M.S. in their own fields and earn a Certificate in Rehabilitation Technology by completing a specialized set of courses. People with advanced degrees are also eligible for the certificate programs.

The department offers a balance between traditional instruction and clinical rehabilitation preceptorship. An emphasis is placed upon the team approach to rehabilitation. The curriculum covers basic science, engineering principles, assistive technology, pathology, rehabilitation, and consumer advocacy. All students must complete a common set of core courses before pursuing specialized educational tracks. Students participate in clinics and rounds, work with consumer groups, perform research, and present at seminars and conferences.

Core courses are taught by distinguished faculty members from the department. Assistance is provided by the Departments of Occupational Therapy, Physical Therapy, Bioengineering, and Physical Medicine and Rehabilitation. Advanced courses are provided by appropriate departments across the entire University. The curriculum is designed to accommodate the knowledge and experience of practicing rehabilitation professionals who are returning for an advanced degree. Students with training from different disciplines are required to take courses that complement their previous training. The specific choice of courses required for graduation depends upon each student's advisory committee and the background of the student within the framework of the University requirements. The department offers both thesis and nonthesis options for the master's degree. The doctoral degree requires a dissertation.

Research Facilities

Extensive research facilities are available to students enrolled in the various programs of the department. The Department of Rehabilitation Science and Technology provides research funding for 15 graduate students on average. The faculty have active research programs in rehabilitation engineering, assistive technology, rehabilitation science, biomechanics, standards development, and outcomes measures. The department houses the National Institute for Disability and Rehabilitation Research (NIDRR) Rehabilitation Engineering Research Center on Wheeled Mobility. The department also participates in collaborative research with the VA Pittsburgh Healthcare System. Opportunities exist at the Pitt/VA Human Engineering Research Laboratories and the Rehabilitative Neuroscience Laboratory. The department also houses the Center for Assistive Technology, which provides clinical services, performs research, and participates in education. Departmental faculty members receive research funding from NIH, NIDRR, the VA, and private foundations.

Students may also receive research training from a number of centers and laboratories that are affiliated with the department. Opportunities exist at the Musculoskeletal Research Center, the Department of Orthopaedic Surgery, the Vestibular Dysfunction Laboratory, the Department of Otolaryngology, the Neurogenic Speech and Language Lab, the Department of Communication Science and Disorders, and the Pain Evaluation and Treatment Institute–Department of Anesthesiology. Other opportunities exist within the Division of Physical Medicine and Rehabilitation at the University of Pittsburgh Medical Center. Department faculty members also collaborate with many regional hospitals and clinics.

Financial Aid

Students may receive financial support in the form of fellowships, research assistantships, and teaching assistantships. The department has a strong record of providing financial support for research and clinical training. Currently, the department has training grants from NIDRR, RSA, and NIH. Support is awarded on the basis of financial need, academic record, and potential for contributing to the field. Some assistantships have additional criteria. There are also opportunities for employment on and around campus.

Cost of Study

Tuition and fees vary with the school selected. Students should contact the admissions officer for specific details.

Living and Housing Costs

Students can rent furnished and unfurnished rooms and apartments near campus. The Community Resource Center has listings of available housing near campus. The Office of Property Management organizes University housing for students.

Student Group

The department has an active Ph.D. program through the School of Health and Rehabilitation Sciences, with approximately 15 students enrolled at any given time. There are also a number of students pursuing a Ph.D. within the School of Engineering who work with the Department of Rehabilitation Science and Technology faculty members. Enrollment in the Master of Science degree program is currently about 15 students.

Location

Pittsburgh is one of the most livable cities in the United States. It is a cultural city that has a long history of industrial and technological innovation. Pittsburgh has recently undergone a new renaissance emphasizing high technology. The region has also instituted a number of initiatives designed to increase employment of people with disabilities. Pittsburgh has one of the nation's largest collections of corporate headquarters. It offers many cultural and recreational opportunities, such as the excellent symphony, opera company, and ballet theater and several major sports teams.

The University

The University of Pittsburgh is located in the Oakland section of the city. The University was founded in 1787 and is one of the oldest universities in the country. The University of Pittsburgh is a major research and teaching university with world-class faculty members, students, and facilities. The University has approximately 28,500 students enrolled in sixteen schools. The University of Pittsburgh Medical Center is one of the world's leading research and teaching hospitals.

Applying

Applicants must be accepted by the School of Health and Rehabilitation Sciences or the School of Engineering graduate program. Potential candidates must have a B.S. or M.S. degree from an accredited college or university. A degree in a health profession, science, or engineering is preferred. Applicants should complete the GRE General Test.

Correspondence and Information

Louise C. Tkach, Student Coordinator
Department of Rehabilitation Science and Technology
Forbes Tower, Suite 5044
University of Pittsburgh
Pittsburgh, Pennsylvania 15260

Telephone: 412-647-1270
Fax: 412-647-1277
E-mail: rehabsci@pitt.edu
World Wide Web: http://pft5xx36.ft90.upmc.edu/RST/RSTHome.html

University of Pittsburgh

THE FACULTY AND THEIR RESEARCH

Jennifer Angelo, Assistant Professor of Occupational Therapy; Ph.D., Wisconsin–Madison, 1987. Input devices used in assistive technology for persons with physical disabilities, augmentative communication.
Bruce R. Baker, Adjunct Associate Professor of Rehabilitation Engineering; A.M., Middlebury, 1976. System design in augmentative communication, natural language processing, machine translation, sociology of disability.
Gina E. Bertocci, Assistant Professor of Rehabilitation Science and Technology; Ph.D., Pittsburgh, 1997. Wheelchair transportation safety, biodynamics modeling, injury biomechanics, soft-tissue biomechanics.
Michael L. Boninger, Assistant Professor of Orthopaedic Surgery and Rehabilitation Science and Technology; M.D., Ohio State, 1989. Rehabilitation engineering, wheelchair design, injury prevention, fall prevention, assistive devices, electromyography.
David M. Brienza, Assistant Professor of Rehabilitation Science and Technology and Electrical Engineering; Ph.D, Virginia, 1991. Rehabilitation science, wheelchair mobility and seating, control theory, soft tissue biomechanics.
Clifford E. Brubaker, Professor and Dean, School of Health and Rehabilitation Sciences, and Professor of Industrial Engineering; Ph.D., Oregon, 1968. Rehabilitative engineering, disability and assistive devices, technologies for disabilities of mobility and seating.
Al Condeluci, Adjunct Professor of Rehabilitation Science and Technology and Executive Director, United Cerebral Palsy of Pittsburgh; Ph.D., Pittsburgh, 1984. Project Success: identifying, teaming, and placing of middle school children with and without disabilities to learn and serve projects around the community.
Rory A. Cooper, Associate Professor and Chair of Rehabilitation Science and Technology, of Physical Medicine and Rehabilitation, and of Mechanical and Bioengineering, and Director of the Pitt/VA Human Engineering Research Laboratories; Ph.D., California, Santa Barbara, 1989. Rehabilitation engineering, assistive technology standards and testing, design, upper extremity biomechanics, advocacy, medical instrumentation.
John Coltellaro, Clinical Adjunct Instructor in Rehabilitation Science and Technology; M.S., California State, 1990. Direct service delivery.
Kennerly Digges, Adjunct Assistant Professor of Rehabilitation Science and Technology; Ph.D., Ohio State, 1982. Motor vehicle safety standards.
John D. Durrant, Professor of Otolaryngology, Communication, and Rehabilitation Science and Technology, and Director of the Center for Audiology; Ph.D., Northwestern, 1972. Audiologic methods, physiological acoustics (auditory-evoked electric responses and otacoustic emissions), electrodiagnostics (clinical and intraoperative), rehabilitation technology (implanted devices and hearing aids).
Kimberly Henry, Clinical Adjunct Instructor in Rehabilitation Science and Technology; B.S., Pittsburgh, 1993. Rehabilitative engineering, microprocessor-based assistive technologies, user interface and controller design.
Douglas A. Hobson, Associate Professor of Rehabilitation Science and Technology and Mechanical Engineering, and Director of the Rehabilitation Technology Program; Ph.D., Strathclyde (Scotland), 1989. Specialized seating, wheelchairs, standards development, service delivery models, program management.
Andrew F. Jinks, Clinical Adjunct Instructor of Rehabilitation Science and Technology; M.A., Bowling Green State, 1978. Augmentative communication, rehabilitation technology service delivery.
Peter C. Johnson, Adjunct Associate Professor of Rehabilitation Science and Technology, M.D., SUNY Health Science Center at Syracuse, 1980. Tissue engineering of skeletal muscle.
Paul Kornblith, Professor; M.D., Jefferson Medical, 1962. Cellular and molecular biology of neural-normal and neoplastic cells.
Jorge E. Letechipia, Assistant Professor of Rehabilitation Science and Technology, and Director of the Center for Assistive Technology; M.Sc., Case Western Reserve, 1980. Rehabilitation engineering, assistive devices, implementation of service delivery models, international appropriate rehabilitation technology.
Robert Dale Lynch, Senior Lecturer in Rehabilitation Science and Technology, B. Arch. Catholic University, 1967; FAIA. Building accessibility design standards on the American National Standards Institute A117.1 Committee (1998).
Arthur F. T. Mak, Professor, Hong Kong Polytechnic University; Ph.D., Northwestern, 1980. Seating biomechanics, peripheral joint rehabilitation, prosthetic and orthotic bioengineering, fracture rehabilitation, tissue engineering, biomaterials.
Louis E. Penrod, Assistant Professor of Orthopaedics/Division of Physical Medicine and Rehabilitation; M.D., Pittsburgh, 1984. Outcomes research in neurological trauma, spinal cord injury.
Mark S. Redfern, Associate Professor of Otolaryngology, of Industrial Engineering, and of Rehabilitation Science and Technology; Ph.D., Michigan, 1988. Biomechanics of human movement, postural control, ergonomics and rehabilitation engineering.
Richard Robertson, Associate Professor of Orthopedic Surgery and Rehabilitation Science and Technology; Ph.D., Illinois at Urbana-Champaign, 1985. Biomechanics of injury: automobile collisions and workplace settings.
Charles J. Robinson, Professor of Rehabilitation Science and Technology, of Electrical Engineering, and of Orthopaedic Surgery; D.Sc., Washington (St. Louis), 1979. Biomedical engineering; rehabilitation science; rehabilitation engineering; neurophysiology, with a particular emphasis on spinal cord injury and the sensation of touch.
Mark R. Schmeler, Instructor of Rehabilitation Science and Technology; M.S., SUNY at Buffalo, 1993. Assistive technology service delivery, wheelchair seating and mobility.
Nigel Shapcott, Assistant Professor of Rehabilitation Science and Technology; M.Sc., Surrey, 1976. Wheelchair mobility and seating, service delivery model development, technology transfer to developing countries, export systems for wheelchair prescription.
Lucy C. Spruill, Adjunct Instructor and Research Associate; M.S.W., Pittsburgh, 1969. Prevention of secondary disabilities in wheelchair users, curriculum development in disability studies.
Changfeng Tai, Visiting Research Assistant Professor of Rehabilitation Science and Technology; Ph.D., Institute of Xi'an Jiaotong University (China), 1992.
Elaine Trefler, Assistant Professor of Rehabilitation Science and Technology and of Occupational Therapy; M.Ed., Memphis State; 1977. Assistive technologies, seating and wheeled mobility, functional applications.
William C. Welch, Assistant Professor of Neurologic Surgery, Orthopaedic Surgery, and Health and Rehabilitation Sciences; M.D., SUNY Downstate Medical Center, 1985. Spinal surgery, tumor oncology, spinal biomechanics.
Savio L.-Y. Woo, Ferguson Professor and Director, Musculoskeletal Research Center, and Professor of Orthopaedic Surgery, of Mechanical and Civil Engineering, and of Rehabilitation Science and Technology; Ph.D.; Washington (Seattle), 1971. Ligament and tendon biomechanics, soft tissue growth, development, aging and healing and joint kinematics.
Ying-Wei Yuan, Adjunct Professor of Rehabilitation Science and Technology and Director of Engineering, Dymax Corporation; Ph.D., Penn State, 1988. Medical ultrasonics, bioinstrumentation, tissue characterization with ultrasound.

SELECTED RECENT PUBLICATIONS

Bertocci, G. E., P. E. Karg, and **D. A. Hobson.** Wheeled mobility device database for transportation safety research and standards. *Assistive Technol.* 9(2):102–15, 1997.
Boninger, M. L., R. A. Cooper, R. N. Robertson, and T. E. Rudy. Wrist biomechanics during two speeds of wheelchair propulsion: An analysis using a local coordinate system. *Arch. Phys. Med. Rehabil.* 78(4):364–72, 1997.
Brienza, D. M., and P. E. Karg. Seat cushion optimization: A comparison of interface pressure and tissue stiffness characteristics for spinal cord injured and elderly patients. *Arch. Phys. Med. Rehabil.* 79:388–94, 1998.
Cooper, R. A. Awareness of disability culture in research. *Technol. Disabil.* 7:211–8, 1997.
VanSickle, D. P., et al. **(R. A. Cooper** and **M. L. Boninger).** A unified method for calculating the center of pressure during wheelchair propulsion. *Ann. Biomed. Eng. Soc.* 26(2):328–36, 1997.
Cooper, R. A., E. Trefler, and **D. A. Hobson.** Wheelchair and seating: Issues and practices. *Tech. Disabil.* 5:3–26, 1996.
Hobson, D. A., ed. Wheelchair transit: An unresolved challenge in a maturing technology. *J. Rehabil. Res. Dev.* 34(2), 1997.
Robinson, C. J., R. D. Wurster, and J. S. Walter. Testing peripheral somatosensory neuroprostheses by recording from raccoon cortex. *IEEE Trans. Rehabil. Eng.* 5(1):75–80, 1997.
Trefler, E., and **D. A. Hobson.** Assistive technology. In *Occupational Therapy: Enabling Function and Well-Being,* chapter 20, pp. 484–506. Thorofare, N.J.: SLACK Incorporated, 1997.

WASHINGTON UNIVERSITY IN ST. LOUIS

School of Medicine
Program in Occupational Therapy

Programs of Study

The Washington University Program in Occupational Therapy has earned a national reputation for quality, ranking as one of the top three occupational therapy programs in the country. It offers an entry-level master's degree for students with a variety of academic backgrounds who wish to apply their education to a fast-growing applied science profession. It also provides good preparation for doctoral work. Begun in 1918, the Washington University Program in Occupational Therapy is known for its strong scientific base of practice centered on the concept of human performance, the opportunity to learn from professors who are scholars and researchers in their respective fields, and a fully integrated academic and clinical program. In addition to the traditional method of matriculation, a student may choose the 3-2 option. This method blends three years at a contracted liberal arts college with two years at Washington University, allowing the student to earn a B.S. in the original major and an M.S. in occupational therapy in only five years.

A research Master of Arts degree in disability and rehabilitation studies is also offered. This program offers advanced study to occupational therapists, physical therapists, nurses, speech language pathologists, audiologists, psychologists, and related practitioners. Students choose one of three study tracks: developmental performance and neuroscience, work performance and occupational competence, or aging and human performance.

Research Facilities

The Program in Occupational Therapy houses nationally recognized research labs in pediatrics, social participation, return-to-work, and cognitive rehabilitation. Research questions center on understanding mechanisms that support daily life. Research questions center on understanding mechanisms that support daily life. Research is conducted at Barnes-Jewish and St. Louis Children's Hospitals and in community practice sites. The Washington University library system has worldwide access and holds more than 2 million volumes.

Financial Aid

Students are eligible for various University, state, and federal scholarships and loans. One merit scholarship and one minority merit scholarship are awarded annually. Minority student book scholarships are available. Tuition reimbursement is available from various institutions. A cost stabilization plan is an option.

Cost of Study

The professional degree (entry-level master's) program tuition for 1998–99 is $650 per credit hour.

Living and Housing Costs

Convenient on-campus housing costs $2590 per year (August to May) for a single room or a suite with double occupancy.

Student Group

The Washington University Program in Occupational Therapy enrolls approximately 200 students in the professional M.S. degree program and the research degree program. Ninety percent are women, and 10 percent are members of minority groups.

Location

The program is part of the School of Medicine, which is situated west of downtown St. Louis and just east of Forest Park, one of the largest municipal parks in America. Forest Park is the home of the St. Louis Zoo, the St. Louis Art Museum, and the MUNY (Municipal Opera, an outdoor summer theater). The park has biking and jogging trails, a skating rink, racquetball and handball courts, and many other recreational opportunities. Also adjacent to the campus is the Central West End District, an unusual collection of cafés, art galleries, shops, and carefully restored turn-of-the-century mansions. Other cultural opportunities include the St. Louis Symphony Orchestra, the Opera Theatre of St. Louis, and the Repertory Theatre. St. Louis is the home of three professional sports teams: Cardinals baseball, Blues hockey, and Rams football. The Ozark Mountains are a few hours' drive from campus and offer canoeing streams and hiking trails.

The University

Washington University is an independent, medium-sized nondenominational university that offers eighty major areas of concentration and more than 1,600 courses. It was founded in 1853 and is one of only twenty-six institutions that have achieved membership in the Association of American Universities. The Washington University School of Medicine is ranked third in the country, as is the Program in Occupational Therapy.

Applying

Admission is in the fall semester. Each applicant must provide a completed application form, official transcripts of all degrees and advanced course work, three letters of recommendation, three essays as specified on the application form, a resume, GRE scores, and a $50 application fee. At least 30 hours of work/volunteer experience or observation in an occupational therapy facility or community practice site is recommended.

Correspondence and Information

For information about the entry-level M.S. program:

Karina Shenderov, Recruitment Manager
Program in Occupational Therapy
Campus Box 8505
Washington University School of Medicine
4444 Forest Park Avenue
St. Louis, Missouri 63108-2292
Telephone: 314-286-1600
800-279-3229 (toll-free)
Fax: 314-286-1601
E-mail: wuotinfo@ot-link.wustl.edu
World Wide Web: http://www.ot.wustl.edu
Gopher: gopher.ot.wustl.edu
Anonymous ftp to: ftp.ot.wustl.edu

For information about the research M.A. program:

Dr. Gerald Popelka, Associate Director of Advanced Graduate Studies
Program in Occupational Therapy
Campus Box 8505
Washington University School of Medicine
4444 Forest Park Avenue
St. Louis, Missouri 63108-2292
Telephone: 314-286-1600
800-279-3229 (toll-free)
Fax: 314-286-1601
E-mail: wuotinfo@ot-link.wustl.edu
World Wide Web: http://www.ot.wustl.edu
Gopher: gopher.ot.wustl.edu
Anonymous ftp to: ftp.ot.wustl.edu

Washington University in St. Louis

THE FACULTY AND THEIR RESEARCH

M. Carolyn Baum, Assistant Professor in Occupational Therapy and Neurology and Elias Michael Director; Ph.D., Washington (St. Louis), 1993; OTR/L, FAOTA. Occupational performance of the cognitively impaired individual, family-centered care, relationship of occupation and health.

Associate Directors

Carol A. Brownson, Associate Director, Community Health; M.S.P.H., P.H.L.C., Missouri–Columbia, 1979. Public health.

Mary Ann Bruce, Associate Director, Professional Program; Ph.D., USC, 1997. Educational psychology, adult learning and problem solving in occupational therapy, psychosocial occupational therapy.

David B. Gray, Associate Director of Research; Ph.D., Minnesota, 1974. Assistive technology to support independence, disability policy.

Gerald R. Popelka, Associate Director of Advanced Graduate Studies; Ph.D., Wisconsin, 1974. Clinical diagnosis and rehabilitation related to peripheral auditory systems.

Faculty Members

C. Robert Almli, Associate Professor in Occupational Therapy, Neurology, Pediatrics, Neuroscience, and Psychology; Ph.D., Michigan State, 1970. Early development, pediatrics, developmental neuropsychobiology.

Cynthia Ballentine, Instructor; M.S., Washington (St. Louis), 1991; OTR/L. Adult acute rehabilitation, with an emphasis on orthopedics.

Christine Berg, Instructor; M.S., Boston University, 1979: OTR/L. Maternal-child interactions, pediatric rehabilitation.

Ellen Binder, Assistant Professor in Medicine and Occupational Therapy; M.D., Washington (St. Louis), 1981. Impact of exercise on prevention of falls in older adults, effectiveness of rehabilitation methods, relationship of cognitive deficits and discharge placement.

Paula C. Bohr, Instructor; Ph.D., Oklahoma, 1993; OTR/L, FAOTA. Ergonomics, cumulative trauma disorders.

Jeanenne Dallas, Community Practice Occupational Therapist and Lecturer; M.A., Arkansas, 1987; OTR/L. Clinical experience in acute and community phases of mental health treatment, geropsychiatry and management.

Karen Parker Davis, Instructor; M.A., Webster, 1983; OTR/L. Minority recruitment, diversity issues in occupational therapy.

Michael Diringer, Assistant Professor in Neurology, Neurosurgery, and Occupational Therapy; M.D., Kentucky, 1982. Long-term recovery in persons with neurological injury.

Alexander Dromerick, Assistant Professor in Neurology and Occupational Therapy; M.D., Maryland, 1986. Development of measures of recovery of function, rehabilitation outcomes.

Janet M. Duchek, Professor in Occupational Therapy and Neurology; Ph.D., South Carolina, 1982. Cognition, memory and aging.

Dorothy F. Edwards, Assistant Professor in Occupational Therapy and Neurology; Ph.D., Washington (St. Louis), 1980. Functional assessment in acute neurology, psychological aspects of disease and trauma, caregiver burden across stages of dementia.

Bradley Evanoff, Assistant Professor in Medicine and Occupational Therapy; M.D., Washington (St. Louis), 1986. Prevention of work-related injuries.

Mary M. Evert, Adjunct Assistant Professor in Occupational Therapy; M.B.A., National, 1980; OTR/L, FAOTA. Policy, reimbursement.

Shan Pin Fanchiang, Instructor and OT Lead Therapist at Barnes-Jewish Hospital; Ph.D. candidate, USC; OTR/L. Pediatrics (early intervention, autism, and learning disability) and rehabilitation (traumatic brain injury and Parkinson's disease).

Robert Hanlon, Assistant Professor in Neurology and Occupational Therapy; Ph.D., CUNY, City College, 1988; CRC, OTR/L. Effects of neurological deficits on performance.

Phillip E. Higgs, Assistant Professor in Surgery and Occupational Therapy; M.D., Florida, 1974. Upper extremity surgery, upper extremity trauma disorders, fractures.

Kathy Kniepmann, Instructor; M.P.H., Ed.M.; Harvard, 1981; OTR/L. Health promotion, community practice and prevention.

Luci Kohn, Assistant Professor in Occupational Therapy and Anatomy; Ph.D., Wisconsin–Madison, 1989. Assessment of morphology, effects of abnormal growth or nerve injury in craniofacial growth.

Patricia D. LaVesser, Instructor; M.A.T., Webster, 1987; OTR/L. Pediatric rehabilitation.

Susan E. Mackinnon, Professor in Surgery (Plastic and Reconstructive) and Occupational Therapy; M.D., Queen's at Kingston, 1975. Nerve injury and cumulative trauma disorders.

Leonard N. Matheson, Assistant Professor; Ph.D., USC, 1979. Industrial rehabilitation, psychological impact of worker injury.

J. Gail Neely, Professor and Director, Otolaryngology/Neurotology; M.D., Oklahoma, 1965; F.A.C.S. Otolaryngology, head and neck surgery, facial paralysis.

Peggy A. Neufeld, Instructor; M.A., NYU, 1976; OTR/L. Adult physical rehabilitation, social psychological impact of physical disability.

Christine B. Novak, Assistant Professor in Occupational Therapy and Surgery (Plastic and Reconstructive); M.S., Toronto, 1992; PT. Sensory testing and reeducation.

Monica Perlmutter, Instructor; M.A., Washington (St. Louis), 1989; OTR/L. Physical disabilities, functional performance and assessment.

Jay Piccirillo, Assistant Professor in Otolaryngology and Occupational Therapy; M.D., Vermont, 1985. Otolaryngology, head and neck surgery, sleep apnea, hearing loss.

Mary K. Seaton, Instructor; B.S., Missouri, 1977; OTR/L, CHT. Hand rehabilitation, cumulative, and industry.

Susan L. Stark, Instructor; Ph.D., Columbia, 1998; OTR/L. Environmental interventions that support occupational performance, accessibility.

Donna Whitehouse, Instructor; M.H.A., Missouri, 1996; OTR/L. Professional behavior and development issues.

WASHINGTON UNIVERSITY IN ST. LOUIS/ CENTRAL INSTITUTE FOR THE DEAF

Department of Speech and Hearing Professional Education and Communication Sciences Program

Programs of Study

The Department of Speech and Hearing offers degrees in three areas: audiology, education of the hearing-impaired, and communication sciences.

The audiology program offers an M.S. degree. The graduate is qualified to be a certified and licensed clinical audiologist. Unparalleled opportunities exist for students at the Central Institute for the Deaf (CID) to explore the most recent technologies available with the clinicians and scientists who are engaged in the development and evaluation of new devices such as digital hearing aids, cochlear implants, and tactile aids. Association of the audiology program with a school for hearing-impaired children allows for extensive practicum experience in educational and diagnostic audiology for the severely and profoundly hearing-impaired child.

The program in education of the hearing-impaired offers an M.S. degree in speech and hearing and prepares graduates for teaching hearing-impaired children at the infant, preschool, elementary, and secondary school levels. The program emphasizes the teaching of speech, language, and auditory skills. Students receive two full semesters of practice teaching, working closely with experienced cooperating teachers in classrooms with children of all ages. Both course work and practicum occur on the premises, so students have the opportunity to observe and participate in all facets of the program.

The program in communication sciences is a multidisciplinary M.A. and Ph.D. program that prepares students for careers in research, academic teaching, and professional administration. The program includes course work relevant to the scientific study of speech, language, and hearing that is offered in a variety of Washington University departments. Core areas in which the student's dissertation research is carried out are biophysics and neurophysiology of hearing, acoustics and electroacoustics, psychoacoustics, sensory behavior of animals, speech and phonetics, psycholinguistics, or research applied to audiology and/or the education of the hearing-impaired.

Research Facilities

The Central Institute for the Deaf is an internationally known facility dedicated to basic and applied research in all areas of auditory communication and its disorders. Scientists direct research in human psychoacoustics, sensory neuroscience, speech perception, neuroanatomy, digital hearing-aid design, effects of noise on hearing, animal psychoacoustics, and design and evaluation of assistive listening devices. Also housed in the Institute is one of the nation's outstanding libraries devoted to speech, hearing, and related fields.

Financial Aid

Tuition scholarships are available for qualified students who are accepted into the graduate programs. Free housing and food services are also available on the CID campus in exchange for after-school and weekend work in service to the Institute. Opportunities for employment at the Institute include extracurricular supervision of children, clerical work, and participation as subjects in research projects. Students may be eligible for loans through CID and other granting agencies.

Cost of Study

For 1998–99, tuition is $11,500. For part-time students, tuition is charged at the rate of $960 per semester unit. Degree candidates are required to provide evidence of possessing health insurance or to participate in the University's health insurance plan. The cost of books and supplies usually does not exceed $600–$800 for the entire course. All costs are subject to change.

Living and Housing Costs

It is estimated that a student requires approximately $19,000 per year for accommodations, food, utilities, clothing, and entertainment. A limited number of rooms are available on campus for $3430 per school term. Meal contracts for the school dining room range from $318 to $1640 per semester. Apartments are available within walking distance of CID and can be located through the off-campus Housing Office of Washington University. (These costs are for 1998–99 and are subject to change.)

Student Group

The students in the programs are men and women carefully selected on the basis of academic qualifications and professional promise. Students from most of the states of the Union have been enrolled at one time or another, and each class usually includes a number of international students. The influence of the Institute's programs is, therefore, truly international.

Location

St. Louis offers excellent opportunities for recreational and cultural activities. CID adjoins Forest Park, which is the site of a zoo, an art museum, and the St. Louis Science Center. There are facilities for sports activities nearby. CID is located in the Central West End of St. Louis, near shops, restaurants, and residential areas where many young professionals live.

The University and The Program

CID is part of the Washington University Medical School complex, and students have full use of the University's facilities. From its founding in 1914, CID has conducted a program of preparation for professional personnel in the field of speech, hearing, and language disorders. The Institute was a pioneer in this area of specialized professional education and played a major role in developing educational methods and standards. The Institute was first affiliated with Washington University in 1931 and now comprises the Department of Speech and Hearing of the University. The program is located at the Central Institute for the Deaf, where hearing-impaired children are taught, clinical work is conducted, and associated research is carried on every day. Washington University is a member of several college and university associations, including the North Central Association of Colleges and Secondary Schools. The program in education of the hearing-impaired is accredited by the National Commission on the Accreditation of Teacher Education and the Council on the Education of the Deaf. The program in audiology is certified by the Educational Standards Board of the American Speech-Language-Hearing Association.

Applying

All students seeking admission should apply well in advance of the time set for registration, preferably before March 15. There are no midyear admissions. A form statement of purpose is included on the application, requiring the applicant to outline reasons why he or she is seeking admission into the program. To apply, a student needs to submit the application form, official undergraduate transcripts, letters of recommendation, and scores from the General Test of the Graduate Record Examinations. Central Institute and Washington University give full consideration to all applicants for admission and financial aid without regard to sex, race, color, creed, age, disability, or national origin. A $35 filing fee must accompany the application.

Correspondence and Information

Karen Benton
Registrar, Professional Education Program
Central Institute for the Deaf
818 South Euclid
St. Louis, Missouri 63110-1549
Telephone: 314-997-0240

Washington University in St. Louis/Central Institute for the Deaf

THE FACULTY AND THEIR RESEARCH

Lynda C. Berkowitz, Lecturer in Education of the Hearing Impaired; M.S., Washington (St. Louis), 1983. Parenting issues in families with hearing impaired children, effects of early intervention on hearing-impaired children and their families, reading instruction.

Carl D. Bohl, Adjunct Assistant Professor of Environmental Health; D.Sc., Cincinnati, 1973. Hearing conservation in the industrial environment, federal regulation of programs to control noise exposure, workers' compensation activities. In plant practices for job related health hazards control. In *Engineering Aspects,* eds. L. V. Cralley and L. J. Cralley. New York: John Wiley, 1988.

Barbara A. Bohne, Research Professor of Anatomy and Physiology; Ph.D., Washington (St. Louis), 1971. Degeneration and repair in the inner ear using mutant mice with inner-ear anomalies and noise-damaged chinchillas and mice as models. Time course of nerve-fiber regeneration in the noise-damaged chinchilla cochlea. *Int. J. Dev. Neurol.* 15:601–17, 1997.

Donald G. Brennan, Adjunct Professor of Speech Pathology; Ph.D., Oklahoma Health Sciences Center, 1974. Cultural diversity for educating speech and language pathologists and audiologists. Serving African-American children: Preservice training to meet the needs of people from diverse cultural backgrounds. *ASHA,* December 1992 (with Campbell and Steckol).

Sarah C. Cantwell, Lecturer in Education of the Hearing Impaired; M.S., Washington (St. Louis), 1991. Speech and language evaluation, cochlear implants, speech and language development of the young child.

Deborah L. Carter, Lecturer in Education of the Hearing Impaired; M.A.T., Webster, 1992. Mainstreaming, curriculum development, reading instruction, cochlear implants in children, training. *Around the U.S. in 180 Days: A Social Studies Curriculum,* A. G. Bell Convention, Rochester, New York, 1994.

William W. Clark, Professor of Physiological Acoustics; Ph.D., Michigan, 1975. Effects of noise on hearing, industrial hearing conservation, animal psychophysics, cochlear biomechanics, effects of aging on the auditory system. Hearing levels of US industrial workers employed in low-noise environments. In *Scientific Basis of Noise-Induced Hearing Loss,* chap. 31, pp. 397–415, eds. A. Axelsson et al. New York: Thieme Medical Publishing, 1996 (with Bohl).

Lisa A. Davidson, Assistant Professor of Audiology; M.S., Washington (St. Louis), 1987. Cochlear implants in children.

Ann E. Geers, Professor of Psychology; Ph.D., Washington (St. Louis), 1977. Clinical evaluation of hearing-impaired children, cochlear implants, literacy in hearing-impaired children, communication mode and English-language acquisition. Effectiveness of cochlear implants and tactile aids for deaf children: The sensory aids study at CID. *Volta Rev.* 96:5, eds. J. Moog and A. Geers, 1994.

Ira J. Hirsh, Professor of Psychology; Ph.D., Harvard, 1948. Temporal aspects of hearing. Auditory psychophysics and perception. *Annu. Rev. Psychol.* 47:461–84, 1996 (with Watson).

Roanne K. Karzon, Clinical Assistant Professor of Audiology; Ph.D., Washington (St. Louis), 1982. Assessment of auditory sensitivity and processing in children, early identification of hearing loss, pediatric audiology. Growth of the 2 fi-f2 distortion product otoacoustic emission for low-level stimuli in human neonates. *Ear Hear.* 16(2):159–65 (with Popelka).

Victoria J. Kozak, Assistant Professor of Education of the Hearing Impaired; M.A.Ed., Washington (St. Louis), 1979. Language development and auditory stimulation of hearing-impaired children, needs of families of hearing-impaired children, sudden onset deafness, environmental and genetic causes of hearing impairment, educational evaluation of hearing-impaired children, cochlear implants for hearing-impaired children, literature-based reading, thematic teaching. Development of communicative function in young hearing-impaired and normally hearing children. *Volta Rev.* 96(2):113–35, 1994.

Barbara A. Lanfer, Lecturer in Education of the Hearing Impaired; M.A.Ed., Missouri–St. Louis, 1998. Instruction of learning-disabled, hearing-impaired children; reading and literature instruction; and curriculum development for children with hearing impairment. *Literature Based Reading for Hearing Impaired Children,* A. G. Bell Convention, June 1998.

David I. Mason, Assistant Professor of Audiology; Ph.D., Tennessee, 1983. Hearing aids and hearing aid fittings. Factors which affect measures of speech audibility with hearing aids. *Ear Hear.* 8(5):109S, 1987 (with Popelka).

Laura W. McCann, Lecturer in Education of the Hearing Impaired; M.S., Washington (St. Louis), 1977. Mainstreaming, reading instruction, written language development, cochlear implants in children.

James D. Miller, Professor of Psychology; Ph.D., Indiana, 1957. Acoustic bases of speech perception studied by measurement of natural speech, responses to synthetic speech, and interpretation of the results in terms of a computational model of human perceptual processes; speech production by deaf speakers; communication over multimedia telecommunication networks; biological repair of the inner ear. Acoustic correlation of the perceived vowels of American English. *J. Acoust. Soc. Am.* 95(5), 2949(A).

Johanna G. Nicholas, Assistant Professor of Psychology; Ph.D., Washington (St. Louis), 1990. Development of the social uses of language by preschool-age children. Communication of oral deaf and normally hearing children at 36 months of age. *J. Speech Lang. Hear. Res.* 40:1314–27, 1998.

Donald W. Nielsen, Professor of Psychology; Ph.D., Wayne State, 1968. Cochlear micromechanics and transduction, regeneration of cochlear hair cells and nerves, genetics of hearing loss. Sterocilia. In *Neurobiology of Hearing: The Cochlea,* pp. 23–46, eds. R. A. Altschuler, D. W. Hoffman, and R. P. Bobbin. New York: Raven Press, 1986 (with Slepecky).

Judith M. Ogilvie, Assistant Professor of Neurobiology; Ph.D., Harvard, 1983. Molecular mechanisms and neurotrophic factors in sensory cell atrophy and rescue; development and degeneration of retina in organ culture; gene expression in the neurodegenerative model of mouse retina. *Bax* knockout mice have an increased survival of retinal neurons. *Invest. Ophthalmol. Vis. Sci. Suppl.* 1997 (with Peckwerth et al.).

Kevin K. Ohlemiller, Assistant Professor of Auditory Physiology; Ph.D., Northwestern, 1990. The relationship between presbycusis genes, vulnerability of the cochlea to noise and ototoxic compounds, and free radical production and regulation within sensory cells. *In vivo* measurement of cochlear reactive oxygen species in mice: Effects of noise exposure and cochlear ischemia. Abstract of the 1998 *Midwinter Meeting of the Association of Research in Otolaryngology* (with Dugan).

Terlander K. Parthasarathy, Adjunct Associate Professor of Audiology; Ph.D., Texas at Dallas, 1987. Rate, frequency, and intensity effects on early auditory evoked potentials and binaural interaction component in humans. *J. Am. Acad. Aud.* 4:229–37, 1993 (with Moushegian).

Laura Blewer Roberts, Lecturer in Education of the Hearing Impaired; M.S., Fontbonne, 1991. Speech and language evaluation of hearing-impaired children, various modes of communication, cochlear implants in children.

Marlene B. Salas-Provance, Adjunct Assistant Professor of Speech Pathology; Ph.D., Illinois at Urbana-Champaign, 1990. Acoustic characteristics of prespeech vocalizations in babies with cleft palate, laryngeal symptomatology, and the sleep apnea syndrome. Orofacial, physiological, and acoustical characteristics: Implications for speech of African-American children. In *Communication Development and Disorders of African American Children,* pp. 155–87, eds. A. Kamhi, K. Pollock, and J. Harris. James T. Brooks, 1996.

Margaret W. Skinner, Professor of Audiology; Ph.D., Washington (St. Louis), 1976. Optimizing the benefit obtained by patients with cochlear implants. Identification of speech by cochlear implant recipients with the multipeak (MPEAK) and spectral peak (SPEAK) speech coding strategies 1: Vowels. *Ear Hear.* 17:182–97, 1996 (with Fourakis, T. A. Holden, L. K. Holden, and Demarest).

Nancy Tye-Murray, Professor of Audiology; Ph.D., Iowa, 1984. Aural rehabilitation; speech production of deaf talkers. Acquisition of speech by children who have prolonged cochlear implant experience. *J. Speech Hear. Res.* 38:327–37, 1995 (with Spencer and Woodworth).

Rosalie M. Uchanski, Assistant Professor of Electrical Engineering; Ph.D., MIT, 1988. Finding objective acoustic measures that are correlated with the speech intelligibility of deaf children; development of a children's speech database with both normal-hearing and hearing-impaired talkers, speech perception. Speaking clearly for the hard of hearing IV. *J. Speech Hear Res.* 39:494–509, 1996 (with Choi, Braida, Reed, and Durlach).

Elizabeth H. Vrugtman, Lecturer in Education of the Hearing Impaired; M.Ed., Missouri–St. Louis, 1978. Professional and parent training in behavior management of exceptional children, counseling needs of families with handicapped children.

Christine Wood, Lecturer in Audiology; M.S., Washington (St. Louis), 1970. Programming strategies with children with implants, pediatric audiology, sudden onset hearing loss/progressive hearing loss. *Asymmetrical Audiograms and Sudden Onset Hearing Loss.* Missouri Speech and Hearing Association, 1993.

Pamela R. Zacher, Lecturer in Education of the Hearing Impaired; M.S.Ed., Missouri–St. Louis, 1991. Clinical evaluation of hearing-impaired children, social skills training for hearing-impaired children, computer instruction and curriculum development. *Reach for the S.T.A.R.S–Social Training Activities and Resources,* A. G. Bell Convention, Salt Lake City, Utah, 1996.

Section 27
Health Sciences

This section contains directories of institutions offering graduate work in health physics/radiological health and medical physics, followed by in-depth entries submitted by institutions that chose to prepare detailed program descriptions. Additional information about programs listed in the directories but not augmented by an in-depth entry may be obtained by writing directly to the dean of a graduate school or chair of a department at the address given in the directory.

For programs offering related work, see also in this book Dentistry and Dental Sciences, Health Services, Medicine, Nursing, and Public Health; in Book 3, Biological and Biomedical Sciences and Biophysics (Radiation Biology); in Book 4, Physics; and in Book 5, Bioengineering, Biomedical Engineering, and Biotechnology; and Energy and Power Engineering (Nuclear Engineering).

CONTENTS

Health Physics/Radiological Health

Allegheny University of the Health Sciences, School of Medicine, Biomedical Graduate Programs, Department of Radiation Oncology and Nuclear Medicine, Philadelphia, PA 19102-1192. Offers programs in medical physics (MS, PhD), radiation science (MS, PhD). Part-time programs available. Faculty: 19 full-time (3 women). Students: 6 full-time (1 woman); includes 1 minority (African American), 1 international. Average age 29. 16 applicants, 6% accepted. In 1997, 1 master's awarded. Terminal master's awarded for partial completion of doctoral program. *Degree requirements:* For master's, thesis, comprehensive exam required, foreign language not required; for doctorate, 1 foreign language (computer language can substitute), dissertation, qualifying exam. *Entrance requirements:* For master's, GRE General Test (minimum combined score of 1410 on three sections), TOEFL, minimum GPA of 2.75; for doctorate, GRE General Test (minimum combined score of 1650 on three sections), TOEFL, minimum GPA of 3.0. Application deadline: 4/1 (rolling processing). Application fee: $50. *Expenses:* Tuition $10,950 per year. Fees $60 per year. *Financial aid:* Fellowships, research assistantships, teaching assistantships, Federal Work-Study, institutionally sponsored loans, and career-related internships or fieldwork available. Aid available to part-time students. Financial aid application deadline: 5/1; applicants required to submit FAFSA. *Faculty research:* Mechanisms for improving use of radiolabeled antibodies for cancer diagnosis and therapy; improved cancer therapy by linear accelerators and internal, sealed radiation sources; algorithms for improved superminicomputer-assisted radiation therapy simulation and tumor imaging; molecular and cellular mechanisms of radiation damage. • Dr. Fong Y. Tsai, Chairman, 215-762-8722. Application contact: Dr. Jacqueline Emrich, Program Director.

Colorado State University, College of Veterinary Medicine and Biomedical Sciences and Graduate School, Graduate Programs in Veterinary Medicine and Biomedical Sciences, Department of Radiological Health Sciences, Health Physics Training Program, Fort Collins, CO 80523-0015. Awards MS, PhD. Faculty: 17 full-time (1 woman). *Degree requirements:* For master's, thesis required, foreign language not required; for doctorate, dissertation. *Entrance requirements:* GRE General Test, TOEFL, minimum GPA of 3.0. Application deadline: 2/1 (rolling processing). Application fee: $30. Electronic applications accepted. *Expenses:* Tuition $2632 per year full-time, $109 per credit hour part-time for state residents; $10,216 per year full-time, $425 per credit hour part-time for nonresidents. Fees $708 per year full-time, $32 per semester (minimum) part-time. *Financial aid:* In 1997–98, 9 research assistantships, 10 traineeships were awarded; fellowships, Federal Work-Study, and career-related internships or fieldwork also available. *Faculty research:* Radiation therapy; cell, molecular, and tissue mechanisms in radiation biology; diagnostic radiology; radioecology. • Dr. E. L. Gillette, Chairman, Department of Radiological Health Sciences, 970-491-5222. Fax: 970-491-0623. E-mail: lwiedeman@vines.colostate.edu.

Emory University, Graduate School of Arts and Sciences, Department of Physics, Atlanta, GA 30322-1100. Offerings include physics (MA, MS, PhD), with options in biophysics, radiological physics, solid-state physics. Terminal master's awarded for partial completion of doctoral program. Department faculty: 17 full-time (1 woman), 3 part-time (0 women). *Degree requirements:* For master's, thesis required, foreign language not required; for doctorate, dissertation, comprehensive exams required, foreign language not required. *Entrance requirements:* GRE General Test, TOEFL, minimum GPA of 3.0. Application deadline: 1/20 (priority date). Application fee: $45. *Expenses:* Tuition $21,770 per year. Fees $300 per year. • Dr. Vincent Huynh, Director of Graduate Studies, 404-727-4295. E-mail: phsbhh@physics.emory.edu. Application contact: Brenda J. Wingo, Coordinator of Academic Services, 404-727-8037. Fax: 404-727-8073. E-mail: phsbw@physics.emory.edu.

Emory University, School of Medicine, Programs in Allied Health Professions, Program in Radiation Oncology Physics, Atlanta, GA 30322-1100. Awards MM Sc. Faculty: 2 full-time (0 women). Students: 12 full-time (2 women), 1 part-time (0 women); includes 2 African Americans, 1 Asian American, 1 international. Average age 30. 8 applicants, 50% accepted. In 1997, 6 degrees awarded (100% found work related to degree). *Entrance requirements:* GRE General Test (minimum combined score of 1500 on three sections). Application fee: $35. *Financial aid:* Federal Work-Study, institutionally sponsored loans available. Aid available to part-time students. Financial aid application deadline: 3/15; applicants required to submit CSS PROFILE or FAFSA. • Dr. Pat McGinley, Director, 404-778-3535.

Georgetown University, Programs in Biomedical Sciences, Department of Health Physics, Washington, DC 20057. Offers programs in health physics (MS), radiobiology (MS). *Degree requirements:* Thesis. *Entrance requirements:* TOEFL (minimum score 550 required, 600 for teaching assistants). Application deadline: 8/1 (12/15 for spring admission). Application fee: $50 ($55 for international students). *Expenses:* Tuition $19,128 per year full-time, $797 per credit part-time. Fees $99 (one-time charge).

Georgia Institute of Technology, College of Engineering, George W. Woodruff School of Mechanical Engineering, Nuclear Engineering and Health Physics Programs, Atlanta, GA 30332-0001. Offerings in health physics (MSHP), nuclear engineering (MSNE, PhD). Part-time programs available. Faculty: 8 full-time (1 woman). Students: 33 full-time (11 women), 45 part-time (12 women); includes 7 minority (3 African Americans, 1 Asian American, 3 Hispanics), 9 international. Average age 28. 72 applicants, 40% accepted. In 1997, 16 master's, 8 doctorates awarded. Terminal master's awarded for partial completion of doctoral program. *Degree requirements:* For master's, thesis optional, foreign language not required; for doctorate, dissertation, exams required, foreign language not required. *Entrance requirements:* GRE General Test (recommended), TOEFL (minimum score 580). Application deadline: 2/1 (priority date; rolling processing; 11/1 for spring admission). Application fee: $50. *Expenses:* Tuition $2670 per year full-time, $98 per credit hour part-time for state residents; $10,680 per year full-time, $298 per credit hour part-time for nonresidents. Fees $681 per year full-time, $23 per credit hour (minimum) part-time. *Financial aid:* In 1997–98, 37 students received aid, including 21 research assistantships, 4 teaching assistantships; fellowships, partial tuition waivers, Federal Work-Study, institutionally sponsored loans, and career-related internships or fieldwork also available. Aid available to part-time students. Financial aid application deadline: 4/10. *Faculty research:* Reactor engineering and systems, radiation technology, nuclear materials, environmental engineering, plasma physics. • Application contact: Dr. William Wepfer, Graduate Coordinator, 404-894-3204. Fax: 404-894-8336. E-mail: bill.wepfer@me.gatech.edu.

Johns Hopkins University, School of Hygiene and Public Health, Department of Environmental Health Sciences, Division of Radiation Health Sciences, Baltimore, MD 21205. Awards MHS, Sc M, Dr PH, PhD, Sc D. *Degree requirements:* For master's, thesis (for some programs); for doctorate, dissertation, 1 year full-time residency, oral and written exams required, foreign language not required. *Entrance requirements:* GRE General Test. Application deadline: 2/1 (priority date; rolling processing). Application fee: $60. *Financial aid:* Scholarships, Federal Work-Study, institutionally sponsored loans available. Aid available to part-time students. Financial aid application deadline: 4/15. *Faculty research:* Nuclear medicine, radio chemistry, positron emission tomography, radiobiology, neurotoxins, risk assessments, NMR imaging. • Dr. John R. Lever Jr., Director, 410-955-3350.

See in-depth description on page 1499.

Massachusetts Institute of Technology, School of Engineering, Department of Nuclear Engineering, Cambridge, MA 02139-4307. Offerings include health physics (SM), radiation science and technology (SM, PhD, Sc D), radiological health and industrial radiation engineering (M Eng), radiological sciences (PhD, Sc D). Department faculty: 19 full-time (1 woman). *Degree requirements:* For doctorate, dissertation, comprehensive exams. *Entrance requirements:* For doctorate, GRE General Test, TOEFL (minimum score 577). Application deadline: 1/15 (priority date; rolling processing; 11/1 for spring admission). Application fee: $55. *Tuition:* $24,050 per year. • Dr. Jeffrey Freidberg, Head, 617-253-3801. E-mail: kazimi@mit.edu. Application contact: Clare Egan, Graduate Office Administrator, 617-253-3814. Fax: 617-258-7437. E-mail: cegan@mit.edu.

Massachusetts Institute of Technology, Department of Nuclear Engineering and Whitaker College of Health Sciences and Technology, Program in Radiological Sciences, Cambridge, MA 02139-4307. Awards PhD, Sc D. Faculty: 5 full-time (1 woman). Students: 29 full-time (5 women); includes 1 minority (Asian American), 18 international. Average age 23. 23 applicants, 57% accepted. In 1997, 3 degrees awarded (33% entered university research/teaching, 67% found other work related to degree). *Degree requirements:* Dissertation, comprehensive exams. *Entrance requirements:* GRE General Test, TOEFL (minimum score 577). Application deadline: 1/15 (priority date; 11/1 for spring admission). Application fee: $55. *Tuition:* $24,050 per year. *Financial aid:* In 1997–98, 29 students received aid, including 2 fellowships (1 to a first-year student), 18 research assistantships (1 to a first-year student), 9 teaching assistantships (7 to first-year students). Financial aid application deadline: 2/15. *Faculty research:* Imaging science, biomedical applications of NMR, radiation therapy, medical imaging, health physics. • Application contact: Clare Egan, Graduate Office Administrator, 617-253-3814. Fax: 617-258-7437. E-mail: cegan@mit.edu.

See in-depth description on page 1281.

McGill University, Faculty of Graduate Studies and Research, Faculty of Medicine, Medical Radiation Physics Unit, Montréal, PQ H3A 2T5, Canada. Awards M Sc, PhD. Faculty: 16 full-time (3 women). Students: 33 full-time (5 women), 2 part-time (0 women); includes 6 international. Average age 25. 30 applicants, 50% accepted. In 1997, 9 master's awarded (45% found work related to degree, 55% continued full-time study); 1 doctorate awarded. *Degree requirements:* Thesis/dissertation. *Average time to degree:* master's–2.5 years full-time; doctorate–3.5 years full-time. *Entrance requirements:* For master's, TOEFL (minimum score 550), B Sc in physics, minimum GPA of 3.0. Application deadline: 3/1. Application fee: $60. *Expenses:* Tuition $1668 per year for Canadian residents; $8268 per year for nonresidents. Fees $828 per year for Canadian residents; $1216 per year for nonresidents. *Financial aid:* Research assistantships, teaching assistantships available. *Faculty research:* Radiation dosimetry, biodegradable polymers, stereotactic radiosurgery, brachytherapy, functional MR brain imaging. • E. B. Podgorsak, Director, 514-934-8052. Fax: 514-934-8229. E-mail: epodgorsak@medphys.mgh.mcgill.ca. Application contact: Margery Knewstubb, Graduate Secretary. E-mail: mak@medphys.mgh.mcgill.ca.

McMaster University, Faculty of Science, Department of Physics and Astronomy, Program in Health and Radiation Physics, Hamilton, ON L8S 4M2, Canada. Awards M Sc. Part-time programs available. Faculty: 14 (0 women). Students: 0. Average age 28. 3 applicants, 0% accepted. *Degree requirements:* Thesis or alternative required, foreign language not required. *Entrance requirements:* Minimum B+ average. Application deadline: 3/31 (priority date; rolling processing). Application fee: $50. *Expenses:* Tuition $4422 per year full-time, $1590 per year part-time for Canadian residents; $12,000 per year full-time, $6165 per year part-time for nonresidents. Fees $257 per year full-time, $188 per year part-time. *Financial aid:* Application deadline 3/31. *Faculty research:* Imaging, toxicology, dosimetry, body composition, medical lasers. Total annual research expenditures: $800,000. • Dr. David R. Chettle, Coordinator, 905-525-9140 Ext. 27340. E-mail: chettle@mcmail.cis.mcmaster.ca. Application contact: Dr. Harold Haugen, Associate Chair, 905-525-9140 Ext. 24558. Fax: 905-546-1252. E-mail: physics@mcmaster.ca.

Medical College of Ohio, Department of Radiation Therapy, Toledo, OH 43699-0008. Awards MS. Part-time programs available. Faculty: 2 full-time (0 women), 1 part-time (0 women). Students: 4 full-time (0 women), 3 part-time (0 women); includes 1 minority (Asian American), 2 international. Average age 34. 14 applicants, 29% accepted. In 1997, 1 degree awarded (100% found work related to degree). *Degree requirements:* Thesis, qualifying exam required, foreign language not required. *Entrance requirements:* GRE General Test, minimum undergraduate GPA of 3.0. Application fee: $30. *Expenses:* Tuition $5939 per year full-time, $189 per credit hour part-time for state residents; $13,699 per year full-time, $428 per credit hour part-time for nonresidents. Fees $519 per year full-time, $356 per year part-time. *Financial aid:* In 1997–98, 2 fellowships (1 to a first-year student) averaging $1,000 per month and totaling $24,000 were awarded; Federal Work-Study, institutionally sponsored loans also available. Financial aid applicants required to submit FAFSA. *Faculty research:* 3-D treatment planning, stereotactic radiosurgery. • Dr. Ayyangar Komanduri, Head, 419-383-4117. E-mail: mcogradschool@mco.edu. Application contact: Joann Braatz, Clerk, 419-383-4117. Fax: 419-383-6140. E-mail: mcogradschool@mco.edu.

Medical College of Ohio, Department of Radiological Science, Toledo, OH 43699-0008. Awards MS. Part-time programs available. Faculty: 4 full-time (0 women), 5 part-time (0 women). Students: 5 full-time (0 women), 3 part-time (0 women). Average age 35. 11 applicants, 9% accepted. *Degree requirements:* Thesis, qualifying exam required, foreign language not required. *Entrance requirements:* GRE General Test, minimum undergraduate GPA of 3.0. Application fee: $30. *Expenses:* Tuition $5939 per year full-time, $189 per credit hour part-time for state residents; $13,699 per year full-time, $428 per credit hour part-time for nonresidents. Fees $519 per year full-time, $356 per year part-time. *Financial aid:* In 1997–98, 2 fellowships (1 to a first-year student) averaging $1,000 per month and totaling $24,000 were awarded; Federal Work-Study, institutionally sponsored loans also available. Financial aid applicants required to submit FAFSA. *Faculty research:* Radiation dosimetry, digital image processing, mathematical modeling, magnetic resonance imaging. Total annual research expenditures: $38,859. • Application contact: Joann Braatz, Clerk, 419-383-4117. Fax: 419-383-6140. E-mail: mcogradschool@mco.edu.

Midwestern State University, Division of Health Sciences, Program in Radiology, Wichita Falls, TX 76308-2096. Offers radiologic administration (MS), radiologic education (MS). Faculty: 2 full-time (both women). Students: 2 full-time, 56 part-time. Average age 35. 45 applicants, 89% accepted. *Entrance requirements:* GRE General Test, MAT (average 46), TOEFL (average 550). Application deadline: 8/7 (12/15 for spring admission). Application fee: $0 ($50 for international students). *Expenses:* Tuition $44 per hour for state residents; $259 per hour for nonresidents. Fees $90 per year (minimum) full-time, $9 per semester (minimum) part-time. • Dr. Nadia Bugg, Coordinator, 940-397-4571.

National Technological University, Programs in Engineering, Fort Collins, CO 80526-1842. Offerings include health physics (MS). Faculty: 600 part-time (20 women). *Entrance requirements:* BS in engineering or related field. Application deadline: rolling. Application fee: $50. *Tuition:* $585 per credit (minimum). • Lionel V. Baldwin, President, 970-495-6400. Fax: 970-484-0668. E-mail: baldwin@ntu.edu.

New York University, Graduate School of Arts and Science, Nelson Institute of Environmental Medicine, Program in Environmental Health Sciences, New York, NY 10012-1019. Offerings include environmental radiation (PhD). Program faculty: 26 full-time (7 women). *Degree requirements:* 1 foreign language, dissertation, oral and written exams. *Entrance requirements:* GRE General Test, GRE Subject Test, TOEFL, minimum GPA of 3.0; bachelor's degree in biological, physical, or engineering science. Application deadline: 8/1 (12/1 for spring admission). Application fee: $60. *Expenses:* Tuition $715 per credit. Fees $1048 per year full-time, $229 per semester (minimum) part-time. • Application contact: Richard Schlesinger, Director of Graduate Studies, 914-885-5281.

Northwestern University, Robert R. McCormick School of Engineering and Applied Science, Department of Civil Engineering, Evanston, IL 60208. Offerings include health physics/radiological health (MS, PhD). MS and PhD admissions and degrees offered through The Graduate School. Terminal master's awarded for partial completion of doctoral program. Department faculty: 25 full-time (2 women). *Degree requirements:* For doctorate, dissertation. *Entrance requirements:* For doctorate, GRE General Test. Application fee: $50 ($55 for international students). *Tuition:* $20,430 per year full-time, $2424 per course part-time. • Joseph

L. Schofer, Chair, 847-491-3257. E-mail: j-schofer@nwu.edu. Application contact: Liz Inouye, Secretary, 847-491-3257. Fax: 847-491-4011. E-mail: eel@nwu.edu.

Oregon State University, Graduate School, College of Engineering, Department of Nuclear Engineering, Interdisciplinary Program in Radiation Health Physics, Corvallis, OR 97331. Awards MS. Part-time programs available. Faculty: 5 full-time (1 woman), 4 part-time (0 women). Students: 12 full-time (2 women); includes 1 minority (Asian American), 2 international. Average age 30. 7 applicants, 57% accepted. In 1997, 8 degrees awarded (33% entered university research/teaching, 67% found other work related to degree). *Degree requirements:* Thesis, minimum GPA of 3.0 required, foreign language not required. *Entrance requirements:* GRE General Test, TOEFL (minimum score 500), minimum GPA of 3.0 in last 90 hours. Application deadline: 6/15 (rolling processing). Application fee: $50. *Tuition:* $6207 per year full-time, $810 per quarter (minimum) part-time for state residents; $10,551 per year full-time, $1293 per quarter (minimum) part-time for nonresidents. *Financial aid:* In 1997–98, 6 students received aid, including 5 research assistantships (2 to first-year students), 1 teaching assistantship (to a first-year student); fellowships, institutionally sponsored loans also available. Aid available to part-time students. Financial aid application deadline: 2/1. *Faculty research:* Radioactive material transport, research reactor health physics, radiation instrumentation, radiation shielding, environmental monitoring. • Dr. Jack F. Higginbotham, Program Coordinator, 541-737-7046. Fax: 541-737-0480. E-mail: nuc_engr@ne.orst.edu.

Purdue University, Graduate School and School of Pharmacy and Pharmacal Sciences, School of Health Sciences, Program in Health Physics, West Lafayette, IN 47907. Awards MS, PhD, MS/PhD. *Degree requirements:* For master's, thesis optional, foreign language not required; for doctorate, 1 foreign language (computer language can substitute), dissertation. *Entrance requirements:* GRE General Test, minimum B average. Application deadline: rolling. Application fee: $30. Electronic applications accepted. *Tuition:* $3500 per year full-time, $126 per credit hour part-time for state residents; $11,720 per year full-time, $387 per credit hour part-time for nonresidents. *Financial aid:* Fellowships, research assistantships, teaching assistantships available. Aid available to part-time students. Financial aid applicants required to submit FAFSA. *Faculty research:* Radiation dosimetry, radon emanation rates, radioactive waste management. • Dr. P. L. Ziemer, Head, School of Health Sciences, 765-494-1435. Application contact: Dr. Robert Landolt, Graduate Chairperson, 765-494-1440.

See in-depth description on page 1511.

San Diego State University, College of Sciences, Department of Physics, Program in Radiological Health Physics, San Diego, CA 92182. Awards MS. Students: 7 full-time (1 woman), 3 part-time (0 women); includes 2 minority (1 Asian American, 1 Hispanic), 1 international. Average age 29. In 1997, 4 degrees awarded. *Degree requirements:* Oral or written exam required, thesis optional, foreign language not required. *Entrance requirements:* GRE General Test (minimum combined score of 950), TOEFL (minimum score 550). Application deadline: 6/1 (priority date; rolling processing; 12/1 for spring admission). Application fee: $55. *Expenses:* Tuition $0 for state residents; $246 per unit for nonresidents. Fees $1932 per year full-time, $1266 per year part-time. *Financial aid:* Career-related internships or fieldwork available. *Faculty research:* Computational radiological physics, medical physics. • Application contact: Patrick Papin, Graduate Adviser, 619-594-6154. Fax: 619-594-5485. E-mail: ppapin@sciences.sdsu.edu.

Texas A&M University, College of Engineering, Department of Nuclear Engineering, Program in Health Physics/Radiological Health, College Station, TX 77843. Offers health physics (MS), industrial hygiene (MS), safety engineering (MS). Students: 8 full-time (3 women), 11 part-time (2 women); includes 6 minority (3 Asian Americans, 3 Hispanics), 5 international. Average age 28. 234 applicants, 53% accepted. In 1997, 8 degrees awarded. *Degree requirements:* Thesis or alternative required, foreign language not required. *Entrance requirements:* GRE General Test, TOEFL. Application fee: $35 ($75 for international students). *Financial aid:* Fellowships, research assistantships, teaching assistantships available. • Application contact: Dr. Yassin A. Hassan, Graduate Coordinator, 409-845-7090.

Announcement: Facilities: 1-MW Triga reactor with pulsing capabilities and associated laboratories, AGN-201M reactor, subcritical facility, nuclear measurement labs, radiochemistry labs, charged-particle accelerators, 3-GeV cyclotron, 2-phase flow research laboratories. Research areas: reactor safety, aerosols, thermal hydraulics, fusion reactor technology, advanced nuclear reactors, space reactors, zero gravity 2-phase flow, laser flow visualization, numerical methods, radiation dosimetry, nuclear fuels/materials, neutron transmutation doping, ion-beam–solid interactions, waste management.

University of Alberta, Faculties of Medicine and Oral Health Sciences and Graduate Studies and Research, Graduate Programs in Medicine, Department of Radiology and Diagnostic Imaging, Edmonton, AB T6G 2E1, Canada. Offers programs in medical sciences (PhD), radiology and diagnostic imaging (M Sc). Faculty: 2 full-time. Students: 6; includes 1 minority (Asian American), 2 international. Average age 25. 50 applicants, 4% accepted. In 1997, 1 master's, 1 doctorate awarded. Terminal master's awarded for partial completion of doctoral program. *Degree requirements:* Thesis/dissertation required, foreign language not required. *Average time to degree:* master's–3 years full-time; doctorate–3 years full-time. *Entrance requirements:* For master's, minimum GPA of 6.5 on a 9.0 scale. Application deadline: 7/1 (priority date). Application fee: $60. *Financial aid:* In 1997–98, 2 students received aid, including 1 fellowship (to a first-year student) totaling $12,000; career-related internships or fieldwork also available. Financial aid application deadline: 3/31. *Faculty research:* Spectroscopic attenuation correction, nuclear medicine technology, monoclonal antibody labelling, bone mineral analysis using ultrasound, diagnostic imaging. Total annual research expenditures: $1.2 million. • Dr. A. J. B. McEwan, Chair, 403-492-6907. E-mail: smcewan@raddi.uah.ualberta.ca. Application contact: Dr. L. J. Filipow, Graduate Coordinator, 403-492-4094. Fax: 403-492-6176. E-mail: filipow@raddi.uah.ualberta.ca.

University of Cincinnati, College of Engineering, Department of Mechanical, Industrial and Nuclear Engineering, Program in Health Physics, Cincinnati, OH 45221. Awards MS, PhD. Students: 4 full-time (0 women), 1 (woman) part-time; includes 2 minority (1 African American, 1 Asian American). *Degree requirements:* For master's, computer language, thesis or alternative required, foreign language not required; for doctorate, computer language, dissertation. *Entrance requirements:* GRE General Test, TOEFL (minimum score 550). Application deadline: 2/1 (priority date). Application fee: $40. *Tuition:* $7228 per year full-time, $185 per credit hour part-time for state residents; $13,812 per year full-time, $352 per credit hour part-time for nonresidents. *Financial aid:* Fellowships, graduate assistantships, full tuition waivers available. Aid available to part-time students. Financial aid application deadline: 2/1. • Application contact: John Valentine, Graduate Program Director, 513-556-2482. Fax: 513-556-3390. E-mail: john.valentine@uc.edu.

University of Cincinnati, College of Medicine, Graduate Programs in Medicine, Department of Radiological Sciences, Cincinnati, OH 45267. Awards MS. Faculty: 6 full-time. Students: 5 full-time (1 woman), 1 part-time (0 women); includes 1 minority (African American). 9 applicants, 22% accepted. In 1997, 3 degrees awarded. *Degree requirements:* Thesis required, foreign language not required. *Average time to degree:* master's–1.9 years full-time. *Entrance requirements:* GRE General Test. Application deadline: 2/1 (priority date; rolling processing). Application fee: $30. *Tuition:* $7228 per year full-time, $185 per credit hour part-time for state residents; $13,812 per year full-time, $352 per credit hour part-time for nonresidents. *Financial aid:* Graduate assistantships, full tuition waivers available. Financial aid application deadline: 5/1. • Robert R. Lukin, Director, 513-558-4396. Fax: 513-558-4867. E-mail: robert.lukin@uc.edu. Application contact: Howard Elson, Graduate Program Director, 513-558-9092. Fax: 513-558-4007. E-mail: howard.elson@uc.edu.

University of Florida, College of Engineering, Department of Nuclear and Radiological Engineering, Gainesville, FL 32611. Offerings include health physics (MS, PhD). Department faculty: 31. *Degree requirements:* For doctorate, 1 foreign language, dissertation. *Entrance requirements:* For doctorate, GRE General Test, TOEFL, minimum GPA of 3.0. Application deadline: 6/5 (priority date; rolling processing). Application fee: $20. *Tuition:* $138 per credit hour for state residents; $481 per credit hour for nonresidents. • James S. Tulenko, Chair, 352-392-1401. Fax: 352-392-3380. E-mail: tulenko@sun-robot.nuceng.ufl.edu.

University of Illinois at Urbana–Champaign, College of Engineering, Department of Nuclear Engineering, Urbana, IL 61801. Offerings include health physics (MS, PhD). Department faculty: 14 full-time (0 women). *Degree requirements:* Thesis/dissertation required, foreign language not required. *Application deadline:* rolling. *Application fee:* $40 ($50 for international students). • Barclay G. Jones, Head, 217-333-3535.

University of Kentucky, Graduate School Programs from the College of Allied Health, Program in Radiation Sciences, Lexington, KY 40536-0080. Offers health physics (MSHP), radiological medical physics (MSRMP). Offered in cooperation with Graduate Programs in Medicine. Part-time programs available. Faculty: 6 full-time (0 women). Students: 8 full-time (3 women), 2 part-time (1 woman); includes 1 minority (African American), 2 international. 9 applicants, 78% accepted. In 1997, 9 degrees awarded. *Degree requirements:* Comprehensive exam required, foreign language and thesis not required. *Entrance requirements:* GRE General Test, minimum undergraduate GPA of 2.5. Application deadline: 7/19 (rolling processing). Application fee: $30 ($35 for international students). *Financial aid:* In 1997–98, 4 fellowships were awarded; teaching assistantships, Federal Work-Study, institutionally sponsored loans also available. Aid available to part-time students. *Faculty research:* Dosimetry, manpower studies, diagnostic imaging physics, shielding. • Dr. Ralph Christensen, Director of Graduate Studies, 606-323-1100 Ext. 248. Fax: 606-258-1058. E-mail: rechri1@pop.uky.edu. Application contact: Dr. Constance L. Wood, Associate Dean, 606-257-4613. Fax: 606-323-1928.

University of Massachusetts Lowell, College of Arts and Sciences, Department of Physics and Applied Physics, Program in Radiological Sciences and Protection, 1 University Avenue, Lowell, MA 01854-2881. Awards MS, PhD. Faculty: 4 full-time (0 women). Students: 20 full-time (9 women), 21 part-time (4 women); includes 2 minority (1 Asian American, 1 Hispanic), 7 international. 31 applicants, 77% accepted. In 1997, 16 master's awarded. Terminal master's awarded for partial completion of doctoral program. *Degree requirements:* For master's, 1 foreign language, thesis; for doctorate, 2 foreign languages (computer language can substitute for one), dissertation. *Entrance requirements:* GRE General Test. Application deadline: 4/1 (priority date; rolling processing; 10/1 for spring admission). Application fee: $20 ($35 for international students). *Tuition:* $4867 per year full-time, $618 per semester (minimum) part-time for state residents; $10,276 per year full-time, $1294 per semester (minimum) part-time for nonresidents. *Financial aid:* In 1997–98, 7 fellowships, 7 teaching assistantships were awarded; research assistantships and career-related internships or fieldwork also available. Financial aid application deadline: 4/1. • Dr. Clayton French, Coordinator, 978-934-3286. E-mail: clayton_french@woods.uml.edu.

University of Miami, School of Medicine and Graduate School, Graduate Programs in Medicine, Department of Radiology, Coral Gables, FL 33124. Awards MS. Faculty: 13 full-time (2 women), 2 part-time (0 women). Students: 0. *Degree requirements:* Thesis optional, foreign language not required. *Entrance requirements:* GRE General Test (minimum combined score of 1000), TOEFL (minimum score 550). Application deadline: 7/1 (priority date; rolling processing; 11/1 for spring admission). Application fee: $35. *Expenses:* Tuition $815 per credit hour. Fees $174 per year. *Faculty research:* Magnetic resource spectroscopy of central nervous system, spinal cord imaging, spinal cord angiography. • Dr. Robert M. Quencer, Chairman. Application contact: Dr. Pradip Pattany, Director of Graduate Program, 305-243-3920. Fax: 305-243-4673. E-mail: fred@cmiami.med.miami.edu.

University of Michigan, College of Engineering, Department of Nuclear Engineering and Radiological Sciences, Ann Arbor, MI 48109. Offerings include radiological health engineering (M Eng). Department faculty: 15 full-time, 3 part-time. *Average time to degree:* master's–1.5 years full-time; doctorate–3.5 years full-time. *Application deadline:* 2/1 (priority date; rolling processing). *Application fee:* $55. Electronic applications accepted. • Dr. Gary S. Was, Chair, 734-764-4260. Application contact: Helen Lum, Administrative Associate II, 734-764-4260. Fax: 734-763-7863. E-mail: helenlum@engin.umich.edu.

University of Missouri–Columbia, College of Engineering, Nuclear Engineering Program, Columbia, MO 65211. Offerings include nuclear engineering (MS, PhD), with options in health physics (MS), medical physics (MS), nuclear engineering (MS). Program faculty: 5 full-time (0 women), 1 part-time (0 women). *Degree requirements:* Research project. *Entrance requirements:* GRE General Test, TOEFL. Application deadline: 3/15. Application fee: $25 ($50 for international students). *Expenses:* Tuition $3240 per year full-time, $180 per credit hour part-time for state residents; $9108 per year full-time, $506 per credit hour part-time for nonresidents. Fees $55 per year full-time. • Dr. Tushar Ghosh, Director of Graduate Studies, 573-882-8201.

University of Nevada, Las Vegas, College of Health Sciences, Department of Health Physics, Las Vegas, NV 89154-9900. Awards MS. Faculty: 3 full-time (0 women). Students: 4 full-time (2 women), 4 part-time (0 women); includes 1 minority (Asian American), 1 international. 0 applicants. *Degree requirements:* Comprehensive exam required, thesis optional, foreign language not required. *Entrance requirements:* GRE General Test (minimum combined score of 1000), minimum GPA of 2.75. Application deadline: 6/15 (priority date; rolling processing; 11/15 for spring admission). Application fee: $40 ($95 for international students). *Expenses:* Tuition $93 per credit for state residents; $93 per credit full-time, $190 per credit part-time for nonresidents. Fees $5570 per year full-time for nonresidents. *Financial aid:* In 1997–98, 1 research assistantship was awarded; teaching assistantships also available. Financial aid application deadline: 3/1. • Dr. Mark Rudin, Chair, 702-895-3299. Application contact: Graduate College Admissions Evaluator, 702-895-3320.

University of Oklahoma Health Sciences Center, College of Medicine and Graduate College, Graduate Programs in Medicine, Department of Radiological Sciences, Oklahoma City, OK 73190. Offerings include medical radiation physics (MS, PhD), with options in diagnostic radiology, nuclear medicine, radiation therapy, ultrasound. Terminal master's awarded for partial completion of doctoral program. Department faculty: 9 full-time (0 women), 3 part-time (1 woman). *Degree requirements:* Thesis/dissertation required, foreign language not required. *Entrance requirements:* GRE General Test (minimum score 600 on each section), TOEFL (minimum score 550). Application deadline: 7/1 (priority date; rolling processing; 12/1 for spring admission). Application fee: $25 ($50 for international students). • Dr. Bob Eaton, Head, 405-271-5132. Application contact: Dr. Robert Y. L. Chu, Graduate Liaison, 405-271-5641.

University of Pittsburgh, Graduate School of Public Health, Department of Environmental and Occupational Health, Program in Radiation Health, Pittsburgh, PA 15260. Awards Certificate. *Application deadline:* rolling. *Application fee:* $50 ($60 for international students). *Expenses:* Tuition $9402 per year full-time, $388 per credit part-time for state residents; $19,372 per year full-time, $799 per credit part-time for nonresidents. Fees $480 per year full-time, $180 per year part-time. • Dr. Herbert S. Rosenkranz, Chairman, Department of Environmental and Occupational Health, 412-967-6510. Application contact: Joanne E. Buffo, Student Affairs Administrator, 412-967-6521. Fax: 412-624-1020. E-mail: stdntaff@vms.cis.pitt.edu.

The University of Texas at Arlington, College of Science, Department of Physics, Program in Radiological Physics, Arlington, TX 76019-0407. Awards MS. Offered jointly with the University of Texas Southwestern Medical Center at Dallas. Students: 0. 0 applicants. *Degree requirements:* Comprehensive exam required, foreign language and thesis not required. *Entrance requirements:* GRE General Test, TOEFL. Application deadline: rolling. Application fee: $25 ($50 for international students). *Tuition:* $3206 per year full-time, $468 per semester (minimum) part-time for state residents; $8612 per year full-time, $1137 per semester (minimum) part-time for nonresidents. • Application contact: Dr. John L. Fry, Graduate Adviser, 817-272-2461.

The University of Texas Health Science Center at San Antonio, Graduate School of Biomedical Sciences, Radiological Sciences Graduate Program, San Antonio, TX 78284-6200. Awards MS, PhD. *Application deadline:* 4/1 (rolling processing). *Application fee:* $10.

Directories: Health Physics/Radiological Health; Medical Physics

Wayne State University, School of Medicine and Graduate School, Graduate Programs in Medicine, Department of Radiation Oncology, Detroit, MI 48202. Offers programs in medical physics (PhD), radiological physics (MS). Offered jointly with the Department of Radiology. Part-time and evening/weekend programs available. Faculty: 33. Students: 4 full-time (0 women), 6 part-time (2 women); includes 2 minority (both African Americans), 6 international. Average age 28. 5 applicants, 80% accepted. In 1997, 6 master's, 1 doctorate awarded. Terminal master's awarded for partial completion of doctoral program. *Degree requirements:* For master's, thesis, essay, exit exam; for doctorate, dissertation, qualifying exam. *Entrance requirements:* For master's, GRE General Test (minimum combined score of 1815 on three sections; average 1850), BS in physics or related area; for doctorate, GRE General Test (score in 70th percentile or higher), GRE Subject Test (score in 70th percentile or higher), BS in physics or related area. Application deadline: 1/15 (1/15 for spring admission). Application fee: $20 ($30 for international students). *Expenses:* Tuition $163 per credit hour for state residents; $355 per credit hour for nonresidents. Fees $498 per year full-time, $114 per semester (minimum) part-time. *Financial aid:* In 1997–98, 6 students received aid, including 2 fellowships averaging $1,000 per month and totaling $24,000, 2 teaching assistantships averaging $1,000 per month and totaling $24,000; research assistantships and career-related internships or fieldwork also available. Aid available to part-time students. Financial aid application deadline: 1/15. *Faculty research:* Radiotherapy physics, hyperthermia, magnetic resonance imaging and spectroscopy, clinical ultrasound, x-ray physics. Total annual research expenditures: $320,000. • Dr. Arthur Porter, Chairperson, 313-745-2101. Application contact: Dr. Colin Orton, Graduate Committee Chair, 313-745-2486. Fax: 313-745-2314. E-mail: orton@kcl.wayne.edu.

Wayne State University, School of Medicine and Graduate School, Graduate Programs in Medicine, Department of Radiology, Detroit, MI 48202. Offers programs in medical physics (PhD), radiological physics (MS). Offered jointly with the Department of Radiation Oncology. Part-time and evening/weekend programs available. Faculty: 2. Students: 5 full-time (1 woman), 6 part-time (2 women). Average age 27. 6 applicants, 67% accepted. In 1997, 7 master's awarded. *Degree requirements:* For master's, essay, exam; for doctorate, dissertation. *Entrance requirements:* For master's, GRE General Test (score in 50th percentile or higher), BS in physics or related area; for doctorate, GRE. Application deadline: 4/1. Application fee: $20 ($30 for international students). *Expenses:* Tuition $163 per credit hour for state residents; $355 per credit hour for nonresidents. Fees $498 per year full-time, $114 per semester (minimum) part-time. *Financial aid:* Fellowships, research assistantships, teaching assistantships, and career-related internships or fieldwork available. Aid available to part-time students. Financial aid application deadline: 3/1. *Faculty research:* Radiotherapy and imaging physics, hyperthermia, magnetic resonance imaging and spectroscopy, clinical ultrasound, lasers in medicine. • Dr. George Kling, Chairperson, 313-745-3430. Application contact: Al Goldstein, Graduate Committee Chair, 313-745-3430.

Medical Physics

Allegheny University of the Health Sciences, School of Medicine, Biomedical Graduate Programs, Department of Radiation Oncology and Nuclear Medicine, Philadelphia, PA 19102-1192. Offerings include medical physics (MS, PhD). Terminal master's awarded for partial completion of doctoral program. Department faculty: 19 full-time (3 women). *Degree requirements:* For master's, thesis, comprehensive exam required, foreign language not required; for doctorate, 1 foreign language (computer language can substitute), dissertation, qualifying exam. *Entrance requirements:* For master's, GRE General Test (minimum combined score of 1410 on three sections), TOEFL, minimum GPA of 2.75; for doctorate, GRE General Test (minimum combined score of 1650 on three sections), TOEFL, minimum GPA of 3.0. Application deadline: 4/1 (rolling processing). Application fee: $50. *Expenses:* Tuition $10,950 per year. Fees $60 per year. • Dr. Fong Y. Tsai, Chairman, 215-762-8722. Application contact: Dr. Jacqueline Emrich, Program Director.

Columbia University, School of Public Health, Division of Environmental Health Sciences, Program in Medical Physics/Health Physics, New York, NY 10027. Offers public health (MPH, Dr PH), including health, medical physics. Offered jointly with the College of Physicians and Surgeons. Part-time programs available. Faculty: 10. *Degree requirements:* For doctorate, dissertation required, foreign language not required. *Entrance requirements:* For master's, GRE General Test, bachelor's degree in physics, engineering, or mathematics; for doctorate, GRE General Test, bachelor's degree in physics, engineering, or mathematics; MPH or equivalent (Dr PH). Application deadline: 4/10 (rolling processing; 11/15 for spring admission). Application fee: $60. *Tuition:* $22,320 per year full-time, $744 per credit part-time. *Financial aid:* Federal Work-Study and career-related internships or fieldwork available. Aid available to part-time students. Financial aid application deadline: 3/15; applicants required to submit FAFSA. *Faculty research:* Health effects of radiation and other physical agents. • Dr. Marco Zaider, Professor of Clinical Radiation Oncology and Public Health, 212-305-7387. Fax: 212-305-5935. E-mail: zaider@curaob.ccc.columbia.edu.

East Carolina University, College of Arts and Sciences, Department of Physics, Program in Medical Physics, Greenville, NC 27858-4353. Awards MS. *Degree requirements:* 1 foreign language (computer language can substitute), comprehensive exam required, thesis optional. *Entrance requirements:* GRE General Test, TOEFL. Application deadline: 6/1 (priority date; rolling processing; 10/15 for spring admission). Application fee: $40. *Tuition:* $1886 per year full-time, $472 per semester (minimum) part-time for state residents; $9156 per year full-time, $2289 per semester (minimum) part-time for nonresidents. *Financial aid:* Available to part-time students. Financial aid application deadline: 6/1. • Application contact: Dr. Xin-Hua Hu, Director of Graduate Studies, 252-328-1860. Fax: 252-328-6314. E-mail: hux@mail.ecu.edu.

Finch University of Health Sciences/The Chicago Medical School, Department of Medical Radiation Physics, North Chicago, IL 60064-3095. Awards MS, PhD. Faculty: 3 full-time, 5 part-time. Students: 26 full-time (5 women). Average age 23. In 1997, 18 master's, 1 doctorate awarded. Terminal master's awarded for partial completion of doctoral program. *Degree requirements:* For master's, computer language required, thesis not required; for doctorate, computer language, dissertation. *Entrance requirements:* For master's, GRE General Test, TOEFL; for doctorate, GRE General Test, TOEFL, MS in physics. Application deadline: 6/1 (priority date; rolling processing). Application fee: $25. *Tuition:* $20,058 per year (minimum). *Financial aid:* Career-related internships or fieldwork available. Financial aid application deadline: 8/19; applicants required to submit FAFSA. • Dr. John Levan, Chairman, 847-578-8318. Application contact: Dana Frederick, Admissions Officer, 847-578-3209.

Harvard University, Divisions of Health Sciences and Technology and Engineering and Applied Sciences and Department of Physics, Program in Medical Engineering/Medical Physics, Cambridge, MA 02138. Offers applied physics (PhD), engineering sciences (PhD), medical engineering/medical physics (Sc D), physics (PhD). Offered jointly with Massachusetts Institute of Technology. Students: 74 full-time (19 women); includes 17 minority (1 African American, 15 Asian Americans, 1 Hispanic), 21 international. 108 applicants, 12% accepted. In 1997, 15 degrees awarded. *Degree requirements:* Dissertation, oral and written qualifying exams required, foreign language not required. *Application deadline:* 1/15 (rolling processing). *Application fee:* $55. *Expenses:* Tuition $24,050 per year (minimum). Fees $645 per year. • Dr. Martha Gray, Director, 617-253-7470.

Illinois Institute of Technology, Armour College of Engineering and Sciences, Department of Biological, Chemical and Physical Sciences, Physics Division, Chicago, IL 60616-3793. Offerings include health/medical physics (MS, PhD). MS and PhD (health/medical physics) offered jointly with Finch University of Health Sciences/The Chicago Medical School. Terminal master's awarded for partial completion of doctoral program. Division faculty: 13 full-time (0 women), 2 part-time (0 women), 14 FTE. *Degree requirements:* For master's, thesis (for some programs), comprehensive exam required, foreign language not required; for doctorate, dissertation, qualifying comprehensive exam required, foreign language not required. *Entrance requirements:* GRE, TOEFL (minimum score 550). Application deadline: 7/1 (rolling processing; 11/1 for spring admission). Application fee: $30. Electronic applications accepted. *Expenses:* Tuition $17,250 per year full-time, $575 per credit hour part-time. Fees $60 per year full-time, $1.50 per credit hour part-time. • Application contact: Graduate College, 312-567-3024. Fax: 312-567-7517. E-mail: grad@minna.cas.iit.edu.

Massachusetts Institute of Technology, Whitaker College of Health Sciences and Technology, Division of Health Sciences and Technology, Medical Engineering/Medical Physics Program, Cambridge, MA 02139-4307. Offers medical engineering (PhD), medical engineering and medical physics (Sc D), medical physics (PhD). Offered jointly with Harvard University. Students: 74 full-time (19 women); includes 17 minority (1 African American, 15 Asian Americans, 1 Hispanic), 21 international. 108 applicants, 12% accepted. In 1997, 15 degrees awarded. *Degree requirements:* Dissertation, oral and written departmental qualifying exams required, foreign language not required. *Application deadline:* 1/15 (rolling processing). *Application fee:* $55. *Expenses:* Tuition $24,050 per year (minimum). Fees $645 per year. *Financial aid:* Fellowships, research assistantships, teaching assistantships available. Financial aid application deadline: 1/15. • Application contact: Dr. Martha L. Gray, Director of Admissions, 617-253-4378. E-mail: martha@rlf.mit.edu.

McGill University, Faculty of Graduate Studies and Research, Faculty of Medicine, Medical Radiation Physics Unit, Montréal, PQ H3A 2T5, Canada. Awards M Sc, PhD. Faculty: 16 full-time (3 women). Students: 33 full-time (5 women), 2 part-time (0 women); includes 6 international. Average age 25. 30 applicants, 50% accepted. In 1997, 9 master's awarded (45% found work related to degree, 55% continued full-time study); 1 doctorate awarded. *Degree requirements:* Thesis/dissertation. *Average time to degree:* master's–2.5 years full-time; doctorate–3.5 years full-time. *Entrance requirements:* For master's, TOEFL (minimum score 550), B Sc in physics, minimum GPA of 3.0. Application deadline: 3/1. Application fee: $60. *Expenses:* Tuition $1668 per year for Canadian residents; $8268 per year for nonresidents. Fees $828 per year for Canadian residents; $1216 per year for nonresidents. *Financial aid:* Research assistantships, teaching assistantships available. *Faculty research:* Radiation dosimetry, biodegradable polymers, stereotactic radiosurgery, brachytherapy, functional MR brain imaging. • E. B. Podgorsak, Director, 514-934-8052. Fax: 514-934-8229. E-mail: epodgorsak@medphys.mgh.mcgill.ca. Application contact: Margery Knewstubb, Graduate Secretary. E-mail: mak@medphys.mgh.mcgill.ca.

Oakland University, College of Arts and Sciences, Department of Physics, Rochester, MI 48309-4401. Offerings include medical physics (PhD). Department faculty: 11 full-time. *Degree requirements:* Dissertation. *Entrance requirements:* GRE Subject Test. Application deadline: 7/15 (3/15 for spring admission). Application fee: $30. *Expenses:* Tuition $3852 per year full-time, $214 per credit hour part-time for state residents; $8532 per year full-time, $474 per credit hour part-time for nonresidents. Fees $420 per year. • Dr. Beverly Berger, Chair, 248-370-3410. Application contact: Dr. Gopalan Srinivasan, Coordinator, 248-370-3416.

Purdue University, Graduate School and School of Pharmacy and Pharmacal Sciences, School of Health Sciences, Program in Medical Physics, West Lafayette, IN 47907. Awards MS, PhD. *Degree requirements:* For master's, thesis optional, foreign language not required; for doctorate, 1 foreign language (computer language can substitute), dissertation. *Entrance requirements:* GRE General Test, minimum B average. Application deadline: rolling. Application fee: $30. Electronic applications accepted. *Tuition:* $3500 per year full-time, $126 per credit hour part-time for state residents; $11,720 per year full-time, $387 per credit hour part-time for nonresidents. • Dr. P. L. Ziemer, Head, School of Health Sciences, 765-494-1435. Application contact: Dr. Robert Landolt, Graduate Chairperson, 765-494-1440.

See in-depth description on page 1511.

Rush University, Division of Medical Physics, Chicago, IL 60612-3832. Awards MS, PhD, MD/PhD. Faculty: 7 full-time (0 women), 5 part-time (0 women). Students: 8 full-time (0 women), 1 part-time (0 women); includes 4 international. 15 applicants, 13% accepted. In 1997, 1 doctorate awarded (100% entered university research/teaching). Terminal master's awarded for partial completion of doctoral program. *Degree requirements:* For master's, thesis, qualifying exam required, foreign language not required; for doctorate, dissertation, preliminary and qualifying exams required, foreign language not required. *Average time to degree:* doctorate–10 years part-time. *Entrance requirements:* For master's, GRE General Test (minimum combined score of 1500 on three sections), BS in physics or physical science; for doctorate, GRE General Test, GRE Subject Test, TOEFL (minimum score 550). Application deadline: 2/15 (priority date). Application fee: $25. *Tuition:* $8450 per year full-time, $370 per credit hour part-time for state residents; $8470 per year full-time, $370 per credit hour part-time for nonresidents. *Financial aid:* In 1997–98, 5 students received aid, including 1 research assistantship, 5 clinical assistantships; full tuition waivers, Federal Work-Study, institutionally sponsored loans also available. Financial aid application deadline: 2/15. *Faculty research:* Radiation therapy treatment planning, dosimetry, diagnostic radiology and nuclear imaging. • Dr. James Chu, Director, 312-942-5751. Application contact: Thyra Jackson, Coordinator of Admissions, 312-942-6247. Fax: 312-9422100. E-mail: tjackson@rushu.rush.edu.

University of Alberta, Faculty of Graduate Studies and Research, Department of Physics, Edmonton, AB T6G 2E1, Canada. Offerings include medical physics (M Sc, PhD). Department faculty: 33 full-time (0 women), 7 part-time (0 women). *Degree requirements:* Thesis/dissertation. *Average time to degree:* master's–2.2 years full-time; doctorate–4.5 years full-time. *Entrance requirements:* TOEFL (minimum score 550), minimum GPA of 7.0 on a 9.0 scale. Application deadline: 2/15 (priority date; rolling processing). Application fee: $45. *Expenses:* Tuition $390 per course for Canadian residents; $781 per course for nonresidents. Fees $500 per year full-time, $184 per year part-time. • Dr. John Beamish, Associate Chair, 403-492-3518. Application contact: Lynn Chandler, Department Office, 403-492-1072. Fax: 403-492-0714. E-mail: lynn@phys.ualberta.ca.

University of California, Los Angeles, School of Medicine and Graduate Division, Graduate Programs in Medicine, Program in Biomedical Physics, Los Angeles, CA 90095. Awards MS, PhD. Faculty: 17 (5 women). Students: 38 full-time (7 women); includes 11 minority (10 Asian Americans, 1 Hispanic), 5 international. 48 applicants, 15% accepted. *Degree requirements:* For master's, comprehensive exam or thesis required, foreign language not required; for doctorate, dissertation, oral and written qualifying exams required, foreign language not required. *Entrance requirements:* GRE General Test, TOEFL. Application fee: $40. *Expenses:* Tuition $0 for state residents; $9384 per year for nonresidents. Fees $4551 per year. *Financial aid:* In 1997–98, 37 students received aid, including fellowships totaling $143,782, research assistantships totaling $317,062, teaching assistantships totaling $9,098, scholarships totaling $22,182;

full and partial tuition waivers, Federal Work-Study, institutionally sponsored loans also available. Financial aid application deadline: 3/1. • Dr. Edward Hoffman, Chair, 310-825-7811. Application contact: Departmental Office, 310-825-7811. E-mail: lbrookes@mail.rad.ucla.edu.

University of Chicago, Division of the Biological Sciences, Graduate Program in Medical Physics, Chicago, IL 60637-1513. Awards SM, PhD. Faculty: 18 full-time (2 women), 7 part-time (0 women). Students: 19 full-time (5 women); includes 2 minority (both Asian Americans). Average age 26. 18 applicants, 17% accepted. In 1997, 5 doctorates awarded (100% entered university research/teaching). Terminal master's awarded for partial completion of doctoral program. *Degree requirements:* For master's, qualifying exam, thesis or 7 reports required, foreign language not required; for doctorate, dissertation, comprehensive and qualifying exams. *Average time to degree:* doctorate–6 years full-time. *Entrance requirements:* GRE General Test, GRE Subject Test (physics), TOEFL (minimum score 550). Application deadline: 1/15 (priority date). Application fee: $55. *Expenses:* Tuition $23,616 per year full-time, $3258 per course part-time. Fees $378 per year. *Financial aid:* Fellowships, research assistantships, institutionally sponsored loans available. Financial aid application deadline: 6/1. *Faculty research:* Medical imaging, radiation therapy, computer vision. Total annual research expenditures: $5 million. • Dr. Kunio Doi, Director, 773-702-6954. E-mail: k-doi@uchicago.edu. Application contact: Evelyn Ruzich, Student Affairs Administrator, 773-702-6154. Fax: 773-702-0371. E-mail: e-ruzich@uchicago.edu.

See in-depth description on page 1283.

University of Colorado at Boulder, College of Arts and Sciences, Department of Physics, Boulder, CO 80309. Offerings include medical physics (PhD). Terminal master's awarded for partial completion of doctoral program. Department faculty: 35 full-time (2 women). *Degree requirements:* Dissertation, comprehensive exam. *Entrance requirements:* GRE General Test, GRE Subject Test, TOEFL (minimum score 575). Application deadline: 1/31 (priority date; rolling processing; 11/1 for spring admission). Application fee: $40 ($60 for international students). *Expenses:* Tuition $3170 per year full-time, $531 per semester (minimum) part-time for state residents; $14,652 per year full-time, $2442 per semester (minimum) part-time for nonresidents. Fees $667 per year full-time, $130 per semester (minimum) part-time. • John Cumalat, Chair, 303-492-6952. Application contact: Susan Thompson, Graduate Secretary, 303-492-6954. Fax: 303-492-3352. E-mail: susan.thompson@colorado.edu.

University of Colorado Health Sciences Center, Programs in Biological and Medical Sciences, Program in Medical Physics, Denver, CO 80262. Awards MS. In 1997, 8 degrees awarded. *Degree requirements:* Comprehensive final exam, project required, foreign language and thesis not required. *Entrance requirements:* GRE General Test, minimum GPA of 2.75, previous course work in mathematics and physics. Application deadline: 3/1. Application fee: $30. *Financial aid:* Application deadline 3/1. • Dr. Timothy Johnson, Director, 303-315-8065.

University of Florida, College of Engineering, Department of Nuclear and Radiological Engineering, Gainesville, FL 32611. Offerings include medical physics (MS, PhD). Department faculty: 31. *Degree requirements:* For doctorate, 1 foreign language, dissertation. *Entrance requirements:* For doctorate, GRE General Test, TOEFL, minimum GPA of 3.0. Application deadline: 6/5 (priority date; rolling processing). Application fee: $20. *Tuition:* $138 per credit hour for state residents; $481 per credit hour for nonresidents. • James S. Tulenko, Chair, 352-392-1401. Fax: 352-392-3380. E-mail: tulenko@sun-robot.nuceng.ufl.edu.

University of Kentucky, Graduate School Programs from the College of Allied Health, Program in Radiation Sciences, Lexington, KY 40536-0080. Offers health physics (MSHP), radiological medical physics (MSRMP). Offered in cooperation with Graduate Programs in Medicine. Part-time programs available. Faculty: 6 full-time (0 women). Students: 8 full-time (3 women), 2 part-time (1 woman); includes 1 minority (African American), 2 international. 9 applicants, 78% accepted. In 1997, 9 degrees awarded. *Degree requirements:* Comprehensive exam required, foreign language and thesis not required. *Entrance requirements:* GRE General Test, minimum undergraduate GPA of 2.5. Application deadline: 7/19 (rolling processing). Application fee: $30 ($35 for international students). *Financial aid:* In 1997–98, 4 fellowships were awarded; teaching assistantships, Federal Work-Study, institutionally sponsored loans also available. Aid available to part-time students. *Faculty research:* Dosimetry, manpower studies, diagnostic imaging physics, shielding. • Dr. Ralph Christensen, Director of Graduate Studies, 606-323-1100 Ext. 248. Fax: 606-258-1058. E-mail: rechri1@pop.uky.edu. Application contact: Dr. Constance L. Wood, Associate Dean, 606-257-4613. Fax: 606-323-1928.

Announcement: Two-year MS in radiological medical physics emphasizing clinical and laboratory training in therapy and imaging physics. Equipment includes modern linacs, treatment planning systems, Gammaknife, and MRI, SPECT, CT, and oncology imaging systems. Campus visits welcomed. For information and application materials, contact 606-323-1100 Ext. 248, e-mail at rcchri1@pop.uky.edu, or visit the Web site at http://radweb.hosp.uky.edu

University of Massachusetts Medical Center at Worcester, Graduate School of Biomedical Sciences, Program in Biomedical Engineering and Medical Physics, Worcester, MA 01655-0115. Awards PhD. Offered jointly with Worcester Polytechnic Institute. Faculty: 20 full-time (1 woman). Students: 1 (woman) full-time. *Degree requirements:* Dissertation required, foreign language not required. *Entrance requirements:* GRE General Test, GRE Subject Test. Application deadline: 2/1 (priority date; rolling processing). Application fee: $25 ($50 for international students). *Financial aid:* Graduate assistantships available. • Dr. Peter Grigg, Director, 508-856-2457.

University of Minnesota, Twin Cities Campus, Program in Biophysical Sciences and Medical Physics, Minneapolis, MN 55455-0213. Awards MS, PhD. *Degree requirements:* For master's, research paper, oral exam required, thesis optional, foreign language not required; for doctorate, 1 foreign language, computer language, dissertation, oral/written preliminary exam, oral final exam. *Faculty research:* Theoretical biophysics, radiological physics, cellular and molecular biophysics.

Announcement: This interdisciplinary program provides research training and experience in biophysics, medical imaging, magnetic resonance imaging and spectroscopy, radiobiology, and radiation therapy physics. Thirty-one faculty members from 11 departments provide diverse opportunities for multidisciplinary research. A strong undergraduate physics background is desirable. Limited financial aid is available.

See in-depth description on page 1285.

University of Missouri–Columbia, College of Engineering, Nuclear Engineering Program, Columbia, MO 65211. Offerings include nuclear engineering (MS, PhD), with options in health physics (MS), medical physics (MS), nuclear engineering (MS). Program faculty: 5 full-time (0 women), 1 part-time (0 women). *Degree requirements:* Research project. *Entrance requirements:* GRE General Test, TOEFL. Application deadline: 3/15. Application fee: $25 ($50 for international students). *Expenses:* Tuition $3240 per year full-time, $180 per credit hour part-time for state residents; $9108 per year full-time, $506 per credit hour part-time for nonresidents. Fees $55 per year full-time. • Dr. Tushar Ghosh, Director of Graduate Studies, 573-882-8201.

University of Oklahoma Health Sciences Center, College of Medicine and Graduate College, Graduate Programs in Medicine, Department of Radiological Sciences, Oklahoma City, OK 73190. Offers program in medical radiation physics (MS, PhD), including diagnostic radiology, nuclear medicine, radiation therapy, ultrasound. Part-time programs available. Faculty: 9 full-time (0 women), 3 part-time (1 woman). Students: 2 full-time (both women), 5 part-time (1 woman); includes 1 minority (Asian American), 2 international. Average age 33. 14 applicants, 50% accepted. In 1997, 1 master's awarded (100% found work related to degree). Terminal master's awarded for partial completion of doctoral program. *Degree requirements:* Thesis/dissertation required, foreign language not required. *Entrance requirements:* GRE General Test (minimum score 600 on each section), TOEFL (minimum score 550). Application deadline: 7/1 (priority date; rolling processing; 12/1 for spring admission). Application fee: $25 ($50 for international students). *Financial aid:* Fellowships, research assistantships, institutionally sponsored loans, and career-related internships or fieldwork available. Aid available to part-time students. Financial aid application deadline: 7/1. *Faculty research:* Monte Carlo applications in radiation therapy, observer performed studies in diagnostic radiology, error analysis in gated cardiac nuclear medicine studies, nuclear medicine absorbed fraction determinations. • Dr. Bob Eaton, Head, 405-271-5132. Application contact: Dr. Robert Y. L. Chu, Graduate Liaison, 405-271-5641.

The University of Texas–Houston Health Science Center, Graduate School of Biomedical Sciences, Program in Medical Physics, Houston, TX 77225-0036. Awards MS, PhD, MD/PhD. Faculty: 20 full-time (2 women). Students: 8 full-time (1 woman). Average age 27. 37 applicants, 24% accepted. In 1997, 3 master's awarded. *Degree requirements:* Thesis/dissertation required, foreign language not required. *Entrance requirements:* GRE General Test, TOEFL (minimum score 550), TWE (minimum score 4). Application deadline: 1/15 (priority date; rolling processing; 11/1 for spring admission). Application fee: $10. Electronic applications accepted. *Financial aid:* Fellowships, research assistantships, institutionally sponsored loans available. Financial aid application deadline: 1/15. *Faculty research:* Three dimensional and conformal radiotherapy, stereotaxic radiosurgery, image processing and PACS, magnetic resonance imaging. Total annual research expenditures: $2 million. • Dr. Kenneth R. Hogstrom, Director, 713-792-3216. Fax: 713-794-5272. E-mail: khogstro@notes.mdacc.tmc.edu. Application contact: Anne Baronitis, Director of Admissions, 713-500-9860. Fax: 713-500-9877. E-mail: abaron@gsbs.gs.uth.tmc.edu.

University of Wisconsin–Madison, Medical School and Graduate School, Graduate Programs in Medicine, Department of Medical Physics, Madison, WI 53706. Offers programs in health physics (MS), medical physics (MS, PhD). Faculty: 18. Students: 41 full-time (8 women), 4 part-time (0 women); includes 5 international. In 1997, 10 master's, 10 doctorates awarded. *Entrance requirements:* GRE General Test, GRE Subject Test (physics), TOEFL. Application fee: $45. *Tuition:* $4928 per year full-time, $926 per semester (minimum) part-time for state residents; $15,190 per year full-time, $2849 per semester (minimum) part-time for nonresidents. *Financial aid:* In 1997–98, 41 students received aid, including 5 fellowships (2 to first-year students), 24 research assistantships (5 to first-year students), 6 teaching assistantships (2 to first-year students); traineeships also available. • Dr. Paul De Luca, Chair, 608-262-2171. E-mail: pmd@cema.medphysics.wisc.edu. Application contact: Kathy McSherry, Graduate Coordinator, 608-265-6504. Fax: 608-262-2413. E-mail: mcsherry@cema.medphysics.wisc.edu.

Wayne State University, School of Medicine and Graduate School, Graduate Programs in Medicine, Department of Radiation Oncology, Detroit, MI 48202. Offerings include medical physics (PhD). Offered jointly with the Department of Radiology. Terminal master's awarded for partial completion of doctoral program. Department faculty: 33. *Degree requirements:* Dissertation, qualifying exam. *Entrance requirements:* GRE General Test (score in 70th percentile or higher), GRE Subject Test (score in 70th percentile or higher), BS in physics or related area. Application deadline: 1/15 (1/15 for spring admission). Application fee: $20 ($30 for international students). *Expenses:* Tuition $163 per credit hour for state residents; $355 per credit hour for nonresidents. Fees $498 per year full-time, $114 per semester (minimum) part-time. • Dr. Arthur Porter, Chairperson, 313-745-2101. Application contact: Dr. Colin Orton, Graduate Committee Chair, 313-745-2486. Fax: 313-745-2314. E-mail: orton@kcl.wayne.edu.

Wayne State University, School of Medicine and Graduate School, Graduate Programs in Medicine, Department of Radiology, Detroit, MI 48202. Offerings include medical physics (PhD). Offered jointly with the Department of Radiation Oncology. Department faculty: 2. *Degree requirements:* Dissertation. *Entrance requirements:* GRE. Application deadline: 4/1. Application fee: $20 ($30 for international students). *Expenses:* Tuition $163 per credit hour for state residents; $355 per credit hour for nonresidents. Fees $498 per year full-time, $114 per semester (minimum) part-time. • Dr. George Kling, Chairperson, 313-745-3430. Application contact: Al Goldstein, Graduate Committee Chair, 313-745-3430.

Wright State University, College of Science and Mathematics, Department of Physics, Program in Physics, Dayton, OH 45435. Offerings include medical physics (MS). *Degree requirements:* Computer language, thesis required, foreign language not required. *Entrance requirements:* TOEFL (minimum score 550). Application deadline: 3/1 (priority date; rolling processing). Application fee: $25. *Tuition:* $5109 per year full-time, $161 per credit hour part-time for state residents; $9039 per year full-time, $282 per credit hour part-time for nonresidents. • Dr. Gust Bambakidis, Chair, Department of Physics, 937-775-2954. Fax: 937-775-3301.

MASSACHUSETTS INSTITUTE OF TECHNOLOGY

Department of Nuclear Engineering and the Harvard-MIT Division of Health Sciences and Technology Radiological Sciences Doctoral Program

Program of Study

The Radiological Sciences Doctoral Program has been developed to provide students with advanced training in the diverse applications of radiation in medicine and to expand the frontiers of research in this area. Radiological sciences encompasses both ionizing radiation and more recent technologies employing other forms of radiation for diagnosis and therapy, such as nuclear magnetic resonance and ultrasound. The curriculum in radiological sciences entails four to five years of study and leads to the Ph.D. degree in radiological sciences, awarded jointly by MIT's Department of Nuclear Engineering and the Harvard-MIT Division of Health Sciences and Technology.

Students in radiological sciences may pursue their academic and research objectives in the areas of medical imaging, radiation biophysics, computer applications to diagnostic technology, and radiation therapy. Although most core radiological sciences subjects are taken at MIT, students may conduct research at MIT, Harvard, or affiliated Boston-area hospitals, depending on their area of specialization.

The curriculum in radiological sciences is structured to include advanced course work in radiation physics and biophysics, medical imaging, signal processing, and biomedical anatomy and physiology. These courses are taken during the first two years in preparation for the doctoral examination. After successful completion of the doctoral examination, thesis research is conducted under the supervision of faculty members and scientists in associated institutions. Doctoral research usually requires two to three years to complete and culminates in a thesis defense before the program faculty.

Research Facilities

Support for research is extensive and includes laboratories at MIT, Harvard Medical School, and Harvard-affiliated hospitals. Among the facilities at MIT are the Whitaker College Biomedical Imaging and Computation Laboratory; medical imaging centers, including NMR and MRI laboratories in the National Magnet Laboratory; the Spatial NMR Laboratory; the MIT Nuclear Reactor Laboratory; and a variety of state-of-the-art computers. Laboratories in affiliated institutions support many areas of medical imaging and therapy.

Financial Aid

Financial aid to graduate students in the program is available through fellowships, scholarships, teaching and research assistantships, and other sources. In addition, there are Institute and department funds from the U.S. Department of Energy, other governmental sources, and other agencies. In general, students receive awards that are sufficient to cover the costs of tuition as well as living expenses. Potential applicants should explore all other sources of support, such as direct NIH and NSF grants and funding from industry.

Cost of Study

Tuition for the 1998–99 academic year is $24,050; the accident and hospital insurance fee is $636.

Living and Housing Costs

In 1998–99, living expenses, including room and meal costs and miscellaneous expenses, average $1200 per month for single graduate students and slightly more for married students. Single students may live in Ashdown House, Tang Hall, or Edgerton House. Married graduate students live either in on-campus apartments or houses in the surrounding communities.

Student Group

The Radiological Sciences Doctoral Program currently has about 25 students; enrollment is anticipated to reach a level of 30 students. A number of undergraduate students are in related programs.

Location

MIT is located in Cambridge, across the Charles River from Boston. The campus provides excellent facilities for many indoor and outdoor sports, including sailing, swimming, and crew. The Cambridge-Boston area is the home of a number of leading universities such as Harvard, Boston University, Boston College, and Northeastern University. Cultural and educational opportunities abound in the area. Performances of the Boston Symphony Orchestra, Boston Pops, and Boston Opera Company are held only a short distance from the MIT campus.

The Institute

MIT, founded in 1861 as a privately endowed institution, has grown to be one of the foremost institutes of technology in the world. About 9,000 students are enrolled, half of whom are in the graduate school.

The Department of Nuclear Engineering covers many areas of application of nuclear physics to science and engineering, including medical applications. The Whitaker College was established to serve as a focus for the growing interest at MIT in biology and medicine. Although the College has a strong interest in the neurosciences, it is developing a broad program of research and teaching in all biological and medical areas.

Applying

To be considered for admission, students must have completed a baccalaureate degree in physical science or engineering. Additional preparation in physics, mathematics, computer science, biology, and biochemistry is highly recommended. The GRE General Test is required. Students from non-English-speaking countries must demonstrate proficiency in English by earning a TOEFL score of at least 577.

Students who are admitted with a master's degree must, as a minimum, complete the radiological sciences subject requirements during the initial phase of the program.

Students may apply to the program through the MIT Department of Nuclear Engineering and the Harvard-MIT Division of Health Sciences and Technology, specifying the radiological sciences joint program. Applications may be obtained from the MIT Office of Admissions. The application deadline is January 15. Requests for support should be indicated on the application.

Correspondence and Information

For information:

Radiological Sciences Graduate Program
c/o Nuclear Engineering Graduate Office
Room 24-102
Massachusetts Institute of Technology
77 Massachusetts Avenue
Cambridge, Massachusetts 02139

Telephone: 617-253-3814
E-mail: cegan@mit.edu

For applications:

Office of Admissions
Room 3-103
Massachusetts Institute of Technology
77 Massachusetts Avenue
Cambridge, Massachusetts 02139

Massachusetts Institute of Technology

THE FACULTY AND THEIR RESEARCH

David G. Cory, Associate Professor, Department of Nuclear Engineering; Ph.D., Case Western Reserve, 1987. NMR imaging and spectroscopy, new methodology and applications of NMR techniques for the study of spatial properties of matter.

Bruce R. Rosen, Visiting Associate Professor, Department of Nuclear Engineering and Division of Health Sciences and Technology; M.D., Hahnemann, 1982; Ph.D., MIT, 1984. Magnetic resonance imaging (MRI), including functional imaging of the brain and heart; chemical shift spectroscopy and imaging.

Jacquelyn C. Yanch, Associate Professor, Department of Nuclear Engineering and Whitaker College; Ph.D., London, 1988. Nuclear medical imaging, computational modeling in both therapy and image restoration, radiation health physics, and neutron dosimetry.

In addition, other faculty members of the Department of Nuclear Engineering and of other departments participate in this program on a part-time basis.

THE UNIVERSITY OF CHICAGO

Pritzker School of Medicine
Division of the Biological Sciences
Graduate Program in Medical Physics

Program of Study

The Department of Radiology and the Department of Radiation and Cellular Oncology offer a joint program leading to an M.S. or a Ph.D. degree in medical physics. These training programs prepare graduates for research careers in academic institutions, national laboratories, hospitals, and private industry. The first year of study is devoted to course work in the areas of basic interactions of radiation with matter, physics of radiation therapy, nuclear medicine, diagnostic radiology, and health physics. During that year, students are also introduced to research methods. At the end of the first year, qualifying examinations are given. Second-year courses include elective subjects and research courses. At the end of the second year, comprehensive examinations are given for Ph.D. candidates. Thesis research completes the requirements for the advanced degree. Students are encouraged and are given support to present their results at national meetings. The M.S. degree is only granted as a terminal degree or as a transitional degree en route to the Ph.D. Two years of residency are required, during which students may elect specialized training directed toward either research or clinical-support applications of physics in radiology or radiation oncology.

Research Facilities

As leading research facilities, the Departments of Radiology and of Radiation and Cellular Oncology are equipped for state-of-the-art research in medical physics. Advanced imaging equipment in the Department of Radiology includes CT scanners (including spiral units), magnetic resonance imagers, a computed-radiography system, a PET scanner, and advanced nuclear-medicine imaging systems. The Department of Radiation and Cellular Oncology operates ten linear accelerators, multi-leaf collimators, and an electronic portal imager. The varied and numerous computers (DEC, Sun, SGI, and IBM) in the departments are linked with a high-speed network. There are also several specialized image processing computers, such as a PIXAR, a Pixel Machine, an SGI Onyx, and virtual reality devices such as an Immersa Desk.

Financial Aid

Most graduate students in the department receive full support and tuition remission from various faculty research grants and University funds. This financial aid is available to candidates on a competitive basis. Stipends for 1998–99 are approximately $17,000; these stipends also cover tuition and health fees. In some cases, support is restricted to citizens and permanent residents of the United States.

Cost of Study

In 1998–99, full-time tuition is approximately $32,000. Students are charged full tuition for three quarters. Usually, tuition is waived for students who have reached the master's degree level if a proper arrangement for a research assistantship is established. Additional mandatory fees of approximately $400 per quarter include health insurance and activities fees.

Living and Housing Costs

Living expenses for a single student are approximately $11,000 per year. Housing information can be obtained through the Graduate Student Assignment Office, the University of Chicago, 824 East 58th Street, Chicago, Illinois 60637.

Student Group

In spring 1998, there were 20 graduate students (5 women and 15 men) in the program. All received financial assistance. After completion of study, many graduates join academic institutions, hospitals, and private industry. Three new graduate students were accepted for admission with financial aid for fall 1997.

Student Outcomes

Since 1992, there have been 16 doctoral graduates from the programs. Eleven of the graduates have academic positions at institutions such as the Universities of Chicago, California at San Francisco, and Michigan; MIT; and Stanford. Four of these involve a combination of clinical service and research, while the other seven are pure academic positions. Two graduates are working in industry with medical imaging companies.

Location

The University of Chicago is located in an urban setting in Hyde Park, a culturally rich and ethnically diverse neighborhood adjacent to Lake Michigan, seven miles south of downtown Chicago. The city has numerous theaters, museums, and restaurants that are easily accessible by public transportation. The University of Chicago operates a shuttle service on campus.

The University

Since its inception in 1892, the University of Chicago has been one of the premier educational institutions in the world. The Pritzker School of Medicine is part of the Division of the Biological Sciences, which offers opportunities for interdisciplinary research and collaboration between the basic sciences and clinical staff members. As a result, the University of Chicago is recognized internationally for its innovative and advanced research in the life sciences.

Applying

Application forms may be obtained from the address listed below. The application form, all undergraduate and graduate school transcripts (official copies), and three letters of recommendation must be submitted by the second week of January for admission in the following autumn. Students are also required to provide official reports of scores on the GRE General Test and the Subject Test in physics. International students whose native language is not English are required to submit an official report of a TOEFL score that is no more than five years old. A minimum score of 550 is required to be considered for admission. The program encourages applications from women and minority students. While the program grants both M.S. and Ph.D. degrees, the training is designed for individuals desiring a Ph.D. in medical physics. As a result, students seeking only an M.S. degree are discouraged from applying.

Correspondence and Information

Kunio Doi, Ph.D.
Director, Graduate Program in Medical Physics
The University of Chicago
5841 South Maryland Avenue, MC-2026
Chicago, Illinois 60637
Telephone: 773-702-6154
Fax: 773-702-0371
E-mail: k-doi@uchicago.edu

The University of Chicago

THE FACULTY AND THEIR RESEARCH

S. G. Armato, Instructor; Ph.D., Chicago, 1997.
R. N. Beck, Professor; B.S., Chicago, 1955.
F. M. Behlen, Assistant Professor; Ph.D., Chicago, 1980.
C. T. Chen, Associate Professor; Ph.D., Chicago, 1986.
G. T. Y. Chen, Professor; Ph.D., Brown, 1972.
K. Doi, Professor; Ph.D., Waseda (Japan), 1969.
M. L. Giger, Associate Professor; Ph.D., Chicago, 1985.
H. Halpern, Associate Professor; Ph.D., Wisconsin, 1976; M.D., Miami (Florida), 1980.
K. R. Hoffmann, Associate Professor; Ph.D., Brandeis, 1984.
Y. Jiang, Instructor; Ph.D., Chicago, 1997.
L. S. Johnson, Instructor; Ph.D., MIT, 1994.
G. S. Karczmar, Associate Professor; Ph.D., Berkeley, 1984.
F. T. Kuchnir, Associate Professor; Ph.D., Illinois, 1965.
D. N. Levin, Professor; Ph.D., Harvard, 1970; M.D., Chicago, 1981.
Y. Lu, Assistant Professor; Ph.D., Ohio State, 1990.
C. E. Metz, Professor; Ph.D., Pennsylvania, 1969.
L. Myrianthopoulos, Assistant Professor; Ph.D., Chicago, 1978.
R. M. Nishikawa, Assistant Professor; Ph.D., Toronto, 1990.
B. C. O'Brien-Penney, Associate Professor; Ph.D., Worcester Polytechnic, 1979.
X. Pan, Assistant Professor; Ph.D., Chicago, 1991.
C. A. Pelizzari, Associate Professor; Ph.D., Michigan, 1974.
C. S. Reft, Assistant Professor; Ph.D., Pittsburgh, 1973.
J. Roeske, Assistant Professor; Ph.D., Chicago, 1992.
R. A. Schmidt, Associate Professor; M.D., Chicago, 1982.
L. Skaggs, Emeritus Professor; Ph.D., Chicago, 1939.
C. J. Vyborny, Associate Professor; Ph.D., 1976, M.D., 1980, Chicago.
H. Yoshida, Assistant Professor; Ph.D., Tokyo, 1989.

CURRENT RESEARCH PROJECTS

X-ray Imaging

Image feature analysis (using artificial neural networks, wavelet transforms, etc.) and computer-aided diagnosis in digital radiography:
- chest radiography: detection of lung nodules and pneumothoraces, classification of normal and abnormal lungs with interstitial disease, quantification of abnormal heart size, image registration for temporal subtraction, correlation of chest radiographs with radioisotope images, detection of asymmetries and CP angle blunting
- mammography: detection of breast masses and clustered microcalcifications, differential diagnosis of breast lesions, assessment of cancer risk
- angiography: automated vessel size measurements in DSA and coronary arteriography, automated tracking and characterization of the vessel tree in DSA and coronary arteriography, determination and rendering of 3-D vascular structures from two or more views
- CT angiography: segmentation, description and rendering of aorta and its branches
- musculoskeletal radiology: quantification of osteoporosis and bone strength
- CT: detection of lung nodules, temporal subtraction, 3-D visualization

Clinical impact of digital radiography:
- effect of image compression on detection of abnormalities in chest radiographs
- development and evaluation of picture archiving and communications systems (PACS)
- improvements in diagnostic image quality using density correction and unsharp masking

Investigation of basic imaging properties of screen-film systems, film digitizers, and digital radiography systems

Magnetic Resonance Imaging (MRI)

Functional MR imaging of the brain
Analysis of dynamic MR images of brain and cerebrospinal fluid pulsations
Development and application of MR for measurement of tumor blood flow, metabolism, and response to therapy
Computer-assisted electroencephalography using 3-D multimodality images of the brain
New algorithms for constrained MR image acquisition and reconstruction
Development of new targeted MR contrast agents
Computerized analyses of lesions in MR images of the breast

Nuclear Medicine

Instrumentation: development of advanced PET and miniature gamma camera
Physics: investigation of photon attenuation, scattered radiation, spatial blurring, and noise properties in PET and SPECT
Image reconstruction and processing: development of novel methods for reconstruction of 2-D and 3-D tomographic images
development of statistical methods for image reconstruction and processing
development of methods for 3-D image visualization
Radiopharmaceuticals: PET radiopharmaceuticals for the study of flow, metabolism, and neurotransmitter-receptor systems
SPECT radiopharmaceuticals for neurotransmitter-receptor systems
Functional imaging: drug interactions with enzyme receptors and neuroreceptors
neurotransmitter-receptor interactions
brain mapping

Ultrasound Imaging

Ultrasound imaging physics
Tomographic ultrasound imaging
Ultrasound image processing and analysis

Radiation Oncology

Development of advanced computerized treatment-planning tools
Computer techniques for multimodality image correlation and volume visualization
Case-based reasoning in radiotherapy planning
Dosimetry of photons, electrons, and radioactive isotopes and for radioimmunotherapy
Imaging and oxymetry of tumor physiology with low-frequency electron paramagnetic resonance (EPR)
Dosimetry for radioimmunotherapy
Free radical toxicity via spin trapping and genetic engineering
Applications of computer vision in radiotherapy treatment delivery
High-quality volume rendering from 3-D medical image datasets
Biological modeling of tumor control and normal tissue complication
Intensity-modulated radiotherapy
Monte Carlo simulation of radiation transport

Objective Evaluation of Diagnostic Performance

Development and applications of receiver operating characteristic (ROC) analysis
Methodology for optimal utilization of diagnostic tests

UNIVERSITY OF MINNESOTA

UNIVERSITY OF MINNESOTA

Graduate Program in Biophysical Sciences and Medical Physics

Programs of Study

The Graduate Program in Biophysical Sciences and Medical Physics is interdisciplinary, with faculty members having primary appointments in departments that include radiology, physics, engineering, computer science, physiology, dentistry, genetics, and biochemistry. Programs lead to the M.S. and Ph.D. degrees. Students concentrate in research areas that include molecular biophysics, medical imaging, magnetic resonance imaging and spectroscopy, radiobiology, radiation therapy physics, and mathematical biophysics and computation. A limited number of students prepare for employment as hospital-based medical physicists through a program that includes opportunities for course work, laboratories, and directed study to provide experience in areas such as purchase specification, acceptance testing, quality assurance, and radiation safety. The majority of students prepare for research careers in the basic sciences.

Candidates for the M.S. degree may pursue either thesis or nonthesis plans of study. The thesis plan is considered suitable for students with full-time employment if their thesis can be related to their work assignments. The nonthesis plan is more suitable for students planning to work in government or hospital settings where technical knowledge is more germane than research experience. Students in the nonthesis plan perform a research project under the direction of a faculty member and present the work to their faculty committee in an oral exam.

Candidates for the Ph.D. take preliminary written exams at the end of the first year of study or as soon as possible after completing the core course sequence—topics in physics for medicine and biology. An oral preliminary exam focuses on the plan for thesis research and the student's grasp of related information and is taken by the fall of the third year of full-time registration or its equivalent.

The program reports to the Basic Science Policy and Review Council of the Graduate School and receives a small amount of funding in the form of block grants from the Graduate School. However, graduate student support is almost exclusively obtained through grants and contracts held by the faculty members.

Research Facilities

Students have access to personal computers and workstations (SGI, SUN, DEC, Kontron) as well as the facilities of the Minnesota Supercomputer Institute. Separate research facilities exist for the Center for Magnetic Resonance Research, the Center for Immunotherapy, Radiobiology, Radiation Therapy, Diagnostic Radiology, and the School of Dentistry.

Financial Aid

The majority of students receive some sort of financial aid, typically a 50 percent time research assistantship with full tuition waiver. The sources of funds are NIH awards, departmental grants and contracts, and graduate school block grants. For details on need-based awards, students should contact the Office of Student Financial Aid, 210 Fraser Hall, University of Minnesota, 106 Pleasant Street, SE, Minneapolis, Minnesota 55455-0422 (telephone: 612-624-1665). Applications as early as January for the following fall quarter are encouraged.

Cost of Study

Quarterly tuition for full-time students (7–15 quarter credits) is $1700 for residents and $3300 for nonresidents in 1998–99. On average, tuition rises about 5 percent annually and is usually determined in July. A quarterly student services fee of $160 covers basic outpatient health care, student organization fees, and the student newspaper.

Living and Housing Costs

The cost of living is comparable to that of other Midwestern urban areas. The University offers dormitory housing for single and married graduate students. Information about housing in the Twin Cities area may be obtained from University of Minnesota Housing Services, Comstock Hall-East, 210 Delaware Street Southeast, Minneapolis, Minnesota 55455-0307.

Student Group

In 1998–99, there are 24 graduate students in the program—20 doctoral students and 4 master's candidates. Women comprise 23 percent of the current student population, international students, 31 percent. Four to 6 new students are admitted each year. The total Graduate School enrollment consists of 9,000 graduate students in 170 major fields.

Location

The Graduate School of the University of Minnesota is located on the banks of the Mississippi River in the Twin Cities of Minneapolis (the largest city in Minnesota) and St. Paul (the state capital). The Twin Cities area, with a population of 2.3 million, provides an unusual combination of the personal and the cosmopolitan. It is home to the Tyrone Guthrie Theatre and the St. Paul Chamber orchestra, as well as a rich array of locally cherished theater, music, and arts organizations. It is also a thriving center of commerce, with major corporate headquarters in electronics and computers, food processing, retailing, and transportation. The area consistently ranks near the top on quality-of-life and residential satisfaction ratings, thanks in part to an extensive park system that covers 12,500 acres and includes more than 200 lakes. Residents may also drive a few hours north to the Boundary Waters Canoe Area Wilderness, one of the most unsullied wilderness areas in the nation.

The University and The Program

The University of Minnesota awarded its first Ph.D. in 1988. The biophysical sciences program, dating back to the early 1950s, is administered by the Graduate School of the University of Minnesota but involves collaborative teaching and research efforts from the University Hospital and Medical School. The program offers opportunities for interdisciplinary research and collaboration among clinical faculty members from the University Hospital, basic sciences departments, engineering, statistics, and computer science. Faculty members and students interact in University Hospital and Medical School and Graduate School projects. The University Hospital and Medical School is internationally known for programs in bone marrow transplant, artificial organ development, and functional neurological imaging.

Applying

Applicants are required to possess strong backgrounds in physics and math with some course work in chemistry, biology or anatomy, and physiology. The applicant's GPA should exceed 3.0. GRE General Test scores and three letters of recommendation are required. International applicants must receive TOEFL scores above 550. Applicants are encouraged to submit materials before March 1. Earlier applications are considered.

Correspondence and Information

E. Russell Ritenour
University of Minnesota School of Medicine
Department of Radiology, Box 292 UMHC
420 Delaware Street Southeast
Minneapolis, Minnesota 55455

Telephone: 612-626-0131
Fax: 612-626-4102
E-mail: riter@rad-gate.drad.umn.edu

University of Minnesota

THE FACULTY AND THEIR RESEARCH

Dean E. Abrahamson, M.D., Ph.D. Analysis of energy policy, environmental implications of various technologies, climate change, occupational health.
Dwight L. Anderson, Ph.D. Structure and assembly of bacterial viruses.
Vincent Barnett, Ph.D. Correlation of mechanical response and molecular dynamics of muscle proteins, studies of the biochemical and physiological interaction of myosin and actin and the elasticity of titin. Techniques include electron paramagnetic resonance spectroscopy (EPR), measurement of muscle stiffness, and force generation.
Victor A. Bloomfield, Ph.D. Ion-induced transition in DNA, hydrodynamic theory, quasi-electric light scattering, dynamics of concentrated biopolymer solutions.
Bianca M. Conti-Fine, M.D. Neurobiochemistry and neuropharmacology.
Ralph DeLong, Ph.D. Robotics as applied to reproducing mandibular movement, three-dimensional digitalization of anatomic structures and computer graphics, wear of dental materials and oral anatomic structures, computer modeling of the masticatory system.
William H. Douglas, Ph.D. Robotics as applied to reproducing mandibular movement, three-dimensional digitalization of anatomic structures and computer graphics, wear of dental materials and oral anatomic structures, computer modeling of masticatory system.
Stanley M. Finkelstein, Ph.D. Hemodynamic impedance properties of peripheral vasculature, respiratory and cardiovascular simulation, monitoring of long-term care for chronic diseases, biomedical signal processing.
John E. Foker, M.D., Ph.D. Myocardial metabolism.
Michael G. Garwood, Ph.D. Magnetic resonance imaging and spectroscopy methods, the design of improved radio frequency pulses, pulse sequences to localize spectroscopic signals to specific tissues or organs of interest, fast imaging, application of these methods to investigate brain tumor metabolism in animals and humans.
Richard A. Geise, Ph.D. Radiation dose determination, particularly bone dosimetry from high-dose interventional procedures; evaluation of radiologic equipment performance, particularly mammography and computer tomography systems; dosimetry and performance evaluation of shock wave lithotripters, particularly by measurement of cavitation.
Bruce J. Gerbi, Ph.D. Ionization chamber response characteristics in high-energy proton and electron beams, electron contamination determination in high-energy proton beams, deposition of radiation dose for obliquely incident photon beams.
Rolf Gruetter, Ph.D. Study of biochemical pathways and physiology using NMR spectroscopy (MRI); interdisciplinary approaches to study regulation of metabolism in health and disease, such as combining MRS with PET, MRS with functional anatomic imaging, and MRS with molecular biology/gene therapy.
Bruce Hammer, Ph.D. Nuclear magnetic resonance imaging and spectroscopy.
Bruce E. Hasselquiest, Ph.D. Computer modeling of imaging in nuclear medicine, including the effects of attenuation and scatter in single photon emission computer tomography; simultaneous dual isotope imaging in nuclear medicine.
Patrick Higgins, Ph.D., Radiation dosimetry, basic mechanisms of radiation interaction with matter using measurements and computer models, quantification of dose distributions in tissues against biological or clinical endpoints, thermal dosimetry and heat transport modeling for hyperthermia.
Russell K. Hobbie, Ph.D. Radiological physics.
James Holte, Ph.D. Technologies that support the delivery of high-quality health care at lower costs, including instrumentation, biological system modeling, and the creation of readily searchable database structures; flow of information, material, and people in the medical enterprise, using sensors, signal analysis, information capture, and storage (real-time measurement and long-term archiving).
Xiaoping Hu, Ph.D. Acquisition, reconstruction, processing, and visualization of medical imaging data and application of medical imaging techniques, with emphasis on magnetic resonance imaging and spectroscopy.
Michael Jerosch-Herold, Ph.D. Magnetic resonance imaging methods for functional evaluation of tissues or organs, in particular the heart; magnetic resonance perfusion imaging; tracer kinetic modeling for quantification of tissue blood flow; image processing for evaluation of heart function; application of MRI methods to experimental models of coronary artery disease.
Faiz M. Khan, Ph.D. Dorimetry of electron and photon beams radiotherapy treatment planning, portal electron imaging.
Seong-Gi Kim, Ph.D.
Jeih-San Liow, Ph.D. Optimization of data acquisition, image reconstruction/processing, compartmental modeling and statistical analysis techniques for quantitative positron emission tomography (PET).
Merle K. Loken, M.D., Ph.D. Development and evaluation of radiopharmaceutical and instrumentation (including use of computers) for establishing new procedures in the practice of nuclear medicine.
Rex E. Lovrien, Ph.D. Enzymology, calorimetry, thermochemistry of biochemical reactions, development of new legends and methods for separations, protection, confirmation control, cocrystallization of proteins.
Robert Margolis, Ph.D. Biophysics of the middle ear: measuring the impedance in the ear canal of human and animal subjects with normal auditory function and with various ear pathologies; inner ear electrophysiology: auditory-evoked potentials that originate in the inner ear and auditory neural pathway.
Scott M. O'Grady, M.D. Mechanisms and regulation of electrolyte transport across epithelial tissues, role of electroneutral cotransport and exchange mechanisms in vectorial salt and water transport in epithelia, regulation of cell volume and intracellular pH.
Richard E. Poppele, Ph.D. Mammalian muscle spindles, mechanical properties of muscle, the nature of the transduction mechanism, encoding of muscle receptor information within the central nervous system.
Kelly Rehm, Ph.D. Digital image processing and evaluation; analysis and visualization of 3-dimensional brain image volumes acquired by PET, MRI, and fMRI.
Stephen J. Riederer, Ph.D. The physics and engineering of diagnostic medical imaging systems, especially magnetic resonance imaging (MRI). High-speed MR image acquisition and reconstruction, vascular MRI and MR angiography, compensation for motion during MR image acquisition.
E. Russell Ritenour, Ph.D. Performance evaluation of radiologic imaging systems, specific absorption rate calculation for magnetic resonance imaging (MRI), ultrasound-induced mutation in mammalian cells, ultrasound dosimetry.
Andreas Rosenberg, Ph.D. Dynamics of protein structure, studies by methods such as fluorescence quenching and isotope exchange kinetics, structure-function relationships in red-cell cytoskeleton, studies by partial reconstruction of membrane structures.
Chang W. Song, Ph.D. Biological effects of radiation, vascular function in tumors and normal tissues, radiosensitization and radioprotection, microelectrode method to measure tissue pH and p02, ion transport through the cell membrane.
Arthur E. Stillman, M.D., Ph.D. Proton magnetic resonance spectroscopy of the brain for following treatment effects, functional magnetic resonance imaging of the brain for therapy planning.
Stephen Strother, Ph.D. Medical imaging, particularly positron emission tomography (PET) and magnetic resonance imaging (MRI), with emphasis on parameter estimation, optimal model selection, and artificial neural networks for functional activation studies of the brain.
David D. Thomas, Ph.D. Spectroscopic studies of molecular dynamics in energy transducing ATPase of muscle; myosin, actin, muscle fibers, sarcoplasmic reticulum, calcium transport, ATPase; electron paramagnetic resonance (EPR), phosphorescence, fluorescence.
Kamil Ugurbil, Ph.D. Development of magnetic resonance methods and their applications in vivo for obtaining physiological, functional, anatomical, and biochemical information noninvasively; functional mapping in the human brain; cardiac bioenergetics.
Warren J. Warwick, Ph.D. New models of the function of the lung, noninvasive measurements of physiologic functions, integration of computer technology in the practice of medicine, mucous transport in the airway, water balance in the lungs, total body water and body composition analysis, allometric effects seen in physiologic tests during growth.
Clare K. Woodward, Ph.D. Protein structure and dynamics, protein folding, construction and physical-chemical characterization of protein variants produced by site-directed mutagenesis, NMR, hydrogen exchange, colorimetry, protein engineering, computer-based molecular modeling of proteins, molecular graphics of proteins.

Section 28
Health Services

This section contains directories of institutions offering graduate work in health services management and hospital administration and health services research, followed by in-depth entries submitted by institutions that chose to prepare detailed program descriptions. Additional information about programs listed in the directories but not augmented by an in-depth entry may be obtained by writing directly to the dean of a graduate school or chair of a department at the address given in the directory.

For programs offering related work, see also in this book Allied Health, Business Administration and Management, Nursing, and Public Health.

CONTENTS

Program Directories

Announcements

Cross-Discipline Announcements

In-Depth Descriptions

See also:

Health Services Management and Hospital Administration

Arizona State University, College of Business, School of Health Administration and Policy, Tempe, AZ 85287. Awards MHSA, JD/MHSA, MBA/MHSA, MS/MHSA. Accredited by ACEHSA. MS/MHSA offered jointly with College of Nursing. Faculty: 5 full-time (1 woman). Students: 37 full-time (15 women); includes 5 minority (2 African Americans, 1 Asian American, 2 Hispanics), 1 international. Average age 27. 73 applicants, 77% accepted. In 1997, 22 degrees awarded. *Entrance requirements:* GMAT. Application fee: $45. *Expenses:* Tuition $2088 per year full-time, $110 per hour part-time for state residents; $9040 per year full-time, $377 per hour part-time for nonresidents. Fees $72 per year full-time, $18 per semester (minimum) part-time. *Faculty research:* Medical care delivery systems, institutional management concepts, consumer participation in hospitals via organizational development technologies. • Dr. Eugene Schneller, Director, 602-965-7778. E-mail: asuhap@asuvm.inre.asu.edu.

See in-depth description on page 1305.

Armstrong Atlantic State University, School of Graduate Studies, Program in Health Science, Major in Administration, Savannah, GA 31419-1997. Awards MHS. *Expenses:* Tuition $83 per quarter hour for state residents; $250 per quarter hour for nonresidents. Fees $145 per quarter hour for state residents; $228 per quarter hour for nonresidents. • Dr. James Streater, Department Head, Program in Health Science, 912-921-5480.

Baker College Center for Graduate Studies, Programs in Business, Flint, MI 48507. Offerings include health and recreation services management (MBA), health care management (EMBA, MBA). MBA (health and recreation services management) enrollment limited to international students. Faculty: 8 full-time, 73 part-time. *Application deadline:* rolling. *Application fee:* $25. *Tuition:* $215 per quarter hour. • Dr. Michael Heberling, President, 800-469-3165. Application contact: Chuck Gurden, Director of Admissions, 800-469-3165. Fax: 810-766-4399.

Baldwin-Wallace College, Division of Business Administration, Program in Executive Health Care Management, Berea, OH 44017-2088. Awards MBA. Faculty: 8 full-time (1 woman), 11 part-time (2 women). Students: 33 part-time (25 women); includes 1 African American. Average age 42. 37 applicants, 89% accepted. *Entrance requirements:* Interview, work experience. Application deadline: 8/1 (priority date). Application fee: $15. *Financial aid:* Available to part-time students. Financial aid applicants required to submit FAFSA. • Application contact: Linda Suffron, Graduate Coordinator, 440-826-2064. Fax: 440-826-3868. E-mail: lsuffron@bw.edu.

Barry University, School of Natural and Health Sciences, Program in Health Services Administration, Miami Shores, FL 33161-6695. Awards MS. Part-time and evening/weekend programs available. Postbaccalaureate distance learning degree programs offered (minimal on-campus study). Faculty: 7 full-time (3 women), 5 part-time (3 women), 8.75 FTE. Students: 3 full-time (1 woman), 47 part-time (28 women); includes 32 minority (13 African Americans, 2 Asian Americans, 17 Hispanics), 2 international. Average age 36. 12 applicants, 83% accepted. In 1997, 23 degrees awarded. *Degree requirements:* Minimum GPA of 3.0, oral or written comprehensive exam required, foreign language and thesis not required. *Entrance requirements:* GMAT or GRE General Test, 3 years of health field experience, minimum GPA of 3.0, 1 semester of course work in computer applications for business or equivalent. Application deadline: 8/1 (priority date; rolling processing). Application fee: $30. *Tuition:* $450 per credit (minimum). *Financial aid:* 24 students received aid; career-related internships or fieldwork available. Aid available to part-time students. Financial aid application deadline: 5/1; applicants required to submit FAFSA. *Faculty research:* Managed care, provider/patient relationships. • Dr. Dennis M. Toback, Director, 305-899-3237. E-mail: dtoback@mail.barry.edu. Application contact: Beatrice Aubery, Administrative Assistant, 305-899-3237. Fax: 305-899-3543. E-mail: health@mail.barry.edu.

Baruch College of the City University of New York, School of Business, Program in Health Care Administration, 17 Lexington Avenue, New York, NY 10010-5585. Awards MBA. Accredited by ACEHSA. Offered jointly with the Mount Sinai School of Medicine of the City University of New York. Part-time and evening/weekend programs available. Faculty: 4 full-time (1 woman), 2 part-time (1 woman). Students: 2 full-time (0 women), 89 part-time (37 women). In 1997, 31 degrees awarded. *Degree requirements:* Computer language required, foreign language and thesis not required. *Average time to degree:* master's–3 years part-time. *Entrance requirements:* GMAT, TOEFL (minimum score 570), TWE (minimum score 4.5). Application deadline: 6/15. Application fee: $40. *Expenses:* Tuition $4350 per year full-time, $185 per credit part-time for state residents; $7600 per year full-time, $320 per credit part-time for nonresidents. Fees $53 per year. *Financial aid:* Research assistantships, Federal Work-Study available. Aid available to part-time students. Financial aid application deadline: 5/3; applicants required to submit FAFSA. • Nancy Aries, Director, 212-802-6960. Application contact: Michael S. Wynne, Office of Graduate Admissions, 212-802-2330. Fax: 212-802-2335. E-mail: graduate_admissions@baruch.cuny.edu.

Baylor University, Academy of Health Sciences, Program in Health Care Administration, Fort Sam Houston, TX 78234. Awards MHA. Accredited by ACEHSA. Offered jointly with the U.S. Army. Students: 105 full-time (27 women); includes 12 minority (3 African Americans, 3 Asian Americans, 6 Hispanics). In 1997, 53 degrees awarded (100% found work related to degree). *Entrance requirements:* GRE General Test (minimum combined score of 1000), minimum GPA of 2.7. Application deadline: 6/15 (rolling processing). Application fee: $25. *Faculty research:* Data quality, public health policy, organizational behavior, AIDS. • Col. Clarence E. Maxwell, Director, 210-221-6935 Ext. 6443. Application contact: Maj. Lawrence M. Leahy, Program Administrator, 210-221-6443 Ext. 6136.

Bellevue University, Graduate School, Bellevue, NE 68005-3098. Offerings include health care administration (MS). Postbaccalaureate distance learning degree programs offered (no on-campus study). School faculty: 22 full-time (9 women), 13 part-time (5 women). *Average time to degree:* master's–2 years full-time, 3 years part-time. *Application deadline:* 7/15 (priority date; rolling processing; 11/15 for spring admission). *Application fee:* $50. • Dr. Douglas Frost, Dean, 402-293-2025. E-mail: frostd@scholars.bellevue.edu. Application contact: Elizabeth Wall, Director of Marketing and Enrollment, 402-293-3702. Fax: 402-293-3730. E-mail: eaw@scholars.bellevue.edu.

Boston University, School of Management, Program in Health-care Management, Boston, MA 02215. Awards MBA, JD/MBA, MBA/MA, MBA/MS, MBA/MPH, MBA/MSMIS. Accredited by ACEHSA. Part-time and evening/weekend programs available. Faculty: 7 full-time (2 women), 5 part-time (1 woman). Students: 41 full-time (16 women), 53 part-time (27 women); includes 18 minority (3 African Americans, 15 Asian Americans), 3 international. Average age 31. 93 applicants, 65% accepted. *Degree requirements:* Internship required, foreign language and thesis not required. *Entrance requirements:* GMAT (average 581). Application deadline: 4/15 (rolling processing; 11/15 for spring admission). Application fee: $50. Electronic applications accepted. *Expenses:* Tuition $22,830 per year full-time, $713 per credit part-time. Fees $218 per year full-time, $40 per semester part-time. *Financial aid:* Federal Work-Study, institutionally sponsored loans, and career-related internships or fieldwork available. Aid available to part-time students. Financial aid application deadline: 3/15; applicants required to submit FAFSA. *Faculty research:* Managed care, healthcare technology, physician behavior, effects of public policy on health care, health care finance. • Alan B. Cohen, Director, 617-353-2730. Application contact: Brigitte Bowen-Cordero, Assistant Director, 617-353-2730. Fax: 617-353-9498.

Boston University, School of Medicine, School of Public Health, Health Services Department, Boston, MA 02215. Offers program in health services (MPH). Students: 34 full-time (23 women), 68 part-time (52 women); includes 16 minority (3 African Americans, 10 Asian Americans, 3 Hispanics), 6 international. Average age 33. *Entrance requirements:* GRE General Test, TOEFL. Application deadline: 4/15 (rolling processing; 10/25 for spring admission). Application fee: $50. *Financial aid:* Federal Work-Study, institutionally sponsored loans, and career-related internships or fieldwork available. Aid available to part-time students. • Dr. Mark Prashker, Chairman, 617-638-5042. Application contact: Barbara St. Onge, Director of Admissions, 617-638-4640. Fax: 617-638-5299. E-mail: sphadmis@bu.edu.

See in-depth description on page 1487.

Brandeis University, The Heller Graduate School, Program in Management, Waltham, MA 02454-2728. Offerings include health care administration (MBA, MM). *Average time to degree:* master's–1 year full-time, 3 years part-time. *Entrance requirements:* GRE General Test or GMAT (MM), GRE General Test (MBA). Application fee: $50. *Expenses:* Tuition $22,390 per year full-time, $1940 per course part-time. Fees $45 per year (minimum). • Application contact: Karen Cooney, Admissions Officer, 781-736-3820. Fax: 781-736-3881. E-mail: cooney@binah.cc.brandeis.edu.

Brooklyn College of the City University of New York, Department of Health and Nutrition Science, Program in Community Health, 2900 Bedford Avenue, Brooklyn, NY 11210-2889. Offerings include health care management (MA, MPH), health care policy and administration (MA, MPH). *Application deadline:* 3/1 (11/1 for spring admission). *Application fee:* $40. *Expenses:* Tuition $4350 per year full-time, $185 per credit part-time for state residents; $7600 per year full-time, $320 per credit part-time for nonresidents. Fees $500 per year for state residents; $806 per year for nonresidents. • Dr. Erika Friedmann, Chairperson, Department of Health and Nutrition Science, 718-951-5026. E-mail: erikaf@brooklyn.cuny.edu. Application contact: Jerrold Mirotznik, Deputy Chairperson for Graduate Studies, 718-951-4197. Fax: 718-951-4670.

Bryant College, College of Business Administration, Programs in Health Services Management and Hospital Administration, Smithfield, RI 02917-1284. Awards MBA, CAGS. Part-time and evening/weekend programs available. Faculty: 4 part-time (1 woman). Students: 1 full-time (0 women), 27 part-time (15 women). Average age 38. 8 applicants, 88% accepted. In 1997, 6 master's awarded. *Entrance requirements:* For master's, GMAT (minimum score 480; average 520). Application deadline: 7/1 (priority date; rolling processing; 11/15 for spring admission). Application fee: $55 ($70 for international students). *Tuition:* $1025 per course. *Financial aid:* Research assistantships, graduate assistantships, and career-related internships or fieldwork available. Aid available to part-time students. Financial aid applicants required to submit FAFSA. • Cathy Lalli, Assistant Director of Graduate Programs, Graduate School, 401-232-6230. Fax: 401-232-6494. E-mail: gradprog@bryant.edu.

California College for Health Sciences, Program in Community Health Administration and Wellness Promotion, 222 West 24th Street, National City, CA 91950-6605. Awards MS. Part-time and evening/weekend programs available. Postbaccalaureate distance learning degree programs offered (no on-campus study). Faculty: 2 full-time (both women), 4 part-time (all women). Students: 788 part-time; includes 58 international. Average age 30. In 1997, 40 degrees awarded. *Degree requirements:* Fieldwork, internship required, foreign language and thesis not required. *Average time to degree:* master's–3 years part-time. *Entrance requirements:* Previous course work in psychology. Application deadline: rolling. Application fee: $35. *Expenses:* Tuition $335 per course. Fees $35 per course. • Lisa J. Davis, Dean of Student Affairs, 800-221-7374. E-mail: admissns@cchs.edu. Application contact: Admissions and Records Department, 619-477-4800. Fax: 619-477-2257. E-mail: admissns@cchs.edu.

California Lutheran University, School of Business Administration, Thousand Oaks, CA 91360-2787. Offerings include healthcare management (MBA). School faculty: 8 full-time (3 women), 29 part-time (4 women). *Entrance requirements:* GMAT, minimum GPA of 3.0, interview. Application deadline: 8/1 (priority date; rolling processing). Application fee: $50. *Tuition:* $395 per unit. • Dr. Ronald Hagler, Director, 805-493-3371.

California School of Professional Psychology–Los Angeles, Program in Behavioral Health Care Management, Alhambra, CA 91803-1360. Awards MBHCM. Students: 5 full-time (2 women); includes 2 minority (1 Asian American, 1 Hispanic), 1 international. Average age 28. 6 applicants, 83% accepted. *Application deadline:* 1/2. *Application fee:* $50. *Financial aid:* 5 students received aid. Financial aid application deadline: 2/15. • Dr. Michael Jospe, Coordinator of Program Development and Implementation, 626-284-2777. Application contact: Patricia J. Mullen, Vice President, Marketing and Enrollment, 800-457-1273. Fax: 415-931-8322. E-mail: admissions@mail.cspp.edu.

California State University, Bakersfield, School of Business and Public Administration, Department of Public Policy and Administration, Program in Health Care Management, 9001 Stockdale Highway, Bakersfield, CA 93311-1099. Awards MSA. Students: 5 full-time (3 women), 1 (woman) part-time; includes 3 minority (1 Asian American, 2 Hispanics), 1 international. 4 applicants, 100% accepted. *Entrance requirements:* GRE. Application deadline: rolling. Application fee: $55. *Expenses:* Tuition $0 for state residents; $246 per unit full-time, $164 per unit part-time for nonresidents. Fees $1584 per year full-time, $918 per year part-time. • Dr. Jack Goldsmith, Graduate Coordinator, 805-664-2323. Fax: 805-664-2438.

California State University, Chico, College of Behavioral and Social Sciences, Department of Political Science, Program in Public Administration, Option in Health Administration, Chico, CA 95929-0722. Awards MPA. *Degree requirements:* Thesis or alternative required, foreign language not required. *Application deadline:* 4/1 (rolling processing). *Application fee:* $55. *Expenses:* Tuition $0 for state residents; $246 per unit for nonresidents. Fees $2108 per year full-time, $1442 per year part-time. • Dr. Jon Ebeling, Graduate Coordinator, Program in Public Administration, 530-898-5301.

California State University, Fresno, Division of Graduate Studies, School of Health and Social Work, Department of Public Health, 5241 North Maple Avenue, Fresno, CA 93740. Offerings include health administration (MPH). Department faculty: 8 full-time (1 woman). *Degree requirements:* Thesis or alternative required, foreign language not required. *Average time to degree:* master's–3.5 years full-time. *Entrance requirements:* GRE General Test, TOEFL (minimum score 550), minimum GPA of 2.5. Application deadline: 3/1 (priority date; rolling processing). Application fee: $55. Electronic applications accepted. *Expenses:* Tuition $0 for state residents; $246 per unit for nonresidents. Fees $1872 per year full-time, $1206 per year part-time. • Dr. Sanford Brown, Graduate Program Coordinator, 209-278-4747. E-mail: sanford_brown@csufresno.edu.

California State University, Long Beach, College of Health and Human Services, Program in Health Care Administration, Long Beach, CA 90840-4902. Awards MS, Certificate. Students: 25 full-time (13 women), 34 part-time (19 women); includes 28 minority (6 African Americans, 18 Asian Americans, 3 Hispanics, 1 Native American), 1 international. Average age 36. 27 applicants, 70% accepted. In 1997, 18 master's awarded. *Degree requirements:* For master's, comprehensive exam or thesis required, foreign language not required. *Entrance requirements:* For master's, minimum GPA of 3.0. Application deadline: 8/1 (rolling processing; 12/1 for spring admission). Application fee: $55. *Expenses:* Tuition $0 for state residents; $246 per unit for nonresidents. Fees $1846 per year full-time, $1180 per year part-time. *Financial aid:* Application deadline 3/2. *Faculty research:* Long-term care, Immigration Reform Act and health care, physician reimbursement. • Dr. Harold Hunter, Director, 562-985-5304. Fax: 562-985-2384. E-mail: hhunter@csulb.edu.

Directory: Health Services Management and Hospital Administration

California State University, Los Angeles, School of Business and Economics, Program in Health Care Management, Los Angeles, CA 90032-8530. Awards MS. Part-time and evening/weekend programs available. Students: 10 full-time (5 women), 23 part-time (15 women). In 1997, 11 degrees awarded. *Degree requirements:* Comprehensive exam required, foreign language and thesis not required. *Entrance requirements:* GMAT, TOEFL (minimum score 550), minimum GPA of 2.5 during previous 2 years. Application deadline: 6/30 (rolling processing; 11/30 for spring admission). Application fee: $55. *Expenses:* Tuition $0 for state residents; $164 per unit for nonresidents. Fees $1763 per year full-time, $1097 per year part-time. *Financial aid:* 3 students received aid; Federal Work-Study and career-related internships or fieldwork available. Aid available to part-time students. Financial aid application deadline: 3/1. • Dr. Paul Washburn, Coordinator, 213-343-2890.

California State University, Northridge, College of Health and Human Development, Department of Health Sciences, Program in Health Administration, Northridge, CA 91330. Awards MS. 20 applicants, 85% accepted. *Degree requirements:* Thesis or alternative required, foreign language not required. *Entrance requirements:* TOEFL, GRE General Test or minimum GPA of 3.0. Application deadline: 11/30. Application fee: $55. *Expenses:* Tuition $0 for state residents; $246 per unit for nonresidents. Fees $1970 per year full-time, $1304 per year part-time. *Financial aid:* Application deadline 3/1. • Dr. Miriam Cotler, Chair, Department of Health Sciences, 818-677-3101. Application contact: Dr. Roberta Madison, Graduate Coordinator, 818-677-2015 Ext. 3101.

California State University, San Bernardino, Graduate Studies, School of Natural Sciences, Program in Health Services Administration, San Bernardino, CA 92407-2397. Awards MS. Faculty: 5 full-time (2 women). Students: 31 full-time (24 women), 18 part-time (14 women); includes 16 minority (10 African Americans, 2 Asian Americans, 3 Hispanics, 1 Native American), 3 international. 33 applicants, 94% accepted. In 1997, 11 degrees awarded. *Degree requirements:* Thesis or alternative required, foreign language not required. *Application deadline:* 8/31 (priority date). *Application fee:* $55. *Expenses:* Tuition $0 for state residents; $164 per unit for nonresidents. Fees $1922 per year full-time, $1256 per year part-time. *Financial aid:* Fellowships, research assistantships, teaching assistantships available. *Faculty research:* Smoking and health, oral hygiene, menopause, health services research. • Dr. Joseph Lovett, Coordinator, 909-880-5393.

Cardinal Stritch University, College of Business and Management, Programs in Management for Adults, Milwaukee, WI 53217-3985. Offerings include health services administration (MS). *Application deadline:* 4/1 (priority date; rolling processing). *Application fee:* $20. *Expenses:* Tuition $338 per credit. Fees $25 per semester. • Application contact: Shirley Hansen, Director of Marketing, 414-410-4315.

Carlow College, Division of Professional Leadership, Pittsburgh, PA 15213-3165. Offerings include health service education (MS). Division faculty: 2 full-time (both women), 16 part-time (14 women). *Degree requirements:* Thesis or alternative required, foreign language not required. *Average time to degree:* master's–2 years part-time. *Entrance requirements:* Interview, minimum GPA of 3.0. Application deadline: 6/1 (priority date; 11/1 for spring admission). Application fee: $35. • Dr. M. Sandie Turner, Director, 412-578-6669. Application contact: Bonnie Potthoff, Office Manager, Graduate Studies, 412-578-8764. Fax: 412-578-8822.

Carnegie Mellon University, H. John Heinz III School of Public Policy and Management, Program in Health Care Policy and Management, Pittsburgh, PA 15213-3891. Awards MSHCPM. *Degree requirements:* Internship required, foreign language and thesis not required. *Application deadline:* 3/15 (priority date; rolling processing). *Application fee:* $50. Electronic applications accepted. *Expenses:* Tuition $21,275 per year full-time, $295 per unit part-time. Fees $130 per year. *Financial aid:* Scholarships available. Financial aid application deadline: 3/15. • Application contact: Mark Wessel, Associate Dean, 412-268-3841. E-mail: mw4f@andrew.cmu.edu.

Central Michigan University, College of Extended Learning, Program in Administration, Mount Pleasant, MI 48859. Offerings include health services administration (MSA, Certificate). Postbaccalaureate distance learning degree programs offered. *Entrance requirements:* For master's, minimum GPA of 2.5 in major. Application fee: $50. *Tuition:* $211 per credit hour. • Dr. Susan Smith, Director, 517-774-4373. Application contact: Marketing Office, 800-950-1144. Fax: 517-774-2461.

Central Michigan University, College of Health Professions, Department of Health Promotion and Rehabilitation, Mount Pleasant, MI 48859. Offerings include health services administration (MSA). Department faculty: 41 full-time (13 women). *Application deadline:* 2/15. *Application fee:* $30. *Expenses:* Tuition $139 per credit hour (minimum) for state residents; $276 per credit hour (minimum) for nonresidents. Fees $260 per year full-time, $150 per semester part-time. • Dr. Herman Triezenberg, Chairperson, 517-774-3541. E-mail: 320ss5j@cmich.edu.

Chapman University, Department of Biology and Health Sciences, Orange, CA 92866. Offers program in health administration (MHA). Part-time programs available. Students: 24. *Degree requirements:* Comprehensive exam required, foreign language and thesis not required. *Entrance requirements:* GRE General Test (minimum combined score of 900) or MAT (minimum score 45). Application deadline: rolling. Application fee: $40. *Financial aid:* Application deadline 3/1. • Dr. Harry Schuler, Vice Provost, 714-997-6730. Application contact: Pamela Davidson, Chair, 714-744-0156.

Chapman University, Professional Studies, Orange, CA 92866. Offerings include health administration (MHA). Faculty: 3 full-time (2 women). *Application deadline:* rolling. *Application fee:* $40. • Harry J. Schuler, Vice Provost, 714-997-6730.

Charleston Southern University, Program in Business, Charleston, SC 29423-8087. Offerings include health care administration (MBA). Program faculty: 8 full-time (0 women), 1 (woman) part-time, 8.33 FTE. *Entrance requirements:* GMAT. Application deadline: rolling. Application fee: $25. *Tuition:* $3821 per year full-time, $173 per hour (minimum) part-time. • Dr. Al Parish, MBA Director, 803-863-7904. Fax: 803-863-7919. E-mail: aparish@awdd.com. Application contact: Terri Jordan, MBA Coordinator, 803-863-7955. Fax: 803-863-7922.

Clarkson College, Graduate Programs, Department of Health Services Management, 101 South 42nd Street, Omaha, NE 68131-2739. Awards MS. Part-time and evening/weekend programs available. Faculty: 2. Students: 15. In 1997, 4 degrees awarded. *Degree requirements:* Practicum required, foreign language not required. *Entrance requirements:* GMAT, minimum GPA of 3.0. Application deadline: rolling. Application fee: $17. *Expenses:* Tuition $314 per credit hour. Fees $16 per credit hour. *Financial aid:* Scholarships, institutionally sponsored loans available. • Dr. Carol Kleinman, Director, 402-552-6123. Fax: 402-552-6019. Application contact: Jeff Beals, Director of Enrollment Management, 402-552-3100. Fax: 402-552-6057. E-mail: admiss@clrkcol.crhsnet.edu.

Clark University, Graduate School of Management, Program in Health Administration, Worcester, MA 01610-1477. Awards MHA. Program being phased out; applicants no longer accepted. Part-time and evening/weekend programs available. Students: 10 full-time (4 women), 27 part-time (18 women). In 1997, 10 degrees awarded. *Degree requirements:* Computer language, thesis or alternative required, foreign language not required. *Financial aid:* Fellowships, research assistantships, Federal Work-Study, and career-related internships or fieldwork available. *Faculty research:* Management information systems, financial management, legal aspects, organizational behavior, policy analysis. • Dr. Robert Bradbury, Director, 508-793-7667.

Clemson University, College of Health, Education, and Human Development, Department of Public Health, Clemson, SC 29634. Awards MHA. Offered jointly with the Medical University of South Carolina. Students: 5 full-time (3 women), 15 part-time (8 women); includes 2 minority (1 African American, 1 Asian American). 13 applicants, 69% accepted. *Entrance requirements:* GRE General Test, TOEFL. Application fee: $35. *Expenses:* Tuition $3154 per year full-time, $130 per credit hour part-time for state residents; $6452 per year full-time, $264 per credit hour part-time for nonresidents. Fees $190 per year. • Dr. Carol Schwartz, Chair, 864-656-5865. Fax: 864-656-5488. E-mail: carol@clemson.edu.

College of Mount Saint Vincent, Program in Allied Health, Riverdale, NY 10471-1093. Offerings include allied health studies (MS), with options in addictions, child and family health, community health education, counseling, health care management, health care systems and policies; health care management (Certificate); health care systems and policies (Certificate). Program faculty: 1 (woman) full-time, 8 part-time (4 women), 3.6 FTE. *Degree requirements:* For master's, thesis or alternative required, foreign language not required. *Average time to degree:* master's–2 years part-time. *Entrance requirements:* For master's, sample of written work. Application deadline: 9/23 (priority date; rolling processing). Application fee: $50. • Dr. Rita Scher Dytell, Director, 718-405-3788. Fax: 718-405-3249.

College of Saint Elizabeth, Department of Health Professions and Related Sciences, Morristown, NJ 07960-6989. Offers program in health care management (MS). Part-time and evening/weekend programs available. Faculty: 5 full-time (3 women). Students: 17 part-time (15 women); includes 3 minority (1 African American, 1 Asian American, 1 Hispanic). Average age 40. 38 applicants, 45% accepted. *Degree requirements:* Thesis optional, foreign language not required. *Application deadline:* rolling. *Application fee:* $35. *Expenses:* Tuition $364 per credit. Fees $455 per year full-time, $70 per semester part-time. *Financial aid:* Research assistantships, teaching assistantships, and career-related internships or fieldwork available. Aid available to part-time students. Financial aid application deadline: 3/15; applicants required to submit FAFSA. *Faculty research:* Health promotion, outcomes evaluation. • Dr. Anne M. Hewitt, Director of Graduate Program, 973-290-4040. Fax: 973-290-4167. E-mail: healthcare@liza.st-elizabeth.edu.

Colorado Technical University, Graduate Studies, Program in Management, 4435 North Chestnut Street, Colorado Springs, CO 80907-3896. Offerings include health science management (MSM). Program faculty: 8 full-time (2 women), 8 part-time (1 woman), 12 FTE. *Average time to degree:* master's–2 years full-time. *Application deadline:* 10/4 (rolling processing; 4/5 for spring admission). *Application fee:* $100. *Expenses:* Tuition $230 per quarter hour. Fees $6 per quarter. • Dr. Mark Pieffer, Dean, 719-590-6765. Application contact: Judy Galante, Graduate Admissions, 719-590-6720. Fax: 719-598-3740.

Columbia University, School of Public Health, Division of Health Policy and Management, New York, NY 10032. Awards Exec MPH, MPH, Dr PH. Evening/weekend programs available. Students: 221. In 1997, 123 master's, 1 doctorate awarded. *Degree requirements:* For master's, thesis optional, foreign language not required; for doctorate, dissertation required, foreign language not required. *Average time to degree:* master's–1.5 years full-time, 3 years part-time; doctorate–4 years full-time, 7 years part-time. *Entrance requirements:* For master's, GRE General Test; for doctorate, GRE General Test, MPH or equivalent (Dr PH). Application deadline: 4/10 (11/15 for spring admission). Application fee: $60. *Tuition:* $22,320 per year full-time, $744 per credit part-time. *Financial aid:* Research assistantships, teaching assistantships, Federal Work-Study, and career-related internships or fieldwork available. Aid available to part-time students. Financial aid application deadline: 3/15; applicants required to submit FAFSA. *Faculty research:* Health care reform, health care cost containment, improving quality of health care, assessment of health care technology. • Dr. Lawrence Brown, Head, 212-305-3924. Application contact: Dr. Sheila Gorman, Deputy Head, 212-305-3724. Fax: 212-305-3405.

Concordia University Wisconsin, Division of Graduate Studies, MBA Program, Mequon, WI 53097-2402. Offerings include health care administration (MBA). Postbaccalaureate distance learning degree programs offered (minimal on-campus study). *Degree requirements:* Thesis or alternative, comprehensive exam. *Average time to degree:* master's–2 years part-time. *Entrance requirements:* TOEFL (minimum score 550). Application deadline: 8/1 (priority date; rolling processing; 1/15 for spring admission). Application fee: $50. *Tuition:* $300 per credit. • David Borst, Director, 414-243-4298. Fax: 414-243-4428. E-mail: dborst@bach.cuw.edu.

Cornell University, Graduate Fields of Human Ecology, Field of Human Service Studies, Program in Health Services Administration, Ithaca, NY 14853-0001. Awards MHA. Accredited by ACEHSA. *Entrance requirements:* GMAT or GRE General Test, TOEFL. Application deadline: 3/15. Application fee: $65. • Director of Graduate Studies, Field of Human Service Studies, 607-255-7772. Application contact: Graduate Field Assistant, 607-255-7772. Fax: 607-255-4071. E-mail: hss_grad@cornell.edu.

See in-depth description on page 1307.

Dalhousie University, Faculty of Health Professions, School of Health Services Administration, Halifax, NS B3H 3J5, Canada. Awards MHSA, LL B/MHSA, MN/MHSA. Accredited by ACEHSA. Part-time programs available. Faculty: 3 full-time (1 woman), 10 part-time (4 women). Students: 19 full-time (13 women), 21 part-time (19 women); includes 8 minority (all Asian Americans). Average age 30. 27 applicants, 81% accepted. In 1997, 15 degrees awarded. *Entrance requirements:* GMAT, TOEFL (minimum score 580). Application deadline: 5/1 (rolling processing). Application fee: $55. *Financial aid:* Fellowships, teaching assistantships available. *Faculty research:* Hospital, nursing, long-term, public, and community health administration; government administration in health areas. • Dr. Thomas A. Rathwell, Director, 902-494-7097. Fax: 902-494-6849. E-mail: health.services.administration@dal.ca.

DePaul University, College of Liberal Arts and Sciences, Programs in Public Services, Program in Health Law and Policy, Chicago, IL 60604-2287. Awards MS. Students: 7 full-time (5 women), 8 part-time (7 women); includes 5 minority (2 African Americans, 3 Asian Americans). Average age 35. 12 applicants, 83% accepted. In 1997, 2 degrees awarded. *Degree requirements:* Practicum or thesis required, foreign language not required. *Entrance requirements:* Minimum GPA of 3.0, experience in related field, interview. Application deadline: 7/1 (rolling processing; 1/20 for spring admission). Application fee: $25. *Expenses:* Tuition $320 per credit hour. Fees $30 per year. *Financial aid:* In 1997–98, 2 research assistantships (1 to a first-year student) averaging $500 per month and totaling $10,000 were awarded; partial tuition waivers also available. Financial aid application deadline: 7/1. *Faculty research:* Physicians in group practice, nonprofit organizations, community policing. Total annual research expenditures: $90,000. • Application contact: Graduate Information, 312-362-5367. Fax: 312-362-5749.

See in-depth description on page 619.

Duke University, Fuqua School of Business, Concentration in Health Services Management, Durham, NC 27708-0586. Awards MBA. Evening/weekend programs available. Faculty: 10 full-time (3 women), 6 part-time (1 woman), 11 FTE. Students: 50 full-time (20 women). Average age 27. In 1997, 20 degrees awarded (100% found work related to degree). *Average time to degree:* master's–2 years full-time. *Entrance requirements:* GMAT, TOEFL, 1 semester of calculus. Application deadline: 4/20 (priority date; rolling processing). Application fee: $125. *Expenses:* Tuition $25,250 per year. Fees $1235 per year. *Financial aid:* 38 students received aid; fellowships available. Financial aid application deadline: 3/1. *Faculty research:* Surgery costs, malpractice, law and costs, physician incentives, alcohol and teenagers. • Sim Sitkin, Director, 919-660-7946. Fax: 919-681-6245. Application contact: Robert R. Williams, Director of Admissions, 919-660-7705. Fax: 919-681-8026.

Duquesne University, John G. Rangos, Sr. School of Health Sciences, Pittsburgh, PA 15282-0001. Offerings include health management systems (MHMS). School faculty: 30 full-time (17 women), 12 part-time (6 women), 34.8 FTE. *Average time to degree:* master's–2 years full-time. *Application deadline:* 12/1 (priority date). *Application fee:* $45. Electronic applications accepted. *Expenses:* Tuition $510 per credit. Fees $39 per credit. • Dr. Jerome L. Martin, Dean, 412-396-6012. E-mail: martin2@duq2.cc.duq.edu. Application contact: Deborah L. Durica, Director of Student and Alumni Services, 412-396-6652. Fax: 412-396-5554. E-mail: durica@duq2.cc.duq.edu.

Directory: Health Services Management and Hospital Administration

Duquesne University, School of Pharmacy, Graduate School of Pharmaceutical Sciences, Program in Pharmaceutical Administration, Pittsburgh, PA 15282-0001. Awards MS. Faculty: 4 full-time. 4 applicants, 0% accepted. *Degree requirements:* Thesis required, foreign language not required. *Entrance requirements:* GRE General Test, TOEFL, TSE, degree in pharmacy from an ACPE-accredited program. Application deadline: 3/1 (priority date; rolling processing). Application fee: $40. *Expenses:* Tuition $530 per credit. Fees $39 per credit. *Financial aid:* Teaching assistantships available. • Dr. Aleem Gangjee, Director, Graduate School of Pharmaceutical Sciences, 412-396-5662.

See in-depth description on page 1791.

D'Youville College, Division of Business, Buffalo, NY 14201-1084. Offerings include health services administration (MS). MS (international business) new for fall 1998. Division faculty: 3 full-time (all women), 9 part-time (3 women). *Degree requirements:* Computer language, thesis required, foreign language not required. *Entrance requirements:* Minimum GPA of 3.0 in major. Application deadline: rolling. Application fee: $25. *Expenses:* Tuition $357 per credit hour. Fees $350 per year. • Dr. Jayanti Sen, Interim Director, 716-881-3200. Application contact: Joseph Syracuse, Graduate Admissions Director, 716-881-7676. Fax: 716-881-7790.

Eastern Kentucky University, College of Social and Behavioral Sciences, Department of Government, Program in General Public Administration, Richmond, KY 40475-3101. Offerings include community health administration (MPA). *Degree requirements:* Computer language required, foreign language and thesis not required. *Entrance requirements:* GRE General Test (minimum combined score of 1000; average 1420), minimum GPA of 2.5. Application fee: $0. *Tuition:* $2390 per year full-time, $133 per credit hour part-time for state residents; $6630 per year full-time, $365 per credit hour part-time for nonresidents. • Dr. Richard Vance, Chair, Department of Government, 606-622-5931.

Emory University, The Rollins School of Public Health, Department of Health Policy and Management, Atlanta, GA 30322-1100. Awards MPH. *Degree requirements:* Thesis (for some programs), practicum required, foreign language not required. *Entrance requirements:* GRE General Test. Application deadline: 2/15 (priority date; rolling processing). Application fee: $50. *Expenses:* Tuition $14,136 per year full-time, $589 per credit hour part-time. Fees $200 per year. *Financial aid:* Application deadline 2/15. • Application contact: Susan Daniel, Director of Admissions, 404-727-5481. Fax: 404-727-3996. E-mail: admit@sph.emory.edu.

Finch University of Health Sciences/The Chicago Medical School, School of Related Health Sciences, Department of Healthcare Risk Management, North Chicago, IL 60064-3095. Awards MS. Part-time programs available. Postbaccalaureate distance learning degree programs offered (minimal on-campus study). Faculty: 2 full-time (both women), 8 part-time (2 women). Students: 23 part-time (21 women); includes 1 minority (Hispanic). Average age 40. 12 applicants, 92% accepted. In 1997, 11 degrees awarded (100% found work related to degree). *Degree requirements:* Thesis required, foreign language not required. *Average time to degree:* master's–2.5 years part-time. *Entrance requirements:* Minimum GPA of 2.8, risk management experience, professional certificate or license. Application deadline: 7/1 (priority date; rolling processing). Application fee: $25. *Tuition:* $370 per credit hour. *Financial aid:* Partial tuition waivers, institutionally sponsored loans available. Aid available to part-time students. Financial aid application deadline: 2/1. *Faculty research:* Impact on medical malpractice claims, quantifying impact on claim activity and hospital finances, impact of risk management activities on reducing claims. • Kathleen Ruroede, Chair, 847-578-3310. E-mail: ruroedek@mis.finchcms.edu. Application contact: Julie Perrault, Administrative Assistant, 847-578-3310. Fax: 847-578-8641. E-mail: perraulj@mis.finchcms.edu.

See in-depth description on page 1237.

Florida Institute of Technology, School of Extended Graduate Studies, Program in Management, Melbourne, FL 32901-6975. Offerings include health management (MS). *Application fee:* $50. *Tuition:* $550 per credit hour. • Application contact: Carolyn P. Farrior, Associate Dean of Graduate Admissions, 407-674-7118. Fax: 407-723-9468. E-mail: cfarrior@fit.edu.

Florida International University, College of Urban and Public Affairs, School of Policy and Management, Department of Health Services Administration, Miami, FL 33199. Awards MHSA. Accredited by ACEHSA. Part-time and evening/weekend programs available. Faculty: 8 full-time (3 women). Students: 22 full-time (15 women), 40 part-time (33 women); includes 32 minority (19 African Americans, 1 Asian American, 12 Hispanics), 7 international. Average age 31. 45 applicants, 44% accepted. In 1997, 39 degrees awarded. *Entrance requirements:* GRE General Test (minimum combined score of 1000), TOEFL (minimum score 500), interview, minimum GPA of 3.0. Application deadline: 4/1 (priority date; rolling processing; 10/1 for spring admission). Application fee: $20. *Expenses:* Tuition $138 per credit hour for state residents; $482 per credit hour for nonresidents. Fees $46 per semester. • Dr. David Bergwall, Director, School of Policy and Management, 305-919-5890. Fax: 305-919-5848. E-mail: bergwall@fiu.edu.

Framingham State College, Graduate Programs, Program in Health Care Administration, Framingham, MA 01701-9101. Awards MA. Part-time and evening/weekend programs available. Faculty: 2 full-time, 4 part-time. Students: 92 part-time. In 1997, 31 degrees awarded. *Tuition:* $4184 per year full-time, $523 per course part-time for state residents; $4848 per year full-time, $606 per course part-time for nonresidents. • Dr. George Jarnis, Adviser, 508-620-1220. Application contact: Graduate Office, 508-626-4550.

Gannon University, School of Graduate Studies, College of Sciences, Engineering, and Health Sciences, School of Health Sciences, Program in Health Services Administration, Erie, PA 16541. Awards MS, Certificate. Program being phased out; applicants no longer accepted. Part-time and evening/weekend programs available. Students: 3 part-time (2 women). Average age 34. In 1997, 10 master's awarded. *Degree requirements:* For master's, thesis, comprehensive exam, research project. *Financial aid:* Scholarships and career-related internships or fieldwork available. Aid available to part-time students. Financial aid applicants required to submit FAFSA. • Holly Nishimura, Director, 814-871-7789.

The George Washington University, School of Public Health and Health Services, Department of Health Services Management and Policy, Washington, DC 20052. Awards MHSA, Specialist, JD/MHSA. One or more programs accredited by ACEHSA. Faculty: 8 full-time (2 women), 7 part-time (3 women), 10 FTE. Students: 69 full-time (37 women), 78 part-time (51 women); includes 43 minority (20 African Americans, 20 Asian Americans, 3 Hispanics), 8 international. Average age 28. 129 applicants, 96% accepted. In 1997, 36 master's, 3 Specialists awarded. *Degree requirements:* For master's, internship or residency required, foreign language and thesis not required. *Entrance requirements:* For master's, GMAT or GRE, TOEFL (minimum score 550); for Specialist, GMAT or GRE, TOEFL (minimum score 550), master's degree in related field. Application deadline: 5/15 (priority date; rolling processing; 11/15 for spring admission). Application fee: $50. *Expenses:* Tuition $680 per semester hour. Fees $35 per semester hour. *Financial aid:* Federal Work-Study, institutionally sponsored loans, and career-related internships or fieldwork available. Financial aid application deadline: 6/1. *Faculty research:* Hospital administration, ambulatory health care, social gerontology, health care financing, health care ethics. • Dr. Richard Southby, Chairman, 202-994-6220. Fax: 202-944-3773. Application contact: Michelle Sparacino, Director of Recruitment, 202-994-2160. Fax: 202-994-3773. E-mail: sphhs-info@gwumc.edu.

Announcement: Health Services Management and Policy Program offers an ACEHSA-accredited Master in Health Services Administration degree program with specialization in management or policy. Administrative medicine track in CEPH-accredited MPH program, as well as a post-master's specialist degree. New 48-credit-hour curriculum offers options in managed care and long-term care in conjunction with the School's Wertlieb Institute for Long-Term Care Management. Bachelor's degree required for admission to MHSA. Graduate degree required for admission to administrative medicine track in MPH. JD/MPH and JD/MHSA degrees and specialization in health services offered within the MBA program. Visit the Web site (http://www.gwumc.edu/sphhs).

See in-depth description on page 1495.

The George Washington University, School of Public Health and Health Services, Master's Program in Public Health, Track in Administrative Medicine, Washington, DC 20052. Offers programs in management (MPH), policy (MPH). *Degree requirements:* Case study or special project required, thesis not required. *Entrance requirements:* GMAT, GRE General Test, or MCAT; TOEFL. Application deadline: 5/15 (priority date; rolling processing; 11/15 for spring admission). Application fee: $50. *Expenses:* Tuition $680 per semester hour. Fees $35 per semester hour. • Application contact: Michelle Sparacino, Director of Recruitment, 202-994-2160. Fax: 202-994-3773. E-mail: sphhs-info@gwumc.edu.

See in-depth description on page 1495.

Georgia Institute of Technology, College of Engineering, School of Industrial and Systems Engineering, Program in Health Systems, Atlanta, GA 30332-0001. Awards MSHS. Faculty: 47 full-time (6 women). Students: 5 full-time (3 women), 1 part-time (0 women); includes 1 international. Average age 26. 14 applicants, 36% accepted. In 1997, 18 degrees awarded. *Degree requirements:* Computer language required, foreign language and thesis not required. *Entrance requirements:* GRE General Test, TOEFL (minimum score 550), minimum GPA of 3.0. Application deadline: 7/1 (priority date; rolling processing; 2/1 for spring admission). Application fee: $50. Electronic applications accepted. *Expenses:* Tuition $2670 per year full-time, $98 per credit hour part-time for state residents; $10,680 per year full-time, $298 per credit hour part-time for nonresidents. Fees $681 per year full-time, $23 per credit hour (minimum) part-time. *Financial aid:* In 1997–98, 5 students received aid, including 5 research assistantships (all to first-year students) averaging $633 per month and totaling $28,500; teaching assistantships, Federal Work-Study, institutionally sponsored loans, and career-related internships or fieldwork also available. Aid available to part-time students. Financial aid application deadline: 2/1. *Faculty research:* Emergency medical services, health development planning, health services evaluations. • Dr. Justin Myrick, Coordinator, 404-894-4551. Application contact: ISYE Graduate Office, 404-894-4289. Fax: 404-894-2301. E-mail: gradstudies@isye.gatech.edu.

Georgia State University, College of Business Administration, Institute of Health Administration, Atlanta, GA 30303-3083. Awards MHA, MSHA, MBA/MHA. Accredited by ACEHSA. Faculty: 4 full-time. Students: 97 (49 women); includes 14 minority (10 African Americans, 3 Asian Americans, 1 Hispanic), 5 international. Average age 28. In 1997, 29 degrees awarded. *Entrance requirements:* GMAT (average 566), TOEFL. Application deadline: 5/1 (rolling processing; 10/1 for spring admission). Application fee: $25. *Expenses:* Tuition $2673 per year full-time, $99 per semester hour part-time for state residents; $10,692 per year full-time, $396 per semester hour part-time for nonresidents. Fees $228 per year. *Financial aid:* Partial tuition waivers and career-related internships or fieldwork available. Aid available to part-time students. Financial aid applicants required to submit FAFSA. • Dr. Everett A. Johnson, Director, 404-651-2637. Fax: 404-651-1230. Application contact: Office of Academic Assistance and Master's Admissions, 404-651-1913. Fax: 404-651-0219.

Golden Gate University, School of Liberal Studies and Public Affairs, Programs in Urban and Public Affairs, Program in Health Care Management, San Francisco, CA 94105-2968. Awards MHM, Certificate. Part-time and evening/weekend programs available. *Degree requirements:* For master's, thesis or alternative required, foreign language not required. *Entrance requirements:* For master's, GMAT (MBA), TOEFL (minimum score 550), minimum GPA of 2.5, appropriate bachelor's degree. Application deadline: 7/1 (priority date; rolling processing). Application fee: $55 ($70 for international students). *Tuition:* $996 per course (minimum). *Financial aid:* Fellowships, Federal Work-Study, institutionally sponsored loans, and career-related internships or fieldwork available. Aid available to part-time students. • Application contact: Enrollment Services, 415-442-7800. Fax: 415-442-7807. E-mail: info@ggu.edu.

Governors State University, College of Health Professions, Division of Health Administration and Human Services, Program in Health Administration, University Park, IL 60466. Awards MHA. Accredited by ACEHSA. In 1997, 17 degrees awarded. *Degree requirements:* Computer language, comprehensive exam, field experience or internship required, foreign language and thesis not required. *Entrance requirements:* Minimum GPA of 3.0 in last 60 hours of undergraduate course work or 9 hours of graduate course work. Application deadline: 7/15 (priority date; rolling processing; 11/10 for spring admission). Application fee: $0. *Expenses:* Tuition $1140 per trimester full-time, $95 per credit hour part-time for state residents; $3420 per trimester full-time, $285 per credit hour part-time for nonresidents. Fees $95 per trimester. *Financial aid:* Research assistantships, scholarships, full and partial tuition waivers, Federal Work-Study, institutionally sponsored loans, and career-related internships or fieldwork available. Financial aid application deadline: 5/1. • Dr. Sang-O Rhee, Chairperson, Division of Health Administration and Human Services, 708-534-4030.

Harvard University, Graduate School of Arts and Sciences, Committee on Higher Degrees in Health Policy, Cambridge, MA 02138. Awards PhD. Students: 33 full-time (22 women); includes 3 minority (2 African Americans, 1 Asian American), 5 international. 63 applicants, 17% accepted. In 1997, 4 degrees awarded. *Degree requirements:* Dissertation required, foreign language not required. *Entrance requirements:* GRE General Test, GMAT, or MCAT, TOEFL (minimum score 550). Application deadline: 12/30. Application fee: $60. *Expenses:* Tuition $21,342 per year. Fees $686 per year. *Financial aid:* Fellowships, research assistantships, teaching assistantships, Federal Work-Study, and career-related internships or fieldwork available. Financial aid application deadline: 12/30; applicants required to submit FAFSA. • Dr. Joseph Newhouse, Chair, 617-495-1325. Application contact: Office of Admissions and Financial Aid, 617-495-5315.

Harvard University, School of Public Health, Department of Health Policy and Management, Boston, MA 02115. Awards SM, DPH, SD. Part-time programs available. Faculty: 22 full-time (6 women), 37 part-time (7 women). Students: 61 full-time (41 women), 13 part-time (12 women); includes 17 minority (2 African Americans, 15 Asian Americans), 11 international. Average age 29. 138 applicants, 56% accepted. In 1997, 36 master's awarded. *Entrance requirements:* For master's, GRE, TOEFL (minimum score 550). Application deadline: 1/4. Application fee: $60. *Expenses:* Tuition $21,895 per year full-time, $10,948 per year part-time. Fees $686 per year. *Financial aid:* Fellowships, partial tuition waivers, Federal Work-Study available. Aid available to part-time students. Financial aid application deadline: 2/12; applicants required to submit FAFSA. *Faculty research:* Management of health care institutions and systems, management of health hazards, international health, financing health care and insurance. • Dr. Arnold Epstein, Chairman, 617-432-1090. Application contact: Kristine Forsgard, Deputy Director, 617-432-1090.

Harvard University, School of Public Health, Master of Public Health Program, Boston, MA 02115. Offerings include health care and organizational management (MPH). *Average time to degree:* master's–1 year full-time, 2.5 years part-time. *Entrance requirements:* GRE, TOEFL (minimum score 550). Application deadline: 1/4 (priority date). Application fee: $60. *Expenses:* Tuition $21,895 per year full-time, $10,948 per year part-time. Fees $686 per year. • Dr. Gareth M. Green, Associate Dean for Professional Education, 617-432-0090. Application contact: Carrie Daniels, Assistant Director of Admissions, 617-432-1031. Fax: 617-432-2009. E-mail: admisofc@sph.harvard.edu.

Hofstra University, School of Education and Allied Human Services, Department of Health, Physical Education and Recreation, Program in Health Administration, Hempstead, NY 11549. Awards MA. Part-time and evening/weekend programs available. Faculty: 4 full-time (1 woman), 10 part-time (4 women). Students: 16 full-time (11 women), 113 part-time (86 women); includes 11 minority (5 African Americans, 3 Asian Americans, 2 Hispanics, 1 Native American), 1 international. Average age 31. 57 applicants, 56% accepted. In 1997, 38 degrees awarded. *Degree requirements:* Departmental qualifying exam, final essay. *Entrance requirements:*

Interview, minimum GPA of 2.75. Application deadline: rolling. Application fee: $40 ($75 for international students). *Expenses:* Tuition $10,968 per year full-time, $457 per credit hour part-time. Fees $670 per year full-time, $112 per semester (minimum) part-time. *Financial aid:* 10 students received aid; institutionally sponsored loans available. Financial aid applicants required to submit FAFSA. • Dr. Estelle Weinstein, Coordinator, 516-463-5817. Fax: 516-463-4810. E-mail: hprezw@hofstra.edu. Application contact: Mary Beth Carey, Dean of Admissions, 516-463-6700. Fax: 516-560-7660. E-mail: hofstra@hofstra.edu.

Houston Baptist University, Center for Health Studies, Program in Health Administration, Houston, TX 77074-3298. Awards MS. Faculty: 3 full-time (2 women), 6 part-time (3 women). Students: 40 full-time (28 women), 5 part-time (4 women); includes 22 minority (4 African Americans, 11 Asian Americans, 7 Hispanics). 30 applicants, 77% accepted. *Entrance requirements:* GRE General Test (minimum combined score of 900), MAT (minimum score 45), minimum GPA of 2.5. Application deadline: 7/1 (priority date; rolling processing; 1/1 for spring admission). Application fee: $25 ($85 for international students). *Expenses:* Tuition $300 per semester hour. Fees $235 per quarter. • Dr. Betty Souther, Director, Center for Health Studies, 281-649-3000 Ext. 2364.

Howard University, School of Business, Department of Health Services Administration, 2400 Sixth Street, NW, Washington, DC 20059-0002. Awards MBA. Part-time and evening/weekend programs available. *Degree requirements:* Computer language, internship required, foreign language and thesis not required. *Entrance requirements:* GMAT. Application deadline: 4/1. Application fee: $45. *Expenses:* Tuition $10,200 per year full-time, $567 per credit hour part-time. Fees $405 per year. *Financial aid:* Research assistantships, teaching assistantships, grants, institutionally sponsored loans, and career-related internships or fieldwork available. Financial aid application deadline: 4/1. • Dr. Sterling King, Chairman, 202-806-1579.

Idaho State University, College of Pharmacy, Department of Pharmacy Practice and Administrative Sciences, Pocatello, ID 83209. Offerings include pharmacy administration (MS, PhD). Department faculty: 20 full-time (10 women), 1 (woman) part-time. *Degree requirements:* For master's, 1 foreign language, thesis. *Entrance requirements:* GRE General Test. Application deadline: 8/1 (priority date). Application fee: $30. • Dr. Vaughn Culbertson, Chairman, 208-236-2586.

Illinois School of Professional Psychology, Chicago Campus, Program in Health Services Administration, 20 South Clark Street, Chicago, IL 60603. Awards MS. *Degree requirements:* Comprehensive exam required, foreign language and thesis not required. *Application deadline:* 5/15. *Application fee:* $55.

See in-depth description on page 1309.

Indiana State University, School of Health and Human Performance, Department of Health and Safety, Terre Haute, IN 47809-1401. Offerings include health program and facility administration (MA, MS), occupational safety management (MA, MS). Department faculty: 11 full-time (4 women). *Application deadline:* rolling. *Application fee:* $20. *Tuition:* $143 per credit hour for state residents; $325 per credit hour for nonresidents. • Dr. Portia Plummer, Chairperson, 812-237-3071. Application contact: Dr. Richard Spear, Graduate Adviser, 812-237-3107.

Indiana University Northwest, Division of Public and Environmental Affairs, Gary, IN 46408-1197. Offerings include health services administration (MPA). Division faculty: 7 full-time (2 women), 5 part-time (2 women), 8.25 FTE. *Entrance requirements:* GRE General Test. Application deadline: 8/15 (priority date; rolling processing). Application fee: $25. • Joseph M. Pellicciotti, Director, 219-980-6695. E-mail: jpelli@iunhaw1.iun.indiana.edu. Application contact: Suzanne Green, Recorder, 219-980-6695. Fax: 219-980-6737. E-mail: sgreen@iunhaw1.iun.indiana.edu.

Indiana University–Purdue University Indianapolis, School of Public and Environmental Affairs, Graduate Program in Health Administration, Indianapolis, IN 46202-2896. Awards MHA, JD/MHA, MBA/MHA, MSN/MHA. Accredited by ACEHSA. Part-time and evening/weekend programs available. Faculty: 6 full-time (3 women), 3 part-time (0 women). Students: 76 full-time (38 women), 25 part-time (13 women); includes 16 minority (6 African Americans, 9 Asian Americans, 1 Hispanic), 4 international. Average age 31. 60 applicants, 77% accepted. In 1997, 15 degrees awarded (100% found work related to degree). *Degree requirements:* Research or residency required, foreign language and thesis not required. *Average time to degree:* master's–2 years full-time, 4 years part-time. *Entrance requirements:* GRE General Test (minimum combined score of 1000), minimum GPA of 3.0 preferred. Application deadline: 7/15 (priority date; rolling processing; 11/15 for spring admission). Application fee: $35 ($50 for international students). *Expenses:* Tuition $3602 per year full-time, $150 per credit hour part-time for state residents; $10,392 per year full-time, $433 per credit hour part-time for nonresidents. Fees $100 per year (minimum) full-time, $40 per year (minimum) part-time. *Financial aid:* In 1997–98, 5 research assistantships (3 to first-year students) averaging $650 per month were awarded; fellowships, Federal Work-Study, and career-related internships or fieldwork also available. Aid available to part-time students. Financial aid application deadline: 3/1. *Faculty research:* Health care financing, health economics, health policy, aging, organization design and structure. • Dr. John Ottensmann, Director, 317-274-7361. Application contact: Office of Student Services, 317-274-4656. Fax: 317-274-5153. E-mail: speainfo@speanet.iupui.edu.

See in-depth description on page 1311.

Iona College, School of Arts and Science, Program in Health Service Administration, 715 North Avenue, New Rochelle, NY 10801-1890. Awards MS, Certificate. Faculty: 4 full-time (3 women), 11 part-time (4 women). Students: 4 full-time (2 women), 58 part-time (47 women); includes 14 minority (10 African Americans, 1 Asian American, 2 Hispanics, 1 Native American). Average age 38. In 1997, 28 master's awarded. *Degree requirements:* For master's, thesis. *Entrance requirements:* For master's, minimum undergraduate GPA of 2.75. Application deadline: rolling. Application fee: $25. *Expenses:* Tuition $455 per credit hour. Fees $25 per semester. *Financial aid:* Graduate assistantships and career-related internships or fieldwork available. Aid available to part-time students. *Faculty research:* Quality management, quantitative methods, health industry analysis. • Vincent Maher, Chair, 914-633-2192. Application contact: Arlene Melillo, Director of Graduate Recruitment, 914-633-2328. Fax: 914-633-2023.

ISIM University, Programs in Information Management, Program in Business Administration, Denver, CO 80246. Offerings include health care management (MBA). *Application deadline:* rolling. *Application fee:* $50. Electronic applications accepted.

Johns Hopkins University, School of Continuing Studies, Division of Business and Management, Baltimore, MD 21218-2699. Offerings include the business of medicine (Certificate), the business of nursing (Certificate). Division faculty: 12 full-time, 190 part-time. *Application deadline:* rolling. *Application fee:* $50. • Dr. Jon Heggan, Director, 410-516-0755. Application contact: Lenora Henry, Admissions Coordinator, 410-872-1234. Fax: 410-872-1251. E-mail: adv_mail@jhuvms.hcf.jhu.edu.

Johns Hopkins University, School of Hygiene and Public Health, Department of Health Policy and Management, Baltimore, MD 21205. Offers programs in health and public policy (MHS, Dr PH, PhD, Sc D), health services research (MHS, Dr PH, PhD, Sc D), social and behavioral sciences (MHS, Sc M, Dr PH, PhD, Sc D). One or more programs accredited by ACEHSA. Part-time and evening/weekend programs available. Faculty: 74 full-time, 170 part-time. Students: 263 (189 women); includes 57 minority (17 African Americans, 28 Asian Americans, 11 Hispanics, 1 Native American), 28 international. 425 applicants, 40% accepted. In 1997, 64 master's, 25 doctorates awarded. *Degree requirements:* For master's, thesis (for some programs), comprehensive exam, internship required, foreign language not required; for doctorate, dissertation, 1 year full-time residency, comprehensive exam, oral and written exams required, foreign language not required. *Entrance requirements:* GRE General Test, TOEFL (minimum score 600), work experience in health-related field. Application deadline: 2/1 (priority date; rolling processing). Application fee: $60. *Financial aid:* Scholarships, stipends, Federal Work-Study, institutionally sponsored loans available. Financial aid application deadline: 4/15. *Faculty research:* Quality of care and health outcomes, health care finance and technology, innovative health care systems, vulnerable populations, prevention of disease and injury. Total annual research expenditures: $16.9 million. • Donald M. Steinwachs, Chairman, 410-955-3625. Application contact: Judith Holzer, Academic Administrator, 410-955-2488. E-mail: jholzer@jhsph.edu.

See in-depth description on page 1313.

Johns Hopkins University, School of Hygiene and Public Health, Program in Public Health, Baltimore, MD 21205. Offerings include health policy and management (MPH). *Entrance requirements:* GRE General Test, TOEFL (minimum score 550), 2 years of work related experience. Application deadline: 2/1 (priority date; rolling processing). Application fee: $60. • Dr. Miriam Alexander, Director, 410-955-1291. Application contact: Lenora Davis, Administrator, 410-955-1291. Fax: 410-955-4749. E-mail: lrdavis@jhsph.edu.

Johns Hopkins University, School of Hygiene and Public Health, Department of International Health, Division of Health Systems, Baltimore, MD 21205. Awards MHS, Dr PH, PhD, Sc D. One or more programs accredited by ACEHSA. *Degree requirements:* For master's, internship required, foreign language not required; for doctorate, dissertation, 1 year full-time residency, oral and written exams required, foreign language not required. *Entrance requirements:* GRE General Test. Application deadline: 2/1 (priority date; rolling processing). Application fee: $60. *Financial aid:* Scholarships, Federal Work-Study, institutionally sponsored loans available. Aid available to part-time students. Financial aid application deadline: 4/15. *Faculty research:* Health manpower planning, infectious disease control, health information systems. • Dr. Richard H. Morrow, Director, 410-614-1419. Application contact: Nancy Stephens, Student Coordinator, 410-955-3734. Fax: 410-955-8734. E-mail: nstephen@jhsph.edu.

Kean University, School of Business, Government, and Technology, Department of Public Administration, Union, NJ 07083. Offerings include health services administration (MPA). *Entrance requirements:* GRE General Test. Application deadline: 6/15 (11/15 for spring admission). Application fee: $35. *Tuition:* $5926 per year full-time, $248 per credit part-time for state residents; $7312 per year full-time, $304 per credit part-time for nonresidents. • Dr. Jon Erickson, Coordinator, 908-527-3022. Application contact: Joanne Morris, Director of Graduate Admissions, 908-527-2665. Fax: 908-527-2286. E-mail: grad_adm@turbo.kean.edu.

King's College, William G. McGowan School of Business, Wilkes-Barre, PA 18711-0801. Offerings include health care administration (MS). School faculty: 7 full-time (1 woman), 3 part-time (0 women). *Average time to degree:* master's–2.5 years part-time. *Entrance requirements:* GMAT. Application deadline: 7/31 (priority date; rolling processing; 12/1 for spring admission). Application fee: $35. *Tuition:* $460 per credit. • Dr. Edward J. Schoen, Dean, 717-208-5932. Fax: 717-826-5989. E-mail: ejschoen@rs01.kings.edu. Application contact: Dr. Elizabeth S. Lott, Director of Graduate Programs, 717-208-5991. Fax: 717-825-9049. E-mail: eslott@rs02.kings.edu.

Lesley College, School of Management, Cambridge, MA 02138-2790. Offerings include health services management (MSM). Postbaccalaureate distance learning degree programs offered (no on-campus study). School faculty: 10 full-time (4 women), 204 part-time (78 women). *Application deadline:* rolling. *Application fee:* $45. *Tuition:* $425 per credit. • Dr. Earl Potter, Dean, 617-349-8682. Fax: 617-349-8678. Application contact: Marilyn Gove, Associate Director, 617-349-8690. Fax: 617-349-8313. E-mail: mgove@mail.lesley.edu.

Lindenwood University, Programs in Individualized Education, St. Charles, MO 63301-1695. Offerings include health management (MS). Faculty: 10 full-time (7 women), 23 part-time (6 women). *Application deadline:* 6/30 (priority date; rolling processing; 12/1 for spring admission). *Application fee:* $25. *Tuition:* $5880 per year full-time, $245 per credit hour part-time. • Dr. Dan Kemper, Dean, 314-916-9125. Application contact: John Guffey, Director of Graduate Admissions, 314-949-4933. Fax: 314-949-4910.

Loma Linda University, School of Public Health, Programs in Health Administration, Loma Linda, CA 92350. Awards MHA, MPH. 22 applicants, 59% accepted. In 1997, 15 degrees awarded. *Entrance requirements:* GMAT (MHA), Michigan Test of English Language Proficiency (minimum score 92) or TOEFL (minimum score 600). Application deadline: rolling. Application fee: $100. *Tuition:* $380 per unit. *Financial aid:* Career-related internships or fieldwork available. Financial aid application deadline: 5/15. • Dr. C. Torben Thomsen, Chair, 909-824-4573. Fax: 909-824-4087. Application contact: Terri Tamayose, Director of Admissions and Academic Records, 909-824-4694. Fax: 909-824-8087. E-mail: ttamayose@sph.llu.edu.

Long Island University, Brooklyn Campus, School of Health Professions, Department of Community Health, Brooklyn, NY 11201-8423. Offerings include health management (MS). Department faculty: 3 full-time (2 women), 15 part-time (4 women). *Application deadline:* rolling. *Application fee:* $30. Electronic applications accepted. *Expenses:* Tuition $480 per credit. Fees $415 per year full-time, $73 per semester (minimum) part-time. • Enna Crosman, Chair, 718-488-1067. Application contact: Bernard W. Sullivan, Associate Director of Admissions, 718-488-1011.

Long Island University, Brooklyn Campus, Arnold and Marie Schwartz College of Pharmacy and Health Sciences, Graduate Programs in Pharmacy, Division of Pharmacy Administration, Brooklyn, NY 11201-8423. Offers programs in drug regulatory affairs (MS), hospital pharmacy administration (MS), pharmaceutical and health care marketing administration (MS). Part-time and evening/weekend programs available. Faculty: 7 full-time (1 woman), 8 part-time (1 woman). Students: 5 full-time (4 women), 25 part-time (13 women); includes 12 minority (5 African Americans, 7 Asian Americans), 7 international. Average age 28. In 1997, 4 degrees awarded. *Degree requirements:* Thesis optional, foreign language not required. *Average time to degree:* master's–2 years full-time, 5 years part-time. *Entrance requirements:* Minimum GPA of 3.0. Application deadline: rolling. Application fee: $30. *Expenses:* Tuition $480 per credit. Fees $415 per year full-time, $73 per semester (minimum) part-time. *Financial aid:* In 1997–98, 4 students received aid, including 4 teaching assistantships averaging $350 per month. • Dr. Steven Strauss, Director, 718-488-1105. Application contact: Bernard W. Sullivan, Associate Director of Admissions, 718-488-1011.

Long Island University, C.W. Post Campus, College of Management, School of Public Service, Department of Health Care and Public Administration, Brookville, NY 11548-1300. Awards MPA, Certificate, CG, JD/MPA. Programs in gerontology (CG), health administration (MPA), health administration/gerontology (MPA), health systems finance (MPA, Certificate), public administration (MPA). JD/MPA offered jointly with Touro College. Part-time and evening/weekend programs available. Faculty: 10 full-time (3 women), 23 part-time (3 women). Students: 23 full-time (10 women), 174 part-time (120 women). 96 applicants, 92% accepted. In 1997, 43 master's, 1 other advanced degree awarded. *Degree requirements:* For master's, computer language, thesis required, foreign language not required. *Entrance requirements:* For master's, minimum GPA of 3.0; for other advanced degree, minimum GPA of 2.75. Application deadline: rolling. Application fee: $30. Electronic applications accepted. *Expenses:* Tuition $480 per credit. Fees $316 per year full-time, $71 per semester (minimum) part-time. *Financial aid:* Graduate assistantships available. Aid available to part-time students. Financial aid application deadline: 5/15; applicants required to submit FAFSA. • Dr. Thomas Webster, Chair, 516-299-2716. Application contact: Sally Luzader, Associate Director of Graduate Admissions, 516-299-2417. Fax: 516-299-2137. E-mail: admissions@collegehall.liunet.edu.

Lynn University, School of Graduate Studies, Department of Gerontology and Health Services, Boca Raton, FL 33431-5598. Offers programs in aging studies (Certificate); biomechanical trauma (MS); health care administration (MS, Certificate), including nursing home administrator licensure (MS). Part-time and evening/weekend programs available. Faculty: 6 full-time (4 women), 2 part-time (0 women). Students: 22 full-time (16 women), 18 part-time (12 women); includes 1 international. 39 applicants, 67% accepted. In 1997, 16 master's awarded. *Degree requirements:* For master's, computer language, internship, comprehensive exam (nursing

Directory: Health Services Management and Hospital Administration

Lynn University (continued)
home administrator licensure), thesis/dissertation (biomechanical trauma) required, foreign language not required. *Average time to degree:* master's–1.9 years full-time, 3.6 years part-time. *Entrance requirements:* For master's, MAT, minimum undergraduate GPA of 3.0. Application deadline: rolling. Application fee: $50. Electronic applications accepted. *Expenses:* Tuition $375 per credit hour. Fees $60 per year. *Financial aid:* In 1997–98, 21 students received aid, including 1 graduate assistantship (to a first-year student); partial tuition waivers and career-related internships or fieldwork also available. Financial aid application deadline: 6/15; applicants required to submit FAFSA. *Faculty research:* Alzheimer's disease, therapeutic programming, physician training in geriatrics, case management, long term care administration. • Dr. Rita Gugel, Associate Dean, 561-994-0770 Ext. 194. Fax: 561-994-5827. Application contact: Pat Sieredcki, Graduate Admissions Coordinator, 800-544-8035. Fax: 561-241-3552. E-mail: admission@lynn.edu.

Madonna University, Program in Health Services, Livonia, MI 48150-1173. Awards MS. Faculty: 4 full-time, 2 part-time. Students: 15 full-time (11 women), 14 part-time (12 women). *Degree requirements:* Thesis optional, foreign language not required. *Entrance requirements:* TOEFL (minimum score 550), GRE General Test or minimum GPA of 3.25. Application deadline: 8/1 (priority date; rolling processing; 4/1 for spring admission). *Expenses:* Tuition $260 per credit hour (minimum). Fees $50 per semester. • Ellen Oliver Smith, Dean, 734-432-5515. E-mail: smith-e@smtp.munet.edu. Application contact: Sandra Kellums, Coordinator of Graduate Admissions, 734-432-5666. Fax: 734-432-5393. E-mail: kellums@smtp.munet.edu.

Marshall University, Graduate School of Management, Program in Health Care Administration, South Charleston, WV 25303-1600. Awards MSM. Part-time and evening/weekend programs available. Faculty: 1 full-time (0 women). Students: 5 full-time (2 women), 62 part-time (41 women); includes 4 minority (2 African Americans, 2 Asian Americans). Average age 37. In 1997, 29 degrees awarded. *Degree requirements:* Comprehensive exam required, foreign language and thesis not required. *Entrance requirements:* GMAT (minimum score 450) or GRE General Test (minimum combined score of 1000), minimum GPA of 2.5. Application deadline: 8/1 (priority date; rolling processing). Application fee: $0. *Financial aid:* Full tuition waivers and career-related internships or fieldwork available. Aid available to part-time students. Financial aid applicants required to submit FAFSA. • Dr. Kurt Olmosk, Associate Dean, Graduate School of Management, 304-746-1958. Fax: 304-746-2503.

Marymount University, School of Business Administration, Program in Health Care Management, Arlington, VA 22207-4299. Awards MS. Part-time and evening/weekend programs available. Students: 54. *Degree requirements:* Thesis optional, foreign language not required. *Entrance requirements:* GMAT or GRE General Test, interview. Application deadline: rolling. Application fee: $35. *Expenses:* Tuition $465 per credit hour. Fees $120 per year full-time, $5 per credit hour part-time. *Financial aid:* Career-related internships or fieldwork available. Aid available to part-time students. Financial aid applicants required to submit FAFSA. • Dr. Donald Lavanty, Chair, 703-284-5910. Fax: 703-527-3815.

Marywood University, Graduate School of Arts and Sciences, Department of Public Administration, Program in Health Services Administration, Scranton, PA 18509-1598. Awards MHSA. Students: 3 full-time (all women), 6 part-time (5 women). Average age 36. 2 applicants, 100% accepted. *Degree requirements:* Thesis or alternative, internship/practicum required, foreign language not required. *Entrance requirements:* TOEFL (minimum score 550; average 590). Application deadline: 7/15 (priority date; rolling processing; 12/1 for spring admission). Application fee: $20. *Expenses:* Tuition $449 per credit hour. Fees $530 per year full-time, $180 per year part-time. *Financial aid:* Research assistantships, scholarships/tuition reductions, partial tuition waivers, and career-related internships or fieldwork available. Aid available to part-time students. Financial aid application deadline: 2/15; applicants required to submit FAFSA. • Application contact: Deborah M. Flynn, Coordinator of Admissions, 717-340-6002. Fax: 717-961-4745. E-mail: gsas_adm@ac.marywood.edu.

McGill University, Faculty of Graduate Studies and Research, Faculty of Medicine, Department of Epidemiology and Biostatistics, Montréal, PQ H3A 2T5, Canada. Offerings include health care evaluation (M Sc). Department faculty: 35 full-time (7 women), 23 part-time (6 women). *Degree requirements:* Thesis optional, foreign language not required. *Entrance requirements:* GRE, minimum GPA of 3.0. Application deadline: 3/1 (rolling processing). Application fee: $60. *Expenses:* Tuition $1668 per year for Canadian residents; $8268 per year for nonresidents. Fees $828 per year for Canadian residents; $1216 per year for nonresidents. • Dr. G. Theriault, Chair, Graduate Committee, 514-398-6259. E-mail: gtheri@epid.lan.mcgill.ca. Application contact: Marlene Abrams, Secretary for Graduate Studies, 514-398-6269. Fax: 514-398-4503. E-mail: marlene@epid.lan.mcgill.ca.

Medical University of South Carolina, College of Health Professions, Program in Health Sciences, Charleston, SC 29425-0002. Offerings include health information administration (MHS). Postbaccalaureate distance learning degree programs offered (minimal on-campus study). Program faculty: 12 (7 women). *Entrance requirements:* GRE General Test, interview, minimum GPA of 3.0. Application deadline: rolling. Application fee: $55. *Expenses:* Tuition $4072 per year full-time, $221 per semester hour part-time for state residents; $7064 per year full-time, $387 per semester hour part-time for nonresidents. Fees $150 per year (minimum). • Dr. Valerie T. West, Associate Dean, 843-792-3326. E-mail: westvt@musc.edu. Application contact: Fran Clement, Student Services, 843-792-3326. Fax: 843-792-4024. E-mail: clementf@musc.edu.

Medical University of South Carolina, College of Health Professions, Department of Health Administration and Policy, Doctoral Program in Health Administration, Charleston, SC 29425-0002. Awards DHA. Postbaccalaureate distance learning degree programs offered (minimal on-campus study). Faculty: 7 full-time (2 women). *Degree requirements:* Dissertation, minimum GPA of 3.0 in each course required, foreign language not required. *Average time to degree:* doctorate–3 years full-time. *Entrance requirements:* GRE General Test (minimum combined score of 1500 on three sections), GMAT (minimum score 500), minimum 10 years experience in health care, interview. *Expenses:* Tuition $4072 per year full-time, $221 per semester hour part-time for state residents; $7064 per year full-time, $387 per semester hour part-time for nonresidents. Fees $150 per year (minimum). *Faculty research:* Strategic planning, management and health information systems, health policy analysis, health economics and finance, AIDS research and development. • Dr. James A. Johnson, Director, 843-792-3324. E-mail: johnsnja@musc.edu. Application contact: Kurt Komlos, Program Manager, 843-792-2115. Fax: 843-792-3327. E-mail: komlosk@musc.edu.

Medical University of South Carolina, College of Health Professions, Department of Health Administration and Policy, Master's Program in Health Administration, Charleston, SC 29425-0002. Awards MHA, MHA/MHS. Accredited by ACEHSA. Offered jointly with Clemson University. Part-time and evening/weekend programs available. Postbaccalaureate distance learning degree programs offered (minimal on-campus study). Faculty: 12 full-time (2 women), 5 part-time (2 women), 14 FTE. Students: 1 (woman) full-time, 1 part-time (0 women). Average age 35. 0 applicants. In 1997, 38 degrees awarded (98% found work related to degree, 2% continued full-time study). *Degree requirements:* Minimum GPA of 3.0 in each course, 30 to 40 hours of community service required, foreign language and thesis not required. *Average time to degree:* master's–2 years full-time, 4 years part-time. *Entrance requirements:* GRE General Test (minimum combined score of 1500 on three sections), GMAT (minimum score 500), TOEFL (minimum score 500), minimum GPA of 3.0. Application deadline: rolling. Application fee: $55. *Expenses:* Tuition $4072 per year full-time, $221 per semester hour part-time for state residents; $7064 per year full-time, $387 per semester hour part-time for nonresidents. Fees $150 per year (minimum). *Financial aid:* In 1997–98, 1 fellowship was awarded; research assistantships and career-related internships or fieldwork also available. Aid available to part-time students. Financial aid application deadline: 4/1; applicants required to submit FAFSA. *Faculty research:* Strategic planning, management and health information systems, health policy analysis, health economics and finance, AIDS research and development. Total annual research expenditures: $99,000. • Application contact: Kelly Long, Student Services Coordinator, 843-792-8510. Fax: 843-792-3327. E-mail: longk@musc.edu.

Medical University of South Carolina, College of Health Professions, Department of Health Administration and Policy, Program in Health Information Administration, Charleston, SC 29425-0002. Awards MHS, MHA/MHS. Part-time and evening/weekend programs available. Postbaccalaureate distance learning degree programs offered. Faculty: 10 full-time (4 women), 2 part-time (1 woman), 10.9 FTE. In 1997, 9 degrees awarded (100% found work related to degree). *Degree requirements:* Minimum GPA of 3.0 in each course, 30 to 40 hours of community service required, foreign language and thesis not required. *Average time to degree:* master's–2 years full-time, 4 years part-time. *Entrance requirements:* GRE General Test (minimum combined score of 1000), MAT (minimum score 42) (MHS), minimum GPA of 3.0. Application fee: $55. *Expenses:* Tuition $4072 per year full-time, $221 per semester hour part-time for state residents; $7064 per year full-time, $387 per semester hour part-time for nonresidents. Fees $150 per year (minimum). *Financial aid:* 14 students received aid; fellowships, research assistantships, Federal Work-Study available. Aid available to part-time students. Financial aid application deadline: 4/1; applicants required to submit FAFSA. *Faculty research:* Computer-based patient records, Internet use in health care, health information networks, continuous quality improvement, organizational behavior. Total annual research expenditures: $21,294. • Karen A. Wager, Director, 843-792-4491. E-mail: wagerka@musc.edu. Application contact: Kelly Long, Student Services Coordinator, 843-792-8510. Fax: 843-792-3327. E-mail: longk@musc.edu.

Medical University of South Carolina, College of Health Professions, Department of Health Administration and Policy, Program in Health Management, Charleston, SC 29425-0002. Awards Certificate. Postbaccalaureate distance learning degree programs offered (no on-campus study). Faculty: 10 full-time (1 woman), 1 (woman) part-time, 10.25 FTE. Students: 8 full-time (6 women); includes 1 minority (African American). Average age 34. 8 applicants, 100% accepted. *Degree requirements:* Minimum GPA of 3.0 in each course required, foreign language and thesis not required. *Entrance requirements:* GMAT, GRE, enrollment in a participating MBA program. Application fee: $55. *Expenses:* Tuition $4072 per year full-time, $221 per semester hour part-time for state residents; $7064 per year full-time, $387 per semester hour part-time for nonresidents. Fees $150 per year (minimum). *Financial aid:* Fellowships, research assistantships, Federal Work-Study available. Aid available to part-time students. Financial aid application deadline: 4/1; applicants required to submit FAFSA. *Faculty research:* Strategic planning, management and health information systems, health policy analysis, health economics and finance, AIDS. Total annual research expenditures: $99,000. • David S. Snyder, Coordinator, 843-792-3776. Fax: 843-792-3327. E-mail: snyderds@musc.edu.

Meharry Medical College, Division of Community Health Sciences, Nashville, TN 37208-9989. Offers programs in general preventive medicine (MSPH), health services administration (MSPH), occupational medicine (MSPH), public health administration (MSPH). Accredited by ACEHSA. Part-time and evening/weekend programs available. Faculty: 12 full-time (4 women), 10 part-time (5 women). Students: 47 full-time (26 women); includes 39 minority (35 African Americans, 3 Asian Americans, 1 Hispanic), 4 international. Average age 32. 45 applicants, 51% accepted. In 1997, 19 degrees awarded. *Degree requirements:* Thesis, externship required, foreign language not required. *Average time to degree:* master's–2 years full-time, 4 years part-time. *Entrance requirements:* GRE General Test (minimum combined score of 800). Application deadline: 6/30 (rolling processing). Application fee: $45. *Expenses:* Tuition $7020 per year. Fees $1633 per year. *Financial aid:* Scholarships, Federal Work-Study, institutionally sponsored loans, and career-related internships or fieldwork available. Aid available to part-time students. Financial aid application deadline: 7/15; applicants required to submit FAFSA. *Faculty research:* Policy and management, health care financing, health education and promotion. • Dr. Herman Ellis, Interim Director, 615-327-5530. Application contact: Dr. Otis Cosby, Assistant Director, 615-327-6069. Fax: 615-327-6717.

Mercer University, Cecil B. Day Campus, Stetson School of Business and Economics, 3001 Mercer University Drive, Atlanta, GA 30341-4155. Offerings include health care policy and administration (MS). School faculty: 24 full-time (11 women), 14 part-time (5 women). *Average time to degree:* master's–1.5 years full-time, 2.5 years part-time. *Application deadline:* 8/1 (rolling processing; 12/1 for spring admission). *Application fee:* $35 ($50 for international students). *Tuition:* $327 per semester hour. • Dr. W. Carl Joiner, Dean, 912-752-2832. Application contact: Dr. Victoria Johnson, Associate Dean, 770-986-3235. Fax: 770-986-3337. E-mail: johnson_v@mercer.edu.

Mississippi College, College of Arts and Sciences, Department of Biological Sciences, Program in Health Science, Clinton, MS 39058. Offers health care administration (MHS). *Degree requirements:* Oral comprehensive exam required, foreign language and thesis not required. *Entrance requirements:* GRE General Test (minimum combined score of 850), minimum GPA of 2.5. Application deadline: 8/15 (priority date; rolling processing). Application fee: $25 ($75 for international students). *Expenses:* Tuition $6624 per year full-time, $276 per hour part-time. Fees $230 per year full-time, $35 per semester (minimum) part-time. *Financial aid:* Career-related internships or fieldwork available. Aid available to part-time students. Financial aid application deadline: 4/1. • Dr. Ted Snazelle, Head, Department of Biological Sciences, 601-925-3339.

Montana State University–Billings, College of Education and Human Services, Department of Health and Human Services, Program in Health Care Administration, Billings, MT 59101-9984. Awards MS. *Degree requirements:* Thesis or professional paper and/or field experience required, foreign language not required. *Entrance requirements:* GRE General Test (minimum combined score of 1350 on three sections) or MAT (minimum score 38), minimum GPA of 3.0 (undergraduate), 3.25 (graduate). Application deadline: 8/1 (priority date; rolling processing; 1/1 for spring admission). Application fee: $30. *Expenses:* Tuition $2253 per year full-time, $397 per semester (minimum) part-time for state residents; $5313 per year full-time, $907 per semester (minimum) part-time for nonresidents. Fees $378 per year full-time, $105 per semester (minimum) part-time.

Montana State University–Bozeman, College of Nursing, 211 Montana Hall, Bozeman, MT 59717. Offerings include health administration (MHA). College faculty: 20 full-time (all women). *Application deadline:* 6/1 (priority date; rolling processing; 11/1 for spring admission). *Application fee:* $50. *Tuition:* $3994 per year full-time, $367 per semester (minimum) part-time for state residents; $9507 per year full-time, $957 per semester (minimum) part-time for nonresidents. • Dr. Lea Acord, Dean, 406-994-3783. Fax: 406-994-6020. E-mail: znu7003@montana.edu.

National University, School of Management and Technology, Department of Professional Studies, Program in Health Care Administration, La Jolla, CA 92037-1011. Awards MHCA. Students: 14 full-time (10 women), 9 part-time (6 women); includes 11 minority (4 African Americans, 4 Asian Americans, 3 Hispanics), 1 international. Average age 34. *Entrance requirements:* Interview, minimum GPA of 2.5. Application deadline: rolling. Application fee: $60 ($100 for international students). *Tuition:* $7830 per year full-time, $870 per course part-time. *Financial aid:* Application deadline 5/1. • Harold Hartman, Head, 619-642-8417. Application contact: Nancy Rohland, Director of Enrollment Management, 619-563-7100. Fax: 619-563-7393.

New England College, Program in Organizational Management, 7 Main Street, Henniker, NH 03242-3293. Offerings include health care (MS), health care management (Certificate). College faculty: 7 full-time, 13 part-time. *Degree requirements:* For master's, independent research project required, foreign language not required. *Application deadline:* rolling. *Application fee:* $25. *Expenses:* Tuition $175 per credit. Fees $20 per semester. • Dr. Patricia Prinz, Director of Graduate and Continuing Studies, 603-428-2252. Fax: 603-428-2266. Application contact: Robert Godard, Associate Director, 603-428-2483.

New Hampshire College, Graduate School of Business, Program in Business Administration, Manchester, NH 03106-1045. Offerings include health administration (Certificate). Program faculty: 7 full-time (1 woman), 66 part-time (11 women), 47 FTE. *Average time to degree:* master's–1.5 years full-time, 4.5 years part-time. *Application deadline:* rolling. *Application fee:* $0. *Expenses:* Tuition $17,044 per year full-time, $945 per course part-time. Fees $530 per year full-time, $80 per year part-time. • Dr. Paul Schneiderman, Acting Dean, Graduate School of Business, 603-644-3102. Fax: 603-644-3150.

New Jersey City University, School of Professional Studies and Education, Department of Health Sciences, Jersey City, NJ 07305-1957. Offerings include health administration (MS). *Degree requirements:* Thesis or alternative, internship required, foreign language not required. *Entrance requirements:* GRE, TOEFL or MAT. Application deadline: 8/1 (priority date; rolling processing; 12/1 for spring admission). Application fee: $0.

New School University, Robert J. Milano Graduate School of Management and Urban Policy, Program in Health Services Management and Policy, New York, NY 10011-8603. Offers health services management and policy (MS), management of medical services (Adv C), materials management (Adv C), mental health administration (Adv C). Part-time and evening/weekend programs available. Faculty: 6 full-time (3 women), 95 part-time (69 women). Students: 30 full-time (24 women), 278 part-time (222 women); includes 113 minority (72 African Americans, 25 Asian Americans, 16 Hispanics), 1 international. Average age 33. In 1997, 125 master's awarded. *Degree requirements:* For master's, computer language, thesis required, foreign language not required. *Average time to degree:* master's–1.5 years full-time, 3 years part-time. *Entrance requirements:* For master's, interview. Application deadline: 9/1 (priority date; rolling processing). Application fee: $30. *Tuition:* $622 per credit. *Financial aid:* In 1997–98, 44 scholarships (18 to first-year students) totaling $168,320 were awarded; teaching assistantships, full and partial tuition waivers, Federal Work-Study, and career-related internships or fieldwork also available. Aid available to part-time students. Financial aid application deadline: 3/1; applicants required to submit FAFSA. *Faculty research:* Health care economics. • Dr. Howard Berliner, Chair, 212-229-5337. E-mail: hberline@newschool.edu. Application contact: Susan Morris, Assistant Dean, 212-229-5388. Fax: 212-229-8935. E-mail: smorris@newschool.edu.

New York Medical College, Graduate School of Health Sciences, Program in Clinical Research Administration, Valhalla, NY 10595-1691. Awards MS. *Degree requirements:* Thesis required, foreign language not required. *Entrance requirements:* TOEFL. *Tuition:* $415 per credit. • Dr. Peter Cervoni, Director, 914-594-4804.

New York Medical College, Graduate School of Health Sciences, Program in Health Policy and Management, Valhalla, NY 10595-1691. Awards MPH, MS. Part-time and evening/weekend programs available. *Degree requirements:* Computer language required, foreign language not required. *Entrance requirements:* TOEFL. Application deadline: 7/20 (priority date; rolling processing; 12/1 for spring admission). Application fee: $35 ($60 for international students). *Tuition:* $415 per credit. *Financial aid:* Federal Work-Study, institutionally sponsored loans, and career-related internships or fieldwork available. Financial aid application deadline: 6/15. • Annette Choolthian, Director, 914-594-4250.

See in-depth description on page 1507.

New York University, Robert F. Wagner Graduate School of Public Service, Program in Health Policy and Management, New York, NY 10012-1019. Awards MPA, PhD, AMPC, APC, MS/AMPC. Offerings include financial management (MPA, APC), health policy analysis (MPA, APC), health policy and management (PhD, AMPC), health services management (MPA, APC). Part-time and evening/weekend programs available. Faculty: 12 full-time (4 women), 17 part-time (9 women), 15 FTE. Students: 102 full-time (76 women), 196 part-time (141 women); includes 105 minority (47 African Americans, 30 Asian Americans, 26 Hispanics, 2 Native Americans), 21 international. Average age 28. 219 applicants, 69% accepted. In 1997, 98 master's, 1 other advanced degree awarded. *Degree requirements:* For master's, thesis or alternative, residency (internship); for doctorate, 1 foreign language, dissertation. *Average time to degree:* master's–2 years full-time, 4 years part-time; other advanced degree–1 year full-time. *Entrance requirements:* For master's, GRE General Test (recommended), minimum undergraduate GPA of 3.0; for doctorate, GMAT or GRE General Test, minimum GPA of 3.5. Application deadline: 8/1 (rolling processing; 1/1 for spring admission). Application fee: $50 ($70 for international students). *Financial aid:* In 1997–98, 122 students received aid, including 5 research assistantships averaging $850 per month, 117 scholarships; full and partial tuition waivers, Federal Work-Study, institutionally sponsored loans, and career-related internships or fieldwork also available. Aid available to part-time students. Financial aid application deadline: 2/15; applicants required to submit FAFSA. • Beth Weitzman, Director, 212-998-7440. Fax: 212-995-4162. Application contact: Hedy Flanders, Director, Admissions and Financial Aid, 212-998-7414. Fax: 212-995-4164. E-mail: wagner.admissions@nyu.edu.

New York University, Robert F. Wagner Graduate School of Public Service, Program in Management, New York, NY 10012-1019. Offerings include health policy and management (MS). MA/MS offered jointly with the Division of Nursing. Program faculty: 29 full-time (11 women), 69 part-time (30 women), 42 FTE. *Degree requirements:* Thesis or alternative. *Average time to degree:* master's–1 year full-time, 2 years part-time. *Entrance requirements:* Minimum undergraduate GPA of 3.0. Application deadline: 8/1 (rolling processing; 1/1 for spring admission). Application fee: $50 ($70 for international students). • Application contact: Hedy Flanders, Director, Admissions and Financial Aid, 212-998-7414. Fax: 212-995-4164. E-mail: wagner.admissions@nyu.edu.

Northeastern University, Bouvé College of Pharmacy and Health Sciences Graduate School, Programs in Health Professions, Boston, MA 02115-5096. Offerings include health policy (MHP). Faculty: 11 full-time (4 women). *Degree requirements:* Comprehensive exam required, foreign language not required. *Entrance requirements:* Minimum GPA of 3.0, bachelor's degree in science. Application deadline: (3/1 for spring admission). Application fee: $50. *Expenses:* Tuition $440 per credit hour. Fees $55 per quarter full-time, $13.25 per quarter part-time. • Judith Barr, Director, 617-373-4188. Application contact: Bill Purnell, Director of Graduate Admissions, 617-373-2708. Fax: 617-373-4701. E-mail: w.purnell@nunet.neu.edu.

See in-depth description on page 1797.

Northeastern University, Graduate School of Arts and Sciences, Department of Political Science, Program in Public Administration, Boston, MA 02115-5096. Offerings include health administration and policy (MPA). Program faculty: 8 full-time (0 women), 7 part-time (1 woman). *Application deadline:* 2/15 (rolling processing; 2/15 for spring admission). *Application fee:* $50. *Expenses:* Tuition $440 per credit hour. Fees $55 per quarter full-time, $13.25 per quarter part-time. • Dr. John Portz, Chair, 617-373-2796. Application contact: Mary Churchill, Administrative Assistant for Graduate Programs, 617-373-4404. Fax: 617-373-5311. E-mail: mchurch@neu.edu.

Northwestern University, J. L. Kellogg Graduate School of Management, Programs in Management, Program in Health Services Management, Evanston, IL 60208. Awards MM. Accredited by ACEHSA. *Entrance requirements:* GMAT, TOEFL, interview. Application fee: $125. *Tuition:* $25,872 per year. *Financial aid:* Institutionally sponsored loans and career-related internships or fieldwork available. Financial aid application deadline: 2/1; applicants required to submit FAFSA. *Faculty research:* Strategy, structure, and performance of integrated health systems; application of total quality management to health care organizations; structure and effects of hospital market competition; effects of technology acquisition and technological competition; assessing the implications of patient outcome research and development of practice guidelines. • Dr. Joel Shalowitz, Director, 847-491-5540. Fax: 847-491-2683. Application contact: Office of Admissions and Financial Aid, 847-491-3308.

Nova Southeastern University, School of Business and Entrepreneurship, Program in Health Services Administration, Fort Lauderdale, FL 33314-7721. Offers health services administration (MS). Part-time and evening/weekend programs available. Students: 5 full-time (3 women), 85 part-time (64 women); includes 29 minority (21 African Americans, 1 Asian American, 7 Hispanics), 5 international. 1 applicant. In 1997, 29 degrees awarded. *Degree requirements:* Internship, thesis or workshop. *Entrance requirements:* GMAT (minimum score 450), GRE General Test (minimum combined score of 1000), prerequisites in psychology, accounting, finance, and statistics; work experience; computer literacy. Application deadline: 8/15 (priority date; rolling processing; 2/10 for spring admission). Application fee: $50. *Tuition:* $270 per credit hour (minimum). *Faculty research:* Strategic management, health policy analysis. • Dr. Daniel Austin, Director, 954-262-5145. Application contact: Shane Strum, Marketing Manager, 954-262-5035.

The Ohio State University, College of Medicine and Public Health and Graduate School, Graduate Programs in the Basic Medical Sciences, Division of Health Services Management and Policy, Columbus, OH 43210. Awards MHA, PhD, JD/MHA, MD/MHA, MHA/MBA, MHA/MPA, MHA/MS. Program in health administration (MHA, PhD). One or more programs accredited by ACEHSA. Part-time programs available. Faculty: 7 full-time (2 women), 5 part-time (2 women). Students: 46 full-time (26 women), 9 part-time (8 women); includes 15 minority (6 African Americans, 5 Asian Americans, 3 Hispanics, 1 Native American). Average age 26. 113 applicants, 32% accepted. In 1997, 23 master's awarded (100% found work related to degree). *Average time to degree:* master's–2 years full-time, 4 years part-time. *Entrance requirements:* For master's, GMAT or GRE General Test. Application deadline: 3/15 (priority date; rolling processing). Application fee: $30 ($40 for international students). *Tuition:* $5472 per year full-time, $554 per quarter (minimum) part-time for state residents; $14,172 per year full-time, $1424 per quarter (minimum) part-time for nonresidents. *Financial aid:* In 1997–98, 3 fellowships (all to first-year students), 24 administrative assistantships, associateships, traineeships (4 to first-year students) were awarded; research assistantships, Federal Work-Study, institutionally sponsored loans also available. Aid available to part-time students. Financial aid application deadline: 2/1; applicants required to submit FAFSA. *Faculty research:* Patient satisfaction, health care costs in Ohio, health care financial management, health care policy, restructuring of health care operations. Total annual research expenditures: $750,000. • Dr. Stephen F. Loebs, Chairman, 614-292-9708. Application contact: Sandra L. Daly, Director of Admissions, 614-292-8193. Fax: 614-292-3572.

See in-depth descriptions on pages 1315 and 1509.

The Ohio State University, College of Pharmacy and Graduate School, Graduate Programs in Pharmacy, Division of Pharmacy Practice and Administration, Columbus, OH 43210. Offers programs in hospital pharmacy (MS), pharmaceutical administration (MS, PhD). Part-time programs available. Faculty: 3 full-time (0 women). Students: 20 full-time (11 women), 2 part-time (both women); includes 6 minority (5 African Americans, 1 Hispanic), 3 international. Average age 25. 21 applicants, 29% accepted. In 1997, 5 master's awarded (80% found work related to degree, 20% continued full-time study); 1 doctorate awarded (100% found work related to degree). *Degree requirements:* For doctorate, 1 foreign language, dissertation. *Average time to degree:* master's–2 years full-time; doctorate–4 years full-time. *Entrance requirements:* For master's, GRE General Test, TOEFL (minimum score 600), TSE (minimum score 60); for doctorate, GRE General Test, TOEFL (minimum score 600), TSE (minimum score 60), minimum GPA of 3.0. Application deadline: 1/15 (priority date; 1/1 for spring admission). Application fee: $30 ($40 for international students). *Tuition:* $5472 per year full-time, $554 per quarter (minimum) part-time for state residents; $14,172 per year full-time, $1424 per quarter (minimum) part-time for nonresidents. *Financial aid:* In 1997–98, 1 fellowship averaging $2,208 per month, 9 research assistantships (4 to first-year students) averaging $1,990 per month, 6 teaching assistantships averaging $1,175 per month, 1 administrative associateship averaging $1,108 per month were awarded. Financial aid application deadline: 1/15. *Faculty research:* Pharmacoeconomic analysis, finance, institutional behavior, drug distribution and public policy. • Dr. Dev S. Pathak, Chairman, 614-292-0540. Fax: 614-292-1335. E-mail: pathak.1@osu.edu.

See in-depth description on page 1799.

Ohio University, Graduate Studies, College of Health and Human Services, School of Health Sciences, Athens, OH 45701-2979. Awards MHA. Part-time programs available. Faculty: 10 full-time (5 women), 8 part-time (7 women). Students: 22 full-time (17 women), 6 part-time (all women); includes 2 minority (both African Americans), 5 international. 28 applicants, 39% accepted. In 1997, 14 degrees awarded. *Degree requirements:* Internship required, foreign language and thesis not required. *Entrance requirements:* GMAT, GRE General Test. Application deadline: 6/1 (priority date). Application fee: $30. *Tuition:* $5430 per year full-time, $216 per quarter hour part-time for state residents; $10,431 per year full-time, $423 per quarter hour part-time for nonresidents. *Financial aid:* In 1997–98, 11 students received aid, including 4 research assistantships (all to first-year students) averaging $625 per month, 7 teaching assistantships (all to first-year students) averaging $625 per month; full tuition waivers, Federal Work-Study, institutionally sponsored loans, and career-related internships or fieldwork also available. Financial aid application deadline: 3/15. *Faculty research:* Health care management, gerontology, stress reduction, health policy, managed care, long term care administration. • Dr. Paul Fitzgerald, Director, 740-593-4675. Fax: 740-593-0555. E-mail: fitzgera@oak.cats.ohiou.edu. Application contact: Dr. Douglas Bolon, Coordinator, 614-593-0750. Fax: 614-593-0555. E-mail: bolon@ohiou.edu.

Oklahoma City University, School of Management and Business Sciences, Program in Business Administration, Oklahoma City, OK 73106-1402. Offerings include health administration (MBA). *Degree requirements:* Comprehensive exam required, foreign language and thesis not required. *Entrance requirements:* TOEFL, minimum GPA of 2.5. Application deadline: rolling. Application fee: $35 ($55 for international students). *Expenses:* Tuition $350 per hour. Fees $124 per year. • Application contact: Laura L. Rahhal, Director of Graduate Admissions, 800-633-7242 Ext. 2. Fax: 405-521-5356. E-mail: lrahhal1@frodo.okcu.edu.

Old Dominion University, College of Health Sciences, Program in Urban Services/Urban Health Services, Norfolk, VA 23529. Awards PhD. Students: 6 full-time (all women), 20 part-time (15 women); includes 7 minority (6 African Americans, 1 Asian American), 3 international. Average age 41. In 1997, 1 degree awarded. *Degree requirements:* Dissertation, comprehensive exams required, foreign language not required. *Entrance requirements:* GMAT (minimum score 500), GRE General Test (minimum combined score of 1100), MAT, minimum GPA of 3.0. Application deadline: 7/1 (rolling processing; 11/1 for spring admission). Application fee: $30. Electronic applications accepted. *Expenses:* Tuition $180 per credit hour for state residents; $477 per credit hour for nonresidents. Fees $140 per year full-time, $32 per semester part-time. *Financial aid:* In 1997–98, 8 students received aid, including 1 fellowship totaling $1,500, 7 research assistantships totaling $66,672; teaching assistantships, tuition grants, partial tuition waivers, and career-related internships or fieldwork also available. Aid available to part-time students. Financial aid application deadline: 2/15; applicants required to submit FAFSA. *Faculty research:* Grief, sports, minority issues, access to health services, health outcomes. • Dr. Clare Houseman, Director, 757-683-4259. Fax: 757-683-5674. E-mail: chousema@odu.edu.

Old Dominion University, College of Health Sciences, School of Community Health Professions and Physical Therapy, Norfolk, VA 23529. Offerings include long-term care administration (Certificate). School faculty: 9 full-time (7 women), 5 part-time (3 women), 10.7 FTE. *Application deadline:* 2/15 (rolling processing). *Application fee:* $30. *Expenses:* Tuition $180 per credit hour for state residents; $477 per credit hour for nonresidents. Fees $140 per year full-time, $32 per semester part-time. • Dr. George Maihafer, Chair, 757-683-4520. E-mail: gmaihafer@odu.edu.

Oregon State University, Graduate School, College of Health and Human Performance, Department of Public Health, Program in Health and Safety Administration, Corvallis, OR 97331. Awards MAIS, MS. Faculty: 10 full-time (5 women), 1 (woman) part-time. Students: 5 full-time, 1 part-time; includes 2 international. Average age 41. 9 applicants, 44% accepted. In

Directory: Health Services Management and Hospital Administration

Oregon State University (continued)

1997, 1 degree awarded. *Degree requirements:* Thesis, minimum GPA of 3.0 required, foreign language not required. *Entrance requirements:* GRE General Test, TOEFL (minimum score 550), minimum GPA of 3.0 in last 90 hours. Application deadline: 3/1 (rolling processing). Application fee: $50. *Tuition:* $6207 per year full-time, $810 per quarter (minimum) part-time for state residents; $10,551 per year full-time, $1293 per quarter (minimum) part-time for nonresidents. *Financial aid:* Research assistantships, teaching assistantships, Federal Work-Study, institutionally sponsored loans, and career-related internships or fieldwork available. Aid available to part-time students. Financial aid application deadline: 2/1. *Faculty research:* Safety management, health promotion, health care administration, health policy. • Dr. David C. Lawson, Director, 541-737-3826.

Our Lady of the Lake University of San Antonio, School of Business and Public Administration, 411 Southwest 24th Street, San Antonio, TX 78207-4689. Offerings include health care management (MBA). School faculty: 15 full-time (2 women), 15 part-time (2 women). *Degree requirements:* Thesis optional. *Entrance requirements:* GMAT, GRE General Test, or MAT. Application deadline: rolling. Application fee: $15. *Expenses:* Tuition $371 per credit hour. Fees $57 per semester full-time, $32 per semester part-time. • Dr. W. Earl Walker, Dean, 210-434-6711 Ext. 281. Application contact: Quentin W. Korte, MBA Adviser, 210-434-6711 Ext. 491. Fax: 210-434-0821.

Pace University, Dyson College of Arts and Sciences, Department of Public Administration, New York, NY 10038. Offerings include health care administration (MPA). *Entrance requirements:* GRE General Test. Application deadline: 7/31 (priority date; rolling processing; 11/30 for spring admission). Application fee: $60. *Expenses:* Tuition $520 per credit. Fees $360 per year full-time, $53 per semester (minimum) part-time.

Pace University, Lubin School of Business, Health Systems Management Program, New York, NY 10038. Awards MBA. Part-time and evening/weekend programs available. *Degree requirements:* Computer language required, foreign language not required. *Entrance requirements:* GMAT. Application deadline: 7/31 (priority date; rolling processing; 11/30 for spring admission). Application fee: $60. *Expenses:* Tuition $545 per credit. Fees $360 per year full-time, $53 per semester (minimum) part-time.

Pennsylvania State University Great Valley School of Graduate Professional Studies, Graduate Studies and Continuing Education, Program in Health Care Administration, Malvern, PA 19355-1488. Awards MBA. *Entrance requirements:* GMAT, TOEFL (minimum score 550). Application fee: $40. *Financial aid:* Research assistantships, Federal Work-Study available. • Dr. Madlyn Hanes, Campus Executive Officer and Associate Dean, Graduate Studies and Continuing Education, 610-648-3200.

See in-depth description on page 1319.

Pennsylvania State University Harrisburg Campus of the Capital College, School of Public Affairs, Program in Health Administration, Middletown, PA 17057-4898. Awards MHA. Students: 3 full-time (1 woman), 44 part-time (27 women). *Degree requirements:* Computer language, thesis, fieldwork or previous experience required, foreign language not required. *Entrance requirements:* GMAT or GRE General Test, minimum GPA of 3.0 during previous 2 years. Application deadline: 7/26. Application fee: $40. *Expenses:* Tuition $6534 per year full-time, $276 per credit part-time for state residents; $12,516 per year full-time, $523 per credit part-time for nonresidents. Fees $232 per year (minimum) full-time, $40 per semester (minimum) part-time. • Dr. James Ziegenfuss, Coordinator, 717-948-6050.

Pennsylvania State University University Park Campus, College of Health and Human Development, Department of Health Policy and Administration, University Park, PA 16802-1503. Awards MHA, MS, PhD. One or more programs accredited by ACEHSA. Students: 22 full-time (12 women), 9 part-time (4 women). In 1997, 15 master's, 1 doctorate awarded. *Entrance requirements:* GMAT or GRE General Test. Application fee: $40. *Expenses:* Tuition $6534 per year full-time, $276 per credit part-time for state residents; $13,460 per year full-time, $561 per credit part-time for nonresidents. Fees $252 per year (minimum) full-time, $43 per semester (minimum) part-time. • Dr. S. Diane Brannon, Interim Head, 814-863-2900.

Announcement: The MS and PhD programs in health policy and administration prepare students for research/analyst positions in health-care organizations, government, and academia. The cross-disciplinary curriculum has a heavy emphasis on research methods and statistics. MS graduates provide analytic support for health services research in a variety of settings; PhD graduates direct research enterprises or serve in academic positions. Feedback from recent alumni documents the program's distinctive competencies as useable knowledge and strong mentoring. Graduate assistantships and traineeships provide financial support for MS/PhD students. For additional information about the MBA/MHA program, see Business Administration and Management cross-discipline announcement.

See in-depth description on page 1317.

Philadelphia College of Textiles and Science, School of Business, Program in Business, Philadelphia, PA 19144-5497. Offerings include health care management (MBA). *Entrance requirements:* GMAT, minimum GPA of 2.85. Application deadline: rolling. Application fee: $35. *Tuition:* $448 per credit hour. • Rita Powell, Director, 215-951-2950. Fax: 215-951-2652. E-mail: powellr@phila.col.edu. Application contact: Robert J. Reed, Director of Graduate Admissions, 215-951-2943. Fax: 215-951-2907. E-mail: gradadm@phila.col.edu.

Portland State University, College of Urban and Public Affairs, School of Government, Division of Public Administration, Concentration in Health Administration, Portland, OR 97207-0751. Offers programs in health administration (MPA), health administration and policy (MPH). Part-time and evening/weekend programs available. Faculty: 13 full-time (3 women), 14 part-time (2 women), 14 FTE. Students: 24 full-time (17 women), 46 part-time (34 women); includes 7 minority (4 Asian Americans, 2 Hispanics, 1 Native American), 7 international. Average age 36. 39 applicants, 85% accepted. *Degree requirements:* Internship (MPA), practicum (MPH) required, foreign language and thesis not required. *Entrance requirements:* TOEFL (minimum score 550), minimum GPA of 3.0 in upper-division course work or 2.75 overall. Application deadline: 4/1 (11/1 for spring admission). Application fee: $50. *Tuition:* $6101 per year full-time, $689 per semester (minimum) part-time for state residents; $10,445 per year full-time, $689 per semester (minimum) part-time for nonresidents. *Financial aid:* Fellowships, research assistantships, teaching assistantships, Federal Work-Study, institutionally sponsored loans, and career-related internships or fieldwork available. Aid available to part-time students. Financial aid application deadline: 3/1; applicants required to submit FAFSA. • Dr. Ronald C. Cease, Chair, Division of Public Administration, 503-725-3920. E-mail: ron@upa.pdx.edu. Application contact: Betty Lewis, 503-725-3920. Fax: 503-725-8250. E-mail: betty@upa.pdx.edu.

Queen's University at Kingston, Faculty of Medicine and School of Graduate Studies and Research, Graduate Programs in Medicine, Department of Community Health and Epidemiology, Kingston, ON K7L 3N6, Canada. Offerings include health-care systems (M Sc). *Degree requirements:* Thesis required, foreign language not required. *Entrance requirements:* TOEFL (minimum score 550). Application fee: $60. Electronic applications accepted. *Tuition:* $3803 per year (minimum) full-time, $1901 per year (minimum) part-time for Canadian residents; $7330 per year (minimum) for nonresidents. • Dr. J. L. Pater, Graduate Coordinator, 613-545-2901. Application contact: R. E. M. Lees, Graduate Coordinator, 613-545-4954.

Quinnipiac College, School of Business, Program in Business Administration, Hamden, CT 06518-1904. Offerings include health management (MBA). Program faculty: 17 full-time (2 women), 4 part-time (1 woman). *Degree requirements:* Thesis optional, foreign language not required. *Average time to degree:* master's–2 years full-time, 4 years part-time. *Entrance requirements:* GMAT (minimum score 400; average 470), interview, minimum GPA of 2.5. Application deadline: 8/1 (priority date; rolling processing). Application fee: $45. Electronic applications accepted. *Expenses:* Tuition $395 per credit hour. Fees $380 per year full-time. • Dr. Earl Chrysler, Director, 203-281-8799. Fax: 203-281-8664. E-mail: chrysler@quinnipiac.edu. Application contact: Scott Farber, Director of Graduate Admissions, 203-281-8795. Fax: 203-287-5238. E-mail: qcgradadmi@quinnipiac.edu.

Quinnipiac College, School of Business, Program in Health Administration, Hamden, CT 06518-1904. Awards MHA, JD/MHA. Offerings include health administration (MHA), long-term care administration (MHA). Part-time and evening/weekend programs available. Faculty: 2 full-time (0 women), 4 part-time (2 women). Students: 2 full-time (1 woman), 20 part-time (11 women). Average age 30. 12 applicants, 83% accepted. In 1997, 9 degrees awarded (100% found work related to degree). *Degree requirements:* Thesis or alternative, internship. *Average time to degree:* master's–2 years full-time, 4 years part-time. *Entrance requirements:* GMAT (minimum score 400; average 470), interview, minimum GPA of 2.5. Application deadline: 8/1 (priority date; rolling processing). Application fee: $45. Electronic applications accepted. *Expenses:* Tuition $395 per credit hour. Fees $380 per year full-time. *Financial aid:* In 1997–98, 1 research assistantship was awarded; career-related internships or fieldwork also available. Aid available to part-time students. Financial aid applicants required to submit FAFSA. *Faculty research:* Health care financing, health policy, health care marketing, health economics, health care management information systems. • Dr. Ramon Castellblanch, Director, 203-287-5276. Fax: 203-281-8664. E-mail: castellblanch@quinnipiac.edu. Application contact: Scott Farber, Director of Graduate Admissions, 203-281-8795. Fax: 203-287-5238. E-mail: qcgradadmi@quinnipiac.edu.

See in-depth description on page 1321.

Robert Morris College, Program in Business Administration, 881 Narrows Run Road, Moon Township, PA 15108-1189. Offerings include health services management (MBA, MS). Only part-time programs offered. Program faculty: 35 full-time (6 women), 35 part-time (5 women). *Entrance requirements:* GMAT (minimum score 450), minimum GPA of 2.5. Application deadline: 8/1 (priority date; rolling processing; 11/30 for spring admission). Application fee: $25 ($35 for international students). *Expenses:* Tuition $328 per credit. Fees $15 per credit. • Dr. Joseph F. Constable, Dean, School of Management, 412-262-8451. Fax: 412-262-8494. E-mail: constabl@robert-morris.edu. Application contact: Vincent J. Kane, Recruiting Coordinator, 412-262-8535. Fax: 412-299-2425.

Rochester Institute of Technology, College of Applied Science and Technology, Center for Multidisciplinary Studies, Program in Health Systems Administration, Rochester, NY 14623-5604. Offers health systems administration (MS), health systems-finance (AC). Students: 2 full-time (both women), 51 part-time (39 women). 11 applicants, 82% accepted. *Entrance requirements:* For master's, minimum GPA of 3.0; for AC, GRE, TOEFL (minimum score 550), minimum GPA of 3.0. Application deadline: 3/1 (priority date; rolling processing). Application fee: $40. *Expenses:* Tuition $18,765 per year full-time, $527 per credit hour part-time. Fees $126 per year full-time. • William Walence, Chair, 716-475-7359.

See in-depth description on page 1323.

Rush University, College of Health Sciences, Department of Health Systems Management, Chicago, IL 60612-3832. Awards MS. Accredited by ACEHSA. Part-time programs available. Faculty: 3 full-time (2 women), 110 part-time (58 women). Students: 30 full-time (20 women), 5 part-time (2 women); includes 5 minority (1 African American, 4 Asian Americans), 3 international. Average age 27. 57 applicants, 32% accepted. In 1997, 14 degrees awarded. *Degree requirements:* Thesis required, foreign language not required. *Entrance requirements:* GMAT or GRE, previous course work in accounting and statistics. Application deadline: rolling. Application fee: $40. *Tuition:* $8480 per year full-time, $370 per credit hour part-time. *Financial aid:* Career-related internships or fieldwork available. Financial aid application deadline: 4/15. *Faculty research:* Economics of aging, organizational performance, occupational health, breast cancer epidemiology. • James T. Frankenbach, Chairman, 312-942-2169. Fax: 312-942-2055. E-mail: jfranken@rpslmc.edu. Application contact: Leslie Compere, Program Coordinator, 312-942-5402. Fax: 312-942-4957.

See in-depth description on page 1325.

Rutgers, The State University of New Jersey, Camden, Program in Public Administration, Camden, NJ 08102-1401. Offerings include health care management and policy (MPA). MPA (health care management and policy) offered jointly with the University of Medicine and Dentistry of New Jersey. Program faculty: 11 full-time, 15 part-time. *Entrance requirements:* GMAT, GRE General Test, LCAT, or MCAT. Application deadline: 5/1 (rolling processing; 12/1 for spring admission). Application fee: $40. *Expenses:* Tuition $6492 per year full-time, $268 per credit part-time for state residents; $9520 per year full-time, $395 per credit part-time for nonresidents. Fees $891 per year full-time, $160 per semester (minimum) part-time. • Dr. James L. Garnett, Director, 609-225-6359.

Rutgers, The State University of New Jersey, Newark, Department of Public Administration, Newark, NJ 07102-3192. Offerings include health care administration (MPA). Department faculty: 11 full-time (3 women), 6 part-time (1 woman), 12 FTE. *Degree requirements:* Thesis or alternative, comprehensive exam. *Average time to degree:* master's–2 years full-time, 3 years part-time. *Entrance requirements:* GRE, minimum undergraduate B average. Application deadline: 7/1 (priority date; rolling processing; 12/1 for spring admission). Application fee: $40. *Expenses:* Tuition $6248 per year full-time, $257 per credit part-time for state residents; $9160 per year full-time, $380 per credit part-time for nonresidents. Fees $738 per year full-time, $107 per semester (minimum) part-time. • Dr. Marcia Whicker, Director, 973-353-5093. E-mail: whicker@andromeda.rutgers.edu.

Sacred Heart University, College of Business, 5151 Park Avenue, Fairfield, CT 06432-1000. Offerings include health care administration (MBA), health systems management (MA). MA new for fall 1998. College faculty: 24 full-time (4 women), 38 part-time (10 women). *Application deadline:* rolling. *Application fee:* $40 ($100 for international students). *Expenses:* Tuition $395 per credit. Fees $78 per semester. • Scott Colvin, Director, 203-371-7850. Application contact: Brian Ihlefeld, Graduate Admissions Counselor, 203-371-7880. Fax: 203-365-4732. E-mail: gradstudies@sacredheart.edu.

Sage Graduate School, Graduate School, Division of Management Studies, Program in Health Services Administration, Troy, NY 12180-4115. Offers gerontology (MS), health education (MS), management (MS), nutrition and dietetics (MS). Part-time and evening/weekend programs available. Faculty: 1 full-time (0 women), 4 part-time (1 woman). Students: 11 full-time, 89 part-time. *Entrance requirements:* Minimum GPA of 2.75. Application deadline: 8/1 (rolling processing; 12/15 for spring admission). Application fee: $25. *Expenses:* Tuition $360 per credit hour. Fees $50 per semester. *Financial aid:* Career-related internships or fieldwork available. Aid available to part-time students. Financial aid application deadline: 7/1; applicants required to submit FAFSA. • Application contact: Melissa Robertson, Associate Director of Admissions, 518-244-6878. Fax: 518-244-6880. E-mail: sgsadm@sage.edu.

St. Ambrose University, College of Business, Program in Health Care Administration, Davenport, IA 52803-2898. Awards MHCA. Part-time and evening/weekend programs available. *Degree requirements:* Capstone Seminar required, foreign language and thesis not required. *Average time to degree:* master's–4.5 years part-time. *Entrance requirements:* GMAT. Application deadline: 8/15 (priority date; rolling processing). Application fee: $25. Electronic applications accepted.

St. John's University, College of Pharmacy and Allied Health Professions, Graduate Programs in Pharmacy, Program in Pharmacy Administration, Jamaica, NY 11439. Offers pharmaceutical (MS), pharmacy administration (MS). Part-time and evening/weekend programs available. Students: 9 full-time (4 women), 10 part-time (5 women); includes 3 minority (all Asian Americans), 9 international. Average age 31. 19 applicants, 74% accepted. In 1997, 7 degrees awarded. *Degree requirements:* Comprehensive exam required, thesis optional, foreign language not required. *Entrance requirements:* Minimum GPA of 3.0. Application deadline: 6/1 (priority date; rolling processing; 10/1 for spring admission). Application fee: $40. *Expenses:* Tuition $675 per credit. Fees $150 per year. *Financial aid:* Fellowships, teaching assistantships, clinical assistantships, Federal Work-Study, and career-related internships or fieldwork available. Aid available to part-time students. Financial aid application deadline: 3/1; applicants required to submit FAFSA. • Dr. Robert Sause, Chair, 718-990-6679. Application contact: Shamus J. McGrenra, TOR, Associate Director, Graduate Admissions, 718-990-6107. Fax: 718-990-5736. E-mail: mcgrenrs@stjohns.edu.

Saint Joseph's College, Program in Health Services Administration, Standish, ME 04084-5263. Awards MHSA. Degree program is external; available only by correspondence. Part-time programs available. Postbaccalaureate distance learning degree programs offered (minimal on-campus study). Faculty: 2 full-time (1 woman), 26 part-time (6 women), 8.5 FTE. Students: 1,020 part-time (715 women); includes 305 minority (175 African Americans, 50 Asian Americans, 80 Hispanics), 27 international. Average age 43. 170 applicants, 90% accepted. In 1997, 54 degrees awarded. *Degree requirements:* Thesis, summer residency required, foreign language not required. *Average time to degree:* master's–2 years full-time, 6 years part-time. *Application fee:* $50. *Tuition:* $220 per credit hour. *Financial aid:* Institutionally sponsored loans available. Aid available to part-time students. *Faculty research:* Health care organization, policy, and management; long-term care. • Dr. Paul L. Selbst, Director, 207-893-7981. Fax: 207-893-7987. E-mail: pselbst@sjcme.edu. Application contact: Admissions Department, 800-752-4723. Fax: 207-892-7480.

Saint Joseph's University, Department of Health Services, Program in Health Administration, Philadelphia, PA 19131-1395. Awards MS. Evening/weekend programs available. Students: 219 (161 women). In 1997, 71 degrees awarded. *Entrance requirements:* TOEFL, GRE General Test or minimum undergraduate GPA of 2.5. Application deadline: 7/15. Application fee: $30. *Tuition:* $470 per credit hour. *Financial aid:* Career-related internships or fieldwork available. • Dr. David White, Chair, Department of Health Services, 610-660-1582.

Saint Joseph's University, Erivan K. Haub School of Business, Programs in Graduate Business, Program in Health and Medical Services Administration, Philadelphia, PA 19131-1395. Awards MBA. Students: 25 (5 women). *Entrance requirements:* GMAT, TOEFL. Application deadline: 7/15 (priority date; rolling processing; 11/15 for spring admission). Application fee: $35. *Tuition:* $510 per credit hour. *Financial aid:* Graduate assistantships available. Financial aid application deadline: 5/1. • Adele C. Foley, Associate Dean, Programs in Graduate Business, 610-660-1690. Fax: 610-660-1599. E-mail: afoley@sju.edu.

St. Louis College of Pharmacy, Program in Pharmacy Administration, St. Louis, MO 63110-1088. Offers managed care pharmacy (MS), pharmacy administration (MS). Part-time and evening/weekend programs available. Faculty: 3 full-time (1 woman), 4 part-time (0 women). Students: 20 part-time (6 women). Average age 35. 2 applicants, 0% accepted. In 1997, 1 degree awarded (100% found work related to degree). *Degree requirements:* Thesis or alternative required, foreign language not required. *Average time to degree:* master's–4 years part-time. *Entrance requirements:* GMAT (average 506). Application deadline: 8/1 (priority date; rolling processing). Application fee: $35. *Tuition:* $300 per credit hour. *Faculty research:* Geriatric pharmacy, health economics, pharmacoeconomics, job satisfaction, managed care and insurance. • Dr. Kenneth Schafermeyer, Director of Graduate Studies, 314-367-8700 Ext. 1743. Fax: 314-367-8132. E-mail: kschafermeyer@slcop.stlcop.edu.

Saint Louis University, School of Public Health, Program in Health Administration, St. Louis, MO 63108. Awards MHA, JD/MHA, MHA/MBA. Accredited by ACEHSA. Students: 44 full-time (20 women), 21 part-time (14 women); includes 11 minority (5 African Americans, 5 Asian Americans, 1 Hispanic), 7 international. 60 applicants, 72% accepted. In 1997, 21 degrees awarded. *Degree requirements:* Comprehensive oral exam required, thesis not required. *Entrance requirements:* GMAT or GRE General Test. Application deadline: 7/1 (rolling processing; 11/1 for spring admission). Application fee: $40. *Tuition:* $542 per credit hour. *Financial aid:* Career-related internships or fieldwork available. Financial aid application deadline: 4/1. *Faculty research:* Quality improvement in health administration, health services utilization, managed care impacts, health economics, financial performance. • Dr. Claudia Campbell, Acting Chairperson, 314-977-8106. Fax: 314-977-8150. Application contact: Dr. Marcia Buresch, Assistant Dean of the Graduate School, 314-977-2240. Fax: 314-977-3943.

Saint Mary's College of California, School of Extended Education, Department of Health Services Administration, Moraga, CA 94575. Awards MS. Part-time and evening/weekend programs available. Faculty: 3 full-time (2 women), 38 part-time (10 women). Students: 74 part-time (63 women); includes 12 minority (3 African Americans, 7 Asian Americans, 2 Hispanics). Average age 41. 52 applicants, 96% accepted. In 1997, 52 degrees awarded. *Entrance requirements:* 3 years of related work experience. Application deadline: 8/25 (priority date; rolling processing; 2/26 for spring admission). Application fee: $35. *Tuition:* $7632 per year. *Faculty research:* Medical sociology, medical rehabilitation, health care future, cultural diversity, medical ethics, bioethics. • Dr. William Frey, Chair, 925-631-4021. Fax: 925-631-9214. Application contact: Office of Admissions, 925-631-4900. Fax: 925-631-9869.

Saint Mary's University of Minnesota, Program in Human and Health Services Administration, Minneapolis, MN 55404. Awards MA, MA/MA. MA/MA offered jointly with the Program in Management. Part-time and evening/weekend programs available. *Degree requirements:* Thesis, colloquium presentation required, foreign language not required. *Entrance requirements:* Interview, minimum GPA of 2.75. Application deadline: rolling. Application fee: $20.

St. Thomas University, School of Graduate Studies, Department of Professional Management, Specialization in Health Management, Miami, FL 33054-6459. Awards MBA, MSM, Certificate. Part-time and evening/weekend programs available. *Degree requirements:* For master's, comprehensive exam required, foreign language and thesis not required. *Average time to degree:* master's–1 year full-time. *Entrance requirements:* For master's, TOEFL (minimum score 550), interview, minimum GPA of 3.0 or GMAT. Application deadline: 6/15 (priority date; rolling processing; 11/15 for spring admission). Application fee: $30. *Tuition:* $410 per credit.

Saint Xavier University, Graham School of Management, Chicago, IL 60655-3105. Offerings include health care management (MBA), healthcare management (Certificate). School faculty: 15 full-time (2 women), 6 part-time (3 women). *Entrance requirements:* For master's, GMAT, minimum GPA of 3.0, 2 years of work experience. Application deadline: 8/15. Application fee: $35. *Expenses:* Tuition $455 per hour. Fees $50 per year. • Dr. John Eber, Dean, 773-298-3601. Fax: 773-298-3610. E-mail: eber@sxu.edu. Application contact: Sr. Evelyn McKenna, Vice President of Enrollment Management, 773-298-3050. Fax: 773-298-3076. E-mail: mckenna@sxu.edu.

Salve Regina University, Program in Health Services Administration, Newport, RI 02840-4192. Awards MS. Part-time and evening/weekend programs available. Faculty: 1 (woman) full-time, 4 part-time (0 women), 2 FTE. Students: 3 full-time (1 woman), 61 part-time (53 women). Average age 31. 14 applicants, 57% accepted. In 1997, 18 degrees awarded. *Average time to degree:* master's–2 years full-time, 3 years part-time. *Entrance requirements:* GMAT, GRE General Test, or MAT. Application deadline: rolling. Application fee: $35. *Expenses:* Tuition $275 per credit hour. Fees $70 per year. *Financial aid:* Federal Work-Study and career-related internships or fieldwork available. Aid available to part-time students. Financial aid application deadline: 3/1. • Dr. Joan Chapdelaine, Director, 401-847-6650 Ext. 3190. Fax: 401-847-0372. Application contact: Laura E. McPhie, Dean of Enrollment Services, 401-847-6650 Ext. 2908. Fax: 401-848-2823. E-mail: sruadmis@salve.edu.

San Diego State University, College of Health and Human Services, Graduate School of Public Health, San Diego, CA 92182. Offerings include health services administration (MPH). Accredited by ACEHSA. School faculty: 25 full-time (9 women), 36 part-time (21 women). *Application deadline:* 5/15 (priority date; rolling processing; 10/15 for spring admission). *Application fee:* $55. *Expenses:* Tuition $0 for state residents; $246 per unit for nonresidents. Fees $1932 per year full-time, $1266 per year part-time. • Dr. Kenneth Bart, Director, 619-594-6317. Application contact: Brenda Fass-Holmes, Coordinator, Admissions and Student Affairs, 619-594-6317. E-mail: bholmes@mail.sdsu.edu.

San Jose State University, College of Applied Arts and Sciences, Department of Health Science, San Jose, CA 95192-0001. Offerings include health administration (Certificate). Department faculty: 5 full-time (1 woman), 2 part-time (1 woman). *Application deadline:* 6/1 (rolling processing). *Application fee:* $59. *Expenses:* Tuition $0 for state residents; $246 per unit for nonresidents. Fees $2017 per year full-time, $1351 per year part-time. • Dr. William Washington, Chair, 408-924-2970. Application contact: Dr. Kathy Roe, Graduate Coordinator, 408-924-2976.

Seton Hall University, College of Arts and Sciences, Center for Public Service, Program in Healthcare Administration, South Orange, NJ 07079-2697. Awards MHA. Part-time and evening/weekend programs available. Postbaccalaureate distance learning degree programs offered (minimal on-campus study). *Entrance requirements:* GMAT, GRE General Test, or LSAT. Application fee: $50. *Expenses:* Tuition $500 per credit. Fees $610 per year full-time, $185 per semester part-time. *Financial aid:* Assistantships, scholarships available. • Application contact: Barbara Metelsky, Assistant Director, 973-761-9510. Fax: 973-275-2463. E-mail: metelsba@lanmail.shu.edu.

See in-depth description on page 1327.

Seton Hall University, College of Arts and Sciences, Center for Public Service, Program in Health Policy and Management, South Orange, NJ 07079-2697. Awards MPA. Part-time and evening/weekend programs available. *Degree requirements:* Research project. *Entrance requirements:* GMAT, GRE General Test, or LSAT. Application deadline: rolling. Application fee: $50. *Expenses:* Tuition $500 per credit. Fees $610 per year full-time, $185 per semester part-time. *Financial aid:* Research assistantships, nonprofit management scholarships, and career-related internships or fieldwork available. • Application contact: Barbara Metelsky, Assistant Director, 973-761-9510. Fax: 973-275-2463. E-mail: metelsba@lanmail.shu.edu.

See in-depth description on page 1327.

Simmons College, Graduate School for Health Studies, Program in Health Care Administration, Boston, MA 02115. Awards MS, CAGS. One or more programs accredited by ACEHSA. Part-time and evening/weekend programs available. Faculty: 4 full-time (3 women), 12 part-time (7 women). Students: 1 (woman) full-time, 88 part-time (74 women); includes 9 minority (7 African Americans, 2 Asian Americans), 3 international. Average age 32. 64 applicants, 59% accepted. In 1997, 29 master's awarded. *Degree requirements:* For master's, practicum required, thesis optional, foreign language not required. *Entrance requirements:* For master's, GMAT or GRE, TOEFL (minimum score 550). Application deadline: 7/1 (priority date; rolling processing; 11/1 for spring admission). Application fee: $50. *Expenses:* Tuition $587 per credit hour. Fees $20 per year. *Financial aid:* Federal Work-Study, institutionally sponsored loans available. Aid available to part-time students. Financial aid application deadline: 3/1; applicants required to submit FAFSA. *Faculty research:* International science/technology policies, middle managers in health care organizations. • Linda Roemer, Director, 617-521-2377. Fax: 617-521-3046. E-mail: lroemer@simmons.edu. Application contact: Christine Keuleyan, Admission Coordinator, 617-521-2650. Fax: 617-521-3137. E-mail: keuleyan@simmons.edu.

See in-depth description on page 1329.

Southeastern University, Program in Health Services Administration, Washington, DC 20024-2788. Awards MPA. Part-time and evening/weekend programs available. Faculty: 13 part-time (2 women). Students: 7 full-time (6 women), 8 part-time (6 women); includes 11 minority (all African Americans), 4 international. Average age 37. 6 applicants, 100% accepted. In 1997, 7 degrees awarded. *Degree requirements:* Computer language required, foreign language not required. *Entrance requirements:* TOEFL. Application deadline: rolling. Application fee: $45. *Expenses:* Tuition $228 per credit hour. Fees $175 per quarter. *Financial aid:* Federal Work-Study and career-related internships or fieldwork available. Aid available to part-time students. • Dr. Mohammed Safa, Head, 202-488-8162. Application contact: Jack Flinter, Director of Admissions, 202-265-5343. Fax: 202-488-8093.

Southeast Missouri State University, Program in Administrative Science, Cape Girardeau, MO 63701-4799. Offerings include health care administration (MSA). *Degree requirements:* Thesis or alternative required, foreign language not required. *Entrance requirements:* Minimum GPA of 2.5. Application deadline: 4/1 (priority date; rolling processing; 11/21 for spring admission). Application fee: $20 ($100 for international students). *Tuition:* $2034 per year full-time, $113 per credit hour part-time for state residents; $3672 per year full-time, $204 per credit hour part-time for nonresidents. • Application contact: Office of Graduate Studies, 573-651-2192.

Southern Adventist University, School of Business, Collegedale, TN 37315-0370. Offerings include health care administration (MBA). *Application fee:* $25. *Tuition:* $275 per credit hour. • Don Van Ornam, Dean, 423-238-2750.

Southwest Baptist University, School of Graduate Studies, School of Business, 1600 University Avenue, Bolivar, MO 65613-2597. Offerings include administration (MS), with options in accounting, business administration, health services. School faculty: 11 part-time (3 women). *Average time to degree:* master's–1.2 years full-time. *Entrance requirements:* Interviews, minimum GPA of 2.75. Application deadline: rolling. Application fee: $25. *Tuition:* $145 per credit hour. • Dr. Michael Awad, Interim Dean, 417-326-1751. Fax: 417-326-1887. E-mail: business@sbuniv.edu. Application contact: Dr. Rodney Oglesby, Director of Graduate Studies, 417-326-1756.

Southwest Texas State University, School of Health Professions, Department of Health Administration, San Marcos, TX 78666. Offers program in health care administration (MSHP). Accredited by ACEHSA. Part-time and evening/weekend programs available. Faculty: 10 full-time (1 woman). Students: 38 full-time (22 women), 37 part-time (24 women); includes 15 minority (1 African American, 4 Asian Americans, 9 Hispanics, 1 Native American), 2 international. Average age 29. In 1997, 17 degrees awarded. *Degree requirements:* Committee review, comprehensive exam required, foreign language not required. *Entrance requirements:* GRE General Test (minimum combined score of 900), TOEFL (minimum score 550), minimum GPA of 2.75 in last 60 hours. Application deadline: 7/15 (priority date; rolling processing; 11/15 for spring admission). Application fee: $25 ($50 for international students). *Expenses:* Tuition $648 per year full-time, $120 per semester (minimum) part-time for state residents; $4500 per year full-time, $750 per semester (minimum) part-time for nonresidents. Fees $1264 per year full-time, $314 per semester (minimum) part-time. *Financial aid:* In 1997–98, 19 stipends averaging $800 per month were awarded; Federal Work-Study, institutionally sponsored loans, and career-related internships or fieldwork also available. Aid available to part-time students. Financial aid application deadline: 4/1; applicants required to submit FAFSA. *Faculty research:* Managerial ethics, health care financial management, health services delivery in rural areas, health services delivery in medically underserved areas, telemedicine. • Dr. Wayne Sorensen, Chair, 512-245-3556. Fax: 512-245-8712. E-mail: ws06@swt.edu. Application contact: Dr. J. Michael Willoughby, Dean of the Graduate School, 512-245-2581. Fax: 512-245-8365. E-mail: jw02@swt.edu.

Southwest Texas State University, School of Health Professions, Department of Health Services and Research, Program in Healthcare Human Resources, San Marcos, TX 78666. Awards MSHP. Accredited by ACEHSA. Part-time and evening/weekend programs available. Students: 2 full-time (both women), 11 part-time (7 women); includes 3 minority (2 African Americans, 1 Hispanic). Average age 33. In 1997, 6 degrees awarded. *Degree requirements:* Thesis (for some programs), committee review, comprehensive exam required, foreign language not required. *Entrance requirements:* GRE General Test (minimum combined score of 900), TOEFL (minimum score 550), minimum GPA of 2.75 in last 60 hours. Application deadline: 7/15 (priority date; rolling processing; 11/15 for spring admission). Application fee: $25 ($50 for international students). *Expenses:* Tuition $648 per year full-time, $120 per semester (minimum) part-time for state residents; $4500 per year full-time, $750 per semester (minimum) part-time for nonresidents. Fees $1264 per year full-time, $314 per semester (minimum) part-time.

Directory: Health Services Management and Hospital Administration

Southwest Texas State University (continued)
Financial aid: Research assistantships, teaching assistantships, Federal Work-Study, institutionally sponsored loans, and career-related internships or fieldwork available. Aid available to part-time students. Financial aid application deadline: 4/1; applicants required to submit FAFSA. *Faculty research:* Human resource development, health institutions. • Dr. Charles Johnson, Chair, Department of Health Services and Research, 512-245-3494. Fax: 512-245-8712. E-mail: cj01@swt.edu. Application contact: Dr. J. Michael Willoughby, Dean of the Graduate School, 512-245-2581. Fax: 512-245-8365. E-mail: jw02@swt.edu.

Springfield College, Program in Health Care Management, Springfield, MA 01109-3797. Awards M Ed, MS. Part-time and evening/weekend programs available. Faculty: 6 full-time (2 women). Students: 8 full-time (2 women), 1 part-time (0 women); includes 1 international. Average age 25. 9 applicants, 89% accepted. *Degree requirements:* Comprehensive exam required, foreign language and thesis not required. *Application deadline:* (12/1 for spring admission). *Application fee:* $40. *Expenses:* Tuition $474 per credit. Fees $25 per year. *Financial aid:* Fellowships, Federal Work-Study, institutionally sponsored loans, and career-related internships or fieldwork available. Financial aid application deadline: 3/1; applicants required to submit FAFSA. • Dr. John Doyle, Director, 413-748-3199. Application contact: Donald J. Shaw Jr., Director of Graduate Admissions, 413-748-3225. Fax: 413-748-3694. E-mail: dshaw@spfldcol.edu.

State University of New York at Albany, School of Public Health, Department of Health Policy and Management, Executive Park South, Albany, NY 12203-3727. Awards MS. Faculty: 5 full-time (3 women). Students: 12 full-time (7 women), 17 part-time (11 women); includes 4 minority (1 African American, 2 Asian Americans, 1 Hispanic), 1 international. 24 applicants, 75% accepted. In 1997, 8 degrees awarded. *Degree requirements:* Thesis. *Entrance requirements:* GRE General Test. Application fee: $50. *Expenses:* Tuition $5100 per year full-time, $213 per credit hour part-time for state residents; $8416 per year full-time, $351 per credit hour part-time for nonresidents. Fees $705 per year full-time, $26.85 per credit hour part-time. • Dr. Edward Hannan, Chair, 518-402-0333.

State University of New York at Binghamton, School of Management, Program in Business Administration, Binghamton, NY 13902-6000. Offerings include health care professional executive (MBA). MBA/MA offered jointly with the Department of History. *Degree requirements:* Computer language required, thesis not required. *Entrance requirements:* GMAT, TOEFL. Application deadline: 4/15 (priority date; rolling processing; 11/1 for spring admission). Application fee: $50. Electronic applications accepted. *Expenses:* Tuition $5100 per year full-time, $213 per credit hour part-time for state residents; $8416 per year full-time, $351 per credit hour part-time for nonresidents. Fees $654 per year full-time, $75 per semester (minimum) part-time. • Frances Yammarino, Coordinator of Graduate Admissions, 607-777-2306.

State University of New York at Stony Brook, Health Sciences Center, School of Health Technology and Management, Stony Brook, NY 11794. Offers programs in health care management (Advanced Certificate), health care policy and management (MS). Part-time programs available. Faculty: 32 full-time, 11 part-time. Students: 1 (woman) full-time, 43 part-time (28 women); includes 4 minority (2 Asian Americans, 2 Hispanics). 68 applicants, 90% accepted. In 1997, 18 master's, 21 Advanced Certificates awarded. *Degree requirements:* For master's, thesis required, foreign language not required. *Entrance requirements:* For master's, GRE General Test, minimum GPA of 3.0, work experience in field. Application deadline: 1/15. Application fee: $50. *Expenses:* Tuition $5100 per year full-time, $213 per credit hour part-time for state residents; $8416 per year full-time, $351 per credit hour part-time for nonresidents. Fees $529 per year full-time, $77 per semester (minimum) part-time. *Financial aid:* Federal Work-Study, institutionally sponsored loans, and career-related internships or fieldwork available. Financial aid application deadline: 3/15. *Faculty research:* Health promotion and disease prevention. Total annual research expenditures: $468,363. • Dr. Lorna McBarnette, Dean, 516-444-2251. Application contact: Nanci C. Rice, Director of Health Care Policy and Management, 516-444-3240. Fax: 516-444-7621. E-mail: nrice@epo.hsc.sunysb.edu.

Suffolk University, Sawyer School of Management, Department of Public Management, Boston, MA 02108-2770. Offerings include health administration (MHA, MPA). MPA/MS offered jointly with Department of Education and Human Services. Department faculty: 7 full-time (2 women), 20 part-time (12 women). *Application deadline:* 6/15 (priority date; rolling processing; 11/15 for spring admission). *Application fee:* $50. *Expenses:* Tuition $16,122 per year full-time, $1611 per course part-time. Fees $50 per year full-time, $20 per year part-time. • Michael Lavin, Chair, 617-573-8317. Fax: 617-573-8345. E-mail: mlavin@acad.suffolk.edu. Application contact: Judy Reynolds, Acting Director of Graduate Admissions, 617-573-8302. Fax: 617-523-0116. E-mail: grad.admission@admin.suffolk.edu.

Suffolk University, Sawyer School of Management, Program in Health Administration, Boston, MA 02108-2770. Awards MBAH, MHA, MPA. Part-time and evening/weekend programs available. Faculty: 7 full-time (2 women), 20 part-time (12 women). Students: 8 part-time (3 women). Average age 30. 4 applicants, 100% accepted. In 1997, 11 degrees awarded. *Application deadline:* 6/15 (priority date; rolling processing; 11/15 for spring admission). *Application fee:* $50. *Expenses:* Tuition $16,122 per year full-time, $1611 per course part-time. Fees $50 per year full-time, $20 per year part-time. *Financial aid:* In 1997–98, 2 students received aid, including 1 fellowship; Federal Work-Study, institutionally sponsored loans, and career-related internships or fieldwork also available. Aid available to part-time students. Financial aid application deadline: 4/1; applicants required to submit FAFSA. *Faculty research:* Mental health, federal policy, health care. • Michael Lavin, Chair, 617-573-8317. Fax: 617-573-8345. E-mail: mlavin@acad.suffolk.edu. Application contact: Judy Reynolds, Acting Director of Graduate Admissions, 617-573-8302. Fax: 617-523-0116. E-mail: grad.admission@admin.suffolk.edu.

Announcement: To meet the continuing need for well-trained managers in agencies doing health planning and oversight, Suffolk University offers 4 degree options: (1) Master of Business Administration/Health Administration; (2) Master of Health Administration; (3) Master of Public Administration in health administration; (4) Master of Public Administration in disability studies. Courses are available on weekdays, early evenings, or Saturdays. Programs are intended to help students develop the skills they need for advancement or for preparation for careers in public or private health administration.

Temple University, School of Business and Management, Master's Program in Business Administration, Concentration in Healthcare Management, Philadelphia, PA 19122-6096. Awards MBA, MS, MBA/MS. Programs in healthcare financial management (MS), healthcare management (MBA). One or more programs accredited by ACEHSA. Evening/weekend programs available. *Entrance requirements:* GMAT (average 500), TOEFL (minimum score 575), minimum GPA of 3.0 during previous 2 years, 2.8 overall. Application fee: $40. *Expenses:* Tuition $323 per semester hour for state residents; $444 per semester hour for nonresidents. Fees $170 per year full-time, $28 per semester (minimum) part-time. • Dr. Charles P. Hall, Chair, 215-204-8156.

Announcement: Temple's MBA program in healthcare management and MS program in healthcare financial management have educated students for leadership positions in healthcare management for more than 30 years. Its 750 alumni work in all aspects of the healthcare industry, and the program is nationally recognized. Its strengths are threefold—a strong curriculum that prepares students for innovative and responsible management, a flexible fieldwork option that meets professional development objectives, and a job-placement program. The program accepts no more than 30 full-time students a year and offers evening, part-time study for healthcare managers and professionals. An undergraduate degree in business from an accredited institution may allow the student to waive the business core. A joint MBA/MS in healthcare management and financial management is also offered.

See in-depth description on page 1331.

Texas Tech University, Graduate School, College of Business Administration, Program in Health Organization Management, PO Box 42101, Lubbock, TX 79409-2101. Awards MBA, MSA, Certificate, JD/MBA, MBA/MSN, MD/MBA. Offerings include health organization management (MBA, Certificate), health organization management/controllership (MSA). One or more programs accredited by ACEHSA. Offered jointly with Texas Tech University Health Sciences Center, School of Medicine. Faculty: 6 full-time (1 woman). Students: 40 (18 women); includes 4 minority (1 African American, 2 Asian Americans, 1 Hispanic), 5 international. Average age 29. 12 applicants, 33% accepted. In 1997, 14 master's awarded (100% found work related to degree). *Degree requirements:* For master's, computer language, comprehensive exam, internship required, foreign language and thesis not required. *Average time to degree:* master's–2 years full-time, 5 years part-time. *Entrance requirements:* For master's, GMAT (average 544), TOEFL, average GPA of 3.37. Application deadline: 4/15 (priority date; rolling processing; 9/30 for spring admission). Application fee: $25 ($50 for international students). *Expenses:* Tuition $68 per credit hour for state residents; $250 per credit hour for nonresidents. Fees $1454 per year full-time, $412 per semester (minimum) part-time. *Financial aid:* Fellowships, scholarships, Federal Work-Study, and career-related internships or fieldwork available. Financial aid applicants required to submit FAFSA. • Dr. Grant Savage, Director, 806-742-3164. Application contact: Nancy Dodge, Director, 806-742-3184. Fax: 806-742-3958.

Announcement: The Texas Tech Graduate Program in Health Organization Management (HOM) offers the MBA (HOM), MSA (HOM), MS/MIS (HOM), MSN (HOM), and the PhD in business administration (Management-HOM). Joint degrees include the JD/MBA (HOM) and the MD/MBA (HOM). For more information, visit the Web site at http://www.ba.ttu.edu (Graduate Programs in Business Administration) or http://www.ba.ttu.edu/hom

Texas Woman's University, College of Health Sciences, Program in Health Care Administration-Dallas Parkland, Denton, TX 76204. Awards MS. Accredited by ACEHSA. Part-time and evening/weekend programs available. Faculty: 3 full-time (1 woman), 3 part-time (2 women). Students: 31 full-time (18 women), 49 part-time (33 women); includes 16 minority (5 African Americans, 5 Asian Americans, 5 Hispanics, 1 Native American), 2 international. Average age 32. 35 applicants, 89% accepted. In 1997, 22 degrees awarded (100% found work related to degree). *Degree requirements:* Thesis required, foreign language not required. *Average time to degree:* master's–2.5 years full-time. *Entrance requirements:* GRE, GMAT, or MAT. Application deadline: 6/30 (priority date; rolling processing; 10/30 for spring admission). Application fee: $25. *Financial aid:* 10 students received aid; Federal Work-Study, institutionally sponsored loans available. Aid available to part-time students. Financial aid application deadline: 4/1; applicants required to submit FAFSA. *Faculty research:* Managed care contracting, asset pricing models, econometric models, risk management, employer/employee relations. • Dr. Michael Laman, Coordinator, 214-689-6600. Application contact: Health Care Administration Department, 214-689-6560. Fax: 214-689-6587.

Texas Woman's University, College of Health Sciences, Program in Health Care Administration-Houston Center, Denton, TX 76204. Awards MS. Accredited by ACEHSA. Part-time and evening/weekend programs available. Faculty: 6 full-time (3 women), 5 part-time (1 woman). Students: 9 full-time (7 women), 66 part-time (48 women); includes 26 minority (12 African Americans, 9 Asian Americans, 5 Hispanics), 2 international. Average age 35. 30 applicants, 50% accepted. In 1997, 11 degrees awarded (100% found work related to degree). *Degree requirements:* Thesis required, foreign language not required. *Entrance requirements:* GMAT, GRE, or MAT, minimum GPA of 3.0 (for unconditional admission). Application fee: $25. *Financial aid:* Federal Work-Study, institutionally sponsored loans, and career-related internships or fieldwork available. Aid available to part-time students. Financial aid application deadline: 4/1. *Faculty research:* Health economics, health finance, quality improvement, gerontology. Total annual research expenditures: $5000. • Dr. K. Moseley, Director, 713-794-2061.

Thunderbird, The American Graduate School of International Management, Program in International Health Management, Glendale, AZ 85306-3236. Awards MIHM. *Degree requirements:* 1 foreign language required, thesis optional. *Entrance requirements:* GMAT (minimum score 500; average 590), TOEFL (average 610). Application deadline: 1/31 (priority date; rolling processing; 7/31 for spring admission). Application fee: $50. *Expenses:* Tuition $21,000 per year full-time, $1000 per credit hour part-time. Fees $200 per year. *Financial aid:* Available to part-time students. Financial aid application deadline: 4/1; applicants required to submit FAFSA. • Application contact: Judy Johnson, Director of Admissions, 602-978-7100. Fax: 602-439-5432. E-mail: johnsonj@t-bird.edu.

See in-depth description on page 555.

Touro College, Barry Z. Levine School of Health Sciences, Health Information Management Program, 27-33 West 23rd Street, New York, NY 10010. Awards Certificate. Students: 3 full-time (2 women), 3 part-time (all women). *Entrance requirements:* Minimum GPA of 2.5. Application deadline: rolling. Application fee: $40. • William Merryman, Director, 212-746-4390.

Trinity University, Division of Behavioral and Administrative Studies, Department of Health Care Administration, San Antonio, TX 78212-7200. Awards MS. Accredited by ACEHSA. Part-time programs available. Faculty: 6 full-time (1 woman), 4 part-time (1 woman), 7 FTE. Students: 48 full-time (21 women), 55 part-time (25 women); includes 15 minority (3 African Americans, 5 Asian Americans, 7 Hispanics), 1 international. Average age 29. 85 applicants, 49% accepted. In 1997, 31 degrees awarded (100% found work related to degree). *Degree requirements:* Research projects required, foreign language not required. *Entrance requirements:* GMAT (minimum score 500 preferred), GRE General Test (minimum combined score of 1000 preferred), previous course work in accounting, economics, statistics. Application deadline: 5/1 (priority date; rolling processing). Application fee: $25. *Expenses:* Tuition $14,580 per year full-time, $608 per hour part-time. Fees $18 per year full-time, $6 per hour part-time. *Financial aid:* Research assistantships, graduate assistantships, institutionally sponsored loans, and career-related internships or fieldwork available. Financial aid application deadline: 6/1. • Dr. William McCaughrin, Chair, 210-736-8107. E-mail: wmccaugh@trinity.edu.

See in-depth description on page 1333.

Tulane University, School of Public Health and Tropical Medicine, Department of Health Systems Management, New Orleans, LA 70118-5669. Awards MHA, MMM, MPH, Dr PH, JD/MHA, MBA/MPH, MD/MPH. One or more programs accredited by ACEHSA. Students: 178 full-time (60 women), 28 part-time (15 women); includes 26 minority (12 African Americans, 7 Asian Americans, 6 Hispanics, 1 Native American), 20 international. Average age 30. Terminal master's awarded for partial completion of doctoral program. *Degree requirements:* For master's, 1 foreign language required, thesis not required; for doctorate, 1 foreign language, dissertation. *Average time to degree:* master's–1.5 years full-time; doctorate–4 years full-time. *Entrance requirements:* For master's, GRE General Test (minimum combined score of 1000; average 1100), TOEFL (minimum score 525); for doctorate, GRE General Test (minimum combined score of 1000; average 1250), TOEFL (minimum score 525). Application deadline: 4/15 (priority date; rolling processing; 10/15 for spring admission). Application fee: $40. *Financial aid:* Application deadline 2/1. *Faculty research:* Health policy, organizational governance, international health administration. • David J. Fine, Chairman, 504-588-5428.

See in-depth description on page 1335.

Union College, Graduate and Continuing Studies, Graduate Management Institute, Health Studies Center, Schenectady, NY 12308-2311. Offers programs in health systems administration (MBA), health systems management (MS). One or more programs accredited by ACEHSA. Part-time and evening/weekend programs available. Students: 22 full-time (8 women), 25 part-time (10 women); includes 5 minority (1 African American, 2 Asian Americans, 2 Hispanics). 25 applicants, 92% accepted. In 1997, 19 degrees awarded. *Degree requirements:* Computer language, internships (MBA), comprehensive exam required, foreign language and thesis not required. *Entrance requirements:* GMAT. Application deadline: 5/15 (rolling processing). Application fee: $35. *Tuition:* $1434 per course. *Financial aid:* Fellowships, research assistantships, full and partial tuition waivers, and career-related internships or fieldwork available. Financial aid application deadline: 5/15. • Dr. James Lambrinos, Director, 518-388-6253. Application contact: Carolyn Micklas, Recruiting and Admissions Coordinator, 518-388-6239.

Université de Montréal, Faculties of Medicine and Graduate Studies, Graduate Programs in Medicine, Department of Health Administration, Montréal, PQ H3C 3J7, Canada. Awards M Sc. Accredited by ACEHSA. Faculty: 29 full-time (8 women). Students: 41 full-time (23 women), 41 part-time (26 women). 83 applicants, 30% accepted. In 1997, 27 degrees awarded. *Degree requirements:* Thesis. *Entrance requirements:* Proficiency in French, knowledge of English. Application deadline: 2/1 (priority date; rolling processing). Application fee: $30. *Financial aid:* Institutionally sponsored loans and career-related internships or fieldwork available. • A. Pierre Contandriopoulos, Chairman, 514-343-6175. Application contact: Jean-Louis Denis, Graduate Chairman, 514-343-6031.

The University of Alabama at Birmingham, School of Health Related Professions and Graduate School of Management, Program in Administration-Health Services, Birmingham, AL 35294. Awards PhD. Students: 16 full-time (9 women), 9 part-time (3 women); includes 6 minority (5 African Americans, 1 Asian American). 11 applicants, 100% accepted. In 1997, 5 degrees awarded. *Degree requirements:* Dissertation. *Entrance requirements:* GMAT or GRE General Test. Application deadline: 4/15 (priority date). Application fee: $30 ($60 for international students). Electronic applications accepted. *Expenses:* Tuition $129 per credit hour for state residents; $258 per credit hour for nonresidents. Fees $627 per year (minimum) full-time, $110 per quarter (minimum) part-time. *Financial aid:* In 1997–98, 11 students received aid, including 4 fellowships (1 to a first-year student), 6 research assistantships (3 to first-year students), 1 teaching assistantship; assistantships, institutionally sponsored loans, and career-related internships or fieldwork also available. Financial aid application deadline: 4/15. *Faculty research:* Healthcare strategic management, marketing, and organization studies. Total annual research expenditures: $1.5 million. • Dr. S. Robert Hernandez, Chair, 205-934-5665. E-mail: busf023@uabdpo.dpo.uab.edu.

See in-depth description on page 1337.

The University of Alabama at Birmingham, Graduate School, School of Health Related Professions, Program in Health Administration, Birmingham, AL 35294. Awards MSHA. Accredited by ACEHSA. Students: 76 full-time (27 women), 17 part-time (6 women); includes 11 minority (8 African Americans, 3 Asian Americans). 59 applicants, 100% accepted. In 1997, 24 degrees awarded. *Degree requirements:* Thesis or alternative required, foreign language not required. *Entrance requirements:* GMAT, GRE General Test or MAT, minimum GPA of 3.0. Application deadline: rolling. Application fee: $30 ($60 for international students). Electronic applications accepted. *Expenses:* Tuition $129 per credit hour for state residents; $258 per credit hour for nonresidents. Fees $627 per year (minimum) full-time, $110 per quarter (minimum) part-time. *Financial aid:* Career-related internships or fieldwork available. • Dr. Robert A. McLean, Director, 205-934-1583.

See in-depth description on page 1337.

The University of Alabama at Birmingham, Graduate School, School of Public Health, Department of Health Care Organization and Policy, Birmingham, AL 35294. Awards MPH, MSPH, JD/MPH, MBA/MPH, MPH/PhD, OD/MPH. JD/MPH offered jointly with Samford University. *Degree requirements:* Fieldwork, research project required, foreign language and thesis not required. *Entrance requirements:* GRE General Test or MAT. Application deadline: rolling. Application fee: $30 ($60 for international students). Electronic applications accepted. *Expenses:* Tuition $3672 per year full-time, $102 per credit hour part-time for state residents; $7344 per year full-time, $204 per credit hour part-time for nonresidents. Fees $699 per year (minimum) full-time, $116 per quarter (minimum) part-time. *Financial aid:* Career-related internships or fieldwork available. *Faculty research:* Public health administration and policy, health education, maternal and child health. • Dr. Peter M. Ginter, Chair, 205-935-8970. Application contact: Nancy Pinson, Coordinator of Student Admissions, 205-934-4993. Fax: 205-975-5484. E-mail: osas@ms.soph.uab.edu.

See in-depth description on page 1523.

University of Alberta, Faculty of Graduate Studies and Research, Program in Business Administration, Edmonton, AB T6G 2E1, Canada. Offerings include health administration (MBA). Accredited by ACEHSA. *Degree requirements:* Thesis or alternative required, foreign language not required. *Entrance requirements:* GMAT, TOEFL. Application deadline: 5/31 (priority date; rolling processing). Application fee: $60. *Expenses:* Tuition $390 per course for Canadian residents; $781 per course for nonresidents. Fees $500 per year full-time, $184 per year part-time. • Dr. Kay Devine, Associate Dean, 403-492-3946. E-mail: kay.devine@ualberta.ca. Application contact: Darren Bondar, Assistant Director, 403-492-3946. Fax: 403-492-7825. E-mail: darren.bondar@ualberta.ca.

University of Alberta, Faculties of Medicine and Oral Health Sciences and Graduate Studies and Research, Graduate Programs in Medicine, Department of Public Health Sciences, Edmonton, AB T6G 2E1, Canada. Offerings include health policy and management (MPH, PhD), health services administration (Postgraduate Diploma). Terminal master's awarded for partial completion of doctoral program. Department faculty: 20 full-time, 11 part-time. *Degree requirements:* For doctorate, dissertation required, foreign language not required. *Average time to degree:* master's–2 years full-time, 4 years part-time; doctorate–4 years full-time, 6 years part-time. *Application deadline:* 2/1 (priority date; rolling processing). *Application fee:* $60. • Dr. T. W. Noseworthy, Chair, 403-492-6408. Application contact: Felicity Hey, Graduate Programs Administrator, 403-492-6407. Fax: 403-492-0364. E-mail: felicity.hey@ualberta.ca.

University of Arkansas at Little Rock, College of Professional Studies, Department of Health Services Administration, Little Rock, AR 72204-1099. Awards MHSA. Accredited by ACEHSA. Part-time and evening/weekend programs available. Students: 20 full-time (9 women), 18 part-time (8 women); includes 2 minority (both African Americans), 5 international. Average age 27. 28 applicants, 71% accepted. In 1997, 16 degrees awarded. *Degree requirements:* Directed study or residency required, foreign language and thesis not required. *Entrance requirements:* GMAT (minimum score 500) or GRE General Test (minimum combined score of 1500 on three sections), interview, minimum GPA of 2.75. Application deadline: 6/15 (priority date; rolling processing). Application fee: $25 ($30 for international students). *Expenses:* Tuition $2466 per year full-time, $137 per credit hour part-time for state residents; $5256 per year full-time, $292 per credit hour part-time for nonresidents. Fees $216 per year full-time, $36 per semester (minimum) part-time. *Financial aid:* Research assistantships, Federal Work-Study, institutionally sponsored loans, and career-related internships or fieldwork available. Aid available to part-time students. Financial aid application deadline: 6/15. • Dr. John B. Wayne, Chairperson, 501-569-3293.

University of British Columbia, Faculties of Medicine and Graduate Studies, Graduate Programs in Medicine, Department of Health Care and Epidemiology, Vancouver, BC V6T 1W5, Canada. Offerings include health administration (MHA). *Average time to degree:* master's–3 years full-time, 4 years part-time. *Application deadline:* 3/31 (rolling processing). *Application fee:* $50.

University of California, Berkeley, Group in Health Services and Policy Analysis, Berkeley, CA 94720-1500. Awards PhD. Students: 26 full-time (15 women); includes 5 minority (1 African American, 3 Asian Americans, 1 Hispanic), 3 international. 27 applicants, 30% accepted. In 1997, 3 degrees awarded. *Degree requirements:* Dissertation, qualifying exam. *Entrance requirements:* GRE General Test, minimum GPA of 3.0. Application deadline: 1/12. Application fee: $40. *Expenses:* Tuition $0 for state residents; $9384 per year for nonresidents. Fees $4409 per year. *Financial aid:* Application deadline 12/15. • James Robinson, Chair. Application contact: Holly Wilson, Graduate Assistant for Admission, 510-643-8571. Fax: 510-643-6981. E-mail: hwilson@uclink2.berkeley.edu.

University of California, Berkeley, School of Public Health, Division of Health Policy and Administration, Berkeley, CA 94720-1500. Awards MPH, MBA/MPH, MCP/MPH, MPP/MPH. *Degree requirements:* Comprehensive exam. *Entrance requirements:* GRE General Test, minimum GPA of 3.0. Application deadline: 1/5 (rolling processing). Application fee: $40. *Expenses:* Tuition $0 for state residents; $9384 per year for nonresidents. Fees $4409 per year. *Financial aid:* Fellowships, research assistantships, teaching assistantships, Federal Work-Study available. Financial aid application deadline: 3/2. • Dr. Ralph Catalano, Deputy. Application contact: Holly Wilson, Administrative Assistant, 510-643-8571. Fax: 510-643-6981. E-mail: hwilson@uclink2.berkeley.edu.

University of California, Los Angeles, School of Public Health, Department of Health Services, Los Angeles, CA 90095. Awards MS, PhD. Faculty: 10 (2 women). Students: 35 full-time (23 women); includes 7 minority (1 African American, 3 Asian Americans, 3 Hispanics), 2 international. 21 applicants, 43% accepted. *Degree requirements:* For master's, comprehensive exam or thesis required, foreign language not required; for doctorate, dissertation, oral and written qualifying exams required, foreign language not required. *Entrance requirements:* For master's, GRE General Test (minimum combined score of 1100), minimum GPA of 3.0; for doctorate, GRE General Test (minimum combined score of 1200), minimum undergraduate GPA of 3.0. Application deadline: 12/15. Application fee: $40. Electronic applications accepted. *Expenses:* Tuition $0 for state residents; $9384 per year for nonresidents. Fees $4551 per year. *Financial aid:* In 1997–98, 30 students received aid, including fellowships totaling $65,185, research assistantships totaling $8,963, teaching assistantships totaling $66,082, federal fellowships and scholarships totaling $186,638. Financial aid application deadline: 3/1. • Dr. Thomas Rice, Chair, 310-825-7863. Application contact: Departmental Office, 310-825-7863. E-mail: app_hs@admin.ph.ucla.edu.

University of Central Florida, College of Health and Public Affairs, Program in Health Sciences, Orlando, FL 32816. Offers health services administration (MS). Part-time and evening/weekend programs available. Students: 71 full-time (52 women), 58 part-time (42 women); includes 22 minority (10 African Americans, 2 Asian Americans, 10 Hispanics), 2 international. Average age 34. 56 applicants, 70% accepted. In 1997, 46 degrees awarded. *Degree requirements:* Thesis or alternative required, foreign language not required. *Entrance requirements:* GRE General Test. Application deadline: 7/15 (rolling processing; 12/15 for spring admission). Application fee: $20. *Expenses:* Tuition $3288 per year full-time, $137 per credit hour part-time for state residents; $11,520 per year full-time, $480 per credit hour part-time for nonresidents. Fees $105 per year. *Financial aid:* Teaching assistantships, Federal Work-Study, institutionally sponsored loans, and career-related internships or fieldwork available. Aid available to part-time students. • Dr. Gregory Frazer, Chair, 407-823-2359.

University of Chicago, Graduate Program in Health Administration and Policy, 969 East 60th Street, Office 6011, Chicago, IL 60637-1513. Awards AM, MBA, Certificate. MBA available through the Graduate School of Business; AM available through The Irving B. Harris Graduate School of Public Policy Studies or the School of Social Service Administration. Faculty: 18 full-time (3 women). Students: 50 full-time (31 women), 4 part-time (3 women); includes 20 minority (9 African Americans, 11 Asian Americans). In 1997, 22 master's awarded. *Average time to degree:* master's–2 years full-time. *Application deadline:* 10/1 (priority date; rolling processing). *Application fee:* $0. *Financial aid:* Fellowships, research assistantships, teaching assistantships, institutionally sponsored loans, and career-related internships or fieldwork available. Financial aid application deadline: 2/2. *Faculty research:* Maternal and child health, oral health, health policy research. • Dr. Edward F. Lawlor, Director, 773-702-7104. Application contact: Margarita M. O'Connell, Administrator, 773-702-7107. Fax: 773-702-7222. E-mail: marg@chas.uchicago.edu.

See in-depth description on page 1339.

University of Cincinnati, College of Design, Architecture, Art and Planning, School of Planning, Program in Health Planning/Administration, Cincinnati, OH 45221. Awards MS, JD/MS. Students: 16 full-time (13 women), 21 part-time (14 women); includes 7 minority (6 African Americans, 1 Asian American), 7 international. 0 applicants. In 1997, 5 degrees awarded. *Degree requirements:* Thesis required, foreign language not required. *Average time to degree:* master's–2.2 years full-time. *Entrance requirements:* GRE General Test. Application deadline: 2/1. Application fee: $30. *Tuition:* $7228 per year full-time, $185 per credit hour part-time for state residents; $13,812 per year full-time, $352 per credit hour part-time for nonresidents. *Financial aid:* Application deadline 5/1. • Jack Kleymeyer, Director, 513-556-0214. Fax: 513-556-1274.

University of Colorado at Denver, Graduate School of Business Administration, Executive Program in Health Administration, Denver, CO 80248-0006. Awards Exec MS. Accredited by ACEHSA. Evening/weekend programs available. Postbaccalaureate distance learning degree programs offered (minimal on-campus study). Faculty: 17 full-time (5 women). *Entrance requirements:* GMAT (minimum score 400), TOEFL (minimum score 525; average 560). Application deadline: 4/15 (priority date; rolling processing). Application fee: $0. *Financial aid:* Need-based scholarships available. Financial aid application deadline: 4/1. • W. Scott Guthrie, Director, 303-623-1888. Fax: 303-623-9228. E-mail: sguthrie@conan.cudenver.edu. Application contact: Pete Taffe, Program Manager, 303-623-1888. Fax: 303-623-6228. E-mail: peter_taffe@together.cudenver.edu.

University of Colorado at Denver, Graduate School of Business Administration, Program in Health Administration, Denver, CO 80217-3364. Awards MS, MBA/MS. Accredited by ACEHSA. Part-time and evening/weekend programs available. Faculty: 4 full-time. Students: 89. In 1997, 29 degrees awarded. *Entrance requirements:* GMAT (minimum score 400; average 520), TOEFL (minimum score 525; average 560). Application deadline: 7/1 (priority date; rolling processing; 11/1 for spring admission). Application fee: $50 ($60 for international students). *Expenses:* Tuition $3754 per year full-time, $225 per semester hour part-time for state residents; $12,962 per year full-time, $777 per semester hour part-time for nonresidents. Fees $252 per year. *Financial aid:* In 1997–98, 16 tuition grant traineeships (8 to first-year students) totaling $32,000 were awarded. Financial aid application deadline: 4/1. *Faculty research:* Cost containment, financial management, governance, rural health care delivery systems. • Errol Biggs, Director, 303-556-5845. Fax: 303-556-5899. Application contact: Lori Cain, Graduate Business Admissions Office, 303-556-5900. Fax: 303-556-5904. E-mail: lori_cain@maroon.cudenver.edu.

See in-depth description on page 1341.

University of Connecticut, School of Business Administration, Storrs, CT 06269. Offerings include health care management (MBA). School faculty: 63. *Entrance requirements:* GMAT. Application deadline: 6/1 (priority date; rolling processing; 11/1 for spring admission). Application fee: $40 ($45 for international students). *Expenses:* Tuition $5272 per year full-time, $293 per credit part-time for state residents; $13,696 per year full-time, $761 per credit part-time for nonresidents. Fees $948 per year full-time, $640 per year part-time. • Thomas G. Gutteridge, Dean, 860-486-3096. Application contact: David W. Palmer, Chairperson, 860-486-3096.

University of Dallas, Graduate School of Management, Program in Health Services Management, Irving, TX 75062-4799. Awards MBA, MM. Part-time programs available. Students: 75 (46 women). In 1997, 68 degrees awarded. *Average time to degree:* master's–1.3 years full-time, 2.5 years part-time. *Entrance requirements:* GMAT (minimum score 400), TOEFL (average 520), minimum GPA of 3.0. Application deadline: 8/6 (priority date; rolling processing; 12/8 for spring admission). Application fee: $25 ($50 for international students). *Expenses:* Tuition $380 per credit hour. Fees $125 per year. *Financial aid:* Application deadline 2/15. • Robert Lynch, Director, 972-721-5173. Fax: 972-721-5130. Application contact: Roxanne Del Rio, Director of Admissions, 972-721-5174. Fax: 972-721-4009. E-mail: admiss@gsm.udallas.edu.

Directory: Health Services Management and Hospital Administration

University of Denver, University College, Denver, CO 80208. Offerings include healthcare systems (MHS). *Average time to degree:* master's–1.5 years full-time, 2.7 years part-time. *Application deadline:* 8/10 (rolling processing; 2/22 for spring admission). *Application fee:* $25. *Expenses:* Tuition $245 per quarter hour for state residents; $310 per quarter hour for nonresidents. Fees $165 per quarter hour (minimum).

University of Denver, Daniels College of Business, General Business Administration Program, Denver, CO 80208. Offerings include health care management (MSM), public health management (MSM). MSMGEN offered jointly with the Department of Engineering; MSMC new for fall 1998. Program faculty: 76 full-time (15 women). *Application deadline:* 5/1 (priority date; rolling processing; 1/1 for spring admission). *Application fee:* $50. *Expenses:* Tuition $18,216 per year full-time, $506 per credit hour part-time. Fees $159 per year. • Dr. Tom Howard, Director, 303-871-4402. Application contact: Jan Johnson, Executive Director, Student Services, 303-871-3416. Fax: 303-871-4466. E-mail: dcb@du.edu.

University of Detroit Mercy, College of Health Professions, Program in Health Services Administration, Detroit, MI 48219-0900. Awards MS. *Degree requirements:* Thesis. *Entrance requirements:* GRE General Test (minimum combined score of 1200), minimum GPA of 3.0. Application fee: $25. *Faculty research:* Health systems issues, organizational theory.

University of Evansville, Graduate Programs, Department of Nursing, Program in Health Services Administration, Evansville, IN 47722-0002. Awards MS. Faculty: 1 (woman) full-time, 2 part-time (0 women). Students: 13 part-time (11 women). Average age 33. *Entrance requirements:* GRE General Test. Application deadline: 7/1. Application fee: $20. *Expenses:* Tuition $395 per credit hour. Fees $30 per year. *Financial aid:* Research assistantships available. Financial aid application deadline: 7/1. • Dr. Rita Behnke, Director, Department of Nursing, 812-479-2550.

University of Florida, Colleges of Health Professions and Business Administration, Program in Health and Hospital Administration, Gainesville, FL 32611. Awards MHA, MBA/MHA. Accredited by ACEHSA. Faculty: 5. Students: 16 full-time (4 women), 18 part-time (8 women); includes 5 minority (1 African American, 1 Asian American, 3 Hispanics), 1 international. 40 applicants, 38% accepted. In 1997, 18 degrees awarded. *Entrance requirements:* GMAT (minimum score 500), minimum GPA of 3.0. Application deadline: 4/1 (rolling processing). Application fee: $60. *Tuition:* $138 per credit hour for state residents; $481 per credit hour for nonresidents. *Financial aid:* In 1997–98, 4 students received aid, including 1 fellowship averaging $820 per month, 3 research assistantships averaging $412 per month; teaching assistantships, graduate assistantships, and career-related internships or fieldwork also available. *Faculty research:* Hospital profitability, indigent care, rural health care systems, AIDS education, managed care, outcomes. • Dr. Niccie L. McKay, Chair, 352-395-8042. Fax: 352-395-8043. E-mail: nmckay@hp.ufl.edu.

University of Florida, College of Pharmacy and Graduate School, Graduate Programs in Pharmacy, Department of Pharmacy Health Care Administration, Gainesville, FL 32611. Awards MS, PhD, Pharm D/PhD. Part-time programs available. Faculty: 7 full-time (3 women). Students: 8 full-time (1 woman); includes 3 minority (1 African American, 2 Asian Americans). Average age 31. 36 applicants, 8% accepted. In 1997, 2 doctorates awarded (100% entered university research/teaching). *Degree requirements:* For doctorate, dissertation. *Entrance requirements:* For master's, minimum GPA of 3.0; for doctorate, GRE General Test (minimum combined score of 1000; average 1171), TOEFL (minimum score 600), minimum GPA of 3.0. Application deadline: 3/1 (priority date; rolling processing). Application fee: $20. *Tuition:* $138 per credit hour for state residents; $481 per credit hour for nonresidents. *Financial aid:* In 1997–98, 1 fellowship averaging $986 per month, 8 teaching assistantships averaging $828 per month were awarded; research assistantships, full tuition waivers also available. Financial aid application deadline: 2/1. *Faculty research:* Pharmaceutical care, drug use systems, drug-related morbidity, pharmacy law. • Dr. Richard Segal, Chair, 352-392-5270. E-mail: segal@cop.health.ufl.edu. Application contact: Dr. Carole Kimberlin, Graduate Coordinator, 352-392-9120. Fax: 352-392-7782. E-mail: kimber@cop.health.ufl.edu.

University of Georgia, College of Pharmacy, Department of Clinical and Administrative Sciences, Athens, GA 30602. Offers programs in experimental therapeutics (PhD), experimental therapeutics (MS), pharmacy care administration (MS, PhD). *Degree requirements:* For master's, thesis required, foreign language not required; for doctorate, 1 foreign language (computer language can substitute), dissertation. *Entrance requirements:* GRE General Test, minimum GPA of 3.0. Application fee: $30. *Financial aid:* Application deadline 2/15. • Dr. Joseph T. DiPiro, Head. Application contact: Dr. Randall L. Tackett, Graduate Coordinator, 706-542-7400.

See in-depth description on page 1813.

University of Hawaii at Manoa, College of Health Sciences and Social Welfare, School of Public Health, Program in Health Services Administration and Planning, Honolulu, HI 96822. Awards MPH, MS. Part-time programs available. Faculty: 4 full-time (1 woman). Students: 30 full-time (15 women), 31 part-time (16 women); includes 30 minority (1 African American, 28 Asian Americans, 1 Hispanic). 37 applicants, 65% accepted. In 1997, 33 degrees awarded. *Degree requirements:* Thesis (for some programs). *Average time to degree:* master's–1.2 years full-time, 3 years part-time. *Application deadline:* 3/1 (9/1 for spring admission). *Application fee:* $25 ($50 for international students). *Tuition:* $4029 per year full-time, $214 per credit hour part-time for state residents; $9957 per year full-time, $461 per credit hour part-time for nonresidents. *Financial aid:* Career-related internships or fieldwork available. *Faculty research:* Politics of health care, worksite wellness, public administration, health promotion, international health and community development. • Dr. Walter Patrick, Head, 808-956-7587. Application contact: Nancy Kilonsky, Assistant Dean, 808-956-8267.

University of Houston, College of Pharmacy, Department of Clinical Sciences and Administration, 4800 Calhoun, Houston, TX 77204-2163. Offerings include pharmacy administration (MSPHR). Department faculty: 5 full-time (1 woman). *Degree requirements:* Thesis required, foreign language not required. *Entrance requirements:* GRE General Test, TOEFL (minimum score 550), bachelor's degree in pharmacy. Application deadline: 5/1 (priority date). Application fee: $25 ($100 for international students). *Expenses:* Tuition $1152 per year full-time, $120 per semester (minimum) part-time for state residents; $4482 per year full-time, $249 per credit hour part-time for nonresidents. Fees $977 per year full-time, $119 per semester (minimum) part-time. • Dr. Mark Stratton, Chair, 713-795-8387. Application contact: Dr. William McCormick, 713-795-8367. Fax: 713-795-8383.

University of Houston–Clear Lake, School of Business and Public Administration, Program in Public Affairs, Houston, TX 77058-1098. Offerings include administration of health services (MS), healthcare administration (MHA). One or more programs accredited by ACEHSA. Program faculty: 15. *Application deadline:* 8/1 (rolling processing; 12/1 for spring admission). *Application fee:* $30 ($60 for international students). *Tuition:* $207 per credit hour for state residents; $336 per credit hour for nonresidents. • Dr. Richard Allison, Chair, 281-283-3251. Application contact: Dr. Sue Neeley, Associate Dean, 281-283-3110.

University of Illinois at Chicago, School of Public Health, Program in Health Resources Management, Chicago, IL 60607-7128. Awards MPH, MS, Dr PH, PhD. MS and PhD offered jointly with Graduate College. *Degree requirements:* For master's, thesis, field practicum required, foreign language not required; for doctorate, dissertation, independent research, internship required, foreign language not required. *Entrance requirements:* GRE General Test (minimum combined score of 1000), TOEFL (minimum score 550), minimum GPA of 3.75 on a 5.0 scale. Application deadline: 7/3 (11/8 for spring admission). Application fee: $40 ($50 for international students). • Dr. Bernard Baum, Director, 312-996-7816. Application contact: Dr. Babette Neuberger, Assistant Dean, 312-996-6625.

The University of Iowa, College of Medicine and Graduate College, Graduate Programs in Medicine, Program in Hospital and Health Administration, Iowa City, IA 52242-1316. Awards MA, PhD, JD/MA, MA/MA, MBA/MA, MS/MA. One or more programs accredited by ACEHSA. MA/MA and MS/MA offered jointly with the Program in Urban and Regional Planning. Faculty: 9 full-time (1 woman), 9 part-time (3 women). Students: 53 full-time (25 women); includes 7 minority (4 African Americans, 3 Asian Americans), 8 international. Average age 25. 100 applicants, 22% accepted. In 1997, 27 master's awarded (100% found work related to degree). *Degree requirements:* For doctorate, dissertation required, foreign language not required. *Average time to degree:* master's–2 years full-time; doctorate–3 years full-time. *Entrance requirements:* For master's, GRE General Test (minimum combined score of 1050) or GMAT (minimum score 550), minimum GPA of 3.0; for doctorate, GRE General Test (minimum combined score of 1110) or GMAT (minimum score 550), minimum GPA of 3.25. Application deadline: 5/1 (rolling processing). Application fee: $20. *Expenses:* Tuition $3166 per year full-time, $176 per semester hour part-time for state residents; $10,202 per year full-time, $176 per semester hour part-time for nonresidents. Fees $202 per year. *Financial aid:* In 1997–98, 23 students received aid, including 5 fellowships (3 to first-year students) averaging $525 per month and totaling $26,250, 17 research assistantships (6 to first-year students) averaging $525 per month and totaling $89,250, 1 teaching assistantship, 10 traineeships, minority scholarships, alumni scholarships, scholarships (5 to first-year students); Federal Work-Study, institutionally sponsored loans, and career-related internships or fieldwork also available. Financial aid application deadline: 5/1; applicants required to submit FAFSA. *Faculty research:* Health policy, quality assessment, outcomes and appropriateness of care, organizational behavior, rural health. • Dr. Douglas S. Wakefield, Interim Director, 319-335-9822. E-mail: douglas-wakefield@uiowa.edu. Application contact: Michelle Thien, Admissions Coordinator, 319-335-9817. Fax: 319-335-9772.

See in-depth description on page 1343.

University of Kansas, School of Pharmacy, Department of Health Services Administration, Lawrence, KS 66045. Awards MHSA, JD/MHSA. Accredited by ACEHSA. Part-time and evening/weekend programs available. Faculty: 4 full-time. Students: 36 full-time (15 women), 58 part-time (31 women); includes 16 minority (5 African Americans, 7 Asian Americans, 2 Hispanics, 2 Native Americans), 4 international. Average age 27. 70 applicants, 54% accepted. In 1997, 27 degrees awarded. *Entrance requirements:* GMAT, GRE General Test, TOEFL (minimum score 600). Application deadline: 4/1. Application fee: $20. *Expenses:* Tuition $2400 per year full-time, $100 per credit hour part-time for state residents; $7890 per year full-time, $329 per credit hour part-time for nonresidents. Fees $428 per year full-time, $31 per credit hour part-time. *Financial aid:* In 1997–98, 9 fellowships (5 to first-year students) averaging $425 per month, 1 research assistantship averaging $600 per month were awarded; teaching assistantships and career-related internships or fieldwork also available. *Faculty research:* Rural health, outcomes, health policy. • Robert Lee, Interim Chair, 785-864-3212. Fax: 785-864-5089. Application contact: Rodney McAdams, Graduate Director, 785-864-3259.

University of Kentucky, Program in Health Administration, Lexington, KY 40506-0032. Awards MHA. Accredited by ACEHSA. Faculty: 8 full-time (0 women), 1 part-time (0 women). Students: 26 full-time (13 women), 23 part-time (14 women); includes 3 minority (all African Americans). 49 applicants, 88% accepted. In 1997, 18 degrees awarded. *Degree requirements:* Comprehensive exam. *Application deadline:* 4/1 (9/1 for spring admission). *Application fee:* $30 ($35 for international students). *Financial aid:* In 1997–98, 2 fellowships were awarded; research assistantships also available. *Faculty research:* Health economy, health finance, health policy. Total annual research expenditures: $822,349. • Dr. Douglas Scutchfield, Director of Graduate Studies, 606-323-1100. Application contact: Dr. Constance L. Wood, Associate Dean, 606-257-4613. Fax: 606-323-1928.

University of La Verne, School of Organizational Management, Department of Health Care Management, La Verne, CA 91750-4443. Offers program in health administration (MHA). Part-time and evening/weekend programs available. *Entrance requirements:* TOEFL (minimum score 550), minimum GPA of 2.5. Application fee: $25. *Expenses:* Tuition $315 per unit (minimum). Fees $60 per year. *Faculty research:* Patient care management.

University of Mary Hardin–Baylor, Graduate Program in Health Services Management, Belton, TX 76513. Awards MHSM. Part-time and evening/weekend programs available. Faculty: 4 full-time (2 women), 7 part-time (3 women). Students: 3 full-time (2 women), 98 part-time (75 women); includes 29 minority (14 African Americans, 5 Asian Americans, 9 Hispanics, 1 Native American), 1 international. Average age 38. 31 applicants, 84% accepted. In 1997, 18 degrees awarded. *Degree requirements:* Thesis or alternative, competency exam, management project required, foreign language not required. *Average time to degree:* master's–2 years full-time, 3 years part-time. *Entrance requirements:* GRE General Test (minimum combined score of 850). Application deadline: 8/1 (priority date; rolling processing). Application fee: $35 ($135 for international students). *Expenses:* Tuition $270 per semester hour. Fees $15 per semester hour. *Financial aid:* Career-related internships or fieldwork available. Aid available to part-time students. Financial aid application deadline: 6/1. *Faculty research:* Ambulatory care management, professional continuing education; curriculum innovation, alternative medicine. • Dr. Michael P. West, Chair, 254-295-4558. Fax: 254-933-3300.

University of Maryland, Baltimore, Graduate School, Graduate Programs in Pharmacy, Department of Pharmacy Practice and Science, Baltimore, MD 21201-1627. Offerings include pharmacy administration (PhD). Terminal master's awarded for partial completion of doctoral program. Department faculty: 10 full-time (2 women). *Degree requirements:* Dissertation required, foreign language not required. *Average time to degree:* doctorate–3 years full-time. *Entrance requirements:* GRE General Test, minimum GPA of 3.0. Application deadline: 4/1 (priority date; rolling processing). Application fee: $45. *Expenses:* Tuition $253 per credit hour for state residents; $454 per credit hour for nonresidents. Fees $317 per year. • Dr. Gary Smith, Chair, 410-706-2963. Application contact: Dr. Julie Zito, Director, Graduate Programs, 410-706-0524. Fax: 410-706-4725. E-mail: jzito@pharmacy.ab.umd.edu.

University of Maryland, Baltimore County, Graduate School, Department of Emergency Health Services, Baltimore, MD 21250-5398. Offers programs in administration, planning, and policy (MS); education (MS); preventive medicine and epidemiology (MS). Part-time programs available. *Entrance requirements:* GRE General Test, minimum GPA of 3.0. Application deadline: 7/1. Application fee: $40. *Expenses:* Tuition $260 per credit hour for state residents; $468 per credit hour for nonresidents. Fees $39 per credit hour.

University of Massachusetts Lowell, College of Health Professions, Department of Health Services Administration, 1 University Avenue, Lowell, MA 01854-2881. Awards MS. Part-time programs available. Faculty: 4 full-time (3 women). Students: 9 full-time (6 women), 36 part-time (30 women); includes 1 minority (Asian American), 3 international. 30 applicants, 63% accepted. In 1997, 8 degrees awarded. *Degree requirements:* Thesis optional, foreign language not required. *Entrance requirements:* GRE General Test. Application deadline: 4/1 (priority date; rolling processing; 10/1 for spring admission). Application fee: $20 ($35 for international students). *Tuition:* $4867 per year full-time, $618 per semester (minimum) part-time for state residents; $10,276 per year full-time, $1294 per semester (minimum) part-time for nonresidents. *Financial aid:* In 1997–98, 3 teaching assistantships were awarded; Federal Work-Study, institutionally sponsored loans, and career-related internships or fieldwork also available. Financial aid application deadline: 4/1. *Faculty research:* Alzheimer's disease, total quality management systems, information systems, market analysis. • Dr. Beverly Volicer, Chair, 978-934-4479. Application contact: Dr. Vincent Pivnicny, Coordinator, 978-934-4482. E-mail: vincent_pivnicny@woods.uml.edu.

The University of Memphis, College of Arts and Sciences, Department of Political Science, Program in Health Administration, Memphis, TN 38152. Awards MHA. Accredited by ACEHSA. Students: 15 full-time (7 women), 22 part-time (16 women); includes 3 minority (all African Americans), 5 international. Average age 32. 39 applicants, 38% accepted. In 1997, 9 degrees awarded. *Degree requirements:* Thesis or alternative, comprehensive exam, internship. *Entrance requirements:* GRE General Test (minimum combined score of 1000) or GMAT (minimum score 500), minimum GPA of 3.0. Application deadline: 8/1 (rolling processing; 12/1 for spring admission). Application fee: $25 ($50 for international students). *Tuition:* $2862 per year full-time, $166 per credit hour part-time for state residents; $6696 per year full-time, $379 per credit hour part-time for nonresidents. • Dr. Winsor C. Schmidt, Coordinator, 901-678-3369. E-mail: wschmidt@cc.memphis.edu. Application contact: James R. Carruth, Coordinator of Graduate Studies, 901-678-3360. Fax: 901-678-2983. E-mail: jrcarrth@memphis.edu.

The University of Memphis, College of Arts and Sciences, Department of Political Science, Program in Public Administration, Memphis, TN 38152. Offerings include health services administration (MPA). *Degree requirements:* Thesis or alternative, comprehensive exam, internship. *Entrance requirements:* GRE General Test (minimum combined score of 1000) or GMAT (minimum score 500), minimum GPA of 3.0. Application deadline: 8/1 (rolling processing; 12/1 for spring admission). Application fee: $25 ($50 for international students). *Tuition:* $2862 per year full-time, $166 per credit hour part-time for state residents; $6696 per year full-time, $379 per credit hour part-time for nonresidents. • Dr. Dorothy Norris-Tirrell, Coordinator, 901-678-3360. E-mail: dnrrstrr@memphis.edu. Application contact: James R. Carruth, Coordinator of Graduate Studies, 901-678-3360. Fax: 901-678-2983. E-mail: jrcarrth@memphis.edu.

University of Miami, School of Business Administration, Department of Management Science, Coral Gables, FL 33124. Offerings include health administration (Certificate). Postbaccalaureate distance learning degree programs offered. Department faculty: 11 full-time (2 women). *Average time to degree:* master's–2 years full-time, 4 years part-time. *Entrance requirements:* TOEFL (minimum score 550). Application deadline: 6/30 (priority date; rolling processing; 10/31 for spring admission). Application fee: $35. *Expenses:* Tuition $815 per credit hour. Fees $174 per year. • Dr. Edward Baker, Chairman, 305-284-6599. E-mail: ebaker@umiami.ir.miami.edu. Application contact: Dr. Ronny Aboudi, Director of MS Programs, 305-284-1966. Fax: 305-281-2321.

University of Michigan, School of Public Health, Department of Health Management and Policy, Ann Arbor, MI 48109. Awards MHSA, MPH, Dr PH, PhD, JD/MHSA, MD/MPH, MHSA/AM, MHSA/MBA, MHSA/MPP, MHSA/MS, MPH/MPP. Programs in health management and policy (MHSA, MPH), health policy (Dr PH), health services organization and policy (PhD). One or more programs accredited by ACEHSA. PhD offered through the Horace H. Rackham School of Graduate Studies. Faculty: 19. *Degree requirements:* For doctorate, oral defense of dissertation, preliminary exam. *Entrance requirements:* For master's, GMAT, GRE General Test; for doctorate, GRE General Test. Application deadline: 3/1 (priority date; rolling processing). Application fee: $55. *Financial aid:* Fellowships, research assistantships, teaching assistantships available. Financial aid application deadline: 3/1. • William G. Weissert, Chair, 734-936-1191.

See in-depth description on page 1535.

University of Michigan, College of Pharmacy and Horace H. Rackham School of Graduate Studies, Graduate Programs in Pharmaceutical Sciences, Program in Pharmacy Administration, Ann Arbor, MI 48109. Awards MS, PhD. *Degree requirements:* For doctorate, dissertation, oral defense of dissertation, preliminary exam required, foreign language not required. *Entrance requirements:* For master's, GRE General Test, TOEFL (miminum score of 560); for doctorate, GRE General Test. Application deadline: rolling. Application fee: $55. Electronic applications accepted. *Financial aid:* Fellowships, research assistantships, teaching assistantships available. • Application contact: Denise Smith, Administrative Assistant, 734-764-7312. Fax: 734-763-2022.

University of Minnesota, Twin Cities Campus, Program in Health Informatics, Minneapolis, MN 55455-0213. Awards MS, PhD. Part-time programs available. Faculty: 15 full-time (5 women), 8 part-time (0 women). Students: 20 full-time (9 women), 9 part-time (6 women); includes 1 minority (Hispanic), 14 international. Average age 38. 18 applicants, 50% accepted. In 1997, 5 master's awarded (20% entered university research/teaching, 60% found other work related to degree, 20% continued full-time study); 2 doctorates awarded (100% found work related to degree). *Degree requirements:* For master's, thesis or alternative, project paper; for doctorate, dissertation. *Average time to degree:* master's–2.4 years full-time, 4 years part-time. *Entrance requirements:* For master's, GRE General Test, previous course work in calculus, linear algebra, life sciences, programming, and biology; for doctorate, GRE General Test, previous course work in life sciences, programming, and differential equations. Application deadline: 6/30 (rolling processing). Application fee: $40 ($50 for international students). *Financial aid:* In 1997–98, 18 students received aid, including 1 fellowship (to a first-year student), 11 research assistantships (5 to first-year students), 2 teaching assistantships (1 to a first-year student), 5 grants, traineeships; full and partial tuition waivers, Federal Work-Study also available. Financial aid application deadline: 1/15. *Faculty research:* Medical decision making, physiological control systems, population studies, clinical information systems, telemedicine. • Dr. Stuart Speedie, Director, 612-625-8440.

University of Minnesota, Twin Cities Campus, Carlson School of Management, Department of Healthcare Management, Minneapolis, MN 55455-0213. Awards MHA, MHA/MBA. Accredited by ACEHSA. *Entrance requirements:* GMAT or GRE General Test. Application deadline: 3/30. Application fee: $50 ($75 for international students).

Announcement: Minnesota's MHA has earned a national reputation for excellence in training leaders for the health-care industry. A strong curriculum, blending advanced management theory with practical experience in health-care settings, draws upon the rich resources of a dynamic and innovative health-care community in Minneapolis–St. Paul. Paid residency, individualized placement, and a dual degree with business available. Multidisciplinary, research-based curriculum includes concentrations in such areas as medical sociology, policy analysis, strategic management, finance, and long-term care.

See in-depth description on page 1345.

University of Minnesota, Twin Cities Campus, School of Public Health, Major in Health Services Research, Policy, and Administration, Minneapolis, MN 55455-0213. Awards PhD. Students: 35 (17 women). In 1997, 4 degrees awarded. *Degree requirements:* Dissertation required, foreign language not required. *Entrance requirements:* GRE General Test (minimum combined score of 1800 on three sections). Application deadline: 3/1 (rolling processing). Application fee: $50 ($75 for international students). *Financial aid:* Research assistantships, teaching assistantships, Federal Work-Study, institutionally sponsored loans available. • Dr. Will Manning, Chair, 612-624-6151. E-mail: wmanning@vx.cis.umn.edu. Application contact: Janet Shapiro, Student Coordinator, 612-624-9432. E-mail: j-shap@maroon.tc.umn.edu.

See in-depth description on page 1537.

University of Minnesota, Twin Cities Campus, School of Public Health, Major in Public Health Administration, Minneapolis, MN 55455-0213. Awards MPH. Part-time programs available. Faculty: 5 full-time. Students: 28. In 1997, 14 degrees awarded. *Entrance requirements:* GRE General Test (minimum combined score of 1500 on three sections), minimum GPA of 3.0. Application deadline: 4/15 (priority date; rolling processing). Application fee: $50 ($75 for international students). *Financial aid:* Federal Work-Study, institutionally sponsored loans, and career-related internships or fieldwork available. Financial aid applicants required to submit FAFSA. *Faculty research:* Community health service organizations, nursing services, dental services, the elderly. • Dr. Mila Aroskar, Chair, 612-625-0615. E-mail: arosk001@tc.umn.edu. Application contact: Ria Dickhausen, Coordinator, 612-625-9480. E-mail: m-greg@tc.umn.edu.

See in-depth description on page 1537.

University of Missouri–Columbia, Department of Health Management and Informatics, Columbia, MO 65211. Offers program in health services management (MHA). Part-time programs available. Faculty: 11 full-time (9 women), 4 part-time (3 women). Students: 79 full-time (36 women); includes 5 minority (3 African Americans, 1 Asian American, 1 Hispanic), 3 international. In 1997, 34 degrees awarded. *Entrance requirements:* GRE General Test, minimum GPA of 3.0. Application deadline: 7/15. Application fee: $25 ($50 for international students). *Expenses:* Tuition $3240 per year full-time, $180 per credit hour part-time for state residents; $9108 per year full-time, $506 per credit hour part-time for nonresidents. Fees $55 per year full-time. • Dr. Gordon Brown, Director of Graduate Studies, 573-882-6179.

University of New Hampshire, School of Health and Human Services, Department of Health Management and Policy, Durham, NH 03824. Awards MHA. Accredited by ACEHSA. Evening/weekend programs available. Faculty: 8 full-time. Students: 35 full-time (24 women), 2 part-time (both women). Average age 29. 28 applicants. In 1997, 18 degrees awarded. *Entrance requirements:* GMAT or GRE General Test. Application deadline: 7/1 (priority date; rolling processing). Application fee: $50. *Expenses:* Tuition $7461 per year full-time, $388 per credit hour part-time for state residents; $8207 per year full-time, $427 per credit hour part-time for nonresidents. Fees $789 per year full-time, $15 per semester part-time. *Financial aid:* In 1997–98, 4 fellowships (2 to first-year students) were awarded; research assistantships, teaching assistantships, scholarships also available. Financial aid application deadline: 2/15. • Dr. James B. Lewis, Chairperson, 603-862-2733.

Announcement: The Department of Health Management and Policy at the University of New Hampshire offers the Master of Health Administration degree especially for students who wish to pursue their graduate professional education while continuing to work full-time. Classes meet on alternate weekends (Fridays and Saturdays) from September through May, plus 2 residential weeks, 1 in late August, the other in late May. The 2-year program prepares students for management careers in health-care networks, hospitals, nursing-care facilities, ambulatory care, mental health services, managed care, health-care financing organizations, planning and regulatory agencies, professional associations, and private industry.

See in-depth description on page 1347.

University of New Haven, School of Business, Program in Business Administration, West Haven, CT 06516-1916. Offerings include health care management (MBA). *Degree requirements:* Thesis or alternative required, foreign language not required. *Application deadline:* rolling. *Application fee:* $50. *Expenses:* Tuition $1125 per course. Fees $13 per trimester. • Dr. Omid Nodoushani, Coordinator, 203-932-7123.

University of New Haven, School of Business, Program in Health Care Administration, West Haven, CT 06516-1916. Awards MS. Students: 13 full-time (8 women), 77 part-time (64 women); includes 7 minority (4 African Americans, 1 Asian American, 2 Hispanics), 7 international. 34 applicants, 74% accepted. *Degree requirements:* Thesis or alternative required, foreign language not required. *Application deadline:* rolling. *Application fee:* $50. *Expenses:* Tuition $1125 per course. Fees $13 per trimester. *Financial aid:* Application deadline 5/1. • Charles Coleman, Chairman, 203-932-7375.

University of New Haven, School of Business, Program in Public Administration, West Haven, CT 06516-1916. Offerings include health care management (MPA). *Degree requirements:* Thesis or alternative required, foreign language not required. *Application deadline:* rolling. *Application fee:* $50. *Expenses:* Tuition $1125 per course. Fees $13 per trimester. • Charles Coleman, Chairman, 203-932-7375.

The University of North Carolina at Chapel Hill, School of Public Health, Department of Health Policy and Administration, Chapel Hill, NC 27599. Awards MHA, MPH, MSPH, Dr PH, PhD. One or more programs accredited by ACEHSA. Part-time programs available. Faculty: 23 full-time (9 women), 72 part-time (17 women). Students: 131 full-time (81 women), 130 part-time (84 women); includes 34 minority (14 African Americans, 13 Asian Americans, 4 Hispanics, 3 Native Americans), 25 international. Average age 35. 325 applicants, 51% accepted. In 1997, 43 master's, 9 doctorates awarded. *Degree requirements:* For master's, Capstone Course or major paper, comprehensive exam required, foreign language and thesis not required; for doctorate, dissertation, comprehensive exam required, foreign language not required. *Entrance requirements:* GRE General Test (minimum combined score of 1000), minimum GPA of 3.0. Application deadline: 1/1 (priority date; rolling processing). Application fee: $55. *Expenses:* Tuition $2008 per year full-time, $502 per semester (minimum) part-time for state residents; $10,414 per year full-time, $2604 per semester (minimum) part-time for nonresidents. Fees $782 per year full-time, $332 per semester (minimum) part-time. *Financial aid:* In 1997–98, 19 fellowships, 20 research assistantships, 32 teaching assistantships were awarded; graduate assistantships, Federal Work-Study, institutionally sponsored loans, and career-related internships or fieldwork also available. Financial aid application deadline: 1/1. *Faculty research:* Data-based intervention for cancer control, dental sealant technology on Medicaid programs, hospital efficiency, international culture and management. Total annual research expenditures: $639,556. • Dr. Kerry E. Kilpatrick, Chair, 919-966-7350. E-mail: kerry_kilpatrick@unc.edu. Application contact: Pam McDonald, Registrar, 919-966-7391. Fax: 919-966-6961. E-mail: pam_mcdonald@unc.edu.

University of North Carolina at Charlotte, Program in Health Administration, Charlotte, NC 28223-0001. Awards MHA, MSN/MHA. Faculty: 1 full-time (0 women), 7 part-time (3 women), 3 FTE. Students: 12 full-time (8 women), 54 part-time (40 women); includes 8 minority (4 African Americans, 3 Asian Americans, 1 Hispanic). Average age 33. 36 applicants, 94% accepted. *Application deadline:* 7/1. *Application fee:* $35. *Tuition:* $1786 per year full-time, $339 per semester (minimum) part-time for state residents; $8914 per year full-time, $2121 per semester (minimum) part-time for nonresidents. *Financial aid:* Application deadline 4/1. • Dr. Carolyn Thompson, Coordinator, 704-547-4522. Application contact: Kathy Barringer, Assistant Director of Graduate Admissions, 704-547-3366. Fax: 704-547-3279. E-mail: gradadm@email.uncc.edu.

University of North Florida, College of Health, Jacksonville, FL 32224-2645. Offerings include employee health services (MS), health administration (MHA), health care administration (MS). MSN new for fall 1998. College faculty: 14 full-time (9 women). *Application deadline:* rolling. *Application fee:* $20. *Tuition:* $3388 per year full-time, $141 per credit hour part-time for state residents; $11,634 per year full-time, $485 per credit hour part-time for nonresidents. • Dr. Joan Farrell, Dean, 904-646-2840.

University of North Texas, School of Community Service, Department of Applied Gerontology, Denton, TX 76203-6737. Offerings include administration of aging organizations (MA, MS). Department faculty: 4 full-time (0 women). *Degree requirements:* Thesis, internship required, foreign language not required. *Entrance requirements:* GRE General Test (minimum combined score of 800). Application deadline: 7/17 (rolling processing; 12/1 for spring admission). Application fee: $25 ($50 for international students). *Tuition:* $2063 per year full-time, $815 per year part-time for state residents; $5897 per year full-time, $2100 per year part-time for nonresidents. • Dr. Richard A. Lusky, Director, 940-565-2765. Application contact: Phyllis Eccleston, Academic Program Coordinator, 940-565-3449. Fax: 940-565-4370.

University of Oklahoma Health Sciences Center, College of Public Health, Department of Health Administration and Policy, Oklahoma City, OK 73190. Awards MHA, MPH, MS, Dr PH, PhD, MPH/JD, MPH/MBA. MPH/JD and MPH/MBA offered jointly with Oklahoma State University and the University of Oklahoma. Part-time programs available. Faculty: 13 full-time (3 women), 17 part-time (6 women). Students: 49 full-time (31 women), 114 part-time (67 women); includes 34 minority (8 African Americans, 4 Asian Americans, 9 Hispanics, 13 Native Americans), 8 international. Average age 36. 117 applicants, 58% accepted. In 1997, 52 master's awarded. *Degree requirements:* For master's, computer language, thesis (for some programs), comprehensive exam required, foreign language not required; for doctorate, 2 foreign languages, computer language, dissertation, oral and written comprehensive exam. *Entrance requirements:* For master's, TOEFL (minimum score 550); for doctorate, GRE General Test, TOEFL (minimum score 550). Application deadline: 7/1 (rolling processing; 12/1 for spring admission). Application fee: $25 ($50 for international students). *Financial aid:* Fellowships, research assistantships, traineeships, partial tuition waivers, institutionally sponsored loans, and career-related

Directory: Health Services Management and Hospital Administration

University of Oklahoma Health Sciences Center (continued)

internships or fieldwork available. Aid available to part-time students. Financial aid application deadline: 5/1. *Faculty research:* Public health administration, health institutions management, public policy and the aged, injury control. • Dr. Keith Curtis, Interim Chair, 405-271-2114.

University of Osteopathic Medicine and Health Sciences, College of Health Sciences, Des Moines, IA 50312-4104. Offerings include health care administration (MS). College faculty: 21. *Entrance requirements:* Minimum GPA of 3.0. Application deadline: 12/31 (rolling processing). Application fee: $35. *Expenses:* Tuition $265 per credit hour. Fees $75 per year. • Dr. Susan Cigelman, Interim Dean, 515-271-1634. Application contact: Dr. Dennis L. Bates, Director of Admissions, 515-271-1450. Fax: 515-271-1578.

University of Ottawa, Faculty of Administration, Health Administration Program, Ottawa, ON K1N 6N5, Canada. Awards MHA. Accredited by ACEHSA. Part-time programs available. Faculty: 2. Students: 31 full-time (18 women), 17 part-time (12 women); includes 2 international. Average age 34. In 1997, 31 degrees awarded. *Degree requirements:* Administrative residency required, thesis optional, foreign language not required. *Entrance requirements:* GMAT (score in 50th percentile or higher), honors degree or equivalent, minimum B average. Application deadline: 4/15 (rolling processing). Application fee: $60. *Expenses:* Tuition $4677 per year for Canadian residents; $9900 per year for nonresidents. Fees $230 per year. *Financial aid:* Fellowships, full tuition waivers, Federal Work-Study, and career-related internships or fieldwork available. *Faculty research:* Information systems, health care policy, health systems, comparative health care system. • Douglas Angus, Director, 613-562-5800 Ext. 4722. Application contact: Diane Sarrazin, Administrator, 613-562-5800 Ext. 4713. Fax: 613-562-5164.

University of Pennsylvania, Wharton School, Health Care Systems Department, Philadelphia, PA 19104. Awards MBA, PhD. One or more programs accredited by ACEHSA. Terminal master's awarded for partial completion of doctoral program. *Entrance requirements:* For master's, GMAT; for doctorate, GMAT or GRE. Application fee: $125. • Dr. Mark Pauly, Chairperson, 215-898-2838. Application contact: June Kinney, Director, 215-898-6861.

University of Pittsburgh, School of Health and Rehabilitation Sciences, Interdisciplinary Program in Health and Rehabilitation Sciences, Pittsburgh, PA 15260. Offers clinical laboratory sciences (MS), health care supervision and management (MS), health information systems (MS), occupational therapy (MS), physical therapy (MS), rehabilitation science (PhD), rehabilitation science and technology (MS), rehabilitation technology (Certificate), rehabilitation technology service delivery (Certificate). Part-time and evening/weekend programs available. Students: 23 full-time (16 women), 83 part-time (55 women); includes 10 minority (6 African Americans, 2 Asian Americans, 2 Hispanics), 7 international. 74 applicants, 85% accepted. In 1997, 28 master's awarded. *Degree requirements:* For doctorate, dissertation required, foreign language not required. *Entrance requirements:* For master's, GRE General Test, TOEFL, minimum QPA of 3.0; for doctorate, GRE General Test, TOEFL. Application deadline: rolling. Application fee: $30 ($40 for international students). *Expenses:* Tuition $9402 per year full-time, $388 per credit part-time for state residents; $19,372 per year full-time, $799 per credit part-time for nonresidents. Fees $480 per year full-time, $180 per year part-time. *Financial aid:* In 1997–98, 7 research assistantships (4 to first-year students) averaging $1,200 per month, 1 teaching assistantship (to a first-year student) averaging $1,286 per month, 3 assistantships averaging $1,049 per month were awarded; Federal Work-Study, institutionally sponsored loans also available. Aid available to part-time students. Financial aid applicants required to submit FAFSA. *Faculty research:* Assistive technology, seating and wheeled mobility, cellular neurophysiology, low back syndrome, augmentative communication. Total annual research expenditures: $1.941 million. • Dr. George Carvell, Associate Dean of Graduate Studies, 412-647-1296. E-mail: shrsadmit+@pitt.edu. Application contact: Shameem Gangjee, Director of Admissions, 412-647-1258. Fax: 412-647-1255. E-mail: shrsadmit+@pitt.edu.

See in-depth description on page 1351.

University of Pittsburgh, Graduate School of Public Health, Department of Health Services Administration, Program in Health Administration, Pittsburgh, PA 15260. Awards MHA, MPH/MHA. Accredited by ACEHSA. Offered jointly with the Joseph M. Katz Graduate School of Business. Part-time programs available. Faculty: 18 full-time (10 women). Students: 33 full-time (14 women), 24 part-time (7 women); includes 11 minority (4 African Americans, 6 Asian Americans, 1 Hispanic). 51 applicants, 45% accepted. In 1997, 22 degrees awarded. *Degree requirements:* Thesis required (for some programs), foreign language not required. *Average time to degree:* master's–2 years full-time, 4 years part-time. *Entrance requirements:* GMAT (average 585), TOEFL, previous course work in business calculus. Application deadline: rolling. Application fee: $50 ($60 for international students). *Expenses:* Tuition $9402 per year full-time, $388 per credit part-time for state residents; $19,372 per year full-time, $799 per credit part-time for nonresidents. Fees $480 per year full-time, $180 per year part-time. *Financial aid:* In 1997–98, 6 students received aid, including 4 assistantships, scholarships (all to first-year students) averaging $1,049 per month and totaling $34,000; Federal Work-Study, institutionally sponsored loans, and career-related internships or fieldwork also available. Financial aid applicants required to submit FAFSA. *Faculty research:* Managed care, child health insurance, women's health benefits, cost effectiveness of clinical services. Total annual research expenditures: $1.9 million. • Dr. Judith R. Lave, Interim Co-Director, 412-624-0898. E-mail: lave@vms.cis.pitt.edu. Application contact: Duane S. Kavinsky, Coordinator, 412-624-3125. Fax: 412-624-3146. E-mail: dukek+@pitt.edu.

See in-depth description on page 1349.

University of Pittsburgh, Graduate School of Public Health, Department of Health Services Administration, Program in Health Services Administration, Pittsburgh, PA 15260. Awards Dr PH. Part-time programs available. Faculty: 18 full-time (10 women). Students: 11 full-time (5 women), 21 part-time (16 women); includes 5 minority (3 African Americans, 1 Hispanic, 1 Native American), 4 international. In 1997, 3 degrees awarded. *Degree requirements:* Dissertation, comprehensive and preliminary exams required, foreign language not required. *Average time to degree:* doctorate–4 years full-time, 8 years part-time. *Entrance requirements:* GRE, TOEFL (minimum score 550), master's degree in public health or related field. Application deadline: 3/30. Application fee: $50 ($60 for international students). *Expenses:* Tuition $9402 per year full-time, $388 per credit part-time for state residents; $19,372 per year full-time, $799 per credit part-time for nonresidents. Fees $480 per year full-time, $180 per year part-time. *Financial aid:* Research assistantships, scholarships, partial tuition waivers, Federal Work-Study, institutionally sponsored loans available. Aid available to part-time students. *Faculty research:* Maternal and child health, health education and promotion, evaluation of prevention programs, public health and aging. • Application contact: Lynette Spataro, Student Affairs Assistant, 412-624-3107. Fax: 412-624-5510. E-mail: popph@vms.cis.pitt.edu.

See in-depth description on page 1545.

University of Puerto Rico, Medical Sciences Campus, College of Health Related Professions, Department of Administrative and Community Health Programs, Program in Medical Records Administration, San Juan, PR 00936-5067. Awards MS. Part-time programs available. *Degree requirements:* 1 foreign language, thesis, internship. *Average time to degree:* master's–2 years full-time, 4 years part-time. *Entrance requirements:* PAEG (minimum score 295; average 521), interview. Application deadline: 2/15 (priority date; rolling processing). Application fee: $15.

University of Puerto Rico, Medical Sciences Campus, Graduate School of Public Health, Department of Health Services Administration, Program in Health Services Administration, San Juan, PR 00936-5067. Awards MHSA. Accredited by ACEHSA. Part-time programs available. Faculty: 6 full-time (3 women). Students: 55 (31 women). 48 applicants, 50% accepted. In 1997, 11 degrees awarded. *Degree requirements:* Thesis required, foreign language not required. *Entrance requirements:* GRE, previous course work in accounting, statistics, economics, algebra, and managerial finance. Application deadline: 3/3. Application fee: $15. *Financial aid:* Federal Work-Study and career-related internships or fieldwork available. Financial aid application deadline: 4/30. • Prof. Dharma Vázquez, Coordinator, 787-758-2525 Ext. 1440. Application contact: Mayra E. Santiago-Vargas, Counselor, 787-756-5244. Fax: 787-759-6719.

University of Regina, Faculty of Graduate Studies and Research, Interdisciplinary Studies, Program in Health Administration, Regina, SK S4S 0A2, Canada. Awards MHA. *Entrance requirements:* TOEFL (minimum score 580). Application fee: $0. *Tuition:* $1875 per year full-time, $187 per credit part-time for Canadian residents; $2812 per year full-time, $374 per credit part-time for nonresidents. *Financial aid:* Application deadline 6/15. • Dr. J. Ito, Coordinator, 306-585-4714. Fax: 306-585-4805. E-mail: jack.ito@uregina.ca.

University of St. Francis, Graduate Studies, Program in Health Services Administration, Joliet, IL 60435-6188. Offers health services administration (MS), long-term care administration (Certificate). Part-time and evening/weekend programs available. Faculty: 3 full-time (0 women), 55 part-time (24 women). Students: 184 full-time (120 women), 929 part-time (772 women). Average age 39. 225 applicants, 85% accepted. In 1997, 199 master's awarded (100% found work related to degree). *Degree requirements:* For master's, computer language, comprehensive exam required, foreign language not required. *Entrance requirements:* For master's, minimum GPA of 2.75, 2 years of professional experience. Application deadline: rolling. Application fee: $25. *Tuition:* $285 per credit hour. *Financial aid:* Available to part-time students. • Dr. F. William Kelley Jr., Dean, Graduate Studies, 800-735-4723. Fax: 815-740-3537. E-mail: grdinfo@stfrancis.edu.

University of St. Thomas, Graduate School of Business, Day MBA Program, St. Paul, MN 55105-1096. Offerings include health care management (MBA). Program faculty: 13 part-time. *Degree requirements:* Computer language required, foreign language and thesis not required. *Entrance requirements:* GMAT (score in 50th percentile or higher). Application deadline: 5/1 (priority date; rolling processing). Application fee: $30. *Tuition:* $473 per credit hour. • Application contact: Jim O'Connor, Student Adviser, 612-962-4233. Fax: 612-962-4260.

University of St. Thomas, Graduate School of Business, Evening MBA Program, St. Paul, MN 55105-1096. Offerings include health care management (MBA, Certificate). Program faculty: 16 full-time (2 women), 89 part-time (17 women). *Degree requirements:* For master's, computer language required, foreign language and thesis not required. *Entrance requirements:* For master's, GMAT (score in 50th percentile or higher). Application deadline: 8/1 (priority date; rolling processing; 12/1 for spring admission). Application fee: $30. *Tuition:* $416 per credit hour. • Dr. Stanford Nyquist, MBA Director, 612-962-4242. Application contact: Martha Ballard, Director of Student Services, 612-962-4226. Fax: 612-962-4260.

University of St. Thomas, Graduate School of Business, Program in Medical Group Management, St. Paul, MN 55105-1096. Awards MBA. Part-time and evening/weekend programs available. Postbaccalaureate distance learning degree programs offered. Faculty: 1 full-time (0 women), 6 part-time (0 women). Students: 14 full-time (5 women), 24 part-time (13 women); includes 2 minority (1 Asian American, 1 Hispanic). Average age 41. 27 applicants, 100% accepted. In 1997, 9 degrees awarded. *Degree requirements:* Computer language required, foreign language and thesis not required. *Entrance requirements:* GMAT. Application deadline: 5/1 (priority date; rolling processing). Application fee: $30. *Tuition:* $424 per credit hour. *Financial aid:* Career-related internships or fieldwork available. Aid available to part-time students. Financial aid application deadline: 4/1; applicants required to submit FAFSA. • Tom Gilliam, Director, 612-962-4131. Application contact: Stephanie Hagel, Program Coordinator, 612-962-4135. Fax: 612-962-4410.

University of San Francisco, McLaren School of Business, Program in Rehabilitation Administration, San Francisco, CA 94117-1080. Awards EMRA. Faculty: 5 full-time (3 women), 4 part-time (3 women). Students: 24 full-time (13 women), 22 part-time (16 women); includes 3 minority (2 African Americans, 1 Asian American). Average age 37. 31 applicants, 94% accepted. In 1997, 27 degrees awarded. *Entrance requirements:* GMAT (average 540), TOEFL (minimum score 600), minimum undergraduate GPA of 3.2. Application deadline: 7/1 (priority date; rolling processing; 11/30 for spring admission). *Tuition:* $658 per unit (minimum). *Financial aid:* 24 students received aid. Financial aid application deadline: 3/2. *Faculty research:* International finance, technology transfer licensing, international marketing, strategic management. Total annual research expenditures: $50,000. • Jeanette Harvey, Director, 415-422-6333.

University of San Francisco, College of Professional Studies, Department of Public Management, Program in Public Administration, Concentration in Health Services Administration, San Francisco, CA 94117-1080. Awards MPA. Part-time and evening/weekend programs available. Faculty: 3 full-time (1 woman), 17 part-time (5 women). Students: 110 full-time (82 women); includes 32 minority (9 African Americans, 15 Asian Americans, 8 Hispanics). Average age 39. 68 applicants, 81% accepted. In 1997, 52 degrees awarded. *Degree requirements:* Thesis optional, foreign language not required. *Entrance requirements:* Minimum GPA of 3.0. Application fee: $35. *Financial aid:* 40 students received aid. Financial aid application deadline: 3/2. • Maurice Penner, Director, 415-422-2144. Application contact: Advising Office, 415-422-6000.

University of Scranton, Department of Health Administration and Human Resources, Program in Health Administration, Scranton, PA 18510-4622. Awards MHA. Accredited by ACEHSA. Part-time and evening/weekend programs available. Students: 11 full-time (6 women), 36 part-time (22 women); includes 1 minority (Asian American), 1 international. Average age 30. 22 applicants, 95% accepted. In 1997, 16 degrees awarded. *Degree requirements:* Comprehensive exam required, foreign language and thesis not required. *Entrance requirements:* TOEFL (minimum score 575), minimum GPA of 2.75. Application deadline: 4/15 (priority date). Application fee: $35. *Expenses:* Tuition $465 per credit. Fees $25 per semester. *Financial aid:* Teaching assistantships, teaching fellowships available. Financial aid application deadline: 3/1. • Dr. Peter C. Olden, Director, 717-941-4242. Fax: 717-941-4201. E-mail: oldenp1@uofs.edu.

University of South Carolina, Graduate School, School of Public Health, Department of Health Administration, Columbia, SC 29208. Awards MHA, MPH, Dr PH, PhD, MPH/MSN, MSW/MPH. One or more programs accredited by ACEHSA. Faculty: 7 full-time (3 women), 2 part-time (both women). Students: 74 full-time (42 women), 27 part-time (15 women); includes 16 minority (12 African Americans, 3 Asian Americans, 1 Hispanic), 19 international. Average age 33. 144 applicants, 41% accepted. In 1997, 27 master's, 3 doctorates awarded. *Degree requirements:* For master's, thesis or alternative, internship (MHA) required, foreign language not required; for doctorate, dissertation. *Entrance requirements:* For master's, GMAT (MHA), GRE General Test (MPH); for doctorate, GRE General Test. Application deadline: rolling. Application fee: $35. Electronic applications accepted. *Expenses:* Tuition $4480 per year full-time, $220 per credit hour part-time for state residents; $9338 per year full-time, $457 per credit hour part-time for nonresidents. Fees $125 per year full-time, $37 per semester (minimum) part-time. *Financial aid:* Research assistantships, teaching assistantships, traineeships, and career-related internships or fieldwork available. *Faculty research:* Health systems management, evaluation, and planning; forecast applications in health care; Medicaid process to health care services. • Dr. Carleen Stoskopf, Interim Chair, 803-777-6096. Application contact: Dr. Roger Amidon, Graduate Director, 803-777-6096. Fax: 803-777-4783.

University of Southern California, Graduate School, School of Public Administration, Program in Health Administration, Los Angeles, CA 90089. Awards MHA, MHA/MS. Accredited by ACEHSA. Students: 100 full-time (61 women), 21 part-time (13 women); includes 57 minority (11 African Americans, 33 Asian Americans, 13 Hispanics), 11 international. Average age 26. 97 applicants, 65% accepted. In 1997, 36 degrees awarded. *Entrance requirements:* GRE General Test. Application deadline: 7/1 (priority date; 12/1 for spring admission). Application fee: $55. *Expenses:* Tuition $16,944 per year full-time, $706 per unit part-time. Fees $414 per year full-time, $32 per year part-time. *Financial aid:* In 1997–98, 45 fellowships, 2 research assistantships, 1 teaching assistantship, 34 scholarships were awarded; Federal Work-Study, institutionally sponsored loans also available. Aid available to part-time students. Financial aid application deadline: 2/15; applicants required to submit FAFSA. • Jane Ferris, Chair.

University of Southern Maine, Edmund S. Muskie School of Public Service, Program in Health Policy and Management, Portland, ME 04104-9300. Awards MS. Faculty: 4 full-time (2 women), 5 part-time (2 women). Students: 5 full-time (3 women), 15 part-time (11 women); includes 2 minority (1 African American, 1 Hispanic). Average age 30. 20 applicants, 75% accepted. *Degree requirements:* Computer language, thesis, Capstone Project required, foreign language not required. *Entrance requirements:* GRE General Test. Application deadline: 4/1 (priority date; rolling processing; 12/1 for spring admission). Application fee: $25. Electronic applications accepted. *Expenses:* Tuition $178 per credit hour for state residents; $267 per credit hour (minimum) for nonresidents. Fees $282 per year full-time, $83 per semester (minimum) part-time. *Financial aid:* In 1997–98, 4 students received aid, including 3 research assistantships (all to first-year students) averaging $600 per month and totaling $15,400; Federal Work-Study and career-related internships or fieldwork also available. Aid available to part-time students. Financial aid application deadline: 4/1; applicants required to submit CSS PROFILE. *Faculty research:* Health care, child welfare, social services, aging, substance abuse, mental health, developmental disabilities. • David Hartley, Director, 207-780-4513. E-mail: davidh@usm.maine.edu. Application contact: Carlene R. Goldman, Coordinator of Student Affairs, 207-780-4864. Fax: 207-780-4417.

University of Southern Mississippi, College of Health and Human Sciences, Center for Community Health, Hattiesburg, MS 39406-5167. Offerings include health policy/administration (MPH). Center faculty: 6 full-time (3 women), 1 (woman) part-time. *Degree requirements:* Comprehensive exam required, foreign language and thesis not required. *Entrance requirements:* GRE General Test, minimum GPA of 2.75. Application deadline: 8/9 (priority date; rolling processing). Application fee: $0 ($25 for international students). *Tuition:* $2870 per year full-time, $137 per credit hour part-time for state residents; $5972 per year full-time, $172 per credit hour part-time for nonresidents. • Dr. Agnes Hinton, Interim Director, 601-266-5437.

University of South Florida, College of Public Health, Department of Health Policy and Management, Tampa, FL 33620-9951. Awards MHA, MPH, MSPH, PhD. Part-time and evening/weekend programs available. Faculty: 9 full-time (1 woman). 54 applicants, 56% accepted. *Degree requirements:* Thesis/dissertation required, foreign language not required. *Entrance requirements:* For master's, GRE General Test (minimum combined score of 1000), TOEFL (minimum score 550), minimum GPA of 3.0 in upper-level course work; for doctorate, GRE General Test (minimum combined score of 1100), TOEFL (minimum score 550), minimum GPA of 3.0 in upper-level course work. Application deadline: 6/1 (rolling processing; 10/15 for spring admission). Application fee: $20. *Tuition:* $142 per credit hour for state residents; $486 per credit hour for nonresidents. *Financial aid:* Federal Work-Study, institutionally sponsored loans available. Financial aid applicants required to submit FAFSA. *Faculty research:* Tracking community health, inpatient care, discharge policies, stroke education, leadership practices. Total annual research expenditures: $241,113. • Dr. Lois Nixon, Interim Chair, 813-974-5131. E-mail: lnixon@com1.med.usf.edu. Application contact: Magdalene Argiry, Director of Student Services, 813-974-6665. Fax: 813-974-4718. E-mail: margiry@com1.med.usf.edu.

University of Southwestern Louisiana, College of Business Administration, Lafayette, LA 70503. Offerings include health care administration (MBA). College faculty: 41 full-time (8 women). *Degree requirements:* Computer language required, foreign language and thesis not required. *Entrance requirements:* GMAT (minimum score 425), minimum GPA of 2.75. Application deadline: 8/15. Application fee: $5 ($15 for international students). *Tuition:* $2012 per year full-time, $300 per semester (minimum) part-time for state residents; $7244 per year full-time, $300 per semester (minimum) part-time for nonresidents. • Dr. C. William Roe, Graduate Coordinator, 318-482-5882.

The University of Texas at Tyler, School of Business Administration, Tyler, TX 75799-0001. Offerings include health care (MBA). School faculty: 12 full-time (3 women), 1 part-time (0 women). *Degree requirements:* Computer language required, thesis optional, foreign language not required. *Entrance requirements:* Minimum AACSB index of 1000. Application fee: $0 ($50 for international students). *Tuition:* $2144 per year full-time, $337 per semester (minimum) part-time for state residents; $7256 per year full-time, $964 per semester (minimum) part-time for nonresidents. • Dr. Jim Tarter, Dean, 903-566-7360. Application contact: Martha D. Wheat, Director of Admissions and Student Records, 903-566-7201. Fax: 903-566-7068.

University of the Sciences in Philadelphia, Program in Health Policy, Philadelphia, PA 19104-4495. Awards PhD. Program new for fall 1998. *Degree requirements:* Dissertation required, foreign language not required. *Entrance requirements:* GRE General Test, TOEFL. Application deadline: 5/1 (rolling processing; 10/1 for spring admission). Application fee: $30. • Dr. Ruth Schemm, Director, 215-596-8767.

See in-depth description on page 1821.

University of the Sciences in Philadelphia, Program in Pharmacy Administration, Philadelphia, PA 19104-4495. Awards MS. Part-time programs available. Faculty: 3 full-time (0 women). Students: 1 (woman) full-time, 6 part-time (3 women). Average age 33. 0 applicants. In 1997, 1 degree awarded. *Entrance requirements:* GRE General Test, TOEFL. Application deadline: 5/1 (rolling processing; 10/1 for spring admission). Application fee: $30. *Financial aid:* Full tuition waivers, institutionally sponsored loans available. *Faculty research:* Cost-effect analysis, pharmaceutical economics, pharmaceutical care, marketing research, health communications. • Dr. William McGhan, Director, 215-596-8852. E-mail: w.mcghan@pcps.edu. Application contact: Dr. Charles W. Gibley Jr., Dean, 215-596-8937. Fax: 215-596-8764. E-mail: graduate@pcps.edu.

See in-depth description on page 1821.

University of Virginia, Graduate School of Arts and Sciences, Department of Health Evaluation Sciences, Charlottesville, VA 22903. Offers programs in clinical investigation (MS), epidemiology (MS), health care informatics (MS), health care resource management (MS), health services research and outcomes evaluation (MS). Part-time programs available. Faculty: 10 full-time (2 women), 12 part-time (8 women), 12 FTE. Students: 7 full-time (4 women), 5 part-time (1 woman); includes 3 minority (2 African Americans, 1 Asian American), 1 international. Average age 30. 32 applicants, 78% accepted. In 1997, 3 degrees awarded. *Degree requirements:* Thesis required (for some programs), foreign language not required. *Entrance requirements:* GRE or MCAT. Application deadline: 3/1 (priority date). Application fee: $40. *Tuition:* $4870 per year full-time, $941 per semester (minimum) part-time for state residents; $15,818 per year full-time, $2745 per semester (minimum) part-time for nonresidents. *Financial aid:* Career-related internships or fieldwork available. Financial aid applicants required to submit FAFSA. • Dr. Paige Hornsby, Director, 804-924-0496. E-mail: pph8c@virginia.edu. Application contact: Robyn Kells, Program Coordinator, 804-924-8646. Fax: 804-924-8437. E-mail: ms-hes@virginia.edu.

See in-depth description on page 1353.

University of Washington, School of Public Health and Community Medicine, Health Services Administration and Planning Group, Seattle, WA 98195. Awards MHA, MBA/MHA. Accredited by ACEHSA. Offered jointly with the School of Business Administration. Evening/weekend programs available. *Degree requirements:* Thesis or alternative required, foreign language not required. *Entrance requirements:* GRE General Test, TOEFL (minimum score 580), minimum GPA of 3.0. Application deadline: 2/15. Application fee: $45. *Tuition:* $5433 per year full-time, $775 per quarter (minimum) part-time for state residents; $13,479 per year full-time, $1925 per quarter (minimum) part-time for nonresidents. *Financial aid:* Teaching assistantships, Federal Work-Study, institutionally sponsored loans, and career-related internships or fieldwork available. *Faculty research:* Managed care, interorganizational analysis, quality assurance, cost and outcomes of health care. • Mary Richardson, Director, 206-543-8778. Application contact: Aline Wilson, Student Services Coordinator, 206-543-8778.

See in-depth description on page 1549.

University of Wisconsin–Madison, School of Pharmacy and Graduate School, Graduate Programs in Pharmacy, Department of Pharmacy Administration, Madison, WI 53706-1380. Awards PhD. *Degree requirements:* Dissertation. *Application fee:* $38.

University of Wisconsin–Madison, Medical School and Graduate School, Graduate Programs in Medicine, Population Health Program, Administrative Medicine Program, Madison, WI 53706-1380. Awards MS, PhD. One or more programs accredited by ACEHSA. *Application fee:* $45. *Tuition:* $4928 per year full-time, $926 per semester (minimum) part-time for state residents; $15,190 per year full-time, $2849 per semester (minimum) part-time for nonresidents. • Dr. David Kindig, Director, 608-263-4886. Fax: 608-263-4885. E-mail: dakindig@facstaff.wisc.edu.

University of Wisconsin–Oshkosh, College of Letters and Science, Department of Public Affairs, Oshkosh, WI 54901-8602. Offerings include health care (MPA). Department faculty: 3 full-time (1 woman), 4 part-time (2 women). *Degree requirements:* Thesis required, foreign language not required. *Entrance requirements:* Public service-related experience, sample of written work, GRE General Test or minimum GPA of 2.75. Application deadline: 3/1 (priority date; 8/1 for spring admission). Application fee: $45. *Tuition:* $3638 per year full-time, $609 per semester (minimum) part-time for state residents; $11,282 per year full-time, $1884 per semester (minimum) part-time for nonresidents. • Dr. David Jones, Chair, 920-424-3230. Application contact: Dr. Stephen Hintz, Coordinator, 920-424-3230. E-mail: hintz@uwosh.edu.

Villanova University, Graduate School of Liberal Arts and Sciences, Program in Human Organization Science, Health Care Administration Option, Villanova, PA 19085-1699. Awards MS. Students: 4 part-time (3 women). Average age 35. *Degree requirements:* Comprehensive exam required, foreign language and thesis not required. *Entrance requirements:* GRE General Test, minimum GPA of 3.0. Application deadline: 8/1 (priority date; 12/1 for spring admission). Application fee: $40. *Expenses:* Tuition $400 per credit. Fees $60 per year. *Financial aid:* Federal Work-Study and career-related internships or fieldwork available. Financial aid application deadline: 4/1. • Dr. Theresa M. Valiga, Coordinator, 610-519-4934.

Virginia Commonwealth University, School of Allied Health Professions, Department of Health Administration, Executive Master's Program in Health Administration, Richmond, VA 23284-9005. Awards MSHA. Accredited by ACEHSA. Faculty: 15 full-time. Students: 53 full-time (23 women), 2 part-time (both women); includes 4 minority (all African Americans). Average age 39. 39 applicants, 87% accepted. In 1997, 27 degrees awarded. *Degree requirements:* Residency required, thesis not required. *Entrance requirements:* GMAT or GRE General Test. Application deadline: 5/15. Application fee: $30 ($0 for international students). *Tuition:* $4960 per year full-time, $257 per credit part-time for state residents; $12,652 per year full-time, $684 per credit part-time for nonresidents. • Dr. Jan Clement, Director, 804-828-1886. Fax: 804-828-8194. E-mail: jpclemen@vcu.edu.

See in-depth description on page 1355.

Virginia Commonwealth University, School of Allied Health Professions, Department of Health Administration, Program in Health Administration, Richmond, VA 23284-9005. Awards MHA, JD/MHA. Accredited by ACEHSA. JD/MHA offered jointly with the University of Richmond. Students: 52 full-time (20 women), 23 part-time (13 women); includes 11 minority (9 African Americans, 2 Asian Americans), 1 international. Average age 26. 82 applicants, 52% accepted. In 1997, 35 degrees awarded. *Degree requirements:* Residency required, thesis not required. *Entrance requirements:* GMAT or GRE General Test. Application deadline: 5/15 (priority date). Application fee: $30 ($0 for international students). *Tuition:* $4960 per year full-time, $257 per credit part-time for state residents; $12,652 per year full-time, $684 per credit part-time for nonresidents. • Dr. Jan Clement, Director, 804-828-1886. Fax: 804-828-1894. E-mail: jpclemen@vcu.edu.

Announcement: The Department of Health Administration at the Virginia Commonwealth University, Medical College of Virginia Campus, prepares health-care professionals who will assume leadership positions in a wide variety of health-care institutions, public agencies, and academic centers. The department offers 4 graduate degree programs: the MHA; a dual MHA/JD; the MSHA, an innovative executive program for working professionals; and the PhD in health services organization and research. The department's educational programs are fully accredited and are recognized as being among the best in the country. For detailed information, contact Department of Health Administration, Virginia Commonwealth University, PO Box 980203, Richmond, VA 23298-0203; 804-828-0719; fax: 804-828-1894.

See in-depth description on page 1355.

Virginia Commonwealth University, School of Allied Health Professions, Department of Health Administration, Program in Health Services Organization and Research, Richmond, VA 23284-9005. Awards PhD. Students: 11 full-time (6 women), 21 part-time (11 women); includes 1 minority (African American), 9 international. Average age 38. 15 applicants, 47% accepted. In 1997, 5 degrees awarded. *Degree requirements:* Dissertation, residency. *Entrance requirements:* GMAT or GRE General Test. Application deadline: 1/31. Application fee: $30 ($0 for international students). *Tuition:* $4960 per year full-time, $257 per credit part-time for state residents; $12,652 per year full-time, $684 per credit part-time for nonresidents. • Dr. Michael McCue, Director, 804-828-1893. Fax: 804-828-1894. E-mail: mjmccue@vcu.edu.

See in-depth description on page 1355.

Walden University, Graduate Programs, Program in Health Services, 155 Fifth Avenue South, Minneapolis, MN 55401. Awards PhD. Part-time and evening/weekend programs available. Postbaccalaureate distance learning degree programs offered. *Degree requirements:* Dissertation, brief dispersed residency sessions required, foreign language not required. *Entrance requirements:* 3 years of professional experience, master's degree. Application fee: $50. Electronic applications accepted. *Tuition:* $3125 per quarter.

Washington University in St. Louis, School of Medicine, Graduate Programs in Medicine, Health Administration Program, St. Louis, MO 63110. Awards MHA, JD/MHA, MBA/MHA, MD/MHA, MHA/MHRM, MHA/MIM, MHA/MSW. Accredited by ACEHSA. Faculty: 5 full-time (0 women), 13 part-time (2 women). Students: 62 full-time (29 women), 5 part-time (4 women); includes 20 minority (5 African Americans, 13 Asian Americans, 2 Hispanics), 3 international. Average age 25. In 1997, 28 degrees awarded (100% found work related to degree). *Degree requirements:* Thesis optional, foreign language not required. *Entrance requirements:* GMAT or GRE General Test, TOEFL (minimum score 550), minimum GPA of 3.0, 1 semester of course work in basic accounting. Application deadline: rolling. Application fee: $30. *Tuition:* $20,500 per year. *Financial aid:* Institutionally sponsored loans available. Aid available to part-time students. Financial aid application deadline: 5/1; applicants required to submit FAFSA. • Dr. James O. Hepner, Director, 314-362-4277. Application contact: Marilyn Hummert, Coordinator of Student Services, 314-362-3274.

See in-depth description on page 1357.

Webster University, School of Business and Technology, Department of Business, St. Louis, MO 63119-3194. Offerings include health care management (MA), health services management (MA, MBA). Department faculty: 5 full-time (1 woman). *Application deadline:* rolling. *Application fee:* $25 ($50 for international students). *Tuition:* $350 per credit hour. • Lucille Berry, Chair, 314-968-7022. Fax: 314-968-7077. E-mail: berrylm@webster.edu. Application contact: Beth Russell, Director of Graduate Admissions, 314-968-7089. Fax: 314-968-7166. E-mail: russellmb@webster.edu.

West Chester University of Pennsylvania, School of Business and Public Affairs, Program in Administration, West Chester, PA 19383. Offerings include health services (MSA), longterm care (MSA). Program faculty: 8 part-time. *Degree requirements:* Comprehensive exams required, foreign language and thesis not required. *Entrance requirements:* GMAT, GRE General Test, or MAT, interview, minimum GPA of 3.0. Application deadline: 4/15 (priority date; rolling

West Chester University of Pennsylvania (continued)

processing); 10/15 for spring admission). Application fee: $25. *Expenses:* Tuition $3468 per year full-time, $193 per credit part-time for state residents; $6236 per year full-time, $346 per credit part-time for nonresidents. Fees $660 per year full-time, $38 per credit part-time. • Dr. James Milne, Graduate Coordinator, 610-436-2448.

Western Carolina University, College of Applied Science, Department of Health Sciences, Cullowhee, NC 28723. Awards MHS. Part-time and evening/weekend programs available. Faculty: 9 (5 women). Students: 8 full-time (all women), 38 part-time (34 women); includes 1 minority (Hispanic). 22 applicants, 68% accepted. In 1997, 6 degrees awarded. *Degree requirements:* Comprehensive exam required, thesis optional, foreign language not required. *Entrance requirements:* GRE General Test. Application deadline: rolling. Application fee: $35. *Tuition:* $1799 per year full-time, $144 per credit hour (minimum) part-time for state residents; $9069 per year full-time, $1053 per credit hour (minimum) part-time for nonresidents. *Financial aid:* In 1997–98, 4 students received aid, including 1 research assistantship (to a first-year student) totaling $2,000, 3 teaching assistantships (2 to first-year students) totaling $7,600; fellowships, Federal Work-Study, institutionally sponsored loans also available. Financial aid application deadline: 3/15. • Barbara K. Lovin, Head, 828-227-7113. Application contact: Kathleen Owen, Assistant to the Dean, 828-227-7398. Fax: 828-227-7480.

Western International University, Program in Health Care Management, 9215 North Black Canyon Highway, Phoenix, AZ 85021-2718. Awards MBA. Evening/weekend programs available. *Degree requirements:* Thesis, research project. *Entrance requirements:* GMAT (strongly recommended), minimum GPA of 2.75. Application deadline: rolling. Application fee: $50 ($100 for international students). • Dr. Susan Roe, Chair, 602-943-2311. Application contact: Enrollment Department, 602-943-2311. Fax: 602-371-8637.

Western Kentucky University, Ogden College of Science, Technology, and Health, Department of Public Health, Bowling Green, KY 42101-3576. Offerings include health care administration (MS). Department faculty: 11 full-time (4 women). *Application deadline:* 8/1 (priority date; rolling processing; 12/1 for spring admission). *Application fee:* $20. *Tuition:* $2460 per year full-time, $133 per credit hour part-time for state residents; $6700 per year full-time, $369 per credit hour part-time for nonresidents. • Dr. J. David Dunn, Head, 502-745-4797. Fax: 502-745-4437. E-mail: david.dunn@wku.edu.

Western New England College, School of Business, Program in Health Care Management, Springfield, MA 01119-2654. Awards MBA. *Application deadline:* rolling. *Application fee:* $30. *Expenses:* Tuition $353 per credit hour. Fees $44 per semester (minimum). *Financial aid:* Application deadline 4/1. • Application contact: Rod Pease, Director of Student Administrative Services, 413-796-2080.

Widener University, School of Business Administration, Program in Health and Medical Services Administration, Chester, PA 19013-5792. Awards MBA, MHA, MD/MBA, MD/MHA, Psy D/MBA, Psy D/MHA. One or more programs accredited by ACEHSA. MD/MBA and MD/MHA offered jointly with Thomas Jefferson University. Part-time and evening/weekend programs available. Faculty: 3 full-time (1 woman), 6 part-time (1 woman). Students: 32 full-time, 77 part-time; includes 10 minority (6 African Americans, 2 Asian Americans, 2 Hispanics). Average age 29. 23 applicants, 78% accepted. In 1997, 25 degrees awarded. *Degree requirements:* Clerkship, residency required, foreign language and thesis not required. *Average time to degree:* master's–2 years full-time, 4 years part-time. *Entrance requirements:* GMAT (minimum score 450), interview, minimum GPA of 2.5. Application deadline: 8/1 (priority date; rolling processing; 12/1 for spring admission). Application fee: $25 ($300 for international students). *Tuition:* $455 per credit. *Financial aid:* Research assistantships, traineeships, and career-related internships or fieldwork available. Aid available to part-time students. *Faculty research:* Cost containment in health care, reimbursement of hospitals, strategic behavior. • Dr. Caryl Carpenter, Director, 610-499-4322.

Widener University, School of Human Service Professions, Institute for Graduate Clinical Psychology, Program in Clinical Psychology and Health and Medical Services Administration, Chester, PA 19013-5792. Awards Psy D/MBA, Psy D/MHA. Jointly administered through the Program in Health and Medical Services Administration. Faculty: 15 full-time (6 women), 120 part-time (37 women). Students: 29 full-time (11 women). *Application deadline:* 12/31 (rolling processing). *Application fee:* $60. *Tuition:* $14,300 per year full-time, $595 per credit hour part-time. *Financial aid:* Federal Work-Study, institutionally sponsored loans, and career-related internships or fieldwork available. Financial aid application deadline: 5/31. *Faculty research:* Psychosocial competence, family systems, medical care systems and financing. • Dr. Marshall S. Swift, Director, 610-499-1206.

Wilkes University, Program in Health Administration, Wilkes-Barre, PA 18766-0002. Awards MHA. Evening/weekend programs available. Faculty: 2 full-time. Students: 1 full-time (0 women), 16 part-time (12 women); includes 1 minority (Asian American). In 1997, 12 degrees awarded. *Application deadline:* rolling. *Application fee:* $30. *Expenses:* Tuition $12,552 per year full-time, $523 per credit hour part-time. Fees $240 per year full-time, $10 per credit hour part-time. *Financial aid:* Application deadline 2/28; applicants required to submit FAFSA. • Dr. Robert Seeley, Director, 717-408-4717.

Wilkes University, Programs in Business Administration, Wilkes-Barre, PA 18766-0002. Offerings include health care (MBA). MBA (management, management information systems) being phased out; applicants no longer accepted. Faculty: 11 full-time, 2 part-time. *Entrance requirements:* GMAT. Application deadline: rolling. Application fee: $30. *Expenses:* Tuition $12,552 per year full-time, $523 per credit hour part-time. Fees $240 per year full-time, $10 per credit hour part-time. • Dr. Robert Seeley, Director, 717-408-4717.

Wright State University, College of Business and Administration, Department of Management, Dayton, OH 45435. Offerings include health care management (MBA). *Entrance requirements:* GMAT, TOEFL (minimum score 550), minimum AACSB index of 1000. Application fee: $25. *Tuition:* $5109 per year full-time, $161 per credit hour part-time for state residents; $9039 per year full-time, $282 per credit hour part-time for nonresidents. • Dr. Crystal Owen, Chair, 937-775-2290. Application contact: James Crawford, Director of Graduate Programs, 937-775-2437. Fax: 937-775-3301.

Xavier University, College of Social Sciences, Program in Health Services Administration, Cincinnati, OH 45207-2111. Awards MHSA, MBA/MHSA. Accredited by ACEHSA. Part-time and evening/weekend programs available. Faculty: 6 full-time (1 woman), 7 part-time (3 women), 7.75 FTE. Students: 48 full-time (26 women), 50 part-time (32 women); includes 10 minority (3 African Americans, 4 Asian Americans, 2 Hispanics, 1 Native American), 1 international. Average age 30. 89 applicants, 65% accepted. In 1997, 31 degrees awarded (100% found work related to degree). *Degree requirements:* Thesis, administrative residency required, foreign language not required. *Average time to degree:* master's–2.5 years full-time, 3 years part-time. *Entrance requirements:* GMAT (minimum score 500) or GRE, minimum undergraduate GPA of 3.0, interview. Application deadline: 8/15 (priority date; rolling processing). Application fee: $25. *Tuition:* $400 per credit hour. *Financial aid:* In 1997–98, 10 research assistantships were awarded; teaching assistantships, scholarships, residency stipends, and career-related internships or fieldwork also available. Financial aid application deadline: 5/1. *Faculty research:* Quality and outcomes of care, physician resource allocation and utilization, community health status and information networks, managerial ethics, corporate culture and strategic management. • Dr. Ira Critelli Schick, Interim Director, 513-745-1912. E-mail: schicki@xavier.xu.edu. Application contact: Cyrina Wolf, Assistant to Director, 513-745-3687. Fax: 513-745-4301. E-mail: wolf@xavier.xu.edu.

See in-depth description on page 1359.

Yale University, School of Medicine, Department of Epidemiology and Public Health, Division of Health Policy and Administration, New Haven, CT 06520. Awards MPH, Dr PH, PhD. PhD offered through the Graduate School. Part-time programs available. Faculty: 7 full-time (4 women), 3 part-time (1 woman). Students: 85 full-time (58 women), 8 part-time (4 women); includes 21 minority (5 African Americans, 13 Asian Americans, 3 Hispanics), 6 international. Average age 27. 181 applicants, 56% accepted. In 1997, 32 master's, 2 doctorates awarded. Terminal master's awarded for partial completion of doctoral program. *Degree requirements:* For master's, thesis, internship required, foreign language not required; for doctorate, dissertation, comprehensive exams, residency period required, foreign language not required. *Entrance requirements:* For master's, GMAT, GRE, LSAT, or MCAT; TOEFL, previous undergraduate course work in mathematics and science; for doctorate, GRE General Test (minimum combined score of 1200), TOEFL (minimum score 570). Application deadline: rolling. Application fee: $60. *Financial aid:* Scholarships, Federal Work-Study, institutionally sponsored loans, and career-related internships or fieldwork available. Aid available to part-time students. Financial aid application deadline: 4/15. *Faculty research:* Health politics, policy, and regulation; mental health and substance abuse; consumer choice and decision making; determinants of clinical decision making. • Dr. Mark Schlesinger, Associate Professor of Public Health, 203-785-4619. Fax: 203-785-6287. E-mail: mark.schlesinger@yale.edu. Application contact: Joan Stenner, Admissions Officer, 203-785-2844. Fax: 203-785-4845. E-mail: joan.stenner@yale.edu.

See in-depth description on page 1551.

Youngstown State University, College of Health and Human Services, Department of Health Professions, Youngstown, OH 44555-0002. Offers program in health and human services (MHHS). Part-time and evening/weekend programs available. Faculty: 2 full-time (1 woman). Students: 8 full-time (6 women), 12 part-time (10 women). 21 applicants, 100% accepted. *Degree requirements:* Thesis optional, foreign language not required. *Entrance requirements:* GRE General Test, TOEFL (minimum score 550), minimum GPA of 3.0. Application deadline: 8/15 (priority date; rolling processing; 2/15 for spring admission). Application fee: $30 ($75 for international students). *Expenses:* Tuition $90 per credit hour for state residents; $144 per credit hour (minimum) for nonresidents. Fees $528 per year full-time, $244 per year (minimum) part-time. *Financial aid:* In 1997–98, 2 students received aid, including 2 scholarships totaling $2,580; Federal Work-Study, institutionally sponsored loans also available. Aid available to part-time students. Financial aid application deadline: 3/1. *Faculty research:* Drug prevention, multiskilling in health care, organizational behavior, health care management, health behaviors, research management. • Joseph J. Mistovich, Chair, 330-742-3327. Application contact: Dr. Peter J. Kasvinsky, Dean of Graduate Studies, 330-742-3091. Fax: 330-742-1580. E-mail: amgrad03@ysub.ysu.edu.

Health Services Research

Arizona State University, College of Business, Program in Business Administration, Tempe, AZ 85287. Offerings include health services research (PhD). Program faculty: 93 full-time (21 women), 10 part-time (1 woman). *Degree requirements:* Dissertation. *Application fee:* $45. *Expenses:* Tuition $2088 per year full-time, $110 per hour part-time for state residents; $9040 per year full-time, $377 per hour part-time for nonresidents. Fees $72 per year full-time, $18 per semester (minimum) part-time. • Dr. Lee R. McPheters, Associate Dean, 602-965-9377. Fax: 602-965-3368. Application contact: Judy Heilala, Director of MBA, 602-965-3331.

Brown University, Division of Biology and Medicine, Department of Community Health, Program in Biostatistics, Providence, RI 02912. Offerings include health services research (MS, PhD). *Degree requirements:* For doctorate, dissertation, preliminary exam. *Entrance requirements:* GRE General Test. Application deadline: 1/2 (priority date; rolling processing). Application fee: $60. *Expenses:* Tuition $23,616 per year. Fees $436 per year. • Dr. Constantine Gatsonis, Director, Department of Community Health, 401-863-1106. E-mail: gatsonis@jenny.biomed.brown.edu.

Brown University, Division of Biology and Medicine, Department of Community Health, Program in Epidemiology, Providence, RI 02912. Offerings include health services research (MS, PhD). *Degree requirements:* For doctorate, dissertation, preliminary exam. *Entrance requirements:* GRE General Test. Application deadline: 1/2 (priority date; rolling processing). Application fee: $60. *Expenses:* Tuition $23,616 per year. Fees $436 per year. • Dr. Constantine Gatsonis, Director, Department of Community Health, 401-863-1106. E-mail: gatsonis@jenny.biomed.brown.edu.

Case Western Reserve University, Schools of Medicine and Graduate Studies, Graduate Programs in Medicine, Department of Epidemiology and Biostatistics, Program in Health Services Research, Cleveland, OH 44106. Awards MS, PhD. Part-time programs available. Terminal master's awarded for partial completion of doctoral program. *Degree requirements:* For doctorate, dissertation required, foreign language not required. *Entrance requirements:* GRE General Test, TOEFL (minimum score 500). Application deadline: 2/1 (priority date; rolling processing). Application fee: $25. *Tuition:* $18,400 per year full-time, $767 per credit hour part-time. *Financial aid:* Fellowships, research assistantships, partial tuition waivers, and career-related internships or fieldwork available. Financial aid application deadline: 4/1. • Application contact: Joan Marold, Admissions Secretary, 216-368-3195. Fax: 216-368-3970.

Cornell University, Graduate School of Medical Sciences, Program in Clinical Epidemiology and Health Services Research, New York, NY 10031. Awards MS. Faculty: 18 full-time (7 women), 3 part-time (0 women). Students: 4 full-time (2 women); includes 1 minority (African American). *Degree requirements:* Thesis. *Entrance requirements:* MD or RN certificate, 3 years of work experience. Application deadline: 1/15. Application fee: $50. *Tuition:* $18,290 per year. *Financial aid:* Grants available. • Application contact: Valerie Blake, Administrator.

Dartmouth College, School of Arts and Sciences, Program in Evaluative Clinical Science, Hanover, NH 03755. Awards MS, PhD. Part-time programs available. Faculty: 16 part-time (2 women). Students: 40 full-time (21 women), 38 part-time (22 women); includes 4 minority (1 African American, 2 Asian Americans, 1 Hispanic), 6 international. 83 applicants, 86% accepted. In 1997, 37 master's awarded (87% found work related to degree, 13% continued full-time study); 1 doctorate awarded (100% entered university research/teaching). *Degree requirements:* For master's, research project required, thesis not required; for doctorate, dissertation. *Average time to degree:* master's–1 year full-time, 2 years part-time. *Entrance requirements:* For doctorate, GRE General Test, GRE Subject Test. Application fee: $10. *Tuition:* $31,719 per year. *Financial aid:* 40 students received aid; fellowships, research assistantships, training grants, institutionally sponsored loans available. Financial aid application deadline: 4/15; applicants required to submit FAFSA. • Gerry O'Connor, Head, 603-650-1782. Application contact: Susan Benson, Coordinator of Educational Programs, 603-650-1782.

Johns Hopkins University, School of Hygiene and Public Health, Department of Health Policy and Management, Faculty of Health Services Research, Baltimore, MD 21205. Awards MHS, Dr PH, PhD, Sc D. Dr PH being phased out; applicants no longer accepted. *Degree requirements:* For master's, comprehensive exam, internship required, foreign language not required; for doctorate, dissertation, 1 year full-time residency, comprehensive exam, oral and written exams required, foreign language not required. *Entrance requirements:* GRE General Test, TOEFL (minimum score 600), work experience in health-related field. Application deadline: 2/1 (priority date; rolling processing). Application fee: $60. *Financial aid:* Scholarships, stipends, Federal Work-Study, institutionally sponsored loans available. Financial aid application deadline: 4/15. *Faculty research:* Outcomes measurement, health services evaluation, emergency medical services, women's health care, managed care. • Dr. Carol Weisman, Associate Chair, 410-955-5315. Application contact: Judith Holzer, Academic Administrator, 410-955-2488. E-mail: jholzer@jhsph.edu.

McMaster University, Faculty of Health Sciences and School of Graduate Studies, Program in Clinical Health Sciences/Health Research Methodology, Hamilton, ON L8S 4M2, Canada. Awards M Sc, PhD. Part-time programs available. Students: 11 full-time, 94 part-time. In 1997, 12 master's awarded. *Degree requirements:* For master's, thesis required, foreign language not required; for doctorate, dissertation, comprehensive exam required, foreign language not required. *Entrance requirements:* For master's, honors B Sc, McMaster equivalent to B+ in last year of study; for doctorate, M Sc with McMaster equivalent to B+, students with proven research experience and an A average may be admitted with a B Sc degree. Application deadline: 2/28 (priority date). Application fee: $50. *Tuition:* $7199 per year for Canadian residents; $32,954 per year for nonresidents. *Financial aid:* Teaching assistantships available. • Dr. Chris Woodward, Coordinator, 905-525-9140 Ext. 22218. Application contact: Dr. R. Haslam, Chair, Graduate Programs in Health Sciences, 905-525-9140 Ext. 22983. Fax: 905-546-1129.

MGH Institute of Health Professions, Program in Clinical Investigation, 101 Merrimac Street, Boston, MA 02114-4719. Awards MS. Part-time and evening/weekend programs available. Faculty: 2 full-time (1 woman). Students: 5 part-time (1 woman); includes 1 minority (Asian American). Average age 30. 11 applicants, 55% accepted. *Entrance requirements:* GRE General Test. Application deadline: 8/1 (rolling processing; 12/1 for spring admission). Application fee: $50. *Expenses:* Tuition $20,320 per year full-time, $530 per credit part-time. Fees $300 per year. *Financial aid:* Partial tuition waivers and career-related internships or fieldwork available. Financial aid application deadline: 3/6; applicants required to submit FAFSA. *Faculty research:* Management of clinical research studies, outcomes research, operations research in data management and analysis, clinical trials research. • Dr. Richard Ferraro, Director, 617-724-6327. Fax: 617-726-8022. E-mail: ferraro.richard@mgh.harvard.edu. Application contact: Office of Student Affairs, 617-726-3140. Fax: 617-726-8010.

See in-depth description on page 1435.

Saint Louis University, School of Public Health, Program in Health Services Research, St. Louis, MO 63108. Awards PhD, MPH/PhD. Students: 6 full-time (2 women), 15 part-time (8 women); includes 2 minority (1 African American, 1 Asian American), 6 international. 19 applicants, 16% accepted. In 1997, 3 degrees awarded. *Degree requirements:* Dissertation, preliminary exams. *Entrance requirements:* GMAT or GRE General Test, interview. Application deadline: 3/1 (rolling processing). Application fee: $40. *Tuition:* $542 per credit hour. *Financial aid:* In 1997–98, 5 research assistantships were awarded. Financial aid application deadline: 4/1. *Faculty research:* Utilization of health services, aging, AIDS, health economics, outcomes, prevention. • Dr. James C. Romeis, Director, 314-977-8148. Fax: 314-977-8150. Application contact: Dr. Marcia Buresch, Assistant Dean of the Graduate School, 314-977-2240. Fax: 314-977-3943.

Southwest Texas State University, School of Health Professions, Department of Health Services and Research, Program in Allied Health Research, San Marcos, TX 78666. Awards MSHP. Part-time and evening/weekend programs available. Students: 7 full-time (5 women), 15 part-time (8 women); includes 5 minority (2 African Americans, 2 Asian Americans, 1 Hispanic), 1 international. Average age 32. In 1997, 3 degrees awarded. *Degree requirements:* Thesis (for some programs), committee review, comprehensive exam required, foreign language not required. *Entrance requirements:* GRE General Test (minimum combined score of 900), TOEFL (minimum score 550), minimum GPA of 2.75 in last 60 hours. Application deadline: 7/15 (priority date; rolling processing; 11/15 for spring admission). Application fee: $25 ($50 for international students). *Expenses:* Tuition $648 per year full-time, $120 per semester (minimum) part-time for state residents; $4500 per year full-time, $750 per semester (minimum) part-time for nonresidents. Fees $1264 per year full-time, $314 per semester (minimum) part-time. *Financial aid:* Research assistantships, teaching assistantships, Federal Work-Study, institutionally sponsored loans, and career-related internships or fieldwork available. Aid available to part-time students. Financial aid application deadline: 4/1; applicants required to submit FAFSA. *Faculty research:* Computer applications, quantitative management science technology, philosophy and methodology of research, evaluation. • Dr. Charles Johnson, Chair, 512-245-3494. Fax: 512-245-8712. E-mail: cj01@swt.edu.

Stanford University, School of Medicine, Graduate Programs in Medicine, Division of Health Services Research, Stanford, CA 94305-9991. Awards MS. Division accepts internal applicants only. Faculty: 11 full-time (5 women). Students: 6 full-time (2 women), 10 part-time (5 women); includes 3 minority (all Asian Americans). Average age 31. 4 applicants, 75% accepted. In 1997, 3 degrees awarded. *Degree requirements:* Thesis. *Application deadline:* 1/31. *Application fee:* $65 ($75 for international students). *Expenses:* Tuition $22,110 per year. Fees $156 per year. *Faculty research:* Cost and quality of life in cardiovascular disease, technology assessment, physician decision making. • Application contact: Admissions Office, 650-723-2460.

University of Alberta, Faculties of Medicine and Oral Health Sciences and Graduate Studies and Research, Graduate Programs in Medicine, Department of Public Health Sciences, Edmonton, AB T6G 2E1, Canada. Offerings include health policy research (MPH). Department faculty: 20 full-time, 11 part-time. *Average time to degree:* master's–2 years full-time, 4 years part-time; doctorate–4 years full-time, 6 years part-time. *Application deadline:* 2/1 (priority date; rolling processing). *Application fee:* $60. • Dr. T. W. Noseworthy, Chair, 403-492-6408. Application contact: Felicity Hey, Graduate Programs Administrator, 403-492-6407. Fax: 403-492-0364. E-mail: felicity.hey@ualberta.ca.

University of British Columbia, Faculties of Medicine and Graduate Studies, Graduate Programs in Medicine, Department of Health Care and Epidemiology, Vancouver, BC V6T 1W5, Canada. Offerings include health services research (M Sc, PhD). *Degree requirements:* For doctorate, dissertation. *Average time to degree:* master's–3 years full-time, 4 years part-time. *Entrance requirements:* For doctorate, work experience. Application deadline: 3/31 (rolling processing). Application fee: $50.

University of Michigan, School of Public Health, Interdepartmental Program in Clinical Research Design and Statistical Analysis, Ann Arbor, MI 48109. Awards MS. Offered through the Horace H. Rackham School of Graduate Studies. Program admits applicants in odd calendar years. Part-time and evening/weekend programs available. Faculty: 6. Students: 42 full-time. 49 applicants, 92% accepted. *Degree requirements:* Thesis required, foreign language not required. *Entrance requirements:* GRE General Test. Application deadline: 3/1 (priority date; rolling processing). Application fee: $55. • Jonathan Raz, Program Director, 734-936-1009.

University of Minnesota, Twin Cities Campus, School of Public Health, Major in Health Services Research and Policy, Minneapolis, MN 55455-0213. Awards MS. Faculty: 15 full-time, 2 part-time. Students: 8; includes 1 minority (African American), 2 international. 13 applicants, 69% accepted. In 1997, 3 degrees awarded. *Entrance requirements:* GRE General Test (minimum combined score of 1800 on three sections), minimum GPA of 3.0. Application fee: $50 ($75 for international students). *Financial aid:* Fellowships, research assistantships, teaching assistantships, Federal Work-Study, institutionally sponsored loans available. *Faculty research:* Quality, access, and cost of health services. • Dr. Bryan Dowd, Chair, 612-624-6151. E-mail: dowdx001@maroon.tc.umn.edu. Application contact: Janet Shapiro, Student Coordinator, 612-624-9432. E-mail: j-shap@maroon.tc.umn.edu.

See in-depth description on page 1537.

University of Minnesota, Twin Cities Campus, School of Public Health, Major in Health Services Research, Policy, and Administration, Minneapolis, MN 55455-0213. Awards PhD. Students: 35 (17 women). In 1997, 4 degrees awarded. *Degree requirements:* Dissertation required, foreign language not required. *Entrance requirements:* GRE General Test (minimum combined score of 1800 on three sections). Application deadline: 3/1 (rolling processing). Application fee: $50 ($75 for international students). *Financial aid:* Research assistantships, teaching assistantships, Federal Work-Study, institutionally sponsored loans available. • Dr. Will Manning, Chair, 612-624-6151. E-mail: wmanning@vx.cis.umn.edu. Application contact: Janet Shapiro, Student Coordinator, 612-624-9432. E-mail: j-shap@maroon.tc.umn.edu.

See in-depth description on page 1537.

University of Puerto Rico, Medical Sciences Campus, Graduate School of Public Health, Department of Health Services Administration, Program in Evaluation Research of Health Systems, San Juan, PR 00936-5067. Awards MS. Part-time programs available. Students: 35 (28 women); includes 1 international. 24 applicants, 54% accepted. In 1997, 1 degree awarded. *Degree requirements:* Computer language, thesis required, foreign language not required. *Entrance requirements:* GRE, previous course work in algebra and statistics. Application deadline: 3/3. Application fee: $15. *Financial aid:* Research assistantships, teaching assistantships, Federal Work-Study, institutionally sponsored loans, and career-related internships or fieldwork available. Financial aid application deadline: 4/30. • Dr. Carmen Albizu, Coordinator, 787-758-2525 Ext. 1422. Application contact: Mayra E. Santiago-Vargas, Counselor, 787-756-5244. Fax: 787-759-6719.

University of Rochester, School of Medicine and Dentistry, Graduate Programs in Medicine and Dentistry, Department of Community and Preventive Medicine, Program in Health Services Research, Rochester, NY 14627-0001. Awards PhD, MPH/PhD. Students: 6 full-time (5 women), 5 part-time (4 women). 7 applicants, 43% accepted. Terminal master's awarded for partial completion of doctoral program. *Degree requirements:* For doctorate, dissertation, qualifying exam required, foreign language not required. *Entrance requirements:* For doctorate, GRE General Test. Application deadline: 2/1. Application fee: $25. *Expenses:* Tuition $21,485 per year full-time, $672 per credit hour part-time. Fees $336 per year. *Financial aid:* Fellowships, research assistantships, teaching assistantships, full and partial tuition waivers available. Financial aid application deadline: 2/1. • Dr. Jack Zwanziger, Director, 716-275-2192.

See in-depth description on page 1547.

University of Southern California, School of Medicine and Graduate School, Graduate Programs in Medicine, Department of Preventive Medicine, Program in Health Behavior Research, Los Angeles, CA 90089. Awards PhD. Faculty: 12 full-time (6 women). Students: 23 full-time (18 women); includes 6 minority (1 African American, 2 Asian Americans, 3 Hispanics), 3 international. Average age 33. 33 applicants, 24% accepted. In 1997, 4 degrees awarded (50% found work related to degree, 50% continued full-time study). *Degree requirements:* Computer language, dissertation required, foreign language not required. *Average time to degree:* doctorate–5.5 years full-time. *Entrance requirements:* GRE General Test (minimum combined score of 1000), GRE Subject Test, TOEFL, minimum GPA of 3.0. Application deadline: 2/1. Application fee: $55. *Expenses:* Tuition $16,944 per year full-time, $706 per unit part-time. Fees $414 per year full-time, $32 per year part-time. *Financial aid:* In 1997–98, 20 students received aid, including 2 fellowships (1 to a first-year student), 11 research assistantships (7 to first-year students), 4 teaching assistantships, 4 training grants; Federal Work-Study, institutionally sponsored loans, and career-related internships or fieldwork also available. Financial aid application deadline: 2/1. *Faculty research:* Substance abuse prevention, cancer and heart disease prevention, mass media and health communication research, health promotion, treatment compliance. • Dr. C. Anderson Johnson, Director, 213-342-2628. Application contact: Dr. Luanne Rohrbach, Director, Graduate Studies, 213-342-2686. Fax: 213-342-2601.

Announcement: The PhD program in preventive medicine, health behavior research, offers training in a multidisciplinary program encompassing theory and methods from allied fields, including preventive medicine, epidemiology, psychology, communication, public health, and biostatistics. In addition to course work, students become meaningfully involved in supervised as well as independent research activities. The program prepares students for academic and applied health research careers. It is not intended for students planning to become practitioners or administrators.

University of Virginia, Graduate School of Arts and Sciences, Department of Health Evaluation Sciences, Charlottesville, VA 22903. Offers programs in clinical investigation (MS), epidemiology (MS), health care informatics (MS), health care resource management (MS), health services research and outcomes evaluation (MS). Part-time programs available. Faculty: 10 full-time (2 women), 12 part-time (8 women), 12 FTE. Students: 7 full-time (4 women), 5 part-time (1 woman); includes 3 minority (2 African Americans, 1 Asian American), 1 international. Average age 30. 32 applicants, 78% accepted. In 1997, 3 degrees awarded. *Degree requirements:* Thesis required (for some programs), foreign language not required. *Entrance requirements:* GRE or MCAT. Application deadline: 3/1 (priority date). Application fee: $40. *Tuition:* $4870 per year full-time, $941 per semester (minimum) part-time for state residents; $15,818 per year full-time, $2745 per semester (minimum) part-time for nonresidents. *Financial aid:* Career-related internships or fieldwork available. Financial aid applicants required to submit FAFSA. • Dr. Paige Hornsby, Director, 804-924-0496. E-mail: pph8c@virginia.edu. Application contact: Robyn Kells, Program Coordinator, 804-924-8646. Fax: 804-924-8437. E-mail: ms-hes@virginia.edu.

See in-depth description on page 1353.

University of Wisconsin–Madison, Medical School and Graduate School, Graduate Programs in Medicine, Population Health Program, Madison, WI 53706-1380. Offerings include health services research (MS, PhD). *Application fee:* $45. *Tuition:* $4928 per year full-time, $926 per semester (minimum) part-time for state residents; $15,190 per year full-time, $2849 per semester (minimum) part-time for nonresidents. • Donn D'Alessio, Chair, 608-263-2881. Fax: 608-263-2820. E-mail: dalessio@facstaff.wisc.edu.

Virginia Commonwealth University, School of Allied Health Professions, Department of Health Administration, Program in Health Services Organization and Research, Richmond, VA 23284-9005. Awards PhD. Students: 11 full-time (6 women), 21 part-time (11 women); includes 1 minority (African American), 9 international. Average age 38. 15 applicants, 47% accepted. In 1997, 5 degrees awarded. *Degree requirements:* Dissertation, residency. *Entrance requirements:* GMAT or GRE General Test. Application deadline: 1/31. Application fee: $30 ($0 for international students). *Tuition:* $4960 per year full-time, $257 per credit part-time for state

Directory: Health Services Research; Cross-Discipline Announcements

Virginia Commonwealth University (continued)
residents; $12,652 per year full-time, $684 per credit part-time for nonresidents. • Dr. Michael McCue, Director, 804-828-1893. Fax: 804-828-1894. E-mail: mjmccue@vcu.edu.

See in-depth description on page 1355.

Wake Forest University, School of Medicine and Graduate School, Graduate Programs in Medicine, Program in Health Services Research, Winston-Salem, NC 27109. Awards MS. Students: 3 full-time (2 women). 7 applicants, 57% accepted. *Degree requirements:* Thesis. *Entrance requirements:* GRE General Test, GRE Subject Test. Application deadline: 2/15 (priority date; rolling processing). Application fee: $25. *Tuition:* $17,450 per year. *Financial aid:* In 1997–98, 3 students received aid, including 3 tuition scholarships (all to first-year students) totaling $24,900. Financial aid application deadline: 2/15. • Dr. Michelle Naughton, Director, 336-716-2918.

Cross-Discipline Announcements

Brandeis University, The Heller Graduate School, Waltham, MA 02454-2728.

The Heller Graduate School at Brandeis University offers health-care administration concentrations in its Master of Management (MM) and Master of Business Administration (MBA) programs. Master's degree students benefit from cross-training in health policy and cutting-edge management education for careers as leaders in not-for-profit, for-profit, and public health services organizations, foundations, and think tanks. See in-depth description for the MM and MBA degree options in Book 6, Business Administration and Management section and in *Peterson's Guide to MBA Programs.*

The George Washington University, School of Business and Public Management, Department of Public Administration, Washington, DC 20052.

The George Washington University's Master of Public Administration (MPA) program is known for its exceptional faculty, distinctive curricular approaches, and well-established links with business, government, and nonprofit organizations. Located 4 blocks from the White House and 6 subway stops from the US Congress, The George Washington University MPA program places graduates in think tanks, policy advocacy and lobbying organizations, national associations, nonprofit organizations, businesses, and international organizations as well as local, state, and federal government agencies. Students can begin or enhance their career with an MPA or PhD in public administration from The George Washington University School of Business and Public Management.

Monmouth University, School of Business Administration, West Long Branch, NJ 07764-1898.

The MBA in health-care management prepares managers, health-care professionals, and business graduates for executive responsibilities in hospitals and health agencies. The program also prepares nurses to move from patient care to administration and doctors, dentists, and other health-care professionals for the business aspects of private practice or administration.

Saint Louis University, School of Law, St. Louis, MO 63108.

Saint Louis University School of Law offers a JD degree with a certificate option in health law. The School also offers a 4-year joint degree program in law and health administration and an LL M in health law. The health law faculty members are involved in conducting research projects on a wide range of issues. Opportunities are available for students to participate in these projects or to conduct their own work, under supervision, for directed research credit. The School's endowed library collection in health law provides an outstanding research facility.

State University of New York at Albany, School of Public Health, Executive Park South, Albany, NY 12203-3727.

The MS in health policy, management, and behavior and the MPH with concentrations in health administration and behavioral science combine the teaching of theory with contemporary public health practice. The participation of the NYS Department of Health provides outstanding training for careers in health policy analysis and program development and evaluation. MS students can select from 3 tracks: health systems, management, and social behavior and community health. See the in-depth description of the School of Public Health.

University of Southern California, Graduate School, Leonard Davis School of Gerontology, Los Angeles, CA 90089.

The School of Gerontology provides the opportunity for students to specialize in health-care administration (profit and nonprofit) through the dual degree with the USC School of Public Administration Health Services Administration program. This degree is designed to provide in-depth training for administrators of gerontology programs in hospitals and other acute-care settings, in addition to the administration of nursing homes, hospitals, long-term-care facilities, and other health services for older persons.

Walden University, Graduate Programs, 155 Fifth Avenue South, Minneapolis, MN 55401.

The distance learning doctoral program (PhD) in health services offers a specialization in health administration. Students may concentrate either in a specific functional management area, on the management of services/organizations dedicated to 1 stage in the continuum of care, or on 1 institutional/industry-specific management area that cuts across different levels of care. This specialization must be studied within the context of the integrated delivery system model. For more information, see Book 1 of this series.

ARIZONA STATE UNIVERSITY

College of Business
School of Health Administration and Policy

Programs of Study

Ranked twelfth by *U.S. News & World Report,* the School of Health Administration and Policy offers a Master of Health Services Administration (M.H.S.A.) and concurrent M.H.S.A./M.B.A. degree programs. These are designed to prepare qualified individuals who seek management careers in hospitals, group practices, health maintenance organizations, long-term care facilities, consulting firms, health departments, and other health-care organizations. The curriculum supports the belief that health services administrators share with their business colleagues a need for managerial skills. Beyond this commonality, however, lies a critical difference: the professional growth of health services administrators must be patient oriented as well as management oriented.

Students' skills are developed in a two-year, full-time, lockstep sequence. School faculty members are supported by a number of College of Business faculty members, many of whom have specific interests in health within their particular subject areas, e.g., marketing, economics, accounting, management, and finance.

The School also offers concurrent master's degree programs with the College of Law (M.H.S.A./J.D.) and the College of Nursing (M.H.S.A./M.S. in nursing administration). Separate applications are required, and admission requirements of both programs must be met for all concurrent degrees.

The School offers the Master in Public Health (M.P.H.) concentration in health administration and policy through the Arizona Graduate Program in Public Health. The M.P.H. is offered to full- or part-time students, with the degree being completed in no more than four years.

Research Facilities

Arizona State University was awarded the prestigious Research I University status in 1994, recognizing ASU as a premier research institution. The School of Health Administration and Policy offers a core of faculty expertise for the study of health-care delivery issues. The School is a member of the Center for Health Management Research. This academic-industry collaborative research center is the first one in the field funded by the National Science Foundation. The proximity of business faculty members provides opportunities for focusing research on the management practices and administrative needs of the health-care delivery system. The compilation of data needed for decision making, the analysis and evaluation of programs and processes, and the development of new systems or new applications are areas appropriate to the School's research mission.

The collections of the University's libraries comprise more than 3 million volumes, 35,000 periodical and serial subscriptions, and approximately 6.3 million microform units. Computer access to commercially and locally produced databases and the ability to borrow research materials from other libraries enhance local resources. Extensive computer facilities in the College of Business and on the ASU mainframe system are available to students.

Financial Aid

Financial assistance for M.H.S.A. students is available through private scholarships, public health traineeships, Graduate College tuition-waiver scholarships, loans, and fellowships. Approximately two thirds of the students receive some form of financial assistance. Graduate research assistantships are available to students admitted with regular status, and out-of-state tuition is waived for assistants working one-quarter time or more. The College of Business has a strong commitment to the financial aid program and assists graduate students to the extent that funds are available.

Cost of Study

Full-time graduate tuition for 1998–99 is $2988 per year for Arizona residents and $9640 for nonresidents. Books and supplies average $350 per semester.

Living and Housing Costs

There are residence halls for graduate students, although the majority of them prefer to live in available off-campus apartments. More information regarding University and off-campus housing can be obtained from the Office of Residence Life at 602-965-3515.

Student Group

Entering classes in the School number 25–35 students, facilitating the development of a cohesive, interacting group. Representing the entire country, students come from a variety of undergraduate backgrounds, including nursing, business, sociology, and psychology. Approximately 50 percent of the students have had prior experience in diverse professional and clinical environments. Students applying to the dual M.H.S.A./M.B.A. must have a minimum of two years of full-time work experience. An active student chapter of the American College of Healthcare Executives (ACHE-ASU) sponsors professional development seminars, field trips, and social functions for student members.

Location

Arizona State University's main campus is located near the heart of metropolitan Phoenix in the city of Tempe (population 156,844), just 5 miles from Phoenix Sky Harbor International Airport. The metropolitan area is serviced by more than twenty hospitals. Several HMOs, preferred provider options, and free-standing clinics are part of a very competitive health-care environment. The Phoenix area is also the home of the Arizona Department of Health, the Arizona Health Care Cost Containment System (AHCCCS) program, the western satellite of the Mayo Clinic, and several nationally recognized health-care consulting firms.

The University and The School

Arizona State University's 700-acre main campus is among the largest of the nation's institutions of higher education. With approximately 43,000 students, ASU is the fifth-largest university in the nation. Graduate students make up nearly one third of the University's on-campus enrollment. The College of Business is one of eleven colleges that compose the University and is accredited by the American Assembly of Collegiate Schools of Business.

The School of Health Administration and Policy is a nationally ranked academic unit within the College of Business, created in 1974 to offer a master's degree program for individuals seeking management careers in hospitals and other health-care organizations. The M.H.S.A. program is accredited by the Accrediting Commission on Education for Health Services Administration and is a member of the Association of University Programs in Health Administration. The M.B.A. program is accredited by the AACSB and the M.P.H. is accredited by the CEPH

Applying

Admission is granted to applicants who have earned a bachelor's or graduate degree from an accredited college or university. Applications for admission to the M.H.S.A. degree program must include a personal essay expressing career interest in health services administration, a grade point average of at least 3.0 (4.0 = A) in all work leading to the bachelor's degree, and three recommendations. Applicants are also required to take the Graduate Management Admission Test (GMAT) or Graduate Record Examinations (GRE). Only the GMAT is accepted for the M.H.S.A./M.B.A. degree program. The application deadlines are December 15, March 1, and May 1 for fall admission. Preference for departmental financial awards will be given to students who are admitted to the M.H.S.A. program by March 15. Applicants interested in being considered for graduate assistantships must also be admitted by March 15. A brochure is available upon request by writing directly to the School or by calling 602-965-7778. Interviews are encouraged for students interested in visiting the campus. Students may request a telephone interview with the director upon completion of their admission file, if they reside more than 250 miles from ASU.

Correspondence and Information

School of Health Administration and Policy
College of Business
Arizona State University
Box 874506
Tempe, Arizona 85287-4506

Telephone: 602-965-7778
Fax: 602-965-6654
E-mail: asuhap@asu.edu
World Wide Web: http://www.asu.edu/bus/ache (ACHE Student Chapter)
http://www.cob.asu.edu:80/hap/index.html (ASU Business School of Health Administration and Policy)

Arizona State University

THE FACULTY AND THEIR RESEARCH

Montague Brown, Visiting Professor of Health Services Administration; Dr.P.H., 1972, J.D., 1981, North Carolina at Chapel Hill. Strategic issues and policies, including the integration of delivery systems, managed care, strategic alliances, delivery networks, and joint ventures. Dr. Brown is the editor of the *Health Care Management Review* and has held research and teaching positions at the University of Chicago, Northwestern University, and Duke University.

William G. Johnson, Professor of Health Economics; Ph.D., Rutgers, 1971. Health economics. Research interests include graduate medical education, medical malpractice, disability, and occupational health. Dr. Johnson serves as principal investigator on projects to assess graduate medical education in Arizona (supported by the Flinn Foundation), to report on the employment effects of wage discrimination against black men (with colleagues at the University of East Carolina), and to report on labor market discrimination against women with disabilities. He is a Fellow for Employment Benefit Research Institute, the Collegium Ramazzini, and a member of the National Academy of Social Insurance. He is also appointed as the Clinical Professor of the Arizona Graduate Program in Public Health, Allied Health Sciences Center.

Bradford L. Kirkman-Liff, Professor of Health Administration and Policy; Dr.P.H., North Carolina at Chapel Hill, 1980. Financial, marketing, and medical care utilization management in managed care plans; primary care group practice management; health-care systems in industrialized nations. His U.S. research has examined access to preventative services, including prenatal care, family planning services, and breast and cervical cancer screening for women enrolled in Medicaid managed care plans. His comparative policy research is focused on the Netherlands, Germany, England, and Canada. In these locations he has examined health-care reform, physician payment, and hospital organization. He is the Visiting Professor at the Institute for Health Care Policy and Management, Rotterdam, the Netherlands, and the Centre for Health Care Planning and Management, Keel, England.

Jennie J. Kronenfeld, Professor of Health Services Administration; Ph.D., Brown, 1976. Medical sociology, health policy, medical care organization. Much of her research is in health behavior, prevention, and use of health care. Other research deals with general health policy issues. Currently involved in research activities that include evaluating projects' delivery extended health-care services at school settings, supported by the Flinn Foundation. She has recently directed projects, with collaborators from UCLA and the University of South Carolina, on perceived risks of AIDS (funded by the South Carolina Department of Health and Environmental Control) and on perceptions of risk injury to young children (supported by the National Institute of Child Health and Human Development). She has continued her efforts in procedure health behaviors and exploring "well-roles" among adults. Other research interests are variations in preventative health behavior, use of health care, and student health care by ethnicity and social class differences.

Lawrence S. Mayer, Research Physician; M.D., 1970, Ph.D., 1971, Ohio State. Development and application of biostatistical methods for analyzing data related to the development of the brain and human behavior; attributable risk type-measures and their application to intermediate end-point studies in internal medicine, psychiatry, and health services research.

Eugene S. Schneller, Professor of Health Services Administration; Ph.D., NYU, 1973. Medical sociology, organizational behavior. Research interests include issues related to the medical division of labor with a focus on the changing nature of professions, emerging health-care occupations, and the roles of physicians in management in the U.S., England, and the New Independent States. Other projects focus on the changing role of public relations in integrated delivery systems, physician leadership in emerging systems, and strategic adaptation in the professions.

Stuart A. Wesbury Jr., Professor of Health Services Administration and Director, Executive Education Programs, College of Business; Ph.D., Florida, 1972. Economics and management. Research interests include health policy, health-care delivery trends, and management issues. Dr. Wesbury was codirector of a series of Delphi studies exploring the future of the health care of the U.S., a joint project of the American College of Healthcare Executives and Arthur Andersen & Co., 1983–1991. Other completed works include: hospital CEO turnover, hospital smoking policies, patient confidentiality issues, and career development in health administration. As president/CEO of the American College of Healthcare Executives, 1979 to 1991, Dr. Wesbury directed a number of studies and evaluations of the credentialing of health-care executives.

Frank G. Williams, Professor of Health Services Administration; Ph.D., Iowa, 1975. Long-term care, finance, rural health. Clinical Professor in the Arizona Graduate Program in Public Health, University of Arizona Health Sciences Center. His research interests are in the areas of long-term care, rural health, and reimbursement policy. In the last ten years, he has obtained nearly 1.5 million dollars in external research grants. He serves on the Arizona Board of Regents Student Health Advisory Committee and was recently appointed by the board to represent the three Arizona Universities on the Legislative Oversight Health Insurance Benefits Review Committee. He is an executive member of the Board of Directors of the Arizona Affordable Health Care Foundation, a board member of the EMPACT Suicide Prevention Center, a board member of the Network for Education in Health Services Administration, and a former board member of the CIGNA Health Plan of Arizona, Desert Samaritan Hospital, and the Jane Wayland Community Mental Health Center. He is also a faculty associate of the American College of Health Care Executives and a site visitor and past Fellow of the Accrediting Commission on Education for Health Services Administration. In 1992, Dr. Williams was inducted into Beta Gamma Sigma, the Honor Society for Collegiate Schools of Business.

Affiliated Faculty

Ben Forsyth, Senior Executive Assistant to the President and Professor of Health Services Administration; M.D., NYU, 1957. Research interest is in areas of infectious diseases.

Jeffrey Rupert Wilson, Associate Professor of Statistics; Ph.D., Iowa State, 1984. Research interests focus on longitudinal, categorical, logistic regression, and other binary models and on generalized linear models for overdispersion and its applications to biomedical research and epidemiologic data. Current research includes a National Science Foundation grant to study overdispersed models and a USDA grant to estimate usage in public faculties. He is the author of several publications based on categorical and survey sampling models and is the recipient of several teaching awards, including the Golden Key National Honor Society Award.

Adjunct Faculty

Armaity V. Austin, M.P.H., Indiana, 1980; M.D., St. George's University School of Medicine, 1984.
Douglas Campos-Outcalt, M.D., 1979, M.P.A., 1985, Arizona State.
Meyer W. Cohen, M.P.H., Baylor, 1970.
Dorothy L. Faulkner, M.P.H., Alabama, 1987; Ph.D., Michigan, 1994.
Barbara P. McCool, M.H.A., Minnesota, 1967; Ph.D., Ohio State, 1972.
Mary A. Paterson, Ph.D., Berkeley, 1992.
John R. Rivers, B.A., Notre Dame, 1968.
Gail Silverstein, Ph.D., Arizona State, 1993.
Edward A. Smith, M.D., Arizona, 1974.
Rosalyn P. Sterling-Scott, M.D., NYU, 1974.
Jonathan B. Weisbuch, M.D., NYU, 1963; M.P.H., Harvard, 1967.

CORNELL UNIVERSITY

Sloan Program in Health Services Administration

Program of Study

The Sloan Program has been at the forefront of health services management education and research for more than forty years. Originally endowed by Alfred P. Sloan in the 1950s, the program was the first of its kind to recognize the importance of integrating management tools with population-based health sciences in educating future health-care leaders. Today, it continues to provide a curriculum acknowledged internationally for its creativity and rigor. The Sloan Program consists of a 60-credit hour ACEHSA-accredited curriculum culminating in a Master of Health Administration (M.H.A.) degree. This is a two-year, nonthesis, in-residence graduate program that matriculates 15–20 students annually from around the world. Course work in management, health services systems, epidemiology, quantitative methods, law and ethics, insurance and managed care, health-care financing and economics, health policy, and strategic management is practically applied during the required ten-week summer practicum, which is undertaken between the first and second years. Students select and secure summer residencies with health-care organizations from around the world. The curriculum is supplemented by the Sloan Symposia, which bring practitioners and researchers to Cornell throughout the academic year for seminars and presentations, and by the winter intersession trips, in which students meet with national policy makers and health-care leaders. Sloan students have numerous opportunities to interface with a very active alumni association, numbering 800 strong and represented by a 10-member executive board that visits the campus several times a year. The Sloan Alumni Association sponsors the Mentor Program, in which students match their professional interests with participating alumni. Sloan alumni also are consistently seen in positions of national prominence. Reginald Ballantyne (Sloan '67) serves as Chair of the American Hospital Association, and Alan Weinstein (Sloan '66) is President of Premier, Inc., the largest managed care firm in the U.S.

Research Facilities

Cornell has sixteen campus libraries with nearly 5 million volumes and subscriptions to more than 50,000 periodicals; it also serves as a depository for government documents. Research facilities include the Cornell Institute for Social and Economic Research; the Center for International Studies; the Cornell Institute for Public Affairs; the Bronfenbrenner Life Course Center; the Center for Environmental Research; the Program on Science, Technology and Society; and numerous other specialized programs. State-of-the-art computer facilities include mainframe and microcomputers, a developing intracollege high-speed network, instructional software and workshops, and consultant services.

Financial Aid

A very limited number of highly competitive college and program fellowship and scholarship awards are available based on academic merit and professional promise. Some minority fellowships also exist. Faculty members conduct interviews for a limited number of assistantships, which cover tuition and pay a stipend. Other institutional support includes loans and a work-study program. Ninety-seven percent of summer residencies held by Sloan students are paid positions.

Cost of Study

Tuition for the 1998–99 academic year is approximately $11,550.

Living and Housing Costs

The estimated cost of living for the 1998–99 academic year (books, room and board, and personal expenses) for a single student is $8500–$10,500.

Student Group

Sloan students are a diverse group, with approximately 30 percent representing ethnic minorities. Of the 30 students enrolled in the spring 1998 semester, 1 is a physician, 2 are dentists, and 5 are international students. A majority of students come to the Sloan Program with professional experience in health care or other business sectors. Approximately one third hold undergraduate degrees in business, and nearly 30 percent have degrees in health care or biological sciences. Another 20 percent hold undergraduate degrees in the social sciences.

Student Outcomes

Sloan graduates experience outstanding employment and fellowship opportunities. On average, more than 95 percent are placed in positions of their choice within three months of graduation, and more than a third of all alumni hold senior management positions in health-care systems and institutions around the world. Current graduates migrate toward management positions with managed care organizations and consulting firms or pursue fellowships with national health-care systems. Of those graduating in the past two years, 4 have been awarded postgraduate fellowships with health-care organization, 11 have selected management positions with managed care organizations or health-care systems, 5 have taken positions with consulting firms, 1 has taken a position as a CEO of a large orthopedic practice, 1 has secured a position with an investment banking and equity firm, and 2 manage hospital departments.

Location

The program is located in the Department of Policy Analysis and Management on the Cornell campus in Ithaca, a city of more than 30,000 (Tompkins County—65,000), which overlooks Cayuga Lake in upstate New York. Syracuse is 1 hour away by car, and New York City can be reached in 5 hours by car. Flights from the local airport connect with major cities in the U.S. and abroad. The beautiful and culturally rich community was selected in 1997 as the most progressive "best place" to live and offers abundant recreational resources the year round, including three state parks within 10 miles, as well as lectures, music, theater, dance, and the arts. The Herbert F. Johnson Museum of Art is also located on the Cornell campus.

The University

Founded in 1865, Cornell University is a member of the Ivy League. It is part land-grant college and part private university. There are 12,000 undergraduate and 5,000 graduate and professional students enrolled in the University.

Applying

Students are only admitted in the fall semester. There is a rolling admissions process that begins in November, but for students interested in University Fellowships, the deadline is January 10. To be considered, applicants must submit all of the following: a completed application form; a statement of purpose; two letters of recommendation; transcripts of all academic work completed, including evidence of an undergraduate degree; and GMAT or GRE General Test scores. International students also must submit TOEFL scores.

Correspondence and Information

Andrea Parrot, Ph.D., Director of Graduate Studies
Department of Policy Analysis and Management
College of Human Ecology
Cornell University
Ithaca, New York 14853-4401

Telephone: 607-255-7772
Fax: 607-255-4071
E-mail: gms3@cornell.edu
World Wide Web: http://www.human.cornell.edu/pam/sloan

Cornell University

THE FACULTY

Henry Allen, Adjunct Professor; M.B.A., J.D., Cornell. Health law.
Roger Battistella, Professor; Ph.D., Michigan. Organization, financing, and planning of personal and public health services, managed care delivery systems, health services restructuring, international health policy and management.
Laura Dimmler, Lecturer and Associate Director, Sloan Program in Health Services Administration; M.P.A., Harvard. Health-care marketing, social marketing, management and strategic planning.
John Ford, Professor; Ph.D., Michigan. Health systems planning, social epidemiology, community mental health.
Margaret Hubbert, Senior Lecturer; M.B.A., SUNY at Binghamton. Finance and accounting.
Andrea Kabcenell, Senior Research Associate; M.P.H., Michigan. Provision of long-term health care and quality of care, managed care and people with chronic disabilities, processes that will spread innovative ideas to new organizations.
Donald Kenkel, Associate Professor; Ph.D., Chicago. Health economics and public policy economics, consumer health behavior.
John Kuder, Associate Professor and Director, Sloan Program in Health Services Administration; Ph.D., Michigan. Health economics; corporate finance; managed care, especially public programs; evaluation of the changing institutional mechanisms for the delivery and financing of medical care in the U.S.
Andrea Parrot, Associate Professor; Ph.D., Cornell. Health services; women's health and medical ethics; human sexuality, teenage pregnancy, acquaintance rape, sexuality education, and infertility.
Eunice Rodriguez, Associate Professor; Ph.D., Berkeley. Epidemiology, planning and evaluation of health-care services, impact of environmental change on health status, health promotion and disease prevention.
William Trochim, Professor; Ph.D., Northwestern. Experimental and quasi-experimental research design; computer simulations of novel statistical analytic approaches; investigations of quality, implementation, and conceptualizations of research.
Stephen Walston, Assistant Professor; Ph.D., Pennsylvania. Health-care management, organizational theory and strategy, organization design, hospital renewal through reengineering strategy.
Jerome Ziegler, Professor Emeritus; M.A., Chicago. Policy analysis of current political and socioeconomic issues in the context of the intergovernmental system.

ILLINOIS SCHOOL OF PROFESSIONAL PSYCHOLOGY AT CHICAGO

Graduate Program in Health Services Administration

Program of Study

The Graduate Program in Health Services Administration (HSA) provides a comprehensive course of graduate study that prepares health service providers and managers for the challenges of modern health care. Within this framework, the program is designed to accommodate the needs of current practitioners as well as full-time students. Students are taught to recognize the value of applied research in solving the problems of today's health systems, and course work encourages the acquisition of sustainable research methods and skills. The HSA program combines theory from the worlds of science and business, building on the School's practitioner-based clinical training programs and its research in behavioral modeling, the foundation of consumer economics. The result is the integration of behavior theories with traditional health-care management applications in solving the problems of modern health-care delivery.

A commitment to the interdisciplinary nature of effective health-care delivery is a hallmark of the program. As students progress, they are exposed to major theories and developments in health care originating from a variety of academic disciplines. Understanding how to integrate and adapt these diverse ideas in solving practical problems in health delivery is a main goal of the program. Areas of current research interest include merger and consolidation of corporate health-care providers, factors in managed care profitability, economic credentialing, quality assessment and cost analysis by employers and self-insured purchasers, the growth and impact of telemedical technologies, use of outcomes data and practice guidelines in litigation, single payer systems: organization and regional trends, and gender and cultural aspects of health care.

The master's degree is awarded after successful completion of a two-year course of study, with required core courses in health-care organizations, health financing, accounting and business practices, health behaviors, and management. Additional course work is designed to develop skills in health outcomes measurement, information systems, and applied research methods. Limited elective courses are permitted to allow concentrated study in a particular area.

Research Facilities

Research in topics relevant to current trends and practices, taught by working practitioners, is a major strength of the program. The school library and computer facilities, as well as online databases, are available to all students. The program is offered through the American Schools of Professional Psychology, with campuses in five different states and located in a variety of metropolitan settings. Online interactive capabilities between campuses provide unprecedented research opportunities in studying geographically diverse health systems.

Financial Aid

Loans and scholarships are available through a variety of sources. Part-time or full-time employment opportunities are abundant near the campus, which is located in the heart of Chicago's business district. The School maintains a fully staffed financial aid office to assist students.

Cost of Study

Tuition for 1998–99 is $396 per trimester hour, with most courses receiving 3 hours of credit. Total costs vary according to the student's desired course load.

Living and Housing Costs

On-campus housing is not available. Housing costs vary widely in the greater Chicago area, and many students choose to live in the culturally rich, and less expensive neighborhoods surrounding downtown Chicago.

Student Group

A multidisciplinary approach that encourages student enrollment from a variety of educational backgrounds is favored. The program seeks to limit class size to 20 new students per year, encouraging diversity in academic backgrounds and work experiences. Students come from social sciences, humanities, business, law, and clinical and ancillary health-care professions. Integration of students into professional life is highly encouraged through involvement with local and national professional associations.

Student Outcomes

The program is designed to train health administrators, managers, and practitioners to provide immediate leadership in today's health-care delivery systems. Through affiliations and close interaction with major health-care provider corporations and service organizations, students are continuously exposed to real-world problems faced by industry professionals. Employment is seen as an extension of the program training, rather than a starting point for learning health-care management. Graduates can expect opportunities to work in managed care systems, multi-institutional care systems, employer-based health-care management, health-care consulting firms, government, the financial services industry, universities, not-for-profit agencies, and the pharmaceutical industry.

Location

The program is offered by the Illinois School of Professional Psychology at Chicago. The campus is located in the heart of downtown Chicago, minutes from the city's main transportation lines and suburban commuter trains. Within immediate walking distance is the Chicago City Library, as well as a number of national health-care associations and corporate headquarters for a number of major health-care providers.

The School

The programs offered by ISPP/Chicago are based upon accepted and tested educational principles and practices within professional psychology and have as a goal the development of skilled practitioners who can provide psychological services to diverse populations. The Illinois School of Professional Psychology at Chicago was originated as a master's and doctoral degree granting institution. The succeeding years have seen the institution develop additional campuses and provide a greater variety of degree programs and curricula, including the Master in Health Services Administration. The School is fully accredited by the North Central Association of Colleges and Schools.

Applying

An undergraduate degree from an accredited college is required for admission to the program. Applicants are selected based on academic transcripts, test scores, work experience, and letters of recommendation. Applicants are advised to take the GRE or GMAT. Students may obtain a program description and application from the address below.

Correspondence and Information

Graduate Program in Health Services Administration
Illinois School of Professional Psychology at Chicago
Two First National Plaza
20 South Clark Street, Third Floor
Chicago, Illinois 60603
Telephone: 312-201-0200

Illinois School of Professional Psychology at Chicago

THE FACULTY

A commitment to the interdisciplinary nature of effective health-care delivery is a hallmark of the program. Faculty members who can contribute a unique perspective to the program are chosen from diverse backgrounds. As students progress, they are exposed to major theories and developments in health care, originating from a variety of academic disciplines and organizational settings brought to the program through faculty experience. Understanding how to integrate and adapt these diverse ideas in solving practical problems in health delivery is one of the biggest challenges managers face. Working-theory development and applied research are encouraged from the faculty members throughout the program.

Current areas of faculty research interest include the following: merger and consolidation of corporate health-care providers: effects on delivery of services; factors in managed care profitability, economic credentialing, and the provider role; quality assessment and cost analysis by employers and self-insured purchasers-HEDIS measurement; growth and impact of telemedical technologies on health-care organization; use of outcomes data and practice guidelines in litigation; single payer systems: organization and structure, regional trends; comparative analysis of patient satisfaction instruments; gender and cultural aspects of health care; online services, EDI, and the Internet; and new roles for nontraditional providers of care.

INDIANA UNIVERSITY–PURDUE UNIVERSITY INDIANAPOLIS

School of Public and Environmental Affairs
Graduate Program in Health Administration

Program of Study

The Graduate Program in Health Administration in the School of Public and Environmental Affairs (SPEA) provides an advanced course of study leading to the Master of Health Administration (M.H.A.) degree. The program is designed to prepare individuals for leadership positions in the health services. It is especially appealing to those who have a mix of education and employment in their backgrounds. It provides a broadly balanced foundation of theoretical and practical knowledge and technical skills necessary to succeed in the complex and changing health field. The program consists of a 60-credit-hour, interdisciplinary curriculum, which accommodates a wide range of career interests and backgrounds. The M.H.A. program is fully accredited by the Accrediting Commission on Education for Health Services Administration.

Areas of emphasis in the M.H.A. program curriculum include management, health finance and economics, community assessment and strategic planning, program and outcome evaluation, managed care and integrated networks, and marketing, among others. Students have the opportunity to participate in an optional third-year administrative residency in a health agency. A Washington, D.C.–based advanced health policy project option is also available. Those not selecting the residency conduct a challenging health research project during the final portion of their program.

Research Facilities

SPEA maintains a number of centers for the encouragement and coordination of research. The Bowen Research Center, as well as related research centers in the School of Medicine, provides exciting research opportunities for students. Recent projects have focused on the cost-effectiveness of new medical devices and on improving patient outcomes. Other research projects include the evaluation of the Campaign for Healthy Babies, the evaluation of the Indiana Choice Program, the Indiana Physician Distribution Study, and an evaluation of the Ohio Medicaid HMO Program. A fully electronic library stands as a model for university libraries across the country.

Financial Aid

Graduate assistantships (research and administrative) are available. These provided a stipend of $650 per month for a period of nine months in 1997–98. Some also provide tuition fee remission. The total financial value of the awards is in excess of $9500. The School makes every effort to continue financial support for each student who is academically eligible (minimum GPA of 3.0 on a 4.0 scale for 18 credits) for a second year. In addition, frequently there are research opportunities through which the student can continue employment during the summer months. (Part-time students are not eligible for assistantships.) March 1 is the priority date for consideration for graduate assistantships.

Cost of Study

In 1997–98, the tuition for in-state students was $144.30 per credit hour. Out-of-state students paid $416.30 per credit hour of study. Other costs included $27 per semester for parking, a technology fee of $80, miscellaneous fees of $40 per semester, and $400–$600 per semester for books.

Living and Housing Costs

On-campus housing is limited; however, a variety of privately owned apartments are available nearby. Rent ranges from about $400 to $650 per month. A flexible campus meal plan is available through the campus housing office.

Student Group

Approximately half of the M.H.A. students have a health-related background. The program is small, accepting 25–35 new part-time and full-time students annually.

Student Outcomes

Health administration students leave the M.H.A. program with a comprehensive understanding of the health-care system, focusing on issues and techniques in organizational and financial management, public policy, and statistical methods. The opportunity to participate in a one-year residency or undertake an applied research project completes the M.H.A. degree program.

Graduates of the program have entered nearly every type of health-care organization. Alumni can be found across the country in hospitals, long-term-care facilities, public health agencies, mental health centers, physician group practices, ambulatory and managed care, preventive medicine, voluntary health agencies, rehabilitation facilities, consulting firms, corporate health programs, insurance companies, and government and other regulatory agencies. The list of recent residency placements in this program summary illustrates the utility of the M.H.A. and its ability to open a variety of doors to the health-care sector.

Location

Indiana University–Purdue University Indianapolis (IUPUI) is located on the western periphery of a dynamically changing downtown Indianapolis, which is within easy walking distance. Recently completed downtown area attractions include the 100-shop Circle Centre Mall, Victory Field (a 13,000-seat baseball stadium), an impressive IMAX theater, White River State Park, and Canal Walk. Indianapolis is also noted for its world-class symphony, ballet, theater, and opera companies and is home to the world's largest children's museum. Indianapolis is known as well for its sports, playing host to the NBA's Pacers, NFL's Colts, minor league baseball's Indians (AAA), ice hockey's ICE, and the Indianapolis 500 and Brickyard 400 auto races. The men's professional tennis tour also makes a stop every summer for the RCA Championships at the Indianapolis Tennis Center, located on the IUPUI campus. Eagle Creek Park, on the city's northwest side, has more than 3,800 acres of woods, a 1,300-acre reservoir, and a variety of recreational facilities.

The University

IUPUI demonstrates a model partnership between government, community, and university. It was formed in 1969 by combining the city facilities and the programs of Indiana University and Purdue University under one name and administration. IUPUI is a campus of change, diversity, and achievement, with nineteen schools offering more than 200 programs to 27,000 students. The University attracts many in-service students who attend evening classes and enhance the graduate experience by sharing their experiences and expertise.

Applying

All applicants must have a baccalaureate degree from an accredited institution. A GPA of 3.0 or higher on a 4.0 scale is preferred. Undergraduate prerequisites include one course each in accounting, statistics, and microeconomics. An application form, three references, transcripts, and GRE scores must be submitted along with a nonrefundable $35 application fee. Applications should be received no later than July 15 for fall admission. Students who wish to be considered for graduate assistantships should have their completed applications on file by March 1.

Correspondence and Information

Graduate Program in Health Administration
School of Public and Environmental Affairs
Indiana University–Purdue University Indianapolis
801 West Michigan Street, BS 3027
Indianapolis, Indiana 46202-5152

Telephone: 317-274-4656
E-mail: speainfo@speanet.iupui.edu
World Wide Web: http://www.spea.iupui.edu

Indiana University–Purdue University Indianapolis

THE FACULTY AND THEIR RESEARCH

Thomas DeCoster, Ph.D., Notre Dame, 1968. Self-managed work teams, organizational behavior.
Deborah Freund, Ph.D., Michigan, 1980. Health economics, health-care financing, health policy.
Michael Gleeson, Ph.D., Syracuse, 1973. Management science.
Karen Harlow, Ph.D., Texas at Arlington, 1981. Applied health policy, community assessment, long-term care.
Ann Holmes, Ph.D., British Columbia, 1993. Health economics, measurement of health outcomes, welfare implications of health-care decision statistics.
John Ottensmann, Ph.D., North Carolina at Chapel Hill, 1974. Urban planning, public policy, application of personal computers and management information systems to public planning and management.
Gerard Wedig, Ph.D., Harvard, 1987. Industrial organization, econometrics, health economics, business investment and finance, economics of technological change.
Terrell Zollinger, Dr.P.H., Loma Linda, 1979. Health services research, maternal and child health, child abuse.

Recent Preceptors and Residency Placements
Jack Basler and Blake Dye, Vice Presidents, Henry County Memorial Hospital, New Castle, Indiana.
James Bigogno, President, Howard County Community Hospital, Kokomo, Indiana.
Robert Brodhead, President, Ball Memorial Hospital, Muncie, Indiana.
David Cantrell, Business Manager and Chief Financial Officer, and Marjorie Albohm, Director, Orthopedic Research, The Center for Hip and Knee Surgery, Mooresville, Indiana.
Greg Carlson, President and CEO, Owensboro Mercy Health System, Owensboro, Kentucky.
Jack Corey, President, DeKalb Memorial Hospital, Inc., Auburn, Indiana.
Gary Ford, President, VHA Tristate, Inc., Indianapolis, Indiana.
James Jones, Director, VA Medical Center, Danville, Illinois.
Richard Keenan, President, Baptist Homes of Indiana, Indianapolis, Indiana.
Richard Kohr, President, Bloomington Hospital, Bloomington, Indiana.
Thomas Kramer, President, Deaconess Hospital, Evansville, Indiana.
Marsha Life, Administrator, Four Seasons Retirement Center, Columbus, Indiana.
Steven Linerode, Vice President, St. Joseph's Hospital and Health Center, Kokomo, Indiana.
John McGinty Jr., President and CEO, Columbus Regional Hospital, Columbus, Indiana.
Susan Palmer, Associate Director, VA Medical Center, Indianapolis, Indiana.
Beth Sharer, Vice President, Memorial Hospital, Jasper, Indiana.
Thomas Steinmetz, Executive Director, Nasser, Smith and Pinkerton Cardiology, Inc., Indianapolis, Indiana.
Christy Tidwell, Administrator, Obstetrics and Gynecology, Indiana University Medical Center, Indianapolis, Indiana.
John Walling, President, and John Barry, Senior Vice President, Home Hospital, Lafayette, Indiana.

Recent Placements of M.H.A. Graduates in Fellowship and Career Appointments
Hyeson Bang, The Mayo Foundation, Rochester, Minnesota.
Mike Cohen, Michigan Children's Hospital/Detroit Medical Center, Detroit, Michigan.
Julie Dezarn, Rural Health Group, Inc., Jackson, North Carolina.
Katie Diefenthaler, Washington Hospital Center, Washington, D.C.
John Gaskey, Veterans Administration, Portland, Oregon.
Djallon Hatchett, Kaiser Permanente, Los Angeles, California.
Janet Henderson, Parkland Hospital, Dallas, Texas.
Chip Hubbs, Mt. Sinai Hospital Medical Center, Chicago, Illinois.
Cheryl Kopec, Franklin Hospital, Franklin, Pennsylvania.
Wright Lassiter, Methodist Hospital, Dallas, Texas.
Charles Nefkens, Veterans Administration, Long Beach, California.
Monica Perkins, V.A. Medical Center, Chicago, Illinois.
Trisha Seib, The American College of Healthcare Executives, Chicago, Illinois.
Jennifer Stephenson, Oxmar Group Practice, Baton Rouge, Louisiana.
Jeff Zeh, The Cleveland Clinic, Cleveland, Ohio.

JOHNS HOPKINS UNIVERSITY

School of Hygiene and Public Health
Department of Health Policy and Management

Programs of Study

The Department of Health Policy and Management educates master's, doctoral, and postdoctoral students to assume leadership roles in management, education, research, and public policy. The department has a multidisciplinary faculty that teaches and conducts research related to the promotion and maintenance of health; the prevention of injury, disease, and disability; and the organization, financing, and delivery of health-care services. The department provides doctoral-level education in three broad areas—Social and Behavioral Sciences, Health Services Research, and Health and Public Policy—culminating in the Ph.D. or Sc.D. degree. Doctoral degree candidates are expected to complete core course requirements and pass written qualifying examinations by the end of their first year of study and to pass departmental and School oral examinations on their dissertation protocol by the end of their second year. Many doctoral degree candidates complete their dissertation research and pass a final oral examination by the end of their fourth year of study.

Master of Health Science (M.H.S.) degree programs are offered in the areas of health education, health finance and management, and health policy. These programs prepare graduates for positions as health educators, managers, planners, evaluators, and policy analysts in health organizations, government units, and private corporations. The M.H.S. programs are offered both full-time and part-time. Generally, the full-time programs consist of one academic year of course work followed by a supervised field placement in an appropriate organization. A joint program in genetic counseling is offered by the Department of Health Policy and Management and the National Center of Human Genome Research at the National Institutes of Health (NIH) and leads to a Master of Science (Sc.M.) degree. The program requires 2½ years of full-time study; course work is taken at both the Johns Hopkins University in Baltimore and the NIH in Bethesda, Maryland. Postdoctoral study is available for students who wish to pursue advanced research training with an individual faculty member. Generally, postdoctoral fellows must seek their own funding.

Research Facilities

The Health Services Research and Development Center, the Center for Hospital Finance and Management, the Center for Injury Research and Policy, the Center for Gun Policy and Research, the Center for Research on Services for Severe Mental Illness, the Risk Sciences and Public Policy Institute, the Primary Care Policy Center for Underserved Populations, and the Bioethics Institute of the Johns Hopkins University are multidisciplinary research units within the department that are resources for research and technical assistance to students and faculty. Students have access to all University library facilities, which provide more than 2.5 million volumes. The Welch Medical Library and the Lilenfeld Library are the central facilities serving the needs of the Johns Hopkins Medical Institutions. Extensive computer facilities are also available.

Financial Aid

Doctoral students accepted to the program receive tuition scholarship assistance from the department. Funding for M.H.S. applicants is available for the internship year. The School's Office of Student Financial Services provides information and applications for various loans available to graduate students.

Cost of Study

Tuition for 1998–99 is $22,680. Medical insurance for a single person ranges from $130 to $175 per month; the cost of books and course supplies averages $150 per month.

Living and Housing Costs

Minimum living expenses for a single person, including rent, utilities, food, supplies, public transportation, and miscellaneous items, total approximately $1800 per month.

Student Group

The department's enrollment consists of more than 350 students from across the United States and around the world. Students in the department come with various backgrounds, including sociology, economics, law, history, medicine, and business. Many have several years of health-related experience before enrolling for graduate work.

Student Outcomes

Recent graduates hold positions as health policy analysts and planners, managers, educators, and researchers in federal and state government, private foundations and consulting firms, health-care organizations, and academic and research institutions.

Location

Baltimore is a heterogeneous metropolis that is rich in American history and cultural and recreational opportunities. The city is situated on the mid-Atlantic corridor, 45 minutes from Washington, D.C., and 4 hours' driving time from New York City. The School of Public Health is located 1 mile from the Inner Harbor of the Chesapeake Bay, the nation's largest tidewater bay. The Inner Harbor is the home of the National Aquarium, the Maryland Science Center, the U.S. Frigate *Constellation,* Oriole Park at Camden Yards, and a 2-mile waterfront promenade with shopping pavilions.

The School

The School of Hygiene and Public Health of the Johns Hopkins University, the oldest school of public health in the world, was established in 1916 by persons of vision who planned a school of the biological, physical, social, and behavioral sciences. Its goal is to preserve and improve the health of the public. The School provides the highest quality of education in public health and the sciences basic to it for those individuals who have the potential to excel in education, research, and public health practice. The School addresses current and future health problems at the local, national, and international levels. Proximity to Washington, D.C., presents the opportunity to utilize national resources in the executive and legislative branches of government to further an understanding of functional public health policy. In addition, there are opportunities to observe and interact with state and local health agencies.

Applying

Admission consideration to the programs offered in this department requires: an application from the School, a statement of intent, a curriculum vitae or resume, proof of a baccalaureate degree, and three letters of reference. GRE scores are required for all degree-seeking applicants; GMAT scores will be accepted for applicants to the M.H.S. program in Health Finance and Management only. For applicants whose native language is not English, a minimum TOEFL score of 600 is required. Nonnative English-speaking applicants are also required to submit scores from the Test of Written English (TWE). A minimum score of 4.5 is required on this exam. Some departmental programs may have additional requirements. Doctoral (Sc.D. and Ph.D.) applications and all supporting documents must be received by January 2. Applications submitted and/or completed after this date are not considered for admission. Applicants are notified by mail of the outcomes of the application in mid-to-late March. Sc.M. (genetic counseling) applications and all supporting documents must be received by January 15. Applications submitted and/or completed after this date may not be considered for admission. Invitations for interviews are presented in early March, with final decisions and offers being made on May 1. M.H.S. applications and all supporting documents must be received by February 1. Applications submitted and/or completed after this date may not be considered for admission.

Correspondence and Information

Judith L. Holzer, M.B.A. Academic Administrator
Hampton House, Room 492
Department of Health Policy and Management
The Johns Hopkins School of Hygiene and Public Health
624 North Broadway
Baltimore, Maryland 21205-2179
Telephone: 410-955-2488
E-mail: jholzer@jhsph.edu
World Wide Web: http://www.sph.jhu.edu/Departments/HPM/

Johns Hopkins University

THE FACULTY AND THEIR RESEARCH

Donald M. Steinwachs, Ph.D., Chair of the Department.

Health and Public Policy. Susan P. Baker, M.P.H., Associate Chair.

Susan P. Baker, M.P.H., Professor. Injury epidemiology and prevention, aviation safety, occupational safety, injury severity measurement.
Thomas A. Burke, Ph.D., M.P.H., Associate Professor. Environmental health policy, risk assessment and communication, environmental epidemiology.
Ruth Faden, Ph.D., M.P.H., Professor. Public health ethics; ethical, psychological, and social issues in health policy; risk perception and protective behavior.
Mark Farfel, Sc.D., Associate Professor. Lead poisoning, community-based interventions.
Lawrence Gostin, J.D., Professor. Health law.
Nancy Kass, Sc.D., Associate Professor. Bioethics; AIDS reproduction decision making, insurance, genetics, and public policy.
Thomas LaVeist, Ph.D., Associate Professor. Social determinants of mortality and morbidity, comparative health and aging, minority health, life course studies.
Robert Lawrence, M.D., Professor. Evidence-based decision rules for prevention policy, assessing risk for health-damaging and health-promoting behaviors.
Vicente Navarro, M.D., D.M.S.A., Dr.P.H., Professor. Health and social policy, international health, health-care policy.
Thomas Oliver, Ph.D., Assistant Professor. Political science, evolution of Medicare policy, Medicaid reform.
Leiyu Shi, Dr.P.H., M.B.A., Associate Professor. Primary care, managed care.
Edyth H. Schoenrich, M.D., M.P.H., Professor. Public health administration, program planning, implementation of planned change, services to the chronically ill and aging.
Gordon Smith, M.B., CHP, M.P.H., Associate Professor. Epidemiology and control of injuries, alcohol/drugs and relationship to injury, injuries in developing countries, trauma.
Barbara Starfield, M.D., M.P.H., University Distinguished Service Professor. Evaluation of health-care organization, practice, and quality; primary care; child and adolescent health status measurement; child health policy.
Stephen P. Teret, J.D., M.P.H., Professor. Public health law and injury control.
Nga Lien Tran, Dr.P.H., M.P.H., M.B.A., Assistant Scientist. Environmental policy analysis, risk assessment.
Jon S. Vernick, J.D., M.P.H., Assistant Professor. Injury control, gun policy, public health law, motor vehicle injuries.
Daniel Webster, Sc.D., M.P.H., Assistant Professor. Violence prevention, gun policy, public health advocacy, evaluation.

Health Services Research. Gerard Anderson, Ph.D., Associate Chair.

Gerard F. Anderson, Ph.D., Professor. Health care/finance, outcomes research, comparative health insurance systems, technology assessment.
Charles D. Flagle, Dr.Eng., Professor Emeritus. Health systems analysis, evaluation, planning.
Christopher Forrest, Ph.D., M.D., Assistant Professor. Referral-consultation process, primary-care services research, methods for assessing child health outcomes, managed care, practice-based research, child health policy.
Kevin Frick, Ph.D., M.A., Assistant Professor. Health insurance, managed-care coverage decisions, cost-effectiveness analysis, economics of prevention.
Pearl German, Sc.D., Professor Emerita. Organization of health-care services for the elderly, drug patterns among elderly, health status and independent functioning among the elderly.
Judith Kasper, Ph.D., Associate Professor. Health policy in long-term care, disability and disease in older women, expenditures/access to care for vulnerable populations.
Monroe Lerner, Ph.D., Professor Emeritus. Health status indices and measurements.
C. Alan Lyles, Sc.D., M.P.H., Assistant Professor. Outcomes research on the use of pharmaceuticals, access, cost and appropriateness of use of health-care services.
Ellen J. MacKenzie, Ph.D., Professor. Emergency medical services and trauma care evaluation, epidemiology of injuries, health status measurement, rehabilitation.
Laura Morlock, Ph.D., Professor. Health-care organization and management, medical liability and risk management.
Anne W. Riley, Ph.D., Assistant Professor. Psychosocial factors in health-care utilization, detection of mental disorder in general medical/pediatric settings, health services outcomes measurement.
David S. Salkever, Ph.D., Professor. Health economics, mental health economics, disability studies.
Sam Shapiro, B.S., Professor Emeritus. Health services evaluation, organization of services, quality of care.
Eric P. Slade, Ph.D., Assistant Professor. Health economics, economics of work injuries and disabilities, economics of children's mental health.
Donald M. Steinwachs, Ph.D., Professor. Health services evaluation, health manpower, primary care, hospital payment systems, determinants of utilization, management information systems.
William J. Ward Jr., M.B.A., Associate Scientist. Health-care accounting and finance, hospital organization and management, facilities planning and design.
Jonathan P. Weiner, Dr.P.H., Professor. HMOs/managed care, ambulatory/primary-care health services research and evaluation methods, quality of care, workforce planning.
Albert Wu, M.D., M.P.H., Associate Professor. Health status measurement, outcome measurement in AIDS, effectiveness in treatments for HIV disease, physician error and iatrogenic illness.

Social and Behavioral Sciences. Debra Roter, Dr.P.H., Associate Chair.

Janice Bowie, Ph.D., M.P.H., Assistant Professor. Urban health, community health education.
M. Harvey Brenner, Ph.D., Professor. Effects of social and economic changes on morbidity, mortality, and health services utilization.
Barbara Curbow, Ph.D., Associate Professor. Social psychology of health and illness, quality of life, job stress, persuasive communications.
Margaret E. Ensminger, Ph.D., Associate Professor. Life-span development and health, childhood and adolescence, social structure and health, substance use, aggressive and violent behavior.
Andrea Gielen, Sc.D., Associate Professor. Behavioral science and health education strategies for injury prevention, women's health, issues of HIV/AIDS and violence.
Jeffrey V. Johnson, Ph.D., Associate Professor. Psychosocial work environment and health, social epidemiology of chronic disease, sociology of work.
D. Lawrence Kincaid, Ph.D., Associate Scientist. Communications research, family planning, evaluation research.
Carl Latkin, Ph.D., Associate Scientist. Risk behaviors for HIV acquisition and transmission.
Suezanne T. Orr, Ph.D., Associate Professor. Psychosocial aspects of maternal and child health, low birth rate and preterm delivery, well child care, depressive symptoms among women.
Debra Roter, Dr.P.H., Professor. Analysis of patient-provider communication, health education and health promotion, CME training.
Lawrence Wissow, M.D., M.P.H., Associate Professor. Patient-provider communication, especially as it relates to disclosure of sensitive psychosocial issues and family violence; cultural and developmental differences in disclosure; Native Americans and children.

THE OHIO STATE UNIVERSITY

College of Medicine and Public Health, School of Public Health
Division of Health Services Management and Policy

Program of Study

The Division of Health Services Management and Policy offers the Master of Health Administration degree. Graduates move directly into careers in management and policy analysis in health-care facilities (including hospitals, nursing homes, and clinics), management services and consulting, insurance, comprehensive financing and delivery organizations (HMOs, etc.), regulatory agencies, public health-care programs, and a variety of other settings. The program is accredited by the Accrediting Commission on Education for Health Services Administration.

The 84-credit-hour program requires two academic years of full-time study. Beyond the required core courses, students may pursue individual areas of concentration through course work or research. Most students choose to develop a specialization either around functional lines (such as finance, strategic planning, or marketing) or in an area of application (such as gerontology and long-term care). Unique areas of specialization may be developed, with faculty permission, by drawing from many other departments and colleges of the University. Faculty members are actively engaged in research and welcome student participation.

Paid administrative residency opportunities between the first and second year of course work are available throughout the nation. Preceptors, faculty, and students mutually arrange placement in these positions to blend career and location interests.

Formal dual-degree programs are available with the College of Medicine and Public Health (M.H.A./M.D.), the College of Business (M.H.A./M.B.A.), the College of Law (M.H.A./J.D.), the School of Public Policy and Management (M.H.A./M.P.A.), and the College of Nursing (M.H.A./M.S.N.), reducing the time necessary to receive both degrees. Other combinations may be arranged on an individual basis.

Research Facilities

The University Libraries system contains more than 4 million volumes and provides a full range of services for classwork and research. The University provides students with access to several mainframe computers as well as microcomputer laboratories with a variety of equipment. Students in the graduate program have access to a special departmental microcomputer resource area to assist in research and course work. Free workshops are offered for those who wish to expand their knowledge of computing.

Financial Aid

There are four primary resources for financial aid for students: University Fellowships, Graduate Enrichment Fellowships for members of underrepresented groups, U.S. Public Health Service Traineeships, and Divisional Scholarships. Applicants who express an interest in financial aid are automatically considered for all these sources. Many students work part-time in local health service organizations, as research associates to faculty members, or in other University positions.

Cost of Study

Instructional and general fees for full-time study were $5214 for Ohio residents and $13,500 for nonresidents for the nine-month 1997–98 academic year. All fees are subject to change.

Living and Housing Costs

University graduate student housing is available, with many options for single and married students; a typical dormitory and meal arrangement for a single student costs approximately $5000 for the academic year. Off-campus housing in a wide variety of styles and prices is easily available within walking or driving distance of the campus.

Student Group

The program admits approximately 25 students each year from varied academic, regional, and professional backgrounds. The class usually includes individuals directly out of college as well as experienced managers, physicians, lawyers, and other professionals. Opportunities for women and members of minority groups in health services management are excellent.

Student Outcomes

According to recent surveys, new graduates have had impressive success in career placement, with 90 percent reporting that they were able to get their first-choice job. Recent graduates are working for organizations such as hospitals and integrated health-care delivery systems, academic medical centers, consulting firms, public agencies responsible for health services, and a variety of related settings, such as insurance and long-term care.

Location

The Columbus metropolitan area (population more than 1 million) has a wide variety of health institutions and agencies that work closely with the graduate program. The state capital, Columbus, is a large city with headquarters for many major corporations, thriving programs in the arts, and entertainment and recreation of all kinds.

The University and The Program

One of the foremost centers of graduate and professional education in the nation, Ohio State excels in the breadth and depth of its resources. On the same campus are all the typical liberal arts departments and a full complement of professional schools.

The program is located within the College of Medicine and Public Health/University Hospitals complex, immediately adjacent to the central campus. Required courses are taken in the College of Medicine and Public Health, and elective courses are available in many departments. Faculty members with health-related interests can be found in departments all over campus.

Applying

Admission is highly competitive. The program seeks applicants who can demonstrate both the academic potential to succeed in a rigorous curriculum and the maturity to succeed in a demanding professional career. Each application is reviewed by the faculty, and the most promising applicants are invited for an interview. There is a $30 fee for domestic applications; a $40 fee is charged for international applications.

Students are admitted once a year to begin study in the autumn quarter. All applicants must complete either the GMAT or the GRE General Test. Applications must be completed by January 15 to be eligible for all sources of financial aid. The overall application deadline is March 15.

Correspondence and Information

Admissions Coordinator
Division of Health Services Management and Policy
SAMP Building, Room 246
The Ohio State University
1583 Perry Street
Columbus, Ohio 43210-1234
Telephone: 614-292-9708
E-mail: hsmp@osu.edu

The Ohio State University

THE FACULTY AND THEIR RESEARCH

Stephen F. Loebs, Associate Professor and Chairman of the Division of Health Services Management and Policy; Ph.D., Michigan. Health-care organization, health-care policy and politics, alternative delivery systems. Principal investigator for comprehensive study of health-care costs in Ohio. Research interests include the development of alternative delivery systems and models of consumer choice of health-care plans. Has served as chairman of the board of a health maintenance organization and of the Association of University Programs in Health Administration.

Robert J. Caswell, Associate Professor of Health Services Management and Policy; Ph.D., Michigan. Economics of health and medical care, business forecasting. Has published on a range of topics such as the economics of medical residency training, forecasting in medical records administration, and the cost of nursing home services. Special interests include regulation and measures of market structure in the health-care industry. Current research includes studies of Medicaid, access problems, and competition in hospital markets.

William O. Cleverley, Professor of Health Services Management and Policy; Ph.D., Berkeley. Health-care financial management. Former senior editor for the journal *Topics in Health Care Financing* and author of three leading textbooks and numerous articles in health-care financial management. Special interest in measurement of performance by health-care firms and prediction of performance using financial variables. Director of the Center for Healthcare Industry Performance Studies, a nationwide financial analysis system for the health-care industry.

Timothy S. Jost, Professor of Law and of Health Services Management and Policy; J.D., Chicago. Administrative law and regulation, quality assurance. Recipient of a Fulbright award to study regulation of health care in European countries. Coauthor of a leading casebook on health law, as well as numerous articles and book chapters dealing with legal issues in health care. Special interests include quality assurance and enforcement in the nursing home industry and private regulation of health care, such as the Joint Commission on Accreditation of Healthcare Organizations.

Dev S. Pathak, Merrell Dow Professor of Pharmaceutical Administration and Professor of Health Services Management and Policy; Ph.D., Michigan State. Health-care marketing management, pharmacoeconomics, economic evaluation of health practices. Research interests include total quality management, marketing professional services, and utility analysis of health programs.

Sharon B. Schweikhart, Assistant Professor of Health Services Management and Policy; Ph.D., Minnesota. Operations management, management science. Research interests include health-care operations, quality management and improvement, service operations, and location decisions. Has published articles in *Decision Sciences* and the *Journal of Operations Management*. Current research includes facility location and design decisions, service recovery in health-care organizations, and total quality management programs.

Sandra Tanenbaum, Assistant Professor of Health Services Management and Policy; Ph.D., MIT. Health policy and politics. Publications on disability, social policy, and Medicaid. Current research interests include kinship and aging policy, history of the Medicaid program, and physician decision making. Author of *Engineering Disability: Public Policy and Compensatory Technology* (Temple).

PENNSTATE

PENNSYLVANIA STATE UNIVERSITY

College of Health and Human Development

Programs of Study

Penn State's College of Health and Human Development is unlike any other college in the country. It is the first to combine the study of health and the prevention of illness with the study of human development through the life span. Graduate degrees are available in eight programs: Biobehavioral Health; Communication Disorders; Health Policy and Administration; Hotel, Restaurant, and Institutional Management; Human Development and Family Studies; Kinesiology; Leisure Studies; and Nursing. In addition, the College is the home of an intercollege graduate program in Nutrition; College faculty members also participate in the Genetics graduate program. The College has many distinguished faculty members who are carrying out research on a wide range of issues such as child language development, cardiovascular disease, diabetes, vitamin metabolism, aging, leisure behavior, health-care cost containment and quality improvement, human locomotion, exercise, genetic basis of behavior, role of attitudes and education in treating AIDS, and effects of day care on children's development.

The College's faculty members were involved in externally funded projects that generated $16 million in funding last year. Some of the projects included Empowering People who Stutter, A Treatment Program; Dietetic Technician Program for WIC Paraprofessionals, Otitis Media; Behavior and Attention in Daycare; Vitamin A Nutritional Status and Immune Function; Defining Comfort for the Improvement of Nursing Care; Fluid Ability Training Among Elderly; Impact of Prospective Drug Use Review on Health Outcomes; Origins of Variance in the Old-Old-Octogenarian Twins; Insulin and Protein Synthesis after Resistance Exercise; Gene Mapping for Quantitative Traits; Movement Dynamic Analysis of Akathisia; and Posture in the Neuropathic Diabetic Elderly and Center for Study of Prevention Through Innovative Methods.

Research Facilities

The College has several research centers, clinics, institutes, and laboratories, including the Center for Locomotion Studies, the Prevention Research Center for the Promotion of Human Development, the Center for Developmental and Health Genetics, the Methodology Center, the Center for Special Populations and Health, the Gerontology Center, and the Noll Physiological Research Center. In addition, the College collaborates with the College of Medicine and with the Department of Intercollegiate Athletics to support the Center for Sports Medicine. Among the University's other major resources are libraries and computer centers for instruction and research.

Financial Aid

Financial support other than loans is provided for 64 percent of the College's full-time students and 41 percent of its part-time students. Students may apply for grants, loans, fellowships, scholarships, assistantships, veterans' benefits, traineeships, instructorships, resident assistant positions, and work-study positions. Teaching and research assistantships offer students a stipend and a grant-in-aid for tuition. Employment is also possible at the University and in the community. Financial aid application deadlines vary, but in general it is best to apply by February 1 for the next academic year. Information can be obtained from each department or from the Graduate School Information Center, Pennsylvania State University, 113 Kern Graduate Building, University Park, Pennsylvania 16802-3300.

Cost of Study

Tuition for 12 or more credits was $3151 per semester for Pennsylvania residents and $6490 for non-Pennsylvanians for the 1997–98 academic year. Tuition for fewer than 12 credits per semester was calculated at $266 per credit for Pennsylvanians and $541 for non-Pennsylvanians. Students are also charged a $75 computer fee and a $25 activity fee.

Living and Housing Costs

The cost of living at the University Park Campus and in surrounding areas is moderate. The University offers on-campus apartments as well as dormitory rooms. Dormitory residents may purchase meal plans ranging in price from about $1035 to $1290 per semester. On-campus housing rates range from about $1075 to $1285 per semester. For those who prefer off-campus housing, private homes and apartment complexes in the area offer accommodations at a wide range of prices.

Student Group

More than 500 graduate students are enrolled in the College; 67 percent are women, 14 percent are international, and 7 percent belong to minority groups.

Student Outcomes

Graduates enter such diverse fields as rehabilitation; work-site health promotion; public- and private-sector human services, including day care and employee assistance programs; health-care administration; nursing specialties; park and recreation planning; nutrition science and education; physiology; private practice; consulting; research; education; speech-language pathology; and audiology. The College helps prepare students for research, teaching, managerial, and policy roles in a variety of settings, including the health care field, government agencies, universities, and large and small corporations. Graduates work in hospitals, rehabilitation centers, long-term care facilities, or research laboratories. Some work in human service agencies, health organizations, or insurance companies. Others work in the food and pharmaceutical industries, while others work in restaurants, hotels, resorts, and parks.

Location

State College, in the middle of an area of more than 100,000 residents, is the major cultural center of central Pennsylvania. The town has a collegiate atmosphere and is within a 5-hour drive of New York; Washington, D.C.; and Philadelphia. There is bus and air commuting service to all major cities. The University and the community sponsor cultural, athletic, professional, and scholarly events. There are excellent recreational opportunities on campus and in the surrounding open countryside and mountain forests.

The University and The College

Founded in 1855, Penn State is Pennsylvania's land-grant university. It is a major research institution and a member of the Association of American Universities. The University enrolls approximately 10,500 graduate students. Most of the graduate programs are offered at the University Park Campus.

The College of Health and Human Development is the first in the country to take a comprehensive approach to the health, development, and well-being of individuals and families. Several of its programs are among the oldest of their type and are consistently ranked among the nation's best. Many of its faculty members are internationally renowned.

Applying

For admission to a graduate program, applicants must have a baccalaureate degree and must submit transcripts of all prior college work. Applicants also must meet department requirements for course work in specific fields and for the minimum grade point average. Most departments also require letters of recommendation, a statement of the applicant's research and career interests, and scores from the Graduate Record Examinations or an approved equivalent test.

Correspondence and Information

Information about a particular graduate program may be obtained by contacting that program directly. Information can also be obtained by accessing the College's Web site or by e-mail (addresses listed below).

Herberta Lundegren, Senior Associate Dean—Academic Studies
201 Henderson Building
Pennsylvania State University
University Park, Pennsylvania 16802-6501
Telephone: 814-865-1427
E-mail: health@psu.edu
World Wide Web: http://www.hhdev.psu.edu

Pennsylvania State University

GRADUATE PROGRAMS AND PROGRAM HEADS

GRADUATE PROGRAMS OF THE COLLEGE OF HEALTH AND HUMAN DEVELOPMENT

Biobehavioral Health (Ph.D.): Dr. John Graham, Professor-in-Charge of the Graduate Program; 315 Health and Human Development Building East. This program helps prepare students to focus on how biological, behavioral, sociocultural, and environmental variables interact to influence health in individuals as well as groups. Because the level of health often is a product of variables that interact, understanding effective interventions may require combinations of biological, behavioral, sociocultural, and environmental strategies. Scholars and professionals who can bring this integrated perspective to their work are needed in research, teaching, and policy roles in a variety of settings, including the health-care field, research laboratories, government agencies, universities, and medical schools. Students should contact Shannon Seiner (telephone: 814-863-7256; e-mail: sls9@psu.edu) for more information. World Wide Web: http://bbh.hhdev.psu.edu

Communication Disorders (M.S., Ph.D.): Dr. Gordon W. Blood, Department Head; 122 Moore Building (telephone: 814-865-0971). The program prepares professionals to work with people who have a communication disorder. Program requirements emphasize a clinical research approach to speech-language pathology and audiology. The M.S. program is accredited by the Educational Standards Board, and the Speech and Hearing Clinic is accredited by the Professional Service Board of the American Speech-Language-Hearing Association. Settings for student training and research include therapy and diagnostic services in the in-house Speech and Hearing Clinic and laboratories in speech science, audiology, speech/language pathology, assistive devices (technology transfer), and environmental acoustics. Most M.S. graduates take positions in health-related settings such as clinics, hospitals, and rehabilitation centers; others work in schools. Ph.D. graduates work in universities, hospitals, and rehabilitation centers. A growing number of graduates enter private practice. World Wide Web: http://www.hhdev.psu.edu/cmdis/cmdis.htm

Health Policy and Administration (M.B.A./M.H.A., M.S., Ph.D.): Dr. Larry Gamm (M.B.A./M.H.A.) and Dr. Diane Brannon (M.S., Ph.D.), Professors-in-Charge; 116 Henderson Building (telephone: 814-863-5421). The M.H.A. program is offered concurrently with the M.B.A. (the M.B.A. is offered through the Smeal College of Business Administration) as a two-year course of study. The M.H.A. is accredited by the Accrediting Commission on Education in Health Services Administration with a combined credit requirement of 63 credits, including an intervening summer course and internship experience. The M.B.A./M.H.A. concurrent degrees program prepares students for management positions in hospitals, health systems, multigroup practices, nursing homes, managed care organizations, health insurance companies, consulting firms, and government health organizations. The M.S. in health policy and administration is a 41-credit program that provides research training for individuals to provide research support for the types of organizations listed above. The Ph.D. degree provides advanced training in health services research, with disciplinary foundations in economics and organizational theory. The department works closely on interdisciplinary projects with faculty members throughout the University, including faculty members in the Center for Health Policy Research and the Gerontology Center. World Wide Web: http://www.hhdev.psu.edu/hpa/hpa.htm

Hotel, Restaurant, and Institutional Management (M.H.R.I.M., M.S., Ph.D.): Dr. Rick Andrew, Professor-in-Charge of the Graduate Program; 201 Mateer Building (telephone: 814-863-0272). This program prepares students for executive, research, or educational roles in the hospitality industry or academic institutions. The program emphasizes the design and management of services related to providing lodging and food in both the private and public sectors. The M.H.R.I.M. degree emphasizes advanced hospitality management theory and cutting edge applications to the hospitality industry. The M.S. and Ph.D. degrees are focused on conceptual and research issues in the field of hospitality management. Students entering the program are expected to have at least two years of experience in a relevant field. World Wide Web: http://www.hrrm.psu.edu

Human Development and Family Studies (Ph.D.): Dr. David Eggebeen, Professor-in-Charge of the Graduate Program; 110 Henderson Building South (telephone: 814-863-0241). Students in this interdisciplinary program are trained to design and conduct research that advances knowledge about individual and family development. Interventions that promote healthy development are an additional focus of research. The program takes a life-span perspective on development in infancy, childhood, adolescence, adulthood, and old age. Understanding the familial, cultural, and community context of development is integral to this perspective. Ph.D. graduates of the program are research scientists, educators, and administrators of agencies and programs. HDFS faculty are affiliated with four centers that promote research and graduate training: the Prevention Research Center for the Promotion of Human Development, Child Development Laboratory, Gerontology Center, and Methodology Center. World Wide Web: http://www.psu.edu/dept/HDFS

Kinesiology (M.S., Ph.D.): Graduate Program Director; 146 Recreation Building (telephone: 814-863-0847; e-mail: alb1@psu.edu). The program offers four areas of specialization: biomechanics and locomotion studies, exercise physiology, history and philosophy of sport, and motor behavior. All areas stress research and the completion of a scholarly thesis under the direction of a faculty adviser. Graduates pursue careers in academia and private industry. The Biomechanics and Motor Behavior Laboratories are based in the department. Students also have access to the College's Noll Physiological Research Center and to the Center for Locomotion Studies. World Wide Web: http://www.hhdev.psu.edu/kines/kines.htm

Leisure Studies (M.S., M.Ed., Ph.D.): Dr. Linda Caldwell, Professor-in-Charge of the Graduate Program; 201 Mateer Building (telephone: 814-863-8983). This program prepares students for careers in administration, research, and teaching. Students work in the community, including public park and recreation systems, voluntary agencies, and private commercial enterprises; in therapeutic settings; and in park planning, interpretive services, outdoor education, and outdoor recreation. The program emphasizes research in leisure behavior, with concentration on field application and innovative approaches and practices in recreation and leisure services. This program is administered by the School of Hotel, Restaurant, and Recreation Management, which also houses the Center for Hospitality, Recreation and Tourism Outreach and Research, and is affiliated with the Shaver's Creek Environmental Center. World Wide Web: http://www.hrrm.psu.edu

Nursing (M.S.): Dr. Frieda M. Holt, Interim Associate Director for Graduate Programs; 203 Health and Human Development East Building (telephone: 814-863-2211). The graduate program of the School of Nursing has four options that prepare nurses for advanced practice as family nurse practitioners, neonatal nurse practitioners, adult/older adult clinical nurse specialists, or community health clinical nurse specialists. All options can be completed in four semesters of full-time study or as individually planned in part-time study. Post-master's study is available for the nurse practitioner options. The program combines advanced knowledge and nursing research with input from a rich multidisciplinary environment and emphasizes advanced practice in rural and medically underserved communities. Graduates serve in hospitals, clinics, and community and other health-care delivery settings. A doctoral minor in nursing is available, and the faculty is currently planning a doctoral program. World Wide Web: http://www.hhdev.psu.edu/nurs/nurs.htm

INTERCOLLEGE GRADUATE PROGRAMS BASED IN THE COLLEGE OF HEALTH AND HUMAN DEVELOPMENT

Nutrition (M.Ed., M.S., Ph.D.): Dr. John A. Milner, Department Head; 126 Henderson Building South (telephone: 814-863-0772). This program offers four emphases: nutrition science, applied human and animal nutrition, nutrition education, and nutrition in public health. Faculty from Health and Human Development, Agriculture, and other units participate in the program. Facilities include well-equipped nutrition science laboratories; the Nutrition Clinic, providing experience and research in nutrition counseling skills; and the Nutrition Center, where nutrition education programs and materials are developed, evaluated, and disseminated. Collaboration with faculty in the College of Medicine also provides additional opportunities for clinical research. Graduates of the program work in the food, fitness, and pharmaceutical industries; government and community-based projects; and teaching and research. World Wide Web: http://www.nutrition.hhdev.psu.edu

PENNSYLVANIA STATE UNIVERSITY GREAT VALLEY SCHOOL OF GRADUATE PROFESSIONAL STUDIES

Graduate Study in Health Care Administration

Programs of Study

Graduate Study in Health Care Administration is offered through the Department of Business and Management and is designed to prepare professionals for administrative, management, and leadership positions in the health-care field. These interdisciplinary programs include an M.B.A. degree program in health-care administration and a post-master's Certificate of Advanced Study in Health Policy and Administration.

A major strength of these programs is the integration of study in business and management from a health-care-industry perspective. The programs emphasize the development of solid expertise in a wide array of skills required for executive management positions. Course work focuses on business methods, procedures, and techniques in finance, accounting, marketing, economics, computing, statistics, strategy development, and managerial communications, among other areas. Case studies and applications link these management tools to the health-care industry. Elective courses address industry-specific topics, such as clinical outcomes research and management, diversity leadership in health-care organizations, quality assessment, health services reimbursement, and health services information systems.

Students are prepared for management positions in a variety of organizations, including hospitals, HMOs, long-term-care facilities, pharmaceutical and biopharmaceutical firms, health insurance and health information systems firms, regulatory agencies, rehabilitation services, accounting and law firms, and trade associations.

The master's degree requires the completion of 42 credits of course work and can be completed in about three years on a part-time basis. Post-master's certificate programs can be completed in one year and are for physicians and other professionals who already hold a master's, Ph.D., or related advanced degree and want to upgrade or expand their knowledge.

Research Facilities

The Computer Center provides laboratories and classroom networks of more than 150 Pentium-class and Macintosh microcomputer workstations. These are connected to the campus's Local Area Network (LAN) and the University's Wide Area Network (WAN), which allows student access to the Internet and the World Wide Web. Students have e-mail accounts and dial-up access to facilitate the remote use of University-wide computer resources, libraries, and the World Wide Web.

The library has more than 24,000 books; 360 current professional, trade, and popular periodicals; and a collection of government publications, microfiche, CD-ROMs, and books on audiotape. The Great Valley library is part of Penn State's University Libraries system, a nationally leading library system with more than 4 million cataloged volumes, 1.4 million government publications, and 32,000 current journals and serials, plus a number of informational materials in various formats, from maps to microforms. Students can access materials at all Big Ten university libraries, other national research centers, and the Tri-State College Library Cooperative, which includes the library resources of more than thirty colleges in the Philadelphia area.

Financial Aid

Financial assistance at Penn State Great Valley exists in the form of scholarships, grants, Federal Stafford Student Loans, graduate research assistantships, a minority fellowship, and Federal Work-Study. For more information, students should contact the Financial Aid Office at Great Valley. Many students receive tuition reimbursement from their employers.

Cost of Study

Part-time tuition for 1998–99 is $343 per graduate semester credit for Pennsylvania residents. Tuition for non-Pennsylvania residents is $611 per graduate semester credit. Books and supplies cost approximately $80 per course. An administrative computing fee, charged to all students in the fall and spring, is based on the number of credits taken in a semester and averages $50 per semester.

Living and Housing Costs

Most graduate students are enrolled at Penn State Great Valley on a part-time basis and take evening or Saturday courses. They live and are employed in the greater Philadelphia region.

Student Group

More than 500 part-time students at Great Valley pursue graduate study in health-care administration and business and management. They have a wide range of experience, and many hold advanced degrees in areas of clinical specialization. A typical health-care class includes practicing physicians; managers of clinical and operational areas; nurse supervisors, clinicians, and allied health professionals; and reimbursement, finance, accounting, and information specialists. They enroll to keep up with technological challenges, build academic credentials to advance their careers, and redirect their career paths into emerging fields.

Location

The campus is situated in the Great Valley Corporate Center, along the Philadelphia region's high-technology corridor. The campus is the nation's first university facility that is permanently housed in a corporate park, sitting shoulder to shoulder with world-class companies.

The University and The School

Penn State Great Valley is one of twenty-five campuses of Pennsylvania State University, an internationally known teaching and research university. The University's programs in health and human development and business administration are consistently ranked among the nation's best.

Since its inception in 1988, interdisciplinary graduate study in business, management, and health-care administration has grown rapidly.

Penn State Great Valley is designed specifically for adult learners. To meet the needs of working adults, most courses meet in seven-week sessions. This allows students to take one course at a time and complete two courses each semester. Students may complete as many as five graduate courses (15 credits) in one year and earn their degree in about three years on a part-time basis. Evening or Saturday classes enable students to maintain full-time professional positions.

Applying

Applicants must hold a bachelor's degree from a regionally accredited U.S. institution or a comparable degree from a recognized college or university outside the United States.

New students are admitted in the beginning of the fall or spring semesters. To apply, students must submit an application, a $40 application fee, two official transcripts from each institution attended, a current resume, two recommendation forms, a statement of career objectives, and GMAT scores. TOEFL scores of at least 550 are required of international applicants. Individuals with a broad undergraduate background may apply.

Correspondence and Information

Admissions Office
Pennsylvania State University Great Valley School of Graduate Professional Studies
30 East Swedesford Road
Malvern, Pennsylvania 19355
Telephone: 610-648-3248
Fax: 610-889-1334
E-mail: gvmba@psu.edu
World Wide Web: http://www.gv.psu.edu

Pennsylvania State University Great Valley School of Graduate Professional Studies

THE FACULTY AND THEIR RESEARCH

Faculty members are drawn from diverse disciplines and reflect the program's interdisciplinary approach to effective health-care administration and leadership.

Janice L. Dreachslin, Associate Professor of Health Policy and Administration; Ph.D., Wayne State. Management implications of workforce diversity and comparative health systems.
David J. Fritzsche, Professor of Management and Organization and Academic Division Head; D.B.A., Indiana. Role of business ethics in strategy, values, and ethics in decision making, strategic management, and business policy.
Veronica M. Godshalk, Assistant Professor of Management and Organization; Ph.D., Drexel. Career management, mentoring, stress, intersection of work and nonwork domains, organizational behavior and change, communication skills.
Xiaohua Lin, Assistant Professor of Marketing; Ph.D., Oklahoma State. International marketing strategies, management of strategic alliances, cross-cultural consumer behavior, business-to-business marketing.
Effy Oz, Associate Professor of Management Science and Information Systems; Ph.D., Boston University. Strategic information systems, ethical issues in information technology, impact of information technology on decision making, management of information technology.
Denise Potosky, Assistant Professor of Management and Organization; Ph.D., Rutgers. Individual differences and measurement, human-computer interaction, development of computer expertise in organizations, selection and training functions in organizations, organizational communications.
Hindupur V. Ramakrishna, Associate Professor of Management Science and Information Systems; Ph.D., Georgia State. Management of information systems, problem solving, managerial statistics, development and management of small businesses.
I. Donald Snook, Senior Lecturer; Ph.D., Pennsylvania. Hospital management, hospital marketing.
John J. Sosik, Assistant Professor of Management and Organization; Ph.D., SUNY at Binghamton. Transformational/charismatic leadership, computer-assisted work groups/teams, creativity, organizational behavior, managerial and financial accounting.
Joan Scattone Spira, Assistant Professor of Marketing; Ph.D., NYU. Cognitive structure underlying consumers' brand attitudes, attitude strength and its influence on information processing, persuasion, and marketing management.
Eric W. Stein, Associate Professor of Management Science and Information Systems; Ph.D., Pennsylvania. Organizational memory and learning, human expertise, application of artificial intelligence to business problems, software entrepreneurship.
Roger C. Vergin, Professor of Business Administration; Ph.D., Minnesota. Entrepreneurship, operations management.
Premal P. Vora, Assistant Professor of Finance; Ph.D., Penn State. Optimal financial contracts, capital structure, leasing, tax-deferred investing, finance.

Affiliate and Adjunct Faculty

J. Brian Adams, Ph.D., Delaware. Statistics.
Kathleen Anderson, Ed.D., Widener. Communications.
Rocco Ballerini, Ph.D., Colorado State. Statistics.
George Benscoter, Ph.D., Penn State. Human resources.
Brian Bower, Ph.D., Oklahoma. Management, MIS, business environment.
Albert S. Camardella, M.B.A., LaSalle. International business.
John Cameron, J.D., Widener. Health-care law, business law.
Dean Croushore, Ph.D., Ohio State. Economics.
Refik Culpan, Ph.D., NYU. Strategic management.
Janet Duck, Ph.D., Penn State. Communications.
Michael Fitzgerald, M.P.S., Cornell. Communications, human resources management.
Kerry Go, Ph.D., Rice. Statistics.
Robert Hancox, Ph.D., Pace. Management, marketing.
Sharon Hellwig, Ed.D., Columbia. Health care.
Mahmond Kaboudan, Ph.D., West Virginia. Economics, statistics.
M. S. Khalil, M.S., Temple. Statistics.
Robert Kokat, Ph.D., Indiana. Marketing, statistics.
Patrick Lee, Ph.D., Carnegie Mellon. MIS.
John Mason, Ph.D., Michigan State. Economics, finance.
Ali Naggar, Ph.D., Oklahoma. Accounting.
Tahany Naggar, Ph.D., Oklahoma. Statistics, economics.
Albert Olenzak, Ph.D., Princeton. Human resources.
Louis J. Petriello, J.D., Widener. Accounting.
Edward M. Quinn, M.B.A., Rutgers. Health-care finance.
Jeffrey C. Rinehart, Ph.D., Penn State. Management, human resources, business environment.
Nicholas Rongione, Ph.D., NYU. Business environment.
Michael Rudolph, M.B.A., Philadelphia College of Textiles and Science. Health care.
Stephen Thorpe, Ed.D., Delaware. MIS.
Robert Vito, M.B.A., Widener. Accounting.

QUINNIPIAC COLLEGE

Master of Health Administration Program

Programs of Study

The Master of Health Administration (M.H.A.) degree program at Quinnipiac College offers both qualified active practitioners and new career entrants the opportunity to improve their theoretical and practical knowledge and acquire the professional techniques needed to assume positions of greater responsibility in health services administration. Two concentrations are offered: general health services administration and long-term-care administration (nursing home administration). Students interested in nursing home administration may also choose a nondegree certificate program. A dual-degree program that confers the J.D./M.H.A. is also offered in conjunction with the School of Law.

The program in health administration provides students with the background and skills needed to assume management positions in hospitals, health maintenance organizations, group practices, and in other organizations concerned with health-care needs, such as those that handle employee benefits and health insurance. Graduates are well versed in federal regulations and policy and are familiar with the ever-widening range of health providers. Students gain a view of the health-care industry from the inside out through internships with local organizations such as Planned Parenthood, United Way, Pfizer, Aetna, Blue Cross/Blue Shield, Bayer, Prudential, Travelers', and CIGNA and through residencies in hospitals and nursing homes.

Quinnipiac is one of the largest health administration centers in the Northeast corridor between New York City and Boston. The College has integrated its programs with community health-care facilities through its clinical affiliations and its professional associations. Courses are taught by faculty members who hold advanced degrees and who have extensive professional experience in health services administration.

Quinnipiac is addressing the changing needs of health-care providers. Because of the rapid changes in the country's health-care system, medical practitioners are finding that they need to know more about the business side of health care. Quinnipiac's health administration program, combined with the College's expertise in entrepreneurship, offers doctors and other health-care providers an opportunity to acquire the skills they need to manage their own businesses.

The general curriculum consists of four components. The first is prerequisite courses (9 credit hours). These may be waived if evidence is provided of completion of appropriate undergraduate work in the subject matter or if a waiver examination is passed. The second component comprises the business core courses (12 credit hours). The third component of the curriculum encompasses specific health management courses geared to each concentration (27 credit hours). The fourth is the residency or the consulting practicum portion of the program. The residency in general health services administration (500 clock hours, 6 credit hours) involves an internship in either a general acute-care hospital or a health maintenance organization setting. Other facilities may be used with the permission of the program director. The consulting practicum consists of a group of students working with a faculty member in an actual consulting engagement to solve real problems for a health organization. In lieu of this requirement, students may pursue two additional electives and a comprehensive examination, with permission of the program director.

Research Facilities

The Quinnipiac College Library features a growing collection of health-care administration journals and related periodicals as well as a wide collection of health sciences publications. For those publications not available on campus, interlibrary loan and document delivery service are provided. There are several full-text databases on line, including LEXIS-NEXIS.

Financial Aid

Several avenues are available to help both full- and part-time students fund their education. Students may be eligible for Federal Stafford Student Loans. Graduate assistantships are available on a limited basis to both full- and part-time students.

Cost of Study

In 1998–99, the tuition rate is $395 per credit hour. Part-time students pay a $20 registration fee each semester. Full-time students are charged a student fee of $185 each semester. The College offers a variety of payment plans, including deferred payment and installment programs, and coordinates employer reimbursement programs.

Living and Housing Costs

On-campus housing is available during the summer. Privately owned housing is available near the campus. For more information concerning off-campus housing, interested students should contact the Office of Residential Life at 203-281-8666.

Student Group

There are 22 full- and part-time students enrolled in the M.H.A. program.

Location

Quinnipiac is located on a beautiful campus in Hamden, Connecticut, a suburb of New Haven. It is 30 minutes from Hartford, 1½ hours from New York City, and 2 hours from Boston.

The College

Quinnipiac enrolls 3,310 full-time undergraduates and approximately 1,300 graduate students. The College comprises the Schools of Health Sciences, Business, Law, and Liberal Arts and the College for Adults. A dean, reporting to the Provost/Vice President for Academic Affairs, heads each of these units, and a distinguished faculty of 170 full-time members and nearly 100 adjunct members provides instruction for the programs of the College.

Applying

Applications for this program are accepted on a rolling basis for fall, spring, and summer. Admission is selective, but there is no entering class limit.

Applicants to the M.H.A. program need to submit their GMAT score, bachelor's degree transcripts, recommendations, and a resume as well as their application. An interview with the Chair of the M.H.A. Program faculty graduate admissions committee, either in person or by telephone, is also required.

Correspondence and Information

Office of Graduate Admissions
Quinnipiac College
275 Mount Carmel Avenue
Hamden, Connecticut 06518

Telephone: 203-281-8672
800-462-1944 (toll-free)
Fax: 203-287-5238
E-mail: qcgradadmi@quinnipiac.edu

Quinnipiac College

THE FACULTY AND THEIR RESEARCH

Ramón Castellblanch, Chair; M.P.P., Harvard; Ph.D., Johns Hopkins. Group purchasing of health care, health-care regulation and legislation.
James Marshall, M.B.A., Wisconsin; Ph.D., Arizona State. Health-care informatics, marketing.
Ronald Rozett, M.P.H., M.D., Harvard. Management of health-care professionals, quality management in health care.
Teresa Tai, Ph.D., Texas A&M. Health services research, international health, management of health-care professionals.

R·I·T

ROCHESTER INSTITUTE OF TECHNOLOGY

Program in Health Systems Administration

Program of Study

The Master of Science degree in health systems administration is a flexible distance learning program designed to meet the needs and demands of professionals who desire a degree specific to the health-care field. Employing a leading-edge, systems approach, the program capitalizes on RIT's experience and skill in delivering creative academic offerings using technology. In addition, students benefit from faculty experience with the resources found in Rochester, New York, which has received national recognition for its low-cost, community-wide health-care programs.

The curriculum is centered on business management (tailored to health systems professionals), total quality, computer technology, and health systems planning and issues. Courses link themes, including ethics and social responsibility, systems perspective, communication skills, managing change, quality, and computer literacy. The degree requires 57 quarter credit hours and can be completed in less than two years, with only three to five days on campus each year. Teaching methods include computer networking, video lectures and seminars, audiotaped lectures and discussions, and teleconferences. An internship is required for students who have less than three years of professional experience in a health-care or health-related organization or business environment.

Courses follow the same eleven-week quarter periods as on-campus classes. Distance learning frees students from commuting to campus and allows them to schedule classes around work and family. Although the program is designed to be completed at a rate of two courses per quarter, students may elect to participate in just one course at a time.

Research Facilities

The Wallace Library is a combination of electronic networks and quality staff coupled with a modern, accessible multimedia facility. The library houses more than 350,000 books, 4,700 journals, 2,300 audio recordings, 4,800 film and video recordings, and 380,000 microforms. It offers group study rooms and seating for 1,000. The online infoNet menu provides 24-hour access to the Internet, Einstein (Wallace's holdings), CD-ROM products, and interlibrary loan and book requests. VIA (the VAX Internet Area) provides graphic interface workstations, image scanning, and interactive CD titles.

Additional supporting features include extensive research and laboratory facilities for imaging science and engineering (CAE/CAD, vibrations, dynamic systems, fluid flow), the Mason E. Westcott Laboratory for statistics, the W. A. Weiss Book Testing Laboratory, the American Airlines Sabre Laboratory, the VAX/VMS and VAX/Ultrix (UNIX) computer systems and microcomputers, and a networked laboratory of AT&T minicomputers, microcomputers, and workstations, which is dedicated to graduate computer science students. Most RIT colleges have specialized computing facilities for their students. Computers, systems, and terminals are networked for in-house and worldwide access via the BITNET network.

Financial Aid

Graduate teaching and research assistantships, externally funded stipends, and scholarships are available and may be held concurrently. Further information on assistantships and stipends can be obtained from the appropriate department chairperson. Scholarship applications may be submitted to the department head.

In 1998–99, RIT graduate scholarships are offered in all colleges. New York State residents who are full-time students may apply for TAP awards that range from $75 to $550. Students may also apply for federal financial aid by completing the Free Application for Federal Student Aid (FAFSA) and having the results sent to RIT.

Cost of Study

In 1997–98, the cost of full-time study (12–18 credit hours) was $6018 per quarter. Those taking more than 18 credit hours paid the rate for full-time study plus $507 per credit hour for each hour of study exceeding 18. Full-time students were required to pay a nonrefundable Student Association Fee of $42 per quarter. The cost of part-time study (11 credit hours or fewer) was $507 per credit hour. The rate for those on graduate internships was $290 per hour.

Living and Housing Costs

The Center for Residence Life (716-475-2572 or 716-475-2113 TTY) handles assignments for university-operated residence halls and more than 960 campus apartment units. Apartment rents begin at $543 per month for one-bedroom units for the academic year; reduced summer rates are available. In addition, there are several large local apartment complexes and individual living quarters within a short distance of the campus. Students electing to live off campus may need their own transportation. Further information regarding off-campus accommodations and roommates may be obtained from the Housing Connection Office at 716-475-2575 or 716-475-7721 TTY.

Student Group

The total enrollment at the Institute is 12,933. Enrollment in the graduate degree programs is 1,800.

Location

RIT's campus in suburban Rochester occupies 400 acres on a 1,300-acre site and is located close to the cultural and entertainment attractions of Rochester. Gallery and museum exhibits, a philharmonic orchestra, and theaters are located in metropolitan Rochester.

The Institute

RIT is accredited by the Middle States Association of Colleges and Schools and the New York State Board of Regents. It is a privately endowed, nonsectarian institution of higher education. RIT has been a pioneer in professional and career development programs since its founding in 1829. Its principal task is preparing men and women with the knowledge, skills, and attitudes required for technological, managerial, and aesthetic competence. It strives to assist them to mature as perceptive, skilled, and incisive professionals. The hallmark of the graduate programs is diversity. Each program is built as a freestanding unit and is designed to fill a specific demand in a given field. The thrust of the graduate programs is toward state-of-the-art technology and business, as well as the aesthetic areas of the fine arts, photography, printing, and the science of psychology.

Applying

Applicants are considered without regard to race, color, national origin, sex, age, handicap, or veteran's status. Each graduate program has its own requirements for acceptance, and a description of these may be obtained by writing to the appropriate department chairperson or graduate coordinator.

Admission application forms and graduate catalogs may be obtained from the Office of Admissions.

Correspondence and Information

Dr. William W. Walence, Chair
Health Systems Administration
Center for Multidisciplinary Studies
Rochester Institute of Technology
31 Lomb Memorial Drive
Rochester, New York 14623-5603
Telephone: 716-475-7359
Fax: 716-475-5595
E-mail: wwwcad@rit.edu

Rochester Institute of Technology

THE FACULTY

William W. Walence, Associate Professor and Program Chair, Health Systems Administration, Ph.D.
Thomas McCaffery, Associate Professor, J.D., M.H.A.

Adjunct Faculty
Richard Cowen, M.B.A., Health Care Consultant, Rochester, New York.
Christopher Davis, M.D., Physician, Rochester, New York.
Reese Davis, M.S., Director, Education and Health Promotion, Blue Cross and Blue Shield of Rochester.
James Fatula, Ph.D., Consultant, Health Care Management, Rochester, New York.
Arnold S. Gissin, M.P.H., Administrator, Jewish Home of Rochester.
Katherine Hiltunen, M.B.A., B.S.N., Director, QM/UM Analysis, Blue Cross and Blue Shield of Rochester.
Patricia Houghton, M.H.A., CPHQ–Administrative Director of Quality, Rochester General Hospital; RN.
Michael O'Connor, M.S., Executive Director, Rochester Community Individual Practice Association.
Larry A. Rice, M.P.H., RMS Associates, Rochester, New York.
Michael Tarcinale, Ph.D., Vice President, Randamax, Inc., Rochester, New York; RN.
Arthur G. Tweet, Ph.D., Consultant, CQI Associates, Rochester, New York.
Beverly Voos, M.S., President and Chief Executive Officer, Rochester Health Care Information Group, Rochester, New York.

RIT, a pioneer of distance learning education, has been offering innovative courses using electronic forms of communication for nearly twenty years.

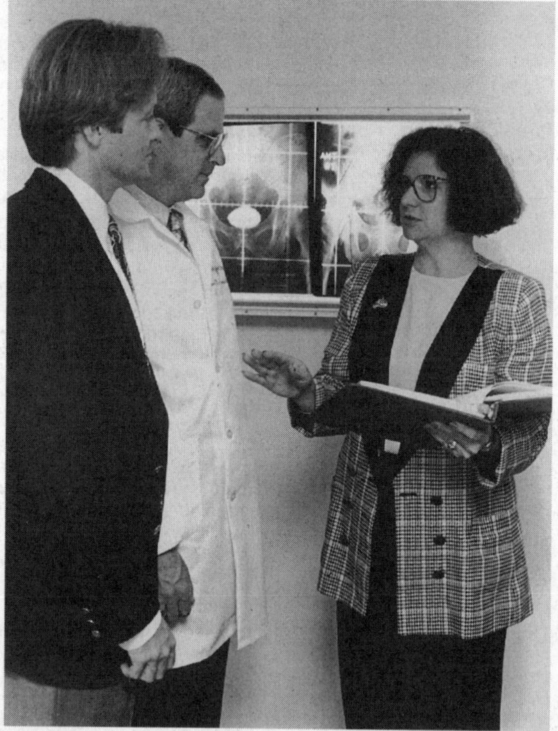

RIT's M.S. degree in health systems administration, offered through distance learning, features a systems approach to understanding complex health-care issues.

RUSH

RUSH UNIVERSITY

Department of Health Systems Management

Program of Study

The Graduate Program in Health Systems Management at Rush University offers an applied study experience in the environment of a major health system. Rush–Presbyterian–St. Luke's Medical Center is one of the most advanced, vertically integrated multi-institutional systems in the United States. Faculty members are practicing professionals who combine teaching and research with responsibilities for administration, management consulting, finance, law, human resources, and information systems. By virtue of their concurrent management responsibilities, the faculty bring a special understanding to the classroom and a practical perspective to the entire academic process. This synthesis produces graduates with highly marketable management skills.

The program is predominantly offered on a full-time basis and is a two-year course of study leading to a Master of Science degree. A part-time option is available on a limited basis. The curriculum consists of a series of well-integrated learning sequences that focus on the development of health-care management professionals with an emphasis upon the development of analytical and quantitative skills. The curriculum represents a comprehensive array of studies in organizational behavior, information systems, finance, quantitative methods, human resources management, health law, planning, and marketing related to the management of health-care organizations.

Students have opportunities for employment within the health-care system while enrolled in the program. Most of the first-year students are employed at Rush for the academic year. Students also receive assistance from the Placement Committee in finding a work experience for the summer quarter between the first and second years of the program. Students have been employed in a variety of organizations including St. Thomas Hospital in London, Deloitte and Touche, the American Hospital Association, Henry Ford Medical Center, and the Joint Commission on the Accreditation of Hospital Organizations. Employment opportunities continue into the second year of academic study, allowing the students to benefit from three different employment experiences.

The health systems management program at Rush University is accredited by the Accrediting Commission on Education for Health Services Administration (ACEHSA).

Research Facilities

The Rush University Library is one of the oldest in Chicago. Its collection includes more than 137,193 total volumes, a rare book collection, and more than 1,989 periodicals. It acquires new monographs and reference books at the rate of more than 4,000 a year. The Center for Health Management Studies is involved in the conduct of applied research in the health-care industry. Research findings are shared with health systems management students, faculty, and practicing managers through seminars, presentations, and publications. As a result, the student is well prepared to deal with the health-care industry as it exists today and as it will change in the future.

Financial Aid

Traineeships and scholarships are available for selected full-time students. The Rush University Financial Aid Office provides assistance for all admitted students in need, so that Rush University can be a viable choice for all who desire to attend. Students are given the opportunity for employment within the health-care system while enrolled in the program.

Cost of Study

Tuition for the 1998–99 academic year is $12,720 per year or $370 per credit.

Living and Housing Costs

The student living on campus should allow $950 per month for rent, food, transportation, and personal expenses. The student living off campus should allow $1100 per month.

Student Group

The program matriculates about 15 students a year. The entering students have varied backgrounds. Many have had full-time work experience before entering the program.

Student Outcomes

Graduates of the program possess a highly marketable set of management skills; the majority take positions in hospitals, hospital-based systems, consulting firms, and ambulatory health-care organizations or pursue further study in postgraduate fellowships. Health systems management graduates are working in health care throughout the nation.

Location

Rush University is located at Rush–Presbyterian–St. Luke's Medical Center on Chicago's Near West Side. Facilities on campus include Rush University, the academic component, with some 1,300 students and 3,000 faculty members; Presbyterian–St. Luke's Hospital, a 903-bed major referral center; and the Johnston R. Bowman Health Center for the Elderly, with 176 beds. Easily accessible by rapid transit, which has stops on campus, are the Loop (downtown Chicago) and the western suburbs, both 15 minutes away. Lake Michigan is nearby, and sports and numerous cultural activities are available in the exciting Chicago area.

The University

Rush University includes the College of Health Sciences, the Graduate College, the College of Nursing, and Rush Medical College. Because the University believes that education of health professionals is best achieved in an institution committed to both education and service, all faculty members are teacher-practitioners.

Applying

The program accepts students for the fall term only. All applicants must have a baccalaureate degree from an accredited institution and should have completed basic course work in accounting and statistics. Candidates for the program should submit the completed application form, official transcripts from all colleges and universities attended, scores on the GRE or GMAT, and three letters of recommendation. International students should take the TOEFL prior to applying.

Correspondence and Information

Department of Health Systems Management
Rush University
1700 West Van Buren
TOB 126
Chicago, Illinois 60612
Telephone: 312-942-5402
Fax: 312-942-4957
E-mail: rushhsm@hsmsun.tob.rpslmc.edu
World Wide Web: http://www.rushu.rush.edu/hsm

Rush University

THE FACULTY

James Frankenbach, M.B.A., Assistant Professor, Chairman of the Department of Health Systems Management, and Senior Vice President of Corporate and Hospital Affairs.
John E. Trufant, Ed.D., Associate Professor, Vice President of Academic Resources, Dean of the College of Health Sciences, and Dean of the Graduate College.
Gerald Glandon, Ph.D., Associate Professor, Program Director of the Department of Health Systems Management, and Associate Director of the Center for Health Management Studies.
Max D. Brown, J.D., Associate Professor and Vice President of Legal Affairs.
Laurel Burton, Th.D., Professor and Chairperson of Religion, Health and Human Values.
Bruce Campbell, Dr.P.H., Associate Professor and President of the Illinois Masonic Medical Center.
Leslie Compere, M.S., Instructor and Program Coordinator of the Department of Health Systems Management.
Anthony Cutilletta, M.D., Assistant Professor and Medical Director of Rush Children's Heart Center.
Thomas Cutting, M.B.A., Instructor and Assistant Vice President of Finance.
Andrew Davis, M.D., Assistant Professor and Associate Medical Director of Rush Prudential Health Plans.
Paula Douglass, M.A., Assistant Professor and Associate Vice President of Corporate Planning.
Rebecca Dowling, Ph.D., Assistant Professor and Assistant Vice President of Support Services.
G. Thomas Ferguson, M.P.H., Assistant Professor and Assistant Vice President of Human Resources.
Trudy Gardner, Ph.D., Assistant Professor, Assistant Dean for Educational Resources/Director of Rush Library.
Mary Gregoire, Ph.D., Professor and Associate Director of Food and Nutrition.
Bradley Hinrichs, M.M., Assistant Professor and Assistant Vice President and Administrator of Surgical Hospital.
Catherine Jacobson, Instructor and Associate Vice President of Program Evaluation.
Michael Kearns, M.B.A., Instructor and Vice President of Marketing of Rush System for Health.
Barbara Kovel, M.M., Assistant Professor and Assistant Vice President of Corporate Finance.
Christopher Leeds, M.B.A., Assistant Professor and Project Director of the Department of Health Systems Management.
Ryan Meade, J.D., Assistant Professor and General Counsel of Katten, Muchin and Zavis.
Avery Miller, Instructor and Senior Vice President of Corporate and External Affairs.
Dennis Millirons, M.S., Assistant Professor, President and CEO of Riverside Medical Center.
Kevin Necas, M.B.A., Assistant Professor and Vice President of Finance.
Donald R. Oder, M.B.A., Professor Emeritus.
Richard Odwazny, M.S., M.B.A., Assistant Professor and Assistant Vice President of Information Services.
Denise Oleske, Ph.D., Associate Professor and Research Associate of the Center for Health Management Studies.
Mayur Patel, M.S., Instructor and Partner for NextSource Consulting, Inc.
Paul Pierpaoli, M.S., Assistant Professor and Director of In-Patient Pharmacy.
Yvette Reiner, M.S., Instructor, Assistant Vice President of the Rush Cancer Institute and Administrator of Professional Affairs.
David Rice, J.D., Instructor and Associate General Counsel of Legal Affairs.
Dale Sietsema, M.B.A., Instructor and Associate Vice President of Health Care Finance.
Marie Sinioris, M.P.H., Professor, Corporate Vice President, and President and CEO of ArcVentures.
Patricia Skarulis, M.A., Assistant Professor, Vice President and Chief Information Officer.
Stacy Sochacki, M.S., Assistant Professor and Vice President of Administration at the Rush North Shore Medical Center.
Mari Terman, M.B.A., Assistant Professor and Director of Patient Access.
Lee Thompson, Ph.D., Assistant Professor and Information Center Consultant.
John Webb, M.A., Instructor and Director of Materials Management.
Vicki Wilson, M.P.H., Instructor and Assistant Vice President of Finance.
Karen Williams, Instructor and Director of Financial Services.

The Center for Health Management Studies

The Center for Health Management Studies was established in 1982 within the Department of Health Systems Management as the department's research division. The mission of the center is to advance knowledge in health-care management by conducting applied research in health-care organizations through collaborative efforts involving researchers from diverse disciplines, such as economics, epidemiology, finance, management science, marketing, medicine, nursing, organizational behavior, planning, and statistics/quantitative methods. Research and evaluation activities are primarily focused upon a select group of primary program areas: impacts of changes in health-care organization, delivery, and financing; assessment of clinical and managerial technology utilized by health-care organizations; aging and long-term care (in conjunction with the Center for Research on Healthy Aging); occupational health; and quality of health care. Research and evaluation projects conducted by the center staff members emphasize significant issues within the Rush System for Health.

SETON HALL UNIVERSITY

Center for Public Service
Healthcare Administration and
Health Policy and Management Programs

Programs of Study

The Center for Public Service offers a Master of Public Administration (M.P.A.) degree program with a concentration in health policy and management and a Master of Healthcare Administration (M.H.A.) degree program.

The M.P.A. program is designed for students who seek careers in public or nonprofit organizations that focus on health-care services and health policy. The program is accredited by the National Association of Schools of Public Affairs and Administration (NASPAA). Other M.P.A. concentrations are available in public service administration and policy, nonprofit organization management, criminal justice, and court administration. Students who wish to gain expertise in more than one concentration may select elective courses from any concentration area.

The M.H.A. program (offered both on campus and on line via the Internet) is designed for professionals who wish to advance in their management careers or individuals interested in a health-care management career. The degree prepares students to assume leadership positions in a variety of health-care organizations, including health-care systems, hospitals, long-term-care facilities, alternative delivery systems, ambulatory care facilities, planning agencies, the pharmaceutical industry, health-care insurance companies, managed-care corporations, health-care consulting firms, and private medical practices.

The M.H.A. online program allows the student to study "any time, any place." The twenty-month program centers on a learning team of 30 students who begin at the same time and then continue as "virtual classmates." Three weekend residencies are required. The online M.H.A. program is open to individuals with a minimum of five years of health-care management experience.

A 12-credit graduate certificate in health-care administration is also offered as well as certificates in nonprofit organization management and law and justice management.

The curriculum stresses the development of managerial and analytical skills, as well as ethical and professional values. All classes meet late afternoons, evenings, and on alternate Saturdays for the convenience of working students. To allow for study throughout the year, Wintersession and summer session courses are offered in addition to the fall and spring semester course offerings.

Research Facilities

A library opened in 1994 and houses 410,000 titles and 2,200 current periodicals. It is equipped with listening tables and more than 2,500 phonodiscs, a microform room with six reader/printers and microfilm reelers, and five copying machines. Personal computers are available for student use. Corrigan Hall houses the University Computer Center, which is supported by time-sharing and microcomputer terminals located throughout the campus.

In addition to its academic programs, the Center conducts applied public policy research and provides technical assistance to community-based organizations. The Center houses the Local Advisory Board for Healthcare Planning (LAB), which conducts applied research on community health issues. Students are given opportunities to participate in research projects and to gain hands-on management experience through a number of the Center's academic and technical assistance programs.

Financial Aid

Assistantships, scholarships, and federal financial aid are available to M.H.A. and M.P.A. students. A limited number of graduate assistantships are available for full-time students. Those who receive this assistance are normally assigned administrative and/or research duties in one of the University's offices for 20 hours per week in exchange for full tuition and a monthly stipend. Partial Goya Scholarships are available based on financial need and on a competitive basis to Hispanic students studying in the M.H.A. program or in any M.P.A. concentration area. Additional scholarship programs are available to those who presently work in or who are seeking careers in nonprofit organization management, including Nonprofit Management Scholarships, Reiner Scholarships, and Nonprofit Management and Leadership Opportunity Scholarships. Applications and information on assistantships and scholarships can be received from the Center for Public Service. Students interested in applying for federal financial aid should contact Seton Hall's Office of Enrollment Services (telephone: 973-761-9350).

Cost of Study

Graduate tuition for 1998–99 is $500 per semester hour. There is an additional registration fee of $85 per semester for part-time students and $105 per semester for full-time students.

Living and Housing Costs

Seton Hall offers graduate housing both on and off campus (in the village of South Orange). Also, the South Orange area provides a broad selection of private housing options. For information about University and private housing options, interested students should contact the Office of Housing and Residence Life (telephone: 973-761-9172).

Student Group

A student chapter of the American College of Healthcare Executives (ACHE) is housed at the Center, as is a chapter of the National Honor Society of Public Administration's Pi Alpha Alpha and the North Jersey Chapter of the American Society of Public Administration (ASPA).

Location

South Orange is situated about half an hour from Manhattan, where many distinguished libraries, museums, theaters, concert halls, and sports arenas are located. Areas for summer and winter sports are easily accessible.

The University

Founded in 1856, Seton Hall is a private coeducational Catholic institution—the first diocesan college in the United States. It is made up of the College of Arts and Sciences, the College of Education and Human Services, Stillman School of Business, the College of Nursing, Immaculate Conception Seminary School of Theology, the School of Graduate Medical Education, and the School of Law. The total enrollment is about 9,000. The main campus comprises 58 acres in the village of South Orange. Seton Hall is accredited by the Middle States Association of Colleges and Schools and holds additional accreditations by the National Council for Accreditation of Teacher Education, AACSB–The International Association for Management Education, National League for Nursing, and American Bar Association. The M.P.A. program is accredited by the National Association of Schools of Public Affairs and Administration.

Applying

Applicants must forward the following to the office of graduate admissions: a completed application with a $50 application fee, official transcripts from all colleges and universities attended, and scores on either the Graduate Record Examinations (GRE), Graduate Management Admission Test (GMAT), or Law School Admission Test (LSAT). These scores are only required of students who have completed their undergraduate work within the past five years. Three letters of reference concerning the applicant's work experience and academic performance, a letter of intent from the applicant describing career goals and reasons for applying to the M.P.A. program, and a current resume are also required.

Correspondence and Information

Christopher Gonzalez, Assistant Director of
Recruitment and Student Support Services
Center for Public Service
Seton Hall University
South Orange, New Jersey 07079

Telephone: 973-761-9510
Fax: 973-275-2463
E-mail: gonzalch@shu.edu
World Wide Web: http://www.shu.edu/~centerps/
http://www.setonworldwide.net (for information on the online M.H.A. program)

Seton Hall University

THE FACULTY AND THEIR RESEARCH

Philip S. DiSalvio, Associate Professor of Public Administration; Ed.D., Harvard. Public/nonprofit financial management, budgeting, management information systems, and health-care administration. Former Robert Wood Johnson Faculty Fellow in Healthcare Finance. Author of *Managing Computers and Information in Public and Health Care Organizations.*

Jonathan Engel, Assistant Professor of Public Administration; Ph.D, Yale. Research methods and health-care systems and policy. Former Research Analyst, Advisory Committee on Human Radiation Experiments, Washington, D.C.

William Kleintop, Assistant Professor of Public Administration; Ph.D., Temple. Computers, organizational theory, human resources, uses of information technology by local governments and nonprofit organizations.

Pamela J. Leland, Assistant Professor of Public Administration; Ph.D., Delaware. Nonprofit management and urban public policy. Research interests include issues in homelessness and affordable housing, charitable tax exemption at the state and local levels, and the dynamics between and among the public, private, and nonprofit sectors in the development of public policy.

Roseanne Mirabella, Assistant Professor of Public Administration and Director of Nonprofit Sector Resource Institute of New Jersey; Ph.D., NYU. Public policy, organization theory and behavior, and nonprofit management.

Naomi Bailin Wish, Professor of Public Administration, Chair of the Graduate Department of Public Administration, and Director of the Center for Public Service; Ph.D., Rutgers. Policy analysis, program evaluation, quantitative methods. Author of articles in *Public Administration Review, International Journal of Public Administration, American Journal of Economics and Sociology,* and the *Municipal Yearbook.*

John Abbott Worthley, University Professor of Public Administration; D.P.A., SUNY at Albany. Management information systems, budgets and finance, administrative ethics, health care. Author of more than twenty articles and four books, including *Managing Computers and Information in Public and Health Care Organizations* and *Zero-base Budgeting in State and Local Government.*

SIMMONS COLLEGE

Graduate School for Health Studies

Programs of Study

The Graduate School for Health Studies offers coeducational programs of study leading to the M.S. degree in health-care administration, nutrition and health promotion, primary health-care nursing, and physical therapy. A postbaccalaureate Dietetic Internship Program is also offered.

The graduate program in health-care administration prepares women and men for leadership in the management of effective, efficient, and equitable health services. The program is accredited by the Accrediting Commission on Education for Health Services Administration. The curriculum is designed so that students obtain the required knowledge and skills, apply critical-analytic thinking to the management of health services, bring ethical considerations to the decision-making process, and anticipate the health-care system of the future. Intensive learning experiences encourage students to share knowledge and experience. Classes are scheduled in the evening and are kept small to ensure that learning is interactive. The program also offers a Certificate of Advanced Graduate Study for individuals who hold advanced degrees in other fields.

The graduate nutrition program offers an M.S. degree in nutrition and health promotion and can be completed in one year of full-time study.

The graduate nursing program provides students with specialized education in primary health-care nursing and the foundation necessary for leadership, research, and doctoral study. The program is NLN-accredited and has seven nurse practitioner concentration options available: in adult primary care—adult, gerontologic, and occupational health; in parent-child primary care—pediatrics, school, or women's health; and family health. Two dual-degree programs exist with the Harvard School of Public Health, one in parent-child health and one in occupational health. Graduates receive a master's degree in primary health-care nursing from Simmons College and a Master of Science in maternal-child health or environmental-occupational health from the Harvard School of Public Health. A dual-degree program is also available in primary health-care nursing and health-care administration. Other study options include a master's degree program for currently practicing nurse practitioners; a nurse practitioner certificate program; and an R.N./M.S. program for nurses with diplomas or associate degrees. An off-site weekend college option is offered at the University of New England/Westbrook College in Portland, Maine.

The graduate program in physical therapy is an accredited, innovative, integrated, three-year, entry-level master's program. The curriculum is designed to educate men and women who can serve clients in a variety of settings and meet the challenges of today's evolving health-care system. Within the three years, students complete three 8-week clinical affiliations at a variety of sites across the country. Students are provided the option of completing a thesis under the guidance of a faculty member.

The Dietetic Internship Program is approved by the American Dietetic Association and is designed for students who hold a baccalaureate degree and meet the Didactic Program in Dietetics requirements of the association. Upon completion of the program, the student is expected to pass the Commission on Dietetic Registration examination.

Research Facilities

The Simmons College library system consists of Beatley Library, the main facility, as well as the libraries of the Graduate Schools of Management, Library and Information Science, and Social Work. The library system also includes a Media Center, a Microcomputer Laboratory, a state-of-the-art language laboratory, a Career Resource Library, and the College Archives. Comprehensive reference service, which includes interlibrary loans and computerized searching, is available at Beatley Library.

Financial Aid

College awards in the 1997–98 academic year included merit-based scholarships in some programs, Professional Nursing Traineeship Grants, and scholarships for minority students. Need-based financial aid, primarily grants, loans, scholarships, and work-study employment, is offered for qualified students. Aid is available on a prorated basis for students who enroll in at least 6 semester credit hours.

Cost of Study

Tuition for the 1998–99 academic year at the Graduate School for Health Studies is $587 per credit hour for all programs or $1761 per 3-credit course.

Living and Housing Costs

A single student should allow a nine-month budget of approximately $11,500 for housing, food, and moderate personal expenses if he or she plans to live off campus. Graduate students can be accommodated in residence halls. Residence charges for 1998–99, including room and board, are $8474 for the academic year. Summer housing is available.

Student Group

In fall 1997, the total enrollment at Simmons College was 3,480, including 2,243 graduate students. The Graduate School for Health Studies enrolled 500 students. All of the physical therapy students attend full-time, while most of the students in the health-care administration, graduate nursing, and graduate nutrition programs attend on a part-time basis. Simmons' graduate students are professionals who seek to enhance their knowledge and professional skills either to advance in their current professions or to change careers.

Location

Simmons College is located in the heart of the Longwood Medical area and is neighbor to notable medical institutions such as Beth Israel/Deaconess, Brigham and Women's, and Children's Hospitals. These and other health-care organizations provide excellent clinical and field study placements as well as career opportunities in health-related programs. Within a mile of the campus are the Museum of Fine Arts, the Gardner Museum, the Boston Public and Countway Medical libraries, Symphony Hall, and Fenway Park, all of which provide a rich context for both course work and leisure activities.

The College

Graduate education has been offered at Simmons since the founding of the College at the turn of the century. At the undergraduate level, Simmons is a women's college that embodies the principles of a liberal arts and sciences education combined with professional preparation. At the graduate level, Simmons is coeducational and is committed to preparing women and men for personal and professional growth. The graduate schools and programs have developed naturally from the mission of the College as well as from the strengths of its curriculum. In addition to the Graduate School for Health Studies, Simmons's graduate-level education includes the Graduate School of Library and Information Science, the Graduate School of Social Work, the Graduate School of Management, and nine Graduate Studies Programs administered through departments of the College.

Applying

The application deadline for the physical therapy program is February 1. Applications for the Dietetic Internship Program must be postmarked no later than February 15. Health-care administration, nursing, and nutrition program applications are accepted throughout the year. Admissions procedures, entry dates, and options for full-time and part-time study are described in the graduate school catalog.

Correspondence and Information

Graduate School for Health Studies
Simmons College
300 The Fenway
Boston, Massachusetts 02115

Telephone: 617-521-2650
Fax: 617-521-3137
E-mail: gshsadm@simmons.edu
World Wide Web: http://www.simmons.edu/programs/gshs

Simmons College

THE FACULTY

Harriet G. Tolpin, Dean; Ph.D., Boston College.

Health Care Administration
Linda Roemer, Director; Ph.D., Tufts.
John M. Lowe, Ph.D., Illinois at Chicago.
Leslie Pearlman, D.B.A., Boston University.
Alice Sapienza, D.B.A., Harvard.

Physical Therapy
Diane Jette, Director; D.Sc., Boston University; PT.
Shelley Goodgold-Edwards, D.Sc., Boston University; PT.
Deborah Heller, M.S., Boston University; PT.
Stephanie Johnson, M.B.A., Houston.
Regina Kaufman, M.S., MGH Institute of Health Professions; PT.
Steven Morrison, Ph.D., Penn State.
Elizabeth Ratcliffe, M.S., O.C.S., MGH Institute of Health Professions; PT.
Joanne Rivard, M.S., Boston University; PT.
Clare Safran, M.S., O.C.S., Boston University; PT.
Mary Slavin, Ph.D., Clark; PT.
Antoinette Tasker, O.C.S., Russell Sage; PT.

Primary Health Care Nursing
Carol Frazier-Love, Director; Ph.D., Cincinnati.
Judy Beal, D.N.Sc., Boston University.
Kimberly Boothby-Ballantyne, M.S., Simmons.
Rebecca Donohue, Ph.D., Rhode Island.
Susan Neary, Ph.D., Boston College.
Patricia Rissmiller, D.N.Sc., Boston University.
Beverly Rothfeld, M.S., Wisconsin.
Patricia White, M.S., Boston College.

Nutrition
Nancie Herbold, Director; Ed.D., Boston University; RD.
Kristy Hendricks, Ph.D., Boston University; RD.
Janet Lacey, Dr.P.H., North Carolina at Chapel Hill; RD.
Paul Taylor, Ph.D., Maine.

Simmons College is located in the heart of the Longwood Medical Area, neighbor to notable medical institutions.

TEMPLE UNIVERSITY

of the Commonwealth System of Higher Education

School of Business and Management
Program in Healthcare Management

Programs of Study

Temple University, with the oldest healthcare management program in the region, is accredited by both the AACSB–The International Association for Management Education and the Accrediting Commission on Education for Health Services (ACEHSA).

The basic M.B.A. program consists of nineteen courses and can be completed in two years. Business courses such as finance, accounting, and computer science give the student the management tools necessary to make decisions. An undergraduate degree or courses in business administration may allow the student to waive the basic courses. Minimum completion time is twelve months. Eight health-care courses are required, including accounting, epidemiology, finance, insurance and risk, law, marketing, operations, and planning and policy. The strong emphasis on finance and the integration of health-care courses in the M.B.A. are two of the strengths of the program. The student leaves the program prepared to assume management positions in HMOs, hospitals, consulting, ambulatory facilities, and long-term care. An M.S. program in healthcare financial management is also offered. A dual M.B.A./M.S. in healthcare financial management is available with one additional semester.

Temple is located in one of the largest and most innovative health-care markets in the United States. Students meet with the chief executive officer to learn hands-on, practical knowledge from the top executives in the field. A series of seminars is also offered featuring local, national, and international health-care leaders dealing with current issues. The residency is a paid work experience in a health-care setting that typically occurs between the first and second year. The department manages residency placement through its extensive network of cooperating agencies and facilities.

The support of the student does not end with graduation. The 700-plus Temple alumni have their own active Alumni Association, which is very helpful for job placement. In recent years, all graduates have been placed. In addition, a Job Bank is maintained by the program.

Research Facilities

Student have access to Temple's Paley library as well as the libraries of the other universities in the area. They also have access to excellent library facilities at Blue Cross and the College of Physicians. The department maintains its own bank of computers for exclusive use of Health Administration students, and students also have access to the University's mainframe computer, with worldwide access via all standard software.

Financial Aid

The Shirley Rock Scholarship, Alumni Endowment Scholarship, and USPHS funds, as well as the McGraw Scholarship, offered in conjunction with the AUPHA, make it possible to grant limited financial aid to those who demonstrate need and promise. With the exception of graduate assistants, students must be prepared to pay for their own personal living expenses with guaranteed loans, earnings, or savings. Financial aid decisions are made separately from admission, and early application is encouraged.

Cost of Study

Tuition for a 30-semester-hour academic year in 1997–98 was $9240 ($308 per hour) for Pennsylvania residents and $12,870 ($429 per hour) for nonresidents.

Living and Housing Costs

A student moving to Philadelphia should budget a minimum of $800 a month for books, transportation, and living expenses. Rent is very reasonable for a major city, and mass transit makes it convenient to live in the Center City, Queen Village, Germantown, or Chestnut Hill neighborhoods or in outlying areas in Montgomery County and southern New Jersey.

Student Group

Enrollment is limited to no more than 30 full-time admissions per year. There is a larger, part-time population that serves current professionals. The student body is diverse in age, experience, and ethnic background, and more than half are women. The active student association leads to a very cohesive group.

Student Outcomes

The program graduates about 40 students each year. Of that number, close to half have jobs prior to graduation. Many of these graduates are currently working in health care or have job offers related to their summer residencies. Within six months of graduation, close to 100 percent of graduates are placed, thanks to the School's Placement Office and strong alumni network. Most new entrants into health management are employed in consulting firms, integrated health delivery systems, hospitals, long-term care, community health, or physician practice management. These jobs are typically in program development or entrepreneurial enterprises and require strong teamwork skills.

Location

Temple's location in Philadelphia allows the student access to a range of health-care opportunities and to the richness of one of the largest, most historic and diverse cities in the United States.

The University

Temple has 30,000 students on its eight campuses, with more than 1,600 graduate business students attending classes at three campuses: Center City (16th and Walnut), suburban Ambler, and Main (2 miles north of City Hall). The departmental office is in Speakman Hall on the Main Campus.

Applying

Full-time students who are admitted only in the fall semester should apply by April 15 and have complete transcripts and test scores submitted by June 1. Part-time students may apply for any semester and may enroll for up to three courses on a nonmatriculated basis.

Correspondence and Information

Director of Admissions
Program in Healthcare Management
School of Business and Management
Temple University 006-00
Philadelphia, Pennsylvania 19122

Telephone: 215-204-8468
E-mail: dbsmith@astro.ocis.temple.edu
World Wide Web: http://www.sbm.temple.edu/hamba.htm

Temple University

THE FACULTY AND THEIR RESEARCH

William E. Aaronson, Associate Professor; Ph.D., Temple. Epidemiology, geriatrics and health services management.
Thomas E. Getzen, Professor and Director of Health Care Financial Management Program; Ph.D., Washington (Seattle). Health economics, finance, and forecasting.
Charles P. Hall Jr., Professor and Director of IMBA (International M.B.A.) Program in France, 1996–97; Ph.D., Pennsylvania; FACHE. Health economics, insurance, risk management and policy.
David Barton Smith, Program Director and Professor; Ph.D., Michigan. Medical-care organization, planning and information systems.
Michael A. Valenza, Assistant Professor; J.D., Temple. Malpractice, health-care law.
Jacqueline Zinn, Associate Professor; Ph.D., Pennsylvania (Wharton). Health-care systems, long-term care, business policy, organization and strategy.

Adjunct Faculty and Staff
H. Robert Cathcart, FACHE Administrator-in-Residence. Hospital administration.
Michael L. Dolfman, Adjunct Professor, Ph.D. Health-care marketing and planning.
Donald Friel, Adjunct Professor, M.B.A., CPA. Health-care accounting.
Soon W. Lee, Affiliate Professor, M.B.A., CPA, FHFMA. Health-care accounting, medicare reimbursement, tax compliance, reporting for nonprofit health-care institutions.
Robert M. Sigmond, Scholar-in-Residence, M.A. Community benefit standards, planning and administration.

Graduate classroom.

Meryle Stephanie Ostroff, Vice President of Episcopal Hospital.

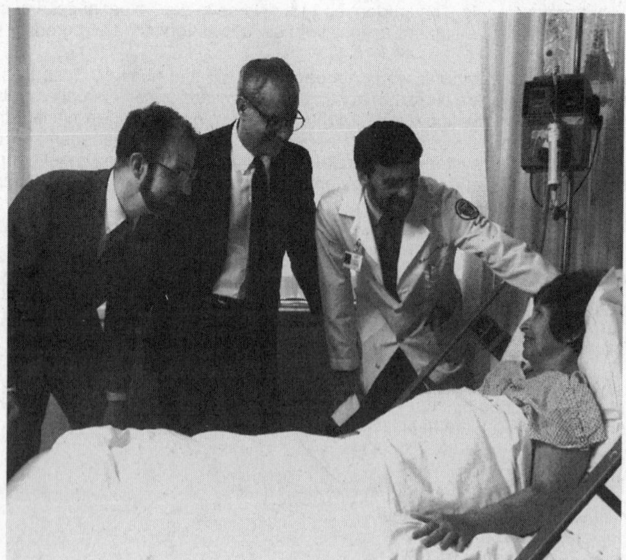

Faculty members discuss care with one of the patients in the Medical-Economic Rounds/Clinical Decision-Making course.

TRINITY UNIVERSITY

Department of Health Care Administration

Programs of Study

Trinity University offers two graduate programs leading to an M.S. in health-care administration. The faculty has designed the curriculum to provide the theoretical knowledge and practical skills necessary for leadership in health-care organizations and institutions, focusing on the interpersonal and organizational skills that facilitate critical thinking in the analysis and resolution of problems particular to the complex and competitive field of health-care management.

The On-Campus Program prepares students, through varied and comprehensive courses in health-care administration and the Administrative Residency, to make sound, informed professional decisions at the highest levels of the field. The full-time program consists of 51 semester hours: 45 hours of on-campus courses (usually requiring sixteen months—four semesters—for completion) and a stipend-supported residency carrying 6 hours of academic credit (usually completed in an additional twelve months). The Administrative Residency offers students the opportunity to balance administrative experience and education by applying theories and techniques learned through course work in a carefully selected health-care system setting. Students are guided in their residencies by an on-site experienced health-care administrator and by a faculty member from the Department of Health Care Administration.

The department also offers an Executive Program, which recognizes both the desire for further education among individuals currently working in health-care management positions and the importance and value of practical experience to professional education. This program is designed for individuals currently holding responsible positions in a health-care setting who are searching for a part-time distance learning experience. The core curriculum includes fourteen courses totaling 42 semester hours of graduate credit. Each semester begins with a three-day intensive on-campus session, followed by written assignments and regular telephone conferences. The Executive Program usually takes three years to complete.

Research Facilities

The Elizabeth Coates Maddux Library affords ample resources and space for graduate study. The growing holdings already number more than 1 million volumes of books and bound periodicals, in addition to microfilm collections, government documents, and audiovisual materials, and include a comprehensive collection in health-care administration. Graduate students also have access to specialized research collections in San Antonio and, through the interlibrary loan program, to facilities at such nearby institutions as the University of Texas at Austin and the University of Texas Health Science Center at San Antonio.

Trinity's Computer Center provides excellent support for graduate course work and research. Its resources include an IBM mainframe and four microcomputer laboratories. Graduate students have access to the Internet and letter-quality impact, laser, and color plotter printers. In addition, the department maintains a microcomputer for student use.

Financial Aid

Trinity University's Financial Aid and Business offices facilitate student applications for loans and deferred-payment plans. The department offers both graduate assistantships and traineeships to students enrolled in the On-Campus Program through University endowment funds and grants received from the U.S. Department of Health and Human Services. Most financial aid determinations are made on the basis of scholarship, financial need, and available funds. Executive Program students are encouraged to inquire about educational reimbursement that may be available through their current employer.

Cost of Study

The 1998–99 tuition is $607.50 per semester hour, or $7290 per semester, for full-time students. The activities fee for graduate students is $1 per semester hour.

Living and Housing Costs

Most graduate students live within a short driving distance of the campus. While the responsibility for securing housing rests with the student, the University Housing Office offers assistance whenever possible. Living expenses average $13,000 per year for a single student.

Student Group

The On-Campus and Executive programs can each admit approximately 25 students each year. The 1997–98 mean age for on-campus students was 23; 61 percent were women. Students enter this program with a variety of undergraduate degrees and health-care experience. The Executive Program attracts older students—the mean age was 41—from a wide range of geographical locations and health-care management positions. The department's active Alumni Association provides a support base and network for program graduates.

Student Outcomes

Trinity graduates have been highly successful at securing jobs at appropriate levels for their backgrounds. Many of Trinity's health-care administration program graduates begin their careers in operational management positions. Examples of job placements for recent graduates include hospitals, hospital systems, long-term care organizations, managed care organizations, medical group practice management, insurance organizations, and consulting firms.

Location

The San Antonio community is Texas's most historic metropolitan area and the nation's ninth-largest city. Its warm semitropical climate and historic charm have attracted many growth industries, including biomedical research. The Alamo, surrounded by downtown skyscrapers, stands near the popular San Antonio River Walk. In addition, the Gulf Coast beach, Texas hill country, and the colorful country of Mexico are only a short drive from Trinity's campus.

The University and The Department

Trinity is a private, highly selective institution that emphasizes undergraduate liberal arts and select M.S. programs in professional fields. The University was founded in 1869, but the Skyline Campus is only about 44 years old.

The graduate program in Health Care Administration admitted its first class in 1965. More than 1,100 alumni are now in key administrative roles in the health-care industry. The department has been accredited by the Accrediting Commission on Education for Health Services Administration (ACEHSA) since 1969.

Applying

All applicants must have a bachelor's degree from an accredited college or university; the degree may be in any undergraduate major. Applicants are required to take either the GRE General Test or the GMAT. Prerequisite courses include 3 hours of undergraduate credit in each of the fields of accounting, economics, and statistics. Applicants are evaluated on the basis of transcripts, standardized test scores, letters of recommendation, a résumé, a statement of purpose, and a required personal interview. Application for the fall should be made by June 1. Earlier applications for admission and departmental financial aid will be given priority.

Correspondence and Information

William C. McCaughrin, Ph.D.
Chair, Department of Health Care Administration
Trinity University
715 Stadium Drive
San Antonio, Texas 78212-7200

Telephone: 210-736-8107
Fax: 210-736-8108
E-mail: epitluk@trinity.edu

Trinity University

THE FACULTY AND THEIR RESEARCH

William C. McCaughrin, Associate Professor and Department Chair; Ph.D., Michigan. Organization theory and its uses in health services delivery, quality of care, individual and organizational decision making, health policy analysis.

Stephen L. Tucker, Professor; Fellow, American College of Healthcare Executives; D.B.A., George Washington. Strategic planning and marketing, institutional management. Extensive work with hospitals and multi-institutional health-care systems.

Mary E. Stefl, Professor and Dean, Division of Behavioral and Administrative Studies; 1991–92 Chairman of the Board of Directors, Association of University Programs in Health Administration; Ph.D., Cincinnati. Quality control management, managerial epidemiology, community health.

Ted R. Sparling, Associate Professor; Fellow, American College of Healthcare Executives; Dr.P.H., Texas. Management theory, strategic planning, human resource management, health-care ethics, managed care.

Murray J. Côté, Assistant Professor; Ph.D., Texas A&M. Stochastic modeling and performance measures of health care, nonlinear and integer programming, queuing networks.

James S. Hahn, Assistant Professor; Ph.D., Stanford. Economic evaluation of health-care programs, comparative analyses of health-care systems, health economics, and health-care financial management.

On-campus program students spend sixteen months completing course work followed by a twelve-month administrative residency.

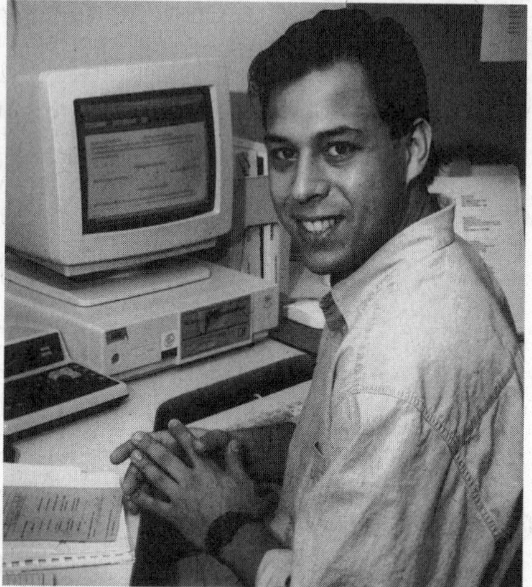

Trinity University has four microcomputer labs and a departmental microcomputer for graduate students to use. The computer facilities offer Internet access and letter-quality impact and laser and color plotter printers.

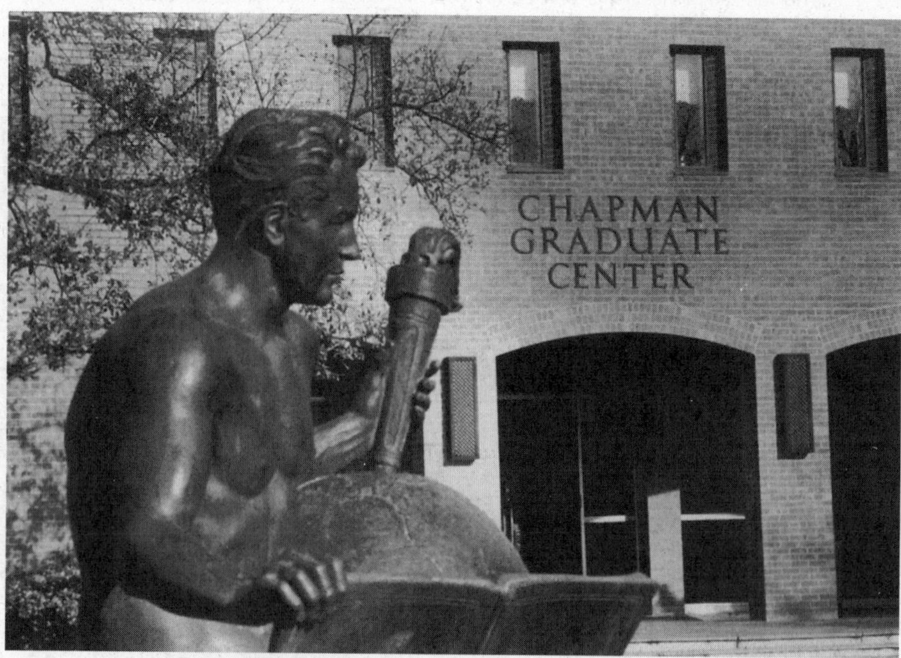

The Department of Health Care Administration is located on the fourth floor of Chapman Graduate Center.

TULANE UNIVERSITY

Department of Health Systems Management

Programs of Study

Tulane's Department of Health Systems Management prepares individuals for a broad range of management careers in health-care systems. The department is organized following a unique practitioner-educator model integrating the academic curriculum offered through the Tulane University School of Public Health and Tropical Medicine and the management practice environment of the local health-care market. The departmental degree programs include Master of Health Administration, Executive Master of Health Administration, Master of Business Administration/Master of Public Health, Juris Doctor/Master of Health Administration, Medical Doctor/Master of Public Health, Master of Medical Management, and Doctor of Public Health.

Tulane's M.H.A. program involves a 60-credit-hour curriculum. The management core and elective studies, which comprise 54 credit hours of the program, are complemented by 6 credit hours of administrative internship and residency experience. The M.H.A. curriculum is developed on the premise that effectiveness in health systems management requires the understanding of health and health systems in addition to business skills. The M.H.A. Policy Track provides students with the analytical skills necessary to conduct health policy analyses in both the public and private sectors. The curriculum is designed to develop a detailed understanding of major public and private health policy issues, the options available for addressing these issues, the potential solutions and their impacts, and practical concerns regarding their implementation. Applicants to the M.H.A. Policy Track should complete undergraduate courses in statistics and economics prior to enrollment. The Executive Master of Health Administration Program is a 50-credit-hour course of study following a rigorous twenty-six-month, nontraditional schedule of classes held every other weekend. Because Executive M.H.A. students are experienced health-care professionals, no residency is required. The Master of Public Health Program requires 36 credit hours of study with emphasis on the department's management curriculum. The curriculum consists of 20 credit hours of public health and management core courses, allowing for 16 credit hours of elective credits in health systems management. The M.B.A./M.P.H. program is offered jointly by Health Systems Management and the Tulane A. B. Freeman School of Business. It allows the exceptional student to earn both an M.B.A. and an M.P.H. in 91 semester hours in approximately three years. Tulane's joint J.D./M.H.A. program coordinates the curricula and faculties of the Tulane Law School and the School of Public Health and Tropical Medicine so that the joint degree can be obtained after completion of 126 semester hours in four academic years. The Joint M.D./M.P.H. program provides a strong management background for medical students. It requires 28 credit hours of study in the department's management curriculum pursued concurrently with Tulane Medical School studies. The M.M.M. program requires 36 credit hours in a distance learning format. The program is open to physicians who have completed the ACPE certificate program in medical management. Tulane's Dr.P.H. program provides graduates with the knowledge and credentials necessary for teaching at the university level and for careers in applied health services research. Students in the Dr.P.H. program must complete a minimum of 72 graduate credit hours and successfully defend a dissertation.

Research Facilities

The department's Institute for Health Services Research provides impartial research, technical assistance, and education for policy makers and other key members of the health-care community. The institute serves as a resource for these leaders to improve the health of the community and to refine the organization, financing, and delivery of health services. The institute serves as a forum for critical thinking and discussion of relevant health-care issues.

The Tulane University Medical Center Library has public health, clinical medicine, and basic science collections totaling more than 140,000 volumes and more than 1,000 medical and scientific journals. The library provides access to numerous online computer services and databases. Students also have access to Tulane University's nine libraries, which hold more than 7 million volumes and 16,000 periodicals. In addition, the department maintains a small library containing a collection of health administration and general management periodicals along with key reference materials.

The School of Public Health and Tropical Medicine maintains computer facilities that are available for graduate student use. The department maintains a personal computer laboratory for health systems management students, with computers that are linked to the University computer system.

Financial Aid

Most students finance their education through a combination of governmentally subsidized loans, scholarships, savings, part-time and summer employment, and family support. A complete packet of financial aid information is available through the Medical Center Financial Aid Office (telephone: 504-584-2962). Outstanding students in the Department of Health Systems Management compete for need- and merit-based scholarships. Most students in the M.H.A. program receive tuition scholarships for 8 credit hours and a summer stipend through the administrative residency placement.

Cost of Study

In the 1998–99 academic year, Tulane's School of Public Health and Tropical Medicine tuition is $390 per credit, and fees are $20 per credit. Tuition and fees are payable within thirty days of registration each semester. An activity fee of $208 per semester is also assessed to full-time students. These fees are subject to change.

Living and Housing Costs

The University provides space in an apartment complex that is located near the School of Public Health and Tropical Medicine. All units are furnished and air conditioned. Utilities are furnished except for a telephone, which must be individually arranged. Rent for one bedroom ranges from $650 per month for a private room to $490 per month for a bedroom within a two-bedroom, three-bedroom, or four-bedroom configuration.

Student Group

A baccalaureate degree is required for admission to all H.S.M. programs. The ages and work experience of H.S.M. students vary greatly. As a rule, however, new graduates comprise one third of students pursuing the full-time M.H.A., M.B.A./M.P.H., J.D./M.H.A., and M.D./M.P.H. programs.

Location

New Orleans is a city like no other. Its distinctive culture, cuisine, and musical heritage give New Orleans a flavor all its own. With a metropolitan population of more than 1 million people, New Orleans has also become a major medical center. The city is home to more than thirty-five hospitals, two medical schools, a dental school, and many ancillary services.

The University

Tulane University is one of the major research universities in the South. It includes eleven schools and colleges and enrolls more than 11,000 students, 4,600 of whom are graduate students. Tulane is one of the twenty-five most selective private universities in the nation.

Applying

Students wishing to pursue the nationally competitive, full-time M.H.A. and M.B.A./M.P.H. programs should note that all admissions are for the fall semester and that applicants are encouraged to submit all materials by March 1. Admissions to H.S.M. programs are approved by a department admissions committee. Applications for other H.S.M. programs are received throughout the year. A $40 application fee must be included with each application for admission.

Correspondence and Information

Department of Health Systems Management (SL-29)
School of Public Health and Tropical Medicine
Tulane University
1430 Tulane Avenue
New Orleans, Louisiana 70112
Telephone: 504-588-5429
Fax: 504-584-3783
E-mail: hsm@mailhost.tcs.tulane.edu

Tulane University

THE FACULTY AND THEIR RESEARCH

David J. Fine, M.H.A., Regents Professor and Chairman. Managed care, hospital efficiency and costs.
E. Gordon Whyte, Ph.D., Clinical Associate Professor, Vice Chairman, and Director, Master Programs. Strategic management, health-care marketing, long-term care.

Gail Bopp Agrawal, J.D., Clinical Associate Professor. Health law.
Lisa Amoss, M.B.A., Adjunct Instructor. Organizational behavior.
Roy M. Arnold, M.D., M.H.A., Clinical Assistant Professor. Outcomes management.
Doreen L. Babo, M.B.A., Dr.P.H., Clinical Assistant Professor. Clinical outcomes measurement, international health services.
Antonio Barrios, M.D., Adjunct Assistant Professor. International health-care management.
Peter J. Betts, M.H.A., Adjunct Instructor. Hospital administration.
Eugene Beyt, M.D., Clinical Associate Professor. Physician leadership.
Walter M. Burnett, Ph.D., Associate Professor. Strategic management, managed care, health policy.
Linda A. Burns, M.H.A., M.B.A., Clinical Assistant Professor. Ambulatory care.
Ann H. Butcher, Ph.D., Assistant Professor. Organizational theory and behavior, primary care, public health management.
Cielle Clemenceau, M.B.A., Clinical Instructor. Administrative residencies, career development.
Jaquetta B. Clemons, M.B.A., M.P.H., Adjunct Instructor. Accounting, finance.
Richard Culbertson, Ph.D., Associate Professor. Ethics, managed care, academic health centers.
Charlotte C. Cunliffe, M.B.A., M.P.H., Ph.D., Research Assistant Professor. International health.
Peter J. Fos, D.D.S., M.P.H., Ph.D., Associate Professor. Expert systems, decision modeling, negotiations, comparative health systems, managerial epidemiology.
Curtis Florence, Ph.D., Research Assistant Professor. Health-care economics and policy.
Donna D. Fraiche, J.D., Adjunct Assistant Professor. Health law.
Gary Frentz, M.D., Adjunct Professor. Clinical outcomes.
Jeffrey S. Friedman, M.P.H., Clinical Assistant Professor. Physician group practice management.
J. T. Hamrick, M.D., Professor. Community medicine.
Katherine Harris, Ph.D., Assistant Professor. Institute for Health Services Research.
Julia A. Hughes, M.B.A., Dr.P.H., Clinical Assistant Professor. Women's health services, executive education.
Charles N. Kahn III, M.P.H., Clinical Professor. Health policy analysis.
Timothy Keogh, Ph.D., Clinical Associate Professor. Management communication.
M. Mahmud Khan, Ph.D., Associate Professor. Behavior of health-care cost, comparative health systems, nutritional surveillance, health economics.
Joseph Kimbrell Jr., M.S.W., Adjunct Instructor. Public health administration.
Susan L. Krinsky, J.D., Lecturer. Health law, ethics.
Karen Lauterbach, Ph.D., Adjunct Assistant Professor. Organizational behavior and human resources.
John J. Lefante Jr., Ph.D., Adjunct Professor. Biostatistics and epidemiology.
Hugh W. Long, Ph.D., J.D., Associate Professor. Health-care financial management, physician executive administration.
William F. Martin, Psy.D., Clinical Assistant Professor. Organizational behavior, employee assistance, health-care management.
Ray G. Newman, Ph.D., Clinical Associate Professor. Finance, accounting.
Gregory M. St. L. O'Brien, Ph.D., Adjunct Professor. Organizational behavior.
Judith W. Overall, J.D., Clinical Assistant Professor. Long-term care, health policy analysis, health law, management.
Stephen Pickett, M.P.H., CPA, Adjunct Clinical Instructor. Hospital administration.
David R. Pitts, M.H.A., Clinical Professor. Health-care consultation.
Benjamin M. Pulimood, M.B.B.S., Adjunct Professor. International health services administration.
Dahlia Remler, D.Phil., Ph.D., Assistant Professor. Institute for Health Services Research.
Paul Rodenhauser, M.D., Adjunct Professor. Administrative psychiatry.
Alex B. Smith III, M.H.A., Ph.D., Adjunct Assistant Professor. Hospital administration.
Joni Steinberg, Ph.D., Clinical Associate Professor. Operation research.
Kenneth Thorpe, Ph.D., Professor and Director, Institute for Health Services Research, health policy analysis.
Vinod K. Thukral, Ph.D., Associate Professor. Health-care marketing, international health, health status and health education.
Margaret M. Van Bree, M.H.A., Dr.P.H., Clinical Assistant Professor. Health-care administration, quality management.
Neal Vanselow, M.D., Adjunct Professor. Health manpower and policy.
Subramanian Venkateswaran, Ph.D., Adjunct Professor. Operations research.
Stephen F. Verderber, Arch.D., Adjunct Associate Professor. Design of health-care facilities.
David J. Ward, M.H.S.A., Adjunct Instructor. Health services management, community health development.
Bryan Weiner, Ph.D., Assistant Professor. Organizational behavior.
Miguel Zuniga, M.D., M.H.A., Dr.P.H., Adjunct Associate Professor. Clinical outcomes measurement.

THE UNIVERSITY OF ALABAMA AT BIRMINGHAM

School of Health Related Professions
Department of Health Services Administration

Programs of Study

The Department of Health Services Administration offers a unique selection of three graduate programs in health services administration and health informatics. The mission of the department is to improve health administration practice through the acquisition, development, and dissemination of knowledge about the organization, financing, and delivery of health services.

The Ph.D. program in administration—health services is jointly sponsored by the Department of Health Services Administration and the School of Business and includes specialization in strategic management. The purpose of the program is to improve research and instruction in health administration through the training of academicians with a specific disciplinary competency. The program prepares students for university teaching and research as well as other research positions. Students work closely with faculty members on joint publications and paper presentations. Students with a master's degree in a closely related field generally need at least three years of full-time study for completion of the program.

The Master of Science in Health Administration (M.S.H.A.) is ranked in the top ten health administration programs nationally by *U.S. News & World Report*. The purpose of the program is to train individuals for senior executive positions in health services organizations. The program is accredited by the Accrediting Commission on Education for Health Services Administration. For the M.S.H.A. degree, fifteen months (five quarters) of course work is followed by nine months in an administrative residency. In collaboration with the School of Business, the department also offers a program leading to both the M.S.H.A. and M.B.A. degrees that requires 21 months (seven quarters) of course work and a 9-month residency. Students may also complete a Certificate in Gerontology.

The Master of Science in Health Informatics (M.S.H.I.) is one of very few programs worldwide that offers a curriculum that integrates the domains of information science, information resources management, and health-care organization and management. The purpose of the program is to train broadly educated individuals who are concerned with the introduction and enhancement of information technology in health-care organizations and are prepared to assume senior-level positions in the strategic planning, management, design, integration, implementation, and evaluation of clinical and administrative information systems in health-care enterprises. The program involves a 62-credit-hour curriculum, including an administrative internship, and offers both part-time and full-time options.

Research Facilities

Classified as a Carnegie Research University I, UAB has more than $200 million in external grants and contracts support. UAB ranks 15th among all U.S. universities in total extramural dollars received from the National Institutes of Health. UAB has more than seventy Centers of Excellence that provide opportunities for interdisciplinary collaboration in research, health care, and education.

Financial Aid

In addition to federal financial aid programs administered by UAB's Financial Aid Office, the Department of Health Services Administration has limited scholarship and traineeship funds available to students in the M.S.H.A. program. The Ph.D. program awards assistantships, fellowships, and full-tuition scholarships based on merit.

Cost of Study

The 1998–99 tuition for in-state students is $126 per credit hour for graduate students. Out-of-state students pay $222 per credit hour for graduates. There may be additional special fees when applicable.

Living and Housing Costs

UAB offers a range of housing facilities, including traditional residence halls, apartments, and suites. Housing is centrally located and within walking distance of all classroom buildings, libraries, and the medical center. The housing cost ranges from $168 to $494 per month.

Student Group

Students enter the programs in the Department of Health Services Administration from all over the U.S. and several other countries. The graduate programs admit students with a variety of undergraduate degrees and health-care experience. The M.S.H.I. and M.S.H.A. programs each admit approximately 30 students per year. The Ph.D. program admits approximately 5 students per year.

Location

Greater Birmingham is a busy urban center with a population of nearly 1 million people located in the foothills of the Appalachian Mountains. Health care and education have replaced heavy industry as Birmingham's economic base, and UAB is the city's leading employer and the largest employer in Alabama. The five-county area has more than twenty-one hospitals. Birmingham is known for its great natural beauty, the hospitality of its people, and its temperate climate.

The University

The University of Alabama at Birmingham is a comprehensive, urban research university and academic health center in Alabama's major city and is an autonomous campus of the University of Alabama System. Student enrollment exceeds 15,500 and faculty and staff members number more than 15,800. The campus encompasses a seventy-block area near downtown, with more than 100 major buildings. The University of Alabama at Birmingham is accredited by the Commission on Colleges of the Southern Association of Colleges and Schools to award degrees at the bachelor's, master's, specialist, and doctoral levels.

Applying

Enrollment in the Ph.D. and M.S.H.A. programs is only in the fall term. Ph.D. applicants must submit a satisfactory GMAT or GRE score, transcripts, three evaluation letters, an application, and a statement of career goals by April 15. Applications received by March 1 receive priority consideration. Admitted students typically score in the top 25 percent on the GMAT or GRE. M.S.H.A. applicants must have a baccalaureate degree from an accredited academic institution with a GPA of 3.0 (on a 4.0 scale) in the last 60 hours, a GRE score of at least 1500 or a GMAT score of at least 480, three letters of recommendation, a personal statement, and an interview. Prior to matriculation, M.S.H.A. students must successfully complete 6 credit hours of accounting and 3 credit hours of statistics. Applications must be completed by March 1. Early application is encouraged. M.S.H.I. applicants must have a bachelor's degree from a regionally accredited academic institution with a GPA of 3.0 out of 4.0, a score of at least 50 on the MAT or 1500 on the GRE or 480 on the GMAT. Prior to matriculation, accepted students must have completed program prerequisites (courses in computing fundamentals, introduction to programming, and principles of accounting), and three letters of recommendation.

Correspondence and Information

For General Information:

Department of Health Services Administration
School of Health Related Professions
The University of Alabama at Birmingham
Birmingham, Alabama 35294-3361

For the Ph.D. Program:

Dr. Myron D. Fottler
Director, Ph.D. Program in
Administration—Health Services
Telephone: 205-934-3113
Fax: 205-975-6608
E-mail: phdha@uab.edu

For the M.S.H.A. Program:

Dr. Cynthia Carter Haddock
Director, M.S.H.A. Program
Telephone: 205-934-1669
Fax: 205-975-6608
E-mail: msha@uab.edu

For the M.S.H.I. Program:

Director, M.S.H.I. Program
Telephone: 205-934-3509
Fax: 205-975-6608
E-mail: mshi@uab.edu

The University of Alabama at Birmingham

THE FACULTY

Eta S. Berner, Ed.D., Professor.
Michael R. Bowers, Ph.D, Professor.
Jerome H. Carter, M.D., Assistant Professor.
W. Jack Duncan, Ph.D., Professor.
Myron D. Fottler, Ph.D., Professor and Director, Ph.D. Program.
Peter M. Ginter, Ph.D., Professor.
Cynthia Carter Haddock, Ph.D., Professor and Director, M.S.H.A. Program.
J. Michael Hardin, Ph.D., Professor.
Mahmud Hassan, Ph.D., Professor.
S. Robert Hernandez, Dr.P.H., Professor and Chair.
Howard W. Houser, Ph.D., Professor.
Charles L. Joiner, Ph.D., Professor.
L. R. Jordan, M.A., Professor.
Gail W. McGee, Ph.D., Professor.
Robert A. McLean, Ph.D., Associate Professor.
Michael A. Morrisey, Ph.D., Professor.
Jose B. Quintana, Ph.D., Assistant Professor.
John E. Sheridan, Ph.D., L. R. Jordan Professor of Health Services Administration.
Richard M. Shewchuk, Ph.D., Associate Professor and Director, Gerontology Program.
John E. Swan, D.B.A., Professor.
Norman Weissman, Ph.D., Professor.

UNIVERSITY OF CHICAGO

Graduate Program in Health Administration and Policy

Program of Study

The Graduate Program in Health Administration and Policy admits students from three professional schools at the University of Chicago. Students may pursue a two-year course of study leading to an M.A. degree in the School of Social Service Administration (SSA) or the Irving B. Harris Graduate School of Public Policy Studies (HGSPPS). Students may also pursue a two-year course of study leading to an M.B.A. degree in the Graduate School of Business (GSB). The purpose of the program is to educate students for leadership in the health-care field by developing their critical-analytical, problem-solving, and decision-making capabilities. The respective schools emphasize different applications of these capabilities. SSA focuses on the delivery of health and social services, HGSPPS on health policy design and evaluation, and GSB on the management of health-care organizations. The common core courses, combined with the individual perspectives of each school, allow students both flexibility and focus in preparing for their chosen careers. Certification recognizing successful completion of the program is provided.

A typical course of study includes nine or ten courses satisfying basic M.A. or M.B.A. requirements, four specifically health-related courses, and five or six electives that may include additional health studies. Students are required to take one course that assesses organization and financing of health services, one course in which students use concepts and skills developed in the classroom to address actual management or planning problems in health-care organizations, and one course in managerial accounting.

Research Facilities

The program is allied with the Center for Health Administration Studies, an interdisciplinary unit with a thirty-year tradition of vanguard studies in the organization and financing of medical care. In the classroom, students are exposed to the latest in research and are often taught by the researchers. Students are sometimes employed part-time to assist with ongoing research projects. The University's extensive library and computer facilities, as well as additional computer facilities maintained by the graduate schools, are available to all students.

Financial Aid

No prospective student should refrain from applying to the program for financial reasons. Loans and fellowships are available from each of the schools. Also, research assistantships and other part-time employment are sometimes available through the program.

Cost of Study

Tuition for 1998–99 is $26,200 for GSB, $22,680 for HGSPPS, and $20,370 for SSA.

Living and Housing Costs

Annual room and board expenses for a single student attending the University of Chicago are approximately $9600 in 1998–99.

Student Group

Approximately 20 students from all parts of the country enter the program each year. The majority have full-time work experience, but talented people coming directly from undergraduate programs are also encouraged to apply. The program seeks persons from a broad range of undergraduate majors, including the social sciences, the humanities, business, and the biological sciences, as well as those with degrees in such health professions as medicine and nursing. An active organization of graduate students interested in health policy and administration—The Health Services Management Association—enriches the academic and social life of students in the program.

Student Outcomes

Program graduates are in demand for positions in a variety of organizations in the health field. Although the majority of graduates have accepted positions with hospitals or management consulting firms, increasing numbers are now employed by health maintenance organizations, multi-institutional health-care systems, pharmaceutical and supplier industries, investment banks, foundations, the government, and professional associations. Graduates are assisted in placement by the program's extensive network of alumni as well as by the placement office of the graduate schools. Health administration has been offered at the University since 1934, and alumni occupy senior management positions in all parts of the country.

Location

Chicago is the headquarters for most national organizations in the health-care field, including the American Hospital Association, the American Medical Association, the American College of Healthcare Executives, and the Blue Cross and Blue Shield Association. The University of Chicago is located in Hyde Park, an attractive lakefront residential area only 15 minutes from the center of town.

The University and The Program

The University of Chicago is best known as a center for advanced research and training. Graduate and professional students make up more than 70 percent of the University's total enrollment of more than 11,000 students.

The University's small size and its emphasis on graduate studies encourage interaction among disciplines. The faculty of the program includes many individuals who are prominent in a variety of academic disciplines. Joint appointments and the cross-listing of courses are common. In addition to the three participating professional schools, the Schools of Medicine and Law and the Departments of Economics, Sociology, Anthropology, and Human Development all offer course work that is of interest to students in the program. The Graduate School of Business and the Medical School offer a joint M.D./M.B.A. degree that can be completed in five years, and GSB, SSA, and HGSPPS offer joint master's degrees that can be completed in three years.

Applying

Students must first be accepted to a participating school and then complete an application to be considered for the program. Students may obtain applications for all the schools from the address below. A bachelor's degree from an accredited college is generally required for admission. There are no specific course prerequisites. The GSB and HGSPPS require and the SSA recommends that applicants take the GMAT or the GRE. Student selection criteria include previous educational record, test scores, letters of recommendation, and work experience. Applications completed after February are at a disadvantage in competing for places in the class and for scholarships.

Correspondence and Information

Graduate Program in Health Administration and Policy
University of Chicago
969 East 60th Street, Office 6011
Chicago, Illinois 60637
Telephone: 773-753-8220

University of Chicago

THE FACULTY

George Bateman, M.B.A., Senior Lecturer. Quality management.
Meei-shia Chen, Ph.D., Associate Professor. Health education.
Marshall Chin, M.D., M.P.H., Assistant Professor. Outcomes, quality of care.
Nicholas A. Christakis, M.D., Assistant Professor. Geriatric care and medical ethics.
Thomas D'Aunno, Ph.D., Associate Professor. Organizational psychology.
Peter Friedmann, M.D., Assistant Professor. Physician decision making and clinical epidemiology.
Sarah Gehlert, Ph.D., Assistant Professor. Maternal and child health, adaptation to neurologic illness.
Michael Koetting, Ph.D., Lecturer and Vice President, University of Chicago Hospitals. Health and society.
John Lantos, M.D., Associate Professor. Indigent care.
Edward Lawlor, Ph.D., Associate Professor and Director. Health policy and planning.
Laurence E. Lynn Jr., Ph.D., Professor. Policy analysis and public management.
Willard G. Manning Jr., Ph.D., Professor. Health insurance and managed care.
David Meltzer, M.D., Ph.D., Assistant Professor. Health economics and public policy.
Ralph Muller, M.A., Lecturer and President, University of Chicago Hospitals and Health System. Hospital administration.
Tomas J. Philipson, Ph.D., Associate Professor. Economics and health care.
William Pollak, Ph.D., Associate Professor. Health services finance.
Kristiana Raube, Ph.D., Assistant Professor. Health policy and health services delivery.
Michael Roizen, M.D., Professor. Medical-care organization.
Richard Sewell, M.P.H., Executive Director, Chicago Health Policy Research Council. Health planning and urban health care.
Mark Siegler, M.D., Professor. Issues of ethics in physician decision making.
Min-Woong Sohn, Ph.D., Assistant Professor. Network analysis of hospital markets and organization theory and behavior.
Henry Webber, M.P.P., Vice President, Community Affairs, University of Chicago. Financial management.

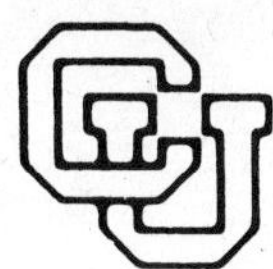

UNIVERSITY OF COLORADO AT DENVER

Graduate School of Business Administration
Master of Science Program in Health Administration

Program of Study

The Graduate Program in Health Administration is dedicated to preparing women and men who, after appropriate practical experience in management, are capable of assuming positions as chief executive officers or senior-level managers in the health-care industry. The program offers a course of study leading to the Master of Science in Health Administration (M.S.H.A.) degree or to both the Master of Science (M.S.) and Master of Business Administration (M.B.A.) degrees. Either course of study may be completed full- or part-time.

The Graduate Program in Health Administration at the University of Colorado at Denver is part of the Graduate School of Business Administration and builds on a base of expertise in management concepts and techniques to address issues unique to one of the nation's most complex and rapidly growing industries. A full-time faculty with distinguished research records and a select group of managers who practice in the field join in bringing the latest thinking on the most important issues confronting the field of health administration into the classroom. The program attracts students who have a variety of backgrounds and experience levels, which further enriches the classroom experience.

To graduate with the Master of Science in Health Administration, students must complete a minimum of 57 graduate semester hours in business and health administration management. The curriculum is based on a series of structured learning sequences, beginning with a year of course work primarily from the M.B.A. curriculum, that provide the student with a broad base in management theory, along with introductory courses in health administration. The second half of the course work focuses more particularly on advanced health administration topics. All courses are taught in the evening to enable working students to pursue the degree on a part-time basis.

After graduation, a management residency is optional but recommended for all students, especially those with limited health-care experience. Program faculty members provide assistance in securing the residency and provide consultation during the residency period.

The Graduate Program in Health Administration is accredited by the Accrediting Commission on Education for Health Services Administration, the only agency recognized by the U.S. Department of Education for accreditation of health administration programs. The only program of its kind in the Rocky Mountain region, the CU-Denver Health Administration Program has carried this accreditation since 1968. The Graduate School of Business Administration is accredited by AACSB–The International Association for Management Education.

Because so many of the M.B.A. core courses are included as requirements for the Master of Science in Health Administration degree, many students elect to complete a dual-degree program, which combines the M.B.A. with the M.S.H.A.; only three additional courses are needed for a dual degree. The course requirement for the M.S.H.A./M.B.A. dual degree option is 66 semester hours.

The Executive Program in Health Administration provides practicing health-care professionals with a graduate degree in health administration in twenty-five months. The program consists of intensive on-campus sessions held approximately every six months and computer-based instruction during the off-campus sessions. The Executive Program provides high-quality instruction and utilizes faculty from fourteen accredited health administration programs that are part of the Network for Health Care Management. Drawing upon this exceptionally broad resource base, the program offers the student an educational environment impossible for a single institution to produce.

Research Facilities

All students in business administration have access to four computer labs equipped with IBM-compatible machines that are part of a local area network (LAN) and are linked to the Internet. One lab is reserved exclusively for business students.

Financial Aid

The University of Colorado at Denver participates in all forms of federally subsidized financial aid for degree-seeking students who are U.S. residents or citizens. Information on how and when to apply for financial aid through the University is included in the packet that also includes the application for admission and other information about the program.

Cost of Study

The 1997–98 Colorado state resident tuition was $222 per credit hour. Full-time residents paid no more than $1853 per semester for up to 15 credit hours. Nonresident students were charged $752 per credit hour up to a semester maximum of $6274.

Living and Housing Costs

Single students should budget approximately $9000 per academic year for housing, food, and moderate entertainment expenses. No on-campus housing is provided, but students can find reasonably priced accommodations in neighborhoods close to the campus or in the greater Denver area.

Student Group

The Graduate Program in Health Administration appeals to students nationwide and attracts a student enrollment that represents a broad diversity of background and experience. Work experience is not required for admission to the program. The average Master of Science in Health Administration candidate is 28 years old, achieved a 3.0 grade point average in his or her undergraduate program, and brings to the classroom an average of five years of work experience. Admission to the program is open to international students.

Location

The University of Colorado at Denver is part of the Auraria Higher Education Consortium, which is a safe, 171-acre campus located in booming downtown Denver, the heart of a five-county metropolitan area of more than 2 million residents. Because of the school's location on the edge of the central downtown business district, students have ready access to a vibrant business community and a wealth of cultural opportunities that are easily accessible through good public transportation and highway systems. Colorado's mild climate and access to the Rocky Mountains provide many recreational opportunities that entice people to participate in outdoor activities. The new Denver International Airport makes access to the region convenient for world business and pleasure travelers.

The School

The Graduate School of Business Administration is the largest graduate business program in Colorado. Its high-quality programs are nationally certified by AACSB–The International Association for Management Education, which granted the school additional specialized accreditation in accounting in 1996. The health administration program is accredited by the Accrediting Commission on Education for Health Services Administration. CU-Denver has distinguished itself as an urban center of international excellence.

Applying

Students admitted to degree candidacy in health administration may begin a program in the Graduate School of Business Administration in the fall, spring, or summer term. A two-part application form, optional resume, personal essay, required GMAT score, two original transcripts from each institution of higher education attended, letters of recommendation, and an application fee (M.B.A. or M.S. applicants, $50; M.B.A./M.S. dual-degree applicants, $80; international applicants, $60) must be submitted by the published deadlines. International students whose native language is not English must submit TOEFL scores. Four letters of recommendation are required for all international students and M.S. in Health Administration applicants. Application forms may be downloaded from the Internet at the Web site listed below, or students may inquire through the Graduate School of Business Administration.

Correspondence and Information

Graduate School of Business Administration
University of Colorado at Denver
P.O. Box 173364-Campus Box 165
Denver, Colorado 80217-3364

Telephone: 303-556-5900
Fax: 303-556-5904
E-mail: lori_cain@maroon.cudenver.edu
World Wide Web: http://www.cudenver.edu/public/business

University of Colorado at Denver

THE FACULTY

Yash P. Gupta, Dean and Professor of Management; Ph.D., Bradford (England).
Marlene A. Smith, Associate Dean and Associate Professor of Quantitative Methods; Ph.D., Florida.
Jean-Claude Bosch, Associate Dean and Professor of Finance; Ph.D., Washington (Seattle).

Health Administration Professors

Heidi Boerstler, Professor of Health Administration and Management; Dr.P.H., Yale; J.D., Denver.
Bruce R. Neumann, Professor of Accounting and Health Administration; Ph.D., Illinois.
Richard W. Foster, Associate Professor of Finance and Health Administration; Ph.D., Chicago.
Blair D. Gifford, Assistant Professor of Management and Health Administration; Ph.D., Chicago.
Errol Biggs, Senior Instructor in Health Administration and Management and Health Services Administration Program Director; Ph.D., Penn State.

Professors

Marcelle V. Arak, Professor of Finance; Ph.D., MIT.
Peter G. Bryant, Professor of Management and Information Systems; Ph.D., Stanford.
Wayne F. Cascio, Professor of Management; Ph.D., Rochester.
Lawrence F. Cunningham, Professor of Marketing and Transportation; D.B.A., Tennessee.
E. Woodrow Eckard Jr., Professor of Business Economics; Ph.D., UCLA.
Jahangir Karimi, Professor of Information Systems and Management Information Systems Program Director; Ph.D., Arizona.
Gary A. Kochenberger, Professor of Operations Management; Ph.D., Colorado at Boulder.
James O. Morris, Professor of Finance; Ph.D., Berkeley.
Dennis F. Murray, Professor of Accounting and Accounting Program Director; Ph.D., Massachusetts.
Edward J. O'Connor, Professor of Management; Ph.D., Akron.
John C. Ruhnka, Professor of Management and Business Law; J.D., Yale; L.L.M., Cambridge.
Donald L. Stevens, Professor of Finance and Director of the Center for International Business; Ph.D., Michigan State.
Dean G. Taylor, Professor of Finance and Finance Program Director; Ph.D., Chicago.
Raymond F. Zammuto, Professor of Management; Ph.D., Illinois.

Associate Professors

Kang Rae Cho, Associate Professor of Management and International Business; Ph.D., Washington (Seattle).
Edward J. Conry, Associate Professor of Business Law and Ethics; J.D., California, Davis.
Elizabeth S. Cooperman, Associate Professor of Finance; Ph.D., Georgia.
C. Marlena Fiol, Associate Professor of Management; Ph.D., Illinois.
James H. Gerlach, Associate Professor of Information Systems; Ph.D., Purdue.
Susan M. Keaveney, Associate Professor of Marketing and MBA Program Director; Ph.D., Colorado at Boulder.
Fen Yang "Bob" Kuo, Associate Professor of Information Systems; Ph.D., Arizona.
Manuel Serapio Jr., Associate Professor of Management and International Business and International Business Program Director; Ph.D., Illinois.
Clifford E. Young, Associate Professor of Marketing and Marketing Program Director; Ph.D., Utah.

Assistant Professors

Ajeyo Banerjee, Assistant Professor of Finance; Ph.D., Massachusetts.
Kenneth L. Bettenhausen, Assistant Professor of Management; Ph.D., Illinois.
Anol Bhattacherjee, Assistant Professor of Information Systems; Ph.D., Houston.
John W. Byrd, Assistant Professor of Finance; Ph.D., Oregon.
Gary J. Colbert, Assistant Professor of Accounting; Ph.D., Oregon.
Richard E. Cook, Assistant Professor of Finance; Ph.D., Washington (St. Louis).
David A. Forlani, Assistant Professor of Marketing; Ph.D., Minnesota.
John Jacob, Assistant Professor of Accounting; Ph.D., Northwestern.
Deborah L. Kellogg, Assistant Professor of Operations Management; Ph.D., USC.
Vickie Ratcliff Lane, Assistant Professor of Marketing; Ph.D., Washington (Seattle).
Linda G. Levy, Assistant Professor of Accounting; Ph.D., Colorado at Boulder.
L. Ann Martin, Assistant Professor of Accounting; Ph.D., Minnesota.
Sara Kovoor-Misra, Assistant Professor of Management; Ph.D., USC.
Madhavan Parthasarathy, Assistant Professor of Marketing; Ph.D., Nebraska.
Michele L. Wingate, Assistant Professor of Accounting; Ph.D., Oregon.

Senior Instructors

Elizabeth S. Conner, Senior Instructor in Accounting; M.S., Colorado State.
Charles M. Franks, Senior Instructor in Quantitative Methods; Ph.D., Colorado at Boulder.
Gary Giese, Senior Instructor in Business Law and Organization and Management Program Director; J.D., Nebraska.
Robert D. Hockenbury, Senior Instructor in Accounting; M.S., Houston.
Lawrence F. Johnston, Senior Instructor in Finance; Ph.D., Colorado at Boulder.
Paul J. Patinka, Senior Instructor in Management; Ph.D., Purdue.
Barbara A. Pelter, Senior Instructor in Finance; M.A., California, Davis.
Marianne Plunkert, Senior Instructor in Finance; M.B.A., Ohio State.
Eric J. Thompson, Senior Instructor in Information Systems; M.S., Colorado at Boulder.
John Turner, Senior Instructor in Finance; Ph.D., Saint Louis.

Instructors

Michael D. Harper, Instructor in Operations Management; Ph.D., Rensselaer.
Chen Ji, Instructor in Finance; M.B.A., Denver; M.S., Colorado at Boulder.
Charles A. Rice, Instructor in Management; M.B.A., Denver.
Gary R. Schornack, Instructor in Marketing; Ed.D., Nova.
M. Catherine Volland, Instructor in Management; M.A., Colorado at Boulder.

UNIVERSITY OF IOWA

Graduate Program in Hospital and Health Administration

Programs of Study

The Graduate Program in Hospital and Health Administration, administered by the College of Medicine and the Graduate College, is accredited by the Accrediting Commission on Education for Health Services Administration (ACEHSA). The program awards M.H.A. and Ph.D. degrees in hospital and health administration. Joint-degree programs are available with the College of Business Administration (M.H.A./M.B.A.), the College of Law (M.H.A./J.D.), and the Department of Urban and Regional Planning (M.H.A./M.A.). Affiliation with the University's College of Business Administration, the Center for Health Services Research, and the University of Iowa Hospitals and Clinics—the nation's largest university-owned teaching hospital—provides students with a firsthand understanding of the health-care industry and with business, technical, and managerial skills. Students benefit from the program's extensive, nationwide alumni network. Alumni serve as career counselors and preceptors for summer internships and postgraduate residencies and fellowships. The master's curriculum is a two-year, 60-credit-hour program. Students may concentrate in general health management courses such as alternative delivery systems, ambulatory-care management, finance, hospital operations, and long-term-care administration. Alternatively, students may select electives in the health analysis area, which emphasizes health systems analysis, population-based planning, quality assessment, and utilization review. The doctoral program is oriented toward careers in health services research, teaching, and policy analysis. The program's close ties to the Center for Health Services Research and the University of Iowa Hospitals and Clinics promote student participation in a dynamic learning environment that involves interaction with both a multidisciplinary research-oriented faculty and senior-level health-care administrators. The curriculum usually consists of two years of full-time, post-master's course work followed by comprehensive examinations and completion of a dissertation. Support for dissertation research is available.

Research Facilities

The Center for Health Services Research is a University-wide interdisciplinary research facility. Faculty from the Colleges of Medicine, Dentistry, Nursing, Pharmacy, Business Administration, and Liberal Arts are involved in research related to appropriateness and quality of clinical practice, health of the elderly and long-term care, and rural health. The University's library system includes more than 2 million volumes in the main library and more than 800,000 volumes in eleven specialty libraries. The Hardin Library for the Health Sciences, the largest of the specialty libraries, provides a computerized literature search system that is free to students. Computing facilities range from the University's mainframe computers to the departmental student computer resource area housed in the program's facilities. Funds for computing are available to all students, as are free workshops. Iowa City health-care institutions include the 845-bed University of Iowa Hospitals and Clinics, the 159-bed Department of Veterans Affairs Medical Center, and Mercy Hospital, a 222-bed community hospital. The area also has a significant number of long-term care and community-based service providers.

Financial Aid

Information on financial aid, including scholarships, grants, and loan programs, is available through the Office of Student Financial Aid (http://www.uiowa.edu~finaid/). Departmental research assistantships provide stipends and qualify out-of-state students for in-state tuition rates. Traineeships, scholarships, and minority scholarships and fellowships are also available. Some awards are offered in recognition of outstanding scholarship and experience, independent of need. Financial need should not deter students from applying.

Cost of Study

Tuition for the nine-month 1998–99 academic year is $3166 for Iowa residents and $10,202 for nonresidents. The student health fee is $50 per semester, and the computer fee is $51 per semester.

Living and Housing Costs

The cost of living in Iowa City is very reasonable. Designated graduate student University housing (single or married) is available. Students interested in on-campus housing information should contact the Family Housing/University Apartments Office, 100 Housing Service Building, Iowa City, Iowa 52242 (telephone: 319-335-9199 or 800-553-IOWA Ext. 5-9199 (toll-free). The student contact for off-campus information is Housing Clearinghouse, 172 IMU, University of Iowa, Iowa City, Iowa 52242 (telephone: 319-335-3055 or 800-553-IOWA Ext. 5-3055 (toll-free); Web site: http://www.imuis.uiowa.edu/cic/). The University Cambus system is free.

Student Group

The master's program annually enrolls between 20 and 25 students with a variety of undergraduate backgrounds, some with clinical/professional experience. The number of doctoral students averages approximately 10.

Student Outcomes

The placement record is excellent for M.H.A. summer internships, postgraduate residencies/fellowships/positions, and doctoral placement. Graduates are placed in diverse facilities, including hospitals, consulting and research firms, group practices, insurance agencies, rehabilitation centers, government agencies, public health departments, and colleges and universities. They include Arthur Anderson & Company; Blue Cross/Blue Shield of Iowa; Daughters of Charity Health System; Duke University Medical Center; Ernst & Young; Fallon Clinic; Henry Ford Health Systems; John Deere Health Care, Inc.; Johns Hopkins University Medical Center; Lake Forest Hospital; Massachusetts General; Mayo Foundation; Mercy Health Systems; Ohio State University Children's Hospital; Ochsner Clinic; University of Iowa Hospitals and Clinics; University of Wisconsin Hospitals and Clinics; and Veterans Affairs Medical Centers.

Location

The Iowa City area provides a wealth of cultural, recreational, and entertainment opportunities. The Iowa Center for the Arts offers regular performances and exhibitions by national and international artists, while the nearby Coralville Reservoir and Lake Macbride recreational areas provide ample opportunities for year-round outdoor activities. Iowa City lies within 300 miles of Chicago, Minneapolis, Kansas City, and St. Louis.

The University

Chartered in 1847, the University was the first state university to admit women on an equal basis with men. The first African Americans to earn a law degree and Ph.D.'s in history and music did so at Iowa. It is one of the nation's premier research centers.

Applying

Applicants to the master's program must hold a baccalaureate degree with a cumulative GPA of at least 3.0 on a 4.0 scale. It is preferred that applicants earn at least a 550 on the GMAT or a combined verbal and quantitative score above 1050 on the GRE General Test. Experience and aptitude are also considered. Courses in accounting, economics, and statistics as well as competence in the use of a personal computer are recommended prior to entering the program. Applicants for the Ph.D. program are generally expected to hold a master's degree in a health-related field, although other degrees will be considered. A minimum score of 600 on the TOEFL is required of applicants whose native language is not English. The program publishes a separate brochure and application forms. Completed applications should be received by May 1.

Correspondence and Information

Student Affairs Administrator
Graduate Program in Hospital and Health Administration
2700 Steindler Building
University of Iowa
Iowa City, Iowa 52242
Telephone: 319-335-9817
800-553-IOWA Ext. 5-9817 (toll-free)
World Wide Web: http://www.pmeh.uiowa.edu/hha

University of Iowa

THE FACULTY AND THEIR RESEARCH

Primary Faculty

Douglas S. Wakefield, Professor and Interim Director, Graduate Program in Hospital and Health Administration and Center for Health Services Research; Ph.D. (hospital and health administration), Iowa. Health services management, organizational behavior, development of telemedicine services and quality assessment and enhancement.

Peter E. Hilsenrath, Associate Professor; Ph.D. (economics), Texas at Austin. Health economics, health policy, technology assessment.

Samuel Levey, Gerhard Hartman Professor; Ph.D. (hospital and health administration), Iowa; S.M. (public health), Harvard. Health policy studies, organizational leadership and restructuring.

Liam O'Neill, Associate; Ph.D. (operations management), Penn State. Efficiency measurement, outcomes research and quality, hospital information systems, data envelopment analysis, quantitative methods.

James E. Rohrer, Professor; Ph.D. (health services organization and policy), Michigan. Medical care organization, quality assessment, policy and planning.

Thomas E. Vaughn, Assistant Professor; Ph.D. (health services organization and policy), Michigan. Substance abuse treatment organizations, rural hospitals, physician-organization relations.

Marcia M. Ward, Associate Professor; Ph.D. (clinical psychology), Ohio State. Health services research, health outcomes, health economics, health behavior and promotion.

David K. Wyant, Associate; Ph.D. (health services research policy and administration), Minnesota. Health finance and health economics.

Secondary Faculty

James L. Price, Professor, Department of Sociology; Ph.D. (sociology), Columbia. Employee absenteeism and turnover.

Gerard Rushton, Professor, Department of Geography; Ph.D. (geography), Iowa. Medical geography and location theory.

Emmett J. Vaughan, Professor, Division of Continuing Education; Ph.D. (economics and insurance), Nebraska. Health insurance and claims.

Adjunct Faculty

William W. Hesson, Adjunct Associate Professor and Associate Director, External Relations and Legal Services, University of Iowa Hospitals and Clinics; J.D., Iowa.

R. Edward Howell, Adjunct Professor and Director and CEO, University of Iowa Hospitals and Clinics; M.S. (hospital and health services administration), Ohio State.

Todd C. Linden, Adjunct Lecturer and President and CEO, Grinnell Regional Medical Center; M.A. (hospital and health administration), Iowa.

Richard R. Murphy, Adjunct Assistant Professor and Associate Director of Financial Management and Control, University of Iowa Hospitals and Clinics; M.B.A., Drake.

Ann O'Brien, Adjunct Lecturer and Lecturer, College of Business, University of Iowa; M.B.A., Texas at Austin; CPA.

John H. Staley, Adjunct Associate Professor and Associate Director and COO, University of Iowa Hospitals and Clinics; Ph.D. (hospital and health administration), Iowa.

Tanya M. Uden-Holman, Adjunct Assistant Professor and Director, Institute for Quality Healthcare Resource Center, University of Iowa; Ph.D. (sociology), Iowa.

James R. Wagner, Adjunct Assistant Professor and Director, Information Systems, University of Iowa Hospitals and Clinics; M.S. (computer science), Iowa.

The Health Sciences Campus, showing the Colleges of Medicine, Dentistry, Nursing, and Pharmacy; the University of Iowa Hospitals and Clinics; and the Department of Veterans Affairs Medical Center.

UNIVERSITY OF MINNESOTA

Program in Healthcare Management

Program of Study

Students choose the University of Minnesota program because of its strengths in four key areas: its national reputation for excellence in health-care education; its innovative curriculum that blends advanced management theory with current issues in health care and practical experience; the diversity and quality of job and fellowship placements available to its graduates; and its alumni network, the largest of its kind in the country, which actively supports the program's activities. Students in the Minnesota program also benefit greatly from its location in the dynamic health-care community of the Minneapolis–St. Paul area, which provides students with access to organizations pioneering the health-care systems of tomorrow.

The Minnesota Master of Healthcare Administration (M.H.A.) program is a professional management program designed to prepare students for executive and leadership positions in health-care organizations and corporations. The curriculum consists of two academic years (eighteen months) of classroom preparation and a three-month administrative residency between the two years. The first year provides students with an orientation to health care, management theory, and important health-care organizations and corporations. The second phase of the curriculum, the summer residency and clerkship, gives students a chance to apply theory to actual health-care organizations. During the second year of the program, students complete advanced required course work, a research thesis, and 25 hours of electives in an area of concentration. Students may concentrate in a wide variety of areas—for example, finance, marketing, management information systems, and long-term care.

For the required residency, students are placed in health-care organizations throughout the country. After graduation, students may accept positions or fellowships.

Dual M.H.A./M.B.A. degrees are possible for students who are accepted by the Carlson School of Management.

Research Facilities

Diehl Hall, one of fourteen libraries on campus, subscribes to more than 3,300 periodicals and has more than 300,000 bound volumes. The Sabra Hamilton Library—the M.H.A. library located within the program's facilities—contains a collection of health administration and general management periodicals along with key reference materials. The University maintains numerous computer facilities that are available for instruction, training, and use by graduate students. In addition, the computer laboratory, specifically for use by graduate students in the Carlson School of Management, contains personal computers linked to the main University computer system.

Financial Aid

The program offers many awards and scholarships that have been established by alumni and friends of the program. These are based upon promise of early achievement, academic performance, and/or financial need.

The University of Minnesota Alumni Association has developed an educational trust fund that makes $4000 available for every M.H.A. student to borrow once he or she has successfully completed the first quarter of study. Students may also work within the Division of Health Management and Policy as research assistants.

Cost of Study

Full-time graduate tuition for residents in 1998–99 is approximately $6000. Resident tuition applies to students from Minnesota, North Dakota, South Dakota, Wisconsin, and Manitoba. Nonresident tuition for 1998–99 is approximately $10,000. Books and mandatory health insurance cost approximately $400 per quarter.

Living and Housing Costs

Annual room and board expenses for a single student are about $700 per month. Married students should expect to pay about $940 per month, plus $150 per month for each child.

Student Group

Twenty-five students from throughout the United States enter the program each fall. Most have some health-care and/or management experience. Ages range from 22 to 41. About half of the students are women. Students have had a wide range of undergraduate majors.

Location

Minneapolis and St. Paul make up an attractive metropolitan area of 2 million people. The University of Minnesota benefits from access to a health-care community that leads the nation in the development of new ideas in health-care organization. The metropolitan area is also known for outstanding cultural and recreational activities, parks, and lakes.

The Program

The University of Minnesota Program in Healthcare Management is one of the nation's first academic programs in health administration. Since its beginning, the Minnesota program has been widely recognized for its leadership in the field, for its academic excellence, and for the quality and success of its graduates. The Alumni Association, the country's largest health administration alumni group, provides financial support to the program and its students and conducts a placement service for students and graduates. The program is housed in the new, state-of-the-art Carlson School of Management.

Applying

The M.H.A. program accepts students to enter in the fall quarter for twenty-one months of full-time study. Admission to the program is highly selective. Although academic ability is a principal criterion, experience and aptitude are given serious consideration.

Applicants to the M.H.A. program must hold a baccalaureate degree from an accredited institution. Course work in accounting, statistics, and microeconomics is required prior to entering the program but not prior to application. Applicants must submit scores on the General Test of the GRE or on the GMAT. It is recommended that M.H.A. applications be submitted as early as January, although they will be accepted through March 30, for entrance the following fall. The program publishes a separate admissions brochure and application form; interested applicants are encouraged to request it.

Correspondence and Information

Program in Healthcare Management
3-140 Carlson School of Management
University of Minnesota
Minneapolis, Minnesota 55455
Telephone: 612-624-8818
Fax: 612-624-8804

University of Minnesota

THE FACULTY

James Begun, Professor; Ph.D. (sociology), North Carolina.
Jon B. Christiansen, Professor; Ph.D. (economics), Wisconsin.
Robert Connor, Assistant Professor; Ph.D. (health-care finance), Pennsylvania (Wharton).
N. Tor Dahl, Lecturer; M.B.A. (health-care economics), Norwegian School of Economics.
Bright Dornblaser, Professor; M.H.A. (total quality management and strategic planning), Minnesota.
David Feinwach, J.D., Ph.D. (health-care law), Minnesota.
Leslie Grant, Assistant Professor; Ph.D. (human development and aging), California, San Francisco.
Gregory W. Hart, Clinical Assistant Professor; M.H.A., Minnesota; Senior Associate Director and Director of Operations, University of Minnesota Hospital and Clinics.
Steve G. Hillestad, Instructor; M.A. (health administration), M.A. (public affairs), Wisconsin.
Steve Housh, Instructor; M.H.A. (health-care administration), Minnesota.
George O. Johnson, Associate Professor and Director, Division of Healthcare Management; Ph.D. (hospital and health-care administration), Minnesota.
Geoffrey L. Kaufmann, Instructor; M.A. (health-care management), Chicago.
John Kralewski, William Wallace Professor of Health Services Research and Administration and Director, Center for Health Services Research; Ph.D. (hospital and health-care administration), Minnesota.
Patrick Langan, Instructor; M.B.A. (human resources), St. Thomas (Minnesota).
Margaret Le Bien, J.D., M.P.H. (mediation and negotiation), Minnesota.
Theodor J. Litman, Professor; Ph.D. (sociology), Minnesota.
Richard Norling, Instructor; M.H.A. (health-care administration), Minnesota.
John A. Nyman, Assistant Professor; Ph.D. (economics), Wisconsin.
David PeKarna, Adjunct Instructor; M.H.A. (health-care administration), Minnesota.
Sandra Potthoff, Assistant Professor; Ph.D. (operations research), Wisconsin.
John Reiling, Lecturer; M.H.A. (health-care administration), Minnesota; M.A. (teaching), St. Thomas (Minnesota).
Michael Resnick, Associate Professor; Ph.D. (hospital and health-care administration), Minnesota.
James A. Rice, Adjunct Lecturer; M.H.A. (international health care), Minnesota.
William Riley, Instructor; Ph.D. (health-care finance), Minnesota.
John Sweetland, Adjunct Assistant Professor; M.H.A., Minnesota; President, Hamilton/KSA Associates, Inc.
Vernon E. Weckwerth, Professor and Coordinator, Alternative Studies Program; Ph.D. (biometry), Minnesota.
Helen Yates, Instructor; M.A. (public administration), Harvard.

UNIVERSITY OF NEW HAMPSHIRE

Department of Health Management and Policy

Program of Study

The Department of Health Management and Policy is accredited by the Accrediting Commission on Education for Health Services Administration and is a member of the Association of University Programs in Health Administration. It offers an executive Master of Health Administration (M.H.A.) primarily, but not exclusively, for individuals currently working in the field of health services who wish to pursue their graduate professional education while continuing to work full-time. As the only graduate program of its kind in a New England public institution, the M.H.A. program at the University of New Hampshire (UNH) links competencies from the functional areas of management with skill courses involving the planning, administration, and evaluation of health services. This two-year program's objective is to enable students to improve their effectiveness and performance in the management of health-care services, programs, institutions, organizations, and policies in hospitals, networks, nursing care facilities, ambulatory care organizations, mental health organizations, alternative health-care delivery systems, managed care programs, consulting firms, public health and social welfare agencies, professional associations, private industry, health-care financing organizations, planning and regulatory agencies, and others.

To graduate, students must complete twenty courses during the two years, including a health-care management core involving courses in managerial accounting, health-care finance, statistics and quantitative methods, organization theory, marketing, management information systems, human resources management; a health-care core consisting of courses in the organization, delivery, and financing of health services plus courses in health economics, ethics, health-care planning, health policy, quality assurance and assessment, epidemiology, and health law; and courses in interest areas such as hospital management, long-term-care management and policy, managed care, health-care reimbursement, and others.

Each student in the M.H.A. program has a faculty adviser to assist in planning the interest area appropriate to the student's career objectives. To relate theory to practice, each student undertakes a field experience (praxis/internship) during the summer between the first and second years. This experience frequently takes place at the student's place of employment. Students attend classes on alternate weekends (Fridays and Saturdays) from September through May and during two residential weeks, one in late August and another in late May.

Research Facilities

Through a generous gift from the McKerley Foundation, the department maintains a dedicated computer laboratory with IBM-compatible personal computers, numerous printers and software programs, plus additional computer-related equipment. Students also have access both to the University's mainframes and to microcomputers. The University of New Hampshire's library system includes holdings in the Dimond Library as well as in several specialized libraries. The collection totals in excess of 1 million volumes and 6,000 periodicals. Within this collection is an assemblage of books and periodicals available to students in areas of management, economics, finance, psychology, sociology, organization theory and behavior, government and public policy, and other subjects allied with the health management field. Specifically within health management, there are more than 40 periodical subscriptions and 400 books. The library system staff members provide valuable assistance to students undertaking literature searches and accessing information databases. Participation in regional and national library services allows the University library system to provide a comprehensive range of services.

Financial Aid

Financial aid consists primarily of student loans, supplemented by a limited number of partial scholarships. Most aid is offered on a financial need basis. When available, fellowship and trainee support from federal funds is limited to citizens and permanent residents of the United States.

Cost of Study

Full-time tuition costs for 1998–99 for the M.H.A. program are $7461 in-state and $8207 out-of-state. The one-time cost of the praxis between the first and second years is $860. Per-course tuition for part-time students is $1164 in-state and $1280 out-of-state.

Living and Housing Costs

Classes are at the New England Center (NEC), a highly respected conference facility on the UNH campus, during the August and May residential weeks. The cost is approximately $1000 for both weeks and includes all meals; a room for the two weeks is an extra $1000. Most Friday/Saturday classes are in the Memorial Union Building; these room costs and break food are covered by tuition. There are a number of options for meals and sleeping rooms, including UNH Dining Services debit cards, the graduate student dorm, and the NEC. The approximate cost of textbooks and reading packets is $1200.

Student Group

The M.H.A. program admits between 10 and 20 students per class. Students come from a variety of backgrounds, which include unit and department managers; mid-level managers; and care givers such as nurses, occupational therapists, physical therapists, recreational therapists, and others, including physicians; heads of quality assurance programs; planners; and financial managers. The majority of the students are women. Most students seek to become health-care managers at either entry-level or mid-level positions. The diversity in the backgrounds, positions, and ages of the students stimulates the sharing of ideas and experiences in and out of the classroom.

Student Outcomes

Graduates of the M.H.A. program secure employment in all areas of the health-care delivery system, including direct-care management, insurance and managed care, long-term care, and in the business world, which supplies and supports health care. Students often are promoted within their current jobs during the course of the program, secure new positions, or use the program to redirect themselves into new career paths on graduation. Examples of positions that students have moved into include manager of primary care, director of physician practices, long-term care administrator, assistant program director for ambulatory care, director of quality assessment and risk management, and director of development.

Location

The University is located in Durham, a semirural town in the seacoast region of New Hampshire, 10 miles west of Portsmouth. The 200-acre campus is surrounded by nearly 4,000 acres of University-owned fields, farms, and woodlands. Its proximity to Boston (65 miles), Concord, New Hampshire (25 miles), and Portland, Maine (75 miles), makes Durham an especially accessible place to pursue a graduate professional education.

The University

The University of New Hampshire is a land-grant institution originally founded in connection with Dartmouth College. It moved to Durham in 1923, where it now enrolls more than 11,000 students, has a full-time faculty of about 600, and offers ninety-five undergraduate and seventy-seven graduate programs. The student body includes more than 1,400 graduate students.

Applying

The M.H.A. program typically reviews applications between February and July. Applicants should have a baccalaureate degree from an accredited college or university; submit competitive scores from either the Graduate Management Admission Test (GMAT) or the Graduate Record Examinations (GRE), which should be taken before July; have successfully completed at least one course in accounting plus one course in statistics; preferably have satisfactory health-related professional experience of at least two years; and have acceptable recommendations from 3 individuals, one of whom must be a member of an academic faculty and another who must be experienced in the field of health management and policy.

Correspondence and Information

Director, Master of Health Administration Program
Department of Health Management and Policy
University of New Hampshire
Four Library Way
Durham, New Hampshire 03824
Telephone: 603-862-2733
Fax: 603-862-3461
E-mail: mha.info@unh.edu

University of New Hampshire

THE FACULTY AND THEIR RESEARCH

W. David Bradford, Associate Professor; Ph.D., LSU. Health economics.
Raymond T. Coward, Professor and Dean, School of Health and Human Services; Ph.D., Purdue. Gerontology and geriatrics, rural health, minority health.
Marc D. Hiller, Associate Professor; Dr.P.H., Pittsburgh. Health-care ethics, long-term-care policy.
William J. Irvine, Instructor; M.Ed., Rhode Island College. Human resources management.
James B. Lewis, Associate Professor, Department Chair, and Graduate Program Director; Sc.D., Johns Hopkins. Finance, marketing, managed care.
Richard J. A. Lewis, Associate Professor; M.B.A., Ohio State; FACHE. Financial management.
Martin D. Merry, Associate Professor; M.D., McGill. Quality of care, quality management.
David A. Pearson, Professor; Ph.D., Yale. Health-care strategy and structure, epidemiology.
Theodore D. Peters, Assistant Professor; Ph.D., SUNY at Albany. Organizations, health-care organizational behavior.
Jeffrey C. Salloway, Professor; Ph.D., Boston University. Medical sociology, health-care behavior.
John W. Seavey, Professor; Ph.D., Arizona. Health planning, health policy, rural hospitals and health care.
Lee F. Seidel, Professor; Ph.D., Penn State. Hospital and health services management, strategic planning.
Albert F. Shamash, Assistant Professor; J.D., Stanford. Health law.
Michele R. Solloway, Research Associate Professor; Ph.D., Berkeley. Health-care reform, maternity and child health, health systems finance and delivery.
David W. Towne, Instructor; M.H.A., New Hampshire. Health-care management information services.

UNIVERSITY OF PITTSBURGH

Graduate Schools of Business and Public Health
Health Administration Program

Program of Study

The Health Administration Program offers the unique advantage that comes from the united resources of two outstanding schools. The Master of Health Administration (M.H.A.) degree is awarded jointly by the University's Joseph M. Katz Graduate School of Business and the Graduate School of Public Health. Students also have two dual degree options: M.H.A./M.B.A. and M.H.A./M.P.H.

Conceptually, the curriculum is designed to expose students first to the disciplines of management and then to the application of these disciplines to the health sector. Here, one will find strong students interacting with excellent faculty members. The program integrates full-time faculty members focused on cutting-edge research with adjunct faculty members, often leaders in health care, who focus on application of knowledge in today's dynamic world of health management. Students develop the enduring and transferable skills, values, and conceptual abilities so necessary for success in health-care management.

The curriculum requires sixteen months of full-time study; students may also pursue the degree on a part-time basis over a longer period. The curriculum consists of 56 credits divided among three academic terms. A series of preprogram workshops in accounting, economics, statistics, finance, and computing allows students to reach parity in those areas.

A management residency is served in the summer and generally includes a stipend. Placement for the residency is facilitated by program staff and faculty members, exposing students to excellent management role models. The program is accredited by the Accrediting Commission on Education for Health Services Administration (ACEHSA).

Research Facilities

A rich array of research facilities is available to the program's faculty and students. Research institutes of particular relevance to the program include the Health Policy Institute, which conducts a range of policy studies on the cost and quality of health care; the Pittsburgh Research Institute for Studies in Marketing, which applies the latest in marketing concepts and research techniques to management problems; the Program in Corporate Culture, which focuses on methods for managing corporate culture (ideologies, beliefs, attitudes, and norms); the Health Services Research Unit, which conducts studies on public health issues; the Strategic Management Institute, which does leading-edge research on corporate and business planning techniques and strategies; and the Business, Government, and Society Research Institute, which conducts research of national distinction on the ways in which organizations interact with their political and social environments.

Financial Aid

The program administers an extensive set of financial aid opportunities, including scholarships, fellowships, and loans. While financial aid is not guaranteed, no student should refrain from applying to the program for financial reasons. In addition to aid based on financial need or academic excellence, students generally receive a stipend during their management residency. Applications for financial assistance are considered independently and only after decisions regarding admission to the program have been made.

Cost of Study

Tuition for 1998–99 is $9403 per two-term year for Pennsylvania residents and $19,373 for nonresidents. The cost per credit hour for part-time students is $389 for state residents and $800 for nonresidents. The transitional module is $1500. Tuition charges are subject to change. Students should generally allow $500 per term for textbooks and supplies. Mandatory costs in addition to tuition and books are a student activity fee, a health service fee, a security fee, and a computer fee, all of which total about $225 per term. A health insurance plan is available.

Living and Housing Costs

There is some housing available on campus for graduate students, but most choose to live in privately owned accommodations nearby. Students should budget a minimum of $10,000 per year for room, board, and miscellaneous expenses. Individual needs and preferences create a wide variance in actual living costs.

Student Group

The program admits 20–25 full-time and an equal number of part-time students each year. Ages range from 20s to 40s, with 27 the average. While most have had at least two years' full-time work experience, many come directly from undergraduate schools. Enrollment includes approximately equal numbers of men and women. Students can join several professional organizations during M.H.A. work, including the Pitt Chapter of American College of Healthcare Executives and the Health Executive Forum of Southwest Pennsylvania.

Student Outcomes

Graduates of the program assume management positions in hospitals and multiunit systems, health maintenance organizations, preferred provider organizations, medical group practices, health affairs divisions of corporations, consulting firms, insurance organizations, and policy and planning organizations. Recent examples of graduate employment are: Group Practice Administrator at Network Management Services, Springfield, Vermont; Health Care Management Consultant at Deloitte & Touche, Pittsburgh, Pennsylvania; Practice Analyst at Highmark Blue Cross Blue Shield, Pittsburgh, Pennsylvania; Senior Consultant at Ernst & Young, Detroit, Michigan; Administrative Fellow at Johns Hopkins Health System, Baltimore, Maryland.

Location

The University's main campus occupies sixty buildings on 131 acres in Oakland, the educational and cultural center of the city of Pittsburgh. The program is located on the campus of a leading academic medical center. There is ready access to the Carnegie Museum–Library–Music Hall–Fine Arts complex, a botanical garden, and a 456-acre public park. Cultural opportunities in Pittsburgh include the symphony, ballet, and opera.

The University

Founded in 1787, the University of Pittsburgh is one of the oldest universities in the United States. In 1974, the University was elected to membership in the Association of American Universities, an elite group of fifty of the most respected research institutions in the country. The Health Administration Program was established in 1950. M.H.A. students have access to the resources of a nationally recognized university and the University of Pittsburgh Medical Center (UPMC), one of the world's leading academic medical centers.

Applying

A bachelor's degree from an accredited college or university is required for admission. Undergraduate performance is an important factor in the admissions committee's decision, as are scores on the Graduate Management Admission Test and letters of recommendation. The committee looks for evidence of good interpersonal and communication skills in applicants. One course in calculus is the only specific course requirement. Students are encouraged to apply as early as possible; completed applications are reviewed as they are received, and decisions are made quickly.

Correspondence and Information

Duane S. Kavinsky, Program Coordinator
Health Administration Program
A-646 Crabtree Hall
University of Pittsburgh
Pittsburgh, Pennsylvania 15261

Telephone: 412-624-3123 or 412-624-3125
Fax: 412-624-3146
E-mail: dschultz@vms.cis.pitt.edu
World Wide Web: http://www.pitt.edu/~pittmha

University of Pittsburgh

THE FACULTY AND THEIR RESEARCH

Michael D. Busch, Adjunct Assistant Professor; M.P.M., Carnegie Mellon. Group practice management.
John H. Evans III, Professor; Ph.D., Carnegie Mellon. Accounting.
Lawrence J. Feick, Professor; Ph.D., Penn State. Marketing.
Daniel Fogel, Professor; Ph.D., Wisconsin. Organizational behavior.
Thomas Heatherington, Adjunct Professor; M.H.A., M.B.A., Pittsburgh. Reengineering operations.
Nathan Hershey, Professor; LL.B., Harvard. Health law.
George A. Huber, Adjunct Associate Professor; J.D., Duquesne. Organization theory.
Judith R. Lave, Director and Professor; Ph.D., Harvard. Economics.
Beaufort B. Longest Jr., Professor; Ph.D., Georgia State. Health policy.
Gordon K. MacLeod, Professor; M.D., Cincinnati. Medical-care organization.
Franklin L. McCarthy, Associate Professor; Ph.D., Minnesota. Health accounting and finance, third-party reimbursement.
Robert Nachtmann, Associate Professor; Ph.D., Indiana. Finance.
Margaret A. Potter, Research Associate; J.D., Rutgers. Health policy.
Charles Pruitt, Adjunct Assistant Professor; M.B.A., Florida; FACHE. Long-term care.
Wesley M. Rohrer III, Assistant Professor; Ph.D., Pittsburgh. Human resources management.
Jeffrey A. Romoff, Adjunct Assistant Professor; M.Phil., Yale. Strategic management.
Robert J. Schuler, Adjunct Professor; M.B.A., Pittsburgh. Health insurance.
Carl W. Smollinger, Adjunct Professor; M.B.A., Shippensburg. Managed care.
George Yeckel, Adjunct Assistant Professor; M.S.H.A., Northwestern. Continuous quality improvement.

UNIVERSITY OF PITTSBURGH

School of Health and Rehabilitation Sciences

Programs of Study

The School of Health and Rehabilitation Sciences offers entry-level and postprofessional programs with concentrations in clinical dietetics and nutrition, communication science and disorders, health information management, occupational therapy, physical therapy, and rehabilitation science and technology. In addition, the school offers two Ph.D. programs: rehabilitation sciences or communication science and disorders.

The entry-level program in physical therapy leads to a Master of Physical Therapy (M.P.T.) degree and prepares students with bachelor's degrees to be self-directed, self-accountable general physical therapists who practice in a variety of settings.

The postprofessional Master of Science and Master of Arts programs are designed for professionals experienced in a health-care or rehabilitation field who wish to acquire knowledge regarding advanced clinical services, research, teaching, and administration in the health-care and rehabilitation systems. The Department of Clinical Dietetics and Nutrition offers an M.S. program for dietitians and nutritionists. The Department of Communication Science and Disorders offers programs in speech-language pathology and audiology that lead to an M.A. or M.S. degree. The Department of Health Information Management offers two programs leading to the M.S. degree: health information systems (HIS) and health-care supervision and management (HSM). HSM is an interdisciplinary program with concentrations in administration/management and long-term care. The Department of Occupational Therapy offers advanced training leading to an M.S. degree. The Department of Physical Therapy offers graduate study to physical therapists who wish to obtain an advanced knowledge of and skills in musculoskeletal or neuromuscular physical therapy. The Department of Rehabilitation Science and Technology offers an M.S. degree with a concentration in rehabilitation technology.

The Ph.D. program in rehabilitation sciences is available to individuals who have a specific area of expertise related to rehabilitation. Core areas include augmentation of sensory/motor function; biomechanics of movement/ergonomics; epidemiology of disability; neural basis of sensory/motor function and dysfunction; information systems and technology related to rehabilitation science; economic, legal, policy, and organizational issues in rehabilitation and disabilities; and psychosocial, social, and cultural aspects of disability. The Ph.D. program in communication science and disorders is oriented toward the basic scientific questions in the discipline, with an emphasis on basic and applied research training.

Research Facilities

The School is dedicated to developing research opportunities to enable students to meet the growing needs of the health-care and rehabilitation fields. Faculty members and students have access to sophisticated research equipment and laboratories, including facilities for the measurement and study of motion; balance disorders; human performance; hearing disorders; speech; language and cognitive disorders; and neurophysiological parameters. They also have access to facilities for wheelchair performance and design and to the HIM computer laboratory. The School has established the Center for Assistive Technology, the NIDRR Rehabilitation Engineering Research Center, and the Pitt/VA Human Engineering Laboratories. Faculty members provide programmatic direction in a variety of multidisciplinary careers associated with the University of Pittsburgh Medical Center (UPMC), including the Facial Nerve Center, the Jordan Balance and Vestibular Laboratory, and the Comprehensive Spine Center. Students have access to all on-campus health-care facilities, in which graduate students assist in serving clients and conducting research. The University Medical Center includes six schools and several hospitals and clinics. There are twenty-seven library collections on or near the campus that are available to all students and faculty members. The University library system contains more than 6.9 million volumes (including microforms), more than 300,000 government documents, and more than 20,000 periodicals. The library also offers Computerized Information Retrieval Service and a cooperative nationwide interlibrary loan program. Computer facilities are available for student use.

Financial Aid

Tuition assistance is available for full-time graduate students on a competitive basis. The School also awards financial assistance to teaching assistants, teaching fellows, and graduate assistants. Money from external sources for faculty research also provides employment for graduate students in a research capacity.

Cost of Study

For 1997–98, tuition for state residents was $4521 per term for full-time students (9 to 15 credits) and $374 per credit for part-time students (1 to 8 credits). Nonresident tuition was $9314 per term full-time and $769 per credit part-time.

Living and Housing Costs

Most graduate students live in nearby apartments off campus, and costs vary depending upon the accommodations desired. The Commuter Resource Center provides community listings of private rooms and apartments for rent throughout the year. The Office of Property Management lists University-owned rental units. Registered students are eligible for a voluntary board plan on campus.

Student Group

There were approximately 250 graduate students in the School of Health and Rehabilitation Sciences during the 1997–98 year. They represent a wide variety of professionals in the health-care system.

Location

The University of Pittsburgh's main campus, in Pittsburgh's cultural and medical center, is close to the city's central business district. Pittsburgh is a leading metropolitan area known for its recreation, arts, cultural resources, and distinctive ethnic diversity. Entertainment resources include symphony, chamber music, opera, light opera, theater, ballet, museums, galleries, art festivals, folk festivals, and sports events. There are nearby facilities for virtually all indoor and outdoor leisure activities.

The University

The University of Pittsburgh, a private, publicly supported institution completing its 211th year, is a member of the AAU research university organization. It is committed to further enhancing the quality of its programs of teaching, research, and public service and to maintaining the stature and prestige of the University and its schools, faculties, and graduates. Pitt has more than 35,000 enrolled students, who are served by 3,000 faculty members. At the center of the Pittsburgh campus is the Gothic-inspired Cathedral of Learning, a forty-two-story skyscraper that houses administrative offices and classrooms and is one of the tallest school buildings in the country. Its Nationality Rooms, memorials to the city's ethnic heritage, are toured each year by visitors from all over the world. The University's four regional campuses provide programs that complement those at the Pittsburgh campus. The School of Health and Rehabilitation Sciences is one of six schools that make up the schools of the health sciences. These six schools—the Schools of Dental Medicine, Health and Rehabilitation Sciences, Medicine, Nursing, Pharmacy, and the Graduate School of Public Health—have a coordinated program of teaching and research in the health and medical sciences. The schools participate actively as a resource in services to the community, state, and nation.

Applying

GRE scores are required for the entry-level physical therapy (M.P.T.) program, the M.S. and M.A. programs in communication science and disorders, and the Ph.D. programs. None of the other graduate programs require entrance examinations. International applicants whose native language is not English must submit TOEFL scores. Applicants to the occupational therapy and physical therapy programs must have professional certification to be eligible. The admission deadline for the M.S. and M.A. in communication science and disorders is March 20; the deadline for entry-level physical therapy is November 30. Students are accepted into all other programs on a rolling basis.

Correspondence and Information

School of Health and Rehabilitation Sciences
Office of Admissions
4019 Forbes Tower
University of Pittsburgh
Pittsburgh, Pennsylvania 15260

Telephone: 412-647-1252
Fax: 412-647-1255
E-mail: shrsadmi+@pitt.edu
World Wide Web: http://www.shrs.upmc.edu

University of Pittsburgh

THE FACULTY

Department of Clinical Dietetics and Nutrition
Graduate emphasis: clinical dietetics.

Faculty research interests: nutrition intervention in medical nutrition therapy, health promotion, and disease prevention emphasizing athletic training and rehabilitation; nutrition for women's health; pediatric nutrition; pediatric developmental disabilities; alternate feeding modalities; and nutrition in the elderly.

Regina M. Onda, Ph.D., RD, Acting Chairman.
Catherine Connell, M.P.M., RD.
Andrea (Kim) Crawford, M.S., RD.
Judith Dodd, M.S., RD.
Diane Helsel, M.A., RD.
Charles Hollinger, M.Ed.
Lisa McDermott, M.S., RD, CDE.
Mary Miller, M.P.H., RD.

Department of Communication Science and Disorders
Graduate emphases: speech-language pathology, audiology.

Faculty research interests: genetics, fluency, aphasia, auditory rehabilitation, hearing aids, auditory electrophysiology, voice disorders, speech motor control, otitis media, pediatric language disorders, right-hemisphere communication impairment.

Malcolm R. McNeil, Ph.D., CCC-SLP, Chairman.
Ellen Cohn, Ph.D., CCC-SLP.
Thomas Campbell, Ph.D.
Christine A. Dollaghan, Ph.D., CCC-SLP.
Patrick J. Doyle, Ph.D.
John Durrant, Ph.D.
Diane Eger, Ph.D.
Davida Fromm, Ph.D., CCC-SLP.
Judith Grayhack, Ph.D., CCC-SLP.
Aage Moller, Ph.D.
Robert Nebes, Ph.D.
Catherine V. Palmer, Ph.D., CCC-A.
Sheila R. Pratt, Ph.D., CCC-A/SLP.
Diane Sabo, Ph.D.
Susan Shaiman, Ph.D.
Connie Tompkins, Ph.D., CCC-SLP.

Department of Health Information Management
World Wide Web: http://www.pitt.edu/~him
Graduate emphases: health information systems, health-care supervision and management (HSM).

Faculty research interests: medical informatics, computer-based patient records, telemedicine, registries/databases and information retrieval, human resource management, neural networks, policy analysis in health care and long-term care.

Mervat N. Abdelhak, Ph.D., RRA, Chairman.
Patricia Anania-Firouzan, M.S.I.S., RRA.
Frances L. Geigle-Bentz, Ph.D.
Charles Friedman, Ph.D.
John Innocenti, M.B.A.
William Krieger, M.B.A., CPA.
Jane Mazzoni-Maddigan, Ph.D., RRA.
Wilbur McCoy Otto, Esq.
Bambang Parmanto, Ph.D.
Wesley M. Rohrer III, M.B.A., Ph.D.
Melissa Saul, M.S.
Myrna Silverman, Ph.D.
August M. Turano, Ph.D.
Valerie J. M. Watzlaf, Ph.D., RRA.
Sharon Winters, M.S., CTR, RRA.

Department of Occupational Therapy
Graduate emphasis: occupational therapy.

Faculty research interests: assistive technology; fine motor coordination in children; occupational therapy education; functional assessment and rehabilitation of older adults; relationship between impairment and disability.

Jennifer Angelo, Ph.D., OTR/L, Acting Chairman.
Carmela Battaglia, M.S., OTR/L.
Caroline Brayley, Ph.D., OTR/L.
Denise Chisholm, OTR/L.
Joan Rogers, Ph.D., OTR/L.

Department of Physical Therapy
Graduate emphasis: musculoskeletal or neuromuscular.

Faculty research interests: biomechanics of movement, cellular neurophysiology, low back syndrome, biomechanics of the spine and extremities, knee ligament and reconstruction, sports medicine, facial neuromuscular disorders, balance and vestibular rehabilitation, geriatric rehabilitation.

Anthony Delitto, Ph.D., PT, Chairman.
Ray Burdett, Ph.D., PT, Vice Chairman.
George Carvell, Ph.D., PT, Associate Dean of Graduate Studies and Research.
Roberta D'Achille, M.S., PT.
Brian Egloff, M.P.T.
Richard Erhard, D.C., PT.
Katherine Flood, M.D.
Freddie H. Fu, M.D.
Joseph Furman, M.D., Ph.D.
Jere Gallagher, Ph.D.
Elizabeth Hile, M.P.T.
Christopher Hughes, Ph.D., PT.
Jay Irrgang, M.S., PT, ATC, Vice Chairman.
Ray Jurewicz, PT.
Kathy Kelly, M.S., PT.
Greg Marchetti, M.S., PT.
Kenneth Metz, Ph.D.
David Pezzullo, M.S., PT, ATC, SCS.
Mark Redfern, Ph.D.
Fred Schomburg, M.M.Sc., PT.
Rosemary Scully, Ed.D., PT.
Michael Timko, M.S., PT, OMT.
Jessie VanSwearingen, Ph.D., PT.
Mary Kay Walsh, M.S., PT, NCS.
Sherry Warunek-Mascio, M.S., PT.
Susan Whitney, Ph.D., PT, ATC.

Department of Rehabilitation Science and Technology
Graduate emphases: rehabilitation technology and rehabilitation engineering.

Faculty research interests: augmentative communication, rehabilitation engineering, wheelchair design, disability and assistive devices, upper extremity biomechanics, biomedical engineering, audiologic methods, implementation of service delivery models, international appropriate rehabilitation technology, ergonomics and seating.

Rory Cooper, Ph.D., Chairman.
Jennifer Angelo, Ph.D., OTR/L.
Bruce R. Baker, A.M.
Gina Bertocci, Ph.D.
Michael L. Boninger, M.D.
David Brienza, Ph.D.
Clifford E. Brubaker, Ph.D., Dean.
John Coltellaro, M.S.
Allen Condeluci, Ph.D.
Kennerly Diggs, Ph.D.
John Durrant, Ph.D.
Kimberly Henry, B.S.
Douglas A. Hobson, Ph.D.
Andrew F. Jinks, M.A.
Peter Johnson, Ph.D.
Lynda J. Katz, Ph.D.
Paul Kornblith, Ph.D.
Jorge E. Letechipia, M.Sc.
Robert Lynch, AIA.
Arthur Mak, Ph.D.
Michael McCue, Ph.D.
Louis E. Penrod, M.D.
Mark S. Redfern, Ph.D.
Richard Robertson, Ph.D.
Charles J. Robinson, D.Sc., PE.
Mark Schmeler, M.S., OTR/L.
Nigel Shapcott, M.Sc.
Lucy Spruill, M.S.W.
Changfeng Tai, Ph.D.
Elaine Trefler, M.Ed., OTR/L.
William Welch, Ph.D.
Savio L. Y. Woo, Ph.D.
Ying-Wei Yuan, Ph.D.

UNIVERSITY OF VIRGINIA

Graduate School of Arts and Sciences / School of Medicine
Department of Health Evaluation Sciences

Programs of Study

One of the first programs of its kind, the interdisciplinary Master of Science program in health evaluation sciences is an invaluable asset both to new graduate students who seek effective preparation for a career in the modern, dynamic health-care field and to current health professionals who wish to enhance their clinical, research, administrative, or information management skills.

The 30-credit program, designed to be completed in one year of intensive full-time study, provides a broad-based introduction to the basic clinical sciences and provides flexibility for students to choose from among five tracks. Part-time study options are also available. A joint M.D./M.S. in health evaluation sciences is available to UVA medical students. Students should contact the program coordinator for details.

Concentrations are offered in epidemiology, clinical investigation, health services research and outcomes evaluation, health care informatics, and health care resource management. Students complete a core curriculum of five courses in the fall semester; the spring is devoted to completing specialized course work appropriate to a student's chosen concentration and a thesis or project conducted under the supervision of a faculty adviser.

The program's faculty includes internationally recognized leaders in the fields of epidemiology, risk adjustment, clinical trials, medical informatics, and medical decision making. Faculty members from various departments in the School of Medicine and elsewhere at the University of Virginia are closely involved in student advising and research supervision within the program.

Research Facilities

The Department of Health Evaluation Sciences occupies newly renovated space in the University of Virginia Health Sciences Center. The main departmental space includes a modern classroom.

The University of Virginia Health Sciences Library is a fully equipped research library that contains more than 185,000 volumes as well as computer facilities and a variety of online reference services. The Health Sciences Library and Department of Health Evaluation Sciences enjoy a close collaborative relationship in the realms of information management and informatics.

Students also have access to fourteen other University libraries, including Alderman Library, one of the finest research libraries in the country, and numerous network-enabled computing facilities around the University grounds.

Financial Aid

The department actively searches for outside sources of financial support on an ongoing basis. Inquiries about the current availability of outside aid and part-time employment opportunities should be directed to the Program Coordinator.

If no such aid is available, it is recommended that students apply for federal student loans.

Cost of Study

For the 1998–99 academic year, full-time out-of-state tuition is $15,818. Full-time in-state tuition is $4870. Students are also charged a one-time application fee of $40. Total nontuition fees are $958 for all full-time students.

Living and Housing Costs

On-grounds housing costs per academic year range from roughly $2000 (single-student residential housing) to approximately $4000 (married-student housing). The cost of living in Charlottesville is moderate in comparison to larger metropolitan areas. Students should allow an additional $5000 per academic year to cover food, entertainment, and insurance expenses. All students are required to carry hospitalization insurance.

Graduate students are not required to live on grounds and may make any living arrangements they deem suitable.

Student Group

The University of Virginia has a student body of approximately 18,000, of whom nearly one fourth are graduate students. The program in health evaluation sciences is projected to grow to 40 students within five years.

Student Outcomes

An M.S. in health evaluation sciences uniquely equips students to meet the challenges posed by the sweeping changes that are now occurring in the health professions as researchers concerned with traditional questions of disease etiology and prognosis, clinicians interested in the effectiveness and quality of medical treatments and interventions, administrators of health-care organizations concerned with the economically sound and effective use of resources or the evaluation and management of their institutions, or planners of health policy in local, state, or national government agencies. The degree also serves as excellent preparation for M.D. or Ph.D. programs.

Location

The University of Virginia is located in central Charlottesville, beautifully situated in the foothills of the Blue Ridge Mountains. Founded in 1762, Charlottesville, with its growing population of approximately 40,000, combines historical charm and small-town friendliness with a cosmopolitan cultural and economic sophistication normally seen only in much larger cities. The area offers a rich variety of outdoor recreation activities, including hiking, camping, canoeing and rafting, skiing, and rock climbing. Students can easily take advantage of other academic resources, cultural attractions, and sports events in nearby Richmond and Washington, D.C.

The University and The Department

Thomas Jefferson founded the University of Virginia's "Academical Village" in 1819. The beautiful grounds and diverse program offerings are lasting tributes to his aesthetic vision and educational ideals. The University of Virginia encompasses ten schools.

The Schools of Medicine and Nursing rank among the ten highest-funded institutions by the National Institutes of Health. The Master of Science in health evaluation sciences is one of ninety-four master's degrees offered by the University in fifty-six fields.

The Department of Health Evaluation Sciences, the first department of its kind in a U.S. medical school, was formed in 1995 with broad-based support from the University in response to fundamental changes occurring in the medical sciences. Advances in basic research have led to a variety of new therapies that have progressed hand in hand with similarly profound developments in the areas of information processing and sharing. The department's mission is to create an expanded knowledge base and a better understanding of the mechanisms and relationships among basic biological discoveries, patient characteristics, treatment options, system design considerations, and optimal patient outcomes. These new approaches are intended to improve health-care research and delivery and facilitate better communication and sharing of responsibility between clinicians and patients.

Applying

The normal departmental admissions deadline is March 31. Applications received after this date are considered on a space-available basis.

Applicants must submit a two-page application along with a statement of purpose, two letters of recommendation, transcripts of all college-level course work, and official reports of either GRE or MCAT scores. International students must also submit TOEFL scores (minimum acceptable score is 600). Payment of the $40 application fee should accompany application materials. Interviews are optional but encouraged.

Students should submit applications to the Graduate School of Arts and Sciences, 437 Cabell Hall, University of Virginia, Charlottesville, Virginia 22903.

Correspondence and Information

M.S. Program Coordinator
Department of Health Evaluation Sciences
University of Virginia School of Medicine, Box 600
Charlottesville, Virginia 22908

Telephone: 804-924-8646
Fax: 804-924-8437
E-mail: ms-hes@virginia.edu
World Wide Web: http://www.med.virginia.edu/docs/hes/ms-program/

University of Virginia

THE FACULTY AND THEIR RESEARCH

Clinical Investigation Track

Frank E. Harrell, Ph.D., Professor of Biostatistics and Statistics and Head of Clinical Investigation Track. Survival analysis, general linear models, statistical computing, model validation using resampling, modeling strategies, nonparametrics, applied Bayesian methods, statistical graphics, clinical trials, pharmaceutical studies.

Students learn and are able to apply the basic sciences of clinical investigation: measurement, data analysis, computing, and the design/conduct/interpretation of clinical trials.

Epidemiology Track

Paige P. Hornsby, Ph.D., Assistant Professor of Health Evaluation Sciences and Head of Epidemiology Track. Women's health, reproductive epidemiology, health promotion and disease prevention.

Students learn the methods for studying the distribution and determinants of infectious and chronic disease in populations and how to apply these methods to the control of health problems.

Health Care Informatics Track

Robert E. Reynolds, M.D., Dr.P.H., Professor of Medicine and Health Evaluation Sciences, Vice Provost for Health Sciences, and Head of Health Care Informatics Track. Development and evaluation of the Clinical Data Repository, academic and health-care administration, medical informatics and information sciences, primary care.

Students design, implement, and use information systems and tools to assess the quality, effectiveness, and costs of health care.

Health Care Resource Management Track

Armando L. Bolmey, M.B.A., Lecturer, Administrative Director of the Department of Health Evaluation Sciences, and Head of Health Care Resource Management Track. Health-care management and policy, total quality management, use of quantitative methods to improve medical care.

Students learn to accurately measure and comprehensively evaluate, manage, and improve the efficiency, efficacy, and quality performance of a variety of health-care institutions.

Health Services Research and Outcomes Evaluation Track

Alfred F. Connors Jr., M.D., Professor of Health Evaluation Sciences and Medicine and Head of Health Services Research and Outcomes Evaluation Track. Evaluation and measurement of patient outcomes, effectiveness of therapy, effectiveness of processes of care, medical decision making, management of the seriously ill.

Students master the description, analysis, and evaluation of the organization, financing, utilization, and delivery of health care. Students learn the methods of measuring, evaluating, and analyzing outcomes from the perspective of the patient, the caregiver, the third-party payer, and society. The track emphasizes methods for ensuring cost-effective, quality care for populations and individuals.

OTHER PRIMARY FACULTY AND RESEARCH INTERESTS

Robert D. Abbott, Ph.D., Professor of Biostatistics and Statistics. Survival analysis, cardiovascular epidemiology, competing risks, statistical models for dementia and cognitive impairment, repeated measures, nonlinear regression.

Wendy F. Cohn, Ph.D., Assistant Professor of Health Evaluation Sciences. Program evaluation, outcomes research, public health, epidemiology, qualitative research, substance abuse.

Jonathan Einbinder, M.D., M.P.H., Assistant Professor of Health Evaluation Sciences and Medicine. Electronic patient records, quality improvement.

Carolyn L. Engelhard, M.P.A., Lecturer in Health Evaluation Sciences and Executive Director of the Virginia Health Policy Research Center. State government health policy issues: Medicaid (particularly long-term care), regulation of insurance and managed-care plans, and the uninsured; macro health policy issues: quality initiatives, academic health centers, Medicare, and medical education.

Barry M. Farr, M.D., M.Sc., William S. Jordan, Jr. Professor of Medicine and Hospital Epidemiologist. Hospital epidemiology, clinical epidemiology, nosocomial infections, epidemiology of infectious diseases.

Jack M. Gwaltney Jr., M.D., Professor of Medicine and Chief of the Division of Epidemiology and Virology. Acute respiratory disease, common cold, acute sinusitis.

Diane G. Hillman, M.P.A., Lecturer in Health Evaluation Sciences and Assistant Vice President for Health Sciences Planning. Effects of the changing health-care delivery system on use rates and outcomes, use of information systems to change and improve administrative processes and practice patterns, effect of information systems on organizational structure and function.

William A. Knaus, M.D., Evelyn Troup Hobson Professor and Chair of Health Evaluation Sciences. Critical care medicine, severity of illness measurements, medical decision making, clinical outcomes research.

Elizabeth I. Merwin, Ph.D., Associate Professor of Nursing and Health Evaluation Sciences. Mental health delivery systems research, including studies of cost, access, and quality of care.

Mario Peruggia, Ph.D., Associate Professor of Biostatistics and Statistics. Bayesian statistics, with applications in the medical sciences.

Gina R. Petroni, Ph.D., Assistant Professor of Biostatistics and Statistics. Clinical trials design, cancer clinical trials, survival analysis.

John B. Schorling, M.D., Associate Professor of Medicine. Health problems of disadvantaged primary-care patients: diabetes and other cardiovascular risk factors; substance abuse, including cigarette smoking; depression and other mental health problems; association of diarrhea with nutritional status among children in an urban Brazilian slum.

Douglas P. Wagner, Ph.D., Professor of Health Evaluation Sciences. Severity of illness (hospital case mix) measurement, clinical trial design for acutely ill patients, medical decision making, health economics, statistical and econometric methods, cost/benefit analysis.

VIRGINIA COMMONWEALTH UNIVERSITY

Medical College of Virginia Campus
School of Allied Health Professions
Department of Health Administration

Programs of Study

Virginia Commonwealth University is the home of four excellent graduate programs in health services administration. Three master's degree programs are designed to prepare individuals for executive positions in health service organizations: the Master of Health Administration (M.H.A.) degree program; the Executive Program leading to the degree of Master of Science in Health Administration (M.S.H.A.); and a dual-degree program leading to the award of both the M.H.A. and Juris Doctor (J.D.) degrees. The fourth graduate degree program offered by the Department of Health Administration is a Ph.D. degree in health services organization and research.

The M.H.A. degree program is a full-time program completed in four semesters of on-campus study followed by a one-year administrative residency. The Executive Program (M.S.H.A.) is oriented to individuals working full-time, residing anywhere in the United States, who seek graduate management education for continued career development. Utilizing a distance learning model, self-motivated, mature, and experienced professionals interact with faculty members and classmates using state-of-the-art Internet technology throughout a two-year course of study, which includes five on-campus sessions on the Medical College of Virginia (MCV) Campus. The dual M.H.A./J.D. degree program, conducted in cooperation with the T. C. Williams School of Law at the University of Richmond, allows students to combine three-year programs in both law and health administration, completing both degrees in four years by taking courses (including summer residencies) for twelve months each year. The Ph.D. degree program prepares individuals for positions as faculty members, researchers, policy analysts, and top-level staff members in complex health organizations. The Ph.D. course work can be completed in two years of full-time study, exclusive of dissertation requirements.

Research Facilities

The David G. Williamson, Jr. Institute for Health Studies of the Department of Health Administration provides both a financial and structural framework for the research activities of faculty members and students. The department is well equipped with computer technology and has excellent access to relevant databases on which significant and valuable health services research is conducted.

Financial Aid

Students are eligible for limited scholarships and traineeships offered through the School of Allied Health Professions and the Department of Health Administration. In addition, the Department offers employment assistance, which provides opportunities for students to work with faculty members, area alumni, and many other organizations in part-time and summer employment opportunities. During the third year of the M.H.A. program (the administrative residency), students are paid a stipend by their sponsoring organization.

Cost of Study

Tuition and fees for the 1997–98 academic year were $14,657 for nonresidents and $7174 for Virginia residents for the M.S.H.A. and $12,265 for nonresidents and $4782 for Virginia residents for the M.H.A.

Living and Housing Costs

University-sponsored housing includes dormitories located on campus and a number of apartments for married students. Average expenses for on-campus housing are approximately $2000 per semester. Many options for off-campus housing are available throughout the city and surrounding areas, some accessible to campus via public transportation. Off-campus housing ranges from $300 to more than $1000 per month and is available within easy travel distances of the MCV Campus.

Student Group

Approximately 30 students each are admitted annually to the M.H.A. (including M.H.A./J.D.) and M.S.H.A. programs. The Ph.D. program admits approximately 6 students each year. A master's degree is required for admission to the Ph.D. program. While experience in health services is desirable for admission to the graduate programs, it is not a requirement for the M.H.A. program. International students and students from diverse cultural backgrounds are welcomed, and the graduate program classes are approximately 50 percent men and 50 percent women.

Student Outcomes

The demand for professionally prepared health services executives, educators, and researchers remains high. Alumni of the master's-level graduate programs hold leadership positions in hospitals, nursing homes, integrated health systems, managed care organizations, health insurance companies, and management consulting firms. Ph.D. graduates hold positions as university faculty members, health services researchers, and policy analysts. The Department of Health Administration offers its graduates and alumni assistance with placement services throughout their careers.

Location

Richmond, the capital of Virginia, has become a contemporary urban center. Richmond is located along the scenic James River and, with a metropolitan population of 935,000, offers a wide variety of cultural and leisure opportunities, including museums, art galleries, stage and music performances, and sports events. Colonial Williamsburg, Jamestown, and Yorktown are nearby, and Richmond is an easy 2-hour drive from beautiful Atlantic coast beaches, the scenic Blue Ridge Mountains, and the nation's capital, Washington, D.C. The blend of tradition, economic development, temperate climate, and geographic location provides an attractive environment in which to live and work.

The University

Virginia Commonwealth University is the largest urban institution of higher education in Virginia. Approximately 4,700 students are on the MCV Campus, and overall University enrollment is 21,000. The Department of Health Administration's master's degree programs were recently ranked seventh among all U.S. graduate programs in health services administration. The M.H.A. program (founded in 1949) was one of the first programs of its kind in the United States, and the Department of Health Administration has produced approximately 1,700 graduates who have been leaders in the advancement of the profession of health administration and management.

Applying

Admission to the graduate programs is competitive; therefore, applicants are encouraged to apply early. All applications for the academic year must be received by the March 15 of that year for the master's degree programs and by May 15 for the doctoral program.

Correspondence and Information

Director, Professional Graduate Programs or
Director, Ph.D. Program
Department of Health Administration
MCV Campus
Virginia Commonwealth University
P.O. Box 980203
Richmond, Virginia 23298-0203
Telephone: 804-828-0719 (master's degree programs)
804-828-5220 (Ph.D. program)
Fax: 804-828-1894
World Wide Web: http://www.had.vcu.edu

Virginia Commonwealth University

THE FACULTY AND THEIR RESEARCH

Thomas C. Barker, Professor and Dean Emeritus, School of Allied Health Professions; Ph.D. (hospital and health administration), Iowa, 1963. Health policy, long-term care, ethics in health care and health manpower education, distribution and utilization.

Dolores G. Clement, Associate Professor and Associate Dean, School of Allied Health Professions; Dr.P.H. (health policy and administration), Berkeley, 1988. Health-care policy, the management of information for complex health-care organizations, and international health care; examination of patterns of diffusion, growth, and survival among alternative health-care organizations; satisfaction and access to care in Medicare risk contract HMOs; and the use of alternative payment strategies by Medicare.

Jan P. Clement, Associate Professor and Director of Professional Graduate Programs; Ph.D. (health policy and administration), North Carolina, 1986. Financial strategy for health-care firms, the financial behavior of managers of not-for-profit firms, and financial evaluation techniques; empirical research on cost-shifting, uncompensated care, and corporate strategy.

Paul A. Gross, Professor Emeritus; M.H.A. (hospital administration), Virginia Commonwealth, 1964. Strategic management and design of health-care organizations, physician-administration relations.

Robert E. Hurley, Associate Professor; Ph.D. (health policy and administration), North Carolina, 1988. Alternative delivery and financing systems, Medicaid reform, the application of organization theory to health services organizations.

Richard C. Kraus, Professor and Executive in Residence; M.H.A. (hospital administration), Virginia Commonwealth, 1964. Operational and strategic management of health-care organizations.

Roice D. Luke, Professor; Ph.D. (medical care organization, health economics), Michigan, 1976. Strategic management and health-care policy; the structures of local markets and the strategic behaviors of local hospital systems.

Michael J. McCue, Associate Professor; D.B.A. (finance), Kentucky, 1985. Health-care finance and performance of multihospital systems; the financial and operating performance of system-affiliated psychiatric and rehabilitative hospitals.

Yasar A. Ozcan, Associate Professor; Ph.D. (health administrative sciences), Virginia Commonwealth, 1988. Mathematical modeling applications in health care, health-care information systems, general statistical applications; health systems productivity, technical efficiency, financial efficiency, and effectiveness for health-care providers.

Louis F. Rossiter, Professor and Founding Director of the David G. Williamson, Jr., Institute for Health Studies; Ph.D. (economics), North Carolina, 1977. Competition and the financing and delivery of health-care services, particularly in reimbursement incentive policies and their effects on health-care expenditures; strategic and operational issues surrounding Medicaid and Medicare alternative health systems.

Ramesh K. Shukla, Professor and Director of the Williamson Institute for Health Studies; Ph.D. (systems engineering), Wisconsin–Madison, 1977. Manpower utilization and productivity, decision support systems, and hospital information systems; evaluating various strategies for improving manpower productivity without reducing quality of care or employee satisfaction; assessing and separating the effects of people, structures, and systems on manpower performance and productivity in nursing services.

Karen N. Swisher, Associate Professor and Associate Director of the Williamson Institute; J.D., Richmond, 1981. Medical law, medical sociology, business policy, and bioethics.

Thomas T. H. Wan, Professor and Chairman of the Department of Health Administration; Ph.D. (sociology), Georgia, 1970. Managerial epidemiology, long-term care research, health services research and clinical outcome evaluation, and medical sociology.

Kenneth R. White, Assistant Professor and Associate Director of Professional Graduate Programs; Ph.D. (health services organization and research), Virginia Commonwealth, 1996. Organizational theory and design, behavior of Catholic health-care organizations, the strategic direction of the nursing profession.

OTHER UNIVERSITY FACULTY MEMBERS WITH JOINT APPOINTMENTS

Tilahun Adera, Assistant Professor, Ph.D.
Mary N. Blackwood, Instructor, M.H.A.
Viktor E. Bovbjerg, Assistant Professor, Ph.D.
Thomas H. Casey, Assistant Professor, Ph.D.
Robert Cohen, Professor, Ph.D.
John Dayhoff, Associate Professor, M.A.
Anthony J. DeLellis, Associate Professor, Ed.D.
Christopher E. Desch, Associate Professor, M.D.
Carl R. Fischer, Associate Professor, M.H.A.
Donald C. H. Gehring, Assistant Professor, J.D.
Jack Lanier, Professor, Dr.P.H.
Barbara Mark, Professor, Ph.D.; RN.
Paul Mazmanian, Professor, Ph.D.
Michael A. Pyles, Assistant Professor, Ph.D.
Sheldon M. Retchin, Professor, M.D.
Thomas J. Smith, Associate Professor, M.D.
Wally R. Smith, Assistant Professor, M.D.
M. Scott Sullivan, Associate Professor, Ph.D.
Deborah L. Ulmer, Assistant Professor, Ph.D.
David S. Wilkinson, Professor, M.D.
John M. Witherspoon, Professor, M.D., M.P.H.

WASHINGTON UNIVERSITY IN ST. LOUIS

School of Medicine
Graduate Program in Health Administration

Program of Study

Washington University offers a full-time, two-year graduate program in health administration through its School of Medicine. Upon completion of the four semesters of study (60 units), the student receives a Master of Health Administration degree (M.H.A.). The student then has the option of pursuing a postgraduate twelve-month administrative residency, for which a certificate is awarded by Washington University and the affiliated residency organization.

Research Facilities

Students in the Health Administration Program may use the facilities of both the main campus, known as the Hilltop campus, and the medical school campus, including the major affiliated teaching hospitals of the University. The metropolitan area's health-care organizations, hospital association, long-term-care facilities, and community hospitals offer rich learning resources. Library facilities available are the Medical Library, the Olin Library on the Hilltop campus, public libraries of the city and county, and the Catholic Health Association Library. There is a computer center containing IBM microcomputers for the exclusive use of health administration students. Available software includes spreadsheet programs, statistical packages, graphics, word processing, and database management systems.

Financial Aid

Financial assistance is awarded on the basis of documented financial need and upon availability of funds. Approximately 80 percent of the students receive financial aid, awarded in varying amounts, in the form of scholarships and no-interest departmental loans.

Cost of Study

Tuition, which includes mandatory health insurance, is $20,500 for 1998–99.

Living and Housing Costs

Estimated living expenses, including books and supplies, for a single student are $20,000. A dormitory for graduate students in the allied health professions is located on the medical school campus. Apartments are available in the St. Louis area within walking or driving distance.

Student Group

Students in the program are very heterogeneous with respect to their undergraduate majors. Of the approximately 65 students, about half have had full-time work experience, half are women, and the average age is 25. Many of the students work part-time while pursuing their M.H.A. degree. Throughout its more than fifty-year history, the program has produced many leaders in the health-care industry. More than 1,000 graduates are active in health management areas. The program sponsors a successful professional placement program.

Location

The program is located within the Washington University Medical Center and is adjacent to the fashionable Central West End. St. Louis is a major center of industry, commerce, culture, education, sports, and health care.

The University and The Program

Washington University was chartered in 1853 by the state of Missouri, and in 1899 the Washington University School of Medicine was formed by the union of St. Louis Medical College and the Missouri Medical College. At the end of World War II, along with the need for well-trained physicians, a need for knowledgeable managers of health institutions was observed by many administrators at teaching hospitals. In 1946, Washington University established a graduate course in hospital administration under the guidance of Frank R. Bradley, M.D., director of Barnes Hospital. The program began as an academic unit within the School of Medicine because that school was believed to be best equipped to produce such expert managers, and the program is still in this setting today.

Applying

All applicants must have a bachelor's degree from an accredited college or university. No specific undergraduate major is required. A semester of accounting is the only required course. Applicants must submit GMAT or GRE General Test scores, three reference letters, and transcripts of all previous studies. Once the file is complete, an on-site interview in St. Louis is required. Individuals are judged primarily by a critical evaluation of their demonstrated academic ability and potential. Consideration is given to health-care experience, motivation, and leadership.

Correspondence and Information

Admissions
Health Administration Program
School of Medicine
Washington University in St. Louis
4547 Clayton Avenue
St. Louis, Missouri 63110
Telephone: 314-362-3274

Washington University in St. Louis

THE FACULTY AND THEIR RESEARCH

Stuart B. Boxerman, D.Sc., Associate Professor and Deputy Director. Statistics, quantitative methods and information systems.
Ronald E. Gribbins, Ph.D., Assistant Professor. Organizational behavior.
James O. Hepner, Ph.D., Professor and Director. Health-care organization, planning.
Dennis L. Lambert, Ph.D., Instructor. Finance.
Mark A. Schnitzler, Ph.D., Research Lecturer. Statistical research methods.
Robert S. Woodward, Ph.D., Associate Professor. Finance.

Adjunct Faculty
Marlowe W. Erickson, Ph.D., Lecturer. Psychology.
Joan M. Evans, Ph.D., Lecturer. Strategic health-care management and marketing.
Zachary B. Gerbarg, M.D., Lecturer. Managed care.
Michael A. Gross, B.S., Lecturer; CPA. Accounting.
Philip J. Karst, Ph.D., Lecturer. Managed care.
Terry L. Leet, Ph.D., Lecturer. Epidemiology.
Patricia Mueth, M.H.S.M.; RN. Information systems.
Wesley P. Sperr, B.A., Lecturer. Long-term care.
Stuart D. Yoak, Ph.D., Lecturer. Ethics.

XAVIER UNIVERSITY

College of Social Sciences
Graduate Program in Health Services Administration

Program of Study

The Graduate Program in Health Services Administration awards a Master of Health Services Administration (M.H.S.A.) degree. Established in 1958, the Graduate Program has a strong tradition of success and is accredited by the Accrediting Commission on Education for Health Services Administration (ACEHSA).

The program's academic work and administrative residency prepare qualified individuals with the specific knowledge and experience required to achieve high-level management positions and success in today's rapidly changing health-care field. Critical to this success is the understanding of patient, community, governmental, clinical, and ethical influences on health-care management decision making. The program of study develops a strong foundation of business management skills, then further enhances the student's ability to succeed in the health-care field through course work in areas such as applied epidemiology, population-based planning, clinical outcomes management, ethical decision making, health-policy analysis, physician relations, managed care, integrated health delivery systems, and provider payment strategies.

Students may pursue an M.H.S.A./M.B.A. dual degree by completing one to two additional semesters of M.B.A. graduate course work. The Graduate Program also offers a concentration in long-term care administration. After completing an administrative residency under the preceptorship of a licensed nursing home administrator, the student may sit for the State of Ohio licensure exam.

The traditional full-time program involves sixteen months of academic study on campus, followed by an eight- to twelve-month full-time administrative residency in a health-care facility under the supervision of a preceptor. The part-time evening program for health-care professionals consists of nine semesters of academic study along with directed field experiences completed at their places of employment.

Research Facilities

Affiliations with the University of Cincinnati's Institute for Health Policy and Health Services Research and the Greater Cincinnati Health Council provide opportunities for faculty members and students to work cooperatively with a variety of health professionals in addressing vital operational and policy issues. There are more than 130 health-care organizations in greater Cincinnati, ranging from large integrated delivery systems and medical centers to rural health networks, managed-care institutions, group practices, consulting firms, long-term-care facilities, and insurance companies. The program has collaborative relationships with many of these organizations, and these provide additional opportunities for the Graduate Program to conduct applied health-care research.

The McDonald Memorial Library collection at Xavier University numbers more than 350,000 books and periodicals and 600,000 pieces of microfilm and microfiche. The library receives more than 1,500 subscriptions to periodicals, including a comprehensive listing for the M.H.S.A. program. Electronic resources include computerized indexes and online research services such as Medline and HealthSTAR. Xavier University provides state-of-the-art computer–related services and Internet access.

Financial Aid

Students are eligible to apply for graduate assistantships, university and program scholarships, professional association and minority scholarships and grants, U.S. Public Health Service traineeships, deferred tuition payment plans, and loan funds. Students typically receive stipends from their preceptor organizations during the administrative residency. Administrative stipends for the 1997 residency year averaged more than $2000 per month with benefits.

The Graduate Program's relationship with health services organizations throughout the greater Cincinnati area often results in part-time paid research assistantships or internships. These informal arrangements provide students with financial assistance while they gain valuable health-care work experience.

Cost of Study

The 1998–99 tuition fees are $400 per credit hour. The student should also budget approximately $500 per semester for textbooks and other fees. The stipend students receive during the administrative residency typically helps offset the total cost of the academic portion of the degree.

Living and Housing Costs

Graduate students live off-campus throughout the Cincinnati area. Living expenses average $897 per month. This estimate may vary depending on the personal requirements of the individual student. Information about off-campus housing can be obtained by contacting Commuter Services at 513-745-3824.

Student Group

The Graduate Program's first-year student body consists of approximately 25 full-time students and 15 part-time evening students. The class is typically split equally between male and female students, with an average age of 24 for the full-time students and 32 for the evening students.

The students are highly motivated and share a deep sense of social responsibility. Strong interpersonal, communication, and creative problem-solving skills, work experience, community involvement, and personal commitment are characteristics of the Xavier M.H.S.A. student.

Student Outcomes

Upon graduation, students obtain managerial leadership positions in a variety of health-care organizations, including integrated delivery systems; managed care and insurance companies; medical group practices; long-term care facilities; governmental health, policy, and regulatory agencies; and consulting firms.

More than 75 percent of recent graduates were offered a position in the same organization where they did their residency. Half of the students took positions within a hospital or medical center setting, with the rest going into managed care, group practice, long-term care, and consulting.

Location

Cincinnati has been rated as one of the nation's most livable cities. Xavier University, a 10-minute drive from downtown, is ideally situated with easy access to Cincinnati's many attractions. The city offers unlimited dining, recreation, entertainment, and cultural activities.

The University and the Program

Xavier University, a private Jesuit institution established in 1831, and the Graduate Program in Health Services Administration are nationally recognized for preparing individuals who serve as models of appropriate leadership behavior within their organizations, their professions, and their communities.

M.H.S.A. alumni have a national reputation for leadership excellence in health services administration. Individual alumni have been recognized with such prestigious honors as the American College of Healthcare Executives' Young Administrator of the Year award. With more than 1,550 members, the Graduate Program Alumni Association provides strong support to students, including scholarship funding, a mentoring program, and career assistance after graduation.

Applying

A bachelor's degree from an accredited school is required of all applicants. Typically, applicants are considered academically qualified for acceptance into the Graduate Program if their cumulative undergraduate GPA is 3.0 or above and their GMAT total score exceeds 500. Two letters of recommendation, a resume, a $25 application fee, and a statement of intent must be included with the application. A formal interview is required before the final selection. Preference is given to students with strong academic backgrounds and health-related work experience.

Correspondence and Information

Graduate Program in Health Services Administration
Xavier University
3800 Victory Parkway
Cincinnati, Ohio 45207-7331
Telephone: 513-745-1912
800-344-4698 Ext. 1912 (toll-free)
Fax: 513-745-4301
E-mail: xumhsa@xavier.xu.edu

Xavier University

THE FACULTY AND THEIR RESEARCH

Albert A. Bocklet, Associate Professor Emeritus; Ph.D. (adult education), Arizona State, 1974. Quality of care and the application of neural network technologies to clinical and managerial decision making.

Martin B. Gerowitz, Professor; Ph.D. (management), SUNY at Buffalo, 1975. Determinants of organizational culture and the impact of culture on the structure, behavior, and performance of top management teams within and across various health-delivery organizations.

Lin Guo, Assistant Professor; Ph.D. (industrial engineering), Cincinnati, 1995. Development of ergonomic assessment systems for improving health-care productivity and cost-effectiveness, application of quantitative and informational system methods in continuous quality improvement.

Robert W. Hankins, Assistant Professor; Ph.D. (business administration), North Carolina at Chapel Hill, 1985. Processes through which health-care managers and policy makers use information, particularly the application of activity-based costing to the expansion and competitive operation of vertically integrated systems.

N. Martin MacDowell, Associate Professor; Dr.P.H. (community health practice), Texas School of Public Health, 1982. Applied epidemiology in regard to the development of preventive health-care strategies, the application of neural networks for assessing appropriate service utilization and patient outcomes, the implementation of managed care, especially the use of provider profiling.

Jack G. Reamy, Associate Professor; Ph.D. (management and policy sciences), Texas School of Public Health, 1992. Effects of physician resource management plans in Canada on physician supply and distribution.

Ida Critelli Schick, Associate Professor and Interim Chair; Ph.D. (philosophy), Marquette, 1965. Privacy and confidentiality of information in an electronic environment, the needs and roles of ethics committees in health-care organizations; ethical issues in managed care.

Adjunct Faculty

Alan R. Bayowski, M.S. (gerontological studies), Miami (Ohio), 1980. Utilization of community services, both existing and proposed, for chronically ill patients and an aging population.

Linda M. Harpster, J.D. (law), Kentucky, 1978. Balancing both the rights and the obligations of the constituent parties in a health-care system where laws and regulations are cumbersome, confusing, and conflicting.

Diane Lansberry-Shank, J.D. (law), Cincinnati, 1989. Development and analysis of industry-consistent quality indicators to accurately interpret quality of medical outcomes.

M. Douglas Reed, Ph.D. (counseling and personnel services), Maryland, 1970. Assessment and analysis of the behaviors of people and the organizational systems within which they work, physician leadership development.

Richard E. Sexton, Ph.D. (psychology), Arizona, 1981. Psychological, social, and environmental factors that emerge with advancing age and the interplay of these factors with effective means of intervention.

Sue N. Weinstein, M.D. (medicine), Cincinnati, 1986. Application of continuous quality improvement to clinical practice, community health-status assessment.

Mark A. Wellinghoff, M.S. (community health/planning administration), Cincinnati, 1979. Role of the administrator in developing and administering policies and programs to meet the needs of the chronically ill patient in an aging population.

Section 29
Nursing

This section contains directories of institutions that have graduate units in nursing and offer study in advanced practice, gerontological, maternal/child-care, medical-surgical, oncology, psychiatric, public health, and rehabilitation nursing; nurse anesthesia; nurse midwifery; nursing administration; and nursing education, followed by in-depth entries submitted by institutions that chose to prepare detailed program descriptions. Additional information about programs listed in the directories but not augmented by an in-depth entry may be obtained by writing directly to the dean of a school or chair of a department at the address given in the directory.

For programs offering related work, see also in this book Health Services and Public Health; and in Book 2, Home Economics and Family Studies (Gerontology).

CONTENTS

Program Directories

Announcements

Cross-Discipline Announcement

In-Depth Descriptions

See also:

Nursing—General

Abilene Christian University, School of Nursing, Abilene, TX 79699-9100. Awards MS, MSN. Faculty: 4 part-time (all women). Students: 1 (woman) full-time, 10 part-time (8 women). 1 applicant, 100% accepted. In 1997, 6 degrees awarded. *Application deadline:* 4/1 (priority date; rolling processing; 11/1 for spring admission). *Application fee:* $25 ($45 for international students). *Expenses:* Tuition $308 per credit hour. Fees $430 per year full-time, $85 per semester (minimum) part-time. *Financial aid:* Application deadline 4/1. • Dr. Corinne Bonnett, Dean, 915-672-2441. Application contact: Dr. Carley Dodd, Graduate Dean, 915-674-2354. Fax: 915-674-6717. E-mail: gradinfo@nicanor.acu.edu.

Adelphi University, School of Nursing, Garden City, NY 11530. Awards MS, PhD, PMC. One or more programs accredited by NLN. Part-time and evening/weekend programs available. Students: 150 part-time (146 women); includes 56 minority (24 African Americans, 31 Asian Americans, 1 Hispanic), 1 international. Average age 40. In 1997, 42 master's, 6 doctorates, 29 PMCs awarded. *Degree requirements:* For master's, thesis required, foreign language not required; for doctorate, computer language, dissertation required, foreign language not required. *Entrance requirements:* For master's, BSN, clinical experience; for doctorate, GRE General Test or MAT, MSN, 2 years of clinical experience, previous course work in statistics. Application deadline: rolling. Application fee: $50. *Expenses:* Tuition $16,000 per year full-time, $485 per credit part-time. Fees $500 per year full-time, $150 per semester part-time. *Financial aid:* Research assistantships, teaching assistantships, graduate achievement awards, and career-related internships or fieldwork available. Aid available to part-time students. Financial aid application deadline: 3/1. *Faculty research:* Pain-relaxation techniques, bereavement, family grief, historiography, gerontology. • Dr. Caryle G. Wolahan, Director, 516-877-4545.

See in-depth description on page 1421.

Albany State University, School of Nursing and Allied Health Sciences, Albany, GA 31705-2717. Offers program in nursing (MS). Accredited by NLN. Part-time programs available. Faculty: 5 full-time (4 women). Students: 5 full-time (all women), 10 part-time (all women); includes 8 minority (all African Americans). Average age 28. 10 applicants, 80% accepted. In 1997, 5 degrees awarded. *Degree requirements:* Thesis, comprehensive exam required, foreign language not required. *Entrance requirements:* GRE General Test (minimum combined score of 800) or MAT (minimum score 44), BSN; current Georgia RN license; minimum GPA of 3.0; previous course work in health assessment, nursing research, pathophysiology, and statistics. Application deadline: 9/1 (rolling processing). Application fee: $10. • Dr. Lucille B. Wilson, Dean, 912-430-4724. E-mail: lwilson@fld94.alsnet.peachnet.edu. Application contact: Dr. Doris S. Holeman, Coordinator, Graduate Nursing Program, 912-430-4727. Fax: 912-430-3937. E-mail: dholeman@fld94.alsnet.peachnet.edu.

Alcorn State University, School of Nursing, Lorman, MS 39096-9402. Offers program in rural nursing (MSN). *Application deadline:* 7/1 (priority date; rolling processing; 12/1 for spring admission). *Application fee:* $10. *Tuition:* $2470 per year full-time, $378 per semester (minimum) part-time for state residents; $5331 per year full-time, $855 per semester (minimum) part-time for nonresidents.

Allegheny University of the Health Sciences, School of Nursing, Philadelphia, PA 19102-1192. Awards MSN, Certificate. Part-time programs available. Faculty: 30 full-time (27 women), 2 part-time (both women). Students: 21 full-time (16 women), 55 part-time (52 women). Average age 40. 109 applicants, 75% accepted. In 1997, 8 master's, 6 Certificates awarded. *Entrance requirements:* For master's, GRE General Test (minimum combined score of 1410 on three sections), BSN, professional registered nurse license, 1 year of nursing experience, minimum GPA of 2.75. Application deadline: 5/15 (rolling processing). Application fee: $50. *Expenses:* Tuition $11,390 per year full-time, $630 per credit part-time. Fees $125 per year full-time, $31 per semester part-time. *Financial aid:* Federal Work-Study, institutionally sponsored loans, and career-related internships or fieldwork available. Aid available to part-time students. Financial aid application deadline: 5/1; applicants required to submit FAFSA. • Dr. Gloria Donnelly, Dean, 215-762-1336. Application contact: Dr. Mary Lou McHugh, 215-762-4446.

Allentown College of St. Francis de Sales, Graduate Division, Graduate Program in Nursing, Center Valley, PA 18034-9568. Awards MSN. Accredited by NLN. Part-time and evening/weekend programs available. Faculty: 5 full-time (all women), 1 (woman) part-time. Students: 3 full-time (all women), 17 part-time (15 women); includes 2 minority (1 African American, 1 Hispanic). In 1997, 9 degrees awarded. *Degree requirements:* Thesis optional, foreign language not required. *Average time to degree:* master's–2 years full-time, 5 years part-time. *Entrance requirements:* GRE General Test (minimum score 500 on each section), MAT (minimum score 35), minimum B average (undergraduate), basic statistics, health assessment course or equivalent. Application deadline: rolling. Application fee: $35. *Tuition:* $385 per credit. *Faculty research:* Caring, work of clinical specialist, women's health, fibromyalgia, theory validation, needs of homeless, ovarian cancer. • Dr. Karen Moore Schaefer, Director, 610-282-1100 Ext. 1285.

Andrews University, School of Graduate Studies, College of Arts and Sciences, Department of Nursing, Berrien Springs, MI 49104. Awards MS. Accredited by NLN. Part-time and evening/weekend programs available. Faculty: 6 full-time (all women). *Degree requirements:* Thesis. *Entrance requirements:* Minimum GPA of 2.5, 1 year of nursing experience, RN license. Application deadline: 3/15 (rolling processing). Application fee: $30. *Expenses:* Tuition $290 per quarter hour (minimum). Fees $75 per quarter. *Financial aid:* Institutionally sponsored loans available. *Faculty research:* Theory for nursing, salary equitability. • Dr. Patricia Scott, Chairperson, 616-471-7771. Application contact: Dr. Zerita J. Hagerman, Graduate Program Director, 616-471-3361.

Angelo State University, College of Sciences, Program in Nursing, San Angelo, TX 76909. Awards MSN. Faculty: 4 full-time (all women), 5 part-time (2 women). Students: 8 full-time (all women), 20 part-time (19 women); includes 4 minority (2 Hispanics, 2 Native Americans). 11 applicants, 100% accepted. *Degree requirements:* Comprehensive exam required, foreign language not required. *Entrance requirements:* GRE General Test, minimum GPA of 2.5. Application deadline: 8/7 (priority date; rolling processing; 1/2 for spring admission). Application fee: $25 ($50 for international students). *Expenses:* Tuition $1022 per year full-time, $36 per semester hour part-time for state residents; $7382 per year full-time, $246 per semester hour part-time for nonresidents. Fees $1140 per year full-time, $165 per semester (minimum) part-time. *Financial aid:* In 1997–98, 6 fellowships were awarded. Financial aid application deadline: 8/1. • Dr. Leslie Mayrand, Head, 915-942-2224.

Arizona State University, College of Nursing, Tempe, AZ 85287. Awards MS, MS/MHSA. Accredited by NLN. Faculty: 54 full-time (53 women), 10 part-time (all women). Students: 83 full-time (75 women), 35 part-time (34 women); includes 13 minority (1 African American, 3 Asian Americans, 7 Hispanics, 2 Native Americans). Average age 38. 49 applicants, 88% accepted. In 1997, 62 degrees awarded. *Degree requirements:* Thesis, oral and written exams. *Entrance requirements:* GRE. Application fee: $45. *Expenses:* Tuition $2088 per year full-time, $110 per hour part-time for state residents; $9040 per year full-time, $377 per hour part-time for nonresidents. Fees $72 per year full-time, $18 per semester (minimum) part-time. *Faculty research:* Health education, study of family health-illness behavior. • Dr. Barbara H. Durand, Dean, 602-965-3244. Application contact: Dr. Nancy Melvin, Associate Dean, 602-965-3948.

Arkansas State University, College of Nursing and Health Professions, Program in Nursing, State University, AR 72467. Awards MSN. Accredited by NLN. Part-time programs available. Faculty: 8 full-time (7 women), 2 part-time (both women). Students: 6 full-time (5 women), 81 part-time (69 women); includes 14 minority (all African Americans). Average age 37. In 1997, 15 degrees awarded. *Degree requirements:* Thesis or alternative, comprehensive exam. *Entrance requirements:* GRE General Test or MAT, appropriate bachelor's degree. Application deadline: 7/1 (priority date; rolling processing; 11/15 for spring admission). Application fee: $15 ($25 for international students). *Expenses:* Tuition $2760 per year full-time, $115 per credit hour part-time for state residents; $6936 per year full-time, $289 per credit hour part-time for nonresidents. Fees $506 per year full-time, $44 per semester (minimum) part-time. *Financial aid:* Fellowships, teaching assistantships, partial tuition waivers, and career-related internships or fieldwork available. Aid available to part-time students. Financial aid application deadline: 7/1; applicants required to submit FAFSA. • Dr. Thomas A. Kippenbrock, Chair, 870-972-3074. Fax: 870-972-2954. E-mail: tkippen@crow.astate.edu.

Armstrong Atlantic State University, School of Graduate Studies, Program in Nursing, Savannah, GA 31419-1997. Awards MSN. Accredited by NLN. Faculty: 14. *Expenses:* Tuition $83 per quarter hour for state residents; $250 per quarter hour for nonresidents. Fees $145 per quarter hour for state residents; $228 per quarter hour for nonresidents. • Dr. Camille Stern, Department Head, 912-921-5721.

Augustana College, Program in Advanced Nursing Practice in Emerging Health Systems, Sioux Falls, SD 57197. Awards MA. Students: 12 part-time (10 women). *Application deadline:* 6/1 (priority date; rolling processing). *Application fee:* $50. *Tuition:* $14,726 per year full-time, $250 per credit hour part-time. • Dr. Margot Nelson, Head, 605-336-4729. Application contact: Kay West, Secretary, 605-336-4126. Fax: 605-336-4450.

Azusa Pacific University, School of Nursing, Azusa, CA 91702-7000. Awards MSN. Accredited by NLN. Part-time and evening/weekend programs available. Faculty: 10 full-time (all women), 3 part-time (all women), 11 FTE. Students: 95; includes 35 minority (11 African Americans, 14 Asian Americans, 9 Hispanics, 1 Native American). In 1997, 17 degrees awarded. *Degree requirements:* Computer language required, thesis optional, foreign language not required. *Entrance requirements:* BSN. Application deadline: rolling. Application fee: $45 ($65 for international students). *Expenses:* Tuition $350 per unit. Fees $57 per year. *Financial aid:* Teaching assistantships, traineeships available. Financial aid application deadline: 10/15. *Faculty research:* Family adaptation to illness and crisis, bioethical issues in nursing, self-care activities, quality of life issues, home health. • Dr. Rose Liegler, Dean, 626-815-5384. Application contact: Barb Barthelmess, Graduate Program Secretary, 626-815-5391. Fax: 626-815-5414.

Ball State University, College of Applied Science and Technology, School of Nursing, 2000 University Avenue, Muncie, IN 47306-1099. Awards MS. Accredited by NLN. Part-time programs available. Faculty: 20. Students: 3 full-time (all women), 80 part-time (75 women); includes 5 minority (2 African Americans, 3 Asian Americans). Average age 39. 30 applicants, 87% accepted. In 1997, 11 degrees awarded. *Entrance requirements:* Bachelor's degree in nursing with minimum GPA of 2.8 in upper-level course work. Application fee: $15 ($25 for international students). *Expenses:* Tuition $3454 per year full-time, $518 per semester (minimum) part-time for state residents; $9316 per year full-time, $1221 per semester (minimum) part-time for nonresidents. Fees $242 per year full-time, $18 per semester (minimum) part-time. *Financial aid:* Teaching assistantships and career-related internships or fieldwork available. • Dr. Phyllis Irvine, Director, 765-285-5570.

Barry University, School of Nursing, Doctoral Program in Nursing, Miami Shores, FL 33161-6695. Awards PhD. Faculty: 2 full-time (1 woman), 7 part-time (4 women). Students: 4 full-time (all women), 16 part-time (14 women); includes 3 minority (1 African American, 1 Asian American, 1 Hispanic). Average age 47. 21 applicants, 57% accepted. *Degree requirements:* Dissertation required, foreign language not required. *Entrance requirements:* GRE General Test (minimum combined score of 1000) or MAT (minimum score 50), minimum GPA of 3.3, MSN. Application deadline: 5/1 (priority date; rolling processing). Application fee: $30. *Tuition:* $450 per credit (minimum). *Financial aid:* 1 student received aid. Aid available to part-time students. Financial aid application deadline: 5/1. *Faculty research:* Women's studies, phenomenology, contemporary cultural and social studies, postmodernism, HIV/AIDS. • Dr. Diane LaRochelle, Director, 305-899-3838. Fax: 305-899-3831. E-mail: larochelle@diana.barry.edu. Application contact: Angela Scott, Enrollment Services, Assistant Dean, 305-899-3112. Fax: 305-899-3149. E-mail: ascott@jeanne.barry.edu.

Baylor University, School of Nursing, Waco, TX 76798. Offers programs in family nurse practitioner (MSN), patient care management (MSN). Accredited by NLN. Students: 11 full-time (all women), 14 part-time (13 women); includes 5 minority (3 Asian Americans, 2 Hispanics). In 1997, 6 degrees awarded. *Entrance requirements:* GRE General Test. Application deadline: 8/1 (rolling processing; 12/1 for spring admission). Application fee: $25. *Expenses:* Tuition $7392 per year full-time, $308 per semester hour part-time. Fees $1024 per year. • Dr. Phyllis S. Karns, Dean, 254-710-3361.

Bellarmine College, Allan and Donna Lansing School of Nursing, Louisville, KY 40205-0671. Awards MSN. Part-time and evening/weekend programs available. Faculty: 5 full-time (all women), 5 part-time (all women), 7 FTE. Students: 4 full-time (3 women), 95 part-time (90 women); includes 6 minority (2 African Americans, 2 Asian Americans, 2 Hispanics). 33 applicants, 76% accepted. In 1997, 25 degrees awarded. *Degree requirements:* Thesis required, foreign language not required. *Entrance requirements:* GRE General Test (minimum combined score of 800; average 825), minimum undergraduate GPA of 2.75, RN license. Application deadline: 8/1 (priority date; rolling processing; 1/1 for spring admission). Application fee: $25. Electronic applications accepted. *Tuition:* $330 per credit hour. *Faculty research:* Pain, empathy, leadership styles, control. • Dr. Susan Hockenberger, Dean, 800-274-4723 Ext.8217. Application contact: Dr. Margaret E. Miller, Director, 800-274-4723 Ext. 8414. Fax: 502-452-8058.

Belmont University, Graduate Program in Nursing, Nashville, TN 37212-3757. Awards MSN. Accredited by NLN. Part-time programs available. Faculty: 1 (woman) full-time, 5 part-time (all women). Students: 11 full-time (all women), 23 part-time (22 women); includes 1 minority (African American). Average age 35. 41 applicants, 51% accepted. In 1997, 10 degrees awarded. *Degree requirements:* Thesis required, foreign language not required. *Average time to degree:* master's–1.2 years full-time, 2 years part-time. *Entrance requirements:* GRE, BSN. Application deadline: 2/15 (10/15 for spring admission). Application fee: $50. *Financial aid:* In 1997–98, 10 students received aid, including 1 research assistantship; teaching assistantships, advising assistantships also available. *Faculty research:* Postpartum post-operative care, adherence/compliance behavior in chronic illness. • Dr. Debra Wollaber, Acting Dean, 615-460-6106. Fax: 615-460-6125. E-mail: wollaberd@belmont.edu.

Bethel College, Center for Graduate and Continuing Studies, Department of Nursing, 3900 Bethel Drive, St. Paul, MN 55112-6999. Awards MA. Students: 10. *Entrance requirements:* Interview, minimum GPA of 3.0. Application fee: $25. *Expenses:* Tuition $270 per credit. Fees $75 per year. • Dr. Marjorie A. Schaffer, Coordinator of Graduate Education, 612-638-6298. E-mail: schmara@homer.bethel.edu.

Bloomsburg University of Pennsylvania, School of Graduate Studies, College of Professional Studies, School of Health Sciences, Department of Nursing, Bloomsburg, PA 17815-1905. Offers program in nursing (MSN). Accredited by NLN. Faculty: 6 full-time (all women). Students: 8 full-time (7 women), 14 part-time (all women); includes 1 minority (African American). Average age 35. 7 applicants, 100% accepted. In 1997, 5 degrees awarded. *Degree requirements:* Thesis required, foreign language not required. *Entrance requirements:* GRE General Test, minimum QPA of 2.5. Application deadline: rolling. Application fee: $25. *Expenses:* Tuition $3468 per year full-time, $193 per credit part-time for state residents; $6236 per year full-time, $346 per credit part-time for nonresidents. Fees $748 per year full-time, $166 per semester (minimum) part-time. *Faculty research:* Cardiopulmonary nursing, cancer topics, community health, adult health and illness, women's health. • Application contact: Dr. Sharon Haymaker, Coordinator, 717-389-4602. Fax: 717-389-4454. E-mail: haymaker@planetx.bloomu.edu.

Boston College, School of Nursing, Chestnut Hill, MA 02167-9991. Awards MS, PhD, MBA/MS. Programs in adult health nursing (MS); community health nursing (MS); family health (MS); gerontology (MS); maternal/child health nursing (MS), including pediatric and women's health; nursing (PhD); psychiatric-mental health nursing (MS). One or more programs accredited by NLN. Part-time programs available. Faculty: 18 full-time (all women), 1 (woman) part-time. Students: 94 full-time (90 women), 47 part-time (45 women); includes 4 minority (2 African Americans, 1 Asian American, 1 Hispanic), 4 international. 122 applicants, 80% accepted. In 1997, 47 master's awarded; 9 doctorates awarded (100% found work related to degree). *Degree requirements:* For master's, oral comprehensive exam, research project required, foreign language and thesis not required; for doctorate, dissertation, computer literacy exam or foreign language. *Average time to degree:* doctorate–4 years full-time. *Entrance requirements:* For master's, GRE General Test, bachelor's degree in nursing. Application deadline: 3/1 (priority date; 10/15 for spring admission). Application fee: $40. Electronic applications accepted. *Expenses:* Tuition $626 per semester hour. Fees $80 per year (minimum) full-time, $30 per semester part-time. *Financial aid:* In 1997–98, 54 students received aid, including 15 fellowships (5 to first-year students) averaging $940 per month and totaling $112,781, 4 teaching assistantships averaging $886 per month and totaling $28,344, 37 traineeships (27 to first-year students) totaling $62,080; partial tuition waivers, Federal Work-Study, institutionally sponsored loans, and career-related internships or fieldwork also available. Aid available to part-time students. Financial aid application deadline: 3/2. *Faculty research:* Ethics, reduction of risk behaviors, support during chronic illness. • Dr. Barbara Munro, Dean, 617-552-4251. Fax: 617-552-0931. E-mail: barbara.munro@bc.edu. Application contact: Dana Robinson, Administrative Secretary, 617-552-4059. Fax: 617-552-0745. E-mail: dana.robinson@bc.edu.

Bowie State University, Program in Nursing, 14000 Jericho Park Road, Bowie, MD 20715. Offers administration of nursing services (MS), family nurse practitioner (MS), nursing education (MS). Accredited by NLN. *Degree requirements:* Thesis, research paper, written comprehensive exam required, foreign language not required. *Entrance requirements:* Minimum GPA of 2.5. Application deadline: 3/15 (rolling processing). Application fee: $30. *Expenses:* Tuition $169 per credit hour for state residents; $304 per credit hour for nonresidents. Fees $171 per year. *Faculty research:* Minority health, women's health, gerontology, leadership management.

Bradley University, College of Education and Health Sciences, Division of Nursing, Peoria, IL 61625-0002. Awards MSN. Part-time and evening/weekend programs available. *Degree requirements:* Comprehensive exam required, thesis optional. *Entrance requirements:* GRE General Test or MAT, TOEFL (minimum score 500), interview, Illinois RN license. Application deadline: 7/1 (priority date; rolling processing; 11/1 for spring admission). Application fee: $35. *Tuition:* $13,240 per year full-time, $359 per semester hour (minimum) part-time.

Brenau University, Department of Nursing, Gainesville, GA 30501-3697. Offers program in family nurse practitioner (MSN). Part-time programs available. Faculty: 5 full-time (all women), 3 part-time (all women). Students: 29 part-time (all women); includes 4 minority (3 African Americans, 1 Hispanic). Average age 32. *Entrance requirements:* GRE General Test (minimum combined score of 950) or MAT (minimum score 45). Application deadline: rolling. Application fee: $30. *Tuition:* $411 per semester hour. *Financial aid:* Career-related internships or fieldwork available. Financial aid application deadline: 6/1. • Dr. JoAnne Richard, Chair, 770-534-6260. Fax: 770-538-4666. E-mail: jrichard@lib.brenau.edu. Application contact: Kathy Cobb, Director of Graduate Admissions, 770-534-6162. Fax: 770-538-4306. E-mail: kcobb@lib.brenau.edu.

Brigham Young University, College of Nursing, Provo, UT 84602-1001. Awards MS. Accredited by NLN. Part-time programs available. Faculty: 26 full-time (24 women). Students: 20 full-time (13 women), 22 part-time (16 women); includes 3 minority (1 Asian American, 1 Hispanic, 1 Native American). Average age 32. 31 applicants, 68% accepted. In 1997, 16 degrees awarded. *Degree requirements:* Thesis. *Average time to degree:* master's–2.5 years full-time, 5 years part-time. *Entrance requirements:* GRE, minimum GPA of 3.0 in last 60 hours. Application deadline: 12/1 (rolling processing; 12/1 for spring admission). Application fee: $30. *Tuition:* $3200 per year full-time, $178 per credit hour part-time for state residents; $4800 per year full-time, $266 per credit hour part-time for nonresidents. *Financial aid:* 24 students received aid; research assistantships, teaching assistantships, institutionally sponsored loans, and career-related internships or fieldwork available. Aid available to part-time students. Financial aid application deadline: 2/1; applicants required to submit FAFSA. *Faculty research:* Cardiovascular risk factors, stroke patients, nutrition, stress among children, family response to life-threatening illness. • Dr. Sandra Rogers, Dean, 801-378-7204. E-mail: sandra_rogers@byu.edu. Application contact: Mary Williams, Associate Dean, 801-378-5626. Fax: 801-378-3198. E-mail: mary_williams@byu.edu.

California State University, Bakersfield, School of Arts and Sciences, Program in Nursing, 9001 Stockdale Highway, Bakersfield, CA 93311-1099. Awards MS. Accredited by NLN. Students: 3 full-time (all women), 15 part-time (all women); includes 2 minority (both Asian Americans). 12 applicants, 100% accepted. In 1997, 5 degrees awarded. *Degree requirements:* Thesis, cognate in business. *Entrance requirements:* MAT (minimum score 50), BSN from an NLN-accredited program. Application deadline: rolling. Application fee: $55. *Expenses:* Tuition $0 for state residents; $246 per unit full-time, $164 per unit part-time for nonresidents. Fees $1584 per year full-time, $918 per year part-time. *Financial aid:* Scholarships, traineeships available. *Faculty research:* AIDS, gerontological nursing, cultural health beliefs. • Dr. Colette York, Graduate Coordinator, 805-664-3115.

California State University, Chico, College of Natural Sciences, School of Nursing, Chico, CA 95929-0722. Awards MS. Faculty: 13 full-time (all women), 5 part-time (all women), 15 FTE. Students: 1 full-time (0 women), 6 part-time (all women). Average age 42. In 1997, 3 degrees awarded. *Degree requirements:* Thesis required, foreign language not required. *Entrance requirements:* MAT. Application deadline: 4/1 (rolling processing). Application fee: $55. *Expenses:* Tuition $0 for state residents; $246 per unit for nonresidents. Fees $2108 per year full-time, $1442 per year part-time. *Financial aid:* Career-related internships or fieldwork available. • Dr. Sherry D. Fox, Director, 530-898-5891. Application contact: Dr. Shelly Young, Graduate Coordinator, 530-898-6207.

California State University, Dominguez Hills, School of Health, Program in Nursing, Carson, CA 90747-0001. Awards MSN. Accredited by NLN. Students: 38 full-time (all women), 501 part-time (480 women); includes 142 minority (46 African Americans, 56 Asian Americans, 33 Hispanics, 7 Native Americans), 1 international. Average age 39. In 1997, 87 degrees awarded. *Entrance requirements:* Minimum GPA of 2.5. Application deadline: 6/1. Application fee: $55. *Expenses:* Tuition $0 for state residents; $246 per unit for nonresidents. Fees $1896 per year full-time, $1230 per year part-time. • Dr. Peggy Wallace, Chair, 310-243-2050. Application contact: Admissions Office, 310-243-2060.

California State University, Fresno, Division of Graduate Studies, School of Health and Social Work, Department of Nursing, 5241 North Maple Avenue, Fresno, CA 93740. Offers program in nursing (MS), including clinical specialty, primary care nurse practitioner. Accredited by NLN. Part-time and evening/weekend programs available. Faculty: 13 full-time (12 women). Students: 32 full-time (24 women), 47 part-time (39 women); includes 16 minority (6 African Americans, 8 Asian Americans, 2 Hispanics). Average age 31. 17 applicants, 88% accepted. In 1997, 25 degrees awarded. *Degree requirements:* Thesis or alternative required, foreign language not required. *Average time to degree:* master's–3.5 years full-time. *Entrance requirements:* GRE General Test, TOEFL (minimum score 550), 1 year of clinical practice, previous course work in statistics, BSN, minimum GPA of 3.0 in nursing, 2.5 overall. Application deadline: 3/1 (priority date; rolling processing). Application fee: $55. Electronic applications accepted. *Expenses:* Tuition $0 for state residents; $246 per unit for nonresidents. Fees $1872 per year full-time, $1206 per year part-time. *Financial aid:* In 1997–98, 3 teaching assistantships totaling $11,000, 28 traineeships, scholarships totaling $59,027 were awarded; Federal Work-Study and career-related internships or fieldwork also available. Financial aid application deadline: 3/1; applicants required to submit FAFSA. • Dr. Mariamma Mathai, Interim Chair, 209-278-2041. E-mail: mariamma_mathai@csufresno.edu. Application contact: Mike Russler, Graduate Program Coordinator, 209-278-2429. Fax: 209-278-6630. E-mail: mike_russler@csufresno.edu.

California State University, Long Beach, College of Health and Human Services, Department of Nursing, Long Beach, CA 90840-0301. Awards MS, MPH/MS. Programs in nurse anesthesiology (MS), nursing (MS). Accredited by NLN. Faculty: 14 full-time (13 women), 1 (woman) part-time. Students: 94 full-time (79 women), 86 part-time (78 women); includes 59 minority (17 African Americans, 30 Asian Americans, 11 Hispanics, 1 Native American), 2 international. Average age 38. 113 applicants, 58% accepted. In 1997, 80 degrees awarded. *Degree requirements:* Thesis required, foreign language not required. *Entrance requirements:* Minimum GPA of 3.0. Application deadline: 8/1 (rolling processing; 12/1 for spring admission). Application fee: $55. *Expenses:* Tuition $0 for state residents; $246 per unit for nonresidents. Fees $1846 per year full-time, $1180 per year part-time. *Financial aid:* Application deadline 3/2. *Faculty research:* Newborns of drug-dependent mothers, abuse of residents in nursing homes, interventions in care of Alzheimer's patients. Total annual research expenditures: $10,000. • Dr. Christine Talmadge, Chair, 562-985-5250. Application contact: Dr. Judith Smith, Graduate Coordinator, 562-985-4469. Fax: 562-985-2382.

California State University, Los Angeles, School of Health and Human Services, Department of Nursing, Los Angeles, CA 90032-8530. Awards MS. Accredited by NLN. Part-time and evening/weekend programs available. Faculty: 17 full-time, 20 part-time. Students: 33 full-time (31 women), 68 part-time (59 women); includes 44 minority (10 African Americans, 19 Asian Americans, 14 Hispanics, 1 Native American). In 1997, 33 degrees awarded. *Degree requirements:* Comprehensive exam, project, or thesis required, foreign language not required. *Entrance requirements:* TOEFL (minimum score 550), minimum GPA of 3.0 in nursing, previous course work in nursing and statistics. Application deadline: 6/30 (rolling processing; 2/1 for spring admission). Application fee: $55. *Expenses:* Tuition $0 for state residents; $164 per unit for nonresidents. Fees $1763 per year full-time, $1097 per year part-time. *Financial aid:* 31 students received aid; Federal Work-Study available. Aid available to part-time students. Financial aid application deadline: 3/1. *Faculty research:* Family stress, geripsychiatric nursing, self-care counseling, holistic nursing, adult health. • Dr. Judy Papenhausen, Chair, 213-343-4700.

California State University, Sacramento, School of Health and Human Services, Division of Nursing, Sacramento, CA 95819-6048. Awards MS. Accredited by NLN. Part-time programs available. *Degree requirements:* Thesis or alternative, writing proficiency exam. *Entrance requirements:* GRE, TOEFL (minimum score 550), minimum GPA of 3.0, bachelor's degree in nursing. Application deadline: 4/15 (11/1 for spring admission). Application fee: $55. *Expenses:* Tuition $0 for state residents; $246 per unit for nonresidents. Fees $2012 per year full-time, $1346 per year part-time. *Financial aid:* Research assistantships, teaching assistantships, Federal Work-Study, and career-related internships or fieldwork available. Aid available to part-time students. Financial aid application deadline: 3/1. • Dr. Annita Watson, Chair, 916-278-6525. Application contact: Dr. Robyn Nelson, Coordinator, 916-278-7243.

Capital University, School of Nursing, Columbus, OH 43209-2394. Awards MSN, JD/MSN, MBA/MSN, MSN/MA. Programs in administration (MSN), family and community (MSN), legal studies (MSN), theological studies (MSN). Part-time and evening/weekend programs available. Faculty: 17 full-time (10 women), 3 part-time (1 woman). Students: 3 full-time (2 women), 52 part-time (all women); includes 4 minority (1 African American, 2 Asian Americans, 1 Native American), 2 international. *Degree requirements:* Thesis or alternative required, foreign language not required. *Entrance requirements:* GRE General Test (combined average 1350), TOEFL (minimum score 550), BSN, current RN license, minimum GPA of 3.0, 1 year of professional practice. Application deadline: 8/1 (priority date; rolling processing; 12/1 for spring admission). Application fee: $25. *Tuition:* $260 per credit hour. *Financial aid:* Career-related internships or fieldwork available. Financial aid applicants required to submit FAFSA. *Faculty research:* Bereavement, health policy, women's health, health/patient education, wellness/health promotion. Total annual research expenditures: $2000. • Dr. Doris Edwards, Dean, 614-236-6703. Application contact: Dr. Laurel Talabere, Associate Dean, 614-236-6361. Fax: 614-236-6157. E-mail: ltalaber@capital.edu.

Carlow College, Division of Nursing, Pittsburgh, PA 15213-3165. Offers programs in case management (Certificate), gerontological case management/administrator (MSN), home health advanced practice nursing (MSN, Certificate), home health case management/administrator (MSN). Part-time and evening/weekend programs available. Postbaccalaureate distance learning degree programs offered (minimal on-campus study). Faculty: 6 full-time (all women), 14 part-time (12 women). Students: 102 part-time (96 women); includes 9 minority (4 African Americans, 2 Asian Americans, 2 Hispanics, 1 Native American). Average age 35. 60 applicants, 90% accepted. *Degree requirements:* For master's, thesis or alternative required, foreign language not required. *Entrance requirements:* For master's, GRE General Test (minimum combined score of 1000), interview, minimum GPA of 3.0; for Certificate, MSN. Application deadline: 6/30 (rolling processing; 4/25 for spring admission). Application fee: $35. *Financial aid:* Partial tuition waivers and career-related internships or fieldwork available. Aid available to part-time students. Financial aid application deadline: 3/15. *Faculty research:* Breastfeeding, body piercing, depression in the elderly. Total annual research expenditures: $75,000. • Mary Lou Bost, Acting Chair, 412-578-6116. Fax: 412-578-6114. Application contact: Bonnie Potthoff, Office Manager, Graduate Studies, 412-578-8764. Fax: 412-578-8822.

Case Western Reserve University, Frances Payne Bolton School of Nursing, Doctoral Program in Nursing, Cleveland, OH 44106. Awards PhD. Students: 21 full-time (20 women), 59 part-time (55 women); includes 3 minority (all African Americans), 41 international. Average age 35. In 1997, 7 doctorates awarded (100% entered university research/teaching). Terminal master's awarded for partial completion of doctoral program. *Degree requirements:* For doctorate, dissertation required, foreign language not required. *Entrance requirements:* For doctorate, GRE General Test. Application deadline: 3/1 (priority date; rolling processing). Application fee: $35. *Tuition:* $18,400 per year full-time, $767 per credit hour part-time. *Financial aid:* In 1997–98, 2 research assistantships (1 to a first-year student), 7 Dean's scholarships (5 to first-year students) were awarded; teaching assistantships, partial tuition waivers, institutionally sponsored loans also available. Aid available to part-time students. Financial aid application deadline: 6/30; applicants required to submit FAFSA. *Faculty research:* Acute care nursing, parent-child gerontology, information systems, clinical decisions. • Dr. Beverly Roberts, Director, 216-368-2522. Fax: 216-368-3542. Application contact: Keith Auer, Admission Counselor, 216-368-2521.

See in-depth description on page 1423.

Case Western Reserve University, Frances Payne Bolton School of Nursing, Master's Program in Nursing, Cleveland, OH 44106. Awards MSN, MSN/MA, MSN/MBA. Offerings include community health nursing (MSN); critical care nursing (MSN); medical-surgical nursing (MSN); nurse anesthesia (MSN); nurse midwifery (MSN); nurse practitioner (MSN), including acute care adult nurse practitioner, acute care pediatric nurse practitioner, adult practitioner, family nurse practitioner, gerontological nurse practitioner, neonatal practitioner, pediatric nurse practitioner, psychiatric-mental health nurse practitioner, women's health nurse practitioner; oncology nursing (MSN). Accredited by NLN. Part-time programs available. Students: 189 full-time (178 women), 88 part-time (82 women); includes 20 minority (11 African Americans, 7 Asian Americans, 2 Hispanics), 14 international. Average age 35. 206 applicants, 60% accepted. In 1997, 198 degrees awarded. *Degree requirements:* Thesis optional, foreign language not required. *Entrance requirements:* GRE General Test or MAT. Application deadline: rolling. Application fee: $75. *Tuition:* $18,400 per year full-time, $767 per credit hour part-time. *Financial aid:* In 1997–98, 5 teaching assistantships (4 to first-year students) were awarded; fellowships, research assistantships, partial tuition waivers, institutionally sponsored loans also available. Aid available to part-time students. Financial aid application deadline: 6/30. • Dr. Marion Hemstrom, Director, 216-368-2522. Application contact: Molly Blank, Admission Counselor, 216-368-2529. Fax: 216-368-3542. E-mail: mab44@po.cwru.edu.

Directory: Nursing—General

Case Western Reserve University (continued)

Announcement: Comprehensive graduate program leads to these degrees: Master of Science in Nursing (MSN) with specializations in nurse midwifery, nurse anesthesia, nurse practitioner studies (adult acute care, pediatric acute care, adult, family, gerontological, neonatal, pediatric, psychiatric–mental health, and women's health), community health, critical care, medical-surgical, oncology; MSN/MA in anthropology, MSN/MA in bioethics, and MSN/MBA; Doctor of Nursing (ND), a first professional degree for advanced practice with a postlicensure component; Doctor of Philosophy (PhD) in nursing, for those interested in pediatrics, gerontology, and acute care nursing and health systems research.

See in-depth description on page 1423.

Case Western Reserve University, Frances Payne Bolton School of Nursing, MSN/MBA Program, Cleveland, OH 44106. Awards MSN/MBA. Offered jointly with Weatherhead School of Management. Students: 0. Average age 35. 1 applicant, 100% accepted. *Application deadline:* 6/1 (priority date; rolling processing). *Application fee:* $75. *Tuition:* $18,400 per year full-time, $767 per credit hour part-time. *Financial aid:* Application deadline 6/30. *Faculty research:* Organizational costs and length of stay, organizational structure and policy, professionals in bureaucratic organizations. • Application contact: Molly Blank, Admission Counselor, 216-368-2529. Fax: 216-368-3542. E-mail: mab44@po.cwru.edu.

Case Western Reserve University, Frances Payne Bolton School of Nursing and Department of Anthropology, Nursing/Anthropology Program, Cleveland, OH 44106. Awards MSN/MA. Students: 1 (woman) full-time. 0 applicants. *Average time to degree:* master's–2 years full-time, 3 years part-time. *Application fee:* $75. *Tuition:* $18,400 per year full-time, $767 per credit hour part-time. *Financial aid:* Fellowships, research assistantships, teaching assistantships available. Financial aid application deadline: 6/30. • Application contact: Molly Blank, Admission Counselor, 216-368-8855. Fax: 216-368-3542. E-mail: mab44@po.cwru.edu.

Case Western Reserve University, Frances Payne Bolton School of Nursing, Nursing/Bioethics Program, Cleveland, OH 44106. Awards MSN/MA. Offered jointly with the Program in Bioethics. Students: 0. *Application fee:* $75. *Tuition:* $18,400 per year full-time, $767 per credit hour part-time. *Financial aid:* Fellowships, research assistantships, teaching assistantships available. Financial aid application deadline: 6/30. • Application contact: Molly Blank, Admission Counselor, 216-368-2529. Fax: 216-368-3542. E-mail: mab44@po.cwru.edu.

Case Western Reserve University, Frances Payne Bolton School of Nursing, Professional Program in Nursing, Cleveland, OH 44106. Awards ND. Accredited by NLN. Students: 103 full-time (95 women), 39 part-time (37 women); includes 24 minority (9 African Americans, 12 Asian Americans, 1 Hispanic, 2 Native Americans), 1 international. Average age 30. 94 applicants, 73% accepted. In 1997, 10 degrees awarded (100% found work related to degree). *Degree requirements:* Dissertation required, foreign language not required. *Entrance requirements:* GRE General Test. Application deadline: 6/1 (priority date; rolling processing). Application fee: $75. *Tuition:* $18,400 per year full-time, $767 per credit hour part-time. *Financial aid:* In 1997–98, 1 research assistantship, 1 teaching assistantship were awarded; partial tuition waivers, Federal Work-Study, institutionally sponsored loans also available. Aid available to part-time students. Financial aid application deadline: 6/30. *Faculty research:* Clinical nursing, acute care, gerontology, mental health, critical care. • Dr. Theresa Standing, Director, 216-368-5990. Application contact: Molly Blank, Admission Counselor, 216-368-2529. Fax: 216-368-3542. E-mail: mab44@.po.cwru.edu.

See in-depth description on page 1423.

The Catholic University of America, School of Nursing, Washington, DC 20064. Offers programs in advanced practice nursing (MSN), including administration of nursing service, adult nurse practitioner, education, family nurse practitioner, geriatric nurse practitioner, pediatric nurse practitioner, psychiatric-mental health, school health nurse practitioner; clinical nursing (DN Sc). Accredited by NLN. Part-time programs available. Faculty: 18 full-time (all women), 2 part-time (both women), 19 FTE. Students: 77 full-time (74 women), 46 part-time (44 women); includes 19 minority (14 African Americans, 2 Asian Americans, 3 Hispanics), 27 international. Average age 40. 45 applicants, 84% accepted. In 1997, 21 master's, 4 doctorates awarded. *Degree requirements:* For master's, comprehensive exam required, thesis optional, foreign language not required; for doctorate, dissertation, comprehensive exam required, foreign language not required. *Entrance requirements:* For master's, GRE General Test (minimum combined score of 1350 on three sections); for doctorate, GRE General Test (minimum combined score of 1500 on three sections). Application deadline: 8/1 (priority date; rolling processing; 12/1 for spring admission). Application fee: $50. *Expenses:* Tuition $17,325 per year full-time, $668 per credit hour part-time. Fees $680 per year full-time, $360 per year part-time. *Financial aid:* In 1997–98, 25 students received aid, including 2 teaching assistantships (1 to a first-year student); research assistantships, full and partial tuition waivers, Federal Work-Study, institutionally sponsored loans, and career-related internships or fieldwork also available. Aid available to part-time students. Financial aid application deadline: 4/1; applicants required to submit FAFSA. *Faculty research:* Outcome research–readmission of home health care patients with congestive heart failure, spirituality of chronic illness, minority multigravidos utilization of prenatal care. Total annual research expenditures: $5500. • Sr. Mary Jean Flaherty, Dean, 202-319-5403.

Christopher Newport University, Graduate Studies, Department of Nursing, 1 University Place, Newport News, VA 23606-2998. Awards MS. Part-time and evening/weekend programs available. Faculty: 7 full-time (4 women), 1 (woman) part-time. Students: 8 part-time (7 women); includes 2 minority (1 African American, 1 Hispanic). Average age 42. *Degree requirements:* Thesis, comprehensive exam required, foreign language not required. *Entrance requirements:* GRE, 1 year of clinical nursing practice, minimum GPA of 3.0. Application deadline: 8/1 (priority date; rolling processing; 12/15 for spring admission). Application fee: $40. *Expenses:* Tuition $3474 per year full-time, $145 per credit hour part-time for state residents; $8424 per year full-time, $351 per credit hour part-time for nonresidents. Fees $40 per year. *Financial aid:* In 1997–98, 1 research assistantship totaling $2,000 was awarded; Federal Work-Study and career-related internships or fieldwork also available. Aid available to part-time students. Financial aid application deadline: 4/1; applicants required to submit FAFSA. *Faculty research:* Effects of music therapy on pain, case management program evaluation, Alzheimer's disease and psychosociological family effect. • Dr. Karin Polifko-Harris, Chair, 757-594-7252. Fax: 757-594-7862. E-mail: kpolifko@cnu.edu. Application contact: Graduate Admissions, 800-333-4268. Fax: 757-594-7333. E-mail: admit@cnu.edu.

Clarion University of Pennsylvania, School of Nursing, Program in Nursing, Clarion, PA 16214. Awards MSN. Offered jointly with Slippery Rock University of Pennsylvania. Faculty: 3 full-time (all women). Students: 8 full-time (all women), 17 part-time (15 women); includes 2 minority (1 African American, 1 Native American). 20 applicants, 80% accepted. *Degree requirements:* Thesis required, foreign language not required. *Entrance requirements:* GRE, minimum QPA of 2.75. Application fee: $25. *Expenses:* Tuition $3468 per year full-time, $193 per credit hour part-time for state residents; $6236 per year full-time, $346 per credit hour part-time for nonresidents. Fees $921 per year full-time, $90 per credit hour part-time for state residents; $921 per year full-time, $89 per credit hour part-time for nonresidents. • Dr. Joyce White, Coordinator, 412-738-2323.

Clarke College, Program in Nursing, Dubuque, IA 52001-3198. Awards MS. Part-time and evening/weekend programs available. Students: 14 part-time (all women). 14 applicants, 100% accepted. *Entrance requirements:* GRE General Test or MAT, BSN, minimum GPA of 3.0. Application deadline: rolling. Application fee: $25. Electronic applications accepted. *Expenses:* Tuition $12,688 per year full-time, $315 per credit hour part-time. Fees $240 per year. *Financial aid:* Career-related internships or fieldwork available. Aid available to part-time students. Financial aid applicants required to submit FAFSA. • Dr. Nancy Schoofs, Coordinator, 800-224-2736. Application contact: Admissions Office, 800-383-2345. Fax: 319-588-6789. E-mail: graduate@clarke.edu.

Clarkson College, Graduate Programs, Department of Nursing, 101 South 42nd Street, Omaha, NE 68131-2739. Offers programs in administration (MSN), education (MSN), family nurse practitioner (MSN). Accredited by NLN. Part-time and evening/weekend programs available. Faculty: 6. Students: 201. In 1997, 20 degrees awarded. *Degree requirements:* Practicum required, foreign language not required. *Entrance requirements:* GRE General Test, minimum GPA of 3.0. Application deadline: rolling. Application fee: $17. *Expenses:* Tuition $314 per credit hour. Fees $16 per credit hour. *Financial aid:* Scholarships, institutionally sponsored loans available. • Dr. Charles J. Beauchamp, Dean, 402-552-2958. Fax: 402-552-6058. Application contact: Jeff Beals, Director of Enrollment Management, 402-552-3100. Fax: 402-552-6057. E-mail: admiss@clrkcol.crhsnet.edu.

Clemson University, College of Health, Education, and Human Development, School of Nursing, Clemson, SC 29634. Awards MS. Accredited by NLN. Part-time programs available. Postbaccalaureate distance learning degree programs offered. Students: 24 full-time (22 women), 47 part-time (41 women); includes 3 minority (all African Americans), 1 international. Average age 37. 39 applicants, 64% accepted. In 1997, 32 degrees awarded. *Degree requirements:* Thesis or alternative. *Entrance requirements:* GRE General Test (minimum combined score of 1500 on three sections), TOEFL, RN license. Application deadline: 6/1 (12/1 for spring admission). Application fee: $35. Electronic applications accepted. *Expenses:* Tuition $3154 per year full-time, $130 per credit hour part-time for state residents; $6452 per year full-time, $264 per credit hour part-time for nonresidents. Fees $190 per year. *Financial aid:* Fellowships, research assistantships, teaching assistantships, traineeships, and career-related internships or fieldwork available. *Faculty research:* Risk behaviors and chronic risk-taking in early adolescents, stress in older caregivers, home care of elderly, cancer awareness, pain. Total annual research expenditures: $19,547. • Dr. Barbara Logan, Director, 864-656-0383. Fax: 864-656-5488. E-mail: logan@clemson.edu. Application contact: Beth Hearn, Director of Student Services, 864-656-5495. Fax: 864-656-1688. E-mail: mary2@clemson.clemson.edu.

College Misericordia, Division of Health Sciences, Program in Nursing, Dallas, PA 18612-1098. Awards MSN. Accredited by NLN. Part-time and evening/weekend programs available. Faculty: 7 full-time (all women). Students: 65 part-time (57 women). 31 applicants, 84% accepted. In 1997, 31 degrees awarded. *Degree requirements:* Practicum required, thesis optional, foreign language not required. *Entrance requirements:* GRE (score in 35th percentile or higher) or MAT (score in 35th percentile or higher), interview, minimum GPA of 2.5, physical assessment, previous course work in statistics. Application deadline: 8/7 (priority date; rolling processing; 1/3 for spring admission). Application fee: $20. *Tuition:* $445 per credit. *Financial aid:* In 1997–98, 11 students received aid, including 11 traineeships (9 to first-year students); research assistantships, teaching assistantships, and career-related internships or fieldwork also available. Aid available to part-time students. Financial aid application deadline: 8/15. *Faculty research:* Quality of life, maternal-child, spirituality, critical thinking, adult health. • Dr. Helen Streubert, Head, 717-674-6262. Application contact: Barbara Leggat, Continuing Education Specialist, 800-852-7675. Fax: 717-675-2441.

College of Mount Saint Vincent, Department of Nursing, Riverdale, NY 10471-1093. Offers programs in addictions nursing (MS), adult nurse practitioner (MS), nursing administration (MS), nursing for the adult and aged (MS). Accredited by NLN. Part-time programs available. Faculty: 3 full-time (all women), 15 part-time (all women). Students: 10 full-time, 140 part-time. Average age 32. 50 applicants, 90% accepted. In 1997, 8 degrees awarded. *Degree requirements:* Computer language, written research project required, foreign language and thesis not required. *Entrance requirements:* Bachelor's degree from NLN-accredited institution, minimum GPA of 3.0. Application deadline: 6/15 (priority date; rolling processing; 12/1 for spring admission). Application fee: $50. *Financial aid:* Available to part-time students. Financial aid application deadline: 6/1. *Faculty research:* Family support. • Dr. Barbara Cohen, Director, 718-405-3352. Application contact: Dr. Kem Louie, Chairperson, 718-405-3355.

The College of New Jersey, Graduate Division, School of Nursing, Ewing, NJ 08628. Awards MSN. Accredited by NLN. Part-time and evening/weekend programs available. Faculty: 3. Students: 83 part-time (79 women); includes 8 minority (1 African American, 1 Asian American, 6 Hispanics), 2 international. In 1997, 15 degrees awarded. *Degree requirements:* Comprehensive exam required, foreign language and thesis not required. *Average time to degree:* master's–2 years full-time. *Entrance requirements:* GRE General Test, minimum GPA of 3.0 in field or 2.75 overall. Application deadline: 3/15. Application fee: $50. *Expenses:* Tuition $6892 per year full-time, $287 per credit hour part-time for state residents; $9602 per year full-time, $402 per credit hour part-time for nonresidents. Fees $799 per year full-time, $33 per credit hour part-time. *Financial aid:* Graduate assistantships available. Financial aid application deadline: 5/1; applicants required to submit FAFSA. • Dr. Laurie N. Sherwen, Dean, 609-771-2591. Fax: 609-637-5159. E-mail: sherwen@tcnj.edu. Application contact: Dr. Gail Hilbert, Graduate Coordinator, 609-771-2510.

College of New Rochelle, Program in Nursing, New Rochelle, NY 10805-2308. Awards MS, Certificate. One or more programs accredited by NLN. Part-time and evening/weekend programs available. Faculty: 7 full-time (all women), 7 part-time (6 women), 11 FTE. Students: 8 full-time (7 women), 102 part-time (100 women); includes 18 minority (12 African Americans, 4 Asian Americans, 1 Hispanic, 1 Native American). Average age 38. 58 applicants, 48% accepted. In 1997, 15 master's awarded (100% found work related to degree). *Average time to degree:* master's–1.5 years full-time, 3 years part-time. *Entrance requirements:* For master's, GRE General Test or MAT, BSN, malpractice insurance, minimum GPA of 3.0, RN license. Application deadline: 8/1 (priority date; rolling processing). Application fee: $35. *Tuition:* $410 per credit. *Financial aid:* In 1997–98, 6 students received aid, including 6 traineeships (1 to a first-year student) totaling $26,980. Aid available to part-time students. Financial aid application deadline: 8/15. *Faculty research:* Holistic modalities, academic success variables. • Dr. Judith Forker, Assistant Dean, 914-654-5233. Fax: 914-654-5994.

College of St. Catherine, Graduate Program, Program in Nursing, St. Paul, MN 55105-1789. Awards MA. Accredited by NLN. Part-time and evening/weekend programs available. Faculty: 6 full-time (all women), 4 part-time (all women). Students: 40 full-time (all women), 13 part-time (all women). Average age 36. 46 applicants, 74% accepted. In 1997, 28 degrees awarded. *Degree requirements:* Thesis required, foreign language not required. *Entrance requirements:* GRE General Test (score in 50th percentile or higher), Michigan English Language Assessment Battery (minimum score 90) or TOEFL (minimum score 600), minimum GPA of 3.0. Application deadline: 4/1 (priority date). Application fee: $25. *Expenses:* Tuition $460 per credit hour. Fees $60 per year. *Financial aid:* 29 students received aid; institutionally sponsored loans and career-related internships or fieldwork available. Aid available to part-time students. Financial aid application deadline: 4/1; applicants required to submit FAFSA. • Dr. Mary Wright, Director, 612-690-6585. Application contact: Office of Admission, 612-690-6505.

College of St. Scholastica, Program in Nursing, Duluth, MN 55811-4199. Awards MA. Accredited by NLN. Part-time and evening/weekend programs available. Faculty: 4 full-time (all women), 7 part-time (all women). Students: 19 full-time (17 women), 52 part-time (51 women); includes 1 minority (Asian American), 1 international. Average age 32. 23 applicants, 96% accepted. In 1997, 15 degrees awarded. *Degree requirements:* Thesis. *Entrance requirements:* GRE General Test or MAT, bachelor's degree in nursing, RN license. Application deadline: 5/1 (priority date). Application fee: $50. *Tuition:* $7968 per year full-time, $332 per credit part-time. *Financial aid:* 58 students received aid; traineeships available. Aid available to part-time students. Financial aid applicants required to submit FAFSA. • Dr. Marty T. Witrak, Director, 218-723-6021. Application contact: Cheryl Cooke, Graduate Nursing Secretary, 218-723-5975. Fax: 218-723-6472. E-mail: ccooke@css.edu.

Columbia University, School of Nursing, New York, NY 10032. Awards MS, DN Sc, Adv C, MBA/MS, MPH/MS. One or more programs accredited by NLN. Part-time programs available.

Faculty: 33 full-time (31 women), 19 part-time (17 women). Students: 58 full-time (55 women), 401 part-time (375 women); includes 64 minority (22 African Americans, 29 Asian Americans, 13 Hispanics). Average age 34. 368 applicants, 72% accepted. In 1997, 122 master's awarded. *Entrance requirements:* For master's, GRE General Test (minimum score 500 on verbal and analytical sections), BSN, 1 year of clinical experience (preferred), or completion of a clinical residency; for doctorate, GRE General Test, MSN; previous course work in statistics, research, and theory; for Adv C, MSN, previous course work in statistics, clinical preceptorship. Application deadline: 4/1 (rolling processing). *Tuition:* $19,376 per year full-time, $692 per credit (minimum) part-time. *Financial aid:* 109 students received aid; teaching assistantships, Federal Work-Study, institutionally sponsored loans available. Financial aid application deadline: 2/1; applicants required to submit FAFSA. • Dr. Mary O. Mundinger, Dean, 212-305-3582. Application contact: Joseph Tomaino, Assistant Dean for Student Services, 212-305-5756. E-mail: jt238@columbia.edu.

See in-depth description on page 1425.

Concordia University Wisconsin, Division of Graduate Studies, Program in Nursing, Mequon, WI 53097-2402. Offers family nurse practitioner (MSN), geriatric nurse practitioner (MSN), nurse educator (MSN). Postbaccalaureate distance learning degree programs offered (minimal on-campus study). *Degree requirements:* Thesis or alternative, comprehensive exam. *Entrance requirements:* TOEFL (minimum score 550). Application deadline: 8/1 (priority date; rolling processing). *Tuition:* $250 per credit. *Financial aid:* Application deadline 8/1. • Dr. Ruth Gresley, Director, 414-243-4452. E-mail: rgresley@bach.cuw.edu.

Creighton University, School of Nursing, Omaha, NE 68178-0001. Awards MS. Accredited by NLN. Part-time and evening/weekend programs available. Postbaccalaureate distance learning degree programs offered (minimal on-campus study). Faculty: 11 full-time (all women), 2 part-time (both women), 12 FTE. Students: 11 full-time (9 women), 59 part-time (56 women); includes 2 minority (1 African American, 1 Hispanic). Average age 30. 10 applicants, 100% accepted. In 1997, 16 degrees awarded. *Degree requirements:* Thesis optional. *Average time to degree:* master's–2 years full-time, 4.5 years part-time. *Entrance requirements:* GRE General Test, BSN, RN license. Application deadline: 3/15 (10/15 for spring admission). Application fee: $30. *Expenses:* Tuition $402 per credit hour. Fees $536 per year full-time, $28 per semester part-time. *Financial aid:* In 1997–98, 3 traineeships (2 to first-year students) totaling $30,235 were awarded; Federal Work-Study, institutionally sponsored loans, and career-related internships or fieldwork also available. *Faculty research:* Body image alteration, osteoporosis prevention, ethical decision making, cardiac rehabilitation, patient control of visitors. • Dr. Edeth K. Kitchens, Dean, 402-280-2004. E-mail: kitchens@creighton.edu. Application contact: Dr. Linda Lazure, Associate Dean for Student Affairs, 402-280-2001. Fax: 402-280-2045. E-mail: llazure@creighton.edu.

Daemen College, Program in Adult Nurse Practitioner, Amherst, NY 14226-3592. Awards MS. Part-time programs available. Faculty: 2 full-time (both women), 3 part-time (2 women). Students: 15 full-time (14 women), 19 part-time (all women); includes 2 minority (both African Americans). Average age 39. *Degree requirements:* Thesis or alternative required, foreign language not required. *Entrance requirements:* Interview, minimum undergraduate GPA of 3.25, 1 year of medical/surgical experience. Application deadline: 3/1 (priority date; rolling processing; 10/1 for spring admission). Application fee: $25. *Expenses:* Tuition $430 per credit. Fees $13 per credit. *Financial aid:* Available to part-time students. Financial aid application deadline: 2/15; applicants required to submit FAFSA. • Deborah A. Wydysh, Director, 716-839-8408. Application contact: Deborah Fargo, Associate Director of Admissions, 716-839-8225. Fax: 716-839-8516. E-mail: dfargo@daemen.edu.

Dalhousie University, Faculty of Health Professions, School of Nursing, Halifax, NS B3H 3J5, Canada. Awards MN, MN/MHSA. Part-time programs available. Postbaccalaureate distance learning degree programs offered (minimal on-campus study). Faculty: 15 full-time. Students: 16 full-time (all women), 82 part-time (all women); includes 1 international. Average age 32. 21 applicants, 86% accepted. In 1997, 15 degrees awarded. *Degree requirements:* Thesis optional, foreign language not required. *Entrance requirements:* GRE General Test, TOEFL (minimum score 580), minimum GPA of 3.0. Application deadline: 4/1 (rolling processing). Application fee: $55. *Financial aid:* Fellowships, research assistantships, teaching assistantships available. *Faculty research:* Coping, social support, health promotion, aging, feminist studies. • M. E. Ellerton, Acting Director, 902-494-2535. Application contact: Dr. Frances Gregor, Associate Director, 902-494-2642. Fax: 902-494-3487.

Delta State University, School of Nursing, Cleveland, MS 38733-0001. Awards MSN. Part-time programs available. Faculty: 5 full-time (all women), 1 (woman) part-time, 5.25 FTE. Students: 19 full-time (17 women), 12 part-time (11 women); includes 7 minority (all African Americans). Average age 36. 2 applicants, 100% accepted. In 1997, 18 degrees awarded. *Degree requirements:* Thesis optional, foreign language not required. *Entrance requirements:* GRE General Test (minimum combined score of 800). Application deadline: 8/1 (priority date; rolling processing). Application fee: $0. *Tuition:* $2596 per year full-time, $121 per semester hour part-time for state residents; $5546 per year full-time, $285 per semester hour part-time for nonresidents. *Financial aid:* Research assistantships, Federal Work-Study, institutionally sponsored loans, and career-related internships or fieldwork available. Financial aid application deadline: 6/1. • Dr. Maureen Propst, Dean, 601-846-4268. Fax: 601-846-4267. Application contact: Dr. John Thornell, Dean of Graduate Studies and Continuing Education, 601-846-4310. Fax: 601-846-4016. E-mail: thornell@dsu.deltast.edu.

DePaul University, College of Liberal Arts and Sciences, Department of Nursing, Chicago, IL 60604-2287. Offers programs in advanced practice nursing (MS), nurse anesthesia (MS). Accredited by NLN. MS (nurse anesthesia) offered jointly with Ravenswood Hospital Medical Center. Faculty: 5 full-time (all women), 1 (woman) part-time. Students: 16 full-time (13 women), 64 part-time (62 women); includes 32 minority (22 African Americans, 5 Asian Americans, 5 Hispanics). Average age 39. 41 applicants, 88% accepted. In 1997, 16 degrees awarded. *Degree requirements:* Comprehensive written exam required, thesis optional, foreign language not required. *Entrance requirements:* GRE, BSN, RN license, minimum GPA of 2.85. Application fee: $25. *Expenses:* Tuition $320 per credit hour. Fees $30 per year. *Financial aid:* Traineeships available. *Faculty research:* Children's health, women's health, health promotion. • Dr. Susan Poslusny, Chair, 773-325-7280. E-mail: sposlusn@wppost.depaul.edu.

Drake University, College of Pharmacy and Health Sciences, Division of Nursing, Des Moines, IA 50311-4516. Awards MSN. Part-time and evening/weekend programs available. Faculty: 4 full-time (3 women). Students: 19 full-time (18 women), 38 part-time (37 women). Average age 31. 23 applicants, 78% accepted. In 1997, 6 degrees awarded. *Degree requirements:* Computer language, thesis or alternative, oral comprehensive exams required, foreign language not required. *Average time to degree:* master's–2.5 years full-time, 5 years part-time. *Entrance requirements:* GRE General Test (minimum combined score of 1000) or MAT (minimum score 36), 2 years of work experience. Application deadline: 8/15 (priority date; rolling processing). Application fee: $25. *Financial aid:* 12 students received aid. *Faculty research:* Nursing education, program evaluation, rural health care needs, nursing administration, adolescent suicide. • Dr. Linda H. Brady, Chair, 515-271-2830. Fax: 515-271-4569. E-mail: linda.brady@drake.edu.

Duke University, School of Nursing, Durham, NC 27708-0586. Awards MSN, Certificate, MBA/MSN. Programs in acute care adult (Certificate); acute care pediatric (Certificate); adult cardiovascular (Certificate); adult oncological/HIV (Certificate); clinical nurse specialist (MSN), including acute care pediatric, adult oncological/HIV, gerontological, neonatal, pediatric; family (Certificate); gerontological (Certificate); health systems leadership and outcomes (MSN, Certificate); neonatal (Certificate); nurse practitioner (MSN), including acute care adult, acute care pediatric, adult cardiovascular, adult oncological/HIV, family, gerontological, neonatal, pediatric; nursing informatics (Certificate); pediatric (Certificate). One or more programs accredited by NLN. Part-time programs available. Postbaccalaureate distance learning degree programs offered (minimal on-campus study). Faculty: 24 full-time (22 women), 4 part-time (all women). Students: 55 full-time (52 women), 169 part-time (162 women); includes 25 minority (14 African Americans, 3 Asian Americans, 4 Hispanics, 4 Native Americans). Average age 37. 125 applicants, 84% accepted. In 1997, 59 master's, 27 Certificates awarded. *Degree requirements:* For master's, computer language required, thesis optional, foreign language not required. *Average time to degree:* master's–1.5 years full-time, 3 years part-time; other advanced degree–1 year full-time, 2 years part-time. *Entrance requirements:* For master's, GRE General Test or MAT, BSN, minimum GPA of 3.0, previous course work in statistics, RN license, 1 year of nursing experience. Application deadline: 4/1 (priority date; rolling processing; 10/1 for spring admission). Application fee: $50. *Tuition:* $20,976 per year full-time, $552 per unit part-time. *Financial aid:* In 1997–98, 132 students received aid, including 132 scholarships (75 to first-year students) totaling $480,000; institutionally sponsored loans and career-related internships or fieldwork also available. Aid available to part-time students. Financial aid applicants required to submit FAFSA. *Faculty research:* Elder care, cancer prevention, neurotrauma, nursing systems. Total annual research expenditures: $300,000. • Dr. Mary T. Champagne, Dean, 919-684-3786. E-mail: champ001@mc.duke.edu. Application contact: Judith K. Carter, Admissions Officer, 919-684-4248. Fax: 919-681-8899. E-mail: carte026@mc.duke.edu.

Duquesne University, School of Nursing, Pittsburgh, PA 15282-0001. Awards MSN, PhD, MSN/MBA. Programs in family nurse practitioner (MSN), nursing (PhD), nursing administration (MSN), nursing education (MSN). One or more programs accredited by NLN. Part-time programs available. Postbaccalaureate distance learning degree programs offered (minimal on-campus study). Faculty: 5 full-time (all women), 3 part-time (1 woman). Students: 28 full-time (all women), 122 part-time (116 women); includes 5 minority (1 African American, 3 Asian Americans, 1 Hispanic). In 1997, 37 master's awarded. *Degree requirements:* For master's, computer language required, foreign language and thesis not required; for doctorate, computer language, dissertation. *Entrance requirements:* For master's, GMAT (MSN/MBA), MAT, 1 year of work experience (2 years for family nurse practitioner); for doctorate, GRE. Application deadline: 7/31 (priority date; rolling processing; 11/31 for spring admission). Application fee: $40. *Expenses:* Tuition $481 per credit. Fees $39 per credit. *Financial aid:* Professional nurse traineeships, Federal Work-Study, institutionally sponsored loans available. *Faculty research:* Ethics, asthma, needle exchange, alternative medicine, genetics. • Dr. Jeri A. Milstead, Chair, 412-396-4865. E-mail: milstead@duq3.cc.duq.edu. Application contact: Carole Sisul, Administrative Assistant, Graduate Programs, 412-396-6551. Fax: 412-396-6346. E-mail: sisul@duq2.cc.duq.edu.

D'Youville College, Division of Nursing, Buffalo, NY 14201-1084. Offers programs in nurse practitioner (MS), nursing (MSN). Accredited by NLN. Part-time and evening/weekend programs available. Faculty: 9 full-time (8 women), 9 part-time (3 women). Students: 58 full-time, 133 part-time; includes 10 minority (6 African Americans, 2 Asian Americans, 2 Hispanics), 95 international. Average age 41. In 1997, 24 degrees awarded. *Degree requirements:* Computer language, thesis (for some programs), membership on board of community agency, publishable paper required, foreign language not required. *Entrance requirements:* BS in nursing, minimum GPA of 3.0, previous course work in statistics and computers. Application deadline: rolling. Application fee: $25. *Expenses:* Tuition $357 per credit hour. Fees $350 per year. *Financial aid:* In 1997–98, 1 research assistantship (to a first-year student) totaling $3,000, 44 scholarships (28 to first-year students) totaling $35,200 were awarded; Federal Work-Study also available. Aid available to part-time students. Financial aid application deadline: 3/1; applicants required to submit FAFSA. *Faculty research:* Nursing curriculum, nursing theory-testing, wellness research, communication and socialization patterns. • Dr. Carol Gutt, Chairperson, 716-881-3200. Application contact: Joseph Syracuse, Graduate Admissions Director, 716-881-7676. Fax: 716-881-7790.

East Carolina University, School of Nursing, Greenville, NC 27858-4353. Awards MSN. Accredited by NLN. Part-time programs available. Faculty: 21 full-time (19 women). Students: 51 full-time (46 women), 51 part-time (48 women); includes 14 minority (10 African Americans, 2 Asian Americans, 1 Hispanic, 1 Native American). Average age 37. 51 applicants, 73% accepted. In 1997, 41 degrees awarded. *Degree requirements:* Comprehensive exams required, thesis optional, foreign language not required. *Entrance requirements:* GRE General Test or MAT, bachelor's degree in nursing, professional license, minimum B average in nursing. Application deadline: 6/1 (priority date; rolling processing). Application fee: $40. *Tuition:* $1886 per year full-time, $472 per semester (minimum) part-time for state residents; $9156 per year full-time, $2289 per semester (minimum) part-time for nonresidents. *Financial aid:* Research assistantships, teaching assistantships, Federal Work-Study available. Aid available to part-time students. Financial aid application deadline: 6/1. • Dr. Lou Everett, Director of Graduate Studies, 252-328-4302. Fax: 252-328-4300. E-mail: everettl@mail.ecu.edu. Application contact: Dr. Paul D. Tschetter, Associate Dean, 252-328-6012. Fax: 252-328-6071. E-mail: grad@mail.ecu.edu.

Eastern Kentucky University, College of Allied Health and Nursing, Department of Nursing, Richmond, KY 40475-3101. Offers programs in rural community health care (MSN), rural health family nurse practitioner (MSN). Students: 63. In 1997, 16 degrees awarded. *Entrance requirements:* GRE General Test. Application fee: $0. *Tuition:* $2390 per year full-time, $133 per credit hour part-time for state residents; $6630 per year full-time, $365 per credit hour part-time for nonresidents. • Dr. D. Whitehouse, Chair, 606-622-1956.

Eastern Washington University, Intercollegiate Center for Nursing Education, Cheney, WA 99004-2431. Awards MN. Offered jointly with Gonzaga University, Washington State University, and Whitworth College. Faculty: 30 full-time (29 women). Students: 1 (woman) full-time, 1 part-time (0 women). Average age 31. 2 applicants, 50% accepted. *Degree requirements:* Thesis, comprehensive exam. *Entrance requirements:* GRE General Test, minimum GPA of 3.0. Application deadline: 4/1 (priority date; rolling processing). Application fee: $35. *Tuition:* $4200 per year full-time, $140 per credit part-time for state residents; $12,780 per year full-time, $415 per credit part-time for nonresidents. *Financial aid:* Application deadline 2/1. • Dr. Dorothy Detlor, Dean, 509-324-7334. Application contact: Dr. Marian Sheafor, Associate Dean, 509-324-7334.

East Tennessee State University, College of Nursing, Johnson City, TN 37614-0734. Offers programs in advanced nursing practice (Post Master's Certificate), nursing (MSN). One or more programs accredited by NLN. Part-time programs available. Faculty: 21 full-time (20 women). Students: 74 full-time (66 women), 15 part-time (13 women); includes 4 minority (2 Asian Americans, 1 Hispanic, 1 Native American), 2 international. Average age 36. 93 applicants, 70% accepted. In 1997, 14 master's awarded. *Degree requirements:* For master's, oral and written comprehensive exams required, thesis optional, foreign language not required. *Entrance requirements:* For master's, GRE General Test (minimum combined score of 1000), TOEFL (minimum score 550), minimum GPA of 3.0, bachelor's degree in nursing, current RN license. Application deadline: 1/15 (priority date; rolling processing). Application fee: $25 ($35 for international students). *Tuition:* $2944 per year full-time, $158 per credit hour part-time for state residents; $7770 per year full-time, $369 per credit hour part-time for nonresidents. *Financial aid:* In 1997–98, 1 research assistantship (to a first-year student) averaging $600 per month, 14 graduate assistantships, professional nurse traineeships (6 to first-year students) averaging $857 per month were awarded; career-related internships or fieldwork also available. Aid available to part-time students. Financial aid application deadline: 7/1. *Faculty research:* Rural primary care, health care for the homeless, community health problems across the lifespan, nursing education research, school health services. • Dr. Joellen Edwards, Dean, 423-439-6752. E-mail: edwardsj@etsu-tn.edu. Application contact: Dr. Patricia Smith, Associate Dean, Graduate Programs and Research, 423-439-4476. Fax: 423-439-5903. E-mail: smithp@etsu-tn.edu.

Edgewood College, Program in Nursing, Madison, WI 53711-1998. Awards MNA. Faculty: 2 full-time (both women). Students: 23. *Degree requirements:* Practicum, research project required, foreign language and thesis not required. *Application deadline:* 8/1 (priority date; rolling processing). *Application fee:* $25. *Tuition:* $330 per credit. • Dr. Virginia Wirtz, Chair, 608-257-4861 Ext. 2292. Application contact: Sr. Lucille Marie Frost, Assistant Dean of Graduate Programs, 608-257-4861 Ext. 2382. Fax: 608-257-1455.

Directory: Nursing—General

Edinboro University of Pennsylvania, School of Science, Management and Technology, Department of Nursing, Edinboro, PA 16444. Offers program in family nurse practitioner (MSN). Faculty: 4 full-time (all women). Students: 12 full-time (8 women), 28 part-time (all women); includes 2 minority (1 African American, 1 Native American). Average age 37. In 1997, 8 degrees awarded. *Degree requirements:* Thesis required, foreign language not required. *Entrance requirements:* GRE or MAT (score in 30th percentile or higher). Application deadline: rolling. Application fee: $25. *Expenses:* Tuition $3468 per year full-time, $193 per credit part-time for state residents; $6236 per year full-time, $346 per credit part-time for nonresidents. Fees $898 per year full-time, $50 per semester (minimum) part-time. *Financial aid:* In 1997–98, 2 assistantships were awarded; career-related internships or fieldwork also available. • Dr. Mary Louise Keller, Chair, 814-732-2900. E-mail: keller@edinboro.edu. Application contact: Dr. Philip Kerstetter, Dean of Graduate Studies, 814-732-2856. Fax: 814-732-2611. E-mail: kerstetter@edinboro.edu.

Emory University, Nell Hodgson Woodruff School of Nursing, Atlanta, GA 30322-1100. Awards MSN, MSN/MPH. Programs in adult health (MSN), including adult medical/surgical/nurse practitioner, adult oncology/nurse practitioner, critical care/nurse practitioner, psychosocial nurse practitioner; nursing systems (MSN), including family and adult nurse practitioner, gerontologic nurse practitioner, occupational health nurse practitioner; women and children (MSN), including child health/pediatric nurse practitioner, midwifery, pediatric oncology nurse practitioner, perinatal/neonatal nurse. Accredited by NLN. Part-time programs available. Postbaccalaureate distance learning degree programs offered (minimal on-campus study). Faculty: 33 full-time (32 women), 21 part-time (19 women), 48 FTE. Students: 114 full-time (109 women), 82 part-time (75 women); includes 26 minority (19 African Americans, 5 Asian Americans, 2 Hispanics), 3 international. Average age 28. 220 applicants, 50% accepted. In 1997, 86 degrees awarded. *Degree requirements:* Thesis optional, foreign language not required. *Average time to degree:* master's–1.5 years full-time, 3 years part-time. *Entrance requirements:* GRE General Test (minimum combined score of 1500 on three sections) or MAT (minimum score 35), minimum GPA of 3.0, BS in nursing or RN license and additional course work. Application deadline: 2/1 (priority date; rolling processing; 11/1 for spring admission). Application fee: $50. *Expenses:* Tuition $18,050 per year. Fees $200 per year. *Financial aid:* In 1997–98, 96 students received aid, including 5 fellowships (all to first-year students) totaling $32,000, 11 research assistantships averaging $500 per month, 2 teaching assistantships averaging $500 per month; Federal Work-Study, institutionally sponsored loans, and career-related internships or fieldwork also available. Aid available to part-time students. Financial aid application deadline: 2/15; applicants required to submit CSS PROFILE or FAFSA. *Faculty research:* Oncology nursing, women's health, psychosocial responses to pain, stress and coping, adolescent health promotion. Total annual research expenditures: $3.35 million. • Dr. Dyanne D. Affonso, Dean, 404-727-7976. Fax: 404-727-0536. Application contact: Debbie Ashtiani, Director, 404-727-7980.

Fairfield University, School of Nursing, Fairfield, CT 06430-5195. Offers programs in family nurse practitioner (MSN, CAS), psychiatric nurse practitioner (MSN). Part-time programs available. Faculty: 2 full-time (both women), 7 part-time (5 women), 4.3 FTE. Students: 31 full-time (30 women), 27 part-time (26 women); includes 5 minority (4 African Americans, 1 Asian American). Average age 35. 83% of applicants accepted. In 1997, 1 master's awarded (100% found work related to degree). *Degree requirements:* For master's, thesis. *Average time to degree:* master's–2 years full-time, 3 years part-time. *Entrance requirements:* For master's, GMAT or GRE, minimum QPA of 3.0, RN license; for CAS, 1 year of work experience, MSN. Application deadline: 5/1 (priority date; rolling processing; 12/1 for spring admission). Application fee: $50. *Expenses:* Tuition $355 per credit hour. Fees $20 per semester. *Financial aid:* In 1997–98, 17 students received aid, including 17 traineeship grants (5 to first-year students) totaling $31,993; career-related internships or fieldwork also available. *Faculty research:* Empathy, health beliefs, critical care, image of nursing, nursing outcomes, HIV, depression pedagogy. Total annual research expenditures: $34,556. • Dr. Kathleen Wheeler, Director, 203-254-4150. E-mail: kwheeler@fair1.fairfield.edu. Application contact: Kathy Borrelli, Secretary for MSN Program, 203-254-4150. Fax: 203-254-4126. E-mail: kborrelli@fair1.fairfield.edu.

Fairleigh Dickinson University, Teaneck–Hackensack Campus, University College: Arts, Sciences, and Professional Studies, School of Nursing and Allied Health, 1000 River Road, Teaneck, NJ 07666-1914. Offers program in nursing (MS). Faculty: 24 part-time (all women), 1.46 FTE. *Degree requirements:* Thesis optional, foreign language not required. *Entrance requirements:* GRE General Test, RN license. Application deadline: rolling. Application fee: $35. *Expenses:* Tuition $522 per credit. Fees $302 per year full-time, $138 per year part-time. • Dr. Caroline Jordet, Director, 201-692-2888. Fax: 201-692-2388.

Felician College, Program in Advanced Practice Nursing, Lodi, NJ 07644-2198. Awards MSN. *Entrance requirements:* BS in nursing, minimum GPA of 3.0. Application deadline: rolling. Application fee: $35. *Tuition:* $362 per credit. • Dr. Rona Levin, Director, 973-778-1190. Application contact: Debra A. Savage, Administrative Assistant, 973-778-1190 Ext. 6080. Fax: 973-778-4111.

Fitchburg State College, Program in Forensic Nursing, Fitchburg, MA 01420-2697. Awards MS. Part-time and evening/weekend programs available. *Entrance requirements:* GRE General Test or MAT, bachelor's degree in nursing from NLN-accredited program, minimum GPA of 2.8, previous course work in statistics, health assesssment competency, 1 year of clinical practice, Massachusetts license or intention to apply. Application deadline: rolling. Application fee: $10. *Expenses:* Tuition $147 per credit. Fees $55 per semester. *Financial aid:* Graduate assistantships, Federal Work-Study available. Aid available to part-time students. Financial aid application deadline: 3/30; applicants required to submit FAFSA. • Dr. Barbara Madden, Chair, 978-665-3498. Fax: 978-665-3658. E-mail: dgce@fsc.edu. Application contact: James DuPont, Director of Admissions, 978-665-3144. Fax: 978-665-4540. E-mail: admissions@fsc.edu.

See in-depth description on page 1427.

Florida Atlantic University, College of Nursing, Boca Raton, FL 33431-0991. Awards MS, Post Master's Certificate. One or more programs accredited by NLN. Part-time programs available. Faculty: 18 full-time (15 women), 8 part-time (7 women). Students: 25 full-time (all women), 143 part-time (128 women); includes 17 minority (9 African Americans, 1 Asian American, 7 Hispanics), 1 international. Average age 35. 19 applicants, 100% accepted. In 1997, 49 master's awarded. *Degree requirements:* For master's, thesis or alternative required, foreign language not required. *Average time to degree:* master's–2 years full-time, 3 years part-time. *Entrance requirements:* For master's, GRE General Test (minimum combined score of 1000), minimum GPA of 3.0. Application deadline: 6/1 (rolling processing; 10/15 for spring admission). Application fee: $20. *Expenses:* Tuition $2520 per year full-time, $140 per credit hour part-time for state residents; $8712 per year full-time, $484 per credit hour part-time for nonresidents. Fees $5 per year (minimum). *Financial aid:* In 1997–98, 7 research assistantships (2 to first-year students), 15 teaching assistantships (3 to first-year students), 13 scholarships, traineeships (4 to first-year students) were awarded; Federal Work-Study, institutionally sponsored loans, and career-related internships or fieldwork also available. Aid available to part-time students. Financial aid application deadline: 7/1. *Faculty research:* Community-based programs, head lice, genital herpes/HPV, econometrics of nurse-patient relationship, aging, Alzheimer's disease, falls. • Dr. Anne Boykin, Dean, 561-297-3206. Fax: 561-297-3687. E-mail: boykina@acc.fau.edu. Application contact: Dr. Ellis Quinn Youngkin, Graduate Program Coordinator, 561-297-3384. Fax: 561-297-3652. E-mail: eyoungkin@fau.edu.

Florida International University, College of Health, Department of Nursing, Miami, FL 33199. Awards MSN. Accredited by NLN. Part-time programs available. Faculty: 21 full-time (18 women). Students: 72 full-time (63 women), 134 part-time (121 women); includes 111 minority (58 African Americans, 22 Asian Americans, 31 Hispanics), 1 international. Average age 38. 91 applicants, 22% accepted. In 1997, 53 degrees awarded. *Degree requirements:* Thesis. *Application deadline:* 4/1 (priority date; rolling processing; 10/1 for spring admission). *Application fee:* $20. *Expenses:* Tuition $138 per credit hour for state residents; $482 per credit hour for nonresidents. Fees $46 per semester. *Faculty research:* Adult health nursing. • Dr. M. Velasco-Whetsell, Chair, 305-919-5915. Fax: 305-919-5395.

Florida State University, School of Nursing, Tallahassee, FL 32306. Offers program in family nursing (MSN), including adult nurse practitioner, advanced registered nurse practitioner, case manager, family nurse practitioner, nurse educator. Accredited by NLN. Part-time programs available. Faculty: 16 full-time (14 women), 7 part-time (5 women). Students: 13 full-time (9 women), 78 part-time (75 women); includes 13 minority (7 African Americans, 1 Asian American, 3 Hispanics, 2 Native Americans). Average age 38. 35 applicants, 49% accepted. In 1997, 26 degrees awarded (100% found work related to degree). *Degree requirements:* Thesis required, foreign language not required. *Average time to degree:* master's–2 years full-time, 3.5 years part-time. *Entrance requirements:* GRE General Test (minimum combined score of 1000), minimum GPA of 3.0, BSN, Florida RN License, 2 years of work experience. Application deadline: 4/15 (priority date; rolling processing; 7/15 for spring admission). Application fee: $20. *Tuition:* $139 per credit hour for state residents; $482 per credit hour for nonresidents. *Financial aid:* In 1997–98, 18 fellowships (10 to first-year students) were awarded; research assistantships, teaching assistantships, federal nurse traineeships, partial tuition waivers, Federal Work-Study, institutionally sponsored loans, and career-related internships or fieldwork also available. Financial aid application deadline: 4/15. *Faculty research:* Distance learning, maternal/child relationship, gerontology, health promotion, educational strategies. • Dr. Evelyn Singer, Dean, 850-644-3299. Fax: 850-644-7660. E-mail: esinger@mailer.fsu.edu. Application contact: Dr. Deborah I. Frank, Graduate Program Coordinator, 850-644-5974. E-mail: dfrank@mailer.acns.fsu.edu.

Fort Hays State University, College of Health and Life Sciences, Department of Nursing, Hays, KS 67601-4099. Awards MSN. Accredited by NLN. Faculty: 4 full-time (all women). Students: 16 full-time (all women), 54 part-time (51 women); includes 1 minority (Hispanic), 6 international. Average age 29. 12 applicants, 83% accepted. In 1997, 23 degrees awarded. *Degree requirements:* Thesis optional, foreign language not required. *Entrance requirements:* GRE General Test or MAT. Application deadline: 7/1 (priority date; rolling processing). Application fee: $25 ($35 for international students). *Tuition:* $94 per credit hour for state residents; $249 per credit hour for nonresidents. *Financial aid:* Research assistantships, teaching assistantships available. • Dr. Mary Hassett, Chair, 785-628-4498.

Gannon University, School of Graduate Studies, College of Sciences, Engineering, and Health Sciences, School of Health Sciences, Department of Nursing, Erie, PA 16505. Offers programs in administration (MSN), anesthesia (MSN), family nurse practitioner (MSN, Certificate), gerontology (MSN), medical-surgical nursing (MSN). Part-time and evening/weekend programs available. Students: 10 full-time (all women), 39 part-time (33 women); includes 1 minority (Hispanic). Average age 34. 12 applicants, 67% accepted. In 1997, 24 master's awarded. *Degree requirements:* For master's, thesis. *Entrance requirements:* For master's, GRE General Test (minimum score 500 on each section), MAT (minimum score 60), bachelor's degree from a NLN-approved nursing program, interview, Pennsylvania RN license. Application deadline: 4/15. Application fee: $25. *Financial aid:* Traineeships and career-related internships or fieldwork available. Aid available to part-time students. Financial aid application deadline: 3/1; applicants required to submit FAFSA. • Dr. Beverly Bartlett, Director, 814-871-5520. Application contact: Beth Nemenz, Director of Admissions, 814-871-7240. Fax: 814-871-5803. E-mail: admissions@gannon.edu.

Gannon University, School of Graduate Studies, College of Sciences, Engineering, and Health Sciences, School of Health Sciences, MSN/MBA Program, Erie, PA 16541. Awards MSN/MBA. Part-time and evening/weekend programs available. Students: 2 part-time (both women). Average age 30. *Application deadline:* 4/15 (priority date). *Application fee:* $25. *Financial aid:* Career-related internships or fieldwork available. Aid available to part-time students. Financial aid application deadline: 3/1; applicants required to submit FAFSA. • Application contact: Beth Nemenz, Director of Admissions, 814-871-7240. Fax: 814-871-5803. E-mail: admissions@gannon.edu.

George Mason University, College of Nursing and Health Science, Fairfax, VA 22030-4444. Offers programs in advanced clinical nursing (MSN), nurse practitioner (MSN), nursing (MSN, PhD), nursing administration (MSN). One or more programs accredited by NLN. Faculty: 50 full-time (46 women), 26 part-time (24 women), 61.65 FTE. Students: 61 full-time (55 women), 237 part-time (228 women); includes 50 minority (21 African Americans, 21 Asian Americans, 7 Hispanics, 1 Native American), 13 international. Average age 40. 177 applicants, 79% accepted. In 1997, 83 master's, 8 doctorates awarded. *Degree requirements:* For doctorate, dissertation, oral/written exams. *Entrance requirements:* For master's, RN license (MSN), minimum GPA of 3.0 in last 60 hours; for doctorate, MAT, master's degree, minimum GPA of 3.25, 3 years of nursing experience, professional liability insurance. Application deadline: 5/1 (11/1 for spring admission). Application fee: $30. Electronic applications accepted. *Tuition:* $4344 per year full-time, $181 per credit hour part-time for state residents; $12,504 per year full-time, $521 per credit hour part-time for nonresidents. *Financial aid:* Fellowships, research assistantships, teaching assistantships, partial tuition waivers available. Aid available to part-time students. Financial aid application deadline: 3/1; applicants required to submit FAFSA. • Dr. Rita M. Carty, Dean, 703-993-1919. Application contact: Dr. James D. Vail, Associate Dean, Graduate Programs and Research, 703-993-1913. Fax: 703-993-1942. E-mail: jvail@osf1.gmu.edu.

Georgetown University, School of Nursing, Washington, DC 20057. Awards MS. Accredited by NLN. *Degree requirements:* Thesis optional. *Entrance requirements:* GRE General Test or MAT, TOEFL (minimum score 550), bachelor's degree in nursing from NLN accredited school, minimum undergraduate GPA of 3.0. Application fee: $50 ($55 for international students). *Expenses:* Tuition $19,128 per year full-time, $797 per credit part-time. Fees $99 (one-time charge).

See in-depth description on page 1429.

Georgia College and State University, School of Health Sciences, Department of Nursing, Milledgeville, GA 31061. Awards MSN. Accredited by NLN. Students: 5 full-time (all women), 77 part-time (70 women); includes 20 minority (18 African Americans, 2 Asian Americans), 1 international. In 1997, 19 degrees awarded. *Degree requirements:* Thesis or alternative. *Entrance requirements:* GRE General Test or MAT, bachelor's degree in nursing. Application deadline: 7/31 (priority date; rolling processing). Application fee: $10. *Financial aid:* Assistantships available. Financial aid application deadline: 4/15. • Dr. Pamela Levi, Dean, School of Health Sciences, 912-445-4004.

Georgia Southern University, College of Health and Professional Studies, Department of Nursing, Statesboro, GA 30460-8126. Offers programs in rural community health nurse specialist (MSN), rural family nurse practitioner (MSN, Certificate). One or more programs accredited by NLN. Part-time programs available. Postbaccalaureate distance learning degree programs offered (minimal on-campus study). Faculty: 12 full-time (all women). Students: 38 full-time (36 women), 9 part-time (7 women); includes 7 minority (3 African Americans, 1 Asian American, 2 Hispanics, 1 Native American). Average age 37. 20 applicants, 40% accepted. In 1997, 36 master's awarded. *Degree requirements:* For master's, project or thesis required, foreign language not required. *Average time to degree:* master's–1.5 years full-time, 2.5 years part-time. *Entrance requirements:* For master's, GRE General Test (minimum score 450 on each section), minimum GPA of 3.0, nursing license, 2 years of clinical experience; for Certificate, MSN. Application deadline: 7/15 (priority date; rolling processing; 11/15 for spring admission). Application fee: $0. Electronic applications accepted. *Tuition:* $2619 per year full-time, $287 per semester (minimum) part-time for state residents; $8619 per year full-time, $1037 per semester (minimum) part-time for nonresidents. *Financial aid:* In 1997–98, 2 assistantships were awarded; research assistantships, teaching assistantships, Federal Work-Study, and career-related internships or fieldwork also available. Aid available to part-time students. Financial aid application deadline: 4/15. *Faculty research:* Caring, HIV disease, qualitative health research, health policy, rural. • Dr. Kaye Herth, Chair, 912-681-5479. Application contact:

Dr. John R. Diebolt, Associate Graduate Dean, 912-681-5384. Fax: 912-681-0740. E-mail: gradschool@gsvms2.cc.gasou.edu.

Georgia State University, College of Health and Human Sciences, School of Nursing, Atlanta, GA 30303-3083. Offers programs in adult health (MS); child health/pediatric nurse practitioner (MS); community nursing (PhD); family nurse practitioner (MS); family nursing (PhD); gerontology (MS); health promotion, protection, and restoration (PhD); perinatal women's health/practitioner (MS); psychiatric/mental health nursing (MS), including child and adolescent psychology. One or more programs accredited by NLN. MS (child and adolescent psychology, gerontology) and PhD (community nursing, family nursing) being phased out; applicants no longer accepted. Part-time and evening/weekend programs available. Faculty: 26 full-time (all women), 3 part-time (all women). Students: 117 full-time (106 women), 132 part-time (128 women); includes 59 minority (47 African Americans, 4 Asian Americans, 8 Hispanics), 1 international. Average age 38. 123 applicants, 47% accepted. In 1997, 90 master's, 9 doctorates awarded. *Degree requirements:* For master's, research project or thesis required, thesis optional, foreign language not required; for doctorate, dissertation required, foreign language not required. *Entrance requirements:* For master's, interview, RN license; for doctorate, GRE General Test. Application deadline: 4/15. Application fee: $25. *Expenses:* Tuition $2862 per year full-time, $106 per semester hour part-time for state residents; $11,448 per year full-time, $424 per semester hour part-time for nonresidents. Fees $228 per year. *Financial aid:* Fellowships, research assistantships, teaching assistantships, minority fellowships, Federal Work-Study, institutionally sponsored loans available. Aid available to part-time students. Financial aid application deadline: 4/15; applicants required to submit FAFSA. *Faculty research:* Health restoration, child abuse, vulnerable populations, health promotion. • Dr. Dee Baldwin, Director of Graduate Programs, 404-651-3040. Application contact: Barbara Smith, Admissions Counselor, 404-651-3064. Fax: 404-651-4871.

Gonzaga University, Graduate School, School of Professional Studies, Program in Nursing, Spokane, WA 99258-0001. Awards MSN. Accredited by NLN. *Entrance requirements:* MAT, TOEFL (minimum score 550), minimum B average in undergraduate course work. Application deadline: 7/20 (priority date; rolling processing; 11/1 for spring admission). Application fee: $40. *Tuition:* $7380 per year (minimum) full-time, $410 per credit (minimum) part-time. *Financial aid:* Application deadline 3/1. • Application contact: Dr. Joseph Albert, 509-328-4220 Ext. 3564.

Governors State University, College of Health Professions, Division of Nursing and Health Science, Program in Nursing, University Park, IL 60466. Awards MSN. Accredited by NLN. Faculty: 7 full-time (6 women), 1 (woman) part-time. Average age 37. In 1997, 22 degrees awarded. *Degree requirements:* Thesis or alternative, comprehensive exam, practicum required, foreign language not required. *Entrance requirements:* GRE General Test, minimum GPA of 3.0 in upper-division nursing courses, 2.5 overall; BSN verification of AAS or employment as a registered nurse; Illinois licensure; BSN degree from an institution accredited by the National League for Nursing. Application deadline: 7/15 (priority date; rolling processing; 11/10 for spring admission). Application fee: $0. *Expenses:* Tuition $1140 per trimester full-time, $95 per credit hour part-time for state residents; $3420 per trimester full-time, $285 per credit hour part-time for nonresidents. Fees $95 per trimester. *Financial aid:* Research assistantships, full and partial tuition waivers, Federal Work-Study, institutionally sponsored loans, and career-related internships or fieldwork available. Aid available to part-time students. Financial aid application deadline: 5/1. • Dr. Connie Edwards, Chairperson, Division of Nursing and Health Science, 708-534-4040.

Graceland College, Master's in Nursing Program, 221 West Lexington, Suite 110, Independence, MO 64050. Offers clinical nurse specialist/family nursing (educator) (MSN), family nurse practitioner (MSN, PMC), health care administration (MSN). Part-time programs available. Postbaccalaureate distance learning degree programs offered (minimal on-campus study). Faculty: 6 full-time (all women), 1 (woman) part-time, 6.5 FTE. Students: 5 full-time (all women), 59 part-time (50 women); includes 5 minority (2 African Americans, 1 Asian American, 1 Hispanic, 1 Native American). Average age 42. 39 applicants, 85% accepted. In 1997, 6 master's, 3 PMCs awarded. *Degree requirements:* For master's, thesis optional, foreign language not required. *Average time to degree:* master's–2 years full-time, 2.5 years part-time; other advanced degree–1 year full-time, 1.5 years part-time. *Entrance requirements:* For master's, BSN from nationally accredited program. Application deadline: rolling. Application fee: $80. *Tuition:* $350 per credit hour (minimum). *Financial aid:* 12 students received aid; institutionally sponsored loans available. Aid available to part-time students. Financial aid applicants required to submit FAFSA. *Faculty research:* International nursing, family care-giving, health promotion. • Dr. Karen Fernengel, Chair, 816-833-0524. Fax: 816-833-2990. E-mail: karenf@graceland.edu. Application contact: Lewis Smith, Director, Student Information Service, 800-537-6276. Fax: 540-344-1508.

Grambling State University, School of Nursing, Grambling, LA 71245. Awards MSN. Evening/weekend programs available. Faculty: 6 full-time (all women). Students: 7 full-time (4 women); includes 1 minority (African American). Average age 30. 41 applicants, 20% accepted. *Degree requirements:* Thesis optional, foreign language not required. *Entrance requirements:* GRE. Application deadline: rolling. Application fee: $15. *Tuition:* $1960 per year full-time, $297 per semester (minimum) part-time for state residents; $7110 per year full-time, $297 per semester (minimum) part-time for nonresidents. *Financial aid:* Application deadline 5/31. • Dr. Betty E. Smith, Dean, 318-274-3234. Application contact: Rhonda Hensley, Coordinator, 318-274-2672.

Grand Valley State University, Russell B. Kirkhof School of Nursing, Allendale, MI 49401-9403. Awards MSN. Accredited by NLN. Part-time programs available. Faculty: 15 full-time (all women). Students: 13 full-time (all women), 132 part-time (127 women); includes 3 minority (1 African American, 1 Hispanic, 1 Native American). Average age 39. 75 applicants, 71% accepted. In 1997, 26 degrees awarded. *Degree requirements:* Thesis required, foreign language not required. *Average time to degree:* master's–2 years full-time, 3 years part-time. *Entrance requirements:* GRE, minimum GPA of 3.0, previous course work in statistics. Application deadline: 3/15 (priority date; rolling processing). Application fee: $20. Electronic applications accepted. *Financial aid:* In 1997–98, 6 research assistantships (2 to first-year students) totaling $12,900, 19 traineeships (11 to first-year students) totaling $29,696 were awarded; Federal Work-Study, institutionally sponsored loans, and career-related internships or fieldwork also available. *Faculty research:* Asian-American cancer control survey; osteoporosis study: elderly, adolescents, and ethnic minorities. • Dr. Lorraine Rodrigues-Fisher, Dean, 616-895-3558. Fax: 616-895-2510.

Gwynedd–Mercy College, Graduate Program in Nursing, Gwynedd Valley, PA 19437-0901. Offers gerontology (MSN); nurse practitioner (MSN), including adult, pediatric; oncology (MSN); pediatrics (MSN). Accredited by NLN. MSN (pediatrics, oncology) admissions temporarily suspended. Part-time programs available. Faculty: 9 full-time (all women), 8 part-time (6 women). Students: 20 full-time (all women), 68 part-time (65 women); includes 4 minority (1 African American, 1 Asian American, 1 Hispanic, 1 Native American). Average age 38. 36 applicants, 89% accepted. In 1997, 47 degrees awarded (17% entered university research/teaching, 83% found other work related to degree). *Degree requirements:* Thesis or research project required, foreign language not required. *Average time to degree:* master's–2.5 years full-time, 3.5 years part-time. *Entrance requirements:* GRE General Test (minimum combined score of 1350; average 1401), MAT (minimum score 40; average 48), 1 year of experience, physical assessment, previous course work in statistics. Application deadline: 8/1 (priority date; rolling processing). Application fee: $25. *Expenses:* Tuition $375 per credit. Fees $150 per year full-time, $80 per year part-time. *Financial aid:* In 1997–98, 25 students received aid, including 25 traineeships totaling $59,800. Financial aid application deadline: 8/30. *Faculty research:* Critical thinking, therapeutic touch, self-care, multiculturalism, breast self-examination. Total annual research expenditures: $6400. • Dr. Mary Dressler, Dean, 215-641-5533. E-mail: dressler.m@gmc.edu. Application contact: Dr. Barbara A. Jones, Associate Professor, 215-646-7300 Ext. 407. Fax: 215-641-5517.

Hampton University, Department of Nursing, Hampton, VA 23668. Awards MS. Accredited by NLN. Part-time and evening/weekend programs available. Faculty: 10 full-time (all women), 1 part-time (0 women). Students: 32 full-time (30 women), 30 part-time (27 women); includes 43 minority (40 African Americans, 1 Asian American, 2 Hispanics), 1 international. In 1997, 18 degrees awarded. *Degree requirements:* Thesis optional, foreign language not required. *Entrance requirements:* GRE General Test (minimum score 450 on verbal section). Application deadline: 6/1 (priority date; rolling processing; 11/1 for spring admission). Application fee: $25. *Expenses:* Tuition $9038 per year full-time, $220 per credit part-time. Fees $70 per year. *Financial aid:* Fellowships, research assistantships, teaching assistantships, scholarships, Federal Work-Study, institutionally sponsored loans, and career-related internships or fieldwork available. Aid available to part-time students. Financial aid application deadline: 5/1; applicants required to submit FAFSA. *Faculty research:* Curriculum development, physical and mental assessment. • Johnnie Bunch, Chair, 757-727-5991. Application contact: Erika Henderson, Director, Graduate Programs, 757-727-5454. Fax: 757-727-5084.

Hardin–Simmons University, School of Nursing, Abilene, TX 79698-0001. Awards MSN. Offered jointly with Abilene Christian University and McMurry University. Part-time programs available. Faculty: 3 full-time (all women). Students: 1 (woman) full-time, 3 part-time (all women). Average age 42. In 1997, 2 degrees awarded. *Degree requirements:* Thesis or alternative required, foreign language not required. *Application deadline:* 8/15 (priority date; rolling processing; 1/5 for spring admission). *Application fee:* $25. *Financial aid:* 3 students received aid; full and partial tuition waivers, Federal Work-Study, and career-related internships or fieldwork available. Aid available to part-time students. Financial aid application deadline: 3/15; applicants required to submit FAFSA. *Faculty research:* Adolescent pregnancy, spirituality, psyche/mental health, care of aged. • Dr. Corine Bonnet, Dean, 915-672-2441. Application contact: Dr. J. Paul Sorrels, Dean of Graduate Studies, 915-670-1298. Fax: 915-670-1564.

Hawaii Pacific University, School of Nursing, 1166 Fort Street, Honolulu, HI 96813-2785. Offers programs in community clinical nurse specialist (MSN), family nurse practitioner (MSN). Program new for fall 1998. *Degree requirements:* Practicum, professional paper. *Entrance requirements:* Bachelor's degree in nursing. Application deadline: rolling. Application fee: $50. *Tuition:* $7920 per year full-time, $330 per credit part-time. • Dr. Carol Winters, Dean, 808-236-3552. Application contact: Leina Danao, Admissions Coordinator, 808-544-1120. Fax: 808-544-0280. E-mail: gradservetr@hpu.edu.

Holy Family College, Graduate Studies, Program in Nursing, Philadelphia, PA 19114-2094. Awards MSN. Faculty: 2 full-time (both women). Students: 8 part-time (7 women); includes 1 minority (Asian American). Average age 37. 7 applicants, 100% accepted. *Degree requirements:* Thesis or alternative required, foreign language not required. *Entrance requirements:* GRE or MAT, bachelor's degree in nursing or RN license. Application deadline: (11/15 for spring admission). Application fee: $25. *Expenses:* Tuition $320 per credit hour. Fees $65 per semester. *Financial aid:* Research assistantships available. Aid available to part-time students. Financial aid application deadline: 2/15; applicants required to submit FAFSA. • Phyllis Marshall, Graduate Coordinator, 215-637-7700 Ext. 3295. Application contact: Joseph Canaday, Graduate Coordinator, 215-637-7203. Fax: 215-637-1478. E-mail: jcanaday@hfc.edu.

Holy Names College, Department of Nursing, 3500 Mountain Boulevard, Oakland, CA 94619-1699. Offers programs in community health nursing/case manager (MS), family nurse practitioner (MS). Part-time and evening/weekend programs available. Faculty: 6 full-time (all women), 1 (woman) part-time. Students: 28 part-time (25 women); includes 10 minority (6 African Americans, 2 Asian Americans, 1 Hispanic, 1 Native American). 36 applicants, 94% accepted. *Entrance requirements:* TOEFL (minimum score 550), bachelor's degree in nursing or related field, California RN license or eligibility, minimum GPA of 3.0, previous coursework in research or statistics. Application deadline: 8/1 (rolling processing; 12/1 for spring admission). Application fee: $35. *Tuition:* $7650 per year full-time, $425 per unit part-time. *Financial aid:* 9 students received aid; Federal Work-Study and career-related internships or fieldwork available. Aid available to part-time students. Financial aid application deadline: 3/2; applicants required to submit FAFSA. *Faculty research:* Women's reproductive health, gerontology, attitudes about aging, schizophrenic families, international health issues, substance abuse, high-risk populations. • Aida Sahud, Program Director, 510-436-1239. Application contact: Graduate Admissions Office, 800-430-1321. Fax: 510-436-1317. E-mail: garner@admin.hnc.edu.

Houston Baptist University, Center for Health Studies, Program in Nursing, Houston, TX 77074-3298. Offers congregational care nurse (MSN), family nurse practitioner (MSN), family nurse practitioner-congregational nurse (MSN). Faculty: 7 full-time (all women), 3 part-time (2 women). Students: 6 full-time (4 women), 10 part-time (all women); includes 7 minority (4 African Americans, 1 Asian American, 2 Hispanics). 11 applicants, 73% accepted. *Entrance requirements:* GRE General Test (minimum combined score of 900), MAT (minimum score 45), minimum GPA of 2.5. Application deadline: 7/1 (priority date; rolling processing; 1/1 for spring admission). Application fee: $25 ($85 for international students). *Expenses:* Tuition $350 per semester hour (minimum). Fees $235 per quarter. *Financial aid:* Federal Work-Study available. • Dr. Brenda Binder, Head, 281-649-3000 Ext. 2385.

Howard University, College of Pharmacy, Nursing and Allied Health Sciences, Division of Nursing, 2400 Sixth Street, NW, Washington, DC 20059-0002. Offers programs in nurse practitioner (Certificate), primary family health nursing (MSN). One or more programs accredited by NLN. Part-time programs available. Faculty: 4 full-time (all women), 2 part-time (both women), 4.75 FTE. Students: 10 full-time (all women), 13 part-time (12 women); includes 16 minority (all African Americans), 5 international. Average age 36. 32 applicants, 78% accepted. In 1997, 9 master's awarded (66% found work related to degree); 1 Certificate awarded. *Degree requirements:* For master's, thesis or alternative required, foreign language not required. *Average time to degree:* master's–2.5 years full-time, 4 years part-time; other advanced degree–1.5 years full-time, 2 years part-time. *Entrance requirements:* For master's, RN license, minimum GPA of 3.0, BS in nursing. Application deadline: 4/1 (priority date; rolling processing; 11/1 for spring admission). Application fee: $45. *Expenses:* Tuition $10,200 per year full-time, $567 per credit hour part-time. Fees $405 per year. *Financial aid:* In 1997–98, 8 grants (6 to first-year students) averaging $861 per month and totaling $55,098 were awarded; teaching assistantships, institutionally sponsored loans, and career-related internships or fieldwork also available. Financial aid application deadline: 4/1. *Faculty research:* Urinary incontinence, breast cancer prevention, depression in the elderly, adolescent pregnancy. • Dr. Dorothy L. Powell, Associate Dean, 202-806-7456. Application contact: Dr. Coralease C. Ruff, Assistant Dean, Graduate Program, 202-806-7460. Fax: 202-806-5958.

Hunter College of the City University of New York, Hunter-Bellevue School of Nursing, 695 Park Avenue, New York, NY 10021-5085. Awards MS, AC, MS/MPH. One or more programs accredited by NLN. Part-time programs available. Faculty: 19 full-time (18 women), 2 part-time (1 woman). Students: 17 full-time (14 women), 267 part-time (247 women); includes 108 minority (61 African Americans, 31 Asian Americans, 16 Hispanics), 3 international. Average age 38. 152 applicants, 71% accepted. In 1997, 64 master's awarded (100% found work related to degree); 9 ACs awarded. *Degree requirements:* For master's, practicum required, foreign language and thesis not required. *Average time to degree:* master's–1.5 years full-time, 3 years part-time. *Entrance requirements:* For master's, TOEFL (minimum score 550), minimum GPA of 3.0, New York RN license; for AC, MSN, minimum GPA of 3.0. Application deadline: 4/27 (rolling processing; 11/21 for spring admission). Application fee: $40. *Expenses:* Tuition $4350 per year full-time, $185 per credit part-time for state residents; $7600 per year full-time, $320 per credit part-time for nonresidents. Fees $26 per year. *Financial aid:* In 1997–98, 6 traineeships (5 to first-year students) averaging $500 per month were awarded; partial tuition waivers, Federal Work-Study also available. Aid available to part-time students. Financial aid application deadline: 5/1; applicants required to submit FAFSA. *Faculty research:* Aging, high-risk mothers and babies, adolescent health, care of HIV/AIDS clients, critical care nursing, primary care, homeless families. • Dr. Evelynn Gioiella, Dean, 212-481-4312. Fax:

Directory: Nursing—General

Hunter College of the City University of New York (continued)
212-481-5078. E-mail: egioiell@shiva.hunter.cuny.edu. Application contact: Audrey Berman, Associate Director for Graduate Admissions, 212-772-4490.

Husson College, Program in Nursing, Bangor, ME 04401-2999. Offers family nurse practioner (MSN), nursing (MSN), psychiatric nursing (MSN). Faculty: 2. Students: 41. *Entrance requirements:* MAT, BSN. Application deadline: 7/15 (priority date; rolling processing). Application fee: $25. • Dr. Barbara Higgins, Director, Nurse Practitioner Program, 207-947-7057.

Idaho State University, College of Health Professions, Department of Nursing, Pocatello, ID 83209. Awards MS, Certificate. One or more programs accredited by NLN. Part-time programs available. Faculty: 6 full-time (4 women). Students: 16 full-time (11 women), 25 part-time (22 women). Average age 39. In 1997, 19 master's, 1 Certificate awarded. *Degree requirements:* For master's, thesis optional, foreign language not required. *Entrance requirements:* For master's, GRE General Test (score in 35th percentile or higher); for Certificate, GRE General Test. Application deadline: 5/1 (priority date; rolling processing; 11/15 for spring admission). Application fee: $30. *Tuition:* $3130 per year full-time, $136 per credit hour part-time for state residents; $9370 per year full-time, $226 per credit hour part-time for nonresidents. *Financial aid:* In 1997–98, 1 teaching assistantship (to a first-year student), 10 traineeships (all to first-year students) totaling $29,631 were awarded. Aid available to part-time students. Financial aid application deadline: 3/1. *Faculty research:* Health promotions, health of homeless, exercise and elderly, student stress, midwifery. • Dr. Pamela Clarke, Chair, 208-286-2185.

Indiana State University, School of Nursing, Terre Haute, IN 47809-1401. Awards MS, MBA/MS. Accredited by NLN. Part-time programs available. Faculty: 13 full-time (all women), 2 part-time (both women). Students: 7 full-time (6 women), 35 part-time (34 women); includes 1 minority (African American). Average age 40. 28 applicants, 89% accepted. In 1997, 14 degrees awarded. *Entrance requirements:* GRE General Test, BSN, RN license, CPR certificate. Application deadline: rolling. Application fee: $20. *Tuition:* $143 per credit hour for state residents; $325 per credit hour for nonresidents. *Financial aid:* In 1997–98, 1 research assistantship was awarded; teaching assistantships, Federal Work-Study, and career-related internships or fieldwork also available. Aid available to part-time students. Financial aid application deadline: 3/1. *Faculty research:* Nursing faculty-student interactions, clinical evaluation, program evaluation, sexual dysfunction, faculty attitudes. • Dr. Judith Alexander, Acting Dean, 812-237-2320.

Indiana University of Pennsylvania, College of Health and Human Services, Department of Nursing, Indiana, PA 15705-1087. Awards MS. Accredited by NLN. Part-time programs available. Students: 9 full-time (6 women), 35 part-time (all women); includes 4 international. Average age 40. 10 applicants, 90% accepted. In 1997, 10 degrees awarded. *Degree requirements:* Thesis optional, foreign language not required. *Entrance requirements:* TOEFL (minimum score 500). Application deadline: 7/1 (priority date; rolling processing; 11/1 for spring admission). Application fee: $30. *Expenses:* Tuition $3468 per year full-time, $193 per credit part-time for state residents; $6236 per year full-time, $346 per credit part-time for nonresidents. Fees $313 per year (minimum) full-time, $84 per year part-time. *Financial aid:* Research assistantships, Federal Work-Study available. Aid available to part-time students. Financial aid application deadline: 3/15. • Jodell Kuzneski, Chairperson, 724-357-2557. E-mail: kuzneski@grove.iup.edu. Application contact: Dr. Nashat Zuraikat, Graduate Coordinator, 724-357-7647. E-mail: zuraikat@grove.iup.edu.

Indiana University–Purdue University Indianapolis, School of Nursing, Indianapolis, IN 46202-2896. Awards MSN, PhD, MSN/MHA, MSN/MPA. One or more programs accredited by NLN. Part-time programs available. Faculty: 47 full-time (45 women), 1 (woman) part-time. Students: 55 full-time (50 women), 296 part-time (291 women); includes 24 minority (14 African Americans, 5 Asian Americans, 4 Hispanics, 1 Native American), 10 international. Average age 28. 74 applicants, 62% accepted. In 1997, 90 master's, 6 doctorates awarded. Terminal master's awarded for partial completion of doctoral program. *Degree requirements:* For master's, thesis required, foreign language not required; for doctorate, computer language, dissertation required, foreign language not required. *Average time to degree:* master's–2 years full-time, 6 years part-time; doctorate–3 years full-time, 6 years part-time. *Entrance requirements:* For master's, GRE General Test (minimum score 400 on each section), minimum GPA of 3.0, RN; for doctorate, GRE General Test (minimum score 550 on each section), minimum GPA of 3.5, MSN, RN. Application fee: $35. *Expenses:* Tuition $3602 per year full-time, $150 per credit hour part-time for state residents; $10,392 per year full-time, $433 per credit hour part-time for nonresidents. Fees $100 per year (minimum) full-time, $40 per year (minimum) part-time. *Financial aid:* In 1997–98, 93 students received aid, including 16 fellowships (5 to first-year students) totaling $10,000, 47 research assistantships (15 to first-year students), 15 teaching assistantships (1 to a first-year student), 15 scholarships (5 to first-year students); Federal Work-Study also available. Aid available to part-time students. Financial aid application deadline: 5/1. *Faculty research:* Chronic illness, cancer, health services research, family health. Total annual research expenditures: $2.572 million. • Dr. Linda Finke, Associate Dean for Graduate Programs, 317-274-2806. Application contact: Academic Counselor, Graduate Programs, 317-274-2806. Fax: 317-274-2996.

See in-depth description on page 1431.

Indiana Wesleyan University, Division of Nursing Education, Marion, IN 46953-4999. Offers programs in community health development (MS), community health nursing (MS), nursing education (MS), primary care nursing (MS). Accredited by NLN. Part-time and evening/weekend programs available. Faculty: 4 full-time (3 women). Students: 54. Average age 37. In 1997, 38 degrees awarded. *Degree requirements:* Thesis required, foreign language not required. *Entrance requirements:* MAT, RN license, 1 year of related experience. Application fee: $10. *Tuition:* $402 per hour. *Financial aid:* In 1997–98, 4 teaching assistantships, 1 scholarship were awarded; career-related internships or fieldwork also available. Aid available to part-time students. Financial aid application deadline: 3/15. *Faculty research:* Primary health care with international emphasis, international nursing. • Dr. DeAnne Messias, Director of Graduate Nursing, 765-677-2148.

Jewish Hospital College of Nursing and Allied Health, Program in Nursing, St. Louis, MO 63110-1091. Offers programs in adult nurse practitioner (MSN), education (MSN), gerontology nurse practitioner (MSN), holistics (MSN), neonatal nurse practitioner (MSN). Faculty: 10. Students: 125. *Application deadline:* rolling. *Application fee:* $25. *Tuition:* $320 per credit hour. • Dr. Sandra A. Jones, Director, 314-454-8416. Application contact: Connie Stohlman, Chief Admissions Officer, 314-454-7538.

Johns Hopkins University, School of Nursing, Baltimore, MD 21218-2699. Awards MSN, PhD, Certificate, MPH/MSN, MSN/MS. One or more programs accredited by NLN. Part-time programs available. Faculty: 38 full-time (37 women), 9 part-time (8 women), 41.7 FTE. Students: 27 full-time (21 women), 99 part-time (92 women); includes 20 minority (13 African Americans, 6 Asian Americans, 1 Hispanic). Average age 31. 209 applicants, 57% accepted. In 1997, 35 master's awarded. *Degree requirements:* For master's, scholarly project required, foreign language not required; for doctorate, dissertation required, foreign language not required. *Average time to degree:* master's–1 year full-time, 2 years part-time; doctorate–4 years full-time. *Entrance requirements:* For master's and doctorate, GRE, interview, minimum GPA of 3.0. Application deadline: 3/1 (priority date; rolling processing). Application fee: $40. *Financial aid:* In 1997–98, 57 students received aid, including 8 fellowships totaling $87,650, 39 merit scholarships (26 to first-year students) totaling $104,770; Federal Work-Study, institutionally sponsored loans, and career-related internships or fieldwork also available. Aid available to part-time students. Financial aid application deadline: 5/1; applicants required to submit FAFSA. *Faculty research:* Pain management, hypertension, AIDS, asthma, violence, cardiovascular risk symptom management. Total annual research expenditures: $3 million. • Sue K. Donaldson, Dean, 410-955-7544. Fax: 410-955-4890. E-mail: suek@son.jhmi.edu. Application contact: Mary O'Rourke, Director of Admissions/Student Services, 410-955-7548. Fax: 410-614-7086. E-mail: orourke@son.jhmi.edu.

See in-depth description on page 1433.

Johns Hopkins University, School of Nursing and Division of Business and Management, Dual Program in Nursing and Business, Baltimore, MD 21218-2699. Awards MSN/MS. Part-time programs available. Faculty: 13 full-time (12 women), 3 part-time (all women), 14 FTE. Students: 7 part-time (all women); includes 1 minority (African American). 8 applicants, 50% accepted. *Application deadline:* 3/1 (priority date; rolling processing; 11/15 for spring admission). *Application fee:* $40. *Financial aid:* Merit scholarships, Federal Work-Study, institutionally sponsored loans, and career-related internships or fieldwork available. Aid available to part-time students. Financial aid application deadline: 5/1; applicants required to submit FAFSA. *Faculty research:* Program evaluation, outcomes, staff satisfaction, program development. • Jacqueline Dienemann, Head, 410-614-5301. Fax: 410-955-7463. E-mail: jackied@son.jhmi.edu. Application contact: Mary O'Rourke, Director of Admissions/Student Services, 410-955-7548. Fax: 410-614-7086. E-mail: orourke@son.jhmi.edu.

Kean University, School of Natural Sciences, Mathematics, and Nursing, Department of Nursing, Union, NJ 07083. Awards MS. Students: 1 (woman) full-time, 36 part-time (32 women); includes 14 minority (7 African Americans, 4 Asian Americans, 3 Hispanics). Average age 42. In 1997, 15 degrees awarded. *Degree requirements:* Thesis or alternative required, foreign language not required. *Entrance requirements:* GRE General Test or MAT. Application deadline: 6/15 (11/15 for spring admission). Application fee: $35. *Tuition:* $5926 per year full-time, $248 per credit part-time for state residents; $7312 per year full-time, $304 per credit part-time for nonresidents. • Dr. Susan Salmond, Coordinator, 908-527-2608. Application contact: Joanne Morris, Director of Graduate Admissions, 908-527-2665. Fax: 908-527-2286. E-mail: grad_adm@turbo.kean.edu.

Kennesaw State University, School of Nursing, Kennesaw, GA 30144-5591. Offers program in primary care nurse practitioner (MSN). Part-time and evening/weekend programs available. Faculty: 8 full-time (7 women), 8 part-time (7 women). Students: 70 full-time (65 women), 4 part-time (all women); includes 12 African Americans. Average age 34. 87 applicants, 57% accepted. In 1997, 16 degrees awarded. *Entrance requirements:* GRE General Test (minimum combined score of 1350 on three sections), minimum GPA of 2.5, RN license, 3 years of professional experience. Application deadline: 7/1 (rolling processing; 2/20 for spring admission). Application fee: $20. *Expenses:* Tuition $2398 per year full-time, $83 per credit hour part-time for state residents; $8398 per year full-time, $333 per credit hour part-time for nonresidents. Fees $338 per year. *Financial aid:* Federal Work-Study available. Aid available to part-time students. Financial aid application deadline: 6/15; applicants required to submit FAFSA. • Dr. Julia Perkins, Dean, 770-423-6565. Fax: 770-423-6627. E-mail: jperkins@ksumail.kennesaw.edu. Application contact: Susan N. Barrett, Administrative Specialist, Admissions, 770-423-6500. Fax: 770-423-6541. E-mail: sbarrett@ksumail.kennesaw.edu.

Kent State University, School of Nursing, Kent, OH 44242-0001. Offers programs in clinical nursing (MSN), including nursing of the adult (medical/surgical nursing), psychiatric mental health nursing; nursing administration (MSN); nursing education (MSN); parent-child nursing (MSN). Accredited by NLN. Faculty: 29 full-time. Students: 53 full-time (46 women), 78 part-time (76 women). 56 applicants, 100% accepted. In 1997, 31 degrees awarded. *Degree requirements:* Thesis optional, foreign language not required. *Entrance requirements:* Minimum GPA of 2.75. Application deadline: 7/12 (rolling processing; 11/29 for spring admission). Application fee: $30. *Tuition:* $4752 per year full-time, $216 per credit hour part-time for state residents; $9213 per year full-time, $419 per credit hour part-time for nonresidents. *Financial aid:* Research assistantships, teaching assistantships, full tuition waivers, Federal Work-Study, institutionally sponsored loans available. Financial aid application deadline: 2/1. • Dr. Davina Gosnell, Dean, 330-672-7930. Fax: 330-672-2433.

La Roche College, Program in Nursing, Pittsburgh, PA 15237-5898. Offers community health nursing (MSN), critical care nursing (MSN), family nurse practitioner (MSN), gerontological nursing (MSN), nursing management (MSN). Part-time and evening/weekend programs available. Faculty: 5 full-time (all women), 2 part-time (both women). Students: 84. *Degree requirements:* Internship, practicum required, thesis optional, foreign language not required. *Entrance requirements:* GRE General Test (minimum combined score of 1200), TOEFL (minimum score 500). Application fee: $25. *Tuition:* $431 per credit. *Financial aid:* Graduate assistantships and career-related internships or fieldwork available. Aid available to part-time students. Financial aid applicants required to submit FAFSA. *Faculty research:* Patient education, perception. • Dr. Kathleen Sullivan, Division Chair, 412-536-1169. Application contact: Judy Henry, Manager of Nursing Student Enrollment, 412-536-1267. Fax: 412-536-1283.

La Salle University, Program in Nursing, 1900 West Olney Avenue, Philadelphia, PA 19141-1199. Awards MSN, MSN/MBA. Offerings include clinical nurse specialist, adult health and illness (MSN); nurse practitioner/primary care of adults (MSN); nursing administration (MSN); nursing education (MSN); nursing informatics (MSN); public health nursing (MSN); wound, ostomy, and continence nursing (MSN). Accredited by NLN. MSN (wound, ostomy, and continence nursing) new for fall 1998. Part-time programs available. Faculty: 13 full-time (12 women), 8 part-time (all women). Students: 56 full-time (54 women), 83 part-time (75 women); includes 16 minority (13 African Americans, 3 Hispanics). Average age 40. 39 applicants, 90% accepted. In 1997, 56 degrees awarded. *Entrance requirements:* GRE or MAT, BSN, Pennsylvania RN license. Application deadline: rolling. Application fee: $30. *Financial aid:* In 1997–98, 48 students received aid, including teaching assistantships averaging $300 per month; scholarships, traineeships, institutionally sponsored loans also available. Aid available to part-time students. Financial aid application deadline: 7/1. *Faculty research:* Medical errors, wound care, dying in the intensive care unit, teaching-learning, metacognition. • Dr. Zane R. Wolf, Dean, 215-951-1430. E-mail: wolf@lasalle.edu. Application contact: Dr. Janice Beitz, Graduate Director, 215-951-1430. Fax: 215-951-1896. E-mail: beitz@lasalle.edu.

Lehman College of the City University of New York, Division of Natural and Social Sciences, Department of Nursing, 250 Bedford Park Boulevard West, Bronx, NY 10468-1589. Offers programs in adult health nursing (MS), nursing of old adults (MS), parent-child nursing (MS), pediatric nurse practitioner (MS). Accredited by NLN. Part-time and evening/weekend programs available. Faculty: 13 full-time (12 women). Students: 4 full-time (all women), 103 part-time (98 women). *Entrance requirements:* Bachelor's degree in nursing, New York RN license. Application deadline: 4/1 (rolling processing; 11/1 for spring admission). Application fee: $40. *Expenses:* Tuition $4350 per year full-time, $185 per credit part-time for state residents; $7600 per year full-time, $320 per credit part-time for nonresidents. Fees $120 per year full-time, $80 per year part-time. *Financial aid:* Partial tuition waivers, Federal Work-Study, and career-related internships or fieldwork available. Aid available to part-time students. Financial aid application deadline: 5/15; applicants required to submit FAFSA. • Ngo Nkongho, Chair, 718-960-8374. Application contact: Keville Frederickson, Director of Graduate Studies, 718-960-8378. Fax: 718-960-8488.

Lewis University, College of Nursing, Romeoville, IL 60446. Offers programs in community health (MSN), nursing administration (MSN, Certificate), nursing education (MSN). One or more programs accredited by NLN. *Entrance requirements:* For master's, GRE General Test (minimum combined score of 850) or College of Nursing Writing Exam, minimum GPA of 2.5. Application deadline: rolling. Application fee: $35. *Faculty research:* Cancer prevention, phenomenological methods, public policy analysis, history of nursing, nursing informatics.

Loma Linda University, Graduate School, Department of Graduate Nursing, Loma Linda, CA 92350. Offers programs in adult and aging family nursing (MS); growing family nursing (MS); nursing administration (MS, Certificate), including nursing administration (MS), nursing management (Certificate). One or more programs accredited by NLN. Part-time programs available. *Degree requirements:* For master's, thesis or alternative required, foreign language not required. *Entrance requirements:* For master's, GRE General Test (minimum combined score of 1500).

Application fee: $40. *Tuition:* $380 per unit. *Financial aid:* Grants, Federal Work-Study, institutionally sponsored loans, and career-related internships or fieldwork available. Aid available to part-time students. Financial aid application deadline: 6/1. • Dr. Lois Van Cleve, Director, 909-824-4360.

Long Island University, Brooklyn Campus, School of Nursing, Brooklyn, NY 11201-8423. Awards MS. Faculty: 4. Students: 13 full-time (10 women), 48 part-time (44 women); includes 45 minority (37 African Americans, 3 Asian Americans, 5 Hispanics). 36 applicants, 53% accepted. *Entrance requirements:* New York RN license. Application deadline: rolling. Application fee: $30. Electronic applications accepted. *Expenses:* Tuition $480 per credit. Fees $415 per year full-time, $73 per semester (minimum) part-time. *Financial aid:* In 1997–98, 2 students received aid, including 2 assistantships. Financial aid applicants required to submit FAFSA. • Dr. Esther Siegel, Dean, 718-488-1508. Application contact: Bernard W. Sullivan, Associate Director of Admissions, 718-488-1011.

Long Island University, C.W. Post Campus, School of Health Professions, Program in Nursing, Brookville, NY 11548-1300. Offers advanced practical nursing (MS), family nurse practitioner (MS, Certificate). Part-time and evening/weekend programs available. Faculty: 4 full-time (all women), 5 part-time (3 women). Students: 24 part-time (22 women). Average age 25. 21 applicants, 81% accepted. *Degree requirements:* For master's, computer language, thesis required, foreign language not required. *Entrance requirements:* For master's, TOEFL (minimum score 500), minimum GPA of 3.0 in major. Application deadline: rolling. Application fee: $30. Electronic applications accepted. *Expenses:* Tuition $480 per credit. Fees $316 per year full-time, $71 per semester (minimum) part-time. *Financial aid:* Assistantships available. Aid available to part-time students. Financial aid application deadline: 5/15; applicants required to submit FAFSA. *Faculty research:* Lactation/breast cancer, early discharge in maternity. • Dr. Theodora Grauer, Chairperson, 516-299-2320. Fax: 516-299-2527. E-mail: ttgrauer@hornet.liu.edu. Application contact: Robin Steadman, Graduate Adviser, 516-299-2337.

Louisiana State University Medical Center, School of Nursing, 433 Bolivar Street, New Orleans, LA 70112-2223. Offers programs in adult health and illness (MN), adult health and nursing (DNS), neonatal nurse practitioner (MN), nursing (MN), nursing service administration (MN, DNS), parent-child health nursing (MN), primary care nurse practitioner (MN), psychiatric/community mental health nursing (MN, DNS), public health/community health nursing (MN, DNS). One or more programs accredited by NLN. Part-time programs available. Faculty: 10 full-time (all women), 4 part-time (3 women). Students: 41 full-time (37 women), 107 part-time (101 women); includes 36 minority (32 African Americans, 3 Asian Americans, 1 Hispanic). Average age 37. 65 applicants, 52% accepted. In 1997, 31 master's, 8 doctorates awarded. *Degree requirements:* For master's, thesis optional, foreign language not required; for doctorate, dissertation required, foreign language not required. *Entrance requirements:* For master's, GRE General Test, MAT (minimum score 50), TOEFL, minimum GPA of 3.0; for doctorate, GRE General Test (minimum combined score of 1500 on three sections), TOEFL (minimum score 550), minimum GPA of 3.5. Application deadline: 3/17. Application fee: $50. *Expenses:* Tuition $2878 per year full-time, $421 per semester (minimum) part-time for state residents; $6003 per year full-time, $838 per semester (minimum) part-time for nonresidents. Fees $350 per year full-time, $90 per semester (minimum) part-time. *Financial aid:* In 1997–98, 10 fellowships (all to first-year students) averaging $500 per month, 1 research assistantship (to a first-year student) averaging $600 per month, 1 teaching assistantship (to a first-year student) averaging $600 per month, 3 graduate assistantships (all to first-year students) averaging $600 per month were awarded; Federal Work-Study, institutionally sponsored loans also available. Aid available to part-time students. *Faculty research:* Advanced clinical practice, nursing education, health, social support, nursing administration. • Dr. Elizabeth Humphrey, Dean, 504-568-4106. Application contact: Dr. Barbara C. Donlon, Acting Director, 504-568-4137. Fax: 504-568-3308. E-mail: bdonlo@lsumc.edu.

Loyola University Chicago, Graduate School, Marcella Niehoff School of Nursing, 820 North Michigan Avenue, Chicago, IL 60611-2196. Awards MSN, PhD, M Div/MSN, MSN/MBA. Programs in adult nurse clinical nursing specialist (MSN), adult nurse practitioner (MSN), cardiac health/rehabilitation clinical nursing specialist (MSN), critical care/trauma clinical nursing specialist (MSN), critical care/trauma nurse practitioner (MSN), nursing (PhD), nursing service administration (MSN), nursing/pastoral studies (M Div/MSN), oncology clinical nursing specialist (MSN), pediatric nurse practitioner (MSN), women's health nurse practitioner (MSN). One or more programs accredited by NLN. Part-time programs available. Postbaccalaureate distance learning degree programs offered (no on-campus study). Faculty: 30 full-time (all women), 1 part-time (0 women). Students: 7 full-time (6 women), 201 part-time (196 women); includes 7 minority (3 African Americans, 3 Asian Americans, 1 Hispanic). Average age 29. 107 applicants, 92% accepted. In 1997, 31 master's, 5 doctorates awarded. Terminal master's awarded for partial completion of doctoral program. *Degree requirements:* For master's, comprehensive exam or oral thesis defense required, foreign language not required; for doctorate, dissertation, preliminary exam required, foreign language not required. *Entrance requirements:* For master's, GRE General Test (minimum combined score of 1350 on three sections), BSN, minimum GPA of 3.0, professional license; for doctorate, GRE General Test (minimum combined score of 1500 on three sections), BSN, minimum GPA of 3.0, professional license. Application deadline: rolling. Application fee: $35. Electronic applications accepted. *Tuition:* $467 per semester hour. *Financial aid:* In 1997–98, 18 students received aid, including 1 fellowship averaging $1,000 per month and totaling $8,000, 13 research assistantships (4 to first-year students) averaging $1,000 per month, 4 assistantships, traineeships (2 to first-year students); teaching assistantships, Federal Work-Study, institutionally sponsored loans, and career-related internships or fieldwork also available. Aid available to part-time students. Financial aid applicants required to submit FAFSA. *Faculty research:* Immunology, neonatal sepsis, osteoporosis, women and heart disease, PNI. • Dr. Shirley Dooling, Dean, 773-508-3254. Application contact: Dr. Marcia Maurer, Associate Dean and Director of Graduate Programs, 773-508-3261. Fax: 773-508-3241. E-mail: mmaurer@luc.edu.

Loyola University New Orleans, Program in Nursing, New Orleans, LA 70118-6195. Offers family nurse practitioner (MSN). Faculty: 5 full-time (all women). Students: 16 part-time (14 women); includes 2 minority (1 African American, 1 Hispanic), 1 international. Average age 36. 19 applicants, 100% accepted. *Degree requirements:* 735 hours of clinical practice, comprehensive exam required, foreign language and thesis not required. *Entrance requirements:* GRE. Application deadline: 3/1. Application fee: $20. *Expenses:* Tuition $386 per credit hour. Fees $556 per year full-time, $164 per year part-time. *Financial aid:* 11 students received aid; Federal Work-Study available. Aid available to part-time students. Financial aid application deadline: 5/1; applicants required to submit FAFSA. *Faculty research:* Increasing compliance with treatment, patient satisfaction with care provided by nurse practitioners. • Dr. Billie Ann Wilson, Director, 504-865-3142. Fax: 504-865-3254. E-mail: bwilson@loyno.edu.

Madonna University, Program in Nursing, Livonia, MI 48150-1173. Awards MSN, MSN/MSBA. Offerings include adult health: chronic health conditions (MSN), nursing administration (MSN). Accredited by NLN. Part-time programs available. Faculty: 13 full-time (all women), 3 part-time (1 woman). Students: 4 full-time (all women), 92 part-time (86 women). Average age 36. 8 applicants, 88% accepted. In 1997, 9 degrees awarded. *Degree requirements:* Thesis or alternative required, foreign language not required. *Entrance requirements:* GRE General Test. Application deadline: 8/1 (priority date; rolling processing; 4/1 for spring admission). *Expenses:* Tuition $260 per credit hour (minimum). Fees $50 per semester. *Financial aid:* Federal Work-Study and career-related internships or fieldwork available. *Faculty research:* Coping, caring. • Dr. Mary Eddy, Coordinator of Graduate Nursing, 734-432-5461. Fax: 734-432-5463. E-mail: eddy@smtp.munet.edu. Application contact: Sandra Kellums, Coordinator of Graduate Admissions, 734-432-5666. Fax: 734-432-5393. E-mail: kellums@smtp.munet.edu.

Mankato State University, College of Allied Health and Nursing, Department of Nursing, South Rd and Ellis Ave, PO Box 8400, Mankato, MN 56002-8400. Offers programs in family nursing (MSN), including clinical nurse specialist, educator, family nurse practitioner, manager; managed care (MSN), including clinical nurse specialist, educator, family nurse practitioner, manager. Accredited by NLN. Offered jointly with Metropolitan State University. Faculty: 13 full-time (all women). Students: 20 full-time (all women), 9 part-time (all women). Average age 39. 24 applicants, 29% accepted. In 1997, 10 degrees awarded. *Degree requirements:* Computer language, comprehensive exam, internships, research project or thesis required, foreign language not required. *Entrance requirements:* GRE General Test (minimum combined score of 1350) or MAT, minimum GPA of 3.0 during previous 2 years, BSN or equivalent. Application deadline: 7/10 (priority date; rolling processing; 10/30 for spring admission). Application fee: $20. *Tuition:* $126 per credit (minimum) for state residents; $200 per credit for nonresidents. *Financial aid:* Research assistantships, teaching assistantships available. Financial aid application deadline: 3/15; applicants required to submit FAFSA. *Faculty research:* Psychosocial nursing, computers in nursing, family adaptation. • Mary Huntley, Director, 507-389-6022. Application contact: Collaborative MSN Program Admissions, 507-389-6022.

Marquette University, College of Nursing, Milwaukee, WI 53201-1881. Offers programs in adult nurse practitioner (Certificate); advanced practice nursing (MSN), including adult, children, neonatal nurse practitioner, nurse-midwifery, older adult; gerontological nurse practitioner (Certificate); neonatal nurse practitioner (Certificate); nurse-midwifery (Certificate); pediatric nurse practitioner (Certificate). One or more programs accredited by NLN. Part-time and evening/weekend programs available. Faculty: 24 full-time (23 women), 5 part-time (4 women). Students: 51 full-time (47 women), 120 part-time (118 women); includes 1 international. Average age 36. 67 applicants, 85% accepted. In 1997, 42 master's awarded. *Degree requirements:* For master's, thesis or alternative, comprehensive exam required, foreign language not required. *Entrance requirements:* For master's, GRE General Test, TOEFL (minimum score 550), BSN, RN, Wisconsin license. Application fee: $40. *Tuition:* $490 per credit. *Financial aid:* In 1997–98, 6 research assistantships, 1 teaching assistantship were awarded; scholarships, full and partial tuition waivers, Federal Work-Study, institutionally sponsored loans, and career-related internships or fieldwork also available. Aid available to part-time students. Financial aid application deadline: 2/15. *Faculty research:* Psychosocial adjustment to chronic illness, gerontology, reminiscence, health policy: uninsured and access, hospital care delivery systems. Total annual research expenditures: $30,413. • Dr. Madeline Wake, Dean, 414-288-3812. Application contact: Dr. Gregory Olson, Associate Dean, 414-288-3808. Fax: 414-288-1578.

Marshall University, School of Nursing, Huntington, WV 25755-2020. Awards MSN. Accredited by NLN. Faculty: 15 (14 women). Students: 5 full-time (all women), 56 part-time (54 women); includes 1 minority (Hispanic). In 1997, 15 degrees awarded. *Entrance requirements:* GRE General Test (minimum combined score of 1200 on three sections). *Tuition:* $2364 per year full-time, $132 per hour part-time for state residents; $6894 per year full-time, $383 per hour part-time for nonresidents. • Dr. Lynne Welch, Dean, 304-696-6750. Application contact: Dr. James Harless, Director of Admissions, 304-696-3160.

Marymount University, School of Health Professions, Programs in Nursing, Arlington, VA 22207-4299. Offerings in critical care nursing (MSN), nursing administration (MSN), nursing education (MSN), primary care family practitioner (MSN). Accredited by NLN. Part-time programs available. Students: 64. *Degree requirements:* Thesis or alternative required, foreign language not required. *Entrance requirements:* 2 years of clinical experience, minimum GPA of 3.0, RN license. Application deadline: rolling. Application fee: $35. *Expenses:* Tuition $465 per credit hour. Fees $120 per year full-time, $5 per credit hour part-time. *Financial aid:* Research assistantships and career-related internships or fieldwork available. Aid available to part-time students. Financial aid applicants required to submit FAFSA. • Dr. Catherine Connelly, Dean, School of Health Professions, 703-284-1580. Fax: 703-284-3819. E-mail: catherine.connelly@marymount.edu.

McGill University, Faculty of Graduate Studies and Research, Faculty of Medicine, School of Nursing, Montréal, PQ H3A 2T5, Canada. Awards M Sc, M Sc A, PhD. PhD offered jointly with the Université du Québec à Montréal. Part-time programs available. Faculty: 7 full-time (all women), 73 part-time (3 women). Students: 37 full-time (35 women), 17 part-time (15 women). *Degree requirements:* For master's, thesis required (for some programs), foreign language not required; for doctorate, dissertation required, foreign language not required. *Entrance requirements:* For master's, GRE General Test, TOEFL (minimum score 580), minimum GPA of 3.0; for doctorate, GRE General Test, TOEFL (minimum score 580). Application deadline: 3/1 (priority date; rolling processing). Application fee: $60. *Expenses:* Tuition $1668 per year for Canadian residents; $8268 per year for nonresidents. Fees $828 per year for Canadian residents; $1216 per year for nonresidents. *Faculty research:* Pain, maternal-child nursing , women's health, children in hospitals, elderly. • Dr. L. Gottlieb, Associate Dean, Director, 514-398-4145. Application contact: Anna Santandrea, Coordinator, 514-398-4151. Fax: 514-398-8455. E-mail: asantand@wilson.lan.mcgill.ca.

McMaster University, Faculty of Health Sciences and School of Graduate Studies, Program in Clinical Health Sciences/Nursing, Hamilton, ON L8S 4M2, Canada. Awards M Sc, PhD. Part-time programs available. Students: 11 full-time, 16 part-time. *Degree requirements:* For master's, thesis required, foreign language not required; for doctorate, dissertation, comprehensive exam required, foreign language not required. *Entrance requirements:* For master's, honors B Sc N, McMaster equivalent to B+ in last year of study; for doctorate, M Sc with McMaster equivalent to B+, students with proven research experience and an A average may be admitted with a B Sc degree. Application deadline: 1/31 (priority date). Application fee: $50. *Tuition:* $7199 per year for Canadian residents; $32,954 per year for nonresidents. • Dr. Jo Anne Fox-Threlkeld, Coordinator, 905-525-9140 Ext. 22408. Fax: 905-521-0667. Application contact: Dr. R. Haslam, Chair, Graduate Programs in Health Sciences, 905-525-9140 Ext. 22983. Fax: 905-546-1129.

McNeese State University, College of Nursing, Lake Charles, LA 70609-2495. Awards MSN. Accredited by NLN. Offered jointly with Southeastern Louisiana University and Southern University and Agricultural and Mechanical College. Faculty: 4 full-time (all women). Students: 5 full-time (2 women), 28 part-time (25 women). In 1997, 1 degree awarded. *Application deadline:* 7/15 (priority date; rolling processing). *Application fee:* $10 ($25 for international students). *Tuition:* $2118 per year full-time, $344 per semester (minimum) part-time for state residents; $7308 per year full-time, $344 per semester (minimum) part-time for nonresidents. • Dr. Anita Fields, Dean, 318-475-5820.

Medical College of Georgia, Graduate Programs in Nursing, Augusta, GA 30912-1500. Offerings in adult nursing (MSN), community nursing (MSN), mental health nursing (MSN), nurse anesthesia (MN), nurse practitioner (MN), nursing (PhD), parent-child nursing (MSN). PhD offered jointly with Georgia State University. Part-time programs available. Faculty: 17 full-time (14 women). Students: 46 full-time (36 women), 42 part-time (37 women); includes 9 minority (6 African Americans, 3 Hispanics), 2 international. Average age 36. 81 applicants, 57% accepted. In 1997, 22 master's, 10 doctorates awarded. *Degree requirements:* Thesis/dissertation required, foreign language not required. *Entrance requirements:* GRE General Test (minimum combined score of 900), TOEFL (minimum score 600). Application deadline: 6/30 (priority date; rolling processing). Application fee: $0. *Expenses:* Tuition $2670 per year full-time, $111 per credit part-time for state residents; $10,680 per year full-time, $445 per credit part-time for nonresidents. Fees $286 per year. *Financial aid:* Federal Work-Study, institutionally sponsored loans available. Financial aid application deadline: 5/1. • Dr. Virginia Kemp, Associate Dean, 706-721-4710. E-mail: vkemp@mail.mcg.edu. Application contact: Dr. Gary C. Bond, Associate Dean, 706-721-3278. Fax: 706-721-6829. E-mail: gradstud@mail.mcg.edu.

Medical College of Ohio, School of Nursing, Toledo, OH 43699-0008. Awards MSN, Post Master's Certificate. Program in advanced practice nursing (MSN), including clinical nurse specialist, family nurse practitioner. One or more programs accredited by NLN. Part-time programs available. Faculty: 27 full-time (25 women). Students: 12 full-time (all women), 146 part-time (139 women); includes 7 minority (5 African Americans, 1 Asian American, 1 Hispanic). 54 applicants, 87% accepted. In 1997, 43 master's awarded. *Degree requirements:* For master's, thesis or scholarly project required, foreign language not required. *Average time to*

Directory: Nursing—General

Medical College of Ohio (continued)

degree: master's–2 years full-time, 3 years part-time. *Entrance requirements:* For master's, GRE General Test, BS in nursing, minimum undergraduate GPA of 3.0. Application deadline: 5/1 (9/1 for spring admission). Application fee: $30. *Financial aid:* Scholarships, Federal Work-Study, institutionally sponsored loans available. *Faculty research:* Sexuality issues, prenatal testing, health care of homeless, nursing education, chronic/acute pain, eating disorders, low birth weight infants. • Dr. Jeri Millstead, Dean, 419-383-5858. E-mail: mcogradschool@mco.edu. Application contact: Joann Braatz, Clerk, 419-383-4117. Fax: 419-383-6140. E-mail: mcogradschool@mco.edu.

Medical University of South Carolina, College of Nursing, Charleston, SC 29425-0002. Awards MSN, PhD. One or more programs accredited by NLN. Part-time programs available. Faculty: 47 full-time. Students: 61 full-time (60 women), 76 part-time (69 women); includes 11 minority (9 African Americans, 1 Asian American, 1 Hispanic), 1 international. Average age 33. 90 applicants, 78% accepted. In 1997, 64 master's awarded. *Degree requirements:* For master's, computer language required, thesis optional, foreign language not required. *Entrance requirements:* For master's, GRE General Test (minimum combined score of 1000), BSN, previous course work in statistics and physical assessment, 1 year nursing experience, license; for doctorate, GRE General Test (minimum combined score of 1500 on three sections). Application deadline: 2/15 (10/15 for spring admission). Application fee: $55. Electronic applications accepted. *Expenses:* Tuition $3760 per year full-time, $173 per semester hour part-time for state residents; $5672 per year full-time, $270 per semester hour part-time for nonresidents. Fees $280 per year (minimum). *Financial aid:* In 1997–98, 30 federal professional nurse traineeships were awarded; teaching assistantships, Federal Work-Study, institutionally sponsored loans also available. Financial aid application deadline: 5/1. *Faculty research:* Vulnerable populations (aged, chronically mentally ill, high-risk children and families, homeless persons, and rural poor), organizational effectiveness (health care). • Maureen Keefe, Dean, 843-792-8515. Fax: 843-792-9258. Application contact: Office of Enrollment Services, 843-792-3281.

Memorial University of Newfoundland, School of Graduate Studies, School of Nursing, St. John's, NF A1C 5S7, Canada. Awards MN. Part-time programs available. Students: 15 full-time (all women), 25 part-time (all women). 17 applicants, 71% accepted. In 1997, 9 degrees awarded. *Degree requirements:* Thesis. *Entrance requirements:* Bachelor's degree in nursing. Application deadline: 12/31 (priority date). Application fee: $40. *Expenses:* Tuition $1896 per year (minimum). Fees $60 per year for Canadian residents; $621 per year for nonresidents. *Financial aid:* Fellowships, research assistantships, teaching assistantships available. Financial aid application deadline: 12/31. • Dr. M. Lamb, Director, 709-737-6695. Fax: 709-737-7037. E-mail: mlamb@morgan.ucs.mun.ca. Application contact: Shirley Solberg, Graduate Officer, 709-737-6272.

Mennonite College of Nursing, Program in Nursing, Bloomington, IL 61701-3078. Awards MS. Part-time programs available. Faculty: 6 full-time (all women), 8 part-time (all women). Students: 16 full-time (all women), 19 part-time (all women); includes 2 minority (both African Americans). Average age 40. 34 applicants, 82% accepted. In 1997, 3 degrees awarded (100% found work related to degree). *Degree requirements:* Project required, foreign language and thesis not required. *Average time to degree:* master's–3 years full-time. *Entrance requirements:* GRE, BSN, minimum GPA of 3.0, RN license, 2 years of related experience. Application deadline: 2/1. Application fee: $0. Electronic applications accepted. *Tuition:* $455 per semester hour. *Financial aid:* 29 students received aid; Federal Work-Study, institutionally sponsored loans available. Aid available to part-time students. Financial aid application deadline: 4/1; applicants required to submit FAFSA. *Faculty research:* FNP track development, caring, support groups for families, nurse practitioner, teaching models, readiness for graduate studies. Total annual research expenditures: $225,000. • Dr. Karen Kapke, Director, 309-829-0715 Ext. 3591. Application contact: Mary Ann Watkins, Director of Admissions and Financial Aid, 309-829-0718. Fax: 309-829-0765. E-mail: mwatkins@mcon.edu.

Mercy College, Department of Nursing, Dobbs Ferry, NY 10522-1189. Offers program in family health nursing (MS). Accredited by NLN. Part-time programs available. Students: 41 part-time (all women). Average age 36. *Degree requirements:* Thesis. *Entrance requirements:* GRE General Test or MAT, BSN, minimum GPA of 3.0. Application deadline: 8/15 (priority date; rolling processing). Application fee: $35. *Tuition:* $390 per credit. *Financial aid:* Federal Work-Study, institutionally sponsored loans, and career-related internships or fieldwork available. Aid available to part-time students. *Faculty research:* Program evaluation, cost and home care, children of alcoholic parents, clinical decision making. • Dr. Carolyn Lansberry, Chairperson, 914-674-9331 Ext. 552.

Metropolitan State University, School of Nursing, St. Paul, MN 55106-5000. Awards MSN. Part-time programs available. Faculty: 6 full-time (all women). Students: 2 full-time (both women), 22 part-time (21 women); includes 2 minority (both African Americans). Average age 34. 20 applicants, 90% accepted. In 1997, 2 degrees awarded. *Degree requirements:* Thesis or alternative required, foreign language not required. *Entrance requirements:* GRE General Test (minimum combined score of 1200; average 1500) or MAT (minimum score 45; average 50), minimum GPA of 3.0, RN license. Application deadline: 4/1. Application fee: $20. *Tuition:* $133 per credit for state residents; $208 per credit for nonresidents. *Financial aid:* Federal Work-Study, institutionally sponsored loans, and career-related internships or fieldwork available. *Faculty research:* Women's health, gerontology. Total annual research expenditures: $12,480. • Marilyn T. Molen, Dean, 612-772-7705. E-mail: marilynmolen@metro2.edu. Application contact: Jan Mitchell, Office Manager, 612-772-7712. Fax: 612-772-7738. E-mail: janmitchell@metro2.edu.

MGH Institute of Health Professions, Program in Nursing, 101 Merrimac Street, Boston, MA 02114-4719. Awards MSN, Certificate. One or more programs accredited by NLN. Part-time and evening/weekend programs available. Faculty: 22 full-time (21 women), 1 (woman) part-time, 22.7 FTE. Students: 145 full-time (132 women), 43 part-time (40 women); includes 15 minority (4 African Americans, 9 Asian Americans, 1 Hispanic, 1 Native American). Average age 34. 181 applicants, 49% accepted. In 1997, 79 master's awarded (100% found work related to degree). *Degree requirements:* For master's, thesis or alternative required, foreign language not required. *Average time to degree:* master's–3 years full-time. *Entrance requirements:* For master's, GRE General Test, minimum GPA of 3.0. Application deadline: 1/23 (11/1 for spring admission). Application fee: $50. *Expenses:* Tuition $20,320 per year full-time, $530 per credit part-time. Fees $300 per year. *Financial aid:* In 1997–98, 143 students received aid, including 27 assistantships, traineeships; full and partial tuition waivers and career-related internships or fieldwork also available. Aid available to part-time students. Financial aid application deadline: 3/6; applicants required to submit FAFSA. *Faculty research:* Biobehavioral nursing; psychoimmunology; hardiness, social support, and health in HIV; critical thinking; diagnostic reasoning; strengthened parenting. • Dr. Arlene Lowenstein, Director, 617-726-3163. Fax: 617-726-8022. E-mail: lowenstein.arlene@mgh.harvard.edu. Application contact: Office of Student Affairs, 617-726-3140. Fax: 617-726-8010.

See in-depth description on page 1435.

Michigan State University, College of Nursing, East Lansing, MI 48824-1020. Awards MSN. Accredited by NLN. Part-time programs available. Faculty: 21 full-time (19 women). Students: 189 (176 women); includes 18 minority (8 African Americans, 8 Asian Americans, 1 Hispanic, 1 Native American), 4 international. In 1997, 54 degrees awarded. *Degree requirements:* Scholarly project or thesis required, foreign language not required. *Average time to degree:* master's–2 years full-time, 3 years part-time. *Entrance requirements:* GRE General Test, minimum GPA of 3.0, 1 year of professional nursing experience, previous course work in statistics. Application deadline: 1/15 (rolling processing). Application fee: $30 ($40 for international students). *Expenses:* Tuition $4609 per year full-time, $223 per credit hour (minimum) part-time for state residents; $8704 per year full-time, $450 per credit hour (minimum) part-time for nonresidents. Fees $576 per year full-time, $476 per year part-time. *Financial aid:* Fellowships, research assistantships, teaching assistantships, Federal Work-Study available. Aid available to part-time students. *Faculty research:* Decision making, home care, cancer care, prenatal care, aging. • Dr. Marilyn Rothert, Dean, 517-355-6527. Application contact: Reneé Canady, Acting Director of Student Affairs, 517-353-4827. Fax: 517-353-9553.

Announcement: Michigan State University, a leader in primary-care-oriented, community-based nursing education, offers a Master of Science in Nursing (MSN) with advanced practice nurse studies tracks in family and gerontology. Clinical experiences are available in primary-care sites throughout the state, and students are involved in interdisciplinary management of health-care services for clients and their families. Graduates are qualified for ANA certification in adult care, family care, or gerontology and for Michigan nurse practitioner licensure. More than 50% of nursing faculty members are in clinical practice. Federally funded research focuses on health status and health outcomes in diverse populations. Contact 517-353-4827, fax: 517-353-9553, e-mail: nurse@pilot.msu.edu, WWW: http://pilot.msu.edu/unit/nurse

Midwestern State University, Division of Health Sciences, Nursing Program, Wichita Falls, TX 76308-2096. Offers family nurse practitioner (MSN), nurse educator (MSN). Offered jointly with Texas Tech University. Faculty: 5 full-time (all women). Students: 5 full-time, 31 part-time; includes 5 minority (1 African American, 1 Asian American, 2 Hispanics, 1 Native American). Average age 35. 1 applicant, 100% accepted. *Entrance requirements:* GRE General Test, TOEFL (average 550). Application deadline: 8/7 (12/15 for spring admission). Application fee: $0 ($50 for international students). *Expenses:* Tuition $44 per hour for state residents; $259 per hour for nonresidents. Fees $90 per year (minimum) full-time, $9 per semester (minimum) part-time. • Sandra Church, Coordinator, 940-397-4597.

Millersville University of Pennsylvania, School of Science and Mathematics, Department of Nursing, Millersville, PA 17551-0302. Awards MSN. Faculty: 4 full-time (all women), 9 part-time (8 women). Students: 51 part-time (48 women). Average age 37. 43 applicants, 67% accepted. *Entrance requirements:* GRE, BSN, minimum GPA of 3.0, RN license, 1 year of clinical experience, undergraduate research. Application deadline: 5/1 (priority date; rolling processing). Application fee: $25. *Tuition:* $3468 per year full-time, $234 per credit part-time for state residents; $6236 per year full-time, $387 per credit part-time for nonresidents. *Financial aid:* In 1997–98, 2 graduate assistantships (1 to a first-year student) averaging $445 per month and totaling $8,000 were awarded; Federal Work-Study, institutionally sponsored loans also available. Aid available to part-time students. Financial aid application deadline: 5/1. *Faculty research:* Nursing practitioner-patterns of practice, health beliefs and practices of women and Amish, nursing centers, case/care management seamless care delivery, critical thinking abilities of students. Total annual research expenditures: $10,000. • Dr. Ruth E. Davis, Coordinator, 717-872-2183. Fax: 717-872-3985. Application contact: Dr. Robert Labriola, Dean of Graduate Studies, 717-872-3030. Fax: 717-871-2022.

Mississippi University for Women, Division of Nursing, Columbus, MS 39701-9998. Awards MSN, Certificate. One or more programs accredited by NLN. Part-time programs available. Faculty: 6 full-time (all women), 1 (woman) part-time. Students: 27 full-time (25 women), 14 part-time (all women); includes 7 minority (all African Americans), 1 international. Average age 37. 54 applicants, 93% accepted. In 1997, 26 master's awarded. *Degree requirements:* For master's, thesis, comprehensive exam required, foreign language not required. *Entrance requirements:* For master's, GRE General Test (minimum combined score of 900), appropriate bachelor's degree, previous course work in statistics, proficiency in English. Application deadline: 4/1. Application fee: $0 ($25 for international students). *Tuition:* $2556 per year full-time, $142 per hour part-time for state residents; $5546 per year full-time, $308 per hour part-time for nonresidents. *Financial aid:* In 1997–98, 10 students received aid, including 10 fellowships averaging $1,100 per month and totaling $110,000; federal traineeships, Federal Work-Study, institutionally sponsored loans also available. Financial aid application deadline: 4/1. • Dr. Sheila Adams, Head, 601-329-7299. E-mail: sadams@muw.edu. Application contact: Dr. Mary Pat Curtis, Director, 601-329-7323. Fax: 601-329-8555.

Molloy College, Department of Nursing, 1000 Hempstead Avenue, Rockville Centre, NY 11571-5002. Offers programs in adult nurse practitioner (MSN, Advanced Certificate), family nurse practitioner (MSN, Advanced Certificate), nurse practitioner psychiatry (MSN, Advanced Certificate), nursing (MSN), nursing administration (Advanced Certificate), nursing education (Advanced Certificate), pediatric nurse practitioner (MSN, Advanced Certificate). Part-time and evening/weekend programs available. Faculty: 16 full-time (14 women), 12 part-time (9 women). Students: 12 full-time (10 women), 213 part-time (204 women); includes 60 minority (31 African Americans, 22 Asian Americans, 7 Hispanics). Average age 36. 110 applicants, 51% accepted. In 1997, 16 master's awarded (50% entered university research/teaching, 50% found other work related to degree); 19 Advanced Certificates awarded. *Degree requirements:* For master's, thesis optional, foreign language not required. *Average time to degree:* master's–2.2 years full-time, 3.7 years part-time; other advanced degree–1 year full-time, 2 years part-time. *Entrance requirements:* For master's, BS in nursing, minimum undergraduate GPA of 3.0; for Advanced Certificate, master's degree in nursing. Application deadline: 9/2 (priority date; rolling processing; 1/20 for spring admission). Application fee: $60. *Expenses:* Tuition $430 per credit. Fees $430 per year full-time, $165 per semester (minimum) part-time. *Financial aid:* In 1997–98, 2 students received aid, including 1 research assistantship averaging $95 per month and totaling $375, 1 teaching assistantship averaging $95 per month and totaling $375; partial tuition waivers, institutionally sponsored loans also available. Aid available to part-time students. Financial aid application deadline: 5/1; applicants required to submit FAFSA. *Faculty research:* Hardiness and aging, alcoholism, current ethics, breast cancer, nurse role perception. • Dr. Carol A. Clifford, Director, Graduate Program, 516-256-2218. Fax: 516-678-9718. E-mail: clica01@molloy.edu. Application contact: Wayne James, Vice President for Enrollment and Management, 516-678-5000 Ext. 240. Fax: 516-256-2247.

Monmouth University, Program in Nursing, West Long Branch, NJ 07764-1898. Awards MSN. Part-time and evening/weekend programs available. Faculty: 2 full-time (both women), 2 part-time (1 woman). Students: 3 full-time (all women), 55 part-time (53 women); includes 2 minority (both Asian Americans). Average age 42. 34 applicants, 91% accepted. *Entrance requirements:* GRE General Test, RN license, 1 year of work experience. Application deadline: 8/1 (priority date; rolling processing; 12/1 for spring admission). Application fee: $35. *Expenses:* Tuition $459 per credit. Fees $274 per semester full-time, $137 per semester part-time. *Financial aid:* In 1997–98, 11 students received aid, including 3 assistantships averaging $270 per month and totaling $6,060; partial tuition waivers, Federal Work-Study, and career-related internships or fieldwork also available. Aid available to part-time students. Financial aid application deadline: 3/1; applicants required to submit FAFSA. • Marilyn Lauria, Director, 732-571-4494. Fax: 732-571-5131. Application contact: Office of Graduate Admissions, 732-571-3452. Fax: 732-571-5123.

Announcement: The Master of Science in Nursing program prepares registered nurses for increased responsibilities and opportunities as advanced practice nurses in a variety of health-care environments. Students may select from four areas of clinical specialization: adult nurse practitioner, family nurse practitioner, gerontological nurse practitioner, and acute-care clinical nurse practitioner.

Montana State University–Bozeman, College of Nursing, 211 Montana Hall, Bozeman, MT 59717. Offers programs in health administration (MHA), nursing (MN). Part-time programs available. Faculty: 20 full-time (all women). Students: 19 full-time (17 women), 6 part-time (all women). Average age 39. 25 applicants, 60% accepted. In 1997, 14 degrees awarded. *Degree requirements:* Thesis required, foreign language not required. *Entrance requirements:* GRE General Test, TOEFL (minimum score 580), previous course work in statistics. Application deadline: 6/1 (priority date; rolling processing; 11/1 for spring admission). Application fee: $50. *Tuition:* $3994 per year full-time, $367 per semester (minimum) part-time for state residents; $9507 per year full-time, $957 per semester (minimum) part-time for nonresidents. *Financial aid:* In 1997–98, 5 teaching assistantships (2 to first-year students) averaging $469 per month and totaling $9,610 were awarded. Financial aid application deadline: 3/1. *Faculty research:* Rural health, gerontology, health of Native Americans, clinical problems. Total annual research expenditures: $370,428. • Dr. Lea Acord, Dean, 406-994-3783. Fax: 406-994-6020. E-mail: znu7003@montana.edu.

Announcement: Montana State University–Bozeman offers a Master of Nursing (MN) degree with a rural family nurse practitioner studies option and an interdisciplinary MN/Master of Health Administration degree. Both programs can be accessed through the College's main campus in Bozeman or through any of the off-campus sites in Billings, Great Falls, or Missoula, Montana.

Mount Marty College, Graduate Studies Division, 3109 South Kiwanis Avenue, Sioux Falls, SD 57105. Offers program in nursing anesthesia (MS). Faculty: 2 full-time (0 women), 7 part-time (1 woman). Students: 43 full-time (16 women); includes 3 minority (1 African American, 1 Asian American, 1 Hispanic). Average age 28. 40 applicants, 63% accepted. In 1997, 21 degrees awarded (100% found work related to degree). *Degree requirements:* Thesis or alternative required, foreign language not required. *Average time to degree:* master's–2 years full-time. *Entrance requirements:* GRE General Test (minimum combined score of 1200), BSN or RN, minimum GPA of 3.0, 1 year of clinical nursing experience in acute care within the last 3 years. Application deadline: 12/15 (priority date; rolling processing). Application fee: $10. *Tuition:* $12,305 per year. *Financial aid:* 19 students received aid; grants, scholarships, institutionally sponsored loans, and career-related internships or fieldwork available. Financial aid application deadline: 8/1; applicants required to submit FAFSA. *Faculty research:* Clinical anesthesia, professional characteristics, motivations of applicants. • Dr. Larry L. Dahlen, Director, 605-357-9802. Application contact: J. C. Crane, Director of Admissions, 800-658-4552. Fax: 605-668-1357.

Mount Saint Mary College, Division of Nursing, Newburgh, NY 12550-3494. Offers programs in adult nurse practitioner (MS), including nursing education, nursing management; clinical nurse specialist-adult health (MS), including nursing education, nursing management. MS (adult nurse practitioner) new for fall 1998. Part-time and evening/weekend programs available. Faculty: 6 full-time (5 women), 1 (woman) part-time. Students: 25 part-time (24 women); includes 2 minority (1 Asian American, 1 Hispanic). Average age 41. *Degree requirements:* Computer language, research project required, foreign language and thesis not required. *Entrance requirements:* GRE General Test (minimum combined score of 1200; average 1400) or MAT (minimum score 40), BSN, minimum GPA of 3.0, RN license. Application deadline: 5/3 (priority date; 10/31 for spring admission). Application fee: $20. *Expenses:* Tuition $367 per credit. Fees $30 per year. • Sr. Leona DeBoer, Coordinator, 914-569-3138. Fax: 914-562-6762. E-mail: deboer@msmc.edu.

Murray State University, College of Sciences, Department of Nursing, Murray, KY 42071-0009. Offers programs in nurse anesthesia (MSNA), nursing (MSN). Accredited by NLN. Part-time programs available. Faculty: 7 full-time (5 women). Students: 37 full-time (31 women), 29 part-time (28 women). 19 applicants, 89% accepted. In 1997, 26 degrees awarded. *Degree requirements:* Thesis required, foreign language not required. *Entrance requirements:* GRE General Test, TOEFL (minimum score 500). Application deadline: rolling. Application fee: $20. *Expenses:* Tuition $2500 per year full-time, $124 per hour part-time for state residents; $6740 per year full-time, $357 per hour part-time for nonresidents. Fees $360 per year full-time, $180 per year part-time. *Financial aid:* Research assistantships, teaching assistantships, Federal Work-Study available. Financial aid application deadline: 4/1. • Application contact: Dr. Nancey France, Graduate Coordinator, 502-762-6671. Fax: 502-762-6662.

Nazareth College of Rochester, Graduate Studies, Department of Nursing, Rochester, NY 14618-3790. Offers program in gerontological nurse practitioner (MS). Part-time programs available. Faculty: 5 full-time (all women), 1 part-time (0 women). Students: 11 part-time (all women). 2 applicants, 100% accepted. *Entrance requirements:* GRE General Test or MAT, minimum GPA of 2.7. Application deadline: 6/1 (priority date; rolling processing; 11/1 for spring admission). Application fee: $40. *Expenses:* Tuition $436 per credit hour. Fees $20 per semester. *Financial aid:* Career-related internships or fieldwork available. Aid available to part-time students. Financial aid applicants required to submit FAFSA. • Dr. Margaret Andrews, Head, 716-389-2710. Application contact: Dr. Kay F. Marshman, Dean, 716-389-2815. Fax: 716-389-2452.

Neumann College, Program in Nursing, Aston, PA 19014-1298. Awards MS. Part-time programs available. Faculty: 3 full-time (all women), 1 part-time (0 women). Students: 1 (woman) full-time, 9 part-time (all women); includes 1 minority (African American). *Entrance requirements:* GRE or MAT, TOEFL. Application deadline: rolling. Application fee: $50. *Tuition:* $530 per credit. *Financial aid:* Available to part-time students. Financial aid application deadline: 3/15; applicants required to submit FAFSA. • Dr. Jill Derstine, Chair, Division of Nursing and Health Services, 610-558-5561. Fax: 610-459-1370. Application contact: Denise Ewing, Admissions Counselor, 610-558-5531. Fax: 610-558-5652. E-mail: neucoladm@hslc.org.

Newman University, Division of Nursing, Wichita, KS 67213-2084. Awards MS. Faculty: 2 full-time. Students: 9. *Application deadline:* 8/15. *Application fee:* $25. *Tuition:* $257 per credit hour. • Dr. Jeanette Jeffers, Program Director, 316-942-4291 Ext. 267. Fax: 316-942-4483.

New Mexico State University, College of Health and Social Services, Department of Nursing, Las Cruces, NM 88003-8001. Awards MSN. Accredited by NLN. Faculty: 9 full-time (8 women). Students: 8 full-time (6 women), 11 part-time (9 women); includes 5 minority (1 African American, 1 Asian American, 3 Hispanics). Average age 38. 13 applicants, 69% accepted. In 1997, 4 degrees awarded. *Degree requirements:* Clinical practice required, thesis optional, foreign language not required. *Entrance requirements:* GRE or MAT, BSN, minimum GPA of 3.0, previous course work in statistics. Application deadline: 7/1 (priority date; rolling processing; 11/1 for spring admission). Application fee: $15 ($35 for international students). Electronic applications accepted. *Tuition:* $2514 per year full-time, $105 per credit hour part-time for state residents; $7848 per year full-time, $327 per credit hour part-time for nonresidents. *Financial aid:* Fellowships, research assistantships, teaching assistantships, Federal Work-Study, and career-related internships or fieldwork available. Financial aid application deadline: 3/1. *Faculty research:* Advanced practice nursing, evidence-based nursing practice, health policy, community outreach, clinical judgement. • Judith Karshmer, Head, 505-646-3812. Fax: 505-646-2167. E-mail: jkarshme@nmsu.edu.

New York University, School of Education, Division of Nursing, New York, NY 10012-1019. Awards MA, PhD, AC, MA/MS. One or more programs accredited by NLN. Part-time and evening/weekend programs available. Faculty: 27 full-time (24 women), 9 part-time. Students: 23 full-time, 432 part-time. 147 applicants, 69% accepted. In 1997, 69 master's, 7 doctorates, 33 ACs awarded. Terminal master's awarded for partial completion of doctoral program. *Degree requirements:* For doctorate, dissertation. *Entrance requirements:* For master's, TOEFL; for doctorate, GRE General Test, TOEFL, interview; for AC, TOEFL, master's degree. Application deadline: 2/1 (priority date; rolling processing; 12/1 for spring admission). Application fee: $40 ($60 for international students). *Financial aid:* Partial tuition waivers, Federal Work-Study, institutionally sponsored loans, and career-related internships or fieldwork available. Aid available to part-time students. Financial aid application deadline: 3/1; applicants required to submit FAFSA. *Faculty research:* Gerontology, geriatric nursing, breast cancer, Alzheimer's disease, diabetes, bioethics, AIDS care, uses of technology in nursing. • Diane McGivern, Chairperson, 212-998-5300. Application contact: Office of Graduate Admissions, 212-998-5030. Fax: 212-995-4328.

See in-depth description on page 757.

Niagara University, Graduate Division of Nursing, Niagara University, NY 14109. Offers program in family nurse practitioner (MS). Students: 7 full-time (all women), 14 part-time (all women); includes 3 minority (2 African Americans, 1 Asian American), 4 international. In 1997, 2 degrees awarded. *Application deadline:* 8/1 (rolling processing). *Application fee:* $30. *Expenses:* Tuition $7740 per year full-time, $430 per credit hour part-time. Fees $25 per semester. *Financial aid:* Federal Work-Study and career-related internships or fieldwork available. Aid available to part-time students. • Nancy Shaffer, Acting Dean, 716-286-8312.

Northeastern University, Graduate School of Nursing, Boston, MA 02115-5096. Awards MS, CAS, MS/MBA. One or more programs accredited by NLN. Part-time programs available. Faculty: 25 full-time (all women), 13 part-time (11 women). Students: 55 full-time (54 women), 249 part-time (240 women). Average age 37. 178 applicants, 76% accepted. In 1997, 75 master's awarded. *Degree requirements:* For master's, thesis or alternative required, foreign language not required. *Entrance requirements:* For master's, GRE General Test, minimum GPA of 3.0, previous course work in statistics, 1-2 years nursing experience, RN license, ICU experience. Application deadline: (2/1 for spring admission). Application fee: $50. *Expenses:* Tuition $440 per credit hour. Fees $55 per quarter full-time, $13.25 per quarter part-time. *Financial aid:* In 1997–98, 34 students received aid, including 1 fellowship (to a first-year student), 11 research assistantships (5 to first-year students), 5 teaching assistantships (4 to first-year students), 7 graduate assistantships (2 to first-year students); full and partial tuition waivers, institutionally sponsored loans, and career-related internships or fieldwork also available. Aid available to part-time students. Financial aid application deadline: 7/1. *Faculty research:* Community-based health care delivery, coping and adaptation, functional disability in the elderly, psychological trauma. Total annual research expenditures: $15,000. • Carole A. Shea, Director and Associate Dean, 617-373-3125. E-mail: cshea@lynx.edu. Application contact: Molly Schnabel, Admissions Coordinator, 617-373-3590. Fax: 617-373-8672. E-mail: mschnabe@lynx.neu.edu.

See in-depth description on page 1437.

Northern Arizona University, College of Health Professions, Department of Nursing, Flagstaff, AZ 86011. Awards MSN. Faculty: 8 full-time (all women), 2 part-time (both women). Students: 15 full-time (all women), 10 part-time (8 women); includes 3 minority (all Hispanics). Average age 28. 24 applicants, 42% accepted. In 1997, 4 degrees awarded. *Entrance requirements:* GRE General Test, minimum GPA of 3.0. Application deadline: 2/15 (priority date). Application fee: $45. *Expenses:* Tuition $2088 per year full-time, $330 per semester (minimum) part-time for state residents; $8004 per year full-time, $1002 per semester (minimum) part-time for nonresidents. Fees $72 per year full-time, $18 per semester (minimum) part-time. *Financial aid:* In 1997–98, 2 research assistantships were awarded. • Dr. Eileen Breslin, Chair, 520-523-2671.

Northern Illinois University, College of Health and Human Sciences, School of Nursing, De Kalb, IL 60115-2854. Awards MS. Accredited by NLN. Part-time programs available. Faculty: 12 full-time (all women). Students: 16 full-time (15 women), 89 part-time (all women); includes 4 minority (2 African Americans, 2 Asian Americans). Average age 38. 26 applicants, 65% accepted. In 1997, 27 degrees awarded. *Degree requirements:* Comprehensive exam required, thesis optional, foreign language not required. *Entrance requirements:* GRE General Test, TOEFL (minimum score 550), minimum GPA of 2.75 in last 60 hours, BA in nursing, nursing license. Application deadline: 6/1 (rolling processing; 11/1 for spring admission). Application fee: $30. *Tuition:* $3984 per year full-time, $154 per credit hour part-time for state residents; $8160 per year full-time, $328 per credit hour part-time for nonresidents. *Financial aid:* In 1997–98, 7 research assistantships, 5 teaching assistantships, 1 staff assistantship were awarded; fellowships, full tuition waivers, Federal Work-Study, and career-related internships or fieldwork also available. Aid available to part-time students. • Dr. Marilyn Frank-Stromborg, Chair, 815-753-6550.

Northern Kentucky University, Program in Nursing, Highland Heights, KY 41099. Awards MSN. Accredited by NLN. Faculty: 19 full-time (18 women). Students: 8 full-time (7 women), 44 part-time (40 women); includes 1 minority (Asian American). Average age 38. 39 applicants, 87% accepted. In 1997, 18 degrees awarded. *Degree requirements:* Comprehensive exam, investigative project. *Entrance requirements:* GRE, minimum GPA of 3.0. Application deadline: 11/15 (priority date; rolling processing). Application fee: $25. *Tuition:* $2420 per year full-time, $132 per semester hour part-time for state residents; $6660 per year full-time, $368 per semester hour part-time for nonresidents. • Dr. Margaret Anderson, Chair, 606-572-5248. Application contact: Peg Griffin, Coordinator, Graduate Program, 606-572-6364.

Northern Michigan University, College of Nursing and Allied Health Science, Department of Nursing, Marquette, MI 49855-5301. Awards MSN. Accredited by NLN. Part-time and evening/weekend programs available. Faculty: 7 full-time (6 women), 1 (woman) part-time. Students: 11 full-time (9 women), 48 part-time (all women); includes 1 minority (Native American). 19 applicants, 100% accepted. In 1997, 17 degrees awarded. *Degree requirements:* Thesis or alternative required, foreign language not required. *Entrance requirements:* GRE General Test, minimum GPA of 3.0. Application deadline: 4/15 (priority date; rolling processing; 11/1 for spring admission). Application fee: $25. *Expenses:* Tuition $135 per credit hour for state residents; $215 per credit hour for nonresidents. Fees $183 per year full-time, $94 per year (minimum) part-time. *Financial aid:* In 1997–98, 2 graduate assistantships averaging $770 per month were awarded; Federal Work-Study, institutionally sponsored loans also available. Financial aid application deadline: 3/1. • Dr. Elmer W. Moisio, Head, 906-227-2834. Application contact: Dr. Sara Doubledee, Coordinator.

North Georgia College & State University, Graduate School, Program in Family Practitioner, Dahlonega, GA 30597-1001. Awards MSN. Program new for fall 1998. *Degree requirements:* Thesis optional, foreign language not required. *Entrance requirements:* Minimum GPA of 2.75. Application deadline: rolling. Application fee: $25. *Financial aid:* Application deadline 5/1. • Dr. Linda Roberts-Betsch, Head, 706-864-1930. Fax: 706-864-1845. E-mail: lrbetsch@nugget.ngc.peachnet.edu.

North Park University, Department of Nursing, Chicago, IL 60625-4895. Awards MS, MBA/MS. Part-time and evening/weekend programs available. *Degree requirements:* Thesis. *Entrance requirements:* GMAT (minimum score 500), GRE General Test (minimum combined score of 1500), MAT (minimum score 47). Application deadline: 8/31 (rolling processing). Application fee: $20. *Faculty research:* Aging, consultation roles, critical thinking skills, family breakdown, science of caring.

Northwestern State University of Louisiana, Division of Nursing, Natchitoches, LA 71497. Awards MSN. Accredited by NLN. Part-time programs available. Faculty: 5 full-time (all women). Students: 11 full-time (10 women), 86 part-time (80 women); includes 9 minority (all African Americans). Average age 37. In 1997, 27 degrees awarded. *Degree requirements:* Thesis or alternative, oral and written comprehensive exams required, foreign language not required. *Entrance requirements:* GRE General Test (minimum combined score of 800), BS in nursing, minimum GPA of 3.0, 6 months of clinical nursing experience. Application deadline: 8/1 (priority date; rolling processing; 1/10 for spring admission). Application fee: $15 ($25 for international students). *Tuition:* $2147 per year full-time, $336 per semester (minimum) part-time for state residents; $6437 per year full-time, $336 per semester (minimum) part-time for nonresidents. *Financial aid:* Federal Work-Study and career-related internships or fieldwork available. Aid available to part-time students. Financial aid application deadline: 7/15. • Dr. Norann Planchock, Director, 318-677-3100. Application contact: Dr. Tom Hanson, Dean, Graduate Studies and Research, 318-357-5851. Fax: 318-357-5019.

Oakland University, School of Nursing, Rochester, MI 48309-4401. Awards MSN. Accredited by NLN. Part-time and evening/weekend programs available. Faculty: 18 full-time. Students: 15 full-time (11 women), 83 part-time (79 women); includes 7 minority (1 African American, 4 Asian Americans, 1 Hispanic, 1 Native American). 54 applicants, 89% accepted. In 1997, 35 degrees awarded. *Entrance requirements:* GRE General Test, minimum GPA of 3.0 for unconditional admission. Application deadline: 7/15 (3/15 for spring admission). Application fee: $30. *Expenses:* Tuition $3852 per year full-time, $214 per credit hour part-time for state residents; $8532 per year full-time, $474 per credit hour part-time for nonresidents. Fees $420 per year. *Financial aid:* Full tuition waivers, Federal Work-Study, institutionally sponsored loans

Directory: Nursing—General

Oakland University (continued)

available. Financial aid application deadline: 3/1; applicants required to submit FAFSA. • Dr. Justine Speer, Dean, 248-370-4071. Application contact: Dr. Diane Wilson, Coordinator, 248-370-4484.

The Ohio State University, College of Nursing, Columbus, OH 43210. Awards MS, PhD, MBA/MS, MHA/MS. One or more programs accredited by NLN. Part-time programs available. Faculty: 34. Students: 94 full-time (91 women), 124 part-time (116 women); includes 20 minority (14 African Americans, 4 Asian Americans, 2 Hispanics), 6 international. 107 applicants, 72% accepted. In 1997, 51 master's, 3 doctorates awarded. *Degree requirements:* For master's, thesis optional, foreign language not required; for doctorate, dissertation. *Entrance requirements:* GRE General Test. Application deadline: 5/1 (priority date; rolling processing; 2/1 for spring admission). Application fee: $30 ($40 for international students). *Tuition:* $5472 per year full-time, $554 per quarter (minimum) part-time for state residents; $14,172 per year full-time, $1424 per quarter (minimum) part-time for nonresidents. *Financial aid:* Fellowships, research assistantships, teaching assistantships, administrative assistantships, Federal Work-Study, institutionally sponsored loans available. Aid available to part-time students. • Dr. Carole A. Anderson, Dean, 614-292-8900. E-mail: anderson.32@osu.edu. Application contact: Dr. Connie Brown, Office of Student Affairs, 614-292-4041. Fax: 614-292-4535. E-mail: brown.106@osu.edu.

Old Dominion University, College of Health Sciences, School of Nursing, Norfolk, VA 23529. Awards MSN, Certificate. One or more programs accredited by NLN. Part-time programs available. Postbaccalaureate distance learning degree programs offered (no on-campus study). Faculty: 9 full-time (all women), 11 part-time (7 women), 12.7 FTE. Students: 124 full-time (102 women), 43 part-time (40 women); includes 18 minority (9 African Americans, 7 Asian Americans, 2 Native Americans), 7 international. Average age 37. 110 applicants, 78% accepted. In 1997, 83 master's awarded. *Degree requirements:* For master's, comprehensive exam required, foreign language and thesis not required. *Entrance requirements:* For master's, GRE or MAT, BSN; minimum GPA of 3.0 in nursing, 2.5 overall. Application deadline: 7/1 (rolling processing). Application fee: $30. *Expenses:* Tuition $180 per credit hour for state residents; $477 per credit hour for nonresidents. Fees $140 per year full-time, $32 per semester part-time. *Financial aid:* In 1997–98, 76 students received aid, including 1 fellowship (to a first-year student) totaling $1,500, 3 research assistantships (all to first-year students) totaling $11,322, 56 tuition grants (13 to first-year students) totaling $444,224; teaching assistantships, partial tuition waivers, and career-related internships or fieldwork also available. Aid available to part-time students. Financial aid application deadline: 2/15; applicants required to submit FAFSA. *Faculty research:* Oncology nursing, rural health primary care nursing, perinatal nursing, adolescent health, homeless health. Total annual research expenditures: $191,373. • Dr. Brenda Nichols, Chair, 757-683-4297. E-mail: bnichols@odu.edu. Application contact: Dr. Richardean Benjamin-Coleman, Director, 757-683-4298. Fax: 757-683-5253. E-mail: rcoleman@odu.edu.

Oregon Health Sciences University, School of Nursing, 3181 SW Sam Jackson Park Road, Portland, OR 97201-3098. Awards MN, MPH, MS, PhD, Post Master's Certificate. One or more programs accredited by NLN. Part-time programs available. Faculty: 50 full-time (49 women), 16 part-time (14 women). Students: 118 full-time (108 women), 71 part-time (69 women); includes 8 minority (6 Asian Americans, 1 Hispanic, 1 Native American), 8 international. Average age 34. 155 applicants, 41% accepted. In 1997, 102 master's awarded. *Degree requirements:* For master's, thesis optional, foreign language not required; for doctorate, dissertation. *Entrance requirements:* For master's, GRE General Test (minimum combined score of 1000), bachelor's degree in nursing, minimum undergraduate GPA of 3.0; for doctorate, GRE General Test (minimum combined score of 1000), master's degree in nursing, minimum undergraduate GPA of 3.0, graduate, 3.5; for Post Master's Certificate, master's degree in nursing. Application deadline: 1/15. Application fee: $40. *Financial aid:* In 1997–98, 10 fellowships (5 to first-year students), 42 research assistantships (12 to first-year students), 8 teaching assistantships, 75 traineeships averaging $200 per month were awarded; career-related internships or fieldwork also available. *Faculty research:* Nursing care of older persons; families in health, illness, and transition; family caregiving; end of life care/decision making; mother-infant interactions; pregnancy outcomes; enteral feeding; psychoactive drugs in long-term care. Total annual research expenditures: $1.282 million. • Dr. Kathleen Potempa, Dean, 503-494-7790. Application contact: Office of Recruitment, 503-494-7725. Fax: 503-494-4350. E-mail: proginfo@ohsu.edu.

Otterbein College, Program in Nursing, Westerville, OH 43081. Offers adult health care (MSN), adult health practitioner (Certificate), family nurse practitioner (Certificate), nurse service administration (MSN). Postbaccalaureate distance learning degree programs offered. Students: 124. In 1997, 19 master's awarded. *Application deadline:* rolling. *Application fee:* $35. *Tuition:* $5216 per quarter. • Dr. Judy Strayer, Chair, 614-823-1614. Fax: 614-823-3131.

Pace University, Lienhard School of Nursing, Pleasantville, NY 10570. Awards MS, Advanced Certificate. One or more programs accredited by NLN. Part-time and evening/weekend programs available. *Entrance requirements:* For master's, GRE General Test or MAT. Application deadline: 7/31 (priority date; rolling processing; 11/30 for spring admission). Application fee: $60. *Expenses:* Tuition $500 per credit. Fees $360 per year full-time, $53 per semester (minimum) part-time.

See in-depth description on page 1439.

Pacific Lutheran University, School of Nursing, Tacoma, WA 98447. Awards MSN. Accredited by NLN. Part-time and evening/weekend programs available. Faculty: 11 full-time (10 women), 1 (woman) part-time. Students: 21 full-time (20 women), 16 part-time (15 women); includes 4 minority (1 African American, 2 Asian Americans, 1 Hispanic). Average age 38. 28 applicants, 86% accepted. In 1997, 32 degrees awarded. *Degree requirements:* Thesis optional, foreign language not required. *Entrance requirements:* GRE General Test, TOEFL (minimum score 550), bachelor's degree in nursing, minimum undergraduate GPA of 3.0. Application deadline: 4/1 (priority date; rolling processing). Application fee: $35. *Tuition:* $490 per semester hour. *Financial aid:* Research assistantships, scholarships, Federal Work-Study available. Financial aid application deadline: 3/1. • Dr. Terry Miller, Dean, 253-535-7674. Application contact: Marjo Burdick, Office of Admissions, 253-535-7151. Fax: 253-535-8320. E-mail: admissions@plu.edu.

Pennsylvania State University University Park Campus, College of Health and Human Development, Department of Nursing, University Park, PA 16802-1503. Awards MS. Accredited by NLN. Students: 25 full-time (24 women), 30 part-time (28 women). In 1997, 20 degrees awarded. *Entrance requirements:* GRE General Test. Application fee: $40. *Expenses:* Tuition $6534 per year full-time, $276 per credit part-time for state residents; $13,460 per year full-time, $561 per credit part-time for nonresidents. Fees $252 per year (minimum) full-time, $43 per semester (minimum) part-time. • Dr. Sarah H. Gueldner, Director, 814-863-0245. Application contact: Dr. Elanor Crowder, Associate Director, 814-863-2211.

See in-depth description on page 1317.

Pittsburg State University, College of Arts and Sciences, Department of Nursing, Pittsburg, KS 66762-5880. Awards MSN. Faculty: 7 full-time. Students: 19 full-time (16 women), 27 part-time (24 women); includes 1 international. In 1997, 5 degrees awarded. *Entrance requirements:* GRE General Test. Application fee: $40. *Tuition:* $2418 per year full-time, $103 per credit hour part-time for state residents; $6130 per year full-time, $258 per credit hour part-time for nonresidents. • Dr. Jo-Ann Marrs, Chair, 316-235-4432.

Pontifical Catholic University of Puerto Rico, College of Sciences, Department of Nursing, Ponce, PR 00731-6382. Offers programs in medical-surgical nursing (MS), mental health and psychiatric nursing (MS). Accredited by NLN. Part-time and evening/weekend programs available. Faculty: 3 full-time (all women), 2 part-time (both women). Students: 3 full-time (all women), 58 part-time (49 women); includes 61 minority (all Hispanics). Average age 35. 15 applicants, 100% accepted. In 1997, 12 degrees awarded. *Degree requirements:* Clinical research paper. *Entrance requirements:* GRE General Test, minimum GPA of 2.5, BSN, 2 years of work experience, RN license. Application deadline: 4/30 (priority date; rolling processing). Application fee: $15. Electronic applications accepted. *Financial aid:* Fellowships, partial tuition waivers, Federal Work-Study available. Aid available to part-time students. Financial aid application deadline: 7/15. • Dr. Carmen L. Madera, Director, 787-841-2000 Ext. 261. Application contact: Manuel Luciano, Director of Admissions, 787-841-2000 Ext. 426. Fax: 787-840-4295.

Purdue University Calumet, School of Professional Studies, Department of Nursing, Hammond, IN 46323-2094. Awards MS. Accredited by NLN. *Entrance requirements:* TOEFL. Application fee: $30. *Faculty research:* Adult health, cardiovascular and renal nursing.

Queens College, Hayworth College, Division of Nursing, 1900 Selwyn Avenue, Charlotte, NC 28274-0002. Offers program in nursing management (MSN). MSN new for fall 1998. *Degree requirements:* Research project required, thesis not required. *Entrance requirements:* Minimum GPA of 3.0. Application deadline: rolling. Application fee: $25. *Expenses:* Tuition $225 per credit hour. Fees $40 per year. • Dr. Joan McGill, Chair, 704-337-2295. Application contact: Anne Duplessis, Director of Admissions, 704-337-2314. Fax: 704-337-2415.

Queen's University at Kingston, Faculty of Health Sciences, School of Nursing, Kingston, ON K7L 3N6, Canada. Awards M Sc. Faculty: 15 full-time (all women). Students: 23 full-time (all women). Average age 30. In 1997, 10 degrees awarded (100% found work related to degree). *Degree requirements:* Thesis required, foreign language not required. *Average time to degree:* master's–2.5 years full-time. *Entrance requirements:* TOEFL. Application deadline: 9/1 (rolling processing; 2/1 for spring admission). Application fee: $60. Electronic applications accepted. *Tuition:* $3803 per year (minimum) full-time, $1901 per year (minimum) part-time for Canadian residents; $7330 per year (minimum) for nonresidents. *Financial aid:* In 1997–98, 1 fellowship totaling $8,000, 2 research assistantships totaling $3,000, 7 teaching assistantships totaling $20,000 were awarded; institutionally sponsored loans also available. Financial aid application deadline: 2/1. *Faculty research:* Women and children's health, health and chronic illness. • Dr. S. Eastabrook, Dean. Fax: 613-545-4755. Application contact: Prof. R. Maloney, Graduate Program Committee Coordinator. Fax: 613-545-4751.

Quinnipiac College, School of Health Sciences, Nurse Practitioner Program, Hamden, CT 06518-1904. Awards MSN. *Degree requirements:* Thesis optional. *Application fee:* $45. *Expenses:* Tuition $395 per credit hour. Fees $380 per year full-time. • Dr. Joy Cohen, Director, 203-287-5366. E-mail: cohen@quinnipiac.edu. Application contact: Scott Farber, Director of Graduate Admissions, 203-281-8795. Fax: 203-287-5238. E-mail: qcgradadmi@quinnipiac.edu.

See in-depth description on page 1441.

Radford University, Graduate College, College of Nursing and Health Services, School of Nursing, Radford, VA 24142. Awards MS. Accredited by NLN. Part-time programs available. Postbaccalaureate distance learning degree programs offered (minimal on-campus study). Faculty: 19 full-time (18 women), 1 (woman) part-time, 19.2 FTE. Students: 18 full-time (17 women), 25 part-time (all women); includes 6 minority (2 African Americans, 1 Asian American, 3 Hispanics). Average age 39. 25 applicants, 80% accepted. In 1997, 5 degrees awarded. *Degree requirements:* Thesis or alternative, comprehensive exam required, foreign language not required. *Entrance requirements:* GMAT, GRE General Test, MAT, or NTE; TOEFL (minimum score 550), minimum GPA of 2.7. Application deadline: 2/1 (priority date; rolling processing; 10/1 for spring admission). Application fee: $25. Electronic applications accepted. *Expenses:* Tuition $2302 per year full-time, $147 per credit hour part-time for state residents; $5672 per year full-time, $287 per credit hour part-time for nonresidents. Fees $1222 per year full-time. *Financial aid:* In 1997–98, 30 students received aid, including 2 fellowships totaling $6,700, 3 research assistantships totaling $10,718, 6 teaching assistantships totaling $14,676, scholarships/grants totaling $100,995; Federal Work-Study, institutionally sponsored loans, and career-related internships or fieldwork also available. Financial aid application deadline: 2/1; applicants required to submit FAFSA. • Dr. Janet H. Boettcher, Chairperson, 540-831-5415. Fax: 540-831-6299. E-mail: jboettch@runet.edu.

Regis College, Division of Nursing, Weston, MA 02493. Awards MS, Certificate. Faculty: 6 full-time (5 women), 12 part-time (10 women). Students: 74 full-time (71 women), 124 part-time (121 women); includes 3 minority (2 Asian Americans, 1 Hispanic). 149 applicants, 46% accepted. In 1997, 8 master's, 9 Certificates awarded. *Degree requirements:* For master's, thesis required, foreign language not required. *Average time to degree:* master's–3 years part-time; other advanced degree–2 years part-time. *Entrance requirements:* For master's, GRE or MAT, minimum GPA of 3.0. Application deadline: rolling. Application fee: $30. *Expenses:* Tuition $390 per credit hour. Fees $95 per semester. *Financial aid:* 68 students received aid. Aid available to part-time students. Financial aid applicants required to submit FAFSA. *Faculty research:* Health policy, education, aging, job satisfaction, psychiatric nursing. • Dr. Amy Anderson, Chair, 781-768-7090. E-mail: amynurse@aol.com. Application contact: Patricia Andaloro, Representative, 781-768-7188. Fax: 781-768-8339.

Regis University, School for Healthcare Professions, Program in Nursing, Denver, CO 80221-1099. Awards MSN. Accredited by NLN. Offered at Northwest Denver Campus. Students: 52 full-time (50 women); includes 9 minority (1 African American, 1 Asian American, 5 Hispanics, 2 Native Americans). *Degree requirements:* Thesis or alternative. *Entrance requirements:* MAT. Application deadline: 1/15 (rolling processing; 9/15 for spring admission). Application fee: $60. *Tuition:* $250 per semester hour. *Financial aid:* Nursing internships available. • Dr. Nancy Case, Director. Application contact: Admissions Counselor, 303-458-4344.

Research College of Nursing, Nursing Program, Kansas City, MO 64132. Offers program in family nurse practitioner (MSN). Faculty: 12 full-time (all women). Students: 3 part-time (2 women). Average age 30. *Degree requirements:* Research project required, foreign language and thesis not required. *Entrance requirements:* GRE General Test or MAT, minimum GPA of 3.0, interview. Application deadline: 10/1 (priority date). Application fee: $25. • Dr. Nancy De Basio, President and Dean, 816-276-4721. Application contact: Dr. Charles F. Dorlac, Associate Dean, 816-276-4729. Fax: 816-276-3526.

The Richard Stockton College of New Jersey, Graduate Programs, Program in Nursing, Pomona, NJ 08240-9988. Awards MSN. Part-time programs available. Faculty: 3 full-time (all women). Students: 9 part-time (all women); includes 1 minority (African American). Average age 39. *Application deadline:* 6/1 (rolling processing). *Application fee:* $35. *Financial aid:* Federal Work-Study and career-related internships or fieldwork available. Aid available to part-time students. Financial aid application deadline: 3/1; applicants required to submit FAFSA. *Faculty research:* Psychoneuroimmunology, relationship of nutrition and disease, mental health as affected by chronic disease states. • Cheryle Eisele, Head, 609-652-4496. E-mail: iaprod210@pollux.stockton.edu. Application contact: Alison Henry, Associate Director of Admissions, 609-652-4261. Fax: 609-748-5541. E-mail: siprod42@pollux.stockton.edu.

Rivier College, Department of Nursing, Nashua, NH 03060-5086. Awards MS. Accredited by NLN. *Entrance requirements:* GRE, MAT. Application deadline: rolling. Application fee: $25.

Rush University, College of Nursing, Chicago, IL 60612-3832. Awards MSN, DN Sc, ND. One or more programs accredited by NLN. Part-time programs available. Faculty: 48 full-time (45 women), 69 part-time (all women), 52 FTE. Students: 10 full-time, 355 part-time; includes 48 minority (21 African Americans, 21 Asian Americans, 5 Hispanics, 1 Native American), 3 international. Average age 36. 178 applicants, 76% accepted. In 1997, 39 master's awarded (100% found work related to degree); 34 doctorates awarded. *Degree requirements:* For master's, practicum required, foreign language not required; for doctorate, dissertation, practicum required, foreign language not required. *Entrance requirements:* For master's, GRE General Test, interview; for doctorate, interview, previous course work in statistics. Application deadline: 8/1 (rolling processing; 2/15 for spring admission). Application fee: $40. *Tuition:* $8560 per year full-time, $370 per credit hour part-time. *Financial aid:* 260 students received aid; fellowships, research assistantships, teaching assistantships, Federal Work-Study, institutionally sponsored loans, and career-related internships or fieldwork available. Aid available to part-time students. Financial aid applicants required to submit FAFSA. *Faculty research:* Psychoneuroimmunology, HIV/AIDS, parenting skills, geropsychiatric home care, quality of life, nursing service, pain intervention studies. • Dr. Kathleen Andreoli, Dean, 312-942-7117. Application contact: Hicela Castruita, Director, College Admissions Services, 312-942-7100. Fax: 312-942-2219.

See in-depth description on page 1443.

Rutgers, The State University of New Jersey, Newark, College of Nursing, Newark, NJ 07102-3192. Offers programs in acute care of adults and aged (MS), advanced practice in pediatric nursing (MS), advanced practice with childbearing families (MS), community health nursing (MS), family nurse practitioner (MS), nursing research (PhD), primary care of adults and aged (MS), psychiatric/mental health nursing (MS). One or more programs accredited by NLN. Part-time programs available. Faculty: 23 full-time (all women). Students: 14 full-time (12 women), 295 part-time (289 women); includes 32 minority (12 African Americans, 16 Asian Americans, 3 Hispanics, 1 Native American). Average age 35. 118 applicants, 51% accepted. In 1997, 48 master's awarded (2% entered university research/teaching, 98% found other work related to degree); 1 doctorate awarded (100% found work related to degree). *Degree requirements:* For master's, comprehensive exam required, foreign language and thesis not required; for doctorate, computer language, dissertation required, foreign language not required. *Average time to degree:* master's–1.3 years full-time, 3.5 years part-time; doctorate–7 years part-time. *Entrance requirements:* For master's, GRE General Test, TOEFL, RN license, minimum B average, BS in nursing; for doctorate, GRE General Test (minimum combined score of 1500 on three sections), TOEFL, master's degree in nursing, minimum B average, RN license. Application deadline: 8/15 (rolling processing; 12/15 for spring admission). Application fee: $40. Electronic applications accepted. *Expenses:* Tuition $6248 per year full-time, $257 per credit part-time for state residents; $9160 per year full-time, $380 per credit part-time for nonresidents. Fees $738 per year full-time, $107 per semester (minimum) part-time. *Financial aid:* In 1997–98, 1 fellowship (to a first-year student), 1 research assistantship, 1 teaching assistantship were awarded; traineeships, Federal Work-Study, institutionally sponsored loans, and career-related internships or fieldwork also available. Financial aid application deadline: 4/15. *Faculty research:* HIV/AIDS, quality of life—MS and breast cancer, sleep patterns of cardiac patients. • Dr. Hurdis Griffith, Dean/Director, 973-353-5018. E-mail: griffith@nightingale.rutgers.edu. Application contact: Dr. Elaine Dolinsky, Associate Dean for Student Life and Services, 973-353-5060. Fax: 973-353-1277. E-mail: dolinsky@nightingale.rutgers.edu.

Sacred Heart University, College of Education and Health Professions, Faculty of Science and Mathematics, 5151 Park Avenue, Fairfield, CT 06432-1000. Awards MSN, MSN/MBA. Program in nursing administration (MSN). Accredited by NLN. Part-time and evening/weekend programs available. Faculty: 5 full-time (all women), 5 part-time (all women). Students: 1 (woman) full-time, 65 part-time (63 women); includes 7 minority (5 African Americans, 1 Asian American, 1 Hispanic). Average age 36. 4 applicants, 100% accepted. In 1997, 10 degrees awarded. *Entrance requirements:* MAT (minimum score 52), BSN, minimum GPA of 3.0. Application deadline: rolling. Application fee: $40 ($100 for international students). *Expenses:* Tuition $365 per credit. Fees $78 per semester. • Dr. Constance Young, Acting Director, Graduate Program in Nursing, 203-371-7715. Application contact: Elizabeth Nugent, Graduate Admissions Counselor, 203-371-7880. Fax: 203-365-4732. E-mail: gradstudies@sacredheart.edu.

Sage Graduate School, Graduate School, Division of Nursing, Troy, NY 12180-4115. Awards MS, PMC, MBA/MS. Programs in community health nursing (MS), family nurse practitioner (MS), medical-surgical nursing (MS), nursing (MS, PMC), psychiatric–mental health nurse practitioner (MS). One or more programs accredited by NLN. Part-time and evening/weekend programs available. Faculty: 8 full-time (all women), 5 part-time (4 women). Students: 58 full-time, 109 part-time. *Degree requirements:* For master's, thesis or alternative required, foreign language not required. *Entrance requirements:* For master's, BS in nursing, minimum GPA of 2.75. Application deadline: 8/1 (rolling processing; 12/15 for spring admission). Application fee: $25. *Expenses:* Tuition $360 per credit hour. Fees $50 per semester. *Financial aid:* Scholarships, assistantships, Federal Work-Study, and career-related internships or fieldwork available. Financial aid application deadline: 7/1; applicants required to submit FAFSA. • Dr. Glenda Kelman, Director, 518-244-2046. Fax: 518-244-4545. Application contact: Melissa Robertson, Associate Director of Admissions, 518-244-6878. Fax: 518-244-6880. E-mail: sgsadm@sage.edu.

Saginaw Valley State University, College of Nursing, University Center, MI 48710. Awards MSN. Accredited by NLN. Part-time programs available. Faculty: 5 full-time (all women). Students: 5 full-time (all women), 44 part-time (43 women); includes 3 minority (1 African American, 2 Hispanics), 1 international. In 1997, 9 degrees awarded. *Degree requirements:* Thesis. *Average time to degree:* master's–3 years part-time. *Entrance requirements:* GRE. Application deadline: rolling. Application fee: $25. *Expenses:* Tuition $159 per credit hour for state residents; $311 per credit hour for nonresidents. Fees $8.70 per credit hour. *Financial aid:* Federal Work-Study available. Financial aid applicants required to submit FAFSA. *Faculty research:* Adolescent pregnancy, nursing administration, bone loss and women's health, family caregiving, family context: children's health behavior. • Dr. Cheryl Easley, Dean, 517-790-4145. Application contact: Dr. Janalou Blecke, Assistant Dean, 517-790-4130. Fax: 517-790-1978. E-mail: jblecke@tardis.svsu.edu.

St. John Fisher College, School of Adult and Graduate Education, Nursing Program, Rochester, NY 14618-3597. Offers family nurse practitioner (Certificate), nursing (MS). One or more programs accredited by NLN. Part-time and evening/weekend programs available. Faculty: 6 full-time (all women), 3 part-time (1 woman). Students: 4 full-time (0 women), 139 part-time (127 women); includes 5 minority (3 African Americans, 1 Asian American, 1 Native American). Average age 38. 47 applicants, 74% accepted. In 1997, 22 master's awarded. *Degree requirements:* For master's, computer language required, foreign language and thesis not required. *Entrance requirements:* For master's, BSN, minimum GPA of 3.0. Application deadline: 8/1 (priority date; rolling processing; 1/1 for spring admission). Application fee: $30. *Tuition:* $13,500 per year full-time, $375 per credit hour part-time. • Dr. Cynthia McCloskey, Graduate Director, 716-385-8241. Fax: 716-385-8466. E-mail: mccloskey@sjfc.edu. Application contact: Steven T. Hoskins, Director, Graduate Admissions, 716-385-8161. Fax: 716-385-8344. E-mail: hoskins@sjfc.edu.

Saint Joseph College, Division of Nursing, West Hartford, CT 06117-2700. Offers programs in family health nursing (MS), psychiatric/mental health nursing (MS). Accredited by NLN. Part-time programs available. Faculty: 10 full-time (9 women), 2 part-time (both women). Students: 65 (63 women); includes 5 minority (all African Americans). Average age 32. In 1997, 23 degrees awarded. *Degree requirements:* Thesis or alternative required, foreign language not required. *Application deadline:* 8/29 (rolling processing). *Application fee:* $25. *Tuition:* $395 per credit. *Financial aid:* Application deadline 8/31. • Dr. Virginia Knowlden, Director, 860-232-4571 Ext. 258.

Saint Joseph's College, Department of Nursing, Standish, ME 04084-5263. Awards MS. Offered only through faculty directed independent study. Part-time programs available. Postbaccalaureate distance learning degree programs offered (minimal on-campus study). Faculty: 4 full-time (all women), 2 part-time (1 woman). Students: 149 part-time (138 women); includes 2 minority (both African Americans). Average age 41. 53 applicants, 96% accepted. *Degree requirements:* Thesis, summer residency required, foreign language not required. *Average time to degree:* master's–2 years full-time, 6 years part-time. *Entrance requirements:* GRE or MAT. Application fee: $50. *Tuition:* $220 per credit hour. *Financial aid:* Institutionally sponsored loans available. Aid available to part-time students. • Dr. Holley S. Gimpel, Chair, 207-893-7956. Fax: 207-892-7423. E-mail: hgimpel@sjcme.edu. Application contact: Admissions Department, 800-752-4723. Fax: 207-892-7480.

Saint Louis University, School of Nursing, Doctoral Program in Nursing, St. Louis, MO 63103-2097. Awards PhD. Students: 10 full-time, 34 part-time. 7 applicants, 71% accepted. In 1997, 7 degrees awarded. *Degree requirements:* Dissertation, preliminary exams required, foreign language not required. *Entrance requirements:* GRE General Test. Application deadline: 7/1 (rolling processing; 11/1 for spring admission). Application fee: $40. *Tuition:* $542 per credit hour. *Financial aid:* Traineeships available. Financial aid application deadline: 4/1. • Dr. Irene Riddle, Program Director, 314-577-8971. Application contact: Dr. Marcia Buresch, Assistant Dean of the Graduate School, 314-977-2240. Fax: 314-977-3943.

Saint Martin's College, Graduate Programs, Program in Nursing, Lacey, WA 98503-7500. Offers family nurse practitioner (MSN), leadership in health policy (MSN). Program being phased out; applicants no longer accepted. • Dr. Maura Egan, Director, 360-438-4560.

Saint Peter's College, Program in Nursing, 2641 Kennedy Boulevard, Jersey City, NJ 07306-5997. Awards MSN. Part-time and evening/weekend programs available. Faculty: 4 full-time (3 women), 2 part-time (both women). Students: 13 part-time (12 women); includes 5 minority (all Asian Americans). Average age 45. 16 applicants, 100% accepted. *Entrance requirements:* GRE or MAT. Application deadline: 8/1 (priority date; rolling processing). Application fee: $20. *Tuition:* $516 per credit. *Financial aid:* In 1997–98, 1 research assistantship (to a first-year student) was awarded. *Faculty research:* Battered women's perceptions of the emergency department experience. • Dr. Marylou Yam, Director, 201-915-9412. Fax: 201-915-9062. Application contact: Nancy P. Campbell, Associate Vice President for Enrollment, 201-915-9213. Fax: 201-432-5360. E-mail: admissions@spcvxa.spc.edu.

Saint Xavier University, School of Nursing, Chicago, IL 60655-3105. Awards MS, PMC, MBA/MS. Programs in adult health clinical nurse specialist (MS), family nurse practitioner (MS, PMC), leadership in community health nursing (MS), psychiatric/mental health clinical nurse specialist (MS). One or more programs accredited by NLN. MBA/MS offered in cooperation with the Graham School of Management. Part-time and evening/weekend programs available. Faculty: 10 full-time (all women), 2 part-time (both women). Students: 87. In 1997, 33 master's awarded. *Entrance requirements:* For master's, MAT or GRE General Test, minimum GPA of 3.0, RN license. Application deadline: 2/15 (9/15 for spring admission). Application fee: $35. *Expenses:* Tuition $450 per hour. Fees $50 per year. *Financial aid:* Available to part-time students. Financial aid applicants required to submit FAFSA. • Dr. Mary Lebold, Dean, 773-298-3700. Fax: 773-779-9061. E-mail: lebold@sxu.edu. Application contact: Sr. Evelyn McKenna, Vice President of Enrollment Management, 773-298-3050. Fax: 773-298-3076. E-mail: mckenna@sxu.edu.

Salem State College, Nursing Department, Salem, MA 01970-5353. Awards MSN, MBA/MSN. Accredited by NLN. *Entrance requirements:* GRE General Test. Application deadline: rolling. Application fee: $25. *Expenses:* Tuition $140 per credit hour for state residents; $230 per credit hour for nonresidents. Fees $20 per credit hour.

Salisbury State University, Program in Nursing, Salisbury, MD 21801-6837. Awards MS. Accredited by NLN. Part-time programs available. Faculty: 7 full-time (all women), 4 part-time (2 women). Students: 7 full-time (6 women), 36 part-time (34 women); includes 3 minority (all African Americans). Average age 33. 10 applicants, 80% accepted. In 1997, 16 degrees awarded. *Entrance requirements:* Minimum GPA of 2.75. Application deadline: 8/1 (rolling processing). Application fee: $30. *Expenses:* Tuition $158 per credit hour for state residents; $310 per credit hour for nonresidents. Fees $4 per credit hour. *Financial aid:* 9 students received aid; graduate assistantships, grants available. *Faculty research:* Female health and maternity, adolescent health, family health, school health. • Dr. Ruth Carroll, Acting Director, 410-546-6420. Fax: 410-548-3313. E-mail: rmcarroll@ssu.edu.

Samford University, Ida V. Moffett School of Nursing, Birmingham, AL 35229-0002. Awards MSN, MBA/MSN. Part-time programs available. Faculty: 27 full-time (all women), 2 part-time (both women). Students: 13 full-time (9 women), 12 part-time (all women); includes 6 minority (5 African Americans, 1 Asian American). Average age 38. 16 applicants, 50% accepted. *Degree requirements:* Thesis required, foreign language not required. *Average time to degree:* master's–2 years full-time. *Entrance requirements:* GRE General Test (minimum combined score of 1000), MAT (minimum score 50), Alabama RN license, BSN from an NLN-accredited school, minimum GPA of 3.2. Application deadline: 8/1 (priority date; rolling processing; 1/2 for spring admission). Application fee: $25. *Tuition:* $354 per credit hour. *Financial aid:* 14 students received aid; Federal Work-Study, institutionally sponsored loans, and career-related internships or fieldwork available. Financial aid application deadline: 3/1; applicants required to submit FAFSA. *Faculty research:* Diversity, transcultural quality improvement, spirituality, adolescent issues, portfolio development. • Dr. Marian K. Baur, Dean, 205-870-2861. Application contact: Dr. Joyce Jones, Director, 205-870-2863. Fax: 205-870-2219.

Samuel Merritt College, Department of Nursing, Oakland, CA 94609-3108. Offers programs in case management (MSN), family nurse practitioner (Certificate), nurse anesthetist (Certificate), nursing (MSN). Faculty: 11 full-time (9 women), 5 part-time (3 women), 13.37 FTE. Students: 121 full-time (101 women), 51 part-time (45 women); includes 51 minority (18 African Americans, 23 Asian Americans, 7 Hispanics, 3 Native Americans). Average age 36. 72 applicants, 71% accepted. In 1997, 30 master's awarded. *Degree requirements:* For master's, thesis or alternative required, foreign language not required. *Average time to degree:* master's–2.2 years full-time. *Entrance requirements:* For master's, TOEFL (minimum score 600), minimum GPA of 2.5 in science, 3.0 overall. Application deadline: 2/1 (rolling processing). Application fee: $50. *Expenses:* Tuition $605 per unit. Fees $25 per year. *Financial aid:* Scholarships, Federal Work-Study, and career-related internships or fieldwork available. Financial aid application deadline: 3/2; applicants required to submit FAFSA. *Faculty research:* Gerontology, community health, maternal-child health, sexually transmitted diseases, substance abuse. Total annual research expenditures: $5000. • Dr. Audrey Berman, Graduate Coordinator, 510-869-6733. Application contact: John Garten-Schuman, Director of Admissions, 510-869-6576. Fax: 510-869-6525.

San Diego State University, College of Health and Human Services, School of Nursing, San Diego, CA 92182. Awards MS. Accredited by NLN. Part-time and evening/weekend programs available. Faculty: 18 (16 women). Students: 64 full-time (62 women), 52 part-time (49 women); includes 19 minority (1 African American, 11 Asian Americans, 7 Hispanics). Average age 31. In 1997, 25 degrees awarded. *Degree requirements:* Thesis required (for some programs), foreign language not required. *Average time to degree:* master's–2 years full-time, 4 years part-time. *Entrance requirements:* GRE General Test (minimum combined score of 950), TOEFL (minimum score 550), previous course work in statistics and physical assessment. Application deadline: 1/15 (rolling processing; 11/1 for spring admission). Application fee: $55. *Expenses:* Tuition $0 for state residents; $246 per unit for nonresidents. Fees $1932 per year full-time, $1266 per year part-time. *Financial aid:* In 1997–98, 18 traineeships (10 to first-year students) were awarded; career-related internships or fieldwork also available. *Faculty research:* Health promotion, nursing systems and leadership, physiologic nursing, maternal-child nursing, advanced practice nursing. Total annual research expenditures: $115,000. • Patricia Wahl, Director, 619-594-6384. E-mail: pwahl@sciences.sdsu.edu. Application contact: Carolyn Walker, Graduate Coordinator, 619-594-6386. Fax: 619-594-2765. E-mail: cwalker@mail.sdsu.edu.

San Francisco State University, College of Health and Human Services, School of Nursing, San Francisco, CA 94132-1722. Offers programs in case management (MS), including long-term care, primary care/family nurse practitioner; nursing administration (MS); nursing education (MS). Accredited by NLN. Part-time programs available. *Degree requirements:* Thesis required, foreign language not required. *Entrance requirements:* Minimum GPA of 3.0. Application deadline: 11/30 (priority date; rolling processing; 5/31 for spring admission). Application fee: $55. *Expenses:* Tuition $0 for state residents; $246 per unit for nonresidents. Fees $1982 per year full-time, $1316 per year part-time. *Faculty research:* Nursing case management and clinical outcomes, outcome of undergraduate and graduate education in nursing, patient education strategies and learning outcomes.

Directory: Nursing—General

San Jose State University, College of Applied Arts and Sciences, School of Nursing, San Jose, CA 95192-0001. Offers programs in community health nursing (MS), including nursing administration, nursing education; gerontology nurse practitioner (MS). Accredited by NLN. Part-time and evening/weekend programs available. Faculty: 26 full-time (24 women), 13 part-time (12 women). Students: 7 full-time (all women), 67 part-time (63 women); includes 20 minority (3 African Americans, 13 Asian Americans, 3 Hispanics, 1 Native American). Average age 42. 66 applicants, 73% accepted. In 1997, 17 degrees awarded. *Degree requirements:* Thesis required, foreign language not required. *Entrance requirements:* BS in nursing, RN license. Application deadline: 6/1 (rolling processing). Application fee: $59. *Expenses:* Tuition $0 for state residents; $246 per unit for nonresidents. Fees $2017 per year full-time, $1351 per year part-time. *Financial aid:* In 1997–98, 2 scholarships (1 to a first-year student) were awarded; institutionally sponsored loans and career-related internships or fieldwork also available. Aid available to part-time students. *Faculty research:* Nurse-managed clinics, computers in nursing. • Dr. Bobbye Gorenberg, Director, 408-924-3130. Application contact: Dr. Colleen Saylor, Graduate Coordinator, 408-924-3134.

Seattle Pacific University, School of Health Sciences, Seattle, WA 98119-1997. Offers program in leadership in advanced nursing practice (MSN). Accredited by NLN. Part-time and evening/weekend programs available. Faculty: 2 full-time (both women), 8 part-time (all women). Students: 6 full-time (5 women), 56 part-time (52 women); includes 1 minority (Asian American), 2 international. Average age 38. In 1997, 15 degrees awarded (100% found work related to degree). *Degree requirements:* Thesis, internships required, foreign language not required. *Average time to degree:* master's–1.3 years full-time, 2 years part-time. *Entrance requirements:* GRE General Test (minimum combined score of 950), interview, Washington RN license, BS or BSN degree from a National League of Nursing accredited program. Application deadline: 9/1 (priority date; rolling processing). Application fee: $50. *Tuition:* $310 per credit. *Financial aid:* In 1997–98, 32 students received aid, including 6 teaching assistantships (4 to first-year students), scholarships totaling $50,000; institutionally sponsored loans and career-related internships or fieldwork also available. Aid available to part-time students. *Faculty research:* Health promotion, intercultural/international education, empathy/spiritual care, social policy, critical care/quality of life. • Dr. Annalee Oakes, Dean, 206-281-2233. E-mail: aoakes@spu.edu. Application contact: Jan Boyd, Graduate Admissions Counselor, 206-281-2888. Fax: 206-281-2767. E-mail: msninfo@spu.edu.

Seattle University, School of Nursing, Seattle, WA 98122. Awards MSN, Certificate. Part-time and evening/weekend programs available. Faculty: 9 full-time (8 women). Students: 15 full-time (14 women), 17 part-time (16 women); includes 5 minority (3 African Americans, 1 Asian American, 1 Native American). Average age 36. 20 applicants, 65% accepted. In 1997, 7 master's awarded. *Degree requirements:* For master's, thesis optional, foreign language not required. *Entrance requirements:* For master's, GRE General Test, bachelor's degree in nursing, minimum GPA of 3.0. Application deadline: 6/1. Application fee: $55. *Expenses:* Tuition $367 per credit hour. Fees $70 per year. *Financial aid:* Fellowships, research assistantships, Federal Work-Study, and career-related internships or fieldwork available. Aid available to part-time students. Financial aid applicants required to submit FAFSA. *Faculty research:* Pain, asthma in African-American children, midlife women, quality of life. • Dr. Constance Nakao, Director, 206-296-5660. Fax: 206-296-5544. E-mail: cnakao@seattleu.edu. Application contact: Michael McKeon, Dean of Admissions, 206-296-5900. Fax: 206-296-5656. E-mail: admissions@seattleu.edu.

Seton Hall University, College of Nursing, South Orange, NJ 07079-2697. Awards MA, MSN, MSN/MA. Accredited by NLN. Part-time programs available. Faculty: 11 full-time (all women), 15 part-time (12 women). Students: 26 full-time (all women), 176 part-time (172 women); includes 12 minority (4 African Americans, 3 Asian Americans, 4 Hispanics, 1 Native American). Average age 28. 167 applicants, 82% accepted. In 1997, 48 degrees awarded. *Degree requirements:* Research project required, foreign language and thesis not required. *Entrance requirements:* GRE or MAT, BSN. Application deadline: 5/15 (priority date; rolling processing; 11/15 for spring admission). Application fee: $50. *Expenses:* Tuition $500 per credit. Fees $610 per year full-time, $185 per semester part-time. *Financial aid:* Graduate assistantships, traineeships, partial tuition waivers, institutionally sponsored loans available. Aid available to part-time students. Financial aid application deadline: 7/15. *Faculty research:* Parent/child, adult, and gerontological nursing. • Dr. Barbara Beeker, Dean, 973-761-9015. E-mail: beekerba@shu.edu. Application contact: Mary Jo Bugel, Director of Recruitment, 973-761-9285. Fax: 973-761-9607. E-mail: bugelmar@shu.edu.

Shenandoah University, Division of Nursing, 1460 University Drive, Winchester, VA 22601-5195. Awards MSN. Part-time programs available. Faculty: 6 full-time (all women), 1 (woman) part-time. Students: 21 full-time (18 women), 3 part-time (all women); includes 1 minority (African American). Average age 32. 21 applicants, 90% accepted. *Degree requirements:* Research project required, foreign language and thesis not required. *Entrance requirements:* GRE General Test, previous course work in statistics, community nursing, and health assessment. Application deadline: 7/15. Application fee: $30. Electronic applications accepted. *Tuition:* $470 per credit. *Faculty research:* Family health promotion, well-woman, maternal/child nursing. • Dr. Martha Erbach, Interim Chair, 540-678-4374. Fax: 540-665-5519. E-mail: merbach@su.edu. Application contact: Michael Carpenter, Director of Admissions, 540-665-4581. Fax: 540-665-4627. E-mail: admit@su.edu.

Simmons College, Graduate School for Health Studies, Program in Primary Health Care Nursing, Boston, MA 02115. Awards MS, CAGS. Accredited by NLN. Part-time programs available. Faculty: 7 full-time (all women), 9 part-time (all women). Students: 253 part-time (244 women); includes 9 minority (6 African Americans, 2 Asian Americans, 1 Hispanic), 5 international. Average age 30. 99 applicants, 69% accepted. In 1997, 81 master's awarded. *Entrance requirements:* For master's, GRE General Test, TOEFL (minimum score 550), 1 year of full-time clinical experience. Application deadline: 1/15 (rolling processing). Application fee: $50. *Expenses:* Tuition $587 per credit hour. Fees $20 per year. *Financial aid:* Traineeships, Federal Work-Study, institutionally sponsored loans available. Aid available to part-time students. Financial aid application deadline: 3/1; applicants required to submit FAFSA. *Faculty research:* Nursing leadership and mentoring, gerontology/homecare, nurse practitioner in occupational health. • Dr. Carol Love, Director, 617-521-2141. Fax: 617-521-3045. E-mail: clove@simmons.edu. Application contact: Christine Keuleyan, Admission Coordinator, 617-521-2650. Fax: 617-521-3137. E-mail: keuleyan@simmons.edu.

See in-depth description on page 1329.

Slippery Rock University of Pennsylvania, College of Human Service Professions, Program in Nursing, Slippery Rock, PA 16057. Awards MSN. Offered jointly with Clarion University of Pennsylvania. Part-time and evening/weekend programs available. Faculty: 13 part-time (12 women). Students: 11 full-time (10 women), 51 part-time (48 women); includes 5 minority (all African Americans), 1 international. Average age 34. 15 applicants, 67% accepted. In 1997, 10 degrees awarded (100% found work related to degree). *Degree requirements:* Thesis or alternative required, foreign language not required. *Average time to degree:* master's–2 years full-time, 2.5 years part-time. *Entrance requirements:* GRE, minimum QPA of 2.75. Application deadline: 4/15 (priority date; 11/15 for spring admission). Application fee: $25. *Tuition:* $4484 per year full-time, $247 per credit part-time for state residents; $7667 per year full-time, $423 per credit part-time for nonresidents. *Financial aid:* In 1997–98, 1 student received aid, including 1 graduate assistantship averaging $445 per month and totaling $4,000; institutionally sponsored loans and career-related internships or fieldwork also available. Financial aid applicants required to submit FAFSA. *Faculty research:* Sexually transmitted disease prevention, grief, informatics, decision making. • Dr. Joyce White, Coordinator, 724-738-2323. Fax: 724-738-2881. E-mail: joyce.white@sru.edu. Application contact: Jan McClaine, Coordinator, 724-226-2337. Fax: 724-226-2722. E-mail: mcclaine@mail.clarion.edu.

South Dakota State University, College of Nursing, Brookings, SD 57007. Awards MS. Accredited by NLN. Faculty: 8 full-time (all women). Students: 22 full-time (16 women), 55 part-time (48 women); includes 2 minority (1 Hispanic, 1 Native American). 15 applicants, 93% accepted. In 1997, 39 degrees awarded. *Degree requirements:* Thesis, oral exam required, foreign language not required. *Average time to degree:* master's–2 years full-time, 4 years part-time. *Entrance requirements:* TOEFL. Application deadline: rolling. Application fee: $15. *Financial aid:* Fellowships, research assistantships, teaching assistantships, Federal Work-Study available. *Faculty research:* Rural health, aging, parents of children with fetal alcohol syndrome, health promotion, Native American health, woman's health. • Dr. Roberta Olson, Dean, 605-688-5178. Application contact: Barbara Heater, Graduate Head, 605-688-4114.

Southeastern Louisiana University, College of Nursing, Hammond, LA 70402. Awards MSN. Accredited by NLN. Part-time programs available. Faculty: 10 full-time, 1 part-time. Students: 3 full-time (all women), 17 part-time (all women); includes 3 minority (all African Americans). Average age 36. In 1997, 8 degrees awarded. *Degree requirements:* Thesis required, foreign language not required. *Entrance requirements:* GRE General Test (minimum combined score of 1200), previous course work in statistics, physical assessment. Application deadline: 7/15 (priority date; rolling processing; 12/15 for spring admission). Application fee: $10 ($25 for international students). Electronic applications accepted. *Expenses:* Tuition $2010 per year full-time, $287 per semester (minimum) part-time for state residents; $5232 per year full-time, $287 per semester (minimum) part-time for nonresidents. Fees $5 per year. *Financial aid:* Research assistantships, administrative assistantships, Federal Work-Study, and career-related internships or fieldwork available. Aid available to part-time students. Financial aid application deadline: 5/1; applicants required to submit FAFSA. *Faculty research:* Community health, social support, homelessness, psychosocial health, psychophysiology. Total annual research expenditures: $2000. • Dr. S. Kay A. Thornhill, Director, Graduate Nursing, 504-549-5045. Fax: 504-549-5087. E-mail: sthornhill@selu.edu. Application contact: Stephen C. Soutullo, Registrar and Director of Enrollment Services, 504-549-2066. Fax: 504-549-5632. E-mail: ssoutullo@selu.edu.

Southeast Missouri State University, Department of Nursing, Cape Girardeau, MO 63701-4799. Awards MSN. Accredited by NLN. *Degree requirements:* Thesis required, foreign language not required. *Entrance requirements:* Minimum GPA of 3.0, nursing license. Application deadline: 4/1 (priority date; rolling processing; 11/21 for spring admission). Application fee: $20 ($100 for international students). *Tuition:* $2034 per year full-time, $113 per credit hour part-time for state residents; $3672 per year full-time, $204 per credit hour part-time for nonresidents. *Financial aid:* Research assistantships available. • Louise Hart, Chairperson, 573-651-2585. Application contact: Office of Graduate Studies, 573-651-2192.

Southern Connecticut State University, School of Professional Studies, Department of Nursing, New Haven, CT 06515-1355. Awards MSN. Faculty: 3 full-time, 1 part-time. Students: 3 full-time (2 women), 60 part-time (56 women); includes 3 minority (2 African Americans, 1 Hispanic). 43 applicants, 5% accepted. In 1997, 8 degrees awarded. *Entrance requirements:* GRE, MAT, interview, minimum QPA of 2.8, RN license. Application deadline: 7/15 (priority date; rolling processing). Application fee: $40. *Expenses:* Tuition $2632 per year full-time, $188 per credit part-time for state residents; $7200 per year full-time, $188 per credit part-time for nonresidents. Fees $1806 per year full-time, $45 per semester part-time for state residents; $2703 per year full-time, $45 per semester part-time for nonresidents. • Dr. Cesarina Thompson, Chairperson, 203-392-6487. Application contact: Dr. Susan Killion, Graduate Coordinator, 203-392-6482.

Southern Illinois University at Edwardsville, School of Nursing, Edwardsville, IL 62026-0001. Offers programs in community health nursing (MS), medical-surgical nursing (MS), nurse anesthesia (MS), nurse practitioner nursing (MS), psychiatric nursing (MS). Accredited by NLN. Part-time programs available. Faculty: 30 full-time (29 women), 18 part-time (17 women). Students: 85 full-time (73 women), 69 part-time (65 women); includes 16 minority (11 African Americans, 3 Asian Americans, 1 Hispanic, 1 Native American). 68 applicants, 54% accepted. In 1997, 35 degrees awarded. *Degree requirements:* Thesis or alternative, final exam required, foreign language not required. *Entrance requirements:* Appropriate bachelor's degree, RN license. Application deadline: 7/24. Application fee: $25. *Expenses:* Tuition $1716 per year full-time, $95 per credit hour part-time for state residents; $5149 per year full-time, $286 per credit hour part-time for nonresidents. Fees $463 per year full-time, $433 per year part-time. *Financial aid:* In 1997–98, 2 fellowships, 3 assistantships were awarded; research assistantships, teaching assistantships, Federal Work-Study, institutionally sponsored loans also available. Aid available to part-time students. • Dr. Felissa Lashley, Dean, 618-692-3956.

Southern University and Agricultural and Mechanical College, School of Nursing, Baton Rouge, LA 70813. Awards MSN. Accredited by NLN. Part-time programs available. Faculty: 5 full-time (all women), 2 part-time (both women). Students: 4 full-time (all women), 39 part-time (36 women); includes 43 minority (31 African Americans, 12 Asian Americans). Average age 35. 6 applicants, 83% accepted. In 1997, 7 degrees awarded (71% entered university research/teaching, 29% found other work related to degree). *Degree requirements:* Thesis required, foreign language not required. *Average time to degree:* master's–2 years full-time, 2.5 years part-time. *Entrance requirements:* GRE General Test (minimum combined score of 1200), BSN, minimum GPA of 2.7. Application deadline: 9/8 (1/21 for spring admission). Application fee: $5. *Tuition:* $2226 per year full-time, $267 per semester (minimum) part-time for state residents; $6262 per year full-time, $267 per semester (minimum) part-time for nonresidents. *Financial aid:* 1 student received aid; research assistantships, graduate assistantships, institutionally sponsored loans available. *Faculty research:* Self-cure habits of African-American families. • Dr. Janet Rami, Dean, 504-771-2166. Application contact: Dr. Elaine C. Vallette, Graduate Chairperson, 504-771-2663. Fax: 504-771-2641.

Southwest Missouri State University, College of Health and Human Services, Department of Nursing, Springfield, MO 65804-0094. Awards MSN. Faculty: 3 full-time (2 women). Students: 13 full-time (12 women), 13 part-time (10 women). *Degree requirements:* Comprehensive exam required, foreign language not required. *Entrance requirements:* Minimum GPA of 3.0. Application fee: $25. *Expenses:* Tuition $1980 per year full-time, $110 per credit hour part-time for state residents; $3960 per year full-time, $220 per credit hour part-time for nonresidents. Fees $274 per year full-time, $73 per semester part-time. • Dr. Alex Trombetta, Head, 417-836-5416. Fax: 417-836-5484. E-mail: adt964f@wpgate.smsu.edu.

Spalding University, School of Nursing and Health Sciences, Louisville, KY 40203-2188. Offers programs in administration (MSN), family nurse practitioner (MSN). Accredited by NLN. Part-time and evening/weekend programs available. Faculty: 5 full-time (4 women). Students: 30 full-time (28 women), 29 part-time (27 women); includes 2 minority (both African Americans). Average age 36. 42 applicants, 98% accepted. In 1997, 16 degrees awarded. *Entrance requirements:* GRE General Test, BSN. Application deadline: 8/15 (priority date; rolling processing). Application fee: $30. *Expenses:* Tuition $350 per credit hour (minimum). Fees $48 per year full-time, $4 per credit hour part-time. *Financial aid:* In 1997–98, 36 students received aid, including 30 scholarships, traineeships totaling $61,783; research assistantships and career-related internships or fieldwork also available. Aid available to part-time students. Financial aid application deadline: 3/15; applicants required to submit FAFSA. *Faculty research:* Nurse educational administration, maternal/child nursing, nursing history. • Dr. Cynthia Crabtree, Dean, 502-585-7125. E-mail: nursing@spalding10.win.net. Application contact: Jeanne Anderson, Assistant to the Provost and Director of Graduate Office, 502-585-7105. Fax: 502-585-7158. E-mail: gradoffc@spalding6.win.net.

State University of New York at Binghamton, School of Nursing, Binghamton, NY 13902-6000. Awards MS, PhD, Certificate. PhD new for fall 1998. Part-time and evening/weekend programs available. Students: 55 full-time (51 women), 41 part-time (36 women); includes 5 minority (3 African Americans, 1 Asian American, 1 Hispanic), 1 international. Average age 37. 44 applicants, 93% accepted. In 1997, 51 master's, 29 Certificates awarded. *Degree requirements:* For master's, thesis, comprehensive exam; for doctorate, dissertation. *Entrance requirements:* For master's, GRE General Test, TOEFL; for doctorate, TOEFL. Application deadline: 4/15 (priority date; rolling processing; 11/1 for spring admission). Application fee: $50. Electronic applications accepted. *Expenses:* Tuition $5100 per year full-time, $213 per credit hour part-time for state residents; $8416 per year full-time, $351 per credit hour part-time for nonresidents. Fees $654 per year full-time, $75 per semester (minimum) part-time. *Financial aid:* In 1997–98, 48 students received aid, including 1 fellowship averaging $650 per month and totaling $6,500, 3 research assistantships (2 to first-year students) averaging $680 per month and totaling $20,400, 7 teaching assistantships (4 to first-year students) averaging $680 per month and totaling $47,300, 34 graduate assistantships, traineeships (8 to first-year students) averaging $395 per month and totaling $105,900; Federal Work-Study, institutionally sponsored loans, and career-related internships or fieldwork also available. Aid available to part-time students. Financial aid application deadline: 2/15. • Dr. Mary Collins, Dean, 607-777-2354.

State University of New York at Buffalo, Graduate School, School of Nursing, Buffalo, NY 14260. Offers programs in adult health nursing (MS), including clinical specialist, nurse practitioner; child health nursing (MS), including clinical nurse specialist, pediatric nurse practitioner; nurse anesthesia (MS); nursing (DNS). Part-time programs available. Postbaccalaureate distance learning degree programs offered (minimal on-campus study). Faculty: 28 full-time (25 women), 13 part-time (12 women). Students: 79 full-time (70 women), 181 part-time (167 women); includes 18 minority (5 African Americans, 2 Asian Americans, 3 Hispanics, 8 Native Americans), 15 international. Average age 28. 121 applicants, 68% accepted. In 1997, 84 master's, 6 doctorates awarded. Terminal master's awarded for partial completion of doctoral program. *Degree requirements:* For doctorate, dissertation required, foreign language not required. *Entrance requirements:* For master's, GRE General Test (minimum score 450 on each section), TOEFL (minimum score 550), interview, minimum GPA of 3.0, RN license; for doctorate, GRE General Test (minimum score 500 on each section), TOEFL (minimum score 550), minimum GPA of 3.2, RN license. Application deadline: 5/1 (priority date; rolling processing; 10/15 for spring admission). Application fee: $35. *Tuition:* $5970 per year full-time, $288 per credit hour part-time for state residents; $9286 per year full-time, $426 per credit hour part-time for nonresidents. *Financial aid:* In 1997–98, 1 fellowship averaging $834 per month and totaling $10,008, 2 research assistantships (1 to a first-year student) averaging $991 per month and totaling $8,920, 12 teaching assistantships (7 to first-year students) averaging $1,050 per month and totaling $104,400 were awarded; full and partial tuition waivers, Federal Work-Study also available. Financial aid application deadline: 3/1. *Faculty research:* Stress and coping in chronic illness, healthful outcomes and quality of life, symptom management, technology, nursing and patient care. Total annual research expenditures: $804,000. • Dr. Mecca S. Cranley, Dean, 716-829-2533. E-mail: mcranley@nurse.buffalo.edu. Application contact: Dr. William P. Harden, Assistant Dean, 716-829-3314. Fax: 716-829-2021. E-mail: wharden@nurse.buffalo.edu.

State University of New York at New Paltz, Faculty of Liberal Arts and Sciences, Department of Nursing, New Paltz, NY 12561-2499. Offers program in gerontological nursing (MS). Accredited by NLN. Students: 12 full-time (all women), 26 part-time (25 women); includes 2 minority (both African Americans). In 1997, 3 degrees awarded. *Entrance requirements:* GRE General Test, minimum GPA of 3.0. Application deadline: 3/15 (priority date; rolling processing). Application fee: $50. *Expenses:* Tuition $5100 per year full-time, $213 per credit hour part-time for state residents; $8416 per year full-time, $351 per credit hour part-time for nonresidents. Fees $493 per year full-time, $48 per semester (minimum) part-time. • Dr. Ide Katims, Director, 914-257-2922.

State University of New York at Stony Brook, Health Sciences Center, School of Nursing, Stony Brook, NY 11794. Awards MS, Certificate. Faculty: 29 full-time, 25 part-time. Students: 182 full-time (175 women), 323 part-time (302 women); includes 68 minority (29 African Americans, 24 Asian Americans, 14 Hispanics, 1 Native American), 1 international. Average age 30. 430 applicants, 69% accepted. In 1997, 166 master's, 44 Certificates awarded. *Degree requirements:* For master's, thesis required, foreign language not required. *Entrance requirements:* For master's, BSN, minimum GPA of 3.0, previous course work in statistics. Application deadline: 1/15. Application fee: $50. *Expenses:* Tuition $5100 per year full-time, $213 per credit hour part-time for state residents; $8416 per year full-time, $351 per credit hour part-time for nonresidents. Fees $529 per year full-time, $77 per semester (minimum) part-time. *Financial aid:* Traineeships, Federal Work-Study, institutionally sponsored loans, and career-related internships or fieldwork available. Financial aid application deadline: 3/15. *Total annual research expenditures:* $204,216. • Dr. Lenora J. McClean, Dean, 516-444-3262. Fax: 516-444-3136.

State University of New York Health Science Center at Brooklyn, College of Nursing, Graduate Program in Nursing, 450 Clarkson Avenue, Brooklyn, NY 11203-2098. Offers nurse practitioner (MS, Post Master's Certificate), nursing (MS). One or more programs accredited by NLN. Part-time programs available. *Degree requirements:* For master's, thesis, clinical research project required, foreign language not required. *Average time to degree:* master's–1.5 years full-time, 3 years part-time. *Entrance requirements:* For master's, GRE, BSN, minimum GPA of 3.0; for Post Master's Certificate, BSN, minimum GPA of 3.0. Application deadline: 5/1 (priority date; rolling processing). Application fee: $35. *Expenses:* Tuition $5100 per year full-time, $213 per credit hour part-time for state residents; $8416 per year full-time, $351 per credit hour part-time for nonresidents. Fees $225 per year full-time, $75 per semester (minimum) part-time. *Faculty research:* AIDS, continuity of care, case management, self-care.

State University of New York Health Science Center at Syracuse, College of Nursing, Syracuse, NY 13210-2334. Awards MS. Accredited by NLN. Part-time programs available. Faculty: 7 full-time (6 women). Students: 19 full-time (all women), 54 part-time (49 women). 102 applicants, 48% accepted. In 1997, 15 degrees awarded. *Degree requirements:* Thesis or alternative required, foreign language not required. *Average time to degree:* master's–2 years full-time, 4 years part-time. *Entrance requirements:* GRE General Test, GRE Subject Test (minimum score 600), TOEFL (minimum score 550), TSE. Application deadline: 3/1 (rolling processing). Application fee: $40. *Expenses:* Tuition $5100 per year full-time, $213 per credit hour part-time for state residents; $8416 per year full-time, $351 per credit hour part-time for nonresidents. Fees $405 per year full-time, $108 per semester (minimum) part-time. *Financial aid:* 73 students received aid; Federal Work-Study available. Aid available to part-time students. Financial aid application deadline: 4/1; applicants required to submit FAFSA. • Dr. Jorge Grimes, Chair, 315-464-4276.

State University of New York Institute of Technology at Utica/Rome, School of Nursing, PO Box 3050, Utica, NY 13504-3050. Offers programs in adult nurse practitioner (MS, Certificate), nursing administration (MS). One or more programs accredited by NLN. Part-time programs available. Faculty: 9 full-time (all women), 6 part-time (5 women). Students: 15 full-time (all women), 64 part-time (61 women); includes 2 minority (both African Americans). Average age 35. 29 applicants, 72% accepted. In 1997, 18 master's awarded. *Degree requirements:* For master's, thesis or alternative required, foreign language not required. *Average time to degree:* master's–2 years full-time, 4 years part-time. *Entrance requirements:* For master's, GRE General Test, minimum GPA of 3.0 in last 30 hours of undergraduate course work, bachelor's degree in nursing, 1 year of professional experience. Application deadline: 6/15 (priority date; rolling processing). Application fee: $50. *Expenses:* Tuition $5100 per year full-time, $213 per credit hour part-time for state residents; $8416 per year full-time, $351 per credit hour part-time for nonresidents. Fees $570 per year full-time, $17.60 per credit hour part-time. *Financial aid:* In 1997–98, 43 students received aid, including 1 research assistantship; fellowships, Federal Work-Study, and career-related internships or fieldwork also available. Aid available to part-time students. Financial aid applicants required to submit FAFSA. *Faculty research:* Moral reasoning, Myers-Briggs personality, home care, critical thinking, public health. • Dr. Elizabeth Kellogg Walker, Dean, 315-792-7295. Fax: 315-792-7555. E-mail: aekw@sunyit.edu. Application contact: Marybeth Lyons, Director of Admissions, 315-792-7500. Fax: 315-792-7837. E-mail: smbl@sunyit.edu.

Syracuse University, College of Nursing, Syracuse, NY 13244-0003. Awards MS. Accredited by NLN. Part-time and evening/weekend programs available. Faculty: 14 full-time, 49 part-time. Students: 23 full-time (21 women), 128 part-time (120 women); includes 8 minority (5 African Americans, 2 Hispanics, 1 Native American), 4 international. 55 applicants, 87% accepted. In 1997, 22 degrees awarded. *Degree requirements:* Thesis or alternative, comprehensive exam. *Entrance requirements:* GRE General Test, BSN, competence in basic statistics. Application deadline: rolling. Application fee: $40. *Tuition:* $13,320 per year full-time, $555 per credit hour part-time. *Financial aid:* In 1997–98, 2 teaching assistantships were awarded; partial tuition waivers, Federal Work-Study, and career-related internships or fieldwork also available. Financial aid application deadline: 3/1. *Faculty research:* Medical-surgical nursing, community health, psychiatric-mental health, childbearing, family. • Grace Chickadonz, Dean, 315-443-2141. Application contact: Jan Pedersen, 315-443-4272.

Temple University, Health Sciences Center and Graduate School, College of Allied Health Professions, Department of Nursing, Philadelphia, PA 19140. Awards MSN. Accredited by NLN. Faculty: 7 full-time (6 women). Students: 64 (55 women); includes 18 minority (13 African Americans, 1 Asian American, 3 Hispanics, 1 Native American). 68 applicants, 66% accepted. In 1997, 19 degrees awarded. *Degree requirements:* Thesis or research project required, foreign language not required. *Entrance requirements:* GRE General Test, current RN license, interview. Application deadline: 2/15 (priority date). Application fee: $40. *Expenses:* Tuition $323 per semester hour for state residents; $444 per semester hour for nonresidents. Fees $170 per year full-time, $28 per semester (minimum) part-time. *Financial aid:* Teaching assistantships, traineeships, institutionally sponsored loans, and career-related internships or fieldwork available. Aid available to part-time students. *Faculty research:* Osteoporosis, sensory deprivation in elderly, child abuse, attitudes towards AIDS, management styles. Total annual research expenditures: $310,492. • Dr. Catherine A. Bevil, Chair, 215-707-4687. Application contact: Dr. Jean A. Woods, Interim Director of Graduate Studies in Nursing, 215-707-4626. Fax: 215-707-1599.

See in-depth description on page 1263.

Tennessee State University, School of Nursing, Nashville, TN 37209-1561. Awards MS. Accredited by NLN. *Entrance requirements:* GRE General Test (minimum combined score of 900) or MAT (minimum score 30), BSN, current RN license, minimum GPA of 3.0. Application deadline: rolling. Application fee: $15. *Tuition:* $2962 per year full-time, $182 per credit hour part-time for state residents; $7788 per year full-time, $393 per credit hour part-time for nonresidents. • Dr. Marion Anema, Dean, 615-963-5254.

Texas A&M University–Corpus Christi, College of Science and Technology, Program in Nursing, Corpus Christi, TX 78412-5503. Offers nursing administration (MSN). Accredited by NLN. Part-time and evening/weekend programs available. Students: 10 full-time (8 women), 68 part-time (60 women); includes 26 minority (3 African Americans, 22 Hispanics, 1 Native American). Average age 40. In 1997, 6 degrees awarded. *Degree requirements:* Thesis optional, foreign language not required. *Entrance requirements:* GRE General Test. Application deadline: 7/15 (priority date; rolling processing; 11/15 for spring admission). Application fee: $10 ($30 for international students). *Expenses:* Tuition $648 per year full-time, $120 per semester (minimum) part-time for state residents; $4482 per year full-time, $747 per semester (minimum) part-time for nonresidents. Fees $1010 per year full-time, $205 per semester part-time. *Financial aid:* Federal Work-Study, institutionally sponsored loans, and career-related internships or fieldwork available. Aid available to part-time students. Financial aid application deadline: 3/15; applicants required to submit FAFSA. • Dr. Rebecca Jones, Director, 512-994-2649. E-mail: addst014@tamucc.edu. Application contact: Mary Margaret Dechant, Director of Admissions, 512-994-2624. Fax: 512-994-5887.

Texas Tech University Health Sciences Center, School of Nursing, Lubbock, TX 79430-0002. Offers programs in administration (MSN), community health (MSN), education (MSN), family nurse practitioner (MSN), gerontics (MSN). Accredited by NLN. Part-time programs available. Postbaccalaureate distance learning degree programs offered (minimal on-campus study). Faculty: 14 full-time (all women). Students: 9 full-time (6 women), 27 part-time (all women); includes 5 minority (1 African American, 3 Asian Americans, 1 Hispanic). Average age 35. 18 applicants, 33% accepted. In 1997, 7 degrees awarded. *Degree requirements:* Thesis required, foreign language not required. *Average time to degree:* master's–2 years full-time, 3 years part-time. *Entrance requirements:* GRE General Test (minimum combined score of 1000), MAT (minimum score 50), minimum GPA of 3.0, sample of written work. Application deadline: 6/1 (rolling processing; 10/1 for spring admission). Application fee: $30 ($50 for international students). *Expenses:* Tuition $36 per credit hour for state residents; $249 per credit hour for nonresidents. Fees $1348 per year full-time for state residents; $1349 per year full-time for nonresidents. *Financial aid:* In 1997–98, 14 students received aid, including 4 teaching assistantships, 7 traineeships averaging $400 per month and totaling $34,000; research assistantships, institutionally sponsored loans also available. Aid available to part-time students. Financial aid application deadline: 5/1; applicants required to submit FAFSA. *Faculty research:* Primary health care, family, rural health care. Total annual research expenditures: $55,500. • Dr. Pat S. Yoder Wise, Dean, 806-743-2738. E-mail: sonpsy@ttuhsc.edu. Application contact: Nancy Ridenour, Associate Dean for Education, 806-743-2737. Fax: 806-743-1622. E-mail: sonnar@ttuhsc.edu.

Texas Woman's University, College of Nursing, Denton, TX 76204. Offers programs in adult health nurse (MS), adult health nurse practitioner (MS), community health nursing (MS), family nurse practitioner (MS), nursing (PhD), pediatric nurse practitioner (MS), pediatric nursing (MS), psychiatric-mental health nursing (MS), women's health nurse (PhD), women's health nurse practitioner (PhD). One or more programs accredited by NLN. Part-time programs available. Faculty: 30 full-time (29 women), 12 part-time (10 women). Students: 60 full-time (53 women), 390 part-time (375 women); includes 71 minority (27 African Americans, 21 Asian Americans, 23 Hispanics), 1 international. Average age 39. 71 applicants, 83% accepted. In 1997, 66 master's, 24 doctorates awarded. *Degree requirements:* For master's, thesis or alternative required, foreign language not required; for doctorate, 1 foreign language (computer language can substitute), dissertation. *Entrance requirements:* For master's, GRE General Test (minimum combined score of 750), minimum GPA of 3.0; for doctorate, GRE General Test (minimum combined score of 1000), MS in nursing, minimum GPA of 3.0. Application deadline: rolling. Application fee: $25. *Financial aid:* In 1997–98, 3 research assistantships (2 to first-year students), 5 teaching assistantships (3 to first-year students), 19 graduate traineeships (5 to first-year students) averaging $500 per month were awarded. Financial aid application deadline: 4/1. *Faculty research:* Prevention of battering during pregnancy, teen pregnancy, support and stressors in lower income expectant females, AIDS risk behaviors of street children. • Dr. Carolyn S. Gunning, Dean, 940-898-2401.

Thomas Jefferson University, Program in Nursing, Philadelphia, PA 19107. Awards MS. Accredited by NLN. Part-time programs available. Faculty: 9 full-time (all women). Students: 11 full-time (all women), 57 part-time (54 women); includes 4 minority (1 African American, 1 Asian American, 2 Hispanics), 2 international. 48 applicants, 67% accepted. In 1997, 23 degrees awarded. *Entrance requirements:* GRE or MAT, BSN or equivalent, CPR certification, professional RN license, 1 year of professional experience, previous undergraduate course work in statistics and nursing research. Application deadline: rolling. Application fee: $30. *Tuition:* $18,100 per year full-time, $625 per credit part-time. *Financial aid:* In 1997–98, 3 training grants (all to first-year students) averaging $560 per month were awarded; fellowships, research assistantships, Federal Work-Study, institutionally sponsored loans also available. Aid available to part-time students. Financial aid application deadline: 5/1; applicants required to submit FAFSA. *Faculty research:* Interdisciplinary primary care, women and HIV, health promotion and disease prevention, psychosocial impact of disability. • Dr. Mary Schaal, Graduate Director, 215-503-7937. Fax: 215-503-0376. E-mail: mary.schaal@mail.tju.edu. Application contact: Jessie F. Pervall, Director of Admissions, 215-503-4400. Fax: 215-503-3433. E-mail: cgs-info@mail.tju.edu.

Troy State University, Graduate School, College of Health and Human Services, Program in Nursing, Troy, AL 36082. Awards MS. Accredited by NLN. Part-time and evening/weekend programs available. Students: 21 full-time (20 women), 90 part-time (83 women); includes 51 minority (50 African Americans, 1 Asian American). Average age 30. In 1997, 41 degrees awarded. *Entrance requirements:* Minimum GPA of 2.5. Application deadline: rolling. Applica-

Directory: Nursing—General

Troy State University (continued)

tion fee: $20. Electronic applications accepted. *Expenses:* Tuition $2040 per year full-time, $68 per hour part-time for state residents; $4200 per year full-time, $140 per hour part-time for nonresidents. Fees $240 per year full-time, $27 per quarter (minimum) part-time. *Financial aid:* Available to part-time students. Financial aid applicants required to submit FAFSA. • Application contact: Teresa Rodgers, Director of Graduate Admissions, 334-670-3188. Fax: 334-670-3733. E-mail: trodgers@trojan.troyst.edu.

Uniformed Services University of the Health Sciences, Graduate School of Nursing, Bethesda, MD 20814-4799. Awards MSN. Accredited by NLN. Available to military officers only. Faculty: 15 full-time (10 women), 5 part-time (4 women), 18.3 FTE. Students: 58 full-time (33 women); includes 6 minority (3 African Americans, 1 Asian American, 2 Hispanics). Average age 35. In 1997, 18 degrees awarded (100% found work related to degree). *Degree requirements:* Thesis required, foreign language not required. *Average time to degree:* master's–2 years full-time. *Entrance requirements:* Minimum GPA of 3.0, clinical experience, BSN, previous course work in science. Application deadline: rolling. Application fee: $0. *Tuition:* $0. • Dr. Faye G. Abdellah, Dean, 301-295-1993. E-mail: fabdella@usuhs.mil. Application contact: Bernadette Hoover, Recording Secretary for Admissions Committee, 301-295-9893. Fax: 301-295-9006. E-mail: bhoover@usuhs.mil.

Université de Montréal, Faculty of Nursing, Montréal, PQ H3C 3J7, Canada. Awards M Sc, PhD. PhD offered jointly with McGill University. Part-time programs available. Faculty: 41 full-time (37 women). 91 applicants, 47% accepted. In 1997, 22 master's awarded. *Degree requirements:* For master's, 1 foreign language required, thesis optional; for doctorate, dissertation, general exam. *Entrance requirements:* For master's, proficiency in English and French. Application deadline: 2/1 (priority date; rolling processing). Application fee: $30. *Financial aid:* Fellowships, research assistantships, teaching assistantships, Federal Work-Study, institutionally sponsored loans, and career-related internships or fieldwork available. *Faculty research:* Mental and physical care of chronic patients, care of the hospitalized aged, cancer nursing, home care of caregivers, AIDS patients. • Suzanne Kerouac, Dean, 514-343-6436. Application contact: Nicole Ricard, Assistant to the Dean for Graduate Studies, 514-343-6379.

Université Laval, Faculty of Nursing, Sainte-Foy, PQ G1K 7P4, Canada. Awards M Sc. Students: 14 full-time (13 women), 44 part-time (43 women). Average age 36. 29 applicants, 72% accepted. In 1997, 5 degrees awarded. *Application deadline:* 3/1. *Application fee:* $30. *Expenses:* Tuition $1334 per year (minimum) full-time, $56 per credit (minimum) part-time for Canadian residents; $5966 per year (minimum) full-time, $249 per credit (minimum) part-time for nonresidents. Fees $150 per year full-time, $6.25 per credit part-time. • Linda Lepage, Dean, 418-656-2131 Ext. 2128. Fax: 418-656-7747. E-mail: fsi@fsi.ulaval.ca.

The University of Akron, College of Nursing, Akron, OH 44325-0001. Offers programs in nursing administration (MSN), nursing clinical specialist (MSN), nursing education (MSN). Accredited by NLN. Part-time programs available. Faculty: 19 full-time, 13 part-time. Students: 69 full-time (52 women), 134 part-time (122 women); includes 16 minority (8 African Americans, 5 Hispanics, 3 Native Americans), 1 international. Average age 39. In 1997, 87 degrees awarded. *Degree requirements:* Thesis optional, foreign language not required. *Entrance requirements:* GRE or MAT, minimum GPA of 3.0. Application deadline: 8/15 (rolling processing). Application fee: $25 ($50 for international students). *Expenses:* Tuition $178 per credit hour for state residents; $333 per credit hour for nonresidents. Fees $145 per year full-time, $32 per semester (minimum) part-time. *Financial aid:* In 1997–98, 54 students received aid, including 22 fellowships, 12 research assistantships; teaching assistantships, Federal Work-Study, and career-related internships or fieldwork also available. Financial aid application deadline: 5/15. *Faculty research:* Gerontological nursing, adolescent drug abuse, oncology nursing, neurological nursing, cardiovascular nursing. • Cynthia Capers, Dean, 330-972-7552. Application contact: Dr. Linda Linc, Interim Associate Dean of the Graduate Program, 330-972-7553.

The University of Alabama at Birmingham, Graduate School, School of Nursing, Birmingham, AL 35294. Awards MSN, DSN, MBA/MSN. Accredited by NLN. Students: 150 full-time (130 women), 170 part-time (161 women); includes 66 minority (38 African Americans, 25 Asian Americans, 2 Hispanics, 1 Native American). 116 applicants, 97% accepted. In 1997, 101 master's, 15 doctorates awarded. Terminal master's awarded for partial completion of doctoral program. *Degree requirements:* For master's, thesis or alternative, comprehensive exam required, foreign language not required; for doctorate, dissertation, comprehensive and qualifying exams required, foreign language not required. *Entrance requirements:* For master's, GRE General Test (minimum combined score of 1000), interview; for doctorate, GRE General Test (minimum combined score of 1150), interview. Application deadline: rolling. Application fee: $30 ($60 for international students). Electronic applications accepted. *Expenses:* Tuition $119 per credit hour for state residents; $238 per credit hour for nonresidents. Fees $627 per year (minimum) full-time, $110 per quarter (minimum) part-time. *Financial aid:* In 1997–98, 3 fellowships, 1 research assistantship averaging $438 per month were awarded; Federal Work-Study also available. Aid available to part-time students. • Dr. Rachel Z. Booth, Dean, 205-934-5360.

See in-depth description on page 1445.

The University of Alabama in Huntsville, College of Nursing, Huntsville, AL 35899. Awards MSN. Accredited by NLN. Part-time and evening/weekend programs available. Faculty: 14 full-time (all women), 5 part-time (all women), 15.25 FTE. Students: 97 full-time (85 women), 90 part-time (81 women); includes 18 minority (14 African Americans, 3 Asian Americans, 1 Hispanic). Average age 39. 140 applicants, 56% accepted. In 1997, 57 degrees awarded. *Degree requirements:* Thesis or alternative, oral and written exams required, foreign language not required. *Entrance requirements:* MAT (minimum score 50), Alabama RN license, BSN, minimum GPA of 3.0. Application deadline: 7/24 (priority date; rolling processing; 11/15 for spring admission). Application fee: $20. Electronic applications accepted. *Tuition:* $2886 per year full-time, $540 per semester (minimum) part-time for state residents; $5298 per year full-time, $1098 per semester (minimum) part-time for nonresidents. *Financial aid:* In 1997–98, 41 fellowships (20 to first-year students) averaging $118 per month and totaling $42,215, 6 teaching assistantships (3 to first-year students) averaging $712 per month and totaling $38,448 were awarded; research assistantships, scholarships, full and partial tuition waivers, Federal Work-Study, institutionally sponsored loans, and career-related internships or fieldwork also available. Aid available to part-time students. Financial aid application deadline: 4/1; applicants required to submit FAFSA. *Faculty research:* Home health care, gerontology, pediatric nursing, family nurse practitioner, adult acute care administration. Total annual research expenditures: $8624. • Dr. Fay Raines, Dean, 205-890-6345. E-mail: rainesc@email.uah.edu. Application contact: Mary Beth Magathan, Director of Student Affairs, 205-890-6742. Fax: 205-890-6026. E-mail: magathanm@email.uah.edu.

University of Alaska Anchorage, College of Health, Education and Social Welfare, School of Nursing and Health Science, Anchorage, AK 99508-8060. Awards MS. Accredited by NLN. Part-time programs available. Students: 13 full-time (12 women), 33 part-time (30 women); includes 2 minority (1 Hispanic, 1 Native American). 24 applicants, 58% accepted. In 1997, 27 degrees awarded. *Degree requirements:* Thesis required, foreign language not required. *Entrance requirements:* GRE or MAT, BA in nursing, interview, minimum GPA of 3.0, RN license, 1.5 years of clinical experience. Application deadline: 3/1. Application fee: $45. *Expenses:* Tuition $2988 per year full-time, $1990 per year part-time for state residents; $5814 per year full-time, $3876 per year part-time for nonresidents. Fees $298 per year. *Financial aid:* In 1997–98, 13 graduate traineeships were awarded; Federal Work-Study and career-related internships or fieldwork also available. Aid available to part-time students. Financial aid application deadline: 4/1. • Dr. Tina De Lapp, Interim Director, 907-786-4571. Fax: 907-786-4558. Application contact: Linda Berg Smith, Associate Vice Chancellor for Enrollment Services, 907-786-1529.

University of Alberta, Faculty of Graduate Studies and Research, Faculty of Nursing, Edmonton, AB T6G 2E1, Canada. Awards MN, PhD. Part-time programs available. Students: 55 full-time (53 women), 76 part-time (74 women). 39 applicants, 54% accepted. In 1997, 30 master's awarded (16% continued full-time study); 5 doctorates awarded. *Degree requirements:* For master's, clinical practice required, thesis optional, foreign language not required; for doctorate, dissertation required, foreign language not required. *Average time to degree:* master's–3.2 years full-time, 3.2 years part-time. *Entrance requirements:* For master's, B Sc N, 1 year of experience; for doctorate, MN. Application deadline: 6/30 (priority date; rolling processing). Application fee: $60. *Expenses:* Tuition $390 per course for Canadian residents; $781 per course for nonresidents. Fees $500 per year full-time, $184 per year part-time. *Financial aid:* In 1997–98, 58 students received aid, including 58 fellowships (13 to first-year students) totaling $332,401, 37 research assistantships (9 to first-year students) totaling $38,530, 36 teaching assistantships (8 to first-year students) totaling $61,197, 23 research grants, tuition scholarships (1 to a first-year student) totaling $26,800; institutionally sponsored loans also available. *Faculty research:* Bioethics, perinatal, qualitative research, substance abuse, gerontolgy, social support. • Dr. M. J. Wood, Dean, 403-492-6251. Application contact: Elaine Carswell, Administrative Assistant, 403-492-6251. Fax: 403-492-2551. E-mail: ecarswel@ua-nursing.ualberta.ca.

The University of Arizona, College of Nursing, Tucson, AZ 85721. Awards MS, PhD. Accredited by NLN. Part-time programs available. Terminal master's awarded for partial completion of doctoral program. *Degree requirements:* Computer language, thesis/dissertation required, foreign language not required. *Entrance requirements:* GRE General Test, TOEFL (minimum score 550), Arizona RN license. Application deadline: 4/1 (rolling processing). Application fee: $35. *Tuition:* $2162 per year full-time, $337 per semester (minimum) part-time for state residents; $6860 per year full-time, $1138 per semester (minimum) part-time for nonresidents. *Faculty research:* Gerontological nursing, health promotion strategies, family health, nursing systems, managing chronic illness.

University of Arkansas for Medical Sciences, Graduate School, College of Nursing, 4301 West Markham, Little Rock, AR 72205-7199. Awards MN Sc, PhD. Accredited by NLN. Part-time programs available. Faculty: 41 full-time (36 women). Students: 29 full-time (24 women), 172 part-time (157 women); includes 19 minority (14 African Americans, 4 Asian Americans, 1 Native American), 2 international. In 1997, 52 master's awarded. *Entrance requirements:* For master's, MAT. Application fee: $0. *Tuition:* $3060 per year full-time, $153 per credit hour part-time for state residents; $6560 per year full-time, $328 per credit hour part-time for nonresidents. *Financial aid:* In 1997–98, 13 traineeships were awarded; career-related internships or fieldwork also available. Aid available to part-time students. • Dr. Linda C. Hodges, Dean, 501-686-5374. Application contact: Dr. Patricia E. Thompson, 501-686-5374.

University of British Columbia, Faculty of Applied Science, School of Nursing, Vancouver, BC V6T 1Z2, Canada. Awards MSN, PhD. Part-time programs available. *Degree requirements:* For master's, essay or thesis; for doctorate, dissertation, comprehensive exam. *Average time to degree:* master's–2.5 years full-time, 4.5 years part-time. *Entrance requirements:* For master's, TOEFL, bachelor's degree in nursing; for doctorate, TOEFL, master's degree in nursing. Application deadline: 4/30 (1/30 for spring admission). Application fee: $60. *Faculty research:* Women and children, aging, critical care, cross-cultural.

The University of Calgary, Faculty of Nursing, Calgary, AB T2N 1N4, Canada. Awards MN, PhD. PhD offered in special cases only. Part-time programs available. Faculty: 32 full-time (31 women), 62 part-time (60 women). Students: 32 full-time (all women), 28 part-time (all women). Average age 30. 38 applicants, 55% accepted. In 1997, 19 master's, 1 doctorate awarded. *Degree requirements:* For master's, comprehensive exams (course-based MN) or thesis; for doctorate, dissertation. *Average time to degree:* master's–2 years full-time, 3.5 years part-time; doctorate–2.5 years full-time. *Entrance requirements:* For master's, BN, AARN registration; for doctorate, master's degree, AARN registration. Application deadline: 2/1. Application fee: $60. *Expenses:* Tuition $5448 per year full-time, $908 per course part-time for Canadian residents; $10,896 per year full-time, $1816 per course part-time for nonresidents. Fees $285 per year full-time, $119 per semester (minimum) part-time. *Financial aid:* In 1997–98, 18 teaching assistantships (9 to first-year students) averaging $730 per month and totaling $52,560, 16 scholarships (6 to first-year students) totaling $33,550 were awarded; research assistantships also available. *Faculty research:* Nursing in adult health, family systems nursing, community health, women's health. • Dr. L. Watson, Associate Dean, 403-220-6618. E-mail: lwatson@acs.ucalgary.ca. Application contact: P. Jolly, Graduate Administrator, 403-220-6241. Fax: 403-284-4803. E-mail: pjolly@acs.ucalgary.ca.

University of California, Los Angeles, School of Nursing, Los Angeles, CA 90095. Awards MSN, PhD, MBA/MSN, MD/PhD. Accredited by NLN. Faculty: 22 (all women). Students: 268 full-time (254 women); includes 104 minority (14 African Americans, 60 Asian Americans, 24 Hispanics, 6 Native Americans), 8 international. 235 applicants, 63% accepted. *Degree requirements:* For master's, comprehensive exam required, foreign language not required; for doctorate, dissertation, oral and written qualifying exams required, foreign language not required. *Entrance requirements:* For master's, Commission on Graduates of Foreign Nursing School Exam, TOEFL, minimum GPA of 3.0; for doctorate, GRE General Test, Commissions on Graduates of Foreign Nursing School exam, minimum undergraduate GPA of 3.0. Application deadline: 2/1. Application fee: $40. Electronic applications accepted. *Expenses:* Tuition $0 for state residents; $9384 per year for nonresidents. Fees $4551 per year. *Financial aid:* In 1997–98, 217 students received aid, including fellowships totaling $142,044, research assistantships totaling $7,717, teaching assistantships totaling $44,916, federal fellowships and scholarships totaling $270,347; full and partial tuition waivers, Federal Work-Study, institutionally sponsored loans also available. Financial aid application deadline: 3/1. *Faculty research:* AIDS, adolescents, gerontology, homeless, activity/mobility. • Donna Vredevoe, Acting Dean, 310-825-7181. Application contact: Departmental Office, 310-825-7181. E-mail: sonsaff@sonnet.ucla.edu.

University of California, San Francisco, School of Nursing, Program in Nursing, San Francisco, CA 94143. Awards MS, PhD. Accredited by NLN. Faculty: 76. Students: 564 full-time (512 women); includes 107 minority (20 African Americans, 50 Asian Americans, 31 Hispanics, 6 Native Americans), 23 international. 754 applicants, 34% accepted. In 1997, 191 master's, 14 doctorates awarded. *Degree requirements:* For master's, thesis or alternative, comprehensive exam; for doctorate, dissertation. *Entrance requirements:* GRE General Test. Application deadline: 3/1. Application fee: $40. *Expenses:* Tuition $0 for state residents; $9384 per year for nonresidents. Fees $6294 per year. *Financial aid:* Fellowships, Federal Work-Study available. Aid available to part-time students. Financial aid application deadline: 1/10. • Application contact: Jeff Kilmer, Director, Office of Student and Curricular Affairs, 415-476-1435.

University of Central Arkansas, College of Health and Applied Sciences, Department of Nursing, Conway, AR 72035-0001. Awards MSN. Accredited by NLN. Faculty: 7 full-time (all women), 2 part-time (both women), 7.66 FTE. Students: 9 full-time (8 women), 34 part-time (31 women); includes 5 minority (all African Americans). 14 applicants, 79% accepted. In 1997, 14 degrees awarded. *Degree requirements:* Comprehensive exam required, thesis optional, foreign language not required. *Entrance requirements:* GRE General Test, minimum GPA of 2.7. Application deadline: 3/1 (priority date; rolling processing; 10/1 for spring admission). Application fee: $15 ($40 for international students). *Expenses:* Tuition $161 per credit hour for state residents; $298 per credit hour for nonresidents. Fees $150 per year. *Financial aid:* In 1997–98, 2 assistantships were awarded; Federal Work-Study also available. Financial aid application deadline: 2/15. • Dr. Barbara Williams, Chairperson, 501-450-3119. Fax: 501-450-5503. E-mail: barbaraw@mail.uca.edu.

University of Central Florida, College of Health and Public Affairs, Program in Nursing, Orlando, FL 32816. Awards MSN. Faculty: 20. Students: 54 full-time (51 women), 5 part-time (all women); includes 10 minority (1 African American, 5 Asian Americans, 4 Hispanics). Average age 39. 43 applicants, 63% accepted. In 1997, 24 degrees awarded. *Entrance requirements:* GRE General Test. Application deadline: 2/15. Application fee: $20. *Expenses:* Tuition $3288 per year full-time, $137 per credit hour part-time for state residents; $11,520 per year full-time, $480 per credit hour part-time for nonresidents. Fees $105 per year. • E.

Stullenbarger, Chair, 407-823-2744. E-mail: stullenbarger@pegasus.cc.ucf.edu. Application contact: Dr. Mary Lou Sole, Coordinator, 407-823-5133. E-mail: mnoll@pegasus.cc.ucf.edu.

University of Cincinnati, College of Nursing and Health, Cincinnati, OH 45221-0038. Awards MSN, PhD, MBA/MSN. Programs in adult health nursing (MSN), community health nursing (MSN), nurse anesthesia (MSN), nurse midwifery (MSN), nurse practitioner studies (MSN), nursing (PhD), nursing administration (MSN), parent/child nursing (MSN), psychiatric nursing (MSN). Part-time programs available. Faculty: 26 full-time. Students: 138 full-time (121 women), 170 part-time (162 women); includes 23 minority (16 African Americans, 4 Asian Americans, 2 Hispanics, 1 Native American), 5 international. Average age 28. 175 applicants, 69% accepted. In 1997, 86 master's, 7 doctorates awarded. *Degree requirements:* For master's, project or thesis required, foreign language not required; for doctorate, variable foreign language requirement, computer language, dissertation, comprehensive exam. *Average time to degree:* master's–1.5 years full-time, 2.5 years part-time; doctorate–4 years full-time, 6 years part-time. *Entrance requirements:* GRE General Test. Application deadline: 1/1 (priority date; rolling processing). Application fee: $30. *Tuition:* $7228 per year full-time, $185 per credit hour part-time for state residents; $13,812 per year full-time, $352 per credit hour part-time for nonresidents. *Financial aid:* Fellowships, research assistantships, teaching assistantships, full and partial tuition waivers available. Aid available to part-time students. Financial aid application deadline: 5/1. *Faculty research:* Alcohol/trauma, fetal alcohol syndrome, work redesign, cardiovascular science. Total annual research expenditures: $1.2 million. • Dr. Andrea Lindell, Dean, 513-558-5330. Application contact: Tom West, Program Coordinator, 513-558-3600. Fax: 513-558-7523. E-mail: tom.west@uc.edu.

University of Colorado at Colorado Springs, Department of Graduate Nursing, Colorado Springs, CO 80933-7150. Offers programs in adult health nurse practitioner and clinical specialist (MSN); family practitioner (MSN), including community clinical specialist, forensic clinical specialist, holistic clinical specialist; neonatal nurse practitioner and clinical specialist (MSN). Accredited by NLN. Part-time programs available. Postbaccalaureate distance learning degree programs offered (minimal on-campus study). Faculty: 9 full-time (8 women). Students: 38 full-time (33 women), 50 part-time (47 women); includes 4 minority (1 African American, 1 Asian American, 2 Hispanics). Average age 47. 9 applicants, 100% accepted. In 1997, 9 degrees awarded (100% found work related to degree). *Degree requirements:* Thesis optional, foreign language not required. *Average time to degree:* master's–2.5 years full-time, 5 years part-time. *Entrance requirements:* GRE General Test (minimum combined score of 1400) or MAT (minimum score 50), BSN, GPA of 3.0. Application deadline: 2/15 (priority date; 10/15 for spring admission). Application fee: $40. Electronic applications accepted. *Expenses:* Tuition $4644 per year full-time, $193 per credit hour part-time for state residents; $10,254 per year full-time, $420 per credit hour part-time for nonresidents. Fees $399 per year (minimum) full-time, $106 per year (minimum) part-time. *Financial aid:* In 1997–98, 22 fellowships totaling $22,000 were awarded; Federal Work-Study, institutionally sponsored loans, and career-related internships or fieldwork also available. Aid available to part-time students. *Faculty research:* Women's health, uncertainty, empowerment, family experience in chronic illness. • Barbara Joyce-Nagata, Chair, 719-262-4430. Fax: 719-262-4416.

University of Colorado Health Sciences Center, School of Nursing, Program in Nursing, Denver, CO 80262. Awards ND. Part-time programs available. Students: 93 full-time (84 women), 3 part-time (all women); includes 7 minority (3 Asian Americans, 3 Hispanics, 1 Native American). Average age 31. 62 applicants, 61% accepted. In 1997, 12 degrees awarded. *Application fee:* $40. *Financial aid:* Fellowships, research assistantships, teaching assistantships, Federal Work-Study, institutionally sponsored loans, and career-related internships or fieldwork available. Aid available to part-time students. Financial aid application deadline: 3/15. • Application contact: Office of Admissions, 303-315-5592.

University of Colorado Health Sciences Center, School of Nursing, Programs in Nursing, Denver, CO 80262. Awards MS, PhD. Accredited by NLN. Offered through Graduate School. Students: 212 full-time (206 women), 42 part-time (41 women); includes 12 minority (3 African Americans, 4 Asian Americans, 4 Hispanics, 1 Native American), 5 international. Average age 40. 192 applicants, 57% accepted. In 1997, 98 master's, 18 doctorates awarded. *Degree requirements:* For doctorate, dissertation required, foreign language not required. *Entrance requirements:* For master's, GRE General Test (minimum combined score of 900), minimum GPA of 2.75. Application deadline: 12/1. Application fee: $30. *Financial aid:* Federal Work-Study, institutionally sponsored loans, and career-related internships or fieldwork available. Aid available to part-time students. Financial aid application deadline: 3/15. • Dr. Marlaine Smith, Co-Director. Application contact: Mary Lepley, Director of Admissions, 303-315-5592.

Announcement: MS options: nurse practitioner studies (adult, gerontological, family, pediatric, women's health), clinical specialist studies (adult health, oncology, critical care, community health, school nursing, psychiatric mental health), nursing administration (including dual MBA), nurse midwifery, PhD focus: nursing theory and research. Requirements: MS: undergraduate GPA 2.75; PhD: postbaccalaureate GPA 3.5. MS and PhD require GRE. Center for Nursing Research. NLN accredited.

University of Connecticut, School of Nursing, Storrs, CT 06269. Offers programs in nurse education (MS), nursing (PhD), nursing management (MS). Accredited by NLN. Faculty: 26. Students: 48 full-time (46 women), 93 part-time (86 women); includes 9 minority (4 African Americans, 3 Hispanics, 2 Native Americans), 3 international. Average age 38. 71 applicants, 73% accepted. In 1997, 67 master's awarded. *Entrance requirements:* For master's, TOEFL. Application deadline: 4/1 (priority date; rolling processing; 11/1 for spring admission). Application fee: $40 ($45 for international students). *Expenses:* Tuition $5272 per year full-time, $293 per credit part-time for state residents; $13,696 per year full-time, $761 per credit part-time for nonresidents. Fees $948 per year full-time, $640 per year part-time. *Financial aid:* In 1997–98, 5 fellowships totaling $20,000, 5 research assistantships (4 to first-year students) totaling $32,725, 8 teaching assistantships (2 to first-year students) totaling $39,319 were awarded. Financial aid application deadline: 2/15. • Barbara K. Redman, Dean, 860-486-3716. Application contact: Jane E. Murdock, Chairperson, 860-486-3821.

University of Delaware, College of Health and Nursing Sciences, Department of Nursing, Newark, DE 19716. Offers programs in cardiopulmonary (MSN, Certificate); clinical nurse specialist (MSN, Certificate); clinical nurse specialist/nurse practitioner (Certificate), including cardiopulmonary, gerontology, oncology/immune deficiency, pediatrics, women's health; family nurse practitioner (MSN, Certificate); gerontology (MSN, Certificate); nursing (MSN); nursing administration (MSN, Certificate); oncology/immune deficiency (MSN, Certificate); pediatrics (MSN, Certificate); women's health (MSN, Certificate). One or more programs accredited by NLN. Part-time and evening/weekend programs available. Faculty: 10 full-time (9 women), 5 part-time (all women), 12.25 FTE. Students: 16 full-time (14 women), 107 part-time (105 women); includes 3 African Americans, 2 Asian Americans, 3 Hispanics. Average age 30. 50 applicants, 92% accepted. In 1997, 27 master's awarded. *Degree requirements:* For master's, thesis optional, foreign language not required. *Average time to degree:* master's–2 years full-time, 3 years part-time. *Entrance requirements:* For master's, GRE General Test. Application deadline: 7/1. Application fee: $45. *Expenses:* Tuition $4250 per year full-time, $236 per credit hour part-time for state residents; $12,250 per year full-time, $681 per credit hour part-time for nonresidents. Fees $466 per year full-time, $15 per semester (minimum) part-time. *Financial aid:* In 1997–98, 19 students received aid, including 16 fellowships (9 to first-year students), 3 teaching assistantships (2 to first-year students), 1 tuition scholarship (to a first-year student); institutionally sponsored loans also available. Aid available to part-time students. *Faculty research:* Pediatric restraint use, killer cell activity in breast cancer, smoking and pregnancy, body image and cancer. • Application contact: Betty Bonavita, Graduate Secretary, 302-831-1255. Fax: 302-831-2382. E-mail: elizabeth.bonavita@mvs.udel.edu.

University of Evansville, Graduate Programs, Department of Nursing, Program in Nursing, Evansville, IN 47722-0002. Awards MS. Accredited by NLN. Faculty: 1 (woman) full-time, 1 (woman) part-time. Students: 8 part-time (all women). Average age 30. *Entrance requirements:* GRE General Test. Application deadline: 7/1. Application fee: $20. *Expenses:* Tuition $395 per credit hour. Fees $30 per year. *Financial aid:* Application deadline 7/1. • Dr. Rita Behnke, Director, Department of Nursing, 812-479-2550.

University of Florida, College of Nursing, Gainesville, FL 32611. Awards MS Nsg, PhD. Accredited by NLN. Part-time programs available. Faculty: 35. Students: 53 full-time (45 women), 211 part-time (199 women); includes 26 minority (11 African Americans, 3 Asian Americans, 9 Hispanics, 3 Native Americans), 2 international. 160 applicants, 61% accepted. In 1997, 128 master's, 6 doctorates awarded. *Degree requirements:* For master's, thesis required, foreign language not required; for doctorate, dissertation. *Entrance requirements:* GRE General Test, minimum GPA of 3.0. Application deadline: 3/1 (priority date; rolling processing). Application fee: $20. *Tuition:* $138 per credit hour for state residents; $481 per credit hour for nonresidents. *Financial aid:* Fellowships, research assistantships, teaching assistantships, Federal Work-Study, and career-related internships or fieldwork available. Aid available to part-time students. *Faculty research:* Health care systems, wellness in the elderly, high risk behavior, women's health. • Dr. Kathleen Long, Dean, 352-392-3752. E-mail: kal.vpha@mail.health.ufl.edu. Application contact: Dr. Myrna Courage, Graduate Coordinator, 352-392-4366. Fax: 352-392-8100. E-mail: couramm.ufcon@shands.ufl.edu.

University of Hartford, College of Education, Nursing, and Health Professions, Program in Nursing, West Hartford, CT 06117-1599. Awards MSN, MSN/MSOB. Accredited by NLN. Part-time and evening/weekend programs available. Faculty: 6 full-time (all women). Students: 1 full-time (0 women), 121 part-time (120 women); includes 3 minority (2 African Americans, 1 Native American), 1 international. Average age 41. 47 applicants, 94% accepted. In 1997, 18 degrees awarded. *Degree requirements:* Research project required, foreign language and thesis not required. *Entrance requirements:* BSN, Connecticut RN license. Application deadline: 4/30 (priority date; rolling processing). Application fee: $40 ($55 for international students). Electronic applications accepted. *Financial aid:* Federal Work-Study available. Aid available to part-time students. Financial aid application deadline: 6/1; applicants required to submit FAFSA. *Faculty research:* Child development, women in doctoral study, applying feminist theory in teaching methods, near death experience, grandmothers as primary care providers. • Dr. Barbara Witt, Director, 860-768-4214. Application contact: Marlene Hall, Counselor, 860-768-4213. E-mail: galvin@mail.hartford.edu.

University of Hawaii at Manoa, College of Health Sciences and Social Welfare, School of Nursing, Honolulu, HI 96822. Offers programs in clinical nurse specialist (MS), including adult health, community mental health; nurse practitioner (MS), including adult health, community mental health, family nurse practitioner; nursing (Certificate); nursing administration (MS). One or more programs accredited by NLN. Faculty: 27 full-time (24 women). Students: 47 full-time (46 women), 62 part-time (52 women); includes 36 minority (1 African American, 34 Asian Americans, 1 Hispanic), 3 international. *Entrance requirements:* For master's, Hawaii RN license. *Tuition:* $4029 per year full-time, $214 per credit hour part-time for state residents; $9957 per year full-time, $461 per credit hour part-time for nonresidents. • Dr. Rosanne Harrigan, Dean, 808-956-8522. Application contact: Office of Student Services, 808-956-8939.

University of Illinois at Chicago, College of Nursing, Chicago, IL 60607-7128. Awards MS, PhD, MBA/MS, MPH/MS. One or more programs accredited by NLN. Part-time programs available. Faculty: 63 full-time (61 women), 9 part-time (8 women). Students: 81 full-time (75 women), 395 part-time (383 women); includes 71 minority (34 African Americans, 30 Asian Americans, 5 Hispanics, 2 Native Americans), 21 international. Average age 37. 277 applicants, 58% accepted. In 1997, 113 master's, 24 doctorates awarded. *Degree requirements:* For master's, thesis or alternative required, foreign language not required; for doctorate, dissertation required, foreign language not required. *Entrance requirements:* GRE General Test, TOEFL (minimum score 550), minimum GPA of 3.75 on a 5.0 scale. Application deadline: 5/15 (10/15 for spring admission). Application fee: $40 ($50 for international students). *Financial aid:* Fellowships, research assistantships, teaching assistantships, partial tuition waivers, Federal Work-Study, institutionally sponsored loans, and career-related internships or fieldwork available. • Dr. Kathleen Potempa, Dean, 312-996-7800. Application contact: Kathleen Knafl, Director of Graduate Studies, 312-996-2159.

The University of Iowa, College of Nursing, Iowa City, IA 52242-1316. Awards MSN, PhD, MBA/MSN. One or more programs accredited by NLN. Faculty: 39 full-time, 5 part-time. Students: 61 full-time (58 women), 154 part-time (147 women); includes 8 minority (2 African Americans, 3 Asian Americans, 1 Hispanic, 2 Native Americans), 11 international. 71 applicants, 59% accepted. In 1997, 53 master's, 6 doctorates awarded. *Degree requirements:* For master's, thesis optional; for doctorate, dissertation, comprehensive exam. *Entrance requirements:* GRE General Test. Application fee: $30 ($50 for international students). *Expenses:* Tuition $3166 per year full-time, $176 per semester hour part-time for state residents; $10,202 per year full-time, $176 per semester hour part-time for nonresidents. Fees $202 per year full-time, $52 per year (minimum) part-time. *Financial aid:* In 1997–98, 19 fellowships (7 to first-year students), 9 research assistantships (3 to first-year students), 16 teaching assistantships (4 to first-year students) were awarded. Financial aid applicants required to submit FAFSA. • Melanie Dreher, Dean, 319-335-7018. Fax: 319-335-9990.

University of Kansas, School of Nursing, Kansas City, KS 66160. Awards MS, PhD. One or more programs accredited by NLN. Part-time programs available. Postbaccalaureate distance learning degree programs offered (minimal on-campus study). Faculty: 34 full-time (all women), 7 part-time (all women). Students: 49 full-time (45 women), 118 part-time (111 women); includes 16 minority (5 African Americans, 6 Asian Americans, 3 Hispanics, 2 Native Americans), 2 international. Average age 39. 24 applicants, 96% accepted. In 1997, 85 master's, 3 doctorates awarded. Terminal master's awarded for partial completion of doctoral program. *Degree requirements:* For master's, general oral exam required, foreign language and thesis not required; for doctorate, variable foreign language requirement, dissertation, comprehensive oral and written exam. *Entrance requirements:* For master's, GRE General Test, TOEFL (minimum score 570), bachelor's degree in nursing, minimum GPA of 3.0, RN license, 1 year of clinical experience; for doctorate, GRE General Test, TOEFL (minimum score 570), master's degree in nursing, minimum GPA of 3.5. Application deadline: 4/1 (9/1 for spring admission). Application fee: $25. *Expenses:* Tuition $2400 per year full-time, $100 per credit hour part-time for state residents; $7890 per year full-time, $329 per credit hour part-time for nonresidents. Fees $428 per year full-time, $31 per credit hour part-time. *Financial aid:* 35 students received aid; research assistantships, teaching assistantships, traineeships, Federal Work-Study, institutionally sponsored loans, and career-related internships or fieldwork available. Aid available to part-time students. Financial aid application deadline: 4/3; applicants required to submit FAFSA. • Dr. Karen Miller, Dean, 913-588-1619. Application contact: Dr. Rita Clifford, Associate Dean, Student Affairs, 913-588-1619. Fax: 913-588-1615. E-mail: soninfo@kumc.edu.

University of Kentucky, College of Nursing, Doctoral Program in Nursing, Lexington, KY 40506-0032. Awards PhD. 10 applicants, 60% accepted. In 1997, 1 degree awarded. *Degree requirements:* Dissertation, exam required, foreign language not required. *Entrance requirements:* GRE General Test, minimum graduate GPA of 3.0. Application deadline: 2/15 (rolling processing; 11/15 for spring admission). Application fee: $30 ($35 for international students). *Financial aid:* Application deadline 3/1. • Dr. Lynne Hall, Director of Graduate Studies, 606-323-8076. Application contact: Dr. Constance L. Wood, Associate Dean, 606-257-4613. Fax: 606-323-1928.

See in-depth description on page 1447.

University of Kentucky, College of Nursing, Master's Program in Nursing, Lexington, KY 40506-0032. Awards MSN. Accredited by NLN. 73 applicants, 56% accepted. In 1997, 65 degrees awarded. *Degree requirements:* Comprehensive exam, research project required, thesis optional, foreign language not required. *Entrance requirements:* GRE General Test, minimum undergraduate GPA of 2.5. Application deadline: 7/1 (rolling processing; 11/15 for spring admission). Application fee: $30 ($35 for international students). *Financial aid:* Fellowships, research assistantships, teaching assistantships, Federal Work-Study, institutionally

Directory: Nursing—General

University of Kentucky (continued)

sponsored loans available. Aid available to part-time students. Financial aid application deadline: 3/1. *Faculty research:* Women's and children's health, health services research, injury prevention, coping with acute and chronic illness, health promotion. Total annual research expenditures: $318,100. • Dr. Juliann Sebastian, Director of Graduate Studies, 606-323-6685. Application contact: Dr. Constance L. Wood, Associate Dean, 606-257-4613. Fax: 606-323-1928.

See in-depth description on page 1447.

University of Louisville, School of Nursing, Louisville, KY 40292-0001. Awards MSN. Accredited by NLN. Part-time programs available. Faculty: 19 full-time (all women), 17 part-time (all women), 25 FTE. Students: 7 full-time (all women), 73 part-time (67 women); includes 8 minority (5 African Americans, 2 Asian Americans, 1 Hispanic). Average age 37. In 1997, 110 degrees awarded. *Degree requirements:* Thesis (for some programs). *Entrance requirements:* GRE General Test. Application deadline: rolling. Application fee: $25. • Dr. Mary H. Mundt, Dean, 502-852-5366.

University of Maine, College of Business, Public Policy and Health, School of Nursing, Orono, ME 04469. Awards MS, CAS. One or more programs accredited by NLN. Faculty: 4. Students: 8 (7 women). *Entrance requirements:* For master's, GRE General Test, TOEFL (minimum score 550). Application deadline: 2/1 (priority date; rolling processing; 10/15 for spring admission). Application fee: $50. *Expenses:* Tuition $194 per credit hour for state residents; $548 per credit hour for nonresidents. Fees $378 per year full-time, $33 per semester (minimum) part-time. *Financial aid:* Full and partial tuition waivers, Federal Work-Study, institutionally sponsored loans, and career-related internships or fieldwork available. Aid available to part-time students. Financial aid application deadline: 3/1. • Dr. Therese Shipps, Interim Director, 207-581-2592. Fax: 207-581-2585. Application contact: Scott Delcourt, Director of the Graduate School, 207-581-3218. Fax: 207-581-3232. E-mail: graduate@maine.edu.

University of Manitoba, Faculty of Nursing, Winnipeg, MB R3T 2N2, Canada. Awards MN. *Degree requirements:* Thesis. *Application deadline:* 3/1.

University of Mary, Division of Nursing, 7500 University Drive, Bismarck, ND 58504-9652. Offers programs in family nurse practitioner (MSN), nursing administration (MSN), nursing education (MSN). Accredited by NLN. Part-time programs available. Faculty: 10 full-time (9 women). Students: 24 full-time (22 women), 22 part-time (20 women); includes 3 minority (2 Asian Americans, 1 Native American). Average age 30. 25 applicants, 56% accepted. In 1997, 12 degrees awarded. *Degree requirements:* Thesis (for some programs), internship (family nurse practitioner) required, foreign language not required. *Average time to degree:* master's–2.5 years full-time, 4 years part-time. *Entrance requirements:* Minimum GPA of 3.0 in nursing course work. Application fee: $15. *Tuition:* $265 per credit. *Financial aid:* In 1997–98, 7 fellowships (5 to first-year students), 2 teaching assistantships (both to first-year students) were awarded; institutionally sponsored loans also available. Aid available to part-time students. Financial aid application deadline: 7/1. *Faculty research:* Gerontology issues, rural nursing, health policy, primary care, health care financing. • Dr. Betty Rembur, Chair, 701-255-7500 Ext. 470. Application contact: Dr. Diane Fladeland, Director, Graduate Programs, 701-255-7500. Fax: 701-255-7687.

University of Maryland, Baltimore, Graduate School, School of Nursing, Baltimore, MD 21201-1627. Awards MS, PhD, MS/MBA. Programs in community health nursing (MS); gerontological nursing (MS); maternal-child nursing (MS); medical-surgical nursing (MS); nursing (PhD), including direct nursing, indirect nursing; nursing administration (MS); nursing education (MS); nursing health policy (MS); primary care nursing (MS); psychiatric nursing (MS). One or more programs accredited by NLN. MS/MBA offered jointly with the University of Baltimore. Part-time programs available. Faculty: 49 (45 women). Students: 148 full-time (135 women), 498 part-time (469 women); includes 74 minority (47 African Americans, 17 Asian Americans, 7 Hispanics, 3 Native Americans), 28 international. Average age 33. 287 applicants, 69% accepted. In 1997, 204 master's, 19 doctorates awarded. *Degree requirements:* For master's, thesis or alternative required, foreign language not required; for doctorate, dissertation required, foreign language not required. *Entrance requirements:* For master's, GRE General Test, TOEFL, minimum GPA of 2.75, previous course work in statistics, BS in nursing; for doctorate, GRE General Test, TOEFL, minimum GPA of 3.0, MS in nursing. Application fee: $42. *Expenses:* Tuition $253 per credit hour for state residents; $454 per credit hour for nonresidents. Fees $317 per year. *Financial aid:* Fellowships, research assistantships, teaching assistantships, nurse traineeships, and career-related internships or fieldwork available. Aid available to part-time students. Financial aid application deadline: 2/15. • Dr. Barbara Heller, Dean, 410-706-6741. Application contact: Dr. Susan Wozenski, Assistant Dean for Student Affairs, 410-706-0501. Fax: 410-706-7238.

University of Massachusetts Amherst, School of Nursing, Amherst, MA 01003-0001. Awards MS, PhD. One or more programs accredited by NLN. Part-time programs available. Faculty: 16 full-time (all women). Students: 37 full-time (36 women), 77 part-time (70 women); includes 2 minority (1 Asian American, 1 Hispanic), 1 international. Average age 39. 56 applicants, 75% accepted. In 1997, 52 master's, 3 doctorates awarded. *Degree requirements:* For master's, thesis optional, foreign language not required; for doctorate, dissertation. *Entrance requirements:* For master's, GRE General Test, minimum GPA of 3.0, previous course work in statistics and physical assessment, interview. Application deadline: 3/1 (priority date; rolling processing; 10/1 for spring admission). Application fee: $40. *Expenses:* Tuition $2640 per year full-time, $110 per credit part-time for state residents; $3690 per year (minimum) full-time, $165 per credit (minimum) part-time for nonresidents. Fees $2856 per year full-time, $422 per semester part-time for state residents; $3204 per year full-time, $480 per semester part-time for nonresidents. *Financial aid:* In 1997–98, 63 fellowships, 1 research assistantship, 26 teaching assistantships were awarded; full tuition waivers, Federal Work-Study also available. Aid available to part-time students. Financial aid application deadline: 3/1. *Faculty research:* Health of older adults and their caretakers, mental health of individuals and families, health of children and adolescents, power and decision making, transcultural health. • Dr. Brenda Millette, Dean, 413-545-5092. Fax: 413-545-0086.

University of Massachusetts Boston, College of Nursing, Boston, MA 02125-3393. Awards MS, PhD, MS/MBA. One or more programs accredited by NLN. Part-time and evening/weekend programs available. Students: 44 full-time (40 women), 91 part-time (83 women); includes 11 minority (6 African Americans, 4 Asian Americans, 1 Hispanic). 110 applicants, 60% accepted. In 1997, 44 master's awarded. *Degree requirements:* For master's, comprehensive exams required, foreign language not required; for doctorate, dissertation, comprehensive exams required, foreign language not required. *Entrance requirements:* For master's, GRE General Test, minimum GPA of 2.75; for doctorate, GRE General Test, master's degree, minimum GPA of 3.3. Application deadline: 3/1 (priority date; 11/1 for spring admission). Application fee: $25 ($35 for international students). *Expenses:* Tuition $2640 per year full-time, $110 per credit part-time for state residents; $8930 per year full-time, $373 per credit part-time for nonresidents. Fees $2650 per year full-time, $420 per semester (minimum) part-time for state residents; $2736 per year full-time, $420 per semester (minimum) part-time for nonresidents. *Financial aid:* In 1997–98, 1 research assistantship averaging $225 per month, 13 teaching assistantships (6 to first-year students) averaging $225 per month and totaling $18,000 were awarded; administrative assistantships also available. Financial aid application deadline: 3/1; applicants required to submit FAFSA. • Dr. Brenda Cherry, Dean, 617-287-7500. Application contact: Lisa Lavely, Director of Graduate Admissions and Records, 617-287-6400. Fax: 617-287-6236.

University of Massachusetts Dartmouth, Graduate School, College of Nursing, North Dartmouth, MA 02747-2300. Awards MS. Accredited by NLN. Faculty: 18 full-time (all women). Students: 3 full-time (all women), 77 part-time (72 women); includes 4 minority (2 African Americans, 2 Hispanics). 39 applicants, 67% accepted. In 1997, 26 degrees awarded. *Degree requirements:* Thesis required, foreign language not required. *Entrance requirements:* GRE General Test, BSN, minimum undergraduate GPA of 3.0. Application deadline: 4/20 (priority date; rolling processing; 11/15 for spring admission). Application fee: $40. *Expenses:* Tuition $2950 per year full-time, $82 per credit part-time for state residents; $10,249 per year full-time, $285 per credit part-time for nonresidents. Fees $5002 per year full-time, $143 per credit part-time for state residents; $6830 per year full-time, $194 per credit part-time for nonresidents. *Financial aid:* In 1997–98, 1 research assistantship totaling $3,000, 6 teaching assistantships totaling $17,000, 1 graduate assistantship totaling $5,176 were awarded; Federal Work-Study also available. Aid available to part-time students. Financial aid application deadline: 3/15; applicants required to submit FAFSA. • Dr. Elisabeth Pennington, Dean, 508-999-8556. Fax: 508-999-9127. Application contact: Carol A. Novo, Graduate Admissions Office, 508-999-8604. Fax: 508-999-8375. E-mail: graduate@umassd.edu.

University of Massachusetts Lowell, College of Health Professions, Department of Nursing, 1 University Avenue, Lowell, MA 01854-2881. Offers programs in administration of nursing services (PhD), including health promotion; family and community health nursing (MS); gerontological nursing (MS); occupational health nursing (MS), including adult psychiatric nursing, occupational health nursing. One or more programs accredited by NLN. Faculty: 15 full-time (all women). Students: 43 full-time (41 women), 78 part-time (75 women); includes 3 minority (2 African Americans, 1 Asian American), 1 international. Average age 30. 118 applicants, 65% accepted. In 1997, 40 master's awarded. *Degree requirements:* For master's, thesis optional, foreign language not required; for doctorate, dissertation. *Entrance requirements:* GRE General Test. Application deadline: 4/1 (priority date; rolling processing; 10/1 for spring admission). Application fee: $20 ($35 for international students). *Tuition:* $4867 per year full-time, $618 per semester (minimum) part-time for state residents; $10,276 per year full-time, $1294 per semester (minimum) part-time for nonresidents. *Financial aid:* In 1997–98, 37 fellowships, 10 teaching assistantships were awarded; Federal Work-Study, institutionally sponsored loans, and career-related internships or fieldwork also available. Financial aid application deadline: 4/1. *Faculty research:* Gerontology, women's health issues, long-term care, alcoholism, health promotion. • Dr. May Futrell, Chair, 978-934-4467. E-mail: may_futrell@woods.uml.edu.

University of Massachusetts Medical Center at Worcester, Graduate School of Nursing, Worcester, MA 01655-0115. Offers programs in adult acute/critical care (MS, Certificate), adult ambulatory/community care (MS, Certificate), adult nurse practitioner (MS), nursing (PhD). One or more programs accredited by NLN. Part-time programs available. Faculty: 6 full-time (5 women), 4 part-time (all women), 8 FTE. Students: 22 full-time (all women), 61 part-time (57 women); includes 2 minority (1 African American, 1 Asian American), 1 international. Average age 40. 66 applicants, 61% accepted. In 1997, 30 master's, 3 doctorates, 17 Certificates awarded. *Degree requirements:* For doctorate, dissertation. *Average time to degree:* master's–2 years part-time; doctorate–3 years full-time; other advanced degree–1 year full-time. *Entrance requirements:* For master's, GRE General Test, BSN, previous course work in statistics; for Certificate, master's degree. Application deadline: 3/15 (rolling processing). Application fee: $18 ($25 for international students). *Financial aid:* In 1997–98, 36 traineeships were awarded; research assistantships, teaching assistantships, Federal Work-Study, and career-related internships or fieldwork also available. Financial aid application deadline: 3/23; applicants required to submit FAFSA. *Faculty research:* HIV among chronically ill, management of health services, stress management and coping, treatment of delirium in cardiac care patients. • Dr. Lillian R. Goodman, Dean, 508-856-5801. E-mail: lillian.goodman@banyan.ummed.edu. Application contact: Kathleen Trumpaitis, Student Coordinator, 508-856-5801. Fax: 508-856-6552. E-mail: kathleen.trumpaitis@banyan.ummed.edu.

University of Medicine and Dentistry of New Jersey, School of Nursing, Newark, NJ 07107-3001. Offers programs in nursing (MSN, PMC), nursing informatics (MSN). One or more programs accredited by NLN. MSN (nursing informatics) offered jointly with New Jersey Institute of Technology. Part-time programs available. Faculty: 30 full-time (28 women), 6 part-time (all women), 32.6 FTE. Students: 41 full-time (38 women), 118 part-time (107 women); includes 40 minority (17 African Americans, 16 Asian Americans, 7 Hispanics). 101 applicants, 64% accepted. In 1997, 44 master's, 7 PMCs awarded. *Entrance requirements:* For master's, GRE, TOEFL, RN license; basic life support, statistics, and health assessment experience. Application deadline: 5/15 (rolling processing; 10/15 for spring admission). Application fee: $30. *Financial aid:* Teaching assistantships, academic scholarships, institutionally sponsored loans available. Aid available to part-time students. *Faculty research:* HIV/AIDS, diabetes education, learned helplessness, nursing science, psychoeducation. • Dr. Frances W. Quinless, Dean, 973-972-4322. Fax: 973-972-3225. Application contact: Peter R. Falk, Manager, Enrollment and Student Services, 973-972-5447. Fax: 973-972-7453.

University of Miami, School of Nursing, Coral Gables, FL 33124. Offers programs in nursing (PhD); primary health care (MSN), including adult nurse practitioner, family nurse practitioner, nurse midwifery. Accredited by NLN. Part-time programs available. Faculty: 28 full-time (27 women), 1 (woman) part-time. Students: 40 full-time (38 women), 64 part-time (61 women); includes 33 minority (16 African Americans, 1 Asian American, 16 Hispanics), 4 international. Average age 36. 42 applicants, 52% accepted. In 1997, 21 master's awarded (5% entered university research/teaching, 90% found other work related to degree, 5% continued full-time study); 7 doctorates awarded (71% entered university research/teaching, 29% found other work related to degree). *Degree requirements:* For master's, thesis optional, foreign language not required; for doctorate, dissertation required, foreign language not required. *Average time to degree:* master's–2 years full-time, 35 years part-time; doctorate–6.7 years full-time. *Entrance requirements:* For master's, GRE General Test, TOEFL (minimum score 550), BSN, minimum GPA of 3.0, RN experience; for doctorate, GRE General Test, TOEFL (minimum score 550), BSN or MSN, minimum GPA of 3.0. Application deadline: 3/1 (priority date; rolling processing; 10/1 for spring admission). Application fee: $35. *Expenses:* Tuition $815 per credit hour. Fees $174 per year. *Financial aid:* In 1997–98, 15 students received aid, including 5 research assistantships averaging $864 per month, 10 teaching assistantships (2 to first-year students) averaging $864 per month; fellowships, graduate assistantships, Federal Work-Study, institutionally sponsored loans also available. Aid available to part-time students. Financial aid application deadline: 3/1; applicants required to submit FAFSA. *Faculty research:* Transcultural nursing. • Dr. Diane Horner, Dean, 305-284-2107. Application contact: Heidi McInnis, Director of Student Services, 305-284-4325. Fax: 305-284-5686. E-mail: lemieux@miami.edu.

University of Michigan, School of Nursing, Ann Arbor, MI 48109. Awards MS, PhD, Certificate, MBA/MS. One or more programs accredited by NLN. Part-time programs available. Faculty: 40 full-time (37 women), 6 part-time (all women). Students: 159 full-time (149 women), 151 part-time (146 women); includes 31 minority (14 African Americans, 9 Asian Americans, 6 Hispanics, 2 Native Americans), 16 international. 242 applicants, 79% accepted. In 1997, 69 master's, 9 doctorates awarded. Terminal master's awarded for partial completion of doctoral program. *Degree requirements:* For master's, thesis required, foreign language not required; for doctorate, dissertation, oral defense of dissertation, preliminary exam required, foreign language not required. *Average time to degree:* master's–2 years full-time, 4 years part-time; doctorate–4 years full-time, 7 years part-time. *Entrance requirements:* For master's and doctorate, GRE General Test. Application fee: $55. *Financial aid:* In 1997–98, 150 fellowships, 6 research assistantships, 9 teaching assistantships were awarded; traineeships, partial tuition waivers, Federal Work-Study, institutionally sponsored loans also available. Aid available to part-time students. *Faculty research:* Preparation of clinical nurse-researchers. • Dr. Ada Sue Hinshaw, Dean, 734-764-9454.

University of Minnesota, Twin Cities Campus, School of Nursing, Minneapolis, MN 55455-0213. Awards MS, PhD. One or more programs accredited by NLN. Part-time programs available. Faculty: 60. Students: 122 full-time, 163 part-time; includes 7 minority (4 African Americans, 3 Asian Americans), 7 international. Average age 37. 196 applicants, 82% accepted. In 1997, 93 master's, 7 doctorates awarded. *Degree requirements:* For master's, final oral exam, project or thesis; for doctorate, dissertation. *Entrance requirements:* For doctorate, GRE General Test. Application deadline: 12/15 (rolling processing). Application fee: $40 ($50 for international students). *Financial aid:* Fellowships, research assistantships, teaching assistantships, professional nurse traineeships, and career-related internships or fieldwork available.

• Sandra Edwardson, Dean, 612-624-4454. Fax: 612-626-2359. Application contact: Kate Hanson, Nursing Recruiter, 612-624-9494. Fax: 612-624-3174. E-mail: hanso041@maroon.tc.umn.edu.

University of Mississippi Medical Center, School of Nursing, Jackson, MS 39216-4505. Awards MSN. Accredited by NLN. Part-time and evening/weekend programs available. Faculty: 10 full-time (9 women), 3 part-time (1 woman). Students: 45 full-time (42 women), 57 part-time (50 women); includes 18 minority (all African Americans). Average age 38. 110 applicants, 51% accepted. In 1997, 41 degrees awarded. *Degree requirements:* Computer language required, thesis optional, foreign language not required. *Average time to degree:* master's–1 year full-time, 2 years part-time. *Entrance requirements:* GRE, 1 year of clinical experience, RN license. Application deadline: 2/15 (priority date). Application fee: $10. Electronic applications accepted. *Tuition:* $2378 per year full-time, $132 per hour part-time for state residents; $4698 per year full-time, $261 per hour part-time for nonresidents. *Financial aid:* In 1997–98, 28 students received aid, including 28 federal traineeships (all to first-year students); Federal Work-Study, institutionally sponsored loans also available. Aid available to part-time students. Financial aid application deadline: 4/1. *Faculty research:* Quality of life, neuroscience nursing, adult learning, gerontology, child birthing/parenting education. Total annual research expenditures: $107,835. • Dr. Anne G. Peirce, Dean, 601-984-6220. Application contact: Dr. Theresa Doddato, Associate Dean for Administrative Affairs.

University of Missouri–Columbia, School of Nursing, Columbia, MO 65211. Awards MS, PhD. One or more programs accredited by NLN. PhD offered jointly with the University of Missouri–Kansas City and the University of Missouri–St. Louis. Part-time programs available. Faculty: 40 full-time (39 women), 1 (woman) part-time. Students: 48 full-time (43 women), 75 part-time (71 women); includes 4 minority (1 African American, 2 Asian Americans, 1 Native American), 1 international. In 1997, 43 master's, 2 doctorates awarded. *Degree requirements:* For master's, thesis, non-thesis, or practicum; oral exam required, foreign language not required; for doctorate, dissertation. *Entrance requirements:* For master's, GRE General Test (minimum combined score of 1500 on three sections), BSN, minimum GPA of 3.0 during last 60 hours, nursing license. Application deadline: 8/1 (priority date; rolling processing). Application fee: $25 ($50 for international students). *Expenses:* Tuition $3240 per year full-time, $180 per credit hour part-time for state residents; $9108 per year full-time, $506 per credit hour part-time for nonresidents. Fees $55 per year full-time. *Financial aid:* Fellowships, research assistantships, teaching assistantships, professional nurse traineeships, full tuition waivers, Federal Work-Study, and career-related internships or fieldwork available. Aid available to part-time students. *Faculty research:* Pain, stepfamilies, chemotherapy-related nausea and vomiting, stress management, self-care deficit theory. • Dr. Rose Porter, Associate Dean, 573-882-0278.

See in-depth description on page 1449.

University of Missouri–Kansas City, School of Nursing, Kansas City, MO 64110-2499. Offers programs in nurse practitioner (MSN), including health care for adults, health care for children, health care for women; nursing (PhD). One or more programs accredited by NLN. Part-time programs available. Faculty: 17 full-time (15 women), 40 part-time (all women), 37 FTE. Students: 24 full-time (22 women), 206 part-time (191 women); includes 9 minority (5 African Americans, 3 Asian Americans, 1 Hispanic). Average age 39. 193 applicants, 82% accepted. In 1997, 86 master's awarded. *Degree requirements:* For master's, thesis or alternative required, foreign language not required. *Entrance requirements:* For master's, minimum undergraduate GPA of 3.0. Application deadline: 2/1 (9/15 for spring admission). Application fee: $25. *Expenses:* Tuition $182 per credit hour for state residents; $508 per credit hour for nonresidents. Fees $60 per year. *Financial aid:* 30 students received aid; fellowships, teaching assistantships, full and partial tuition waivers, Federal Work-Study, institutionally sponsored loans, and career-related internships or fieldwork available. Aid available to part-time students. Financial aid application deadline: 6/30. *Faculty research:* Geriatrics/gerontology, children's pain, neonatology, Alzheimer's care, cancer caregivers. • Dr. Nancy Mills, Dean, 816-235-1700. Application contact: Brenda Cain, Student Services Assistant, 816-235-1710. Fax: 816-235-1701.

Announcement: The University of Missouri–Kansas City (UMKC) School of Nursing provides high-quality education. Programs offered include BSN completion, RN to MSN, MSN, and PhD. MSN clinical emphasis in nursing care for adults, women, and children; functional role options include educator, administrator, clinical nurse specialist, nurse practitioner, and family nurse practitioner. National League for Nursing accreditation. For information, call 816-235-1700.

University of Missouri–St. Louis, School of Nursing, St. Louis, MO 63121-4499. Awards MSN, ND, PhD. One or more programs accredited by NLN. Faculty: 22 (20 women). Students: 32 full-time (28 women), 220 part-time (204 women); includes 21 minority (13 African Americans, 5 Asian Americans, 2 Hispanics, 1 Native American). 8 applicants, 75% accepted. In 1997, 107 master's awarded. *Degree requirements:* For master's, thesis or alternative; for doctorate, dissertation. *Entrance requirements:* For doctorate, GRE General Test. Application deadline: 7/1 (priority date; rolling processing; 10/1 for spring admission). Application fee: $0. Electronic applications accepted. *Expenses:* Tuition $3903 per year full-time, $167 per credit hour part-time for state residents; $11,745 per year full-time, $489 per credit hour part-time for nonresidents. Fees $816 per year full-time, $34 per credit hour part-time. *Financial aid:* In 1997–98, 3 teaching assistantships were awarded; fellowships also available. *Faculty research:* Health promotion and restoration, family disruption, violence abuse, battered women, health survey methods, infant apnea. • Dr. Jean Bachman, Associate Dean, 314-516-6075. E-mail: sjhbach@umslvma.umsl.edu. Application contact: Graduate Admissions, 314-516-5458. Fax: 314-516-6759. E-mail: gradadm@umslvma.umsl.edu.

University of Mobile, Graduate Programs, Program in Nursing, Mobile, AL 36663-0220. Awards MSN. Accredited by NLN. Part-time and evening/weekend programs available. Faculty: 11 part-time (10 women). Students: 34 full-time (30 women), 19 part-time (18 women); includes 16 minority (all African Americans). Average age 36. 47 applicants, 87% accepted. In 1997, 18 degrees awarded (100% found work related to degree). *Degree requirements:* Thesis or alternative, comprehensive exam. *Entrance requirements:* GMAT, GRE, or MAT; TOEFL (minimum score 550). Application deadline: 8/3 (priority date; rolling processing; 12/23 for spring admission). Application fee: $30. *Tuition:* $160 per semester hour. *Financial aid:* 44 students received aid; partial tuition waivers, Federal Work-Study available. Aid available to part-time students. Financial aid application deadline: 8/1. *Faculty research:* Nursing management, transcultural nursing, spiritual aspects, educational expectations. • Dr. Rosemary Adams, Dean, School of Nursing, 334-675-5990 Ext. 227. Fax: 334-679-0875. Application contact: Kaye F. Brown, Dean, Graduate and Special Programs, 334-675-5990 Ext. 270. Fax: 334-675-9816.

University of Nebraska Medical Center, Graduate Program in Nursing, Omaha, NE 68198-0001. Awards MSN, PhD. One or more programs accredited by NLN. Part-time programs available. Faculty: 41 full-time. Students: 66 full-time (62 women), 97 part-time (95 women); includes 2 minority (both African Americans). Average age 35. 93 applicants, 85% accepted. In 1997, 51 master's, 3 doctorates awarded. *Degree requirements:* For doctorate, dissertation required, foreign language not required. *Entrance requirements:* For master's, GRE General Test; for doctorate, GRE General Test (minimum combined score of 1000), minimum GPA of 3.2. Application deadline: 5/1 (priority date; rolling processing; 12/1 for spring admission). Application fee: $25. *Financial aid:* In 1997–98, 46 students received aid, including 22 fellowships (4 to first-year students) averaging $400 per month and totaling $64,302, 24 teaching assistantships (10 to first-year students) averaging $450 per month; research assistantships, institutionally sponsored loans also available. Aid available to part-time students. Financial aid application deadline: 2/1. *Faculty research:* Endotrachial suctioning, health beliefs, pressure sore etiology, paternal role acquisition, attachment behavior and life satisfaction of the elderly. • Dr. Nancy Bergstrom, Associate Dean, 402-559-7457. Fax: 402-559-7570. Application contact: Jo Wagner, Associate Director of Admissions, 402-559-4206.

University of Nevada, Las Vegas, College of Health Sciences, Department of Nursing, Las Vegas, NV 89154-9900. Offers programs in acute and chronic health problems (MS), family nurse practitioner (MS), terminal illness (MS). Faculty: 12 full-time (10 women), 3 part-time (1 woman). Students: 16 full-time (15 women), 22 part-time (20 women); includes 3 minority (2 Asian Americans, 1 Hispanic). 16 applicants, 75% accepted. In 1997, 11 degrees awarded. *Degree requirements:* Comprehensive exam required, thesis optional, foreign language not required. *Entrance requirements:* GRE General Test (minimum combined score of 1000), minimum GPA of 2.75. Application deadline: 4/15 (10/15 for spring admission). Application fee: $40 ($95 for international students). *Expenses:* Tuition $93 per credit for state residents; $93 per credit full-time, $190 per credit part-time for nonresidents. Fees $5570 per year full-time for nonresidents. *Financial aid:* In 1997–98, 1 research assistantship, 4 teaching assistantships were awarded. Financial aid application deadline: 3/1. • Dr. Rosemary Witt, Chair, 702-895-3415. Application contact: Graduate College Admissions Evaluator, 702-895-3320.

University of Nevada, Reno, College of Human and Community Sciences, Orvis School of Nursing, Reno, NV 89557. Awards MS. Faculty: 5 (all women). Students: 16 full-time (15 women), 13 part-time (11 women); includes 2 minority (both Hispanics). Average age 43. 17 applicants, 53% accepted. In 1997, 16 degrees awarded. *Degree requirements:* Thesis optional, foreign language not required. *Entrance requirements:* GRE General Test (minimum combined score of 1000) or MAT, TOEFL (minimum score 500), minimum GPA of 2.75. Application deadline: 3/1 (priority date; rolling processing). Application fee: $40. *Expenses:* Tuition $0 for state residents; $5770 per year full-time, $200 per credit part-time for nonresidents. Fees $93 per credit. *Financial aid:* Research assistantships, teaching assistantships available. Financial aid application deadline: 3/1. • Dr. Julie E. Johnson, Director, 702-784-6841. Application contact: Dr. Jdee Richardson, Director of Graduate Studies, 702-784-6841. E-mail: jkr@equinex.unr.edu.

University of New Hampshire, School of Health and Human Services, Department of Nursing, Durham, NH 03824. Awards MS. Accredited by NLN. Faculty: 12 full-time. Students: 22 full-time (20 women), 46 part-time (all women). Average age 40. 26 applicants, 65% accepted. In 1997, 19 degrees awarded. *Degree requirements:* Thesis or alternative required, foreign language not required. *Entrance requirements:* GRE General Test or MAT. Application deadline: 7/1 (priority date; rolling processing). Application fee: $50. *Expenses:* Tuition $5440 per year full-time, $302 per credit hour part-time for state residents; $8160 per year (minimum) full-time, $453 per credit hour (minimum) part-time for nonresidents. Fees $868 per year full-time, $15 per year part-time. *Financial aid:* In 1997–98, 6 fellowships (2 to first-year students), 2 teaching assistantships, 14 scholarships (2 to first-year students) were awarded; full and partial tuition waivers, Federal Work-Study also available. Financial aid application deadline: 2/15. *Faculty research:* Adult health, nursing administration, family nurse practitioner. • Dr. Ann Kelley, Chairperson, 603-862-2216. Application contact: Dr. Juliette Petillo, 603-862-4123.

University of New Mexico, College of Nursing, Albuquerque, NM 87131-2039. Awards MSN, Certificate, MSN/MALAS. Programs in administration of nursing (MSN, Certificate); advanced nurse practice (Certificate); advanced nursing practice (MSN), including adult health nursing, gerontological nursing, parent-child nursing, psychiatric-mental health nursing; community health nursing (MSN); primary care nursing (MSN), including family nurse practitioner, nurse midwifery. One or more programs accredited by NLN. Part-time programs available. Faculty: 38 full-time (36 women), 23 part-time (all women), 46.57 FTE. Students: 58 full-time (50 women), 59 part-time (54 women); includes 17 minority (2 African Americans, 5 Asian Americans, 8 Hispanics, 2 Native Americans). Average age 42. 97 applicants, 52% accepted. In 1997, 49 master's awarded. *Degree requirements:* For master's, thesis optional, foreign language not required. *Entrance requirements:* For master's, GRE General Test, interview, minimum GPA of 3.0, previous course work in statistics. Application deadline: 7/15 (11/1 for spring admission). Application fee: $25. *Expenses:* Tuition $2442 per year full-time, $103 per credit hour part-time for state residents; $8691 per year full-time, $103 per credit hour (minimum) part-time for nonresidents. Fees $32 per year. *Financial aid:* Fellowships, research assistantships, teaching assistantships, full tuition waivers, Federal Work-Study, and career-related internships or fieldwork available. *Faculty research:* Health outcomes. Total annual research expenditures: $162,757. • Dr. Sandra Ferketich, Dean, 505-272-6284. Application contact: Anne-Marie Oechsler, Director, Academic Advisement, 505-272-4224. Fax: 505-272-3970. E-mail: annmarie@unm.edu.

The University of North Carolina at Chapel Hill, School of Nursing, Chapel Hill, NC 27599. Awards MSN, PhD. One or more programs accredited by NLN. Part-time programs available. Faculty: 50 full-time (47 women). Students: 70 full-time (64 women), 76 part-time (69 women); includes 11 minority (5 African Americans, 5 Asian Americans, 1 Native American), 3 international. Average age 34. 125 applicants, 56% accepted. In 1997, 48 master's, 5 doctorates awarded. Terminal master's awarded for partial completion of doctoral program. *Degree requirements:* For master's, thesis, comprehensive exam required, foreign language not required; for doctorate, computer language, dissertation, 3 exams required, foreign language not required. *Entrance requirements:* For master's, GRE General Test (minimum combined score of 1000), minimum GPA of 3.0; for doctorate, GRE General Test (minimum combined score of 1100), minimum GPA of 3.0 (undergraduate nursing), 3.5 (MSN). Application deadline: 1/1 (priority date; rolling processing; 10/15 for spring admission). Application fee: $55. *Expenses:* Tuition $1428 per year full-time, $357 per semester (minimum) part-time for state residents; $10,414 per year full-time, $2604 per semester (minimum) part-time for nonresidents. Fees $782 per year full-time, $332 per semester (minimum) part-time. *Financial aid:* In 1997–98, 51 fellowships averaging $445 per month, 7 research assistantships averaging $900 per month, 5 teaching assistantships averaging $660 per month were awarded; Federal Work-Study, institutionally sponsored loans also available. Financial aid application deadline: 2/1; applicants required to submit FAFSA. *Faculty research:* Chronic illness parenting, cardiovascular health in children, acute confusion and physical frailty in elderly. Total annual research expenditures: $3 million. • Dr. Cynthia M. Freund, Dean, 919-966-3731. Application contact: Dr. Carol C. Hogue, Associate Dean for Graduate Studies, 919-966-3733. Fax: 919-966-3540. E-mail: chogue.uncson@mhs.unc.edu.

University of North Carolina at Charlotte, College of Nursing and Health Professions, Department of Nursing, Charlotte, NC 28223-0001. Awards MSN, MSN/MHA. Accredited by NLN. Faculty: 14 full-time (12 women), 1 (woman) part-time, 14.25 FTE. Students: 36 full-time (26 women), 125 part-time (114 women); includes 20 minority (15 African Americans, 2 Asian Americans, 3 Hispanics). Average age 36. 122 applicants, 76% accepted. In 1997, 37 degrees awarded. *Entrance requirements:* GRE General Test, minimum GPA of 3.0 in undergraduate major. Application deadline: 7/1. Application fee: $35. *Tuition:* $1786 per year full-time, $339 per semester (minimum) part-time for state residents; $8914 per year full-time, $2121 per semester (minimum) part-time for nonresidents. *Financial aid:* Federal Work-Study available. Financial aid application deadline: 4/1. • Application contact: Kathy Barringer, Assistant Director of Graduate Admissions, 704-547-3366. Fax: 704-547-3279. E-mail: gradadm@email.uncc.edu.

University of North Carolina at Greensboro, School of Nursing, Greensboro, NC 27412-0001. Offers programs in administration of nursing in health agencies (MSN), gerontological nurse practitioner (PMC), nurse anesthesia (MSN, PMC). Accredited by NLN. Faculty: 22 full-time (all women), 7 part-time (all women). Students: 134 full-time (123 women), 96 part-time (95 women); includes 37 minority (32 African Americans, 1 Asian American, 2 Hispanics, 2 Native Americans). 117 applicants, 84% accepted. In 1997, 85 master's awarded. *Degree requirements:* For master's, thesis or alternative required, foreign language not required. *Entrance requirements:* For master's, GRE General Test or MAT, BSN, clinical experience, liability insurance, RN license; for PMC, liability insurance, MSN, RN license. Application fee: $35. *Expenses:* Tuition $1842 per year full-time, $370 per semester (minimum) part-time for state residents; $10,296 per year full-time, $2484 per semester (minimum) part-time for

Directory: Nursing—General

University of North Carolina at Greensboro (continued)
nonresidents. Fees $806 per year full-time, $111 per semester (minimum) part-time. *Financial aid:* In 1997–98, 8 research assistantships totaling $40,000, 71 traineeships totaling $140,913 were awarded. • Dr. Lynne Pearcey, Dean, 336-334-5010.

University of North Dakota, School of Nursing, Grand Forks, ND 58202. Awards MS. Part-time programs available. Postbaccalaureate distance learning degree programs offered (minimal on-campus study). Faculty: 16 full-time (all women). Students: 52 full-time (41 women), 63 part-time (59 women). 47 applicants, 68% accepted. In 1997, 38 degrees awarded. *Degree requirements:* Thesis or alternative required, foreign language not required. *Entrance requirements:* TOEFL (minimum score 550), minimum GPA of 3.0. Application deadline: 1/1 (rolling processing). Application fee: $20. *Financial aid:* In 1997–98, 11 students received aid, including 6 fellowships totaling $14,400, 5 teaching assistantships totaling $45,910; research assistantships, traineeships, full and partial tuition waivers, Federal Work-Study, institutionally sponsored loans also available. Financial aid application deadline: 3/15. • Dr. Regina Monnig, Director, 701-777-4552. Fax: 701-777-4096. E-mail: regina_monnig@mail.und.nodak.edu.

University of Northern Colorado, College of Health and Human Sciences, School of Nursing, Greeley, CO 80639. Offers programs in family nurse practitioner (MS), nursing education (MS). Accredited by NLN. Faculty: 10 full-time (all women), 1 (woman) part-time. Students: 42 full-time (35 women), 6 part-time (5 women); includes 5 minority (4 Hispanics, 1 Native American). Average age 40. 36 applicants, 75% accepted. In 1997, 28 degrees awarded. *Degree requirements:* Thesis or alternative, comprehensive exams. *Application deadline:* rolling. *Application fee:* $35. *Expenses:* Tuition $2327 per year full-time, $129 per credit hour part-time for state residents; $9578 per year full-time, $532 per credit hour part-time for nonresidents. Fees $752 per year full-time, $184 per semester (minimum) part-time. *Financial aid:* In 1997–98, 35 students received aid, including 4 fellowships (all to first-year students) totaling $3,275, 2 graduate assistantships (1 to a first-year student) totaling $7,312; teaching assistantships also available. Financial aid application deadline: 3/1. • Dr. Sandy Baird, Director, 970-351-2293.

University of Oklahoma Health Sciences Center, College of Nursing, Oklahoma City, OK 73190. Awards MS, MS/MBA. Accredited by NLN. MS/MBA offered jointly with Oklahoma State University and the University of Oklahoma. Part-time programs available. Faculty: 31 full-time (29 women), 26 part-time (all women). Students: 41 full-time (39 women), 191 part-time (181 women); includes 26 minority (2 African Americans, 2 Asian Americans, 4 Hispanics, 18 Native Americans). 109 applicants, 83% accepted. In 1997, 80 degrees awarded. *Degree requirements:* Comprehensive exam required, thesis optional, foreign language not required. *Entrance requirements:* GRE General Test, TOEFL (minimum score 550). Application deadline: 6/1 (rolling processing; 11/1 for spring admission). Application fee: $25 ($50 for international students). *Financial aid:* Research assistantships, teaching assistantships, scholarships, traineeships, institutionally sponsored loans available. Aid available to part-time students. Financial aid application deadline: 8/1. *Faculty research:* Parenting and Native Americans, elderly reminiscence, diabetes in Native Americans. • Dr. Patricia Forni, Dean, 405-271-2420.

University of Ottawa, Faculty of Health Sciences, School of Nursing, Ottawa, ON K1N 6N5, Canada. Awards M Sc. Part-time and evening/weekend programs available. Faculty: 11 full-time, 2 part-time. Students: 15 full-time (all women), 22 part-time (all women). Average age 39. In 1997, 7 degrees awarded. *Degree requirements:* Thesis or alternative. *Entrance requirements:* Honors degree or equivalent, minimum B average. Application fee: $35. *Expenses:* Tuition $4677 per year for Canadian residents; $9900 per year for nonresidents. Fees $230 per year. *Financial aid:* Fellowships, research assistantships, teaching assistantships, Federal Work-Study available. • Betty Cragg, Director and Associate Dean, 613-562-5423. Application contact: France Proulx, Academic Administrator, 613-562-5800 Ext. 8417. Fax: 613-562-5443.

University of Pennsylvania, School of Nursing, Philadelphia, PA 19104. Awards MSN, PhD, Certificate, MBA/MSN, MBA/PhD, MSN/PhD. One or more programs accredited by NLN. Part-time programs available. Postbaccalaureate distance learning degree programs offered. Faculty: 44 full-time, 81 part-time. Students: 182 full-time (172 women), 243 part-time (236 women); includes 31 minority (18 African Americans, 9 Asian Americans, 3 Hispanics, 1 Native American), 22 international. Average age 32. 297 applicants, 66% accepted. In 1997, 201 master's, 11 doctorates awarded. Terminal master's awarded for partial completion of doctoral program. *Degree requirements:* For doctorate, dissertation required, foreign language not required. *Entrance requirements:* For master's, GRE General Test, GMAT (MBA/MSN), BSN, minimum GPA of 3.0; for doctorate, GRE General Test, GMAT (MBA/PhD), BSN or MSN, minimum GPA of 3.0. Application deadline: rolling. Application fee: $65. *Financial aid:* In 1997–98, 26 research assistantships, 37 teaching assistantships were awarded; fellowships, Federal Work-Study, institutionally sponsored loans, and career-related internships or fieldwork also available. Aid available to part-time students. Financial aid application deadline: 1/2; applicants required to submit FAFSA. *Faculty research:* Nursing and patient outcomes research. Total annual research expenditures: $5.3 million. • Dr. Marla Salmon, Associate Dean and Director of Graduate Studies, 215-898-8286. Fax: 215-573-6659. Application contact: Susan K. Ogle, Associate Director of Admissions and Student Affairs, 215-898-3301. Fax: 215-573-8439. E-mail: sogle@pobox.upenn.edu.

University of Phoenix, Graduate Programs, Nursing Programs, 4615 East Elwood St, PO Box 52069, Phoenix, AZ 85072-2069. Offerings in nursing administration (MN), women's health nurse practitioner (MN). Accredited by NLN. Evening/weekend programs available. Postbaccalaureate distance learning degree programs offered (no on-campus study). Students: 756 full-time (722 women); includes 221 minority (111 African Americans, 64 Asian Americans, 36 Hispanics, 10 Native Americans). Average age 40. In 1997, 137 degrees awarded. *Degree requirements:* Thesis or alternative required, foreign language not required. *Entrance requirements:* TOEFL (minimum score 520), minimum GPA of 2.5, RN license, 3 years of work experience in field, comprehensive cognitive assessment (COCA). Application deadline: rolling. Application fee: $50. *Tuition:* $248 per credit hour. • Dr. Sandra Pepicello, Dean, 602-966-9577. Application contact: Campus Information Center, 602-966-9577.

University of Pittsburgh, School of Nursing, Pittsburgh, PA 15260. Awards MSN, PhD. One or more programs accredited by NLN. Part-time programs available. Postbaccalaureate distance learning degree programs offered. Faculty: 33 full-time (29 women), 1 part-time (0 women). Students: 97 full-time (81 women), 247 part-time (236 women); includes 21 minority (12 African Americans, 7 Asian Americans, 2 Hispanics), 3 international. 200 applicants, 58% accepted. In 1997, 103 master's, 4 doctorates awarded. *Degree requirements:* For doctorate, dissertation required, foreign language not required. *Average time to degree:* master's–2 years full-time, 5 years part-time; doctorate–3 years full-time, 8 years part-time. *Entrance requirements:* For master's, TOEFL, BSN, RN license, nursing experience; for doctorate, GRE General Test, TOEFL, BSN, MSN. Application deadline: 2/1 (priority date; rolling processing; 9/15 for spring admission). Application fee: $35 ($40 for international students). *Financial aid:* In 1997–98, 152 students received aid, including 5 fellowships, 25 research assistantships (5 to first-year students) averaging $1,050 per month, 10 teaching assistantships (1 to a first-year student) averaging $1,286 per month, 57 scholarships, tuition aid (26 to first-year students); Federal Work-Study, institutionally sponsored loans, and career-related internships or fieldwork also available. Aid available to part-time students. Financial aid application deadline: 6/1; applicants required to submit FAFSA. *Faculty research:* Chronic disease, critical care, adolescent health, biobehavioral emphasis. Total annual research expenditures: $2.915 million. • Dr. Ellen B. Rudy, Dean, 412-624-2400. Fax: 412-624-2401. E-mail: nursao+@pitt.edu. Application contact: Dr. Kathy Lucke, Director, Student Services, 412-624-2405. Fax: 412-624-2409. E-mail: nursao+@pitt.edu.

Announcement: The University of Pittsburgh School of Nursing is known nationally for its clinical and research programs. The School's nurse practitioner and nurse anesthetist programs have achieved national prominence. Nonclinical programs are available in administration, education, research, and informatics. Current faculty and student research reflects the breadth of patient populations and health-care problems under investigation, including focused areas in critical care, adolescent health, chronic illness, and health-care outcomes. Students in all programs benefit from the variety and excellence of available clinical sites, including many institutions of UPMC and 3 nurse-managed practitioner clinics.

See in-depth description on page 1451.

University of Portland, School of Nursing, Portland, OR 97203-5798. Offers programs in family nurse practitioner (Post Master's Certificate), leadership in health care systems (Post Master's Certificate), nursing (MS). One or more programs accredited by NLN. Part-time and evening/weekend programs available. Postbaccalaureate distance learning degree programs offered (minimal on-campus study). Faculty: 11 full-time (10 women). Students: 11 full-time (10 women), 11 part-time (10 women). 22 applicants, 95% accepted. In 1997, 31 master's awarded. *Entrance requirements:* For master's, GRE General Test, Oregon RN license, BSN, previous course work in statistics. Application deadline: rolling. Application fee: $40. *Tuition:* $540 per semester hour. *Financial aid:* Fellowships, research assistantships, institutionally sponsored loans available. Aid available to part-time students. Financial aid application deadline: 3/15. • Dr. Terry Misener, Dean, 503-283-7211. Fax: 503-283-7399. E-mail: misener@up.edu.

University of Puerto Rico, Medical Sciences Campus, School of Nursing, San Juan, PR 00936-5067. Offers programs in anesthesia (MSN), clinical specialist (MSN), nursing administration (MSN), teaching nursing (MSN). Accredited by NLN. *Degree requirements:* 1 foreign language, thesis, research project. *Entrance requirements:* GRE, BSN, interview, (Puerto Rico) RN license, 2 years of nursing experience, previous course work in physical examination. Application deadline: 3/16. Application fee: $25. *Faculty research:* HIV and AIDS, teen pregnancy, cancer and therapeutic touch, substance abuse.

University of Rhode Island, College of Nursing, Kingston, RI 02881. Offers programs in nursing (PhD), nursing service administration (MS), teaching of nursing (MS). One or more programs accredited by NLN. *Application deadline:* 4/15. *Application fee:* $35. *Expenses:* Tuition $3446 per year full-time, $191 per credit part-time for state residents; $9850 per year full-time, $547 per credit part-time for nonresidents. Fees $1276 per year full-time, $135 per semester (minimum) part-time.

See in-depth description on page 1453.

University of Rochester, School of Nursing, Rochester, NY 14642. Awards MS, PhD, MBA/MS. One or more programs accredited by NLN. Part-time programs available. Faculty: 21 full-time (all women), 255 part-time (235 women). Students: 108 full-time (103 women), 108 part-time (103 women); includes 13 minority (9 African Americans, 3 Asian Americans, 1 Hispanic), 13 international. 78 applicants, 72% accepted. In 1997, 66 master's, 3 doctorates awarded. *Degree requirements:* For master's, thesis optional, foreign language not required; for doctorate, dissertation required, foreign language not required. *Entrance requirements:* For master's, GRE General Test or MAT, interview; for doctorate, GRE General Test, interview. Application deadline: 2/15 (9/15 for spring admission). Application fee: $25. *Expenses:* Tuition $21,485 per year full-time, $672 per credit hour part-time. Fees $336 per year. *Financial aid:* 200 students received aid; scholarships, traineeships, full and partial tuition waivers, Federal Work-Study available. Financial aid application deadline: 6/15. *Faculty research:* Interdisciplinary collaboration in treatment decisions of the critically ill, HIV prevention in school aged children, symptom monitoring in childhood asthma, community intervention/developmental outcomes for children and families, parents coping with critically ill children. • Sheila A. Ryan, Dean, 716-275-5451. Application contact: Elaine Andolina, Student Affairs Office, 716-275-2375. E-mail: eand@son.rochester.edu.

University of Saint Francis, Department of Nursing, Fort Wayne, IN 46808-3994. Awards MSN. Faculty: 3 full-time, 1 part-time. Students: 1 full-time, 60 part-time; includes 5 minority (all African Americans). 26 applicants, 77% accepted. In 1997, 20 degrees awarded. *Degree requirements:* Research project. *Entrance requirements:* MAT (average 40), minimum GPA of 3.0. Application deadline: 7/1 (priority date; rolling processing; 11/1 for spring admission). Application fee: $20. *Expenses:* Tuition $350 per semester hour. Fees $390 per year full-time, $69 per semester (minimum) part-time. • Dr. Nancy Gillespie, Chair, 219-434-3240. Fax: 219-434-3183. E-mail: ngillespi@sfc.edu.

University of San Diego, Philip Y. Hahn School of Nursing, San Diego, CA 92110-2492. Awards MSN, DNS, MBA/MSN, MIB/MSN. Programs in adult health nurse practitioner (MSN), family health nurse practitioner (MSN), nursing administration (MSN), nursing science (DNS), school health nurse practitioner (MSN). Part-time and evening/weekend programs available. Faculty: 12 full-time (all women), 4 part-time (all women). Students: 45 full-time (41 women), 119 part-time (109 women); includes 21 minority (4 African Americans, 6 Asian Americans, 11 Hispanics). Average age 35. 90 applicants, 81% accepted. In 1997, 52 master's awarded (100% found work related to degree); 12 doctorates awarded (100% found work related to degree). *Degree requirements:* For doctorate, dissertation, administrative residency required, foreign language not required. *Entrance requirements:* For master's, GRE or MAT, TOEFL (minimum score 580), TWE, BSN, minimum GPA of 3.0; for doctorate, GRE or MAT, minimum GPA of 3.5, MSN. Application deadline: 5/1 (priority date; rolling processing; 11/15 for spring admission). Application fee: $45. *Expenses:* Tuition $585 per unit (minimum). Fees $50 per year full-time, $30 per year part-time. *Financial aid:* Fellowships, scholarships, traineeships, Federal Work-Study, institutionally sponsored loans available. Aid available to part-time students. Financial aid application deadline: 5/1; applicants required to submit FAFSA. *Faculty research:* Health promotion, decision making, psychogeriatric nursing, historical nursing, leadership behavior. Total annual research expenditures: $26,000. • Dr. Janet Rodgers, Dean, 619-260-4550. Fax: 619-260-6814. Application contact: Mary Jane Tiernan, Director of Graduate Admissions, 619-260-4524. Fax: 619-260-4158. E-mail: grads@acusd.edu.

University of San Francisco, School of Nursing, San Francisco, CA 94117-1080. Awards MSN, MSN/MBA. Programs in advanced practice nursing-nurse practitioner and clinical nurse specialist (MSN), including adult health nursing; nursing administration (MSN). Accredited by NLN. Part-time programs available. Faculty: 9 full-time (8 women), 1 (woman) part-time. Students: 16 full-time (14 women), 8 part-time (all women); includes 6 minority (2 African Americans, 3 Asian Americans, 1 Hispanic). Average age 39. 14 applicants, 79% accepted. In 1997, 8 degrees awarded. *Average time to degree:* master's–2 years full-time, 2.5 years part-time. *Entrance requirements:* Minimum GPA of 3.0. Application deadline: rolling. Application fee: $40. *Tuition:* $658 per unit (minimum). *Financial aid:* 14 students received aid; institutionally sponsored loans available. Financial aid application deadline: 3/2. *Faculty research:* Direct patient/client care; providers of health care. • Dr. John Lantz, Interim Dean, 415-422-6681. Fax: 415-422-6877. E-mail: lantzj@usfca.edu.

University of Saskatchewan, College of Nursing, Saskatoon, SK S7N 5A2, Canada. Awards MN. Part-time programs available. *Degree requirements:* Thesis (for some programs). *Entrance requirements:* CANTEST (minimum score 4.5) or International English Language Testing System (minimum score 6) or Michigan English Language Assessment Battery (minimum score 80), or TOEFL (minimum score 550; average 560). Application deadline: 7/1 (priority date; rolling processing). Application fee: $0.

University of Scranton, Department of Nursing, Scranton, PA 18510-4622. Offers program in family nurse practitioner (MS). Applicants accepted in odd-numbered years only. Part-time and evening/weekend programs available. Faculty: 12 full-time (all women), 2 part-time (1 woman). Students: 4 full-time (all women), 30 part-time (29 women). Average age 40. 29 applicants, 83% accepted. In 1997, 6 degrees awarded. *Entrance requirements:* BSN, minimum GPA of 3.0, Pennsylvania RN license. Application deadline: rolling. Application fee: $35. *Expenses:* Tuition $465 per credit. Fees $25 per semester. *Financial aid:* In 1997–98, 1 teaching assistantship (to a first-year student) averaging $648 per month and totaling $5,035 was awarded. Financial aid application deadline: 3/1. *Faculty research:* Home care, doctoral education, health care of women and children, pain, health promotion and adolescence. • Dr. Patricia

Harrington, Chair, 717-941-7673. E-mail: harringtonp1@uofs.edu. Application contact: Dr. Mary Jane Hanson, Director, 717-941-4060. Fax: 717-941-4201. E-mail: hansonm2@uofs.edu.

University of South Alabama, College of Nursing, Mobile, AL 36688-0002. Offers programs in adult health nursing (MSN), community mental health nursing (MSN), maternal child nursing (MSN). Accredited by NLN. Part-time and evening/weekend programs available. Faculty: 9 full-time (all women), 1 (woman) part-time. Students: 124 full-time (106 women), 161 part-time (143 women); includes 30 minority (19 African Americans, 3 Asian Americans, 3 Hispanics, 5 Native Americans), 6 international. 101 applicants, 71% accepted. In 1997, 89 degrees awarded. *Degree requirements:* Written comprehensive exam, research project or thesis required, foreign language not required. *Entrance requirements:* GRE General Test (minimum combined score of 1000) or MAT (minimum score 45), BSN, minimum GPA of 3.0, 1 year of nursing experience, interview, nursing license. Application deadline: 9/1 (priority date; rolling processing). Application fee: $25. *Financial aid:* In 1997–98, 31 traineeships were awarded; research assistantships also available. Aid available to part-time students. Financial aid application deadline: 4/1. • Dr. Amanda Baker, Dean, 334-434-3415.

University of South Carolina, Graduate School, College of Nursing, Program in Clinical Nursing, Columbia, SC 29208. Awards MSN. Accredited by NLN. Students: 13 full-time (11 women), 37 part-time (34 women); includes 2 minority (both African Americans), 1 international. Average age 37. In 1997, 15 degrees awarded. *Degree requirements:* Oral or written comprehensive exam required, foreign language not required. *Entrance requirements:* GRE General Test, BS in nursing, previous course work in statistics. Application deadline: 4/15 (rolling processing; 10/15 for spring admission). Application fee: $35. Electronic applications accepted. *Expenses:* Tuition $4480 per year full-time, $220 per credit hour part-time for state residents; $9338 per year full-time, $457 per credit hour part-time for nonresidents. Fees $125 per year full-time, $37 per semester (minimum) part-time. *Financial aid:* Application deadline 2/1. • Application contact: Office of Academic and Student Affairs, 803-777-7412. Fax: 803-777-0616.

University of South Carolina, Graduate School, College of Nursing, Program in Nursing Science, Columbia, SC 29208. Awards PhD. Students: 10 full-time (9 women), 27 part-time (26 women); includes 4 minority (3 African Americans, 1 Asian American). Average age 46. In 1997, 4 degrees awarded. *Degree requirements:* Computer language, dissertation, oral comprehensive exams required, foreign language not required. *Entrance requirements:* GRE, previous course work in nursing theory and statistics, RN license. Application deadline: 4/15 (rolling processing; 10/15 for spring admission). Application fee: $35. Electronic applications accepted. *Expenses:* Tuition $4480 per year full-time, $220 per credit hour part-time for state residents; $9338 per year full-time, $457 per credit hour part-time for nonresidents. Fees $125 per year full-time, $37 per semester (minimum) part-time. *Financial aid:* Application deadline 2/1. • Application contact: Office of Academic and Student Affairs, 803-777-7412. Fax: 803-777-0616.

University of Southern California, Graduate School, School of Health Affairs, Department of Nursing, Los Angeles, CA 90089. Awards MS, Certificate, MBA/MS. Accredited by NLN. Students: 37 full-time (35 women), 23 part-time (21 women); includes 20 minority (3 African Americans, 10 Asian Americans, 7 Hispanics), 1 international. Average age 36. 43 applicants, 63% accepted. In 1997, 14 master's awarded. *Entrance requirements:* For master's, GRE General Test. Application deadline: 8/1 (priority date; 12/1 for spring admission). Application fee: $55. *Expenses:* Tuition $16,944 per year full-time, $706 per unit part-time. Fees $414 per year full-time, $32 per year part-time. *Financial aid:* In 1997–98, 30 fellowships, 14 teaching assistantships, 2 scholarships were awarded; research assistantships, Federal Work-Study, institutionally sponsored loans also available. Aid available to part-time students. Financial aid application deadline: 2/15; applicants required to submit FAFSA. • Adele Pillitteri, Chair, 213-342-2001.

University of Southern Indiana, Graduate Studies, School of Nursing and Health Professions, Evansville, IN 47712-3590. Awards MSN. Faculty: 8 full-time (7 women), 1 part-time (0 women). Students: 9 full-time (8 women), 34 part-time (31 women); includes 2 minority (both African Americans). Average age 37. 31 applicants, 35% accepted. In 1997, 6 degrees awarded. *Entrance requirements:* Minimum GPA of 3.0. Application deadline: rolling. Application fee: $25. *Tuition:* $129 per credit hour for state residents; $260 per credit hour for nonresidents. • Dr. Nadine Coudret, Dean, 812-465-1151. E-mail: ncoudret.usc@smtp.usi.edu.

University of Southern Maine, College of Nursing, Portland, ME 04104-9300. Offers programs in adult health nursing (MS, PMC), family nursing (MS, PMC), management (MS), psychiatric-mental health nursing (MS, PMC). One or more programs accredited by NLN. Part-time programs available. Postbaccalaureate distance learning degree programs offered (minimal on-campus study). Faculty: 11 full-time (all women), 5 part-time (all women). Students: 41 full-time (35 women), 77 part-time (76 women); includes 2 minority (1 Asian American, 1 Native American), 1 international. Average age 35. 75 applicants, 69% accepted. In 1997, 30 master's awarded. *Degree requirements:* For master's, thesis optional, foreign language not required. *Average time to degree:* master's–2.5 years full-time, 4 years part-time. *Entrance requirements:* For master's, GRE General Test (minimum combined score of 1000 on verbal and quantitative sections) or MAT (minimum score 45), minimum GPA of 3.0. Application deadline: 3/1. Application fee: $25. *Expenses:* Tuition $178 per credit hour for state residents; $267 per credit hour (minimum) for nonresidents. Fees $282 per year full-time, $83 per semester (minimum) part-time. *Financial aid:* In 1997–98, 16 research assistantships, 19 traineeships totaling $31,114 were awarded; fellowships, teaching assistantships, full and partial tuition waivers, Federal Work-Study, and career-related internships or fieldwork also available. Aid available to part-time students. *Faculty research:* Women's health, urinary incontinence, nursing history, weight control, community services, spirituality, substance abuse. • Dr. Marianne W. Rodgers, Interim Dean, 207-780-4808. Fax: 207-780-4997. E-mail: mrodgers@usm.maine.edu. Application contact: Mary Sloan, Assistant Director of Graduate Studies, 207-780-4386. Fax: 207-780-4969. E-mail: msloan@usm.maine.edu.

University of Southern Mississippi, College of Nursing, Hattiesburg, MS 39406-5167. Offers programs in community health nursing (MSN), nursing service administration (MSN), psychiatric nursing (MSN). Accredited by NLN. Part-time programs available. Faculty: 18 full-time (all women). Students: 39 full-time (38 women), 91 part-time (85 women); includes 18 minority (17 African Americans, 1 Hispanic). Average age 38. 73 applicants, 71% accepted. In 1997, 28 degrees awarded. *Degree requirements:* Thesis optional, foreign language not required. *Entrance requirements:* GRE General Test, minimum GPA of 2.75. Application deadline: 8/9 (priority date; rolling processing). Application fee: $0 ($25 for international students). *Tuition:* $2870 per year full-time, $137 per credit hour part-time for state residents; $5972 per year full-time, $172 per credit hour part-time for nonresidents. *Financial aid:* Research assistantships, traineeships, Federal Work-Study available. Financial aid application deadline: 3/15. *Faculty research:* Gerontology, stress, chronic illness, disasters, chemical dependency. • Dr. Gerry Cadenhead, Director, 601-266-5509. Fax: 601-266-5927.

University of South Florida, College of Nursing, Tampa, FL 33620-9951. Awards MS, PhD. One or more programs accredited by NLN. Part-time and evening/weekend programs available. Faculty: 40 full-time (39 women). Students: 79 full-time (77 women), 122 part-time (114 women); includes 20 minority (8 African Americans, 6 Asian Americans, 6 Hispanics). 74 applicants, 69% accepted. In 1997, 83 master's awarded. *Degree requirements:* For master's, thesis optional; for doctorate, dissertation. *Entrance requirements:* GRE General Test (minimum combined score of 1000) or minimum GPA of 3.0 in last 60 hours. Application deadline: 6/1 (rolling processing; 10/15 for spring admission). Application fee: $20. *Tuition:* $142 per credit hour for state residents; $486 per credit hour for nonresidents. *Financial aid:* In 1997–98, 55 students received aid, including 2 fellowships averaging $369 per month and totaling $6,650, 4 research assistantships averaging $500 per month and totaling $17,994, 3 teaching assistantships averaging $462 per month and totaling $12,480; Federal Work-Study, institutionally sponsored loans also available. Aid available to part-time students. Financial aid applicants required to submit FAFSA. *Faculty research:* Aging, oncology, substance abuse, domestic violence, acute and chronic illness, women's health issues. Total annual research expenditures: $521,240. • Patricia A. Burns, Dean, 813-974-2191. E-mail: pburns@com1.med.usf.edu. Application contact: Dr. Barbara Redding, 813-974-2191. Fax: 813-974-5418. E-mail: bredding@com1.med.usf.edu.

University of Southwestern Louisiana, College of Nursing, Lafayette, LA 70503. Awards MSN. Accredited by NLN. Offered jointly with McNeese State University, Southeastern Louisiana University, and Southern University and Agricultural and Mechanical College. Faculty: 11 full-time (10 women). Students: 12 full-time (11 women), 16 part-time (15 women); includes 3 minority (all African Americans), 1 international. 21 applicants, 81% accepted. In 1997, 4 degrees awarded. *Entrance requirements:* GRE General Test, minimum GPA of 2.75. Application deadline: 8/15. Application fee: $5 ($15 for international students). *Tuition:* $2012 per year full-time, $300 per semester (minimum) part-time for state residents; $7244 per year full-time, $300 per semester (minimum) part-time for nonresidents. • Dr. Gail Poirrier, Acting Dean, 318-482-6808. Application contact: Dr. Carolyn P. Delahoussaye, Graduate Coordinator, 318-482-6683.

The University of Tampa, Nursing Program, Tampa, FL 33606-1490. Offers family nurse practitioner (MSN), nursing administration (MSN). Part-time and evening/weekend programs available. Postbaccalaureate distance learning degree programs offered (minimal on-campus study). Faculty: 5 full-time (4 women), 7 part-time (6 women). Students: 15 full-time (11 women), 116 part-time (105 women); includes 7 minority (3 African Americans, 1 Asian American, 3 Hispanics). Average age 36. 35 applicants, 80% accepted. In 1997, 35 degrees awarded. *Degree requirements:* Oral exam, practicum required, thesis optional. *Entrance requirements:* GRE General Test (minimum combined score of 1000), minimum GPA of 3.0, RN license. Application deadline: 8/20 (priority date; rolling processing). Application fee: $35. Electronic applications accepted. *Financial aid:* Research assistantships and career-related internships or fieldwork available. Aid available to part-time students. Financial aid applicants required to submit FAFSA. *Faculty research:* Domestic violence (assessment in emergency departments, changing demographics), transcultural health assessment, priorities in maintaining autonomy of elderly. • Dr. Nancy Ross, Director, 813-253-6223. Fax: 813-258-7214. Application contact: Barbara P. Strickler, Vice President for Enrollment, 800-733-4773. Fax: 813-254-4955. E-mail: admissions@alpha.utampa.edu.

University of Tennessee at Chattanooga, School of Human Services, School of Nursing, Chattanooga, TN 37403-2598. Offers programs in administration (MSN), adult health (MSN), education (MSN), family nurse practitioner (MSN), nurse anesthesia (MSN). Faculty: 8 full-time (7 women), 4 part-time (3 women). Students: 56 full-time (35 women), 26 part-time (19 women); includes 5 minority (3 African Americans, 2 Asian Americans). Average age 38. 46 applicants, 91% accepted. In 1997, 24 degrees awarded. *Degree requirements:* Qualifying exams required, foreign language and thesis not required. *Entrance requirements:* GRE General Test (combined average 1485 on three sections). Application deadline: rolling. Application fee: $25. *Tuition:* $2864 per year full-time, $160 per credit hour part-time for state residents; $6806 per year full-time, $379 per credit hour part-time for nonresidents. *Financial aid:* Application deadline 4/1. • Dr. Maria Smith, Director, 423-755-4646. Fax: 423-755-4668. E-mail: msmith@utcvm.utc.edu. Application contact: Dr. Deborah Arfken, Assistant Provost for Graduate Studies, 423-755-4667. Fax: 423-755-4478.

University of Tennessee, Knoxville, College of Nursing, Knoxville, TN 37996. Awards MSN, PhD. One or more programs accredited by NLN. Part-time programs available. Faculty: 27 full-time (all women). Students: 110 full-time (88 women), 40 part-time (34 women); includes 5 minority (2 Asian Americans, 3 Hispanics), 1 international. 128 applicants, 52% accepted. In 1997, 43 master's, 1 doctorate awarded. *Degree requirements:* For master's, thesis or alternative required, foreign language not required; for doctorate, dissertation required, foreign language not required. *Entrance requirements:* GRE General Test, TOEFL (minimum score 550), minimum GPA of 2.7. Application deadline: 2/1 (priority date; rolling processing). Application fee: $35. Electronic applications accepted. *Tuition:* $3354 per year full-time, $181 per semester hour part-time for state residents; $8410 per year full-time, $462 per semester hour part-time for nonresidents. *Financial aid:* In 1997–98, 1 fellowship was awarded; research assistantships, teaching assistantships, graduate assistantships, Federal Work-Study, institutionally sponsored loans also available. Financial aid application deadline: 2/1. • Dr. Joan L. Creasia, Dean, 423-974-4151. Fax: 423-974-3569. E-mail: jcreasia@utk.edu. Application contact: Dr. Martha Alligood, Graduate Representative, 423-974-7607. E-mail: malligoo@utk.edu.

University of Tennessee, Memphis, Colleges of Graduate Health Sciences and Nursing, PhD Program in Nursing, Memphis, TN 38163-0002. Awards PhD. Part-time programs available. Terminal master's awarded for partial completion of doctoral program. *Degree requirements:* For doctorate, dissertation, oral and written preliminary and comprehensive exams required, foreign language not required. *Entrance requirements:* For doctorate, GRE General Test (minimum combined score of 1500), TOEFL, minimum GPA of 3.0. Application fee: $0.

The University of Texas at Arlington, School of Nursing, Arlington, TX 76019-0407. Offers programs in administration/supervision of nursing (MSN), teaching of nursing (MSN). Accredited by NLN. Faculty: 20 full-time (all women), 4 part-time (all women). Students: 38 full-time (33 women), 184 part-time (161 women); includes 21 minority (9 African Americans, 4 Asian Americans, 8 Hispanics), 1 international. 125 applicants, 83% accepted. In 1997, 72 degrees awarded. *Degree requirements:* Comprehensive exam or thesis required, foreign language not required. *Entrance requirements:* GRE General Test (minimum combined score of 1000 on verbal and analytical sections). Application deadline: rolling. Application fee: $25 ($50 for international students). *Tuition:* $3206 per year full-time, $468 per semester (minimum) part-time for state residents; $8612 per year full-time, $1137 per semester (minimum) part-time for nonresidents. *Financial aid:* In 1997–98, 23 fellowships (7 to first-year students), 1 research assistantship, 6 teaching assistantships (2 to first-year students) were awarded; traineeships and career-related internships or fieldwork also available. • Dr. Elizabeth C. Poster, Dean, 817-272-2885. Application contact: Dr. Susan Grove, Graduate Adviser, 817-272-2776. Fax: 817-272-5006.

The University of Texas at Austin, Graduate School, School of Nursing, Austin, TX 78712. Awards MSN, PhD, MBA/MSN. One or more programs accredited by NLN. Faculty: 39 full-time (38 women), 4 part-time (all women), 41 FTE. Students: 267 (239 women); includes 33 minority (5 African Americans, 7 Asian Americans, 19 Hispanics, 2 Native Americans), 29 international. 97 applicants, 66% accepted. In 1997, 48 master's, 28 doctorates awarded. *Degree requirements:* For master's, thesis optional, foreign language not required; for doctorate, dissertation required, foreign language not required. *Entrance requirements:* For master's, GRE General Test (minimum combined score of 1000; average 1125); for doctorate, GRE General Test (minimum combined score of 1000; average 1090). Application deadline: 2/1. Application fee: $50 ($75 for international students). Electronic applications accepted. *Expenses:* Tuition $2592 per year full-time, $324 per semester (minimum) part-time for state residents; $7704 per year full-time, $963 per semester (minimum) part-time for nonresidents. Fees $778 per year full-time, $161 per semester (minimum) part-time. *Financial aid:* In 1997–98, 2 fellowships (both to first-year students) were awarded; research assistantships, teaching assistantships also available. Financial aid application deadline: 2/1. *Faculty research:* Diabetes and chronic illness, ethics, health promotion, nursing interventions, women's and adolescents' health. • Dr. Dolores Sands, Dean, 512-471-7311. Application contact: Dr. Lynn Rew, Graduate Adviser, 512-471-7311.

The University of Texas at El Paso, College of Nursing and Health Science, Program in Nursing, 500 West University Avenue, El Paso, TX 79968-0001. Offers adult health (MSN), community health (MSN), community health/family nurse practitioner (MSN), nurse midwifery (MSN), nursing administration (MSN), parent-child nursing (MSN), psychiatric/mental health nursing (MSN), womens health care/nurse practitioner (MSN). Part-time and evening/weekend programs available. *Degree requirements:* Thesis optional, foreign language not required. *Entrance requirements:* GRE General Test or MAT (minimum score 50), TOEFL (minimum

Directory: Nursing—General

The University of Texas at El Paso (continued)

score 550), BSN, course work in statistics. Application deadline: 7/1 (rolling processing; 11/1 for spring admission). Application fee: $15 ($65 for international students). Electronic applications accepted. *Tuition:* $2063 per year full-time, $284 per credit hour part-time for state residents; $5753 per year full-time, $425 per credit hour part-time for nonresidents. *Faculty research:* Clinical research, administrative research, education.

The University of Texas at Tyler, School of Nursing, Tyler, TX 75799-0001. Awards MSN, MSN/MBA. Accredited by NLN. Part-time programs available. Postbaccalaureate distance learning degree programs offered (minimal on-campus study). Faculty: 8 full-time (all women), 2 part-time (both women), 8.5 FTE. Students: 12 full-time (10 women), 49 part-time (45 women); includes 9 minority (8 African Americans, 1 Hispanic). Average age 40. In 1997, 12 degrees awarded. *Degree requirements:* Computer language, thesis or alternative required, foreign language not required. *Average time to degree:* master's–2 years full-time, 4 years part-time. *Entrance requirements:* GRE General Test (minimum combined score of 1000; average 1057) or MAT (average 50th percentile), minimum undergraduate GPA of 3.0; previous course work in statistics, accounting, and computer programming; RN license. Application deadline: 3/1 (priority date; rolling processing; 10/1 for spring admission). Application fee: $0. *Tuition:* $2144 per year full-time, $337 per semester (minimum) part-time for state residents; $7256 per year full-time, $964 per semester (minimum) part-time for nonresidents. *Financial aid:* 8 students received aid; fellowships, Federal Work-Study, institutionally sponsored loans available. Financial aid application deadline: 7/1. *Faculty research:* Psychosocial adjustment, aging, support/commitment of caregivers, psychological abuse and violence. Total annual research expenditures: $5000. • Dr. Linda Klotz, Dean, 903-566-7320. Application contact: Martha D. Wheat, Director of Admissions and Student Records, 903-566-7201. Fax: 903-566-7068.

The University of Texas Health Science Center at San Antonio, Graduate School of Biomedical Sciences, School of Nursing, San Antonio, TX 78284-6200. Awards MSN, PhD. One or more programs accredited by NLN. Part-time and evening/weekend programs available. *Entrance requirements:* For master's, GRE General Test (minimum combined score of 1000), MAT (minimum score 50), minimum GPA of 3.0. Application deadline: 4/1 (10/1 for spring admission). Application fee: $15. *Faculty research:* Pain, wound healing, thermoregulation, aging, AIDS.

The University of Texas–Houston Health Science Center, School of Nursing, Doctoral Program in Nursing, Houston, TX 77225-0036. Awards DSN. Part-time programs available. Faculty: 65 full-time, 24 part-time, 76.9 FTE. Students: 10 full-time (all women), 3 part-time (all women); includes 3 minority (2 African Americans, 1 Native American), 1 international. Average age 34. 14 applicants, 29% accepted. *Degree requirements:* Dissertation required, foreign language not required. *Entrance requirements:* GRE, interview, MSN, Texas RN license. Application deadline: 5/1 (priority date; rolling processing). Application fee: $10. Electronic applications accepted. *Financial aid:* In 1997–98, 5 federal nurse traineeships were awarded; research assistantships, institutionally sponsored loans also available. Aid available to part-time students. *Faculty research:* Malnutrition in institutionalized elderly, defining nursing, sensitive outcome measures, substance abuse in mothers during pregnancy, psychoeducational intervention among caregivers of stroke patients. Total annual research expenditures: $150,000. • Dr. Janet Meininger, Coordinator, 713-500-2124. Fax: 713-500-2142. E-mail: jmeining@son1.nur.tmc.edu. Application contact: Marisa Mundey, Student Affairs, 713-500-2106. Fax: 713-500-2107. E-mail: mmundey@son1.nur.tmc.edu.

The University of Texas–Houston Health Science Center, School of Nursing, Master's Program in Nursing, Houston, TX 77225-0036. Awards MSN, MSN/MPH. Offerings include acute care (MSN), emergency care nursing (MSN), gerontology nursing (MSN), neonatal (MSN), nurse anesthesia (MSN), oncology nursing (MSN), pediatric nurse practitioner (MSN), perinatal (MSN), psychiatric health nursing (MSN), women's health care (MSN). Accredited by NLN. Part-time programs available. Students: 207 full-time (130 women), 168 part-time (154 women); includes 90 minority (33 African Americans, 35 Asian Americans, 21 Hispanics, 1 Native American), 4 international. Average age 34. 496 applicants, 57% accepted. In 1997, 87 degrees awarded. *Degree requirements:* Thesis required, foreign language not required. *Entrance requirements:* GRE or MAT, BSN, Texas RN license. Application deadline: 5/1 (priority date; rolling processing; 9/1 for spring admission). Application fee: $10. Electronic applications accepted. *Financial aid:* Research assistantships, teaching assistantships, federal nurse traineeships, full tuition waivers, institutionally sponsored loans available. • Frank Cole, Chair, Graduate Curriculum Committee, 713-500-2153. Fax: 713-500-2171. E-mail: fcole@son1.nur.uth.tmc.edu. Application contact: Eleanor Evans, Pre-Admissions Counselor, 713-500-2104. Fax: 713-500-2107. E-mail: eevans@son1.nur.uth.tmc.edu.

The University of Texas Medical Branch at Galveston, Master's Program in Nursing, Galveston, TX 77555. Awards MSN, PhD. One or more programs accredited by NLN. Part-time programs available. Postbaccalaureate distance learning degree programs offered (minimal on-campus study). Faculty: 28 full-time (26 women), 1 part-time (0 women). Students: 61 full-time (55 women), 95 part-time (87 women); includes 17 minority (8 African Americans, 3 Asian Americans, 5 Hispanics, 1 Native American), 1 international. 90 applicants, 48% accepted. In 1997, 72 master's awarded. *Degree requirements:* For master's, thesis optional, foreign language not required. *Entrance requirements:* For master's, GRE General Test (minimum combined score of 1100), MAT (minimum score 45), BSN, minimum GPA of 3.0, 1 year of nursing experience. Application deadline: 2/1 (rolling processing; 8/1 for spring admission). Application fee: $25. *Expenses:* Tuition $36 per credit hour for state residents; $249 per credit hour for nonresidents. Fees $146 per year full-time, $124 per semester (minimum) part-time. *Financial aid:* Traineeships, Federal Work-Study, institutionally sponsored loans available. Aid available to part-time students. • Jeanette Hartshorn, Director, 409-772-7311. Fax: 409-747-1519. E-mail: hartsho@utmb.edu. Application contact: Richard Louis, Registrar, 409-772-1215. Fax: 409-772-5056.

The University of Texas Medical Branch at Galveston, Graduate School of Biomedical Sciences, Doctoral Program in Nursing, Galveston, TX 77555. Awards PhD. Part-time programs available. Faculty: 14 full-time (13 women). Students: 7 full-time (6 women), 1 (woman) part-time. Average age 46. 16 applicants, 56% accepted. *Degree requirements:* Dissertation required, foreign language not required. *Entrance requirements:* GRE General Test (minimum combined score of 1100), MSN, minimum GPA of 3.0. Application deadline: rolling. Application fee: $25 ($50 for international students). *Expenses:* Tuition $36 per credit hour for state residents; $249 per credit hour for nonresidents. Fees $146 per year full-time, $124 per semester (minimum) part-time. *Financial aid:* Research assistantships, traineeships, Federal Work-Study, institutionally sponsored loans available. Financial aid applicants required to submit FAFSA. *Faculty research:* Quality of life, epilepsy, feeding pre-term infants, teen pregnancy prevention, student retention. • Dr. Phyllis Kritek, Director, 409-747-1528. E-mail: pkritek@utmb.edu. Application contact: Chandra Ganesan, Secretary, 409-747-1528. Fax: 409-747-1550. E-mail: cganesan@utmb.edu.

The University of Texas–Pan American, College of Health and Human Services, Department of Nursing, Edinburg, TX 78539-2999. Awards MSN. Part-time and evening/weekend programs available. Faculty: 5 full-time (4 women), 3 part-time (1 woman), 6 FTE. Students: 21 part-time (20 women); includes 18 minority (all Hispanics), 2 international. In 1997, 10 degrees awarded (10% entered university research/teaching, 70% found other work related to degree, 20% continued full-time study). *Degree requirements:* Computer language required, thesis optional, foreign language not required. *Average time to degree:* master's–1.5 years full-time, 2.5 years part-time. *Entrance requirements:* GRE General Test (minimum combined score of 1000), minimum GPA of 3.0. Application deadline: rolling. Application fee: $0. *Tuition:* $2156 per year full-time, $283 per semester (minimum) part-time for state residents; $6788 per year full-time, $862 per semester (minimum) part-time for nonresidents. *Financial aid:* Scholarships and career-related internships or fieldwork available. Aid available to part-time students. *Faculty research:* Health promotion, adolescent pregnancy, herbal and nontraditional approaches. • Dr. Carolina G. Huerta, Chair, 956-381-3495. Fax: 956-381-2384. E-mail: chuerta@panam.edu. Application contact: Student Development Committee, 956-316-7082.

University of the Incarnate Word, School of Graduate Studies, College of Professional Studies, Program in Nursing, San Antonio, TX 78209-6397. Awards MSN, MBA/MSN. Accredited by NLN. Part-time and evening/weekend programs available. Faculty: 9 full-time (7 women), 1 part-time (0 women), 9.12 FTE. *Degree requirements:* Comprehensive exam or thesis required, foreign language not required. *Average time to degree:* master's–2 years full-time, 4 years part-time. *Entrance requirements:* GRE General Test (minimum combined score of 1200), MAT (minimum score 43), TOEFL (minimum score 550), minimum GPA of 3.0. Application deadline: 8/15 (priority date; rolling processing; 12/31 for spring admission). Application fee: $20. *Expenses:* Tuition $350 per semester hour. Fees $180 per year full-time, $111 per semester (minimum) part-time. *Financial aid:* Federal traineeships available. Aid available to part-time students. Financial aid application deadline: 3/1. *Faculty research:* Learning styles, epilepsy, menopausal women, addictive behavior, adolescent pregnancy. • Dr. Sara E. Kolb, Graduate Director, 210-829-6029.

University of Toronto, School of Graduate Studies, Life Sciences Division, Department of Nursing Science, Toronto, ON M5S 1A1, Canada. Awards MN, M Sc, PhD. Part-time programs available. Faculty: 39. Students: 75 full-time (74 women), 181 part-time (174 women); includes 1 international. 128 applicants, 74% accepted. In 1997, 29 master's awarded. *Degree requirements:* For doctorate, dissertation. *Application fee:* $75. *Expenses:* Tuition $4070 per year for Canadian residents; $7870 per year for nonresidents. Fees $628 per year. *Financial aid:* Career-related internships or fieldwork available. • J. Graydon, Chair, 416-978-2853. Application contact: Secretary, 416-978-2067. Fax: 416-978-8222. E-mail: graduate.nursing@utoronto.ca.

University of Utah, College of Nursing, Program in Nursing, Salt Lake City, UT 84112-1107. Awards MS, PhD. One or more programs accredited by NLN. Part-time programs available. Students: 131 full-time (114 women), 69 part-time (58 women); includes 8 minority (1 Asian American, 5 Hispanics, 2 Native Americans), 4 international. In 1997, 75 master's, 7 doctorates awarded. *Degree requirements:* For master's, thesis or project required, foreign language not required; for doctorate, dissertation required, foreign language not required. *Entrance requirements:* For master's, GRE, TOEFL (minimum score 500), Utah RN license; for doctorate, GRE, TOEFL (minimum score 500), interview, Utah RN license. Application deadline: 7/1. Application fee: $30 ($50 for international students). *Tuition:* $2045 per year full-time, $562 per semester (minimum) part-time for state residents; $6129 per year full-time, $1607 per semester (minimum) part-time for nonresidents. • Application contact: Joyce Rathbun, Graduate Adviser, 801-581-8798. E-mail: jrathbun@nursac.nurs.utah.edu.

University of Vermont, School of Nursing, Burlington, VT 05405-0160. Awards MS. Accredited by NLN. Students: 50; includes 1 international. 26 applicants, 65% accepted. In 1997, 2 degrees awarded. *Entrance requirements:* GRE General Test, TOEFL (minimum score 550). Application deadline: 4/1 (priority date; rolling processing). Application fee: $25. *Expenses:* Tuition $302 per credit for state residents; $755 per credit for nonresidents. Fees $434 per year full-time, $46 per semester (minimum) part-time. *Financial aid:* Application deadline 3/1. • M. McGrath, Interim Dean, 802-656-3399. Application contact: C. Gilbert, Coordinator, 802-656-3399.

University of Virginia, School of Nursing, Charlottesville, VA 22903. Awards MSN, PhD, MSN/MBA. One or more programs accredited by NLN. Faculty: 46 full-time (40 women), 5 part-time (4 women), 48 FTE. Students: 77 full-time (71 women), 55 part-time (50 women); includes 5 minority (3 African Americans, 2 Asian Americans), 3 international. Average age 36. 113 applicants, 72% accepted. In 1997, 43 master's, 4 doctorates awarded. *Entrance requirements:* For master's, GRE General Test, MAT. Application deadline: 4/1 (12/1 for spring admission). Application fee: $40. *Tuition:* $4906 per year full-time, $959 per semester (minimum) part-time for state residents; $15,854 per year full-time, $2763 per semester (minimum) part-time for nonresidents. *Financial aid:* Fellowships, Federal Work-Study available. • B. Jeanette Lancaster, Dean, 804-924-0063. Application contact: Gregg E. Newschwander, Admissions and Advisement, 804-924-0067. E-mail: nur-osa@virginia.edu.

University of Washington, School of Nursing, Seattle, WA 98195. Awards MN, MS, PhD, MN/MPH. One or more programs accredited by NLN. Part-time programs available. *Entrance requirements:* For master's, GRE, TOEFL, minimum GPA of 3.0; for doctorate, GRE, TOEFL (minimum score 500), minimum GPA of 3.0. Application deadline: 2/1. Application fee: $45. *Tuition:* $5433 per year full-time, $775 per quarter (minimum) part-time for state residents; $13,479 per year full-time, $1925 per quarter (minimum) part-time for nonresidents.

The University of Western Ontario, Social Sciences Division, Faculty of Nursing, London, ON N6A 5B8, Canada. Awards M Sc N. Part-time programs available. Faculty: 10 full-time (all women), 12 part-time (all women). Students: 14 full-time (all women), 30 part-time (all women). 17 applicants, 76% accepted. *Degree requirements:* Research project required, thesis optional. *Average time to degree:* master's–2.5 years full-time, 4.5 years part-time. *Entrance requirements:* Minimum B average, BA in nursing. Application deadline: 2/1. Application fee: $50. *Financial aid:* 13 students received aid; research assistantships available. Financial aid application deadline: 4/1. *Faculty research:* Empowerment, self-efficacy, family health, community health, gerontology. • Dr. Carroll Iwasiw, Acting Director, 519-661-6592.

University of Windsor, Faculty of Science, Department of Nursing, Windsor, ON N9B 3P4, Canada. Awards M Sc. *Degree requirements:* Thesis optional. *Entrance requirements:* TOEFL (minimum score 550). Application deadline: 2/15 (priority date; rolling processing). Application fee: $50. *Expenses:* Tuition $4370 per year (minimum) full-time, $345 per course (minimum) part-time for Canadian residents; $8453 per year (minimum) full-time, $915 per course (minimum) part-time for nonresidents. Fees $462 per year (minimum) full-time, $141 per year (minimum) part-time.

University of Wisconsin–Eau Claire, College of Professional Studies, School of Nursing, Eau Claire, WI 54702-4004. Awards MSN. Accredited by NLN. Part-time programs available. Students: 29 full-time (all women), 84 part-time (80 women); includes 6 minority (1 African American, 3 Asian Americans, 2 Native Americans). Average age 37. In 1997, 26 degrees awarded. *Degree requirements:* Thesis, oral and written exams required, foreign language not required. *Entrance requirements:* GRE General Test. Application deadline: 7/1 (rolling processing; 12/1 for spring admission). Application fee: $45. *Tuition:* $3651 per year full-time, $611 per semester (minimum) part-time for state residents; $11,295 per year full-time, $1886 per semester (minimum) part-time for nonresidents. *Financial aid:* Federal Work-Study available. Aid available to part-time students. Financial aid application deadline: 3/1. • Dr. Marjorie Bottoms, Associate Dean, 715-836-5287.

University of Wisconsin–Madison, School of Nursing, Madison, WI 53792-2455. Awards MS, PhD. One or more programs accredited by NLN. Part-time programs available. Faculty: 22 full-time (all women), 1 (woman) part-time, 22.7 FTE. Students: 67 full-time (65 women), 94 part-time (all women); includes 8 minority (1 African American, 2 Asian Americans, 4 Hispanics, 1 Native American), 10 international. Average age 37. 69 applicants, 35% accepted. In 1997, 71 master's awarded; 6 doctorates awarded (100% entered university research/teaching). *Degree requirements:* For master's, research practicum required, thesis not required; for doctorate, dissertation. *Average time to degree:* master's–1.7 years full-time, 2.5 years part-time; doctorate–4 years full-time, 5 years part-time. *Entrance requirements:* For master's, GRE General Test, BS in nursing from an NLN-accredited program, minimum GPA of 3.0 in last 60 credits, professional nursing license, course work in statistics during previous 2 years, 1 year of professional experience; for doctorate, GRE General Test (minimum combined score of 1200), BS in nursing from an NLN-accredited program, minimum undergraduate GPA of 3.0 in last 60 credits, 2 samples of scholarly written work. Application deadline: 3/1 (10/1 for spring admission). Application fee: $45. Electronic applications accepted. *Tuition:* $4928 per year full-time, $926 per semester (minimum) part-time for state residents; $15,190 per year full-time, $2849 per semester (minimum) part-time for nonresidents. *Financial aid:* In 1997–98, 25 fellowships, 4 research assistantships, 5 teaching assistantships, 33 scholarships totaling $30,000 were awarded; Federal Work-Study, institutionally sponsored loans, and career-related internships or fieldwork also available. Aid available to part-time students. Financial aid application deadline: 5/1. *Faculty research:* Nursing informatics to promote self-care and disease management skills among patients and caregivers; quality of care to frail, vulnerable, and chronically ill populations; coping with cancer, especially pain and symptom management; family resilience and adaptation to chronic illness; study of health-related and health-seeking behaviors; anorexia as a human response to illness or injury. Total annual research expenditures: $1.635 million. • Dr. Vivian M. Littlefield, Dean, 608-263-5155. Fax: 608-263-5323. E-mail: vmlittle@facstaff.wisc.edu. Application contact: Susan Kosharek, Program Assistant, 608-263-5180. Fax: 608-263-5332. E-mail: sjkoshar@facstaff.wisc.edu.

University of Wisconsin–Milwaukee, School of Nursing, Milwaukee, WI 53201-0413. Awards MS, PhD. One or more programs accredited by NLN. Part-time programs available. Faculty: 34 full-time (all women). Students: 48 full-time (45 women), 128 part-time (122 women); includes 13 minority (8 African Americans, 3 Asian Americans, 1 Hispanic, 1 Native American), 2 international. 81 applicants, 54% accepted. In 1997, 38 master's, 6 doctorates awarded. *Degree requirements:* For master's, thesis required, foreign language not required; for doctorate, dissertation. *Entrance requirements:* For master's, GRE General Test or MAT. Application deadline: 1/1 (priority date; rolling processing; 9/1 for spring admission). Application fee: $45 ($75 for international students). *Tuition:* $4996 per year full-time, $1030 per semester (minimum) part-time for state residents; $15,216 per year full-time, $2947 per semester (minimum) part-time for nonresidents. *Financial aid:* In 1997–98, 2 fellowships, 1 research assistantship, 3 teaching assistantships, 5 project assistantships were awarded; Federal Work-Study and career-related internships or fieldwork also available. Aid available to part-time students. Financial aid application deadline: 4/15. • Sharon Hoffman, Dean, 414-229-5468. Application contact: Ellen K. Murphy, Representative, 414-229-5468.

University of Wisconsin–Oshkosh, College of Nursing, Oshkosh, WI 54901-8602. Offers programs in family nurse practitioner (MSN), primary health care (MSN). Accredited by NLN. Part-time programs available. Faculty: 5 full-time (all women), 12 part-time (11 women). Students: 39 full-time (37 women), 32 part-time (all women); includes 3 minority (1 African American, 1 Asian American, 1 Hispanic). Average age 33. 30 applicants, 100% accepted. In 1997, 48 degrees awarded (100% found work related to degree). *Degree requirements:* Thesis or alternative required, foreign language not required. *Entrance requirements:* RN license, BSN, course work in statistics and health assessment in past 5 years, minimum undergraduate GPA of 3.0. Application deadline: 1/15. Application fee: $45. *Tuition:* $3638 per year full-time, $609 per semester (minimum) part-time for state residents; $11,282 per year full-time, $1884 per semester (minimum) part-time for nonresidents. *Financial aid:* In 1997–98, 39 federal traineeships (13 to first-year students) totaling $57,686 were awarded; Federal Work-Study and career-related internships or fieldwork also available. Aid available to part-time students. Financial aid application deadline: 3/15. *Faculty research:* Gerontology, nurse practitioners practice, health care service, advanced practitioner roles. • Dr. Merritt Knox, Dean, 920-424-3089. Application contact: Dr. Michael Morgan, Director of Graduate Programs, 920-424-2106. E-mail: morganm@uwosh.edu.

University of Wyoming, College of Health Sciences, School of Nursing, Laramie, WY 82071. Awards MS. Accredited by NLN. Part-time programs available. Faculty: 14 full-time (all women). Students: 22 full-time (19 women), 31 part-time (29 women); includes 3 minority (all Hispanics), 1 international. 43 applicants, 42% accepted. In 1997, 10 degrees awarded. *Entrance requirements:* GRE General Test (minimum combined score of 900), BSN from NLN-accredited school, minimum GPA of 3.0. Application deadline: 11/15 (priority date). Application fee: $40. *Expenses:* Tuition $2430 per year full-time, $135 per credit hour part-time for state residents; $7518 per year full-time, $418 per credit hour part-time for nonresidents. Fees $386 per year full-time, $9.25 per credit hour part-time. *Financial aid:* Research assistantships, teaching assistantships, scholarships, traineeships, institutionally sponsored loans, and career-related internships or fieldwork available. Aid available to part-time students. Financial aid application deadline: 3/1. *Faculty research:* Rural health, strokes, support systems for the elderly, breastfeeding, fetal alcohol syndrome, teen pregnancy, selfcare responses, interventions/outcomes in homecare. • Dr. Marcia Dale, Dean, 307-766-6569. E-mail: marcia@uwyo.edu. Application contact: Debbie Shoefelt, Office Associate, 307-766-4292. Fax: 307-766-4294. E-mail: shoefelt@uwyo.edu.

Ursuline College, Graduate Studies, Graduate Program in Nursing, Pepper Pike, OH 44124-4398. Awards MSN. Program new for fall 1998. *Entrance requirements:* Minimum undergraduate GPA of 3.0. Application deadline: 8/1 (priority date; rolling processing). Application fee: $25. *Expenses:* Tuition $405 per credit hour. Fees $22 per credit hour. *Financial aid:* Application deadline 3/1. • Dr. Carole Cashion, Dean, 440-646-8166.

Valdosta State University, College of Nursing, Valdosta, GA 31698. Offers programs in administration (MSN), community health nursing (MSN). Accredited by NLN. Part-time programs available. Faculty: 3 full-time (all women). Students: 22 full-time (20 women), 4 part-time (3 women); includes 6 minority (3 African Americans, 3 Hispanics). Average age 32. 15 applicants, 80% accepted. In 1997, 20 degrees awarded. *Entrance requirements:* GRE General Test (minimum combined score of 800), minimum GPA of 2.8. Application deadline: 8/1 (rolling processing; 11/15 for spring admission). Application fee: $10. *Expenses:* Tuition $2472 per year full-time, $83 per semester hour part-time for state residents; $8472 per year full-time, $333 per semester hour part-time for nonresidents. Fees $236 per year full-time. *Financial aid:* Federal Work-Study available. Aid available to part-time students. Financial aid application deadline: 7/1. *Faculty research:* Nutrition, children's health beliefs, alternative treatment modalities, job satisfaction, leadership. • Dr. Maryann Reichenbach, Dean, 912-333-5959. E-mail: mreichenb@grits.valdosta.peachnet.edu.

Valparaiso University, College of Nursing, Valparaiso, IN 46383-6493. Awards MSN. Accredited by NLN. Faculty: 12 (all women). Students: 3 full-time (all women), 23 part-time (20 women). Average age 42. 0% of applicants accepted. In 1997, 31 degrees awarded. *Entrance requirements:* Minimum GPA of 3.0. Application deadline: rolling. Application fee: $30. *Financial aid:* Federal Work-Study, institutionally sponsored loans, and career-related internships or fieldwork available. Financial aid applicants required to submit FAFSA. • Dr. Cynthia Russell, Acting Dean, 219-464-5289. Fax: 219-464-5425.

Vanderbilt University, School of Nursing, Nashville, TN 37240-1001. Awards MSN, PhD, MBA/MSN. Programs in adult acute care nurse practitioner (MSN), family nurse practitioner (MSN), gerontology nurse practitioner (MSN), health systems management (MSN), neonatal critical care practitioner (MSN), neonatal nurse practitioner (MSN), nurse midwifery (MSN), nursing science (PhD), occupational health/adult health nurse practitioner (MSN), pediatric nurse practitioner (MSN), psychiatric-mental health nurse practitioner (MSN), women's health nurse practitioner (MSN). One or more programs accredited by NLN. Part-time programs available. Postbaccalaureate distance learning degree programs offered (minimal on-campus study). Faculty: 76 full-time (66 women), 253 part-time (224 women). Students: 376 full-time (323 women), 89 part-time (84 women); includes 33 minority (17 African Americans, 11 Asian Americans, 1 Hispanic, 4 Native Americans), 4 international. Average age 29. 649 applicants, 67% accepted. In 1997, 259 master's, 1 doctorate awarded. *Degree requirements:* For master's, terminal course required, thesis not required; for doctorate, dissertation. *Average time to degree:* master's–2 years full-time, 4 years part-time; doctorate–4 years full-time, 5 years part-time. *Entrance requirements:* For master's, GMAT, GRE, or MAT, minimum B average; for doctorate, GRE. Application deadline: rolling. Application fee: $50. Electronic applications accepted. *Financial aid:* Fellowships, research assistantships, teaching assistantships, full tuition waivers, Federal Work-Study, institutionally sponsored loans available. Aid available to part-time students. Financial aid application deadline: 3/15; applicants required to submit CSS PROFILE or FAFSA. *Faculty research:* Stress and coping in children and adults, health promotion, chronic illness, health care delivery systems and patient outcomes. Total annual research expenditures: $506,304. • Dr. Colleen Conway-Welch, Dean, 615-343-3243. Fax: 615-343-7711. Application contact: Patricia Peerman, Assistant Dean of Admissions, 615-322-3800. Fax: 615-343-0333. E-mail: vusn-admission@mcmail.vanderbilt.edu.

Vanderbilt University, Graduate School, Program in Nursing Science, Nashville, TN 37240-1001. Awards PhD. Offered jointly with the School of Nursing. Faculty: 11 full-time (8 women). Students: 7 full-time (all women), 4 part-time (3 women); includes 1 minority (African American). Average age 38. 12 applicants, 67% accepted. In 1997, 1 degree awarded. *Degree requirements:* Dissertation, final and qualifying exams required, foreign language not required. *Entrance requirements:* GRE General Test. Application deadline: 1/15. Application fee: $40. *Expenses:* Tuition $16,452 per year full-time, $914 per semester hour part-time. Fees $236 per year. *Financial aid:* 11 students received aid; research assistantships, teaching assistantships, full and partial tuition waivers, and career-related internships or fieldwork available. Financial aid application deadline: 1/15. *Faculty research:* Adaptation to chronic illness/conditions, health problems related to stress and coping, vulnerable childbearing and childrearing families. • Dr. Colleen Conway-Welch, Dean, School of Nursing, 615-343-8876. E-mail: colleen.conway.welch@mcmail.vanderbilt.edu. Application contact: Gail L. Ingersoll, Director, 615-343-4173. Fax: 615-343-7711. E-mail: gail.ingersoll@mcmail.vanderbilt.edu.

Villanova University, College of Nursing, Villanova, PA 19085-1690. Offers programs in adult nurse practitioner (MSN), clinical case management (MSN, Post Master's Certificate), health care administration (MSN), nurse anesthetist (MSN, Post Master's Certificate), nurse practitioner (Post Master's Certificate), nursing education (MSN), pediatric nurse practitioner (MSN). Accredited by NLN. MSN (pediatric nurse practitioner), Post Master's Certificate (nurse practitioner, nurse anesthetist, clinical case management) new for fall 1998. Part-time and evening/weekend programs available. Faculty: 30 full-time (all women). Students: 17 full-time (13 women), 98 part-time (95 women); includes 1 African American, 3 Asian Americans, 2 Hispanics, 3 international. Average age 35. 30 applicants, 77% accepted. In 1997, 52 master's awarded. *Degree requirements:* For master's, independent study project required, foreign language and thesis not required. *Entrance requirements:* For master's, GRE General Test (verbal section) or MAT, BSN, 1 year of recent experience, physical assessment, previous course work in statistics. Application deadline: 7/1 (priority date; rolling processing; 12/1 for spring admission). Application fee: $25. *Expenses:* Tuition $445 per credit. Fees $60 per year. *Financial aid:* In 1997–98, 15 students received aid, including 6 graduate assistantships, tuition scholarships (3 to first-year students); institutionally sponsored loans and career-related internships or fieldwork also available. Financial aid application deadline: 3/1. *Faculty research:* Women's health issues, leadership, genetics, clinical ethics, cognitive development of students. • Dr. Claire Manfredi, Graduate Director, 610-519-4907. Fax: 610-519-7997. E-mail: cmanfred@email.vill.edu.

Announcement: The College offers 45-credit, NLN-accredited master's program, preparing primary care adult nurse practitioners, nurse anesthetists, nurse educators, health service administrators, and clinical case managers. Subspecialty in community health administration available. Program focuses on nursing leadership, advanced nursing knowledge, clinical practice, role development, and preparation for doctoral study.

Virginia Commonwealth University, School of Nursing, Richmond, VA 23284-9005. Offers programs in adult health nursing (MS); biology of health and illness (PhD); child health nursing (MS); family health nursing (MS); human health and illness (PhD); nurse practitioner (Certificate); nursing administration (MS), including clinical nurse manager, nurse executive; nursing systems (PhD); psychiatric-mental health nursing (MS); women's health nursing (MS). One or more programs accredited by NLN. Part-time and evening/weekend programs available. Faculty: 50 full-time (all women), 5 part-time (all women). Students: 116 full-time (108 women), 118 part-time (113 women); includes 22 minority (12 African Americans, 7 Asian Americans, 2 Hispanics, 1 Native American), 5 international. Average age 37. 202 applicants, 55% accepted. In 1997, 38 master's, 6 doctorates, 14 Certificates awarded. *Entrance requirements:* For master's, GRE General Test, BSN, minimum GPA of 2.8; for doctorate, GRE General Test. Application deadline: 2/1. Application fee: $30 ($0 for international students). *Tuition:* $4960 per year full-time, $257 per credit part-time for state residents; $12,652 per year full-time, $684 per credit part-time for nonresidents. *Financial aid:* Fellowships, research assistantships, teaching assistantships, institutionally sponsored loans, and career-related internships or fieldwork available. • Dr. Nancy F. Langston, Dean, 804-828-5174. E-mail: nflangst@vcu.edu. Application contact: Susan Lipp, Admissions Counselor, 804-828-5171. Fax: 804-828-7743. E-mail: sllipp@vcu.edu.

Viterbo College, Graduate Program in Nursing, La Crosse, WI 54601-4797. Awards MSN. Program new for fall 1998. *Entrance requirements:* GRE General Test or MAT, bachelor's degree in nursing, minimum GPA of 3.0, RN license. Application deadline: 3/1 (priority date; rolling processing). Application fee: $25. • Bonnie Nesbitt, Director, 608-796-3688. E-mail: bjnesbitt@mail.viterbo.edu. Application contact: School of Nursing, 608-796-3670.

Wagner College, Department of Nursing, Program in Nursing, Staten Island, NY 10301. Awards MS. Accredited by NLN. Part-time and evening/weekend programs available. Faculty: 5 full-time (4 women), 1 (woman) part-time. Students: 11 full-time (9 women), 75 part-time (70 women); includes 4 minority (3 African Americans, 1 Asian American). 24 applicants, 88% accepted. In 1997, 14 degrees awarded. *Degree requirements:* Thesis optional, foreign language not required. *Entrance requirements:* BS in nursing, current clinical experience, minimum GPA of 2.75. Application deadline: 8/1 (priority date; rolling processing; 12/10 for spring admission). Application fee: $50 ($65 for international students). *Tuition:* $580 per credit. *Financial aid:* In 1997–98, 4 teaching assistantships (1 to a first-year student) averaging $300 per month and totaling $9,600, 6 alumni fellowships (4 to first-year students) were awarded. • Application contact: Admissions Office, 718-390-3411.

Washington State University, School of Nursing, Pullman, WA 99164-1610. Awards M Nurs. Offered jointly with Eastern Washington University and Whitworth College. Part-time programs available. Faculty: 22 full-time (21 women). Students: 20 full-time (18 women), 25 part-time (21 women); includes 2 minority (1 Asian American, 1 Hispanic). Average age 39. In 1997, 23 degrees awarded. *Degree requirements:* Thesis or alternative, oral exam required, foreign language not required. *Average time to degree:* master's–2 years full-time, 4 years part-time. *Entrance requirements:* BSN, minimum GPA of 3.0. Application deadline: 3/1 (priority date; rolling processing; 11/15 for spring admission). Application fee: $35. Electronic applications accepted. *Tuition:* $5334 per year full-time, $267 per credit hour part-time for state residents; $13,380 per year full-time, $677 per credit hour part-time for nonresidents. *Financial aid:* In 1997–98, 2 teaching assistantships were awarded; research assistantships, partial tuition waivers, Federal Work-Study, institutionally sponsored loans also available. Financial aid application deadline: 4/1; applicants required to submit FAFSA. *Faculty research:* Home health care, nursing informatics, primary care of homeless, ethics, violence against women. Total annual research expenditures: $102,183. • Dr. Dorothy Detlor, Dean, 509-324-7333. Application contact: Margaret Ruby, Administrative Assistant, 509-324-7334. Fax: 509-324-7336. E-mail: mruby@wsu.edu.

Wayne State University, College of Nursing, Detroit, MI 48202. Awards MSN, PhD, Certificate. One or more programs accredited by NLN. Part-time programs available. Faculty: 69. Students: 64 full-time (62 women), 255 part-time (249 women); includes 42 minority (38 African Americans, 1 Asian American, 2 Hispanics, 1 Native American), 19 international. Average age 39. 81 applicants, 59% accepted. In 1997, 49 master's, 18 doctorates, 5 Certificates awarded. Terminal master's awarded for partial completion of doctoral program. *Degree requirements:* For master's, computer language, thesis or alternative required, foreign language not required; for doctorate, computer language, dissertation required, foreign language not required. *Entrance requirements:* For master's, GRE General Test (minimum combined score of 800), minimum GPA of 2.8; for doctorate, GRE General Test (minimum score 400 on each section, 1000 combined), minimum GPA of 3.3. Application deadline: rolling. Application fee: $20 ($30 for international students). *Expenses:* Tuition $163 per credit hour for state residents; $355 per

Directory: Nursing—General

Wayne State University (continued)
credit hour for nonresidents. Fees $498 per year full-time, $114 per semester (minimum) part-time. *Financial aid:* In 1997–98, 47 students received aid, including 4 fellowships, 10 research assistantships, 2 teaching assistantships, 31 scholarships, traineeships (5 to first-year students); Federal Work-Study, institutionally sponsored loans also available. Aid available to part-time students. Financial aid application deadline: 7/1; applicants required to submit FAFSA. *Faculty research:* Self-care; transcultural care; adaptation to acute and chronic illness; urban health and health care systems. • Dr. Barbara Redman, Dean, 313-577-4070. Application contact: Vickie Radoye, Administrative Assistant Dean, Student Affairs, 313-577-4082. Fax: 313-577-6949.

Webster University, College of Arts and Sciences, Department of Nursing, St. Louis, MO 63119-3194. Offers program in family systems nursing (MSN). Faculty: 3 full-time (all women). Students: 13 full-time (all women), 12 part-time (11 women); includes 1 minority (African American). 19 applicants, 74% accepted. *Entrance requirements:* 1 year of clinical experience, BSN, interview, minimum C+ in statistics and physical assessment, minimum GPA of 3.0, RN license. Application deadline: rolling. Application fee: $25 ($50 for international students). *Tuition:* $350 per credit hour. *Financial aid:* Federal Work-Study available. Aid available to part-time students. Financial aid application deadline: 4/1; applicants required to submit FAFSA. *Faculty research:* Health teaching. • Janice Hooper, Chair, 314-968-7488. Fax: 314-963-6101. E-mail: hooperjl@webster.edu. Application contact: Beth Russell, Director of Graduate Admissions, 314-968-7089. Fax: 314-968-7166. E-mail: russelmb@webster.edu.

West Chester University of Pennsylvania, School of Health Sciences, Department of Nursing, West Chester, PA 19383. Offers programs in community health nursing (MSN), nursing (MS). Accredited by NLN. Students: 9 full-time (all women), 23 part-time (22 women); includes 2 minority (both Asian Americans). Average age 30. 4 applicants, 75% accepted. In 1997, 8 degrees awarded. *Degree requirements:* Comprehensive exam required, foreign language not required. *Entrance requirements:* GRE General Test or MAT, RN license. Application deadline: 4/15 (priority date; rolling processing; 10/15 for spring admission). Application fee: $25. *Expenses:* Tuition $3468 per year full-time, $193 per credit part-time for state residents; $6236 per year full-time, $346 per credit part-time for nonresidents. Fees $660 per year full-time, $38 per credit part-time. *Financial aid:* Research assistantships available. Financial aid application deadline: 2/15. • Anne Coghlan Stowe, Chair, 610-436-2219. Application contact: Jan Hickman, Graduate Coordinator, 610-436-2219.

Western Connecticut State University, School of Professional Studies, Program in Nursing, Danbury, CT 06810-6885. Awards MSN. Accredited by NLN. Part-time and evening/weekend programs available. Students: 5 full-time (all women), 14 part-time (all women). In 1997, 30 degrees awarded. *Degree requirements:* Thesis. *Entrance requirements:* MAT (minimum score 51), bachelor's degree in nursing, minimum GPA of 3.0, previous course work in statistics and nursing research, RN license. Application deadline: 8/1 (priority date; rolling processing). Application fee: $40. *Expenses:* Tuition $4127 per year (minimum) full-time, $178 per credit hour part-time for state residents; $9581 per year (minimum) full-time, $178 per credit hour part-time for nonresidents. Fees $25 per year part-time. *Financial aid:* Federal Work-Study and career-related internships or fieldwork available. Aid available to part-time students. Financial aid application deadline: 5/1. • Dr. Barbara Piscopo, Chairperson, 203-837-8557.

Western Kentucky University, Ogden College of Science, Technology, and Health, Department of Nursing, Bowling Green, KY 42101-3576. Awards MSN. Part-time programs available. Faculty: 7 full-time (all women). Students: 8 full-time (all women), 11 part-time (10 women). Average age 33. 18 applicants, 89% accepted. In 1997, 6 degrees awarded (100% found work related to degree). *Degree requirements:* Thesis optional, foreign language not required. *Average time to degree:* master's–2.5 years part-time. *Entrance requirements:* GRE General Test. Application deadline: 8/1 (priority date; rolling processing; 4/14 for spring admission). Application fee: $20. *Tuition:* $2460 per year full-time, $133 per credit hour part-time for state residents; $6700 per year full-time, $369 per credit hour part-time for nonresidents. *Financial aid:* In 1997–98, 1 research assistantship (to a first-year student) totaling $5,000, 2 traineeships averaging $731 per month and totaling $13,174 were awarded; Federal Work-Study, institutionally sponsored loans also available. Aid available to part-time students. Financial aid application deadline: 4/1; applicants required to submit FAFSA. • Dr. Kay Carr, Interim Head, 502-745-3391. Fax: 502-745-3392.

Western University of Health Sciences, Program in Nursing, Pomona, CA 91766-1854. Offers family nurse practitioner (MSN). Students: 10. *Application deadline:* rolling. *Application fee:* $60. *Tuition:* $17,150 per year. • Dr. Ted Wendel, Chancellor, 916-898-7020. Application contact: Susan M. Hanson, Director of Admissions, 909-469-5335.

Westminster College of Salt Lake City, St. Mark's-Westminster School of Nursing and Health Sciences, Program in Nursing, Salt Lake City, UT 84105-3697. Awards MSN. Part-time and evening/weekend programs available. Faculty: 4 full-time (all women), 3 part-time (2 women), 4.5 FTE. Students: 27 full-time (25 women), 5 part-time (4 women); includes 2 minority (1 African American, 1 Hispanic), 1 international. Average age 39. 44 applicants, 39% accepted. In 1997, 12 degrees awarded. *Degree requirements:* Thesis or alternative, project or thesis required, foreign language not required. *Average time to degree:* master's–2 years full-time, 4 years part-time. *Entrance requirements:* Resume, Utah RN license. Application deadline: 3/1 (priority date; rolling processing). Application fee: $25. Electronic applications accepted. *Expenses:* Tuition $448 per credit hour. Fees $200 per year full-time, $65 per semester (minimum) part-time. *Financial aid:* In 1997–98, 19 students received aid, including 2 scholarships, tuition remissions totaling $8,405; Federal Work-Study also available. Aid available to part-time students. Financial aid applicants required to submit FAFSA. • Dr. Sharon Bator, Interim Director, 801-488-1648. Fax: 801-467-8601. E-mail: s-bator@wcslc.edu. Application contact: Philip J. Alletto, Vice President for Student Development and Enrollment Management, 801-488-4200. Fax: 801-484-3252. E-mail: admispub@wcslc.edu.

West Texas A&M University, College of Agriculture, Nursing, and Natural Sciences, Division of Nursing, Canyon, TX 79016-0001. Awards MSN. Accredited by NLN. Part-time programs available. Faculty: 3 full-time (all women), 2 part-time (both women). Students: 4 full-time (3 women), 64 part-time (55 women); includes 3 minority (all Hispanics). Average age 34. 19 applicants, 42% accepted. In 1997, 43 degrees awarded. *Degree requirements:* Comprehensive exam required, thesis optional, foreign language not required. *Average time to degree:* master's–3 years full-time, 6 years part-time. *Entrance requirements:* GRE General Test (minimum combined score of 950; average 964), bachelor's degree in nursing, minimum GPA of 3.0 in last 60 hours. Application deadline: rolling. Application fee: $0 ($50 for international students). Electronic applications accepted. *Expenses:* Tuition $46 per semester hour for state residents; $259 per semester hour for nonresidents. Fees $156 per semester (minimum). *Financial aid:* Partial tuition waivers, Federal Work-Study, institutionally sponsored loans, and career-related internships or fieldwork available. Aid available to part-time students. Financial aid applicants required to submit FAFSA. *Faculty research:* Family-focused nursing, nursing traineeship. • Dr. Heidi Taylor, Head, 806-651-2630. Fax: 806-651-2632. E-mail: heidi.taylor@wtamu.edu. Application contact: Rebecca Robinson, Graduate Adviser, 806-651-2629. E-mail: rebecca.robinson@wtamu.edu.

West Virginia University, School of Nursing, Morgantown, WV 26506. Offers programs in nurse practitioner (Certificate), nursing (MSN). Part-time programs available. Postbaccalaureate distance learning degree programs offered (minimal on-campus study). Faculty: 38 full-time (37 women). Students: 37 full-time (36 women), 59 part-time (55 women); includes 2 minority (1 Asian American, 1 Hispanic). Average age 36. 43 applicants, 93% accepted. In 1997, 24 master's awarded. *Degree requirements:* For master's, thesis or alternative required, foreign language not required. *Average time to degree:* master's–2 years full-time, 4 years part-time. *Entrance requirements:* For master's, GRE General Test (minimum score 400 on verbal section, 350 on qualitative, 400 on analytical), TOEFL (minimum score 550), minimum GPA of 3.0, current U.S. RN license, BSN degree, previous course work in statistics and physical assessment. Application deadline: 6/1 (10/1 for spring admission). Application fee: $45. *Tuition:* $3452 per year for state residents; $9908 per year for nonresidents. *Financial aid:* In 1997–98, 18 students received aid, including 2 research assistantships, 1 graduate administrative assistantship; full and partial tuition waivers, Federal Work-Study, institutionally sponsored loans, and career-related internships or fieldwork also available. Financial aid application deadline: 2/1; applicants required to submit FAFSA. *Faculty research:* Rural primary health/health promotion, parent/child/women's health, cardiovascular risk reduction, complementary health modalities, breast cancer detection-care. Total annual research expenditures: $32,846. • Dr. E. Jane Martin, Dean, 304-293-4831. Application contact: Jacqueline W. Riley, Assistant Dean for Student and Alumni Affairs, 304-293-1386. Fax: 304-293-6826. E-mail: jriley@wvu.edu.

Wheeling Jesuit University, Department of Nursing, Wheeling, WV 26003-6295. Awards MSN. Accredited by NLN. Part-time and evening/weekend programs available. Faculty: 5 full-time (all women). Students: 27 part-time (all women); includes 1 minority (Hispanic). *Degree requirements:* Thesis required, foreign language not required. *Entrance requirements:* GRE General Test (minimum combined score of 900), BSN, minimum GPA of 3.0, previous course work in research and statistics. Application deadline: 8/1 (priority date; rolling processing; 12/15 for spring admission). Application fee: $25. *Tuition:* $360 per credit hour. *Financial aid:* Assistantships, Federal Work-Study available. Financial aid applicants required to submit FAFSA. *Faculty research:* Children with asthma, homelessness, group decision making. • Dr. Judith A. Lemire, Coordinator, 304-243-2215. Fax: 304-243-2243. Application contact: Carol Carroll, Graduate Secretary, 304-243-2344. Fax: 304-243-4441.

Wichita State University, College of Health Professions, School of Nursing, Wichita, KS 67260. Awards MSN, MSN/MBA. Programs in clinical specialization (MSN), including adult nursing, maternal-child nursing, psychiatric/mental health nursing; nursing administration (MSN); teaching of nursing (MSN). Accredited by NLN. Part-time programs available. Faculty: 11 full-time (all women). Students: 41 full-time (34 women), 183 part-time (169 women); includes 10 minority (2 African Americans, 3 Asian Americans, 2 Hispanics, 3 Native Americans), 3 international. Average age 38. 46 applicants, 76% accepted. In 1997, 30 degrees awarded. *Degree requirements:* Comprehensive exam required, thesis optional, foreign language not required. *Entrance requirements:* GRE, TOEFL (minimum score 550), BSN, minimum undergraduate GPA of 2.75. Application deadline: 6/30 (priority date; rolling processing; 1/1 for spring admission). Application fee: $25 ($40 for international students). Electronic applications accepted. *Expenses:* Tuition $2303 per year full-time, $96 per credit hour part-time for state residents; $7691 per year full-time, $321 per credit hour part-time for nonresidents. Fees $490 per year full-time, $75 per semester (minimum) part-time. *Financial aid:* In 1997–98, 2 research assistantships averaging $900 per month, 4 teaching assistantships averaging $703 per month and totaling $18,794 were awarded; Federal Work-Study, institutionally sponsored loans, and career-related internships or fieldwork also available. Financial aid application deadline: 4/1; applicants required to submit FAFSA. *Faculty research:* Adolescent pregnancy, alcoholism, arthritis and chronic disease, health practices of elderly, diabetes. • Dr. Bonnie Holaday, Interim Dean, 316-978-3610. E-mail: holaday@chp.twsu.edu. Application contact: Dr. Donna Hawley, Graduate Coordinator, 316-978-3610. Fax: 316-978-3094. E-mail: hawley@chp.twsu.edu.

Widener University, School of Nursing, Chester, PA 19013-5792. Awards MSN, DN Sc, PMC. One or more programs accredited by NLN. Part-time and evening/weekend programs available. Faculty: 15 full-time (all women), 18 part-time (15 women). Students: 38 full-time (all women), 131 part-time (129 women). Average age 34. 56 applicants, 93% accepted. In 1997, 54 master's awarded (100% found work related to degree); 11 doctorates awarded (100% entered university research/teaching). *Degree requirements:* For doctorate, dissertation required, foreign language not required. *Entrance requirements:* For master's, GRE, BSN, previous course work in statistics; for doctorate, GRE, MSN, previous course work in statistics. Application deadline: 7/1 (rolling processing; 11/1 for spring admission). Application fee: $25. *Financial aid:* In 1997–98, 4 traineeships were awarded; Federal Work-Study and career-related internships or fieldwork also available. Aid available to part-time students. Financial aid application deadline: 4/1. *Faculty research:* Women's health leadership, nursing education, research utilization, program evaluation, health promotion. • Dr. Mary B. Walker, Assistant Dean for Graduate Studies, 610-499-4208.

Wilkes University, Program in Nursing, Wilkes-Barre, PA 18766-0002. Awards MSN. Accredited by NLN. Faculty: 10 full-time. Students: 14 full-time (7 women), 7 part-time (5 women); includes 1 minority (Asian American). In 1997, 7 degrees awarded. *Entrance requirements:* GRE, MAT. Application deadline: rolling. Application fee: $30. *Expenses:* Tuition $12,552 per year full-time, $523 per credit hour part-time. Fees $240 per year full-time, $10 per credit hour part-time. *Financial aid:* Application deadline 2/28; applicants required to submit FAFSA. • Dr. Ann Marie Kolanowski, Chair, 717-408-4070. Application contact: Dr. Mary Ann Saueraker, Coordinator, 717-408-4070.

William Paterson University of New Jersey, College of Science and Health, Department of Nursing, Wayne, NJ 07470-8420. Awards MSN. Part-time and evening/weekend programs available. Faculty: 5 full-time (4 women), 2 part-time (0 women). Students: 3 full-time (all women), 43 part-time (40 women); includes 6 minority (2 African Americans, 3 Asian Americans, 1 Hispanic). Average age 40. 29 applicants, 62% accepted. *Entrance requirements:* GRE General Test, minimum GPA of 2.75. Application deadline: 4/1 (rolling processing; 10/15 for spring admission). Application fee: $35. *Expenses:* Tuition $230 per credit for state residents; $327 per credit for nonresidents. Fees $3.25 per credit. *Financial aid:* In 1997–98, 1 graduate assistantship totaling $6,000 was awarded. Financial aid application deadline: 4/1. • Dr. Sandra DeYoung, Chairperson, 973-720-2673. Application contact: Office of Graduate Studies, 973-720-2237. Fax: 973-720-2035.

Wilmington College, Division of Nursing, New Castle, DE 19720-6491. Offers programs in family nurse practitioner (MSN), nursing (MSN). Accredited by NLN. Part-time programs available. *Entrance requirements:* BSN, RN license. Application deadline: 1/24 (priority date). Application fee: $25. *Expenses:* Tuition $4410 per year full-time, $735 per course part-time. Fees $50 per year. • Dr. Betty Caffo, Chair, 302-328-9401. Application contact: Michael Lee, Director of Admissions and Financial Aid, 302-328-9401 Ext. 102.

Winona State University, Graduate Studies, College of Nursing, Winona, MN 55987-5838. Awards MSN. Accredited by NLN. Faculty: 5 full-time (4 women). Students: 31 full-time (29 women), 68 part-time (67 women); includes 1 minority (Hispanic), 2 international. 67 applicants, 54% accepted. In 1997, 25 degrees awarded. *Degree requirements:* Thesis required, foreign language not required. *Entrance requirements:* GRE General Test (minimum combined score of 900). Application deadline: 3/1. Application fee: $20. *Financial aid:* In 1997–98, 3 research assistantships, 5 traineeships were awarded. • Dr. Marjorie Smith, Graduate Director, 507-285-7473. E-mail: mjs@vax2.winona.msus.edu.

Announcement: Master's program in advanced nursing practice is offered at the WSU Rochester Center, Rochester, Minnesota. Students select a focus of nurse educator studies, clinical nurse specialist studies, nurse administrator studies, or adult/family nurse practitioner studies. Course work is available for full-time, part-time, and post-master's study. Block scheduling on Thursdays facilitates inclusion of working professional nurses. Program requirements individualized to student characteristics. Partnership with Mayo Clinic's School of Health-Related Sciences. Collaborative programs in rural nurse practitioner (NP) project with graduate nursing schools at University of Minnesota and all other NP programs in Minnesota. Areas served: southeast Minnesota, northeast Iowa, and southwest Wisconsin. World Wide Web address: http://www.winona.msus.edu.

Wright State University, College of Nursing and Health, Program in Nursing, Dayton, OH 45435. Awards MS, MBA/MS. Offerings include adult health and illness (MS), child and adolescent health (MS), community health (MS), family nurse practitioner (MS), nursing administration (MS), nursing education (MS). Accredited by NLN. Part-time and evening/weekend programs available. Students: 50 full-time (46 women), 168 part-time (164 women); includes 29 minority (26 African Americans, 1 Hispanic, 2 Native Americans). Average age 39. 76 applicants, 72% accepted. In 1997, 58 degrees awarded. *Degree requirements:* Thesis or alternative required, foreign language not required. *Average time to degree:* master's–2 years full-time, 5 years part-time. *Entrance requirements:* GRE General Test, TOEFL (minimum score 550), BSN from NLN-accredited college, Ohio RN license. Application deadline: 4/15 (priority date). Application fee: $25. *Tuition:* $5109 per year full-time, $161 per credit hour part-time for state residents; $9039 per year full-time, $282 per credit hour part-time for nonresidents. *Financial aid:* In 1997–98, 5 fellowships (3 to first-year students) averaging $300 per month and totaling $18,000, 11 graduate assistantships (8 to first-year students) averaging $620 per month and totaling $62,000 were awarded; research assistantships, teaching assistantships, Federal Work-Study, institutionally sponsored loans also available. Aid available to part-time students. Financial aid application deadline: 6/1; applicants required to submit FAFSA. *Faculty research:* Clinical nursing and health, teaching, caring, pain administration, informatics and technology. • Application contact: Theresa Haghnazarian, Director of Student and Alumni Affairs, 937-775-3133. Fax: 937-775-4571.

Xavier University, College of Social Sciences, Department of Nursing, Cincinnati, OH 45207-2111. Offers program in nursing administration (MSN). Part-time and evening/weekend programs available. Faculty: 10 full-time (all women). Students: 11 part-time (all women). Average age 43. 0 applicants. In 1997, 4 degrees awarded. *Degree requirements:* Computer language required, thesis optional, foreign language not required. *Entrance requirements:* MAT. Application deadline: 8/26 (priority date; rolling processing; 1/10 for spring admission). Application fee: $25. *Tuition:* $400 per credit hour. *Financial aid:* In 1997–98, 2 students received aid, including 2 scholarships totaling $900. Aid available to part-time students. Financial aid application deadline: 4/1. *Faculty research:* Stroke rehabilitation, informatics, history, gerontology, hope and its cultural influences on health, healing touch. • Dr. Susan Schmidt, Interim Chair, 513-745-3814. E-mail: schmidts@xu.edu. Application contact: Marilyn Gomez, Coordinator, 513-745-4392. Fax: 513-745-1087. E-mail: gomez@admin.xu.edu.

Yale University, School of Nursing, New Haven, CT 06536-0740. Awards MSN, DN Sc, Post Master's Certificate, MSN/MPH, MSN/MPPM. One or more programs accredited by NLN. Part-time programs available. Faculty: 55 full-time (51 women), 39 part-time (35 women), 62.66 FTE. Students: 199 full-time (179 women), 67 part-time (62 women); includes 40 minority (10 African Americans, 25 Asian Americans, 5 Hispanics), 3 international. Average age 30. 325 applicants, 42% accepted. In 1997, 75 master's awarded. *Degree requirements:* For master's and doctorate, thesis/dissertation. *Average time to degree:* master's–2 years full-time, 3.5 years part-time; doctorate–4 years full-time, 7 years part-time. *Entrance requirements:* For master's, GRE General Test; for doctorate, GRE General Test, MSN. Application deadline: rolling. Application fee: $50. *Financial aid:* In 1997–98, 72 students received aid, including 9 research assistantships (4 to first-year students) averaging $1,112 per month, 63 traineeships, scholarships (30 to first-year students) totaling $818,845; Federal Work-Study, institutionally sponsored loans also available. Aid available to part-time students. Financial aid application deadline: 5/24; applicants required to submit FAFSA. *Faculty research:* Family-based care, chronic illness, primary care, development, policy. • Judith B. Krauss, Dean, 203-785-2393. Fax: 203-785-6455. E-mail: judith.krauss@yale.edu. Application contact: Barbara F. Reif, Director of Student/Alumni Affairs, 203-785-2389. Fax: 203-737-5409. E-mail: barbara.reif@yale.edu.

See in-depth description on page 1455.

Youngstown State University, College of Health and Human Services, Department of Nursing, Youngstown, OH 44555-0002. Awards MSN. Part-time and evening/weekend programs available. Faculty: 4 full-time (all women). Students: 12 part-time (10 women). 5 applicants, 100% accepted. *Degree requirements:* Thesis optional, foreign language not required. *Entrance requirements:* TOEFL (minimum score 550), GRE General Test, BSN, CPR certification. Application deadline: 8/15 (priority date; rolling processing; 2/15 for spring admission). Application fee: $30 ($75 for international students). *Expenses:* Tuition $90 per credit hour for state residents; $144 per credit hour (minimum) for nonresidents. Fees $528 per year full-time, $244 per year (minimum) part-time. *Financial aid:* In 1997–98, 1 student received aid, including 1 scholarship totaling $344; Federal Work-Study, institutionally sponsored loans also available. Aid available to part-time students. Financial aid application deadline: 3/1. • Dr. Patricia McCarthy, Chair. Application contact: Dr. Peter J. Kasvinsky, Dean of Graduate Studies, 330-742-3091. Fax: 330-742-1580. E-mail: amgrad03@ysub.ysu.edu.

Advanced Practice Nursing

Barry University, School of Nursing, Advanced Nursing Completion Program, Miami Shores, FL 33161-6695. Awards MSN. Students: 1 (woman) part-time; includes 1 minority (African American). Average age 44. 5 applicants, 100% accepted. In 1997, 1 degree awarded. *Degree requirements:* Research project or thesis required, foreign language not required. *Entrance requirements:* GRE General Test (minimum combined score of 900) or MAT (minimum score 40), BSN, minimum GPA of 3.0, previous course work in statistics. Application deadline: 5/1 (priority date; rolling processing). Application fee: $30. *Tuition:* $450 per credit (minimum). *Financial aid:* Institutionally sponsored loans and career-related internships or fieldwork available. Aid available to part-time students. Financial aid application deadline: 5/1; applicants required to submit FAFSA. • Dr. Claudia Hauri, Director, 305-899-3800. Fax: 305-899-3831. Application contact: Angela Scott, Enrollment Services, Assistant Dean, 305-899-3112. Fax: 305-899-3149. E-mail: ascott@jeanne.barry.edu.

Barry University, School of Nursing, Program in Nurse Practitioner, Miami Shores, FL 33161-6695. Awards MSN. Part-time and evening/weekend programs available. Faculty: 3 full-time (all women), 6 part-time (all women), 4 FTE. Students: 30 full-time (all women), 80 part-time (76 women); includes 53 minority (36 African Americans, 5 Asian Americans, 12 Hispanics), 2 international. Average age 38. 24 applicants, 79% accepted. In 1997, 41 degrees awarded. *Degree requirements:* Research project or thesis required, foreign language not required. *Entrance requirements:* GRE General Test (minimum combined score of 900) or MAT (minimum score 40), BSN, minimum GPA of 3.0, previous course work in statistics. Application deadline: 5/1 (priority date; rolling processing). Application fee: $30. *Tuition:* $450 per credit (minimum). *Financial aid:* 31 students received aid; full tuition waivers, institutionally sponsored loans, and career-related internships or fieldwork available. Aid available to part-time students. Financial aid application deadline: 5/1; applicants required to submit FAFSA. *Faculty research:* Child abuse, health beliefs, teenage pregnancy, stroke rehabilitation. • Dr. Claudia Hauri, Director, 305-899-3800. Application contact: Angela Scott, Enrollment Services, Assistant Dean, 305-899-3112. Fax: 305-899-3149. E-mail: ascott@jeanne.barry.edu.

Baylor University, School of Nursing, Waco, TX 76798. Offerings include family nurse practitioner (MSN). Accredited by NLN. *Entrance requirements:* GRE General Test. Application deadline: 8/1 (rolling processing; 12/1 for spring admission). Application fee: $25. *Expenses:* Tuition $7392 per year full-time, $308 per semester hour part-time. Fees $1024 per year. • Dr. Phyllis S. Karns, Dean, 254-710-3361.

Bowie State University, Program in Nursing, 14000 Jericho Park Road, Bowie, MD 20715. Offerings include family nurse practitioner (MS). Accredited by NLN. *Degree requirements:* Thesis, research paper, written comprehensive exam required, foreign language not required. *Entrance requirements:* Minimum GPA of 2.5. Application deadline: 3/15 (rolling processing). Application fee: $30. *Expenses:* Tuition $169 per credit hour for state residents; $304 per credit hour for nonresidents. Fees $171 per year.

Brenau University, Department of Nursing, Gainesville, GA 30501-3697. Offers program in family nurse practitioner (MSN). Part-time programs available. Faculty: 5 full-time (all women), 3 part-time (all women). Students: 29 part-time (all women); includes 4 minority (3 African Americans, 1 Hispanic). Average age 32. *Entrance requirements:* GRE General Test (minimum combined score of 950) or MAT (minimum score 45). Application deadline: rolling. Application fee: $30. *Tuition:* $411 per semester hour. *Financial aid:* Career-related internships or fieldwork available. Financial aid application deadline: 6/1. • Dr. JoAnne Richard, Chair, 770-534-6260. Fax: 770-538-4666. E-mail: jrichard@lib.brenau.edu. Application contact: Kathy Cobb, Director of Graduate Admissions, 770-534-6162. Fax: 770-538-4306. E-mail: kcobb@lib.brenau.edu.

California State University, Fresno, Division of Graduate Studies, School of Health and Social Work, Department of Nursing, 5241 North Maple Avenue, Fresno, CA 93740. Offerings include nursing (MS), with options in clinical specialty, primary care nurse practitioner. Accredited by NLN. Department faculty: 13 full-time (12 women). *Degree requirements:* Thesis or alternative required, foreign language not required. *Average time to degree:* master's–3.5 years full-time. *Entrance requirements:* GRE General Test, TOEFL (minimum score 550), 1 year of clinical practice, previous course work in statistics, BSN, minimum GPA of 3.0 in nursing, 2.5 overall. Application deadline: 3/1 (priority date; rolling processing). Application fee: $55. Electronic applications accepted. *Expenses:* Tuition $0 for state residents; $246 per unit for nonresidents. Fees $1872 per year full-time, $1206 per year part-time. • Dr. Mariamma Mathai, Interim Chair, 209-278-2041. E-mail: mariamma_mathai@csufresno.edu. Application contact: Mike Russler, Graduate Program Coordinator, 209-278-2429. Fax: 209-278-6630. E-mail: mike_russler@csufresno.edu.

Carlow College, Division of Nursing, Pittsburgh, PA 15213-3165. Offerings include home health advanced practice nursing (MSN, Certificate). Postbaccalaureate distance learning degree programs offered (minimal on-campus study). Division faculty: 6 full-time (all women), 14 part-time (12 women). *Degree requirements:* For master's, thesis or alternative required, foreign language not required. *Entrance requirements:* For master's, GRE General Test (minimum combined score of 1000), interview, minimum GPA of 3.0; for Certificate, MSN. Application deadline: 6/30 (rolling processing; 4/25 for spring admission). Application fee: $35. • Mary Lou Bost, Acting Chair, 412-578-6116. Fax: 412-578-6114. Application contact: Bonnie Potthoff, Office Manager, Graduate Studies, 412-578-8764. Fax: 412-578-8822.

Case Western Reserve University, Frances Payne Bolton School of Nursing, Master's Program in Nursing, Nurse Practitioner Program, Cleveland, OH 44106. Offers acute care adult nurse practitioner (MSN), acute care pediatric nurse practitioner (MSN), adult practitioner (MSN), family nurse practitioner (MSN), gerontological nurse practitioner (MSN), neonatal practitioner (MSN), pediatric nurse practitioner (MSN), psychiatric-mental health nurse practitioner (MSN), women's health nurse practitioner (MSN). Accredited by NLN. Students: 82 full-time (77 women), 73 part-time (69 women); includes 15 minority (8 African Americans, 5 Asian Americans, 1 Hispanic, 1 Native American), 11 international. Average age 35. 136 applicants, 63% accepted. In 1997, 83 degrees awarded. *Degree requirements:* Thesis optional, foreign language not required. *Entrance requirements:* GRE General Test or MAT. Application deadline: 6/1 (rolling processing). Application fee: $75. *Tuition:* $18,400 per year full-time, $767 per credit hour part-time. *Financial aid:* Research assistantships, teaching assistantships, partial tuition waivers, institutionally sponsored loans available. Aid available to part-time students. Financial aid application deadline: 6/30. • Application contact: Molly Blank, Admission Counselor, 216-368-2529. Fax: 216-368-3542. E-mail: mab44@po.cwru.edu.

The Catholic University of America, School of Nursing, Washington, DC 20064. Offerings include advanced practice nursing (MSN), with options in administration of nursing service, adult nurse practitioner, education, family nurse practitioner, geriatric nurse practitioner, pediatric nurse practitioner, psychiatric-mental health, school health nurse practitioner. Accredited by NLN. School faculty: 18 full-time (all women), 2 part-time (both women), 19 FTE. *Degree requirements:* Comprehensive exam required, thesis optional, foreign language not required. *Entrance requirements:* GRE General Test (minimum combined score of 1350 on three sections). Application deadline: 8/1 (priority date; rolling processing; 12/1 for spring admission). Application fee: $50. *Expenses:* Tuition $17,325 per year full-time, $668 per credit hour part-time. Fees $680 per year full-time, $360 per year part-time. • Sr. Mary Jean Flaherty, Dean, 202-319-5403.

Clarkson College, Graduate Programs, Department of Nursing, 101 South 42nd Street, Omaha, NE 68131-2739. Offerings include family nurse practitioner (MSN). Accredited by NLN. Department faculty: 6. *Degree requirements:* Practicum required, foreign language not required. *Entrance requirements:* GRE General Test, minimum GPA of 3.0. Application deadline: rolling. Application fee: $17. *Expenses:* Tuition $314 per credit hour. Fees $16 per credit hour. • Dr. Charles J. Beauchamp, Dean, 402-552-2958. Fax: 402-552-6058. Application contact: Jeff Beals, Director of Enrollment Management, 402-552-3100. Fax: 402-552-6057. E-mail: admiss@clrkcol.crhsnet.edu.

Columbia University, School of Nursing, Program in Adult Nurse Practitioner, New York, NY 10032. Awards MS, Adv C. One or more programs accredited by NLN. Part-time programs available. Faculty: 4 full-time (all women), 3 part-time (all women). Students: 90 part-time (83 women); includes 28 minority (8 African Americans, 17 Asian Americans, 3 Hispanics). Average age 36. 66 applicants, 76% accepted. In 1997, 20 master's awarded. *Entrance requirements:* For master's, GRE General Test (minimum score 500 on verbal and analytical sections), BSN, 1 year of clinical experience (preferred), or completion of a clinical residency; for Adv C, MSN, previous course work in statistics, clinical preceptorship. Application deadline: 4/1 (rolling processing; 10/1 for spring admission). Application fee: $60. *Tuition:* $19,376 per year full-time, $692 per credit (minimum) part-time. *Financial aid:* Teaching assistantships available. Financial aid application deadline: 2/1. • Prof. Joanne Falletta, Director, 212-305-2804. Application contact: Joseph Tomaino, Assistant Dean for Student Services, 212-305-5756. E-mail: jt238@columbia.edu.

Columbia University, School of Nursing, Program in Critical Care Nurse Practitioner, New York, NY 10032. Awards MS. Accredited by NLN. Part-time programs available. Faculty: 1 (woman) full-time, 3 part-time (all women). Students: 45 part-time (41 women); includes 26 minority (5 African Americans, 20 Asian Americans, 1 Hispanic). Average age 30. 28 applicants, 86% accepted. In 1997, 18 degrees awarded. *Entrance requirements:* GRE General Test (minimum score 500 on verbal and analytical sections), BSN, 1 year of clinical experience (preferred), or completion of a clinical residency. Application deadline: 4/1 (priority date; rolling processing; 10/1 for spring admission). Application fee: $60. *Tuition:* $19,376 per year full-time, $692 per credit (minimum) part-time. *Financial aid:* Teaching assistantships available. Financial aid application deadline: 2/1. • Prof. Joan Valas, Director, 212-305-8563. Application contact: Joseph Tomaino, Assistant Dean for Student Services, 212-305-5756. E-mail: jt238@columbia.edu.

Directory: Advanced Practice Nursing

Columbia University, School of Nursing, Program in Emergency Nurse Practitioner, New York, NY 10032. Awards MS, Adv C. One or more programs accredited by NLN. Part-time programs available. Faculty: 1 (woman) full-time, 3 part-time (all women). *Entrance requirements:* For master's, GRE General Test (minimum score 500 on verbal and analytical sections), BSN, 1 year of clinical experience (preferred), or completion of a clinical residency. Application deadline: 4/1 (priority date; rolling processing; 10/1 for spring admission). Application fee: $60. *Tuition:* $19,376 per year full-time, $692 per credit (minimum) part-time. *Financial aid:* Teaching assistantships available. Financial aid application deadline: 2/1. • Prof. Joan Vaias, Director, 212-305-8563. Application contact: Joseph Tomaino, Assistant Dean for Student Services, 212-305-5756. E-mail: jt238@columbia.edu.

Columbia University, School of Nursing, Program in Family Nurse Practitioner, New York, NY 10032. Awards MS, Adv C. One or more programs accredited by NLN. Part-time programs available. Faculty: 3 full-time (all women). Students: 3 full-time (all women), 69 part-time (66 women); includes 9 minority (4 African Americans, 1 Asian American, 4 Hispanics). Average age 34. 56 applicants, 64% accepted. In 1997, 16 master's awarded. *Entrance requirements:* For master's, GRE General Test (minimum score 500 on verbal and analytical sections), BSN, 1 year of clinical experience (preferred), or completion of a clinical residency; for Adv C, MSN, previous course work in statistics, clinical preceptorship. Application deadline: 4/1 (rolling processing; 10/1 for spring admission). Application fee: $60. *Tuition:* $19,376 per year full-time, $692 per credit (minimum) part-time. *Financial aid:* Teaching assistantships available. Financial aid application deadline: 2/1. • Elizabeth Hall, Director, 212-305-2806. Application contact: Joseph Tomaino, Assistant Dean for Student Services, 212-305-5756. E-mail: jt238@columbia.edu.

Columbia University, School of Nursing, Program in Geriatric Nurse Practitioner, New York, NY 10032. Awards MS, Adv C. One or more programs accredited by NLN. Part-time programs available. Faculty: 1 (woman) full-time. Students: 1 (woman) full-time, 12 part-time (all women); includes 5 minority (3 African Americans, 2 Asian Americans). Average age 36. 8 applicants, 88% accepted. In 1997, 1 master's awarded. *Entrance requirements:* For master's, GRE General Test (minimum score 500 on verbal and analytical sections), BSN, 1 year of clinical experience (preferred), or completion of a clinical residency; for Adv C, MSN, previous course work in statistics, clinical preceptorship. Application deadline: 4/1 (priority date; rolling processing; 10/1 for spring admission). Application fee: $60. *Tuition:* $19,376 per year full-time, $692 per credit (minimum) part-time. *Financial aid:* Teaching assistantships available. Financial aid application deadline: 2/1. • Dr. Carolyn Auerhahn, Director, 212-305-3471. Application contact: Joseph Tomaino, Assistant Dean for Student Services, 212-305-5756. E-mail: jt238@columbia.edu.

Columbia University, School of Nursing, Program in Neonatal Nurse Practitioner, New York, NY 10032. Awards MS, Adv C. One or more programs accredited by NLN. Part-time programs available. Students: 1 (woman) full-time, 23 part-time (all women); includes 15 minority (4 African Americans, 10 Asian Americans, 1 Hispanic). Average age 32. 15 applicants, 93% accepted. In 1997, 6 master's awarded. *Entrance requirements:* For master's, GRE General Test (minimum score 500 on verbal and analytical sections), BSN, 1 year of clinical experience (preferred), or completion of a clinical residency; for Adv C, MSN, previous course work in statistics, clinical preceptorship. Application deadline: 4/1 (10/1 for spring admission). Application fee: $50. *Tuition:* $19,376 per year full-time, $692 per credit (minimum) part-time. *Financial aid:* Application deadline 2/1. • Application contact: Joseph Tomaino, Assistant Dean for Student Services, 212-305-5756. E-mail: jt238@columbia.edu.

Columbia University, School of Nursing, Program in Pediatric Nurse Practitioner, New York, NY 10032. Awards MS, Adv C. One or more programs accredited by NLN. Part-time programs available. Faculty: 1 (woman) full-time, 1 (woman) part-time. Students: 13 full-time (all women), 45 part-time (42 women); includes 17 minority (15 African Americans, 2 Asian Americans). Average age 32. 38 applicants, 68% accepted. In 1997, 15 master's awarded. *Entrance requirements:* For master's, GRE General Test (minimum score 500 on verbal and analytical sections), BSN, 1 year of clinical experience (preferred), or completion of a clinical residency; for Adv C, MSN, previous course work in statistics, clinical preceptorship. Application deadline: 4/1 (priority date; rolling processing; 10/1 for spring admission). Application fee: $50. *Tuition:* $19,376 per year full-time, $692 per credit (minimum) part-time. *Financial aid:* Teaching assistantships available. Financial aid application deadline: 2/1. • Dr. Judy Honig, Director, 212-305-2816. Application contact: Joseph Tomaino, Assistant Dean for Student Services, 212-305-5756. E-mail: jt238@columbia.edu.

Columbia University, School of Nursing, Program in Women's Health Nurse Practitioner, New York, NY 10032. Awards MS, Adv C. One or more programs accredited by NLN. Part-time programs available. Faculty: 1 (woman) full-time. Students: 1 (woman) full-time, 10 part-time (all women); includes 2 minority (1 Asian American, 1 Hispanic). Average age 32. 5 applicants, 100% accepted. In 1997, 3 master's awarded. *Entrance requirements:* For master's, GRE General Test (minimum score 500 on verbal and analytical sections), BSN, 1 year of clinical experience (preferred), or completion of a clinical residency. Application deadline: 4/1 (priority date; rolling processing; 10/1 for spring admission). Application fee: $60. *Tuition:* $19,376 per year full-time, $692 per credit (minimum) part-time. *Financial aid:* Teaching assistantships available. Financial aid application deadline: 2/1. • Dr. Noreen Esposito, Director, 212-305-2280. Application contact: Joseph Tomaino, Assistant Dean for Student Services, 212-305-5756. E-mail: jt238@columbia.edu.

Concordia University Wisconsin, Division of Graduate Studies, Program in Nursing, Mequon, WI 53097-2402. Offerings include family nurse practitioner (MSN). Postbaccalaureate distance learning degree programs offered (minimal on-campus study). *Degree requirements:* Thesis or alternative, comprehensive exam. *Entrance requirements:* TOEFL (minimum score 550). Application deadline: 8/1 (priority date; rolling processing). *Tuition:* $250 per credit. • Dr. Ruth Gresley, Director, 414-243-4452. E-mail: rgresley@bach.cuw.edu.

Daemen College, Program in Adult Nurse Practitioner, Amherst, NY 14226-3592. Awards MS. Part-time programs available. Faculty: 2 full-time (both women), 3 part-time (2 women). Students: 15 full-time (14 women), 19 part-time (all women); includes 2 minority (both African Americans). Average age 39. *Degree requirements:* Thesis or alternative required, foreign language not required. *Entrance requirements:* Interview, minimum undergraduate GPA of 3.25, 1 year of medical/surgical experience. Application deadline: 3/1 (priority date; rolling processing; 10/1 for spring admission). Application fee: $25. *Expenses:* Tuition $430 per credit. Fees $13 per credit. *Financial aid:* Available to part-time students. Financial aid application deadline: 2/15; applicants required to submit FAFSA. • Deborah A. Wydysh, Director, 716-839-8408. Application contact: Deborah Fargo, Associate Director of Admissions, 716-839-8225. Fax: 716-839-8516. E-mail: dfargo@daemen.edu.

DePaul University, College of Liberal Arts and Sciences, Department of Nursing, Chicago, IL 60604-2287. Offerings include advanced practice nursing (MS). MS (nurse anesthesia) offered jointly with Ravenswood Hospital Medical Center. Department faculty: 5 full-time (all women), 1 (woman) part-time. *Degree requirements:* Comprehensive written exam required, thesis optional, foreign language not required. *Entrance requirements:* GRE, BSN, RN license, minimum GPA of 2.85. Application fee: $25. *Expenses:* Tuition $320 per credit hour. Fees $30 per year. • Dr. Susan Poslusny, Chair, 773-325-7280. E-mail: sposlusn@wppost.depaul.edu.

Duke University, School of Nursing, Durham, NC 27708-0586. Offerings include nurse practitioner (MSN), with options in acute care adult, acute care pediatric, adult cardiovascular, adult oncological/HIV, family, gerontological, neonatal, pediatric. Accredited by NLN. Postbaccalaureate distance learning degree programs offered (minimal on-campus study). School faculty: 24 full-time (22 women), 4 part-time (all women). *Degree requirements:* Computer language required, thesis optional, foreign language not required. *Average time to degree:* master's–1.5 years full-time, 3 years part-time; other advanced degree–1 year full-time, 2 years part-time. *Entrance requirements:* GRE General Test or MAT, BSN, minimum GPA of 3.0, previous course work in statistics, RN license, 1 year of nursing experience. Application deadline: 4/1 (priority date; rolling processing; 10/1 for spring admission). Application fee: $50. *Tuition:* $20,976 per year full-time, $552 per unit part-time. • Dr. Mary T. Champagne, Dean, 919-684-3786. E-mail: champ001@mc.duke.edu. Application contact: Judith K. Carter, Admissions Officer, 919-684-4248. Fax: 919-681-8899. E-mail: carte026@mc.duke.edu.

Duquesne University, School of Nursing, Pittsburgh, PA 15282-0001. Offerings include family nurse practitioner (MSN). Accredited by NLN. Postbaccalaureate distance learning degree programs offered (minimal on-campus study). School faculty: 5 full-time (all women), 3 part-time (1 woman). *Degree requirements:* Computer language required, foreign language and thesis not required. *Entrance requirements:* GMAT (MSN/MBA), MAT, 1 year of work experience (2 years for family nurse practitioner). Application deadline: 7/31 (priority date; rolling processing; 11/31 for spring admission). Application fee: $40. *Expenses:* Tuition $481 per credit. Fees $39 per credit. • Dr. Jeri A. Milstead, Chair, 412-396-4865. E-mail: milstead@duq3.cc.duq.edu. Application contact: Carole Sisul, Administrative Assistant, Graduate Programs, 412-396-6551. Fax: 412-396-6346. E-mail: sisul@duq2.cc.duq.edu.

D'Youville College, Division of Nursing, Buffalo, NY 14201-1084. Offerings include nurse practitioner (MS). Accredited by NLN. Division faculty: 9 full-time (8 women), 9 part-time (3 women). *Application deadline:* rolling. *Application fee:* $25. *Expenses:* Tuition $357 per credit hour. Fees $350 per year. • Dr. Carol Gutt, Chairperson, 716-881-3200. Application contact: Joseph Syracuse, Graduate Admissions Director, 716-881-7676. Fax: 716-881-7790.

Eastern Kentucky University, College of Allied Health and Nursing, Department of Nursing, Richmond, KY 40475-3101. Offerings include rural health family nurse practitioner (MSN). *Entrance requirements:* GRE General Test. Application fee: $0. *Tuition:* $2390 per year full-time, $133 per credit hour part-time for state residents; $6630 per year full-time, $365 per credit hour part-time for nonresidents. • Dr. D. Whitehouse, Chair, 606-622-1956.

East Tennessee State University, College of Nursing, Johnson City, TN 37614-0734. Offerings include advanced nursing practice (Post Master's Certificate). College faculty: 21 full-time (20 women). *Application deadline:* 1/15 (priority date; rolling processing). *Application fee:* $25 ($35 for international students). *Tuition:* $2944 per year full-time, $158 per credit hour part-time for state residents; $7770 per year full-time, $369 per credit hour part-time for nonresidents. • Dr. Joellen Edwards, Dean, 423-439-6752. E-mail: edwardsj@etsu-tn.edu. Application contact: Dr. Patricia Smith, Associate Dean, Graduate Programs and Research, 423-439-4476. Fax: 423-439-5903. E-mail: smithp@etsu-tn.edu.

Edinboro University of Pennsylvania, School of Science, Management and Technology, Department of Nursing, Edinboro, PA 16444. Offerings include family nurse practitioner (MSN). Department faculty: 4 full-time (all women). *Degree requirements:* Thesis required, foreign language not required. *Entrance requirements:* GRE or MAT (score in 30th percentile or higher). Application deadline: rolling. Application fee: $25. *Expenses:* Tuition $3468 per year full-time, $193 per credit part-time for state residents; $6236 per year full-time, $346 per credit part-time for nonresidents. Fees $898 per year full-time, $50 per semester (minimum) part-time. • Dr. Mary Louise Keller, Chair, 814-732-2900. E-mail: keller@edinboro.edu. Application contact: Dr. Philip Kerstetter, Dean of Graduate Studies, 814-732-2856. Fax: 814-732-2611. E-mail: kerstetter@edinboro.edu.

Emory University, Nell Hodgson Woodruff School of Nursing, Atlanta, GA 30322-1100. Offerings include adult health (MSN), with options in adult medical/surgical/nurse practitioner, adult oncology/nurse practitioner, critical care/nurse practitioner, psychosocial nurse practitioner; nursing systems (MSN), with options in family and adult nurse practitioner, gerontologic nurse practitioner, occupational health nurse practitioner. One or more programs accredited by NLN. Postbaccalaureate distance learning degree programs offered (minimal on-campus study). School faculty: 33 full-time (32 women), 21 part-time (19 women), 48 FTE. *Degree requirements:* Thesis optional, foreign language not required. *Average time to degree:* master's–1.5 years full-time, 3 years part-time. *Entrance requirements:* GRE General Test (minimum combined score of 1500 on three sections) or MAT (minimum score 35), minimum GPA of 3.0, BS in nursing or RN license and additional course work. Application deadline: 2/1 (priority date; rolling processing; 11/1 for spring admission). Application fee: $50. *Expenses:* Tuition $18,050 per year. Fees $200 per year. • Dr. Dyanne D. Affonso, Dean, 404-727-7976. Fax: 404-727-0536. Application contact: Debbie Ashtiani, Director, 404-727-7980.

Fairfield University, School of Nursing, Fairfield, CT 06430-5195. Offerings include family nurse practitioner (MSN, CAS), psychiatric nurse practitioner (MSN). School faculty: 2 full-time (both women), 7 part-time (5 women), 4.3 FTE. *Degree requirements:* For master's, thesis. *Average time to degree:* master's–2 years full-time, 3 years part-time. *Entrance requirements:* For master's, GMAT or GRE, minimum QPA of 3.0, RN license; for CAS, 1 year of work experience, MSN. Application deadline: 5/1 (priority date; rolling processing; 12/1 for spring admission). Application fee: $50. *Expenses:* Tuition $355 per credit hour. Fees $20 per semester. • Dr. Kathleen Wheeler, Director, 203-254-4150. E-mail: kwheeler@fair1.fairfield.edu. Application contact: Kathy Borrelli, Secretary for MSN Program, 203-254-4150. Fax: 203-254-4126. E-mail: kborrelli@fair1.fairfield.edu.

Felician College, Program in Advanced Practice Nursing, Lodi, NJ 07644-2198. Awards MSN. *Entrance requirements:* BS in nursing, minimum GPA of 3.0. Application deadline: rolling. Application fee: $35. *Tuition:* $362 per credit. • Dr. Rona Levin, Director, 973-778-1190. Application contact: Debra A. Savage, Administrative Assistant, 973-778-1190 Ext. 6080. Fax: 973-778-4111.

Florida Atlantic University, College of Nursing, Programs in Adult and Family Care Practitioner, Boca Raton, FL 33431-0991. Offerings in adult health (MS), adult practitioner (MS, Post Master's Certificate), family health (MS), family practitioner (MS, Post Master's Certificate), nursing administration (MS). One or more programs accredited by NLN. Part-time programs available. Faculty: 18 full-time (15 women), 8 part-time (7 women). Students: 25 full-time (all women), 143 part-time (128 women); includes 17 minority (9 African Americans, 1 Asian American, 7 Hispanics), 1 international. Average age 35. 19 applicants, 100% accepted. In 1997, 49 master's awarded. *Degree requirements:* For master's, thesis or alternative required, foreign language not required. *Average time to degree:* master's–2 years full-time, 3 years part-time. *Entrance requirements:* For master's, GRE General Test (minimum combined score of 1000), minimum GPA of 3.0. Application deadline: 6/1 (rolling processing; 10/15 for spring admission). Application fee: $20. *Expenses:* Tuition $2520 per year full-time, $140 per credit hour part-time for state residents; $8712 per year full-time, $484 per credit hour part-time for nonresidents. Fees $5 per year (minimum). *Financial aid:* In 1997–98, 7 research assistantships (2 to first-year students), 15 teaching assistantships (3 to first-year students), 13 scholarships, traineeships (4 to first-year students) were awarded; Federal Work-Study, institutionally sponsored loans, and career-related internships or fieldwork also available. Aid available to part-time students. Financial aid application deadline: 7/1. *Faculty research:* Sandwich generation, menopause HRT, nursing history, self-healing. • Dr. Ellis Quinn Youngkin, Graduate Program Coordinator, 561-297-3384. Fax: 561-297-3652. E-mail: eyoungkin@fau.edu.

Florida State University, School of Nursing, Tallahassee, FL 32306. Offerings include family nursing (MSN), with options in adult nurse practitioner, advanced registered nurse practitioner, case manager, family nurse practitioner, nurse educator. Accredited by NLN. School faculty: 16 full-time (14 women), 7 part-time (5 women). *Degree requirements:* Thesis required, foreign language not required. *Average time to degree:* master's–2 years full-time, 3.5 years part-time. *Entrance requirements:* GRE General Test (minimum combined score of 1000), minimum GPA of 3.0, BSN, Florida RN License, 2 years of work experience. Application deadline: 4/15 (priority date; rolling processing; 7/15 for spring admission). Application fee: $20. *Tuition:* $139 per credit hour for state residents; $482 per credit hour for nonresidents. • Dr. Evelyn Singer, Dean, 850-644-3299. Fax: 850-644-7660. E-mail: esinger@mailer.fsu.edu. Application contact: Dr. Deborah I. Frank, Graduate Program Coordinator, 850-644-5974. E-mail: dfrank@mailer.acns.fsu.edu.

Gannon University, School of Graduate Studies, College of Sciences, Engineering, and Health Sciences, School of Health Sciences, Department of Nursing, Erie, PA 16505. Offerings include family nurse practitioner (MSN, Certificate). Accredited by NLN. *Degree requirements:* For master's, thesis. *Entrance requirements:* For master's, GRE General Test (minimum score 500 on each section), MAT (minimum score 60), bachelor's degree from a NLN-approved nursing program, interview, Pennsylvania RN license. Application deadline: 4/15. Application fee: $25. • Dr. Beverly Bartlett, Director, 814-871-5520. Application contact: Beth Nemenz, Director of Admissions, 814-871-7240. Fax: 814-871-5803. E-mail: admissions@gannon.edu.

George Mason University, College of Nursing and Health Science, Fairfax, VA 22030-4444. Offerings include nurse practitioner (MSN). Accredited by NLN. College faculty: 50 full-time (46 women), 26 part-time (24 women), 61.65 FTE. *Entrance requirements:* RN license (MSN), minimum GPA of 3.0 in last 60 hours. Application deadline: 5/1 (11/1 for spring admission). Application fee: $30. Electronic applications accepted. *Tuition:* $4344 per year full-time, $181 per credit hour part-time for state residents; $12,504 per year full-time, $521 per credit hour part-time for nonresidents. • Dr. Rita M. Carty, Dean, 703-993-1919. Application contact: Dr. James D. Vail, Associate Dean, Graduate Programs and Research, 703-993-1913. Fax: 703-993-1942. E-mail: jvail@osf1.gmu.edu.

Georgia Southern University, College of Health and Professional Studies, Department of Nursing, Statesboro, GA 30460-8126. Offerings include rural family nurse practitioner (MSN, Certificate). Accredited by NLN. Postbaccalaureate distance learning degree programs offered (minimal on-campus study). Department faculty: 12 full-time (all women). *Degree requirements:* For master's, project or thesis required, foreign language not required. *Average time to degree:* master's–1.5 years full-time, 2.5 years part-time. *Entrance requirements:* For master's, GRE General Test (minimum score 450 on each section), minimum GPA of 3.0, nursing license, 2 years of clinical experience; for Certificate, MSN. Application deadline: 7/15 (priority date; rolling processing; 11/15 for spring admission). Application fee: $0. Electronic applications accepted. *Tuition:* $2619 per year full-time, $287 per semester (minimum) part-time for state residents; $8619 per year full-time, $1037 per semester (minimum) part-time for nonresidents. • Dr. Kaye Herth, Chair, 912-681-5479. Application contact: Dr. John R. Diebolt, Associate Graduate Dean, 912-681-5384. Fax: 912-681-0740. E-mail: gradschool@gsvms2.cc.gasou.edu.

Graceland College, Master's in Nursing Program, 221 West Lexington, Suite 110, Independence, MO 64050. Offerings include clinical nurse specialist/family nursing (educator) (MSN), family nurse practitioner (MSN, PMC). Postbaccalaureate distance learning degree programs offered (minimal on-campus study). Program faculty: 6 full-time (all women), 1 (woman) part-time, 6.5 FTE. *Degree requirements:* For master's, thesis optional, foreign language not required. *Average time to degree:* master's–2 years full-time, 2.5 years part-time; other advanced degree–1 year full-time, 1.5 years part-time. *Entrance requirements:* For master's, BSN from nationally accredited program. Application deadline: rolling. Application fee: $80. *Tuition:* $350 per credit hour (minimum). • Dr. Karen Fernengel, Chair, 816-833-0524. Fax: 816-833-2990. E-mail: karenf@graceland.edu. Application contact: Lewis Smith, Director, Student Information Service, 800-537-6276. Fax: 540-344-1508.

Gwynedd–Mercy College, Graduate Program in Nursing, Gwynedd Valley, PA 19437-0901. Offerings include nurse practitioner (MSN), with options in adult, pediatric. Accredited by NLN. MSN (pediatrics, oncology) admissions temporarily suspended. Program faculty: 9 full-time (all women), 8 part-time (6 women). *Degree requirements:* Thesis or research project required, foreign language not required. *Average time to degree:* master's–2.5 years full-time, 3.5 years part-time. *Entrance requirements:* GRE General Test (minimum combined score of 1350; average 1401), MAT (minimum score 40; average 48), 1 year of experience, physical assessment, previous course work in statistics. Application deadline: 8/1 (priority date; rolling processing). Application fee: $25. *Expenses:* Tuition $375 per credit. Fees $150 per year full-time, $80 per year part-time. • Dr. Mary Dressler, Dean, 215-641-5533. E-mail: dressler.m@gmc.edu. Application contact: Dr. Barbara A. Jones, Associate Professor, 215-646-7300 Ext. 407. Fax: 215-641-5517.

Hawaii Pacific University, School of Nursing, 1166 Fort Street, Honolulu, HI 96813-2785. Offerings include family nurse practitioner (MSN). Program new for fall 1998. *Degree requirements:* Practicum, professional paper. *Entrance requirements:* Bachelor's degree in nursing. Application deadline: rolling. Application fee: $50. *Tuition:* $7920 per year full-time, $330 per credit part-time. • Dr. Carol Winters, Dean, 808-236-3552. Application contact: Leina Danao, Admissions Coordinator, 808-544-1120. Fax: 808-544-0280. E-mail: gradservetr@hpu.edu.

Holy Names College, Department of Nursing, 3500 Mountain Boulevard, Oakland, CA 94619-1699. Offerings include family nurse practitioner (MS). Department faculty: 6 full-time (all women), 1 (woman) part-time. *Entrance requirements:* TOEFL (minimum score 550), bachelor's degree in nursing or related field, California RN license or eligibility, minimum GPA of 3.0, previous coursework in research or statistics. Application deadline: 8/1 (rolling processing; 12/1 for spring admission). Application fee: $35. *Tuition:* $7650 per year full-time, $425 per unit part-time. • Aida Sahud, Program Director, 510-436-1239. Application contact: Graduate Admissions Office, 800-430-1321. Fax: 510-436-1317. E-mail: garner@admin.hnc.edu.

Houston Baptist University, Center for Health Studies, Program in Nursing, Houston, TX 77074-3298. Offerings include family nurse practitioner (MSN), family nurse practitioner-congregational nurse (MSN). Program faculty: 7 full-time (all women), 3 part-time (2 women). *Entrance requirements:* GRE General Test (minimum combined score of 900), MAT (minimum score 45), minimum GPA of 2.5. Application deadline: 7/1 (priority date; rolling processing; 1/1 for spring admission). Application fee: $25 ($85 for international students). *Expenses:* Tuition $350 per semester hour (minimum). Fees $235 per quarter. • Dr. Brenda Binder, Head, 281-649-3000 Ext. 2385.

Howard University, College of Pharmacy, Nursing and Allied Health Sciences, Division of Nursing, 2400 Sixth Street, NW, Washington, DC 20059-0002. Offerings include nurse practitioner (Certificate). Division faculty: 4 full-time (all women), 2 part-time (both women), 4.75 FTE. *Average time to degree:* master's–2.5 years full-time, 4 years part-time; other advanced degree–1.5 years full-time, 2 years part-time. *Application deadline:* 4/1 (priority date; rolling processing; 11/1 for spring admission). *Application fee:* $45. *Expenses:* Tuition $10,200 per year full-time, $567 per credit hour part-time. Fees $405 per year. • Dr. Dorothy L. Powell, Associate Dean, 202-806-7456. Application contact: Dr. Coralease C. Ruff, Assistant Dean, Graduate Program, 202-806-7460. Fax: 202-806-5958.

Hunter College of the City University of New York, Hunter-Bellevue School of Nursing, Gerontological Nurse Practitioner Program, 695 Park Avenue, New York, NY 10021-5085. Awards MS. Accredited by NLN. Part-time programs available. Faculty: 9 full-time (all women), 2 part-time (both women). Students: 3 full-time (2 women), 68 part-time (63 women); includes 30 minority (14 African Americans, 11 Asian Americans, 5 Hispanics), 1 international. Average age 39. 18 applicants, 72% accepted. In 1997, 14 degrees awarded (100% found work related to degree). *Degree requirements:* Practicum required, foreign language and thesis not required. *Average time to degree:* master's–2 years full-time, 4 years part-time. *Entrance requirements:* TOEFL (minimum score 550), minimum GPA of 3.0, New York RN license, 2 years of professional practice experience. Application deadline: 4/27 (rolling processing; 11/21 for spring admission). Application fee: $40. *Expenses:* Tuition $4350 per year full-time, $185 per credit part-time for state residents; $7600 per year full-time, $320 per credit part-time for nonresidents. Fees $26 per year. *Financial aid:* Traineeships, partial tuition waivers, Federal Work-Study available. Aid available to part-time students. Financial aid application deadline: 5/1; applicants required to submit FAFSA. *Faculty research:* Relationship between psychological factors and cognitive changes in the elderly. • Dr. Maura C. Ryan, Coordinator, 212-481-4420. Fax: 212-481-5078. E-mail: mryan@hejira.hunter.cuny.edu. Application contact: Audrey Berman, Associate Director for Graduate Admissions, 212-772-4490.

Hunter College of the City University of New York, Hunter-Bellevue School of Nursing, Pediatric Nurse Practitioner Program, 695 Park Avenue, New York, NY 10021-5085. Awards MS, AC. One or more programs accredited by NLN. Part-time programs available. Faculty: 7 full-time (all women), 1 part-time (0 women). Students: 1 (woman) full-time, 34 part-time (31 women); includes 10 minority (8 African Americans, 2 Hispanics). Average age 36. 20 applicants, 70% accepted. In 1997, 12 master's, 9 ACs awarded. *Degree requirements:* For master's, practicum required, foreign language and thesis not required. *Average time to degree:* master's–2 years full-time, 3.5 years part-time. *Entrance requirements:* For master's, TOEFL (minimum score 550), BSN, minimum GPA of 3.0, New York RN license, 2 years of professional practice experience; for AC, MSN, minimum GPA of 3.0. Application deadline: 4/27 (rolling processing; 11/21 for spring admission). Application fee: $40. *Expenses:* Tuition $4350 per year full-time, $185 per credit part-time for state residents; $7600 per year full-time, $320 per credit part-time for nonresidents. Fees $26 per year. *Financial aid:* Traineeships, partial tuition waivers, Federal Work-Study available. Aid available to part-time students. Financial aid application deadline: 5/1; applicants required to submit FAFSA. *Faculty research:* Primary care: infants, children, and adolescents. • Dr. Janet N. Natapoft, Coordinator, 212-481-5070. Fax: 212-481-5078. E-mail: jnatapof@hejira.hunter.cuny.edu. Application contact: Audrey Berman, Associate Director for Graduate Admissions, 212-772-4490.

Husson College, Program in Nursing, Bangor, ME 04401-2999. Offerings include family nurse practioner (MSN). Program faculty: 2. *Entrance requirements:* MAT, BSN. Application deadline: 7/15 (priority date; rolling processing). Application fee: $25. • Dr. Barbara Higgins, Director, Nurse Practitioner Program, 207-947-7057.

Jewish Hospital College of Nursing and Allied Health, Program in Nursing, St. Louis, MO 63110-1091. Offerings include adult nurse practitioner (MSN), gerontology nurse practitioner (MSN), neonatal nurse practitioner (MSN). College faculty: 10. *Application deadline:* rolling. *Application fee:* $25. *Tuition:* $320 per credit hour. • Dr. Sandra A. Jones, Director, 314-454-8416. Application contact: Connie Stohlman, Chief Admissions Officer, 314-454-7538.

Johns Hopkins University, School of Nursing, Dual Major in Clinical Specialist/Management, Baltimore, MD 21218-2699. Offers programs in adult health (MSN), AIDS/HIV (MSN), oncology nursing (MSN). Accredited by NLN. Part-time programs available. Faculty: 13 full-time (12 women), 3 part-time (2 women), 15 FTE. Students: 1 (woman) full-time, 3 part-time (all women). Average age 35. 3 applicants, 67% accepted. In 1997, 1 degree awarded (1% found work related to degree). *Degree requirements:* Scholarly project required, thesis optional, foreign language not required. *Average time to degree:* master's–5 years part-time. *Entrance requirements:* GRE, interview, minimum GPA of 3.0. Application deadline: 3/1 (priority date; rolling processing; 11/15 for spring admission). Application fee: $40. *Financial aid:* In 1997–98, 2 students received aid, including 2 merit scholarships (1 to a first-year student) totaling $7,000; Federal Work-Study, institutionally sponsored loans, and career-related internships or fieldwork also available. Aid available to part-time students. Financial aid application deadline: 5/1; applicants required to submit FAFSA. *Faculty research:* HIV/AIDS symptoms, outcomes, cardiovascular disease, fatigue, program evaluation. • Jacqueline Dienemann, Associate Professor, 410-614-5301. Fax: 410-955-7463. E-mail: jackied@son.jhmi.edu. Application contact: Mary O'Rourke, Director of Admissions/Student Services, 410-955-7548. Fax: 410-614-7086. E-mail: orourke@son.jhmi.edu.

Johns Hopkins University, School of Nursing, Program in Advanced Practice Nursing/Clinical Specialist, Baltimore, MD 21218-2699. Offers adult health (MSN), AIDS/HIV (MSN), oncology nursing (MSN). Accredited by NLN. Part-time programs available. Faculty: 10 full-time (9 women), 2 part-time (1 woman), 11 FTE. Students: 1 (woman) full-time, 11 part-time (10 women); includes 6 minority (4 African Americans, 2 Asian Americans). Average age 38. 18 applicants, 83% accepted. In 1997, 4 degrees awarded (75% found work related to degree, 25% continued full-time study). *Degree requirements:* Scholarly project required, thesis optional, foreign language not required. *Average time to degree:* master's–1.5 years full-time, 4 years part-time. *Entrance requirements:* GRE, interview, minimum GPA of 3.0. Application deadline: 3/1 (priority date; rolling processing). Application fee: $40. *Financial aid:* In 1997–98, 5 students received aid, including 1 merit scholarship totaling $3,000; Federal Work-Study, institutionally sponsored loans, and career-related internships or fieldwork also available. Aid available to part-time students. Financial aid application deadline: 5/1; applicants required to submit FAFSA. *Faculty research:* Pediatric pain, outcomes, rehabilitation, psychosocial oncology, symptom management. Total annual research expenditures: $653,577. • Patricia Grimm, Head, 410-614-5302. Fax: 410-955-7463. E-mail: pgrimm@son.jhmi.edu. Application contact: Mary O'Rourke, Director of Admissions/Student Services, 410-955-7548. Fax: 410-614-7086. E-mail: orourke@son.jhmi.edu.

See in-depth description on page 1433.

Johns Hopkins University, School of Nursing, Program in Advanced Practice Nursing (Nurse Practitioner), Baltimore, MD 21218-2699. Offers advanced practice nursing-nurse practitioner (MSN), including adult acute/critical care, adult and pediatric primary care, family primary care; nurse practitioner (Certificate), including adult acute/critical care, adult or pediatric primary care, family primary care. One or more programs accredited by NLN. MSN, Certificate (family primary care) new for fall 1998. Part-time programs available. Faculty: 16 full-time (15 women), 9 part-time (8 women), 18 FTE. Students: 8 full-time (4 women), 50 part-time (49 women). Average age 31. 73 applicants, 63% accepted. In 1997, 21 master's awarded (95% found work related to degree, 5% continued full-time study). *Degree requirements:* For master's, scholarly project required, thesis optional, foreign language not required. *Average time to degree:* master's–1 year full-time, 2 years part-time. *Entrance requirements:* For master's, GRE, interview, minimum GPA of 3.0. Application deadline: 3/1. Application fee: $40. *Financial aid:* In 1997–98, 25 students received aid, including 25 merit scholarships (15 to first-year students) totaling $58,677; Federal Work-Study also available. Aid available to part-time students. Financial aid application deadline: 5/1; applicants required to submit FAFSA. *Faculty research:* Community outreach, primary care of underserved populations, substance abusing individuals, childhood violence. Total annual research expenditures: $243,758. • Stella Shiber, Head, 410-614-4081. Fax: 410-955-7463. E-mail: sshiber@son.jhmi.edu. Application contact: Mary O'Rourke, Director of Admissions/Student Services, 410-955-7548. Fax: 410-614-7086. E-mail: orourke@son.jhmi.edu.

See in-depth description on page 1433.

Kennesaw State University, School of Nursing, Program in Primary Care Nurse Practitioner, Kennesaw, GA 30144-5591. Awards MSN. Part-time and evening/weekend programs available. Faculty: 8 full-time (7 women), 8 part-time (7 women). Students: 70 full-time (65 women), 4 part-time (all women); includes 12 minority (all African Americans). Average age 34. 87 applicants, 57% accepted. In 1997, 16 degrees awarded. *Entrance requirements:* GRE General Test (minimum combined score of 1350 on three sections), minimum GPA of 2.5, RN license, 3 years of professional experience. Application deadline: 7/1 (rolling processing; 2/20 for spring admission). Application fee: $20. *Expenses:* Tuition $2398 per year full-time, $83 per credit hour part-time for state residents; $8398 per year full-time, $333 per credit hour part-time for nonresidents. Fees $338 per year. *Financial aid:* Federal Work-Study available. Aid available to part-time students. Financial aid application deadline: 6/15; applicants required to submit FAFSA. • Dr. B. Regina Dorman, Director, 770-423-6172. Fax: 770-423-6627. E-mail: gdorman@ksumail.kennesaw.edu. Application contact: Susan N. Barrett, Administrative Specialist, Admissions, 770-423-6500. Fax: 770-423-6541.

La Roche College, Program in Nursing, Pittsburgh, PA 15237-5898. Offerings include family nurse practitioner (MSN). Accredited by NLN. Program faculty: 5 full-time (all women), 2 part-time (both women). *Degree requirements:* Internship, practicum required, thesis optional, foreign language not required. *Entrance requirements:* GRE General Test (minimum combined score of 1200), TOEFL (minimum score 500). Application fee: $25. *Tuition:* $431 per credit. • Dr. Kathleen Sullivan, Division Chair, 412-536-1169. Application contact: Judy Henry, Manager of Nursing Student Enrollment, 412-536-1267. Fax: 412-536-1283.

Directory: Advanced Practice Nursing

La Salle University, Program in Nursing, 1900 West Olney Avenue, Philadelphia, PA 19141-1199. Offerings include nurse practitioner/primary care of adults (MSN). Accredited by NLN. MSN (wound, ostomy, and continence nursing) new for fall 1998. Program faculty: 13 full-time (12 women), 8 part-time (all women). *Entrance requirements:* GRE or MAT, BSN, Pennsylvania RN license. Application deadline: rolling. Application fee: $30. • Dr. Zane R. Wolf, Dean, 215-951-1430. E-mail: wolf@lasalle.edu. Application contact: Dr. Janice Beitz, Graduate Director, 215-951-1430. Fax: 215-951-1896. E-mail: beitz@lasalle.edu.

Long Island University, Brooklyn Campus, School of Nursing, Department of Adult Nurse Practitioner, Brooklyn, NY 11201-8423. Awards MS. Faculty: 4. Students: 13 full-time (10 women), 48 part-time (44 women); includes 45 minority (37 African Americans, 3 Asian Americans, 5 Hispanics). 36 applicants, 53% accepted. *Entrance requirements:* New York RN license. Application deadline: rolling. Application fee: $30. Electronic applications accepted. *Expenses:* Tuition $480 per credit. Fees $415 per year full-time, $73 per semester (minimum) part-time. *Financial aid:* In 1997–98, 3 students received aid, including 3 assistantships. • Dawn Kilts, Director, 718-488-1508. Application contact: Bernard W. Sullivan, Associate Director of Admissions, 718-488-1011.

Long Island University, C.W. Post Campus, School of Health Professions, Program in Nursing, Brookville, NY 11548-1300. Offerings include advanced practical nursing (MS), family nurse practitioner (MS, Certificate). Program faculty: 4 full-time (all women), 5 part-time (3 women). *Degree requirements:* For master's, computer language, thesis required, foreign language not required. *Entrance requirements:* For master's, TOEFL (minimum score 500), minimum GPA of 3.0 in major. Application deadline: rolling. Application fee: $30. Electronic applications accepted. *Expenses:* Tuition $480 per credit. Fees $316 per year full-time, $71 per semester (minimum) part-time. • Dr. Theodora Grauer, Chairperson, 516-299-2320. Fax: 516-299-2527. E-mail: ttgrauer@hornet.liu.edu. Application contact: Robin Steadman, Graduate Adviser, 516-299-2337.

Louisiana State University Medical Center, School of Nursing, 433 Bolivar Street, New Orleans, LA 70112-2223. Offerings include primary care nurse practitioner (MN). Accredited by NLN. School faculty: 10 full-time (all women), 4 part-time (3 women). *Degree requirements:* Thesis optional, foreign language not required. *Entrance requirements:* GRE General Test, MAT (minimum score 50), TOEFL, minimum GPA of 3.0. Application deadline: 3/17. Application fee: $50. *Expenses:* Tuition $2878 per year full-time, $421 per semester (minimum) part-time for state residents; $6003 per year full-time, $838 per semester (minimum) part-time for nonresidents. Fees $350 per year full-time, $90 per semester (minimum) part-time. • Dr. Elizabeth Humphrey, Dean, 504-568-4106. Application contact: Dr. Barbara C. Donlon, Acting Director, 504-568-4137. Fax: 504-568-3308. E-mail: bdonlo@lsumc.edu.

Loyola University Chicago, Graduate School, Marcella Niehoff School of Nursing, Critical Care/Trauma Nurse Practitioner Program, 820 North Michigan Avenue, Chicago, IL 60611-2196. Awards MSN. Accredited by NLN. Part-time programs available. Students: 2 full-time (1 woman), 14 part-time (12 women); includes 1 African American. 5 applicants, 60% accepted. In 1997, 6 degrees awarded. *Degree requirements:* Comprehensive exam or oral thesis defense required, foreign language not required. *Entrance requirements:* GRE General Test (minimum combined score of 1350 on three sections), BSN, minimum GPA of 3.0, professional license. Application deadline: rolling. Application fee: $35. *Tuition:* $467 per semester hour. *Financial aid:* In 1997–98, 1 traineeship (to a first-year student) was awarded. Financial aid application deadline: 3/1. *Faculty research:* Critical care/trauma recidivism. • Application contact: Dr. Marcia Maurer, Associate Dean and Director of Graduate Programs, 773-508-3261. Fax: 773-508-3241. E-mail: mmaurer@luc.edu.

Loyola University Chicago, Graduate School, Marcella Niehoff School of Nursing, Women's Health Nurse Practitioner Program, 820 North Michigan Avenue, Chicago, IL 60611-2196. Awards MSN. Accredited by NLN. Students: 1 (woman) full-time, 13 part-time (all women). Average age 29. 7 applicants, 71% accepted. In 1997, 5 degrees awarded. *Degree requirements:* Comprehensive exam or oral thesis defense required, foreign language not required. *Entrance requirements:* GRE General Test (minimum combined score of 1350 on three sections), BSN, clinical experience, minimum GPA of 3.0, professional licensure. Application deadline: rolling. Application fee: $35. *Tuition:* $467 per semester hour. *Financial aid:* In 1997–98, 1 assistantship was awarded; teaching assistantships also available. Financial aid application deadline: 3/1. *Faculty research:* Breast feeding, postpartum depression, pre-term labor tocolysis. • Application contact: Dr. Marcia Maurer, Associate Dean and Director of Graduate Programs, 773-508-3261. Fax: 773-508-3241. E-mail: mmaurer@luc.edu.

Loyola University New Orleans, Program in Nursing, New Orleans, LA 70118-6195. Offerings include family nurse practitioner (MSN). Program faculty: 5 full-time (all women). *Degree requirements:* 735 hours of clinical practice, comprehensive exam required, foreign language and thesis not required. *Entrance requirements:* GRE. Application deadline: 3/1. Application fee: $20. *Expenses:* Tuition $386 per credit hour. Fees $556 per year full-time, $164 per year part-time. • Dr. Billie Ann Wilson, Director, 504-865-3142. Fax: 504-865-3254. E-mail: bwilson@loyno.edu.

Mankato State University, College of Allied Health and Nursing, Department of Nursing, South Rd and Ellis Ave, PO Box 8400, Mankato, MN 56002-8400. Offerings include family nursing (MSN), with options in clinical nurse specialist, educator, family nurse practitioner, manager; managed care (MSN), with options in clinical nurse specialist, educator, family nurse practitioner, manager. One or more programs accredited by NLN. Offered jointly with Metropolitan State University. Department faculty: 13 full-time (all women). *Degree requirements:* Computer language, comprehensive exam, internships, research project or thesis required, foreign language not required. *Entrance requirements:* GRE General Test (minimum combined score of 1350) or MAT, minimum GPA of 3.0 during previous 2 years, BSN or equivalent. Application deadline: 7/10 (priority date; rolling processing; 10/30 for spring admission). Application fee: $20. *Tuition:* $126 per credit (minimum) for state residents; $200 per credit for nonresidents. • Mary Huntley, Director, 507-389-6022. Application contact: Collaborative MSN Program Admissions, 507-389-6022.

Marquette University, College of Nursing, Milwaukee, WI 53201-1881. Offerings include advanced practice nursing (MSN), with options in adult, children, neonatal nurse practitioner, nurse-midwifery, older adult. Accredited by NLN. College faculty: 24 full-time (23 women), 5 part-time (4 women). *Degree requirements:* Thesis or alternative, comprehensive exam required, foreign language not required. *Entrance requirements:* GRE General Test, TOEFL (minimum score 550), BSN, RN, Wisconsin license. Application fee: $40. *Tuition:* $490 per credit. • Dr. Madeline Wake, Dean, 414-288-3812. Application contact: Dr. Gregory Olson, Associate Dean, 414-288-3808. Fax: 414-288-1578.

Marymount University, School of Health Professions, Programs in Nursing, Program in Primary Care Family Practitioner, Arlington, VA 22207-4299. Awards MSN. Accredited by NLN. *Degree requirements:* Thesis or alternative required, foreign language not required. *Entrance requirements:* 2 years of clinical experience, interview, minimum GPA of 3.0, RN license. Application deadline: rolling. Application fee: $35. *Expenses:* Tuition $465 per credit hour. Fees $120 per year full-time, $5 per credit hour part-time. • Dr. Catherine Connelly, Dean, School of Health Professions, 703-284-1580. Fax: 703-284-3819. E-mail: catherine.connelly@marymount.edu.

Medical College of Georgia, Graduate Programs in Nursing, Augusta, GA 30912-1500. Offerings include nurse practitioner (MN). Accredited by NLN. Faculty: 17 full-time (14 women). *Application deadline:* 6/30 (priority date; rolling processing). *Application fee:* $0. *Expenses:* Tuition $2670 per year full-time, $111 per credit part-time for state residents; $10,680 per year full-time, $445 per credit part-time for nonresidents. Fees $286 per year. • Dr. Virginia Kemp, Associate Dean, 706-721-4710. E-mail: vkemp@mail.mcg.edu. Application contact: Dr. Gary C. Bond, Associate Dean, 706-721-3278. Fax: 706-721-6829. E-mail: gradstud@mail.mcg.edu.

Medical College of Ohio, School of Nursing, Toledo, OH 43699-0008. Offerings include advanced practice nursing (MSN), with options in clinical nurse specialist, family nurse practitioner. Accredited by NLN. School faculty: 27 full-time (25 women). *Degree requirements:* Thesis or scholarly project required, foreign language not required. *Average time to degree:* master's–2 years full-time, 3 years part-time. *Entrance requirements:* GRE General Test, BS in nursing, minimum undergraduate GPA of 3.0. Application deadline: 5/1 (9/1 for spring admission). Application fee: $30. • Dr. Jeri Millstead, Dean, 419-383-5858. E-mail: mcogradschool@mco.edu. Application contact: Joann Braatz, Clerk, 419-383-4117. Fax: 419-383-6140. E-mail: mcogradschool@mco.edu.

Medical University of South Carolina, College of Nursing, Program in Nursing, Family Nurse Practitioner Program, Charleston, SC 29425-0002. Awards MSN. Accredited by NLN. Faculty: 7 full-time (all women), 5 part-time (all women). *Degree requirements:* Computer language required, thesis optional, foreign language not required. *Entrance requirements:* GRE General Test (minimum combined score of 1000), BSN, previous course work in statistics and physical assessment, 1 year nursing experience, license. Application deadline: 2/15. Application fee: $55. *Expenses:* Tuition $3760 per year full-time, $173 per semester hour part-time for state residents; $5672 per year full-time, $270 per semester hour part-time for nonresidents. Fees $280 per year (minimum). • Liz Erkel, Track Coordinator, 843-792-8515. Application contact: Office of Enrollment Services, 843-792-3281.

Midwestern State University, Division of Health Sciences, Nursing Program, Wichita Falls, TX 76308-2096. Offerings include family nurse practitioner (MSN). Offered jointly with Texas Tech University. Program faculty: 5 full-time (all women). *Entrance requirements:* GRE General Test, TOEFL (average 550). Application deadline: 8/7 (12/15 for spring admission). Application fee: $0 ($50 for international students). *Expenses:* Tuition $44 per hour for state residents; $259 per hour for nonresidents. Fees $90 per year (minimum) full-time, $9 per semester (minimum) part-time. • Sandra Church, Coordinator, 940-397-4597.

Molloy College, Department of Nursing, 1000 Hempstead Avenue, Rockville Centre, NY 11571-5002. Offerings include family nurse practitioner (MSN, Advanced Certificate). Department faculty: 16 full-time (14 women), 12 part-time (9 women). *Degree requirements:* For master's, thesis optional, foreign language not required. *Average time to degree:* master's–2.2 years full-time, 3.7 years part-time; other advanced degree–1 year full-time, 2 years part-time. *Entrance requirements:* For master's, BS in nursing, minimum undergraduate GPA of 3.0; for Advanced Certificate, master's degree in nursing. Application deadline: 9/2 (priority date; rolling processing; 1/20 for spring admission). Application fee: $60. *Expenses:* Tuition $430 per credit. Fees $430 per year full-time, $165 per semester (minimum) part-time. • Dr. Carol A. Clifford, Director, Graduate Program, 516-256-2218. Fax: 516-678-9718. E-mail: clica01@molloy.edu. Application contact: Wayne James, Vice President for Enrollment and Management, 516-678-5000 Ext. 240. Fax: 516-256-2247.

Mount Saint Mary College, Division of Nursing, Newburgh, NY 12550-3494. Offerings include adult nurse practitioner (MS), with options in nursing education, nursing management. MS (adult nurse practitioner) new for fall 1998. Division faculty: 6 full-time (5 women), 1 (woman) part-time. *Degree requirements:* Computer language, research project required, foreign language and thesis not required. *Entrance requirements:* GRE General Test (minimum combined score of 1200; average 1400) or MAT (minimum score 40), BSN, minimum GPA of 3.0, RN license. Application deadline: 5/3 (priority date; 10/31 for spring admission). Application fee: $20. *Expenses:* Tuition $367 per credit. Fees $30 per year. • Sr. Leona DeBoer, Coordinator, 914-569-3138. Fax: 914-562-6762. E-mail: deboer@msmc.edu.

New York University, School of Education, Division of Nursing, Programs in Advanced Practice Nursing, New York, NY 10012-1019. Awards MA, AC, MA/MS. Offerings include adult nurse practitioner acute care (MA); adult nurse practitioner primary care (MA); advanced practice nursing: adult (AC); advanced practice nursing: elderly (MA, AC); advanced practice nursing: infants, children, and adolescents (MA, AC); advanced practice nursing: mental health (MA, AC); delivery of nursing services (MA); nurse midwifery (MA, AC); teaching of nursing (MA). One or more programs accredited by NLN. MA/MS offered jointly with the Program in Management in the Robert F. Wagner Graduate School of Public Service. Part-time and evening/weekend programs available. Faculty: 25 full-time, 9 part-time. Students: 18 full-time, 362 part-time. 127 applicants, 73% accepted. In 1997, 69 master's, 33 ACs awarded. *Entrance requirements:* For master's, TOEFL; for AC, TOEFL, master's degree. Application deadline: 2/1 (priority date; rolling processing; 12/1 for spring admission). Application fee: $40 ($60 for international students). *Financial aid:* Partial tuition waivers, Federal Work-Study, institutionally sponsored loans, and career-related internships or fieldwork available. Aid available to part-time students. Financial aid application deadline: 3/1; applicants required to submit FAFSA. *Faculty research:* Elderly black diabetics, families and illness, public health nursing, parent-child nursing, health policy costs. • Judi Haber, Director, 212-998-5300. Application contact: Office of Graduate Admissions, 212-998-5030. Fax: 212-995-4328.

Niagara University, Graduate Division of Nursing, Niagara University, NY 14109. Offers program in family nurse practitioner (MS). Students: 7 full-time (all women), 14 part-time (all women); includes 3 minority (2 African Americans, 1 Asian American), 4 international. In 1997, 2 degrees awarded. *Application deadline:* 8/1 (rolling processing). *Application fee:* $30. *Expenses:* Tuition $7740 per year full-time, $430 per credit hour part-time. Fees $25 per semester. *Financial aid:* Federal Work-Study and career-related internships or fieldwork available. Aid available to part-time students. • Nancy Shaffer, Acting Dean, 716-286-8312.

Northeastern University, Graduate School of Nursing, Program in Critical Care-Acute Care Nurse Practitioner, Boston, MA 02115-5096. Awards MS, CAS. One or more programs accredited by NLN. *Degree requirements:* For master's, thesis or alternative required, foreign language not required. *Entrance requirements:* For master's, GRE General Test, minimum GPA of 3.0, previous course work in statistics, 1-2 years nursing experience, RN license, ICU experience. Application deadline: 4/1 (priority date; rolling processing; 2/1 for spring admission). Application fee: $50. *Expenses:* Tuition $440 per credit hour. Fees $55 per quarter full-time, $13.25 per quarter part-time. • Dr. Elizabeth Howard, Coordinator, 617-373-4590. Application contact: Molly Schnabel, Admissions Coordinator, 617-373-3590. Fax: 617-373-8672. E-mail: mschnabe@lynx.neu.edu.

Announcement: Master's program in critical-care nursing (52 quarter hours), with concentration in acute-care NP role. Includes interventions for primary care and emphasis on advanced critical care and rehabilitation. Trauma nursing elective. Full- and part-time study. Preceptorships available in Boston's top health-care organizations. For application, contact Molly Schnabel, Admissions Coordinator, at 617-373-3590.

Northeastern University, Graduate School of Nursing, Program in Critical Care-Neonatal Nurse Practitioner, Boston, MA 02115-5096. Awards MS, CAS. One or more programs accredited by NLN. *Degree requirements:* For master's, thesis or alternative required, foreign language not required. *Entrance requirements:* For master's, GRE General Test, minimum GPA of 3.0, previous course work in statistics, 1-2 years nursing experience, RN license, ICU experience. Application deadline: 4/1 (priority date; rolling processing; 2/1 for spring admission). Application fee: $50. *Expenses:* Tuition $440 per credit hour. Fees $55 per quarter full-time, $13.25 per quarter part-time. *Faculty research:* Critical thinking and diagnostic reasoning, clinical outcomes of acute and critical health problems. • Dr. Elizabeth Howard, Coordinator, 617-373-4590. Fax: 617-373-8672. Application contact: Molly Schnabel, Admissions Coordinator, 617-373-3590. Fax: 617-373-8672. E-mail: mschnabe@lynx.neu.edu.

Northeastern University, Graduate School of Nursing, Program in Primary Care Nursing, Boston, MA 02115-5096. Awards MS, CAS. One or more programs accredited by NLN. *Entrance requirements:* For master's, GRE General Test, minimum GPA of 3.0, previous course work in statistics, 1-2 years nursing experience, RN license, ICU experience. Application deadline: 4/1 (priority date; rolling processing; 2/1 for spring admission). Application fee: $50. *Expenses:* Tuition $440 per credit hour. Fees $55 per quarter full-time, $13.25 per quarter part-time. *Faculty research:* Pediatric witness to violences. • Dr. Michelle A. Beauchesne, Coordinator, 617-373-3621. Fax: 617-373-3050. Application contact: Molly Schnabel, Admissions Coordinator, 617-373-3590. Fax: 617-373-8672. E-mail: mschnabe@lynx.neu.edu.

Announcement: Master's program in primary-care nursing for adult or pediatric NP (52 quarter hours) and family NP (76 quarter hours). Includes advanced community-based primary-care interventions. Certificate programs for MS-prepared nurses. Full- and part-time study. Preceptorships available in Boston's top health-care agencies. For application, contact Molly Schnabel, Admissions Coordinator, at 617-373-3590.

North Georgia College & State University, Graduate School, Program in Family Practitioner, Dahlonega, GA 30597-1001. Awards MSN. Program new for fall 1998. *Degree requirements:* Thesis optional, foreign language not required. *Entrance requirements:* Minimum GPA of 2.75. Application deadline: rolling. Application fee: $25. *Financial aid:* Application deadline 5/1. • Dr. Linda Roberts-Betsch, Head, 706-864-1930. Fax: 706-864-1845. E-mail: lrbetsch@nugget.ngc.peachnet.edu.

Oregon Health Sciences University, School of Nursing, Acute Care Nurse Practitioner Program, 3181 SW Sam Jackson Park Road, Portland, OR 97201-3098. Awards Post Master's Certificate. *Entrance requirements:* Master's degree in nursing. Application deadline: 1/15. Application fee: $40. • Dr. Charold Baer, Processor, 503-494-3741. E-mail: baerc@ohsu.edu. Application contact: Office of Recruitment, 503-494-7725. Fax: 503-494-4350.

Oregon Health Sciences University, School of Nursing, Program in Primary Health Care, 3181 SW Sam Jackson Park Road, Portland, OR 97201-3098. Offers adult nurse practitioner (MN, MS, Post Master's Certificate), family nurse practitioner (MN, MS, Post Master's Certificate), geriatric nurse practitioner (Post Master's Certificate), pediatric nurse practitioner (MN, MS, Post Master's Certificate). *Degree requirements:* For master's, thesis optional, foreign language not required. *Entrance requirements:* For master's, GRE General Test (minimum combined score of 1000), bachelor's degree in nursing, minimum undergraduate GPA of 3.0; for Post Master's Certificate, master's degree in nursing. Application deadline: 1/15. Application fee: $40. • Application contact: Office of Recruitment, 503-494-7725. Fax: 503-494-4350.

Oregon Health Sciences University, School of Nursing, Women's Health Care Nurse Practitioner Program, 3181 SW Sam Jackson Park Road, Portland, OR 97201-3098. Awards MN, MS, Post Master's Certificate. One or more programs accredited by NLN. *Degree requirements:* For master's, thesis optional, foreign language not required. *Entrance requirements:* For master's, GRE General Test (minimum combined score of 1000), bachelor's degree in nursing, minimum undergraduate GPA of 3.0; for Post Master's Certificate, master's degree in nursing. Application deadline: 1/15. Application fee: $40. • Application contact: Office of Recruitment, 503-494-7725. Fax: 503-494-4350.

Otterbein College, Program in Nursing, Westerville, OH 43081. Offerings include family nurse practitioner (Certificate). Postbaccalaureate distance learning degree programs offered. *Application deadline:* rolling. *Application fee:* $35. *Tuition:* $5216 per quarter. • Dr. Judy Strayer, Chair, 614-823-1614. Fax: 614-823-3131.

Pacific Lutheran University, School of Nursing, Program in Nurse Practitioner, Tacoma, WA 98447. Offers family nurse practitioner (MSN), gerontology (MSN), women's health care (MSN). Accredited by NLN. Part-time and evening/weekend programs available. Faculty: 11 full-time (10 women), 1 (woman) part-time. Students: 17 full-time (16 women), 8 part-time (all women); includes 4 minority (1 African American, 2 Asian Americans, 1 Hispanic). Average age 37. 21 applicants, 81% accepted. In 1997, 20 degrees awarded. *Degree requirements:* Thesis optional, foreign language not required. *Entrance requirements:* GRE General Test, TOEFL (minimum score 550), bachelor's degree in nursing, minimum undergraduate GPA of 3.0. Application deadline: 4/1 (priority date; rolling processing). Application fee: $35. *Tuition:* $490 per semester hour. *Financial aid:* Research assistantships, scholarships, Federal Work-Study available. Financial aid application deadline: 3/1. • Application contact: Marjo Burdick, Office of Admissions, 253-535-7151. Fax: 253-535-8320. E-mail: admissions@plu.edu.

Quinnipiac College, School of Health Sciences, Nurse Practitioner Program, Hamden, CT 06518-1904. Awards MSN. *Degree requirements:* Thesis optional. *Application fee:* $45. *Expenses:* Tuition $395 per credit hour. Fees $380 per year full-time. • Dr. Joy Cohen, Director, 203-287-5366. E-mail: cohen@quinnipiac.edu. Application contact: Scott Farber, Director of Graduate Admissions, 203-281-8795. Fax: 203-287-5238. E-mail: qcgradadmi@quinnipiac.edu.

See in-depth description on page 1441.

Research College of Nursing, Nursing Program, Kansas City, MO 64132. Offerings include family nurse practitioner (MSN). College faculty: 12 full-time (all women). *Degree requirements:* Research project required, foreign language and thesis not required. *Entrance requirements:* GRE General Test or MAT, minimum GPA of 3.0, interview. Application deadline: 10/1 (priority date). Application fee: $25. • Dr. Nancy De Basio, President and Dean, 816-276-4721. Application contact: Dr. Charles F. Dorlac, Associate Dean, 816-276-4729. Fax: 816-276-3526.

Rush University, College of Nursing, Department of Community Health Nursing, Chicago, IL 60612-3832. Offerings include family/community nurse practitioner (ND). Department faculty: 10 full-time (all women), 11 part-time (all women), 17.18 FT *Application deadline:* 8/1 (rolling processing; 2/1 for spring admission). *Application fee:* $40. *Tuition:* $8560 per year full-time, $370 per credit hour part-time. • Dr. Kathleen Andveoli, Dean and Acting Chairperson, 312-942-7117. Application contact: Hicela Castruita, Director, College Admissions Services, 312-942-7100. Fax: 312-942-2219.

Rush University, College of Nursing, Department of Gerontological Nursing, Chicago, IL 60612-3832. Offerings include adult/gerontological nurse practitioner (MSN, DN Sc, ND), gerontological nurse practitioner (MSN, DN Sc, ND). Department faculty: 6 full-time (all women), 3 part-time (all women), 7 FTE. *Degree requirements:* For doctorate, dissertation required, foreign language not required. *Entrance requirements:* For master's, GRE General Test, interview; for doctorate, interview, previous course work in statistics. Application deadline: 8/1 (rolling processing; 2/1 for spring admission). Application fee: $40. *Tuition:* $8560 per year full-time, $370 per credit hour part-time. • Jane Ulsafer-Van Lanen, Acting Chairperson, 312-942-3480. Application contact: Hicela Castruita, Director, College Admissions Services, 312-942-7100. Fax: 312-942-2219.

Rush University, College of Nursing, Department of Maternal-Child Nursing, Chicago, IL 60612-3832. Offerings include high risk perinatal nurse practioner (ND), high risk perinatal nurse practitioner (MSN, DN Sc), neonatal nurse practitioner (MSN, DN Sc, ND), pediatric critical care nurse practitioner (MSN, DN Sc, ND), pediatric nurse practitioner (MSN, DN Sc, ND). Department faculty: 7 full-time (6 women), 12 part-time (all women), 14.11 FTE. *Entrance requirements:* For master's, GRE General Test, interview. Application deadline: 8/1 (rolling processing; 2/1 for spring admission). Application fee: $40. *Tuition:* $8560 per year full-time, $370 per credit hour part-time. • Dr. Karren Kowalski, Chairperson, 312-942-6604. Application contact: Hicela Castruita, Director, College Admissions Services, 312-942-7100. Fax: 312-942-2219.

Rush University, College of Nursing, Department of Medical/Surgical Nursing, Chicago, IL 60612-3832. Offerings include acute care nurse practitioner (MSN, DN Sc, ND), adult nurse practitioner (MSN, DN Sc, ND), anesthesia nurse practitioner (MSN, DN Sc, ND). Department faculty: 14 full-time (13 women), 17 part-time (all women), 25.18 FTE *Degree requirements:* For doctorate, dissertation required, foreign language not required. *Entrance requirements:* For master's, GRE General Test, interview, previous course work in statistics; for doctorate, MS or GRE General Test, interview, previous course work in statistics. Application deadline: 8/1 (rolling processing; 2/1 for spring admission). Application fee: $40. *Tuition:* $8560 per year full-time, $370 per credit hour part-time. • Dr. Jane Llewellyn, Chairperson, 312-942-7112. Application contact: Hicela Castruita, Director, College Admissions Services, 312-942-7100. Fax: 312-942-2219.

Rush University, College of Nursing, Department of Psychiatric Nursing, Chicago, IL 60612-3832. Offerings include psychiatric nurse practitioner (MSN, DN Sc, ND), psychiatric/adult nurse practitioner (MSN, DN Sc, ND). Department faculty: 6 full-time (5 women), 4 part-time (all women), 8 FTE. *Degree requirements:* For doctorate, dissertation required, foreign language not required. *Entrance requirements:* For master's, GRE General Test, interview; for doctorate, MS or GRE General Test, interview, previous course work in statistics. Application deadline: 8/1 (rolling processing; 2/1 for spring admission). Application fee: $40. *Tuition:* $8560 per year full-time, $370 per credit hour part-time. • Jane Ulsafer-Van Lanen, Acting Chairperson, 312-942-3480. Application contact: Hicela Castruita, Director, College Admissions Services, 312-942-7100. Fax: 312-942-2219.

Rutgers, The State University of New Jersey, Newark, College of Nursing, Graduate Program in Advanced Practice in Pediatric Nursing, Newark, NJ 07102-3192. Awards MS. Accredited by NLN. Part-time programs available. *Degree requirements:* Comprehensive exam required, foreign language and thesis not required. *Entrance requirements:* GRE General Test, TOEFL, RN license, minimum B average, BS in nursing. Application deadline: 8/15 (rolling processing; 12/15 for spring admission). Application fee: $40. Electronic applications accepted. *Expenses:* Tuition $6248 per year full-time, $257 per credit part-time for state residents; $9160 per year full-time, $380 per credit part-time for nonresidents. Fees $738 per year full-time, $107 per semester (minimum) part-time. *Financial aid:* Federal Work-Study, institutionally sponsored loans, and career-related internships or fieldwork available. • Application contact: Dr. Elaine Dolinsky, Associate Dean for Student Life and Services, 973-353-5060. Fax: 973-353-1277.

Rutgers, The State University of New Jersey, Newark, College of Nursing, Graduate Program in Advanced Practice with Childbearing Families, Newark, NJ 07102-3192. Awards MS. Accredited by NLN. Part-time programs available. *Degree requirements:* Comprehensive exam required, foreign language and thesis not required. *Entrance requirements:* GRE General Test, TOEFL, RN license, minimum B average, BS in nursing. Application deadline: 8/15 (rolling processing; 12/15 for spring admission). Application fee: $40. Electronic applications accepted. *Expenses:* Tuition $6248 per year full-time, $257 per credit part-time for state residents; $9160 per year full-time, $380 per credit part-time for nonresidents. Fees $738 per year full-time, $107 per semester (minimum) part-time. *Financial aid:* Federal Work-Study, institutionally sponsored loans, and career-related internships or fieldwork available. Financial aid application deadline: 3/1. • Application contact: Dr. Elaine Dolinsky, Associate Dean for Student Life and Services, 973-353-5060. Fax: 973-353-1277.

Rutgers, The State University of New Jersey, Newark, College of Nursing, Graduate Program in Family Nurse Practitioner, Newark, NJ 07102-3192. Awards MS. Accredited by NLN. *Degree requirements:* Comprehensive exam required, foreign language and thesis not required. *Entrance requirements:* GRE General Test, TOEFL, RN license, minimum B average, BS in nursing. Application deadline: 8/15 (rolling processing; 12/15 for spring admission). Application fee: $40. Electronic applications accepted. *Expenses:* Tuition $6248 per year full-time, $257 per credit part-time for state residents; $9160 per year full-time, $380 per credit part-time for nonresidents. Fees $738 per year full-time, $107 per semester (minimum) part-time. *Financial aid:* Federal Work-Study, institutionally sponsored loans, and career-related internships or fieldwork available. • Application contact: Dr. Elaine Dolinsky, Associate Dean for Student Life and Services, 973-353-5060. Fax: 973-353-1277.

Sage Graduate School, Graduate School, Division of Nursing, Program in Family Nurse Practitioner, Troy, NY 12180-4115. Awards MS. Accredited by NLN. Part-time and evening/weekend programs available. *Degree requirements:* Thesis or alternative required, foreign language not required. *Entrance requirements:* BS in nursing, minimum GPA of 2.75. Application deadline: 8/1 (rolling processing; 12/15 for spring admission). Application fee: $25. *Expenses:* Tuition $360 per credit hour. Fees $50 per semester. *Financial aid:* Career-related internships or fieldwork available. Financial aid application deadline: 7/1; applicants required to submit FAFSA. • Application contact: Melissa Robertson, Associate Director of Admissions, 518-244-6878. Fax: 518-244-6880. E-mail: sgsadm@sage.edu.

Sage Graduate School, Graduate School, Division of Nursing, Program in Psychiatric–Mental Health Nurse Practitioner, Troy, NY 12180-4115. Awards MS. Accredited by NLN. Part-time and evening/weekend programs available. *Degree requirements:* Thesis or alternative required, foreign language not required. *Entrance requirements:* BS in nursing, minimum GPA of 2.75. Application deadline: 8/1 (rolling processing; 12/15 for spring admission). Application fee: $25. *Expenses:* Tuition $360 per credit hour. Fees $50 per semester. *Financial aid:* Career-related internships or fieldwork available. Financial aid application deadline: 7/1; applicants required to submit FAFSA. • Application contact: Melissa Robertson, Associate Director of Admissions, 518-244-6878. Fax: 518-244-6880. E-mail: sgsadm@sage.edu.

Saginaw Valley State University, College of Nursing, Program in Clinical Nurse Specialist, University Center, MI 48710. Awards MSN. Accredited by NLN. Students: 0. *Degree requirements:* Thesis. *Entrance requirements:* GRE. Application deadline: rolling. Application fee: $25. *Expenses:* Tuition $159 per credit hour for state residents; $311 per credit hour for nonresidents. Fees $8.70 per credit hour. • Application contact: Dr. Janalou Blecke, Assistant Dean, 517-790-4130. Fax: 517-790-1978. E-mail: jblecke@tardis.svsu.edu.

Saginaw Valley State University, College of Nursing, Program in Nurse Practitioner, University Center, MI 48710. Awards MSN. Accredited by NLN. Part-time programs available. Faculty: 5 full-time (all women). Students: 18 part-time (17 women). *Degree requirements:* Thesis. *Entrance requirements:* GRE. Application deadline: rolling. Application fee: $25. *Expenses:* Tuition $159 per credit hour for state residents; $311 per credit hour for nonresidents. Fees $8.70 per credit hour. • Application contact: Dr. Janalou Blecke, Assistant Dean, 517-790-4130. Fax: 517-790-1978. E-mail: jblecke@tardis.svsu.edu.

St. John Fisher College, School of Adult and Graduate Education, Nursing Program, Rochester, NY 14618-3597. Offerings include family nurse practitioner (Certificate). Program faculty: 6 full-time (all women), 3 part-time (1 woman). *Application deadline:* 8/1 (priority date; rolling processing; 1/1 for spring admission). *Application fee:* $30. *Tuition:* $13,500 per year full-time, $375 per credit hour part-time. • Dr. Cynthia McCloskey, Graduate Director, 716-385-8241. Fax: 716-385-8466. E-mail: mccloskey@sjfc.edu. Application contact: Steven T. Hoskins, Director, Graduate Admissions, 716-385-8161. Fax: 716-385-8344. E-mail: hoskins@sjfc.edu.

Saint Louis University, School of Nursing, Program in Adult Nursing, St. Louis, MO 63103-2097. Offerings include adult nurse practitioner (MSN, MSN(R), Certificate). One or more programs accredited by NLN. *Degree requirements:* For master's, comprehensive oral exam required, thesis optional, foreign language not required. *Entrance requirements:* For master's, GRE General Test. Application deadline: 7/1 (rolling processing; 11/1 for spring admission). Application fee: $40. *Tuition:* $542 per credit hour. • Dr. S. Ann Perry, Program Director, 314-577-8948. Application contact: Dr. Marcia Buresch, Assistant Dean of the Graduate School, 314-977-2240. Fax: 314-977-3943.

Saint Louis University, School of Nursing, Program in Family and Community Health Nursing, St. Louis, MO 63103-2097. Offerings include family nurse practitioner (MSN, MSN(R), Certificate). One or more programs accredited by NLN. *Degree requirements:* For master's, comprehensive oral exam required, thesis optional, foreign language not required. *Entrance requirements:* For master's, GRE General Test. Application deadline: 7/1 (rolling processing; 11/1 for spring admission). Application fee: $40. *Tuition:* $542 per credit hour. • Dr. Cordie Reese, Program Director, 314-577-8932. Application contact: Dr. Marcia Buresch, Assistant Dean of the Graduate School, 314-977-2240. Fax: 314-977-3943.

Saint Louis University, School of Nursing, Program in Gerontological Nursing, St. Louis, MO 63103-2097. Offerings include gerontological nurse practitioner (MSN, MSN(R), Certificate).

Directory: Advanced Practice Nursing

Saint Louis University (continued)

One or more programs accredited by NLN. *Degree requirements:* For master's, comprehensive oral exam required, thesis optional, foreign language not required. *Entrance requirements:* For master's, GRE General Test. Application deadline: 7/1 (rolling processing; 11/1 for spring admission). Application fee: $40. *Tuition:* $542 per credit hour. • Dr. Margie Edel, Program Director, 314-577-8931. Application contact: Dr. Marcia Buresch, Assistant Dean of the Graduate School, 314-977-2240. Fax: 314-977-3943.

Saint Louis University, School of Nursing, Program in Nursing of Children, St. Louis, MO 63103-2097. Offerings include pediatric nurse practitioner (MSN, MSN(R), Certificate). One or more programs accredited by NLN. *Degree requirements:* For master's, comprehensive oral exam required, thesis optional, foreign language not required. *Entrance requirements:* For master's, GRE General Test. Application deadline: 7/1 (rolling processing; 11/1 for spring admission). Application fee: $40. *Tuition:* $542 per credit hour. • Dr. Irene Riddle, Program Director, 314-577-8971. Application contact: Dr. Marcia Buresch, Assistant Dean of the Graduate School, 314-977-2240. Fax: 314-977-3943.

Saint Martin's College, Graduate Programs, Program in Nursing, Lacey, WA 98503-7500. Offerings include family nurse practitioner (MSN). Program being phased out; applicants no longer accepted. • Dr. Maura Egan, Director, 360-438-4560.

Saint Xavier University, School of Nursing, Chicago, IL 60655-3105. Offerings include adult health clinical nurse specialist (MS), family nurse practitioner (MS, PMC). One or more programs accredited by NLN and NLN. MBA/MS offered in cooperation with the Graham School of Management. School faculty: 10 full-time (all women), 2 part-time (both women). *Entrance requirements:* For master's, MAT or GRE General Test, minimum GPA of 3.0, RN license. Application deadline: 2/15 (9/15 for spring admission). Application fee: $35. *Expenses:* Tuition $450 per hour. Fees $50 per year. • Dr. Mary Lebold, Dean, 773-298-3700. Fax: 773-779-9061. E-mail: lebold@sxu.edu. Application contact: Sr. Evelyn McKenna, Vice President of Enrollment Management, 773-298-3050. Fax: 773-298-3076. E-mail: mckenna@sxu.edu.

Samuel Merritt College, Department of Nursing, Oakland, CA 94609-3108. Offerings include family nurse practitioner (Certificate). Department faculty: 11 full-time (9 women), 5 part-time (3 women), 13.37 FTE. *Average time to degree:* master's–2.2 years full-time. *Application deadline:* 2/1 (rolling processing). *Application fee:* $50. *Expenses:* Tuition $605 per unit. Fees $25 per year. • Dr. Audrey Berman, Graduate Coordinator, 510-869-6733. Application contact: John Garten-Schuman, Director of Admissions, 510-869-6576. Fax: 510-869-6525.

San Francisco State University, College of Health and Human Services, School of Nursing, San Francisco, CA 94132-1722. Offerings include case management (MS), with options in long-term care, primary care/family nurse practitioner. Accredited by NLN. *Degree requirements:* Thesis required, foreign language not required. *Entrance requirements:* Minimum GPA of 3.0. Application deadline: 11/30 (priority date; rolling processing; 5/31 for spring admission). Application fee: $55. *Expenses:* Tuition $0 for state residents; $246 per unit for nonresidents. Fees $1982 per year full-time, $1316 per year part-time.

San Jose State University, College of Applied Arts and Sciences, School of Nursing, San Jose, CA 95192-0001. Offerings include gerontology nurse practitioner (MS). Accredited by NLN. School faculty: 26 full-time (24 women), 13 part-time (12 women). *Degree requirements:* Thesis required, foreign language not required. *Entrance requirements:* BS in nursing, RN license. Application deadline: 6/1 (rolling processing). Application fee: $59. *Expenses:* Tuition $0 for state residents; $246 per unit for nonresidents. Fees $2017 per year full-time, $1351 per year part-time. • Dr. Bobbye Gorenberg, Director, 408-924-3130. Application contact: Dr. Colleen Saylor, Graduate Coordinator, 408-924-3134.

Seattle Pacific University, School of Health Sciences, Seattle, WA 98119-1997. Offers program in leadership in advanced nursing practice (MSN). Accredited by NLN. Part-time and evening/weekend programs available. Faculty: 2 full-time (both women), 8 part-time (all women). Students: 6 full-time (5 women), 56 part-time (52 women); includes 1 minority (Asian American), 2 international. Average age 38. In 1997, 15 degrees awarded (100% found work related to degree). *Degree requirements:* Thesis, internships required, foreign language not required. *Average time to degree:* master's–1.3 years full-time, 2 years part-time. *Entrance requirements:* GRE General Test (minimum combined score of 950), interview, Washington RN license, BS or BSN degree from a National League of Nursing accredited program. Application deadline: 9/1 (priority date; rolling processing). Application fee: $50. *Tuition:* $310 per credit. *Financial aid:* In 1997–98, 32 students received aid, including 6 teaching assistantships (4 to first-year students), scholarships totaling $50,000; institutionally sponsored loans and career-related internships or fieldwork also available. Aid available to part-time students. *Faculty research:* Health promotion, intercultural/international education, empathy/spiritual care, social policy, critical care/quality of life. • Dr. Annalee Oakes, Dean, 206-281-2233. E-mail: aoakes@spu.edu. Application contact: Jan Boyd, Graduate Admissions Counselor, 206-281-2888. Fax: 206-281-2767. E-mail: msninfo@spu.edu.

Seton Hall University, College of Nursing, Department of Graduate Nursing, Advanced Practice in Acute Care Nursing Program, South Orange, NJ 07079-2697. Offers acute care nurse practitioner (MSN). Accredited by NLN. Part-time programs available. Faculty: 1 (woman) full-time, 5 part-time (all women). *Degree requirements:* Research project required, foreign language and thesis not required. *Entrance requirements:* GRE or MAT, BSN. Application deadline: 5/15 (priority date; rolling processing; 11/15 for spring admission). Application fee: $50. *Expenses:* Tuition $500 per credit. Fees $610 per year full-time, $185 per semester part-time. *Financial aid:* Graduate assistantships, traineeships, partial tuition waivers, institutionally sponsored loans available. Financial aid application deadline: 7/15. *Faculty research:* Pulmonary infections, stress, patient-nurse environmental interactions, open-heart surgery. • Dr. Leona Kleinman, Director, 973-761-9286. Fax: 973-761-9607. E-mail: kleinmle@shu.edu.

Seton Hall University, College of Nursing, Department of Graduate Nursing, Advanced Practice in Primary Health Care Program, South Orange, NJ 07079-2697. Offers adult nurse practitioner (MSN), gerontological nurse practitioner (MSN), pediatric nurse practitioner (MSN), school nurse practitioner (MSN), women's health nurse practitioner (MSN). Accredited by NLN. Part-time programs available. Faculty: 6 full-time (all women), 4 part-time (all women). *Degree requirements:* Research project required, foreign language and thesis not required. *Entrance requirements:* GRE or MAT, BSN. Application deadline: 5/15 (priority date; rolling processing; 11/15 for spring admission). Application fee: $50. *Expenses:* Tuition $500 per credit. Fees $610 per year full-time, $185 per semester part-time. *Financial aid:* Graduate assistantships, traineeships, institutionally sponsored loans available. Financial aid application deadline: 7/15. *Faculty research:* Health promotion in well aged, practice outcomes, collaborative practice. • Dr. Cynthia Hughes, Director, 973-761-9273. Fax: 973-761-9607. E-mail: hughesci@shu.edu.

Simmons College, Graduate School for Health Studies, Program in Primary Health Care Nursing, Boston, MA 02115. Awards MS, CAGS. Accredited by NLN. Part-time programs available. Faculty: 7 full-time (all women), 9 part-time (all women). Students: 253 part-time (244 women); includes 9 minority (6 African Americans, 2 Asian Americans, 1 Hispanic), 5 international. Average age 30. 99 applicants, 69% accepted. In 1997, 81 master's awarded. *Entrance requirements:* For master's, GRE General Test, TOEFL (minimum score 550), 1 year of full-time clinical experience. Application deadline: 1/15 (rolling processing). Application fee: $50. *Expenses:* Tuition $587 per credit hour. Fees $20 per year. *Financial aid:* Traineeships, Federal Work-Study, institutionally sponsored loans available. Aid available to part-time students. Financial aid application deadline: 3/1; applicants required to submit FAFSA. *Faculty research:* Nursing leadership and mentoring, gerontology/homecare, nurse practitioner in occupational health. • Dr. Carol Love, Director, 617-521-2141. Fax: 617-521-3045. E-mail: clove@simmons.edu. Application contact: Christine Keuleyan, Admission Coordinator, 617-521-2650. Fax: 617-521-3137. E-mail: keuleyan@simmons.edu.

See in-depth description on page 1329.

Sonoma State University, School of Natural Sciences, Family Nurse Practitioner Program, Rohnert Park, CA 94928-3609. Awards MS. Accredited by NLN. Part-time programs available. Faculty: 10 full-time (8 women), 8 part-time (all women). Students: 46 full-time (43 women), 22 part-time (18 women); includes 4 minority (3 Asian Americans, 1 Native American). Average age 40. 51 applicants, 61% accepted. In 1997, 52 degrees awarded. *Degree requirements:* Thesis or alternative, comprehensive and oral exams. *Entrance requirements:* GRE General Test, minimum GPA of 3.0, previous course work in statistics, physical assessment, RN license, BSN. Application deadline: 11/30. Application fee: $55. *Expenses:* Tuition $0 for state residents; $246 per unit for nonresidents. Fees $2130 per year full-time, $1464 per year part-time. *Financial aid:* In 1997–98, 22 students received aid, including 1 fellowship; career-related internships or fieldwork also available. Financial aid application deadline: 3/2. *Faculty research:* Pain management, collaborative practice. • Dr. Elizabeth Close, Head, 707-664-2465. E-mail: elizabeth.close@sonoma.edu. Application contact: Wendy Smith, Coordinator, 707-664-2276.

Southern Illinois University at Edwardsville, School of Nursing, Program in Nurse Practitioner Nursing, Edwardsville, IL 62026-0001. Awards MS. Accredited by NLN. Students: 38 full-time (33 women); includes 3 minority (1 African American, 1 Asian American, 1 Hispanic). 5 applicants, 0% accepted. *Degree requirements:* Thesis or alternative, final exam required, foreign language not required. *Entrance requirements:* Appropriate bachelor's degree, RN license. Application deadline: 7/24. Application fee: $25. *Expenses:* Tuition $1716 per year full-time, $95 per credit hour part-time for state residents; $5149 per year full-time, $286 per credit hour part-time for nonresidents. Fees $463 per year full-time, $433 per year part-time. *Financial aid:* Fellowships, Federal Work-Study, institutionally sponsored loans available. Aid available to part-time students. • Dr. Felissa Lashley, Dean, School of Nursing, 618-692-3956.

Spalding University, School of Nursing and Health Sciences, Louisville, KY 40203-2188. Offerings include family nurse practitioner (MSN). Accredited by NLN. School faculty: 5 full-time (4 women). *Entrance requirements:* GRE General Test, BSN. Application deadline: 8/15 (priority date; rolling processing). Application fee: $30. *Expenses:* Tuition $350 per credit hour (minimum). Fees $48 per year full-time, $4 per credit hour part-time. • Dr. Cynthia Crabtree, Dean, 502-585-7125. E-mail: nursing@spalding10.win.net. Application contact: Jeanne Anderson, Assistant to the Provost and Director of Graduate Office, 502-585-7105. Fax: 502-585-7158. E-mail: gradoffc@spalding6.win.net.

State University of New York at Stony Brook, Health Sciences Center, School of Nursing, Program in Adult Health/Primary Care Nursing, Stony Brook, NY 11794. Offerings include adult health nurse practitioner (Certificate). *Application deadline:* 1/15. *Application fee:* $50. *Expenses:* Tuition $5100 per year full-time, $213 per credit hour part-time for state residents; $8416 per year full-time, $351 per credit hour part-time for nonresidents. Fees $529 per year full-time, $77 per semester (minimum) part-time. • Dr. Kathleen Shurpin, Chair, 516-444-3276. Fax: 516-444-3136. E-mail: kathy_shurpin@notes2.nursing.sunysb.edu.

State University of New York at Stony Brook, Health Sciences Center, School of Nursing, Program in Child Health Nursing, Stony Brook, NY 11794. Offerings include child health nurse practitioner (Certificate). *Application deadline:* 1/15. *Application fee:* $50. *Expenses:* Tuition $5100 per year full-time, $213 per credit hour part-time for state residents; $8416 per year full-time, $351 per credit hour part-time for nonresidents. Fees $529 per year full-time, $77 per semester (minimum) part-time. • Dr. Carole L. Blair, Chair, 516-444-3258. Fax: 516-444-3136. E-mail: carole_blair@notes2.nursing.sunysb.edu.

State University of New York at Stony Brook, Health Sciences Center, School of Nursing, Program in Mental Health/Psychiatric Nursing, Stony Brook, NY 11794. Offerings include mental health nurse practitioner (Certificate). *Application deadline:* 1/15. *Application fee:* $50. *Expenses:* Tuition $5100 per year full-time, $213 per credit hour part-time for state residents; $8416 per year full-time, $351 per credit hour part-time for nonresidents. Fees $529 per year full-time, $77 per semester (minimum) part-time. • Dr. Patricia Long, Chair, 516-444-3269. Fax: 516-444-3136. E-mail: pat_long@notes2.nursing.sunysb.edu.

State University of New York at Stony Brook, Health Sciences Center, School of Nursing, Program in Neonatal Nursing, Stony Brook, NY 11794. Offerings include neonatal nurse practitioner (Certificate). *Application deadline:* 1/15. *Application fee:* $50. *Expenses:* Tuition $5100 per year full-time, $213 per credit hour part-time for state residents; $8416 per year full-time, $351 per credit hour part-time for nonresidents. Fees $529 per year full-time, $77 per semester (minimum) part-time. • Dr. Carole Blair, Chair, 516-444-3258. Fax: 516-444-3136. E-mail: carole_blair@notes2.nursing.sunysb.edu.

State University of New York at Stony Brook, Health Sciences Center, School of Nursing, Program in Perinatal/Women's Health Nursing, Stony Brook, NY 11794. Offerings include perinatal/women's health nurse practitioner (Certificate). *Application deadline:* 1/15. *Application fee:* $50. *Expenses:* Tuition $5100 per year full-time, $213 per credit hour part-time for state residents; $8416 per year full-time, $351 per credit hour part-time for nonresidents. Fees $529 per year full-time, $77 per semester (minimum) part-time. • Dr. Carole L. Blair, Coordinator, 516-444-3258. Fax: 516-444-3136. E-mail: carole_blair@notes2.nursing.sunysb.edu.

State University of New York Health Science Center at Brooklyn, College of Nursing, Graduate Program in Nursing, Nurse Practitioner Program, 450 Clarkson Avenue, Brooklyn, NY 11203-2098. Awards MS, Post Master's Certificate. One or more programs accredited by NLN. Part-time programs available. *Degree requirements:* For master's, thesis required, foreign language not required. *Entrance requirements:* For master's, GRE, BSN, minimum GPA of 3.0; for Post Master's Certificate, BSN, minimum GPA of 3.0. Application deadline: 5/1 (priority date; rolling processing). Application fee: $35. *Expenses:* Tuition $5100 per year full-time, $213 per credit hour part-time for state residents; $8416 per year full-time, $351 per credit hour part-time for nonresidents. Fees $225 per year full-time, $75 per semester (minimum) part-time. *Faculty research:* Women's health.

State University of New York Institute of Technology at Utica/Rome, School of Nursing, Program in Adult Nurse Practitioner, PO Box 3050, Utica, NY 13504-3050. Awards MS, Certificate. One or more programs accredited by NLN. Part-time programs available. Faculty: 6 full-time (all women), 3 part-time (2 women). Students: 10 full-time (all women), 51 part-time (49 women); includes 2 minority (both African Americans). Average age 35. 18 applicants, 67% accepted. In 1997, 9 master's awarded. *Degree requirements:* For master's, thesis or alternative required, foreign language not required. *Average time to degree:* master's–2 years full-time, 4 years part-time. *Entrance requirements:* For master's, GRE General Test, minimum GPA of 3.0 in last 30 hours of undergraduate course work, bachelor's degree in nursing, 1 year of professional experience. Application deadline: 6/15 (priority date; rolling processing). Application fee: $50. *Expenses:* Tuition $5100 per year full-time, $213 per credit hour part-time for state residents; $8416 per year full-time, $351 per credit hour part-time for nonresidents. Fees $570 per year full-time, $17.60 per credit hour part-time. *Financial aid:* 34 students received aid; Federal Work-Study and career-related internships or fieldwork available. Aid available to part-time students. Financial aid applicants required to submit FAFSA. *Faculty research:* Moral reasoning, Myers-Briggs personality, home care, critical thinking, public health. • Application contact: Marybeth Lyons, Director of Admissions, 315-792-7500. Fax: 315-792-7837. E-mail: smbl@sunyit.edu.

Texas Tech University Health Sciences Center, School of Nursing, Lubbock, TX 79430-0002. Offerings include family nurse practitioner (MSN). Accredited by NLN. Postbaccalaureate distance learning degree programs offered (minimal on-campus study). School faculty: 14 full-time (all women). *Degree requirements:* Thesis required, foreign language not required. *Average time to degree:* master's–2 years full-time, 3 years part-time. *Entrance requirements:*

GRE General Test (minimum combined score of 1000), MAT (minimum score 50), minimum GPA of 3.0, sample of written work. Application deadline: 6/1 (rolling processing; 10/1 for spring admission). Application fee: $30 ($50 for international students). *Expenses:* Tuition $36 per credit hour for state residents; $249 per credit hour for nonresidents. Fees $1348 per year full-time for state residents; $1349 per year full-time for nonresidents. • Dr. Pat S. Yoder Wise, Dean, 806-743-2738. E-mail: sonpsy@ttuhsc.edu. Application contact: Nancy Ridenour, Associate Dean for Education, 806-743-2737. Fax: 806-743-1622. E-mail: sonrar@ttuhsc.edu.

Texas Woman's University, College of Nursing, Denton, TX 76204. Offerings include adult health nurse practitioner (MS), family nurse practitioner (MS), pediatric nurse practitioner (MS), women's health nurse practitioner (PhD). One or more programs accredited by NLN. College faculty: 30 full-time (29 women), 12 part-time (10 women). *Degree requirements:* For master's, thesis or alternative required, foreign language not required; for doctorate, 1 foreign language (computer language can substitute), dissertation. *Entrance requirements:* For master's, GRE General Test (minimum combined score of 750), minimum GPA of 3.0; for doctorate, GRE General Test (minimum combined score of 1000), MS in nursing, minimum GPA of 3.0. Application deadline: rolling. Application fee: $25. • Dr. Carolyn S. Gunning, Dean, 940-898-2401.

Uniformed Services University of the Health Sciences, Graduate School of Nursing, Department of Nurse Practitioner, Bethesda, MD 20814-4799. Awards MSN. Accredited by NLN. Available to military officers only. Faculty: 5 full-time (all women), 3 part-time (all women), 6.8 FTE. Students: 21 full-time (17 women); includes 2 minority (both African Americans). Average age 27. 7 applicants. In 1997, 7 degrees awarded (100% found work related to degree). *Degree requirements:* Thesis required, foreign language not required. *Average time to degree:* master's–2 years full-time. *Entrance requirements:* Minimum GPA of 3.0, clinical experience, BSN, previous course work in science. Application deadline: rolling. Application fee: $0. *Tuition:* $0. *Faculty research:* Women's health in the military, management of menopausal symptoms in mastectomy patients. • Dr. Carol Ledbetter, Chair, 301-295-1992. Fax: 301-295-1094. E-mail: cledbell@usuhs.mil. Application contact: Bernadette Hoover, Recording Secretary for Admissions Committee, 301-295-9893. Fax: 301-295-9006. E-mail: bhoover@usuhs.mil.

University of Cincinnati, College of Nursing and Health, Cincinnati, OH 45221-0038. Offerings include nurse practitioner studies (MSN). Accredited by NLN. College faculty: 26 full-time. *Degree requirements:* Project or thesis required, foreign language not required. *Average time to degree:* master's–1.5 years full-time, 2.5 years part-time; doctorate–4 years full-time, 6 years part-time. *Entrance requirements:* GRE General Test. Application deadline: 1/1 (priority date; rolling processing). Application fee: $30. *Tuition:* $7228 per year full-time, $185 per credit hour part-time for state residents; $13,812 per year full-time, $352 per credit hour part-time for nonresidents. • Dr. Andrea Lindell, Dean, 513-558-5330. Application contact: Tom West, Program Coordinator, 513-558-3600. Fax: 513-558-7523. E-mail: tom.west@uc.edu.

University of Colorado at Colorado Springs, Department of Graduate Nursing, Colorado Springs, CO 80933-7150. Offerings include adult health nurse practitioner and clinical specialist (MSN); family practitioner (MSN), with options in community clinical specialist, forensic clinical specialist, holistic clinical specialist; neonatal nurse practitioner and clinical specialist (MSN). One or more programs accredited by NLN. Postbaccalaureate distance learning degree programs offered (minimal on-campus study). Department faculty: 9 full-time (8 women). *Degree requirements:* Thesis optional, foreign language not required. *Average time to degree:* master's–2.5 years full-time, 5 years part-time. *Entrance requirements:* GRE General Test (minimum combined score of 1400) or MAT (minimum score 50), BSN, GPA of 3.0. Application deadline: 2/15 (priority date; 10/15 for spring admission). Application fee: $40. Electronic applications accepted. *Expenses:* Tuition $4644 per year full-time, $193 per credit hour part-time for state residents; $10,254 per year full-time, $420 per credit hour part-time for nonresidents. Fees $399 per year (minimum) full-time, $106 per year (minimum) part-time. • Barbara Joyce-Nagata, Chair, 719-262-4430. Fax: 719-262-4416.

University of Delaware, College of Health and Nursing Sciences, Department of Nursing, Newark, DE 19716. Offerings include clinical nurse specialist/nurse practitioner (Certificate), with options in cardiopulmonary, gerontology, oncology/immune deficiency, pediatrics, women's health; family nurse practitioner (MSN, Certificate). One or more programs accredited by NLN. Department faculty: 10 full-time (9 women), 5 part-time (all women), 12.25 FTE. *Degree requirements:* For master's, thesis optional, foreign language not required. *Average time to degree:* master's–2 years full-time, 3 years part-time. *Entrance requirements:* For master's, GRE General Test. Application deadline: 7/1. Application fee: $45. *Expenses:* Tuition $4250 per year full-time, $236 per credit hour part-time for state residents; $12,250 per year full-time, $681 per credit hour part-time for nonresidents. Fees $466 per year full-time, $15 per semester (minimum) part-time. • Application contact: Betty Bonavita, Graduate Secretary, 302-831-1255. Fax: 302-831-2382. E-mail: elizabeth.bonavita@mvs.udel.edu.

University of Hawaii at Manoa, College of Health Sciences and Social Welfare, School of Nursing, Honolulu, HI 96822. Offerings include nurse practitioner (MS), with options in adult health, community mental health, family nurse practitioner. Accredited by NLN. School faculty: 27 full-time (24 women). *Entrance requirements:* Hawaii RN license. *Tuition:* $4029 per year full-time, $214 per credit hour part-time for state residents; $9957 per year full-time, $461 per credit hour part-time for nonresidents. • Dr. Rosanne Harrigan, Dean, 808-956-8522. Application contact: Office of Student Services, 808-956-8939.

University of Mary, Division of Nursing, Program in Family Nurse Practitioner, 7500 University Drive, Bismarck, ND 58504-9652. Awards MSN. Accredited by NLN. 20 applicants, 60% accepted. *Degree requirements:* Internship required, foreign language not required. *Entrance requirements:* Minimum GPA of 3.0 in nursing course work. Application deadline: 3/1 (priority date). Application fee: $15. *Tuition:* $265 per credit. *Financial aid:* Institutionally sponsored loans available. Aid available to part-time students. Financial aid application deadline: 7/1. • Application contact: Dr. Diane Fladeland, Director, Graduate Programs, 701-255-7500. Fax: 701-255-7687.

University of Massachusetts Medical Center at Worcester, Graduate School of Nursing, Worcester, MA 01655-0115. Offerings include adult nurse practitioner (MS). Accredited by NLN. School faculty: 6 full-time (5 women), 4 part-time (all women), 8 FTE. *Average time to degree:* master's–2 years part-time; doctorate–3 years full-time; other advanced degree–1 year full-time. *Entrance requirements:* GRE General Test, BSN, previous course work in statistics. Application deadline: 3/15 (rolling processing). Application fee: $18 ($25 for international students). • Dr. Lillian R. Goodman, Dean, 508-856-5801. E-mail: lillian.goodman@banyan.ummed.edu. Application contact: Kathleen Trumpaitis, Student Coordinator, 508-856-5801. Fax: 508-856-6552. E-mail: kathleen.trumpaitis@banyan.ummed.edu.

University of Miami, School of Nursing, Coral Gables, FL 33124. Offerings include primary health care (MSN), with options in adult nurse practitioner, family nurse practitioner, nurse midwifery. Accredited by NLN. School faculty: 28 full-time (27 women), 1 (woman) part-time. *Degree requirements:* Thesis optional, foreign language not required. *Average time to degree:* master's–2 years full-time, 35 years part-time; doctorate–6.7 years full-time. *Entrance requirements:* GRE General Test, TOEFL (minimum score 550), BSN, minimum GPA of 3.0, RN experience. Application deadline: 3/1 (priority date; rolling processing; 10/1 for spring admission). Application fee: $35. *Expenses:* Tuition $815 per credit hour. Fees $174 per year. • Dr. Diane Horner, Dean, 305-284-2107. Application contact: Heidi McInnis, Director of Student Services, 305-284-4325. Fax: 305-284-5686. E-mail: lemieux@miami.edu.

University of Michigan, School of Nursing, Division of Health Promotion and Risk Reduction, Ann Arbor, MI 48109. Offerings include community health nursing (MS), with options in adult primary care/adult nurse practitioner, community care/home care, family nurse practitioner, occupational health nursing; parent-child nursing (MS), with options in acute care pediatric nurse practitioner, infant, child, adolescent health nursepractitioner, nurse midwifery, women's health/child-bearing families nurse practitioner. One or more programs accredited by NLN. *Degree requirements:* Thesis required, foreign language not required. *Entrance requirements:* GRE General Test. Application deadline: 2/1. Application fee: $55. • Dr. Carol Loveland-Cherry, Director, 734-763-0016.

University of Michigan, School of Nursing, Division of Acute, Critical and Long-Term Care, Program in Adult Acute Care Nurse Practitioner, Ann Arbor, MI 48109. Awards MS. Accredited by NLN. *Degree requirements:* Thesis required, foreign language not required. *Entrance requirements:* GRE General Test. Application deadline: 2/1. Application fee: $55. • Dr. Bonnie Metzger, Director, Division of Acute, Critical and Long-Term Care, 734-763-0010.

University of Michigan, School of Nursing, Division of Acute, Critical and Long-Term Care, Program in Psychiatric Mental Health Nursing, Ann Arbor, MI 48109. Offerings include psychiatric mental health nurse practitioner (MS). *Degree requirements:* Thesis required, foreign language not required. *Entrance requirements:* GRE General Test. Application deadline: rolling. Application fee: $55. • Application contact: Graduate Program Secretary, 734-763-0010. Fax: 734-936-5525.

University of Minnesota, Twin Cities Campus, School of Nursing, Children with Special Health Needs Nurse Practitioner Program, Minneapolis, MN 55455-0213. Offers advanced clinical specialist in children with special health needs (MS). Accredited by NLN. Students: 8 full-time. 8 applicants, 75% accepted. *Degree requirements:* Final oral exam, project or thesis. *Application deadline:* 12/15 (rolling processing). *Application fee:* $40 ($50 for international students). *Financial aid:* Fellowships, research assistantships, teaching assistantships, traineeships, and career-related internships or fieldwork available. • Barbara Leonard, Head, 612-624-9950. Fax: 612-626-2359. Application contact: Kate Hanson, Nursing Recruiter, 612-624-9494. Fax: 612-624-3174. E-mail: hanso041@maroon.tc.umn.edu.

University of Minnesota, Twin Cities Campus, School of Nursing, Family Nurse Practitioner Program, Minneapolis, MN 55455-0213. Awards MS. Accredited by NLN. Students: 15 full-time, 14 part-time. 46 applicants, 33% accepted. *Degree requirements:* Final oral exam, project or thesis. *Application deadline:* 12/15 (rolling processing). *Application fee:* $40 ($50 for international students). *Financial aid:* Fellowships, research assistantships, teaching assistantships, professional nurse traineeships, and career-related internships or fieldwork available. • Head, 612-624-7653. Fax: 612-626-2359. Application contact: Kate Hanson, Nursing Recruiter, 612-624-9494. Fax: 612-624-3174. E-mail: hanso041@maroon.tc.umn.edu.

University of Minnesota, Twin Cities Campus, School of Nursing, Gerontology Nurse Practitioner Program, Minneapolis, MN 55455-0213. Awards MS. Accredited by NLN. Part-time programs available. Students: 10 full-time, 12 part-time. 19 applicants, 53% accepted. *Degree requirements:* Final oral exam, project or thesis. *Application deadline:* 12/15 (rolling processing). *Application fee:* $40 ($50 for international students). *Financial aid:* Fellowships, research assistantships, teaching assistantships, professional nurse traineeships, and career-related internships or fieldwork available. • Mariah Snyder, Head, 612-626-3478. Fax: 612-626-2359. Application contact: Kate Hanson, Nursing Recruiter, 612-624-9494. Fax: 612-624-3174. E-mail: hanso041@maroon.tc.umn.edu.

University of Minnesota, Twin Cities Campus, School of Nursing, Pediatric Nurse Practitioner Program, Minneapolis, MN 55455-0213. Awards MS. Accredited by NLN. Students: 16 full-time. *Degree requirements:* Final oral exam, project or thesis. *Application deadline:* 12/15 (rolling processing). *Application fee:* $40 ($50 for international students). *Financial aid:* Fellowships, research assistantships, teaching assistantships, professional nurse traineeships, and career-related internships or fieldwork available. • Barbara Leonard, Head, 612-629-9950. Fax: 612-626-2359. Application contact: Kate Hanson, Nursing Recruiter, 612-624-9494. Fax: 612-624-3174. E-mail: hanso041@maroon.tc.umn.edu.

University of Missouri–Kansas City, School of Nursing, Kansas City, MO 64110-2499. Offerings include nurse practitioner (MSN), with options in health care for adults, health care for children, health care for women. Accredited by NLN. School faculty: 17 full-time (15 women), 40 part-time (all women), 37 FTE. *Degree requirements:* Thesis or alternative required, foreign language not required. *Entrance requirements:* Minimum undergraduate GPA of 3.0. Application deadline: 2/1 (9/15 for spring admission). Application fee: $25. *Expenses:* Tuition $182 per credit hour for state residents; $508 per credit hour for nonresidents. Fees $60 per year. • Dr. Nancy Mills, Dean, 816-235-1700. Application contact: Brenda Cain, Student Services Assistant, 816-235-1710. Fax: 816-235-1701.

University of Nevada, Las Vegas, College of Health Sciences, Department of Nursing, Las Vegas, NV 89154-9900. Offerings include family nurse practitioner (MS). Department faculty: 12 full-time (10 women), 3 part-time (1 woman). *Degree requirements:* Comprehensive exam required, thesis optional, foreign language not required. *Entrance requirements:* GRE General Test (minimum combined score of 1000), minimum GPA of 2.75. Application deadline: 4/15 (10/15 for spring admission). Application fee: $40 ($95 for international students). *Expenses:* Tuition $93 per credit for state residents; $93 per credit full-time, $190 per credit part-time for nonresidents. Fees $5570 per year full-time for nonresidents. • Dr. Rosemary Witt, Chair, 702-895-3415. Application contact: Graduate College Admissions Evaluator, 702-895-3320.

University of New Mexico, College of Nursing, Albuquerque, NM 87131-2039. Offerings include advanced nurse practice (Certificate); advanced nursing practice (MSN), with options in adult health nursing, gerontological nursing, parent-child nursing, psychiatric-mental health nursing; primary care nursing (MSN), with options in family nurse practitioner, nurse midwifery. One or more programs accredited by NLN. College faculty: 38 full-time (36 women), 23 part-time (all women), 46.57 FTE. *Degree requirements:* For master's, thesis optional, foreign language not required. *Entrance requirements:* For master's, GRE General Test, interview, minimum GPA of 3.0, previous course work in statistics. Application deadline: 7/15 (11/1 for spring admission). Application fee: $25. *Expenses:* Tuition $2442 per year full-time, $103 per credit hour part-time for state residents; $8691 per year full-time, $103 per credit hour (minimum) part-time for nonresidents. Fees $32 per year. • Dr. Sandra Ferketich, Dean, 505-272-6284. Application contact: Anne-Marie Oechsler, Director, Academic Advisement, 505-272-4224. Fax: 505-272-3970. E-mail: annmarie@unm.edu.

University of Northern Colorado, College of Health and Human Sciences, School of Nursing, Greeley, CO 80639. Offerings include family nurse practitioner (MS). Accredited by NLN. School faculty: 10 full-time (all women), 1 (woman) part-time. *Degree requirements:* Thesis or alternative, comprehensive exams. *Application deadline:* rolling. *Application fee:* $35. *Expenses:* Tuition $2327 per year full-time, $129 per credit hour part-time for state residents; $9578 per year full-time, $532 per credit hour part-time for nonresidents. Fees $752 per year full-time, $184 per semester (minimum) part-time. • Dr. Sandy Baird, Director, 970-351-2293.

University of North Florida, College of Health, Jacksonville, FL 32224-2645. Offerings include advanced practice nursing (MSN). MSN new for fall 1998. College faculty: 14 full-time (9 women). *Application deadline:* rolling. *Application fee:* $20. *Tuition:* $3388 per year full-time, $141 per credit hour part-time for state residents; $11,634 per year full-time, $485 per credit hour part-time for nonresidents. • Dr. Joan Farrell, Dean, 904-646-2840.

University of Pennsylvania, School of Nursing, Adult Acute/Tertiary Nurse Practitioner Program, Philadelphia, PA 19104. Offers tertiary nurse practitioner (MSN), including cardiopulmonary, neuroscience, renal metabolic, surgical. Accredited by NLN. Part-time programs available. Students: 7 full-time (6 women), 17 part-time (all women). Average age 32. 19 applicants, 79% accepted. In 1997, 15 degrees awarded. *Entrance requirements:* GRE General Test, BSN, minimum GPA of 3.0, previous course work in statistics. Application deadline: 9/1 (rolling processing). Application fee: $65. *Financial aid:* In 1997–98, 1 fellowship, 5 teaching assistantships were awarded; research assistantships, Federal Work-Study, institutionally sponsored loans also available. Aid available to part-time students. *Faculty research:* Post-injury disability, bereavement and attributions in fire survivors, stress in staff nurses. • Dr. Anne Keane, Director, 215-898-5766. Fax: 215-573-7492. E-mail: akeane@pobox.upenn.edu. Application

Directory: Advanced Practice Nursing

University of Pennsylvania (continued)
contact: Susan K. Ogle, Associate Director of Admissions and Student Affairs, 215-898-3301. Fax: 215-573-8439. E-mail: sogle@pobox.upenn.edu.

University of Pennsylvania, School of Nursing, Adult Critical Care Nurse Practitioner Program, Philadelphia, PA 19104. Awards MSN. Accredited by NLN. Part-time programs available. Students: 1 full-time (0 women), 11 part-time (all women); includes 2 minority (1 Asian American, 1 Hispanic). Average age 34. 27 applicants, 63% accepted. In 1997, 9 degrees awarded. *Degree requirements:* 2 years of experience required, foreign language and thesis not required. *Entrance requirements:* GRE General Test, BSN, minimum GPA of 3.0, previous course work in statistics. Application deadline: 9/1 (rolling processing). Application fee: $65. *Financial aid:* Fellowships, research assistantships, teaching assistantships, Federal Work-Study, institutionally sponsored loans, and career-related internships or fieldwork available. Aid available to part-time students. *Faculty research:* Stress; coping with illness, sexuality, and health; quality of life and sexual function in burn victims. • Dr. Rosalyn J. Watts, Director, 215-898-4727. Fax: 215-573-7492 Ext. 7496. E-mail: rwatts@pobox.upenn.edu. Application contact: Susan K. Ogle, Associate Director of Admissions and Student Affairs, 215-898-3301. Fax: 215-573-8439. E-mail: sogle@pobox.upenn.edu.

University of Pennsylvania, School of Nursing, Gerontological Nurse Practitioner Program, Philadelphia, PA 19104. Awards MSN. Accredited by NLN. Part-time programs available. Students: 7 full-time (4 women), 20 part-time (all women); includes 2 international. Average age 35. 22 applicants, 77% accepted. In 1997, 14 degrees awarded. *Entrance requirements:* GRE General Test, BSN, minimum GPA of 3.0, previous course in basic statistics. Application deadline: 9/1 (rolling processing). Application fee: $65. *Financial aid:* In 1997–98, 1 fellowship, 19 research assistantships, 5 teaching assistantships were awarded; Federal Work-Study, institutionally sponsored loans, and career-related internships or fieldwork also available. Aid available to part-time students. *Faculty research:* Restraints, incontinence, discharge planning, frail elders, quality of life across continuum of care. • Dr. Neville Strumpf, Director, 215-898-8802. Fax: 215-573-7492 Ext. 7496. E-mail: strumpf@pobox.upenn.edu. Application contact: Susan K. Ogle, Associate Director of Admissions and Student Affairs, 215-898-3301. Fax: 215-573-8439. E-mail: sogle@pobox.upenn.edu.

University of Pennsylvania, School of Nursing, Health Care of Women Nurse Practitioner Program, Philadelphia, PA 19104. Awards MSN. Accredited by NLN. Part-time programs available. Postbaccalaureate distance learning degree programs offered (minimal on-campus study). Students: 6 full-time (all women), 15 part-time (all women); includes 2 minority (both African Americans), 3 international. Average age 28. 22 applicants, 64% accepted. In 1997, 19 degrees awarded. *Entrance requirements:* GRE General Test, BSN, minimum GPA of 3.0, previous course in statistics, physical assessment experience. Application deadline: 5/20 (rolling processing). Application fee: $65. *Financial aid:* In 1997–98, 2 fellowships, 3 research assistantships, 1 teaching assistantship were awarded; Federal Work-Study, institutionally sponsored loans, and career-related internships or fieldwork also available. Aid available to part-time students. *Faculty research:* New mother and infant healthcare follow up, adequacy of antepartum care, models of healthcare. • Dr. Ruth York, Director, 215-898-5323. Fax: 215-573-7291. E-mail: yorkr@pobox.upenn.edu. Application contact: Susan K. Ogle, Associate Director of Admissions and Student Affairs, 215-898-3301. Fax: 215-573-8439. E-mail: sogle@pobox.upenn.edu.

University of Pennsylvania, School of Nursing, Neonatal Nurse Practitioner Program, Philadelphia, PA 19104. Awards MSN. Accredited by NLN. Part-time programs available. Students: 4 full-time (all women), 9 part-time (8 women). Average age 30. 11 applicants, 55% accepted. In 1997, 3 degrees awarded (100% found work related to degree). *Average time to degree:* master's–1 year full-time, 2 years part-time. *Entrance requirements:* GRE General Test, BSN, minimum GPA of 3.0, previous course work in statistics, 1 year of experience in a neonatal intensive care unit. Application deadline: 9/1 (rolling processing). Application fee: $65. *Financial aid:* In 1997–98, 2 research assistantships, 1 teaching assistantship were awarded; fellowships, Federal Work-Study, institutionally sponsored loans, and career-related internships or fieldwork also available. Aid available to part-time students. *Faculty research:* Neurobehavioral development, temperament, newborn sucking behaviors, parenting pre-term infants. • Dr. Susan Gennaro, Director, 215-898-1844. Fax: 215-898-6320. E-mail: gennaro@pobox.upenn.edu. Application contact: Susan K. Ogle, Associate Director of Admissions and Student Affairs, 215-898-3301. Fax: 215-573-8439. E-mail: sogle@pobox.upenn.edu.

University of Pennsylvania, School of Nursing, Occupational Health Nurse Practitioner Program, Philadelphia, PA 19104. Offers administration/consulting (MSN), primary care (MSN). Accredited by NLN. Part-time programs available. Students: 9 part-time (8 women); includes 1 international. Average age 33. 4 applicants, 0% accepted. In 1997, 3 degrees awarded. *Average time to degree:* master's–1.5 years full-time, 3 years part-time. *Entrance requirements:* GRE General Test, BSN, minimum GPA of 3.0, previous course work in statistics. Application deadline: 9/1 (rolling processing). Application fee: $65. *Financial aid:* In 1997–98, 6 research assistantships, 1 teaching assistantship were awarded; Federal Work-Study, institutionally sponsored loans, and career-related internships or fieldwork also available. Aid available to part-time students. *Faculty research:* Injury prevention. • Kay M. Arendasky, Associate Director, 215-898-2194. Fax: 215-573-7381. E-mail: arendask@pobox.upenn.edu. Application contact: Susan K. Ogle, Associate Director of Admissions and Student Affairs, 215-898-3301. Fax: 215-573-8439. E-mail: sogle@pobox.upenn.edu.

University of Pennsylvania, School of Nursing, Oncology Advanced Practice Nurse Program, Philadelphia, PA 19104. Awards MSN. Accredited by NLN. Part-time programs available. Students: 5 full-time (all women), 21 part-time (all women); includes 3 international. Average age 29. 16 applicants, 50% accepted. In 1997, 9 degrees awarded. *Entrance requirements:* GRE General Test, BSN, minimum GPA of 3.0, previous course work in statistics. Application deadline: 9/1 (rolling processing). Application fee: $65. *Financial aid:* Fellowships, research assistantships, teaching assistantships, Federal Work-Study, institutionally sponsored loans, and career-related internships or fieldwork available. Aid available to part-time students. *Faculty research:* Randomized clinical trials to evaluate advanced nursing practice in oncology patients and their caregivers, symptoms management. • Dr. Ruth McCorkle, Director, 215-898-9134. Fax: 215-898-1868. E-mail: mccorkle@pobox.upenn.edu. Application contact: Susan K. Ogle, Associate Director of Admissions and Student Affairs, 215-898-3301. Fax: 215-573-8439. E-mail: sogle@pobox.upenn.edu.

University of Pennsylvania, School of Nursing, Pediatric Acute/Chronic Care Nurse Practitioner Program, Philadelphia, PA 19104. Awards MSN. Accredited by NLN. Part-time programs available. Postbaccalaureate distance learning degree programs offered. Students: 2 full-time (both women), 19 part-time (all women); includes 2 minority (1 African American, 1 Hispanic), 1 international. Average age 30. 10 applicants, 70% accepted. In 1997, 17 degrees awarded. *Entrance requirements:* GRE General Test, BSN, minimum GPA of 3.0, previous course work in statistics, 1 year of clinical course work. Application deadline: 2/15 (rolling processing). Application fee: $65. *Financial aid:* In 1997–98, 1 research assistantship, 1 teaching assistantship were awarded; institutionally sponsored loans and career-related internships or fieldwork also available. Aid available to part-time students. *Faculty research:* Hispanic health, bereavement, pediatric AIDS, chronically ill children and their families. • Dr. Janet Deatrick, Director, 215-898-1799. Fax: 215-573-7507. E-mail: deatrick@pobox.upenn.edu. Application contact: Susan K. Ogle, Associate Director of Admissions and Student Affairs, 215-898-3301. Fax: 215-573-8439. E-mail: sogle@pobox.upenn.edu.

University of Pennsylvania, School of Nursing, Pediatric Critical Care Nurse Practitioner Program, Philadelphia, PA 19104. Awards MSN. Accredited by NLN. Students: 6 full-time (all women), 3 part-time (all women); includes 1 international. 9 applicants, 89% accepted. In 1997, 3 degrees awarded. *Entrance requirements:* GRE General Test, BSN, minimum GPA of 3.0, previous course work in statistics, 1 year of clinical course work. Application deadline: 2/15. Application fee: $65. • Dr. Janet Deatrick, Director, 215-898-1799. Fax: 215-573-7507. E-mail: deatrick@pobox.upenn.edu. Application contact: Susan K. Ogle, Associate Director of Admissions and Student Affairs, 215-898-3301. Fax: 215-573-8439. E-mail: sogle@pobox.upenn.edu.

University of Pennsylvania, School of Nursing, Pediatric Oncology Nurse Practitioner Program, Philadelphia, PA 19104. Awards MSN. Accredited by NLN. Students: 0. 1 applicant, 100% accepted. *Entrance requirements:* GRE General Test, BSN, minimum GPA of 3.0, previous course work in statistics. Application deadline: 9/1. Application fee: $5. • Dr. Ruth McCorkle, Director, 215-898-9134. Fax: 215-898-1868. E-mail: mccorkle@pobox.upenn.edu. Application contact: Susan K. Ogle, Associate Director of Admissions and Student Affairs, 215-898-3301. Fax: 215-573-8439. E-mail: sogle@pobox.upenn.edu.

University of Pennsylvania, School of Nursing, Perinatal Advanced Practice Nurse Specialist Program, Philadelphia, PA 19104. Awards MSN. Accredited by NLN. Part-time programs available. Students: 1 (woman) part-time; includes 1 minority (African American). 0 applicants. *Entrance requirements:* GRE General Test, BSN, minimum GPA of 3.0, previous course work in statistics. Application deadline: 9/1 (rolling processing). Application fee: $65. *Financial aid:* Fellowships, research assistantships, teaching assistantships, Federal Work-Study, institutionally sponsored loans, and career-related internships or fieldwork available. Aid available to part-time students. • Application contact: Susan K. Ogle, Associate Director of Admissions and Student Affairs, 215-898-3301. Fax: 215-573-8439. E-mail: sogle@pobox.upenn.edu.

University of Pennsylvania, School of Nursing, Perinatal Nurse Practitioner Program, Philadelphia, PA 19104. Awards MSN. Accredited by NLN. Part-time programs available. Students: 3 full-time (all women), 2 part-time (both women). Average age 31. 4 applicants, 75% accepted. In 1997, 7 degrees awarded. *Average time to degree:* master's–1 year full-time, 2 years part-time. *Entrance requirements:* GRE General Test, BSN, minimum GPA of 3.0, previous course work in statistics. Application deadline: 9/1 (rolling processing). Application fee: $65. *Financial aid:* Fellowships, research assistantships, teaching assistantships, Federal Work-Study, institutionally sponsored loans, and career-related internships or fieldwork available. Aid available to part-time students. *Faculty research:* Low-birth weight prevention and care. • Susan Gennaro, Director, 215-898-1844. Fax: 215-898-6320. E-mail: gennaro@pobox.upenn.edu. Application contact: Susan K. Ogle, Associate Director of Admissions and Student Affairs, 215-898-3301. Fax: 215-573-8439. E-mail: solge@pobox.upenn.edu.

University of Pennsylvania, School of Nursing, Primary Care Nurse Practitioner Program: Adult, Philadelphia, PA 19104. Awards MSN. Accredited by NLN. Part-time programs available. Students: 3 full-time (all women), 14 part-time (13 women); includes 2 minority (both Asian Americans). 19 applicants, 63% accepted. In 1997, 14 degrees awarded. *Average time to degree:* master's–1 year full-time, 2 years part-time. *Entrance requirements:* GRE General Test, BSN, minimum GPA of 3.0, previous course work in statistics, 1 year of clinical experience in area of interest. Application deadline: 2/15 (priority date; rolling processing). Application fee: $65. *Financial aid:* Teaching assistantships, Federal Work-Study, institutionally sponsored loans, and career-related internships or fieldwork available. Aid available to part-time students. *Faculty research:* Payment structures for nurse practitioners, delirium in older adults. • Dr. Eileen Sullivan-Marx, Director, 215-898-4063. Fax: 215-573-7381. E-mail: eileens@pobox.upenn.edu. Application contact: Susan K. Ogle, Associate Director of Admissions and Student Affairs, 215-898-3301. Fax: 215-573-8439. E-mail: sogle@pobox.upenn.edu.

University of Pennsylvania, School of Nursing, Primary Care Nurse Practitioner Program: Family, Philadelphia, PA 19104. Awards MSN, Certificate. Accredited by NLN. Part-time programs available. Students: 25 full-time (22 women), 10 part-time (9 women); includes 5 minority (4 African Americans, 1 Asian American), 1 international. Average age 32. 19 applicants, 68% accepted. In 1997, 15 master's awarded. *Average time to degree:* master's–1 year full-time, 2 years part-time. *Entrance requirements:* For master's, GRE General Test, BSN, minimum GPA of 3.0, previous course work in statistics, 1 year of clinical experience in area of interest. Application deadline: 2/15 (rolling processing). Application fee: $65. *Financial aid:* In 1997–98, 6 research assistantships, 1 teaching assistantship were awarded; Federal Work-Study, institutionally sponsored loans, and career-related internships or fieldwork also available. Aid available to part-time students. *Faculty research:* Evaluation of primary care practitioner practice, access to primary care. • Dr. Melinda Jenkins, Director, 215-898-4043. Fax: 215-573-7381. E-mail: mjenkins@pobox.upenn.edu. Application contact: Susan K. Ogle, Associate Director of Admissions and Student Affairs, 215-898-3301. Fax: 215-573-8439. E-mail: sogle@pobox.upenn.edu.

University of Pennsylvania, School of Nursing, Primary Care Nurse Practitioner Program: Pediatrics, Philadelphia, PA 19104. Awards MSN. Accredited by NLN. Part-time programs available. Students: 11 full-time (all women), 18 part-time (all women); includes 1 international. 15 applicants, 93% accepted. In 1997, 25 degrees awarded. *Entrance requirements:* GRE General Test, BSN, minimum GPA of 3.0, previous course work in statistics, 1 year of clinical experience in area of interest. Application deadline: 2/1 (rolling processing). Application fee: $65. *Financial aid:* In 1997–98, 3 research assistantships, 1 teaching assistantship were awarded; Federal Work-Study, institutionally sponsored loans, and career-related internships or fieldwork also available. Aid available to part-time students. *Faculty research:* Adolescent behavior change, prevention of teenage pregnancy, community schools. Total annual research expenditures: $500,000. • Dr. Ann O'Sullivan, Director, 215-898-4043. Fax: 215-573-7381. E-mail: osull@pobox.upenn.edu. Application contact: Susan K. Ogle, Associate Director of Admissions and Student Affairs, 215-898-3301. Fax: 215-573-8439. E-mail: sogle@pobox.upenn.edu.

University of Pennsylvania, School of Nursing, Psychiatric Mental Health Advanced Practice Nurse Program, Philadelphia, PA 19104. Offers adult and special populations (MSN), child and family (MSN), geropsychiatrics (MSN). Accredited by NLN. Part-time programs available. Students: 5 full-time (all women), 18 part-time (17 women); includes 1 minority (African American). Average age 34. 13 applicants, 69% accepted. In 1997, 13 degrees awarded. *Entrance requirements:* GRE General Test, BSN, minimum GPA of 3.0, previous course work in statistics. Application deadline: 9/1 (rolling processing). Application fee: $65. *Financial aid:* In 1997–98, 5 research assistantships, 8 teaching assistantships were awarded; fellowships, Federal Work-Study, institutionally sponsored loans, and career-related internships or fieldwork also available. Aid available to part-time students. *Faculty research:* Use of restraints in psychiatry, victims of trauma, spiritual use of prayer by cancer patients, coping strategies of African-Americans, urban health care. • Dr. Freida Outlaw, Director, 215-898-5730. Fax: 215-898-6320. E-mail: foutlaw@pobox.upenn.edu. Application contact: Susan K. Ogle, Associate Director of Admissions and Student Affairs, 215-898-3301. Fax: 215-573-8439. E-mail: sogle@pobox.upenn.edu.

University of Phoenix, Graduate Programs, Nursing Programs, Track in Women's Health Nurse Practitioner, 4615 East Elwood St, PO Box 52069, Phoenix, AZ 85072-2069. Awards MN. Accredited by NLN. Programs offered at campuses in Phoenix, Sacramento, and Southern California. Postbaccalaureate distance learning degree programs offered (no on-campus study). *Degree requirements:* Thesis or alternative required, foreign language not required. *Entrance requirements:* TOEFL (minimum score 520), minimum GPA of 2.5, RN license, 3 years of work experience in field, comprehensive cognitive assessment (COCA). Application deadline: rolling. Application fee: $50. *Tuition:* $248 per credit hour. • Application contact: Campus Information Center, 602-966-9577.

University of Pittsburgh, School of Nursing, Advanced Specialized Role Program, Pittsburgh, PA 15260. Offers administration (MSN), individualized options (MSN), informatics (MSN), nursing education (MSN), research (MSN). Accredited by NLN. *Degree requirements:* Thesis optional, foreign language not required. *Entrance requirements:* GRE or MAT, TOEFL, BSN, RN license, nursing experience. Application deadline: 2/1 (priority date; rolling processing; 9/15 for spring admission). Application fee: $35 ($40 for international students). *Financial aid:* Application deadline 6/1. • Judith A. Tate, Coordinator, 412-624-5872. Fax: 412-383-7227.

E-mail: jtaloo+@pitt.edu. Application contact: Dr. Kathy Lucke, Director, Student Services, 412-624-2405. Fax: 412-624-2409. E-mail: nursao+@pitt.edu.

See in-depth description on page 1451.

University of Pittsburgh, School of Nursing, Program in Nurse Practitioner Studies, Pittsburgh, PA 15260. Offers acute and tertiary care (MSN), including acute care nurse practitioner; health and community systems (MSN), including psychiatric primary care nurse practitioner; health promotion and development (MSN), including family nurse practitioner, pediatric nurse practitioner, women's health nurse practitioner. Accredited by NLN. Part-time programs available. Students: 56 full-time, 182 part-time. 97 applicants, 64% accepted. In 1997, 87 degrees awarded. *Degree requirements:* Thesis or alternative required, foreign language not required. *Average time to degree:* master's–2 years full-time, 5 years part-time. *Entrance requirements:* GRE General Test or MAT, TOEFL, BSN, RN license, 1 to 3 years of nursing experience. Application deadline: 2/1 (priority date; rolling processing; 9/15 for spring admission). Application fee: $35 ($40 for international students). *Financial aid:* Application deadline 6/1. • Application contact: Dr. Kathy Lucke, Director, Student Services, 412-624-2405. Fax: 412-624-2409. E-mail: nursao+@pitt.edu.

See in-depth description on page 1451.

University of Portland, School of Nursing, Portland, OR 97203-5798. Offerings include family nurse practitioner (Post Master's Certificate). Postbaccalaureate distance learning degree programs offered (minimal on-campus study). School faculty: 11 full-time (10 women). *Application deadline:* rolling. *Application fee:* $40. *Tuition:* $540 per semester hour. • Dr. Terry Misener, Dean, 503-283-7211. Fax: 503-283-7399. E-mail: misener@up.edu.

University of San Diego, Philip Y. Hahn School of Nursing, San Diego, CA 92110-2492. Offerings include adult health nurse practitioner (MSN), family health nurse practitioner (MSN). One or more programs accredited by NLN. School faculty: 12 full-time (all women), 4 part-time (all women). *Entrance requirements:* GRE or MAT, TOEFL (minimum score 580), TWE, BSN, minimum GPA of 3.0. Application deadline: 5/1 (priority date; rolling processing; 11/15 for spring admission). Application fee: $45. *Expenses:* Tuition $585 per unit (minimum). Fees $50 per year full-time, $30 per year part-time. • Dr. Janet Rodgers, Dean, 619-260-4550. Fax: 619-260-6814. Application contact: Mary Jane Tiernan, Director of Graduate Admissions, 619-260-4524. Fax: 619-260-4158. E-mail: grads@acusd.edu.

University of San Francisco, School of Nursing, San Francisco, CA 94117-1080. Offerings include advanced practice nursing-nurse practitioner and clinical nurse specialist (MSN), with option in adult health nursing. Accredited by NLN. School faculty: 9 full-time (8 women), 1 (woman) part-time. *Average time to degree:* master's–2 years full-time, 2.5 years part-time. *Entrance requirements:* Minimum GPA of 3.0. Application deadline: rolling. Application fee: $40. *Tuition:* $658 per unit (minimum). • Dr. John Lantz, Interim Dean, 415-422-6681. Fax: 415-422-6877. E-mail: lantzj@usfca.edu.

University of Scranton, Department of Nursing, Scranton, PA 18510-4622. Offerings include family nurse practitioner (MS). Applicants accepted in odd-numbered years only. Department faculty: 12 full-time (all women), 2 part-time (1 woman). *Entrance requirements:* BSN, minimum GPA of 3.0, Pennsylvania RN license. Application deadline: rolling. Application fee: $35. *Expenses:* Tuition $465 per credit. Fees $25 per semester. • Dr. Patricia Harrington, Chair, 717-941-7673. E-mail: harringtonp1@uofs.edu. Application contact: Dr. Mary Jane Hanson, Director, 717-941-4060. Fax: 717-941-4201. E-mail: hansonm2@uofs.edu.

University of South Carolina, Graduate School, College of Nursing, Program in Advanced Practice Nursing, Columbia, SC 29208. Awards Certificate. Students: 45 part-time (all women); includes 5 minority (3 African Americans, 1 Asian American, 1 Hispanic). Average age 45. In 1997, 30 degrees awarded. *Application deadline:* 4/15 (rolling processing; 10/15 for spring admission). *Application fee:* $35. Electronic applications accepted. *Expenses:* Tuition $4480 per year full-time, $220 per credit hour part-time for state residents; $9338 per year full-time, $457 per credit hour part-time for nonresidents. Fees $125 per year full-time, $37 per semester (minimum) part-time. *Financial aid:* Application deadline 2/1. • Application contact: Office of Academic and Student Affairs, 803-777-7412. Fax: 803-777-0616.

The University of Tampa, Nursing Program, Tampa, FL 33606-1490. Offerings include family nurse practitioner (MSN). Postbaccalaureate distance learning degree programs offered (minimal on-campus study). Program faculty: 5 full-time (4 women), 7 part-time (6 women). *Degree requirements:* Oral exam, practicum required, thesis optional. *Entrance requirements:* GRE General Test (minimum combined score of 1000), minimum GPA of 3.0, RN license. Application deadline: 8/20 (priority date; rolling processing). Application fee: $35. Electronic applications accepted. • Dr. Nancy Ross, Director, 813-253-6223. Fax: 813-258-7214. Application contact: Barbara P. Strickler, Vice President for Enrollment, 800-733-4773. Fax: 813-254-4955. E-mail: admissions@alpha.utampa.edu.

University of Tennessee at Chattanooga, School of Human Services, School of Nursing, Chattanooga, TN 37403-2598. Offerings include family nurse practitioner (MSN). Accredited by NLN. School faculty: 8 full-time (7 women), 4 part-time (3 women). *Degree requirements:* Qualifying exams required, foreign language and thesis not required. *Entrance requirements:* GRE General Test (combined average 1485 on three sections). Application deadline: rolling. Application fee: $25. *Tuition:* $2864 per year full-time, $160 per credit hour part-time for state residents; $6806 per year full-time, $379 per credit hour part-time for nonresidents. • Dr. Maria Smith, Director, 423-755-4646. Fax: 423-755-4668. E-mail: msmith@utcvm.utc.edu. Application contact: Dr. Deborah Arfken, Assistant Provost for Graduate Studies, 423-755-4667. Fax: 423-755-4478.

The University of Texas at El Paso, College of Nursing and Health Science, Program in Nursing, 500 West University Avenue, El Paso, TX 79968-0001. Offerings include community health/family nurse practitioner (MSN), womens health care/nurse practitioner (MSN). One or more programs accredited by NLN. *Degree requirements:* Thesis optional, foreign language not required. *Entrance requirements:* GRE General Test or MAT (minimum score 50), TOEFL (minimum score 550), BSN, course work in statistics. Application deadline: 7/1 (rolling processing; 11/1 for spring admission). Application fee: $15 ($65 for international students). Electronic applications accepted. *Tuition:* $2063 per year full-time, $284 per credit hour part-time for state residents; $5753 per year full-time, $425 per credit hour part-time for nonresidents.

University of Wisconsin–Oshkosh, College of Nursing, Oshkosh, WI 54901-8602. Offerings include family nurse practitioner (MSN). Accredited by NLN. College faculty: 5 full-time (all women), 12 part-time (11 women). *Degree requirements:* Thesis or alternative required, foreign language not required. *Entrance requirements:* RN license, BSN, course work in statistics and health assessment in past 5 years, minimum undergraduate GPA of 3.0. Application deadline: 1/15. Application fee: $45. *Tuition:* $3638 per year full-time, $609 per semester (minimum) part-time for state residents; $11,282 per year full-time, $1884 per semester (minimum) part-time for nonresidents. • Dr. Merritt Knox, Dean, 920-424-3089. Application contact: Dr. Michael Morgan, Director of Graduate Programs, 920-424-2106. E-mail: morganm@uwosh.edu.

Vanderbilt University, School of Nursing, Nashville, TN 37240-1001. Offerings include family nurse practitioner (MSN), gerontology nurse practitioner (MSN), neonatal critical care practitioner (MSN), neonatal nurse practitioner (MSN), occupational health/adult health nurse practitioner (MSN), pediatric nurse practitioner (MSN), psychiatric-mental health nurse practitioner (MSN), women's health nurse practitioner (MSN). One or more programs accredited by NLN. Postbaccalaureate distance learning degree programs offered (minimal on-campus study). School faculty: 76 full-time (66 women), 253 part-time (224 women). *Degree requirements:* Terminal course required, thesis not required. *Average time to degree:* master's–2 years full-time, 4 years part-time; doctorate–4 years full-time, 5 years part-time. *Entrance requirements:* GMAT, GRE, or MAT, minimum B average. Application deadline: rolling. Application fee: $50. Electronic applications accepted. • Dr. Colleen Conway-Welch, Dean, 615-343-3243. Fax: 615-343-7711. Application contact: Patricia Peerman, Assistant Dean of Admissions, 615-322-3800. Fax: 615-343-0333. E-mail: vusn-admission@mcmail.vanderbilt.edu.

Villanova University, College of Nursing, Villanova, PA 19085-1690. Offerings include nurse practitioner (Post Master's Certificate). MSN (pediatric nurse practitioner), Post Master's Certificate (nurse practitioner, nurse anesthetist, clinical case management) new for fall 1998. College faculty: 30 full-time (all women). *Application deadline:* 7/1 (priority date; rolling processing; 12/1 for spring admission). *Application fee:* $25. *Expenses:* Tuition $445 per credit. Fees $60 per year. • Dr. Claire Manfredi, Graduate Director, 610-519-4907. Fax: 610-519-7997. E-mail: cmanfred@email.vill.edu.

Virginia Commonwealth University, School of Nursing, Nurse Practitioner Program, Richmond, VA 23284-9005. Awards Certificate. Students: 2 full-time (both women), 29 part-time (28 women); includes 1 minority (Asian American). Average age 43. 30 applicants, 80% accepted. In 1997, 14 degrees awarded. *Application deadline:* 2/1. *Application fee:* $30 ($0 for international students). *Tuition:* $4960 per year full-time, $257 per credit part-time for state residents; $12,652 per year full-time, $684 per credit part-time for nonresidents. • Application contact: Dr. W. Richard Cowling III, Associate Dean for Graduate Programs, 804-828-0836. Fax: 804-828-7743. E-mail: wrcowlin@vcu.edu.

Wagner College, Department of Nursing, Program in Family Nurse Practitioner, Staten Island, NY 10301. Awards Certificate. Part-time and evening/weekend programs available. Faculty: 1 (woman) full-time, 1 part-time (0 women). Students: 12 part-time (all women). 4 applicants, 75% accepted. In 1997, 5 degrees awarded. *Entrance requirements:* Master's degree in nursing from an NLN-accredited program, minimum GPA of 3.0. Application deadline: 8/1 (priority date; rolling processing; 12/10 for spring admission). Application fee: $50 ($65 for international students). *Tuition:* $580 per credit. • Application contact: Admissions Office, 718-390-3411.

Wayne State University, College of Nursing, Department of Adult Health and Administration, Program in Adult Primary Care Nursing, Detroit, MI 48202. Awards MSN. Accredited by NLN. Part-time programs available. Students: 16 full-time (all women), 47 part-time (43 women); includes 6 minority (all African Americans). Average age 35. 41 applicants, 68% accepted. In 1997, 18 degrees awarded. *Degree requirements:* Computer language, thesis or alternative required, foreign language not required. *Entrance requirements:* GRE General Test (minimum combined score of 800), minimum GPA of 2.8. Application deadline: 7/1 (priority date; rolling processing; 11/1 for spring admission). Application fee: $20 ($30 for international students). *Expenses:* Tuition $163 per credit hour for state residents; $355 per credit hour for nonresidents. Fees $498 per year full-time, $114 per semester (minimum) part-time. *Financial aid:* In 1997–98, 3 students received aid, including 3 traineeships (1 to a first-year student); research assistantships also available. Aid available to part-time students. Financial aid application deadline: 7/1; applicants required to submit FAFSA. *Faculty research:* Nurse practitioner interventions, health promotion in elders and low-income adults. • Dr. Dawn Hameister, Assistant Dean, 313-577-4386. Fax: 313-577-4571. Application contact: Vickie Radoye, Administrative Assistant Dean, Student Affairs, 313-577-4082. Fax: 313-577-6949.

Wayne State University, College of Nursing, Department of Family, Community and Mental Health, Neonatal Nurse Practitioner Program, Detroit, MI 48202. Awards Certificate. Students: 2 part-time (both women). Average age 30. 1 applicant, 0% accepted. In 1997, 3 degrees awarded. *Entrance requirements:* Admission to MSN program and 3000 hours of neonatal experience including 1800 hours in a level 3 neonatal ICU. Application deadline: 7/1 (priority date; rolling processing; 11/1 for spring admission). Application fee: $20 ($30 for international students). *Expenses:* Tuition $163 per credit hour for state residents; $355 per credit hour for nonresidents. Fees $498 per year full-time, $114 per semester (minimum) part-time. *Financial aid:* Application deadline 7/1. *Faculty research:* High-risk pregnancy, infant developmental/cocaine abuse. • Dr. Marie-Luise Friedemann, Assistant Dean, 313-577-4092. Fax: 313-577-4571. Application contact: Vickie Radoye, Administrative Assistant Dean, Student Affairs, 313-577-4082. Fax: 313-577-6949.

Western University of Health Sciences, Program in Nursing, Pomona, CA 91766-1854. Offerings include family nurse practitioner (MSN). *Application deadline:* rolling. *Application fee:* $60. *Tuition:* $17,150 per year. • Dr. Ted Wendel, Chancellor, 916-898-7020. Application contact: Susan M. Hanson, Director of Admissions, 909-469-5335.

West Virginia University, School of Nursing, Morgantown, WV 26506. Offerings include nurse practitioner (Certificate). Postbaccalaureate distance learning degree programs offered (minimal on-campus study). School faculty: 38 full-time (37 women). *Average time to degree:* master's–2 years full-time, 4 years part-time. *Application deadline:* 6/1 (10/1 for spring admission). *Application fee:* $45. *Tuition:* $3452 per year for state residents; $9908 per year for nonresidents. • Dr. E. Jane Martin, Dean, 304-293-4831. Application contact: Jacqueline W. Riley, Assistant Dean for Student and Alumni Affairs, 304-293-1386. Fax: 304-293-6826. E-mail: jriley@wvu.edu.

Wilmington College, Division of Nursing, New Castle, DE 19720-6491. Offerings include family nurse practitioner (MSN). Accredited by NLN. *Entrance requirements:* BSN, RN license. Application deadline: 1/24 (priority date). Application fee: $25. *Expenses:* Tuition $4410 per year full-time, $735 per course part-time. Fees $50 per year. • Dr. Betty Caffo, Chair, 302-328-9401. Application contact: Michael Lee, Director of Admissions and Financial Aid, 302-328-9401 Ext. 102.

Wright State University, College of Nursing and Health, Program in Nursing, Dayton, OH 45435. Offerings include family nurse practitioner (MS). Accredited by NLN. *Degree requirements:* Thesis or alternative required, foreign language not required. *Average time to degree:* master's–2 years full-time, 5 years part-time. *Entrance requirements:* GRE General Test, TOEFL (minimum score 550), BSN from NLN-accredited college, Ohio RN license. Application deadline: 4/15 (priority date). Application fee: $25. *Tuition:* $5109 per year full-time, $161 per credit hour part-time for state residents; $9039 per year full-time, $282 per credit hour part-time for nonresidents. • Application contact: Theresa Haghnazarian, Director of Student and Alumni Affairs, 937-775-3133. Fax: 937-775-4571.

Gerontological Nursing

Boston College, School of Nursing, Chestnut Hill, MA 02167-9991. Offerings include gerontology (MS). Accredited by NLN. School faculty: 18 full-time (all women), 1 (woman) part-time. *Degree requirements:* Oral comprehensive exam, research project required, foreign language and thesis not required. *Average time to degree:* doctorate–4 years full-time. *Entrance requirements:* GRE General Test, bachelor's degree in nursing. Application deadline: 3/1 (priority date; 10/15 for spring admission). Application fee: $40. Electronic applications accepted. *Expenses:* Tuition $626 per semester hour. Fees $80 per year (minimum) full-time, $30 per semester part-time. • Dr. Barbara Munro, Dean, 617-552-4251. Fax: 617-552-0931. E-mail: barbara.munro@bc.edu. Application contact: Dana Robinson, Administrative Secretary, 617-552-4059. Fax: 617-552-0745. E-mail: dana.robinson@bc.edu.

Case Western Reserve University, Frances Payne Bolton School of Nursing, Master's Program in Nursing, Nurse Practitioner Program, Cleveland, OH 44106. Offerings include gerontological nurse practitioner (MSN). *Degree requirements:* Thesis optional, foreign language not required. *Entrance requirements:* GRE General Test or MAT. Application deadline: 6/1 (rolling processing). Application fee: $75. *Tuition:* $18,400 per year full-time, $767 per credit hour part-time. • Application contact: Molly Blank, Admission Counselor, 216-368-2529. Fax: 216-368-3542. E-mail: mab44@po.cwru.edu.

The Catholic University of America, School of Nursing, Washington, DC 20064. Offerings include advanced practice nursing (MSN), with options in administration of nursing service, adult nurse practitioner, education, family nurse practitioner, geriatric nurse practitioner, pediatric nurse practitioner, psychiatric-mental health, school health nurse practitioner. Accredited by NLN. School faculty: 18 full-time (all women), 2 part-time (both women), 19 FTE. *Degree requirements:* Comprehensive exam required, thesis optional, foreign language not required. *Entrance requirements:* GRE General Test (minimum combined score of 1350 on three sections). Application deadline: 8/1 (priority date; rolling processing; 12/1 for spring admission). Application fee: $50. *Expenses:* Tuition $17,325 per year full-time, $668 per credit hour part-time. Fees $680 per year full-time, $360 per year part-time. • Sr. Mary Jean Flaherty, Dean, 202-319-5403.

College of Mount Saint Vincent, Department of Nursing, Riverdale, NY 10471-1093. Offerings include nursing for the adult and aged (MS). Accredited by NLN. Department faculty: 3 full-time (all women), 15 part-time (all women). *Degree requirements:* Computer language, written research project required, foreign language and thesis not required. *Entrance requirements:* Bachelor's degree from NLN-accredited institution, minimum GPA of 3.0. Application deadline: 6/15 (priority date; rolling processing; 12/1 for spring admission). Application fee: $50. • Dr. Barbara Cohen, Director, 718-405-3352. Application contact: Dr. Kem Louie, Chairperson, 718-405-3355.

Columbia University, School of Nursing, Program in Geriatric Nurse Practitioner, New York, NY 10032. Awards MS, Adv C. One or more programs accredited by NLN. Part-time programs available. Faculty: 1 (woman) full-time. Students: 1 (woman) full-time, 12 part-time (all women); includes 5 minority (3 African Americans, 2 Asian Americans). Average age 36. 8 applicants, 88% accepted. In 1997, 1 master's awarded. *Entrance requirements:* For master's, GRE General Test (minimum score 500 on verbal and analytical sections), BSN, 1 year of clinical experience (preferred), or completion of a clinical residency; for Adv C, MSN, previous course work in statistics, clinical preceptorship. Application deadline: 4/1 (priority date; rolling processing; 10/1 for spring admission). Application fee: $60. *Tuition:* $19,376 per year full-time, $692 per credit (minimum) part-time. *Financial aid:* Teaching assistantships available. Financial aid application deadline: 2/1. • Dr. Carolyn Auerhahn, Director, 212-305-3471. Application contact: Joseph Tomaino, Assistant Dean for Student Services, 212-305-5756. E-mail: jt238@columbia.edu.

Concordia University Wisconsin, Division of Graduate Studies, Program in Nursing, Mequon, WI 53097-2402. Offerings include geriatric nurse practitioner (MSN). Postbaccalaureate distance learning degree programs offered (minimal on-campus study). *Degree requirements:* Thesis or alternative, comprehensive exam. *Entrance requirements:* TOEFL (minimum score 550). Application deadline: 8/1 (priority date; rolling processing). *Tuition:* $250 per credit. • Dr. Ruth Gresley, Director, 414-243-4452. E-mail: rgresley@bach.cuw.edu.

Duke University, School of Nursing, Durham, NC 27708-0586. Offerings include clinical nurse specialist (MSN), with options in acute care pediatric, adult oncological/HIV, gerontological, neonatal, pediatric; gerontological (Certificate); nurse practitioner (MSN), with options in acute care adult, acute care pediatric, adult cardiovascular, adult oncological/HIV, family, gerontological, neonatal, pediatric. One or more programs accredited by NLN. Postbaccalaureate distance learning degree programs offered (minimal on-campus study). School faculty: 24 full-time (22 women), 4 part-time (all women). *Degree requirements:* For master's, computer language required, thesis optional, foreign language not required. *Average time to degree:* master's–1.5 years full-time, 3 years part-time; other advanced degree–1 year full-time, 2 years part-time. *Entrance requirements:* For master's, GRE General Test or MAT, BSN, minimum GPA of 3.0, previous course work in statistics, RN license, 1 year of nursing experience. Application deadline: 4/1 (priority date; rolling processing; 10/1 for spring admission). Application fee: $50. *Tuition:* $20,976 per year full-time, $552 per unit part-time. • Dr. Mary T. Champagne, Dean, 919-684-3786. E-mail: champ001@mc.duke.edu. Application contact: Judith K. Carter, Admissions Officer, 919-684-4248. Fax: 919-681-8899. E-mail: carte026@mc.duke.edu.

Emory University, Nell Hodgson Woodruff School of Nursing, Atlanta, GA 30322-1100. Offerings include nursing systems (MSN), with options in family and adult nurse practitioner, gerontologic nurse practitioner, occupational health nurse practitioner. Accredited by NLN. Postbaccalaureate distance learning degree programs offered (minimal on-campus study). School faculty: 33 full-time (32 women), 21 part-time (19 women), 48 FTE. *Degree requirements:* Thesis optional, foreign language not required. *Average time to degree:* master's–1.5 years full-time, 3 years part-time. *Entrance requirements:* GRE General Test (minimum combined score of 1500 on three sections) or MAT (minimum score 35), minimum GPA of 3.0, BS in nursing or RN license and additional course work. Application deadline: 2/1 (priority date; rolling processing; 11/1 for spring admission). Application fee: $50. *Expenses:* Tuition $18,050 per year. Fees $200 per year. • Dr. Dyanne D. Affonso, Dean, 404-727-7976. Fax: 404-727-0536. Application contact: Debbie Ashtiani, Director, 404-727-7980.

Gannon University, School of Graduate Studies, College of Sciences, Engineering, and Health Sciences, School of Health Sciences, Department of Nursing, Erie, PA 16505. Offerings include gerontology (MSN). Accredited by NLN. *Degree requirements:* Thesis. *Entrance requirements:* GRE General Test (minimum score 500 on each section), MAT (minimum score 60), bachelor's degree from a NLN-approved nursing program, interview, Pennsylvania RN license. Application deadline: 4/15. Application fee: $25. • Dr. Beverly Bartlett, Director, 814-871-5520. Application contact: Beth Nemenz, Director of Admissions, 814-871-7240. Fax: 814-871-5803. E-mail: admissions@gannon.edu.

Georgia State University, College of Health and Human Sciences, School of Nursing, Atlanta, GA 30303-3083. Offerings include gerontology (MS). One or more programs accredited by NLN. MS (child and adolescent psychology, gerontology) and PhD (community nursing, family nursing) being phased out; applicants no longer accepted. School faculty: 26 full-time (all women), 3 part-time (all women). *Degree requirements:* Research project or thesis required, thesis optional, foreign language not required. *Entrance requirements:* Interview, RN license. Application deadline: 4/15. Application fee: $25. *Expenses:* Tuition $2862 per year full-time, $106 per semester hour part-time for state residents; $11,448 per year full-time, $424 per semester hour part-time for nonresidents. Fees $228 per year. • Dr. Dee Baldwin, Director of Graduate Programs, 404-651-3040. Application contact: Barbara Smith, Admissions Counselor, 404-651-3064. Fax: 404-651-4871.

Gwynedd–Mercy College, Graduate Program in Nursing, Gwynedd Valley, PA 19437-0901. Offerings include gerontology (MSN). Accredited by NLN. MSN (pediatrics, oncology) admissions temporarily suspended. Program faculty: 9 full-time (all women), 8 part-time (6 women). *Degree requirements:* Thesis or research project required, foreign language not required. *Average time to degree:* master's–2.5 years full-time, 3.5 years part-time. *Entrance requirements:* GRE General Test (minimum combined score of 1350; average 1401), MAT (minimum score 40; average 48), 1 year of experience, physical assessment, previous course work in statistics. Application deadline: 8/1 (priority date; rolling processing). Application fee: $25. *Expenses:* Tuition $375 per credit. Fees $150 per year full-time, $80 per year part-time. • Dr. Mary Dressler, Dean, 215-641-5533. E-mail: dressler.m@gmc.edu. Application contact: Dr. Barbara A. Jones, Associate Professor, 215-646-7300 Ext. 407. Fax: 215-641-5517.

Hunter College of the City University of New York, Hunter-Bellevue School of Nursing, Gerontological Nurse Practitioner Program, 695 Park Avenue, New York, NY 10021-5085. Awards MS. Accredited by NLN. Part-time programs available. Faculty: 9 full-time (all women), 2 part-time (both women). Students: 3 full-time (2 women), 68 part-time (63 women); includes 30 minority (14 African Americans, 11 Asian Americans, 5 Hispanics), 1 international. Average age 39. 18 applicants, 72% accepted. In 1997, 14 degrees awarded (100% found work related to degree). *Degree requirements:* Practicum required, foreign language and thesis not required. *Average time to degree:* master's–2 years full-time, 4 years part-time. *Entrance requirements:* TOEFL (minimum score 550), minimum GPA of 3.0, New York RN license, 2 years of professional practice experience. Application deadline: 4/27 (rolling processing; 11/21 for spring admission). Application fee: $40. *Expenses:* Tuition $4350 per year full-time, $185 per credit part-time for state residents; $7600 per year full-time, $320 per credit part-time for nonresidents. Fees $26 per year. *Financial aid:* Traineeships, partial tuition waivers, Federal Work-Study available. Aid available to part-time students. Financial aid application deadline: 5/1; applicants required to submit FAFSA. *Faculty research:* Relationship between psychological factors and cognitive changes in the elderly. • Dr. Maura C. Ryan, Coordinator, 212-481-4420. Fax: 212-481-5078. E-mail: mryan@hejira.hunter.cuny.edu. Application contact: Audrey Berman, Associate Director for Graduate Admissions, 212-772-4490.

Jewish Hospital College of Nursing and Allied Health, Program in Nursing, St. Louis, MO 63110-1091. Offerings include gerontology nurse practitioner (MSN). College faculty: 10. *Application deadline:* rolling. *Application fee:* $25. *Tuition:* $320 per credit hour. • Dr. Sandra A. Jones, Director, 314-454-8416. Application contact: Connie Stohlman, Chief Admissions Officer, 314-454-7538.

La Roche College, Program in Nursing, Pittsburgh, PA 15237-5898. Offerings include gerontological nursing (MSN). Accredited by NLN. Program faculty: 5 full-time (all women), 2 part-time (both women). *Degree requirements:* Internship, practicum required, thesis optional, foreign language not required. *Entrance requirements:* GRE General Test (minimum combined score of 1200), TOEFL (minimum score 500). Application fee: $25. *Tuition:* $431 per credit. • Dr. Kathleen Sullivan, Division Chair, 412-536-1169. Application contact: Judy Henry, Manager of Nursing Student Enrollment, 412-536-1267. Fax: 412-536-1283.

Lehman College of the City University of New York, Division of Natural and Social Sciences, Department of Nursing, 250 Bedford Park Boulevard West, Bronx, NY 10468-1589. Offerings include nursing of old adults (MS). Accredited by NLN. Department faculty: 13 full-time (12 women). *Entrance requirements:* Bachelor's degree in nursing, New York RN license. Application deadline: 4/1 (rolling processing; 11/1 for spring admission). Application fee: $40. *Expenses:* Tuition $4350 per year full-time, $185 per credit part-time for state residents; $7600 per year full-time, $320 per credit part-time for nonresidents. Fees $120 per year full-time, $80 per year part-time. • Ngo Nkongho, Chair, 718-960-8374. Application contact: Keville Frederickson, Director of Graduate Studies, 718-960-8378. Fax: 718-960-8488.

Loma Linda University, Graduate School, Department of Graduate Nursing, Program in Adult and Aging Family Nursing, Loma Linda, CA 92350. Awards MS. Accredited by NLN. Part-time programs available. *Degree requirements:* Thesis or alternative required, foreign language not required. *Entrance requirements:* GRE General Test (minimum combined score of 1500). Application fee: $40. *Tuition:* $380 per unit. *Financial aid:* Grants, Federal Work-Study, institutionally sponsored loans, and career-related internships or fieldwork available. Aid available to part-time students. Financial aid application deadline: 6/1. *Faculty research:* Coping, integration of research. • Dr. Pat Jones, Coordinator, 909-824-4360.

Marquette University, College of Nursing, Milwaukee, WI 53201-1881. Offerings include gerontological nurse practitioner (Certificate). College faculty: 24 full-time (23 women), 5 part-time (4 women). *Application fee:* $40. *Tuition:* $490 per credit. • Dr. Madeline Wake, Dean, 414-288-3812. Application contact: Dr. Gregory Olson, Associate Dean, 414-288-3808. Fax: 414-288-1578.

Medical University of South Carolina, College of Nursing, Program in Nursing, Charleston, SC 29425-0002. Offerings include gerontological nursing (MSN). Accredited by NLN. *Degree requirements:* Computer language required, thesis optional, foreign language not required. *Entrance requirements:* GRE General Test (minimum combined score of 1000), BSN, previous course work in statistics and physical assessment, 1 year nursing experience, license. Application deadline: 2/15 (10/15 for spring admission). Application fee: $55. *Expenses:* Tuition $3760 per year full-time, $173 per semester hour part-time for state residents; $5672 per year full-time, $270 per semester hour part-time for nonresidents. Fees $280 per year (minimum). • Dr. Jean Leuner, Associate Dean, 843-792-8515. Application contact: Office of Enrollment Services, 843-792-3281.

Nazareth College of Rochester, Graduate Studies, Department of Nursing, Gerontological Nurse Practitioner Program, Rochester, NY 14618-3790. Awards MS. Part-time programs available. Faculty: 5 full-time (all women), 1 part-time (0 women). Students: 11 part-time (all women). 2 applicants, 100% accepted. *Entrance requirements:* GRE General Test or MAT, minimum GPA of 2.7. Application deadline: 6/1 (priority date; rolling processing; 11/1 for spring admission). Application fee: $40. *Expenses:* Tuition $436 per credit hour. Fees $20 per semester. *Financial aid:* Career-related internships or fieldwork available. Aid available to part-time students. Financial aid applicants required to submit FAFSA. • Patricia Hanson, Director, 716-389-2711. Fax: 716-389-4252. Application contact: Dr. Kay F. Marshman, Dean, 716-389-2815. Fax: 716-389-2452.

New York University, School of Education, Division of Nursing, Programs in Advanced Practice Nursing, New York, NY 10012-1019. Offerings include advanced practice nursing: elderly (MA, AC). One or more programs accredited by NLN. MA/MS offered jointly with the Program in Management in the Robert F. Wagner Graduate School of Public Service. Faculty: 25 full-time, 9 part-time. *Entrance requirements:* For master's, TOEFL; for AC, TOEFL, master's degree. Application deadline: 2/1 (priority date; rolling processing; 12/1 for spring admission). Application fee: $40 ($60 for international students). • Judi Haber, Director, 212-998-5300. Application contact: Office of Graduate Admissions, 212-998-5030. Fax: 212-995-4328.

Oregon Health Sciences University, School of Nursing, PhD Nursing Program, 3181 SW Sam Jackson Park Road, Portland, OR 97201-3098. Offerings include gerontological nursing (PhD). *Degree requirements:* Dissertation required, foreign language not required. *Entrance requirements:* GRE General Test (minimum combined score of 1000), master's degree in nursing; minimum GPA of 3.0 (undergraduate), 3.5 (graduate). Application deadline: 1/15. Application fee: $40. • Application contact: Office of Recruitment, 503-494-7725. Fax: 503-494-4350.

Oregon Health Sciences University, School of Nursing, Program in Gerontological Nursing, 3181 SW Sam Jackson Park Road, Portland, OR 97201-3098. Awards MN, MS, Post Master's Certificate. One or more programs accredited by NLN. *Degree requirements:* For master's, thesis optional, foreign language not required. *Entrance requirements:* For master's, GRE General Test (minimum combined score of 1000), bachelor's degree in nursing, minimum undergraduate GPA of 3.0; for Post Master's Certificate, master's degree in nursing. Application deadline: 1/15. Application fee: $40. • Application contact: Office of Recruitment, 503-494-7725. Fax: 503-494-4350.

Pacific Lutheran University, School of Nursing, Program in Nurse Practitioner, Tacoma, WA 98447. Offerings include gerontology (MSN). Accredited by NLN. Program faculty: 11 full-time (10 women), 1 (woman) part-time. *Degree requirements:* Thesis optional, foreign language not required. *Entrance requirements:* GRE General Test, TOEFL (minimum score 550), bachelor's degree in nursing, minimum undergraduate GPA of 3.0. Application deadline: 4/1 (priority date; rolling processing). Application fee: $35. *Tuition:* $490 per semester hour. • Application contact: Marjo Burdick, Office of Admissions, 253-535-7151. Fax: 253-535-8320. E-mail: admissions@plu.edu.

Rush University, College of Nursing, Department of Gerontological Nursing, Chicago, IL 60612-3832. Offers programs in adult/gerontological nurse practitioner (MSN, DN Sc, ND), gerontological nurse practitioner (MSN, DN Sc, ND), rehabilitation nursing (MSN, DN Sc, ND). One or more programs accredited by NLN. Part-time programs available. Faculty: 6 full-time (all women), 3 part-time (all women), 7 FTE. Students: 31 part-time. Average age 36. *Degree requirements:* For doctorate, dissertation required, foreign language not required. *Entrance requirements:* For master's, GRE General Test, interview; for doctorate, interview, previous course work in statistics. Application deadline: 8/1 (rolling processing; 2/1 for spring admission). Application fee: $40. *Tuition:* $8560 per year full-time, $370 per credit hour part-time. *Financial aid:* Federal Work-Study, institutionally sponsored loans, and career-related internships or fieldwork available. Aid available to part-time students. Financial aid applicants required to submit FAFSA. *Faculty research:* Use of restraints, depression and environmental control in elderly hospitalized, attitude barriers to rehabilitation of elderly, interdisciplinary training for geriatric health professionals. • Jane Ulsafer-Van Lanen, Acting Chairperson, 312-942-3480. Application contact: Hicela Castruita, Director, College Admissions Services, 312-942-7100. Fax: 312-942-2219.

Rutgers, The State University of New Jersey, Newark, College of Nursing, Graduate Program in Acute Care of Adults and Aged, Newark, NJ 07102-3192. Awards MS. Accredited by NLN. Part-time programs available. *Degree requirements:* Comprehensive exam required, foreign language and thesis not required. *Entrance requirements:* GRE General Test, TOEFL, RN license, minimum B average, BS in nursing. Application deadline: 8/15 (rolling processing; 12/15 for spring admission). Application fee: $40. Electronic applications accepted. *Expenses:* Tuition $6248 per year full-time, $257 per credit part-time for state residents; $9160 per year full-time, $380 per credit part-time for nonresidents. Fees $738 per year full-time, $107 per semester (minimum) part-time. *Financial aid:* Application deadline 3/1. • Application contact: Dr. Elaine Dolinsky, Associate Dean for Student Life and Services, 973-353-5060. Fax: 973-353-1277.

Rutgers, The State University of New Jersey, Newark, College of Nursing, Graduate Program in Primary Care of Adults and Aged, Newark, NJ 07102-3192. Awards MS. Accredited by NLN. Part-time programs available. *Degree requirements:* Comprehensive exam required, foreign language and thesis not required. *Entrance requirements:* GRE General Test, TOEFL, RN license, minimum B average, BS in nursing. Application deadline: 8/15 (rolling processing; 12/15 for spring admission). Application fee: $40. Electronic applications accepted. *Expenses:* Tuition $6248 per year full-time, $257 per credit part-time for state residents; $9160 per year full-time, $380 per credit part-time for nonresidents. Fees $738 per year full-time, $107 per semester (minimum) part-time. *Financial aid:* Federal Work-Study, institutionally sponsored loans, and career-related internships or fieldwork available. • Application contact: Dr. Elaine Dolinsky, Associate Dean for Student Life and Services, 973-353-5060. Fax: 973-353-1277.

Saint Louis University, School of Nursing, Program in Gerontological Nursing, St. Louis, MO 63103-2097. Awards MSN, MSN(R), Certificate, MPH/MSN, MSN/MBA. Offerings include clinical health specialist/case manager (MSN, MSN(R), Certificate), gerontological nurse practitioner (MSN, MSN(R), Certificate). One or more programs accredited by NLN. *Degree requirements:* For master's, comprehensive oral exam required, thesis optional, foreign language not required. *Entrance requirements:* For master's, GRE General Test. Application deadline: 7/1 (rolling processing; 11/1 for spring admission). Application fee: $40. *Tuition:* $542 per credit hour. *Financial aid:* Traineeships available. Financial aid application deadline: 4/1. • Dr. Margie Edel, Program Director, 314-577-8931. Application contact: Dr. Marcia Buresch, Assistant Dean of the Graduate School, 314-977-2240. Fax: 314-977-3943.

San Jose State University, College of Applied Arts and Sciences, School of Nursing, San Jose, CA 95192-0001. Offerings include gerontology nurse practitioner (MS). Accredited by NLN. School faculty: 26 full-time (24 women), 13 part-time (12 women). *Degree requirements:* Thesis required, foreign language not required. *Entrance requirements:* BS in nursing, RN license. Application deadline: 6/1 (rolling processing). Application fee: $59. *Expenses:* Tuition $0 for state residents; $246 per unit for nonresidents. Fees $2017 per year full-time, $1351 per year part-time. • Dr. Bobbye Gorenberg, Director, 408-924-3130. Application contact: Dr. Colleen Saylor, Graduate Coordinator, 408-924-3134.

Seton Hall University, College of Nursing, Department of Graduate Nursing, Advanced Practice in Primary Health Care Program, South Orange, NJ 07079-2697. Offerings include gerontological nurse practitioner (MSN). Accredited by NLN. Program faculty: 6 full-time (all women), 4 part-time (all women). *Degree requirements:* Research project required, foreign language and thesis not required. *Entrance requirements:* GRE or MAT, BSN. Application deadline: 5/15 (priority date; rolling processing; 11/15 for spring admission). Application fee: $50. *Expenses:* Tuition $500 per credit. Fees $610 per year full-time, $185 per semester part-time. • Dr. Cynthia Hughes, Director, 973-761-9273. Fax: 973-761-9607. E-mail: hughesci@shu.edu.

State University of New York at New Paltz, Faculty of Liberal Arts and Sciences, Department of Nursing, New Paltz, NY 12561-2499. Offerings include gerontological nursing (MS). Accredited by NLN. *Entrance requirements:* GRE General Test, minimum GPA of 3.0. Application deadline: 3/15 (priority date; rolling processing). Application fee: $50. *Expenses:* Tuition $5100 per year full-time, $213 per credit hour part-time for state residents; $8416 per year full-time, $351 per credit hour part-time for nonresidents. Fees $493 per year full-time, $48 per semester (minimum) part-time. • Dr. Ide Katims, Director, 914-257-2922.

State University of New York at Stony Brook, Health Sciences Center, School of Nursing, Program in Gerontological Nursing, Stony Brook, NY 11794. Awards MS. Accredited by NLN. Students: 0. In 1997, 4 degrees awarded. *Degree requirements:* Thesis required, foreign language not required. *Entrance requirements:* BSN, minimum GPA of 3.0, previous course work in statistics. Application deadline: 1/15. Application fee: $50. *Expenses:* Tuition $5100 per year full-time, $213 per credit hour part-time for state residents; $8416 per year full-time, $351 per credit hour part-time for nonresidents. Fees $529 per year full-time, $77 per semester (minimum) part-time. *Financial aid:* Application deadline 3/15. • Dr. Carole L. Blair, Coordinator, 516-444-3258. Fax: 516-444-3136. E-mail: carole_blair@notes2.nursing.sunysb.edu.

Texas Tech University Health Sciences Center, School of Nursing, Lubbock, TX 79430-0002. Offerings include geronitics (MSN). Accredited by NLN. Postbaccalaureate distance learning degree programs offered (minimal on-campus study). School faculty: 14 full-time (all women). *Degree requirements:* Thesis required, foreign language not required. *Average time to degree:* master's–2 years full-time, 3 years part-time. *Entrance requirements:* GRE General Test (minimum combined score of 1000), MAT (minimum score 50), minimum GPA of 3.0, sample of written work. Application deadline: 6/1 (rolling processing; 10/1 for spring admission). Application fee: $30 ($50 for international students). *Expenses:* Tuition $36 per credit hour for state residents; $249 per credit hour for nonresidents. Fees $1348 per year full-time for state residents; $1349 per year full-time for nonresidents. • Dr. Pat S. Yoder Wise, Dean, 806-743-2738. E-mail: sonpsy@ttuhsc.edu. Application contact: Nancy Ridenour, Associate Dean for Education, 806-743-2737. Fax: 806-743-1622. E-mail: sonnar@ttuhsc.edu.

University of Delaware, College of Health and Nursing Sciences, Department of Nursing, Newark, DE 19716. Offerings include clinical nurse specialist/nurse practitioner (Certificate), with options in cardiopulmonary, gerontology, oncology/immune deficiency, pediatrics, women's health; gerontology (MSN, Certificate). Department faculty: 10 full-time (9 women), 5 part-time (all women), 12.25 FTE. *Degree requirements:* For master's, thesis optional, foreign language not required. *Average time to degree:* master's–2 years full-time, 3 years part-time. *Entrance requirements:* For master's, GRE General Test. Application deadline: 7/1. Application fee: $45. *Expenses:* Tuition $4250 per year full-time, $236 per credit hour part-time for state residents; $12,250 per year full-time, $681 per credit hour part-time for nonresidents. Fees $466 per year full-time, $15 per semester (minimum) part-time. • Application contact: Betty Bonavita, Graduate Secretary, 302-831-1255. Fax: 302-831-2382. E-mail: elizabeth.bonavita@mvs.udel.edu.

University of Maryland, Baltimore, Graduate School, School of Nursing, Baltimore, MD 21201-1627. Offerings include gerontological nursing (MS). Accredited by NLN. MS/MBA offered jointly with the University of Baltimore. School faculty: 49 (45 women). *Degree requirements:* Thesis or alternative required, foreign language not required. *Entrance requirements:* GRE General Test, TOEFL, minimum GPA of 2.75, previous course work in statistics, BS in nursing. Application fee: $42. *Expenses:* Tuition $253 per credit hour for state residents; $454 per credit hour for nonresidents. Fees $317 per year. • Dr. Barbara Heller, Dean, 410-706-6741. Application contact: Dr. Susan Wozenski, Assistant Dean for Student Affairs, 410-706-0501. Fax: 410-706-7238.

University of Massachusetts Lowell, College of Health Professions, Department of Nursing, Program in Gerontological Nursing, 1 University Avenue, Lowell, MA 01854-2881. Awards MS. Accredited by NLN. Students: 15 full-time (all women), 11 part-time (10 women); includes 1 minority (African American), 1 international. 19 applicants, 74% accepted. In 1997, 5 degrees awarded. *Degree requirements:* Thesis optional, foreign language not required. *Entrance requirements:* GRE General Test. Application deadline: 4/1 (priority date; rolling processing; 10/1 for spring admission). Application fee: $20 ($35 for international students). *Tuition:* $4867 per year full-time, $618 per semester (minimum) part-time for state residents; $10,276 per year full-time, $1294 per semester (minimum) part-time for nonresidents. *Financial aid:* Fellowships, teaching assistantships, Federal Work-Study, and career-related internships or fieldwork available. Financial aid application deadline: 4/1. • Dr. May Futrell, Chair, Department of Nursing, 978-934-4467. E-mail: may_futrell@woods.uml.edu.

University of Michigan, School of Nursing, Division of Acute, Critical and Long-Term Care, Program in Gerontology Nursing, Ann Arbor, MI 48109. Awards MS. One or more programs accredited by NLN. Part-time programs available. *Degree requirements:* Thesis required, foreign language not required. *Entrance requirements:* GRE General Test. Application deadline: 2/1 (priority date; rolling processing). Application fee: $55. *Financial aid:* Fellowships, research assistantships, teaching assistantships, partial tuition waivers, Federal Work-Study available. • Application contact: Graduate Program Secretary, 734-763-0010. Fax: 734-936-5525.

University of Minnesota, Twin Cities Campus, School of Nursing, Gerontology Nurse Practitioner Program, Minneapolis, MN 55455-0213. Awards MS. Accredited by NLN. Part-time programs available. Students: 10 full-time, 12 part-time. 19 applicants, 53% accepted. *Degree requirements:* Final oral exam, project or thesis. *Application deadline:* 12/15 (rolling processing). *Application fee:* $40 ($50 for international students). *Financial aid:* Fellowships, research assistantships, teaching assistantships, professional nurse traineeships, and career-related internships or fieldwork available. • Mariah Snyder, Head, 612-626-3478. Fax: 612-626-2359. Application contact: Kate Hanson, Nursing Recruiter, 612-624-9494. Fax: 612-624-3174. E-mail: hanso041@maroon.tc.umn.edu.

University of Minnesota, Twin Cities Campus, School of Nursing, Program in Gerontological Nursing, Minneapolis, MN 55455-0213. Offers advanced clinical specialist in gerontology (MS). Accredited by NLN. Part-time programs available. Students: 2 full-time, 2 part-time. 4 applicants, 50% accepted. *Degree requirements:* Final oral exam, project or thesis. *Application deadline:* 12/15 (rolling processing). *Application fee:* $40 ($50 for international students). *Financial aid:* Fellowships, research assistantships, teaching assistantships, and career-related internships or fieldwork available. • Mariah Snyder, Head, 612-626-3478. Fax: 612-626-2359. Application contact: Kate Hanson, Nursing Recruiter, 612-624-9494. Fax: 612-624-3174. E-mail: hanso041@maroon.tc.umn.edu.

University of New Mexico, College of Nursing, Albuquerque, NM 87131-2039. Offerings include advanced nursing practice (MSN), with options in adult health nursing, gerontological nursing, parent-child nursing, psychiatric-mental health nursing. Accredited by NLN. College faculty: 38 full-time (36 women), 23 part-time (all women), 46.57 FTE. *Degree requirements:* Thesis optional, foreign language not required. *Entrance requirements:* GRE General Test, interview, minimum GPA of 3.0, previous course work in statistics. Application deadline: 7/15 (11/1 for spring admission). Application fee: $25. *Expenses:* Tuition $2442 per year full-time, $103 per credit hour part-time for state residents; $8691 per year full-time, $103 per credit hour (minimum) part-time for nonresidents. Fees $32 per year. • Dr. Sandra Ferketich, Dean, 505-272-6284. Application contact: Anne-Marie Oechsler, Director, Academic Advisement, 505-272-4224. Fax: 505-272-3970. E-mail: annmarie@unm.edu.

University of North Carolina at Greensboro, School of Nursing, Greensboro, NC 27412-0001. Offerings include gerontological nurse practitioner (PMC). School faculty: 22 full-time (all women), 7 part-time (all women). *Entrance requirements:* Liability insurance, MSN, RN license. Application fee: $35. *Expenses:* Tuition $1842 per year full-time, $370 per semester (minimum) part-time for state residents; $10,296 per year full-time, $2484 per semester (minimum) part-time for nonresidents. Fees $806 per year full-time, $111 per semester (minimum) part-time. • Dr. Lynne Pearcey, Dean, 336-334-5010.

University of Pennsylvania, School of Nursing, Gerontological Nurse Practitioner Program, Philadelphia, PA 19104. Awards MSN. Accredited by NLN. Part-time programs available. Students: 7 full-time (4 women), 20 part-time (all women); includes 2 international. Average age 35. 22 applicants, 77% accepted. In 1997, 14 degrees awarded. *Entrance requirements:* GRE General Test, BSN, minimum GPA of 3.0, previous course in basic statistics. Application deadline: 9/1 (rolling processing). Application fee: $65. *Financial aid:* In 1997–98, 1 fellowship, 19 research assistantships, 5 teaching assistantships were awarded; Federal Work-Study, institutionally sponsored loans, and career-related internships or fieldwork also available. Aid available to part-time students. *Faculty research:* Restraints, incontinence, discharge planning, frail elders, quality of life across continuum of care. • Dr. Neville Strumpf, Director, 215-898-8802. Fax: 215-573-7492 Ext. 7496. E-mail: strumpf@pobox.upenn.edu. Application contact: Susan K. Ogle, Associate Director of Admissions and Student Affairs, 215-898-3301. Fax: 215-573-8439. E-mail: sogle@pobox.upenn.edu.

The University of Texas–Houston Health Science Center, School of Nursing, Master's Program in Nursing, Houston, TX 77225-0036. Offerings include gerontology nursing (MSN). Accredited by NLN. *Degree requirements:* Thesis required, foreign language not required. *Entrance requirements:* GRE or MAT, BSN, Texas RN license. Application deadline: 5/1 (priority date; rolling processing; 9/1 for spring admission). Application fee: $10. Electronic applications accepted. • Frank Cole, Chair, Graduate Curriculum Committee, 713-500-2153. Fax: 713-500-2171. E-mail: fcole@son1.nur.uth.tmc.edu. Application contact: Eleanor Evans, Pre-Admissions Counselor, 713-500-2104. Fax: 713-500-2107. E-mail: eevans@son1.nur.uth.tmc.edu.

University of Utah, College of Nursing, Gerontology Center, Salt Lake City, UT 84112-1107. Awards MS, Certificate. Part-time programs available. Faculty: Students: 6 full-time (5 women), 18 part-time (11 women). Average age 34. In 1997, 3 master's awarded. *Degree requirements:* For master's, thesis optional, foreign language not required. *Entrance requirements:* For master's, GRE General Test, TOEFL (minimum score 500). Application deadline: 4/15 (priority

Directories: Gerontological Nursing; Maternal/Child-Care Nursing

University of Utah (continued)

date). Application fee: $30 ($50 for international students). *Tuition:* $2045 per year full-time, $562 per semester (minimum) part-time for state residents; $6129 per year full-time, $1607 per semester (minimum) part-time for nonresidents. *Financial aid:* Fellowships, research assistantships, teaching assistantships, scholarships available. *Faculty research:* Family caregiving, bereavement, *Video Respite* (a resource developed by center faculty to assist family and professional caregivers of persons with Alzheimer's Disease) research and applications. • Dr. Dale A. Lund, Director, 801-581-8198. E-mail: dale@nurfac.nurs.utah.edu. Application contact: Scott D. Wright, Coordinator of Graduate Studies, 801-585-9542. Fax: 801-581-4642. E-mail: swright@nurfac.nurs.utah.edu.

Vanderbilt University, School of Nursing, Nashville, TN 37240-1001. Offerings include gerontology nurse practitioner (MSN). Accredited by NLN. Postbaccalaureate distance learning degree programs offered (minimal on-campus study). School faculty: 76 full-time (66 women), 253 part-time (224 women). *Degree requirements:* Terminal course required, thesis not required. *Average time to degree:* master's–2 years full-time, 4 years part-time; doctorate–4 years full-time, 5 years part-time. *Entrance requirements:* GMAT, GRE, or MAT, minimum B average. Application deadline: rolling. Application fee: $50. Electronic applications accepted. • Dr. Colleen Conway-Welch, Dean, 615-343-3243. Fax: 615-343-7711. Application contact: Patricia Peerman, Assistant Dean of Admissions, 615-322-3800. Fax: 615-343-0333. E-mail: vusn-admission@mcmail.vanderbilt.edu.

Maternal/Child-Care Nursing

Adelphi University, School of Nursing, Program in Parent-Child Nursing, Garden City, NY 11530. Awards MS, PMC. One or more programs accredited by NLN. Part-time and evening/weekend programs available. Students: 19 part-time (all women); includes 6 minority (2 African Americans, 4 Asian Americans). Average age 36. *Degree requirements:* For master's, thesis required, foreign language not required. *Entrance requirements:* For master's, BSN, clinical experience. Application deadline: rolling. Application fee: $50. *Expenses:* Tuition $16,000 per year full-time, $485 per credit part-time. Fees $500 per year full-time, $150 per semester part-time. *Financial aid:* Research assistantships, teaching assistantships, graduate achievement awards, and career-related internships or fieldwork available. Aid available to part-time students. Financial aid application deadline: 3/1. • Dr. Caryle G. Wolahan, Director, School of Nursing, 516-877-4545.

Baylor University, School of Nursing, Waco, TX 76798. Offerings include family nurse practitioner (MSN). Accredited by NLN. *Entrance requirements:* GRE General Test. Application deadline: 8/1 (rolling processing; 12/1 for spring admission). Application fee: $25. *Expenses:* Tuition $7392 per year full-time, $308 per semester hour part-time. Fees $1024 per year. • Dr. Phyllis S. Karns, Dean, 254-710-3361.

Boston College, School of Nursing, Chestnut Hill, MA 02167-9991. Offerings include maternal/child health nursing (MS), with option in pediatric and women's health. Accredited by NLN. School faculty: 18 full-time (all women), 1 (woman) part-time. *Degree requirements:* Oral comprehensive exam, research project required, foreign language and thesis not required. *Average time to degree:* doctorate–4 years full-time. *Entrance requirements:* GRE General Test, bachelor's degree in nursing. Application deadline: 3/1 (priority date; 10/15 for spring admission). Application fee: $40. Electronic applications accepted. *Expenses:* Tuition $626 per semester hour. Fees $80 per year (minimum) full-time, $30 per semester part-time. • Dr. Barbara Munro, Dean, 617-552-4251. Fax: 617-552-0931. E-mail: barbara.munro@bc.edu. Application contact: Dana Robinson, Administrative Secretary, 617-552-4059. Fax: 617-552-0745. E-mail: dana.robinson@bc.edu.

Case Western Reserve University, Frances Payne Bolton School of Nursing, Master's Program in Nursing, Nurse Practitioner Program, Cleveland, OH 44106. Offerings include acute care pediatric nurse practitioner (MSN), neonatal practitioner (MSN), pediatric nurse practitioner (MSN). One or more programs accredited by NLN. *Degree requirements:* Thesis optional, foreign language not required. *Entrance requirements:* GRE General Test or MAT. Application deadline: 6/1 (rolling processing). Application fee: $75. *Tuition:* $18,400 per year full-time, $767 per credit hour part-time. • Application contact: Molly Blank, Admission Counselor, 216-368-2529. Fax: 216-368-3542. E-mail: mab44@po.cwru.edu.

The Catholic University of America, School of Nursing, Washington, DC 20064. Offerings include advanced practice nursing (MSN), with options in administration of nursing service, adult nurse practitioner, education, family nurse practitioner, geriatric nurse practitioner, pediatric nurse practitioner, psychiatric-mental health, school health nurse practitioner. Accredited by NLN. School faculty: 18 full-time (all women), 2 part-time (both women), 19 FTE. *Degree requirements:* Comprehensive exam required, thesis optional, foreign language not required. *Entrance requirements:* GRE General Test (minimum combined score of 1350 on three sections). Application deadline: 8/1 (priority date; rolling processing; 12/1 for spring admission). Application fee: $50. *Expenses:* Tuition $17,325 per year full-time, $668 per credit hour part-time. Fees $680 per year full-time, $360 per year part-time. • Sr. Mary Jean Flaherty, Dean, 202-319-5403.

Columbia University, School of Nursing, Program in Neonatal Nurse Practitioner, New York, NY 10032. Awards MS, Adv C. One or more programs accredited by NLN. Part-time programs available. Students: 1 (woman) full-time, 23 part-time (all women); includes 15 minority (4 African Americans, 10 Asian Americans, 1 Hispanic). Average age 32. 15 applicants, 93% accepted. In 1997, 6 master's awarded. *Entrance requirements:* For master's, GRE General Test (minimum score 500 on verbal and analytical sections), BSN, 1 year of clinical experience (preferred), or completion of a clinical residency; for Adv C, MSN, previous course work in statistics, clinical preceptorship. Application deadline: 4/1 (10/1 for spring admission). Application fee: $50. *Tuition:* $19,376 per year full-time, $692 per credit (minimum) part-time. *Financial aid:* Application deadline 2/1. • Application contact: Joseph Tomaino, Assistant Dean for Student Services, 212-305-5756. E-mail: jt238@columbia.edu.

Columbia University, School of Nursing, Program in Pediatric Nurse Practitioner, New York, NY 10032. Awards MS, Adv C. One or more programs accredited by NLN. Part-time programs available. Faculty: 1 (woman) full-time, 1 (woman) part-time. Students: 13 full-time (all women), 45 part-time (42 women); includes 17 minority (15 African Americans, 2 Asian Americans). Average age 32. 38 applicants, 68% accepted. In 1997, 15 master's awarded. *Entrance requirements:* For master's, GRE General Test (minimum score 500 on verbal and analytical sections), BSN, 1 year of clinical experience (preferred), or completion of a clinical residency; for Adv C, MSN, previous course work in statistics, clinical preceptorship. Application deadline: 4/1 (priority date; rolling processing; 10/1 for spring admission). Application fee: $50. *Tuition:* $19,376 per year full-time, $692 per credit (minimum) part-time. *Financial aid:* Teaching assistantships available. Financial aid application deadline: 2/1. • Dr. Judy Honig, Director, 212-305-2816. Application contact: Joseph Tomaino, Assistant Dean for Student Services, 212-305-5756. E-mail: jt238@columbia.edu.

Columbia University, School of Nursing, Program in Women's Health Nurse Practitioner, New York, NY 10032. Awards MS, Adv C. One or more programs accredited by NLN. Part-time programs available. Faculty: 1 (woman) full-time. Students: 1 (woman) full-time, 10 part-time (all women); includes 2 minority (1 Asian American, 1 Hispanic). Average age 32. 5 applicants, 100% accepted. In 1997, 3 master's awarded. *Entrance requirements:* For master's, GRE General Test (minimum score 500 on verbal and analytical sections), BSN, 1 year of clinical experience (preferred), or completion of a clinical residency. Application deadline: 4/1 (priority date; rolling processing; 10/1 for spring admission). Application fee: $60. *Tuition:* $19,376 per year full-time, $692 per credit (minimum) part-time. *Financial aid:* Teaching assistantships available. Financial aid application deadline: 2/1. • Dr. Noreen Esposito, Director, 212-305-2280. Application contact: Joseph Tomaino, Assistant Dean for Student Services, 212-305-5756. E-mail: jt238@columbia.edu.

Duke University, School of Nursing, Durham, NC 27708-0586. Offerings include acute care pediatric (Certificate); clinical nurse specialist (MSN), with options in acute care pediatric, adult oncological/HIV, gerontological, neonatal, pediatric; neonatal (Certificate); nurse practitioner (MSN), with options in acute care adult, acute care pediatric, adult cardiovascular, adult oncological/HIV, family, gerontological, neonatal, pediatric; pediatric (Certificate). One or more programs accredited by NLN. Postbaccalaureate distance learning degree programs offered (minimal on-campus study). School faculty: 24 full-time (22 women), 4 part-time (all women). *Degree requirements:* For master's, computer language required, thesis optional, foreign language not required. *Average time to degree:* master's–1.5 years full-time, 3 years part-time; other advanced degree–1 year full-time, 2 years part-time. *Entrance requirements:* For master's, GRE General Test or MAT, BSN, minimum GPA of 3.0, previous course work in statistics, RN license, 1 year of nursing experience. Application deadline: 4/1 (priority date; rolling processing; 10/1 for spring admission). Application fee: $50. *Tuition:* $20,976 per year full-time, $552 per unit part-time. • Dr. Mary T. Champagne, Dean, 919-684-3786. E-mail: champ001@mc.duke.edu. Application contact: Judith K. Carter, Admissions Officer, 919-684-4248. Fax: 919-681-8899. E-mail: carte026@mc.duke.edu.

Emory University, Nell Hodgson Woodruff School of Nursing, Atlanta, GA 30322-1100. Offerings include women and children (MSN), with options in child health/pediatric nurse practitioner, midwifery, pediatric oncology nurse practitioner, perinatal/neonatal nurse. Accredited by NLN. Postbaccalaureate distance learning degree programs offered (minimal on-campus study). School faculty: 33 full-time (32 women), 21 part-time (19 women), 48 FTE. *Degree requirements:* Thesis optional, foreign language not required. *Average time to degree:* master's–1.5 years full-time, 3 years part-time. *Entrance requirements:* GRE General Test (minimum combined score of 1500 on three sections) or MAT (minimum score 35), minimum GPA of 3.0, BS in nursing or RN license and additional course work. Application deadline: 2/1 (priority date; rolling processing; 11/1 for spring admission). Application fee: $50. *Expenses:* Tuition $18,050 per year. Fees $200 per year. • Dr. Dyanne D. Affonso, Dean, 404-727-7976. Fax: 404-727-0536. Application contact: Debbie Ashtiani, Director, 404-727-7980.

Florida Atlantic University, College of Nursing, Programs in Adult and Family Care Practitioner, Boca Raton, FL 33431-0991. Offerings include family health (MS), family practitioner (MS, Post Master's Certificate). One or more programs accredited by NLN and NLN. Faculty: 18 full-time (15 women), 8 part-time (7 women). *Degree requirements:* For master's, thesis or alternative required, foreign language not required. *Average time to degree:* master's–2 years full-time, 3 years part-time. *Entrance requirements:* For master's, GRE General Test (minimum combined score of 1000), minimum GPA of 3.0. Application deadline: 6/1 (rolling processing; 10/15 for spring admission). Application fee: $20. *Expenses:* Tuition $2520 per year full-time, $140 per credit hour part-time for state residents; $8712 per year full-time, $484 per credit hour part-time for nonresidents. Fees $5 per year (minimum). • Dr. Ellis Quinn Youngkin, Graduate Program Coordinator, 561-297-3384. Fax: 561-297-3652. E-mail: eyoungkin@fau.edu.

Georgia State University, College of Health and Human Sciences, School of Nursing, Atlanta, GA 30303-3083. Offerings include child health/pediatric nurse practitioner (MS), perinatal women's health/practitioner (MS). One or more programs accredited by NLN. MS (child and adolescent psychology, gerontology) and PhD (community nursing, family nursing) being phased out; applicants no longer accepted. School faculty: 26 full-time (all women), 3 part-time (all women). *Degree requirements:* Research project or thesis required, thesis optional, foreign language not required. *Entrance requirements:* Interview, RN license. Application deadline: 4/15. Application fee: $25. *Expenses:* Tuition $2862 per year full-time, $106 per semester hour part-time for state residents; $11,448 per year full-time, $424 per semester hour part-time for nonresidents. Fees $228 per year. • Dr. Dee Baldwin, Director of Graduate Programs, 404-651-3040. Application contact: Barbara Smith, Admissions Counselor, 404-651-3064. Fax: 404-651-4871.

Gwynedd–Mercy College, Graduate Program in Nursing, Gwynedd Valley, PA 19437-0901. Offerings include nurse practitioner (MSN), with options in adult, pediatric; pediatrics (MSN). One or more programs accredited by NLN. MSN (pediatrics, oncology) admissions temporarily suspended. Program faculty: 9 full-time (all women), 8 part-time (6 women). *Degree requirements:* Thesis or research project required, foreign language not required. *Average time to degree:* master's–2.5 years full-time, 3.5 years part-time. *Entrance requirements:* GRE General Test (minimum combined score of 1350; average 1401), MAT (minimum score 40; average 48), 1 year of experience, physical assessment, previous course work in statistics. Application deadline: 8/1 (priority date; rolling processing). Application fee: $25. *Expenses:* Tuition $375 per credit. Fees $150 per year full-time, $80 per year part-time. • Dr. Mary Dressler, Dean, 215-641-5533. E-mail: dressler.m@gmc.edu. Application contact: Dr. Barbara A. Jones, Associate Professor, 215-646-7300 Ext. 407. Fax: 215-641-5517.

Hunter College of the City University of New York, Hunter-Bellevue School of Nursing, Pediatric Nurse Practitioner Program, 695 Park Avenue, New York, NY 10021-5085. Awards MS, AC. One or more programs accredited by NLN. Part-time programs available. Faculty: 7 full-time (all women), 1 part-time (0 women). Students: 1 (woman) full-time, 34 part-time (31 women); includes 10 minority (8 African Americans, 2 Hispanics). Average age 36. 20 applicants, 70% accepted. In 1997, 12 master's, 9 ACs awarded. *Degree requirements:* For master's, practicum required, foreign language and thesis not required. *Average time to degree:* master's–2 years full-time, 3.5 years part-time. *Entrance requirements:* For master's, TOEFL (minimum score 550), BSN, minimum GPA of 3.0, New York RN license, 2 years of professional practice experience; for AC, MSN, minimum GPA of 3.0. Application deadline: 4/27 (rolling processing; 11/21 for spring admission). Application fee: $40. *Expenses:* Tuition $4350 per year full-time, $185 per credit part-time for state residents; $7600 per year full-time, $320 per credit part-time for nonresidents. Fees $26 per year. *Financial aid:* Traineeships, partial tuition waivers, Federal Work-Study available. Aid available to part-time students. Financial aid application deadline: 5/1; applicants required to submit FAFSA. *Faculty research:* Primary care: infants, children, and adolescents. • Dr. Janet N. Natapoff, Coordinator, 212-481-5070. Fax: 212-481-5078. E-mail: jnatapof@hejira.hunter.cuny.edu. Application contact: Audrey Berman, Associate Director for Graduate Admissions, 212-772-4490.

Hunter College of the City University of New York, Hunter-Bellevue School of Nursing, Program in Maternal Child-Health Nursing, 695 Park Avenue, New York, NY 10021-5085. Awards MS. Accredited by NLN. Part-time programs available. Faculty: 9 full-time (all women). Students: 12 part-time (all women); includes 6 minority (4 African Americans, 1 Asian American, 1 Hispanic), 1 international. Average age 32. 7 applicants, 71% accepted. In 1997, 5 degrees awarded (100% found work related to degree). *Degree requirements:* Practicum required, foreign language and thesis not required. *Average time to degree:* master's–1.5 years full-time, 3 years part-time. *Entrance requirements:* TOEFL (minimum score 550), minimum GPA of 3.0, New York RN license. Application deadline: 4/27 (rolling processing; 11/21 for spring admission). Application fee: $40. *Expenses:* Tuition $4350 per year full-time, $185 per credit part-time for state residents; $7600 per year full-time, $320 per credit part-time for nonresidents. Fees $26 per year. *Financial aid:* Traineeships, partial tuition waivers, Federal Work-Study available. Aid available to part-time students. Financial aid application deadline: 5/1; applicants required to submit FAFSA. *Faculty research:* Maternal-infant attachment, children's perception of health, accident prevention in children. • Dr. Janet N. Natapoff, Coordinator, 212-481-5070. Fax: 212-481-5078. E-mail: jnatapof@hejira.hunter.cuny.edu. Application contact: Audrey Berman, Associate Director for Graduate Admissions, 212-772-4490.

Jewish Hospital College of Nursing and Allied Health, Program in Nursing, St. Louis, MO 63110-1091. Offerings include neonatal nurse practitioner (MSN). College faculty: 10. *Application deadline:* rolling. *Application fee:* $25. *Tuition:* $320 per credit hour. • Dr. Sandra A. Jones, Director, 314-454-8416. Application contact: Connie Stohlman, Chief Admissions Officer, 314-454-7538.

Johns Hopkins University, School of Nursing, Program in Advanced Practice Nursing (Nurse Practitioner), Baltimore, MD 21218-2699. Offerings include advanced practice nursing-nurse practitioner (MSN), with options in adult acute/critical care, adult and pediatric primary care, family primary care; nurse practitioner (Certificate), with options in adult acute/critical care, adult or pediatric primary care, family primary care. One or more programs accredited by NLN. MSN, Certificate (family primary care) new for fall 1998. Program faculty: 16 full-time (15 women), 9 part-time (8 women), 18 FTE. *Degree requirements:* For master's, scholarly project required, thesis optional, foreign language not required. *Average time to degree:* master's–1 year full-time, 2 years part-time. *Entrance requirements:* For master's, GRE, interview, minimum GPA of 3.0. Application deadline: 3/1. Application fee: $40. • Stella Shiber, Head, 410-614-4081. Fax: 410-955-7463. E-mail: sshiber@son.jhmi.edu. Application contact: Mary O'Rourke, Director of Admissions/Student Services, 410-955-7548. Fax: 410-614-7086. E-mail: orourke@son.jhmi.edu.

See in-depth description on page 1433.

Kent State University, School of Nursing, Kent, OH 44242-0001. Offerings include parent-child nursing (MSN). Accredited by NLN. School faculty: 29 full-time. *Degree requirements:* Thesis optional, foreign language not required. *Entrance requirements:* Minimum GPA of 2.75. Application deadline: 7/12 (rolling processing; 11/29 for spring admission). Application fee: $30. *Tuition:* $4752 per year full-time, $216 per credit hour part-time for state residents; $9213 per year full-time, $419 per credit hour part-time for nonresidents. • Dr. Davina Gosnell, Dean, 330-672-7930. Fax: 330-672-2433.

Lehman College of the City University of New York, Division of Natural and Social Sciences, Department of Nursing, 250 Bedford Park Boulevard West, Bronx, NY 10468-1589. Offerings include parent-child nursing (MS), pediatric nurse practitioner (MS). One or more programs accredited by NLN. Department faculty: 13 full-time (12 women). *Entrance requirements:* Bachelor's degree in nursing, New York RN license. Application deadline: 4/1 (rolling processing; 11/1 for spring admission). Application fee: $40. *Expenses:* Tuition $4350 per year full-time, $185 per credit part-time for state residents; $7600 per year full-time, $320 per credit part-time for nonresidents. Fees $120 per year full-time, $80 per year part-time. • Ngo Nkongho, Chair, 718-960-8374. Application contact: Keville Frederickson, Director of Graduate Studies, 718-960-8378. Fax: 718-960-8488.

Loma Linda University, Graduate School, Department of Graduate Nursing, Program in Growing Family Nursing, Loma Linda, CA 92350. Awards MS. Accredited by NLN. Part-time programs available. *Degree requirements:* Thesis or alternative required, foreign language not required. *Entrance requirements:* GRE General Test (minimum combined score of 1500). Application fee: $40. *Tuition:* $380 per unit. *Financial aid:* Grants, Federal Work-Study, institutionally sponsored loans, and career-related internships or fieldwork available. Aid available to part-time students. Financial aid application deadline: 6/1. *Faculty research:* Family coping in chronic illness; women, identity, and career/family issues. • Dr. Lois Van Cleve, Director, Department of Graduate Nursing, 909-824-4360.

Louisiana State University Medical Center, School of Nursing, 433 Bolivar Street, New Orleans, LA 70112-2223. Offerings include neonatal nurse practitioner (MN), parent-child health nursing (MN). One or more programs accredited by NLN. School faculty: 10 full-time (all women), 4 part-time (3 women). *Degree requirements:* Thesis optional, foreign language not required. *Entrance requirements:* GRE General Test, MAT (minimum score 50), TOEFL, minimum GPA of 3.0. Application deadline: 3/17. Application fee: $50. *Expenses:* Tuition $2878 per year full-time, $421 per semester (minimum) part-time for state residents; $6003 per year full-time, $838 per semester (minimum) part-time for nonresidents. Fees $350 per year full-time, $90 per semester (minimum) part-time. • Dr. Elizabeth Humphrey, Dean, 504-568-4106. Application contact: Dr. Barbara C. Donlon, Acting Director, 504-568-4137. Fax: 504-568-3308. E-mail: bdonlo@lsumc.edu.

Loyola University Chicago, Graduate School, Marcella Niehoff School of Nursing, Pediatric Nurse Practitioner Program, 820 North Michigan Avenue, Chicago, IL 60611-2196. Awards MSN. Accredited by NLN. Students: 20 part-time (all women); includes 1 minority (Hispanic). Average age 29. 18 applicants, 67% accepted. *Degree requirements:* Comprehensive exam or oral thesis defense required, foreign language not required. *Entrance requirements:* GRE General Test (minimum combined score of 1350 on three sections), BSN, minimum GPA of 3.0, professional license. Application deadline: rolling. Application fee: $35. *Tuition:* $467 per semester hour. *Financial aid:* Traineeships available. Financial aid application deadline: 3/1. *Faculty research:* Ethics, self care. • Application contact: Dr. Marcia Maurer, Associate Dean and Director of Graduate Programs, 773-508-3261. Fax: 773-508-3241. E-mail: mmaurer@luc.edu.

Marquette University, College of Nursing, Milwaukee, WI 53201-1881. Offerings include advanced practice nursing (MSN), with options in adult, children, neonatal nurse practitioner, nurse-midwifery, older adult; neonatal nurse practitioner (Certificate); pediatric nurse practitioner (Certificate). One or more programs accredited by NLN. College faculty: 24 full-time (23 women), 5 part-time (4 women). *Degree requirements:* For master's, thesis or alternative, comprehensive exam required, foreign language not required. *Entrance requirements:* For master's, GRE General Test, TOEFL (minimum score 550), BSN, RN, Wisconsin license. Application fee: $40. *Tuition:* $490 per credit. • Dr. Madeline Wake, Dean, 414-288-3812. Application contact: Dr. Gregory Olson, Associate Dean, 414-288-3808. Fax: 414-288-1578.

Medical College of Georgia, Graduate Programs in Nursing, Augusta, GA 30912-1500. Offerings include parent-child nursing (MSN). Accredited by NLN. Faculty: 17 full-time (14 women). *Application deadline:* 6/30 (priority date; rolling processing). *Application fee:* $0. *Expenses:* Tuition $2670 per year full-time, $111 per credit part-time for state residents; $10,680 per year full-time, $445 per credit part-time for nonresidents. Fees $286 per year. • Dr. Virginia Kemp, Associate Dean, 706-721-4710. E-mail: vkemp@mail.mcg.edu. Application contact: Dr. Gary C. Bond, Associate Dean, 706-721-3278. Fax: 706-721-6829. E-mail: gradstud@mail.mcg.edu.

Medical University of South Carolina, College of Nursing, Program in Nursing, Charleston, SC 29425-0002. Offerings include neonatal nurse practitioner (MSN), parent-child nursing (MSN). One or more programs accredited by NLN. *Degree requirements:* Computer language required, thesis optional, foreign language not required. *Entrance requirements:* GRE General Test (minimum combined score of 1000), BSN, previous course work in statistics and physical assessment, 1 year nursing experience, license. Application deadline: 2/15 (10/15 for spring admission). Application fee: $55. *Expenses:* Tuition $3760 per year full-time, $173 per semester hour part-time for state residents; $5672 per year full-time, $270 per semester hour part-time for nonresidents. Fees $280 per year (minimum). • Dr. Jean Leuner, Associate Dean, 843-792-8515. Application contact: Office of Enrollment Services, 843-792-3281.

Molloy College, Department of Nursing, 1000 Hempstead Avenue, Rockville Centre, NY 11571-5002. Offerings include pediatric nurse practitioner (MSN, Advanced Certificate). Department faculty: 16 full-time (14 women), 12 part-time (9 women). *Degree requirements:* For master's, thesis optional, foreign language not required. *Average time to degree:* master's–2.2 years full-time, 3.7 years part-time; other advanced degree–1 year full-time, 2 years part-time. *Entrance requirements:* For master's, BS in nursing, minimum undergraduate GPA of 3.0; for Advanced Certificate, master's degree in nursing. Application deadline: 9/2 (priority date; rolling processing; 1/20 for spring admission). Application fee: $60. *Expenses:* Tuition $430 per credit. Fees $430 per year full-time, $165 per semester (minimum) part-time. • Dr. Carol A. Clifford, Director, Graduate Program, 516-256-2218. Fax: 516-678-9718. E-mail: clica01@molloy.edu. Application contact: Wayne James, Vice President for Enrollment and Management, 516-678-5000 Ext. 240. Fax: 516-256-2247.

New York University, School of Education, Division of Nursing, Programs in Advanced Practice Nursing, New York, NY 10012-1019. Offerings include advanced practice nursing: infants, children, and adolescents (MA, AC). One or more programs accredited by NLN. MA/MS offered jointly with the Program in Management in the Robert F. Wagner Graduate School of Public Service. Faculty: 25 full-time, 9 part-time. *Entrance requirements:* For master's, TOEFL; for AC, TOEFL, master's degree. Application deadline: 2/1 (priority date; rolling processing; 12/1 for spring admission). Application fee: $40 ($60 for international students). • Judi Haber, Director, 212-998-5300. Application contact: Office of Graduate Admissions, 212-998-5030. Fax: 212-995-4328.

Northeastern University, Graduate School of Nursing, Program in Critical Care-Neonatal Nurse Practitioner, Boston, MA 02115-5096. Awards MS, CAS. One or more programs accredited by NLN. *Degree requirements:* For master's, thesis or alternative required, foreign language not required. *Entrance requirements:* For master's, GRE General Test, minimum GPA of 3.0, previous course work in statistics, 1-2 years nursing experience, RN license, ICU experience. Application deadline: 4/1 (priority date; rolling processing; 2/1 for spring admission). Application fee: $50. *Expenses:* Tuition $440 per credit hour. Fees $55 per quarter full-time, $13.25 per quarter part-time. *Faculty research:* Critical thinking and diagnostic reasoning, clinical outcomes of acute and critical health problems. • Dr. Elizabeth Howard, Coordinator, 617-373-4590. Fax: 617-673-8672. Application contact: Molly Schnabel, Admissions Coordinator, 617-373-3590. Fax: 617-373-8672. E-mail: mschnabe@lynx.neu.edu.

Announcement: Master's program in critical-care nursing (52 quarter hours), with concentration in neonatal NP role. Includes theory and interventions for critically ill infants and emphasis on family and cultural issues. Full- and part-time study. Preceptorships available in Boston's top neonatal intensive care units. For application, call Molly Schnabel, Admissions Coordinator, at 617-373-3590.

Oregon Health Sciences University, School of Nursing, Program in Family Nursing, 3181 SW Sam Jackson Park Road, Portland, OR 97201-3098. Awards MN, MS. One or more programs accredited by NLN. Students: 4 full-time (all women), 9 part-time (all women); includes 1 minority (Native American), 1 international. 10 applicants, 90% accepted. In 1997, 2 degrees awarded. *Degree requirements:* Thesis optional, foreign language not required. *Entrance requirements:* GRE General Test (minimum combined score of 1000), bachelor's degree in nursing, minimum undergraduate GPA of 3.0. Application deadline: 1/15. Application fee: $40. *Financial aid:* Career-related internships or fieldwork available. • Application contact: Office of Recruitment, 503-494-7725. Fax: 503-494-4350.

Oregon Health Sciences University, School of Nursing, Women's Health Care Nurse Practitioner Program, 3181 SW Sam Jackson Park Road, Portland, OR 97201-3098. Awards MN, MS, Post Master's Certificate. One or more programs accredited by NLN. *Degree requirements:* For master's, thesis optional, foreign language not required. *Entrance requirements:* For master's, GRE General Test (minimum combined score of 1000), bachelor's degree in nursing, minimum undergraduate GPA of 3.0; for Post Master's Certificate, master's degree in nursing. Application deadline: 1/15. Application fee: $40. • Application contact: Office of Recruitment, 503-494-7725. Fax: 503-494-4350.

Rush University, College of Nursing, Department of Maternal-Child Nursing, Chicago, IL 60612-3832. Offers programs in genetics health clinical nurse specialist (MSN, DN Sc, ND), high risk perinatal nurse practioner (ND), high risk perinatal nurse practitioner (MSN, DN Sc), neonatal nurse practitioner (MSN, DN Sc, ND), pediatric clinical nurse specialist (MSN, DN Sc, ND), pediatric critical care nurse practitioner (MSN, DN Sc, ND), pediatric nurse practitioner (MSN, DN Sc, ND), women's health clinical nurse specialist (MSN, DN Sc, ND). One or more programs accredited by NLN. Part-time programs available. Faculty: 7 full-time (6 women), 12 part-time (all women), 14.11 FTE. Students: 2 full-time, 88 part-time. Average age 36. *Degree requirements:* For doctorate, dissertation required, foreign language not required. *Entrance requirements:* For master's, GRE General Test, interview; for doctorate, interview, previous course work in statistics. Application deadline: 8/1 (rolling processing; 2/1 for spring admission). Application fee: $40. *Tuition:* $8560 per year full-time, $370 per credit hour part-time. *Financial aid:* Federal Work-Study, institutionally sponsored loans, and career-related internships or fieldwork available. Aid available to part-time students. Financial aid applicants required to submit FAFSA. *Faculty research:* Outcomes assessment in asthma, family-centered care, pediatric pain measurement and management, women's health, socialization among adolescents. • Dr. Karren Kowalski, Chairperson, 312-942-6604. Application contact: Hicela Castruita, Director, College Admissions Services, 312-942-7100. Fax: 312-942-2219.

Rutgers, The State University of New Jersey, Newark, College of Nursing, Graduate Program in Advanced Practice in Pediatric Nursing, Newark, NJ 07102-3192. Awards MS. Accredited by NLN. Part-time programs available. *Degree requirements:* Comprehensive exam required, foreign language and thesis not required. *Entrance requirements:* GRE General Test, TOEFL, RN license, minimum B average, BS in nursing. Application deadline: 8/15 (rolling processing; 12/15 for spring admission). Application fee: $40. Electronic applications accepted. *Expenses:* Tuition $6248 per year full-time, $257 per credit part-time for state residents; $9160 per year full-time, $380 per credit part-time for nonresidents. Fees $738 per year full-time, $107 per semester (minimum) part-time. *Financial aid:* Federal Work-Study, institutionally sponsored loans, and career-related internships or fieldwork available. • Application contact: Dr. Elaine Dolinsky, Associate Dean for Student Life and Services, 973-353-5060. Fax: 973-353-1277.

Rutgers, The State University of New Jersey, Newark, College of Nursing, Graduate Program in Advanced Practice with Childbearing Families, Newark, NJ 07102-3192. Awards MS. Accredited by NLN. Part-time programs available. *Degree requirements:* Comprehensive exam required, foreign language and thesis not required. *Entrance requirements:* GRE General Test, TOEFL, RN license, minimum B average, BS in nursing. Application deadline: 8/15 (rolling processing; 12/15 for spring admission). Application fee: $40. Electronic applications accepted. *Expenses:* Tuition $6248 per year full-time, $257 per credit part-time for state residents; $9160 per year full-time, $380 per credit part-time for nonresidents. Fees $738 per year full-time, $107 per semester (minimum) part-time. *Financial aid:* Federal Work-Study, institutionally sponsored loans, and career-related internships or fieldwork available. Financial aid application deadline: 3/1. • Application contact: Dr. Elaine Dolinsky, Associate Dean for Student Life and Services, 973-353-5060. Fax: 973-353-1277.

Saint Joseph College, Division of Nursing, West Hartford, CT 06117-2700. Offerings include family health nursing (MS). Accredited by NLN. Division faculty: 10 full-time (9 women), 2 part-time (both women). *Degree requirements:* Thesis or alternative required, foreign language not required. *Application deadline:* 8/29 (rolling processing). *Application fee:* $25. *Tuition:* $395 per credit. • Dr. Virginia Knowlden, Director, 860-232-4571 Ext. 258.

Directory: Maternal/Child-Care Nursing

Saint Louis University, School of Nursing, Program in Nursing of Children, St. Louis, MO 63103-2097. Awards MSN, MSN(R), Certificate, MPH/MSN, MSN/MBA. Offerings include clinical health specialist/case manager (MSN, MSN(R), Certificate), pediatric nurse practitioner (MSN, MSN(R), Certificate). One or more programs accredited by NLN. *Degree requirements:* For master's, comprehensive oral exam required, thesis optional, foreign language not required. *Entrance requirements:* For master's, GRE General Test. Application deadline: 7/1 (rolling processing; 11/1 for spring admission). Application fee: $40. *Tuition:* $542 per credit hour. *Financial aid:* Traineeships available. Financial aid application deadline: 4/1. • Dr. Irene Riddle, Program Director, 314-577-8971. Application contact: Dr. Marcia Buresch, Assistant Dean of the Graduate School, 314-977-2240. Fax: 314-977-3943.

Saint Louis University, School of Nursing, Program in Perinatal Nursing, St. Louis, MO 63103-2097. Awards MSN, MSN(R), Certificate, MPH/MSN, MSN/MBA. Offerings include clinical health specialist/case manager (MSN, MSN(R), Certificate). One or more programs accredited by NLN. *Degree requirements:* For master's, comprehensive oral exam required, thesis optional, foreign language not required. *Entrance requirements:* For master's, GRE General Test. Application deadline: 7/1 (rolling processing; 11/1 for spring admission). Application fee: $40. *Tuition:* $542 per credit hour. *Financial aid:* Traineeships available. Financial aid application deadline: 4/1. • Dr. Patsy Ruchala, Program Director, 314-577-8970. Application contact: Dr. Marcia Buresch, Assistant Dean of the Graduate School, 314-977-2240. Fax: 314-977-3943.

Seton Hall University, College of Nursing, Department of Graduate Nursing, Advanced Practice in Primary Health Care Program, South Orange, NJ 07079-2697. Offerings include pediatric nurse practitioner (MSN). Accredited by NLN. Program faculty: 6 full-time (all women), 4 part-time (all women). *Degree requirements:* Research project required, foreign language and thesis not required. *Entrance requirements:* GRE or MAT, BSN. Application deadline: 5/15 (priority date; rolling processing; 11/15 for spring admission). Application fee: $50. *Expenses:* Tuition $500 per credit. Fees $610 per year full-time, $185 per semester part-time. • Dr. Cynthia Hughes, Director, 973-761-9273. Fax: 973-761-9607. E-mail: hughesci@shu.edu.

State University of New York at Buffalo, Graduate School, School of Nursing, Buffalo, NY 14260. Offerings include child health nursing (MS), with options in clinical nurse specialist, pediatric nurse practitioner. Accredited by NLN. Postbaccalaureate distance learning degree programs offered (minimal on-campus study). School faculty: 28 full-time (25 women), 13 part-time (12 women). *Entrance requirements:* GRE General Test (minimum score 450 on each section), TOEFL (minimum score 550), interview, minimum GPA of 3.0, RN license. Application deadline: 5/1 (priority date; rolling processing; 10/15 for spring admission). Application fee: $35. *Tuition:* $5970 per year full-time, $288 per credit hour part-time for state residents; $9286 per year full-time, $426 per credit hour part-time for nonresidents. • Dr. Mecca S. Cranley, Dean, 716-829-2533. E-mail: mcranley@nurse.buffalo.edu. Application contact: Dr. William P. Harden, Assistant Dean, 716-829-3314. Fax: 716-829-2021. E-mail: wharden@nurse.buffalo.edu.

State University of New York at Stony Brook, Health Sciences Center, School of Nursing, Program in Child Health Nursing, Stony Brook, NY 11794. Offers child health nurse practitioner (Certificate), child health nursing (MS). One or more programs accredited by NLN. Students: 14 full-time (12 women), 49 part-time (48 women); includes 8 minority (1 African American, 2 Asian Americans, 5 Hispanics). In 1997, 22 master's, 8 Certificates awarded. *Degree requirements:* For master's, thesis required, foreign language not required. *Entrance requirements:* For master's, BSN, minimum GPA of 3.0, previous course work in statistics. Application deadline: 1/15. Application fee: $50. *Expenses:* Tuition $5100 per year full-time, $213 per credit hour part-time for state residents; $8416 per year full-time, $351 per credit hour part-time for nonresidents. Fees $529 per year full-time, $77 per semester (minimum) part-time. *Financial aid:* Application deadline 3/15. • Dr. Carole L. Blair, Chair, 516-444-3258. Fax: 516-444-3136. E-mail: carole_blair@notes2.nursing.sunysb.edu.

State University of New York at Stony Brook, Health Sciences Center, School of Nursing, Program in Neonatal Nursing, Stony Brook, NY 11794. Offers neonatal nurse practitioner (Certificate), neonatal nursing (MS). One or more programs accredited by NLN. Students: 17 full-time (all women), 10 part-time (all women); includes 4 minority (1 African American, 3 Asian Americans). In 1997, 6 master's, 2 Certificates awarded. *Degree requirements:* For master's, thesis required, foreign language not required. *Entrance requirements:* For master's, BSN, minimum GPA of 3.0, previous course work in statistics. Application deadline: 1/15. Application fee: $50. *Expenses:* Tuition $5100 per year full-time, $213 per credit hour part-time for state residents; $8416 per year full-time, $351 per credit hour part-time for nonresidents. Fees $529 per year full-time, $77 per semester (minimum) part-time. *Financial aid:* Application deadline 3/15. • Dr. Carole Blair, Chair, 516-444-3258. Fax: 516-444-3136. E-mail: carole_blair@notes2.nursing.sunysb.edu.

State University of New York at Stony Brook, Health Sciences Center, School of Nursing, Program in Perinatal/Women's Health Nursing, Stony Brook, NY 11794. Offers perinatal/women's health nurse practitioner (Certificate), perinatal/women's health nursing (MS). One or more programs accredited by NLN. Students: 8 full-time (all women), 28 part-time (all women); includes 9 minority (6 African Americans, 3 Asian Americans). In 1997, 4 master's, 4 Certificates awarded. *Degree requirements:* For master's, thesis required, foreign language not required. *Entrance requirements:* For master's, BSN, minimum GPA of 3.0, previous course work in statistics. Application deadline: 1/15. Application fee: $50. *Expenses:* Tuition $5100 per year full-time, $213 per credit hour part-time for state residents; $8416 per year full-time, $351 per credit hour part-time for nonresidents. Fees $529 per year full-time, $77 per semester (minimum) part-time. *Financial aid:* Application deadline 3/15. • Dr. Carole L. Blair, Coordinator, 516-444-3258. Fax: 516-444-3136. E-mail: carole_blair@notes2.nursing.sunysb.edu.

Texas Woman's University, College of Nursing, Denton, TX 76204. Offerings include pediatric nursing (MS). Accredited by NLN. College faculty: 30 full-time (29 women), 12 part-time (10 women). *Degree requirements:* Thesis or alternative required, foreign language not required. *Entrance requirements:* GRE General Test (minimum combined score of 750), minimum GPA of 3.0. Application deadline: rolling. Application fee: $25. • Dr. Carolyn S. Gunning, Dean, 940-898-2401.

University of Cincinnati, College of Nursing and Health, Cincinnati, OH 45221-0038. Offerings include parent/child nursing (MSN). Accredited by NLN. College faculty: 26 full-time. *Degree requirements:* Project or thesis required, foreign language not required. *Average time to degree:* master's–1.5 years full-time, 2.5 years part-time; doctorate–4 years full-time, 6 years part-time. *Entrance requirements:* GRE General Test. Application deadline: 1/1 (priority date; rolling processing). Application fee: $30. *Tuition:* $7228 per year full-time, $185 per credit hour part-time for state residents; $13,812 per year full-time, $352 per credit hour part-time for nonresidents. • Dr. Andrea Lindell, Dean, 513-558-5330. Application contact: Tom West, Program Coordinator, 513-558-3600. Fax: 513-558-7523. E-mail: tom.west@uc.edu.

University of Colorado at Colorado Springs, Department of Graduate Nursing, Colorado Springs, CO 80933-7150. Offerings include family practitioner (MSN), with options in community clinical specialist, forensic clinical specialist, holistic clinical specialist; neonatal nurse practitioner and clinical specialist (MSN). One or more programs accredited by NLN. Postbaccalaureate distance learning degree programs offered (minimal on-campus study). Department faculty: 9 full-time (8 women). *Degree requirements:* Thesis optional, foreign language not required. *Average time to degree:* master's–2.5 years full-time, 5 years part-time. *Entrance requirements:* GRE General Test (minimum combined score of 1400) or MAT (minimum score 50), BSN, GPA of 3.0. Application deadline: 2/15 (priority date; 10/15 for spring admission). Application fee: $40. Electronic applications accepted. *Expenses:* Tuition $4644 per year full-time, $193 per credit hour part-time for state residents; $10,254 per year full-time, $420 per credit hour part-time for nonresidents. Fees $399 per year (minimum) full-time, $106 per year (minimum) part-time. • Barbara Joyce-Nagata, Chair, 719-262-4430. Fax: 719-262-4416.

University of Delaware, College of Health and Nursing Sciences, Department of Nursing, Newark, DE 19716. Offerings include clinical nurse specialist/nurse practitioner (Certificate), with options in cardiopulmonary, gerontology, oncology/immune deficiency, pediatrics, women's health; pediatrics (MSN, Certificate). One or more programs accredited by NLN. Department faculty: 10 full-time (9 women), 5 part-time (all women), 12.25 FTE. *Degree requirements:* For master's, thesis optional, foreign language not required. *Average time to degree:* master's–2 years full-time, 3 years part-time. *Entrance requirements:* For master's, GRE General Test. Application deadline: 7/1. Application fee: $45. *Expenses:* Tuition $4250 per year full-time, $236 per credit hour part-time for state residents; $12,250 per year full-time, $681 per credit hour part-time for nonresidents. Fees $466 per year full-time, $15 per semester (minimum) part-time. • Application contact: Betty Bonavita, Graduate Secretary, 302-831-1255. Fax: 302-831-2382. E-mail: elizabeth.bonavita@mvs.udel.edu.

University of Illinois at Chicago, College of Nursing, Program in Maternal-Child Nursing, Chicago, IL 60607-7128. Offers maternity nursing/nurse midwifery (MS), pediatric nursing (MS), perinatal nursing (MS). Accredited by NLN. Faculty: 9 full-time (all women). Students: 9 full-time (all women), 83 part-time (81 women); includes 14 minority (9 African Americans, 3 Asian Americans, 1 Hispanic, 1 Native American). Average age 35. 53 applicants, 43% accepted. In 1997, 6 degrees awarded. *Degree requirements:* Thesis or alternative required, foreign language not required. *Entrance requirements:* GRE General Test, TOEFL (minimum score 550), minimum GPA of 3.75 on a 5.0 scale. Application deadline: 5/15 (10/15 for spring admission). Application fee: $40 ($50 for international students). *Financial aid:* Fellowships, research assistantships, teaching assistantships, partial tuition waivers, Federal Work-Study, institutionally sponsored loans, and career-related internships or fieldwork available. • Arlene Burroughs, Head, 312-996-7935. Application contact: Kathleen Knafl, Director of Graduate Studies, 312-996-2159.

University of Maryland, Baltimore, Graduate School, School of Nursing, Baltimore, MD 21201-1627. Offerings include maternal-child nursing (MS). Accredited by NLN. MS/MBA offered jointly with the University of Baltimore. School faculty: 49 (45 women). *Degree requirements:* Thesis or alternative required, foreign language not required. *Entrance requirements:* GRE General Test, TOEFL, minimum GPA of 2.75, previous course work in statistics, BS in nursing. Application fee: $42. *Expenses:* Tuition $253 per credit hour for state residents; $454 per credit hour for nonresidents. Fees $317 per year. • Dr. Barbara Heller, Dean, 410-706-6741. Application contact: Dr. Susan Wozenski, Assistant Dean for Student Affairs, 410-706-0501. Fax: 410-706-7238.

University of Michigan, School of Nursing, Division of Health Promotion and Risk Reduction, Program in Parent-Child Nursing, Ann Arbor, MI 48109. Offers acute care pediatric nurse practitioner (MS); infant, child, adolescent health nurse practitioner (MS); nurse midwifery (MS); women's health/child-bearing families nurse practitioner (MS). Accredited by NLN. Part-time programs available. *Degree requirements:* Thesis required, foreign language not required. *Entrance requirements:* GRE General Test, BS in nursing. Application deadline: 2/1 (priority date). Application fee: $55. *Financial aid:* Fellowships, traineeships, partial tuition waivers, Federal Work-Study available. • Application contact: Graduate Program Secretary, 734-763-0016. Fax: 734-647-0351.

University of Minnesota, Twin Cities Campus, School of Nursing, Children with Special Health Needs Nurse Practitioner Program, Minneapolis, MN 55455-0213. Offers advanced clinical specialist in children with special health needs (MS). Accredited by NLN. Students: 8 full-time. 8 applicants, 75% accepted. *Degree requirements:* Final oral exam, project or thesis. *Application deadline:* 12/15 (rolling processing). *Application fee:* $40 ($50 for international students). *Financial aid:* Fellowships, research assistantships, teaching assistantships, traineeships, and career-related internships or fieldwork available. • Barbara Leonard, Head, 612-624-9950. Fax: 612-626-2359. Application contact: Kate Hanson, Nursing Recruiter, 612-624-9494. Fax: 612-624-3174. E-mail: hanso041@maroon.tc.umn.edu.

University of Minnesota, Twin Cities Campus, School of Nursing, Pediatric Nurse Practitioner Program, Minneapolis, MN 55455-0213. Awards MS. Accredited by NLN. Students: 16 full-time. *Degree requirements:* Final oral exam, project or thesis. *Application deadline:* 12/15 (rolling processing). *Application fee:* $40 ($50 for international students). *Financial aid:* Fellowships, research assistantships, teaching assistantships, professional nurse traineeships, and career-related internships or fieldwork available. • Barbara Leonard, Head, 612-629-9950. Fax: 612-626-2359. Application contact: Kate Hanson, Nursing Recruiter, 612-624-9494. Fax: 612-624-3174. E-mail: hanso041@maroon.tc.umn.edu.

University of Minnesota, Twin Cities Campus, School of Nursing, Program in Child and Family Nursing, Minneapolis, MN 55455-0213. Offers advanced clinical specialist in child and family nursing (MS). Accredited by NLN. Part-time programs available. Students: 4 part-time. 5 applicants, 100% accepted. *Degree requirements:* Final oral exam, project or thesis. *Application deadline:* 12/15 (rolling processing). *Application fee:* $40 ($50 for international students). *Financial aid:* Fellowships, research assistantships, teaching assistantships, professional nurse traineeships, and career-related internships or fieldwork available. • Patricia Tomlinson, Head, 612-624-6684. Fax: 612-626-2359. Application contact: Kate Hanson, Nursing Recruiter, 612-624-9494. Fax: 612-624-3174. E-mail: hanso041@maroon.tc.umn.edu.

University of Missouri–Kansas City, School of Nursing, Kansas City, MO 64110-2499. Offerings include nurse practitioner (MSN), with options in health care for adults, health care for children, health care for women. Accredited by NLN. School faculty: 17 full-time (15 women), 40 part-time (all women), 37 FTE. *Degree requirements:* Thesis or alternative required, foreign language not required. *Entrance requirements:* Minimum undergraduate GPA of 3.0. Application deadline: 2/1 (9/15 for spring admission). Application fee: $25. *Expenses:* Tuition $182 per credit hour for state residents; $508 per credit hour for nonresidents. Fees $60 per year. • Dr. Nancy Mills, Dean, 816-235-1700. Application contact: Brenda Cain, Student Services Assistant, 816-235-1710. Fax: 816-235-1701.

University of New Mexico, College of Nursing, Albuquerque, NM 87131-2039. Offerings include advanced nursing practice (MSN), with options in adult health nursing, gerontological nursing, parent-child nursing, psychiatric-mental health nursing. Accredited by NLN. College faculty: 38 full-time (36 women), 23 part-time (all women), 46.57 FTE. *Degree requirements:* Thesis optional, foreign language not required. *Entrance requirements:* GRE General Test, interview, minimum GPA of 3.0, previous course work in statistics. Application deadline: 7/15 (11/1 for spring admission). Application fee: $25. *Expenses:* Tuition $2442 per year full-time, $103 per credit hour part-time for state residents; $8691 per year full-time, $103 per credit hour (minimum) part-time for nonresidents. Fees $32 per year. • Dr. Sandra Ferketich, Dean, 505-272-6284. Application contact: Anne-Marie Oechsler, Director, Academic Advisement, 505-272-4224. Fax: 505-272-3970. E-mail: annmarie@unm.edu.

University of Pennsylvania, School of Nursing, Health Care of Women Nurse Practitioner Program, Philadelphia, PA 19104. Awards MSN. Accredited by NLN. Part-time programs available. Postbaccalaureate distance learning degree programs offered (minimal on-campus study). Students: 6 full-time (all women), 15 part-time (all women); includes 2 minority (both African Americans), 3 international. Average age 28. 22 applicants, 64% accepted. In 1997, 19 degrees awarded. *Entrance requirements:* GRE General Test, BSN, minimum GPA of 3.0, previous course in statistics, physical assessment experience. Application deadline: 5/20 (rolling processing). Application fee: $65. *Financial aid:* In 1997–98, 2 fellowships, 3 research assistantships, 1 teaching assistantship were awarded; Federal Work-Study, institutionally sponsored loans, and career-related internships or fieldwork also available. Aid available to part-time students. *Faculty research:* New mother and infant healthcare follow up, adequacy of antepartum care, models of healthcare. • Dr. Ruth York, Director, 215-898-5323. Fax: 215-573-7291. E-mail: yorkr@pobox.upenn.edu. Application contact: Susan K. Ogle, Associate Director of Admissions and Student Affairs, 215-898-3301. Fax: 215-573-8439. E-mail: sogle@pobox.upenn.edu.

University of Pennsylvania, School of Nursing, Neonatal Nurse Practitioner Program, Philadelphia, PA 19104. Awards MSN. Accredited by NLN. Part-time programs available. Students: 4 full-time (all women), 9 part-time (8 women). Average age 30. 11 applicants, 55% accepted. In 1997, 3 degrees awarded (100% found work related to degree). *Average time to degree:* master's–1 year full-time, 2 years part-time. *Entrance requirements:* GRE General Test, BSN, minimum GPA of 3.0, previous course work in statistics, 1 year of experience in a neonatal intensive care unit. Application deadline: 9/1 (rolling processing). Application fee: $65. *Financial aid:* In 1997–98, 2 research assistantships, 1 teaching assistantship were awarded; fellowships, Federal Work-Study, institutionally sponsored loans, and career-related internships or fieldwork also available. Aid available to part-time students. *Faculty research:* Neurobehavioral development, temperament, newborn sucking behaviors, parenting pre-term infants. • Dr. Susan Gennaro, Director, 215-898-1844. Fax: 215-898-6320. E-mail: gennaro@pobox.upenn.edu. Application contact: Susan K. Ogle, Associate Director of Admissions and Student Affairs, 215-898-3301. Fax: 215-573-8439. E-mail: sogle@pobox.upenn.edu.

University of Pennsylvania, School of Nursing, Pediatric Acute/Chronic Care Nurse Practitioner Program, Philadelphia, PA 19104. Awards MSN. Accredited by NLN. Part-time programs available. Postbaccalaureate distance learning degree programs offered. Students: 2 full-time (both women), 19 part-time (all women); includes 2 minority (1 African American, 1 Hispanic), 1 international. Average age 30. 10 applicants, 70% accepted. In 1997, 17 degrees awarded. *Entrance requirements:* GRE General Test, BSN, minimum GPA of 3.0, previous course work in statistics, 1 year of clinical course work. Application deadline: 2/15 (rolling processing). Application fee: $65. *Financial aid:* In 1997–98, 1 research assistantship, 1 teaching assistantship were awarded; institutionally sponsored loans and career-related internships or fieldwork also available. Aid available to part-time students. *Faculty research:* Hispanic health, bereavement, pediatric AIDS, chronically ill children and their families. • Dr. Janet Deatrick, Director, 215-898-1799. Fax: 215-573-7507. E-mail: deatrick@pobox.upenn.edu. Application contact: Susan K. Ogle, Associate Director of Admissions and Student Affairs, 215-898-3301. Fax: 215-573-8439. E-mail: sogle@pobox.upenn.edu.

University of Pennsylvania, School of Nursing, Pediatric Critical Care Nurse Practitioner Program, Philadelphia, PA 19104. Awards MSN. Accredited by NLN. Students: 6 full-time (all women), 3 part-time (all women); includes 1 international. 9 applicants, 89% accepted. In 1997, 3 degrees awarded. *Entrance requirements:* GRE General Test, BSN, minimum GPA of 3.0, previous course work in statistics, 1 year of clinical course work. Application deadline: 2/15. Application fee: $65. • Dr. Janet Deatrick, Director, 215-898-1799. Fax: 215-573-7507. E-mail: deatrick@pobox.upenn.edu. Application contact: Susan K. Ogle, Associate Director of Admissions and Student Affairs, 215-898-3301. Fax: 215-573-8439. E-mail: sogle@pobox.upenn.edu.

University of Pennsylvania, School of Nursing, Perinatal Advanced Practice Nurse Specialist Program, Philadelphia, PA 19104. Awards MSN. Accredited by NLN. Part-time programs available. Students: 1 (woman) part-time; includes 1 minority (African American). 0 applicants. *Entrance requirements:* GRE General Test, BSN, minimum GPA of 3.0, previous course work in statistics. Application deadline: 9/1 (rolling processing). Application fee: $65. *Financial aid:* Fellowships, research assistantships, teaching assistantships, Federal Work-Study, institutionally sponsored loans, and career-related internships or fieldwork available. Aid available to part-time students. • Application contact: Susan K. Ogle, Associate Director of Admissions and Student Affairs, 215-898-3301. Fax: 215-573-8439. E-mail: sogle@pobox.upenn.edu.

University of Pennsylvania, School of Nursing, Perinatal Nurse Practitioner Program, Philadelphia, PA 19104. Awards MSN. Accredited by NLN. Part-time programs available. Students: 3 full-time (all women), 2 part-time (both women). Average age 31. 4 applicants, 75% accepted. In 1997, 7 degrees awarded. *Average time to degree:* master's–1 year full-time, 2 years part-time. *Entrance requirements:* GRE General Test, BSN, minimum GPA of 3.0, previous course work in statistics. Application deadline: 9/1 (rolling processing). Application fee: $65. *Financial aid:* Fellowships, research assistantships, teaching assistantships, Federal Work-Study, institutionally sponsored loans, and career-related internships or fieldwork available. Aid available to part-time students. *Faculty research:* Low-birth weight prevention and care. • Susan Gennaro, Director, 215-898-1844. Fax: 215-898-6320. E-mail: gennaro@pobox.upenn.edu. Application contact: Susan K. Ogle, Associate Director of Admissions and Student Affairs, 215-898-3301. Fax: 215-573-8439. E-mail: solge@pobox.upenn.edu.

University of Pennsylvania, School of Nursing, Primary Care Nurse Practitioner Program: Family, Philadelphia, PA 19104. Awards MSN, Certificate. Accredited by NLN. Part-time programs available. Students: 25 full-time (22 women), 10 part-time (9 women); includes 5 minority (4 African Americans, 1 Asian American), 1 international. Average age 32. 19 applicants, 68% accepted. In 1997, 15 master's awarded. *Average time to degree:* master's–1 year full-time, 2 years part-time. *Entrance requirements:* For master's, GRE General Test, BSN, minimum GPA of 3.0, previous course work in statistics, 1 year of clinical experience in area of interest. Application deadline: 2/15 (rolling processing). Application fee: $65. *Financial aid:* In 1997–98, 6 research assistantships, 1 teaching assistantship were awarded; Federal Work-Study, institutionally sponsored loans, and career-related internships or fieldwork also available. Aid available to part-time students. *Faculty research:* Evaluation of primary care practitioner practice, access to primary care. • Dr. Melinda Jenkins, Director, 215-898-4043. Fax: 215-573-7381. E-mail: mjenkins@pobox.upenn.edu. Application contact: Susan K. Ogle, Associate Director of Admissions and Student Affairs, 215-898-3301. Fax: 215-573-8439. E-mail: sogle@pobox.upenn.edu.

University of Pennsylvania, School of Nursing, Primary Care Nurse Practitioner Program: Pediatrics, Philadelphia, PA 19104. Awards MSN. Accredited by NLN. Part-time programs available. Students: 11 full-time (all women), 18 part-time (all women); includes 1 international. 15 applicants, 93% accepted. In 1997, 25 degrees awarded. *Entrance requirements:* GRE General Test, BSN, minimum GPA of 3.0, previous course work in statistics, 1 year of clinical experience in area of interest. Application deadline: 2/1 (rolling processing). Application fee: $65. *Financial aid:* In 1997–98, 3 research assistantships, 1 teaching assistantship were awarded; Federal Work-Study, institutionally sponsored loans, and career-related internships or fieldwork also available. Aid available to part-time students. *Faculty research:* Adolescent behavior change, prevention of teenage pregnancy, community schools. Total annual research expenditures: $500,000. • Dr. Ann O'Sullivan, Director, 215-898-4043. Fax: 215-573-7381. E-mail: osull@pobox.upenn.edu. Application contact: Susan K. Ogle, Associate Director of Admissions and Student Affairs, 215-898-3301. Fax: 215-573-8439. E-mail: sogle@pobox.upenn.edu.

University of Pittsburgh, School of Nursing, Program in Nurse Practitioner Studies, Pittsburgh, PA 15260. Offerings include health promotion and development (MSN), with options in family nurse practitioner, pediatric nurse practitioner, women's health nurse practitioner. Accredited by NLN. *Degree requirements:* Thesis or alternative required, foreign language not required. *Average time to degree:* master's–2 years full-time, 5 years part-time. *Entrance requirements:* GRE General Test or MAT, TOEFL, BSN, RN license, 1 to 3 years of nursing experience. Application deadline: 2/1 (priority date; rolling processing; 9/15 for spring admission). Application fee: $35 ($40 for international students). • Application contact: Dr. Kathy Lucke, Director, Student Services, 412-624-2405. Fax: 412-624-2409. E-mail: nursao+@pitt.edu.

See in-depth description on page 1451.

University of South Alabama, College of Nursing, Mobile, AL 36688-0002. Offerings include maternal child nursing (MSN). Accredited by NLN. College faculty: 9 full-time (all women), 1 (woman) part-time. *Degree requirements:* Written comprehensive exam, research project or thesis required, foreign language not required. *Entrance requirements:* GRE General Test (minimum combined score of 1000) or MAT (minimum score 45), BSN, minimum GPA of 3.0, 1 year of nursing experience, interview, nursing license. Application deadline: 9/1 (priority date; rolling processing). Application fee: $25. • Dr. Amanda Baker, Dean, 334-434-3415.

The University of Texas at El Paso, College of Nursing and Health Science, Program in Nursing, 500 West University Avenue, El Paso, TX 79968-0001. Offerings include parent-child nursing (MSN). Accredited by NLN. *Degree requirements:* Thesis optional, foreign language not required. *Entrance requirements:* GRE General Test or MAT (minimum score 50), TOEFL (minimum score 550), BSN, course work in statistics. Application deadline: 7/1 (rolling processing; 11/1 for spring admission). Application fee: $15 ($65 for international students). Electronic applications accepted. *Tuition:* $2063 per year full-time, $284 per credit hour part-time for state residents; $5753 per year full-time, $425 per credit hour part-time for nonresidents.

The University of Texas–Houston Health Science Center, School of Nursing, Master's Program in Nursing, Houston, TX 77225-0036. Offerings include neonatal (MSN), pediatric nurse practitioner (MSN), perinatal (MSN). One or more programs accredited by NLN. *Degree requirements:* Thesis required, foreign language not required. *Entrance requirements:* GRE or MAT, BSN, Texas RN license. Application deadline: 5/1 (priority date; rolling processing; 9/1 for spring admission). Application fee: $10. Electronic applications accepted. • Frank Cole, Chair, Graduate Curriculum Committee, 713-500-2153. Fax: 713-500-2171. E-mail: fcole@son1.nur.uth.tmc.edu. Application contact: Eleanor Evans, Pre-Admissions Counselor, 713-500-2104. Fax: 713-500-2107. E-mail: eevans@son1.nur.uth.tmc.edu.

Vanderbilt University, School of Nursing, Nashville, TN 37240-1001. Offerings include neonatal critical care practitioner (MSN), neonatal nurse practitioner (MSN), pediatric nurse practitioner (MSN), women's health nurse practitioner (MSN). One or more programs accredited by NLN. Postbaccalaureate distance learning degree programs offered (minimal on-campus study). School faculty: 76 full-time (66 women), 253 part-time (224 women). *Degree requirements:* Terminal course required, thesis not required. *Average time to degree:* master's–2 years full-time, 4 years part-time; doctorate–4 years full-time, 5 years part-time. *Entrance requirements:* GMAT, GRE, or MAT, minimum B average. Application deadline: rolling. Application fee: $50. Electronic applications accepted. • Dr. Colleen Conway-Welch, Dean, 615-343-3243. Fax: 615-343-7711. Application contact: Patricia Peerman, Assistant Dean of Admissions, 615-322-3800. Fax: 615-343-0333. E-mail: vusn-admission@mcmail.vanderbilt.edu.

Villanova University, College of Nursing, Villanova, PA 19085-1690. Offerings include pediatric nurse practitioner (MSN). Accredited by NLN. MSN (pediatric nurse practitioner), Post Master's Certificate (nurse practitioner, nurse anesthetist, clinical case management) new for fall 1998. College faculty: 30 full-time (all women). *Degree requirements:* Independent study project required, foreign language and thesis not required. *Entrance requirements:* GRE General Test (verbal section) or MAT, BSN, 1 year of recent experience, physical assessment, previous course work in statistics. Application deadline: 7/1 (priority date; rolling processing; 12/1 for spring admission). Application fee: $25. *Expenses:* Tuition $445 per credit. Fees $60 per year. • Dr. Claire Manfredi, Graduate Director, 610-519-4907. Fax: 610-519-7997. E-mail: cmanfred@email.vill.edu.

Virginia Commonwealth University, School of Nursing, Richmond, VA 23284-9005. Offerings include child health nursing (MS). Accredited by NLN. School faculty: 50 full-time (all women), 5 part-time (all women). *Entrance requirements:* GRE General Test, BSN, minimum GPA of 2.8. Application deadline: 2/1. Application fee: $30 ($0 for international students). *Tuition:* $4960 per year full-time, $257 per credit part-time for state residents; $12,652 per year full-time, $684 per credit part-time for nonresidents. • Dr. Nancy F. Langston, Dean, 804-828-5174. E-mail: nflangst@vcu.edu. Application contact: Susan Lipp, Admissions Counselor, 804-828-5171. Fax: 804-828-7743. E-mail: slipp@vcu.edu.

Wayne State University, College of Nursing, Department of Family, Community and Mental Health, Neonatal Nurse Practitioner Program, Detroit, MI 48202. Awards Certificate. Students: 2 part-time (both women). Average age 30. 1 applicant, 0% accepted. In 1997, 3 degrees awarded. *Entrance requirements:* Admission to MSN program and 3000 hours of neonatal experience including 1800 hours in a level 3 neonatal ICU. Application deadline: 7/1 (priority date; rolling processing; 11/1 for spring admission). Application fee: $20 ($30 for international students). *Expenses:* Tuition $163 per credit hour for state residents; $355 per credit hour for nonresidents. Fees $498 per year full-time, $114 per semester (minimum) part-time. *Financial aid:* Application deadline 7/1. *Faculty research:* High-risk pregnancy, infant developmental/cocaine abuse. • Dr. Marie-Luise Friedemann, Assistant Dean, 313-577-4092. Fax: 313-577-4571. Application contact: Vickie Radoye, Administrative Assistant Dean, Student Affairs, 313-577-4082. Fax: 313-577-6949.

Wayne State University, College of Nursing, Department of Family, Community and Mental Health, Program in Nursing, Parenting and Families, Detroit, MI 48202. Awards MSN. Accredited by NLN. Part-time programs available. Students: 10 full-time (all women), 48 part-time (all women); includes 7 minority (all African Americans), 2 international. Average age 36. 20 applicants, 55% accepted. In 1997, 16 degrees awarded. *Degree requirements:* Computer language, thesis or alternative required, foreign language not required. *Entrance requirements:* GRE General Test (minimum combined score of 800), minimum GPA of 2.8. Application deadline: 7/1 (priority date; rolling processing; 11/1 for spring admission). Application fee: $20 ($30 for international students). *Expenses:* Tuition $163 per credit hour for state residents; $355 per credit hour for nonresidents. Fees $498 per year full-time, $114 per semester (minimum) part-time. *Financial aid:* In 1997–98, 17 students received aid, including 2 research assistantships, 15 scholarships, traineeships (4 to first-year students); institutionally sponsored loans also available. Financial aid application deadline: 7/1; applicants required to submit FAFSA. *Faculty research:* Biophysiologic measurement, infant mental health, postoperative pain in children, women's health, chronic childhood illness, parenting across age groups and pregnancy. • Dr. Marie-Luise Friedemann, Assistant Dean, 313-577-4092. Fax: 313-577-4571. Application contact: Vickie Radoye, Administrative Assistant Dean, Student Affairs, 313-577-4082. Fax: 313-577-6949.

Wichita State University, College of Health Professions, School of Nursing, Wichita, KS 67260. Offerings include clinical specialization (MSN), with options in adult nursing, maternal-child nursing, psychiatric/mental health nursing. Accredited by NLN. School faculty: 11 full-time (all women). *Degree requirements:* Comprehensive exam required, thesis optional, foreign language not required. *Entrance requirements:* GRE, TOEFL (minimum score 550), BSN, minimum undergraduate GPA of 2.75. Application deadline: 6/30 (priority date; rolling processing; 1/1 for spring admission). Application fee: $25 ($40 for international students). Electronic applications accepted. *Expenses:* Tuition $2303 per year full-time, $96 per credit hour part-time for state residents; $7691 per year full-time, $321 per credit hour part-time for nonresidents. Fees $490 per year full-time, $75 per semester (minimum) part-time. • Dr. Bonnie Holaday, Interim Dean, 316-978-3610. E-mail: holaday@chp.twsu.edu. Application contact: Dr. Donna Hawley, Graduate Coordinator, 316-978-3610. Fax: 316-978-3094. E-mail: hawley@chp.twsu.edu.

Wright State University, College of Nursing and Health, Program in Nursing, Dayton, OH 45435. Offerings include child and adolescent health (MS). *Degree requirements:* Thesis or alternative required, foreign language not required. *Average time to degree:* master's–2 years full-time, 5 years part-time. *Entrance requirements:* GRE General Test, TOEFL (minimum score 550), BSN from NLN-accredited college, Ohio RN license. Application deadline: 4/15 (priority date). Application fee: $25. *Tuition:* $5109 per year full-time, $161 per credit hour part-time for state residents; $9039 per year full-time, $282 per credit hour part-time for nonresidents. • Application contact: Theresa Haghnazarian, Director of Student and Alumni Affairs, 937-775-3133. Fax: 937-775-4571.

Medical/Surgical Nursing

Adelphi University, School of Nursing, Program in Adult Health Nursing, Garden City, NY 11530. Awards MS, PMC. One or more programs accredited by NLN. Part-time and evening/weekend programs available. Students: 19 part-time (18 women); includes 7 minority (1 African American, 6 Asian Americans). Average age 39. *Degree requirements:* For master's, thesis required, foreign language not required. *Entrance requirements:* For master's, BSN, clinical experience. Application deadline: rolling. Application fee: $50. *Expenses:* Tuition $16,000 per year full-time, $485 per credit part-time. Fees $500 per year full-time, $150 per semester part-time. *Financial aid:* Research assistantships, teaching assistantships, graduate achievement awards, and career-related internships or fieldwork available. Aid available to part-time students. Financial aid application deadline: 3/1. • Dr. Caryle G. Wolahan, Director, School of Nursing, 516-877-4545.

Boston College, School of Nursing, Chestnut Hill, MA 02167-9991. Offerings include adult health nursing (MS). Accredited by NLN. School faculty: 18 full-time (all women), 1 (woman) part-time. *Degree requirements:* Oral comprehensive exam, research project required, foreign language and thesis not required. *Average time to degree:* doctorate–4 years full-time. *Entrance requirements:* GRE General Test, bachelor's degree in nursing. Application deadline: 3/1 (priority date; 10/15 for spring admission). Application fee: $40. Electronic applications accepted. *Expenses:* Tuition $626 per semester hour. Fees $80 per year (minimum) full-time, $30 per semester part-time. • Dr. Barbara Munro, Dean, 617-552-4251. Fax: 617-552-0931. E-mail: barbara.munro@bc.edu. Application contact: Dana Robinson, Administrative Secretary, 617-552-4059. Fax: 617-552-0745. E-mail: dana.robinson@bc.edu.

Case Western Reserve University, Frances Payne Bolton School of Nursing, Master's Program in Nursing, Nurse Practitioner Program, Cleveland, OH 44106. Offerings include acute care adult nurse practitioner (MSN), adult practitioner (MSN). One or more programs accredited by NLN. *Degree requirements:* Thesis optional, foreign language not required. *Entrance requirements:* GRE General Test or MAT. Application deadline: 6/1 (rolling processing). Application fee: $75. *Tuition:* $18,400 per year full-time, $767 per credit hour part-time. • Application contact: Molly Blank, Admission Counselor, 216-368-2529. Fax: 216-368-3542. E-mail: mab44@po.cwru.edu.

Case Western Reserve University, Frances Payne Bolton School of Nursing, Master's Program in Nursing, Program in Critical Care Nursing, Cleveland, OH 44106. Awards MSN. Accredited by NLN. Students: 5 part-time; includes 3 international. 3 applicants, 67% accepted. In 1997, 3 degrees awarded. *Degree requirements:* Thesis optional, foreign language not required. *Entrance requirements:* GRE General Test or MAT. Application deadline: 6/1 (priority date; rolling processing). Application fee: $75. *Tuition:* $18,400 per year full-time, $767 per credit hour part-time. *Financial aid:* Fellowships, research assistantships, teaching assistantships, partial tuition waivers, institutionally sponsored loans available. Aid available to part-time students. Financial aid application deadline: 6/30. • Application contact: Molly Blank, Admission Counselor, 216-368-2529. Fax: 216-368-3542. E-mail: mab44@po.cwru.edu.

Case Western Reserve University, Frances Payne Bolton School of Nursing, Master's Program in Nursing, Program in Medical-Surgical Nursing, Cleveland, OH 44106. Awards MSN. Accredited by NLN. Students: 4 full-time, 12 part-time; includes 3 international. 2 applicants, 50% accepted. In 1997, 2 degrees awarded. *Degree requirements:* Thesis optional, foreign language not required. *Entrance requirements:* GRE General Test or MAT. Application deadline: 6/1 (priority date; rolling processing). Application fee: $75. *Tuition:* $18,400 per year full-time, $767 per credit hour part-time. *Financial aid:* Fellowships, research assistantships, teaching assistantships, partial tuition waivers, institutionally sponsored loans available. Aid available to part-time students. Financial aid application deadline: 6/30. *Faculty research:* Clinical nursing, oncology, acute care, critical care. • Application contact: Molly Blank, Admission Counselor, 216-368-2529. Fax: 216-368-3542. E-mail: mab44@po.cwru.edu.

The Catholic University of America, School of Nursing, Washington, DC 20064. Offerings include advanced practice nursing (MSN), with options in administration of nursing service, adult nurse practitioner, education, family nurse practitioner, geriatric nurse practitioner, pediatric nurse practitioner, psychiatric-mental health, school health nurse practitioner. Accredited by NLN. School faculty: 18 full-time (all women), 2 part-time (both women), 19 FTE. *Degree requirements:* Comprehensive exam required, thesis optional, foreign language not required. *Entrance requirements:* GRE General Test (minimum combined score of 1350 on three sections). Application deadline: 8/1 (priority date; rolling processing; 12/1 for spring admission). Application fee: $50. *Expenses:* Tuition $17,325 per year full-time, $668 per credit hour part-time. Fees $680 per year full-time, $360 per year part-time. • Sr. Mary Jean Flaherty, Dean, 202-319-5403.

College of Mount Saint Vincent, Department of Nursing, Riverdale, NY 10471-1093. Offerings include adult nurse practitioner (MS), nursing for the adult and aged (MS). One or more programs accredited by NLN. Department faculty: 3 full-time (all women), 15 part-time (all women). *Degree requirements:* Computer language, written research project required, foreign language and thesis not required. *Entrance requirements:* Bachelor's degree from NLN-accredited institution, minimum GPA of 3.0. Application deadline: 6/15 (priority date; rolling processing; 12/1 for spring admission). Application fee: $50. • Dr. Barbara Cohen, Director, 718-405-3352. Application contact: Dr. Kem Louie, Chairperson, 718-405-3355.

Columbia University, School of Nursing, Program in Adult Nurse Practitioner, New York, NY 10032. Awards MS, Adv C. One or more programs accredited by NLN. Part-time programs available. Faculty: 4 full-time (all women), 3 part-time (all women). Students: 90 part-time (83 women); includes 28 minority (8 African Americans, 17 Asian Americans, 3 Hispanics). Average age 36. 66 applicants, 76% accepted. In 1997, 20 master's awarded. *Entrance requirements:* For master's, GRE General Test (minimum score 500 on verbal and analytical sections), BSN, 1 year of clinical experience (preferred), or completion of a clinical residency; for Adv C, MSN, previous course work in statistics, clinical preceptorship. Application deadline: 4/1 (rolling processing; 10/1 for spring admission). Application fee: $60. *Tuition:* $19,376 per year full-time, $692 per credit (minimum) part-time. *Financial aid:* Teaching assistantships available. Financial aid application deadline: 2/1. • Prof. Joanne Falletta, Director, 212-305-2804. Application contact: Joseph Tomaino, Assistant Dean for Student Services, 212-305-5756. E-mail: jt238@columbia.edu.

Columbia University, School of Nursing, Program in Critical Care Nurse Practitioner, New York, NY 10032. Awards MS. Accredited by NLN. Part-time programs available. Faculty: 1 (woman) full-time, 3 part-time (all women). Students: 45 part-time (41 women); includes 26 minority (5 African Americans, 20 Asian Americans, 1 Hispanic). Average age 30. 28 applicants, 86% accepted. In 1997, 18 degrees awarded. *Entrance requirements:* GRE General Test (minimum score 500 on verbal and analytical sections), BSN, 1 year of clinical experience (preferred), or completion of a clinical residency. Application deadline: 4/1 (priority date; rolling processing; 10/1 for spring admission). Application fee: $60. *Tuition:* $19,376 per year full-time, $692 per credit (minimum) part-time. *Financial aid:* Teaching assistantships available. Financial aid application deadline: 2/1. • Prof. Joan Valas, Director, 212-305-8563. Application contact: Joseph Tomaino, Assistant Dean for Student Services, 212-305-5756. E-mail: jt238@columbia.edu.

Columbia University, School of Nursing, Program in Emergency Nurse Practitioner, New York, NY 10032. Awards MS, Adv C. One or more programs accredited by NLN. Part-time programs available. Faculty: 1 (woman) full-time, 3 part-time (all women). *Entrance requirements:* For master's, GRE General Test (minimum score 500 on verbal and analytical sections), BSN, 1 year of clinical experience (preferred), or completion of a clinical residency. Application deadline: 4/1 (priority date; rolling processing; 10/1 for spring admission). Application fee: $60. *Tuition:* $19,376 per year full-time, $692 per credit (minimum) part-time. *Financial aid:* Teaching assistantships available. Financial aid application deadline: 2/1. • Prof. Joan Vaias, Director, 212-305-8563. Application contact: Joseph Tomaino, Assistant Dean for Student Services, 212-305-5756. E-mail: jt238@columbia.edu.

Duke University, School of Nursing, Durham, NC 27708-0586. Offerings include acute care adult (Certificate); adult cardiovascular (Certificate); adult oncological/HIV (Certificate); clinical nurse specialist (MSN), with options in acute care pediatric, adult oncological/HIV, gerontological, neonatal, pediatric; nurse practitioner (MSN), with options in acute care adult, acute care pediatric, adult cardiovascular, adult oncological/HIV, family, gerontological, neonatal, pediatric. One or more programs accredited by NLN. Postbaccalaureate distance learning degree programs offered (minimal on-campus study). School faculty: 24 full-time (22 women), 4 part-time (all women). *Degree requirements:* For master's, computer language required, thesis optional, foreign language not required. *Average time to degree:* master's–1.5 years full-time, 3 years part-time; other advanced degree–1 year full-time, 2 years part-time. *Entrance requirements:* For master's, GRE General Test or MAT, BSN, minimum GPA of 3.0, previous course work in statistics, RN license, 1 year of nursing experience. Application deadline: 4/1 (priority date; rolling processing; 10/1 for spring admission). Application fee: $50. *Tuition:* $20,976 per year full-time, $552 per unit part-time. • Dr. Mary T. Champagne, Dean, 919-684-3786. E-mail: champ001@mc.duke.edu. Application contact: Judith K. Carter, Admissions Officer, 919-684-4248. Fax: 919-681-8899. E-mail: carte026@mc.duke.edu.

Emory University, Nell Hodgson Woodruff School of Nursing, Atlanta, GA 30322-1100. Offerings include adult health (MSN), with options in adult medical/surgical/nurse practitioner, adult oncology/nurse practitioner, critical care/nurse practitioner, psychosocial nurse practitioner. Accredited by NLN. Postbaccalaureate distance learning degree programs offered (minimal on-campus study). School faculty: 33 full-time (32 women), 21 part-time (19 women), 48 FTE. *Degree requirements:* Thesis optional, foreign language not required. *Average time to degree:* master's–1.5 years full-time, 3 years part-time. *Entrance requirements:* GRE General Test (minimum combined score of 1500 on three sections) or MAT (minimum score 35), minimum GPA of 3.0, BS in nursing or RN license and additional course work. Application deadline: 2/1 (priority date; rolling processing; 11/1 for spring admission). Application fee: $50. *Expenses:* Tuition $18,050 per year. Fees $200 per year. • Dr. Dyanne D. Affonso, Dean, 404-727-7976. Fax: 404-727-0536. Application contact: Debbie Ashtiani, Director, 404-727-7980.

Florida Atlantic University, College of Nursing, Programs in Adult and Family Care Practitioner, Boca Raton, FL 33431-0991. Offerings include adult health (MS), adult practitioner (MS, Post Master's Certificate). One or more programs accredited by NLN and NLN. Faculty: 18 full-time (15 women), 8 part-time (7 women). *Degree requirements:* For master's, thesis or alternative required, foreign language not required. *Average time to degree:* master's–2 years full-time, 3 years part-time. *Entrance requirements:* For master's, GRE General Test (minimum combined score of 1000), minimum GPA of 3.0. Application deadline: 6/1 (rolling processing; 10/15 for spring admission). Application fee: $20. *Expenses:* Tuition $2520 per year full-time, $140 per credit hour part-time for state residents; $8712 per year full-time, $484 per credit hour part-time for nonresidents. Fees $5 per year (minimum). • Dr. Ellis Quinn Youngkin, Graduate Program Coordinator, 561-297-3384. Fax: 561-297-3652. E-mail: eyoungkin@fau.edu.

Gannon University, School of Graduate Studies, College of Sciences, Engineering, and Health Sciences, School of Health Sciences, Department of Nursing, Erie, PA 16505. Offerings include medical-surgical nursing (MSN). Accredited by NLN. *Degree requirements:* Thesis. *Entrance requirements:* GRE General Test (minimum score 500 on each section), MAT (minimum score 60), bachelor's degree from a NLN-approved nursing program, interview, Pennsylvania RN license. Application deadline: 4/15. Application fee: $25. • Dr. Beverly Bartlett, Director, 814-871-5520. Application contact: Beth Nemenz, Director of Admissions, 814-871-7240. Fax: 814-871-5803. E-mail: admissions@gannon.edu.

George Mason University, College of Nursing and Health Science, Fairfax, VA 22030-4444. Offerings include advanced clinical nursing (MSN). Accredited by NLN. College faculty: 50 full-time (46 women), 26 part-time (24 women), 61.65 FTE. *Entrance requirements:* RN license (MSN), minimum GPA of 3.0 in last 60 hours. Application deadline: 5/1 (11/1 for spring admission). Application fee: $30. Electronic applications accepted. *Tuition:* $4344 per year full-time, $181 per credit hour part-time for state residents; $12,504 per year full-time, $521 per credit hour part-time for nonresidents. • Dr. Rita M. Carty, Dean, 703-993-1919. Application contact: Dr. James D. Vail, Associate Dean, Graduate Programs and Research, 703-993-1913. Fax: 703-993-1942. E-mail: jvail@osf1.gmu.edu.

Gwynedd–Mercy College, Graduate Program in Nursing, Gwynedd Valley, PA 19437-0901. Offerings include nurse practitioner (MSN), with options in adult, pediatric. Accredited by NLN. MSN (pediatrics, oncology) admissions temporarily suspended. Program faculty: 9 full-time (all women), 8 part-time (6 women). *Degree requirements:* Thesis or research project required, foreign language not required. *Average time to degree:* master's–2.5 years full-time, 3.5 years part-time. *Entrance requirements:* GRE General Test (minimum combined score of 1350; average 1401), MAT (minimum score 40; average 48), 1 year of experience, physical assessment, previous course work in statistics. Application deadline: 8/1 (priority date; rolling processing). Application fee: $25. *Expenses:* Tuition $375 per credit. Fees $150 per year full-time, $80 per year part-time. • Dr. Mary Dressler, Dean, 215-641-5533. E-mail: dressler.m@gmc.edu. Application contact: Dr. Barbara A. Jones, Associate Professor, 215-646-7300 Ext. 407. Fax: 215-641-5517.

Hunter College of the City University of New York, Hunter-Bellevue School of Nursing, Program in Adult Nurse Practitioner, 695 Park Avenue, New York, NY 10021-5085. Awards MS. Accredited by NLN. Faculty: 6 full-time (all women). Students: 3 full-time (1 woman), 32 part-time (29 women); includes 11 minority (2 African Americans, 8 Asian Americans, 1 Hispanic). Average age 35. 53 applicants, 72% accepted. *Degree requirements:* Practicum required, foreign language and thesis not required. *Entrance requirements:* TOEFL (minimum score 550), minimum GPA of 3.0, New York RN license. Application deadline: 4/27 (rolling processing; 11/21 for spring admission). Application fee: $40. *Expenses:* Tuition $4350 per year full-time, $185 per credit part-time for state residents; $7600 per year full-time, $320 per credit part-time for nonresidents. Fees $26 per year. *Financial aid:* Application deadline 5/1. *Faculty research:* Adult primary care, critical care. • Dr. Carole Birdsall, Coordinator, 212-481-4454. Fax: 212-481-5078. E-mail: cbirdsal@hejira.hunter.cuny.edu. Application contact: Audrey Berman, Associate Director for Graduate Admissions, 212-772-4490.

Hunter College of the City University of New York, Hunter-Bellevue School of Nursing, Program in Medical/Surgical Nursing, 695 Park Avenue, New York, NY 10021-5085. Awards MS. Accredited by NLN. Part-time programs available. Faculty: 10 full-time (all women). Students: 3 full-time (all women), 33 part-time (30 women); includes 15 minority (9 African Americans, 4 Asian Americans, 2 Hispanics). Average age 35. 19 applicants, 63% accepted. In 1997, 6 degrees awarded (100% found work related to degree). *Degree requirements:* Practicum required, foreign language and thesis not required. *Average time to degree:* master's–1.5 years full-time, 3 years part-time. *Entrance requirements:* TOEFL (minimum score 550), minimum GPA of 3.0, New York RN license. Application deadline: 4/27 (rolling processing; 11/21 for spring admission). Application fee: $40. *Expenses:* Tuition $4350 per year full-time, $185 per credit part-time for state residents; $7600 per year full-time, $320 per credit part-time for nonresidents. Fees $26 per year. *Financial aid:* Traineeships, partial tuition waivers, Federal Work-Study available. Aid available to part-time students. Financial aid application deadline: 5/1; applicants required to submit FAFSA. *Faculty research:* Relationship of activity and self-concept in patients after bypass surgery, health focus of control in patients with pacemakers. • Dr. Steven Baumann, Coordinator, 212-481-4457. Fax: 212-481-5078. E-mail: sbaumann@shiva.hunter.cuny.edu. Application contact: Audrey Berman, Associate Director for Graduate Admissions, 212-772-4490.

Jewish Hospital College of Nursing and Allied Health, Program in Nursing, St. Louis, MO 63110-1091. Offerings include adult nurse practitioner (MSN). College faculty: 10. *Application deadline:* rolling. *Application fee:* $25. *Tuition:* $320 per credit hour. • Dr. Sandra A. Jones, Director, 314-454-8416. Application contact: Connie Stohlman, Chief Admissions Officer, 314-454-7538.

Johns Hopkins University, School of Nursing, Dual Major in Clinical Specialist/Management, Baltimore, MD 21218-2699. Offerings include adult health (MSN). Accredited by NLN. Faculty: 13 full-time (12 women), 3 part-time (2 women), 15 FTE. *Degree requirements:* Scholarly project required, thesis optional, foreign language not required. *Average time to degree:* master's–5 years part-time. *Entrance requirements:* GRE, interview, minimum GPA of 3.0. Application deadline: 3/1 (priority date; rolling processing; 11/15 for spring admission). Application fee: $40. • Jacqueline Dienemann, Associate Professor, 410-614-5301. Fax: 410-955-7463. E-mail: jackied@son.jhmi.edu. Application contact: Mary O'Rourke, Director of Admissions/Student Services, 410-955-7548. Fax: 410-614-7086. E-mail: orourke@son.jhmi.edu.

Johns Hopkins University, School of Nursing, Program in Advanced Practice Nursing/Clinical Specialist, Baltimore, MD 21218-2699. Offerings include adult health (MSN). Accredited by NLN. Program faculty: 10 full-time (9 women), 2 part-time (1 woman), 11 FTE. *Degree requirements:* Scholarly project required, thesis optional, foreign language not required. *Average time to degree:* master's–1.5 years full-time, 4 years part-time. *Entrance requirements:* GRE, interview, minimum GPA of 3.0. Application deadline: 3/1 (priority date; rolling processing). Application fee: $40. • Patricia Grimm, Head, 410-614-5302. Fax: 410-955-7463. E-mail: pgrimm@son.jhmi.edu. Application contact: Mary O'Rourke, Director of Admissions/Student Services, 410-955-7548. Fax: 410-614-7086. E-mail: orourke@son.jhmi.edu.

See in-depth description on page 1433.

Johns Hopkins University, School of Nursing, Program in Advanced Practice Nursing (Nurse Practitioner), Baltimore, MD 21218-2699. Offerings include advanced practice nursing-nurse practitioner (MSN), with options in adult acute/critical care, adult and pediatric primary care, family primary care; nurse practitioner (Certificate), with options in adult acute/critical care, adult or pediatric primary care, family primary care. One or more programs accredited by NLN. MSN, Certificate (family primary care) new for fall 1998. Program faculty: 16 full-time (15 women), 9 part-time (8 women), 18 FTE. *Degree requirements:* For master's, scholarly project required, thesis optional, foreign language not required. *Average time to degree:* master's–1 year full-time, 2 years part-time. *Entrance requirements:* For master's, GRE, interview, minimum GPA of 3.0. Application deadline: 3/1. Application fee: $40. • Stella Shiber, Head, 410-614-4081. Fax: 410-955-7463. E-mail: sshiber@son.jhmi.edu. Application contact: Mary O'Rourke, Director of Admissions/Student Services, 410-955-7548. Fax: 410-614-7086. E-mail: orourke@son.jhmi.edu.

See in-depth description on page 1433.

Kent State University, School of Nursing, Kent, OH 44242-0001. Offerings include clinical nursing (MSN), with options in nursing of the adult (medical/surgical nursing), psychiatric mental health nursing. Accredited by NLN. School faculty: 29 full-time. *Degree requirements:* Thesis optional, foreign language not required. *Entrance requirements:* Minimum GPA of 2.75. Application deadline: 7/12 (rolling processing; 11/29 for spring admission). Application fee: $30. *Tuition:* $4752 per year full-time, $216 per credit hour part-time for state residents; $9213 per year full-time, $419 per credit hour part-time for nonresidents. • Dr. Davina Gosnell, Dean, 330-672-7930. Fax: 330-672-2433.

La Roche College, Program in Nursing, Pittsburgh, PA 15237-5898. Offerings include critical care nursing (MSN). Accredited by NLN. Program faculty: 5 full-time (all women), 2 part-time (both women). *Degree requirements:* Internship, practicum required, thesis optional, foreign language not required. *Entrance requirements:* GRE General Test (minimum combined score of 1200), TOEFL (minimum score 500). Application fee: $25. *Tuition:* $431 per credit. • Dr. Kathleen Sullivan, Division Chair, 412-536-1169. Application contact: Judy Henry, Manager of Nursing Student Enrollment, 412-536-1267. Fax: 412-536-1283.

La Salle University, Program in Nursing, 1900 West Olney Avenue, Philadelphia, PA 19141-1199. Offerings include clinical nurse specialist, adult health and illness (MSN); nurse practitioner/primary care of adults (MSN). One or more programs accredited by NLN. MSN (wound, ostomy, and continence nursing) new for fall 1998. Program faculty: 13 full-time (12 women), 8 part-time (all women). *Entrance requirements:* GRE or MAT, BSN, Pennsylvania RN license. Application deadline: rolling. Application fee: $30. • Dr. Zane R. Wolf, Dean, 215-951-1430. E-mail: wolf@lasalle.edu. Application contact: Dr. Janice Beitz, Graduate Director, 215-951-1430. Fax: 215-951-1896. E-mail: beitz@lasalle.edu.

Lehman College of the City University of New York, Division of Natural and Social Sciences, Department of Nursing, 250 Bedford Park Boulevard West, Bronx, NY 10468-1589. Offerings include adult health nursing (MS). Accredited by NLN. Department faculty: 13 full-time (12 women). *Entrance requirements:* Bachelor's degree in nursing, New York RN license. Application deadline: 4/1 (rolling processing; 11/1 for spring admission). Application fee: $40. *Expenses:* Tuition $4350 per year full-time, $185 per credit part-time for state residents; $7600 per year full-time, $320 per credit part-time for nonresidents. Fees $120 per year full-time, $80 per year part-time. • Ngo Nkongho, Chair, 718-960-8374. Application contact: Keville Frederickson, Director of Graduate Studies, 718-960-8378. Fax: 718-960-8488.

Louisiana State University Medical Center, School of Nursing, 433 Bolivar Street, New Orleans, LA 70112-2223. Offerings include adult health and illness (MN), adult health and nursing (DNS). One or more programs accredited by NLN. School faculty: 10 full-time (all women), 4 part-time (3 women). *Degree requirements:* For master's, thesis optional, foreign language not required; for doctorate, dissertation required, foreign language not required. *Entrance requirements:* For master's, GRE General Test, MAT (minimum score 50), TOEFL, minimum GPA of 3.0; for doctorate, GRE General Test (minimum combined score of 1500 on three sections), TOEFL (minimum score 550), minimum GPA of 3.5. Application deadline: 3/17. Application fee: $50. *Expenses:* Tuition $2878 per year full-time, $421 per semester (minimum) part-time for state residents; $6003 per year full-time, $838 per semester (minimum) part-time for nonresidents. Fees $350 per year full-time, $90 per semester (minimum) part-time. • Dr. Elizabeth Humphrey, Dean, 504-568-4106. Application contact: Dr. Barbara C. Donlon, Acting Director, 504-568-4137. Fax: 504-568-3308. E-mail: bdonlo@lsumc.edu.

Loyola University Chicago, Graduate School, Marcella Niehoff School of Nursing, Adult Nurse Clinical Nursing Specialist Program, 820 North Michigan Avenue, Chicago, IL 60611-2196. Awards MSN. Accredited by NLN. Part-time programs available. Students: 16 part-time (all women); includes 1 minority (African American). Average age 29. 16 applicants, 69% accepted. In 1997, 6 degrees awarded. *Degree requirements:* Comprehensive exam or oral thesis defense required, foreign language not required. *Entrance requirements:* GRE General Test (minimum combined score of 1350 on three sections), BSN, minimum GPA of 3.0, professional license, clinical experience. Application deadline: rolling. Application fee: $35. *Tuition:* $467 per semester hour. *Financial aid:* Teaching assistantships, assistantships, traineeships available. Financial aid application deadline: 3/1; applicants required to submit FAFSA. *Faculty research:* Oncology nursing, coping/quality of life in cardiac transplant, osteoporosis, hormone replacement, women and heart disease. • Application contact: Dr. Marcia Maurer, Associate Dean and Director of Graduate Programs, 773-508-3261. Fax: 773-508-3241. E-mail: mmaurer@luc.edu.

Loyola University Chicago, Graduate School, Marcella Niehoff School of Nursing, Adult Nurse Practitioner Program, 820 North Michigan Avenue, Chicago, IL 60611-2196. Awards MSN. Accredited by NLN. Part-time programs available. Students: 3 full-time (all women), 36 part-time (34 women); includes 1 minority (African American). Average age 29. 12 applicants, 83% accepted. In 1997, 3 degrees awarded. *Degree requirements:* Comprehensive exam or oral thesis defense required, foreign language not required. *Entrance requirements:* GRE General Test (minimum combined score of 1350 on three sections), BSN, minimum GPA of 3.0, professional license. Application deadline: rolling. Application fee: $35. *Tuition:* $467 per semester hour. *Financial aid:* In 1997–98, 2 traineeships (both to first-year students) were awarded. Financial aid application deadline: 3/1. *Faculty research:* Menopause. • Application contact: Dr. Marcia Maurer, Associate Dean and Director of Graduate Programs, 773-508-3261. Fax: 773-508-3241. E-mail: mmaurer@luc.edu.

Madonna University, Program in Nursing, Livonia, MI 48150-1173. Offerings include adult health: chronic health conditions (MSN). Accredited by NLN. Program faculty: 13 full-time (all women), 3 part-time (1 woman). *Degree requirements:* Thesis or alternative required, foreign language not required. *Entrance requirements:* GRE General Test. Application deadline: 8/1 (priority date; rolling processing; 4/1 for spring admission). *Expenses:* Tuition $260 per credit hour (minimum). Fees $50 per semester. • Dr. Mary Eddy, Coordinator of Graduate Nursing, 734-432-5461. Fax: 734-432-5463. E-mail: eddy@smtp.munet.edu. Application contact: Sandra Kellums, Coordinator of Graduate Admissions, 734-432-5666. Fax: 734-432-5393. E-mail: kellums@smtp.munet.edu.

Marquette University, College of Nursing, Milwaukee, WI 53201-1881. Offerings include adult nurse practitioner (Certificate); advanced practice nursing (MSN), with options in adult, children, neonatal nurse practitioner, nurse-midwifery, older adult. One or more programs accredited by NLN. College faculty: 24 full-time (23 women), 5 part-time (4 women). *Degree requirements:* For master's, thesis or alternative, comprehensive exam required, foreign language not required. *Entrance requirements:* For master's, GRE General Test, TOEFL (minimum score 550), BSN, RN, Wisconsin license. Application fee: $40. *Tuition:* $490 per credit. • Dr. Madeline Wake, Dean, 414-288-3812. Application contact: Dr. Gregory Olson, Associate Dean, 414-288-3808. Fax: 414-288-1578.

Marymount University, School of Health Professions, Programs in Nursing, Program in Critical Care Nursing, Arlington, VA 22207-4299. Awards MSN. Accredited by NLN. *Degree requirements:* Thesis or alternative required, foreign language not required. *Entrance requirements:* 2 years of clinical experience, interview, minimum GPA of 3.0, RN license. Application deadline: rolling. Application fee: $35. *Expenses:* Tuition $465 per credit hour. Fees $120 per year full-time, $5 per credit hour part-time. • Dr. Catherine Connelly, Dean, School of Health Professions, 703-284-1580. Fax: 703-284-3819. E-mail: catherine.connelly@marymount.edu.

Medical College of Georgia, Graduate Programs in Nursing, Augusta, GA 30912-1500. Offerings include adult nursing (MSN). Accredited by NLN. Faculty: 17 full-time (14 women). *Application deadline:* 6/30 (priority date; rolling processing). *Application fee:* $0. *Expenses:* Tuition $2670 per year full-time, $111 per credit part-time for state residents; $10,680 per year full-time, $445 per credit part-time for nonresidents. Fees $286 per year. • Dr. Virginia Kemp, Associate Dean, 706-721-4710. E-mail: vkemp@mail.mcg.edu. Application contact: Dr. Gary C. Bond, Associate Dean, 706-721-3278. Fax: 706-721-6829. E-mail: gradstud@mail.mcg.edu.

Medical University of South Carolina, College of Nursing, Program in Nursing, Charleston, SC 29425-0002. Offerings include adult health nursing (MSN). Accredited by NLN. *Degree requirements:* Computer language required, thesis optional, foreign language not required. *Entrance requirements:* GRE General Test (minimum combined score of 1000), BSN, previous course work in statistics and physical assessment, 1 year nursing experience, license. Application deadline: 2/15 (10/15 for spring admission). Application fee: $55. *Expenses:* Tuition $3760 per year full-time, $173 per semester hour part-time for state residents; $5672 per year full-time, $270 per semester hour part-time for nonresidents. Fees $280 per year (minimum). • Dr. Jean Leuner, Associate Dean, 843-792-8515. Application contact: Office of Enrollment Services, 843-792-3281.

Molloy College, Department of Nursing, 1000 Hempstead Avenue, Rockville Centre, NY 11571-5002. Offerings include adult nurse practitioner (MSN, Advanced Certificate). Department faculty: 16 full-time (14 women), 12 part-time (9 women). *Degree requirements:* For master's, thesis optional, foreign language not required. *Average time to degree:* master's–2.2 years full-time, 3.7 years part-time; other advanced degree–1 year full-time, 2 years part-time. *Entrance requirements:* For master's, BS in nursing, minimum undergraduate GPA of 3.0; for Advanced Certificate, master's degree in nursing. Application deadline: 9/2 (priority date; rolling processing; 1/20 for spring admission). Application fee: $60. *Expenses:* Tuition $430 per credit. Fees $430 per year full-time, $165 per semester (minimum) part-time. • Dr. Carol A. Clifford, Director, Graduate Program, 516-256-2218. Fax: 516-678-9718. E-mail: clica01@molloy.edu. Application contact: Wayne James, Vice President for Enrollment and Management, 516-678-5000 Ext. 240. Fax: 516-256-2247.

Mount Saint Mary College, Division of Nursing, Newburgh, NY 12550-3494. Offerings include adult nurse practitioner (MS), with options in nursing education, nursing management; clinical nurse specialist-adult health (MS), with options in nursing education, nursing management. MS (adult nurse practitioner) new for fall 1998. Division faculty: 6 full-time (5 women), 1 (woman) part-time. *Degree requirements:* Computer language, research project required, foreign language and thesis not required. *Entrance requirements:* GRE General Test (minimum combined score of 1200; average 1400) or MAT (minimum score 40), BSN, minimum GPA of 3.0, RN license. Application deadline: 5/3 (priority date; 10/31 for spring admission). Application fee: $20. *Expenses:* Tuition $367 per credit. Fees $30 per year. • Sr. Leona DeBoer, Coordinator, 914-569-3138. Fax: 914-562-6762. E-mail: deboer@msmc.edu.

New York University, School of Education, Division of Nursing, Programs in Advanced Practice Nursing, New York, NY 10012-1019. Offerings include adult nurse practitioner acute care (MA), adult nurse practitioner primary care (MA), advanced practice nursing: adult (AC). One or more programs accredited by NLN. MA/MS offered jointly with the Program in Management in the Robert F. Wagner Graduate School of Public Service. Faculty: 25 full-time, 9 part-time. *Entrance requirements:* For master's, TOEFL; for AC, TOEFL, master's degree. Application deadline: 2/1 (priority date; rolling processing; 12/1 for spring admission). Application fee: $40 ($60 for international students). • Judi Haber, Director, 212-998-5300. Application contact: Office of Graduate Admissions, 212-998-5030. Fax: 212-995-4328.

Oakland University, School of Nursing, Program in Adult Health, Rochester, MI 48309-4401. Awards MSN. Students: 3 full-time (all women), 69 part-time (66 women); includes 4 minority (1 African American, 3 Asian Americans). Average age 37. 36 applicants, 86% accepted. In 1997, 19 degrees awarded. *Entrance requirements:* GRE General Test, minimum GPA of 3.0 for unconditional admission. Application deadline: 7/15 (3/15 for spring admission). Application fee: $30. *Expenses:* Tuition $3852 per year full-time, $214 per credit hour part-time for state residents; $8532 per year full-time, $474 per credit hour part-time for nonresidents. Fees $420 per year. *Financial aid:* Full tuition waivers, Federal Work-Study, institutionally sponsored loans available. Financial aid application deadline: 3/1; applicants required to submit FAFSA. • Dr. Diane Wilson, Director, 248-370-4484.

Oregon Health Sciences University, School of Nursing, Program in Adult Health and Illness Nursing, 3181 SW Sam Jackson Park Road, Portland, OR 97201-3098. Awards MN, MS, Post Master's Certificate. One or more programs accredited by NLN. Students: 4 full-time (all women), 12 part-time (11 women); includes 2 minority (1 Asian American, 1 Hispanic). 12 applicants, 50% accepted. In 1997, 8 master's awarded. *Degree requirements:* For master's, thesis optional, foreign language not required. *Entrance requirements:* For master's, GRE General Test (minimum combined score of 1000), bachelor's degree in nursing, minimum undergraduate GPA of 3.0; for Post Master's Certificate, master's degree in nursing. Application deadline: 1/15. Application fee: $40. *Financial aid:* Career-related internships or fieldwork available. • Application contact: Office of Recruitment, 503-494-7725. Fax: 503-494-4350.

Otterbein College, Program in Nursing, Westerville, OH 43081. Offerings include adult health care (MSN), adult health practitioner (Certificate). Postbaccalaureate distance learning degree

Directory: Medical/Surgical Nursing

Otterbein College (continued)
programs offered. *Application deadline:* rolling. *Application fee:* $35. *Tuition:* $5216 per quarter. • Dr. Judy Strayer, Chair, 614-823-1614. Fax: 614-823-3131.

Pontifical Catholic University of Puerto Rico, College of Sciences, Department of Nursing, Ponce, PR 00731-6382. Offerings include medical-surgical nursing (MS). Accredited by NLN. Department faculty: 3 full-time (all women), 2 part-time (both women). *Degree requirements:* Clinical research paper. *Entrance requirements:* GRE General Test, minimum GPA of 2.5, BSN, 2 years of work experience, RN license. Application deadline: 4/30 (priority date; rolling processing). Application fee: $15. Electronic applications accepted. • Dr. Carmen L. Madera, Director, 787-841-2000 Ext. 261. Application contact: Manuel Luciano, Director of Admissions, 787-841-2000 Ext. 426. Fax: 787-840-4295.

Rush University, College of Nursing, Department of Medical/Surgical Nursing, Chicago, IL 60612-3832. Offers programs in acute care nurse practitioner (MSN, DN Sc, ND), adult nurse practitioner (MSN, DN Sc, ND), altered immunocompetence clinical specialist (MSN, DN Sc, ND), anesthesia nurse practitioner (MSN, DN Sc, ND), critical care clinical specialist (MSN, DN Sc, ND), medical surgical clinical specialist (MSN, DN Sc, ND). One or more programs accredited by NLN. Part-time programs available. Faculty: 14 full-time (13 women), 17 part-time (all women), 25.18 FTE. Students: 5 full-time, 125 part-time. Average age 36. *Degree requirements:* For doctorate, dissertation required, foreign language not required. *Entrance requirements:* For master's, GRE General Test, interview, previous course work in statistics; for doctorate, MS or GRE General Test, interview, previous course work in statistics. Application deadline: 8/1 (rolling processing; 2/1 for spring admission). Application fee: $40. *Tuition:* $8560 per year full-time, $370 per credit hour part-time. *Financial aid:* Federal Work-Study, institutionally sponsored loans, and career-related internships or fieldwork available. Aid available to part-time students. Financial aid applicants required to submit FAFSA. *Faculty research:* Clinical nutrition in HIV, post-anesthesia care, ostomies and skin care, transplant surgery, critical care pathways. • Dr. Jane Llewellyn, Chairperson, 312-942-7112. Application contact: Hicela Castruita, Director, College Admissions Services, 312-942-7100. Fax: 312-942-2219.

Rutgers, The State University of New Jersey, Newark, College of Nursing, Graduate Program in Acute Care of Adults and Aged, Newark, NJ 07102-3192. Awards MS. Accredited by NLN. Part-time programs available. *Degree requirements:* Comprehensive exam required, foreign language and thesis not required. *Entrance requirements:* GRE General Test, TOEFL, RN license, minimum B average, BS in nursing. Application deadline: 8/15 (rolling processing; 12/15 for spring admission). Application fee: $40. Electronic applications accepted. *Expenses:* Tuition $6248 per year full-time, $257 per credit part-time for state residents; $9160 per year full-time, $380 per credit part-time for nonresidents. Fees $738 per year full-time, $107 per semester (minimum) part-time. *Financial aid:* Application deadline 3/1. • Application contact: Dr. Elaine Dolinsky, Associate Dean for Student Life and Services, 973-353-5060. Fax: 973-353-1277.

Rutgers, The State University of New Jersey, Newark, College of Nursing, Graduate Program in Primary Care of Adults and Aged, Newark, NJ 07102-3192. Awards MS. Accredited by NLN. Part-time programs available. *Degree requirements:* Comprehensive exam required, foreign language and thesis not required. *Entrance requirements:* GRE General Test, TOEFL, RN license, minimum B average, BS in nursing. Application deadline: 8/15 (rolling processing; 12/15 for spring admission). Application fee: $40. Electronic applications accepted. *Expenses:* Tuition $6248 per year full-time, $257 per credit part-time for state residents; $9160 per year full-time, $380 per credit part-time for nonresidents. Fees $738 per year full-time, $107 per semester (minimum) part-time. *Financial aid:* Federal Work-Study, institutionally sponsored loans, and career-related internships or fieldwork available. • Application contact: Dr. Elaine Dolinsky, Associate Dean for Student Life and Services, 973-353-5060. Fax: 973-353-1277.

Sage Graduate School, Graduate School, Division of Nursing, Program in Medical-Surgical Nursing, Troy, NY 12180-4115. Awards MS. Accredited by NLN. Part-time and evening/weekend programs available. *Degree requirements:* Thesis or alternative required, foreign language not required. *Entrance requirements:* BS in nursing, minimum GPA of 2.75. Application deadline: 8/1 (rolling processing; 12/15 for spring admission). Application fee: $25. *Expenses:* Tuition $360 per credit hour. Fees $50 per semester. *Financial aid:* Career-related internships or fieldwork available. Financial aid application deadline: 7/1; applicants required to submit FAFSA. • Application contact: Melissa Robertson, Associate Director of Admissions, 518-244-6878. Fax: 518-244-6880. E-mail: sgsadm@sage.edu.

Saint Louis University, School of Nursing, Program in Adult Nursing, St. Louis, MO 63103-2097. Awards MSN, MSN(R), Certificate, MPH/MSN, MSN/MBA. Offerings include adult nurse practitioner (MSN, MSN(R), Certificate), clinical health care specialist/case manager (MSN, MSN(R), Certificate). One or more programs accredited by NLN. *Degree requirements:* For master's, comprehensive oral exam required, thesis optional, foreign language not required. *Entrance requirements:* For master's, GRE General Test. Application deadline: 7/1 (rolling processing; 11/1 for spring admission). Application fee: $40. *Tuition:* $542 per credit hour. *Financial aid:* Traineeships available. Financial aid application deadline: 4/1. • Dr. S. Ann Perry, Program Director, 314-577-8948. Application contact: Dr. Marcia Buresch, Assistant Dean of the Graduate School, 314-977-2240. Fax: 314-977-3943.

Saint Xavier University, School of Nursing, Chicago, IL 60655-3105. Offerings include adult health clinical nurse specialist (MS). Accredited by NLN. MBA/MS offered in cooperation with the Graham School of Management. School faculty: 10 full-time (all women), 2 part-time (both women). *Entrance requirements:* MAT or GRE General Test, minimum GPA of 3.0, RN license. Application deadline: 2/15 (9/15 for spring admission). Application fee: $35. *Expenses:* Tuition $450 per hour. Fees $50 per year. • Dr. Mary Lebold, Dean, 773-298-3700. Fax: 773-779-9061. E-mail: lebold@sxu.edu. Application contact: Sr. Evelyn McKenna, Vice President of Enrollment Management, 773-298-3050. Fax: 773-298-3076. E-mail: mckenna@sxu.edu.

Seton Hall University, College of Nursing, Department of Graduate Nursing, Advanced Practice in Primary Health Care Program, South Orange, NJ 07079-2697. Offerings include adult nurse practitioner (MSN). Accredited by NLN. Program faculty: 6 full-time (all women), 4 part-time (all women). *Degree requirements:* Research project required, foreign language and thesis not required. *Entrance requirements:* GRE or MAT, BSN. Application deadline: 5/15 (priority date; rolling processing; 11/15 for spring admission). Application fee: $50. *Expenses:* Tuition $500 per credit. Fees $610 per year full-time, $185 per semester part-time. • Dr. Cynthia Hughes, Director, 973-761-9273. Fax: 973-761-9607. E-mail: hughesci@shu.edu.

Southern Illinois University at Edwardsville, School of Nursing, Program in Medical-Surgical Nursing, Edwardsville, IL 62026-0001. Awards MS. Accredited by NLN. Students: 12 full-time (10 women), 35 part-time (33 women); includes 6 minority (4 African Americans, 1 Asian American, 1 Native American). 17 applicants, 71% accepted. In 1997, 10 degrees awarded. *Degree requirements:* Thesis or alternative, final exam required, foreign language not required. *Entrance requirements:* Appropriate bachelor's degree, RN license. Application deadline: 7/24. Application fee: $25. *Expenses:* Tuition $1716 per year full-time, $95 per credit hour part-time for state residents; $5149 per year full-time, $286 per credit hour part-time for nonresidents. Fees $463 per year full-time, $433 per year part-time. *Financial aid:* Fellowships, Federal Work-Study, institutionally sponsored loans available. Aid available to part-time students. • Dr. Felissa Lashley, Dean, School of Nursing, 618-692-3956.

State University of New York at Buffalo, Graduate School, School of Nursing, Buffalo, NY 14260. Offerings include adult health nursing (MS), with options in clinical specialist, nurse practitioner. Accredited by NLN. Postbaccalaureate distance learning degree programs offered (minimal on-campus study). School faculty: 28 full-time (25 women), 13 part-time (12 women). *Entrance requirements:* GRE General Test (minimum score 450 on each section), TOEFL (minimum score 550), interview, minimum GPA of 3.0, RN license. Application deadline: 5/1 (priority date; rolling processing; 10/15 for spring admission). Application fee: $35. *Tuition:* $5970 per year full-time, $288 per credit hour part-time for state residents; $9286 per year full-time, $426 per credit hour part-time for nonresidents. • Dr. Mecca S. Cranley, Dean, 716-829-2533. E-mail: mcranley@nurse.buffalo.edu. Application contact: Dr. William P. Harden, Assistant Dean, 716-829-3314. Fax: 716-829-2021. E-mail: wharden@nurse.buffalo.edu.

State University of New York at Stony Brook, Health Sciences Center, School of Nursing, Program in Adult Health/Primary Care Nursing, Stony Brook, NY 11794. Offers adult health nurse practitioner (Certificate), adult health/primary care nursing (MS). One or more programs accredited by NLN. Students: 53 full-time (50 women), 179 part-time (166 women); includes 30 minority (11 African Americans, 14 Asian Americans, 4 Hispanics, 1 Native American), 1 international. In 1997, 66 master's, 20 Certificates awarded. *Degree requirements:* For master's, thesis required, foreign language not required. *Entrance requirements:* For master's, BSN, minimum GPA of 3.0, previous course work in statistics. Application deadline: 1/15. Application fee: $50. *Expenses:* Tuition $5100 per year full-time, $213 per credit hour part-time for state residents; $8416 per year full-time, $351 per credit hour part-time for nonresidents. Fees $529 per year full-time, $77 per semester (minimum) part-time. *Financial aid:* Application deadline 3/15. • Dr. Kathleen Shurpin, Chair, 516-444-3276. Fax: 516-444-3136. E-mail: kathy_shurpin@notes2.nursing.sunysb.edu.

Texas Woman's University, College of Nursing, Denton, TX 76204. Offerings include adult health nurse (MS), women's health nurse (PhD). One or more programs accredited by NLN. College faculty: 30 full-time (29 women), 12 part-time (10 women). *Degree requirements:* For master's, thesis or alternative required, foreign language not required; for doctorate, 1 foreign language (computer language can substitute), dissertation. *Entrance requirements:* For master's, GRE General Test (minimum combined score of 750), minimum GPA of 3.0; for doctorate, GRE General Test (minimum combined score of 1000), MS in nursing, minimum GPA of 3.0. Application deadline: rolling. Application fee: $25. • Dr. Carolyn S. Gunning, Dean, 940-898-2401.

University of Cincinnati, College of Nursing and Health, Cincinnati, OH 45221-0038. Offerings include adult health nursing (MSN). Accredited by NLN. College faculty: 26 full-time. *Degree requirements:* Project or thesis required, foreign language not required. *Average time to degree:* master's–1.5 years full-time, 2.5 years part-time; doctorate–4 years full-time, 6 years part-time. *Entrance requirements:* GRE General Test. Application deadline: 1/1 (priority date; rolling processing). Application fee: $30. *Tuition:* $7228 per year full-time, $185 per credit hour part-time for state residents; $13,812 per year full-time, $352 per credit hour part-time for nonresidents. • Dr. Andrea Lindell, Dean, 513-558-5330. Application contact: Tom West, Program Coordinator, 513-558-3600. Fax: 513-558-7523. E-mail: tom.west@uc.edu.

University of Colorado at Colorado Springs, Department of Graduate Nursing, Colorado Springs, CO 80933-7150. Offerings include adult health nurse practitioner and clinical specialist (MSN). Accredited by NLN. Postbaccalaureate distance learning degree programs offered (minimal on-campus study). Department faculty: 9 full-time (8 women). *Degree requirements:* Thesis optional, foreign language not required. *Average time to degree:* master's–2.5 years full-time, 5 years part-time. *Entrance requirements:* GRE General Test (minimum combined score of 1400) or MAT (minimum score 50), BSN, GPA of 3.0. Application deadline: 2/15 (priority date; 10/15 for spring admission). Application fee: $40. Electronic applications accepted. *Expenses:* Tuition $4644 per year full-time, $193 per credit hour part-time for state residents; $10,254 per year full-time, $420 per credit hour part-time for nonresidents. Fees $399 per year (minimum) full-time, $106 per year (minimum) part-time. • Barbara Joyce-Nagata, Chair, 719-262-4430. Fax: 719-262-4416.

University of Hawaii at Manoa, College of Health Sciences and Social Welfare, School of Nursing, Honolulu, HI 96822. Offerings include clinical nurse specialist (MS), with options in adult health, community mental health; nurse practitioner (MS), with options in adult health, community mental health, family nurse practitioner. One or more programs accredited by NLN. School faculty: 27 full-time (24 women). *Entrance requirements:* Hawaii RN license. *Tuition:* $4029 per year full-time, $214 per credit hour part-time for state residents; $9957 per year full-time, $461 per credit hour part-time for nonresidents. • Dr. Rosanne Harrigan, Dean, 808-956-8522. Application contact: Office of Student Services, 808-956-8939.

University of Illinois at Chicago, College of Nursing, Program in Medical-Surgical Nursing, Chicago, IL 60607-7128. Awards MS. Accredited by NLN. Faculty: 16 full-time (14 women). Students: 2 full-time (both women), 70 part-time (67 women); includes 14 minority (7 African Americans, 7 Asian Americans), 1 international. 54 applicants, 61% accepted. In 1997, 21 degrees awarded. *Degree requirements:* Thesis or alternative required, foreign language not required. *Entrance requirements:* GRE General Test, TOEFL (minimum score 550), minimum GPA of 3.75 on a 5.0 scale. Application deadline: 5/15 (10/15 for spring admission). Application fee: $40 ($50 for international students). *Financial aid:* In 1997–98, 2 teaching assistantships were awarded; fellowships, research assistantships, partial tuition waivers, Federal Work-Study, institutionally sponsored loans, and career-related internships or fieldwork also available. • Dr. Felissa Cohen, Head, 312-996-7955. Application contact: Kathleen Knafl, Director of Graduate Studies, 312-996-2159.

University of Maryland, Baltimore, Graduate School, School of Nursing, Baltimore, MD 21201-1627. Offerings include medical-surgical nursing (MS). Accredited by NLN. MS/MBA offered jointly with the University of Baltimore. School faculty: 49 (45 women). *Degree requirements:* Thesis or alternative required, foreign language not required. *Entrance requirements:* GRE General Test, TOEFL, minimum GPA of 2.75, previous course work in statistics, BS in nursing. Application fee: $42. *Expenses:* Tuition $253 per credit hour for state residents; $454 per credit hour for nonresidents. Fees $317 per year. • Dr. Barbara Heller, Dean, 410-706-6741. Application contact: Dr. Susan Wozenski, Assistant Dean for Student Affairs, 410-706-0501. Fax: 410-706-7238.

University of Massachusetts Medical Center at Worcester, Graduate School of Nursing, Worcester, MA 01655-0115. Offerings include adult acute/critical care (MS, Certificate), adult ambulatory/community care (MS, Certificate), adult nurse practitioner (MS). One or more programs accredited by NLN. School faculty: 6 full-time (5 women), 4 part-time (all women), 8 FTE. *Average time to degree:* master's–2 years part-time; doctorate–3 years full-time; other advanced degree–1 year full-time. *Entrance requirements:* For master's, GRE General Test, BSN, previous course work in statistics; for Certificate, master's degree. Application deadline: 3/15 (rolling processing). Application fee: $18 ($25 for international students). • Dr. Lillian R. Goodman, Dean, 508-856-5801. E-mail: lillian.goodman@banyan.ummed.edu. Application contact: Kathleen Trumpaitis, Student Coordinator, 508-856-5801. Fax: 508-856-6552. E-mail: kathleen.trumpaitis@banyan.ummed.edu.

University of Miami, School of Nursing, Coral Gables, FL 33124. Offerings include primary health care (MSN), with options in adult nurse practitioner, family nurse practitioner, nurse midwifery. Accredited by NLN. School faculty: 28 full-time (27 women), 1 (woman) part-time. *Degree requirements:* Thesis optional, foreign language not required. *Average time to degree:* master's–2 years full-time, 35 years part-time; doctorate–6.7 years full-time. *Entrance requirements:* GRE General Test, TOEFL (minimum score 550), BSN, minimum GPA of 3.0, RN experience. Application deadline: 3/1 (priority date; rolling processing; 10/1 for spring admission). Application fee: $35. *Expenses:* Tuition $815 per credit hour. Fees $174 per year. • Dr. Diane Horner, Dean, 305-284-2107. Application contact: Heidi McInnis, Director of Student Services, 305-284-4325. Fax: 305-284-5686. E-mail: lemieux@miami.edu.

University of Michigan, School of Nursing, Division of Acute, Critical and Long-Term Care, Program in Adult Acute Care Nurse Practitioner, Ann Arbor, MI 48109. Awards MS. Accredited by NLN. *Degree requirements:* Thesis required, foreign language not required. *Entrance requirements:* GRE General Test. Application deadline: 2/1. Application fee: $55. • Dr. Bonnie Metzger, Director, Division of Acute, Critical and Long-Term Care, 734-763-0010.

University of Michigan, School of Nursing, Division of Acute, Critical and Long-Term Care, Program in Medical-Surgical Nursing, Ann Arbor, MI 48109. Awards MS. One or more programs accredited by NLN. Part-time programs available. *Degree requirements:* Thesis required, foreign language not required. *Entrance requirements:* GRE General Test. Application deadline: rolling. Application fee: $55. *Financial aid:* Fellowships, research assistantships, teaching assistantships, partial tuition waivers, Federal Work-Study available. • Application contact: Graduate Program Secretary, 734-763-0010. Fax: 734-936-5525.

University of Michigan, School of Nursing, Division of Health Promotion and Risk Reduction, Program in Community Health Nursing, Ann Arbor, MI 48109. Offerings include adult primary care/adult nurse practitioner (MS). Accredited by NLN. *Degree requirements:* Thesis required, foreign language not required. *Entrance requirements:* GRE General Test, BS in nursing. Application deadline: 2/1. Application fee: $55. • Dr. Carol Loveland-Cherry, Chairperson, 734-763-0016. Application contact: Graduate Program Secretary, 734-763-0016. Fax: 734-647-0351.

University of Minnesota, Twin Cities Campus, School of Nursing, Program in Adult Health Nursing, Minneapolis, MN 55455-0213. Offers advanced clinical specialist in adult health nursing (MS). Accredited by NLN. Part-time programs available. Students: 2 full-time, 24 part-time. 22 applicants, 77% accepted. *Degree requirements:* Final oral exam, project or thesis. *Application deadline:* 12/15 (rolling processing). *Application fee:* $40 ($50 for international students). *Financial aid:* Fellowships, research assistantships, teaching assistantships available. • Ruth Lindquist, Head, 612-624-5646. Application contact: Kate Hanson, Nursing Recruiter, 612-624-9494. Fax: 612-624-3174. E-mail: hanso041@maroon.tc.umn.edu.

University of Missouri–Kansas City, School of Nursing, Kansas City, MO 64110-2499. Offerings include nurse practitioner (MSN), with options in health care for adults, health care for children, health care for women. Accredited by NLN. School faculty: 17 full-time (15 women), 40 part-time (all women), 37 FTE. *Degree requirements:* Thesis or alternative required, foreign language not required. *Entrance requirements:* Minimum undergraduate GPA of 3.0. Application deadline: 2/1 (9/15 for spring admission). Application fee: $25. *Expenses:* Tuition $182 per credit hour for state residents; $508 per credit hour for nonresidents. Fees $60 per year. • Dr. Nancy Mills, Dean, 816-235-1700. Application contact: Brenda Cain, Student Services Assistant, 816-235-1710. Fax: 816-235-1701.

University of New Mexico, College of Nursing, Albuquerque, NM 87131-2039. Offerings include advanced nursing practice (MSN), with options in adult health nursing, gerontological nursing, parent-child nursing, psychiatric-mental health nursing. Accredited by NLN. College faculty: 38 full-time (36 women), 23 part-time (all women), 46.57 FTE. *Degree requirements:* Thesis optional, foreign language not required. *Entrance requirements:* GRE General Test, interview, minimum GPA of 3.0, previous course work in statistics. Application deadline: 7/15 (11/1 for spring admission). Application fee: $25. *Expenses:* Tuition $2442 per year full-time, $103 per credit hour part-time for state residents; $8691 per year full-time, $103 per credit hour (minimum) part-time for nonresidents. Fees $32 per year. • Dr. Sandra Ferketich, Dean, 505-272-6284. Application contact: Anne-Marie Oechsler, Director, Academic Advisement, 505-272-4224. Fax: 505-272-3970. E-mail: annmarie@unm.edu.

University of Pennsylvania, School of Nursing, Adult Acute/Tertiary Nurse Practitioner Program, Philadelphia, PA 19104. Offerings include tertiary nurse practitioner (MSN), with options in cardiopulmonary, neuroscience, renal metabolic, surgical. Accredited by NLN. *Entrance requirements:* GRE General Test, BSN, minimum GPA of 3.0, previous course work in statistics. Application deadline: 9/1 (rolling processing). Application fee: $65. • Dr. Anne Keane, Director, 215-898-5766. Fax: 215-573-7492. E-mail: akeane@pobox.upenn.edu. Application contact: Susan K. Ogle, Associate Director of Admissions and Student Affairs, 215-898-3301. Fax: 215-573-8439. E-mail: sogle@pobox.upenn.edu.

University of Pennsylvania, School of Nursing, Adult Critical Care Nurse Practitioner Program, Philadelphia, PA 19104. Awards MSN. Accredited by NLN. Part-time programs available. Students: 1 full-time (0 women), 11 part-time (all women); includes 2 minority (1 Asian American, 1 Hispanic). Average age 34. 27 applicants, 63% accepted. In 1997, 9 degrees awarded. *Degree requirements:* 2 years of experience required, foreign language and thesis not required. *Entrance requirements:* GRE General Test, BSN, minimum GPA of 3.0, previous course work in statistics. Application deadline: 9/1 (rolling processing). Application fee: $65. *Financial aid:* Fellowships, research assistantships, teaching assistantships, Federal Work-Study, institutionally sponsored loans, and career-related internships or fieldwork available. Aid available to part-time students. *Faculty research:* Stress; coping with illness, sexuality, and health; quality of life and sexual function in burn victims. • Dr. Rosalyn J. Watts, Director, 215-898-4727. Fax: 215-573-7492 Ext. 7496. E-mail: rwatts@pobox.upenn.edu. Application contact: Susan K. Ogle, Associate Director of Admissions and Student Affairs, 215-898-3301. Fax: 215-573-8439. E-mail: sogle@pobox.upenn.edu.

University of Pennsylvania, School of Nursing, Primary Care Nurse Practitioner Program: Adult, Philadelphia, PA 19104. Awards MSN. Accredited by NLN. Part-time programs available. Students: 3 full-time (all women), 14 part-time (13 women); includes 2 minority (both Asian Americans). 19 applicants, 63% accepted. In 1997, 14 degrees awarded. *Average time to degree:* master's–1 year full-time, 2 years part-time. *Entrance requirements:* GRE General Test, BSN, minimum GPA of 3.0, previous course work in statistics, 1 year of clinical experience in area of interest. Application deadline: 2/15 (priority date; rolling processing). Application fee: $65. *Financial aid:* Teaching assistantships, Federal Work-Study, institutionally sponsored loans, and career-related internships or fieldwork available. Aid available to part-time students. *Faculty research:* Payment structures for nurse practitioners, delirium in older adults. • Dr. Eileen Sullivan-Marx, Director, 215-898-4063. Fax: 215-573-7381. E-mail: eileens@pobox.upenn.edu. Application contact: Susan K. Ogle, Associate Director of Admissions and Student Affairs, 215-898-3301. Fax: 215-573-8439. E-mail: sogle@pobox.upenn.edu.

University of San Francisco, School of Nursing, San Francisco, CA 94117-1080. Offerings include advanced practice nursing-nurse practitioner and clinical nurse specialist (MSN), with option in adult health nursing. Accredited by NLN. School faculty: 9 full-time (8 women), 1 (woman) part-time. *Average time to degree:* master's–2 years full-time, 2.5 years part-time. *Entrance requirements:* Minimum GPA of 3.0. Application deadline: rolling. Application fee: $40. *Tuition:* $658 per unit (minimum). • Dr. John Lantz, Interim Dean, 415-422-6681. Fax: 415-422-6877. E-mail: lantzj@usfca.edu.

University of South Alabama, College of Nursing, Mobile, AL 36688-0002. Offerings include adult health nursing (MSN). Accredited by NLN. College faculty: 9 full-time (all women), 1 (woman) part-time. *Degree requirements:* Written comprehensive exam, research project or thesis required, foreign language not required. *Entrance requirements:* GRE General Test (minimum combined score of 1000) or MAT (minimum score 45), BSN, minimum GPA of 3.0, 1 year of nursing experience, interview, nursing license. Application deadline: 9/1 (priority date; rolling processing). Application fee: $25. • Dr. Amanda Baker, Dean, 334-434-3415.

University of Southern Maine, College of Nursing, Portland, ME 04104-9300. Offerings include adult health nursing (MS, PMC). One or more programs accredited by NLN. Postbaccalaureate distance learning degree programs offered (minimal on-campus study). College faculty: 11 full-time (all women), 5 part-time (all women). *Degree requirements:* For master's, thesis optional, foreign language not required. *Average time to degree:* master's–2.5 years full-time, 4 years part-time. *Entrance requirements:* For master's, GRE General Test (minimum combined score of 1000 on verbal and quantitative sections) or MAT (minimum score 45), minimum GPA of 3.0. Application deadline: 3/1. Application fee: $25. *Expenses:* Tuition $178 per credit hour for state residents; $267 per credit hour (minimum) for nonresidents. Fees $282 per year full-time, $83 per semester (minimum) part-time. • Dr. Marianne W. Rodgers, Interim Dean, 207-780-4808. Fax: 207-780-4997. E-mail: mrodgers@usm.maine.edu. Application contact: Mary Sloan, Assistant Director of Graduate Studies, 207-780-4386. Fax: 207-780-4969. E-mail: msloan@usm.maine.edu.

University of Tennessee at Chattanooga, School of Human Services, School of Nursing, Chattanooga, TN 37403-2598. Offerings include adult health (MSN). Accredited by NLN. School faculty: 8 full-time (7 women), 4 part-time (3 women). *Degree requirements:* Qualifying exams required, foreign language and thesis not required. *Entrance requirements:* GRE General Test (combined average 1485 on three sections). Application deadline: rolling. Application fee: $25. *Tuition:* $2864 per year full-time, $160 per credit hour part-time for state residents; $6806 per year full-time, $379 per credit hour part-time for nonresidents. • Dr. Maria Smith, Director, 423-755-4646. Fax: 423-755-4668. E-mail: msmith@utcvm.utc.edu. Application contact: Dr. Deborah Arfken, Assistant Provost for Graduate Studies, 423-755-4667. Fax: 423-755-4478.

The University of Texas at El Paso, College of Nursing and Health Science, Program in Nursing, 500 West University Avenue, El Paso, TX 79968-0001. Offerings include adult health (MSN). Accredited by NLN. *Degree requirements:* Thesis optional, foreign language not required. *Entrance requirements:* GRE General Test or MAT (minimum score 50), TOEFL (minimum score 550), BSN, course work in statistics. Application deadline: 7/1 (rolling processing; 11/1 for spring admission). Application fee: $15 ($65 for international students). Electronic applications accepted. *Tuition:* $2063 per year full-time, $284 per credit hour part-time for state residents; $5753 per year full-time, $425 per credit hour part-time for nonresidents.

Vanderbilt University, School of Nursing, Nashville, TN 37240-1001. Offerings include adult acute care nurse practitioner (MSN), occupational health/adult health nurse practitioner (MSN). One or more programs accredited by NLN. Postbaccalaureate distance learning degree programs offered (minimal on-campus study). School faculty: 76 full-time (66 women), 253 part-time (224 women). *Degree requirements:* Terminal course required, thesis not required. *Average time to degree:* master's–2 years full-time, 4 years part-time; doctorate–4 years full-time, 5 years part-time. *Entrance requirements:* GMAT, GRE, or MAT, minimum B average. Application deadline: rolling. Application fee: $50. Electronic applications accepted. • Dr. Colleen Conway-Welch, Dean, 615-343-3243. Fax: 615-343-7711. Application contact: Patricia Peerman, Assistant Dean of Admissions, 615-322-3800. Fax: 615-343-0333. E-mail: vusn-admission@mcmail.vanderbilt.edu.

Villanova University, College of Nursing, Villanova, PA 19085-1690. Offerings include adult nurse practitioner (MSN). Accredited by NLN. MSN (pediatric nurse practitioner), Post Master's Certificate (nurse practitioner, nurse anesthetist, clinical case management) new for fall 1998. College faculty: 30 full-time (all women). *Degree requirements:* Independent study project required, foreign language and thesis not required. *Entrance requirements:* GRE General Test (verbal section) or MAT, BSN, 1 year of recent experience, physical assessment, previous course work in statistics. Application deadline: 7/1 (priority date; rolling processing; 12/1 for spring admission). Application fee: $25. *Expenses:* Tuition $445 per credit. Fees $60 per year. • Dr. Claire Manfredi, Graduate Director, 610-519-4907. Fax: 610-519-7997. E-mail: cmanfred@email.vill.edu.

Virginia Commonwealth University, School of Nursing, Richmond, VA 23284-9005. Offerings include adult health nursing (MS). Accredited by NLN. School faculty: 50 full-time (all women), 5 part-time (all women). *Entrance requirements:* GRE General Test, BSN, minimum GPA of 2.8. Application deadline: 2/1. Application fee: $30 ($0 for international students). *Tuition:* $4960 per year full-time, $257 per credit part-time for state residents; $12,652 per year full-time, $684 per credit part-time for nonresidents. • Dr. Nancy F. Langston, Dean, 804-828-5174. E-mail: nflangst@vcu.edu. Application contact: Susan Lipp, Admissions Counselor, 804-828-5171. Fax: 804-828-7743. E-mail: sllipp@vcu.edu.

Wayne State University, College of Nursing, Department of Adult Health and Administration, Program in Advanced Medical-Surgical Nursing, Detroit, MI 48202. Awards MSN. Accredited by NLN. Part-time programs available. Students: 12 full-time (all women), 44 part-time (43 women); includes 8 minority (7 African Americans, 1 Hispanic), 3 international. Average age 36. 1 applicant, 0% accepted. In 1997, 8 degrees awarded. *Degree requirements:* Computer language, thesis or alternative required, foreign language not required. *Entrance requirements:* GRE General Test (minimum combined score of 800), minimum GPA of 2.8. Application deadline: 7/1 (priority date; rolling processing; 11/1 for spring admission). Application fee: $20 ($30 for international students). *Expenses:* Tuition $163 per credit hour for state residents; $355 per credit hour for nonresidents. Fees $498 per year full-time, $114 per semester (minimum) part-time. *Financial aid:* In 1997–98, 5 students received aid, including 5 scholarships, traineeships; research assistantships, institutionally sponsored loans also available. Financial aid application deadline: 7/1; applicants required to submit FAFSA. *Faculty research:* Wound healing, ostomy care, cognitive mapping and compliance in patients, caregiving planning. • Dr. Dawn Hameister, Assistant Dean, 313-577-4386. Fax: 313-577-4571. Application contact: Vickie Radoye, Administrative Assistant Dean, Student Affairs, 313-577-4082. Fax: 313-577-6949.

Wichita State University, College of Health Professions, School of Nursing, Wichita, KS 67260. Offerings include clinical specialization (MSN), with options in adult nursing, maternal-child nursing, psychiatric/mental health nursing. Accredited by NLN. School faculty: 11 full-time (all women). *Degree requirements:* Comprehensive exam required, thesis optional, foreign language not required. *Entrance requirements:* GRE, TOEFL (minimum score 550), BSN, minimum undergraduate GPA of 2.75. Application deadline: 6/30 (priority date; rolling processing; 1/1 for spring admission). Application fee: $25 ($40 for international students). Electronic applications accepted. *Expenses:* Tuition $2303 per year full-time, $96 per credit hour part-time for state residents; $7691 per year full-time, $321 per credit hour part-time for nonresidents. Fees $490 per year full-time, $75 per semester (minimum) part-time. • Dr. Bonnie Holaday, Interim Dean, 316-978-3610. E-mail: holaday@chp.twsu.edu. Application contact: Dr. Donna Hawley, Graduate Coordinator, 316-978-3610. Fax: 316-978-3094. E-mail: hawley@chp.twsu.edu.

Wright State University, College of Nursing and Health, Program in Nursing, Dayton, OH 45435. Offerings include adult health and illness (MS). Accredited by NLN. *Degree requirements:* Thesis or alternative required, foreign language not required. *Average time to degree:* master's–2 years full-time, 5 years part-time. *Entrance requirements:* GRE General Test, TOEFL (minimum score 550), BSN from NLN-accredited college, Ohio RN license. Application deadline: 4/15 (priority date). Application fee: $25. *Tuition:* $5109 per year full-time, $161 per credit hour part-time for state residents; $9039 per year full-time, $282 per credit hour part-time for nonresidents. • Application contact: Theresa Haghnazarian, Director of Student and Alumni Affairs, 937-775-3133. Fax: 937-775-4571.

Nurse Anesthesia

Albany Medical College, Graduate Programs in Biological and Medical Sciences, Program in Nurse Anesthesiology, Albany, NY 12208-3479. Awards MS. Accredited by CANAEP. *Degree requirements:* Thesis, thesis/clinical research required, foreign language not required. *Average time to degree:* master's–2 years full-time. *Entrance requirements:* GRE General Test, TOEFL (minimum score 550), BSN or appropriate bachelor's degree, current RN license, critical care experience. Application deadline: rolling. Application fee: $60.

Barry University, School of Natural and Health Sciences, Program in Anesthesiology, Miami Shores, FL 33161-6695. Awards MS. Accredited by CANAEP. Part-time and evening/weekend programs available. Postbaccalaureate distance learning degree programs offered (minimal on-campus study). Faculty: 4 full-time (2 women), 2 part-time (1 woman). Students: 18 full-time (9 women), 28 part-time (18 women); includes 15 minority (2 African Americans, 2 Asian Americans, 10 Hispanics, 1 Native American). Average age 36. In 1997, 24 degrees awarded. *Degree requirements:* Oral and written comprehensive exam required, foreign language and thesis not required. *Entrance requirements:* GRE General Test (minimum combined score of 1000), minimum GPA of 3.0; 2 courses in chemistry (1 with lab); minimum 1 year critical care experience; BSN or RN; 4 year baccalaureate in health sciences, nursing, biology, or chemistry. Application deadline: (9/1 for spring admission). Application fee: $30. *Tuition:* $450 per credit (minimum). *Financial aid:* Career-related internships or fieldwork available. Aid available to part-time students. Financial aid application deadline: 5/1; applicants required to submit FAFSA. • Dr. Norman Wolford, Director, 305-899-3230. E-mail: wolford@buaxp1.barry.edu. Application contact: Mercedes Diaz-Rodriguez, Graduate Health Administrative Assistant, 305-899-3230. Fax: 305-899-3366. E-mail: mrodriguez@diana.barry.edu.

Baylor College of Medicine, Medical School, Program in Nurse Anesthesia, Houston, TX 77030-3498. Awards MS. Accredited by CANAEP. Faculty: 4 (2 women). Students: 34 full-time (28 women); includes 9 minority (1 African American, 2 Asian Americans, 5 Hispanics, 1 Native American). Average age 31. 30 applicants, 37% accepted. In 1997, 13 degrees awarded (100% found work related to degree). *Average time to degree:* master's–2 years full-time. *Entrance requirements:* GRE General Test, Texas nursing license, 1 year of work experience in acute care nursing. Application deadline: 1/1. Application fee: $30. *Expenses:* Tuition $8200 per year. Fees $502 per year (minimum). *Financial aid:* 30 students received aid; Federal Work-Study, institutionally sponsored loans, and career-related internships or fieldwork available. Financial aid application deadline: 5/8; applicants required to submit FAFSA. *Faculty research:* Roles of nurse anesthetists, protocol for use of Sufonta-continuous infusion. • James R. Walker, Director, 713-793-2860. Fax: 713-793-2867. E-mail: jrwalker@bcm.tmc.edu. Application contact: Dr. L. Leighton Hill, Assistant Dean, 713-798-4842.

California State University, Long Beach, College of Health and Human Services, Department of Nursing, Program in Nurse Anesthesiology, 1250 Bellflower Boulevard, Long Beach, CA 90840-0119. Awards MS. Offered jointly with Kaiser-Permante School of Anesthesia for Nurses. Faculty: 6 full-time (5 women). *Degree requirements:* Thesis required, foreign language not required. *Entrance requirements:* Minimum GPA of 3.0. Application deadline: 8/1 (rolling processing; 12/1 for spring admission). Application fee: $55. *Expenses:* Tuition $0 for state residents; $246 per unit for nonresidents. Fees $1846 per year full-time, $1180 per year part-time. *Financial aid:* Application deadline 3/2. • Dr. Joyce Kelly, Director, 213-667-8861.

Case Western Reserve University, Frances Payne Bolton School of Nursing, Master's Program in Nursing, Program in Nurse Anesthesia, Cleveland, OH 44106. Awards MSN. Accredited by CANAEP. Students: 17 full-time, 26 part-time. 33 applicants, 48% accepted. In 1997, 20 degrees awarded. *Degree requirements:* Thesis optional, foreign language not required. *Entrance requirements:* GRE General Test or MAT. Application deadline: 1/15 (rolling processing). Application fee: $75. *Tuition:* $18,400 per year full-time, $767 per credit hour part-time. *Financial aid:* Research assistantships, teaching assistantships, partial tuition waivers, institutionally sponsored loans available. Aid available to part-time students. Financial aid application deadline: 6/30. • Application contact: Molly Blank, Admission Counselor, 216-368-2529. Fax: 216-368-3542. E-mail: mab44@po.cwru.edu.

Columbia University, School of Nursing, Program in Nurse Anesthesia, New York, NY 10032. Awards MS. Accredited by CANAEP. Faculty: 1 (woman) full-time, 3 part-time (2 women). Students: 18 full-time (15 women), 15 part-time (10 women); includes 9 minority (1 African American, 5 Asian Americans, 3 Hispanics). Average age 32. 50 applicants, 34% accepted. In 1997, 10 degrees awarded. *Entrance requirements:* GRE General Test (minimum score 500 on verbal and analytical sections), BSN, 1 year of clinical experience (preferred), or completion of a clinical residency. Application deadline: 4/1 (priority date; rolling processing; 10/1 for spring admission). Application fee: $60. *Tuition:* $19,376 per year full-time, $692 per credit (minimum) part-time. *Financial aid:* Application deadline 2/1. • Prof. Sherry Ikalowych, Director, 212-305-4196. Application contact: Joseph Tomaino, Assistant Dean for Student Services, 212-305-5756. E-mail: jt238@columbia.edu.

DePaul University, College of Liberal Arts and Sciences, Department of Nursing, Chicago, IL 60604-2287. Offerings include nurse anesthesia (MS). Accredited by CANAEP. MS (nurse anesthesia) offered jointly with Ravenswood Hospital Medical Center. Department faculty: 5 full-time (all women), 1 (woman) part-time. *Degree requirements:* Comprehensive written exam required, thesis optional, foreign language not required. *Entrance requirements:* GRE, BSN, RN license, minimum GPA of 2.85. Application fee: $25. *Expenses:* Tuition $320 per credit hour. Fees $30 per year. • Dr. Susan Poslusny, Chair, 773-325-7280. E-mail: sposlusn@wppost.depaul.edu.

Emory University, School of Medicine, Programs in Allied Health Professions, Program in Anesthesiology/Patient Monitoring Systems, Atlanta, GA 30322-1100. Offers anesthesiology/patient monitoring systems (MM Sc), critical care medicine (MM Sc). MM Sc (critical care medicine) admissions temporarily suspended. Faculty: 7 part-time (1 woman). Students: 61 full-time (21 women); includes 15 minority (3 African Americans, 12 Asian Americans). Average age 24. 98 applicants, 36% accepted. In 1997, 27 degrees awarded (100% found work related to degree). *Entrance requirements:* GRE General Test (minimum combined score of 1500 on three sections) or MCAT. Application deadline: 5/1 (priority date; rolling processing). Application fee: $50. *Financial aid:* Federal Work-Study, institutionally sponsored loans available. Aid available to part-time students. Financial aid application deadline: 3/15; applicants required to submit CSS PROFILE or FAFSA. • Wesley T. Frazier, Director, 404-727-5910.

Gannon University, School of Graduate Studies, College of Sciences, Engineering, and Health Sciences, School of Health Sciences, Department of Nursing, Erie, PA 16505. Offerings include anesthesia (MSN). Accredited by CANAEP. *Degree requirements:* Thesis. *Entrance requirements:* GRE General Test (minimum score 500 on each section), MAT (minimum score 60), bachelor's degree from a NLN-approved nursing program, interview, Pennsylvania RN license. Application deadline: 4/15. Application fee: $25. • Dr. Beverly Bartlett, Director, 814-871-5520. Application contact: Beth Nemenz, Director of Admissions, 814-871-7240. Fax: 814-871-5803. E-mail: admissions@gannon.edu.

Gonzaga University, Graduate School, School of Education, Program in Anesthesiology Education, Spokane, WA 99258-0001. Awards M Anesth Ed. Accredited by CANAEP. Faculty: 3 full-time (2 women), 5 part-time (2 women). Students: 11 full-time (8 women). Average age 33. In 1997, 6 degrees awarded. *Degree requirements:* Comprehensive exam required, foreign language and thesis not required. *Entrance requirements:* GRE General Test or MAT, TOEFL (minimum score 550). Application deadline: 12/1. Application fee: $40. *Tuition:* $7380 per year (minimum) full-time, $410 per credit (minimum) part-time. *Financial aid:* Application deadline 3/1. • Dr. Janet Brougher, Academic Director, 509-328-4220 Ext. 3502.

Gooding Institute of Nurse Anesthesia, Program in Nurse Anesthesia, Panama City, FL 32401. Awards MS. Accredited by CANAEP. Postbaccalaureate distance learning degree programs offered (no on-campus study). Faculty: 21 full-time (5 women), 1 (woman) part-time. Students: 20 full-time (11 women). Average age 28. 50 applicants, 20% accepted. In 1997, 9 degrees awarded. *Degree requirements:* Thesis. *Average time to degree:* master's–2 years full-time. *Entrance requirements:* GRE General Test (minimum combined score of 1300 on three sections; average 1500), BSN, RN license. Application deadline: 3/1 (priority date; rolling processing). Application fee: $35. *Expenses:* Tuition $17,000 per year. Fees $1225 per year. *Financial aid:* 18 students received aid. Financial aid application deadline: 8/1. • David Ely, Director, 850-747-6918. Fax: 850-747-6115.

La Roche College, Program in Health Sciences, Pittsburgh, PA 15237-5898. Offers nurse anesthesia (MS). Accredited by CANAEP. Faculty: 2 full-time (0 women), 4 part-time (1 woman). Students: 78. *Degree requirements:* Thesis optional, foreign language not required. *Entrance requirements:* GRE General Test (minimum combined score of 1200), MAT (minimum score 50), TOEFL (minimum score 500). Application deadline: 12/31. Application fee: $25. *Tuition:* $385 per credit. *Financial aid:* Available to part-time students. Financial aid applicants required to submit FAFSA. • Dr. Don Fujito, Coordinator, 412-536-1157. Application contact: Roland Gagne, Director of Graduate Studies, 412-536-1265. Fax: 412-536-1283.

Mayo School of Health-Related Sciences, Program in Nurse Anesthesia, Rochester, MN 55905. Awards MNA. Accredited by CANAEP. Students: 56 full-time. *Degree requirements:* Comprehensive exam, research project required, foreign language and thesis not required. *Entrance requirements:* GRE General Test, minimum GPA of 3.0, minimum 1 year of critical care experience. Application deadline: 10/15. Application fee: $50. • Mary E. Marienau, Director, 507-284-3293. Application contact: Tammy Neis, Secretary, 507-284-8331.

Medical College of Georgia, Graduate Programs in Nursing, Augusta, GA 30912-1500. Offerings include nurse anesthesia (MN). Accredited by NLN and CANAEP. Faculty: 17 full-time (14 women). *Application deadline:* 6/30 (priority date; rolling processing). *Application fee:* $0. *Expenses:* Tuition $2670 per year full-time, $111 per credit part-time for state residents; $10,680 per year full-time, $445 per credit part-time for nonresidents. Fees $286 per year. • Dr. Virginia Kemp, Associate Dean, 706-721-4710. E-mail: vkemp@mail.mcg.edu. Application contact: Dr. Gary C. Bond, Associate Dean, 706-721-3278. Fax: 706-721-6829. E-mail: gradstud@mail.mcg.edu.

Medical University of South Carolina, College of Health Professions, Program in Health Sciences, Anesthesia for Nurses Program, Charleston, SC 29425-0002. Awards MHS. One or more programs accredited by CANAEP. Faculty: 2 full-time (0 women). Students: 29 full-time (20 women); includes 2 minority (1 Asian American, 1 Hispanic). Average age 34. 27 applicants, 67% accepted. In 1997, 15 degrees awarded (100% found work related to degree). *Degree requirements:* Research proposal required, foreign language and thesis not required. *Average time to degree:* master's–2.2 years full-time. *Entrance requirements:* GRE General Test (minimum combined score of 1000), interview, minimum GPA of 3.0, 2 years of RN (ICU) experience, RN license. Application deadline: 12/1 (priority date). Application fee: $55. *Expenses:* Tuition $4072 per year full-time, $221 per semester hour part-time for state residents; $7064 per year full-time, $387 per semester hour part-time for nonresidents. Fees $150 per year (minimum). *Financial aid:* Federal Work-Study available. Aid available to part-time students. Financial aid application deadline: 4/1; applicants required to submit FAFSA. *Faculty research:* Pharmacology, surgery, pathophysiology. • Larry Truver, Director, 843-792-3785. E-mail: truverl@musc.edu. Application contact: Jerri Snider, Administrative Specialist, 843-792-3785. Fax: 843-792-1984. E-mail: sniderj@musc.edu.

Middle Tennessee School of Anesthesia, Program in Nurse Anesthesia, Madison, TN 37116. Awards MS. Accredited by CANAEP. Faculty: 6 full-time (2 women), 16 part-time (3 women). Students: 72 (36 women); includes 3 minority (2 African Americans, 1 Asian American). Average age 30. 166 applicants, 22% accepted. In 1997, 37 degrees awarded (100% found work related to degree). *Degree requirements:* Project. *Average time to degree:* master's–3 years part-time. *Entrance requirements:* MAT, RN license, 1 year of critical-care nursing experience. Application deadline: 10/31. Application fee: $25. *Tuition:* $6000 per year. • Mary E. DeVasher, Vice President and Dean, 615-868-6503. Fax: 615-868-9885.

Mount Marty College, Graduate Studies Division, 3109 South Kiwanis Avenue, Sioux Falls, SD 57105. Offers program in nursing anesthesia (MS). One or more programs accredited by CANAEP. Faculty: 2 full-time (0 women), 7 part-time (1 woman). Students: 43 full-time (16 women); includes 3 minority (1 African American, 1 Asian American, 1 Hispanic). Average age 28. 40 applicants, 63% accepted. In 1997, 21 degrees awarded (100% found work related to degree). *Degree requirements:* Thesis or alternative required, foreign language not required. *Average time to degree:* master's–2 years full-time. *Entrance requirements:* GRE General Test (minimum combined score of 1200), BSN or RN, minimum GPA of 3.0, 1 year of clinical nursing experience in acute care within the last 3 years. Application deadline: 12/15 (priority date; rolling processing). Application fee: $10. *Tuition:* $12,305 per year. *Financial aid:* 19 students received aid; grants, scholarships, institutionally sponsored loans, and career-related internships or fieldwork available. Financial aid application deadline: 8/1; applicants required to submit FAFSA. *Faculty research:* Clinical anesthesia, professional characteristics, motivations of applicants. • Dr. Larry L. Dahlen, Director, 605-357-9802. Application contact: J. C. Crane, Director of Admissions, 800-658-4552. Fax: 605-668-1357.

Murray State University, College of Sciences, Department of Nursing, Murray, KY 42071-0009. Offerings include nurse anesthesia (MSNA). Accredited by CANAEP. Department faculty: 7 full-time (5 women). *Application deadline:* rolling. *Application fee:* $20. *Expenses:* Tuition $2500 per year full-time, $124 per hour part-time for state residents; $6740 per year full-time, $357 per hour part-time for nonresidents. Fees $360 per year full-time, $180 per year part-time. • Application contact: Dr. Nancey France, Graduate Coordinator, 502-762-6671. Fax: 502-762-6662.

Northeastern University, Graduate School of Nursing, Program in Nurse Anesthesia, Boston, MA 02115-5096. Awards MS. Accredited by CANAEP. *Degree requirements:* Thesis or alternative required, foreign language not required. *Entrance requirements:* GRE General Test, minimum GPA of 3.0, previous course work in statistics, 1-2 years nursing experience, RN license, ICU experience. Application deadline: 10/1 (priority date; rolling processing; 2/1 for spring admission). Application fee: $50. *Expenses:* Tuition $440 per credit hour. Fees $55 per quarter full-time, $13.25 per quarter part-time. • Janet Dewan, Coordinator. E-mail: janet.dewan@es.nemc.org. Application contact: Molly Schnabel, Admissions Coordinator, 617-373-3590. Fax: 617-373-8672. E-mail: mschnabe@lynx.neu.edu.

Announcement: Master's program in nurse anesthesia (54 quarter hours) offered in conjunction with New England Medical Center in Boston. Includes advanced academic and clinical preparation for CRNA role. Full-time study for 27 months. Master's completion program for CRNAs and certificate program for MS-prepared nurses. For application, contact Admissions Coordinator Molly Schnabel at 617-373-3590.

Oakland University, School of Nursing, Program in Nurse Anesthetist, Rochester, MI 48309-4401. Awards MSN. Accredited by CANAEP. Offered jointly with Beaumont Hospital Corporation. Students: 12 full-time (8 women), 7 part-time (6 women); includes 3 minority (1 Asian American, 1 Hispanic, 1 Native American). 10 applicants, 100% accepted. In 1997, 9 degrees awarded. *Entrance requirements:* GRE General Test, minimum GPA of 3.0 for unconditional admission. Application deadline: 7/15 (3/15 for spring admission). Application fee: $30. *Expenses:* Tuition $3852 per year full-time, $214 per credit hour part-time for state residents; $8532 per year full-time, $474 per credit hour part-time for nonresidents. Fees $420 per year. *Financial aid:* Full tuition waivers, Federal Work-Study, institutionally sponsored loans available. Financial aid application deadline: 3/1; applicants required to submit FAFSA. • Dr. Diane Wilson, Director, 248-370-4484.

Rush University, College of Nursing, Department of Medical/Surgical Nursing, Chicago, IL 60612-3832. Offerings include anesthesia nurse practitioner (MSN, DN Sc, ND). One or more programs accredited by CANAEP. Department faculty: 14 full-time (13 women), 17 part-time (all women), 25.18 FTE *Degree requirements:* For doctorate, dissertation required, foreign language not required. *Entrance requirements:* For master's, GRE General Test, interview, previous course work in statistics; for doctorate, MS or GRE General Test, interview, previous course work in statistics. Application deadline: 8/1 (rolling processing; 2/1 for spring admission). Application fee: $40. *Tuition:* $8560 per year full-time, $370 per credit hour part-time. • Dr. Jane Llewellyn, Chairperson, 312-942-7112. Application contact: Hicela Castruita, Director, College Admissions Services, 312-942-7100. Fax: 312-942-2219.

Saint Joseph's University, Department of Health Services, Program in Nurse Anesthesia, Philadelphia, PA 19131-1395. Awards MS. Students: 116 (83 women). In 1997, 38 degrees awarded. *Degree requirements:* Thesis required (for some programs), foreign language not required. *Entrance requirements:* TOEFL, Pennsylvania RN license, 1 year of nursing experience. Application deadline: 7/15. Application fee: $30. *Tuition:* $470 per credit hour. • Dr. Laura Frank, Director, 610-660-1580.

Saint Mary's University of Minnesota, Nurse Anesthesia Program, Minneapolis, MN 55404. Awards MS. Accredited by CANAEP. Offered jointly with Abbott-Northwestern School of Anesthesia and the Minneapolis School of Anesthesia. *Degree requirements:* Thesis or alternative, research presentation required, foreign language not required. *Entrance requirements:* Interview, minimum GPA of 2.75, RN license. Application deadline: rolling. Application fee: $20.

Saint Mary's University of Minnesota, Program in Nurse Anesthesia for CRNA's, Minneapolis, MN 55404. Awards MS. Accredited by CANAEP. Part-time and evening/weekend programs available. *Degree requirements:* Thesis or alternative, research presentation required, foreign language not required. *Entrance requirements:* Minimum GPA of 2.75, RN license. Application deadline: rolling. Application fee: $20.

Samuel Merritt College, Department of Nursing, Oakland, CA 94609-3108. Offerings include nurse anesthetist (Certificate). One or more programs accredited by CANAEP. Department faculty: 11 full-time (9 women), 5 part-time (3 women), 13.37 FTE. *Average time to degree:* master's–2.2 years full-time. *Application deadline:* 2/1 (rolling processing). *Application fee:* $50. *Expenses:* Tuition $605 per unit. Fees $25 per year. • Dr. Audrey Berman, Graduate Coordinator, 510-869-6733. Application contact: John Garten-Schuman, Director of Admissions, 510-869-6576. Fax: 510-869-6525.

Southern Illinois University at Edwardsville, School of Nursing, Program in Nurse Anesthesia, Edwardsville, IL 62026-0001. Awards MS. Accredited by CANAEP. Students: 19 full-time (15 women), 9 part-time (7 women); includes 2 minority (1 African American, 1 Asian American). 32 applicants, 38% accepted. In 1997, 10 degrees awarded. *Degree requirements:* Thesis or alternative, final exam required, foreign language not required. *Entrance requirements:* Appropriate bachelor's degree, RN license. Application deadline: 7/24. Application fee: $25. *Expenses:* Tuition $1716 per year full-time, $95 per credit hour part-time for state residents; $5149 per year full-time, $286 per credit hour part-time for nonresidents. Fees $463 per year full-time, $433 per year part-time. *Financial aid:* In 1997–98, 2 fellowships, 2 assistantships were awarded; research assistantships, teaching assistantships also available. • Dr. Felissa Lashley, Dean, School of Nursing, 618-692-3956.

Southwest Missouri State University, College of Health and Human Services, Department of Biomedical Sciences, Springfield, MO 65804-0094. Offers program in nurse anesthesia (MS). One or more programs accredited by CANAEP. Part-time programs available. Faculty: 7 full-time (0 women). Students: 13 full-time (7 women), 4 part-time (all women). *Degree requirements:* Thesis or alternative required, foreign language not required. *Entrance requirements:* GRE General Test, minimum GPA of 3.0. Application deadline: 8/7 (priority date; rolling processing; 12/7 for spring admission). Application fee: $25. *Expenses:* Tuition $1980 per year full-time, $110 per credit hour part-time for state residents; $3960 per year full-time, $220 per credit hour part-time for nonresidents. Fees $274 per year full-time, $73 per semester part-time. *Financial aid:* In 1997–98, 5 graduate assistantships totaling $26,250 were awarded. • Dr. Harold Falls, Head, 417-836-5603. Fax: 417-836-5588. E-mail: hbf931f@wpgate.smsu.edu.

State University of New York at Buffalo, Graduate School, School of Nursing, Buffalo, NY 14260. Offerings include nurse anesthesia (MS). Accredited by CANAEP. Postbaccalaureate distance learning degree programs offered (minimal on-campus study). School faculty: 28 full-time (25 women), 13 part-time (12 women). *Entrance requirements:* GRE General Test (minimum score 450 on each section), TOEFL (minimum score 550), interview, minimum GPA of 3.0, RN license. Application deadline: 5/1 (priority date; rolling processing; 10/15 for spring admission). Application fee: $35. *Tuition:* $5970 per year full-time, $288 per credit hour part-time for state residents; $9286 per year full-time, $426 per credit hour part-time for nonresidents. • Dr. Mecca S. Cranley, Dean, 716-829-2533. E-mail: mcranley@nurse.buffalo.edu. Application contact: Dr. William P. Harden, Assistant Dean, 716-829-3314. Fax: 716-829-2021. E-mail: wharden@nurse.buffalo.edu.

Texas Wesleyan University, Program in Nurse Anesthesia, Fort Worth, TX 76105-1536. Awards MHS. One or more programs accredited by CANAEP. Faculty: 3 full-time (0 women), 2 part-time (0 women). Students: 132 full-time (54 women), 3 part-time (1 woman); includes 12 minority (4 African Americans, 1 Asian American, 6 Hispanics, 1 Native American), 1 international. Average age 34. In 1997, 61 degrees awarded (100% found work related to degree). *Average time to degree:* master's–2 years full-time. *Entrance requirements:* GRE General Test (minimum combined score of 1500 on three sections), minimum GPA of 3.0 in final 60 hours of undergraduate course work, RN. Application deadline: rolling. Application fee: $20. *Expenses:* Tuition $360 per hour. Fees $200 per semester. *Financial aid:* 94 students received aid; institutionally sponsored loans available. Financial aid application deadline: 3/15; applicants required to submit FAFSA. • Kay K. Sanders, Director, 817-531-4406. Application contact: Joyce Breeden, Dean of Admissions, 817-531-4458. Fax: 817-531-4231.

Uniformed Services University of the Health Sciences, Graduate School of Nursing, Department of Nurse Anesthesia, Bethesda, MD 20814-4799. Awards MSN. Accredited by CANAEP. Available to military officers only. Faculty: 7 full-time (3 women). Students: 37 full-time (16 women); includes 4 minority (1 African American, 1 Asian American, 2 Hispanics). Average age 35. In 1997, 11 degrees awarded (100% found work related to degree). *Degree requirements:* Thesis required, foreign language not required. *Average time to degree:* master's–2 years full-time. *Entrance requirements:* GRE General Test (minimum combined score of 1000), MAT, minimum GPA of 3.0, clinical experience, BSN, previous course work in science. Application deadline: rolling. Application fee: $0. *Tuition:* $0. *Faculty research:* International nurse anesthesia practice, pharmacology, neuroscience, malignant hyperthermia. • Capt. E. Jane McCarthy, Chair, 301-295-6565. Fax: 301-295-2228. E-mail: jmccarth@usuhs.mil. Application contact: Bernadette Hoover, Recording Secretary for Admissions Committee, 301-295-9893. Fax: 301-295-9006. E-mail: bhoover@usuhs.mil.

Université de Montréal, Faculties of Medicine and Graduate Studies, Graduate Programs in Medicine, Program in Specialized Studies, Montréal, PQ H3C 3J7, Canada. Offerings include anesthesia-resuscitation (DES). Program faculty: 204 full-time (32 women), 36 part-time (1 woman). *Application deadline:* 10/1. *Application fee:* $30. • Dr. Jean-Paul Perreault, Vice Dean, 514-343-7798.

The University of Alabama at Birmingham, Graduate School, School of Health Related Professions, Program in Nurse Anesthesia, Birmingham, AL 35294. Awards MNA. Accredited by CANAEP. Students: 66 full-time (34 women), 1 part-time (0 women); includes 7 minority (3 African Americans, 1 Asian American, 2 Hispanics, 1 Native American). 44 applicants, 100% accepted. In 1997, 35 degrees awarded. *Entrance requirements:* GRE, MAT, minimum GPA of 3.0, RN license, 1 year of critical care experience. Application fee: $30 ($60 for international students). Electronic applications accepted. *Expenses:* Tuition $129 per credit hour for state residents; $258 per credit hour for nonresidents. Fees $627 per year (minimum) full-time, $110 per quarter (minimum) part-time. • Joe R. Williams, Director, 205-934-3209.

University of Cincinnati, College of Nursing and Health, Cincinnati, OH 45221-0038. Offerings include nurse anesthesia (MSN). Accredited by CANAEP. College faculty: 26 full-time. *Degree requirements:* Project or thesis required, foreign language not required. *Average time to degree:* master's–1.5 years full-time, 2.5 years part-time; doctorate–4 years full-time, 6 years part-time. *Entrance requirements:* GRE General Test. Application deadline: 1/1 (priority date; rolling processing). Application fee: $30. *Tuition:* $7228 per year full-time, $185 per credit hour part-time for state residents; $13,812 per year full-time, $352 per credit hour part-time for nonresidents. • Dr. Andrea Lindell, Dean, 513-558-5330. Application contact: Tom West, Program Coordinator, 513-558-3600. Fax: 513-558-7523. E-mail: tom.west@uc.edu.

University of Detroit Mercy, College of Health Professions, Program in Nurse Anesthesiology, Detroit, MI 48219-0900. Awards MS. Accredited by CANAEP. *Entrance requirements:* GRE General Test (minimum combined score of 1200), minimum GPA of 3.0. Application fee: $25.

University of Kansas, School of Allied Health, Department of Nurse Anesthesia, Kansas City, KS 66160. Awards MS. Accredited by CANAEP. Part-time programs available. Faculty: 5 full-time (3 women). Students: 55 full-time (25 women), 3 part-time (1 woman); includes 5 minority (1 African American, 1 Asian American, 1 Hispanic, 2 Native Americans). Average age 35. 85 applicants, 22% accepted. In 1997, 24 degrees awarded. *Degree requirements:* Thesis, comprehensive exam required, foreign language not required. *Entrance requirements:* GRE General Test, TOEFL (minimum score 570), BS in nursing, RN license, 1 year of work experience, minimum GPA of 2.75. Application deadline: 1/1 (rolling processing). Application fee: $25. *Expenses:* Tuition $2400 per year full-time, $100 per credit hour part-time for state residents; $7890 per year full-time, $329 per credit hour part-time for nonresidents. Fees $428 per year full-time, $31 per credit hour part-time. *Financial aid:* 47 students received aid; traineeships, Federal Work-Study, institutionally sponsored loans, and career-related internships or fieldwork available. Aid available to part-time students. Financial aid application deadline: 4/3; applicants required to submit FAFSA. • Carol Elliott, Chair, 913-588-6612. Fax: 913-588-3334. E-mail: nanesthe@kumc.edu.

University of Michigan–Flint, School of Health Professions and Studies, Program in Anesthesia, Flint, MI 48502-1950. Awards MSA. Accredited by CANAEP. Part-time programs available. Faculty: 4 full-time (2 women), 28 part-time (9 women). Students: 13 full-time (7 women). 20 applicants, 40% accepted. In 1997, 7 degrees awarded. *Degree requirements:* Thesis required, foreign language not required. *Entrance requirements:* GRE, BSN or BS in science, critical care experience, RN license. Application deadline: 9/1. Application fee: $30. *Financial aid:* Career-related internships or fieldwork available. Aid available to part-time students. Financial aid application deadline: 4/1. *Faculty research:* Effects of muscle relaxants, pediatric sedation, nausea and vomiting courses, effect of epidural analgesia on nemostasis. Total annual research expenditures: $5000. • Dr. Francis Gerbasi, Director, 810-762-7264. Fax: 810-760-0839.

University of New England, College of Health Professions, Program in Nurse Anesthesia, Biddeford, ME 04005-9526. Awards MS. Accredited by CANAEP. Offered in association with Eastern Maine Medical Center, St. Joseph Hospital, and Harlem Hospital. Faculty: 4 full-time (0 women), 2 part-time (both women). Students: 105 full-time (73 women); includes 19 minority (10 African Americans, 7 Asian Americans, 1 Hispanic, 1 Native American). Average age 37. 42 applicants, 83% accepted. In 1997, 45 degrees awarded. *Degree requirements:* Practicum required, foreign language and thesis not required. *Entrance requirements:* GRE, BSN, RN, 2-5 years of general practice experience. Application deadline: 11/1 (rolling processing). Application fee: $40. *Expenses:* Tuition $360 per credit. Fees $230 per year. *Financial aid:* Federal Work-Study and career-related internships or fieldwork available. Aid available to part-time students. Financial aid application deadline: 5/1; applicants required to submit FAFSA. • Dr. Carl Spirito, Director, 207-283-0171 Ext. 2203. Fax: 207-282-6379. Application contact: Patricia T. Cribby, Dean of Admissions and Enrollment Management, 207-283-0171 Ext. 2297. Fax: 207-286-3678. E-mail: jshea@mailbox.une.edu.

University of North Carolina at Greensboro, School of Nursing, Greensboro, NC 27412-0001. Offerings include nurse anesthesia (MSN, PMC). Accredited by CANAEP. School faculty: 22 full-time (all women), 7 part-time (all women). *Degree requirements:* For master's, thesis or alternative required, foreign language not required. *Entrance requirements:* For master's, GRE General Test or MAT, BSN, clinical experience, liability insurance, RN license; for PMC, liability insurance, MSN, RN license. Application fee: $35. *Expenses:* Tuition $1842 per year full-time, $370 per semester (minimum) part-time for state residents; $10,296 per year full-time, $2484 per semester (minimum) part-time for nonresidents. Fees $806 per year full-time, $111 per semester (minimum) part-time. • Dr. Lynne Pearcey, Dean, 336-334-5010.

University of Pittsburgh, School of Nursing, Program in Anesthesia Nursing, Pittsburgh, PA 15260. Awards MSN. Accredited by CANAEP. Part-time programs available. Students: 53 full-time, 1 part-time. 31 applicants, 58% accepted. In 1997, 16 degrees awarded. *Degree requirements:* Thesis or alternative required, foreign language not required. *Entrance requirements:* GRE General Test, TOEFL, BSN, RN license, 2 years of specified critical care experience. Application deadline: 2/1 (priority date; rolling processing; 9/15 for spring admission). Application fee: $35 ($40 for international students). *Financial aid:* Application deadline 6/1. • John O'Donnell, Director, 412-624-4860. Fax: 412-624-2401. Application contact: Dr. Kathy Lucke, Director, Student Services, 412-624-2405. Fax: 412-624-2409. E-mail: nursao+@pitt.edu.

See in-depth description on page 1451.

University of Puerto Rico, Medical Sciences Campus, School of Nursing, San Juan, PR 00936-5067. Offerings include anesthesia (MSN). Accredited by CANAEP. *Degree requirements:* 1 foreign language, thesis, research project. *Entrance requirements:* GRE, BSN, interview, (Puerto Rico) RN license, 2 years of nursing experience, previous course work in physical examination. Application deadline: 3/16. Application fee: $25.

University of South Carolina, School of Medicine and Graduate School, Graduate Programs in Medicine, Graduate Program in Biomedical Science, Program in Nurse Anesthesia, Columbia, SC 29208. Awards MBS. Students: 45 full-time (29 women); includes 2 minority (both African Americans). Average age 32. 47 applicants, 38% accepted. In 1997, 12 degrees awarded (100% found work related to degree). *Average time to degree:* master's–2.5 years full-time. *Entrance requirements:* GRE, RN license, 1 year of critical care experience. Application fee: $35. Electronic applications accepted. *Expenses:* Tuition $4480 per year full-time, $220 per credit hour part-time for state residents; $9338 per year full-time, $457 per credit hour part-time for nonresidents. Fees $125 per year full-time, $37 per semester (minimum) part-time. *Financial aid:* Institutionally sponsored loans available. • Dr. Donald O. Allen, Chair, Department of Pharmacology, 803-733-3254. E-mail: doa@dcsmserver.med.sc.edu. Application contact: Mary Sue Poole, Program Coordinator, 803-733-3100. Fax: 803-733-3168. E-mail: biomed@dcsmserver.med.sc.edu.

University of Tennessee at Chattanooga, School of Human Services, School of Nursing, Chattanooga, TN 37403-2598. Offerings include nurse anesthesia (MSN). Accredited by CANAEP. School faculty: 8 full-time (7 women), 4 part-time (3 women). *Degree requirements:* Qualifying exams required, foreign language and thesis not required. *Entrance requirements:* GRE General Test (combined average 1485 on three sections). Application deadline: rolling. Application fee: $25. *Tuition:* $2864 per year full-time, $160 per credit hour part-time for state residents; $6806 per year full-time, $379 per credit hour part-time for nonresidents. • Dr. Maria Smith, Director, 423-755-4646. Fax: 423-755-4668. E-mail: msmith@utcvm.utc.edu. Application contact: Dr. Deborah Arfken, Assistant Provost for Graduate Studies, 423-755-4667. Fax: 423-755-4478.

Directories: Nurse Anesthesia; Nurse Midwifery

The University of Texas–Houston Health Science Center, School of Nursing, Master's Program in Nursing, Houston, TX 77225-0036. Offerings include nurse anesthesia (MSN). Accredited by CANAEP. *Degree requirements:* Thesis required, foreign language not required. *Entrance requirements:* GRE or MAT, BSN, Texas RN license. Application deadline: 5/1 (priority date; rolling processing; 9/1 for spring admission). Application fee: $10. Electronic applications accepted. • Frank Cole, Chair, Graduate Curriculum Committee, 713-500-2153. Fax: 713-500-2171. E-mail: fcole@son1.nur.uth.tmc.edu. Application contact: Eleanor Evans, Pre-Admissions Counselor, 713-500-2104. Fax: 713-500-2107. E-mail: eevans@son1.nur.uth.tmc.edu.

University of Wisconsin–La Crosse, College of Science and Allied Health, Department of Biology and Microbiology, La Crosse, WI 54601-3742. Offerings include nurse anesthetist (MS). Accredited by CANAEP. Department faculty: 18 full-time (2 women). *Degree requirements:* Thesis (for some programs), oral comprehensive exam required, foreign language not required. *Entrance requirements:* GRE General Test, minimum GPA of 3.0 during previous 2 years or 2.85 overall. Application deadline: 3/1 (priority date; rolling processing). Application fee: $38. *Tuition:* $3737 per year full-time, $208 per credit part-time for state residents; $11,921 per year full-time, $633 per credit part-time for nonresidents. • Dr. Mark Sandheinrich, Coordinator, 608-785-8261. E-mail: sandheinrich@mail.uwlax.edu. Application contact: Tim Lewis, Director of Admissions, 608-785-8939. Fax: 608-785-6695. E-mail: admissions@mail.uwlax.edu.

Villanova University, College of Nursing, Villanova, PA 19085-1690. Offerings include nurse anesthetist (MSN, Post Master's Certificate). MSN (pediatric nurse practitioner), Post Master's Certificate (nurse practitioner, nurse anesthetist, clinical case management) new for fall 1998. College faculty: 30 full-time (all women). *Degree requirements:* For master's, independent study project required, foreign language and thesis not required. *Entrance requirements:* For master's, GRE General Test (verbal section) or MAT, BSN, 1 year of recent experience, physical assessment, previous course work in statistics. Application deadline: 7/1 (priority date; rolling processing; 12/1 for spring admission). Application fee: $25. *Expenses:* Tuition $445 per credit. Fees $60 per year. • Dr. Claire Manfredi, Graduate Director, 610-519-4907. Fax: 610-519-7997. E-mail: cmanfred@email.vill.edu.

Virginia Commonwealth University, School of Allied Health Professions, Department of Nurse Anesthesia, Richmond, VA 23284-9005. Awards MSNA. Accredited by CANAEP. Faculty: 16 (4 women). Students: 59 full-time (42 women), 2 part-time (both women); includes 7 minority (2 African Americans, 2 Asian Americans, 3 Hispanics). Average age 33. 36 applicants, 78% accepted. In 1997, 24 degrees awarded. *Degree requirements:* Thesis required, foreign language not required. *Entrance requirements:* GRE General Test, BSN, current state RPN license. Application deadline: 1/31. Application fee: $30 ($0 for international students). *Tuition:* $4960 per year full-time, $257 per credit part-time for state residents; $12,652 per year full-time, $684 per credit part-time for nonresidents. *Faculty research:* Obstetrical anesthesia, ambulatory anethesia, regional anesthesia, practice profiles, clinical practice. • Dr. James P. Embrey, Chair, 804-828-6738. Fax: 804-828-0581. E-mail: jpembrey@vcu.edu.

Wayne State University, College of Pharmacy and Allied Health Professions, Faculty of Allied Health Professions, Department of Anesthesia, Detroit, MI 48202. Awards MS. Students: 15 full-time (10 women), 2 part-time (both women). 4 applicants, 50% accepted. In 1997, 22 degrees awarded. *Degree requirements:* Thesis optional, foreign language not required. *Entrance requirements:* GRE General Test, BSN, 1 year of ICU experience. Application fee: $20 ($30 for international students). *Expenses:* Tuition $163 per credit hour for state residents; $355 per credit hour for nonresidents. Fees $498 per year full-time, $114 per semester (minimum) part-time. *Financial aid:* Scholarships and career-related internships or fieldwork available. Aid available to part-time students. *Faculty research:* Cardiac hemodynamics, hypocalcemia trauma/CA+, K+. • Prudentia Worth, Chairperson, 313-745-3610.

Webster University, College of Arts and Sciences, Department of Science, Program in Nurse Anesthesia, St. Louis, MO 63119-3194. Awards MS. Accredited by CANAEP. Faculty: 8 full-time (2 women), 5 part-time (1 woman). Students: 10 full-time (7 women), 1 part-time (0 women). *Degree requirements:* Thesis required, foreign language not required. *Entrance requirements:* 1 year of work related experience, 75 hours of graduate course work, BSN, interview. Application deadline: 9/2 (rolling processing). Application fee: $40 ($50 for international students). *Tuition:* $350 per credit hour. *Faculty research:* Clinical anesthesia, substance abuse education in the health professions, technology and education, clinical pharmacology. • Gary Clark, Director, 314-968-7075. E-mail: clarkga@webster.edu. Application contact: Beth Russell, Director of Graduate Admissions, 314-968-7089. Fax: 314-968-7166. E-mail: russelmb@webster.edu.

Xavier University of Louisiana, Nurse Anesthesia Program, New Orleans, LA 70125-1098. Awards MS. Accredited by CANAEP. Offered jointly with the Charity Hospital School of Nurse Anesthesiology. Students: 86 full-time (38 women); includes 13 minority (11 African Americans, 2 Asian Americans). Average age 30. 187 applicants, 26% accepted. In 1997, 55 degrees awarded. *Degree requirements:* Comprehensive exam required, foreign language and thesis not required. *Average time to degree:* master's–2.2 years full-time. *Entrance requirements:* GRE General Test (minimum combined score of 800), MAT (minimum score 30), minimum GPA of 2.5. Application fee: $30. *Tuition:* $200 per semester hour. *Financial aid:* 82 students received aid. Financial aid application deadline: 1/3. • Dr. Richard Barrow, Director, 504-568-2816. Fax: 504-568-4976. Application contact: Dr. Alvin J. Richard, Dean of the Graduate School, 504-483-7487. Fax: 504-485-7921. E-mail: arichard@xula.edu.

Nurse Midwifery

Baylor College of Medicine, Medical School, Nurse Midwifery Program, Houston, TX 77030-3498. Awards MS. Preaccredited by ACNM. Students: 2 full-time (both women). Average age 27. 8 applicants, 25% accepted. In 1997, 3 degrees awarded. *Average time to degree:* master's–2 years full-time. *Entrance requirements:* GRE General Test (minimum combined score of 900; average 990), minimum GPA of 3.0. Application deadline: 1/1 (rolling processing). Application fee: $30. *Expenses:* Tuition $8200 per year. Fees $467 per year (minimum). *Financial aid:* 1 student received aid; Federal Work-Study, institutionally sponsored loans available. Financial aid application deadline: 5/8; applicants required to submit FAFSA. • Dr. Susan Wente, Director, 713-798-7594.

Boston University, School of Medicine, School of Public Health, Maternal and Child Health Department, Boston, MA 02215. Offerings include nurse midwifery education (Certificate). Accredited by ACNM. *Application deadline:* 4/15 (rolling processing; 10/25 for spring admission). *Application fee:* $50. • Dr. Lisa Paine, Chairman, 617-638-5012. Fax: 617-638-5370. Application contact: Barbara St. Onge, Director of Admissions, 617-638-4640. Fax: 617-638-5299.

See in-depth description on page 1487.

Case Western Reserve University, Frances Payne Bolton School of Nursing, Master's Program in Nursing, Program in Nurse Midwifery, Cleveland, OH 44106. Awards MSN. Accredited by ACNM. Students: 50 full-time, 7 part-time. 15 applicants, 40% accepted. In 1997, 83 degrees awarded. *Degree requirements:* Thesis optional, foreign language not required. *Entrance requirements:* GRE General Test or MAT. Application deadline: 2/15 (rolling processing). Application fee: $75. *Tuition:* $18,400 per year full-time, $767 per credit hour part-time. *Financial aid:* Fellowships, research assistantships, teaching assistantships, partial tuition waivers, institutionally sponsored loans available. Aid available to part-time students. Financial aid application deadline: 6/30. *Faculty research:* Clinical nursing, normal childbearing, descriptive studies of care. • Application contact: Molly Blank, Admission Counselor, 216-368-2529. Fax: 216-368-3542. E-mail: mab44@po.cwru.edu.

Columbia University, School of Nursing, Program in Nurse Midwifery, New York, NY 10032. Awards MS. Accredited by ACNM and NLN. Part-time programs available. Faculty: 2 full-time (both women), 2 part-time (both women). Students: 11 full-time (all women), 29 part-time (all women); includes 9 minority (5 African Americans, 2 Asian Americans, 2 Hispanics). Average age 28. 35 applicants, 77% accepted. In 1997, 16 degrees awarded. *Entrance requirements:* GRE General Test (minimum score 500 on verbal and analytical sections), BSN, 1 year of clinical experience (preferred), or completion of a clinical residency. Application deadline: 4/1 (10/1 for spring admission). Application fee: $60. *Tuition:* $19,376 per year full-time, $692 per credit (minimum) part-time. *Financial aid:* Teaching assistantships available. Financial aid application deadline: 2/1. • Prof. Jennifer Dohrn, Director, 212-305-5236. Application contact: Joseph Tomaino, Assistant Dean for Student Services, 212-305-5756. E-mail: jt238@columbia.edu.

Emory University, Nell Hodgson Woodruff School of Nursing, Atlanta, GA 30322-1100. Offerings include women and children (MSN), with options in child health/pediatric nurse practitioner, midwifery, pediatric oncology nurse practitioner, perinatal/neonatal nurse. Accredited by ACNM. Postbaccalaureate distance learning degree programs offered (minimal on-campus study). School faculty: 33 full-time (32 women), 21 part-time (19 women), 48 FTE. *Degree requirements:* Thesis optional, foreign language not required. *Average time to degree:* master's–1.5 years full-time, 3 years part-time. *Entrance requirements:* GRE General Test (minimum combined score of 1500 on three sections) or MAT (minimum score 35), minimum GPA of 3.0, BS in nursing or RN license and additional course work. Application deadline: 2/1 (priority date; rolling processing; 11/1 for spring admission). Application fee: $50. *Expenses:* Tuition $18,050 per year. Fees $200 per year. • Dr. Dyanne D. Affonso, Dean, 404-727-7976. Fax: 404-727-0536. Application contact: Debbie Ashtiani, Director, 404-727-7980.

Marquette University, College of Nursing, Milwaukee, WI 53201-1881. Offerings include advanced practice nursing (MSN), with options in adult, children, neonatal nurse practitioner, nurse-midwifery, older adult; nurse-midwifery (Certificate). One or more programs accredited by ACNM. College faculty: 24 full-time (23 women), 5 part-time (4 women). *Degree requirements:* For master's, thesis or alternative, comprehensive exam required, foreign language not required. *Entrance requirements:* For master's, GRE General Test, TOEFL (minimum score 550), BSN, RN, Wisconsin license. Application fee: $40. *Tuition:* $490 per credit. • Dr. Madeline Wake, Dean, 414-288-3812. Application contact: Dr. Gregory Olson, Associate Dean, 414-288-3808. Fax: 414-288-1578.

Medical University of South Carolina, College of Nursing, Program in Nurse-Midwifery, Charleston, SC 29425-0002. Awards MSN. Faculty: 7 full-time (all women), 1 (woman) part-time. Students: 11 full-time (all women), 6 part-time (all women); includes 1 minority (African American). Average age 35. 22 applicants, 41% accepted. In 1997, 4 degrees awarded. *Degree requirements:* Computer language required, thesis optional, foreign language not required. *Entrance requirements:* GRE General Test (minimum combined score of 1000), BSN, previous course work in statistics and physical assessment, 2 years nursing experience, license, interview. Application deadline: 2/15. Application fee: $55. *Expenses:* Tuition $3760 per year full-time, $173 per semester hour part-time for state residents; $5672 per year full-time, $270 per semester hour part-time for nonresidents. Fees $280 per year (minimum). *Financial aid:* Federal Work-Study, institutionally sponsored loans available. Financial aid application deadline: 5/1. • Deborah Williamson, Track Coordinator, 843-792-8515. Application contact: Office of Enrollment Services, 843-792-3281.

Medical University of South Carolina, College of Nursing, Program in Nursing, Charleston, SC 29425-0002. Offerings include nurse-midwifery (MSN). Accredited by ACNM. *Degree requirements:* Computer language required, thesis optional, foreign language not required. *Entrance requirements:* GRE General Test (minimum combined score of 1000), BSN, previous course work in statistics and physical assessment, 1 year nursing experience, license. Application deadline: 2/15 (10/15 for spring admission). Application fee: $55. *Expenses:* Tuition $3760 per year full-time, $173 per semester hour part-time for state residents; $5672 per year full-time, $270 per semester hour part-time for nonresidents. Fees $280 per year (minimum). • Dr. Jean Leuner, Associate Dean, 843-792-8515. Application contact: Office of Enrollment Services, 843-792-3281.

New York University, School of Education, Division of Nursing, Programs in Advanced Practice Nursing, Program in Nurse Midwifery, New York, NY 10012-1019. Awards MA, AC. Preaccredited by ACNM. Part-time and evening/weekend programs available. Faculty: 25 full-time, 9 part-time. Students: 1 full-time, 25 part-time. 8 applicants, 75% accepted. *Degree requirements:* For master's, thesis required (for some programs), foreign language not required. *Entrance requirements:* For master's, TOEFL; for AC, TOEFL, master's degree. Application deadline: 2/1 (priority date; rolling processing; 12/1 for spring admission). Application fee: $40 ($60 for international students). *Financial aid:* Partial tuition waivers, Federal Work-Study, institutionally sponsored loans available. Financial aid application deadline: 3/1; applicants required to submit FAFSA. • Patricia Burkhardt, Director, 212-998-5895. Fax: 212-995-3143. Application contact: Office of Graduate Admissions, 212-998-5030. Fax: 212-995-4328.

Oregon Health Sciences University, School of Nursing, Program in Nurse Midwifery, 3181 SW Sam Jackson Park Road, Portland, OR 97201-3098. Awards MN, MS, Post Master's Certificate. One or more programs accredited by ACNM and NLN. *Degree requirements:* For master's, thesis optional, foreign language not required. *Entrance requirements:* For master's, GRE General Test (minimum combined score of 1000), bachelor's degree in nursing, minimum undergraduate GPA of 3.0; for Post Master's Certificate, master's degree in nursing. Application deadline: 1/15. Application fee: $40. • Application contact: Office of Recruitment, 503-494-7725. Fax: 503-494-4350.

Philadelphia College of Textiles and Science, School of Science and Health, Program in Midwifery, Philadelphia, PA 19144-5497. Awards MS. Part-time and evening/weekend programs available. *Entrance requirements:* GRE or MAT, minimum GPA of 2.85. Application deadline: rolling. Application fee: $35. *Tuition:* $448 per credit hour. *Financial aid:* Research assistantships, graduate assistantships, residential assistantships, Federal Work-Study, and career-related internships or fieldwork available. Financial aid applicants required to submit FAFSA. • Kate McHugh, Director, 215-951-2528. Fax: 215-951-2615. E-mail: mchugh@phila.col.edu. Application contact: Robert J. Reed, Director of Graduate Admissions, 215-951-2943. Fax: 215-951-2907. E-mail: gradadm@phila.col.edu.

State University of New York at Stony Brook, Health Sciences Center, School of Nursing, Program in Nurse-Midwifery, Stony Brook, NY 11794. Awards MS, Certificate. Preaccredited by ACNM. Students: 87 full-time (86 women), 14 part-time (all women); includes 7 minority (4 African Americans, 3 Hispanics). In 1997, 45 master's, 10 Certificates awarded. *Degree requirements:* For master's, thesis required, foreign language not required. *Entrance* *requirements:* For master's, BSN, minimum GPA of 3.0, previous course work in statistics. Application deadline: 1/15. Application fee: $50. *Expenses:* Tuition $5100 per year full-time, $213 per credit hour part-time for state residents; $8416 per year full-time, $351 per credit hour part-time for nonresidents. Fees $529 per year full-time, $77 per semester (minimum) part-time. *Financial aid:* Application deadline 3/15. • Dr. Judith Treistman, Director, 516-444-8444. Fax: 516-444-3136. E-mail: judith_treistman@notes2.nursing.sunysb.edu.

University of Cincinnati, College of Nursing and Health, Cincinnati, OH 45221-0038. Offerings include nurse midwifery (MSN). Preaccredited by ACNM. College faculty: 26 full-time. *Degree requirements:* Project or thesis required, foreign language not required. *Average time to degree:* master's–1.5 years full-time, 2.5 years part-time; doctorate–4 years full-time, 6 years part-time. *Entrance requirements:* GRE General Test. Application deadline: 1/1 (priority date; rolling processing). Application fee: $30. *Tuition:* $7228 per year full-time, $185 per credit hour part-time for state residents; $13,812 per year full-time, $352 per credit hour part-time for nonresidents. • Dr. Andrea Lindell, Dean, 513-558-5330. Application contact: Tom West, Program Coordinator, 513-558-3600. Fax: 513-558-7523. E-mail: tom.west@uc.edu.

University of Illinois at Chicago, College of Nursing, Program in Maternal-Child Nursing, Chicago, IL 60607-7128. Offerings include maternity nursing/nurse midwifery (MS). Accredited by ACNM. Program faculty: 9 full-time (all women). *Degree requirements:* Thesis or alternative required, foreign language not required. *Entrance requirements:* GRE General Test, TOEFL (minimum score 550), minimum GPA of 3.75 on a 5.0 scale. Application deadline: 5/15 (10/15 for spring admission). Application fee: $40 ($50 for international students). • Arlene Burroughs, Head, 312-996-7935. Application contact: Kathleen Knafl, Director of Graduate Studies, 312-996-2159.

University of Medicine and Dentistry of New Jersey, School of Health Related Professions, Newark, NJ 07107-3001. Offerings include nurse midwifery (Certificate). Accredited by ACNM. School faculty: 44 full-time (36 women), 15 part-time (10 women), 51.55 FTE. *Entrance requirements:* RN license (nurse midwifery). Application deadline: rolling. Application fee: $35. • Dr. David M. Gibson, Dean, 973-972-4276. Application contact: Dr. Laura Nelson, Associate Dean of Academic and Student Services, 973-972-5453. Fax: 973-972-7028. E-mail: shrp.adm@umdnj.edu.

See in-depth description on page 1267.

University of Miami, School of Nursing, Coral Gables, FL 33124. Offerings include primary health care (MSN), with options in adult nurse practitioner, family nurse practitioner, nurse midwifery. Accredited by ACNM. School faculty: 28 full-time (27 women), 1 (woman) part-time. *Degree requirements:* Thesis optional, foreign language not required. *Average time to degree:* master's–2 years full-time, 35 years part-time; doctorate–6.7 years full-time. *Entrance requirements:* GRE General Test, TOEFL (minimum score 550), BSN, minimum GPA of 3.0, RN experience. Application deadline: 3/1 (priority date; rolling processing; 10/1 for spring admission). Application fee: $35. *Expenses:* Tuition $815 per credit hour. Fees $174 per year. • Dr. Diane Horner, Dean, 305-284-2107. Application contact: Heidi McInnis, Director of Student Services, 305-284-4325. Fax: 305-284-5686. E-mail: lemieux@miami.edu.

University of Michigan, School of Nursing, Division of Health Promotion and Risk Reduction, Program in Parent-Child Nursing, Ann Arbor, MI 48109. Offerings include nurse midwifery (MS). Accredited by ACNM. *Degree requirements:* Thesis required, foreign language not required. *Entrance requirements:* GRE General Test, BS in nursing. Application deadline: 2/1 (priority date). Application fee: $55. • Application contact: Graduate Program Secretary, 734-763-0016. Fax: 734-647-0351.

University of Minnesota, Twin Cities Campus, School of Nursing, Nurse Midwifery Program, Minneapolis, MN 55455-0213. Awards MS. Accredited by ACNM. Students: 26 full-time; includes 1 minority (African American). 15 applicants, 47% accepted. *Degree requirements:* Final oral exam, project or thesis. *Application deadline:* 12/15 (rolling processing). *Application fee:* $40 ($50 for international students). *Financial aid:* Fellowships, research assistantships, teaching assistantships, professional nurse traineeships, and career-related internships or fieldwork available. • Melissa Avery, Head, 612-624-6494. Fax: 612-626-2359. Application contact: Kate Hanson, Nursing Recruiter, 612-624-9494. Fax: 612-624-3174. E-mail: hanso041@maroon.tc.umn.edu.

University of New Mexico, College of Nursing, Albuquerque, NM 87131-2039. Offerings include primary care nursing (MSN), with options in family nurse practitioner, nurse midwifery. Accredited by ACNM and NLN. College faculty: 38 full-time (36 women), 23 part-time (all women), 46.57 FTE. *Degree requirements:* Thesis optional, foreign language not required. *Entrance requirements:* GRE General Test, interview, minimum GPA of 3.0, previous course work in statistics. Application deadline: 7/15 (11/1 for spring admission). Application fee: $25. *Expenses:* Tuition $2442 per year full-time, $103 per credit hour part-time for state residents; $8691 per year full-time, $103 per credit hour (minimum) part-time for nonresidents. Fees $32 per year. • Dr. Sandra Ferketich, Dean, 505-272-6284. Application contact: Anne-Marie Oechsler, Director, Academic Advisement, 505-272-4224. Fax: 505-272-3970. E-mail: annmarie@unm.edu.

University of Pennsylvania, School of Nursing, Program in Nurse Midwifery, Philadelphia, PA 19104. Awards MSN. Part-time programs available. Students: 35 full-time (all women), 5 part-time (all women); includes 2 minority (1 African American, 1 Asian American). Average age 33. 28 applicants, 57% accepted. In 1997, 17 degrees awarded. *Average time to degree:* master's–1 year full-time, 2 years part-time. *Entrance requirements:* GRE General Test, BSN, minimum GPA of 3.0, previous course work in statistics, physical assessment. Application deadline: 2/15 (rolling processing). Application fee: $65. *Financial aid:* In 1997–98, 8 fellowships were awarded; research assistantships, teaching assistantships, Federal Work-Study, institutionally sponsored loans, and career-related internships or fieldwork also available. Aid available to part-time students. *Faculty research:* Breast-feeding protocols, history of midwifery, hydrotherapy in labor, cocaine abuse during pregnancy, stress in pregnancy. • Dr. Joyce Thompson, Director, 215-898-4335. Fax: 215-573-7291. E-mail: thompsoj@pobox.upenn.edu. Application contact: Susan K. Ogle, Associate Director of Admissions and Student Affairs, 215-898-3301. Fax: 215-573-8439. E-mail: sogle@pobox.upenn.edu.

The University of Texas at El Paso, College of Nursing and Health Science, Program in Nursing, 500 West University Avenue, El Paso, TX 79968-0001. Offerings include nurse midwifery (MSN). Accredited by ACNM. *Degree requirements:* Thesis optional, foreign language not required. *Entrance requirements:* GRE General Test or MAT (minimum score 50), TOEFL (minimum score 550), BSN, course work in statistics. Application deadline: 7/1 (rolling processing; 11/1 for spring admission). Application fee: $15 ($65 for international students). Electronic applications accepted. *Tuition:* $2063 per year full-time, $284 per credit hour part-time for state residents; $5753 per year full-time, $425 per credit hour part-time for nonresidents.

Vanderbilt University, School of Nursing, Nashville, TN 37240-1001. Offerings include nurse midwifery (MSN). Preaccredited by ACNM. Postbaccalaureate distance learning degree programs offered (minimal on-campus study). School faculty: 76 full-time (66 women), 253 part-time (224 women). *Degree requirements:* Terminal course required, thesis not required. *Average time to degree:* master's–2 years full-time, 4 years part-time; doctorate–4 years full-time, 5 years part-time. *Entrance requirements:* GMAT, GRE, or MAT, minimum B average. Application deadline: rolling. Application fee: $50. Electronic applications accepted. • Dr. Colleen Conway-Welch, Dean, 615-343-3243. Fax: 615-343-7711. Application contact: Patricia Peerman, Assistant Dean of Admissions, 615-322-3800. Fax: 615-343-0333. E-mail: vusn-admission@mcmail.vanderbilt.edu.

Virginia Commonwealth University, School of Nursing, Richmond, VA 23284-9005. Offerings include women's health nursing (MS). Accredited by NLN. School faculty: 50 full-time (all women), 5 part-time (all women). *Entrance requirements:* GRE General Test, BSN, minimum GPA of 2.8. Application deadline: 2/1. Application fee: $30 ($0 for international students). *Tuition:* $4960 per year full-time, $257 per credit part-time for state residents; $12,652 per year full-time, $684 per credit part-time for nonresidents. • Dr. Nancy F. Langston, Dean, 804-828-5174. E-mail: nflangst@vcu.edu. Application contact: Susan Lipp, Admissions Counselor, 804-828-5171. Fax: 804-828-7743. E-mail: sllipp@vcu.edu.

Nursing Administration

Adelphi University, School of Nursing, Program in Nursing Service Administration, Garden City, NY 11530. Awards MS, PMC. One or more programs accredited by NLN. Part-time and evening/weekend programs available. Students: 23 part-time (22 women); includes 7 minority (3 African Americans, 4 Asian Americans). Average age 41. *Degree requirements:* For master's, thesis required, foreign language not required. *Entrance requirements:* For master's, BSN, clinical experience. Application deadline: rolling. Application fee: $50. *Expenses:* Tuition $16,000 per year full-time, $485 per credit part-time. Fees $500 per year full-time, $150 per semester part-time. *Financial aid:* Research assistantships, teaching assistantships, graduate achievement awards, and career-related internships or fieldwork available. Aid available to part-time students. Financial aid application deadline: 3/1. • Dr. Caryle G. Wolahan, Director, School of Nursing, 516-877-4545.

Barry University, School of Nursing, Program in Nursing Administration, Miami Shores, FL 33161-6695. Awards MSN. Part-time and evening/weekend programs available. Faculty: 1 (woman) full-time, 3 part-time (all women). Students: 1 (woman) full-time, 21 part-time (20 women); includes 8 minority (5 African Americans, 1 Asian American, 2 Hispanics). Average age 41. 2 applicants, 100% accepted. In 1997, 12 degrees awarded. *Degree requirements:* Research project or thesis required, foreign language not required. *Entrance requirements:* GRE General Test (minimum combined score of 900) or MAT (minimum score 40), BSN, minimum GPA of 3.0, previous course work in statistics. Application deadline: 5/1 (priority date; rolling processing). Application fee: $30. *Tuition:* $450 per credit (minimum). *Financial aid:* 4 students received aid. Aid available to part-time students. Financial aid application deadline: 5/1; applicants required to submit FAFSA. *Faculty research:* Power/empowerment, health delivery systems, managed care, employee health and well being. Total annual research expenditures: $2000. • Dr. Diane LaRochelle, Associate Dean, 305-899-3800. Fax: 305-899-3831. E-mail: larochelle@diana.barry.edu. Application contact: Angela Scott, Enrollment Services, Assistant Dean, 305-899-3112. Fax: 305-899-3149. E-mail: ascott@jeanne.barry.edu.

Barry University, Schools of Nursing and Business, Program in Nursing Administration and Business Administration, Miami Shores, FL 33161-6695. Awards MBA/MSN. Part-time and evening/weekend programs available. Faculty: 1 (woman) full-time, 3 part-time (all women). Students: 1 (woman) full-time, 5 part-time (all women); includes 1 minority (Hispanic). Average age 41. 0 applicants. *Application deadline:* 5/1 (priority date; rolling processing). *Application fee:* $30. *Tuition:* $450 per credit (minimum). *Financial aid:* 2 students received aid. Aid available to part-time students. Financial aid application deadline: 5/1; applicants required to submit FAFSA. *Faculty research:* Power/empowerment, health delivery systems, managed care, employee health well-being. • Dr. Diane LaRochelle, Associate Dean, 305-899-3800. Fax: 305-899-3831. E-mail: larochelle@diana.barry.edu. Application contact: Angela Scott, Enrollment Services, Assistant Dean, 305-899-3112. Fax: 305-899-3149. E-mail: ascott@jeanne.barry.edu.

Baylor University, School of Nursing, Waco, TX 76798. Offerings include patient care management (MSN). *Entrance requirements:* GRE General Test. Application deadline: 8/1 (rolling processing; 12/1 for spring admission). Application fee: $25. *Expenses:* Tuition $7392 per year full-time, $308 per semester hour part-time. Fees $1024 per year. • Dr. Phyllis S. Karns, Dean, 254-710-3361.

Bellarmine College, Allan and Donna Lansing School of Nursing, Department of Graduate Nursing, Louisville, KY 40205-0671. Offerings include nursing administration (MSN). Department faculty: 5 full-time (all women), 5 part-time (all women), 7 FTE. *Degree requirements:* Thesis required, foreign language not required. *Entrance requirements:* GRE General Test (minimum combined score of 800; average 825), minimum undergraduate GPA of 2.75, RN license. Application deadline: 8/1 (priority date; rolling processing; 1/1 for spring admission). Application fee: $25. Electronic applications accepted. *Tuition:* $330 per credit hour. • Dr. Margaret E. Miller, Director, 800-274-4723 Ext. 8414. Fax: 502-452-8058.

Bowie State University, Program in Nursing, 14000 Jericho Park Road, Bowie, MD 20715. Offerings include administration of nursing services (MS). Accredited by NLN. *Degree requirements:* Thesis, research paper, written comprehensive exam required, foreign language not required. *Entrance requirements:* Minimum GPA of 2.5. Application deadline: 3/15 (rolling processing). Application fee: $30. *Expenses:* Tuition $169 per credit hour for state residents; $304 per credit hour for nonresidents. Fees $171 per year.

Capital University, School of Nursing, Columbus, OH 43209-2394. Offerings include administration (MSN). School faculty: 17 full-time (10 women), 3 part-time (1 woman). *Degree requirements:* Thesis or alternative required, foreign language not required. *Entrance requirements:* GRE General Test (combined average 1350), TOEFL (minimum score 550), BSN, current RN license, minimum GPA of 3.0, 1 year of professional practice. Application deadline: 8/1 (priority date; rolling processing; 12/1 for spring admission). Application fee: $25. *Tuition:* $260 per credit hour. • Dr. Doris Edwards, Dean, 614-236-6703. Application contact: Dr. Laurel Talabere, Associate Dean, 614-236-6361. Fax: 614-236-6157. E-mail: ltalaber@capital.edu.

Carlow College, Division of Nursing, Pittsburgh, PA 15213-3165. Offerings include case management (Certificate), gerontological case management/administrator (MSN), home health case management/administrator (MSN). Postbaccalaureate distance learning degree programs offered (minimal on-campus study). Division faculty: 6 full-time (all women), 14 part-time (12 women). *Degree requirements:* For master's, thesis or alternative required, foreign language not required. *Entrance requirements:* For master's, GRE General Test (minimum combined score of 1000), interview, minimum GPA of 3.0; for Certificate, MSN. Application deadline: 6/30 (rolling processing; 4/25 for spring admission). Application fee: $35. • Mary Lou Bost, Acting Chair, 412-578-6116. Fax: 412-578-6114. Application contact: Bonnie Potthoff, Office Manager, Graduate Studies, 412-578-8764. Fax: 412-578-8822.

The Catholic University of America, School of Nursing, Washington, DC 20064. Offerings include advanced practice nursing (MSN), with options in administration of nursing service, adult nurse practitioner, education, family nurse practitioner, geriatric nurse practitioner, pediatric nurse practitioner, psychiatric-mental health, school health nurse practitioner. Accredited by

Directory: Nursing Administration

The Catholic University of America (continued)
NLN. School faculty: 18 full-time (all women), 2 part-time (both women), 19 FTE. *Degree requirements:* Comprehensive exam required, thesis optional, foreign language not required. *Entrance requirements:* GRE General Test (minimum combined score of 1350 on three sections). Application deadline: 8/1 (priority date; rolling processing; 12/1 for spring admission). Application fee: $50. *Expenses:* Tuition $17,325 per year full-time, $668 per credit hour part-time. Fees $680 per year full-time, $360 per year part-time. • Sr. Mary Jean Flaherty, Dean, 202-319-5403.

Clarkson College, Graduate Programs, Department of Nursing, 101 South 42nd Street, Omaha, NE 68131-2739. Offerings include administration (MSN). Accredited by NLN. Department faculty: 6. *Degree requirements:* Practicum required, foreign language not required. *Entrance requirements:* GRE General Test, minimum GPA of 3.0. Application deadline: rolling. Application fee: $17. *Expenses:* Tuition $314 per credit hour. Fees $16 per credit hour. • Dr. Charles J. Beauchamp, Dean, 402-552-2958. Fax: 402-552-6058. Application contact: Jeff Beals, Director of Enrollment Management, 402-552-3100. Fax: 402-552-6057. E-mail: admiss@clrkcol.crhsnet.edu.

College of Mount Saint Vincent, Department of Nursing, Riverdale, NY 10471-1093. Offerings include nursing administration (MS). Accredited by NLN. Department faculty: 3 full-time (all women), 15 part-time (all women). *Degree requirements:* Computer language, written research project required, foreign language and thesis not required. *Entrance requirements:* Bachelor's degree from NLN-accredited institution, minimum GPA of 3.0. Application deadline: 6/15 (priority date; rolling processing; 12/1 for spring admission). Application fee: $50. • Dr. Barbara Cohen, Director, 718-405-3352. Application contact: Dr. Kem Louie, Chairperson, 718-405-3355.

Duke University, School of Nursing, Durham, NC 27708-0586. Offerings include health systems leadership and outcomes (MSN, Certificate). One or more programs accredited by NLN. Postbaccalaureate distance learning degree programs offered (minimal on-campus study). School faculty: 24 full-time (22 women), 4 part-time (all women). *Degree requirements:* For master's, computer language required, thesis optional, foreign language not required. *Average time to degree:* master's–1.5 years full-time, 3 years part-time; other advanced degree–1 year full-time, 2 years part-time. *Entrance requirements:* For master's, GRE General Test or MAT, BSN, minimum GPA of 3.0, previous course work in statistics, RN license, 1 year of nursing experience. Application deadline: 4/1 (priority date; rolling processing; 10/1 for spring admission). Application fee: $50. *Tuition:* $20,976 per year full-time, $552 per unit part-time. • Dr. Mary T. Champagne, Dean, 919-684-3786. E-mail: champ001@mc.duke.edu. Application contact: Judith K. Carter, Admissions Officer, 919-684-4248. Fax: 919-681-8899. E-mail: carte026@mc.duke.edu.

Duquesne University, School of Nursing, Pittsburgh, PA 15282-0001. Offerings include nursing administration (MSN). Accredited by NLN. Postbaccalaureate distance learning degree programs offered (minimal on-campus study). School faculty: 5 full-time (all women), 3 part-time (1 woman). *Degree requirements:* Computer language required, foreign language and thesis not required. *Entrance requirements:* GMAT (MSN/MBA), MAT, 1 year of work experience (2 years for family nurse practitioner). Application deadline: 7/31 (priority date; rolling processing; 11/31 for spring admission). Application fee: $40. *Expenses:* Tuition $481 per credit. Fees $39 per credit. • Dr. Jeri A. Milstead, Chair, 412-396-4865. E-mail: milstead@duq3.cc.duq.edu. Application contact: Carole Sisul, Administrative Assistant, Graduate Programs, 412-396-6551. Fax: 412-396-6346. E-mail: sisul@duq2.cc.duq.edu.

Florida Atlantic University, College of Nursing, Programs in Adult and Family Care Practitioner, Boca Raton, FL 33431-0991. Offerings include nursing administration (MS). Accredited by NLN. Faculty: 18 full-time (15 women), 8 part-time (7 women). *Degree requirements:* Thesis or alternative required, foreign language not required. *Average time to degree:* master's–2 years full-time, 3 years part-time. *Entrance requirements:* GRE General Test (minimum combined score of 1000), minimum GPA of 3.0. Application deadline: 6/1 (rolling processing; 10/15 for spring admission). Application fee: $20. *Expenses:* Tuition $2520 per year full-time, $140 per credit hour part-time for state residents; $8712 per year full-time, $484 per credit hour part-time for nonresidents. Fees $5 per year (minimum). • Dr. Ellis Quinn Youngkin, Graduate Program Coordinator, 561-297-3384. Fax: 561-297-3652. E-mail: eyoungkin@fau.edu.

Gannon University, School of Graduate Studies, College of Sciences, Engineering, and Health Sciences, School of Health Sciences, Department of Nursing, Erie, PA 16505. Offerings include administration (MSN). Accredited by NLN. *Degree requirements:* Thesis. *Entrance requirements:* GRE General Test (minimum score 500 on each section), MAT (minimum score 60), bachelor's degree from a NLN-approved nursing program, interview, Pennsylvania RN license. Application deadline: 4/15. Application fee: $25. • Dr. Beverly Bartlett, Director, 814-871-5520. Application contact: Beth Nemenz, Director of Admissions, 814-871-7240. Fax: 814-871-5803. E-mail: admissions@gannon.edu.

George Mason University, College of Nursing and Health Science, Fairfax, VA 22030-4444. Offerings include nursing administration (MSN). Accredited by NLN. College faculty: 50 full-time (46 women), 26 part-time (24 women), 61.65 FTE. *Entrance requirements:* RN license (MSN), minimum GPA of 3.0 in last 60 hours. Application deadline: 5/1 (11/1 for spring admission). Application fee: $30. Electronic applications accepted. *Tuition:* $4344 per year full-time, $181 per credit hour part-time for state residents; $12,504 per year full-time, $521 per credit hour part-time for nonresidents. • Dr. Rita M. Carty, Dean, 703-993-1919. Application contact: Dr. James D. Vail, Associate Dean, Graduate Programs and Research, 703-993-1913. Fax: 703-993-1942. E-mail: jvail@osf1.gmu.edu.

Graceland College, Master's in Nursing Program, 221 West Lexington, Suite 110, Independence, MO 64050. Offerings include health care administration (MSN). Postbaccalaureate distance learning degree programs offered (minimal on-campus study). Program faculty: 6 full-time (all women), 1 (woman) part-time, 6.5 FTE. *Degree requirements:* Thesis optional, foreign language not required. *Average time to degree:* master's–2 years full-time, 2.5 years part-time; other advanced degree–1 year full-time, 1.5 years part-time. *Entrance requirements:* BSN from nationally accredited program. Application deadline: rolling. Application fee: $80. *Tuition:* $350 per credit hour (minimum). • Dr. Karen Fernengel, Chair, 816-833-0524. Fax: 816-833-2990. E-mail: karenf@graceland.edu. Application contact: Lewis Smith, Director, Student Information Service, 800-537-6276. Fax: 540-344-1508.

Hunter College of the City University of New York, Hunter-Bellevue School of Nursing, Program in Nursing Administration, 695 Park Avenue, New York, NY 10021-5085. Awards MS. Accredited by NLN. Part-time programs available. Faculty: 10 full-time (all women). Students: 16 part-time (14 women); includes 6 minority (3 African Americans, 2 Asian Americans, 1 Hispanic). Average age 38. 6 applicants, 33% accepted. In 1997, 12 degrees awarded (100% found work related to degree). *Degree requirements:* Thesis or alternative, practicum required, foreign language not required. *Average time to degree:* master's–1.5 years full-time, 3 years part-time. *Entrance requirements:* TOEFL (minimum score 550), minimum GPA of 3.0, New York RN license. Application deadline: 4/27 (rolling processing; 11/21 for spring admission). Application fee: $40. *Expenses:* Tuition $4350 per year full-time, $185 per credit part-time for state residents; $7600 per year full-time, $320 per credit part-time for nonresidents. Fees $26 per year. *Financial aid:* Partial tuition waivers, Federal Work-Study available. Aid available to part-time students. Financial aid application deadline: 5/1; applicants required to submit FAFSA. *Faculty research:* Leadership characteristics of nurse managers. • Dr. Donna Nickitas, Coordinator, 212-481-4376. Fax: 212-481-5078. E-mail: dnickita@hejira.hunter.cuny.edu. Application contact: Audrey Berman, Associate Director for Graduate Admissions, 212-772-4490.

Indiana University–Purdue University Fort Wayne, School of Health Sciences, Fort Wayne, IN 46805-1499. Offers program in nursing administration (MS). Part-time and evening/weekend programs available. Faculty: 8 full-time (7 women). Students: 1 (woman) full-time, 9 part-time (all women). Average age 32. *Application deadline:* 8/1 (priority date; rolling processing; 12/1 for spring admission). *Application fee:* $30. *Expenses:* Tuition $2356 per year full-time, $131 per credit hour part-time for state residents; $5253 per year full-time, $292 per credit hour part-time for nonresidents. Fees $183 per year full-time, $10.15 per credit hour part-time. *Financial aid:* Application deadline 3/1. • James E. Jones, Dean, 219-481-6967. Application contact: Elaine N. Cowen, Chair, Department of Nursing, 219-481-6816.

Johns Hopkins University, School of Nursing, Dual Major in Clinical Specialist/Management, Baltimore, MD 21218-2699. Offers programs in adult health (MSN), AIDS/HIV (MSN), oncology nursing (MSN). Accredited by NLN. Part-time programs available. Faculty: 13 full-time (12 women), 3 part-time (2 women), 15 FTE. Students: 1 (woman) full-time, 3 part-time (all women). Average age 35. 3 applicants, 67% accepted. In 1997, 1 degree awarded (1% found work related to degree). *Degree requirements:* Scholarly project required, thesis optional, foreign language not required. *Average time to degree:* master's–5 years part-time. *Entrance requirements:* GRE, interview, minimum GPA of 3.0. Application deadline: 3/1 (priority date; rolling processing; 11/15 for spring admission). Application fee: $40. *Financial aid:* In 1997–98, 2 students received aid, including 2 merit scholarships (1 to a first-year student) totaling $7,000; Federal Work-Study, institutionally sponsored loans, and career-related internships or fieldwork also available. Aid available to part-time students. Financial aid application deadline: 5/1; applicants required to submit FAFSA. *Faculty research:* HIV/AIDS symptoms, outcomes, cardiovascular disease, fatigue, program evaluation. • Jacqueline Dienemann, Associate Professor, 410-614-5301. Fax: 410-955-7463. E-mail: jackied@son.jhmi.edu. Application contact: Mary O'Rourke, Director of Admissions/Student Services, 410-955-7548. Fax: 410-614-7086. E-mail: orourke@son.jhmi.edu.

Johns Hopkins University, School of Nursing, Program in Nursing Systems and Management, Baltimore, MD 21218-2699. Awards MSN. Accredited by NLN. Part-time programs available. Faculty: 9 full-time (8 women), 3 part-time (all women), 10 FTE. Students: 14 part-time (12 women); includes 4 minority (all African Americans). Average age 31. 11 applicants, 64% accepted. In 1997, 6 degrees awarded (100% found work related to degree). *Degree requirements:* Scholarly project required, thesis optional, foreign language not required. *Average time to degree:* master's–1 year full-time, 2 years part-time. *Entrance requirements:* GRE, interview, minimum GPA of 3.0. Application deadline: 3/1 (priority date; rolling processing). Application fee: $40. *Financial aid:* In 1997–98, 3 students received aid, including 2 merit scholarships totaling $2,100; research assistantships, teaching assistantships, Federal Work-Study, institutionally sponsored loans, and career-related internships or fieldwork also available. Aid available to part-time students. Financial aid application deadline: 5/1; applicants required to submit FAFSA. *Faculty research:* Violence, cultural competence, models of nursing care delivery, nurse satisfaction, nursing care costs. Total annual research expenditures: $23,356. • Jacqueline Dienemann, Head, 410-614-5301. Fax: 410-955-7463. E-mail: jackied@sonnet.nsg.jhu.edu. Application contact: Mary O'Rourke, Director of Admissions/Student Services, 410-955-7548. Fax: 410-614-7086. E-mail: orourke@son.jhmi.edu.

See in-depth description on page 1433.

Kent State University, School of Nursing, Kent, OH 44242-0001. Offerings include nursing administration (MSN). Accredited by NLN. School faculty: 29 full-time. *Degree requirements:* Thesis optional, foreign language not required. *Entrance requirements:* Minimum GPA of 2.75. Application deadline: 7/12 (rolling processing; 11/29 for spring admission). Application fee: $30. *Tuition:* $4752 per year full-time, $216 per credit hour part-time for state residents; $9213 per year full-time, $419 per credit hour part-time for nonresidents. • Dr. Davina Gosnell, Dean, 330-672-7930. Fax: 330-672-2433.

La Roche College, Program in Nursing, Pittsburgh, PA 15237-5898. Offerings include nursing management (MSN). Accredited by NLN. Program faculty: 5 full-time (all women), 2 part-time (both women). *Degree requirements:* Internship, practicum required, thesis optional, foreign language not required. *Entrance requirements:* GRE General Test (minimum combined score of 1200), TOEFL (minimum score 500). Application fee: $25. *Tuition:* $431 per credit. • Dr. Kathleen Sullivan, Division Chair, 412-536-1169. Application contact: Judy Henry, Manager of Nursing Student Enrollment, 412-536-1267. Fax: 412-536-1283.

La Salle University, Program in Nursing, 1900 West Olney Avenue, Philadelphia, PA 19141-1199. Offerings include nursing administration (MSN). Accredited by NLN. MSN (wound, ostomy, and continence nursing) new for fall 1998. Program faculty: 13 full-time (12 women), 8 part-time (all women). *Entrance requirements:* GRE or MAT, BSN, Pennsylvania RN license. Application deadline: rolling. Application fee: $30. • Dr. Zane R. Wolf, Dean, 215-951-1430. E-mail: wolf@lasalle.edu. Application contact: Dr. Janice Beitz, Graduate Director, 215-951-1430. Fax: 215-951-1896. E-mail: beitz@lasalle.edu.

Lewis University, College of Nursing, Romeoville, IL 60446. Offerings include nursing administration (MSN, Certificate). One or more programs accredited by NLN. *Entrance requirements:* For master's, GRE General Test (minimum combined score of 850) or College of Nursing Writing Exam, minimum GPA of 2.5. Application deadline: rolling. Application fee: $35.

Loma Linda University, Graduate School, Department of Graduate Nursing, Program in Nursing Administration, Loma Linda, CA 92350. Offers nursing administration (MS), nursing management (Certificate). One or more programs accredited by NLN. Part-time programs available. *Degree requirements:* For master's, thesis or alternative required, foreign language not required. *Entrance requirements:* For master's, GRE General Test (minimum combined score of 1500). Application fee: $40. *Tuition:* $380 per unit. *Financial aid:* Grants, Federal Work-Study, institutionally sponsored loans, and career-related internships or fieldwork available. Aid available to part-time students. Financial aid application deadline: 6/1. *Faculty research:* Job aspects contributing to satisfaction among leaders in health care institutions, leadership content significant to RN graduates. • Dr. Ruth Weber, Director, 909-824-4360.

Louisiana State University Medical Center, School of Nursing, 433 Bolivar Street, New Orleans, LA 70112-2223. Offerings include nursing service administration (MN, DNS). One or more programs accredited by NLN. School faculty: 10 full-time (all women), 4 part-time (3 women). *Degree requirements:* For master's, thesis optional, foreign language not required; for doctorate, dissertation required, foreign language not required. *Entrance requirements:* For master's, GRE General Test, MAT (minimum score 50), TOEFL, minimum GPA of 3.0; for doctorate, GRE General Test (minimum combined score of 1500 on three sections), TOEFL (minimum score 550), minimum GPA of 3.5. Application deadline: 3/17. Application fee: $50. *Expenses:* Tuition $2878 per year full-time, $421 per semester (minimum) part-time for state residents; $6003 per year full-time, $838 per semester (minimum) part-time for nonresidents. Fees $350 per year full-time, $90 per semester (minimum) part-time. • Dr. Elizabeth Humphrey, Dean, 504-568-4106. Application contact: Dr. Barbara C. Donlon, Acting Director, 504-568-4137. Fax: 504-568-3308. E-mail: bdonlo@lsumc.edu.

Loyola University Chicago, Graduate School, Marcella Niehoff School of Nursing, Nursing Service Administration Program, 820 North Michigan Avenue, Chicago, IL 60611-2196. Awards MSN, MSN/MBA. Accredited by NLN. Students: 2 full-time (1 woman), 17 part-time (all women). Average age 36. 2 applicants, 100% accepted. In 1997, 6 degrees awarded. *Degree requirements:* Comprehensive exam or oral thesis defense required, foreign language not required. *Entrance requirements:* GRE General Test (minimum combined score of 1350 on three sections), BSN, minimum GPA of 3.0, professional license, clinical experience. Application deadline: rolling. Application fee: $35. *Tuition:* $467 per semester hour. *Financial aid:* Teaching assistantships, assistantships, traineeships available. Financial aid application deadline: 3/1. *Faculty research:* Patient classification systems, career/job mobility. • Application contact: Dr. Marcia Maurer, Associate Dean and Director of Graduate Programs, 773-508-3261. Fax: 773-508-3241. E-mail: mmaurer@luc.edu.

Madonna University, Program in Nursing, Livonia, MI 48150-1173. Offerings include nursing administration (MSN). Accredited by NLN. Program faculty: 13 full-time (all women), 3 part-time (1 woman). *Degree requirements:* Thesis or alternative required, foreign language not required. *Entrance requirements:* GRE General Test. Application deadline: 8/1 (priority date; rolling processing; 4/1 for spring admission). *Expenses:* Tuition $260 per credit hour (minimum). Fees $50 per semester. • Dr. Mary Eddy, Coordinator of Graduate Nursing, 734-432-5461. Fax: 734-432-5463. E-mail: eddy@smtp.munet.edu. Application contact: Sandra Kellums, Coordinator of Graduate Admissions, 734-432-5666. Fax: 734-432-5393. E-mail: kellums@smtp.munet.edu.

Mankato State University, College of Allied Health and Nursing, Department of Nursing, South Rd and Ellis Ave, PO Box 8400, Mankato, MN 56002-8400. Offerings include family nursing (MSN), with options in clinical nurse specialist, educator, family nurse practitioner, manager; managed care (MSN), with options in clinical nurse specialist, educator, family nurse practitioner, manager. One or more programs accredited by NLN. Offered jointly with Metropolitan State University. Department faculty: 13 full-time (all women). *Degree requirements:* Computer language, comprehensive exam, internships, research project or thesis required, foreign language not required. *Entrance requirements:* GRE General Test (minimum combined score of 1350) or MAT, minimum GPA of 3.0 during previous 2 years, BSN or equivalent. Application deadline: 7/10 (priority date; rolling processing; 10/30 for spring admission). Application fee: $20. *Tuition:* $126 per credit (minimum) for state residents; $200 per credit for nonresidents. • Mary Huntley, Director, 507-389-6022. Application contact: Collaborative MSN Program Admissions, 507-389-6022.

Marymount University, School of Health Professions, Programs in Nursing, Program in Nursing Administration, Arlington, VA 22207-4299. Awards MSN. Accredited by NLN. *Degree requirements:* Thesis or alternative required, foreign language not required. *Entrance requirements:* 2 years of clinical experience, interview, minimum GPA of 3.0, RN license. Application deadline: rolling. Application fee: $35. *Expenses:* Tuition $465 per credit hour. Fees $120 per year full-time, $5 per credit hour part-time. • Dr. Catherine Connelly, Dean, School of Health Professions, 703-284-1580. Fax: 703-284-3819. E-mail: catherine.connelly@marymount.edu.

Medical University of South Carolina, College of Nursing, Program in Nursing, Charleston, SC 29425-0002. Offerings include administration in nursing (MSN). Accredited by NLN. *Degree requirements:* Computer language required, thesis optional, foreign language not required. *Entrance requirements:* GRE General Test (minimum combined score of 1000), BSN, previous course work in statistics and physical assessment, 1 year nursing experience, license. Application deadline: 2/15 (10/15 for spring admission). Application fee: $55. *Expenses:* Tuition $3760 per year full-time, $173 per semester hour part-time for state residents; $5672 per year full-time, $270 per semester hour part-time for nonresidents. Fees $280 per year (minimum). • Dr. Jean Leuner, Associate Dean, 843-792-8515. Application contact: Office of Enrollment Services, 843-792-3281.

Molloy College, Department of Nursing, 1000 Hempstead Avenue, Rockville Centre, NY 11571-5002. Offerings include nursing administration (Advanced Certificate). Department faculty: 16 full-time (14 women), 12 part-time (9 women). *Average time to degree:* master's–2.2 years full-time, 3.7 years part-time; other advanced degree–1 year full-time, 2 years part-time. *Entrance requirements:* Master's degree in nursing. Application deadline: 9/2 (priority date; rolling processing; 1/20 for spring admission). Application fee: $60. *Expenses:* Tuition $430 per credit. Fees $430 per year full-time, $165 per semester (minimum) part-time. • Dr. Carol A. Clifford, Director, Graduate Program, 516-256-2218. Fax: 516-678-9718. E-mail: clica01@molloy.edu. Application contact: Wayne James, Vice President for Enrollment and Management, 516-678-5000 Ext. 240. Fax: 516-256-2247.

Mount Saint Mary College, Division of Nursing, Newburgh, NY 12550-3494. Offerings include adult nurse practitioner (MS), with options in nursing education, nursing management; clinical nurse specialist-adult health (MS), with options in nursing education, nursing management. MS (adult nurse practitioner) new for fall 1998. Division faculty: 6 full-time (5 women), 1 (woman) part-time. *Degree requirements:* Computer language, research project required, foreign language and thesis not required. *Entrance requirements:* GRE General Test (minimum combined score of 1200; average 1400) or MAT (minimum score 40), BSN, minimum GPA of 3.0, RN license. Application deadline: 5/3 (priority date; 10/31 for spring admission). Application fee: $20. *Expenses:* Tuition $367 per credit. Fees $30 per year. • Sr. Leona DeBoer, Coordinator, 914-569-3138. Fax: 914-562-6762. E-mail: deboer@msmc.edu.

Northeastern University, Graduate School of Nursing, Program in Nursing Administration, Boston, MA 02115-5096. Awards MS, MS/MBA. *Degree requirements:* Thesis or alternative required, foreign language not required. *Entrance requirements:* GRE General Test, minimum GPA of 3.0, previous course work in statistics, 1-2 years nursing experience, RN license, ICU experience. Application deadline: 4/1 (priority date; rolling processing; 2/1 for spring admission). Application fee: $50. *Expenses:* Tuition $440 per credit hour. Fees $55 per quarter full-time, $13.25 per quarter part-time. *Faculty research:* Nursing informatics. • Dr. Jane Aroian, Coordinator, 617-373-3128. Application contact: Molly Schnabel, Admissions Coordinator, 617-373-3590. Fax: 617-373-8672. E-mail: mschnabe@lynx.neu.edu.

Announcement: Master's program in nursing administration (52 quarter hours) for nurse managers and MS/MBA program (88 quarter hours) for nurse executives. Includes advanced health-care informatics and the latest transformations in the health-care systems. Full- and part-time study. Preceptorships available in Boston's top health-care organizations. For application, contact Molly Schnabel, Admissions Coordinator, at 617-373-3590.

Oakland University, School of Nursing, Program in Nursing Administration, Rochester, MI 48309-4401. Awards MSN. Accredited by NLN. Students: 7 part-time (all women). 0 applicants. In 1997, 7 degrees awarded. *Degree requirements:* Thesis. *Entrance requirements:* GRE General Test, minimum GPA of 3.0 for unconditional admission. Application deadline: 7/15 (3/15 for spring admission). Application fee: $30. *Expenses:* Tuition $3852 per year full-time, $214 per credit hour part-time for state residents; $8532 per year full-time, $474 per credit hour part-time for nonresidents. Fees $420 per year. *Financial aid:* Full tuition waivers, Federal Work-Study, institutionally sponsored loans available. Financial aid application deadline: 3/1; applicants required to submit FAFSA. • Dr. Diane Wilson, Director, 248-370-4484.

Otterbein College, Program in Nursing, Westerville, OH 43081. Offerings include nurse service administration (MSN). Postbaccalaureate distance learning degree programs offered. *Application deadline:* rolling. *Application fee:* $35. *Tuition:* $5216 per quarter. • Dr. Judy Strayer, Chair, 614-823-1614. Fax: 614-823-3131.

Pacific Lutheran University, School of Nursing, Program in Health Care Management, Tacoma, WA 98447. Offers client systems management (MSN), health care systems management (MSN). Accredited by NLN. Part-time and evening/weekend programs available. Faculty: 11 full-time (10 women), 1 (woman) part-time. Students: 4 full-time (all women), 8 part-time (7 women). Average age 41. 7 applicants, 100% accepted. In 1997, 12 degrees awarded. *Degree requirements:* Thesis optional, foreign language not required. *Entrance requirements:* GRE General Test, TOEFL (minimum score 550), bachelor's degree in nursing, minimum undergraduate GPA of 3.0. Application deadline: 4/1 (priority date; rolling processing). Application fee: $35. *Tuition:* $490 per semester hour. *Financial aid:* Research assistantships, scholarships, Federal Work-Study available. Financial aid application deadline: 3/1. • Application contact: Marjo Burdick, Office of Admissions, 253-535-7151. Fax: 253-535-8320. E-mail: admissions@plu.edu.

Queens College, Hayworth College, Division of Nursing, 1900 Selwyn Avenue, Charlotte, NC 28274-0002. Offerings include nursing management (MSN). MSN new for fall 1998. *Degree requirements:* Research project required, thesis not required. *Entrance requirements:* Minimum GPA of 3.0. Application deadline: rolling. Application fee: $25. *Expenses:* Tuition $225 per credit hour. Fees $40 per year. • Dr. Joan McGill, Chair, 704-337-2295. Application contact: Anne Duplessis, Director of Admissions, 704-337-2314. Fax: 704-337-2415.

Sacred Heart University, College of Education and Health Professions, Faculty of Science and Mathematics, 5151 Park Avenue, Fairfield, CT 06432-1000. Awards MSN, MSN/MBA. Program in nursing administration (MSN). Accredited by NLN. Part-time and evening/weekend programs available. Faculty: 5 full-time (all women), 5 part-time (all women). Students: 1 (woman) full-time, 65 part-time (63 women); includes 7 minority (5 African Americans, 1 Asian American, 1 Hispanic). Average age 36. 4 applicants, 100% accepted. In 1997, 10 degrees awarded. *Entrance requirements:* MAT (minimum score 52), BSN, minimum GPA of 3.0. Application deadline: rolling. Application fee: $40 ($100 for international students). *Expenses:* Tuition $365 per credit. Fees $78 per semester. • Dr. Constance Young, Acting Director, Graduate Program in Nursing, 203-371-7715. Application contact: Elizabeth Nugent, Graduate Admissions Counselor, 203-371-7880. Fax: 203-365-4732. E-mail: gradstudies@sacredheart.edu.

Saginaw Valley State University, College of Nursing, Program in Nursing Client Care Management, University Center, MI 48710. Awards MSN. Accredited by NLN. Part-time programs available. Faculty: 5 full-time (all women). Students: 4 full-time (all women), 13 part-time (all women); includes 1 minority (African American), 1 international. In 1997, 2 degrees awarded. *Degree requirements:* Thesis. *Entrance requirements:* GRE. Application deadline: rolling. Application fee: $25. *Expenses:* Tuition $159 per credit hour for state residents; $311 per credit hour for nonresidents. Fees $8.70 per credit hour. • Application contact: Dr. Janalou Blecke, Assistant Dean, 517-790-4130. Fax: 517-790-1978. E-mail: jblecke@tardis.svsu.edu.

Saint Louis University, School of Nursing, Program in Administration of Nursing and Patient Care Systems, St. Louis, MO 63103-2097. Awards MSN, MSN(R), Certificate, MPH/MSN, MSN/MBA. Offerings include informatics nurse (MSN, MSN(R), Certificate). *Degree requirements:* For master's, comprehensive oral exam required, thesis optional, foreign language not required. *Entrance requirements:* For master's, GRE General Test. Application deadline: 7/1 (rolling processing; 11/1 for spring admission). Application fee: $40. *Tuition:* $542 per credit hour. *Financial aid:* Traineeships available. Financial aid application deadline: 4/1. • Dr. Sandra Blaesing, Program Director, 314-577-8962. Application contact: Dr. Marcia Buresch, Assistant Dean of the Graduate School, 314-977-2240. Fax: 314-977-3943.

Saint Martin's College, Graduate Programs, Program in Nursing, Lacey, WA 98503-7500. Offerings include leadership in health policy (MSN). Program being phased out; applicants no longer accepted. • Dr. Maura Egan, Director, 360-438-4560.

Saint Xavier University, School of Nursing, Chicago, IL 60655-3105. Offerings include leadership in community health nursing (MS). Accredited by NLN. MBA/MS offered in cooperation with the Graham School of Management. School faculty: 10 full-time (all women), 2 part-time (both women). *Entrance requirements:* MAT or GRE General Test, minimum GPA of 3.0, RN license. Application deadline: 2/15 (9/15 for spring admission). Application fee: $35. *Expenses:* Tuition $450 per hour. Fees $50 per year. • Dr. Mary Lebold, Dean, 773-298-3700. Fax: 773-779-9061. E-mail: lebold@sxu.edu. Application contact: Sr. Evelyn McKenna, Vice President of Enrollment Management, 773-298-3050. Fax: 773-298-3076. E-mail: mckenna@sxu.edu.

Samuel Merritt College, Department of Nursing, Oakland, CA 94609-3108. Offerings include case management (MSN). Department faculty: 11 full-time (9 women), 5 part-time (3 women), 13.37 FTE. *Degree requirements:* Thesis or alternative required, foreign language not required. *Average time to degree:* master's–2.2 years full-time. *Entrance requirements:* TOEFL (minimum score 600), minimum GPA of 2.5 in science, 3.0 overall. Application deadline: 2/1 (rolling processing). Application fee: $50. *Expenses:* Tuition $605 per unit. Fees $25 per year. • Dr. Audrey Berman, Graduate Coordinator, 510-869-6733. Application contact: John Garten-Schuman, Director of Admissions, 510-869-6576. Fax: 510-869-6525.

San Francisco State University, College of Health and Human Services, School of Nursing, San Francisco, CA 94132-1722. Offerings include nursing administration (MS). Accredited by NLN. *Degree requirements:* Thesis required, foreign language not required. *Entrance requirements:* Minimum GPA of 3.0. Application deadline: 11/30 (priority date; rolling processing; 5/31 for spring admission). Application fee: $55. *Expenses:* Tuition $0 for state residents; $246 per unit for nonresidents. Fees $1982 per year full-time, $1316 per year part-time.

San Jose State University, College of Applied Arts and Sciences, School of Nursing, San Jose, CA 95192-0001. Offerings include community health nursing (MS), with options in nursing administration, nursing education. Accredited by NLN. School faculty: 26 full-time (24 women), 13 part-time (12 women). *Degree requirements:* Thesis required, foreign language not required. *Entrance requirements:* BS in nursing, RN license. Application deadline: 6/1 (rolling processing). Application fee: $59. *Expenses:* Tuition $0 for state residents; $246 per unit for nonresidents. Fees $2017 per year full-time, $1351 per year part-time. • Dr. Bobbye Gorenberg, Director, 408-924-3130. Application contact: Dr. Colleen Saylor, Graduate Coordinator, 408-924-3134.

Seton Hall University, College of Nursing, Department of Graduate Nursing, Nursing Administration Program, South Orange, NJ 07079-2697. Awards MSN. Accredited by NLN. Part-time programs available. Faculty: 1 (woman) full-time, 2 part-time (1 woman). *Degree requirements:* Research project required, foreign language and thesis not required. *Entrance requirements:* GRE or MAT, BSN. Application deadline: 5/15 (priority date; rolling processing; 11/15 for spring admission). Application fee: $50. *Expenses:* Tuition $500 per credit. Fees $610 per year full-time, $185 per semester part-time. *Financial aid:* Graduate assistantships, traineeships, partial tuition waivers, institutionally sponsored loans available. Financial aid application deadline: 7/15. • Dr. Joan Trofino, Director, 973-761-9280. Fax: 973-761-9670. E-mail: trofinjo@shu.edu.

Seton Hall University, College of Nursing, Department of Graduate Nursing, Nursing Case Management Program, South Orange, NJ 07079-2697. Awards MSN. Accredited by NLN. Faculty: 1 (woman) full-time, 2 part-time (1 woman). *Degree requirements:* Research project required, foreign language and thesis not required. *Entrance requirements:* GRE or MAT. Application deadline: 5/15 (priority date; rolling processing; 11/15 for spring admission). Application fee: $50. *Expenses:* Tuition $500 per credit. Fees $610 per year full-time, $185 per semester part-time. *Financial aid:* Graduate assistantships, traineeships, partial tuition waivers, institutionally sponsored loans available. Financial aid application deadline: 7/15. • Dr. Joan Trofino, Director, 973-761-9280. Fax: 973-761-9607. E-mail: trofinjo@shu.edu.

Spalding University, School of Nursing and Health Sciences, Louisville, KY 40203-2188. Offerings include administration (MSN). Accredited by NLN. School faculty: 5 full-time (4 women). *Entrance requirements:* GRE General Test, BSN. Application deadline: 8/15 (priority date; rolling processing). Application fee: $30. *Expenses:* Tuition $350 per credit hour (minimum). Fees $48 per year full-time, $4 per credit hour part-time. • Dr. Cynthia Crabtree, Dean, 502-585-7125. E-mail: nursing@spalding10.win.net. Application contact: Jeanne Anderson, Assistant to the Provost and Director of Graduate Office, 502-585-7105. Fax: 502-585-7158. E-mail: gradoffc@spalding6.win.net.

State University of New York Institute of Technology at Utica/Rome, School of Nursing, Program in Nursing Administration, PO Box 3050, Utica, NY 13504-3050. Awards MS. Accredited by NLN. Part-time programs available. Faculty: 3 full-time (all women), 2 part-time (both women). Students: 5 full-time (all women), 12 part-time (11 women). Average age 35. 11 applicants, 82% accepted. In 1997, 9 degrees awarded. *Degree requirements:* Thesis or alternative required, foreign language not required. *Average time to degree:* master's–2 years full-time, 4 years part-time. *Entrance requirements:* GRE General Test, minimum GPA of 3.0 in last 30 hours of undergraduate course work, bachelor's degree in nursing, RN license, 1 year of professional experience. Application deadline: 6/15 (priority date; rolling processing). Application fee: $50. *Expenses:* Tuition $5100 per year full-time, $213 per credit hour part-time for state residents; $8416 per year full-time, $351 per credit hour part-time for nonresidents. Fees $570 per year full-time, $17.60 per credit hour part-time. *Financial aid:* 9 students received aid; Federal Work-Study and career-related internships or fieldwork available. Aid available to part-time students. Financial aid applicants required to submit FAFSA. *Faculty research:* Moral

Directory: Nursing Administration

State University of New York Institute of Technology at Utica/Rome (continued)

reasoning, Myers-Briggs personality, home care, critical thinking, public health. • Application contact: Marybeth Lyons, Director of Admissions, 315-792-7500. Fax: 315-792-7837. E-mail: smbl@sunyit.edu.

Texas A&M University–Corpus Christi, College of Science and Technology, Program in Nursing, Corpus Christi, TX 78412-5503. Offers nursing administration (MSN). Accredited by NLN. Part-time and evening/weekend programs available. Students: 10 full-time (8 women), 68 part-time (60 women); includes 26 minority (3 African Americans, 22 Hispanics, 1 Native American). Average age 40. In 1997, 6 degrees awarded. *Degree requirements:* Thesis optional, foreign language not required. *Entrance requirements:* GRE General Test. Application deadline: 7/15 (priority date; rolling processing; 11/15 for spring admission). Application fee: $10 ($30 for international students). *Expenses:* Tuition $648 per year full-time, $120 per semester (minimum) part-time for state residents; $4482 per year full-time, $747 per semester (minimum) part-time for nonresidents. Fees $1010 per year full-time, $205 per semester part-time. *Financial aid:* Federal Work-Study, institutionally sponsored loans, and career-related internships or fieldwork available. Aid available to part-time students. Financial aid application deadline: 3/15; applicants required to submit FAFSA. • Dr. Rebecca Jones, Director, 512-994-2649. E-mail: addst014@tamucc.edu. Application contact: Mary Margaret Dechant, Director of Admissions, 512-994-2624. Fax: 512-994-5887.

Texas Tech University Health Sciences Center, School of Nursing, Lubbock, TX 79430-0002. Offerings include administration (MSN). Accredited by NLN. Postbaccalaureate distance learning degree programs offered (minimal on-campus study). School faculty: 14 full-time (all women). *Degree requirements:* Thesis required, foreign language not required. *Average time to degree:* master's–2 years full-time, 3 years part-time. *Entrance requirements:* GRE General Test (minimum combined score of 1000), MAT (minimum score 50), minimum GPA of 3.0, sample of written work. Application deadline: 6/1 (rolling processing; 10/1 for spring admission). Application fee: $30 ($50 for international students). *Expenses:* Tuition $36 per credit hour for state residents; $249 per credit hour for nonresidents. Fees $1348 per year full-time for state residents; $1349 per year full-time for nonresidents. • Dr. Pat S. Yoder Wise, Dean, 806-743-2738. E-mail: sonpsy@ttuhsc.edu. Application contact: Nancy Ridenour, Associate Dean for Education, 806-743-2737. Fax: 806-743-1622. E-mail: sonnar@ttuhsc.edu.

The University of Akron, College of Nursing, Akron, OH 44325-0001. Offerings include nursing administration (MSN). Accredited by NLN. College faculty: 19 full-time, 13 part-time. *Degree requirements:* Thesis optional, foreign language not required. *Entrance requirements:* GRE or MAT, minimum GPA of 3.0. Application deadline: 8/15 (rolling processing). Application fee: $25 ($50 for international students). *Expenses:* Tuition $178 per credit hour for state residents; $333 per credit hour for nonresidents. Fees $145 per year full-time, $32 per semester (minimum) part-time. • Cynthia Capers, Dean, 330-972-7552. Application contact: Dr. Linda Linc, Interim Associate Dean of the Graduate Program, 330-972-7553.

University of Cincinnati, College of Nursing and Health, Cincinnati, OH 45221-0038. Offerings include nursing administration (MSN). Accredited by NLN. College faculty: 26 full-time. *Degree requirements:* Project or thesis required, foreign language not required. *Average time to degree:* master's–1.5 years full-time, 2.5 years part-time; doctorate–4 years full-time, 6 years part-time. *Entrance requirements:* GRE General Test. Application deadline: 1/1 (priority date; rolling processing). Application fee: $30. *Tuition:* $7228 per year full-time, $185 per credit hour part-time for state residents; $13,812 per year full-time, $352 per credit hour part-time for nonresidents. • Dr. Andrea Lindell, Dean, 513-558-5330. Application contact: Tom West, Program Coordinator, 513-558-3600. Fax: 513-558-7523. E-mail: tom.west@uc.edu.

University of Connecticut, School of Nursing, Storrs, CT 06269. Offerings include nursing management (MS). Accredited by NLN. School faculty: 26. *Entrance requirements:* TOEFL. Application deadline: 4/1 (priority date; rolling processing; 11/1 for spring admission). Application fee: $40 ($45 for international students). *Expenses:* Tuition $5272 per year full-time, $293 per credit part-time for state residents; $13,696 per year full-time, $761 per credit part-time for nonresidents. Fees $948 per year full-time, $640 per year part-time. • Barbara K. Redman, Dean, 860-486-3716. Application contact: Jane E. Murdock, Chairperson, 860-486-3821.

University of Delaware, College of Health and Nursing Sciences, Department of Nursing, Newark, DE 19716. Offerings include nursing administration (MSN, Certificate). One or more programs accredited by NLN. Department faculty: 10 full-time (9 women), 5 part-time (all women), 12.25 FTE. *Degree requirements:* For master's, thesis optional, foreign language not required. *Average time to degree:* master's–2 years full-time, 3 years part-time. *Entrance requirements:* For master's, GRE General Test. Application deadline: 7/1. Application fee: $45. *Expenses:* Tuition $4250 per year full-time, $236 per credit hour part-time for state residents; $12,250 per year full-time, $681 per credit hour part-time for nonresidents. Fees $466 per year full-time, $15 per semester (minimum) part-time. • Application contact: Betty Bonavita, Graduate Secretary, 302-831-1255. Fax: 302-831-2382. E-mail: elizabeth.bonavita@mvs.udel.edu.

University of Hawaii at Manoa, College of Health Sciences and Social Welfare, School of Nursing, Honolulu, HI 96822. Offerings include nursing administration (MS). Accredited by NLN. School faculty: 27 full-time (24 women). *Entrance requirements:* Hawaii RN license. *Tuition:* $4029 per year full-time, $214 per credit hour part-time for state residents; $9957 per year full-time, $461 per credit hour part-time for nonresidents. • Dr. Rosanne Harrigan, Dean, 808-956-8522. Application contact: Office of Student Services, 808-956-8939.

University of Illinois at Chicago, College of Nursing, Program in Administrative Studies in Nursing, Chicago, IL 60607-7128. Awards MS. Accredited by NLN. Faculty: 6 full-time (all women). Students: 2 full-time (both women), 23 part-time (22 women); includes 5 minority (3 African Americans, 2 Asian Americans), 1 international. 5 applicants, 100% accepted. In 1997, 4 degrees awarded. *Degree requirements:* Thesis or alternative required, foreign language not required. *Entrance requirements:* GRE General Test, TOEFL (minimum score 550), minimum GPA of 3.75 on a 5.0 scale. Application deadline: 5/15 (10/15 for spring admission). Application fee: $40 ($50 for international students). *Financial aid:* Fellowships, research assistantships, teaching assistantships, partial tuition waivers, Federal Work-Study, institutionally sponsored loans, and career-related internships or fieldwork available. • Gloria Henderson, Head, 312-996-7889. Application contact: Kathleen Knafl, Director of Graduate Studies, 312-996-2159.

University of Mary, Division of Nursing, Program in Nursing Administration, 7500 University Drive, Bismarck, ND 58504-9652. Awards MSN. Accredited by NLN. *Entrance requirements:* Minimum GPA of 3.0 in nursing course work. Application deadline: 8/1 (priority date). Application fee: $15. *Tuition:* $265 per credit. *Financial aid:* Institutionally sponsored loans available. Aid available to part-time students. Financial aid application deadline: 7/1. • Application contact: Dr. Diane Fladeland, Director, Graduate Programs, 701-255-7500. Fax: 701-255-7687.

University of Maryland, Baltimore, Graduate School, School of Nursing, Baltimore, MD 21201-1627. Offerings include nursing administration (MS). Accredited by NLN. MS/MBA offered jointly with the University of Baltimore. School faculty: 49 (45 women). *Degree requirements:* Thesis or alternative required, foreign language not required. *Entrance requirements:* GRE General Test, TOEFL, minimum GPA of 2.75, previous course work in statistics, BS in nursing. Application fee: $42. *Expenses:* Tuition $253 per credit hour for state residents; $454 per credit hour for nonresidents. Fees $317 per year. • Dr. Barbara Heller, Dean, 410-706-6741. Application contact: Dr. Susan Wozenski, Assistant Dean for Student Affairs, 410-706-0501. Fax: 410-706-7238.

University of Massachusetts Lowell, College of Health Professions, Department of Nursing, Program in Administration of Nursing Services, 1 University Avenue, Lowell, MA 01854-2881. Offers health promotion (PhD). Students: 4 full-time (2 women), 9 part-time (8 women); includes 2 minority (both African Americans). *Degree requirements:* Dissertation. *Entrance requirements:* GRE General Test. Application deadline: 4/1 (priority date; rolling processing; 10/1 for spring admission). Application fee: $20 ($35 for international students). *Tuition:* $4867 per year full-time, $618 per semester (minimum) part-time for state residents; $10,276 per year full-time, $1294 per semester (minimum) part-time for nonresidents. *Financial aid:* Application deadline 4/1. • Dr. May Futrell, Chair, Department of Nursing, 978-934-4467. E-mail: may_futrell@woods.uml.edu.

University of Michigan, School of Nursing, Division of Nursing and Health Care Systems Administration, Ann Arbor, MI 48109. Awards MS, MBA/MS. Program in administration of nursing and patient care services (MS). Accredited by NLN. Part-time programs available. Postbaccalaureate distance learning degree programs offered (minimal on-campus study). Students: 16 full-time (14 women); includes 3 minority (1 African American, 1 Asian American, 1 Hispanic), 2 international. Average age 25. 5 applicants, 80% accepted. In 1997, 3 degrees awarded. *Degree requirements:* Thesis required, foreign language not required. *Entrance requirements:* GRE General Test. Application deadline: 2/1 (rolling processing). Application fee: $55. *Financial aid:* Partial tuition waivers, Federal Work-Study available. Financial aid application deadline: 3/15. *Faculty research:* Outcomes research. • Dr. Katherine R. Jones, Director, 734-936-3683.

University of Minnesota, Twin Cities Campus, School of Nursing, Program in Nursing Management, Minneapolis, MN 55455-0213. Awards MS. Accredited by NLN. Part-time programs available. Students: 3 full-time, 7 part-time. 5 applicants, 80% accepted. *Degree requirements:* Final oral exam, project or thesis. *Application deadline:* 12/15 (rolling processing). *Application fee:* $40 ($50 for international students). *Financial aid:* Fellowships, research assistantships, teaching assistantships available. • Helen Hansen, Head, 612-624-3102. Application contact: Kate Hanson, Nursing Recruiter, 612-624-9494. Fax: 612-624-3174. E-mail: hanso041@maroon.tc.umn.edu.

University of New Mexico, College of Nursing, Albuquerque, NM 87131-2039. Offerings include administration of nursing (MSN, Certificate). One or more programs accredited by NLN. College faculty: 38 full-time (36 women), 23 part-time (all women), 46.57 FTE. *Degree requirements:* For master's, thesis optional, foreign language not required. *Entrance requirements:* For master's, GRE General Test, interview, minimum GPA of 3.0, previous course work in statistics. Application deadline: 7/15 (11/1 for spring admission). Application fee: $25. *Expenses:* Tuition $2442 per year full-time, $103 per credit hour part-time for state residents; $8691 per year full-time, $103 per credit hour (minimum) part-time for nonresidents. Fees $32 per year. • Dr. Sandra Ferketich, Dean, 505-272-6284. Application contact: Anne-Marie Oechsler, Director, Academic Advisement, 505-272-4224. Fax: 505-272-3970. E-mail: annmarie@unm.edu.

University of North Carolina at Greensboro, School of Nursing, Greensboro, NC 27412-0001. Offerings include administration of nursing in health agencies (MSN). School faculty: 22 full-time (all women), 7 part-time (all women). *Degree requirements:* Thesis or alternative required, foreign language not required. *Entrance requirements:* GRE General Test or MAT, BSN, clinical experience, liability insurance, RN license. Application fee: $35. *Expenses:* Tuition $1842 per year full-time, $370 per semester (minimum) part-time for state residents; $10,296 per year full-time, $2484 per semester (minimum) part-time for nonresidents. Fees $806 per year full-time, $111 per semester (minimum) part-time. • Dr. Lynne Pearcey, Dean, 336-334-5010.

University of Pennsylvania, School of Nursing, Occupational Health Administration/Consultation Program, Philadelphia, PA 19104. Awards MSN. Accredited by NLN. Students: 1 (woman) full-time, 2 part-time (both women); includes 1 international. 0 applicants. *Entrance requirements:* GRE General Test, BSN, minimum GPA of 3.0, previous course work in statistics. Application deadline: 9/1. Application fee: $65. • Kay M. Arendasky, Associate Director, 215-898-2194. Fax: 215-573-7381. E-mail: arendask@pobox.upenn.edu. Application contact: Susan K. Ogle, Associate Director of Admissions and Student Affairs, 215-898-3301. Fax: 215-573-8439. E-mail: sogle@pobox.upenn.edu.

University of Pennsylvania, School of Nursing, Program in Nursing Administration, Philadelphia, PA 19104. Awards MSN, PhD, MBA/MSN. One or more programs accredited by NLN. Part-time programs available. Students: 13 full-time (12 women), 18 part-time (16 women); includes 5 minority (1 African American, 4 Asian Americans), 3 international. Average age 31. 17 applicants, 88% accepted. In 1997, 10 master's awarded. Terminal master's awarded for partial completion of doctoral program. *Degree requirements:* For doctorate, dissertation required, foreign language not required. *Entrance requirements:* For master's, GRE General Test, GMAT (MBA/MSN), BSN, minimum GPA of 3.0, previous course work in statistics; for doctorate, GRE General Test, GMAT (MBA/PhD), BSN or MSN, minimum GPA of 3.0. Application deadline: 9/1 (rolling processing). Application fee: $65. *Financial aid:* In 1997–98, 2 research assistantships, 8 teaching assistantships were awarded; Federal Work-Study, institutionally sponsored loans, and career-related internships or fieldwork also available. Aid available to part-time students. Financial aid application deadline: 1/2. *Faculty research:* Nursing services and policy, home health services utilization. • Dr. Cynthia Scalzi, Director, 215-898-4721. Fax: 215-573-7496. E-mail: scalzi@pobox.upenn.edu. Application contact: Susan K. Ogle, Associate Director of Admissions and Student Affairs, 215-898-3301. Fax: 215-573-8439. E-mail: sogle@pobox.upenn.edu.

University of Phoenix, Graduate Programs, Nursing Programs, Program in Nursing Administration, 4615 East Elwood St, PO Box 52069, Phoenix, AZ 85072-2069. Awards MN. Accredited by NLN. Programs offered at campuses in Colorado, Colorado Springs, Florida, Hawaii, Louisiana, Michigan, New Mexico, Northern California, Phoenix, Sacramento, San Diego, Southern California, Tucson, Utah, and at the Center for Distance Education. Postbaccalaureate distance learning degree programs offered (no on-campus study). *Degree requirements:* Thesis or alternative required, foreign language not required. *Entrance requirements:* TOEFL (minimum score 520), minimum GPA of 2.5, RN license, 3 years of work experience in field, comprehensive cognitive assessment (COCA). Application deadline: rolling. Application fee: $50. *Tuition:* $248 per credit hour. • Application contact: Campus Information Center, 602-966-9577.

University of Pittsburgh, School of Nursing, Advanced Specialized Role Program, Pittsburgh, PA 15260. Offerings include administration (MSN). Accredited by NLN. *Degree requirements:* Thesis optional, foreign language not required. *Entrance requirements:* GRE or MAT, TOEFL, BSN, RN license, nursing experience. Application deadline: 2/1 (priority date; rolling processing; 9/15 for spring admission). Application fee: $35 ($40 for international students). • Judith A. Tate, Coordinator, 412-624-5872. Fax: 412-383-7227. E-mail: jtaloo+@pitt.edu. Application contact: Dr. Kathy Lucke, Director, Student Services, 412-624-2405. Fax: 412-624-2409. E-mail: nursao+@pitt.edu.

See in-depth description on page 1451.

University of Portland, School of Nursing, Portland, OR 97203-5798. Offerings include leadership in health care systems (Post Master's Certificate). Postbaccalaureate distance learning degree programs offered (minimal on-campus study). School faculty: 11 full-time (10 women). *Application deadline:* rolling. *Application fee:* $40. *Tuition:* $540 per semester hour. • Dr. Terry Misener, Dean, 503-283-7211. Fax: 503-283-7399. E-mail: misener@up.edu.

University of Puerto Rico, Medical Sciences Campus, School of Nursing, San Juan, PR 00936-5067. Offerings include nursing administration (MSN). Accredited by NLN. *Degree requirements:* 1 foreign language, thesis, research project. *Entrance requirements:* GRE, BSN, interview, (Puerto Rico) RN license, 2 years of nursing experience, previous course work in physical examination. Application deadline: 3/16. Application fee: $25.

University of Rhode Island, College of Nursing, Kingston, RI 02881. Offerings include nursing service administration (MS). One or more programs accredited by NLN. *Application deadline:* 4/15. *Application fee:* $35. *Expenses:* Tuition $3446 per year full-time, $191 per credit part-time for state residents; $9850 per year full-time, $547 per credit part-time for nonresidents. Fees $1276 per year full-time, $135 per semester (minimum) part-time.

See in-depth description on page 1453.

University of San Diego, Philip Y. Hahn School of Nursing, San Diego, CA 92110-2492. Offerings include nursing administration (MSN). Accredited by NLN. School faculty: 12 full-time (all women), 4 part-time (all women). *Entrance requirements:* GRE or MAT, TOEFL (minimum score 580), TWE, BSN, minimum GPA of 3.0. Application deadline: 5/1 (priority date; rolling processing; 11/15 for spring admission). Application fee: $45. *Expenses:* Tuition $585 per unit (minimum). Fees $50 per year full-time, $30 per year part-time. • Dr. Janet Rodgers, Dean, 619-260-4550. Fax: 619-260-6814. Application contact: Mary Jane Tiernan, Director of Graduate Admissions, 619-260-4524. Fax: 619-260-4158. E-mail: grads@acusd.edu.

University of San Francisco, School of Nursing, San Francisco, CA 94117-1080. Offerings include nursing administration (MSN). Accredited by NLN. School faculty: 9 full-time (8 women), 1 (woman) part-time. *Average time to degree:* master's–2 years full-time, 2.5 years part-time. *Entrance requirements:* Minimum GPA of 3.0. Application deadline: rolling. Application fee: $40. *Tuition:* $658 per unit (minimum). • Dr. John Lantz, Interim Dean, 415-422-6681. Fax: 415-422-6877. E-mail: lantzj@usfca.edu.

University of South Carolina, Graduate School, College of Nursing, Program in Nursing Administration, Columbia, SC 29208. Awards MSN, Certificate. One or more programs accredited by NLN. Students: 3 full-time (all women), 12 part-time (all women); includes 3 minority (2 African Americans, 1 Hispanic). Average age 42. In 1997, 4 master's awarded. *Degree requirements:* For master's, oral or written comprehensive exam required, foreign language not required. *Entrance requirements:* For master's, GRE General Test, BS in nursing, previous course work in statistics. Application deadline: 4/15 (rolling processing; 10/15 for spring admission). Application fee: $35. Electronic applications accepted. *Expenses:* Tuition $4480 per year full-time, $220 per credit hour part-time for state residents; $9338 per year full-time, $457 per credit hour part-time for nonresidents. Fees $125 per year full-time, $37 per semester (minimum) part-time. *Financial aid:* Application deadline 2/1. • Application contact: Office of Academic and Student Affairs, 803-777-7412. Fax: 803-777-0616.

University of Southern Maine, College of Nursing, Portland, ME 04104-9300. Offerings include management (MS). Postbaccalaureate distance learning degree programs offered (minimal on-campus study). College faculty: 11 full-time (all women), 5 part-time (all women). *Degree requirements:* Thesis optional, foreign language not required. *Average time to degree:* master's–2.5 years full-time, 4 years part-time. *Entrance requirements:* GRE General Test (minimum combined score of 1000 on verbal and quantitative sections) or MAT (minimum score 45), minimum GPA of 3.0. Application deadline: 3/1. Application fee: $25. *Expenses:* Tuition $178 per credit hour for state residents; $267 per credit hour (minimum) for nonresidents. Fees $282 per year full-time, $83 per semester (minimum) part-time. • Dr. Marianne W. Rodgers, Interim Dean, 207-780-4808. Fax: 207-780-4997. E-mail: mrodgers@usm.maine.edu. Application contact: Mary Sloan, Assistant Director of Graduate Studies, 207-780-4386. Fax: 207-780-4969. E-mail: msloan@usm.maine.edu.

University of Southern Mississippi, College of Nursing, Hattiesburg, MS 39406-5167. Offerings include nursing service administration (MSN). Accredited by NLN. College faculty: 18 full-time (all women). *Degree requirements:* Thesis optional, foreign language not required. *Entrance requirements:* GRE General Test, minimum GPA of 2.75. Application deadline: 8/9 (priority date; rolling processing). Application fee: $0 ($25 for international students). *Tuition:* $2870 per year full-time, $137 per credit hour part-time for state residents; $5972 per year full-time, $172 per credit hour part-time for nonresidents. • Dr. Gerry Cadenhead, Director, 601-266-5509. Fax: 601-266-5927.

The University of Tampa, Nursing Program, Tampa, FL 33606-1490. Offerings include nursing administration (MSN). Postbaccalaureate distance learning degree programs offered (minimal on-campus study). Program faculty: 5 full-time (4 women), 7 part-time (6 women). *Degree requirements:* Oral exam, practicum required, thesis optional. *Entrance requirements:* GRE General Test (minimum combined score of 1000), minimum GPA of 3.0, RN license. Application deadline: 8/20 (priority date; rolling processing). Application fee: $35. Electronic applications accepted. • Dr. Nancy Ross, Director, 813-253-6223. Fax: 813-258-7214. Application contact: Barbara P. Strickler, Vice President for Enrollment, 800-733-4773. Fax: 813-254-4955. E-mail: admissions@alpha.utampa.edu.

University of Tennessee at Chattanooga, School of Human Services, School of Nursing, Chattanooga, TN 37403-2598. Offerings include administration (MSN). Accredited by NLN. School faculty: 8 full-time (7 women), 4 part-time (3 women). *Degree requirements:* Qualifying exams required, foreign language and thesis not required. *Entrance requirements:* GRE General Test (combined average 1485 on three sections). Application deadline: rolling. Application fee: $25. *Tuition:* $2864 per year full-time, $160 per credit hour part-time for state residents; $6806 per year full-time, $379 per credit hour part-time for nonresidents. • Dr. Maria Smith, Director, 423-755-4646. Fax: 423-755-4668. E-mail: msmith@utcvm.utc.edu. Application contact: Dr. Deborah Arfken, Assistant Provost for Graduate Studies, 423-755-4667. Fax: 423-755-4478.

The University of Texas at Arlington, School of Nursing, Arlington, TX 76019-0407. Offerings include administration/supervision of nursing (MSN). Accredited by NLN. School faculty: 20 full-time (all women), 4 part-time (all women). *Degree requirements:* Comprehensive exam or thesis required, foreign language not required. *Entrance requirements:* GRE General Test (minimum combined score of 1000 on verbal and analytical sections). Application deadline: rolling. Application fee: $25 ($50 for international students). *Tuition:* $3206 per year full-time, $468 per semester (minimum) part-time for state residents; $8612 per year full-time, $1137 per semester (minimum) part-time for nonresidents. • Dr. Elizabeth C. Poster, Dean, 817-272-2885. Application contact: Dr. Susan Grove, Graduate Adviser, 817-272-2776. Fax: 817-272-5006.

The University of Texas at El Paso, College of Nursing and Health Science, Program in Nursing, 500 West University Avenue, El Paso, TX 79968-0001. Offerings include nursing administration (MSN). Accredited by NLN. *Degree requirements:* Thesis optional, foreign language not required. *Entrance requirements:* GRE General Test or MAT (minimum score 50), TOEFL (minimum score 550), BSN, course work in statistics. Application deadline: 7/1 (rolling processing; 11/1 for spring admission). Application fee: $15 ($65 for international students). Electronic applications accepted. *Tuition:* $2063 per year full-time, $284 per credit hour part-time for state residents; $5753 per year full-time, $425 per credit hour part-time for nonresidents.

University of Tulsa, College of Business Administration, Program in Nursing Administration, Tulsa, OK 74104-3189. Awards MNA, MNA/MBA. Part-time and evening/weekend programs available. Faculty: 4 full-time (all women). Students: 0. 0 applicants. In 1997, 2 degrees awarded. *Degree requirements:* Thesis optional, foreign language not required. *Entrance requirements:* GRE General Test (minimum combined score of 1100), TOEFL (minimum score 575), bachelor's degree in nursing, RN license. Application deadline: rolling. Application fee: $30. Electronic applications accepted. *Expenses:* Tuition $480 per credit hour. Fees $2 per credit hour. *Financial aid:* Fellowships, research assistantships, teaching assistantships, Federal Work-Study available. Financial aid application deadline: 2/1; applicants required to submit FAFSA. *Faculty research:* Substance abuse, international health policy, transcultural nursing, denial in stroke patients. • Dr. Susan K. Gaston, Chairperson, 918-631-3116. Application contact: Dr. Donna M. Wing, Adviser, 918-631-2934. Fax: 918-631-2068.

Valdosta State University, College of Nursing, Valdosta, GA 31698. Offerings include administration (MSN). Accredited by NLN. College faculty: 3 full-time (all women). *Entrance requirements:* GRE General Test (minimum combined score of 800), minimum GPA of 2.8. Application deadline: 8/1 (rolling processing; 11/15 for spring admission). Application fee: $10. *Expenses:* Tuition $2472 per year full-time, $83 per semester hour part-time for state residents; $8472 per year full-time, $333 per semester hour part-time for nonresidents. Fees $236 per year full-time. • Dr. Maryann Reichenbach, Dean, 912-333-5959. E-mail: mreichenb@grits.valdosta.peachnet.edu.

Villanova University, College of Nursing, Villanova, PA 19085-1690. Offerings include clinical case management (MSN, Post Master's Certificate), health care administration (MSN). One or more programs accredited by NLN. MSN (pediatric nurse practitioner), Post Master's Certificate (nurse practitioner, nurse anesthetist, clinical case management) new for fall 1998. College faculty: 30 full-time (all women). *Degree requirements:* For master's, independent study project required, foreign language and thesis not required. *Entrance requirements:* For master's, GRE General Test (verbal section) or MAT, BSN, 1 year of recent experience, physical assessment, previous course work in statistics. Application deadline: 7/1 (priority date; rolling processing; 12/1 for spring admission). Application fee: $25. *Expenses:* Tuition $445 per credit. Fees $60 per year. • Dr. Claire Manfredi, Graduate Director, 610-519-4907. Fax: 610-519-7997. E-mail: cmanfred@email.vill.edu.

Virginia Commonwealth University, School of Nursing, Richmond, VA 23284-9005. Offerings include nursing administration (MS), with options in clinical nurse manager, nurse executive. Accredited by NLN. School faculty: 50 full-time (all women), 5 part-time (all women). *Entrance requirements:* GRE General Test, BSN, minimum GPA of 2.8. Application deadline: 2/1. Application fee: $30 ($0 for international students). *Tuition:* $4960 per year full-time, $257 per credit part-time for state residents; $12,652 per year full-time, $684 per credit part-time for nonresidents. • Dr. Nancy F. Langston, Dean, 804-828-5174. E-mail: nflangst@vcu.edu. Application contact: Susan Lipp, Admissions Counselor, 804-828-5171. Fax: 804-828-7743. E-mail: sllipp@vcu.edu.

Wayne State University, College of Nursing, Department of Adult Health and Administration, Program in Nursing Care Administration, Detroit, MI 48202. Awards MSN. Accredited by NLN. Students: 1 (woman) full-time, 4 part-time (all women); includes 1 minority (African American), 3 international. Average age 41. 2 applicants, 50% accepted. In 1997, 2 degrees awarded. *Application deadline:* 7/1 (priority date; rolling processing; 11/1 for spring admission). *Application fee:* $20 ($30 for international students). *Expenses:* Tuition $163 per credit hour for state residents; $355 per credit hour for nonresidents. Fees $498 per year full-time, $114 per semester (minimum) part-time. *Financial aid:* Research assistantships, scholarships, traineeships, institutionally sponsored loans available. Financial aid application deadline: 7/1. *Faculty research:* Health care systems, program evaluation, extended care data system. • Dr. Dawn Hameister, Assistant Dean, 313-577-4386. Fax: 313-577-4571. Application contact: Vickie Radoye, Administrative Assistant Dean, Student Affairs, 313-577-4082. Fax: 313-577-6949.

Wichita State University, College of Health Professions, School of Nursing, Wichita, KS 67260. Offerings include nursing administration (MSN). Accredited by NLN. School faculty: 11 full-time (all women). *Degree requirements:* Comprehensive exam required, thesis optional, foreign language not required. *Entrance requirements:* GRE, TOEFL (minimum score 550), BSN, minimum undergraduate GPA of 2.75. Application deadline: 6/30 (priority date; rolling processing; 1/1 for spring admission). Application fee: $25 ($40 for international students). Electronic applications accepted. *Expenses:* Tuition $2303 per year full-time, $96 per credit hour part-time for state residents; $7691 per year full-time, $321 per credit hour part-time for nonresidents. Fees $490 per year full-time, $75 per semester (minimum) part-time. • Dr. Bonnie Holaday, Interim Dean, 316-978-3610. E-mail: holaday@chp.twsu.edu. Application contact: Dr. Donna Hawley, Graduate Coordinator, 316-978-3610. Fax: 316-978-3094. E-mail: hawley@chp.twsu.edu.

Wright State University, College of Nursing and Health, Program in Nursing, Dayton, OH 45435. Offerings include nursing administration (MS). Accredited by NLN. *Degree requirements:* Thesis or alternative required, foreign language not required. *Average time to degree:* master's–2 years full-time, 5 years part-time. *Entrance requirements:* GRE General Test, TOEFL (minimum score 550), BSN from NLN-accredited college, Ohio RN license. Application deadline: 4/15 (priority date). Application fee: $25. *Tuition:* $5109 per year full-time, $161 per credit hour part-time for state residents; $9039 per year full-time, $282 per credit hour part-time for nonresidents. • Application contact: Theresa Haghnazarian, Director of Student and Alumni Affairs, 937-775-3133. Fax: 937-775-4571.

Xavier University, College of Social Sciences, Department of Nursing, Cincinnati, OH 45207-2111. Offers program in nursing administration (MSN). Part-time and evening/weekend programs available. Faculty: 10 full-time (all women). Students: 11 part-time (all women). Average age 43. 0 applicants. In 1997, 4 degrees awarded. *Degree requirements:* Computer language required, thesis optional, foreign language not required. *Entrance requirements:* MAT. Application deadline: 8/26 (priority date; rolling processing; 1/10 for spring admission). Application fee: $25. *Tuition:* $400 per credit hour. *Financial aid:* In 1997–98, 2 students received aid, including 2 scholarships totaling $900. Aid available to part-time students. Financial aid application deadline: 4/1. *Faculty research:* Stroke rehabilitation, informatics, history, gerontology, hope and its cultural influences on health, healing touch. • Dr. Susan Schmidt, Interim Chair, 513-745-3814. E-mail: schmidts@xu.edu. Application contact: Marilyn Gomez, Coordinator, 513-745-4392. Fax: 513-745-1087. E-mail: gomez@admin.xu.edu.

Nursing Education

Adelphi University, School of Nursing, Program in Teaching, Garden City, NY 11530. Awards MS, PMC. One or more programs accredited by NLN. Part-time and evening/weekend programs available. Students: 5 part-time (all women); includes 3 minority (all African Americans). Average age 50. *Degree requirements:* For master's, thesis required, foreign language not required. *Entrance requirements:* For master's, BSN, clinical experience. Application deadline: rolling. Application fee: $50. *Expenses:* Tuition $16,000 per year full-time, $485 per credit part-time. Fees $500 per year full-time, $150 per semester part-time. *Financial aid:* Research assistantships, teaching assistantships, graduate achievement awards, and career-related internships or fieldwork available. Aid available to part-time students. Financial aid application deadline: 3/1. • Dr. Caryle G. Wolahan, Director, School of Nursing, 516-877-4545.

Barry University, School of Nursing, Program in Nursing Education, Miami Shores, FL 33161-6695. Awards MSN. Part-time and evening/weekend programs available. Faculty: 1

Directory: Nursing Education

Barry University (continued)

(woman) full-time, 3 part-time (all women). Students: 1 (woman) full-time, 13 part-time (all women); includes 7 minority (5 African Americans, 2 Hispanics). Average age 39. 7 applicants, 86% accepted. In 1997, 12 degrees awarded. *Degree requirements:* Research project or thesis required, foreign language not required. *Entrance requirements:* GRE General Test (minimum combined score of 900) or MAT (minimum score 40), BSN, minimum GPA of 3.0, previous course work in statistics. Application deadline: 5/1 (priority date; rolling processing). Application fee: $30. *Tuition:* $450 per credit (minimum). *Financial aid:* 9 students received aid. Aid available to part-time students. Financial aid application deadline: 5/1; applicants required to submit FAFSA. *Faculty research:* HIV/AIDS, gerontology. • Dr. Diane LaRochelle, Associate Dean, 305-899-3800. Fax: 305-899-3831. E-mail: larochelle@diana.barry.edu. Application contact: Angela Scott, Enrollment Services, Assistant Dean, 305-899-3112. Fax: 305-899-3149. E-mail: ascott@jeanne.barry.edu.

Bellarmine College, Allan and Donna Lansing School of Nursing, Department of Graduate Nursing, Louisville, KY 40205-0671. Offerings include nursing education (MSN). Department faculty: 5 full-time (all women), 5 part-time (all women), 7 FTE. *Degree requirements:* Thesis required, foreign language not required. *Entrance requirements:* GRE General Test (minimum combined score of 800; average 825), minimum undergraduate GPA of 2.75, RN license. Application deadline: 8/1 (priority date; rolling processing; 1/1 for spring admission). Application fee: $25. Electronic applications accepted. *Tuition:* $330 per credit hour. • Dr. Margaret E. Miller, Director, 800-274-4723 Ext. 8414. Fax: 502-452-8058.

Bowie State University, Program in Nursing, 14000 Jericho Park Road, Bowie, MD 20715. Offerings include nursing education (MS). Accredited by NLN. *Degree requirements:* Thesis, research paper, written comprehensive exam required, foreign language not required. *Entrance requirements:* Minimum GPA of 2.5. Application deadline: 3/15 (rolling processing). Application fee: $30. *Expenses:* Tuition $169 per credit hour for state residents; $304 per credit hour for nonresidents. Fees $171 per year.

The Catholic University of America, School of Nursing, Washington, DC 20064. Offerings include advanced practice nursing (MSN), with options in administration of nursing service, adult nurse practitioner, education, family nurse practitioner, geriatric nurse practitioner, pediatric nurse practitioner, psychiatric-mental health, school health nurse practitioner. Accredited by NLN. School faculty: 18 full-time (all women), 2 part-time (both women), 19 FTE. *Degree requirements:* Comprehensive exam required, thesis optional, foreign language not required. *Entrance requirements:* GRE General Test (minimum combined score of 1350 on three sections). Application deadline: 8/1 (priority date; rolling processing; 12/1 for spring admission). Application fee: $50. *Expenses:* Tuition $17,325 per year full-time, $668 per credit hour part-time. Fees $680 per year full-time, $360 per year part-time. • Sr. Mary Jean Flaherty, Dean, 202-319-5403.

Clarkson College, Graduate Programs, Department of Nursing, 101 South 42nd Street, Omaha, NE 68131-2739. Offerings include education (MSN). Accredited by NLN. Department faculty: 6. *Degree requirements:* Practicum required, foreign language not required. *Entrance requirements:* GRE General Test, minimum GPA of 3.0. Application deadline: rolling. Application fee: $17. *Expenses:* Tuition $314 per credit hour. Fees $16 per credit hour. • Dr. Charles J. Beauchamp, Dean, 402-552-2958. Fax: 402-552-6058. Application contact: Jeff Beals, Director of Enrollment Management, 402-552-3100. Fax: 402-552-6057. E-mail: admiss@clrkcol.crhsnet.edu.

Concordia University Wisconsin, Division of Graduate Studies, Program in Nursing, Mequon, WI 53097-2402. Offerings include nurse educator (MSN). Postbaccalaureate distance learning degree programs offered (minimal on-campus study). *Degree requirements:* Thesis or alternative, comprehensive exam. *Entrance requirements:* TOEFL (minimum score 550). Application deadline: 8/1 (priority date; rolling processing). *Tuition:* $250 per credit. • Dr. Ruth Gresley, Director, 414-243-4452. E-mail: rgresley@bach.cuw.edu.

Duquesne University, School of Nursing, Pittsburgh, PA 15282-0001. Offerings include nursing education (MSN). Accredited by NLN. Postbaccalaureate distance learning degree programs offered (minimal on-campus study). School faculty: 5 full-time (all women), 3 part-time (1 woman). *Degree requirements:* Computer language required, foreign language and thesis not required. *Entrance requirements:* GMAT (MSN/MBA), MAT, 1 year of work experience (2 years for family nurse practitioner). Application deadline: 7/31 (priority date; rolling processing; 11/31 for spring admission). Application fee: $40. *Expenses:* Tuition $481 per credit. Fees $39 per credit. • Dr. Jeri A. Milstead, Chair, 412-396-4865. E-mail: milstead@duq3.cc.duq.edu. Application contact: Carole Sisul, Administrative Assistant, Graduate Programs, 412-396-6551. Fax: 412-396-6346. E-mail: sisul@duq2.cc.duq.edu.

Eastern Michigan University, College of Health and Human Services, Program in Nursing Education, Ypsilanti, MI 48197. Awards MSN. Faculty: 14 full-time (all women). 30 applicants, 53% accepted. In 1997, 2 degrees awarded. *Degree requirements:* Thesis optional, foreign language not required. *Entrance requirements:* GRE General Test, TOEFL (minimum score 500), Michigan RN license. Application deadline: 5/15 (rolling processing; 3/15 for spring admission). Application fee: $30. *Expenses:* Tuition $2691 per year full-time, $150 per credit hour part-time for state residents; $6300 per year full-time, $350 per credit hour part-time for nonresidents. Fees $368 per year full-time, $88 per semester (minimum) part-time. *Financial aid:* Fellowships, teaching assistantships available. Aid available to part-time students. Financial aid application deadline: 3/15; applicants required to submit FAFSA. • Dr. Regina Williams, Head, 734-487-2310.

Eastern Washington University, Intercollegiate Center for Nursing Education, Cheney, WA 99004-2431. Awards MN. Offered jointly with Gonzaga University, Washington State University, and Whitworth College. Faculty: 30 full-time (29 women). Students: 1 (woman) full-time, 1 part-time (0 women). Average age 31. 2 applicants, 50% accepted. *Degree requirements:* Thesis, comprehensive exam. *Entrance requirements:* GRE General Test, minimum GPA of 3.0. Application deadline: 4/1 (priority date; rolling processing). Application fee: $35. *Tuition:* $4200 per year full-time, $140 per credit part-time for state residents; $12,780 per year full-time, $415 per credit part-time for nonresidents. *Financial aid:* Application deadline 2/1. • Dr. Dorothy Detlor, Dean, 509-324-7334. Application contact: Dr. Marian Sheafor, Associate Dean, 509-324-7334.

Florida State University, School of Nursing, Tallahassee, FL 32306. Offerings include family nursing (MSN), with options in adult nurse practitioner, advanced registered nurse practitioner, case manager, family nurse practitioner, nurse educator. Accredited by NLN. School faculty: 16 full-time (14 women), 7 part-time (5 women). *Degree requirements:* Thesis required, foreign language not required. *Average time to degree:* master's–2 years full-time, 3.5 years part-time. *Entrance requirements:* GRE General Test (minimum combined score of 1000), minimum GPA of 3.0, BSN, Florida RN License, 2 years of work experience. Application deadline: 4/15 (priority date; rolling processing; 7/15 for spring admission). Application fee: $20. *Tuition:* $139 per credit hour for state residents; $482 per credit hour for nonresidents. • Dr. Evelyn Singer, Dean, 850-644-3299. Fax: 850-644-7660. E-mail: esinger@mailer.fsu.edu. Application contact: Dr. Deborah I. Frank, Graduate Program Coordinator, 850-644-5974. E-mail: dfrank@mailer.acns.fsu.edu.

Georgia State University, College of Health and Human Sciences, School of Nursing, Atlanta, GA 30303-3083. Offerings include health promotion, protection, and restoration (PhD). MS (child and adolescent psychology, gerontology) and PhD (community nursing, family nursing) being phased out; applicants no longer accepted. School faculty: 26 full-time (all women), 3 part-time (all women). *Degree requirements:* Dissertation required, foreign language not required. *Entrance requirements:* GRE General Test. Application deadline: 4/15. Application fee: $25. *Expenses:* Tuition $2862 per year full-time, $106 per semester hour part-time for state residents; $11,448 per year full-time, $424 per semester hour part-time for nonresidents. Fees $228 per year. • Dr. Dee Baldwin, Director of Graduate Programs, 404-651-3040. Application contact: Barbara Smith, Admissions Counselor, 404-651-3064. Fax: 404-651-4871.

Graceland College, Master's in Nursing Program, 221 West Lexington, Suite 110, Independence, MO 64050. Offerings include clinical nurse specialist/family nursing (educator) (MSN). Postbaccalaureate distance learning degree programs offered (minimal on-campus study). Program faculty: 6 full-time (all women), 1 (woman) part-time, 6.5 FTE. *Degree requirements:* Thesis optional, foreign language not required. *Average time to degree:* master's–2 years full-time, 2.5 years part-time; other advanced degree–1 year full-time, 1.5 years part-time. *Entrance requirements:* BSN from nationally accredited program. Application deadline: rolling. Application fee: $80. *Tuition:* $350 per credit hour (minimum). • Dr. Karen Fernengel, Chair, 816-833-0524. Fax: 816-833-2990. E-mail: karenf@graceland.edu. Application contact: Lewis Smith, Director, Student Information Service, 800-537-6276. Fax: 540-344-1508.

Indiana Wesleyan University, Division of Nursing Education, Marion, IN 46953-4999. Offerings include nursing education (MS). Accredited by NLN. Division faculty: 4 full-time (3 women). *Degree requirements:* Thesis required, foreign language not required. *Entrance requirements:* MAT, RN license, 1 year of related experience. Application fee: $10. *Tuition:* $402 per hour. • Dr. DeAnne Messias, Director of Graduate Nursing, 765-677-2148.

Jewish Hospital College of Nursing and Allied Health, Program in Nursing, St. Louis, MO 63110-1091. Offerings include education (MSN). College faculty: 10. *Application deadline:* rolling. *Application fee:* $25. *Tuition:* $320 per credit hour. • Dr. Sandra A. Jones, Director, 314-454-8416. Application contact: Connie Stohlman, Chief Admissions Officer, 314-454-7538.

Kent State University, School of Nursing, Kent, OH 44242-0001. Offerings include nursing education (MSN). Accredited by NLN. School faculty: 29 full-time. *Degree requirements:* Thesis optional, foreign language not required. *Entrance requirements:* Minimum GPA of 2.75. Application deadline: 7/12 (rolling processing; 11/29 for spring admission). Application fee: $30. *Tuition:* $4752 per year full-time, $216 per credit hour part-time for state residents; $9213 per year full-time, $419 per credit hour part-time for nonresidents. • Dr. Davina Gosnell, Dean, 330-672-7930. Fax: 330-672-2433.

La Salle University, Program in Nursing, 1900 West Olney Avenue, Philadelphia, PA 19141-1199. Offerings include nursing education (MSN). Accredited by NLN. MSN (wound, ostomy, and continence nursing) new for fall 1998. Program faculty: 13 full-time (12 women), 8 part-time (all women). *Entrance requirements:* GRE or MAT, BSN, Pennsylvania RN license. Application deadline: rolling. Application fee: $30. • Dr. Zane R. Wolf, Dean, 215-951-1430. E-mail: wolf@lasalle.edu. Application contact: Dr. Janice Beitz, Graduate Director, 215-951-1430. Fax: 215-951-1896. E-mail: beitz@lasalle.edu.

Lewis University, College of Nursing, Romeoville, IL 60446. Offerings include nursing education (MSN). Accredited by NLN. *Entrance requirements:* GRE General Test (minimum combined score of 850) or College of Nursing Writing Exam, minimum GPA of 2.5. Application deadline: rolling. Application fee: $35.

Mankato State University, College of Allied Health and Nursing, Department of Nursing, South Rd and Ellis Ave, PO Box 8400, Mankato, MN 56002-8400. Offerings include family nursing (MSN), with options in clinical nurse specialist, educator, family nurse practitioner, manager; managed care (MSN), with options in clinical nurse specialist, educator, family nurse practitioner, manager. One or more programs accredited by NLN. Offered jointly with Metropolitan State University. Department faculty: 13 full-time (all women). *Degree requirements:* Computer language, comprehensive exam, internships, research project or thesis required, foreign language not required. *Entrance requirements:* GRE General Test (minimum combined score of 1350) or MAT, minimum GPA of 3.0 during previous 2 years, BSN or equivalent. Application deadline: 7/10 (priority date; rolling processing; 10/30 for spring admission). Application fee: $20. *Tuition:* $126 per credit (minimum) for state residents; $200 per credit for nonresidents. • Mary Huntley, Director, 507-389-6022. Application contact: Collaborative MSN Program Admissions, 507-389-6022.

Marymount University, School of Health Professions, Programs in Nursing, Program in Nursing Education, Arlington, VA 22207-4299. Awards MSN. Accredited by NLN. *Degree requirements:* Thesis or alternative required, foreign language not required. *Entrance requirements:* 2 years of clinical experience, interview, minimum GPA of 3.0, RN license. Application deadline: rolling. Application fee: $35. *Expenses:* Tuition $465 per credit hour. Fees $120 per year full-time, $5 per credit hour part-time. • Dr. Catherine Connelly, Dean, School of Health Professions, 703-284-1580. Fax: 703-284-3819. E-mail: catherine.connelly@marymount.edu.

Midwestern State University, Division of Health Sciences, Nursing Program, Wichita Falls, TX 76308-2096. Offerings include nurse educator (MSN). Offered jointly with Texas Tech University. Program faculty: 5 full-time (all women). *Entrance requirements:* GRE General Test, TOEFL (average 550). Application deadline: 8/7 (12/15 for spring admission). Application fee: $0 ($50 for international students). *Expenses:* Tuition $44 per hour for state residents; $259 per hour for nonresidents. Fees $90 per year (minimum) full-time, $9 per semester (minimum) part-time. • Sandra Church, Coordinator, 940-397-4597.

Molloy College, Department of Nursing, 1000 Hempstead Avenue, Rockville Centre, NY 11571-5002. Offerings include nursing education (Advanced Certificate). Department faculty: 16 full-time (14 women), 12 part-time (9 women). *Average time to degree:* master's–2.2 years full-time, 3.7 years part-time; other advanced degree–1 year full-time, 2 years part-time. *Entrance requirements:* Master's degree in nursing. Application deadline: 9/2 (priority date; rolling processing; 1/20 for spring admission). Application fee: $60. *Expenses:* Tuition $430 per credit. Fees $430 per year full-time, $165 per semester (minimum) part-time. • Dr. Carol A. Clifford, Director, Graduate Program, 516-256-2218. Fax: 516-678-9718. E-mail: clica01@molloy.edu. Application contact: Wayne James, Vice President for Enrollment and Management, 516-678-5000 Ext. 240. Fax: 516-256-2247.

Mount Saint Mary College, Division of Nursing, Newburgh, NY 12550-3494. Offerings include adult nurse practitioner (MS), with options in nursing education, nursing management; clinical nurse specialist-adult health (MS), with options in nursing education, nursing management. MS (adult nurse practitioner) new for fall 1998. Division faculty: 6 full-time (5 women), 1 (woman) part-time. *Degree requirements:* Computer language, research project required, foreign language and thesis not required. *Entrance requirements:* GRE General Test (minimum combined score of 1200; average 1400) or MAT (minimum score 40), BSN, minimum GPA of 3.0, RN license. Application deadline: 5/3 (priority date; 10/31 for spring admission). Application fee: $20. *Expenses:* Tuition $367 per credit. Fees $30 per year. • Sr. Leona DeBoer, Coordinator, 914-569-3138. Fax: 914-562-6762. E-mail: deboer@msmc.edu.

New York University, School of Education, Division of Nursing, Programs in Advanced Practice Nursing, New York, NY 10012-1019. Offerings include teaching of nursing (MA). Accredited by NLN. MA/MS offered jointly with the Program in Management in the Robert F. Wagner Graduate School of Public Service. Faculty: 25 full-time, 9 part-time. *Entrance requirements:* TOEFL. Application deadline: 2/1 (priority date; rolling processing; 12/1 for spring admission). Application fee: $40 ($60 for international students). • Judi Haber, Director, 212-998-5300. Application contact: Office of Graduate Admissions, 212-998-5030. Fax: 212-995-4328.

Saginaw Valley State University, College of Nursing, Program in Nursing Education, University Center, MI 48710. Awards MSN. Accredited by NLN. Part-time programs available. Faculty: 5 full-time (all women). Students: 1 (woman) full-time, 13 part-time (all women); includes 2 minority (both Hispanics). In 1997, 7 degrees awarded. *Degree requirements:* Thesis. *Entrance requirements:* GRE. Application deadline: rolling. Application fee: $25. *Expenses:* Tuition $159 per credit hour for state residents; $311 per credit hour for nonresidents. Fees $8.70 per credit hour. • Application contact: Dr. Janalou Blecke, Assistant Dean, 517-790-4130. Fax: 517-790-1978. E-mail: jblecke@tardis.svsu.edu.

San Francisco State University, College of Health and Human Services, School of Nursing, San Francisco, CA 94132-1722. Offerings include nursing education (MS). Accredited by NLN. *Degree requirements:* Thesis required, foreign language not required. *Entrance requirements:* Minimum GPA of 3.0. Application deadline: 11/30 (priority date; rolling processing; 5/31 for spring admission). Application fee: $55. *Expenses:* Tuition $0 for state residents; $246 per unit for nonresidents. Fees $1982 per year full-time, $1316 per year part-time.

San Jose State University, College of Applied Arts and Sciences, School of Nursing, San Jose, CA 95192-0001. Offerings include community health nursing (MS), with options in nursing administration, nursing education. Accredited by NLN. School faculty: 26 full-time (24 women), 13 part-time (12 women). *Degree requirements:* Thesis required, foreign language not required. *Entrance requirements:* BS in nursing, RN license. Application deadline: 6/1 (rolling processing). Application fee: $59. *Expenses:* Tuition $0 for state residents; $246 per unit for nonresidents. Fees $2017 per year full-time, $1351 per year part-time. • Dr. Bobbye Gorenberg, Director, 408-924-3130. Application contact: Dr. Colleen Saylor, Graduate Coordinator, 408-924-3134.

Seton Hall University, College of Nursing, Department of Graduate Nursing, Nursing Education Program, South Orange, NJ 07079-2697. Awards MA, MSN/MA. Accredited by NLN. Part-time programs available. Faculty: 1 (woman) full-time. *Degree requirements:* Research project required, foreign language and thesis not required. *Entrance requirements:* GRE or MAT, BSN. Application deadline: 5/15 (priority date; rolling processing; 11/15 for spring admission). Application fee: $50. *Expenses:* Tuition $500 per credit. Fees $610 per year full-time, $185 per semester part-time. *Financial aid:* Partial tuition waivers, institutionally sponsored loans available. Financial aid application deadline: 7/15. *Faculty research:* Teaching methods for adult learners. • Dr. Gloria Caliandro-Hegy, Director, 973-761-9295. Fax: 973-761-9607. E-mail: caliangl@shu.edu.

State University of New York College at Oneonta, Department of Education, Program in School Nurse Teacher, Oneonta, NY 13820-4015. Awards MS Ed. Part-time and evening/weekend programs available. Students: 0. In 1997, 1 degree awarded. *Entrance requirements:* GRE General Test. Application deadline: 4/15. Application fee: $50. *Expenses:* Tuition $5100 per year full-time, $213 per credit hour part-time for state residents; $8416 per year full-time, $351 per credit hour part-time for nonresidents. Fees $482 per year full-time, $6.85 per credit hour part-time. • James Baker, Chair, Department of Physical Education, 607-436-3595.

Teachers College, Columbia University, Graduate Faculty of Education, Department of Health and Behavior Studies, Program in Nursing, Professional Role, 525 West 120th Street, New York, NY 10027-6696. Awards Ed M, MA, Ed D. Faculty: 1 (woman) full-time. Students: 10 full-time (9 women), 14 part-time (13 women); includes 6 minority (3 African Americans, 3 Asian Americans), 1 international. Average age 47. 7 applicants, 86% accepted. In 1997, 2 master's, 3 doctorates awarded. *Degree requirements:* For master's, Capstone Project required, foreign language not required; for doctorate, dissertation required, foreign language not required. *Entrance requirements:* For master's, BSN, nursing license; for doctorate, GRE General Test or MAT (minimum score 54), BSN, nursing license. Application deadline: 5/15 (12/1 for spring admission). Application fee: $50. *Expenses:* Tuition $640 per credit. Fees $120 per semester. *Financial aid:* Traineeships, full and partial tuition waivers, Federal Work-Study, institutionally sponsored loans, and career-related internships or fieldwork available. Aid available to part-time students. Financial aid application deadline: 2/1. *Faculty research:* Empathy in nurses, clinical teaching for basic nursing students, interdisciplinary health care team. • Application contact: Ursula Felton, Office of Admissions, 212-678-3710. Fax: 212-678-4171.

Teachers College, Columbia University, Graduate Faculty of Education, Department of Organization and Leadership, Program in Nurse Executive, 525 West 120th Street, New York, NY 10027-6696. Awards Ed M, MA, Ed D. Faculty: 2 full-time (both women), 2 part-time (1 woman), 2.8 FTE. Students: 27 full-time (24 women), 10 part-time (all women); includes 10 minority (6 African Americans, 2 Asian Americans, 2 Hispanics). Average age 43. 0 applicants. In 1997, 2 master's, 3 doctorates awarded. *Degree requirements:* For master's, Capstone Project required, foreign language not required; for doctorate, dissertation required, foreign language not required. *Entrance requirements:* For master's, BSN; for doctorate, GRE General Test or MAT (minimum score 54), BSN, nursing license. Application deadline: 5/15 (12/1 for spring admission). Application fee: $50. *Expenses:* Tuition $640 per credit. Fees $120 per semester. *Financial aid:* Traineeships, full and partial tuition waivers, Federal Work-Study, institutionally sponsored loans, and career-related internships or fieldwork available. Aid available to part-time students. Financial aid application deadline: 2/1. *Faculty research:* Health care administration, health care law, nursing administration and education, consumer satisfaction with health care. • Application contact: Christine Souders, Office of Admissions, 212-678-3710. Fax: 212-678-4171.

Texas Tech University Health Sciences Center, School of Nursing, Lubbock, TX 79430-0002. Offerings include education (MSN). Accredited by NLN. Postbaccalaureate distance learning degree programs offered (minimal on-campus study). School faculty: 14 full-time (all women). *Degree requirements:* Thesis required, foreign language not required. *Average time to degree:* master's–2 years full-time, 3 years part-time. *Entrance requirements:* GRE General Test (minimum combined score of 1000), MAT (minimum score 50), minimum GPA of 3.0, sample of written work. Application deadline: 6/1 (rolling processing; 10/1 for spring admission). Application fee: $30 ($50 for international students). *Expenses:* Tuition $36 per credit hour for state residents; $249 per credit hour for nonresidents. Fees $1348 per year full-time for state residents; $1349 per year full-time for nonresidents. • Dr. Pat S. Yoder Wise, Dean, 806-743-2738. E-mail: sonpsy@ttuhsc.edu. Application contact: Nancy Ridenour, Associate Dean for Education, 806-743-2737. Fax: 806-743-1622. E-mail: sonnar@ttuhsc.edu.

The University of Akron, College of Nursing, Akron, OH 44325-0001. Offerings include nursing education (MSN). Accredited by NLN. College faculty: 19 full-time, 13 part-time. *Degree requirements:* Thesis optional, foreign language not required. *Entrance requirements:* GRE or MAT, minimum GPA of 3.0. Application deadline: 8/15 (rolling processing). Application fee: $25 ($50 for international students). *Expenses:* Tuition $178 per credit hour for state residents; $333 per credit hour for nonresidents. Fees $145 per year full-time, $32 per semester (minimum) part-time. • Cynthia Capers, Dean, 330-972-7552. Application contact: Dr. Linda Linc, Interim Associate Dean of the Graduate Program, 330-972-7553.

University of Connecticut, School of Nursing, Storrs, CT 06269. Offerings include nurse education (MS). Accredited by NLN. School faculty: 26. *Entrance requirements:* TOEFL. Application deadline: 4/1 (priority date; rolling processing; 11/1 for spring admission). Application fee: $40 ($45 for international students). *Expenses:* Tuition $5272 per year full-time, $293 per credit part-time for state residents; $13,696 per year full-time, $761 per credit part-time for nonresidents. Fees $948 per year full-time, $640 per year part-time. • Barbara K. Redman, Dean, 860-486-3716. Application contact: Jane E. Murdock, Chairperson, 860-486-3821.

University of Mary, Division of Nursing, Program in Nursing Education, 7500 University Drive, Bismarck, ND 58504-9652. Awards MSN. Accredited by NLN. *Entrance requirements:* Minimum GPA of 3.0 in nursing course work. Application deadline: 8/1 (priority date). Application fee: $15. *Tuition:* $265 per credit. *Financial aid:* Institutionally sponsored loans available. Aid available to part-time students. Financial aid application deadline: 7/1. • Application contact: Dr. Diane Fladeland, Director, Graduate Programs, 701-255-7500. Fax: 701-255-7687.

University of Maryland, Baltimore, Graduate School, School of Nursing, Baltimore, MD 21201-1627. Offerings include nursing education (MS). Accredited by NLN. MS/MBA offered jointly with the University of Baltimore. School faculty: 49 (45 women). *Degree requirements:* Thesis or alternative required, foreign language not required. *Entrance requirements:* GRE General Test, TOEFL, minimum GPA of 2.75, previous course work in statistics, BS in nursing. Application fee: $42. *Expenses:* Tuition $253 per credit hour for state residents; $454 per credit hour for nonresidents. Fees $317 per year. • Dr. Barbara Heller, Dean, 410-706-6741. Application contact: Dr. Susan Wozenski, Assistant Dean for Student Affairs, 410-706-0501. Fax: 410-706-7238.

University of Minnesota, Twin Cities Campus, School of Nursing, Program in Nursing Education, Minneapolis, MN 55455-0213. Awards MS. Accredited by NLN. Part-time programs available. Students: 6 full-time, 18 part-time. 11 applicants, 91% accepted. *Degree requirements:* Final oral exam, project or thesis. *Application deadline:* 12/15 (rolling processing). *Application fee:* $40 ($50 for international students). *Financial aid:* Research assistantships, teaching assistantships, and career-related internships or fieldwork available. • Kathleen Keichbaum, Head, 612-624-7697. Application contact: Kate Hanson, Nursing Recruiter, 612-624-9494. Fax: 612-624-3174. E-mail: hanso041@maroon.tc.umn.edu.

University of Northern Colorado, College of Health and Human Sciences, School of Nursing, Greeley, CO 80639. Offerings include nursing education (MS). Accredited by NLN. School faculty: 10 full-time (all women), 1 (woman) part-time. *Degree requirements:* Thesis or alternative, comprehensive exams. *Application deadline:* rolling. *Application fee:* $35. *Expenses:* Tuition $2327 per year full-time, $129 per credit hour part-time for state residents; $9578 per year full-time, $532 per credit hour part-time for nonresidents. Fees $752 per year full-time, $184 per semester (minimum) part-time. • Dr. Sandy Baird, Director, 970-351-2293.

University of Pittsburgh, School of Nursing, Advanced Specialized Role Program, Pittsburgh, PA 15260. Offerings include nursing education (MSN). Accredited by NLN. *Degree requirements:* Thesis optional, foreign language not required. *Entrance requirements:* GRE or MAT, TOEFL, BSN, RN license, nursing experience. Application deadline: 2/1 (priority date; rolling processing; 9/15 for spring admission). Application fee: $35 ($40 for international students). • Judith A. Tate, Coordinator, 412-624-5872. Fax: 412-383-7227. E-mail: jtaloo+@pitt.edu. Application contact: Dr. Kathy Lucke, Director, Student Services, 412-624-2405. Fax: 412-624-2409. E-mail: nursao+@pitt.edu.

See in-depth description on page 1451.

University of Puerto Rico, Medical Sciences Campus, School of Nursing, San Juan, PR 00936-5067. Offerings include teaching nursing (MSN). Accredited by NLN. *Degree requirements:* 1 foreign language, thesis, research project. *Entrance requirements:* GRE, BSN, interview, (Puerto Rico) RN license, 2 years of nursing experience, previous course work in physical examination. Application deadline: 3/16. Application fee: $25.

University of Rhode Island, College of Nursing, Kingston, RI 02881. Offerings include teaching of nursing (MS). One or more programs accredited by NLN. *Application deadline:* 4/15. *Application fee:* $35. *Expenses:* Tuition $3446 per year full-time, $191 per credit part-time for state residents; $9850 per year full-time, $547 per credit part-time for nonresidents. Fees $1276 per year full-time, $135 per semester (minimum) part-time.

See in-depth description on page 1453.

University of Tennessee at Chattanooga, School of Human Services, School of Nursing, Chattanooga, TN 37403-2598. Offerings include education (MSN). Accredited by NLN. School faculty: 8 full-time (7 women), 4 part-time (3 women). *Degree requirements:* Qualifying exams required, foreign language and thesis not required. *Entrance requirements:* GRE General Test (combined average 1485 on three sections). Application deadline: rolling. Application fee: $25. *Tuition:* $2864 per year full-time, $160 per credit hour part-time for state residents; $6806 per year full-time, $379 per credit hour part-time for nonresidents. • Dr. Maria Smith, Director, 423-755-4646. Fax: 423-755-4668. E-mail: msmith@utcvm.utc.edu. Application contact: Dr. Deborah Arfken, Assistant Provost for Graduate Studies, 423-755-4667. Fax: 423-755-4478.

The University of Texas at Arlington, School of Nursing, Arlington, TX 76019-0407. Offerings include teaching of nursing (MSN). Accredited by NLN. School faculty: 20 full-time (all women), 4 part-time (all women). *Degree requirements:* Comprehensive exam or thesis required, foreign language not required. *Entrance requirements:* GRE General Test (minimum combined score of 1000 on verbal and analytical sections). Application deadline: rolling. Application fee: $25 ($50 for international students). *Tuition:* $3206 per year full-time, $468 per semester (minimum) part-time for state residents; $8612 per year full-time, $1137 per semester (minimum) part-time for nonresidents. • Dr. Elizabeth C. Poster, Dean, 817-272-2885. Application contact: Dr. Susan Grove, Graduate Adviser, 817-272-2776. Fax: 817-272-5006.

Villanova University, College of Nursing, Villanova, PA 19085-1690. Offerings include nursing education (MSN). Accredited by NLN. MSN (pediatric nurse practitioner), Post Master's Certificate (nurse practitioner, nurse anesthetist, clinical case management) new for fall 1998. College faculty: 30 full-time (all women). *Degree requirements:* Independent study project required, foreign language and thesis not required. *Entrance requirements:* GRE General Test (verbal section) or MAT, BSN, 1 year of recent experience, physical assessment, previous course work in statistics. Application deadline: 7/1 (priority date; rolling processing; 12/1 for spring admission). Application fee: $25. *Expenses:* Tuition $445 per credit. Fees $60 per year. • Dr. Claire Manfredi, Graduate Director, 610-519-4907. Fax: 610-519-7997. E-mail: cmanfred@email.vill.edu.

Wayne State University, College of Nursing, Department of Adult Health and Administration, Program in Nursing Education, Detroit, MI 48202. Awards Certificate. Students: 1 (woman) part-time. 1 applicant, 100% accepted. In 1997, 2 degrees awarded. *Entrance requirements:* GRE General Test (minimum combined score of 800), minimum GPA of 2.8. Application deadline: 7/1 (priority date; rolling processing; 11/1 for spring admission). Application fee: $20 ($30 for international students). *Expenses:* Tuition $163 per credit hour for state residents; $355 per credit hour for nonresidents. Fees $498 per year full-time, $114 per semester (minimum) part-time. *Financial aid:* Scholarships, traineeships, institutionally sponsored loans available. Financial aid application deadline: 7/1. *Faculty research:* Clinical teaching, curriculum development and evaluation, teaching methodology. • Dr. Dawn Hameister, Assistant Dean, 313-577-4386. Fax: 313-577-4571. Application contact: Vickie Radoye, Administrative Assistant Dean, Student Affairs, 313-577-4082. Fax: 313-577-6949.

Wichita State University, College of Health Professions, School of Nursing, Wichita, KS 67260. Offerings include teaching of nursing (MSN). Accredited by NLN. School faculty: 11 full-time (all women). *Degree requirements:* Comprehensive exam required, thesis optional, foreign language not required. *Entrance requirements:* GRE, TOEFL (minimum score 550), BSN, minimum undergraduate GPA of 2.75. Application deadline: 6/30 (priority date; rolling processing; 1/1 for spring admission). Application fee: $25 ($40 for international students). Electronic applications accepted. *Expenses:* Tuition $2303 per year full-time, $96 per credit hour part-time for state residents; $7691 per year full-time, $321 per credit hour part-time for nonresidents. Fees $490 per year full-time, $75 per semester (minimum) part-time. • Dr. Bonnie Holaday, Interim Dean, 316-978-3610. E-mail: holaday@chp.twsu.edu. Application contact: Dr. Donna Hawley, Graduate Coordinator, 316-978-3610. Fax: 316-978-3094. E-mail: hawley@chp.twsu.edu.

Wright State University, College of Nursing and Health, Program in Nursing, Dayton, OH 45435. Offerings include nursing education (MS). Accredited by NLN. *Degree requirements:* Thesis or alternative required, foreign language not required. *Average time to degree:* master's–2 years full-time, 5 years part-time. *Entrance requirements:* GRE General Test, TOEFL (minimum score 550), BSN from NLN-accredited college, Ohio RN license. Application deadline: 4/15 (priority date). Application fee: $25. *Tuition:* $5109 per year full-time, $161 per credit hour part-time for state residents; $9039 per year full-time, $282 per credit hour part-time for nonresidents. • Application contact: Theresa Haghnazarian, Director of Student and Alumni Affairs, 937-775-3133. Fax: 937-775-4571.

Oncology Nursing

Case Western Reserve University, Frances Payne Bolton School of Nursing, Master's Program in Nursing, Program in Oncology Nursing, Cleveland, OH 44106. Awards MSN. Accredited by NLN. Part-time programs available. 1 applicant, 0% accepted. In 1997, 5 degrees awarded. *Degree requirements:* Thesis optional, foreign language not required. *Entrance requirements:* GRE General Test or MAT. Application deadline: 6/1 (priority date; rolling processing). Application fee: $75. *Tuition:* $18,400 per year full-time, $767 per credit hour part-time. *Financial aid:* Research assistantships, teaching assistantships, partial tuition waivers, institutionally sponsored loans available. Aid available to part-time students. Financial aid application deadline: 6/30. *Faculty research:* Clinical nursing, social support, infection control. • Application contact: Molly Blank, Admission Counselor, 216-368-2529. Fax: 216-368-3542. E-mail: mab44@po.cwru.edu.

Columbia University, School of Nursing, Program in Oncology Nursing, New York, NY 10032. Awards MS, Adv C. One or more programs accredited by NLN. Part-time programs available. Faculty: 1 (woman) full-time. Students: 1 (woman) full-time, 20 part-time (19 women); includes 4 minority (1 African American, 3 Asian Americans). Average age 34. 9 applicants, 89% accepted. In 1997, 5 master's awarded. *Entrance requirements:* For master's, GRE General Test (minimum score 500 on verbal and analytical sections), BSN, 1 year of clinical experience (preferred), or completion of a clinical residency; for Adv C, MSN, previous course work in statistics, clinical preceptorship. Application deadline: 4/1 (priority date; rolling processing; 10/1 for spring admission). Application fee: $60. *Tuition:* $19,376 per year full-time, $692 per credit (minimum) part-time. *Financial aid:* Teaching assistantships available. Financial aid application deadline: 2/1. *Faculty research:* Human sexuality. • Marianne Glasel, Director, 212-305-4196. Application contact: Joseph Tomaino, Assistant Dean for Student Services, 212-305-5756. E-mail: jt238@columbia.edu.

Duke University, School of Nursing, Durham, NC 27708-0586. Offerings include adult oncological/HIV (Certificate); clinical nurse specialist (MSN), with options in acute care pediatric, adult oncological/HIV, gerontological, neonatal, pediatric; nurse practitioner (MSN), with options in acute care adult, acute care pediatric, adult cardiovascular, adult oncological/HIV, family, gerontological, neonatal, pediatric. One or more programs accredited by NLN. Postbaccalaureate distance learning degree programs offered (minimal on-campus study). School faculty: 24 full-time (22 women), 4 part-time (all women). *Degree requirements:* For master's, computer language required, thesis optional, foreign language not required. *Average time to degree:* master's–1.5 years full-time, 3 years part-time; other advanced degree–1 year full-time, 2 years part-time. *Entrance requirements:* For master's, GRE General Test or MAT, BSN, minimum GPA of 3.0, previous course work in statistics, RN license, 1 year of nursing experience. Application deadline: 4/1 (priority date; rolling processing; 10/1 for spring admission). Application fee: $50. *Tuition:* $20,976 per year full-time, $552 per unit part-time. • Dr. Mary T. Champagne, Dean, 919-684-3786. E-mail: champ001@mc.duke.edu. Application contact: Judith K. Carter, Admissions Officer, 919-684-4248. Fax: 919-681-8899. E-mail: carte026@mc.duke.edu.

Emory University, Nell Hodgson Woodruff School of Nursing, Atlanta, GA 30322-1100. Offerings include adult health (MSN), with options in adult medical/surgical/nurse practitioner, adult oncology/nurse practitioner, critical care/nurse practitioner, psychosocial nurse practitioner; women and children (MSN), with options in child health/pediatric nurse practitioner, midwifery, pediatric oncology nurse practitioner, perinatal/neonatal nurse. One or more programs accredited by NLN. Postbaccalaureate distance learning degree programs offered (minimal on-campus study). School faculty: 33 full-time (32 women), 21 part-time (19 women), 48 FTE. *Degree requirements:* Thesis optional, foreign language not required. *Average time to degree:* master's–1.5 years full-time, 3 years part-time. *Entrance requirements:* GRE General Test (minimum combined score of 1500 on three sections) or MAT (minimum score 35), minimum GPA of 3.0, BS in nursing or RN license and additional course work. Application deadline: 2/1 (priority date; rolling processing; 11/1 for spring admission). Application fee: $50. *Expenses:* Tuition $18,050 per year. Fees $200 per year. • Dr. Dyanne D. Affonso, Dean, 404-727-7976. Fax: 404-727-0536. Application contact: Debbie Ashtiani, Director, 404-727-7980.

Gwynedd–Mercy College, Graduate Program in Nursing, Gwynedd Valley, PA 19437-0901. Offerings include oncology (MSN). Accredited by NLN. MSN (pediatrics, oncology) admissions temporarily suspended. Program faculty: 9 full-time (all women), 8 part-time (6 women). *Degree requirements:* Thesis or research project required, foreign language not required. *Average time to degree:* master's–2.5 years full-time, 3.5 years part-time. *Entrance requirements:* GRE General Test (minimum combined score of 1350; average 1401), MAT (minimum score 40; average 48), 1 year of experience, physical assessment, previous course work in statistics. Application deadline: 8/1 (priority date; rolling processing). Application fee: $25. *Expenses:* Tuition $375 per credit. Fees $150 per year full-time, $80 per year part-time. • Dr. Mary Dressler, Dean, 215-641-5533. E-mail: dressler.m@gmc.edu. Application contact: Dr. Barbara A. Jones, Associate Professor, 215-646-7300 Ext. 407. Fax: 215-641-5517.

Johns Hopkins University, School of Nursing, Dual Major in Clinical Specialist/Management, Baltimore, MD 21218-2699. Offerings include oncology nursing (MSN). Accredited by NLN. Faculty: 13 full-time (12 women), 3 part-time (2 women), 15 FTE. *Degree requirements:* Scholarly project required, thesis optional, foreign language not required. *Average time to degree:* master's–5 years part-time. *Entrance requirements:* GRE, interview, minimum GPA of 3.0. Application deadline: 3/1 (priority date; rolling processing; 11/15 for spring admission). Application fee: $40. • Jacqueline Dienemann, Associate Professor, 410-614-5301. Fax: 410-955-7463. E-mail: jackied@son.jhmi.edu. Application contact: Mary O'Rourke, Director of Admissions/Student Services, 410-955-7548. Fax: 410-614-7086. E-mail: orourke@son.jhmi.edu.

Johns Hopkins University, School of Nursing, Program in Advanced Practice Nursing/Clinical Specialist, Baltimore, MD 21218-2699. Offerings include oncology nursing (MSN). Accredited by NLN. Program faculty: 10 full-time (9 women), 2 part-time (1 woman), 11 FTE. *Degree requirements:* Scholarly project required, thesis optional, foreign language not required. *Average time to degree:* master's–1.5 years full-time, 4 years part-time. *Entrance requirements:* GRE, interview, minimum GPA of 3.0. Application deadline: 3/1 (priority date; rolling processing). Application fee: $40. • Patricia Grimm, Head, 410-614-5302. Fax: 410-955-7463. E-mail: pgrimm@son.jhmi.edu. Application contact: Mary O'Rourke, Director of Admissions/Student Services, 410-955-7548. Fax: 410-614-7086. E-mail: orourke@son.jhmi.edu.

See in-depth description on page 1433.

Loyola University Chicago, Graduate School, Marcella Niehoff School of Nursing, Oncology Clinical Nursing Specialist Program, 820 North Michigan Avenue, Chicago, IL 60611-2196. Awards MSN. Students: 3 part-time (all women). Average age 29. 2 applicants, 100% accepted. In 1997, 2 degrees awarded. *Degree requirements:* Comprehensive exam or oral thesis defense required, foreign language not required. *Entrance requirements:* GRE General Test (minimum combined score of 1350 on three sections), BSN, minimum GPA of 3.0, professional license. Application deadline: rolling. Application fee: $35. *Tuition:* $467 per semester hour. *Financial aid:* Teaching assistantships, assistantships, traineeships available. Financial aid application deadline: 3/1. *Faculty research:* Breast cancer, coping with cancer, pain. • Application contact: Dr. Marcia Maurer, Associate Dean and Director of Graduate Programs, 773-508-3261. Fax: 773-508-3241. E-mail: mmaurer@luc.edu.

University of Delaware, College of Health and Nursing Sciences, Department of Nursing, Newark, DE 19716. Offerings include clinical nurse specialist/nurse practitioner (Certificate), with options in cardiopulmonary, gerontology, oncology/immune deficiency, pediatrics, women's health; oncology/immune deficiency (MSN, Certificate). One or more programs accredited by NLN. Department faculty: 10 full-time (9 women), 5 part-time (all women), 12.25 FTE. *Degree requirements:* For master's, thesis optional, foreign language not required. *Average time to degree:* master's–2 years full-time, 3 years part-time. *Entrance requirements:* For master's, GRE General Test. Application deadline: 7/1. Application fee: $45. *Expenses:* Tuition $4250 per year full-time, $236 per credit hour part-time for state residents; $12,250 per year full-time, $681 per credit hour part-time for nonresidents. Fees $466 per year full-time, $15 per semester (minimum) part-time. • Application contact: Betty Bonavita, Graduate Secretary, 302-831-1255. Fax: 302-831-2382. E-mail: elizabeth.bonavita@mvs.udel.edu.

University of Minnesota, Twin Cities Campus, School of Nursing, Program in Oncology Nursing, Minneapolis, MN 55455-0213. Awards MS. Accredited by NLN. Part-time programs available. Students: 3 full-time, 9 part-time. 6 applicants, 100% accepted. *Degree requirements:* Final oral exam, project or thesis. *Application deadline:* 12/15 (rolling processing). *Application fee:* $40 ($50 for international students). *Financial aid:* Fellowships, research assistantships, teaching assistantships, and career-related internships or fieldwork available. • Janice Post White, Head, 612-624-1921. Application contact: Kate Hanson, Nursing Recruiter, 612-624-9494. Fax: 612-624-3174. E-mail: hanso041@maroon.tc.umn.edu.

University of Pennsylvania, School of Nursing, Oncology Advanced Practice Nurse Program, Philadelphia, PA 19104. Awards MSN. Accredited by NLN. Part-time programs available. Students: 5 full-time (all women), 21 part-time (all women); includes 3 international. Average age 29. 16 applicants, 50% accepted. In 1997, 9 degrees awarded. *Entrance requirements:* GRE General Test, BSN, minimum GPA of 3.0, previous course work in statistics. Application deadline: 9/1 (rolling processing). Application fee: $65. *Financial aid:* Fellowships, research assistantships, teaching assistantships, Federal Work-Study, institutionally sponsored loans, and career-related internships or fieldwork available. Aid available to part-time students. *Faculty research:* Randomized clinical trials to evaluate advanced nursing practice in oncology patients and their caregivers, symptoms management. • Dr. Ruth McCorkle, Director, 215-898-9134. Fax: 215-898-1868. E-mail: mccorkle@pobox.upenn.edu. Application contact: Susan K. Ogle, Associate Director of Admissions and Student Affairs, 215-898-3301. Fax: 215-573-8439. E-mail: sogle@pobox.upenn.edu.

University of Pennsylvania, School of Nursing, Pediatric Oncology Nurse Practitioner Program, Philadelphia, PA 19104. Awards MSN. Accredited by NLN. Students: 0. 1 applicant, 100% accepted. *Entrance requirements:* GRE General Test, BSN, minimum GPA of 3.0, previous course work in statistics. Application deadline: 9/1. Application fee: $5. • Dr. Ruth McCorkle, Director, 215-898-9134. Fax: 215-898-1868. E-mail: mccorkle@pobox.upenn.edu. Application contact: Susan K. Ogle, Associate Director of Admissions and Student Affairs, 215-898-3301. Fax: 215-573-8439. E-mail: sogle@pobox.upenn.edu.

The University of Texas–Houston Health Science Center, School of Nursing, Master's Program in Nursing, Houston, TX 77225-0036. Offerings include oncology nursing (MSN). Accredited by NLN. *Degree requirements:* Thesis required, foreign language not required. *Entrance requirements:* GRE or MAT, BSN, Texas RN license. Application deadline: 5/1 (priority date; rolling processing; 9/1 for spring admission). Application fee: $10. Electronic applications accepted. • Frank Cole, Chair, Graduate Curriculum Committee, 713-500-2153. Fax: 713-500-2171. E-mail: fcole@son1.nur.uth.tmc.edu. Application contact: Eleanor Evans, Pre-Admissions Counselor, 713-500-2104. Fax: 713-500-2107. E-mail: eevans@son1.nur.uth.tmc.edu.

Psychiatric Nursing

Adelphi University, School of Nursing, Program in Psychiatric Nursing, Garden City, NY 11530. Awards MS, PMC. One or more programs accredited by NLN. Part-time and evening/weekend programs available. Students: 16 part-time (all women); includes 5 minority (3 African Americans, 1 Asian American, 1 Hispanic). Average age 45. *Degree requirements:* For master's, thesis required, foreign language not required. *Entrance requirements:* For master's, BSN, clinical experience. Application deadline: rolling. Application fee: $50. *Expenses:* Tuition $16,000 per year full-time, $485 per credit part-time. Fees $500 per year full-time, $150 per semester part-time. *Financial aid:* Research assistantships, teaching assistantships, graduate achievement awards, and career-related internships or fieldwork available. Aid available to part-time students. Financial aid application deadline: 3/1. • Dr. Caryle G. Wolahan, Director, School of Nursing, 516-877-4545.

Boston College, School of Nursing, Chestnut Hill, MA 02167-9991. Offerings include psychiatric-mental health nursing (MS). Accredited by NLN. School faculty: 18 full-time (all women), 1 (woman) part-time. *Degree requirements:* Oral comprehensive exam, research project required, foreign language and thesis not required. *Average time to degree:* doctorate–4 years full-time. *Entrance requirements:* GRE General Test, bachelor's degree in nursing. Application deadline: 3/1 (priority date; 10/15 for spring admission). Application fee: $40. Electronic applications accepted. *Expenses:* Tuition $626 per semester hour. Fees $80 per year (minimum) full-time, $30 per semester part-time. • Dr. Barbara Munro, Dean, 617-552-4251. Fax: 617-552-0931. E-mail: barbara.munro@bc.edu. Application contact: Dana Robinson, Administrative Secretary, 617-552-4059. Fax: 617-552-0745. E-mail: dana.robinson@bc.edu.

Case Western Reserve University, Frances Payne Bolton School of Nursing, Master's Program in Nursing, Nurse Practitioner Program, Cleveland, OH 44106. Offerings include psychiatric-mental health nurse practitioner (MSN). Accredited by NLN. *Degree requirements:* Thesis optional, foreign language not required. *Entrance requirements:* GRE General Test or MAT. Application deadline: 6/1 (rolling processing). Application fee: $75. *Tuition:* $18,400 per year full-time, $767 per credit hour part-time. • Application contact: Molly Blank, Admission Counselor, 216-368-2529. Fax: 216-368-3542. E-mail: mab44@po.cwru.edu.

The Catholic University of America, School of Nursing, Washington, DC 20064. Offerings include advanced practice nursing (MSN), with options in administration of nursing service, adult nurse practitioner, education, family nurse practitioner, geriatric nurse practitioner, pediatric nurse practitioner, psychiatric-mental health, school health nurse practitioner. Accredited by NLN. School faculty: 18 full-time (all women), 2 part-time (both women), 19 FTE. *Degree requirements:* Comprehensive exam required, thesis optional, foreign language not required. *Entrance requirements:* GRE General Test (minimum combined score of 1350 on three sections).

Application deadline: 8/1 (priority date; rolling processing; 12/1 for spring admission). Application fee: $50. *Expenses:* Tuition $17,325 per year full-time, $668 per credit hour part-time. Fees $680 per year full-time, $360 per year part-time. • Sr. Mary Jean Flaherty, Dean, 202-319-5403.

Columbia University, School of Nursing, Program in Psychiatric-Community Mental Health Nursing, New York, NY 10032. Awards MS, Adv C. One or more programs accredited by NLN. Part-time programs available. Faculty: 3 full-time (all women), 2 part-time (both women). Students: 3 full-time (all women), 40 part-time (37 women); includes 9 minority (4 African Americans, 4 Asian Americans, 1 Hispanic). Average age 35. 31 applicants, 84% accepted. In 1997, 13 master's awarded. *Entrance requirements:* For master's, GRE General Test (minimum score 500 on verbal and analytical sections), BSN, 1 year of clinical experience (preferred), or completion of a clinical residency; for Adv C, MSN, previous course work in statistics, clinical preceptorship. Application deadline: 4/1 (priority date; rolling processing; 10/1 for spring admission). Application fee: $60. *Tuition:* $19,376 per year full-time, $692 per credit (minimum) part-time. *Financial aid:* Teaching assistantships available. Financial aid application deadline: 2/1. • Prof. Penny Buschman, Director, 212-305-3199. Application contact: Joseph Tomaino, Assistant Dean for Student Services, 212-305-5756. E-mail: jt238@columbia.edu.

Emory University, Nell Hodgson Woodruff School of Nursing, Atlanta, GA 30322-1100. Offerings include adult health (MSN), with options in adult medical/surgical/nurse practitioner, adult oncology/nurse practitioner, critical care/nurse practitioner, psychosocial nurse practitioner. Accredited by NLN. Postbaccalaureate distance learning degree programs offered (minimal on-campus study). School faculty: 33 full-time (32 women), 21 part-time (19 women), 48 FTE. *Degree requirements:* Thesis optional, foreign language not required. *Average time to degree:* master's–1.5 years full-time, 3 years part-time. *Entrance requirements:* GRE General Test (minimum combined score of 1500 on three sections) or MAT (minimum score 35), minimum GPA of 3.0, BS in nursing or RN license and additional course work. Application deadline: 2/1 (priority date; rolling processing; 11/1 for spring admission). Application fee: $50. *Expenses:* Tuition $18,050 per year. Fees $200 per year. • Dr. Dyanne D. Affonso, Dean, 404-727-7976. Fax: 404-727-0536. Application contact: Debbie Ashtiani, Director, 404-727-7980.

Georgia State University, College of Health and Human Sciences, School of Nursing, Atlanta, GA 30303-3083. Offerings include psychiatric/mental health nursing (MS), with option in child and adolescent psychology. One or more programs accredited by NLN. MS (child and adolescent psychology, gerontology) and PhD (community nursing, family nursing) being phased out; applicants no longer accepted. School faculty: 26 full-time (all women), 3 part-time (all women). *Degree requirements:* Research project or thesis required, thesis optional, foreign language not required. *Entrance requirements:* Interview, RN license. Application deadline: 4/15. Application fee: $25. *Expenses:* Tuition $2862 per year full-time, $106 per semester hour part-time for state residents; $11,448 per year full-time, $424 per semester hour part-time for nonresidents. Fees $228 per year. • Dr. Dee Baldwin, Director of Graduate Programs, 404-651-3040. Application contact: Barbara Smith, Admissions Counselor, 404-651-3064. Fax: 404-651-4871.

Hunter College of the City University of New York, Hunter-Bellevue School of Nursing, Program in Psychiatric Nursing, 695 Park Avenue, New York, NY 10021-5085. Awards MS. Accredited by NLN. Part-time programs available. Faculty: 10 full-time (9 women). Students: 4 full-time (all women), 15 part-time (all women); includes 5 minority (3 African Americans, 2 Asian Americans). Average age 42. 7 applicants, 86% accepted. In 1997, 6 degrees awarded (100% found work related to degree). *Degree requirements:* Practicum required, foreign language and thesis not required. *Average time to degree:* master's–1.5 years full-time, 3 years part-time. *Entrance requirements:* TOEFL (minimum score 550), minimum GPA of 3.0, New York RN license. Application deadline: 4/27 (rolling processing; 11/21 for spring admission). Application fee: $40. *Expenses:* Tuition $4350 per year full-time, $185 per credit part-time for state residents; $7600 per year full-time, $320 per credit part-time for nonresidents. Fees $26 per year. *Financial aid:* Traineeships, partial tuition waivers, Federal Work-Study available. Aid available to part-time students. Financial aid application deadline: 5/1; applicants required to submit FAFSA. *Faculty research:* Nursing approaches with the homeless, chronic mentally ill, and depressed; power and empathy. • Dr. Steven Baumann, Coordinator, 212-481-4457. Fax: 212-481-5078. E-mail: sbaumann@shiva.hunter.cuny.edu. Application contact: Audrey Berman, Associate Director for Graduate Admissions, 212-772-4490.

Husson College, Program in Nursing, Bangor, ME 04401-2999. Offerings include psychiatric nursing (MSN). Program faculty: 2. *Entrance requirements:* MAT, BSN. Application deadline: 7/15 (priority date; rolling processing). Application fee: $25. • Dr. Barbara Higgins, Director, Nurse Practitioner Program, 207-947-7057.

Kent State University, School of Nursing, Kent, OH 44242-0001. Offerings include clinical nursing (MSN), with options in nursing of the adult (medical/surgical nursing), psychiatric mental health nursing. Accredited by NLN. School faculty: 29 full-time. *Degree requirements:* Thesis optional, foreign language not required. *Entrance requirements:* Minimum GPA of 2.75. Application deadline: 7/12 (rolling processing; 11/29 for spring admission). Application fee: $30. *Tuition:* $4752 per year full-time, $216 per credit hour part-time for state residents; $9213 per year full-time, $419 per credit hour part-time for nonresidents. • Dr. Davina Gosnell, Dean, 330-672-7930. Fax: 330-672-2433.

Louisiana State University Medical Center, School of Nursing, 433 Bolivar Street, New Orleans, LA 70112-2223. Offerings include nursing (MN), psychiatric/community mental health nursing (MN, DNS). One or more programs accredited by NLN and NLN. School faculty: 10 full-time (all women), 4 part-time (3 women). *Degree requirements:* For master's, thesis optional, foreign language not required; for doctorate, dissertation required, foreign language not required. *Entrance requirements:* For master's, GRE General Test, MAT (minimum score 50), TOEFL, minimum GPA of 3.0; for doctorate, GRE General Test (minimum combined score of 1500 on three sections), TOEFL (minimum score 550), minimum GPA of 3.5. Application deadline: 3/17. Application fee: $50. *Expenses:* Tuition $2878 per year full-time, $421 per semester (minimum) part-time for state residents; $6003 per year full-time, $838 per semester (minimum) part-time for nonresidents. Fees $350 per year full-time, $90 per semester (minimum) part-time. • Dr. Elizabeth Humphrey, Dean, 504-568-4106. Application contact: Dr. Barbara C. Donlon, Acting Director, 504-568-4137. Fax: 504-568-3308. E-mail: bdonlo@lsumc.edu.

Medical College of Georgia, Graduate Programs in Nursing, Augusta, GA 30912-1500. Offerings include mental health nursing (MSN). Accredited by NLN. Faculty: 17 full-time (14 women). *Application deadline:* 6/30 (priority date; rolling processing). *Application fee:* $0. *Expenses:* Tuition $2670 per year full-time, $111 per credit part-time for state residents; $10,680 per year full-time, $445 per credit part-time for nonresidents. Fees $286 per year. • Dr. Virginia Kemp, Associate Dean, 706-721-4710. E-mail: vkemp@mail.mcg.edu. Application contact: Dr. Gary C. Bond, Associate Dean, 706-721-3278. Fax: 706-721-6829. E-mail: gradstud@mail.mcg.edu.

Medical University of South Carolina, College of Nursing, Program in Nursing, Charleston, SC 29425-0002. Offerings include psychiatric-mental health nursing (MSN). Accredited by NLN. *Degree requirements:* Computer language required, thesis optional, foreign language not required. *Entrance requirements:* GRE General Test (minimum combined score of 1000), BSN, previous course work in statistics and physical assessment, 1 year nursing experience, license. Application deadline: 2/15 (10/15 for spring admission). Application fee: $55. *Expenses:* Tuition $3760 per year full-time, $173 per semester hour part-time for state residents; $5672 per year full-time, $270 per semester hour part-time for nonresidents. Fees $280 per year (minimum). • Dr. Jean Leuner, Associate Dean, 843-792-8515. Application contact: Office of Enrollment Services, 843-792-3281.

Molloy College, Department of Nursing, 1000 Hempstead Avenue, Rockville Centre, NY 11571-5002. Offerings include nurse practitioner psychiatry (MSN, Advanced Certificate). Department faculty: 16 full-time (14 women), 12 part-time (9 women). *Degree requirements:* For master's, thesis optional, foreign language not required. *Average time to degree:* master's–2.2 years full-time, 3.7 years part-time; other advanced degree–1 year full-time, 2 years part-time. *Entrance requirements:* For master's, BS in nursing, minimum undergraduate GPA of 3.0; for Advanced Certificate, master's degree in nursing. Application deadline: 9/2 (priority date; rolling processing; 1/20 for spring admission). Application fee: $60. *Expenses:* Tuition $430 per credit. Fees $430 per year full-time, $165 per semester (minimum) part-time. • Dr. Carol A. Clifford, Director, Graduate Program, 516-256-2218. Fax: 516-678-9718. E-mail: clica01@molloy.edu. Application contact: Wayne James, Vice President for Enrollment and Management, 516-678-5000 Ext. 240. Fax: 516-256-2247.

New York University, School of Education, Division of Nursing, Programs in Advanced Practice Nursing, Program in Advanced Practice Nursing: Mental Health, New York, NY 10012-1019. Awards MA, AC. One or more programs accredited by NLN. Faculty: 25 full-time, 9 part-time. Students: 3 full-time, 15 part-time. 12 applicants, 92% accepted. *Degree requirements:* For master's, thesis required (for some programs), foreign language not required. *Entrance requirements:* For master's, TOEFL; for AC, TOEFL, master's degree. Application deadline: 2/1 (priority date; rolling processing; 12/1 for spring admission). Application fee: $40 ($60 for international students). *Financial aid:* Partial tuition waivers, Federal Work-Study, institutionally sponsored loans, and career-related internships or fieldwork available. Financial aid application deadline: 3/1; applicants required to submit FAFSA. *Faculty research:* Addiction, HIV, substance abuse. • Madeline Naegle, Coordinator, 212-998-5321. Fax: 212-995-4359. Application contact: Office of Graduate Admissions, 212-998-5030. Fax: 212-995-4328.

Northeastern University, Graduate School of Nursing, Program in Psychiatric-Mental Health Nursing, Boston, MA 02115-5096. Awards MS, CAS. One or more programs accredited by NLN. *Degree requirements:* For master's, thesis or alternative required, foreign language not required. *Entrance requirements:* For master's, GRE General Test, minimum GPA of 3.0, previous course work in statistics, 1-2 years nursing experience, RN license, ICU experience. Application deadline: 4/1 (priority date; rolling processing; 2/1 for spring admission). Application fee: $50. *Expenses:* Tuition $440 per credit hour. Fees $55 per quarter full-time, $13.25 per quarter part-time. *Faculty research:* Clinical psychopharmacology, access to mental health care, child abuse, seasonal affect ive disorder (SAD), chronic and persistant mental illness, crisis intervention. • Dr. Margery Chisholm, Coordinator, 617-373-4603. Application contact: Molly Schnabel, Admissions Coordinator, 617-373-3590. Fax: 617-373-8672. E-mail: mschnabe@lynx.neu.edu.

Announcement: Master's program in psychiatric–mental health nursing (52 quarter hours). Advanced preparation as clinical specialist or nurse practitioner with adult or child concentration. Health assessment, psychodynamic therapies, psychobiology interventions, and psychopharmacology. Full- and part-time study. Preceptorships available in Boston's top mental health–care agencies. Certificate program for MS-prepared nurses. For application, contact Admissions Coordinator Molly Schnabel at 617-373-3590.

Oregon Health Sciences University, School of Nursing, Program in Mental Health Nursing, 3181 SW Sam Jackson Park Road, Portland, OR 97201-3098. Awards MN, MS, Post Master's Certificate. One or more programs accredited by NLN. Students: 26 full-time (22 women), 17 part-time (16 women); includes 3 minority (2 Asian Americans, 1 Native American), 2 international. 32 applicants, 59% accepted. In 1997, 8 master's awarded. *Degree requirements:* For master's, thesis optional, foreign language not required. *Entrance requirements:* For master's, GRE General Test (minimum combined score of 1000), bachelor's degree in nursing, minimum undergraduate GPA of 3.0; for Post Master's Certificate, master's degree in nursing. Application deadline: 1/15. Application fee: $40. *Financial aid:* Career-related internships or fieldwork available. • Application contact: Office of Recruitment, 503-494-7725. Fax: 503-494-4350.

Pontifical Catholic University of Puerto Rico, College of Sciences, Department of Nursing, Ponce, PR 00731-6382. Offerings include mental health and psychiatric nursing (MS). Accredited by NLN. Department faculty: 3 full-time (all women), 2 part-time (both women). *Degree requirements:* Clinical research paper. *Entrance requirements:* GRE General Test, minimum GPA of 2.5, BSN, 2 years of work experience, RN license. Application deadline: 4/30 (priority date; rolling processing). Application fee: $15. Electronic applications accepted. • Dr. Carmen L. Madera, Director, 787-841-2000 Ext. 261. Application contact: Manuel Luciano, Director of Admissions, 787-841-2000 Ext. 426. Fax: 787-840-4295.

Rush University, College of Nursing, Department of Psychiatric Nursing, Chicago, IL 60612-3832. Offers programs in psychiatric nurse practitioner (MSN, DN Sc, ND), psychiatric/adult nurse practitioner (MSN, DN Sc, ND). One or more programs accredited by NLN. Part-time programs available. Faculty: 6 full-time (5 women), 4 part-time (all women), 8 FTE. Students: 25 part-time. Average age 36. *Degree requirements:* For doctorate, dissertation required, foreign language not required. *Entrance requirements:* For master's, GRE General Test, interview; for doctorate, MS or GRE General Test, interview, previous course work in statistics. Application deadline: 8/1 (rolling processing; 2/1 for spring admission). Application fee: $40. *Tuition:* $8560 per year full-time, $370 per credit hour part-time. *Financial aid:* Federal Work-Study, institutionally sponsored loans, and career-related internships or fieldwork available. Aid available to part-time students. Financial aid applicants required to submit FAFSA. *Faculty research:* Outcomes of child in-patient hospitalization, self-efficacy of depressed patients, parenting skills, outcomes of geropsychiatric home care. • Jane Ulsafer-Van Lanen, Acting Chairperson, 312-942-3480. Application contact: Hicela Castruita, Director, College Admissions Services, 312-942-7100. Fax: 312-942-2219.

Rutgers, The State University of New Jersey, Newark, College of Nursing, Graduate Program in Psychiatric/Mental Health Nursing, Newark, NJ 07102-3192. Awards MS. Accredited by NLN. Part-time programs available. *Degree requirements:* Comprehensive exam required, foreign language and thesis not required. *Entrance requirements:* GRE General Test, TOEFL, RN license, minimum B average, BS in nursing. Application deadline: 8/15 (rolling processing; 12/15 for spring admission). Application fee: $40. Electronic applications accepted. *Expenses:* Tuition $6248 per year full-time, $257 per credit part-time for state residents; $9160 per year full-time, $380 per credit part-time for nonresidents. Fees $738 per year full-time, $107 per semester (minimum) part-time. *Financial aid:* Federal Work-Study, institutionally sponsored loans, and career-related internships or fieldwork available. Financial aid application deadline: 3/1. • Application contact: Dr. Elaine Dolinsky, Associate Dean for Student Life and Services, 973-353-5060. Fax: 973-353-1277.

Sage Graduate School, Graduate School, Division of Nursing, Program in Psychiatric–Mental Health Nurse Practitioner, Troy, NY 12180-4115. Awards MS. Accredited by NLN. Part-time and evening/weekend programs available. *Degree requirements:* Thesis or alternative required, foreign language not required. *Entrance requirements:* BS in nursing, minimum GPA of 2.75. Application deadline: 8/1 (rolling processing; 12/15 for spring admission). Application fee: $25. *Expenses:* Tuition $360 per credit hour. Fees $50 per semester. *Financial aid:* Career-related internships or fieldwork available. Financial aid application deadline: 7/1; applicants required to submit FAFSA. • Application contact: Melissa Robertson, Associate Director of Admissions, 518-244-6878. Fax: 518-244-6880. E-mail: sgsadm@sage.edu.

Saint Joseph College, Division of Nursing, West Hartford, CT 06117-2700. Offerings include psychiatric/mental health nursing (MS). Accredited by NLN. Division faculty: 10 full-time (9 women), 2 part-time (both women). *Degree requirements:* Thesis or alternative required, foreign language not required. *Application deadline:* 8/29 (rolling processing). *Application fee:* $25. *Tuition:* $395 per credit. • Dr. Virginia Knowlden, Director, 860-232-4571 Ext. 258.

Saint Louis University, School of Nursing, Program in Psychiatric-Mental Health Nursing, St. Louis, MO 63103-2097. Awards MSN, MSN(R), Certificate, MPH/MSN, MSN/MBA. Offerings include clinical health specialist/case manager (MSN, MSN(R), Certificate). One or more programs accredited by NLN. *Degree requirements:* For master's, comprehensive oral exam required, thesis optional, foreign language not required. *Entrance requirements:* For master's,

Directory: Psychiatric Nursing

Saint Louis University (continued)

GRE General Test. Application deadline: 7/1 (rolling processing; 11/1 for spring admission). Application fee: $40. *Tuition:* $542 per credit hour. *Financial aid:* Traineeships available. Financial aid application deadline: 4/1. • Dr. Ruth Murray, Program Director, 314-577-8956. Application contact: Dr. Marcia Buresch, Assistant Dean of the Graduate School, 314-977-2240. Fax: 314-977-3943.

Saint Xavier University, School of Nursing, Chicago, IL 60655-3105. Offerings include psychiatric/mental health clinical nurse specialist (MS). Accredited by NLN. MBA/MS offered in cooperation with the Graham School of Management. School faculty: 10 full-time (all women), 2 part-time (both women). *Entrance requirements:* MAT or GRE General Test, minimum GPA of 3.0, RN license. Application deadline: 2/15 (9/15 for spring admission). Application fee: $35. *Expenses:* Tuition $450 per hour. Fees $50 per year. • Dr. Mary Lebold, Dean, 773-298-3700. Fax: 773-779-9061. E-mail: lebold@sxu.edu. Application contact: Sr. Evelyn McKenna, Vice President of Enrollment Management, 773-298-3050. Fax: 773-298-3076. E-mail: mckenna@sxu.edu.

Southern Illinois University at Edwardsville, School of Nursing, Program in Psychiatric Nursing, Edwardsville, IL 62026-0001. Awards MS. Accredited by NLN. Students: 11 full-time (10 women), 9 part-time (all women); includes 4 minority (all African Americans). 8 applicants, 100% accepted. In 1997, 2 degrees awarded. *Degree requirements:* Thesis or alternative, final exam required, foreign language not required. *Entrance requirements:* Appropriate bachelor's degree, RN license. Application deadline: 7/24. Application fee: $25. *Expenses:* Tuition $1716 per year full-time, $95 per credit hour part-time for state residents; $5149 per year full-time, $286 per credit hour part-time for nonresidents. Fees $463 per year full-time, $433 per year part-time. *Financial aid:* Fellowships, Federal Work-Study, institutionally sponsored loans available. Aid available to part-time students. • Dr. Felissa Lashley, Dean, School of Nursing, 618-692-3956.

State University of New York at Stony Brook, Health Sciences Center, School of Nursing, Program in Mental Health/Psychiatric Nursing, Stony Brook, NY 11794. Offers mental health nurse practitioner (Certificate), mental health/psychiatric nursing (MS). One or more programs accredited by NLN. Students: 3 full-time (2 women), 43 part-time (36 women); includes 10 minority (6 African Americans, 2 Asian Americans, 2 Hispanics). In 1997, 19 master's awarded. *Degree requirements:* For master's, thesis required, foreign language not required. *Entrance requirements:* For master's, BSN, minimum GPA of 3.0, previous course work in statistics. Application deadline: 1/15. Application fee: $50. *Expenses:* Tuition $5100 per year full-time, $213 per credit hour part-time for state residents; $8416 per year full-time, $351 per credit hour part-time for nonresidents. Fees $529 per year full-time, $77 per semester (minimum) part-time. *Financial aid:* Application deadline 3/15. • Dr. Patricia Long, Chair, 516-444-3269. Fax: 516-444-3136. E-mail: pat_long@notes2.nursing.sunysb.edu.

Texas Woman's University, College of Nursing, Denton, TX 76204. Offerings include psychiatric-mental health nursing (MS). Accredited by NLN. College faculty: 30 full-time (29 women), 12 part-time (10 women). *Degree requirements:* Thesis or alternative required, foreign language not required. *Entrance requirements:* GRE General Test (minimum combined score of 750), minimum GPA of 3.0. Application deadline: rolling. Application fee: $25. • Dr. Carolyn S. Gunning, Dean, 940-898-2401.

University of Cincinnati, College of Nursing and Health, Cincinnati, OH 45221-0038. Offerings include psychiatric nursing (MSN). Accredited by NLN. College faculty: 26 full-time. *Degree requirements:* Project or thesis required, foreign language not required. *Average time to degree:* master's–1.5 years full-time, 2.5 years part-time; doctorate–4 years full-time, 6 years part-time. *Entrance requirements:* GRE General Test. Application deadline: 1/1 (priority date; rolling processing). Application fee: $30. *Tuition:* $7228 per year full-time, $185 per credit hour part-time for state residents; $13,812 per year full-time, $352 per credit hour part-time for nonresidents. • Dr. Andrea Lindell, Dean, 513-558-5330. Application contact: Tom West, Program Coordinator, 513-558-3600. Fax: 513-558-7523. E-mail: tom.west@uc.edu.

University of Illinois at Chicago, College of Nursing, Program in Psychiatric Nursing, Chicago, IL 60607-7128. Awards MS. Accredited by NLN. Faculty: 5 full-time (all women). Students: 21; includes 1 minority (Asian American), 1 international. Average age 41. 5 applicants, 80% accepted. In 1997, 5 degrees awarded. *Degree requirements:* Thesis or alternative required, foreign language not required. *Entrance requirements:* GRE General Test, TOEFL (minimum score 550), minimum GPA of 3.75 on a 5.0 scale. Application deadline: 5/15 (10/15 for spring admission). Application fee: $40 ($50 for international students). *Financial aid:* In 1997–98, 1 research assistantship was awarded; fellowships, teaching assistantships, partial tuition waivers, Federal Work-Study, institutionally sponsored loans, and career-related internships or fieldwork also available. • Dr. Barbara Logan, Head, 312-996-8008. Application contact: Kathleen Knafl, Director of Graduate Studies, 312-996-2159.

University of Maryland, Baltimore, Graduate School, School of Nursing, Baltimore, MD 21201-1627. Offerings include psychiatric nursing (MS). Accredited by NLN. MS/MBA offered jointly with the University of Baltimore. School faculty: 49 (45 women). *Degree requirements:* Thesis or alternative required, foreign language not required. *Entrance requirements:* GRE General Test, TOEFL, minimum GPA of 2.75, previous course work in statistics, BS in nursing. Application fee: $42. *Expenses:* Tuition $253 per credit hour for state residents; $454 per credit hour for nonresidents. Fees $317 per year. • Dr. Barbara Heller, Dean, 410-706-6741. Application contact: Dr. Susan Wozenski, Assistant Dean for Student Affairs, 410-706-0501. Fax: 410-706-7238.

University of Massachusetts Lowell, College of Health Professions, Department of Nursing, Program in Occupational Health Nursing, 1 University Avenue, Lowell, MA 01854-2881. Offerings include adult psychiatric nursing (MS). Accredited by NLN. *Degree requirements:* Thesis optional, foreign language not required. *Entrance requirements:* GRE General Test. Application deadline: 4/1 (priority date; rolling processing; 10/1 for spring admission). Application fee: $20 ($35 for international students). *Tuition:* $4867 per year full-time, $618 per semester (minimum) part-time for state residents; $10,276 per year full-time, $1294 per semester (minimum) part-time for nonresidents. • Dr. May Futrell, Chair, Department of Nursing, 978-934-4467. E-mail: may_futrell@woods.uml.edu.

University of Michigan, School of Nursing, Division of Acute, Critical and Long-Term Care, Program in Psychiatric Mental Health Nursing, Ann Arbor, MI 48109. Offers psychiatric mental health nurse practitioner (MS), psychiatric mental health nursing (MS). One or more programs accredited by NLN. Part-time programs available. *Degree requirements:* Thesis required, foreign language not required. *Entrance requirements:* GRE General Test. Application deadline: rolling. Application fee: $55. *Financial aid:* Fellowships, research assistantships, teaching assistantships available. • Application contact: Graduate Program Secretary, 734-763-0010. Fax: 734-936-5525.

University of New Mexico, College of Nursing, Albuquerque, NM 87131-2039. Offerings include advanced nursing practice (MSN), with options in adult health nursing, gerontological nursing, parent-child nursing, psychiatric-mental health nursing. Accredited by NLN. College faculty: 38 full-time (36 women), 23 part-time (all women), 46.57 FTE. *Degree requirements:* Thesis optional, foreign language not required. *Entrance requirements:* GRE General Test, interview, minimum GPA of 3.0, previous course work in statistics. Application deadline: 7/15 (11/1 for spring admission). Application fee: $25. *Expenses:* Tuition $2442 per year full-time, $103 per credit hour part-time for state residents; $8691 per year full-time, $103 per credit hour (minimum) part-time for nonresidents. Fees $32 per year. • Dr. Sandra Ferketich, Dean, 505-272-6284. Application contact: Anne-Marie Oechsler, Director, Academic Advisement, 505-272-4224. Fax: 505-272-3970. E-mail: annmarie@unm.edu.

University of Pennsylvania, School of Nursing, Psychiatric Mental Health Advanced Practice Nurse Program, Philadelphia, PA 19104. Offers adult and special populations (MSN), child and family (MSN), geropsychiatrics (MSN). Accredited by NLN. Part-time programs available. Students: 5 full-time (all women), 18 part-time (17 women); includes 1 minority (African American). Average age 34. 13 applicants, 69% accepted. In 1997, 13 degrees awarded. *Entrance requirements:* GRE General Test, BSN, minimum GPA of 3.0, previous course work in statistics. Application deadline: 9/1 (rolling processing). Application fee: $65. *Financial aid:* In 1997–98, 5 research assistantships, 8 teaching assistantships were awarded; fellowships, Federal Work-Study, institutionally sponsored loans, and career-related internships or fieldwork also available. Aid available to part-time students. *Faculty research:* Use of restraints in psychiatry, victims of trauma, spiritual use of prayer by cancer patients, coping strategies of African-Americans, urban health care. • Dr. Freida Outlaw, Director, 215-898-5730. Fax: 215-898-6320. E-mail: foutlaw@pobox.upenn.edu. Application contact: Susan K. Ogle, Associate Director of Admissions and Student Affairs, 215-898-3301. Fax: 215-573-8439. E-mail: sogle@pobox.upenn.edu.

University of Pittsburgh, School of Nursing, Program in Nurse Practitioner Studies, Pittsburgh, PA 15260. Offerings include health and community systems (MSN), with option in psychiatric primary care nurse practitioner. Accredited by NLN. *Degree requirements:* Thesis or alternative required, foreign language not required. *Average time to degree:* master's–2 years full-time, 5 years part-time. *Entrance requirements:* GRE General Test or MAT, TOEFL, BSN, RN license, 1 to 3 years of nursing experience. Application deadline: 2/1 (priority date; rolling processing; 9/15 for spring admission). Application fee: $35 ($40 for international students). • Application contact: Dr. Kathy Lucke, Director, Student Services, 412-624-2405. Fax: 412-624-2409. E-mail: nursao+@pitt.edu.

See in-depth description on page 1451.

University of South Alabama, College of Nursing, Mobile, AL 36688-0002. Offerings include community mental health nursing (MSN). Accredited by NLN. College faculty: 9 full-time (all women), 1 (woman) part-time. *Degree requirements:* Written comprehensive exam, research project or thesis required, foreign language not required. *Entrance requirements:* GRE General Test (minimum combined score of 1000) or MAT (minimum score 45), BSN, minimum GPA of 3.0, 1 year of nursing experience, interview, nursing license. Application deadline: 9/1 (priority date; rolling processing). Application fee: $25. • Dr. Amanda Baker, Dean, 334-434-3415.

University of South Carolina, Graduate School, College of Nursing, Program in Community Mental Health and Psychiatric Health Nursing, Columbia, SC 29208. Awards MSN. Accredited by NLN. Students: 4 full-time (all women), 17 part-time (15 women); includes 2 minority (1 African American, 1 Hispanic). Average age 44. *Degree requirements:* Oral or written comprehensive exam required, foreign language not required. *Entrance requirements:* GRE General Test, BS in nursing, previous course work in statistics. Application deadline: 4/15 (rolling processing; 10/15 for spring admission). Application fee: $35. Electronic applications accepted. *Expenses:* Tuition $4480 per year full-time, $220 per credit hour part-time for state residents; $9338 per year full-time, $457 per credit hour part-time for nonresidents. Fees $125 per year full-time, $37 per semester (minimum) part-time. *Financial aid:* Application deadline 2/1. • Application contact: Office of Academic and Student Affairs, 803-777-7412. Fax: 803-777-0616.

University of Southern Maine, College of Nursing, Portland, ME 04104-9300. Offerings include psychiatric-mental health nursing (MS, PMC). One or more programs accredited by NLN. Postbaccalaureate distance learning degree programs offered (minimal on-campus study). College faculty: 11 full-time (all women), 5 part-time (all women). *Degree requirements:* For master's, thesis optional, foreign language not required. *Average time to degree:* master's–2.5 years full-time, 4 years part-time. *Entrance requirements:* For master's, GRE General Test (minimum combined score of 1000 on verbal and quantitative sections) or MAT (minimum score 45), minimum GPA of 3.0. Application deadline: 3/1. Application fee: $25. *Expenses:* Tuition $178 per credit hour for state residents; $267 per credit hour (minimum) for nonresidents. Fees $282 per year full-time, $83 per semester (minimum) part-time. • Dr. Marianne W. Rodgers, Interim Dean, 207-780-4808. Fax: 207-780-4997. E-mail: mrodgers@usm.maine.edu. Application contact: Mary Sloan, Assistant Director of Graduate Studies, 207-780-4386. Fax: 207-780-4969. E-mail: msloan@usm.maine.edu.

University of Southern Mississippi, College of Nursing, Hattiesburg, MS 39406-5167. Offerings include psychiatric nursing (MSN). Accredited by NLN. College faculty: 18 full-time (all women). *Degree requirements:* Thesis optional, foreign language not required. *Entrance requirements:* GRE General Test, minimum GPA of 2.75. Application deadline: 8/9 (priority date; rolling processing). Application fee: $0 ($25 for international students). *Tuition:* $2870 per year full-time, $137 per credit hour part-time for state residents; $5972 per year full-time, $172 per credit hour part-time for nonresidents. • Dr. Gerry Cadenhead, Director, 601-266-5509. Fax: 601-266-5927.

The University of Texas at El Paso, College of Nursing and Health Science, Program in Nursing, 500 West University Avenue, El Paso, TX 79968-0001. Offerings include psychiatric/mental health nursing (MSN). Accredited by NLN. *Degree requirements:* Thesis optional, foreign language not required. *Entrance requirements:* GRE General Test or MAT (minimum score 50), TOEFL (minimum score 550), BSN, course work in statistics. Application deadline: 7/1 (rolling processing; 11/1 for spring admission). Application fee: $15 ($65 for international students). Electronic applications accepted. *Tuition:* $2063 per year full-time, $284 per credit hour part-time for state residents; $5753 per year full-time, $425 per credit hour part-time for nonresidents.

The University of Texas–Houston Health Science Center, School of Nursing, Master's Program in Nursing, Houston, TX 77225-0036. Offerings include psychiatric health nursing (MSN). Accredited by NLN. *Degree requirements:* Thesis required, foreign language not required. *Entrance requirements:* GRE or MAT, BSN, Texas RN license. Application deadline: 5/1 (priority date; rolling processing; 9/1 for spring admission). Application fee: $10. Electronic applications accepted. • Frank Cole, Chair, Graduate Curriculum Committee, 713-500-2153. Fax: 713-500-2171. E-mail: fcole@son1.nur.uth.tmc.edu. Application contact: Eleanor Evans, Pre-Admissions Counselor, 713-500-2104. Fax: 713-500-2107. E-mail: eevans@son1.nur.uth.tmc.edu.

Vanderbilt University, School of Nursing, Nashville, TN 37240-1001. Offerings include psychiatric-mental health nurse practitioner (MSN). Accredited by NLN. Postbaccalaureate distance learning degree programs offered (minimal on-campus study). School faculty: 76 full-time (66 women), 253 part-time (224 women). *Degree requirements:* Terminal course required, thesis not required. *Average time to degree:* master's–2 years full-time, 4 years part-time; doctorate–4 years full-time, 5 years part-time. *Entrance requirements:* GMAT, GRE, or MAT, minimum B average. Application deadline: rolling. Application fee: $50. Electronic applications accepted. • Dr. Colleen Conway-Welch, Dean, 615-343-3243. Fax: 615-343-7711. Application contact: Patricia Peerman, Assistant Dean of Admissions, 615-322-3800. Fax: 615-343-0333. E-mail: vusn-admission@mcmail.vanderbilt.edu.

Virginia Commonwealth University, School of Nursing, Richmond, VA 23284-9005. Offerings include psychiatric-mental health nursing (MS). Accredited by NLN. School faculty: 50 full-time (all women), 5 part-time (all women). *Entrance requirements:* GRE General Test, BSN, minimum GPA of 2.8. Application deadline: 2/1. Application fee: $30 ($0 for international students). *Tuition:* $4960 per year full-time, $257 per credit part-time for state residents; $12,652 per year full-time, $684 per credit part-time for nonresidents. • Dr. Nancy F. Langston, Dean, 804-828-5174. E-mail: nflangst@vcu.edu. Application contact: Susan Lipp, Admissions Counselor, 804-828-5171. Fax: 804-828-7743. E-mail: sllipp@vcu.edu.

Wayne State University, College of Nursing, Department of Family, Community and Mental Health, Program in Adult Psychiatric-Mental Health Nursing, Detroit, MI 48202. Awards MSN. Accredited by NLN. Part-time programs available. Students: 3 full-time (1 woman), 4 part-time (3 women); includes 6 minority (4 African Americans, 1 Asian American, 1 Native American). Average age 43. 3 applicants, 67% accepted. In 1997, 3 degrees awarded. *Degree requirements:*

Computer language, thesis or alternative required, foreign language not required. *Entrance requirements:* GRE General Test (minimum combined score of 800), minimum GPA of 2.8. Application deadline: 7/1 (priority date; rolling processing; 11/1 for spring admission). Application fee: $20 ($30 for international students). *Expenses:* Tuition $163 per credit hour for state residents; $355 per credit hour for nonresidents. Fees $498 per year full-time, $114 per semester (minimum) part-time. *Financial aid:* In 1997–98, 1 student received aid, including 1 scholarship averaging $360 per month; research assistantships, institutionally sponsored loans also available. Aid available to part-time students. Financial aid application deadline: 7/1; applicants required to submit FAFSA. *Faculty research:* Substance abuse, sleep disorders, family functioning, coping with cancer, family care giving, family instrument development. • Dr. Marie-Luise Friedemann, Assistant Dean, 313-577-4092. Fax: 313-577-4571. Application contact: Vickie Radoye, Administrative Assistant Dean, Student Affairs, 313-577-4082. Fax: 313-577-6949.

Wayne State University, College of Nursing, Department of Family, Community and Mental Health, Program in Child/Adolescent Psychiatric Nursing, Detroit, MI 48202. Awards MSN. Accredited by NLN. Part-time programs available. Students: 3 part-time (all women); includes 3 minority (all African Americans). Average age 41. 0 applicants. In 1997, 1 degree awarded. *Degree requirements:* Computer language, thesis or alternative required, foreign language not required. *Entrance requirements:* GRE General Test (minimum combined score of 800), minimum GPA of 2.8. Application deadline: 7/1 (priority date; rolling processing; 11/1 for spring admission). Application fee: $20 ($30 for international students). *Expenses:* Tuition $163 per credit hour for state residents; $355 per credit hour for nonresidents. Fees $498 per year full-time, $114 per semester (minimum) part-time. *Financial aid:* Research assistantships, scholarships, traineeships, institutionally sponsored loans available. Financial aid application deadline: 7/1; applicants required to submit FAFSA. *Faculty research:* Attachment in cocaine using mothers and their infants, fostering ego development and self-care in high-risk children. • Dr. Marie-Luise Friedemann, Assistant Dean, 313-577-4092. Fax: 313-577-4571. Application contact: Vickie Radoye, Administrative Assistant Dean, Student Affairs, 313-577-4082. Fax: 313-577-6949.

Wichita State University, College of Health Professions, School of Nursing, Wichita, KS 67260. Offerings include clinical specialization (MSN), with options in adult nursing, maternal-child nursing, psychiatric/mental health nursing. Accredited by NLN. School faculty: 11 full-time (all women). *Degree requirements:* Comprehensive exam required, thesis optional, foreign language not required. *Entrance requirements:* GRE, TOEFL (minimum score 550), BSN, minimum undergraduate GPA of 2.75. Application deadline: 6/30 (priority date; rolling processing; 1/1 for spring admission). Application fee: $25 ($40 for international students). Electronic applications accepted. *Expenses:* Tuition $2303 per year full-time, $96 per credit hour part-time for state residents; $7691 per year full-time, $321 per credit hour part-time for nonresidents. Fees $490 per year full-time, $75 per semester (minimum) part-time. • Dr. Bonnie Holaday, Interim Dean, 316-978-3610. E-mail: holaday@chp.twsu.edu. Application contact: Dr. Donna Hawley, Graduate Coordinator, 316-978-3610. Fax: 316-978-3094. E-mail: hawley@chp.twsu.edu.

Public Health Nursing

Bellarmine College, Allan and Donna Lansing School of Nursing, Department of Graduate Nursing, Louisville, KY 40205-0671. Offerings include advanced community health nursing (MSN). Department faculty: 5 full-time (all women), 5 part-time (all women), 7 FTE. *Degree requirements:* Thesis required, foreign language not required. *Entrance requirements:* GRE General Test (minimum combined score of 800; average 825), minimum undergraduate GPA of 2.75, RN license. Application deadline: 8/1 (priority date; rolling processing; 1/1 for spring admission). Application fee: $25. Electronic applications accepted. *Tuition:* $330 per credit hour. • Dr. Margaret E. Miller, Director, 800-274-4723 Ext. 8414. Fax: 502-452-8058.

Boston College, School of Nursing, Chestnut Hill, MA 02167-9991. Offerings include community health nursing (MS). Accredited by NLN. School faculty: 18 full-time (all women), 1 (woman) part-time. *Degree requirements:* Oral comprehensive exam, research project required, foreign language and thesis not required. *Average time to degree:* doctorate–4 years full-time. *Entrance requirements:* GRE General Test, bachelor's degree in nursing. Application deadline: 3/1 (priority date; 10/15 for spring admission). Application fee: $40. Electronic applications accepted. *Expenses:* Tuition $626 per semester hour. Fees $80 per year (minimum) full-time, $30 per semester part-time. • Dr. Barbara Munro, Dean, 617-552-4251. Fax: 617-552-0931. E-mail: barbara.munro@bc.edu. Application contact: Dana Robinson, Administrative Secretary, 617-552-4059. Fax: 617-552-0745. E-mail: dana.robinson@bc.edu.

Case Western Reserve University, Frances Payne Bolton School of Nursing, Master's Program in Nursing, Program in Community Health Nursing, Cleveland, OH 44106. Awards MSN. Accredited by NLN. Part-time programs available. Students: 2 full-time, 6 part-time. Average age 35. 7 applicants, 71% accepted. In 1997, 2 degrees awarded. *Degree requirements:* Thesis optional, foreign language not required. *Entrance requirements:* GRE General Test or MAT. Application deadline: 6/1 (priority date; rolling processing). Application fee: $75. *Tuition:* $18,400 per year full-time, $767 per credit hour part-time. *Financial aid:* Research assistantships, teaching assistantships, partial tuition waivers, institutionally sponsored loans available. Aid available to part-time students. Financial aid application deadline: 6/30. *Faculty research:* Clinical nursing, international health, aging, home care. • Application contact: Molly Blank, Admission Counselor, 216-368-2529. Fax: 216-368-3542. E-mail: mab44@po.cwru.edu.

Georgia Southern University, College of Health and Professional Studies, Department of Nursing, Statesboro, GA 30460-8126. Offerings include rural community health nurse specialist (MSN). Postbaccalaureate distance learning degree programs offered (minimal on-campus study). Department faculty: 12 full-time (all women). *Degree requirements:* Project or thesis required, foreign language not required. *Average time to degree:* master's–1.5 years full-time, 2.5 years part-time. *Entrance requirements:* GRE General Test (minimum score 450 on each section), minimum GPA of 3.0, nursing license, 2 years of clinical experience. Application deadline: 7/15 (priority date; rolling processing; 11/15 for spring admission). Application fee: $0. Electronic applications accepted. *Tuition:* $2619 per year full-time, $287 per semester (minimum) part-time for state residents; $8619 per year full-time, $1037 per semester (minimum) part-time for nonresidents. • Dr. Kaye Herth, Chair, 912-681-5479. Application contact: Dr. John R. Diebolt, Associate Graduate Dean, 912-681-5384. Fax: 912-681-0740. E-mail: gradschool@gsvms2.cc.gasou.edu.

Georgia State University, College of Health and Human Sciences, School of Nursing, Atlanta, GA 30303-3083. Offerings include community nursing (PhD). One or more programs accredited by NLN. MS (child and adolescent psychology, gerontology) and PhD (community nursing, family nursing) being phased out; applicants no longer accepted. School faculty: 26 full-time (all women), 3 part-time (all women). *Degree requirements:* Dissertation required, foreign language not required. *Entrance requirements:* GRE General Test. Application deadline: 4/15. Application fee: $25. *Expenses:* Tuition $2862 per year full-time, $106 per semester hour part-time for state residents; $11,448 per year full-time, $424 per semester hour part-time for nonresidents. Fees $228 per year. • Dr. Dee Baldwin, Director of Graduate Programs, 404-651-3040. Application contact: Barbara Smith, Admissions Counselor, 404-651-3064. Fax: 404-651-4871.

Hawaii Pacific University, School of Nursing, 1166 Fort Street, Honolulu, HI 96813-2785. Offerings include community clinical nurse specialist (MSN). Program new for fall 1998. *Degree requirements:* Practicum, professional paper. *Entrance requirements:* Bachelor's degree in nursing. Application deadline: rolling. Application fee: $50. *Tuition:* $7920 per year full-time, $330 per credit part-time. • Dr. Carol Winters, Dean, 808-236-3552. Application contact: Leina Danao, Admissions Coordinator, 808-544-1120. Fax: 808-544-0280. E-mail: gradservetr@hpu.edu.

Holy Names College, Department of Nursing, 3500 Mountain Boulevard, Oakland, CA 94619-1699. Offerings include community health nursing/case manager (MS). Department faculty: 6 full-time (all women), 1 (woman) part-time. *Entrance requirements:* TOEFL (minimum score 550), bachelor's degree in nursing or related field, California RN license or eligibility, minimum GPA of 3.0, previous coursework in research or statistics. Application deadline: 8/1 (rolling processing; 12/1 for spring admission). Application fee: $35. *Tuition:* $7650 per year full-time, $425 per unit part-time. • Aida Sahud, Program Director, 510-436-1239. Application contact: Graduate Admissions Office, 800-430-1321. Fax: 510-436-1317. E-mail: garner@admin.hnc.edu.

Hunter College of the City University of New York, Hunter-Bellevue School of Nursing, Community Health Nursing Program, 695 Park Avenue, New York, NY 10021-5085. Awards MS. Accredited by NLN. Part-time programs available. Faculty: 9 full-time (8 women), 1 part-time (0 women). Students: 33 part-time (30 women). Average age 39. 14 applicants, 79% accepted. In 1997, 4 degrees awarded (100% found work related to degree). *Degree requirements:* Practicum required, foreign language and thesis not required. *Average time to degree:* master's–1.5 years full-time, 3 years part-time. *Entrance requirements:* TOEFL (minimum score 550), minimum GPA of 3.0, New York RN license. Application deadline: 4/27 (rolling processing; 11/21 for spring admission). Application fee: $40. *Expenses:* Tuition $4350 per year full-time, $185 per credit part-time for state residents; $7600 per year full-time, $320 per credit part-time for nonresidents. Fees $26 per year. *Financial aid:* Traineeships, partial tuition waivers, Federal Work-Study available. Aid available to part-time students. Financial aid application deadline: 5/1; applicants required to submit FAFSA. *Faculty research:* HIV/AIDS, health promotion with vulnerable populations. • Dr. Kathleen Nokes, Coordinator, 212-481-7594. Fax: 212-481-5078. E-mail: knokes@hejira.hunter.cuny.edu. Application contact: Audrey Berman, Associate Director for Graduate Admissions, 212-772-4490.

Hunter College of the City University of New York, Hunter-Bellevue School of Nursing, Community Health Nursing/Community Health Education Program, 695 Park Avenue, New York, NY 10021-5085. Awards MS/MPH. Offered jointly with the School of Health Sciences. Part-time programs available. Faculty: 11 full-time (9 women), 1 part-time (0 women). Students: 3 full-time (all women), 14 part-time (13 women); includes 8 minority (5 African Americans, 2 Asian Americans, 1 Hispanic), 1 international. Average age 40. 8 applicants, 88% accepted. *Application deadline:* 4/27 (rolling processing; 11/21 for spring admission). *Application fee:* $40. *Expenses:* Tuition $4350 per year full-time, $185 per credit part-time for state residents; $7600 per year full-time, $320 per credit part-time for nonresidents. Fees $26 per year. *Financial aid:* Partial tuition waivers, Federal Work-Study available. Aid available to part-time students. Financial aid application deadline: 5/1; applicants required to submit FAFSA. *Faculty research:* HIV/AIDS, health promotion with vulnerable populations, immigrant health. • Dr. Kathleen Nokes, Coordinator, 212-481-7594. Fax: 212-481-5078. E-mail: knokes@hejira.hunter.cuny.edu. Application contact: Audrey Berman, Associate Director for Graduate Admissions, 212-772-4490.

Indiana Wesleyan University, Division of Nursing Education, Marion, IN 46953-4999. Offerings include community health development (MS), community health nursing (MS). One or more programs accredited by NLN. Division faculty: 4 full-time (3 women). *Degree requirements:* Thesis required, foreign language not required. *Entrance requirements:* MAT, RN license, 1 year of related experience. Application fee: $10. *Tuition:* $402 per hour. • Dr. DeAnne Messias, Director of Graduate Nursing, 765-677-2148.

Johns Hopkins University, Schools of Nursing and Hygiene and Public Health, Joint Program in Nursing and Public Health, Baltimore, MD 21218-2699. Awards MPH/MSN. Part-time programs available. Faculty: 27 full-time (17 women), 11 part-time (10 women), 30 FTE. Students: 9 full-time (8 women), 5 part-time (all women); includes 3 minority (1 African American, 2 Asian Americans). Average age 31. 26 applicants, 46% accepted. *Average time to degree:* master's–1.5 years full-time, 3 years part-time. *Application deadline:* 1/31 (priority date; rolling processing; 11/15 for spring admission). *Application fee:* $40. *Financial aid:* In 1997–98, 8 students received aid, including 8 merit scholarships (5 to first-year students) totaling $31,500; Federal Work-Study also available. Aid available to part-time students. Financial aid application deadline: 5/1; applicants required to submit FAFSA. *Faculty research:* Asthma, tuberculosis control, injury: education development, violence, international health, women's health, substance abuse. Total annual research expenditures: $348,879. • Martha Neff-Smith, Head, 410-614-5311. Fax: 410-955-7463. E-mail: mnsmith@son.jhmi.edu. Application contact: Mary O'Rourke, Director of Admissions/Student Services, 410-955-7548. Fax: 410-614-7086. E-mail: orourke@son.jhmi.edu.

Johns Hopkins University, School of Nursing, Program in Community Health Nursing, Baltimore, MD 21218-2699. Awards MSN. Accredited by NLN. Part-time programs available. Faculty: 7 full-time (6 women), 2 part-time (both women), 8 FTE. Students: 1 (woman) full-time, 2 part-time (both women). Average age 31. 6 applicants, 67% accepted. *Degree requirements:* Scholarly project required, foreign language and thesis not required. *Entrance requirements:* GRE, interview, minimum GPA of 3.0. Application deadline: 3/1 (priority date; rolling processing). Application fee: $40. *Financial aid:* In 1997–98, 1 student received aid, including 1 merit scholarship (to a first-year student) totaling $2,500; Federal Work-Study, institutionally sponsored loans, and career-related internships or fieldwork also available. Aid available to part-time students. Financial aid application deadline: 5/1; applicants required to submit FAFSA. *Faculty research:* Violence, community outreach, outcomes, asthma, HIV. Total annual research expenditures: $438,585. • Joan Kub, Head, 410-955-7763. Fax: 410-955-7463. E-mail: jkub@son.jhmi.edu. Application contact: Mary O'Rourke, Director of Admissions/Student Services, 410-955-7548. Fax: 410-614-7086. E-mail: orourke@son.jhmi.edu.

See in-depth description on page 1433.

La Roche College, Program in Nursing, Pittsburgh, PA 15237-5898. Offerings include community health nursing (MSN). Accredited by NLN. Program faculty: 5 full-time (all women), 2 part-time (both women). *Degree requirements:* Internship, practicum required, thesis optional, foreign language not required. *Entrance requirements:* GRE General Test (minimum combined score of 1200), TOEFL (minimum score 500). Application fee: $25. *Tuition:* $431 per credit. • Dr. Kathleen Sullivan, Division Chair, 412-536-1169. Application contact: Judy Henry, Manager of Nursing Student Enrollment, 412-536-1267. Fax: 412-536-1283.

La Salle University, Program in Nursing, 1900 West Olney Avenue, Philadelphia, PA 19141-1199. Offerings include public health nursing (MSN). Accredited by NLN. MSN (wound, ostomy, and continence nursing) new for fall 1998. Program faculty: 13 full-time (12 women), 8 part-time (all women). *Entrance requirements:* GRE or MAT, BSN, Pennsylvania RN license. Application deadline: rolling. Application fee: $30. • Dr. Zane R. Wolf, Dean, 215-951-1430.

Directory: Public Health Nursing

La Salle University (continued)

E-mail: wolf@lasalle.edu. Application contact: Dr. Janice Beitz, Graduate Director, 215-951-1430. Fax: 215-951-1896. E-mail: beitz@lasalle.edu.

Lewis University, College of Nursing, Romeoville, IL 60446. Offerings include community health (MSN). Accredited by NLN. *Entrance requirements:* GRE General Test (minimum combined score of 850) or College of Nursing Writing Exam, minimum GPA of 2.5. Application deadline: rolling. Application fee: $35.

Louisiana State University Medical Center, School of Nursing, 433 Bolivar Street, New Orleans, LA 70112-2223. Offerings include public health/community health nursing (MN, DNS). One or more programs accredited by NLN. School faculty: 10 full-time (all women), 4 part-time (3 women). *Degree requirements:* For master's, thesis optional, foreign language not required; for doctorate, dissertation required, foreign language not required. *Entrance requirements:* For master's, GRE General Test, MAT (minimum score 50), TOEFL, minimum GPA of 3.0; for doctorate, GRE General Test (minimum combined score of 1500 on three sections), TOEFL (minimum score 550), minimum GPA of 3.5. Application deadline: 3/17. Application fee: $50. *Expenses:* Tuition $2878 per year full-time, $421 per semester (minimum) part-time for state residents; $6003 per year full-time, $838 per semester (minimum) part-time for nonresidents. Fees $350 per year full-time, $90 per semester (minimum) part-time. • Dr. Elizabeth Humphrey, Dean, 504-568-4106. Application contact: Dr. Barbara C. Donlon, Acting Director, 504-568-4137. Fax: 504-568-3308. E-mail: bdonlo@lsumc.edu.

Medical College of Georgia, Graduate Programs in Nursing, Augusta, GA 30912-1500. Offerings include community nursing (MSN). Accredited by NLN. Faculty: 17 full-time (14 women). *Application deadline:* 6/30 (priority date; rolling processing). *Application fee:* $0. *Expenses:* Tuition $2670 per year full-time, $111 per credit part-time for state residents; $10,680 per year full-time, $445 per credit part-time for nonresidents. Fees $286 per year. • Dr. Virginia Kemp, Associate Dean, 706-721-4710. E-mail: vkemp@mail.mcg.edu. Application contact: Dr. Gary C. Bond, Associate Dean, 706-721-3278. Fax: 706-721-6829. E-mail: gradstud@mail.mcg.edu.

Northeastern University, Graduate School of Nursing, Program in Community Health Nursing, Boston, MA 02115-5096. Awards MS, CAS, MS/MBA. One or more programs accredited by NLN. Faculty: 23 full-time (all women), 12 part-time (11 women). *Degree requirements:* For master's, thesis or alternative required, foreign language not required. *Entrance requirements:* For master's, GRE General Test, minimum GPA of 3.0, previous course work in statistics, 1-2 years nursing experience, RN license, ICU experience. Application deadline: 4/1 (priority date; rolling processing; 2/1 for spring admission). Application fee: $50. *Expenses:* Tuition $440 per credit hour. Fees $55 per quarter full-time, $13.25 per quarter part-time. • Dr. Margaret Mahoney, Coordinator. Application contact: Molly Schnabel, Admissions Coordinator, 617-373-3590. Fax: 617-373-8672. E-mail: mschnabe@lynx.neu.edu.

Announcement: Master's program in community health nursing (52 quarter hours), with concentrations in adult NP role and public health. Includes community-based primary care, clinical decision making, family violence interventions, and program planning. Full- and part-time study. Preceptorships available in Boston's top health-care agencies. For application, contact Molly Schnabel, Admissions Coordinator, at 617-373-3590.

Oregon Health Sciences University, School of Nursing, Program in Community Health Care Systems, 3181 SW Sam Jackson Park Road, Portland, OR 97201-3098. Awards MN, MS, Post Master's Certificate. One or more programs accredited by NLN. Students: 11 full-time (all women), 14 part-time (all women); includes 1 international. 18 applicants, 50% accepted. In 1997, 8 master's awarded. *Degree requirements:* For master's, thesis optional, foreign language not required. *Entrance requirements:* For master's, GRE General Test (minimum combined score of 1000), bachelor's degree in nursing, minimum undergraduate GPA of 3.0. Application deadline: 1/15. Application fee: $40. *Financial aid:* Career-related internships or fieldwork available. • Application contact: Office of Recruitment, 503-494-7725. Fax: 503-494-4350.

Oregon Health Sciences University, School of Nursing, Program in Public Health Nursing, 3181 SW Sam Jackson Park Road, Portland, OR 97201-3098. Awards MPH. *Degree requirements:* Thesis optional, foreign language not required. *Entrance requirements:* GRE General Test (minimum combined score of 1000), bachelor's degree in nursing, minimum undergraduate GPA of 3.0. Application deadline: 1/15. Application fee: $40. • Application contact: Office of Recruitment, 503-494-7725. Fax: 503-494-4350.

Rush University, College of Nursing, Department of Community Health Nursing, Chicago, IL 60612-3832. Offers programs in community health nursing (MSN, DN Sc, ND), family/community nurse practitioner (ND). One or more programs accredited by NLN. Part-time programs available. Faculty: 10 full-time (all women), 11 part-time (all women), 17.18 FTE. Students: 3 full-time, 86 part-time. Average age 36. *Degree requirements:* For master's, practicum required, foreign language and thesis not required; for doctorate, dissertation, practicum required, foreign language not required. *Entrance requirements:* For master's, GRE General Test, interview; for doctorate, interview, previous course work in statistics. Application deadline: 8/1 (rolling processing; 2/1 for spring admission). Application fee: $40. *Tuition:* $8560 per year full-time, $370 per credit hour part-time. *Financial aid:* Federal Work-Study, institutionally sponsored loans, and career-related internships or fieldwork available. Aid available to part-time students. Financial aid applicants required to submit FAFSA. *Faculty research:* Health promotion, health policy, prevalence of diabetics and TB in minority populations. • Dr. Kathleen Andveoli, Dean and Acting Chairperson, 312-942-7117. Application contact: Hicela Castruita, Director, College Admissions Services, 312-942-7100. Fax: 312-942-2219.

Rutgers, The State University of New Jersey, Newark, College of Nursing, Graduate Program in Community Health Nursing, Newark, NJ 07102-3192. Awards MS. Accredited by NLN. Part-time programs available. *Degree requirements:* Comprehensive exam required, foreign language and thesis not required. *Entrance requirements:* GRE General Test, TOEFL, RN license, minimum B average, BS in nursing. Application deadline: 8/15 (rolling processing; 12/15 for spring admission). Application fee: $40. Electronic applications accepted. *Expenses:* Tuition $6248 per year full-time, $257 per credit part-time for state residents; $9160 per year full-time, $380 per credit part-time for nonresidents. Fees $738 per year full-time, $107 per semester (minimum) part-time. *Financial aid:* Federal Work-Study, institutionally sponsored loans, and career-related internships or fieldwork available. Financial aid application deadline: 3/1. • Application contact: Dr. Elaine Dolinsky, Associate Dean for Student Life and Services, 973-353-5060. Fax: 973-353-1277.

Sage Graduate School, Graduate School, Division of Nursing, Program in Community Health Nursing, Troy, NY 12180-4115. Awards MS. Accredited by NLN. Part-time programs available. *Degree requirements:* Thesis or alternative required, foreign language not required. *Entrance requirements:* BS in nursing, minimum GPA of 2.75. Application deadline: 8/1 (rolling processing; 12/15 for spring admission). Application fee: $25. *Expenses:* Tuition $360 per credit hour. Fees $50 per semester. *Financial aid:* Federal Work-Study and career-related internships or fieldwork available. Financial aid application deadline: 7/1; applicants required to submit FAFSA. • Application contact: Melissa Robertson, Associate Director of Admissions, 518-244-6878. Fax: 518-244-6880. E-mail: sgsadm@sage.edu.

Saint Louis University, School of Nursing, Program in Family and Community Health Nursing, St. Louis, MO 63103-2097. Awards MSN, MSN(R), Certificate, MPH/MSN, MSN/MBA. Offerings include family nurse practitioner (MSN, MSN(R), Certificate), public health nurse manager (MSN, MSN(R), Certificate), public health nurse practice (MSN, MSN(R), Certificate). One or more programs accredited by NLN. *Degree requirements:* For master's, comprehensive oral exam required, thesis optional, foreign language not required. *Entrance requirements:* For master's, GRE General Test. Application deadline: 7/1 (rolling processing; 11/1 for spring admission). Application fee: $40. *Tuition:* $542 per credit hour. *Financial aid:* Traineeships available. Financial aid application deadline: 4/1. • Dr. Cordie Reese, Program Director, 314-577-8932. Application contact: Dr. Marcia Buresch, Assistant Dean of the Graduate School, 314-977-2240. Fax: 314-977-3943.

Saint Xavier University, School of Nursing, Chicago, IL 60655-3105. Offerings include leadership in community health nursing (MS). Accredited by NLN. MBA/MS offered in cooperation with the Graham School of Management. School faculty: 10 full-time (all women), 2 part-time (both women). *Entrance requirements:* MAT or GRE General Test, minimum GPA of 3.0, RN license. Application deadline: 2/15 (9/15 for spring admission). Application fee: $35. *Expenses:* Tuition $450 per hour. Fees $50 per year. • Dr. Mary Lebold, Dean, 773-298-3700. Fax: 773-779-9061. E-mail: lebold@sxu.edu. Application contact: Sr. Evelyn McKenna, Vice President of Enrollment Management, 773-298-3050. Fax: 773-298-3076. E-mail: mckenna@sxu.edu.

San Jose State University, College of Applied Arts and Sciences, School of Nursing, San Jose, CA 95192-0001. Offerings include community health nursing (MS), with options in nursing administration, nursing education. Accredited by NLN. School faculty: 26 full-time (24 women), 13 part-time (12 women). *Degree requirements:* Thesis required, foreign language not required. *Entrance requirements:* BS in nursing, RN license. Application deadline: 6/1 (rolling processing). Application fee: $59. *Expenses:* Tuition $0 for state residents; $246 per unit for nonresidents. Fees $2017 per year full-time, $1351 per year part-time. • Dr. Bobbye Gorenberg, Director, 408-924-3130. Application contact: Dr. Colleen Saylor, Graduate Coordinator, 408-924-3134.

Southern Illinois University at Edwardsville, School of Nursing, Program in Community Health Nursing, Edwardsville, IL 62026-0001. Awards MS. Accredited by NLN. Students: 5 full-time (all women), 16 part-time (all women); includes 1 minority (African American). 6 applicants, 83% accepted. In 1997, 13 degrees awarded. *Degree requirements:* Thesis or alternative, final exam required, foreign language not required. *Entrance requirements:* Appropriate bachelor's degree, RN license. Application deadline: 7/24. Application fee: $25. *Expenses:* Tuition $1716 per year full-time, $95 per credit hour part-time for state residents; $5149 per year full-time, $286 per credit hour part-time for nonresidents. Fees $463 per year full-time, $433 per year part-time. *Financial aid:* In 1997–98, 1 assistantship was awarded; fellowships, Federal Work-Study, institutionally sponsored loans also available. Aid available to part-time students. • Dr. Felissa Lashley, Dean, School of Nursing, 618-692-3956.

Texas Tech University Health Sciences Center, School of Nursing, Lubbock, TX 79430-0002. Offerings include community health (MSN). Accredited by NLN. Postbaccalaureate distance learning degree programs offered (minimal on-campus study). School faculty: 14 full-time (all women). *Degree requirements:* Thesis required, foreign language not required. *Average time to degree:* master's–2 years full-time, 3 years part-time. *Entrance requirements:* GRE General Test (minimum combined score of 1000), MAT (minimum score 50), minimum GPA of 3.0, sample of written work. Application deadline: 6/1 (rolling processing; 10/1 for spring admission). Application fee: $30 ($50 for international students). *Expenses:* Tuition $36 per credit hour for state residents; $249 per credit hour for nonresidents. Fees $1348 per year full-time for state residents; $1349 per year full-time for nonresidents. • Dr. Pat S. Yoder Wise, Dean, 806-743-2738. E-mail: sonpsy@ttuhsc.edu. Application contact: Nancy Ridenour, Associate Dean for Education, 806-743-2737. Fax: 806-743-1622. E-mail: sonnar@ttuhsc.edu.

Texas Woman's University, College of Nursing, Denton, TX 76204. Offerings include community health nursing (MS). Accredited by NLN. College faculty: 30 full-time (29 women), 12 part-time (10 women). *Degree requirements:* Thesis or alternative required, foreign language not required. *Entrance requirements:* GRE General Test (minimum combined score of 750), minimum GPA of 3.0. Application deadline: rolling. Application fee: $25. • Dr. Carolyn S. Gunning, Dean, 940-898-2401.

University of Cincinnati, College of Nursing and Health, Cincinnati, OH 45221-0038. Offerings include community health nursing (MSN). Accredited by NLN. College faculty: 26 full-time. *Degree requirements:* Project or thesis required, foreign language not required. *Average time to degree:* master's–1.5 years full-time, 2.5 years part-time; doctorate–4 years full-time, 6 years part-time. *Entrance requirements:* GRE General Test. Application deadline: 1/1 (priority date; rolling processing). Application fee: $30. *Tuition:* $7228 per year full-time, $185 per credit hour part-time for state residents; $13,812 per year full-time, $352 per credit hour part-time for nonresidents. • Dr. Andrea Lindell, Dean, 513-558-5330. Application contact: Tom West, Program Coordinator, 513-558-3600. Fax: 513-558-7523. E-mail: tom.west@uc.edu.

University of Hawaii at Manoa, College of Health Sciences and Social Welfare, School of Nursing, Honolulu, HI 96822. Offerings include clinical nurse specialist (MS), with options in adult health, community mental health; nurse practitioner (MS), with options in adult health, community mental health, family nurse practitioner. One or more programs accredited by NLN. School faculty: 27 full-time (24 women). *Entrance requirements:* Hawaii RN license. *Tuition:* $4029 per year full-time, $214 per credit hour part-time for state residents; $9957 per year full-time, $461 per credit hour part-time for nonresidents. • Dr. Rosanne Harrigan, Dean, 808-956-8522. Application contact: Office of Student Services, 808-956-8939.

University of Illinois at Chicago, College of Nursing, Program in Public Health Nursing, Chicago, IL 60607-7128. Awards MS. Accredited by NLN. Faculty: 9 full-time (all women), 1 (woman) part-time. Students: 28 full-time (24 women), 148 part-time (142 women); includes 22 minority (6 African Americans, 11 Asian Americans, 4 Hispanics, 1 Native American), 1 international. Average age 37. 138 applicants, 61% accepted. In 1997, 36 degrees awarded. *Degree requirements:* Thesis or alternative required, foreign language not required. *Entrance requirements:* GRE General Test, TOEFL (minimum score 550), minimum GPA of 3.75 on a 5.0 scale. Application deadline: 5/15 (10/15 for spring admission). Application fee: $40 ($50 for international students). *Financial aid:* In 1997–98, 1 fellowship, 2 research assistantships, 1 teaching assistantship, 4 traineeships were awarded; partial tuition waivers, Federal Work-Study, institutionally sponsored loans, and career-related internships or fieldwork also available. • Dr. Naomi Ervin, Acting Head, 312-996-7969. Application contact: Kathleen Knafl, Director of Graduate Studies, 312-996-2159.

University of Maryland, Baltimore, Graduate School, School of Nursing, Baltimore, MD 21201-1627. Offerings include community health nursing (MS). Accredited by NLN. MS/MBA offered jointly with the University of Baltimore. School faculty: 49 (45 women). *Degree requirements:* Thesis or alternative required, foreign language not required. *Entrance requirements:* GRE General Test, TOEFL, minimum GPA of 2.75, previous course work in statistics, BS in nursing. Application fee: $42. *Expenses:* Tuition $253 per credit hour for state residents; $454 per credit hour for nonresidents. Fees $317 per year. • Dr. Barbara Heller, Dean, 410-706-6741. Application contact: Dr. Susan Wozenski, Assistant Dean for Student Affairs, 410-706-0501. Fax: 410-706-7238.

University of Massachusetts Lowell, College of Health Professions, Department of Nursing, Program in Family and Community Health Nursing, 1 University Avenue, Lowell, MA 01854-2881. Awards MS. Accredited by NLN. Students: 21 full-time (all women), 20 part-time (all women); includes 1 minority (African American). 48 applicants, 38% accepted. In 1997, 12 degrees awarded. *Degree requirements:* Thesis optional, foreign language not required. *Entrance requirements:* GRE General Test. Application deadline: 4/1 (priority date; rolling processing; 10/1 for spring admission). Application fee: $20 ($35 for international students). *Tuition:* $4867 per year full-time, $618 per semester (minimum) part-time for state residents; $10,276 per year full-time, $1294 per semester (minimum) part-time for nonresidents. *Financial aid:* Fellowships, teaching assistantships available. Financial aid application deadline: 4/1. • Dr. May Futrell, Chair, Department of Nursing, 978-934-4467. E-mail: may_futrell@woods.uml.edu.

University of Massachusetts Lowell, College of Health Professions, Department of Nursing, Program in Occupational Health Nursing, 1 University Avenue, Lowell, MA 01854-2881. Offers adult psychiatric nursing (MS), occupational health nursing (MS). Accredited by NLN. *Degree requirements:* Thesis optional, foreign language not required. *Entrance requirements:* GRE General Test. Application deadline: 4/1 (priority date; rolling processing; 10/1 for spring admission). Application fee: $20 ($35 for international students). *Tuition:* $4867 per year full-time, $618 per semester (minimum) part-time for state residents; $10,276 per year full-time, $1294 per semester (minimum) part-time for nonresidents. *Financial aid:* Fellowships, teaching assistantships, Federal Work-Study, institutionally sponsored loans, and career-related internships or fieldwork available. Financial aid application deadline: 4/1. • Dr. May Futrell, Chair, Department of Nursing, 978-934-4467. E-mail: may_futrell@woods.uml.edu.

University of Massachusetts Medical Center at Worcester, Graduate School of Nursing, Worcester, MA 01655-0115. Offerings include adult ambulatory/community care (MS, Certificate). Accredited by NLN. School faculty: 6 full-time (5 women), 4 part-time (all women), 8 FTE. *Average time to degree:* master's–2 years part-time; doctorate–3 years full-time; other advanced degree–1 year full-time. *Entrance requirements:* For master's, GRE General Test, BSN, previous course work in statistics; for Certificate, master's degree. Application deadline: 3/15 (rolling processing). Application fee: $18 ($25 for international students). • Dr. Lillian R. Goodman, Dean, 508-856-5801. E-mail: lillian.goodman@banyan.ummed.edu. Application contact: Kathleen Trumpaitis, Student Coordinator, 508-856-5801. Fax: 508-856-6552. E-mail: kathleen.trumpaitis@banyan.ummed.edu.

University of Michigan, School of Nursing, Division of Health Promotion and Risk Reduction, Program in Community Health Nursing, Ann Arbor, MI 48109. Offers adult primary care/adult nurse practitioner (MS), community care/home care (MS), family nurse practitioner (MS), occupational health nursing (MS). Accredited by NLN. Part-time programs available. *Degree requirements:* Thesis required, foreign language not required. *Entrance requirements:* GRE General Test, BS in nursing. Application deadline: 2/1. Application fee: $55. *Financial aid:* Fellowships, research assistantships, teaching assistantships, traineeships, partial tuition waivers, Federal Work-Study available. • Dr. Carol Loveland-Cherry, Chairperson, 734-763-0016. Application contact: Graduate Program Secretary, 734-763-0016. Fax: 734-647-0351.

University of Minnesota, Twin Cities Campus, School of Nursing, Program in Public Health Nursing, Minneapolis, MN 55455-0213. Awards MS. Accredited by NLN. Part-time programs available. Students: 12 full-time, 26 part-time. 27 applicants, 93% accepted. *Degree requirements:* Final oral exam, project or thesis. *Application deadline:* 12/15 (rolling processing). *Application fee:* $40 ($50 for international students). *Financial aid:* Fellowships, research assistantships, teaching assistantships available. • L. Josten, Head, 612-624-5139. Application contact: Kate Hanson, Nursing Recruiter, 612-624-9494. Fax: 612-624-3174. E-mail: hanso041@maroon.tc.umn.edu.

University of Minnesota, Twin Cities Campus, School of Public Health, Division of Environmental and Occupational Health, Area in Occupational Health Nursing, Minneapolis, MN 55455-0213. Awards MPH, MS, PhD, MPH/MS. *Degree requirements:* For doctorate, dissertation required, foreign language not required. *Entrance requirements:* GRE General Test (minimum combined score of 1500 on three sections), minimum GPA of 3.0. Application deadline: 4/15 (priority date; rolling processing). Application fee: $50 ($75 for international students). *Financial aid:* Fellowships, research assistantships, and career-related internships or fieldwork available. Financial aid application deadline: 4/15. • Application contact: Kathy Soupir, Student Coordinator, 612-625-0622. Fax: 612-626-4837. E-mail: ksoupir@mail.eoh.umn.edu.

University of New Mexico, College of Nursing, Albuquerque, NM 87131-2039. Offerings include community health nursing (MSN); primary care nursing (MSN), with options in family nurse practitioner, nurse midwifery. One or more programs accredited by NLN. College faculty: 38 full-time (36 women), 23 part-time (all women), 46.57 FTE. *Degree requirements:* Thesis optional, foreign language not required. *Entrance requirements:* GRE General Test, interview, minimum GPA of 3.0, previous course work in statistics. Application deadline: 7/15 (11/1 for spring admission). Application fee: $25. *Expenses:* Tuition $2442 per year full-time, $103 per credit hour part-time for state residents; $8691 per year full-time, $103 per credit hour (minimum) part-time for nonresidents. Fees $32 per year. • Dr. Sandra Ferketich, Dean, 505-272-6284. Application contact: Anne-Marie Oechsler, Director, Academic Advisement, 505-272-4224. Fax: 505-272-3970. E-mail: annmarie@unm.edu.

The University of North Carolina at Chapel Hill, School of Public Health, Public Health Nursing Program, Chapel Hill, NC 27599. Awards MPH, MS. Accredited by NLN. Part-time programs available. Postbaccalaureate distance learning degree programs offered (minimal on-campus study). Faculty: 10 full-time (9 women), 23 part-time (22 women). Students: 4 full-time (all women), 9 part-time (all women). 6 applicants, 50% accepted. In 1997, 7 degrees awarded. *Degree requirements:* Thesis (MS), paper (MPH), comprehensive exam required, foreign language not required. *Entrance requirements:* GRE General Test (minimum combined score of 1000), TOEFL, minimum GPA of 3.0. Application deadline: 1/1 (rolling processing; 10/15 for spring admission). Application fee: $55. *Expenses:* Tuition $2008 per year full-time, $502 per semester (minimum) part-time for state residents; $10,414 per year full-time, $2604 per semester (minimum) part-time for nonresidents. Fees $782 per year full-time, $332 per semester (minimum) part-time. *Financial aid:* In 1997–98, 10 traineeships were awarded; institutionally sponsored loans and career-related internships or fieldwork also available. Financial aid application deadline: 2/1. *Total annual research expenditures:* $278,595. • Dr. Arnold Kaluzny, Director, 919-966-5285. E-mail: arnold_kalkuzny@unc.edu. Application contact: Sharon Pickard, Registrar, 919-966-5305. Fax: 919-966-0981. E-mail: spickard@sph.unc.edu.

University of San Diego, Philip Y. Hahn School of Nursing, San Diego, CA 92110-2492. Offerings include school health nurse practitioner (MSN). Accredited by NLN. School faculty: 12 full-time (all women), 4 part-time (all women). *Entrance requirements:* GRE or MAT, TOEFL (minimum score 580), TWE, BSN, minimum GPA of 3.0. Application deadline: 5/1 (priority date; rolling processing; 11/15 for spring admission). Application fee: $45. *Expenses:* Tuition $585 per unit (minimum). Fees $50 per year full-time, $30 per year part-time. • Dr. Janet Rodgers, Dean, 619-260-4550. Fax: 619-260-6814. Application contact: Mary Jane Tiernan, Director of Graduate Admissions, 619-260-4524. Fax: 619-260-4158. E-mail: grads@acusd.edu.

University of South Carolina, Graduate School, College of Nursing, Program in Health Nursing, Columbia, SC 29208. Awards MSN. One or more programs accredited by NLN. Students: 47 full-time (44 women), 81 part-time (74 women); includes 19 minority (16 African Americans, 3 Asian Americans). Average age 36. In 1997, 20 degrees awarded. *Application fee:* $35. Electronic applications accepted. *Expenses:* Tuition $4480 per year full-time, $220 per credit hour part-time for state residents; $9338 per year full-time, $457 per credit hour part-time for nonresidents. Fees $125 per year full-time, $37 per semester (minimum) part-time. • Application contact: Office of Academic and Student Affairs, 803-777-7412. Fax: 803-777-0616.

University of Southern Mississippi, College of Nursing, Hattiesburg, MS 39406-5167. Offerings include community health nursing (MSN). Accredited by NLN. College faculty: 18 full-time (all women). *Degree requirements:* Thesis optional, foreign language not required. *Entrance requirements:* GRE General Test, minimum GPA of 2.75. Application deadline: 8/9 (priority date; rolling processing). Application fee: $0 ($25 for international students). *Tuition:* $2870 per year full-time, $137 per credit hour part-time for state residents; $5972 per year full-time, $172 per credit hour part-time for nonresidents. • Dr. Gerry Cadenhead, Director, 601-266-5509. Fax: 601-266-5927.

The University of Texas at El Paso, College of Nursing and Health Science, Program in Nursing, 500 West University Avenue, El Paso, TX 79968-0001. Offerings include community health (MSN), community health/family nurse practitioner (MSN). One or more programs accredited by NLN. *Degree requirements:* Thesis optional, foreign language not required. *Entrance requirements:* GRE General Test or MAT (minimum score 50), TOEFL (minimum score 550), BSN, course work in statistics. Application deadline: 7/1 (rolling processing; 11/1 for spring admission). Application fee: $15 ($65 for international students). Electronic applications accepted. *Tuition:* $2063 per year full-time, $284 per credit hour part-time for state residents; $5753 per year full-time, $425 per credit hour part-time for nonresidents.

Valdosta State University, College of Nursing, Valdosta, GA 31698. Offerings include community health nursing (MSN). Accredited by NLN. College faculty: 3 full-time (all women). *Entrance requirements:* GRE General Test (minimum combined score of 800), minimum GPA of 2.8. Application deadline: 8/1 (rolling processing; 11/15 for spring admission). Application fee: $10. *Expenses:* Tuition $2472 per year full-time, $83 per semester hour part-time for state residents; $8472 per year full-time, $333 per semester hour part-time for nonresidents. Fees $236 per year full-time. • Dr. Maryann Reichenbach, Dean, 912-333-5959. E-mail: mreichenb@grits.valdosta.peachnet.edu.

Wayne State University, College of Nursing, Department of Family, Community and Mental Health, Program in Community Health Nursing, Detroit, MI 48202. Awards MSN. Accredited by NLN. Part-time programs available. Students: 11 part-time (all women); includes 5 minority (all African Americans), 1 international. Average age 40. 3 applicants, 33% accepted. In 1997, 1 degree awarded. *Degree requirements:* Computer language, thesis or alternative required, foreign language not required. *Entrance requirements:* GRE General Test (minimum combined score of 800), minimum GPA of 2.8. Application deadline: 7/1 (priority date; rolling processing; 11/1 for spring admission). Application fee: $20 ($30 for international students). *Expenses:* Tuition $163 per credit hour for state residents; $355 per credit hour for nonresidents. Fees $498 per year full-time, $114 per semester (minimum) part-time. *Financial aid:* In 1997–98, 2 students received aid, including 2 scholarships, traineeships; research assistantships, institutionally sponsored loans also available. Aid available to part-time students. Financial aid application deadline: 7/1; applicants required to submit FAFSA. *Faculty research:* Literacy, technology dependence with children, transcultural, violence in families. • Dr. Marie-Luise Friedemann, Assistant Dean, 313-577-4092. Fax: 313-577-4571. Application contact: Vickie Radoye, Administrative Assistant Dean, Student Affairs, 313-577-4082. Fax: 313-577-6949.

West Chester University of Pennsylvania, School of Health Sciences, Department of Nursing, West Chester, PA 19383. Offerings include community health nursing (MSN). Accredited by NLN. *Application deadline:* 4/15 (priority date; rolling processing; 10/15 for spring admission). *Application fee:* $25. *Expenses:* Tuition $3468 per year full-time, $193 per credit part-time for state residents; $6236 per year full-time, $346 per credit part-time for nonresidents. Fees $660 per year full-time, $38 per credit part-time. • Anne Coghlan Stowe, Chair, 610-436-2219. Application contact: Jan Hickman, Graduate Coordinator, 610-436-2219.

Wright State University, College of Nursing and Health, Program in Nursing, Dayton, OH 45435. Offerings include community health (MS). Accredited by NLN. *Degree requirements:* Thesis or alternative required, foreign language not required. *Average time to degree:* master's–2 years full-time, 5 years part-time. *Entrance requirements:* GRE General Test, TOEFL (minimum score 550), BSN from NLN-accredited college, Ohio RN license. Application deadline: 4/15 (priority date). Application fee: $25. *Tuition:* $5109 per year full-time, $161 per credit hour part-time for state residents; $9039 per year full-time, $282 per credit hour part-time for nonresidents. • Application contact: Theresa Haghnazarian, Director of Student and Alumni Affairs, 937-775-3133. Fax: 937-775-4571.

Rehabilitation Nursing

College of Mount Saint Vincent, Department of Nursing, Riverdale, NY 10471-1093. Offerings include addictions nursing (MS). Accredited by NLN. Department faculty: 3 full-time (all women), 15 part-time (all women). *Degree requirements:* Computer language, written research project required, foreign language and thesis not required. *Entrance requirements:* Bachelor's degree from NLN-accredited institution, minimum GPA of 3.0. Application deadline: 6/15 (priority date; rolling processing; 12/1 for spring admission). Application fee: $50. • Dr. Barbara Cohen, Director, 718-405-3352. Application contact: Dr. Kem Louie, Chairperson, 718-405-3355.

Loyola University Chicago, Graduate School, Marcella Niehoff School of Nursing, Cardiac Health/Rehabilitation Clinical Nursing Specialist Program, 820 North Michigan Avenue, Chicago, IL 60611-2196. Awards MSN. Accredited by NLN. Part-time programs available. Students: 6 part-time (all women). 4 applicants, 100% accepted. *Degree requirements:* Comprehensive exam or oral thesis defense required, foreign language not required. *Entrance requirements:* GRE General Test (minimum combined score of 1350 on three sections), BSN, minimum GPA of 3.0, professional license. Application deadline: rolling. Application fee: $35. *Tuition:* $467 per semester hour. *Financial aid:* Application deadline 3/1. *Faculty research:* Cardiac exercise. • Application contact: Dr. Marcia Maurer, Associate Dean and Director of Graduate Programs, 773-508-3261. Fax: 773-508-3241. E-mail: mmaurer@luc.edu.

Rush University, College of Nursing, Department of Gerontological Nursing, Chicago, IL 60612-3832. Offerings include rehabilitation nursing (MSN, DN Sc, ND). Department faculty: 6 full-time (all women), 3 part-time (all women), 7 FTE. *Degree requirements:* For doctorate, dissertation required, foreign language not required. *Entrance requirements:* For master's, GRE General Test, interview; for doctorate, interview, previous course work in statistics. Application deadline: 8/1 (rolling processing; 2/1 for spring admission). Application fee: $40. *Tuition:* $8560 per year full-time, $370 per credit hour part-time. • Jane Ulsafer-Van Lanen, Acting Chairperson, 312-942-3480. Application contact: Hicela Castruita, Director, College Admissions Services, 312-942-7100. Fax: 312-942-2219.

Cross-Discipline Announcement

Walden University, Graduate Programs, 155 Fifth Avenue South, Minneapolis, MN 55401.

The distance learning doctoral program (PhD) in health services includes a specialization in health and human behavior that allows students to concentrate in one of the following areas: health and healing, health and the life span, health and organizational behavior, health and social behavior, and health and professional behavior. The last area's focus is on the education and training of health professionals. For more information, see Book 1 of this series.

ADELPHI UNIVERSITY

School of Nursing

Program of Study

The Master of Science program in the School of Nursing prepares advanced practice nurses for the roles of nursing service administrator, nurse practitioner, and clinical specialist in adult-health, mental health-psychiatric, or parent-child nursing. Planned educational experiences include study of people in health and illness and practice of nursing intervention with individuals, families, groups, and communities. Through this rich and cohesive curriculum, students emerge as leaders able to solve problems, make decisions, and initiate change. Candidates for the degree of Master of Science must satisfactorily complete a program of study that contains 42–48 credit hours and submit a master's project. The Post-Master's Certificate program is designed for students who already hold a master's degree in nursing. Post-master's certificates are awarded in nursing service administration, nursing education, and advanced practice (clinical specialist or nurse practitioner).

Research Facilities

The School of Nursing Research Committee offers occasional colloquia and other lectures and provides research consultation and assistance to faculty and students. The Swirbul Library has a collection of more than 1.2 million bound volumes and microfilms as well as documents, manuscripts, and other items in nonprint media. A wide variety of community-based agencies and health-care facilities provide resources for nursing research.

Financial Aid

A limited number of graduate assistantships and appointments as teaching or research assistants are offered. Federal and state loan programs, special scholarships, and deferred-payment options are also available. Information about funding agencies, including foundations and government sources, is available from the Financial Aid Office as a guide for students seeking financial assistance.

Cost of Study

In 1997–98, tuition was $465 per credit hour. Special fees included a nonrefundable application fee of $50; University fees of $100 to $300, depending on the number of credits taken; a $15 voice mail fee; and laboratory or workshop fees specific to courses. The fees for master's project advisement approximate the cost of a 3-credit course. Any student who is academically inactive in any fall or spring semester is charged a continuous matriculation fee.

Living and Housing Costs

The cost of living is comparable to that in New York City. Information about a full range of housing is available from the Student Housing Department.

Student Group

The approximately 200 students in the master's program are a heterogeneous group, including both men and women whose ages range from 22 to 60. Many are employed by health agencies, and most are active in professional organizations, including Adelphi's Alpha Omega chapter of Sigma Theta Tau, the international honor society in nursing.

Location

Garden City, a suburban residential community in Nassau County, Long Island, is less than an hour from midtown Manhattan by car or train. Both the county and nearby New York City offer a wide variety of athletic, cultural, and social resources to meet the many needs of a large and diverse population.

The University

Adelphi University was founded in Brooklyn and chartered by the state of New York in 1896 as Adelphi College. The first degree-granting liberal arts institution of higher education on Long Island, it was granted university status in 1963. It is private, nonsectarian, and coeducational. The University is composed of eight divisions: the College of Arts and Sciences, the Graduate School of Arts and Sciences, the University College, the School of Management and Business, the School of Nursing, the School of Social Work, the Institute of Advanced Psychological Studies, and the School of Education. On-campus facilities include a cafeteria, a rathskeller, and a nursery school for preschoolers. The student health center is capable of handling emergency health needs and minor health problems and offers counseling and health instruction. Psychological services are available.

Applying

To be considered for admission to the master's program in nursing, an applicant must be a currently licensed registered professional nurse holding a baccalaureate degree from a NLN-accredited baccalaureate program, which must include upper division theory and practice in parent-child, adult-health, psychiatric, and community health nursing. Applicants are required to have completed a basic statistics course within three years prior to admission, earning a grade of B or better. Applicants must meet all prerequisites for the specialty. Two years of clinical practice in nursing and an undergraduate average of at least a B are required. Completed application forms, official transcripts of all post-high school academic work, and four letters of reference must be submitted.

In order to be admitted to the Post-Master's Certificate program, the applicant must be a registered professional nurse and provide evidence of an earned master's degree in nursing.

Correspondence and Information

Graduate Admissions
Adelphi University
1 South Avenue
Garden City, New York 11530
Telephone: 800-ADELPHI (toll-free)
Fax: 516-877-3039
E-mail: admissions@adelphi.edu
World Wide Web: http://www.adelphi.edu

Adelphi University

THE FACULTY

Caryle G. Wolahan, Ed.D., Professor and Dean; RN.

E. Judith Ackerhalt, Ed.D., Associate Professor; RN.
A. Campagna, M.S., Associate Professor; RN.
D. Hays, Ed.D., Professor; RN.
M. Klainberg, Ed.D., Assistant Professor; RN.
C. Lamanno, Ed.D., Associate Professor; RN.
G. Malloy, Ph.D., Professor; RN.
M. McLaughlin, Ed.D., Assistant Professor; RN.
N. Noel, Ed.D., Associate Professor; RN.
E. Pasquali, Ph.D., Professor; RN.
M. Ryan, Ph.D., Associate Professor; RN.
M. Silver, M.S., Assistant Professor; RN.
A. Trolman, Ed.D., Associate Professor; RN.
E. Udofia, Ph.D., Assistant Professor; PNP.
C. Windwer, Ph.D., Professor; RN.
J. Winter, Ed.D., Assistant Professor; RN.

CWRU

CASE WESTERN RESERVE UNIVERSITY

Frances Payne Bolton School of Nursing

Programs of Study

The Frances Payne Bolton School of Nursing offers a comprehensive graduate program leading to three advanced degrees in nursing: the Master of Science in Nursing (M.S.N.), the Doctor of Nursing (N.D.), and the Doctor of Philosophy in nursing (Ph.D.). Graduates of the School hold leadership positions in nursing practice, education, administration, and research at local, state, regional, national, and international levels.

The Master of Science in Nursing (M.S.N.) program emphasizes preparation of advanced practice nurses. Nurses from all basic nursing programs accredited by the National League for Nursing (NLN) are eligible to apply. Graduates of nursing baccalaureate programs complete the M.S.N. requirements in approximately two years. Specialization is offered in nurse midwifery, nurse anesthesia, nurse practitioner studies (adult acute care, pediatric acute care, adult, pediatric, neonatal, women's health, family, gerontological, and psychiatric–mental health), medical-surgical nursing, community health nursing, and oncology nursing. Three dual-degree programs are also offered: an M.S.N./M.A. in anthropology, an M.S.N./M.A. in bioethics, and an M.S.N./M.B.A. in conjunction with the Weatherhead School of Management of Case Western Reserve University. The master's program prepares graduates to provide comprehensive nursing care to a defined client population, demonstrate beginning competence in scientific inquiry, and provide leadership in the advancement of nursing practice.

The Doctor of Nursing (N.D.) degree program is a four-year professional program designed for college graduates with a baccalaureate degree in a discipline other than nursing, or for individuals who have completed a minimum of 90 semester hours of undergraduate course work and have approval of their college or university to complete baccalaureate requirements at the Bolton School of Nursing. This program includes strong preparation in professional nursing; specialization in a selected area of advanced practice nursing, such as midwifery or adult or family nurse practitioner studies; clinical investigation; and health planning, policy, and information management. Graduates with a B.S.N. degree may enter the N.D. program and complete its third and fourth year to obtain the N.D. degree. Certified advanced practice nurses with the M.S.N. degree may obtain the N.D. in approximately one year of study. The N.D. program prepares graduates to enter professional nursing at an advanced level of practice and to demonstrate clinical leadership and scholarship.

The Doctor of Philosophy in nursing (Ph.D.) degree program is designed for individuals who seek preparation in research, and who have completed either an M.S.N. degree with a clinical nursing major or at least 24 semester hours of graduate study, including 12 semester hours of supervised clinical nursing practice. The Ph.D. student concentrates on the organization and development of knowledge requisite to nursing practice for service to a delineated client/patient population. Research, which focuses on acute care, pediatric nursing, gerontological nursing, and health systems, is conducted by an internationally known faculty. Opportunities for postdoctoral study and combined-degree programs also are available.

Research Facilities

The School of Nursing is located in the Health Sciences Center, which has modern research and laboratory space, computer and audiovisual facilities, and library resources. The Health Sciences Center is adjacent to the University Hospitals of Cleveland, an aggregate of specialized hospitals with more than 900 beds.

Financial Aid

Financial assistance is awarded through grants, scholarships, loans, and work agreements. Information may be obtained from the Registrar's office at the School of Nursing.

Cost of Study

For 1998–99, tuition is $767 per credit hour for students taking 1 to 11 credit hours per semester and $18,400 for students taking 12 to 17 credit hours per semester. Books and supplies cost approximately $800.

Living and Housing Costs

A variety of housing exists both on and off campus. In University graduate housing, a single-occupancy room ranged from $3470 to $3890 for the 1997–98 academic year. University meal plans are $985 per semester.

Student Group

During 1997–98, the School of Nursing enrolled 690 graduate students, of whom 424 were M.S.N., 174 were N.D., and 92 were Ph.D. students; their average age was 35. About 10 percent were members of ethnic minority groups and/or men. Students come from forty-four states and eight countries.

Student Outcomes

Graduates of the Frances Payne Bolton School of Nursing are prepared to be future leaders in the nursing profession, assuming roles as nurse practitioners, clinical specialists, administrators, educators, and researchers.

Location

The University is located in Cleveland's 500-acre University Circle area, a complex of world-renowned educational, scientific, medical, and cultural institutions.

The University and The School

Case Western Reserve University was established in 1967 by the federation of Western Reserve University and Case Institute of Technology. The University is engaged in instruction and research, at the undergraduate and graduate levels, in the physical, biological, mathematical, and behavioral sciences; the humanities; and engineering, dentistry, law, management, medicine, nursing, and social work. The present School of Nursing was established in 1923 as an autonomous unit of the University.

Applying

Applicants to the School of Nursing must submit transcripts of all postsecondary course work, three letters of recommendation, and a statement describing their educational objectives. An overall average of at least B should have been achieved in undergraduate and other graduate courses. Applicants for M.S.N. and Ph.D. study must have completed a nursing program accredited by the NLN and present evidence of RN licensure. Candidates for the N.D. and Ph.D. programs must submit satisfactory scores on the GRE General Test; M.S.N. candidates must submit satisfactory scores on either the Miller Analogies Test or the GRE General Test. M.S.N./M.B.A. applicants must submit satisfactory GMAT scores and be accepted by both the School of Nursing and the Weatherhead School of Management. Nurses who have a B.A. or B.S. in another discipline but lack a B.S.N. may be admitted directly into the M.S.N. program if they meet certain requirements. M.S.N. candidates who hold associate degrees or diplomas in nursing must complete specified prerequisite course work. Personal interviews are highly recommended for applicants to all programs and are required for applicants to the Ph.D. program. International applicants must also submit scores on the TOEFL and must show evidence of adequate financial resources. The academic year begins in late August. M.S.N. and Ph.D. study may begin in August, January, or June; N.D. study begins in the fall term only. Further information and application forms for all programs may be obtained from the Admissions Office of the School of Nursing.

Correspondence and Information

Office of Student and Alumni Services
Frances Payne Bolton School of Nursing
Case Western Reserve University
10900 Euclid Avenue
Cleveland, Ohio 44106-4904

Telephone: 216-368-2529
800-825-2540 Ext. 2529 (toll-free)
E-mail: admissions@fpb.cwru.edu
World Wide Web: http://fpb.cwru.edu

Case Western Reserve University

THE FACULTY AND THEIR RESEARCH

MANAGED CARE

Research to Improve or Maintain Health

Improving Health Behaviors and Functional Status of Elders
Marie Haug, Ph.D., Professor Emerita.
Graham J. McDougall, Ph.D., Assistant Professor; RNC.
Diana Lynn Morris, Ph.D., Assistant Professor; RN, FAAN.
Beverly L. Roberts, Ph.D., Associate Professor; RN, FAAN.
May L. Wykle, Ph.D., Florence Cellar Professor of Gerontological Nursing, Associate Dean for Community Affairs, and Director of the University Center on Aging and Health; RN, FAAN.
Jaclene A. Zauszniewski, Ph.D., Associate Professor; RNC.

Improving Health Behaviors of Those with Cardiac Disease and Chronic Conditions
Laura L. Hayman, Ph.D., Carl W. and Margaret Walter Davis Professor; RN, FAAN.
Patricia Higgins, Ph.D., Assistant Professor; RN.
Hae-Ok Lee, D.N.Sc., Assistant Professor; RN.
Patricia E. McDonald, Ph.D., Assistant Professor; RN.
Shirley M. Moore, Ph.D., Associate Professor; RN.

Research to Limit Episodes of Illness

Pain Management
Susan Auvil-Novak, Ph.D., Assistant Professor; RN.
Marion P. Good, Ph.D., Assistant Professor; RN.

High-Technology Care
Barbara J. Daly, Ph.D., Associate Professor; RN, CCRN, FAAN.
Sara L. Douglas, Ph.D., Assistant Professor; RN.
Shyang-Yun Pamela Shiao, Ph.D., Assistant Professor; RN.
Ronald Wright, Ph.D., Associate Professor.

Self-Regulatory Care
Gene Cranston Anderson, Ph.D., Edward J. and Louise Mellen Professor of Nursing; RN, FAAN.
Donna Dowling, Ph.D., Assistant Professor; RN.

Models of Practice
Mary K. Anthony, Ph.D., Assistant Professor; RN.

Research in Home and Community Care, Caregiver Health, and Long-Term Care

Home Care
Dorothy Brooten, Ph.D., John Burry Jr. Professor of Nursing and Dean; RN, FAAN.
Elizabeth Madigan, Ph.D., Assistant Professor; RN.
Jeanne M. Novotny, Ph.D., Assistant Professor and Assistant Dean; RN.

Community Care
Daisy Alford-Smith, Ph.D., Assistant Professor and Director of the Center for Urban and Minority Health; RN, FAAN.
Claire Andrews, Ph.D., Associate Professor; RN, CNM, FAAN.
Joyce J. Fitzpatrick, Ph.D., Elizabeth Brooks Ford Professor of Nursing; RN, FAAN.
Marion Hemstrom, D.N.Sc., Assistant Professor and Director of the Master of Science in Nursing (M.S.N.) program; RN, CS.
Doris Modly, Ph.D., Professor and Director of the School's WHO Collaborating Center; RN, FAAN.
Grayce M. Sills, Ph.D., Independence Foundation Visiting Professor of Nursing Education; RN, FAAN.

Caregiver Health
Carol M. Musil, Ph.D., Assistant Professor; RN.
Sandra Fulton Picot, Ph.D., Associate Professor; RN.
Theresa Standing, Ph.D., Assistant Professor and Director of the Doctor of Nursing (N.D.) program; RN.
JoAnne M. Youngblut, Ph.D., Associate Professor; RN, FAAN.

Long-Term Care
Kimberly Adams-Davis, N.D., Assistant Professor; RN, FAAN.
M. Linda Workman, Ph.D., Associate Professor; RN, FAAN.

MINORITY HEALTH RESEARCH

Daisy Alford-Smith, Ph.D., Assistant Professor and Director of the Center for Urban and Minority Health; RN, FAAN.
Dorothy Brooten, Ph.D., John Burry Jr. Professor of Nursing and Dean; RN, FAAN.
Hae-Ok Lee, D.N.Sc., Assistant Professor; RN.
Patricia E. McDonald, Ph.D., Assistant Professor; RN.
Sandra Fulton Picot, Ph.D., Associate Professor; RN.
May L. Wykle, Ph.D., Florence Cellar Professor of Gerontological Nursing, Associate Dean for Community Affairs, and Director of the University Center on Aging and Health; RN, FAAN.

INNOVATIVE MODELS OF CARE DELIVERY

Mary K. Anthony, Ph.D., Assistant Professor; RN.
Dorothy Brooten, Ph.D., John Burry Jr. Professor of Nursing and Dean; RN, FAAN.
Barbara J. Daly, Ph.D., Associate Professor; RN, CCRN, FAAN.
Sara L. Douglas, Ph.D., Assistant Professor; RN.
Marion Hemstrom, D.N.Sc., Assistant Professor and Director of the Master of Science in Nursing (M.S.N.) program; RN, CS.
Elizabeth Madigan, Ph.D., Assistant Professor; RN.

PATIENT EDUCATION RESEARCH

Laura L. Hayman, Ph.D., Carl W. and Margaret Walter Davis Professor; RN, FAAN.
Graham J. McDougall, Ph.D., Associate Professor; RNC.
Shirley M. Moore, Ph.D., Associate Professor; RN.
Beverly L. Roberts, Ph.D., Associate Professor; RN, FAAN.
Jaclene A. Zauszniewski, Ph.D., Associate Professor; RNC.

POPULATION GROUPS

Elderly
Marie Haug, Ph.D., Professor Emerita.
Marion Hemstrom, D.N.Sc., Assistant Professor and Director of the Master of Science in Nursing (M.S.N.) program; RN, CS.
Elizabeth Madigan, Ph.D., Assistant Professor; RN.
Graham J. McDougall, Ph.D., Associate Professor; RNC.
Diana Lynn Morris, Ph.D., Assistant Professor; RN, FAAN.
Beverly L. Roberts, Ph.D., Associate Professor; RN, FAAN.
May L. Wykle, Ph.D., Florence Cellar Professor of Gerontological Nursing, Associate Dean for Community Affairs, and Director of the University Center on Aging and Health; RN, FAAN.
Jaclene A. Zauszniewski, Ph.D., Associate Professor; RNC.

Adults
Daisy Alford-Smith, Ph.D., Assistant Professor and Director of the Center for Urban and Minority Health; RN, FAAN.
Mary K. Anthony, Ph.D., Assistant Professor; RN.
Susan Auvil-Novak, Ph.D., Assistant Professor; RN.
Barbara J. Daly, Ph.D., Associate Professor; RN, CCRN, FAAN.
Sara L. Douglas, Ph.D., Assistant Professor; RN.
Joyce J. Fitzpatrick, Ph.D., Elizabeth Brooks Ford Professor of Nursing; RN, FAAN.
Marion P. Good, Ph.D., Assistant Professor; RN.
Patricia Higgins, Ph.D., Assistant Professor; RN.
Hae-Ok Lee, D.N.Sc., Assistant Professor; RN.
Patricia E. McDonald, Ph.D., Assistant Professor; RN.
Shirley M. Moore, Ph.D., Associate Professor; RN.
Grayce M. Sills, Ph.D., Independence Foundation Visiting Professor of Nursing Education; RN, FAAN.
M. Linda Workman, Ph.D., Associate Professor; RN, FAAN.

Women
Kimberly Adams-Davis, N.D., Assistant Professor; RN, FAAN.
Claire Andrews, Ph.D., Associate Professor; RN, CNM, FAAN.
Dorothy Brooten, Ph.D., John Burry Jr. Professor of Nursing and Dean; RN, FAAN.
Elizabeth Madigan, Ph.D., Assistant Professor; RN.
Shirley M. Moore, Ph.D., Associate Professor; RN.
Carol M. Musil, Ph.D., Assistant Professor; RN.
Sandra Fulton Picot, Ph.D., Associate Professor; RN.
Theresa Standing, Ph.D., Assistant Professor and Director of the Doctor of Nursing (N.D.) program; RN.
JoAnne M. Youngblut, Ph.D., Associate Professor; RN, FAAN.

Children
Gene Cranston Anderson, Ph.D., Edward J. and Louise Mellen Professor of Nursing; RN, FAAN.
Donna Dowling, Ph.D., Assistant Professor; RN.
Laura L. Hayman, Ph.D., Carl W. and Margaret Walter Davis Professor; RN, FAAN.
Jeanne M. Novotny, Ph.D., Assistant Professor and Assistant Dean; RN.
Shyang-Yun Pamela Shiao, Ph.D., Assistant Professor; RN.
JoAnne M. Youngblut, Ph.D., Associate Professor; RN, FAAN.

COLUMBIA UNIVERSITY

School of Nursing

Program of Study

The School of Nursing offers four levels of educational programs. The Entry To Practice (ETP) Program is an accelerated combined-degree program (B.S./M.S.) for nonnurse baccalaureate-prepared graduates, designed to prepare the student for a career as a professional nurse. Academic studies are closely integrated with clinical experience. Phase I of the program consists of 60 credits that are completed in twelve months of full-time study. Upon completion, the B.S. degree is granted and the graduate is eligible to take the professional nurse licensure examination in any state. In Phase II, the postlicensure M.S. phase, the student follows the curriculum for a clinical specialty. Part-time study is available. The Accelerated Master's Program (AMP) is also a combined-degree program (B.S./M.S.), designed to further the educational and career goals of RNs who have a diploma or associate degree in nursing and 60 liberal arts credits. Phase I consists of 31 credits of course work and 30 credits granted through the successful completion of the NLN's Nursing Mobility Profile II exams. Part-time study is available for both phases. The Graduate Program, leading to the M.S. degree, affords B.S.N.-prepared nurses the opportunity to increase their knowledge in advanced nursing practice. The School currently offers ten clinical specialties, all providing eligibility for certification as a nurse practitioner as well as dual certification for some as clinical nurse specialists. Majors include anesthesia, critical-care, midwifery, oncology, and psychiatric–mental health nursing and the primary-care specialties (adult, family, geriatric, women's health, and pediatric). The credit requirements range from 45 to 50 credits. Joint degrees are available with the Schools of Public Health and Business. The Certificate Program allows RNs with a master's degree in nursing to pursue an advanced practice program. The credit requirements range from 26 to 38 credits. The Doctor of Nursing Science Program is designed to prepare clinical nurse scholars to examine, shape, and refine the health-care delivery system. The program consists of 90 credits beyond the baccalaureate degree. Of these, 45 are master's-level credits earned in a clinical specialist/nurse practitioner program. All students are expected to be certified in a clinical specialty.

Research Facilities

The center of clinical activity at the Health Science Campus is the Columbia–Presbyterian Medical Center, which includes a number of world-renowned facilities. Among the most notable are the Neurological Institute, the Eye Institute, Babies Hospital, Sloane Hospital for Women, the Center for Geriatrics and Gerontology, the Organ Transplant Center, and the Center for Health Promotion and Disease Prevention. In addition, approximately 150 other sites in the tristate area are available for clinical education. The Augustus C. Long Library is the fourth-largest academic medical library in the country and is part of the Columbia University Library system, which encompasses approximately forty libraries and more than 4 million volumes. The Long Library houses more than 400,000 volumes and receives more than 4,500 journals, most of which can be accessed through online computer search programs. The Media and Computer Center contains more than 3,000 audiovisual and computer-assisted instruction programs, including slides, videodiscs, tapes, and a wide variety of personal computer applications. The Special Collections Section houses several thousand rare and unique works, including the Florence Nightingale Collection, which is featured at exhibitions along with rare holdings of Freud and Webster. The School of Nursing's Technology Learning Center contains seven patient units, which provide a hands-on environment for developing psychomotor skills, as well as state-of-the-art computer-assisted monitoring equipment that simulates a real clinical environment.

Financial Aid

The goal of the School of Nursing financial aid program is to provide as many students as possible with sufficient resources to meet their needs and to distribute funds to eligible students in a fair and equitable manner. Financial aid is met through a combination of scholarships, grants, work, and loans. Students should be able to meet all expenses for the academic year through a combination of these resources.

Cost of Study

During the 1997–98 academic year, graduate tuition was $660 per didactic credit and $833 per clinical credit.

Living and Housing Costs

Housing costs on the Health Science Campus range from $3733 to $5984. Other expenses, including health fees, books, personal expenses, transportation, and uniforms, are estimated at $4872.

Student Group

The nearly 600 students enrolled in the School of Nursing represent a diverse group of nursing professionals. They come from all over the country, but most are from the tristate area.

Location

The School of Nursing is located on the Health Science Campus, a 20-acre campus overlooking the Hudson River on Manhattan's Upper West Side. Students can avail themselves of the recreational, cultural, educational, and entertainment events and sites that have made New York City famous.

The University and The School

By royal charter of King George II of England, Columbia University was founded in 1754 as King's College. It is the oldest institution of higher learning in New York State and the fifth-largest in the nation. A private, nonsectarian institution, Columbia University is organized into fifteen schools and is associated with more than seventy research and public service institutions and twenty-two scholarly journals. The School of Nursing is part of the Health Science Division, which includes the Schools of Medicine, Dental and Oral Surgery, and Public Health and the programs in physical therapy, nutrition, and occupational therapy. Founded in 1892 as the Presbyterian Hospital School of Nursing, the School began offering baccalaureate degrees when it joined Columbia University's Faculty of Medicine in 1937. In 1956, it became the first nursing program in the country to award a master's degree in a clinical nursing specialty.

Applying

Applications are accepted for programs beginning in September, January, and May. Admission is based on past academic and professional performance. Admission requirements include an application form with fee, a typed personal statement describing professional goals and aspirations, three letters of reference, official transcripts from all postsecondary schools, official scores on the GRE or MAT, an undergraduate course in statistics, and an interview (by invitation). Applicants must have a minimum cumulative grade point average of 3.0. Applicants to the ETP program must have 9–12 credits of science (i.e., biology, chemistry, and microbiology). All RN applicants must submit a copy of their current license and registration and have a course in physical assessment and a minimum of one year of clinical experience in nursing in an area relevant to their chosen clinical major. There are additional requirements for the D.N.Sc. program.

Correspondence and Information

Carolyn Auerhahn, Assistant Dean
Office of Student Services
School of Nursing
Columbia University
630 West 168th Street
New York, New York 10032

Telephone: 212-305-5756

Columbia University

THE FACULTY

Joyce Anastasi, Assistant Professor and Director, HIV/AIDS Program; Ph.D., Adelphi. AIDS, HIV symptomology.
Carolyn Auerhahn, Assistant Professor, Director, Geriatric Nurse Practitioner Programs, and Assistant Dean, Student Services; Ed.D., Columbia Teachers College.
Mary Byrne, Assistant Professor; Ph.D., Adelphi. High-risk families.
Sarah Sheets Cook, Assistant Professor and Vice Dean; M.Ed., Columbia.
Jennifer Dohrn, Instructor; M.S.N., Columbia; CNM.
Donna A. Gaffney, Assistant Professor; D.N.Sc., Pennsylvania; Certified Child and Adolescent Psychiatric Clinical Specialist. Children's fears, adolescent suicide.
Richard Garfield, Assistant Professor; Dr.P.H., Columbia. Health policy and community access patterns for health care, epidemiology.
Kristine Gebbie, Assistant Professor of Nursing; Dr.P.H., Michigan.
Marianne Glasel, Instructor and Director, Oncology; M.S., CUNY, Hunter.
Libby Hall, Assistant Professor of Clinical Nursing; M.S., Pace; FNP.
Judy Honig, Instructor and Director, Pediatric Nurse Practitioner Program; Ed.D., Columbia; PNP.
Sherry Ikalowych, Instructor in Clinical Nursing; M.S.N., Columbia; CRNA.
Elizabeth Lenz, Professor of Nursing Research and Associate Dean/Director of Doctoral Program; Ph.D., Delaware.
Marlene McHugh, Assistant Professor of Clinical Nursing; M.S.N., Columbia; FNP.
Mary O. Mundinger, Dean and Professor; Dr.P.H., Columbia. Health policy, family care of the frail elderly, technology assessment in home care.
Jo Sapp, Instructor, Director, Continuing Education, and Director, AMP Program; M.S., Columbia; Certified Psychiatric Nurse Specialist.
Jan Weingrad Smith, Instructor; M.S./M.P.H., Columbia; CNM.
Edwidge Thomas, Instructor of Clinical Nursing; M.S., Columbia; ANP.
Joan Valas, Assistant Professor of Clinical Nursing and Director, Critical Care Nurse Practitioner Program; M.S., Columbia; CCRN, ANP.

FITCHBURG STATE COLLEGE

Department of Nursing
Master of Science (Forensic Nursing)

Program of Study

The College's Master of Science (M.S.) program (forensic nursing speciality) is designed for registered nurses who wish to pursue advanced leadership positions in the community and health-care system. The program, which consists of 39 credits, is currently planned on a part-time, two-year calendar through evening, weekend, intersession, or summer courses. Course sequence is flexible, but is designed to complete core nursing courses (with the exception of the Scholarly Inquiry requirement prior to, or concurrent with, any clinical specialty nursing career), support the clinical specialty nursing courses through prerequisite cognate courses, and cap the program with a practicum in which enrollees also apply research skills. Through course work and clinical practice, graduates are prepared to handle the challenges of advanced practice in the field; influence policy-making; actively promote professional standards, ethics, and legal principles; contribute to the advancement of nursing as a result of their studies and research; and assume a leadership role with health-care consumers and providers to improve the planning and delivery of health care. The curriculum adds aspects of study and research into fields of support for victims of violent crime and trauma and investigations related to such situations along with how the nursing profession relates to the legalities of dealing with various work- and community-related agencies and the judicial system.

Research Facilities

The College Library provides 96 hours of weekly service, online access to the library's catalog, and more than sixty databases via the library's home page. A CD-ROM local area network provides ready access to heavily utilized subscription services. There are approximately 263,000 volumes and 1,467 current periodicals, supplemented by the 404,000-item Educational Resources Information Center (ERIC). Additional services include interlibrary loans, reciprocal borrowing privileges, and specialized collections for criminal justice and nursing.

The College Computer Center serves the general administrative, educational, and research needs of the campus. The Tricord ES8000 and CDC Cyber 932-32 mainframes serve the administrative computer needs of the College. An Alpha Server 2100 acts as the central locus for faculty and staff members and students, providing an enhanced environment for computer science applications and e-mail and Internet access capabilities. A Proliant DHCP server hosts TCP/IP to the entire campus. Five accessible general-purpose labs, five residence hall labs, and one VAX terminal lab exist for general use. Falcon Net, FSC's major telecommuncations upgrade, offers each classroom and residence hall high-speed T-1 network connectivity, making possible the full potential of distance learning and videoconferencing and a scalable infrastructure prepared for the growth of tomorrow.

Financial Aid

Graduate scholarships are available in amounts ranging from $110 to $1790 per year. Scholarships are awarded annually in the form of tuition and fee waivers. The application deadline is February 1 of each academic year. Students admitted to a graduate or C.A.G.S. program may apply for graduate assistantships in the areas of teaching, research, or administration. Graduate assistants are paid $5500 for the academic year, awarded a tuition waiver for 24 semester hours over a two-year period, must carry a load of 6 semester hours per semester, and are required to work 20 hours per week. Applications for graduate assistantships can be obtained from the Graduate Office and are due by May 15. Many students receive tuition reimbursement from their current employers.

Cost of Study

Graduate tuition for 1998–99 is $140 per credit. A comprehensive registration fee of $55 per student and a capital projects fee of $7 per credit is charged at the time of enrollment.

Living and Housing Costs

Fitchburg State College assists students in arranging housing in residence halls or private accommodations. Campus housing is available in double-occupancy rooms within suites. A few single rooms are available. Efforts are made to meet requests pending availability of spaces. Listings for potential off-campus housing can be found in the Office of Residence Life. On-campus housing costs for 1997–98 were $2590 per year. Board plans range from $1500 to $1800 per year.

Student Group

Since the master's program focuses on currently employed professional nurses, students complete their course of study on a part-time basis. Students have significant work experience and attend the program to enhance their existing practice through preparation as a clinical nurse specialist. Some students at certificate levels have completed a master's in nursing and wish to focus on the specialty track in forensic nursing.

Student Outcomes

Since this is a new program, with the first graduating class expected in 1999, alumni surveys for job acquisition and student satisfaction with outcomes have yet to be initiated. It is expected that employment opportunities will be available in a variety of settings in the areas of prevention, treatment, and rehabilitation of forensic victims and perpetrators and in education, consultation, and other medicolegal services.

Location

The College is located in the attractive Montachusett region of north-central Massachusetts, an hour's drive west of Boston and just minutes from some of New England's finest camping, hiking, and fishing spots. The 90-acre campus includes academic and administrative buildings, the library/campus center, an auditorium/theater, a dining commons, and a gymnasium.

The Department

The Department of Nursing has forty years of experience in collegiate nursing education, with continuing accreditation by the National League for Nursing at the undergraduate level since the 1960s. The philosophy of the department includes a holistic approach to individual clients and groups. The graduate program builds on the knowledge and competencies acquired in baccalaureate education and prepares graduate students to assume leadership in the health-care system and contribute to the development of nursing science. The faculty is a diverse group, including researchers, teachers, and scholars, some internationally recognized. Their role at the graduate level is to facilitate the student's creative inquiry and achievement of specialized role competencies using group discussion, student projects, and internships.

Applying

To enroll in the M.S. in Nursing degree program, a student must submit a completed application, an official transcript as a graduate of an NLN-accredited baccalaureate nursing program, official results of the Miller Analogies Test (MAT) or the Graduate Record Examinations (GRE), letters of recommendation documenting a minimum of one year of recent successful clinical practice or part-time equivalent, a license as an RN in Massachusetts (or indication of intent to apply for same), a professional resume, and a written personal statement of career goals.

Correspondence and Information

Division of Graduate and Continuing Education
Fitchburg State College
160 Pearl Street
Fitchburg, Massachusetts 01420-2697

Telephone: 978-665-3181
Fax: 978-665-3658
E-mail: dgce@fsc.edu
World Wide Web: http://www.fsc.edu

Fitchburg State College

THE FACULTY AND THEIR RESEARCH

Graduate Dean and Program Chair

Michele Moran Zide, Associate Vice President, Academic Affairs, and Dean, Graduate and Continuing Education; Ed.D., Massachusetts. (telephone: 978-665-3185)

Barbara Madden, Program Chair; Ed.D., Northeastern. (telephone: 978-665-3498)

Distinguished Scholars, Teachers, and Practitioners in the Fitchburg State College Master of Science (Nursing) Degree Program

Barbara A. Cammuso, Associate Professor; Ph.D., Clark; Ph.D., Dunsbuch.
Anne Marie Catalano, Instructor; Ph.D., Boston College.
Elizabeth Fisk, Associate Professor; M.S.N., Boston University; M.O.E., New Hampshire.
Sophia Harrell, Department Chairperson and Professor; Ed.D., Massachusetts Amherst.
Tayna Ratney, Associate Professor; Ed.D., Boston University.
Ann Scannell, Assistant Professor; N.D., Case Western Reserve.
Andrea Wallen, Professor; Ed.D., Massachusetts Amherst.

GEORGETOWN UNIVERSITY

School of Nursing

Programs of Study

Georgetown University School of Nursing awards the Master of Science degree in five specialty areas: family nurse practitioner, nurse anesthesia, nurse midwifery, acute care nurse practitioner, and management of integrated health systems. Students who complete the nurse midwifery specialty are specialists in women's health care and normal childbearing. Nurse midwifery students earn 45 credits in either sixteen months of full-time study or twenty-seven months of part-time study and are eligible to take the American College of Nurse-Midwives' certifying examination. The acute care nurse practitioner (ACNP) track prepares nurses to provide comprehensive, consistent care to patients with complex problems in acute and critical care settings. The ACNP track integrates advanced pathophysiology, nurse practitioner skills, and the advanced practice nursing roles required to meet complex patient needs. Graduates are eligible to sit for the certification exam through the American Nurses Association as an ACNP. The ACNP track can be completed in one year of intensive full-time study or up to three years of part-time study. The family nurse practitioner program is designed to prepare competent, caring practitioners that manage the health care of families in primary care settings. Emphasis is placed on health advocacy and attaining the knowledge and skills necessary for disease prevention, assessment, and management of common acute and chronic illnesses. Upon completion of the program, the graduate is eligible to take the certification examination for family nurse practitioners. The program can be completed in fifteen months of full-time study or up to three years of part-time study. The nurse anesthesia program is designed to prepare graduates to provide one-on-one care to their patients before, during, and after operations by delivering quality anesthesia services for surgical and obstetric procedures, combined with a personal concern for the health and welfare of the individual. Upon completion, students are eligible to take the certification examination of the Council on Certification of Nurse Anesthesia. The program offers only a full-time, 27-month option for study. The Management of Integrated Health Systems program is designed to prepare graduates to assume leadership roles in the changing organizational structures of integrated delivery systems. The program is jointly taught by faculty members in the School of Nursing and the School of Business and provides students with the business skills needed to manage complex, multidivisional organizations. On completion of the program, the nursing graduates are prepared with the didactic content necessary to sit for the American Nurses Association Certification exam in nursing administration. The program of study may be completed in one calendar year of intense study or up to three years of part-time study. It emphasizes the acquisition of business skills in a collaborative, multidisciplinary learning environment. Interactive teaching strategies that are oriented toward the adult learner are used in both classroom and field experiences. A B.S.N. is not required for admission.

Research Facilities

The Academic Computer Center provides computer hardware, software, and consultative support for all faculty and students. The School of Nursing has its own computer resource center to facilitate computer-assisted learning. All students are expected to use computers for their research activities. Six libraries on campus provide support. The Medical Library has an Integrated Academic Information Management System to expedite bibliographic searches and access to multiple databases.

Financial Aid

Professional Nurse Traineeship and grant funds are available on a limited basis. Loans are available. Students requesting financial aid of any kind must complete a Georgetown financial aid form and the FAF. Georgetown University Hospital offers a tuition remission plan to nurses who are employed while they study.

Cost of Study

During the 1998–99 academic year, the cost of one year of full-time study is estimated at $20,682. The cost of books averages $500 per semester.

Living and Housing Costs

Living costs in Washington, D.C., Maryland, and Virginia vary depending on location and individual needs. A University off-campus housing office helps students to find suitable housing.

Student Group

The diverse student body is composed of men and women from a broad geographic area. Many are full-time students whose relocation to Washington is temporary; others are part-time students who may be employed by local health-care agencies. Students range in age from approximately 22 to 55 and are professional nurses who wish to expand their knowledge and skills in order to provide client care of high quality and to function as more effective leaders in a variety of situations.

Location

The Washington, D.C., metropolitan area is rich in educational, governmental, political, and cultural resources. The Metro system links the city-suburban area efficiently and provides access to the National Institutes of Health, the National Medical Library, Capitol Hill, the National Airport, and many historic areas such as Old Town in Alexandria, Virginia. Excellent restaurants, interesting boutiques, and lively entertainment centers are within walking distance.

The University and The School

Established in 1789, Georgetown University is the oldest Catholic university in the United States. Founded by the Jesuits, it is composed of four undergraduate schools—the College of Arts and Sciences and the Schools of Business Administration, Foreign Service, and Nursing—and three graduate and professional schools—Law, Medicine, and the Graduate School. The School of Summer and Continuing Education offers academic and certificate programs year-round.

The School of Nursing opened in 1903 and is one of the largest privately operated centers for nursing education in the United States. The NLN Graduate Program was established in 1980 and emphasizes individualized education of the highest quality.

Applying

Requirements for admission include a bachelor's degree in nursing from an NLN-accredited school, a GPA of 3.0 on a 4.0 scale in undergraduate studies, registered nurse licensure, one year of professional nursing practice, scores on the Graduate Record Examinations or the Miller Analogies Test (with the exception of the nurse anesthesia program, which requires the GRE), and a background course in basic statistics. The deadline to apply for fall admission to the nurse anesthesia, family nurse practitioner, and nurse midwifery programs is February 1. Students applying to the acute care nurse practitioner program must do so before June 15. Admission to the spring semester is offered on a limited basis, and the deadline for applying for spring admission is November 15.

Correspondence and Information

Georgetown University School of Nursing
Box 571107
3700 Reservoir Road, NW
Washington, D.C. 20007
Telephone: 202-687-2781

Georgetown University

THE FACULTY

Elaine Larson, Professor and Dean; Ph.D., Washington (Seattle); RN, FAAN.
Denise Korniewicz, Associate Professor and Associate Dean for Academic Development; Ph.D., Catholic University; RN, FAAN.
Judith Baigis-Smith, Professor and Associate Dean for Research and Scholarship; Ph.D., NYU; RN, FAAN.
Dorrie Fontaine, Director of Academic Programs and Coordinator of Acute Care Nurse Practitioner Program; D.N.Sc., Catholic University; RN, CCRN.

Program Coordinators

Deborah Bash, Assistant Professor and Coordinator of Nurse Midwifery Program; Ed.D., George Washington; RN, CNM.
Patricia Cloonan, Assistant Professor and Coordinator of Management of Integrated Health Systems Program; Ph.D., Virginia; RN.
Donna Jasinski, Instructor and Coordinator of Nurse Anesthesia Program; M.S., Georgetown; RN, CRNA.
Jean Kelley, Assistant Professor and Academic Coordinator of Family Nurse Practitioner Program; Ph.D., Texas Woman's, RN, CFNP.
Mary Ann Zakutney, Assistant Professor and Clinical Coordinator of Family Nurse Practitioner Program; Ph.D., Utah; RN, CFNP.

Areas of Research Interest and Related Special Expertise

Faculty research interests span a broad range of topics important to advanced nursing practice. These interests include caring behaviors of nurses; clinical performance evaluation of nurse midwifery students; stress and illness; reimbursement for nurse practitioner services; nurse midwifery pain management: influence of values and beliefs; effects of open-heart surgery on the elderly: acute confusional states; methods to classify home-care needs; national survey of nurse practitioners; validation of nursing diagnoses; and nursing management of the client with cancer and HIV.

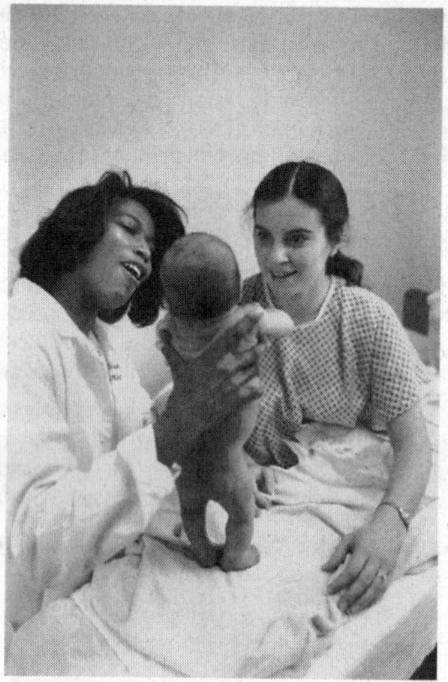

Nurse midwifery student and mother approvingly assess a newborn's strength and reflexes.

Built shortly after the Civil War, Healy Hall remains in active use and is a treasured campus landmark.

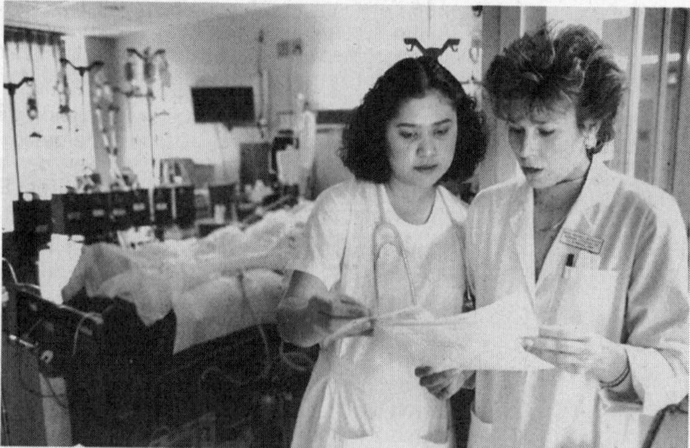

Student reviews the patient's status and nursing needs with her mentor.

INDIANA UNIVERSITY–PURDUE UNIVERSITY INDIANAPOLIS

School of Nursing

Programs of Study

Indiana University School of Nursing (IUSON) graduate offerings include a Master of Science in Nursing (M.S.N.) program, with ten majors, and a Ph.D. in nursing science. The goal of the M.S.N. program is to prepare its graduates for leadership roles in advanced nursing practice, clinical specialization, and nursing administration. Majors are offered in ten areas: adult nurse practitioner, adult psychiatric/mental health nursing, child/adolescent psychiatric/mental health nursing, community health nursing, family nurse practitioner, nursing administration, nursing of adults, nursing of children at risk, OB/GYN practitioner, and pediatric nurse practitioner. Post-master's options are available in all clinical areas as well as nursing administration and teacher education. Students select a major area of study when they apply for admission. Students may elect to follow a full- or part-time course of study. All majors require 42 credits. Selected master's courses are offered over the Indiana Higher Education Telecommunications System (IHETS) and the Internet. All majors include the following areas of study: (1) core courses: one course each in research methodology, policy and practice perspectives in advanced nursing practice, ethical and legal perspectives in advanced nursing practice, advanced nursing practice roles, and nursing theory, for a total of 12 credit hours; (2) courses in nursing major: between 15 and 20 credit hours in speciality content from the major; (3) focus area courses: between 6 and 12 credits of electives chosen by the student with advisement by faculty adviser; (4) nursing study/thesis option: the nursing study earns 3 credit hours; the thesis, 6 credit hours. The Ph.D. program, which builds on baccalaureate or master's nursing education, is based on the belief that professional nursing is a scientific discipline and that it has a unique role and body of knowledge. This body of knowledge can be expanded, applied, and validated through recognized methods of scholarly inquiry. As students progress through the program, they become socialized to the value of research and interdisciplinary inquiry and acquire the skills necessary to conduct independent research. The primary goal of the Ph.D. program is the preparation of scholars in the following fields of study: environments for health, acute and chronic health problems, health promotion, and family health adaptation. Graduates create and disseminate to the public new knowledge related to these fields of study. Students pursue study and related research in one of four focus areas of the programs. These focus areas were chosen on the basis of faculty research strengths and funding priorities of the National Institute of Nursing Research. The program is not developed to meet every need but to prepare graduates with skills in the areas of faculty strength. The 90-credit curriculum includes the following four concentrations: theory, research, and statistics (24 credits); nursing science and research (30 credits); external cognate minor (12 credits); and dissertation (24 credits). Thirty credits of the 90-credit curriculum may be met by completed Master of Science course work.

Research Facilities

The IUSON has a Center of Nursing Research, which provides research and statistical consultation for students. Computer clusters and software are also available to assist students in research and grant writing. The center is also the home of the Mary Margaret Walther Cancer Program.

Financial Aid

A limited number of fellowships/traineeships are available on a competitive basis for full-time study. Research assistant and teaching assistant positions are also available for full-time and part-time students.

Cost of Study

The estimated 1997–98 costs for graduate study were $143 per credit hour. Students also paid technology, clinical, and activity fees. Approximate costs for a clinical specialist or nurse practitioner major was $5000–$8000, depending on the major.

Living and Housing Costs

There is limited on-campus housing available to students. Admission to the University does not guarantee campus housing accommodations. Students must file separate applications for housing in order to reserve spaces and should apply as soon as they decide to attend school at the Indianapolis campus.

Student Group

The IUSON meets the needs of more than 600 graduate students pursuing their professional goals. Eighty percent of the students are studying part-time. The School has a mentoring program for international students and students of color.

Student Outcomes

The graduates of the master's and doctoral degree programs are in high demand for positions in health-care settings, academia, and research. The opportunities for employment far exceed the large graduation numbers.

Location

Indianapolis, the capital of Indiana, is known as a center for business, amateur sports, and culture. In recent national surveys, Indianapolis has been named one of the safest and most livable cities in the United States. The city has a fine symphony and excellent theater and opera as well as outstanding museums. There are also fine residential areas, parks, and recreational facilities.

The University and The School

The IUSON graduate program is located on the campus of Indiana University–Purdue University Indianapolis (IUPUI). Created in 1969, when the programs of Indiana and Purdue Universities merged, IUPUI offers 169 degree programs. The Medical Center located on the IUPUI campus includes the Schools of Nursing, Medicine, Social Work, Allied Health, and Dentistry. The Medical Center's extensive diagnostic clinics and its five teaching hospitals—University, Riley (the only children's hospital in the state), Wishard, Veterans Administration, and LaRue Carter Psychiatric Hospital—are the state's primary referral hospitals and its chief centers for clinical instruction in the health professions. More than 800,000 patients visit these clinics and hospitals annually.

IUSON was founded in 1914. With 8,000 students and 244 faculty members at eight campuses throughout the state (Bloomington, Columbus, Gary, Indianapolis, Kokomo, New Albany, Richmond, and South Bend), it is the largest multipurpose school of nursing in the country offering a full range of programs from the associate degree through the doctoral degree. The School has outstanding faculty members who are actively involved in scholarship as well as professional and community service. The headquarters of Sigma Theta Tau International, founded at IUSON in 1922, are located on the Indianapolis campus. The School's commitment to excellence is reflected in the number of its innovative programs and its ongoing cutting-edge research. The IUSON graduate programs are ranked in the top fourteen in the country (*U.S. News & World Report,* 1995). IUSON has been a leader in graduate education since 1945 when the master's degree program was begun.

Applying

Applications for the master's program are considered twice a year. Completed applications are due April 1 and October 1. Applicants for the Ph.D. program are considered once a year and are due January 15.

Correspondence and Information

Application forms:
Office of Educational Services
Indiana University School of Nursing
1111 Middle Drive
Indianapolis, Indiana 46202-5107
Fax: 317-274-2996
World Wide Web: http://www.iupui.edu/~nursing/index.html

International applicants:
IUPUI Office of International Affairs
620 Union Drive, Room 207
Indianapolis, Indiana 46202-5167

Indiana University–Purdue University Indianapolis

THE FACULTY

Margaret Applegate, Professor; Ed.D., Indiana, 1980; RN.
Joan Austin, Professor; D.N.S.; Indiana, 1981; RN, FAAN.
Jane Backer, Associate Professor; D.N.S., Indiana, 1990; RN.
Constance M. Baker, Professor; Ed.D., Columbia, 1977; RN.
Cheryl Bean, Associate Professor; D.S.N., Alabama, 1987; RN.
Janis Beckstrand, Associate Professor; Ph.D., Texas at Austin, 1978; RN, FAAN.
Susan Bennett, Associate Professor; D.N.S., Indiana, 1990; RN.
Diane Billings, Professor; Ed.D., Indiana, 1986; RN, FAAN.
Donna Boland, Associate Professor; Ph.D., Utah, 1986; RN.
Sandra Burgener, Associate Professor; Ph.D., Wayne State, 1989; RN.
Victoria Champion, Professor; D.N.S., Indiana, 1981; RN, FAAN.
Karen Cobb, Assistant Professor; M.S.N., Indiana, 1982; RN.
Nancy Dayhoff, Associate Professor; Ed.D., Indiana, 1987; RN.
Eleanor Donnelly, Associate Professor; Ph.D., SUNY at Buffalo, 1984; RN.
Linda Finke, Professor; Ph.D., Miami (Ohio), 1985; RN.
Mary Fisher, Associate Professor; Ph.D., Kent State, 1984; RN.
Beverly Flynn, Professor; Ph.D., Wisconsin, 1972; RN, FAAN.
Sharon Holmberg, Associate Professor; Ph.D., Rochester, 1994; RN.
Betsy Joyce, Associate Professor; Ed.D., Indiana, 1988; RN.
Juanita Keck, Associate Professor; D.N.S., Indiana, 1983; RN.
M. Jan Keffer, Associate Professor; Ph.D., Illinois at Chicago, 1990; RN.
Beverly Linde, Assistant Professor; Ph.D., Michigan, 1989; RN.
Brenda Lyon, Associate Professor; D.N.S., Indiana, 1981; RN, FAAN.
Joanne Martin, Assistant Professor; Dr.P.H., Berkeley, 1985; RN, FAAN.
Rose Mays, Associate Professor; Ph.D., Texas at Austin, 1987; RN.
Angela Barron McBride, Distinguished Professor; Ph.D., Purdue, 1978; RN, FAAN.
Anna McDaniel, Assistant Professor; D.N.S., Indiana, 1991; RN.
Suzanne Morrissey, Associate Professor; D.N.S., Indiana, 1984; RN.
Nancy Opie, Professor; D.N.S., Indiana, 1982; RN, FAAN.
Joanne Rains, Associate Professor; D.N.S., Indiana, 1990; RN.
Dixie Ray, Associate Professor; Ph.D., Indiana, 1992.
Beverly Richards, Associate Professor; D.N.S., Indiana, 1984; RN.
Virginia Richardson, Associate Professor; D.N.S., Indiana, 1994; RN.
Linda A. Rooda, Associate Professor; Ph.D., Purdue, 1990; RN.
Lee Schwecke, Associate Professor; Ed.D., Indiana, 1992; RN.
Mary Lou DeLeon Siantz, Associate Professor; Ph.D., Maryland, 1984; RN, FAAN.
Sharon Sims, Associate Professor; Ph.D., Utah, 1986; RN.
Rebecca Sloan, Assistant Professor; Ph.D., Kentucky, 1995; RN.
Roberta Smith, Professor; Ph.D., George Peabody, 1976; RN, FAAN.
Phyllis Stern, Professor; D.N.S., California, San Francisco, 1976; RN, FAAN.
Melinda Swenson, Associate Professor; Ph.D., Indiana, 1991; RN.

IUPUI campus by night.

JOHNS HOPKINS UNIVERSITY

School of Nursing

Program of Study

The purpose of the master's program is to prepare nurses for leadership positions in advanced nursing practice and/or health-care management in a variety of settings. The master's program emphasizes flexibility and is designed to accommodate individual professional objectives. Johns Hopkins provides unsurpassed opportunities for personal and professional development in advanced clinical practice, the research process, and leadership management of health-care environments. Core courses taken by all students include nursing theory, computer applications in nursing, biostatistics, research, and ethics.

Graduates of the Master of Science in Nursing (M.S.N.) program in advanced practice nursing with an adult, family, or pediatric focus are eligible to apply for ANCC certification as an adult, family, or pediatric nurse practitioner and/or clinical specialist. An acute/critical-care nurse practitioner program is also available. Nurses with master's degrees in nursing are eligible to apply to the Post-Master's Nurse Practitioner Program. Other majors offered in the M.S.N. degree program are nursing systems and management; a dual M.S.N. in nursing systems and management/M.S. in business, offered with the School of Continuing Studies; community health nursing; a joint M.S.N. in community health nursing/M.P.H., offered with the School of Hygiene and Public Health; and an advanced practice nursing clinical specialty in HIV/AIDS, oncology, and adult health. The Business of Nursing, a 12-credit graduate certificate program, is also available in conjunction with the School of Continuing Studies.

A Ph.D. in nursing is available to prepare nurse scholars to conduct research that advances the theoretical foundation of nursing practice and health-care delivery.

Research Facilities

In the spring 1998 semester, the School of Nursing opened its doors to a newly built, state-of-the-art education and research facility. The Johns Hopkins Medical Institutions (JHMI) campus is part of a world-renowned academic health center that includes the Schools of Nursing, Medicine, and Hygiene and Public Health; the Johns Hopkins Hospital; and the William H. Welch Medical Library. The William H. Welch Medical Library is a central resource library that serves the Johns Hopkins Medical Institutions. Students gain free 24-hour-a-day access to the Welch Library Gateway. The Nursing Information Resource Center (NIRC), located in the School of Nursing, is managed by the Welch Library. The NIRC maintains a core collection of books to support student course work, a reprint file of material used in the students' courses, a pamphlet file of material from the National League for Nursing, and clinical skills videocassettes. In addition, the facilities and 2 million volumes of the University's Milton S. Eisenhower Library on the Homewood Campus are available to students at the School of Nursing. The Center for Nursing Research (CNR) provides students and faculty members with such support services as consultation on research design and conduct, including data management and analysis; information on funding sources and grant application processes; and advice on career development and continuing education, research, and other resources. The 3,000 square feet of the state-of-the-art School of Nursing Research Lab supports biological-based nursing research.

The Johns Hopkins Health System includes, in addition to the Johns Hopkins Hospital, three other hospital campuses, one of which houses the National Institute on Aging Gerontology Center and the National Institute on Drug Abuse Addiction Research Center.

Financial Aid

Financial assistance includes merit-based scholarships and student loans. Merit scholarships are awarded to applicants who demonstrate exceptional scholastic and leadership ability. The awards are not based on financial need.

A loan program is available to assist students in financing the cost of education. Further information on loans and scholarships is available through the Office of Financial Student Services.

Cost of Study

Tuition for full-time study is $16,750 for the 1998–99 academic year. Degree candidates are assessed a one-time matriculation fee of $500 upon entering the program.

Living and Housing Costs

A variety of University-owned housing is available to full-time graduate students. Convenient off-campus housing is also readily available. The cost of living in Baltimore varies with location and needs. More information can be obtained by contacting the Office of Student Services at the School of Nursing.

Student Group

In 1997–98, enrollment was approximately 6,250 full-time students and 6,450 part-time students. Enrollment on the East Baltimore Campus—the academic health center—consists mainly of graduate students.

Location

Baltimore is a national showcase of urban renewal and ethnic tradition and provides students with a wide variety of social and cultural opportunities. The School of Nursing is located near downtown Baltimore, on the academic health center campus.

The University

Johns Hopkins is a privately endowed, coeducational institution for higher education based in Baltimore. The Baltimore divisions of the University are the School of Arts and Sciences, Whiting School of Engineering, School of Medicine, School of Hygiene and Public Health, School of Nursing, School of Continuing Studies, and Peabody Institute. The University operates separate divisions in Howard County, Maryland, Washington, D.C., and Bologna, Italy. The University was incorporated in 1867 under a bequest from Johns Hopkins, a Quaker merchant from Baltimore, who directed that the funds be divided equally and used for the establishment of the University and the Johns Hopkins Hospital, which is a separate corporate entity. At its opening in 1876, the University was the first educational institution in the United States established with advanced studies and research as its primary goals.

Applying

Admission requirements include graduation from a baccalaureate or master's degree program in nursing with a GPA of 3.0 or above, a current license to practice nursing, preferably a year of nursing practice, and competitive scores on the Graduate Record Examinations (GRE). Academic and professional references, official transcripts from all previous schools attended, completed application forms, and GRE results must be submitted prior to March 1 to ensure scholarship eligibility. Provisional admission is offered to some students. Personal interviews are preferred and may be requested.

Correspondence and Information

Office of Admissions and Student Services
Johns Hopkins University School of Nursing
Suite 113
525 North Wolfe Street
Baltimore, Maryland 21205-2110

Telephone: 410-955-7548
E-mail: jhuson@son.jhmi.edu
World Wide Web: http://www.son.jhmi.edu

Johns Hopkins University

THE FACULTY AND THEIR RESEARCH

Jerilyn Allen, Associate Professor; Sc.D., Johns Hopkins, 1988. Primary and secondary prevention of cardiovascular disease, cardiovascular disease in women, functional status and quality of life, behavioral interventions.

Lynn Baxendale-Cox, Assistant Professor, Physiology, and Director of School of Nursing Research Lab; Ph.D., Indiana, 1983. Postdoctoral Research Associate, Boston University, 1983–84; Postdoctoral Fellow, University of Illinois at Urbana-Champaign, 1984–87; SURGIKOS Postdoctoral Fellow, Johns Hopkins University, 1989–90: electrophysiology, membrane transport processes, wound healing, biological modeling of behavioral systems.

Ronald A. Berk, Professor and Statistician in Residence; Ph.D., Maryland, 1973. Research methodology.

Betsy Brock, Instructor; Ph.D., Johns Hopkins, 1995; FNP.

Jacquelyn Campbell, Anna D. Wolf Professor; Ph.D., Rochester, 1986. Family violence.

Mary K. Cresci, Instructor; Ph.D., Wayne State, 1997; CCRN. Computers in nursing education and adult health.

Ada Romaine Davis, Associate Professor; Ph.D., Maryland, 1979. Advanced practice nursing, history of nursing, cognitive intervention with older adults to maintain independence.

Jacqueline Dienemann, Associate Professor and Coordinator of Nursing Systems, Management and Care, M.S.N./M.P.H., and M.S.N./M.S.B.; Ph.D., Catholic University, 1983. Nursing management, research development, domestic violence.

Ernest Robert Feroli, Associate Director of Clinical Practice, Department of Pharmacy Services, Johns Hopkins Hospital; Pharm.Dr., Maryland, 1978. Clinical practice.

Fannie Gaston-Johansson, Associate Professor, Elsie M. Lawler Chair, and Director of International and Extramural Programs; D.Med.Sc., Goteborg (Sweden), 1985. Pain assessment and pain management.

Patricia Grimm, Associate Professor and Mary Edna Busch American Cancer Society Professor of Oncology Nursing; Coordinator, Advanced Practice Clinical Specialist Nursing Track and Program Coordinator, Oncology Clinical Specialist; Ph.D., Maryland, 1989. Psychosocial oncology, symptom management, bone marrow transplant outcomes.

Karen B. Haller, Associate Professor, Nursing Administration; Ph.D., Michigan, 1982. Quality assurance and clinical ethics.

Martha N. Hill, Professor and Director, Center for Nursing Research; Director, Post-Doctoral Programs; and Interim Director, Doctoral Program; Ph.D., Johns Hopkins, 1986. Postdoctoral Fellow, Robert Wood Johnson Clinical Nurse Scholars Program, University of Pennsylvania, 1986–88: patient and professional education and behavior, hypertension control in minorities.

Karen Huss, Associate Professor, joint appointment with the Department of Medicine, Johns Hopkins; D.M.Sc., Catholic University, 1990; CANP 1981–present. Sandoz Postdoctoral Research Fellow, Johns Hopkins University, 1992–94: patient and professional education, asthma, allergy, immunology.

Cris Kasper, Associate Professor; Ph.D., Michigan, 1982. Postdoctoral Fellow, Rush University, 1982–84: skeletal muscle physiology.

Myong Kim, Instructor; Ph.D., Arizona, 1995. Postdoctoral Fellow, University of Arizona, 1996: nursing instrumentation/evaluation.

Joan Kub, Assistant Professor, Community Health Nursing; Ph.D., Johns Hopkins, 1992. Adolescent mental health, violence, tuberculosis, models of community care.

Linda Lewandowski, Assistant Professor and clinical psychologist and pediatric clinical nurse specialist; Ph.D., Massachusetts Amherst, 1988. Advanced practice acute and critical-care pediatrics, children's responses to violence and other types of trauma.

Victoria Mock, Associate Professor and Director of Oncology Nursing Research, Johns Hopkins Hospital; D.N.Sc., Catholic University, 1988. Symptom management and quality of life.

Candis Morrison, Associate Professor; Ph.D., Maryland, 1994; CRNP. Cancer detection/screening, substance abuse, domestic violence, depression, women's health.

Martha Neff-Smith, Professor and Program Coordinator of M.S.N./M.P.H. and Community Health Nursing; Ph.D., Michigan, 1978. Epidemiologic methods to study and evaluate disease and injury internationally.

Marie Nolan, Assistant Professor; D.N.Sc., Catholic University, 1988. Stress and coping, gerontological nursing, ethical issues.

Linda Rose, Assistant Professor, Psychiatric/Mental Health Nursing; Ph.D., Maryland, 1992. Caregiver stress, coping, chronic psychiatric illness, qualitative research methodology.

Cynthia Rushton, Assistant Professor; D.N.Sc., Catholic University, 1994. Bioethics.

Stella M. Shiber, Associate Dean, Professional Education Programs and Practice; Ph.D., Maryland, 1983. Social welfare, psychiatric–mental health nursing, substance abuse.

Carol Smith, Assistant Professor; Ph.D., Cornell, 1990. Pediatric primary care, health care of adolescents and underserved populations.

Margaret Soderstrom, Assistant Professor, Psychiatric/Mental Health Nursing; Ph.D., Maryland, 1990. Post-traumatic stress, alcoholism, family systems.

Elaine Stashinko, Assistant Professor; Ph.D., Pennsylvania, 1987. Children's health behaviors, pediatric pain.

Judith A. Vessey, Professor and Coordinator, Advanced Practice Nursing, Nurse Practitioner Programs; Ph.D., Pennsylvania, 1986. Primary care, children with chronic conditions.

Margaret A. Vettese, Lecturer and Program Coordinator of HIV/AIDS Clinical Specialist Nursing; Ph.D., Case Western Reserve, 1991. Terminal illness, end-of-life decision making, symptom management, loneliness/social isolation.

Benita Walton-Moss, Assistant Professor and Program Coordinator of Family Nurse Practitioner Program; D.N.Sc., California, San Francisco, 1994.

MGH INSTITUTE OF HEALTH PROFESSIONS

Graduate Programs in Nursing, Physical Therapy, Communication Sciences and Disorders, and Clinical Investigation

Programs of Study

The graduate programs offered at the Institute combine a rigorous academic curriculum with clinical practica in multiple settings, designed to prepare graduates for leadership positions in their respective professions. Founded by, and affiliated with, Massachusetts General Hospital (MGH) in Boston, the Institute offers an interdisciplinary curriculum as well as different tracks and specialties within a field. Opportunities for postprofessional certification (Certificates of Advanced Study) exist in several of the programs.

The Master of Science in Nursing degree program accepts both nonregistered nurse college graduates and nurses with bachelor's degrees in nursing or other fields. The nonregistered nurse program requires three years of full-time study and consists of generalist and advanced practice nursing courses, with opportunities to develop specializations in a variety of areas: women's health, gerontology, and HIV/AIDS. Pediatric, adult, and family nurse practitioner tracks allow all students to prepare for certification. RN-prepared students may complete the program on a full- or part-time basis, with courses offered in the daytime, evening, and during the summer.

The Master of Science degree program in physical therapy offers both professional (entry-level) and postprofessional (advanced) curricula. The Professional Program in Physical Therapy, which prepares students who hold a bachelor's degree in another field to become physical therapists, is a full-time, two-year program, followed by a one-year clinical internship. The Post-Professional Program in Physical Therapy, offered on a full- or part-time basis, admits licensed physical therapists who have had one year of clinical experience. Specialty areas include cardiopulmonary, neurologic, and orthopaedic physical therapy, or a student may design an individualized program of study. A thesis is required.

The Master of Science degree program in speech-language pathology offers a curriculum based on a solid foundation in the normal processes and disorders of human communication across the life span. The Graduate Program in Communication Sciences and Disorders prepares students to provide speech-language pathology services in multiple settings, including acute care, rehabilitation, long-term care, community clinics, and both special and regular public schools. Unique features of the program include the opportunity to pursue additional certification in written language (reading) and cross-registration with the Harvard Graduate School of Education.

The Master of Science degree program in clinical investigation is a new, three-semester program that prepares health-care professionals and other qualified students to be team members and leaders in clinical research through participation in the development of new and improved therapies and interventions, implementation of clinical trials, data management, regulatory affairs, medical writing, outcomes research, and study oversight.

Research Facilities

Clinical and research opportunities are provided at MGH and in more than 500 other major health-care centers and community settings in the greater Boston area. Through MGH's Treadwell Library, with major basic science, medical, and nursing collections, students may access online computer databases and an extensive reference and periodical collection. Students working on research projects may also access the Countway Library of Medicine at Harvard Medical School. In addition, the Institute houses the Ruth Sleeper Learning Center, which provides computers and modern technology for interactive learning.

Financial Aid

Financial assistance is supplemental to the student's financial resources. Whenever possible, financial need is met through a combination of sources that may include federal loans, partial scholarships, graduate assistantships, and federal traineeships.

Cost of Study

Tuition for the 1998–99 academic year is $530 per credit hour, with the number of credits dependent on individual program requirements. Fees include a clinical education fee, a computer fee, and a student services fee. Books and supplies are estimated to cost about $1500 per year.

Living and Housing Costs

The Institute does not provide housing for students; however, the Office of Students Affairs does provide limited assistance to students who are relocating. Rents in the area vary. It is estimated that annual expenses for a single student living alone in Boston will run $12,000 a year.

Student Group

Fall 1997 enrollment was 530, 50 percent of whom were full-time students. With many of these students making career changes, the student body is composed of highly talented individuals from diverse backgrounds who wish to become leaders in the health professions.

Student Outcomes

Graduates of the Institute are equipped to meet the challenges of managed care in a variety of settings: major teaching hospitals, ambulatory health-care environments, educational institutions, hospital-based systems, and private practice. Many continue their education at the doctoral level.

Location

Located in the heart of Boston, near Massachusetts General Hospital, the Institute offers students a stimulating environment. There are numerous opportunities for extracurricular activities—theaters, museums, concerts, and professional sports events. Boston has an excellent public transportation system and is located in proximity to rivers, lakes, mountains, and parks.

The Institute

The Institute was founded in 1977 by the Massachusetts General Hospital and maintains a close affiliation with the hospital while being separately incorporated. The Institute's faculty members are engaged in teaching, clinical practice, and research. As model practitioners, faculty members integrate theory with the care of patients, evaluation of that care, and the design and implementation of student research to improve health care. Students test theories through clinical application with faculty assistance. Interdisciplinary study is an integral part of the Institute's educational philosophy.

Applying

All applicants must submit a completed application along with a $50 fee, official transcripts from all colleges and universities attended, GRE General Test scores (taken within the last five years), three letters of recommendation, and a biographical summary with a statement of purpose and career objectives. International applicants and applicants who did not receive their undergraduate degree from an English-speaking institution are required to submit Test of English as a Foreign Language (TOEFL) scores.

Correspondence and Information

Office of Student Affairs
MGH Institute of Health Professions
P.O. Box 6357
Boston, Massachusetts 02114-0016
Telephone: 617-726-3140
Fax: 617-726-8010

MGH Institute of Health Professions

FACULTY AND RESEARCH AREAS

NURSING

Linda Andrist, Assistant Professor; Ph.D., Brandeis.
Elizabeth Blackington, Clinical Assistant Professor; M.S.N., Simmons.
Christine Bridges, Clinical Assistant Professor; D.N.Sc., Boston University.
Cheryl Cahill, Amelia Peabody Professor of Nursing Research; Ph.D., Michigan.
Meredith Censullo, Associate Professor; Ph.D., Boston College.
Emily Chandler, Assistant Professor; Ph.D., Claremont.
Inge Corless, Associate Professor; Ph.D., Brown.
Carol Kammer, Associate Professor and Director, RN Programs; Ed.D., Indiana.
Veronica Kane, Clinical Assistant Professor; M.S., Yale.
Arlene J. Lowenstein, Professor and Director; Ph.D., Pittsburgh.
Talli McCormick, Clinical Instructor; M.S.N., MGH Institute of Health Professions.
Janice Bell Meisenhelder, Associate Professor; D.N.Sc., Boston University.
Patrice Nicholas, Associate Professor; D.N.Sc., Boston University.
Hollie T. Noveletsky-Rosenthal, Assistant Professor; Ph.D., Boston College.
Alexandra Paul-Simon, Assistant Professor and Academic Coordinator of Clinical Education; Ph.D., Boston College.
Kathleen Solomon, Clinical Instructor; M.S., Massachusetts.
Jean E. Steel, Professor; Ph.D., Boston University.
Nancy M. Terres, Assistant Professor; M.S., Boston University.
JoAnn Trybulski, Clinical Assistant Professor; M.S., Simmons.
John Twomey, Assistant Professor; Ph.D., Virginia.
Barbara K. Willson, Assistant Professor; Ph.D., Brandeis.
Christine M. Wilson, Assistant Professor; Ph.D., Boston College.
Karen A. Wolf, Clinical Associate Professor; Ph.D., Brandeis.
Elaine Young, Associate Professor; Ph.D., Penn State.

Stress and coping, menstrual cycle, HIV-AIDS, fatigue, family studies, maternal-infant relationships, diagnostic reasoning, pain, gerontology, high-risk newborns, ethics, quality of life, women's health issues, cultural diversity.

PHYSICAL THERAPY

Marianne Beninato, Assistant Professor; Ph.D., Virginia Commonwealth.
Russell Butler, Associate Professor; M.D., Chicago.
Lisa Cohen, Clinical Instructor; M.S., Columbia.
Kathleen Gill-Body, Assistant Professor; M.S., MGH Institute of Health Professions.
Kathleen Grimes, Clinical Assistant Professor; M.S., C.C.S., Virginia Commonwealth.
Bette Ann Harris, Assistant Professor and Program Director; M.S., MGH Institute of Health Professions.
Colleen Kigin, Assistant Professor; M.S., Boston University.
Aimee Klein, Clinical Assistant Professor; M.S., Boston University.
Mary Knab, Assistant Professor; M.S., Texas Woman's.
David Krebs, Professor; Ph.D., NYU.
Leroy Lavine, Professor; M.D., NYU.
Claire McCarthy, Associate Professor; M.S., Boston University.
Chris McGibbon, Assistant Professor; Ph.D., New Brunswick.
Theresa Hoskins Michel, Assistant Professor; M.S., Boston University.
Diane Plante, Clinical Assistant Professor; M.S., MGH Institute of Health Professions.
Leslie Portney, Associate Professor and Director, Professional Program; Ph.D., Boston University.
Linda Steiner, Clinical Assistant Professor; M.S., MGH Institute of Health Professions.
Patricia E. Sullivan, Associate Professor; Ph.D., Boston University.
Mary P. Watkins, Clinical Associate Professor; M.S., Boston University.
Cynthia Coffin Zadai, Assistant Professor; M.S., Northeastern.

Physical therapy management of pain, epidemiology and assessment of physical disability among the elderly, cost effectiveness of physical therapy interventions, quantitative analysis of posture and gait in the elderly and the neurologically impaired, prosthetics and orthotics in physical therapy, determinants of falls in the elderly, benefits of exercise in cardiopulmonary patients, effectiveness of strengthening programs in the elderly.

COMMUNICATION SCIENCES AND DISORDERS

Julie Atwood, Professor; M.Ed., Boston University.
Lynne Davis, Assistant Professor; Ph.D., Ohio State.
Charles Haynes, Assistant Professor; Ed.D., Harvard.
Robert Hillman, Professor and Program Director; Ph.D., Purdue.
Pamela Hook, Assistant Professor; Ph.D., Northwestern.
Gregory L. Lof, Assistant Professor; Ph.D., Wisconsin.
Lesley Maxwell, Clinical Assistant Professor, Coordinator of Clinical Education, and Director of Language Laboratory; M.S., Boston University.
Howard Shane, Professor; Ph.D., Syracuse.
Kenneth Stevens, Professor; Sc.D., MIT.
Aaron Thornton, Professor; Ph.D., Iowa.
Katherine Verdolini, Associate Professor; Ph.D., Washington (St. Louis).

Developmental and acquired disorders of voice, speech, and language (spoken and written).

CLINICAL INVESTIGATION

Cheryl Cahill, Amelia Peabody Professor of Nursing Research; Ph.D., Michigan.
Richard H. Ferraro, Clinical Associate Professor and Director; D.M.D., Tufts.
David Krebs, Professor; Ph.D., NYU.

Management of clinical research studies, outcomes research including pharmacoeconomics, operations research in data management and analysis, and clinical trials research in various therapeutic areas.

NORTHEASTERN UNIVERSITY

Graduate School of Nursing

Program of Study

The Graduate School of Nursing offers a Master of Science degree in nursing that is designed to prepare nurses with a general background as nurse practitioners, specialists, managers, and educators. The NLN-accredited master's program includes clinical specialization in administration, anesthesia, community health, critical-care, neonatal, primary-care, and psychiatric–mental health nursing. Within the framework of nursing science, the concepts of knowledge, competence, and role provide the foundation for advanced professional practice. Learning experiences encompass both critical inquiry in the academic environment and application of clinical theory and research in health-care settings. Professional socialization and interdisciplinary collaboration are emphasized throughout the program.

The 52- to 54-quarter-hour curriculum is designed so that students may pursue either a full-time or part-time program of study. Full-time students may expect to complete the degree requirements in one calendar year. Part-time students may take up to five years to complete the program. Classes are offered in the late afternoon and evening. There are some modifications in the curriculum for nurse anesthesia students.

The School also offers an RN to M.S. program for diploma or associate degree nurses. The curriculum encompasses graduate courses in one of the areas of specialization, the foundation courses, and specified courses that address topics such as pathophysiology, cultural diversity, nursing informatics, and public health nursing. The program may be completed in two years on a full-time basis or up to five years on a part-time basis. The 85-quarter-hour program offers an innovative pathway to earning a joint B.S.N./M.S. degree.

The M.S./M.B.A. joint-degree program is offered in conjunction with Northeastern's Graduate School of Business Administration. The 88-quarter-hour program may be taken on a part-time basis.

Post-master's certificate programs are available for study in primary care and psychiatric–mental health nursing.

Research Facilities

Interdisciplinary centers and institutes that engage in research in collaboration with academic departments include the Center for Communications and Digital Signal Processing; Center for Drug Targeting and Analysis; Center for Innovation in Urban Education; Center for Technology Management; Center for Vertebrate Studies; Center for European Economic Studies; Institute on Learning, Work, and the Workplace; Urban Law and Public Policy Institute; Marine Science Center; Barnett Institute of Chemical Analysis and Materials Science; Electron Microscopy Center; Center for Electromagnetic Research; Center for the Study of Sport in Society; Center for Applied Social Research; Center for Labor Market Studies; and Center for Biotechnology Engineering. The Division of Academic Computing provides access to computing resources. A high-speed data network links users and facilities on the central campus and on three satellite campuses. The campus network is also connected via the global Internet to computing resources around the world. Students have access to DEC VAX systems, public access microcomputer labs (PC and Macintosh), a computer and conferencing system, a multimedia lab, and specialized computing equipment. University libraries contain more than 829,000 volumes, 1.9 million microforms, 170,000 government documents, 8,900 serial subscriptions, and 17,000 audio, video, and software titles. A central library contains technologically sophisticated services, including online catalog and circulation systems, a gateway to external networked information resources, and a network of CD-ROM optical disc databases. Students have access to major research collections through the Boston Library Consortium.

Financial Aid

Northeastern awards need-based aid through the Federal Perkins Loan, Federal Work-Study, and Federal Stafford Student Loan programs and also offers minority fellowships and Martin Luther King Jr. Scholarships. The graduate schools offer assistance through teaching, research, and administrative assistantship awards that include tuition remission and a stipend typically ranging between $9000 and $11,500 and requiring a maximum of 20 hours of work per week. Also available are tuition assistantships that provide partial or full tuition remission and require a maximum of 10 hours of work per week.

Cost of Study

The cost of study for the 1998–99 academic year in the Graduate School of Nursing is $415 per quarter hour of credit. Where applicable, special tuition charges are made for theses.

Living and Housing Costs

In 1998–99, quarterly on-campus room rates for a single bedroom range from $1425 to $1600 within an apartment. A single efficiency apartment is $1960. A shared bedroom in an apartment ranges from $1300 to $1390 per quarter. While there are several board options available, graduate students typically pay approximately $1000 per quarter for ten meals per week. An off-campus referral service is available.

Student Group

In fall 1997, 19,780 undergraduate and 4,799 graduate students were enrolled at Northeastern University. They represent a wide variety of academic, professional, geographic, and cultural backgrounds. Nursing students include those from Asia, Europe, and Africa as well as students from all across the United States.

Location

Boston, the capital of Massachusetts, offers many academic, cultural, and recreational opportunities. In addition to the abundant resources available within Northeastern University, students have access to the resources of the other educational and cultural institutions of the Greater Boston area. The city is home to people of every intellectual, political, economic, racial, ethnic, and religious background. Boston is a mixture of Colonial tradition and modern technology. It is a place where the past is appreciated, the present enjoyed, and the future anticipated.

The University

Founded in 1898, Northeastern University is a privately endowed nonsectarian institution of higher learning and one of the largest private universities in the country. Northeastern University has seven undergraduate colleges, nine graduate and professional schools, two part-time undergraduate divisions, a number of continuing and special education programs and institutes, several suburban campuses, and an extensive research division.

Applying

Applicants should have an earned baccalaureate degree in nursing from a program accredited by the National League for Nursing. As part of their degree program, students should have taken an elementary statistics course. Additional requirements include a satisfactory scholastic record, an official copy of all college transcripts, satisfactory scores on the General Test of the Graduate Record Examinations, three letters of reference, a personal goal statement, and current registration to practice nursing in a state or territory. There are some modifications in the program requirements for international students, including their submission of TOEFL scores. The B.S.N./M.S. degree program allows diploma and A.D. nurses to pursue graduate study.

There is a rolling admission policy for some specializations. However, students interested in full-time study and all international students should submit their application by April 1 for admission in the fall quarter.

Correspondence and Information

Graduate School of Nursing
Robinson Hall 205
Northeastern University
Boston, Massachusetts 02115-5096
Telephone: 617-373-3590
Fax: 617-373-8672

Northeastern University

THE FACULTY

Jane F. Aroian, Associate Professor; Ed.D., Northeastern; RN.
Lynn Babington, Associate Professor; Ph.D., Washington (Seattle); RN.
Anne Bateman, Assistant Professor; Ed.D., Massachusetts; RN.
Michelle A. Beauchesne, Assistant Professor; D.N.Sc., Boston University; RN, PNP.
Carol Bova, Graduate Lecturer; M.S., Boston College; RN.
Olivia Breton, M.Ed., Boston University; RN.
Rosanne Buck, Part-time Instructor; M.S., Northeastern; RN, NNP.
Janet Carroll, Associate Professor; M.S.N., Boston College; RN.
Margery M. Chisholm, Associate Professor; Ed.D., Boston University; RN.
Margaret Christiansen, Assistant Professor; Ph.D., Michigan; RN.
Margaret Curtin, Part-time Instructor; MSN, California, San Francisco; RNC, FNP.
Rosanna De Marco, Instructor; Ph.D. candidate, Wayne State; RN.
Janet Dewan, Adjunct Assistant Professor; M.S., New York Medical College; RN, CRNA.
Karen Flynn, Part-time Instructor; M.S., Boston University; RN.
Mary Anne Gauthier, Associate Professor; Ed.D., Vanderbilt; RN, GNP.
Alice Gervasini, Part-time Instructor; Ph.D., Boston College; RN.
Carol Glod, Assistant Professor; Ph.D., Boston College; MS/RN, CS.
Martha Griffin, Clinical Specialist; Ph.D., Rhode Island; RN.
Patricia Hollen, Associate Professor; Ph.D., Rochester; RN.
Dorett Hope, Associate Professor; Ed.D., Boston University.
Elizabeth P. Howard, Associate Professor; Ph.D., Boston College; RN, ANP.
Barbara R. Kelley, Assistant Professor; Ed.D., Boston University; RN, PNP.
Ann Kennedy, Clinical Specialist; M.S., Catholic University; RN.
Marcia Lynch, Associate Professor; D.N.Sc., Boston University; RN.
Margaret Mahoney, Assistant Professor; Ph.D., Boston College; RN, ANP.
Peggy S. Matteson, Assistant Professor; Ph.D., Boston College; RN.
Patricia M. Meservey, Associate Professor; Ph.D., Boston College; RN.
Kathleen Miller, Assistant Professor; Ed.D., Boston University; RN, ANP.
Virginia Minichiello, Part-time Instructor; M.S.N., Simmons; RNC, COHN.
Abraham Ndiwane, Assistant Professor; Ed.D., Boston Unversity; RN.
Carolyn O'Brien, Lecturer; M.S., Northeastern; RN, ANP.
Frank Palin, Lecturer; M.S.N., Yale; RN, PNP.
Carol Patsdaughter, Assistant Professor; Ph.D., Washington (Seattle); RN.
Howard Rivenson, Part-time Instructor; M.B.A., NYU; CPA.
Susan Roberts, Associate Professor; D.N.Sc., Boston University; RN, ANP.
Carole A. Shea, Associate Professor, Associate Dean, and Director of the Graduate School of Nursing; Ph.D., Rutgers; RN, FAAN.
Lynne Swindler, Adjunct Instructor; M.S., Northeastern; RN, CRNA.
Mary Suzanne Tarmina, Associate Professor; Ph.D., Utah; RN, FNP.
Bruce Weiner, Associate Clinical Professor; M.S., Florida.
Pamela Whitting, Clinical Placement Coordinator; M.S., Adelphi; RN.
Delaine Williamson, Associate Professor; M.P.H., Harvard; RD.
Rachel Zachariah, Associate Professor; D.N.Sc., California, San Francisco.
Eileen H. Zungolo, Professor and Dean of the College of Nursing; Ed.D., Columbia; RN.

PACE UNIVERSITY

Lienhard School of Nursing

Programs of Study The Lienhard School of Nursing offers the M.S. degree, the B.S.N./M.S. Combined Degree Program, the Bridge Program for RNs with a nonnursing bachelor's degree, an accelerated B.S./M.S. program for RNs, and the Certificate of Advanced Graduate Study. The master's program is designed for registered nurses who hold a first professional degree in nursing. Major areas of concentration include adult nursing, family nurse practitioner, psychiatric–mental health nursing, and case management. The program requires completion of 36 credits (39 credits for the family nurse practitioner program) and is open to both full-time and part-time students. It is divided into core courses, functional role courses, and clinical specialty courses. The graduate department also offers a Bridge Program for registered nurses with bachelor's degrees in fields other than nursing. After validation of first professional degree knowledge in nursing, students may enter the M.S. program. The B.S.N./M.S. Combined Degree Program is an accelerated course of study that offers non-nurse college graduates an opportunity to complete baccalaureate education in nursing and to follow through with graduate education in the nursing specialty of their choice in seven semesters of full-time study. (Part-time study is also available.) After completing the B.S.N. in one calendar year, students are eligible to sit for the RN licensure examination (NCLEX). The accelerated B.S./M.S. program for RNs can be completed in as few as six semesters. The Certificate of Advanced Graduate Study, an 18-credit program (24 credits for family nurse practitioner concentration) with a formal route to additional specialization at the master's level, is awarded to students who hold a second professional degree in nursing. Students are prepared for advanced roles in case management, adult and psychiatric–mental health nursing, or as family nurse practitioners. The adult and psychiatric programs are offered at the Pleasantville campus. The family nurse practitioner and case management programs (M.S. and Certificate of Advanced Graduate Study) are offered at the New York City and Pleasantville campuses.

Research Facilities Pace University's totally integrated online library system holds approximately 825,000 volumes and subscribes to nearly 4,000 serial publications. Electronic access to internal and external information and knowledge sources, including locally mounted CD-ROM databases, online retrieval systems, and the Internet, is available. The Pace libraries annually contract with Dialog, BRS, LEXIS-NEXIS, and Dow Jones/News Retrieval to access statistical, bibliographic, directory, and full-text databases covering all major subjects. The University computing network provides access to a range of both mainframe and microcomputing hardware and software. Currently, more than 250 computers are located in academic computing facilities. Pace University's wide-area network (Pace Net) can be accessed from labs, dormitory rooms, and offices. The Center for Nursing Research and Clinical Practice is responsible for facilitating nursing research and clinical practice for the Lienhard School. Its University Health Care Unit offers health-care services to the University community. Inpatient, outpatient, and community health facilities, including medical teaching centers and community hospitals, are used by the School for clinical experience and fieldwork. Geographically, they include sites in Westchester County, Connecticut, the Bronx, Queens, and Manhattan.

Financial Aid A number of graduate scholarships and assistantships are available. Awards are made on the basis of outstanding academic performance. Graduate assistantships are available for full-time and part-time students. Graduate assistants received stipends of up to $5300 for 1997–98 and remission of tuition for up to 24 credits. A variety of deferred payment and loan programs are offered. For further information, students should contact the Financial Aid Office, Pace University, Bedford Road, Pleasantville, New York 10570 or One Pace Plaza, New York, New York 10038.

Cost of Study Tuition for graduate courses in the Lienhard School of Nursing is $500 per credit in 1998–99. Lab fees are charged for clinical courses.

Living and Housing Costs Dormitory rooms at the Pleasantville and New York City campuses of Pace University cost $4520 for the 1998–99 academic year. A wide variety of off-campus housing in the vicinity of either campus is available to graduate students.

Student Group Students in the master's program are experienced nurses who are pursuing advanced knowledge in an area of specialization. Students in the accelerated RN/B.S./M.S. track are practicing RNs seeking to earn their baccalaureate and master's degrees as quickly as possible. Students in the B.S.N./M.S. Combined Degree Program of the Graduate Department are highly motivated individuals with diverse educational backgrounds who seek to enter the nursing profession. Graduates are employed throughout the United States and abroad.

Location The suburban Pleasantville campus is easily accessible by car, bus, and railroad commuter service and is surrounded by towns and villages that have gifted artisans, musical and theatrical groups, museums, retail centers, and corporate headquarters. The New York City campus is located in downtown Manhattan near the South Street Seaport and the World Trade Center. Pace's new state-of-the-art Midtown Center is located on Fifth Avenue in proximity to the landmark Grand Central Station.

The University Founded in 1906, Pace University is a comprehensive, diversified, coeducational institution with campuses in New York City and Westchester County. In 1948, Pace Institute became Pace College; in 1973, the State Board of Regents approved a charter change to designate Pace a university, offering degrees through the Dyson College of Arts and Sciences, the School of Computer Science and Information Systems, the Lubin School of Business Administration, the College of White Plains, the School of Education, the Lienhard School of Nursing, the Lubin Graduate School of Business, and the School of Law.

Applying Admission to the B.S.N./M.S. Combined Degree Program requires satisfactory completion of a baccalaureate program at an accredited institution and completion of the GRE General Test or the Miller Analogies Test. Applications for the B.S.N./M.S. Combined Degree Program must be filed by March 1 to start the nursing sequence in the summer. Applicants for the master's program must have satisfactorily completed an NLN-approved baccalaureate nursing program and the GRE General Test or the Miller Analogies Test, and must have RN licensure. Completion of one year of nursing practice is also recommended. Registered nurses with a bachelor's degree in an area other than nursing are admitted to a Bridge Program pending satisfactory validation of first-professional-degree knowledge in nursing. Applications for the M.S. program must be completed by August 1 for the fall, December 1 for the spring, and May 1 for the summer semester.

Correspondence and Information

Office of Graduate Admission
Pace University
1 Martine Avenue
White Plains, New York 10606
Telephone: 914-422-4283
Fax: 914-422-4287
E-mail: gradwp@pace.edu

Office of Graduate Admission
Pace University
1 Pace Plaza
New York, New York 10038
Telephone: 212-346-1531
Fax: 212-346-1585
E-mail: gradnyc@pace.edu

Pace University

THE FACULTY AND THEIR RESEARCH

Patricia Blagman, Associate Professor and Chairperson, Combined Degree Program; Ed.D., Columbia Teachers College, 1979. Decision making in professional practice, pain, healing.
David Ekstrom, Assistant Professor; Ph.D., NYU, 1995. Gender and nurse caring, nursing via the Internet, international exchanges in nursing education.
Harriet R. Feldman, Professor; Ph.D., NYU, 1984; FAAN. Pain perception and management.
Louise Gallagher, Associate Professor; Ed.D., Columbia Teachers College, 1985. Clinical performance examination, health promotion.
Susan Gordon, Professor and Chairperson, RN/B.S. Program; Ed.D., Columbia Teachers College, 1972. Medical/surgical nursing, psychiatric nursing, stress and aging, baccalaureate education for registered nurses.
Martha Greenberg, Assistant Professor; Ph.D., NYU, 1995. Humor, displaced nurses.
Karen Anderson Keith, Assistant Professor; Ph.D., Adelphi, 1992. Family primary care, primary health care.
Catherine Kelleher, Associate Professor and Director of Research and Project Evaluation; Sc.D., Johns Hopkins, 1985. Health services research.
Suwersh Khanna, Assistant Professor; Ed.D., Columbia Teachers College, 1979. History of nursing in India, AIDS.
Sandra Lewenson, Associate Professor; Ed.D., Columbia Teachers College, 1989. Historical research, nursing's role in the women's movement, community health, accreditation.
Diana J. Mason, Professor; Ph.D., NYU, 1987; FAAN. Health services research, health policy.
Helen P. Neuhs, Professor; Ph.D., NYU, 1984. Self-esteem and aging, women and retirement, variables influencing adjustment in retirement.
Alice O'Flynn, Associate Professor and Chairperson, CNS Program; Ph.D., Connecticut, 1982. Evaluative research, eating disorders.
Ellen Rich, Assistant Professor and Chairperson, Family Nurse Practitioner Program; Ph.D., Adelphi, 1997; FNP. Primary care, health promotion, stress management, self-efficiency.
Paula Scharf, Associate Professor; Ph.D., NYU, 1986. Burnout, predictors of success for baccalaureate students.
Lillie Shortridge-Baggett, Professor and Director of the Center for Scholarship, Development and International Affairs; Ed.D., Columbia Teachers College, 1977; FAAN. Family stress and coping, health behaviors, nurse practitioner clinical competencies, homeless families.
Joanne Singleton, Assistant Professor; Ph.D., Adelphi, 1993. Family primary care, self-care.
Barbara Stewart, Professor; Ph.D., NYU, 1973. Psychosocial responses to cancer, family communication patterns during the cancer experience, effects on families of persons with AIDS.
Shirlee A. Stokes, Professor; Ed.D., Columbia Teachers College, 1972; FAAN. Stress and aging, health promotion for the aged.
Edilma Yearwood, Instructor; Ph.D., Adelphi, 1997. Child-rearing practices among immigrant and minority populations, resilience in at-risk children and adolescents, factors affecting minority mental health

QUINNIPIAC COLLEGE

Nurse Practitioner Program

Programs of Study

The Nurse Practitioner Program at Quinnipiac College prepares professional nurses for advanced practice in nursing within diverse health-care facilities and to assume clinical management and leadership positions as primary health-care providers across the adult life span. Interdisciplinary in nature, this challenging curriculum combines classroom learning, hands-on practice, and supervised clinical experiences to provide registered nurses with a broad-based appreciation of the holistic nature of care and caring. One outstanding characteristic of the program is the deliberate focus on collaborative education across multiple health-care disciplines. Nursing, pathologists' assistant studies, and physician assistant studies students find themselves learning together in preparation for the realities of working together in clinical settings.

Upon successful completion of the program, students earn a Master of Science in Nursing (M.S.N.) degree, and they are prepared to take the ANA's Nurse Practitioner Adult Health Certification exam. They are also qualified to take the pharmacology exam to become licensed as advanced practice registered nurses (APRN).

Designed to span two full-time summers and two full-time or four half-time academic years, the curriculum comprises a required sequence of core courses, clinical practicums and an internship, and a thesis or integrated research project, for a total of 58 credit hours. The course of study is divided into three broad areas. The graduate core involves the study of research, policy, theory, role, organizational theory, family theory, community-based care, cultural diversity, ethics, health-care economics, and managed care. The advanced practice clinical core covers health assessment, pharmacology, pathophysiology, clinical decision making, health promotion/disease prevention, and community-based practice. The nurse practitioner core addresses specialty management content and specialty role content.

Because nurses today work in a wide variety of health-care environments and in a time marked by profound changes in the organization and financing of health care, attention is also given to the cultural, social, technological, and economic influences on public policy and health-care management. Those already in nursing find that the diversity and wealth of the curriculum significantly advance their knowledge and skills in the areas of critical thinking, judgment, collaboration, consultation, and inquiry.

Research Facilities

Quinnipiac College has all of the facilities and support systems essential for a professional graduate program in nursing. The state-of-the-art Clinical Skills Laboratory, Computer Laboratory, and Echlin Health Sciences Center, all on the main campus, are the primary sites for clinical skills practice and some of the course work. The Clinical Skills Laboratory is a well-equipped simulation of a hospital setting, complete with interactive television, monitor equipment, mannequins, and patient care areas. Two of the rooms can be adjusted to simulate other clinical settings, such as intensive care.

Financial Aid

Several avenues are available to help both full- and part-time students fund their education. Students may be eligible for Federal Stafford Student Loans. Graduate assistantships are available on a limited basis to both full- and part-time students.

Cost of Study

In 1998–99, the tuition rate is $395 per credit hour. Part-time students pay a $20 registration fee each semester. Full-time students are charged a student fee of $185 per semester. The College offers a variety of payment plans, including deferred payment and installment programs, and coordinates employer reimbursement programs.

Living and Housing Costs

On-campus housing is available during the summer. Privately owned housing is available near the campus. For more information concerning off-campus housing, interested students should contact the Office of Residential Life at 203-281-8666.

Student Group

The Nurse Practitioner Program at Quinnipiac began in the fall of 1998.

Location

Quinnipiac is located on a beautiful campus in Hamden, Connecticut, a suburb of New Haven. It is 30 minutes from Hartford, 1½ hours from New York City, and 2 hours from Boston.

The College

Quinnipiac enrolls 3,310 full-time undergraduates and approximately 1,300 graduate students. The College comprises the Schools of Health Sciences, Business, Law, and Liberal Arts and the College for Adults. A dean, reporting to the Provost/Vice President for Academic Affairs, heads each of these units, and a distinguished faculty of 170 full-time members and nearly 100 adjunct members provides instruction for the programs of the College.

Applying

Applicants to the Nurse Practitioner Program must be graduates of accredited baccalaureate programs of nursing who are registered and licensed nurses and who have been in clinical practice for at least one year. Confirmation of licensure must be on file in the Department of Nursing.

In addition to submitting the Quinnipiac College Graduate School application and official college transcripts, candidates for this program are required to provide information specific to their nursing careers, such as current license number(s) and evidence of malpractice insurance, and to submit the results of the Miller Analogies Test and three letters of recommendation. Candidates should have an overall GPA of at least 3.0. International applicants must also submit an official copy of recent results of the TOEFL.

As of 1999, classes will begin in the summer only for this program. The application deadline is April 15. Interviews are scheduled on a selected basis and may occur on a weekend.

Correspondence and Information

Office of Graduate Admissions
Quinnipiac College
275 Mount Carmel Avenue
Hamden, Connecticut 06518
Telephone: 203-281-8672
800-462-1944 (toll-free)
Fax: 203-287-5238
E-mail: qcgradadmi@quinnipiac.edu

Quinnipiac College

THE FACULTY AND THEIR RESEARCH

Joy Ruth Cohen, Ph.D., Walden; RN, CNM, CNAA. Transformational leadership, rehabilitation nursing.
Jeanne LeVasseur, M.S.N., Ph.D., Connecticut; APRN. Art of nursing, women's health.

RUSH UNIVERSITY

College of Nursing

Programs of Study

Rush University's College of Nursing is committed to providing excellence in professional education for nurses. The education of students is facilitated by the unification of the academic and clinical practice components of the health-care system. This unique integration stimulates excellence in education, practice, scholarly activities, and professional leadership by the faculty members and the graduates of the College of Nursing.

The College of Nursing offers four graduate options: the Master of Science in Nursing (M.S.N.) degree, the Post-Master's Option, the Doctor of Nursing (N.D.) degree, and the Doctor of Nursing Science (D.N.Sc.) degree. The master's degree study option focuses on clinical specialist and nurse practitioner roles, with intensive examination of the biological and behavioral sciences and their application within the context of nursing practice, education, and research. Degree requirements include courses in nursing theory, advanced practice role, biostatistics, research, and biological and behavioral sciences. Clinical seminars and practice are required in the area of concentration. Advanced practice options include acute-care, adult, anesthesia, critical-care, community health, genetic health, gerontology, high-risk perinatal, HIV/oncology, medical-surgical, neonatal, pediatric, psychiatric, rehabilitation, and women's health nursing. A minimum of 55 quarter hours of credit are needed for the M.S.N. degree. Graduates are eligible for certification exams in the various areas of specialization. A dual M.S.N./M.M. degree is available in conjunction with the Kellogg School of Management at Northwestern University. Post-master's nurse practitioner preparation is available in the areas of acute-care, adult, gerontologic, neonatal, and pediatric nursing.

The Doctor of Nursing option prepares nurses to function as advanced practitioners, integrating the role of teacher, consultant, and manager of clinical practice. Doctor of Nursing students learn to initiate clinical research utilization studies. The same specialty areas available at the master's level are available at the N.D. level. The community (family) nurse practitioner option is available at the N.D. level only. A minimum of 85 quarter hours of postbaccalaureate graduate study are needed to complete the N.D. degree.

The Doctor of Nursing Science curriculum prepares expert clinicians with the investigative skills of researchers and the leadership skills necessary to influence health-care systems and develop health policy. Core courses in research, theory, and role development are combined with cognate studies and clinical practicums. The clinical practicums are individually designed courses to help students explore their phenomena of interest. The D.N.Sc. degree can be pursued in a summer option. Summer D.N.Sc. students must enroll full-time their first three summers in the College. At least 125 quarter hours of postbaccalaureate graduate study, exclusive of the dissertation, are required for the D.N.Sc. degree.

Research Facilities

Excellent facilities for clinical nursing research include the Rush-Presbyterian–St. Luke's Medical Center inpatient, outpatient, and home-care units; the interdisciplinary biological science laboratories; and the resources of the Rush System for Health. Also, a well-equipped McCormick Educational Technology Center and Rush University Library are used by all D.N.Sc. students. The Department of Nursing Services Research and Support is a resource for students and faculty members in research efforts.

Financial Aid

Financial aid at Rush is awarded on the basis of demonstrated financial need. Financial aid includes state, federal, institutional, and other funds that may be available. Full- and part-time students may apply for assistance. All who seek aid must complete the Free Application for Federal Student Aid for determination of financial need. Federal Professional Nurse Traineeships and some institutional awards are available for qualified graduate students. Predoctoral and postdoctoral research fellowships are also available.

Cost of Study

Tuition rates for the 1997–98 school year were $4035 per year or $354 per quarter hour for graduate students. The cost for books was approximately $880 per year. Medical insurance is required.

Living and Housing Costs

The student living on campus should allow $1020 per month for rent, food, transportation, and personal expenses. The student living off campus should allow $1300 per month.

Student Group

Students in the College are a diverse group in terms of age, ethnic background, and experience. Most of the graduate students hold full-time positions in health-care organizations and attend school on a part-time basis. The students actively participate in College governance by serving on faculty committees. Students also maintain their own organizations and participate in many public service activities, sometimes in collaboration with other University students and outside professional organizations. Enrollment in the College continues to grow. The current enrollment of 650 includes 345 graduate students.

Graduates have assumed a wide variety of professional positions both locally and nationally, including clinical, education, research, and administration employment opportunities.

Location

The main campus of the University/Medical Center is located on the west side of Chicago, not far from downtown and the lakefront, where numerous cultural and recreational activities can be found. Rush is in the Medical Center District, which includes the University of Illinois West Campus, Cook County Hospital, Westside Veterans Administration Hospital, and the Illinois State Psychiatric Institute. Rush is surrounded by new town homes, condominiums, restaurants, and businesses. The area provides easy access to public transportation.

The University

Rush University is the academic component of Rush-Presbyterian–St. Luke's Medical Center. Founded in 1972, the University has expanded from one college and fewer than 100 students to four colleges and more than 1,400 students. It includes Rush Medical College, the College of Nursing, the College of Health Sciences, and the Graduate College. The purpose of Rush University is to educate students as practitioners, scientists, and teachers who will become leaders in advancing health care and to further the advancement of knowledge through research. As a major component of Rush-Presbyterian–St. Luke's Medical Center, the University integrates patient care, education, and research through the practitioner-teacher model. Rush University encourages the growth of its students by committing itself to the pursuit of excellence, to free inquiry, and to the highest intellectual and ethical standards.

Applying

Each applicant must provide the Admissions Office with a complete application, a $40 application fee, three recommendations, official transcripts of all undergraduate and graduate work, results of the GRE General Test (unless the student has earned a master's degree), and a photocopy of his or her nursing license. If a major portion of prior education was not taken in an English-speaking school, successful completion of the TOEFL and TWE are required.

Correspondence and Information

College Admissions Services
Rush University
600 South Paulina, Suite 440
Chicago, Illinois 60612-3824

Telephone: 312-942-7100
World Wide Web: http://www.rpslmc.edu/RushU/nursing.html

Rush University

FACULTY RESEARCH AREAS

Faculty members of the College of Nursing embrace Rush University's commitment to achieving national and international leadership in setting standards of excellence in patient care, education, research, and management. Faculty members are currently involved in a variety of research studies, including individual and interdisciplinary collaborative projects that will have an impact on current health practices. Research projects, publications, and scholarly presentations attest to the faculty's regional, national, and international involvement.

Faculty members of the College of Nursing at Rush University maintain a high level of research and scholarly productivity. Current faculty research endeavors include twenty-one federally funded grants; thirty-one foundation, government, or association-funded grants; eighteen College of Nursing–funded grants; and seven department-supported projects. The following list provides some examples of the research and training projects in which the faculty members are currently involved.

Physiological Responses in Health and Illness

Using the Braden Scale to Predict Ulcer Risk in a Critically Ill Population. E. Carlson, M. Kemp (American Association of Critical Care Nurses; Kinetics Concepts, Inc.).

Nutritional Support in Early HIV Infection. R. Hershow, J. Keithly, S. Leurgans, B. Sha, B. Swanson, P. Urbanski, J. Zeller (University of Illinois at Chicago); M. Schwarber (University of Illinois); R. Novak (University of Illinois at Chicago); J. Fitzpatrick (Cook County Hospital). (National Institute of Nursing Research, NIH).

cAMP and Protection Against Endothelial Barrier Dysfunction. J. Podolski (American Lung Association and American Lung Association of Metropolitan Chicago).

Functional Benefits to Aerobic Training After Stroke. K. Potempa (University of Illinois), L. Braun, M. Lopez, P. Szidon (National Institute of Nursing Research, NIH).

Pilot Study of Physiological Markers of Chronic Stress in Premenopausal Women. A. Baum, W. Lovallo, K. Matthews, J. McCann, R. Midgley, M. Ory, L. Powell, A. Stone (Fitzer Institute).

The Impact of Early, Minimal Enteral Feedings on Gut Colonization and Infection in Low Birth-Weight Infants. F. Strodbeck (Foundation for Neonatal Research and Education).

Altered Immunocompetence Nursing Specialization Training Grant. S. Brozenec, C. Farran, A. Keenan, J. Keithley, P. Kelly, R. Wickham, J. Zeller (Division of Nursing, Department of Health and Human Services).

Behavioral and Psychological Responses in Health and Illness

Alzheimer's Disease Center Core Grant. L. Beckett, D. Bennett, E. Cochran, D. Evans, C. J. Farran (National Institute of Aging).

Ethical Decision-Making By Certified Registered Nurse Anesthetists. M. Bosek (American Association of Nurse Anesthetists Foundation).

Managing Cognitive Impairment in Hospitalized Elderly. D. Cronin-Stubbs (National Institute of Mental Health).

Longitudinal Study of Four Types of AD Special-Care Units. D. Bennett, D. Evans, C. Farran, D. Gilley, J. McCann, R. Wilson (National Institute on Aging).

Perceptions of Physicians Regarding Neonatal Resuscitation of Very Low and Extremely Low Birth-Weight Infants. A. Catlin, S. Faux (American Academy of Pediatrics).

Efficacy of Community-Based Parent/Teacher Training. L. Fogg, J. Grady, D. Gross (National Institute for Nursing Research).

Parent Participation in a Prevention Trial. D. Gross (National Institute for Nursing Research).

Needs and Interventions of Early-Stage Alzheimer's Disease Caregivers. C. Farran, D. Kuhn, D. Lindeman (Helen Bader Foundation).

Pain Intervention for Children with Sickle Cell Disease. M. Broome, V. Maikler (National Institutes of Health).

Health-Care Services Research

Nurse Anesthetist Training Program. M. Faut-Callahan (Department of Health and Human Services, Health Resources Services Administration, Division of Nursing).

Improving Patient-Centered Care Through Initiatives in Nursing: Phase Two. A. Minnick (The Picker/Commonwealth Fund).

Pilsen Homeless Clinic. L. Edwards, K. Scoulis (VNA Foundation of Chicago).

Quality-of-Life Outcomes in Patients with a HeartMate LVAD. M. Costanza-Nordin, D. Dressler, K. Grady, A. Kaan, A. Mattea, L. Ohler, W. Piccione, B. Todd, C. White-Williams (American Heart Association National Grant-in-Aid).

Age and Gender Differences in Heart Transplant Outcomes. R. Bourge, M. Costanza-Nordin, K. Grady, A. Jalowiec, J. Kirklin, R. Pifarre, C. White-Williams (National Institutes of Health; National Institute of Nursing Research).

Exploring Outcomes After Critical Illness in the Elderly. R. Kleinpell (National Institute of Nursing Research).

Longitudinal Study of Acute Care Nurse Practitioners. R. Kleinpell (American Nurses Foundation; College of Nursing Research Resource Fund).

Acute Care Nurse Practitioner Training Grant. S. Brozenec, L. Hollinger-Smith, J. Keithley, K. Kowalski, D. LaRochelle, K. Lauer, J. Llewellyn, S. Naber, F. Strodtbeck (National Institute of Nursing Research, NIH).

Implications of the Geneticization of Health Care for Primary Care Practitioners. M. Lessick, M. Mahowald (University of Chicago) (U.S. Department of Energy, Office of Health and Environmental Research, Human Genome Program).

Breast-Feeding Services for Low Birth-Weight Infants: Outcome and Cost. P. Meier (National Institute for Nursing Research through the University of Pennsylvania).

Physical Restraint Reduction in Acute Care Settings. K. Lamb, A. Minnick, L. Mion, R. Palmer (Community Foundations).

Parent Perceptions of the Needs of Physically, Mentally or Handicapped Children in the School System. S. Faux, J. Smith (Beta Omega Chapter, Sigma Theta Tau).

UNIVERSITY OF ALABAMA AT BIRMINGHAM

School of Nursing

Program of Study

The School of Nursing offers graduate studies leading to the Master of Science of Nursing (M.S.N.) and Doctor of Science in Nursing (D.S.N.). The master's program educates baccalaureate-prepared nurses for advanced nursing practice as nurse practitioners or for positions dealing with outcomes measurement and health-care improvement. Advanced study is available for those selecting primary care in one of the following areas: adult nursing, family nursing, gerontological nursing, pediatric nursing, and women's health nursing. Students in adult nursing may elect further concentration in occupational health or oncology. Students selecting acute care and continuing care as their practice area must concentrate their advanced study in adult nursing and may select an area of focus such as cardiovascular, neuroscience, or trauma nursing. Clinical experiences and support courses that complement the focus area are determined for the individual student's program of study and are based on availability of experiences and courses. In addition, a coordinated degree offering between the School of Nursing and the School of Public Health is available; this degree allows the student to complete the master's degree as a pediatric or women's health practitioner jointly with the public health offering in maternal child health. Postmaster's study for M.S.N. graduates who are seeking nurse practitioner preparation is available in primary care. Master's graduates who have clinical specialization preparation may focus on adult, pediatric, or family nursing. The doctoral program educates persons with the master's degree in nursing for professional practice as educators, administrators, and health policy analysts or as leaders in the practitioner role. The doctoral curriculum includes course work in nursing, research, and role preparation and prepares graduates to contribute to nursing and human knowledge of the health field, make connections across disciplines, apply nursing and health-related knowledge responsibly to consequential health problems, and acquire, transform, and transmit nursing knowledge. To help evaluate the progress of doctoral study, a qualifying examination is given after 12 credits of required course work is completed, and a comprehensive exam is given during the final quarter of course work. Upon successful completion of the comprehensive examination and approval of a dissertation proposal by the student's graduate committee, the student is admitted to candidacy and completes the dissertation. The degree is awarded primarily on the basis of the dissertation, which describes original research in an area related to the student's professional preparation in the program. The usual length of the entire D.S.N. program is four years.

Research Facilities

The School of Nursing houses a state-of-the-art Center for Nursing Research (CNR), which promotes research in nursing and supports the research goals of the school and the University. The CNR provides office, work, and conference space for research activities, and a research suite for clinical nursing research. The research suite includes examining rooms, utility space, a wet laboratory, and a video suite. Services provided to faculty members and graduate students through the CNR include assistance and consultation for all phases of the research process, research funding, and research dissemination. In addition to the School of Nursing's resources, strong collaborative relationships exist with many other research centers across campus, including the Center for Health Promotion, the Center for Aging, the Comprehensive Cancer Center, and the Civitan International Research Center. Numerous health-care facilities on the UAB campus provide opportunities for clinical nursing research. In addition, School of Nursing faculty provide health screening services to City of Birmingham employees and are involved in health-care research in the community.

Financial Aid

Appointments as graduate teaching (annual stipend of $5250) or research assistantships (annual stipend of $8000) are available to graduate students, and UAB Academic Health Center Fellowships are available to doctoral students. When professional nurse traineeships funds are available and students are eligible, these supplementary funds provide support for tuition and fees for master's and doctoral students. Additional sources of support include scholarships from the Alabama Board of Nursing, the School of Nursing, and Sigma Theta Tau; national research service awards for predoctoral nursing fellowships; and part-time employment.

Cost of Study

The 1997–98 cost of tuition was $96 per semester hour for Alabama residents and $192 per semester hour for out-of-state residents. Additional fees (such as professional nursing tuition and student services) are levied on a per semester hour basis, and others (such as building, student health, and liability insurance fees) on a per term basis. In addition, an annual fee is charged for hospitalization insurance. Certain other special fees are billed for circumstances such as applying for admission and graduation. Tuition and fees are subject to change at the beginning of any term.

Living and Housing Costs

UAB offers a number of reasonably priced apartment units for on-campus residence, including Hixson Hall, a dormitory facility adjacent to the School of Nursing. The Housing Office also provides information on off-campus housing. For information, students can contact the Housing Office (1604 Ninth Avenue South; telephone: 205-934-2092). Since there is a waiting list, students should apply early for on-campus housing.

Student Group

The total number of students enrolled in master's study in nursing is currently about 200. Doctoral students number about 100. A wide variety of academic, ethnic, national and international backgrounds, and life circumstances are represented among these students. About two thirds of master's students are enrolled full-time; one third of doctoral students are enrolled full-time. The School of Nursing seeks qualified applicants from diverse backgrounds.

Student Outcomes

Master's graduates hold positions as nurse practitioners in the health-care delivery system in both urban and rural settings, in institutional and community sectors, in acute and primary care divisions or as outcomes managers, case managers, or quality review managers. Doctoral graduates are employed in academic or health-care delivery settings and serve as leaders and scholars.

Location

UAB is a comprehensive institution in Birmingham, an exciting, growing city in the foothills of the Appalachians and an urban center of great natural beauty. The hospitality of the people and the temperate climate complement a wide variety of educational offerings, cultural and entertainment activities, and sporting events. Health care and education have replaced heavy industry as Birmingham's economic base, and UAB is now the city's leading employer.

The University and The School

UAB, a city within a city covering 70 square blocks, was established in 1969 as an autonomous university within the University of Alabama System. It now serves as one of the nation's top-ranked universities in research support, higher education, and the provision of world-class health care. The School of Nursing is one of six schools in the UAB Academic Health Sciences Center. The master's program was established in 1955, and the Doctor of Science in Nursing degree was approved by the Board of Trustees in 1975. The School of Nursing was ranked seventeenth by *U.S. News & World Report* among more than 200 graduate nursing programs in the nation and is one of seven World Health Organizations Collaborating Centers for International Nursing in the United States.

Applying

Complete official transcripts, GRE scores, and references and interviews are required of all applicants for graduate study. All applicants to graduate study should contact UAB Student Affairs Office, 1701 University Boulevard, School of Nursing Building, Room 105, Birmingham, Alabama 35294-1210. M.S.N. application materials must be received by December 5, 1997 for spring 1998 admission. Applications for post-master's study must be received by September 13, 1997 for spring 1998 admission. D.S.N. applicants should contact UAB Graduate School, 1400 University Boulevard, Hill University Center 511, Birmingham, Alabama 35294-1150. D.S.N. application materials must be received by July 7, 1998 for fall 1998 admission. Other deadlines are available on request.

Correspondence and Information

Dr. Lynda Harrison, Associate Dean of Graduate Studies
School of Nursing Building, Room 108
University of Alabama at Birmingham
1701 University Boulevard
Birmingham, Alabama 35294-1210
Telephone: 205-934-3485
E-mail: harrisol@admin.son.uab.edu
World Wide Web: http://www.uab.edu/son/sonintr2.htm

University of Alabama at Birmingham

THE FACULTY AND THEIR RESEARCH

Rachel Booth, Professor; Ph.D., Maryland, 1978; Administration of higher education, leadership, primary care.
Kathleen Brown, Professor; Ph.D., Case Western Reserve, 1981. Community health nursing, occupational health, back injury prevention.
Joan Carlisle, Assistant Professor; D.S.N., Alabama at Birmingham, 1991. Child health promotion.
Ann Clark, Associate Professor; Ph.D., Chicago, 1981. Women's health, alternative therapies.
Ruth Cox, Assistant Professor; Ph.D., Florida State, 1990. Delinquency, family health.
Priscilla Daffin, Assistant Professor; D.S.N., Alabama at Birmingham, 1988. Oncology prevention and screening; pain and suffering.
Carol Dashiff, Professor; Ph.D., Florida State, 1978. Family processes, parenting, adolescent autonomy, and chronic conditions.
Linda Davis, Professor; Ph.D., Maryland, 1985. Family systems, caregiving and chronic illness.
Anne Edgil, Professor; D.S.N., Alabama at Birmingham, 1980. Adolescent health care, school health nursing.
Juanzetta Flowers, Associate Professor; D.S.N., Alabama at Birmingham, 1985. Women's health, health policy, international nursing.
Anne Foote, Associate Professor; D.S.N., Alabama at Birmingham, 1985. Nursing education, neuroscience nursing.
Pamela Fordham, Assistant Professor; D.S.N., Alabama at Birmingham, 1989. Primary health care, death and dying, nursing education.
Dorothy Gauthier, Associate Professor; Ph.D., Massachusetts, 1967. Pathophysiology, psychoneuroimmunology, nursing interventions.
Joyce Newman Giger, Professor; Ed.D., Ball State, 1986. Risk reduction in African-American women.
Joan Grant, Associate Professor; D.S.N., Alabama at Birmingham, 1989. Nursing diagnosis, family caregiving.
Lynda Harrison, Professor; Ph.D., Tennessee, 1982. Effects of human touch on pre-term infants, maternal-child health, parenting.
Gail Hill, Assistant Professor; Ph.D., Alabama at Birmingham, 1984. Health systems, acute care.
Duck-Hee Kang, Assistant Professor; Ph.D., Wisconsin, 1993. Psychoneuroimmunology, immune responses and stress in asthmatic children and adolescents and in cancer patients.
Norman Keltner, Associate Professor; Ed.D., San Francisco, 1981. Psychopharmacology, psychiatric nursing.
Mable Lamb, Associate Professor; D.S.N., Alabama at Birmingham, 1983. Nursing service and job motivation, nursing care of children.
Alberta McCaleb, Assistant Professor; D.S.N., Alabama at Birmingham, 1991. Self-care activities and health promotion in adolescents.
Linda Miers, Assistant Professor; D.S.N., Alabama at Birmingham, 1993. Nurse caring behaviors, Roy adaptation model.
Kathleen Mikan, Professor; Ph.D., Michigan State, 1972. Instructional development, health education media, informatics, telehealth.
Marilyn Musacchio, Associate Professor; Ph.D., Case Western Reserve, 1993. Nurse-midwifery.
Penelope Paul, Associate Professor; D.S.N., Alabama at Birmingham, 1981. Gerontology, elders with dementia and their caregivers.
Judy Pemberton, Assistant Professor; Ph.D., Alabama at Birmingham, 1993. Outcomes measurement, quality improvement, patient/ stakeholder satisfaction.
Jennan Phillips, Assistant Professor; D.S.N., Alabama at Birmingham, 1991. Occupational health.
Victoria Poole, Assistant Professor; D.S.N., Alabama at Birmingham, 1991. Pregnancy intendedness, women's health, family planning.
Mary Lynn Reilly, Assistant Professor; D.S.N., Alabama at Birmingham, 1985. Nursing education, maternal infant nursing.
Marti Rice, Assistant Professor; Ph.D., Georgia State, 1990. Anger, stress, blood pressure, exercise, and cardiovascular risk in children and adolescents.
Barbara A. Smith, Professor and O'Koren Endowed Chair; Ph.D., Ohio State, 1986. Exercise physiology and health promotion in children and patients with AIDS.
Mary Colette Smith, Professor; Ph.D., Maryland, 1970. Adult health, meta-analysis, Orem theory in research.
Ann Turner-Henson, Associate Professor; D.S.N., Alabama at Birmingham, 1992. Children with special health-care needs, caregiving within families.
Joan Turner, Professor; D.S.N., Alabama at Birmingham, 1983. Prevention and control of infectious and communicable diseases.
Mary Umlauf, Associate Professor; Ph.D., Texas, Austin, 1983. Gerontology, incontinence.
Michael Weaver, Associate Professor; Ph.D., Toledo, 1990. Health promotion, community health, biostatistics.
Anne Williams, Assistant Professor; Ph.D., Austin, 1986. Stroke victims, caregiving.
Roma Williams, Assistant Professor; Ph.D., Texas Woman's, 1986. Women's health, health promotion, disease prevention.
Penelope Wright, Associate Professor; Ph.D., Northwestern, 1988. Pediatric oncology, quality of life.

University of Alabama School of Nursing.

Dr. Rachel Booth (center), Dean, and four doctoral student honorees.

UNIVERSITY OF KENTUCKY

College of Nursing

Programs of Study

A Master of Science in Nursing degree prepares nurses for the advanced practice of nursing in a particular clinical specialty. The program leading to the degree is designed to build on the first professional degree and focuses on nursing theory, research, and practice.

Students may specialize in adult nursing (adult client, gerontology, critical care, oncology, ER/trauma, nurse case manager, or acute care nurse practitioner), psychiatric nursing (adult client, geropsychiatric, or substance abuse), parent-child nursing (children, adolescents, and families; pediatric nurse practitioner; or neonatal-perinatal), or community health (community health administration, family nurse practitioner, geriatric nurse practitioner, adult nurse practitioner, community nursing clinical specialist, or nurse case manager).

Many University of Kentucky (UK) College of Nursing students continue to pursue their nursing careers while working toward a graduate degree. Through flexible scheduling and selected evening courses, such graduate students are able to obtain a degree.

The Post Graduate Clinical Scholars program offers nurses who have master's and doctoral degrees an opportunity to obtain knowledge and skills necessary to become nationally certified as family nurse practitioners, gerontological nurse practitioners, adult nurse practitioners (primary care), pediatric nurse practitioners, acute care nurse practitioners, nurse case managers, or advanced practice psychiatric nurses. This program offers graduate credit.

The Doctor of Philosophy in Nursing prepares nurse scholars to assume roles as researchers, educators, and administrators. Doctoral course work is interdisciplinary. It provides a foundation for the development of nursing knowledge through the conduct of clinical research significant to nursing practice. Graduate education at the doctoral level is an immersion into a community of scholars. It requires a commitment to the advancement of nursing knowledge through research. Mentoring by faculty members and collegial interactions among doctoral students support the development of nurse scholars. Student dissertation research has focused on topics such as pain in the preterm neonate, rehabilitation of amputee farmers, coping of women with breast cancer, caregivers of the chronically mentally ill, and the effectiveness of critical pathways in providing nursing care. Research within the College focuses on two emphasis areas: prevention and management of chronic health problems and health services care delivery research.

Research Facilities

The nationally ranked College of Nursing is located in the Chandler Medical Center, which includes the Colleges of Allied Health Professions, Dentistry, Medicine, and Pharmacy as well as the 470-bed University of Kentucky Hospital. The College of Nursing occupies a modern facility that contains research and computer laboratories staffed with faculty and support personnel. Information and consultation services in grant and research issues are available for students and faculty members. In addition to the University of Kentucky Hospital, a large Veterans Affairs Hospital, five community hospitals, and numerous local health-care agencies offer rich teaching and research opportunities. Libraries on campus provide on-site support and computer capability to expedite bibliographic searches.

Financial Aid

A limited number of Professional Nurse Traineeships from the Division of Nursing, United States Public Health Service, are available to graduate students. The traineeship pays tuition for two full-time students who are enrolled in the program. A limited number of fellowships and assistantships are available. The assistantships provide wages for guided research and teaching; tuition grants may be awarded for meritorious scholarship.

Doctoral students are assisted in applying for National Research Service Awards from the National Institute of Nursing Research, National Institutes of Health, and other fellowship and dissertation awards. The University is a member of the Academic Common Market.

Cost of Study

In 1997–98, graduate registration fees were $147 per semester hour up to a maximum of $1320 per semester for Kentucky residents and $440 per semester hour up to a maximum of $3960 for nonresidents. A $168 mandatory registration fee is charged to all full-time students each semester.

Living and Housing Costs

The cost of an on-campus food plan for single students was $650 per semester in 1997–98. On-campus apartment housing, which includes adequate basic furnishings, utilities, and maintenance, costs an estimated $322 per month for an efficiency, $403 for one bedroom, and $420–$520 for two bedrooms.

Student Group

The University student body is made up of 17,099 undergraduates, 5,399 graduate students, and 1,834 professional students on the campus in Lexington. The College of Nursing has 165 M.S.N. graduate students, 18 postgraduate students, and 35 doctoral students.

Location

The University is located in Lexington, in the heart of the Kentucky Bluegrass country. More than 400 horse farms are located within a 20-mile radius of the city, which has a population of approximately 250,000. Kentucky's scenic Cumberland Mountains are 30 miles east of Lexington, and both Louisville and Cincinnati are within a 2-hour drive of the campus. Kentucky's forty state and national parks include some of the finest in the nation. Three of these parks, Boonesboro, Natural Bridge, and Old Fort Harrod, are within a 45-minute drive of the University. Lexington has an average annual temperature of 55°F.

The University

The University of Kentucky is a land-grant university founded in 1865. It began offering graduate work in 1870 and first awarded graduate degrees in 1876. The Chandler Medical Center is located on the main campus of the University, thus providing easy access to all of the University's resources. The University is committed to programs of teaching, research, and public service. It is particularly interested in improving and expanding its programs of advanced study and research and is designated a Research I University by the Carnegie Foundation, one of only fifty-nine public universities in the country designated as research-intensive. Students have an opportunity for specialization and the pursuit of a particular interest in ten colleges, including the College of Nursing.

Applying

Applications for admission to the master's program should be completed by March 1. After this date, applicants are considered on a space-available basis. Applications for admission to the doctoral program should be completed by August 15 for spring admission and January 15 for fall admission. Applications are processed as received and completed. Criteria for entry include, but are not limited to, graduation from a B.S.N. program accredited by the NLN or its equivalent, a GPA of at least 2.7 postbaccalaureate or 3.3 post-master's, nursing licensure, and completion of the General Test of the Graduate Record Examinations. Admission is based upon qualifications as evidenced in the application, transcripts, professional references, and interviews. Admission to the Ph.D. program is based on the application, including a goal statement, GRE scores, GPA (master's), professional references, and faculty interviews.

Correspondence and Information

Office of Student Services
College of Nursing
University of Kentucky
Lexington, Kentucky 40536-0232
Telephone: 606-323-5108
World Wide Web: http://www.uky.edu/Nursing/

University of Kentucky

THE FACULTY AND THEIR RESEARCH

Carolyn A. Williams, Professor and Dean; Ph.D., North Carolina, Chapel Hill, 1969; FAAN. Evaluation of community-based health services, nursing contributions to primary care.

Sharon J. Barton, Assistant Professor; Ph.D., Loyola Chicago, 1994. Infant feeding practices.
Dorothy Y. Brockopp, Professor; Ph.D., SUNY at Buffalo, 1981. Psychological/spiritual attributes of acute and cancer pain.
Norma J. Christman, Associate Professor; Ph.D., Wayne State, 1980; FAAN. Effects of uncertainty on stress and coping, effects of preparatory interventions on coping outcomes, psychosocial oncology.
Mary C. DeLetter, Assistant Professor; Ph.D., Kentucky, 1991. Quality of life, chronic disease, chronic airflow limitation.
Juanita W. Fleming, Professor; Ph.D., Catholic University, 1969; FAAN. Health-care needs of young children.
Teresa A. Free, Associate Professor; Ph.D., Texas at Austin, 1988. Effects of maternal substance abuse on infants and children.
Margaret R. Grier, Professor; Ph.D., Texas Woman's, 1975; FAAN. Information processing and decision making in nursing practice.
Ellen J. Hahn, Assistant Professor; D.N.S., Indiana, 1992. School- and home-based health promotion; alcohol, tobacco, and other drug prevention with families and young children; tobacco policy research.
Lynne A. Hall, Associate Professor and Assistant Dean for Research and Doctoral Studies; Dr.P.H., North Carolina, Chapel Hill, 1983. Social support, stress, and depression in vulnerable populations; single-parent families; the effect of mothers' mental health on child outcomes.
Margaret J. Hickman, Associate Professor; Ed.D., Ball State, 1982. Long-term home health care for adults in rural areas, community strategies for health promotion.
Vicki P. Hines-Martin, Assistant Professor; Ph.D., Kentucky, 1994. Mental health/illness in African-American adults, community mental health, minority health policy.
Patricia B. Howard, Assistant Professor; Ph.D., Kentucky, 1992. Family caregiving for the chronically mentally ill, consumer satisfaction with mental health services.
Pamela A. Kidd, Associate Professor; Ph.D., Arizona, 1989. Trauma/emergency nursing, injury prevention.
Marilyn G. King, Associate Professor; D.N.Sc., Boston University, 1987. Women's health, early detection of breast cancer and caregiving, nursing history.
Gwendolen Lee, Professor; Ed.D., Tennessee, Memphis, 1973. Neonatal behaviors and transition to parenthood.
Ann R. Peden, Associate Professor; D.S.N., Alabama at Birmingham, 1991. Depression in women, women's mental health.
Barbara A. Sachs, Professor; Ph.D., Wayne State, 1981; FAAN. Adolescent reproduction and parenthood, low-birth-weight children and their families.
Juliann G. Sebastian, Associate Professor and Assistant Dean for Advanced Practice Nursing; Ph.D., Kentucky, 1994. Community health nursing administration, health-care delivery systems and outcomes, integrated delivery networks.
Sharon L. Sheahan, Associate Professor; Ph.D., Kentucky, 1990. Substance abuse across the life span.
Marcia Stanhope, Professor and Associate Dean; D.S.N., Alabama at Birmingham, 1981; FAAN. Nursing care for the homeless, resource use in home care, education and practice of nurse practitioners.
L. Sherry Warden, Associate Professor; Ph.D., Kentucky, 1990. Psychosocial issues in the management of pain, spirituality, healing and alternative/complimentary health care.

UNIVERSITY OF MISSOURI–COLUMBIA

School of Nursing

Program of Study

The University of Missouri–Columbia (MU) School of Nursing offers graduate study at master's (M.S.) and doctoral (Ph.D.) levels in three areas: health restoration and support, health protection and promotion, and health-care systems.

Master's students prepare for advanced practice nursing as clinical nurse specialists/case managers in specialty areas such as critical care, oncology, gerontics, and rehabilitation. Public health nursing also offers the clinical nurse specialist role. Students may choose to focus on the role of educator, administrator, or some combination of these. Preparation for advanced practice nursing as family nurse practitioners, gerontological nurse practitioners, mental health nurse practitioners, or nurse-midwives is also available. Other master's students may pursue nursing administration as their focus.

Doctoral students may focus their studies in one or more of the three areas of study. Individual design of programs of studies in conjunction with faculty is the hallmark of the Ph.D. program. The Ph.D. program prepares nurse scholars to conduct essential nursing research and to assume leadership roles in social, political, and ethical issues in nursing and health care.

Research Facilities

The University of Missouri–Columbia School of Nursing is part of a health sciences complex located on a comprehensive university campus. The University, rated as a Carnegie Foundation Research 1 University, provides numerous resources for support and research. The J. Otto Lottes Health Sciences Library, one of nine branch libraries on campus, contains nearly 200,000 volumes and maintains approximately 2,000 journal subscriptions. Eighteen computer labs throughout campus, with software available for checkout, technician support, and access to the University's mainframe computer system, make computing accessible for all.

Financial Aid

The School of Nursing offers a variety of assistance programs for full- and part-time students, including teaching and research assistantships, Division of Health and Human Services Professional Nurse Traineeships, scholarships, and fellowships. The community offers many professional nursing employment opportunities along with tuition reimbursement programs.

Cost of Study

Required fees for in-state students are $180.15 per credit hour in 1998–99. Out-of-state students pay $506.65 per credit hour. A $57.50 per semester health fee is assessed for full-time graduate students (enrolled in 9 or more hours). Fees are subject to change.

Living and Housing Costs

University-supervised or off-campus housing is available for graduate students. Students may request information about University-owned housing by writing to Residential Life, 125 Jesse Hall, Columbia, Missouri 65211.

Student Group

A graduate student profile indicates that more than 115 students worked toward their Master of Science degree in the School of Nursing during the 1997–98 academic year. The average age of the students was 37, and 73 percent were part-time students. Thirty students were enrolled in the Ph.D. program. The average age was 42, 77 percent were part-time students, and 23 percent were full-time. Both male and female students from a variety of cultures are working on their graduate degrees in the School of Nursing. Part-time students often continue in their professional nursing practice endeavors while completing their graduate work. An active Graduate Student Association is represented on faculty councils and participates in School of Nursing and campuswide graduate student activities.

Location

Columbia is in the heart of Missouri, equidistant from St. Louis, 125 miles to the east, and Kansas City, 125 miles to the west. The scenic Lake of the Ozarks is 80 miles south of the city. Columbia is a progressive community of 77,000 and has a nationally recognized public school system.

The University and The School

Founded as the first state university west of the Mississippi River in 1839, the University of Missouri–Columbia is one of the most comprehensive institutions of higher learning in the nation, offering many different undergraduate, graduate, and professional degrees. MU's graduate school is a member of the Association of Graduate Schools and the Council of Graduate Schools.

The School of Nursing celebrated its seventieth anniversary in 1990 and has offered a graduate program since 1968. The nursing school is located in the Health Sciences Center, which includes the University Hospital and Clinics, Ellis Fischel Cancer Center, the Rusk Rehabilitation Center, the Children's Hospital, the School of Medicine, the J. Otto Lottes Health Sciences Library, the Mason Institute of Ophthalmology, the Cosmopolitan International Diabetes Center, the Arthritis Center, the Mid-Missouri Health Center, and the Harry S. Truman Veterans Administration Hospital.

Applying

To be considered for admission to the Master's Program, an applicant must be a registered nurse with a baccalaureate degree in nursing from an NLN-accredited program. Applicants submit a departmental application, including a statement of goals, two references, and Graduate Record Examinations (GRE) scores. A personal interview may be requested. A one-time $25 nonrefundable application fee is required by the University. Applications may be received at any time. Admissions are made on a rolling basis for fall, winter, and summer sessions.

To be considered for the Ph.D. program, applicants must be graduates of NLN-accredited master's programs. Graduates of NLN-accredited baccalaureate programs may be considered for provisional admission, with full admission criteria decided according to campus guidelines. Applicants must submit a departmental application, GRE scores (minimum composite score of 1500 expected), three letters of reference, and an original essay outlining goals of doctoral study and research interests. An interview by invitation will be contingent on ranking related to the applicant's material received. Applications may be received at any time. Admissions are made on a rolling basis for fall, winter, and summer sessions.

Correspondence and Information

Student Affairs Office
Graduate Recruitment and Progression
School of Nursing
University of Missouri–Columbia
Columbia, Missouri 65211

Telephone: 573-882-0277
800-437-4339 (toll-free)

University of Missouri–Columbia

THE FACULTY AND THEIR RESEARCH

Jane Armer (Community Health Nursing, Gerontic Nursing); Ph.D., Rochester. Relocation adjustment among community-dwelling rural elderly, health promotion and emotional well-being among culturally diverse rural elders; perceptions of crisis in health care and response to alternative modes of health-care delivery, perceptions of control and choice of alternative treatments in chronic illness.

JoAnne Banks-Wallace (Public Health); Ph.D., Washington (Seattle). Storytelling as an emancipatory tool among women of African descent.

Cheryl L. Bausler (Adult Health); Ph.D., Missouri–Columbia. Gender differences associated with self-care practices following open-heart surgery, burnout related to faculty and students.

Linda Bullock (Public Health, Maternal and Child Nursing); Ph.D., New Zealand. Battering during pregnancy, effect of stress and social support during pregnancy, health promotion from an international perspective.

Vicki Conn (Aged Adult Nursing, Acute/Critical Care); Ph.D., Missouri–Columbia. Medication-taking behaviors in elderly, self-management of cardiac diseases.

Deborah L. Finfgeld (Mental Health); Ph.D., Texas at Austin. Self-resolution of alcohol problems, courage and the management of long-term health concerns, grounded theory research.

Lawrence Ganong (Family Dynamics Communication); Ph.D., Missouri–Columbia. Stepfamily dynamics, stereotyping and therapy.

Elizabeth Geden (Family Nurse Practitioner); Ph.D., Missouri–Columbia. Nonpharmacologic pain reduction, research, energy expenditure, self-care agency.

Victoria Grando (Community Mental Health); Ph.D., Kansas. Women's mental health issues, nursing history, feminist theory, relationship violence.

Alice Kuehn (Family/Gerontology Nurse Practitioner); Ph.D., Missouri–Columbia. Clinical gerontology nursing; research focus: mobility and balance in the older adult, self-care of older adults, falls and hip fracture in the elderly; educational focus: nurse practitioner education, clinical teaching.

Priscilla LeMone (Adult Health); D.S.N., Alabama at Birmingham. Health assessment, sexuality in adults with diabetes mellitus, nursing diagnosis, women with heart disease.

Kay Libbus (Community Health); Dr.P.H., Texas Health Science Center at Houston. Factors affecting prenatal care, breastfeeding and health care for low-income women, contraceptive decision making, end-of-life decision making.

Roxanne McDaniel (Adult Nursing, Oncology); Ph.D., Texas at Austin. Quality of life, symptom distress.

Eileen Porter (Community Health Nursing); Ph.D., Wisconsin–Milwaukee. Phenomenological research, gerontology.

Rosemary Porter, Associate Dean (Nursing Service Administration, Adult Nursing); Ph.D., Missouri–Columbia. Work environment, images of nursing, career development, health policy.

Marilyn Rantz (Nursing Administration, Chronic Care); Ph.D., Wisconsin–Milwaukee. Health policy, quality, long-term care, management effectiveness.

Donna Scheideberg (Nurse Midwifery); Ph.D., Michigan State. Perinatal case management.

Toni Sullivan, Dean (Community Health Nursing and Gerontology); Ed.D., Columbia Teachers College. Self-care deficit nursing theory, policy/future research, nursing service delivery model.

Susan Taylor (Adult Nursing, Gerontic Nursing, Theory Elaboration); Ph.D., Catholic University. Self-care agency, nursing ethics, self-management.

Deidre d'Amour Wipke-Tevis (Adult Health); Ph.D., California, San Francisco. Wound healing and wound care, care of cardiovascular patients, nutrition.

UNIVERSITY OF PITTSBURGH

School of Nursing

Programs of Study

Graduate programs of study lead to the M.S.N. and Ph.D. degrees. Professional nurses who want to pursue a graduate degree have several choices at the School. In the advanced practice arena, the School of Nursing prepares students for the role of a nurse anesthetist or nurse practitioner. There are currently five nurse practitioner options: acute-care nurse practitioner, with a concentration in cardiopulmonary, critical care, oncology, or a directed option; and primary-care nurse practitioner, with options in family, pediatrics, psychiatric, or women's health. A second option is the specialized role. This role could include a focus in administration, education, informatics, or research. Options are also available for an individually designed program tailored to a student's educational and career objectives.

The advanced practice option varies from 49 to 52 credits. The curriculum consists of core courses, advanced nursing practice specialty courses, role development courses, and electives. Core courses include health promotion, pathophysiology, physical diagnosis, pharmacology, nursing theory and research, and the research practicum. The specialized role option is 40 credits in length. The curriculum consists of core courses, specialty cognates, and focused electives. Core courses include research theory and practicum, health-care outcomes, informatics, and a specialized practicum. Minors in nursing education or nursing systems (administration) are also available, as are the school nurse certificate and management certificate for health professionals. For those who have a current master's degree, a second master's option is also available, and a thesis is optional.

The Ph.D. program prepares scholars to extend scientific knowledge that advances the science and practice of nursing and to contribute to the scientific base of other disciplines. The curriculum includes courses in history and philosophy of science, nursing theory development, the structure of nursing knowledge, advanced statistics, quantitative research methods, research methodologies, instrumentation, and several research practicums with experienced researchers. An area of research emphasis, which matches a faculty member's research emphasis, is selected by the student early in the program. Current faculty research initiatives include adolescent health, chronic disorders, critical care, and chronic disorders. The culminating requirement is a dissertation.

Two tracks exist for completing the Ph.D. degree: the B.S.N./Ph.D. track and the M.S.N./Ph.D. track. The B.S.N./Ph.D. track is a 95- to 97-credit option that includes eight full-time semesters of course work and the completion of a dissertation. This track is for B.S.N. graduate students who want to focus on research and prepare for a research career. It does not require nor lead to a master's degree with a clinical specialty focus. The M.S.N./Ph.D. track is a 64-credit option that includes five full-time semesters of course work and the completion of a dissertation. This track builds on a traditional M.S.N. degree with a clinical specialty focus. Students who wish to enroll in part-time course work can do so in the M.S.N./Ph.D. track.

Research Facilities

The University of Pittsburgh is a major research institution in the health care field, and the School of Nursing actively encourages research activity among faculty and students, including research with interdisciplinary colleagues across the campus. The Center for Nursing Research within the school offers support services to faculty preparing research proposals, including design and proposal development consultation, assistance with data management and analysis, and critiques and technical preparation of proposals. Doctoral degree students consult with statisticians from the Center for Nursing Research and the Departments of Biostatistics or Statistics for help with data design and analysis. Research opportunities for students are also available with faculty members throughout the school as well as with health related-studies across the campus.

Financial Aid

Master's students have a variety of financial aid options available including Professional Nurse Traineeships for full-time study, University tuition aid for part-time study, specified scholarships, and loans. Research assistantships are available to qualified graduate students.

Most full-time doctoral degree students have graduate student researcher, graduate student assistant, teaching assistant, or teaching fellow positions, which are primarily merit-based, pay a stipend, and include a tuition scholarship and individual health insurance. Students in these positions work 10–20 hours per week, and many have excellent experiences working with faculty research projects or teaching. Workshops to assist students in applying for pre- and postdoctoral training grant fellowships are provided. Other scholarships and part-time tuition aid are also available.

Cost of Study

Tuition per term for 1997–98 for full-time study was $4521 for in-state and $9314 for out-of-state students. Tuition per credit for part-time study was $374 for in-state and $769 for out-of-state students. Full-time fees were $258 and part-time student fees were $72 per term. Doctoral degree students from out-of-state who enroll full-time pay in-state tuition rates due to school-based scholarships.

Living and Housing Costs

The cost of living is reasonable in comparison to other large metropolitan areas. The University has some apartment facilities available, but most graduate students live in privately owned off-campus housing. A variety of housing options are available in neighborhoods surrounding the University. Some of these areas are served by the free University shuttle bus system.

Student Group

In 1997–98, 268 master's and 52 Ph.D. students were enrolled for a total graduate student population of 320.

Location

The campus is situated in the heart of the city's civic center in Oakland. Surrounding the 125-acre campus are museums, libraries, concert halls, and other institutions of higher education. Within the past 15 years, Pittsburgh has earned a reputation as an up-and-coming center for industry, science, health care, and education. With a rich cultural heritage in music and the arts, Pittsburgh is also a major sports town. It is located at the confluence of three major rivers with a variety of recreational opportunities nearby.

The University and The School

Founded in 1787, the University of Pittsburgh is an independent, state-related, research institution offering a variety of undergraduate, graduate and adult education programs. Total enrollment on the main campus is about 30,000, including almost 10,000 graduate and professional students. The School of Nursing is one of six schools of the health sciences located in the heart of the University of Pittsburgh Medical Center.

Applying

Master's applicants must have a baccalaureate degree in nursing, a current license to practice and one to two years of experience (for full-time study). Admission decisions are based upon a faculty interview, professional goals, previous academic performance, and GRE or MAT scores. Applications should be received by February 1.

Ph.D. applicants must have a baccalaureate degree in nursing, documentation of academic success in an appropriate master's program (for the M.S.N./Ph.D. program), evidence of competence in scholarly research and the ability to communicate in writing, and satisfactory GRE scores.

Correspondence and Information

Becky Carr
Director of Student Recruitment and Placement
University of Pittsburgh, School of Nursing
3500 Victoria Street
Pittsburgh, Pennsylvania 15261
Telephone: 412-624-2407
Fax: 412-624-2409
E-mail: nursao+@pitt.edu
World Wide Web: http://www.pitt.edu/~nursing

University of Pittsburgh

THE FACULTY

Susan A. Albrecht, Assistant Professor; Ph.D., Pittsburgh; RN. Smoking cessation, adolescent health, pregnant adolescents.
Patricia Bartone, Instructor; M.S.N., Pittsburgh; CRNP. Psychiatric Primary Care Nurse Practitioner Program.
Catherine Bender, Assistant Professor; Ph.D., Pittsburgh; RN. Cognitive function associated with cancer and cancer therapy, neuroendocrine hormone function in cancer therapy, quality of life in cancer and cancer therapy.
Lisa M. Bernardo, Assistant Professor; Ph.D., NYU; RN, CEN. Community health nursing, pediatric emergency nursing.
Patricia Bohachick, Associate Professor; Ph.D., Pittsburgh; RN. Cardiovascular nursing, quality of life, social support.
Denise Charron-Prochownik, Assistant Professor; Ph.D., Michigan; RN. Behavior and chronic illness, child and adolescent health, juvenile diabetes.
John M. Clochesy, Associate Professor and Associate Dean; Ph.D., Case Western Reserve; RN, FAAN, FCCM. Weaning from mechanical ventilatory support, care of chronically critically ill adults, biophysical measurement in critical care.
Rose Constantino, Associate Professor; Ph.D., Pittsburgh; RN, FAAN. Bereavement, mourning, and biobehavioral-phychosocial responses of suicide survivors; nursing care needs of battered and abused women.
Mary Cothran, Assistant Professor; Ph.D., Tennessee; CRNP.
Lynda Davidson, Assistant Professor and Assistant Dean; Ph.D., Case Western Reserve; RN. Nutrition and the MICU patient, outcomes related to nursing care.
Bettina Dixon, Instructor; M.S.N., Pittsburgh; CRNA.
Lorah Dorn, Assistant Professor; Ph.D., Penn State; CPNP. Behavioral endocrinology and the stress system, adolescent health and development, puberty.
Willa Doswell, Assistant Professor; Ph.D., NYU; RN, FAAN. Effects of swaddling in neonates; stress, immunity, and hypertensive African-American women; stress, personality, and puberty in African-American preteens.
Jacqeline Dunbar-Jacob, Professor; Ph.D., Stanford; RN, FAAN. Adherence to health-care regimens, behavioral interventions in physical illness, adherence in clinical trial research.
Janyce Dyer, Assistant Professor; D.N.Sc., Catholic University; RN, CS, CRNP. Psychiatric Primary Care Nurse Practitioner Program; families of the mentally ill, familial influence on risk and protective factors in major depression, neuropsychiatric predictors of course and outcome in major depression, schizophrenia.
Sandra Engberg, Assistant Professor; Ph.D., Pittsburgh; CRNP. Women's health.
Judith Erlen, Associate Professor; Ph.D., Texas Women's; RN. Ethical decision making, quality of care, quality of life.
Karen Evanczuk, Assistant Professor; Ph.D., Pittsburgh; CRNP. Psychiatric Primary Care Nurse Practitioner Program; critical incident stress debriefing.
Robbi Ewell, Instructor and Director, Learning Resources Center; M.P.S., Cornell.
Donna Falsetti, Instructor; M.S.N., Pittsburgh; CRNP.
Richard Henker, Assistant Professor; Ph.D., Washington (Seattle); RN. Human responses to treatment of fever, theories underlying fever development, clinical thermometry.
Pamela P. Hepple, Assistant Professor; Ph.D., Northwestern.
Mary Christina Hines, Assistant Professor; Ph.D., Louisville. Physiology.
Leslie Hoffman, Professor and Chairperson of the Department of Acute and Tertiary Care; Ph.D., Pittsburgh; RN, FAAN. Pulmonary dysfunction, weaning from mechanical ventilation, functional ability.
Marilyn Hravnak, Instructor; M.S.N., Pittsburgh; CRNP.
Lynette Jack, Associate Professor and Director of the Graduate Program; Ph.D., Pittsburgh; RN, CARN. Psychiatric mental health and addictions nursing specialist.
Judith Kaufmann, Instructor; M.S.N., Pittsburgh; CRNA.
Mary E. Kerr, Assistant Professor and Director of the Center for Nursing Research; Ph.D., Case Western Reserve; RN. Physiologic response to routine nursing intervention, head injuries, critical care.
Jacqueline Lamb, Assistant Professor; Ph.D., Pittsburgh; RN. School-based intervention to promote mental health in rural teens, smoking cessation intervention for pregnant teens.
Kathleen Lucke, Assistant Professor and Director of Student Services; Ph.D., Maryland; RN. Neuroscience nursing.
Kathy Magdic, Instructor; M.S.N., Pittsburgh; CRNP.
Judith T. Matthews, Instructor; M.S., Boston University; RN. Community health nursing.
Beatrice J. McDowell, Associate Professor; Ph.D., Pittsburgh; CRNP, FAAN. Gerontology, urinary incontinence, health care delivery.
Ann Mitchell, Assistant Professor; Ph.D., Pittsburgh; RN. Bereavement, psychosocial needs, adjustment of survivors of the violent death of a relative or significant other, efficacy of CISD intervention.
Donna G. Nativio, Associate Professor; Ph.D., Pittsburgh; CRNP.
John O'Donnell, Instructor and Director of Nurse Anesthesia Program; M.S.N., Pittsburgh; CRNA.
Laura Palmer, Instructor; M.N.Ed., Pittsburgh; CRNA.
Patrice Peebles, Instructor; M.N.Ed., Pittsburgh; RN. RN Options faculty.
Ellen Piper-Caulkins, Instructor; M.N., M.B.A., UCLA; RN. Weaning from ventilatory support, care of chronically critically ill adults, biophysical measurement in critical care.
Kathryn R. Puskar, Associate Professor; Ph.D., Pittsburgh; RN, FAAN. Adolescent stress and coping; stress, coping, and women's health; health promotion for teens.
Sara J. Reeder, Assistant Professor; Ph.D., Maryland; RN. Outcomes of critically ill, patients with acute renal failure.
Ellen B. Rudy, Professor and Dean; Ph.D., Case Western Reserve; RN. Interventions for the care of critically ill patients, effects of exercise on women's physical and psychosocial health.
Deborah Rust, Instructor and Program Coordinator of the Acute Care Nurse Practitioner Program; M.S.N., Pittsburgh; CRNP.
Elizabeth Schlenk, Assistant Professor and Assistant Director, Center for Research in Chronic Disorders; Ph.D., Michigan; RN.
Susan Sereika, Research Assistant Professor; Ph.D., Michigan. Survival analysis, longitudinal data analysis, nonparametric statistics.
Barbara Spier, Assistant Professor; Ph.D., Pittsburgh; RN. Adherence to exercise among healthy older adults, maintaining function in the elderly, prevention of disruptive behaviors in the cognitively impaired elderly.
Clement Stone, Assistant Professor and Statistician; Ph.D., Arizona.
Valerie Swigart, Assistant Professor; Ph.D., Pittsburgh; CRNP. Biomedical ethics, surrogate ethical decision making, death and dying.
Susan Van Cleve, Instructor; M.S.N., Boston College; CPNP, CRNP.
Gayle Whitman, Assistant Professor; M.S.N., Case Western; RN. Outcomes research.
Gail Wolf, Assistant Professor and Associate Dean; D.N.Sc., Indiana–Purdue at Indianapolis; RN.
Joyce Yasko, Professor and Associate Director of Pittsburgh Cancer Institute; Ph.D., Pittsburgh; RN, FAAN. Family caregivers of cancer patients, management of cancer symptoms, economics of health care delivery.
Ann Yurick, Associate Professor and Chairperson of the Department of Health and Community Systems; Ph.D., Pittsburgh; RN. Functional vision changes in the elderly, disruptive behaviors in cognitively impaired elderly, peer support and exercise adherence in osteo-arthritic patients.

UNIVERSITY OF RHODE ISLAND

College of Nursing

Programs of Study

The College of Nursing offers graduate programs leading to the M.S. and Ph.D. degrees in nursing. The M.S. program prepares professional nurses to assume leadership roles in improving the quality of professional nursing practice in a variety of settings. The curriculum offers advanced practice in primary-health-care nursing, nurse midwifery, mental health nursing, critical-care nursing, gerontological nursing, parent-child health nursing, nursing administration, and teaching in nursing. Most concentrations require 41 credits of study; primary health care requires 42 and nurse midwifery requires 46. A core of nursing courses addresses nursing theory, nursing research, and leadership. The program, designed to accommodate both full- and part-time students, requires the equivalent of four semesters of full-time work. Students may begin graduate study in fall or spring, but fall matriculation is preferable. The program is NLN- accredited.

The Ph.D. program prepares nurse scholars and researchers to advance nursing knowledge through the development and testing of theory and the conduct of research in clinical practice. The 61-credit program comprises core courses in nursing and the cognates (25 credits), nursing electives (9 credits), other electives (9 credits), and a dissertation (18 credits). The nursing electives allow students in-depth study in at least two theoretical domains of nursing. Doctoral students may attend classes part-time, but they are required to have two consecutive semesters of at least 6 credits.

Research Facilities

The College of Nursing has a research center in the nursing building, and the campus has a supporting research office, as well as computer services. The library has extensive holdings in nursing, as well as relevant materials in other disciplines. Nurses from nearby hospitals and community health agencies frequently work with faculty and students to develop nursing research projects.

Financial Aid

Several forms of financial assistance are available to graduate students; detailed information is available from the Graduate School Office and is included in the *Graduate Student Manual.* Fellowships and scholarships are awarded by the dean of the Graduate School to students selected from nominees submitted by the director of graduate programs in the College of Nursing. Students are advised to request nomination from the director. A limited number of research assistantships are also available.

Cost of Study

For the 1998–99 academic year, the tuition for full-time study is estimated at $5217 for Rhode Island residents ($196 per credit), $6983 for students participating in the New England Regional Student Program ($294 per credit), and $11,535 ($548 per credit) for out-of-state residents. Fees are an additional $1027.

Living and Housing Costs

The cost of living is comparable to that in other New England states and is less than that in Boston or New York City. Students often live on or near the beach in rental houses that are available from September to May.

Student Group

Approximately 100 M.S. and 40 Ph.D. students are enrolled in the College. Two thirds are enrolled part-time. Students from all parts of the United States, as well as from other countries, have been enrolled in the programs.

Student Outcomes

Graduates of the administration and education options are employed in a variety of health-care settings. Several have assumed management positions in hospitals, VNA's, and other health-care settings. Nurse practitioner studies, nurse-midwife studies, and psych-mental health graduates have found employment in private practice, HMO's, hospitals, and clinics. Graduates in the clinical practice options work in geriatric, intensive care, and other health-care settings.

Location

The University of Rhode Island is a medium-sized state university located in the southern part of Rhode Island, in the village of Kingston. Kingston is a small campus community; nearby residents frequently participate in cultural events sponsored by the University. Kingston is about 15 minutes from the scenic beaches of Narragansett, 25 minutes from the beautiful beaches in Newport, 90 miles from Boston, 180 miles from New York City, and about 30 miles from Providence, Rhode Island's capital.

The University

As a land-grant college since its founding in 1892, the University of Rhode Island emphasizes preparation for earning a living and for responsible citizenship, carries on research, and takes its expertise to the community through its extension programs. In part because of its location 6 miles from Narragansett Bay, the University has developed strong marine programs and has been designated one of the national sea-grant colleges. The University has nine colleges and three schools: the Colleges of Arts and Science, Business Administration, Continuing Education, Engineering, Human Science and Services, Nursing, Pharmacy, and Resource Development; University College; the Graduate School; the Graduate School of Library and Information Studies; and the Graduate School of Oceanography.

About 12,000 students are enrolled on the Kingston campus and another 3,000 in credit courses throughout the state. Of the total, about 3,200 are graduate students, including approximately 950 in full-time residence. The full-time teaching faculty numbers about 750.

Applying

All applicants for admission to M.S. and Ph.D. programs in nursing are processed through the Graduate School. Prospective applicants should request application materials from the Graduate Admissions Office.

To be admitted to the M.S. program, applicants should have completed an NLN-accredited baccalaureate-degree nursing program with an upper-division major in nursing. In addition, the College of Nursing requires an undergraduate GPA of at least 3.0, satisfactory scores on either the MAT or the GRE General Test, three references, a registered nurse license and/or eligibility for licensure in Rhode Island, and an undergraduate course in statistics. Applications must be submitted by April 15 for entry in the fall and November 15 for entry in the spring. Students concentrating in primary health care and nurse midwifery must have two years of clinical nursing practice. No new students can be accepted into the advanced practice critical-care and parent-child health concentrations for the 1998–99 academic year.

Applicants to the Ph.D. program must have a bachelor's degree from an NLN-accredited program and a master's degree in nursing and must have completed a course in statistics, including inferential statistics. Applicants must submit two scholarly papers (one theoretical, one empirical) or a master's thesis or its equivalent, GRE General Test scores, and three letters of reference. Applications must be submitted by April 15 or November 15.

Correspondence and Information

Dr. Donna Schwartz-Barcott
Director of Graduate Studies
College of Nursing
University of Rhode Island
2 Heathman Road
Kingston, Rhode Island 02881-0814
Telephone: 401-874-2766
Fax: 401-874-2061

University of Rhode Island

THE FULL-TIME FACULTY AND THEIR RESEARCH

Patricia Burbank, Associate Professor; D.N.Sc., Boston University. Gerontology, meaning in life.
Rebecca Carley, Assistant Professor; M.S., Boston University. Primary health care, women's health care.
Denise Coppa, Assistant Professor; M.S., Colorado. Primary health care, children's primary health care, healing, chaos theory.
Marlene Dufault, Associate Professor; Ph.D., Connecticut; Research utilization, pain assessment, patient education.
Ginette Ferszt, Lecturer; M.S., Pennsylvania. Psychiatric/mental health nursing.
Jacqueline Fortin, Associate Professor; D.N.Sc., Boston University. Research methodology, critical care, pain.
Diane Gersevitz, Assistant Professor; M.S., Rhode Island; Certified Family Nurse Practitioner. Primary health care.
Janet Hirsch, Professor; Ed.D., Boston University. Maternal-child health, nursing education, client education.
Dayle Joseph, Associate Professor and Interim Dean; Ed.D., Boston University. Clinical decision making, decision making in diabetic clients.
Holly Kennedy, Assistant Professor; M.S.N., Medical College of Georgia; Certified Nurse Midwife. Theory development in nurse midwifery from critical theory and feminist theory.
Hesook Suzie Kim, Professor; Ph.D., Brown. Metatheory, collaborative decision making, gerontology.
Margaret McGrath, Professor; D.N.Sc., Boston University. Parent-child interaction, high-risk families, maternity.
Jean Miller, Professor and Weyker Endowed Chair in Thanatology; Ph.D., Washington (Seattle). Family, decision making, mind-body-spirit relationships, spiritual care, inner-city health care, cross-cultural issues.
Norma Jean Schmieding, Professor; Ed.D., Boston University. Nursing administration, reflective practice.
Donna Schwartz-Barcott, Professor and Director of Graduate Studies; Ph.D., North Carolina at Chapel Hill. Qualitative research, inductive theory development, common concepts in nursing.
Evelyn Yeaw, Associate Professor; Ph.D., Boston College. Medical-surgical critical care, confusion, positioning, hypoxia.

YALE UNIVERSITY

School of Nursing

Programs of Study

The Yale School of Nursing offers the M.S.N. and the D.N.Sc. (Doctor of Nursing Science) degrees and a post-master's certification program. The School of Nursing admits both registered nurses who have a baccalaureate degree and college graduates with no previous nursing education. The graduate moves directly into a chosen area of clinical specialization. The full-time student is expected to complete the requirements for the M.S.N. degree in two academic years. Scheduled part-time study is also available. The graduate entry program in nursing requires two terms and one summer session in addition to the two-year specialization sequence. The curriculum places emphasis on clinical competence and nursing research. Each student is educated to function in an expanded role in the clinical area of his or her choice.

The M.S.N. program emphasizes clinical specialization. The programs of study offered are adult/family nurse practitioner studies, psychiatric–mental health nursing, nurse-midwifery, adult advanced practice nursing (which includes gerontological and acute care nurse practitioner options), pediatric nurse practitioner studies (with both primary care and chronic illness tracks), and the nursing management and policy program. The D.N.Sc. degree program is designed to prepare nurse scientists who are expert in clinical research to advance knowledge development for the discipline of nursing by conducting research on nursing phenomena. Graduates of the program will assume major leadership roles in extending the theoretical base of nursing, including shaping responses to political, economic, ethical, and other health-care issues.

Research Facilities

The major collection of the Yale School of Nursing is in the Yale Medical Library, which serves the entire Yale–New Haven Medical Center as well as others in the University. A Reference Room with state-of-the-art technology is also available on site. The collections, covering nursing, clinical medicine and its specialties, public health, and related fields, number more than 380,000 volumes. About 90,000 or more are source materials or supporting works in the historical collections. More than 2,500 current journals are received regularly. Sterling Memorial Library (Yale's main library), Beincke Rare Book and Manuscript Library, Cross Campus Library, and Seeley Mudd Library contain about 5.6 million volumes. The Kline Science Library has 358,000 volumes and about 1,900 current journals.

The combined facilities of the Yale School of Medicine, the Yale–New Haven Hospital, the Yale Child Study Center, the Yale School of Nursing, and the Yale Psychiatric Institute constitute the Yale–New Haven Medical Center. The Connecticut Mental Health Center is closely affiliated with this complex. In addition, a large number of community agencies are utilized, including schools, visiting nurses' associations, and community clinics.

Financial Aid

Financial aid is not a consideration in the admissions process. The School of Nursing accepts applications for financial aid from candidates prior to their acceptance in order to expedite notification of awards upon acceptance. Financial need is met by a combination of scholarships, nurse traineeships, graduate assistantships, and federal loans.

Cost of Study

In 1998–99, tuition is $9890 per term for fall and spring terms. Tuition for students in the first year of the Graduate Entry Program in Nursing is $13,795 per term, which includes the twelve-week summer term.

Living and Housing Costs

Room and board and other personal expenses are about $10,270 to $13,500 for the 1998–99 academic year. Other educational expenses, including books, health insurance, and student fees, total approximately $1390 to $1680.

Student Group

The Yale School of Nursing currently enrolls 275 students, of whom 199 are full-time students and 76 are part-time. Approximately three quarters of YSN graduates seek a first position in the advanced clinical practice specialty for which they were educated. Graduates of YSN have gone on to distinguished positions in clinical practice, health service administration, the federal government, and academia.

Student Outcomes

Recent graduates hold positions as nurse clinicians, clinical specialists, or nurse practitioners in a variety of health-care facilities. Their responsibilities include direct patient care, supervision and teaching of others involved in caring for patients, interdisciplinary planning, and execution and evaluation of services. Graduates from former years are also in administrative and teaching and/or research positions in educational institutions, foundations, or the federal government. Some hold positions as consultants to public and private agencies.

Location

Yale's effort to help students feel at home in the University is reflected by its central location. The Yale University Art Gallery, Peabody Museum of Natural History, Yale Center for British Art, and Payne Whitney Gymnasium are all accessible to YSN students. In addition, the city of New Haven has long been known for its theater life, music, art, and a range of other cultural activities. An entertainment district adjacent to Yale's Old Campus includes the renovated Shubert and Palace theaters.

The University and The School

Yale University was chartered in 1701. The central mission of the University is to preserve, disseminate, and advance knowledge through teaching and research. This mission is carried out in its undergraduate school, Yale College, and its eleven graduate and professional schools.

The Yale School of Nursing was started in 1923. Under the direction of its first dean, Annie W. Goodrich, the School established a new pattern for nursing education with student instruction and experience based upon an educational plan rather than an apprenticeship system.

Applying

Students are admitted to the graduate program in nursing once a year in September. The minimum requirement for admission to the Graduate Entry Program in Nursing is a baccalaureate degree from a recognized college or university. No specific major is required. Collegiate courses in biological and social sciences are recommended, and an undergraduate course in statistics is required. The minimum requirement for the M.S.N. program is a baccalaureate degree from a recognized college or university and graduation from a school of nursing. Personal experience is desirable but not required. Applicants must be licensed to practice nursing in at least one state. An undergraduate course in statistics is required. Applicants to the D.N.Sc. program are admitted once a year in September and must hold an M.S.N. degree. Previous course work in research methods and statistics is required, and students must pass a minimum competency examination in statistics. All students must submit official transcripts of all previous college records, an official transcript of GRE test scores, personal references from three individuals, and an admission essay. Qualified candidates are asked to come to the School for an interview. Students should contact the Student Affairs Office for application deadlines.

Correspondence and Information

Yale University School of Nursing
Office of Student Affairs
P.O. Box 9740
New Haven, Connecticut 06536-0740
Telephone: 203-785-2389

Yale University

THE FACULTY

Nina Adams, Lecturer; M.S.N., Yale, 1977.
Ivy Alexander, Program Instructor; M.S., Northeastern, 1992.
Ann Ameling, Professor; M.S.N., Yale, 1967.
Lynette Ament, Assistant Professor; Ph.D., Wisconsin–Milwaukee, 1996; CNM.
Katharine Bailey, Assistant Professor; M.S., Boston College, 1979.
Patricia Polgar Bailey, Program Instructor; M.S.N., Simmons, 1991.
Margaret Beal, Associate Professor; M.S.N., Yale, 1982; CNM.
Clarice M. Begemann, Program Instructor; M.S.N., M.P.P.M., Yale, 1990.
Helen Varney Burst, Professor; M.S.N., Yale, 1963; CNM.
Deborah Chyun, Assistant Professor; M.S.N., Yale, 1982.
Sally Solomon Cohen, Assistant Professor; Ph.D., Columbia, 1993; FAAN.
Susan Cohen, Associate Professor; D.S.N., Alabama, 1983.
Sarah Cohn, Lecturer; M.S.N., Yale, 1973; J.D., Yale, 1983; CNM.
Maureen Cook, Lecturer; M.S.N., Columbia, 1992.
Jessica Coviello, Lecturer; M.S.N., Yale, 1982.
Angela Crowley, Associate Professor; M.S.N., NYU, 1975.
Susan E. Devine, Lecturer; M.S.N., Yale, 1991.
Donna Diers, Professor; M.S.N., Yale, 1964; FAAN.
Jane Dixon, Professor; Ph.D., Connecticut, 1973.
J. Deborah Ferholt, Lecturer; M.D., Rochester, 1966.
Marjorie Funk, Associate Professor; Ph.D., Yale, 1992.
Geriann Gallagher, Lecturer; M.S.N., Rush, 1992; N.D., Rush, 1992.
Margaret Grey, Professor and Associate Dean for Research and Doctoral Studies; Dr.P.H., Columbia, 1984; FAAN.
Elaine Gustafson, Program Instructor; M.S.N., Yale, 1986.
Barbara Hackley, Program Instructor; M.S.N., Columbia, 1980; CNM.
Wendy Holmes, Associate Professor; M.S.N., Boston University, 1976.
Carrie Klima, Assistant Professor; M.S., Illinois, 1986; CNM.
Mary Kathryn Knobf, Associate Professor; M.S.N., Yale, 1982; FAAN.
Judith Krauss, Professor and Dean; M.S.N., Yale, 1970; FAAN.
Melva D. Kravitz, Associate Professor; Ph.D., Utah, 1984.
Jerilynn Lamb-Pagone, Lecturer; M.S.N., CUNY, Hunter, 1980.
Robin Leger, Assistant Professor; M.S., Syracuse, 1984.
Courtney H. Lyder, Associate Professor; N.D., Rush, 1990.
Donna Mahrenholz, Associate Professor; Ph.D., Maryland, 1990.
Gail Melkus, Associate Professor; Ed.D., Columbia Teachers College, 1989.
Paula Milone-Nuzzo, Associate Professor; Ph.D., Connecticut, 1989.
Pamela Minarik, Associate Professor; M.S., California, San Francisco, 1981; FAAN.
Catharine Moffett, Program Instructor; M.S.N., Yale, 1982.
Alison Moriarty, Assistant Professor; M.S.N., Yale, 1994.
Beth Muller, Program Instructor; M.S.N., Yale, 1987.
Leslie Nield-Anderson, Associate Professor; Ph.D., NYU, 1991.
Douglas Olsen, Assistant Professor; Ph.D., Boston College, 1994.
Jeannie Pasacreta, Associate Professor; Ph.D., Pennsylvania, 1993.
Valentine Pascale, Lecturer; B.S., Connecticut, 1994.
Carole Passarelli, Associate Professor; M.S., Connecticut, 1977.
Linda Honan Pellico, Lecturer; M.S.N., Yale, 1989.
Cassy D. Pollack, Assistant Professor and Associate Dean for Students and Master's Studies; M.S.N., M.P.P.M., Yale, 1983.
Elisabeth Reilly, Program Instructor; M.S.N., Yale, 1990.
Heather Reynolds, Associate Professor; M.S.N., Yale, 1980; CNM.
Leslie Robinson, Lecturer; M.S.N., Yale, 1981; CNM.
Mary Ellen Rousseau, Associate Professor; M.S.N., Columbia, 1975; CNM.
Patricia Ryan-Krause, Program Instructor; M.S.N., Yale, 1981.
Ann Powers, Program Instructor; M.S.N., Connecticut, 1984.
Lois Sadler, Assistant Professor; Ph.D., Connecticut, 1997.
Lawrence Scahill, Assistant Professor; Ph.D., Yale, 1997.
Lynne Schilling, Research Scientist; Ph.D., Syracuse, 1977.
Dorothy Sexton, Professor; Ed.D., Boston University, 1974.
Gail Simonson, Lecturer; M.S.N., Rochester, 1982.
Geralyn Spollett, Assistant Professor; M.S.N., Boston College, 1982.
Martha Swartz, Associate Professor; M.S., Michigan, 1981.
Ann Williams, Associate Professor; Ed.D., Columbia Teachers College, 1989; FAAN.
Walter Zawalich, Research Scientist; Ph.D., Florida State, 1971.

Section 30
Public Health

This section contains directories of institutions that have graduate units in public health and offer programs in community health, environmental and occupational health, epidemiology, health promotion, industrial hygiene, international health, and maternal and child health, followed by in-depth entries submitted by institutions that chose to prepare detailed program descriptions. Additional information about programs listed in the directories but not augmented by an in-depth entry may be obtained by writing directly to the dean of a graduate school or chair of a department at the address given in the directory.

For programs offering related work, see also in this book Allied Health, Education, Health Services Management and Hospital Administration, and Nursing; in Book 2, Home Economics and Family Studies (Gerontology) and Sociology, Anthropology, and Archaeology (Demography and Population Studies); in Book 3, Biological and Biomedical Sciences; Ecology, Environmental Biology, and Evolutionary Biology; Microbiological Sciences; and Nutrition; in Book 4, Mathematical Sciences and Environmental Sciences and Management; and in Book 5, Bioengineering, Biomedical Engineering, and Biotechnology; Civil and Environmental Engineering; Industrial Engineering; Energy and Power Engineering (Nuclear Engineering); and Management of Engineering and Technology.

CONTENTS

Public Health—General

Allegheny University of the Health Sciences, School of Public Health, Philadelphia, PA 19102-1192. Awards MPH. Faculty: 11 full-time (8 women). Students: 41 full-time (29 women); includes 18 minority (7 African Americans, 7 Asian Americans, 4 Hispanics). Average age 27. 98 applicants, 66% accepted. *Entrance requirements:* GMAT, GRE, LSAT, or MCAT; TOEFL, previous course work in statistics and word processing. Application deadline: 2/1 (rolling processing). Application fee: $50. *Expenses:* Tuition $17,500 per year. Fees $60 per year full-time. *Faculty research:* Epidemiology, behavioral and social sciences, problem-based learning. • William E. Welton, Acting Dean. Application contact: Lenore Sherman, Associate Director of Student Affairs and Public Health, 215-762-8251. Fax: 215-762-4088.

See in-depth description on page 1485.

Armstrong Atlantic State University, School of Graduate Studies, Program in Health Science, Major in Public Health, Savannah, GA 31419-1997. Awards MPH. *Expenses:* Tuition $83 per quarter hour for state residents; $250 per quarter hour for nonresidents. Fees $145 per quarter hour for state residents; $228 per quarter hour for nonresidents. • Dr. James Streater, Department Head, Program in Health Science, 912-921-5480.

Benedictine University, Program in Public Health, Lisle, IL 60532-0900. Awards MPH, MBA/MPH, MPH/MS. MPH/MS offered jointly with the Program in Management and Organizational Behavior and the Program in Management Information Systems. Part-time and evening/weekend programs available. Faculty: 3 full-time (1 woman), 11 part-time (3 women). Students: 213 (172 women). *Entrance requirements:* MAT. Application fee: $30. *Financial aid:* Available to part-time students. • Dr. Ruth Ann Althaus, Director, 630-829-6225. Fax: 630-960-1126. Application contact: Dr. James Hagen, 630-829-6224. Fax: 630-829-6226. E-mail: jhagen@ben.edu.

Boise State University, College of Health Science, Program in Health Science, Boise, ID 83725-0399. Awards MHS. Part-time programs available. Faculty: 10 full-time (5 women), 4 part-time (2 women). Students: 2 full-time (1 woman), 15 part-time (12 women); includes 1 minority (Native American). Average age 38. 9 applicants, 89% accepted. *Entrance requirements:* GRE General Test (minimum combined score of 1000), minimum GPA of 3.0 in last 60 hours. Application deadline: 7/26 (priority date; rolling processing; 11/29 for spring admission). Application fee: $20 ($30 for international students). Electronic applications accepted. *Tuition:* $3020 per year full-time, $135 per credit part-time for state residents; $8900 per year full-time, $135 per credit part-time for nonresidents. *Financial aid:* In 1997–98, 2 students received aid, including 2 graduate assistantships; Federal Work-Study, institutionally sponsored loans, and career-related internships or fieldwork also available. Aid available to part-time students. Financial aid application deadline: 3/1. • Dr. Gary Shook, Graduate Director, 208-385-3795. Fax: 208-385-3469.

Boston University, School of Medicine, School of Public Health, Boston, MA 02215. Awards MA, MPH, M Sc, D Sc, PhD, Certificate, JD/MPH, MBA/MPH, MD/MPH, MPH/MA, MSW/MPH. Accredited by CEPH. Part-time and evening/weekend programs available. Faculty: 25 full-time (6 women), 79 part-time (19 women). Students: 253 full-time (193 women), 296 part-time (218 women); includes 96 minority (20 African Americans, 53 Asian Americans, 22 Hispanics, 1 Native American), 52 international. Average age 31. In 1997, 265 master's, 4 doctorates awarded. *Degree requirements:* For doctorate, 1 foreign language, dissertation, comprehensive written and oral exams. *Entrance requirements:* For master's, GRE General Test, TOEFL; for doctorate, GRE General Test, MPH or equivalent. Application deadline: 4/15 (rolling processing; 10/25 for spring admission). Application fee: $50. *Financial aid:* Federal Work-Study, institutionally sponsored loans, and career-related internships or fieldwork available. Aid available to part-time students. *Faculty research:* Chemical carcinogenesis, patients' rights, health services, elderly medical care, substance use and abuse, AIDS. • Robert F. Meenan, Director, 617-638-4640. Application contact: Barbara St. Onge, Director of Admissions, 617-638-4640. Fax: 617-638-5299. E-mail: sphadmis@bu.edu.

See in-depth description on page 1487.

Bowling Green State University, College of Health and Human Services, Program in Public Health, Bowling Green, OH 43403. Awards MPH. Offered jointly with the Medical College of Ohio and the University of Toledo. Part-time programs available. Students: 13 part-time (6 women); includes 1 minority (African American). 22 applicants, 100% accepted. *Degree requirements:* Thesis or alternative. *Entrance requirements:* GRE General Test, TOEFL (minimum score 550), minimum GPA of 3.0. Application deadline: 3/15. Application fee: $30. *Tuition:* $6070 per year full-time, $284 per credit hour part-time for state residents; $11,358 per year full-time, $536 per credit hour part-time for nonresidents. *Financial aid:* Application deadline 2/15; applicants required to submit FAFSA. • Dr. Clyde Willis, Dean, College of Health and Human Services, 419-372-8242.

Brooklyn College of the City University of New York, Department of Health and Nutrition Science, Program in Community Health, 2900 Bedford Avenue, Brooklyn, NY 11210-2889. Offers community health (MA, MPH), computer science and health science (MS), health care management (MA, MPH), health care policy and administration (MA, MPH), nutrition (MS), thanatology (MA). MS (computer science and health science) offered jointly with the Department of Computer and Information Science. Students: 2 full-time (0 women), 34 part-time (25 women); includes 19 minority (17 African Americans, 2 Hispanics). In 1997, 12 degrees awarded. *Degree requirements:* Thesis or alternative required, foreign language not required. *Entrance requirements:* TOEFL (minimum score 500), 18 credits in health-related areas. Application deadline: 3/1 (11/1 for spring admission). Application fee: $40. *Expenses:* Tuition $4350 per year full-time, $185 per credit part-time for state residents; $7600 per year full-time, $320 per credit part-time for nonresidents. Fees $500 per year for state residents; $806 per year for nonresidents. *Financial aid:* Application deadline 5/1; applicants required to submit FAFSA. *Faculty research:* Diet restriction, religious practices in bereavement, diabetes, stress management, palliative care. • Dr. Erika Friedmann, Chairperson, Department of Health and Nutrition Science, 718-951-5026. E-mail: erikaf@brooklyn.cuny.edu. Application contact: Jerrold Mirotznik, Deputy Chairperson for Graduate Studies, 718-951-4197. Fax: 718-951-4670.

California State University, Fresno, Division of Graduate Studies, School of Health and Social Work, Department of Public Health, 5241 North Maple Avenue, Fresno, CA 93740. Offers programs in environmental/occupational health (MPH), health administration (MPH), health promotion (MPH). Preaccredited by CEPH. Part-time and evening/weekend programs available. Faculty: 8 full-time (1 woman). Students: 31 full-time (23 women), 51 part-time (28 women); includes 30 minority (6 African Americans, 15 Asian Americans, 9 Hispanics), 2 international. Average age 31. 46 applicants, 80% accepted. In 1997, 6 degrees awarded. *Degree requirements:* Thesis or alternative required, foreign language not required. *Average time to degree:* master's–3.5 years full-time. *Entrance requirements:* GRE General Test, TOEFL (minimum score 550), minimum GPA of 2.5. Application deadline: 3/1 (priority date; rolling processing). Application fee: $55. Electronic applications accepted. *Expenses:* Tuition $0 for state residents; $246 per unit for nonresidents. Fees $1872 per year full-time, $1206 per year part-time. *Financial aid:* In 1997–98, 3 fellowships totaling $13,500, 19 graduate assistantships, scholarships totaling $30,972 were awarded; research assistantships, Federal Work-Study, and career-related internships or fieldwork also available. Financial aid application deadline: 3/1; applicants required to submit FAFSA. • Dr. Sanford Brown, Graduate Program Coordinator, 209-278-4747. E-mail: sanford_brown@csufresno.edu.

California State University, Northridge, College of Health and Human Development, Department of Health Sciences, Program in Public Health, Northridge, CA 91330. Awards MPH. Students: 23 full-time (18 women), 25 part-time (24 women); includes 15 minority (3 African Americans, 4 Asian Americans, 7 Hispanics, 1 Native American). Average age 32. 39 applicants, 77% accepted. *Entrance requirements:* TOEFL, GRE General Test or minimum GPA of 3.0. Application deadline: 11/30. Application fee: $55. *Expenses:* Tuition $0 for state residents; $246 per unit for nonresidents. Fees $1970 per year full-time, $1304 per year part-time. *Financial aid:* Application deadline 3/1. • Dr. Miriam Cotler, Chair, Department of Health Sciences, 818-677-3101. Application contact: Dr. Roberta Madison, Graduate Coordinator, 818-677-2015 Ext. 3101.

Columbia University, School of Public Health, New York, NY 10032. Awards Exec MPH, MPH, MS, Dr PH, PhD, DDS/MPH, MBA/MPH, MD/MPH, MPA/MPH, MPH/MIA, MPH/MS. One or more programs accredited by CEPH. MPH/MS offered jointly with the School of Nursing, the School of Social Work, the Program in Urban Planning, and the Program in Occupational Therapy; PhD offered in cooperation with the Graduate School of Arts and Sciences. Part-time and evening/weekend programs available. Faculty: 103 full-time (50 women), 201 part-time (91 women). Students: 292 full-time (230 women), 337 part-time (214 women); includes 219 minority (70 African Americans, 109 Asian Americans, 39 Hispanics, 1 Native American), 52 international. Average age 31. 1,116 applicants, 56% accepted. In 1997, 238 master's, 8 doctorates awarded. *Degree requirements:* For doctorate, dissertation required, foreign language not required. *Average time to degree:* master's–1.5 years full-time, 3 years part-time; doctorate–4 years full-time, 7 years part-time. *Entrance requirements:* For master's, GRE General Test; for doctorate, GRE General Test, MPH or equivalent (Dr PH). Application deadline: 4/10 (11/15 for spring admission). Application fee: $60. *Tuition:* $22,320 per year full-time, $744 per credit part-time. *Financial aid:* 377 students received aid; fellowships, research assistantships, teaching assistantships, Federal Work-Study, and career-related internships or fieldwork available. Aid available to part-time students. Financial aid application deadline: 3/15; applicants required to submit FAFSA. • Dr. Allan Rosenfield, Dean, 212-305-3927. Application contact: Office of Admissions, 212-305-3927. Fax: 212-305-6450. E-mail: ph-admit@columbia.edu.

See in-depth description on page 1489.

Eastern Virginia Medical School, Program in Public Health, Norfolk, VA 23501-1980. Awards MPH. Part-time and evening/weekend programs available. Students: 13 part-time (8 women); includes 2 minority (both African Americans). 31 applicants, 42% accepted. *Entrance requirements:* GRE General Test (minimum combined score of 1000), TOEFL (minimum score 550). Application fee: $50. *Expenses:* Tuition $9285 per year. Fees $198 per year. *Financial aid:* 8 students received aid; institutionally sponsored loans and career-related internships or fieldwork available. Financial aid application deadline: 4/1; applicants required to submit FAFSA. • Don Combs, Vice President for Planning and Program Development, 757-446-6090.

East Stroudsburg University of Pennsylvania, School of Health Sciences and Human Performance, East Stroudsburg, PA 18301-2999. Awards M Ed, MPH, MS. One or more programs accredited by CEPH. Part-time and evening/weekend programs available. *Degree requirements:* Comprehensive exam required, foreign language not required. *Application deadline:* 7/31 (priority date; rolling processing; 11/30 for spring admission). *Application fee:* $15 ($25 for international students). *Expenses:* Tuition $3468 per year full-time, $193 per credit part-time for state residents; $6236 per year full-time, $346 per credit part-time for nonresidents. Fees $700 per year full-time, $39 per credit part-time.

East Tennessee State University, College of Public and Allied Health, Department of Public Health, Johnson City, TN 37614-0734. Awards MPH. Part-time programs available. Faculty: 9 full-time (6 women). Students: 15 full-time (11 women), 12 part-time (10 women); includes 4 minority (3 African Americans, 1 Native American), 3 international. Average age 32. 21 applicants, 62% accepted. In 1997, 11 degrees awarded. *Degree requirements:* Comprehensive written exam required, thesis optional, foreign language not required. *Entrance requirements:* GRE General Test (minimum combined score of 1440 on three sections), TOEFL (minimum score 550), 2 years of community health experience. Application deadline: 7/15 (priority date; rolling processing). Application fee: $25 ($35 for international students). *Tuition:* $2944 per year full-time, $158 per credit hour part-time for state residents; $7770 per year full-time, $369 per credit hour part-time for nonresidents. *Financial aid:* In 1997–98, 2 research assistantships (both to first-year students) were awarded; teaching assistantships, full tuition waivers, institutionally sponsored loans, and career-related internships or fieldwork also available. • Dr. Richard Wissell, Chair and MPH Coordinator, 423-439-4427. Fax: 423-439-5238. E-mail: wissell@etsu-tn.edu.

Emerson College, School of Communication, Management, and Public Policy, Department of Communication, Program in Health Communication, Boston, MA 02116-1511. Awards MA. Offered jointly with Tufts University. Part-time and evening/weekend programs available. Students: 29 full-time (24 women), 12 part-time (all women); includes 1 international. Average age 26. 29 applicants, 83% accepted. *Degree requirements:* Thesis, comprehensive exam. *Entrance requirements:* GMAT or GRE General Test, minimum GPA of 3.0. Application deadline: 7/1 (rolling processing; 12/1 for spring admission). Application fee: $45 ($75 for international students). *Expenses:* Tuition $566 per credit. Fees $30 per semester (minimum). *Financial aid:* Career-related internships or fieldwork available. Aid available to part-time students. Financial aid application deadline: 2/15; applicants required to submit FAFSA. • Dr. Scott Ratzan, Program Director, 617-824-8737. Application contact: Lynn Terrell, Director of Graduate Admissions, 617-824-8610. Fax: 617-824-8614. E-mail: gradapp@emerson.edu.

Announcement: The Emerson-Tufts program in health communication is designed to educate professionals who can craft and deliver campaigns that promote good health and disease prevention, participate in the planning and implementation of health-care policy, and employ ethical decision making that will enhance the quality of life for individuals and communities around the globe. The program builds upon the application of theoretical models from communication, medicine, social marketing, negotiation, management, epidemiology, psychology, government, and public health. Boston, as a media center as well as a mecca for medical care and research, offers a broad range of internship opportunities.

Emory University, The Rollins School of Public Health, Atlanta, GA 30322-1100. Awards MPH, MS, MSPH, PhD, JD/MPH, MBA/MPH, MD/MPH, MSN/MPH. One or more programs accredited by CEPH. PhD offered jointly with the Department of Biostatistics and the Division of Epidemiology in the Graduate School of Arts and Sciences. Part-time programs available. Faculty: 94 full-time (43 women), 223 part-time (73 women), 127.5 FTE. Students: 420 full-time (311 women), 285 part-time (201 women); includes 231 minority (115 African Americans, 96 Asian Americans, 18 Hispanics, 2 Native Americans), 43 international. Average age 26. 883 applicants, 67% accepted. In 1997, 237 master's, 6 doctorates awarded. *Degree requirements:* For master's, thesis (for some programs), practicum required, foreign language not required. *Entrance requirements:* GRE General Test. Application deadline: 2/15 (priority date; rolling processing). Application fee: $50. *Expenses:* Tuition $14,136 per year full-time, $589 per credit hour part-time. Fees $200 per year. *Financial aid:* In 1997–98, 485 students received aid, including scholarships totaling $907,495; fellowships, research assistantships, teaching assistantships, Federal Work-Study, institutionally sponsored loans, and career-related internships or fieldwork also available. Aid available to part-time students. Financial aid application deadline: 2/15; applicants required to submit CSS PROFILE or FAFSA. *Faculty research:* Cancer risk and occurrence, AIDS prevention, infectious disease models, violence prevention, minority health. Total annual research expenditures: $14 million. • Dr. James W. Curran, Dean, 404-727-8720. Fax: 404-727-9853. E-mail: curran@sph.emory.edu. Application contact: Susan Daniel, Director of Admissions, 404-727-5481. Fax: 404-727-3996. E-mail: admit@sph.emory.edu.

See in-depth description on page 1493.

Florida International University, College of Health, Department of Public Health, Miami, FL 33199. Awards MPH. Accredited by CEPH. Offered jointly with the University of Miami. Part-time programs available. Faculty: 5 full-time (0 women), 1 (woman) part-time, 5.5 FTE.

Students: 37 full-time (26 women), 42 part-time (29 women); includes 48 minority (32 African Americans, 2 Asian Americans, 14 Hispanics), 2 international. Average age 34. 62 applicants, 52% accepted. In 1997, 25 degrees awarded. *Degree requirements:* Computer language required, thesis optional, foreign language not required. *Entrance requirements:* GRE General Test (minimum combined score of 1000), minimum GPA of 3.0. Application deadline: 4/1 (priority date; rolling processing; 10/1 for spring admission). Application fee: $20. *Expenses:* Tuition $138 per credit hour for state residents; $482 per credit hour for nonresidents. Fees $46 per semester. *Faculty research:* Drugs/AIDS intervention among migrant workers, provision of services for active/recovering drug users with HIV. • Dr. William J. Keppler, Chairperson, 305-940-5877. Fax: 305-919-5507.

The George Washington University, School of Public Health and Health Services, Doctoral Program in Public Health, Washington, DC 20052. Awards Dr PH. Terminal master's awarded for partial completion of doctoral program. *Application deadline:* 5/15 (priority date; rolling processing; 11/15 for spring admission). *Application fee:* $50. *Expenses:* Tuition $680 per semester hour. Fees $35 per semester hour. • Dr. Donna Lind Infeld, Director, 202-994-1514. Fax: 202-994-4067. E-mail: dlind@gwis2.circ.gwu.edu. Application contact: Michelle Sparacino, Director of Recruitment, 202-994-2160. Fax: 202-994-3773. E-mail: sphhs-info@gwumc.edu.

Announcement: The Dr PH educates future leaders in public health and health services. Students specialize in health systems, health policy, health behavior, or international health and development. Program requires 72 credit hours. Research opportunities available at GW research centers and other Washington sites, including the Institute of Medicine. Graduates prepared for professional careers in public and private organizations that deliver, finance, purchase, regulate, and set health services policy nationally and internationally. Visit the Web site (http://www.gwumc.edu/sphhs).

See in-depth description on page 1495.

The George Washington University, School of Public Health and Health Services, Master's Program in Public Health, Washington, DC 20052. Awards MPH, JD/MPH, LL M/MPH, MD/MPH, MSHS/MPH. Offerings include administrative medicine (MPH), including management, policy; community-oriented primary care (MPH); environmental-occupational health (MPH); epidemiology-biostatistics (MPH); health promotion-disease prevention (MPH); international health (MPH), including health promotion, policy and programs; maternal and child health (MPH). Accredited by CEPH. *Degree requirements:* Case study or special project required, thesis not required. *Entrance requirements:* GMAT, GRE General Test, or MCAT; TOEFL. Application deadline: 5/15 (priority date; rolling processing; 11/15 for spring admission). Application fee: $50. *Expenses:* Tuition $680 per semester hour. Fees $35 per semester hour. • Dr. Daniel Hoffman, Associate Dean, 202-994-7770. E-mail: sphdah@gwumc.edu. Application contact: Michelle Sparacino, Director of Recruitment, 202-994-2160. Fax: 202-994-3773. E-mail: sphhs-info@gwumc.edu.

See in-depth description on page 1495.

Harvard University, Extension School, Cambridge, MA 02138-3722. Offerings include public health (CPH). School faculty: 400 part-time. *Application deadline:* rolling. *Application fee:* $75. • Michael Shinagel, Dean. Application contact: Program Director, 617-495-4024. Fax: 617-495-9176.

Harvard University, School of Public Health, Boston, MA 02115. Awards MOH, MPH, SM, DPH, PhD, SD, MD/MPH. One or more programs accredited by CEPH. SM (occupational health, maternal and child health) offered jointly with Simmons College. Part-time programs available. Faculty: 160 full-time (46 women), 154 part-time (40 women). Students: 544 full-time (346 women), 210 part-time (118 women); includes 135 minority (31 African Americans, 80 Asian Americans, 19 Hispanics, 5 Native Americans), 192 international. Average age 32. 1,211 applicants, 56% accepted. In 1997, 293 master's, 48 doctorates awarded. *Degree requirements:* For doctorate, dissertation, qualifying exam. *Entrance requirements:* GRE, TOEFL (minimum score 550). Application deadline: 1/4. Application fee: $60. *Expenses:* Tuition $21,895 per year full-time, $10,948 per year part-time. Fees $686 per year. *Financial aid:* Fellowships, research assistantships, teaching assistantships, partial tuition waivers, Federal Work-Study available. Aid available to part-time students. Financial aid application deadline: 2/12; applicants required to submit FAFSA. • Dr. James Ware, Acting Dean, 617-432-1025. Application contact: Carrie Daniels, Assistant Director of Admissions, 617-432-1031. Fax: 617-432-2009. E-mail: admisofc@sph.harvard.edu.

See in-depth description on page 1497.

Harvard University, Graduate School of Arts and Sciences, Program in Biological Sciences in Public Health (BPH), Boston, MA 02115. Awards PhD. Terminal master's awarded for partial completion of doctoral program. *Degree requirements:* For doctorate, dissertation, qualifying exam required, foreign language not required. *Entrance requirements:* For doctorate, GRE General Test, GRE Subject Test, TOEFL (minimum score 550). Application deadline: 12/15. Application fee: $60. *Expenses:* Tuition $21,342 per year. Fees $686 per year. *Financial aid:* Fellowships, research assistantships, teaching assistantships, full tuition waivers, institutionally sponsored loans available. Financial aid application deadline: 1/1. *Faculty research:* Nutrition biochemistry, molecular and cellular toxicology, cardiovascular disease, cancer biology, tropical public health, environmental health physiology. • Dyann Wirth, Director, 617-432-4470. Application contact: Leah Simons, Manager of Student Affairs, 617-432-0162.

Hunter College of the City University of New York, School of Health Sciences, Program in Community Health Education, 695 Park Avenue, New York, NY 10021-5085. Awards MPH, MS/MPH. Accredited by CEPH. Faculty: 6 full-time (3 women), 12 part-time (6 women). Students: 13 full-time (12 women), 115 part-time (99 women); includes 64 minority (35 African Americans, 12 Asian Americans, 14 Hispanics, 3 Native Americans), 1 international. Average age 33. In 1997, 35 degrees awarded. *Degree requirements:* Comprehensive exam required, foreign language and thesis not required. *Entrance requirements:* GRE General Test, TOEFL (minimum score 550), 2 years of health-related experience. Application deadline: 4/7 (11/7 for spring admission). Application fee: $40. *Expenses:* Tuition $4350 per year full-time, $185 per credit part-time for state residents; $7600 per year full-time, $320 per credit part-time for nonresidents. Fees $26 per year. *Financial aid:* Application deadline 3/1. *Faculty research:* Gerontology, occupational and environmental epidemiology, AIDS policy, sexuality, urban health, women's health. • Marilyn Auerbach, Director, 212-481-5111.

Idaho State University, College of Health Professions, Department of Health and Nutrition Sciences, Pocatello, ID 83209. Offers programs in health education (MHE), public health (MPH). Part-time programs available. Faculty: 7 full-time (2 women), 2 part-time (0 women). Students: 23 full-time (14 women), 25 part-time (24 women); includes 1 minority (African American). Average age 33. In 1997, 9 degrees awarded. *Entrance requirements:* GRE General Test (score in 35th percentile or higher). Application deadline: 7/1 (priority date; rolling processing; 12/1 for spring admission). Application fee: $30. *Tuition:* $3130 per year full-time, $136 per credit hour part-time for state residents; $9370 per year full-time, $226 per credit hour part-time for nonresidents. *Financial aid:* Teaching assistantships and career-related internships or fieldwork available. • Dr. James Girvan, Chairman, 208-236-2656. Fax: 208-236-4000.

Indiana University Bloomington, School of Health, Physical Education and Recreation, Program in Applied Health Science, Bloomington, IN 47405. Offers health and safety studies (HSD, HS Dir), health behavior (PhD), health promotion (MS), human development/family studies (MS), nutrition science (MS), public health (MPH), public health education (HS Dir), safety management (MS), school and college health education (HS Dir), school health education (MS). One or more programs accredited by CEPH. PhD offered through the University Graduate School. Part-time programs available. Faculty: 14 full-time (6 women). Students: 14 full-time (11 women), 11 part-time (7 women); includes 3 minority (2 African Americans, 1 Hispanic), 5 international. In 1997, 9 master's, 2 doctorates awarded. Terminal master's awarded for partial completion of doctoral program. *Degree requirements:* For master's, thesis optional, foreign language not required; for doctorate, dissertation; for HS Dir, thesis or alternative required, foreign language not required. *Entrance requirements:* For master's, GRE or minimum GPA of 2.8, 12 hours of course work in health education; for doctorate and HS Dir, GRE. Application deadline: rolling. Application fee: $35. *Expenses:* Tuition $153 per credit hour for state residents; $446 per credit hour for nonresidents. Fees $343 per year. *Financial aid:* Fellowships, teaching assistantships, fee scholarships, fee remissions, partial tuition waivers, Federal Work-Study, institutionally sponsored loans, and career-related internships or fieldwork available. Financial aid application deadline: 3/1. *Faculty research:* Cancer education, HIV/AIDS and drug education, public health, parent-child interactions, safety education. • James W. Crowe, Chair, 812-855-3627. Application contact: Mohammad Torabi, Graduate Coordinator, 812-855-4806. Fax: 812-855-3936.

Johns Hopkins University, School of Hygiene and Public Health, Baltimore, MD 21205. Awards MHS, MPH, Sc M, Dr PH, PhD, Sc D, MD/PhD, MHS/MA, MPH/MSN. One or more programs accredited by CEPH. MHS/MA offered jointly with the Paul H. Nitze School of Advanced International Studies; MPH/MSN offered jointly with the School of Nursing. Part-time and evening/weekend programs available. Faculty: 386 full-time, 529 part-time. Students: 1,196 (757 women); includes 257 minority (73 African Americans, 140 Asian Americans, 41 Hispanics, 3 Native Americans), 260 international. Average age 31. 2,091 applicants, 56% accepted. In 1997, 426 master's, 89 doctorates awarded. *Degree requirements:* For doctorate, dissertation, 1 year full-time residency, oral and written exams. *Entrance requirements:* GRE General Test. Application deadline: 2/1 (rolling processing). Application fee: $60. *Financial aid:* In 1997–98, 1,105 scholarships (306 to first-year students) averaging $458 per month and totaling $9 were awarded; Federal Work-Study, institutionally sponsored loans also available. Aid available to part-time students. Financial aid application deadline: 4/15; applicants required to submit FAFSA. *Total annual research expenditures:* $159.6 million. • Dr. Alfred Sommer, Dean, 410-955-3540. Fax: 410-955-0121. Application contact: Linda R. Myers, Director of Admissions, 410-955-3543. Fax: 410-955-0464. E-mail: lmyers@jhsph.edu.

See in-depth description on page 1501.

Loma Linda University, School of Public Health, Loma Linda, CA 92350. Awards MHA, MPH, MS, MSPH, Dr PH. One or more programs accredited by CEPH. Part-time programs available. Faculty: 62 full-time (28 women), 6 part-time (3 women). Students: 239 full-time (143 women), 175 part-time (119 women); includes 143 minority (32 African Americans, 67 Asian Americans, 39 Hispanics, 5 Native Americans), 57 international. 284 applicants, 79% accepted. In 1997, 123 master's, 6 doctorates awarded. Terminal master's awarded for partial completion of doctoral program. *Degree requirements:* For doctorate, dissertation. *Entrance requirements:* For master's, Michigan English Language Assessment Battery (minimum score 92) or TOEFL (minimum score 600); for doctorate, GRE General Test (minimum combined score of 1500 on three sections). Application deadline: rolling. Application fee: $100. *Tuition:* $380 per unit. *Financial aid:* In 1997–98, 80 students received aid, including 2 graduate assistantships (both to first-year students); fellowships, research assistantships, teaching assistantships, partial tuition waivers, Federal Work-Study, institutionally sponsored loans, and career-related internships or fieldwork also available. Aid available to part-time students. Financial aid application deadline: 5/15. *Faculty research:* Lifestyle and health, nutrition and cancer, nutrition and cardiovascular disease, smoking and health, aging and longevity. • Dr. Richard Hart, Dean, 909-824-4578. Fax: 909-824-4087. Application contact: Terri Tamayose, Director of Admissions and Academic Records, 909-824-4694. Fax: 909-824-8087. E-mail: ttamayose@sph.llu.edu.

Louisiana State University Medical Center, School of Graduate Studies in New Orleans, Department of Public Health and Preventive Medicine, 433 Bolivar Street, New Orleans, LA 70112-2223. Awards MPH. Open only to currently enrolled medical students. Program new for fall 1998. Part-time and evening/weekend programs available. Faculty: 4 full-time (2 women). Students: 11 part-time (3 women); includes 2 minority (1 African American, 1 Asian American). Average age 24. 14 applicants, 79% accepted. *Degree requirements:* Thesis required, foreign language not required. *Average time to degree:* master's–0 years part-time. *Entrance requirements:* Interview. Application deadline: 4/1. Application fee: $30. *Expenses:* Tuition $2878 per year full-time, $421 per semester (minimum) part-time for state residents; $6003 per year full-time, $838 per semester (minimum) part-time for nonresidents. Fees $350 per year full-time, $90 per semester (minimum) part-time. *Faculty research:* Health care outcomes, occupational medicine, health status measurement, Rasch measurement, civil rights litigation. • Dr. Anne Jordan, Program Administrator, 504-568-6864. Fax: 504-568-6905. E-mail: ajorda@lsumc.edu.

Medical College of Ohio, Program in Public Health, Toledo, OH 43699-0008. Awards MPH, MD/MPH. Offered jointly in a consortium with Bowling Green State University and the University of Toledo. Part-time and evening/weekend programs available. 29 applicants, 79% accepted. *Average time to degree:* master's–2.5 years part-time. *Entrance requirements:* GRE General Test, minimum undergraduate GPA of 3.0. Application deadline: rolling. Application fee: $30. *Expenses:* Tuition $5939 per year full-time, $189 per credit hour part-time for state residents; $13,699 per year full-time, $428 per credit hour part-time for nonresidents. Fees $519 per year full-time, $356 per year part-time. *Financial aid:* Scholarships, Federal Work-Study, institutionally sponsored loans available. Financial aid applicants required to submit FAFSA. *Faculty research:* Public health administration, health promotion and education, environmental and occupational health. • Dr. Stephen Roberts, Director, 419-530-2765. E-mail: srobert@utnet.utoledo.edu. Application contact: Theresa Langenderfer, Secretary, 419-383-4160. Fax: 419-383-6140. E-mail: mcogradschool@mco.edu.

Medical College of Wisconsin, Medical School, Department of Preventive Medicine, Milwaukee, WI 53226-0509. Offers programs in general preventive medicine and public health (MPH), occupational medicine (MPH). Accredited by CEPH. Part-time programs available. Postbaccalaureate distance learning degree programs offered (no on-campus study). *Degree requirements:* Project in occupational medicine or public health required, foreign language and thesis not required. *Average time to degree:* master's–3.3 years part-time. *Entrance requirements:* TOEFL, MD/DO license to practice medicine in U. S. or Canada. Application deadline: 7/15 (priority date; rolling processing; 3/15 for spring admission). Application fee: $125. *Tuition:* $16,264 per year for state residents; $26,355 per year for nonresidents. *Faculty research:* Environmental medicine, ergonomics, epidemiology, surveillance, distance education.

Morehouse School of Medicine, Master of Public Health Program, Atlanta, GA 30310-1495. Awards MPH, MPH/MBA, MPH/MD, MPH/M Div, MPH/MIAD, MPH/MSW. MPH/MBA, MPH/MSW, and MPH/MIAD offered jointly with Clark Atlanta University; MPH/M Div offered jointly with the Interdenomination Theological Center. Part-time programs available. Faculty: 4 full-time (2 women), 45 part-time (23 women), 24 FTE. Students: 14 full-time (5 women), 4 part-time (all women); includes 18 minority (all African Americans). Average age 32. 39 applicants, 26% accepted. *Degree requirements:* Thesis. *Entrance requirements:* GMAT, GRE General Test (MPH/MBA), public health or human service experience. Application deadline: 4/1 (rolling processing; 8/1 for spring admission). Application fee: $45. *Financial aid:* In 1997–98, 10 students received aid, including 2 research assistantships (1 to a first-year student) averaging $800 per month and totaling $8,000; teaching assistantships, Federal Work-Study, institutionally sponsored loans, and career-related internships or fieldwork also available. Financial aid application deadline: 4/20. *Faculty research:* Women's and adolescent health, violence prevention, environmental justice, literacy and development. Total annual research expenditures: $45,000. • Dr. Janice Vaughn, Program Director, 404-752-1898. Application contact: Karen A. Lewis, Assistant Director of Admissions, 404-752-1650. Fax: 404-752-1512. E-mail: karen@link.msm.edu.

New Mexico State University, College of Health and Social Services, Department of Health Science, Las Cruces, NM 88003-8001. Awards MPH. Faculty: 5 full-time (2 women), 1 (woman) part-time. Students: 12 full-time (8 women), 11 part-time (9 women); includes 9 minority (3 African Americans, 1 Asian American, 5 Hispanics), 1 international. Average age 35. 19 applicants, 68% accepted. *Degree requirements:* Thesis optional, foreign language not required.

Directory: Public Health—General

New Mexico State University (continued)

Entrance requirements: GRE or MAT, 6 hours in psychosocial course work, 4 hours in biology, 3 hours in statistics. Application deadline: 7/1 (priority date; rolling processing; 11/1 for spring admission). Application fee: $15 ($35 for international students). Electronic applications accepted. *Tuition:* $2514 per year full-time, $105 per credit hour part-time for state residents; $7848 per year full-time, $327 per credit hour part-time for nonresidents. *Financial aid:* Research assistantships, teaching assistantships, and career-related internships or fieldwork available. Financial aid application deadline: 3/1. *Faculty research:* Community health education, health issues of U.S.-Mexico border, health policy and management, victims of violence (spatial abuse), environmental and occupational health issues. • Jeffrey E. Brandon, Associate Dean, 505-646-4300. Fax: 505-646-4343. E-mail: jbrandon@nmsu.edu.

New York Medical College, Graduate School of Health Sciences, Valhalla, NY 10595-1691. Awards MPH, MS. Part-time and evening/weekend programs available. Faculty: 11 full-time (7 women), 120 part-time (63 women). Students: 117 full-time, 509 part-time. Average age 33. In 1997, 50 degrees awarded. *Degree requirements:* Computer language required, foreign language not required. *Entrance requirements:* TOEFL. Application fee: $35 ($60 for international students). *Tuition:* $415 per credit. *Financial aid:* In 1997–98, 65 students received aid, including 8 tuition reimbursements totaling $18,240; Federal Work-Study, institutionally sponsored loans, and career-related internships or fieldwork also available. Aid available to part-time students. Financial aid applicants required to submit FAFSA. *Faculty research:* Etiology of Alzheimer's, colorectal cancer, medical managed care, biomechanical analysis of shoulder, neurobehavioral analysis of reaching movements in the neurologically impaired. • Sheila M. Smythe, Dean, 914-594-4531. Application contact: Marian McGowan, Director of Admissions, 914-594-4510.

See in-depth description on page 1507.

New York University, School of Education, Department of Health Studies, New York, NY 10012-1019. Offers programs in deafness rehabilitation (MA); health education (MA, MPH, Ed D, PhD, CAS), including administrators and supervisors of health education (CAS), community health education (MPH, Ed D, PhD), human sexuality education (MA, Ed D, PhD), school and college health education (MA, Ed D, PhD); recreation and leisure studies (MA, PhD, CAS); rehabilitation counseling (MA, PhD). One or more programs accredited by CEPH. Part-time and evening/weekend programs available. Faculty: 10 full-time (5 women), 37 part-time. Students: 100 full-time, 116 part-time. 173 applicants, 60% accepted. In 1997, 59 master's, 8 doctorates awarded. Terminal master's awarded for partial completion of doctoral program. *Degree requirements:* For doctorate, dissertation. *Entrance requirements:* For master's, TOEFL; for doctorate, GRE General Test, TOEFL, interview; for CAS, TOEFL, master's degree. Application deadline: 2/1 (priority date; rolling processing; 12/1 for spring admission). Application fee: $40 ($60 for international students). *Financial aid:* Partial tuition waivers, Federal Work-Study, institutionally sponsored loans, and career-related internships or fieldwork available. Aid available to part-time students. Financial aid application deadline: 3/1; applicants required to submit FAFSA. *Faculty research:* HIV/AIDS education, HIV infection among intravenous drug users, international health education. • Vivian P. J. Clarke, Chairperson, 212-998-5780. Application contact: Office of Graduate Admissions, 212-998-5030. Fax: 212-995-4328.

See in-depth description on page 757.

Northern Arizona University, College of Health Professions, Department of Health, Physical Education, Exercise Science, and Nutrition, Program in Public Health, Flagstaff, AZ 86011. Offers health education and health promotion (MPH). Accredited by CEPH. Offered jointly with University of Arizona. *Degree requirements:* Thesis or alternative required, foreign language not required. *Entrance requirements:* GRE General Test, minimum GPA of 3.0. Application fee: $45. *Expenses:* Tuition $2088 per year full-time, $330 per semester (minimum) part-time for state residents; $8004 per year full-time, $1002 per semester (minimum) part-time for nonresidents. Fees $72 per year full-time, $18 per semester (minimum) part-time. • Dr. John P. Sciacca, Director, 520-523-4122.

Northern Illinois University, College of Health and Human Sciences, School of Allied Health Professions, De Kalb, IL 60115-2854. Offers program in public health (MPH). Accredited by CEPH. Part-time programs available. Faculty: 12 full-time (9 women), 1 (woman) part-time. Students: 14 full-time (12 women), 17 part-time (12 women); includes 4 minority (2 African Americans, 1 Asian American, 1 Hispanic), 2 international. Average age 34. 34 applicants, 53% accepted. In 1997, 11 degrees awarded. *Degree requirements:* Comprehensive exam, internship, research paper required, thesis optional, foreign language not required. *Entrance requirements:* GRE General Test, TOEFL (minimum score 550), minimum GPA of 2.75. Application deadline: 6/1 (rolling processing; 11/1 for spring admission). Application fee: $30. *Tuition:* $3984 per year full-time, $154 per credit hour part-time for state residents; $8160 per year full-time, $328 per credit hour part-time for nonresidents. *Financial aid:* In 1997–98, 13 research assistantships, 3 staff assistantships were awarded; fellowships, teaching assistantships, full tuition waivers, Federal Work-Study, and career-related internships or fieldwork also available. Aid available to part-time students. • Dr. Sherilynn Spear, Chair, 815-753-6329.

Northwestern University, Program in Public Health, Evanston, IL 60208. Awards MPH. Faculty: 16 full-time (8 women), 27 part-time (18 women). Students: 2 part-time (0 women). 3 applicants, 100% accepted. *Entrance requirements:* GRE General Test, TOEFL. Application fee: $50 ($55 for international students). *Tuition:* $20,430 per year full-time, $2424 per course part-time. *Faculty research:* Cardiovascular epidemiology, cancer epidemiology, nutritional interventions for the prevention of cardiovascular disease and cancer, women's health, outcomes research. Total annual research expenditures: $3.844 million. • Roland Chang, Director. Application contact: Maureen Moran, Associate Director, 847-503-0500. Fax: 847-908-9588. E-mail: m-moran@nwu.edu.

Northwestern University, Division of Interdepartmental Programs, Combined MD/MPH Program in Public Health, Evanston, IL 60208. Awards MD/MPH. Application must be made to both The Graduate School and the Medical School. 6 applicants, 100% accepted. *Application fee:* $50 ($55 for international students). *Tuition:* $20,430 per year full-time, $2424 per course part-time. *Financial aid:* Institutionally sponsored loans and career-related internships or fieldwork available. Financial aid application deadline: 1/15; applicants required to submit FAFSA. *Faculty research:* Cardiovascular epidemiology, cancer epidemiology, nutritional interventions for the prevention of cardiovascular disease and cancer, women's health, outcomes research. • Roland Chang, Director. Application contact: Maureen Moran, Associate Director, 847-503-0500. Fax: 847-908-9588. E-mail: m.moran@nwu.edu.

The Ohio State University, College of Medicine and Public Health and Graduate School, Graduate Programs in the Basic Medical Sciences, School of Public Health, Columbus, OH 43210. Awards MPH, MS, PhD, MD/MPH. Preaccredited by CEPH. Part-time and evening/weekend programs available. Faculty: 15 full-time (6 women), 2 part-time (0 women). Students: 49 full-time (37 women), 33 part-time (23 women); includes 17 minority (7 African Americans, 10 Asian Americans), 8 international. Average age 25. 71 applicants, 55% accepted. In 1997, 19 master's awarded (10% entered university research/teaching, 58% found other work related to degree, 32% continued full-time study); 6 doctorates awarded (33% entered university research/teaching, 67% found other work related to degree). Terminal master's awarded for partial completion of doctoral program. *Degree requirements:* For master's, thesis optional, foreign language not required; for doctorate, dissertation required, foreign language not required. *Entrance requirements:* GRE General Test, TOEFL. Application deadline: rolling. Application fee: $30 ($40 for international students). *Tuition:* $5472 per year full-time, $554 per quarter (minimum) part-time for state residents; $14,172 per year full-time, $1424 per quarter (minimum) part-time for nonresidents. *Financial aid:* In 1997–98, 13 research assistantships (2 to first-year students) averaging $842 per month, 2 assistantships, traineeships averaging $876 per month were awarded; fellowships, Federal Work-Study, institutionally sponsored loans also available. Aid available to part-time students. Financial aid application deadline: 7/1. *Faculty research:* Occupational epidemiology, carcinogenesis and chemoprevention, cancer epidemiology and control, environmental exposure and the health of rural populations. Total annual research expenditures: $1.340 million. • Dr. Antoinette Eaton, Chairperson, 614-293-3907. Application contact: Judy Dawson, Graduate Studies Office, 614-293-3907. Fax: 614-293-3937. E-mail: dawson.6@osu.edu.

See in-depth description on page 1509.

Old Dominion University, College of Health Sciences, School of Community Health Professions and Physical Therapy, Norfolk, VA 23529. Offers programs in community health professions (MS), long-term care administration (Certificate), physical therapy (MS), professional preparation (MS), public health (MPH). MPH offered jointly with Eastern Virginia Medical School. Part-time programs available. Faculty: 9 full-time (7 women), 5 part-time (3 women), 10.7 FTE. Students: 143 full-time (94 women), 39 part-time (27 women); includes 30 minority (19 African Americans, 7 Asian Americans, 1 Hispanic, 3 Native Americans), 9 international. Average age 29. In 1997, 86 master's awarded. *Degree requirements:* For master's, oral exam required, thesis optional, foreign language not required. *Entrance requirements:* For master's, GRE General Test, minimum GPA of 2.75. Application deadline: 2/15 (rolling processing). Application fee: $30. *Expenses:* Tuition $180 per credit hour for state residents; $477 per credit hour for nonresidents. Fees $140 per year full-time, $32 per semester part-time. *Financial aid:* In 1997–98, 94 students received aid, including 6 research assistantships (1 to a first-year student) totaling $45,954, 2 tuition grants totaling $3,226; fellowships, teaching assistantships, partial tuition waivers, and career-related internships or fieldwork also available. Aid available to part-time students. Financial aid application deadline: 2/15; applicants required to submit FAFSA. *Faculty research:* Electromyography, nerve conduction, gait analysis, patient-provider communication. • Dr. George Maihafer, Chair, 757-683-4520. E-mail: gmaihafer@odu.edu.

Oregon State University, Graduate School, College of Health and Human Performance, Department of Public Health, Program in Public Health, Corvallis, OR 97331. Awards MPH. Students: 0. *Degree requirements:* Minimum GPA of 3.0 required, foreign language not required. *Entrance requirements:* TOEFL (minimum score 550), minimum GPA of 3.0 in last 90 hours. Application deadline: 3/1 (rolling processing). Application fee: $50. *Tuition:* $6207 per year full-time, $810 per quarter (minimum) part-time for state residents; $10,551 per year full-time, $1293 per quarter (minimum) part-time for nonresidents. *Financial aid:* Application deadline 2/1. • Dr. Rebecca Donatelle, Chair, Department of Public Health, 541-737-3824. Fax: 541-737-4001.

Portland State University, College of Urban and Public Affairs, School of Community Health, Division of Health Education, Portland, OR 97207-0751. Offers programs in health education (MA, MS), health education and health promotion (MPH). MPH offered jointly with Oregon Health Sciences University and Oregon State University. Part-time programs available. Faculty: 8 full-time (5 women), 25 part-time (17 women), 10 FTE. Students: 15 full-time (12 women), 19 part-time (18 women); includes 2 minority (1 African American, 1 Hispanic), 1 international. Average age 32. 18 applicants, 67% accepted. In 1997, 14 degrees awarded. *Degree requirements:* Variable foreign language requirement, oral and written exams required, thesis not required. *Entrance requirements:* TOEFL (minimum score 550), minimum GPA of 3.0 in upper-division course work or 2.75 overall. Application deadline: 4/1 (11/1 for spring admission). Application fee: $50. *Tuition:* $6101 per year full-time, $689 per semester (minimum) part-time for state residents; $10,445 per year full-time, $689 per semester (minimum) part-time for nonresidents. *Financial aid:* In 1997–98, 3 research assistantships (1 to a first-year student) were awarded; fellowships, teaching assistantships, Federal Work-Study, institutionally sponsored loans, and career-related internships or fieldwork also available. Aid available to part-time students. Financial aid application deadline: 3/1; applicants required to submit FAFSA. *Faculty research:* Health and wholeness, exercise physiology, health promotion campaigns, comprehensive health education, maternal/child health. • Application contact: Elizabeth Bull, 503-725-4401. Fax: 503-725-5100. E-mail: eliz@upa.pdx.edu.

Rutgers, The State University of New Jersey, New Brunswick, Edward J. Bloustein School of Planning and Public Policy, Program in Public Health, New Brunswick, NJ 08903. Awards MPH, Dr PH, PhD, MBA/MPH, MD/MPH. Offered jointly with the University of Medicine and Dentistry of New Jersey. Part-time and evening/weekend programs available. Students: 44 full-time (25 women), 187 part-time (116 women); includes 64 minority (19 African Americans, 37 Asian Americans, 7 Hispanics, 1 Native American). Average age 33. 161 applicants, 74% accepted. In 1997, 37 master's awarded; 3 doctorates awarded (100% found work related to degree). *Degree requirements:* For master's, internship required, foreign language and thesis not required; for doctorate, dissertation required, foreign language not required. *Entrance requirements:* For master's, GRE General Test, TOEFL; for doctorate, GRE General Test, MPH (Dr PH); MPH, MA, or MS (PhD). Application deadline: 3/15 (11/1 for spring admission). Application fee: $40. *Expenses:* Tuition $6492 per year full-time, $268 per credit part-time for state residents; $9520 per year full-time, $395 per credit part-time for nonresidents. Fees $208 per year (minimum). *Financial aid:* In 1997–98, fellowships totaling $2,699, 3 teaching assistantships averaging $1,166 per month and totaling $10,500 were awarded; career-related internships or fieldwork also available. Financial aid application deadline: 3/1. *Faculty research:* Epidemiology, risk perception, statistical research design, health care utilization, health promotion. • George G. Rhoads, Director, 732-445-0193. Application contact: Tina Greco, Administrator, 732-445-0199. Fax: 732-445-0917.

See in-depth description on page 1531.

Saint Louis University, School of Public Health, St. Louis, MO 63108. Awards MHA, MPH, PhD, JD/MHA, JD/MPH, MD/MPH, MHA/MBA, MPH/MS, MPH/MSN, MPH/MSW, MPH/PhD. One or more programs accredited by CEPH. Faculty: 23 full-time (8 women), 85 part-time (31 women). Students: 107 full-time (60 women), 109 part-time (78 women); includes 57 minority (28 African Americans, 24 Asian Americans, 5 Hispanics), 18 international. 199 applicants, 66% accepted. In 1997, 50 master's, 3 doctorates awarded. *Degree requirements:* For master's, comprehensive oral exam required, thesis not required; for doctorate, dissertation, preliminary exams. *Entrance requirements:* For master's, GMAT or GRE General Test; for doctorate, GMAT or GRE General Test, interview. Application deadline: rolling. Application fee: $40. *Tuition:* $542 per credit hour. *Financial aid:* In 1997–98, 1 fellowship, 6 research assistantships were awarded; career-related internships or fieldwork also available. Financial aid application deadline: 4/1. *Faculty research:* Health services utilization, health care economics, quality of care, AIDS, homelessness. • Dr. Richard S. Kurz, Dean, 314-977-8111. Application contact: Dr. Marcia Buresch, Assistant Dean of the Graduate School, 314-977-2240. Fax: 314-977-3943.

San Diego State University, College of Health and Human Services, Graduate School of Public Health, San Diego, CA 92182. Awards MPH, MS, PhD, MSW/MPH. Programs in environmental health (MPH, MS); epidemiology (MPH, PhD), including biostatistics (MPH); health promotion (MPH); health services administration (MPH); industrial hygiene (MS); toxicology (MS). Part-time programs available. Faculty: 25 full-time (9 women), 36 part-time (21 women). Students: 237 full-time (156 women), 128 part-time (85 women); includes 116 minority (11 African Americans, 47 Asian Americans, 54 Hispanics, 4 Native Americans), 6 international. 370 applicants, 49% accepted. In 1997, 96 master's, 2 doctorates awarded. *Degree requirements:* For master's, thesis required (for some programs), foreign language not required; for doctorate, dissertation required, foreign language not required. *Entrance requirements:* For master's, GMAT (health services administration), GRE General Test; for doctorate, GRE General Test. Application deadline: 5/15 (priority date; rolling processing; 10/15 for spring admission). Application fee: $55. *Expenses:* Tuition $0 for state residents; $246 per unit for nonresidents. Fees $1932 per year full-time, $1266 per year part-time. *Financial aid:* In 1997–98, 66 traineeships (34 to first-year students) totaling $49,196 were awarded; research assistantships, teaching assistantships, Federal Work-Study, and career-related internships or fieldwork also available. Financial aid applicants required to submit FAFSA. *Faculty research:* Evaluation of tobacco, AIDS prevalence and prevention, mammography, infant death project, Alzheimer's in elderly Chinese. • Dr. Kenneth Bart, Director, 619-594-6317. Application contact:

Brenda Fass-Holmes, Coordinator, Admissions and Student Affairs, 619-594-6317. E-mail: bholmes@mail.sdsu.edu.

San Jose State University, College of Applied Arts and Sciences, Department of Health Science, San Jose, CA 95192-0001. Offers programs in gerontology (MS), health administration (Certificate), health science (MA), public health (MPH). One or more programs accredited by CEPH. Faculty: 5 full-time (1 woman), 2 part-time (1 woman). Students: 54 full-time (48 women), 47 part-time (41 women); includes 29 minority (6 African Americans, 15 Asian Americans, 8 Hispanics), 3 international. Average age 38. 109 applicants, 55% accepted. In 1997, 32 master's awarded. *Entrance requirements:* For master's, GRE General Test (minimum combined score of 1000), minimum B average. Application deadline: 6/1 (rolling processing). Application fee: $59. *Expenses:* Tuition $0 for state residents; $246 per unit for nonresidents. Fees $2017 per year full-time, $1351 per year part-time. *Financial aid:* In 1997–98, 4 fellowships (all to first-year students) were awarded; partial tuition waivers, Federal Work-Study, institutionally sponsored loans, and career-related internships or fieldwork also available. Aid available to part-time students. *Faculty research:* Behavioral science in occupational and health care settings, epidemiology in health care settings. • Dr. William Washington, Chair, 408-924-2970. Application contact: Dr. Kathy Roe, Graduate Coordinator, 408-924-2976.

Sarah Lawrence College, Program in Health Advocacy, Bronxville, NY 10708. Awards MA, MPS. *Degree requirements:* Fieldwork. *Average time to degree:* master's–2 years full-time, 3 years part-time. *Entrance requirements:* Previous course work in biology and microeconomics. Application fee: $45. *Expenses:* Tuition $576 per credit. Fees $290 per year.

Announcement: Graduate study offered in theory and practice of advocacy as it relates to health care for careers such as patient representative or community health ombudsman. MA or MPS granted after 40 course credits plus 600 hours of fieldwork. Small classes. Full-time study requires 4 semesters and 1 summer. Part-time study also available. Prerequisites: biology and microeconomics. Financial aid available.

See in-depth description on page 1513.

Southern Connecticut State University, School of Professional Studies, Department of Public Health, New Haven, CT 06515-1355. Awards MPH. One or more programs accredited by CEPH. Faculty: 8 full-time. Students: 28 full-time (27 women), 66 part-time (57 women); includes 14 minority (8 African Americans, 3 Asian Americans, 3 Hispanics). 129 applicants, 28% accepted. In 1997, 37 degrees awarded. *Degree requirements:* Thesis optional, foreign language not required. *Entrance requirements:* Minimum undergraduate QPA of 3.0 in graduate major field or 2.5 overall, interview. Application deadline: 3/15. Application fee: $40. *Expenses:* Tuition $2632 per year full-time, $188 per credit part-time for state residents; $7200 per year full-time, $188 per credit part-time for nonresidents. Fees $1806 per year full-time, $45 per semester part-time for state residents; $2703 per year full-time, $45 per semester part-time for nonresidents. *Financial aid:* In 1997–98, 1 teaching assistantship was awarded; career-related internships or fieldwork also available. • Dr. William Faraclas, Chairman, 203-392-6950. Application contact: Dr. Michael Perlin, Graduate Coordinator, 203-392-6950.

State University of New York at Albany, School of Public Health, Executive Park South, Albany, NY 12203-3727. Awards MPH, MS, Dr PH, PhD. One or more programs accredited by CEPH. Faculty: 11 full-time (4 women), 57 part-time (3 women). Students: 166 full-time (89 women), 80 part-time (42 women); includes 22 minority (10 African Americans, 6 Asian Americans, 6 Hispanics), 65 international. 227 applicants, 60% accepted. In 1997, 57 master's, 10 doctorates awarded. *Degree requirements:* For doctorate, dissertation. *Entrance requirements:* GRE General Test. Application fee: $50. *Expenses:* Tuition $5100 per year full-time, $213 per credit hour part-time for state residents; $8416 per year full-time, $351 per credit hour part-time for nonresidents. Fees $705 per year full-time, $26.85 per credit hour part-time. *Financial aid:* Fellowships, research assistantships available. • Dr. John Conway, Interim Dean, 518-485-5500. Application contact: Jeffrey Collins, Assistant Director, Graduate Admissions, 518-442-3980.

See in-depth description on page 1515.

Temple University, School of Social Administration, Department of Health Studies, Program in Public Health, Philadelphia, PA 19122-6096. Offers community health education (MPH). Part-time programs available. Faculty: 11 full-time (8 women). Students: 23 (12 women); includes 5 minority (3 African Americans, 2 Asian Americans), 1 international. 56 applicants, 43% accepted. In 1997, 6 degrees awarded. *Degree requirements:* Fieldwork, practicum required, foreign language and thesis not required. *Average time to degree:* master's–2 years full-time, 4 years part-time. *Entrance requirements:* GRE General Test, minimum undergraduate GPA of 2.8. Application deadline: 2/1 (10/15 for spring admission). Application fee: $40. *Expenses:* Tuition $323 per semester hour for state residents; $444 per semester hour for nonresidents. Fees $170 per year full-time, $28 per semester (minimum) part-time. *Financial aid:* Fellowships, research assistantships, teaching assistantships, partial tuition waivers, Federal Work-Study, institutionally sponsored loans, and career-related internships or fieldwork available. Financial aid application deadline: 5/1; applicants required to submit FAFSA. *Faculty research:* School health education, violence prevention, HIV/AIDS prevention, women's health. Total annual research expenditures: $68,625. • Dr. Alice J. Hausman, Head, 215-204-5112. E-mail: hausman@vm.temple.edu. Application contact: Joyce Hankins, Administrative Assistant, 215-204-8726. Fax: 215-204-1455.

See in-depth description on page 1517.

Tufts University, School of Medicine, Programs in Public Health, Medford, MA 02155. Awards MPH, MS, MD/MPH. Offerings include health communication (MS), public health (MPH). One or more programs accredited by CEPH. MS offered jointly with Emerson College. Part-time and evening/weekend programs available. In 1997, 17 degrees awarded. *Degree requirements:* Thesis required (for some programs), foreign language not required. *Entrance requirements:* GRE General Test, TOEFL. Application deadline: 6/15 (rolling processing; 11/15 for spring admission). Application fee: $40 ($75 for international students). *Financial aid:* Federal Work-Study and career-related internships or fieldwork available. Aid available to part-time students. Financial aid application deadline: 4/1; applicants required to submit FAFSA. *Faculty research:* Environmental and occupational health, nutrition, epidemiology, health communication, health services management and policy. • Peggy Newell, Associate Dean for Special Programs, 617-636-6767. E-mail: pnewell@infonet.tufts.edu. Application contact: Nicole Di Minico, Secretary, 617-636-6767. Fax: 617-636-0375. E-mail: sschool@infonet.tufts.edu.

See in-depth description on page 1519.

Tulane University, School of Public Health and Tropical Medicine, New Orleans, LA 70118-5669. Awards MADH, MHA, MMM, MPH, MPHTM, MS, MSPH, Dr PH, PhD, Sc D, Diploma, JD/MHA, JD/MPH, JD/MSPH, LL M/MSPH, MBA/MPH, MD/MPH, MD/PhD, MD/MPHTM, MD/MSPH, MSW/MPH. One or more programs accredited by CEPH. MS and PhD offered through the Graduate School. Part-time programs available. Faculty: 108 full-time, 29 part-time. Students: 855 full-time (521 women), 129 part-time (77 women); includes 231 minority (137 African Americans, 53 Asian Americans, 36 Hispanics, 5 Native Americans), 201 international. Average age 33. 765 applicants, 76% accepted. In 1997, 309 master's, 13 doctorates awarded. Terminal master's awarded for partial completion of doctoral program. *Degree requirements:* For master's, 1 foreign language required, thesis not required; for doctorate, 1 foreign language, dissertation. *Entrance requirements:* For master's, GRE General Test (minimum combined score of 1000; average 1100), TOEFL (minimum score 525); for doctorate, GRE General Test (minimum combined score of 1000; average 1250), TOEFL (minimum score 525). Application deadline: 4/15 (priority date; rolling processing; 10/15 for spring admission). Application fee: $40. Electronic applications accepted. *Financial aid:* Fellowships, research assistantships, teaching assistantships, Federal Work-Study, institutionally sponsored loans available. Aid available to part-time students. Financial aid application deadline: 2/1. • Dr. Paul K. Whelton, Dean, 504-588-5397. Fax: 504-588-5718. E-mail: pwhelton@mailhost.tcs.tulane.edu. Application contact: Jeffrey T. Johnson, Director of Admissions, 504-588-5387. Fax: 504-584-1667. E-mail: jjohnso1@mailhost.tcs.tulane.edu.

See in-depth descriptions on pages 1335 and 1521.

Uniformed Services University of the Health Sciences, School of Medicine, Division of Basic Medical Sciences, Department of Preventive Medicine/Biometrics, Program in Public Health, Bethesda, MD 20814-4799. Awards MPH, MSPH, Dr PH. One or more programs accredited by CEPH. MSPH new for fall 1998. Faculty: 52 full-time (9 women), 97 part-time (16 women). Students: 35 full-time (17 women), 14 part-time (3 women); includes 5 minority (1 African American, 4 Asian Americans). Average age 28. 85 applicants, 36% accepted. In 1997, 22 master's awarded (100% found work related to degree). *Degree requirements:* For master's, computer language, comprehensive exam required, foreign language and thesis not required; for doctorate, dissertation, qualifying exam required, foreign language not required. *Average time to degree:* master's–1 year full-time. *Entrance requirements:* For master's, GRE General Test, TOEFL, U.S. citizenship; for doctorate, GRE General Test, GRE Subject Test, TOEFL, minimum GPA of 3.0, U.S. citizenship. Application deadline: 2/15 (rolling processing). Application fee: $0. *Tuition:* $0. *Faculty research:* Epidemiology, biostatistics, health services administration, environmental and occupational health, tropical public health. • Col. Kenneth Dixon, Graduate Program Director, 301-295-3050. Fax: 301-295-1933. Application contact: Janet M. Anastasi, Graduate Program Coordinator, 301-295-9474. Fax: 301-295-6772.

The University of Alabama at Birmingham, Graduate School and School of Dentistry, Graduate Programs in Dentistry, Birmingham, AL 35294. Offerings include dental public health (MPH). *Application deadline:* rolling. *Application fee:* $30 ($60 for international students). Electronic applications accepted. *Expenses:* Tuition $99 per credit hour for state residents; $198 per credit hour for nonresidents. Fees $516 per year (minimum) full-time, $73 per quarter (minimum) part-time for state residents; $516 per year (minimum) full-time, $73 per unit (minimum) part-time for nonresidents. • Dr. Firoz Rahemtulla, Director, 205-934-5426.

The University of Alabama at Birmingham, Graduate School, School of Public Health, Birmingham, AL 35294. Awards MPH, MS, MSPH, Dr PH, PhD, JD/MPH, MBA/MPH, MPA/MPH, MPH/PhD, OD/MPH. One or more programs accredited by CEPH. Part-time programs available. Students: 311 full-time (183 women), 61 part-time (34 women); includes 127 minority (69 African Americans, 53 Asian Americans, 5 Hispanics). 488 applicants, 85% accepted. In 1997, 119 master's, 14 doctorates awarded. *Degree requirements:* For master's, research project; for doctorate, dissertation. *Application deadline:* rolling. *Application fee:* $30 ($60 for international students). Electronic applications accepted. *Expenses:* Tuition $3672 per year full-time, $102 per credit hour part-time for state residents; $7344 per year full-time, $204 per credit hour part-time for nonresidents. Fees $699 per year (minimum) full-time, $116 per quarter (minimum) part-time. *Financial aid:* Fellowships, Federal Work-Study, and career-related internships or fieldwork available. Aid available to part-time students. • Dr. Eli I. Capilouto, Dean, 205-934-4993. Application contact: Nancy Pinson, Coordinator of Student Admissions, 205-934-4993. Fax: 205-975-5484. E-mail: osas@ms.soph.uab.edu.

See in-depth description on page 1523.

University of Alberta, Faculties of Medicine and Oral Health Sciences and Graduate Studies and Research, Graduate Programs in Medicine, Department of Public Health Sciences, Edmonton, AB T6G 2E1, Canada. Offers programs in environmental health (M Sc, PhD), epidemiology (M Sc, PhD), health policy and management (MPH, PhD), health policy research (MPH), health services administration (Postgraduate Diploma), occupational health (M Sc), population health (M Sc, PhD), public health (MPH). One or more programs accredited by CEPH. Faculty: 20 full-time, 11 part-time. Students: 62 full-time (42 women), 22 part-time (14 women). 110 applicants, 32% accepted. In 1997, 3 master's awarded. Terminal master's awarded for partial completion of doctoral program. *Degree requirements:* For master's, thesis required (for some programs), foreign language not required; for doctorate, dissertation required, foreign language not required. *Average time to degree:* master's–2 years full-time, 4 years part-time; doctorate–4 years full-time, 6 years part-time. *Entrance requirements:* For master's, GMAT (minimum score 500) or GRE General Test (minimum combined score of 1500 on three sections). Application deadline: 2/1 (priority date; rolling processing). Application fee: $60. *Financial aid:* In 1997–98, 3 research assistantships totaling $13,610 were awarded; career-related internships or fieldwork also available. Financial aid application deadline: 2/1. *Total annual research expenditures:* $900,000. • Dr. T. W. Noseworthy, Chair, 403-492-6408. Application contact: Felicity Hey, Graduate Programs Administrator, 403-492-6407. Fax: 403-492-0364. E-mail: felicity.hey@ualberta.ca.

The University of Arizona, Arizona Graduate Program in Public Health, Tucson, AZ 85721. Awards MPH. Accredited by CEPH. *Entrance requirements:* TOEFL (minimum score 550). Application fee: $35. *Tuition:* $2162 per year full-time, $337 per semester (minimum) part-time for state residents; $6860 per year full-time, $1138 per semester (minimum) part-time for nonresidents.

Announcement: The Arizona Graduate Program in Public Health (AzGPPH) is an interdisciplinary, interuniversity program. Six concentration areas for the Master of Public Health degree are offered between the University of Arizona, Arizona State University, and Northern Arizona University. For more information, contact: AzGPPH, University of Arizona, Box 245033, Tucson, AZ 85724-5033.

The University of Arizona, College of Medicine, Graduate Programs in Medicine, Program in Public Health, Tucson, AZ 85721. Awards MPH. Accredited by CEPH. *Entrance requirements:* GRE General Test. Application fee: $35. *Tuition:* $2162 per year full-time, $337 per semester (minimum) part-time for state residents; $6860 per year full-time, $1138 per semester (minimum) part-time for nonresidents. *Faculty research:* Prevention, health preparation, epidemiology, nutritional sciences.

University of California, Berkeley, Haas School of Business and School of Public Health, Concurrent MBA/MPH Program, Berkeley, CA 94720-1500. Awards MBA/MPH. Faculty: 11 full-time (3 women). Students: 14 full-time (11 women). Average age 25. 40 applicants, 10% accepted. *Application deadline:* 3/31. *Application fee:* $40. *Expenses:* Tuition $0 for state residents; $9384 per year for nonresidents. Fees $4409 per year. *Financial aid:* In 1997–98, 8 fellowships (4 to first-year students) were awarded; research assistantships, teaching assistantships, Federal Work-Study, institutionally sponsored loans, and career-related internships or fieldwork also available. Financial aid application deadline: 1/31. • Dr. Thomas Rundall, Director, Health Services Management Program, 510-642-5023. Fax: 510-643-6981. E-mail: trundall@uclink2.berkeley.edu. Application contact: Lee Forgue, Program Assistant, 510-642-5023. Fax: 510-643-6659. E-mail: ellis@haas.berkeley.edu.

University of California, Berkeley, School of Public Health, Division of Biostatistics, Berkeley, CA 94720-1500. Offers programs in biostatistics (MA, PhD), epidemiology (MPH), epidemiology/biostatistics (MPH). One or more programs accredited by CEPH. Faculty: 5 full-time (1 woman), 1 part-time (0 women). Students: 16 full-time (8 women); includes 3 minority (1 African American, 2 Asian Americans), 5 international. 42 applicants, 26% accepted. In 1997, 10 master's, 3 doctorates awarded. *Degree requirements:* For master's, oral exam required, foreign language not required; for doctorate, dissertation, oral exam required, foreign language not required. *Entrance requirements:* GRE General Test, minimum GPA of 3.0. Application deadline: 1/12 (rolling processing). Application fee: $40. *Expenses:* Tuition $0 for state residents; $9384 per year for nonresidents. Fees $4409 per year. *Financial aid:* Fellowships, research assistantships, teaching assistantships, full and partial tuition waivers, Federal Work-Study, institutionally sponsored loans, and career-related internships or fieldwork available. Financial aid application deadline: 12/15; applicants required to submit FAFSA. • Dr. Steve Selvin, Head, 510-642-4618. Application contact: Bonnie Hutchings, Graduate Assistant, 510-642-3241. Fax: 510-643-5163. E-mail: bjh@stat.berkeley.edu.

Directory: Public Health—General

University of California, Berkeley, School of Public Health, Division of Environmental Health Sciences, Berkeley, CA 94720-1500. Awards MPH, MS, PhD. One or more programs accredited by CEPH. Faculty: 7 full-time (2 women), 6 part-time (2 women). Students: 49 full-time (26 women). 62 applicants, 45% accepted. In 1997, 18 master's, 6 doctorates awarded. *Degree requirements:* For master's, comprehensive exam (MPH), project or thesis (MS); for doctorate, dissertation, departmental and qualifying exams required, foreign language not required. *Average time to degree:* master's–2 years full-time. *Entrance requirements:* For master's, GRE General Test, TOEFL (minimum score 570), minimum GPA of 3.0; previous course work in biology, calculus, and chemistry; for doctorate, GRE General Test, TOEFL (minimum score 570), master's degree in relevant scientific discipline or engineering; minimum GPA of 3.0; previous course work in biology, calculus, and chemistry. Application deadline: 1/10 (rolling processing). Application fee: $40. Electronic applications accepted. *Expenses:* Tuition $0 for state residents; $9384 per year for nonresidents. Fees $4409 per year. *Financial aid:* Fellowships, research assistantships, teaching assistantships available. Financial aid application deadline: 3/2. *Faculty research:* Toxicology, industrial hygiene, exposure assessment, risk assessment, ergonomics. • Martyn T. Smith, Chair. Application contact: Ramona Brockman, Graduate Assistant for Admission, 510-643-5160. Fax: 510-642-5815. E-mail: ehs_div@uclink4.berkeley.edu.

University of California, Berkeley, School of Public Health, Division of Health Policy and Administration, Berkeley, CA 94720-1500. Awards MPH, MBA/MPH, MCP/MPH, MPP/MPH. Accredited by CEPH. *Degree requirements:* Comprehensive exam. *Entrance requirements:* GRE General Test, minimum GPA of 3.0. Application deadline: 1/5 (rolling processing). Application fee: $40. *Expenses:* Tuition $0 for state residents; $9384 per year for nonresidents. Fees $4409 per year. *Financial aid:* Fellowships, research assistantships, teaching assistantships, Federal Work-Study available. Financial aid application deadline: 3/2. • Dr. Ralph Catalano, Deputy. Application contact: Holly Wilson, Administrative Assistant, 510-643-8571. Fax: 510-643-6981. E-mail: hwilson@uclink2.berkeley.edu.

University of California, Berkeley, School of Public Health, Division of Public Health Biology and Epidemiology, Berkeley, CA 94720-1500. Offers programs in epidemiology (MPH, MS, PhD), epidemiology/biostatistics (MPH), infectious diseases (MA, MPH, PhD). One or more programs accredited by CEPH. *Degree requirements:* For master's, comprehensive exam; for doctorate, dissertation, oral and written exam. *Entrance requirements:* For master's, GRE General Test, minimum GPA of 3.0; MD, DDS, DVM, or PhD in a biomedical science (1 year MPH program); for doctorate, GRE General Test, minimum GPA of 3.0. Application deadline: 12/16 (priority date). Application fee: $40. *Expenses:* Tuition $0 for state residents; $9384 per year for nonresidents. Fees $4409 per year. *Financial aid:* Fellowships, research assistantships, teaching assistantships, Federal Work-Study available. Financial aid application deadline: 12/16. • Dr. Arthur L. Reingold, Head, 510-642-0327. Application contact: Ron Jeremicz, Graduate Assistant, 510-643-9912. Fax: 510-643-5163. E-mail: rtj@uclink2.berkeley.edu.

University of California, Berkeley, School of Public Health, Doctoral Program in Public Health, Berkeley, CA 94720-1500. Awards Dr PH. Accredited by CEPH. Terminal master's awarded for partial completion of doctoral program. *Degree requirements:* For doctorate, dissertation, exam. *Entrance requirements:* For doctorate, GRE General Test, minimum GPA of 3.0. Application deadline: rolling. Application fee: $40. *Expenses:* Tuition $0 for state residents; $9384 per year for nonresidents. Fees $4409 per year. • Jean Morton, Associate Dean for Student Services. Application contact: Rick Love, Student Affairs Officer, 510-643-8452.

University of California, Berkeley, School of Public Health, Master Internationalist Program, Berkeley, CA 94720-1500. Offers community health education (MPH), epidemiology (MPH), interdisciplinary (MPH), maternal and child health (MPH), public health nutrition (MPH). Accredited by CEPH. MA (community health education) admissions temporarily suspended. *Entrance requirements:* GRE General Test, minimum GPA of 3.0. Application deadline: 1/12 (rolling processing). Application fee: $40. *Expenses:* Tuition $0 for state residents; $9384 per year for nonresidents. Fees $4409 per year. *Financial aid:* Fellowships, research assistantships, teaching assistantships, Federal Work-Study available. Financial aid application deadline: 12/15. • Application contact: Sharon Harper, Student Affairs Officer, 510-642-4706. Fax: 510-643-5676. E-mail: sharper@socrates.berkeley.edu.

University of California, Berkeley, School of Public Health, Program in Health and Social Behavior, Berkeley, CA 94720-1500. Awards MPH. Accredited by CEPH. Program new for fall 1999. *Entrance requirements:* GRE General Test, minimum GPA of 3.0. Application deadline: rolling. Application fee: $40. *Expenses:* Tuition $0 for state residents; $9384 per year for nonresidents. Fees $4409 per year. • S. Leonard Syme, Head. Application contact: Laura Spautz, Graduate Assistant, 510-643-2700.

University of California, Los Angeles, School of Public Health, Los Angeles, CA 90095. Awards MPH, MS, D Env, Dr PH, PhD, MBA/MPH, MD/PhD, MPH/MA. Programs in biostatistics (MS, PhD); community health sciences (MS, PhD), including public health; environmental health sciences (MS, PhD); environmental science and engineering (D Env); epidemiology (MS, PhD); health services (MS, PhD); public health (MPH, MS, Dr PH, PhD); public health for health and allied professionals (MPH). One or more programs accredited by CEPH. Faculty: 53 (15 women). Students: 539 full-time (344 women); includes 199 minority (25 African Americans, 127 Asian Americans, 45 Hispanics, 2 Native Americans), 90 international. 788 applicants, 52% accepted. *Degree requirements:* For doctorate, dissertation, oral and written qualifying exams required, foreign language not required. *Entrance requirements:* For master's, GRE General Test (minimum combined score of 1100), minimum GPA of 3.0; for doctorate, GRE General Test (minimum combined score of 1200), minimum undergraduate GPA of 3.0. Application deadline: 12/15. Application fee: $40. Electronic applications accepted. *Expenses:* Tuition $0 for state residents; $9384 per year for nonresidents. Fees $4551 per year. *Financial aid:* In 1997–98, 442 students received aid, including fellowships totaling $834,535, research assistantships totaling $813,236, teaching assistantships totaling $459,227, federal fellowships and scholarships totaling $1.288 million; full and partial tuition waivers, Federal Work-Study, institutionally sponsored loans, and career-related internships or fieldwork also available. Financial aid application deadline: 3/1. • Dr. A. A. Afifi, Dean, 310-825-5524. Application contact: Departmental Office, 310-825-5524. E-mail: app_request@admin.ph.ucla.edu.

University of California, San Diego, Program in Public Health and Epidemiology, 9500 Gilman Drive, La Jolla, CA 92093-5003. Awards PhD. Offered jointly with San Diego State University. Students: 13 (9 women). *Application fee:* $40. *Expenses:* Tuition $0 for state residents; $9384 per year full-time, $4692 per year part-time for nonresidents. Fees $4887 per year full-time, $3344 per year part-time. • Deborah Wingard, Head. Application contact: Graduate Coordinator, 619-534-3720.

University of Colorado Health Sciences Center, Program in Public Health, Denver, CO 80262. Awards MSPH. Accredited by CEPH. Students: 24 full-time (16 women), 27 part-time (20 women); includes 7 minority (1 African American, 4 Asian Americans, 1 Hispanic, 1 Native American). In 1997, 23 degrees awarded (100% found work related to degree). *Degree requirements:* Thesis or alternative required, foreign language not required. *Entrance requirements:* GRE General Test, minimum GPA of 2.75. Application deadline: 2/1. Application fee: $30. *Financial aid:* Fellowships, research assistantships, teaching assistantships, Federal Work-Study, institutionally sponsored loans available. Financial aid application deadline: 3/1. *Faculty research:* Perinatal epidemiology, chronic disease epidemiology, injury epidemiology, statistical methodology. • Dr. Phoebe Lindsey Barton, Director, 303-315-8357. Application contact: Jackie Newnam, Secretary, 303-315-8357.

See in-depth description on page 1529.

University of Connecticut, Field of Public Health, Storrs, CT 06269. Awards MPH, JD/MPH. Faculty: 29. Students: 33 full-time (25 women), 141 part-time (105 women); includes 25 minority (9 African Americans, 8 Asian Americans, 7 Hispanics, 1 Native American), 8 international. Average age 37. 114 applicants, 50% accepted. In 1997, 37 degrees awarded. *Application deadline:* 6/1 (priority date; rolling processing; 11/1 for spring admission). *Application fee:* $40 ($45 for international students). *Expenses:* Tuition $5272 per year full-time, $293 per credit part-time for state residents; $13,696 per year full-time, $761 per credit part-time for nonresidents. Fees $948 per year full-time, $640 per year part-time. *Financial aid:* In 1997–98, 4 research assistantships (2 to first-year students) totaling $44,888, 2 teaching assistantships totaling $8,184 were awarded. • Holger Hansen, Director, 860-674-3402. Application contact: Hal Mark, Chairperson, 860-679-3351. Fax: 860-679-2518.

University of Connecticut Health Center, Programs in Biomedical Sciences, Program in Public Health, Farmington, CT 06030. Awards MPH, MD/MPH. Accredited by CEPH. Part-time and evening/weekend programs available. *Degree requirements:* Thesis optional, foreign language not required. *Entrance requirements:* GRE General Test. Application deadline: 3/1 (priority date; rolling processing). Application fee: $35. *Faculty research:* Cancer epidemiology, birth defects, gerontology, health manpower, health services.

University of Denver, University College, Denver, CO 80208. Offerings include public health (MPH). *Average time to degree:* master's–1.5 years full-time, 2.7 years part-time. *Application deadline:* 8/10 (rolling processing; 2/22 for spring admission). *Application fee:* $25. *Expenses:* Tuition $245 per quarter hour for state residents; $310 per quarter hour for nonresidents. Fees $165 per quarter hour (minimum).

University of Hawaii at Manoa, College of Health Sciences and Social Welfare, School of Public Health, Honolulu, HI 96822. Offers programs in biostatistics (MPH, MS); biostatistics-epidemiology (PhD); community health development and education (MPH, MS); environmental and occupational health (MPH, MS), including environmental health engineering, environmental health management, environmental/occupational health sciences; epidemiology (MPH, MS), including chronic diseases, infectious diseases; health services administration and planning (MPH, MS); health services development (Dr PH); international health (MPH, MS); maternal and child health (MPH, MS); personal and community health maintenance and promotion (Dr PH). Part-time programs available. Faculty: 18 full-time (8 women), 4 part-time (2 women), 19.6 FTE. Students: 111 full-time (70 women), 94 part-time (58 women); includes 125 minority (8 African Americans, 111 Asian Americans, 5 Hispanics, 1 Native American). 181 applicants, 48% accepted. In 1997, 88 master's, 6 doctorates awarded. Terminal master's awarded for partial completion of doctoral program. *Degree requirements:* For master's, thesis (for some programs); for doctorate, computer language, dissertation required, foreign language not required. *Average time to degree:* master's–1.2 years full-time, 3 years part-time. *Entrance requirements:* For doctorate, GRE General Test. Application deadline: 3/1 (9/1 for spring admission). Application fee: $25 ($50 for international students). *Tuition:* $4029 per year full-time, $214 per credit hour part-time for state residents; $9957 per year full-time, $461 per credit hour part-time for nonresidents. *Financial aid:* In 1997–98, 40 traineeships/tuition waivers were awarded; career-related internships or fieldwork also available. • Dr. D. William Wood, Interim Dean, 808-956-8491. Application contact: Nancy Kilonsky, Assistant Dean, 808-956-8267.

University of Illinois at Chicago, School of Public Health, Chicago, IL 60607-7128. Awards MPH, MS, Dr PH, PhD, DDS/MPH, MBA/MPH, MD/PhD, MPH/MS. Programs in biostatistics (MS, PhD), community health sciences (MPH, MS, Dr PH, PhD), environmental and occupational health sciences (MPH, MS, Dr PH, PhD), epidemiology and biostatistics (MPH, MS, Dr PH, PhD), health resources management (MPH, MS, Dr PH, PhD). One or more programs accredited by CEPH. MS and PhD offered jointly with Graduate College. Part-time programs available. Faculty: 46 full-time (13 women), 4 part-time (0 women). Students: 152 full-time (95 women), 306 part-time (200 women); includes 143 minority (66 African Americans, 45 Asian Americans, 31 Hispanics, 1 Native American), 48 international. 150 applicants, 29% accepted. In 1997, 7 master's, 10 doctorates awarded. Terminal master's awarded for partial completion of doctoral program. *Degree requirements:* For master's, thesis, field practicum required, foreign language not required; for doctorate, dissertation, independent research, internship required, foreign language not required. *Entrance requirements:* GRE General Test (minimum combined score of 1000), TOEFL (minimum score 550), minimum GPA of 3.75 on a 5.0 scale. Application deadline: 7/3 (11/8 for spring admission). Application fee: $40 ($50 for international students). *Financial aid:* In 1997–98, 3 fellowships, 13 research assistantships, 3 teaching assistantships, 5 traineeships were awarded; institutionally sponsored loans and career-related internships or fieldwork also available. Aid available to part-time students. • Dr. Susan Scrimshaw, Dean, 312-996-6620. Application contact: Dr. Babette Neuberger, Assistant Dean, 312-996-6625.

University of Illinois at Springfield, School of Health and Human Services, Program in Public Health, Springfield, IL 62794-9243. Awards MPH. Part-time and evening/weekend programs available. Faculty: 2 full-time (1 woman), 1 part-time (0 women), 2.25 FTE. Students: 20 full-time (15 women), 48 part-time (33 women); includes 16 minority (10 African Americans, 3 Asian Americans, 3 Hispanics). Average age 34. 39 applicants, 72% accepted. In 1997, 8 degrees awarded. *Degree requirements:* Thesis or alternative required, foreign language not required. *Entrance requirements:* Minimum GPA of 3.0. Application deadline: rolling. Application fee: $0. *Expenses:* Tuition $99 per credit hour for state residents; $296 per credit hour for nonresidents. Fees $242 per year full-time, $63 per semester (minimum) part-time. *Financial aid:* In 1997–98, 30 students received aid, including 3 assistantships averaging $606 per month; partial tuition waivers, Federal Work-Study, and career-related internships or fieldwork also available. Aid available to part-time students. Financial aid application deadline: 6/1; applicants required to submit FAFSA. *Faculty research:* Health education program evaluation, epidemiology of breast cancer, HIV/AIDS policy. Total annual research expenditures: $50,000. • Michael Quam, Director, 217-786-6301.

The University of Iowa, College of Dentistry and Graduate College, Graduate Programs in Dentistry, Department of Preventive and Community Dentistry, Iowa City, IA 52242-1316. Offers program in dental public health (MS). Faculty: 8 full-time (4 women), 26 part-time (10 women). Students: 6 full-time (4 women), 3 part-time (all women); includes 4 international. In 1997, 2 degrees awarded. *Degree requirements:* Thesis. *Entrance requirements:* GRE, TOEFL, DDS. Application deadline: 7/1. Application fee: $30 ($50 for international students). *Expenses:* Tuition $3166 per year full-time, $176 per semester hour part-time for state residents; $10,202 per year full-time, $176 per semester hour part-time for nonresidents. Fees $202 per year full-time, $52 per year (minimum) part-time. • Dr. Henrietta Logan, Interim Head, 319-335-7184. Application contact: Dr. Steven Levy, Graduate Program Director, 319-335-7185. Fax: 319-335-7155.

University of Kansas, Department of Preventive Medicine, Kansas City, KS 66160. Awards MPH. Part-time programs available. Faculty: 13 full-time (5 women), 1 part-time (0 women). Students: 6 full-time (5 women), 47 part-time (30 women); includes 5 minority (3 Asian Americans, 2 Native Americans), 3 international. Average age 39. 28 applicants, 54% accepted. In 1997, 8 degrees awarded. *Degree requirements:* Thesis, comprehensive oral exam required, foreign language not required. *Entrance requirements:* GRE General Test, TOEFL (minimum score 570), minimum GPA of 3.0. Application deadline: 6/1 (rolling processing; 11/1 for spring admission). Application fee: $25. *Expenses:* Tuition $2400 per year full-time, $100 per credit hour part-time for state residents; $7890 per year full-time, $329 per credit hour part-time for nonresidents. Fees $428 per year full-time, $31 per credit hour part-time. *Financial aid:* Federal Work-Study, institutionally sponsored loans available. Aid available to part-time students. Financial aid application deadline: 4/3; applicants required to submit FAFSA. • Dr. S. Edwards Dismuke, Chairman, 913-588-2627. Fax: 913-588-2695. E-mail: edismuke@kumc.edu. Application contact: Dr. Stanley Edlavitch, Director, 913-588-2790. Fax: 913-588-2780.

University of Kentucky, Graduate School and College of Medicine, Graduate Programs in Medicine, Program in Public Health, Lexington, KY 40506-0032. Awards MSPH. Faculty: 17 full-time (5 women). Students: 11 full-time (2 women), 15 part-time (7 women); includes 1 minority (Asian American), 1 international. 27 applicants, 44% accepted. In 1997, 7 degrees awarded. *Degree requirements:* Comprehensive exam required, foreign language not required.

Entrance requirements: GRE General Test, minimum undergraduate GPA of 2.5, 3.0 graduate. Application deadline: 5/1 (rolling processing; 10/1 for spring admission). Application fee: $30 ($35 for international students). *Financial aid:* In 1997–98, 1 teaching assistantship was awarded; fellowships, research assistantships also available. • Dr. Sanford W. Horstman, Director of Graduate Studies, 606-323-8089. E-mail: thorstma@uklans.uky.edu. Application contact: Dr. Constance L. Wood, Associate Dean, 606-257-4613. Fax: 606-323-1928.

University of Massachusetts Amherst, School of Public Health and Health Sciences, Department of Public Health, Amherst, MA 01003-0001. Awards MPH, MS, PhD. One or more programs accredited by CEPH. Part-time programs available. Faculty: 25 full-time (8 women). Students: 97 full-time (59 women), 69 part-time (40 women); includes 28 minority (7 African Americans, 14 Asian Americans, 6 Hispanics, 1 Native American), 36 international. Average age 31. 211 applicants, 62% accepted. In 1997, 64 master's, 1 doctorate awarded. *Degree requirements:* Thesis/dissertation required, foreign language not required. *Entrance requirements:* GRE General Test. Application deadline: 3/1 (priority date; rolling processing; 10/1 for spring admission). Application fee: $40. *Expenses:* Tuition $2640 per year full-time, $110 per credit part-time for state residents; $3690 per year (minimum) full-time, $165 per credit (minimum) part-time for nonresidents. Fees $2856 per year full-time, $422 per semester part-time for state residents; $3204 per year full-time, $480 per semester part-time for nonresidents. *Financial aid:* In 1997–98, 27 fellowships, 65 research assistantships, 32 teaching assistantships were awarded; traineeships, full tuition waivers also available. Aid available to part-time students. Financial aid application deadline: 3/1. • Dr. Jessie S. Ortiz, Graduate Program Director, 413-545-4271. Fax: 413-545-1264. E-mail: j.ortiz@dpc.umass.edu.

University of Medicine and Dentistry of New Jersey, Robert Wood Johnson Medical School, Program in Public Health, Newark, NJ 07107-3001. Awards MPH, Dr PH, PhD, MBA/MPH, MD/MPH, MD/PhD, MD/Dr PH. One or more programs accredited by CEPH. Offered jointly with Rutgers, The State University of New Jersey, New Brunswick. Part-time and evening/weekend programs available. Students: 53 full-time (30 women), 166 part-time (102 women); includes 62 minority (15 African Americans, 41 Asian Americans, 5 Hispanics, 1 Native American). 240 applicants, 51% accepted. In 1997, 37 master's, 5 doctorates awarded. *Degree requirements:* For master's, internship required, foreign language and thesis not required; for doctorate, dissertation required, foreign language not required. *Entrance requirements:* For master's, GRE General Test, TOEFL; for doctorate, GRE General Test, TOEFL, MPH (Dr PH); MA, MPH, or MS (PhD). Application deadline: 3/15 (11/1 for spring admission). Application fee: $40. *Financial aid:* 21 students received aid; fellowships, teaching assistantships, and career-related internships or fieldwork available. Aid available to part-time students. *Faculty research:* Epidemiology, environmental health, statistical research design, health care utilization, health promotion. • Dr. George G. Rhoads, Director, 732-445-0195. E-mail: rhoads@umdnj.edu. Application contact: Tina Greco, Administrator, 732-445-0199. Fax: 732-445-0122.

See in-depth description on page 1531.

University of Miami, School of Medicine and Graduate School, Graduate Programs in Medicine, Department of Epidemiology and Public Health, Programs in Public Health, Coral Gables, FL 33124. Awards MPH, JD/MPH, MD/MPH, MPA/MPH. Accredited by CEPH. Part-time programs available. Faculty: 18 full-time (6 women), 7 part-time (2 women), 21 FTE. Students: 24 full-time (15 women), 22 part-time (15 women); includes 28 minority (4 African Americans, 8 Asian Americans, 16 Hispanics), 2 international. Average age 35. 32 applicants, 31% accepted. In 1997, 9 degrees awarded. *Degree requirements:* Computer language, project required, foreign language and thesis not required. *Average time to degree:* master's–2 years full-time, 3 years part-time. *Entrance requirements:* GRE General Test (minimum combined score of 1000), TOEFL (minimum score 550), minimum GPA of 3.0. Application deadline: 7/1 (rolling processing; 11/15 for spring admission). Application fee: $35. *Expenses:* Tuition $815 per credit hour. Fees $174 per year. *Financial aid:* In 1997–98, 40 students received aid, including 1 fellowship, 3 research assistantships averaging $420 per month, 2 graduate administrative assistantships averaging $420 per month; partial tuition waivers, Federal Work-Study, institutionally sponsored loans, and career-related internships or fieldwork also available. Aid available to part-time students. Financial aid application deadline: 2/1; applicants required to submit FAFSA. *Faculty research:* Behavioral epidemiology, AIDS, cardiovascular diseases, cancer prevention, subtance abuse epidemiology, women's health. Total annual research expenditures: $11.8 million. • Dr. Peggy O'Hara, Director, 305-243-6759. E-mail: pohara@mednet.med.miami.edu. Application contact: Ana Godur, Administrator, 305-243-6759. Fax: 305-243-5544. E-mail: agodur@mednet.med.miami.edu.

See in-depth description on page 1533.

University of Michigan, School of Public Health, Ann Arbor, MI 48109. Awards MHSA, MPH, MS, Dr PH, PhD, JD/MHSA, MD/MPH, MHSA/AM, MHSA/MBA, MHSA/MPP, MHSA/MS, MPH/AM, MPH/MPP, MSW/MPH. One or more programs accredited by CEPH. MS, PhD, MPH/AM, and MPH/MS offered through the Horace H. Rackham School of Graduate Studies. Part-time and evening/weekend programs available. Terminal master's awarded for partial completion of doctoral program. *Degree requirements:* For doctorate, oral defense of dissertation, preliminary exam. *Entrance requirements:* For doctorate, GRE General Test. Application deadline: 3/1 (priority date; rolling processing). Application fee: $55. *Financial aid:* Fellowships, research assistantships, teaching assistantships, grants, Federal Work-Study, and career-related internships or fieldwork available. Aid available to part-time students. Financial aid application deadline: 3/1. • Noreen M. Clark, Dean, 734-764-5425.

See in-depth description on page 1535.

University of Minnesota, Twin Cities Campus, School of Public Health, Minneapolis, MN 55455-0213. Awards MPH, MS, PhD, MPH/MBA, MPH/MS, MSW/MPH. One or more programs accredited by CEPH. Part-time programs available. Faculty: 87 full-time, 15 part-time. Students: 362; includes 32 minority (5 African Americans, 20 Asian Americans, 6 Hispanics, 1 Native American), 38 international. 552 applicants, 51% accepted. In 1997, 175 master's, 19 doctorates awarded. *Degree requirements:* For doctorate, dissertation required, foreign language not required. *Entrance requirements:* For master's, GRE General Test, minimum GPA of 3.0; for doctorate, GRE General Test. Application deadline: rolling. Application fee: $50 ($75 for international students). *Financial aid:* Fellowships, research assistantships, teaching assistantships, scholarships, Federal Work-Study, institutionally sponsored loans, and career-related internships or fieldwork available. Financial aid applicants required to submit FAFSA. • Dr. Edith Leyasmeyer, Dean, 612-624-6669. Application contact: Student Services Center, 800-774-8636. Fax: 612-626-6931. E-mail: sph_uofm@greg2.sph.umn.edu.

See in-depth description on page 1537.

University of New Mexico, Biomedical Sciences Graduate Committee, Albuquerque, NM 87131-2039. Offerings include public health (MPH). Accredited by CEPH. Faculty: 56 full-time (14 women), 3 part-time (0 women), 56.95 FTE. *Application deadline:* 2/1. *Application fee:* $25. *Expenses:* Tuition $2442 per year full-time, $103 per credit hour part-time for state residents; $8691 per year full-time, $103 per credit hour (minimum) part-time for nonresidents. Fees $32 per year. • William R. Galey Jr., Director, 505-277-1887. Fax: 505-277-1754. Application contact: Kathy Hayden, Administrative Assistant, 505-272-1887. Fax: 505-272-8738. E-mail: khayden@salud.unm.edu.

The University of North Carolina at Chapel Hill, School of Public Health, Chapel Hill, NC 27599. Awards MHA, MPH, MS, MSEE, MSPH, Dr PH, PhD, DDS/MPH, JD/MPH, MD/MPH, MPH/MSW. One or more programs accredited by CEPH. Part-time programs available. Postbaccalaureate distance learning degree programs offered. Faculty: 167 full-time (67 women), 384 part-time (140 women). Students: 579 full-time (381 women), 424 part-time (272 women); includes 139 minority (72 African Americans, 43 Asian Americans, 20 Hispanics, 4 Native Americans), 144 international. Average age 31. 1,489 applicants, 48% accepted. In 1997, 214 master's, 67 doctorates awarded. Terminal master's awarded for partial completion of doctoral program. *Degree requirements:* For master's, comprehensive exam required, foreign language not required; for doctorate, dissertation, comprehensive exam required, foreign language not required. *Average time to degree:* master's–2 years full-time, 4 years part-time; doctorate–3 years full-time, 6 years part-time. *Entrance requirements:* GRE General Test (minimum combined score of 1000), minimum GPA of 3.0. Application deadline: 1/1 (rolling processing). Application fee: $55. *Expenses:* Tuition $2008 per year full-time, $502 per semester (minimum) part-time for state residents; $10,414 per year full-time, $2604 per semester (minimum) part-time for nonresidents. Fees $782 per year full-time, $332 per semester (minimum) part-time. *Financial aid:* In 1997–98, 81 fellowships (26 to first-year students), 224 research assistantships (65 to first-year students), 53 teaching assistantships (5 to first-year students), 117 graduate assistantships, traineeships (20 to first-year students) were awarded; Federal Work-Study, institutionally sponsored loans, and career-related internships or fieldwork also available. Aid available to part-time students. Financial aid applicants required to submit FAFSA. *Faculty research:* Health promotion and disease prevention, injury prevention, international health, environmental studies, occupational health studies. Total annual research expenditures: $26.9 million. • Dr. William L. Roper, Dean, 919-966-3215. E-mail: bill_roper@unc.edu. Application contact: Aundra Shields, Associate Dean, 919-966-3524. Fax: 919-966-6380.

See in-depth description on page 1541.

The University of North Carolina at Chapel Hill, School of Public Health, Department of Health Behavior and Health Education, Chapel Hill, NC 27599. Awards MPH, Dr PH, PhD. One or more programs accredited by CEPH. Faculty: 13 full-time (8 women), 58 part-time (34 women). Students: 92 full-time (76 women), 15 part-time (13 women); includes 24 minority (9 African Americans, 11 Asian Americans, 4 Hispanics), 7 international. Average age 29. 246 applicants, 43% accepted. In 1997, 39 master's, 2 doctorates awarded. *Degree requirements:* For master's, thesis, major paper, comprehensive exam required, foreign language not required; for doctorate, dissertation, comprehensive exam required, foreign language not required. *Average time to degree:* master's–2 years full-time; doctorate–4 years full-time. *Entrance requirements:* GRE General Test (minimum combined score of 1000), minimum GPA of 3.0. Application deadline: 1/1 (rolling processing). Application fee: $55. *Expenses:* Tuition $2008 per year full-time, $502 per semester (minimum) part-time for state residents; $10,414 per year full-time, $2604 per semester (minimum) part-time for nonresidents. Fees $782 per year full-time, $332 per semester (minimum) part-time. *Financial aid:* In 1997–98, 4 fellowships (2 to first-year students), 15 research assistantships (8 to first-year students), 2 teaching assistantships were awarded; graduate assistantships, Federal Work-Study, institutionally sponsored loans, and career-related internships or fieldwork also available. Financial aid application deadline: 1/1; applicants required to submit FAFSA. *Faculty research:* Cancer prevention and control, aging health promotion and disease prevention, adolescent health, nutrition intervention. • Dr. JoAnne L. Earp, Chair, 919-966-3918. E-mail: jearp@sph.unc.edu. Application contact: Linda W. Cook, Registrar, 919-966-5771. Fax: 919-966-2921. E-mail: lcook@sph.unc.edu.

See in-depth description on page 1539.

University of Northern Colorado, College of Health and Human Sciences, Department of Community Health, Greeley, CO 80639. Awards MPH. Accredited by CEPH. Faculty: 3 full-time (1 woman). Students: 42 full-time (33 women), 11 part-time (7 women); includes 4 minority (1 African American, 1 Asian American, 2 Hispanics), 1 international. Average age 32. 26 applicants, 85% accepted. In 1997, 21 degrees awarded. *Degree requirements:* Thesis or alternative, comprehensive exams. *Application deadline:* rolling. *Application fee:* $35. *Expenses:* Tuition $2327 per year full-time, $129 per credit hour part-time for state residents; $9578 per year full-time, $532 per credit hour part-time for nonresidents. Fees $752 per year full-time, $184 per semester (minimum) part-time. *Financial aid:* In 1997–98, 35 students received aid, including 8 fellowships (2 to first-year students) totaling $12,750, 1 teaching assistantship totaling $3,463, 4 graduate assistantships (2 to first-year students) totaling $13,635. Financial aid application deadline: 3/1. • Larry Harrison, Chairperson, 907-351-2755.

University of North Texas Health Science Center at Fort Worth, Graduate School of Biomedical Sciences, Program in Public Health, Fort Worth, TX 76107-2699. Awards MPH, DDS/MPH, DO/MPH, MPH/MS, MPH/PhD. MPH, DO/MPH, MPH/MS, and MPH/PhD offered jointly with the University of North Texas. DDS/MPH offered jointly with Baylor College of Dentistry. Part-time and evening/weekend programs available. Faculty: 15 full-time (6 women), 14 part-time (6 women). Students: 20 full-time (13 women), 50 part-time (33 women); includes 24 minority (10 African Americans, 7 Asian Americans, 7 Hispanics), 3 international. 45 applicants, 62% accepted. In 1997, 16 degrees awarded (63% found work related to degree, 37% continued full-time study). *Degree requirements:* Thesis. *Entrance requirements:* GRE General Test (minimum combined score of 1000), TOEFL (minimum score 550). Application deadline: 6/1 (rolling processing; 11/1 for spring admission). Application fee: $25 ($50 for international students). *Tuition:* $1482 per year full-time, $297 per semester (minimum) part-time for state residents; $5316 per year full-time, $936 per semester (minimum) part-time for nonresidents. *Financial aid:* Federal Work-Study, institutionally sponsored loans available. Aid available to part-time students. Financial aid application deadline: 4/1; applicants required to submit FAFSA. • Dr. Fernando Treviño, Executive Director, 817-735-2401. E-mail: gsbs@hsc.unt.edu. Application contact: Jan Sharp, Administrative Assistant, 817-735-0258. Fax: 817-735-0243. E-mail: gsbs@hsc.unt.edu.

See in-depth description on page 1543.

University of Oklahoma Health Sciences Center, College of Public Health, Oklahoma City, OK 73190. Awards MHA, MPH, MS, Dr PH, PhD, MPH/JD, MPH/MBA, MS/JD. One or more programs accredited by CEPH. Part-time programs available. Faculty: 37 full-time (10 women), 45 part-time (12 women). Students: 138 full-time (78 women), 226 part-time (133 women); includes 85 minority (22 African Americans, 20 Asian Americans, 13 Hispanics, 30 Native Americans), 24 international. Average age 36. 318 applicants, 57% accepted. In 1997, 109 master's, 4 doctorates awarded. *Degree requirements:* For master's, computer language, comprehensive exam required, foreign language not required; for doctorate, computer language, dissertation, oral and written comprehensive exam. *Entrance requirements:* For master's, TOEFL (minimum score 550); for doctorate, GRE, TOEFL (minimum score 550). Application deadline: 7/1 (rolling processing). Application fee: $25 ($50 for international students). *Financial aid:* Fellowships, research assistantships, traineeships, partial tuition waivers, Federal Work-Study, institutionally sponsored loans, and career-related internships or fieldwork available. Aid available to part-time students. Financial aid application deadline: 5/1. • Dr. Elisa Lee, Dean, 405-271-2232.

University of Pittsburgh, Graduate School of Public Health, Pittsburgh, PA 15260. Awards MHA, MHPE, MPH, MS, Dr PH, PhD, Certificate, JD/MPH, MPH/M Div, MPH/MHA, PhD/MPH. One or more programs accredited by CEPH. MPH/M Div offered jointly with the Pittsburgh Theological Seminary; MHPE offered jointly with the School of Education. Part-time programs available. Faculty: 106 full-time (44 women), 7 part-time (5 women). Students: 231 full-time (131 women), 253 part-time (161 women); includes 88 minority (34 African Americans, 37 Asian Americans, 15 Hispanics, 2 Native Americans), 62 international. 546 applicants, 51% accepted. In 1997, 99 master's, 23 doctorates awarded. Terminal master's awarded for partial completion of doctoral program. *Degree requirements:* For doctorate, dissertation. *Average time to degree:* master's–2 years full-time, 4 years part-time; doctorate–3 years full-time, 5 years part-time. *Application fee:* $50 ($60 for international students). *Expenses:* Tuition $9402 per year full-time, $388 per credit part-time for state residents; $19,372 per year full-time, $799 per credit part-time for nonresidents. Fees $480 per year full-time, $180 per year part-time. *Financial aid:* Fellowships, research assistantships, teaching assistantships, assistantships, scholarships, full and partial tuition waivers, Federal Work-Study, institutionally sponsored loans, and career-related internships or fieldwork available. Aid available to part-time students. Financial aid applicants required to submit FAFSA. • Dr. Donald R. Mattison, Dean, 412-624-3002. E-mail: mattison@vms.cis.pitt.edu. Application contact: Office of Student Affairs, 412-624-3002. Fax: 412-624-3755. E-mail: stuaff@gsphedean.gsph.pitt.edu.

Directory: Public Health—General

University of Pittsburgh (continued)

Announcement: Graduate School of Public Health offers master's and doctoral degrees in biostatistics, public health statistics, human genetics, epidemiology, infectious diseases and microbiology, public and community health services, health administration, health promotion and education, risk assessment (with the School of Education), and environmental and occupational health. Certificates in risk assessment and management for health professionals (with the School of Nursing) are available. A multidisciplinary MPH is offered for doctoral-level health professionals, some experienced professionals, and advanced students. Joint-degree programs (JD/MPH, MD/MPH, MHA/MBA) are available, and there is a cooperative program (M Div/MPH) with the Pittsburgh Theological Seminary.

See in-depth description on page 1545.

University of Puerto Rico, Medical Sciences Campus, Graduate School of Public Health, Department of Health Services Administration, Program in Public Health, San Juan, PR 00936-5067. Awards MPH. Accredited by CEPH. Part-time programs available. Students: 78 (50 women); includes 3 international. 56 applicants, 73% accepted. In 1997, 23 degrees awarded. *Degree requirements:* Computer language required, foreign language and thesis not required. *Entrance requirements:* GRE, previous course work in algebra. Application deadline: 3/3. Application fee: $15. *Financial aid:* Research assistantships, teaching assistantships, Federal Work-Study, institutionally sponsored loans available. Financial aid application deadline: 4/30. • Dr. José M. Cobos, Coordinator, 787-758-2525 Ext. 1442. Application contact: Mayra E. Santiago-Vargas, Counselor, 787-756-5244. Fax: 787-759-6719.

University of Rochester, School of Medicine and Dentistry, Graduate Programs in Medicine and Dentistry, Department of Community and Preventive Medicine, Program in Public Health, Rochester, NY 14627-0001. Awards MPH, MBA/MPH, MD/MPH, MPH/MS, MPH/PhD. Accredited by CEPH. Students: 19 full-time (12 women), 45 part-time (27 women); includes 13 minority (4 African Americans, 6 Asian Americans, 3 Hispanics), 1 international. 53 applicants, 70% accepted. In 1997, 12 degrees awarded. *Entrance requirements:* GRE General Test. Application deadline: 2/1. Application fee: $25. *Expenses:* Tuition $21,485 per year full-time, $672 per credit hour part-time. Fees $336 per year. *Financial aid:* Application deadline 2/1. • Sarah Trafton, Director, 716-275-2194.

See in-depth description on page 1547.

University of South Carolina, Graduate School, School of Public Health, Program in General Public Health, Columbia, SC 29208. Awards MPH. Accredited by CEPH. Part-time programs available. Students: 10 full-time (7 women), 9 part-time (4 women); includes 4 minority (2 African Americans, 1 Asian American, 1 Hispanic), 6 international. Average age 41. 11 applicants, 18% accepted. In 1997, 6 degrees awarded. *Degree requirements:* Practicum. *Entrance requirements:* DAT or MCAT, GRE General Test. Application deadline: rolling. Application fee: $35. Electronic applications accepted. *Expenses:* Tuition $4480 per year full-time, $220 per credit hour part-time for state residents; $9338 per year full-time, $457 per credit hour part-time for nonresidents. Fees $125 per year full-time, $37 per semester (minimum) part-time. *Financial aid:* Research assistantships, teaching assistantships, and career-related internships or fieldwork available. • Dr. Roger L. Amidon, Chair, 803-777-5030. Fax: 803-777-4783.

University of Southern California, School of Medicine and Graduate School, Graduate Programs in Medicine, Program in Public Health, Los Angeles, CA 90089. Offers biometry/epidemiology (MPH), health promotion (MPH), preventive nutrition (MPH). Program new for fall 1998. *Entrance requirements:* GRE General Test (minimum combined score of 1000), TOEFL, minimum GPA of 3.0. *Expenses:* Tuition $706 per unit. Fees $414 per year full-time, $32 per year part-time. • Dr. Richard N. Lolley, Associate Dean for Research, Graduate Programs in Medicine, 213-342-1607. Fax: 213-342-1610. E-mail: lolley@hsc.usc.edu.

Announcement: The University of Southern California (USC) offers an MPH program with concentrations in health promotion, biometry/epidemiology, and preventive nutrition. USC's affiliation with a diverse array of health-related institutions and agencies in southern California and the Pacific Rim nations provides for excellent training opportunities. For information, call 323-442-2500 (toll-free) or go on line (http://www.usc.edu/go/ipr).

University of Southern Mississippi, College of Health and Human Sciences, Center for Community Health, Hattiesburg, MS 39406-5167. Offers programs in health education (MPH), health policy/administration (MPH), occupational/environmental health (MPH), public health nutrition (MPH). Accredited by CEPH. Part-time and evening/weekend programs available. Faculty: 6 full-time (3 women), 1 (woman) part-time. Students: 32 full-time (16 women), 29 part-time (19 women); includes 14 minority (10 African Americans, 4 Asian Americans), 2 international. Average age 30. 46 applicants, 65% accepted. In 1997, 20 degrees awarded. *Degree requirements:* Comprehensive exam required, foreign language and thesis not required. *Entrance requirements:* GRE General Test, minimum GPA of 2.75. Application deadline: 8/9 (priority date; rolling processing). Application fee: $0 ($25 for international students). *Tuition:* $2870 per year full-time, $137 per credit hour part-time for state residents; $5972 per year full-time, $172 per credit hour part-time for nonresidents. *Financial aid:* Research assistantships, teaching assistantships available. Financial aid application deadline: 3/15. *Faculty research:* Rural health care delivery, school health, nutrition of pregnant teens, risk factor reduction, sexually transmitted diseases. • Dr. Agnes Hinton, Interim Director, 601-266-5437.

University of South Florida, College of Public Health, Tampa, FL 33612-3805. Awards MHA, MPH, MSPH, PhD. One or more programs accredited by CEPH. Part-time and evening/weekend programs available. Postbaccalaureate distance learning degree programs offered (no on-campus study). Faculty: 54 full-time (20 women). Students: 224 full-time (152 women), 331 part-time (207 women); includes 117 minority (38 African Americans, 27 Asian Americans, 50 Hispanics, 2 Native Americans), 45 international. Average age 34. 325 applicants, 49% accepted. In 1997, 96 master's, 4 doctorates awarded. *Degree requirements:* Thesis/dissertation required, foreign language not required. *Entrance requirements:* For master's, GRE General Test (minimum combined score of 1000), TOEFL (minimum score 550), minimum GPA of 3.0 in upper-level course work; for doctorate, GRE General Test (minimum combined score of 1100), TOEFL (minimum score 550), minimum GPA of 3.0 in upper-level course work. Application deadline: 6/1 (rolling processing; 10/15 for spring admission). Application fee: $20. *Tuition:* $142 per credit hour for state residents; $486 per credit hour for nonresidents. *Financial aid:* In 1997–98, 229 students received aid, including 8 fellowships averaging $729 per month and totaling $52,500, 21 research assistantships (3 to first-year students) averaging $554 per month and totaling $139,527, 2 teaching assistantships averaging $456 per month and totaling $10,945, 72 graduate assistantships (16 to first-year students) averaging $345 per month and totaling $298,246; Federal Work-Study, institutionally sponsored loans, and career-related internships or fieldwork also available. Aid available to part-time students. Financial aid applicants required to submit FAFSA. *Total annual research expenditures:* $2.83 million. • Dr. Charles Mahan, Dean, 813-974-3623. E-mail: cmahan@com1.med.usf.edu. Application contact: Magdalene Argiry, Director of Student Services, 813-974-6665. Fax: 813-974-4718. E-mail: margiry@com1.med.usf.edu.

University of Tennessee, Knoxville, College of Human Ecology, Department of Health and Safety Sciences, Program in Public Health, Knoxville, TN 37996. Offers community health education (MPH), gerontology (MPH), health planning/administration (MPH). Accredited by CEPH. Students: 20 full-time (14 women), 37 part-time (34 women); includes 5 minority (all African Americans), 3 international. 49 applicants, 35% accepted. In 1997, 18 degrees awarded. *Degree requirements:* Thesis optional, foreign language not required. *Entrance requirements:* TOEFL (minimum score 550), minimum GPA of 2.7. Application deadline: 2/1 (priority date; rolling processing). Application fee: $35. Electronic applications accepted. *Tuition:* $3354 per year full-time, $181 per semester hour part-time for state residents; $8410 per year full-time, $462 per semester hour part-time for nonresidents. *Financial aid:* Application deadline 2/1. • Dr. Charles B. Hamilton, Head, Department of Health and Safety Sciences, 423-974-5041. Fax: 423-974-6439. E-mail: cbhamilton@utk.edu.

See in-depth description on page 1185.

The University of Texas–Houston Health Science Center, School of Public Health, Houston, TX 77225-0036. Awards MPH, MS, Dr PH, PhD, JD/MPH, MD/MPH, MD/PhD, MSN/MPH. One or more programs accredited by CEPH. JD/MPH offered jointly with University of Houston. Part-time programs available. Faculty: 113 full-time (40 women), 13 part-time (6 women). Students: 299 full-time (192 women), 567 part-time (380 women); includes 272 minority (81 African Americans, 97 Asian Americans, 88 Hispanics, 6 Native Americans), 81 international. Average age 36. 661 applicants, 54% accepted. In 1997, 129 master's, 37 doctorates awarded. *Degree requirements:* Thesis/dissertation. *Entrance requirements:* For master's, TOEFL (minimum score 565), GRE General Test (minimum combined score of 1000) or minimum GPA of 3.0; for doctorate, TOEFL (minimum score 565), GRE General Test (minimum combined score of 1200) or minimum GPA of 3.0. Application deadline: 3/1 (rolling processing; 9/1 for spring admission). Application fee: $10. Electronic applications accepted. *Financial aid:* In 1997–98, 156 students received aid, including 47 stipends averaging $350 per month and totaling $134,642. Aid available to part-time students. Financial aid applicants required to submit FAFSA. *Faculty research:* Epidemiology of cancer associated with environmental and occupational exposures, water resource development, clinical trials in cardiovascular disease, ethnic food purchase patterns. • Dr. R. Palmer Beasley, Dean, 713-500-9050. Application contact: Dr. Toya Candelari, Office of Student Affairs, 713-500-9030. Fax: 713-500-9068.

University of Toledo, College of Education and Allied Professions, Department of Health Promotion and Human Performance, Toledo, OH 43606-3398. Offerings include public health (M Ed, MPH). MPH offered jointly with Bowling Green State University and Medical College of Ohio. Department faculty: 17 full-time (5 women). *Application deadline:* 8/1 (priority date; rolling processing). *Application fee:* $30. Electronic applications accepted. *Tuition:* $5907 per year full-time, $246 per hour part-time for state residents; $11,835 per year full-time, $493 per hour part-time for nonresidents. • Dr. Carol Plimpton, Chair, 419-530-2747. Fax: 419-530-4759. E-mail: cplimpt@utnet.utoledo.edu.

University of Utah, School of Medicine and Graduate School, Graduate Programs in Medicine, Programs in Public Health, Salt Lake City, UT 84112-1107. Awards MPH, MSPH, M Stat, MD/MPH. Offerings include biostatistics (M Stat), public health (MPH, MSPH). One or more programs accredited by CEPH. MD/MPH new for fall 1998. Part-time programs available. Faculty: 11 full-time (4 women), 22 part-time (3 women). Students: 51 full-time (21 women), 53 part-time (19 women); includes 2 minority (both Hispanics), 4 international. Average age 29. 90 applicants, 58% accepted. In 1997, 41 degrees awarded. *Degree requirements:* Comprehensive exam, thesis or project (MSPH) required, foreign language not required. *Average time to degree:* master's–2.4 years part-time. *Entrance requirements:* GRE General Test, minimum GPA of 3.0. Application deadline: 2/28 (priority date; rolling processing). Application fee: $50. *Tuition:* $2045 per year full-time, $562 per semester (minimum) part-time for state residents; $6129 per year full-time, $1607 per semester (minimum) part-time for nonresidents. *Financial aid:* In 1997–98, 1 fellowship (to a first-year student), 2 research assistantships (1 to a first-year student), 1 teaching assistantship (to a first-year student) averaging $350 per month and totaling $1,750, 15 traineeships (all to first-year students) averaging $734 per month and totaling $85,878 were awarded; Federal Work-Study, institutionally sponsored loans, and career-related internships or fieldwork also available. Aid available to part-time students. *Faculty research:* Health services research, occupational and environmental health, epidemiology of chronic disease, industrial hygiene, ergonomics and safety. • Dr. F. Marian Bishop, Director, 801-581-7234. E-mail: mbishop@dfpm.utah.edu. Application contact: Dorothy Crockett, Coordinator, 801-581-7234. Fax: 801-585-9805. E-mail: dcrockett@dfpm.utah.edu.

University of Washington, School of Public Health and Community Medicine, Seattle, WA 98195. Awards MHA, MPH, MS, PhD, MBA/MHA, MD/MPH, MN/MPH, MPH/MAIS, MPH/MSW. One or more programs accredited by CEPH. Part-time and evening/weekend programs available. Faculty: 172 full-time (60 women), 83 part-time (21 women). Students: 532 (347 women); includes 122 minority (21 African Americans, 76 Asian Americans, 23 Hispanics, 2 Native Americans), 83 international. Average age 30. In 1997, 135 master's, 16 doctorates awarded. Terminal master's awarded for partial completion of doctoral program. *Degree requirements:* For doctorate, dissertation required, foreign language not required. *Average time to degree:* master's–2 years full-time, 4 years part-time; doctorate–5 years full-time. *Entrance requirements:* GRE General Test, TOEFL, minimum GPA of 3.0. Application fee: $45. *Tuition:* $5433 per year full-time, $775 per quarter (minimum) part-time for state residents; $13,479 per year full-time, $1925 per quarter (minimum) part-time for nonresidents. *Financial aid:* Fellowships, research assistantships, teaching assistantships, traineeships, tuition supports, full and partial tuition waivers, Federal Work-Study, institutionally sponsored loans, and career-related internships or fieldwork available. Aid available to part-time students. Financial aid applicants required to submit FAFSA. • Gilbert S. Omenn, Dean, 206-543-1144. Application contact: Marcia Syverson, Student Services Coordinator, 206-543-1144.

See in-depth description on page 1549.

University of Wisconsin–Eau Claire, College of Professional Studies, School of Human Sciences and Services, Division of Allied Health Professions, Program in Environmental and Public Health, Eau Claire, WI 54702-4004. Awards MS. Students: 16 full-time (8 women), 5 part-time (1 woman); includes 3 minority (2 African Americans, 1 Asian American). In 1997, 11 degrees awarded. *Degree requirements:* Thesis, oral and written exams required, foreign language not required. *Application deadline:* 3/1 (rolling processing). *Application fee:* $45. *Tuition:* $3651 per year full-time, $611 per semester (minimum) part-time for state residents; $11,295 per year full-time, $1886 per semester (minimum) part-time for nonresidents. *Financial aid:* Federal Work-Study available. Financial aid application deadline: 3/1. • Dr. Dale Taylor, Director, Division of Allied Health Professions, 715-836-2628.

University of Wisconsin–La Crosse, College of Health, Physical Education and Recreation, Department of Health Education, La Crosse, WI 54601-3742. Offers programs in community health (MS), community health education (MPH), school health (MS). One or more programs accredited by CEPH. Part-time and evening/weekend programs available. Faculty: 8 full-time (2 women). Students: 17 full-time (12 women), 14 part-time (10 women); includes 3 minority (2 Asian Americans, 1 Hispanic). Average age 28. 21 applicants, 76% accepted. In 1997, 16 degrees awarded (100% found work related to degree). *Degree requirements:* Thesis (for some programs), community health education preceptorship required, foreign language not required. *Entrance requirements:* GRE General Test, GRE Subject Test (MPH), minimum GPA of 3.0 during previous 2 years (MPH), minimum GPA of 2.85 (MS). Application fee: $38. *Tuition:* $3737 per year full-time, $208 per credit part-time for state residents; $11,921 per year full-time, $633 per credit part-time for nonresidents. *Financial aid:* In 1997–98, 5 students received aid, including 5 research assistantships (3 to first-year students) averaging $546 per month and totaling $24,570; career-related internships or fieldwork also available. Aid available to part-time students. Financial aid application deadline: 2/15; applicants required to submit FAFSA. *Faculty research:* Stress management, wellness inventories, health curriculum, health promotion, drug and alcohol use. • Dr. Gary D. Gilmore, Director, Community and Health Education, 608-785-8163. E-mail: gilmore@mail.uwlax.edu. Application contact: Tim Lewis, Director of Admissions, 608-785-8939. Fax: 608-785-6695. E-mail: admissions@mail.uwlax.edu.

Vanderbilt University, School of Medicine, Department of Preventive Medicine, Nashville, TN 37240-1001. Offers program in public health (MPH). Faculty: 12 full-time. Students: 10 full-time. *Degree requirements:* Research project. *Entrance requirements:* MD or equivalent. Application deadline: 10/15 (rolling processing). Application fee: $50. *Financial aid:* Application deadline 3/1. *Faculty research:* Pharmacoepidemiology, health services research, cancer epidemiology, infectious diseases, public health practice, clinical trials, biostatistics. • Dr. Wayne A. Ray, Director, 615-322-2017. Fax: 615-343-8722. E-mail: wayne.ray@mcmail.vanderbilt.edu.

Virginia Commonwealth University, Schools of Graduate Studies and Medicine, School of Medicine Graduate Programs, Department of Preventive Medicine, Richmond, VA 23284-9005. Awards MPH. Accredited by CEPH. Faculty: 7 full-time. Students: 30 full-time (25 women), 36 part-time (30 women); includes 27 minority (19 African Americans, 4 Asian Americans, 4 Hispanics), 1 international. Average age 31. 83 applicants, 66% accepted. In 1997, 23 degrees awarded. *Entrance requirements:* GMAT or MCAT, DAT or GRE General Test. Application deadline: 4/1. Application fee: $30 ($0 for international students). *Tuition:* $4960 per year full-time, $257 per credit part-time for state residents; $12,652 per year full-time, $684 per credit part-time for nonresidents. • Dr. Jack Lanier, Chair, 804-828-9785. E-mail: jlanier@gems.vcu.edu. Application contact: Lorna Brown, Graduate Program Coordinator, 804-828-9785. Fax: 804-828-9773. E-mail: lobrown@gems.vcu.edu.

Western Kentucky University, Ogden College of Science, Technology, and Health, Department of Public Health, Bowling Green, KY 42101-3576. Offers programs in environmental health (MS), gerontology (MS), health care administration (MS), health education (MA Ed), public health (MS), public health education (MS). Part-time and evening/weekend programs available. Faculty: 11 full-time (4 women). Students: 22 full-time (16 women), 10 part-time (7 women); includes 3 minority (all African Americans), 2 international. Average age 30. 35 applicants, 91% accepted. *Degree requirements:* Variable foreign language requirement, thesis or alternative. *Entrance requirements:* GRE General Test. Application deadline: 8/1 (priority date; rolling processing; 12/1 for spring admission). Application fee: $20. *Tuition:* $2460 per year full-time, $133 per credit hour part-time for state residents; $6700 per year full-time, $369 per credit hour part-time for nonresidents. *Financial aid:* In 1997–98, 13 service awards (7 to first-year students) averaging $485 per month and totaling $34,100 were awarded; research assistantships, Federal Work-Study, institutionally sponsored loans, and career-related internships or fieldwork also available. Aid available to part-time students. Financial aid application deadline: 4/1; applicants required to submit FAFSA. *Faculty research:* Drug alcohol education, health care reform, violence prevention, public health reform, health care policy. • Dr. J. David Dunn, Head, 502-745-4797. Fax: 502-745-4437. E-mail: david.dunn@wku.edu.

West Virginia University, School of Medicine, Graduate Programs in Basic Health Sciences, Public Health Program, Morgantown, WV 26506. Awards MPH. Accredited by CEPH. Part-time programs available. Postbaccalaureate distance learning degree programs offered (minimal on-campus study). Students: 18 full-time (11 women), 19 part-time (10 women); includes 7 minority (all Asian Americans), 2 international. Average age 36. 25 applicants, 20% accepted. In 1997, 1 degree awarded (100% found work related to degree). *Degree requirements:* Computer language, practicum, project required, foreign language and thesis not required. *Average time to degree:* master's–2 years full-time. *Entrance requirements:* MCAT (average 9), GRE General Test (combined average 1250), medical degree, medical internship. Application deadline: 4/15 (priority date; rolling processing; 12/1 for spring admission). Application fee: $45. *Tuition:* $3986 per year for state residents; $10,968 per year for nonresidents. *Financial aid:* In 1997–98, 2 research assistantships, 1 teaching assistantship were awarded. Financial aid application deadline: 2/1; applicants required to submit FAFSA. *Faculty research:* Occupational health, environmental health, clinical epidemiology, health care management, prevention. Total annual research expenditures: $500,000. • Dr. Bill Carlton, MPH Director, 304-293-2502. E-mail: bcearlton@wvu.edu. Application contact: Melissa R. Baker, Program Coordinator, 304-293-2502. Fax: 304-293-6685. E-mail: mbaker@wvu.edu.

Wichita State University, College of Health Professions, School of Health Sciences, Department of Public Health, Wichita, KS 67260. Awards MPH. Offered jointly with the University of Kansas. Faculty: 8 full-time (3 women), 1 (woman) part-time. Students: 7 full-time (4 women), 48 part-time (32 women); includes 4 minority (all African Americans), 3 international. Average age 38. 19 applicants, 53% accepted. In 1997, 4 degrees awarded. *Entrance requirements:* GRE, TOEFL (minimum score 570), bachelor's degree in health, minimum GPA of 3.0, 1 year of work experience. Application deadline: 6/1 (rolling processing; 1/1 for spring admission). Application fee: $25 ($40 for international students). Electronic applications accepted. *Expenses:* Tuition $2303 per year full-time, $96 per credit hour part-time for state residents; $7691 per year full-time, $321 per credit hour part-time for nonresidents. Fees $490 per year full-time, $75 per semester (minimum) part-time. *Financial aid:* In 1997–98, 3 research assistantships averaging $815 per month and totaling $18,320 were awarded; teaching assistantships, graduate assistantships, full and partial tuition waivers, Federal Work-Study, institutionally sponsored loans, and career-related internships or fieldwork also available. Aid available to part-time students. Financial aid application deadline: 4/1; applicants required to submit FAFSA. • Dr. Kenneth Pitetti, Director, 316-978-3661. E-mail: pitetti@chp.twsu.edu. Application contact: Dr. Steven Gladhart, Interim Dean, 316-978-3060. Fax: 316-978-3025. E-mail: gladhart@chp.twsu.edu.

Yale University, School of Medicine, Department of Epidemiology and Public Health, New Haven, CT 06520. Awards MPH, Dr PH, PhD, MD/MPH, MFS/MPH, MPH/MA, MPPM/MPH, MSN/MPH. Programs in biostatistics (MPH, Dr PH, PhD), chronic disease epidemiology (MPH, Dr PH, PhD), environmental health (MPH, Dr PH, PhD), epidemiology of microbial diseases (MPH, Dr PH, PhD), health policy and administration (MPH, Dr PH, PhD), international health (MPH), parasitology (PhD). One or more programs accredited by CEPH. PhD offered through the Graduate School. Part-time programs available. Faculty: 58 full-time (28 women), 35 part-time (9 women). Students: 267 full-time (171 women), 16 part-time (9 women); includes 81 minority (9 African Americans, 58 Asian Americans, 13 Hispanics, 1 Native American), 39 international. Average age 27. 522 applicants, 52% accepted. In 1997, 92 master's, 9 doctorates awarded. Terminal master's awarded for partial completion of doctoral program. *Degree requirements:* For master's, thesis, internship; for doctorate, dissertation, comprehensive exams, residency required, foreign language not required. *Entrance requirements:* For master's, GMAT, GRE, LSAT, or MCAT; TOEFL, previous undergraduate course work in mathematics and science; for doctorate, GRE General Test (minimum combined score of 1200), TOEFL. Application deadline: rolling. Application fee: $60. *Financial aid:* 102 students received aid; fellowships, research assistantships, teaching assistantships, scholarships, full and partial tuition waivers, Federal Work-Study, institutionally sponsored loans, and career-related internships or fieldwork available. Aid available to part-time students. Financial aid application deadline: 4/15; applicants required to submit FAFSA. *Faculty research:* Genetic and emerging infections epidemiology, virology, cost/quality, vector biology, quantitative methods. Total annual research expenditures: $8.2 million. • Dr. Michael H. Merson, Dean and Chairman, 203-785-2867. Fax: 203-785-6103. E-mail: michael.merson@yale.edu. Application contact: Joan Stenner, Admissions Officer, 203-785-2844. Fax: 203-785-4845. E-mail: joan.stenner@yale.edu.

See in-depth description on page 1551.

Community Health

Brooklyn College of the City University of New York, Department of Health and Nutrition Science, Program in Community Health, 2900 Bedford Avenue, Brooklyn, NY 11210-2889. Offers community health (MA, MPH), computer science and health science (MS), health care management (MA, MPH), health care policy and administration (MA, MPH), nutrition (MS), thanatology (MA). MS (computer science and health science) offered jointly with the Department of Computer and Information Science. Students: 2 full-time (0 women), 34 part-time (25 women); includes 19 minority (17 African Americans, 2 Hispanics). In 1997, 12 degrees awarded. *Degree requirements:* Thesis or alternative required, foreign language not required. *Entrance requirements:* TOEFL (minimum score 500), 18 credits in health-related areas. Application deadline: 3/1 (11/1 for spring admission). Application fee: $40. *Expenses:* Tuition $4350 per year full-time, $185 per credit part-time for state residents; $7600 per year full-time, $320 per credit part-time for nonresidents. Fees $500 per year for state residents; $806 per year for nonresidents. *Financial aid:* Application deadline 5/1; applicants required to submit FAFSA. *Faculty research:* Diet restriction, religious practices in bereavement, diabetes, stress management, palliative care. • Dr. Erika Friedmann, Chairperson, Department of Health and Nutrition Science, 718-951-5026. E-mail: erikaf@brooklyn.cuny.edu. Application contact: Jerrold Mirotznik, Deputy Chairperson for Graduate Studies, 718-951-4197. Fax: 718-951-4670.

Brown University, Division of Biology and Medicine, Department of Community Health, Providence, RI 02912. Awards MS, PhD, MD/PhD. Programs in biostatistics (MS, PhD), including health services research; epidemiology (MS, PhD), including health services research. Faculty: 32 full-time (16 women). Students: 9 full-time (6 women). *Degree requirements:* For doctorate, dissertation, preliminary exam. *Entrance requirements:* GRE General Test. Application deadline: 1/2 (priority date; rolling processing). Application fee: $60. *Expenses:* Tuition $23,616 per year. Fees $436 per year. *Financial aid:* Fellowships, research assistantships available. Financial aid application deadline: 1/2. • Dr. Constantine Gatsonis, Director, 401-863-1106. E-mail: gatsonis@jenny.biomed.brown.edu.

Columbia University, School of Public Health, Division of Sociomedical Sciences, New York, NY 10032. Awards MPH, Dr PH, PhD. One or more programs accredited by CEPH. PhD offered in cooperation with the Graduate School of Arts and Sciences. Part-time programs available. Students: 121. In 1997, 32 master's, 1 doctorate awarded. *Degree requirements:* For doctorate, dissertation required, foreign language not required. *Average time to degree:* master's–1.5 years full-time, 3 years part-time; doctorate–4 years full-time, 7 years part-time. *Entrance requirements:* For master's, GRE General Test; for doctorate, GRE General Test, MPH or equivalent (Dr PH). Application deadline: 4/10 (11/15 for spring admission). Application fee: $60. *Tuition:* $22,320 per year full-time, $744 per credit part-time. *Financial aid:* Research assistantships, teaching assistantships, Federal Work-Study, and career-related internships or fieldwork available. Aid available to part-time students. Financial aid application deadline: 3/15; applicants required to submit FAFSA. *Faculty research:* Social and cultural factors in health and health care, health services delivery and utilization, health promotion and disease prevention, AIDS. • Dr. Cheryl Healton, Head, 212-305-5656. Application contact: Rosalie Acinapura, Program Coordinator, 212-305-5656. Fax: 212-305-6832.

Dalhousie University, Faculties of Graduate Studies and Medicine, Graduate Programs in Medicine, Department of Community Health and Epidemiology, Halifax, NS B3H 3J5, Canada. Awards M Sc. Part-time programs available. Faculty: 10 full-time (4 women), 22 part-time (11 women). Students: 25 full-time (21 women), 16 part-time (11 women). Average age 28. 30 applicants, 43% accepted. In 1997, 6 degrees awarded. *Degree requirements:* Thesis. *Entrance requirements:* TOEFL (minimum score 580). Application deadline: 3/1. Application fee: $55. *Financial aid:* Fellowships, research assistantships, partial tuition waivers, and career-related internships or fieldwork available. *Faculty research:* Population health, health promotion, health services utilization, chronic disease epidemiology. • Dr. D. R. MacLean, Head, 902-494-1235. Application contact: Dr. Susan Kirkland, Graduate Coordinator, 902-494-3860. Fax: 902-494-1597.

Emory University, The Rollins School of Public Health, Department of Behavioral Sciences and Health Education, Atlanta, GA 30322-1100. Awards MPH. Accredited by CEPH. *Degree requirements:* Thesis (for some programs), practicum required, foreign language not required. *Entrance requirements:* GRE General Test. Application deadline: 2/15 (priority date; rolling processing). Application fee: $50. *Expenses:* Tuition $14,136 per year full-time, $589 per credit hour part-time. Fees $200 per year. *Financial aid:* Application deadline 2/15. • Dr. Ronald Braithwaite, Chair, 404-727-8093. Application contact: Susan Daniel, Director of Admissions, 404-727-5481. Fax: 404-727-3996. E-mail: admit@sph.emory.edu.

See in-depth description on page 1493.

The George Washington University, School of Public Health and Health Services, Master's Program in Public Health, Track in Community-oriented Primary Care, Washington, DC 20052. Awards MPH. Accredited by CEPH. *Degree requirements:* Case study or special project required, thesis not required. *Entrance requirements:* GMAT, GRE General Test, or MCAT; TOEFL. Application deadline: 5/15 (priority date; rolling processing; 11/15 for spring admission). Application fee: $50. *Expenses:* Tuition $680 per semester hour. Fees $35 per semester hour. • Application contact: Michelle Sparacino, Director of Recruitment, 202-994-2160. Fax: 202-994-3773. E-mail: sphhs-info@gwumc.edu.

See in-depth description on page 1495.

Harvard University, School of Public Health, Master of Public Health Program, Boston, MA 02115. Offerings include public management and community health (MPH). *Average time to degree:* master's–1 year full-time, 2.5 years part-time. *Entrance requirements:* GRE, TOEFL (minimum score 550). Application deadline: 1/4 (priority date). Application fee: $60. *Expenses:* Tuition $21,895 per year full-time, $10,948 per year part-time. Fees $686 per year. • Dr. Gareth M. Green, Associate Dean for Professional Education, 617-432-0090. Application contact: Carrie Daniels, Assistant Director of Admissions, 617-432-1031. Fax: 617-432-2009. E-mail: admisofc@sph.harvard.edu.

Long Island University, Brooklyn Campus, School of Health Professions, Department of Community Health, Brooklyn, NY 11201-8423. Offers programs in community mental health (MS), family health (MS), health management (MS). Part-time and evening/weekend programs available. Faculty: 3 full-time (2 women), 15 part-time (4 women). Students: 25 full-time (20 women), 58 part-time (41 women); includes 60 minority (45 African Americans, 9 Asian Americans, 6 Hispanics). 36 applicants, 81% accepted. In 1997, 28 degrees awarded. *Application deadline:* rolling. *Application fee:* $30. Electronic applications accepted. *Expenses:* Tuition $480 per credit. Fees $415 per year full-time, $73 per semester (minimum) part-time. *Financial aid:* In 1997–98, 4 students received aid, including 4 assistantships. • Enna Crosman, Chair, 718-488-1067. Application contact: Bernard W. Sullivan, Associate Director of Admissions, 718-488-1011.

Mankato State University, College of Allied Health and Nursing, Department of Health Science, South Rd and Ellis Ave, PO Box 8400, Mankato, MN 56002-8400. Offerings include community health (MS). Department faculty: 8 full-time (4 women). *Application deadline:* 7/10 (priority date; rolling processing; 10/30 for spring admission). *Application fee:* $20. *Tuition:* $126 per credit (minimum) for state residents; $200 per credit for nonresidents. • Dr. Harold Slobof, Chairperson, 507-389-1528. Application contact: Joni Roberts, Admissions Coordinator, 507-389-2321. Fax: 507-389-5974. E-mail: grad@mankato.msus.edu.

McGill University, Faculty of Graduate Studies and Research, Faculty of Medicine, Department of Epidemiology and Biostatistics, Montréal, PQ H3A 2T5, Canada. Offerings include

Directory: Community Health

McGill University (continued)
community health (M Sc). Department faculty: 35 full-time (7 women), 23 part-time (6 women). *Degree requirements:* Thesis optional, foreign language not required. *Entrance requirements:* GRE, minimum GPA of 3.0. Application deadline: 3/1 (rolling processing). Application fee: $60. *Expenses:* Tuition $1668 per year for Canadian residents; $8268 per year for nonresidents. Fees $828 per year for Canadian residents; $1216 per year for nonresidents. • Dr. G. Theriault, Chair, Graduate Committee, 514-398-6259. E-mail: gtheri@epid.lan.mcgill.ca. Application contact: Marlene Abrams, Secretary for Graduate Studies, 514-398-6269. Fax: 514-398-4503. E-mail: marlene@epid.lan.mcgill.ca.

Meharry Medical College, Division of Community Health Sciences, Nashville, TN 37208-9989. Offers programs in general preventive medicine (MSPH), health services administration (MSPH), occupational medicine (MSPH), public health administration (MSPH). Part-time and evening/weekend programs available. Faculty: 12 full-time (4 women), 10 part-time (5 women). Students: 47 full-time (26 women); includes 39 minority (35 African Americans, 3 Asian Americans, 1 Hispanic), 4 international. Average age 32. 45 applicants, 51% accepted. In 1997, 19 degrees awarded. *Degree requirements:* Thesis, externship required, foreign language not required. *Average time to degree:* master's–2 years full-time, 4 years part-time. *Entrance requirements:* GRE General Test (minimum combined score of 800). Application deadline: 6/30 (rolling processing). Application fee: $45. *Expenses:* Tuition $7020 per year. Fees $1633 per year. *Financial aid:* Scholarships, Federal Work-Study, institutionally sponsored loans, and career-related internships or fieldwork available. Aid available to part-time students. Financial aid application deadline: 7/15; applicants required to submit FAFSA. *Faculty research:* Policy and management, health care financing, health education and promotion. • Dr. Herman Ellis, Interim Director, 615-327-5530. Application contact: Dr. Otis Cosby, Assistant Director, 615-327-6069. Fax: 615-327-6717.

Memorial University of Newfoundland, Faculty of Medicine and School of Graduate Studies, Graduate Programs in Medicine, Division of Community Health, St. John's, NF A1C 5S7, Canada. Offers programs in clinical epidemiology (M Sc, PhD, Diploma), community health (M Sc, PhD, Diploma). Part-time programs available. Faculty: 15 full-time (3 women), 2 part-time (1 woman). Students: 9 full-time (7 women), 44 part-time (29 women). 25 applicants, 80% accepted. In 1997, 6 master's awarded. *Degree requirements:* For master's, thesis required, foreign language not required; for doctorate, comprehensive exam, oral defense of thesis required, foreign language not required. *Entrance requirements:* For master's, TOEFL, MD or B Sc; for doctorate, TOEFL, MD or M Sc. Application deadline: 3/31 (priority date; rolling processing). Application fee: $40. *Expenses:* Tuition $1896 per year (minimum). Fees $60 per year for Canadian residents; $621 per year for nonresidents. *Financial aid:* Fellowships, research assistantships available. Financial aid application deadline: 3/31. *Faculty research:* Epidemiology of chronic diseases, especially hypertension; health care delivery and administration. • Dr. Roy West, Associate Dean, 709-737-6693.

Old Dominion University, College of Health Sciences, School of Community Health Professions and Physical Therapy, Norfolk, VA 23529. Offerings include community health professions (MS). School faculty: 9 full-time (7 women), 5 part-time (3 women), 10.7 FTE. *Application deadline:* 2/15 (rolling processing). *Application fee:* $30. *Expenses:* Tuition $180 per credit hour for state residents; $477 per credit hour for nonresidents. Fees $140 per year full-time, $32 per semester part-time. • Dr. George Maihafer, Chair, 757-683-4520. E-mail: gmaihafer@odu.edu.

Queen's University at Kingston, Faculty of Medicine and School of Graduate Studies and Research, Graduate Programs in Medicine, Department of Community Health and Epidemiology, Kingston, ON K7L 3N6, Canada. Offers programs in biostatistics (M Sc), environmental and occupational health (M Sc), epidemiology (M Sc), general community health (M Sc), health-care systems (M Sc), preventive medicine (M Sc). Part-time programs available. Students: 21 full-time (16 women), 16 part-time (11 women). In 1997, 16 degrees awarded. *Degree requirements:* Thesis required, foreign language not required. *Entrance requirements:* TOEFL (minimum score 550). Application fee: $60. Electronic applications accepted. *Tuition:* $3803 per year (minimum) full-time, $1901 per year (minimum) part-time for Canadian residents; $7330 per year (minimum) for nonresidents. *Financial aid:* Fellowships, institutionally sponsored loans available. Financial aid application deadline: 3/1. • Dr. J. L. Pater, Graduate Coordinator, 613-545-2901. Application contact: R. E. M. Lees, Graduate Coordinator, 613-545-4954.

Sage Graduate School, Graduate School, Division of Psychology, Troy, NY 12180-4115. Offerings include community psychology (MA), with options in chemical dependency, child care and children's services, community counseling, community health educator, general psychology, visual art therapy. Division faculty: 2 full-time (1 woman), 2 part-time (both women). *Degree requirements:* Thesis or alternative required, foreign language not required. *Entrance requirements:* GRE General Test, minimum GPA of 2.75. Application deadline: 8/1 (rolling processing; 12/15 for spring admission). Application fee: $25. *Expenses:* Tuition $360 per credit hour. Fees $50 per semester. • Dr. Patricia O'Connor, Director, 518-244-2221. Fax: 518-244-4545. E-mail: occonp@sage.edu. Application contact: Melissa Robertson, Associate Director of Admissions, 518-244-6878. Fax: 518-244-6880. E-mail: sgsadm@sage.edu.

Sage Graduate School, Graduate School, Division of Education, Program in Health Education, Troy, NY 12180-4115. Offerings include community health (MS). *Degree requirements:* Thesis optional, foreign language not required. *Entrance requirements:* Minimum GPA of 2.75. Application deadline: 8/1 (rolling processing; 12/15 for spring admission). Application fee: $25. *Expenses:* Tuition $360 per credit hour. Fees $50 per semester. • Dr. John J. Pelizza, Adviser, 518-244-2051. Fax: 218-244-2334. Application contact: Melissa Robertson, Associate Director of Admissions, 518-244-6878. Fax: 518-244-6880. E-mail: sgsadm@sage.edu.

Saint Louis University, School of Public Health, Program in Community Health, St. Louis, MO 63108. Awards MPH, JD/MPH, MD/MPH, MPH/MS, MPH/MSN, MPH/MSW, MPH/PhD. Accredited by CEPH. Students: 57 full-time (38 women), 73 part-time (56 women); includes 44 minority (22 African Americans, 18 Asian Americans, 4 Hispanics), 5 international. 120 applicants, 72% accepted. In 1997, 29 degrees awarded. *Degree requirements:* Comprehensive oral exam required, thesis not required. *Entrance requirements:* GRE General Test. Application deadline: 7/1 (rolling processing; 11/1 for spring admission). Application fee: $40. *Tuition:* $542 per credit hour. *Financial aid:* In 1997–98, 1 fellowship, 1 research assistantship were awarded. Financial aid application deadline: 4/1. *Faculty research:* Environmental health, epidemiology, health promotion, evaluative research methods, toxicology. • Dr. Ross Brownson, Chairman, 314-977-8110. Application contact: Dr. Marcia Buresch, Assistant Dean of the Graduate School, 314-977-2240. Fax: 314-977-3943.

State University of New York at Buffalo, Graduate School, School of Medicine, Graduate Programs in Medicine, Department of Social and Preventive Medicine, Buffalo, NY 14214. Offerings include epidemiology and community health (PhD). Department faculty: 12 full-time (4 women), 3 part-time (1 woman). *Degree requirements:* Dissertation. *Entrance requirements:* GRE General Test, TOEFL. Application deadline: 4/15 (priority date; rolling processing; 10/1 for spring admission). Application fee: $35. *Tuition:* $5970 per year full-time, $288 per credit hour part-time for state residents; $9286 per year full-time, $426 per credit hour part-time for nonresidents. • Dr. Maurizio Trevisan, Chairman, 716-829-2975. Application contact: Dr. John E. Vena, Director of Graduate Studies, 716-829-2975. Fax: 716-829-2979. E-mail: jvena@acsu.buffaol.edu.

Temple University, School of Social Administration, Department of Health Studies, Program in Public Health, Philadelphia, PA 19122-6096. Offerings include community health education (MPH). Accredited by CEPH. Program faculty: 11 full-time (8 women). *Degree requirements:* Fieldwork, practicum required, foreign language and thesis not required. *Average time to degree:* master's–2 years full-time, 4 years part-time. *Entrance requirements:* GRE General Test, minimum undergraduate GPA of 2.8. Application deadline: 2/1 (10/15 for spring admission). Application fee: $40. *Expenses:* Tuition $323 per semester hour for state residents; $444 per semester hour for nonresidents. Fees $170 per year full-time, $28 per semester (minimum) part-time. • Dr. Alice J. Hausman, Head, 215-204-5112. E-mail: hausman@vm.temple.edu. Application contact: Joyce Hankins, Administrative Assistant, 215-204-8726. Fax: 215-204-1455.

See in-depth description on page 1517.

Trinity College, School of Professional Studies, Program in Health, Washington, DC 20017-1094. Offers community health promotion and education (MA). Faculty: 1 (woman) full-time. Students: 38 (37 women); includes 17 minority (15 African Americans, 1 Asian American, 1 Hispanic). *Degree requirements:* Thesis or alternative. *Entrance requirements:* Minimum GPA of 2.8. Application deadline: rolling. Application fee: $35. *Tuition:* $460 per credit hour. • Application contact: Karen Goodwin, Director of Graduate Admissions, 202-884-9400. Fax: 202-884-9229.

Université de Montréal, Faculties of Medicine and Graduate Studies, Graduate Programs in Medicine, Department of Social and Preventive Medicine, Montréal, PQ H3C 3J7, Canada. Offers program in community health (M Sc, PhD, DESS). Faculty: 22 full-time (13 women). Students: 134 full-time (81 women), 30 part-time (19 women). 86 applicants, 37% accepted. In 1997, 8 master's, 5 doctorates, 8 DESSs awarded. Terminal master's awarded for partial completion of doctoral program. *Degree requirements:* For master's, thesis; for doctorate, dissertation, general exam. *Entrance requirements:* For master's and doctorate, proficiency in French, knowledge of English; for DESS, proficiency in French. Application fee: $30. • Pierre Fournier, Director, 514-343-6140.

Université Laval, Faculties of Medicine and Graduate Studies, Graduate Programs in Medicine, Department of Social and Preventive Medicine, Program in Community Health, Sainte-Foy, PQ G1K 7P4, Canada. Awards M Sc. Students: 17 full-time (15 women), 35 part-time (26 women). 53 applicants, 81% accepted. In 1997, 16 degrees awarded. *Application deadline:* 3/1. *Application fee:* $30. *Expenses:* Tuition $1334 per year (minimum) full-time, $56 per credit (minimum) part-time for Canadian residents; $5966 per year (minimum) full-time, $249 per credit (minimum) part-time for nonresidents. Fees $150 per year full-time, $6.25 per credit part-time. • Therese Morais, Director, 418-656-2131 Ext. 3720. Fax: 418-656-7759. E-mail: therese.morais@msp.ulaval.ca.

University of British Columbia, Faculties of Medicine and Graduate Studies, Graduate Programs in Medicine, Department of Health Care and Epidemiology, Vancouver, BC V6T 1W5, Canada. Offerings include community health (MH Sc). *Average time to degree:* master's–3 years full-time, 4 years part-time. *Application deadline:* 3/31 (rolling processing). *Application fee:* $50.

The University of Calgary, Faculties of Medicine and Graduate Studies, Department of Community Health Sciences, Calgary, AB T2N 1N4, Canada. Awards M Sc, PhD. Faculty: 23 full-time (8 women), 26 part-time (16 women). Students: 39 full-time (28 women), 9 part-time (4 women); includes 6 international. Average age 34. 77 applicants, 10% accepted. In 1997, 3 master's awarded (100% found work related to degree); 3 doctorates awarded (67% entered university research/teaching, 33% found other work related to degree). *Degree requirements:* For master's, computer language, thesis required, foreign language not required; for doctorate, computer language, dissertation, candidacy exam required, foreign language not required. *Average time to degree:* master's–2.6 years full-time; doctorate–3.6 years full-time. *Entrance requirements:* TOEFL (minimum score 580), minimum GPA of 3.2. Application deadline: 3/1. Application fee: $60. Electronic applications accepted. *Tuition:* $6110 per year for Canadian residents; $30,000 per year for nonresidents. *Financial aid:* In 1997–98, 17 students received aid, including 7 research assistantships (1 to a first-year student) averaging $980 per month and totaling $25,640, 2 teaching assistantships averaging $1,303 per month and totaling $10,428, 7 scholarships (all to first-year students) totaling $41,000; full and partial tuition waivers also available. Financial aid application deadline: 2/1. *Faculty research:* Epidemiology, health care research, biostatistics, occupational and environmental health, mental health. Total annual research expenditures: $4.939 million. • Gordon H. Fick, Graduate Coordinator, 403-220-6939. E-mail: lsutherl@acs.ucalgary.ca. Application contact: Crystal Elliott, Graduate Secretary, 403-220-4288. Fax: 403-270-7307. E-mail: chsgrad@acs.ucalgary.ca.

The University of Calgary, Faculty of Education, Graduate Division of Educational Research, Calgary, AB T2N 1N4, Canada. Offerings include community rehabilitation (MA, M Ed, M Sc, Ed D, PhD). Postbaccalaureate distance learning degree programs offered (minimal on-campus study). Division faculty: 60 full-time, 25 part-time. *Degree requirements:* For master's, thesis (for some programs), comprehensive exam required, foreign language not required; for doctorate, dissertation. *Entrance requirements:* For master's, minimum GPA of 3.0; for doctorate, minimum GPA of 3.5. Application deadline: 2/1. Application fee: $60. Electronic applications accepted. *Expenses:* Tuition $5448 per year full-time, $908 per course part-time for Canadian residents; $10,896 per year full-time, $1816 per course part-time for nonresidents. Fees $285 per year full-time, $119 per semester (minimum) part-time. • Dr. Bryant Griffith, Assistant Dean, 403-220-5675. Fax: 403-282-3005. E-mail: griffith@acs.ucalgary.ca.

University of California, Los Angeles, School of Public Health, Department of Community Health Sciences, Los Angeles, CA 90095. Offers program in public health (MS, PhD). Faculty: 17 (10 women). Students: 340 full-time (240 women); includes 156 minority (19 African Americans, 98 Asian Americans, 37 Hispanics, 2 Native Americans), 31 international. 576 applicants, 54% accepted. *Degree requirements:* For master's, comprehensive exam or thesis required, foreign language not required; for doctorate, dissertation, oral and written qualifying exams required, foreign language not required. *Entrance requirements:* For master's, GRE General Test (minimum combined score of 1100), minimum GPA of 3.0; for doctorate, GRE General Test (minimum combined score of 1200), minimum undergraduate GPA of 3.0. Application deadline: 12/15. Application fee: $40. Electronic applications accepted. *Expenses:* Tuition $0 for state residents; $9384 per year for nonresidents. Fees $4551 per year. *Financial aid:* In 1997–98, 275 students received aid, including fellowships totaling $454,295, research assistantships totaling $120,871, teaching assistantships totaling $244,911, federal fellowships and scholarships totaling $558,690. Financial aid application deadline: 3/1. • Dr. Gail Harrison, Chair, 310-825-5524. Application contact: Departmental Office, 310-825-5524. E-mail: app_request@admin.ph.ucla.edu.

University of Hawaii at Manoa, College of Health Sciences and Social Welfare, School of Public Health, Program in Community Health Development and Education, Honolulu, HI 96822. Awards MPH, MS. Part-time programs available. Faculty: 2 full-time (1 woman), 1 (woman) part-time, 2.85 FTE. Students: 25 full-time (19 women), 9 part-time (5 women); includes 19 minority (2 African Americans, 15 Asian Americans, 2 Hispanics). 48 applicants, 40% accepted. In 1997, 17 degrees awarded. *Degree requirements:* Thesis (for some programs). *Average time to degree:* master's–1.2 years full-time, 3 years part-time. *Application deadline:* 3/1 (9/1 for spring admission). *Application fee:* $25 ($50 for international students). *Tuition:* $4029 per year full-time, $214 per credit hour part-time for state residents; $9957 per year full-time, $461 per credit hour part-time for nonresidents. *Financial aid:* Career-related internships or fieldwork available. *Faculty research:* Gerontology, community-based health professional education. • Dr. Jerome Grossman, Head, 808-956-5769. Application contact: Nancy Kilonsky, Assistant Dean, 808-956-8267.

University of Illinois at Chicago, School of Public Health, Program in Community Health Sciences, Chicago, IL 60607-7128. Awards MPH, MS, Dr PH, PhD. One or more programs accredited by CEPH. MS and PhD offered jointly with Graduate College. *Degree requirements:* For master's, thesis, field practicum required, foreign language not required; for doctorate, dissertation, independent research, internship required, foreign language not required. *Entrance requirements:* GRE General Test (minimum combined score of 1000), TOEFL (minimum score 550), minimum GPA of 3.75 on a 5.0 scale. Application deadline: 7/3 (11/8 for spring admission). Application fee: $40 ($50 for international students). • Dr. Naomi Harris, Director, 312-996-8866. Application contact: Dr. Babette Neuberger, Assistant Dean, 312-996-6625.

Directory: Community Health

University of Illinois at Urbana–Champaign, College of Applied Life Studies, Department of Community Health, Urbana, IL 61801. Offers programs in community health (MSPH, PhD); rehabilitation education services (MS), including rehabilitation. One or more programs accredited by CEPH. Faculty: 10 full-time (4 women). Students: 39 full-time (29 women); includes 8 minority (4 African Americans, 2 Asian Americans, 1 Hispanic, 1 Native American), 4 international. Average age 28. 31 applicants, 39% accepted. In 1997, 6 master's, 3 doctorates awarded. *Degree requirements:* Thesis/dissertation. *Entrance requirements:* For master's, GRE General Test, minimum GPA of 4.0 on a 5.0 scale; for doctorate, GRE General Test, minimum graduate GPA of 4.5 on a 5.0 scale, interview. Application deadline: 3/8 (priority date; rolling processing). Application fee: $40 ($50 for international students). *Financial aid:* In 1997–98, 6 research assistantships, 23 teaching assistantships were awarded; fellowships, full and partial tuition waivers, Federal Work-Study, institutionally sponsored loans, and career-related internships or fieldwork also available. Financial aid application deadline: 2/15. *Faculty research:* Epidemiology, health behavior, health services research, health policy. • Lee Alden Crandall, Head, 217-244-0502.

The University of Iowa, College of Medicine and Graduate College, Graduate Programs in Medicine, Department of Preventive Medicine and Environmental Health, Iowa City, IA 52242-1316. Offerings include community health (MS). MS/MA and MS/MS offered jointly with the Program in Urban and Regional Planning. Department faculty: 27 full-time (5 women), 11 part-time (4 women). *Degree requirements:* Computer language (biostatistics) required, thesis optional, foreign language not required. *Average time to degree:* master's–2 years full-time, 6 years part-time; doctorate–5 years full-time, 9 years part-time. *Entrance requirements:* GRE General Test (minimum combined score of 1050), TOEFL (minimum score 600), minimum GPA of 2.7. Application deadline: 1/15 (priority date; rolling processing; 10/1 for spring admission). Application fee: $30 ($50 for international students). *Expenses:* Tuition $3166 per year full-time, $176 per credit hour part-time for state residents; $10,202 per year full-time, $567 per credit hour part-time for nonresidents. Fees $101 per year full-time, $51 per year (minimum) part-time. • Dr. James Merchant, Interim Head, 319-335-9833. Fax: 319-335-9772. E-mail: james-merchant@uiowa.edu. Application contact: Barbara Scott, Graduate Studies Coordinator, 319-335-8992. Fax: 319-335-9200. E-mail: barbara-scott@uiowa.edu.

University of Manitoba, Faculties of Medicine and Graduate Studies, Graduate Programs in Medicine, Department of Community Health Sciences, Winnipeg, MB R3T 2N2, Canada. Awards M Sc, PhD. *Degree requirements:* Thesis/dissertation required, foreign language not required. *Average time to degree:* master's–4 years full-time; doctorate–3 years full-time. *Entrance requirements:* Minimum GPA of 3.0. Application deadline: 4/11 (priority date). Application fee: $50. *Faculty research:* Health services, aboriginal health, health policy, epidemiology, environmental and occupational health.

University of Minnesota, Twin Cities Campus, School of Public Health, Major in Community Health Education, Minneapolis, MN 55455-0213. Awards MPH. Accredited by CEPH. Part-time programs available. Faculty: 14 full-time. Students: 43; includes 4 minority (1 African American, 2 Asian Americans, 1 Native American). 94 applicants, 33% accepted. In 1997, 15 degrees awarded. *Entrance requirements:* GRE General Test (minimum combined score of 1500 on three sections), minimum GPA of 3.0. Application deadline: 2/28 (rolling processing). Application fee: $50 ($75 for international students). *Financial aid:* Fellowships, research assistantships, teaching assistantships, Federal Work-Study, institutionally sponsored loans, and career-related internships or fieldwork available. *Faculty research:* Community-based programs, public policy, social change. • Dr. Leslie Lytle, Chair, 612-626-1818. Application contact: Andrea Kish, Student Coordinator, 612-626-8802. Fax: 612-624-0315. E-mail: kish@epivax.epi.umn.edu.

University of Minnesota, Twin Cities Campus, Medical School and Graduate School, Graduate Programs in Medicine, Department of Family Practice and Community Health, Minneapolis, MN 55455-0213. Awards MS. Part-time programs available. *Degree requirements:* Paper. *Entrance requirements:* MD. Application deadline: 7/15 (rolling processing; 12/15 for spring admission). Application fee: $40 ($50 for international students). *Faculty research:* Geriatic clinical care, clinical trials for hypercholesterolemia, obstetrical risk management, curriculum design and evaluation, projecting health personnel needs.

University of Missouri–Columbia, School of Medicine and Graduate School, Graduate Programs in Medicine, Department of Family and Community Medicine, Columbia, MO 65211. Awards MSPH, MBA/MSPH, MPA/MSPH. Part-time programs available. Faculty: 27 full-time (8 women), 5 part-time (3 women). Students: 8 full-time (1 woman). In 1997, 1 degree awarded. *Entrance requirements:* GRE General Test, TOEFL, minimum GPA of 3.0. Application deadline: 5/1. Application fee: $25 ($50 for international students). *Tuition:* $3240 per year full-time, $180 per credit hour part-time for state residents; $9108 per year full-time, $506 per credit hour part-time for nonresidents. *Financial aid:* Fellowships, Federal Work-Study available. Aid available to part-time students. • Dr. Michael C. Hosokawa, Director of Graduate Studies, 573-882-4992.

University of North Carolina at Greensboro, School of Health and Human Performance, Department of Public Health Education, Greensboro, NC 27412-0001. Awards MPH. Faculty: 6 full-time (3 women), 4 part-time. Students: 48 full-time (44 women), 14 part-time (12 women); includes 8 minority (all African Americans), 1 international. 55 applicants, 76% accepted. In 1997, 8 degrees awarded. *Degree requirements:* Thesis or alternative, comprehensive exam required, foreign language not required. *Entrance requirements:* GRE General Test or MAT. Application deadline: 7/1 (priority date; rolling processing; 11/1 for spring admission). Application fee: $35. *Expenses:* Tuition $1842 per year full-time, $370 per semester (minimum) part-time for state residents; $10,296 per year full-time, $2484 per semester (minimum) part-time for nonresidents. Fees $806 per year full-time, $111 per semester (minimum) part-time. *Financial aid:* In 1997–98, 7 research assistantships totaling $49,477 were awarded; fellowships also available. *Faculty research:* Peer facilitator training, innovative health education approaches. • Dr. Keith Howell, Head, 336-334-5708.

University of Northern Colorado, College of Health and Human Sciences, Department of Community Health, Greeley, CO 80639. Awards MPH. Accredited by CEPH. Faculty: 3 full-time (1 woman). Students: 42 full-time (33 women), 11 part-time (7 women); includes 4 minority (1 African American, 1 Asian American, 2 Hispanics), 1 international. Average age 32. 26 applicants, 85% accepted. In 1997, 21 degrees awarded. *Degree requirements:* Thesis or alternative, comprehensive exams. *Application deadline:* rolling. *Application fee:* $35. *Expenses:* Tuition $2327 per year full-time, $129 per credit hour part-time for state residents; $9578 per year full-time, $532 per credit hour part-time for nonresidents. Fees $752 per year full-time, $184 per semester (minimum) part-time. *Financial aid:* In 1997–98, 35 students received aid, including 8 fellowships (2 to first-year students) totaling $12,750, 1 teaching assistantship totaling $3,463, 4 graduate assistantships (2 to first-year students) totaling $13,635. Financial aid application deadline: 3/1. • Larry Harrison, Chairperson, 907-351-2755.

University of North Texas, College of Education, Department of Kinesiology, Health Promotion, and Recreation, Program in Health Promotion, Denton, TX 76203-6737. Offerings include community health (MS). *Degree requirements:* Thesis required (for some programs), foreign language not required. *Entrance requirements:* GRE General Test (minimum score 375 on each section; 800 combined). Application deadline: 7/17. Application fee: $25 ($50 for international students). *Tuition:* $2063 per year full-time, $815 per year part-time for state residents; $5897 per year full-time, $2100 per year part-time for nonresidents. • Application contact: Chwee L. Chng, Adviser, 940-565-2651.

University of Ottawa, Faculty of Medicine, Department of Epidemiology and Community Medicine, Ottawa, ON K1N 6N5, Canada. Awards M Sc. Offered jointly with Carleton University. Faculty: 18 full-time, 8 part-time. Students: 12 full-time (5 women), 24 part-time (10 women). Average age 34. In 1997, 5 degrees awarded. *Degree requirements:* Thesis required, foreign language not required. *Entrance requirements:* Honors degree or equivalent, minimum B average. Application deadline: 2/28. Application fee: $35. *Expenses:* Tuition $4677 per year for Canadian residents; $9900 per year for nonresidents. Fees $230 per year. *Financial aid:* Teaching assistantships and career-related internships or fieldwork available. Financial aid application deadline: 2/28. *Faculty research:* Health systems research, community health. Total annual research expenditures: $4.5 million. • Ian W. McDowell, Chair, 613-562-5427. Application contact: Mariella Peca, Administrative Officer, 613-562-5800 Ext. 8281. Fax: 613-562-5465.

University of Pittsburgh, Graduate School of Public Health, Department of Health Services Administration, Program in Community Health Services, Pittsburgh, PA 15260. Awards MPH. Accredited by CEPH. Part-time programs available. Faculty: 18 full-time (10 women). Students: 16 full-time (12 women), 22 part-time (16 women); includes 15 minority (8 African Americans, 6 Asian Americans, 1 Hispanic), 1 international. 73 applicants, 75% accepted. In 1997, 24 degrees awarded. *Degree requirements:* Computer language, thesis required, foreign language not required. *Entrance requirements:* GRE General Test, TOEFL, bachelor's degree in public health or related field. Application deadline: 5/1 (rolling processing; 10/1 for spring admission). Application fee: $50 ($60 for international students). *Expenses:* Tuition $9402 per year full-time, $388 per credit part-time for state residents; $19,372 per year full-time, $799 per credit part-time for nonresidents. Fees $480 per year full-time, $180 per year part-time. *Financial aid:* In 1997–98, 10 students received aid, including 8 research assistantships averaging $1,116 per month, 2 assistantships averaging $1,049 per month; Federal Work-Study, institutionally sponsored loans, and career-related internships or fieldwork also available. Aid available to part-time students. *Faculty research:* Public health and aging, maternal and child health, substance abuse, privatization of health service. • Dr. Ravi K. Sharma, Director, 412-624-3615. E-mail: rks1946+@pitt.edu. Application contact: Gabriele E. M. Amersbach, Coordinator, 412-624-3124. Fax: 412-624-5510. E-mail: amers@vms.cis.pitt.edu.

See in-depth description on page 1545.

University of Saskatchewan, Colleges of Medicine and Graduate Studies and Research, Graduate Programs in Medicine, Department of Community Health and Epidemiology, Saskatoon, SK S7N 5A2, Canada. Awards M Sc, PhD. Faculty: 6 full-time, 6 part-time. Students: 12 full-time, 16 part-time. *Degree requirements:* Thesis/dissertation. *Entrance requirements:* International English Language Testing System (minimum score 6) or Michigan English Language Assessment Battery (mimimum score of 80) or TOEFL (minimum score 550). Application deadline: 7/1 (priority date; rolling processing). Application fee: $0 ($100 for international students). *Financial aid:* Fellowships, research assistantships, teaching assistantships available. Financial aid application deadline: 1/31. • Dr. L. Tan, Head, 306-966-7945. Fax: 306-966-7920.

University of South Florida, College of Public Health, Department of Community and Family Health, Tampa, FL 33620-9951. Awards MPH, MSPH, PhD. One or more programs accredited by CEPH. Part-time and evening/weekend programs available. Faculty: 15 full-time (8 women). 83 applicants, 57% accepted. *Degree requirements:* For master's, thesis required, foreign language not required; for doctorate, computer language, dissertation required, foreign language not required. *Entrance requirements:* For master's, GRE General Test (minimum combined score of 1000), TOEFL (minimum score 550), minimum GPA of 3.0 in upper-level course work; for doctorate, GRE General Test (minimum combined score of 1100), TOEFL (minimum score 550), minimum GPA of 3.0 in upper-level course work. Application deadline: 6/1 (rolling processing; 10/15 for spring admission). Application fee: $20. *Tuition:* $142 per credit hour for state residents; $486 per credit hour for nonresidents. *Financial aid:* Federal Work-Study, institutionally sponsored loans available. Aid available to part-time students. Financial aid applicants required to submit FAFSA. *Faculty research:* Family violence, high-risk infant, medical material and child health, healthy start, social marketing, adolesent health, high-risk behaviors. Total annual research expenditures: $1.558 million. • Dr. Robert J. McDermott, Chairperson, 813-974-6700. E-mail: rmcdermo@com1.med.usf.edu. Application contact: Magdalene Argiry, Director of Student Services, 813-974-6665. Fax: 813-974-4718. E-mail: margiry@com1.med.usf.edu.

University of Tennessee, Knoxville, College of Human Ecology, Program in Human Ecology, Knoxville, TN 37996. Offerings include community health (PhD). *Degree requirements:* Dissertation required, foreign language not required. *Entrance requirements:* GRE General Test, TOEFL (minimum score 550), minimum GPA of 2.7. Application deadline: 2/1 (priority date; rolling processing). Application fee: $35. Electronic applications accepted. *Tuition:* $3354 per year full-time, $181 per semester hour part-time for state residents; $8410 per year full-time, $462 per semester hour part-time for nonresidents. • Dr. James D. Moran III, Chair, 423-974-5224. Fax: 423-974-2617. E-mail: jmoran@utk.edu.

University of Tennessee, Knoxville, College of Human Ecology, Department of Health and Safety Sciences, Program in Public Health, Knoxville, TN 37996. Offerings include community health education (MPH). *Degree requirements:* Thesis optional, foreign language not required. *Entrance requirements:* TOEFL (minimum score 550), minimum GPA of 2.7. Application deadline: 2/1 (priority date; rolling processing). Application fee: $35. Electronic applications accepted. *Tuition:* $3354 per year full-time, $181 per semester hour part-time for state residents; $8410 per year full-time, $462 per semester hour part-time for nonresidents. • Dr. Charles B. Hamilton, Head, Department of Health and Safety Sciences, 423-974-5041. Fax: 423-974-6439. E-mail: cbhamilton@utk.edu.

See in-depth description on page 1185.

The University of Texas Medical Branch at Galveston, Graduate School of Biomedical Sciences, Program in Preventive Medicine and Community Health, Galveston, TX 77555. Awards MS, PhD. Faculty: 47 full-time (14 women). Students: 25 full-time (11 women), 5 part-time (3 women); includes 6 minority (4 Asian Americans, 2 Native Americans), 6 international. Average age 35. 16 applicants, 44% accepted. In 1997, 4 doctorates awarded. *Degree requirements:* For master's, thesis or alternative required, foreign language not required; for doctorate, dissertation required, foreign language not required. *Entrance requirements:* For master's, GRE General Test (minimum combined score of 1100) or MAT (minimum score 45); for doctorate, GRE General Test (minimum combined score of 1100). Application deadline: 5/15 (priority date; rolling processing). Application fee: $25 ($50 for international students). *Expenses:* Tuition $36 per credit hour for state residents; $249 per credit hour for nonresidents. Fees $146 per year full-time, $124 per semester (minimum) part-time. *Financial aid:* Fellowships, research assistantships, Federal Work-Study, institutionally sponsored loans available. Financial aid applicants required to submit FAFSA. *Faculty research:* Environmental toxicology and sociomedical sciences, aging, health behavior, epidemiology and biostatistics, nutrition through the life cycle. • James A. Hokanson, Director, 409-772-3732. Fax: 409-772-5272. E-mail: james.hokanson@utmb.edu.

University of Toronto, School of Graduate Studies, Life Sciences Division, Department of Community Health, Toronto, ON M5S 1A1, Canada. Awards MH Sc, M Sc, PhD. Part-time programs available. Faculty: 189. Students: 401 full-time (267 women), 65 part-time (45 women); includes 14 international. 586 applicants, 39% accepted. In 1997, 107 master's, 11 doctorates awarded. *Degree requirements:* For master's, thesis (for some programs); for doctorate, dissertation. *Application fee:* $75. *Expenses:* Tuition $4070 per year for Canadian residents; $7870 per year for nonresidents. Fees $628 per year. *Financial aid:* Career-related internships or fieldwork available. • H. A. Skinner, Acting Chair, 416-978-1552. Application contact: Secretary, 416-978-2058. Fax: 416-978-1883. E-mail: chl.grad@utoronto.ca.

University of Wisconsin–La Crosse, College of Health, Physical Education and Recreation, Department of Health Education, La Crosse, WI 54601-3742. Offerings include community health (MS), community health education (MPH). One or more programs accredited by CEPH. Department faculty: 8 full-time (2 women). *Application fee:* $38. *Tuition:* $3737 per year full-time, $208 per credit part-time for state residents; $11,921 per year full-time, $633 per credit part-time for nonresidents. • Dr. Gary D. Gilmore, Director, Community and Health Education, 608-785-8163. E-mail: gilmore@mail.uwlax.edu. Application contact: Tim Lewis, Director of Admissions, 608-785-8939. Fax: 608-785-6695. E-mail: admissions@mail.uwlax.edu.

Directories: Community Health; Environmental and Occupational Health

Wayne State University, School of Medicine and Graduate School, Graduate Programs in Medicine, Department of Community Medicine, Detroit, MI 48202. Offers programs in community health (MS), community health services (Certificate). Faculty: 17. Students: 4 full-time (3 women), 19 part-time (18 women). Average age 29. 19 applicants, 63% accepted. In 1997, 4 master's awarded. *Degree requirements:* For master's, computer language, thesis (for some programs) required, foreign language not required. *Entrance requirements:* For master's, GRE, minimum GPA of 2.6. Application deadline: 8/1. Application fee: $20 ($30 for international students). *Expenses:* Tuition $163 per credit hour for state residents; $355 per credit hour for nonresidents. Fees $498 per year full-time, $114 per semester (minimum) part-time. *Financial aid:* Scholarships, Federal Work-Study, and career-related internships or fieldwork available. Aid available to part-time students. Financial aid application deadline: 6/1. *Faculty research:* Chronic disease, geriatric health, chemical dependency, maternal-child health, violence and medicine. • Dr. John Waller, Chairperson, 313-577-1033. Application contact: Dr. Rosalie Young, Graduate Officer, 313-577-1033. Fax: 313-577-0316.

West Virginia University, School of Medicine, Graduate Programs in Basic Health Sciences, Community Health Promotion Program, Morgantown, WV 26506. Awards MS. Part-time and evening/weekend programs available. Postbaccalaureate distance learning degree programs offered (no on-campus study). Students: 33 full-time (22 women), 188 part-time (161 women); includes 17 minority (13 African Americans, 3 Asian Americans, 1 Hispanic), 2 international. Average age 37. 110 applicants, 87% accepted. In 1997, 45 degrees awarded (100% found work related to degree). *Degree requirements:* Thesis required (for some programs), foreign language not required. *Entrance requirements:* TOEFL (minimum score 550), minimum GPA of 3.0. Application deadline: 3/1 (priority date; rolling processing). Application fee: $45. *Financial aid:* In 1997–98, 5 students received aid, including 2 research assistantships (both to first-year students) averaging $589 per month, 2 teaching assistantships (both to first-year students) averaging $589 per month; partial tuition waivers, Federal Work-Study, institutionally sponsored loans, and career-related internships or fieldwork also available. Financial aid application deadline: 2/1; applicants required to submit FAFSA. *Faculty research:* Program design, injury control, human sexuality, substance abuse, fitness/health promotion education. • Dr. Kenard McPherson, Program Director, 304-293-7510 Ext. 277. E-mail: kmcphers@wvu.edu. Application contact: Linda A. Lilly, Administrative Secretary, 304-293-7510 Ext. 0. Fax: 304-293-8969. E-mail: llilly@wvu.edu.

Environmental and Occupational Health

Anna Maria College, Program in Occupational and Environmental Health and Safety, Paxton, MA 01612. Awards MS. Part-time and evening/weekend programs available. Faculty: 7. In 1997, 5 degrees awarded. *Degree requirements:* Thesis required, foreign language not required. *Application fee:* $30. *Tuition:* $730 per course. • Dr. Paul Erickson, Director, 508-849-3432.

Boston University, School of Medicine, School of Public Health, Environmental Health Department, Boston, MA 02215. Awards MPH, D Sc. One or more programs accredited by CEPH. Students: 9 full-time (7 women), 31 part-time (20 women); includes 2 minority (1 Asian American, 1 Hispanic), 4 international. Average age 32. *Degree requirements:* For doctorate, 1 foreign language, dissertation, comprehensive written and oral exams. *Entrance requirements:* For master's, GRE General Test, TOEFL; for doctorate, GRE General Test, MPH or equivalent. Application deadline: 4/15 (rolling processing; 10/25 for spring admission). Application fee: $50. *Financial aid:* Federal Work-Study, institutionally sponsored loans, and career-related internships or fieldwork available. Aid available to part-time students. • Dr. David M. Ozonoff, Chairman, 617-638-4620. Application contact: Barbara St. Onge, Director of Admissions, 617-638-4640. Fax: 617-638-5299. E-mail: sphadmis@bu.edu.

See in-depth description on page 1487.

California State University, Fresno, Division of Graduate Studies, School of Health and Social Work, Department of Public Health, 5241 North Maple Avenue, Fresno, CA 93740. Offerings include environmental/occupational health (MPH). Preaccredited by CEPH. Department faculty: 8 full-time (1 woman). *Degree requirements:* Thesis or alternative required, foreign language not required. *Average time to degree:* master's–3.5 years full-time. *Entrance requirements:* GRE General Test, TOEFL (minimum score 550), minimum GPA of 2.5. Application deadline: 3/1 (priority date; rolling processing). Application fee: $55. Electronic applications accepted. *Expenses:* Tuition $0 for state residents; $246 per unit for nonresidents. Fees $1872 per year full-time, $1206 per year part-time. • Dr. Sanford Brown, Graduate Program Coordinator, 209-278-4747. E-mail: sanford_brown@csufresno.edu.

California State University, Northridge, College of Health and Human Development, Department of Family Environmental Sciences, Northridge, CA 91330. Awards MS. Part-time and evening/weekend programs available. Faculty: 14 full-time, 20 part-time. Students: 45 full-time (all women), 37 part-time (35 women); includes 11 minority (5 African Americans, 5 Asian Americans, 1 Hispanic), 5 international. Average age 34. 46 applicants, 91% accepted. *Degree requirements:* Thesis or alternative required, foreign language not required. *Entrance requirements:* TOEFL, GRE General Test or minimum GPA of 3.0. Application deadline: 11/30. Application fee: $55. *Expenses:* Tuition $0 for state residents; $246 per unit for nonresidents. Fees $1970 per year full-time, $1304 per year part-time. *Financial aid:* Teaching assistantships, Federal Work-Study, institutionally sponsored loans, and career-related internships or fieldwork available. Financial aid application deadline: 3/1. • Dr. Alyce Blackmon, Chair, 818-677-3051. Application contact: Dr. Ann Stasch, Graduate Coordinator, 818-677-3116.

California State University, Northridge, College of Health and Human Development, Department of Health Sciences, Program in Environmental Health, Northridge, CA 91330. Awards MS. Accredited by NEHSPAC. Students: 19 full-time (11 women), 19 part-time (10 women); includes 11 minority (7 Asian Americans, 4 Hispanics). Average age 30. 16 applicants, 94% accepted. *Expenses:* Tuition $0 for state residents; $246 per unit for nonresidents. Fees $1970 per year full-time, $1304 per year part-time. • Thomas Hatfield, Professor, 818-677-4708.

Central Missouri State University, College of Applied Sciences and Technology, Department of Safety Science Technology, Warrensburg, MO 64093. Offers programs in human services/public services (Ed S), industrial hygiene (MS), industrial safety management (MS), occupational safety management (MS), public services administration (MS), secondary education/safety education (MSE), security (MS), transportation safety (MS). MS (industrial safety management, public services administration, security, transportation safety) being phased out; applicants no longer accepted. MS (occupational safety management) new for fall 1998. Part-time programs available. Faculty: 9 full-time. Students: 37 full-time (14 women), 59 part-time (18 women). In 1997, 61 master's, 1 Ed S awarded. *Degree requirements:* For master's, comprehensive exam (MS), comprehensive exam or thesis (MSE); for Ed S, thesis. *Entrance requirements:* For master's, GRE General Test, minimum GPA of 2.5, 15 hours in related area (MS); minimum GPA of 2.75, teaching certificate (MSE); for Ed S, master's degree in related field. Application deadline: 6/30 (priority date; rolling processing). Application fee: $25 ($50 for international students). *Tuition:* $3288 per year full-time, $137 per credit hour part-time for state residents; $5928 per year full-time, $274 per credit hour part-time for nonresidents. *Financial aid:* In 1997–98, 4 research assistantships, 1 teaching assistantship, 5 administrative and laboratory assistantships were awarded; Federal Work-Study also available. Aid available to part-time students. Financial aid application deadline: 3/1; applicants required to submit FAFSA. • Dr. John Prince, Interim Chair, 660-543-4626. Fax: 660-543-8142. E-mail: safety@cmsuvmb.cmsu.edu.

Colorado State University, College of Applied Human Sciences, Department of Manufacturing Technology and Construction Management, Fort Collins, CO 80523-0015. Offerings include automotive pollution control (MS). Department faculty: 16 full-time (1 woman), 4 part-time (1 woman). *Degree requirements:* Computer language, thesis (for some programs) required, foreign language not required. *Entrance requirements:* GRE General Test, TOEFL. Application deadline: 2/1 (priority date; rolling processing). Application fee: $30. Electronic applications accepted. *Expenses:* Tuition $2632 per year full-time, $109 per credit hour part-time for state residents; $10,216 per year full-time, $425 per credit hour part-time for nonresidents. Fees $708 per year full-time, $32 per semester (minimum) part-time. • Larry Grosse, Head, 970-491-7958. Application contact: Linda Burrous, Department Secretary, 970-491-7355. Fax: 970-491-2473. E-mail: burrous@cahs.colostate.edu.

Colorado State University, College of Veterinary Medicine and Biomedical Sciences and Graduate School, Graduate Programs in Veterinary Medicine and Biomedical Sciences, Department of Environmental Health, Fort Collins, CO 80523-0015. Awards MS, PhD. Faculty: 18 full-time (3 women), 19 part-time (2 women). Students: 41 full-time (22 women), 31 part-time (18 women); includes 3 minority (2 Hispanics, 1 Native American), 5 international. Average age 34. 84 applicants, 39% accepted. In 1997, 16 master's awarded (100% found work related to degree). *Degree requirements:* For master's, thesis (for some programs), publishable paper required, foreign language not required; for doctorate, dissertation, publishable paper required, foreign language not required. *Entrance requirements:* GRE General Test (minimum combined score of 1650 on three sections), TOEFL (minimum score 550), 1 year of course work in biology lab, chemistry lab; 1 semester of course work in organic chemistry. Application deadline: 2/1 (10/1 for spring admission). Application fee: $30. Electronic applications accepted. *Expenses:* Tuition $2632 per year full-time, $109 per credit hour part-time for state residents; $10,216 per year full-time, $425 per credit hour part-time for nonresidents. Fees $708 per year full-time, $32 per semester (minimum) part-time. *Financial aid:* In 1997–98, 45 students received aid, including 1 fellowship (to a first-year student), 20 research assistantships (5 to first-year students), 3 teaching assistantships (2 to first-year students), 7 traineeships (1 to a first-year student); Federal Work-Study, institutionally sponsored loans, and career-related internships or fieldwork also available. Aid available to part-time students. Financial aid application deadline: 2/1. *Faculty research:* Epidemiology, toxicology, industrial hygiene, occupational health. Total annual research expenditures: $3.4 million. • Dr. John S. Reif, Head, 970-491-7038. E-mail: jreif@cvmbs.colostate.edu. Application contact: J. Calder-Emanuel, Graduate Coordinator, 970-491-0294. Fax: 970-491-2940. E-mail: emanuel@vines.colostate.edu.

Announcement: MS and PhD programs are offered with specialization in occupational health and safety, epidemiology, and environmental toxicology. The curriculum combines training in interdisciplinary environmental health sciences with a strong background in relevant basic physical and biological sciences. Individual attention to educational and professional interests of students is emphasized. Research opportunities include in vitro, chemical-mixture, analytical, and wildlife toxicology; carcinogenesis; pharmacokinetic modeling; risk assessment; industrial hygiene; agricultural safety and health; aerosol technology; noise and air pollution; geographic information systems; and environmental, veterinary, cancer, occupational, and injury epidemiology. Research and teaching assistantships are available. Visit the Web site at http://www.cvmbs.colostate.edu/cvmbs/environhealth/homepage.htm

Columbia University, School of Public Health, Division of Environmental Health Sciences, New York, NY 10032. Awards MPH, Dr PH, PhD. One or more programs accredited by CEPH. PhD offered in cooperation with the Graduate School of Arts and Sciences. Part-time programs available. Students: 57. In 1997, 12 master's, 4 doctorates awarded. *Degree requirements:* For master's, thesis optional, foreign language not required; for doctorate, dissertation required, foreign language not required. *Average time to degree:* master's–1.5 years full-time, 3 years part-time; doctorate–4 years full-time, 7 years part-time. *Entrance requirements:* For master's, GRE General Test, 1 year of course work in biology, general chemistry, organic chemistry, and mathematics; for doctorate, GRE General Test, MPH or equivalent (Dr PH). Application deadline: 4/10 (rolling processing; 11/15 for spring admission). Application fee: $60. *Tuition:* $22,320 per year full-time, $744 per credit part-time. *Financial aid:* Research assistantships, teaching assistantships, Federal Work-Study, and career-related internships or fieldwork available. Aid available to part-time students. Financial aid application deadline: 3/15; applicants required to submit FAFSA. *Faculty research:* Health effects of environmental and occupational exposure to chemicals and radiation, molecular epidemiology, risk assessment. • Dr. Joseph Graziano, Head, 212-305-3464. E-mail: jg24@columbia.edu. Application contact: Dr. Paul Brandt-Rauf, Director of Educational Affairs, 212-305-3464. Fax: 212-305-4012. E-mail: prvb1@columbia.edu.

East Carolina University, School of Allied Health Sciences, Department of Environmental Health, Greenville, NC 27858-4353. Awards MSEH. Accredited by NEHSPAC. Part-time programs available. Faculty: 4 full-time (0 women). Students: 12 full-time (3 women), 3 part-time (1 woman); includes 2 minority (both African Americans), 1 international. Average age 30. 12 applicants, 58% accepted. In 1997, 4 degrees awarded. *Degree requirements:* Computer language, thesis, comprehensive exams. *Entrance requirements:* GRE General Test, TOEFL. Application deadline: 6/1 (priority date; rolling processing; 10/15 for spring admission). Application fee: $40. *Tuition:* $1886 per year full-time, $472 per semester (minimum) part-time for state residents; $9156 per year full-time, $2289 per semester (minimum) part-time for nonresidents. *Financial aid:* Research assistantships, teaching assistantships, Federal Work-Study available. Aid available to part-time students. Financial aid application deadline: 6/1. • Dr. Bernard Kane, Director of Graduate Studies, 252-328-4430. Fax: 252-328-4470. E-mail: kaneb@mail.ecu.edu. Application contact: Dr. Paul D. Tschetter, Associate Dean, 252-328-6012. Fax: 252-328-6071. E-mail: grad@mail.ecu.edu.

East Tennessee State University, College of Public and Allied Health, Department of Environmental Health, Johnson City, TN 37614-0734. Awards MSEH. Accredited by NEHSPAC. Part-time programs available. Faculty: 6 full-time (1 woman). Students: 16 full-time (10 women), 35 part-time (14 women); includes 4 minority (2 African Americans, 2 Asian Americans). Average age 30. 23 applicants, 61% accepted. In 1997, 17 degrees awarded. *Degree requirements:* Comprehensive oral exam required, thesis optional, foreign language not required. *Entrance requirements:* TOEFL (minimum score 550), minimum GPA of 2.5, 30 hours of course work in natural and physical sciences. Application deadline: 7/15 (priority date; rolling processing; 11/1 for spring admission). Application fee: $25 ($35 for international students). *Tuition:* $2944 per year full-time, $158 per credit hour part-time for state residents; $7770 per year full-time, $369 per credit hour part-time for nonresidents. *Financial aid:* In 1997–98, 6 research assistantships (3 to first-year students), 12 assistantships, grants (6 to first-year students) were awarded; teaching assistantships and career-related internships or fieldwork also available. Financial aid application deadline: 5/1. *Faculty research:* Water quality, ecotoxicology, occupational health. Total annual research expenditures: $325,000. • Dr. Lawrence Curtis, Chair, 423-439-7066. E-mail: curtisl@etsu-tn.edu. Application contact: Dr. Albert F. Iglar, Graduate Coordinator, 423-439-4268. Fax: 423-439-5238.

Emory University, The Rollins School of Public Health, Department of Environmental/Occupational Health, Atlanta, GA 30322-1100. Awards MPH. Accredited by CEPH. *Degree*

requirements: Thesis (for some programs), practicum required, foreign language not required. *Entrance requirements:* GRE General Test. Application deadline: 2/15 (priority date; rolling processing). Application fee: $50. *Expenses:* Tuition $14,136 per year full-time, $589 per credit hour part-time. Fees $200 per year. *Financial aid:* Application deadline 2/15. • Dr. Howard Frumkin, Chair, 404-727-3697. Application contact: Susan Daniel, Director of Admissions, 404-727-5481. Fax: 404-727-3996. E-mail: admit@sph.emory.edu.

See in-depth description on page 1493.

The George Washington University, School of Public Health and Health Services, Master's Program in Public Health, Track in Environmental-Occupational Health, Washington, DC 20052. Awards MPH. Accredited by CEPH. *Degree requirements:* Case study or special project required, thesis not required. *Entrance requirements:* GMAT, GRE General Test, or MCAT; TOEFL. Application deadline: 5/15 (priority date; rolling processing; 11/15 for spring admission). Application fee: $5. *Expenses:* Tuition $680 per semester hour. Fees $35 per semester hour. • Application contact: Michelle Sparacino, Director of Recruitment, 202-994-2160. Fax: 202-994-3773. E-mail: sphhs-info@gwumc.edu.

See in-depth description on page 1495.

Harvard University, School of Public Health, Department of Environmental Health, Boston, MA 02115. Offers programs in environmental epidemiology (SM, SD); environmental health (SM); environmental health science (DPH); environmental science and engineering (SM, SD), including environmental health sciences, environmental science and risk management, industrial hygiene and occupational safety; occupational health (MOH, SM, DPH, SD). Accredited by CEPH. Part-time programs available. Faculty: 33 full-time (5 women), 20 part-time (3 women). Students: 56 full-time (30 women), 7 part-time (5 women); includes 9 minority (1 African American, 8 Asian Americans), 26 international. Average age 32. 76 applicants, 68% accepted. In 1997, 16 master's, 5 doctorates awarded. *Degree requirements:* For doctorate, dissertation, qualifying exam. *Entrance requirements:* GRE, TOEFL (minimum score 550). Application deadline: 1/4. Application fee: $60. *Expenses:* Tuition $21,895 per year full-time, $10,948 per year part-time. Fees $686 per year. *Financial aid:* Fellowships, research assistantships, teaching assistantships, partial tuition waivers, Federal Work-Study available. Aid available to part-time students. Financial aid application deadline: 2/12; applicants required to submit FAFSA. *Faculty research:* Identification and prevention of occupational exposures, air pollution, environmental health management. • Dr. Joseph D. Brain, Chairman, 617-432-1272. Application contact: Carrie Daniels, Assistant Director of Admissions, 617-432-1031. Fax: 617-432-2009. E-mail: admisofc@sph.harvard.edu.

See in-depth description on page 1497.

Harvard University, School of Public Health, Master of Public Health Program, Boston, MA 02115. Offerings include occupational and environmental health (MPH). *Average time to degree:* master's–1 year full-time, 2.5 years part-time. *Entrance requirements:* GRE, TOEFL (minimum score 550). Application deadline: 1/4 (priority date). Application fee: $60. *Expenses:* Tuition $21,895 per year full-time, $10,948 per year part-time. Fees $686 per year. • Dr. Gareth M. Green, Associate Dean for Professional Education, 617-432-0090. Application contact: Carrie Daniels, Assistant Director of Admissions, 617-432-1031. Fax: 617-432-2009. E-mail: admisofc@sph.harvard.edu.

Hunter College of the City University of New York, School of Health Sciences, Program in Environmental and Occupational Health Sciences, 695 Park Avenue, New York, NY 10021-5085. Awards MS. Part-time and evening/weekend programs available. Faculty: 3 full-time (0 women), 5 part-time (1 woman). Students: 16 full-time (10 women), 38 part-time (18 women); includes 15 minority (7 African Americans, 2 Asian Americans, 6 Hispanics), 4 international. Average age 34. In 1997, 23 degrees awarded. *Degree requirements:* Comprehensive exam, internship required, thesis optional, foreign language not required. *Average time to degree:* master's–2 years full-time, 3.5 years part-time. *Entrance requirements:* GRE General Test, TOEFL (minimum score 550), previous course work in biology, chemistry, and mathematics. Application deadline: 4/28 (11/21 for spring admission). Application fee: $40. *Expenses:* Tuition $4350 per year full-time, $185 per credit part-time for state residents; $7600 per year full-time, $320 per credit part-time for nonresidents. Fees $26 per year. *Financial aid:* In 1997–98, 6 fellowships (all to first-year students) averaging $500 per month were awarded; partial tuition waivers, Federal Work-Study, institutionally sponsored loans, and career-related internships or fieldwork also available. Aid available to part-time students. Financial aid application deadline: 3/1. *Faculty research:* Hazardous waste, asbestos, lead exposures, worker training, public employees. • Jack Caravanos, Director, 212-481-5119. Application contact: Audrey Berman, Associate Director for Graduate Admissions, 212-772-4490.

Indiana University of Pennsylvania, College of Health and Human Services, Department of Safety Sciences, Indiana, PA 15705-1087. Awards MS. Part-time programs available. Students: 10 full-time (2 women), 38 part-time (11 women); includes 1 minority (Asian American), 2 international. Average age 32. 15 applicants, 80% accepted. In 1997, 20 degrees awarded. *Degree requirements:* Thesis optional, foreign language not required. *Entrance requirements:* TOEFL (minimum score 500). Application deadline: 7/1 (priority date; rolling processing; 11/1 for spring admission). Application fee: $30. *Expenses:* Tuition $3468 per year full-time, $193 per credit part-time for state residents; $6236 per year full-time, $346 per credit part-time for nonresidents. Fees $313 per year (minimum) full-time, $84 per year part-time. *Financial aid:* Research assistantships, Federal Work-Study, and career-related internships or fieldwork available. Aid available to part-time students. Financial aid application deadline: 3/15. • Dr. Robert Soule, Chairperson, 724-357-3017. E-mail: bobsoule@grove.iup.edu. Application contact: Dr. Lon H. Ferguson, Graduate Coordinator, 724-357-3018. E-mail: ferguson@grove.iup.edu.

Johns Hopkins University, School of Hygiene and Public Health, Program in Public Health, Baltimore, MD 21205. Offerings include environmental health sciences (MPH). Accredited by CEPH. *Entrance requirements:* GRE General Test, TOEFL (minimum score 550), 2 years of work related experience. Application deadline: 2/1 (priority date; rolling processing). Application fee: $60. • Dr. Miriam Alexander, Director, 410-955-1291. Application contact: Lenora Davis, Administrator, 410-955-1291. Fax: 410-955-4749. E-mail: lrdavis@jhsph.edu.

Johns Hopkins University, School of Hygiene and Public Health, Department of Environmental Health Sciences, Division of Occupational and Environmental Health, Baltimore, MD 21205. Awards Dr PH, PhD. *Degree requirements:* Dissertation, 1 year full-time residency, oral and written exams required, foreign language not required. *Entrance requirements:* GRE General Test. Application deadline: 2/1 (priority date; rolling processing). Application fee: $60. *Financial aid:* Scholarships, Federal Work-Study, institutionally sponsored loans available. Aid available to part-time students. Financial aid application deadline: 4/15. *Faculty research:* Respiratory diseases, air pollutant effects, occupational health management, occupational health nursing, epidemiology and medical monitoring. • Dr. Paul Strickland, Director, 410-955-4456.

See in-depth description on page 1499.

Loma Linda University, School of Public Health, Programs in Environmental and Occupational Health, Loma Linda, CA 92350. Awards MPH, MSPH. Accredited by CEPH. Students: 3 full-time (1 woman), 4 part-time (1 woman); includes 2 international. 10 applicants, 80% accepted. In 1997, 3 degrees awarded. *Entrance requirements:* Michigan English Language Assessment Battery (minimum score 92) or TOEFL (minimum score 600). Application deadline: rolling. Application fee: $100. *Tuition:* $380 per unit. *Financial aid:* Application deadline 5/15. *Faculty research:* Human exposure to toxins, smog. • Dr. David Dyjack, Chair, 909-824-4918. Fax: 909-824-4087. Application contact: Terri Tamayose, Director of Admissions and Academic Records, 909-824-4694. Fax: 909-824-8087. E-mail: ttamayose@sph.llu.edu.

McGill University, Faculty of Graduate Studies and Research, Faculty of Medicine, Department of Epidemiology and Biostatistics, Montréal, PQ H3A 2T5, Canada. Offerings include environmental health (M Sc), occupational health (M Sc). Department faculty: 35 full-time (7 women), 23 part-time (6 women). *Degree requirements:* Thesis optional, foreign language not required. *Entrance requirements:* GRE, minimum GPA of 3.0. Application deadline: 3/1 (rolling processing). Application fee: $60. *Expenses:* Tuition $1668 per year for Canadian residents; $8268 per year for nonresidents. Fees $828 per year for Canadian residents; $1216 per year for nonresidents. • Dr. G. Theriault, Chair, Graduate Committee, 514-398-6259. E-mail: gtheri@epid.lan.mcgill.ca. Application contact: Marlene Abrams, Secretary for Graduate Studies, 514-398-6269. Fax: 514-398-4503. E-mail: marlene@epid.lan.mcgill.ca.

McGill University, Faculty of Graduate Studies and Research, Faculty of Medicine, Department of Occupational Health, Montréal, PQ H3A 2T5, Canada. Offers program in occupational health (M Sc A, PhD). M Sc A also offered as distance education program. Part-time programs available. Postbaccalaureate distance learning degree programs offered (minimal on-campus study). Faculty: 5 full-time (1 woman), 12 part-time (2 women). Students: 17 full-time (7 women), 52 part-time (17 women); includes 3 international. Average age 37. 47 applicants, 79% accepted. In 1997, 17 master's awarded; 3 doctorates awarded (100% entered university research/teaching). *Degree requirements:* For doctorate, dissertation. *Average time to degree:* master's–1 year full-time, 3 years part-time; doctorate–4 years full-time, 7 years part-time. *Entrance requirements:* For master's, TOEFL (minimum score 550), B Sc in chemistry, engineering physics, environmental sciences, medicine, nursing, or other health science (for occupational health); MD or B Sc in nursing (for distance education), minimum GPA of 3.0; for doctorate, TOEFL (minimum score 550), M Sc in environmental health, chemistry, engineering, community health, physics, epidemiology, medicine, nursing, or occupational health. Application deadline: 3/1 (priority date; rolling processing). Application fee: $60. *Expenses:* Tuition $1668 per year for Canadian residents; $8268 per year for nonresidents. Fees $828 per year for Canadian residents; $1216 per year for nonresidents. *Financial aid:* Fellowships, research assistantships, scholarships, full and partial tuition waivers available. Financial aid application deadline: 10/1. *Faculty research:* Epidemiology of occupational diseases and cancer, effect of the environment on respiratory health, industrial safety. • G. Theriault, Chair, 514-398-6259. E-mail: gtheri@epid.lan.mcgill.ca. Application contact: Suzanne Larivière, Graduate Secretary, 514-398-4229. Fax: 514-398-7435.

Medical College of Ohio, School of Allied Health, Department of Public Health, Toledo, OH 43699-0008. Offers program in occupational health (MS, Certificate). Part-time programs available. Faculty: 3 full-time, 8 part-time. Average age 30. 28 applicants, 86% accepted. In 1997, 12 master's awarded. *Degree requirements:* For master's, scholarly project required, foreign language not required. *Entrance requirements:* For master's, GRE General Test, minimum undergraduate GPA of 3.0. Application deadline: rolling. Application fee: $30. *Financial aid:* Scholarships, Federal Work-Study, institutionally sponsored loans available. Financial aid applicants required to submit FAFSA. *Faculty research:* Exposure assessment of physical, chemical, and biological agents; ergonomics; toxicology. Total annual research expenditures: $15,000. • Dr. Michael Bisesi, Chair, 419-383-5356. E-mail: mcogradschool@mco.edu. Application contact: Theresa Langenderfer, Secretary, 419-383-4160. Fax: 419-383-6140. E-mail: mcogradschool@mco.edu.

See in-depth description on page 1503.

Medical College of Wisconsin, Medical School, Department of Preventive Medicine, Milwaukee, WI 53226-0509. Offerings include occupational medicine (MPH). Accredited by CEPH. *Degree requirements:* Project in occupational medicine or public health required, foreign language and thesis not required. *Average time to degree:* master's–3.3 years part-time. *Entrance requirements:* TOEFL, MD/DO license to practice medicine in U. S. or Canada. Application deadline: 7/15 (priority date; rolling processing; 3/15 for spring admission). Application fee: $125. *Tuition:* $16,264 per year for state residents; $26,355 per year for nonresidents.

Meharry Medical College, Division of Community Health Sciences, Nashville, TN 37208-9989. Offerings include occupational medicine (MSPH). Division faculty: 12 full-time (4 women), 10 part-time (5 women). *Degree requirements:* Thesis, externship required, foreign language not required. *Average time to degree:* master's–2 years full-time, 4 years part-time. *Entrance requirements:* GRE General Test (minimum combined score of 800). Application deadline: 6/30 (rolling processing). Application fee: $45. *Expenses:* Tuition $7020 per year. Fees $1633 per year. • Dr. Herman Ellis, Interim Director, 615-327-5530. Application contact: Dr. Otis Cosby, Assistant Director, 615-327-6069. Fax: 615-327-6717.

Mississippi Valley State University, Department of Natural Science and Environmental Health, Program in Environmental Health, Itta Bena, MS 38941-1400. Awards MS. Evening/weekend programs available. *Application deadline:* rolling. *Application fee:* $0. *Expenses:* Tuition $97 per hour for state residents; $139 per hour for nonresidents. Fees $30 per hour. • Application contact: Office of Admissions, 601-254-3344.

Montclair State University, College of Science and Mathematics, Department of Earth and Environmental Studies, Upper Montclair, NJ 07043-1624. Offerings include environmental studies (MS), with options in environmental education, environmental health, environmental management, environmental science. Department faculty: 11 full-time. *Degree requirements:* Comprehensive exam required, foreign language not required. *Entrance requirements:* GRE General Test. Application deadline: 4/1 (rolling processing; 11/1 for spring admission). Application fee: $40. *Expenses:* Tuition $201 per credit for state residents; $257 per credit for nonresidents. Fees $22.05 per credit. • Dr. Jonathan Lincoln, Chairperson, 973-655-4448.

Murray State University, College of Industry and Technology, Department of Occupational Safety and Health, Murray, KY 42071-0009. Awards MS. Part-time programs available. Faculty: 7 full-time (2 women). Students: 34 full-time (8 women), 26 part-time (9 women); includes 5 minority (3 African Americans, 1 Hispanic, 1 Native American), 1 international. 14 applicants, 100% accepted. In 1997, 30 degrees awarded. *Entrance requirements:* GRE General Test, TOEFL (minimum score 500). Application deadline: rolling. Application fee: $20. *Expenses:* Tuition $2500 per year full-time, $124 per hour part-time for state residents; $6740 per year full-time, $357 per hour part-time for nonresidents. Fees $360 per year full-time, $180 per year part-time. *Financial aid:* Research assistantships, teaching assistantships, Federal Work-Study available. Financial aid application deadline: 4/1. • Dr. Bassam Atieh, Director, 502-762-6652. Fax: 502-762-3630.

New York Medical College, Graduate School of Health Sciences, Program in Environmental and Occupational Health Sciences, Valhalla, NY 10595-1691. Awards MPH, MS. Part-time and evening/weekend programs available. *Degree requirements:* Computer language required, foreign language not required. *Entrance requirements:* TOEFL. Application deadline: 7/20 (priority date; rolling processing; 12/1 for spring admission). Application fee: $35 ($60 for international students). *Tuition:* $415 per credit. *Financial aid:* Federal Work-Study, institutionally sponsored loans, and career-related internships or fieldwork available. Financial aid application deadline: 6/15. • Dr. Denton Brosius, Director, 914-594-4804.

See in-depth description on page 1507.

New York University, Graduate School of Arts and Science, Nelson Institute of Environmental Medicine, Program in Environmental Health Sciences, New York, NY 10012-1019. Offers aquatic toxicology (PhD), environmental biology (PhD), environmental carcinogenesis (PhD), environmental epidemiology and biostatistics (PhD), environmental radiation (PhD), environmental-occupational hygiene (MS), ergonomics and biomechanics (PhD), molecular toxicology (PhD), occupational-environmental hygiene (PhD), systemic toxicology (PhD), toxicology (MS). Faculty: 26 full-time (7 women). *Degree requirements:* For master's, thesis or alternative required, foreign language not required; for doctorate, 1 foreign language, dissertation, oral and written exams. *Entrance requirements:* GRE General Test, GRE Subject Test, TOEFL, minimum GPA of 3.0; bachelor's degree in biological, physical, or engineering science. Application deadline: 8/1 (12/1 for spring admission). Application fee: $60. *Expenses:* Tuition $715 per credit. Fees $1048 per year full-time, $229 per semester (minimum) part-time. *Financial aid:* Partial tuition waivers, Federal Work-Study, institutionally sponsored loans available. Financial aid application deadline: 1/4; applicants required to submit FAFSA. *Faculty research:* Pulmonary toxicol-

Directory: Environmental and Occupational Health

New York University (continued)
ogy, environmental/industrial hygiene. • Application contact: Richard Schlesinger, Director of Graduate Studies, 914-885-5281.

Northwestern University, Robert R. McCormick School of Engineering and Applied Science, Department of Civil Engineering, Evanston, IL 60208. Offerings include environmental health engineering (MS, PhD). MS and PhD admissions and degrees offered through The Graduate School. Terminal master's awarded for partial completion of doctoral program. Department faculty: 25 full-time (2 women). *Degree requirements:* For doctorate, dissertation. *Entrance requirements:* For doctorate, GRE General Test. Application fee: $50 ($55 for international students). *Tuition:* $20,430 per year full-time, $2424 per course part-time. • Joseph L. Schofer, Chair, 847-491-3257. E-mail: j-schofer@nwu.edu. Application contact: Liz Inouye, Secretary, 847-491-3257. Fax: 847-491-4011. E-mail: eel@nwu.edu.

Old Dominion University, College of Health Sciences, School of Medical Laboratory Sciences and Environmental Health, Norfolk, VA 23529. Awards MS. Program being phased out; applicants no longer accepted. Part-time programs available. Faculty: 7 full-time (3 women). Students: 3 part-time (all women); includes 1 minority (African American). Average age 40. In 1997, 2 degrees awarded. *Degree requirements:* Thesis required, foreign language not required. *Entrance requirements:* BS in medical technology or related area; minimum GPA of 3.0 in major, 2.5 overall; professional certification. *Expenses:* Tuition $180 per credit hour for state residents; $477 per credit hour for nonresidents. Fees $140 per year full-time, $32 per semester part-time. *Financial aid:* Research assistantships, teaching assistantships, tuition grants available. Financial aid applicants required to submit FAFSA. *Faculty research:* Instructional methods, student recruitment, retention effects of environmental pollution on marine life, sports physiology, breast cancer criteria. Total annual research expenditures: $3600. • Dr. C. Thomas Somma, Chair, 757-683-3589. E-mail: tsomma@odu.edu.

Oregon State University, Graduate School, College of Health and Human Performance, Department of Public Health, Program in Environmental Health Management, Corvallis, OR 97331. Awards MAIS, MS. Faculty: 10 full-time (5 women), 1 (woman) part-time. Students: 0. Average age 35. 4 applicants, 75% accepted. *Degree requirements:* Thesis, minimum GPA of 3.0 required, foreign language not required. *Entrance requirements:* GRE General Test, TOEFL (minimum score 550), minimum GPA of 3.0 in last 90 hours. Application deadline: 3/1 (rolling processing). Application fee: $50. *Tuition:* $6207 per year full-time, $810 per quarter (minimum) part-time for state residents; $10,551 per year full-time, $1293 per quarter (minimum) part-time for nonresidents. *Financial aid:* Research assistantships, teaching assistantships, Federal Work-Study, institutionally sponsored loans, and career-related internships or fieldwork available. Aid available to part-time students. Financial aid application deadline: 2/1. *Total annual research expenditures:* $500,000. • Dr. Rebecca Donatelle, Chair, Department of Public Health, 541-737-3824. Fax: 541-737-4001.

Polytechnic University, Brooklyn Campus, Department of Civil and Environmental Engineering, Major in Environmental Health Science, Six Metrotech Center, Brooklyn, NY 11201-2990. Awards MS. Part-time and evening/weekend programs available. Students: 1 full-time (0 women), 7 part-time (2 women); includes 2 minority (1 Asian American, 1 Hispanic), 2 international. 6 applicants, 83% accepted. In 1997, 2 degrees awarded. *Degree requirements:* Thesis or alternative. *Application deadline:* rolling. *Application fee:* $45. Electronic applications accepted. *Expenses:* Tuition $19,530 per year full-time, $675 per credit part-time. Fees $600 per year full-time, $135 per semester part-time. *Financial aid:* Fellowships, research assistantships, teaching assistantships, institutionally sponsored loans available. Aid available to part-time students. Financial aid applicants required to submit FAFSA. • Application contact: John S. Kerge, Dean of Admissions, 718-260-3200. Fax: 718-260-3446. E-mail: admitme@poly.edu.

Purdue University, Graduate School and School of Pharmacy and Pharmacal Sciences, School of Health Sciences, Program in Environmental Health, West Lafayette, IN 47907. Awards MS, PhD. *Degree requirements:* For master's, thesis optional, foreign language not required; for doctorate, 1 foreign language (computer language can substitute), dissertation. *Entrance requirements:* GRE General Test, minimum B average. Application deadline: rolling. Application fee: $30. Electronic applications accepted. *Tuition:* $3500 per year full-time, $126 per credit hour part-time for state residents; $11,720 per year full-time, $387 per credit hour part-time for nonresidents. • Dr. P. L. Ziemer, Head, School of Health Sciences, 765-494-1435. Application contact: Dr. Robert Landolt, Graduate Chairperson, 765-494-1440.

See in-depth description on page 1511.

Queen's University at Kingston, Faculty of Medicine and School of Graduate Studies and Research, Graduate Programs in Medicine, Department of Community Health and Epidemiology, Kingston, ON K7L 3N6, Canada. Offerings include environmental and occupational health (M Sc). *Degree requirements:* Thesis required, foreign language not required. *Entrance requirements:* TOEFL (minimum score 550). Application fee: $60. Electronic applications accepted. *Tuition:* $3803 per year (minimum) full-time, $1901 per year (minimum) part-time for Canadian residents; $7330 per year (minimum) for nonresidents. • Dr. J. L. Pater, Graduate Coordinator, 613-545-2901. Application contact: R. E. M. Lees, Graduate Coordinator, 613-545-4954.

Saint Joseph's University, Erivan K. Haub School of Business, Programs in Graduate Business, Program in Environmental Protection and Safety Management, Philadelphia, PA 19131-1395. Offerings include public safety (MS). Program faculty: 2 full-time (0 women), 9 part-time (3 women), 5 FTE. *Average time to degree:* master's–3 years part-time. *Entrance requirements:* GMAT, TOEFL, interview. Application deadline: 7/15 (priority date; rolling processing; 11/15 for spring admission). Application fee: $35. *Tuition:* $510 per credit hour. • Dr. Vincent P. McNally Jr., Director, 610-660-1641. Fax: 610-660-2903. E-mail: vmcnally@sju.edu.

San Diego State University, College of Health and Human Services, Graduate School of Public Health, San Diego, CA 92182. Offerings include environmental health (MPH, MS). One or more programs accredited by CEPH. School faculty: 25 full-time (9 women), 36 part-time (21 women). *Degree requirements:* Thesis required (for some programs), foreign language not required. *Entrance requirements:* GMAT (health services administration), GRE General Test. Application deadline: 5/15 (priority date; rolling processing; 10/15 for spring admission). Application fee: $55. *Expenses:* Tuition $0 for state residents; $246 per unit for nonresidents. Fees $1932 per year full-time, $1266 per year part-time. • Dr. Kenneth Bart, Director, 619-594-6317. Application contact: Brenda Fass-Holmes, Coordinator, Admissions and Student Affairs, 619-594-6317. E-mail: bholmes@mail.sdsu.edu.

State University of New York at Albany, School of Public Health, Department of Environmental Health and Toxicology, Executive Park South, Albany, NY 12203-3727. Offers programs in environmental and occupational health (MS, PhD), environmental chemistry (MS, PhD), toxicology (MS, PhD). Faculty: 1 full-time (0 women). Students: 28 full-time (11 women), 8 part-time (2 women); includes 26 international. 16 applicants, 63% accepted. In 1997, 2 master's, 5 doctorates awarded. *Degree requirements:* Thesis/dissertation. *Entrance requirements:* GRE General Test, GRE Subject Test. Application fee: $50. *Expenses:* Tuition $5100 per year full-time, $213 per credit hour part-time for state residents; $8416 per year full-time, $351 per credit hour part-time for nonresidents. Fees $705 per year full-time, $26.85 per credit hour part-time. *Financial aid:* Fellowships, research assistantships available. • Dr. Kenneth Jackson, Chair, 518-473-7553.

State University of New York at Stony Brook, School of Professional Development and Continuing Studies, Stony Brook, NY 11794. Offerings include environmental/occupational health and safety (Certificate). School faculty: 1 full-time, 101 part-time. *Application deadline:* 1/15. *Application fee:* $50. *Expenses:* Tuition $5100 per year full-time, $213 per credit hour part-time for state residents; $8416 per year full-time, $351 per credit hour part-time for nonresidents. Fees $529 per year full-time, $77 per semester (minimum) part-time. • Dr. Paul J. Edelson, Dean, 516-632-7052. E-mail: paul.edelson@sunysb.edu. Application contact: Sandra Romansky, Director of Admissions and Advisement, 516-632-7050. Fax: 516-632-9046. E-mail: sandra.romansky@sunysb.edu.

Temple University, College of Science and Technology, College of Engineering, Program in Environmental Health Sciences, Philadelphia, PA 19140. Offers environmental health (MS). Part-time programs available. Students: 29 (10 women); includes 4 minority (3 African Americans, 1 Hispanic). 22 applicants, 91% accepted. In 1997, 17 degrees awarded. *Entrance requirements:* GRE General Test, TOEFL (minimum score 575). Application deadline: 7/1 (rolling processing; 11/1 for spring admission). Application fee: $40. *Expenses:* Tuition $323 per semester hour for state residents; $444 per semester hour for nonresidents. Fees $170 per year full-time, $28 per semester (minimum) part-time. *Financial aid:* In 1997–98, 7 students received aid, including 5 fellowships (all to first-year students), 2 teaching assistantships (both to first-year students) averaging $1,044 per month; Federal Work-Study, institutionally sponsored loans, and career-related internships or fieldwork also available. Financial aid application deadline: 2/15. *Faculty research:* Air pollution, industrial hygiene, exposure assessment, nonionizing radiation. • Dr. Robert M. Patterson, Director of Graduate Studies, College of Engineering, 215-204-1665. Fax: 215-204-6936. E-mail: rpatters@thunder.ocis.temple.edu.

Tufts University, Division of Graduate and Continuing Studies and Research, Graduate School of Arts and Sciences, College of Engineering, Department of Civil and Environmental Engineering, Medford, MA 02155. Offerings include environmental engineering (MS, PhD), with options in environmental engineering and environmental sciences, environmental geotechnology, environmental health, environmental science and management, hazardous materials management, water resources engineering. Terminal master's awarded for partial completion of doctoral program. Department faculty: 13 full-time, 7 part-time. *Degree requirements:* For master's, thesis or alternative required, foreign language not required; for doctorate, dissertation required, foreign language not required. *Entrance requirements:* GRE General Test, TOEFL (minimum score 550). Application deadline: 2/15 (rolling processing; 10/15 for spring admission). Application fee: $50. *Expenses:* Tuition $20,859 per year. Fees $1200 per year. • Dr. Lewis Edgers, Chair, 617-627-3211.

Tulane University, School of Public Health and Tropical Medicine, Department of Environmental Health Sciences, New Orleans, LA 70112. Awards MPH, MSPH, Sc D, JD/MPH, JD/MSPH, LL M/MSPH, MBA/MPH. One or more programs accredited by CEPH. Students: 88 full-time (37 women), 13 part-time (5 women); includes 29 minority (21 African Americans, 5 Asian Americans, 3 Hispanics), 21 international. Average age 29. *Degree requirements:* For master's, 1 foreign language required, thesis not required; for doctorate, 1 foreign language, dissertation. *Entrance requirements:* For master's, GRE General Test (minimum combined score of 1000; average 1100), TOEFL (minimum score 525); for doctorate, GRE General Test (minimum combined score of 1000; average 1250), TOEFL (minimum score 525). Application deadline: 4/15 (priority date; rolling processing; 10/15 for spring admission). Application fee: $40. *Financial aid:* Application deadline 2/1. • Dr. William Toscano, Chairman, 504-588-5374.

Université de Montréal, Faculties of Medicine and Graduate Studies, Graduate Programs in Medicine, Department of Environmental Health and Industrial and Environmental Hygiene, Montréal, PQ H3C 3J7, Canada. Awards M Sc, DESS. Faculty: 9 full-time (0 women). Students: 22 full-time (12 women), 5 part-time (1 woman). 7 applicants, 29% accepted. In 1997, 18 master's awarded. *Degree requirements:* For master's, thesis. *Entrance requirements:* For master's, proficiency in French, knowledge of English; for DESS, proficiency in French. Application fee: $30. *Faculty research:* Metabolism of chemical substances, toxicity, biological surveillance, nephrotoxicity, hepatotoxicity. • Joseph Zayed, Director, 514-343-6134.

Université du Québec à Montréal, Program in Ergonomics in Occupational Health and Safety, Montréal, PQ H3C 3P8, Canada. Awards Diploma. Part-time programs available. *Entrance requirements:* Appropriate bachelor's degree or equivalent and proficiency in French. Application deadline: 5/15. Application fee: $50.

Université Laval, Faculties of Medicine and Graduate Studies, Graduate Programs in Medicine, Department of Social and Preventive Medicine, Program in Occupational Health and Safety, Sainte-Foy, PQ G1K 7P4, Canada. Awards Diploma. Students: 5 full-time (3 women), 28 part-time (17 women). 22 applicants, 100% accepted. In 1997, 14 degrees awarded. *Application deadline:* 3/1. *Application fee:* $30. *Expenses:* Tuition $1334 per year (minimum) full-time, $56 per credit (minimum) part-time for Canadian residents; $5966 per year (minimum) full-time, $249 per credit (minimum) part-time for nonresidents. Fees $150 per year full-time, $6.25 per credit part-time. • Fernand Turcotte, Director, 418-656-2131 Ext. 5975. Fax: 418-656-7759. E-mail: fernand.turcotte@msp.ulaval.ca.

The University of Alabama at Birmingham, Graduate School, School of Public Health, Department of Environmental Health Sciences, Birmingham, AL 35294. Offers programs in environmental health (MPH, MSPH, Dr PH, PhD), environmental toxicology (MSPH, PhD), industrial hygiene (MPH, MSPH, Dr PH, PhD), occupational health and safety (MPH, MSPH, Dr PH). One or more programs accredited by CEPH. Faculty: 9. Students: 8 full-time (1 woman); includes 2 minority (both Asian Americans). 3 applicants, 100% accepted. In 1997, 4 doctorates awarded. *Degree requirements:* For master's, internship, project research (MSPH); for doctorate, dissertation. *Entrance requirements:* GRE General Test, TOEFL. Application deadline: 4/1. Application fee: $30 ($60 for international students). Electronic applications accepted. *Expenses:* Tuition $3672 per year full-time, $102 per credit hour part-time for state residents; $7344 per year full-time, $204 per credit hour part-time for nonresidents. Fees $699 per year (minimum) full-time, $116 per quarter (minimum) part-time. *Financial aid:* Fellowships, assistantships, scholarships, and career-related internships or fieldwork available. *Faculty research:* Aquatic toxicology, virology. • Dr. R. Kent Oestenstad, Interim Chair, 205-934-6208. Application contact: Nancy Pinson, Coordinator of Student Admissions, 205-934-4993. Fax: 205-975-5484. E-mail: osas@ms.soph.uab.edu.

See in-depth description on page 1523.

University of Alberta, Faculties of Medicine and Oral Health Sciences and Graduate Studies and Research, Graduate Programs in Medicine, Department of Public Health Sciences, Edmonton, AB T6G 2E1, Canada. Offerings include environmental health (M Sc, PhD), occupational health (M Sc). Terminal master's awarded for partial completion of doctoral program. Department faculty: 20 full-time, 11 part-time. *Degree requirements:* For doctorate, dissertation required, foreign language not required. *Average time to degree:* master's–2 years full-time, 4 years part-time; doctorate–4 years full-time, 6 years part-time. *Application deadline:* 2/1 (priority date; rolling processing). *Application fee:* $60. • Dr. T. W. Noseworthy, Chair, 403-492-6408. Application contact: Felicity Hey, Graduate Programs Administrator, 403-492-6407. Fax: 403-492-0364. E-mail: felicity.hey@ualberta.ca.

University of Arkansas for Medical Sciences, College of Medicine and Graduate School, Graduate Programs in Medicine, Occupational and Environmental Health Program, 4301 West Markham, Little Rock, AR 72205-7199. Awards MS. Offered jointly with the University of Arkansas at Little Rock and the National Center for Toxicological Research. Faculty: 20 full-time (1 woman). Students: 0. In 1997, 4 degrees awarded. *Degree requirements:* Thesis or alternative required, foreign language not required. *Entrance requirements:* GRE General Test. Application fee: $0. *Tuition:* $3060 per year full-time, $153 per credit hour part-time for state residents; $6560 per year full-time, $328 per credit hour part-time for nonresidents. *Financial aid:* Fellowships available. • Dr. Jack A. Hinson, Director, 501-686-5766. Application contact: Dr. Jay Jandy, 501-686-5289.

University of British Columbia, Occupational Hygiene Program, Vancouver, BC V6T 1Z2, Canada. Awards M Sc. Part-time programs available. *Degree requirements:* Thesis optional, foreign language not required. *Average time to degree:* master's–2 years full-time. *Entrance requirements:* GRE, TOEFL. Application deadline: 3/31. Application fee: $60. *Faculty research:* Industrial acoustics, air pollution, biological markers of workplace exposure, exposure assessment for epidemiology, occupational lung disease.

Directory: Environmental and Occupational Health

University of British Columbia, Faculties of Medicine and Graduate Studies, Graduate Programs in Medicine, Department of Health Care and Epidemiology, Vancouver, BC V6T 1W5, Canada. Offerings include occupational and environmental health (M Sc, PhD), occupational health (MH Sc). *Degree requirements:* For doctorate, dissertation. *Average time to degree:* master's–3 years full-time, 4 years part-time. *Entrance requirements:* For doctorate, work experience. Application deadline: 3/31 (rolling processing). Application fee: $50.

University of California, Berkeley, School of Public Health, Division of Environmental Health Sciences, Berkeley, CA 94720-1500. Awards MPH, MS, PhD. One or more programs accredited by CEPH. Faculty: 7 full-time (2 women), 6 part-time (2 women). Students: 49 full-time (26 women). 62 applicants, 45% accepted. In 1997, 18 master's, 6 doctorates awarded. *Degree requirements:* For master's, comprehensive exam (MPH), project or thesis (MS); for doctorate, dissertation, departmental and qualifying exams required, foreign language not required. *Average time to degree:* master's–2 years full-time. *Entrance requirements:* For master's, GRE General Test, TOEFL (minimum score 570), minimum GPA of 3.0; previous course work in biology, calculus, and chemistry; for doctorate, GRE General Test, TOEFL (minimum score 570), master's degree in relevant scientific discipline or engineering; minimum GPA of 3.0; previous course work in biology, calculus, and chemistry. Application deadline: 1/10 (rolling processing). Application fee: $40. Electronic applications accepted. *Expenses:* Tuition $0 for state residents; $9384 per year for nonresidents. Fees $4409 per year. *Financial aid:* Fellowships, research assistantships, teaching assistantships available. Financial aid application deadline: 3/2. *Faculty research:* Toxicology, industrial hygiene, exposure assessment, risk assessment, ergonomics. • Martyn T. Smith, Chair. Application contact: Ramona Brockman, Graduate Assistant for Admission, 510-643-5160. Fax: 510-642-5815. E-mail: ehs_div@uclink4.berkeley.edu.

University of California, Irvine, School of Social Ecology, Department of Environmental Analysis and Design, Irvine, CA 92697. Offerings include environmental health science and policy (MS, PhD). Terminal master's awarded for partial completion of doctoral program. *Degree requirements:* For doctorate, dissertation, research project. *Entrance requirements:* For doctorate, GRE General Test. Application deadline: 1/15 (priority date; rolling processing). Application fee: $40. Electronic applications accepted. *Expenses:* Tuition $0 for state residents; $9384 per year full-time, $1564 per quarter part-time for nonresidents. Fees $4998 per year full-time, $1152 per quarter part-time. • John Whiteley, Acting Chair, 949-824-5576. Application contact: Jeanne Haynes, Office of Student Affairs, 949-824-5917.

University of California, Los Angeles, School of Public Health, Department of Environmental Health Sciences, Los Angeles, CA 90095. Awards MS, PhD. Faculty: 9 (1 woman). Students: 50 full-time (30 women); includes 11 minority (1 African American, 8 Asian Americans, 2 Hispanics), 14 international. 47 applicants, 60% accepted. *Degree requirements:* For master's, comprehensive exam or thesis required, foreign language not required; for doctorate, dissertation, oral and written qualifying exams required, foreign language not required. *Entrance requirements:* For master's, GRE General Test (minimum combined score of 1100), minimum GPA of 3.0; for doctorate, GRE General Test (minimum combined score of 1200), minimum undergraduate GPA of 3.0. Application deadline: 12/15. Application fee: $40. Electronic applications accepted. *Expenses:* Tuition $0 for state residents; $9384 per year for nonresidents. Fees $4551 per year. *Financial aid:* In 1997–98, 46 students received aid, including fellowships totaling $97,795, research assistantships totaling $230,434, teaching assistantships totaling $41,648, federal fellowships and scholarships totaling $46,040. Financial aid application deadline: 3/1. • Dr. John Froines, Chair, 310-206-1619. Application contact: Departmental Office, 310-206-1619. E-mail: app_ehs@admin.ph.ucla.edu.

See in-depth description on page 1525.

University of Cincinnati, College of Medicine, Graduate Programs in Medicine, Department of Environmental Health, Cincinnati, OH 45267. Offers programs in environmental and industrial hygiene (MS), environmental and occupational medicine (MS), environmental health (PhD), environmental hygiene science and engineering (MS, PhD), epidemiology and biostatistics (MS), occupational safety (MS), toxicology (MS, PhD). Faculty: 23 full-time. Students: 72 full-time (33 women), 78 part-time (46 women); includes 26 minority (13 African Americans, 11 Asian Americans, 2 Hispanics), 33 international. 129 applicants, 22% accepted. In 1997, 17 master's, 9 doctorates awarded. Terminal master's awarded for partial completion of doctoral program. *Degree requirements:* For master's, thesis required, foreign language not required; for doctorate, 1 foreign language, dissertation, qualifying exam. *Average time to degree:* master's–2.8 years full-time; doctorate–8.8 years full-time. *Entrance requirements:* For master's, GRE General Test, TOEFL, bachelor's degree in science; for doctorate, GRE General Test, TOEFL. Application deadline: 2/1 (priority date; rolling processing). Application fee: $30. *Tuition:* $7228 per year full-time, $185 per credit hour part-time for state residents; $13,812 per year full-time, $352 per credit hour part-time for nonresidents. *Financial aid:* Graduate assistantships, full tuition waivers, Federal Work-Study, and career-related internships or fieldwork available. Financial aid application deadline: 5/1. *Faculty research:* Carcinogens and mutagenesis, pulmonary studies, reproduction and development. • Dr. Marshall W. Anderson, Chairman, 513-558-5701. Fax: 513-558-4397. E-mail: marshall.anderson@uc.edu. Application contact: Judy Jarell, 513-558-1729. E-mail: judy.jarell@uc.edu.

See in-depth description on page 1527.

University of Georgia, College of Agricultural and Environmental Sciences, Department of Food Science, Program in Environmental Health Science, Athens, GA 30602. Awards MS. Faculty: 5 full-time (2 women). Students: 13 full-time (6 women), 1 part-time (0 women); includes 2 international. 11 applicants, 55% accepted. In 1997, 4 degrees awarded. *Degree requirements:* Thesis required, foreign language not required. *Entrance requirements:* GRE General Test. Application deadline: 7/1 (priority date; 11/15 for spring admission). Application fee: $30. Electronic applications accepted. *Tuition:* $3290 per year full-time, $643 per semester (minimum) part-time for state residents; $11,300 per year full-time, $1645 per semester (minimum) part-time for nonresidents. • Phillip L. Williams, Coordinator, 706-542-2454. Fax: 706-542-7472.

University of Hawaii at Manoa, College of Health Sciences and Social Welfare, School of Public Health, Program in Environmental and Occupational Health, Honolulu, HI 96822. Offers environmental health engineering (MPH, MS), environmental health management (MPH, MS), environmental/occupational health sciences (MPH, MS). Part-time programs available. Faculty: 2 full-time (1 woman), 2 part-time (1 woman), 2.625 FTE. Students: 12 full-time (4 women), 17 part-time (10 women); includes 23 minority (all Asian Americans). 25 applicants, 76% accepted. In 1997, 26 degrees awarded. *Degree requirements:* Thesis (for some programs). *Average time to degree:* master's–1.2 years full-time, 3 years part-time. *Application deadline:* 3/1 (9/1 for spring admission). *Application fee:* $0. *Tuition:* $4029 per year full-time, $214 per credit hour part-time for state residents; $9957 per year full-time, $461 per credit hour part-time for nonresidents. *Financial aid:* Career-related internships or fieldwork available. *Faculty research:* Industrial hygiene and toxicology, environmental physiology, heavy metal pollution, disasters. • Dr. Arthur Kodama, Head, 808-956-5740. Application contact: Nancy Kilonsky, Assistant Dean, 808-956-8267.

University of Illinois at Chicago, School of Public Health, Program in Environmental and Occupational Health Sciences, Chicago, IL 60607-7128. Awards MPH, MS, Dr PH, PhD. One or more programs accredited by CEPH. MS and PhD offered jointly with Graduate College. *Degree requirements:* For master's, thesis, field practicum required, foreign language not required; for doctorate, dissertation, independent research, internship required, foreign language not required. *Entrance requirements:* GRE General Test (minimum combined score of 1000), TOEFL (minimum score 550), minimum GPA of 3.75 on a 5.0 scale. Application deadline: 7/3 (11/8 for spring admission). Application fee: $40 ($50 for international students). • Dr. Richard A. Wadden, Director, 312-996-8856. Application contact: Dr. Babette Neuberger, Assistant Dean, 312-996-6625.

The University of Iowa, College of Medicine and Graduate College, Graduate Programs in Medicine, Department of Preventive Medicine and Environmental Health, Iowa City, IA 52242-1316. Awards MS, PhD, MS/MA, MS/MS. Programs in biostatistics (MS, PhD), community health (MS), epidemiology (MS, PhD), industrial hygiene (MS), occupational and environmental health (MS, PhD). MS/MA and MS/MS offered jointly with the Program in Urban and Regional Planning. Part-time programs available. Faculty: 27 full-time (5 women), 11 part-time (4 women). Students: 49 full-time (21 women), 50 part-time (23 women); includes 4 minority (1 African American, 3 Asian Americans), 29 international. Average age 30. 86 applicants, 57% accepted. In 1997, 21 master's awarded (43% entered university research/teaching, 29% found other work related to degree, 28% continued full-time study); 3 doctorates awarded (33% entered university research/teaching, 67% found other work related to degree). Terminal master's awarded for partial completion of doctoral program. *Degree requirements:* For master's, computer language (biostatistics) required, thesis optional, foreign language not required; for doctorate, dissertation, computer language (biostatistics and epidemiology) required, foreign language not required. *Average time to degree:* master's–2 years full-time, 6 years part-time; doctorate–5 years full-time, 9 years part-time. *Entrance requirements:* For master's, GRE General Test (minimum combined score of 1050), TOEFL (minimum score 600), minimum GPA of 2.7; for doctorate, GRE General Test (minimum combined score of 1050), TOEFL (minimum score 600), minimum GPA of 3.0. Application deadline: 1/15 (priority date; rolling processing; 10/1 for spring admission). Application fee: $30 ($50 for international students). *Expenses:* Tuition $3166 per year full-time, $176 per credit hour part-time for state residents; $10,202 per year full-time, $567 per credit hour part-time for nonresidents. Fees $101 per year full-time, $51 per year (minimum) part-time. *Financial aid:* In 1997–98, 64 students received aid, including 7 fellowships (3 to first-year students) averaging $3,357 per month and totaling $282,008, 43 research assistantships (3 to first-year students) averaging $1,049 per month and totaling $541,059, 5 teaching assistantships (1 to a first-year student) averaging $780 per month and totaling $39,040, 9 traineeships, staff positions (6 to first-year students) averaging $3,718 per month and totaling $125,252; Federal Work-Study, institutionally sponsored loans also available. Aid available to part-time students. Financial aid application deadline: 1/15. *Faculty research:* Chronic disease epidemiology, clinical trials, analytical methods in epidemiology, industrial hygiene, agricultural health. Total annual research expenditures: $15.3 million. • Dr. James Merchant, Interim Head, 319-335-9833. Fax: 319-335-9772. E-mail: james-merchant@uiowa.edu. Application contact: Barbara Scott, Graduate Studies Coordinator, 319-335-8992. Fax: 319-335-9200. E-mail: barbara-scott@uiowa.edu.

University of Miami, College of Engineering, Department of Industrial Engineering, Program in Environmental Health and Safety, Coral Gables, FL 33124. Offers environmental health and safety (MSEH), occupational ergonomics and safety (MS). Faculty: 7 full-time (0 women). Students: 8 full-time (3 women), 2 part-time (1 woman); includes 2 international. Average age 28. 4 applicants, 100% accepted. In 1997, 2 degrees awarded. *Degree requirements:* Thesis optional, foreign language not required. *Average time to degree:* master's–2 years full-time. *Entrance requirements:* GRE General Test (minimum combined score of 1000), TOEFL (minimum score 550), minimum GPA of 3.0. Application deadline: 5/1. Application fee: $35. *Expenses:* Tuition $815 per credit hour. Fees $174 per year. *Financial aid:* Fellowships, research assistantships, teaching assistantships, Federal Work-Study available. Financial aid application deadline: 3/1; applicants required to submit FAFSA. *Faculty research:* Noise, heat stress, water pollution, survey pain. Total annual research expenditures: $335,804. • Dr. Shihab S. Asfour, Graduate Officer, 305-284-2344. Fax: 305-284-4040.

University of Michigan, School of Public Health, Department of Environmental and Industrial Health, Program in Environmental Health, Ann Arbor, MI 48109. Awards MPH, MS, PhD. One or more programs accredited by CEPH. MS and PhD offered through the Horace H. Rackham School of Graduate Studies. *Degree requirements:* For doctorate, variable foreign language requirement, oral defense of dissertation, preliminary exam. *Entrance requirements:* GRE General Test. Application deadline: 3/1 (priority date; rolling processing). Application fee: $55. *Financial aid:* Application deadline 3/1. • Dr. Jerome Nriagu, Program Director, 734-936-0706. E-mail: jnriagu@umich.edu.

See in-depth description on page 1535.

University of Michigan, School of Public Health, Department of Environmental and Industrial Health, Program in Occupational Health, Ann Arbor, MI 48109. Offers industrial hygiene (MS, PhD), occupational medicine (MPH). One or more programs accredited by CEPH. MS and PhD offered through the Horace H. Rackham School of Graduate Studies. *Degree requirements:* For doctorate, variable foreign language requirement, oral defense of dissertation, preliminary exam. *Entrance requirements:* GRE General Test. Application deadline: 3/1 (priority date; rolling processing). Application fee: $55. *Financial aid:* Application deadline 3/1. • Dr. Thomas G. Robbins, Program Director, 734-936-0757. E-mail: trobins@umich.edu.

See in-depth description on page 1535.

University of Minnesota, Twin Cities Campus, School of Public Health, Division of Environmental and Occupational Health, Area in Environmental Health Policy, Minneapolis, MN 55455-0213. Awards MPH, MS, PhD. One or more programs accredited by CEPH. *Degree requirements:* For doctorate, dissertation required, foreign language not required. *Entrance requirements:* GRE General Test (minimum combined score of 1500 on three sections), minimum GPA of 3.0. Application deadline: 4/15 (priority date; rolling processing). Application fee: $50 ($75 for international students). *Financial aid:* Application deadline 4/15. • Application contact: Kathy Soupir, Student Coordinator, 612-625-0622. Fax: 612-626-4837. E-mail: ksoupir@mail.eoh.umn.edu.

See in-depth description on page 1537.

University of Minnesota, Twin Cities Campus, School of Public Health, Division of Environmental and Occupational Health, Area in Occupational Medicine, Minneapolis, MN 55455-0213. Awards MPH. Accredited by CEPH. *Entrance requirements:* GRE General Test (minimum combined score of 1500 on three sections), minimum GPA of 3.0. Application deadline: 4/15 (priority date; rolling processing). Application fee: $50 ($75 for international students). *Financial aid:* Application deadline 4/15. • Application contact: Kathy Soupir, Student Coordinator, 612-625-0622. Fax: 612-626-4837. E-mail: ksoupir@mail.eoh.umn.edu.

See in-depth description on page 1537.

University of Nevada, Reno, Center for Environmental Sciences and Engineering, Graduate Program in Environmental Sciences and Health, Reno, NV 89557. Awards MS, PhD. Students: 14 full-time (9 women), 23 part-time (8 women); includes 1 minority (Asian American), 4 international. Average age 33. 30 applicants, 40% accepted. In 1997, 2 master's, 1 doctorate awarded. *Degree requirements:* Thesis/dissertation. *Entrance requirements:* For master's, GRE General Test (minimum combined score of 1000), TOEFL (minimum score 600), minimum GPA of 2.75; for doctorate, GRE General Test (minimum combined score of 1000), TOEFL (minimum score 600), minimum GPA of 3.0. Application deadline: 3/1 (rolling processing; 11/1 for spring admission). Application fee: $40. *Expenses:* Tuition $0 for state residents; $5770 per year full-time, $200 per credit part-time for nonresidents. Fees $93 per credit. *Financial aid:* Fellowships, research assistantships, teaching assistantships available. Financial aid application deadline: 3/1. • Dr. Glenn C. Miller, Graduate Director, 702-784-6460. Fax: 702-784-1142. E-mail: gmiller@scs.unr.edu.

University of New Haven, School of Public Safety and Professional Studies, Program in Occupational Safety and Health Management, West Haven, CT 06516-1916. Awards MS. Students: 3 full-time (2 women), 39 part-time (14 women); includes 3 minority (2 African Americans, 1 Asian American), 1 international. 11 applicants, 64% accepted. *Degree requirements:* Thesis or alternative required, foreign language not required. *Application deadline:* rolling. *Application fee:* $50. *Expenses:* Tuition $1125 per course. Fees $13 per trimester. *Financial aid:* Federal Work-Study and career-related internships or fieldwork available. Aid

Directory: Environmental and Occupational Health

University of New Haven (continued)
available to part-time students. Financial aid application deadline: 5/1; applicants required to submit FAFSA. • Dr. Brad T. Garber, Director, 203-932-7175.

University of Oklahoma, College of Engineering, School of Civil Engineering and Environmental Science, Program in Environmental Science, Norman, OK 73019-0390. Offerings include occupational safety and health (M Env Sc). *Degree requirements:* Comprehensive and oral exams required, foreign language and thesis not required. *Entrance requirements:* GRE General Test, TOEFL (minimum score 575), minimum GPA of 3.0. Application deadline: 4/1 (priority date; rolling processing). Application fee: $25. *Expenses:* Tuition $1920 per year full-time, $80 per credit hour part-time for state residents; $6108 per year full-time, $255 per credit hour part-time for nonresidents. Fees $468 per year full-time, $12 per semester (minimum) part-time. • Application contact: Larry Canter, Graduate Liaison, 405-325-5911. Fax: 405-325-7508.

University of Oklahoma Health Sciences Center, College of Public Health, Department of Occupational and Environmental Health, Oklahoma City, OK 73190. Awards MPH, MS, Dr PH, PhD, MPH/JD, MS/JD. One or more programs accredited by CEPH. MPH/JD and MS/JD offered jointly with Oklahoma State University and the University of Oklahoma. Part-time programs available. Faculty: 10 full-time (2 women), 16 part-time (4 women). Students: 40 full-time (18 women), 39 part-time (15 women); includes 19 minority (9 African Americans, 5 Asian Americans, 1 Hispanic, 4 Native Americans), 1 international. Average age 36. 55 applicants, 65% accepted. In 1997, 34 master's awarded. *Degree requirements:* For master's, computer language, thesis (for some programs), comprehensive exam required, foreign language not required; for doctorate, computer language, dissertation, oral and written comprehensive exam required, foreign language not required. *Entrance requirements:* For master's, TOEFL (minimum score 550); for doctorate, GRE, TOEFL (minimum score 550). Application deadline: 7/1 (rolling processing; 12/1 for spring admission). Application fee: $25 ($50 for international students). *Financial aid:* Research assistantships, traineeships, partial tuition waivers, institutionally sponsored loans, and career-related internships or fieldwork available. Aid available to part-time students. Financial aid application deadline: 5/1. *Faculty research:* Environmental safety, accident prevention and injury control. • Dr. Nurtan Esmon, Interim Chair, 405-271-2070.

University of Pittsburgh, Graduate School of Public Health, Department of Environmental and Occupational Health, Program in Environmental and Occupational Health, Pittsburgh, PA 15260. Awards MPH, MS, PhD. One or more programs accredited by CEPH. Part-time programs available. Faculty: 21 full-time (4 women), 2 part-time (0 women). Students: 18 full-time (12 women), 16 part-time (10 women); includes 8 minority (2 African Americans, 2 Asian Americans, 4 Hispanics), 8 international. 27 applicants, 70% accepted. In 1997, 5 master's, 2 doctorates awarded. Terminal master's awarded for partial completion of doctoral program. *Degree requirements:* For master's, computer language, thesis; for doctorate, computer language, dissertation, comprehensive and preliminary exams. *Average time to degree:* master's–3 years full-time, 5 years part-time; doctorate–4 years full-time, 8 years part-time. *Entrance requirements:* For master's, GRE General Test, minimum QPA of 3.0; for doctorate, GRE General Test, minimum QPA of 3.4. Application deadline: 7/31 (priority date; rolling processing; 11/30 for spring admission). Application fee: $50 ($60 for international students). *Expenses:* Tuition $9402 per year full-time, $388 per credit part-time for state residents; $19,372 per year full-time, $799 per credit part-time for nonresidents. Fees $480 per year full-time, $180 per year part-time. *Financial aid:* In 1997–98, 23 students received aid, including 3 fellowships averaging $975 per month and totaling $31,997, 9 research assistantships (4 to first-year students) averaging $1,050 per month, 1 teaching assistantship averaging $1,286 per month; Federal Work-Study, institutionally sponsored loans also available. Financial aid application deadline: 4/30; applicants required to submit FAFSA. *Faculty research:* Molecular toxicology, risk assessment, occupational medicine, radiation health, computational toxicology. Total annual research expenditures: $3.4 million. • Application contact: Joanne E. Buffo, Student Affairs Administrator, 412-967-6521. Fax: 412-624-1020. E-mail: stdntaff@vms.cis.pitt.edu.

See in-depth description on page 1545.

University of Pittsburgh, Graduate School of Public Health, Department of Environmental and Occupational Health, Program in Occupational Medicine, Pittsburgh, PA 15260. Awards MPH. Accredited by CEPH. Program restricted to licensed physicians. Students: 4 full-time (0 women), 4 part-time (1 woman); includes 2 minority (1 Asian American, 1 Native American), 1 international. 9 applicants, 67% accepted. In 1997, 2 degrees awarded. *Average time to degree:* master's–2 years full-time, 4 years part-time. *Application fee:* $50 ($60 for international students). *Expenses:* Tuition $9402 per year full-time, $388 per credit part-time for state residents; $19,372 per year full-time, $799 per credit part-time for nonresidents. Fees $480 per year full-time, $180 per year part-time. • Dr. William F. Gauss, Interim Director, 412-624-3155. Fax: 412-624-3040.

University of Puerto Rico, Medical Sciences Campus, Graduate School of Public Health, Department of Environmental Health, Program in Environmental Health, San Juan, PR 00936-5067. Awards MS. Part-time programs available. Students: 136 (83 women). 85 applicants, 65% accepted. In 1997, 17 degrees awarded. *Degree requirements:* Computer language, thesis required, foreign language not required. *Entrance requirements:* GRE, previous course work in biology, chemistry, mathematics, and physics. Application deadline: 3/3. Application fee: $15. *Financial aid:* Research assistantships, teaching assistantships, Federal Work-Study, institutionally sponsored loans available. Financial aid application deadline: 4/30. • Application contact: Mayra E. Santiago-Vargas, Counselor, 787-756-5244. Fax: 787-759-6719.

University of Rochester, School of Medicine and Dentistry, Graduate Programs in Medicine and Dentistry, Department of Environmental Medicine, Program in Environmental Studies and Industrial Hygiene, Rochester, NY 14642. Awards MS. Part-time programs available. Students: 39 part-time (15 women); includes 1 minority (African American). 2 applicants, 100% accepted. In 1997, 2 degrees awarded. *Entrance requirements:* GRE General Test. Application deadline: 2/1. Application fee: $25. *Expenses:* Tuition $21,485 per year full-time, $672 per credit hour part-time. Fees $336 per year. *Financial aid:* Application deadline 2/1. • Dr. Victor Laties, Director, 716-275-4453. Application contact: Joyce Morgan, Graduate Program Secretary, 716-275-6702.

University of South Carolina, Graduate School, School of Public Health, Department of Environmental Health Sciences, Program in Environmental Quality, Columbia, SC 29208. Awards MPH, MSPH, PhD. One or more programs accredited by CEPH. *Degree requirements:* For master's, thesis, practicum (MPH) required, foreign language not required; for doctorate, 1 foreign language, dissertation. *Entrance requirements:* GRE. Application deadline: rolling. Application fee: $35. Electronic applications accepted. *Expenses:* Tuition $4480 per year full-time, $220 per credit hour part-time for state residents; $9338 per year full-time, $457 per credit hour part-time for nonresidents. Fees $125 per year full-time, $37 per semester (minimum) part-time. *Faculty research:* Environmental assessment and planning; environmental toxicology; ecosystems analysis; air quality monitoring and modeling. • Application contact: Dr. Edward Oswald, Graduate Director, 803-777-6994. Fax: 803-777-3391.

University of Southern Mississippi, College of Health and Human Sciences, Center for Community Health, Hattiesburg, MS 39406-5167. Offerings include occupational/environmental health (MPH). Accredited by CEPH. Center faculty: 6 full-time (3 women), 1 (woman) part-time. *Degree requirements:* Comprehensive exam required, foreign language and thesis not required. *Entrance requirements:* GRE General Test, minimum GPA of 2.75. Application deadline: 8/9 (priority date; rolling processing). Application fee: $0 ($25 for international students). *Tuition:* $2870 per year full-time, $137 per credit hour part-time for state residents; $5972 per year full-time, $172 per credit hour part-time for nonresidents. • Dr. Agnes Hinton, Interim Director, 601-266-5437.

University of South Florida, College of Public Health, Department of Environmental and Occupational Health, Tampa, FL 33620-9951. Awards MPH, MSPH, PhD. One or more programs accredited by CEPH. Part-time and evening/weekend programs available. Faculty: 8 full-time (1 woman). 49 applicants, 76% accepted. *Degree requirements:* For master's, thesis required, foreign language not required; for doctorate, computer language, dissertation required, foreign language not required. *Entrance requirements:* For master's, GRE General Test (minimum combined score of 1000), TOEFL (minimum score 550), minimum GPA of 3.0 in upper-level course work; for doctorate, GRE General Test (minimum combined score of 1100), TOEFL (minimum score 550), minimum GPA of 3.0 in upper-level course work. Application deadline: 6/1 (rolling processing; 10/15 for spring admission). Application fee: $20. *Tuition:* $142 per credit hour for state residents; $486 per credit hour for nonresidents. *Financial aid:* Federal Work-Study, institutionally sponsored loans available. Aid available to part-time students. Financial aid applicants required to submit FAFSA. *Faculty research:* Biomedical assessment/stress test, risk impact, nitrobenzes on mammalism glutathion transferases, lysimeter research management, independent hygiene development. Total annual research expenditures: $529,580. • Dr. Yehia Hammad, Chairperson, 813-974-3144. E-mail: yhammad@com1.med.usf.edu. Application contact: Magdalene Argiry, Director of Student Services, 813-974-6665. Fax: 813-974-4718. E-mail: margiry@com1.med.usf.edu.

University of Washington, School of Public Health and Community Medicine, Department of Environmental Health, Seattle, WA 98195. Offers programs in industrial hygiene (PhD), industrial hygiene and safety (MS), occupational medicine (MPH), preventive medicine (MPH), technology (MS), toxicology (MS, PhD). One or more programs accredited by CEPH. Part-time programs available. Faculty: 37 full-time (7 women), 9 part-time (0 women). Students: 63 full-time (28 women), 6 part-time (4 women); includes 10 minority (2 African Americans, 6 Asian Americans, 2 Hispanics), 16 international. 97 applicants, 26% accepted. In 1997, 18 master's, 5 doctorates awarded. Terminal master's awarded for partial completion of doctoral program. *Degree requirements:* Thesis/dissertation required, foreign language not required. *Average time to degree:* master's–2 years full-time; doctorate–5 years full-time. *Entrance requirements:* GRE General Test, TOEFL (minimum score 500), minimum GPA of 3.0. Application deadline: 2/1 (priority date). Application fee: $45. *Tuition:* $5433 per year full-time, $775 per quarter (minimum) part-time for state residents; $13,479 per year full-time, $1925 per quarter (minimum) part-time for nonresidents. *Financial aid:* In 1997–98, 61 students received aid, including 5 fellowships (2 to first-year students), 33 research assistantships (12 to first-year students), 6 teaching assistantships, 18 traineeships (11 to first-year students); Federal Work-Study, institutionally sponsored loans, and career-related internships or fieldwork also available. Financial aid application deadline: 2/28. *Faculty research:* Developmental toxicology, biochemical toxicology, exposure assessment, hazardous waste, industrial chemistry. • Dr. Thomas Burbacher, Graduate Coordinator, 206-543-3199. Application contact: Sara E. Griggs, Manager, Student Services, 206-543-3199. Fax: 206-543-9616. E-mail: ehgrad@u.washington.edu.

See in-depth description on page 1549.

University of Wisconsin–Eau Claire, College of Professional Studies, School of Human Sciences and Services, Division of Allied Health Professions, Program in Environmental and Public Health, Eau Claire, WI 54702-4004. Awards MS. Students: 16 full-time (8 women), 5 part-time (1 woman); includes 3 minority (2 African Americans, 1 Asian American). In 1997, 11 degrees awarded. *Degree requirements:* Thesis, oral and written exams required, foreign language not required. *Application deadline:* 3/1 (rolling processing). *Application fee:* $45. *Tuition:* $3651 per year full-time, $611 per semester (minimum) part-time for state residents; $11,295 per year full-time, $1886 per semester (minimum) part-time for nonresidents. *Financial aid:* Federal Work-Study available. Financial aid application deadline: 3/1. • Dr. Dale Taylor, Director, Division of Allied Health Professions, 715-836-2628.

Virginia Commonwealth University, Center for Environmental Studies, Richmond, VA 23284-9005. Offerings include environmental health (MIS). *Entrance requirements:* GRE General Test. Application fee: $30 ($0 for international students). *Tuition:* $4960 per year full-time, $257 per credit part-time for state residents; $12,652 per year full-time, $684 per credit part-time for nonresidents. • Greg Garman, Director, 804-828-7202. E-mail: gcgarman@vcu.edu. Application contact: Andrew Lacatell, Assistant Director, 804-828-7202. Fax: 804-828-0503. E-mail: adlacate@vcu.edu.

Wayne State University, College of Pharmacy and Allied Health Professions, Faculty of Allied Health Professions, Department of Occupational and Environmental Health Sciences, Detroit, MI 48202. Offers program in occupational health sciences (MS), including industrial hygiene, industrial toxicology, occupational medicine. Part-time and evening/weekend programs available. Faculty: 3 full-time (1 woman), 20 part-time (3 women), 5 FTE. Students: 6 full-time (2 women), 34 part-time (17 women); includes 7 minority (4 African Americans, 3 Asian Americans), 10 international. Average age 30. 23 applicants, 70% accepted. In 1997, 13 degrees awarded. *Degree requirements:* Thesis optional, foreign language not required. *Average time to degree:* master's–2 years full-time, 3.5 years part-time. *Entrance requirements:* GRE General Test, 1 year of course work in biology, mathematics, and physics; 2 years of course work in chemistry. Application deadline: 6/15 (priority date). Application fee: $20 ($30 for international students). *Expenses:* Tuition $163 per credit hour for state residents; $355 per credit hour for nonresidents. Fees $498 per year full-time, $114 per semester (minimum) part-time. *Financial aid:* 4 students received aid; teaching assistantships, scholarships, and career-related internships or fieldwork available. Financial aid application deadline: 7/1. *Faculty research:* Air sampling: methods and development, pulmonary, toxicity oxidant air pollutants, inflammatory reactions, DNA damage and repair. Total annual research expenditures: $637,402. • Dr. David J. P. Bassett, Chairperson, 313-577-1551. Fax: 313-577-5589.

Western Kentucky University, Ogden College of Science, Technology, and Health, Department of Public Health, Bowling Green, KY 42101-3576. Offerings include environmental health (MS). Department faculty: 11 full-time (4 women). *Application deadline:* 8/1 (priority date; rolling processing; 12/1 for spring admission). *Application fee:* $20. *Tuition:* $2460 per year full-time, $133 per credit hour part-time for state residents; $6700 per year full-time, $369 per credit hour part-time for nonresidents. • Dr. J. David Dunn, Head, 502-745-4797. Fax: 502-745-4437. E-mail: david.dunn@wku.edu.

Western Washington University, Huxley College of Environmental Studies, Bellingham, WA 98225-5996. Offerings include behavioral toxicology (MS). College faculty: 9 (2 women). *Degree requirements:* Thesis. *Entrance requirements:* GRE General Test, TOEFL, minimum GPA of 3.0 in last 60 semester hours or last 90 quarter hours. Application deadline: 2/1. Application fee: $35. *Expenses:* Tuition $4200 per year full-time, $140 per credit part-time for state residents; $12,780 per year full-time, $426 per credit part-time for nonresidents. Fees $249 per year full-time, $83 per quarter part-time. • Dr. Brad Smith, Dean, 360-650-3521. Application contact: Dr. John Hardy, Chair, Graduate Program Committee, 360-650-3520.

Yale University, School of Medicine, Department of Epidemiology and Public Health, Division of Environmental Health, New Haven, CT 06520. Awards MPH, Dr PH, PhD. One or more programs accredited by CEPH. PhD offered through the Graduate School. Faculty: 3 full-time (0 women), 9 part-time (2 women). Students: 14 full-time (7 women), 1 (woman) part-time; includes 2 minority (1 African American, 1 Hispanic), 4 international. Average age 27. 34 applicants, 65% accepted. In 1997, 3 master's, 2 doctorates awarded. Terminal master's awarded for partial completion of doctoral program. *Degree requirements:* For master's, thesis, internship required, foreign language not required; for doctorate, dissertation, comprehensive exams, residency period required, foreign language not required. *Entrance requirements:* For master's, GMAT, GRE, LSAT, or MCAT; TOEFL, previous undergraduate course work in mathematics and science; for doctorate, GRE General Test (minimum combined score of 1200), TOEFL, MPH or equivalent and professional experience (Dr PH). Application deadline: rolling. Application fee: $60. *Financial aid:* Scholarships, Federal Work-Study, institutionally sponsored loans, and career-related internships or fieldwork available. Aid available to part-time students. Financial aid application deadline: 4/15. *Faculty research:* Asthma and environmental agents, environmental epidemiology, sensory perceptions, indoor/outdoor air quality, exercise physiology. • Dr. Brian P. Leaderer, Professor of Epidemiology and Public Health, 203-785-2880. Fax: 203-737-6023. Application contact: Joan Stenner, Admissions Officer, 203-785-2844. Fax: 203-785-4845. E-mail: joan.stenner@yale.edu.

See in-depth description on page 1551.

Epidemiology

Boston University, School of Medicine, School of Public Health, Epidemiology and Biostatistics Department, Boston, MA 02215. Offers programs in biostatistics (MA, MPH, PhD), epidemiology (MPH, M Sc, D Sc). One or more programs accredited by CEPH. MA and PhD offered jointly with the Department of Mathematics. Students: 73 full-time (52 women), 97 part-time (68 women); includes 28 minority (5 African Americans, 18 Asian Americans, 4 Hispanics, 1 Native American), 10 international. Average age 30. *Degree requirements:* For doctorate, 1 foreign language, dissertation, comprehensive written and oral exams. *Entrance requirements:* For master's, GRE General Test, TOEFL; for doctorate, GRE General Test, MPH or equivalent. Application deadline: 4/15 (rolling processing; 10/25 for spring admission). Application fee: $50. *Financial aid:* Federal Work-Study, institutionally sponsored loans, and career-related internships or fieldwork available. Aid available to part-time students. • Dr. Theodore Colton, Chairman, 617-638-5172. Application contact: Barbara St. Onge, Director of Admissions, 617-638-4640. Fax: 617-638-5299. E-mail: sphadmis@bu.edu.

See in-depth description on page 1487.

Brown University, Division of Biology and Medicine, Program in Epidemiology and Gerontology, Providence, RI 02912. Awards Sc M, PhD, MD/PhD. Part-time programs available. Faculty: 5 full-time (1 woman). Students: 10 full-time (7 women); includes 1 minority (African American), 1 international. Average age 28. 2 applicants, 100% accepted. In 1997, 1 doctorate awarded. Terminal master's awarded for partial completion of doctoral program. *Degree requirements:* For master's, thesis required, foreign language not required; for doctorate, dissertation, preliminary exam. *Entrance requirements:* GRE General Test, GRE Subject Test. Application deadline: 1/2 (priority date; rolling processing). Application fee: $60. *Expenses:* Tuition $23,616 per year. Fees $436 per year. *Financial aid:* In 1997–98, 1 fellowship (to a first-year student), 1 research assistantship were awarded. Financial aid application deadline: 1/2. • Dr. Constantine Gatsonis, Director, 401-863-1106.

Brown University, Division of Biology and Medicine, Department of Community Health, Program in Epidemiology, Providence, RI 02912. Awards MS, PhD, MD/PhD. Offerings include health services research (MS, PhD). *Degree requirements:* For doctorate, dissertation, preliminary exam. *Entrance requirements:* GRE General Test. Application deadline: 1/2 (priority date; rolling processing). Application fee: $60. *Expenses:* Tuition $23,616 per year. Fees $436 per year. *Financial aid:* Application deadline 1/2. • Dr. Constantine Gatsonis, Director, Department of Community Health, 401-863-1106. E-mail: gatsonis@jenny.biomed.brown.edu.

Announcement: The graduate program in the Department of Community Health is designed to provide methodologic and subject-matter training in the study of the multiplicity of biological, behavioral, and social factors that influence the determinants of disease, its treatment, and its consequences and outcomes, with particular emphasis on health services research. The program offers comprehensive instruction leading to master's and Ph.D. degrees in biostatistics or epidemiology. The program also features an intensive 1-year professional master's degree in each track. For additional information, students may visit the Web site (http://BioMedCS.biomed.brown.edu/Commhlth/index.html) or may write (Graduate Program in Epidemiology, Biostatistics and Health Services Research, Department of Community Health, Brown University, Box G-A4, Providence, Rhode Island 02912).

California State University, Long Beach, College of Natural Sciences, Department of Biological Sciences, Program in Microbiology, Long Beach, CA 90840-3702. Offerings include nurse epidemiology (MPH). Program faculty: 11 full-time. *Application deadline:* 8/1 (rolling processing; 12/1 for spring admission). *Application fee:* $55. *Expenses:* Tuition $0 for state residents; $246 per unit for nonresidents. Fees $1846 per year full-time, $1180 per year part-time. • Dr. Laura Kingsford, Acting Chair, Department of Biological Sciences, 562-985-4807. E-mail: lkingsfo@csulb.edu. Application contact: Dr. Charles Collins, Graduate Coordinator, 562-985-8503. Fax: 562-985-8878. E-mail: ccollins@csulb.edu.

Case Western Reserve University, Schools of Medicine and Graduate Studies, Graduate Programs in Medicine, Department of Epidemiology and Biostatistics, Program in Epidemiology, Cleveland, OH 44106. Awards MS, PhD. Part-time programs available. Faculty: 6 full-time (3 women). Students: 14 full-time (8 women), 12 part-time (8 women). Average age 38. 18 applicants, 83% accepted. In 1997, 7 master's awarded (71% found work related to degree, 29% continued full-time study). Terminal master's awarded for partial completion of doctoral program. *Degree requirements:* Thesis/dissertation required, foreign language not required. *Average time to degree:* master's–2 years full-time, 3 years part-time. *Entrance requirements:* GRE General Test, TOEFL (minimum score 550). Application deadline: 2/1 (priority date; rolling processing). Application fee: $25. *Tuition:* $18,400 per year full-time, $767 per credit hour part-time. *Financial aid:* In 1997–98, 18 students received aid, including 8 fellowships (4 to first-year students), 6 research assistantships (3 to first-year students), 4 teaching assistantships; partial tuition waivers and career-related internships or fieldwork also available. Aid available to part-time students. Financial aid application deadline: 2/1. *Faculty research:* Cardiovascular epidemiology, cancer risk factors, HIV in underserved populations, effectiveness studies in Medicare patients. • Dr. Alfred A. Rimm, Director, 216-368-3197. E-mail: rimm@hal.cwru.edu. Application contact: Joan Marold, Admissions Secretary, 216-368-3195. Fax: 216-368-3970. E-mail: marold@hal.cwru.edu.

Announcement: The department's scientific disciplines include (1) biostatistics: the design and analysis of biomedical research in humans and in laboratory experiments, (2) epidemiology: the search for factors causing disease in humans and the study of the occurrence and distribution of disease in human populations, (3) molecular and genetic epidemiology: the study of genetic factors that determine the distributions and dynamics of disease in populations, and (4) health services research: the description, analysis, and evaluation of the organization, staffing, financing, utilization, and delivery of health care. Faculty members in the department, with grants exceeding $2 million annually, conduct collaborative research with the basic and clinical science departments of the School of Medicine.

Columbia University, School of Public Health, Division of Epidemiology, New York, NY 10032. Awards MPH, MS, Dr PH, PhD. One or more programs accredited by CEPH. PhD offered in cooperation with the Graduate School of Arts and Sciences. Part-time programs available. Students: 98. In 1997, 28 master's, 1 doctorate awarded. *Degree requirements:* Thesis/dissertation required, foreign language not required. *Average time to degree:* master's–1.5 years full-time, 3 years part-time; doctorate–4 years full-time, 7 years part-time. *Entrance requirements:* For master's, GRE General Test; for doctorate, GRE General Test, MPH or equivalent (Dr PH). Application deadline: 4/10. Application fee: $60. *Tuition:* $22,320 per year full-time, $744 per credit part-time. *Financial aid:* Research assistantships, teaching assistantships, Federal Work-Study, and career-related internships or fieldwork available. Aid available to part-time students. Financial aid application deadline: 3/15; applicants required to submit FAFSA. *Faculty research:* Psychiatric epidemiology; epidemiology of neurological disorders, cancer, and cardiovascular disease. • Dr. Geoffrey Howe, Head, 212-305-9412. E-mail: gh68@columbia.edu. Application contact: Liliane Zaretsky, Program Coordinator, 212-305-9412. Fax: 212-305-9413. E-mail: lz3@columbia.edu.

Columbia University, Graduate School of Arts and Sciences, Division of Natural Sciences, Department of Epidemiology, New York, NY 10027. Awards MA, M Phil, PhD, MD/PhD. Faculty: 13 full-time. Students: 15 full-time (13 women), 13 part-time (7 women); includes 3 minority (2 Asian Americans, 1 Hispanic), 4 international. Average age 36. 37 applicants, 32% accepted. In 1997, 5 doctorates awarded. *Degree requirements:* For master's, thesis required, foreign language not required; for doctorate, dissertation, M Phil required, foreign language not required. *Entrance requirements:* GRE General Test, TOEFL. Application deadline: 1/3 (11/30 for spring admission). Application fee: $65. *Tuition:* $22,700 per year full-time, $12,844 per year part-time. *Financial aid:* Fellowships, Federal Work-Study, institutionally sponsored loans available. Aid available to part-time students. Financial aid application deadline: 1/5; applicants required to submit FAFSA. *Faculty research:* Biomedical, social, and statistical epidemiology. • Bruce Link, Chair, 212-305-3921. Fax: 212-305-9413.

Cornell University, Graduate School of Medical Sciences, Program in Clinical Epidemiology and Health Services Research, New York, NY 10031. Awards MS. Faculty: 18 full-time (7 women), 3 part-time (0 women). Students: 4 full-time (2 women); includes 1 minority (African American). *Degree requirements:* Thesis. *Entrance requirements:* MD or RN certificate, 3 years of work experience. Application deadline: 1/15. Application fee: $50. *Tuition:* $18,290 per year. *Financial aid:* Grants available. • Application contact: Valerie Blake, Administrator.

Dalhousie University, Faculties of Graduate Studies and Medicine, Graduate Programs in Medicine, Department of Community Health and Epidemiology, Halifax, NS B3H 3J5, Canada. Awards M Sc. Part-time programs available. Faculty: 10 full-time (4 women), 22 part-time (11 women). Students: 25 full-time (21 women), 16 part-time (11 women). Average age 28. 30 applicants, 43% accepted. In 1997, 6 degrees awarded. *Degree requirements:* Thesis. *Entrance requirements:* TOEFL (minimum score 580). Application deadline: 3/1. Application fee: $55. *Financial aid:* Fellowships, research assistantships, partial tuition waivers, and career-related internships or fieldwork available. *Faculty research:* Population health, health promotion, health services utilization, chronic disease epidemiology. • Dr. D. R. MacLean, Head, 902-494-1235. Application contact: Dr. Susan Kirkland, Graduate Coordinator, 902-494-3860. Fax: 902-494-1597.

Emory University, Graduate School of Arts and Sciences, Division of Epidemiology, Atlanta, GA 30322-1100. Offers program in quantitative epidemiology (PhD). Offered jointly with The Rollins School of Public Health. Part-time programs available. Faculty: 20 full-time (5 women). Students: 25 full-time (14 women); includes 3 minority (all Asian Americans), 4 international. 47 applicants, 9% accepted. In 1997, 3 doctorates awarded. Terminal master's awarded for partial completion of doctoral program. *Degree requirements:* For doctorate, computer language, dissertation, comprehensive exam required, foreign language not required. *Entrance requirements:* For doctorate, GRE General Test, TOEFL, minimum GPA of 3.0. Application deadline: 1/20 (priority date; rolling processing). Application fee: $45. *Expenses:* Tuition $21,770 per year. Fees $300 per year. *Financial aid:* In 1997–98, 25 fellowships (5 to first-year students) averaging $1,240 per month and totaling $248,200, 20 tuition scholarships (5 to first-year students) totaling $259,625 were awarded; partial tuition waivers, institutionally sponsored loans, and career-related internships or fieldwork also available. Financial aid application deadline: 1/20. *Faculty research:* Epidemiologic study design and analysis, surgery methodology, research data management, epidemic modeling, categorical data analysis. • Dr. John Boring, Director, 404-727-8710. Application contact: Dollie Daniels, Associate Director, 404-727-8712.

See in-depth description on page 1491.

Emory University, The Rollins School of Public Health, Department of Epidemiology, Atlanta, GA 30322-1100. Awards MPH. Accredited by CEPH. *Degree requirements:* Thesis (for some programs), practicum required, foreign language not required. *Entrance requirements:* GRE General Test. Application deadline: 2/15 (priority date; rolling processing). Application fee: $50. *Expenses:* Tuition $14,136 per year full-time, $589 per credit hour part-time. Fees $200 per year. *Financial aid:* Application deadline 2/15. • Dr. John R. Boring, Chair, 404-727-8711. Application contact: Susan Daniel, Director of Admissions, 404-727-5481. Fax: 404-727-3996. E-mail: admit@sph.emory.edu.

See in-depth descriptions on pages 1491 and 1493.

Georgetown University, Programs in Biomedical Sciences, Division of Biostatistics and Epidemiology, Washington, DC 20007. Awards MS. *Entrance requirements:* GRE General Test, TOEFL (minimum score 550). Application deadline: 7/15 (rolling processing). Application fee: $50 ($55 for international students). *Expenses:* Tuition $19,128 per year full-time, $797 per credit part-time. Fees $99 (one-time charge). *Faculty research:* Occupation epidemiology, cancer.

Announcement: Georgetown University offers a revitalized M Sc program in biostatistics and epidemiology. This 2-year program is structured to accommodate concurrently employed professional and technical workers. The program includes a supervised research experience in a clinical or laboratory setting either at Georgetown or in outside laboratories (e.g., at NIH). Areas of application include design of gene therapy trials, genetic aspects of mental disorders, statistical problems in pathology and laboratory medicine, and mathematical problems in cognitive science. Faculty members include Gary A. Chase, PhD, Director; Leonard Chiazze Jr., Sc D; Manning Feinleib, MD, Dr PH; Mildred E. Francis, PhD; Edmund A. Gehan, PhD; Karen F. Gold, PhD; and John Hanfelt, PhD. For application materials, students should contact the Office of the Dean of Research and Graduate Education, NW103 Medical-Dental Building, 3900 Reservoir Road, NW, Washington, DC 20007-2197; 202-687-3690.

The George Washington University, Columbian School of Arts and Sciences, Program in Epidemiology, Washington, DC 20052. Awards MS, PhD. Faculty: 8 full-time (2 women), 1 (woman) part-time. Students: 2 full-time (both women), 4 part-time (all women); includes 1 minority (Hispanic), 2 international. Average age 30. *Degree requirements:* For master's, comprehensive exams required, thesis not required; for doctorate, dissertation, general exam. *Entrance requirements:* GRE General Test, minimum GPA of 3.0. Application fee: $50. *Expenses:* Tuition $680 per semester hour. Fees $35 per semester hour. *Financial aid:* Fellowships, teaching assistantships available. Financial aid application deadline: 2/1. • Robert Hirsch, Director and Adviser, 202-994-7893.

The George Washington University, School of Public Health and Health Services, Master's Program in Public Health, Track in Epidemiology-Biostatistics, Washington, DC 20052. Awards MPH. Accredited by CEPH. *Degree requirements:* Case study or special project required, thesis not required. *Entrance requirements:* GMAT, GRE General Test, or MCAT; TOEFL. Application deadline: 5/15 (priority date; rolling processing; 11/15 for spring admission). Applica-

Directory: Epidemiology

The George Washington University (continued)

tion fee: $50. *Expenses:* Tuition $680 per semester hour. Fees $35 per semester hour. • Application contact: Michelle Sparacino, Director of Recruitment, 202-994-2160. Fax: 202-994-3773. E-mail: sphhs-info@gwumc.edu.

Announcement: MPH program offers specialty track in epidemiology-biostatistics. MS and PhD in epidemiology and in biostatistics offered in collaboration with statistics department and George Washington Biostatistics Center. Field experience and research opportunities in nations's capital, including the National Cancer Institute. Evening and late afternoon classes. Visit the Web site (http://www.gwumc.edu/sphhs).

See in-depth description on page 1495.

Harvard University, School of Public Health, Department of Epidemiology, Boston, MA 02115. Awards SM, DPH, SD. Part-time programs available. Faculty: 13 full-time (5 women), 28 part-time (9 women). Students: 88 full-time (61 women), 36 part-time (16 women); includes 16 minority (2 African Americans, 11 Asian Americans, 3 Hispanics), 37 international. Average age 32. 178 applicants, 55% accepted. In 1997, 34 master's, 4 doctorates awarded. *Degree requirements:* For doctorate, dissertation, qualifying exam. *Entrance requirements:* GRE, TOEFL (minimum score 550). Application deadline: 1/4. Application fee: $60. *Expenses:* Tuition $21,895 per year full-time, $10,948 per year part-time. Fees $686 per year. *Financial aid:* Fellowships, partial tuition waivers, Federal Work-Study available. Aid available to part-time students. Financial aid application deadline: 2/12; applicants required to submit FAFSA. *Faculty research:* Breast, kidney, and pancreas cancer; Hodgkin's disease; nutritional epidemiology; congenital abnormalities; international variations in disease abnormalities. • Dr. Alexander Walker, Chairman, 617-432-1050. Application contact: Carrie Daniels, Assistant Director of Admissions, 617-432-1031. Fax: 617-432-2009. E-mail: admisofc@sph.harvard.edu.

Harvard University, School of Public Health, Department of Nutrition, Boston, MA 02115. Offers program in epidemiology/international nutrition (DPH, SD). Faculty: 8 full-time (2 women), 7 part-time (2 women). Students: 14 full-time (12 women), 2 part-time (both women); includes 5 minority (all Asian Americans), 8 international. Average age 30. 22 applicants, 36% accepted. In 1997, 2 degrees awarded. *Degree requirements:* Dissertation, qualifying exam. *Entrance requirements:* GRE, TOEFL (minimum score 550). Application deadline: 1/4. Application fee: $60. *Expenses:* Tuition $21,895 per year full-time, $10,948 per year part-time. Fees $686 per year. *Financial aid:* Fellowships, partial tuition waivers, Federal Work-Study available. Aid available to part-time students. Financial aid application deadline: 2/12; applicants required to submit FAFSA. *Faculty research:* Regulation of cell growth by hormonal growth factors, mechanisms of vitamin D, effects of diet on metabolism by gut flora. • Dr. Walter Willett, Chairman, 617-432-1333. Application contact: Carrie Daniels, Assistant Director of Admissions, 617-432-1031. Fax: 617-432-2009. E-mail: admisofc@sph.harvard.edu.

Harvard University, School of Public Health, Department of Environmental Health, Program in Environmental Epidemiology, Boston, MA 02115. Awards SM, SD. *Degree requirements:* For doctorate, dissertation, qualifying exam. *Entrance requirements:* GRE, TOEFL (minimum score 550). Application deadline: 1/4. Application fee: $60. *Expenses:* Tuition $21,895 per year full-time, $10,948 per year part-time. Fees $686 per year. *Financial aid:* Federal Work-Study available. Aid available to part-time students. Financial aid application deadline: 2/12; applicants required to submit FAFSA. • Dr. Frank Speizer, Director, 617-432-4640.

Johns Hopkins University, School of Hygiene and Public Health, Department of Epidemiology, Baltimore, MD 21205. Offers programs in chronic disease epidemiology (MHS, Sc M, Dr PH, PhD, Sc D), clinical epidemiology (MHS, Sc M, Dr PH, PhD, Sc D), epidemiology (MHS, Sc M, Dr PH, PhD, Sc D), genetics (MHS, Sc M, Dr PH, PhD, Sc D), infectious disease (MHS, Sc M, Dr PH, PhD, Sc D), occupational/environmental epidemiology (MHS, Sc M, Dr PH, PhD, Sc D). Faculty: 49 full-time, 57 part-time. Students: 170 (113 women); includes 34 minority (6 African Americans, 23 Asian Americans, 5 Hispanics), 42 international. 258 applicants, 53% accepted. In 1997, 14 master's, 14 doctorates awarded. *Degree requirements:* For master's, thesis (for some programs); for doctorate, dissertation, 1 year full-time residency, oral and written exams required, foreign language not required. *Entrance requirements:* GRE General Test. Application deadline: 2/1 (priority date; rolling processing). Application fee: $60. *Financial aid:* Scholarships, Federal Work-Study, institutionally sponsored loans available. Aid available to part-time students. Financial aid application deadline: 4/15. *Faculty research:* Cancer and congenital malformations, nutritional epidemiology, AIDS, tuberculosis, cardiovascular disease, risk assessment. Total annual research expenditures: $33.2 million. • Dr. Jonathan Samet, Chairman, 410-955-3286. Application contact: Dr. Adolfo Correa, Chair, Admissions/Credentials Committee, 410-955-3483. Fax: 410-955-0863. E-mail: acorrea@jhsph.edu.

Johns Hopkins University, School of Hygiene and Public Health, Program in Public Health, Baltimore, MD 21205. Offerings include epidemiology (MPH). Accredited by CEPH. *Entrance requirements:* GRE General Test, TOEFL (minimum score 550), 2 years of work related experience. Application deadline: 2/1 (priority date; rolling processing). Application fee: $60. • Dr. Miriam Alexander, Director, 410-955-1291. Application contact: Lenora Davis, Administrator, 410-955-1291. Fax: 410-955-4749. E-mail: lrdavis@jhsph.edu.

Johns Hopkins University, School of Hygiene and Public Health, Department of International Health, Division of Disease Control, Baltimore, MD 21205. Awards MHS, Dr PH, PhD, Sc D. *Degree requirements:* For master's, internship; for doctorate, dissertation, 1 year full-time residency, oral and written exams required, foreign language not required. *Entrance requirements:* GRE General Test. Application deadline: 2/1 (priority date; rolling processing). Application fee: $60. *Financial aid:* Scholarships, Federal Work-Study, institutionally sponsored loans available. Aid available to part-time students. Financial aid application deadline: 4/15. *Faculty research:* AIDS epidemiology and control, diarrheal diseases, vaccine development, immunization programs. • Dr. Neal Halsey, Director, 410-955-6964. Application contact: Nancy Stephens, Student Coordinator, 410-955-3734. Fax: 410-955-8734. E-mail: nstephen@jhsph.edu.

Loma Linda University, School of Public Health, Programs in Epidemiology, Loma Linda, CA 92350. Awards MPH, Dr PH. One or more programs accredited by CEPH. Students: 22 full-time (6 women), 14 part-time (7 women); includes 6 international. 22 applicants, 68% accepted. In 1997, 6 master's awarded. Terminal master's awarded for partial completion of doctoral program. *Degree requirements:* For doctorate, dissertation. *Entrance requirements:* For master's, Michigan English Language Assessment Battery (minimum score 92) or TOEFL (minimum score 600); for doctorate, GRE General Test (minimum combined score of 1500 on three sections). Application deadline: rolling. Application fee: $100. *Tuition:* $380 per unit. *Financial aid:* Application deadline 5/15. *Faculty research:* Aging (Alzheimer's disease), CDV, nutrition and chronic disease, smoking. • Dr. Synnove Knutsen, Chair, 909-824-4753. Fax: 909-824-4087. Application contact: Terri Tamayose, Director of Admissions and Academic Records, 909-824-4694. Fax: 909-824-8087. E-mail: ttamayose@sph.llu.edu.

Announcement: The department offers Master of Public Health (MPH) degrees in biostatistics, environmental epidemiology, epidemiology, health services research, medical epidemiology, and nutritional epidemiology as well as a Doctor of Public Health degree in epidemiology. Students learn skills necessary to function in public health departments, in research, or as research/statistical consultants. Major research areas include the effect of lifestyle on occurrence of chronic diseases such as coronary heart disease, cancer, and osteoporosis as well as the effect of air pollution on respiratory health and cancer. Students with varied backgrounds and quantitative skills are encouraged to apply to the biostatistics program. The epidemiology programs are open to students with prior course work in biological sciences. An MPH in epidemiology or biostatistics is an excellent complement to other health professional degrees (MD, DDS, RN, etc.) and can be taken either en route to these studies or subsequent to them. The MPH may also be the terminal degree for the health professional.

McGill University, Faculty of Graduate Studies and Research, Faculty of Medicine, Department of Epidemiology and Biostatistics, Montréal, PQ H3A 2T5, Canada. Offers programs in community health (M Sc), environmental health (M Sc), epidemiology (M Sc), epidemiology and biostatistics (PhD, Diploma), health care evaluation (M Sc), medical statistics (M Sc), occupational health (M Sc). One or more programs accredited by CEPH. Faculty: 35 full-time (7 women), 23 part-time (6 women). Students: 49 full-time (33 women), 32 part-time (17 women); includes 14 international. Average age 30. 86 applicants, 79% accepted. In 1997, 14 master's, 6 doctorates awarded. *Degree requirements:* For master's, thesis optional, foreign language not required; for doctorate, dissertation required, foreign language not required. *Entrance requirements:* For master's, GRE, minimum GPA of 3.0; for doctorate, GRE. Application deadline: 3/1 (rolling processing). Application fee: $60. *Expenses:* Tuition $1668 per year for Canadian residents; $8268 per year for nonresidents. Fees $828 per year for Canadian residents; $1216 per year for nonresidents. *Financial aid:* Full tuition waivers available. Financial aid application deadline: 2/1. *Faculty research:* Chronic and infectious disease epidemiology, health services research, pharmacoepidemiology. • Dr. G. Theriault, Chair, Graduate Committee, 514-398-6259. E-mail: gtheri@epid.lan.mcgill.ca. Application contact: Marlene Abrams, Secretary for Graduate Studies, 514-398-6269. Fax: 514-398-4503. E-mail: marlene@epid.lan.mcgill.ca.

Medical College of Wisconsin, Program in Epidemiology, Milwaukee, WI 53226-0509. Awards MS. Part-time programs available. Faculty: 1 (woman) full-time, 7 part-time (0 women). Students: 3 full-time (0 women), 8 part-time (2 women); includes 6 international. Average age 30. 6 applicants, 67% accepted. In 1997, 2 degrees awarded (100% found work related to degree). *Degree requirements:* Computer language, thesis required, foreign language not required. *Average time to degree:* master's–2 years full-time, 4 years part-time. *Entrance requirements:* GRE General Test, TOEFL (minimum score 580), interview. Application deadline: 2/15 (priority date; rolling processing). Application fee: $40. *Expenses:* Tuition $9135 per year full-time, $509 per credit part-time. Fees $115 per year. *Financial aid:* Available to part-time students. Financial aid application deadline: 2/15; applicants required to submit FAFSA. *Faculty research:* Descriptive epidemiology of health care delivery using large databases. • Dr. Richard A. Cooper, Director, 414-456-8762. E-mail: rcooper@post.its.mcw.edu. Application contact: Dr. Craig Beam, Program Director, 414-456-4320. Fax: 414-266-8444.

Medical University of South Carolina, Department of Biometry and Epidemiology, Charleston, SC 29425-0002. Awards MS, PhD, MD/PhD. Programs in biometrics (MS, PhD), biostatistics (MS, PhD), epidemiology (MS, PhD). Faculty: 16 part-time (3 women). Students: 37 full-time (18 women); includes 1 minority (African American), 8 international. Average age 33. 21 applicants, 67% accepted. In 1997, 6 master's, 7 doctorates awarded. Terminal master's awarded for partial completion of doctoral program. *Degree requirements:* For master's, thesis, research seminar; for doctorate, dissertation, teaching and research seminar, oral and written exams. *Entrance requirements:* GRE General Test (minimum combined score of 1650 on three sections), GRE Subject Test (international applicants), TOEFL, interview. Application deadline: rolling. Application fee: $55. Electronic applications accepted. *Expenses:* Tuition $3212 per year (minimum) full-time, $1515 per year (minimum) part-time for state residents; $4112 per year (minimum) full-time, $2015 per year (minimum) part-time for nonresidents. Fees $80 per year (minimum). *Financial aid:* In 1997–98, 9 fellowships (6 to first-year students) averaging $1,250 per month were awarded; research assistantships, teaching assistantships, partial tuition waivers, Federal Work-Study also available. Aid available to part-time students. Financial aid application deadline: 4/1; applicants required to submit FAFSA. *Faculty research:* Statistical modeling, survival analysis, cardiovascular epidemiology, biomathematics, biomedical computing. • Dr. John Dunbar III, Interim Chairman, 843-876-1100. Application contact: Julie Johnston, Director of Admissions, 843-792-8710.

Memorial University of Newfoundland, Faculty of Medicine and School of Graduate Studies, Graduate Programs in Medicine, Division of Community Health, St. John's, NF A1C 5S7, Canada. Offerings include clinical epidemiology (M Sc, PhD, Diploma). Division faculty: 15 full-time (3 women), 2 part-time (1 woman). *Degree requirements:* For master's, thesis required, foreign language not required; for doctorate, comprehensive exam, oral defense of thesis required, foreign language not required. *Entrance requirements:* For master's, TOEFL, MD or B Sc; for doctorate, TOEFL, MD or M Sc. Application deadline: 3/31 (priority date; rolling processing). Application fee: $40. *Expenses:* Tuition $1896 per year (minimum). Fees $60 per year for Canadian residents; $621 per year for nonresidents. • Dr. Roy West, Associate Dean, 709-737-6693.

Michigan State University, College of Human Medicine and Graduate School, Graduate Programs in Human Medicine, Department of Epidemiology, East Lansing, MI 48824-1316. Awards MS. Faculty: 3 (1 woman). Students: 29 (18 women); includes 5 minority (all Asian Americans), 6 international. In 1997, 2 degrees awarded. *Degree requirements:* Thesis, oral exam. *Entrance requirements:* GRE General Test, MCAT or ECFMG, TOEFL, minimum GPA of 3.0. Application fee: $30 ($40 for international students). *Expenses:* Tuition $4609 per year (minimum) full-time, $223 per credit hour (minimum) part-time for state residents; $8704 per year (minimum) full-time, $450 per credit hour (minimum) part-time for nonresidents. Fees $576 per year full-time, $476 per year part-time. • Dr. Nigel Paneth, Chairperson, 517-432-1130. E-mail: paneth@pilot.msu.edu. Application contact: Lora A. McAdams, Graduate Secretary, 517-432-3921. Fax: 517-432-1130. E-mail: kemler@pilot.msu.edu.

See in-depth description on page 1505.

New York Medical College, Graduate School of Health Sciences, Program in Biostatistics and Epidemiology, Valhalla, NY 10595-1691. Awards MPH, MS. Part-time and evening/weekend programs available. *Degree requirements:* Computer language required, foreign language not required. *Entrance requirements:* TOEFL. Application deadline: 7/20 (priority date; rolling processing; 12/1 for spring admission). Application fee: $35 ($60 for international students). *Tuition:* $415 per credit. *Financial aid:* Federal Work-Study, institutionally sponsored loans, and career-related internships or fieldwork available. Financial aid application deadline: 6/15. • Dr. Paul Visintainer, Director, 914-594-4817.

See in-depth description on page 1507.

New York University, Graduate School of Arts and Science, Nelson Institute of Environmental Medicine, Program in Environmental Health Sciences, New York, NY 10012-1019. Offerings include environmental epidemiology and biostatistics (PhD). Program faculty: 26 full-time (7 women). *Degree requirements:* 1 foreign language, dissertation, oral and written exams. *Entrance requirements:* GRE General Test, GRE Subject Test, TOEFL, minimum GPA of 3.0; bachelor's degree in biological, physical, or engineering science. Application deadline: 8/1 (12/1 for spring admission). Application fee: $60. *Expenses:* Tuition $715 per credit. Fees $1048 per year full-time, $229 per semester (minimum) part-time. • Application contact: Richard Schlesinger, Director of Graduate Studies, 914-885-5281.

North Carolina State University, College of Veterinary Medicine and Graduate School, Graduate Programs in Comparative Biomedical Sciences, Raleigh, NC 27695. Offerings include epidemiology and population medicine (MS, PhD). Faculty: 116 full-time (27 women), 51 part-time (7 women). *Degree requirements:* Thesis/dissertation. *Entrance requirements:* GRE General Test (minimum combined score of 1100). Application deadline: 6/25 (rolling processing; 11/25 for spring admission). Application fee: $45. *Tuition:* $2370 per year full-time, $517 per semester (minimum) part-time for state residents; $11,536 per year full-time, $2809 per semester (minimum) part-time for nonresidents. • Dr. Jack H. Britt, Associate Dean, 919-829-4213. Fax: 919-829-4222. E-mail: jack_britt@ncsu.edu.

Oregon Health Sciences University, School of Medicine, Department of Public Health and Preventive Medicine, 3181 SW Sam Jackson Park Road, Portland, OR 97201-3098. Awards MPH, MD/MPH. Program in epidemiology and biostatistics (MPH). Preaccredited by CEPH. Part-time programs available. Faculty: 26 part-time (8 women), 4.61 FTE. Students: 39 full-time (24 women); includes 3 minority (all Asian Americans), 1 international. Average age 27. 106 applicants, 19% accepted. *Degree requirements:* Thesis, fieldwork/internship required, foreign language not required. *Average time to degree:* master's–1.5 years full-time, 3 years part-time. *Entrance requirements:* GRE General Test (minimum combined score of 1000; average 1200), TOEFL, previous undergraduate course work in statistics. Application deadline: 1/16 (rolling processing). Application fee: $40. *Financial aid:* In 1997–98, 2 research assistantships averaging $729 per month and totaling $17,496 were awarded; Federal Work-Study, institutionally sponsored loans, and career-related internships or fieldwork also available. Aid available to part-time students. Financial aid applicants required to submit FAFSA. *Faculty research:* Health services, health care access, health policy, environmental and occupational health. Total annual research expenditures: $276,453. • Dr. Merwyn R. Greenlick, Professor and Chair, 503-494-8257. E-mail: mitchg@ohsu.edu. Application contact: Dr. Katherine J. Riley, Department Administrator, 503-494-2556. Fax: 503-494-4981. E-mail: rileyk@ohsu.edu.

Purdue University, School of Veterinary Medicine and Graduate School, Graduate Programs in Veterinary Medicine, Department of Veterinary Pathobiology, West Lafayette, IN 47907. Offerings include epidemiology (MS, PhD). Terminal master's awarded for partial completion of doctoral program. Department faculty: 26 full-time (3 women). *Degree requirements:* For master's, thesis required (for some programs), foreign language not required; for doctorate, dissertation required, foreign language not required. *Entrance requirements:* GRE General Test, TOEFL (minimum score 575). Application fee: $30. • Dr. H. L. Thacker, Interim Head, 765-494-7543.

Queen's University at Kingston, Faculty of Medicine and School of Graduate Studies and Research, Graduate Programs in Medicine, Department of Community Health and Epidemiology, Kingston, ON K7L 3N6, Canada. Offers programs in biostatistics (M Sc), environmental and occupational health (M Sc), epidemiology (M Sc), general community health (M Sc), health-care systems (M Sc), preventive medicine (M Sc). Part-time programs available. Students: 21 full-time (16 women), 16 part-time (11 women). In 1997, 16 degrees awarded. *Degree requirements:* Thesis required, foreign language not required. *Entrance requirements:* TOEFL (minimum score 550). Application fee: $60. Electronic applications accepted. *Tuition:* $3803 per year (minimum) full-time, $1901 per year (minimum) part-time for Canadian residents; $7330 per year (minimum) for nonresidents. *Financial aid:* Fellowships, institutionally sponsored loans available. Financial aid application deadline: 3/1. • Dr. J. L. Pater, Graduate Coordinator, 613-545-2901. Application contact: R. E. M. Lees, Graduate Coordinator, 613-545-4954.

San Diego State University, College of Health and Human Services, Graduate School of Public Health, San Diego, CA 92182. Offerings include epidemiology (MPH, PhD), with option in biostatistics (MPH). One or more programs accredited by CEPH. School faculty: 25 full-time (9 women), 36 part-time (21 women). *Degree requirements:* For doctorate, dissertation required, foreign language not required. *Entrance requirements:* For doctorate, GRE General Test. Application deadline: 5/15 (priority date; rolling processing; 10/15 for spring admission). Application fee: $55. *Expenses:* Tuition $0 for state residents; $246 per unit for nonresidents. Fees $1932 per year full-time, $1266 per year part-time. • Dr. Kenneth Bart, Director, 619-594-6317. Application contact: Brenda Fass-Holmes, Coordinator, Admissions and Student Affairs, 619-594-6317. E-mail: bholmes@mail.sdsu.edu.

Stanford University, School of Medicine, Graduate Programs in Medicine, Department of Epidemiology, Stanford, CA 94305-9991. Awards MS, PhD. Students: 12 full-time (7 women), 2 part-time (both women); includes 4 minority (2 African Americans, 2 Asian Americans). Average age 30. 28 applicants, 7% accepted. In 1997, 7 master's awarded. *Degree requirements:* Thesis/dissertation. *Entrance requirements:* GRE General Test, TOEFL. Application deadline: 1/15. Application fee: $65 ($75 for international students). *Expenses:* Tuition $22,110 per year. Fees $156 per year. • Application contact: Jill Galinus, Admissions Officer, 650-723-5456.

State University of New York at Albany, School of Public Health, Department of Epidemiology, Executive Park South, Albany, NY 12203-3727. Awards MS, PhD. Faculty: 3 full-time (2 women). Students: 13 full-time (9 women), 13 part-time (8 women); includes 4 international. 25 applicants, 56% accepted. In 1997, 5 master's awarded. *Degree requirements:* For master's, thesis, computer application in epidemiology; for doctorate, dissertation. *Entrance requirements:* GRE General Test. Application fee: $50. *Expenses:* Tuition $5100 per year full-time, $213 per credit hour part-time for state residents; $8416 per year full-time, $351 per credit hour part-time for nonresidents. Fees $705 per year full-time, $26.85 per credit hour part-time. • Dr. David Strogatz, Chair, 518-402-0400.

State University of New York at Buffalo, Graduate School, School of Medicine, Graduate Programs in Medicine, Department of Social and Preventive Medicine, Buffalo, NY 14214. Offers programs in epidemiology (MS), epidemiology and community health (PhD). Part-time programs available. Faculty: 12 full-time (4 women), 3 part-time (1 woman). Students: 24 full-time (14 women), 38 part-time (26 women); includes 6 minority (1 African American, 4 Asian Americans, 1 Hispanic), 13 international. Average age 27. 24 applicants, 58% accepted. In 1997, 3 master's, 4 doctorates awarded. *Degree requirements:* Thesis/dissertation. *Entrance requirements:* For master's, GRE General Test, TOEFL (minimum score 550); for doctorate, GRE General Test, TOEFL. Application deadline: 4/15 (priority date; rolling processing; 10/1 for spring admission). Application fee: $35. *Tuition:* $5970 per year full-time, $288 per credit hour part-time for state residents; $9286 per year full-time, $426 per credit hour part-time for nonresidents. *Financial aid:* In 1997–98, 4 fellowships, 4 research assistantships, 1 teaching assistantship were awarded; full and partial tuition waivers, Federal Work-Study, institutionally sponsored loans also available. Financial aid application deadline: 2/28. *Faculty research:* Health services research, cancer and nutrition, cardiovascular disease, reproductive. • Dr. Maurizio Trevisan, Chairman, 716-829-2975. Application contact: Dr. John E. Vena, Director of Graduate Studies, 716-829-2975. Fax: 716-829-2979. E-mail: jvena@acsu.buffaol.edu.

Texas A&M University, College of Veterinary Medicine and Office of Graduate Studies, Graduate Programs in Veterinary Medicine, Department of Veterinary Anatomy and Public Health, College Station, TX 77843. Offerings include epidemiology (MS). Department faculty: 33 full-time (9 women), 7 part-time (2 women), 37.6 FTE. *Degree requirements:* Thesis required, foreign language not required. *Entrance requirements:* GRE General Test, TOEFL. Application deadline: 7/15 (priority date; rolling processing; 10/1 for spring admission). Application fee: $35 ($75 for international students). • Gerald Bratton, Head, 409-845-2828. Fax: 409-847-8981.

Tulane University, School of Public Health and Tropical Medicine, Department of Epidemiology, New Orleans, LA 70118-5669. Awards MPH, MS, Dr PH, PhD. One or more programs accredited by CEPH. MS and PhD offered through the Graduate School. Part-time programs available. Students: 50 full-time (25 women), 7 part-time (4 women); includes 17 minority (9 African Americans, 4 Asian Americans, 4 Hispanics), 12 international. Average age 31. 22 applicants, 45% accepted. In 1997, 2 doctorates awarded. Terminal master's awarded for partial completion of doctoral program. *Degree requirements:* For master's, 1 foreign language required, thesis not required; for doctorate, 1 foreign language, dissertation, comprehensive exam. *Entrance requirements:* For master's, GRE General Test (minimum combined score of 1000; average 1100), TOEFL (minimum score 525); for doctorate, GRE General Test (minimum combined score of 1000; average 1250), TOEFL (minimum score 525). Application deadline: 4/15 (priority date; rolling processing; 10/15 for spring admission). Application fee: $40. *Financial aid:* In 1997–98, 2 research assistantships (both to first-year students) were awarded; teaching assistantships, Federal Work-Study, institutionally sponsored loans also available. Financial aid application deadline: 2/1. *Faculty research:* Environment, cancer, cardiovascular epidemiology, women's health. • Dr. Larry Webber, Chairman, 504-588-5164. Fax: 504-584-1706.

Université Laval, Faculties of Medicine and Graduate Studies, Graduate Programs in Medicine, Department of Medicine, Program in Epidemiology, Sainte-Foy, PQ G1K 7P4, Canada. Awards M Sc, PhD. Students: 41 full-time (23 women), 31 part-time (20 women). 36 applicants, 89% accepted. In 1997, 11 master's, 1 doctorate awarded. *Application deadline:* 3/1. *Application fee:* $30. *Expenses:* Tuition $1334 per year (minimum) full-time, $56 per credit (minimum) part-time for Canadian residents; $5966 per year (minimum) full-time, $249 per credit (minimum) part-time for nonresidents. Fees $150 per year full-time, $6.25 per credit part-time. • Francois Meyer, Director, 418-682-7615. Fax: 418-682-7949. E-mail: francois.meyer@gre.ulaval.ca.

The University of Alabama at Birmingham, Graduate School, School of Public Health, Department of Epidemiology, Birmingham, AL 35294. Awards MPH, MSPH, Dr PH, PhD, MPH/PhD. One or more programs accredited by CEPH. Students: 13 full-time (9 women), 7 part-time (4 women); includes 3 minority (1 African American, 2 Asian Americans). 15 applicants, 100% accepted. In 1997, 1 doctorate awarded. *Degree requirements:* For master's, fieldwork, research project required, foreign language and thesis not required; for doctorate, dissertation required, foreign language not required. *Entrance requirements:* For master's, GRE General Test or MAT; for doctorate, GRE General Test or MAT, MPH or MSPH. Application deadline: rolling. Application fee: $30 ($60 for international students). Electronic applications accepted. *Expenses:* Tuition $3672 per year full-time, $102 per credit hour part-time for state residents; $7344 per year full-time, $204 per credit hour part-time for nonresidents. Fees $699 per year (minimum) full-time, $116 per quarter (minimum) part-time. *Financial aid:* Career-related internships or fieldwork available. *Faculty research:* Biometry. • Dr. Sten Vermund, Chairman, 205-934-6707. Application contact: Nancy Pinson, Coordinator of Student Admissions, 205-934-4993. Fax: 205-975-5484. E-mail: osas@ms.soph.uab.edu.

See in-depth description on page 1523.

University of Alberta, Faculties of Medicine and Oral Health Sciences and Graduate Studies and Research, Graduate Programs in Medicine, Department of Public Health Sciences, Edmonton, AB T6G 2E1, Canada. Offerings include epidemiology (M Sc, PhD). Terminal master's awarded for partial completion of doctoral program. Department faculty: 20 full-time, 11 part-time. *Degree requirements:* For doctorate, dissertation required, foreign language not required. *Average time to degree:* master's–2 years full-time, 4 years part-time; doctorate–4 years full-time, 6 years part-time. *Application deadline:* 2/1 (priority date; rolling processing). *Application fee:* $60. • Dr. T. W. Noseworthy, Chair, 403-492-6408. Application contact: Felicity Hey, Graduate Programs Administrator, 403-492-6407. Fax: 403-492-0364. E-mail: felicity.hey@ualberta.ca.

The University of Arizona, Graduate Interdisciplinary Programs, Graduate Interdisciplinary Program in Epidemiology, Tucson, AZ 85721. Awards MS, PhD. *Entrance requirements:* TOEFL. Application fee: $35. *Tuition:* $2162 per year full-time, $337 per semester (minimum) part-time for state residents; $6860 per year full-time, $1138 per semester (minimum) part-time for nonresidents.

University of British Columbia, Faculties of Medicine and Graduate Studies, Graduate Programs in Medicine, Department of Health Care and Epidemiology, Vancouver, BC V6T 1W5, Canada. Offers programs in clinical epidemiology (MH Sc), community health (MH Sc), epidemiology/clinical epidemiology (M Sc, PhD), health administration (MHA), health services research (M Sc, PhD), occupational and environmental health (M Sc, PhD), occupational health (MH Sc). One or more programs accredited by CEPH. Part-time programs available. *Degree requirements:* Thesis/dissertation. *Average time to degree:* master's–3 years full-time, 4 years part-time. *Entrance requirements:* For master's, GRE General Test (minimum score 500 on each section required for M Sc), (minimum combined score of 1500 required for MHA), MD or equivalent (MH Sc); for doctorate, work experience. Application deadline: 3/31 (rolling processing). Application fee: $50. *Faculty research:* AIDS, public health, environmental toxicology, infectious diseases, health evaluation.

The University of Calgary, Faculties of Medicine and Graduate Studies, Department of Microbiology and Infectious Diseases, Calgary, AB T2N 1N4, Canada. Awards M Sc, PhD. Faculty: 26 full-time (4 women), 10 part-time (0 women). Students: 24 full-time (10 women). Average age 28. 20 applicants, 20% accepted. In 1997, 1 master's, 4 doctorates awarded. *Degree requirements:* For master's, thesis required, foreign language not required; for doctorate, dissertation, candidacy exam required, foreign language not required. *Entrance requirements:* TOEFL (minimum score 580), minimum GPA of 3.2. Application deadline: 5/31 (priority date; rolling processing; 1/31 for spring admission). Application fee: $60. Electronic applications accepted. *Tuition:* $6110 per year for Canadian residents; $30,000 per year for nonresidents. *Financial aid:* 3 students received aid. Financial aid application deadline: 2/1. *Faculty research:* Bacteriology, virology, parasitology, immunology. Total annual research expenditures: $3.5 million. • Dr. Patrick W. K. Lee, Graduate Coordinator, 403-220-7548. E-mail: hartd@acs.ucalgary.ca. Application contact: Susan Dooley, Secretary, 403-220-4572. Fax: 403-270-2772. E-mail: midgrad@acs.ucalgary.ca.

University of California, Berkeley, Group in Epidemiology, Berkeley, CA 94720-1500. Awards MPH, MS, PhD. Accredited by CEPH. Students: 34 full-time (29 women); includes 5 minority (1 African American, 2 Asian Americans, 2 Hispanics), 5 international. 52 applicants, 12% accepted. In 1997, 8 doctorates awarded. *Degree requirements:* For master's, comprehensive exam; for doctorate, dissertation, oral and written qualifying exams. *Entrance requirements:* For master's, GRE General Test, minimum GPA of 3.0; MD, DDS, DVM, or PhD in biomedical science (1 year MPH program); for doctorate, GRE General Test, minimum GPA of 3.0. Application deadline: 1/12. Application fee: $40. *Expenses:* Tuition $0 for state residents; $9384 per year for nonresidents. Fees $4409 per year. *Financial aid:* Fellowships, research assistantships, teaching assistantships available. Financial aid application deadline: 12/15. • Dr. Arthur L. Reingold, Chair, 510-642-0327. Application contact: Ron Jeremicz, Graduate Assistant, 510-643-9912. Fax: 510-643-5163. E-mail: rtj@uclink2.berkeley.edu.

University of California, Berkeley, School of Public Health, Division of Public Health Biology and Epidemiology, Berkeley, CA 94720-1500. Offers programs in epidemiology (MPH, MS, PhD), epidemiology/biostatistics (MPH), infectious diseases (MA, MPH, PhD). One or more programs accredited by CEPH. *Degree requirements:* For master's, comprehensive exam; for doctorate, dissertation, oral and written exam. *Entrance requirements:* For master's, GRE General Test, minimum GPA of 3.0; MD, DDS, DVM, or PhD in a biomedical science (1 year MPH program); for doctorate, GRE General Test, minimum GPA of 3.0. Application deadline: 12/16 (priority date). Application fee: $40. *Expenses:* Tuition $0 for state residents; $9384 per year for nonresidents. Fees $4409 per year. *Financial aid:* Fellowships, research assistantships, teaching assistantships, Federal Work-Study available. Financial aid application deadline: 12/16. • Dr. Arthur L. Reingold, Head, 510-642-0327. Application contact: Ron Jeremicz, Graduate Assistant, 510-643-9912. Fax: 510-643-5163. E-mail: rtj@uclink2.berkeley.edu.

University of California, Davis, Programs in the Biological Sciences, Program in Epidemiology, Davis, CA 95616. Awards MS, PhD. Faculty: 39 full-time (8 women). Students: 21 full-time (13 women), 2 part-time (both women); includes 1 minority (Hispanic), 3 international. 21 applicants, 52% accepted. *Entrance requirements:* GRE General Test, GRE Subject Test (biology), minimum GPA of 3.0. Application deadline: 2/15 (rolling processing). Application fee: $40. *Expenses:* Tuition $0 for state residents; $9384 per year for nonresidents. Fees $4466 per year full-time, $2923 per year part-time. *Financial aid:* Federal Work-Study, institutionally sponsored loans available. Financial aid application deadline: 3/1; applicants required to submit FAFSA. *Faculty research:* Environmental/occupational wildlife, reproductive and veterinary epidemiology, infectious/chronic disease epidemiology, public health. • Tim E. Carpenter, Chair, 530-752-9174. E-mail: tecarpenter@ucdavis.edu. Application contact: Lorna McAdam, Graduate Program Staff, 530-752-8340. Fax: 530-752-0414. E-mail: ljmcadam@ucdavis.edu.

University of California, Los Angeles, School of Public Health, Department of Epidemiology, Los Angeles, CA 90095. Awards MS, PhD. Faculty: 6 (0 women). Students: 37 full-time (15 women); includes 6 minority (1 African American, 4 Asian Americans, 1 Hispanic), 15 international. 49 applicants, 27% accepted. *Degree requirements:* For master's, comprehensive exam or thesis required, foreign language not required; for doctorate, dissertation, oral and written qualifying exams required, foreign language not required. *Entrance requirements:* For master's, GRE General Test (minimum combined score of 1100), minimum GPA of 3.0; for doctorate, GRE General Test (minimum combined score of 1200), minimum undergraduate GPA of 3.0. Application deadline: 12/15. Application fee: $40. Electronic applications accepted.

Directory: Epidemiology

University of California, Los Angeles (continued)

Expenses: Tuition $0 for state residents; $9384 per year for nonresidents. Fees $4551 per year. *Financial aid:* In 1997–98, 31 students received aid, including fellowships totaling $35,069, research assistantships totaling $2,397, teaching assistantships totaling $26,440, federal fellowships and scholarships totaling $435,807. Financial aid application deadline: 3/1. • Dr. Ralph R. Frerichs, Chair, 310-206-3901. Application contact: Departmental Office, 310-206-3901. E-mail: app_epid@admin.ph.ucla.edu.

University of California, San Diego, Program in Public Health and Epidemiology, 9500 Gilman Drive, La Jolla, CA 92093-5003. Awards PhD. Offered jointly with San Diego State University. Students: 13 (9 women). *Application fee:* $40. *Expenses:* Tuition $0 for state residents; $9384 per year full-time, $4692 per year part-time for nonresidents. Fees $4887 per year full-time, $3344 per year part-time. • Deborah Wingard, Head. Application contact: Graduate Coordinator, 619-534-3720.

University of Cincinnati, College of Medicine, Graduate Programs in Medicine, Department of Environmental Health, Cincinnati, OH 45267. Offerings include epidemiology and biostatistics (MS). Department faculty: 23 full-time. *Degree requirements:* Thesis required, foreign language not required. *Average time to degree:* master's–2.8 years full-time; doctorate–8.8 years full-time. *Entrance requirements:* GRE General Test, TOEFL, bachelor's degree in science. Application deadline: 2/1 (priority date; rolling processing). Application fee: $30. *Tuition:* $7228 per year full-time, $185 per credit hour part-time for state residents; $13,812 per year full-time, $352 per credit hour part-time for nonresidents. • Dr. Marshall W. Anderson, Chairman, 513-558-5701. Fax: 513-558-4397. E-mail: marshall.anderson@uc.edu. Application contact: Judy Jarell, 513-558-1729. E-mail: judy.jarrell@uc.edu.

See in-depth description on page 1527.

University of Guelph, Ontario Veterinary College and Faculty of Graduate Studies, Graduate Programs in Veterinary Sciences, Department of Population Medicine, Guelph, ON N1G 2W1, Canada. Offerings include epidemiology (M Sc, DV Sc, PhD). Department faculty: 23 full-time (4 women), 1 (woman) part-time. *Degree requirements:* Thesis/dissertation. *Application deadline:* 2/1 (rolling processing). *Application fee:* $60. *Expenses:* Tuition $4725 per year full-time, $3165 per year part-time for Canadian residents; $6999 per year for nonresidents. Fees $612 per year full-time, $38 per year (minimum) part-time for Canadian residents; $612 per year for nonresidents. • Dr. S. W. Martin, Chair, 519-827-8800 Ext. 4746. Application contact: Dr. P. Physick-Sheard, Graduate Coordinator, 519-827-8800 Ext. 4053.

University of Hawaii at Manoa, College of Health Sciences and Social Welfare, School of Public Health, Honolulu, HI 96822. Offerings include biostatistics-epidemiology (PhD); epidemiology (MPH, MS), with options in chronic diseases, infectious diseases. Terminal master's awarded for partial completion of doctoral program. School faculty: 18 full-time (8 women), 4 part-time (2 women), 19.6 FTE. *Degree requirements:* For master's, thesis (for some programs). *Average time to degree:* master's–1.2 years full-time, 3 years part-time. *Application deadline:* 3/1 (9/1 for spring admission). *Application fee:* $25 ($50 for international students). *Tuition:* $4029 per year full-time, $214 per credit hour part-time for state residents; $9957 per year full-time, $461 per credit hour part-time for nonresidents. • Dr. D. William Wood, Interim Dean, 808-956-8491. Application contact: Nancy Kilonsky, Assistant Dean, 808-956-8267.

University of Hawaii at Manoa, School of Public Health and Graduate Programs in Biomedical Sciences, Program in Biostatistics-Epidemiology, Honolulu, HI 96822. Awards PhD. Part-time programs available. Faculty: 5 full-time (0 women), 5 part-time (1 woman), 5.35 FTE. Students: 4 full-time (2 women), 6 part-time (5 women); includes 7 minority (all Asian Americans). 7 applicants, 0% accepted. In 1997, 2 doctorates awarded. Terminal master's awarded for partial completion of doctoral program. *Degree requirements:* For doctorate, computer language, dissertation required, foreign language not required. *Entrance requirements:* For doctorate, GRE General Test. Application deadline: 3/1 (9/1 for spring admission). Application fee: $25 ($50 for international students). *Tuition:* $4029 per year full-time, $214 per credit hour part-time for state residents; $9957 per year full-time, $461 per credit hour part-time for nonresidents. *Financial aid:* Career-related internships or fieldwork available. *Faculty research:* Genetic epidemiology, demography, infections and chronic disease epidemiology. • Dr. John Grove, Chairman, 808-956-8577. Application contact: Nancy Kilonsky, Assistant Dean, 808-956-8267.

University of Illinois at Chicago, School of Public Health, Program in Epidemiology and Biostatistics, Chicago, IL 60607-7128. Awards MPH, MS, Dr PH, PhD. One or more programs accredited by CEPH. MS and PhD offered jointly with Graduate College. *Degree requirements:* For master's, thesis, field practicum required, foreign language not required; for doctorate, dissertation, independent research, internship required, foreign language not required. *Entrance requirements:* GRE General Test (minimum combined score of 1000), TOEFL (minimum score 550), minimum GPA of 3.75 on a 5.0 scale. Application deadline: 7/3 (11/8 for spring admission). Application fee: $40 ($50 for international students). • Dr. Paul S. Levy, Director, 312-996-8860. Application contact: Dr. Babette Neuberger, Assistant Dean, 312-996-6625.

The University of Iowa, College of Medicine and Graduate College, Graduate Programs in Medicine, Department of Preventive Medicine and Environmental Health, Iowa City, IA 52242-1316. Offerings include epidemiology (MS, PhD). MS/MA and MS/MS offered jointly with the Program in Urban and Regional Planning. Terminal master's awarded for partial completion of doctoral program. Department faculty: 27 full-time (5 women), 11 part-time (4 women). *Degree requirements:* For master's, computer language (biostatistics) required, thesis optional, foreign language not required; for doctorate, dissertation, computer language (biostatistics and epidemiology) required, foreign language not required. *Average time to degree:* master's–2 years full-time, 6 years part-time; doctorate–5 years full-time, 9 years part-time. *Entrance requirements:* For master's, GRE General Test (minimum combined score of 1050), TOEFL (minimum score 600), minimum GPA of 2.7; for doctorate, GRE General Test (minimum combined score of 1050), TOEFL (minimum score 600), minimum GPA of 3.0. Application deadline: 1/15 (priority date; rolling processing; 10/1 for spring admission). Application fee: $30 ($50 for international students). *Expenses:* Tuition $3166 per year full-time, $176 per credit hour part-time for state residents; $10,202 per year full-time, $567 per credit hour part-time for nonresidents. Fees $101 per year full-time, $51 per year (minimum) part-time. • Dr. James Merchant, Interim Head, 319-335-9833. Fax: 319-335-9772. E-mail: james-merchant@uiowa.edu. Application contact: Barbara Scott, Graduate Studies Coordinator, 319-335-8992. Fax: 319-335-9200. E-mail: barbara-scott@uiowa.edu.

University of Maryland, Baltimore, Graduate School, Graduate Programs in Medicine, Department of Epidemiology and Preventive Medicine, Baltimore, MD 21201-1627. Awards MS, PhD, MD/MS, MD/PhD. Part-time programs available. Faculty: 58. Students: 18 full-time (10 women), 11 part-time (4 women); includes 8 minority (2 African Americans, 6 Asian Americans), 2 international. 66 applicants, 39% accepted. In 1997, 6 master's awarded. *Degree requirements:* For doctorate, 1 foreign language, computer language, dissertation, qualifying exam. *Entrance requirements:* GRE General Test, TOEFL, minimum GPA of 3.0. Application deadline: 7/1. Application fee: $42. *Expenses:* Tuition $253 per credit hour for state residents; $454 per credit hour for nonresidents. Fees $317 per year. *Financial aid:* Fellowships, research assistantships, teaching assistantships, and career-related internships or fieldwork available. Aid available to part-time students. Financial aid application deadline: 2/15. *Faculty research:* Chronic and infectious disease epidemiology, environmental and occupational health, biostatistics, gerontology. • Dr. Paul Stolley, Chairperson, 410-706-7867. Application contact: Dr. Trudy Bush, Program Director, 410-706-2865.

University of Maryland, Baltimore County, Graduate School, Department of Emergency Health Services, Baltimore, MD 21250-5398. Offerings include preventive medicine and epidemiology (MS). *Entrance requirements:* GRE General Test, minimum GPA of 3.0. Application deadline: 7/1. Application fee: $40. *Expenses:* Tuition $260 per credit hour for state residents; $468 per credit hour for nonresidents. Fees $39 per credit hour.

University of Miami, School of Medicine and Graduate School, Graduate Programs in Medicine, Department of Epidemiology and Public Health, Program in Epidemiology, Coral Gables, FL 33124. Awards PhD. Faculty: 18 full-time (6 women), 7 part-time (2 women), 21 FTE. Students: 7 full-time (3 women); includes 3 minority (2 Asian Americans, 1 Hispanic), 2 international. Average age 35. 7 applicants, 14% accepted. *Degree requirements:* Computer language, dissertation required, foreign language not required. *Entrance requirements:* GRE General Test (minimum score 500 on each section), TOEFL (minimum score 550), minimum GPA of 3.0, previous course work in epidemiology and statistics. Application deadline: 4/1 (rolling processing). Application fee: $35. *Expenses:* Tuition $815 per credit hour. Fees $174 per year. *Financial aid:* In 1997–98, 7 students received aid, including 1 fellowship averaging $1,250 per month, 1 research assistantship averaging $1,250 per month; full tuition waivers, Federal Work-Study, institutionally sponsored loans, and career-related internships or fieldwork also available. Financial aid application deadline: 2/1. *Faculty research:* Behavioral epidemiology, nutrition, AIDS, cardiovascular diseases, cancer epidemiology. • Edward Trapido, Director, 305-243-3356. Fax: 305-243-4871. E-mail: etrapido@mednet.med.miami.edu. Application contact: Ana Godur, Administrator, 305-243-6759. Fax: 305-243-5544. E-mail: agodvr@mednet.med.miami.edu.

See in-depth description on page 1533.

University of Michigan, School of Public Health, Department of Epidemiology, Ann Arbor, MI 48109. Offers programs in dental public health (MPH), epidemiologic science (PhD), epidemiology (MPH, Dr PH), hospital and molecular epidemiology (MPH), international health (MPH). One or more programs accredited by CEPH. PhD offered through the Horace H. Rackham School of Graduate Studies. Terminal master's awarded for partial completion of doctoral program. *Degree requirements:* For doctorate, variable foreign language requirement, oral defense of dissertation, preliminary exam. *Entrance requirements:* GRE General Test, MCAT. Application deadline: 3/1 (priority date; rolling processing). Application fee: $55. *Financial aid:* Fellowships, research assistantships, teaching assistantships available. Financial aid application deadline: 3/1. • Dr. George A. Kaplan, Chair, 734-764-5435. E-mail: gkaplan@sph.umich.edu.

See in-depth description on page 1535.

University of Minnesota, Twin Cities Campus, School of Public Health, Major in Epidemiology, Minneapolis, MN 55455-0213. Awards MPH, PhD. One or more programs accredited by CEPH. Part-time programs available. Faculty: 15 full-time. Students: 87; includes 10 minority (2 African Americans, 5 Asian Americans, 3 Hispanics), 7 international. 163 applicants, 48% accepted. In 1997, 21 master's, 5 doctorates awarded. *Degree requirements:* For doctorate, dissertation required, foreign language not required. *Entrance requirements:* For master's, GRE General Test (minimum combined score of 1500 on three sections), minimum GPA of 3.0; for doctorate, GRE General Test (minimum combined score of 1500 on three sections). Application deadline: 2/28 (rolling processing). Application fee: $50 ($75 for international students). *Financial aid:* Research assistantships, teaching assistantships, Federal Work-Study, institutionally sponsored loans available. *Faculty research:* Cardiovascular disease, cancer, infectious diseases, genetic epidemiology. • Dr. John Finnegan, Chair, 612-624-1818. E-mail: finnegan@epivax.epi.umn.edu. Application contact: Andrea Kish, Graduate Studies Coordinator, 612-626-8802. Fax: 612-624-0315. E-mail: kish@epivax.epi.umn.edu.

University of Minnesota, Twin Cities Campus, School of Public Health, Division of Environmental and Occupational Health, Area in Environmental and Occupational Epidemiology, Minneapolis, MN 55455-0213. Awards MPH, MS, PhD. One or more programs accredited by CEPH. *Degree requirements:* For doctorate, dissertation required, foreign language not required. *Entrance requirements:* For master's, GRE General Test (minimum combined score of 1500 on three sections), minimum GPA of 3.0; for doctorate, GRE General Test (minimum combined score of 1500 on three sections). Application deadline: 4/15 (priority date; rolling processing). Application fee: $50 ($75 for international students). *Financial aid:* Application deadline 4/15. • Application contact: Kathy Soupir, Student Coordinator, 612-625-0622. Fax: 612-626-4837. E-mail: ksoupir@mail.eoh.umn.edu.

See in-depth description on page 1537.

University of Mississippi Medical Center, Department of Preventive Medicine, Program in Epidemiology, Jackson, MS 39216-4505. Awards MS, PhD. Faculty: 3 full-time (0 women). Students: 1 (woman) part-time. Terminal master's awarded for partial completion of doctoral program. *Degree requirements:* For master's, thesis required, foreign language not required; for doctorate, dissertation, first authored publication required, foreign language not required. *Entrance requirements:* GRE General Test, minimum GPA of 3.0. Application deadline: 7/1 (rolling processing). Application fee: $10. *Expenses:* Tuition $2196 per year full-time, $122 per hour part-time for state residents; $3470 per year full-time, $193 per hour part-time for nonresidents. Fees $176 per year. *Financial aid:* Research assistantships, Federal Work-Study available. Financial aid application deadline: 4/1. *Faculty research:* Cardiovascular disease, cancer, health administration, epidemiologic methodology. • Dr. Edward F. Meydrech, Chairman, Department of Preventive Medicine, 601-984-1935. Fax: 601-984-1939. E-mail: meydrech@fiona.umsmed.edu.

The University of North Carolina at Chapel Hill, School of Dentistry and Graduate School, Graduate Programs in Dentistry, Chapel Hill, NC 27599. Offerings include oral epidemiology (PhD). Faculty: 82 full-time (15 women). *Degree requirements:* Dissertation required, foreign language not required. *Average time to degree:* master's–3 years full-time. *Entrance requirements:* GRE General Test. Application deadline: 10/1. Application fee: $55. Electronic applications accepted. *Expenses:* Tuition $2502 per year full-time, $626 per semester (minimum) part-time for state residents; $12,764 per year full-time, $3191 per semester (minimum) part-time for nonresidents. Fees $1041 per year full-time, $461 per semester (minimum) part-time. • Dr. Ronald Hunt, Associate Dean for Academic Affairs, 919-966-4451. Fax: 919-966-7007. Application contact: Kim Miller, Admissions Office, School of Dentistry, 919-966-4451.

See in-depth description on page 1711.

The University of North Carolina at Chapel Hill, School of Public Health, Department of Epidemiology, Chapel Hill, NC 27599. Awards MPH, MSPH, Dr PH, PhD. One or more programs accredited by CEPH. Part-time programs available. Faculty: 28 full-time (13 women), 109 part-time (27 women). Students: 81 full-time (55 women), 82 part-time (54 women); includes 27 minority (19 African Americans, 5 Asian Americans, 3 Hispanics), 31 international. Average age 34. 222 applicants, 39% accepted. In 1997, 24 master's, 25 doctorates awarded. Terminal master's awarded for partial completion of doctoral program. *Degree requirements:* For master's, computer language, major paper, comprehensive exam required, foreign language and thesis not required; for doctorate, computer language, dissertation, comprehensive exam required, foreign language not required. *Average time to degree:* master's–2 years full-time; doctorate–4.5 years full-time. *Entrance requirements:* GRE General Test (minimum combined score of 1000), minimum GPA of 3.0. Application deadline: 1/1 (priority date; rolling processing). Application fee: $55. *Expenses:* Tuition $2008 per year full-time, $502 per semester (minimum) part-time for state residents; $10,414 per year full-time, $2604 per semester (minimum) part-time for nonresidents. Fees $782 per year full-time, $332 per semester (minimum) part-time. *Financial aid:* In 1997–98, 23 fellowships (11 to first-year students), 62 research assistantships (17 to first-year students), 46 traineeships (7 to first-year students) were awarded; teaching assistantships, Federal Work-Study, institutionally sponsored loans, and career-related internships or fieldwork also available. Aid available to part-time students. Financial aid application deadline: 1/1. *Total annual research expenditures:* $6.564 million. • Dr. David A. Savitz, Chair, 919-966-7428. E-mail: david_savitz@unc.edu. Application contact: Nancy Colvin, Student Services Manager, 919-966-7459. Fax: 919-966-2089. E-mail: ncolvin@unc.edu.

Announcement: The Department of Epidemiology offers master's and doctoral training emphasizing research skills as developed by working closely with faculty members in areas of chronic and infectious disease, environmental and occupational exposures, health care, and reproductive epidemiology. Interested students with preparation in biological and social sciences are encouraged to apply.

University of Oklahoma Health Sciences Center, College of Public Health, Program in Biostatistics and Epidemiology, Oklahoma City, OK 73190. Offers biostatistics (MPH, MS, Dr PH, PhD), epidemiology (MPH, MS, Dr PH, PhD). One or more programs accredited by CEPH. Part-time programs available. Faculty: 8 full-time (2 women), 7 part-time (1 woman). Students: 30 full-time (14 women), 45 part-time (26 women); includes 15 minority (1 African American, 7 Asian Americans, 7 Native Americans), 12 international. Average age 36. 81 applicants, 41% accepted. In 1997, 14 master's, 4 doctorates awarded. *Degree requirements:* For master's, computer language, thesis (for some programs), comprehensive exam required, foreign language not required; for doctorate, computer language, dissertation, oral and written comprehensive exam required, foreign language not required. *Entrance requirements:* For master's, TOEFL (minimum score 550); for doctorate, GRE, TOEFL (minimum score 550). Application deadline: 7/1 (rolling processing; 12/1 for spring admission). Application fee: $25 ($50 for international students). *Financial aid:* Research assistantships, traineeships, institutionally sponsored loans, and career-related internships or fieldwork available. Aid available to part-time students. Financial aid application deadline: 5/1. *Faculty research:* Statistical methodology, applied statistics, acute and chronic disease epidemiology. • Dr. Willis Owen, Interim Chair, 405-271-2229.

University of Ottawa, Faculty of Medicine, Department of Epidemiology and Community Medicine, Ottawa, ON K1N 6N5, Canada. Awards M Sc. Offered jointly with Carleton University. Faculty: 18 full-time, 8 part-time. Students: 12 full-time (5 women), 24 part-time (10 women). Average age 34. In 1997, 5 degrees awarded. *Degree requirements:* Thesis required, foreign language not required. *Entrance requirements:* Honors degree or equivalent, minimum B average. Application deadline: 2/28. Application fee: $35. *Expenses:* Tuition $4677 per year for Canadian residents; $9900 per year for nonresidents. Fees $230 per year. *Financial aid:* Teaching assistantships and career-related internships or fieldwork available. Financial aid application deadline: 2/28. *Faculty research:* Health systems research, community health. Total annual research expenditures: $4.5 million. • Ian W. McDowell, Chair, 613-562-5427. Application contact: Mariella Peca, Administrative Officer, 613-562-5800 Ext. 8281. Fax: 613-562-5465.

University of Pennsylvania, School of Medicine, Center for Clinical Epidemiology and Biostatistics, Philadelphia, PA 19104. Offers programs in clinical epidemiology (MSCE), epidemiology (PhD). PhD offered through the School of Arts and Sciences. Part-time programs available. Faculty: 25 full-time (8 women), 45 part-time (15 women). Students: 37 full-time (17 women), 14 part-time (5 women); includes 2 international. Average age 33. 30 applicants, 80% accepted. In 1997, 5 master's awarded (100% entered university research/teaching). *Degree requirements:* For master's, thesis, comprehensive exam required, foreign language not required; for doctorate, dissertation, qualifying exam, preliminary exam required, foreign language not required. *Average time to degree:* master's–3 years full-time, 5 years part-time. *Entrance requirements:* For master's, GRE General Test or MCAT, advanced degree, clinical background; for doctorate, GRE General Test or MCAT. Application deadline: 1/15 (priority date; rolling processing). Application fee: $0. *Expenses:* Tuition $28,470 per year. Fees $1170 per year. *Financial aid:* In 1997–98, 51 students received aid, including 22 fellowships (15 to first-year students), 7 faculty tuition assistantships, international traineeships (4 to first-year students); career-related internships or fieldwork also available. Financial aid application deadline: 1/15. *Faculty research:* Health services research, pharmacoepidemiology, women's health, cancer epidemiology, emergency department, utilization issues, biostatistics. Total annual research expenditures: $5.8 million. • Dr. Brian L. Strom, Director, 215-898-2368. E-mail: strom@cceb.med.upenn.edu. Application contact: Thomas O. Kelly, Program Coordinator, 215-898-0861. Fax: 215-573-5315. E-mail: kelly@cceb.med.upenn.edu.

University of Pittsburgh, Graduate School of Public Health, Department of Epidemiology, Pittsburgh, PA 15260. Awards MPH, MS, Dr PH, PhD. One or more programs accredited by CEPH. Faculty: 24 full-time (13 women), 4 part-time (all women). Students: 48 full-time (31 women), 56 part-time (42 women); includes 22 minority (10 African Americans, 9 Asian Americans, 3 Hispanics), 11 international. 73 applicants, 36% accepted. In 1997, 17 master's, 7 doctorates awarded. Terminal master's awarded for partial completion of doctoral program. *Degree requirements:* For master's, thesis required, foreign language not required; for doctorate, 1 foreign language (computer language can substitute), dissertation. *Average time to degree:* master's–1 year full-time, 2 years part-time; doctorate–4 years full-time. *Entrance requirements:* For master's, DCAT, GRE General Test (minimum combined score of 1800 on three sections), MCAT, minimum QPA of 3.0, 3 credits in biology and mathematics, 6 credits in behavioral science; for doctorate, DCAT, GRE General Test (minimum combined score of 1800 on three sections), MCAT. Application deadline: 7/1 (priority date; rolling processing; 11/1 for spring admission). Application fee: $50 ($60 for international students). *Expenses:* Tuition $9402 per year full-time, $388 per credit part-time for state residents; $19,372 per year full-time, $799 per credit part-time for nonresidents. Fees $480 per year full-time, $180 per year part-time. *Financial aid:* In 1997–98, 44 students received aid, including 12 fellowships (2 to first-year students) averaging $1,667 per month, 31 research assistantships (7 to first-year students) averaging $1,050 per month and totaling $390,600, 1 teaching assistantship averaging $1,339 per month and totaling $10,712; Federal Work-Study, institutionally sponsored loans, and career-related internships or fieldwork also available. Aid available to part-time students. *Faculty research:* Aging, cardiovascular epidemiology, women's health, environmental epidemiology, diabetes. Total annual research expenditures: $12.05 million. • Dr. Lewis H. Kuller, Chairman, 412-624-3054. Application contact: Dr. Russell R. Rycheck, Associate Professor, 412-624-3141. Fax: 412-624-1736. E-mail: rrrteach@vms.cis.pitt.edu.

See in-depth description on page 1545.

University of Puerto Rico, Medical Sciences Campus, Graduate School of Public Health, Department of Biostatistics and Epidemiology, Program in Epidemiology, San Juan, PR 00936-5067. Awards MPH, MS. One or more programs accredited by CEPH. Part-time programs available. Students: 38 (31 women). 40 applicants, 68% accepted. In 1997, 16 degrees awarded. *Degree requirements:* Computer language required, foreign language and thesis not required. *Entrance requirements:* GRE, previous course work in biology, chemistry, physics, mathematics, and social sciences. Application deadline: 3/3. Application fee: $15. *Financial aid:* Research assistantships, teaching assistantships, Federal Work-Study, institutionally sponsored loans available. Financial aid application deadline: 4/30. • Application contact: Mayra E. Santiago-Vargas, Counselor, 787-756-5244. Fax: 787-759-6719.

University of Saskatchewan, Colleges of Medicine and Graduate Studies and Research, Graduate Programs in Medicine, Department of Community Health and Epidemiology, Saskatoon, SK S7N 5A2, Canada. Awards M Sc, PhD. Faculty: 6 full-time, 6 part-time. Students: 12 full-time, 16 part-time. *Degree requirements:* Thesis/dissertation. *Entrance requirements:* International English Language Testing System (minimum score 6) or Michigan English Language Assessment Battery (mimimum score of 80) or TOEFL (minimum score 550). Application deadline: 7/1 (priority date; rolling processing). Application fee: $0 ($100 for international students). *Financial aid:* Fellowships, research assistantships, teaching assistantships available. Financial aid application deadline: 1/31. • Dr. L. Tan, Head, 306-966-7945. Fax: 306-966-7920.

University of South Carolina, Graduate School, School of Public Health, Department of Epidemiology/Biostatistics, Program in Epidemiology, Columbia, SC 29208. Awards MPH, MSPH, Dr PH, PhD. One or more programs accredited by CEPH. Part-time programs available. Faculty: 6 full-time (4 women). Students: 61 full-time (41 women), 17 part-time (11 women); includes 20 minority (13 African Americans, 4 Asian Americans, 3 Hispanics), 12 international. Average age 30. 49 applicants, 76% accepted. In 1997, 8 master's, 3 doctorates awarded. *Degree requirements:* For master's, thesis, practicum (MPH) required, foreign language not required; for doctorate, dissertation. *Entrance requirements:* GRE General Test. Application deadline: rolling. Application fee: $35. Electronic applications accepted. *Expenses:* Tuition $4480 per year full-time, $220 per credit hour part-time for state residents; $9338 per year full-time, $457 per credit hour part-time for nonresidents. Fees $125 per year full-time, $37 per semester (minimum) part-time. *Financial aid:* Fellowships, research assistantships, teaching assistantships, traineeships, and career-related internships or fieldwork available. *Faculty research:* Cancer epidemiology, infectious disease epidemiology, mental health epidemiology, health effects of physical activity. • Application contact: Dr. Francisco Sy, Graduate Director, 803-777-7353. Fax: 803-777-2524.

University of Southern California, School of Medicine and Graduate School, Graduate Programs in Medicine, Program in Public Health, Los Angeles, CA 90089. Offerings include biometry/epidemiology (MPH). Program new for fall 1998. *Entrance requirements:* GRE General Test (minimum combined score of 1000), TOEFL, minimum GPA of 3.0. *Expenses:* Tuition $706 per unit. Fees $414 per year full-time, $32 per year part-time. • Dr. Richard N. Lolley, Associate Dean for Research, Graduate Programs in Medicine, 213-342-1607. Fax: 213-342-1610. E-mail: lolley@hsc.usc.edu.

University of Southern California, School of Medicine and Graduate School, Graduate Programs in Medicine, Department of Preventive Medicine, Program in Biometry, Los Angeles, CA 90089. Offerings include applied biometry/epidemiology (MS), epidemiology (PhD). Terminal master's awarded for partial completion of doctoral program. Program faculty: 41 full-time (15 women), 4 part-time (3 women). *Degree requirements:* Thesis/dissertation required, foreign language not required. *Average time to degree:* master's–2 years full-time; doctorate–5 years full-time. *Entrance requirements:* For master's, GRE General Test (minimum combined score of 1000), GRE Subject Test, TOEFL, minimum GPA of 3.0; for doctorate, GRE General Test (minimum combined score of 1250), GRE Subject Test, TOEFL, minimum GPA of 3.0. Application deadline: 1/15 (priority date; rolling processing). Application fee: $55. *Expenses:* Tuition $16,944 per year full-time, $706 per unit part-time. Fees $414 per year full-time, $32 per year part-time. • Dr. Stanley P. Azen, Director, 213-442-1810. Fax: 213-442-2993. E-mail: mtrujill@hsc.usc.edu.

University of South Florida, College of Public Health, Department of Epidemiology and Biostatistics, Tampa, FL 33620-9951. Awards MPH, MSPH, PhD. One or more programs accredited by CEPH. Part-time and evening/weekend programs available. Faculty: 9 full-time (2 women). 51 applicants, 41% accepted. *Degree requirements:* Thesis/dissertation required, foreign language not required. *Entrance requirements:* For master's, GRE General Test (minimum combined score of 1000), TOEFL (minimum score 550), minimum GPA of 3.0 in upper-level course work; for doctorate, GRE General Test (minimum combined score of 1100), TOEFL (minimum score 550), minimum GPA of 3.0 in upper-level course work. Application deadline: 6/1 (rolling processing; 10/15 for spring admission). Application fee: $20. *Tuition:* $142 per credit hour for state residents; $486 per credit hour for nonresidents. *Financial aid:* Federal Work-Study, institutionally sponsored loans available. Aid available to part-time students. Financial aid applicants required to submit FAFSA. *Faculty research:* Dementia, mental illness, mental health preventative trails, rural health outreach, clinical and administrative studies. Total annual research expenditures: $498,638. • Dr. Thomas J. Mason, Chairperson, 813-974-4860. E-mail: tmason@com1.med.usf.edu. Application contact: Magdalene Argiry, Director of Student Services, 813-974-6665. Fax: 813-974-4718. E-mail: margiry@com1.med.usf.edu.

University of Virginia, Graduate School of Arts and Sciences, Department of Health Evaluation Sciences, Charlottesville, VA 22903. Offerings include epidemiology (MS). Department faculty: 10 full-time (2 women), 12 part-time (8 women), 12 FTE. *Degree requirements:* Thesis required (for some programs), foreign language not required. *Entrance requirements:* GRE or MCAT. Application deadline: 3/1 (priority date). Application fee: $40. *Tuition:* $4870 per year full-time, $941 per semester (minimum) part-time for state residents; $15,818 per year full-time, $2745 per semester (minimum) part-time for nonresidents. • Dr. Paige Hornsby, Director, 804-924-0496. E-mail: pph8c@virginia.edu. Application contact: Robyn Kells, Program Coordinator, 804-924-8646. Fax: 804-924-8437. E-mail: ms-hes@virginia.edu.

See in-depth description on page 1353.

University of Washington, School of Public Health and Community Medicine, Department of Epidemiology, Seattle, WA 98195. Awards MPH, MS, PhD. One or more programs accredited by CEPH. Faculty: 54 full-time (27 women), 103 part-time (39 women). Students: 96 full-time (68 women), 33 part-time (21 women); includes 32 minority (4 African Americans, 23 Asian Americans, 5 Hispanics), 14 international. Average age 34. 202 applicants, 43% accepted. In 1997, 26 master's awarded (50% entered university research/teaching, 27% found other work related to degree, 23% continued full-time study); 14 doctorates awarded. Terminal master's awarded for partial completion of doctoral program. *Degree requirements:* For master's, thesis, practicum (MPH) required, foreign language not required; for doctorate, dissertation required, foreign language not required. *Average time to degree:* master's–2.2 years full-time; doctorate–5.5 years full-time. *Entrance requirements:* For master's, GRE General Test (combined average 2003 on three sections), TOEFL (minimum score 500), experience in health sciences preferred, minimum GPA of 3.0; for doctorate, GRE General Test (combined average 1890 on three sections), TOEFL (minimum score 500), experience in health sciences preferred, minimum GPA of 3.0. Application deadline: 1/15. Application fee: $45. *Tuition:* $5433 per year full-time, $775 per quarter (minimum) part-time for state residents; $13,479 per year full-time, $1925 per quarter (minimum) part-time for nonresidents. *Financial aid:* In 1997–98, 113 students received aid, including 70 fellowships (26 to first-year students), 26 research assistantships (6 to first-year students) averaging $1,100 per month, 5 teaching assistantships (3 to first-year students) averaging $1,100 per month, 12 tuition supports (2 to first-year students); partial tuition waivers, Federal Work-Study, and career-related internships or fieldwork also available. Aid available to part-time students. Financial aid application deadline: 2/28; applicants required to submit FAFSA. *Faculty research:* Cancer, cardiovascular disease, sexually transmitted diseases, injury epidemiology, maternal and child health. Total annual research expenditures: $7.21 million. • Dr. Thomas D. Koepsell, Chair, 206-543-1065. E-mail: koepsell@u.washington.edu. Application contact: Kate O'Brien, Graduate Student Services Counselor, 206-685-1762. Fax: 206-543-8525. E-mail: kobrien@u.washington.edu.

See in-depth description on page 1549.

The University of Western Ontario, Biosciences Division, Department of Epidemiology and Biostatistics, London, ON N6A 5B8, Canada. Awards M Sc, PhD. One or more programs accredited by CEPH. Part-time programs available. Students: 28. In 1997, 3 master's, 1 doctorate awarded. *Degree requirements:* For master's, thesis required, foreign language not required; for doctorate, comprehensive exam, thesis proposal defense required, foreign language not required. *Entrance requirements:* For master's, BA or B Sc honors degree, minimum B+ average in last 10 courses; for doctorate, M Sc or equivalent, minimum B+ average in last 10 courses. Application deadline: 2/1. Application fee: $20. *Financial aid:* Research assistantships, teaching assistantships, and career-related internships or fieldwork available. Financial aid application deadline: 4/1. *Faculty research:* Chronic disease epidemiology, clinical epidemiology. • Dr. Karen Campbell, Acting Chair, 519-661-2162.

University of Wisconsin–Madison, Medical School and Graduate School, Graduate Programs in Medicine, Population Health Program, Madison, WI 53706-1380. Offerings include epidemiology (MS, PhD). *Application fee:* $45. *Tuition:* $4928 per year full-time, $926 per semester (minimum) part-time for state residents; $15,190 per year full-time, $2849 per semester (minimum) part-time for nonresidents. • Donn D'Alessio, Chair, 608-263-2881. Fax: 608-263-2820. E-mail: dalessio@facstaff.wisc.edu.

Wake Forest University, School of Medicine and Graduate School, Graduate Programs in Medicine, Program in Epidemiology, Winston-Salem, NC 27109. Awards MS, MD/MS. Students: 4 full-time (1 woman), 13 part-time (7 women); includes 2 minority (both African Americans), 2 international. 5 applicants, 80% accepted. In 1997, 3 degrees awarded. *Degree requirements:* Thesis. *Entrance requirements:* GRE General Test, GRE Subject Test. Application deadline: 2/15 (priority date; rolling processing). Application fee: $25. *Tuition:* $17,450 per year. *Financial*

Directories: Epidemiology; Health Promotion

Wake Forest University (continued)

aid: In 1997–98, 4 students received aid, including 4 fellowships (all to first-year students) totaling $66,400; training grants, tuition scholarships also available. Financial aid application deadline: 2/15. *Faculty research:* Geriatrics, cardiovascular disease, cerebrovascular disease, health services utilization. Total annual research expenditures: $13.1 million. • Dr. Curt Furberg, Chairman, Public Health Sciences, 336-716-3730. Application contact: Dr. Lynn Wagenknechv, Director, 336-716-7652.

Announcement: The Master of Science degree is offered in clinical epidemiology, with training specifically designed for health-care professionals, including (but not limited to) physicians, nurses, and nutritionists. Course work broadly includes epidemiology, research methods, biostatistics, and computing. A master's thesis is required. Thirty graduate faculty members in the department have research interests in chronic disease epidemiology, clinical trials, social sciences, and biostatistics. Graduate faculty members from clinical departments also participate. Training grants may be available. For more information, visit the Web site at http://www.phs.bgsm.edu/epi/epigrad.htm

Yale University, School of Medicine, Department of Epidemiology and Public Health, Division of Chronic Disease Epidemiology, New Haven, CT 06520. Awards MPH, Dr PH, PhD. One or more programs accredited by CEPH. PhD offered through the Graduate School. Part-time programs available. Faculty: 17 full-time (13 women), 8 part-time (1 woman). Students: 60 full-time (39 women), 2 part-time (1 woman); includes 16 minority (1 African American, 13 Asian Americans, 2 Hispanics), 8 international. Average age 29. 93 applicants, 55% accepted. In 1997, 18 master's, 3 doctorates awarded. Terminal master's awarded for partial completion of doctoral program. *Degree requirements:* For master's, thesis, internship, thesis required, foreign language not required; for doctorate, dissertation, comprehensive exams, residency period required, foreign language not required. *Entrance requirements:* For master's, GMAT, GRE, LSAT, or MCAT; TOEFL, previous undergraduate course work in mathematics and science; for doctorate, GRE General Test (minimum combined score of 1200), TOEFL, MPH or equivalent and professional experience (Dr PH). Application deadline: rolling. Application fee: $60. *Financial aid:* Fellowships, research assistantships, teaching assistantships, scholarships, full and partial tuition waivers, Federal Work-Study, institutionally sponsored loans, and career-related internships or fieldwork available. Aid available to part-time students. Financial aid application deadline: 4/15; applicants required to submit FAFSA. *Faculty research:* Perinatal epidemiology, epidemiology of aging, psychiatric and social epidemiology, cancer and cardiovascular epidemiology, pharmaco epidemiology. • Dr. Michael B. Bracken, Professor of Epidemiology, 203-785-2846. Fax: 203-785-6279. E-mail: brackenmb@maspo3.mas.yale.edu. Application contact: Joan Stenner, Admissions Officer, 203-785-2844. Fax: 203-785-4845. E-mail: joan.stenner@yale.edu.

See in-depth description on page 1551.

Yale University, School of Medicine, Department of Epidemiology and Public Health, Division of Epidemiology of Microbial Diseases, New Haven, CT 06520. Awards MPH, Dr PH, PhD. One or more programs accredited by CEPH. PhD offered through the Graduate School. Part-time programs available. Faculty: 20 full-time (7 women), 12 part-time (3 women). Students: 57 full-time (34 women), 2 part-time (1 woman); includes 21 minority (2 African Americans, 14 Asian Americans, 4 Hispanics, 1 Native American), 9 international. Average age 28. 92 applicants, 52% accepted. In 1997, 18 master's awarded. Terminal master's awarded for partial completion of doctoral program. *Degree requirements:* For master's, thesis, internship required, foreign language not required; for doctorate, dissertation, comprehensive exams, residency period required, foreign language not required. *Entrance requirements:* For master's, GMAT, GRE, LSAT, or MCAT; TOEFL, previous undergraduate course work in mathematics and science; for doctorate, GRE General Test (minimum combined score of 1200), TOEFL, MPH or equivalent and professional experience (Dr PH). Application deadline: rolling. Application fee: $60. *Financial aid:* Scholarships, Federal Work-Study, institutionally sponsored loans, and career-related internships or fieldwork available. Aid available to part-time students. Financial aid application deadline: 4/15. *Faculty research:* Insect vector competence, vector biology, emerging infections, parasitology, microbial diseases and defense. • Dr. Nancy H. Ruddle, Professor, 203-785-2915. Application contact: Joan Stenner, Admissions Officer, 203-785-2844. Fax: 203-785-4845. E-mail: joan.stenner@yale.edu.

See in-depth description on page 1551.

Health Promotion

Ball State University, College of Applied Science and Technology, Interdepartmental Program in Wellness Management, 2000 University Avenue, Muncie, IN 47306-1099. Offers applied gerontology (MA), wellness management (MS). Faculty: 5. Students: 40 full-time (34 women), 20 part-time (17 women); includes 4 minority (1 African American, 1 Asian American, 1 Hispanic, 1 Native American). Average age 30. 37 applicants, 73% accepted. In 1997, 18 degrees awarded. *Entrance requirements:* GRE General Test. Application fee: $15 ($25 for international students). *Expenses:* Tuition $3454 per year full-time, $518 per semester (minimum) part-time for state residents; $9316 per year full-time, $1221 per semester (minimum) part-time for nonresidents. Fees $242 per year full-time, $18 per semester (minimum) part-time. • Dr. Neil Schmottlach, Director, Institute for Wellness, 765-285-8259.

Boston University, School of Medicine, School of Public Health, Social and Behavioral Sciences Department, Boston, MA 02215. Offers program in health behavior, health promotion, and disease prevention (MPH). Accredited by CEPH. Students: 40 full-time (35 women), 53 part-time (47 women); includes 21 minority (6 African Americans, 10 Asian Americans, 5 Hispanics), 2 international. Average age 28. *Entrance requirements:* GRE General Test, TOEFL. Application deadline: 4/15 (rolling processing; 10/25 for spring admission). Application fee: $50. *Financial aid:* Federal Work-Study, institutionally sponsored loans, and career-related internships or fieldwork available. Aid available to part-time students. • Dr. Ralph W. Hingson, Chairman, 617-638-5160. Application contact: Barbara St. Onge, Director of Admissions, 617-638-4640. Fax: 617-638-5299. E-mail: sphadmis@bu.edu.

See in-depth description on page 1487.

Bridgewater State College, School of Education, Department of Movement Arts, Health Promotion, and Leisure Studies, Program in Health Promotion, Bridgewater, MA 02325-0001. Awards M Ed. Evening/weekend programs available. *Entrance requirements:* GRE General Test. Application deadline: 4/1 (10/1 for spring admission). Application fee: $25. *Expenses:* Tuition $1675 per year full-time, $70 per credit part-time for state residents; $6450 per year full-time, $269 per credit part-time for nonresidents. Fees $1588 per year full-time, $66 per credit hour part-time for state residents; $1588 per year full-time, $66 per credit part-time for nonresidents. *Financial aid:* Career-related internships or fieldwork available. • Application contact: Graduate School, 508-697-1300.

Brigham Young University, College of Physical Education, Department of Physical Education, Provo, UT 84602-1001. Offerings include health promotion (M Ed, MS). M Ed and PhD (corrective physical education) being phased out; applicants no longer accepted. Department faculty: 23 full-time (8 women). *Degree requirements:* Thesis (for some programs), oral exam required, foreign language not required. *Entrance requirements:* GRE General Test (minimum combined score of 1380 on three sections), minimum GPA of 3.0 in last 60 hours. Application deadline: 2/1 (rolling processing). Application fee: $30. *Tuition:* $3200 per year full-time, $178 per credit hour part-time for state residents; $4800 per year full-time, $266 per credit hour part-time for nonresidents. • Dr. Earlene Durrant, Chair, 801-378-2547. Application contact: A. Garth Fisher, Graduate Coordinator, 801-378-3981. Fax: 801-378-8389.

California College for Health Sciences, Program in Community Health Administration and Wellness Promotion, 222 West 24th Street, National City, CA 91950-6605. Awards MS. Part-time and evening/weekend programs available. Postbaccalaureate distance learning degree programs offered (no on-campus study). Faculty: 2 full-time (both women), 4 part-time (all women). Students: 788 part-time; includes 58 international. Average age 30. In 1997, 40 degrees awarded. *Degree requirements:* Fieldwork, internship required, foreign language and thesis not required. *Average time to degree:* master's–3 years part-time. *Entrance requirements:* Previous course work in psychology. Application deadline: rolling. Application fee: $35. *Expenses:* Tuition $335 per course. Fees $35 per course. • Lisa J. Davis, Dean of Student Affairs, 800-221-7374. E-mail: admissns@cchs.edu. Application contact: Admissions and Records Department, 619-477-4800. Fax: 619-477-2257. E-mail: admissns@cchs.edu.

California State University, Fresno, Division of Graduate Studies, School of Health and Social Work, Department of Public Health, 5241 North Maple Avenue, Fresno, CA 93740. Offerings include health promotion (MPH). Preaccredited by CEPH. Department faculty: 8 full-time (1 woman). *Degree requirements:* Thesis or alternative required, foreign language not required. *Average time to degree:* master's–3.5 years full-time. *Entrance requirements:* GRE General Test, TOEFL (minimum score 550), minimum GPA of 2.5. Application deadline: 3/1 (priority date; rolling processing). Application fee: $55. Electronic applications accepted. *Expenses:* Tuition $0 for state residents; $246 per unit for nonresidents. Fees $1872 per year full-time, $1206 per year part-time. • Dr. Sanford Brown, Graduate Program Coordinator, 209-278-4747. E-mail: sanford_brown@csufresno.edu.

Central Michigan University, College of Health Professions, Department of Health Promotion and Rehabilitation, Mount Pleasant, MI 48859. Offers programs in health promotion and program management (MA), health services administration (MSA), physical therapy (MS), physician assistant (MS). Faculty: 41 full-time (13 women). Students: 213 full-time (141 women), 22 part-time (19 women); includes 8 minority (all Asian Americans), 2 international. Average age 27. In 1997, 57 degrees awarded. *Degree requirements:* Thesis or alternative required, foreign language not required. *Entrance requirements:* 21 hours of undergraduate health-related programs. Application deadline: 2/15. Application fee: $30. *Expenses:* Tuition $139 per credit hour (minimum) for state residents; $276 per credit hour (minimum) for nonresidents. Fees $260 per year full-time, $150 per semester part-time. *Financial aid:* In 1997–98, 3 fellowships (all to first-year students), 15 teaching assistantships (8 to first-year students) were awarded; Federal Work-Study and career-related internships or fieldwork also available. Financial aid application deadline: 3/7. *Faculty research:* Children's fitness and active video games, obesity and weight control, international health education, school health education. • Dr. Herman Triezenberg, Chairperson, 517-774-3541. E-mail: 320ss5j@cmich.edu.

The George Washington University, School of Public Health and Health Services, Master's Program in Public Health, Track in Health Promotion-Disease Prevention, Washington, DC 20052. Awards MPH. Accredited by CEPH. *Degree requirements:* Case study or special project required, thesis not required. *Entrance requirements:* GMAT, GRE General Test, or MCAT; TOEFL. Application deadline: 5/15 (priority date; rolling processing; 11/15 for spring admission). Application fee: $50. *Expenses:* Tuition $680 per semester hour. Fees $35 per semester hour. • Application contact: Michelle Sparacino, Director of Recruitment, 202-994-2160. Fax: 202-994-3773. E-mail: sphhs-info@gwumc.edu.

See in-depth description on page 1495.

The George Washington University, School of Public Health and Health Services, Master's Program in Public Health, Track in International Health, Washington, DC 20052. Offerings include health promotion (MPH). *Degree requirements:* Case study or special project required, thesis not required. *Entrance requirements:* GMAT, GRE General Test, or MCAT; TOEFL. Application deadline: 5/15 (priority date; rolling processing; 11/15 for spring admission). Application fee: $50. *Expenses:* Tuition $680 per semester hour. Fees $35 per semester hour. • Application contact: Michelle Sparacino, Director of Recruitment, 202-994-2160. Fax: 202-994-3773. E-mail: sphhs-info@gwumc.edu.

See in-depth description on page 1495.

Harvard University, School of Public Health, Department of Health and Social Behavior, Boston, MA 02115. Awards SM, DPH, SD. Part-time programs available. Faculty: 12 full-time (7 women), 7 part-time (3 women). Students: 74 full-time (61 women), 11 part-time (10 women); includes 17 minority (6 African Americans, 8 Asian Americans, 2 Hispanics, 1 Native American), 10 international. Average age 30. 123 applicants, 50% accepted. In 1997, 9 master's, 5 doctorates awarded. *Degree requirements:* For doctorate, dissertation, qualifying exam. *Entrance requirements:* GRE, TOEFL (minimum score 550). Application deadline: 1/4. Application fee: $60. *Expenses:* Tuition $21,895 per year full-time, $10,948 per year part-time. Fees $686 per year. *Financial aid:* Fellowships, partial tuition waivers, Federal Work-Study available. Aid available to part-time students. Financial aid application deadline: 2/12; applicants required to submit FAFSA. *Faculty research:* Design and evaluation of health promotion programs and child health services, ethnic variations in response to health care. • Dr. Lisa Berkman, Chairman, 617-432-1135. Application contact: Carrie Daniels, Assistant Director of Admissions, 617-432-1031. Fax: 617-432-2009. E-mail: admisofc@sph.harvard.edu.

Idaho State University, College of Health Professions, Department of Health and Nutrition Sciences, Pocatello, ID 83209. Offerings include health education (MHE). Department faculty: 7 full-time (2 women), 2 part-time (0 women). *Application deadline:* 7/1 (priority date; rolling processing; 12/1 for spring admission). *Application fee:* $30. *Tuition:* $3130 per year full-time, $136 per credit hour part-time for state residents; $9370 per year full-time, $226 per credit hour part-time for nonresidents. • Dr. James Girvan, Chairman, 208-236-2656. Fax: 208-236-4000.

Indiana University Bloomington, School of Health, Physical Education and Recreation, Program in Applied Health Science, Bloomington, IN 47405. Offerings include health promotion (MS). Program faculty: 14 full-time (6 women). *Application deadline:* rolling. *Application fee:* $35. *Expenses:* Tuition $153 per credit hour for state residents; $446 per credit hour for nonresidents. Fees $343 per year. • James W. Crowe, Chair, 812-855-3627. Application contact: Mohammad Torabi, Graduate Coordinator, 812-855-4806. Fax: 812-855-3936.

Lehman College of the City University of New York, Division of Natural and Social Sciences, Department of Health Services, Program in Health Education and Promotion, 250 Bedford Park Boulevard West, Bronx, NY 10468-1589. Awards MA. Part-time and evening/weekend programs available. Faculty: 2 full-time (1 woman). Students: 25 part-time (12 women). *Degree requirements:* Thesis or alternative. *Entrance requirements:* Minimum GPA of

2.7. Application deadline: 4/1 (priority date; rolling processing; 11/1 for spring admission). Application fee: $40. *Expenses:* Tuition $4350 per year full-time, $185 per credit part-time for state residents; $7600 per year full-time, $320 per credit part-time for nonresidents. Fees $120 per year full-time, $80 per year part-time. *Financial aid:* Full and partial tuition waivers, Federal Work-Study available. Aid available to part-time students. Financial aid application deadline: 5/15; applicants required to submit FAFSA. • Nicholas Galli, Adviser, 718-960-8775.

Loma Linda University, School of Public Health, Programs in Health Promotion and Education, Loma Linda, CA 92350. Awards MPH, Dr PH. One or more programs accredited by CEPH. Students: 29 full-time (18 women), 115 part-time (87 women). 41 applicants, 85% accepted. In 1997, 64 master's awarded. *Degree requirements:* For doctorate, dissertation. *Entrance requirements:* For master's, Michigan English Language Assessment Battery (minimum score 92) or TOEFL (minimum score 600); for doctorate, GRE General Test (minimum combined score of 1500 on three sections). Application deadline: rolling. Application fee: $100. *Tuition:* $380 per unit. *Financial aid:* Application deadline 5/15. • Dr. Christine Neish, Chair, 909-824-4575. Fax: 909-824-4087. Application contact: Terri Tamayose, Director of Admissions and Academic Records, 909-824-4694. Fax: 909-824-8087. E-mail: ttamayose@sph.llu.edu.

Marymount University, School of Health Professions, Program in Health Promotion Management, Arlington, VA 22207-4299. Awards MS. Part-time and evening/weekend programs available. Students: 20. In 1997, 6 degrees awarded. *Degree requirements:* Thesis or alternative required, foreign language not required. *Entrance requirements:* GRE General Test or MAT, interview. Application deadline: rolling. Application fee: $35. *Expenses:* Tuition $465 per credit hour. Fees $120 per year full-time, $5 per credit hour part-time. • Dr. Liane Summerfield, Chairperson, 703-284-1620. Fax: 703-284-1631. E-mail: liane.summerfield@marymount.edu.

Mississippi State University, College of Education, Department of Physical Health, Education, Recreation, and Sports, Mississippi State, MS 39762. Offerings include physical education (MS), with options in exercise science, health education/health promotion, sport administration, teaching/coaching. Department faculty: 9 full-time (2 women), 1 part-time (0 women). *Degree requirements:* Comprehensive oral or written exam required, thesis optional, foreign language not required. *Entrance requirements:* Minimum QPA of 2.75 in last 2 years. Application deadline: 7/26 (priority date; rolling processing; 11/10 for spring admission). Application fee: $0 ($25 for international students). *Tuition:* $3017 per year full-time, $168 per credit hour part-time for state residents; $6119 per year full-time, $340 per credit hour part-time for nonresidents. • Dr. Robert Boling, Head, 601-325-2963. Fax: 601-325-4525. E-mail: rbb4@ra.msstate.edu.

Nebraska Methodist College of Nursing and Allied Health, Program in Health Promotion, 8501 West Dodge Road, Omaha, NE 68114-3426. Awards MS. Evening/weekend programs available. Postbaccalaureate distance learning degree programs offered (minimal on-campus study). Faculty: 1 (woman) full-time, 14 part-time (7 women). Students: 15 full-time (14 women). 22 applicants, 95% accepted. *Degree requirements:* Thesis required, foreign language not required. *Entrance requirements:* Interview. Application deadline: 6/1 (rolling processing). Application fee: $25. *Financial aid:* In 1997–98, 4 research assistantships were awarded. • Dr. Kay Ryan, Chairperson, 402-354-4953. E-mail: kyan@nmns.org. Application contact: Deann Sterner, Director of Admissions, 402-354-4879. Fax: 402-354-8875. E-mail: dsterne@nmns.org.

New York Medical College, Graduate School of Health Sciences, Program in Behavioral Sciences and Health Promotion, Valhalla, NY 10595-1691. Awards MPH. Part-time and evening/weekend programs available. *Degree requirements:* Computer language required, foreign language not required. *Entrance requirements:* TOEFL. Application deadline: 7/20 (priority date; rolling processing; 12/1 for spring admission). Application fee: $35 ($60 for international students). *Tuition:* $415 per credit. *Financial aid:* Federal Work-Study, institutionally sponsored loans, and career-related internships or fieldwork available. Financial aid application deadline: 6/15. • Dr. Rhea Dornbush, Director, 914-285-7120.

Northern Arizona University, College of Health Professions, Department of Health, Physical Education, Exercise Science, and Nutrition, Program in Public Health, Flagstaff, AZ 86011. Offerings include health education and health promotion (MPH). Accredited by CEPH. Offered jointly with University of Arizona. *Degree requirements:* Thesis or alternative required, foreign language not required. *Entrance requirements:* GRE General Test, minimum GPA of 3.0. Application fee: $45. *Expenses:* Tuition $2088 per year full-time, $330 per semester (minimum) part-time for state residents; $8004 per year full-time, $1002 per semester (minimum) part-time for nonresidents. Fees $72 per year full-time, $18 per semester (minimum) part-time. • Dr. John P. Sciacca, Director, 520-523-4122.

Northwestern State University of Louisiana, Department of Health and Human Performance, Program in Health Promotion, Natchitoches, LA 71497. Awards M Ed. *Degree requirements:* Thesis or alternative required, foreign language not required. *Entrance requirements:* GRE General Test (minimum combined score of 800), minimum undergraduate GPA of 2.5. Application deadline: 8/1 (priority date; rolling processing; 1/10 for spring admission). Application fee: $15 ($25 for international students). *Tuition:* $2147 per year full-time, $336 per semester (minimum) part-time for state residents; $6437 per year full-time, $336 per semester (minimum) part-time for nonresidents. *Financial aid:* Career-related internships or fieldwork available. Financial aid application deadline: 7/15. • Application contact: Dr. Tom Hanson, Dean, Graduate Studies and Research, 318-357-5851. Fax: 318-357-5019.

Portland State University, College of Urban and Public Affairs, School of Community Health, Division of Health Education, Portland, OR 97207-0751. Offerings include health education and health promotion (MPH). MPH offered jointly with Oregon Health Sciences University and Oregon State University. Division faculty: 8 full-time (5 women), 25 part-time (17 women), 10 FTE. *Application deadline:* 4/1 (11/1 for spring admission). *Application fee:* $50. *Tuition:* $6101 per year full-time, $689 per semester (minimum) part-time for state residents; $10,445 per year full-time, $689 per semester (minimum) part-time for nonresidents. • Application contact: Elizabeth Bull, 503-725-4401. Fax: 503-725-5100. E-mail: eliz@upa.pdx.edu.

Purdue University, School of Liberal Arts, Department of Health, Kinesiology and Leisure Studies, West Lafayette, IN 47907. Offerings include health promotion (MS, PhD). Department faculty: 18 full-time (5 women), 2 part-time (1 woman). *Degree requirements:* For master's, thesis required (for some programs), foreign language not required; for doctorate, dissertation required, foreign language not required. *Entrance requirements:* GRE General Test, TOEFL (minimum score 550). Application deadline: 2/15 (priority date; rolling processing). Application fee: $30. Electronic applications accepted. *Tuition:* $3500 per year full-time, $126 per credit hour part-time for state residents; $11,720 per year full-time, $387 per credit hour part-time for nonresidents. • Dr. T. J. Templin, Head, 765-494-3178. Application contact: W. A. Harper, Graduate Committee Chair, 765-494-1518. Fax: 765-496-1239. E-mail: wharper@purdue.edu.

San Diego State University, College of Health and Human Services, Graduate School of Public Health, San Diego, CA 92182. Offerings include health promotion (MPH). One or more programs accredited by CEPH. School faculty: 25 full-time (9 women), 36 part-time (21 women). *Application deadline:* 5/15 (priority date; rolling processing; 10/15 for spring admission). *Application fee:* $55. *Expenses:* Tuition $0 for state residents; $246 per unit for nonresidents. Fees $1932 per year full-time, $1266 per year part-time. • Dr. Kenneth Bart, Director, 619-594-6317. Application contact: Brenda Fass-Holmes, Coordinator, Admissions and Student Affairs, 619-594-6317. E-mail: bholmes@mail.sdsu.edu.

Simmons College, Graduate School for Health Studies, Program in Nutrition and Health Promotion, Boston, MA 02115. Awards MS. Part-time and evening/weekend programs available. Faculty: 4 full-time (3 women). Students: 15 full-time (14 women), 13 part-time (all women); includes 2 international. 71 applicants, 66% accepted. *Degree requirements:* Research project required, foreign language not required. *Entrance requirements:* GRE General Test, TOEFL (minimum score 550). Application deadline: rolling. Application fee: $50. *Expenses:* Tuition $587 per credit hour. Fees $20 per year. *Financial aid:* Application deadline 3/1. *Faculty research:* Nutrition supplements of athletes' nutrition and health-related behaviors of college-age women, glutamine supplementation in AIDS. • Dr. Nancie Herbold, Program Director, 617-521-2711. E-mail: nherbold@simmons.edu. Application contact: Christine Keuleyan, Admission Coordinator, 617-521-2650. Fax: 617-521-3137. E-mail: keuleyan@simmons.edu.

Southwest Missouri State University, College of Health and Human Services, Department of Health, Physical Education, and Recreation, Springfield, MO 65804-0094. Offers program in health promotion and wellness management (MS). Students: 8 full-time (5 women), 6 part-time (5 women). *Degree requirements:* Comprehensive exam required, foreign language not required. *Entrance requirements:* Minimum GPA of 3.0. Application fee: $25. *Expenses:* Tuition $1980 per year full-time, $110 per credit hour part-time for state residents; $3960 per year full-time, $220 per credit hour part-time for nonresidents. Fees $274 per year full-time, $73 per semester part-time. • Thomas H. Burnett, Head, 417-836-5370. E-mail: thb427f@vma.smsu.edu. Application contact: Dalen Duitsmane, Graduate Adviser, 417-836-5550. Fax: 417-836-5371. E-mail: dmd271f@wpgate.smsu.edu.

Springfield College, Program in Health Promotion/Wellness Management, Springfield, MA 01109-3797. Awards M Ed, MS, CAS. Part-time programs available. Faculty: 3 full-time (2 women), 1 (woman) part-time. Students: 21 full-time (14 women), 10 part-time (6 women); includes 4 international. Average age 26. 27 applicants, 93% accepted. In 1997, 15 master's awarded. *Degree requirements:* For master's, comprehensive exam, research project required, foreign language and thesis not required. *Application deadline:* (12/1 for spring admission). *Application fee:* $40. *Expenses:* Tuition $474 per credit. Fees $25 per year. *Financial aid:* In 1997–98, 2 teaching assistantships (both to first-year students) were awarded; fellowships, full and partial tuition waivers, Federal Work-Study, and career-related internships or fieldwork also available. Financial aid application deadline: 3/1. • Dr. Carol Wargula, Director, 413-788-2421. Application contact: Donald J. Shaw Jr., Director of Graduate Admissions, 413-748-3225. Fax: 413-748-3694. E-mail: dshaw@spfldcol.edu.

Trinity College, School of Professional Studies, Program in Health, Washington, DC 20017-1094. Offers community health promotion and education (MA). Faculty: 1 (woman) full-time. Students: 38 (37 women); includes 17 minority (15 African Americans, 1 Asian American, 1 Hispanic). *Degree requirements:* Thesis or alternative. *Entrance requirements:* Minimum GPA of 2.8. Application deadline: rolling. Application fee: $35. *Tuition:* $460 per credit hour. • Application contact: Karen Goodwin, Director of Graduate Admissions, 202-884-9400. Fax: 202-884-9229.

The University of Alabama, College of Education, Area of Professional Studies, Program in Health Education and Promotion, Tuscaloosa, AL 35487. Awards MA, PhD. PhD offered jointly with the University of Alabama at Birmingham. *Degree requirements:* For doctorate, 1 foreign language, computer language, dissertation. *Average time to degree:* doctorate–3 years full-time, 6 years part-time. *Entrance requirements:* GRE General Test, MAT (score in 50th percentile or higher), or NTE (minimum score 658 on each core battery test), minimum GPA of 3.0. Application deadline: 7/6 (rolling processing). Application fee: $25. *Financial aid:* Fellowships, research assistantships, teaching assistantships, Federal Work-Study, institutionally sponsored loans, and career-related internships or fieldwork available. Financial aid application deadline: 7/14. • Dr. James Eddy, Head, 205-348-2956. Fax: 205-348-7568. E-mail: jeddy@bamaed.ua.edu.

The University of Alabama at Birmingham, Graduate School, School of Public Health, Department of Health Behavior, Birmingham, AL 35294. Offerings include health education/promotion (PhD). One or more programs accredited by CEPH. PhD offered jointly with The University of Alabama–Tuscaloosa. *Application deadline:* rolling. *Application fee:* $30 ($60 for international students). Electronic applications accepted. *Expenses:* Tuition $3672 per year full-time, $102 per credit hour part-time for state residents; $7344 per year full-time, $204 per credit hour part-time for nonresidents. Fees $699 per year (minimum) full-time, $116 per quarter (minimum) part-time. • Dr. James Raczynski, Chair, 205-934-6021. Application contact: Nancy Pinson, Coordinator of Student Admissions, 205-934-4993. Fax: 205-975-5484. E-mail: osas@ms.soph.uab.edu.

See in-depth description on page 1523.

The University of Alabama at Birmingham, Graduate School, School of Education, Department of Human Studies, Program in Health Education/Health Promotion, Birmingham, AL 35294. Awards PhD, Ed S. Offered jointly with The University of Alabama–Tuscaloosa. Students: 10 full-time (7 women), 5 part-time (4 women); includes 6 minority (5 African Americans, 1 Asian American). 26 applicants, 92% accepted. In 1997, 4 doctorates awarded. *Degree requirements:* For doctorate, dissertation; for Ed S, comprehensive exam. *Application fee:* $30 ($55 for international students). Electronic applications accepted. *Expenses:* Tuition $99 per credit hour for state residents; $198 per credit hour for nonresidents. Fees $516 per year (minimum) full-time, $73 per quarter (minimum) part-time for state residents; $516 per year (minimum) full-time, $73 per unit (minimum) part-time for nonresidents. • Dr. David M. Macrina, Chairperson, Department of Human Studies, 205-934-2446.

University of Alberta, Faculty of Graduate Studies and Research, Centre for Health Promotion Studies, Edmonton, AB T6G 2E1, Canada. Awards M Sc, Postgraduate Diploma. Part-time programs available. Postbaccalaureate distance learning degree programs offered (minimal on-campus study). Students: 14 full-time (12 women), 33 part-time (31 women). 49 applicants, 57% accepted. *Degree requirements:* For master's, thesis required, foreign language not required. *Entrance requirements:* For master's, minimum GPA of 7.0 on a 9.0 scale. Application deadline: 3/1 (priority date). Application fee: $60. *Expenses:* Tuition $390 per course for Canadian residents; $781 per course for nonresidents. Fees $500 per year full-time, $184 per year part-time. *Financial aid:* In 1997–98, 7 research assistantships (all to first-year students) averaging $550 per month and totaling $16,856, 1 tuition scholarship were awarded; career-related internships or fieldwork also available. *Faculty research:* Healthy public policy development, effectiveness of community-based health promotion programs, evaluation of changes in health determinants. • Dr. M. Stewart, Director, 403-492-9413. E-mail: miriam.stewart@ualberta.ca. Application contact: R. G. Glassford, Coordinator, 403-492-9347. Fax: 403-492-9579.

University of Delaware, College of Health and Nursing Sciences, Department of Health and Exercise Scien ces, Newark, DE 19716. Offerings include health promotion (MS). Department faculty: 12 full-time (3 women). *Average time to degree:* master's–2.5 years full-time, 4.5 years part-time. *Application deadline:* 7/1 (priority date; rolling processing; 12/1 for spring admission). *Application fee:* $45. *Expenses:* Tuition $4250 per year full-time, $236 per credit hour part-time for state residents; $12,250 per year full-time, $681 per credit hour part-time for nonresidents. Fees $466 per year full-time, $15 per semester (minimum) part-time. • Application contact: Gail E. Manogue, Administrative Assistant, 302-831-8370.

University of Georgia, College of Education, School of Health and Human Performance, Department of Health Promotion and Behavior, Athens, GA 30602. Offers programs in education (MA), health promotion and behavior (PhD), health promotion and behavior and safety education (M Ed), safety education (Ed S). Faculty: 5 full-time (1 woman). Students: 30 full-time, 9 part-time (all women); includes 4 minority (all African Americans), 3 international. 44 applicants, 43% accepted. In 1997, 13 master's awarded. *Degree requirements:* For master's, thesis (MA) required, foreign language not required; for doctorate, dissertation required, foreign language not required. *Entrance requirements:* For master's and Ed S, GRE General Test or MAT; for doctorate, GRE General Test. Application deadline: 7/1 (priority date; 11/15 for spring admission). Application fee: $30. Electronic applications accepted. *Tuition:* $3290 per year full-time, $643 per semester (minimum) part-time for state residents; $11,300 per year full-time, $1645 per semester (minimum) part-time for nonresidents. *Financial aid:* Fellowships, research assistantships, teaching assistantships, assistantships available. • Dr. Mark G. Wilson, Graduate Coordinator, 706-542-3313. Fax: 706-542-4956.

University of Hawaii at Manoa, College of Health Sciences and Social Welfare, School of Public Health, Honolulu, HI 96822. Offerings include personal and community health

Directory: Health Promotion

University of Hawaii at Manoa (continued)
maintenance and promotion (Dr PH). Terminal master's awarded for partial completion of doctoral program. School faculty: 18 full-time (8 women), 4 part-time (2 women), 19.6 FTE. *Average time to degree:* master's–1.2 years full-time, 3 years part-time. *Application deadline:* 3/1 (9/1 for spring admission). *Application fee:* $25 ($50 for international students). *Tuition:* $4029 per year full-time, $214 per credit hour part-time for state residents; $9957 per year full-time, $461 per credit hour part-time for nonresidents. • Dr. D. William Wood, Interim Dean, 808-956-8491. Application contact: Nancy Kilonsky, Assistant Dean, 808-956-8267.

University of Kentucky, Graduate School Programs from the College of Education, Program in Kinesiology and Health Promotion, Lexington, KY 40506-0032. Awards MS, Ed D. Faculty: 12 full-time (3 women), 2 part-time (0 women). Students: 59 full-time (26 women), 26 part-time (12 women); includes 4 minority (3 African Americans, 1 Hispanic), 6 international. 69 applicants, 77% accepted. In 1997, 30 master's, 1 doctorate awarded. Terminal master's awarded for partial completion of doctoral program. *Degree requirements:* For master's, comprehensive exam required, thesis optional, foreign language not required; for doctorate, dissertation, comprehensive exam required, foreign language not required. *Entrance requirements:* For master's, GRE General Test, minimum undergraduate GPA of 2.5; for doctorate, GRE General Test, minimum graduate GPA of 3.0. Application deadline: 7/19 (rolling processing). Application fee: $30 ($35 for international students). *Financial aid:* In 1997–98, 3 fellowships, 1 research assistantship, 8 teaching assistantships, 8 graduate assistantships were awarded; Federal Work-Study, institutionally sponsored loans, and career-related internships or fieldwork also available. Aid available to part-time students. • Dr. Richard Riggs, Director of Graduate Studies, 606-257-3645. E-mail: rsrigg01@ukcc.uky.edu. Application contact: Dr. Constance L. Wood, Associate Dean, 606-257-4613. Fax: 606-323-1928.

University of Massachusetts Lowell, College of Health Professions, Department of Nursing, Program in Administration of Nursing Services, 1 University Avenue, Lowell, MA 01854-2881. Offerings include health promotion (PhD). *Degree requirements:* Dissertation. *Entrance requirements:* GRE General Test. Application deadline: 4/1 (priority date; rolling processing; 10/1 for spring admission). Application fee: $20 ($35 for international students). *Tuition:* $4867 per year full-time, $618 per semester (minimum) part-time for state residents; $10,276 per year full-time, $1294 per semester (minimum) part-time for nonresidents. • Dr. May Futrell, Chair, Department of Nursing, 978-934-4467. E-mail: may_futrell@woods.uml.edu.

The University of Memphis, College of Education, Department of Human Movement Sciences and Education, Memphis, TN 38152. Offerings include health promotion (MS). Department faculty: 16 full-time (4 women), 6 part-time (0 women). *Degree requirements:* Thesis, comprehensive exam required, foreign language not required. *Entrance requirements:* GRE General Test (minimum combined score of 750) or MAT (minimum score 33). Application deadline: 5/1 (priority date; rolling processing; 11/1 for spring admission). Application fee: $25 ($50 for international students). *Tuition:* $2862 per year full-time, $166 per credit hour part-time for state residents; $6696 per year full-time, $379 per credit hour part-time for nonresidents. • Dr. Ralph C. Wilcox, Chairman, 901-678-2324. Application contact: Dr. Mary D. Fry, Coordinator of Graduate Studies in Health, 901-678-4986.

University of Michigan, School of Public Health, Department of Health Behavior and Health Education, Ann Arbor, MI 48109. Awards MPH, PhD, MSW/MPH. One or more programs accredited by CEPH. PhD offered through the Horace H. Rackham School of Graduate Studies. Faculty: 18 full-time (11 women). Students: 140 full-time. 282 applicants, 48% accepted. In 1997, 42 master's, 5 doctorates awarded. Terminal master's awarded for partial completion of doctoral program. *Degree requirements:* For doctorate, variable foreign language requirement, oral defense of dissertation, preliminary exam. *Entrance requirements:* GRE General Test. Application deadline: 3/1 (priority date; rolling processing). Application fee: $55. *Financial aid:* In 1997–98, 7 fellowships, 1 research assistantship, 1 teaching assistantship were awarded. Financial aid application deadline: 3/1. *Faculty research:* Asthma management, women and heart disease, cancer prevention and control. • Dr. Barbara A. Israel, Chair, 734-764-9494. Application contact: Jackie Cormany, Student Services Assistant, 734-763-9938. E-mail: sph.hbhe.inquiries@umich.edu.

See in-depth description on page 1535.

University of North Texas, College of Education, Department of Kinesiology, Health Promotion, and Recreation, Program in Health Promotion, Denton, TX 76203-6737. Offers community health (MS), school health (MS). Part-time programs available. *Degree requirements:* Thesis required (for some programs), foreign language not required. *Entrance requirements:* GRE General Test (minimum score 375 on each section; 800 combined). Application deadline: 7/17. Application fee: $25 ($50 for international students). *Tuition:* $2063 per year full-time, $815 per year part-time for state residents; $5897 per year full-time, $2100 per year part-time for nonresidents. *Financial aid:* Teaching assistantships, Federal Work-Study, institutionally sponsored loans, and career-related internships or fieldwork available. Financial aid application deadline: 4/1. • Application contact: Chwee L. Chng, Adviser, 940-565-2651.

University of Oklahoma Health Sciences Center, College of Public Health, Department of Health Promotion Sciences, Oklahoma City, OK 73190. Awards MPH, MS, Dr PH, PhD. One or more programs accredited by CEPH. Part-time programs available. Faculty: 6 full-time (3 women), 6 part-time (1 woman). Students: 19 full-time (15 women), 28 part-time (25 women); includes 17 minority (4 African Americans, 4 Asian Americans, 3 Hispanics, 6 Native Americans), 3 international. Average age 38. 65 applicants, 69% accepted. In 1997, 9 master's awarded. *Degree requirements:* For master's, computer language, thesis (for some programs), comprehensive exam required, foreign language not required; for doctorate, 2 foreign languages, computer language, dissertation, oral and written comprehensive exam. *Entrance requirements:* For master's, TOEFL (minimum score 550); for doctorate, GRE, TOEFL (minimum score 550). Application deadline: 7/1 (rolling processing). Application fee: $25 ($50 for international students). *Financial aid:* Research assistantships, traineeships, partial tuition waivers, institutionally sponsored loans, and career-related internships or fieldwork available. Aid available to part-time students. Financial aid application deadline: 5/1. *Faculty research:* Health education, school health, health behavior, American Indian health. • Dr. Kenneth McLeroy, Chair, 405-271-2017.

University of Pittsburgh, School of Education, Department of Health, Physical, and Recreation Education, Pittsburgh, PA 15260. Offerings include movement science (MHPE, MS, PhD), with options in developmental movement (MS, PhD), exercise physiology (MS, PhD), health promotion and education (MHPE), sports medicine (MS, PhD). MHPE offered jointly with the Graduate School of Public Health. Department faculty: 10 full-time (6 women). *Average time to degree:* master's–2 years full-time, 4 years part-time; doctorate–4 years full-time, 6 years part-time. *Application deadline:* 2/1. *Application fee:* $30 ($40 for international students). *Expenses:* Tuition $8018 per year full-time, $329 per credit part-time for state residents; $16,508 per year full-time, $680 per credit part-time for nonresidents. Fees $480 per year full-time, $180 per year part-time. • Dr. Louis A. Pingel, Associate Dean, 412-648-1775. E-mail: pingel1+@pitt.edu. Application contact: Jackie Harden, Manager, 412-648-7060. Fax: 412-648-1899. E-mail: jackie@sched.fsl.pitt.edu.

University of South Carolina, Graduate School, School of Public Health, Department of Health Promotion and Education, Columbia, SC 29208. Offers programs in alcohol and drug studies (Certificate), health education administration (Ed D), health promotion and education (MAT, MPH, MS, MSPH, Dr PH, PhD), school health education (Certificate). One or more programs accredited by CEPH. MAT and Ed D offered in cooperation with the College of Education. Faculty: 11 full-time (3 women). Students: 86 full-time (73 women), 55 part-time (52 women); includes 24 minority (22 African Americans, 1 Asian American, 1 Hispanic), 12 international. Average age 32. 99 applicants, 64% accepted. In 1997, 46 master's, 10 doctorates, 10 Certificates awarded. *Degree requirements:* For master's, thesis or alternative, practicum (MPH), project (MS) required, foreign language not required; for doctorate, dissertation. *Entrance requirements:* For master's and doctorate, GRE General Test. Application deadline: rolling. Application fee: $35. Electronic applications accepted. *Expenses:* Tuition $4480 per year full-time, $220 per credit hour part-time for state residents; $9338 per year full-time, $457 per credit hour part-time for nonresidents. Fees $125 per year full-time, $37 per semester (minimum) part-time. *Financial aid:* Research assistantships, teaching assistantships, traineeships, and career-related internships or fieldwork available. *Faculty research:* Implementation and evaluation of health behavior change programs, nutrition behavior, work site health promotion, AIDS education. • Dr. Donna L. Richter, Chair, 803-777-6558. Application contact: Dr. Murray Vincent, Graduate Director, 803-777-7096. Fax: 803-777-4783.

University of Southern California, School of Medicine and Graduate School, Graduate Programs in Medicine, Program in Public Health, Los Angeles, CA 90089. Offerings include health promotion (MPH). Program new for fall 1998. *Entrance requirements:* GRE General Test (minimum combined score of 1000), TOEFL, minimum GPA of 3.0. *Expenses:* Tuition $706 per unit. Fees $414 per year full-time, $32 per year part-time. • Dr. Richard N. Lolley, Associate Dean for Research, Graduate Programs in Medicine, 213-342-1607. Fax: 213-342-1610. E-mail: lolley@hsc.usc.edu.

University of Tennessee, Knoxville, College of Human Ecology, Department of Health and Safety Sciences, Program in Health Promotion and Health Education, Knoxville, TN 37996. Awards MS. Part-time programs available. Students: 3 full-time (2 women), 11 part-time (9 women); includes 2 minority (both African Americans), 1 international. 7 applicants, 71% accepted. In 1997, 8 degrees awarded. *Degree requirements:* Thesis optional, foreign language not required. *Entrance requirements:* TOEFL (minimum score 550), minimum GPA of 2.7. Application deadline: 2/1 (priority date; rolling processing). Application fee: $35. Electronic applications accepted. *Tuition:* $3354 per year full-time, $181 per semester hour part-time for state residents; $8410 per year full-time, $462 per semester hour part-time for nonresidents. *Financial aid:* Application deadline 2/1. • Dr. Jack Ellison, Graduate Representative, 423-974-5041.

See in-depth description on page 1185.

The University of Texas Medical Branch at Galveston, Graduate School of Biomedical Sciences, Program in Allied Health Sciences, Galveston, TX 77555. Offerings include health education and promotion (MS). Program faculty: 15 full-time (4 women). *Degree requirements:* Thesis or alternative required, foreign language not required. *Entrance requirements:* GRE General Test (minimum combined score of 1100). Application deadline: 8/15 (rolling processing). Application fee: $25 ($50 for international students). *Expenses:* Tuition $36 per credit hour for state residents; $249 per credit hour for nonresidents. Fees $146 per year full-time, $124 per semester (minimum) part-time. • Dr. David Chiriboga, Director, 409-772-3038. Fax: 409-747-1610. E-mail: dchiribo@utmb.edu.

University of Utah, College of Health, Department of Health Promotion and Education, Salt Lake City, UT 84112-1107. Awards M Phil, MS, Ed D, PhD. Part-time programs available. Faculty: 6 full-time (3 women), 15 part-time (11 women). Students: 19 full-time (10 women), 14 part-time (9 women); includes 1 minority (Asian American). Average age 34. In 1997, 2 master's, 3 doctorates awarded. Terminal master's awarded for partial completion of doctoral program. *Degree requirements:* Thesis/dissertation or alternative, comprehensive exam, field experience required, foreign language not required. *Entrance requirements:* For master's, GRE General Test (minimum combined score of 1000), TOEFL (minimum score 500), minimum GPA of 3.0; for doctorate, GRE General Test (minimum combined score of 1000) or MAT (minimum score 51), TOEFL (minimum score 500), minimum GPA of 3.2, 2 years of teaching experience, writing sample. Application deadline: 7/1. Application fee: $30 ($50 for international students). *Tuition:* $2045 per year full-time, $562 per semester (minimum) part-time for state residents; $6129 per year full-time, $1607 per semester (minimum) part-time for nonresidents. *Financial aid:* In 1997–98, 4 teaching assistantships were awarded; Federal Work-Study, institutionally sponsored loans, and career-related internships or fieldwork also available. Financial aid application deadline: 3/28. *Faculty research:* Health behavior and counseling, health service administration, evaluation of health programs. • Iona R. Grosshans, Chair, 801-581-8095. Application contact: Eric Trunnell, Director of Graduate Studies, 801-581-4462.

Western Illinois University, College of Education and Human Services, Department of Health Education and Promotion, Macomb, IL 61455-1390. Awards MS. Part-time programs available. Faculty: 13 full-time (3 women). Students: 15 full-time (12 women), 27 part-time (21 women); includes 5 minority (4 African Americans, 1 Asian American), 5 international. Average age 36. 21 applicants, 81% accepted. In 1997, 14 degrees awarded. *Degree requirements:* Thesis or alternative required, foreign language not required. *Entrance requirements:* Minimum GPA of 2.75. Application deadline: rolling. Application fee: $0 ($25 for international students). *Expenses:* Tuition $2304 per year full-time, $96 per semester hour part-time for state residents; $6912 per year full-time, $288 per semester hour part-time for nonresidents. Fees $944 per year full-time, $33 per semester hour part-time. *Financial aid:* In 1997–98, 10 students received aid, including 10 research assistantships averaging $610 per month; full tuition waivers also available. Financial aid applicants required to submit FAFSA. *Faculty research:* Alcohol-impaired DUI program, rural health, lead poisoning prevention, fire safety. • Dr. B. Nicholas DiGrino, Interim Chairperson, 309-298-1076. Application contact: Barbara Baily, Director of Graduate Studies, 309-298-1806. Fax: 309-298-2245. E-mail: barb_baily@ccmail.wiu.edu.

West Virginia University, School of Medicine, Graduate Programs in Basic Health Sciences, Community Health Promotion Program, Morgantown, WV 26506. Awards MS. Part-time and evening/weekend programs available. Postbaccalaureate distance learning degree programs offered (no on-campus study). Students: 33 full-time (22 women), 188 part-time (161 women); includes 17 minority (13 African Americans, 3 Asian Americans, 1 Hispanic), 2 international. Average age 37. 110 applicants, 87% accepted. In 1997, 45 degrees awarded (100% found work related to degree). *Degree requirements:* Thesis required (for some programs), foreign language not required. *Entrance requirements:* TOEFL (minimum score 550), minimum GPA of 3.0. Application deadline: 3/1 (priority date; rolling processing). Application fee: $45. *Financial aid:* In 1997–98, 5 students received aid, including 2 research assistantships (both to first-year students) averaging $589 per month, 2 teaching assistantships (both to first-year students) averaging $589 per month; partial tuition waivers, Federal Work-Study, institutionally sponsored loans, and career-related internships or fieldwork also available. Financial aid application deadline: 2/1; applicants required to submit FAFSA. *Faculty research:* Program design, injury control, human sexuality, substance abuse, fitness/health promotion education. • Dr. Kenard McPherson, Program Director, 304-293-7510 Ext. 277. E-mail: kmcphers@wvu.edu. Application contact: Linda A. Lilly, Administrative Secretary, 304-293-7510 Ext. 0. Fax: 304-293-8969. E-mail: llilly@wvu.edu.

Industrial Hygiene

Central Missouri State University, College of Applied Sciences and Technology, Department of Safety Science Technology, Warrensburg, MO 64093. Offerings include industrial hygiene (MS). MS (industrial safety management, public services administration, security, transportation safety) being phased out; applicants no longer accepted. MS (occupational safety management) new for fall 1998. Department faculty: 9 full-time. *Application deadline:* 6/30 (priority date; rolling processing). *Application fee:* $25 ($50 for international students). *Tuition:* $3288 per year full-time, $137 per credit hour part-time for state residents; $5928 per year full-time, $274 per credit hour part-time for nonresidents. • Dr. John Prince, Interim Chair, 660-543-4626. Fax: 660-543-8142. E-mail: safety@cmsuvmb.cmsu.edu.

Harvard University, School of Public Health, Department of Environmental Health, Program in Environmental Science and Engineering, Boston, MA 02115. Offerings include industrial hygiene and occupational safety (SM, SD). *Degree requirements:* For doctorate, dissertation, qualifying exam. *Entrance requirements:* GRE, TOEFL (minimum score 550). Application deadline: 1/4. Application fee: $60. *Expenses:* Tuition $21,895 per year full-time, $10,948 per year part-time. Fees $686 per year. • Dr. John D. Spengler, Director, 617-432-1255.

Montana Tech of The University of Montana, Graduate School, Industrial Hygiene Program, Butte, MT 59701-8997. Awards MS. Part-time programs available. Faculty: 5 full-time (1 woman). Students: 10 full-time (5 women), 6 part-time (5 women). 7 applicants, 86% accepted. In 1997, 9 degrees awarded. *Degree requirements:* Thesis required, foreign language not required. *Entrance requirements:* GRE General Test, TOEFL (minimum score 525), minimum GPA of 3.25. Application deadline: 4/1 (priority date; rolling processing; 10/1 for spring admission). Application fee: $30. *Tuition:* $2976 per year full-time, $373 per semester (minimum) part-time for state residents; $8857 per year full-time, $1118 per semester (minimum) part-time for nonresidents. *Financial aid:* In 1997–98, 16 students received aid, including 4 teaching assistantships (2 to first-year students) averaging $266 per month and totaling $8,500; fellowships, research assistantships, full and partial tuition waivers, Federal Work-Study, institutionally sponsored loans, and career-related internships or fieldwork also available. Aid available to part-time students. Financial aid application deadline: 4/1; applicants required to submit FAFSA. *Faculty research:* Ergonomics, metal bioavailability, aerosols, particulate sizing, respiration protection. Total annual research expenditures: $75,000. • Julie Norman, Department Head, 406-496-4393. Fax: 406-496-4650. E-mail: jnorman@po1.mtech.edu. Application contact: Cindy Dunstan, Administrative Assistant, 406-496-4128. Fax: 406-496-4334. E-mail: cdunstan@po1.mtech.edu.

Purdue University, Graduate School and School of Pharmacy and Pharmacal Sciences, School of Health Sciences, Program in Industrial Hygiene, West Lafayette, IN 47907. Awards MS, PhD. *Degree requirements:* For master's, thesis optional, foreign language not required; for doctorate, 1 foreign language (computer language can substitute), dissertation. *Entrance requirements:* GRE General Test, minimum B average. Application deadline: rolling. Application fee: $30. Electronic applications accepted. *Tuition:* $3500 per year full-time, $126 per credit hour part-time for state residents; $11,720 per year full-time, $387 per credit hour part-time for nonresidents. *Financial aid:* Available to part-time students. Financial aid applicants required to submit FAFSA. • Dr. P. L. Ziemer, Head, School of Health Sciences, 765-494-1435. Application contact: Dr. Robert Landolt, Graduate Chairperson, 765-494-1440.

See in-depth description on page 1511.

San Diego State University, College of Health and Human Services, Graduate School of Public Health, San Diego, CA 92182. Offerings include industrial hygiene (MS). School faculty: 25 full-time (9 women), 36 part-time (21 women). *Application deadline:* 5/15 (priority date; rolling processing; 10/15 for spring admission). *Application fee:* $55. *Expenses:* Tuition $0 for state residents; $246 per unit for nonresidents. Fees $1932 per year full-time, $1266 per year part-time. • Dr. Kenneth Bart, Director, 619-594-6317. Application contact: Brenda Fass-Holmes, Coordinator, Admissions and Student Affairs, 619-594-6317. E-mail: bholmes@mail.sdsu.edu.

Texas A&M University, College of Engineering, Department of Nuclear Engineering, Program in Health Physics/Radiological Health, College Station, TX 77843. Offerings include industrial hygiene (MS). *Degree requirements:* Thesis or alternative required, foreign language not required. *Entrance requirements:* GRE General Test, TOEFL. Application fee: $35 ($75 for international students). • Application contact: Dr. Yassin A. Hassan, Graduate Coordinator, 409-845-7090.

Université du Québec à Trois-Rivières, Program in Industrial Safety and Hygiene, Trois-Rivières, PQ G9A 5H7, Canada. Awards M Sc A. Part-time programs available. Students: 5 full-time (3 women). 9 applicants, 89% accepted. *Entrance requirements:* Appropriate bachelor's degree, proficiency in French. Application deadline: 2/1. Application fee: $30. *Financial aid:* Fellowships, research assistantships, teaching assistantships available. • Pierre C. Dessureault, Director, 819-376-5070. Fax: 819-376-5012. E-mail: pierre_dessureault@uqtr.uquebec.ca. Application contact: Suzanne Camirand, Admissions Officer, 819-376-5045 Ext. 2591. Fax: 819-376-5210. E-mail: suzanne_camirand@uqtr.uquebec.ca.

The University of Alabama at Birmingham, Graduate School, School of Public Health, Department of Environmental Health Sciences, Birmingham, AL 35294. Offerings include industrial hygiene (MPH, MSPH, Dr PH, PhD). One or more programs accredited by CEPH. Department faculty: 9. *Degree requirements:* For master's, internship, project research (MSPH); for doctorate, dissertation. *Entrance requirements:* GRE General Test, TOEFL. Application deadline: 4/1. Application fee: $30 ($60 for international students). Electronic applications accepted. *Expenses:* Tuition $3672 per year full-time, $102 per credit hour part-time for state residents; $7344 per year full-time, $204 per credit hour part-time for nonresidents. Fees $699 per year (minimum) full-time, $116 per quarter (minimum) part-time. • Dr. R. Kent Oestenstad, Interim Chair, 205-934-6208. Application contact: Nancy Pinson, Coordinator of Student Admissions, 205-934-4993. Fax: 205-975-5484. E-mail: osas@ms.soph.uab.edu.

See in-depth description on page 1523.

University of Cincinnati, College of Medicine, Graduate Programs in Medicine, Department of Environmental Health, Cincinnati, OH 45267. Offerings include environmental and industrial hygiene (MS). Department faculty: 23 full-time. *Degree requirements:* Thesis required, foreign language not required. *Average time to degree:* master's–2.8 years full-time; doctorate–8.8 years full-time. *Entrance requirements:* GRE General Test, TOEFL, bachelor's degree in science. Application deadline: 2/1 (priority date; rolling processing). Application fee: $30. *Tuition:* $7228 per year full-time, $185 per credit hour part-time for state residents; $13,812 per year full-time, $352 per credit hour part-time for nonresidents. • Dr. Marshall W. Anderson, Chairman, 513-558-5701. Fax: 513-558-4397. E-mail: marshall.anderson@uc.edu. Application contact: Judy Jarell, 513-558-1729. E-mail: judy.jarrell@uc.edu.

See in-depth description on page 1527.

The University of Iowa, College of Medicine and Graduate College, Graduate Programs in Medicine, Department of Preventive Medicine and Environmental Health, Iowa City, IA 52242-1316. Offerings include industrial hygiene (MS). MS/MA and MS/MS offered jointly with the Program in Urban and Regional Planning. Department faculty: 27 full-time (5 women), 11 part-time (4 women). *Degree requirements:* Computer language (biostatistics) required, thesis optional, foreign language not required. *Average time to degree:* master's–2 years full-time, 6 years part-time; doctorate–5 years full-time, 9 years part-time. *Entrance requirements:* GRE General Test (minimum combined score of 1050), TOEFL (minimum score 600), minimum GPA of 2.7. Application deadline: 1/15 (priority date; rolling processing; 10/1 for spring admission). Application fee: $30 ($50 for international students). *Expenses:* Tuition $3166 per year full-time, $176 per credit hour part-time for state residents; $10,202 per year full-time, $567 per credit hour part-time for nonresidents. Fees $101 per year full-time, $51 per year (minimum) part-time. • Dr. James Merchant, Interim Head, 319-335-9833. Fax: 319-335-9772. E-mail: james-merchant@uiowa.edu. Application contact: Barbara Scott, Graduate Studies Coordinator, 319-335-8992. Fax: 319-335-9200. E-mail: barbara-scott@uiowa.edu.

University of Michigan, School of Public Health, Department of Environmental and Industrial Health, Program in Occupational Health, Ann Arbor, MI 48109. Offerings include industrial hygiene (MS, PhD). MS and PhD offered through the Horace H. Rackham School of Graduate Studies. *Degree requirements:* For doctorate, variable foreign language requirement, oral defense of dissertation, preliminary exam. *Entrance requirements:* For doctorate, GRE General Test. Application deadline: 3/1 (priority date; rolling processing). Application fee: $55. • Dr. Thomas G. Robbins, Program Director, 734-936-0757. E-mail: trobins@umich.edu.

See in-depth description on page 1535.

University of Minnesota, Twin Cities Campus, School of Public Health, Division of Environmental and Occupational Health, Area in Industrial Hygiene, Minneapolis, MN 55455-0213. Awards MPH, MS, PhD. One or more programs accredited by CEPH. Faculty: 20 full-time (8 women). *Degree requirements:* For doctorate, dissertation required, foreign language not required. *Entrance requirements:* For master's, GRE General Test (minimum combined score of 1500 on three sections), minimum GPA of 3.0; for doctorate, GRE General Test (minimum combined score of 1500 on three sections). Application deadline: 4/15 (priority date; rolling processing). Application fee: $50 ($75 for international students). *Financial aid:* Federal Work-Study, institutionally sponsored loans, and career-related internships or fieldwork available. Financial aid application deadline: 4/15. • Application contact: Kathy Soupir, Student Coordinator, 612-625-0622. Fax: 612-626-4837. E-mail: ksoupir@mail.eoh.umn.edu.

See in-depth description on page 1537.

University of New Haven, School of Public Safety and Professional Studies, Program in Industrial Hygiene, West Haven, CT 06516-1916. Awards MS. Students: 2 full-time (0 women), 16 part-time (4 women); includes 3 minority (1 African American, 1 Asian American, 1 Hispanic). 3 applicants, 33% accepted. *Degree requirements:* Thesis or alternative required, foreign language not required. *Application deadline:* rolling. *Application fee:* $50. *Expenses:* Tuition $1125 per course. Fees $13 per trimester. *Financial aid:* Application deadline 5/1; applicants required to submit FAFSA. • Dr. Brad T. Garber, Director, 203-932-7175.

University of Puerto Rico, Medical Sciences Campus, Graduate School of Public Health, Department of Environmental Health, Program in Industrial Hygiene, San Juan, PR 00936-5067. Awards MS. Part-time programs available. Students: 44 (30 women). 33 applicants, 33% accepted. In 1997, 4 degrees awarded. *Degree requirements:* Computer language, thesis required, foreign language not required. *Entrance requirements:* GRE, previous course work in biology, chemistry, mathematics, and physics. Application deadline: 3/3. Application fee: $15. *Financial aid:* Research assistantships, teaching assistantships, Federal Work-Study, institutionally sponsored loans available. Financial aid application deadline: 4/30. • Application contact: Mayra E. Santiago-Vargas, Counselor, 787-756-5244. Fax: 787-759-6719.

University of South Carolina, Graduate School, School of Public Health, Department of Environmental Health Sciences, Program in Industrial Hygiene, Columbia, SC 29208. Awards MPH, MSPH, PhD. One or more programs accredited by CEPH. *Degree requirements:* For master's, thesis, practicum (MPH) required, foreign language not required; for doctorate, 1 foreign language, dissertation. *Entrance requirements:* GRE. Application deadline: rolling. Application fee: $35. Electronic applications accepted. *Expenses:* Tuition $4480 per year full-time, $220 per credit hour part-time for state residents; $9338 per year full-time, $457 per credit hour part-time for nonresidents. Fees $125 per year full-time, $37 per semester (minimum) part-time. *Faculty research:* Sampling and calibration method development, exposure and risk assessment, respirator and dermal protective equipment, ergonomics, air cleaning methods and devices. • Application contact: Dr. Edward Oswald, Graduate Director, 803-777-6994. Fax: 803-777-3391.

University of Washington, School of Public Health and Community Medicine, Department of Environmental Health, Seattle, WA 98195. Offerings include industrial hygiene (PhD), industrial hygiene and safety (MS). Terminal master's awarded for partial completion of doctoral program. Department faculty: 37 full-time (7 women), 9 part-time (0 women). *Degree requirements:* For doctorate, dissertation required, foreign language not required. *Average time to degree:* master's–2 years full-time; doctorate–5 years full-time. *Entrance requirements:* For doctorate, GRE General Test, TOEFL (minimum score 500), minimum GPA of 3.0. Application deadline: 2/1 (priority date). Application fee: $45. *Tuition:* $5433 per year full-time, $775 per quarter (minimum) part-time for state residents; $13,479 per year full-time, $1925 per quarter (minimum) part-time for nonresidents. • Dr. Thomas Burbacher, Graduate Coordinator, 206-543-3199. Application contact: Sara E. Griggs, Manager, Student Services, 206-543-3199. Fax: 206-543-9616. E-mail: ehgrad@u.washington.edu.

See in-depth description on page 1549.

Wayne State University, College of Pharmacy and Allied Health Professions, Faculty of Allied Health Professions, Department of Occupational and Environmental Health Sciences, Detroit, MI 48202. Offerings include occupational health sciences (MS), with options in industrial hygiene, industrial toxicology, occupational medicine. Department faculty: 3 full-time (1 woman), 20 part-time (3 women), 5 FTE. *Degree requirements:* Thesis optional, foreign language not required. *Average time to degree:* master's–2 years full-time, 3.5 years part-time. *Entrance requirements:* GRE General Test, 1 year of course work in biology, mathematics, and physics; 2 years of course work in chemistry. Application deadline: 6/15 (priority date). Application fee: $20 ($30 for international students). *Expenses:* Tuition $163 per credit hour for state residents; $355 per credit hour for nonresidents. Fees $498 per year full-time, $114 per semester (minimum) part-time. • Dr. David J. P. Bassett, Chairperson, 313-577-1551. Fax: 313-577-5589.

International Health

Boston University, School of Medicine, School of Public Health, International Health Department, Boston, MA 02215. Awards MPH, Certificate. One or more programs accredited by CEPH. Students: 44 full-time (26 women), 13 part-time (8 women); includes 8 minority (1 African American, 4 Asian Americans, 3 Hispanics), 25 international. Average age 31. *Degree requirements:* For master's, thesis required, foreign language not required. *Entrance requirements:* For master's, GRE General Test, TOEFL. Application deadline: 4/15 (rolling processing; 10/25 for spring admission). Application fee: $50. *Financial aid:* Federal Work-Study, institutionally sponsored loans, and career-related internships or fieldwork available. • Dr. William J. Bicknell, Chairman, 617-638-5234. Application contact: Amy Gluckin, 617-638-5234. Fax: 617-638-4476. E-mail: cih@bu.edu.

See in-depth description on page 1487.

Emory University, The Rollins School of Public Health, Department of International Health, Atlanta, GA 30322-1100. Awards MPH. Accredited by CEPH. *Degree requirements:* Thesis (for some programs), practicum required, foreign language not required. *Entrance requirements:* GRE General Test. Application deadline: 2/15 (priority date; rolling processing). Application fee: $50. *Expenses:* Tuition $14,136 per year full-time, $589 per credit hour part-time. Fees $200 per year. *Financial aid:* Application deadline 2/15. • Application contact: Susan Daniel, Director of Admissions, 404-727-5481. Fax: 404-727-3996. E-mail: admit@sph.emory.edu.

See in-depth description on page 1493.

The George Washington University, School of Public Health and Health Services, Master's Program in Public Health, Track in International Health, Washington, DC 20052. Offers programs in health promotion (MPH), policy and programs (MPH). Accredited by CEPH. *Degree requirements:* Case study or special project required, thesis not required. *Entrance requirements:* GMAT, GRE General Test, or MCAT; TOEFL. Application deadline: 5/15 (priority date; rolling processing; 11/15 for spring admission). Application fee: $50. *Expenses:* Tuition $680 per semester hour. Fees $35 per semester hour. • Application contact: Michelle Sparacino, Director of Recruitment, 202-994-2160. Fax: 202-994-3773. E-mail: sphhs-info@gwumc.edu.

Announcement: Master of Public Health program offers an international health track with concentrations in policy and health promotion as part of the Department of International Public Health in the School of Public Health and Health Services. The George Washington University Center for International Health is the first WHO Collaborating Center in International Health and Development. Visit the Web site (http://www.gwumc.edu/sphhs).

See in-depth description on page 1495.

Harvard University, School of Public Health, Department of Population and International Health, Boston, MA 02115. Awards SM, DPH, SD. Part-time programs available. Faculty: 16 full-time (3 women), 8 part-time (3 women). Students: 40 full-time (28 women), 8 part-time (6 women); includes 6 minority (1 African American, 2 Asian Americans, 3 Hispanics), 19 international. Average age 31. 100 applicants, 30% accepted. In 1997, 12 master's, 11 doctorates awarded. *Degree requirements:* For master's, thesis; for doctorate, dissertation, qualifying exam. *Entrance requirements:* GRE, TOEFL (minimum score 550). Application deadline: 1/4. Application fee: $60. *Expenses:* Tuition $21,895 per year full-time, $10,948 per year part-time. Fees $686 per year. *Financial aid:* Fellowships, partial tuition waivers, Federal Work-Study available. Aid available to part-time students. Financial aid application deadline: 2/12; applicants required to submit FAFSA. *Faculty research:* Fertility, population and development in Latin America, demographic and regional planning models, international health policy. • Dr. Michael Reich, Acting Chair, 617-432-0687. Application contact: Carrie Daniels, Assistant Director of Admissions, 617-432-1031. Fax: 617-432-2009. E-mail: admisofc@sph.harvard.edu.

Harvard University, School of Public Health, Master of Public Health Program, Boston, MA 02115. Offerings include international health (MPH). *Average time to degree:* master's–1 year full-time, 2.5 years part-time. *Entrance requirements:* GRE, TOEFL (minimum score 550). Application deadline: 1/4 (priority date). Application fee: $60. *Expenses:* Tuition $21,895 per year full-time, $10,948 per year part-time. Fees $686 per year. • Dr. Gareth M. Green, Associate Dean for Professional Education, 617-432-0090. Application contact: Carrie Daniels, Assistant Director of Admissions, 617-432-1031. Fax: 617-432-2009. E-mail: admisofc@sph.harvard.edu.

Johns Hopkins University, School of Hygiene and Public Health, Department of International Health, Baltimore, MD 21205. Offers programs in disease control (MHS, Dr PH, PhD, Sc D); health systems (MHS, Dr PH, PhD, Sc D); human nutrition (MHS, Dr PH, PhD, Sc D); international health policy, planning, and implementation (MHS, Dr PH, PhD, Sc D); social sciences and public health (MHS, Dr PH, Sc D); vaccine sciences (Dr PH, PhD, Sc D). Faculty: 81 full-time, 149 part-time. Students: 119 (77 women); includes 20 minority (5 African Americans, 13 Asian Americans, 2 Hispanics), 40 international. 192 applicants, 51% accepted. In 1997, 18 master's, 12 doctorates awarded. *Degree requirements:* For master's, thesis (for some programs), internship required, foreign language not required; for doctorate, dissertation, 1 year full-time residency, oral and written exams required, foreign language not required. *Entrance requirements:* GRE General Test. Application deadline: 2/1 (priority date; rolling processing). Application fee: $60. *Financial aid:* Scholarships, Federal Work-Study, institutionally sponsored loans available. Aid available to part-time students. Financial aid application deadline: 4/15. *Faculty research:* Respiratory diseases, oral rehydration programs, vitamin A deficiency, infant malnutrition, health manpower planning. Total annual research expenditures: $22.6 million. • Dr. Robert E. Black, Chairman, 410-955-3934. E-mail: rblack@jhsph.edu. Application contact: Nancy Stephens, Student Coordinator, 410-955-3734. Fax: 410-955-8734. E-mail: nstephen@jhsph.edu.

Johns Hopkins University, School of Hygiene and Public Health, Program in Public Health, Baltimore, MD 21205. Offerings include international health (MPH). Accredited by CEPH. *Entrance requirements:* GRE General Test, TOEFL (minimum score 550), 2 years of work related experience. Application deadline: 2/1 (priority date; rolling processing). Application fee: $60. • Dr. Miriam Alexander, Director, 410-955-1291. Application contact: Lenora Davis, Administrator, 410-955-1291. Fax: 410-955-4749. E-mail: lrdavis@jhsph.edu.

Loma Linda University, School of Public Health, Programs in International Health, Loma Linda, CA 92350. Awards MPH. One or more programs accredited by CEPH. Students: 26 full-time (13 women), 24 part-time (16 women). 21 applicants, 71% accepted. In 1997, 20 degrees awarded. *Entrance requirements:* Michigan English Language Assessment Battery (minimum score 92) or TOEFL (minimum score 600). Application deadline: rolling. Application fee: $100. *Tuition:* $380 per unit. *Financial aid:* Application deadline 5/15. • Dr. Jayakaran Job, Chair, 909-824-4902. Application contact: Terri Tamayose, Director of Admissions and Academic Records, 909-824-4694. Fax: 909-824-8087. E-mail: ttamayose@sph.llu.edu.

New York Medical College, Graduate School of Health Sciences, Programs in International and Public Health, Valhalla, NY 10595-1691. Offerings include international health (MPH, MS). *Degree requirements:* Computer language required, foreign language not required. *Entrance requirements:* TOEFL. Application deadline: 7/20 (priority date; rolling processing; 12/1 for spring admission). Application fee: $35 ($60 for international students). *Tuition:* $415 per credit. • Dr. Cathey Falvo, Director, 914-594-4250.

Thunderbird, The American Graduate School of International Management, Program in International Health Management, Glendale, AZ 85306-3236. Awards MIHM. *Degree requirements:* 1 foreign language required, thesis optional. *Entrance requirements:* GMAT (minimum score 500; average 590), TOEFL (average 610). Application deadline: 1/31 (priority date; rolling processing; 7/31 for spring admission). Application fee: $50. *Expenses:* Tuition $21,000 per year full-time, $1000 per credit hour part-time. Fees $200 per year. *Financial aid:* Available to part-time students. Financial aid application deadline: 4/1; applicants required to submit FAFSA. • Application contact: Judy Johnson, Director of Admissions, 602-978-7100. Fax: 602-439-5432. E-mail: johnsonj@t-bird.edu.

See in-depth description on page 555.

Tulane University, School of Public Health and Tropical Medicine, Department of International Health and Development, New Orleans, LA 70118-5669. Awards MADH, MPH, Dr PH. One or more programs accredited by CEPH. Students: 207 full-time (138 women), 18 part-time (12 women); includes 36 minority (11 African Americans, 11 Asian Americans, 13 Hispanics, 1 Native American), 60 international. Average age 28. Terminal master's awarded for partial completion of doctoral program. *Degree requirements:* For master's, 1 foreign language required, thesis not required; for doctorate, 1 foreign language, dissertation. *Average time to degree:* master's–1.5 years full-time; doctorate–4 years full-time. *Entrance requirements:* For master's, GRE General Test (minimum combined score of 1000; average 1100), TOEFL (minimum score 525); for doctorate, GRE General Test (minimum combined score of 1000; average 1250), TOEFL (minimum score 525). Application deadline: 4/15 (priority date; rolling processing; 10/15 for spring admission). Application fee: $40. *Financial aid:* Application deadline 2/1. *Faculty research:* Reproductive health, HIV/AIDS, nutrition and food security, health financing, program evaluation. Total annual research expenditures: $2.367 million. • Dr. Jane Bertrand, Head, 504-587-7318. Application contact: Penny Jessop, Coordinator, 504-588-5399. Fax: 504-584-3653. E-mail: pjessop@mailhost.tcs.tulane.edu.

Uniformed Services University of the Health Sciences, School of Medicine, Division of Basic Medical Sciences, Department of Preventive Medicine/Biometrics, Program in Tropical Medicine and Hygiene, Bethesda, MD 20814-4799. Awards MTMH. Faculty: 52 full-time (9 women), 97 part-time (16 women). Students: 0. 3 applicants, 33% accepted. *Degree requirements:* Computer language, comprehensive exam required, foreign language and thesis not required. *Entrance requirements:* GRE General Test, TOEFL, MD, U.S. citizenship. Application deadline: 2/15 (rolling processing). Application fee: $0. *Tuition:* $0. *Faculty research:* Epidemiology, biostatistics, tropical public health. • Col. Kenneth Dixon, Graduate Program Director, 301-295-3050. Fax: 301-295-1933. Application contact: Janet M. Anastasi, Graduate Program Coordinator, 301-295-9474. Fax: 301-295-6772.

The University of Alabama at Birmingham, Graduate School, School of Public Health, Department of International Health, Birmingham, AL 35294. Offers programs in international health (MPH, Dr PH), public health nutrition (MPH, Dr PH). One or more programs accredited by CEPH. *Degree requirements:* For master's, research project; for doctorate, dissertation. *Entrance requirements:* GRE General Test, TOEFL. Application deadline: 4/1. Application fee: $30 ($60 for international students). Electronic applications accepted. *Expenses:* Tuition $3672 per year full-time, $102 per credit hour part-time for state residents; $7344 per year full-time, $204 per credit hour part-time for nonresidents. Fees $699 per year (minimum) full-time, $116 per quarter (minimum) part-time. • Dr. Charles B. Stephensen, Interim Chair, 205-934-1732. Fax: 205-975-3329. E-mail: soph-ih@crl.soph.uab.edu. Application contact: Nancy Pinson, Coordinator of Student Admissions, 205-934-4993. Fax: 205-975-5484. E-mail: osas@ms.soph.uab.edu.

Announcement: The department offers MPH and Dr PH degrees in international health. Primary interests of the faculty include nutrition and infectious diseases; vitamin A and other micronutrient deficiencies; tuberculosis, STDs, and AIDS; environmental sanitation; reproductive health; and program management. Overseas internships and projects are required for some MPH programs. Current research sites include Bangladesh, Guatemala, Jamaica, Peru, and Zambia. For more information, students may send e-mail (soph-ih@crl.soph.uab.edu) or access the department's Web site (http://www.uab.edu/PublicHealth).

See in-depth description on page 1523.

University of Hawaii at Manoa, College of Health Sciences and Social Welfare, School of Public Health, Honolulu, HI 96822. Offerings include international health (MPH, MS). School faculty: 18 full-time (8 women), 4 part-time (2 women), 19.6 FTE. *Degree requirements:* Thesis (for some programs). *Average time to degree:* master's–1.2 years full-time, 3 years part-time. *Application deadline:* 3/1 (9/1 for spring admission). *Application fee:* $25 ($50 for international students). *Tuition:* $4029 per year full-time, $214 per credit hour part-time for state residents; $9957 per year full-time, $461 per credit hour part-time for nonresidents. • Dr. D. William Wood, Interim Dean, 808-956-8491. Application contact: Nancy Kilonsky, Assistant Dean, 808-956-8267.

University of Michigan, School of Public Health, Department of Epidemiology, Ann Arbor, MI 48109. Offerings include international health (MPH). Accredited by CEPH. *Entrance requirements:* GRE General Test, MCAT. Application deadline: 3/1 (priority date; rolling processing). Application fee: $55. • Dr. George A. Kaplan, Chair, 734-764-5435. E-mail: gkaplan@sph.umich.edu.

See in-depth description on page 1535.

Yale University, School of Medicine, Department of Epidemiology and Public Health, Division of International Health, New Haven, CT 06520. Awards MPH. Accredited by CEPH. Faculty: 2 full-time (1 woman), 1 (woman) part-time. Students: 39 full-time (25 women), 1 (woman) part-time; includes 17 minority (14 Asian Americans, 3 Hispanics), 6 international. Average age 25. 85 applicants, 48% accepted. In 1997, 17 degrees awarded. *Degree requirements:* 1 foreign language, thesis, internship. *Entrance requirements:* GMAT, GRE, LSAT, or MCAT; TOEFL, previous undergraduate course work in mathematics and science. Application deadline: rolling. Application fee: $60. *Financial aid:* Scholarships, Federal Work-Study, institutionally sponsored loans, and career-related internships or fieldwork available. Aid available to part-time students. Financial aid application deadline: 4/15. *Faculty research:* International health promotion and healthy public policy, community health planning, health of elderly and disabled persons. • Dr. Lowell S. Levin, Professor, 203-785-2861. Fax: 203-785-6193. Application contact: Joan Stenner, Admissions Officer, 203-785-2844. Fax: 203-785-4845. E-mail: joan.stenner@yale.edu.

See in-depth description on page 1551.

Maternal and Child Health

Boston University, School of Medicine, School of Public Health, Maternal and Child Health Department, Boston, MA 02215. Offers programs in maternal and child health (MPH), nurse midwifery education (Certificate). Students: 40 full-time (39 women), 12 part-time (11 women); includes 17 minority (5 African Americans, 9 Asian Americans, 3 Hispanics), 4 international. Average age 30. *Entrance requirements:* For master's, GRE General Test, TOEFL. Application deadline: 4/15 (rolling processing; 10/25 for spring admission). Application fee: $50. • Dr. Lisa Paine, Chairman, 617-638-5012. Fax: 617-638-5370. Application contact: Barbara St. Onge, Director of Admissions, 617-638-4640. Fax: 617-638-5299.

See in-depth description on page 1487.

Columbia University, School of Public Health, Division of Population and Family Health, New York, NY 10032. Awards MPH. One or more programs accredited by CEPH. Part-time programs available. Students: 60. In 1997, 35 degrees awarded. *Average time to degree:* master's–1.5 years full-time, 3 years part-time. *Entrance requirements:* GRE General Test. Application deadline: 4/10. Application fee: $60. *Tuition:* $22,320 per year full-time, $744 per credit part-time. *Financial aid:* Research assistantships, Federal Work-Study, and career-related internships or fieldwork available. Financial aid application deadline: 3/15; applicants required to submit FAFSA. *Faculty research:* Women's sexual and reproductive health, adolescent sexual and reproductive behavior, infant and child health, maternal mortality, reproductive rights. • Dr. James McCarthy, Head, 212-304-5200. E-mail: jm25@columbia.edu. Application contact: Caroline Kay, Program Coordinator, 212-304-5261. Fax: 212-305-7024. E-mail: cck11@columbia.edu.

The George Washington University, School of Public Health and Health Services, Master's Program in Public Health, Track in Maternal and Child Health, Washington, DC 20052. Awards MPH. Accredited by CEPH. *Degree requirements:* Case study or special project required, thesis not required. *Entrance requirements:* GMAT, GRE General Test, or MCAT; TOEFL. Application deadline: 5/15 (priority date; rolling processing; 11/15 for spring admission). Application fee: $50. *Expenses:* Tuition $680 per semester hour. Fees $35 per semester hour. • Application contact: Michelle Sparacino, Director of Recruitment, 202-994-2160. Fax: 202-994-3773. E-mail: sphhs-info@gwumc.edu.

See in-depth description on page 1495.

Harvard University, School of Public Health, Department of Maternal and Child Health, Boston, MA 02115. Awards SM, DPH, SD. SM offered jointly with Simmons College. Part-time programs available. Faculty: 6 full-time (3 women), 20 part-time (7 women). Students: 15 full-time (13 women), 11 part-time (all women); includes 4 minority (3 Asian Americans, 1 Hispanic), 3 international. Average age 35. 44 applicants, 55% accepted. In 1997, 7 master's, 3 doctorates awarded. *Degree requirements:* For doctorate, dissertation, qualifying exam. *Entrance requirements:* GRE, TOEFL (minimum score 550). Application deadline: 1/4. Application fee: $60. *Expenses:* Tuition $21,895 per year full-time, $10,948 per year part-time. Fees $686 per year. *Financial aid:* Fellowships, partial tuition waivers, Federal Work-Study available. Aid available to part-time students. Financial aid application deadline: 2/12; applicants required to submit FAFSA. *Faculty research:* Childhood determinants of adult health, childhood injury, adolescent suicide, children with special needs. • Dr. Marie McCormick, Chairman, 617-432-1080. Application contact: Carrie Daniels, Assistant Director of Admissions, 617-432-1031. Fax: 617-432-2009. E-mail: admisofc@sph.harvard.edu.

Johns Hopkins University, School of Hygiene and Public Health, Department of Maternal and Child Health, Baltimore, MD 21205. Offers programs in public health/maternal and child health program planning, evaluation, and administration (MHS, Dr PH, PhD, Sc D); research, administration, and teaching (PhD). Faculty: 22 full-time, 15 part-time. Students: 35 (33 women); includes 10 minority (5 African Americans, 3 Asian Americans, 2 Hispanics), 2 international. 75 applicants, 24% accepted. In 1997, 6 master's, 3 doctorates awarded. *Degree requirements:* For master's, essay, fieldwork required, foreign language not required; for doctorate, dissertation, 1 year full-time residency, oral and written exams required, foreign language not required. *Entrance requirements:* GRE General Test. Application deadline: 2/1 (priority date; rolling processing). Application fee: $60. *Financial aid:* Scholarships, Federal Work-Study, institutionally sponsored loans available. Aid available to part-time students. Financial aid application deadline: 4/15. *Faculty research:* Child welfare, juvenile justice and child victimization, women's health, HIV infection, immunization, neonatal behavior. Total annual research expenditures: $6.2 million. • Dr. Bernard Guyer, Chair, 410-955-3384. Application contact: Sharon Hall, Academic Coordinator, 410-955-1116. Fax: 410-955-2303. E-mail: shall@jhsph.edu.

Johns Hopkins University, School of Hygiene and Public Health, Program in Public Health, Baltimore, MD 21205. Offerings include maternal and child health (MPH). Accredited by CEPH. *Entrance requirements:* GRE General Test, TOEFL (minimum score 550), 2 years of work related experience. Application deadline: 2/1 (priority date; rolling processing). Application fee: $60. • Dr. Miriam Alexander, Director, 410-955-1291. Application contact: Lenora Davis, Administrator, 410-955-1291. Fax: 410-955-4749. E-mail: lrdavis@jhsph.edu.

New York Medical College, Graduate School of Health Sciences, Programs in International and Public Health, Valhalla, NY 10595-1691. Offerings include maternal and child health (MPH). *Application deadline:* 7/20 (priority date; rolling processing; 12/1 for spring admission). *Application fee:* $35 ($60 for international students). *Tuition:* $415 per credit. • Dr. Cathey Falvo, Director, 914-594-4250.

Tulane University, School of Public Health and Tropical Medicine, Department of Community Health Sciences, Program in Maternal and Child Health, New Orleans, LA 70118-5669. Awards MPH, Dr PH, MSW/MPH. One or more programs accredited by CEPH. Students: 60 full-time (49 women), 11 part-time (8 women); includes 30 minority (22 African Americans, 4 Asian Americans, 3 Hispanics, 1 Native American), 16 international. Average age 29. *Degree requirements:* For master's, 1 foreign language required, thesis not required; for doctorate, 1 foreign language, dissertation. *Entrance requirements:* For master's, GRE General Test (minimum combined score of 1000; average 1100), TOEFL (minimum score 525); for doctorate, GRE General Test (minimum combined score of 1000; average 1250), TOEFL (minimum score 525). Application deadline: 4/15 (priority date; rolling processing; 10/15 for spring admission). Application fee: $40. *Financial aid:* Application deadline 2/1. • Dr. Judith La Rosa, Chair, Department of Community Health Sciences, 504-588-5391.

The University of Alabama at Birmingham, Graduate School, School of Public Health, Department of Maternal and Child Health, Birmingham, AL 35294. Awards MSPH. Accredited by CEPH. *Degree requirements:* Research project. *Application deadline:* rolling. *Application fee:* $30 ($60 for international students). Electronic applications accepted. *Expenses:* Tuition $3672 per year full-time, $102 per credit hour part-time for state residents; $7344 per year full-time, $204 per credit hour part-time for nonresidents. Fees $699 per year (minimum) full-time, $116 per quarter (minimum) part-time. • Dr. Lorraine V. Klerman, Chair, 205-934-7161. Application contact: Nancy Pinson, Coordinator of Student Admissions, 205-934-4993. Fax: 205-975-5484. E-mail: osas@ms.soph.uab.edu.

See in-depth description on page 1523.

University of California, Berkeley, School of Public Health, Master Internationalist Program, Berkeley, CA 94720-1500. Offerings include maternal and child health (MPH). Accredited by CEPH. MA (community health education) admissions temporarily suspended. *Entrance requirements:* GRE General Test, minimum GPA of 3.0. Application deadline: 1/12 (rolling processing). Application fee: $40. *Expenses:* Tuition $0 for state residents; $9384 per year for nonresidents. Fees $4409 per year. • Application contact: Sharon Harper, Student Affairs Officer, 510-642-4706. Fax: 510-643-5676. E-mail: sharper@socrates.berkeley.edu.

University of Hawaii at Manoa, College of Health Sciences and Social Welfare, School of Public Health, Program in Maternal and Child Health, Honolulu, HI 96822. Awards MPH, MS. Part-time programs available. Faculty: 3 full-time (all women), 3 part-time (2 women), 4.12 FTE. Students: 17 full-time (14 women), 10 part-time (9 women); includes 19 minority (3 African Americans, 15 Asian Americans, 1 Hispanic). 25 applicants, 64% accepted. In 1997, 14 degrees awarded. *Degree requirements:* Thesis (for some programs). *Average time to degree:* master's–1.2 years full-time, 3 years part-time. *Application deadline:* 3/1 (9/1 for spring admission). *Application fee:* $25 ($50 for international students). *Tuition:* $4029 per year full-time, $214 per credit hour part-time for state residents; $9957 per year full-time, $461 per credit hour part-time for nonresidents. *Financial aid:* Career-related internships or fieldwork available. *Faculty research:* High risk in pregnancy/neonatal period, early development screening/assessment, child maltreatment and family violence, nutrition for children with special needs. • Dr. Gigliola Baruffi, Head, 808-956-5756. Application contact: Nancy Kilonsky, Assistant Dean, 808-956-8267.

University of Minnesota, Twin Cities Campus, School of Public Health, Major in Maternal and Child Health, Minneapolis, MN 55455-0213. Awards MPH. Accredited by CEPH. Part-time programs available. Faculty: 5 full-time, 2 part-time. Students: 28; includes 4 international. 38 applicants, 66% accepted. In 1997, 12 degrees awarded. *Entrance requirements:* GRE General Test (minimum combined score of 1500 on three sections), minimum GPA of 3.0. Application deadline: 4/15 (priority date; rolling processing). Application fee: $50 ($75 for international students). *Financial aid:* Federal Work-Study, institutionally sponsored loans available. *Faculty research:* Childhood chronic illness and disability, perinatal and adolescent health. • Dr. Joän Patterson, Chair, 612-625-3660. E-mail: jasu@maroon.tc.umn.edu. Application contact: Christina Olson, Student Coordinator, 612-625-3660. Fax: 612-624-5920. E-mail: olson032@maroon.tc.umn.edu.

See in-depth description on page 1537.

The University of North Carolina at Chapel Hill, School of Public Health, Department of Maternal and Child Health, Chapel Hill, NC 27599. Awards MPH, MSPH, Dr PH, MPH/MSW. One or more programs accredited by CEPH. Faculty: 11 full-time (6 women), 23 part-time (9 women). Students: 60 full-time (51 women), 22 part-time (19 women); includes 20 minority (11 African Americans, 5 Asian Americans, 4 Hispanics), 9 international. Average age 32. 106 applicants, 47% accepted. In 1997, 27 master's, 4 doctorates awarded. *Degree requirements:* For master's, major paper, comprehensive exam required, foreign language and thesis not required; for doctorate, dissertation, comprehensive exam required, foreign language not required. *Entrance requirements:* GRE General Test (minimum combined score of 1000), minimum GPA of 3.0. Application deadline: 1/1 (rolling processing; 1/1 for spring admission). Application fee: $55. *Expenses:* Tuition $2008 per year full-time, $502 per semester (minimum) part-time for state residents; $10,414 per year full-time, $2604 per semester (minimum) part-time for nonresidents. Fees $782 per year full-time, $332 per semester (minimum) part-time. *Financial aid:* In 1997–98, 58 research assistantships (10 to first-year students) averaging $1,000 per month, 5 teaching assistantships averaging $750 per month, 23 graduate assistantships, traineeships (20 to first-year students) averaging $500 per month were awarded; fellowships, institutionally sponsored loans, and career-related internships or fieldwork also available. Financial aid application deadline: 1/31. *Faculty research:* Women's health, prenatal health, family planning, program evaluation, child health policy and priorities. Total annual research expenditures: $2.27 million. • Dr. Pierre M. Buekens, Chair, 919-966-5981. E-mail: pierre_buekens@unc.edu. Application contact: Sherry Rhodes, Registrar, 919-966-2018. Fax: 919-966-0455. E-mail: srhodes@sph.unc.edu.

University of Puerto Rico, Medical Sciences Campus, Graduate School of Public Health, Department of Human Development, Program in Mother and Child Health, San Juan, PR 00936-5067. Awards MPH. Accredited by CEPH. Part-time programs available. Students: 7 (6 women). 9 applicants, 67% accepted. In 1997, 9 degrees awarded. *Degree requirements:* Computer language required, foreign language and thesis not required. *Entrance requirements:* GRE, previous course work in algebra. Application deadline: 3/3. Application fee: $15. *Financial aid:* Research assistantships, teaching assistantships, Federal Work-Study, institutionally sponsored loans available. Financial aid application deadline: 4/30. • Dr. Jose J. Gorrín, Coordinator, 787-758-2525 Ext. 1445. Application contact: Mayra E. Santiago-Vargas, Counselor, 787-756-5244. Fax: 787-759-6719.

Wheelock College, Graduate School, Program in Child Life and Family Centered Care, Boston, MA 02215. Awards MS, CAGS. Students: 23 full-time (all women). 35 applicants, 66% accepted. *Degree requirements:* For CAGS, thesis. *Entrance requirements:* For CAGS, interview. Application deadline: 2/15 (priority date; rolling processing). Application fee: $35 ($40 for international students). Electronic applications accepted. *Tuition:* $525 per credit. *Financial aid:* Graduate assistantships, grants, Federal Work-Study, institutionally sponsored loans, and career-related internships or fieldwork available. Aid available to part-time students. Financial aid application deadline: 4/1; applicants required to submit FAFSA. *Faculty research:* Families affected by life-threatening illness. • Marcia Hartley, Coordinator, 617-734-5200 Ext. 270. E-mail: mhartley@wheelock.edu. Application contact: Martha Sheehan, Director of Graduate Admissions, 617-734-5200 Ext. 212. Fax: 617-232-7127. E-mail: msheehan@wheelock.edu.

Cross-Discipline Announcements

University of New Hampshire, School of Health and Human Services, Department of Health Management and Policy, Durham, NH 03824.

The department offers the Master of Health Administration degree primarily for students working full-time in the health field. Classes are held on alternate Fridays and Saturdays from September through May, plus 2 residential weeks, 1 in late August and the other in late May. See in-depth description in Section 28 of this volume.

Walden University, Graduate Programs, 155 Fifth Avenue South, Minneapolis, MN 55401.

The distance learning doctoral program (PhD) in health services includes a specialization in community health. Students may concentrate in community health assessment, community health policy, and community health assurance. For more information, see Book 1 of this series.

ALLEGHENY UNIVERSITY OF THE HEALTH SCIENCES

School of Public Health

Programs of Study

The School of Public Health of Allegheny University of the Health Sciences (formerly Medical College of Pennsylvania and Hahnemann University) offers a full-time, two-year program and a part-time, thirty-six–month program leading to the Master of Public Health (M.P.H.), as well as a five-year M.D./M.P.H. program. The program provides the conceptual foundation to identify conditions that ensure that people can be healthy and builds the skills necessary for promoting and protecting public health through a commitment to social justice. The program's problem-based learning format, based on case studies of existing problems, trains professionals with the knowledge and independent thinking skills to develop and implement plans to ameliorate conditions of disease, disability, and premature death in communities. Students must complete a community-based practicum and defend a master's project. The part-time program is designed for mid-career–level professionals with work experience. All programs feature small-group learning. A joint Master of Science in Nursing and Master of Public Health degree (M.S.N./M.P.H.) and a Doctor of Public Health degree (Dr.P.H.) are under development. The School's educational and research programs are built upon partnerships with communities and the organizations that serve them. Graduates are well prepared for managerial and other leadership roles in the five disciplines of public health.

Research Facilities

For clinical research, students have ready access to the University's comprehensive system of health care, including tertiary-care hospitals, a specialty children's hospital, community hospitals, a large number of practice sites, and active community outreach programs. The libraries and supporting services provide specialized facilities for a variety of research projects, and microcomputer facilities and online search capabilities are available to all students. The University's location in Philadelphia provides access to other excellent libraries as well.

Financial Aid

All University students may apply for financial assistance through the Office of University Student Financial Affairs.

Cost of Study

Tuition in the School of Public Health in 1997–98 was $17,500. All students must maintain adequate medical insurance. Particulars relating to tuition, fees, or financial aid are subject to change.

Living and Housing Costs

Stiles Alumni Hall, a sixteen-story apartment building located on the Center City Campus, has 195 apartment-type units. The estimated cost for room and board is $7200 to $9200 per academic year. Other rooming and apartment facilities are located within easy commuting distance of the Center City Campus and within walking distance of the East Falls Campus.

Student Group

Forty-one full-time and 12 part-time students are enrolled in the School of Public Health. Approximately 74 percent are women.

Location

The School is located at the University's Center City Campus in Philadelphia, with easy access to all central Philadelphia attractions. Students can partake of the many historic, cultural, scientific, sports, entertainment, and dining advantages of the city, many of which are within walking distance. The University is convenient to and accessible by bus, rail, and subway lines. New York City, Atlantic City and other New Jersey shore points, the Pocono Mountains, and Washington, D.C., are but a few of the recreational areas within a 1- to 4-hour commute.

The University

Allegheny University of the Health Sciences is an academic health center that includes more than 3,200 students in the MCP ♦ Hahnemann School of Medicine, School of Health Professions, School of Nursing, and School of Public Health and grants degrees from the associate through the doctorate in more than forty programs. The University, with campuses in Philadelphia and Pittsburgh and more than 4,000 faculty members, was formed through the 1993 consolidation of Medical College of Pennsylvania and Hahnemann University and was given its present name in June 1996. The University is not affiliated with Allegheny College, the liberal arts college located in Meadville, Pennsylvania.

Applying

The application fee is $50; the deadline is February 15. Prerequisites for admission include results of the GRE (preferred), GMAT, MCAT, or LSAT, taken within the last five years; TOEFL results (if applicable); completion of a survey course in statistics before matriculation; and proficiency in word processing. One to two years of work experience in a related field is highly recommended. Six undergraduate or graduate credits in the social or behavioral sciences and 3 in the biological sciences are preferred.

Correspondence and Information

University Office of Admissions and Recruitment
Allegheny University of the Health Sciences
Broad and Vine, Mail Stop 472
Philadelphia, Pennsylvania 19102-1192
Telephone: 215-762-8288
Fax: 215-762-6194
World Wide Web: http://www.auhs.edu

Allegheny University of the Health Sciences

THE FACULTY AND THEIR RESEARCH

Nathalie Bartle, Associate Professor; Ed.D., Harvard, 1994. Maternal child health, women's health, adolescent health.
Phyllis Blumberg, Professor; Ph.D., Pittsburgh, 1976. Education, program evaluation.
Eddy Bresnitz, Professor; M.D., McGill, 1974. Prevention, epidemiology, occupational/environmental health, internal medicine, pulmonary medicine.
Jeffrey Coben, Associate Professor; M.D., Pittsburgh, 1984. Emergency medicine, trauma and injury prevention, domestic violence, fire arm relative injuries.
Michael Faucher, Assistant Professor; M.B.A., Temple, 1983. Hospital administration, mental health administration, nursing home administration.
Janie Gittleman, Assistant Professor; Ph.D., Cornell, 1989. Occupational epidemiology, lead poisoning prevention, surveillance systems, adolescent injuries.
Edward J. Gracely, Associate Professor; Ph.D., Temple, 1986. Statistics.
Michael Greenberg, Associate Professor; M.D., Temple, 1976. Occupational health.
Jonathan Mann, Professor and Dean; M.D., Washington (St. Louis), 1974; M.P.H., Harvard, 1980. Health and human rights, HIV/AIDS.
Jana Mossey, Professor; Ph.D., North Carolina at Chapel Hill, 1976. Aging, epidemiology, research design and methods, psychosocial aspects of health.
Bonnie Blair O'Connor, Assistant Professor; Ph.D., Pennsylvania, 1990. Cultural issues, health belief and behavior/complementary medicine.
Grace Paranzino, Instructor; M.S., Saint Joseph's (Philadelphia), 1991; M.S., Holy Family, 1979; RN. Occupational and environmental health, literacy, health education, program planning, implementation and evaluation, outcomes assessment, prevention, environmental risk communication.
Kim C. Pham, Assistant Professor; M.D., Columbia, 1991. Biostatistics, epidemiology, evidence-based medicine, maternal child health.
Marcia Polansky, Associate Professor; Sc.D., Harvard, 1984. Biostatistics, experimental design/research methods and statistical analysis, clinical trials, asthma epidemiology and interventions, transitional educational programs from high school to college and literacy.
Virginia Rauh, Associate Professor; Sc.D., Harvard, 1982. Maternal and child health, child development, perinatal epidemiology, urban ecology and health effects of poverty.
Renee Royak-Schaler, Associate Professor; Ph.D., Maryland, 1982. Health behavior and health education, women's health, cancer prevention and control, breast cancer, community-based interventions and education programs (design, implementation, and evaluation), health promotion/design prevention in African-American communities.
Harriet L. Rubenstein, Assistant Professor; J.D., Northeastern, 1979; M.P.H., North Carolina, 1975. Occupational and environmental health, student service learning projects, adult education.
Lenore Sherman, Assistant Professor; M.B.A., Temple, 1979. Hospital administration, mental health administration, managed care.
David J. Tollerud, Professor; M.D., Mayo, 1978. Pulmonary medicine/respiratory disease, lead poisoning, occupational hazards, blood-borne pathogens, occupational medicine history, accidental injury, air pollution—indoor/outdoor.
Malin VanAntwerp, Assistant Professor; J.D., Michigan, 1955. Health law.
F. Wayne Vaught, Assistant Professor; Ph.D., Tennessee, 1996. Ethics.
Augusta M. Villanueva, Assistant Professor; Ph.D., Texas at Austin, 1985. Sociology/social sciences, cultural competency and human diversity, health policy.
William E. Welton, Associate Professor; M.H.A., Michigan, 1972. Health policy, business policy and strategy, health economics, organizational theory, managed care.

Allegheny University of the Health Sciences is not affiliated with Allegheny College, the liberal arts college in Meadville, Pennsylvania.

BOSTON UNIVERSITY

School of Public Health

Programs of Study

Boston University School of Public Health provides an educational program of high quality in a flexible format that permits students to obtain a Master of Public Health (M.P.H.) degree with concentrations in environmental health; epidemiology and biostatistics; health behavior, health promotion, and disease prevention; health law; health services; international health; and maternal and child health (MCH). The MCH Department houses an interdisciplinary Maternal and Child Health Leadership Program and a Nurse-Midwifery Education Program for experienced registered nurses. A Master of Science (M.Sc.) in epidemiology and doctoral programs (D.Sc.) in epidemiology and environmental health are also offered. M.A. and Ph.D. programs in biostatistics are offered jointly with the Department of Mathematics in the Graduate School. Several dual-degree programs are available: M.D./M.P.H., J.D./M.P.H., M.S.W./M.P.H., M.B.A./M.P.H., and M.A. (in medical sciences)/M.P.H. A program incorporating Peace Corps experience with the M.P.H. degree has also been established. In addition, the International Health Department runs several short-term training programs. The School's full- and part-time faculty members represent diverse interests and specialties, providing both an academic and a practical dimension to students' educational experience.

To earn the M.P.H. degree, students must complete 48 credit hours. The degree may be completed in 1½ years of full-time study (one calendar year may be possible with careful planning) or in 2½ to 3 years of part-time study. All students are required to complete six core courses (16 credits) that provide the fundamental skills and knowledge necessary for a career in public health. Students must also complete elective courses and the requirements of at least one concentration. Field practice placements are available to augment classroom instruction. Certain concentrations have application requirements that stress relevant work experience as well as academic achievement.

Applicants to the M.Sc. in epidemiology program are expected to have a clinical master's or doctoral degree. Students must complete 32 credits of course work and a thesis. Applicants to the D.Sc. programs should hold a graduate degree in a relevant field. Exceptional candidates without such a degree may be accepted but will be required to complete additional course work. The D.Sc. programs entail 32 credit hours beyond the master's degree. A thesis is required, along with a comprehensive qualifying exam.

Research Facilities

Students have access to all of Boston University's libraries. The Medical Library, which has a substantial collection in public health, also offers computerized literature services. The Office of Information Technology operates a cluster of IBM RS/6000's for instructional and research activities. Boston University maintains a liberal policy on computing services for students, who are given a research account that allows them to use computer resources as needed. In addition, the Learning Resources Center at the Medical Center gives students an opportunity to use current computer hardware and software.

Financial Aid

There are several loan programs available to full- and part-time students. There is no financial aid available for international students.

Cost of Study

Full-time tuition for 1998–99 is $11,415 per semester. Medical insurance is available.

Living and Housing Costs

Most graduate students live off campus. The Office of Orientation and Off-Campus Services maintains listings of off-campus apartments, as well as of students seeking roommates. Housing costs may range from $350 to $600 per month per person.

Student Group

Approximately 600 graduate students are enrolled in the School of Public Health. About 15 percent are international students. Students come from a variety of backgrounds, depending on their concentration. Some have previous graduate degrees; others are just beginning their public health careers.

Location

Boston is one of the country's leading centers of health care and technology. Home to numerous institutions at the forefront of progressive and innovative medical-care delivery and research activity, the city offers public health students a wide variety of opportunities to interact and work with other health-care professionals.

Boston is also known for its historical and cultural attractions and is home to professional sports teams. Beaches lie a short distance to the north and south, and mountains are only a 2-hour drive away.

The University and The School

Founded in 1839, Boston University is an independent, coeducational, nonsectarian university. Its fifteen schools and colleges are evidence of its academic diversity. The School of Public Health, a part of the School of Medicine, was established in 1976. It is located in the Boston University Medical Center, in the city's South End.

Applying

M.P.H. students and doctoral students in environmental health are admitted in September and January. Application deadlines are October 25 for January admission and March 1 (early decision) or April 15 for September admission. M.P.H. applications received after the deadlines are considered on a space-available basis. Doctoral and M.Sc. students in epidemiology are admitted only in September; D.Sc. application deadlines are March 1 (early decision) and April 15; the M.Sc. application deadline is April 15.

Candidates without doctoral-level degrees must submit scores on the GRE General Test. GMAT, LSAT, MCAT, or DAT scores may be substituted. All M.Sc. applicants must submit either GRE, MCAT, GMAT, or DAT scores. Applicants from countries where English is not the language of instruction must submit TOEFL scores.

Correspondence and Information

Office of Admissions
Boston University School of Public Health
715 Albany Street
Boston, Massachusetts 02118
Telephone: 617-638-4640
Fax: 617-638-5299
E-mail: sphadmis@bu.edu
World Wide Web: http://www-busph.bu.edu

Boston University

FACULTY HEADS AND RESEARCH AREAS

Environmental Health
Chair: David M. Ozonoff, M.D., M.P.H.

The Environmental Health Department conducts research on the epidemiology of environmental cancer and other diseases, health effects of toxic chemical exposures, molecular biology, and the economics of compensating victims for environmental and workplace diseases. Some current projects involve conducting community health surveys around hazardous-waste sites and investigating mechanisms of chemical mutagenesis, the effects of chemicals on the immune system, lead exposures in construction workers, use of computer graphics systems in epidemiology, a primary prevention program for lead poisoning in urban neighborhoods, new methods to detect geographic "hot spots" of cancer, and the use of expert evidence in litigation.

Epidemiology and Biostatistics
Chair: Theodore Colton, Sc.D.

Research interests of the faculty encompass preventive oncology, cancer epidemiology, and infectious disease epidemiology. Among the specific research projects currently under investigation are the epidemiology of AIDS; the genetic epidemiology of Huntington's disease and Alzheimer's disease; the relationship of breast cancer to drinking polluted water on Cape Cod; the evaluation of home monitoring among infants at risk for SIDS; the health effects of mothers, daughters, and sons exposed to diethylstilbestrol; the health effects among women who received cosmetic breast implants; and a randomized clinical trial to assess the effect of inhaled steroids in the treatment of infants with bronchopulmonary dysplasia. In addition, faculty members are involved in ongoing studies of the cohorts of the Framingham Heart Study.

The Slone Epidemiology Unit, a part of the School of Public Health, is engaged in the epidemiologic evaluation of drug safety; it is also at the forefront of the national effort to identify and quantify the occurrence of environmentally induced diseases and to document the absence of causal relationships.

Health Law
Chair: George J. Annas, J.D., M.P.H.

Research is carried out primarily in areas in which public policy, as defined by legislation, regulation, and court decisions, has a major impact on the public's health or the health-care system. In recent years, this research has included studies in the following areas: the rights of patients and of human subjects of research, including informed consent, refusal to participate in treatment or research, and claims of entitlement to experimental procedures and products; codes of biomedical research and their relevance to current biotechnology and to HIV drug and vaccine research; access to health care, including the duty of professionals to treat people with AIDS, patients' rights to treatment, and the effect of insurance coverage; biomedical technology resource allocation; child abuse and neglect and religious exemptions; product liability and medical malpractice and their effect on the availability of health-care resources; screening for HIV and illegal drugs; new reproductive technologies and their effect on the status of women and fetuses; uses of criminal law to achieve public health goals, such as criminal penalties to deter illegal drug use and child neglect; scientific evidence in the courtroom; corporate risk management; and the community's right to know of toxic hazards. The Health Law Department is the site for the Center for Patients Rights and Global Attorneys and Physicians for Human Rights.

Health Services
Chair: Mark J. Prashker, M.D., M.P.H.

The Health Services Department prepares students for careers in such areas as management, financing, and service delivery in the public and private sectors. Areas of major importance to the public's health are examined from the perspective of who receives services, what is provided, who pays for it, and how quality is monitored. Enhancing the student's capacity to identify and solve problems in a practical way within a sound conceptual framework is an emphasis throughout the health services concentration. Some faculty members are involved in research in health economics, health quality assessment, and health outcomes measurement. Other current projects include restructuring health-care environments, community-teaching hospital collaborations, appropriateness of and access to health-care services, designing Medicaid managed care programs, evaluating hospital closings and reconfigurations, and new financing and care delivery models for disabled and chronically ill populations.

International Health
Chair: William J. Bicknell, M.D., M.P.H.

The International Health Department coordinates a range of international programs and is the international health teaching arm of the School of Public Health. These programs include courses in the School of Public Health as well as annual certificate courses, three of which provide graduate credit. The credit-bearing courses are twelve weeks long and focus on Health Care in Developing Countries, Financing Health Care in Developing Countries, and Management Methods for International Health. Other short courses include Strengthening Public Hospitals in Developing Nations and Human Resource Development and Health Sector Reform. The department conducts research, consults, and organizes service projects in a range of developing countries; recent projects have involved work in Indonesia, Jamaica, Lesotho, Nepal, Turkey, Sri Lanka, Egypt, Haiti, Vietnam, Zimbabwe, Eritrea, the Marshall Islands, Russia, and Barbados. The department administers a joint program integrating Peace Corps volunteer service and health projects with the M.P.H. degree. The department also coordinates a network of medical schools, schools of public health, and service-delivery sites for student placements, teaching, and collaborative research in countries such as Indonesia, Egypt, Nepal, Zambia, Jamaica, Cameroon, and China.

Maternal and Child Health
Chair: Lisa L. Paine, C.N.M., Dr.P.H.

The Maternal and Child Health Department prepares graduate students for careers aimed at improving the health and well-being of women, mothers, children, and families through public health practice, research, education, and advocacy. Faculty research interests include primary-care services for women and children; maternal and infant mortality; perinatal epidemiology; perinatal technology assessment; early postpartum hospital discharge; development of obstetric and perinatal databases; substance abuse treatment programs for pregnant women; race, ethnicity, and class disparities in perinatal and women's health outcomes; community-based immunization programs for women and children; evaluation of comprehensive family health programs; comparative maternal and child health policy analysis; development of culturally competent systems of care; midwifery care for vulnerable populations; regulation and practice patterns of maternal and child health professionals; and evaluation of competency-based education.

Social and Behavioral Sciences
Chair: Ralph W. Hingson, Sc.D.

Research being carried out by the department includes evaluations of a community program to reduce drunk driving; assessing the efficacy of treatment for alcoholism in large industrial plants; developing and evaluating an intervention for fear of falling among the community-dwelling elderly; risk factors associated with substance use and depression among Hispanics in the United States; the extent to which maternal health habits are associated with adverse fetal development; adolescent pregnancy and parenthood; child abuse etiology; and a study of African-American adolescent drinking and sexual behaviors that put them at potential risk for HIV infection.

COLUMBIA UNIVERSITY

Faculty of Medicine
Columbia School of Public Health

Programs of Study

The Columbia School of Public Health offers programs leading to the Master of Public Health (M.P.H.), Master of Science (M.S.), and Doctor of Public Health (Dr.P.H.). The Doctor of Philosophy (Ph.D.) degree is also offered in collaboration with the Graduate School of Arts and Sciences. Concentrations are available in biostatistics, environmental health sciences, epidemiology, health policy and management, population and family health, and sociomedical sciences. Some courses are taught in the evening, and there is a summer session. The M.P.H. program requires 45 course credits and practical training (practicum) equivalent to one term. A two-year Weekend Executive M.P.H. program in health services management is also available for working professionals. The course requirements for the M.S. and doctoral programs vary, depending on each candidate's program. Part-time study is an option in many of the School's programs.

Formal dual-degree programs exist with the Schools of Business (M.B.A./M.P.H.), Architecture and Urban Planning (M.S.U.P./M.P.H.), Dentistry (D.D.S./M.P.H.), Medicine (M.D./M.P.H.), Nursing (M.S.N./M.P.H.), International Affairs (M.I.A./M.P.H., M.P.A./M.P.H.), Social Work (M.S.S.W./M.P.H.), and Occupational Therapy (M.S.O.T./M.P.H.). A dual-degree program in health services management is available for medical and dental students (M.S./M.D., M.S./D.D.S.).

Research Facilities

Faculty members in all divisions of the School of Public Health are involved in research programs, many of which afford opportunities for student participation. Faculty involvement in research projects enriches classroom and tutorial experiences and contributes to the body of knowledge on health issues. The facilities of the Health Sciences Center are available through faculty members with appointments in the various schools, institutes, centers, and hospitals of the Columbia-Presbyterian Medical Center. The Health Sciences Library is one of the largest medical center libraries in the United States, with more than 500,000 volumes, 4,400 periodicals, and computerized literature searching on several databases, including MEDLARS.

Financial Aid

A limited number of assistantships, traineeships, and student loans are available. Applicants requesting financial aid are encouraged to contact the School's Financial Aid Office early in the application process.

Cost of Study

The full-time tuition was $703 per credit in 1997–98. Health services and hospital insurance plans are available for individual students and members of their family, and are required for full-time students. Health coverage for individual students was $1277 in 1997–98.

Living and Housing Costs

There is some housing available for single students and for couples at or near the Health Sciences campus. Estimated personal and living expenses for students maintaining their own residence were approximately $13,000 for the nine-month academic year in 1997–98. New York offers a wide variety of living options, and actual expenses may vary.

Student Group

In fall 1997, the School enrolled approximately 750 graduate students. While the majority are pursuing the M.P.H. degree, approximately 25 percent are engaged in doctoral studies. Entering students averaged 30 years of age. Their backgrounds reflect the broad range of public health issues. About 40 percent entered with prior professional training, primarily in medicine and nursing. Approximately 15 percent of the student body are from minority groups; 15 percent are international students. Approximately half of the students are engaged in part-time study. Many of these students are mid-career professionals broadening their knowledge base and acquiring new skills. Students at the School of Public Health are part of the Health Sciences Division of Columbia University. Approximately 2,500 students in medicine, dentistry, nursing, public health, and occupational and physical therapy study at this site.

Location

New York City offers the world's most comprehensive networks of private and public health care and social services. Students have the opportunity to study and observe the latest in their area of interest and to work with the leaders in the field, both in the classroom and through the practicum. The campus, located in upper Manhattan a few blocks south of the George Washington Bridge, offers outstanding resources: the College of Physicians and Surgeons; the School of Dental and Oral Surgery; the School of Nursing; the Center for Geriatrics and Gerontology; the Institute of Human Nutrition; the Center for Population and Family Health; the Columbia-Presbyterian Cancer Center; the Sergievsky Center for epidemiological research; the Upper West Side Health Center; and the clinical programs of the Presbyterian Hospital and the New York State Psychiatric Institute. The School has close ties to the New York City Department of Health (NYCDOH), providing excellent opportunities for student field experience. It also participates with Harlem Hospital in a major Prevention Center activity.

The University and The School

Columbia's role is that of education for excellence—a term that embraces high quality in teaching and the furtherance of knowledge through research, preeminence in the professions, and leadership in community and national affairs. Columbia's status as a private institution, its location, its faculty, and its international reputation provide the basis for this diversified educational purpose.

The Columbia School of Public Health is one of the first three schools of public health in the country. In 1997–98, it celebrated its seventy-fifth anniversary. It was founded originally as an institute of the medical school, reflecting an early concern in the Faculty of Medicine with the principles of the health of populations and the administrative sciences of health care. It became the School of Public Health in 1945 and today encompasses global as well as national and community health perspectives. Although the School's offerings are diverse and the breadth of preparation provided is wide, the School of Public Health remains small. A dedicated faculty upholds a basic tenet of the School—the importance of the individual student—and shares a major commitment to flexibility in the learning process.

Applying

The application deadline for regular fall admission is April 10 and for the Executive M.P.H. program, June 15. All applicants must have a bachelor's degree from a recognized university or college, show evidence of satisfactory preparation in quantitative subject areas, and have an acceptable academic record. The program is designed for applicants with appropriate professional or other work experience. Some programs have specific preadmission requirements. The GRE General Test, or another appropriate objective test (MCAT, DAT, LSAT) is required for admission. The TOEFL is required of all applicants whose native language is not English. Applicants with significant deficiencies in written and/or spoken English may be required to take language courses before beginning studies in the School.

Correspondence and Information

Office of Student Services
Columbia School of Public Health
600 West 168th Street
New York, New York 10032

Telephone: 212-305-3927
Fax: 212-305-6450
E-mail: ph-admit@columbia.edu
World Wide Web: http://cpmcnet.columbia.edu/dept/sph/

Columbia University

DIVISIONS AND PROGRAMS

Biostatistics. (M.P.H., M.S., Dr.P.H., Ph.D.) Acting Division Head: Bruce Levin, Ph.D. The collection, analysis, and presentation of data have wide applicability to every area of public health. The Biostatistics Division programs provide a strong base of statistical techniques used to measure and evaluate health status, health hazards, and health measures in the public and private sectors. This diversity is reflected in the backgrounds of those entering the program. Some are mathematicians, others are from the natural or social sciences, still others are professionals in such areas as medicine or dentistry. The common thread is an affinity for quantitative methods and pleasure in the utilization of mathematics to solve practical problems. A knowledge of calculus is strongly recommended. Courses in statistical methodology cover such areas as applied probability theory, vital statistics, analysis of categorical data, regression analysis, multivariate analysis, and sampling. The Division has just introduced a new track in clinical research methods that leads to an M.S. degree. It will be of special interest to clinicians pursuing careers in academic medicine who need formal, rigorous training in skills essential for the design, conduct, and analysis of clinical research studies. Contact for this track is Dr. Melissa Begg (telephone: 212-305-9398; e-mail: clinical_ms@biostat.columbia.edu).

Environmental Health Sciences. (M.P.H., Dr.P.H., Ph.D.) Division Head: Joseph Graziano, Ph.D. This rapidly expanding field requires a broad range of basic and applied scientific skills. The program is primarily oriented at understanding and predicting the health effects of environmental and occupational exposure to chemicals and radiation. Research activities of the faculty strive to generate scientific data that ultimately serve as the underpinnings of environmental policy decisions. Because the field is so broad, students are encouraged to focus on particular areas, including medical/health physics, occupational medicine, environmental or molecular epidemiology, or toxicology. Each of these is taught with some consideration of national, international, and global policy issues. The program typically attracts students with a wide variety of backgrounds and interests. Several academic prerequisites are required for admission, such as one year each of undergraduate biology and mathematics (which must be calculus for the medical/health physics track) and one year each of general and organic chemistry. Admission may be contingent upon completing any of the missing prerequisites during the first year.

Epidemiology. (M.P.H., M.S., Dr.P.H., Ph.D.) Division Head: Geoffrey Howe, Ph.D. Epidemiology is an integral part of human ecology. Its area of concern includes the distribution, determinants, and dynamics of health and disease in populations—from communicable and chronic diseases, child health and development, and mental retardation to stress in health disorders, psychiatric problems, and evaluation of programs and services. The diseases of interest to faculty members include cancer, schizophrenia, coronary heart disease, and neurological disorders. Epidemiologic methodology is also applied to social problems such as homelessness. Special resources available to the student of epidemiology include the Gertrude H. Sergievsky Center for epidemiologic research. The center focuses on the study of epilepsy, cerebral palsy, and the development of brain disorders and provides a rich resource in epidemiologic research and training in neuroepidemiology. An academic background in health, the biological or social sciences, or mathematics and statistics is desirable for candidates wishing to enter this field.

Health Policy and Management. (M.P.H., Executive M.P.H., M.S., Dr.P.H.) Division Head: Lawrence Brown, Ph.D. This program encompasses studies in the formulation and implementation of health-care policy and the planning and management of the increasingly diverse range of institutions that provide health care. The growth of the health services sector demands a better understanding of the production and distribution of care and how to gauge its effectiveness in relation to costs. Just as policymakers should be trained to examine the feasibility of their goals in the light of managers' capacities and constraints, so too managers should be equipped to understand the policy projects that increasingly define the environment in which they work. The Division's programs provide students with analytical skills and methodological tools useful to policymakers and managers in the public, voluntary, and private sectors. Students focusing on management take courses in accounting and budgeting, financial management, health economics, and organizational theory. Students focusing on policy substitute advanced health economics and applied regression for the finance sequence. For students interested in specializing in a particular area of health policy and management, the Division offers the opportunity for specific concentrations, such as the economics of health care and a track in effectiveness and outcomes research leading to an M.P.H. (Contact: Dr. Jane Sisk, telephone: 212-305-4081; e-mail: jes19@columbia.edu). An Executive M.P.H. Program in health services management, a two-year course of study, is available for employed health professionals seeking to advance in management positions (Program Director: Sheila Gorman, Ph.D.).

Population and Family Health. (M.P.H.) Division Head: James McCarthy, Ph.D. This program aims to provide leadership in the search for solutions to the critical public health problems in population and family health, including reproductive, adolescent, and child health in developed and developing countries. The curriculum, which combines theory and practice, provides the necessary base of knowledge and skills to develop and implement policies, programs, and research that address the important issues within these areas. The program is designed for professionals representing the disciplines of pediatrics, obstetrics, nursing, social work, health-care delivery, management, law, and social sciences as well as for those with other relevant professional background or field experience. Prior to admission, students must have work experience in the field. The community- and school-based programs developed and run by the Center for Population and Family Health provide rich and varied training opportunities where students can apply their knowledge and skills. A program option in refugee studies will be introduced beginning in 1998–99.

Sociomedical Sciences. (M.P.H., Ph.D., Dr.P.H.) Division Head: Cheryl Healton, Dr.P.H. The Division brings together a multidisciplinary faculty of social scientists and health professionals who study the influence of social and cultural factors on health and health-care delivery. Major areas of interest include preventive health behavior, social and economic determinants of health and disease, sexuality and policy, the role of social supports, ethical issues in health, research methods, health and human rights, evaluation of health-care programs, organization and delivery of health care, HIV/AIDS, adolescent health, and disability. The Division has three M.P.H. programs. The first focuses on public health research with a strong social science orientation. The second concentrates on health promotion and disease prevention, including program planning, implementation, and evaluation. Applicants to this program should have prior work experience in public health or a related field. An evening M.P.H. program in health promotion and disease prevention is open to working professionals. The third M.P.H. program, the history of public health and medicine, focuses on historical approaches and responses to public health and the insights that history can offer to those concerned with contemporary policy. In addition, the Division offers the Ph.D. degree, with study divided between the School of Public Health and one social science department in Columbia University's Graduate School of Arts and Sciences (Anthropology, Economics, History, Philosophy, Political Science, or Sociology). Students may also obtain the Dr.P.H., focusing on research issues in public health.

General Public Health. (M.P.H.) Program Director: Bernard Challenor, M.D. This program is intended for candidates who already have professional health training and/or considerable public health experience and are generally seeking formal training in methods and issues addressed by several public health disciplines that would allow them broader participation in the field. Since their career needs often require an interdisciplinary approach going beyond the scope of any single Division, applicants to this program need to identify their substantive area(s) of interest and the technical skills (administration, research, program development, etc.) they want to acquire from two or more of the School's Divisions. This program is also available to students in the dual-degree programs offered by the School, and to students with other professional degrees (e.g., law, journalism) where an individualized, interdisciplinary curriculum is deemed particularly suitable.

EMORY UNIVERSITY

Graduate School of Arts and Sciences
Rollins School of Public Health
Department of Epidemiology

Programs of Study

The Department of Epidemiology at Emory University Rollins School of Public Health offers a program of study leading to the Doctor of Philosophy degree through the Graduate School of Arts and Sciences. The department also offers study leading to the Master of Public Health degree with a concentration in epidemiology. The programs are designed for individuals with a strong background and interest in the biological and mathematical sciences. Graduates are pursuing various career options in academia and in public and private health organizations.

The department provides a number of outstanding opportunities for student education and research. Students interested in studying chronic diseases, infectious diseases, or nutritional epidemiology can take advantage of the department's close working relationship with the Centers for Disease Control and Prevention (CDC) by participating in collaborative research projects. Those interested in developing methodology for cancer epidemiology can pursue research opportunities with the National Cancer Institute–supported Surveillance, Epidemiology and End Results (SEER) Program or with the American Cancer Society, whose national headquarters is located on the University campus. In addition, research opportunities are available in other departments of the Rollins School of Public Health, the Carter Center of Emory University, the Georgia Department of Human Resources, the Morehouse School of Medicine, the five large teaching hospitals affiliated with Emory University, and several local health departments. These resources, as well as others in the clinical and basic science departments of Emory School of Medicine, provide students with a range of areas in which to study and do research. Students are required to complete a core curriculum that consists of graduate courses in epidemiology and biostatistics. Advanced course work and research are tailored to the experience, training, and area of concentration of each individual. Students generally need twelve to fifteen months to earn the M.P.H. degree; this program includes at least three semesters of course work and a thesis. The Ph.D. degree program normally requires four calendar years to complete, including approximately five semesters of course work. Some qualified health professionals, such as those with an M.P.H. or a doctoral-level degree, may be able to satisfy the Ph.D. requirements in a shorter period of time.

Research Facilities

The Department of Epidemiology conducts active research programs in nutritional, reproductive, cancer, molecular, and infectious disease epidemiology. In addition, the department has a strong analytical methods faculty. The Rollins School of Public Health, which recently moved into a building on the Clifton Health Corridor, is equipped with state-of-the-art computers and microcomputers. A network of mainframe computers is accessible to the School through high-speed telecommunications lines. Extensive research laboratories are housed at the CDC. Health sciences libraries are conveniently located at Emory University, the national headquarters of the American Cancer Society, and the CDC.

Financial Aid

Ph.D. students are supported by Graduate School Fellowships that include full tuition and a nationally competitive stipend. Financial aid information is available through the Emory Office of Financial Aid.

Cost of Study

Graduate School tuition for 1997–98 was $10,385 per semester for full-time students, or $865 per credit hour. For M.P.H. students, the cost was $6635 per semester for full-time students, or $545 per credit hour. Student activity and athletic fees totaled $95 per semester. The cost of books and supplies averages $650 per year.

Living and Housing Costs

Living expenses for a single person are estimated at $12,500 per year. Information regarding University and off-campus housing may be obtained from the Housing Office of Emory University.

Student Group

Emory University has a total enrollment of 9,300 students. Enrollment in the various schools of the University, including the Rollins School of Public Health, is restricted in order to maintain a favorable balance between resources, faculty members, and students. There are approximately 5,400 students in the undergraduate college and 3,900 in the eight graduate and professional schools. The student body represents all areas of the United States and many other countries.

Location

The Atlanta metropolitan area has a population of nearly 3 million. With eight major universities, it is the major academic center in the Southeast. Atlanta is green the year round, with numerous parks and a temperate climate. Professional, athletic, cultural, and recreational activities are available throughout the year.

The University and The School

Emory University ranks among the twenty-five most distinguished centers for higher education in the United States. The heavily wooded 550-acre campus features a blend of traditional and contemporary architecture. A main corridor through the campus incorporates the expanding health sciences complex with the headquarters of the federal CDC and the recently relocated national offices of the American Cancer Society. Within a short drive of the main campus are a variety of affiliated resources, such as the Georgia Mental Health Institute, the Georgia Department of Human Resources, the Carter Center of Emory University, and Grady Memorial Hospital, which is the teaching facility of the medical school. The Emory University School of Public Health, officially constituted in 1990, is the newest accredited school of public health in the United States and Canada. Establishment of the school was made possible because of a strong community health-delivery base in the metropolitan area and because of Emory's flexibility in developing mutually beneficial institutional affiliations. The school has five academic departments, each of which offers an M.P.H. degree: Biostatistics, Behavioral Sciences and Health Education, Environmental/Occupational Health, Epidemiology, and Health Policy and Management. The Center for International Health is an interdisciplinary program of the Rollins School of Public Health. The Biostatistics Department offers the M.S. and Ph.D. degrees through the Graduate School of Arts and Science.

Applying

General requirements for admission include a baccalaureate degree and satisfactory performance on the GRE. For admission to the M.P.H. program, college biology and college algebra are required; calculus is recommended. For the Ph.D., a background in the biological sciences and mathematics through integral calculus is required. Detailed information and application forms for admission to the Ph.D. program may be obtained from the Graduate School of Arts and Sciences, Emory University, Atlanta, Georgia 30322. International students whose schooling has not been in English must submit a TOEFL score.

Correspondence and Information

Dollie Daniels, M.P.H.
Associate Director of Graduate Studies
Department of Epidemiology
Emory University, Rollins School of Public Health
1518 Clifton Road, NE
Atlanta, Georgia 30322
Telephone: 404-727-8712

Emory University

THE FACULTY AND THEIR RESEARCH

John R. Boring III, Professor and Director; Ph.D., Florida, 1961. Infectious disease epidemiology, molecular biology.
Harland D. Austin, Associate Professor; D.Sc., Harvard, 1983. Quantitative methods, cancer epidemiology.
Carolyn D. Drews-Botsch, Associate Professor; Ph.D., UCLA, 1988. Reproductive and ophthalmic epidemiology, methods.
John William Eley, Assistant Professor; M.D., 1983, M.P.H., 1990, Emory. Cancer epidemiology and control.
Elaine W. Flagg, Assistant Professor; Ph.D., Emory, 1992. Sample survey conduct and analysis, nutritional epidemiology.
W. Dana Flanders, Professor; M.D., Vermont, 1977; D.Sc., Harvard, 1982. Quantitative epidemiology, methods.
Holly A. Hill, Instructor; M.D., 1987, Ph.D., 1992, North Carolina. Cancer epidemiology and prevention.
David G. Kleinbaum, Professor; Ph.D., North Carolina, 1970. Quantitative epidemiology, methods.
Jonathan M. Liff, Associate Professor; Ph.D., Washington (Seattle), 1984. Cancer epidemiology and surveillance.
Michele Marcus, Associate Professor; Ph.D., Columbia, 1986. Reproductive epidemiology, environmental epidemiology, and neuroepidemiology.
Kevin Sullivan, Assistant Professor; Ph.D., Michigan, 1990. Epidemiologic methods, microcomputers in epidemiology.

Visiting Assistant Professors
Anne B. Dilley, Ph.D., Emory, 1994. Hemophilia epidemiology.
J. Michael Soucie, Ph.D., Emory, 1995. Hemophilia epidemiology.

Associate Faculty
J. Elaine Brockman, Senior Associate; M.P.H., Emory, 1988. Cancer epidemiology and surveillance.
John Carter, Senior Associate; Ph.D., Rice, 1968. Perinatal epidemiology, nutrition, and cancer.
Lorie A. Click, Senior Associate; M.N., 1982, M.P.H., 1989, Emory. Cancer and nutritional epidemiology.

Jointly Appointed Faculty
John E. McGowan Jr., Professor; M.D., Harvard, 1967. Infectious disease epidemiology.
Sally E. McNagny, Assistant Professor of Medicine; M.D., Harvard, 1984. Clinical epidemiology.
Ruth M. Parker, Assistant Professor of Medicine; M.D., North Carolina, 1981. Clinical epidemiology.
Aziz R. Samadi, Associate Professor; M.D., Kabul (Afghanistan), 1956. Maternal and child health, tropical diseases in children.
Stephanie L. Sherman, Assistant Professor of Pediatrics; Ph.D., Indiana, 1981. Population and medical genetics.
Nancy Thompson, Assistant Professor; Ph.D., Georgia State, 1988. Behavioral and psychiatric epidemiology, injury and violence prevention and control, applications of psychological theory.

Adjunct Faculty
Melissa Adams, Adjunct Assistant Professor; Ph.D., Washington (Seattle), 1985. Centers for Disease Control and Prevention.
Hani Atrash, Adjunct Assistant Professor; M.D., American (Beirut), 1976. Centers for Disease Control and Prevention.
John V. Bennett, Adjunct Professor; M.D., Jefferson, 1961. The Carter Center of Emory University.
Dan Blumenthal, Adjunct Professor; M.D., Chicago, 1968. Morehouse School of Medicine.
Leslie Boss, Adjunct Assistant Professor; Ph.D., Hawaii, 1981. Centers for Disease Control and Prevention.
Coleen Boyle, Adjunct Assistant Professor; Ph.D., Pittsburgh, 1981. Centers for Disease Control and Prevention.
Tim E. Byers, Adjunct Associate Professor, M.D., Indiana, 1973. Centers for Disease Control and Prevention.
Eugenia Calle, Adjunct Assistant Professor; Ph.D., Ohio State, 1982. American Cancer Society.
Ward Cates, Adjunct Professor; M.D., Yale, 1971. Centers for Disease Control and Prevention.
Lyle J. Conrad, Adjunct Professor; M.D., George Washington, 1961. Centers for Disease Control and Prevention.
Richard C. Dicker, Adjunct Associate Professor; M.D., Massachusetts Medical Center, 1979; M.Sc., Harvard, 1983. Centers for Disease Control and Prevention.
William Elsea, Adjunct Professor; M.D., Washington (St. Louis) 1959. Fulton County Health Department.
William Foege, Adjunct Professor; M.D., Washington (Seattle), 1961. The Carter Center of Emory University.
David Freeman, Adjunct Assistant Professor; Ph.D., North Carolina, 1983. Centers for Disease Control and Prevention.
Richard A. Goodman, Adjunct Associate Professor; M.D., Michigan, 1975. Centers for Disease Control and Prevention.
Clark W. Heath Jr., Adjunct Professor; M.D., Johns Hopkins, 1958. American Cancer Society.
Muin J. Khoury, Adjunct Associate Professor; Ph.D., Johns Hopkins, 1985. Centers for Disease Control and Prevention.
Jeffrey P. Koplan, Adjunct Professor; M.D., NYU, 1970. Centers for Disease Control and Prevention.
Brian McCarthy, Adjunct Associate Professor; M.D., SUNY, 1973. Centers for Disease Control and Prevention.
Adriene Mims, Adjunct Assistant Professor; M.D., Stanford, 1982.
Virgil J. Peavy, Adjunct Assistant Professor; M.S., Georgia, 1963. Centers for Disease Control and Prevention.
Roger W. Rochat, Adjunct Associate Professor; M.D., Washington, 1966. Centers for Disease Control and Prevention.
Audrey F. Saftlas, Adjunct Assistant Professor; Ph.D., Johns Hopkins, 1986. Centers for Disease Control and Prevention.
Myron G. Schultz, Adjunct Professor; M.D., Albany Medical College, 1962, Centers for Disease Control and Prevention.
Mary K. Serdula, Adjunct Assistant Professor; M.D., Minnesota, 1975. Centers for Disease Control and Prevention.
Dixie E. Snider Jr., Adjunct Instructor; M.D., Louisville, 1969. Centers for Disease Control and Prevention.
Stephen B. Thacker, Adjunct Associate Professor; M.D., Mount Sinai, 1977; M.Sc., London, 1984. Centers for Disease Control and Prevention.
Michael J. Thun, Adjunct Associate Professor; M.D., Pennsylvania, 1975. American Cancer Society.
Frederick L. Trowbridge, Adjunct Associate Professor; M.D., Harvard, 1968. Centers for Disease Control and Prevention.
Paul Wiesner, Adjunct Associate Professor; M.D., Wisconsin, 1967. DeKalb County Health Department.
David Forrest Williamson, Adjunct Assistant Professor; Ph.D., Cornell, 1984. Centers for Disease Control and Prevention.
John L. Wilson, Adjunct Assistant Professor; Ph.D., SUNY, 1981. American Cancer Society.

ROLLINS SCHOOL OF PUBLIC HEALTH

EMORY UNIVERSITY

Rollins School of Public Health

Programs of Study

The Rollins School of Public Health (RSPH) of Emory University offers programs leading to the Master of Public Health (M.P.H.) degree with concentrations in behavioral sciences and health education, biostatistics, environmental and occupational health, epidemiology, international health, and health policy and management. The M.S.P.H. is also available in some departments. Several dual-degree programs are available with the Schools of Nursing (M.N./M.P.H.), Business Administration (M.B.A./M.P.H.), Law (J.D./M.P.H.), and Medicine (M.D./M.P.H.). Ph.D. programs in biostatistics and epidemiology and an M.S. program in biostatistics are administered through the Graduate School of Arts and Sciences. A residency program in occupational and environmental medicine is offered by the Rollins School of Public Health. The M.P.H. program meets the needs of both full-time and part-time students and is intended for recent baccalaureate degree graduates who have a strong interest in a health career, physicians and other health professionals who wish to link advanced study in public health with another academic or professional field, international health professionals seeking career development, and currently employed health professionals desiring advanced studies. Evening courses and courses available at other institutions provide flexibility in scheduling a program of study. Each student's program is determined individually. An interdisciplinary approach is emphasized, along with practical public health experiences.

Research Facilities

The ten-story Grace Crum Rollins Public Health Building offers 137,000 square feet of state-of-the-art public health research and training facilities, including advanced computer technology with laboratories for programs in toxicology, biochemistry, molecular biology, and infectious diseases.

Financial Aid

Information about federal loans is available through the Office of Financial Aid (404-727-6039). Non-U.S. citizens are ineligible for federal loans. The Rollins School of Public Health also offers several financial assistance programs. All applicants with complete admission materials received by the financial assistance deadline are considered for these awards. Eligible applicants are reviewed for need-based grants. The Graduate School of Arts and Sciences Fellowship provides full tuition coverage for eligible Ph.D. students.

Cost of Study

The 1998–99 tuition for M.P.H. students is $590 per semester hour.

Living and Housing Costs

Living expenses for a single person attending Emory University are estimated at $13,125 per year. Information regarding University and off-campus housing in the surrounding area may be obtained from the Housing Office at 404-727-8830.

Student Group

Approximately 660 M.P.H. students and 40 Ph.D. students are enrolled in the School. Approximately 12 percent are international students, representing 41 different countries.

Student Outcomes

The RSPH offers a newly created Career Action Center, which assists recent graduates in finding employment as researchers, policy analysts, consultants, health educators, administrators, and clinicians in local, state, and federal health agencies, universities, business enterprises, state and federal government offices, private health organizations, managed-care corporations, professional associations, nongovernmental international health organizations, and health ministries around the world.

Location

Often described as the "public health capital of the world," Atlanta is home to the Centers for Disease Control and Prevention, CARE, the national home office of the American Cancer Society, the Carter Center, the Arthritis Foundation, numerous state and regional health agencies, and the patient-care, teaching, and health-related research programs of Emory University's Robert W. Woodruff Health Sciences Center. With a metropolitan population of nearly three million, a strong corporate base, and wide array of cultural, sports, and entertainment activities, Atlanta is one of the leading cities of the Southeast.

The University and The School

Emory University's student body of 11,109 men and women includes 5,996 undergraduates, 3,433 graduate students, and 1,680 students in professional schools. The Robert W. Woodruff Health Sciences Center of Emory University includes the Schools of Medicine, Nursing, and Public Health. A main corridor through the campus incorporates the expanding medical complex with the headquarters of the CDC and the American Cancer Society. Affiliated resources, such as the Georgia Mental Health Institute, the Georgia Department of Human Resources, the Carter Center, and Grady Memorial Hospital, are nearby. The Rollins School of Public Health, established in 1990, is located in suburban Atlanta on the main University campus. The M.P.H. degree programs and the School are accredited by the Council on Education for Public Health.

Applying

Requirements for admission include satisfactory completion of a four-year baccalaureate degree program and a strong interest in a health career. Applicants are admitted for studies beginning in the fall semester. A complete application consists of the application form, college transcripts, appropriate test scores, and reference letters. All applicants not holding a doctoral-level degree are required to submit GRE scores. In some cases, applicants may submit MCAT scores. Applicants who have completed doctoral-level degrees are not required to submit test scores unless otherwise specified by the department. Applicants to the M.S., M.S.P.H., and Ph.D. programs should have a strong undergraduate background in the mathematical and biological sciences. For all programs, international students whose native language is not English must submit TOEFL scores.

Correspondence and Information

For additional information and applications for M.P.H. programs:

Office of Admissions
The Rollins School of Public Health
1518 Clifton Road, NE
Atlanta, Georgia 30322

Telephone: 404-727-5481

For additional information on M.S. and Ph.D. programs:

Academic Coordinator
Department of (Epidemiology or Biostatistics)
The Rollins School of Public Health
1518 Clifton Road, NE
Atlanta, Georgia 30322

Telephone: 404-727-8710 (Epidemiology)
404-727-3968 (Biostatistics)

Emory University

THE FACULTY AND THEIR RESEARCH

Behavioral Sciences and Health Education. Martha Alexander, M.P.H., Emory, 1986: education and training program development. Melissa Alperin, M.P.H., Emory, 1991: applied evaluation of community-based programs. Ronald Braithwaite, Ph.D., Michigan State, 1974: substance abuse prevention, HIV in prisons, community organization and development, minority health issues. Colleen K. DiIorio, Ph.D., NYU, 1981; HIV/AIDS prevention, epilepsy self-management, application of social cognitive theory, behavioral instrument development. Colleen Doyle, M.S., Ohio State, 1987: community and worksite health promotion, training, and development, health communication. William N. Dudley, Ph.D., Georgia, 1991: application of structural equation modeling to measurement and evaluation research. James P. Griffin Jr., Ph.D., Georgia State, 1991: program evaluation, team building and organizational intervention, resiliency building, and substance abuse prevention. Joan M. Herold, Ph.D., Pennsylvania, 1982: demographic and survey research; migration, fertility, and family planning, with a focus on Latin American and U.S. Hispanic populations. Jeffrey B. Kingree, Ph.D., Georgia State, 1993: substance abuse prevention and treatment. Richard Letz, Ph.D., Texas at Austin, 1979: neurobehavioral assessment in epidemiologic studies, development of neuropsychological testing methods. Richard M. Levinson, Ph.D., Wisconsin, 1975: social determinants of health-risk behavior, access to health care. Kathleen R. Miner, Ph.D., Georgia State, 1984: design and evaluation of community-based interventions related to adolescent health, maternal and child health, chronic disease prevention, and health information systems. Ken Resnicow, Ph.D., Yeshiva, 1985: school health promotion, the relationship between ethnicity and health behavior, and the relationship between personality and health. Jennifer Sharpe-Potter, M.P.H., Emory, 1994: social cognitive theory and its applications in HIV/AIDS prevention. Torrance Stephens, Ph.D., Clark Atlanta, 1992: child survival and maternal health (Nigeria and Senegal), patient education and counseling, qualitative analysis, computer-assisted patient education, African-American men, African and American history. Claire Sterk, Doctoral Anthropology/Sociology, Utrecht, 1983; Ph.D., Rotterdam/CUNY, 1990: women's and children's health, HIV/AIDS, substance abuse, community health. Stephen B. Thomas, Ph.D., Southern Illinois, 1985: minority populations, community-based program planning and evaluation, public health policy, AIDS, violence, addiction. Nancy J. Thompson, Ph.D., Georgia State, 1988: behavioral and psychiatric epidemiology, injury and violence prevention and control, applications of psychological theory. Jane Trowbridge, M.P.H., Emory, 1986: community-based needs assessments and applied evaluation.
Biostatistics. Huiman X. Barnhart, Ph.D., Pittsburgh, 1992: analysis for repeated measures, categorical data analysis, clinical trials. Donna J. Brogan, Ph.D., Iowa State, 1967: sample survey design and analysis, breast cancer epidemiology. W. Scott Clark, Ph.D., Emory, 1990: models of infectious diseases, biostatistical consulting. Danni S. Daniels, M.S., Washington (Seattle), 1990: clinical trials in biostatistical consulting. Lisa Elon, M.P.H., Emory, 1997: sample survey analysis, retrospective cohort study of industrial mercury exposure. Michael J. Haber, Ph.D., Hebrew (Jerusalem), 1976: statistical theory, categorical data analysis, models of infectious diseases. M. Elizabeth Halloran, M.D., Berlin, 1983; M.P.H., 1985, D.Sc., 1989, Harvard: infectious diseases, epidemic modeling, vaccine efficacy, population dynamics, vector-borne diseases, survival analysis. Vicki S. Hertzberg, Ph.D., Washington (Seattle), 1980: categorical data analysis, clinical trials, reproductive epidemiology, DNA fingerprint. Andrzej S. Kosinski, Ph.D., Washington (Seattle), 1990: linear models, cardiovascular clinical trials, statistical computing, survival analysis. Ira M. Longini Jr., Ph.D., Minnesota, 1977: stochastic processes, models for infectious diseases. Michael J. Lynn, M.S., Mississippi State, 1976: clinical trials, applications in ophthalmic research, statistical computing. Amita K. Manatunga, Ph.D., Rochester, 1990: multivariate survival analysis, frailty models, categorical data analysis, longitudinal data. Azhar Nizam, M.S., South Carolina, 1987: multiple comparisons, statistical education. Yannan Shen, M.S., Florida, 1992: data management, analysis of cardiovascular data.
Environmental and Occupational Health. Mary J. DeLong, Ph.D., Notre Dame, 1970: toxicology, occupational and environmental carcinogenesis. Howard Frumkin, M.D., Pennsylvania, 1982; Dr.P.H., Harvard, 1993: clinical occupational medicine, occupational and environmental epidemiology. Edward I. Galaid, M.D., SUNY Downstate Medical Center, 1983: medical information systems and surveillance of occupational disease. Fredric Gerr, M.D., SUNY at Stony Brook, 1982: occupational neurotoxicity and nerve entrapment syndromes, upper extremity musculoskeletal disorders of occupational origin, heavy metal toxicity. Philip L. Graitcer, D.M.D., Temple, 1970: bicycle helmet promotions, surveillance of injuries, impact of injuries on health in developing countries. Arthur Kellermann, M.D., Emory, 1980: injury control, firearm injury prevention, health services. Ricardo Martinez, M.D., LSU, 1980: injury control, motor vehicle injury prevention, trauma care, trauma systems development. P. Barry Ryan, Ph.D., Wesleyan, 1979: environmental exposure assessment, environmental epidemiology, environmental chemistry. Paige Tolbert, Ph.D., North Carolina, 1989: environmental and occupational epidemiology.
Epidemiology. Harland D. Austin, D.Sc., Harvard, 1983: quantitative methods, cancer epidemiology. John R. Boring III, Ph.D., Florida, 1961: infectious disease epidemiology, molecular epidemiology. J. Elaine Brockman, M.P.H., Emory, 1988: cancer epidemiology and surveillance. John Carter, Ph.D., Rice, 1968; M.P.H., Emory, 1991: perinatal epidemiology, nutrition and cancer. Lorie A. Click, M.N., 1982, M.P.H., 1989, Emory: cancer and nutritional epidemiology. Ralph J. Coates, Ph.D., Washington (Seattle), 1986: nutritional and cancer epidemiology. James Curran, M.D., Michigan, 1970: epidemiology of HIV/AIDS. Carolyn D. Drews-Botsch, Ph.D., UCLA, 1988: ophthalmic and reproductive epidemiology, methods. John William Eley, M.D., 1983, M.P.H., 1990, Emory: cancer epidemiology and control. Elaine W. Flagg, Ph.D., Emory, 1992: sample survey conduct and analysis, nutritional epidemiology. W. Dana Flanders, M.D., Vermont, 1977; D.Sc., Harvard, 1979: quantitative epidemiology, methods. Dawna S. Fuqua-Whitley, M.A., Pittsburgh, 1992: medical anthropology, medical geography/geographic information systems, youth violence, public health program evaluation. Holly A. Hill, M.D., 1987, Ph.D., 1992, North Carolina: cancer epidemiology and prevention. David G. Kleinbaum, Ph.D., North Carolina, 1970: quantitative epidemiology, methods. Jonathan M. Liff, Ph.D., Washington (Seattle), 1984: cancer epidemiology and surveillance. Michele Marcus, Ph.D., Columbia, 1986: reproductive and environmental epidemiology, neuroepidemiology. John E. McGowan Jr., M.D., Harvard, 1967: infectious disease epidemiology. Stephen R. Pitts, M.D., Texas Southwestern Medical Center at Dallas, 1979; M.P.H., Emory, 1992: clinical epidemiology. Kevin Sullivan, Ph.D., Michigan, 1990: epidemiologic methods, microcomputers in epidemiology. Knox H. Todd, M.D., Southwestern Medical School, 1983: program evaluation, alcohol use and abuse, pain management, emergency medical services.
Health Policy and Management. E. Kathleen Adams, Ph.D., Colorado, 1979: Medicaid, provider supply, hospital market analysis and public finance. Edmund R. Becker, Ph.D., Vanderbilt, 1981: health-care organization and financing, physician behavior, payment and productivity, unions and labor relations. Steven D. Culler, Ph.D., Illinois, 1981: financial management, cost-effectiveness analysis and health economics. Joyce D. K. Essien, M.D., Wayne State, 1971: health reform and public health policy, continuous quality improvement planning/implementation, preventive health systems. Anthony A. Hudgins, M.A.S., Georgia State, 1981: efficiency/effectiveness of ambulatory care. Fredric D. Kennedy, Ph.D., North Carolina, 1974: clinic operations, large-scale databases for decision support systems, strategic planning. Deborah A. McFarland, M.P.H., North Carolina, 1973; Ph.D., Tennessee, 1987: U.S. health policy, health-care financing in the United States and developing countries, comparative health policy, economic evaluation, public health economics. Victoria L. Phillips, D. Phil., Oxford, 1991: labor and econometrics, health economics, comparative health systems, financing and delivery of long-term and community-based care. Richard B. Saltman, Ph.D., Stanford, 1980: comparative health policy, organization theory, U.S. health policy, health systems reform, accountability, and governance.
International Health. Rachel Albalak, Ph.D., Michigan, 1997: growth and development, evaluation of nutritional interventions. Philip S. Brachman, M.D. Wisconsin, 1953: public health surveillance, preventive medicine, infectious diseases, hospital infections. Stanley O. Foster, M.D., Rochester, 1960: international policy, health program planning, child survival issues. Eugene J. Gangarosa, M.D., Rochester, 1954: control of food-borne and waterborne diseases, child survival issues, primary health care, minority health issues, migrant health. Glen F. Maberly, M.D. New South Wales (Sydney), 1983: micronutrient malnutrition, endocrinology. Reynaldo Martorell, Ph.D., Washington (Seattle), 1973: protein-energy malnutrition, maternal and child nutrition, child growth, nutrition and infection, functional consequences of malnutrition, design and evaluation of nutrition interventions, food and nutrition policy. Rose Nathan, J.D., George Washington, 1983: public health law, micronutrient malnutrition. Claudia Fishman Parvanta, Ph.D., Pennsylvania, 1986: anthropology and public health communication, maternal and child nutrition. Usha Ramakrishnan, Ph.D., Cornell, 1993: childhood malnutrition, maternal and child nutrition, micronutrient malnutrition. Dirk G. Schroeder, Sc.D., Johns Hopkins, 1992: child feeding practices in developing countries, epidemiology of diarrheal disease, dietary management of diarrheal diseases. James Setzer, M.P.H., Tulane, 1983: program planning and management, health finance. Jose Augusto de Aguiar Carrazedo Taddei, Dr.P.H., Sao Paulo School of Public Health, 1988: epidemiology applied to planning and evaluation of health and nutrition policies and programs. Frits van der Haar, Ph.D., Agricultural University (Netherlands), 1977: human nutrition, micronutrient malnutrition. Clive E. West, D.Sc., Agricultural University (Netherlands), 1986: micronutrient malnutrition, food composition and intake.
Women's and Children's Center. Karen N. Bell, M.P.H., Columbia, 1976: child health programs and policies, integration of health and other services for young children. Sheana E. Bull, M.P.H., Tulane, 1992: adolescent reproductive health, family planning, multicultural issues in women's and children's health. Carol J. R. Hogue, Ph.D., North Carolina, 1973: reproductive epidemiology, women's and children's health. Fleda M. Jackson, Ph.D., Illinois, 1991: health status of black children, the church and health services. Alan P. Kendal, Ph.D., University College Hospital Medical School, 1969: childhood immunization, virology.

THE GEORGE WASHINGTON UNIVERSITY

School of Public Health and Health Services

Programs of Study

The School of Public Health and Health Services offers a Council on Education for Public Health–accredited Master of Public Health (M.P.H.) plus an M.S. and Ph.D. program in epidemiology and biostatistics. A master's degree in health services administration (M.H.S.A.), accredited by the Accreditation Commission for Health Services Administration, is also offered, as is an M.S. degree in exercise science. Specializations in the M.P.H. program are offered in the following fields: administrative medicine (management or policy), community-oriented primary care, environmental-occupational health, epidemiology-biostatistics, health promotion–disease prevention, international health (health promotion or policy and programs), and maternal and child health. Students in the M.H.S.A. program select an administrative or policy specialization. Joint J.D./M.P.H., LL.M./M.P.H., M.D./M.P.H., and physician assistant/M.P.H. degrees are also offered, as is the Master's Internationalist Program in the Peace Corps. Close integration and cross-crediting of course work allows students to complete the M.D./M.P.H. program in four years and the J.D./M.P.H. program in three years. Certificate programs are available, and credits can be transferred to the corresponding track of the M.P.H. program. The graduate certificate program may be taken via distance education. The M.S. and Ph.D. Program in epidemiology and biostatistics is offered in cooperation with the Department of Statistics and the George Washington Biostatistics Center. The M.P.H. program may be completed on an intensive basis in one year or part-time in two to four years. Classes are generally scheduled on weekday evenings, late afternoons, and Saturday mornings. A Doctor of Public Health degree is also offered.

Research Facilities

The public health programs cooperate with the University's research centers and institutes, including the new Institute for Health Policy Outcomes and Human Values; the Center for International Health; the Biostatistics Center; and Children's National Medical Center. The centers provide opportunities for master's-level special project research and doctoral dissertations. The Himmelfarb Library contains more than 100,000 volumes and more than 1,500 periodicals. The library offers extensive computer search and educational facilities. Students also have access to the other University libraries and computer facilities.

Financial Aid

Student loans, scholarships, and faculty assistant positions are available, including Public Health traineeships. A limited number of need-based and academic scholarships are available through the program to partially cover tuition. Teaching assistantships and other financial aid is available to doctoral students. Residency and fellowship programs are available in occupational medicine and primary care specialties, which include tuition benefits. Information on financial aid should be requested from the Office of Student Financial Assistance, The George Washington University, Washington, D.C. 20052 (telephone: 202-994-6620).

Cost of Study

Current tuition is $680 per credit hour for the 33-credit M.P.H. and the M.S. programs and the 72-credit doctoral programs. Students may be required to complete 3 to 6 credit hours of additional course requirements. Additional fees include a University fee of $34 per credit hour up to a maximum of $457.50 per semester. Joint M.D./M.P.H. and J.D./M.P.H. students pay tuition, which reduces the overall cost of the M.P.H. program.

Living and Housing Costs

The cost of living in the Washington metropolitan area is comparable to that of other major urban centers in the United States. A wide variety of off-campus housing is available; information on apartments and houses in the metropolitan area may be obtained from the Off-Campus Housing Resource Center, Marvin Center, 800 21st Street, NW, Washington, D.C. 20037 (telephone: 202-994-7221).

Student Group

The student body includes a growing number of full-time students from throughout the nation as well as international students. A substantial number of students are health professionals or joint-degree students. In addition, a large number of students have recently completed their bachelor's degrees. The programs and the University sponsor a large number of student activities, including International Week and Career Week. Many of the approximately 600 students work part-time in the greater Washington metropolitan area.

Student Outcomes

Recent graduates of the programs are employed in health maintenance organizations, national associations, federal government agencies, state health departments, consulting firms, major corporations, and international organizations.

Location

The George Washington University is located in the Foggy Bottom area of Washington, D.C., in proximity to the White House, the Pan American Health Organization, the World Bank, and the Kennedy Center. Subway access to the metropolitan area is available on campus. Course work is also offered at Children's National Medical Center.

The University

The George Washington University, chartered by Congress in 1821, is private and nonsectarian. It holds regional accreditation from the Middle States Association of Colleges and Schools. The George Washington University Medical Center includes the School of Medicine and Health Sciences, the Medical Faculty Associates, and the George Washington University Health Plan, as well as the School of Public Health and Health Services. Affiliated institutions include the Children's National Medical Center.

Applying

Students are admitted for the fall, spring, or summer. Application for the summer must be postmarked before April 1; for the fall, before May 15; and for the spring, before November 15. Late applications and distance education applications will be processed on a space-available basis. Students applying for a scholarship through the Public Health Programs must have completed their application by March 15. A bachelor's degree and specific prerequisites are required except for the administrative medicine program, which generally requires a previous graduate degree. GRE, MCAT, or GMAT test scores are required for those who have not completed a graduate degree. The TOEFL is required of students from countries where English is not an official language and who do not hold a degree from an accredited U.S. institution of higher education. Physicians may substitute the English validation examination of the FMGEMS or ECFMG. M.S. and Ph.D. applicants will be reviewed until all openings have been filled with qualified students.

Correspondence and Information

School of Public Health and Health Services
The George Washington University
2300 K Street, NW
Washington, D.C. 20037

Telephone: 202-994-2807
Fax: 202-994-1299
E-mail: hspmlp@gwunix2.gwu.edu
World Wide Web: http://www.gwumc.edu/sphhs

The George Washington University

DEPARTMENTS AND RESEARCH AREAS

Environmental-Occupational Health
Acting Chair: John Balbus, M.D., M.P.H.
Track Director: Katherine Hunting, Ph.D., M.P.H.
Faculty: James Weeks, Sc.D.; George Carlo, Ph.D.

Faculty research and expertise include studies of occupational and environmental exposures, injury control, occupational epidemiology, and effects of global environmental change. Recent studies include research on repetitive motion injuries and lead exposures. Faculty members provide consultation to a large number of federal agencies, labor unions, and international labor and health organizations. The EPA has recently awarded the School a five-year cooperative agreement. This agreement provides new research initiatives in water safety and other environmental issues.

Epidemiology-Biostatistics
Acting Chair: Daniel Hoffman, Ph.D., M.S.P.H.
Faculty: Robert Hirsch, Ph.D.; Karl Klontz, M.D., M.P.H.; Paul Levine, M.D.; Richard Riegelman, M.D., M.P.H., Ph.D.; Samuel Simmens, Ph.D.; Robert Smythe, Ph.D.; Dante Verme, Ph.D.

The GW Biostatistics Center and the research program of the George Washington University Medical Center provide opportunities for research and statistical consultation. The Biostatistics Center has more than 90 faculty and staff members and serves as the coordinating center for a large number of multicenter controlled clinical trials. The Children's National Medical Center and the Epidemiology Program of the National Cancer Institute provide additional research opportunities. The Biostatistics Center is also responsible for the GW Medical Center Biostatistics unit which provides opportunities for supervised training experience conducting medical research. Faculty expertise includes clinical epidemiology, environmental epidemiology, controlled clinical trial design, cancer epidemiology, sequential analysis, Bayesian analysis, and psychosocial research techniques.

Health Services Management and Policy
Chair: Richard Southby, Ph.D.
Faculty: Kurt Darr, J.D., Sc.D.; Steven Eastaugh, D.Sc., M.S.P.H.; Warren Greenberg, Ph.D.; Bernard Horak, Ph.D.; Donna Lind Infeld, Ph.D.; Nancy Alfred Persily, M.P.H.; Sara Rosenbaum, J.D.; Shoshanna Sofaer, Dr.Ph.; Stephanie Spernak, J.D.

The GW Center for Health Policy Research and the Institute for Health Policy Outcomes and Human Values provides a research base. The center and its parent institute serve as a resource for health policy programs and provide outstanding opportunities for interactions between the University and the many public officials and individuals in the private sector who are directly involved in health policy making in the Washington area. Research expertise of the faculty includes national health-care policy legislation, managed care, disabilities, and long-term care. Tobacco policy and outcomes research are additional areas of faculty expertise.

International Public Health
Chair: Rosalia Rodriguez-Garcia, Ph.D.
Faculty: James Banta, M.D., M.P.H.; Abdel Omran, M.D., M.P.H., Dr.P.H.; Jorge Rios, M.D.; Tomas Silber, M.D.

The GW Center for International Health serves as the research base for the international health track. The center's research focuses on international health and development. Cooperative research and service projects are coordinated with Project HOPE, the Aga Khan Foundation, and a growing list of other international organizations. The center was recently designated as a WHO collaborating center. Faculty expertise includes program evaluation, demography, international adolescent health, and international technology transfer.

Prevention and Community Health
Interim Chair: Lawrence D'Angelo, M.D., M.P.H.
Faculty: Brad Boekaloo, Ph.D., Sc.M.; Letitia Carlson, M.D., M.P.H.; James Cawley, M.P.H., PA-C; Tina Cheng, M.D., M.P.H.; Denise Cora-Bramble, M.D.; Ayman El-Mohandes, M.D., M.P.H.; Joyce Evan, M.D.; Bo Fernhall, Ph.D.; John Grossman, M.D., Ph.D.; Wayne Miller, Ph.D.; Brad Moore, M.D., M.P.H.; Khairia Omran, M.B.Ch.B., Dr.P.H., M.P.H.; Donald Paup, Ph.D.; Mona Sarfaty, M.D.; Peter Scheidt, M.D.; W. Scott Schroth, M.D., M.P.H.; Patricia Sullivan, Ph.D.

Prevention research focuses on behavior change at the individual and community levels. Research is conducted in collaboration with the Center for Health Promotion and other centers of the Institute for Health Policy Outcomes and Human Values as well as Children's National Medical Center. Collaborative service projects funded by the Kellogg Foundation and the PEW Charitable Trust provide additional opportunities for student involvement. The NIH Preventative Research Branch Contract has recently been awarded to the GW Medical Center, which is expected to dramatically increase the research base in maternal and child health.

HARVARD UNIVERSITY

School of Public Health

Programs of Study

The School of Public Health offers programs leading to the graduate degrees of Master of Public Health (M.P.H.), Doctor of Public Health (D.P.H.), Master of Occupational Health (M.O.H.), Master of Science in a specified field (S.M. in that field), and Doctor of Science in a specified field (S.D. in that field). Programs are offered in biostatistics, cancer cell biology, environmental health, epidemiology, health and social behavior, health policy and management, immunology and infectious diseases, international health, maternal and child health, nutrition, occupational health, and population sciences. Some programs are designed for physicians, lawyers, managers, and other health-care professionals; some for college graduates who wish to train for health careers; and others for individuals who hold graduate degrees in medicine, law, business, government, education, and other fields who wish to apply their special skills to public health problems. Special programs include the Master of Science in occupational health or maternal and child health nursing, administered jointly by HSPH and Simmons College; the doctoral program in oral epidemiology, administered jointly by HSPH and the Harvard School of Dental Medicine; and the combined M.D./M.P.H. program offered in conjunction with medical schools. Through its Office of Continuing Education, the School offers professional development courses. The School offers residency training leading to certification by the American Board of Preventive Medicine in occupational medicine.

Research Facilities

The main buildings of the School are the Health Sciences Laboratories at 665 Huntington Avenue, the Sebastian S. Kresge Educational Facilities Building at 677 Huntington Avenue, and the François-Xavier Bagnoud Building at 651 Huntington Avenue. The School maintains well-equipped research laboratories containing sophisticated instrumentation and supporting animal facilities. Computing and data processing resources are also available to students through the Instructional Computing Facility. The Francis A. Countway Library serves the library needs of the School. Its holdings of more than 545,000 volumes and 4,000 periodicals in addition to its extensive collection of historical materials make it the largest library in the country serving a medical and health-related school.

Financial Aid

Financial aid at the School of Public Health can come from a variety of sources. Some departments have training grants offering students full tuition plus a stipend. Through need- and merit-based programs, other students are offered grants that range from half to full tuition. To supplement other aid, many students borrow through one or more of the federal educational loan programs and work at part-time jobs at Harvard and in the community. Eligibility for most financial aid requires U.S. citizenship or permanent resident status.

Cost of Study

Full-time tuition for 1998–99 is $21,895 a year. Hospitalization insurance is required and costs $686. Books and supplies cost approximately $1200 in 1997–98.

Living and Housing Costs

For the academic year 1998–99, it is estimated that a single student needs a minimum of $14,675: $560 for health insurance, $7500 for rent and utilities, and $6615 for other expenses. Limited housing is available in the Shattuck International House, with preference given to international students. Most students arrange for housing in the adjacent communities.

Student Group

There were 752 graduate students (460 women and 292 men) enrolled in 1997–98. About fifty nations are represented.

Student Outcomes

Graduates from the Harvard School of Public Health find employment in a variety of settings, depending in part upon their previous experience and in part upon department and degree programs from which they graduate. Recent graduates have found positions in research institutes, with pharmaceutical companies and governmental and nongovernmental agencies, within the health-care industry, and as faculty members of universities.

Location

Boston is a heterogeneous metropolis rich in history and charm. Athletic, cultural, and recreational activities are abundant. The School is within walking distance of museums, colleges and universities, waterways, and parks.

The University and The School

Harvard College was founded in 1636, and, until the establishment of professorships in medicine in 1782, it comprised the whole of the institution now called Harvard University. In addition to the College, ten graduate schools are now part of the University.

Activity in professional education in the field of public health had been steadily increasing at Harvard University for more than two decades before the actual founding of the School in 1922. The primary mission of the School is to carry out teaching and research aimed at improving the health of population groups throughout the world. The School emphasizes not only the development and implementation of disease prevention and treatment programs but also the planning and management of systems involved in the delivery of health services in this country and abroad. The School cooperates with the Medical School in teaching and research and has close ties with other Harvard faculties. The School has more than 200 full-time and part-time faculty members and eleven academic departments representing major biomedical and social disciplines.

Applying

Applicants must submit a completed application form including all postsecondary and graduate school transcripts, at least three letters of recommendation, a $60 nonrefundable application fee, and a self-addressed notification card. All applicants to the School are required to submit scores from the GRE. Applicants may submit the DAT, GMAT, or MCAT, as appropriate to the applicant's background, in lieu of the GRE. Lawyers applying to the M.P.H. program may submit LSAT scores. In very unusual cases, written requests to waive the test requirement are considered but not necessarily granted. Applicants are urged to take the test no later than November, since applications will not be considered without the scores. Applicants with prior test scores may submit them with their application materials. In addition, applicants must persuade the Committee on Admissions and Degrees of their ability to meet academic standards and of their overall qualifications to undertake advanced study at a graduate level. Students should contact the Admissions Office for information concerning the deadline to apply for admission.

As a matter of policy, law, and commitment, Harvard University does not discriminate against applicants or students in admission, educational policies, or scholarship and loan programs on the basis of race, religion, sex, sexual orientation, marital or parental status, veteran status, national origin, color, creed, handicap, or age. Members of minority groups are strongly encouraged to apply.

Correspondence and Information

Catalogs and applications:

Admissions Office
Harvard School of Public Health
677 Huntington Avenue
Boston, Massachusetts 02115
Telephone: 617-432-1030
Fax: 617-432-2009
E-mail: admisofc@sph.harvard.edu

Counseling and program information:

Caroline Daniels
Assistant Director of Admissions
Harvard School of Public Health
677 Huntington Avenue
Boston, Massachusetts 02115
Telephone: 617-432-1031
Fax: 617-432-2009
E-mail: admisofc@sph.harvard.edu

Harvard University

FACULTY CHAIRS AND DEPARTMENTAL ACTIVITIES

Biostatistics (617-432-1056)
Chair: Nan Laird, Ph.D. The program combines both theory and practice of biostatistics and is aimed at preparing students to be biostatistical scientists pursuing faculty careers in universities and research institutes. Emphasis is on the doctoral program. Faculty research spans both methodological developments on new statistical techniques and important subject matter applications that lead to significant advances in the health sciences. Current interests include AIDS modeling, clinical trials in both AIDS and cancer, computing algorithms, discrete data analysis, empirical Bayes methods, environmental health, health policy, longitudinal studies, risk assessment, and statistical computing.

Cancer Cell Biology (617-432-0054)
Chair: Jack B. Little, M.D. The department has two component divisions, which are radiation biology and toxicology. They feature laboratory research that combines knowledge of recent advances and techniques in biochemistry, molecular and cell biology, and genetics to focus on the mechanisms involved in the development of cancer and the means for its prevention. Specific emphases include the growth control of cancer cells; the damage and repair of DNA, particularly in response to chemicals and oxidants that are present in the environment; chemical and radiation carcinogenesis; receptor-mediated toxicity; and the biological effects of low dose radiation exposure. This research involves the development and use of animal and human cell culture models.

Environmental Health (617-432-1270)
Chair: Joseph Brain, S.D. The department has five programs: The Program in Environmental Health and Public Policy provides opportunities for scholars from the natural and social sciences to work toward solutions to critical environmental problems; the Occupational Health Program has as its goal the training of multidisciplinary teams of professionals to identify and prevent occupational exposures; the Environmental Exposure Assessment and Engineering Program offers concentrations in air pollution, environmental health management, industrial hygiene, and radiological health; the Respiratory Biology Program is a multidisciplinary program emphasizing predoctoral and postdoctoral training in such areas as mechanisms of lung injury, environmental lung disease, aerosol deposition and clearance, macrophage biology, respiratory mechanics, airway pharmacology, and comparative respiratory biology; and the Environmental Epidemiology Program offers predoctoral and postdoctoral training in preparation for research careers in environmental epidemiology with special emphasis on respiratory diseases.

Epidemiology (617-432-1055)
Chair: Alexander Walker, M.D., Dr.P.H. Research involves studies on cancer of the breast, with respect to possible hormonal causes; cancer of the kidney and pancreas; Hodgkin's disease; nutritional epidemiology; causes of congenital abnormalities, such as the possible role of therapeutic drugs; and international variations in the frequency of disease.

Health and Social Behavior (617-432-1135)
Chair: Lisa Berkman, Ph.D. Research carried out by the department includes the design and evaluation of health promotion/education programs aimed at altering unhealthy lifestyles (e.g., smoking, substance abuse), diet, and exercise patterns; identification of child health problems and the design and evaluation of child health services; studies on ethnic variations in response to health care; opiate addiction among street addicts, medical professionals, and medical patients; and the role of stress and social support systems in the utilization of primary-care health services.

Health Policy and Management (617-432-1090)
Chair: Arnold Epstein, M.D. The department prepares students for careers in health management, health research, and design of health programs and policies. Relevant theory and concepts from the social and behavioral sciences, including fields such as economics, law, medicine, political science, anthropology, sociology, and public and business administration, are adapted to the practical problems of public health. Since many wide-ranging problems must be studied through quantitative and analytic methods and administrative techniques, the resources of multiple disciplines and several Harvard faculties are carefully integrated into the master's and doctoral programs. Current research includes management of health-care institutions and systems, management of health hazards, international health, and financing health care and insurance.

Immunology and Infectious Diseases (617-432-1023)
Chair: M. E. Essex, D.V.M., Ph.D. The department focuses on the biological, immunological, epidemiological, and ecological aspects of viral, bacterial, protozoan, and helminthic diseases of animals and humans and the vectors that transmit some of these infectious agents. Emphasis is on research identifying basic pathogenic mechanisms that may lead to better diagnostic tools and the development of vaccines and other immune interventions for prevention and control of infections and disease as well as the identification of new targets for antiviral and antiparasite drugs.

Maternal and Child Health (617-432-1080)
Chair: Marie McCormick, M.D., Sc.D. The department offers an academic program for experienced professionals whose interest is the maintenance and enhancement of the health of mothers and children. It provides fundamental skills in planning, developing, implementing, and evaluating services. The curriculum focuses on factors influencing the attainment of optimal health and development and on health-related services needed by children and by women of childbearing age. Research includes childhood determinants of adult health, epidemiology and control of childhood injury, adolescent suicide, and determinants of functioning for children with special needs and their families.

Nutrition (617-432-1333)
Chair: Walter C. Willett, M.D., Dr.P.H. The research of the department involves various aspects of nutrition ranging from cell biology and metabolism to animal pathophysiology, clinical studies, and policy planning at domestic and international levels. Some specific studies are regulation of cell growth by hormonal growth factors obtained from human blood components, mechanism of action of vitamin D, effects of diet on the metabolism of nutrients and drugs by gut flora, the etiology of sudden death ischemic heart disease, and the regulation of gene expression by dietary factors.

Population and International Health (617-432-2253)
Chair: Lincoln C. Chen, M.D., M.P.H. Research and training activities involve demography and social change; women's and reproductive health (including sexually transmitted diseases); community-oriented approaches to fertility and mortality; international health policy and management; human ecology and the control of tropical diseases; and nutrition and food policy.

Division of Biological Sciences (617-432-4089)
Director: Edgar Haber, M.D. The division offers a multidisciplinary program designed for doctoral students committed to a career in the biological sciences who have not yet selected a field of concentration. About 60 participating faculty members represent the fields of cancer biology, environmental science and physiology, molecular biology, nutrition, toxicology, and tropical public health. The two-year program includes flexible course opportunities, interdisciplinary seminars, and three or four laboratory rotations in students' selected areas of interest. Students then pursue thesis research in the department or laboratory of their choice.

Master of Public Health Program (617-432-0090)
Director: Gareth M. Green, M.D., Associate Dean for Professional Education. The program is designed to provide both a general background and flexibility of specialization in public health. The five areas of concentration are health care and organizational management, international health, occupational and environmental health, public management and community health, and quantitative methods.

JOHNS HOPKINS UNIVERSITY

School of Hygiene and Public Health
Department of Environmental Health Sciences

Programs of Study

The Department of Environmental Health Sciences offers both specialized and more general training at the master's and doctoral levels. At the master's level, specialized training programs lead to the M.H.S. degree in environmental engineering or radiation health sciences, and a broader interdisciplinary departmental program leads to the M.H.S. degree in environmental health. The specialized M.H.S. programs, which can lead to certification eligibility in industrial hygiene or health physics, require up to two years of full-time study. The departmental M.H.S. program may be taken on a part-time basis and requires the equivalent of one year of full-time study. These programs do not require a written comprehensive examination or a research thesis.

At the doctoral level, specialized Ph.D. programs in environmental engineering, occupational health, physiology, radiation health, and toxicology are available, as well as an interdisciplinary departmental program leading to the Dr.P.H. degree in environmental health. The doctoral programs require at least one year of course work, followed by approximately three years of research, culminating in a thesis. These programs require a written comprehensive examination, an oral examination prior to thesis research, and a final, oral thesis defense. Under special circumstances, a student may transfer from a doctoral program into an Sc.M. program in the same discipline. Such a program requires a more modest research thesis.

The M.H.S. programs emphasize formal course work, although laboratory rotations are available. All students are expected to participate in seminars, journal clubs, and other opportunities for faculty-student interactions. The doctoral programs emphasize individual research. Examples of current research include identification of the gene responsible for airways inflammation in subjects exposed to ozone, the effect of electromagnetic fields on workers, investigation of the impact of lead poisoning on brain receptors, assessment of ultraviolet light and its role in skin cancer in Maryland watermen, early detection of lung cancer, and chemoprevention of liver cancer in human populations.

Research Facilities

The department currently occupies 54,000 square feet of space in the School of Public Health. This space includes many specialized laboratories, such as the Human Exposure Assessment Laboratory, in which human physiologic monitoring and radiographic imaging studies are performed to assess the response to environmental agents, and the Inhalation Toxicology Facility for animal exposures to oxidants, solvents, particles, and biologic agents.

Financial Aid

A variety of aid is available from the government, the private sector, and the School itself; a Financial Aid Office coordinates aid. Financial assistance includes scholarships, fellowships, traineeships, student employment, student loans, and Federal Work-Study funds. Financial aid is awarded based on merit, need, and the availability of funds. Demonstrated financial need is required for some programs and is determined in conjunction with federal need analysis.

Cost of Study

Tuition for 1998–99 is $22,680 for full-time students and $473 per credit for part-time students. Yearly increases are expected.

Living and Housing Costs

In general, the cost of living in the Baltimore area is less than that of other major cities in the United States. Total living expenses, excluding tuition and fees, for students living off campus for eleven months are approximately $16,000. The School of Public Health provides residence hall living accommodations in Reed Hall for single or married students not accompanied by their spouses.

Student Group

In 1997–98, there were a total of 105 graduate students—71 Ph.D., 12 Dr.P.H., 20 M.H.S., and 2 Sc.M. The School of Public Health has more than 1,300 graduate students, representing most states of the Union and seventy-eight other countries.

Graduates of the program enter academic, public, or industrial careers. Most of the master's graduates are involved in public or private environmental endeavors, such as in state environment departments and the EPA, or as industrial hygienists or health physicists in industry. Doctoral graduates are typically in academic settings.

Location

Baltimore is ranked among the largest of the industrial and seaport cities. It offers a lively mix of tradition and progress with an easy, pleasant lifestyle. Its neighborhoods represent many ethnic and racial backgrounds. The School of Public Health is located 1 mile from the inner harbor of the Chesapeake Bay, the nation's largest tidewater bay. Inner Harbor is home of many shopping pavilions; the National Aquarium; the Maryland Science Center; the U.S. Frigate *Constellation;* the baseball stadium, Oriole Park at Camden Yards; and a 2-mile waterfront promenade. Nearby are the Morris Mechanic, Lyric, and Center Stage theaters; the Walters Art Gallery; and Meyerhoff Hall, home of the Baltimore Symphony Orchestra.

The University and The Department

Johns Hopkins University was founded on the European model of graduate research education. The School of Public Health, ranked first in the nation, emphasizes the inseparability of graduate-level education, basic research, and professional practice. Accordingly, the Department of Environmental Health Sciences' mission is to perform high-quality, mechanism-based research focused on the adverse effects on human health caused by chemical, physical, and biological agents either occurring naturally or introduced into the environment by man and to apply this knowledge to train graduate research scientists and public health professionals.

Applying

A strong background in the physical sciences is typically required for the specialized degree programs. Greater flexibility is available for the interdisciplinary programs. Students are selected on the basis of academic background and performance, work experience, GRE scores, letters of recommendation, and interviews with the faculty. Students are strongly encouraged to apply by March 1.

Correspondence and Information

Kay Castleberry
Department of Environmental Health Sciences
Johns Hopkins School of Hygiene and Public Health
615 North Wolfe Street
Baltimore, Maryland 21205
Telephone: 410-955-2212
Fax: 410-955-0617

Johns Hopkins University

THE FACULTY AND THEIR RESEARCH

Jacqueline Agnew, M.P.H., Ph.D., Associate Professor of Occupational and Environmental Health. Neurobehavioral testing, occupational health nursing.
Kwamena Baidoo, Ph.D., Assistant Professor of Radiation Health Sciences. Development of recognition site-specific radiopharmaceuticals.
Joseph Bressler, Ph.D., Assistant Professor of Toxicological Sciences. Interaction of lead with signal transduction mechanisms, role of the blood-brain barrier in neurotoxicity.
Patrick N. Breysse, Ph.D., Associate Professor of Environmental Health Engineering. Industrial hygiene, asbestos exposure assessment, man-made mineral fibers, air cleaning adsorbents, electric and magnetic fields, airborne allergens.
Timothy J. Buckley, M.H.S., Ph.D., Assistant Professor of Environmental Health Engineering. Multimedia exposure and measurement and assessment, biomarkers of exposure, dermal exposure.
Srinivasan Chandrasegaran, Ph.D., Associate Professor of Environmental Health Sciences. Study of protein–nucleic acid recognition using restriction enzymes as model systems.
Jacqueline K. Corn, D.A., Associate Professor Emeritus of Environmental Health Sciences.
Morton Corn, Ph.D., Professor Emeritus of Environmental Health Engineering. Occupational safety and health management, risk assessment and management.
Thomas Croxton, M.D., Ph.D., Assistant Professor of Physiology. Electrophysiology, ion fluxes in cells.
Valeria Culotta, Ph.D., Associate Professor of Toxicological Sciences. Transition metals and oxygen-free radicals, molecular genetics of the oxidative stress response.
Arthur M. Dannenberg Jr., M.D., Ph.D., Professor of Environmental Health Sciences. Mechanisms of inflammatory response in the skin and the lung, including tuberculosis.
Walter Ehrlich, M.D., Associate Professor Emeritus of Physiology. Regulations of the cardiovascular system, autoregulations.
Robert S. Fitzgerald, Ph.D., Professor of Physiology. Cardiopulmonary physiology.
Sheila T. Fitzgerald, Ph.D., Assistant Professor of Occupational and Environmental Health. Maintenance of employment, return to work, occupational health nursing, stress and asthma, adolescents and work.
William Michael Foster, Ph.D., Associate Professor of Physiology. Physics and physiology of human exposure to environmental agents.
Robert Frank, M.D., Professor Emeritus of Physiology. Effects of inhaled pollutants in man.
Arthur Freed, Ph.D., Associate Professor of Physiology. Mechanisms of airway reactivity, airflow-induced bronchoconstriction.
Allison Fryer, Ph.D., Associate Professor of Physiology. Effects of viral infections on cell membrane receptors.
Robyn Gershon, D.P.H., Assistant Scientist of Environmental Health Sciences. Biohazards, occupational health and safety of health-care workers.
Alan M. Goldberg, Ph.D., Professor of Toxicological Sciences, Director of the Center for Alternatives to Animal Testing, and Associate Dean for Corporate Affairs. Alternative test methods to the use of animals.
John D. Groopman, Ph.D., Anna M. Baetjer Professor and Chair of Environmental Health Sciences and Director of NIEHS Johns Hopkins Center in Urban Environmental Health. Molecular dosimetry and biomarkers of human carcinogens and mechanisms of chemical carcinogens, DNA adduct formation, chemoprevention.
Tomás R. Guilarte, Ph.D., Professor of Radiation Health Sciences. Developmental changes in the brain following exposure to environmental toxins and nutritional deprivation, role of neuroreceptors in Pb neurotoxicity.
John Howell, B.S., Instructor of Physiology. Electronic instrumentation.
George J. Jakab, Ph.D., Professor of Physiology. Interaction between airborne pollutants and respiratory infections.
David Jett, Ph.D., Assistant Professor of Toxicological Sciences. Neurotoxicology, lead and organophosphate pesticides, cholinergic receptors, signal transduction, learning and memory and the CNS.
Thomas W. Kensler, Ph.D., Professor of Toxicological Sciences. Molecular mechanisms of chemical carcinogenesis, reactive oxygen, cancer chemoprotection.
Steven R. Kleeberger, Ph.D., Associate Professor of Physiology. Airways inflammation and genetics, susceptibility factors in oxidant inhalation.
Peter S. J. Lees, Ph.D., Associate Professor of Environmental Health Engineering. Industrial hygiene, surface contamination, retrospective exposure assessment, man-made vitreous fibers, lead.
John R. Lever, Ph.D., Associate Professor of Radiation Health Sciences. Design, synthesis, and application of organic radiotracers; radiopharmacology; neuroreceptors; neurotoxins.
Susan Z. Lever, Ph.D., Associate Professor of Radiation Health Sciences. Synthetic organic and inorganic chemistry and radiochemistry for the preparation of radiotracers for use in biological experiments; lead toxicity.
Jonathan M. Links, Ph.D., Associate Professor of Radiation Health Sciences. Radiation-based biomarkers, emission computed tomography, dosimetry.
Clifford Mitchell, M.D., M.P.H., Assistant Professor of Occupational and Environmental Health. Evaluation of preventive interventions, using musculoskeletal injuries and indoor air as models.
Wayne Mitzner, Ph.D., Professor and Director of Physiology. In vivo lung imaging, respiratory structure and function, pulmonary circulation.
Jonathan Patz, M.D., M.P.H., Assistant Scientist in Occupational and Environmental Health. Health effects of global climate and ecological change, policy implications.
Donald F. Proctor, M.D., Professor Emeritus of Physiology. Nasal, upper-airway physiology.
Terence Risby, Ph.D., Professor of Toxicological Sciences. Characterization of chemical agents, combustion mechanisms, chemical basis of bioavailability, bioaccumulation and bioactivity, noninvasive biomarkers of tissue injury.
Robert J. Rubin, Ph.D., Professor Emeritus of Environmental Health Sciences. Environmental and occupational toxicology, risk assessment.
Brian S. Schwartz, M.D., Associate Professor and Director of Occupational and Environmental Health and Director of Occupational Medicine Residents. Occupational epidemiology, Lyme disease in outdoor workers, effects of chemicals on neurobehavioral and olfactory function, biomarkers of lead exposure and susceptibility.
Shelley S. Sehnert, Ph.D., Instructor of Environmental Health Sciences. Analytical chemistry, noninvasive biomarkers of toxicity.
Machiko Shirahata, M.D., Assistant Professor of Physiology. Electrophysiology, control of ventilation.
Ernst Wm. Spannhake, Ph.D., Professor of Physiology and Associate Chair of the Department of Environmental Health Sciences. Effects of environmental airborne pollutants on airway reactivity, inflammation, viral infectivity and allergic airways disease.
Paul T. Strickland, Ph.D., Professor of Occupational and Environmental Health. Occupational carcinogenesis, biomarkers of cancer, molecular epidemiology.
Thomas R. Sutter, Ph.D., Associate Professor of Toxicological Sciences. Mechanisms of receptor-mediated carcinogenesis, isolation and characterization of xenobiotic responsive genes.
Clarke Tankersley, Ph.D., Assistant Scientist of Physiology. Genetic control of respiration.
Michael A. Trush, Ph.D., Professor of Toxicological Sciences and Deputy Director of NIEHS Johns Hopkins Center in Urban Environmental Health. Biochemical and molecular toxicology, toxicology of leukocyte and bone marrow, oxidative mechanisms of toxicity, free-radical mechanisms of chemical activation.
Henry N. Wagner Jr., M.D., Professor and Director of Radiation Health Sciences and Director of the Center for the Advancement of Radiation Education and Research. Nuclear medicine, radiochemistry, instrumentation development.
Jia-Sheng Wang, M.D., Ph.D., Assistant Scientist in Toxicological Sciences. Biomarkers for chemical carcinogens and mechanisms for liver cancer.
Virginia Weaver, M.D., M.P.H., Assistant Professor of Occupational and Environmental Health. Biomarkers of exposure and early biological effect of occupational and environmental toxins, molecular epidemiology of lead and benzene.
Marsha Wills-Karp, Ph.D., Associate Professor of Physiology. Second-messenger and G-protein regulation of cell function.
M. Gordon Wolman, Ph.D., Professor of Geography, Department of Geography and Environmental Engineering, and Director of the Division of Environmental Health Engineering.
James D. Yager, Ph.D., Professor and Director of Toxicological Sciences and Director of the Research Training Programs in Environmental Health Sciences. Mechanisms of estrogen carcinogenesis, genetic and environmental susceptibility to breast cancer, tumor promotion and growth regulation in liver.
Joanne Zurlo, Ph.D., Associate Scientist of Toxicological Sciences and Associate Director of the Center for Alternatives to Animal Testing.

JOHNS HOPKINS UNIVERSITY

School of Hygiene and Public Health

Programs of Study The School of Hygiene and Public Health offers programs leading to the Doctor of Public Health (Dr.P.H.), Doctor of Science (Sc.D.), Doctor of Philosophy (Ph.D.), and Master of Science (Sc.M.) degrees. These programs emphasize the acquisition of research capabilities in specialized areas of science as they apply to health and disease. The Master of Public Health (M.P.H.), offered on a full- or part-time basis, is a broad-based degree program to prepare selected professionals for administrative and academic careers in public health. It is intended mainly for those who already possess professional qualifications in medicine, dentistry, veterinary medicine, engineering, nursing, or the sciences and those who have had considerable work experience in the health or human services field. Recent baccalaureate recipients with general backgrounds and those without extensive work experience in the health field should consider applying for admission to the Master of Health Science (M.H.S.) degree program, which provides specialized training in several departments. A number of departments offer postdoctoral training as well as approved residency programs in general preventive medicine or occupational medicine.

Research Facilities Well-equipped research laboratories are available for use by graduate students in the various departments of the School. There also are opportunities for field training in many local, state, national, and international health and medical care organizations.

The School has access to all the University library facilities, which provide more than 2.5 million volumes selected to support the studies of all departments and divisions of the University. The William H. Welch Medical Library coordinates access to biomedical literature and online databases for the Johns Hopkins Medical Institutions. The Abraham M. Lilienfeld Library is the primary information resource within the School of Public Health. Extensive computer facilities also are available to students.

Financial Aid Financial assistance includes scholarships, traineeships, student loans, Federal Work-Study funds, or a combination of these. Aid is offered on the basis of merit, financial need, and availability of funds and is independent of the admission decision. All scholarships are awarded upon the recommendation of the individual's departmental chair or the M.P.H. program director. Requests for consideration for scholarships should be submitted directly to the appropriate department or program.

The Office of Student Financial Services offers personal and confidential service to applicants and students. It certifies and awards student loans and Federal Work-Study funds. Applicants requesting loans or Federal Work-Study funds are required to submit a financial aid application.

Cost of Study Tuition will be $22,680 for the nine-month 1999–2000 academic year; tuition will be $28,350 for the eleven-month M.P.H. program. All new full-time students are assessed a one-time matriculation fee of $500. Books and instructional supplies average $1200 per year.

Living and Housing Costs Yearly living expenses for an individual are estimated at $15,000 for 1999–2000. The cost of living is comparable to that in most urban centers in the United States, and students may choose from a wide variety of affordable housing. Information on apartments and houses as well as University accommodations may be obtained from the Office of Housing, Reed Hall, 1620 McElderry Street.

Student Group The School of Hygiene and Public Health has more than 1,500 graduate students representing most states of the Union and more than seventy-five other countries. Doctoral and postdoctoral students constitute one half of the student body. More than half of the resident students are women; 27 percent of Americans are members of minority groups.

Student Outcomes Graduates are readily absorbed into the job market and find employment at all levels of the U.S. or international governments, academic institutions, hospitals, and other health-care facilities; profit, nonprofit, and nongovernmental organizations; managed care organizations; and consulting firms. Selected job titles include primary health-care project evaluator, public health specialist, health educator, epidemiologist, technical support manager, community education facilitator, public health officer, director of maternal and child health program, and public health associate.

Location Baltimore is a heterogeneous metropolis that is rich in American history and offers many cultural and recreational opportunities. The city is conveniently situated on the mid-Atlantic corridor, 45 minutes from Washington, D.C., and 4 hours' driving time from New York. Because Baltimore is close to both the Chesapeake Bay and mountainous areas, year-round recreational opportunities are available.

The University and The School Recognized as the first true university in America, Johns Hopkins University was incorporated in 1867 by Johns Hopkins, a Quaker merchant of Baltimore. The medical campus in East Baltimore is composed of the School of Hygiene and Public Health, the School of Medicine, the School of Nursing, the Welch Medical Library, and the Johns Hopkins Hospital. The area adjoining the medical institutions includes a residence hall. The Denton A. Cooley Center has an indoor jogging track; a sauna; racquetball, squash, and tennis courts; and an outdoor swimming pool. Excellent athletics and cultural facilities also are available at the nearby Homewood campus.

The School of Hygiene and Public Health is the oldest school of public health in the world. It was established in 1916 by persons of vision who planned a school of the biological, physical, social, and behavioral sciences. Its goal, now as then, is to preserve and improve the health of the public through the advancement of knowledge and the preparation of students for a variety of careers in public health. A 376-member full-time faculty represents major biomedical and social disciplines; ten academic departments offer graduate training.

Applying A baccalaureate degree is required. All applicants are required to submit scores of the GRE General Test, with the exception of M.P.H. applicants who have prior doctoral degrees; TOEFL scores must be submitted by international applicants whose native language is not English. Applications are processed on a rolling basis between October 1 and February 1. Early application is strongly encouraged. The nonrefundable application fee of $60 may be waived for U.S. students with financial need, upon receipt of a letter from the financial aid officer of the undergraduate institution currently attended.

Correspondence and Information

Director of Admissions
School of Hygiene and Public Health
Johns Hopkins University
615 North Wolfe Street
Baltimore, Maryland 21205

Telephone: 410-955-3543
Fax: 410-955-0464
E-mail: admiss@jhsph.edu
World Wide Web: http://www.jhsph.edu

Johns Hopkins University

DEPARTMENTAL HEADS AND ACTIVITIES

Biochemistry. Chair: Roger McMacken, Ph.D. The Ph.D. program emphasizes basic research in biochemistry, molecular and cell biology, and biophysics. Specific areas of concentration in research and training include enzyme mechanisms, DNA replication, recombination and repair, gene cloning and expression, gene regulation in plants, mechanism and regulation of eukaryotic mRNA synthesis, signal transduction mechanisms, heat-shock proteins and molecular chaperones, mechanism and regulation of proteolysis, assembly and function of nucleoprotein complexes, glycobiology, molecular genetics, organic and enzymatic synthesis of oligonucleotides, and mechanisms of cell transformation and of carcinogenesis.

Biostatistics. Chair: Scott L. Zeger, Ph.D. Programs involve course work in statistical methods and theory as well as supervised research. Faculty research includes theory of inference, regression, stochastic processes, sampling, survival analysis, and multivariate analysis; applications of statistics to biology, epidemiology, health care, demography, public health practice, clinical research, and genetics; and statistical computing. Applicants should have had preparation in the natural sciences and mathematics. Programs lead to the M.H.S. (one year), Sc.M. (two years), and Ph.D. degrees. Special training programs for doctoral students in the application of biostatistics to mental health, psychiatry, and aging are also available.

Environmental Health Sciences. Chair: John D. Groopman, Ph.D. The department seeks to understand and define the mechanisms by which chemical, physical, and biological agents, either naturally occurring or introduced into the environment, cause disability and disease and the means of preventing and controlling the effects of these agents. Training and research are offered in the scientific disciplines that contribute to an understanding of broad health-related issues pertaining to the environment. These include toxicological sciences, environmental health engineering, physiology, occupational and environmental health, and radiation health sciences. Professional education emphasizes the analysis and management of problems of air and water pollution; toxic substances, hazardous wastes, and radiation; and occupational safety and health. Master's and doctoral degrees are offered.

Epidemiology. Chair: Jonathan Samet, M.D., M.S. The broad educational and research program covers six main areas: clinical epidemiology; chronic disease epidemiology, including cardiovascular diseases and cancer; infectious disease epidemiology; human genetics/genetic epidemiology; occupational and environmental epidemiology; and clinical trials. Students generally specialize in a selected area, but every effort is made to provide a broad background in the methods and content of epidemiology. Working relationships with the Johns Hopkins School of Medicine and the Johns Hopkins Hospital add much to the students' experiences. Master's and doctoral degrees and postdoctoral fellowship training are offered.

Health Policy and Management. Chair: Donald M. Steinwachs, Ph.D. The Department of Health Policy and Management has a multidisciplinary faculty that teaches and conducts research related to the promotion and maintenance of health; the prevention of injury, disease, and disability; and the organization, financing, and delivery of health-care services. The department provides educational programs at the master's (full- and part-time), doctoral (full-time), and postdoctoral levels.

International Health. Chair: Robert E. Black, M.D., M.P.H. This is the most comprehensive training program in international health offered by any university. Focusing largely on the needs of the poorest countries, degree programs are offered with specialization in health systems management; social sciences and public health; disease prevention and control; vaccine development, evaluation, and policy; and human nutrition. Students are encouraged to do fieldwork in an overseas setting. Master's and doctoral degrees are offered.

Maternal and Child Health. Chair: Bernard Guyer, M.D., M.P.H. Maternal and child health encompasses all aspects of human growth and development during infancy, childhood, adolescence, and the reproductive period and includes individuals with special needs. The department identifies and addresses the multifaceted problems facing children and families, particularly those living in adverse environmental conditions. To address these concerns, the faculty members apply a broad array of disciplinary skills, including developmental psychology, behavioral sciences, epidemiology and quantitative science, health services research, social work, sociology, demography, policy analysis, political and administrative sciences, nutrition, and various clinical disciplines. The department's work encompasses such fields as nutrition, policy, health services research, social work, behavioral sciences, public health practice, and the influence of the contemporary role of women on childbearing, child rearing, and work. Master's, doctoral, and postdoctoral programs are offered.

Mental Hygiene. Chair: John C. S. Breifner, M.D., M.P.H. The department's research and training programs focus on measurement and understanding of the prevalence of mental disorders, alcohol and other substance abuse and dependence, and the disability that they produce in populations. This epidemiologic research serves as the basis for experimental community-based prevention and mental health services and service system research designed to promote mental health and prevent specific disorders. Research is done on the life-span developmental paths leading to mental health or disorder; sociological, biological, psychological, and behavioral aspects are part of the perspective. Training is provided for both scientists and administrators. Ph.D., Sc.D., Dr.P.H., Sc.M., and M.H.S. degrees are offered, as well as opportunities for M.P.H. specialization in mental hygiene and postdoctoral fellowships.

Molecular Microbiology and Immunology. Chair: Diane E. Griffin, M.D., Ph.D. This interdisciplinary department investigates fundamental mechanisms involved in the pathogenesis of infectious diseases of public health significance. The disciplines of virology, bacteriology, parasitology, immunology, biochemistry, molecular biology, vector biology, and ecology are used to gain a deeper understanding of host-pathogen interactions. The department's major focus is on laboratory research, but opportunities are also available for field investigations. Programs leading to master's and doctoral degrees are offered.

Population Dynamics. Chair: W. Henry Mosley, M.D., M.P.H. This interdisciplinary department trains scientists, policymakers, and administrators for careers concerned with population problems and programs. The faculty represents four major fields: demography and related social sciences, reproductive health, family planning, and reproductive biology. Students in demography examine social determinants and consequences of population trends and pursue the mathematical and statistical study of population dynamics. Reproductive health takes an epidemiological approach to the health aspects of reproduction and contraception. The emphasis in family planning is on policy determination, program planning, management, and evaluation. The reproductive biology group undertakes basic laboratory investigations of the male and female reproductive processes. Master's and doctoral degrees as well as postdoctoral study are offered. Joint-degree programs are available.

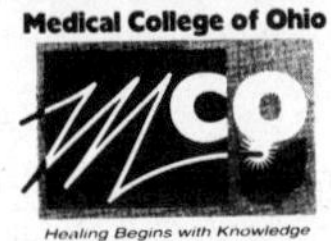

MEDICAL COLLEGE OF OHIO

School of Allied Health
Department of Public Health

Programs of Study

Located in the Howard L. Collier Nursing and Allied Health Building, the Department of Public Health in the School of Allied Health at the Medical College of Ohio (MCO) in Toledo offers Master of Science in Occupational Health (M.S.O.H.) degree and Certificate in Occupational Health (C.O.H.) programs. The department consists of 3 full-time faculty members and 15 part-time supporting faculty members.The M.S.O.H. and C.O.H. programs feature tracks in industrial hygiene and safety. The M.S.O.H. degree programs consist of a 40-semester-credit curriculum, with 26 semester credits of core course work that includes 4–8 semester credits of a thesis or project and 14 semester credits of track-specific course work. The M.S.O.H. degree can be completed in twelve to fifteen months with full-time study and twenty-four to thirty months with part-time study. The C.O.H. programs consist of a 14-semester-credit curriculum that is composed of courses from the M.S.O.H. curriculum.

The core courses for the M.S.O.H. and C.O.H. programs are environmental and occupational health law, environmental health, epidemiology, ergonomics, hazardous materials, occupational health, occupational safety, research methods, statistics, and thesis or project. Track-specific courses for industrial hygiene are air monitoring and analytical methods, hazard control, human systems and occupational diseases, physical agents, and toxicology. Track-specific courses for safety are accident causation and investigation, fire safety and emergency planning, general and mechanical hazards, safety programs and risk management, and system safety analysis.

Research Facilities

Approximately 1,200 square feet of laboratory space is allocated for M.S.O.H. instructional and research use in the Collier Building. Within this space, there is one dedicated student teaching lab where the students can use state-of-the-art field and analytical equipment for research projects or classroom assignments. Available equipment includes a gas chromatograph, a UV/VIS spectrophotometer, an inductively coupled plasma spectrometer, microscopes, sound and light meters, air-monitoring equipment, and ionizing and nonionizing radiation meters.

Financial Aid

Three graduate school tuition waivers are offered to qualified full-time applicants on a competitive basis.

Cost of Study

Projected tuition for full-time M.S.O.H. graduate students is $5822 per year for in-state students and $13,385 per year for out-of-state students. The mandatory student general fee is $194 per term.

Living and Housing Costs

Many apartments are available within walking distance of the MCO campus. Prices range from $350 to $700 per month. Housing information can be obtained from the Office of Student Services, Mulford Library Building, 3000 Arlington Avenue, Toledo, Ohio 43614.

Student Group

The M.S.O.H. student group consists of approximately 50 individuals from varied academic and professional backgrounds. Most students are part-time, nontraditional students who are employed in related fields. M.S.O.H. students are eligible for membership in the MCO Student Local Section of the American Industrial Hygiene Association. Since 1988, 61 students have graduated from the program.

Location

MCO is located in Toledo, Ohio, which is situated In northwestern Ohio, at the western-most point of Lake Erie. The city has a world-class art museum, ballet, theater, the Center of Science and Industry (COSI), professional baseball and hockey teams, and exceptional metropark system and recreational facilities.

The College

MCO was founded in 1964 and is currently composed of four schools: the Schools of Medicine, Nursing, and Allied Health and the Graduate School. MCO employs approximately 3,400 employees and operates a 270-bed teaching hospital. The student body is composed of approximately 560 medical students, 125 nursing students, and 260 other students who are engaged in graduate studies.

Applying

Application materials and credentials are accepted year-round. The application fee is $30. Materials should be submitted at least four weeks prior to the anticipated matriculation date. Applicants must have an earned baccalaureate degree from an accredited college or university, which includes 21 semester credits in communications, humanities, and social sciences and 63 semester credits in undergraduate- or graduate-level science, mathematics, and/or technical courses. A minimum GPA of 3.0 (based on a 4.0 scale) is required for regular admission; a minimum GPA of 2.5 is required for possible conditional admission. The GRE General Test or its equivalent is required for all applicants. International applicants must submit a TOEFL score of 550 or higher to be considered for admission.

Correspondence and Information

Michael Bisesi, Ph.D., RS, CIH
Department of Public Health
Medical College of Ohio
3015 Arlington Avenue
Toledo, Ohio 43614-5803
Telephone: 419-383-4235
Fax: 419-383-5880
E-mail: mbisesi@mco.edu
World Wide Web: http://www.mco.edu/allh/pubhealth

Mary E. Alderman, A.A.B.
Department of Public Health
Medical College of Ohio
3015 Arlington Avenue
Toledo, Ohio 43614-5803
Telephone: 419-383-5356
Fax: 419-383-5880
E-mail: malderman@mco.edu

Medical College of Ohio

THE FACULTY AND THEIR RESEARCH

Michael Bisesi, Professor and Chairman of the Department of Public Health; Ph.D., SUNY College of Environmental Science and Forestry, 1987; RS, CIH. Biological and chemical exposure assessment, environmental toxicology.

Laurie Abrams, Adjunct Assistant Professor of Public Health; Ph.D., Michigan, 1996. Occupational exposure assessment.

Farhang Akbar, Professor of Public Health; Ph.D., Newcastle (England), 1978; CSP, CIH. Exposure assessment, hazard control methods, relationship between harmful agents and their adverse health effect on exposed employees.

Douglas Clutts, Adjunct Instructor of Public Health; M.S., Central Missouri State, 1976. Federal regulations and statutes.

Michael Dennis, Assistant Professor of Radiology; Ph.D., Texas, 1979. Diagnostic imaging methods: magnetic resonance imaging (MRI), digital tomosynthesis, image processing, radiation doses from diagnostic procedures.

Robert Forney Jr., Associate Professor of Pathology and Public Health; Ph.D., Indiana, 1974. Methods in toxicology, drug testing.

Jeffrey Jablonski, Assistant Professor of Public Health; Ph.D., Toledo, 1990. Educational technology, research measurement.

Bradley Joseph, Adjunct Assistant Professor of Public Health; Ph.D., Michigan, 1986. Ergonomics, surveillance to identify high risk, high-priority jobs for intervention.

Charles Keil, Adjunct Assistant Professor of Public Health; Ph.D., Illinois, 1994. Pollution control modeling, exposure assessment.

Sadik Khuder, Assistant Professor of Medicine and Public Health; Ph.D., Alabama at Birmingham, 1992; CIH. Cancer epidemiology, occupational health.

Ashok Kumar, Adjunct Professor of Public Health; Ph.D., Waterloo, 1977; PE. Air pollution control and ventilation.

Kenneth Mauer, Adjunct Assistant Professor of Public Health; J.D., Toledo, 1985. Environmental and occupational health law.

Eric Schaub, Assistant Professor of Medicine and Public Health; M.D., Northeastern Ohio College of Medicine, 1985, M.P.H., John Hopkins, 1990. Epidemiology, meta-analysis.

Gary Silverman, Adjunct Associate Professor of Public Health; D.Env., UCLA, 1983. Water quality, international environmental education.

Tracy Willcoxon, Adjunct Instructor of Public Health; M.S., Air Force Tech, 1988. Industrial water treatment, indoor air quality.

Sandra Woolley, Associate Professor of Public Health; Ph.D., SUNY at Buffalo, 1989. Functional abilities of elderly individuals, ergonomics.

MICHIGAN STATE UNIVERSITY

College of Human Medicine Department of Epidemiology

Program of Study

The Department of Epidemiology, located in the Michigan State University College of Human Medicine, offers a program leading to a Master of Science degree in epidemiology. The degree requires 40 semester credits, including a thesis, and may be completed within eighteen months. Core courses give students a firm grounding in the principles and concepts of epidemiology and relevant biostatistics. Electives are available in the epidemiology of nutritional and cardiovascular disorders, reproductive and perinatal health, cancer, aging, communicable and zoonotic diseases, spatial epidemiology and medical geography, and epidemiologic modeling. The program in epidemiology was established in 1989 and achieved departmental status in 1997. The Master of Science degree program was initiated in 1994.

A partial listing of the faculty's research interests includes the etiology and preventability of reproductive and child health disorders, nutritional and cardiovascular diseases, cancer, and communicable diseases. Research programs in occupational health and the assessment of medical care effectiveness are actively pursued. Faculty members are developing methodological innovations in epidemiologic modeling, disease mapping, and biostatistical procedures. A focus on the public health relevance and impact of research findings is a central departmental emphasis.

Research Facilities

The College of Human Medicine is a community-based medical school utilizing a network of practice sites and hospitals across Michigan. Medical facilities of six Michigan communities are linked to the College as community campuses. These communities, serving more than 2 million people, provide large patient populations suitable for epidemiologic investigations. Proximity to the Michigan Department of Community Health creates numerous opportunities for collaboration. Community-based research is supported by both an electronic infrastructure, which links all six campus sites, and a network of family practice groups that collaborate in research. Two suites of offices for graduate assistants are furnished with networked computer terminals in cubicles with desks and storage facilities.

Financial Aid

A limited number of research assistantships are awarded on a competitive basis to successful applicants who have completed at least one semester of graduate work. Stipends for half-time appointments range from $1004 to $1464 per month. Health insurance coverage is provided. Graduate assistants receive a 6-credit tuition waiver during fall and spring semesters and a 4-credit waiver during summer and are exempt from out-of-state fees.

Cost of Study

Tuition for Michigan residents in 1998–99 is $216 per credit hour; tuition for nonresidents is $437 per credit hour. Students usually register for 6 or more credits per semester.

Living and Housing Costs

Excellent housing is available on campus. Unmarried men and women graduate students may rent accommodations in Owen Hall, where furnished rooms are available with maid service, bed linen, and telephones. The semester rate for single room and board in 1998–99 is $1873. The University operates more than 1,200 one- and two-bedroom furnished apartments on campus to meet the needs of married students. These rent for $381 to $454 per month. Privately owned off-campus rooms and apartments are also readily available. The cost of living in East Lansing is considered moderate by national standards.

Student Group

On-campus enrollment at Michigan State University in 1997–98 was 40,369, including nearly 8,000 graduate and professional students. The majority of graduate students are from out of state, and a substantial number are international students.

Student Outcomes

Program alumni are involved in a variety of activities, including employment in university research projects and pursuit of higher education in medicine.

Location

East Lansing is a residential city adjacent to the Michigan State University campus and close to Lansing, the state capital. Opportunities for cultural and social development include nationally recognized regional theater ensembles. The University's Wharton Center is one of the nation's top-grossing theaters. The surrounding area has excellent recreational facilities, including sites for camping, canoeing, and skiing. The University maintains a year-round ice arena, two golf courses, and numerous tennis courts, swimming pools, and playing fields.

The University

Michigan State University, prototype of the land-grant college, was founded in 1855. It has grown to be one of America's largest universities, with many educational innovations to its credit. Through its fourteen colleges and more than 100 departments, it offers more than 200 different programs leading to undergraduate and graduate degrees.

Applying

Applicants are required to have a bachelor's degree from a recognized college or university, along with a sufficiently strong academic record to give evidence of the capacity for graduate study. One year of college-level biology and of mathematics or statistics are ordinarily required. Satisfactory GRE, MCAT, or ECFMG scores are required of applicants lacking a doctoral degree from a university in the U.S. or Canada. The Test of English as a Foreign Language (TOEFL) is required of students for whom English is not the first language.

Additional information and application forms may be obtained by writing to the Graduate Secretary. The application deadline is May 1 of each year for fall admission. Three letters of recommendation, including one from a source familiar with the applicant's recent academic work, are required. Previous work experience in a health field is recommended. Applications are reviewed by the Admissions Committee as applicants' files are completed, and students are notified as decisions are made.

Correspondence and Information

Dr. Nigel Paneth
Chair
Department of Epidemiology
College of Human Medicine
A-206 E. Fee Hall
Michigan State University
East Lansing, Michigan 48824-1316
Telephone: 517-353-8623
Fax: 517-432-1130
E-mail: paneth@pilot.msu.edu

Lora Kemler McAdams
Graduate Secretary
Department of Epidemiology
College of Human Medicine
A-214 E. Fee Hall
Michigan State University
East Lansing, Michigan 48824-1316
Telephone: 517-432-3921
Fax: 517-432-1130
E-mail: kemler@pilot.msu.edu

Michigan State University

THE FACULTY AND THEIR RESEARCH

Program Faculty

Michael Collins, M.D., Assistant Professor of Epidemiology. Communicable disease modeling, reproductive epidemiology.
Wenjiang Fu, Ph.D., Assistant Professor of Epidemiology. Shrinkage models, smoothing techniques, longitudinal models.
Joseph Gardiner, Ph.D., Professor of Statistics and Director, Division of Biostatistics. Survival analysis, censoring problems, and sequential trials; cost-effective analyses; interval-censored data.
Claudia Holzman, D.V.M., M.P.H., Ph.D., Assistant Professor of Epidemiology. Reproductive epidemiology, particularly birth defects; prematurity prevention; zoonotic diseases.
Alka Indurkhya, Ph.D., Assistant Professor of Epidemiology. Residual analysis in mixture models, assessing power of designs, design and evaluation of primary and secondary prevention interventions in mental health.
Nigel Paneth, M.D., M.P.H., Professor of Pediatrics and Epidemiology and Chair, Department of Epidemiology. Reproductive, perinatal, and child health epidemiology; outcomes research; history of epidemiology and public health.
Dorothy Pathak, Ph.D., Associate Professor of Family Practice and Epidemiology. Breast cancer epidemiology, statistical methods in epidemiology research.
Pramod Pathak, Ph.D., Professor of Statistics and Epidemiology. Complex sample surveys, resampling methods, mathematical statistics.
Michael Rip, M.P.H., Ph.D., Assistant Professor of Geography and Epidemiology. Disease mapping techniques, the geographic distribution of health services, and the application of statistical methods for areal analysis to health problems; child health issues.
Aryeh Stein, M.P.H., Ph.D., Assistant Professor of Epidemiology and Medicine. Reliability and consistency of dietary assessment methods, determinants of cardiovascular risk factors in children, educational and behavioral strategies for reducing cardiovascular disease risk.

Adjunct Faculty Appointed in Other Departments

Paul Bartlett, D.V.M., Ph.D., Professor of Veterinary Epidemiology and Preventive Medicine and Epidemiology. Veterinary public health, zoonoses, dairy cattle epidemiology, veterinary food animal epidemiology, antibiotic resistance, food hygiene, and foodborne disease control.
Cathy Bradley, Ph.D., Assistant Professor of Medicine and Epidemiology. Economics and cost-effectiveness analysis.
Ruth Ann Dunn, M.D., Assistant Professor of Pediatrics and Human Development and Epidemiology. Child health, immunization initiatives.
Charles Given, Ph.D., Professor of Family Practice. Health problems of the elderly, cancer management in the community.
Michael Harrison, Ph.D., Professor of Physics and Epidemiology. Mathematical modeling of epidemics, especially HIV/AIDS.
Andrew Hogan, Ph.D., Associate Professor of Medicine and Epidemiology. Health economics.
John Kaneene, D.V.M., Ph.D., Professor of Large Animal Clinical Science and Epidemiology and Director, Population Medicine Center. Dairy herd health monitoring, statistical methods in epidemiologic research, food-borne health hazards.
John M. Lorenz, M.D., Associate Professor of Pediatrics and Human Development and Epidemiology. Neonatal intensive care decision making and outcomes.
Kenneth Rosenman, M.D., Professor of Medicine and Epidemiology. Occupational medicine.
Blake Smith, Ph.D., Professor of Family Practice. Methods for estimating practice size, mathematical modeling in health.
G. Marie Swanson, Ph.D., M.P.H., Professor of Family Practice and Epidemiology; Director, MSU Cancer Center; and Co-Principal Investigator, Greater Detroit SEER Program. Cancer epidemiology, occupational hazards to health.
Howard Teitelbaum, D.O., Ph.D., M.P.H., Professor of Osteopathic Medicine. Sexually transmitted diseases, clinical epidemiology.
Linda Beth Tiedje, Ph.D., Associate Professor of Human Medicine and Epidemiology; RN. Women's health, health behavior in pregnancy, stress and coping in employed women.

Adjunct Faculty at Other Institutions

William Hall, M.D., M.P.H., Associate Clinical Professor of Epidemiology and Chief, Disease Control Division, Michigan Department of Community Health. Communicable disease epidemiology.
David Johnson, M.D., M.P.H., Assistant Clinical Professor of Epidemiology and Acting Chief Medical Officer, Michigan Department of Community Health. Outbreak investigation, child health, infectious disease epidemiology.
Harry McGee, M.P.H., Assistant Adjunct Professor of Epidemiology and Chief, Chronic Disease Epidemiology Section, Michigan Department of Community Health. Survey research, communicable diseases, international health.
Jonathan Ramlow, Ph.D., M.P.H., Assistant Adjunct Professor of Epidemiology and Project Leader, Epidemiology/Health and Environmental Sciences, The Dow Chemical Company. Occupational and industrial epidemiology.
Mathew Reeves, B.V.Sc., Ph.D., Assistant Adjunct Professor of Epidemiology and Chief, Division of Epidemiological Services, Michigan Department of Community Health. Evidence-based medicine, chronic disease epidemiology.
Dean Sienko, M.D., Associate Clinical Professor of Epidemiology and Medical Director, Ingham County Health Department. Preventive medicine in public health.
Kenneth Wilcox, M.D., Dr.P.H., Clinical Professor of Medicine and Epidemiology; State Epidemiologist; and Chief, Division of Epidemiology, Michigan Department of Community Health. Chronic disease epidemiology, epidemiology in health policy.

NEW YORK MEDICAL COLLEGE

Graduate School of Health Sciences

Programs of Study

The Graduate School of Health Sciences offers the M.P.H. degree in behavioral sciences and health promotion, biostatistics, developmental disabilities, emergency medical services, environmental and occupational health sciences, epidemiology, gerontology, health informatics, health services management and policy, international health, maternal and child health, and public health. Candidates for the M.P.H. degree must complete a minimum of 45 credits.

The M.S. degree is offered in biostatistics, clinical research administration, developmental disabilities, emergency medical services, environmental and occupational health sciences, epidemiology, health services management and policy, international health, and physical therapy. Candidates for the M.S. degree must complete a minimum of 36 credits, except in physical therapy, which requires 80 credits.

An individual may apply for a degree program as a matriculated student or take courses on a nonmatriculated basis. Similarly, a student enrolled in a graduate degree program at another institution may enroll as a nonmatriculated student.

Research Facilities

Research facilities include the Alumni Computer Learning Laboratory and the Medical Sciences Library, which maintains a collection of more than 169,000 volumes and 2,100 journal titles. Online CD-ROM and network databases include MEDLINE, PsychLIT, HealthPLAN, Reference Update, PDR, Entrez, and Grateful Med. The graduate programs, as well as research in environmental health and health promotion, are enhanced by an affiliation between the Graduate School and the American Health Foundation, which has research facilities located on the College campus. The program in developmental disabilities draws upon the professional resources of the Westchester Institute for Human Development.

In addition, the Graduate School of Health Sciences benefits from the presence of the basic science laboratories that serve the medical school and the Graduate School of Basic Medical Sciences and from eight research centers and institutes that focus on such issues as AIDS, Lyme disease, and adolescent health.

Financial Aid

Financial aid is available for full-time students. Students are encouraged to talk to the financial aid staff, who are available to assist them in planning financial aid packages.

Cost of Study

For 1998–99, tuition is $415 per credit hour; the matriculation fee is $100 and the computer lab fee, when applicable, is $100. Tuition for the physical therapy program is $17,000 per year.

Living and Housing Costs

Students must be full-time matriculants to be eligible for housing on the Valhalla campus. Matriculating students, full-time or part-time, are eligible for housing at College-owned housing in Manhattan (depending on availability). Assistance in obtaining off-campus housing is available from the Housing Office. Housing costs are approximately $6000 per year.

Student Group

Approximately 600 students are enrolled in the Graduate School of Health Sciences. The majority of these students attend part-time and many work full-time in the health care system as administrators, physicians, nurses, corporate benefits administrators, nutritionists, technologists, engineers, and researchers.

Graduates work in a variety of settings, including government, private practice, nursing homes, home health agencies, public health agencies, corporations, environmental and pharmaceutical laboratories, and community service organizations.

Location

New York Medical College is located on a 565-acre campus shared with Westchester County Medical Center in Valhalla, New York. Its suburban site in the center of Westchester County is approximately 20 miles north of New York City. There are ample educational, recreational, and cultural opportunities available locally and in the New York metropolitan area. Courses are also offered at Good Samaritan Hospital in Suffern, New York.

The University and The School

Founded in 1860, New York Medical College has a strong history of involvement in medical and health education and in training, research, and professional and community service. It is chartered by the Regents of the state of New York and is a member of the Middle States Association of Colleges and Secondary Schools.

The scope of the College's earliest mission—to prepare physicians to be outstanding clinicians—has been broadened to include the educational preparation of scientists and health-care professionals. Today it is chartered as a health sciences university, and its mission is carried out through three schools: the Medical School; the Graduate School of Basic Medical Sciences, originated in 1963; and the Graduate School of Health Sciences, which began in 1981. The Graduate School of Health Sciences seeks to respond to the growing need for well-educated health professionals on the local, national, and international levels.

Applying

Applicants must hold a baccalaureate degree from an accredited college or university. Prerequisite requirements will vary by program. Two to three years of relevant work experience is desirable, although not required.

The admission decision is based on the information provided in the applicant's completed application. This includes past academic performance (undergraduate and graduate, if any), a personal statement, recommendations, work experience, community involvement, and school extracurricular activities. The application fee is $35.

International applicants should be prepared to furnish TOEFL scores, proof of health insurance, statement of planned residence, affidavit of support, and accompanying U.S. bank statements to cover all school and living expenses. The application fee for international students is $60.

Students are admitted for the fall, spring, and summer terms, except for the physical therapy program, which admits new students in April for the academic year that begins in May. Review of new applications begins in February for the fall term and in late September for the spring term.

Correspondence and Information

Director of Admissions and Recruitment
Graduate School of Health Sciences
Learning Center
New York Medical College
Valhalla, New York 10595
Telephone: 914-594-4510
Fax: 914-594-4292
E-mail: gshs_admissions@nymc.edu

New York Medical College

PROGRAM AND TRACK DIRECTORS

Ansley Bacon, Ph.D., Developmental Disabilities Program Director.
Denton Brosius, Ph.D., Environmental and Occupational Health Sciences and Health Informatics Track Director.
C. Gene Cayten, M.D., M.P.H., Emergency Medical Services Track Director.
Peter Cervoni, Ph.D., Clinical Research Administration Track Director.
Annette Choolfaian, M.P.A., Health Services, Management and Policy Program Director; RN.
Rhea L. Dornbush, Ph.D., Behavioral Sciences and Health Promotion Track Director.
Jeffrey Escher, M.D., Gerontology Track Director.
Cathey E. Falvo, M.D., M.P.H., International and Public Health Program Director.
Raymond Fink, Ph.D., Health Services Research Director.
James Gordon, Ed.D., Physical Therapy Program Director; PT.
Paul F. Visintainer, Ph.D., Health Quantitative Sciences (including Biostatistics and Epidemiology) Program Director.

THE OHIO STATE UNIVERSITY

School of Public Health

Programs of Study

The Ohio State University (OSU) School of Public Health is the first and only such school in the state of Ohio. The School is situated within one of the largest comprehensive medical centers in the United States, on a university campus that includes the disciplines relevant to public health. Consequently, the School is a center for the integration of public health and medicine. The degrees offered by the School are the Master of Public Health (M.P.H.), the Master of Health Administration (M.H.A.), the Master of Science (M.S.), and the Doctor of Philosophy (Ph.D.).

Both the M.P.H. and the M.H.A. are practitioner-oriented degrees that have as their emphasis the improvement of policy and practice. Competencies related to these professional degrees focus on application and on policy leadership. The M.S. and the Ph.D. are research-oriented degrees that have as their emphasis the advancement of knowledge. Competencies related to these academic degrees focus on research methodologies and on scholarly leadership.

Research Facilities

The School maintains a Biometrics Laboratory to serve students and faculty members of the College of Medicine, other departments in the University, and many health agencies. Students have the opportunity to serve as assistants in this laboratory. Extensive computer facilities and data processing equipment are available. Students may work in research programs initiated in the School, the clinical departments of the College of Medicine, the Ohio Department of Health, the Columbus Health Department, and other health agencies. The University libraries, with holdings of more than 4 million print volumes and 2.7 million microforms, are available to all students.

Financial Aid

The School offers graduate associate appointments, which are awarded on the basis of scholastic merit and provide a monthly stipend and payment of tuition for three quarters of full-time enrollment. Faculty members with research funding often offer student stipends based upon the individual researcher's needs and interests. The Graduate School at OSU administers internal University fellowships as well as graduate fellowships and traineeships funded through national and local agencies. Federal Work-Study, Federal Perkins Loans, Federal Stafford Student Loans, and University loans are other sources of support for graduate study.

Cost of Study

For the 1997–98 year, tuition for Ohio residents enrolled full-time was $1738 per quarter; for nonresidents, the fee was $4500 per quarter. Health insurance for a student was $191 per quarter. It is estimated that textbooks cost approximately $180 per quarter.

Living and Housing Costs

A range of housing options is available for single students and for families. The surrounding community also has many housing opportunities at reasonable costs.

Student Group

The students currently enrolled in graduate programs come from many parts of the United States and from several other countries. They represent a variety of undergraduate disciplines and experiences.

Student Outcomes

The Office for Practice Placements and Employment Services provides assistance to students who wish to pursue field experience, with preceptors representing local health agencies, hospitals, insurance companies, and other relevant organizations. This office also assists students in job placement and career development. Graduates of the School's programs have competed successfully for a variety of positions in health organizations at local, state, national, and international levels in both the public and private sectors.

Location

Columbus is among the twenty largest cities in the United States. It ranks as the third-largest research and information center in the world, behind only Moscow and Washington, D.C. Columbus is the capital of Ohio, and, thus, major health and health-related agencies are located within the city. An excellent public school system, efficient public transportation, and a reasonable cost of living make Columbus an attractive place to live and study. Columbus supports major music, dance, and theater groups. The Columbus Museum of Art and the Wexner Center for Contemporary Arts make Columbus a major focus for the visual and performing arts in the Midwest.

The University

The Ohio State University is a land-grant institution with an international reputation for excellence. It is the major comprehensive university in the state of Ohio. As the major graduate institution of the state, the Ohio State University plays an important role in the generation of new knowledge through research and other creative work and in the preparation of mature scholars.

Applying

Applicants must hold a baccalaureate, master's, or professional degree from an accredited college or university. All applicants for the M.P.H., M.S., or Ph.D. programs must take the General Test of the Graduate Record Examinations (GRE), and final consideration for admission requires submission of the examination scores. Applicants to the M.H.A. program may take the Graduate Management Admission Test (GMAT) or the GRE. An interview on campus with the M.H.A. faculty is required. No specific major is required. For the M.H.A., one 5-credit-hour course in financial accounting is required as a prerequisite to course work (the course may be taken after applying to the program). The M.H.A. faculty also recommends that prospective students take an additional course in managerial accounting and courses in the areas of statistics and economics.

Entry into the School's programs is normally in the autumn quarter. The application deadline is March 1. Applications received after March 1 will be considered only if space permits. All M.H.A. applicants must complete and return application materials by March 15. Applications received after March 15 will be considered if space permits.

Correspondence and Information

Interested applicants to the M.P.H., M.S., and Ph.D. programs should contact:

Office of Graduate Studies
M-120 Starling Loving
320 West 10th Avenue
The Ohio State University
Columbus, Ohio 43210-1240

Telephone: 614-293-3907
Fax: 614-293-3937
E-mail: dawson.6@osu.edu

Interested applicants for the M.H.A. program should contact:

Graduate Program in Health Services Management and Policy
1583 Perry Street, Room 246
The Ohio State University
Columbus, Ohio 43210-1234

Telephone: 614-292-8193
E-mail: hsmp@osu.edu

The Ohio State University

THE FACULTY AND THEIR RESEARCH

Antoinette P. Eaton, Interim Dean; M.D. Pediatrics, maternal and child health.

Franklin R. Banks, Ph.D. Behavioral sciences and health.
Deborah Burr, Ph.D. Statistical computing, survival analysis.
Robert Caswell, Ph.D. Forecasting methods, cost, performance, regulation.
Moon S. Chen Jr., M.P.H., Ph.D. Health education, promotion, minority health issues.
William Cleverley, Ph.D. Health-care financial management.
Randall E. Harris, M.D., Ph.D. Cancer epidemiology, cancer control, chronic disease risk factors.
Catherine Heaney, M.P.H., Ph.D. Disease prevention and health promotion, worksite stress management.
Benita Jackson, M.D., M.P.H. Infectious disease epidemiology, community disease control, vaccine preventable diseases.
Martin D. Keller, M.D., M.P.H., Ph.D. Epidemiology, health services, international health.
Richard R. Lanese, Ph.D. Epidemiology, behavioral science, research methodology.
Stephen Loebs, M.H.A., Ph.D. Health-care costs and cost containment strategies in Ohio.
Randi Love, Ph.D. Health education and promotion, substance abuse and prevention, HIV disease and related issues.
Melvin L. Moeschberger, Ph.D. Applied statistics, survival analysis, competing risks.
Mark A. Morse, Ph.D. Cancer chemoprevention, biochemical toxicology.
Gilbert Nestel, M.S. Hazards in the workplace, effect of benefits/retirement.
Judith A. Schwartzbaum, Ph.D. Cancer epidemiology, biostatistics.
Sharon Schweikhart, M.B.A., Ph.D.. Locations decisions, quality management, performance.
Gary D. Stoner, Ph.D. Molecular carcinogenesis, cancer chemoprevention.
Sandra Tanenbaum, Ph.D. Health policy and aging, politics, long-term care.
Christopher Weghorst, Ph.D. Molecular biology of cancer.
John R. Wilkins III, Dr.P.H. Environmental and cancer epidemiology, health and hazard survey.

PURDUE UNIVERSITY

School of Health Sciences

Programs of Study

The School of Health Sciences offers programs leading to the M.S. or Ph.D. degree in health physics, industrial hygiene, medical physics, toxicology, and environmental health. These training programs prepare graduates for research, clinical, or professional careers in academic institutions, national laboratories, medical facilities, federal agencies, or private industry. Two types of master's degrees are available. For the nonthesis option, the student takes a minimum of 33 semester hours of course work, including 18 hours in the student's primary area of interest, with the remaining courses chosen from appropriate supporting areas. A special project or critical essay is required in lieu of the thesis. The thesis master's degree program consists of a minimum of 24 semester hours of courses and a research-based thesis. The doctoral program normally requires approximately 48 semester hours of credit in the students's primary and related areas of interest, together with the preparation of an acceptable scholarly thesis.

Research Facilities

The School is equipped with state-of-the-art instruments for training and research in the areas specified. The equipment and facilities available include intrinsic Ge detectors with PC-based multichannel analysis capabilities, liquid scintillation counters, gamma counters, thermoluminescent dosimeter readers, gamma cameras, high-level gamma irradiators, portable radiation monitoring equipment, calibrated radon standards, nonionizing radiation and electromagnetic field monitoring equipment, gas chromatograph units, high-pressure liquid chromatographs, high-speed and ultracentrifuges, UV-visible spectrophotometers, a particle size spectrometer, a monodisperse aerosol generator, and instruments to measure pulmonary function. Also available on campus are a nuclear reactor, a linear accelerator, an accelerator mass spectrometer, electron microscopes, supercomputing facilities, and accredited animal facilities. Graduate students have access to all the University's library facilities, including computer-based online search capabilities. The diagnostic X-ray and radiation oncology facilities of the Indiana University School of Medicine, Indianapolis, are utilized in the medical physics program.

Financial Aid

Most graduate students receive support and tuition remission from various teaching assistantships, faculty research grants, or University and federal fellowships. Such support is available on a competitive basis and is based on academic record. Stipends for teaching assistants were $13,200 per year for 1997–98. Fellowships vary depending on the sponsor providing the support.

Cost of Study

For 1998–99, full-time tuition and fees total $5860 per semester for out-of-state students and $1750 per semester for in-state students. Tuition and fees are waived for students who hold assistantships except for a mandatory fee of $308 per semester.

Living and Housing Costs

Living expenses vary according to the individual's housing needs. Single rooms run approximately $300 per month (excluding board). Rental apartments range from about $350 to $700 per month. Housing information can be obtained from Off-campus Housing Services, Office of the Dean of Students, Schleman Hall, Room 207, Purdue University, West Lafayette, Indiana 47907.

Student Group

In fall 1997, there were 22 graduate students (5 women and 17 men) in the health sciences graduate program. Eight of these were international students. The Graduate School at Purdue enrolls some 6,200 graduate students.

Student Outcomes

All individuals completing their graduate programs during the past three years were successful in finding positions in their area of professional interest. One third of these graduates were at the Ph.D. level and two thirds were at the M.S. level. The distribution of job types was as follows: 33 percent went to medical or clinical facilities, 33 percent entered private industry, 20 percent took positions in federal or military facilities, and 13 percent went to academic institutions.

Location

Purdue University is located in West Lafayette, Indiana, approximately 65 miles northwest of Indianapolis and 125 miles southeast of Chicago. The population of the greater Lafayette–West Lafayette area is about 140,000. The community is served by two airlines as well as by major bus lines and by Amtrak rail service. There are extensive offerings of cultural and athletic events at the University and in the community.

The University

Purdue University is a state-supported institution and is Indiana's land-grant university. With a student body of some 36,000 students on the West Lafayette campus, Purdue is a major research university. Research funding for 1996–97 totaled more than $135 million.

Applying

Interested individuals may obtain application forms from the address listed below. The application form must be submitted together with all previous undergraduate and graduate transcripts, GRE General Test scores, and three letters of recommendation. The application fee is $30. International students whose native language is not English must submit a TOEFL score of 550 or higher to be considered for admission. Application materials should be submitted by February 1 to ensure consideration for the fall semester.

Correspondence and Information

Paul L. Ziemer, Ph.D.
Head, School of Health Sciences, CIVL 1338
Purdue University
West Lafayette, Indiana 47907

Telephone: 765-494-1419
Fax: 765-496-1377
E-mail: ziemer@purdue.edu

Purdue University

THE FACULTY

D. R. Black, Professor of Health Promotion; Ph.D., Stanford, 1978.
C. Bloch, Adjunct Assistant Professor of Medical Physics; Ph.D., Michigan State, 1987.
G. S. Born, Professor of Health Sciences; Ph.D., Purdue, 1966.
G. P. Carlson, Professor of Toxicology and Associate Head; Ph.D., Chicago, 1969.
H. Cember, Adjunct Professor of Health Physics; Ph.D., Pittsburgh, 1960.
J. E. Christian, Professor Emeritus and Hovde Distinguished Service Professor Emeritus; Ph.D., Purdue, 1944.
M. A. Green, Professor of Medicinal Chemistry; Ph.D., Indiana, 1982.
G. D. Hutchens, Adjunct Associate Professor of Medical Physics; Ph.D., Wisconsin, 1984.
S. G. Johnson, Adjunct Assistant Professor of Health Sciences; Ph.D., Iowa State, 1990.
R. A. Kruger, Adjunct Professor of Medical Physics; Ph.D., Wisconsin, 1978.
R. R. Landolt, Professor of Health Physics; Ph.D., Purdue, 1968.
R. E. Langford, Adjunct Professor of Industrial Hygiene; Ph.D., Georgia, 1973.
Y. Liang, Assistant Professor of Medical Physics; Ph.D., SUNY at Stony Brook, 1991.
J. D. McGlothlin, Associate Professor of Occupational Safety and Health; Ph.D., Michigan, 1988.
L. Papiez, Adjunct Associate Professor of Medical Physics; Ph.D., Silesian, 1976.
G. F. Perry, Adjunct Professor of Occupational Medicine; M.D., Indiana, 1970.
T. O. Peyton, Adjunct Associate Professor of Environmental Health; Ph.D., Purdue, 1974.
F. S. Rosenthal, Associate Professor of Occupational and Environmental Health Sciences; Ph.D., Columbia, 1971.
G. A. Sandison, Adjunct Professor of Medical Physics; Ph.D., Manitoba, 1987.
J. F. Schweitzer, Assistant Professor of Health Physics; Ph.D., Purdue, 1985.
S. M. Shaw, Professor of Nuclear Pharmacy; Ph.D., Purdue, 1962.
R. M. Witt, Adjunct Assistant Professor of Medicinal Chemistry; Ph.D., Wisconsin–Madison, 1975.
R. E. Zelac, Adjunct Professor of Health Physics; Ph.D., Florida, 1970.
P. L. Ziemer, Professor of Health Physics and Head; Ph.D., Purdue, 1962.
J. D. Zimbrick, Professor of Radiation Biophysics; Ph.D., Kansas, 1967.
N. J. Zimmerman, Associate Professor of Occupational Safety and Health; Ph.D., North Carolina, 1980.

CURRENT RESEARCH PROJECTS

Radiation Dosimetry
Determination of radiation doses to accidentally exposed individuals by means of electron spin resonance measurements.

Decommissioning and Nuclear Power Health Physics
Characterization of aerosols generated during the demolition of concrete reactor shields.

Indoor Air Quality
Evaluation of an acceptable indoor carbon dioxide concentration with respect to indoor air quality.
Odor formulation from residential fumigation with methyl bromide: factors and identification.

Inhalation Toxicology
Aerosol probes of lung injury; aerosol disposition in lung disease.
Particle size distributions in exhaled breath.
Distribution of inhaled particles to pulmonary airways and alveoli.

Biochemical Toxicology
Metabolism and toxicity of xenobiotics in lung.
Pulmonary metabolism of benzene.
Biotransformation of styrene and its toxicity in lung and liver.

SPECT and PET Imaging
Generator-based radiopharmaceuticals for positron emission tomography.
Receptor-targeted metal radiopharmaceuticals.

Radiopharmaceuticals
Dosage for formulations and dissolution characteristics.
Factors resulting in undesired biodistribution and/or pharmacokinetics.

Radiation Oncology
New dose algorithm for electron radiotherapy.
A compound Poisson process model for multiple scattering of electrons.
Proton therapy considerations for the I.U. cyclotron.

Medical Imaging
Isotropic imaging by spiral computed tomography.
Thermoacoustic spectroscopy in medical imaging.

Ergonomics
Evaluation of workplace exposure using real-time assessment techniques

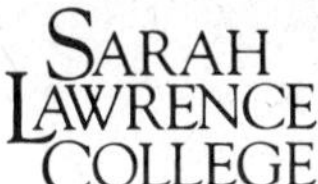

SARAH LAWRENCE COLLEGE

Genetic Counseling and Health Advocacy Graduate Programs

Programs of Study

The Human Genetics Program and the Health Advocacy Program, both leading to a master's degree, train health professionals devoted to the concerns of patients facing medical crises. The required interdisciplinary curriculum in each program consists of 40 academic course credits and 600 hours of clinical practicum. The proximity of Sarah Lawrence College to the Metropolitan New York area offers a rich network of settings—hospitals, clinics, and community agencies—in which on-site supervised training enables students to integrate theoretical knowledge with actual patient care. The faculty includes experts drawn from the well-known medical centers in the New York area as well as from Sarah Lawrence College. Small classes and close faculty-student interaction offer a productive and stimulating environment for professional growth.

In 1969, Sarah Lawrence College established the first master's-level program in genetic counseling, which has set the standard for the field; it is called the Human Genetics Program. The program fulfills all the requirements for certification of genetic counselors; such certification is available through the American Board of Medical Genetics. The genetic counselor, as a member of a medical genetics team, provides individuals and families with genetic information, emotional support, and help with crucial decisions at times of emotional distress. The required curriculum can be completed on a full-time basis in two years or part-time in three years. The program leads to the Master of Science or Master of Professional Studies degree. From courses, seminars, and fieldwork experiences, the students acquire competence in both medical genetics and genetic counseling. There is a strong emphasis on psychological counseling. The program offers a guest lecture series exposing students to current information and breakthroughs in this rapidly developing field.

In 1980, Sarah Lawrence College established the first and only master's-level program in health advocacy to meet the education requirements for this challenging new profession—the Health Advocacy Program. The program's focus is on preparation of students for professional roles as ombudsmen in hospitals, industry, categorical disease foundations, nursing homes, voluntary health organizations, and other institutions where there is concern for the individual and his or her interaction with the health-care provider in the broader sense. Advocacy often involves working directly with the patient and family but also requires the ability to negotiate with other health-care providers, administrators of health-care facilities, and even politicians. The theory and practice of health advocacy is based on concepts from medical care, law, economics, social work, and health administration. The required curriculum can be completed on a full-time basis in sixteen months (three semesters and one summer) or part-time in two to three years. The program leads to the Master of Arts or Master of Professional Studies degree. Course work is conducted in seminars and tutorials with an emphasis on student participation, library research, and fieldwork.

Research Facilities

Sarah Lawrence College has established affiliations with more than thirty medical and research centers in the Metropolitan New York area. Placement with leading researchers at area institutions is readily available for students with research interests. A well-equipped human genetics lab serves the Human Genetics Program. The College maintains a library of books, periodicals, and reference materials of interest to students in the Human Genetics and Health Advocacy programs. In addition, students in both programs have access to the rich resources of libraries, hospitals, and community agencies throughout Metropolitan New York.

Financial Aid

Most students in these programs receive partial or full financial aid in the form of scholarships and/or loans. Students are accepted regardless of ability to pay. Financial aid is available based on need as determined by the Financial Aid PROFILE and FAFSA.

Cost of Study

Tuition for the Human Genetics Program in 1998–99 is $591 per academic credit. Tuition for the Health Advocacy Program is $576 per academic credit and $200 per field placement.

Living and Housing Costs

Although housing is not available on campus, off-campus single rooms are available for $300 to $500 per month; sharing an apartment ranges from $500 to $700 per month. The minimum cost for an apartment in the area is $500 per month. Housing information is available from the Office of Graduate Studies. Meals at reasonable rates are available at the College's dining room.

Student Group

Of the 250 graduate students at Sarah Lawrence College, 50 are in the Human Genetics Program and 30 are in the Health Advocacy Program. Other graduate programs are Art of Teaching, Child Development, Dance, Women's History, Writing, and Theatre.

Location

The College is located in Bronxville, New York, 15 miles from midtown Manhattan. This location offers students the comforts of suburban living within a 30-minute commute of the city. Regular vans to New York City, notices of special events, and general information about New York City are all provided by the Office of Student Affairs. The commuter train station is a short walk from campus.

The College

Founded in 1926, Sarah Lawrence College is a small, liberal arts college for men and women. It is a lively community of students, scholars, and artists and is nationally renowned for its unique academic structure, which combines small classes with individual student-faculty conferences.

Applying

The Human Genetics Program seeks qualified applicants who can demonstrate a well-developed interest in medical genetic services. Prerequisites for admission are general biology, developmental biology (vertebrate embryology), genetics (Mendelian and molecular), basic chemistry, and probability and statistics. Other recommended courses include organic chemistry, psychology of personality, and Spanish. A personal interview is required. GRE scores are not required. The deadline for applications and all supporting documents is February 1.

The Health Advocacy Program seeks qualified applicants who can demonstrate a commitment to improving people's access to and use of health care. Prerequisites for admission are completion of a bachelor's degree with a strong undergraduate record, which includes courses in introductory biology and microeconomics (may be completed as corequisite) and intermediate-level work in the social sciences. Facility in a second language, especially Spanish, is considered advantageous. A personal interview is required. GRE scores are not required. The application deadline is February 1.

Correspondence and Information

Susan Guma
Graduate Programs
Sarah Lawrence College
Bronxville, New York 10708

Sarah Lawrence College

THE FACULTY AND THEIR RESEARCH

Health Advocacy Program
Diana Borst, M.B.A., NYU.
Marvin Frankel, Ph.D., Chicago.
Gretchen G. Harris, B.A., Grinnell.
Alice Herb, LL.M., NYU.
Marsha Hurst, Ph.D., Columbia.
Margaret Keller, J.D., M.S., Columbia.
Janice Levy, M.A., Sarah Lawrence.
Terry Mizrahi, Ph.D., Virginia.
Lucy Schmolka, M.A., Sarah Lawrence.
Michael J. Smith, D.S.W., Columbia.

Human Genetics Program
Ellen R. Batt, Ph.D., Columbia.
Linda Brzustowicz, M.D., Columbia.
Jessica Davis, M.D., Columbia.
Marvin Frankel, Ph.D., Chicago.
Eva Griepp, M.D., NYU.
Susan Gross, M.D., Toronto.
Elisabeth Guthrie, M.D., Yeshiva (Einstein).
Caroline Lieber, M.A., Sarah Lawrence.
Robert Marin, M.D., Yeshiva (Einstein).
Elsa Reich, M.S., Sarah Lawrence.
Piero Rinaldo, M.D., Padova (Italy).

Sarah Lawrence is in suburban Westchester, 15 miles from New York City.

STATE UNIVERSITY OF NEW YORK AT ALBANY

School of Public Health

Programs of Study

The School of Public Health, University at Albany, State University of New York, is accredited by the national Council on Education for Public Health. The School encompasses five graduate academic departments that offer graduate degrees in the basic disciplines that constitute public health: biomedical sciences, environmental health and toxicology, epidemiology, biometry and statistics, and health policy and management, including social behavior and community health. The School also offers a number of professional programs, including the Master of Public Health and the Doctor of Public Health. The Preventive Medicine Residency Program and the Residency in Dental Public Health are available to physicians and dentists interested in acquiring the academic and practical skills necessary to work in the field of public health.

The School's unique partnership between academia and the world of public health practice offers great intellectual growth for students and results in high employment rates in their areas of concentration. The School opened in 1985 as a joint venture between the University and the New York State Department of Health; Albany Medical College later became an affiliate. This partnership is unparalleled and one that richly benefits the School's diverse student body. Many of the 200 faculty members work on a daily basis within the field of public health, administering major health programs for the state of New York or studying scientific or policy-oriented public health problems of national significance. Students have regular access to these health experts as teachers and mentors. Students have immediate access to a vast array of internship opportunities at a wide variety of public and private health agencies and institutions throughout New York State, the nation, and the world.

Research Facilities

The School of Public Health provides an unusually impressive array of educational, scientific, and policy-related resources. Students find some of the most sophisticated, state-of-the-art laboratory equipment available in the world. Several excellent libraries are available with extensive information retrieval services. The School also offers advanced mainframe and personal computing facilities, and students have ready access to a large number of unique databases that open many lines of epidemiological, statistical, and policy-related research. The Wadsworth Center for Laboratories and Research is the third-largest public health research facility in the U.S. after the National Institutes of Health and the Centers for Disease Control and Prevention.

Financial Aid

To help defray educational expenses, the School provides a limited number of graduate assistantships and tuition scholarships. The graduate assistantships, awarded to qualified students, carry an obligation of up to 20 hours per week of research, teaching, or administrative duties. Full or partial tuition scholarships, as well as paid internships and field placements, are available. Increasingly, students are supported by training grants and other external funding sources.

All M.S. and M.P.H. applicants are eligible to compete for the Axelrod Fellowship. The stipend of $10,000 is supplemented by full tuition support. The award is designed to encourage outstanding students in public health, and applications are reviewed by the faculty and the Axelrod Endowment Committee. The deadline for applications is March 15.

Outstanding Ph.D. applicants may qualify for the University's Presidential Fellowships. The stipend associated with the award is $13,000 for the academic year, and all recipients are eligible for a full tuition scholarship. These appointments are for a continuous three-year period, assuming the student makes satisfactory academic progress. Applicants who are interested in being nominated for this award must submit their applications before February 1.

Cost of Study

Tuition for New York State residents for the 1997–98 academic year was $2550 per semester for full-time graduate students (those carrying 12 or more credit hours) or $213 per credit hour for those carrying less than 12 credit hours per semester. Full-time out-of-state students and international students paid $4208 per semester or $351 per credit hour when carrying less than 12 credit hours a semester. Mandatory fees for transportation and technology services were $411 for full-time students.

Living and Housing Costs

Campus lodging options include dormitory rooms at $1649 per semester and double occupancy apartments at $1860 per person per semester. Affordable housing is also available in Albany and throughout the surrounding Capital Region.

Student Group

The University at Albany is northeastern New York's educational centerpiece. The largest of the fifteen colleges and universities in the immediate area, the University at Albany enrolls approximately 17,000 students, including 5,000 graduate students. Within the University's total student body, 18 percent are students from minority groups. The School of Public Health has 280 enrolled students and anticipates growth to approximately 650 students over the next ten years. The School is deeply committed to maintaining and increasing the diversity of its student enrollment. The University offers a variety of counseling and other services as well as student associations, which allow for social, professional, and academic interaction.

Location

Albany is an exciting setting in which to study, work, and live. The Albany area, with a population of 1 million, offers a rich variety of musical, dance, and theatrical performances at many local and nearby locations.

The countryside surrounding Albany offers much natural beauty and many opportunities for skiing, boating, camping, hiking, and other outdoor activities. The Catskill Mountains are a 30-minute drive south, the Adirondack Mountains are 60 minutes north, and Vermont and the Berkshire Mountains of western Massachusetts are less than an hour east. The University is also only 150 miles from New York City, 165 miles from Boston, and 242 miles from Montreal.

The University and The School

The University at Albany is the senior campus of the largest centrally managed system of public higher education in the nation. Three traditional obligations guide the University: teaching, research, and community service. Students are encouraged to challenge themselves, to explore freely the world about them, and to accept the responsibility that comes with challenge and freedom. The University actively assists and encourages its members to engage in scholarly and creative research and to make the results widely known.

The educational programs offered by the School of Public Health are designed with the complex public health needs of the next century in mind. The opportunities for research and practical experience are rich, varied, and virtually unlimited in scope and possibility. Students of all ethnic, cultural, and racial backgrounds are encouraged to apply to the School, where they will join a cadre of faculty members deeply committed to addressing the difficult health problems of a broad range of social groups. The School regards all of New York State as a laboratory for the study of public health problems that affect the country as a whole.

Applying

Application for admission can be made for any semester during the year. Admission standards and requirements for each department and professional program differ, but all applicants must hold a bachelor's degree and be able to demonstrate ability and potential to complete graduate work of high quality. Appropriate undergraduate transcripts and GRE or GMAT scores, as well as TOEFL scores for students from non-English-speaking countries, are required. Three letters of recommendation are also required.

Correspondence and Information

Applicants may call or write for applications and other information related to the School of Public Health. Preapplication questions can be referred to individual departments. Additional information is available at the School's Web site listed below.

School of Public Health
State University of New York at Albany
One University Place
Rensselaer, New York 12144-3456
World Wide Web: http://www.albany.edu

State University of New York at Albany

THE FACULTY

Department of Biomedical Sciences (518-473-7553)

Carmen Mannella, Chair (518-474-2462)

The Department of Biomedical Sciences offers programs leading to the M.S. or Ph.D. degree in four areas of specialization: structural and cell biology, immunology and infectious diseases, molecular genetics, and neuroscience. Training is individualized, with course selection based on the area of specialization and on the background and interests of each student. Emphasis is placed on informal instruction and interaction between students and faculty members in the laboratories, seminars, colloquia, and journal clubs. The Department of Biomedical Sciences has its home base in the Wadsworth Center, the central laboratory complex of the New York State Department of Health. The laboratories are spacious, modern facilities that are among the most technologically advanced and comprehensive laboratory complexes in the country. Facilities include cryoelectron and high-voltage electron microscopes with extensive computer image analysis systems, X-ray protein crystallography, multidimensional NMR (500 and 650 MHz spectrometers), and biological mass spectroscopy. Core facilities are available for peptide and oligonucleotide synthesis, protein microsequencing, DNA sequencing, and gene knockouts.

Department of Environmental Health and Toxicology (518-473-7553)

Kenneth Jackson, Chair (518-474-4197)

The Department of Environmental Health and Toxicology offers programs leading to the M.S. and Ph.D. degrees in three broad areas of specialization: environmental chemistry, toxicology, and environmental and occupational health. The environmental chemistry track focuses on the effect of chemicals on the environment and human health. The toxicology track combines studies on the effects of environmental toxic substances that pose human health hazards. The environmental and occupational health track focuses on environmental health sciences in programs directed at evaluating and controlling occupational and environmental health risks. Graduate programs are individualized; courses are selected in accordance with both the track requirements and the background and interests of the individual student. The programs benefit from being based in the Wadsworth Center, the central laboratory complex of the New York State Department of Health. The laboratories provide scientific expertise and analytical support for numerous environmental and public health problems, including the greenhouse effect, acid rain, toxic waste, PCBs in the Hudson River, indoor air pollution, and the combustion of hazardous/municipal waste.

Department of Epidemiology (518-402-0400)

David S. Strogatz, Chair (518-402-0400)

Epidemiology describes the occurrence of disorders of health, especially those affecting large numbers of people, so that steps can be taken to prevent disease and promote public health. Epidemiologists perform research and conduct field investigations, and their findings are available to policy makers for guidance in actions to improve public health. Biostatistics is an essential tool for the understanding and practice of epidemiology and is integrated into much of the teaching in these graduate programs. The student of epidemiology must be able to apply a background in biology, social sciences, natural sciences, and clinical sciences to contemporary public health problems. Most of the faculty members are senior-level public health epidemiologists in the New York State Department of Health and also hold University at Albany appointments. These faculty researchers are actively engaged in their own investigations and research. Faculty research interests include communicable disease epidemiology, cancer epidemiology, environmental health and injury epidemiology, fertility patterns and women's health, and the epidemiology of vaccine-preventable diseases. Other organizations also offer learning experiences, including Albany Medical Center and a number of state and local health organizations. The department offers M.S. and Ph.D. degrees.

Department of Biometry and Statistics (518-402-0400)

Timothy Lance, Interim Chair (518-402-0400)

Students in the Department of Biometry and Statistics prepare for careers in public health, government statistics, biostatistics for clinical research, and environmental statistics as well as academically oriented careers in teaching and research. Course work is coupled with formal involvement in research projects, often in multidisciplinary collaborations with researchers at the New York State Department of Health, the Albany Medical Center, with faculty members in other University at Albany departments and institutes, and local industry. The faculty of the Department of Biometry and Statistics includes employees in the New York State Department of Health and University at Albany faculty members in the Departments of Mathematics and Statistics, Economics, and Educational Psychology and Statistics. Faculty members work with students individually to find the particular balance of course work, the area of application or collaboration, and the program breadth to suit each student's interest and goals. The department offers M.S. and Ph.D. degrees.

Department of Health Policy, Management and Behavior (518-402-0333)

Edward Hannan, Chair (518-402-0333)

The M.S. degree in health policy, management, and behavior is intended for those who wish to pursue careers in public health policy formulation and analysis, health services research, program development and evaluation, research on social and behavioral aspects of health, and management of health organizations. It provides students with strong analytical skills and public health experience that prepares them to analyze, develop, implement, and evaluate health policy and programs. The educational experience is enhanced through study with senior-level health practitioners and researchers who are directly involved in the formulation and implementation of health policy. Three concentrations are offered in the program: health systems, management, and social behavior and community health. Currently, graduate placement in related health fields is nearly 100 percent within six months of graduation.

Professional Education Programs (518-402-0404)

John Conway, Director (518-402-0404)

The Professional Education Programs (PEP) are designed to be interdepartmental programs. Students are admitted to the program rather than to a department. The areas of concentration are behavioral sciences, biomedical sciences, biostatistics, environmental health, epidemiology, and health administration. Students take core courses that provide the breadth of knowledge necessary for an understanding of public health and then complete additional courses in a concentration. The capstone experiences of the program are provided by internship rotations through areas of public health as practiced in state government or other health related agencies. All students are expected to complete at least one internship (two or more if they do not have previous experience relevant to public health).

The goal of the Preventive Medicine Residency Program is to provide residents with a broad background in the academic and practical skills necessary to work effectively in the field of preventive medicine and public health. The educational setting is the New York State Department of Health, which has a wide variety of public health programs in place or in the planing stages. At the end of this program, residents have fulfilled the residency requirements to sit for the Preventive Medicine/Public Health Board Certification exam.

The goal of the Residency Program in Dental Public Health is to provide training and experience to qualified dentists in dental public health administration and research. The program is designed to provide residents with a broad range of instruction and practical experience in dental public health practice. The program in Dental Public Health is accredited by the Commission on Dental Accreditation, which is recognized by the Commission on Postsecondary Accreditation and the United States Department of Education.

The Dr.P.H. program prepares leaders in the public health profession who address the complex public health issues society continues to face throughout the coming decades. Graduates are expected to combine sophisticated analytical and research skills with a broad-based understanding of the political, scientific, medical, statistical, psychosocial, ethical, and economic factors that contribute to health problems. The Dr.P.H. curriculum is predicated upon intensive practical instruction, offering the opportunity to do four internships in a range of public health programs, and culminates in a professional dissertation. The Dr.P.H. program is highly individualized and tailored to the interests of the student and to advisers and mentors with matching interests.

TEMPLE UNIVERSITY

Department of Health Studies

Programs of Study

The Department of Health Studies strives to advance and disseminate new knowledge in the multidisciplinary field of health studies. The departmental mission emphasizes advancing the principles and practices of the applied social-behavioral sciences of health education and therapeutic recreation by creating and evaluating applied interventions, programs, curricula, and policies designed to improve health status and quality of life. The Department of Health Studies offers four graduate programs: the Ph.D. in health studies, the Master of Public Health (M.P.H.) in community health education, and the Master of Education (Ed.M.) in health studies with concentrations in school health or therapeutic recreation.

The Ph.D. degree is an 82-semester-hour program with areas of specialization in health education and therapeutic recreation. The academic focus of the Ph.D. program is to prepare students to integrate social and behavioral health sciences with substantive knowledge of particular populations (e.g., children, youth, elderly, physically challenged) and specific intervention modalities (e.g., patient education, therapeutic recreation). The integration of knowledge and skills is achieved through specialized cognate areas that emphasize multidisciplinary approaches to social, behavioral, and educational research that have applications in a wide variety of settings and diverse populations. There is a commitment to conduct basic and applied research, thereby contributing to national, state, and regional policy bodies that are actively involved in the delivery of health education and therapeutic recreation services.

The M.P.H. is a 45-semester-hour program designed to give students a working knowledge of core areas in public health, including health-care organization and administration, epidemiology, biostatistics, program planning (using appropriate educational theory and services), and skills to evaluate health education programs. In the final year of the program, students complete an in-depth community fieldwork practicum in one of a wide range of approved local health agencies in order to gain experience in applying skills acquired in the academic program. The program is fully accredited by the Council on Education for Public Health (CEPH).

The Ed.M. is a 36-semester-hour program that concentrates on training practitioners to work primarily in therapeutic recreation or health education in school settings. Students in therapeutic recreation are eligible to take the national certification exam administered by the National Council on Therapeutic Recreation Certification (NCTRC) upon completion of their degree (and any supportive course work required for NCTRC eligibility). Health education students may take courses to become eligible for teacher certification in the commonwealth of Pennsylvania.

Research Facilities

Temple University students have access to a sophisticated computer center. Through several computer laboratories, students have access to word processing, statistical programs, and Internet and e-mail services. In addition, the Computer Center offers numerous training opportunities through a regular series of workshops. Temple's libraries are comprehensive and offer a full range of computer-assisted search facilities, interlibrary loans, and extensive microform holdings. The Sponsored Projects Office of Temple University and the Graduate School are available to assist with grant-making activities. The department's extensive relationship with community agencies enables access to community-based research activities.

Financial Aid

University aid in the form of scholarships, grants, and loans is awarded based on academic promise or need, as calculated by Student Financial Services. Candidates in the Ph.D. or M.P.H. programs may be nominated by the department for University, Russell Conwell, Presidential, or Future Faculty fellowships, which provide a twelve-month stipend and full tuition remission for a maximum of two years. The department also offers teaching assistantships to a limited number of graduate students. A graduate teaching assistant is required to teach or assist in teaching 20 hours per week in exchange for a stipend and tuition remission.

Cost of Study

Graduate tuition for 1997–98 was $308 per credit hour for Pennsylvania residents and $429 per credit hour for nonresidents; a $50 computer fee, a $25 activity fee, and a $35 health fee were also required.

Living and Housing Costs

There is limited on-campus housing available for graduate students. Rooms, apartments, and houses are available for students in the surrounding city and suburbs.

Student Group

Temple University has an enrollment of approximately 28,000 students in fourteen schools and colleges. The Department of Health Studies has more than 200 students enrolled in its undergraduate and graduate programs.

Student Outcomes

Ph.D. graduates are trained to become faculty members in departments of health education, therapeutic recreation, and other related fields where the applied social-behavioral sciences are central to the preparation of students (e.g., nursing, physical therapy, and dental hygiene).

Graduates of the M.P.H. in community health education program become practitioners in a wide range of health-related settings, such as public health departments, voluntary health agencies, health maintenance organizations, hospitals, clinics, schools, and work sites. Students completing the Ed.M. with a therapeutic recreation major find employment as recreation therapists and administrators in diverse health-care agencies, such as physical rehabilitation hospitals, adult day-care centers, nursing homes, and behavioral health agencies. Students with a school health major find employment in diverse school-related agencies providing health education programs. Students who specialize in health education also meet the requirements for community health education specialist (CHES) certification.

Location

Philadelphia is a culturally diverse city that is consistently listed among the country's most livable cities. In addition to Independence Hall and the Liberty Bell, the birthplace of the nation also has world-renowned art museums, two opera companies, a ballet company, one of the finest symphony orchestras in the world, outstanding theaters, and America's oldest zoo. Philadelphia is also the home of several medical research centers with which there are many opportunities to work collaboratively. Temple University's location provides access to medical and governmental libraries and resources as well as a variety of rehabilitation and human services agencies in the Delaware Valley. In addition, easy travel to Baltimore, New York, and Washington, D.C., offers access to a wide range of public health and patient service scholars and related professional organizational meetings.

The University and The Department

Temple University was founded in 1884 by Dr. Russell Conwell on the premise that those who have the imagination to dream and the desire to work should also have the opportunity to make their dreams come true. Temple University has become one of America's premier senior comprehensive universities.

The Department of Health Studies faculty includes 11 full-time and 11 part-time faculty members. In addition, more than 50 fieldwork supervisors work with students in the master's program.

Applying

Deadlines for admission to the M.P.H. and Ed.H. programs are February 1 for fall and October 15 for spring. Doctoral students are admitted only in the fall. The department takes a portfolio approach to admission, looking at standardized test scores (GRE), grade point average, evidence of writing skill, a personal statement, and previous experience.

Correspondence and Information

Joyce Hankins
Department of Health Studies
304 Vivacqua Hall (062-00)
Temple University
Philadelphia, Pennsylvania 19122-0843

Telephone: 215-204-8726
Fax: 215-204-1455
E-mail: jhankins@nimbus.temple.edu.

Temple University

THE FACULTY AND THEIR RESEARCH

Rosangela Boyd, Associate Professor; Ph.D., Clemson. Aging, developmental disabilities, therapeutic recreation, multicultural issues.
Catherine Coyle, Associate Professor; Ph.D., Temple. Therapeutic recreation in rehabilitation, transitional skills in school learning theory.
Nikki Franke, Associate Professor; Ed.D., Temple. African-American health issues, sports nutrition, community health program development.
Clara Haignere, Assistant Professor; Ph.D., Denver; M.P.H., Columbia. HIV/AIDS, international health, health behavior, adolescent health.
Alice Hausman, Associate Professor; Ph.D., SUNY at Binghamton; M.P.H., Harvard. Youth violence prevention, adolescent health, program evaluation.
Terry Kinney, Professor; Ph.D., NYU. Psychosocial aspects of disability and illness, therapeutic recreation, program evaluation.
Patricia M. Legos, Professor and Chair; Ed.D., Temple; CHES. School health education, curriculum and instruction, teacher behavior.
Xueqin Grace Ma, Assistant Professor; Ph.D., Oklahoma. Substance abuse prevention, community and family health, ethnic/transcultural health issues, program planning and evaluation.
Sheryl B. Ruzek, Professor; Ph.D., California, Davis; M.P.H., Berkeley. Women's health, maternal and child health, medical technology/risk assessment and communication, epidemiology.
Jay S. Segal, Professor; Ph.D., Ohio State. Stress management, health counseling, human sexuality.
John Shank, Professor; Ed.D., Boston University. Therapeutic recreation, community-based play and recreation, social psychology of leisure.

TUFTS UNIVERSITY

School of Medicine
Program in Public Health and Program in Health Communication

Programs of Study

The Master of Public Health (M.P.H.) and the Master of Science (M.S.) in Health Communication Programs at Tufts University School of Medicine are designed to allow for full-time study or for part-time evening study by persons who wish to remain employed while attending graduate school.

The Master of Science in Health Communication Program was developed in conjunction with Emerson College. Founded in 1880, Emerson College is the only four-year undergraduate and graduate college in the United States that is totally devoted to the study of the communication arts and sciences. This program prepares students to develop, deliver, and evaluate health promotion and disease prevention strategies and campaigns, as well as disseminate information and participate in the formulation and implementation of health policy initiatives. Tufts and Emerson have long-standing traditions of academic excellence in communication and health sciences. Combining each institution's unique resources synergistically strengthens their ability to educate students to play an active role in this burgeoning field.

The Master of Public Health Program is offered by the medical school in cooperation with Tufts School of Nutrition Science and Policy and Faculty of Arts and Sciences. Its mission is to provide a sound foundation in the fundamental disciplines of public health: epidemiology and biostatistics, environmental health, social and behavioral science, health services, and public health policy. In addition to receiving a strong foundation in the core disciplines, students gain additional depths in a chosen substantive area of public health. Core concentration areas include epidemiology and biostatistics, health services management and policy, nutrition, and environmental health. Graduates of this program have the necessary and appropriate knowledge and skills to practice in the broad arena of public health. Employment settings may include nongovernmental or governmental health organizations at the local, state, national, or international level; health-based consulting agencies, health insurers; and community health centers.

The Master of Public Health/Master of Science in Nutrition is a collaborative program offered by the School of Medicine and the School of Nutrition Science and Policy. This program prepares students for careers that combine applied nutrition and public health and offers a strong public policy focus. Applicants to the dual degree program must also apply to the School of Nutrition Science and Policy. Contact the Office of Special Programs for application materials.

Research Facilities

Library resources at Tufts University and Emerson College include electronic online services, more than 800,000 volumes, and 1,500 journal subscriptions. Media facilities and equipment at Emerson and at Tufts' Arthur M. Sackler Center for Health Communications are available for student use in the study and application of strategic health communication, marketing, and advertising and public relations concepts, such as public service announcements, commercial advertisements, and spokesperson training.

Financial Aid

Financial aid opportunities available to qualified students include scholarships, college work-study, and several subsidized and unsubsidized loan programs.

Cost of Study

Tuition for both programs is $570 per credit hour for the 1998–99 academic year. Students may attend full-time or part-time.

Living and Housing Costs

The residential sections of Beacon Hill and Back Bay are within easy walking distance of both Tufts University School of Medicine and Emerson College. Housing in Cambridge, Brookline, and Brighton is easily accessible by public transportation or bicycle. Dormitory housing is also available.

Student Group

In the Boston facilities of Tufts University, approximately 1,500 students are preparing for the medical, dental, and veterinary professions, and approximately 250 students are pursing graduate degrees.

Location

Tufts University School of Medicine is located adjacent to New England Medical Center near Boston's Chinatown section. Metropolitan Boston's well-known cultural resources include theaters, a symphony orchestra, museums, historic sites, and major-league sports teams. Easy access to many ocean beaches in Massachusetts, New Hampshire, Maine, and Rhode Island and to mountains in New Hampshire and Vermont makes the area a recreational center. The concentration of academic excellence in the Boston area facilitates exchange and collaboration between individuals at different institutions. Tufts University has interlibrary loan agreements with a number of other universities in the area.

The University

Tufts University, founded in 1852, spans three campuses. The Medford campus consists of the Tufts College of Liberal Arts for Men and Jackson College for Women, the College of Engineering, the Graduate School of Arts and Sciences, the Boston School of Occupational Therapy, the School of Nutrition, and the Fletcher School of Law and Diplomacy. On the Boston campus are the Schools of Medicine, Dental Medicine, and Veterinary Medicine; the USDA Human Nutrition Research Center; and the Sackler School of Graduate Biomedical Sciences. The clinical facilities of the School of Veterinary Medicine are located on the Grafton campus.

Applying

Admission is based on academic performance, personal and professional experience, letters of reference, GRE General Test scores, and potential for contribution to the field. Applicants from abroad must demonstrate competence in English by means of TOEFL scores or comparable credentials. Admission is on a rolling basis. Applicants are encouraged to submit application forms and all supporting materials by May 15 for the fall semester and November 15 for the spring. Applications that arrive after these dates will be considered at the discretion of the admissions committee as long as space is available in the program.

Correspondence and Information

Office of Special Programs
School of Medicine
Tufts University
136 Harrison Avenue
Boston, Massachusetts 02111
Telephone: 617-636-0935
E-mail: sprograms@infonet.tufts.edu

Tufts University

THE FACULTY AND THEIR RESEARCH

Elizabeth Barbeau, M.P.H., D.Sc., Associate Director of the Master of Public Health Program and Assistant Professor of Family Medicine and Community Health. Professor Barbeau's research is focused on public health policy issues including the tobacco industry's targeting of adolescents through marketing and advertising practices, prevention of childhood and occupational lead poisoning in the U.S. and abroad, workplace tobacco control policies, and other environmental and occupational health issues. She is chair of the Epidemiology and Lab Sciences Section of the Massachusetts Public Health Association and is a member of the editorial board of the Journal of Public Health Policy.

Richard Glickman-Simon, M.D., Assistant Professor of Family Medicine and Community Health. In addition to practicing medicine, Dr. Glickman-Simon teaches in the traditional M.D. degree program, the combined M.D./M.P.H. program, and the M.S. in Health Communication Program. His interests include predoctoral medical education, clinical prevention, and mind-body medicine.

Jeffrey K. Griffiths, M.D., M.P.H.T.M., Associate Director of the M.D./M.P.H. and D.V.M./M.P.H. Program, Assistant Professor of Family Medicine and Community Health and Biomedical Sciences of the Tufts University Schools of Medicine and Veterinary Medicine. Dr. Griffiths received his M.D. at Albert Einstein and his M.P.H.T.M. at Tulane. His clinical training in internal medicine and pediatrics was at Yale and in infectious diseases was at Tufts. His major research interests are in diarrheal diseases in the developing world and in people with AIDS. He represents the National Association of People with AIDS to the EPA, and is a member of the National Drinking Water Advisory Council.

David Gute, M.P.H., Ph.D., Environmental Health Concentration Leader and Associate Professor of Civil and Environmental Engineering and of Family Medicine and Community Health. Prior to joining Tufts, Dr. Gute served as Assistant Commissioner and Director of the Center for Health Promotion and Disease Prevention at the Massachusetts Department of Public Health. Dr. Gute's primary research interests are in the area of environmental and occupational risk factors in human disease. He has served as a core instructor in the combined M.D./M.P.H. program, as co-principal investigator in the dissemination of principles of epidemiology to state and local elected officials, and as a consultant to the World Health Organization.

Catherine Hayes, D.M.D., D.M.Sc., Assistant Professor of General Dentistry and of Family Medicine and Community Health, Associate Director of Graduate Studies, and Head of the Division of Dental Public Health at Tufts University School of Dental Medicine. Professor Hayes's research and professional interests are in the areas of dental medicine, dental public health, epidemiology, and biostatistics.

James N. Hyde, M.A., M.Sc., Associate Director of the Tufts-Emerson Program and Associate Professor of Family Medicine and Community Health. Professor Hyde currently directs NIH and EPA-funded research activities that span the areas of prevention and primary care practice, environmental health policy, and tobacco control. Prior to his appointment at Tufts, Professor Hyde spent four years as Director of the Division of Preventive Medicine in the Massachusetts Department of Public Health and four years at Boston's Children's Hospital as a Research Associate in the Harvard Medical School Department of Pediatrics. He has developed and maintains close working relationships with public sector colleagues at both state and local levels while serving as a consultant and working with federal agencies, including AHCPR, CDC, and EPA.

Mary L. Joyce, D.B.A., Associate Professor of Communication Studies at Emerson College. Professor Joyce is an expert in health-care marketing campaigns and has helped design and deliver health promotion and disease prevention campaigns nationally and internationally. Her publications and research include determinants of preventive health behavior in breast self-examination, health-care concerns of older consumers, hospital marketing programs and staff trends, institutional change in health care, and blood donation behavior, safety, and delivery.

Aviva Must, M.S., Ph.D., Epidemiology and Biostatistics Concentration Leader and Assistant Professor of Family Medicine and Community Health. Dr. Must also maintains appointments in the Epidemiology Program of the Jean Mayer USDA Human Nutrition Research Center on Aging and the School of Nutrition Science and Policy. She is a Research Affiliate at the Clinical Research Center of Massachusetts Institute of Technology. Dr. Must's research is in the area of obesity, particularly in the pediatric population. She is interested in the epidemiology, identification, and consequences of obesity in early life, with a particular focus on the interplay of metabolism, diet, and activity.

J. David Naparstek, M.Sc., Assistant Professor of Family Medicine and Community Health. Professor Naparstek has almost twenty years of experience in directing public health programs. He is past president of the Massachusetts Health Officers Association and has received numerous awards for his innovation, dedication, and service, including the National Environmental Health Association's Robert C. Perriello Award.

Eileen O'Neil, J.D., Ph.D., Health Services Management and Policy Concentration Leader and Assistant Professor of Family Medicine and Community Health. In addition to teaching in the medical, public health, and undergraduate programs at Tufts, Dr. O'Neil has lectured nationally to professionals in the health-care field, including hospital administrators, members of boards of directors, physicians, nurses, and pharmacists. She has also practiced law, with a specialization in health-care corporate structuring, contract issues, and risk management.

J. Gregory Payne, M.P.A., Ph.D., Associate Professor and Chair of Communication Studies at Emerson College. Professor Payne's expertise is in political communication, ethics, and docudrama. His most recent work includes published research in the areas of ethics, mass media, health communication, and political communication.

Scott C. Ratzan, M.D., M.P.A., M.A., Director of the Emerson-Tufts Program in Health Communication, Assistant Professor of Communication Studies at Emerson College, and Assistant Professor of Family Medicine and Community Health at Tufts. Dr. Ratzan specializes in health communication and negotiation. He has lectured and chaired panels nationally and internationally on negotiation, information technologies, health communication, ethics, management, public relations, forensics, conflict management, and political communication. Dr. Ratzan is a past recipient of the Robert F. Kennedy Award for Community Service. He is a frequent lecturer and consultant for business and government agencies throughout the world.

Lisa A. Roghaar, M.B.A., Ph.D., Assistant Professor of Communication Studies at Emerson College. Professor Roghaar specializes in interpersonal and family communication, professional communication, and communication theory.

Ronnen Roubenouf, M.D., M.H.S., F.A.C.P., Nutrition Concentration Leader and Assistant Professor of Medicine and of Nutrition. Dr. Roubenoff trained in internal medicine and rheumatology at the Johns Hopkins Hospital and completed a concurrent fellowship in clinical epidemiology at the Johns Hopkins School of Hygiene and Public Health. He then trained in nutrition at Tufts University and currently focuses his research on the interactions of nutrition and immunity in chronic disease and aging in both human diseases and animal models. He is Scientist I at the Jean Mayer USDA Human Nutrition Research Center on Aging and has a clinical practice in rheumatology and nutrition at the New England Medical Center.

TULANE UNIVERSITY

School of Public Health and Tropical Medicine

Programs of Study

Tulane University School of Public Health and Tropical Medicine offers graduate degree programs in biostatistics, environmental health (water quality management, industrial hygiene, toxicology and risk assessment, and occupational health), epidemiology, health-care administration, health communication/education, health systems management, international health and development, maternal and child health, nutrition, parasitology, population studies, and tropical medicine. The degree programs include M.P.H., M.H.A., M.M.M., M.A.D., M.P.H./T.M., M.S.P.H., Dr.P.H., and Sc.D. The Ph.D. and M.S. degrees are available through the Graduate School. The School also offers a residency program in preventive medicine that leads to board eligibility and combined-degree programs with the Schools of Medicine, Law, Business, and Social Work.

Special programs include the Master's Internationalist Program and the joint-degree M.D./M.P.H. In June 1998, Tulane had the largest Master's Internationalist Program in the U.S., with volunteers serving in twenty-one countries. The first year is spent in New Orleans completing academic requirements for the master's degree (approximately 40 credit hours). Under its rules, the U.S. Peace Corps assigns students for two years of service. Successful completion of the academic and Peace Corps service requirements results in a degree in any of the tracks offered in the School of Public Health and Tropical Medicine. Students should contact the School's Master's Internationalist Coordinator (telephone: 800-676-5389, toll-free; e-mail: mastersintl-l@mailhost.tcs.tulane.edu). In addition, Tulane offers joint M.D./M.P.H. degrees for medical students currently enrolled in the Tulane School of Medicine. Current track specializations are in primary care, maternal and child health, epidemiology, biostatistics, tropical medicine, environmental health, health systems management, and international health and development.

Research Facilities

The commitment of the School to research is reflected in the Center for Bioenvironmental Research (CBR) and other research centers, including the Institute for Health Services Research, the International Collaboration in Infectious Disease Research, the Tulane Cancer Center, the Tulane Xavier Center for Women's Health, the International Communication Enhancement Center, the Tulane Center for International Health and Development, and the Tulane Center for Cardiovascular Health.

Financial Aid

Tulane University seeks to offer its educational opportunities to qualified students regardless of their ability to meet expenses. Need-based assistance consists of a package of loans and campus employment as determined by federal eligibility criteria. Remaining financial need can be met through some combination of scholarships, traineeships, Federal Perkins Loans, other loan programs, and Federal Work-Study Program funding. The School offers its own programs of limited financial assistance to qualified students. For further information, students should contact Financial Aid (telephone: 504-585-6135; e-mail: plott@mailhost.tcs.tulane.edu).

Cost of Study

In the 1998–99 academic year, tuition is $400 per credit and fees are $20 per credit. Student health fees are $304 per year, and there is a technology fee of $30 per year. Health insurance may be purchased if needed. Full-time students typically take 15 credits per semester (30 per academic year) at a cost of $6300 per semester. However, full-time students have course loads that range from 9 to 20 credits per semester. Tuition and fees are payable within thirty days of registration each semester. Students are also assessed an activity fee.

Living and Housing Costs

Campus housing is available for graduate public health and medical students at Elk's Place, a newly constructed facility that opened in August 1998. The new structure is located within the Tulane University Medical Center. Housing questions may be directed to Martha Dees (telephone: 504-524-8225). For information regarding off-campus housing, students should visit the School's Web page (listed below).

Student Group

The School is large enough to provide a breadth of educational opportunities for students yet small enough to give individual attention to their needs. In 1997–98, 724 core students enrolled. Approximately 20 percent of them represented more than fifty countries. Designing programs that take into account the past experiences of students and devising courses of study that allow them to pursue individual goals is important to the faculty.

Location

The name New Orleans instantly evokes Mardi Gras, the French Quarter, Creole cuisine, and jazz. The School is located within walking distance of the riverfront, Jackson Square, Riverwalk, Convention Center, Louisiana Superdome, and the Aquarium of the Americas. New Orleans has been called the most European city in America because of its numerous historic landmarks, cuisine, music, and diverse mix of ethnic neighborhoods.

The University

Tulane University is one of the major research universities in the South. It includes eleven schools and colleges and enrolls more than 11,000 students, 4,800 of whom are graduate students. Tulane is one of the twenty-five most selective private universities in the nation.

Applying

Each applicant must apply to a specific program within the School. Requirements listed represent the minimum standards set by the School. Individual departments or programs may stipulate additional requirements. Applicants must have a baccalaureate degree from an accredited institution, official transcripts of all academic work, a grade point average of no less than 3.0 on a 4.0 scale, three letters of recommendation, and GRE scores (required of all graduates of U.S. institutions). When appropriate, GMAT, MCAT, or MAT scores may be substituted. A written statement of career goals and TOEFL scores are required of applicants from non-English speaking nations. A nonrefundable application fee of $40 must accompany each application.

Correspondence and Information

Jeffrey T. Johnson
Director of Admissions
Tulane University School of Public Health and Tropical Medicine
1501 Canal Street, Suite 703
New Orleans, Louisiana 70112-2824
Telephone: 800-676-5389 (toll-free)
Fax: 504-584-1667
E-mail: adminsph-l@mailhost.tcs.tulane.edu
World Wide Web: http://www.sph.tulane.edu

Tulane University

FACULTY HEADS, RESEARCH, AND PROGRAM ACTIVITIES

Community Health Sciences
Chair: Judith LaRosa, Ph.D.
The Department of Community Health Sciences is a coalition of faculty members from a variety of disciplines with a common interest in meeting student learning needs in the area of public health practice. The department is composed of three administrative sections: Health Communication/Education (HCED), Maternal and Child Health (MCHL), and Nutrition (NTRN). The department offers a Master of Public Health degree with specialization in each of these disciplines and dual specialization in HCED/MCHL. A combined M.S.W./M.P.H. degree is available in maternal and child health. Research interests include effectiveness of communication in enhancing utilization of family planning methods, prevention of teenage pregnancy, and effectiveness of health education in reducing the use of tobacco. Contact: Sandy Gray (telephone: 504-584-3539; e-mail: sgray@mailhost.tcs.tulane.edu).

Biostatistics and Epidemiology
Chair: Larry S. Webber, Ph.D.
Biostatistics and epidemiology are complementary disciplines for the understanding of risk factors for disease in human populations. Offerings include the M.P.H., M.S.P.H., Sc.D., and Dr.P.H. Research interests include clinical trials, longitudinal data analysis, quantitative risk assessment, statistical computing, occupational and environmental health studies, sampling and surveying techniques, cardiovascular health, and multivariate methods. Epidemiological studies are in such areas as cancer, infectious diseases, protein energy malnutrition, environmental health, psychiatric disorders, health information systems, and health program evaluation. Contact: Susan Gautier (telephone: 504-587-2102; e-mail: sgautie@mailhost.tcs.tulane.edu).

Environmental Health Sciences
Chair: William A. Toscano Jr., Ph.D.
The Department of Environmental Health Sciences offers a wide array of programs designed to prepare students to effectively prevent and respond to environmental health problems. Focus areas include water quality management, industrial hygiene, occupational health, toxicology and health risk assessment, hazardous-waste management, and environmental health for developing countries. Offerings in environmental health include the M.S.P.H., M.P.H., and Sc.D. The department also offers four joint-degree programs with the Schools of Medicine, Business, and Law and with arts and sciences. Contact: Dr. William Toscano (telephone: 504-584-5374; e-mail: wtoscano@mailhost.tcs.tulane.edu).

Health Systems Management
Chair: David Fine, M.H.A.
The Department of Health Systems Management prepares individuals for management careers in the health-care system. Its program emphasizes generic management concepts and messages as they apply to complex health-care systems. Two basic programs are offered at the master's level: the M.H.A. and the M.P.H. Joint-degree programs are offered with the Schools of Business, Medicine, and Law. The department also offers a program that leads to the Dr.P.H. degree. An executive Master of Medical Management (M.M.M.) degree is available for practicing physicians. Research interests include efficiency and productivity measures in the hospital sector, computer-assisted decision analysis, corporate finance, and health-care policy. Contact: Kathy Haggerty Ammersbach (telephone: 504-585-5428; e-mail: khaggert@mailhost.tcs.tulane.edu).

International Health and Development
Chair: Jane Bertrand, Ph.D.
The Department of International Health and Development is an interdisciplinary department oriented toward individuals who plan to work in developing countries. The program emphasizes the development of skills and the acquisition of applied knowledge in at least one of the following career-track concentrations: epidemiology-based planning and evaluation, population studies, management and health economics, health communication/education, tropical medicine, environmental health, reproductive studies, and nutrition. Combined international health track options in the areas of environmental education, environmental epidemiology, health communication/education, and epidemiology are increasingly popular. Offerings in the program include the M.P.H. and Dr.P.H. Research interests include operations research, disaster mitigation, monitoring and evaluation, information technology (HIS/MIS/GIS), food and nutrition monitoring and surveillance, and health planning policy and finance. Contact: Penny Jessop (telephone: 504-584-3655; e-mail: pjessop@mailhost.tcs.tulane.edu).

Tropical Medicine
Chair: Donald J. Krogstad, M.D.
The Department of Tropical Medicine prepares students for careers in research and control of parasitic and tropical diseases. Programs offered include the M.P.H./T.M. for health professionals, the M.S.P.H. in parasitology, the Sc.D. degree in parasitology, and a Diploma Course in clinical tropical medicine. Current research includes the immunology and cell biology of parasitic infection, molecular strategies to define the clonal nature of parasitic infection, the development of antiparasitic infection, the basis of vector capacity, diagnosis and treatment of diarrheal disease in children, and the development and implementation of effective and economical preventive strategies. Contact: Karen Rachel (telephone: 504-588-5199; e-mail: tropmed@mailhost.tcs.tulane.edu).

Dean Paul Whelton with public health students.

UNIVERSITY OF ALABAMA AT BIRMINGHAM

School of Public Health

Programs of Study

The School of Public Health, one of twenty-seven accredited by the Council on Education for Public Health, offers programs leading to the degrees of Master of Public Health (M.P.H.), Master of Science (M.S.), Master of Science in Public Health (M.S.P.H.), Doctor of Public Health (Dr.P.H.), and Doctor of Philosophy (Ph.D). Specialties include behavioral science, biostatistics, environmental health, environmental toxicology, epidemiology, general theory and practice, health-care organization, health behavior, health education, health promotion, international health, maternal and child health, occupational health and safety, occupational health and safety/hazardous substance, and public health nutrition. The M.S.P.H. program for students without previous experience offers specializations in environmental health sciences, environmental toxicology, epidemiology, and industrial hygiene. An M.S. degree is offered in biostatistics. These programs can be completed in two years. The Dr.P.H. program provides education and training at an advanced level and is more broadly based. Specialty areas are maternal and child health, public health nutrition, international health, environmental health, and health-care organization and policy. The Dr.P.H. can generally be completed in three years. The Ph.D. is offered in environmental toxicology, industrial hygiene, epidemiology, biostatistics, and environmental health. The program prepares scientists for careers in research and teaching and emphasizes research methodology, study design, data analysis, and subject-area expertise. Degree work may be completed in four to five years. The School also offers the following six coordinated degree programs with the University of Alabama at Birmingham (UAB): the M.P.H./M.B.A., M.P.H./O.D., M.P.H./M.P.A., M.P.H./J.D., M.P.H./M.S.N., and M.P.H./Ph.D. (psychology). The M.P.H./Ph.D. (psychology) is also offered with the University of Alabama (UA). Weekend M.P.H. degree programs in health-care organization and maternal and child health are offered for working health professionals. These degree programs can be completed in two years.

Research Facilities

Environmental health laboratories for industrial hygiene; air pollution; microbiology, including virology; bioaccumulation; and analytical chemistry are located in the School. Additional research facilities are the Comprehensive Cancer Center, the Specialized Center for Ischemic Heart Disease, the Center for Aging, the Burn Center, the Cardia Coordinating Center, the Cardiovascular Research and Training Center, the AIDS Research Center, the Diabetes Research and Training Center, the Multipurpose Arthritis Center, and the Injury Prevention Center. The Deep South Occupational Health and Safety Educational Resource Center, the Sparkman Center for International Public Health Education, the Center for Community Health Resource Development, the Lister Hill Center for Health Policy, and the Center for Health Promotion and Disease Prevention are all based in the School of Public Health.

Financial Aid

The School and the University provide financial assistance for more than 50 percent of the student body. The Public Health Education Fund, established by donations from faculty and friends of the School, supports students through assistantships and scholarships. A limited number of fellowships, loans, and work-study awards are also available through the School and the University. Under the Academic Common Market Agreement, qualified students from Arkansas, Florida, Kentucky, Maryland, Mississippi, Tennessee, Texas, Virginia, and West Virginia can enter the program at in-state tuition rates (for some programs, residents of Georgia and South Carolina can as well).

Cost of Study

In 1998–99, tuition and fees for a full-time student are $1188 per term for Alabama residents and $2376 per term for nonresidents. Students enrolled in joint or concurrent degree programs may incur slightly higher tuition costs. These fees are subject to change at the beginning of each quarter. Book expenses add about $300 per quarter, depending on the courses taken. (Figures are subject to change.)

Living and Housing Costs

Birmingham offers a variety of housing choices, ranging from the large old homes near UAB to modern apartment complexes with pools and tennis courts. Commuting time averages less than 30 minutes from a number of surrounding communities. In addition, some apartments are available on campus. Monthly costs for a single student should average about $400 for housing and $300 for food.

Student Group

Approximately 400 students are enrolled in the School. About 53 percent are women, 35 percent are members of minority groups, and 12 percent are international students. Recent graduates are involved in areas as diverse as marketing of health services; epidemiology; monitoring, evaluating, and controlling health hazards in the workplace; smoking cessation; and AIDS education program development.

Location

Birmingham has a civic-center complex that provides exceptional facilities for major musical and theatrical productions. The community offers art and science museums, a botanical garden, the largest zoo in a nine-state area, collegiate and professional sports events, and a modern state park system. Birmingham is Alabama's largest city, with a population of 800,000.

The University

UAB has three major academic units: the undergraduate programs, the Medical Center, and the graduate school. The Medical Center comprises the six health professional schools of Medicine, Dentistry, Optometry, Nursing, Health-Related Professions, and Public Health, as well as the University of Alabama Hospitals, various clinics and outpatient programs, and a number of research and training centers that address specific diseases. The UAB faculty and staff number more than 10,000 and serve a student body exceeding 15,000. More than 28,000 persons are cared for annually in the UAB Hospitals, and the UAB medical complex is the state's largest referral facility.

Applying

Information and application packets are available from the School of Public Health. Results of the GRE General Test, or an equivalent (e.g., GMAT, LSAT, or MCAT), and TOEFL scores from international applicants are required. Personal interviews are recommended. A nonrefundable application fee of $35 for U.S. citizens and permanent residents and $60 for others is required. Admission to the master's programs is offered once a year in the fall. Applications to these programs should be completed by April 1. Applications to the doctoral programs may be submitted at any time.

Correspondence and Information

Donna J. Petersen, M.H.S., Sc.D.
Assistant Dean for Academic Affairs
School of Public Health
University of Alabama at Birmingham
1665 University Boulevard
Birmingham, Alabama 35294-0022

Telephone: 205-934-4993
Fax: 205-975-5484
E-mail: osas@ms.soph.uab.edu
World Wide Web: http://www.uab.edu/PublicHealth

University of Alabama at Birmingham

FACULTY HEADS AND RESEARCH ACTIVITIES

Department of Biostatistics

Interim Chair: Charles R. Katholi, Ph.D. The department provides students with a fundamental understanding of basic statistical principles needed to advance statistical theory and to interact effectively with scientists in other disciplines in order to advance knowledge in those fields. The department works closely with the Department of Epidemiology in the design and analysis of epidemiologic studies.

Department of Environmental Health Sciences

Interim Chair: Kent Oestenstad, Ph.D. Environmental health scientists are essential to our understanding of the environment and its preservation. Research in the department focuses on recognizing, evaluating, and controlling physical, biological, and chemical agents in both the general environment and the workplace. Effects of toxic and hazardous substances on human health, occupational safety and health, the role of the biological environment in infectious disease, biological-waste treatment, and monitoring DNA damage caused by chemicals and radiation are all major research areas.

Department of Epidemiology

Chair: Sten Vermund, M.D., Ph.D. The principal areas of research are (1) the epidemiology and control of cancer, (2) methods of epidemiologic research, (3) the epidemiology and control of infectious diseases, and (4) chronic diseases, including occupational epidemiology, heart disease, genetic disease, diabetes, and injuries.

Department of Health Behavior

Chair: James M. Raczynski, Ph.D. This department is currently involved in a variety of research projects addressing both chronic and infectious disease prevention and health promotion, including HIV/AIDS education and prevention in women and children, cancer prevention and education in minority groups, prevention of sexually transmitted diseases, alcohol use prevention during pregnancy, community health education in prevention of alcohol and drug abuse, smoking cessation, cardiovascular disease prevention, and physical activity and nutrition programs for adolescents.

Department of Health Care Organization and Policy

Chair: Peter M. Ginter, Ph.D. Research focuses on issues of health economics, outcomes research, strategic management, health systems management, and health policy. Current activities include research on health insurance and managed-care issues, clinical decision making, outcomes research, Medicaid, maternal and child health, health-care market structure, health-care quality, and management of public health services organizations. Web site: http://lhcwww.soph.uab.edu/hcop/

Department of International Health

Interim Chair: Charles B. Stephensen, Ph.D. Areas of research currently include nutritional problems affecting mothers, infants, and the growth and development of children in developing nations; vitamin A deficiency, assessment, and metabolism; micronutrient deficiencies in developing countries; water and sanitation-related problems; molecular biology of viruses–vaccine development; nutrition, diet, and infectious disease; risk factors for sexually transmitted diseases and AIDS; tuberculosis and respiratory diseases in developing countries.

Department of Maternal and Child Health

Chair: Lorraine V. Klerman, Dr.P.H. Faculty and students are involved in research on factors associated with low birth weight, including epidemiology, smoking, nutrition and weight gain, psychosocial factors and prenatal care; evaluation of the impact of managed care on women and children; community-based research and evaluation; development of systems to serve diverse cultures and children with chronic conditions; interconception care; unintended pregnancy; prevention of developmental disabilities, including mental retardation; and methods of needs assessment.

Deep South Center for Occupational Health and Safety

Director: Vernon E. Rose, Dr.P.H. This center was created in 1979 and has as its mission the implementation of multidisciplinary educational and research programs that enable students to learn to anticipate, recognize, evaluate, and control hazards found in, or arising from, the workplace that may adversely affect the health and well-being of workers and the general population. It is composed of academic programs in the UAB Schools of Public Health, Nursing, and Medicine, as well as the College of Engineering at Auburn University. In addition to its academic offerings, the center maintains a multidisciplinary continuing education program.

Center for Health Promotion

Director: James M. Raczynski, Ph.D. This center addresses risk reduction through development of the UAB Consortium for Health Promotion and Disease Prevention (HPDP) to link together UAB units engaged in HPDP, other state HPDP advocates, the CDC, and other funding agencies. The UAB Center for Health Promotion supports the activities of the consortium and undertakes specific demonstration and research projects, linkage activities, training, and administrative activities. The primary emphasis of the center is on risk reduction in underserved populations, focusing broadly on the need to develop new models and methods for health promotion and disease prevention and building on family-based cultural values and informal networks.

Lister Hill Center for Health Policy

Director: Michael A. Morrisey, Ph.D. Federally endowed in 1987, the Lister Hill Center has a University-wide mission to facilitate the conduct of health policy research, to disseminate the findings of that research beyond the usual channels of academic publication, and to sponsor the Lister Hill Health Policy Fellows program. The center draws on scholars from throughout the University to address issues of health-care access, financing, organization, delivery, and outcomes, with particular emphasis on prevention strategies. The center publishes UAB Health Policy Research, a precis of policy research for regional and national policymakers, and it sponsors an intramural grants program in health policy/health services research. Current areas of research include health-care markets and managed care, maternal and child health, management in public organizations, and health-care outcomes. Web site: http://lhcwww.soph.uab.edu

Sparkman Center for International Public Health Education

Acting Director: Charles B. Stephensen, Ph.D. Affiliated with the Department of International Health, the John J. Sparkman Center for International Public Health Education (SCIPHE) develops, provides, and promotes educational programs and related activities for public health professionals and researchers in developing countries. Current activities include projects in China, Jamaica, Peru, Bangladesh, Guatemala, Pakistan, Zambia, and Zimbabwe.

Center for Community Health Resource Development

Director: Linda W. Goodson, RN. Established in 1989, the center is a joint venture between the UAB Medical Center and the Alabama Cooperative Extension Service. Its mission is to promote and facilitate community-based organization and resource development for health promotion and disease prevention initiatives. The center serves as a mechanism by which the faculty in the School as well as the University can access the public and develop collaborative initiatives to conduct community-based research projects statewide. Faculty and staff members in the center participate in the academic preparation of students both in the School and throughout the University by serving as lecturers, coursemasters, and preceptors.

UNIVERSITY OF CALIFORNIA, LOS ANGELES

Graduate Programs in Environmental Health Sciences

Programs of Study

The Department of Environmental Health Sciences in the School of Public Health focuses its research and educational activities on the protection of human health from biological, chemical, and physical hazards in the environment. Environmental health sciences graduates are highly trained scientists and professionals capable of identifying and measuring agents of environmental concern; evaluating the health, environmental, and all other impacts of such agents; developing means for their effective management; and evaluating alternative policies directed at improving and protecting environments. Such training is accomplished through several degree programs that offer specialized study in selected academic areas of environmental health sciences such as air pollution, environmental chemistry, environmental management, environmental toxicology, ergonomics, industrial hygiene, and water quality. Graduates of the department pursue careers in the private or public sector as researchers, educators, managers, policy makers, and/or practitioners.

Multidisciplinary campus and community collaborations allow many community and field interactions that add richness to the educational experience. Students and faculty in epidemiology, behavioral sciences and health education, biostatistics, and international studies interact regularly with those in Environmental Health Sciences programs. Interactions at UCLA also exist with the Schools of Medicine, Nursing, Management, Architecture and Urban Planning, Law, and Engineering and Applied Sciences and with the College of Letters and Science. Collaborations include those with L.A. County Departments, regional agencies, state departments and boards, and federal agencies, as well as industry, labor, and consulting groups.

The department offers M.S. and Ph.D. degrees in environmental health sciences and, through the School of Public Health, M.P.H. and Dr.P.H. degrees with a specialization in environmental health sciences. In addition, a unique doctoral degree—the Doctor of Environmental Science and Engineering (D.Env.)—is offered by the interdepartmental Environmental Sciences and Engineering Program, which is administered through the department.

The UCLA School of Public Health is accredited by the Council on Education for Public Health, the Accrediting Commission on Education for Health Services, and the American Board of Preventive Medicine.

Research Facilities

UCLA has some of the finest library resources and computer facilities in the nation. The University libraries, in total, contain more than 6 million volumes and more than 95,000 serial publications. The School of Public Health Microcomputer Instructional Center and the Office of Academic Computing offer computer services with a variety of software to support faculty and students in teaching, learning, and research. In addition, a computer workstation for the visually impaired is located within the Microcomputer Instructional Center. The School has laboratory resources for the studies of air quality, environmental chemistry, ergonomics, industrial hygiene, toxicology, and water quality.

Financial Aid

Awards are based on either academic merit or financial need, but the two are not mutually exclusive. Students are strongly urged to apply in all categories for which they may qualify. Financial aid available to students includes specialized federal traineeships, Graduate Division fellowships and scholarships, Graduate Opportunity Program funding, nonresident tuition fee scholarship, research and teaching assistantships, and loans, grants, and work-study programs administered by the Financial Aid Office.

Cost of Study

The estimated fees for California residents in 1998–99 are $4502 per year; tuition and fees for nonresidents are $13,500 per year.

Living and Housing Costs

Cost for University resident fees, books and educational supplies, housing, food, transportation, and personal items for the nine-month academic year are estimated to be between $17,000 and $20,000 for single students and between $19,000 and $22,000 for married students. For more information about housing, students should contact the UCLA Community Housing Office, 350 De Neve Drive, Los Angeles, California 90095 (telephone: 310-825-4491).

Student Group

There are about 23,620 undergraduate and 11,500 graduate students at UCLA. Each year, the department enrolls 30–40 new students at the master's and doctoral levels. Nineteen percent of the student body received their previous degrees from other countries, 67 percent received their previous degree from an institution in California, and 33 percent received their previous degree outside California.

Location

UCLA is located in the foothills of the Santa Monica Mountains and is just five miles inland from the ocean in one of the most attractive areas of southern California. The many diverse cultural and recreational opportunities in the region are within easy reach, and the University itself is a vigorous community center.

The University

UCLA, established in 1919, is academically ranked among the leading universities in the United States and has attracted distinguished scholars and researchers from all over the world. Undergraduate and graduate programs offered in the colleges and schools cover the academic spectrum. UCLA has also developed research programs and curricula outside the usual departmental structures. Interdisciplinary research facilities include institutes, centers, projects, bureaus, nondepartmental laboratories, stations, and museums. The University's Center for the Health Sciences contains one of the nation's leading hospitals and several nationally known institutes. UCLA's performing arts program of music, dance, theater, film, and lectures is one of the largest and most diverse offered by any university in the country.

Applying

Descriptive brochures and applications for the department may be obtained by writing to the Student Affairs Officer, Department of Environmental Health Sciences, Los Angeles, California 90095-1772.

The GRE General Test is required. TOEFL scores are required for international applicants whose native language is not English. The preferred deadline for graduate application is December 15 for fall quarter admission. Applications received after the deadline have considerably reduced opportunities for admission and financial aid.

Correspondence and Information

Student Affairs Officer
Box 951772
Department of Environmental Health Sciences
School of Public Health
University of California, Los Angeles
Los Angeles, California 90095-1772
Telephone: 310-206-1619

University of California, Los Angeles

THE FACULTY AND THEIR RESEARCH

Richard F. Ambrose, Associate Professor; Ph.D., UCLA, 1982. Ecology, marine biology, and environmental science and engineering.
Michael D. Collins, Associate Professor; Ph.D., Missouri–Columbia, 1982. Toxicology, molecular toxicology.
Climis A. Davos, Professor; Ph.D., Michigan, 1974. Environmental economics, planning, policy and management.
L. Donald Duke, Assistant Professor; Ph.D., Stanford, 1992. Environmental management, environmental science and engineering.
Curtis D. Eckhert, Professor; Ph.D., Cornell, 1974. Biochemistry, molecular biology, toxicology.
John R. Froines, Professor; Ph.D., Yale, 1967. Toxicology, industrial hygiene, risk assessment, pollution prevention, environmental policy.
Philip Harber, Professor; M.D., Pennsylvania, 1972, M.P.H., Johns Hopkins, 1980. Occupational medicine.
William C. Hinds, Professor; Ph.D., Harvard, 1972. Industrial hygiene, aerosol science.
Wen Chen Victor Liu, Assistant Professor In-Residence; Ph.D., UCLA, 1986. Ergonomics, industrial hygiene.
Robert Mah, Emeritus; Ph.D., California, Davis, 1963. Environmental microbiology, water quality.
Mario Panaqua, Lecturer; M.S., California State, Los Angeles, 1972. Analytical measurements.
Diane M. Perry, Assistant Field Program Supervisor; Ph.D., USC, 1983. Ecology, environmental management.
Shane S. Que Hee, Professor; Ph.D., Saskatchewan, 1976. Industrial hygiene, environmental chemistry.
Irwin H. (Mel) Suffet, Professor; Ph.D., Rutgers, 1968. Aquatic chemistry, environmental science and engineering.
Jane L. Valentine, Associate Professor; Ph.D., Texas, 1973. Water quality, environmental health.
Arthur M. Winer, Professor and Director of Environmental Science and Engineering; Ph.D., Ohio State, 1969. Air pollution, environmental science and engineering.

UNIVERSITY OF CINCINNATI

College of Medicine
Department of Environmental Health

Programs of Study

The Department of Environmental Health at the University of Cincinnati is a basic science and clinical department within the College of Medicine. The department emphasizes research on the causal relationship between environmental hazards, human health, and man's ecosystem so that adverse effects may be prevented or controlled. Several programs are offered leading to the M.S. and Ph.D. degrees: epidemiology and biostatistics, environmental and industrial hygiene, occupational safety and ergonomics, occupational medicine, and toxicology. In general, the master's degree requires two years of study beyond the bachelor's degree with the completion of a thesis. The doctoral degree requires four to five years of study beyond the bachelor's degree with the completion of a dissertation that demonstrates the ability to conduct independent research.

The epidemiology program examines physical, chemical, and/or social and psychological associations with disease occurrence and prevention in human populations. There are three focus areas in the program: occupational and environmental, quantitative, and genetic/molecular epidemiology. Soon after arrival, the student becomes engaged in epidemiology research with a faculty adviser. Applied biostatistical methodology is the main focus of the applied biostatistics program. The curriculum for both programs covers the many facets of data collection, analysis, and interpretation of results that relate to environmental and biomedical health research.

The environmental and industrial hygiene and occupational safety and ergonomics programs offer both M.S. and Ph.D. degrees. The M.S. in environmental and industrial hygiene program also has a focus area in hazardous substances academic training as well as other areas of emphasis such as biological monitoring, aerosol measurement, exposure assessment, and worker training. These programs include training in the recognition, identification, evaluation, and control of chemical, biological, and physical factors that may affect health and safety. The M.S. programs take about two years to complete and include a thesis requirement. The Ph.D. programs require between four and five years for completion.

The M.S. program in environmental and industrial hygiene is accredited by the Related Accreditation Commission of the Accreditation Board for Engineering Technology through a program created by the American Academy of Industrial Hygiene.

The occupational medicine program is a clinical and research training program for physicians concerned with the sources, diagnosis, prevention, and treatment of diseases and injuries resulting from exposure to chemical and physical agents, products, or processes at work or within the community. The two-year residency program can lead to certification by the American Board of Preventive Medicine in Occupational Medicine.

The occupational medicine, environmental and industrial hygiene, and occupational safety and ergonomics programs are part of the Education and Research Center supported by the National Institute for Occupational Safety and Health, which also includes programs in occupational health nursing (College of Nursing and Health) and occupational safety (College of Engineering).

The toxicology program is designed to enable students to investigate toxic effects and the mechanisms by which they are produced, develop new methods for the quantitative evaluation of exposure and toxicity, and assess risks of exposure. Areas of research expertise include genetic toxicology, ecogenetics, signal transduction, effects of heavy metals, biotransformation of xenobiotics, and pulmonary toxicology.

Research Facilities

Research and teaching activities are housed primarily at the Medical Center in the Kettering Laboratory and Medical Sciences Building. Among the major research facilities are laboratories for molecular biology, carcinogenesis, inhalation exposure, clinical studies, biomechanics, aerosol science, and analytical instrumentation. Department faculty members collaborate with faculty members from other departments in the Colleges of Medicine and Engineering and from the Departments of Biology, Chemistry, and Mathematics in the College of Arts and Sciences. Cooperative research and training occur with the nearby labs of the National Institute for Occupational Safety and Health and the Environmental Protection Agency.

Financial Aid

Tuition remission and stipend support are available for many full-time students.

Cost of Study

For graduate students enrolled in the Department of Environmental Health, tuition and fees for the year were $7224 for Ohio residents and $13,808 for nonresidents in 1997–98.

Living and Housing Costs

According to national surveys, the cost of living in Cincinnati is below the average for large American cities. Suitable apartments within easy commuting distance of the University rent for $250 and up per month. Some University housing is available for both married and single students.

Student Group

The University has a total student body of approximately 36,000 with about 6,000 enrolled in the Graduate School. In the department there are about 150 full- and part-time students. The departmental Graduate Student Association and the 1,200-member Kettering Fellows alumni group are both active organizations.

Location

Cincinnati provides cultural and entertainment opportunities. Its symphony orchestra, May Festival, summer opera, and College Conservatory of Music are well known. The Playhouse in the Park is a theater with a national reputation. Professional baseball, football, and University sporting events are well attended.

The University

Founded in 1819, the University is a member of the Ohio State University System. It was in Cincinnati in 1906 that the first co-op training program started in the College of Engineering. The University Centers of Environmental Genetics, Risk Assessment, Groundwater Research, Aerosol Processes, and Hazardous Waste Research have faculty from the Colleges of Arts and Sciences, Engineering, and Medicine, with major input of faculty from the Department of Environmental Health. The University is an Equal Opportunity/Affirmative Action employer.

Applying

Application materials and credentials should be submitted as early as possible, preferably before February 15, for fall admission. The GRE General Test is required. Applicants should have a strong undergraduate background in one of the sciences and a year of study in three of the following: biology, chemistry, calculus, engineering, and physics. Students with a baccalaureate or a master's degree in one of the basic biological, chemical, physical, or engineering sciences may qualify for advanced standing in one of the Ph.D. programs.

Correspondence and Information

Graduate Studies
Department of Environmental Health
College of Medicine
University of Cincinnati
P.O. Box 670056
Cincinnati, Ohio 45267-0056

Telephone: 513-558-5704
E-mail: jean.malone@uc.edu

University of Cincinnati

THE FACULTY AND THEIR RESEARCH

Marshall W. Anderson, Professor of Environmental Health and Chairman of the Department; Ph.D., Tennessee, 1966. Molecular genetics of cancer and environmental carcinogenesis.

Professors

Roy E. Albert, M.D., NYU, 1946. Carcinogenic mechanisms in relation to dose-response and risk assessment.
Howard E. Ayer, Professor Emeritus; M.S., Harvard, 1955. Occupational safety and industrial hygiene.
Amit Bhattacharya, Ph.D., Kentucky, 1975. Occupational biomechanics-ergonomics, stress physiology, physical factors, noninvasive methods.
Eula Bingham, Ph.D., Cincinnati, 1958. Risk assessment.
Robert L. Bornschein, Ph.D., Louisville, 1973. Characterization of in utero and early postnatal exposures to environmental agents and their influence on child development.
C. Ralph Buncher, Sc.D., Harvard, 1967. Biostatistics, especially as applied in clinical trials.
C. Scott Clark, Ph.D., Johns Hopkins, 1965. Environmental and industrial hygiene exposure assessment and intervention studies.
Ernest C. Foulkes, D.Phil., Oxford, 1952. Renal physiology, heavy-metal toxicology.
Grace Lemasters, Ph.D., Cincinnati, 1983. Epidemiological studies of man-made mineral fibers, adverse reproductive outcomes from solvent exposure.
James E. Lockey, M.D., Temple, 1972. Research group–population studies of various types of man-made mineral fibers: hypersensitivity pneumonitis, acute and chronic berylliosis, reproductive studies and solvent exposure.
John C. Loper, Professor of Microbiology and Environmental Health; Ph.D., Johns Hopkins, 1960. Microbial genetics, mutagenesis.
Daniel W. Nebert, M.D., Oregon, 1964. Molecular mechanisms regulating expression of eukaryotic genes and gene batteries, use of molecular biological techniques in the study of perturbation of gene expression by toxic chemicals.
Bernard E. Saltzman, Professor Emeritus; Ph.D., Cincinnati, 1958. Industrial hygiene chemistry and exposure modeling.
Pasquale S. Scarpino, Professor of Civil and Environmental Engineering and Environmental Health; Ph.D., Rutgers, 1961. Aquatic microbiology, microbial utilization of solid wastes; bacterial and viral air pollution; toxins.
Richard L. Shell, Professor of Industrial Engineering and Environmental Health; Ph.D., Illinois, 1970. Manufacturing safety; human performance; management.
Raymond R. Suskind, Professor Emeritus; M.D., SUNY Downstate Medical Center, 1943. Absorption and metabolism of phenoxy herbicides and their contaminants, mechanisms of cutaneous responses to chemical irritants and antigenic stimuli.
M. Wilson Tabor, Ph.D., Cincinnati, 1974. Environmental chemistry and biochemical toxicology of xenobiotics and metals, including persistence, fate and transport, and interindividual differences in their metabolism.
David Warshawsky, Ph.D., Cincinnati, 1972. Chemical carcinogenesis, mechanisms of action of carcinogens, chemical and physical binding to DNA metabolism.
Klaus Willeke, Ph.D., Stanford, 1969. Aerosol science and technology; applications of aerosol generation, sampling, and analysis methods to industrial hygiene, air pollution, and toxicology.

Associate Professors

C. Stuart Baxter, Ph.D., London, 1970. Carcinogenesis and mutagenesis; mechanisms of action of carcinogens, mutagens, and tumor-promoting agents in vivo and in vitro.
Ranjan Deka, Ph.D., Dibrugarh (India), 1976. Genetic epidemiology.
Kim Dietrich, Ph.D., Wayne State, 1981. Influence of fetal and postnatal exposure to toxic compounds on neonatal neurological status and development.
Kathleen Dixon, Ph.D., Rochester, 1970. Use of plasmid shuttle vectors and in vitro DNA replication systems to elucidate mechanisms of DNA damage processing by mammalian cells.
Peter S. Gartside, Ph.D., UCLA, 1973. Epidemiological studies of human health and the environment.
Sergey Grinshpun, Ph.D., Odessa, 1987. Aerosol science.
George Leikauf, Ph.D., NYU, 1981. Pulmonary-airway epithelium response to inhaled pollutants, modulatory roles of inflammatory mediators in stimulus-secretion coupling.
Douglas Linz, M.D., Michigan, 1977. Chemical neurotoxicology and cross-sectional epidemiological studies in the workplace.
Marian L. Miller, Ph.D., Cincinnati, 1971. Microscopic observation of tissues exposed to toxic materials.
Ellen J. O'Flaherty, Associate Professor Emeritus; Ph.D., Yale, 1964. Interrelationships among applied dose, toxicokinetic measures of internal or effective dose, and magnitude of effects.
Alvaro Puga, Ph.D., Purdue, 1972. Gene regulation in eukaryotes with emphasis on transcriptional control of cytochrome P-450 gene expression, biological effects of dioxins and oxygen radical metabolism.
Tiina Reponen, Ph.D., Kuopio (Finland), 1994. Physical and microbiological aspects of indoor air research; fungal spores and bacteria in homes and offices; filter performance with bioaerosols.
Carol Rice, Ph.D., North Carolina at Chapel Hill, 1983. Reconstruction of working-lifetime exposures to industrial toxins to evaluate association between exposure and development of disease.
Howard G. Shertzer, Ph.D., UCLA, 1973. Biotransformation and mutagenicity; aspects of drug metabolism, especially as related to mechanisms of toxicity, mutagenesis, and chemoprotection.
Rakesh Shukla, Ph.D., Ohio State, 1983. Combination of applied and theoretical biostatistics, particularly in the area of longitudinal data analysis.
Glenn Talaska, Ph.D., Texas Medical Branch, 1986. Development of methods to monitor carcinogen-DNA adducts in target organs.

Assistant Professors

M. Kathryn Brown, Ph.D., Cincinnati, 1994. Environmental epidemiology, environmental equity and public policy, geographic information systems, ecogenetics, health effects of occupational radiation and chemical exposures.
Michael P. Carty, Ph.D., University College, Galway (Ireland), 1986. Mutagenesis, molecular biology.
Andrew Freeman, M.D., California, San Diego, 1986. Hypersensitivy pneumonitis, medical clearance for respirator use, disability management, ergonomics, biomonitoring of cyanide.
Linda Levin Ph.D., Cincinnati, 1996. Longitudinal data analysis and measurement error in exposure estimation.
Roy McKay, Ph.D., Cincinnati, 1982. Pulmonary toxicology.
Susan M. Pinney, Ph.D., Cincinnati, 1990. Environmental and occupational epidemiology.
Paul Succop, Ph.D., SUNY at Buffalo, 1988. Multivariate analysis, structural equations, covariance structure analysis.
Jonathan S. Wiest, Ph.D., Medical College of Ohio, 1988. Tumorigenesis of lung cancer, the genetic alterations that occur in tumors and genetic susceptibility to lung cancer.

Field Service Faculty

Judy L. Jarrell, Field Service Associate Professor; Ed.D., Cincinnati, 1994. Continuing education.
Koka Jayasimhulu, Field Service Associate Professor; Ph.D., Cincinnati, 1976. Bioanalytical chemistry, biochemistry, mass spectrometry.
Jozef Svetlik, Field Service Assistant Professor Emeritus; B.S., Cincinnati, 1972. Industrial hygiene, respirator fit testing.

UNIVERSITY OF COLORADO HEALTH SCIENCES CENTER

Department of Preventive Medicine and Biometrics Master of Science Program in Public Health

Program of Study

The degree program leading to the Master of Science in Public Health (M.S.P.H.) is intended to provide graduate-level training that introduces students to the core content areas of public health. Specific program emphases include epidemiological research, community needs assessment, public health practice and ethics, environmental and occupational health, and health policy. The program's goals are to provide education for students in the core content and methodological areas of public health (epidemiology, biostatistics, health-care systems, occupational and environmental health, and social and community factors in health); to prepare students for practical application of acquired skills and knowledge to public and community health research, community needs assessment, and program planning and evaluation; to direct students to relevant elective course work and help them to apply all areas of program learning experiences to their individual interests and activities in the health field; to give students an opportunity to demonstrate an integration of acquired skills and knowledge, as well as an ability to organize, synthesize, and communicate these skills orally and in writing, through preparation and defense of a publishable research paper or a thesis; and to enrich graduate medical education programs and continuing education for public health professionals. The program would be of interest to those working or expecting to work in academic or clinical settings, industry, or government health agencies. The program is accredited by the Council on Education for Public Health.

The program includes a core of required courses and a choice of electives that enable the student, in consultation with a faculty adviser, to plan an individual course of study that is responsive to the student's needs and interests. Electives may include departmental offerings as well as a broad range of course offerings in other programs of the Health Sciences Center and on the Boulder and Denver campuses of the University. Independent study may be organized with departmental faculty and through a variety of health agencies with which the department enjoys excellent working relationships. Completion of the degree program requires 50 quarter hours, including 6 hours toward a research project resulting in either a thesis or publishable research paper. Both full- and part-time study is encouraged. Full-time students normally graduate in about two years. Part-time students are allowed up to four years to complete the program. The program is committed to maintaining the high quality of faculty-student interactions and thus will remain relatively small, admitting approximately 25 new students each year.

Research Facilities

The department houses a computer-user room, with personal computers and appropriate analytical software, which is available to students and faculty in the department. The Dennison Memorial Library serves the Health Sciences Center and contains more than 240,000 volumes and 1,900 periodicals. Research opportunities are available both through research projects directed by faculty members and through arrangements with the Colorado Department of Health, county health departments, and community health agencies.

Financial Aid

The department grants a limited number of assistantships through funds available from the Graduate School. Research stipends are also available. Other aid is available through the Office of Financial Aid, to which application can be made only after a student has been admitted to the program. Funds include Federal Perkins Loans and Colorado Graduate Loans. Inquiries regarding financial aid should be addressed to: Office of Financial Aid, UCHSC, 4200 East Ninth Avenue, Box A-088 (telephone: 303-315-8364).

Cost of Study

The tuition for the 1998–99 academic year is $120 per credit hour for Colorado residents and $318 per credit hour for nonresidents. In addition, approximately $1421 is needed for the activity fees, medical insurance, and health-service insurance.

Living and Housing Costs

There is no on-campus housing, but there is an ample supply of apartments, duplexes, and houses in the Denver metropolitan area. Many of these accommodations are within walking distance of the Health Sciences Center and are usually available for immediate occupancy. Average monthly rents for unfurnished housing near campus are $380 for one-bedroom apartments and $575 for two-bedroom apartments. Houses rent for $800 and up per month. Total monthly expenses, including costs of food and moderate entertainment, are estimated at $800 for a single student and $1000 for a couple.

Student Group

Approximately 70 students are currently enrolled in the Master of Science in Public Health program. They have a very broad range of experiences and career goals. Eighty percent are women, and about 20 percent are physicians.

Student Outcomes

A survey conducted in August 1995, with responses representing 50 percent of the total MSPH alumni, indicated that 72 percent of the respondents are currently working in the public health field. The majority of respondents indicated that they are currently working for a state government or in an academic setting. The largest number of respondents (22 percent) described their current position as epidemiological research.

Location

The Health Sciences Center is located in a medical/public health complex approximately 3 miles from downtown Denver and the Colorado state capitol. Denver, with a population of 3 million in the metropolitan area, is located at the foot of the Rocky Mountains. It offers all the cultural, recreational, athletic, and economic opportunities to be found in a major city.

The Center and The Department

The Health Sciences Center is one of the two Denver campuses of the University of Colorado; the University also has a campus in Boulder and one in Colorado Springs. UCHSC includes the dental, medical, pharmacy, and nursing schools, University Hospital, and the graduate programs of the departments in the various schools.

The Department of Preventive Medicine and Biometrics has a multidisciplinary faculty actively involved in medical and graduate education, residency training, research, and service to the public health community and to the medical community at large. Faculty research interests include chronic disease epidemiology, perinatal epidemiology, injury epidemiology, medical care evaluation, health policy, medical ethics, preventive health care, environmental epidemiology, and biostatistics.

Applying

Application materials, which describe the admission requirements in detail, are available from the program office. A baccalaureate degree is required as a minimum. GRE General Test scores or the equivalent are required of all applicants. A brief statement describing the applicant's career goals and reasons for applying to the program is also expected. Interviews with faculty members are highly recommended. All application materials must be received by February 1 for entry in either the summer or fall quarter.

Correspondence and Information

Director
Master of Science in Public Health Program
University of Colorado Health Sciences Center
4200 East Ninth Avenue, Box C-245
Denver, Colorado 80262
Telephone: 303-315-8357

University of Colorado Health Sciences Center

THE FACULTY AND THEIR RESEARCH

Anna E. Barón, Associate Professor; Ph.D., Texas, 1984. Biostatistics, epidemiology, discriminate analysis, survival analysis.
Phoebe Lindsey Barton, Associate Professor and Director of MSPH Program; Ph.D., UCLA, 1987. Health policy, health financing, Medicaid, AIDS.
Judith Baxter, Senior Instructor; M.A., Denver, 1981. Demography, diabetes epidemiology.
Tim Byers, Professor; M.D., M.P.H., Indiana, 1973. Cancer epidemiology.
Lori Crane, Assistant Professor; Ph.D., UCLA, 1991. Behavioral science and cancer.
Judith Glazner, Senior Instructor; M.S.B.A., Denver, 1968. Indigent health care, health-care policy.
Richard F. Hamman, Chairman and Professor; M.D., Case Western Reserve, 1972; Dr.P.H., Johns Hopkins, 1978. Chronic disease epidemiology, environmental radiation, epidemiologic methods, clinical trials.
Laurel Harken, Assistant Professor; M.D., 1969, M.P.H., 1972, Harvard. Pediatric epidemiology, child abuse, developmental disabilities, substance abuse.
Richard H. Jones, Professor and Section Head; Ph.D., Brown, 1961. Time-series analysis, repeated measures analysis.
Dennis C. Lezotte, Associate Professor; Ph.D., SUNY at Buffalo, 1975; Multivariate statistical techniques for clinical laboratory data, decision support systems.
William M. Marine, Professor and Director of General Preventive Medicine Residency Program; M.D., Emory, 1957; M.P.H., Michigan, 1963. Occupational epidemiology, injury epidemiology.
Julie A. Marshall, Assistant Professor; Ph.D., Washington (Seattle), 1987. Epidemiologic methods, diabetes epidemiology, disease etiology, nutrition.
James R. Murphy, Associate Professor; Ph.D., Johns Hopkins, 1977. Clinical trials, nonlinear models of growth curve functions.
Bernard Nelson, Professor; M.D., Stanford, 1961. Health policy.
Jill Norris, Assistant Professor; Ph.D., Pennsylvania, 1990. Diabetes epidemiology, nutrition.
Marian Rewers, Assistant Professor; M.D., 1981, Ph.D., 1986, Poznan (Poland). Pediatrics, diabetes epidemiology.
A. James Ruttenber, Associate Professor; M.D./Ph.D., Emory, 1981. Occupational and environmental health, risk assessment, environmental epidemiology, drug abuse epidemiology.
Mark Yarborough, Assistant Professor Adjoint; Ph.D., Tennessee, 1984. Biomedical ethics.
David Young, Assistant Professor; Ph.D., Colorado Health Sciences Center, 1992. Linear and nonlinear mixed effect models, genetic linkage.
Gary O. Zerbe, Professor; Ph.D., Ohio State, 1973. Growth curve analysis, applied multivariate analysis.

Selected Affiliated and Clinical Faculty

Ned Calonge, Assistant Professor; M.D., Colorado Health Sciences Center, 1981; M.P.H., Washington (Seattle), 1986. Family medicine.
Peter Dawson, Assistant Clinical Professor; M.D., Western Reserve, 1965; M.P.H., North Carolina, 1970. Maternal and child health.
Arthur J. Davidson, Assistant Professor; M.D., Einstein (Yeshiva), 1979; M.S.P.H., Colorado Health Sciences Center, 1988. Communicable disease epidemiology, community health.
Richard Hoffman, Assistant Clinical Professor and State Epidemiologist, Colorado Department of Health; M.D., Texas, 1975; M.P.H., Johns Hopkins, 1983.
Lynn Mason, Assistant Professor; Ph.D., UCLA, 1972. Medical anthropology.
Dann Milne, Assistant Clinical Professor; Ph.D., Texas, 1975. Health economics.
John A. Sbarbaro, Professor; M.D., Johns Hopkins, 1962; M.P.H., Harvard, 1968. Health services management.
John Steiner, Assistant Professor; M.D., Pennsylvania, 1982; M.P.H., Washington (Seattle), 1987. Internal medicine, preventive medicine.

UNIVERSITY OF MEDICINE AND DENTISTRY OF NEW JERSEY/RUTGERS, THE STATE UNIVERSITY OF NEW JERSEY, NEW BRUNSWICK

New Jersey Graduate Program in Public Health

Program of Study

The New Jersey Graduate Program in Public Health offers the Master of Public Health (M.P.H.), Doctor of Public Health (Dr.P.H.), and Doctor of Philosophy (Ph.D.) degrees, conferred jointly by the University of Medicine and Dentistry of New Jersey–Robert Wood Johnson Medical School (UMDNJ–RWJMS) and Rutgers, The State University of New Jersey. The master's degree program requires 45 credit hours. Full-time students may complete the program within two years. Part-time students may take from three to four years. The curriculum requirements include core courses (15 hours), specialty tracks (12–18 hours), electives (5–11 hours), and fieldwork (6 hours). The required core courses include biostatistics-biocomputing, environmental health, epidemiology, health-care organization and administration, and health education and behavioral science. Specialty tracks are offered in environmental-occupational health, epidemiology and quantitative methods, family health, health-care organization and administration, and health education–behavioral science. Electives may be chosen from the wide variety of courses offered within the program and by the various colleges at Rutgers University. Fieldwork is required of all students. The doctoral degree programs require 72 credit hours for completion. Candidates for either doctoral degree are required to complete comprehensive written and oral examinations in major and minor areas and complete and defend original dissertation research. The Dr.P.H. and the Ph.D. in public health differ somewhat in emphasis and requirements. In most cases, Dr.P.H. candidates enter with an M.P.H. degree or fulfill the qualifications for that degree during their course of study (including an internship). Ph.D. candidates may enter with a master's-level degree in a relevant discipline and have the option of completing the M.P.H. requirements prior to fulfilling the core requirements for the Ph.D. degree. Currently, the Ph.D. is offered in environmental-occupational health, epidemiology and quantitative methods, and health education–behavioral science and the Dr.P.H. in environmental-occupational health and health education–behavioral science. A joint M.D./M.P.H. program is available within the New Jersey Graduate Program in Public Health that allows students to complete both the M.P.H. and M.D. degrees in four or five years. Application is restricted to students who have already been admitted to UMDNJ–RWJMS. A special program for M.D.'s is also available for those students who stay at UMDNJ–RWJMS for their residency training without adding a year to their formal training or taking time out of their careers. An M.B.A./M.P.H. is also offered with the School of Management at Rutgers University, and an executive M.S. in health management is slated for fall 1998.

Research Facilities

Research facilities at the two universities are extensive. The Rutgers University Library of Science and Medicine, which serves UMDNJ–RWJMS, is conveniently located in an adjacent building. The library's broad collections now number almost 400,000 books and periodical volumes. Periodical holdings are particularly strong in older journals, but currently published journals are well represented. Interlibrary loans, MEDLINE searches, and access to other materials and services beyond the library can be arranged through the reference department. Students have access to the computing facilities at the Rutgers University Hill Center, including the Center for Computer and Information Services, as well as the data processing capabilities located in the Department of Environmental and Community Medicine. UMDNJ–RWJMS and Rutgers are situated on adjoining campuses, and an extensive bus system permits easy movement among the various facilities.

Financial Aid

In 1997–98, full-time teaching assistantships provided annual stipends of $10,600 plus remission of tuition. Financial aid includes the Federal Perkins Loan Program and the Federal Stafford Student Loan Program. The program currently receives limited traineeship funds from the U.S. Public Health Service to support new students in biostatistics, epidemiology, and environmental health. These funds will be used for tuition remission and will be awarded on the basis of past academic performance, with preference going to full-time students.

Cost of Study

Tuition was $249 per credit hour for the 1997–98 academic year for New Jersey residents. Tuition for out-of-state students was $366 per credit for the 1997–98 academic year. There is an $85.50 registration fee.

Living and Housing Costs

National cost-of-living indices place the New Brunswick area at about the median. A housing office located in the UMDNJ–RWJMS Office of Student Affairs maintains a list of housing in nearby communities, where relatively inexpensive accommodations are available in residences easily accessible to the University.

Student Group

There are 260 full-time and part-time students in the program. This number includes students currently employed in the health field (i.e., dentists, nurses, physicians, and environmental scientists), as well as students who recently received their bachelor's degree and those who are pursuing a dual degree in conjunction with other programs offered at Rutgers University.

Location

New Brunswick, situated in central New Jersey, has a population of nearly 45,000. It has many community health agencies available to students for project work and practicum experiences. New Brunswick is the home of Johnson & Johnson, AT&T, Colgate Palmolive, Revlon, and other technically oriented companies. New Brunswick is within a half-hour drive of New York City, the New Jersey shore, or the rural countryside.

The Universities

Chartered as Queens College in 1776, Rutgers was the eighth institution of higher education to be founded in Colonial America. In 1825, its name was changed to Rutgers College. A graduate faculty was organized in 1932, and the Graduate School was formally established in 1952. The Robert Wood Johnson Medical School (formerly Rutgers Medical School) was founded in 1970 as part of the College of Medicine and Dentistry of New Jersey. The College evolved into the University of Medicine and Dentistry of New Jersey in 1984. The New Jersey Graduate Program in Public Health is conducted on the New Brunswick and Piscataway campuses of the universities.

Applying

A bachelor's degree with at least a B average in academic work is required for admission to the M.P.H. program. Selection is made on the basis of previous academic work, letters of recommendation, and scores on the GRE General Test. A master's degree in a relevant field is required to enter either the Dr.P.H. or the Ph.D. program. In addition, sponsorship, evidenced by a letter of support from the New Jersey Graduate Program in Public Health faculty, is required prior to application. This letter of support is in addition to GRE scores and three letters of recommendation, of which at least two must be from people who have known the candidate in an academic setting. With regard to all the programs of study, TOEFL scores are required of students from countries in which English is not the native language. Applicants for the fall term must submit materials prior to March 15; November 1 is the application deadline for spring.

Correspondence and Information

Director, New Jersey Graduate Program in Public Health
University of Medicine and Dentistry of New Jersey–Robert Wood Johnson Medical School
Environmental and Occupational Health Sciences Institute
170 Frelinghuysen Road, Room 236
Piscataway, New Jersey 08855-1179

Telephone: 732-445-0199
Fax: 732-445-0917
E-mail: mclanejm@umdnj.edu
World Wide Web: http://eohsi.rutgers.edu

University of Medicine and Dentistry of New Jersey/Rutgers, New Brunswick

THE FACULTY AND THEIR RESEARCH

UMDNJ–Robert Wood Johnson Medical School

Daria M. Boccher-Lattimore, Assistant Professor of Family Medicine; M.P.H., 1985, Dr.P.H., 1996, Columbia. HIV prevention and adolescents, health behavior, health services for the undeserved.

Mary B. Breckenridge, Professor of Family Medicine; Ph.D., Princeton, 1976. Medical demography, vulnerable populations, health-care utilization and outcomes assessment.

Ronald Cody, Associate Professor of Environmental and Community Medicine; Ed.D., Rutgers, 1973. Statistical research design.

Michael A. Gallo, Professor of Environmental and Community Medicine, Director of NIEHS Center of Excellence, Associate Director of Cancer Institute of New Jersey; Ph.D., Albany Medical College, 1972. Metabolism of xenobiotics, hormone carcinogenesis, risk assessment.

Michael Gochfeld, Clinical Professor of Environmental and Community Medicine; M.D., Yeshiva (Einstein), 1965; Ph.D., CUNY Graduate Center, 1975. Medical surveillance, biomonitoring of workers, and communities exposed to hazardous wastes; environmental and ecological risk assessment.

Bernard D. Goldstein, Director of Environmental and Occupational Health Sciences Institute and Professor and Chairman of Environmental and Community Medicine; M.D., NYU, 1962. Toxicity of oxidant air pollutants and benzene, environmental health policy, community risk assessment.

Audrey R. Gotsch, Professor of Environmental and Community Medicine, Chief of Division of Consumer Health Education, and Director of Division of Public Education and Risk Communication at the Environmental and Occupational Health Sciences Institute; Dr.P.H., Columbia, 1976. Attitudes and practices of consumers, health professionals, evaluating the training needs of special target groups, compliance, health promotion strategies.

Lois Grau, Associate Professor of Clinical Environmental and Community Medicine and Director of the Health Care Organization and Administration Track, New Jersey Graduate Program in Public Health; Ph.D., Wisconsin–Milwaukee, 1979; RN. Long-term care and gerontology with a focus on patient-provider satisfaction and service utilization issues.

Patrice Gregory, Assistant Professor of Family Medicine; Ph.D., University of Medicine and Dentistry of New Jersey–Robert Wood Johnson Medical School/Rutgers, 1996; M.P.H., Columbia, 1981. Use of health services among special groups such as minority, elderly, maternal, and infant.

Bob Hamer, Associate Professor of Psychiatry; Ph.D., North Carolina at Chapel Hill. Biostatistics, psychiatry, clinical trials.

Jeffrey S. Hammond, Professor of Surgery; M.D., 1975, M.P.H., 1995, Miami (Florida). Injury epidemiology, violence prevention, trauma systems.

David Howarth, Associate Professor of Family Medicine; M.D., St. George's (West Indies), 1983; M.P.H., University of Medicine and Dentistry of New Jersey–Robert Wood Johnson Medical School/Rutgers, 1987. Geriatrics: home care, advanced directives, and dementia.

Howard M. Kipen, Associate Professor of Environmental and Community Medicine and Director of Occupational Medicine; M.D., California, San Francisco, 1979; M.P.H., Columbia, 1983. Clinical epidemiologic studies of occupational asthma, disease diagnosis; chemical sensitivity.

Jane Lewis, Assistant Professor of Environmental and Community Medicine; Dr.P.H., Texas. Planning, implementation, and promotion of programs; development of educational materials; and evaluation research.

Donald W. Light, Professor of Psychiatry, School of Osteopathic Medicine; Ph.D., Brandeis, 1980. Comparative health-care systems and the transformation of the American health-care system.

Robert C. Like, Associate Professor of Family Medicine; M.D., Harvard, 1979; M.S., Case Western Reserve, 1984. Clinically applied anthropology, chronic disabilities, primary-care health services research.

Paul J. Lioy, Professor of Environmental and Community Medicine, Chief of Division of Exposure Measurement and Assessment, and Director of Division of Human Exposure at the Environmental and Occupational Health Sciences Institute; Ph.D., Rutgers, 1975. Human exposure to toxic substances from single and multiple media, health effects of ozone and hazardous wastes.

Laura Micek-Galinat, Associate Professor of Clinical Family Medicine; M.D., University of Medicine and Dentistry of New Jersey, 1983; M.P.H., University of Medicine and Dentistry of New Jersey–Robert Wood Johnson Medical School/Rutgers, 1987. Disease prevention and health promotion, women's health issues, medical education.

Sandra Mohr, Assistant Professor; M.D., Kansas, 1983; M.P.H., Yale, 1994. Following occupational cohorts for ergonomic problems, particularly carpal tunnel syndrome; reactive airways disease and other lung problems due to chemical inhalation.

George G. Rhoads, Professor of Environmental and Community Medicine and Director of New Jersey Graduate Program in Public Health; M.D., Harvard, 1965; M.P.H., Hawaii, 1970. Epidemiology of perinatal, environmental, and noninfectious health problems.

Marian R. Stuart, Clinical Professor of Family Medicine; M.S., 1973, Ph.D., 1975, Rutgers. Doctor/patient relationship, mind/body medicine, attitude.

David E. Swee, Professor and Chairman of Family Medicine; M.D., Dalhousie, 1975. Managed care, prevention, medical education, ethics.

Alfred F. Tallia, Associate Professor and Vice Chair, Family Medicine; M.D., University of Medicine and Dentistry of New Jersey–Robert Wood Johnson Medical School/Rutgers, 1978; M.P.H., University of Medicine and Dentistry of New Jersey–Robert Wood Johnson Medical School/Rutgers, 1988. Graduate medical education, health-care utilization, outcome assessment.

Lynn Waishwell, Assistant Professor of Environmental and Community Medicine; Ph.D., Southern Illinois at Carbondale; M.H.E., Florida. Multicultural issues in health education, models of health behavior, qualitative research methods, community health issues; drugs, environmental education.

Daniel Wartenberg, Associate Professor of Environmental and Community Medicine; Ph.D., SUNY at Stony Brook, 1984. Epidemiologic methods.

Clifford Weisel, Associate Professor of Environmental and Community Medicine, Division of Exposure Measurement and Assessment; Ph.D., Rhode Island, 1981. Human exposure to organic compounds and trace metals.

Bernadette M. West, Adjunct Assistant Professor; M.A., American, 1981; Ph.D., Rutgers, 1992. Community health assessment.

Nicholas Wright, Associate Professor of Environmental and Community Medicine; M.D., NYU, 1961; M.P.H., Michigan, 1967. Maternal health, fertility control, and AIDS in Third World countries.

Rutgers, The State University of New Jersey, New Brunswick

Karen Erstfeld, Assistant Professor; Ph.D., Michigan, 1986; M.S., Michigan, 1981. Environmental fate of chemicals; exposure; biomarkers.

Karen Denard Goldman, Assistant Professor of Urban Studies and Community Health; Ph.D., NYU, 1992. Application of social marketing and diffusion of innovation theories and practices in community health education; training; curriculum development.

Dennis Gorman, Assistant Professor and Director Prevention, Center of Alcohol Studies; Ph.D., Essex, 1988; M.Sc., Essex, 1981. Development, implementation, evaluation of substance abuse prevention programs; community-based initiatives developed for use in inner-city.

Michael Greenberg, Professor of Urban Studies and Community Health and Co-Director of New Jersey Graduate Program in Public Health; Ph.D., Columbia, 1969. Geography of mortality, morbidity, and risk factors; hazardous waste management.

Ellen Idler, Associate Professor of Sociology; Ph.D., Yale, 1985. Social factors in health and mortality.

Richard Lynch, Assistant Professor of Urban Studies and Community Health; Ph.D., University of Medicine and Dentistry of New Jersey–Robert Wood Johnson Medical School/Rutgers, 1995; M.S., Temple, 1988. Industrial hygiene, occupational ergonomics, occupational safety and health.

David Mechanic, University Professor, Rene Dubos Professor of Behavioral Sciences, and Director of the Institute for Health, Health Care Policy and Aging Research; Ph.D., Stanford, 1959. Organization of medical and psychiatric care.

Jane Miller, Assistant Professor of Urban Studies and Community Health and Institute for Health, Health Care Policy and Aging Research; Ph.D., Pennsylvania, 1989. Maternal and child health and nutrition, reproductive health, demography.

Michele Ochsner, Assistant Professor of Urban Studies and Community Health; Ph.D., Columbia, 1992. Environmental occupational health policy.

Mark Robson, Executive Director of the Environmental and Occupational Health Sciences Institute; Ph.D., Rutgers, 1988; M.P.H., University of Medicine and Dentistry of New Jersey, 1995; M.S., Rutgers, 1979. Pesticide use, policy, and regulation and alternative pest control.

Dona Schneider, Associate Professor of Urban Studies and Community Health; Ph.D., Rutgers, 1988; M.P.H., University of Medicine and Dentistry of New Jersey–Robert Wood Johnson Medical School/Rutgers, 1990. Geographic distribution of mortality, disease, and high-risk behaviors among children and young adults.

Shirley Smoyak, Professor of Urban Studies and Community Health and Director of Undergraduate Public Health Administration Program; Ph.D., Rutgers, 1970. Legal and clinical determinants of discharge readiness, barriers to community placement of psychiatric patients.

William Strawderman, Professor of Statistics; Ph.D., Rutgers, 1969. Decision and estimation theory and linear models.

Dong-Churl Suh, Assistant Professor of Pharmacy; M.B.A., SUNY at Buffalo, 1988; Ph.D., Minnesota, 1993. Pharmacoeconomics, outcomes assessment, and pharmaceutical economics.

Meredeth Turshen, Associate Professor of Urban Studies and Community Health and Coordinator, Master of Science Program in Gender and Development Planning; Ph.D., Sussex (England), 1975. International health policy with a focus on Africa, women's health, and occupational health policy in the United States and France.

Nancy Wolff, Assistant Professor of Urban Studies and Community Health and Associate Director of the Center for Research on the Organization and Financing of Care for the Severely Mentally Ill; Ph.D., Iowa State, 1984. Organization, financing, and distribution, of mental health services.

UNIVERSITY OF MIAMI

School of Medicine
Department of Epidemiology and Public Health
Graduate Programs in Public Health

Program of Study

The Department of Epidemiology and Public Health offers course work leading to a Master of Public Health (M.P.H.) degree as well as a Ph.D. degree in epidemiology. The mission of the department is to provide up-to-date educational programs to students, to guide and stimulate research activities relevant to health needs, and to provide assistance to health agencies for disease prevention, health promotion, environmental safety, and the management of health delivery services.

The M.P.H. degree, accredited by the Council on Education for Public Health, is a 45-credit hour program requiring 24 credit hours of core courses and 21 credit hours of electives in one of three concentration areas (epidemiology and biostatistics, health education and behavior, or environmental health). Full-time students can expect to complete the program requirements in two years. Joint degree programs are also offered in conjunction with the School of Medicine (M.D./M.P.H.), School of Law (J.D./M.P.H.), and School of Business (M.P.A./M.P.H.). Contact the Graduate Programs in Public Health directly for further information on these joint programs.

The Ph.D. program in epidemiology is an intensive research training program for students with prior training in epidemiology or related disciplines. All Ph.D. students in the program have extensive contact with faculty members because the program is explicitly designed to be small and interactive. The program takes advantage of South Florida's unique opportunities for epidemiologic research, including our ever-changing mix of races, ethnicities, and cultures. Many of our research programs could not be conducted elsewhere. Since the program is located within the School of Medicine, interactions with basic scientists and clinicians provide opportunities for epidemiologists to develop translational and interdisciplinary research. The program is primarily designed for students who have completed an M.P.H. degree. However, students possessing a master's or professional degree in a related discipline, as well as selected postbaccalaureate students, will be eligible for admission. The Ph.D. curriculum is planned on an individual basis and is based on a core of 24 credit hours, 12 credit hours in elective courses, and a minimum of 24 credit hours in a doctoral dissertation. Formal course work is expected to be completed within two years of admission into the program.

Research Facilities

Laboratories within the Department of Epidemiology and Public Health include a bone mineral density measurement facility and a student computer laboratory. Library facilities include the Calder Medical Library, the Richter Library on the Coral Gables campus, various other libraries located within specific schools, and reference sources available from the Graduate Programs in Public Health office. The Richter Library is also a Federal Government Document Depository. All libraries within the University have combined holdings of 1.97 million volumes, 19,025 serial subscriptions, and 2.94 million microfilms.

Financial Aid

A variety of financial assistance programs are available through the Office of Financial Assistance, including grants, educational loans, student employment, and tuition payment plans. The department has tuition waivers, graduate assistantships, and stipends that are available based on faculty grants and departmental funding.

Cost of Study

Graduate tuition for the 1998–99 academic year is $815 per credit hour. Funds may be available to subsidize the tuition costs of M.P.H. students. Subsidized credits and tuition are subject to change each academic year. For Ph.D. students, tuition may be covered internally.

Living and Housing Costs

The University residence halls, located at the Coral Gables campus, offer various accommodations ranging from $2100 to $2900 per semester, depending on the size and type of accommodation. Some students economize by sharing the rent of a private house or apartment. Meal plans are also offered, ranging from $1248 to $1525 per semester.

Student Group

In 1997–98, there were 3,140 graduate students attending the University of Miami. The Graduate Programs in Public Health enrolled 75 M.P.H. and 8 Ph.D. students, with 55 percent women, 46 percent minorities, and 17 percent international students.

Student Outcomes

Because of the broad nature of the M.P.H. degree, opportunities for employment depend on an individual's previous academic and employment background. Graduates seeking employment have obtained positions as research personnel, administrators, and public health providers for the University, various hospitals, nonprofit organizations, and federal, state, or local public health programs.

Location

Miami is a cosmopolitan, multilingual community. It offers a variety of sporting events, concerts, plays, festivals, and operas. Nearby parks, ocean beaches, tropical gardens, and wildlife sanctuaries offer abundant opportunities for outdoor recreation.

The University

The University, founded in 1925, is an independent, private institution that consists of fourteen colleges and schools. The Department of Epidemiology and Public Health is located in the School of Medicine, near downtown Miami, adjacent to several hospitals. The Coral Gables campus of the University is about 15 minutes away and is easily accessible by Metrorail.

Applying

Admission into the M.P.H. program is held in the fall and spring terms. Application deadlines are July 1 and November 15, respectively. Ph.D. applications are only accepted for enrollment in the fall semester, with a submission deadline of April 1. The criteria for admission into any of the programs include a minimum grade point average of 3.0 and a minimum combined verbal and quantitative score of 1000 on the GRE General Test (minimum score of 500 on each section for the Ph.D. program), taken within the last five years. The Ph.D. program also requires previous course work in epidemiology and biostatistics. Highly qualified Ph.D. candidates for admission will also be contacted to schedule an interview with the department. All applicants are required to submit a completed application, official transcripts of all college work, a written letter of intent, supporting evidence of computer literacy and competency, three letters of recommendation, and an updated resume or curriculum vitae. International applicants are also required to pass the TOEFL test with a minimum score of 550.

Correspondence and Information

Dr. Peggy O'Hara, Director
Graduate Program in Public Health
Department of Epidemiology and Public Health (R-669)
University of Miami School of Medicine
P.O. Box 016069
Miami, Florida 33101

Telephone: 305-243-6759
Fax: 305-243-5544
E-mail: agodur@mednet.med.miami.edu
World Wide Web: http://www.med.miami.edu/epidemiology/

University of Miami

THE FACULTY AND THEIR RESEARCH

Judy A. Bean, Professor; Ph.D., Texas Health Science Center at Houston, 1973. Statistical methods, epidemiology, survey sampling.
Jasenka Demirovic, Associate Professor; M.D., Sarajevo 1971; Ph.D., Belgrade, 1985. Epidemiology and prevention of cardiovascular disease and aging, women's health issues.
Robert C. Duncan, Professor; Ph.D., Oklahoma, 1966. Clinical trials, mathematical modeling.
Lora E. Fleming, Associate Professor; M.D./M.P.H., Harvard, 1984. Occupational and environmental health, epidemiology, medicine.
Michael French, Research Associate Professor; Ph.D., Boston College, 1986. Medical sociology, sociology of aging.
Orlando Gomez-Marin, Associate Professor; Ph.D., Minnesota, 1981. Cardiovascular disease, epidemiology of aging populations.
David J. Lee, Associate Professor; Ph.D., Texas Medical Branch, 1989. Cardiovascular disease epidemiology and prevention, psychosocial factors and health.
Clyde B. McCoy, Professor; Ph.D., Cincinnati, 1970. Substance abuse, cancer, AIDS, demography, community and public health.
Lisa R. Metsch, Research Assistant Professor; Ph.D., Florida, 1994. HIV/AIDS prevention, drug abuse epidemiology, aging, maternal and child health.
Peggy O'Hara, Associate Professor and Director of Graduate Programs in Public Health; Ph.D., Pittsburgh, 1981. Health education, behavioral epidemiology, HIV prevention, women's health intervention, smoking cessation.
James E. Rivers, Research Associate Professor; Ph.D., Kentucky, 1979. Substance abuse, program evaluation, community behavioral epidemiology, geographic information systems, service needs assessments.
Gary Schwartz, Research Associate Professor; Ph.D., SUNY Health Science Center at Brooklyn, 1985; Ph.D., North Carolina at Chapel Hill, 1988, 1993. Molecular epidemiology, cancer epidemiology, prostate cancer and vitamin D.
James M. Shultz, Associate Professor; Ph.D., Minnesota, 1988. AIDS, substance abuse epidemiology, disease impact estimation, media in public health, behavioral epidemiology.
Selina Smith, Research Associate Professor; Ph.D., Howard, 1988. Minority health, chronic disease, nutrition, cancer, diabetes, cardiovascular disease, women's health issues.
Frank W. Stitt, Clinical Professor; M.D., Sydney, 1963. Clinical epidemiology.
Edward J. Trapido, Professor and Director of the Ph.D. Program in Epidemiology; Sc.D., Harvard, 1981. Cancer epidemiology, breast cancer, disease surveillance, cancer prevention.
Norman L. Weatherby, Research Associate Professor; Ph.D., Florida State, 1983. Social and medical demography, quantitative and qualitative research methodology.

UNIVERSITY OF MICHIGAN

School of Public Health

Programs of Study

The mission of the School of Public Health is to create and disseminate knowledge with the aim of preventiing disease and promoting the health of populations in the United States and around the world. Of special concern are the poor, often minority populations, who suffer disproportionately from ailments and disabilities. Among health science schools, the School of Public Health at the University of Michigan is unique in that a strong emphasis is placed on disease prevention and health promotion rather than the treatment of existing illness, and the focus is on the health of populations rather than of individuals. Here, students both learn and help to create integrated approaches to solving public health problems. A full and flexible array of courses, programs of study, and concentrations are offered to meet students' academic and professional goals, including biostatistics; environmental health; occupational health; toxicology; human nutrition; general epidemiology; hospital and molecular epidemiology; dental public health; international health, health behavior, and health education; health management; and health policy. Degrees available include a Master of Public Health (M.P.H.), Master of Health Services Administration (M.H.S.A.), Master of Science (M.S.), Doctor of Public Health (Dr.P.H.), and Doctor of Philosophy (Ph.D.). A number of dual-degree programs exist with other excellent programs at Michigan, combining the public health experience with business administration, social work, public policy, law, and medicine. Dual degrees offered include M.P.H./M.A., M.P.H./M.D., M.H.S.A./M.B.A., M.H.S.A./J.D., M.P.H./M.S.W., M.P.H./M.P.P., and M.H.S.A./M.P.P. Michigan also offers interdepartmental concentrations designed to provide students an opportunity to deepen their understanding of public health topics that have major implications for society as a whole. Two interdepartmental concentrations currently available are public health genetics and women's and reproductive health.

Research Facilities

The University of Michigan is one of the largest public research institutions in the United States. The School of Public Health enjoys a healthy relationship with many University resources and partners, including the Institute for Social Research, ICPSR; thirty-nine libraries, including the School's own extensive Public Health Library, noted for housing one of the most comprehensive collections of public health books and journals in the U.S.; and the University of Michigan Medical Center. Innovative research is one of the strengths of the School of Public Health, with numerous grants and funding agencies working together to find solutions to health problems. The School's Health Media Research Laboratory works to identify new methods of conveying preventive health information to the public. Access to the School's modern microcomputer lab provides students with software programs, statistical applications, and a full suite of communications programs that provide Internet access.

Financial Aid

Tuition assistance awards are available to full-time residential students based on academic merit and maintaining eligibility while in attendance. International students and On Job/On Campus students are not eligible for tuition assistance awards from the School. Some special departmental scholarships are also available, and interested students should contact individual departments for information. Loans and/or work-study awards are available to eligible students through the University's Central Office of Financial Aid. Students applying for loans or work-study must complete a Free Application for Federal Student Aid (FAFSA) in order to be considered. For information regarding loans and work-study awards, students should contact the Central Office of Financial Aid at 734-763-6600.

Cost of Study

Tuition costs for 1997–98 were approximately $9820 for in-state students and $19,930 for out-of-state students. The costs are per academic year (two semesters) and based on full-time enrollment. Fees are approximately $180. Students should budget at least $600 per year for books and supplies.

Living and Housing Costs

The University's Housing Office provides information regarding on-campus housing for graduate students as well as off-campus listings of apartments and houses for rent. Most students elect to live off-campus in one of many residential communities that surround Ann Arbor. Housing costs range from $350 to $800 per month per person.

Student Group

The School of Public Health enrolls approximately 800 students per year. With a strong commitment to diversity, students from every walk of life find their way to Michigan, with approximately 11 percent of the total enrollment representing members of minority groups, 62 percent women, and 12 percent international students. The On Job/On Campus programs bring midcareer professionals back to school while maintaining their full employment.

Student Outcomes

Over the next decade, the demand for public health graduates will increase. According to a recent survey by the Association of Schools of Public Health, graduates find jobs within two months. It is reported that 47 percent work for governmental agencies, 30 percent work for nonprofit agencies, and 19 percent are employed by for-profit firms. Michigan's School of Public Health graduates find a wide range of career possibilities in research, management, community health practice, policy formation, and teaching.

Location

Ann Arbor is a community that blends small-town charm with big-city excitement. With its tree-shaded clapboard houses, open-air Farmer's Market, world-class visiting artists, first-rate restaurants, and outdoor summer concerts and movies, Ann Arbor offers an exceptional blend of riches and resources. Conveniently located just 25 minutes from Detroit Metropolitan Airport, less than an hour from Detroit and Toledo, and less than 5 hours from Chicago, Ann Arbor is easily accessible.

The University and The School

Long known for its academic excellence and superb learning facilities, the University of Michigan is an integral part of the community and the source of a great deal of Ann Arbor's active intellectual and social life. Among Michigan's faculty members are internationally known scientists, celebrated visual and performing artists, widely read novelists and poets, sought after business and technology consultants, filmmakers, Pulitzer Prize winners, and even an astronaut. The School of Public Health celebrated its fifty-year anniversary in 1989.

Applying

Applicants for the M.S. and Ph.D. degree programs must complete a Rackham Graduate School application by February 1. Applicants for the M.P.H., M.H.S.A., and Dr.P.H. degree programs must complete a School of Public Health application by March 1. All applicants should possess a bachelor's degree from an accredited institution and have substantial knowledge in a discipline relevant to public health. Complete applications contain official transcripts for all completed undergraduate and graduate work, GRE scores from the last five years (GMAT, MCAT, and DAT scores are accepted by some departments), three letters of recommendation, and a personal statement.

Correspondence and Information

Office of Academic Affairs
School of Public Health
University of Michigan
109 South Observatory
Ann Arbor, Michigan 48109-2029
Telephone: 734-764-5425
Fax: 734-763-5455
E-mail: sph.inquiries@umich.edu
World Wide Web: http://www.sph.umich.edu

University of Michigan

THE DEPARTMENTS AND DEPARTMENT CHAIRS

Biostatistics

Chair: Roderick J. A. Little, Ph.D.

The Department of Biostatistics prepares students for careers in the development and application of statistical and mathematical methods as they relate to the design and analysis of public health problems and biomedical research. Job opportunities exist in research agencies such as the Centers for Disease Control and Prevention, National Institutes of Health, and the Food and Drug Administration as well as in industry and academic institutions. Because of the broad nature of the fields of application of biostatistics, applicants with a variety of academic backgrounds are accepted into the program; major undergraduate fields such as mathematics, statistics, computer science, biology, sociology, or a behavioral science are especially appropriate.

Environmental and Industrial Health

Chair: James H. Vincent, Ph.D.

The Department of Environmental Health offers four programs of study for students. Environmental health prepares students to meet present and future needs for environmental management as it pertains to human health and disease. This program offers instruction in six areas of specialization: air quality, environmental chemistry, environmental health management, hazardous waste, radiological health, and water quality. Job opportunities are found in governmental health agencies at the local, state, and national levels; private industry; academic institutions; and international health agencies.

Occupational health is concerned with protecting the health of persons in the workplace and community. While working in this profession, students learn about manufacturing processes, disease and injury processes, statistical sampling procedures, chemistry, engineering, environmental and work regulations, and labor-management issues. Two overlapping but separate tracks of study are offered: industrial hygiene for persons with science backgrounds seeking certification as industrial hygienists and occupational medicine for physicians seeking specialty in this field. Industrial hygienists focus on the workplace, studying the manufacturing process to ensure the safety of workers. This includes the safe and proper use of equipment, the noise level and cleanliness of the air inside the plant, and the raw materials used in manufacturing.

Toxicology combines the principles of biology and chemistry to help understand the harmful effects of pollutants, pesticides, and other chemicals on human health. Toxicologists apply their multidisciplinary training to research or testing in academic institutions where they create and maintain centers of education and training as well as conduct original toxicological research. In industry, they participate in all aspects of the life of a chemical product, from development through testing to control and regulation of its ultimate use. In government, they participate in basic and applied research or function in regulatory capacities preparing risk-benefit analyses to ensure the safe manufacture, handling, use, and disposal of many types of chemical products.

The study of human nutrition is essential to the understanding of the mechanisms of health and disease. Research efforts in human nutrition have recently become focused on the problems of nutrient excess and nutrient imbalance. Increased emphasis has been placed on the role of nutrition and diet in the prevention and treatment of chronic diseases, including cardiovascular disease, obesity, diabetes, and cancer. The study of human nutrition has become more interdisciplinary, increasingly drawing on expertise from public health, epidemiology, biostatistics, and the social and behavioral sciences. Graduate study in human nutrition prepares students for career opportunities in such public health agencies as local and state health departments, hospitals, clinics, industry, or private practice.

Epidemiology

Chair: George A. Kaplan, Ph.D.

The Department of Epidemiology offers four programs of study for students. General epidemiology is concerned with analyzing and describing patterns of occurrence and determinants of diseases in human populations. The principles and methods of epidemiology provide knowledge of the natural history of disease processes, the foundation for preventive medical practice, and the basis for rational decisions concerning public health policy. Epidemiologists find positions in governmental agencies such as the Centers for Disease Control and Prevention, National Institutes of Health, and state health departments. Opportunities also exist in academic institutions, private industry, and hospitals.

Hospital and molecular epidemiology focuses on the molecular biology and biochemistry of infectious agents. Besides gaining an understanding of epidemiology, pathology, immunology, and molecular biology, students also develop managerial skills that may be used in laboratory supervision as well as planning and development for public health programs. Students are also qualified to work as an infection control officer or in a senior laboratory services position in academia or research and public health institutions.

Dentists and hygienists with degrees in dental public health are establishing dental health policy at the national level, directing state and local dental programs, conducting research in national agencies, directing the dental plans for major health insurance groups, and teaching and researching in universities across the nation.

The program in international health covers health conditions and health services outside the United States, with the primary focus on developing countries. The program is interdisciplinary and provides training in both the physical and social sciences as they relate to health. Graduates are equipped for employment in international, national, governmental, and nongovernmental agencies involved in health research or health service delivery in developing countries.

Health Behavior and Health Education

Chair: Barbara A. Israel, Dr.P.H.

The Department of Health Behavior and Health Education examines the factors associated with the study of health-related behavior and health status and develops and evaluates educational activities designed to improve individual and community health and quality of life. Graduates are prepared to function in leadership positions in educational, federal, state, and community systems. They learn to apply social and behavioral science content and research methods to the analysis of health problems and their solutions. They are also proficient in the design of health education programs, health promotion initiatives, and social changes focusing on many levels, including individual, family, network, group, organization, community, and policy.

Health Management and Policy

Chair: William G. Weissert, Ph.D.

Rapid changes taking place in both the private and public sectors of health-care and related industries have created a need for a broad spectrum of qualified professionals to manage complex institutions, organizations, and health services delivery programs. Students with backgrounds in the natural, biological, or social sciences; business; marketing; economics; and finance find vast career opportunities, including mid- to executive-level administrative positions in all sectors of the health-care industry. Two overlapping but separate degree tracks are offered at the master's level. The Master of Health Services Administration (M.H.S.A.) degree prepares students for successful careers in the management and planning of health care. For this track, students need to complete a course in the principles of accounting prior to enrollment. The Master of Public Health (M.P.H.) degree is appropriate for students who plan to work in federal, state, local, or international public health agencies, or, alternately, those who envision a public or private sector career in a policy area such as environmental or occupational health, injury prevention, or substance abuse.

UNIVERSITY OF MINNESOTA

School of Public Health

Programs of Study

The School of Public Health offers majors leading to the Master of Public Health (M.P.H.) degree. Master of Science (M.S.) and Doctor of Philosophy (Ph.D.) programs are also offered by the School of Public Health and are administered through the Graduate School. The M.P.H. is an advanced professional degree program providing specialized education in biostatistics, community health education, environmental health, epidemiology, maternal and child health, public health administration, and public health nutrition. The M.S. degree in biostatistics, environmental health, epidemiology, and health services research and policy, and the Ph.D. degree in biostatistics, environmental health, epidemiology, and health services research, policy, and administration are awarded by the Graduate School with teaching, research, and advising through the School of Public Health. Dual M.P.H./M.B.A., M.P.H./M.S.W., and M.P.H./M.S. in nursing degrees are also available. The School does not have a distance education program at the present time. Students in all degree programs may use elective courses and a wide range of University resources to respond to individual needs.

Research Facilities

Students conduct individual and collaborative research both on campus in laboratories or off campus in community settings. The Minnesota State Department of Health, located on campus, and many other health-related organizations in the area offer research and internship opportunities. The Biomedical Library and the Learning Resources Center are located within the Academic Health Center and provide up-to-date materials.

Financial Aid

Several opportunities for financial aid are available including research assistantships and teaching assistantships. The School also offers federally funded traineeships, and fellowships from the Graduate School. Limited funds are available for small loans at no interest to students who are registered for 4 credits or more.

Cost of Study

Tuition for M.P.H. students for 1997–98 was $128 per credit for Minnesota residents and $257 per credit for nonresidents. The University has a reciprocity agreement with the states of North Dakota, South Dakota, and Wisconsin and with the province of Manitoba. Full-time students generally take 16 credits per quarter. Degree programs can be completed in one or two years, depending upon previous relevant experience and/or education.

Living and Housing Costs

Costs vary depending upon students' selection of housing and personal expenses. Housing is available both on and off campus. The University Housing Bureau is available for assistance.

Student Group

In 1997–98, the School of Public Health enrolled approximately 350 graduate students in master's and doctoral degree areas of study. Students came from thirty-nine states and thirteen countries; 60 percent were women. All students are encouraged to participate in the School of Public Health Student Senate as well as to represent students on the Educational Policy Committee; Administrative Council; Research Committee; or Recognition, Awards and Honors Committee. The Council for Health Interdisciplinary Participation (CHIP) is an organization for health sciences students that is dedicated to promoting the team approach to health services delivery through student services and community programs. CHIP offers educational and social activities. Membership in the School of Public Health Alumni Society is available to all students who have completed a minimum of 15 credits, and to all graduates.

Location

With more than 2.3 million residents, the Twin Cities offer all the educational and cultural advantages of a major metropolitan area. Arts and music attractions include the Minnesota Orchestra, the St. Paul Chamber Orchestra, the Minneapolis Institute of Arts, Guthrie Theater, and the Walker Art Center as well as many vigorous new theaters, galleries, and musical groups. The Twin Cities also offer access to abundant natural wildlife areas with plentiful parks, lakes, and rivers. Minnesota's diversity of seasons allows for a variety of outdoor activities including skiing, skating, and hiking in the winter, and swimming, sailing, fishing, cycling, golfing, tennis, jogging, and in-line skating during the other seasons. The Twin Cities area is also home to the Minnesota Twins, Vikings, and Timberwolves professional sports franchises, as well as the Mall of America, the country's largest shopping mall.

The University and The School

The University was chartered in 1851, seven years before the Minnesota Territory became a state. Today, it has about 4,500 full-time faculty members, more than 47,000 students in day school, and thousands more students in evening, continuing education, and noncredit courses. The University has twenty-four colleges and four coordinate campuses. The Board of Regents authorized expansion of the Department of Preventive Medicine and Public Health of the Medical School into the School of Public Health in 1944, although the School's beginnings date to 1918, when the first public health training program was established. The School's mission is to preserve and enhance the health of the public through education, research, and service programs designed to discover and transmit new knowledge aimed at the prevention of disease and disability, the improvement of health, and the planning, analysis, management, and improvement of systems for delivering health services. The School of Public Health and its M.P.H. degree program are accredited by the Council on Education for Public Health. All degree programs offered by the School of Public Health or through the Graduate School are fully accredited by the appropriate national accrediting agencies. The School does not offer the Dr.P.H. degree. The University and the School of Public Health are committed to the policy that all persons shall have equal access to its programs, facilities, and employment without regard to race, religion, color, sex, national origin, handicap, age, veteran status, or sexual orientation.

Applying

Information and applications for admission may be obtained from the Student Services Center of the School of Public Health. Applicants must have a baccalaureate or higher degree from an accredited institution and one of the following: a cumulative undergraduate GPA of at least 3.0 or a Graduate Record Examinations score of not less than 1500; for appropriate majors, a Graduate Management Admission Test score of not less than 500; or a Miller Analogies Test score of not less than 40. International applicants must submit a TOEFL score of no less than 575. Further admission criteria may be required by the individual majors. Application deadlines for the various majors vary from January through May. Applications are also accepted on a space-available basis beyond the usual deadlines. However, early application is recommended.

Correspondence and Information

Student Services Center
School of Public Health
University of Minnesota
420 Delaware Street, SE, Box 819
Minneapolis, Minnesota 55455
Telephone: 612-626-3500
800-SPH-UOFM (toll-free)
E-mail: sph-ssc@tc.umn.edu
World Wide Web: http://www.sph.umn.edu

University of Minnesota

FACULTY HEADS, PROGRAMS, AND RESEARCH ACTIVITIES

Biostatistics (M.P.H., M.S., Ph.D.)
John Connett, Ph.D., Chair. Faculty interests cover the spectrum of biostatistical research, with emphasis on design of risk factor intervention studies, spatial statistics, Bayesian methods, survival analysis, meta analysis, management of large databases, analytic strategies for longitudinal data, stopping rules for clinical trials, and techniques of statistical consultation. Some of these efforts arise from collaborative participation in health sciences research projects, including primary prevention of coronary heart disease, prevention of chronic obstructive pulmonary disease in smokers, treatment of otitis media in children, and the treatment of AIDS in community research settings. The Coordinating Centers for Biometric Research is a subunit devoted to the conduct of large clinical trials and other research studies; a Biostatistics Consulting Laboratory provides on-the-job learning experiences for students interested in research-related careers.

Community Health Education (M.P.H.)
Leslie Lytle, Ph.D., RD, Chair. The community health education major prepares public health professionals who address the social and behavioral factors that influence the health of populations and individuals. Students learn how to implement public health policy approaches, workplace health promotion, school-based strategies, and community-based approaches. The program focuses on developing skills in program evaluation, needs assessment, and program development. Community health education faculty members are currently involved in many research projects, including assessments of population behavior patterns and psychosocial risk factors; community-wide intervention programs for heart disease, cancer, AIDS, tobacco use, and eating behaviors; evaluations of health education efforts in schools, worksites, clinics and hospitals, and communities; and efforts to influence public health policies. These projects provide many opportunities for students to work as research assistants. The knowledge generated by faculty research is incorporated into course work.

Environmental Health (M.P.H., M.S., Ph.D.)
Donald Vesley, Ph.D., Major Chair. This major is designed to prepare students to become leaders and practitioners in the public health arena. Students concentrate in the areas of environmental chemistry, environmental toxicology, environmental health policy, environmental microbiology, environmental and occupational epidemiology, industrial hygiene, occupational health nursing, or occupational and environmental medicine. The multidisciplinary and highly collaborative faculty members provide stimulating educational and research opportunities for students. Research interests include (but are not limited to) occupational and environmental epidemiology, measurement and behavior of airborne particles, mechanisms of toxicity of environmental contaminants, the role of science in environmental decision making, assessment management and communication of environmental risks, microbiological contamination control practices, violence prevention and control, and worker health and safety.

Epidemiology (M.P.H., M.S., Ph.D.)
John Finnegan Jr., Ph.D., Chair. Epidemiology is the science of public health. It observes, describes, quantifies, and theorizes about conditions affecting population health and also designs and tests interventions to prevent disease and to promote public health. Faculty members conduct a wide range of epidemiological research from basic biology and etiology through human behavior and community and health policy interventions. Extensive grant-based research anchors the degree programs with an applied approach through which students receive a thorough grounding in epidemiological methods, design, measurement, quantitative analysis, and inference. Program strengths include cardiovascular disease; cancer; genetic epidemiology; infectious disease; human behavior and health; children's and adolescents' health; tobacco, alcohol, and other substance abuse; and community and policy intervention studies.

Health Services Research and Policy (M.S., Ph.D.)
John E. Kralewski, Ph.D., Director. Faculty research mainly focuses on policy issues related to the organization and financing of health services. The main research streams include the structure of health insurance and the effects of costs, utilization of services, and the effectiveness of care; the structure, function, and effectiveness of HMOs and other managed health-care programs; long-term care and health care for older persons; rural health services, including access to care and the impact of new models for providing services to rural populations; the role of financing and organization in mental health utilization and outcomes; and health-care outcomes. The faculty also sponsors a national research center funded by the Health Care Financing Administration, which addresses issues related to the Medicare and Medicaid programs; a National Long-Term Care Resource Center; a Rural Health Research Center; and a Clinical Outcomes Research Center. As well as cosponsoring a doctoral studies program in health services research, policy, and administration, the program offers a Master of Science program. A postdoctoral traineeship to train physicians interested in a career in health services research is also available.

Maternal and Child Health (M.P.H.)
Joän Patterson, Ph.D., Chair. MCH offers both comprehensive (two-year) and accelerated (one-year) programs that prepare graduates for leadership positions in public, private, and nonprofit sectors to assess the health needs of mothers, children, and families; design, implement, and evaluate innovative programs to meet those needs; develop, analyze, and advocate for public policies to address those needs; and conduct research to improve the health of mothers, children, and families. Faculty member research and service focus on reproductive and perinatal health, child and adolescent mental and physical health (including youth risk-taking behaviors such as early pregnancy, substance abuse, and violence), childhood chronic illness and disability, nutrition, family health, and evaluation of community-based programs. The MCH major includes a Center for Adolescent Pregnancy Prevention, funded by the Centers for Disease Control and Prevention.

Public Health Administration (M.P.H.)
Mila Aroskar, Ed.D., Chair. This major prepares leaders who will be advocates for the public interest and promote health through population-focused administration, the development and implementation of public health–enhancing policy, and evidence-based public health (EBPH). Graduates assume positions in public health organizations, planning agencies, voluntary health organizations, mental health agencies, and alternative health-care delivery settings. They share a strong commitment to preventing disease, promoting health, and serving populations. The curriculum incorporates three major categories of knowledge and skills: administration; policy and program development, implementation, and evaluation; and the core areas of public health. Students choose electives and/or concentrations in areas such as health services management, finance, managed care, and long-term care administration. Faculty member research interests include ethics in health care, public health and health-care administration, health-care reform, competition, regulation, rationing and delivery of health services, use of preventive services, access to care, quality of care, organizational behavior, and management communication.

Public Health Nutrition (M.P.H.)
Lawrence Kushi, Sc.D., Chair. The faculty is engaged in research on community-based nutrition, cancer and cardiovascular disease, maternal nutrition and outcome of pregnancy, and child and adolescent nutrition. Students routinely collaborate with faculty members and field faculty members for active involvement in research and public health practice. Graduates are prepared to provide nutrition leadership in state and local health departments, health-care institutions, community health and social service organizations, and business and industry. A firm grounding in nutritional epidemiology with preparation to enter a Ph.D. program is also available. A twenty-four-month program is available for individuals without a nutrition/dietetics background; sixteen- and ten-month programs are available depending upon previous professional experience in nutrition and dietetics.

UNIVERSITY OF NORTH CAROLINA AT CHAPEL HILL

School of Public Health
Department of Health Behavior and Health Education

Programs of Study

The Department of Health Behavior and Health Education trains students, through group and individual field practice, research, and strong classroom teaching, in multiple aspects of health-related social and behavioral change at the population, community, organization, family, and individual levels. Courses and practicums cover a range of subjects, from understanding public health problems to the design of interventions to prevent or eradicate those problems. In addition to the principles, practices, theories, and methods of health education, faculty research and practice interests include women's health, rural health, ethnic minority health, international health, adolescent health, health of the elderly, and substance abuse.

The department offers four graduate degree programs. The Master of Public Health (M.P.H.) degree is the basic qualification for the professional health education specialist. The program of study prepares candidates for professional roles in community development, social action, health promotion and disease prevention, and domestic and international agencies. Students are prepared for leadership positions in health education planning, management, and evaluation. The focus of the M.P.H. program is on the practice of selecting, applying, and monitoring appropriate strategies for behavioral, social, and political change to enhance people's health. In the second year of study, students may choose an emphasis on developing health education research skills or practice skills. Four semesters plus one summer session are required for this degree.

The Master of Science in Public Health is offered for students who intend to work in planning health behavior and health education programs. Students must have at least seven years of progressively responsible professional positions in health education practice. The degree can be completed within a twelve- to eighteen-month period.

Two doctoral degrees are offered: the Doctor of Philosophy (Ph.D.) and the Doctor of Public Health (Dr.P.H.). In the Ph.D. program, emphasis is on the behavioral and social sciences, theory development, and advanced research methodology. The Dr.P.H. program emphasizes the application of research findings to the solutions of public health problems, policy development, and program administration and evaluation. Four consecutive semesters in full-time residence are required; these doctoral degree programs are generally completed in four years. Applicants are required to have a master's degree in health behavior and/or health education, in one of the social or behavioral sciences, or in a field encompassing comparable training.

Research Facilities

The School has the laboratories and equipment needed to support the wide variety of research conducted by the faculty. In addition to the Graduate and Undergraduate libraries, the Health Sciences Library is located across the street from the School and has automated reference services, including MEDLINE. The Division of Computing and Information Services provides a microcomputing laboratory for student educational use in cooperation with the UNC Microcomputing Support Center. Access to University and regional mainframe computers is available for educational and research use.

Financial Aid

A limited number of federally sponsored nonservice traineeships are available to qualified candidates. A few research and teaching assistantships are also available in the department. Members of minority groups are eligible for special financial assistance. Other work opportunities and some student loan funds are available from the University's Student Aid Office.

Cost of Study

In 1998–99, graduate tuition and fees for legal residents of North Carolina are $1395 per semester. For out-of-state students, tuition and fees are $5600 per semester. Field courses require an additional fee.

Living and Housing Costs

The estimated yearly expense (tuition, fees, books and supplies, room and board, and personal expenses) in 1998–99 is $15,314 for North Carolina residents and $31,546 for nonresidents. Housing for single graduate students and married students is available through the University. The area offers an abundance of off-campus housing possibilities at a range of prices.

Student Group

There are, on the average, 75 master's and 25 doctoral students enrolled annually in the department. The department actively recruits students from all minority groups, all states, and many other countries. Recent graduates have found opportunities in the job market to be plentiful. Most students have a job waiting for them upon graduation.

Location

Chapel Hill is affectionately called the "southern part of heaven" by residents and nonresidents alike. Here, one finds a university and a city that thrive together within a small-town yet cosmopolitan environment. Picturesque University buildings, brick sidewalks, attractive shopping areas, and fine older homes provide a "village" atmosphere for Chapel Hill. Conveniently located near Raleigh, Durham, and Research Triangle Park, the town abounds with cultural, educational, entertainment, and employment opportunities. Chapel Hill is equidistant from the ocean and the mountains and midway between Washington, D.C., and Atlanta, Georgia.

The School

The fourth school of public health in the nation, the UNC-CH School of Public Health was the first school to be established within a state university. It is today, with the Schools of Medicine, Dentistry, Nursing, and Pharmacy, a unit of the Division of Health Affairs. Close affiliations are maintained with other graduate schools and departments of the University of North Carolina campuses, as well as with other schools and universities. Students enrolled in the School of Public Health may take courses in other departments of the University, North Carolina State University, or Duke University.

Applying

Admission to the master's programs is for the fall semester only. Applications should be submitted by January 1, although applications received after that date will be considered as long as space is available. Admission to the doctoral programs is granted for the fall, spring, and summer semesters. There is a $55 nonrefundable application fee for all programs. All applicants are required to take the GRE General Test. Prospective applicants are encouraged to consult with department faculty members and, if possible, to visit the campus to meet with both faculty members and graduate students. Letters of inquiry regarding admission and requests for application forms should be directed to the address below.

Correspondence and Information

Linda Cook, Registrar
Department of Health Behavior and Health Education
Rosenau Hall, CB #7400
School of Public Health
University of North Carolina at Chapel Hill
Chapel Hill, North Carolina 27599-7400

Telephone: 919-966-5771
Fax: 919-966-2921
E-mail: lcook@sph.unc.edu

University of North Carolina at Chapel Hill

THE FACULTY AND THEIR RESEARCH

Listed below are the teaching, research, and service interests of the faculty.

Karl E. Bauman, Professor (Sociology); Ph.D., Florida State, 1965. Social and social-psychological determinants of health behaviors and application to health promotion, research methodology, adolescent health, family planning, program evaluation.

Susan J. Blalock, Research Associate Professor (Health Behavior and Health Education); Ph.D., North Carolina at Chapel Hill, 1987. Psychosocial models of health behavior, individual behavior change, osteoporosis risk-reduction, coping with chronic illness, effect of risk perceptions on health behavior.

J. Michael Bowling, Research Assistant Professor (Sociology) and Associate Director of the UNC Injury Prevention Research Center; Ph.D., North Carolina at Chapel Hill, 1992. Epidemiology of unintentional injury and violence, health surveillance, survey sampling design, developmental disabilities.

Lori Carter-Edwards, Research Assistant Professor (Epidemiology); Ph.D., North Carolina at Chapel Hill, 1995. Investigation of social and behavioral risk factors for hypertension, diabetes, cardiovascular disease in African-American communities; questionnaire and index development; community-based research and intervention in underrepresented populations.

Carolyn E. Crump, Research Assistant Professor (Health Behavior and Health Education); Ph.D., North Carolina at Chapel Hill, 1993. Organizational and environmental correlates of health behavior, implementation and evaluation of worksite health promotion programs, occupational injury, adherence to physical activity recommendations, qualitative research methods.

Brenda DeVellis, Professor (Social Psychology); Ph.D., Vanderbilt (Peabody), 1978. Social psychological aspects of health behavior, coping with chronic disease, behavioral science theory, women's health, health-care provider and patient communication.

Robert F. DeVellis, Research Professor (Social Psychology); Ph.D., Vanderbilt (Peabody), 1977. Social variables and individual differences in health behavior and adaptation to illness, emotions and adaptation to arthritis, social support in chronic illness, advanced research methods.

Jo Anne Earp, Chair and Professor (Medical Sociology); Sc.D., Johns Hopkins, 1974. Social and attitudinal correlates of health behaviors; race, socioeconomic status, and access barriers to breast cancer screening; predictors of repeat infections among rural STD patients; women's health issues; program evaluation and survey research methods.

Eugenia Eng, Associate Professor (Health Education); Dr.P.H., North Carolina at Chapel Hill, 1983. Integration of community development and health education interventions in rural and developing countries, lay health adviser interventions, community-based research, correlates of community competence, community organization, cross-cultural and women's health.

Vangie Foshee, Associate Professor (Health Behavior and Health Education); Ph.D., North Carolina at Chapel Hill, 1989. Investigation of psychological, sociological, and biological factors on adolescent health behavior; adolescent dating violence.

Richard M. House, Clinical Associate Professor (Adult Education) and Director of the Distance Learning and Health Communications Center; Ed.D., North Carolina State, 1983. Program management, public health practice, adult and continuing education programs.

Christine Jackson, Assistant Professor (Social Ecology); Ph.D., California, Irvine, 1985. Health communication, substance-use prevention, community-level intervention.

Fletcher Linder, Research Assistant Professor (Medical Anthropology); Ph.D., North Carolina at Chapel Hill, 1995. Epidemiology of osteoarthritis in rural areas, cognitive models of arthritis suffering in the southern United States, school- and community-based adolescent dating violence prevention programs, exploring gender differences in the etiology and experiences of dating violence among adolescents.

Elizabeth Mutran, Professor (Sociology); Ph.D., Indiana, 1977. Aging and human development, impact of changes in roles on mental and physical health, minority aging and social support.

Carolyn P. Parks, Assistant Professor (Health Education); Ph.D., Tennessee, Knoxville, 1993. Community-based health strategies development and evaluation for African-Americans and poor populations of color, cultural and linguistic relevance of health education materials and research instruments, empowerment education and training, health promotion through African-American churches, community- and church-based assets mapping, lay health adviser strategies, barriers to health communication among groups of color.

Sandra C. Quinn, Assistant Professor (Health Education); Ph.D., Maryland College Park, 1993. Health education interventions and evaluation in community settings; minority health, including the sociopolitical context of health in the African-American community; HIV; history of public health.

Carol Runyan, Associate Professor (Health Education/Epidemiology) and Director of the UNC Injury Prevention Research Center; Ph.D., North Carolina at Chapel Hill, 1983. Epidemiology and prevention of unintentional injury and violence, science and policy development, public health framework.

James R. Sorenson, Professor (Social Psychology and Sociology); Ph.D., Cornell, 1970. Design, evaluation, and ethics of health promotion and disease prevention interventions; applied human genetics; genetics and public health; health promotion in maternal and child health; theory in health education practice, research, and policy.

Allan B. Steckler, Professor (Health Education); Dr.P.H., UCLA, 1971. Evaluation of school and community health promotion programs, qualitative research methods; dissemination of health education programs; program planning and evaluation, organizational change, and models of health education practice.

Current Research Projects

Breast cancer screening program: Community and agency intervention to remove barriers to mammography for older black women.
Sexually Transmitted Epidemic Project: A study of attitudes and behaviors of people with repeat STD infections in a rural county.
Compliance gaining strategies in the medical encounter.
The role of the family in the primary prevention of substance use problems in children.
An evaluation of testing and counseling for hemophilia carriers.
Improving physicians' preventive care activities.
Adherence to cancer preventing materials.
Intervention of NCI's databased Intervention Research Program.
Violence against women.
Environmental and policy changes to enhance physical activity at the community level: Methods development.
Evaluation of LIFE, a worksite health promotion program.
Health Works for Women: Development and evaluation of a worksite health promotion program for women.
Osteoporosis prevention: education and outreach.
Genetic testing for breast cancer susceptibility.
Ministry of Health Initiative: A spiritual and holistic approach to health promotion through African-American churches.
Exploring differences in trust and belief in AIDS as genocide among black and white Southerners.
Evaluation of the first year of replication of the black church week of prayer for the healing of AIDS.
Cognitive/emotional skills in spousal support for arthritis.
Save Our Sisters and Sisters Helping Sisters: lay health adviser and nurse adviser interventions to reduce delay in breast cancer screening.
Evaluation of the statewide minority infant mortality reduction.
A church-based survey of diet and blood pressure knowledge among African Americans.
Lifestyle factors related to blood pressure levels among college youth.
A long-term evaluation of Safe Date, an adolescent dating violence prevention project.
Gender and adolescent dating violence.
Influence of a family program on adolescent drug abuse.
Assessing public attitudes toward needle-exchange programs.
An experimental study to improve risk/benefit assessment in informed consent statements.
Pathways: Obesity prevention among Native American children.

UNIVERSITY OF NORTH CAROLINA AT CHAPEL HILL

School of Public Health

Programs of Study

The School of Public Health offers academic programs in biostatistics, environmental sciences and engineering, epidemiology, health behavior and health education, health policy and administration, maternal and child health, nutrition, and public health nursing.

Master's programs offered include the Master of Public Health (M.P.H.) program, preparing students for positions that require a considerable breadth of knowledge of the whole field of public health; the Master of Science in Public Health (M.S.P.H.), which provides the student with greater depth in specialized areas of public health; the Master of Science (M.S.) degree, offered in biostatistics, environmental sciences and engineering, and public health nursing; the Master of Science in Environmental Engineering (M.S.E.E.); and the Master of Healthcare Administration (M.H.A.).

Two doctoral degrees are offered. The Doctor of Philosophy (Ph.D.) program prepares graduates for research and teaching in academic or related settings, while the Doctor of Public Health (Dr.P.H.) program prepares professionals to conduct and supervise research and to integrate new knowledge and techniques into community and public health practice. Joint-degree programs are available in conjunction with the University's Schools of Medicine, Dentistry, Law, Social Work, and Education.

The School's 174 full-time faculty members are involved in a wide range of research activities. Examples include identifying risk factors in cardiovascular disease; preventing infant mortality; examining environmental risks to reproductive health; evaluation of AIDS clinical research programs; studies of health care cost-containment programs; pollution prevention; evaluating the safety of drinking water disinfectants; risk factors for cancer; and the relationship between nutrition and health. Students work with faculty members in both basic and applied research; collaborative relationships with state, federal, and private agencies offer additional research opportunities.

Research Facilities

School facilities are among the largest and best-equipped of any school of public health in the nation. The School's many state-of-the-art laboratories include a modern microcomputer lab for student educational and research use. The University's 3-million-volume library system is ranked among the best in the nation. The Health Sciences Library supports student use of MEDLINE and other electronic databases. Access to University and regional mainframe computers is readily available.

Financial Aid

About 40 percent of the School's graduate students receive some type of financial aid. Sources of student support include federally sponsored traineeships, teaching and research assistantships, endowment scholarships, special fellowships for minority students, and graduate school merit assistantships. Other work-study opportunities and student loans are available through the University's Office of Scholarships and Student Assistance.

Cost of Study

In 1997–98, graduate tuition and fees were $1395 per semester for North Carolina residents and $5598 for out-of-state students. Contingent upon the selected program of study, additional program fees, which vary by department, may be added to the cost of tuition and fees.

Living and Housing Costs

Estimated expenses for the academic year, including tuition, fees, books and supplies, room and board, and personal expenses, are $15,314 for North Carolina residents and $31,546 for out-of-state students. University housing is available for single graduate students and married students. Many off-campus rental units are available nearby.

Student Group

Approximately 1,000 students enroll in the School each year. Eighty-seven percent of these are graduate students. In 1997–98, students came from forty-two states and thirty countries; 35 percent were men, and 65 percent were women; 11 percent were minority students; 14 percent were international students. The School actively recruits students from minority groups.

Location

Chapel Hill, affectionately called the "southern part of heaven," offers a mild climate, a small-town atmosphere, and a cosmopolitan environment with many cultural, educational, entertainment, and employment opportunities. Chapel Hill is a 3-hour drive from beaches and mountain recreation areas.

The University and The School

UNC is consistently ranked among the "Public Ivies" offering education equivalent to that available at the best Ivy League schools. The University attracts more than 23,000 students each year from North Carolina, many other states, and more than seventy countries.

The UNC School of Public Health is part of the UNC Division of Health Affairs, along with the Schools of Medicine, Dentistry, Pharmacy, and Nursing. Close affiliations with other UNC schools, as well as with nearby North Carolina State University and Duke University, expand students' opportunities for interdisciplinary studies and research.

Applying

Most programs at the School require students to enter in the fall semester. It is advisable to apply by January 1 to the UNC–Chapel Hill Graduate School for fall admission, especially if financial aid is desired.

Correspondence and Information

Requests for information or application forms should be addressed to:

Dean's Office, School of Public Health
Rosenau Hall, CB#7400
University of North Carolina at Chapel Hill
Chapel Hill, North Carolina 27599-7400
Telephone: 919-966-7676

University of North Carolina at Chapel Hill

FACULTY HEADS AND PROGRAMS

Dean of the School: William L. Roper, M.D., M.P.H.

Biostatistics. Interim Chair: C. E. Davis, Ph.D. The degree programs in biostatistics provide students with knowledge of statistical techniques and their application to a variety of fields related to the health problems of people. Specialty options are available in such areas as biometry, cancer, clinical trials, data management, demography and population studies, environmental biostatistics, genetics, health services, and mental health statistics.

Environmental Sciences and Engineering. Acting Chair: Donald L. Fox, Ph.D. This department offers programs in air, radiation, and industrial hygiene; aquatic and atmospheric sciences; environmental health sciences; environmental management and policy; and water resources engineering. Interdisciplinary studies are encouraged through the Institute for Environmental Studies, Water Resources Research Institute, and Institute for Marine Sciences. Research projects contribute to a better understanding of the complex issues that affect the major environmental problems.

Epidemiology. Chair: David Savitz, M.S., Ph.D. The department seeks to advance the knowledge of health and disease in populations in order to discover and evaluate opportunities to reduce illness and improve health. The multidisciplinary faculty is committed to educating students who can both advance epidemiology as a discipline and apply their skills in numerous settings, in both the public and private sectors. This educational research program offers training in a number of specialized areas, including cancer, cardiovascular disease, environmental and occupational epidemiology, health-care epidemiology, infectious diseases, and reproductive epidemiology.

Health Behavior and Health Education. Chair: Jo Anne Earp, Sc.D. The department trains students, through research, group, and individual field practice and strong classroom teaching, in multiple aspects of health-related social and behavioral change at the population, community, organization, family, and individual levels. Courses and practica cover a range of subjects from understanding public health problems to the design of interventions to prevent or eradicate those problems. In addition to the principles, practices, theories, and methods of health education, faculty research and practice interests include women's health, rural health, ethnic minority health, adolescent health, health of the elderly, and substance abuse. Other areas of departmental emphasis include injury prevention, health communication, ethics, program planning and evaluation, and methodological subjects, including measurement issues, survey research, and qualitative methods. The department offers two master's and two doctoral degree programs in response to students' individual professional goals. For additional information, interested students should turn to the in-depth description in this section for the Department of Health Behavior and Health Education (HBHE) or to the Health Behavior and Health Education Web site.

Health Policy and Administration. Chair: Kerry E. Kilpatrick, M.B.A., M.S., Ph.D. The department offers three master's degrees: Master of Healthcare Administrations (M.H.A.), Master of Science in Public Health (M.S.P.H.), and Master of Public Health (M.P.H.). Both residential and nonresidential formats are offered for the M.P.H. and M.H.A., while the M.S.P.H. is available only in a residential format. The M.H.A. is a professional degree program for students pursuing management careers in hospitals, health departments, managed care organizations, group practices, and other health-care settings. It provides strong preparation in management, a comprehensive understanding of the health-care sector, and an opportunity to pursue an area of concentration. The M.S.P.H. is designed to prepare students for careers in analysis, planning, development, evaluation, and advocacy of policy at both the domestic and international levels. Students obtain a comprehensive understanding of the health-care system and master the analysis of health-care policy options while pursuing an area of concentration. The M.P.H. is intended for those students who hold a doctoral or professional degree. Students gain a comprehensive understanding of public health philosophy, methods, and values. The Executive M.P.H. and M.H.A. are designed to meet the needs of working professionals who hold administrative or managerial positions in health-care organizations.

Maternal and Child Health. Chair: Pierre Buekens, M.D., Ph.D. The department is committed to improving the health of women, children and adolescents, and their families through the integration of teaching, research, and service programs. The interdisciplinary nature of the department is one of its key characteristics, with strengths in both U.S. and international maternal and child health. Physicians, nurses, social workers, and other public health professionals are prepared for a broad range of leadership roles in maternity care and family planning, child care and development, comprehensive family-centered health care, international maternal and child health, consumer and community development, public policy, financing, and legislation. The department offers three graduate programs: the Master of Public Health (M.P.H.), Master of Science in Public Health (M.S.P.H.), and Doctor of Public Health (Dr.P.H.).

Nutrition. Chair: Steven H. Zeisel, M.D., Ph.D. The department offers training in nutrition that encourages the integration of public health and medicine. The doctoral degree programs share a common core of training that includes biochemistry, behavior, policy development, and epidemiology. Students develop unique training programs specializing in nutritional biochemistry, intervention and policy, health behavior and policy, or public health practice. The two-year M.P.H. degree program is for students with a bachelor's degree who wish to enter a career in public health nutrition in public or private agencies and companies. This program, accredited by the American Dietetic Association, prepares students for eligibility to take the dietetic registration examination. A one-year program is available for Registered Dietitians and other midcareer professionals. The Professional Practice Program is the only one in the U.S. that provides an opportunity for full-time employed nutritionists to earn an M.P.H. degree while continuing to work. This program allows students to become eligible to take the dietetic registration examination. Additional information on the program can be found on the World Wide Web at http://www.sph.unc.edu/nutr/

Public Health Leadership Program. Director: Arnold D. Kaluzny, M.H.A., Ph.D. The Public Health Leadership Program (PHLP) is a new academic unit devoted to public health practice and leadership. The PHLP currently administers the schoolwide Master of Public Health (M.P.H.) degree program, with areas of concentration in health care and prevention, public health nursing, and distance learning; the Master of Science (M.S.) in public health nursing; and the Public Health Leadership Doctoral Program (Dr.P.H.).

INTERDISCIPLINARY PROGRAMS

Carolina Population Center. Director: Amy O. Tsui, Ph.D. This unique center provides coordination for a University-wide program in population research and research training. Its efforts span the social, behavioral, and health sciences. The training program provides financial support and interdisciplinary training at the postdoctoral level and for predoctoral trainees from many departments.

Center for Health Promotion–Disease Prevention. Director: Alan W. Cross, M.D. A collaborative effort of the UNC Schools of Medicine, Dentistry, Nursing, Public Health and Pharmacy, the center promotes research, innovative demonstration programs, teaching, consultation, and technical assistance. Special emphasis is given to the areas of cardiovascular diseases, cancer, low birth weight, blue-collar work site health promotion, aging, and the education of health professionals. These integrated activities offer opportunities for students to work in a multidisciplinary environment while focusing on critical health issues.

Center for Public Health Practice. Director: Rachel Stevens, Ed.D., RN. The Center for Public Health Practice provides research, technical assistance, and problem analysis on public health problems.

Institute for Environmental Studies. Director: Douglas J. Crawford-Brown, M.S., Ph.D. The purpose of the institute is to foster and coordinate interdisciplinary research, teaching, and service in environmental concerns among the various UNC programs. In addition, the institute facilitates cooperative efforts on environmental matters between the University's main campus and other UNC campuses and with other colleges and universities, as well as with government and private agencies.

Injury Prevention Research Center. Director: Carol W. Runyan, M.P.H., Ph.D. The mission of this center is to stimulate and to participate in interdisciplinary research and to facilitate the translation of research into injury control policies and programs for prevention, acute care, and rehabilitation at the state, regional, and national levels. Research focuses on injuries associated with leisure, work, and violence. Other activities stress development and evaluation of injury prevention efforts and professional education.

Cecil G. Sheps Center for Health Services Research. Director: Gordon H. DeFriese, M.A., Ph.D. Established in 1968, this center conducts organized interdisciplinary research on the structure and impact of health-care services delivery systems. A fundamental interest is the interaction between the medical-care system and vulnerable populations, such as the elderly, people in poverty, rural residents, minority groups, children, the chronically ill, and the mentally ill. Questions about access to care, quality of care, and efficacy and effectiveness of care as they affect health-related quality of life are examined in a variety of studies.

UNIVERSITY OF NORTH TEXAS HEALTH SCIENCE CENTER AT FORT WORTH/ UNIVERSITY OF NORTH TEXAS

Master of Public Health Program

Program of Study

A student interested in graduate work in the public health program at the University of North Texas Health Science Center may pursue a Master of Public Health (M.P.H.) degree. The program is a cooperative program with the University of North Texas (UNT). This degree is awarded with a concentration in one of eight specialty tracks. Specialty tracks include community health, environmental health, epidemiology, health administration, health behavior, health economics, health services research, and occupational health.

The required areas for the core curriculum in public health are biostatistics, epidemiology, health administration, environmental health, and social and behavioral sciences. The public health program is designed to fully utilize, wherever appropriate, existing courses and program resources of the UNT Health Science Center and the University of North Texas.

A unique component of the M.P.H. program allows osteopathic physicians to train for careers in public health/primary care with opportunities to practice in urban and rural communities. The program is designed to be completed in four years if combined with the D.O. degree. The M.P.H. program is designed to provide training in the core areas of public health. Other dual-degree programs include the D.D.S./M.P.H. in cooperation with the Texas A&M University System Baylor College of Dentistry and the M.P.H./M.S. or M.P.H./Ph.D. degrees in cooperation with the UNT School of Community Service and the College of Arts and Sciences.

Research Facilities

UNT Health Science Center has 50,000 square feet of prime research space distributed among the different departments. Offices for the faculty, support staff, and administration occupy 6,000 square feet of additional space. The research facilities include state-of-the-art laboratories in a superb research environment. Support facilities include a large multianimal (AALAC-approved) vivarium and the 53,000-square-foot Gibson D. Lewis Health Science Library. Current holdings include more than 139,000 volumes and 2,200 journal subscriptions. The library's Learning Resource Center contains more than 5,700 audiovisual and computer software programs.

The University of North Texas has outstanding facilities to support the M.P.H. program and specialized tracks. The Science Research Building, with 60,000 square feet dedicated to research, and two additional facilities for geographic information systems (GIS) and remote sensing have direct application to the M.P.H. program and its specialized tracks.

Financial Aid

Students seeking financial assistance should contact the UNT Health Science Center Financial Aid Office for the most current information on availability of programs and eligibility requirements.

Cost of Study

In 1998–99, tuition and fees for residents of Texas are $62 per semester hour, with a $100 minimum for a regular semester. Tuition for nonresidents is $275 per semester hour but is waived for certain qualified graduate students with resident tuition charged. These figures do not include fees for certain courses. (All fees are subject to change.)

Living and Housing Costs

Housing facilities in Fort Worth are moderately priced and range from $300 to $450 for a one-bedroom apartment to $500 to $600 for a two-bedroom apartment. No campus housing is available. General cost-of-living figures are below the national average but are equal to the cost-of-living within the state of Texas.

Student Group

Total enrollment at UNT Health Science Center is approximately 550; graduate students account for some 25 percent of the total enrollment. The public health program graduate students perform their course work at the UNT Health Science Center campus in Fort Worth and, for some tracks, at the UNT campus in Denton.

Student Outcomes

Public health professionals assist in meeting the needs of the growing health-care industry by working in local, state, and national public health agencies and in private organizations, such as hospitals, health management organizations, and clinics. The Master of Public Health degree provides a broad spectrum of expertise that benefits physicians, nurses, dentists, allied health professionals, veterinarians, social workers, health educators, and health-care industry administrators.

Location

UNT Health Science Center is in Fort Worth, a city of 450,000 people known for its colorful western heritage and friendly, casual lifestyle. The campus is near Fort Worth's downtown area and adjacent to its cultural district, which includes the Amon Carter Museum of Western Art, Kimbell Art Museum, Fort Worth Art Museum, and Fort Worth Museum of Science and History. The area is served by the Dallas-Fort Worth International Airport.

The University and The Center

UNT Health Science Center, a public institution, is composed of the Graduate School of Biomedical Sciences and the Texas College of Osteopathic Medicine. The Center is nationally recognized for osteopathic medical education, biomedical sciences education, multidisciplinary biomedical research, and primary and specialized patient care.

UNT, established in 1890, is a multipurpose institution with offerings leading to graduate degrees in more than fifty disciplines, including biology, environmental science, chemistry, psychology, health promotion, and social sciences.

Applying

Applicants should request admission forms from the Graduate School of Biomedical Sciences. Applications may also be downloaded from the Web site listed below. Admission requirements include a baccalaureate degree or its equivalent from a regionally accredited institution, a competitive GPA in undergraduate work, and a competitive GRE score. International students must have a TOEFL score of 550 or better. Two letters of evaluation and a statement of personal career goals are also required.

Correspondence and Information

Graduate School of Biomedical Sciences
UNT Health Science Center
3500 Camp Bowie Boulevard
Fort Worth, Texas 76107-2699

Telephone: 817-735-2401
800-511-GRAD (toll-free)
E-mail: gsbs@hsc.unt.edu
World Wide Web: http://www.hsc.unt.edu

University of North Texas Health Science Center at Fort Worth/University of North Texas

THE ADMINISTRATION AND SPECIALIZED TRACKS

Public Health Advisory Council

Thomas Yorio, Ph.D., Dean of the Graduate School of Biomedical Sciences (telephone: 817-735-2560; e-mail: gsbs@hsc.unt.edu), UNTHSC.
Fernando M. Treviño, Ph.D., M.P.H., Professor and Chair of Public Health and Preventive Medicine, Executive Director of M.P.H. Program, UNTHSC.
Gilbert Ramírez, Dr.P.H., Associate Professor and Vice Chair of Public Health and Preventative Medicine, Associate Director of M.P.H. Program, UNTHSC.
Stephen L. Cobb, Ph.D., Associate Professor and Chair of the Department of Economics, UNT.
Art Goven, Ph.D., Professor of Biological Sciences and Faculty Executive Assistant to the Chancellor (telephone: 940-565-2477; e-mail: goven@abn.unt.edu), UNT.
David W. Hartman, Ph.D., Associate Professor of Anthropology and Dean of the School of Community Service.

Graduate Advisor for M.P.H. Program: Gilbert Ramírez, Dr.P.H., Associate Professor and Vice Chair of Public Health and Preventive Medicine, Associate Director of M.P.H. Program, UNTHSC.

Community Health (UNTHSC): Ximena Urrutia-Rojas, Dr.P.H., Track Director; Claudia Coggin, M.S.; Adela N. Gonzalez, M.P.A.; Sue Lurie, Ph.D. The community health track provides unique learning opportunities through the integration of teaching, research, and service activities. The ultimate goal is to prepare the students to assume leadership in the promotion and preservation of health, applying socially and culturally appropriate approaches in the community.

Environmental Health (UNT): Sam F. Atkinson, Ph.D., Track Director. Students choosing the environmental health track learn to identify, explore, and find solutions to environmental health issues, using such tools as environmental monitoring, risk assessment, and hazardous waste management.

Epidemiology (UNTHSC): Antonio A. René, Ph.D., M.P.H., Track Director. The epidemiology track concentrates on the principles, methods, and application of disease investigation, surveillance, occurrence, and distribution among the population.

Health Administration (UNTHSC): Douglas A. Mains, Dr.P.H., Track Director; Robert Kaman, Ph.D., J.D.; Ken Koelln, Ph.D.; Jeff Rous, Ph.D.; Ximena Urrutia-Rojas, Dr.P.H. The purpose of the health administration track is to prepare professionals to deal with a variety of problems relating to the organization, management, planning, and evaluation of public health and health-care services, with a primary emphasis on the public sector.

Health Behavior (UNT): Joseph A. Doster, Ph.D., Track Director; Eugenia Bodenhamer-Davis, Ph.D.; Joseph Critelli, Ph.D.; Susan Franks, Ph.D.; Sigrid Glenn, Ph.D.; Art Goven, Ph.D.; Charles Guarnaccia, Ph.D.; Jim Hall, Ph.D.; Ernest Harrell, Ph.D.; Kimberly Kelly, Ph.D.; Sander Martin, Ph.D.; Jerry McGill, Ph.D.; Vincent Ramos, Ph.D.; Sheila Reed, Ph.D.; Ray Toledo, Ph.D.; Warren Watson, Ph.D. Students acquire knowledge and skills for careers in the application of behavioral science principles to the investigation and promotion of behavioral health and prevention of illness.

Health Economics (UNT): Kenneth Koelln, Ph.D., and Jeffrey Rous, Ph.D., Track Directors. The health economics track is designed to provide public health professionals with expertise to analyze alternative options for allocating community resources to competing public health programs in order to maximize the benefits to society as a whole.

Health Services Research (UNT): Susan Brown Eve, Ph.D., Track Director; Thomas Barton, Ph.D.; Terry Clower, Ph.D.; Tyson Gibbs, Ph.D.; David Hartman, Ph.D.; Stanely Ingman, Ph.D.; Robert John, Ph.D.; Ann Jordan, Ph.D.; Erma Lawson, Ph.D., Jeffrey Longhofer, Ph.D.; Richard Lusky, Ph.D.; Larry Naylor, Ph.D.; Joseph Oppong, Ph.D.; Vijayan Pillai, Ph.D.; Alicia ReCruz, Ph.D.; Daniel Rodeheaver, Ph.D; Keith Turner, Ph.D.; David Williamson, Ph.D.; Dale Yeatts, Ph.D. The objectives of the health services research track are to train professionals to assess the health status and need for health-care services in target populations and to evaluate the implementation and outcomes of health-care delivery systems.

Occupational Health (UNTHSC): John C. Licciardone, D.O., M.B.A., Track Director. The occupational health M.P.H. track is intended for health practitioners (physicians, nurses, physician assistants, and D.O. and P.A. students) who seek a specialization in occupational health. The major objective of the occupational health track is to expand the fundamental knowledge and experience of health-care practitioners to include public health and occupational health along with clinical practice.

Cooperative Dual Programs

D.O./M.P.H. (UNTHSC): Muriel Marshall, D.O., M.P.H.T.M., Dr.P.H., Course Director/Advisor. This dual-degree option provides osteopathic physicians with specialized training to develop, integrate, and apply culturally competent social, psychological, and biomedical approaches to the promotion and preservation of health.

D.D.S./M.P.H. (Baylor College of Dentistry/UNTHSC): Linda C. Niessen, D.M.D., M.P.H., Advisor. This dual-degree option provides dental health-care providers with specialized training to develop, integrate, and apply social, psychological, and biomedical approaches to the promotion and preservation of oral dental health.

M.S. in Sociology/M.P.H. or M.P.H./Ph.D. in Sociology (UNT/UNTHSC): Susan Brown Eve, Ph.D., Track Director. These dual-degree options prepare students for careers as either academic or professional health services researchers.

M.P.H./Ph.D. in Health Psychology/Behavioral Medicine (UNT/UNTHSC): Joseph A. Doster, Ph.D., Advisor. This dual-degree option provides clinical health psychologists with public health training for careers in behavioral medicine, behavioral health programming, and biopsychosocial research.

UNIVERSITY OF PITTSBURGH

Graduate School of Public Health

Programs of Study

The Graduate School of Public Health offers courses of study and research in many areas, including biostatistics, chronic disease epidemiology, community health services, health administration, health policy analysis, human genetics, genetic counseling, environmental and occupational health, health promotion and education, infectious disease epidemiology, infectious diseases and microbiology, nutritional epidemiology (for registered dietitians), psychiatric epidemiology, public health social work, and public health statistics. Involvement in such specific research units as the Center for Public Health Practice, Center for Minority Health, Health Policy Institute, the Pittsburgh Genetics Institute, and the Health Services Research Unit is possible.

The degrees offered are the Master of Public Health, Master of Health Administration, Master of Health Promotion and Education, Master of Science, Doctor of Public Health, and Doctor of Philosophy. Joint degrees (J.D./M.P.H., M.D./M.P.H., and M.H.A./M.B.A.) are available, and there is a cooperative program (M.Div./M.P.H.) with Pittsburgh Theological Seminary. A multidisciplinary M.P.H. is offered for experienced health professionals and advanced students. A certificate in management for health professionals is given jointly with the School of Nursing, and a certificate in risk assessment is offered.

Research Facilities

The School is equipped with modern research and teaching laboratories. Its specialized facilities include animal facilities, very large population datasets, a whole-body counter, a mass spectrometer, and computer teaching laboratories. Research opportunities exist in local industries, county and state health departments, hospitals, and local health and welfare agencies. The Maurice and Laura Falk Library of the Health Sciences contains approximately 50,000 volumes and 150 journals of particular interest to the Graduate School of Public Health. Supplementing the Library of the Health Sciences are the other libraries in the University library system. The School houses a number of centers, including the new Center for Public Health Practice and the Center for Minority Health.

Financial Aid

The School receives funds each year for a limited number of Public Health Service traineeships. Every eligible student is given consideration for some aid to the extent of funds available. In addition, certain programs have a limited number of fellowships or traineeships for qualified students enrolled in those programs. They include predoctoral and postdoctoral fellowships in aging, alcohol, cardiovascular, diabetes, and psychiatric epidemiology and traineeships for social workers holding the M.S.W. degree who are concentrating in public health social work. Eligibility for the preceding aid requires U.S. citizenship or, in the case of foreign nationals, permanent residence or immigrant status. There is no financial aid for international students.

Cost of Study

For full-time students, the tuition charge per term for 1998–99 is $4701 for state residents and $9686 for out-of-state students. This does not include such costs as student health service fees and student activity fees. For part-time students, the cost per credit hour is $388 for state residents and $799 for nonresidents.

Living and Housing Costs

The University has no housing for graduate students, but the Off-Campus Housing Office assists students in obtaining housing. A conservative estimate of monthly living expenses would include approximately $350–$400 for rent, $250 for food, and $100 for miscellaneous expenses.

Student Group

There are approximately 520 students registered in the School for the current academic year, of whom about 13 percent are from other countries. Thirty-two percent of the students are pursuing doctoral studies. Graduates of the School of Public Health have come from all fifty states and sixty-six countries.

Location

Pittsburgh, the Renaissance City of America, known the world over in years past as a center of steel and coal production, is rapidly moving into new technologies. Among other features of the city are the headquarters of a hundred major industrial concerns; cultural opportunities, including the symphony, the ballet, the opera, shows, concerts, and fairs; many parks and recreational facilities; and the Civic Arena, which has one of the world's largest retractable domes. Recreational opportunities include golf, hunting, and fishing in nearby mountain areas; skiing within a few hours' drive of the city; hiking, camping, and stream and lake sports; and professional baseball, football, and hockey.

The School is located in the Oakland area of Pittsburgh, which also includes the Carnegie Library and Museum, Scaife Galleries, the educational television station, four of the city's colleges and universities, and the University of Pittsburgh Medical Center complex.

The School

The Graduate School of Public Health was established in 1948 by the trustees of the University of Pittsburgh as a result of a gift of $13.6 million from the A. W. Mellon Educational and Charitable Trust. In 1957, the School moved into an eight-story building with a capacity of more than 2 million cubic feet, which it soon outgrew. An extension with 48,000 square feet of floor space has since been added. A building designed specifically for toxicological research houses the Department of Environmental and Occupational Health.

Applying

To be considered for fall admission, students should submit applications before the end of June (some programs have earlier deadlines). Admission to the winter and spring terms is possible under certain circumstances. An undergraduate average of at least 3.0 (on a 4.0 scale) is required, and applicants who do not have a postbaccalaureate degree must send the results of the General Test of the Graduate Record Examinations. Some programs require the GRE of all applicants. In some cases, results of the GMAT, LSAT, MCAT, or DAT may be used. Applicants to the health administration program must submit GMAT results. International students must furnish certification of English proficiency, health status, and financial responsibility. Correspondence and requests for additional information may be directed to the address below.

Correspondence and Information

Office of Admissions
114 Parran Hall
Graduate School of Public Health
University of Pittsburgh
Pittsburgh, Pennsylvania 15261

Telephone: 412-624-3002
Fax: 412-624-3755
World Wide Web: http://www.pitt.edu/~gsphhome

University of Pittsburgh

DEPARTMENT CHAIRS AND RESEARCH ACTIVITIES

Donald R. Mattison, M.D., Dean.
Carol Redmond, Sc.D., Vice Dean.
Margaret Potter, J.D., Associate Dean.
Mary M. Derkach, J.D., Assistant Dean.
Barbara H. Evans, Ed.D., Assistant Dean.
Yvette H. Lamb, M.Ed., Assistant Dean.

Biostatistics. Howard Rockette, Ph.D., Acting Chair. Research is focused in biostatistical theory, methods, and applications. Areas of particular emphasis include the development and application of quantitative methods to evaluate health effects associated with urban and industrial environments; the methodology, design, conduct, and analysis of large-scale collaborative clinical trials; and statistical computing applications in public health and medicine. In addition, the faculty provides expertise in quantitative methods and their applications in public health problems through multidisciplinary projects in collaboration with other departments within the School, University, local and state health departments, and other agencies charged with the promotion of health. Research and teaching assistantships are available. GRE scores are required of all applicants.

Environmental and Occupational Health. Herbert S. Rosenkranz, Ph.D., Chair. The mission of this department is to identify chemicals and physical agents in the environment and the workplace that have the potential to cause a human health risk. Following such identification, studies at the organismic, tissue, cellular, and molecular levels are used to understand the basis of their potential risk. This information together with knowledge of the level of exposure is used to perform a risk assessment. The activities of the department cover a broad range of molecular and toxicological areas including sensory irritation, developmental abnormalities, contact and pulmonary sensitizers, mechanisms of DNA damage, and pathways to cancer. A new track in molecular toxicology has been implemented, in addition to an M.P.H. program and a certificate program in risk assessment. A computational toxicology track for Ph.D. students is planned for 1999. Water quality is addressed from both a biological and a chemical standpoint. Other areas of research include radiation health, radiochemistry, cytogenetics, and biomarkers. In addition, highly sophisticated computer-based expert systems are used to evaluate the structural and mechanistic bases of toxicological effects. Students are encouraged to participate in laboratory-based toxicological studies, computerized analyses, and risk assessments.

Epidemiology. Lewis H. Kuller, M.D., Dr.P.H., Chair. Research is oriented toward the prevention and control of major public health disease problems in the urban community. Areas of investigation cover chronic, infectious, nutritional, and psychiatric diseases as well as diseases associated with aging and behavioral and environmental risks to health. A number of studies address women's health issues, health in minority populations, telecommunications in public health, and molecular epidemiology. An area of investigation in pharmacoepidemiology is planned for the near future. Epidemiology has collaborative arrangements with all departments in the School of Public Health, the University of Pittsburgh Health Center, other schools of the health professions, and both state and local health departments. Currently, the department also is maintaining a number of registries for diseases such as Alzheimer's disease, cardiovascular disease, breast cancer, and diabetes mellitus. A WHO-collaborating diabetes research center is responsible for the maintenance of insulin-dependent diabetes millitus registries, for training in the epidemiology of diabetes, and for research studies in the prevention of diabetic complications and of diabetes itself. The Epidemiology Data Center coordinates multicenter clinical trials and registries, including a Liver Transplantation Database and the Bypass Angioplasty Revascularization Investigation, a clinical trial to compare the long-term outcome of coronary angioplasty and coronary bypass surgery.

Health Services Administration. Edmund M. Ricci, Ph.D., Chair and Director, Health Administration Program. The department offers the Master of Public Health degree with tracks in the social and behavioral sciences and in public health practice, the Master of Health Administration degree (with the School of Business), the Master of Health Promotion and Education degree (with the School of Education), and the Doctor of Public Health degree. The department's faculty is involved in a broad range of research related to health-care evaluation, community health assessment, cost containment, and health policy. The multidisciplinary faculty develops collaborative studies within the School and other areas of the University and with local, state, national, and international health-care agencies and organizations. Numerous projects involve the application of preventive intervention techniques on population subgroups from infants to frail elderly; the study of contemporary public health issues, such as outreach and education efforts for AIDS prevention; the assessment of alternative models for institutional care; the privatization of public health services; substance abuse treatment needs; and managed care models. The Center for Research on Health Care (CRHC) and the Health Policy Institute (HPI) design and conduct health-care–oriented studies. The CRHC's primary goal is the establishment of a focused research program in health services outcomes and cost-effectiveness analysis, including microcosting methodologies and patient preference (utility) analysis, while HPI projects seek to enhance health by improving the policies and decisions that influence health care.

Human Genetics. Michael B. Gorin, M.D., Ph.D., Interim Chair. Training and research in the department are oriented toward identifying genes that contribute to common diseases and understanding the mechanisms by which these genes contribute to disease susceptibility. The faculty includes clinical geneticists who identify and recruit patients and families for genetic studies; molecular and biochemical geneticists and cytogeneticists who characterize individuals at the chromosomal, cellular, and molecular levels; and mathematical geneticists who develop and apply the theories of population genetics and statistical methods to clinical and laboratory data in order to localize genes, to identify specific disease genes, and to quantify their contribution to disease risk. Clinical/medical geneticists and genetic counselors are trained to apply this knowledge to the identification of individuals and families who are at increased risk of disease and to counsel those individuals regarding their risk and their options with respect to genetic testing and medical interventions. Research includes the development and application of gene therapy to the treatment of genetic disease and studies of the prevention of disease based on genetic knowledge. Research and training in the department is multidisciplinary and collaborative, involving investigators from the School of Public Health, the School of Medicine, other schools of the health sciences, and the Faculty of Arts and Sciences. The genetic counseling program is accredited by the American Board of Genetic Counselors. Specialty training in biochemical and molecular genetics and cytogenetics is accredited by the American Board of Medical Genetics, and the M.D. in clinical genetics program is accredited by the Council for Graduate Medical Education.

Infectious Diseases and Microbiology. Charles R. Rinaldo Jr., Ph.D., Chair. The disciplines of molecular biology, immunology, epidemiology, and medicine are merged to provide a unique research environment in which basic scientists and clinicians work together to study the mechanism of pathogenesis of specific infectious diseases at the cellular and molecular levels as well as prevention of the spread of infectious agents through education and vaccine development. This multidisciplinary approach provides the graduate student with an opportunity to focus on a specific infectious agent and to study the host, utilizing a combination of approaches. Close associations are maintained with the Divisions of Infectious Diseases and Clinical Microbiology, the Departments of Molecular Genetics and Biochemistry and Pathology in the School of Medicine, and the University of Pittsburgh Cancer Institute, all of which lend additional flexibility to the design and implementation of graduate research projects. Areas of research include (a) molecular and immunological studies on herpesvirus infections in transplant recipients and the regulation of herpesvirus gene expression, (b) biologiccal and molecular virology and immunological studies on the pathogenesis of AIDS, (c) molecular mechanisms of anti-HIV drug resistance, (d) retrovirus-mediated gene therapy in HIV infection, (e) basic research in the development of vaccines for HIV and other infectious agents, and (f) early intervention and prevention of HIV infection and other sexually transmitted diseases.

Multidisciplinary M.P.H. Program. John G. Benitez, M.D., M.P.H., Director. This program (MMPH) provides doctoral-level health professionals with advanced training to perform in the roles of public health generalists and in public health leadership positions. The program provides an opportunity to meet the needs of health science professionals who wish to practice in a public health or community-based setting where data-based concepts, preventive medicine, health promotion, and public health practice will be of benefit. The program is open to holders of doctoral degrees in the health sciences, to advanced doctoral-level health science students considered on an individual basis, to individuals with extensive experience in health-related fields after review by the MMPH committee, and to holders of doctoral degrees from other professional schools, who are considered on an individual basis.

UNIVERSITY OF ROCHESTER

School of Medicine and Dentistry
Department of Community and Preventive Medicine

Programs of Study

The Department of Community and Preventive Medicine offers programs of study leading to the degrees of Master of Public Health and Doctor of Philosophy in health services research. The Master of Public Health (M.P.H.) is designed to train current and future health professionals by developing and enhancing their planning, evaluative, research, and management skills. The doctoral program trains students to teach and conduct independent research in the organization and delivery of health care.

For the M.P.H., a basic amount of course work is required, with additional elective course work and a master's essay (equivalent to 6 to 12 hours). Required courses include epidemiology, biostatistics, methods of medical-care research, health-care policy, management of health services, program evaluation, and environmental health. The master's essay, a research project in the area of medical care using epidemiological and other analytic methodologies, is designed, carried out, analyzed, and written by the student under the supervision of a faculty preceptor and an advisory committee.

The program of study leading to the Ph.D. in health services research is predicated on the belief that there is a critical need in academia, government, and the private sector for health care researchers. These researchers require backgrounds in statistics, economics, and policy analysis combined with an understanding of the institutions, structure, and functioning of the U.S. health care system. They also require knowledge of the important issues in health services research and a command of the special methods and research approaches that have been developed specifically in this field. In the Ph.D. program offered at the UR, there are special tracks for students interested in using political science or economics in studying the health-care system, as well as a track in general health services research based in the Department of Community and Preventive Medicine. The doctoral program is designed so that students earn the M.P.H. degree and/or the M.S. degree in public policy analysis along the way toward completing the Ph.D. requirements.

The M.P.H. and Ph.D. programs can be combined with the M.S. program in public policy analysis; the M.B.A. program; the Ph.D. program in economics, political science, statistics, education, and nursing; the M.S. program in medical statistics; the M.S. program in environmental studies; the M.S. program in industrial hygiene; or the M.D. program.

Research Facilities

Students have access to the University library system, which has 2.75 million volumes and 16,000 current periodicals. The Medical Center library has more than 225,000 volumes, including important medical periodicals and more than 3,000 current periodicals. Students have access to the University Computing Center, which has a wide variety of computers ranging from DEC VAX systems to IBM 4381. In addition, a large number of Macintoshes, IBM PCs, and UNIX-based workstations are available to students.

Financial Aid

For M.P.H. students, financial aid includes tuition scholarships, loans through the Federal Perkins Loan and federally insured student loan programs, work-study funds, and teaching and research assistantships. The work-study program allows eligible students to earn a portion of their educational expenses by working part-time. Applicants accepted into the program are asked to complete the Graduate and Professional School Financial Aid PROFILE. Full-time Ph.D. students are awarded a stipend, and tuition and health fees are fully covered.

Cost of Study

Tuition was $642 per credit hour for the 1997–98 academic year. First-year students register for 25 credit hours and second-year students register for 25 credit hours. Full-time students paid a health fee of approximately $970 per year.

Living and Housing Costs

National cost-of-living indices place the Rochester area at about the midrange. Several types of University housing, ranging from furnished single rooms to town-house units, are available. There are relatively inexpensive accommodations in private residences within walking distance of the Medical Center.

Student Group

The 65 students enrolled in the M.P.H. program include students currently or previously employed in the health field; students who recently received their bachelor's degree; physicians, dentists, and medical students; and combined-degree candidates who are pursuing a degree in this program as well as a degree in another program offered by the University. There are currently 12 Ph.D. students.

Student Outcomes

After earning the M.P.H. degree, graduates find employment in a variety of positions and settings. For example, recent graduates hold the following positions: executive director, obstetrics and gynecology, Brigham and Women's Hospital, Boston, Massachusetts; director, clinical practice analysis, Health Science Center, Syracuse, New York; program director, mental health association of Rhode Island, Pawtucket, Rhode Island; deputy budget director for Health and Human Services, N.Y.S. Assembly Ways and Means, Albany, New York; district public health director, Santa Fe, New Mexico; senior research director, Project Hope, Bethesda, Maryland.

Location

Located on Lake Ontario and close to the Finger Lakes region, the Rochester area, with a population of nearly 1 million, is large enough to offer opportunities for living, working, and recreation. The Rochester area has many community health agencies that are available to students for project work and practicum experiences.

The University

The University of Rochester is an independent, privately endowed institution founded in 1850. The School of Medicine and Dentistry was established in 1920. The University's other major divisions are Arts and Science, Education and Human Development, Engineering and Applied Science, Nursing, the William E. Simon Graduate School of Business Administration, and the Eastman School of Music. The proximity of the schools to each other allows for considerable interaction among the colleges. Of a total student population of 8,500, about 3,500 are enrolled in advanced-degree programs.

Applying

Applicants must submit transcripts, two letters of recommendation, and GRE General Test scores. TOEFL scores are required from international applicants. Applications for admission in the fall should be submitted by the preceding February 1, although applications received after that date will be considered on a space-available basis. Applicants interested in combined-degree programs are advised to contact the directors of both programs and to make separate application to each program.

Correspondence and Information

Graduate Programs
Box 644, Department of Community and Preventive Medicine
University of Rochester School of Medicine and Dentistry
601 Elmwood Avenue
Rochester, New York 14642-8644

Telephone: 716-275-7882
Fax: 716-461-4532
E-mail: brooks@prevmed.rochester.edu

University of Rochester

THE FACULTY AND THEIR RESEARCH

William H. Barker, Associate Professor; M.D., Johns Hopkins, 1966. Communicable chronic disease epidemiology, geriatric medicine, gerontology/health services, influenza.
Robert L. Berg, Professor Emeritus; M.D., Harvard, 1943. Health status indices, health-care resource allocation, multiphasic screening.
Theodore M. Brown, Professor; Ph.D., Princeton, 1968. History of science and history of medicine.
Timothy Dye, Associate Professor; Ph.D., SUNY at Buffalo. Social epidemiology, medical anthropology, maternal and child health.
Richard Frankel, Professor; Ph.D., CUNY Graduate Center, 1977. Communication and malpractice, role of empathy in medical care.
Johnathan Klein, Assistant Professor; M.D., University of Medicine and Dentistry of New Jersey, 1984; M.P.H., Harvard, 1984. Maternal and child health.
Kerry L. Knox, Assistant Professor; Ph.D., Northwestern, 1989. Biology, anthropology, maternal and child health.
Ruth Kouides, Assistant Professor; M.D., Syracuse, 1987. Preventive services/diffusion of innovation, women's health issues, disability process in primary care settings.
Stephen J. Kunitz, Professor; M.D., Rochester, 1964; Ph.D., Yale, 1970. Social change and disease patterns.
Mark Moss, Adjunct Assistant Professor; D.D.S., Marquette, 1984; Ph.D., North Carolina at Chapel Hill, 1994. Oral health services research, data analysis and methodology for correlated data.
Dana B. Mukamel, Assistant Professor; Ph.D., Rochester, 1993. Behavior of providers and patients in different market environments, impact of financial and nonpecuniary incentives on the provision of health care.
Alvin I. Mushlin, Professor; M.D., Vanderbilt, 1966; Sc.M., Johns Hopkins, 1973. Application of decision and cost-effectiveness analysis to the evaluation of clinical policies and practices.
Thomas Pearson, Albert D. Kraiser Professor and Chair; M.D., 1976, Ph.D., 1983, Johns Hopkins. Preventive cardiology epidemiology.
Charles E. Phelps, Professor; Ph.D., Chicago, 1973. Health-care financing, evaluation of medical technologies and medical practice patterns.
Linda Roberge, Assistant Professor; Ph.D., Syracuse. Management information systems, maternal health and public health information systems.
Sarah Trafton, Assistant Professor and M.P.H. Program Director; J.D., Suffolk, 1978. Health-care regulation, legal issues in the delivery of health-care services, long-term health-care policy.
David Witter, Assistant Professor; M.A. (economics), Washington State, 1970. Health-care organization and financing, application of guidelines and outcomes research, quality management.
James G. Zimmer, Professor Emeritus; M.D., Yale, 1957. Long-term care, utilization and quality review, health services planning.
Jack Zwanziger, Associate Professor and Doctoral Program Director; Ph.D., Rand, 1987. Effects of insurance on provider behavior, cost-effectiveness of health-care interventions.

UNIVERSITY OF WASHINGTON

School of Public Health and Community Medicine

Programs of Study

Programs within the School of Public Health and Community Medicine draw from clinical, basic, quantitative, and social sciences to deal with health and disease within communities. The emphasis is on preventing or ameliorating disease and promoting health among population groups; this emphasis contrasts with the single-patient orientation of other health professional schools. Degree programs are designed to produce academicians qualified in research and teaching, highly trained practitioners, innovative leaders in community health capable of shaping the structure and policies of public health, and environmental health specialists. The programs are characterized by their dependence on the research and service programs of the School, careful selection of students, emphasis on high quality and flexibility for adaptation to the needs and interests of individual students, and utilization of relevant strengths in other units of the University.

The Ph.D. degree is offered in biostatistics, environmental health, epidemiology, nutritional sciences, and pathobiology. A minimum of three years is normally required. A doctoral degree program may also be pursued through the Doctoral Opportunities Program in health services. Combined M.D./M.P.H., M.D./Ph.D., and D.D.S./Ph.D. programs can be arranged.

Several master's degrees are awarded. The Master of Public Health program, designed to prepare public health generalists, is offered in environmental health, epidemiology, nutrition, public health genetics, and health services. Master's degree programs are generally of two years' duration and require the completion of a thesis. An extended M.P.H. degree program, designed for health professionals who remain employed while pursuing the degree, is offered through intensive summer sessions and directed study supplemented with weekend sessions during the academic year. Completion of the extended M.P.H. degree program takes three years; special tuition rates apply. The Master of Science degree is offered in the following areas of specialization: biostatistics, environmental health, epidemiology, health services, nutritional sciences, and pathobiology. A Master in Health Administration (M.H.A.) degree is also available through the School. The M.H.A. program trains health services, hospital, and medical care administrators.

Research Facilities

The Health Sciences Library provides access to more than 345,000 volumes, 4,000 periodicals, and online bibliographic services for all National Library of Medicine and most commercial databases. Well-equipped laboratories contain facilities for work in biochemistry, immunochemistry, microbiology, toxicology, electron microscopy, and industrial hygiene. Facilities for animal experimentation (including experiments with primates) are also available. Computing services include a variety of mainframes and microcomputers, the major programming languages, and applications for word processing, database management, graphics, spreadsheet, and statistical analysis. School relationships include those with the University Hospital and affiliated hospitals, the Group Health Cooperative, and state and local health agencies.

Financial Aid

Many graduate students receive financial assistance from the department, the University, and outside sources.

Cost of Study

Tuition in 1997–98 was $4322 per quarter for nonresident students and $1744 per quarter for state residents. Students residing in the state for one year may be eligible to apply for resident status. Tuition in the extended M.P.H. program was $260 per credit for all students.

Living and Housing Costs

A wide selection of privately owned rental units in various price ranges is available in the area. General information about off-campus housing is available from the Student Housing Affairs Office, 105 HUB. The University's Housing and Food Services Office, 301 Schmitz Hall, offers assistance to students wishing to use campus facilities.

Student Group

In 1997–98, the total enrollment of the School of Public Health and Community Medicine was 659 students; 546 were graduate students, 45 were undergraduates, and 68 were in certificate programs. The group included 400 women and 124 members of minority groups.

Location

Seattle is the cultural center of western Washington, with a professional symphony orchestra, a repertory playhouse, an opera company, and a ballet company. A science center, a bustling farmers' market, and a restored old town are popular attractions for visitors and natives, as are the city's professional football, basketball, and baseball teams. Seattle's temperate climate and its location on Puget Sound, between the Cascade and Olympic mountain ranges, provide superb opportunities for year-round sailing, canoeing, hiking, and mountaineering. Cross-country and downhill ski areas are within an hour's drive.

The University

The University of Washington occupies 680 acres on the shores of Lake Washington in a residential area of Seattle. Established in 1861, it was the first state university on the West Coast. Today, it is recognized for the high quality of its research and graduate programs. The University of Washington has ranked among the top five institutions in the country in the amount of competitive grant and contract support received from federal sources for several years. The 35,000 students at the University represent all ethnic groups, most geographic areas in the nation, and most of the countries in the world; 22 percent are graduate students. There is a Graduate and Professional Student Senate, as well as more than 350 student organizations and an intramural sports program.

Applying

Acceptance by the UW Graduate School, a bachelor's degree, and adequate preparation for the student's particular field of interest are required for admission to the School. Catalogs and application forms are available on request. The Graduate School application deadline is July 1 for the fall quarter, but programs in the School of Public Health and Community Medicine at UW urge candidates to apply by January 15 for evaluation by April 1.

Correspondence and Information

University of Washington
Dean's Office
School of Public Health
Box 357230
Seattle, Washington 98195-7230
Telephone: 206-543-1144
Fax: 206-543-3813

University of Washington

THE FACULTY AND THEIR RESEARCH

BIOSTATISTICS. T. Fleming, Ph.D., Professor and Chair: survival analysis, cancer clinical trials, AIDS research, sequential analysis. **Professors:** N. Breslow, Ph.D.: statistical methods in epidemiology, generalized linear models, childhood cancer. J. Crowley, Ph.D.: survival analysis, cancer clinical trials. K. Davis, Ph.D.: density estimation, cardiovascular data analysis, clinical trials. T. DeRouen, Ph.D.: methods for correlated data and applications in dentistry, epidemiology of sexually transmitted diseases. P. Diehr, Ph.D.: health services, small-area analysis, health status. L. Fisher, Ph.D.: sequential clinical trial analysis, new drugs/biologics in humans, clinical trial methodology. A. Hallstrom, Ph.D.: clinical trial methodologies, especially in cardiovascular and emergency services applications. R. Kronmal, Ph.D.: nonparametric density estimation, computer algorithms, cardiovascular data analysis, clinical trials. B. McKnight, Ph.D.: statistical methods in epidemiology, human genetics, and animal carcinogenicity testing. F. O'Sullivan, Ph.D.: quantitation in emission-computed tomography, image analysis, function estimation. A. Peterson, Ph.D.: survival data methodology, competing risks, design and analysis of disease prevention trials. R. Prentice, Ph.D.: failure time analysis, disease prevention trials, epidemiologic methods. S. Self, Ph.D.: longitudinal data analysis, survival time models, cancer prevention and screening trials. E. Thompson, Ph.D., Sc.D.: population genetics and evolution, statistical genetics, computational biology. G. van Belle, Ph.D.: clinical trials, neuroepidemiology, applied statistics, screening, epidemiology, geriatrics, environmental studies. P. Wahl, Ph.D.: multivariate statistical techniques, especially regression analysis applied to cardiovascular data. J. Wellner, Ph.D.: empirical processes, semiparametric models, asymptotic efficiency, survival analysis, martingales. E. Wijsman, Ph.D.: statistical genetics, population genetics, genetic epidemiology. **Associate Professors:** W. Barlow, Ph.D.: survival analysis, residuals, applications to ophthalmology and cancer screening. J. Benedetti, Ph.D.: statistical methodology in infectious disease research, cancer clinical trials. S. Emerson, M.D., Ph.D.: clinical trials, sequential testing, survival analysis, categorical data, statistical consulting. M. Leblanc, Ph.D.: tree-based methods for regression and exploratory survival analysis. B. Leroux, Ph.D.: toxicology, analysis of random effects models, stochastic processes, dental research. D. Lin, Ph.D.: analysis of failure time data, designs and analysis studies. N. Temkin, Ph.D.: clinical trials, recovery models, statistical modeling of epileptic phenomena, survival analysis. M. L. Thompson, Ph.D.: filtered point processes, diagnostic methods, longitudinal reference ranges. **Assistant Professors:** M. Emond, Ph.D.; P. Heagerty, Ph.D.; J. Hughes, Ph.D.; M. McIntosh, Ph.D.; B. Richardson, Ph.D.; L. Sheppard, Ph.D.; D. Yanez, Ph.D.; Q. Yao, Ph.D.

ENVIRONMENTAL HEALTH. G. van Belle, Ph.D., Professor and Chairman: biostatistics, environmental risk factors for neurodegenerative diseases, environmental statistics. **Professors:** T. Burbacher, Ph.D.: behavioral toxicology of trace metals, biomarkers of metal exposure. H. Checkoway, Ph.D.: occupational and environmental epidemiology. L. Costa, Dott. Pharm.: neurotoxicology, developmental neurotoxicity. D. Eaton, Ph.D.: biochemical toxicology, aflatoxin carcinogenesis. E. Faustman, Ph.D.: molecular mechanisms of developmental/reproductive toxicity, risk assessment. G. Franklin, M.D., M.P.H.: occupational injury, neurological epidemiology, public health nutrition. D. Kalman, Ph.D.: environmental chemistry, detection/fate of chemical hazards. J. Koenig, Ph.D.: health effects/lung response of air pollutants. D. Luchtel, Ph.D.: air pollution, fiber toxicology, microscopy. C. Omiecinski, Ph.D.: molecular toxicology, genetic regulation of biotransformation enzymes. J. Woods, Ph.D.: molecular biochemistry and toxicology of metals. **Associate Professors:** S. Barnhart, M.D., M.P.H.: occupational/environmental and pulmonary medicine. W. Daniell, M.D., M.P.H.: occupational medicine and epidemiology. R. Fenske, Ph.D.: exposure assessment, agricultural health, pesticides, risk analysis. S. Guffey, Ph.D.: industrial ventilation, occupational exposure assessment. J. Kaufman, M.D., M.P.H.: epidemiology of occupational/environmental factors in respiratory, skin, and cardiovascular diseases; occupational lead poisoning. T. Kavanagh, Ph.D.: glutathione metabolism, analytic cytology, in vitro toxicology. J. Kissel, Ph.D.: human/environmental risk assessment, hazardous-waste management treatment. M. Morgan, Sc.D.: applied respiratory physiology and inhalation toxicology. A. Nevissi, Ph.D.: environmental radioactivity, nuclear chemistry, radioecology. M. Thompson, Ph.D.: diagnostic methods, reference ranges. **Assistant Professors:** C. Brodkin, M.D., M.P.H.; M. Keifer, M.D., M.P.H.; S. Liu, Sc.D.; M. Samadpour, Ph.D.; N. Seixas, Ph.D.; E. Sheppard, Ph.D.; Z. Xia, Ph.D.; M. Yost, Ph.D.

EPIDEMIOLOGY. T. Koepsell, M.D., M.P.H., Professor and Chairman: epidemiology of chronic diseases, health services research. **Professors:** E. Alexander, M.D., Ph.D.: infectious disease epidemiology. M. Austin, Ph.D.: genetic epidemiology, coronary artery disease. S. Beresford, Ph.D.: cancer control and health promotion. H. Checkoway, Ph.D.: occupational epidemiology. J. Daling, Ph.D.: maternal and child health, cancer research. S. Davis, Ph.D.: cancer epidemiology, disease etiology. I. Emanuel, M.D., M.S.P.M.: epidemiology of maternal and child health problems and childhood factors in adult diseases. H. Foy, M.D., Ph.D.: epidemiology and control of infectious disease. J. Gale, M.D.: epidemiology and control of infectious disease, international health. J. T. Grayston, M.D.: infectious disease epidemiology and control. J. Kreiss, M.D.: infectious diseases, international health. W. Kukull, Ph.D.: aging and neurodegenerative diseases. A. LaCroix, Ph.D.: epidemiology of aging. S. Moolgavkar, M.B.B.S., Ph.D.: cancer epidemiology, development of quantitative methodology. J. Potter, M.D., Ph.D.: cancer epidemiology. D. Siscovick, M.D., M.P.H.: preventive cardiology. A. Stergachis, Ph.D.: Drug epidemiology, health program evaluation. D. Thomas, M.D., Dr.P.H.: cervix and breast carcinoma epidemiology. T. Vaughan, M.D., M.P.H.: cancer/adverse reproductive outcomes, environmental/occupational exposures. N. Weiss, M.D., Dr.P.H.: cancer epidemiology. E. White, Ph.D.: cancer prevention. **Associate Professors:** B. Alderman, M.D., M.P.H.: epidemiology of birth defects, clinical epidemiology. S. Astley, Ph.D.: fetal alcohol syndrome prevention. G. Goldbaum, M.D., M.P.H.: epidemiology of human behaviors that increase risk for disease. V. Holt, Ph.D.: women's reproductive health and newborn care. J. Hoover, M.D., M.P.H.: cardiovascular epidemiology, public health practice. A. Kimball, M.D., M.P.H.: international health. L. Koutsky, Ph.D.: infectious diseases. A. Kristal, Dr.P.H.: nutrition and chronic disease epidemiology. B. Mueller, Dr.P.H.: pediatric injury and emergency treatment, maternal health. B. Psaty, M.D., M.P.H.: cardiovascular disease, health-care delivery systems. G. Reiber, Ph.D.: prevention of complications of diabetes. S. Schwartz, Ph.D.: cancer and cardiovascular disease etiology. P. Stehr-Green, Dr.P.H.: infectious diseases and immunization. M. Williams, Sc.D.: reproductive and perinatal epidemiology. **Assistant Professors:** C. Bynum, Ph.D.; C. Critchlow, Ph.D.; P. Cummings, M.D., M.P.H.; R. Davis, M.D., M.P.H.; D. Farrow, Ph.D.; S. Heckbert, M.D., Ph.D.; L. Jackson, M.D., M.P.H.; C. Mock, M.D., M.P.H.; M. Rossing, Ph.D., D.V.M., M. Wolf, Ph.D.

HEALTH SERVICES. W. Dowling, Ph.D., Professor and Chairman: health services management, medical care, management and organization theory. **Professors:** D. Buchner, M.D., M.P.H.: health promotion in the elderly, falls, geriatric decision making. M. Chapko, Ph.D.: program evaluation. F. Connell, M.D., M.P.H.: maternal/child health policy, pediatric hospital utilization. D. Conrad, Ph.D.: economic regulation in the hospital industry, health-care finance. S. Curry, Ph.D.: health behavior/behavioral sciences, smoking intervention. R. Day, M.D., Ph.D.: health information systems. R. Deyo, M.D., M.P.H.: patient behavior, clinical epidemiology. P. Diehr, Ph.D.: application of statistics to health services research, small-area analysis. D. Grembowski, Ph.D.: health care, prevention, outcomes of care. S. Hedrick, Ph.D.: long-term care, research design/analysis. T. Koepsell, M.D., M.P.H.: chronic diseases. J. LoGerfo, M.D., M.P.H.: quality of care. C. Madden, Ph.D.: insurance, health policy, health-care organization. D. Martin, Ph.D.: health services cost containment. E. Monsen, Ph.D.: nutrition, dietetics. D. Patrick, Ph.D.: sociology of health and illness. E. Perrin, Ph.D.: health information systems, health-care utilization, outcomes of health promotion. A. Ross, M.P.H.: leadership/management, managed care. N. Urban, Sc.D.: health economics, biostatistics in health services research. E. Wagner, M.D., M.P.H.: health services research. K. Wing, J.D., M.P.H.: public health law. H. Zuckerman, M.B.A., Ph.D.: health management research, health administration. **Associate Professors:** M. Bell, Ph.D.: health and social policy analysis, organization/delivery of community services. A. Cheadle, Ph.D.: health promotion/disease prevention, health economics (organization and finance). S. Gloyd, M.D., M.P.H.: international health. V. Holt, Ph.D., M.P.H.: women's reproductive health. A. Kimball, M.D., M.P.H.: maternal and child health, HIV/AIDS, international health. H. Meischke, Ph.D., M.P.H.: health-related content in mass media. A. Plough, Ph.D., M.P.H.: health policy and management. G. Reiber, Ph.D., M.P.H.: diabetes prevention and control. M. Richardson, Ph.D.: chronic diseases, children's services, mental retardation. C. Spigner, Dr.P.H.: race/ethnic diversity, disadvantaged populations. S. Sullivan, Ph.D.: pharmacy-related health services. E. Thompson, Ph.D.: smoking cessation. T. Wickizer, Ph.D., M.P.H.: health promotion evaluation. **Assistant Professors:** M. Cress, D. Gray, M.P.H., Sc.D.; S. Kinne, Ph.D.; William E. Lafferty, M.D., M.P.H.; D. Lessler, Phyllis Levine, Ph.D., M.Ed.; C. V. M. Taylor, B.M.B.S.; M. Weaver, Ph.D.

PATHOBIOLOGY. Professors: L. A. Campbell, Ph.D.: molecular biology, pathogenic mechanisms of chlamydiae. W. Carter, Ph.D.: elucidation of components in cell attachment. J. T. Grayston, M.D.: infectious disease etiology and epidemiology. S. Hakomori, M.D., D.Sc.: biochemistry of carbohydrate antigens on cells. G. E. Kenny, Ph.D.: mycoplasmas: antibiotic resistance and immune response. S. J. Klebanoff, M.D.: infectious diseases, granulocyte activities. C. Kuo, M.D., Ph.D.: antigenic analysis, immunology, pathogenesis of chlamydiae. M. Parsons, Ph.D.: molecular and cellular biology of protozoan parasites. S. Reed, Ph.D.: immune response to human pathogens. M. Roberts, Ph.D.: mycobacterium, antibiotic resistance genes. K. Stuart, Ph.D.: molecular biology of parasites. G. J. Todaro, M.D.: growth regulation in normal and tumor cells. **Associate Professors:** J. Feagin, Ph.D.: molecular parasitology, emphasizing organelle genome organization and expression and protozoan parasites. M. Kahn, Ph.D.: molecular recognition, protein structure-function relationships. P. Myler, Ph.D.: parasite molecular biology and genomics pathogens. D. Riley, Ph.D.: parasitology, urogenital pathogens. M. Rosenfeld, Ph.D.: mechanisms of atherogenesis gene expression. J. Swindle, Ph.D.: regulated gene expression in *Trypanosoma cruzi*. M. Thouless, Ph.D.: retroviruses, enteric viruses, immunodiagnosis, virus variability. W. van Voorhis, M.D.: pathogenesis of infections with *Trypanosoma cruzi* (chagas disease), *Treponema pallidum* (syphilis), and *Chlamydia trachomatis* (pelvic inflammatory disease). **Assistant Professors:** S. Bartelmez, Ph.D.; M. Bosch, Ph.D.; G. Cangelosi, Ph.D.; R. Howard, Ph.D.; S. J. Kahn, M.D.; P. Lampe, Ph.D.; T. Rose, Ph.D.; T. White, Ph.D.

YALE UNIVERSITY

School of Medicine
Department of Epidemiology and Public Health

Programs of Study

The Yale School of Medicine's Department of Epidemiology and Public Health is also an independently accredited school of public health. It offers the Master of Public Health (M.P.H.) and the Doctor of Public Health (Dr.P.H.) (under faculty review in 1998–99) degrees through the School of Medicine and the Ph.D. degree through the Graduate School. The school is one of the few schools of public health with direct access to clinical and basic science departments, because of its medical school base, as well as direct access to private and public institutions and community health agencies. These multiple-resources allow the school to implement its mission of improving the status of community and individual health. Many specialties are available through the six academic divisions: Biostatistics; Chronic Disease Epidemiology; Environmental Health Sciences; Epidemiology of Microbial Diseases; Health Policy and Administration; and International Health. Some of these specialties are cardiovascular, psychosocial, aging, and cancer epidemiology; tropical diseases; epidemic investigation; AIDS epidemiology; parasitology; environmental risk assessment, management, and policy; and health practice and administration and policy analysis in such fields as health promotion, mental health, and maternal and child health. The school of public health also offers formal joint-degree programs with the Schools of Medicine, Nursing, Management, Forestry and Environmental Studies, and the Department of International and Area Studies in the graduate school.

Most M.P.H. students spend two years in residence, although those with earned health doctorates may be eligible for a shorter program. Doctoral candidates usually receive their degrees within four years, two or three of which are in residence. Postdoctoral fellows are appointed subject to the availability of funds.

Yale is a research-oriented institution. Research is emphasized in the teaching program and culminates in the master's thesis or doctoral dissertation. Faculty advisers help students with all aspects of their programs. A schoolwide M.P.H. core curriculum, combined with divisional requirements, electives, and field experiences, promotes employment flexibility. M.P.H. graduates, aided by an active career services office, secure a wide array of positions in the health field. Doctoral students usually choose academic careers, though a number are employed in research settings.

Research Facilities

The school's facilities include basic science and computer laboratories. Libraries include two within the school as well as the exceptionally well-stocked School of Medicine and University libraries. Several major research centers are also located in the school; for example, the Perinatal Epidemiology Research Unit, the first of its kind in the U.S.; the Cancer Control Research Unit for Connecticut, one of two such centers in the country; the John B. Pierce Foundation; and the Yale–World Health Organization Collaborating Centre for Health Promotion, Policy and Research.

Financial Aid

Financial aid consists primarily of student loans, supplemented by scholarships and work-study funds, or a combination of these. Most aid is offered on the basis of financial need; but, in addition, the Admission Committee awards five merit scholarships equivalent to half tuition. Ph.D. candidates are supported by training grants, research grants, and teaching fellowships. Fellowship and trainee support from federal funds is limited to citizens and permanent residents of the United States.

Cost of Study

Tuition for the academic year of 1998–99 is $19,300. Additional fees for those students in residence include a hospitalization premium of $930 per year, $1430 for books, and a $150 student activity fee.

Living and Housing Costs

For 1998–99, the standard nine-month budget for a single student at Yale University is estimated to be a total of $33,000.

Student Group

The school of public health admits about 115 students each year to its M.P.H. program. About 50 students are enrolled in the doctoral programs. Students vary in age, experience, and interest and come from many different states and countries. Physicians and minority students each account for about 10 to 15 percent of the M.P.H. class. The student diversity stimulates faculty members to share ideas and experiences in seminars and in research and community projects.

Location

New Haven, an industrial and commercial city surrounding the University, is also known for its theater, art, and medical resources. Auto, bus, plane, and train provide links to Boston and New York City. The school, located on the medical school campus, is within easy walking distance of the University campus, where lectures, concerts, art exhibits, and sports events attract both University staff and local residents.

The University and The School

Yale's ten professional schools, Graduate School, and College offer disciplinary depth as well as a remarkable range of course offerings. A notable strength of the University is the attention it pays to the individual student. The schools of medicine and public health carry out research, service, and teaching missions involving the full spectrum of health and disease. Other professional schools—chiefly Law, Management, Forestry and Environmental Studies, and Nursing—broaden the range of courses and research opportunities available to M.P.H. and doctoral students. The school of public health was last accredited in 1993 for a six-year term. It is one of the largest departments in the School of Medicine. The Dean of Public Health and Chair of the department is Michael H. Merson, M.D.

Applying

Prospective M.P.H. students may request a brochure and application package from the Admissions Office. Because the school operates on a rolling admissions plan, applicants benefit from completing the package well before the April 1 deadline for the M.P.H. and Dr.P.H. programs and January 2 for the Ph.D. program. An open house day allows applicants or accepted students to visit classes, meet professors and students, and tour the area. The school requires GRE or other standardized graduate admission scores for M.P.H. applicants and GRE scores for doctoral applicants. The TOEFL is also required of all international applicants. The field of public health can accommodate many interests, and each application is carefully reviewed by a faculty committee. Minority students are encouraged to apply. An application fee of $60 is required. The need for financial aid is not considered in the admission process.

Correspondence and Information

For M.P.H. or Dr.P.H.:
Admissions Office
Department of Epidemiology and Public Health
Yale University School of Medicine
P.O. Box 208034
New Haven, Connecticut 06520-8034
Telephone: 203-785-2844

For Ph.D.:
Admissions Office
Yale Graduate School of Arts and Sciences
P.O. Box 208323
Yale Station
New Haven, Connecticut 06520-8323
Telephone: 203-432-2770

Yale University

THE FACULTY AND THEIR RESEARCH

Biostatistics
Head: Robert W. Makuch, Ph.D.

The research interests of this division are concerned with developing a statistical basis for medical and health policy decisions that may advance public health around the world. Areas include methodological issues in clinical trials, modeling of biomedical time series data, regulatory affairs, statistical methods in epidemiology, analysis of time trends in cancer incidence, categorical data analysis, goodness of fit tests, statistical genetics, genetic epidemiology, cancer genetics, applications of probability and statistics to molecular biology and genetics, regression methods, and issues in multivariable analysis.
Faculty: E. Claus, Ph.D., M.D.; G. Fisch, Ph.D.; T. Holford, Ph.D.; S. Lowenthal, M.P.H., M.D.; R. Makuch, Ph.D.; M. Stowe, Ph.D.; D. Zelterman, Ph.D.; H. Zhang, Ph.D., H. Zhao, Ph.D.

Chronic Disease Epidemiology
Head: Michael B. Bracken, Ph.D., M.P.H.

The five principal areas of faculty research and teaching are cancer epidemiology with an emphasis on cancer control and on etiologic studies in association with the Yale Cancer Center; cardiovascular epidemiology focused on coronary heart disease and hypertension and work with the cardiology division of the Department of Internal Medicine; the epidemiology of aging centered on predictors of disability, hospitalization, nursing home admission, and mortality in association with the program on aging; a perinatal epidemiology unit where research includes effects of tobacco smoke, acid aerosols, and electromagnetic fields on infants and mothers in collaboration with the Departments of Obstetrics and Gynecology and of Pediatrics; and psychosocial epidemiology focusing on bereavement, social support, depression, and other predictors of morbidity and mortality in association with the Department of Psychiatry. Cancer research includes lung cancer in nonsmokers, invasive cervical cancer, multiple primary breast cancer, malignant melanoma, gastrointestinal cancer, male breast cancer, childhood cancers, risk of cancer after exposure to radiation and to herbicides, and changes in cancer trends over time.
Faculty: D. Baker, Ph.D.; K. Belanger, Ph.D.; M. Bracken, Ph.D.; L. Brass, M.D.; K. Brownell, Ph.D.; B. Cartmel, Ph.D.; V. DeVita Jr., M.D.; K. Ethier, Ph.D.; A. Feinstein, M.D.; R. Horwitz, M.D.; J. Ickovics, Ph.D.; B. Jones, Ph.D.; S. Kasl, Ph.D.; H. Krumholz, M.D.; B. Levy, Ph.D.; S. Mayne, Ph.D.; R. McCorkle, Ph.D.; K. Merikangas, Ph.D.; P. Moorman, Ph.D.; H. Risch, M.D., Ph.D.; P. Salovey, Ph.D.; D. Stevens, Ph.D.; M. Tinetti, M.D; V. Vaccarino, Ph.D., M.D.

Environmental Health
Head: Brian P. Leaderer, Ph.D.

Research involves epidemiologic studies of water, air quality, and the residential environment. Environmental factors affecting respiration and circulation, various aspects of thermoregulatory physiology, exercise physiology, sensory processes, aging, human exposures to environmental contaminants, perceptions of risks, and risk management.
Faculty: M. Cullen, M.D.; L. DiPietro, Ph.D.; J. Douglas, Ph.D.; A. DuBois, M.D.; B. Leaderer, Ph.D.; G. Mack, Ph.D.; L. Marks, Ph.D.; E. Nadel, Ph.D.; N. Stachenfeld, Ph.D.; J. Stitt, Ph.D.; J. Wise, Ph.D.; T. Zheng, Sc.D.

Epidemiology of Microbial Diseases
Head: Nancy H. Ruddle, Ph.D.

Research focuses on understanding the epidemiology and biology of parasitic, bacterial, and viral diseases. Emphasis is placed on understanding the interactions of pathogens with their vertebrate hosts and vectors in order to better understand the transmission, maintenance, and pathogenesis of disease. These studies are conducted at both the molecular and organismal level.
Faculty: S. Aksoy, Ph.D.; W. Andiman, M.D.; R. Baltimore, M.D.; D. Bessen, Ph.D.; H. Braig, Ph.D.; M. Cappello, M.D.; D. Fish, Ph.D.; G. Friedland, M.D.; J. Hawdon, Ph.D.; R. Heimer, Ph.D.; W. Hierholzer Jr., M.D.; P. Hotez, M.D., Ph.D.; K. Joiner, M.D.; D. McMahon-Pratt, Ph.D.; I. G. Miller, M.D.; L. Munstermann, Ph.D.; V. Navarro, M.D.; J. Neilan, Ph.D.; J. Niederman, M.D.; S. O'Neill, Ph.D.; C. Patton, Ph.D.; A. Ray, Ph.D.; N. Ruddle, Ph.D.; R. Ryder, M.D., M.Sc.; R. Sacca, Ph.D.; D. Scaramuzzino, Ph.D.; P. Selwyn, M.D., M.P.H.; D. Shapiro, M.D.; G. Tignor, Sc.D.; L. Zheng, Ph.D.; L. Zsak, D.V.M., Ph.D.

Health Policy and Administration
Head: Mark J. Schlesinger, Ph.D.

Research focuses on the joint application of the methods and theory of epidemiology, economics, and political science to public policy analysis, quality of care issues, and management in health-care systems. Areas of emphasis are the organization and financing of health services; mental health (depression and the elderly); the politics of health-care reform; maternal and child health (teenage pregnancy; access, quality, and effectiveness of prenatal care; disabilities; foster care); cost-effectiveness analysis of medical care and health-related programs (e.g., as applied to substance abuse); and the application of the social and behavioral sciences to health-care issues.
Faculty: E. Anderson, M.P.H.; E. Bradley, Ph.D.; H. Chauncey Jr., B.A.; D. Diers, M.S.N.; H. Dove, Ph.D.; B. Druss, M.D.; C. Grogan, Ph.D.; R. Hoff, Ph.D.; S. Horwitz, Ph.D.; E. Kaplan, Ph.D.; D. Kessler, M.D., J.D.; K. Kronebusch, Ph.D.; A. Novick, M.D.; M. Olson, Ph.D.; A. Ortega, Ph.D.; D. Paltiel, Ph.D.; J. Rizzo, Ph.D.; M. Schlesinger, Ph.D.; J. Sindelar, Ph.D.; W. White; Ph.D.

International Health
Head: Ilona S. Kickbusch, Ph.D.

Research projects are developed within the framework of the Yale/World Health Organization Centre on Health Promotion Policy Research. Scholars are appointed for periods of four to twelve months with anticipated continuing research collaboration with the Centre. Topics currently include "health investment" policy studies in Spain and national "health assets" surveys in Slovenia and Hungary; promoting health in schools, workplaces, and medical care settings in the European region of WHO; and environmental toxins in the countries of Central and Eastern Europe.
Faculty: G. Andreopoulos, LL.B., Ph.D.; M. Barry, M.D.; E. Clift, M.A.; Z. Dortbudak, Ph.D.; A. M. Foltz, Ph.D.; N. Groce, Ph.D.; J. Jekel, M.D.; L. Levin, Ed.D. Teaching faculty also are drawn from the several divisions of the Department of Epidemiology and Public Health as well as from other University professional schools and graduate departments.

Academic and Professional Programs in Law

This part of Book 6 consists of one section covering law. This section has a table of contents (listing the program directories, announcements, and in-depth descriptions); a program directory, which consists of brief profiles of programs in this field (and that include 50-word or 100-word announcements following the profiles, if programs have chosen to include them); Cross-Discipline Announcements, if any programs have chosen to submit such entries; and in-depth descriptions, which are more individualized statements included, if programs have chosen to submit them.

Section 31
Law

This section contains directories of institutions that have programs in law and legal and justice studies, followed by in-depth entries submitted by institutions that chose to prepare detailed program descriptions. Additional information about programs listed in the directory but not augmented by an in-depth entry may be obtained by writing directly to the dean of a graduate school or chair of a department at the address given in the directory.

For programs offering related work, see also in this book Business Administration and Management and Social Work; in Book 2 Criminology and Forensics; Public, Regional, and Industrial Affairs; Economics; and Political Science and International Affairs; in Book 4, Environmental Sciences and Management; and in Book 5, Management of Engineering and Technology.

CONTENTS

Program Directories

Announcements

Cross-Discipline Announcements

In-Depth Descriptions

See also:

Law

Albany Law School of Union University, Albany, NY 12208-3494. Awards JD, JD/MBA, JD/MPA. Approved by ABA. Member of AALS. JD/MBA offered jointly with College of Saint Rose, Rensselaer Polytechnic Institute, Sage Graduate School, and Union College. JD/MPA offered jointly with University at Albany, State University of New York. Part-time programs available. Faculty: 45 full-time (21 women), 39 part-time (9 women), 53.5 FTE. Students: 690 full-time (357 women), 42 part-time (28 women); includes 114 minority (47 African Americans, 35 Asian Americans, 28 Hispanics, 4 Native Americans), 10 international. Average age 27. 1,200 applicants, 71% accepted. In 1997, 250 degrees awarded. *Degree requirements:* Upper-class writing requirement required, foreign language and thesis not required. *Average time to degree:* first professional–3 years full-time, 4 years part-time. *Entrance requirements:* LSAT (average 150). Application deadline: 3/15 (priority date; rolling processing). Application fee: $50. *Expenses:* Tuition $19,295 per year full-time, $14,471 per year part-time. Fees $130 per year. *Financial aid:* In 1997–98, 33 research assistantships totaling $50,000, 321 grants, scholarships (106 to first-year students) totaling $1.824 million were awarded; full and partial tuition waivers, Federal Work-Study, institutionally sponsored loans, and career-related internships or fieldwork also available. Aid available to part-time students. Financial aid application deadline: 4/15; applicants required to submit FAFSA. *Faculty research:* Federal tax, constitutional law, secured transactions, international law, American politics. • Thomas H. Sponsler, Dean, 518-445-2321. Fax: 518-472-5865. Application contact: Dawn M. Chamberlaine, Assistant Dean of Admissions and Financial Aid, 518-445-2326. Fax: 518-445-2369. E-mail: admissions@mail.als.edu.

American University, Washington College of Law, Program in International Legal Studies, Washington, DC 20016-8001. Awards LL M. Member of AALS. Part-time and evening/weekend programs available. Faculty: 51 full-time (17 women), 95 part-time (27 women). Students: 45 full-time (21 women), 134 part-time (48 women); includes 2 minority (both Hispanics), 163 international. 387 applicants, 55% accepted. In 1997, 116 degrees awarded. *Entrance requirements:* TOEFL, JD. Application deadline: 6/1 (priority date; rolling processing). Application fee: $55. *Expenses:* Tuition $22,590 per year full-time, $837 per credit part-time. Fees $382 per year full-time, $242 per year part-time. *Financial aid:* Dean's fellowships, partial tuition waivers, and career-related internships or fieldwork available. Financial aid application deadline: 2/15. • Daniel D. Bradlow, Director, 202-274-4110.

American University, Washington College of Law, Program in Law, Washington, DC 20016-8001. Awards JD, JD/MA, JD/MBA, JD/MS. Approved by ABA. Member of AALS. Part-time and evening/weekend programs available. Faculty: 51 full-time (17 women), 95 part-time (27 women). Students: 881 full-time (550 women), 314 part-time (155 women); includes 287 minority (97 African Americans, 117 Asian Americans, 62 Hispanics, 11 Native Americans), 11 international. 4,409 applicants, 43% accepted. In 1997, 354 degrees awarded. *Entrance requirements:* LSAT, BA or BS. Application deadline: 3/1 (rolling processing). Application fee: $55. *Expenses:* Tuition $22,590 per year full-time, $837 per credit part-time. Fees $382 per year full-time, $242 per year part-time. *Financial aid:* Dean's fellowships, partial tuition waivers, Federal Work-Study, institutionally sponsored loans, and career-related internships or fieldwork available. Aid available to part-time students. Financial aid application deadline: 2/15. • Application contact: Sandra J. Oakman, Director of Admissions, 202-274-4101.

American University, Washington College of Law, Program in Law and Government, Washington, DC 20016-8001. Awards LL M. Member of AALS. *Entrance requirements:* TOEFL, JD. Application fee: $55. *Expenses:* Tuition $22,590 per year full-time, $837 per credit part-time. Fees $382 per year full-time, $242 per year part-time. *Financial aid:* Application deadline 2/15. • Jamin Raskin, Co-Director, 202-274-4268. Application contact: Sandra J. Oakman, Director of Admissions, 202-274-4101.

Arizona State University, College of Law, Tempe, AZ 85281. Awards JD, JD/MBA, JD/MS, JD/PhD, JD/MHSA. Approved by ABA. Member of AALS. JD/MS offered jointly with Department of Justice Studies; JD/PhD offered jointly with Interdisciplinary Program in Justice Studies. Faculty: 35 full-time. Students: 458 full-time (226 women); includes 114 minority (20 African Americans, 16 Asian Americans, 49 Hispanics, 29 Native Americans), 10 international. Average age 28. 1,754 applicants, 22% accepted. In 1997, 153 degrees awarded. *Degree requirements:* Research paper required, foreign language and thesis not required. *Average time to degree:* first professional–3 years full-time. *Entrance requirements:* LSAT. Application deadline: 3/1 (rolling processing). Application fee: $35. *Financial aid:* In 1997–98, 42 research assistantships totaling $34,617, 181 legal writing internships, scholarships were awarded; Federal Work-Study, institutionally sponsored loans, and career-related internships or fieldwork also available. Financial aid application deadline: 3/1; applicants required to submit FAFSA. *Faculty research:* Family law, jurisprudence, commercial law, intellectual property, Indian law. Total annual research expenditures: $90,032. • Alan A. Matheson, Interim Dean, 602-965-6188. Application contact: Leslie Mamaghani, Assistant Dean, Student Affairs, 602-965-6181.

Baylor University, School of Law, Waco, TX 76703. Awards JD, JD/MBA, JD/MT. Approved by ABA. Member of AALS. Faculty: 20 full-time (6 women), 35 part-time (3 women). Students: 392 full-time (136 women), 4 part-time (1 woman); includes 36 minority (4 African Americans, 5 Asian Americans, 24 Hispanics, 3 Native Americans), 1 international. 797 applicants, 38% accepted. In 1997, 155 degrees awarded. *Entrance requirements:* LSAT. Application deadline: 3/1 (rolling processing; 11/1 for spring admission). Application fee: $40. Electronic applications accepted. *Expenses:* Tuition $11,357 per year. Fees $482 per year. *Financial aid:* In 1997–98, 384 students received aid, including 319 grants; Federal Work-Study, institutionally sponsored loans, and career-related internships or fieldwork also available. • Dr. Bradley J. B. Toben, Dean, 254-710-2316. Application contact: Becky Beck, Admissions Director, 254-710-1911. Fax: 254-710-2316. E-mail: law_support@baylor.edu.

Boston College, Law School, Newton Center, MA 02159. Awards JD, JD/MA, JD/MBA, JD/MSW. Approved by ABA. Member of AALS. JD/MA offered jointly with the Higher Education Administration Specialization. Faculty: 54 full-time (19 women), 53 part-time (9 women). Students: 829 full-time (425 women); includes 160 minority (64 African Americans, 54 Asian Americans, 41 Hispanics, 1 Native American), 7 international. Average age 25. 4,158 applicants, 27% accepted. In 1997, 272 degrees awarded. *Average time to degree:* first professional–3 years full-time. *Entrance requirements:* LSAT. Application deadline: 3/1 (rolling processing). Application fee: $65. *Expenses:* Tuition $23,420 per year. Fees $60 per year. *Financial aid:* 332 students received aid; full and partial tuition waivers, Federal Work-Study, institutionally sponsored loans, and career-related internships or fieldwork available. Financial aid application deadline: 3/1; applicants required to submit FAFSA. *Faculty research:* Commercial law, labor law, legal history, comparative law, international law. • Aviam Soifer, Dean, 617-552-4340. Application contact: Elizabeth Rosselot, Director of Admissions, 617-552-4350.

Boston University, School of Law, Boston, MA 02215. Awards JD, LL M, JD/MA, JD/MBA, JD/MS, JD/MPH. Programs in American banking law (LL M), international banking law (LL M), law (JD), taxation (LL M). Approved by ABA. Member of AALS. Part-time programs available. Faculty: 60 full-time (20 women), 75 part-time (21 women). Students: 1,103 full-time (495 women), 154 part-time (68 women); includes 191 minority (33 African Americans, 101 Asian Americans, 49 Hispanics, 8 Native Americans), 63 international. Average age 26. 4,103 applicants, 40% accepted. In 1997, 362 JDs, 92 master's awarded. *Degree requirements:* For JD, research project required, foreign language not required. *Average time to degree:* master's–1 year full-time; first professional–3 years full-time. *Entrance requirements:* For JD, LSAT; for master's, JD, ranking in the top half of law school class. Application deadline: 3/1 (rolling processing). Application fee: $50. *Expenses:* Tuition $22,830 per year full-time, $713 per credit part-time. Fees $218 per year full-time, $40 per semester part-time. *Financial aid:* In 1997–98, 800 students received aid, including 3 fellowships totaling $87,759, 488 scholarships (143 to first-year students) totaling $4.641 million; partial tuition waivers, Federal Work-Study, institutionally sponsored loans, and career-related internships or fieldwork also available. Financial aid application deadline: 4/1; applicants required to submit CSS PROFILE or FAFSA. *Faculty research:* Law and technology, biotechnology issues in the law, law and health sciences, medicine and disabilities. • Ronald A. Cass, Dean, 617-353-3112. Application contact: Barbara J. Selmo, Director of Admissions and Financial Aid, 617-353-3100. E-mail: bulawadm@bu.edu.

Brigham Young University, J. Reuben Clark Law School, Provo, UT 84602-1001. Awards JD, LL M, JD/Ed D, JD/MBA, JD/M Ed, JD/MPA, JD/PhD, JD/MOB. Approved by ABA. Member of AALS. JD/M Ed, JD/Ed D, and JD/PhD new for fall 1998. Faculty: 30 full-time (6 women), 27 part-time (9 women). Students: 445 full-time (149 women); includes 57 minority (2 African Americans, 22 Asian Americans, 24 Hispanics, 9 Native Americans), 7 international. Average age 26. 685 applicants, 33% accepted. In 1997, 157 JDs awarded. *Average time to degree:* first professional–3 years full-time. *Entrance requirements:* For JD, LSAT (average 160). Application deadline: 2/1 (rolling processing). Application fee: $30. *Financial aid:* Research assistantships, teaching assistantships, institutionally sponsored loans, and career-related internships or fieldwork available. Financial aid application deadline: 6/1; applicants required to submit FAFSA. *Faculty research:* International law, federal taxation, real property law, constitutional law, business organization law. • Dr. H. Reese Hansen, Dean, 801-378-6383. E-mail: hansenr@lawgate.byu.edu. Application contact: Lola Wilcock, Admissions Director, 801-378-4277. Fax: 801-378-5897. E-mail: wilcockl@lawgate.byu.edu.

Brooklyn Law School, Brooklyn, NY 11201-3798. Awards JD, JD/MA, JD/MBA, JD/MPA, JD/MS, JD/MUP. Approved by ABA. Member of AALS. JD/MBA and JD/MPA offered jointly with Baruch College; JD/MUP offered jointly with Hunter College; JD/MA offered jointly with Brooklyn College of the City University of New York; JD/MS offered jointly with Pratt Institute. Part-time and evening/weekend programs available. Faculty: 63 full-time (25 women), 85 part-time (29 women). Students: 936 full-time (439 women), 534 part-time (239 women); includes 262 minority (77 African Americans, 109 Asian Americans, 73 Hispanics, 3 Native Americans), 7 international. Average age 27. 2,826 applicants, 49% accepted. In 1997, 437 degrees awarded. *Average time to degree:* first professional–3 years full-time, 4 years part-time. *Entrance requirements:* LSAT. Application deadline: 2/1 (priority date; rolling processing). Application fee: $60. *Expenses:* Tuition $22,000 per year full-time, $16,000 per year part-time. Fees $100 per year. *Financial aid:* In 1997–98, 1,350 students received aid, including 29 fellowships (10 to first-year students) totaling $125,000, 60 research assistantships (10 to first-year students) totaling $145,000; partial tuition waivers, Federal Work-Study, institutionally sponsored loans, and career-related internships or fieldwork also available. Aid available to part-time students. Financial aid application deadline: 4/15; applicants required to submit FAFSA. *Faculty research:* Civil procedure, securities regulation, family law, corporate finance, international business and law. • Joan G. Wexler, Dean, 718-780-7900. Fax: 718-780-0393. Application contact: Henry W. Haverstick III, Dean of Admissions and Financial Aid, 718-780-7906. Fax: 718-780-0395. E-mail: admitq@brooklaw.edu.

California Western School of Law, San Diego, CA 92101-3046. Awards JD, JD/MSW, MCL/LL M. Approved by ABA. Member of AALS. JD/MSW offered jointly with San Diego State University; MCL/LL M new for fall 1998. Faculty: 43 full-time (18 women), 48 part-time (14 women). Students: 721 full-time (343 women). Average age 27. 1,779 applicants, 72% accepted. *Average time to degree:* first professional–3 years full-time. *Entrance requirements:* LSAT. Application deadline: 5/1 (priority date; rolling processing; 11/1 for spring admission). Application fee: $45. Electronic applications accepted. *Expenses:* Tuition $10,250 per trimester. Fees $35 per trimester. *Financial aid:* Federal Work-Study, institutionally sponsored loans, and career-related internships or fieldwork available. Aid available to part-time students. Financial aid application deadline: 3/20; applicants required to submit FAFSA. • Steven R. Smith, Dean, 619-239-0391. Application contact: Nancy C. Ramsayer, Assistant Dean for Admissions, 619-525-1401. Fax: 619-685-2916. E-mail: admissions@cwsl.edu.

Announcement: Flexible trimester system allows graduation in 2, 2½, or 3 years (full- and part-time day programs). New students accepted fall and spring. Degrees offered: JD, JD/MSW, MCL/LLM. Student-faculty ratio 16:1. First school to have Center for Creative Problem Solving. Extensive clinical internship program augments curriculum. Law specialty courses in international, biotechnology, family/child advocacy, and telecommunications. Outstanding advocacy training program, including mediation. Diverse student body. Scholarship for academic achievement and diversity. Contact Admissions for more information.

Campbell University, School of Law, Buies Creek, NC 27506. Awards JD. Approved by ABA. Faculty: 17 full-time (1 woman), 23 part-time (6 women). Students: 333 full-time (152 women); includes 20 minority (9 African Americans, 5 Asian Americans, 2 Hispanics, 4 Native Americans), 1 international. Average age 25. 600 applicants, 33% accepted. In 1997, 100 degrees awarded. *Entrance requirements:* LSAT. Application deadline: 3/31 (priority date; rolling processing). Application fee: $40. *Expenses:* Tuition $16,500 per year. Fees $233 per year. *Financial aid:* In 1997–98, 47 research assistantships, 6 teaching assistantships, 112 scholarships were awarded; Federal Work-Study, institutionally sponsored loans, and career-related internships or fieldwork also available. Financial aid application deadline: 4/15. *Faculty research:* Interdisciplinary approaches to legal problems, management and planning for lawyers, church/state constitutional problems, basic research in substantive legal areas. • Patrick K. Hetrick, Dean, 910-893-1750. E-mail: hetrick@webster.campbell.edu. Application contact: Tom T. Lanier, Dean of Admissions, 910-893-1754. Fax: 910-893-1780. E-mail: lanier@webster.campbell.edu.

Capital University, Law School, Columbus, OH 43209-2394. Awards JD, LL M, MT, JD/MBA, JD/LL M, JD/MSA, JD/MSN. Approved by ABA. Member of AALS. JD/MSA offered jointly with Ohio University. Part-time and evening/weekend programs available. Faculty: 30 full-time (9 women), 36 part-time (5 women), 37 FTE. Students: 458 full-time (217 women), 369 part-time (156 women); includes 83 minority (56 African Americans, 8 Asian Americans, 17 Hispanics, 2 Native Americans), 7 international. Average age 27. 857 applicants, 70% accepted. In 1997, 217 JDs, 23 master's awarded. *Degree requirements:* For master's, thesis or alternative required, foreign language not required. *Average time to degree:* first professional–3 years full-time, 4 years part-time. *Entrance requirements:* For JD, LSAT (average 152); for master's, previous course work in accounting, business law, and taxation. Application deadline: 5/1 (priority date; rolling processing). Application fee: $35. *Expenses:* Tuition $530 per credit hour. Fees $200 per year. *Financial aid:* 672 students received aid; fellowships, research assistantships, teaching assistantships, full and partial tuition waivers, Federal Work-Study, and career-related internships or fieldwork available. Aid available to part-time students. Financial aid application deadline: 4/1; applicants required to submit FAFSA. *Faculty research:* Dispute resolution, remedies, taxation, commercial law, election law. Total annual research expenditures: $193,280. • Steven C. Bahls, Dean, 614-236-6500. Application contact: Linda J. Mihely, Assistant Dean of Admissions and Financial Aid, 614-236-6310. Fax: 614-236-6972. E-mail: law-admissions@capital.edu.

Case Western Reserve University, School of Law, Cleveland, OH 44106. Awards JD, LL M, JD/MA, JD/MBA, JD/MD, JD/MNO, JD/MSSA. Programs in law (JD), taxation (LL M), U.S. legal studies (LL M). Approved by ABA. Member of AALS. JD/MD new for fall 1998. Part-time programs available. Faculty: 41 full-time (10 women), 59 part-time (13 women). Students: 634 full-time (278 women), 15 part-time (8 women); includes 99 minority (51 African Americans, 37 Asian Americans, 9 Hispanics, 2 Native Americans). Average age 25. 1,292 applicants, 64% accepted. In 1997, 210 JDs, 43 master's awarded. *Entrance requirements:* For JD, LSAT, LSDAS; for master's, TOEFL. Application deadline: 4/1 (priority date; rolling processing). Application fee: $40. *Expenses:* Tuition $20,500 per year full-time, $854 per credit hour part-time. Fees $600 per year. *Financial aid:* In 1997–98, 558 students received aid, including 255 scholarships (65 to first-year students) totaling $1.86 million; Federal Work-Study and career-related internships or fieldwork also available. Aid available to part-time students. Financial aid application deadline: 3/15; applicants required to submit FAFSA. • Gerald Korngold,

Dean, 216-368-3283. Application contact: Barbara F. Andelman, Assistant Dean for Admissions and Financial Aid, 216-368-3600. Fax: 216-368-6144. E-mail: lawadmissions@po.cwru.edu.

The Catholic University of America, Columbus School of Law, Washington, DC 20064. Awards JD, JD/MA, JD/MSW, JD/JCL, JD/MSLS. Approved by ABA. Member of AALS. Part-time and evening/weekend programs available. Faculty: 50 full-time (15 women), 80 part-time (19 women). Students: 659 full-time (327 women), 282 part-time (120 women); includes 162 minority (105 African Americans, 37 Asian Americans, 20 Hispanics), 11 international. Average age 23. 2,161 applicants, 50% accepted. In 1997, 286 degrees awarded. *Average time to degree:* first professional–3 years full-time, 4 years part-time. *Entrance requirements:* LSAT (average 155). Application deadline: 3/1 (rolling processing). Application fee: $55. *Financial aid:* Research assistantships, Federal Work-Study, institutionally sponsored loans, and career-related internships or fieldwork available. Aid available to part-time students. Financial aid application deadline: 3/1; applicants required to submit FAFSA. • Bernard Dobranski, Dean, 202-319-5144. Fax: 202-319-5473. Application contact: George P. Braxton II, Director of Admissions, 202-319-5151. Fax: 202-319-4498. E-mail: braxton@law.cua.edu.

The Catholic University of America, School of Arts and Sciences, Department of Psychology, Program in Psychology/Law, Washington, DC 20064. Awards JD/MA. Part-time programs available. Students: 0. 0 applicants. *Application deadline:* 7/31 (rolling processing). *Application fee:* $50. *Expenses:* Tuition $17,325 per year full-time, $668 per credit hour part-time. Fees $680 per year full-time, $360 per year part-time. *Financial aid:* Scholarships, full and partial tuition waivers, Federal Work-Study, institutionally sponsored loans, and career-related internships or fieldwork available. Aid available to part-time students. Financial aid application deadline: 2/1. *Faculty research:* Psychological methodology, human memory, social and moral development. • Dr. Martin Safer, Director, 202-319-5750.

Chapman University, School of Law, Orange, CA 92866. Awards JD. Approved by ABA. Faculty: 18 full-time (9 women), 4 part-time, 19 FTE. Students: 160 full-time (68 women), 100 part-time (44 women). *Entrance requirements:* LSAT. Application deadline: rolling. Application fee: $50. *Financial aid:* Application deadline 3/1. • Parham Williams, Dean, 714-517-0303. Application contact: Office of Admissions, 888-242-1913. E-mail: jparamor@chapman.edu.

See in-depth description on page 1573.

City University of New York School of Law at Queens College, Professional Program, 65-21 Main Street, Flushing, NY 11367-1358. Awards JD. Approved by ABA. Faculty: 42 full-time (27 women), 21 part-time (12 women). Students: 461 full-time (276 women), 6 part-time (5 women); includes 184 minority (76 African Americans, 54 Asian Americans, 51 Hispanics, 3 Native Americans). Average age 30. 1,441 applicants, 38% accepted. In 1997, 147 degrees awarded. *Entrance requirements:* LSAT. Application deadline: 3/15 (rolling processing). Application fee: $40. *Financial aid:* In 1997–98, 382 students received aid, including 14 fellowships (all to first-year students) totaling $28,000; Federal Work-Study, institutionally sponsored loans, and career-related internships or fieldwork also available. Financial aid application deadline: 5/1; applicants required to submit FAFSA. • Kristin Booth Glen, Dean, 718-340-4201. Fax: 718-340-4482. E-mail: kbg@maclaw.law.cuny.edu. Application contact: William D. Perez, Director of Admissions, 718-340-4210. Fax: 718-340-4372. E-mail: perez@maclaw.law.cuny.edu.

Cleveland State University, Cleveland-Marshall College of Law, Cleveland, OH 44115-2440. Awards JD, LL M, JD/MBA, JD/MPA. Approved by ABA. Member of AALS. Part-time programs available. Faculty: 41 full-time (13 women). Students: 585 full-time (263 women), 321 part-time (151 women); includes 113 minority (72 African Americans, 26 Asian Americans, 12 Hispanics, 3 Native Americans), 1 international. Average age 29. 1,330 applicants, 58% accepted. In 1997, 256 JDs awarded. *Degree requirements:* For master's, thesis. *Entrance requirements:* For JD, LSAT; for master's, JD or LL B. Application deadline: 3/1 (rolling processing). Application fee: $35. *Expenses:* Tuition $7391 per year full-time, $5685 per year part-time for state residents; $14,782 per year full-time, $11,370 per year part-time for nonresidents. Fees $61 per year full-time, $47 per year part-time for state residents; $122 per year full-time, $94 per year part-time for nonresidents. *Financial aid:* In 1997–98, 59 research assistantships (5 to first-year students) were awarded; partial tuition waivers, Federal Work-Study, institutionally sponsored loans, and career-related internships or fieldwork also available. Aid available to part-time students. Financial aid applicants required to submit FAFSA. *Faculty research:* Jurisprudence, law and medicine, constitutional law, legal ethics, international law. • Steven S. Steinglass, Dean, 216-687-2344. Application contact: Margaret McNally, Assistant Dean for Admissions, 216-687-2304. Fax: 216-687-6881.

College of William and Mary, Marshall-Wythe School of Law, Williamsburg, VA 23187-8795. Awards JD, LL M, JD/MA, JD/MBA, JD/MPP. Approved by ABA. Member of AALS. JD/MPP offered jointly with the Thomas Jefferson Program in Public Policy; JD/MA offered jointly with the Program in American Studies; JD/MBA offered jointly with the School of Business. Faculty: 29 full-time (9 women), 19 part-time (8 women). Students: 527 full-time (241 women); includes 105 minority (78 African Americans, 17 Asian Americans, 7 Hispanics, 3 Native Americans), 9 international. Average age 30. 2,363 applicants, 31% accepted. In 1997, 167 JDs, 3 master's awarded. *Degree requirements:* For master's, thesis optional, foreign language not required. *Average time to degree:* master's–1 year full-time; first professional–3 years full-time. *Entrance requirements:* For JD, LSAT; for master's, LSAT, JD. Application deadline: 3/1 (priority date). Application fee: $40. *Financial aid:* In 1997–98, 225 students received aid, including 38 research assistantships (14 to first-year students) averaging $444 per month and totaling $152,000, 24 teaching assistantships averaging $528 per month and totaling $114,000; fellowships, scholarships, Federal Work-Study, institutionally sponsored loans, and career-related internships or fieldwork also available. Financial aid application deadline: 2/15; applicants required to submit FAFSA. *Faculty research:* Bill of Rights, taxation, environmental law, international law. Total annual research expenditures: $60,285. • Paul Marcus, Acting Dean, 757-221-3800. Application contact: Faye F. Shealy, Associate Dean for Admissions, 757-221-3785. Fax: 757-221-3261.

Columbia University, School of Law, New York, NY 10027. Awards JD, LL M, JSD, JD/MA, JD/MBA, JD/MPA, JD/MS, JD/PhD, JD/MFA, JD/MIA, JD/M Phil. Approved by ABA. Member of AALS. JD/MS offered jointly with the School of Social Work, the Program in Urban Planning, and the School of Journalism; JD/MPA offered jointly with Columbia University School of International and Public Affairs and with Princeton University Woodrow Wilson School of Public and International Affairs. Faculty: 71 full-time (19 women), 30 part-time (3 women). Students: 1,105 full-time (495 women); includes 375 minority (135 African Americans, 148 Asian Americans, 85 Hispanics, 7 Native Americans), 40 international. Average age 24. In 1997, 350 JDs, 124 master's, 6 doctorates awarded. Terminal master's awarded for partial completion of doctoral program. *Degree requirements:* For doctorate, dissertation required, foreign language not required. *Average time to degree:* master's–1 year full-time; doctorate–5 years full-time; first professional–3 years full-time. *Entrance requirements:* For JD, LSAT; for master's, TOEFL. Application deadline: 2/15 (rolling processing). Application fee: $65. Electronic applications accepted. *Tuition:* $26,570 per year. *Financial aid:* Fellowships, research assistantships, teaching assistantships, full and partial tuition waivers, Federal Work-Study, institutionally sponsored loans, and career-related internships or fieldwork available. Financial aid application deadline: 3/1; applicants required to submit FAFSA. *Faculty research:* Women in the legal profession, future of the international corporation, privatization in Eastern Europe, study of future legal systems after Korea's unification. • David W. Leebron, Dean of Faculty of Law, 212-854-2675. Application contact: James Milligan, Dean of Admissions, 212-854-2674.

Cornell University, Professional Field of the Law School, Ithaca, NY 14853-0001. Awards JD, LL M, JD/MA, JD/MBA, JD/MPA, JD/PhD, JD/LL M, JD/Maitrise en Droit, JD/MILR, JD/MRP. Approved by ABA. Member of AALS. JD/PhD offered jointly with the Graduate School. Faculty: 43 full-time (14 women), 9 part-time (0 women). Students: 536 full-time (224 women); includes 153 minority (40 African Americans, 65 Asian Americans, 33 Hispanics, 15 Native Americans), 22 international. Average age 25. In 1997, 181 JDs, 44 master's awarded. *Average time to degree:* master's–1 year full-time; first professional–3 years full-time. *Entrance requirements:* For JD, LSAT. Application deadline: 2/1. Application fee: $65. *Financial aid:* Fellowships, Federal Work-Study, institutionally sponsored loans, and career-related internships or fieldwork available. • Russell K. Osgood, Dean, 607-255-3527. Application contact: Richard D. Geiger, Dean of Admissions, 607-255-5141.

Cornell University, Graduate Field in the Law School, Ithaca, NY 14853-0001. Awards JSD, JD/PhD. JD/PhD offered jointly with the Law School. Faculty: 35 full-time. Students: 57 full-time (15 women); includes 57 international. 458 applicants, 33% accepted. *Degree requirements:* Dissertation. *Entrance requirements:* TOEFL, JD, LL M, or equivalent. Application deadline: 1/10 (priority date). Application fee: $65. *Expenses:* Tuition $24,100 per year. Fees $48 per year. *Financial aid:* In 1997–98, 5 students received aid, including 5 fellowships (all to first-year students); research assistantships, teaching assistantships, full and partial tuition waivers, institutionally sponsored loans also available. Financial aid applicants required to submit FAFSA. • Director of Graduate Studies, 607-255-2362. Application contact: Graduate Field Assistant, 607-255-2362. E-mail: gradlaw@law.mail.cornell.edu.

Creighton University, School of Law, Omaha, NE 68178-0001. Awards JD, JD/MBA. Approved by ABA. Member of AALS. Part-time programs available. Faculty: 24 full-time, 34 part-time. Students: 432 full-time (175 women), 17 part-time (7 women); includes 21 minority (6 African Americans, 3 Asian Americans, 10 Hispanics, 2 Native Americans). Average age 26. 692 applicants, 74% accepted. In 1997, 159 degrees awarded. *Entrance requirements:* LSAT (average 149). Application deadline: 5/1 (priority date; rolling processing). Application fee: $40. *Expenses:* Tuition $15,684 per year full-time, $525 per credit hour part-time. Fees $536 per year full-time, $28 per semester part-time. *Financial aid:* 377 students received aid; institutionally sponsored loans and career-related internships or fieldwork available. Aid available to part-time students. Financial aid application deadline: 7/1; applicants required to submit FAFSA. *Faculty research:* Securities law, evidence, legal negotiation, legal ethics, estates and trusts. • Lawrence Raful, Dean, 402-280-2874. Application contact: Maureen O'Connor, Assistant Dean, 402-280-2872. Fax: 402-280-2244.

Dalhousie University, Faculty of Law, Halifax, NS B3H 3J5, Canada. Awards LL M, JSD, LL B/MBA, LL B/MHSA, LL B/MLIS, LL B/MPA. Part-time programs available. Faculty: 36 full-time, 1 part-time. Students: 41 full-time (19 women), 16 part-time (8 women). *Degree requirements:* For master's, thesis or alternative required, foreign language not required; for doctorate, dissertation required, foreign language not required. *Entrance requirements:* For master's, TOEFL (minimum score 580). Application deadline: rolling. Application fee: $55. *Financial aid:* Fellowships available. *Faculty research:* Marine and environmental law, international comparative law, health law, general public and private law fields. • Dawn Russel, Dean, 902-494-2114. Fax: 902-494-1316. Application contact: Sheila Wile, Graduate Secretary, 902-494-1036.

DePaul University, College of Law, Chicago, IL 60604-2287. Awards JD, LL M, JD/MBA. Approved by ABA. Member of AALS. Part-time programs available. Faculty: 39 full-time (12 women), 90 part-time (27 women). Students: 799 full-time (398 women), 363 part-time (169 women); includes 159 minority (54 African Americans, 45 Asian Americans, 57 Hispanics, 3 Native Americans), 10 international. Average age 27. 2,077 applicants, 70% accepted. In 1997, 346 JDs awarded. *Entrance requirements:* For JD, LSAT, LSDAS. Application deadline: 4/1. Application fee: $40. Electronic applications accepted. *Financial aid:* In 1997–98, 625 students received aid, including 154 scholarships (77 to first-year students) totaling $903,500; full and partial tuition waivers, Federal Work-Study, and career-related internships or fieldwork also available. Aid available to part-time students. Financial aid application deadline: 4/21; applicants required to submit FAFSA. *Faculty research:* Health law, international law, corporate law, constitutional law, human rights law, church-state studies. Total annual research expenditures: $524,000. • Teree E. Foster, Dean, 312-362-8701. Fax: 312-362-5448. Application contact: Dennis Shea, Director of Law Admissions, 312-362-8013. Fax: 312-362-5280. E-mail: dshea@wppost.depaul.edu.

See in-depth description on page 1575.

Detroit College of Law at Michigan State University, East Lansing, MI 48824. Awards JD. Approved by ABA. Member of AALS. Part-time and evening/weekend programs available. Faculty: 23 full-time (9 women), 31 part-time (3 women). Students: 517 full-time (205 women), 231 part-time (91 women); includes 91 minority (57 African Americans, 11 Asian Americans, 18 Hispanics, 5 Native Americans), 27 international. Average age 28. 756 applicants, 61% accepted. In 1997, 185 degrees awarded. *Average time to degree:* first professional–3 years full-time, 4 years part-time. *Entrance requirements:* LSAT. Application deadline: 4/15 (priority date; rolling processing). Application fee: $50. Electronic applications accepted. *Tuition:* $535 per credit hour. *Financial aid:* In 1997–98, 53 scholarships were awarded; research assistantships, teaching assistantships, Federal Work-Study, institutionally sponsored loans, and career-related internships or fieldwork also available. Aid available to part-time students. Financial aid application deadline: 4/15. *Faculty research:* Corporate, international, family, constitutional, and health law. • Jeremy T. Harrison, Dean, 517-432-6804. Fax: 517-432-6801. E-mail: jharriso@pilot.msu.edu. Application contact: Andrea Heatley, Director of Admissions, 517-432-0222. Fax: 517-432-0098. E-mail: heatleya@pilot.msu.edu.

See in-depth description on page 1577.

The Dickinson School of Law of The Pennsylvania State University, Carlisle, PA 17013-2899. Offers programs in comparative law (LL M), law (JD). Approved by ABA. Member of AALS. Faculty: 28 full-time (8 women), 60 part-time (10 women). Students: 515 full-time (208 women), 4 part-time (all women); includes 43 minority (16 African Americans, 13 Asian Americans, 11 Hispanics, 3 Native Americans), 12 international. Average age 25. 1,054 applicants, 53% accepted. In 1997, 182 JDs awarded (100% found work related to degree); 11 master's awarded. *Average time to degree:* master's–1 year full-time; first professional–3 years full-time. *Entrance requirements:* For JD, LSAT (average 154); for master's, TOEFL (minimum score 575). Application deadline: 3/1. Application fee: $50. *Expenses:* Tuition $15,040 per year. Fees $150 per year. *Financial aid:* 177 students received aid; Federal Work-Study, institutionally sponsored loans, and career-related internships or fieldwork available. Financial aid application deadline: 2/15; applicants required to submit FAFSA. *Faculty research:* Protecting religious liberty under state law, immunity for disability discrimination, constitutionality of Pennsylvania's disorderly conduct law, sports agents, right to privacy as a testimonial privilege, tax avoidance and statutory interpretation, Irish divorce law. • Peter G. Glenn, Dean, 717-240-5000. Fax: 717-240-5213. Application contact: Barbara W. Guillaume, Director, Law Admissions, 717-240-5207. Fax: 717-243-4366. E-mail: dsladmit@psu.edu.

Drake University, Law School, Des Moines, IA 50311-4516. Awards JD, JD/MA, JD/MBA, JD/MPA, JD/MS, JD/MSW, JD/Pharm D. Approved by ABA. Member of AALS. JD/MA (political science) and JD/MS (agricultural economics) offered jointly with Iowa State University of Science and Technology; JD/MSW offered jointly with the University of Iowa. Faculty: 26 full-time (5 women), 47 part-time (21 women). Students: 399 full-time (172 women), 8 part-time (2 women); includes 42 minority (14 African Americans, 10 Asian Americans, 13 Hispanics, 5 Native Americans), 4 international. Average age 26. 888 applicants, 44% accepted. In 1997, 142 degrees awarded. *Entrance requirements:* LSAT (average 153), median GPA of 3.2. Application deadline: 3/1 (priority date; rolling processing). Application fee: $35. *Tuition:* $16,950 per year full-time, $565 per hour part-time. *Financial aid:* In 1997–98, 375 students received aid, including 24 research assistantships, 7 teaching assistantships, 10 computer laboratory monitors, tutoring positions; full and partial tuition waivers, Federal Work-Study, institutionally sponsored loans, and career-related internships or fieldwork also available. Aid available to part-time students. Financial aid application deadline: 3/1; applicants required to submit FAFSA. *Faculty research:* Death penalty, same-sex marriage, judicial decision making, modern American agriculture, the jury system. • C. Peter Goplerud III, Dean, 515-271-2824. Application contact:

Directory: Law

Drake University (continued)

J. Kara Blanchard, Director of Admission and Financial Aid, 800-44-DRAKE Ext. 2782. Fax: 515-271-2530. E-mail: lawadmit@drake.edu.

See in-depth description on page 1579.

Duke University, School of Law, Durham, NC 27708-0586. Awards JD, LL M, MLS, SJD, JD/MBA, JD/MS, JD/PhD, JD/AM, JD/LL M, JD/MEM, JD/MF, JD/MPP, JD/MTS, MD/JD. Approved by ABA. Member of AALS. LL M and SJD offered only to international students. Faculty: 35 full-time (10 women), 34 part-time (15 women). Students: 672 full-time (266 women); includes 97 minority (53 African Americans, 27 Asian Americans, 16 Hispanics, 1 Native American), 22 international. Average age 23. In 1997, 195 JDs, 55 master's awarded. *Average time to degree:* master's–1 year full-time; first professional–3 years full-time. *Entrance requirements:* For JD, LSAT; for master's and doctorate, TOEFL. Application deadline: 2/1 (priority date; rolling processing). Application fee: $65. *Financial aid:* In 1997–98, 454 students received aid, including 353 scholarships (114 to first-year students) totaling $1.753 million; Federal Work-Study, institutionally sponsored loans also available. Financial aid application deadline: 3/15; applicants required to submit FAFSA. *Faculty research:* Legal theory and doctrine and law reform, comparative law and international law, law and public policy, corporate and commercial law, conflict and dispute resolution. • Pamela B. Gann, Dean, 919-613-7000. Application contact: Dennis J. Shields, Assistant Dean for Admissions and Financial Aid, 919-613-7020. Fax: 919-613-7231. E-mail: admissions@law.duke.edu.

Duquesne University, School of Law, Pittsburgh, PA 15282-0001. Awards JD, JD/MBA, JD/MS, JD/M Div. Approved by ABA. Member of AALS. JD/M Div offered jointly with the Pittsburgh Theological Seminary. Part-time and evening/weekend programs available. Faculty: 30 full-time (9 women), 45 part-time. Students: 337 full-time (152 women), 330 part-time (137 women); includes 37 minority (29 African Americans, 2 Asian Americans, 6 Hispanics), 1 international. Average age 28. In 1997, 169 degrees awarded. *Average time to degree:* first professional–3 years full-time, 4 years part-time. *Entrance requirements:* LSAT (minimum score 155), minimum QPA of 3.25. Application deadline: 4/1 (rolling processing). Application fee: $50. *Financial aid:* 267 students received aid; research assistantships, teaching assistantships, merit scholarships, grant-in-aid awards, partial tuition waivers, Federal Work-Study, and career-related internships or fieldwork available. Aid available to part-time students. Financial aid application deadline: 5/31. *Faculty research:* Law, clinical legal education, litigation/trial advocacy. Total annual research expenditures: $100,000. • Nicholas P. Cafardi, Dean, 412-396-6280. Application contact: Ronald J. Ricci, Dean of Admissions, 412-396-6300. Fax: 412-396-6283. E-mail: ricci@duq2.cc.duq.edu.

Emory University, School of Law, Atlanta, GA 30322-1100. Awards JD, LL M, JD/MBA, JD/M Div, JD/MPH, JD/MTS. Approved by ABA. Member of AALS. Faculty: 41 full-time (9 women), 55 part-time (16 women). Students: 638 full-time (295 women), 5 part-time (3 women); includes 147 minority (64 African Americans, 35 Asian Americans, 46 Hispanics, 2 Native Americans), 9 international. Average age 24. 2,757 applicants, 38% accepted. In 1997, 253 JDs awarded. *Average time to degree:* first professional–3 years full-time. *Entrance requirements:* For JD, LSAT, TOEFL. Application deadline: 3/1 (rolling processing). Application fee: $50. Electronic applications accepted. *Tuition:* $23,175 per year. *Financial aid:* In 1997–98, 502 students received aid, including 12 fellowships (4 to first-year students); research assistantships, Federal Work-Study, institutionally sponsored loans, and career-related internships or fieldwork also available. Financial aid application deadline: 3/1; applicants required to submit FAFSA. *Faculty research:* Law and economics, law and religion, international law, human rights, criminal law. • Howard O. Hunter, Dean, 404-727-6895. Fax: 404-727-0866. Application contact: Lynell Cadray, Assistant Dean for Admissions, 404-727-6801. Fax: 404-727-2477. E-mail: lcadray@law.emory.edu.

Faulkner University, Jones School of Law, Montgomery, AL 36109-3398. Awards JD. Part-time and evening/weekend programs available. Faculty: 4 full-time (2 women), 35 part-time (6 women). Students: 394 full-time (141 women); includes 45 minority (all African Americans). Average age 32. 200 applicants, 50% accepted. In 1997, 117 degrees awarded. *Entrance requirements:* LSAT. Application deadline: 7/15 (priority date; rolling processing; 11/15 for spring admission). Application fee: $25. *Expenses:* Tuition $9982 per year. Fees $85 per semester. *Financial aid:* 241 students received aid; Federal Work-Study and career-related internships or fieldwork available. Aid available to part-time students. Financial aid application deadline: 5/1; applicants required to submit FAFSA. • Wendell W. Mitchell, Dean, 334-260-6210. Application contact: Paul M. Smith, Director, 334-260-6210. Fax: 334-260-6223.

Florida State University, College of Law, Tallahassee, FL 32306. Awards JD, JD/MA, JD/MBA, JD/MPA, JD/MS, JD/MSW, JD/MSP. Approved by ABA. Member of AALS. JD/MA and JD/MS offered jointly with the Program in International Affairs; JD/MS offered with the Department of Economics; JD/MSP offered with the Department of Urban and Regional Planning. Faculty: 43 full-time (15 women), 12 part-time (4 women). Students: 638 full-time (275 women), 2 part-time (1 woman); includes 162 minority (78 African Americans, 13 Asian Americans, 62 Hispanics, 9 Native Americans), 5 international. Average age 25. 1,896 applicants, 34% accepted. In 1997, 205 degrees awarded. *Average time to degree:* first professional–3 years full-time. *Entrance requirements:* LSAT. Application deadline: 2/15 (rolling processing). Application fee: $20. *Financial aid:* In 1997–98, 148 students received aid, including 148 fellowships (48 to first-year students) totaling $742,581, 35 research assistantships totaling $100,800, 16 teaching assistantships totaling $30,720; Federal Work-Study, institutionally sponsored loans, and career-related internships or fieldwork also available. Financial aid application deadline: 4/1. *Faculty research:* Evidence, constitutional law, international law, environmental law, business associations. • Paul A. Lebel, Dean, 850-644-3400. Fax: 850-644-5487. Application contact: Marie E. Capshew, Director of Admissions and Records, 850-644-3787. Fax: 850-644-7284. E-mail: admissions@law.fsu.edu.

Fordham University, School of Law, New York, NY 10023. Awards JD, LL M, JD/MBA, JD/MSW. Programs in banking, corporate and finance law (LL M); international business and trade law (LL M); law (JD). Approved by ABA. Member of AALS. Part-time and evening/weekend programs available. Faculty: 57 full-time (17 women), 93 part-time (26 women). Students: 1,043 full-time (447 women), 361 part-time (163 women). Average age 27. 4,100 applicants, 31% accepted. In 1997, 519 JDs, 31 master's awarded. *Entrance requirements:* For JD, LSAT (average 162). Application deadline: 3/1 (rolling processing). Application fee: $60. *Financial aid:* 580 students received aid; fellowships, research assistantships, institutionally sponsored loans, and career-related internships or fieldwork available. Aid available to part-time students. Financial aid application deadline: 2/28; applicants required to submit CSS PROFILE or FAFSA. • John Feerick, Dean, 212-636-6875. Application contact: Admissions Office, 212-636-6810.

See in-depth description on page 1581.

Franklin Pierce Law Center, Concord, NH 03301-4197. Awards JD, LL M, MEL, MIP, CAGS, Diploma, JD/CAGS, JD/MEL, JD/MIP. Programs in education law (MEL, CAGS), intellectual property (JD, LL M, MIP, Diploma), law (JD). Approved by ABA. Diploma awarded as part of Intellectual Property Summer Institute. MEL, CAGS, JD/MEL, and JD/CAGS new for fall 1998. Faculty: 19 full-time (5 women), 56 part-time (13 women). Students: 403 full-time (150 women), 4 part-time (3 women); includes 34 minority (6 African Americans, 17 Asian Americans, 9 Hispanics, 2 Native Americans), 40 international. Average age 30. 1,134 applicants, 47% accepted. In 1997, 126 JDs, 47 master's awarded. *Entrance requirements:* For JD, LSAT. Application deadline: 5/1 (rolling processing). Application fee: $45. *Expenses:* Tuition $16,450 per year. Fees $25 per year. *Financial aid:* In 1997–98, 49 teaching assistantships totaling $57,756 were awarded; research assistantships, Federal Work-Study, institutionally sponsored loans, and career-related internships or fieldwork also available. Financial aid application deadline: 4/1; applicants required to submit FAFSA. *Faculty research:* Legal applications of artificial intelligence. • James E. Duggan, Interim Dean, 603-228-1541. Application contact: Lory Attalla, Acting Director of Admissions, 603-228-9217.

George Mason University, School of Law, Arlington, VA 22201. Awards JD. Approved by ABA. Member of AALS. Part-time and evening/weekend programs available. Faculty: 25 full-time (5 women), 24 part-time (3 women), 27.7 FTE. Students: 379 full-time (163 women), 336 part-time (110 women); includes 77 minority (28 African Americans, 35 Asian Americans, 12 Hispanics, 2 Native Americans), 1 international. Average age 30. 2,629 applicants, 29% accepted. In 1997, 179 degrees awarded. *Entrance requirements:* LSAT, LSDAS, minimum undergraduate GPA of 3.4. Application deadline: 5/1 (11/1 for spring admission). Application fee: $30. Electronic applications accepted. *Financial aid:* Fellowships available. • Dr. Mark F. Grady, Dean, 703-993-8085. Fax: 703-993-8088. Application contact: Admissions Office, 703-993-8010.

Georgetown University, Law Center, Washington, DC 20001. Awards JD, LL M, SJD, JD/MA, JD/MBA, JD/MS, JD/PhD, JD/MPH. Programs in advocacy (LL M), common law studies (LL M), general (LL M), international and comparative law (LL M), labor and employment law (LL M), law (JD, SJD), securities regulation (LL M), taxation (LL M). Approved by ABA. Member of AALS. JD/MPH offered jointly with Johns Hopkins University–School of Hygiene and Public Health; JD/PhD offered jointly with Department of Government and Department of Philosophy. Part-time and evening/weekend programs available. *Degree requirements:* For master's and doctorate, thesis/dissertation required, foreign language not required. *Average time to degree:* master's–1 year full-time, 3 years part-time; first professional–3 years full-time, 4 years part-time. *Entrance requirements:* For JD, LSAT (average 166); for master's and doctorate, TOEFL (average 600), JD, LL B, or first law degree earned in country of origin. Application deadline: 2/1 (rolling processing). Application fee: $60. *Expenses:* Tuition $24,530 per year full-time, $855 per credit part-time. Fees $99 (one-time charge). *Faculty research:* Constitutional law, legal history, jurisprudence.

The George Washington University, Law School, Washington, DC 20052. Awards JD, LL M, SJD, JD/MA, JD/MBA, JD/MPA, JD/MHSA, JD/MPH, LL M/MPH. Approved by ABA. Member of AALS. Part-time and evening/weekend programs available. Faculty: 65 full-time (17 women), 184 part-time (57 women). Students: 1,384 full-time (612 women), 363 part-time (138 women); includes 453 minority (187 African Americans, 144 Asian Americans, 113 Hispanics, 9 Native Americans), 34 international. Average age 27. 7,011 applicants. In 1997, 464 JDs, 130 master's awarded. *Entrance requirements:* For JD, LSAT, appropriate bachelor's degree; for master's, JD or equivalent; for doctorate, LL M or equivalent. Application deadline: 3/1 (rolling processing). Application fee: $55. *Financial aid:* 615 students received aid; fellowships, research assistantships, full and partial tuition waivers, Federal Work-Study, institutionally sponsored loans, and career-related internships or fieldwork available. Aid available to part-time students. Financial aid application deadline: 3/1. • Michael Young, Dean, 202-994-6288. Application contact: Robert V. Stanek, Assistant Dean of Admissions and Financial Aid, 202-994-7230.

Georgia State University, College of Law, Atlanta, GA 30303-3083. Awards JD, JD/MBA, JD/MPA. Approved by ABA. Member of AALS. Part-time and evening/weekend programs available. Faculty: 40 full-time (17 women), 28 part-time (9 women), 54 FTE. Students: 392 full-time (187 women), 249 part-time (128 women); includes 138 minority (93 African Americans, 30 Asian Americans, 14 Hispanics, 1 Native American), 5 international. Average age 28. 1,872 applicants, 25% accepted. In 1997, 192 degrees awarded. *Entrance requirements:* LSAT. Application deadline: 3/15 (rolling processing). Application fee: $30. *Expenses:* Tuition $3132 per year for state residents; $12,528 per year for nonresidents. Fees $275 per year. *Financial aid:* In 1997–98, 366 students received aid, including 66 research assistantships averaging $225 per month and totaling $63,500, 12 teaching assistantships averaging $200 per month and totaling $12,000; partial tuition waivers, Federal Work-Study, institutionally sponsored loans, and career-related internships or fieldwork also available. Aid available to part-time students. Financial aid application deadline: 4/1; applicants required to submit FAFSA. *Faculty research:* Corporate/commercial law, tax law, labor law, criminal law, constitutional law. Total annual research expenditures: $171,359. • Dr. Janice C. Griffith, Dean, 404-651-2035. Fax: 404-651-2570. E-mail: jgriffith@gsu.edu. Application contact: Dr. Cheryl Jackson, Director of Admissions, 404-651-2048. Fax: 404-651-1244. E-mail: lawcry@gsusgi2.gsu.edu.

Announcement: The College of Law is in downtown Atlanta, center of legal, financial, and government activity in the Southeast. Programs leading to JD, JD/MBA, and JD/MPA offered for full- and part-time students with day and/or evening classes. Student body is diverse and encompasses broad geographic area. Clinical and workshop experiences available. Career services for students and alumni through Career Service Office. Equal opportunity/affirmative action institution.

Golden Gate University, School of Law, San Francisco, CA 94105-2968. Awards JD, LL M, SJD, JD/MA, JD/MBA, JD/MPA, JD/PhD. Programs in environmental law (LL M), international legal studies (LL M, SJD), law (JD), taxation (LL M), U.S. legal studies (LL M). Approved by ABA. Member of AALS. JD/PhD offered jointly with the Pacific Graduate School of Psychology. Part-time and evening/weekend programs available. Faculty: 35 full-time (13 women), 89 part-time (37 women). Students: 534 full-time (312 women), 326 part-time (151 women); includes 201 minority (36 African Americans, 100 Asian Americans, 65 Hispanics), 50 international. Average age 26. 1,963 applicants, 58% accepted. In 1997, 172 JDs awarded. *Average time to degree:* first professional–3 years full-time, 4 years part-time. *Entrance requirements:* For JD, LSAT (median 154). Application deadline: 4/15 (priority date; rolling processing; 11/15 for spring admission). Application fee: $40. *Expenses:* Tuition $19,981 per year full-time, $13,780 per year part-time. Fees $224 per year. *Financial aid:* In 1997–98, 654 students received aid, including 3 fellowships averaging $2,225 per month and totaling $41,200; research assistantships, teaching assistantships, full and partial tuition waivers, Federal Work-Study, institutionally sponsored loans, and career-related internships or fieldwork also available. Aid available to part-time students. Financial aid application deadline: 3/1; applicants required to submit FAFSA. *Faculty research:* International law; civil rights, particularly minority and gay and lesbian issues; alternative dispute resolution; real estate. • Anthony J. Pagano, Dean, 415-442-6600. Fax: 415-442-6609. Application contact: Cherie Scricca, Assistant Dean of Admissions, 415-442-6630. Fax: 415-442-6631. E-mail: lawadmit@ggu.edu.

See in-depth description on page 1583.

Gonzaga University, School of Law, Spokane, WA 99220. Awards JD, JD/MBA, JD/M Acc. Approved by ABA. Member of AALS. Part-time programs available. Faculty: 35 full-time (10 women), 26 part-time (5 women). Students: 506 full-time (194 women), 13 part-time (8 women); includes 75 minority (12 African Americans, 31 Asian Americans, 20 Hispanics, 12 Native Americans), 1 international. Average age 28. 1,005 applicants, 75% accepted. In 1997, 168 degrees awarded. *Entrance requirements:* LSAT. Application deadline: 3/15 (priority date; rolling processing). Application fee: $40. *Expenses:* Tuition $610 per credit hour. Fees $100 per year. *Financial aid:* In 1997–98, 10 fellowships (all to first-year students) were awarded; research assistantships, teaching assistantships, full tuition waivers, Federal Work-Study, institutionally sponsored loans, and career-related internships or fieldwork also available. Aid available to part-time students. Financial aid application deadline: 3/15; applicants required to submit FAFSA. • John E. Clute, Dean, 509-328-4220 Ext. 6090. Application contact: Sally S. Poutiatine, Assistant Dean, 509-324-5532. Fax: 509-324-5710. E-mail: admissions@lawschool.gonzaga.edu.

Hamline University, School of Law, St. Paul, MN 55104-1284. Awards JD, JD/MAM, JD/MAPA, MD/MANM. Approved by ABA. Member of AALS. JD/MANM and JD/MAM new for fall 1998. Part-time programs available. Faculty: 32 full-time (14 women), 70 part-time (22 women), 48 FTE. Students: 450 full-time (224 women), 49 part-time (21 women); includes 50 minority (25 African Americans, 15 Asian Americans, 5 Hispanics, 5 Native Americans), 8 international. Average age 27. 993 applicants, 53% accepted. In 1997, 178 degrees awarded. *Average time to degree:* first professional–3 years full-time. *Entrance requirements:* LSAT. Application deadline: 5/15 (rolling processing). Application fee: $50. *Tuition:* $16,500 per year full-time, $8200 per year part-time. *Financial aid:* In 1997–98, 201 grants, scholarships (56 to first-year students) totaling $1.345 million were awarded; Federal Work-Study and career-related internships or fieldwork also available. Aid available to part-time students. Financial aid applicants required to submit FAFSA. • Raymond R. Krause, Dean, 651-523-2968. Application contact: Elizabeth Schmitt, Director of Admissions, 800-388-3688. Fax: 651-523-2435.

See in-depth description on page 1585.

Harvard University, Law School, Graduate Programs in Law, Cambridge, MA 02138. Awards LL M, SJD. Member of AALS. Students: 244 full-time. Average age 26. In 1997, 148 master's awarded. Terminal master's awarded for partial completion of doctoral program. *Entrance requirements:* For master's, TOEFL (minimum score 570). Application deadline: 12/1. Application fee: $60. *Financial aid:* Fellowships, research assistantships, teaching assistantships, institutionally sponsored loans, and career-related internships or fieldwork available. Financial aid applicants required to submit FAFSA. *Faculty research:* Corporation finance, national and international law, legal ethics, family law, criminal law, administrative law, constitutional law. • Anne-Marie Slaughter, Co-Director, 617-496-8210. Application contact: Office of Admissions and Financial Aid, 617-496-8214.

Harvard University, Law School, Professional Programs in Law, Cambridge, MA 02138. Awards JD, JD/MBA, JD/PhD, JD/MALD, JD/MPP. Approved by ABA. Member of AALS. JD/MALD offered jointly with the Fletcher School of Law and Diplomacy at Tufts University. Students: 1,658 full-time; includes 423 minority (153 African Americans, 181 Asian Americans, 80 Hispanics, 9 Native Americans), 59 international. In 1997, 546 degrees awarded (98% found work related to degree). *Degree requirements:* Thesis. *Average time to degree:* first professional–3 years full-time. *Entrance requirements:* LSAT. Application deadline: 2/1 (rolling processing). Application fee: $65. *Faculty research:* Constitutional law, voting rights law, cyber law. Total annual research expenditures: $6.8 million. • Application contact: Joyce Curll, Assistant Dean for Admissions and Financial Aid, 617-495-3109.

Hofstra University, School of Law, Hempstead, NY 11549. Awards JD, JD/MBA. Approved by ABA. Member of AALS. Faculty: 35 full-time (9 women), 37 part-time (5 women). Students: 819 full-time (375 women); includes 147 minority (53 African Americans, 41 Asian Americans, 53 Hispanics). Average age 26. 1,689 applicants, 49% accepted. In 1997, 276 degrees awarded. *Average time to degree:* first professional–3 years full-time. *Entrance requirements:* LSAT. Application deadline: 4/15 (priority date; rolling processing). Application fee: $60. *Financial aid:* In 1997–98, 447 fellowships (154 to first-year students) totaling $1.542 million were awarded; research assistantships, full and partial tuition waivers, Federal Work-Study, institutionally sponsored loans, and career-related internships or fieldwork also available. Financial aid application deadline: 5/15; applicants required to submit FAFSA. *Faculty research:* Law, technology, and reproduction; federal sentencing law; legal ethics; legislative process, immigration law and policy. Total annual research expenditures: $422,487. • Dr. Stuart Rabinowitz, Dean, 516-463-5854. E-mail: lawszr@hofstra.edu. Application contact: Amy L. Engle, Assistant Dean for Admissions, 516-463-5916. Fax: 516-463-6091. E-mail: lawaee@hofstra.edu.

Howard University, School of Law, Washington, DC 20008. Awards JD, LL M, JD/MBA. Approved by ABA. Member of AALS. Faculty: 28 full-time (9 women), 13 part-time (5 women). Students: 434 full-time (232 women); includes 388 minority (362 African Americans, 13 Asian Americans, 12 Hispanics, 1 Native American), 15 international. In 1997, 130 JDs, 14 master's awarded. *Degree requirements:* For JD, thesis (for some programs). *Average time to degree:* master's–1 year full-time; first professional–3 years full-time. *Entrance requirements:* For JD, LSAT (average 152). Application deadline: 4/30 (rolling processing). Application fee: $60. *Financial aid:* In 1997–98, 360 students received aid, including 228 grants, scholarships (60 to first-year students) totaling $1.99 million; fellowships, research assistantships, teaching assistantships, Federal Work-Study, institutionally sponsored loans, and career-related internships or fieldwork also available. Financial aid application deadline: 4/30. • Alice Gresham Bullock, Dean, 202-806-8000. Fax: 202-806-8424. Application contact: Ruby Sherrod, Assistant Dean, 202-806-8008. Fax: 202-806-8162.

Humphreys College, School of Law, Stockton, CA 95207-3896. Awards JD. Faculty: 2 full-time (1 woman), 16 part-time (3 women). Students: 66 full-time (30 women). Average age 36. 56 applicants, 55% accepted. In 1997, 18 degrees awarded. *Average time to degree:* first professional–4 years part-time. *Entrance requirements:* LSAT. Application deadline: 8/1 (priority date; rolling processing). Application fee: $20. *Tuition:* $6552 per year full-time, $156 per unit part-time. *Financial aid:* Federal Work-Study available. Aid available to part-time students. Financial aid application deadline: 7/1; applicants required to submit FAFSA. • Nels B. Fransen, Dean, 209-478-0800. Application contact: Lance Hall, Law Registrar, 209-478-0800. Fax: 209-478-8721.

Illinois Institute of Technology, Chicago-Kent College of Law, Chicago, IL 60606. Awards JD, LL M, JD/MBA, JD/MPA, JD/MS, JD/LL M. Approved by ABA. Member of AALS. Part-time and evening/weekend programs available. Faculty: 65 full-time (24 women), 125 part-time (24 women), 148 FTE. Students: 883 full-time (431 women), 387 part-time (172 women); includes 210 minority (54 African Americans, 105 Asian Americans, 46 Hispanics, 5 Native Americans), 3 international. Average age 26. 1,864 applicants, 64% accepted. In 1997, 335 JDs awarded (100% found work related to degree); 15 master's awarded (100% found work related to degree). *Average time to degree:* master's–1 year full-time, 3 years part-time; first professional–3 years full-time, 4 years part-time. *Entrance requirements:* For JD, LSAT, LSDAS; for master's, JD. Application deadline: 4/1 (priority date; rolling processing). Application fee: $45. Electronic applications accepted. *Expenses:* Tuition $20,680 per year full-time, $14,915 per year part-time. Fees $40 per semester (minimum). *Financial aid:* In 1997–98, 958 students received aid, including 109 research assistantships, 29 teaching assistantships, 422 scholarships (135 to first-year students) totaling $2.391 million; full and partial tuition waivers, institutionally sponsored loans, and career-related internships or fieldwork also available. Aid available to part-time students. Financial aid application deadline: 4/15; applicants required to submit FAFSA. *Faculty research:* International law, jurisprudence, contract theory, constitutional law, health law. Total annual research expenditures: $717,885. • Henry H. Perritt Jr., Dean, 312-906-5010. Fax: 312-906-5335. E-mail: heperritt@kentlaw.edu. Application contact: Michael Burns, Assistant Dean, 312-906-5020. E-mail: admitq@kentlaw.edu.

Indiana University Bloomington, School of Law, Bloomington, IN 47401. Awards JD, LL M, MCL, SJD, JD/MBA, JD/MPA, JD/MSES, JD/MLS. Approved by ABA. Member of AALS. Part-time programs available. Faculty: 20 full-time (2 women). Students: 637 full-time (266 women), 33 part-time (16 women); includes 112 minority (54 African Americans, 30 Asian Americans, 27 Hispanics, 1 Native American), 45 international. In 1997, 217 JDs, 15 master's awarded. *Entrance requirements:* For JD, LSAT; for master's, TOEFL. Application deadline: 3/1 (priority date; rolling processing). Application fee: $35. *Expenses:* Tuition $217 per credit hour for state residents; $556 per credit hour for nonresidents. Fees $343 per year. *Financial aid:* Fellowships, research assistantships, teaching assistantships, Federal Work-Study, institutionally sponsored loans, and career-related internships or fieldwork available. Financial aid application deadline: 3/1; applicants required to submit FAFSA. • Alfred C. Aman Jr., Dean, 812-855-7995. Application contact: Frank Motley, Admissions Assistant Dean, 812-855-4765. Fax: 812-855-0555. E-mail: patclark@law.indiana.edu.

Indiana University–Purdue University Indianapolis, School of Law, Indianapolis, IN 46202-2896. Awards JD, JD/MBA, JD/MPA, JD/MHA. Approved by ABA. Member of AALS. Part-time programs available. Faculty: 45 full-time (13 women), 25 part-time (7 women). Students: 563 full-time (258 women), 294 part-time (139 women); includes 94 minority (58 African Americans, 15 Asian Americans, 17 Hispanics, 4 Native Americans), 14 international. Average age 28. 945 applicants, 53% accepted. In 1997, 218 degrees awarded. *Degree requirements:* Thesis required, foreign language not required. *Average time to degree:* first professional–3 years full-time, 4 years part-time. *Entrance requirements:* LSAT (average 156), TOEFL (average 550). Application deadline: 3/1 (priority date; rolling processing). Application fee: $35 ($50 for international students). *Financial aid:* Fellowships, research assistantships, full and partial tuition waivers, Federal Work-Study, and career-related internships or fieldwork available. Aid available to part-time students. Financial aid applicants required to submit FAFSA. *Faculty research:* Law and health, law and education, criminal law, professional responsibility, consumer law, international law, state and local government. Total annual research expenditures: $420,000. • Norman Lefstein, Dean, 317-274-2581. E-mail: niefstel@indyunix.iupui.edu. Application contact: Angela M. Espada, Assistant Dean for Admissions, 317-274-2459. Fax: 317-274-3955. E-mail: amespada@iupui.edu.

Inter American University of Puerto Rico, Metropolitan Campus, School of Law, Hato Rey, PR 00936. Awards JD. Approved by ABA. Part-time and evening/weekend programs available. Faculty: 23 full-time (9 women), 27 part-time (8 women). Students: 377 full-time (210 women), 312 part-time (167 women); includes 689 minority (all Hispanics). Average age 23. 945 applicants, 37% accepted. In 1997, 159 degrees awarded. *Average time to degree:* first professional–3 years full-time, 4 years part-time. *Entrance requirements:* LSAT (minimum score 130; average 140), PAEG (minimum score 575; average 620), minimum GPA of 2.5 (average 3.2). Application deadline: 3/31 (priority date). Application fee: $63. *Expenses:* Tuition $325 per credit. Fees $322 per year. *Financial aid:* 513 students received aid; Federal Work-Study and career-related internships or fieldwork available. Aid available to part-time students. Financial aid application deadline: 4/30; applicants required to submit FAFSA. • Carlos E. Ramos-González, Dean, 787-751-1912 Ext. 2001. E-mail: ceramos@ns.inter.edu. Application contact: Julio Fontanet, Dean of Student Affairs, 787-751-1912 Ext. 2011. Fax: 787-751-2975.

John F. Kennedy University, School of Law, Orinda, CA 94563-2689. Awards JD. Part-time and evening/weekend programs available. Faculty: 3 full-time (1 woman), 74 part-time (33 women). Students: 218 full-time (101 women), 18 part-time (11 women); includes 64 minority (19 African Americans, 22 Asian Americans, 19 Hispanics, 4 Native Americans). Average age 37. 104 applicants, 84% accepted. In 1997, 43 degrees awarded. *Entrance requirements:* LSAT, TOEFL (minimum score 550), interview. Application deadline: 5/30 (rolling processing; 11/30 for spring admission). Application fee: $50. *Expenses:* Tuition $431 per unit. Fees $11 per semester. *Financial aid:* Fellowships, institutionally sponsored loans available. Aid available to part-time students. Financial aid application deadline: 3/2. • Michael Guarino, Dean, 925-295-1800. Application contact: Ellena Bloedorn, Director of Admissions, 925-258-2213. Fax: 925-254-6964.

John Marshall Law School, Chicago, IL 60604-3968. Awards JD, LL M, MS, JD/MA, JD/MBA, JD/MPA, JD/LL M. Programs in comparative legal studies (LL M), information technology (LL M, MS), intellectual property (LL M), international business and trade (LL M), law (JD), real estate (LL M), taxation (LL M). Approved by ABA. Member of AALS. JD/MBA offered jointly with Dominican University; JD/MA (political science) and JD/MPA offered jointly with Roosevelt University. Part-time and evening/weekend programs available. Faculty: 52 full-time (14 women), 230 part-time (43 women). Students: 786 full-time (346 women), 486 part-time (184 women); includes 254 minority (75 African Americans, 62 Asian Americans, 59 Hispanics, 58 Native Americans), 28 international. Average age 27. 1,503 applicants, 63% accepted. In 1997, 328 JDs, 55 master's awarded. *Average time to degree:* master's–1.5 years full-time, 2 years part-time; first professional–3 years full-time, 4 years part-time. *Entrance requirements:* For JD, LSAT; for master's, TOEFL (minimum score 600), TWE (minimum score 415), JD. Application deadline: 3/1 (priority date; rolling processing; 10/1 for spring admission). Application fee: $50 ($60 for international students). *Expenses:* Tuition $675 per credit (minimum). Fees $40 per semester. *Financial aid:* 943 students received aid; full and partial tuition waivers available. Aid available to part-time students. Financial aid applicants required to submit FAFSA. • Robert Gilbert Johnson, Dean, 312-427-2737. Application contact: William B. Powers, Dean of Admission and Student Affairs, 312-987-1403. Fax: 312-427-5136. E-mail: 6alonzo@jmls.edu.

Judge Advocate General's School, U.S. Army, Charlottesville, VA 22903-1781. Offers program in military law (LL M). Approved by ABA. Only active duty military lawyers attend this school. Faculty: 34 full-time (5 women), 11 part-time (2 women). Students: 81 full-time (18 women); includes 4 minority (2 African Americans, 1 Asian American, 1 Hispanic), 4 international. Average age 34. *Entrance requirements:* Active duty military lawyer. *Tuition:* $0. *Faculty research:* Criminal law, administrative and civil law, contract law, international law. • Col. Gerard St. Amand, Commandant, 804-972-6301. Application contact: Lt. Col. Wendell Jewell, Admissions Director, 804-972-6310.

Lewis & Clark College, Northwestern School of Law, Portland, OR 97219-7899. Awards JD, LL M. Approved by ABA. Member of AALS. Part-time and evening/weekend programs available. Faculty: 37 full-time (11 women), 40 part-time (13 women). Students: 464 full-time (203 women), 163 part-time (82 women); includes 91 minority (15 African Americans, 50 Asian Americans, 22 Hispanics, 4 Native Americans), 18 international. Average age 29. 1,687 applicants, 55% accepted. In 1997, 215 JDs, 6 master's awarded. *Average time to degree:* first professional–3 years full-time, 4 years part-time. *Entrance requirements:* For JD, LSAT. Application deadline: 3/15 (priority date; rolling processing). Application fee: $50. *Financial aid:* In 1997–98, 379 scholarships, grants (160 to first-year students) were awarded; partial tuition waivers, Federal Work-Study, and career-related internships or fieldwork also available. Aid available to part-time students. Financial aid application deadline: 2/15; applicants required to submit FAFSA. *Faculty research:* Environmental law, business law, tax law. Total annual research expenditures: $203,928. • James L. Huffman, Dean, 503-768-6602. Application contact: Martha Spence, Associate Dean, 503-768-6634. Fax: 503-768-6671. E-mail: spence@lclark.edu.

Louisiana State University and Agricultural and Mechanical College, Paul M. Hebert Law Center, Baton Rouge, LA 70803. Awards JD, LL M, MCL, JD/MPA. Approved by ABA. Member of AALS. Faculty: 33 full-time, 10 part-time. Students: 624 full-time (280 women); includes 65 minority (54 African Americans, 3 Asian Americans, 5 Hispanics, 3 Native Americans), 10 international. Average age 26. 986 applicants, 54% accepted. In 1997, 194 JDs, 4 master's awarded. *Average time to degree:* master's–1 year full-time; first professional–3 years full-time. *Entrance requirements:* For JD, LSAT (average 153). Application deadline: 2/1 (priority date; rolling processing). Application fee: $25. *Financial aid:* Scholarships, full and partial tuition waivers available. Financial aid application deadline: 4/16. • Howard W. L'Enfant, Chancellor, 504-388-8491. Application contact: Beth Loup, Director of Admissions, 504-388-8646. Fax: 504-388-8202.

Loyola Marymount University, Loyola Law School, Los Angeles, CA 90015. Awards JD, JD/MBA. Approved by ABA. Member of AALS. Part-time and evening/weekend programs available. Faculty: 63 full-time (25 women), 58 part-time (12 women). Students: 927 full-time (436 women), 393 part-time (174 women); includes 529 minority (67 African Americans, 265 Asian Americans, 178 Hispanics, 19 Native Americans), 4 international. Average age 25. 2,638 applicants, 40% accepted. In 1997, 408 degrees awarded. *Average time to degree:* first professional–3 years full-time, 4 years part-time. *Entrance requirements:* LSAT. Application deadline: 2/1 (priority date; rolling processing). Application fee: $50. Electronic applications accepted. *Financial aid:* 1,162 students received aid; Federal Work-Study and career-related internships or fieldwork available. Aid available to part-time students. Financial aid application deadline: 3/2; applicants required to submit CSS PROFILE or FAFSA. *Faculty research:* Law and media, computers and the law, trademark law, euthanasia, three strikes laws. Total annual research expenditures: $815,792. • Gerald T. McLaughlin, Dean, 213-736-1435. Fax: 213-487-6736. E-mail: gmclaugh@lmulaw.lmu.edu. Application contact: Anton P. Mack, Assistant Dean for Admissions, 213-736-1180. Fax: 213-736-6523. E-mail: lawadmission@lmulaw.lmu.edu.

Loyola University Chicago, School of Law, 820 North Michigan Avenue, Chicago, IL 60611-2196. Awards JD, LL M, MJ, D Law, SJD, JD/MA, JD/MBA, JD/MSW, JD/MSIR. Programs in child law (LL M, MJ), corporate law (LL M, MJ), health law (LL M, MJ, D Law, SJD), law (JD). Approved by ABA. Member of AALS. Part-time and evening/weekend programs available. Faculty: 26 full-time (5 women), 72 part-time (29 women). Students: 556 full-time (314 women), 195 part-time (94 women); includes 126 minority (45 African Americans, 52 Asian Americans, 26 Hispanics, 3 Native Americans), 23 international. Average age 26. 2,329 applicants, 41% accepted. In 1997, 227 JDs awarded. *Entrance requirements:* For master's, LSAT (average 158). Application deadline: 4/1 (rolling processing). Application fee: $45. *Tuition:* $22,000 per

Directory: Law

Loyola University Chicago (continued)
year full-time, $16,500 per year part-time. *Financial aid:* 580 students received aid; partial tuition waivers, Federal Work-Study, institutionally sponsored loans available. Aid available to part-time students. Financial aid application deadline: 3/1; applicants required to submit FAFSA. *Faculty research:* International law, commercial law. • Nina S. Appel, Dean, 312-915-7120. Application contact: Pamela A. Bloomquist, Director of Admissions, 312-915-7170.

Loyola University New Orleans, School of Law, New Orleans, LA 70118-6195. Awards JD, JD/MA, JD/MBA. Approved by ABA. Member of AALS. Part-time and evening/weekend programs available. Faculty: 30 full-time (10 women), 18 part-time (2 women). Students: 400 full-time (188 women), 282 part-time (133 women); includes 77 minority (34 African Americans, 12 Asian Americans, 29 Hispanics, 2 Native Americans), 324 international. Average age 27. 1,311 applicants, 54% accepted. In 1997, 196 degrees awarded. *Average time to degree:* first professional–3 years full-time, 4 years part-time. *Entrance requirements:* LSAT. Application deadline: 8/20 (rolling processing). Application fee: $20. Electronic applications accepted. *Expenses:* Tuition $18,330 per year full-time, $611 per credit hour part-time. Fees $556 per year full-time, $164 per year part-time. *Financial aid:* 590 students received aid; research assistantships, teaching assistantships, full and partial tuition waivers, Federal Work-Study, and career-related internships or fieldwork available. Aid available to part-time students. Financial aid application deadline: 5/1; applicants required to submit FAFSA. *Faculty research:* Louisiana civil code, general common law. • John Makdisi Jr., Dean, 504-861-5550. Fax: 504-861-5739. Application contact: Michele Allison-Davis, Director of Admissions, 504-861-5575. Fax: 504-861-5772.

Marquette University, Law School, PO Box 1881, Milwaukee, WI 53201-1881. Awards JD, JD/MA, JD/MBA. Approved by ABA. Member of AALS. JD/MA offered jointly with the Department of Political Science. Part-time and evening/weekend programs available. Faculty: 23 full-time (8 women), 30 part-time (6 women), 30.5 FTE. Students: 415 full-time (172 women), 59 part-time (29 women); includes 50 minority (11 African Americans, 14 Asian Americans, 22 Hispanics, 3 Native Americans). Average age 25. 961 applicants, 53% accepted. In 1997, 157 degrees awarded. *Average time to degree:* first professional–3 years full-time. *Entrance requirements:* LSAT (average 153). Application deadline: 4/1 (rolling processing). Application fee: $35. *Tuition:* $18,370 per year full-time, $760 per credit part-time. *Financial aid:* 378 students received aid; tuition scholarships, Federal Work-Study, and career-related internships or fieldwork available. Aid available to part-time students. Financial aid application deadline: 3/1; applicants required to submit FAFSA. *Faculty research:* Pretrial motion in criminal prosecution, expansion of trademark rights, Wisconsin civil discovery, elder law, ethics and the law school. • Howard B. Eisenberg, Dean, 414-288-1765. Fax: 414-288-6403. E-mail: eisenbergh@vms.csd.mu.edu. Application contact: Assistant Dean for Admissions, 414-288-6767. Fax: 414-288-5914.

McGill University, Faculty of Graduate Studies and Research, Faculty of Law, Montreal, PQ H3A 1W9, Canada. Awards LL M, MCL, DCL, Certificate, MBA/LL B, MSW/LL B. Programs in air and space law (LL M, DCL, Certificate), comparative law (LL M, MCL, DCL, Certificate). Faculty: 23 full-time (5 women), 16 part-time (8 women). Students: 84 full-time (46 women); includes 58 international. Average age 25. 214 applicants, 58% accepted. In 1997, 40 master's, 3 doctorates, 2 Certificates awarded. Terminal master's awarded for partial completion of doctoral program. *Degree requirements:* For master's and doctorate, thesis/dissertation required, foreign language not required. *Average time to degree:* master's–1.2 years full-time; other advanced degree–1 year full-time. *Entrance requirements:* For master's, law degree, minimum GPA of 3.0; for doctorate, LL M. Application deadline: 2/1 (rolling processing). Application fee: $60. *Expenses:* Tuition $1668 per year for Canadian residents; $8268 per year for nonresidents. Fees $828 per year for Canadian residents; $1216 per year for nonresidents. *Financial aid:* 15 students received aid; fellowships, research assistantships, teaching assistantships, full and partial tuition waivers, institutionally sponsored loans available. Financial aid application deadline: 2/1. *Faculty research:* International law, international business law, human rights, legal theory and traditions, regulation and technology, bioethics, air and space law. • Stephen J. Toope, Dean, 514-398-6604. Application contact: G. Blaine Baker, Associate Dean, 514-398-3544. Fax: 514-398-8197.

Mercer University, Walter F. George School of Law, 1400 Coleman Avenue, Macon, GA 31207-0003. Awards JD, JD/MBA. Approved by ABA. Member of AALS. Part-time programs available. Faculty: 28 full-time (6 women), 24 part-time (7 women), 32 FTE. Students: 405 full-time (163 women); includes 45 minority (25 African Americans, 10 Asian Americans, 8 Hispanics, 2 Native Americans), 1 international. Average age 26. 1,071 applicants, 45% accepted. In 1997, 141 degrees awarded. *Average time to degree:* first professional–3 years full-time, 5 years part-time. *Entrance requirements:* LSAT. Application deadline: 3/15 (rolling processing). Application fee: $45. *Tuition:* $18,590 per year full-time, $8995 per year part-time. *Financial aid:* In 1997–98, 353 students received aid, including 1 fellowship totaling $4,000, 97 scholarships (29 to first-year students) totaling $927,131; Federal Work-Study, institutionally sponsored loans, and career-related internships or fieldwork also available. Aid available to part-time students. Financial aid application deadline: 4/1; applicants required to submit FAFSA. *Faculty research:* Banking regulation, European community law, legal ethics, feminist jurisprudence, federal taxation, jurisprudence, constitutional law. Total annual research expenditures: $120,000. • R. Lawrence Dessem, Dean, 912-752-2602. Application contact: Forrest Stanford, Assistant Dean of Admissions and Financial Aid, 912-752-2605. Fax: 912-752-2989.

Mississippi College, School of Law, Jackson, MS 39201. Awards JD, JD/MBA. Approved by ABA. Member of AALS. Faculty: 16 full-time (6 women), 19 part-time (1 woman). Students: 418 full-time (157 women); includes 47 minority (34 African Americans, 7 Asian Americans, 2 Hispanics, 4 Native Americans). 699 applicants, 69% accepted. In 1997, 119 degrees awarded. *Entrance requirements:* LSAT. Application deadline: 5/1 (priority date; rolling processing). Application fee: $25. *Expenses:* Tuition $14,291 per year. Fees $162 per year. *Financial aid:* In 1997–98, 356 students received aid, including 98 scholarships (26 to first-year students) totaling $766,028; Federal Work-Study and career-related internships or fieldwork also available. Financial aid application deadline: 5/1. • J. Richard Hurt, Dean, 601-925-7104. Fax: 601-925-7115. E-mail: hurt@mc.edu. Application contact: Patricia H. Evans, Director of Admissions, 601-925-7150. Fax: 601-925-7117. E-mail: pevans@mc.edu.

New College of California, School of Law, 50 Fell Street, San Francisco, CA 94102-5206. Awards JD. Faculty: 6 full-time (4 women), 18 part-time (6 women). Students: 92 full-time (53 women), 54 part-time (28 women); includes 40 minority (15 African Americans, 9 Asian Americans, 16 Hispanics), 1 international. Average age 30. 171 applicants, 32% accepted. In 1997, 48 degrees awarded. *Entrance requirements:* LSAT. Application deadline: 4/1 (priority date; rolling processing). Application fee: $45. *Tuition:* $9394 per year. *Financial aid:* In 1997–98, 10 scholarships were awarded; Federal Work-Study and career-related internships or fieldwork also available. Aid available to part-time students. Financial aid application deadline: 3/1; applicants required to submit FAFSA. *Faculty research:* Public interest, practical skills development. • Debrenia Madison, Dean, 415-241-1325. Application contact: Arlana P. Spikener, Assistant Dean for Admissions, 415-241-1314. Fax: 415-241-1353.

See in-depth description on page 1587.

New England School of Law, Boston, MA 02116-5687. Awards JD. Approved by ABA. Member of AALS. Part-time and evening/weekend programs available. Faculty: 38 full-time (8 women), 49 part-time (12 women), 43 FTE. Students: 549 full-time (275 women), 392 part-time (181 women); includes 152 minority (47 African Americans, 48 Asian Americans, 47 Hispanics, 10 Native Americans), 10 international. Average age 25. 2,218 applicants, 68% accepted. In 1997, 282 degrees awarded. *Average time to degree:* first professional–3 years full-time, 4 years part-time. *Entrance requirements:* LSAT, LSDAS. Application deadline: 6/1 (rolling processing). Application fee: $50. *Financial aid:* 775 students received aid; full and partial tuition waivers, Federal Work-Study, and career-related internships or fieldwork available. Aid available to part-time students. Financial aid application deadline: 4/15; applicants required to submit FAFSA. • John F. O'Brien, Dean, 617-451-0010. Fax: 617-422-7333. Application contact: Pamela Jorgensen, Director of Admissions, 617-422-7210. Fax: 617-422-7200. E-mail: admit@admin.nesl.edu.

New York Law School, New York, NY 10013-2959. Awards JD, JD/MBA. Approved by ABA. Member of AALS. JD/MBA offered jointly with Baruch College of the City University of New York. Part-time and evening/weekend programs available. Faculty: 52 full-time (16 women), 82 part-time (26 women). Students: 880 full-time (415 women), 488 part-time (218 women); includes 286 minority (106 African Americans, 77 Asian Americans, 97 Hispanics, 6 Native Americans), 8 international. Average age 27. 4,177 applicants, 48% accepted. In 1997, 430 degrees awarded. *Average time to degree:* first professional–3 years full-time, 4 years part-time. *Entrance requirements:* LSAT (average 154). Application deadline: 4/1 (priority date; rolling processing). Application fee: $50. *Tuition:* $22,114 per year full-time, $16,588 per year part-time. *Financial aid:* In 1997–98, 472 scholarships, grants (182 to first-year students) totaling $3.13 million were awarded; research assistantships, teaching assistantships, full and partial tuition waivers, Federal Work-Study, institutionally sponsored loans, and career-related internships or fieldwork also available. Aid available to part-time students. Financial aid application deadline: 4/15; applicants required to submit FAFSA. *Faculty research:* New York City law, communications media law, environmental law, international law, public interest law. • Harry H. Wellington, Dean, 212-431-2840. Application contact: Pamela McKenna, Director of Admissions, 212-431-2888. Fax: 212-966-1522.

New York University, School of Law, New York, NY 10012. Awards JD, LL M, MCJ, JSD, PhD, JD/MA, JD/MBA, JD/MPA, JD/MSW, JD/PhD, JD/LL M, JD/MUP. Approved by ABA. Member of AALS. PhD offered through the Graduate School of Arts and Science. Part-time and evening/weekend programs available. Faculty: 102 full-time (37 women), 123 part-time (30 women). Students: 1,317 full-time (613 women); includes 256 minority (74 African Americans, 119 Asian Americans, 62 Hispanics, 1 Native American), 51 international. 6,185 applicants, 24% accepted. In 1997, 437 JDs, 450 master's, 5 doctorates awarded. *Degree requirements:* For doctorate, dissertation required, foreign language not required. *Average time to degree:* master's–1 year full-time; first professional–3 years full-time. *Entrance requirements:* For JD, LSAT (median 168); for master's, JD; for doctorate, JD, LL M. Application deadline: 2/1 (rolling processing). Application fee: $65. *Financial aid:* 1,124 students received aid; fellowships, research assistantships, teaching assistantships, partial tuition waivers, Federal Work-Study, institutionally sponsored loans, and career-related internships or fieldwork available. Financial aid application deadline: 5/1; applicants required to submit FAFSA. *Faculty research:* Constitutional law, environmental law, corporate law, globalization of law, philosophy of law. Total annual research expenditures: $2.333 million. • John Sexton, Dean, 212-998-6000. Fax: 212-995-3150. Application contact: Nan McNamara, Assistant Dean for Admissions, 212-998-6060.

North Carolina Central University, Division of Academic Affairs, School of Law, Durham, NC 27707-3129. Awards JD, JD/MBA, JD/MLS. Approved by ABA. Part-time and evening/weekend programs available. Faculty: 17 full-time (9 women), 10 part-time (6 women). Students: 379 full-time (209 women), 3 part-time (1 woman); includes 198 minority (182 African Americans, 4 Asian Americans, 4 Hispanics, 8 Native Americans). Average age 31. 1,071 applicants, 24% accepted. In 1997, 85 degrees awarded. *Entrance requirements:* LSAT, LSDAS. Application deadline: 4/15. Application fee: $30. *Tuition:* $2071 per year for state residents; $10,997 per year for nonresidents. *Financial aid:* Federal Work-Study, institutionally sponsored loans, and career-related internships or fieldwork available. Aid available to part-time students. Financial aid application deadline: 5/1. • Percy Luney, Dean, 919-560-6427. Application contact: Adrienne Meddock, Acting Assistant Dean, 919-560-5249.

Northeastern University, School of Law, Boston, MA 02115-5096. Awards JD, JD/MBA, JD/MS, JD/PhD, JD/MS/MBA. Approved by ABA. Member of AALS. JD/MS/MBA offered jointly with the Graduate School of Professional Accounting; JD/MS, JD/PhD offered jointly with Program in Law, Policy and Society. Faculty: 29 full-time (13 women), 42 part-time (14 women). Students: 577 full-time (387 women); includes 152 minority (55 African Americans, 57 Asian Americans, 38 Hispanics, 2 Native Americans), 4 international. Average age 26. 2,167 applicants, 36% accepted. In 1997, 191 degrees awarded. *Average time to degree:* first professional–3 years full-time. *Entrance requirements:* LSAT. Application deadline: 3/1 (rolling processing). Application fee: $55. *Tuition:* $22,500 per year. *Financial aid:* In 1997–98, 480 students received aid, including 15 research assistantships, 44 teaching assistantships; fellowships, full and partial tuition waivers, Federal Work-Study, institutionally sponsored loans, and career-related internships or fieldwork also available. Financial aid application deadline: 3/1; applicants required to submit CSS PROFILE or FAFSA. *Faculty research:* Domestic violence, critical legal studies, feminist jurisprudence, international law, comparative law. • Daniel J. Givelber, Acting Dean. Application contact: Paul D. Bauer, Assistant Dean and Director of Admissions, 617-373-2395. Fax: 617-373-8865. E-mail: pbauer@nunet.neu.edu.

Northern Illinois University, College of Law, De Kalb, IL 60115-2854. Awards JD. Approved by ABA. Member of AALS. Faculty: 19 full-time (6 women). Students: 273 full-time (101 women), 7 part-time (2 women); includes 59 minority (23 African Americans, 19 Asian Americans, 15 Hispanics, 2 Native Americans), 1 international. Average age 29. In 1997, 93 degrees awarded. *Average time to degree:* first professional–3 years full-time. *Entrance requirements:* LSAT. Application deadline: 6/1. Application fee: $35. *Financial aid:* In 1997–98, 14 staff assistantships were awarded; research assistantships, teaching assistantships, full and partial tuition waivers, Federal Work-Study, and career-related internships or fieldwork also available. Aid available to part-time students. • LeRoy Pernell, Dean, 815-753-1067. Application contact: Judith L. Malen, Director of Admissions and Financial Aid, 815-753-1420.

Northern Kentucky University, Salmon P. Chase College of Law, Covington, KY 41011. Awards JD, JD/MBA. Approved by ABA. Member of AALS. Part-time and evening/weekend programs available. Faculty: 24 full-time (7 women). Students: 202 full-time (68 women), 199 part-time (76 women); includes 27 minority (21 African Americans, 1 Asian American, 4 Hispanics, 1 Native American). Average age 31. 699 applicants, 39% accepted. In 1997, 106 degrees awarded. *Entrance requirements:* LSAT. Application deadline: 5/1. Application fee: $20. *Tuition:* $5390 per year full-time, $227 per semester hour part-time for state residents; $14,000 per year full-time, $585 per semester hour part-time for nonresidents. *Financial aid:* In 1997–98, 2 research assistantships (both to first-year students), 80 scholarships (35 to first-year students) were awarded; partial tuition waivers and career-related internships or fieldwork also available. Aid available to part-time students. Financial aid application deadline: 4/1. *Faculty research:* Law of automobile financing and sales, libel law, Ohio corporate law, prepaid legal services. • Prof. David Short, Dean, 606-572-6406. Application contact: Gina Bray, Admissions Specialist, 606-572-5384.

Northwestern University, School of Law, Chicago, IL 60611-3069. Awards JD, LL M, SJD, JD/PhD, JD/MM. Approved by ABA. Member of AALS. Faculty: 56 full-time (16 women), 134 part-time (31 women). Students: 678 full-time (283 women); includes 138 minority (47 African Americans, 48 Asian Americans, 39 Hispanics, 4 Native Americans), 54 international. Average age 25. 3,537 applicants, 21% accepted. In 1997, 208 JDs, 39 master's awarded. *Degree requirements:* For doctorate, dissertation required, foreign language not required. *Average time to degree:* master's–1 year full-time; first professional–3 years full-time. *Entrance requirements:* For JD, LSAT; for master's and doctorate, TOEFL (minimum score 600), law degree or equivalent. Application deadline: 2/16 (rolling processing). Application fee: $65. *Tuition:* $23,974 per year. *Financial aid:* 416 students received aid; fellowships, institutionally sponsored loans, and career-related internships or fieldwork available. Financial aid application deadline: 3/17; applicants required to submit FAFSA. *Faculty research:* Medical malpractice and technological advances; dispute resolution techniques; moral reasoning and alternative constitutional law; game theory, social choice concepts, and the norms of public international law. • David VanZandt, Dean, 312-503-8460. Application contact: Donald Rebstock, Assistant

Dean for Admissions and Financial Aid, 312-503-8465. Fax: 312-503-0178. E-mail: nulawadm@harold.law.nwu.edu.

Nova Southeastern University, Shepard Broad Law Center, Fort Lauderdale, FL 33314-7721. Awards JD, JD/MBA, JD/MS. Approved by ABA. Member of AALS. Part-time and evening/weekend programs available. Faculty: 43 full-time (15 women), 45 part-time (12 women). Students: 780 full-time (322 women), 140 part-time (57 women); includes 170 minority (54 African Americans, 8 Asian Americans, 104 Hispanics, 4 Native Americans), 17 international. Average age 29. 1,448 applicants, 55% accepted. In 1997, 305 degrees awarded. *Degree requirements:* Thesis required, foreign language not required. *Average time to degree:* first professional–3 years full-time, 4 years part-time. *Entrance requirements:* LSAT. Application deadline: 3/1 (priority date). Application fee: $50. *Tuition:* $19,710 per year full-time, $14,780 per year part-time. *Financial aid:* In 1997–98, 200 students received aid, including 182 fellowships (27 to first-year students) totaling $1.142 million, 40 research assistantships, 13 teaching assistantships, 35 mediation programs; full and partial tuition waivers, Federal Work-Study, and career-related internships or fieldwork also available. Aid available to part-time students. Financial aid application deadline: 4/1; applicants required to submit FAFSA. *Faculty research:* Legal issues in family law, civil rights, business associations, criminal law, law and popular culture. • Joseph D. Harbaugh, Dean, 954-262-6101. Fax: 954-262-3834. E-mail: harbaughj@nsu.law.nova.edu. Application contact: Nancy Sanguigni, Director, 954-262-6120. Fax: 954-262-3844. E-mail: sanguinin@nsu.law.nova.edu.

Ohio Northern University, Claude W. Pettit College of Law, Ada, OH 45810-1599. Awards JD. Approved by ABA. Member of AALS. Faculty: 26. Students: 380. *Average time to degree:* first professional–3 years full-time. *Entrance requirements:* LSAT. Application deadline: rolling. Application fee: $40. *Tuition:* $18,980 per year. *Financial aid:* Research assistantships, Federal Work-Study, institutionally sponsored loans, and career-related internships or fieldwork available. Financial aid application deadline: 5/1; applicants required to submit FAFSA. *Faculty research:* Constitutional law, environmental law, business law and taxation, criminal law, public interest law. • Victor L. Streib III, Dean, 419-772-2205. Fax: 419-772-1875. Application contact: Office of Admissions, 419-772-2211.

Announcement: The Icelandic Exchange Program is a unique collaborative effort between the Colleges of Law at Ohio Northern and the University of Iceland. Officials at the schools have devised a study exchange program enabling ONU students the rich opportunity to study at the law school in Reykjavik. In addition, ONU law students and law students from Iceland annually visit Iceland and Ohio, respectively. The students gain international exposure to new judicial, social, and legislative systems.

See in-depth description on page 1589.

The Ohio State University, College of Law, Columbus, OH 43210. Awards JD, JD/MA, JD/MBA, JD/MPA, JD/MS, JD/PhD, JD/MHA. Approved by ABA. Member of AALS. Faculty: 40 full-time (12 women), 46 part-time (16 women). Students: 668 full-time (295 women), 4 part-time (2 women); includes 110 minority (52 African Americans, 40 Asian Americans, 17 Hispanics, 1 Native American), 1 international. Average age 24. 1,364 applicants, 43% accepted. In 1997, 210 degrees awarded. *Average time to degree:* first professional–3 years full-time. *Entrance requirements:* LSAT (average 157). Application deadline: 3/15 (priority date; rolling processing). Application fee: $30 ($40 for international students). *Tuition:* $7692 per year for state residents; $17,086 per year for nonresidents. *Financial aid:* 431 students received aid; Federal Work-Study, institutionally sponsored loans, and career-related internships or fieldwork available. Financial aid application deadline: 3/1; applicants required to submit FAFSA. • Gregory H. Williams, Dean, 614-292-2631. Application contact: Jennifer Beadnell, Office Associate, 614-292-8810. Fax: 614-292-1383.

Oklahoma City University, School of Law, Oklahoma City, OK 73106-1402. Awards JD, JD/MBA. Approved by ABA. Part-time and evening/weekend programs available. Students: 388 full-time (149 women), 170 part-time (66 women); includes 82 minority (16 African Americans, 13 Asian Americans, 19 Hispanics, 34 Native Americans), 1 international. Average age 30. In 1997, 145 degrees awarded. *Average time to degree:* first professional–3 years full-time, 4 years part-time. *Entrance requirements:* LSAT (average 147). Application deadline: 6/1. Application fee: $35. *Expenses:* Tuition $504 per hour. Fees $124 per year. *Financial aid:* Partial tuition waivers, Federal Work-Study, institutionally sponsored loans, and career-related internships or fieldwork available. Aid available to part-time students. Financial aid application deadline: 8/1. • Jay Conison, Interim Dean, 405-521-5329. Application contact: Gary Mercer, Director of Law School Admissions, 800-633-7242. E-mail: gmercer@frodo.okcu.edu.

Pace University, School of Law, White Plains, NY 10603. Awards JD, LL M, SJD, JD/MBA, JD/MPA. Approved by ABA. Member of AALS. Part-time and evening/weekend programs available. *Entrance requirements:* For JD, LSAT. Application deadline: 3/15. Application fee: $55. *Expenses:* Tuition $21,750 per year full-time, $16,324 per year part-time. Fees $80 per year full-time, $60 per year part-time.

See in-depth description on page 1591.

Pepperdine University, School of Law, Professional Program, Malibu, CA 90263-0001. Awards JD, JD/MBA. Approved by ABA. Member of AALS. Students: 651 full-time (291 women), 7 part-time (6 women); includes 108 minority (28 African Americans, 49 Asian Americans, 24 Hispanics, 7 Native Americans), 11 international. Average age 27. 2,265 applicants, 46% accepted. In 1997, 258 degrees awarded. *Entrance requirements:* LSAT. Application deadline: 3/1 (rolling processing). Application fee: $50. • Application contact: Shannon Phillips, Director of Admissions, 310-456-4631.

Pontifical Catholic University of Puerto Rico, School of Law, Ponce, PR 00731-6382. Awards JD, LL M, JD/MBA. Approved by ABA. LL M being phased out; applicants no longer accepted. Part-time and evening/weekend programs available. Faculty: 19 full-time (8 women), 12 part-time (2 women). Students: 505 full-time (260 women), 13 part-time (2 women); includes 518 minority (all Hispanics). Average age 31. 489 applicants, 34% accepted. In 1997, 140 JDs awarded. *Degree requirements:* For master's, thesis or alternative. *Entrance requirements:* For JD, LSAT, PAEG. Application deadline: 4/30 (priority date; rolling processing). Application fee: $25. Electronic applications accepted. *Financial aid:* Fellowships, Federal Work-Study available. Aid available to part-time students. Financial aid application deadline: 7/15. • Charles Cuprill, Dean, 787-841-2000 Ext. 341. Application contact: Manuel Luciano, Director of Admissions, 787-841-2000 Ext. 426. Fax: 787-840-4295.

Queen's University at Kingston, Faculty of Law, Kingston, ON K7L 3N6, Canada. Awards LL B, LL M, LL B/MIR. Part-time programs available. Faculty: 32. Students: 478 full-time, 18 part-time. In 1997, 2 master's awarded. *Degree requirements:* For master's, thesis required, foreign language not required. *Entrance requirements:* For LL B, LSAT, minimum 2 years of college; for master's, TOEFL (minimum score 660), LL B. Application fee: $60. Electronic applications accepted. *Tuition:* $3803 per year (minimum) full-time, $1901 per year (minimum) part-time for Canadian residents; $7330 per year (minimum) for nonresidents. *Financial aid:* Fellowships, research assistantships, institutionally sponsored loans available. Financial aid application deadline: 3/1. *Faculty research:* Feminist legal studies, labour relations law, tax law and policy, legal theory, criminal law and policy. • D. D. Carter, Dean, 613-545-2220. Fax: 613-545-6611. E-mail: llb@qsilver.queensu.ca. Application contact: M. G. Baer, Graduate Coordinator, 613-545-2220. Fax: 613-545-4286. E-mail: llm@qsilver.queensu.ca.

Quinnipiac College, School of Law, Hamden, CT 06518-1904. Awards JD, JD/MBA, JD/MHA. Approved by ABA. Member of AALS. Part-time and evening/weekend programs available. Faculty: 45 full-time (17 women), 34 part-time (8 women). Students: 542 full-time (200 women), 239 part-time (99 women); includes 84 minority (37 African Americans, 15 Asian Americans, 26 Hispanics, 6 Native Americans), 9 international. Average age 26. 1,965 applicants, 55% accepted. In 1997, 244 degrees awarded. *Entrance requirements:* LSAT (average 150). Application deadline: rolling. Application fee: $40. *Financial aid:* 664 students received aid; fellowships, Federal Work-Study, institutionally sponsored loans, and career-related internships or fieldwork available. Aid available to part-time students. Financial aid application deadline: 5/1; applicants required to submit FAFSA. *Faculty research:* Tax, health, public interest, and corporate law. • Neil H. Cogan, Dean, 203-287-3200. Fax: 203-287-3209. E-mail: ladm@quinnipiac.edu. Application contact: John J. Noonan, Dean of Admissions, 203-287-3400. Fax: 203-287-3339. E-mail: ladm@quinnipiac.edu.

See in-depth description on page 1593.

Regent University, Graduate School, School of Law, Virginia Beach, VA 23464-9800. Awards JD, JD/MA, JD/MBA. Approved by ABA. Faculty: 20 full-time (3 women), 39 part-time (7 women). Students: 394 full-time (144 women), 14 part-time (2 women); includes 43 minority (25 African Americans, 10 Asian Americans, 6 Hispanics, 2 Native Americans). Average age 30. 308 applicants, 37% accepted. In 1997, 108 degrees awarded. *Average time to degree:* first professional–3 years full-time. *Entrance requirements:* LSAT, minimum undergraduate GPA of 2.75. Application deadline: 4/1 (rolling processing). Application fee: $40. *Expenses:* Tuition $495 per credit hour. Fees $12 per semester. *Financial aid:* 298 students received aid; full and partial tuition waivers and career-related internships or fieldwork available. Financial aid application deadline: 5/1. *Faculty research:* Religious freedom, tort liability of religious organizations, Christian foundations for law, causation issues in law, academic freedom. • J. Nelson Happy, Dean, 757-226-4040. E-mail: nelshap@regent.edu. Application contact: Diane Fiazza, Director of Law and Government Admissions, 757-226-4119. Fax: 757-226-4595. E-mail: lawschool@regent.edu.

Roger Williams University, School of Law, Bristol, RI 02809. Awards JD, JD/MCP, JD/MMA. Approved by ABA. JD/MCP and JD/MMA offered jointly with the University of Rhode Island. Part-time and evening/weekend programs available. Faculty: 29 full-time (10 women), 27 part-time (5 women). Students: 246 full-time (109 women), 202 part-time (79 women); includes 32 minority (16 African Americans, 4 Asian Americans, 12 Hispanics). Average age 27. 706 applicants, 63% accepted. In 1997, 162 degrees awarded (100% found work related to degree). *Average time to degree:* first professional–3 years full-time, 4 years part-time. *Entrance requirements:* LSAT (average 150). Application deadline: 5/15 (priority date; rolling processing). Application fee: $60. *Expenses:* Tuition $19,050 per year full-time, $14,605 per year part-time. Fees $50 per year. *Financial aid:* In 1997–98, 386 students received aid, including 20 scholarships (10 to first-year students) totaling $54,800; institutionally sponsored loans and career-related internships or fieldwork also available. Aid available to part-time students. Financial aid application deadline: 5/1; applicants required to submit FAFSA. *Faculty research:* Elder, tidelands, admiralty, environmental, and public interest law. • John E. Ryan, Dean and Vice President, 401-254-4500. Fax: 401-254-3525. E-mail: ll@rwulaw.rwu.edu. Application contact: Mary D. Upton, Director of Admissions, 401-254-4555. Fax: 401-254-4516. E-mail: mdu@rwulaw.rwu.edu.

See in-depth description on page 1595.

Rutgers, The State University of New Jersey, Camden, School of Law, Camden, NJ 08102-1401. Awards JD, JD/MA, JD/MBA, JD/MPA, JD/MSW, JD/MCRP, JD/MD. Approved by ABA. Member of AALS. JD/MA, JD/MCRP, JD/MSW offered jointly with Rutgers, The State University of New Jersey, New Brunswick. JD/MBA offered jointly with Rutgers, The State University of New Jersey, Newark. JD/MPA, JD/MD offered jointly with the University of Medicine and Dentistry of New Jersey. JD/MD and JD/MSW new for spr. Part-time and evening/weekend programs available. Faculty: 39 full-time (12 women), 47 part-time (6 women). Students: 549 full-time (265 women), 162 part-time (62 women); includes 132 minority (64 African Americans, 38 Asian Americans, 29 Hispanics, 1 Native American), 15 international. Average age 27. 1,503 applicants, 50% accepted. In 1997, 271 degrees awarded. *Average time to degree:* first professional–3 years full-time, 4 years part-time. *Entrance requirements:* LSAT (average 153). Application deadline: 3/1. Application fee: $40. *Expenses:* Tuition $9682 per year full-time, $401 per credit part-time for state residents; $14,206 per year full-time, $591 per credit part-time for nonresidents. Fees $1099 per year full-time, $212 per semester (minimum) part-time. *Financial aid:* 590 students received aid. *Faculty research:* International law, tax law, commercial law, criminal law, public law. • Jay Feinman, Acting Dean, 609-225-6191. Application contact: Camille Spinello Andrews, Associate Dean of Enrollment, Law Admissions, 609-225-6102.

Rutgers, The State University of New Jersey, Newark, School of Law, Newark, NJ 07102-3192. Awards JD, JD/MA, JD/PhD, JD/MCRP. Approved by ABA. Member of AALS. JD/MCRP and JD/PhD offered jointly with the Graduate School at Rutgers, The State University of New Jersey, New Brunswick. Part-time and evening/weekend programs available. Faculty: 44 full-time (14 women), 39 part-time (9 women), 52.4 FTE. Students: 511 full-time (248 women), 222 part-time (86 women); includes 218 minority (94 African Americans, 48 Asian Americans, 76 Hispanics), 35 international. Average age 28. 2,327 applicants, 33% accepted. In 1997, 247 degrees awarded. *Entrance requirements:* LSAT. Application deadline: 3/15 (rolling processing). Application fee: $40. *Financial aid:* In 1997–98, 585 students received aid, including 4 fellowships (all to first-year students), 15 research assistantships, 16 teaching assistantships; Federal Work-Study, institutionally sponsored loans, and career-related internships or fieldwork also available. Aid available to part-time students. Financial aid application deadline: 3/1; applicants required to submit FAFSA. *Faculty research:* Civil rights and liberties, women and the law, international human rights and world order, alternate dispute resolution, criminal law and procedure, social science and the law. Total annual research expenditures: $45,000. • Eric Neisser, Acting Dean, 973-353-5551. Application contact: Olga Hunczak, Director of Admissions, 973-353-5557. Fax: 973-353-1445.

St. John's University, School of Law, Jamaica, NY 11439. Awards JD, JD/MA, JD/MBA. Approved by ABA. Member of AALS. Part-time and evening/weekend programs available. Faculty: 50 full-time (16 women), 21 part-time (3 women). Students: 771 full-time (320 women), 289 part-time (89 women); includes 257 minority (77 African Americans, 82 Asian Americans, 93 Hispanics, 5 Native Americans), 6 international. Average age 27. 2,398 applicants, 45% accepted. In 1997, 392 degrees awarded. *Average time to degree:* first professional–3 years full-time, 4 years part-time. *Entrance requirements:* LSAT, minimum GPA of 3.2 (recommended). Application deadline: 3/1 (11/1 for spring admission). Application fee: $50. *Expenses:* Tuition $22,000 per year full-time, $16,500 per year part-time. Fees $150 per year. *Financial aid:* Federal Work-Study and career-related internships or fieldwork available. Aid available to part-time students. Financial aid application deadline: 3/1; applicants required to submit FAFSA. *Faculty research:* Jurisprudence, law and literature. • Prof. Brian Tamanaha, Acting Dean, 718-990-6600. Application contact: Mary A. Conlon, Assistant Dean and Director of Admissions, 718-990-6592. Fax: 718-591-1855.

Saint Louis University, School of Law, St. Louis, MO 63108. Awards JD, LL M, JD/MBA, JD/MAPA, JD/MAUA, JD/MHA, JD/MPH. Approved by ABA. Member of AALS. Part-time and evening/weekend programs available. Faculty: 34 full-time (8 women), 37 part-time (4 women). Students: 563 full-time (262 women), 261 part-time (97 women); includes 129 minority (72 African Americans, 34 Asian Americans, 19 Hispanics, 4 Native Americans), 5 international. Average age 27. 1,067 applicants, 63% accepted. In 1997, 219 JDs, 3 master's awarded. *Degree requirements:* For master's, thesis required (for some programs), foreign language not required. *Average time to degree:* first professional–3 years full-time, 4 years part-time. *Entrance requirements:* For JD, LSAT (average 154); for master's, TOEFL (minimum score 575), JD or equivalent of basic law degree. Application deadline: 3/1 (priority date; rolling processing). Application fee: $40. *Tuition:* $19,170 per year full-time, $14,360 per year part-time. *Financial aid:* 670 students received aid; fellowships, partial tuition waivers, Federal Work-Study, and career-related internships or fieldwork available. Aid available to part-time students. Financial aid application deadline: 4/1; applicants required to submit FAFSA. *Faculty research:* Health law, employment law, international comparative law, lawyering skills (clinical). • John B. Attanasio, Dean, 314-977-2760. Fax: 314-977-3333. Application contact: Valerie Lampe-McFarlane, Assistant Dean and Director of Admissions, 314-977-2800.

Directory: Law

Saint Louis University (continued)

Announcement: The Saint Louis University School of Law offers a JD degree with both full- and part-time options. The Jesuit nature of the institution is manifested in a commitment to academic excellence and freedom of inquiry, a genuine concern for the development of each student as a person, and an effort to sensitize students to the moral and ethical dimensions of law and lawyering. It is nationally known for its areas of specialization in health law, employment law, and international and comparative law. Certificates can be earned in each of these areas. There are many opportunities for clinical experience and foreign study.

See in-depth description on page 1597.

St. Mary's University of San Antonio, School of Law, San Antonio, TX 78228-8507. Awards JD, JD/MA, JD/MBA, JD/MPA, JD/MS. Approved by ABA. Member of AALS. *Average time to degree:* first professional–3 years full-time. *Entrance requirements:* LSAT. Application deadline: 4/1 (priority date). Application fee: $35. *Expenses:* Tuition $545 per credit hour. Fees $235 per year. *Faculty research:* Ethics, church and state, exclusionary rule, civil rights and labor issues.

St. Thomas University, School of Law, Miami, FL 33054-6459. Awards JD. Approved by ABA. *Average time to degree:* first professional–3 years full-time. *Entrance requirements:* LSAT. Application deadline: 7/1. Application fee: $30. *Expenses:* Tuition $19,144 per year. Fees $830 per year.

Samford University, Cumberland School of Law, Birmingham, AL 35229-0002. Awards JD, JD/MBA, JD/MPA, JD/M Acc, JD/MAE, JD/M Div, JD/MPH, JD/MSEM. Approved by ABA. Member of AALS. JD/MAE, JD/MPA, and JD/MPH offered jointly with the University of Alabama at Birmingham. Faculty: 34 full-time (7 women), 26 part-time (5 women). Students: 610 full-time (207 women), 4 part-time (3 women); includes 48 minority (40 African Americans, 3 Asian Americans, 5 Hispanics). Average age 26. 999 applicants, 59% accepted. In 1997, 211 degrees awarded. *Entrance requirements:* LSAT (average 153). Application deadline: 2/28 (priority date; rolling processing). Application fee: $40. *Tuition:* $18,350 per year full-time, $612 per credit hour part-time. *Financial aid:* In 1997–98, 505 students received aid, including 34 grants, scholarships; research assistantships, teaching assistantships, Federal Work-Study, institutionally sponsored loans, and career-related internships or fieldwork also available. Financial aid application deadline: 3/1; applicants required to submit FAFSA. *Faculty research:* Commercial law, evidence, torts, legal history, law and religion. • Dr. Barry A. Currier, Dean, 205-870-2704. Application contact: Mitzi S. Davis, Assistant Dean for Admissions, 205-870-2702. Fax: 205-870-2673. E-mail: msdavis@samford.edu.

San Joaquin College of Law, Law Program, 901 5th Street, Clovis, CA 93612-1312. Awards JD. Part-time and evening/weekend programs available. Faculty: 6 full-time (3 women), 50 part-time (10 women). Students: 275. *Average time to degree:* first professional–3 years full-time, 4 years part-time. *Entrance requirements:* LSAT. Application deadline: 6/30 (priority date; rolling processing). Application fee: $40. *Expenses:* Tuition $375 per unit. Fees $40 per semester. *Financial aid:* Federal Work-Study and career-related internships or fieldwork available. Aid available to part-time students. Financial aid application deadline: 8/24. • Sally Ann Perring, Associate Dean of Academic Affairs, 209-323-2100. Application contact: Joyce Morodomi, Registrar/Admissions Officer, 209-323-2100. Fax: 209-323-5566.

Santa Clara University, School of Law, Santa Clara, CA 95053-0001. Awards JD, LL M, Certificate, JD/MBA. Approved by ABA. Member of AALS. Part-time and evening/weekend programs available. Faculty: 35 full-time (13 women), 11 part-time (4 women). Students: 865 full-time (414 women), 62 part-time (25 women); includes 274 minority (38 African Americans, 161 Asian Americans, 66 Hispanics, 9 Native Americans), 30 international. Average age 29. 2,676 applicants, 51% accepted. In 1997, 260 JDs awarded. *Entrance requirements:* For JD, LSAT, LSDAS. Application deadline: 3/1. Application fee: $40. *Financial aid:* Fellowships, research assistantships, Federal Work-Study, and career-related internships or fieldwork available. Aid available to part-time students. Financial aid application deadline: 2/1. • Mack Player, Dean, 408-554-4361. Application contact: Julia Yaffee, Director of Admissions, 408-554-4800. Fax: 408-554-7897.

Seattle University, School of Law, Tacoma, WA 98402. Awards JD, JD/MBA, JD/MAE, JD/MIB, JD/MSF. Approved by ABA. Member of AALS. JD/MBA, JD/MAE, JD/MIB, JD/MSF new for fall 1998. Part-time and evening/weekend programs available. Faculty: 37 full-time (16 women), 28 part-time (10 women). Students: 641 full-time (324 women), 189 part-time (90 women); includes 158 minority (37 African Americans, 74 Asian Americans, 23 Hispanics, 24 Native Americans), 9 international. Average age 30. 1,213 applicants, 65% accepted. In 1997, 279 degrees awarded. *Entrance requirements:* LSAT (score in 67th percentile or higher), minimum GPA of 3.0. Application deadline: 4/1 (rolling processing). Application fee: $50. *Expenses:* Tuition $17,880 per year full-time, $14,900 per year part-time. Fees $46 per year full-time, $32 per year part-time. *Financial aid:* 808 students received aid; scholarships, partial tuition waivers, Federal Work-Study, institutionally sponsored loans, and career-related internships or fieldwork available. Aid available to part-time students. Financial aid application deadline: 4/1; applicants required to submit FAFSA. *Faculty research:* Legal status of homeless mentally ill, health law cost containment, legal writing across the curriculum, study of sentencing patterns. • James E. Bond, Dean, 253-591-2273. Application contact: Geraldine Clausen, Executive Director of Admissions and Financial Aid, 253-591-2252. Fax: 253-591-6313. E-mail: lawadmis@seattleu.edu.

Seton Hall University, School of Law, Newark, NJ 07102. Awards JD, LL M, MSJ, JD/MBA. Approved by ABA. Member of AALS. Part-time and evening/weekend programs available. Faculty: 44 full-time (15 women), 88 part-time (18 women). Students: 917 full-time (408 women), 335 part-time (142 women); includes 200 minority (64 African Americans, 64 Asian Americans, 67 Hispanics, 5 Native Americans). Average age 27. 2,402 applicants, 47% accepted. In 1997, 367 JDs awarded. *Average time to degree:* first professional–3 years full-time, 4 years part-time. *Entrance requirements:* For JD, LSAT (median 155), LSDAS. Application deadline: 4/1 (rolling processing). Application fee: $50. Electronic applications accepted. *Expenses:* Tuition $20,940 per year full-time, $698 per credit part-time. Fees $190 per year full-time, $90 per year part-time. *Financial aid:* In 1997–98, 1,050 students received aid, including 70 research assistantships; Federal Work-Study, institutionally sponsored loans, and career-related internships or fieldwork also available. Aid available to part-time students. Financial aid application deadline: 4/15; applicants required to submit FAFSA. *Faculty research:* Employment law, litigation advocacy, constitutional law and public policy, corporate law, alternative medicine. • Ronald J. Riccio, Dean, 973-642-8750. Fax: 973-642-8734. Application contact: Kenneth G. Stevenson, Dean of Admissions and Financial Resource Management, 973-642-8747. Fax: 973-642-8876. E-mail: admitme@shu.edu.

Southern Illinois University at Carbondale, School of Law, Carbondale, IL 62901-6806. Awards JD, JD/MBA, JD/MPA, JD/MSW, JD/PhD, JD/M Acc, JD/MD. Approved by ABA. Member of AALS. Part-time programs available. Faculty: 30 full-time (12 women), 8 part-time (2 women). Students: 365 full-time (141 women), 4 part-time (1 woman); includes 60 minority (20 African Americans, 26 Asian Americans, 10 Hispanics, 4 Native Americans). Average age 27. 681 applicants, 57% accepted. In 1997, 117 degrees awarded. *Average time to degree:* first professional–3 years full-time. *Entrance requirements:* LSAT (average 153). Application deadline: 3/1 (priority date; rolling processing). Application fee: $25. *Expenses:* Tuition $4620 per year for state residents; $13,860 per year for nonresidents. Fees $1034 per year. *Financial aid:* 300 students received aid; scholarships, Federal Work-Study, institutionally sponsored loans, and career-related internships or fieldwork available. Aid available to part-time students. Financial aid applicants required to submit FAFSA. *Faculty research:* Litigation, health law, environmental law, international law, tort reform. • Thomas F. Guernsey, Dean, 618-536-7711. Application contact: Patricia Caporale, Admissions Assistant, 618-536-7711.

Southern Methodist University, School of Law, Dallas, TX 75275. Awards JD, LL M, SJD, JD/MA, JD/MBA. Programs in comparative and international law (LL M), law (JD, LL M, SJD), taxation (LL M). Approved by ABA. Member of AALS. JD/MA (applied economics) offered jointly with the Department of Economics. Faculty: 42 full-time (10 women), 95 part-time (20 women). Students: 791 full-time (356 women), 37 part-time (13 women); includes 167 minority (51 African Americans, 41 Asian Americans, 64 Hispanics, 11 Native Americans), 10 international. Average age 27. In 1997, 216 JDs, 58 master's awarded. *Degree requirements:* For JD, 30 hours of public service required, thesis not required; for master's, thesis optional; for doctorate, dissertation. *Entrance requirements:* For JD, LSAT; for master's, TOEFL (minimum score 575), JD (LL M in law, taxation), foreign law degree (LL M in comparative and international law); for doctorate, TOEFL, LL M. Application deadline: 2/1 (priority date; rolling processing). Application fee: $45. *Financial aid:* Federal Work-Study available. Financial aid application deadline: 2/1; applicants required to submit FAFSA. *Faculty research:* Securities, international health, taxation. • Dr. Harvey Wingo, Interim Dean, 214-768-2620. Application contact: Lynn Switzer, Director of Admissions, 214-768-2550. Fax: 214-768-2549.

Southern New England School of Law, Professional Program, North Dartmouth, MA 02747-1252. Awards JD. Part-time and evening/weekend programs available. Faculty: 15 full-time (4 women), 21 part-time (2 women). Students: 138 full-time (50 women), 218 part-time (84 women); includes 22 minority (10 African Americans, 8 Asian Americans, 3 Hispanics, 1 Native American), 2 international. Average age 32. 222 applicants, 76% accepted. In 1997, 53 degrees awarded. *Average time to degree:* first professional–3 years full-time, 4.6 years part-time. *Entrance requirements:* LSAT. Application deadline: 6/30 (rolling processing). Application fee: $35. *Financial aid:* In 1997–98, 244 students received aid, including 3 research assistantships totaling $3,000; career-related internships or fieldwork also available. Aid available to part-time students. Financial aid application deadline: 6/30; applicants required to submit FAFSA. *Faculty research:* Tort–smoker's battery, judicial administration, constitutional law, computer law, international law. • Francis J. Larkin, Dean, 508-998-9600 Ext.145. Fax: 508-998-2006. E-mail: ddesirey@snesl.edu. Application contact: Nancy Fitzsimmons Hebert, Director of Admissions, 508-998-9400/800-213-0060. Fax: 508-998-9561. E-mail: nhebert@snesl.edu.

Southern University and Agricultural and Mechanical College, Law Center, Baton Rouge, LA 70813. Awards JD. Approved by ABA. Faculty: 27 full-time (11 women), 10 part-time (2 women). Students: 326 full-time (146 women); includes 211 minority (210 African Americans, 1 Asian American). Average age 27. 700 applicants, 27% accepted. In 1997, 99 degrees awarded. *Entrance requirements:* LSAT. Application deadline: 3/31 (priority date). Application fee: $0. *Tuition:* $3128 per year for state residents; $7728 per year for nonresidents. *Financial aid:* In 1997–98, 254 students received aid, including 29 research assistantships, 20 teaching assistantships, 57 scholarships; Federal Work-Study and career-related internships or fieldwork also available. Financial aid application deadline: 4/15. *Faculty research:* Civil law, comparative law, constitutional law, civil rights law. • Bhishma K. Agnihotri, Chancellor, 504-771-2552. Application contact: Velma Wilkerson, Coordinator of Admissions, 504-771-5341. Fax: 504-771-2474.

See in-depth description on page 1599.

South Texas College of Law Affiliated with Texas A&M University, Houston, TX 77002-7000. Awards JD. Approved by ABA. Member of AALS. Part-time and evening/weekend programs available. Faculty: 59 full-time (15 women), 30 part-time (6 women). Students: 790 full-time (330 women), 423 part-time (185 women); includes 253 minority (65 African Americans, 56 Asian Americans, 118 Hispanics, 14 Native Americans), 1 international. Average age 29. 1,686 applicants, 62% accepted. In 1997, 328 degrees awarded. *Average time to degree:* first professional–3 years full-time, 4.5 years part-time. *Entrance requirements:* LSAT (average 151). Application deadline: 3/1 (10/1 for spring admission). Application fee: $40. *Expenses:* Tuition $14,100 per year full-time, $9400 per year part-time. Fees $600 per year. *Financial aid:* In 1997–98, 1,011 students received aid, including 880 grants, scholarships (395 to first-year students) totaling $2.2 million; partial tuition waivers, Federal Work-Study, institutionally sponsored loans, and career-related internships or fieldwork also available. Aid available to part-time students. Financial aid application deadline: 5/1; applicants required to submit FAFSA. *Faculty research:* Bankruptcy, contracts, torts, federal income tax, environmental law. • Frank T. Read, President and Dean, 713-659-8040 Ext. 1819. Fax: 713-659-2217. E-mail: tread@stcl.edu. Application contact: Alicia K. Cramer, Director of Admissions, 713-646-1810. Fax: 713-646-2929. E-mail: acramer@stcl.edu.

Southwestern University School of Law, Los Angeles, CA 90005-3905. Awards JD. Approved by ABA. Member of AALS. Part-time and evening/weekend programs available. Faculty: 49 full-time (16 women), 45 part-time (9 women). Students: 703 full-time (360 women), 326 part-time (157 women); includes 365 minority (64 African Americans, 187 Asian Americans, 106 Hispanics, 8 Native Americans), 6 international. Average age 27. In 1997, 352 degrees awarded. *Average time to degree:* first professional–3 years full-time, 4 years part-time. *Entrance requirements:* LSAT, LSDAS. Application deadline: 6/30 (rolling processing). Application fee: $50. Electronic applications accepted. *Expenses:* Tuition $20,940 per year full-time, $13,262 per year part-time. Fees $100 per year. *Financial aid:* Research assistantships, scholarships, full and partial tuition waivers, Federal Work-Study, institutionally sponsored loans, and career-related internships or fieldwork available. Aid available to part-time students. Financial aid application deadline: 6/1; applicants required to submit FAFSA. *Faculty research:* International trade and law, mediation/arbitration, ethics, land use and urban planning, antitrust law. • Leigh H. Taylor, Dean, 213-738-6710. Application contact: Anne Wilson, Director of Admissions, 213-738-6717. Fax: 213-383-1688. E-mail: admissions@swlaw.edu.

Stanford University, Law School, Stanford, CA 94305-9991. Awards JD, JSM, MLS, JSD, JD/MBA, JD/PhD. Approved by ABA. Member of AALS. Faculty: 41 full-time (8 women). Students: 565 full-time (237 women), 32 part-time (12 women); includes 174 minority (48 African Americans, 49 Asian Americans, 64 Hispanics, 13 Native Americans), 44 international. Average age 27. 4,127 applicants, 13% accepted. In 1997, 205 JDs awarded. *Degree requirements:* For doctorate, dissertation required, foreign language not required. *Entrance requirements:* For JD, LSAT. Application deadline: 3/1. Application fee: $65. *Financial aid:* In 1997–98, 257 students received aid, including 191 fellowships (71 to first-year students) totaling $1.602 million, 55 research assistantships (1 to a first-year student) totaling $502,512, 11 teaching assistantships totaling $119,515; Federal Work-Study also available. Financial aid application deadline: 3/15; applicants required to submit FAFSA. • Paul A. Brest, Dean, 650-723-4455. Fax: 650-725-0253. E-mail: rg.pbc@forsythe.stanford.edu. Application contact: Faye Deal, Director of Admissions, 650-723-0302.

State University of New York at Buffalo, Graduate School, School of Law, Buffalo, NY 14260. Awards JD, JD/MA, JD/MBA, JD/MSW, JD/PhD. Approved by ABA. Member of AALS. Faculty: 51 full-time (20 women), 35 part-time (13 women). Students: 704 full-time (336 women), 6 part-time (all women); includes 111 minority (46 African Americans, 27 Asian Americans, 34 Hispanics, 4 Native Americans), 5 international. Average age 26. 1,023 applicants, 52% accepted. In 1997, 250 degrees awarded. *Entrance requirements:* LSAT (minimum score 134; average 155), minimum undergraduate GPA of 3.3. Application deadline: 2/1 (rolling processing). Application fee: $50. *Financial aid:* In 1997–98, 399 students received aid, including 91 fellowships (30 to first-year students) averaging $910 per month, 37 research assistantships (3 to first-year students) averaging $339 per month, 7 graduate assistantships averaging $485 per month and totaling $24,360; full and partial tuition waivers, Federal Work-Study, institutionally sponsored loans also available. Financial aid application deadline: 3/1; applicants required to submit FAFSA. *Faculty research:* Dispute resolution and litigation, credit and banking, legal history, environmental and natural resources, federal tax. Total annual research expenditures: $300,000. • Barry B. Boyer, Dean, 716-645-2052. Application contact: Kim DeWaal, Assistant Director of Admissions and Financial Aid, 716-645-2060. Fax: 716-645-2064.

Stetson University, College of Law, St. Petersburg, FL 33707. Awards JD, JD/MBA. Approved by ABA. Member of AALS. Faculty: 36 full-time (12 women), 42 part-time (6 women). Students: 629 full-time (328 women), 16 part-time (10 women); includes 116 minority (42 African Americans, 12 Asian Americans, 56 Hispanics, 6 Native Americans). Average age 26. In 1997, 235 degrees awarded. *Entrance requirements:* LSAT, LSDAS. Application deadline: 3/1 (priority date; 9/1 for spring admission). Application fee: $50. *Expenses:* Tuition $19,750 per year. Fees $135 per year. *Financial aid:* In 1997–98, 39 research assistantships, 39 teaching assistantships, 157 academic scholarships (62 to first-year students) were awarded; institutionally sponsored loans and career-related internships or fieldwork also available. Financial aid application deadline: 4/1; applicants required to submit FAFSA. • Lizabeth A. Moody, Dean, 813-562-7809. Application contact: Alexis Boles, Assistant Director of Admissions and Financial Aid, 813-562-7802. E-mail: lawadmit@hermes.law.stetson.edu.

See in-depth description on page 1601.

Suffolk University, Law School, Boston, MA 02108-2770. Awards JD, JD/MBA, JD/MPA, JD/MSF, JD/MSIE. Programs in civil litigation (JD), financial services (JD), health care/biotechnology law (JD), high technology/intellectual property law (JD), tax law (JD). Approved by ABA. Member of AALS. Part-time and evening/weekend programs available. Students: 1,001 full-time (524 women), 742 part-time (342 women); includes 173 minority (62 African Americans, 60 Asian Americans, 45 Hispanics, 6 Native Americans), 22 international. Average age 25. In 1997, 500 degrees awarded. *Average time to degree:* first professional–3 years full-time, 4 years part-time. *Entrance requirements:* LSAT, LSDAS. Application deadline: 3/1 (priority date; rolling processing). Application fee: $50. *Financial aid:* Research assistantships, Federal Work-Study, institutionally sponsored loans, and career-related internships or fieldwork available. Aid available to part-time students. Financial aid application deadline: 3/1. *Faculty research:* Tort reform/damages, civil rights cases, jurisprudence/international law, family law, public interest law. • Gail N. Ellis, Director of Admissions, 617-573-8144. Fax: 617-573-8706. E-mail: g.ellis@suffolk.admin.edu.

Syracuse University, College of Law, Syracuse, NY 13244-1030. Awards JD, JD/MA, JD/MBA, JD/MPA, JD/MS, JD/MSW, JD/PhD, JD/MLS, JD/MPS, JD/MS Acct. Approved by ABA. Member of AALS. JD/MPS (environmental science) offered jointly with the State University of New York College of Environmental Science and Forestry. Part-time programs available. Faculty: 40 full-time (19 women), 43 part-time (8 women). Students: 716 full-time (322 women), 24 part-time (8 women); includes 150 minority (49 African Americans, 62 Asian Americans, 38 Hispanics, 1 Native American), 23 international. Average age 25. 1,715 applicants. In 1997, 238 degrees awarded. *Average time to degree:* first professional–3 years full-time, 4 years part-time. *Entrance requirements:* LSAT (average 151). Application deadline: 4/1 (priority date; rolling processing). Application fee: $50. *Expenses:* Tuition $21,860 per year full-time, $956 per credit hour part-time. Fees $500 per year full-time, $189 per year part-time. *Financial aid:* 517 students received aid; fellowships, research assistantships, teaching assistantships, scholarships, grants, full and partial tuition waivers, Federal Work-Study, institutionally sponsored loans, and career-related internships or fieldwork available. Financial aid application deadline: 3/1; applicants required to submit FAFSA. *Faculty research:* Interdisciplinary legal studies, law and technology, international law, advocacy training, family law. Total annual research expenditures: $156,000. • Daan Braveman, Dean, 315-443-2524. Fax: 315-443-4213. Application contact: Mary Ellen Oyer, Director of Admissions, 315-443-1962. Fax: 315-443-9568. E-mail: admissions@law.syr.edu.

Temple University, School of Law, Philadelphia, PA 19140. Awards JD, LL M, JD/MBA, JD/LL M. Programs in law (JD), taxation (LL M), transnational law (LL M), trial advocacy (LL M). Approved by ABA. Member of AALS. Part-time and evening/weekend programs available. Faculty: 55 full-time (17 women), 171 part-time (53 women). Students: 770 full-time (385 women), 338 part-time (154 women); includes 306 minority (154 African Americans, 98 Asian Americans, 46 Hispanics, 8 Native Americans). Average age 26. 2,712 applicants, 39% accepted. In 1997, 366 JDs, 82 master's awarded. *Entrance requirements:* For JD, LSAT (average 156), TOEFL (minimum score 600). Application deadline: rolling. Application fee: $50. *Financial aid:* 843 students received aid; research assistantships, teaching assistantships, full and partial tuition waivers, Federal Work-Study, and career-related internships or fieldwork available. Aid available to part-time students. Financial aid application deadline: 3/1; applicants required to submit FAFSA. *Faculty research:* Public health law/AIDS, religious rights, sexual harassment, children's rights, products liability. • Robert J. Reinstein, Dean, 215-204-7863. Application contact: Marylouise C. Esten, Assistant Dean for Admissions, Financial Aid, and Student Affairs, 800-560-1428. Fax: 215-204-1185. E-mail: law@astro.ocis.temple.edu.

See in-depth description on page 1603.

Texas Southern University, Thurgood Marshall School of Law, Houston, TX 77004-4584. Awards JD, JD/MA, JD/MBA, JD/MPA, JD/MCP. Approved by ABA. Faculty: 22 full-time (4 women), 4 part-time (1 woman). Students: 10 full-time (4 women), 1 part-time (0 women). In 1997, 141 degrees awarded (100% found work related to degree). *Average time to degree:* first professional–3 years full-time. *Entrance requirements:* LSAT. Application deadline: 4/1. Application fee: $35 ($75 for international students). *Financial aid:* Fellowships, research assistantships, grants, partial tuition waivers, Federal Work-Study, institutionally sponsored loans, and career-related internships or fieldwork available. Financial aid application deadline: 5/1. *Faculty research:* Clinical legal education, civil rights–discrimination, legal education of minorities, employment contracts, criminal and civil litigation and alternatives. • L. Darnell Weeden, Acting Dean, 713-313-7112. Application contact: Cheryl Hanks Love, Director of Admissions, 713-313-7115.

Texas Tech University, School of Law, Lubbock, TX 79409. Awards JD, JD/MBA, JD/MPA, JD/MS. Approved by ABA. Member of AALS. Faculty: 27 full-time (8 women), 6 part-time (0 women), 29.07 FTE. Students: 635 full-time (265 women), 1 part-time (0 women); includes 82 minority (12 African Americans, 8 Asian Americans, 53 Hispanics, 9 Native Americans), 2 international. Average age 26. 1,144 applicants, 48% accepted. In 1997, 193 degrees awarded. *Entrance requirements:* LSAT (average 157). Application deadline: 2/1 (priority date; rolling processing). Application fee: $50. *Expenses:* Tuition $3840 per year for state residents; $7896 per year for nonresidents. Fees $1457 per year. *Financial aid:* In 1997–98, 570 students received aid, including 8 research assistantships averaging $500 per month and totaling $36,013; fellowships, Federal Work-Study, institutionally sponsored loans, and career-related internships or fieldwork also available. Financial aid application deadline: 5/15; applicants required to submit FAFSA. *Faculty research:* Oral advocacy, oil and gas drilling rights in competition with surface mining, administration of criminal justice, law and language policy. Total annual research expenditures: $7400. • W. Frank Newton, Dean, 806-742-3791. Fax: 806-742-1629.

Texas Wesleyan University, Law School, Fort Worth, TX 76105-1536. Awards JD. Approved by ABA. Part-time and evening/weekend programs available. Faculty: 24 full-time (6 women), 24 part-time (8 women), 35.2 FTE. Students: 376 full-time (123 women), 282 part-time (84 women); includes 120 minority (38 African Americans, 12 Asian Americans, 60 Hispanics, 10 Native Americans), 3 international. Average age 32. In 1997, 75 degrees awarded. *Average time to degree:* first professional–3 years full-time, 4 years part-time. *Entrance requirements:* LSAT. Application deadline: 5/1 (priority date; rolling processing). Application fee: $50. *Expenses:* Tuition $450 per hour. Fees $200 per semester. *Financial aid:* 294 students received aid; career-related internships or fieldwork available. Aid available to part-time students. Financial aid applicants required to submit FAFSA. • Frank Walwer, Dean, 817-212-4000. Fax: 817-212-4199. Application contact: Deborah Fathree, Associate Dean of Students, 817-212-4040. Fax: 817-212-4002.

Thomas Jefferson School of Law, San Diego, CA 92110-2905. Awards JD. Approved by ABA. Part-time and evening/weekend programs available. Faculty: 20 full-time (11 women), 28 part-time (6 women). Students: 297 full-time (112 women), 281 part-time (104 women); includes 128 minority (23 African Americans, 41 Asian Americans, 59 Hispanics, 5 Native Americans), 4 international. Average age 30. 1,045 applicants, 81% accepted. In 1997, 165 degrees awarded. *Entrance requirements:* LSAT. Application deadline: 8/26 (priority date; rolling processing; 1/1 for spring admission). Application fee: $35. *Financial aid:* In 1997–98, 578 students received aid, including 16 research assistantships, 18 teaching assistantships; full and partial tuition waivers, Federal Work-Study, institutionally sponsored loans, and career-related internships or fieldwork also available. Aid available to part-time students. Financial aid application deadline: 4/23; applicants required to submit FAFSA. *Faculty research:* Tenant's rights, fetal rights/medical ethics, bilateral treaties/international law, sexual harassment and gender treatment. • Kenneth L. Vandevelde, Dean, 619-297-9700 Ext. 1404. E-mail: kennethv@tjsl.edu. Application contact: Jennifer Keller, Assistant Dean of Admissions, Records, and Financial Assistance, 619-297-9700 Ext. 1472. Fax: 619-294-4713. E-mail: jkeller@tjsl.edu.

Thomas M. Cooley Law School, Lansing, MI 48901-3038. Awards JD. Approved by ABA. Part-time and evening/weekend programs available. Faculty: 61 full-time (17 women). Students: 228 full-time (88 women), 1,345 part-time (527 women); includes 246 minority (122 African Americans, 56 Asian Americans, 51 Hispanics, 17 Native Americans), 35 international. Average age 26. 2,118 applicants, 76% accepted. In 1997, 386 degrees awarded. *Average time to degree:* first professional–3 years full-time, 4 years part-time. *Entrance requirements:* LSAT, LSDAS. Application deadline: rolling. Application fee: $50. *Financial aid:* 1,321 students received aid; Federal Work-Study and career-related internships or fieldwork available. Aid available to part-time students. Financial aid applicants required to submit FAFSA. • Don LeDuc, Dean, 517-371-5140. Fax: 517-334-5780. E-mail: leducd@cooley.edu. Application contact: Stephanie Gregg, Director of Admissions, 517-371-5140. Fax: 517-334-5718.

Touro College, Jacob D. Fuchsberg Law Center, 27-33 West 23rd Street, New York, NY 10010. Offers programs in law (JD), U.S. law for foreign lawyers (LL M). Approved by ABA. Member of AALS. Part-time and evening/weekend programs available. Faculty: 37 full-time, 14 part-time. Students: 776. *Entrance requirements:* For JD, LSAT. Application deadline: 5/1 (rolling processing). Application fee: $40. *Financial aid:* Fellowships, Federal Work-Study, and career-related internships or fieldwork available. Aid available to part-time students. Financial aid application deadline: 5/1. *Faculty research:* Business law, civil rights, international law, criminal justice. • Howard Glickstein, Dean, 516-421-2244. Application contact: Office of Admissions, 516-421-2244 Ext. 314.

Trinity International University, Trinity Law School, 2200 North Grand Avenue, Santa Ana, CA 92705. Awards JD. *Tuition:* $8760 per year full-time, $438 per hour part-time. • Shannon Verleur, Campus CEO, 714-836-7500. Fax: 714-796-7190.

Tulane University, School of Law, New Orleans, LA 70118-5669. Awards JD, LL M, MCL, SJD, JD/MA, JD/MBA, JD/MSW, JD/MHA, JD/MPH, JD/MSPH, LL M/MSPH, MCL/MA. Approved by ABA. Member of AALS. Faculty: 54 full-time (12 women), 105 part-time (18 women). Students: 1,042 full-time (494 women), 14 part-time (7 women); includes 195 minority (84 African Americans, 48 Asian Americans, 55 Hispanics, 8 Native Americans), 86 international. Average age 25. 2,461 applicants, 58% accepted. In 1997, 326 JDs, 64 master's, 1 doctorate awarded. Terminal master's awarded for partial completion of doctoral program. *Degree requirements:* For doctorate, dissertation required, foreign language not required. *Average time to degree:* master's–1 year full-time; doctorate–3 years full-time; first professional–3 years full-time. *Entrance requirements:* For JD, LSAT (average 159); for master's, TOEFL (minimum score 575; average 600); for doctorate, TOEFL. Application deadline: 3/15 (priority date; rolling processing). Application fee: $45. Electronic applications accepted. *Financial aid:* In 1997–98, 876 students received aid, including 3 fellowships averaging $500 per month; full and partial tuition waivers, Federal Work-Study, institutionally sponsored loans, and career-related internships or fieldwork also available. Aid available to part-time students. Financial aid application deadline: 2/15; applicants required to submit FAFSA. *Faculty research:* Admiralty, environmental, international and comparative, sports, and civil law. Total annual research expenditures: $397,720. • Edward Sherman, Dean, 504-865-5938. Application contact: Susan Krinsky, Associate Dean, 504-865-5930.

Union College, Graduate and Continuing Studies, Graduate Management Institute, Program in Law and Business Administration, Schenectady, NY 12308-2311. Awards JD/MBA. Offered jointly with Albany Law School of Union University. Students: 1 (woman) full-time, 6 part-time (1 woman); includes 1 international. 1 applicant, 100% accepted. *Application deadline:* 5/15 (rolling processing). *Application fee:* $35. *Tuition:* $1434 per course. *Financial aid:* Application deadline 5/15. • Application contact: Carolyn Micklas, Recruiting and Admissions Coordinator, 518-388-6239.

Université de Moncton, Law School, Moncton, NB E1A 3E9, Canada. Awards LL B, Certificate, Diploma, LL B/MBA, LL B/MPA. Programs offered exclusively in French. *Degree requirements:* For LL B, 1 foreign language. *Average time to degree:* first professional–3 years full-time. *Entrance requirements:* For LL B, proficiency in French. Application deadline: 3/31 (priority date; rolling processing). Application fee: $30 ($50 for international students). *Faculty research:* Minority language rights, legal translation, rights of the elderly, student rights, constitutional rights.

Université de Montréal, Faculty of Law, Montréal, PQ H3C 3J7, Canada. Awards LL B, LL M, LL D, DDN, DESS. Part-time programs available. Faculty: 57 full-time (17 women), 3 part-time (2 women). Students: 1,155 full-time (685 women), 112 part-time (64 women). 2,153 applicants, 24% accepted. In 1997, 283 LL Bs, 54 master's, 4 doctorates, 7 other advanced degrees awarded. *Degree requirements:* For master's, thesis; for doctorate, dissertation, project; for other advanced degree, thesis (for some programs). *Entrance requirements:* For master's and other advanced degree, minimum B average. Application deadline: 3/1. Application fee: $30. *Financial aid:* Fellowships, research assistantships, teaching assistantships available. *Faculty research:* Legal theory; constitutional, private, and public law. • Claude Fabien, Acting Dean, 514-343-7200. Application contact: Marie-France Bich, Graduate Chair, 514-343-7203.

Université de Sherbrooke, Faculty of Law, Sherbrooke, PQ J1K 2R1, Canada. Awards LL B, LL M, DDN, Diploma. Faculty: 28 full-time (10 women), 92 part-time (29 women), 51 FTE. Students: 643 full-time (399 women), 100 part-time (71 women); includes 13 minority (2 African Americans, 5 Asian Americans, 6 Hispanics), 6 international. Average age 23. 840 applicants, 83% accepted. In 1997, 142 LL Bs, 9 master's, 31 other advanced degrees awarded. *Degree requirements:* For LL B and other advanced degree, 1 foreign language required, thesis not required; for master's, 1 foreign language, thesis. *Average time to degree:* master's–1 year full-time, 4 years part-time; first professional–3 years full-time; other advanced degree–1 year full-time. *Entrance requirements:* For master's and other advanced degree, LL B. Application deadline: 3/1. Application fee: $30. *Financial aid:* In 1997–98, fellowships totaling $2,000, 4 research assistantships totaling $12,168, 17 teaching assistantships totaling $83,863 were awarded; career-related internships or fieldwork also available. *Faculty research:* Medical, labor, constitutional, administrative, and commercial law. • Jean-Guy Bergeron, Dean, 819-821-7511. E-mail: jean-guy.bergeron@droit.usherb.ca. Application contact: Denise Pratte, Secretary, 819-821-8000 Ext. 3513. Fax: 819-821-7578. E-mail: denise.pratte@droit.usherb.ca.

Université du Québec à Montréal, Program in Social and Labor Law, Montréal, PQ H3C 3P8, Canada. Awards LL M. *Entrance requirements:* Appropriate bachelor's degree or equivalent and proficiency in French. Application deadline: 5/1. Application fee: $50.

Université Laval, Faculty of Law, Sainte-Foy, PQ G1K 7P4, Canada. Awards LL M, LL D, Diploma. Students: 94 full-time (60 women), 78 part-time (45 women); includes 28 international. Average age 31. 143 applicants, 69% accepted. In 1997, 30 master's, 3 doctorates, 21 Diplomas awarded. *Application deadline:* 3/1. *Application fee:* $30. *Expenses:* Tuition $1334 per year (minimum) full-time, $56 per credit (minimum) part-time for Canadian residents; $5966 per year (minimum) full-time, $249 per credit (minimum) part-time for nonresidents.

Directory: Law

Université Laval (continued)

Fees $150 per year full-time, $6.25 per credit part-time. • Pierre Lemieux, Dean, 418-656-2131 Ext. 3511. Fax: 418-656-7230. E-mail: fd@fd.ulaval.ca.

The University of Akron, School of Law, Akron, OH 44325-0001. Awards JD, JD/MBA, JD/MPA, JD/MT. Approved by ABA. Member of AALS. Part-time and evening/weekend programs available. Faculty: 25 full-time, 43 part-time. Students: 598 full-time (264 women), 29 part-time (10 women); includes 48 minority (23 African Americans, 14 Asian Americans, 9 Hispanics, 2 Native Americans), 6 international. Average age 29. 1,170 applicants, 51% accepted. In 1997, 167 degrees awarded. *Entrance requirements:* LSAT, LSDAS. Application fee: $25. *Tuition:* $7769 per year full-time, $4872 per year part-time for state residents; $13,217 per year full-time, $8277 per year part-time for nonresidents. *Financial aid:* Full and partial tuition waivers, Federal Work-Study, and career-related internships or fieldwork available. Aid available to part-time students. Financial aid application deadline: 4/1. • Richard L. Aynes Jr., Dean, 330-972-7331. Application contact: Lauri S. File, Director of Admissions and Financial Assistance, 330-972-7331.

The University of Alabama, School of Law, Tuscaloosa, AL 35487. Awards JD, LL M in Tax, MCL, JD/MBA. Approved by ABA. Member of AALS. Postbaccalaureate distance learning degree programs offered (no on-campus study). Faculty: 30 full-time (6 women), 37 part-time (9 women). Students: 568 full-time (231 women); includes 47 minority (36 African Americans, 4 Asian Americans, 2 Hispanics, 5 Native Americans). Average age 24. 744 applicants, 44% accepted. In 1997, 180 JDs awarded. *Entrance requirements:* For JD, LSAT (average 157), TOEFL. Application deadline: 3/1 (rolling processing). Application fee: $25. *Financial aid:* In 1997–98, 340 students received aid, including 54 research assistantships totaling $137,943; full and partial tuition waivers, Federal Work-Study, institutionally sponsored loans, and career-related internships or fieldwork also available. Financial aid application deadline: 3/15. *Faculty research:* Environmental law, legal history, white-collar crime, pensions, comparative law. • Kenneth C. Randall, Dean, 205-348-5117. E-mail: kcrandal@law.ua.edu. Application contact: Betty McGinley, Admissions Coordinator, 205-348-5440. Fax: 205-348-3917. E-mail: admissions@law.ua.edu.

Announcement: The Law School has a long heritage as a strong state law school. The curriculum is traditional but broad, with strengths in business and tax law, criminal law, and clinical programs. The School also enjoys a national reputation for excellence in teaching. The facilities are some of the best in the country, including an outstanding library. In addition the JD program, there is also a joint MBA program, an LLM in taxation program, and an MCL (Master of Comparative Law). Traditional summer school classes are offered, as well as a 5-week summer program at the University of Fribourg (Switzerland).

University of Alberta, Faculty of Law, Edmonton, AB T6G 2E1, Canada. Awards LL B, LL M, Postgraduate Diploma, MBA/LL B. Part-time programs available. Faculty: 15 full-time. Students: 501 full-time (246 women), 4 part-time (2 women); includes 15 minority (3 African Americans, 12 Native Americans), 3 international. Average age 25. 800 applicants, 22% accepted. In 1997, 165 LL Bs, 3 master's awarded. *Degree requirements:* For master's, thesis, 1 year full-time residency required, foreign language not required. *Entrance requirements:* For LL B, LSAT (average 158); for master's, TOEFL (minimum score 600), minimum GPA of 6.5 (equivalent to B or 3.0 average). Application deadline: 11/1 (rolling processing). Application fee: $60. Electronic applications accepted. *Expenses:* Tuition $390 per course for Canadian residents; $781 per course for nonresidents. Fees $500 per year full-time, $184 per year part-time. *Financial aid:* In 1997–98, 3 students received aid, including 3 research assistantships (all to first-year students). Financial aid application deadline: 3/1. *Faculty research:* Health law, legal theory, environmental law, native law issues. Total annual research expenditures: $15,000. • Linda Reif, Director, 403-492-2800. Application contact: Gloria Strohschein, Admissions Officer, 403-492-3062. Fax: 403-492-4924.

The University of Arizona, College of Law, Tucson, AZ 85721. Awards JD, LL M, JD/MA, JD/MBA, JD/MPA, JD/PhD. Programs in international trade law (LL M), law (JD). Approved by ABA. Member of AALS. JD/MA offered jointly with the Department of Economics and Interdisciplinary Program in American Indian Studies; JD/PhD offered jointly with the Departments of Economics, Philosophy, and Psychology. Faculty: 32 full-time (8 women), 50 part-time (14 women). Students: 458 full-time (221 women); includes 108 minority (14 African Americans, 28 Asian Americans, 54 Hispanics, 12 Native Americans), 3 international. Average age 27. 4,863 applicants, 30% accepted. In 1997, 158 JDs awarded. *Degree requirements:* For JD, publishable paper required, foreign language and thesis not required. *Average time to degree:* first professional–3 years full-time. *Entrance requirements:* For JD, LSAT (average 160). Application deadline: 3/1 (rolling processing). Application fee: $45. *Expenses:* Tuition $4464 per year for state residents; $11,416 per year for nonresidents. Fees $74 per year. *Financial aid:* In 1997–98, 300 students received aid, including 300 scholarships totaling $1; fellowships, full and partial tuition waivers, Federal Work-Study, institutionally sponsored loans, and career-related internships or fieldwork also available. Financial aid application deadline: 3/1; applicants required to submit FAFSA. *Faculty research:* Tax law, employment law, corporate law, torts, trial practice and skills, constitutional law, Indian law, securities, family law, estates and trusts. • Joel Seligman, Dean, 520-621-1498. Fax: 520-621-2050. E-mail: seligman@nt.law.arizona.edu. Application contact: Terry Sue Holpert, Assistant Dean for Admissions, 520-621-3477. Fax: 520-621-9140. E-mail: holpert@nt.law.arizona.edu.

University of Arkansas, School of Law, Fayetteville, AR 72701-1201. Offers programs in agricultural law (LL M), law (JD). Approved by ABA. Member of AALS. Faculty: 31 full-time (8 women), 11 part-time (3 women). Students: 377 full-time (151 women); includes 36 minority (21 African Americans, 7 Asian Americans, 2 Hispanics, 6 Native Americans), 4 international. 647 applicants, 49% accepted. In 1997, 136 JDs, 13 master's awarded. *Average time to degree:* master's–4 years full-time; first professional–3 years full-time. *Entrance requirements:* For JD, LSAT. Application deadline: 4/1 (rolling processing). Application fee: $0. *Financial aid:* Federal Work-Study and career-related internships or fieldwork available. Aid available to part-time students. Financial aid application deadline: 4/1; applicants required to submit FAFSA. • Leonard P. Strickman, Dean, 501-575-5601. Application contact: James K. Miller, Associate Dean for Students, 501-575-3102.

University of Arkansas at Little Rock, School of Law, Little Rock, AR 72201. Awards JD, JD/MBA. Approved by ABA. Member of AALS. Part-time and evening/weekend programs available. Faculty: 26 full-time (10 women), 20 part-time (5 women). Students: 253 full-time (134 women), 151 part-time (62 women); includes 51 minority (34 African Americans, 5 Asian Americans, 9 Hispanics, 3 Native Americans). Average age 27. 460 applicants, 51% accepted. In 1997, 120 degrees awarded. *Entrance requirements:* LSAT. Application deadline: 4/1 (rolling processing). Application fee: $40. *Financial aid:* In 1997–98, 254 students received aid, including 24 research assistantships; Federal Work-Study and career-related internships or fieldwork also available. Aid available to part-time students. Financial aid application deadline: 4/1; applicants required to submit FAFSA. *Faculty research:* Tax policy, employment discrimination, death penalty, legal ethics, statutory interpretation. • Rodney K. Smith, Dean, 501-324-9434. Application contact: Jean M. Probasco, Director of Admissions and Registrar, 501-324-9439. Fax: 501-324-9433.

University of Baltimore, School of Law, Baltimore, MD 21201-5779. Awards JD, LL M, JD/MBA, JD/MPA, JD/MS, JD/PhD, JD/LL M. Programs in law (JD), taxation (LL M). Approved by ABA. Member of AALS. JD/PhD (policy studies) offered jointly with the University of Maryland, Baltimore. JD/MS offered jointly with the Program in Criminal Justice. Part-time and evening/weekend programs available. Faculty: 41 full-time (16 women), 60 part-time (17 women). Students: 659 full-time (338 women), 344 part-time (158 women); includes 201 minority (130 African Americans, 43 Asian Americans, 21 Hispanics, 7 Native Americans). Average age 27. 1,684 applicants, 54% accepted. In 1997, 301 JDs, 10 master's awarded. *Average time to degree:* first professional–3 years full-time, 4.5 years part-time. *Entrance requirements:* For JD, LSAT (average 151). Application deadline: 4/1 (priority date; rolling processing). Application fee: $35. *Expenses:* Tuition $8376 per year full-time, $349 per credit part-time for state residents; $14,136 per year full-time, $589 per credit part-time for nonresidents. Fees $550 per year full-time, $208 per semester (minimum) part-time. *Financial aid:* In 1997–98, 650 students received aid, including 27 teaching assistantships; research assistantships, Federal Work-Study, institutionally sponsored loans, and career-related internships or fieldwork also available. Aid available to part-time students. Financial aid application deadline: 4/1; applicants required to submit FAFSA. *Faculty research:* Plain view doctrine, statute of limitations, bankruptcy, family law, international and comparative law. • John Sebert, Dean, 410-837-4458. Application contact: Claire Valentine, Assistant Director of Law Admissions, 410-837-4459. Fax: 410-837-4450. E-mail: cvalentine@ubmail.ubalt.edu.

University of British Columbia, Faculty of Law, Vancouver, BC V6T 1Z2, Canada. Awards LL M, PhD. Part-time programs available. *Degree requirements:* Variable foreign language requirement, thesis/dissertation, seminar. *Average time to degree:* master's–1.5 years full-time. *Entrance requirements:* For master's, TOEFL (minimum score 600; average 615), LL B 12 with first class/A- credits; for doctorate, TOEFL (minimum score 600; average 620), LL B and LL M. Application deadline: 4/30 (priority date; rolling processing). Application fee: $60. Electronic applications accepted. *Faculty research:* Aboriginal rights/native law, Asian legal studies, feminist legal theory, criminal law, environmental law.

The University of Calgary, Faculty of Law, Calgary, AB T2N 1N4, Canada. Awards LL B, LL M. *Average time to degree:* master's–2 years full-time; first professional–3 years full-time, 6 years part-time. *Entrance requirements:* For LL B, LSAT; for master's, TOEFL (minimum score 600). Application deadline: 2/1. Application fee: $60. *Expenses:* Tuition $4128 per year for Canadian residents; $8256 per year for nonresidents. Fees $400 per year. *Faculty research:* Resources law, family law, legal history, taxation law, human rights, energy and environmental law.

University of California, Berkeley, Boalt Hall School of Law, Berkeley, CA 94720-1500. Awards JD, LL M, JSD, PhD, JD/MA, JD/MBA, JD/MSW, JD/MCP, JD/MJ, JD/MPP. Programs in jurisprudence and social policy (PhD), law (JD, LL M, JSD), law/business administration (JD/MBA). Approved by ABA. Member of AALS. JD/MA offered jointly with the Department of Economics, the Group in Asian Studies, and the Group in International and Area Studies. Faculty: 48 full-time (16 women), 82 part-time (22 women). Students: 852 full-time (433 women); includes 246 minority (43 African Americans, 114 Asian Americans, 80 Hispanics, 9 Native Americans), 29 international. 4,171 applicants, 21% accepted. In 1997, 283 JDs awarded. Terminal master's awarded for partial completion of doctoral program. *Degree requirements:* For doctorate, 1 foreign language, dissertation, oral qualifying exam. *Average time to degree:* first professional–3 years full-time. *Entrance requirements:* For JD, LSAT (average 168); for master's, TOEFL (minimum score 570); for doctorate, GRE General Test. Application deadline: 2/1. Application fee: $40. *Expenses:* Tuition $0 for state residents; $9384 per year for nonresidents. Fees $10,815 per year. *Financial aid:* In 1997–98, 650 students received aid, including 13 fellowships totaling $111,761, 36 research assistantships totaling $259,732, 10 teaching assistantships totaling $84,115; full and partial tuition waivers, Federal Work-Study, institutionally sponsored loans, and career-related internships or fieldwork also available. Aid available to part-time students. Financial aid application deadline: 3/2; applicants required to submit FAFSA. • Herma Hill Kay, Dean, 510-642-6483. Application contact: Office of Admissions, 510-642-2274. Fax: 510-643-6222. E-mail: admissions@boalt.berkeley.edu.

University of California, Berkeley, Group in Asian Studies, Berkeley, CA 94720-1500. Offerings include law-Asian studies (JD/MA). *Application deadline:* 12/15. *Application fee:* $40. *Expenses:* Tuition $0 for state residents; $9384 per year for nonresidents. Fees $4409 per year. • Robert R. Reed, Chair. Application contact: Sue Pruyn, Graduate Assistant for Admission, 510-642-0333. Fax: 510-643-7062. E-mail: asianst@uclink4.berkeley.edu.

University of California, Berkeley, Haas School of Business and Boalt Hall School of Law, Concurrent JD/MBA Program, Berkeley, CA 94720-1500. Awards JD/MBA. Approved by ABA. Member of AALS. Faculty: 76 (12 women). Students: 6 full-time (3 women). Average age 27. 43 applicants, 16% accepted. *Average time to degree:* first professional–4 years full-time. *Application deadline:* 2/1. *Application fee:* $40. *Expenses:* Tuition $0 for state residents; $9384 per year for nonresidents. Fees $4409 per year. *Financial aid:* Fellowships, research assistantships, teaching assistantships available. • Dr. David H. Downes, Director, MBA Programs, 510-642-1405. Fax: 510-643-6659. E-mail: downes@haas.berkeley.edu. Application contact: JD Office of Admissions, 510-642-2274. Fax: 510-643-6222. E-mail: admissions@boalt.berkeley.edu.

University of California, Davis, School of Law, Davis, CA 95616. Awards JD, LL M, JD/MA, JD/MBA. Approved by ABA. Member of AALS. Faculty: 32 full-time (11 women), 23 part-time (8 women), 36.82 FTE. Students: 491 full-time (249 women); includes 137 minority (17 African Americans, 71 Asian Americans, 41 Hispanics, 8 Native Americans), 19 international. Average age 25. 2,095 applicants, 38% accepted. In 1997, 164 JDs awarded. *Entrance requirements:* For JD, LSAT. Application deadline: 2/1 (rolling processing). Application fee: $40. *Expenses:* Tuition $0 for state residents; $9384 per year for nonresidents. Fees $10,859 per year. *Financial aid:* 414 students received aid; research assistantships, teaching assistantships, Federal Work-Study, institutionally sponsored loans, and career-related internships or fieldwork available. Financial aid application deadline: 3/2; applicants required to submit FAFSA. *Faculty research:* International law, international trade, immigration, environmental law, public interest law. • Bruce Wolk, Dean, 530-752-0243. Fax: 530-752-7279. E-mail: bawolk@ucdavis.edu. Application contact: Sharon Pinkney, Director, Admissions, 530-752-6477. Fax: 530-752-4704. E-mail: lawadmissions@ucdavis.edu.

University of California, Hastings College of the Law, San Francisco, CA 94102-4978. Awards JD. Approved by ABA. Member of AALS. Faculty: 46 full-time (13 women), 73 part-time (31 women), 65 FTE. Students: 1,156 full-time (556 women); includes 326 minority (44 African Americans, 194 Asian Americans, 77 Hispanics, 11 Native Americans), 4 international. Average age 28. 3,605 applicants, 35% accepted. In 1997, 397 degrees awarded. *Average time to degree:* first professional–3 years full-time. *Entrance requirements:* LSAT (average 162). Application deadline: 2/16 (rolling processing). Application fee: $40. Electronic applications accepted. *Expenses:* Tuition $0 for state residents; $8770 per year for nonresidents. Fees $11,167 per year. *Financial aid:* In 1997–98, 1,010 students received aid, including fellowships totaling $55,000; partial tuition waivers, Federal Work-Study, institutionally sponsored loans, and career-related internships or fieldwork also available. Aid available to part-time students. Financial aid application deadline: 2/16; applicants required to submit FAFSA. • Mary Kay Kane, Dean, 415-565-4600. Application contact: Cornelius H. Darcy, Director of Admissions, 415-565-4885. Fax: 415-565-4863.

University of California, Los Angeles, School of Law, Los Angeles, CA 90095. Awards JD, LL M, JD/MA, JD/MBA, JD/PhD. Approved by ABA. Member of AALS. Faculty: 50 (12 women). Students: 984 full-time (468 women); includes 348 minority (50 African Americans, 181 Asian Americans, 106 Hispanics, 11 Native Americans), 10 international. 4,139 applicants, 25% accepted. *Entrance requirements:* For JD, LSAT. Application deadline: 1/15. Application fee: $40. *Financial aid:* In 1997–98, 836 students received aid, including fellowships totaling $173,807, research assistantships totaling $12,698, teaching assistantships totaling $8,830; full and partial tuition waivers, Federal Work-Study, institutionally sponsored loans, and career-related internships or fieldwork also available. Financial aid application deadline: 3/1. • Dr. Susan Westerberg-Prager, Dean, 310-825-4841. Application contact: Admissions Office, 310-825-2080.

University of Chicago, Law School, Chicago, IL 60637-1513. Awards JD, LL M, MCL, JSD, JD/MBA, JD/PhD, JD/AM. Approved by ABA. Member of AALS. Faculty: 47. Students: 584 full-time (241 women); includes 126 minority (40 African Americans, 56 Asian Americans, 29 Hispanics, 1 Native American), 42 international. Average age 25. In 1997, 186 JDs, 47 master's, 3 doctorates awarded. Terminal master's awarded for partial completion of doctoral program. *Entrance requirements:* For JD, LSAT; for master's, TOEFL. Application deadline: 2/1 (priority date; rolling processing). Application fee: $60. *Financial aid:* Fellowships, institutionally sponsored loans, and career-related internships or fieldwork available. Financial aid application deadline: 3/15; applicants required to submit FAFSA. • Douglas Baird, Dean, 773-702-9494. Application contact: Richard Badger, Assistant Dean, 773-702-9484.

University of Cincinnati, College of Law, Cincinnati, OH 45221. Awards JD, JD/MA, JD/MBA, JD/MS, JD/MCP. Approved by ABA. Member of AALS. *Entrance requirements:* LSAT. Application deadline: 4/1 (priority date; rolling processing). Application fee: $35. *Financial aid:* Fellowships, graduate assistantships, full and partial tuition waivers, and career-related internships or fieldwork available. Financial aid application deadline: 3/1; applicants required to submit FAFSA. *Faculty research:* Capital market regulation in Hungary, gays in the military, interstate air pollution from an international law perspective, remedy for breach of peace in a repossession, government regulatory policy. Total annual research expenditures: $220,000. • Dr. Joseph Tomain, Dean, 513-556-0121. Fax: 513-556-5550. E-mail: joseph.tomain@uc.edu. Application contact: Al Watson, Assistant Dean and Director of Admissions, 513-556-0077. Fax: 513-556-2391.

University of Colorado at Boulder, School of Law, Boulder, CO 80302. Awards JD, JD/MBA, JD/MPA. Approved by ABA. Member of AALS. JD/MPA offered jointly with the University of Colorado at Denver. Faculty: 32 full-time (6 women). Students: 507 full-time (250 women); includes 88 minority (20 African Americans, 18 Asian Americans, 37 Hispanics, 13 Native Americans). Average age 27. 1,806 applicants, 36% accepted. In 1997, 159 degrees awarded. *Average time to degree:* first professional–3 years full-time. *Entrance requirements:* LSAT (average 163). Application deadline: 2/15 (rolling processing). Application fee: $40. *Expenses:* Tuition $4760 per year full-time, $792 per semester (minimum) part-time for state residents; $16,434 per year full-time, $2739 per semester (minimum) part-time for nonresidents. Fees $667 per year full-time, $130 per semester (minimum) part-time. *Financial aid:* Fellowships, teaching assistantships, Federal Work-Study, institutionally sponsored loans available. Financial aid application deadline: 3/1; applicants required to submit FAFSA. *Total annual research expenditures:* $536,000. • Harold H. Bruff, Dean, 303-492-8047. Fax: 303-492-1757. E-mail: harold.bruff@colorado.edu. Application contact: Carol Nelson-Douglas, Director of Admissions and Financial Aid, 303-492-7203. Fax: 303-492-1200. E-mail: lawadmin@colorado.edu.

University of Connecticut, School of Law, 55 Elizabeth Street, Hartford, CT 06105-2296. Awards JD, JD/MA, JD/MBA, JD/MPA, JD/MSW, JD/MLS, JD/MPH. Approved by ABA. Member of AALS. JD/MA offered jointly with Trinity College; JD/MLS offered jointly with Southern Connecticut State University. Part-time and evening/weekend programs available. *Degree requirements:* Extensive research paper required, foreign language and thesis not required. *Entrance requirements:* LSAT. Application deadline: 3/1 (rolling processing). Application fee: $30. *Faculty research:* International law, clinical practice, American legal history, constitutional law, tax law, labor and employment law.

University of Dayton, School of Law, Dayton, OH 45469-1611. Awards JD, JD/MBA. Approved by ABA. Member of AALS. Faculty: 26 full-time (9 women), 30 part-time (4 women). Students: 495 full-time (199 women); includes 75 minority (41 African Americans, 17 Asian Americans, 15 Hispanics, 2 Native Americans), 2 international. Average age 25. 1,350 applicants, 61% accepted. In 1997, 151 degrees awarded (100% found work related to degree). *Entrance requirements:* LSAT (average 151). Application deadline: 5/1 (priority date; rolling processing). Application fee: $40. Electronic applications accepted. *Financial aid:* 180 students received aid; full and partial tuition waivers and career-related internships or fieldwork available. Financial aid application deadline: 3/1; applicants required to submit FAFSA. *Faculty research:* Bankruptcy, criminal procedure, corporate practice, torts, computer law, intellectual property law. Total annual research expenditures: $20,000. • Francis J. Conte, Dean, 937-229-3211. Application contact: Charles Roboski, Assistant Dean and Director of Admissions/Financial Aid, 937-229-3555. Fax: 937-229-2469. E-mail: lawinfo@udayton.edu.

University of Denver, College of Law, Professional Program, Denver, CO 80208. Awards JD, JD/MA, JD/MBA, JD/MSW, JD/PhD, JD/MIM, JD/Psy D. Approved by ABA. Member of AALS. JD/MA offered jointly with the Departments of Psychology and Sociology and the Graduate School of International Studies; JD/PhD offered jointly with the Department of Psychology. Part-time and evening/weekend programs available. Faculty: 40 full-time (10 women). Students: 992 full-time (481 women), 20 part-time (11 women); includes 110 minority (14 African Americans, 41 Asian Americans, 47 Hispanics, 8 Native Americans), 10 international. 1,864 applicants, 61% accepted. In 1997, 319 degrees awarded. *Entrance requirements:* LSAT. Application deadline: 5/1 (rolling processing). Application fee: $45. *Tuition:* $622 per credit hour. *Financial aid:* In 1997–98, 896 students received aid, including 165 legal research assistantships, tutorships totaling $846,319; Federal Work-Study, institutionally sponsored loans, and career-related internships or fieldwork also available. Aid available to part-time students. Financial aid application deadline: 2/15; applicants required to submit FAFSA. *Faculty research:* Lawyering skills, international and legal studies, natural resources law (domestic and international), transportation law, public interest law, business and commercial law. • Application contact: Claudia Tomlin, Director of Admissions, 303-871-6135. Fax: 303-871-6378.

University of Denver, College of Law, Program in American and Comparative Law, Denver, CO 80208. Awards LL M. Member of AALS. Students: 2 (1 woman). 7 applicants, 57% accepted. *Entrance requirements:* JD from U.S. institution or TOEFL (minimum score 580), TWE (minimum score 4). Application deadline: 5/1 (priority date; rolling processing). Application fee: $45. *Tuition:* $622 per credit hour. *Financial aid:* Federal Work-Study, institutionally sponsored loans available. Aid available to part-time students. Financial aid application deadline: 2/15; applicants required to submit FAFSA. • Paula Rhodes, Director, 303-871-6258. Application contact: Karen Higganbotham, Admissions, 303-871-6434. Fax: 303-871-6378.

University of Denver, College of Law, Program in Natural Resources Law, Denver, CO 80208. Awards LL M, MRLS. Member of AALS. Students: 4 full-time (0 women), 4 part-time (1 woman). 10 applicants, 100% accepted. *Entrance requirements:* JD from U.S. institution or TOEFL (minimum score 580), TWE (minimum score 4). Application deadline: 5/1 (priority date; rolling processing). Application fee: $45. *Tuition:* $622 per credit hour. • Jim Otto, Director, 303-871-6052. Application contact: Karen Higganbotham, Admissions, 303-871-6434. Fax: 303-871-6378.

University of Detroit Mercy, School of Law, Detroit, MI 48226. Awards JD, JD/MBA, JD/LL B. Approved by ABA. Member of AALS. Part-time programs available. *Entrance requirements:* LSAT. Application deadline: 4/15. Application fee: $35.

University of Florida, College of Law, Professional Programs in Law, Gainesville, FL 32611. Awards JD, JD/MA, JD/MBA, JD/PhD, JD/M Acc, JD/MAMC, JD/MAURP, JD/MESS. Approved by ABA. Member of AALS. Faculty: 71 full-time (24 women), 4 part-time (0 women). Students: 1,200 full-time. Average age 26. 1,750 applicants, 28% accepted. In 1997, 383 degrees awarded. *Degree requirements:* Thesis or alternative required, foreign language not required. *Average time to degree:* first professional–3 years full-time. *Entrance requirements:* LSAT (average 159). Application deadline: 2/1 (rolling processing; 5/15 for spring admission). Application fee: $20. *Tuition:* $154 per credit hour for state residents; $512 per credit hour for nonresidents. *Financial aid:* Fellowships, Federal Work-Study, institutionally sponsored loans available. Financial aid application deadline: 4/1; applicants required to submit FAFSA. • Application contact: J. Michael Patrick, Assistant Dean for Admissions, 352-392-2087. Fax: 352-392-8727. E-mail: patrick@law.ufl.edu.

University of Florida, College of Law and Graduate School, Program in Comparative Law, Gainesville, FL 32611. Awards LL M CL. Member of AALS. Open only to graduates of foreign law schools. Faculty: 20. Students: 6 full-time (3 women), 7 part-time (3 women); includes 3 minority (2 Asian Americans, 1 Hispanic), 9 international. 25 applicants, 76% accepted. In 1997, 11 degrees awarded. *Degree requirements:* Thesis required, foreign language not required. *Entrance requirements:* TOEFL (minimum score 600). Application deadline: 2/9. Application fee: $20. *Tuition:* $154 per credit hour for state residents; $512 per credit hour for nonresidents. *Financial aid:* In 1997–98, 3 students received aid, including 1 fellowship averaging $412 per month, 2 research assistantships averaging $320 per month. • Application contact: E. L. Roy Hunt, Director, 352-392-9238. Fax: 352-392-3005. E-mail: reynolds@law.ufl.edu.

University of Georgia, School of Law and Graduate School, Graduate Program in Law, Athens, GA 30602. Awards LL M. Member of AALS. Faculty: 1 full-time (0 women). Students: 32 full-time, 1 part-time (0 women); includes 1 minority (Hispanic), 30 international. 120 applicants, 28% accepted. In 1997, 23 degrees awarded. *Degree requirements:* Thesis required, foreign language not required. *Application deadline:* 3/1. *Application fee:* $30. Electronic applications accepted. *Tuition:* $3290 per year for state residents; $11,300 per year for nonresidents. *Financial aid:* Fellowships, research assistantships, teaching assistantships, assistantships, Federal Work-Study, institutionally sponsored loans available. Financial aid application deadline: 1/31. • Gabriel Wilner, Graduate Coordinator, 706-542-5211. Fax: 706-542-5556.

University of Georgia, School of Law, Professional Program in Law, Athens, GA 30602. Awards JD. Approved by ABA. Member of AALS. *Entrance requirements:* LSAT. • Application contact: Giles Kennedy, Director of Law Admissions, 706-542-7060.

University of Hawaii at Manoa, School of Law, Honolulu, HI 96822. Awards JD, JD/MA, JD/MURP, JD/Certificate, JD/MLIS. Approved by ABA. Member of AALS. JD/MA offered jointly with the Program in Asian Studies. Faculty: 18 full-time (8 women), 28 part-time (7 women), 23 FTE. Students: 238 full-time (124 women); includes 116 minority (3 African Americans, 111 Asian Americans, 2 Hispanics), 18 international. Average age 27. 431 applicants, 36% accepted. In 1997, 67 degrees awarded. *Degree requirements:* 6 semesters of full-time residency required, foreign language and thesis not required. *Average time to degree:* first professional–3.2 years full-time. *Entrance requirements:* LSAT (average 160), TOEFL (average 620). Application deadline: 3/1. Application fee: $30. *Financial aid:* In 1997–98, 130 students received aid, including 22 research assistantships; fellowships, full and partial tuition waivers, Federal Work-Study, institutionally sponsored loans, and career-related internships or fieldwork also available. Financial aid application deadline: 3/1; applicants required to submit FAFSA. *Faculty research:* Law of the sea, Asian and Pacific comparative law, native Hawaiian rights, environmental law. • Lawrence C. Foster, Dean, 808-956-6363. E-mail: lawrence@hawaii.edu. Application contact: Joanne K. Punu, Assistant Dean, 808-956-7966. Fax: 808-956-6402. E-mail: lawadm@hawaii.edu.

University of Houston, College of Law, 4800 Calhoun, Houston, TX 77204-2163. Awards JD, LL M, JD/MA, JD/MBA, JD/PhD, JD/MPH. Approved by ABA. Member of AALS. JD/MPH offered jointly with the University of Texas–Houston Health Science Center; JD/PhD (medical humanities) offered jointly with the University of Texas Medical Branch at Galveston; JD/MA (history) offered jointly with Rice University. Part-time and evening/weekend programs available. Faculty: 47 full-time (8 women), 84 part-time (13 women). Students: 775 full-time (332 women), 329 part-time (130 women); includes 212 minority (52 African Americans, 62 Asian Americans, 89 Hispanics, 9 Native Americans), 26 international. Average age 29. 2,149 applicants, 40% accepted. In 1997, 290 JDs awarded (100% found work related to degree); 50 master's awarded (100% found work related to degree). *Degree requirements:* For JD, research paper required, foreign language and thesis not required; for master's, thesis required, foreign language not required. *Average time to degree:* master's–1 year full-time; first professional–3 years full-time, 4 years part-time. *Entrance requirements:* For JD, LSAT, TOEFL (minimum score 600); for master's, LSAT, TOEFL (minimum score 600), JD. Application deadline: 2/1 (priority date). Application fee: $50 ($75 for international students). *Expenses:* Tuition $3840 per year full-time, $160 per credit hour part-time for state residents; $7680 per year full-time, $320 per credit hour part-time for nonresidents. Fees $1193 per year full-time, $119 per semester (minimum) part-time. *Financial aid:* Federal Work-Study, institutionally sponsored loans, and career-related internships or fieldwork available. Aid available to part-time students. Financial aid application deadline: 4/1; applicants required to submit FAFSA. *Faculty research:* Health, environmental, energy, tax, and international law. • Stephen Zamora, Dean, 713-743-2100. Fax: 713-743-2122. Application contact: Sondra Richardson, Assistant Dean for Admissions, 713-743-2181.

University of Idaho, College of Law, Moscow, ID 83844-4140. Awards JD. Approved by ABA. Member of AALS. Faculty: 14 full-time (3 women). Students: 275 full-time (93 women), 16 part-time (8 women); includes 20 minority (8 African Americans, 9 Asian Americans, 3 Native Americans). Average age 29. In 1997, 95 degrees awarded. *Entrance requirements:* LSAT. Application deadline: 2/1. Application fee: $35 ($45 for international students). *Expenses:* Tuition $0 for state residents; $6000 per year full-time, $95 per credit part-time for nonresidents. Fees $2676 per year full-time, $134 per credit part-time. *Financial aid:* Federal Work-Study, institutionally sponsored loans, and career-related internships or fieldwork available. Financial aid application deadline: 2/15. • Dr. John A. Miller, Dean, 208-885-6208.

University of Illinois at Urbana–Champaign, College of Law, Urbana, IL 61801. Awards JD, LL M, MCL, JSD, JD/MBA, JD/MUP, MD/JD. Approved by ABA. Member of AALS. MD/JD offered jointly with the University of Illinois at Chicago College of Medicine at Urbana-Champaign. Faculty: 32 full-time (8 women), 39 part-time (10 women). Students: 651 full-time (258 women); includes 138 minority (73 African Americans, 36 Asian Americans, 29 Hispanics), 29 international. 1,951 applicants, 27% accepted. In 1997, 28 master's awarded. *Degree requirements:* For master's, thesis. *Entrance requirements:* For JD, LSAT, minimum GPA of 2.5. Application deadline: 3/15 (rolling processing). Application fee: $40 ($50 for international students). *Financial aid:* In 1997–98, 4 research assistantships were awarded; fellowships, teaching assistantships, full and partial tuition waivers also available. • Thomas M. Mengler, Dean, 217-333-9857. Application contact: Pamela Coleman, Director of Admissions, 217-244-6415.

The University of Iowa, College of Law, Iowa City, IA 52242-1316. Awards JD, LL M, JD/MA, JD/MBA, JD/MS, JD/MSW, JD/PhD, JD/M Ac. Approved by ABA. Member of AALS. Faculty: 51 full-time (15 women), 22 part-time (10 women), 55 FTE. Students: 657 full-time (277 women); includes 135 minority (47 African Americans, 36 Asian Americans, 36 Hispanics, 16 Native Americans). 1,118 applicants, 40% accepted. In 1997, 235 JDs, 7 master's awarded. *Entrance requirements:* For JD, LSAT (median 159); for master's, GRE General Test, TOEFL (minimum score 570). Application deadline: 3/1 (rolling processing). Application fee: $30 ($50 for international students). *Expenses:* Tuition $6240 per year for state residents; $16,156 per year for nonresidents. Fees $285 per year. *Financial aid:* In 1997–98, 614 students received aid, including 30 fellowships (all to first-year students), 163 research assistantships; Federal Work-Study, institutionally sponsored loans, and career-related internships or fieldwork also available. Financial aid applicants required to submit FAFSA. *Faculty research:* Administrative law, civil procedure, family estates, international and comparative law, legal history, health law, disability law, business law. • N. William Hines, Dean, 319-335-9034. Application contact: Camille de Jorna, Admissions Director, 319-335-9095. Fax: 319-335-9019. E-mail: law-admissions@uiowa.edu.

University of Kansas, School of Law, Lawrence, KS 66045. Awards JD, JD/MA, JD/MBA, JD/MPA, JD/MSW, JD/MHSA, JD/MUP. Approved by ABA. Member of AALS. JD/MA offered jointly with the Departments of Economics and Philosophy. Faculty: 36 full-time (10 women), 14 part-time (5 women). Students: 533 full-time (206 women); includes 57 minority (18 African Americans, 7 Asian Americans, 20 Hispanics, 12 Native Americans), 5 international. Average age 25. 813 applicants, 50% accepted. In 1997, 149 degrees awarded. *Entrance requirements:* LSAT. Application deadline: 3/15 (rolling processing). Application fee: $40. *Expenses:* Tuition $3100 per year for state residents; $10,191 per year for nonresidents. Fees $2598 per year. *Financial aid:* 424 students received aid; research assistantships, teaching assistantships, Federal Work-Study, institutionally sponsored loans, and career-related internships or fieldwork available. Financial aid application deadline: 3/1; applicants required to submit FAFSA. *Faculty research:* Criminal law, environmental law, elder law, legal history, law and public policy.

Directory: Law

University of Kansas (continued)

• Michael H. Hoeflich, Dean, 785-864-4550. Application contact: Diane Lindeman, Director of Admissions, 785-864-4378. Fax: 785-864-5054. E-mail: lindeman@law.wpo.ukans.edu.

University of Kentucky, College of Law, Lexington, KY 40506-0048. Awards JD, JD/MBA, JD/MPA. Approved by ABA. Member of AALS. Faculty: 28 full-time (8 women), 22 part-time (8 women). Students: 421 full-time (157 women); includes 24 minority (20 African Americans, 4 Asian Americans), 2 international. Average age 23. 750 applicants, 42% accepted. In 1997, 137 degrees awarded. *Average time to degree:* first professional–3 years full-time. *Entrance requirements:* LSAT (average 158). Application deadline: 3/1 (rolling processing). Application fee: $25. *Financial aid:* In 1997–98, 300 students received aid, including 105 scholarships; Federal Work-Study and career-related internships or fieldwork also available. Aid available to part-time students. Financial aid application deadline: 4/1; applicants required to submit FAFSA. • David E. Shipley, Dean, 606-257-1678. Application contact: Drusilla V. Bakert, Associate Dean, 606-257-1678. Fax: 606-323-1061. E-mail: dbakert@pop.uky.edu.

University of La Verne, College of Law, La Verne, CA 91750-4443. Awards JD. Also available at San Fernando Valley Campus, Woodland Hills, CA 91367. Contact Julius Walecki, Director of Admissions, 818-883-0529. Part-time and evening/weekend programs available. Faculty: 14 full-time (1 woman), 25 part-time (5 women). Students: 47 full-time (22 women), 116 part-time (51 women); includes 59 minority (11 African Americans, 16 Asian Americans, 31 Hispanics, 1 Native American). Average age 32. *Average time to degree:* first professional–3 years full-time, 4 years part-time. *Entrance requirements:* LSAT (minimum score 144). Application deadline: 8/1 (priority date; rolling processing). Application fee: $30. *Expenses:* Tuition $450 per unit. Fees $410 per year. *Financial aid:* In 1997–98, 18 grants, scholarships were awarded; fellowships, Federal Work-Study also available. Aid available to part-time students. Financial aid application deadline: 3/2; applicants required to submit FAFSA. • Kenneth Held, Dean, 909-596-1848. Application contact: John W. Osborne, Director of Admissions, 909-596-1848.

See in-depth description on page 1605.

University of Louisville, Louis D. Brandeis School of Law, Louisville, KY 40292. Awards JD, JD/MBA, JD/M Div. Approved by ABA. Member of AALS. Offered jointly with Louisville Presbyterian Theological Seminary. Part-time programs available. Faculty: 25 full-time (7 women), 6 part-time (1 woman), 27 FTE. Students: 459 full-time (198 women); includes 36 minority (19 African Americans, 10 Asian Americans, 6 Hispanics, 1 Native American), 2 international. Average age 29. In 1997, 154 degrees awarded. *Average time to degree:* first professional–3 years full-time, 4 years part-time. *Entrance requirements:* LSAT (average 158). Application deadline: 2/15. Application fee: $30. *Financial aid:* 112 students received aid; research assistantships and career-related internships or fieldwork available. Aid available to part-time students. Financial aid applicants required to submit FAFSA. • Donald L. Burnett Jr., Dean, 502-852-6879. Application contact: Glenda Jackson, Admissions Assistant, 502-852-7390. Fax: 502-852-0862. E-mail: gjjack01@ulkyvm.louisville.edu.

University of Maine School of Law, see University of Southern Maine.

University of Manitoba, Faculty of Law, Winnipeg, MB R3T 2N2, Canada. Offers programs in interdisciplinary studies (MA), law (LL M). Part-time programs available. *Degree requirements:* Thesis. *Application deadline:* 6/1 (rolling processing). *Application fee:* $50. *Faculty research:* Constitutional law, legal history, women in law, aboriginal law, medicine and law.

University of Maryland, Baltimore, School of Law, Baltimore, MD 21201-1627. Awards JD, JD/MA, JD/MBA, JD/MSW, JD/PhD, JD/MPM. Approved by ABA. Member of AALS. JD/MA offered jointly with St. John's College. JD/MA and JD/MPM offered jointly with the University of Maryland, College Park. JD/PhD offered jointly with the University of Maryland, Baltimore County. JD/MBA offered jointly with the University of Baltimore or University of Maryland, College Park. Part-time and evening/weekend programs available. Faculty: 45 full-time (17 women), 34 part-time (10 women). Students: 598 full-time (311 women), 258 part-time (118 women); includes 235 minority (119 African Americans, 86 Asian Americans, 27 Hispanics, 3 Native Americans), 9 international. Average age 26. 2,534 applicants, 38% accepted. In 1997, 257 degrees awarded. *Average time to degree:* first professional–3 years full-time, 4 years part-time. *Entrance requirements:* LSAT. Application deadline: 3/1 (priority date; rolling processing). Application fee: $50. *Financial aid:* 643 students received aid; grants, scholarships, Federal Work-Study, institutionally sponsored loans, and career-related internships or fieldwork available. Aid available to part-time students. Financial aid application deadline: 4/15; applicants required to submit FAFSA. • Donald G. Gifford, Dean, 410-706-7214. Application contact: James Forsyth, Associate Dean and Director of Admissions, 410-706-3492. Fax: 410-706-4045.

University of Maryland, College Park, Robert H. Smith School of Business, Program in Business Management/Law, College Park, MD 20742-5045. Awards JD/MBA. Offered jointly with the University of Maryland, Baltimore. Students: 4 full-time (2 women), 2 part-time (0 women); includes 1 minority (African American), 2 international. 16 applicants, 56% accepted. *Application deadline:* rolling. *Application fee:* $50 ($70 for international students). *Expenses:* Tuition $272 per credit hour for state residents; $400 per credit hour for nonresidents. Fees $564 per year full-time, $342 per year part-time. *Financial aid:* In 1997–98, 1 fellowship was awarded. • Dr. Mark Wellman, Assistant Dean, Graduate Programs, 301-405-2028. Application contact: John Mollish, Director, Graduate Admissions and Records, 301-405-4198. Fax: 301-314-9305.

University of Maryland, College Park, School of Public Affairs, Joint Program in Public Management/Law, College Park, MD 20742-5045. Awards JD/MPM. Offered jointly with the University of Maryland, Baltimore. Students: 2 full-time (both women). 4 applicants, 75% accepted. *Application deadline:* rolling. *Application fee:* $50 ($70 for international students). *Expenses:* Tuition $272 per credit hour for state residents; $400 per credit hour for nonresidents. Fees $564 per year full-time, $342 per year part-time. *Financial aid:* Fellowships available. • Dr. Terri H. Reed, Assistant Dean, 301-405-6338. Fax: 301-403-4675. Application contact: John Mollish, Director, Graduate Admissions and Records, 301-405-4198. Fax: 301-314-9305.

The University of Memphis, Cecil C. Humphreys School of Law, Memphis, TN 38152-6513. Awards JD, JD/MBA. Approved by ABA. Part-time programs available. Faculty: 22 full-time (6 women), 31 part-time (11 women). Students: 479 full-time (205 women), 31 part-time (16 women); includes 59 minority (48 African Americans, 6 Asian Americans, 3 Hispanics, 2 Native Americans). Average age 26. 830 applicants, 54% accepted. In 1997, 137 degrees awarded. *Entrance requirements:* LSAT (average 153). Application deadline: 2/15 (priority date; rolling processing). Application fee: $15 ($35 for international students). *Tuition:* $3654 per year full-time, $210 per credit hour part-time for state residents; $8964 per year full-time, $505 per credit hour part-time for nonresidents. *Financial aid:* In 1997–98, 367 students received aid, including 15 fellowships averaging $800 per month and totaling $108,000, 22 research assistantships averaging $578 per month and totaling $88,434; Federal Work-Study and career-related internships or fieldwork also available. Aid available to part-time students. Financial aid application deadline: 4/1; applicants required to submit FAFSA. *Faculty research:* Income taxation, civil rights, civil procedure, family law, insurance. Total annual research expenditures: $12,000. • Donald J. Polden, Dean, 901-678-2421. E-mail: polden@profnet.law.memphis.edu. Application contact: Dr. Sue Ann McClellan, Director of Law Admissions and Recruitment, 901-678-2073. Fax: 901-678-5210. E-mail: uofmlaw@profnet.law.memphis.edu.

University of Miami, School of Law, Coral Gables, FL 33124. Awards JD, LL M, JD/MBA, JD/MS, JD/MPH. Programs in comparative law (LL M), estate planning (LL M), international law (LL M), law (JD), ocean and coastal law (LL M), real property and development (LL M). Approved by ABA. Member of AALS. JD/MS new for fall 1998. Evening/weekend programs available. Faculty: 50 full-time (12 women), 156 part-time (33 women). Students: 1,236 full-time (527 women), 320 part-time (141 women); includes 433 minority (122 African Americans, 44 Asian Americans, 260 Hispanics, 7 Native Americans), 119 international. Average age 25. 2,501 applicants, 63% accepted. In 1997, 410 JDs, 85 master's awarded. *Degree requirements:* For master's, thesis required, foreign language not required. *Average time to degree:* master's–1 year full-time; first professional–3 years full-time, 4 years part-time. *Entrance requirements:* For JD, LSAT (average 154). Application deadline: 3/8 (priority date; rolling processing). Application fee: $45. *Tuition:* $21,530 per year full-time, $897 per credit hour part-time. *Financial aid:* In 1997–98, 1,308 students received aid, including research assistantships totaling $346,000; Federal Work-Study, institutionally sponsored loans, and career-related internships or fieldwork also available. Aid available to part-time students. Financial aid application deadline: 3/1; applicants required to submit FAFSA. • Michael Goodnight, Assistant Dean of Admissions, 305-284-2527. Application contact: Therese Lambert, Director of Student Recruiting, 305-284-6746. Fax: 305-284-3084.

University of Michigan, Law School, Ann Arbor, MI 48109-1215. Awards JD, LL M, MCL, SJD, JD/MBA, JD/MS, JD/PhD, JD/AM, JD/MHSA, JD/MPP. Programs in comparative law (MCL), international economic law (LL M), international law (LL M), law (JD, LL M, SJD). Approved by ABA. Member of AALS. *Entrance requirements:* LSAT. *Financial aid:* Fellowships, Federal Work-Study, and career-related internships or fieldwork available. Aid available to part-time students. • Jeffrey S. Lehman, Dean, 734-764-1358.

University of Minnesota, Twin Cities Campus, Law School, Minneapolis, MN 55455-0213. Awards JD, LL M, JD/MA, JD/MBA, JD/MPP. Approved by ABA. Member of AALS. Faculty: 42 full-time (15 women), 83 part-time (29 women). Students: 801 full-time (333 women); includes 131 minority (23 African Americans, 68 Asian Americans, 31 Hispanics, 9 Native Americans), 46 international. Average age 26. 1,513 applicants, 43% accepted. *Average time to degree:* first professional–3 years full-time. *Entrance requirements:* For JD, LSAT (median 163). Application deadline: 3/1 (rolling processing). Application fee: $40. *Financial aid:* 765 students received aid; fellowships, research assistantships, teaching assistantships, full and partial tuition waivers, Federal Work-Study, institutionally sponsored loans, and career-related internships or fieldwork available. Financial aid application deadline: 3/15; applicants required to submit FAFSA. *Faculty research:* International law, constitutional law, commercial law, tax law, criminal law. • E. Thomas Sullivan, Dean, 612-625-1000. Application contact: Collins B. Byrd Jr., Director of Admissions, 612-625-5005. Fax: 612-625-2011.

University of Mississippi, School of Law, University, MS 38677-9702. Awards JD, JD/MBA. Approved by ABA. Member of AALS. Faculty: 23 full-time (5 women). Students: 493 full-time (201 women), 4 part-time (1 woman); includes 62 minority (50 African Americans, 4 Asian Americans, 4 Hispanics, 4 Native Americans). Average age 24. In 1997, 147 degrees awarded. *Average time to degree:* first professional–3 years full-time, 5 years part-time. *Entrance requirements:* LSAT, TOEFL (minimum score 625), LSDAS. Application deadline: 3/1. Application fee: $0 ($25 for international students). *Financial aid:* Fellowships, research assistantships, teaching assistantships, Federal Work-Study, institutionally sponsored loans, and career-related internships or fieldwork available. Aid available to part-time students. Financial aid application deadline: 3/1. • Dr. William Champion, Acting Dean, 601-232-7361. Application contact: Barbara Vinson, Coordinator of Admissions, 601-232-7361.

University of Missouri–Columbia, School of Law, Columbia, MO 65201. Awards JD, JD/MA, JD/MBA, JD/MPA. Approved by ABA. Member of AALS. JD/MA offered jointly with Department of Economics and Department of Human Development and Family Studies. Faculty: 33 full-time, 7 part-time. Students: 538 full-time (206 women); includes 48 minority (22 African Americans, 12 Asian Americans, 10 Hispanics, 4 Native Americans). Average age 25. 727 applicants, 57% accepted. In 1997, 131 degrees awarded (98% found work related to degree, 2% continued full-time study). *Average time to degree:* first professional–3 years full-time. *Entrance requirements:* LSAT (minimum score 146; average 155). Application deadline: 8/24 (priority date; rolling processing). Application fee: $40. *Financial aid:* 478 students received aid; fellowships, Federal Work-Study, institutionally sponsored loans available. • Timothy J. Heinsz, Dean, 573-882-3246. E-mail: heinsz@law.missouri.edu. Application contact: Sheryl Gregory, Director of Admissions, 573-882-6042. Fax: 573-882-4984. E-mail: gregory@law.missouri.edu.

University of Missouri–Kansas City, School of Law, Graduate Programs in Law, Kansas City, MO 64110-2499. Awards LL M, JD/LL M, LL M/MPA. Offerings include general (LL M), taxation (LL M). Member of AALS. Faculty: 6 full-time (2 women), 3 part-time (1 woman), 7.5 FTE. Students: 13 full-time (3 women), 11 part-time (6 women); includes 1 minority (African American), 1 international. Average age 32. In 1997, 26 degrees awarded (100% found work related to degree). *Degree requirements:* Thesis (general) required, foreign language not required. *Average time to degree:* master's–1 year full-time, 3 years part-time. *Entrance requirements:* Minimum GPA of 3.0 in law (general), 2.7 (tax). Application deadline: 4/1 (rolling processing). Application fee: $25. *Expenses:* Tuition $345 per credit hour for state residents; $689 per credit hour for nonresidents. Fees $326 per year. *Financial aid:* 8 students received aid. • Dr. Burnele Powell, Dean, School of Law, 816-235-1672.

University of Missouri–Kansas City, School of Law, Professional Program in Law, Kansas City, MO 64110-2499. Awards JD, JD/MBA, JD/LL M. Approved by ABA. Member of AALS. Students: 470 full-time (214 women), 26 part-time (12 women); includes 49 minority (20 African Americans, 8 Asian Americans, 14 Hispanics, 7 Native Americans), 2 international. Average age 28. 931 applicants, 56% accepted. In 1997, 146 degrees awarded (100% found work related to degree). *Average time to degree:* first professional–3 years full-time, 5 years part-time. *Entrance requirements:* LSAT. Application deadline: 4/1 (priority date; rolling processing). Application fee: $25. *Expenses:* Tuition $8274 per year for state residents; $16,548 per year for nonresidents. Fees $326 per year. *Financial aid:* 362 students received aid; institutionally sponsored loans and career-related internships or fieldwork available. • Dr. Burnele Powell, Dean, School of Law, 816-235-1672.

The University of Montana–Missoula, School of Law, Missoula, MT 59812-0002. Awards JD, JD/MPA, JD/MS. Approved by ABA. Member of AALS. JD/MS offered jointly with the Program in Environmental Studies. Faculty: 15 full-time (6 women), 15 part-time (2 women), 17.65 FTE. Students: 235 full-time (100 women); includes 15 minority (2 African Americans, 1 Asian American, 4 Hispanics, 8 Native Americans), 3 international. Average age 29. 413 applicants, 54% accepted. In 1997, 75 degrees awarded. *Average time to degree:* first professional–3 years full-time. *Entrance requirements:* LSAT. Application deadline: 3/1. Application fee: $60. *Tuition:* $6622 per year for state residents; $11,993 per year for nonresidents. *Financial aid:* In 1997–98, 179 students received aid, including 22 research assistantships, 16 teaching assistantships averaging $243 per month and totaling $39,137; partial tuition waivers, Federal Work-Study, institutionally sponsored loans, and career-related internships or fieldwork also available. Financial aid application deadline: 3/1; applicants required to submit FAFSA. *Faculty research:* Legal education curriculum, business and probate law reform, rules of civil procedure reform, tribal courts, women's issues. • E. Edwin Eck, Dean, 406-243-4311. Application contact: Christine Sopko, Admissions Officer, 406-243-4311. Fax: 406-243-2576. E-mail: crs@selway.umt.edu.

University of Nebraska–Lincoln, College of Law, Lincoln, NE 68583. Awards JD, JD/MA, JD/MBA, JD/MPA, JD/PhD, JD/MCRP. Approved by ABA. Member of AALS. Faculty: 14 full-time (1 woman), 1 part-time (0 women), 14.67 FTE. Students: 373 full-time (159 women), 4 part-time (all women); includes 33 minority (10 African Americans, 12 Asian Americans, 8 Hispanics, 3 Native Americans), 5 international. Average age 27. 682 applicants, 51% accepted. In 1997, 130 degrees awarded. *Entrance requirements:* LSAT. Application fee: $25. *Financial aid:* Fellowships, research assistantships, teaching assistantships, full tuition waivers, Federal Work-Study, institutionally sponsored loans, and career-related internships or fieldwork available. *Faculty research:* Water law and policy, trademarks and unfair practices, criminal procedure, international trade, labor and discrimination issues. • Harvey S. Perlman, Dean, 402-472-2161. Application contact: Ruth A. Witherspoon, Assistant Dean, 402-472-2161.

University of New Brunswick, Faculty of Law, Fredericton, NB E3B 5A3, Canada. Awards LL B. Students: 228 full-time (103 women). Average age 24. 630 applicants, 13% accepted. In

1997, 79 degrees awarded. *Entrance requirements:* LSAT (minimum score 145; average 157). Application deadline: 3/1 (rolling processing). Application fee: $50. *Faculty research:* Property studies, legal history, family violence, law and technology. Total annual research expenditures: $150,000. • Anne Warner La Forest, Dean, 506-453-4627. Application contact: Robin Dickson, Admissions Officer, 506-453-4693. Fax: 506-453-4604. E-mail: rjd@unb.ca.

University of New Mexico, School of Law, Albuquerque, NM 87131-2039. Awards JD, JD/MA, JD/MBA, JD/MPA, JD/MS, JD/PhD, JD/MALAS. Approved by ABA. Member of AALS. Faculty: 34 full-time (15 women), 27 part-time (13 women). Students: 341 full-time (173 women); includes 135 minority (10 African Americans, 8 Asian Americans, 92 Hispanics, 25 Native Americans). Average age 29. 732 applicants, 34% accepted. In 1997, 103 degrees awarded. *Degree requirements:* Advanced writing piece required, foreign language and thesis not required. *Entrance requirements:* LSAT (average 156). Application deadline: 2/15 (rolling processing). Application fee: $40. *Expenses:* Tuition $3952 per year for state residents; $13,306 per year for nonresidents. Fees $32 per year. *Financial aid:* Full tuition waivers, Federal Work-Study, and career-related internships or fieldwork available. Financial aid application deadline: 3/1; applicants required to submit FAFSA. • Robert J. Desiderio, Dean, 505-277-4700. Fax: 505-277-1597. E-mail: desiderior@law.unm.edu. Application contact: Susan Mitchell, Director of Admissions and Financial Aid, 505-277-0959. Fax: 505-277-9958. E-mail: mitchell@libra.unm.edu.

The University of North Carolina at Chapel Hill, School of Law, Chapel Hill, NC 27599. Awards JD, JD/MBA, JD/MPA, JD/MSW, JD/MAPPS, JD/MPH, JD/MRP. Approved by ABA. Member of AALS. JD/MAPPS offered jointly with Duke University. Faculty: 44 full-time (17 women), 35 part-time (12 women). Students: 687 full-time (334 women); includes 142 minority (88 African Americans, 30 Asian Americans, 14 Hispanics, 10 Native Americans), 5 international. Average age 25. 1,720 applicants, 34% accepted. In 1997, 223 degrees awarded. *Average time to degree:* first professional–3 years full-time. *Entrance requirements:* LSAT. Application deadline: 2/1 (priority date; rolling processing). Application fee: $60. *Expenses:* Tuition $1428 per year full-time, $357 per semester (minimum) part-time for state residents; $13,290 per year full-time, $3323 per semester (minimum) part-time for nonresidents. Fees $1453 per year full-time, $668 per semester (minimum) part-time. *Financial aid:* Research assistantships, teaching assistantships, Federal Work-Study, and career-related internships or fieldwork available. Aid available to part-time students. Financial aid application deadline: 3/1; applicants required to submit FAFSA. *Faculty research:* Death penalty, feminist legal theory, urban reform risk-based environmental policy, state and US constitutional law. • Judith W. Wegner, Dean, 919-962-4417. Application contact: J. Elizabeth Furr, Assistant Dean for Admissions, 919-962-5109. Fax: 919-962-1170. E-mail: law_admission@unc.edu.

University of North Dakota, School of Law, Grand Forks, ND 58202. Awards JD. Approved by ABA. Member of AALS. Faculty: 14 full-time (5 women), 9 part-time (3 women). Students: 192 full-time (75 women); includes 10 minority (1 African American, 2 Asian Americans, 1 Hispanic, 6 Native Americans), 8 international. 263 applicants, 60% accepted. In 1997, 76 degrees awarded. *Entrance requirements:* LSAT. Application deadline: 4/1. Application fee: $35. *Financial aid:* Full and partial tuition waivers, Federal Work-Study, and career-related internships or fieldwork available. • W. Jeremy Davis, Dean, 701-777-2104. Application contact: Linda Kohoutek, Admissions and Records Officer, 701-777-2104.

University of Notre Dame, Law School, Notre Dame, IN 46556. Offers programs in comparative law (LL M), international law (LL M, JSD), law (JD). Approved by ABA. Member of AALS. Faculty: 39 full-time (10 women), 34 part-time (7 women). Students: 550 full-time (201 women); includes 98 minority (14 African Americans, 35 Asian Americans, 40 Hispanics, 9 Native Americans), 23 international. Average age 24. In 1997, 186 JDs, 24 master's awarded. *Degree requirements:* For master's and doctorate, thesis/dissertation. *Entrance requirements:* For JD, LSAT; for master's, TOEFL (minimum score 600). Application deadline: 3/1 (rolling processing). Application fee: $65. *Financial aid:* In 1997–98, 200 fellowships (63 to first-year students), 20 research assistantships, 10 teaching assistantships were awarded; Federal Work-Study, institutionally sponsored loans, and career-related internships or fieldwork also available. Financial aid application deadline: 3/1; applicants required to submit FAFSA. • Dr. David T. Link, Dean, 219-631-7015. Application contact: Office of Admissions, 219-631-6626. Fax: 219-631-6371. E-mail: law.bulletin.1@nd.edu.

University of Oklahoma, College of Law, Norman, OK 73019-0390. Awards JD, JD/MBA, JD/MS, JD/MPH. Approved by ABA. Member of AALS. JD/MPH and JD/MS (environmental management, health administration, occupational health) offered jointly with the University of Oklahoma Health Sciences Center. Faculty: 35 full-time (11 women), 10 part-time (5 women). Students: 544 full-time (225 women), 7 part-time (4 women); includes 80 minority (15 African Americans, 18 Asian Americans, 20 Hispanics, 27 Native Americans), 1 international. Average age 27. 1,090 applicants, 34% accepted. In 1997, 213 degrees awarded. *Entrance requirements:* LSAT. Application deadline: 3/15 (rolling processing). Application fee: $25. *Expenses:* Tuition $4140 per year full-time, $138 per credit hour part-time for state residents; $12,924 per year full-time, $431 per credit hour part-time for nonresidents. Fees $530 per year full-time, $53 per semester (minimum) part-time. *Financial aid:* Full and partial tuition waivers, Federal Work-Study, institutionally sponsored loans, and career-related internships or fieldwork available. Financial aid application deadline: 3/1. • Dr. Andrew M. Coats, Dean, 405-325-4699. Application contact: Deborah Case, Assistant Director, Law Student Services, 405-325-4729.

University of Oregon, School of Law, Eugene, OR 97403. Awards JD, JD/MBA, JD/MS. Approved by ABA. Member of AALS. Faculty: 22 full-time (9 women), 11 part-time (3 women). Students: 528 full-time (253 women), 7 part-time (5 women); includes 78 minority (12 African Americans, 41 Asian Americans, 22 Hispanics, 3 Native Americans), 4 international. 1,046 applicants, 58% accepted. In 1997, 156 degrees awarded. *Average time to degree:* first professional–3 years full-time. *Entrance requirements:* LSAT. Application deadline: 4/1 (rolling processing). Application fee: $50. *Tuition:* $10,236 per year for state residents; $13,984 per year for nonresidents. *Financial aid:* In 1997–98, 27 teaching assistantships (1 to a first-year student) were awarded; partial tuition waivers, Federal Work-Study, institutionally sponsored loans, and career-related internships or fieldwork also available. Financial aid application deadline: 2/1; applicants required to submit FAFSA. • Rennard Strickland, Dean, 541-346-3852. Application contact: Randi Schnechel, 541-346-1810. Fax: 541-346-1564. E-mail: randisch@law.uoregon.edu.

University of Ottawa, Faculty of Law, Ottawa, ON K1N 6N5, Canada. Offers programs in law (LL M, LL D), legislative drafting (Diploma). Part-time and evening/weekend programs available. Faculty: 49 full-time, 4 part-time. Students: 38 full-time (20 women), 30 part-time (18 women); includes 6 international. Average age 36. In 1997, 28 master's awarded. *Degree requirements:* For master's, thesis or alternative required, foreign language not required; for doctorate, dissertation required, foreign language not required. *Entrance requirements:* For master's, honors degree or equivalent, minimum B average; for doctorate, LL B or LL M, minimum B+ average. Application deadline: 2/1. Application fee: $35. *Expenses:* Tuition $4677 per year for Canadian residents; $9900 per year for nonresidents. Fees $230 per year. *Financial aid:* Research assistantships, Federal Work-Study available. *Faculty research:* International law, constitutional and administrative law, human rights, comparative law. • Sanda Rodgers, Dean, 613-562-5774. Application contact: Ruth Sullivan, Director, 613-562-5897. Fax: 613-562-5124.

University of Pennsylvania, Law School, Philadelphia, PA 19104. Awards JD, LL M, SJD, JD/MBA, JD/MSW, JD/PhD, JD/AM, JD/MCP, JD/MGA, MD/JD. Approved by ABA. Member of AALS. Faculty: 43 full-time (10 women), 53 part-time (17 women). Students: 788 full-time (325 women), 16 part-time (6 women); includes 182 minority (65 African Americans, 58 Asian Americans, 56 Hispanics, 3 Native Americans), 102 international. Average age 24. 3,844 applicants, 30% accepted. In 1997, 292 JDs, 65 master's, 1 doctorate awarded. *Degree requirements:* For master's, thesis optional; for doctorate, dissertation. *Average time to degree:* master's–1 year full-time; first professional–3 years full-time. *Entrance requirements:* For JD, LSAT; for master's, TOEFL; for doctorate, LL M. Application deadline: 3/1 (rolling processing). Application fee: $65. *Expenses:* Tuition $24,150 per year. Fees $1638 per year. *Financial aid:* 319 students received aid; scholarships, Federal Work-Study, institutionally sponsored loans, and career-related internships or fieldwork available. Financial aid application deadline: 3/1; applicants required to submit FAFSA. *Faculty research:* Criminal law theory, individual rights in health care, media regulation, separation of powers, affirmative action. • Colin S. Diver, Dean, 215-898-7061. Fax: 215-573-2025. E-mail: cdiver@law.upenn.edu. Application contact: Janice L. Austin, Assistant Dean of Admissions, 215-898-7743.

University of Pittsburgh, School of Law, Professional Programs in Law, Pittsburgh, PA 15260. Awards JD, JD/MA, JD/MPA, JD/MPIA, JD/MS, JD/MURP, JD/MAM, JD/MPH, JD/MSIA, MBA/JD. Approved by ABA. Member of AALS. JD/MAM, JD/MSIA, and JD/MS (public affairs) offered jointly with Carnegie Mellon University. Faculty: 42 full-time (18 women), 20 part-time (7 women). Students: 694 full-time (290 women), 1 (woman) part-time; includes 68 minority (43 African Americans, 13 Asian Americans, 12 Hispanics), 6 international. 1,184 applicants, 19% accepted. In 1997, 231 degrees awarded. *Average time to degree:* first professional–3 years full-time. *Entrance requirements:* LSAT. Application deadline: 3/1 (rolling processing). Application fee: $40. *Expenses:* Tuition $11,912 per year for state residents; $18,618 per year for nonresidents. Fees $480 per year. *Financial aid:* Federal Work-Study, institutionally sponsored loans, and career-related internships or fieldwork available. Financial aid application deadline: 3/1; applicants required to submit FAFSA. *Faculty research:* International business and trade, feminist legal theory, criminal law, corporate law, computer law and intellectual property. Total annual research expenditures: $220,000. • Application contact: Fredi G. Miller, Assistant Dean, 412-648-1400. Fax: 412-648-2647. E-mail: miller@law.pitt.edu.

University of Pittsburgh, School of Law, Program in International and Comparative Law, Pittsburgh, PA 15260. Awards LL M. Member of AALS. Offered to international students only. Faculty: 42 full-time (18 women), 20 part-time (7 women). Students: 9 full-time (4 women); includes 7 international. 52 applicants. In 1997, 8 degrees awarded. *Degree requirements:* Thesis. *Average time to degree:* master's–1 year full-time. *Entrance requirements:* TOEFL (minimum score 550; average 605), law degree from foreign university. Application deadline: 3/30 (priority date; rolling processing). Application fee: $40. Electronic applications accepted. *Expenses:* Tuition $15,000 per year. Fees $480 per year. *Financial aid:* In 1997–98, 7 students received aid, including 7 fellowships totaling $37,500; Federal Work-Study, institutionally sponsored loans, and career-related internships or fieldwork also available. Financial aid application deadline: 3/30. *Faculty research:* International trade and dispute settlement, artificial intelligence and legal reasoning, alternative dispute resolution in international trade, criminal justice. • Application contact: Jody Hoberek, Administrative Assistant, 412-648-7023. Fax: 412-648-2648. E-mail: cile@law.pitt.edu.

University of Puerto Rico, Río Piedras, School of Law, San Juan, PR 00931. Awards JD. Approved by ABA. Member of AALS. Part-time and evening/weekend programs available. *Entrance requirements:* LSAT, PAEG, minimum GPA of 3.0. Application deadline: 2/21. Application fee: $17. *Faculty research:* Civil code, modern corporate law.

University of Richmond, T. C. Williams School of Law, University of Richmond, VA 23173. Awards JD, JD/MA, JD/MBA, JD/MS, JD/MSW, JD/MURP, JD/MHA. Approved by ABA. Member of AALS. JD/MHA, JD/MSW, and JD/MURP offered jointly with Virginia Commonwealth University; JD/MA offered jointly with the Department of History; JD/MS offered jointly with the Department of Biology. Part-time programs available. Faculty: 27 full-time (10 women), 68 part-time (25 women). Students: 471 full-time (216 women), 1 part-time (0 women); includes 76 minority (41 African Americans, 22 Asian Americans, 10 Hispanics, 3 Native Americans), 5 international. Average age 25. 1,314 applicants, 42% accepted. In 1997, 142 degrees awarded. *Average time to degree:* first professional–3 years full-time, 5 years part-time. *Entrance requirements:* LSAT. Application deadline: 2/1. Application fee: $35. *Financial aid:* Research assistantships, Federal Work-Study, and career-related internships or fieldwork available. Aid available to part-time students. Financial aid application deadline: 2/25; applicants required to submit FAFSA. • John R. Pagan, Dean, 804-289-8183. Application contact: Michelle L. Rahman, Director of Admissions, 804-289-8189. Fax: 804-287-6516.

University of San Diego, School of Law, San Diego, CA 92110-2492. Awards JD, LL M, MCL, Diploma, JD/MA, JD/MBA, JD/MIB. Programs in comparative law (MCL), general studies (LL M), international law (LL M), law (JD), taxation (LL M, Diploma). Approved by ABA. Member of AALS. Part-time and evening/weekend programs available. Faculty: 50 full-time (16 women), 34 part-time (13 women), 55.1 FTE. Students: 781 full-time (323 women), 350 part-time (144 women); includes 235 minority (17 African Americans, 131 Asian Americans, 66 Hispanics, 21 Native Americans), 43 international. Average age 28. 2,786 applicants, 46% accepted. In 1997, 305 JDs awarded (100% found work related to degree); 64 master's awarded. *Degree requirements:* For master's, thesis (for some programs). *Entrance requirements:* For JD, LSAT, LSDAS; for master's, TOEFL (MCL), JD (LL M). Application deadline: 3/1. Application fee: $40. *Expenses:* Tuition $20,980 per year full-time, $710 per unit part-time. Fees $50 per year full-time, $40 per year part-time. *Financial aid:* Fellowships, research assistantships, scholarships, Federal Work-Study, institutionally sponsored loans, and career-related internships or fieldwork available. Aid available to part-time students. Financial aid application deadline: 3/1. *Faculty research:* Administrative law, corporate and commercial law, jurisprudence and legal ethics, criminal law and procedure. Total annual research expenditures: $88,000. • Kristine Strachan, Dean, 619-260-4527. Application contact: Carl Eging, Director of Admissions, 619-260-4528.

University of San Francisco, School of Law, San Francisco, CA 94117-1080. Awards JD, JD/MBA. Approved by ABA. Member of AALS. JD/MBA offered jointly with McLaren School of Business. Part-time and evening/weekend programs available. Faculty: 27 full-time (7 women), 34 part-time (9 women). Students: 534 full-time (287 women), 127 part-time (59 women); includes 174 minority (23 African Americans, 99 Asian Americans, 47 Hispanics, 5 Native Americans), 5 international. Average age 28. 2,459 applicants, 48% accepted. In 1997, 232 degrees awarded. *Average time to degree:* first professional–3 years full-time, 4 years part-time. *Entrance requirements:* LSAT (average 157), minimum undergraduate GPA of 3.2. Application deadline: 4/1 (rolling processing). Application fee: $40. *Financial aid:* 556 students received aid; Federal Work-Study, institutionally sponsored loans, and career-related internships or fieldwork available. Aid available to part-time students. Financial aid application deadline: 3/2; applicants required to submit FAFSA. • Jay Folberg, Dean, 415-422-6304. Application contact: Saralynn T. Ferrara, Director of Admissions, 415-422-6586.

University of Saskatchewan, College of Law, Saskatoon, SK S7N 5A2, Canada. Awards LL B, LL M. *Degree requirements:* For master's, thesis required, foreign language not required. *Entrance requirements:* For LL B, LSAT (minimum score 145; average 156); for master's, TOEFL (minimum score 600), LL B. Application deadline: 7/1 (priority date). Application fee: $50. *Faculty research:* Cooperative, native/aboriginal, constitutional, commercial, consumer, and natural resource law; criminal justice; human rights.

University of South Carolina, Law School, Columbia, SC 29208. Awards JD, JD/MA, JD/MBA, JD/MCJ, JD/MPA, JD/MS, JD/M Acc, JD/MHR, JD/MIBS. Approved by ABA. Member of AALS. Faculty: 45 full-time (2 women), 24 part-time (1 woman). Students: 758 full-time (316 women), 10 part-time (5 women); includes 71 minority (58 African Americans, 7 Asian Americans, 4 Hispanics, 2 Native Americans), 2 international. Average age 27. 1,740 applicants, 25% accepted. In 1997, 242 degrees awarded. *Degree requirements:* Thesis. *Entrance requirements:* LSAT (average 157). Application deadline: 2/15. Application fee: $25 ($35 for international students). Electronic applications accepted. *Expenses:* Tuition $7228 per year full-time, $304 per credit hour part-time for state residents; $14,986 per year full-time, $626 per credit hour part-time for nonresidents. Fees $125 per year full-time, $37 per semester (minimum) part-time. *Financial aid:* In 1997–98, 15 fellowships were awarded; Federal Work-Study and career-related internships or fieldwork also available. Financial aid application deadline: 4/15; applicants required to submit FAFSA. • John Montgomery, Dean, 803-777-6617. Application contact: John S. Benfield, Assistant Dean of Admissions, 803-777-6606. Fax: 803-777-7751.

Directory: Law

University of South Dakota, School of Law, Vermillion, SD 57069-2390. Awards JD, JD/MA, JD/MBA, JD/MPA, JD/MP Acc. Approved by ABA. Member of AALS. Faculty: 15 full-time (3 women), 4 part-time (1 woman). Students: 223 full-time (86 women); includes 12 minority (5 African Americans, 2 Asian Americans, 5 Native Americans). Average age 26. 321 applicants, 54% accepted. In 1997, 75 degrees awarded. *Average time to degree:* first professional–3 years full-time. *Entrance requirements:* LSAT. Application deadline: 3/1 (priority date; rolling processing). Application fee: $15. *Financial aid:* In 1997–98, 90 students received aid, including 17 research assistantships averaging $425 per month; Federal Work-Study, institutionally sponsored loans, and career-related internships or fieldwork also available. Financial aid applicants required to submit FAFSA. *Faculty research:* Indian law, capital formation issues, skills training, environmental law, health care. Total annual research expenditures: $28,000. • Barry R. Vickrey, Dean, 605-677-5443. Application contact: Jean Henriques, Admissions Officer/Registrar, 605-677-5443. Fax: 605-677-5417. E-mail: request@jurist.law.usd.edu.

University of Southern California, Law School, Los Angeles, CA 90089. Awards JD, JD/MA, JD/MBA, JD/MPA, JD/MS, JD/MSW, JD/MBT, JD/MRED. Approved by ABA. Member of AALS. Students: 601 full-time (270 women); includes 242 minority (71 African Americans, 81 Asian Americans, 88 Hispanics, 2 Native Americans), 1 international. Average age 26. In 1997, 166 degrees awarded. *Entrance requirements:* LSAT. Application fee: $60. *Expenses:* Tuition $24,638 per year full-time, $952 per unit part-time. Fees $414 per year. *Financial aid:* In 1997–98, 295 fellowships, 8 teaching assistantships, 105 scholarships were awarded; research assistantships, Federal Work-Study, institutionally sponsored loans also available. Aid available to part-time students. Financial aid application deadline: 2/15; applicants required to submit FAFSA. • Scott H. Bice, Dean, 213-740-6473.

University of Southern Maine, University of Maine School of Law, Portland, ME 04104-9300. Awards JD, JD/MA. Approved by ABA. Member of AALS. Faculty: 16 full-time (5 women). Students: 294 full-time (124 women); includes 18 minority (6 African Americans, 6 Asian Americans, 2 Hispanics, 4 Native Americans), 5 international. Average age 28. 569 applicants, 51% accepted. In 1997, 86 degrees awarded. *Average time to degree:* first professional–3 years full-time, 4 years part-time. *Entrance requirements:* LSAT (average 155). Application deadline: 2/15 (rolling processing). Application fee: $25. *Expenses:* Tuition $9360 per year full-time, $300 per credit hour part-time for state residents; $14,040 per year (minimum) full-time, $450 per credit hour (minimum) part-time for nonresidents. Fees $404 per year full-time, $103 per semester (minimum) part-time. *Financial aid:* 240 students received aid; full tuition waivers, Federal Work-Study, and career-related internships or fieldwork available. Aid available to part-time students. Financial aid application deadline: 2/1; applicants required to submit FAFSA. • Donald Zillman, Dean, 207-780-4344. Application contact: Barbara Gauditz, Assistant Dean, 207-780-4341. Fax: 207-780-4239. E-mail: gauditz@usm.maine.edu.

University of Tennessee, Knoxville, College of Law, Knoxville, TN 37996. Awards JD, JD/MBA, JD/MPA. Approved by ABA. Member of AALS. Faculty: 31 full-time (9 women), 37 part-time (11 women). Students: 494 full-time (224 women); includes 52 minority (40 African Americans, 2 Asian Americans, 4 Hispanics, 6 Native Americans). 1,144 applicants, 34% accepted. In 1997, 139 degrees awarded. *Average time to degree:* first professional–3 years full-time. *Entrance requirements:* LSAT (average 155). Application deadline: 2/1 (priority date). Application fee: $15. *Financial aid:* 379 students received aid; Federal Work-Study, institutionally sponsored loans, and career-related internships or fieldwork available. Aid available to part-time students. Financial aid application deadline: 2/14; applicants required to submit FAFSA. *Faculty research:* Legal expert systems, medical malpractice remedies, professional ethics, insanity defense. • Karen R. Britton, Director of Admissions and Career Services, 423-974-4131. E-mail: lawadmit@libra.law.utk.edu. Application contact: Janet S. Hatcher, Admissions and Financial Aid Counselor, 423-974-4131. Fax: 423-974-1572. E-mail: lawadmit@libra.law.utk.edu.

The University of Texas at Austin, School of Law, Austin, TX 78705. Awards JD, LL M, JD/MA, JD/MBA, JD/MP Aff, JD/MSCRP. Approved by ABA. Member of AALS. JD/MA offered jointly with the Program in Post-Soviet and East European Studies, the Center for Latin American Studies, and the Center for Middle Eastern Studies. Faculty: 73 full-time (18 women), 101 part-time (22 women). Students: 1,451 full-time (640 women). Average age 25. 3,487 applicants, 31% accepted. In 1997, 533 JDs, 20 master's awarded. *Average time to degree:* first professional–3 years full-time. *Entrance requirements:* For JD, LSAT. Application deadline: 2/1. Application fee: $65. *Tuition:* $5468 per year for state residents; $11,732 per year for nonresidents. *Financial aid:* Career-related internships or fieldwork available. Financial aid application deadline: 3/31; applicants required to submit FAFSA. *Faculty research:* Federal courts, bankruptcy, criminal law, constitutional law, conflicts of law, international law, intellectual property law, copyright law, family law. • M. Michael Sharlot, Dean, 512-232-1120. Application contact: Shelli D. Soto, Assistant Dean for Admissions, 512-232-1200. Fax: 512-471-6988. E-mail: admissions@mail.law.utexas.edu.

University of the District of Columbia, School of Law, 4200 Connecticut Avenue, NW, Washington, DC 20008-1175. Awards JD. Approved by ABA. Faculty: 20 full-time (10 women), 9 part-time (3 women). Students: 172 full-time (91 women); includes 127 minority (107 African Americans, 10 Asian Americans, 9 Hispanics, 1 Native American). Average age 30. 330 applicants, 43% accepted. In 1997, 76 degrees awarded. *Average time to degree:* first professional–3 years full-time. *Entrance requirements:* LSAT (minimum score 140; average 150). Application deadline: 4/1 (rolling processing). Application fee: $35. *Expenses:* Tuition $7000 per year for district residents; $14,000 per year for nonresidents. Fees $135 per year. *Financial aid:* 167 students received aid; research assistantships, teaching assistantships, full and partial tuition waivers, Federal Work-Study, and career-related internships or fieldwork available. Financial aid application deadline: 5/1; applicants required to submit FAFSA. *Faculty research:* HIV law, juvenile law. • William L. Robinson, Dean, 202-274-7400. E-mail: wrobinso@udc.edu. Application contact: Vivian W. Canty, Director of Admission, 202-274-7341. Fax: 202-274-5583. E-mail: vcanty@udc.edu.

University of the Pacific, McGeorge School of Law, Sacramento, CA 95817. Awards JD, LL M, JD/MBA. Programs in law (JD), transnational business practice (LL M). Approved by ABA. Member of AALS. Part-time and evening/weekend programs available. Faculty: 46 full-time (13 women), 34 part-time (6 women). Students: 817 full-time (382 women), 322 part-time (154 women); includes 263 minority (29 African Americans, 131 Asian Americans, 82 Hispanics, 21 Native Americans). 1,811 applicants, 68% accepted. In 1997, 355 JDs, 31 master's awarded. *Average time to degree:* master's–1 year full-time, 2 years part-time; first professional–3 years full-time, 4 years part-time. *Entrance requirements:* For JD, LSAT; for master's, JD. Application deadline: 5/1 (priority date; rolling processing). Application fee: $40. *Tuition:* $20,762 per year full-time, $13,324 per year part-time. *Financial aid:* In 1997–98, 420 grants, scholarships (60 to first-year students) were awarded; Federal Work-Study and career-related internships or fieldwork also available. Aid available to part-time students. Financial aid applicants required to submit FAFSA. *Faculty research:* Taxation and business, family and juvenile law, governmental affairs, environmental law. • Gerald M. Caplan, Dean, 916-739-7151. Application contact: Admissions Office, 916-739-7105. Fax: 916-739-7134. E-mail: admissionsmcgeorge@uop.edu.

University of Toledo, College of Law, Toledo, OH 43606-3398. Awards JD, JD/MBA. Approved by ABA. Member of AALS. Part-time and evening/weekend programs available. Faculty: 26 full-time (7 women), 23 part-time (5 women). Students: 457 full-time (191 women), 165 part-time (75 women); includes 55 minority (28 African Americans, 9 Asian Americans, 14 Hispanics, 4 Native Americans), 2 international. Average age 27. 712 applicants, 65% accepted. In 1997, 203 degrees awarded. *Entrance requirements:* LSAT. Application deadline: 5/15 (priority date; rolling processing). Application fee: $30. *Tuition:* $7350 per year full-time, $306 per hour part-time for state residents; $14,168 per year full-time, $591 per hour part-time for nonresidents. *Financial aid:* In 1997–98, 487 students received aid, including 17 research assistantships, 4 teaching assistantships, 169 grants, scholarships (85 to first-year students); Federal Work-Study and career-related internships or fieldwork also available. Aid available to part-time students. Financial aid application deadline: 5/1; applicants required to submit FAFSA. *Faculty research:* Videotaping/human memory, feminist theory of process, Ohio Civil Procedure changes, securities regulation in cyberspace, discriminatory treatment/police. Total annual research expenditures: $90,000. • Albert T. Quick, Dean, 419-530-2379. Application contact: Carol E. Frendt, Assistant Dean of Law Admissions, 419-530-4131. Fax: 419-530-4526. E-mail: law0046@uoft01.utoledo.edu.

University of Toronto, Faculty of Law and School of Graduate Studies, Graduate Programs in Law, Toronto, ON M5S 1A1, Canada. Awards LL M, MSL, SJD. Faculty: 38. Students: 47 full-time (19 women); includes 15 international. 141 applicants, 38% accepted. In 1997, 12 master's, 2 doctorates awarded. *Degree requirements:* For master's, thesis (for some programs); for doctorate, dissertation. *Application fee:* $75. *Expenses:* Tuition $4070 per year for Canadian residents; $7870 per year for nonresidents. Fees $628 per year. *Financial aid:* Fellowships, research assistantships, teaching assistantships available. • Application contact: Admissions Office, 416-978-4337. Fax: 416-978-2648. E-mail: jk.hall@utoronto.ca.

University of Toronto, Faculty of Law, Professional Program in Law, Toronto, ON M5S 1A1, Canada. Awards LL B, LL B/MA, LL B/MBA, LL B/MSW, LL B/PhD. Faculty: 38 full-time (14 women), 72 part-time (20 women). Students: 530 full-time (238 women), 11 part-time (8 women). In 1997, 162 degrees awarded. *Entrance requirements:* LSAT. Application deadline: 11/2. Application fee: $150. *Financial aid:* Institutionally sponsored loans available. • Application contact: Ontario Law School Application Service, 519-823-1940. Fax: 519-823-5232. E-mail: olsas@netserv.ouac.on.ca.

University of Tulsa, College of Law, Tulsa, OK 74104-3189. Awards JD, JD/MA, JD/MBA, JD/MS, JD/M Acct, JD/M Tax. Approved by ABA. Member of AALS. Part-time programs available. Faculty: 37 full-time (14 women), 31 part-time (9 women). Students: 453 full-time (195 women), 132 part-time (60 women); includes 104 minority (21 African Americans, 12 Asian Americans, 17 Hispanics, 54 Native Americans), 7 international. Average age 27. 747 applicants, 78% accepted. In 1997, 195 degrees awarded. *Entrance requirements:* LSAT. Application deadline: 8/19 (priority date; rolling processing). Application fee: $30. Electronic applications accepted. *Financial aid:* Federal Work-Study available. Aid available to part-time students. Financial aid application deadline: 3/1; applicants required to submit FAFSA. • Martin H. Belsky, Dean, 918-631-2400. Fax: 918-631-3126. E-mail: martin-belsky@utulsa.edu. Application contact: Velda Staves, Director of Admissions, 918-631-2709. E-mail: velda-staves@utulsa.edu.

University of Utah, College of Law, Salt Lake City, UT 84112-1107. Awards JD, LL M, JD/MBA, JD/MPA. Approved by ABA. Member of AALS. Faculty: 29 full-time (10 women), 36 part-time (7 women). Students: 371 full-time (130 women); includes 45 minority (3 African Americans, 19 Asian Americans, 19 Hispanics, 4 Native Americans), 6 international. Average age 28. 727 applicants, 41% accepted. In 1997, 130 JDs, 10 master's awarded. *Entrance requirements:* For JD, LSAT (average 88th percentile), LSDAS. Application deadline: 2/1 (rolling processing). Application fee: $40. *Tuition:* $3333 per year for state residents; $7361 per year for nonresidents. *Financial aid:* In 1997–98, 298 students received aid, including 45 fellowships (18 to first-year students), 2 research assistantships; teaching assistantships, full tuition waivers, Federal Work-Study, institutionally sponsored loans, and career-related internships or fieldwork also available. Financial aid application deadline: 2/15; applicants required to submit FAFSA. *Faculty research:* Energy, environment, and natural resources law. • Lee E. Teitelbaum, Dean, 801-581-6571. Application contact: Reyes Aguilar, Assistant Dean for Admission and Financial Aid, 801-581-7479. Fax: 801-581-6897. E-mail: reyes.aguilar@law.utah.edu.

University of Victoria, Faculty of Law, Victoria, BC V8W 2Y2, Canada. Awards LL B, MBA/LL B, MPA/LL B. Part-time programs available. Faculty: 25 full-time (6 women), 30 part-time (11 women). Students: 340 full-time (168 women), 4 part-time (3 women); includes 83 minority (12 African Americans, 42 Asian Americans, 3 Hispanics, 26 Native Americans). Average age 27. 914 applicants, 26% accepted. In 1997, 108 degrees awarded. *Degree requirements:* Major paper required, foreign language and thesis not required. *Entrance requirements:* LSAT (average 164), minimum 3 years of full-time, or part-time equivalent, study leading toward a bachelor's degree. Application deadline: 3/31 (rolling processing). Application fee: $50. Electronic applications accepted. *Expenses:* Tuition $2896 per year full-time, $724 per semester part-time. Fees $235 per year. *Financial aid:* In 1997–98, scholarships, bursaries, awards totaling $220,000 were awarded; institutionally sponsored loans and career-related internships or fieldwork also available. Aid available to part-time students. *Faculty research:* Environmental law and policy, Asian-Pacific law, alternative dispute resolution, intellectual property law, legal history. • David Cohen, Dean, 250-721-8147. Fax: 250-472-7299. E-mail: lawdean@uvic.ca. Application contact: Neela Cumming, Admissions Assistant, 250-721-8191. Fax: 250-721-6390. E-mail: lawadmiss@uvic.ca.

University of Virginia, School of Law, Charlottesville, VA 22901. Awards JD, LL M, SJD, JD/MA, JD/MBA, JD/MS, JD/MP. Approved by ABA. Member of AALS. Faculty: 63 full-time (14 women), 3 part-time (1 woman), 64 FTE. Students: 1,145 full-time (419 women); includes 142 minority (83 African Americans, 45 Asian Americans, 10 Hispanics, 4 Native Americans), 18 international. Average age 25. 3,188 applicants, 31% accepted. In 1997, 397 JDs, 29 master's, 3 doctorates awarded. *Entrance requirements:* For JD, LSAT. Application deadline: 1/15 (priority date). Application fee: $40. *Tuition:* $14,606 per year for state residents; $20,706 per year for nonresidents. *Financial aid:* Fellowships, Federal Work-Study available. • Robert E. Scott, Dean, 804-924-7343. Application contact: Albert R. Turnbull, Associate Dean, 804-924-7351.

University of Washington, School of Law, Seattle, WA 98105. Awards JD, LL M, PhD, JD/MBA, JD/MPA, JD/MS, JD/PhD, JD/MAIS. Programs in Asian law (LL M, PhD), international environmental law (LL M), law (JD), law and marine affairs (LL M), law of sustainable international development (LL M), taxation (LL M). Approved by ABA. Member of AALS. Faculty: 47 full-time (19 women), 46 part-time (14 women). Students: 597 full-time (290 women), 52 part-time (28 women); includes 180 minority (16 African Americans, 100 Asian Americans, 46 Hispanics, 18 Native Americans), 38 international. Average age 25. 1,759 applicants, 27% accepted. In 1997, 177 JDs awarded; 60 master's awarded (10% entered university research/teaching, 90% found other work related to degree). *Degree requirements:* For master's and doctorate, thesis/dissertation required, foreign language not required. *Average time to degree:* master's–1 year full-time, 2 years part-time; first professional–3 years full-time. *Entrance requirements:* For JD, LSAT; for master's, TOEFL (minimum score 580), language proficiency (LL M in Asian law). Application deadline: 1/15. Application fee: $50. *Tuition:* $5763 per year for state residents; $14,169 per year for nonresidents. *Financial aid:* In 1997–98, 277 students received aid, including 3 fellowships, 6 research assistantships; partial tuition waivers, Federal Work-Study, institutionally sponsored loans, and career-related internships or fieldwork also available. Financial aid application deadline: 2/28; applicants required to submit FAFSA. *Faculty research:* History, culture and society. Total annual research expenditures: $1.457 million. • Roland L. Hjorth, Dean, 206-543-9476. Fax: 206-616-5305. E-mail: hjorth@u.washington.edu. Application contact: Sandra Madrid, Assistant Dean, 206-543-0199. Fax: 206-543-5671. E-mail: smadrid@u.washington.edu.

The University of Western Ontario, Faculty of Law, London, ON N6A 5B8, Canada. Awards LL B, Diploma, LL B/MBA. Faculty: 55. Students: 450 full-time (220 women). Average age 24. 2,031 applicants, 29% accepted. In 1997, 150 LL Bs awarded. *Entrance requirements:* For LL B, LSAT (minimum score 152; average 159), minimum B+ average. Application deadline: 11/1 (rolling processing). Application fee: $50. *Faculty research:* Taxation, administrative law, torts, drug and alcohol law and policy, property. • Prof. E. E. Gillese, Dean, 519-661-3346. Application contact: B. E. Theobald, Academic Services Officer, 519-661-3356.

University of West Los Angeles, School of Law, 1155 West Arbor Vitae Street, Inglewood, CA 90301-2902. Awards JD. Part-time and evening/weekend programs available. Faculty: 7 full-time (2 women), 30 part-time (6 women). Students: 109 full-time (35 women), 374 part-time (180 women); includes 221 minority (132 African Americans, 46 Asian Americans, 40

Hispanics, 3 Native Americans), 3 international. Average age 35. 178 applicants, 75% accepted. In 1997, 82 degrees awarded (100% found work related to degree). *Application deadline:* 7/15 (priority date; rolling processing). *Application fee:* $45. *Expenses:* Tuition $370 per unit. Fees $140 per semester. *Financial aid:* 416 students received aid; teaching assistantships and career-related internships or fieldwork available. Aid available to part-time students. Financial aid application deadline: 10/15; applicants required to submit FAFSA. • Benjamin Bycel, Acting Dean, 310-342-5200 Ext. 225. Fax: 310-342-5293. Application contact: Candy Suenaga, Director of Admissions, 310-342-5200 Ext. 209. Fax: 310-342-5295.

University of Wisconsin–Madison, Law School, Graduate Programs in Law, Madison, WI 53706-1380. Awards LL M, SJD. Member of AALS. Students: 30 full-time (7 women); includes 29 minority (3 African Americans, 1 Asian American, 9 Hispanics, 16 Native Americans), 1 international. Average age 27. 52 applicants, 48% accepted. In 1997, 15 master's, 6 doctorates awarded. *Application deadline:* 3/15 (rolling processing; 11/15 for spring admission). *Application fee:* $45. *Tuition:* $4653 per year full-time, $776 per semester (minimum) part-time for state residents; $12,231 per year full-time, $2039 per semester (minimum) part-time for nonresidents. *Financial aid:* In 1997–98, 4 fellowships were awarded; Federal Work-Study, institutionally sponsored loans, and career-related internships or fieldwork also available. Aid available to part-time students. Financial aid application deadline: 3/1. • Peter Carstensen, Chairperson, 608-262-9120.

University of Wisconsin–Madison, Law School, Professional Program in Law, Madison, WI 53706-1380. Awards JD. Approved by ABA. Member of AALS. Part-time programs available. Students: 748 full-time (345 women), 64 part-time (35 women); includes 177 minority (76 African Americans, 27 Asian Americans, 52 Hispanics, 22 Native Americans). Average age 25. 1,550 applicants, 38% accepted. In 1997, 267 degrees awarded. *Average time to degree:* first professional–3 years full-time, 4 years part-time. *Entrance requirements:* LSAT. Application deadline: 2/1 (rolling processing). Application fee: $45. *Tuition:* $4653 per year full-time, $776 per semester (minimum) part-time for state residents; $12,231 per year full-time, $2039 per semester (minimum) part-time for nonresidents. *Financial aid:* In 1997–98, 704 students received aid, including 48 fellowships (20 to first-year students) averaging $1,008 per month and totaling $435,456, 10 research assistantships averaging $1,216 per month and totaling $103,634, 12 teaching assistantships averaging $1,015 per month, 10 project assistantships averaging $636 per month; Federal Work-Study, institutionally sponsored loans, and career-related internships or fieldwork also available. Aid available to part-time students. Financial aid application deadline: 3/1; applicants required to submit FAFSA. • Application contact: Prof. William H. Clune, 608-262-5914.

University of Wyoming, College of Law, Laramie, WY 82071. Awards JD, JD/MPA. Approved by ABA. Member of AALS. Faculty: 15 full-time (5 women), 5 part-time (1 woman). Students: 209 full-time (92 women); includes 10 minority (1 African American, 7 Hispanics, 2 Native Americans). Average age 25. 559 applicants, 46% accepted. In 1997, 75 degrees awarded. *Average time to degree:* first professional–3 years full-time. *Entrance requirements:* LSAT. Application deadline: 4/1 (rolling processing). Application fee: $35. *Expenses:* Tuition $2430 per year full-time, $135 per credit hour part-time for state residents; $7518 per year full-time, $418 per credit hour part-time for nonresidents. Fees $386 per year full-time, $9.25 per credit hour part-time. *Financial aid:* In 1997–98, research assistantships totaling $11,205, 7 teaching assistantships averaging $2,300 per month were awarded; Federal Work-Study, institutionally sponsored loans, and career-related internships or fieldwork also available. Financial aid application deadline: 3/15; applicants required to submit FAFSA. *Faculty research:* Environmental, public land, constitutional,and securities law. • John M. Burman, Dean, 307-766-6416. Application contact: Debra J. Madsen, Associate Dean, 307-766-6416.

Valparaiso University, School of Law, Valparaiso, IN 46383-6493. Awards JD, LL M. Approved by ABA. Member of AALS. LL M new for fall 1998. Part-time programs available. Faculty: 25 full-time (7 women), 37 part-time (13 women). Students: 369 full-time (170 women), 38 part-time (19 women); includes 71 minority (44 African Americans, 8 Asian Americans, 15 Hispanics, 4 Native Americans), 4 international. Average age 26. 674 applicants, 59% accepted. In 1997, 146 JDs awarded. *Entrance requirements:* For JD, LSAT, TOEFL; for master's, TOEFL. Application deadline: 4/15 (priority date; rolling processing). Application fee: $30. Electronic applications accepted. *Expenses:* Tuition $17,100 per year full-time, $660 per credit hour part-time. Fees $480 per year full-time, $250 per year part-time. *Financial aid:* 358 students received aid; fellowships, research assistantships, teaching assistantships, partial tuition waivers, Federal Work-Study, institutionally sponsored loans, and career-related internships or fieldwork available. Financial aid application deadline: 5/1; applicants required to submit FAFSA. • Ivan E. Bodensteiner, Dean, 219-465-7834. Application contact: Heike Spahn, Director of Admissions and Student Relations, 219-465-7829. Fax: 219-465-7872. E-mail: heike.spahn@valpo.edu.

Vanderbilt University, School of Law, Nashville, TN 37240-1001. Awards JD, JD/MA, JD/MBA, JD/PhD, JD/M Div, JD/MTS. Approved by ABA. Member of AALS. Faculty: 30 full-time (7 women), 34 part-time (10 women). Students: 542 full-time (216 women); includes 91 minority (54 African Americans, 27 Asian Americans, 9 Hispanics, 1 Native American), 22 international. Average age 25. In 1997, 190 degrees awarded. *Degree requirements:* Thesis required, foreign language not required. *Entrance requirements:* LSAT. Application deadline: 2/1. Application fee: $50. *Financial aid:* Federal Work-Study, institutionally sponsored loans, and career-related internships or fieldwork available. Financial aid application deadline: 4/1; applicants required to submit FAFSA. • Kent D. Syverud, Dean, 615-322-2615. Application contact: Anne M. Brandt, Assistant Dean of Admissions, 615-322-6452.

Vermont Law School, Law School, Professional Program, Chelsea Street, PO Box 96, South Royalton, VT 05068-0096. Awards JD, JD/MSEL. Approved by ABA. Member of AALS. Students: 475 full-time (235 women); includes 32 minority (5 African Americans, 7 Asian Americans, 17 Hispanics, 3 Native Americans). Average age 27. 927 applicants, 64% accepted. In 1997, 150 degrees awarded. *Average time to degree:* first professional–3 years full-time. *Entrance requirements:* LSAT (score in 50th percentile or higher). Application deadline: 2/15 (priority date; rolling processing; 11/15 for spring admission). Application fee: $50. *Expenses:* Tuition $19,415 per year. Fees $75 per year. *Financial aid:* 428 students received aid; partial tuition waivers, Federal Work-Study, institutionally sponsored loans, and career-related internships or fieldwork available. Financial aid application deadline: 2/15; applicants required to submit FAFSA. • Application contact: Geoffrey R. Smith, Assistant Dean and Director of Admissions, 888-APPLYVLS. Fax: 802-763-7071. E-mail: admiss@vermontlaw.edu.

Villanova University, School of Law, Villanova, PA 19085-1699. Awards JD, LL M in Tax, JD/MBA, JD/PhD. Approved by ABA. Member of AALS. JD/PhD offered jointly with Allegheny University of the Health Sciences; LL M in Tax offered jointly with the College of Commerce and Finance. Faculty: 39 full-time (10 women), 68 part-time (18 women). Students: 697 full-time (324 women), 80 part-time (28 women); includes 111 minority (37 African Americans, 46 Asian Americans, 23 Hispanics, 5 Native Americans), 3 international. 1,282 applicants, 56% accepted. In 1997, 241 JDs, 33 master's awarded. *Average time to degree:* first professional–3 years full-time. *Entrance requirements:* For JD, LSAT (average 158). Application deadline: 3/1 (rolling processing). Application fee: $75. *Financial aid:* In 1997–98, 565 students received aid, including 107 research assistantships totaling $250,000, 6 teaching assistantships totaling $4,800; partial tuition waivers, Federal Work-Study, institutionally sponsored loans, and career-related internships or fieldwork also available. Aid available to part-time students. Financial aid application deadline: 3/15; applicants required to submit FAFSA. *Faculty research:* International law, bankruptcy, privacy/confidentiality, trial practice/evidence, computers and law. Total annual research expenditures: $340,000. • Mark A. Sargent, Dean, 610-519-7007. Fax: 610-519-6472. Application contact: David P. Pallozzi, Director of Admissions, 610-519-7010.

Wake Forest University, School of Law, Winston-Salem, NC 27109. Awards JD, LL M, JD/MBA. Approved by ABA. Member of AALS. LL M for foreign law graduates in American law. Faculty: 28 full-time, 38 part-time. Students: 460 full-time (180 women); includes 44 minority (34 African Americans, 6 Asian Americans, 2 Hispanics, 2 Native Americans), 2 international. Average age 25. 1,218 applicants, 42% accepted. In 1997, 155 JDs awarded. *Average time to degree:* first professional–3 years full-time. *Entrance requirements:* For JD, LSAT. Application deadline: 3/15 (rolling processing). Application fee: $60. *Tuition:* $20,450 per year. *Financial aid:* Scholarships, Federal Work-Study, institutionally sponsored loans, and career-related internships or fieldwork available. Financial aid application deadline: 4/30; applicants required to submit FAFSA. *Faculty research:* Constitutional law, family law, land use planning, torts, taxation, international law, corporations and bankruptcy, environmental law, criminal procedure, trial practice. • Robert K. Walsh, Dean, 336-759-5434. Fax: 336-759-4632. Application contact: Melanie E. Nutt, Director of Admissions and Financial Aid, 336-759-5437. Fax: 336-759-4632. E-mail: admissions@law.wfu.edu.

Washburn University of Topeka, School of Law, Topeka, KS 66621. Awards JD. Approved by ABA. Member of AALS. Part-time programs available. Faculty: 27 full-time (9 women), 31 part-time (7 women), 35 FTE. Students: 441 full-time (192 women); includes 49 minority (16 African Americans, 14 Asian Americans, 16 Hispanics, 3 Native Americans), 12 international. Average age 27. 649 applicants, 60% accepted. In 1997, 132 degrees awarded. *Average time to degree:* first professional–3 years full-time. *Entrance requirements:* LSAT (average 150). Application deadline: 3/15 (priority date; rolling processing; 9/15 for spring admission). Application fee: $30. *Financial aid:* In 1997–98, 397 students received aid, including 15 research assistantships averaging $389 per month and totaling $70,000, 7 teaching assistantships averaging $222 per month and totaling $14,000, 146 scholarships (40 to first-year students) totaling $468,730; Federal Work-Study, institutionally sponsored loans, and career-related internships or fieldwork also available. Aid available to part-time students. Financial aid application deadline: 3/1; applicants required to submit CSS PROFILE or FAFSA. *Faculty research:* Constitutional law, family law. • James M. Concannon, Dean, 785-231-1010 Ext. 1662. E-mail: zzconc@washburn.edu. Application contact: Janet K. Kerr, Director of Admissions, 785-231-1185. Fax: 785-232-8087. E-mail: zzkerr@washburn.edu.

Washington and Lee University, School of Law, Lexington, VA 24450-0303. Awards JD. Approved by ABA. Member of AALS. Faculty: 38 full-time (11 women), 16 part-time (0 women). Students: 367 full-time (149 women); includes 34 minority (15 African Americans, 13 Asian Americans, 3 Hispanics, 3 Native Americans), 1 international. 1,389 applicants, 36% accepted. In 1997, 118 degrees awarded. *Entrance requirements:* LSAT. Application deadline: 2/1 (priority date; rolling processing). Application fee: $40. *Expenses:* Tuition $17,470 per year. Fees $221 per year. *Financial aid:* 313 students received aid; fellowships, Federal Work-Study, institutionally sponsored loans, and career-related internships or fieldwork available. Financial aid application deadline: 2/15; applicants required to submit FAFSA. • Barry Sullivan, Dean, 540-463-8502. Application contact: Susan Palmer, Assistant Dean, 540-463-8503.

Washington University in St. Louis, School of Law, St. Louis, MO 63130-4899. Awards JD, LL M, MJS, JSD, JD/MA, JD/MBA, JD/MSW, JD/PhD, JD/MHA. Approved by ABA. Member of AALS. Faculty: 44 full-time (16 women), 68 part-time (15 women). Students: 647 full-time (255 women), 18 part-time (5 women); includes 117 minority (61 African Americans, 44 Asian Americans, 6 Hispanics, 6 Native Americans), 6 international. Average age 24. 1,357 applicants, 56% accepted. In 1997, 188 JDs, 12 master's, 1 doctorate awarded. Terminal master's awarded for partial completion of doctoral program. *Entrance requirements:* For JD, LSAT. Application deadline: 3/1 (priority date; rolling processing). Application fee: $50. Electronic applications accepted. *Tuition:* $23,080 per year. *Financial aid:* Federal Work-Study, institutionally sponsored loans, and career-related internships or fieldwork available. Aid available to part-time students. Financial aid application deadline: 3/1; applicants required to submit FAFSA. *Faculty research:* International law, environmental law, employment discrimination, reproductive rights, bankruptcy and white-collar crime. • Dorsey D. Ellis Jr., Dean, 314-935-6400. Application contact: Janet Bolin, Director of Admissions, 314-935-4525. Fax: 314-935-6959. E-mail: admiss@wulaw.wustl.edu.

See in-depth description on page 1607.

Wayne State University, Law School, Detroit, MI 48202. Awards JD, LL M, JD/MA, JD/MBA. Approved by ABA. Member of AALS. Part-time and evening/weekend programs available. Faculty: 43. Students: 693 full-time (320 women), 149 part-time (58 women); includes 128 minority (90 African Americans, 4 Asian Americans, 20 Hispanics, 14 Native Americans). 1,102 applicants, 55% accepted. In 1997, 233 JDs, 41 master's awarded. *Degree requirements:* For master's, thesis, minimum GPA of 3.0 required, foreign language not required. *Entrance requirements:* For JD, LSAT; for master's, TOEFL (minimum score 600), JD. Application deadline: 4/15. Application fee: $20 ($30 for international students). *Expenses:* Tuition $237 per credit hour for state residents; $508 per credit hour for nonresidents. Fees $498 per year full-time, $114 per semester (minimum) part-time. *Financial aid:* Federal Work-Study available. Aid available to part-time students. • James K. Robinson, Dean, 313-577-3933. Application contact: Dr. John Friedl, Director of Graduate Studies, 313-577-3947. Fax: 313-577-1060. E-mail: jfriedl@cms.cc.wayne.edu.

See in-depth description on page 1609.

Western New England College, School of Law, Springfield, MA 01119-2654. Awards JD. Approved by ABA. Member of AALS. Part-time and evening/weekend programs available. Faculty: 19 full-time (6 women), 37 part-time (15 women). Students: 379 full-time (182 women), 255 part-time (126 women). Average age 30. 1,406 applicants, 63% accepted. In 1997, 218 degrees awarded. *Average time to degree:* first professional–3 years full-time, 4 years part-time. *Entrance requirements:* LSAT (average 152). Application deadline: 3/15 (priority date; rolling processing). Application fee: $35. *Financial aid:* Merit scholarships, Federal Work-Study, institutionally sponsored loans, and career-related internships or fieldwork available. Aid available to part-time students. Financial aid application deadline: 4/1; applicants required to submit FAFSA. *Faculty research:* Family law, environmental law. • Donald J. Dunn, Interim Dean, 413-782-1412. Application contact: Victoria Dutcher, Assistant Dean and Director of Admissions, 413-782-1406.

Western State University College of Law, Professional Program, Fullerton, CA 92831-3014. Awards JD. Approved by ABA. Part-time and evening/weekend programs available. Faculty: 29 full-time (11 women), 42 part-time (6 women), 43 FTE. Students: 253 full-time (105 women), 641 part-time (283 women); includes 296 minority (59 African Americans, 126 Asian Americans, 103 Hispanics, 8 Native Americans). Average age 32. 288 applicants, 59% accepted. In 1997, 293 degrees awarded (100% found work related to degree). *Average time to degree:* first professional–3 years full-time, 4 years part-time. *Entrance requirements:* LSAT. Application deadline: rolling. Application fee: $35. *Expenses:* Tuition $9400 per semester full-time, $6250 per semester part-time. Fees $50 per semester. *Financial aid:* 760 students received aid; fellowships, research assistantships, teaching assistantships, scholarships, full and partial tuition waivers, Federal Work-Study, institutionally sponsored loans, and career-related internships or fieldwork available. Aid available to part-time students. Financial aid applicants required to submit FAFSA. *Faculty research:* Intellectual property and entertainment law, affirmative action and civil rights, immigration and international law, contract and sales law, California law reform. • Dennis R. Honabach, Dean, 714-738-1000 Ext. 2900. E-mail: dennish@wsulaw.edu. Application contact: Joel H. Goodman, Dean of Admissions, 714-738-1000 Ext. 2911. Fax: 714-526-1062. E-mail: adm@wsulaw.edu.

Announcement: Western State University (WSU) College of Law, founded in 1966, is a dynamic presence in southern California. The College's alumni are prominent in the legal community. Students may intern with respected jurists, prosecutors, public defenders, and civil practitioners. WSU offers full-time and part-time day and evening programs. Students may choose from spring and fall entering classes.

See in-depth description on page 1611.

West Virginia University, College of Law, Morgantown, WV 26506. Awards JD, JD/MBA, JD/MPA. Approved by ABA. Member of AALS. Part-time programs available. Faculty: 23 full-time (8 women), 15 part-time (4 women). Students: 420 full-time (192 women), 18 part-

Directories: Law; Legal and Justice Studies

West Virginia University (continued)

time (10 women); includes 18 minority (9 African Americans, 4 Asian Americans, 4 Hispanics, 1 Native American), 1 international. Average age 27. 511 applicants, 50% accepted. In 1997, 138 degrees awarded (100% found work related to degree). *Average time to degree:* first professional–3 years full-time, 5 years part-time. *Entrance requirements:* LSAT (average 157), TOEFL (minimum score 600). Application deadline: 3/1 (rolling processing). Application fee: $45. *Tuition:* $5476 per year for state residents; $12,748 per year for nonresidents. *Financial aid:* In 1997–98, 355 students received aid, including 6 fellowships (3 to first-year students) averaging $1,111 per month, 1 teaching assistantship, 7 graduate administrative assistantships, graduate resident assistantships averaging $566 per month; full tuition waivers, Federal Work-Study, institutionally sponsored loans, and career-related internships or fieldwork also available. Aid available to part-time students. Financial aid application deadline: 3/1. *Faculty research:* Energy law and policy, ethics, constitutional law, tort law, public interest law. • John W. Fisher II, Interim Dean, 304-293-3199. E-mail: jfisher4@wvu.edu. Application contact: Janet Long Armistead, Assistant Dean for Admissions and Student Affairs, 304-293-5304. Fax: 304-293-6891.

Announcement: West Virginia University, a land-grant, Doctoral I institution, established the College of Law in 1878. WVU is exceptional in its broad skills curriculum, which exposes all students to interviewing, counseling, drafting, negotiation, and trial and appellate advocacy. WVU is on the forefront of computer technology in classrooms and in the library. A journal of law and technology is published exclusively on the Internet. Student organizations provide a wide range of academic experiences beyond the classroom, including a nationally recognized law review, an active moot court program, and 2 intensive clinics providing live-client experiences.

Whittier College, School of Law, 3333 Harbor Boulevard, Costa Mesa, CA 92626. Awards JD. Approved by ABA. Member of AALS. Part-time and evening/weekend programs available. Faculty: 28 full-time (12 women), 12 part-time (1 woman). Students: 369 full-time (190 women), 266 part-time (125 women); includes 237 minority (40 African Americans, 93 Asian Americans, 100 Hispanics, 4 Native Americans). Average age 26. 1,743 applicants, 63% accepted. In 1997, 188 degrees awarded. *Entrance requirements:* LSAT (average 151). Application deadline: 3/15 (priority date; rolling processing; 11/1 for spring admission). Application fee: $50. *Financial aid:* In 1997–98, 574 students received aid, including 11 research assistantships, 44 teaching assistantships; Federal Work-Study and career-related internships or fieldwork also available. Aid available to part-time students. Financial aid application deadline: 6/1; applicants required to submit FAFSA. *Total annual research expenditures:* $120,225. • John A. Fitzrandolph, Dean, 714-444-4141. Fax: 714-444-0855.

Widener University, Widener University School of Law, Wilmington, DE 19803. Awards JD, LL M, JD/MBA, JD/Psy D. Approved by ABA. Member of AALS. Part-time programs available. Faculty: 81 full-time (34 women), 83 part-time (24 women). Students: 1,064 full-time (482 women), 644 part-time (260 women); includes 104 minority (57 African Americans, 26 Asian Americans, 15 Hispanics, 6 Native Americans). Average age 26. 1,963 applicants, 72% accepted. In 1997, 549 JDs awarded. *Entrance requirements:* For JD, LSAT. Application deadline: 5/15 (rolling processing). Application fee: $60. *Financial aid:* Fellowships, research assistantships, Federal Work-Study, institutionally sponsored loans, and career-related internships or fieldwork available. Aid available to part-time students. Financial aid application deadline: 2/15. *Faculty research:* Health law, toxic torts, constitutional law, intellectual property, corporate law. Total annual research expenditures: $125,000. • Dr. Arthur Frakt, Dean, 302-477-2100. Application contact: Barbara L. Ayars, Assistant Dean of Admissions, 302-477-2210. Fax: 302-477-2224. E-mail: barbara.l.ayars@law.widener.edu.

See in-depth description on page 1613.

Widener University, School of Human Service Professions, Institute for Graduate Clinical Psychology, Law-Psychology Program, Chester, PA 19013-5792. Awards JD/Psy D. Faculty: 15 full-time (6 women), 120 part-time (37 women). Students: 13 full-time (10 women); includes 2 minority (both African Americans). *Average time to degree:* doctorate–6 years full-time. *Application deadline:* 2/1 (rolling processing). *Application fee:* $60. *Tuition:* $14,300 per year full-time, $595 per credit hour part-time. *Financial aid:* Federal Work-Study, institutionally sponsored loans, and career-related internships or fieldwork available. Financial aid application deadline: 5/31. • Dr. Amiram Elwork, Director, 610-499-1206.

Willamette University, College of Law, Salem, OR 97301-3931. Awards JD, JD/MM. Approved by ABA. Member of AALS. Part-time programs available. Faculty: 27 full-time (9 women), 21 part-time (9 women), 31.2 FTE. Students: 398 full-time (189 women), 5 part-time (3 women); includes 41 minority (8 African Americans, 21 Asian Americans, 9 Hispanics, 3 Native Americans), 7 international. Average age 26. 778 applicants, 74% accepted. In 1997, 174 degrees awarded. *Degree requirements:* Thesis required, foreign language not required. *Average time to degree:* first professional–3 years full-time. *Entrance requirements:* LSAT (median 154), median GPA of 3.24. Application deadline: 4/1 (rolling processing). Application fee: $50. *Financial aid:* 137 students received aid; research assistantships, full and partial tuition waivers, Federal Work-Study, and career-related internships or fieldwork available. Financial aid applicants required to submit FAFSA. *Faculty research:* Labor law, dispute resolution, environmental law, tax law, commercial law, law and government. Total annual research expenditures: $72,500. • Robert M. Ackerman, Dean, 503-370-6402. E-mail: rackerma@willamette.edu. Application contact: Lawrence Seno Jr., Director of Admission, 503-370-6282. Fax: 503-370-6375. E-mail: lseno@willamette.edu.

See in-depth description on page 1615.

William Mitchell College of Law, St. Paul, MN 55105-3076. Awards JD, LL M. Approved by ABA. Member of AALS. Part-time and evening/weekend programs available. Faculty: 31 full-time (8 women), 86 part-time (19 women). Students: 508 full-time (245 women), 545 part-time (246 women); includes 108 minority (40 African Americans, 41 Asian Americans, 15 Hispanics, 12 Native Americans), 6 international. Average age 30. 937 applicants, 74% accepted. In 1997, 305 JDs, 12 master's awarded. *Degree requirements:* For JD, paper required, foreign language and thesis not required. *Entrance requirements:* For JD, LSAT (median 152); for master's, JD. Application deadline: 7/1 (rolling processing). Application fee: $45. *Expenses:* Tuition $17,226 per year full-time, $12,508 per year part-time. Fees $30 per year. *Financial aid:* In 1997–98, 926 students received aid, including research assistantships totaling $140,920, scholarships totaling $777,790; Federal Work-Study and career-related internships or fieldwork also available. Aid available to part-time students. Financial aid application deadline: 3/15; applicants required to submit FAFSA. *Faculty research:* Employment contracts, academic freedom, technology contracts, redrafting uniform limited partnership statute, use of arbitration and mediation to solve disputes domestically and internatonally. • Harry J. Haynsworth, President and Dean, 612-290-6310. Fax: 612-290-6426. Application contact: James H. Brooks Jr., Dean of Students, 612-290-6362. Fax: 612-290-6414. E-mail: admissions@wmitchell.edu.

Yale University, Law School, PO Box 208329, New Haven, CT 06520-8329. Awards JD, LL M, MSL, JSD, JD/MA, JD/PhD, JD/MAR, JD/MD, JD/MES, JD/MFS, JD/MPPM. Approved by ABA. Member of AALS. Faculty: 68 full-time (14 women), 25 part-time (7 women). Students: 619 full-time (264 women). Average age 24. 3,575 applicants, 9% accepted. In 1997, 219 JDs, 30 master's awarded. *Entrance requirements:* For JD, LSAT; for master's, TOEFL. Application deadline: 2/15 (rolling processing). Application fee: $65. *Financial aid:* Fellowships available. Financial aid application deadline: 3/15; applicants required to submit FAFSA. • Anthony T. Kronman, Dean, 203-432-1660. Application contact: Jean Webb, Director of Admissions, 203-432-4995. E-mail: admissions@mail.law.yale.edu.

Yeshiva University, Benjamin N. Cardozo School of Law, New York, NY 10003. Awards JD. Approved by ABA. Member of AALS. Faculty: 43 full-time (13 women), 89 part-time (24 women). Students: 916 full-time (431 women); includes 180 minority (52 African Americans, 75 Asian Americans, 50 Hispanics, 3 Native Americans), 29 international. Average age 23. 2,330 applicants, 46% accepted. In 1997, 340 degrees awarded. *Entrance requirements:* LSAT. Application deadline: 4/1 (priority date; rolling processing; 12/1 for spring admission). Application fee: $60. *Expenses:* Tuition $21,760 per year full-time, $985 per credit part-time. Fees $270 per year. *Financial aid:* In 1997–98, 536 students received aid, including 50 research assistantships; Federal Work-Study, institutionally sponsored loans, and career-related internships or fieldwork also available. Financial aid application deadline: 4/15; applicants required to submit FAFSA. *Faculty research:* Arts and entertainment, corporate, criminal, and international law; intellectual property. • Paul Verkuil, Dean, 212-790-0310. Fax: 212-790-0203. Application contact: Robert L. Schwartz, Director of Admissions, 212-790-0274. Fax: 212-790-0482. E-mail: robschwa@ymail.yu.edu.

York University, Osgoode Hall Law School, Toronto, ON M3J 1P3, Canada. Awards LL B, LL M, D Jur, MBA/LL B, MES/LL B, MPA/LL B. Part-time and evening/weekend programs available. *Degree requirements:* For master's and doctorate, thesis/dissertation required, foreign language not required. *Entrance requirements:* For LL B, LSAT. Application deadline: 2/1. Application fee: $60.

Legal and Justice Studies

American University, Washington College of Law, Program in International Legal Studies, Washington, DC 20016-8001. Awards LL M. Part-time and evening/weekend programs available. Faculty: 51 full-time (17 women), 95 part-time (27 women). Students: 45 full-time (21 women), 134 part-time (48 women); includes 2 minority (both Hispanics), 163 international. 387 applicants, 55% accepted. In 1997, 116 degrees awarded. *Entrance requirements:* TOEFL, JD. Application deadline: 6/1 (priority date; rolling processing). Application fee: $55. *Expenses:* Tuition $22,590 per year full-time, $837 per credit part-time. Fees $382 per year full-time, $242 per year part-time. *Financial aid:* Dean's fellowships, partial tuition waivers, and career-related internships or fieldwork available. Financial aid application deadline: 2/15. • Daniel D. Bradlow, Director, 202-274-4110.

American University, Washington College of Law, Program in Law and Government, Washington, DC 20016-8001. Awards LL M. *Entrance requirements:* TOEFL, JD. Application fee: $55. *Expenses:* Tuition $22,590 per year full-time, $837 per credit part-time. Fees $382 per year full-time, $242 per year part-time. *Financial aid:* Application deadline 2/15. • Jamin Raskin, Co-Director, 202-274-4268. Application contact: Sandra J. Oakman, Director of Admissions, 202-274-4101.

Arizona State University, Interdisciplinary Program in Justice Studies, Tempe, AZ 85287. Awards PhD, JD/PhD. *Application fee:* $45. *Expenses:* Tuition $2088 per year full-time, $110 per hour part-time for state residents; $9040 per year full-time, $377 per hour part-time for nonresidents. Fees $72 per year full-time, $18 per semester (minimum) part-time. • Dr. Marjorie Zata, Director, 602-965-6008.

Arizona State University, College of Public Programs, School of Justice Studies, Tempe, AZ 85287-0403. Awards MS, MA/MS. MA/MS offered jointly with Department of Anthropology. Faculty: 20 full-time (10 women). Students: 32 full-time (23 women), 31 part-time (15 women); includes 13 minority (4 African Americans, 8 Hispanics, 1 Native American), 4 international. Average age 35. 86 applicants, 31% accepted. In 1997, 9 degrees awarded. *Degree requirements:* Thesis optional. *Entrance requirements:* GRE, TOEFL. Application deadline: 3/15. Application fee: $45. *Expenses:* Tuition $2088 per year full-time, $110 per hour part-time for state residents; $9040 per year full-time, $377 per hour part-time for nonresidents. Fees $72 per year full-time, $18 per semester (minimum) part-time. *Financial aid:* Research assistantships, teaching assistantships, full tuition waivers available. *Faculty research:* White-collar crime, female criminality, comparative legal systems, corrections, criminological theory. • David Goldberg, Director, 602-965-7682.

Boston University, School of Medicine, School of Public Health, Health Law Department, Boston, MA 02215. Awards MPH. Students: 13 full-time (11 women), 22 part-time (12 women); includes 4 minority (1 Asian American, 3 Hispanics), 1 international. Average age 32. *Entrance requirements:* GRE General Test, TOEFL. Application deadline: 4/15 (rolling processing; 10/25 for spring admission). Application fee: $50. *Financial aid:* Federal Work-Study, institutionally sponsored loans, and career-related internships or fieldwork available. Aid available to part-time students. • George J. Annas, Chairman, 617-638-4625. Application contact: Barbara St. Onge, Director of Admissions, 617-638-4640. Fax: 617-638-5299. E-mail: sphadmis@bu.edu.

See in-depth description on page 1487.

Carleton University, Faculty of Social Sciences, Department of Law, Ottawa, ON K1S 5B6, Canada. Offers program in legal studies (MA). *Degree requirements:* Thesis. *Entrance requirements:* TOEFL (minimum score 550), honors degree. Application deadline: 3/1 (priority date; rolling processing). Application fee: $35. *Faculty research:* Legal and social theory; women, law, and gender relations; law, crime, and social order; political economy of law; international law.

Case Western Reserve University, School of Law, Cleveland, OH 44106. Offerings include U.S. legal studies (LL M). School faculty: 41 full-time (10 women), 59 part-time (13 women). *Entrance requirements:* TOEFL. Application deadline: 4/1 (priority date; rolling processing). Application fee: $40. *Expenses:* Tuition $20,500 per year full-time, $854 per credit hour part-time. Fees $600 per year. • Gerald Korngold, Dean, 216-368-3283. Application contact: Barbara F. Andelman, Assistant Dean for Admissions and Financial Aid, 216-368-3600. Fax: 216-368-6144. E-mail: lawadmissions@po.cwru.edu.

The Catholic University of America, School of Religious Studies, Department of Canon Law, Washington, DC 20064. Awards JCD, JCL, JD/JCL. Part-time programs available. Faculty: 7 full-time (1 woman). Students: 32 full-time (6 women), 13 part-time (2 women); includes 2 minority (1 Asian American, 1 Hispanic), 6 international. Average age 39. 20 applicants, 90% accepted. In 1997, 4 doctorates, 27 JCLs awarded. *Degree requirements:* For doctorate, 2 foreign languages, dissertation, comprehensive exam; for JCL, 1 foreign language, thesis, oral comprehensive exam. *Entrance requirements:* For doctorate, GRE, Latin test; for JCL, GRE, MA in theology or equivalent. Application deadline: 8/1 (priority date; rolling processing; 11/1 for spring admission). Application fee: $50. *Expenses:* Tuition $17,325 per year full-time, $668 per credit hour part-time. Fees $680 per year full-time, $360 per year part-time. *Financial aid:* Fellowships, full and partial tuition waivers, Federal Work-Study, institutionally sponsored loans, and career-related internships or fieldwork available. Aid available to part-time students. Financial aid application deadline: 2/1. *Faculty research:* Advocacy rights, rotal jurisprudence, church property, church-state relations. • Dr. James H. Provost, Chairperson, 202-319-5492. Fax: 202-319-4187.

Denver Paralegal Institute, Paralegal Program, Denver, CO 80202. Awards Paralegal Certificate. Evening/weekend programs available. Faculty: 30 part-time (17 women). Students: 260 full-time (188 women), 21 part-time (18 women); includes 35 minority (15 African Americans, 4 Asian Americans, 13 Hispanics, 3 Native Americans). Average age 32. 283 applicants, 99% accepted. In 1997, 262 degrees awarded. *Average time to degree:* other advanced degree–.5 years full-time, 1.7 years part-time. *Application deadline:* rolling. *Application fee:* $150. *Tuition:* $7350 per year full-time, $6250 per year part-time. *Financial aid:* Career-related internships or fieldwork available. Aid available to part-time students. Financial aid applicants required to submit FAFSA. • Betsy O'Neil Covington, Director, 303-295-0550. E-mail: bcovington@paralegal-education.com. Application contact: Grant Fleming, Director of Admissions, 303-295-0550. Fax: 303-295-0102. E-mail: gfleming@paralegal-education.com.

DePaul University, College of Liberal Arts and Sciences, Programs in Public Services, Program in Health Law and Policy, Chicago, IL 60604-2287. Awards MS. Students: 7 full-time (5 women), 8 part-time (7 women); includes 5 minority (2 African Americans, 3 Asian Americans). Average age 35. 12 applicants, 83% accepted. In 1997, 2 degrees awarded. *Degree requirements:* Practicum or thesis required, foreign language not required. *Entrance requirements:* Minimum GPA of 3.0, experience in related field, interview. Application deadline: 7/1 (rolling processing; 1/20 for spring admission). Application fee: $25. *Expenses:* Tuition $320 per credit hour. Fees $30 per year. *Financial aid:* In 1997–98, 2 research assistantships (1 to a first-year student) averaging $500 per month and totaling $10,000 were awarded; partial tuition waivers also available. Financial aid application deadline: 7/1. *Faculty research:* Physicians in group practice, nonprofit organizations, community policing. Total annual research expenditures: $90,000. • Application contact: Graduate Information, 312-362-5367. Fax: 312-362-5749.

See in-depth description on page 619.

Golden Gate University, School of Law, San Francisco, CA 94105-2968. Offerings include environmental law (LL M), international legal studies (LL M, SJD), U.S. legal studies (LL M). School faculty: 35 full-time (13 women), 89 part-time (37 women). *Average time to degree:* first professional–3 years full-time, 4 years part-time. *Application deadline:* 4/15 (priority date; rolling processing; 11/15 for spring admission). *Application fee:* $40. *Expenses:* Tuition $19,981 per year full-time, $13,780 per year part-time. Fees $224 per year. • Anthony J. Pagano, Dean, 415-442-6600. Fax: 415-442-6609. Application contact: Cherie Scricca, Assistant Dean of Admissions, 415-442-6630. Fax: 415-442-6631. E-mail: lawadmit@ggu.edu.

See in-depth description on page 1583.

Governors State University, College of Arts and Sciences, Division of Liberal Arts, Program in Political and Justice Studies, University Park, IL 60466. Awards MA. Part-time and evening/weekend programs available. Faculty: 3 full-time (2 women). Average age 34. In 1997, 14 degrees awarded. *Degree requirements:* Thesis or alternative required, foreign language not required. *Entrance requirements:* Bachelor's degree in related field. Application deadline: 7/15 (priority date; rolling processing; 11/10 for spring admission). Application fee: $0. *Expenses:* Tuition $1140 per trimester full-time, $95 per credit hour part-time for state residents; $3420 per trimester full-time, $285 per credit hour part-time for nonresidents. Fees $95 per trimester. *Financial aid:* Research assistantships, scholarships, Federal Work-Study, institutionally sponsored loans available. Aid available to part-time students. Financial aid application deadline: 5/1. • Dr. Sonny Goldenstein, Chairperson, Division of Liberal Arts, 708-534-4010.

John Jay College of Criminal Justice, the City University of New York, Programs in Criminal Justice, New York, NY 10019-1093. Offerings include law and philosophy (PhD). Terminal master's awarded for partial completion of doctoral program. Faculty: 17 full-time, 6 part-time. *Degree requirements:* 1 foreign language (computer language can substitute), dissertation. *Entrance requirements:* GRE General Test, TOEFL. Application deadline: 6/30 (priority date; rolling processing; 12/1 for spring admission). Application fee: $40. *Expenses:* Tuition $4350 per year full-time, $185 per credit part-time for state residents; $7600 per year full-time, $320 per credit part-time for nonresidents. Fees $63 per year. • Dr. William Heffernan, Co-Program Director, 212-237-8376. Application contact: Dr. Barry Spunt, Co-Program Director, 212-237-8677. Fax: 212-237-8309.

John Marshall Law School, Chicago, IL 60604-3968. Offerings include comparative legal studies (LL M). School faculty: 52 full-time (14 women), 230 part-time (43 women). *Average time to degree:* master's–1.5 years full-time, 2 years part-time; first professional–3 years full-time, 4 years part-time. *Application deadline:* 3/1 (priority date; rolling processing; 10/1 for spring admission). *Application fee:* $50 ($60 for international students). *Expenses:* Tuition $675 per credit (minimum). Fees $40 per semester. • Robert Gilbert Johnson, Dean, 312-427-2737. Application contact: William B. Powers, Dean of Admission and Student Affairs, 312-987-1403. Fax: 312-427-5136. E-mail: 6alonzo@jmls.edu.

Marymount University, School of Business Administration, Program in Legal Administration, Arlington, VA 22207-4299. Awards MA. Part-time and evening/weekend programs available. Students: 28. In 1997, 5 degrees awarded. *Degree requirements:* Thesis optional, foreign language not required. *Entrance requirements:* GMAT or GRE General Test, interview. Application deadline: rolling. Application fee: $35. *Expenses:* Tuition $465 per credit hour. Fees $120 per year full-time, $5 per credit hour part-time. *Financial aid:* Career-related internships or fieldwork available. Aid available to part-time students. Financial aid applicants required to submit FAFSA. • Dr. Donald Lavanty, Chair, 703-284-5910. Fax: 703-527-3815.

Montclair State University, College of Humanities and Social Sciences, Department of Legal Studies, Upper Montclair, NJ 07043-1624. Offers programs in dispute resolution (MA), law office management and technology (MA). Faculty: 5 full-time, 1 part-time. Students: 4 full-time (3 women), 23 part-time (21 women); includes 1 minority (African American). *Entrance requirements:* GRE General Test. Application deadline: 4/1 (rolling processing; 11/1 for spring admission). Application fee: $40. *Expenses:* Tuition $201 per credit for state residents; $257 per credit for nonresidents. Fees $22.05 per credit. *Financial aid:* Application deadline 3/1. • Dr. Marilyn Tayler, Chair, 973-655-4152.

New York University, Graduate School of Arts and Science and School of Law, Institute for Law and Society, New York, NY 10012-1019. Awards PhD, JD/MA, JD/PhD. Faculty: 2 full-time (1 woman). Students: 4 full-time (2 women); includes 1 minority (Asian American). Average age 27. 25 applicants, 48% accepted. *Degree requirements:* 1 foreign language, dissertation. *Entrance requirements:* GRE, TOEFL. Application deadline: 1/4. Application fee: $60. *Expenses:* Tuition $715 per credit. Fees $1048 per year full-time, $229 per semester (minimum) part-time. *Financial aid:* Federal Work-Study, institutionally sponsored loans, and career-related internships or fieldwork available. Financial aid application deadline: 1/4; applicants required to submit FAFSA. *Faculty research:* Politics of law, law and social policy, law in comparative global perspective, rights and social movements. • Paul Chevigny, Director, 212-998-8536. Fax: 212-995-4034. E-mail: lawsoc@turing.law.nyu.edu.

Northeastern University, Graduate School of Arts and Sciences, Program in Law, Policy, and Society, Boston, MA 02115-5096. Awards MS, PhD, JD/MS, JD/PhD. Part-time and evening/weekend programs available. Faculty: 102 full-time (41 women). Students: 34 full-time (18 women), 42 part-time (21 women). Average age 42. 59 applicants, 56% accepted. In 1997, 5 doctorates awarded (80% entered university research/teaching, 20% found other work related to degree). *Degree requirements:* For master's, comprehensive exam required, thesis not required; for doctorate, dissertation, comprehensive exams required, foreign language not required. *Entrance requirements:* For master's, GRE General Test or LSAT, JD or LL B; for doctorate, GRE General Test or LSAT. Application deadline: 2/15. Application fee: $50. *Expenses:* Tuition $440 per credit hour. Fees $55 per quarter full-time, $13.25 per quarter part-time. *Financial aid:* In 1997–98, 15 fellowships, 4 research assistantships (2 to first-year students) averaging $910 per month and totaling $37,000, 2 teaching assistantships (both to first-year students) averaging $910 per month were awarded; tuition assistantships, full and partial tuition waivers also available. Financial aid application deadline: 2/15. *Faculty research:* Policy issues in health, crime, and labor; urban studies; education; law and environmental issues; economic development, international trade and law. • Suzann Thomas-Buckle, Co-Director, 617-373-4689. E-mail: sbuckle@lynx.neu.edu. Application contact: Jeanne Winner, Secretary, 617-373-2891. Fax: 617-373-4691. E-mail: jwinner@lynx.neu.edu.

Rutgers, The State University of New Jersey, New Brunswick, Program in Political Science, New Brunswick, NJ 08903. Offerings include public law (PhD). Terminal master's awarded for partial completion of doctoral program. Program faculty: 36 full-time (8 women). *Degree requirements:* 1 foreign language, dissertation. *Entrance requirements:* GRE General Test. Application deadline: 3/1 (rolling processing). Application fee: $40. *Expenses:* Tuition $6492 per year full-time, $268 per credit part-time for state residents; $9520 per year full-time, $395 per credit part-time for nonresidents. Fees $208 per year (minimum). • Dennis Bathory, Vice Chair, 732-932-9321.

Temple University, School of Business and Management, Master's Program in Business Administration, Philadelphia, PA 19122-6096. Offerings include legal studies (MBA). Program faculty: 72 full-time (13 women). *Application fee:* $40. *Expenses:* Tuition $323 per semester hour for state residents; $444 per semester hour for nonresidents. Fees $170 per year full-time, $28 per semester (minimum) part-time. • Application contact: Linda Whelan, Director, 215-204-7678. Fax: 215-204-8300. E-mail: linda@astro.ocis.temple.edu.

University of Baltimore, College of Liberal Arts, Department of History and Philosophy, Baltimore, MD 21201-5779. Offers program in legal and ethical studies (MA). Part-time and evening/weekend programs available. Faculty: 9 full-time (2 women), 6 part-time (2 women). Students: 22 full-time (14 women), 67 part-time (37 women); includes 43 minority (40 African Americans, 1 Asian American, 1 Hispanic, 1 Native American), 4 international. Average age 37. 35 applicants, 86% accepted. In 1997, 25 degrees awarded. *Average time to degree:* master's–2 years full-time. *Application deadline:* 7/15 (priority date; rolling processing; 11/15 for spring admission). *Application fee:* $30. *Expenses:* Tuition $5592 per year full-time, $233 per credit part-time for state residents; $8544 per year full-time, $356 per credit part-time for nonresidents. Fees $550 per year full-time, $208 per semester (minimum) part-time. *Financial aid:* In 1997–98, 5 research assistantships (1 to a first-year student) were awarded; fellowships, Federal Work-Study, and career-related internships or fieldwork also available. Aid available to part-time students. Financial aid application deadline: 4/1; applicants required to submit FAFSA. *Faculty research:* Morality in law and economics, religion and gender in law making, comparative legal history, law and social change. • Dr. Donald Mulcahey, Director, Program in Legal and Ethical Studies, 410-837-5320. E-mail: dmulcahey@ubmail.ubalt.edu. Application contact: Tracey Jamison, Assistant Director of Admissions, 410-837-4809. Fax: 410-837-4793. E-mail: admissions@ubmail.ubalt.edu.

University of California, Berkeley, Boalt Hall School of Law, Graduate Program in Jurisprudence and Social Policy, Berkeley, CA 94720-1500. Awards PhD. Faculty: 12 full-time (2 women), 9 part-time (1 woman). Students: 35 full-time (20 women); includes 6 minority (1 African American, 4 Asian Americans, 1 Hispanic). 67 applicants, 18% accepted. In 1997, 5 degrees awarded. *Degree requirements:* 1 foreign language, dissertation, oral qualifying exam. *Average time to degree:* doctorate–6 years full-time. *Entrance requirements:* GRE General Test, sample of written work. Application deadline: 1/5. Application fee: $40. *Expenses:* Tuition $0 for state residents; $9384 per year for nonresidents. Fees $10,815 per year. *Financial aid:* Fellowships, research assistantships, teaching assistantships, full and partial tuition waivers, Federal Work-Study, institutionally sponsored loans, and career-related internships or fieldwork available. Aid available to part-time students. Financial aid application deadline: 3/2; applicants required to submit FAFSA. • Harry N. Scheiber, Chair, 510-642-4038. Application contact: Margo Rodriguez, Graduate Assistant for Admission, 510-642-3771. Fax: 510-642-2951. E-mail: mnr@uclink.berkeley.edu.

University of Charleston, South Carolina, School of Humanities and Social Sciences, Program in Bilingual Legal Interpreting, Charleston, SC 29424-0001. Awards MA. Faculty: 1 (woman) full-time. Students: 2 part-time (both women). Average age 38. 8 applicants, 88% accepted. *Entrance requirements:* GRE General Test (minimum combined score of 1000), Interpreting Aptitude Exam. Application deadline: 3/31 (priority date; rolling processing). Application fee: $50. • Dr. Virginia Benmaman, Director, 843-953-5718. Fax: 843-953-6432. Application contact: Laura H. Hines, Graduate School Coordinator, 843-953-5614. Fax: 843-953-1434. E-mail: hinesl@cofc.edu.

University of Denver, College of Law, Program in Legal Administration, Denver, CO 80204. Awards MSLA. Part-time and evening/weekend programs available. Faculty: 12 full-time (2 women). Students: 8 full-time (4 women), 1 (woman) part-time; includes 1 international. 18 applicants, 78% accepted. In 1997, 5 degrees awarded. *Entrance requirements:* GMAT, GRE, or LSAT. Application deadline: 5/1 (rolling processing). Application fee: $25. *Tuition:* $622 per credit hour. *Financial aid:* Federal Work-Study and career-related internships or fieldwork available. Aid available to part-time students. Financial aid application deadline: 2/15; applicants required to submit FAFSA. • Lauren Fenton, Director, 303-871-6308. Application contact: Karen Higganbotham, Admissions, 303-871-6434. Fax: 303-871-6378.

University of Illinois at Springfield, School of Public Affairs and Administration, Program in Legal Studies, Springfield, IL 62794-9243. Awards MA. Faculty: 5 full-time (2 women), 5 part-time (1 woman), 7.19 FTE. Students: 7 full-time (3 women), 26 part-time (18 women); includes 2 international. Average age 32. 23 applicants, 61% accepted. In 1997, 7 degrees awarded. *Degree requirements:* Thesis or alternative required, foreign language not required. *Application deadline:* rolling. *Application fee:* $0. *Expenses:* Tuition $99 per credit hour for state residents; $296 per credit hour for nonresidents. Fees $242 per year full-time, $63 per semester (minimum) part-time. *Financial aid:* In 1997–98, 22 students received aid, including 3 assistantships averaging $606 per month; research assistantships, partial tuition waivers, Federal Work-Study, and career-related internships or fieldwork also available. Aid available to part-time students. Financial aid application deadline: 6/1; applicants required to submit FAFSA. *Faculty research:* Family law, women's studies, arbitration, courts, constitutional law. • Ernest Cowles, Convener, 217-786-6343.

University of Manitoba, Faculty of Law, Winnipeg, MB R3T 2N2, Canada. Offerings include interdisciplinary studies (MA). *Application deadline:* 6/1 (rolling processing). *Application fee:* $50.

University of Nebraska–Lincoln, Department of Legal Studies, Lincoln, NE 68588. Awards MLS. Faculty: 14 full-time (1 woman), 1 part-time (0 women), 14.67 FTE. Students: 1 (woman) full-time, 5 part-time (2 women). Average age 35. 13 applicants, 23% accepted. In 1997, 2 degrees awarded. *Entrance requirements:* GRE General Test or LSAT, TOEFL (minimum score 600). Application deadline: 4/15. Application fee: $35. Electronic applications accepted. *Expenses:* Tuition $110 per credit hour for state residents; $270 per credit hour for nonresidents. Fees $480 per year full-time, $110 per semester part-time. *Financial aid:* In 1997–98, 1 fellowship totaling $10,008 was awarded; research assistantships, Federal Work-Study also available. Financial aid application deadline: 2/15. • Craig M. Lawson, Graduate Committee Chair, 402-472-1247.

University of Nevada, Reno, Interdisciplinary Program in Judicial Studies, Reno, NV 89557. Awards MJS. Offered jointly with the National Judicial College and the National Council of Juvenile and Family Court Judges. Part-time programs available. Faculty: 12 part-time (1 woman). Students: 8 full-time (1 woman), 32 part-time (13 women); includes 4 minority (all African Americans). Average age 49. 42 applicants, 98% accepted. In 1997, 5 degrees awarded (100% found work related to degree). *Degree requirements:* Thesis required, foreign language not required. *Entrance requirements:* TOEFL, sitting judge, law degree from an accredited school. Application deadline: 3/1 (rolling processing). Application fee: $40. *Financial*

Directory: Legal and Justice Studies; Cross-Discipline Announcements

University of Nevada, Reno (continued)
aid: Available to part-time students. *Faculty research:* Jury research, capital punishment, expert testimony, environmental law, medical issues, economics and law. • Dr. James T. Richardson, Director, 702-784-6270. Application contact: Denise Schaar-Buis, Coordinator, 702-784-6270. Fax: 702-784-1300. E-mail: schaar@unr.edu.

University of Ottawa, Faculty of Law, Ottawa, ON K1N 6N5, Canada. Offerings include legislative drafting (Diploma). Faculty: 49 full-time, 4 part-time. *Application deadline:* 2/1. *Application fee:* $35. *Expenses:* Tuition $4677 per year for Canadian residents; $9900 per year for nonresidents. Fees $230 per year. • Sanda Rodgers, Dean, 613-562-5774. Application contact: Ruth Sullivan, Director, 613-562-5897. Fax: 613-562-5124.

University of Pennsylvania, Wharton School, Legal Studies Department, Philadelphia, PA 19104. Awards MBA. Faculty: 15 full-time (3 women), 17 part-time (2 women). *Entrance requirements:* GMAT. Application deadline: 4/10. Application fee: $125. *Faculty research:* Corporate law, business ethics, negotiations, international law, criminology, environmental law. • G. Richard Shell, Chairperson, 215-898-9525. Fax: 215-573-2006. Application contact: Robert J. Alig, Director of Admissions, 215-898-3430. Fax: 215-898-0120.

University of Pittsburgh, School of Law, Program in Health Law, Pittsburgh, PA 15260. Awards Certificate. Faculty: 42 full-time (18 women), 20 part-time (7 women). *Application deadline:* rolling. *Application fee:* $40. • Dr. David Herring, Interim Dean, School of Law, 412-648-1401. E-mail: herring@law.pitt.edu. Application contact: Fredi G. Miller, Assistant Dean, 412-648-1400. Fax: 412-648-2647. E-mail: miller@law.pitt.edu.

University of San Diego, School of Law, San Diego, CA 92110-2492. Offerings include general studies (LL M). School faculty: 50 full-time (16 women), 34 part-time (13 women), 55.1 FTE. *Application deadline:* 3/1. *Application fee:* $40. *Expenses:* Tuition $20,980 per year full-time, $710 per unit part-time. Fees $50 per year full-time, $40 per year part-time. • Kristine Strachan, Dean, 619-260-4527. Application contact: Carl Eging, Director of Admissions, 619-260-4528.

University of the Pacific, McGeorge School of Law, Sacramento, CA 95817. Offerings include transnational business practice (LL M). School faculty: 46 full-time (13 women), 34 part-time (6 women). *Average time to degree:* master's–1 year full-time, 2 years part-time; first professional–3 years full-time, 4 years part-time. *Entrance requirements:* JD. Application deadline: 5/1 (priority date; rolling processing). Application fee: $40. *Tuition:* $20,762 per year full-time, $13,324 per year part-time. • Gerald M. Caplan, Dean, 916-739-7151. Application contact: Admissions Office, 916-739-7105. Fax: 916-739-7134. E-mail: admissionsmcgeorge@uop.edu.

University of Wisconsin–Madison, Law School and Graduate School, Department of Legal Institutions, Madison, WI 53706-1380. Awards MLI. Students: 30 full-time (12 women), 1 part-time (0 women); includes 31 international. Average age 28. 85 applicants, 62% accepted. In 1997, 26 degrees awarded. *Application deadline:* 3/31 (rolling processing). *Application fee:* $45. *Tuition:* $4928 per year full-time, $926 per semester (minimum) part-time for state residents; $15,190 per year full-time, $2849 per semester (minimum) part-time for nonresidents. *Financial aid:* Institutionally sponsored loans and career-related internships or fieldwork available. Aid available to part-time students. Financial aid application deadline: 3/1. • Kenneth B. Davis Jr., Dean, Law School, 608-262-0618. Application contact: Prof. William H. Clune, 608-262-5914.

Vermont Law School, Law School, Environmental Law Center, Chelsea Street, PO Box 96, South Royalton, VT 05068-0096. Awards MSEL, JD/MSEL. Part-time programs available. Faculty: 9 full-time (3 women), 8 part-time (4 women), 13 FTE. Students: 25 full-time (10 women); includes 9 minority (3 African Americans, 1 Hispanic, 5 Native Americans), 5 international. Average age 30. 77 applicants, 74% accepted. In 1997, 60 degrees awarded. *Average time to degree:* master's–1 year full-time, 4 years part-time. *Entrance requirements:* GRE General Test (average 544 verbal, 640 quantitative, 679 analytical) or LSAT, TOEFL (average 600). Application deadline: 2/15 (priority date; rolling processing). Application fee: $50. *Expenses:* Tuition $19,415 per year. Fees $75 per year. *Financial aid:* In 1997–98, 2 fellowships (both to first-year students) averaging $666 per month were awarded; partial tuition waivers, Federal Work-Study, institutionally sponsored loans, and career-related internships or fieldwork also available. Aid available to part-time students. Financial aid application deadline: 2/15; applicants required to submit FAFSA. *Faculty research:* Environment and technology; takings; international environmental law; interaction among science, law, and environmental policy; air pollution; cultural resources protection; law of ecosystems; endangered species. Total annual research expenditures: $52,000. • Patrick Parenteau, Director, 802-763-8303 Ext. 2201. E-mail: pparente@vermontlaw.edu. Application contact: Shari Young, Director of Operations, 802-763-8303 Ext. 2201. Fax: 802-763-2940. E-mail: syoung@vermontlaw.edu.

Webster University, College of Arts and Sciences, Department of History, Politics and Law, Program in Legal Studies, St. Louis, MO 63119-3194. Awards MA. Part-time and evening/weekend programs available. Faculty: 1 (woman) full-time, 25 part-time (13 women). Students: 34 full-time (27 women), 15 part-time (12 women); includes 15 minority (all African Americans). *Degree requirements:* Thesis optional, foreign language not required. *Application deadline:* rolling. *Application fee:* $25 ($50 for international students). *Tuition:* $350 per credit hour. *Financial aid:* Federal Work-Study and career-related internships or fieldwork available. Aid available to part-time students. Financial aid application deadline: 4/1; applicants required to submit FAFSA. *Faculty research:* Intellectual property rights, emerging torts, death penalty, juvenile justice, confidentiality issues in banking. • Tena Hart, Director, 314-961-2260 Ext. 7747. Fax: 314-968-7403. E-mail: harttr@webster.edu. Application contact: Beth Russell, Director of Graduate Admissions, 314-968-7089. Fax: 314-968-7166. E-mail: russelmb@webster.edu.

Webster University, College of Arts and Sciences, Department of History, Politics and Law, Program in Paralegal Studies, St. Louis, MO 63119-3194. Awards Certificate. Part-time and evening/weekend programs available. Faculty: 1 (woman) full-time, 25 part-time (13 women). Students: 12 full-time (8 women), 4 part-time (3 women); includes 4 minority (3 African Americans, 1 Asian American). *Application deadline:* rolling. *Application fee:* $25 ($50 for international students). *Tuition:* $350 per credit hour. *Financial aid:* Application deadline 4/1; applicants required to submit FAFSA. *Faculty research:* Intellectual property rights, emerging torts, death penalty, juvenile justice, confidentiality issues in banking. • Tena Hart, Director, 314-961-2660, Ext. 7747. Fax: 314-968-7403. E-mail: harttr@webster.edu. Application contact: Beth Russell, Director of Graduate Admissions, 314-968-7089. Fax: 314-968-7166. E-mail: russelmb@webster.edu.

Cross-Discipline Announcements

Boston College, Wallace E. Carroll Graduate School of Management, Chestnut Hill, MA 02167-9991.

For students who are interested in combining work in law and business, the Boston College MBA/JD degree provides exceptional management skills and the legal know-how to give students a competitive edge. The 2 degrees can be obtained in just 4 years. See in-depth description in this volume.

Case Western Reserve University, Mandel School of Applied Social Sciences, Cleveland, OH 44106.

The Mandel School of Applied Social Sciences awards a master's degree in social work, a dual degree in social work and law, and a PhD in social welfare for students with an undergraduate degree in related areas who have taken considerable social science course work. Social work career options include public interest or family law, public policy, and advocacy. Contact MSASS at 10900 Euclid Avenue, Cleveland, OH 44106-7164. Telephone: 800-944-2290 Ext. 2280 (toll-free).

Monterey Institute of International Studies, Graduate School of International Policy Studies, Program in Commercial Diplomacy, 425 Van Buren Street, Monterey, CA 93940-2691.

The Master of Arts in Commercial Diplomacy (MACD) focuses on the management of complex issues and relationships connected to international commerce between and among global corporations and governments and on the development of advanced language capability. The program of study integrates a number of diverse fields, including economics, politics, policy analysis, trade law, public advocacy techniques, negotiating strategy and tactics, and foreign languages and cultures. Write to the admissions office or call 408-647-4123.

Nova Southeastern University, School of Social and Systemic Studies, Department of Dispute Resolution, Fort Lauderdale, FL 33314-7721.

The department offers a PhD, an MS, and a graduate certificate. The curriculum combines theory with the advanced skills and techniques necessary for developing reflective practitioners prepared to practice dispute resolution in a variety of professional environments. See in-depth description in volume 2 of this series.

Pepperdine University, School of Public Policy, Malibu, CA 90263-0001.

Pepperdine University's School of Public Policy offers a Master of Public Policy degree, which may be considered an alternative or complement to an MBA, a nonprofit management program, or a law degree. The School plans to offer joint-degree programs with the JD, MBA, and Master of Dispute Resolution. It is the School's firm belief that public policy itself is not limited to the study of government solutions but is broadened to embrace a full range of community-based and free-market approaches to public policy problems. For detailed information, see Book 2 of this series, contact 310-317-7493 or 888-456-1177 (toll-free), fax: 310-317-7494, e-mail: npapen@pepperdine.edu, or visit the Web site: http://www.pepperdine.edu/PublicPolicy

University of Southern California, Graduate School, Annenberg School for Communication, School of Communication, Program in Communication Management, Los Angeles, CA 90089.

The dual degree (JD/MA) in communication management has concentrations in communication law and policy, entertainment management, strategic and corporate communication management, marketing communication, and communication and information technologies. The Annenberg School is a partner in USC's Integrated Media Systems Center, the nation's only university-based multimedia research center, funded by the National Science Foundation. Applicants must apply to both units for admission. Offered jointly by the Annenberg School and the Law Center, the dual degree can be completed in 3 years.

University of Wisconsin–Madison, College of Letters and Science, Industrial Relations Research Institute, Madison, WI 53706-1380.

The Institute offers a joint program with the University of Wisconsin Law School whereby students combine studies in industrial relations and law and earn both an MS and a JD. This dual degree enables them to pursue careers in labor law, labor education and negotiation, human resource management, and law school teaching. Students must be admitted to both programs and satisfy all requirements for both degrees. Many courses count in both programs.

Washington University in St. Louis, School of Medicine, Graduate Programs in Medicine, Health Administration Program, St. Louis, MO 63110.

The health administration program at Washington University School of Medicine in St. Louis is a 2-year graduate program that awards the Master of Health Administration (MHA) degree. Optional paid 12-month postgraduate fellowship, active alumni placement services, and a network of more than 1,000 program graduates provide excellent career opportunities.

CHAPMAN UNIVERSITY

School of Law

Program of Study

The Chapman University School of Law is characterized by its mission: to provide personalized education of distinction in an academically challenging environment that stimulates intellectual inquiry, embraces diverse ideas and viewpoints, and fosters competent and ethical lawyering that enhances the capacity of legal institutions to provide justice. To implement this mission, the School of Law seeks to prepare its graduates to assume positions of responsibility and leadership in the legal, business, and government communities. The goal is to produce competent and ethical practitioners who are cognizant of the public trust that society places in attorneys.

Chapman offers both full-time and part-time programs. A minimum of 88 credit units is required for graduation. The required curriculum includes the study of torts, contracts, criminal law, real property, constitutional law, civil procedure, and ethics. The focus of the required courses is to impart not only the substantive law but also the kind of legal reasoning and skill that attorneys must use in providing competent and exemplary service. The School of Law provides all the elements of a traditional legal education while emphasizing writing, research, and ethics throughout the curriculum.

Research Facilities

The law library contains a core collection of more than 209,000 volumes and volume equivalents and continues to expand each year. The library collection includes all basic research materials for American law, including primary materials of federal, state, and territorial jurisdictions. There are numerous law reviews and an expanding treatise collection to support the research needs of students, faculty members, and practitioners.

The School of Law has a well-equipped computer lab for use by students. Both IBM-compatible and Macintosh personal computers are available for use. LEXIS, WESTLAW, CALI, and Internet access are also available to all students.

Financial Aid

Financial aid is available in the form of private and federal loan funds. In addition, the School of Law has a generous scholarship program; scholarships are awarded on the basis of superior credentials. No application is required for these scholarships as they are awarded at the time of acceptance and, subsequently, as merit scholarships for demonstrated academic excellence in law school.

Cost of Study

Tuition for the academic year 1998–99 is $625 per credit unit. Tuition is payable prior to each semester. The University has a payment plan whereby tuition can be paid monthly over the academic year.

Living and Housing Costs

Limited University housing is available for law students. There are also commercial apartment units conveniently located near the School of Law.

Student Group

Chapman law students are graduates of more than eighty undergraduate colleges and universities throughout the United States. A number of students have advanced degrees. The student body is approximately 57 percent men and 43 percent women. The Student Bar Association actively seeks to enrich the academic program through the sponsorship of various student functions, programs, and groups. In addition, cocurricular and extracurricular activities are available to students.

Location

The law school is located in central Orange County, California. The area has many attractions, including nearby ocean beaches, mountains, parks, hiking trails, and professional baseball and hockey teams.

The University and The School

Chapman University is a 137-year-old independent institution of liberal arts and professional training. The University consists of the Wilkinson College of Letters and Sciences, the School of Business and Economics, the School of Education, the School of Film and Television, the School of Music, the School of Communication Arts, and the School of Law. The University offers more than forty fields of undergraduate study as well as eighteen graduate degree programs and credential programs for educators.

The School of Law enrolled its inaugural class in 1995. The faculty is composed of law teachers recruited from across the United States, several having been named Teacher of the Year at their prior law schools. Many have advanced law degrees, including master's and doctoral degrees. In addition to experience in the classroom, the faculty also produces scholarship of distinction. The new School of Law building is scheduled for occupancy for spring semester 1999. It will bridge the historic landmark legacy of Orange County with twenty-first-century fiber-optics technology.

Chapman University's School of Law is provisionally approved by the American Bar Association (550 West North Street, Indianapolis, Indiana 46202; telephone: 317-264-8340); thus, graduates of the law school may take the bar examination in any state.

Applying

Applicants must possess an American bachelor's degree or its international equivalent, must have completed the Law School Admission Test (LSAT), and must be registered with the Law School Data Assembly Service (LSDAS). Language proficiency evaluation may be required of students who do not speak English as their native language. The application fee is $50. Because admissions decisions are made on a rolling basis, it is to the applicant's advantage to apply early.

Correspondence and Information

Office of Admissions
Chapman University School of Law
1240 South State College Boulevard
Anaheim, California 92806

Telephone: 714-517-0305
888-242-1913 (toll-free)
E-mail: lawadm@chapman.edu

Chapman University

THE FACULTY

Parham H. Williams, Jr., Professor, Vice President, and Dean; LL.B., Mississippi, 1954; LL.M., Yale, 1965.
Leonard J. Nelson III, Professor and Associate Dean for Student Affairs; J.D., Gonzaga, 1974; LL.M., Yale 1984.
Larry O'Neil Putt, Professor and Associate Dean; J.D., 1969, LL.M., 1980, Mississippi.

Craig Anthony (Tony) Arnold, Assistant Professor; J.D., Stanford, 1990.
Denis Binder, Professor; J.D., San Francisco, 1970; LL.M., 1971, S.J.D., 1973, Michigan.
Michael H. Cohen, Associate Professor; J.D., 1986, M.B.A., 1998, Berkeley; M.F.A., Iowa, 1990.
Rebecca D. Cornia, Assistant Professor; J.D., Harvard, 1986.
Frank J. Doti, Professor; J.D., ITT/Chicago-Kent, 1969.
Judith D. Fischer, Associate Professor; J.D., Loyola (California), 1981.
Hugh Hewitt, Associate Professor; J.D., Michigan, 1983. Member, order of the coif.
Scott W. Howe, Professor; J.D., Michigan, 1981.
Francis (Frank) E. Jones Jr., Visiting Professor of Law; LL.B., 1948, LL.M., 1952, Georgetown. Member, order of the coif.
Susanna M. Kim, Assistant Professor; J.D., UCLA, 1994. Member, order of the coif.
Sheryl Summers Kramer, Associate Professor and Library Director; M.S.L.S., Wayne State, 1978; J.D., Detroit, 1989.
Jeremy M. Miller, Professor; J.D., Tulane, 1980; LL.M., Pennsylvania, 1981.
Christopher H. Munch, Distinguished Professor; LL.B., Illinois, 1951. Member, order of the coif.
Sharon C. Nantell, Professor; J.D., Cleveland-Marshall, 1976; LL.M., Georgetown, 1979.
Nancy L. Schultz, Associate Professor; J.D., Pennsylvania, 1981.
William L. Stallworth, Salvatori Professor of Law and Community Service; J.D., Harvard, 1979; Ph.D., Stanford, 1982.
Rafael X. Zahralddin, Assistant Professor; J.D., Widener, 1993; LL.M., Georgetown, 1995.

The $30-million Chapman University School of Law building is under construction, with completion scheduled for spring 1999.

DEPAUL UNIVERSITY

College of Law

Programs of Study

The College offers full-time, part-time, and summer programs of study that combine teaching legal theory with the practicing of professional skills. Degrees offered include the Juris Doctor (J.D.), Master of Laws (LL.M.) in tax law and in health law, and the joint J.D./M.B.A.

A member of The Order of the Coif and the American Association of Law Schools, DePaul is a national law school recognized for leadership among both its teaching faculty members and its practicing alumni.

DePaul was among the first schools to offer a full curriculum in health law and among the first to teach negotiations, to conduct research in products liability, to offer a course in international criminal law, and to include pretrial techniques among its lawyering skills courses. Such innovations continue today in DePaul's Legal Clinic and Extern Program, which offer students hands-on experience in such areas as asylum law, community development, mediation, criminal appellate law, and supervised field work with federal and state judges, various municipal agencies, and not-for-profit organizations. Legal writing and research opportunities are available to students through four student-edited law journals and two law digests—*The DePaul Law Review, Journal of Hospital Law, DePaul-LCA Journal of Art and Entertainment Law, DePaul Business Law Journal, Environmental Law Digest,* and *International Law Digest.*

Leadership also marks DePaul alumni. The College's graduates include managing partners and executive committee members of dozens of major law firms, chief executives and general counsels of America's largest corporations, leaders in public interest, and numerous state and federal judges—as well as two generations of Chicago mayors.

Research Facilities

As a result of a successful $100-million DePaul University Cornerstone Campaign, the College of Law now occupies a number of new legal research sites. One such facility is the Law Library, a three-floor telecommunications-enhanced research site, which houses word processing and computer terminals, media-viewing suites, study carrels, video-enhanced seminar rooms, and small-group study rooms. The Internet, LEXIS, WESTLAW, and e-mail can be accessed from computer labs or from remote sites. Computer Assisted Legal Instruction (CALI) is also available. In addition, a state-of-the-art Lawyering Skills Center, which includes two video-enhanced skills suites and a courtroom equipped with six sound-activated cameras, provides excellent facilities in which students can hone their trial preparation and practice skills. Additional research facilities include suites for three College of Law institutes: the International Human Rights Law Institute, the Health Law Institute, and the Center for Church/State Studies—all of which involve students in their publication, public service, and research activities.

Financial Aid

The College provides a range of financial assistance in the form of loans, tuition grants, and merit scholarships. In addition to federal student loans and a special University alternative financing program, the College of Law annually awards approximately $1.5 million in scholarships. The Free Application for Federal Student Aid (FAFSA) is required for need-based financial aid and should be submitted as early as possible after January 1. No separate application other than the required documents for admission is needed for merit scholarship consideration.

Cost of Study

The 1998–99 tuition package is $19,800 for full-time students and $13,400 for part-time students. Tuition for visiting J.D. and for LL.M. students pursuing graduate studies in health law and tax law is $690 per credit hour. A nonrefundable tuition deposit is required of new J.D. students prior to their enrolling.

Living and Housing Costs

The majority of DePaul law students live on Chicago's Near North Side in such neighborhoods as Wrigleyville, DePaul West, Lakeview, Lincoln Park, and Belmont Harbor. Rents vary based on locale and size of unit. Approximate monthly rent for studios starts in the low to mid-$400s, while rent for one-bedroom apartments might start in the low to mid-$700s. The College has no on-campus residence halls.

Student Group

DePaul educates a student body representing a rich diversity of age, ethnicity, education, and career experience. Students in last year's entering class represented about thirty states and countries. Fifteen percent were members of minority groups; 46 percent were women. The average age of full-time students was 25 years old, while the average age of part-time students was 29 years. Approximately 31 students had earned graduate and professional degrees prior to entering DePaul.

Student Outcomes

DePaul students enjoy tremendous success in obtaining positions in traditional law practice, government organizations, and business. More than 90 percent of 1997 graduates reported employment status and, of those, approximately 90 percent were employed within six months of graduation. More than half of DePaul graduates obtained associate positions in private law firms, and nearly one quarter secured prestigious positions in business, including accounting, banking, and insurance.

Location

DePaul offers legal education conducted in a vibrant urban setting. Located in the heart of Chicago's business, legal, and cultural institutions, the College is a short walk from state, federal, and local courts; major law firms and corporations; Chicago's magnificent lakefront; the Art Institute of Chicago; and Orchestra Hall, home of the Chicago Symphony Orchestra.

The University and The College

DePaul is the second-largest private university in Illinois and in 1998 celebrates its centennial. Among its seven colleges, DePaul combines dedication to excellence with a commitment to equality. DePaul was the first Catholic university in the country to admit women on an equal basis with men. Today, women hold half of the University's administrative and leadership posts. In the College of Law, 45 percent of faculty members are women—an exceptionally high percentage among law schools.

Applying

Applications from new J.D. students are accepted for the fall semester only. However, applications from candidates applying for transfer, visiting, and LL.M. admission in tax law and health law are accepted for the fall, spring, and summer semesters. The recommended application deadline for new J.D. candidates is April 1. For transfer, visiting, and LL.M. candidates, it is one month before the semester begins. Application procedures vary for each program. College of Law faculty members review applications and render admission decisions.

Correspondence and Information

Office of Admission
DePaul University College of Law
25 East Jackson Boulevard
Chicago, Illinois 60604-2287

Telephone: 312-362-6831
800-428-7453 (toll-free)
773-325-7296 (TDD)
Fax: 312-362-5280
World Wide Web: http://www.law.depaul.edu

DePaul University

THE FACULTY

The date in parentheses at the end of each entry indicates the year in which the individual joined the faculty.

Alicia Alvarez, Clinical Associate Professor; J.D., Boston College. (1989)
Philip S. Ashley, Associate Professor; LL.M., NYU. (1977)
William Baker, Professor; J.D., Maryland. (1970)
Susan A. Bandes, Professor; J.D., Michigan. (1990)
M. Cherif Bassiouni, Professor; LL.M., John Marshall Law; S.J.D., George Washington. (1964)
Maureen Berens, Legal Writing Instructor; J.D., SUNY at Buffalo. (1997)
Rodney J. Blackman, Professor; Ph.D., Wisconsin; J.D., Harvard. (1973)
Barbara B. Bressler, Clinical Associate Professor and Associate Director of Legal Services; J.D., DePaul. (1984)
Leonard L. Cavise, Associate Professor; J.D., Georgetown. (1983)
Sumi K. Cho, Assistant Professor; Ph.D., J.D., Berkeley. (1995)
Maureen Collins, Director of the Legal Writing Program; J.D., DePaul. (1990)
James W. Colliton, Professor; LL.M., Georgetown. (1977)
John F. Decker, Professor; LL.M., J.S.D., NYU. (1971)
Katheryn M. Dutenhaver, Associate Professor; J.D., DePaul. (1974)
Teree E. Foster, Professor and Dean; J.D., Loyola (Chicago). (1997)
Lisa J. Freedman, Legal Writing Instructor; J.D., Boston University. (1991)
Jerold A. Friedland, Professor; LL.M., Georgetown. (1979)
Judith A. Gaskell, Assistant Professor and Law Librarian; J.D., DePaul; M.A., Chicago. (1983)
Patty Gerstenblith, Professor; J.D., Northwestern; Ph.D., Harvard. (1984)
Steven R. Greenberger, Associate Professor; J.D., Yale. (1988)
Ray J. Grzebielski, Associate Professor; LL.M., Georgetown. (1979).
Brian F. Havel, Assistant Professor; LL.M., Columbia; M.A., Dublin. (1994)
Donald H. J. Hermann, Professor; Ph.D., Northwestern; LL.M., Harvard. (1972)
Michael Jacobs, Associate Professor; J.D., Yale; M.P.H., Johns Hopkins. (1988)
Suzanne Kanter, Legal Writing Instructor; J.D., Northwestern. (1993)
Barry Kellman, Professor; J.D., Yale. (1990)
Terrence F. Kiely, Professor; LL.M., NYU. (1972)
Roberta Rosenthal Kwall, Professor; J.D., Pennsylvania. (1983)
Stephan A. Landsman, Professor; J.D., Harvard. (1994)
Stephen J. Leacock, Professor; LL.M., King's College (London); Barrister, Middle Temple (London); M.B.L., London Polytechnic; Grad. Cert. Ed., Garnett. (1979)
Wayne K. Lewis, Professor; J.D., Cornell. (1982)
Margit Livingston, Professor; LL.M., Illinois; M.A., Minnesota. (1977)
Marlene Arnold Nicholson, Professor; J.D., UCLA. (1971)
Michelle Oberman, Associate Professor; J.D., M.P.H., Michigan. (1993)
Bruce L. Ottley, Professor and Associate Dean; LL.M., Columbia; M.A., Iowa. (1978)
Judith Reed, Assistant Professor; J.D., Columbia. (1995)
Stephen Resnicoff, Professor; J.D., Yale. (1988)
John C. Roberts, Professor; LL.B., Yale. (1986)
Howard M. Rubin, Director of Legal Services; J.D., DePaul. (1977)
Jane Rutherford, Professor; J.D., Michigan. (1986)
Jeffrey M. Shaman, Professor; LL.M., Georgetown. (1973)
Stephen A. Siegel, Professor; LL.M., Harvard. (1972)
William W. Stuart, Professor; LL.B., Washington and Lee. (1976)
Morrison Torrey, Professor; J.D., Drake. (1986)
Susan Thrower, Legal Writing Instructor; J.D., Wake Forest. (1995)
Vincent F. Vitullo, Professor; LL.M., Yale. (1971)
Mark C. Weber, Professor; J.D., Yale. (1986)
Shelly Weinberg, Legal Writing Instructor; J.D., Harvard. (1995)
Diana C. White, Assistant Dean for Student Affairs; J.D., Wisconsin. (1985)
Clifford Zimmerman, Legal Writing Instructor; J.D., Rutgers, Newark. (1990)

DePaul's newly renovated library provides a comfortable setting for study and research.

The Leonard M. Ring Courtroom, a technologically advanced courtroom whose video system was the first of its kind in any law school, gives students a realistic setting in which to practice advocacy.

DETROIT COLLEGE OF LAW AT MICHIGAN STATE UNIVERSITY

Law School

Programs of Study

Founded in 1891, Detroit College of Law at Michigan State University (DCL/MSU) builds on its long-standing tradition of excellence in legal education and service to the community as one of the nation's oldest independent law schools. Located on the campus of Michigan State University, students can earn their Juris Doctor (J.D.) degree in an intimate environment while enjoying the countless resources, recreational activities, and interesting people who belong to this international community.

The Law School is best known for its successful alumni and quality teaching. More than 7,000 graduates have attended DCL/MSU. It has a reputation for providing a strong curriculum and academic agenda leading to the practice of law in any jurisdiction within the United States. First-year legal study is primarily conducted by the "casebook" method and incorporates the solid development of practical lawyering skills. Extensive study in international and comparative law and taxation is offered as concentrations in these areas. Both J.D./M.B.A. and J.D./M.P.A. dual-degree programs are offered.

Detroit College of Law at Michigan State University also supports the unique interests of its students by offering courses that explore areas such as admiralty law, Chinese law, immigration law, sports law, and wildlife law. DCL/MSU has a nationally competitive moot court, and student publications include the *DCL/MSU Law Review* and the *Journal of International Law and Practice*. The Center for Canadian-United States Law at the College provides internship opportunities and assists with joint-practice preparation for students. Joint programs are available. The College provides an excellent learning and living environment for ambitious law students and is committed to legal research, academic enrichment, and classroom technology. DCL/MSU also offers an electronic casebook course. The professor and students use laptop computers during their regular class period in an effort to master skills in legal technology and improve efficiency of study.

Research Facilities

The library contains more than 200,000 volumes and equivalents. The collection includes full coverage of federal and state of Michigan law, state statutes and basic materials from all fifty states, British and Canadian materials, references in nonlegal disciplines, monographs, legal fiction, video collections, resources in international and comparative law, and more than 2,000 journals.

Occupying two floors of a new law school building, the law library and computer lab utilize telecommunications technology, providing more than 300 "LAN drops," and house an impressive list of software and services. Students have access to the Internet, LEXIS-NEXIS, WESTLAW, computer-aided legal instruction, and personal e-mail through the computer lab or from their personal laptops used in classrooms or library study carrels.

In addition, the MSU library system is available for DCL/MSU students with some 4 million volumes, 5 million pieces of microform, 210,000 maps, 40,000 sound recordings, and 3,600 computer files.

Financial Aid

The Dean Charles H. King Scholarship is awarded to select entering candidates at a rate of at least half tuition for the first year. King scholars receive a total of 4 credits and may graduate with honors upon successful completion. Trustee Scholarships are awarded to entering students from minority groups who demonstrate substantial academic and professional promise. The College awards a select number of full and partial tuition scholarships. The DCL/MSU financial aid staff is committed to assisting students in financing their legal education through combinations of Federal Stafford/Unsubsidized Stafford Loans, College Work-Study, Veterans Educational Benefits, alternative loans, and state grants.

Cost of Study

Tuition for full- and part-time study is estimated at the rate of $535 per credit hour for the 1998–99 academic year. A deposit of $200 is required of accepted students and is credited to their total tuition costs upon registration. Books cost about $400 per semester.

Living and Housing Costs

A variety of on-campus housing options are offered for both single and married DCL/MSU students. The MSU Housing Office handles requests for graduate housing and/or single rooms. Most residence halls have computer labs and ATM machines. Meal plans are also available. The 1998–99 estimated cost of attendance for entering full-time students is $24,936 and includes tuition, fees, books, supplies, housing, transportation, and miscellaneous expenses.

Student Group

DCL/MSU attracts students nationwide and internationally. Faculty members look for high-achieving students with unique interests, experiences, and education. About 623 students are enrolled in the day and evening programs. Women make up 36 percent, and 12 percent of the students classify themselves as being members of minority groups.

Student Outcomes

DCL/MSU trains law students in practical lawyering, ethics, and technology. The Career Services staff helps students enhance their potential for employment and boasts a placement rate of 93 percent. Alumni reside and work in forty-eight states and other countries, including Alaska, Hawaii, Guam, Canada, Greece, and China. They have prestigious occupations such as judges, attorneys, public officials, professors, and corporate CEO's. National government agencies and large corporations also employ a great number of graduates.

Location

The Law School is located on the campus of Michigan State University in East Lansing, Michigan, one of the largest and most diverse of American universities. East Lansing is a pleasant residential community 86 miles from Detroit, 217 miles from Chicago, and just a few miles east of Lansing, the capital city. The greater Lansing area includes many small communities and has a total population of about 300,000.

The University and The College

When the Detroit College of Law opened its doors in 1892 "to all class, without regard to sex, color, age or citizenship," the profile of its first class presaged its eventual affiliation with a great land-grant university that values strength in diversity. Of the 30 enrollees, 6 were working lawyers, 1 was African American, 1 was Asian, and 1 was a woman. The affiliation with Michigan State University has strengthened the law College's commitment to legal education through technology, scholarship, communication, and resources for its students.

Applying

Detroit College of Law at Michigan State University has a selective admissions process. The objective of the process is to select men and women who have the highest potential for advancement in the study of law. Applicants must hold a bachelor's degree from an accredited college or university. All applicants must take the LSAT and subscribe to LSDAS. Only those applicants with a high grade point average and a high score on the LSAT will be considered for admission.

Correspondence and Information

Admissions Office
316 Law College Building
Detroit College of Law at Michigan State University
East Lansing, Michigan 48824

Telephone: 517-432-0222
Fax: 517-432-0098
E-mail: heatleya@pilot.msu.edu
World Wide Web: http://www.dcl.edu

Detroit College of Law at Michigan State University

THE FACULTY

Jeremy T. Harrison, Dean and Professor of Law; J.D., San Francisco; LL.M., Harvard.
Brenda Jones Quick, Associate Dean and Professor of Law; J.D., Louisville.

John P. Apol, Professor of Law; J.D., Michigan.
Susan H. Bitensky, Professor of Law; J.D., Chicago.
Donald F. Campbell, Professor of Law; J.D., Detroit Law.
Mario A. Ceresa, Professor of Law and Director of the Library; D.L., Havana Law School; M.A.L.S., Michigan.
Amy Christian, Associate Professor of Law; J.D., Harvard.
Charles H. Clarke, Professor of Law; J.D., Chicago.
Charles E. Consalus, Professor of Law; J.D., Cincinnati; Ed.D., Columbia.
David S. Favre, Professor of Law; J.D., William and Mary.
Robert M. Filiatrault, Professor of Law; J.D., Detroit Law.
Nancy Heathcote, Professor of Law; J.D., Detroit Law.
Clark C. Johnson, Professor of Law; J.D., Ph.D., Wayne State.
Kevin C. Kennedy, Professor of Law; J.D., Wayne State; LL.M., Harvard.
Christine A. Klein, Associate Professor of Law; J.D., Colorado at Boulder; LL.M., Columbia.
Martin L. Kotch, Professor of Law; J.D., NYU.
Mae Kuykendall, Associate Professor of Law; J.D., Harvard; Ph.D., North Carolina.
Michael Lawrence, Associate Professor of Law; J.D., Wisconsin.
Robert A. McCormick, Professor of Law; J.D., Michigan.
Matthew McKinnon, Professor of Law; J.D., Detroit Law.
Patricia Mell, Professor of Law; J.D., Case Western Reserve.
Kathleen E. Payne, Professor of Law; J.D., Detroit Law; LL.M., Michigan.
Elizabeth Price, Associate Professor of Law; J.D., Tennessee; LL.M., Harvard.
John W. Reifenberg Jr., Professor of Law; J.D., Denver.
C. Nicholas Revelos, Professor of Law; J.D., Duke; LL.M., Berkeley.
John Soave Jr., Professor of Law; J.D., Detroit Law.
Cynthia L. Starnes, Professor of Law; J.D., Indiana; LL.M., Columbia.
Alvin L. Storrs, Professor of Law; J.D., Detroit; LL.M., NYU.

DRAKE UNIVERSITY

Drake Law School

Programs of Study

Drake Law School at Drake University offers top-quality programs leading to the Juris Doctor (J.D.) degree. One of the oldest law schools in the country, Drake combines strong theoretical underpinnings with practical experience and professional skills development. The result is well-prepared students who, upon graduation, are ready to practice law in a variety of settings.

A Drake legal education is not limited to the classroom. Drake's location in Des Moines, Iowa's capital, provides numerous opportunities for internships and clerkships with private firms, government agencies, and federal and state judges at both the trial and appellate levels. Extensive clinical programs, housed in a state-of-the-art clinical facility, allow students to gain practical experience. Plus, prominent lawyers, jurists, and legal scholars visit Drake regularly. In the past seven years, six Supreme Court justices have delivered major lectures at Drake, along with the head of the American Civil Liberties Union, top public officials, and numerous legal scholars.

Through joint-degree programs, students may obtain advanced degrees in business, public administration, mass communication, political science, social work, and agricultural economics.

Research Facilities

Drake Law School's facilities are among the best in the country. Opperman Hall and Law Library, built in 1993, has won several architectural and design awards and has received international recognition. The entire library is wired for computer use and includes two computer labs, WESTLAW and LEXIS legal research training centers, and access to the Internet and CD-ROM-based research. In addition, there are two main reading areas conducive to individual study, eighteen small-group study rooms, and several conference and seminar rooms. The library has a collection of more than 250,000 volumes and adjoins Cartwright Hall, the main classroom building. In addition, the Neal and Bea Smith Legal Clinic also has its own library.

Financial Aid

Drake Law School awards more than $1.4 million annually in scholarship assistance and more than 90 percent of students receive financial aid of some type. Scholarships are available based on both need and academic performance and awards have ranged from 10 percent of tuition to full tuition. Seven full-tuition merit scholarships are awarded annually to entering students. General scholarship assistance is available to entering students as well as to second- and third-year students who did not previously receive awards. Loan programs also are available.

Cost of Study

Tuition for the 1998–99 academic year is $8,475 per semester for students taking 10 or more hours per semester. If a student carries fewer than 10 hours, the tuition rate is $565 per hour.

Living and Housing Costs

The cost of living in Des Moines is low compared to that of many metropolitan areas, particularly in housing expenses. There are numerous apartments within walking distance to campus as well as adult student housing on campus. Rent for one-bedroom apartments ranges from $300 to $400 per month and two-bedroom apartments range from $400 to $600 per month.

Student Group

The enrollment in the Law School is approximately 400 students, about 59 percent men and 41 percent women. The median GPA for the fall 1997 entering class was 3.2 and the median LSAT score was 153. Law School students are a diverse group, representing thirty-eight states, seven other countries, and nearly 200 undergraduate institutions; more than half of the students come from outside of Iowa.

Student Outcomes

Drake Law School has alumni in all fifty states and several other countries in positions ranging from state supreme court justices to practicing attorneys to corporate CEOs. Historically, more than 90 percent of graduates secure employment within six months of graduation, which is above the national average.

Location

The Law School is located on the Drake University campus, a 120-acre community within 10 minutes of downtown Des Moines. With a metropolitan population of approximately 400,000, Des Moines is the hub of the state's legal community as well as the state capital, resulting in opportunities for students in government, insurance, and banking, as well as clerking opportunities.

The University and The Law School

Founded in 1881, Drake University is a private, independent university that offers a strong liberal arts foundation complemented by excellent career-oriented programs. Located on the Drake campus, the Law School is one of the twenty-five oldest law schools in the country and is accredited by the American Bar Association and the Association of American Law Schools.

Applying

Applications may be obtained from the Law School Admission Office. The application form should be returned with a personal statement and a nonrefundable application fee of $35. Although letters of recommendation from academic sources are not required, applicants are strongly encouraged to submit them.

Correspondence and Information

Kara Blanchard
Director of Admission and Financial Aid
Drake Law School
Drake University
2507 University Avenue
Des Moines, Iowa 50311
Telephone: 515-271-2782
800-44-DRAKE Ext. 2782 (toll-free)
Fax: 515-271-2530
Video Visit: 1-800-255-0384
E-mail: lawadmit@drake.edu
Word Wide Web: http://www.drake.edu

Drake University

THE FACULTY

C. Peter Goplerud III, Professor and Dean; J.D., Kansas, 1974.
Jerry L. Anderson, Professor and Associate Dean; J.D., Stanford, 1984.

James A. Adams, Richard M. and Anita Calkins Distinguished Professor of Law; J.D., Duke, 1967.
James A. Albert, Professor; J.D., Notre Dame, 1976.
Thomas E. Baker, James Madison Chair in Constitutional Law and Director of the Constitutional Law Resource Center; J.D., Florida, 1977.
Martin D. Begleiter, Professor; J.D., Cornell, 1970.
Daniel B. Bogart, Professor; J.D., Duke, 1986.
Andrea S. Charlow, Professor; LL.M., Columbia, 1982.
Hunter R. Clark, Associate Professor; J.D., Harvard, 1979.
Laurie Kratky Doré, Associate Professor; J.D., SMU, 1984.
Matthew G. Doré, Professor; J.D., Texas at Austin, 1984.
John D. Edwards, Professor and Director of the Law Library; J.D., Missouri–Kansas City, 1977; M.A.L.S., Missouri–Columbia, 1979.
Sally Frank, Professor; J.D., NYU, 1983.
Neil D. Hamilton, Ellis and Nelle Levitt Distinguished Professor of Law and Director of the Agricultural Law Center; J.D., Iowa, 1979.
Robert C. Hunter, Professor; J.D., Duke, 1967.
Russell E. Lovell II, Professor and Executive Director of the Legal Clinic; LL.M., Missouri–Kansas City, 1971.
Cathy Lesser Mansfield, Associate Professor; J.D., Virginia, 1987.
David E. McCord, Richard M. and Anita Calkins Distinguished Professor of Law; J.D., Harvard, 1978.
Keith C. Miller, Ellis and Nelle Levitt Distinguished Professor of Law; LL.M., Michigan, 1979.
James R. Monroe, Professor; M.B.A., Denver, 1967; LL.M., NYU, 1977.
Lawrence E. Pope, Professor; LL.M., NYU, 1969.
Daniel L. Power, Neal and Bea Smith Distinguished Professor of Law and Clinical Education and Director of the National Training and Resource Center for Public Service Attorneys; LL.M., Georgetown, 1964.
Gregory C. Sisk, Professor; J.D., Washington (Seattle), 1984.
Maura I. Strassberg, Associate Professor; J.D., Columbia, 1984.
David S. Walker, Dwight D. Opperman Distinguished Professor of Law; J.D., Virginia, 1969.

FORDHAM UNIVERSITY

School of Law
Programs in Banking, Corporate, and Finance Law and in International Business and Trade Law

Program of Study

The Graduate Program of Fordham School of Law offers two courses of study leading to graduate degrees: a Master of Laws in banking, corporate, and finance Law (LL.M.) and a Master of Laws in international business and trade law (LL.M.). Students may pursue either course of study on a full- or part-time basis.

International business and trade law, along with banking, corporate, and finance law, are vitally important and expanding areas of law today, given the growing interdependence of the United States and its trading partners and the convergence of the banking, corporate, insurance, and other financial sectors. Fordham School of Law has developed special resources and expertise in these areas. The School's Center on European Community Law and International Antitrust provides an unrivaled teaching and research resource for the Graduate Program. The Graduate Program includes seminars sponsored by the center. These seminars are unique in the United States in that European Community officials regularly lead them as part of the curriculum.

The Graduate Program also benefits from its association with the Fordham Corporate Law Institute, which conducts an annual conference on the antitrust and trade laws of the United States, the European Community and its member states, Canada, Japan, and other trading nations. In addition, the Graduate Program sponsors the Graduate Colloquium as a forum for periodic formal presentations throughout the academic year by leading scholars, government officials, and recognized leaders in practice on cutting-edge issues of particular interest to the Graduate Program.

Research Facilities

The Leo T. Kissam Memorial Library comprises nearly 50 percent of the total area of the School of Law and houses one of the major legal collections in the United States, with 450,000 volumes in print and on microform. This includes an extensive collection of English-language and international periodicals that numbers more than 4,000 titles.

Its holdings include all federal and state reporters, digests, and codes and a rapidly growing collection of international, comparative, and international legal materials. In conjunction with the Fordham Center on European Community and International Antitrust, the law library has developed one of the best collections on the European Common Market.

The Library is the home of a student computer lab and training facility that provides network access to the legal databases LEXIS and WESTLAW, as well as computer-assisted legal instruction exercises, library catalogs from Fordham and other institutions, and word processing.

Financial Aid

At the present time, there are no scholarships or fellowships available for Graduate Program students directly from the School of Law. Students are advised to make use of the various government loan programs that may be available to them, such as the Federal Subsidized Stafford and the Federal Unsubsidized Stafford programs. To be eligible for these loans, the student must be a U.S. citizen/national or an eligible noncitizen.

An applicant from abroad may wish to consult the educational attache at the United States Embassy or consulate in his or her country for information on United States government travel grants under the Fulbright program and other information on fellowship opportunities. Some countries have United States Educational Exchange Commissions.

The Rotary Foundation also awards international scholarships. Interested applicants should contact their local Rotary club to obtain application forms and inquire about the availability of scholarship types.

Cost of Study

The annual tuition cost for 1997–98 was $22,600 ($942 per credit part-time). Other charges included a nonrefundable $60 application fee. Tuition is payable in two equal installments, the first half due in August for the fall semester and the second half due in December of the same year.

Living and Housing Costs

Fordham's residence hall at Lincoln Center offers full-time students apartments overlooking a newly landscaped central plaza and the Hudson River. The hall contains 208 two- and three-bedroom apartments, all of which are carpeted, fully furnished, and equipped with efficiency kitchen appliances. On-campus housing was offered at $6300 to $7400 for the 1997–98 nine-month academic year and includes all utilities, cable TV, 100 laundry tokens per semester, and membership to the fitness center.

Student Group

The School's total student population is approximately 1,400 in the J.D. program. The Master of Laws programs have a student population of approximately 60 and a male-female ratio of 60:40. Students from abroad comprise 75 percent of the population in the master's program and represent twenty-eight nationalities.

Student Outcomes

Graduate students successfully secure employment in a wide variety of settings throughout the world. Many return to their home countries to join law firms, banks, and corporations while others choose to join American organizations. From the World Bank to Wall Street, Fordham LL.M. alumni are well received in today's global marketplace.

Location

The School of Law is located in the heart of New York City, next door to Lincoln Center for the Performing Arts. It is minutes away from the world's legal and financial centers. This fortunate coincidence affords its students an opportunity for personal and professional growth that is rare in American legal education.

The University and The School

Fordham, founded as a Jesuit institution in 1841, is a private university offering instruction in the liberal arts and in selected professional areas on both the graduate and undergraduate levels. Fordham offers the Master of Laws degree in banking, corporate, and finance law and a Master of Laws in international business and trade law to approximately 60 students. Approximately 75 percent of the student body in the master's program are from law faculties around the world. In addition, Fordham offers the J.D. degree to approximately 1,400 students. More than 172 American and international colleges are represented in the student body. The faculty is composed of 58 full-time professors and 150 adjunct professors. The adjunct faculty is drawn from leading jurists, practicing attorneys, and government officials. The atmosphere of the School, however cosmopolitan, is friendly, open, and caring. Each individual student's well-being and future success is Fordham's primary concern. What distinguishes Fordham from other universities is its diversity of academic specialties, a 150-year heritage in New York City, and a 450-year-old Jesuit tradition of quality education.

Applying

For admission to the Master of Laws program, the minimum requirements for American law school graduates are graduation from an accredited, four-year college or university or its equivalent and graduation from an approved American undergraduate school of law. The program also welcomes applications from students who have graduated from a law faculty in an international university and who have demonstrated academic achievement comparable to that of American law school graduates. All international applicants must take the Test of English as a Foreign Language (TOEFL). The method of teaching at the Fordham School of Law requires a high level of comprehension and oral expression in English, and the writing of the thesis, research papers, and examinations requires a high proficiency in the English language. The application deadline is February 28. Applicants to the program are admitted in the fall semester only.

Correspondence and Information

Director of Administration
Fordham University School of Law
Master of Laws Program
140 West 62nd Street
Department "P"
New York, New York 10023
Telephone: 212-636-6883
Fax: 212-636-6922
E-mail: llm@mail.lawnet.fordham.edu

Fordham University

THE FACULTY AND THEIR RESEARCH

Full-Time Faculty

Abraham Abramovsky, Professor of Law; J.S.D., Columbia, 1976. Crimes; New York criminal procedure; organized crime; investigation, prosecution, and defense; professional responsibility; complex criminal litigation; international criminal law; international criminal business law and litigation; Jewish law; drug law and policy; comparative criminal legal systems.

Marc M. Arkin, Professor of Law; Ph.D., Yale, 1983. Criminal law, civil procedure, conflict of laws.

Helen Hadjiyannakis Bender, Associate Professor of Law; J.D., Fordham, 1978. Contracts, commercial transactions, remedies, legal process.

Yung Frank Chiang, Professor of Law; LL.M., Northwestern, 1962. Commercial transactions, commercial paper, comparative law, commercial financing, trade with Asian nations, Far Eastern contract and commercial law.

Jeffrey M. Colon, Associate Professor of Law; M.L.T., Georgetown, 1993. Income taxation and international tax.

Carl Felsenfeld, Professor of Law and Director of the Graduate Program in International Business and Trade Law; J.D., Columbia, 1954. Banking law, bankruptcy, commercial paper (payment systems), graduate seminar.

Jill E. Fisch, Professor of Law; J.D., Yale, 1985. Advanced corporate theory, corporations, securities law.

Roger J. Goebel, Professor of Law; LL.M., NYU, 1961. Agency and partnership, corporations, corporate tender offers, EU law, EC corporate and trade law, EC-US comparative constitutional law, international business contract law.

Whitmore Gray, Visiting Professor of Law; LL.D., Michigan, 1983. Advanced commercial contract law, Asian legal systems, contracts.

Hugh C. Hansen, Associate Professor of Law; LL.M., Yale, 1977. Constitutional law, copyright law, trademark law, EU intellectual property law.

Valentine Korah, Visiting Professor of Law; University College, (London). Competition law and policy in the E.E.C.

Michael R. Lanzarone, Professor of Law; LL.M., NYU, 1973. Civil procedure, labor law, SEC regulations.

Michael T. Madison, Professor of Law; LL.M., NYU, 1971. Property, real estate finance.

Michael M. Martin, Associate Dean and Professor of Law; J.D., Iowa, 1966. Advanced evidence-seminar, evidence, conflicts of laws, complex litigation, torts, civil procedure.

Mark R. Patterson, Associate Professor of Law; J.D., Stanford, 1991. Corporations, antitrust.

Thomas M. Quinn, Norris Professor of Law; LL.M., Harvard, 1956. Uniform commercial code, advanced commercial law, consumer protection, child advocacy, public service.

Joel R. Reidenberg, Professor of Law; D.E.A., Universite de Paris I Pantheon-Sorbonne, 1987. Contract law, regulation of international trade.

David A. Schmudde, Associate Professor of Law; J.D., Florida, 1972. Corporate tax, income tax, partnership tax, federal tax procedure, real estate finance.

Donald L. Sharpe, Associate Professor of Law; LL.M., NYU, 1966. Income tax, business tax, advanced business tax, taxation of estates and trusts.

Andrew B. Sims, Associate Professor of Law; J.D., Harvard, 1973. Constitutional law, mass media law, entertainment law.

Linda Sugin, Associate Professor of Law; J.D., NYU, 1988. Taxation, corporations.

Joseph C. Sweeney, Professor of Law; LL.M., Columbia, 1963. Admiralty, air law, history of the Supreme Court, international law, international business transactions, torts.

Ludwik A. Teclaff, Professor Emeritus of Law; J.S.D., NYU, 1965. International law, law of the sea, international environmental law, jurisprudence.

Steve Thel, Professor of Law and Director of the Graduate Program in Banking, Corporate and Finance Law; J.D., Harvard, 1979. Contracts, corporate finance, corporations, securities regulation.

Chantal Thomas, Associate Professor of Law; J.D., Harvard, 1995. Regulation of international trade.

Adjunct Faculty

Kenneth Anderson, Adjunct Associate Professor of Law; J.D., Harvard. International human rights.

The Honorable Roy Babitt, Adjunct Professor of Law; LL.B., NYU. Bankruptcy.

John W. Belash, Adjunct Associate Professor of Law; LL.M., Georgetown. Investment banking regulation.

Edward S. Binkowski, Adjunct Associate Professor of Law; Ph.D., Princeton. Space law.

Victor Brudney, Adjunct Professor of Law; LL.B., Columbia, 1940. Theory of the firm, corporate finance.

The Honorable Howard C. Buschman III, Adjunct Professor of Law; LL.B., Virginia. Advanced bankruptcy.

Saul S. Cohen, Adjunct Professor of Law; J.D., Yale. Broker dealer.

Richard S. Collins, Adjunct Professor of Law; J.D., NYU. Mergers and acquisitions.

Lloyd Constantine, Adjunct Associate Professor of Law; J.D., Columbia. Antitrust.

Manuel Del Valle, Adjunct Professor of Law; LL.M., London School of Economics. International human rights.

Victor Essien, Adjunct Associate Professor of Law; J.S.D., NYU. Law and international economic development.

Jonny Frank, Adjunct Associate Professor of Law; LL.M., Yale. International criminal law.

James C. Freund, Adjunct Professor of Law; J.D., Harvard. Negotiating deals and disputes.

Lee M. Fuller, Adjunct Associate Professor of Law; J.D., Columbia. Immigration law.

Philip J. Hoblin Jr., Adjunct Professor of Law; J.D., Fordham. Securities regulation.

Karl B. Holtzschue, Adjunct Professor of Law; LL.B., Columbia. Real estate conveyancing.

Paul M. Kaplan, Adjunct Professor of Law; LL.M., London School of Economics. Law and economics.

Jeffrey L. Kessler, Adjunct Associate Professor of Law; J.D., Columbia. U.S. international antitrust and trade law.

James B. Kobak Jr., Adjunct Associate Professor of Law; LL.B., Virginia. Patents and antitrust.

David J. Larkin, Adjunct Associate Professor of Law; J.D., Columbia. Insurance.

Stewart E. Lavey, Adjunct Professor of Law; J.D., Fordham. Registration and reporting under the Securities Act of 1933 and the Securities Exchange Act of 1934.

Joel M. Leifer, Adjunct Professor of Law; LL.B., Brooklyn Law. Securities arbitration.

William T. Lifland, Adjunct Professor of Law; J.D., Harvard. Antitrust.

Judith R. MacDonald, Adjunct Professor of Law; J.D., Fordham. Investment banking regulation.

Joseph T. McLaughlin, Adjunct Professor of Law; J.D., Cornell. International commercial dispute resolution.

Lawrence G. Preble, Adjunct Professor of Law; J.D., Loyola. Advanced real estate financing II.

A. Paul Victor, Adjunct Professor of Law; J.D., Michigan. U.S. international antitrust and trade law.

David Yeres, Adjunct Associate Professor of Law; LL.M., London School of Economics. Commodity futures regulation.

Orientation, fall 1994.

GOLDEN GATE UNIVERSITY

SCHOOL OF LAW

GOLDEN GATE UNIVERSITY

School of Law

Programs of Study

Golden Gate University School of Law is noted for integrating practical skills training with legal theory and for its distinguished faculty members, who share a strong commitment to excellence in teaching and accessibility to students. The Law School offers a full-time and part-time program, with classes held during the day and at night. Full-time students may begin their studies in August or January.

As an alternative to the standard curriculum, the Law School offers the Integrated Professional Apprenticeship Curriculum (IPAC) Program, a special honors program in which students spend two semesters working full-time at law offices or government agencies, integrating legal theory with practical experience.

Areas of concentration include corporate/commercial law, criminal law, entertainment law/intellectual property, environmental law, family law, international law, labor/employment law, litigation and alternative dispute resolution, property/real estate, and public interest. Students first accepted by the law school may earn combined J.D./M.B.A. or J.D./M.P.A. degrees. Through a streamlined program, students can earn the J.D./M.B.A. in three years.

Golden Gate has an extensive clinical legal education program. Students earn academic credit while working either under the supervision of faculty members in one of three on-site clinics or under the supervision of judges or practicing attorneys in one of eight field-placement clinics.

Special programs include an Environmental Law Summer Institute in San Francisco and international law summer programs in Bangkok and Istanbul. The law school also has an exchange program with the University of Paris (Nanterre). Graduate programs include L.L.M. degrees: environmental law, international legal studies, taxation, and U.S. legal studies. Students may also earn an S.J.D. in international legal studies.

Research Facilities

The largest law collection in the San Francisco financial district, the law library houses more than 200,000 volumes, including case law and statutes from all jurisdictions and states and major digests, encyclopedias, periodicals, and treatises in U.S. and international law. All students receive training in LEXIS and WESTLAW legal databases and have access to a computer lab equipped with word processing and spreadsheet applications, CD-ROM databases, and computer-assisted legal instruction. The law library is a selective depository for both federal and California state documents. It is a member of the Research Libraries Information Network and is a charter member of the Consortium of Academic Law Libraries of San Francisco.

Financial Aid

The law school awards a number of full-tuition and partial-tuition scholarships each year based on academic achievement and LSAT score. All applicants are automatically considered for these merit scholarships. Students requiring financial aid should apply for Federal Stafford Loans and state fellowships. The Financial Aid Office evaluates students' financial needs, determines financial aid awards, and provides budget and debt management counseling.

Financial aid information is automatically sent to students who apply for admission to the law school. However, since many financial aid program deadlines are earlier than admissions deadlines, applicants should contact the Financial Aid Office as early as possible.

Cost of Study

For the J.D. program, the annual tuition for 1998–99 is approximately $19,980 for full-time and $13,090 for part-time study. For the LL.M. programs, the 1998–99 anticipated tuition is $689 per unit.

Living and Housing Costs

Although the University does not operate dormitories or residence facilities, the Housing Information Service provides updated computerized listings of housing available in San Francisco. Students have many residential choices near the University and downtown area and in nearby communities. Estimated housing costs for the 1998–99 school year are $7425.

Student Group

There are approximately 850 students in the School of Law. Two thirds are full-time students and one third are part-time. Forty-nine percent of the students are men, and 51 percent are women.

Student Outcomes

Many of the graduates begin their legal careers in small- and medium-size law firms and government agencies. Students also go on to a variety of placements in large firms, public interest positions, and corporations. More than 92 percent of the 1997 graduates completed Golden Gate's survey. Of the 161 graduates who responded, 80 percent reported they were employed.

Location

Golden Gate is in the heart of downtown San Francisco. With the legal and financial district on one side and the new South of Market area on the other, the School is within a short walk of restaurants, shopping, and cultural venues. Students work at law firms and judicial and government offices located only a few blocks away.

The University and The School

Accredited by the Western Association of Schools and Colleges, Golden Gate University is a private nonprofit institution. The School of Law, founded in 1901, is accredited by the American Bar Association, the Association of American Law Schools, and the Committee of Bar Examiners of the State of California. Graduates qualify to take the Bar in fifty states and the District of Columbia.

Applying

Applicants must hold a baccalaureate degree or its equivalent from an accredited college or university, take the LSAT, and register with the Law School Data Assembly Service (LSDAS). A complete application file consists of an application for admission, a personal statement, one letter of recommendation, an LSDAS report, and an application fee or fee waiver. Applications for fall should be received by mid-April; applications for spring should be received by mid-November. The law school has rolling admission.

Correspondence and Information

For program information and applications:

Office of Admissions
Golden Gate University, School of Law
536 Mission Street
San Francisco, California 94105–2968

Telephone: 415-442-6630
Fax: 415-442-6631
E-mail: lawadmit@ggu.edu
World Wide Web: http://www.ggu.edu/law

Golden Gate University

THE FACULTY AND THEIR RESEARCH

Barbara M. Anscher, Associate Professor of Law; J.D. (Order of the Coif), Stanford.
J. Lani Bader, Professor of Law and Dean Emeritus; J.D., Chicago. Alternative dispute resolution.
Roger Bernhardt, Professor of Law; J.D. (Order of the Coif), Chicago. Real property.
Maria Blanco, Associate Professor of Law and Associate Director, Women's Employment Rights Clinic; J.D., Berkeley.
Allan Brotsky, Professor of Law (Emeritus); LL.B., Columbia.
Leslie A. Burton, Lecturer; J.D., Santa Clara.
Allan H. Cadgene, Professor of Law; J.D., Yale.
Robert Calhoun, Professor of Law; LL.B., Yale. Criminal procedure.
Mort P. Cohen, Professor of Law; LL.M., Harvard. Constitutional rights of institutionalized persons.
Markita D. Cooper, Associate Professor of Law; J.D., Virginia.
Anne Lee Eng, Staff Attorney, Environmental Law and Justice Clinic; J.D., Columbia.
Rodney O. Fong, Associate Professor of Law and Director, Academic Assistance Program; J.D., San Francisco.
Catherine Glaze, Associate Dean for Student Services; J.D., Stanford.
Thomas M. Goetzl, Professor of Law; J.D. (Order of the Coif), Berkeley.
Helen E. Hartnell, Visiting Associate Professor of Law; J.D., Illinois.
Constance Kleiner Hood, Lecturer; LL.M., Georgetown.
Joan W. Howarth, Professor of Law; J.D. (Order of the Coif), USC. Death penalty and gender.
Lawrence H. Jones, Professor of Law; J.D., Stanford.
Marci L. Kelly, Associate Dean and Director, LL.M. in Taxation Program; LL.M., NYU.
Janice E. Kosel, Professor of Law; J.D. (Order of the Coif), Berkeley.
Sarah Hooke Lee, Law Librarian; J.D., Maine.
Neil M. Levy, Professor of Law (Emeritus); J.D., Chicago.
Judith G. McKelvey, Professor of Law and Dean Emeritus; J.D., Wisconsin.
Leslie A. Minkus, Professor of Law; LL.B., Stanford. Legal ethics.
Myron Moskovitz, Professor of Law; LL.B. (Order of the Coif), Berkeley. Criminal procedure, landlord and tenant law.
Maria L. Ontiveros, Associate Professor of Law; J.D., Harvard; J.S.D., Stanford; M.I.L.R., Cornell. Labor and employment law.
David B. Oppenheimer, Associate Professor of Law; J.D., Harvard. Civil rights.
Anthony J. Pagano, Professor of Law and Dean; J.D., Michigan.
Alan Ramo, Associate Professor of Law and Co-Director, Environmental Law and Justice Clinic; M.J., Berkeley.
Clifford Rechtschaffen, Associate Professor of Law and Co-Director, Environmental Law and Justice Clinic; J.D., Yale.
Susan Rutberg, Associate Professor of Law; J.D., Golden Gate.
Susan Schechter, Associate Professor of Law and Assistant Dean for Law Career and Alumni Services; J.D., Pittsburgh.
Bernard L. Segal, Professor of Law; J.D., Pennsylvania.
Marci Seville, Associate Professor of Law and Director, Women's Employment Rights Clinic; J.D., Rutgers.
Marc Stickgold, Professor of Law; J.D., Northwestern.
Sompong Sucharitkul, Distinguished Professor of International and Comparative Law and Director, LL.M. in International Legal Studies Program; D.Phil., Oxford; Docteur en Droit, Paris; LL.M., Harvard; Diploma, Hague Academy of International Law.
Jon H. Sylvester, Professor of Law and Associate Dean for Academic Affairs; J.D., Harvard.
John Pasley Wilson, Professor of Law and Dean Emeritus; LL.B., Harvard. Medical ethics.
Wayne S. Woody, Professor of Law; J.D., Tulane.
Michael A. Zamperini, Professor and Director, Writing and Research; J.D., George Washington.

HAMLINE
UNIVERSITY
SCHOOL OF LAW

HAMLINE UNIVERSITY

School of Law

Program of Study

Hamline University School of Law offers the supportive, service orientation of a university-affiliated private school while emphasizing the legal profession's obligation to serve the public competently and ethically in a variety of settings. Hamline's academic programs reflect this mission and effectively integrate a rich, traditional, substantive curriculum with a full complement of skills courses. Of particular note are Hamline's programs in alternative dispute resolution (ADR); business law; children and the law; law and religion; public law, government, and ethics; and moot court and litigation.

Students may choose from either full- or part-time day options, with flexible scheduling for first-year students. Classes may be scheduled in a morning block, afternoon block, or throughout the day. Faculty advisers provide personalized guidance with respect to each student's curricular options.

Unlike many schools, Hamline's intensive first-year program employs full-time research and writing instructors. Upper-division students must complete a rigorous writing requirement in a seminar course and can hone their advocacy through moot court, advanced skills classes, or through the many client-contact and client-simulation options. Hamline's Dispute Resolution Institute provides extensive ADR summer programs and a certificate option.

International academic opportunities include two accredited summer programs: the Norway Program at the University of Bergen and the Institute in Law, Religion, and Ethics at Hebrew University in Jerusalem. There are informal exchanges with the University of Costa Rica and Modena University in Italy.

Law students can also obtain a joint master's degree in public administration (M.A.P.A.) with Hamline's Graduate School or in business (M.B.A.) or accounting (A.M.B.A.) at the University of St. Thomas' Graduate School of Business.

Research Facilities

The recently expanded Hamline University Law Library presents law students and faculty with the best combination of technology, services, and books. The collection includes about 220,000 volume equivalents of books and microforms, which are supplemented with online access to WESTLAW, LEXIS, and FirstSearch databases and several sources on CD-ROM. All students have full access to the Internet. The librarians and support staff help students with library research and assist them in obtaining materials from other libraries in the area. The library's computerized catalog identifies not only materials held in the law library but also collections at Hamline University's Bush Library and six other local college libraries.

Financial Aid

Presidential and Dean's Scholarships are awarded to first-year students on the basis of perceived academic performance as measured by the LSAT, undergraduate grade point average, and the date of application. In addition, renewable tuition scholarships are awarded by the Admissions Committee to selected entering students of color based upon academic promise. Federal and private loans are administered by the Office of Financial Aid.

Cost of Study

Tuition for the 1998–99 academic year is $16,460 for full-time (12–15 credits) students and $11,852 for part-time (8–11 credits) students. If a student carries fewer than 10 hours, the tuition rate is $740 per credit hour.

Living and Housing Costs

A campus residence hall houses law students in primarily single rooms. However, most students live off campus in private homes or apartments located in the residential neighborhood surrounding the campus. During the summer months, the Office of Admissions maintains a listing of off-campus housing available in the area. *USA Today* counts the Twin Cities among the twenty-five most affordable U.S. housing markets.

Student Group

Hamline enrolls 150 students in a first-year class, representing twenty states and more than 100 undergraduate schools throughout the country. The median LSAT score for the 1997 entering class was 153, and the median GPA was 3.2. Students participate in many different activities on campus, from competing on one of the School's award-winning moot court teams to playing on the law school hockey team.

Student Outcomes

Surveys of Hamline graduates from 1992 to 1997 showed that they typically entered the following areas of practice: private practice, 37 percent; judicial clerkships, 16 percent; business/industry, 26 percent; public service, 6 percent; government service, 13 percent; academia, 1 percent; and other, 1 percent. The employment survey of the graduating class of 1996 showed 92 percent employed or enrolled in an advanced degree program within nine months after graduation.

Location

Located in a safe, residential neighborhood, Hamline University is midway between the Twin Cities of St. Paul and Minneapolis, with easy access to a variety of recreational and cultural opportunities. The Twin Cities have been recognized time and time again for their high quality of life.

The University and The School

Founded in 1854 as Minnesota's first university, Hamline University is a high-quality, nationally ranked, private liberal arts university with more than 2,700 degree-seeking students in the College of Liberal Arts, School of Law, and Graduate School. It is affiliated with the United Methodist Church. The School of Law is accredited by the American Bar Association and is a member of the Association of American Law Schools.

Applying

The Admissions Committee strives to maintain a selection process that emphasizes a fair examination of each person as an individual, not merely as a set of credentials. Applications may be obtained from the Office of Admissions.

Correspondence and Information

Office of Admissions
Hamline University School of Law
1536 Hewitt Avenue
St. Paul, Minnesota 55104-1284

Telephone: 612-523-2461
800-388-3688 (toll-free)
Fax: 612-523-2435
E-mail: lawadm@hamline.gw.edu
World Wide Web: http://www.hamline.edu

Hamline University

THE FACULTY

Raymond R. Krause, Professor and Dean; J.D., Georgetown.
Edwin J. Butterfoss, Professor and Associate Dean; J.D., Georgetown.
Larry Bakken, Professor; J.D., North Dakota; LL.M., Manitoba. Professor Bakken is the author of *Justice in the Wilderness* and coauthor of *Minnesota Administrative Procedure.* He was a Fulbright scholar to Lithuania and teaches in Hamline's graduate public administration program.
Len Biernat, Professor; J.D., Hamline; LL.M., NYU. Professor Biernat was recently elected to state legislature. He is the coauthor of *Legal Ethics for Management and Their Counsel.*
James R. Coben, Clinical Instructor; J.D., Northeastern. Mr. Coben is the lead trainer for Hamline Dispute Resolution Institute and the Mediation Center and has established an innovative mediation clinic for students.
David M. Cobin, Professor; J.D., Boston; LL.M., Harvard. Professor Cobin established a popular summer-abroad program in Israel in conjunction with Hebrew University.
Joseph Daly, Professor; J.D., William Mitchell Law. Professor Daly was chosen by the International Bar Association (London) as Lecturer to Developing Countries for 1991–92. He was recently invited by the Vietnamese government to help prepare them for a more democratic society.
Cathryn V. Deal, Professor; J.D., Indiana. Professor Deal created and supervises Hamline's award-winning moot court program, and she is an appeals judge for Minneapolis public housing department disputes.
Marie Failinger, Professor; J.D., Valparaiso; LL.M., Yale. Professor Failinger has been involved in founding professional and community organizations on poverty law, legal services for the poor, and American Indian policy and law.
Mary Jo Brooks Hunter, Clinical Instructor; J.D., UCLA. Ms. Hunter was elected the first chief justice of the Supreme Court of the Ho-Chunk Nation (formerly the Wisconsin Winnebago Nation). She serves as an appellate judge for the Turtle Mountain Chippewa Tribe and conducts workshops on the Indian Child Welfare Act and cultural issues of American Indians. She is the full-time supervisor of the Child Advocacy Clinic.
Susan A. Kiefer, Professor and Director of Library; J.D., Oregon; M.L.S., Oregon. Teaches legal research and writing and advanced legal research.
Robin K. Magee, Associate Professor; J.D., Michigan. Professor Magee was a research fellow at the University of Nairobi, where she examined Kenyan laws regulating the activities of U.S. companies operating in Kenya. She is also involved with the Committee Seeking Equal Justice for the Minnesota Eight.
William E. Martin, Associate Professor; J.D., Wisconsin. Professor Martin is a frequent lecturer in workers' compensation and employment law and is a contributing editor to *The Developing Labor Law.*
Barbara McAdoo, Professor; J.D., George Washington. Professor McAdoo is a member of the Minnesota Supreme Court task force on alternative dispute resolution, and she serves on the Board of Directors of the National Conference on Peacemaking and Conflict Resolution.
Angela McCaffrey, Director of General Practice Clinic; J.D., William Mitchell Law. Ms. McCaffrey is currently a Conciliation Court referee in Ramsey County and serves on the board of Southern Minnesota Regional Legal Services.
Douglas D. McFarland, Professor; J.D., NYU; Ph.D., Minnesota. Professor McFarland is the author of several prize-winning CALI exercises.
Mary Jane Morrison, Professor; J.D., William and Mary; Ph.D., Illinois. Professor Morrison advised the emerging Central European nations of Romania, Lithuania, and Albania on the development of their national constitutions as part of an ABA project.
Richard T. Oakes, Professor; J.D., William Mitchell Law; LL.D. (hon.), Hamline. Professor Oakes was a Fulbright scholar and visiting professor at the University of Tiranë in Albania.
Joseph E. Olson, Professor; J.D., Duke; LL.M., Florida. Professor Olson routinely serves on committees recommending changes to Minnesota's Business Corporation Act.
James R. Pielemeier, Professor; J.D., Indiana. Professor Pielemeier has published extensively in the areas of civil procedure and conflict of laws.
Marilynne K. Roberts, Associate Professor; J.D., Minnesota. Professor Roberts litigated the first acid rain deposition standard in the U.S. She served as presenter to the Global Environmental Issues Commission at the Europe-American Emerging Leaders Conference.
Linda J. Rusch, Professor; J.D., Iowa. Professor Rusch is a member of the ABA committees studying revisions to Articles 2, 7, and 9 of the UCC and is the associate reporter for the Article 2 drafting committee.
Kenneth C. Salzberg, Associate Professor; J.D., UCLA. Professor Salzberg's research interests include landlord/tenant law, water law, medieval property law, and Fifth Amendment "taking" jurisprudence.
Michael V. Scherschligt, Associate Professor; J.D., Valparaiso; M.Div., Concordia Seminary. Professor Scherschligt is the founding editor of Hamline's *Journal of Law and Religion.* He is currently an education consultant to the Society of Certified Insurance Counselors.
Robert J. Sheran, Dean Emeritus; LL.B., Minnesota; LL.D. (hon.), Hamline. Dean Sheran is a former Minnesota Supreme Court Justice and is the only judge to be appointed twice to the Supreme Court.
Carol B. Swanson, Professor; J.D., Vanderbilt. Professor Swanson routinely serves on committees recommending changes to Minnesota's Business Corporation Act.
Steven R. Swanson, Professor; J.D., Vanderbilt; LL.M., Yale. Professor Swanson is chair of AALS maritime law section and has published articles on public international law, international civil litigation, admiralty, the European Economic Community, and trusts.
Peter N. Thompson, Professor; J.D., Michigan. Professor Thompson has published extensively in the areas of evidence and criminal law. He has written a major treatise, *Minnesota Practice: Evidence;* has coauthored books on class action suits and courtroom practice; and has done extensive research on the role and function of the jury.
Howard J. Vogel, Professor; J.D., Minnesota; M.A.R.S., United Theological. Professor Vogel is the managing editor of Hamline's *Journal of Law and Religion.* He is engaged in research on the ethical and religious dimensions of constitutional law and the lawyer's vocation.
John E. Weeks, Professor; J.D., Minnesota. Professor Weeks was an academic visitor at the London School of Economics and did postgraduate study at the Parker School of Foreign and Comparative Law at Columbia University as well as at the Hague Academy of International Law in the Netherlands.

NEW COLLEGE OF CALIFORNIA

School of Law

Program of Study

New College of California School of Law is the oldest public interest law school in the nation. Since 1973, New College has offered an innovative program of legal education, combining practical skills training, rigorous classroom work, and supportive services, all in the pursuit of training talented, creative, and compassionate lawyers who will work in the public interest in new and dynamic ways. There are now hundreds of New College attorneys practicing law in neighborhood offices, government agencies, and community organizations, all sharing a special bond based on their experience at this unique school.

The curriculum centers around courses in fundamental doctrine, trial practice and skills courses, and clinical programs both on and off campus. The Apprenticeship Program places advanced students in law offices and agencies to earn academic credit while learning about the practice of law. The on-campus Criminal Defense Program gives third-year students the opportunity to provide direct legal representation for clients. The Housing Advocacy Clinic trains second- and third-year law students to provide legal assistance to low-income tenants facing wrongful evictions. The fundamental doctrine courses, covering those topics tested on the California bar exam, emphasize the intricacies of existing rules and doctrines while offering a critical perspective on the role of law in promoting or hindering social change.

Academic support services are available to all students, regardless of academic standing, in the form of counseling, tutorials, and workshops. The J.D. degree can be earned through either a full-time (three-year) or part-time (four-year) program of study.

Research Facilities

The Law Library plays a central role in the legal education provided at New College. In addition to its collection of more than 20,000 volumes, the library provides students with unlimited access to computer-assisted legal research through WESTLAW, Dialog, MELVYL, and other databases. The Law Library also maintains interactive video equipment and program and word processing stations. The collection meets the requirements of the State Bar of California and includes an extensive collection of practice-oriented materials. In addition, New College participates in the interlibrary loan network, making more than 20 million titles available on request.

Financial Aid

New College School of Law assists many of its students in obtaining the necessary funding to meet the costs of a legal education. The Financial Aid Office administers various state and federal financial aid programs, including grants, loans, and work-study awards. New College also administers several private financial aid programs, such as the Third World Scholarship Fund for students from minority groups with unmet financial need (made possible with funds from the Leon and Esther Blum Foundation) and the M. Jay Kramer Foundation Awards for students pursuing careers in public interest law.

Cost of Study

For 1998–99, tuition is $9394 per year for full-time students and $7048 per year for part-time students. There is a $45 application fee and a student services fee of $25 per semester.

Living and Housing Costs

San Francisco provides several residential neighborhoods with affordable housing within short distances of the campus. The cost of living varies from student to student, depending on living arrangements and other factors.

Student Group

New College School of Law maintains a small, supportive environment with an overall enrollment of 140 students, with an entering first-year class of about 45 students. The student population is highly diverse, with 55 percent women and more than 40 percent of the students from minority groups. In addition, there is a significant presence of lesbian and gay students. There are more than 600 alumni, the majority practicing law in California in public-sector jobs such as in public defender or legal aid offices or in private practice. Alumni obtained many of these positions through contacts made while they were law students participating in the clinical programs.

Location

New College is housed in a four-story landmark building in the heart of San Francisco's Civic Center, within walking distance of numerous government agencies, state and federal trial courts, appellate courts, and law offices where students apprentice as part of their legal education. The Civic Center is also the site of the San Francisco Opera, Symphony, Ballet, and Museum of Modern Art. All public transportation, including BART and MUNI, serves the area.

The College

New College is fully accredited by the Committee of Bar Examiners of the State Bar of California and by the Western Association of Schools and Colleges. Graduates are qualified to sit for the bar examination in California. New College law graduates may sit for the bar exam in some other states after having practiced in California for a certain number of years. The School of Law is an integral part of New College of California, which was founded in 1971 and which offers a wide range of undergraduate and graduate programs annually serving more than 850 students as an alternative to mainstream education.

Applying

New College School of Law seeks to attract socially concerned students from diverse backgrounds who intend to pursue careers in public interest law. The Admissions Office considers factors such as motivation, work and community experience, maturity, and public interest awareness along with standard academic criteria such as LSAT scores and academic histories. First consideration is given to applicants who apply by March 1 of each year. Applicants are expected to take the LSAT no later than February of the year for which they are applying. Most applicants hold a bachelor's degree, but those with less than four years of college and significant life experience may be eligible for admission. Full details are available from the Admissions Office.

Correspondence and Information

Admissions Office
New College of California School of Law
50 Fell Street
San Francisco, California 94102
Telephone: 800-335-6262 Ext. 353 (toll-free)
E-mail: lawinfo@ncgate.newcollege.edu
World Wide Web: http://www.newcollege.edu/Programs/Law/

New College of California

THE FACULTY

New College law faculty members are dedicated legal practitioners and educators who teach because of their desire to participate in the education of competent public interest lawyers and because of their commitment to social and political change. The faculty has an outstanding reputation in the San Francisco Bay Area legal community for its involvement in public service activities, progressive causes, and for its scholarship in the field of critical legal theory.

The faculty at New College is one of the most diverse law faculties in the nation. Women comprise more than 40 percent of the faculty, and one third of the faculty are members of minority groups. In addition, more than 15 percent of the faculty are gay or lesbian. This multicultural faculty adds an important component to the legal education of socially responsible lawyers.

James Raymond Bell, Professor of Law; J.D., California, Hastings Law.
Hon. Jeff Brown, Professor of Law; J.D., San Francisco Law School.
Martin DeJulia, Professor of Law; J.D., New College of California.
Geoffrey Dryvynsyde, Professor of Law; J.D., Yale.
Peter Gabel, Professor of Law and President of New College of California; J.D., Harvard; Ph.D., Wright Institute.
Michael Ginther, Professor of Law; J.D., Golden Gate.
Paul Harris, Professor of Law; J.D., Berkeley.
Chris Gus Kanios, Professor of Law; J.D., New College of California.
Debrenia Madison, Professor of Law and Dean; J.D., Georgetown.
Akilah Monifa, Professor of Law; J.D., Santa Clara.
John Timothy Philipsborn, Professor of Law; J.D., California, Davis.
Ora Prochovnick, Professor of Law; J.D., New College of California.
Maria Diana Ramos, Professor of Law; J.D., Pennsylvania.
Edward R. Roybal, Professor of Law; J.D., Berkeley.
Dean Ito Taylor, Professor of Law; J.D., San Francisco.

In addition to the senior core and associate faculty, New College has a talented group of adjunct faculty members teaching on a regular, part-time basis.

Kent Brintnall, J.D., Northwestern, 1994. Constitutional law.
Thuy Bui, J.D., Santa Clara, 1994. Legal writing and research.
Diana Bullock, J.D., New College of California, 1987. Criminal Defender Clinic.
Geoff Dryvynsyde, J.D., Yale, 1988. Corporations.
Alex Green, J.D., New College of California, 1984. Associate Director, Criminal Defender Clinic.
Geri Green, J.D., Hastings, 1986. Evidence.
Maya L. Harris, J.D., Stanford, 1992. Contracts.
Kathryn Kendall, J.D., Utah. Legal ethics.
Bridgit Lawley, J.D., California, Hastings Law, 1989. Civil procedure.
Joseph A. Myers, J.D., Berkeley, 1975. Indian justice.
Graham Noyes, J.D., California, Davis, 1991. Criminal procedure.
Christy Susman, J.D., Hastings, 1992. Corporations.
Rebecca Young, J.D, Golden Gate, 1985. Criminal pretrial skills.

Oklahoma Professor Anita Hill delivered New College School of Law's commencement address in May 1992. Hill was awarded an honorary doctorate by the School.

OHIO NORTHERN UNIVERSITY

Claude W. Pettit College of Law

Program of Study

Ohio Northern University offers a well-balanced legal education that combines small classes and a low student-faculty ratio with a solid curriculum, faculty expertise, and a high-quality environment for the study of law. The College of Law offers a three-year, full-time program leading to the Juris Doctor degree. The degree is conferred upon the successful completion of 87 semester hours of legal study.

The educational program provides graduates with a strong foundation in the fundamentals of American law. A program of study with a concentration in certain areas of law is also possible due to the exceptional combination of faculty expertise and experience. The curriculum includes electives in a number of areas, such as business law and taxation, international law, intellectual property law, criminal law, environmental law, pharmacy law, public interest law, and trial law.

The College offers a number of opportunities for practical experience such as the Client-Clinic Program, in which students may represent low-income clients in criminal misdemeanor or civil cases by interviewing and advising clients, preparing legal documents, and representing clients in court. A strong moot court program, opportunities for judicial externships, the Pharmacy-Law Institute, and nationally recognized publications, such as the *ONU Law Review* and *Women's Law Journal*, complement a full selection of academic and professional opportunities.

Research Facilities

The Jay P. Taggart Law Library, a federal government depository, contains more than 260,000 volumes and equivalents in its collection. The library has twenty-five computer terminals equipped with word processing and both LEXIS and WESTLAW available to students for legal research. Current renovations include a substantial increase in computerization throughout the library and classrooms. In addition to excellent computer and network facilities, the library holds an extensive collection of volumes concerning American federal and state law and Commonwealth materials focusing on Canada and the United Kingdom.

Financial Aid

All aid programs are administered by Ohio Northern University's Financial Aid Office. Required documents include an ONU Application for Financial Aid, financial aid transcripts, and the Free Application for Federal Student Aid (FAFSA). Applicants are encouraged to begin a file at the Financial Aid Office as soon as possible after January 1. Federal loans are administered by the office, as well as private loans such as Law Access Loans and Law Loans. Through the Legal Scholar Program, students who have excelled academically may be eligible for scholarships of up to $19,000. Merit Awards of up to $10,000 are based on the cumulative first-year and second-year GPA, and Diversity Awards may be granted to students who will enhance diversity, particularly ethnic diversity, in the student body and in the legal profession. In addition, a $500 grant is made available to a current student who chooses public interest work over the summer.

Cost of Study

Tuition for the 1998–99 year is $18,980 per annum, with $50 of that amount dedicated to student activities fees.

Living and Housing Costs

Students will find that off-campus housing in the Village of Ada is relatively inexpensive, and other living costs are below national averages. The Law Admissions Office maintains a listing of off-campus housing available, such as various apartment communities and homes to rent within a short distance of campus. Limited on-campus housing is available for men and women in the Barristers' Annex, which is located conveniently adjacent to the Law College.

Student Group

The student population of approximately 350 law students is a diverse assemblage of men, women, and minority groups representing more than 200 undergraduate institutions and more than 30 states. Members of an alumni body of more than 3,600 are practicing in fifty states, the District of Columbia, Puerto Rico, England, Taiwan, and Australia, with approximately 175 alumni serving as judges. A full selection of activities is available. Some opportunities include a strong moot court program, the *ONU Law Review,* the *Women's Law Journal,* the *Environmental Law Journal,* the Student Bar Association, Criminal Law Society, Legal Association for Women, Street Law Program, American Trial Lawyers Association, Volunteer Income Tax Assistance, Icelandic Exchange Program, Criminal Dispute Resolution Program, and a variety of honorary societies such as the Order of Barristers and Phi Kappa Phi.

Student Outcomes

Within six months of graduation, approximately 76 percent of the College's graduates from the class of 1996 were employed, with key areas of placement being in private practice, government, judicial clerkships, and business. ONU has an outstanding placement rate in federal judicial clerkships as well as a strong bar-passage rate. Several national firms recently joined the ONU on-campus interviewing program. A successful network of alumni contacts provides students with a direct link to the legal market.

Location

Located in northwest Ohio, the village of Ada is home to the beautiful, collegiate campus of Ohio Northern University. The 280-acre campus is a peaceful environment and is also home to a cultural arts center and the most comprehensive sports center in northwest Ohio. Ada is an ideal setting, having few safety concerns and a low cost of living, with the regional trading centers of Findlay and Lima located within 25 minutes' driving time. Lima affords various practical experience opportunities, such as the ONU Legal Clinic, and the metropolitan areas of Columbus, Dayton, Toledo, and Fort Wayne, Indiana, are between 60 and 90 minutes away.

The College

Founded in 1885, the College of Law has enjoyed a rich and distinguished history. Accredited by the American Bar Association and a member of the Association of American Law Schools, the College of Law was also a founding member of the League of Ohio Law Schools. Many outstanding legal scholars have passed through the College's doors and gone on to serve as lawyers, judges, scholars, senators, governors, and congressmen.

Applying

The College of Law admits students for full-time study only, and first-year students are admitted for classes beginning in the fall of each year. Candidates for admission must submit an application for admission, have a baccalaureate degree from an accredited college or university prior to the start of fall semester, take the Law School Admission Test (LSAT), and register for the Law School Data Assembly Service (LSDAS). The Admissions Committee will review files on a rolling basis beginning in late fall and will make decisions until the entering class is filled. While there is no deadline for applying for admission, students are encouraged to apply early to avail themselves of the most consideration possible for admission and financial aid awards.

Correspondence and Information

Office of Law Admissions
Claude W. Pettit College of Law
Ohio Northern University
525 South Main Street
Ada, Ohio 45810

Telephone: 419-772-2211
E-mail: g-justice@onu.edu
World Wide Web: http://www.law.onu.edu

Ohio Northern University

THE FACULTY AND THEIR INTERESTS

In addition to the full-time faculty listed below, Ohio Northern University draws upon a number of distinguished attorneys who provide special experience and expertise as adjunct professors for upper-level courses.

Andrew Beckerman-Rodau, Professor of Law; J.D., Western New England, LL.M., Temple. Property, antitrust, intellectual property.
David J. Benson, Professor of Law; J.D., Syracuse. Torts, domestic relations, criminal law.
Joanne C. Brant, Associate Professor of Law; J.D., Case Western Reserve. Federal courts, corporations, law and literature, employment discrimination, legal ethics.
John Paul Christoff, Professor of Law; J.D., Ohio Northern. Evidence, criminal law, criminal procedure, juvenile law.
David C. Crago, Associate Professor of Law; J.D., Michigan. Business and commercial law.
William L. Evans, Associate Dean and Professor of Law; J.D., Ohio Northern. Decedents' estates and trusts, real property, law and medicine.
Howard N. Fenton III, Interim Dean and Professor of Law; J.D., Texas. Comparative law, international trade law, international law, contracts.
Bruce Comly French, Professor of Law; J.D., Antioch College. Constitutional law, civil procedure, employment discrimination, labor law, criminal procedure.
Richard L. Haight, Professor of Law; J.D., Suffolk; LL.M., Boston University. Federal income tax, estate and gift tax, decedents' estates, estate planning.
Charles J. Hickey, Legal Scholar in Residence; J.D., Yale. Securities regulation, taxes, pension and employee benefits, business planning.
Paula Hicks-Hudson, Instructor of Legal Research and Writing; J.D., Iowa; M.A., Colorado State. Legal research and writing.
Kevin D. Hill, Professor of Law; J.D., Northern Kentucky; LL.M., Temple. Complex litigation, civil procedure, environmental law, evidence, federal courts.
Gregory Laughlin, Assistant Professor and Director of Law Library; M.S.L.S., Illinois; J.D., Missouri. Legal research and writing.
Louis F. Lobenhofer, Professor of Law; J.D., Colorado; LL.M., Denver. Federal income taxation, taxation of partnerships and partners, taxation of corporations and shareholders, law and accounting.
David W. Raack, Professor of Law; J.D., Missouri; LL.M., Temple; LL.M., Columbia. Contracts, legal ethics, jurisprudence, international law, appellate advocacy.
Victor L. Streib, Dean and Professor of Law; J.D., Indiana Bloomington. Capital punishment, criminal law and procedure, juvenile law, women and law.
Vernon L. Traster, Professor of Law; J.D., Drake. Torts, evidence, insurance law.
Katherine A. VanTassel, Law Clinical Director and Instructor; J.D., Case Western Reserve. Products liability litigation.
George D. Vaubel, Professor of Law; LL.B., Ohio Northern; LL.M., Michigan. Constitutional law, civil rights, municipal corporations.
Stephen C. Veltri, Professor of Law; J.D., Georgetown; LL.M., Columbia. Commercial paper, secured transactions, property.
David R. Warner Jr., Professor of Law; J.D., Nebraska; LL.M., Chicago. Administrative law, contracts, law and computers.
Sherry Young, Associate Professor of Law; J.D., Harvard. Torts, products liability, domestic relations, sports law.

Ohio Northern's active moot court program produces national championship teams while preparing students to be more competitive in the national job market.

The 350 students in the College of Law share the beauty, safety, and small-college atmosphere of the 280-acre Ohio Northern campus.

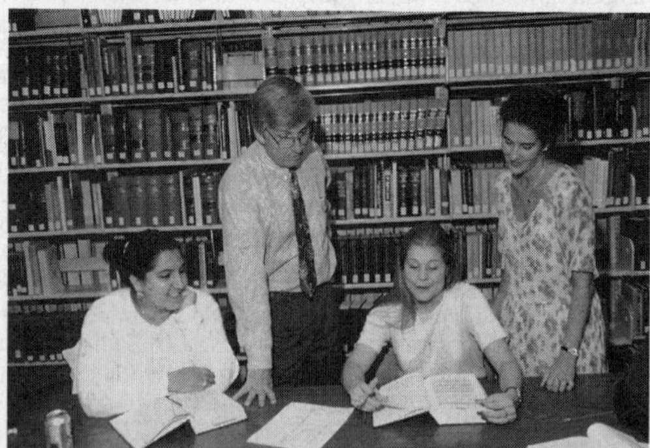

Professor Howard Fenton, an international trade law authority, shares the commitment of Ohio Northern's faculty to help students achieve their highest potential.

PACE UNIVERSITY

School of Law

Programs of Study

Pace School of Law offers a rich array of elective courses covering virtually every facet of law and its interactions with society. Students have the flexibility to build their own programs of legal study on the foundation of basic legal principles and skills, sampling from a variety of areas or focusing in an area of particular interest.

The Juris Doctor (J.D.) program is designed to be completed in three years of full-time study or four years of part-time study in the day or evening division. The curriculum and quality of the day and evening programs do not differ except in scheduling. Full-time faculty members teach courses in both programs. Almost 100 courses are offered each term by School of Law faculty members. In addition, up to 10 credits taken from other graduate programs at Pace University may be applied to the J.D. degree.

Candidates for the J.D. degree may earn certificates demonstrating their proficiency in specialized areas of the law. The certificate programs in environmental law, health law and policy, and international law each require the successful completion of 12 course credits.

Pace offers a program in cooperation with the University of London, University College Faculty of Laws, which provides students with a valuable perspective on European and international law. Students also take part in clinical internships with English law firms and members of Parliament.

The J.D./M.B.A. is a closely integrated program that enables students to pursue graduate studies in law and business administration concurrently.

The J.D./M.P.A. is a combined program in law and public administration that aims to prepare students seeking careers in law, government, and public interest organizations and health care and related fields.

The School of Law offers two graduate programs, the Master of Laws (LL.M.) in environmental law and the Doctor of Juridical Science (S.J.D.).

Research Facilities

The School of Law, recognizing the central role of the law library in legal education, has developed an extensive law library facility that is housed in the Glass Law Center. The Pace Law Library collection contains more than 300,000 volumes, including microform volumes. The collection includes the basic materials necessary for the curriculum and for research in Anglo-American law. These materials include court reports, statutes, and other materials for all fifty states, the federal government, and a number of British Commonwealth countries. The collection contains a special group of international materials with an emphasis on international trade and business law. The law library, designated a federal depository in 1978, receives federal executive, administrative, and Congressional primary materials through this program. Other legal materials, such as encyclopedias, law reviews, loose-leaf services, federal legislative history materials, and legal treatises, are available for use. Each of the library's many computer terminals gives students free access to all the information in the LEXIS, WESTLAW, NEXIS, and Dialog databases. Internet access is also provided over most of the library computers.

Financial Aid

The School of Law feels a responsibility to assist students with financial need to the extent that funds are available. In addition, the School of Law recognizes those students with superior academic achievement. To achieve these goals, a comprehensive aid program has been developed to include grants, employment, scholarships, and loans that may be available on the basis of financial need, academic merit, educational costs, or credit considerations.

Cost of Study

Every effort is made by the University to minimize increases in tuition and fees. Under flat-rate tuition, the tuition amount payable depends on the program in which the student registers and not directly upon the number of credits taken. Tuition for the 1998–99 academic year is $10,875 per semester for the full-time program and $8162 per semester for the part-time program.

Living and Housing Costs

University housing is available for single law students in Dannat Hall, the University's residence hall. It is located on the White Plains campus near the Law Library and an on-campus dining facility. Dannat Hall is a five-story building equipped with a kitchen, a laundry room, and a weight room. Furnished single rooms are available at a cost of $6380 for the nine-month 1998–99 academic year. Double rooms are available for $5160.

A variety of off-campus housing is available in White Plains and the surrounding area. Rates for residential housing vary widely with the type of accommodation provided. While some assistance is provided in locating off-campus housing, final responsibility in securing housing rests with the student.

Location

The White Plains campus on historic North Broadway is the home of the School of Law and satisfies a community need as the only law school between New York City and Albany.

White Plains, the county seat of Westchester County, is an attractive and lively city of some 50,000 inhabitants in which the United States District Court for the Ninth Judicial District, major state courts, and the county government headquarters are situated. The area is the home of a thriving business community that includes the corporate headquarters of many Fortune 500 companies and branches of major New York stores. An extensive city and county park system provides recreational facilities and acres of parkland. The location of White Plains provides easy access both to scenic areas of northern Westchester, the Hudson River Valley, and Connecticut and to the cultural resources of New York City. The center of Manhattan is approximately 25 miles away and can be reached in about 40 minutes.

Student Outcomes

The School's Office of Career Development provides a broad range of services designed to educate students about both various legal career alternatives and the job search process itself. Throughout the academic year, the office holds workshops and panel presentations and each spring holds a networking reception for the School's graduating class. The office administers a fall on-campus interview program and regularly receives notice of opportunities for part-time, summer, full-time (for evening students), and permanent employment.

The University

The School of Law is part of a modern, diversified university. Founded in 1906 with an initial enrollment of 13 students, Pace University's six graduate and undergraduate schools today enroll approximately 15,000 students. More than 1,200 faculty members help students achieve their educational goals in the arts and sciences, computer science and information systems, business administration, nursing, education, and law. The School of Law faculty takes pride in its teaching excellence and its commitment to legal scholarship and community service. In and out of the classroom, the Pace faculty's obvious commitment to students' learning sets the tone for a stimulating and rigorous, yet supportive, academic environment.

Applying

The School of Law received more than 2,800 applications for 1997–98 admission. It enrolls approximately 170 day and 80 evening students annually. Admission is very competitive. The GPAs of the admitted classes average 3.2, and the mean LSAT score is around the 70th percentile. The GPA and LSAT are the two most important factors for admission; however, many additional factors, including school(s) attended, grade progression, and courses taken, are also considered. Students are encouraged to apply by February 15 for equal consideration for admission.

Correspondence and Information

Office of Admissions
Pace University School of Law
78 North Broadway
White Plains, New York 10603

Telephone: 914-422-4210
Fax: 914-422-4010
E-mail: admissions@genesis.law.pace.edu
World Wide Web: http://www.law.pace.edu

Pace University

THE FACULTY

Barbara A. Atwell, Associate Professor of Law; J.D., Columbia.
Eric E. Bergsten, Professor of Commercial Law; J.D., Michigan.
Adele Bernhard, Associate Professor of Law; J.D., NYU.
Barbara Black, Professor of Law; J.D., Columbia.
Jay C. Carlisle, Professor of Law; J.D., California, Davis.
Seymour A. Casper, Professor of Law Emeritus in Residence; LL.M., J.D., NYU.
Karl S. Coplan, Associate Professor of Law; J.D., Columbia.
Donald L. Doernberg, Professor of Law; J.D., Columbia.
David Dorfman, Assistant Professor of Law; J.D., IIT.
James J. Fishman, Professor of Law; J.D., NYU.
Leslie Yalof Garfield, Associate Professor of Law; J.D., Florida.
Bennett L. Gershman, Professor of Law; J.D., NYU.
Steven H. Goldberg, Professor of Law; J.D., Minnesota.
Shelby D. Green, Associate Professor of Law; J.D., Georgetown.
Lissa Griffin, Professor of Law; Law clerkship, 1973–77.
JoAnn Harris, Scholar in Residence; J.D., NYU.
John A. Humbach, Professor of Law; J.D., Ohio State.
Ronald H. Jensen, Professor of Law; LL.B., Harvard.
Irene Johnson, Professor of Law; J.D., Columbia.
Janet A. Johnson, Professor of Law; LL.M., Virginia; J.D., Drake.
Robert F. Kennedy Jr., Professor of Environmental Law; LL.M., Pace; J.D., Virginia.
Josephine Y. King, Professor of Law; J.D., SUNY at Buffalo.
Norman B. Lichtenstein, Professor of Law and Associate Dean for Student Affairs; LL.B., Yale.
M. Stuart Madden, James D. Hopkins Professor of Law; J.D., Georgetown.
Thomas M. McDonnell, Associate Professor of Law; J.D., Fordham.
Vanessa Merton, Professor of Law and Associate Dean for Clinical Education; J.D., NYU.
Jeffrey G. Miller, Professor of Law; LL.B., Harvard.
Gary A. Munneke, Associate Professor of Law; J.D., Texas.
Michael B. Mushlin, Professor of Law and Associate Dean for Academic Affairs; J.D., Northwestern.
John R. Nolon, Professor of Law; J.D., Michigan.
Joseph M. Olivenbaum, Associate Professor of Law; J.D., Northeastern.
Paul O'Neil, Professor of Law; J.D., Oregon.
Richard L. Ottinger, Professor of Law and Dean; LL.B., Harvard.
Ann Powers, Associate Professor of Law; J.D., Georgetown.
Nicholas A. Robinson, Professor of Law; J.D., Columbia.
Audrey Rogers, Associate Professor of Law; J.D., St. John's (New York).
Aaron M. Schreiber, Professor of Law; LL.M., J.S.D., Yale; J.D., Brooklyn Law.
Randolph M. Scott-McLaughlin, Professor of Law; J.D., Harvard.
Michelle S. Simon, Associate Professor of Law; J.D., Syracuse.
David Sive, Professor of Environmental Law; LL.B., Columbia.
Blaine Sloan, Professor Emeritus of International Law and Organization; LL.B., Nebraska; LL.M., Columbia.
William R. Slye, Professor of Law and Director of Environmental Legal Programs; LL.B., Michigan.
Merrill Sobie, Professor of Law; J.D., NYU.
Ralph M. Stein, Professor of Law; J.D., Hofstra.
Nicholas Triffin, Professor of Law, Director of the Law Library, and Director of the Institute for International Commercial Law; M.L.S., Rutgers; J.D., Yale.
Gayl S. Westerman, Professor of Law; LL.M., J.S.D., Yale; J.D., Pace.
David R. Wooley, Professor for Environmental and Energy Law and Executive Director, Center for Environmental Legal Studies; J.D., Rutgers.
Stephen A. Zorn, Associate Professor of Law; J.D., Fordham.

QUINNIPIAC COLLEGE SCHOOL OF LAW

Programs of Study

Quinnipiac College School of Law provides an education in the nature and the function of law and legal institutions in society; in addition, the School of Law trains students in the skills, practices, and technologies of the profession. The School of Law confers the Juris Doctor (J.D.). Candidates are required to take 86 credits, which they complete in six semesters of full-time study (day) or eight semesters of part-time study (day or evening). The educational program at Quinnipiac College School of Law is designed to encourage students to prepare for careers not only in the practice of law but also in teaching, business, industry, politics, the civil service, and the public interest. The curriculum for the first two years is traditional and largely prescribed. After that, students may choose from a variety of courses in order to broaden their legal training or to specialize in their chosen field. Cooperative education programs supplement the classroom curriculum. There are four clinical programs: appellate, civil, health, and tax. The School of Law also offers five externship programs: corporate counsel, judicial, legislative, criminal justice, and public interest. J.D./M.B.A. and J.D./M.H.A. joint degree programs are also available.

Research Facilities

The Law Library contains more than 280,000 volumes and an extensive audiovisual collection. It is equipped with LEXIS and WESTLAW, computerized legal research systems, and IBM PCs for word processing and computer-assisted legal instruction programs.

Financial Aid

Financial aid is received by approximately 80 percent of applicants in the form of scholarships, grants, loans, and work-study awards. Admissions applicants are automatically considered for merit scholarships as determined by the Scholarship Committee. Merit scholarships are also available to upperclass students, based upon performance in law school, and those demonstrating need receive consideration for merit/need-based scholarships. Special consideration is given to students who add diversity to the class.

Cost of Study

Tuition for the academic year 1998–99 is $833 per credit for part-time students (minimum 8 credits) and $19,992 per year for full-time students (12 to 16 credits). The annual Student Bar Association fee for all law students is $75. Students must also pay an annual student fee of $435.

Living and Housing Costs

There is ample, affordable housing available throughout Fairfield and New Haven counties. The School of Law Admissions Office and the Quinnipiac College Office of Residential Life assist in securing off-campus accommodations.

Student Group

The student body of 800 is diverse in terms of geographics, background, education, age, and work experience, and yet it is homogenous in terms of approach and of goals. The first-year class comprises approximately 220 students (65 percent men, 35 percent women) and is taught in three sections: one evening and two day. The mean age of the entering class is 27. About half of the students come directly from undergraduate college. Approximately 13 percent of the class has been out of school for ten or more years, and the mean age of this group is 40; many of them are second-career people and reentering women.

Student boards of the School of Law edit *QLR (The Law Review)* and the *Connecticut Probate Law Journal.* Students also publish a law school newspaper entitled *Quinnipiac Law Times.* Moot Court Board and Mock Trial Society organize intramural competitions and participate in regional and national events. Quinnipiac has a very active Student Bar Association, and its other student organizations include several law fraternities, the Law Women's Association, the Black American Law Students' Association, the Spanish American Student Association, the Jewish American Law Students' Association, the Grotius Society of International Law, the Environmental Law Society, the Sports and Entertainment Law Society, and the Legal Aid Society.

Location

Quinnipiac College School of Law is located in Hamden, Connecticut, only 8 miles from New Haven. The 122,000-square-foot Law Center, which consists of four buildings, is situated on an idyllic 180-acre campus, 90 minutes from New York and 2 hours from Boston.

The School

Dedicated in 1995, the award-winning Law Center is located on the idyllic Hamden Campus of Quinnipiac College, an independent institution founded in 1929. Fully accredited by the American Bar Association, the fundamental strength of the Law School lies in the faculty members' dedication to academic excellence. The rigors of the program are tempered by the personal attention and individual regard that students receive. Faculty members come from a wide variety of distinguished backgrounds in law practice and teaching and have a commitment to excellence in education.

The School of Law has its own Placement Office that provides full placement and counseling services, publishes a monthly job opportunities bulletin, and runs career symposia to expose students to diverse areas of work and to apprise them of employment trends. Most recent placement surveys show that 88 percent of the graduating class is employed within six months of graduation.

Applying

The School employs a rolling admission system: there are no formal application deadlines, although early application is advised. The School of Law offers fall and spring enrollment: full-time students are admitted in the fall; part-time students are admitted in the fall and in the spring (evening classes). Applicants are encouraged to visit the School, to meet with students, and to attend classes.

Admission is based on undergraduate scholastic record, scores on the Law School Admission Test, and other evidence, such as advanced degrees, employment experience, and extracurricular activities, that indicates probable success in the study of law.

Correspondence and Information

Director of Admissions
School of Law
Quinnipiac College
275 Mt. Carmel Avenue
Hamden, Connecticut 06518-1948
Telephone: 203-287-3400
Fax: 203-287-3339

Financial Aid Office
School of Law
Quinnipiac College
275 Mt. Carmel Avenue
Hamden, Connecticut 06518-1948
Telephone: 203-287-3405
Fax: 203-287-3339

Quinnipiac College School of Law

ADMINISTRATIVE OFFICERS AND FACULTY

Administrative Officers

Neil H. Cogan, Professor of Law and Dean; J.D., ca Pennsylvania.
David S. King, Associate Professor of Law and Associate Dean; J.D., Cleveland State; LL.M., Harvard.
Celia-Ann Edwards, Administrative Associate Dean of Students; J.D., Boston University.
John Noonan, Dean of Admissions; M.A., Fairfield.
Deborah Benvenger Assistant Dean of Admissions; M.B.A., Iona.
Anne Traverso, Director of Financial Aid; B.A., Elmira.
Ann DeVeaux, Director of Law Library; J.D., Bridgeport; M.L.S., Southern Connecticut.
Susan Spalter, Director of Career Counseling and Services; J.D., Bridgeport.

Faculty

Melanie Abbott, Assistant Professor of Law; J.D., Bridgeport.
Terence H. Benbow, Professor of Law; J.D., Yale.
Brian Bix, Associate Professor of Law; J.D., Harvard; D.Phil, Oxford.
Jennifer Brown, Associate Professor of Law; J.D., Illinois.
Donald A. Browne, Adjunct Professor of Law; J.D., Connecticut; LL.M., NYU.
Ira B. Charmoy, Adjunct Professor of Law; J.D., Connecticut.
Frederick Tse-Shyang Chen, Professor of Law; J.D., Chicago; LL.M., Yale.
Joseph Corradino, Adjunct Professor of Law; J.D., Catholic University.
Susan Dailey, Writing Specialist; Ph.D., Catholic University.
William Dunlap, Associate Professor of Law; J.D., Yale.
Richard Emmanuel, Assistant Professor of Law; J.D., George Washington.
Steven J. Errante, Adjunct Professor of Law; J.D., SUNY at Buffalo.
Robert Farrell, Professor of Law; J.D., Harvard.
Neil R. Feigenson, Assistant Professor of Law and Director of the Legal Skills Program; J.D., Harvard.
Mary Ferrari, Assistant Professor of Law; J.D., Cornell; LL.M. (taxation), NYU.
Marilyn J. Ford, Professor of Law; J.D., Rutgers.
Samuel S. Freedman, Adjunct Professor of Law; LL.B., Yale; Judge, Connecticut Superior Court.
Stephen Gilles, Associate Professor of Law; J.D., Chicago.
Charles A. Heckman, Professor of Law; J.D., Chicago.
James W. Henderson Jr., Adjunct Professor of Law; J.D., Boston College.
Jon Hirschoff, Adjunct Professor of Law; J.D., Yale.
Joseph Hogan, Legal Skills Instructor; J.D., Widener.
L. Mark Hurley, Adjunct Professor of Law; J.D., Bridgeport.
Carolyn Kaas, Assistant Clinical Professor; J.D., Connecticut.
Thomas E. Lee, Adjunct Professor of Law; J.D., Boston University.
Susan Leighton-Smith, Adjunct Professor; J.D., Chicago.
Richard E. Litvin, Associate Professor of Law; J.D., Temple; LL.M., Yale.
Gregory A. Loken, Associate Professor of Law; J.D., Harvard.
Leonard Long, Associate Professor of Law; J.D., Chicago.
Emanuel Margolis, Adjunct Professor of Law; J.D., Yale.
Martin B. Margulies, Bernard Hersher Professor of Law; LL.M., NYU.
Elizabeth P. Marsh, Associate Professor of Law; J.D., NYU.
Erskine McIntosh, Adjunct Professor of Law; J.D., Catholic University.
Alexander M. Meiklejohn, Associate Professor of Law; J.D., Chicago.
Linda Meyer, Associate Professor of Law; J.D., Ph.D., Berkeley.
John T. Morgan, Professor of Law; J.D., Washington (St. Louis); LL.M., Harvard.
Toni Robinson, Professor of Law; J.D., Columbia; LL.M. (taxation), NYU.
David S. Rosettenstein, Professor of Law; LL.B., Witwatersrand (Johannesburg); D.Phil., Oxford.
Mark Schroeder, Legal Skills Instructor; J.D., Connecticut.
Cindy Slane, Visiting Instructor of Law and Director of Externships; J.D., Yale.
Mark R. Soboslai, Adjunct Professor of Law; J.D., Bridgeport.
Alan Soloway, Adjunct Professor; J.D., Yeshiva.
Evelyn Sommer, Adjunct Professor of Law; J.D., Brooklyn Law.
Carolyn Spencer, Legal Skills Instructor; J.D., Connecticut.
Marcia Speziale, Legal Skills Instructor; J.D., Connecticut.
Gail Stern, Legal Skills Instructor; J.D., Bridgeport.
Sheila Taub, Professor of Law; J.D., Harvard.
Ernest F. Teitell, Adjunct Professor of Law; J.D., Loyola.
W. John Thomas, Associate Professor of Law; J.D., Arizona; LL.M., Yale.
James Trowbridge, Associate Professor of Law and Director of Clinical Programs; LL.B., Georgetown.
Kenneth Votre, Adjunct Professor; J.D., Bridgeport; LL.M., Georgetown.
Mary Moers Wenig, Charles A. Dana Professor of Law; J.D., Columbia.
Jamison V. V. Wilcox, Associate Professor of Law; J.D., Columbia.
Deborah Witkin, Associate Professor of Law; J.D., Connecticut.
Pamela Zeller, Adjunct Professor of Law; J.D., Bridgeport.

ROGER WILLIAMS UNIVERSITY

Ralph R. Papitto School of Law

Programs of Study

The School of Law offers both a regular full-time day division and an extended evening division program. Skills training is an integral component of the legal program at Roger Williams. The goal is to impart the skills necessary for the successful and competent practice of law or in the chosen pursuit of the law student. Students are invited to become part of a young, dynamic, invigorating law school which is building a program of excellence in legal study and affords students the opportunity to be a part of the establishment of traditions.

The School of Law has established a Marine Affairs Institute for the research and study of legal and policy issues surrounding the use of the oceans and coastal zones.

Two joint degrees are offered in conjunction with the University of Rhode Island: Juris Doctor/Master of Community Planning and Juris Doctor/Master of Marine Science.

The School of Law operates the Louis Feinstein Legal Clinic, where senior law students provide legal service to individuals who cannot afford a lawyer and who would otherwise be unrepresented. Students enrolled in the criminal defense or family law clinic represent clients in court and before administrative tribunals as well as counsel clients. Student clerkships are also available with the Rhode Island Attorney General's Office, Public Defender's Office, Office of the Governor, other state agencies, and with judges throughout southeastern New England. Twenty hours of volunteer community service are required for graduation.

Students are invited to participate in summer sessions offered in conjunction with the Inns of Court School of Law in London, England, to study comparative advocacy and international and comparative law.

Roger Williams University School of Law is fully accredited by the American Bar Association. The School of Law received this accreditation in the shortest time possible under ABA guidelines.

Research Facilities

Located on 120 acres of waterfront property, the School of Law is self-contained in a multimillion-dollar building designed exclusively for the study of law. The four-level facility contains class and seminar rooms and is equipped with state-of-the-art audio visual and computer technology. The Law Library holds approximately 200,000 volumes. Legal information is provided via books, periodicals, compact discs, interactive videodiscs, and online databases. Electronic services offered are: INNOPAC, LEXIS, WESTLAW, LegalTrac CD-ROM, and a student computer center, with connections to the Internet, that is also networked to faculty and campus housing.

Financial Aid

Both need-based and credit-based financial aid options are available. The School of Law participates in the William D. Ford Federal Direct Loan Program, Roger Williams Law School Loan Program, the Access Group Programs, and TERI Graduate School Loan Program. Dean's awards, which are merit-based, are available to incoming students. The Office of Financial Aid distributes all the necessary applications and forms.

Cost of Study

Tuition for the 1998–99 academic year is $635 per credit. For a first-year Regular Division student, tuition is $19,100. Extended Division annual student tuition is $14,655, including summer session tuition.

Living and Housing Costs

Affordable housing is within easy commuting distance of the School of Law. The University maintains a limited amount of student housing in a complex located a few minutes from campus. The Admissions Office will gladly provide information to incoming students about the abundant, affordable housing in the community, and the Director of Student Services maintains a list of students seeking roommates.

Student Group

Approximately 300 students are enrolled in the Day Division and approximately 215 students in the Evening Division.

Roger Williams University School of Law sponsors the prestigious cocurricular activities of *Roger Williams University Law Review* and Moot Court Honor Society. Members of the student body actively participate in more than a dozen extracurricular organizations that are either common interest groups, legal practice societies, or legal fraternities. The Student Bar Association, which sponsors such social events as the Barrister's Ball, golf tournament, and spring auction, also appoints members to serve on faculty committees. Students are encouraged to balance their legal education with participation in the academic and social organizations at the School of Law.

Location

The School of Law is centrally located in historic Bristol, Rhode Island, on a 120-acre waterfront campus. This quaint town is only minutes from Providence and Newport, and an hour from Boston. All of New England is easily accessible for sports, cultural and recreational activities, dining, and shopping.

Applying

All applicants must take the Law School Admission Test (LSAT), submit a completed application along with the $60 fee, and register with the Law School Data Assembly Service (LSDAS). The code number for the School of Law is 3081. The priority deadline for applications is May 15; admission is offered on a rolling basis. Letters of recommendation are not required but will certainly be considered by the admissions committee if submitted. Personal interviews are not part of the regular admissions process, but by calling the Office of Admissions, applicants can arrange to visit the School of Law and are encouraged to do so. Tours and classroom visits can be arranged in advance of the visit.

Correspondence and Information

Mary D. Upton, Director of Admissions
Roger Williams University Ralph R. Papitto School of Law
Ten Metacom Avenue
Bristol, Rhode Island 02809-5171
Telephone: 401-254-4555
800-633-2727 (toll-free outside Rhode Island)
E-mail: ll@rwulaw.rwu.edu
World Wide Web: http://www.rwu.edu/law/law.html

Roger Williams University

THE FACULTY AND THEIR RESEARCH

Anthony J. Santoro, University President and Professor of Law; J.D., 1967; LL.M., 1968, Georgetown. Member, State Bar of Massachusetts. Taxation, business planning.
John E. Ryan, Vice President, Dean, and Professor of Law; J.D., University of the Pacific, 1970; LL.M., Illinois, 1976. Member, State Bar of California. Constitutional law, contracts.
Bruce I. Kogan, Associate Dean and Professor of Law; J.D., Dickinson, 1970; LL.M., Georgetown, 1973. Member, State Bar of Pennsylvania. Taxation, legal methods, property, estate planning.

Susan Ayres, Visiting Lecturer in Law; J.D., Baylor, 1998. Member, State Bars of Texas and Rhode Island. Legal methods I and II.
Gary L. Bahr, Professor of Law; J.D., South Dakota, 1969; LL.M., NYU, 1970. Member, State Bar of South Dakota. Contracts, jurisprudence.
Barbara L. Bernier, Associate Professor of Law; J.D., Howard, 1978; LL.M., Temple, 1980. Member, State Bars of District of Columbia, Pennsylvania, and West Virginia. Torts, international law, women and the law, wills and trusts, real estate transactions.
Carl T. Bogus, Associate Professor of Law; J.D., Syracuse, 1972. Member, State Bar of Pennsylvania. Gun control, legal profession, products liability.
Robert A. Chaim, Dean of Students and Director of Academic Support Program; D.A., University of the Pacific, 1980.
Edward J. Eberle, Associate Professor of Law; J.D., Northwestern, 1982. Member, State Bars of Massachusetts, Minnesota, and Rhode Island. Constitutional law, administrative law, international business transactions, professional responsibility.
Christel L. Ertel, University Dean for Institutional Development and Associate Professor of Law; J.D., Widener, 1985. Member, State Bar of Pennsylvania. Client interviewing, counseling, negotiation.
Jose L. Fernandez, Co-Director, Marine Affairs Institute and Associate Professor of Law; J.D., Rutgers, Camden, 1985. Member, State Bar of New Jersey. Property, administrative, environmental, and state constitutional law.
Johnathan M. Gutoff, Assistant Professor of Law; J.D., Chicago, 1987. Member, State Bar of New York. Legal methods, remedies, and federal courts.
Matthew P. Harrington, Co-Director of Marine Affairs Institute and Assistant Professor of Law; J.D., Boston University, 1990; LL.M., Pennsylvania, 1991. Member, State Bars of Pennsylvania and New Jersey. Contracts, sales, secured transactions, bankruptcy, and admiralty.
Diana Hassel, Associate Professor of Law; J.D., Rutgers, Newark, 1985. Member, State Bars of New York and Rhode Island. Clinical education, legal methods.
Andrew Horwitz, Associate Professor of Law; J.D., NYU, 1986. Member, State Bars of Massachusetts, New York, and Rhode Island. Legal methods, trial advocacy, clinical education.
Carol J. King, Associate Professor of Law; J.D., Ohio State, 1979. Member, State Bars of Ohio and Rhode Island. Clinical education, civil litigation, alternative dispute resolution family law.
Peter C. Kostant, Associate Professor of Law; J.D., Fordham, 1978. Member, State Bar of New York. Business organizations, secured transactions, lawyering process, professional responsibility.
Linda Fitts Mischler, Director of the Legal Methods Program and Associate Professor of Law; J.D., Albany Law, 1986. Member, State Bar of New York. Legal methods, law and medicine.
Colleen P. Murphy, Associate Professor of Law; J.D., Yale, 1986. Member, State Bar of Massachusetts. Administrative law and remedies.
David A. Rice, Professor of Law; LL.B., Columbia, 1965. Member, State Bars of Massachusetts and New York. Computer software protection, intellectual property law, contracts.
Larry J. Richie, Professor of Law; J.D., South Carolina, 1967; LL.M., Georgetown, 1972. Member, State Bars of Maryland, South Carolina, and District of Columbia. Criminal law, criminal procedure, legal methods.
Louise E. Teitz, Associate Professor of Law; J.D., SMU, 1981. Member, State Bars of Pennsylvania and Texas and District of Columbia. Civil procedure, complex litigation, antitrust, conflicts of law, federal courts.
Robert H. Whorf, Associate Professor of Law; J.D., Syracuse, 1970. Member, State Bar of New York. Criminal law, criminal procedure, white-collar crime, trial advocacy, criminal defense clinic.
Gail I. Winson, Director of Law Library and Associate Professor of Law; M.S. (library science), Drexel, 1971; J.D., Florida, 1979. Member, State Bars of California and Florida. Advanced legal research.
Michael J. Yelnosky, Associate Professor of Law; J.D., Pennsylvania, 1987. Member, State Bar of Pennsylvania. Legal method, civil procedure, labor law, employment law.
David M. Zlotnick, Assistant Professor of Law; J.D., Harvard, 1986. Member, State Bars of District of Columbia, Florida, and New York. Criminal law, criminal procedure, trial and appellate advocacy.

The Law School was built in 1993 and houses all academic and administrative functions under one roof.

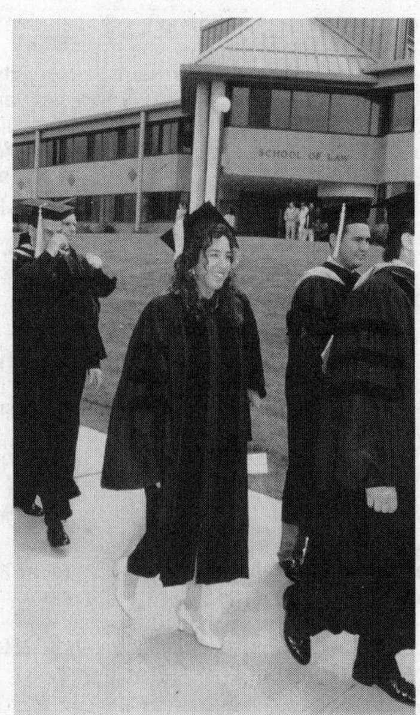

The Law School graduated its first class of day students in 1996 and its first evening division in 1997.

SAINT LOUIS UNIVERSITY

School of Law

Program of Study

Saint Louis University School of Law offers an atmosphere that is the result of a number of factors, including the Jesuit educational traditions, outstanding faculty members and students, and the rich quality of life in a thriving midwestern city. The Jesuit nature of the institution is manifested by a commitment to academic excellence and freedom of inquiry, a genuine concern for the development of each student as a person, and an effort to sensitize students to the moral and ethical dimensions of law and lawyering.

Unique to the School of Law is the special rapport among students, faculty members, and staff. Over the years, the School has built a reputation for an ambience of support and friendship. Faculty members have authored countless casebooks, treatises, monographs, anthologies, articles, essays, and other materials in prominent presses and law journals around the nation and the world.

The School of Law has leading centers in health law, employment law, and international and comparative law, three of the strongest growth areas in the legal profession. Students can earn certificates in each of these specializations. The School also has a strong Professional Skills Program. The School offers a small, highly selective LL.M. program in health law, as well as an LL.M. for international lawyers, which has attracted students from around the world, including Germany, Israel, Russia, China, and Nepal.

Research Facilities

The 485,000-plus–volume collection of the Omer Poos Law Library includes microforms, rare books, audio and video cassettes, computer-assisted learning materials, CD-ROM databases, and computer software. The law library provides access to foreign materials, government documents, legal databases (LEXIS, Westlaw), bibliographic databases (Dialog, MEDLINE, OCLC), Internet connections, and in-house computers for computer-aided instruction and word-processing.

Over the past few years, the law library has received national recognition in the library community through its active participation in several projects. It now ranks twentieth out of 177 accredited law schools for titles (hardcopy) held. Among its numerous distinctions, it was one of eight libraries in the country to receive national-level Enhance status on OCLC and was, in fact, the first law library to receive this authorization. The Law Library houses specialty law centers in health law, employment law, Irish law, Polish law, and Jewish law.

Financial Aid

The majority of law students receive some form of financial assistance. Most awards are need-based (Saint Louis University will accept only the FAFSA), with the exception of the academic merit scholarships and grants. These are administered directly by the School of Law and are awarded on the basis of outstanding academic credentials, exceptional career achievements, and ethnic and cultural diversity. Most scholarships are awarded to students whose academic credentials place them in the top 40–50 percent of the incoming class, as determined by their LSAT score and GPA. These forms of aid are available to both full- and part-time students.

Cost of Study

The tuition for 1998–99 is $19,170 per year for full-time study (12 semester hours or more) and $14,360 for part-time study (8–11 semester hours). There are two tuition deposits of $100 and $200 due on April 15 and June 15, respectively.

Living and Housing Costs

There are many affordable housing opportunities in the surrounding neighborhoods. Rents range from $250 to $500 per month.

Student Group

Enrollment is approximately 570 full-time day students and 260 part-time evening students, representing forty-three states and several countries. The student body includes approximately 43 percent women and 18 percent members of minority groups; the average age is 25 for full-time students and 31 for part-time students. Students publish four distinct law journals. Student organizations play a vital role in meeting the many special interests of the student body.

Student Outcomes

Approximately 52 percent of graduates enter private practice, 14 percent accept judicial clerkships, 10 percent take positions with the government, and nearly 19 percent become employed by the business sector. Smaller numbers enter legal services, public defender offices, graduate education, banks, and accounting firms. Approximately 92 percent of the class of 1996 was employed within six months of graduation. Alumni practice in all fifty states and several other countries; the majority are practicing in the Midwest.

Location

The School of Law is located on the main campus of Saint Louis University in midtown St. Louis, just a few blocks from the Grand Center Arts and Entertainment district and only a couple of miles from the Arch and downtown. St. Louis offers the amenities of urban living without the inconveniences and high costs normally associated with living in a major metropolitan area.

The University and The School

Saint Louis University, founded in 1818, received its University charter in 1832. The School of Law building complex includes the law library, all classrooms, and faculty and administrative offices. The law faculty offices are located in the law library, which contributes significantly to the collegial atmosphere of the School.

Applying

All applicants are required to take the LSAT and subscribe to the LSDAS. First-year students are admitted only in the fall semester. There is a rolling admissions policy with a March 1 preferential deadline. There is a $40 nonrefundable application fee. All applicants are evaluated on their undergraduate GPA, LSAT score, personal statement, letters of recommendation, any graduate work, and other nonacademic background.

Correspondence and Information

Admissions Office
School of Law
Saint Louis University
3700 Lindell Boulevard
St. Louis, Missouri 63108-3478

Telephone: 314-977-2800
Fax: 314-977-3966
E-mail: admissions@lawlib.slu.edu
World Wide Web: http://www.lawlib.slu.edu

Saint Louis University

THE FACULTY

John B. Attanasio, Dean; J.D., NYU; LL.M., Yale; Dipl. in Law, Oxford.
John J. Ammann, Adjunct Assistant Clinical Professor; J.D., Saint Louis.
Charles B. Blackmar, Professor Emeritus; J.D., Michigan.
Myron H. Bright, Professor Emeritus; J.D., Minnesota.
Kent Bunting, Instructor; J.D., Kansas.
Isaak I. Dore, Professor; LL.M., Zambia; LL.M., J.S.D., Yale.
Gerald T. Dunne, Professor Emeritus; J.D., Saint Louis.
John E. Dunsford, Professor; J.D., Saint Louis; LL.M., Harvard.
Susan A. FitzGibbon, Professor; J.D., Saint Louis.
Stanislaw Frankowski, Professor; LL.M., Ph.D., J.S.D., Warsaw; LL.M., NYU.
Christopher W. Frost, Associate Professor; J.D., Kentucky.
Barbara Gilchrist, Associate Clinical Law Professor; J.D., Washington (St. Louis).
Roger L. Goldman, Professor; J.D., Pennsylvania.
Jesse A. Goldner, Professor; J.D., Harvard.
Joel K. Goldstein, Assistant Professor; D.Phil., Oxford; J.D., Harvard.
Thomas L. Greaney, Professor; J.D., Harvard.
John M. Griesbach, Associate Professor; J.D., LL.M., Harvard.
Charisse L. Heath, Assistant Professor; J.D., Yale.
Robert J. Henle, Professor Emeritus; S.J., A.M., Ph.L., S/T.L., Saint Louis; Ph.D., Toronto.
Alan J. Howard, Professor; J.D., Chicago.
Vincent C. Immel, Professor Emeritus; J.D., Michigan.
Sandra Hanneken Johnson, Professor; J.D., NYU; LL.M., Yale.
Nancy H. Kaufman, Associate Professor; J.D., Wisconsin–Madison.
Kathleen A. Kelley, Instructor; J.D., Emory.
Donald B. King, Professor Emeritus; J.D., Harvard; LL.M., NYU; M.S.W., Saint Louis.
Howard S. Levie, Professor Emeritus; J.D., Cornell; LL.M., George Washington.
Matthew C. Mirow, Instructor; J.D., Cornell; Ph.D., Cambridge.
John F. T. Murray, Dean Emeritus; J.D., Harvard.
Carol A. Needham, Assistant Professor; J.D., Northwestern.
Francis M. Nevins, Professor; J.D., NYU.
John C. O'Brien, Professor; J.D., Harvard.
Henry M. Ordower, Professor; J.D., Chicago.
Josef Rohlik, Professor; J.U.Dr., C.Sc., Charles (Czechoslovakia); LL.M., Columbia.
Peter W. Salsich Jr., Professor; J.D., Saint Louis.
Susan Scafidi, Assistant Professor; J.D., Yale.
Craig Schmid, Instructor; J.D., Saint Louis.
Eileen H. Searls, Professor and Librarian; J.D., M.S.L.S., Wisconsin.
Joseph J. Simeone, Professor Emeritus; LL.M., S.J.D., Michigan.
Nicolas P. Terry, Professor; LL.M., Cambridge.
Stephen C. Thaman, Assistant Professor; J.D., Berkeley.
Jeffrey A. Tressler, Assistant Professor; J.D., Yale.
Dennis J. Tuchler, Professor; J.D., Chicago.
Dana E. Underwood, Instructor; J.D., Case Western Reserve.
Constance Wagner, Assistant Professor; J.D., Columbia; LL.M., Konstanz (Germany).
Leland Ware, Professor; J.D., Boston College.
Alan M. Weinberger, Professor; J.D., Michigan.
Douglas R. Williams, Associate Professor; J.D., Duke.
Michael A. Wolff, Professor; J.D., Minnesota.

SOUTHERN UNIVERSITY

Law Center

Program of Study

Southern University Law Center offers a three-year curriculum leading to the Juris Doctor degree. The curriculum is based upon the standard professional courses usually given in member schools accredited by the American Bar Association. It requires the satisfactory completion of at least 96 semester hours, including required courses. The curriculum further requires a full six semesters of residence. Any study undertaken in a summer semester shall not count toward residence requirements. Electives are integrated as part of the curriculum, and students must take courses specified for the respective years.

The program of study is designed to give students a comprehensive knowledge of both the civil law and common law. While emphasis is given to the substantive and procedural law of Louisiana, with its French and Spanish origins, Anglo-American law is strongly integrated into the curriculum. Fundamental differences in method and approach and the results reached in the two systems are analyzed. Students are trained in the art of advocacy, legal research, and the sources and social purposes of legal principles. The teaching of techniques to discipline students' minds in legal reasoning is an important part of the educational objectives of the Center. Students are instructed in the ethics of the legal profession and the professional responsibility of the lawyer to society.

Research Facilities

The Law Library contains 388,614 volumes and offers research assistance and reference service to students, faculty, and the public. The collection of the library is adequate to support the curriculum and conforms to the standards of the American Bar Association and the Association of American Law Schools. Both the federal and the Louisiana state governments have designated the Southern University Law Library an official depository for government documents. A complete collection of Louisiana legal materials, including Continuing Legal Education materials of the Louisiana Bar Association, is provided in the library. Although library acquisitions reflect the civil law tradition of Louisiana, sufficient materials for research in the common law and a substantial number of basic legal reference works are available. The legal periodical collection contains more than 565 titles, and several new titles are added every year. In addition to print materials, the library has collections of microforms and tapes dealing with a wide range of legal subjects. Media equipment in the library includes copying machines for print materials and microforms.

Arrangements have been made with the Louisiana State University Law Center Library, which has one of the largest Anglo-American and civil law collections in the South, to make its resources available for research purposes to the Southern University Law Library.

Financial Aid

A limited number of direct Law Center grants-in-aid are available, based upon students' academic averages and demonstrated financial need. Applications for these scholarships should be directed to the Financial Aid Committee at the Southern University Law Center. Applicants seeking Federal Stafford Student Loans must apply to the Financial Aid Office at Southern University Law Center.

Cost of Study

Tuition per semester is $1564 for Louisiana residents and $3864 for nonresident students in 1998–99.

Living and Housing Costs

Room and board on campus cost approximately $1500 per semester in 1998–99. It costs approximately $1200 per month for a married student living off campus for housing, food, and moderate entertainment in order to live at local standards. It costs a single student about $850 per month for similar expenses.

Student Group

The current enrollment at the Law Center is approximately 335 men and women who have come from colleges and universities across the nation and from international institutions. Students participate in the Student Bar Association; the *Law Review;* the Moot Court Program; the Law Student Division, American Bar Association; the Black Law Students Association; Phi Alpha Delta and Delta Theta Phi law fraternities; *The Public Defender,* the law student newspaper; and other on-campus activities. An active intramural athletic program is well established at Southern.

Location

Baton Rouge, the capital of Louisiana, is a large industrial center and is the fifth-largest port in the United States, with a population of 400,000. The Law Center is located less than 5 miles from the state capitol, and it is situated in the midst of local law firms, a short drive from state and federal court buildings, government law offices, and regulatory agencies, in downtown Baton Rouge. Aside from the cultural, social, and athletic activities on and off campus in Baton Rouge, the fabled city of New Orleans, 85 miles away, offers many attractions. Other tourist attractions and historic sites in southern Louisiana are within easy reach of Baton Rouge.

The University and The Center

Southern University Law Center, established in 1947 as Southern University School of Law, is a progressive, innovative law school. It is located on the eastern bank of the historic Mississippi River in Baton Rouge, Louisiana. The Center is fully approved by the American Bar Association and the Supreme Court of Louisiana and accredited by the Southern Association of Colleges and Schools. It is also fully approved by the Veterans Administration for the training of eligible veterans. The Law Center maintains a high standard of professional education and adheres to the principle of equal opportunity. The University is proud of its rich academic program and culturally diverse student body, and it continues to be receptive to the introduction of new courses in response to a changing society.

Applying

Admission at Southern University Law Center is competitive and is based on a number of factors, including the undergraduate grade point average and scores on the Law School Admission Test (LSAT). All applications for admission are reviewed by a special committee. Among the factors considered by the committee, in addition to those stated above, are work experience, past pursuits, and recommendations.

Students beginning the study of law are admitted only in the fall semester. Applications for admission should be filed at the end of the fall semester of the year prior to the desired date of admission. Applications received later than March 31 may not be processed for admission in August.

Correspondence and Information

Coordinator of Admissions
Southern University Law Center
Baton Rouge, Louisiana 70813
Telephone: 504-771-5341

Southern University

THE FACULTY

Bhishma K. Agnihotri, Professor and Chancellor; LL.M., NYU.
Steve Barbre, Associate Professor; J.D., Chicago.
Cleveland Coon, Assistant Professor; J.D., Southern Law.
Cary deBessonet, Professor; LL.M., Illinois at Urbana-Champaign.
Alfreda S. Diamond, Associate Professor; LL.M., Columbia.
Ernest Easterly III, Associate Professor; J.D., LSU.
Maurice Franks, Associate Professor; J.D., Memphis State.
Michelle R. Ghetti, Assistant Professor; J.D., LSU.
Stanley A. Halpin Jr., Professor; J.D., Tulane.
Nannette Jolizette, Assistant Professor; LL.M., Tulane.
Eileen G. Jones, Assistant Professor; J.D., Temple.
Russell L. Jones, Professor; LL.M., Georgetown.
Virginia Listach, Managing Attorney; J.D., Southern Law.
Washington Marshall, Professor; J.D., Southern Law.
William S. Mayfield, Professor; J.D., Detroit Law.
Arlene McCarthy, Instructor; J.D., Texas.
Ollivette Mencer, Instructor; J.D., Southern Law.
Jacqueline Nash, Managing Attorney; J.D., Southern Law.
Donald North, Managing Attorney; J.D., Southern Law.
Okechukwu Oko, Assistant Professor; J.D., Yale.
Judith Perhay, Instructor; J.D., Loyola (New Orleans).
Cynthia Picou, Professor; J.D., LSU.
John K. Pierre, Assistant Professor; J.D., SMU.
Thomas Richard, Assistant Professor; J.D., LSU.
Winston Riddick, Associate Professor; J.D., LSU.
Arthur E. Stallworth, Professor and Vice Chancellor; J.D., Southern Law.
Clyde C. Tidwell, Professor; J.D., Southern Law.
Roederick White, Assistant Professor; J.D., Wayne State.
Evelyn Wilson, Associate Professor; J.D., LSU.

STETSON UNIVERSITY

College of Law

Program of Study

Stetson's law program offers a comprehensive course of study based on both traditional academic classes and extensive clinical and practical training. The J.D. program requires six semesters of full-time study or five semesters and two 8-week summer sessions. The required curriculum includes business associations, civil procedure, constitutional law, contracts, criminal law, evidence, professional responsibility, property, taxation, torts, and research and writing. Students must also complete courses in the areas of lawyering skills and administrative law and commercial law, fulfill a writing requirement, and provide 20 hours of public service work. A wide range of upper-division electives is offered, enabling students to concentrate in specialty areas of interest. The College's emphasis on practical legal training is supported by a variety of legal clinics and three courtrooms. Summer study abroad is available through the College's program in Tallinn, Estonia, or through programs sponsored by other ABA-approved law schools.

The College of Law and the School of Business Administration offer a combined J.D./M.B.A. degree program. Domestic and international attorneys may also enroll in the College's graduate program, which leads to an LL.M. degree in international law and business.

Research Facilities

Stetson unveiled its new Law Library and Information Center in the 1998–99 academic year. The three-story, 58,000-square-foot structure houses a 350,000-volume collection and provides study rooms, conference rooms, and seminar rooms. The new library offers the latest in research and communications technology, and more than 150 study carrels are equipped for instant access to LEXIS/NEXIS, WESTLAW, the Internet, and other online databases. All students are required to use laptop computers.

Financial Aid

Need-based grants are available from the College of Law, while loans may be obtained from federal and private sources. A limited number of merit scholarships are awarded yearly on the basis of academic excellence. Teaching fellowships and faculty research assistantships are available on a competitive basis to second- and third-year students.

Cost of Study

Stetson's tuition is $9875 per semester for the 1998–99 academic year. The summer term is $4950.

Living and Housing Costs

The College provides dormitory housing for approximately 60 students. Stetson also provides a limited number of single family dwellings and apartments for married and single-parent students. On-campus housing expenses range from $1650 to $2400 per semester for residence halls, apartments, and houses. Other affordable housing is available near the campus.

Student Group

The current enrollment at Stetson is approximately 625 and comprises students from 216 colleges and universities and forty-two states. Students write for the *Stetson Law Review* and other scholarly legal publications and can join any of the College's twenty-two student organizations to help meet their professional and social needs. Students may also try out for Stetson's award-winning moot court and trial teams. Stetson is recognized nationally for having one of the best law school trial and appellate advocacy programs.

Student Outcomes

Approximately 91 percent of Stetson graduates find employment within six months of graduation. While some graduates leave the state for employment opportunities, the majority of Stetson graduates remain in Florida. Some 51 percent of those graduates join private law firms, while an estimated 35 percent take positions in government. A small number of graduates have sought employment in business as in-house counsel or in nonlegal positions. Others have returned to academia to pursue advanced law degrees.

Location

Stetson is located in St. Petersburg on Florida's Gulf of Mexico. St. Petersburg is part of the greater Tampa Bay area, one of the twenty-five largest metropolitan areas in the U.S. With 360 days of sunshine a year, the region's beaches, golf courses, resorts, and waterfronts draw throngs of vacationers and natives alike, as do year-round festivals and major tourist attractions. Orlando, a 90-minute drive from St. Petersburg, is also within easy reach.

The College

Founded as a private law school in 1900, Stetson is Florida's first law school. For more than half a century the College of Law was located on Stetson University's main campus in DeLand, Florida. In 1954, the College was relocated to a 21-acre site in St. Petersburg that was originally a 1920s resort hotel. The College of Law, accredited by the American Bar Association and a member of the Association of American Law Schools since 1931, adheres to a philosophy of dedication to teaching excellence, legal scholarship, law reform, and service to the legal profession.

Applying

All applicants must take the Law School Admission Test (LSAT) and must hold a baccalaureate degree from a regionally accredited college or university. Applicants are evaluated on their undergraduate GPA, LSAT score, personal references, and other factors such as personal accomplishments, graduate or professional training, and extracurricular activities. Deadlines for applications are February 15 for fall, August 15 for spring, and January 15 for summer. Applicants must register with the Law School Data Assembly Service (LSDAS) and may subscribe to the LSDAS Letter of Recommendation Service. Applicants should also submit a completed application, a $50 application fee, and a personal statement.

Correspondence and Information

Director of Admissions
College of Law
Stetson University
1401 61st Street South
St. Petersburg, Florida 33707
Telephone: 813-562-7802
E-mail: lawadmit@hermes.law.stetson.edu
World Wide Web: http://www.law.stetson.edu

Stetson University

THE FACULTY

Thomas E. Allison, Professor and Associate Dean; J.D., Stetson; LL.M., Florida.
Robert Batey, Professor; J.D., Virginia; LL.M., Illinois.
Dorothea Beane, Associate Professor; J.D., Rutgers.
Robert D. Bickel, Professor; J.D., Florida State.
James J. Brown, Professor; J.D., Cleveland State; LL.M., Washington (St. Louis).
Mark R. Brown, Professor; J.D., Louisville; LL.M., Illinois.
John F. Cooper, Professor; J.D., Oklahoma; LL.M., Florida.
A. Darby Dickerson, Associate Professor; J.D., Vanderbilt.
William R. Eleazer, Professor; J.D., George Washington; LL.M., Emory.
Charles M. Elson, Professor; J.D., Virginia.
Stephen M. Everhart, Associate Professor; J.D., Florida.
Michael Finch, Professor; J.D., Boston University; S.J.D., Harvard.
Peter L. Fitzgerald, Assistant Professor; J.D., California, Hastings Law; LL.M., Exeter (United Kingdom).
Roberta K. Flowers, Professor; J.D., Colorado.
Royal C. Gardner, Assistant Professor; J.D., Boston College.
I. Richard Gershon, Professor; J.D., Tennessee; LL.M., Florida.
Bruce R. Jacob, Professor and Dean Emeritus; J.D., Stetson; LL.M., Northwestern; S.J.D., Harvard.
Julian R. Kossow, Visiting Associate Professor; J.D., Georgetown.
Calvin A. Kuenzel, L. LeRoy Highbaugh, Sr. Professor of Law; J.D., Iowa; LL.M., S.J.D., Illinois.
Peter F. Lake, Professor; J.D., Harvard.
Jerome C. Latimer, Professor; J.D., Florida.
Patrick E. Longan, Professor; J.D., Chicago.
Thomas C. Marks Jr., Professor; LL.B., Stetson.
Lizabeth A. Moody, Dean and Professor; J.D., Yale.
Rebecca C. Morgan, Professor; J.D., Stetson.
Luz E. Ortiz Nagle, Assistant Professor; J.D., William and Mary; LL.M., UCLA.
Marleen A. O'Connor, Professor; J.D., Duke.
J. Tim Reilly, Distinguished Professorial Lecturer; J.D., Stetson.
Leslie D. Scharf, Distinguished Professorial Lecturer; LL.B., Wisconsin.
John M. Scheb, Distinguished Professorial Lecturer; J.D., Florida; LL.M., Virginia; D.H.L. (Hon), Florida Southern; LL.D. (Hon), Stetson.
W. McKinley Smiley, Professor; J.D., Emory; LL.M., Miami.
W. Reece Smith Jr., Distinguished Professorial Lecturer; J.D., Florida; LL.D. (Hon), Stetson.
Bradford Stone, Charles A. Dana Professor of Law; J.D., Michigan.
Michael I. Swygert, Professor; J.D., Valparaiso; LL.M., Yale.
Ruth Fleet Thurman, Professor; J.D., Stetson; LL.M., Columbia.
W. Gary Vause, Professor; J.D., Connecticut; LL.M., S.J.D., Virginia.
Darryl C. Wilson, Professor; J.D., Florida; LL.M., John Marshall Law.
J. Lamar Woodard, Librarian and Professor; J.D., Florida.

A view of Stetson University.

LAW

TEMPLE UNIVERSITY

School of Law

Programs of Study

Temple Law School, founded in 1895, offers a three-year full-time and a four-year part-time Juris Doctor (J.D.) program; four 1-year Master of Laws (LL.M.) programs; a flexible, general LL.M. program for overseas law graduates; and three other specialized LL.M. programs in taxation, trial advocacy, and transnational law.

J.D. and general LL.M. students choose from a broad array of courses in traditional legal theory and analysis and advanced courses in every legal discipline. Temple's award-winning trial advocacy program and extensive clinical education courses provide opportunities to learn practical legal skills. Students can concentrate in such areas as commercial law, constitutional law, criminal law, intellectual property, international law, environmental law, taxation, and trial advocacy. The specialized LL.M. programs have defined curricula within their topical areas.

Temple has a unique semester-abroad program in Tokyo, Japan, and six-week summer sessions in Athens, Rome, and Tel Aviv for students in the J.D., LL.M. in transnational law, and general LL.M. programs. J.D. students can also pursue a J.D./M.B.A. degree program.

Research Facilities

The Law Library, with more than 450,000 volumes of statutes, court reports, journals, and treatises, is among the largest libraries in the U.S. Computerized legal databases, the library catalog, Computer Assisted Legal Instruction, Career Planning job postings, the alumni database, a CD-ROM collection, the Internet, WESTLAW, and LEXIS-NEXIS can all be accessed from library carrels and the student computer lab. The lab conducts regular training seminars on e-mail and access to the Internet. Students can rent notebook computers for use at school or home.

Financial Aid

Citizens and permanent U.S. residents can obtain loans from federal and private sources. Need-based grants and some tuition grants based on academic excellence are available for the J.D. and general LL.M. programs. International students who require financial assistance should investigate alternative sources of financial support from their governments, employers, or U.S. sources such as the Fulbright Fellowships.

Cost of Study

Annual tuition for 1997–98 was as follows: for the full-time J.D. program, $8808 for Pennsylvania residents and $15,104 for nonresidents; for the full-time general LL.M. program (for overseas students), $13,326; for the full-time LL.M. in taxation program, $8088 for Pennsylvania residents and $12,000 for nonresidents; for the LL.M. in trial advocacy program, $12,800; and for the LL.M. in transnational law program, $15,104.

Living and Housing Costs

One- and two-bedroom campus housing units with bath and kitchen currently range from $390 to $525 per month. Many affordable and well-maintained rental units are located within an easy commute to the law school by public transportation and are available for a comparable price. Most students prefer to live off campus; half of the international students live on campus. A rough estimate of books, room, and board for a single person without dependents is $12,370 per year.

Student Group

Approximately 1,400 J.D. and LL.M. students attend Temple, with an approximately equal number of men and women. About 450 are part-time and 950 are full-time. Temple is noted for its diverse student body.

Location

Temple University and the School of Law are located less than 2 miles from the commercial and legal district of Philadelphia, a large cosmopolitan city of 5.7 million founded in 1682 and known as the birthplace of the U.S. Constitution. Philadelphia, the second-largest city on the East Coast, has theater, music, and art; major athletic teams (including the school's nationally known basketball team); and wonderful nightlife of every type. It is 1½ hours from New York and 2 hours from Washington, D.C.

The University

The University, founded in 1884, enrolls 32,000 students, including 1,400 law students. It is located in a major East Coast metropolitan area, with branch campuses in Rome and Tokyo.

Applying

Deadlines are as follows: for the J.D. program, April 1; for the general LL.M. program, March 15; and for the LL.M. in trial advocacy program, November 1. The LL.M. in taxation and LL.M. in transnational law programs have a rolling admission policy.

Applicants for the LL.M. in trial advocacy program must hold a degree in law from an A.B.A.-accredited law school. Applicants for the LL.M. in transnational law program must hold a degree in law from a common law country.

Correspondence and Information

For LL.M. programs:
Office of Graduate and International Programs
Room 710
Temple University School of Law
Philadelphia, Pennsylvania 19122-6098
Telephone: 215-204-1448
Fax: 215-204-2282
E-mail: intl-law@vm.temple.edu
World Wide Web: http://www.temple.edu/lawschool/

For J.D. programs:
Office of J.D. Admissions
Temple University School of Law
Philadelphia, Pennsylvania 19122-6098
Telephone: 215-204-5949
Fax: 215-204-9313
E-mail: law@astro.ocis.temple.edu
World Wide Web: http://www.temple.edu/lawschool

Temple University

THE FACULTY

Alice G. Abreu, Professor; J.D., Cornell.
Mark F. Anderson, Associate Professor; J.D., Michigan.
Marina Angel, Professor; J.D., Columbia.
Jane B. Baron, Professor; J.D., Harvard.
Robert J. Bartow, Professor and Associate Dean; LL.M., Yale.
Vicki L. Beyer, Associate Professor and Japan Program Director; J.D., Washington (Seattle).
Anthony J. Bocchino, Jack E. Feinberg Professor; J.D., Connecticut.
Amelia Helen Boss, Professor; J.D., Rutgers.
William L. Bowe, Visiting Professor; J.D., Virginia.
Scott Burris, Associate Professor; J.D., Yale.
Burton Caine, Professor; J.D., Harvard.
Richard B. Cappalli, Professor; LL.M., Yale.
Susan L. DeJarnatt, Assistant Professor; J.D., Temple.
Jeffrey L. Dunoff, Associate Professor; LL.M., Georgetown.
JoAnne A. Epps, I. Herman Stern Professor and Associate Dean; J.D., Yale.
Scott Finet, Associate Professor and Law Librarian; J.D., Illinois.
Theresa Glennon, Associate Professor; J.D., Yale.
Richard K. Greenstein, Peter J. Liacouras Professor; J.D., Vanderbilt.
S. O. Gyandoh Jr., Professor; LL.M., Yale.
Phoebe A. Haddon, Charles Klein Professor; LL.M., Yale.
Sharon S. Harzenski, Professor; J.D., Temple.
Cassandra Jones Havard, Associate Professor; J.D., Pennsylvania.
David Kairys, Professor; LL.M., Pennsylvania.
Nancy J. Knauer, Associate Professor; J.D., Pennsylvania.
Jan M. Levine, Associate Professor and Director; J.D., Boston University.
Peter J. Liacouras, Professor and University President; J.D., Pennsylvania.
Michael E. Libonati, Laura H. Carnell Professor; LL.M., Yale.
Laura E. Little, Professor; J.D., Temple.
Olan B. Lowrey, Professor; LL.B., Baylor.
Diane C. Maleson, Professor and University Vice Provost; J.D., Temple.
Ellie Margolis, Assistant Professor; J.D., Northeastern.
Finbarr McCarthy, Associate Professor; J.D., Tulane.
Frank M. McClellan, Professor; LL.M., Yale.
Stephen L. Mikochik, Professor; J.D., Fordham.
Eleanor W. Myers, Associate Professor; J.D., Pennsylvania.
Louis M. Natali Jr., Professor; J.D., Georgetown.
Edward D. Ohlbaum, Professor and Director; J.D., Temple.
Joseph I. Passon, Professor; LL.B., Temple.
K. G. Jan Pillai, Professor; S.J.D., Yale.
Rafael A. Porrata-Doria Jr., Professor; J.D., Yale.
David G. Post, Associate Professor; J.D., Yale.
Donald R. Price, Professor; J.D., Temple.
Mark C. Rahdert, I. Herman Stern Professor; J.D., Yale.
Robert J. Reinstein, Professor, University Vice President, and Dean; J.D., Harvard.
Henry J. Richardson III, Professor; LL.B., Yale.
Charles H. Rogovin, Professor; LL.B., Columbia.
Peter Sevareid, Professor; J.D., Georgetown.
James A. Shellenberger, Professor; J.D., Villanova.
Carl E. Singley, Professor; J.D., Temple.
David Arthur Skeel Jr., Associate Professor; J.D., Virginia.
Michael R. Smith, Assistant Professor; J.D., Florida.
David A. Sonenshein, Professor; J.D., NYU.
Muriel Morisey Spence, Associate Professor; J.D., Georgetown.
Kathryn M. Stanchi, Assistant Professor; J.D., Boston University.
James A. Strazzella, James G. Schmidt Professor; J.D., Pennsylvania.
Gerald F. Tietz, Professor; J.D., Temple.
Jan Ting, Professor and Director; J.D., Harvard.
William J. Woodward Jr., Professor; J.D., Rutgers.

Emeritus Faculty

Warren M. Ballard, Professor; LL.B., Virginia.
Robert Hachenburg, Professor; LL.B., Pennsylvania.
John M. Lindsey, Professor; J.D., Illinois.
Joseph W. Marshall, Professor; J.D., Temple.
Jerome Sloan, Professor; LL.M., Yale.
William H. Traylor, Professor; J.D., Indiana.
David Weinstein, Professor; LL.B., Yale.
Sidney H. Willig, Professor; LL.B., Brooklyn Law.

UNIVERSITY OF LA VERNE

College of Law

Program of Study

The La Verne and San Fernando Valley campuses of the College of Law offer intellectually stimulating day and evening programs leading to the Juris Doctor (J.D.) degree. The College of Law is accredited by the State Bar of California and the Western Association of Schools and Colleges. The College emphasizes the development of practical skills built on a solid theoretical base. This innovative approach prepares graduates very well for their varied and changing roles in the legal profession.

The course of study leading to the J.D. degree requires satisfactory completion of 84 semester units. Both campuses operate in two 15-week semesters, with an 8-week summer program added for part-time students. Students can attend either full-time day or part-time day or evening classes. Full-time students usually take 15 units per semester, while part-time students take approximately 9 units per regular semester and 4 units in the summer session. The law program can be completed within three years for full-time students and four years for part-time students. The academic curricula at both campuses stress basic required courses in the first two years, with electives increasing in the last half of the program. Both campuses offer a unique 10-unit Lawyering Skills Practicum. This course was created in response to the increasing demand for graduates who are prepared in practical as well as academic skills of the profession. At the College of Law, classes are deliberately kept small—usually between 25 and 40 students—and close contact is maintained between faculty members and the student body. The University of La Verne (ULV) College of Law is proud of its thousands of alumni who are currently practicing law as attorneys and of the more than 60 judges and commissioners in southern California.

Research Facilities

The library holdings of the San Fernando Valley and La Verne campuses total approximately 160,000 volumes, with the resources of each available to the other via messenger and electronic telecopier. The collections include a full range of practice aids and more than 300 law review titles, in addition to statutes, case reporters, encyclopedias, digests, and citators. Both libraries are open daily until late hours. Each campus features WESTLAW computer terminals for legal research, an OCLC terminal, and quiet, roomy study areas. The La Verne campus library has been designated a selective federal and state depository. The San Fernando Valley campus is currently developing a CD-ROM research library for student use.

Financial Aid

At the College of Law, more than half the student body receives financial aid. Entering students who have demonstrated academic excellence, evidenced for the most part by high undergraduate grades and high LSAT scores, are eligible to apply for La Verne scholarships. Continuing students retain their eligibility for scholarships by maintaining a high level of academic achievement over the course of their studies. All students are also eligible to apply for California State Graduate Fellowships and state and federal loan programs, as well as veterans' benefits and many other scholarships at each campus.

Cost of Study

Since the University of La Verne is a nonprofit organization, the College of Law is able to keep the cost of study at a minimum. For the academic year 1998–99, tuition is $450 per semester unit. The College of Law also offers a convenient payment plan with subsidized interest rates to assist students who are not depending on financial aid. Book costs average about $400 per semester for full-time students and about $300 per semester for part-time students. Used books are usually available at substantial savings.

Living and Housing Costs

Students' expenses vary according to marital status, personal needs, and lifestyle. Ample housing in a safe, suburban setting is available to fit a variety of budgets at both campuses.

Student Group

At the College of Law campuses, students from a variety of cultural and religious backgrounds come together to exchange ideas that stem from a multitude of different personal backgrounds. As varied as student lifestyles and opinions may be, there is shared enthusiasm for campus activities, including the Student Bar Association, the publication of the *Journal of Juvenile Law,* Delta Theta Phi International Law Fraternity, and Moot Court Competitions. Women compose almost half of the student body.

Location

The University of La Verne is unique in having two campuses. The central University of La Verne campus occupies 25 acres 30 miles east of downtown Los Angeles, near the San Gabriel Mountain foothills. The law school occupies a distinctive brick building near the center of the campus. The San Fernando Valley campus is housed in a facility at Warner Center in Woodland Hills, an upscale part of Los Angeles's famous suburban area. The College of Law provides a spacious, distinguished, and inviting atmosphere for legal studies. The Los Angeles area offers students virtually every cultural, sports, recreational, and educational attraction imaginable in a world-famous, year-round, favorable climate.

The University

Founded in 1891, the University of La Verne is well-respected by community members and alumni for its tradition of providing quality education. In addition to the College of Law, the University includes the College of Arts and Sciences, the School of Business and Economics, the College of Graduate and Professional Studies, and the School of Continuing Education. Beyond its central campus, the University carries on undergraduate and graduate programs at military bases and other locations throughout California, as well as at distant locations as far away as Alaska, Greece, and Italy. Accredited by the Western Association of Schools and Colleges, ULV is an active member of the Independent Colleges of Southern California and the Association of California Independent Colleges and Universities.

Applying

At the College of Law, the admissions process emphasizes individual attention given to each applicant. Applicants are sought from a wide variety of educational and career backgrounds. Applications are accepted and acted upon on a rolling basis and, although a decision can be made quickly once a file is complete, early application is encouraged to ensure space availability and ample time for financial aid processing.

Correspondence and Information

For the La Verne campus:
Director of Admissions
University of La Verne
College of Law at La Verne
1950 3rd Street
La Verne, California 91750
Telephone: 909-596-1848
Fax: 909-593-5139

For the San Fernando Valley campus:
Director of Admissions
University of La Verne
College of Law at San Fernando Valley
21300 Oxnard Street
Woodland Hills, California 91367
Telephone: 818-883-0529
Fax: 818-883-8142

University of La Verne

THE FACULTY AND THEIR RESEARCH

Kenneth Held, Professor of Law and Dean; J.D., Fordham.
Gregory Fast, Professor of Law and Assistant Dean; J.D., Southwestern Law.
H. Randall Rubin, Associate Professor of Law and Assistant Dean; M.P.A., USC; J.D., Southwestern Law.
Robert S. Ackrich, Professor of Law; M.A., California State, Los Angeles; J.D., Southwestern Law.
Robert Barrett, Assistant Professor of Law; M.S.F.S., J.D., Georgetown.
Caroline A. Chizever, Professor of Law; J.D., La Verne.
Charles S. Doskow, Professor of Law and Dean Emeritus; J.D., Harvard; LL.M., NYU.
Honorable Paul Egly, Professor of Law and Dean Emeritus; LL.B., George Washington.
Gert K. Hirschberg, Associate Professor of Law; J.D., Southwestern Law.
John Huffer, Professor of Law and Dean Emeritus; LL.B., Toledo.
John R. Hultman, Associate of Professor of Law; J.D., La Verne.
George McCormick, Professor of Law; J.D., USC.
Jamal Monono, Assistant Professor of Law; M.B.A., Frostburg State; J.D., Maryland.
Irving Prager, Professor of Law; J.D., Georgetown; LL.M., London School of Economics and Political Science.

WASHINGTON UNIVERSITY IN ST. LOUIS

School of Law

Programs of Study

At Washington University School of Law, students learn the three skills essential to the practice of law: how to obtain all the relevant information, how to analyze the information, and how to communicate these findings clearly and persuasively. The transition to law school is made easier by a law faculty that is genuinely interested in its students' professional education and development and whose teaching and accessibility have been ranked at the top of all American law schools. A student-faculty ratio of 14:1 enables students to get to know the faculty well, with faculty interests extending beyond the law classroom. Throughout the year, faculty members create many opportunities for interaction with students—in basketball games, at end-of-week "happy hours" in the law lounge, one-on-one in their offices, or at potluck dinners in their homes.

Students will find themselves interested in developing close relationships with faculty members so that they can draw on their thorough knowledge of the law. Faculty expertise, developed through practical experiences as well as scholarly research, covers a wide area of law, including environmental, corporate, bankruptcy, tax, land use, consumer protection, labor, immigration, white-collar crime, and international law.

Students interested in practicing exclusively in the emerging areas of business law, environmental law, or international law can pursue studies in these areas or can choose to focus study on their particular areas of interest.

Clinical courses throughout the three-year curriculum emphasize applied lawyering skills such as client counseling, negotiation strategies, adversarial tactics, and legal decision making in the litigative, administrative, legislative, and judicial arenas. The upperclass skills curriculum includes courses on litigation, alternative dispute resolution, and transactional courses.

Students can put legal theory into practice through the School's award-winning Clinical Education program that enhances the simulation courses in the law curriculum by offering opportunities to participate in various lawyering skills competitions. Clinical internships are also available, in which students learn lawyering skills firsthand by working in a private or government law office, a state or federal court, or a congressional office. The Congressional and Federal Administrative Agency Clinics give students practical experience in the nation's complex legislative process. Each spring semester, the School places up to 24 third-year law students in Washington, D.C., where they work full-time for a member of Congress, a congressional committee, or an administrative agency, functioning as a professional staff member.

Research Facilities

The School of Law's Library contains more than 560,000 volumes and acquires approximately 25,000 new volumes each year. Because the collection at the Law Library is so comprehensive, judges, attorneys, and legal scholars in the St. Louis area use the library as the authoritative source for legal research materials.

Eight professional librarians, 11 support staff members, and numerous student assistants maintain the library. The librarians are actively involved in teaching and guiding law students and helping them as they develop their legal research skills. The librarians are also available to help students use all reference materials, government documents, serials, online database searching, microforms, and audiovisual materials.

Financial Aid

The School of Law makes every effort to meet the minimum financial need. It offers merit-based scholarships and administers need- and credit-based loan programs. Most scholarships are given to applicants who have demonstrated the probability that they will be superior law students. Approximately 70 percent of students receive financial assistance.

Cost of Study

The 1997–98 tuition in the School of Law was $21,675 per year. Casebooks and supplies for classes cost approximately $400 per semester.

Living and Housing Costs

The estimated cost of room, board, and other expenses for a single student during the year is $9000 at the Washington University School of Law.

Student Group

More than 9,000 full-time undergraduate, graduate, and professional students come to Washington University from all fifty states and from seventy-four other countries. Students enjoy a university atmosphere characterized by intense intellectual engagement and a wealth of social opportunities.

The student group at Washington University School of Law is diverse. The 665 students enrolled during the 1997–98 academic year hailed from forty-one states, the District of Columbia, and four other countries and attended approximately 150 colleges and universities. These students also share a strong academic record. The class that entered in fall 1997 had a median score of 160 on the Law School Admission Test and a median grade point average of 3.4.

While most of its law students are achievement-oriented, the School fosters a feeling of community. Close student-faculty relationships and supportive friendships are a hallmark of Washington University School of Law.

Location

The Seeley G. Mudd Law Building is located on the beautiful 169-acre Hilltop Campus, which is bordered by Forest Park, the site of the 1904 World's Fair, and by the lovely suburban communities of Clayton and University City. The School of Law's state-of-the-art building was completed in 1996.

The large and impressive corporate and legal communities in St. Louis offer important employment opportunities. St. Louis is headquarters for some of the world's largest corporations, including Anheuser-Busch, the Brown Group, Emerson Electric, Interco, Monsanto, and Ralston Purina. Law firms of all sizes, whose expertise covers all aspects of the legal profession, constitute the city's legal community. The primary business district is located 7 miles from the University on the historic riverfront with its Gateway Arch and Laclede's Landing.

The University and The School

The School of Law is one of several graduate schools at Washington University, an independent institution known internationally for its excellence in teaching and research. The University has ten undergraduate, graduate, and professional divisions, as well as thirty-three research centers and institutes. The Hilltop and Medical campuses, along with the Tyson Research Center and other tracts, comprise 2,211 acres and more than ninety major buildings.

Something is always happening at Washington University. Students can choose from performances by professional theater and dance companies; lectures by prominent and controversial political figures, entertainers, and social commentators; poetry and literature readings by leading writers of the day; impromptu music fests; and ball games.

Applying

First-year students are admitted for full-time study only in the fall of each year. Students may submit the application for admission any time between September 15 and March 1 of the academic year preceding the year in which they plan to enroll. Applications received after March 1 will be considered on a space-available basis. The Admissions Committee also makes a conscientious effort to examine the other more personal variables that have a real impact on the quality of life and the quality of education in this institution: energy, motivation, self-discipline, and character. Insight into these variables can be derived from careful examination of a student's undergraduate record, résumé, personal statement, and other information in the file. Students may also apply online at the World Wide Web address below. To apply for financial assistance, students must complete the Free Application for Federal Student Aid (FAFSA) and related law school forms. If the completed financial aid forms are received by March 1, the School will make every effort to notify students of scholarship and loan awards before the April 15 deadline for first deposit.

Correspondence and Information

Admissions Office
Washington University in St. Louis
School of Law, Campus Box 1120
One Brookings Drive
St. Louis, Missouri 63130-4899

Telephone: 314-935-4525
Fax: 314-935-6959
E-mail: admiss@wulaw.wustl.edu
World Wide Web: http://www.wulaw.wustl.edu/

Washington University in St. Louis

THE FACULTY

Susan Frelich Appleton, Professor; J.D., Berkeley.
Stuart A. Banner, Associate Professor; J.D., Stanford.
David M. Becker, Joseph H. Zumbalen Professor of the Law of Property; J.D., Chicago.
Merton C. Bernstein, Professor Emeritus; LL.B., Columbia.
Neil N. Bernstein, Professor; LL.B., Yale.
Kathleen F. Brickey, James Carr Professor of Criminal Jurisprudence; J.D., Kentucky.
Kathleen Clark, Assistant Professor; J.D., Yale.
Clark D. Cunningham, Professor; Ph.D., Wayne State.
Gray L. Dorsey, Charles Nagel Professor of Jurisprudence and International Law Emeritus; J.S.D., Yale.
John N. Drobak, Professor of Law and Professor of Economics; J.D., Stanford.
Dorsey D. Ellis Jr., Dean and Professor; J.D., Chicago.
Barbara J. Flagg, Professor; J.D., Berkeley.
Frances H. Foster, Professor; J.S.D., Stanford.
Jules B. Gerard, Professor; J.D., Washington (St. Louis).
Katherine Goldwasser, Professor; J.D., Temple.
Michael M. Greenfield, Professor; J.D., Texas at Austin.
Jeffrey Hanslick, Visiting Assistant Professor of Legal Writing; J.D., Northwestern.
William C. Jones, Charles Nagel Professor of International and Comparative Law Emeritus; J.S.D., Chicago.
Daniel L. Keating, Associate Dean and Professor; J.D., Chicago.
Pauline T. Kim, Associate Professor; J.D., Harvard.
Richard B. Kuhns, Professor; S.J.D., Michigan.
D. Bruce La Pierre, Professor; J.D., Columbia.
Stephen H. Legomsky, Walter D. Coles Professor; J.D., San Diego.
Ronald M. Levin, Professor; J.D., Chicago.
Daniel R. Mandelker, Howard A. Stamper Professor; J.S.D., Yale.
Charles R. McManis, Professor; J.D., Duke.
Curtis J. Milhaupt, Associate Professor; J.D., Columbia.
Frank William Miller, James Carr Professor of Criminal Jurisprudence Emeritus; S.J.D., Wisconsin.
A. Peter Mutharika, Professor; J.S.D., Yale.
Kimberly Jade Norwood, Associate Professor; J.D., Missouri–Columbia.
Stanley L. Paulson, Professor of Law and Philosophy; J.D., Harvard.
Karen A. Porter, Associate Professor; J.D., Yale.
Jean M. Scott, Associate Professor; J.D., Georgetown.
Mark W. Smith, Associate Dean; J.D., Washington.
R. Dale Swihart, Professor; J.D., Indiana Bloomington.
Robert B. Thompson, George Alexander Madill Professor; J.D., Virginia.
Karen L. Tokarz, Professor and Director of Clinical Education; LL.M., Berkeley.
Dana Underwood, Visiting Assistant Professor of Legal Writing; J.D., Case Western.
Robin S. Wellford, Visiting Assistant Professor and Director of Legal Writing; J.D., Washington (St. Louis).
Leila Sadat Wexler, Associate Professor; LL.M., Columbia.
Peter J. Wiedenbeck, Professor; J.D., Michigan.

WAYNE STATE UNIVERSITY

Law School

Programs of Study

Wayne State University Law School has educated and trained lawyers for Detroit, the state of Michigan, and the rest of the nation since 1927. The Law School is dedicated to excellence in both legal education and research. Recognized for its strong traditional legal curriculum, the program also emphasizes the development of skills in legal writing and research, litigation, and alternate dispute resolution. The Law School's 9,000 alumni are successful leaders of the bench and bar and respected in the legal and business communities. The Detroit metropolitan area is a center for leading law firms as well as state and federal courts and governmental agencies. The Law School is able to enrich its core curriculum with practical internship opportunities with the courts, judges, prosecutors, and defenders offices as well as in governmental agencies and public interest law firms.

The Juris Doctor (J.D.) degree is awarded upon successful completion of 86 credit hours. The course of study requires three years of full-time study in the day program, four to six years of part-time study in the evening program, or three to four years in the combined day/evening program. Joint J.D./M.A. programs are offered in history, political science, and business administration.

Wayne State University Law School offers Master of Laws (LL.M.) programs in taxation, labor law, and corporate and finance law. Designed for lawyers with some legal experience, this part-time evening program is intended to provide specialization in complex areas requiring education beyond the Juris Doctor degree.

Research Facilities

Wayne State University's Arthur Neef Law Library is the second-largest law library in Michigan and twenty-third in the United States. The Law Library staff emphasizes instruction and service, utilizing varied resources and up-to-date technology. The Law Library is utilized by students, faculty, and alumni, as well as by members of the legal community. The extensive collection includes more than 525,000 books, journals, U.S. government documents, video tapes and audio tapes, microforms, full-text databases, and CD-ROM files. Students may access on-line databases from the Law Library or via modem from home.

Law students have a modern, comfortable thirty-two-station computer facility that includes IBM, IBM-compatible, and Macintosh workstations. The Law Library provides access to and training in Computer Assisted Legal Instruction (CALI), LEXIS-NEXIS, and WESTLAW as well as the Internet, gopher, and the World Wide Web.

Financial Aid

The Law School administers a variety of scholarships and loan funds to assist eligible students. Financial aid awards are designed to supplement the financial contribution of the student and the student's family to his or her education. The financial aid programs available are Board of Governor's Grants, Federal Perkins Loans, Federal College Work-Study, Federal Stafford/Unsubsidized Stafford Loans, and Law Access Private Loans. All programs, with the exception of the Law Access Private Loan program, are need-based. Students must complete the Free Application for Federal Student Aid (FAFSA) form for need-based programs.

Cost of Study

Wayne State University is committed to maintaining an affordable law school tuition rate. In fall 1997, the tuition per year for full-time study was $6834 for residents and $14,364 for nonresidents. Resident tuition is less than one-half that of any other law school in Michigan.

Living and Housing Costs

In fall 1997, the estimated budget for full-time first-year students was $21,416 for residents and $29,444 for nonresidents. These budgets include tuition, room and board, books, transportation, health insurance, and miscellaneous expenses.

Student Group

The Law School has approximately 750 students enrolled in the J.D. program. The median grade point average for the 1996 entering class was 3.27. The median Law School Admissions Test score was 155. The 1996 entering class included 49.3 percent women and 15 percent students of color. The average age was 26.

The survey of the 199 members of the graduating class of 1995 (total responses: 177; 88.9 percent response rate) indicated that six months after graduation 89.8 percent were employed, and of these, 71.8 percent were employed in legal positions. The median salary for all 1995 graduates was $36,555. The Career Services Office offers comprehensive skills training, career information, counseling, and job postings for law students and graduates.

Location

Wayne State University is located 4 miles from downtown Detroit, in the heart of the University Cultural Center and near the Detroit Institute of Arts, the Detroit Public Library, the International Institute, and the Detroit Historical Museum. The campus is easily accessible from all area freeways; safe and convenient parking is readily available.

The University

The Law School was established in 1927 as the Detroit City Law School by the Detroit Board of Education. In 1937, the Law School joined the colleges of liberal arts, education, engineering, medicine, pharmacy, and graduate studies as part of Wayne University. In 1956, Wayne became a public University of the state of Michigan and was renamed Wayne State University. At present, the fifteen schools and colleges enroll more than 30,000 students and grant more than 5,000 doctoral, master's, bachelor's, and professional degrees each year.

Applying

No specific undergraduate major is preferred, but the nature of college work, as well as the grades received, will be considered. The Admissions Committee seeks to enroll a highly qualified, diverse, and talented student body.

Applications for admission are accepted from October 1 through March 15. The Law School requires the LSAT, LSDAS, a personal statement, one letter of recommendation, and a baccalaureate degree awarded by an accredited institution prior to the start of the fall semester. The nonrefundable application fee is $20 for U.S. citizens and $30 for noncitizens.

Correspondence and Information

Admissions Office
Wayne State University Law School
468 West Ferry Mall, Room 195
Detroit, Michigan 48202

Telephone: 313-577-3937
E-mail: inquire@novell.law.wayne.edu
World Wide Web: http://www.law.wayne.edu

Wayne State University

THE FACULTY AND THEIR RESEARCH

Robert H. Abrams, Professor of Law; J.D., Michigan. Civil procedure, environmental law.
David Adamany, Professor of Law and Political Science and President; J.D., Harvard; Ph.D., Wisconsin. Constitutional law, election law.
Martin J. Adelman, Professor of Law; J.D., Michigan. Antitrust, law and economics, patents.
Laura B. Bartell, Associate Professor of Law; J.D., Harvard. Bankruptcy, commercial transactions, property.
Kingsley R. Browne, Associate Professor of Law; J.D., Denver. Employment law, torts.
William Burnham, Professor of Law; J.D., Indiana. Civil procedure, civil rights, federal courts, trial advocacy.
Stephen Calkins, Professor of Law; J.D., Harvard. Antitrust, corporations, torts.
Gennady Danilenko, Professor of Law; Dip. in Law, Rostov-on-Don (Russia); Doctor of Law, Institute of State & Law (USSR). International law, Russian law.
Dennis M. Devaney, Associate Professor of Law; J.D., Georgetown. Labor law, negotiation.
John F. Dolan, Professor of Law; LL.B., Illinois. Bankruptcy, commercial transactions, contracts.
Erica Eisinger, Associate Professor of Law and Director of Clinical Education; Ph.D., Yale; J.D., Wisconsin. Pretrial, trial advocacy.
Zanita E. Fenton, Assistant Professor of Law; J.D., Harvard. Family law, torts.
Janet E. Findlater, Associate Professor of Law; J.D., Michigan. Contracts, criminal law.
John Friedl, Associate Professor of Law, Professor of Anthropology, and Director of the Center for Legal Studies and of the Graduate Program; Ph.D., Berkeley; J.D., Michigan. Education law, intellectual property.
Jane M. Friedman, Professor of Law; J.D., Minnesota. Health law.
Joseph D. Grano, Distinguished Professor of Law; J.D., Temple; LL.M., Illinois. Constitutional law, criminal procedure.
Peter J. Henning, Associate Professor of Law; J.D., Georgetown. Criminal law, corporations, white-collar crime.
Eric Kades, Assistant Professor of Law; J.D., Yale. Corporations, property.
LeRoy Lamborn, Professor Emeritus; LL.B., Case Western Reserve; J.S.D., Columbia. Criminal law and procedure, victims and the law.
Jessica D. Litman, Professor of Law; J.D., Columbia. Intellectual property, trademarks, torts.
Edward Littlejohn, Professor Emeritus; J.D., Detroit Law; J.S.D., Columbia. Torts.
Frederica K. Lombard, Professor of Law and Associate Dean; J.D., Pennsylvania; LL.M., Yale. Civil procedure, family law.
Joan Mahoney, Professor of Law and Dean; J.D., Wayne State; Ph.D., Cambridge. Constitutional law, legal history, jurisprudence.
Lawrence C. Mann, Associate Professor of Law; J.D., Wayne State. Civil procedure, evidence, products liability, trial advocacy.
Michael J. McIntyre, Professor of Law; J.D., Harvard. Federal tax, international taxation, state and local taxation.
John E. Mogk, Professor of Law; J.D., Michigan. Local government law, property, urban housing.
David Moss, Assistant Professor of Law and Assistant Director of Clinical Education; J.D., Columbia. Pretrial advocacy, disability law.
Christopher J. Peters, Assistant Professor of Law; J.D., Michigan. Civil procedure, constitutional law.
James K. Robinson, Professor of Law; J.D., Wayne State. Evidence. (On leave)
Alan Schenk, Professor of Law; J.D., Illinois; LL.M., NYU. Business planning, federal taxation, value added tax.
Robert A. Sedler, Professor of Law; J.D., Pittsburgh. Conflicts of law, constitutional law.
Stephen Schulman, Professor Emeritus; J.D., Columbia; LL.M., NYU. Business planning.
Ralph Slovenko, Professor of Law; Ph.D., LL.B., Tulane. Evidence, law and psychiatry, torts.
Jonathan Weinberg, Associate Professor of Law; J.D., Columbia. Administrative law, constitutional law, mass media law.
Vincent Wellman, Associate Professor of Law; J.D., Yale. Contracts, jurisprudence.
Katherine E. White, Assistant Professor of Law; J.D., Washington (Seattle); LL.M., George Washington. Contracts, intellectual property.
Edward M. Wise, Professor of Law; LL.B., Cornell; LL.M., NYU. Comparative law, criminal law, international law, legal history.

Legal Writing Lecturers

Diana V. Pratt, Director of the Legal Writing Program; J.D., Michigan; Ph.D., Stanford.
Michael McFerren, J.D., Michigan.
Gloria Miller, J.D., Michigan.
Sonal Mithani, J.D., Harvard.
Susanna Peters, J.D., Pennsylvania.

Adjunct Faculty

John R. Axe, LL.B., Harvard. Public finance.
Timothy A. Baughman, J.D., Wayne State. Criminal procedure.
Mary Bedikian, J.D., Detroit Law. Alternate dispute resolution.
Joseph P. Canfield; J.D., Detroit Law. Labor law.
The Honorable Jeffrey G. Collins, J.D., Howard. Trial advocacy.
The Honorable Timothy P. Connors, J.D., Wayne State. Trial advocacy.
Roger Cook, J.D., Wayne State; LL.M., NYU. Taxation.
William H. Dance, LL.B., Michigan. Immigration law.
David J. DeBold, J.D., Harvard. Trial advocacy.
The Honorable Marc L. Goldman, J.D., Wayne State. Trial advocacy.
Michael A. Gruskin, J.D., Harvard. Pretrial advocacy.
Peter Holmes, J.D., Michigan. Environmental law.
Michael A. Indenbaum, J.D., Wayne State; LL.M., NYU. Corporate taxation.
W. David Koeninger, J.D., Michigan
Paul J. Komives, J.D., Michigan. Pretrial advocacy.
Mark C. Larson, J.D., Akron; LL.M., Georgetown. Real estate taxation.
Sheryl Giddings Lendo, J.D., Wayne State. Trusts and estates.
The Honorable Conrad L. Mallett, Jr., J.D., USC. Professional responsibility.
Gerard Mantese, J.D., Saint Louis. Pretrial advocacy.
Mark L. McAlpine, J.D., Detroit Law. Construction law.
Samuel J. McKim III, J.D., Michigan. State and local taxation.
David Moran, J.D., Michigan. Criminal appellate advocacy, criminal procedure.
Anne T. Patton, J.D., Detroit. Arbitration of labor disputes.
Hans H. J. Pijls, M.L., Utrecht (Netherlands); LL.M., Wayne State. Insurance law.
Michael T. Raymond, J.D., John Marhsall Law; LL.M., Georgetown. Securities regulation.
James D. Robb, Assistant Dean for Development and External Relations; J.D., Wayne State. Lawyering.
Louis P. Rochkind, J.D., Michigan. Bankruptcy clinic.
Gail O. Rodwan, J.D., Detroit Law. Criminal appellate advocacy.
Lore A. Rogers, J.D., Michigan. Pretrial advocacy.
The Honorable Gerald E. Rosen, J.D., George Washington. Evidence.
Erwin A. Rubenstein, LL.M., NYU. Tax penalties and prosecution.
John R. Runyan, J.D., Wayne State. Equal employment opportunity.
Lawrence F. Schiller, J.D., Ohio. Employee benefits.
John Sharp, J.D., Wayne State. Trusts and estates.
Stuart L. Sherman, J.D., Wayne State; LL.M., NYU. Estate and gift tax, estate planning.
Michael R. Shpiece, J.D., Michigan. Employee benefits.
Richard S. Soble, J.D., Yale. Partnership tax.
Shlomo Sperka, LL.B., Brooklyn Law. Jewish law.
James Statham, J.D., Detroit; LL.M., NYU. Negotiation.
Peter Sugar, J.D., Wayne State. Corporate finance.
Sandra Van Burkleo, Ph.D., Minnesota. U.S. constitutional history.
Rodger G. Will, J.D., Wayne State. Workers compensation law.
The Honorable Robert P. Young, J.D., Harvard. Pretrial advocacy.

WESTERN STATE UNIVERSITY COLLEGE OF LAW

Program of Study

The curriculum requirements at Western State University College of Law closely follow the guidelines and standards established by the American Bar Association and the Committee of Bar Examiners of the State Bar of California. In tandem with the traditional core curriculum of contracts, civil procedure, property, and torts, first- and second-year students gain insight into the lawyer's role as counselor and problem solver while receiving in-depth training in legal research, alternative dispute resolution, and other essential professional skills. In upper-division electives, professors weave actual courtroom scenarios into the teaching of substantive law via a sequence of integrated advanced-skills texts. Students also have the opportunity to participate in externship programs that allow them to work side by side with prosecutors, public defenders, civil practitioners, and prominent jurists. This focus on the development of professional skills, in concert with law theory, prepares students to function as lawyers from the day they receive their law degrees.

Convenient class scheduling, full-time, part-time, and accelerated course work are available. Students may begin study in either the fall or spring semester. Students must earn 88 units for their Juris Doctor degree, the first professional law degree.

Research Facilities

Western State's new state-of-the-art library houses 144,000 volumes with the capacity for more than 400,000, as the collection continues to grow rapidly. The 31,000-square-foot, three-story building houses a thirty-one-station computer lab, providing full access to the Internet and legal databases. Virtually all study areas in the library are equipped with computer ports. Dedicated multimedia computers enable students to role play as mediators and trial attorneys via interactive CD-ROMs.

Financial Aid

A wide range of financial aid options are available to students with financial need. Programs include state and federally supported scholarship and loan plans as well as private offerings. The law school sponsors an extensive merit scholarship program for both entering and continuing students. The law school participates in the Federal Work-Study Program, which gives students the opportunity to gain law-related work experience. Western State students can also take part in the Veterans Administration Work-Study Program.

Cost of Study

Western State strives to maintain tuition and fee schedules at the lowest possible level. Tuition for law classes is $9400 per semester for full-time students and $6250 per semester for part-time students in 1998–99. A $100 tuition deposit is applied toward the first semester's tuition. Books cost about $600 per year.

Living and Housing Costs

The law school does not provide residence or dormitory housing. Because of its proximity to several universities and colleges, affordable housing is available near the campus. The law school maintains current listings of nearby housing, and can supply entering students with a complete housing packet and individual assistance.

Student Group

There are many active clubs, law fraternities, and organizations available to students. The Western State University *Law Review* is a distinguished publication produced by students. Because of the law school's appeal to those embarking on a second career in law, the student body is a diverse mix of people. Students come from many states but predominately from California and New York.

Location

Western State University is located in one of the nation's most livable and desirable regions—southern California. Beaches, mountains, deserts, and many other recreational attractions are within easy reach, and nearly perfect weather prevails throughout the year. Recently, Orange County was ranked the overall number one most desirable place to live by *Places Rated Almanac.*

The University

Western State is accredited by the Committee of Bar Examiners of the State Bar of California and by the Western Association of Schools and Colleges. Graduates are qualified to take the bar examination in California. Western State graduates may sit for the bar exam in many other states after having practiced law in California for a certain number of years. The law school continues its efforts to seek approval by the American Bar Association under the Standards and Rules of Procedure for the Approval of Law Schools. The ABA is scheduled to act on the law school's application prior to the start of the fall 1998 semester.

Applying

Western State University examines each applicant's overall potential for success in law school by evaluating several factors in addition to numerical indicators. While undergraduate grade point averages and LSAT scores are very important, the Admissions Committee gives considerable weight to other factors, such as maturity, oral expression, employment background, community involvement, and motivation.

Applicants should submit two personal letters of recommendation, college transcripts, and a $35 application fee. An official copy of the Law School Admission Test (LSAT) scores are required. Completed applications are considered on a rolling basis. Preapplication counseling is available without obligation.

Correspondence and Information

Western State University College of Law
1111 North State College Boulevard
Fullerton, California 92831
Telephone: 714-738-1000 Ext. 2600
Fax: 714-441-1748
World Wide Web: http://www.wsulaw.edu

Western State University College of Law

THE FACULTY AND THEIR RESEARCH

Todd Brower, Professor; LL.M., Yale. A stranger to its laws: Homosexuality, schemas, and the lessons and limits of reasoning by analogy. *Santa Clara Law Rev.*, in press.
David Casey, Professor; J.D., Toledo. Conditional checks in California. *Thomas Jefferson Law Rev.*, in press.
Leslie V. Dery, Associate Professor; J.D., California, Hastings Law. Disinterring the good and bad immigrant: A deconstruction of the state court interpreter laws for non-English criminal defense. *45 University Kansas Law Rev.* 837, 1997.
Carol Ebbinghouse, Assistant Professor and Librarian; J.D., Southwestern.
Sidebar—Renaissance librarians. *4 Searcher: Magazine Database Professionals* 8, 1996.
Permission, permission, who's got the permission? *4 Searcher: Magazine Database Professionals* 43, 1996.
Who gets the money? *4 Searcher: Magazine Database Professionals* 51, 1996.
Howard Engelskirchen, Professor; J.D., Berkeley. Consideration as a form for the relinquishment of autonomy. *27 Seton Hall Law Rev.* 490, 1997.
Jon Garon, Associate Dean of Academic Affairs and Associate Professor; J.D., Columbia. Star Wars: Film permitting, prior restraint, and government's role in the entertainment industry. *17 Loyola Entertainment Law J.* 1, 1996.
Neil Gotanda, Professor; LL.M., Harvard. Race, citizenship and the search for political community among 'We the People.' *Oregon Law Rev.*, 1998.
Failure of the color-blind vision: Race, ethnicity, and the California civil rights initiative. *23 Hastings Constitutional Law Q.* 1135, 1996.
Multiculturalism and racial stratification. In *Translating Cultures: The Future of Multiculturalism*, eds. A. Gordon and C. Newfield. University of Minnesota, 1996.
Toward repeal of Asian exclusion, 1943–1950. In *Asian Americans and Congress*, ed. H.-C. Kim, Greendwood Press, 1996.
Dennis Honabach, Dean; J.D., Yale. *Proxy Rules Handbook—1998 Edition.* Clark Boardman Callaghan, 1996. With Sargent.
Maryann Jones, Professor; J.D., IIT. And access for all: Accommodating disabilities in state court. *32 University South Florida Law Rev.* 75, 1997.
Rebecca Jurado, Assistant Professor; J.D., UCLA. Does affirmative action serve a compelling government interest? *Hispanic Bar Assoc. J.* 1996.
Susan Keller, Professor; J.D., Harvard. The rhetoric of marriage, achievement, and power: An analysis of judicial opinions considering the treatment of professional degrees as marital property. *Vermont Law Sch. Law Rev.* 1996.
Glenn Koppel, Professor; J.D., Harvard. Populism, politics, and procedure: The saga of summary judgment and the rulemaking process in California. *Pepperdine Law Sch. Law Rev.* 1996.
Philip L. Merkel, Professor; J.D., Illinois. *Railroad Consolidation and Late 19th Century Constitutionalism: Legal Strategy in Organizing the Southern Pacific System* (completed manuscript).
Kristian Miccio, Associate Professor; LL.M., Columbia. With all due deliberate care: Using international law and the federal violence against mothers in the age de Shaney. *Columbia J. Int. Hum. Rights,* in press.
Stuart Miller, Associate Professor; J.D., NYU. Liability for irresponsible sales of controlled products: An analysis of Macias v. California. *31 University San Francisco Law Rev.* 85, 1996.
Kevin Mohr, Assistant Professor; J.D., Yale. The intersection of patent law and trademark law: Should product configuration disclosed in a utility patent ever qualify for trade dress protection. *COM/ENT—Hastings Commun. Arts Law J.* 1997.
Gloria Sanchez, Associate Professor; J.D., Berkeley. A paradigm shift in legal education: Preparing law students for the twenty-first century: Teaching foreign law, culture, and legal language of the major U.S. trading partners. *University San Diego Law Rev.* 1997.
Michael Schwartz, Associate Professor; J.D., California, Hastings Law *(cum laude)*. Power outage: Amplifying the analysis of a power in legal relations. *33 Williamette Law Sch. Law Rev.* 1996.
Charles Sheppard, Associate Professor; J.D., Loyola. California Code of Civil Procedure Section 580b, anti-deficiency protection regarding purchase money debts: Arguments for the inclusion of refinanced purchase money obligations as being within the anti-deficiency protection of Section 580b. *South. California Interdisciplinary Law J.* 1997.
Edith Warkentine, Professor; J.D., California, Davis. Article 2 revisions: An opportunity to protect consumers and merchant consumers. *John Marshall Law Sch. Law Rev.* 1996.
Kathleen Whitney, Assistant Professor; J.D., Western State. Does the European Convention on Human Rights protect refugees from "safe" countries? *Georgia J. Int. Comp. Law* April 1997.
SIN, FRAPH, and the CIA: U.S. covert action in Haiti. *J. Law Trade Americas* 1997.

Orange County, recently ranked number one overall as the most desirable place to live, is home to Western State University College of Law.

Between classes, students interact with each other to discuss current trends in the legal field.

WIDENER UNIVERSITY

School of Law

Programs of Study

The School of Law confers the Juris Doctor (J.D.) degree and Master of Laws in corporate law and finance and in health law (LL.M.). In addition, joint degrees are offered in conjunction with the Institute of Clinical Psychology (J.D./Psy.D.) and the School of Business Administration (J.D./M.B.A.). All candidates for the J.D. must complete a required 87 semester hours of study. After the first year, this averages a minimum of 14 hours per semester in the Regular Division (3-year program, full-time) and 11 hours per semester in the Extended Division (4-year program, evenings). The LL.M. degree requires 24 semester hours of course work.

The School of Law also develops and conducts programs of continuing legal education primarily directed toward reinforcing the skills and knowledge of attorneys. The School has been certified as an accredited sponsor for continuing legal education in Delaware and by the Pennsylvania Supreme Court as an official provider for continuing legal education in Pennsylvania. The Widener University School of Law is accredited by the ABA and is a member of AALS.

Other course work includes institutes in health law and trial advocacy; clinics in consumer credit, civil law, energy law, environmental law, public interest law, and criminal defense; and international programs in Nairobi, Geneva, and Sydney.

Research Facilities

Located on 40 acres of parklike grounds, the Delaware campus's administrative building was a former Georgian manor house. Expansion and renovation of the facilities on the Delaware campus, to be completed by the fall semester of 1999, will result in a new moot court, classrooms, legal clinic, offices serving students, and additional library space. The 21-acre Harrisburg campus consists of a recently constructed 30,000-square-foot administrative complex with a large moot classroom, a 14,000-square-foot student activities building that was originally a Spanish-styled residence, and a 50,000-square-foot library/classroom building.

The combined libraries of the Delaware and Pennsylvania campuses house one of the most significant legal collections in the region, exceeding 550,000 volumes. The Delaware Campus library has an outstanding collection in taxation and corporate law, with emphasis on Delaware corporate law and health law to support the School's Master of Laws program. A strong health law section also complements the Health Law Institute. The Harrisburg campus collection reflects its proximity to the state capital with emphasis on administrative, legislative, and public interest law. Computers are available for legal research, computer-assisted legal instruction, and word processing at both campuses. All students are instructed in LEXIS and WESTLAW, computer-assisted research software. Dialog and NEXIS databases provide access to nonlegal and interdisciplinary resources. An interactive video station interfaces computer and video to simulate actual trial practice, aiding in the development of courtroom skills. A CD-ROM network and advanced telecommunications permit total linkage between the Delaware and Pennsylvania campuses. Each branch has access to resources on the other campus.

Financial Aid

Students at Widener may receive financial assistance from federal programs, institutional grants, and endowed and other School scholarship funds. All aid programs are administered by the School's Financial Aid Office (telephone: 302-477-2272 for the Delaware campus; 717-541-1924 for the Harrisburg campus). Financial aid is awarded on a rolling basis. Students are encouraged to pursue the following: Federal Work-Study Program, Federal Perkins Loan, Federal Stafford Student Loan, Unsubsidized Federal Stafford Loan, Law Access Loan Program/Law Loan Program, and Delaware State Grants. Financial assistance is also offered directly to students by various organizations or individuals such as state bar associations, veterans' organizations, ethnic and church groups, and alumni associations. Major scholarships are awarded to students with outstanding credentials as well as returning students who have demonstrated high achievement in their law school studies.

Cost of Study

Tuition for 1998–99 is $18,500 for the incoming regular division students for full-time study in the J.D. program. For incoming extended division students, the cost is $13,880 per year. For the combined programs, the cost of Psy.D. courses in the J.D./Psy.D. program is $572 per credit; in the J.D./M.B.A. program, the cost for management courses is $470 per credit. In those combined programs, the J.D. courses are $620 per credit.

Living and Housing Costs

The Delaware campus maintains two student housing facilities available to law students only, which include 135 single-occupancy, fully furnished and air conditioned rooms. Twenty-four one- and two-bedroom townhouses are also available. Although the Harrisburg campus does not maintain on-campus housing, a considerable number of apartment complexes offering a wide range of choices are located within a short distance of campus. Detailed information on available housing on the Harrisburg campus is available by contacting the Admission Office at 717-541-3903.

Student Group

Total enrollment is 1,646 with an alumni body of 7,600 practicing in more than forty-five states, Puerto Rico, and the District of Columbia. Students can take advantage of a variety of cocurricular and extracurricular programs. Cocurricular activities include three law reviews, Moot Court Honor Society, Moe Levine Trial Advocacy Honor Society, American Inns of Court, and Order of Barristers. Extracurricular activities include Student Bar Association; American Trial Lawyers Association; Black Law Student Association, Inc.; Law Forum; National Legal Fraternities; Sports and Entertainment Law Society; State Bar Association Affiliations; and Women's Law Caucus. Other organizations include American Civil Liberties Union, Brehon Law Society, Christian Legal Society, Environmental Law Society, International Law Society, International Student Union, Jewish Law Students Association, Justinian Society, and National Italian-American Bar Association.

Location

Widener University School of Law occupies two campuses: Wilmington, Delaware, and Harrisburg, Pennsylvania. The Delaware campus is in the heart of the Brandywine Valley, minutes from the downtown area that is the corporate capital of the United States. The Harrisburg, Pennsylvania, campus is 7 miles from the downtown area. Most of the major urban legal centers of the eastern United States are within two hours of both campuses.

The School

Founded in 1971 as the Delaware Law School, the School affiliated with Widener University in 1975 and graduated its first class of 163 that same year. At both campus locations, the emphasis is on teaching, and the primary mission is to provide the highest quality legal education to all students.

Applying

The application deadline is May 15 for the fall semester. Admission is on a rolling basis with first acceptances offered in January. Candidates must have a bachelor's degree from an accredited college or university and must submit LSAT scores (LSATs given in June, October, December, and February). A graduate degree, work experience, extracurriculars, and life experiences are also considered.

Correspondence and Information

Office of Admissions
Widener University School of Law
4601 Concord Pike
P.O. Box 7474
Wilmington, Delaware 19803-0474
Telephone: 302-477-2160

Office of Admissions
Widener University School of Law
3800 Vartan Way
P.O. Box 69381
Harrisburg, Pennsylvania 17106-9381
Telephone: 717-541-3903

Widener University

THE ADMINISTRATION

Barry R. Furrow, J.D., Dean of Faculty, Delaware; Director, Health Law Institute; and Professor of Law.
Loren D. Prescott Jr., LL.M., Associate Dean, Administration and Faculty Affairs, Harrisburg, and Associate Professor of Law.
Marion R. Newbold, J.D., Dean of Students, Delaware.
Ann E. Fruth, J.D., Dean of Students and Director of Admissions, Harrisburg.

The Law Library on the Delaware campus. A CD-ROM network permits total linkage between both campuses.

Widener's 21-acre Harrisburg campus contains a 30,000-square-foot administrative complex, a 14,000-square-foot student activities building, and a 50,000-square-foot library/classroom building.

Harrisburg campus.

WILLAMETTE UNIVERSITY

College of Law
Truman Wesley Collins Legal Center

Program of Study

Willamette University College of Law was established in 1883 and is the second oldest law school in the West. Students enroll in a full-time, three-year program leading to the Doctor of Jurisprudence (J.D.) degree. With a first-year class of 150, Willamette is one of the nation's most intellectually intimate law schools. It is approved by the American Bar Association (ABA) and is a member of the Association of American Law Schools (AALS).

The Willamette curriculum is unusually comprehensive for a small law school. Specialties reflect faculty member expertise: environmental and natural resources law, international law, intellectual property, labor and employment law, elder law, alternative dispute resolution, tax law, real estate law, civil litigation, commercial and business law, estate planning, civil and constitutional rights, and criminal law. Practical skills are honed in the externship and clinical law programs, innovative legal research and writing, trial practice, and pre-trial civil litigation courses, and with participation in moot court competition and two academic journals, *Willamette Law Review* and *Willamette Bulletin of International Law & Dispute Resolution.* Students can be court-certified, allowing them to argue in an Oregon courtroom under the supervision of a practicing attorney.

Nationally recognized programs distinguish Willamette from other schools. Through Law & Government, students gain academic and professional benefits using the resources of Oregon's capital city. The Center for Dispute Resolution trains students in negotiation, arbitration, and mediation and offers a specialized certificate. The College of Law, with the Atkinson Graduate School of Management, offers a four-year Joint Degree Program (J.D./M.M.) that enables students to link interests in law, not-for-profit agencies, government, and business. Atkinson is accredited by AACSB-The International Association for Management Education and by the National Association of Schools of Public Affairs and Administration.

Research Facilities

The gracious Truman Wesley Collins Legal Center, home to the College of Law and the J. W. Long Library, underwent an $8-million refurbishment in 1992. In addition to Long Library, the Collins Legal Center also houses the Center for Dispute Resolution, the John Paulus Great Hall, a state-of-the-art courtroom, seven modern classrooms, four student lounges, and student services, career services, admission, and faculty offices. Collins Legal Center stands adjacent to the other Willamette professional schools, the Atkinson Graduate School of Management, and the School of Education. Nearby Haseldorf Apartments and University Apartments, Willamette-owned complexes, house single graduate students and upperclass undergraduates. The Clinical Law Program is in Lee House, just across the street on the undergraduate campus.

The J. W. Long Library, open 24 hours a day, contains a comprehensive collection tailored to the law school curriculum. Its 240,000 volumes and microform equivalents include state and federal primary law sources as well as the leading treatises, periodicals, and other secondary sources that are vital to a full understanding of American law. It also has special collections in tax law, labor law, and public international law, and is a selective federal government documents depository. Three reading lounges are available. Small conference and video rooms are also options for study. Networked personal computers and printers are available in two labs and at two other stations in Long Library. Each networked PC offers access to Windows, MS Word, Pine e-mail system, WordPerfect, Internet via Netscape, LEXIS, WESTLAW, ORLaw (Oregon law), LegalTrac periodicals index, the online catalog, CALI (Computer Assisted Legal Instruction) programs, and other applications. Within blocks of Long Library are Willamette's Mark O. Hatfield Library, the Oregon Supreme Court Library, the Oregon State Library, and the Oregon State Archives.

Financial Aid

A generous scholarship program is available to Willamette first-year students. Approximately 30 percent of the first-year class are Trustee Scholarship recipients, selected on the basis of overall record and academic promise. Scholarships range up to $12,000 and are renewed each year, as long as students are in good academic standing (2.0 GPA on a 4.0 scale). No separate scholarship application is required. Loan programs, administered through the Willamette University Office of Financial Aid, are also available. Students should submit the FAFSA by February 1.

Cost of Study

Willamette University's endowment, in excess of $170 million, ranks it among the West's most financially stable institutions. Annual tuition for the 1998–99 academic year is $17,700. Books and supplies are estimated at $1250 per year. The student body fee is $80.

Living and Housing Costs

Because of the University's location near the metropolitan Portland area, overall costs are less. For the 1998–99 academic year, personal expenses for a single, first-year student are estimated to be $9720 (includes housing, food, utilities, transportation, and medical).

Student Group

In 1997–98, 158 students comprised the first-year class. Sixty percent were residents of states other than Oregon. More than seventy-eight colleges and universities were represented. The average age was 27. Women comprised 48 percent of the class; minority students made up 9 percent. The 75th percentile LSAT score was 158; the 25th percentile was 151. The 75th and 25th GPA percentiles were 3.5 and 3.0, respectively.

Student Outcomes

In the most recent employment survey of the Willamette graduating class, 86 percent reported being employed within one year of graduation. Of these, 63.4 percent were in private practice, 16.1 percent were employed in business, 15.2 percent were in government, and about 4 percent were in public interest positions. The majority of those reporting were living in the Pacific Northwest and California.

Location

The picturesque, peaceful 57-acre Willamette University campus is situated near the heart of the verdant Willamette Valley in Salem, Oregon's capital. Willamette lies adjacent to the Oregon state capitol complex, including the state supreme court, court of appeals, county courthouse, legislature, governor's office, and numerous agencies and departments. Acres of agricultural lands surround the city and include Christmas tree farms, iris fields, and world-class vineyards. Salem is Oregon's third largest city with more than 120,000 residents. Though less than 1 hour from Portland, the pace in Salem is relaxed. The Oregon coast and the Cascade Mountains are within an hour's drive.

The University

Named for one of Oregon's great rivers, Willamette University is a private, independent university and a member of Phi Beta Kappa. Founded in 1842, it is the West's oldest university, and it remains historically affiliated with the United Methodist Church. More than 2,500 students are enrolled in the College of Liberal Arts, the College of Law, the Atkinson Graduate School of Management, and the School of Education.

Applying

Willamette seeks students with strong academic credentials and broad experiences. The Committee on Admission is particularly interested in applicants who desire a smaller environment for their legal education. Willamette requires the LSAT, LSDAS, a personal statement, two letters of reference (submitted through LSDAS), and the baccalaureate degree from an accredited institution. The nonrefundable application fee is $50. The application deadline is April 1.

Correspondence and Information

Office of Admission
Willamette University College of Law
900 State Street
Salem, Oregon 97301
Telephone: 503-370-6282
World Wide Web: http://www.willamette.edu

Willamette University

THE FACULTY AND ADMINISTRATION

Faculty

Robert M. Ackerman, Dean and Professor of Law; J.D., Harvard. Torts, professional responsibility.
Robert C. Art, Professor of Law; LL.M., Columbia. Corporate finance, securities regulation, property.
Richard Birke, Assistant Professor of Law and Director, Center for Dispute Resolution; LL.M., Harvard. Dispute resolution, negotiation, mediation.
Richard F. Breen Jr., Professor of Law and Law Librarian; LL.B., Maine; M.L.S., Oregon.
Claudia Burton, Professor of Law; J.D., UCLA. Real estate transactions, constitutional law, property.
David L. Cameron, Associate Professor of Law; J.D., Northwestern. Federal income tax, property, real estate finance.
Vincent Chiappetta, Associate Professor of Law; J.D., Michigan. Intellectual property, business organizations, sales.
Kathy T. Graham, Professor of Law and Associate Dean for Academic Affairs; J.D., California, Davis. Domestic relations, torts.
Gwendolyn Griffith, Professor of Law; J.D., Stanford. Federal income tax, entities tax.
Richard B. Hagedorn, Professor of Law; J.D., Willamette. Contracts, secured transactions, payment systems.
Robert L. Misner, Professor of Law; J.D., Chicago. Criminal law, criminal procedure, local government.
James A. R. Nafziger, Thomas B. Stoel Professor of Law and Director of International Programs; J.D., Harvard. International business transactions, international law and dispute resolution, comparative law, conflict of laws.
Dean M. Richardson, Professor of Law; J.D., Syracuse. Civil rights, American Indian law, torts.
Ross R. Runkel, Professor of Law; J.D., Washington (Seattle). Labor law, employment discrimination, contracts.
Susan L. Smith, Associate Professor of Law; J.D., Harvard. Environmental law, natural resources law, criminal law, dispute resolution.
Carlton J. Snow, Professor of Law; J.D., Wisconsin. Arbitration, negotiation, contracts.
Jeffrey A. Standen, Associate Professor of Law; J.D., Virginia. Torts, advanced criminal law, jurisprudence.
Yvonne Tamayo, Assistant Professor of Law; J.D., Loyola of New Orleans. Civil procedure.
Leroy J. Tornquist, Professor of Law; J.D., Northwestern. Negotiation, evidence, civil procedure, trial practice.
Donald H. Turner, Professor of Law; J.D., Willamette. Scientific proof, criminal law, criminal procedure, evidence.
Maureen P. VanderMay, Associate Professor of Law; J.D., Chicago. Administrative law, constitutional law, professional responsibility, land-use planning.
Valerie J. Vollmar, Professor of Law; J.D., Willamette. Trusts and estates, estate planning, professional responsibility.
Michael B. Wise, Professor of Law; J.D., Stanford. Constitutional law, civil procedure, law and education.

Emeritus Faculty

Courtney Arthur, Professor of Law Emeritus; J.D., Illinois.
Henry J. Bailey, Professor of Law Emeritus; J.D., Yale.
Edwin W. Butler, Professor of Law Emeritus; J.D., Colorado.
John C. Paulus, Professor of Law Emeritus; J.D., Iowa.

Adjunct Faculty

Nancy E. Brown, Adjunct Professor; J.D. State Conciliator, Oregon Employment Relations Board. Mediation workshop.
Cinda Conroyd, Adjunct Professor; J.D. Attorney, Douglas, Conroyd & McMinimee. Elder law.
Scott J. Horenstein, Adjunct Professor; J.D. Partner, Horenstein & Duggen. Community property.
Nancy J. King, Adjunct Professor; J.D. Partner, Bullard, Korshoj, Smith & Jernstedt. Employment law.
The Hon. Jack L. Landau, Adjunct Professor; J.D. Judge, Oregon Court of Appeals. Legislation.
The Hon. Virginia L. Linder, Adjunct Professor; J.D. Judge, Oregon Court of Appeals. Appellate review.
Paul Lipscomb, Adjunct Professor; J.D. Presiding Judge of Marion County Courts. Insurance law.
Paul E. Loving, Adjunct Professor; J.D. Attorney, NIKE, Inc. Sports law.
Allen W. Lyons, Adjunct Professor; J.D. Partner, Scheminske & Lyons. Workers' compensation.
Reed Marbut, Adjunct Professor; J.D. Oregon Water Resources Department, Federal Water Rights Coordinator. Water law.
Mark M. Meininger, Adjunct Professor; J.D. Partner, Hancock, Meininger & Porter. Patent law.
James A. Perry, Adjunct Professor; LL.B. Attorney, Saalfeld, Griggs, Gorsuch, Alexander & Emerick. Advanced estate planning workshop.
Carol J. Prause, Adjunct Professor; J.D. Partner, Peterson & Prause. Business planning.
C. Kent Roberts, Adjunct Professor; J.D. Partner, Schwabe, Williamson & Wyatt. Admiralty.
Robert B. Rocklin, Adjunct Professor; J.D. Attorney, Oregon Department of Justice. Appellate review.
Helen F. Russon, Adjunct Professor; J.D. Program Coordinator, Oregon Bureau of Labor and Industries. Interviewing and counseling.
Donna Sandoval, Adjunct Professor; J.D. Attorney, Bullivant, Houser & Bailey. Employment law.

Distinguished Visitors-in-Residence

Judy S. Henry, Distinguished Practitioner-in-Residence and Director, Oregon Court of Appeals Appellate Settlement Conference Program; J.D., Lewis & Clark.
The Hon. Hans A. Linde, Distinguished Scholar-in-Residence; J.D., Berkeley. State constitutional law.
The Hon. Edwin J. Peterson, Distinguished Jurist-in-Residence; LL.B., Oregon. Pre-trial civil litigation.

Legal Research and Writing

Edward J. Harri, Instructor and Assistant Dean for Student Affairs; J.D., Willamette.
Marcia (Sam) Jacobson, Instructor; J.D., Iowa.
Helen L. Mazur-Hart, Instructor; J.D., Willamette.

Clinical Law Program

M. David Daniel, Staff Attorney and Instructor; J.D., Willamette.
Mitzi M. Naucler, Staff Attorney and Instructor; J.D., Willamette.
Jennifer Wright, Director and Assistant Professor of Law; J.D., Stanford.

Center for Dispute Resolution

Richard Birke, Director and Assistant Professor of Law; LL.M., Harvard.

Administration

Robert M. Ackerman, Dean and Professor of Law; J.D., Harvard.
Kathy T. Graham, Associate Dean for Academic Affairs and Professor of Law; J.D., California, Davis.
David R. Kenagy, Associate Dean for Administration; J.D., UCLA.
Lawrence Seno Jr., Director of Admission; M.P.R., USC.
Diane Reynolds, Director of Career Services; M.A., Oregon.
Sharon Blus, Director of Development and Alumni Relations; M.M., Willamette.

Academic and Professional Programs in Library and Information Studies

This part of Book 6 consists of one section covering information studies and library science. This section has a table of contents (listing the program directories, announcements, and in-depth descriptions); program directories, which consist of brief profiles of programs in the relevant fields (and that include 50-word or 100-word announcements following the profiles, if programs have chosen to include them); Cross-Discipline Announcements, if any programs have chosen to submit such entries; and in-depth descriptions, which are more individualized statements included, if programs have chosen to submit them.

Section 32
Library and Information Studies

This section contains a directory of institutions offering graduate work in information studies and library science, followed by in-depth entries submitted by institutions that chose to prepare detailed program descriptions. Additional information about programs listed in the directory but not augmented by an in-depth entry may be obtained by writing directly to the dean of a graduate school or chair of a department at the address given in the directory.

For programs offering related work, see also in this book Education; and in Book 5, see Computer Science and Information Technology.

CONTENTS

Program Directories

Announcements

In-Depth Descriptions

See also:

Information Studies

The Catholic University of America, School of Library and Information Science, Washington, DC 20064. Awards MSLS, JD/MSLS, MSLS/MA, MSLS/MS. One or more master's programs accredited by ALA. MSLS/MA jointly administered by the Departments of English, Greek and Latin, History, and the Schools of Music and Religious Studies; MSLS/MS jointly administered by the Department of Biology; JD/MSLS jointly administered with Columbia School of Law. Part-time and evening/weekend programs available. Postbaccalaureate distance learning degree programs offered (minimal on-campus study). Faculty: 8 (all women). Students: 38 full-time (31 women), 253 part-time (201 women); includes 44 minority (31 African Americans, 10 Asian Americans, 1 Hispanic, 2 Native Americans), 17 international. Average age 35. 136 applicants, 79% accepted. In 1997, 161 degrees awarded. *Degree requirements:* Comprehensive exam required, foreign language and thesis not required. *Entrance requirements:* GRE General Test. Application deadline: 7/1 (priority date; rolling processing; 11/1 for spring admission). Application fee: $50. *Expenses:* Tuition $17,326 per year full-time, $668 per credit hour part-time. Fees $680 per year full-time, $180 per semester part-time. *Financial aid:* Fellowships, research assistantships, project assistantships, full and partial tuition waivers, Federal Work-Study, institutionally sponsored loans, and career-related internships or fieldwork available. Aid available to part-time students. Financial aid application deadline: 2/1. *Faculty research:* Information transfer, archives and manuscripts, legal libraries, information seeking, information storage and retrieval, special collections, information systems. Total annual research expenditures: $3000. • Dr. Elizabeth Aversa, Dean, 202-319-5085. Application contact: Dr. Jean L. Preer, Chair, Admissions Committee, 202-319-5085.

See in-depth description on page 1631.

Central Missouri State University, Department of Library Science and Information Services, Warrensburg, MO 64093. Offerings include library science and information services (MS). Department faculty: 2 full-time. *Degree requirements:* Thesis or alternative. *Entrance requirements:* Minimum GPA of 2.75, interview, 2 years of teaching experience. Application deadline: 6/30 (priority date; rolling processing). Application fee: $25 ($50 for international students). *Tuition:* $3288 per year full-time, $137 per credit hour part-time for state residents; $5928 per year full-time, $274 per credit hour part-time for nonresidents. • Dr. Larry Dorrell, Chair, 660-543-8633. Fax: 660-543-8001.

Clark Atlanta University, School of Library and Information Studies, Atlanta, GA 30314. Awards MSLS, SLS. One or more master's programs accredited by ALA. Part-time and evening/weekend programs available. Faculty: 7 full-time (1 woman), 3 part-time (1 woman). Students: 39 full-time (29 women), 43 part-time (31 women); includes 52 minority (45 African Americans, 4 Asian Americans, 3 Hispanics). Average age 34. In 1997, 39 master's awarded. *Degree requirements:* For master's, 1 foreign language required, thesis optional; for SLS, 1 foreign language, thesis. *Entrance requirements:* For master's, GRE, TOEFL. Application deadline: rolling. Application fee: $40. *Expenses:* Tuition $9672 per year full-time, $403 per credit hour part-time. Fees $200 per year. *Financial aid:* In 1997–98, 47 students received aid, including 41 fellowships totaling $133,920, 4 tutorial assistantships totaling $13,500; full and partial tuition waivers, Federal Work-Study, institutionally sponsored loans, and career-related internships or fieldwork also available. Aid available to part-time students. Financial aid application deadline: 6/1. *Faculty research:* International research, public libraries, library history, school media, African-American history. • Dr. Arthur C. Gunn, Acting Dean, 404-880-8698. Fax: 404-880-8977. E-mail: agunn@cau.edu.

College of St. Catherine, Graduate Program, Program in Library and Information Science, St. Paul, MN 55105-1789. Awards MA. Offered in cooperation with Dominican University. Part-time and evening/weekend programs available. Faculty: 16 part-time (8 women). Students: 46 full-time (40 women), 36 part-time (30 women); includes 6 minority (2 African Americans, 1 Asian American, 2 Hispanics, 1 Native American). Average age 36. 72 applicants, 83% accepted. *Degree requirements:* Minimum of 12 credits completed in residence at Rosary College required, foreign language and thesis not required. *Entrance requirements:* Michigan English Language Assessment Battery (minimum score 90) or TOEFL (minimum score 600), minimum GPA of 3.2. Application deadline: 2/15. Application fee: $25. *Expenses:* Tuition $460 per credit hour. Fees $60 per year. *Financial aid:* 39 students received aid; institutionally sponsored loans available. Aid available to part-time students. Financial aid application deadline: 4/1; applicants required to submit FAFSA. • Mary Wagner, Director, 612-690-6802. Application contact: Office of Admission, 612-690-6505.

Dalhousie University, Faculty of Management, School of Library and Information Studies, Halifax, NS B3H 3J5, Canada. Awards MLIS, LL B/MLIS. One or more master's programs accredited by ALA. Faculty: 4 full-time, 5 part-time. Students: 65 full-time (49 women), 10 part-time (9 women). 69 applicants, 49% accepted. In 1997, 26 degrees awarded. *Degree requirements:* 1 foreign language required, thesis optional. *Entrance requirements:* TOEFL (minimum score 580). Application deadline: 6/1 (rolling processing). Application fee: $55. *Financial aid:* In 1997–98, 20 students received aid, including 14 fellowships (7 to first-year students) totaling $58,000, 6 scholarships (3 to first-year students) totaling $8,350; career-related internships or fieldwork also available. Financial aid application deadline: 3/31. *Faculty research:* Information-seeking behavior, electronic text design, browsing in digital environments, information diffusion among scientists. Total annual research expenditures: $65,000. • Dr. B. H. MacDonald, Director, 902-494-3656. Application contact: Judy Dunn, Graduate Coordinator, 902-494-3656.

Dominican University, Graduate School of Library and Information Science, River Forest, IL 60305-1099. Awards MLIS, MSMIS, CSS, MBA/MLIS, MLIS/MA, MLIS/M Div, MLIS/MM. One or more master's programs accredited by ALA. MLIS/M Div offered jointly with McCormick Theological Seminary; MLIS/MA (public history) offered jointly with Loyola University Chicago; MLIS/MM (music history) offered jointly with Northwestern University. Part-time and evening/weekend programs available. Postbaccalaureate distance learning degree programs offered (minimal on-campus study). Faculty: 9 full-time (2 women), 26 part-time (10 women), 14 FTE. Students: 382; includes 17 minority (7 African Americans, 5 Asian Americans, 5 Hispanics), 8 international. Average age 33. *Degree requirements:* For master's, computer language required, foreign language and thesis not required. *Entrance requirements:* For master's, TOEFL (minimum score 600), minimum GPA of 3.0 or GRE General Test (minimum score 550 required on 2 out of 3 sections). Application deadline: 8/15 (priority date; rolling processing; 12/15 for spring admission). Application fee: $25. *Financial aid:* Fellowships, research assistantships, scholarships, partial tuition waivers, Federal Work-Study, and career-related internships or fieldwork available. Aid available to part-time students. Financial aid application deadline: 4/15. *Faculty research:* Productivity and the information environment, bibliometrics, library history, subject access, library materials and services for children. • Prudence Dalrymple, Dean, 708-524-6472. Fax: 708-524-6657.

See in-depth description on page 1633.

Drexel University, College of Information Science and Technology, 3141 Chestnut Street, Philadelphia, PA 19104-2875. Offers programs in information studies (PhD, CAS), information systems (MSIS), library and information science (MS). One or more master's programs accredited by ALA. Part-time and evening/weekend programs available. Faculty: 17 full-time (7 women), 17 part-time (6 women), 22.7 FTE. Students: 76 full-time (51 women), 477 part-time (245 women); includes 59 minority (29 African Americans, 23 Asian Americans, 5 Hispanics, 2 Native Americans), 81 international. Average age 37. 252 applicants, 58% accepted. In 1997, 126 master's, 3 doctorates awarded. *Degree requirements:* For doctorate, dissertation required, foreign language not required. *Entrance requirements:* For master's, GRE General Test, TOEFL (minimum score 600); for doctorate, GRE General Test, TOEFL (minimum score 600), master's degree. Application deadline: 8/21 (rolling processing). Application fee: $35. *Expenses:* Tuition $437 per credit hour. Fees $121 per quarter full-time, $65 per quarter part-time. *Financial aid:* In 1997–98, 2 research assistantships, 5 teaching assistantships, 8 graduate assistantships were awarded; partial tuition waivers, Federal Work-Study, institutionally sponsored loans, and career-related internships or fieldwork also available. Aid available to part-time students. Financial aid application deadline: 2/1. *Faculty research:* Bibliometric analysis, information management, scientific communication, expert systems, man-machine interfaces in information transfer. • Dr. Richard Lytle, Dean, 215-895-2475. Application contact: Anne B. Tanner, Associate Dean, 215-895-2474.

See in-depth description on page 1635.

Emporia State University, School of Graduate Studies, School of Library and Information Management, Emporia, KS 66801-5087. Awards MLS, PhD. One or more master's programs accredited by ALA. Part-time programs available. Faculty: 13 full-time (7 women), 47 part-time (28 women). Students: 53 full-time (41 women), 155 part-time (129 women); includes 9 minority (5 African Americans, 3 Asian Americans, 1 Hispanic), 2 international. 39 applicants, 100% accepted. In 1997, 124 master's, 1 doctorate awarded. *Degree requirements:* For master's, comprehensive exam or thesis required, foreign language not required. *Entrance requirements:* For master's, GRE General Test, TOEFL (minimum score 550); for doctorate, GRE General Test (minimum combined score of 1100), TOEFL (minimum score 650), interview, minimum graduate GPA of 3.5. Application deadline: 8/15 (priority date; rolling processing). Application fee: $30 ($75 for international students). Electronic applications accepted. *Tuition:* $2300 per year full-time, $103 per credit hour part-time for state residents; $6012 per year full-time, $258 per credit hour part-time for nonresidents. *Financial aid:* In 1997–98, 11 research assistantships averaging $558 per month, 7 teaching assistantships averaging $522 per month were awarded; Federal Work-Study, institutionally sponsored loans, and career-related internships or fieldwork also available. Financial aid application deadline: 3/15; applicants required to submit FAFSA. *Faculty research:* Information management in corporate environment. • Dr. Faye N. Vowell, Dean, 316-341-5203. E-mail: vowellfa@emporia.edu.

Florida State University, School of Information Studies, Tallahassee, FL 32306. Offers programs in information studies (Adv M, PhD), library and information studies (MS, PhD). One or more master's programs accredited by ALA. Part-time and evening/weekend programs available. Postbaccalaureate distance learning degree programs offered (minimal on-campus study). Faculty: 14 full-time (6 women), 7 part-time (4 women), 15.75 FTE. Students: 73 full-time (56 women), 368 part-time (261 women); includes 53 minority (30 African Americans, 9 Asian Americans, 13 Hispanics, 1 Native American), 21 international. Average age 38. 190 applicants, 82% accepted. In 1997, 145 master's awarded; 6 doctorates awarded (100% found work related to degree). *Degree requirements:* For doctorate, dissertation required, foreign language not required. *Entrance requirements:* For master's, GRE General Test (minimum combined score of 1000), minimum GPA of 3.0; for doctorate, GRE General Test (minimum combined score of 1000), minimum graduate GPA of 3.5. Application fee: $20. *Tuition:* $139 per credit hour for state residents; $482 per credit hour for nonresidents. *Financial aid:* In 1997–98, 57 students received aid, including 3 fellowships (2 to first-year students) averaging $1,179 per month and totaling $28,304, 21 research assistantships (12 to first-year students) averaging $325 per month and totaling $43,060, 3 teaching assistantships averaging $488 per month and totaling $8,200, 30 assistantships (23 to first-year students) averaging $319 per month and totaling $51,950; Federal Work-Study also available. Financial aid application deadline: 4/1. *Faculty research:* Community information service, needs assessment, disaster preparedness, information policy, usability analysis. • Dr. Jane B. Robbins, Dean, 850-644-5775. Application contact: Marion Davis, Program Assistant, 850-644-8103. Fax: 850-644-9763. E-mail: mdavis@mailer.lis.fsu.edu.

See in-depth description on page 1637.

Indiana University Bloomington, School of Library and Information Science, Bloomington, IN 47405. Awards MIS, MLS, PhD, Spec, DBA/MIS, JD/MLS, MLS/MA, MPA/MLS, PhD/MIS. One or more master's programs accredited by ALA. MLS/MA offered jointly through the School of Fine Arts, School of Journalism, School of Music, Department of Comparative Literature, Department of History, and Department of History and Philosophy of Science. PhD offered through the University Graduate School. Part-time programs available. Faculty: 17 full-time (7 women). Students: 151 full-time (98 women), 147 part-time (109 women); includes 14 minority (2 African Americans, 6 Asian Americans, 4 Hispanics, 2 Native Americans), 20 international. In 1997, 179 master's, 2 doctorates awarded. *Degree requirements:* For doctorate, 1 foreign language (computer language can substitute), dissertation. *Entrance requirements:* For master's, minimum GPA of 3.0; for doctorate, GRE General Test, minimum GPA of 3.5. Application fee: $35. *Expenses:* Tuition $153 per credit hour for state residents; $446 per credit hour for nonresidents. Fees $343 per year. *Financial aid:* Fellowships, partial tuition waivers, and career-related internships or fieldwork available. Aid available to part-time students. *Faculty research:* Scholarly communication, interface design, public library policy, computer-mediated communication, information retrieval. • Dr. Blaise Cronin, Dean, 812-855-2018. Application contact: Rhonda Spencer, Admissions Coordinator, 812-855-2666. Fax: 812-855-6166.

See in-depth description on page 1639.

Long Island University, C.W. Post Campus, Palmer School of Library and Information Science, Brookville, NY 11548-1300. Offers programs in archives (Certificate), information studies (PhD), library and information science (MS), records management (Certificate). One or more master's programs accredited by ALA. Part-time and evening/weekend programs available. Postbaccalaureate distance learning degree programs offered (minimal on-campus study). Faculty: 12 full-time (5 women), 30 part-time (18 women). Students: 61 full-time (50 women), 343 part-time (296 women). 179 applicants, 83% accepted. In 1997, 130 master's awarded. *Degree requirements:* For master's, thesis optional, foreign language not required; for doctorate, dissertation required, foreign language not required. *Entrance requirements:* For master's, GRE or MAT, minimum undergraduate GPA of 3.0. Application fee: $30. Electronic applications accepted. *Expenses:* Tuition $480 per credit. Fees $316 per year full-time, $71 per semester (minimum) part-time. *Financial aid:* Fellowships, research assistantships, partial tuition waivers, Federal Work-Study, institutionally sponsored loans, and career-related internships or fieldwork available. Aid available to part-time students. Financial aid application deadline: 5/15; applicants required to submit FAFSA. *Faculty research:* Managing information technology, bibliographic control, organizational culture, scholarly communication. • Anne Woodsworth, Dean, 516-299-2855. E-mail: woodswor@titan.liunet.edu. Application contact: Graduate Admissions, 516-299-2866. Fax: 516-299-4168. E-mail: palmer@titan.liunet.edu.

Louisiana State University and Agricultural and Mechanical College, School of Library and Information Science, Baton Rouge, LA 70803. Awards MLIS, CLIS. One or more master's programs accredited by ALA. Evening/weekend programs available. Faculty: 6 full-time (4 women). Students: 93 full-time (66 women), 84 part-time (71 women); includes 30 minority (24 African Americans, 2 Asian Americans, 4 Hispanics), 16 international. Average age 34. 74 applicants, 82% accepted. In 1997, 80 master's, 2 CLISs awarded. *Degree requirements:* For master's, comprehensive exam required, thesis optional, foreign language not required. *Entrance requirements:* For master's, GRE General Test (minimum combined score of 1000), minimum GPA of 3.0. Application deadline: 1/25 (priority date; rolling processing). Application fee: $25. *Tuition:* $2736 per year full-time, $285 per semester (minimum) part-time for state residents; $6636 per year full-time, $460 per semester (minimum) part-time for nonresidents. *Financial aid:* In 1997–98, 4 fellowships, 19 research assistantships (7 to first-year students), 20 service assistantships (5 to first-year students) were awarded; teaching assistantships and career-related internships or fieldwork also available. Aid available to part-time students. *Faculty research:* Information retrieval, management, collection development, public libraries. Total annual research expenditures: $200,000. • Dr. Bert R. Boyce, Dean, 504-388-3158. Application contact: Shirley Watson, Admissions Secretary, 504-388-1481.

McGill University, Faculty of Graduate Studies and Research, Faculty of Education, Graduate School of Library and Information Studies, Montréal, PQ H3A 2T5, Canada. Awards MLIS,

PhD, Diploma. One or more master's programs accredited by ALA. Diploma and PhD new for fall 1998. Faculty: 8 full-time (4 women), 12 part-time (4 women). Students: 93 full-time (68 women), 7 part-time (6 women). Average age 32. In 1997, 59 master's awarded. *Degree requirements:* For doctorate, dissertation. *Entrance requirements:* For master's, TOEFL (minimum score 550), minimum GPA of 3.0. Application deadline: 3/1 (rolling processing). Application fee: $60. *Expenses:* Tuition $1668 per year for Canadian residents; $8268 per year for nonresidents. Fees $828 per year for Canadian residents; $1216 per year for nonresidents. *Faculty research:* Thesaurus construction, interface design, bilingual multimedia, organizational structures, bibliographic control. • Jamshid Behesti, Director, 514-398-4204. Fax: 514-398-7193.

Montana State University–Billings, College of Business, Program in Information Processing and Communications, Billings, MT 59101-9984. Awards MSIPC. *Entrance requirements:* GMAT or GRE, minimum GPA of 3.0 (undergraduate), 3.25 (graduate). Application deadline: 8/1 (priority date; rolling processing; 1/1 for spring admission). *Expenses:* Tuition $2253 per year full-time, $397 per semester (minimum) part-time for state residents; $5313 per year full-time, $907 per semester (minimum) part-time for nonresidents. Fees $378 per year full-time, $105 per semester (minimum) part-time.

North Carolina Central University, Division of Academic Affairs, School of Library and Information Sciences, Durham, NC 27707-3129. Awards MIS, MLS, JD/MLS. One or more master's programs accredited by ALA. Part-time and evening/weekend programs available. Faculty: 9 full-time (4 women), 5 part-time (4 women). Students: 26 full-time (22 women), 150 part-time (125 women); includes 63 minority (51 African Americans, 8 Asian Americans, 2 Hispanics, 2 Native Americans). Average age 37. 38 applicants, 100% accepted. In 1997, 82 degrees awarded. *Degree requirements:* 1 foreign language (computer language can substitute), alternate thesis or research paper. *Entrance requirements:* 90 hours in liberal arts, minimum B average. Application deadline: 8/1. Application fee: $30. *Tuition:* $2027 per year full-time, $508 per semester (minimum) part-time for state residents; $9155 per year full-time, $2290 per semester (minimum) part-time for nonresidents. *Financial aid:* Fellowships, research assistantships, state grants, institutionally sponsored loans, and career-related internships or fieldwork available. Aid available to part-time students. Financial aid application deadline: 5/1. *Faculty research:* African-American resources, planning and evaluation, analysis of economic and physical resources, geography of information, artificial intelligence. • Dr. Benjamin F. Speller Jr., Dean, 919-560-6485.

Pratt Institute, School of Information and Library Science, Program in Library and Information Science, Brooklyn, NY 11205-3899. Awards MS, Adv C, JD/MS, MS/MS. One or more master's programs accredited by ALA. JD/MS offered jointly with the Brooklyn Law School; MS/MS offered jointly with the Program in Art History. Part-time and evening/weekend programs available. *Degree requirements:* For master's, thesis required, foreign language not required. *Average time to degree:* master's–2 years full-time. *Entrance requirements:* For master's, TOEFL (minimum score 550). Application deadline: 3/1 (priority date; rolling processing). Application fee: $35 ($80 for international students). *Expenses:* Tuition $14,520 per year full-time, $605 per credit part-time. Fees $480 per year. *Faculty research:* Law and medical librarianship, library computer software, confidentiality.

See in-depth description on page 1641.

Queens College of the City University of New York, Social Science Division, Graduate School of Library and Information Studies, 65-30 Kissena Boulevard, Flushing, NY 11367-1597. Awards MLS, AC. One or more master's programs accredited by ALA. Part-time and evening/weekend programs available. Students: 13 full-time (9 women), 358 part-time (261 women); includes 47 minority (20 African Americans, 10 Asian Americans, 17 Hispanics), 2 international. 163 applicants, 87% accepted. In 1997, 95 master's awarded. *Degree requirements:* For master's, thesis required, foreign language not required; for AC, thesis optional, foreign language not required. *Entrance requirements:* For master's, TOEFL, minimum GPA of 3.0; for AC, TOEFL, master's degree or equivalent. Application deadline: 4/1 (rolling processing; 11/1 for spring admission). Application fee: $40. *Expenses:* Tuition $4350 per year full-time, $185 per credit part-time for state residents; $7600 per year full-time, $320 per credit part-time for nonresidents. Fees $104 per year. *Financial aid:* Partial tuition waivers, Federal Work-Study, institutionally sponsored loans, and career-related internships or fieldwork available. Aid available to part-time students. Financial aid application deadline: 4/1; applicants required to submit FAFSA. *Faculty research:* Multimedia and video studies, ethnicity and librarianship, information science and computer applications. • Dr. Marianne Cooper, Director and Chair, 718-997-3790. Application contact: Dr. Karen Smith, Graduate Adviser, 718-997-3790.

Rutgers, The State University of New Jersey, New Brunswick, Program in Communication, Information and Library Studies, New Brunswick, NJ 08903. Awards PhD. Offered in conjunction with the School of Communication, Information and Library Studies. Part-time programs available. Faculty: 46 full-time (17 women), 1 (woman) part-time. Students: 29 full-time (15 women), 72 part-time (42 women); includes 9 minority (8 African Americans, 1 Hispanic), 19 international. Average age 35. 53 applicants, 58% accepted. In 1997, 6 doctorates awarded. Terminal master's awarded for partial completion of doctoral program. *Degree requirements:* For doctorate, dissertation, qualifying exams required, foreign language not required. *Entrance requirements:* For doctorate, GRE General Test. Application deadline: 5/1. Application fee: $40. Electronic applications accepted. *Expenses:* Tuition $6492 per year full-time, $268 per credit part-time for state residents; $9520 per year full-time, $395 per credit part-time for nonresidents. Fees $208 per year (minimum). *Financial aid:* In 1997–98, 3 fellowships, 7 research assistantships (1 to a first-year student), 17 teaching assistantships (5 to first-year students) were awarded; institutionally sponsored loans also available. Financial aid application deadline: 2/1. *Faculty research:* Information science, information policy, communication media studies, library studies. • Lea P. Stewart, Director, 732-932-7447.

Rutgers, The State University of New Jersey, New Brunswick, School of Communication, Information and Library Studies, Program in Communication and Information Studies, New Brunswick, NJ 08903. Awards MCIS. Part-time programs available. Faculty: 38 full-time (12 women). Students: 19 full-time (12 women), 63 part-time (35 women); includes 6 minority (2 African Americans, 4 Hispanics), 15 international. Average age 30. 94 applicants, 49% accepted. In 1997, 23 degrees awarded. *Degree requirements:* Thesis optional, foreign language not required. *Entrance requirements:* GRE General Test, TOEFL. Application deadline: 5/1 (rolling processing; 11/1 for spring admission). Application fee: $40. Electronic applications accepted. *Expenses:* Tuition $6492 per year full-time, $268 per credit part-time for state residents; $9520 per year full-time, $395 per credit part-time for nonresidents. Fees $208 per year (minimum). *Financial aid:* In 1997–98, 4 fellowships were awarded; Federal Work-Study, institutionally sponsored loans, and career-related internships or fieldwork also available. Aid available to part-time students. Financial aid application deadline: 3/1. *Faculty research:* Communication processes and systems, information process and systems, human information and communication behavior. • Robert W. Kubey, Director, 732-932-6516. Fax: 732-932-8177. E-mail: mcis@scils.rutgers.edu.

St. John's University, Graduate School of Arts and Sciences, Division of Library and Information Science, Jamaica, NY 11439. Offers programs in drug information specialist (MS/MLS), government information specialist (MA/MLS), library and information science (MLS, Adv C). One or more master's programs accredited by ALA. Part-time and evening/weekend programs available. Faculty: 9 full-time (7 women), 2 part-time (0 women). Students: 13 full-time (9 women), 87 part-time (65 women); includes 25 minority (17 African Americans, 2 Asian Americans, 6 Hispanics), 3 international. Average age 35. 65 applicants, 78% accepted. In 1997, 34 master's awarded. *Entrance requirements:* For master's, minimum GPA of 3.0. Application deadline: rolling. Application fee: $40. *Expenses:* Tuition $600 per credit. Fees $150 per year. *Financial aid:* In 1997–98, 3 research assistantships averaging $667 per month were awarded; graduate assistantships, Federal Work-Study, and career-related internships or fieldwork also available. Aid available to part-time students. Financial aid application deadline: 3/1; applicants required to submit FAFSA. *Faculty research:* On-line database management, public library patronage, medieval monastic libraries and archives, children's literature, indexing. • Dr. James Benson, Director, 718-990-6200. Application contact: Shamus J. McGrenra, TOR, Associate Director, Graduate Admissions, 718-990-6107. Fax: 718-990-5736. E-mail: mcgrenrs@stjohns.edu.

San Jose State University, Graduate Studies Program, School of Library and Information Science, San Jose, CA 95192-0001. Awards MLIS. One or more master's programs accredited by ALA. Part-time and evening/weekend programs available. Faculty: 6 full-time (3 women), 4 part-time (3 women). Students: 96 full-time (70 women), 157 part-time (119 women); includes 47 minority (10 African Americans, 25 Asian Americans, 10 Hispanics, 2 Native Americans), 5 international. Average age 36. 250 applicants, 82% accepted. In 1997, 173 degrees awarded. *Degree requirements:* Comprehensive exam required, thesis not required. *Entrance requirements:* Minimum GPA of 3.0. Application deadline: 6/1 (rolling processing). Application fee: $59. *Expenses:* Tuition $0 for state residents; $246 per unit for nonresidents. Fees $2017 per year full-time, $1351 per year part-time. *Financial aid:* In 1997–98, 4 fellowships (all to first-year students), 4 teaching assistantships (all to first-year students) were awarded; Federal Work-Study, institutionally sponsored loans, and career-related internships or fieldwork also available. Aid available to part-time students. Financial aid application deadline: 8/20. *Faculty research:* Evaluation of information services on-line, search strategy, organizational behavior. • Dr. Blanche Woolls, Director, 408-924-2491.

Simmons College, Graduate School of Library and Information Science, Boston, MA 02115. Awards MS, DA, MS Ed/MS, MS/MA. One or more master's programs accredited by ALA. MS Ed/MS offered jointly with the Department of Education; MS/MA offered jointly with the Program in Archives Management. Part-time and evening/weekend programs available. Faculty: 13 full-time, 9 part-time, 17 FTE. Students: 82 full-time (66 women), 392 part-time (320 women); includes 15 minority (7 African Americans, 5 Asian Americans, 3 Hispanics), 13 international. Average age 33. 287 applicants, 90% accepted. In 1997, 192 master's awarded. *Degree requirements:* For master's, technology competency required, foreign language and thesis not required. *Entrance requirements:* For master's, MAT or GRE General Test; for doctorate, interview. Application deadline: 7/1 (priority date; rolling processing; 11/1 for spring admission). Application fee: $25. *Expenses:* Tuition $587 per credit hour. Fees $20 per year. *Financial aid:* 176 students received aid; full and partial tuition waivers, Federal Work-Study, institutionally sponsored loans, and career-related internships or fieldwork available. Aid available to part-time students. Financial aid application deadline: 3/1; applicants required to submit FAFSA. *Faculty research:* Optical technology, visual communications, database management, information policy. • Dr. James Matarazzo, Dean, 617-521-2806. E-mail: jmatarazzo@simmons.edu. Application contact: Judith J. Beals, Director of Admissions, 617-521-2801. Fax: 617-521-3192. E-mail: jbeals@simmons.edu.

See in-depth description on page 1643.

Southern Connecticut State University, School of Communication, Information and Library Science, New Haven, CT 06515-1355. Offerings include library/information studies (Diploma). *Degree requirements:* Thesis or alternative. *Entrance requirements:* Master's degree. Application deadline: 7/15 (priority date; rolling processing). Application fee: $40. *Expenses:* Tuition $2632 per year full-time, $188 per credit part-time for state residents; $7200 per year full-time, $188 per credit part-time for nonresidents. Fees $1806 per year full-time, $45 per semester part-time for state residents; $2703 per year full-time, $45 per semester part-time for nonresidents. • Dr. Nancy Disbrow, Chairperson, 203-392-5781.

See in-depth description on page 1645.

State University of New York at Albany, Nelson A. Rockefeller College of Public Affairs and Policy, School of Information Science and Policy, Albany, NY 12222-0001. Awards MLS, CAS, MLS/MA. One or more master's programs accredited by ALA. Part-time and evening/weekend programs available. Faculty: 10 full-time (3 women), 1 part-time (0 women). Students: 104 full-time (67 women), 143 part-time (106 women); includes 5 minority (4 African Americans, 1 Asian American), 10 international. 115 applicants, 89% accepted. In 1997, 116 master's, 1 CAS awarded. *Application fee:* $50. *Expenses:* Tuition $5100 per year full-time, $213 per credit hour part-time for state residents; $8416 per year full-time, $351 per credit hour part-time for nonresidents. Fees $705 per year full-time, $26.85 per credit hour part-time. *Financial aid:* Fellowships, Federal Work-Study available. • Philip Eppard, Interim Dean, 518-442-5115. Application contact: Gerald Parker, Assistant Provost, 518-442-5200.

State University of New York at Buffalo, Graduate School, School of Information and Library Studies, Buffalo, NY 14260. Awards MLS, Certificate. One or more master's programs accredited by ALA. Part-time and evening/weekend programs available. Faculty: 8 full-time (5 women), 1 part-time (0 women). Students: 103 full-time (74 women), 135 part-time (110 women); includes 11 African Americans, 4 Asian Americans, 1 Hispanic, 5 international. Average age 34. 158 applicants, 67% accepted. In 1997, 105 master's awarded. *Degree requirements:* For master's, thesis optional, foreign language not required; for Certificate, thesis required, foreign language not required. *Entrance requirements:* For master's, minimum GPA of 3.0. Application deadline: 4/1 (priority date; 10/15 for spring admission). Application fee: $35. *Tuition:* $5970 per year full-time, $288 per credit hour part-time for state residents; $9286 per year full-time, $426 per credit hour part-time for nonresidents. *Financial aid:* In 1997–98, 2 fellowships (both to first-year students), 9 graduate assistantships (all to first-year students) were awarded; research assistantships, teaching assistantships, full and partial tuition waivers, Federal Work-Study, institutionally sponsored loans, and career-related internships or fieldwork also available. Aid available to part-time students. Financial aid application deadline: 3/1. *Faculty research:* Information user behavior, storage and information retrieval, digital libraries, information management services to information users. Total annual research expenditures: $13,500. • Dr. George S. Bobinski, Dean, 716-645-2412. Fax: 716-645-3775. E-mail: sils@acsu.buffalo.edu.

Syracuse University, School of Information Studies, Information Resources Management Program, Syracuse, NY 13244-0003. Awards MS, JD/MS. Students: 33 full-time (14 women), 120 part-time (52 women); includes 9 minority (7 African Americans, 1 Asian American, 1 Hispanic), 55 international. 68 applicants, 87% accepted. In 1997, 31 degrees awarded. *Entrance requirements:* GRE General Test (minimum combined score of 1000). Application fee: $40. *Tuition:* $13,320 per year full-time, $555 per credit hour part-time. *Financial aid:* Application deadline 3/1. • Ralf T. Wigand, Director. Application contact: Barbara Settel, Assistant Dean, 315-443-2911.

See in-depth descriptions on pages 589 and 1647.

Syracuse University, School of Information Studies, Information Transfer Program, Syracuse, NY 13244-0003. Awards PhD. Students: 21 full-time (8 women), 10 part-time (7 women); includes 17 international. 15 applicants, 27% accepted. *Degree requirements:* Dissertation. *Entrance requirements:* GRE General Test (minimum score 600 on each section). Application deadline: rolling. Application fee: $40. *Tuition:* $13,320 per year full-time, $555 per credit hour part-time. *Financial aid:* Application deadline 3/1. • Barbara Kwasnik, Director. Application contact: Robert Oddy, Graduate Contact, 315-443-4525.

See in-depth description on page 1647.

Texas Woman's University, School of Library and Information Studies, Denton, TX 76204. Awards MA, MLS, PhD. One or more master's programs accredited by ALA. Part-time and evening/weekend programs available. Faculty: 11 full-time (9 women), 8 part-time (all women). Students: 41 full-time (38 women), 240 part-time (227 women); includes 19 minority (11 African Americans, 4 Asian Americans, 3 Hispanics, 1 Native American), 3 international. Average age 40. 79 applicants, 94% accepted. In 1997, 58 master's, 4 doctorates awarded. *Degree requirements:* For master's, thesis; for doctorate, variable foreign language requirement, dissertation. *Average time to degree:* master's–1 year full-time; doctorate–3 years full-time. *Entrance requirements:* For master's, GRE General Test (minimum score 500 on verbal section, 400 on quantitative, 450 on analytical), minimum GPA of 3.0; for doctorate, GRE General Test (minimum combined score of 1000), minimum GPA of 3.0. Application fee: $25. *Financial aid:* In 1997–98, 43 students received aid, including 5 fellowships (1 to a

Directory: Information Studies

Texas Woman's University (continued)
first-year student), 16 teaching assistantships (4 to first-year students), 11 scholarships (5 to first-year students); research assistantships, Federal Work-Study, institutionally sponsored loans, and career-related internships or fieldwork also available. Aid available to part-time students. Financial aid application deadline: 4/1; applicants required to submit FAFSA. *Faculty research:* Information use studies, children's literature, congitive aspects of information. • Dr. Keith Swigger, Dean, 940-898-2602. Fax: 940-898-2611. E-mail: slis@twu.edu.

See in-depth description on page 1649.

Université de Montréal, Faculty of Arts and Sciences, School of Information and Library Science, Montréal, PQ H3C 3J7, Canada. Offers programs in information and library science (MBSI); information science (PhD), including information systems and resources, information transfer. One or more master's programs accredited by ALA. Faculty: 13 full-time (6 women). Students: 108 full-time (75 women), 8 part-time (6 women). 122 applicants, 59% accepted. In 1997, 53 master's awarded. *Degree requirements:* For master's, computer language required, thesis optional. *Entrance requirements:* For master's, master's degree in library and information science or equivalent, interview. Application deadline: 3/28. Application fee: $30. *Financial aid:* Fellowships available. • Gilles Deschatelets, Director, 514-343-7400. Application contact: Diane Mayar, Assistante á la gestion des dossiers des étudiants, 514-343-6044. Fax: 514-343-5753. E-mail: mayardi@ere.umontreal.ca.

The University of Alabama, College of Communication, School of Library and Information Studies, Tuscaloosa, AL 35487. Offers programs in book arts (MFA), library and information studies (MLIS, Ed S). Faculty: 11 full-time (6 women). Students: 52 full-time (33 women), 92 part-time (78 women); includes 21 minority (13 African Americans, 6 Asian Americans, 2 Native Americans), 7 international. Average age 28. 62 applicants, 92% accepted. In 1997, 81 master's, 3 Ed Ss awarded. *Entrance requirements:* For master's, GRE General Test (minimum combined score of 1500 on three sections) or MAT (minimum score 50), minimum GPA of 3.0. Application deadline: 2/15 (priority date; rolling processing; 11/1 for spring admission). Application fee: $25. Electronic applications accepted. *Tuition:* $2684 per year full-time, $594 per semester (minimum) part-time for state residents; $7216 per year full-time, $1248 per semester (minimum) part-time for nonresidents. *Financial aid:* In 1997–98, 67 students received aid, including 41 fellowships totaling $206,899, 9 research assistantships totaling $41,010, 17 teaching assistantships totaling $67,105; Federal Work-Study and career-related internships or fieldwork also available. Financial aid application deadline: 2/15. *Faculty research:* Instructional design, information equity, youth services, rural information services. • Dr. Joan Atkinson, Director, 205-348-1522. Fax: 205-348-3746. E-mail: jatkinso@slism.slis.ua.edu.

University of Alberta, Faculty of Graduate Studies and Research, School of Library and Information Studies, Edmonton, AB T6G 2E1, Canada. Awards MLIS. One or more master's programs accredited by ALA. Faculty: 6 full-time (4 women), 8 part-time (6 women). Students: 67 full-time (54 women), 26 part-time (22 women). 84 applicants, 56% accepted. In 1997, 29 degrees awarded. *Average time to degree:* master's–2 years full-time, 4 years part-time. *Entrance requirements:* GRE General Test (minimum combined score of 1725 on three sections, 600 on verbal, 525 on quantitative, 600 on analytical). Application deadline: 7/1 (rolling processing). Application fee: $60. *Expenses:* Tuition $390 per course for Canadian residents; $781 per course for nonresidents. Fees $500 per year full-time, $184 per year part-time. *Financial aid:* In 1997–98, 39 students received aid, including 5 tuition scholarships; career-related internships or fieldwork also available. Aid available to part-time students. Financial aid application deadline: 7/1. *Faculty research:* Intellectual freedom, materials for children and young adults, teacher-librarianship, cataloging. • Dr. Alvin Schrader, Director, 403-492-4578. Application contact: Susan Scullion, Student Admissions, 403-492-4578. Fax: 403-492-2430. E-mail: office@slis.ualberta.ca.

The University of Arizona, College of Social and Behavioral Sciences, School of Library Science, Tucson, AZ 85721. Awards MA, PhD. One or more master's programs accredited by ALA. Part-time programs available. *Degree requirements:* For master's, computer language, proficiency in disk operating system (DOS) required, foreign language and thesis not required; for doctorate, dissertation. *Entrance requirements:* For master's, GRE, TOEFL (minimum score 550), minimum GPA of 3.0; for doctorate, GRE General Test, TOEFL (minimum score 550). Application deadline: 2/1 (rolling processing). Application fee: $35. *Tuition:* $2162 per year full-time, $337 per semester (minimum) part-time for state residents; $6860 per year full-time, $1138 per semester (minimum) part-time for nonresidents. *Faculty research:* Microcomputer applications; quantitative methods systems; information transfer, planning, evaluation, and technology.

University of British Columbia, Faculties of Arts and Graduate Studies, School of Library, Archival and Information Studies, Vancouver, BC V6T 1Z2, Canada. Offers programs in archival studies (MAS, CAS), librarianship (MLIS), library and information studies (CAS). One or more master's programs accredited by ALA. Part-time programs available. Faculty: 9 full-time (5 women), 17 part-time (9 women). Students: 66 full-time (51 women), 21 part-time (15 women). Average age 30. 125 applicants, 38% accepted. In 1997, 56 master's awarded. *Degree requirements:* Thesis optional. *Average time to degree:* master's–2 years full-time. *Entrance requirements:* For master's, TOEFL (minimum score 600), interview; for CAS, TOEFL (minimum score 600). Application deadline: 2/1 (priority date). Application fee: $60. *Financial aid:* In 1997–98, 2 fellowships, 3 academic assistantships (1 to a first-year student) were awarded; Federal Work-Study and career-related internships or fieldwork also available. *Faculty research:* Computer systems/database design, library and archival management, archival description and organization, censorship and intellectual freedom, children's literature and youth services. • Dr. Ken Haycock, Director, 604-822-2404. E-mail: ken.haycock@ubc.ca. Application contact: Lynne Lighthall, Graduate Admissions, 604-822-2404. Fax: 604-822-6006. E-mail: admit@slais.ubc.ca.

University of California, Berkeley, School of Information Management and Systems, Berkeley, CA 94720-1500. Awards MIMS, PhD. Faculty: 10 full-time (2 women). Students: 51 full-time (29 women); includes 9 minority (4 Asian Americans, 5 Hispanics), 9 international. 217 applicants, 24% accepted. In 1997, 1 doctorate awarded. *Degree requirements:* For doctorate, dissertation, qualifying exam. *Entrance requirements:* For master's, GRE General Test, TOEFL (minimum score 570), minimum GPA of 3.0, previous coursework in java or C programming; for doctorate, GRE General Test, minimum GPA of 3.0. Application deadline: 1/5. Application fee: $40. *Expenses:* Tuition $0 for state residents; $9384 per year for nonresidents. Fees $4409 per year. *Financial aid:* Fellowships, research assistantships, teaching assistantships available. Financial aid application deadline: 1/5. *Faculty research:* Information retrieval research, design and evaluation of information systems, work practice-based design of information systems, economics of information, intellectual property law. • Dr. Hal R. Varian, Dean, 510-642-9980. Application contact: Michael Hawkins, Student Affairs Officer, 510-642-1465. Fax: 510-642-5814. E-mail: info@sims.berkeley.edu.

University of California, Los Angeles, Graduate School of Education and Information Studies, Department of Library and Information Science, Los Angeles, CA 90095. Awards MLIS, PhD, Certificate, MBA/MLIS. Programs in archive and preservation management (MLIS), information access (MLIS), information organization (MLIS), information policy and management (MLIS), information systems (MLIS), library and information science (PhD, Certificate). One or more master's programs accredited by ALA. Part-time programs available. Faculty: 11 full-time (9 women), 13 part-time (9 women). Students: 121 full-time (84 women), 28 part-time (22 women); includes 29 minority (5 African Americans, 13 Asian Americans, 8 Hispanics, 3 Native Americans), 14 international. Average age 33. 164 applicants, 68% accepted. In 1997, 42 master's, 2 doctorates awarded. Terminal master's awarded for partial completion of doctoral program. *Degree requirements:* For master's, 1 foreign language, professional portfolio required, thesis not required; for doctorate, 1 foreign language, dissertation, oral and written qualifying exams, professional portfolio. *Average time to degree:* master's–2 years full-time, 3 years part-time. *Entrance requirements:* For master's, GRE General Test, TOEFL, TWE, previous course work in computer programming and statistics, proficiency in 1 foreign language; for doctorate, GRE General Test (minimum combined score of 1200), TOEFL, TWE, previous course work in computer programming and statistics, 2 samples of research writing in English. Application deadline: 12/15 (priority date; rolling processing). Application fee: $40. Electronic applications accepted. *Expenses:* Tuition $0 for state residents; $9384 per year for nonresidents. Fees $4551 per year. *Financial aid:* In 1997–98, 119 students received aid, including 23 fellowships totaling $116,471, research assistantships totaling $197,997, teaching assistantships totaling $20,122, federal fellowships and scholarships totaling $41,448; full and partial tuition waivers, Federal Work-Study, institutionally sponsored loans, and career-related internships or fieldwork also available. Aid available to part-time students. Financial aid application deadline: 3/1; applicants required to submit FAFSA. *Faculty research:* Multimedia, digital libraries, archives and electronic records, interface design, information technology and policy, preservation, access. • Dr. Michele V. Cloonan, Chair, 310-825-8799. Fax: 310-206-3076. E-mail: mcloonan@ucla.edu. Application contact: Susan S. Abler, Student Affairs Officer, 310-825-5269. Fax: 310-206-4460. E-mail: abler@gseis.ucla.edu.

University of Denver, University College, Denver, CO 80208. Offerings include library and information services (MLIS). *Average time to degree:* master's–1.5 years full-time, 2.7 years part-time. *Application deadline:* 8/10 (rolling processing; 2/22 for spring admission). *Application fee:* $25. *Expenses:* Tuition $245 per quarter hour for state residents; $310 per quarter hour for nonresidents. Fees $165 per quarter hour (minimum).

University of Hawaii at Manoa, School of Library and Information Studies, Honolulu, HI 96822. Awards MLIS, PhD, Certificate, JD/MLIS, MLIS/MA, MLIS/MS. Programs in advanced library and information studies (Certificate), communication and information science (PhD), library and information studies (MLIS). One or more master's programs accredited by ALA. Part-time programs available. *Degree requirements:* For master's, oral comprehensive exam required, thesis optional, foreign language not required. *Entrance requirements:* For master's, GRE General Test (minimum combined score of 1100), TOEFL (minimum score 600). Application deadline: 3/1 (rolling processing; 9/1 for spring admission). Application fee: $0. *Tuition:* $4029 per year full-time, $214 per credit hour part-time for state residents; $9957 per year full-time, $461 per credit hour part-time for nonresidents. *Faculty research:* Electronic information, retrieval telecommunications, information policy, information needs, database design.

Announcement: Founded in 1965, the ALA-accredited Library and Information Science Program prepares information professionals for work in all types of libraries and organizations through its Master of Library and Information Studies (MLIS) degree and the Certificate in Advanced Library and Information Studies (CALIS) programs. The program is one of 4 sponsors of the interdisciplinary PhD program in communication and information sciences. Dual master's degrees are offered in Pacific Islands studies (MA/MLIS), American studies (MA/MLIS), Asian studies (MA/MLIS), computer science (MS/MLIS), history (MA/MLIS), and law (JD/MLIS). Scholarships and paid internships available. Contact Student Services Officer, Library and Information Science Program, University of Hawaii at Manoa, 2550 The Mall, Honolulu, HI 96822; 808-956-7321; fax: 808-956-5835; e-mail: slis@hawaii.edu

University of Illinois at Urbana–Champaign, Graduate School of Library and Information Science, 501 East Daniel Street, Champaign, IL 61820-6212. Awards MS, PhD, CAS. One or more master's programs accredited by ALA. Faculty: 14 full-time (8 women), 6 part-time (4 women). Students: 234 full-time (158 women); includes 27 minority (10 African Americans, 12 Asian Americans, 5 Hispanics), 34 international. Average age 31. 292 applicants, 61% accepted. In 1997, 123 master's, 4 doctorates awarded. *Degree requirements:* For doctorate, dissertation; for CAS, project. *Entrance requirements:* For master's, GRE General Test, minimum GPA of 4.0 on a 5.0 scale. Application deadline: 6/1 (priority date; rolling processing; 10/1 for spring admission). Application fee: $40 ($50 for international students). *Financial aid:* In 1997–98, 10 fellowships, 140 research assistantships, 11 teaching assistantships were awarded; full and partial tuition waivers also available. Financial aid application deadline: 2/1. • Dr. Leigh S. Estabrook, Dean, 217-333-3280. Application contact: Curt McKay, Assistant Dean, 217-333-3280. Fax: 217-244-3302.

See in-depth description on page 1651.

The University of Iowa, College of Liberal Arts, School of Library and Information Science, Iowa City, IA 52242-1316. Awards MA, JD/MA, MBA/MA. One or more master's programs accredited by ALA. Faculty: 7 full-time, 1 part-time. Students: 53 full-time (40 women), 42 part-time (30 women); includes 2 minority (both Asian Americans), 5 international. 47 applicants, 53% accepted. In 1997, 42 degrees awarded. *Degree requirements:* Thesis optional. *Entrance requirements:* GRE General Test. Application fee: $30 ($50 for international students). *Expenses:* Tuition $3166 per year full-time, $176 per semester hour part-time for state residents; $10,202 per year full-time, $176 per semester hour part-time for nonresidents. Fees $202 per year full-time, $52 per year (minimum) part-time. *Financial aid:* In 1997–98, 12 research assistantships, 4 teaching assistantships were awarded; fellowships also available. Financial aid applicants required to submit FAFSA. • Padmini Srinivasan, Director, 319-335-5707.

University of Maryland, College Park, College of Library and Information Services, College Park, MD 20742-5045. Awards MA, MLS, MS, PhD, MA/MLS. One or more master's programs accredited by ALA. Part-time and evening/weekend programs available. Faculty: 11 full-time (5 women), 14 part-time (6 women). Students: 95 full-time (72 women), 145 part-time (119 women); includes 20 minority (10 African Americans, 6 Asian Americans, 3 Hispanics, 1 Native American), 9 international. 214 applicants, 61% accepted. In 1997, 113 master's, 1 doctorate awarded. Terminal master's awarded for partial completion of doctoral program. *Degree requirements:* For doctorate, dissertation required, foreign language not required. *Entrance requirements:* For master's, GRE General Test, minimum GPA of 3.0; for doctorate, GRE General Test. Application deadline: 8/15 (rolling processing). Application fee: $50 ($70 for international students). *Expenses:* Tuition $272 per credit hour for state residents; $400 per credit hour for nonresidents. Fees $564 per year full-time, $342 per year part-time. *Financial aid:* In 1997–98, 8 fellowships, 20 teaching assistantships were awarded; research assistantships, full and partial tuition waivers, Federal Work-Study, and career-related internships or fieldwork also available. Financial aid application deadline: 2/1. • Dr. Ann E. Prentice, Dean, 301-405-2033. Fax: 301-314-9145. Application contact: John Mollish, Director, Graduate Admissions and Records, 301-405-4198. Fax: 301-314-9305.

See in-depth description on page 1653.

University of Michigan, School of Information, Ann Arbor, MI 48109. Offers programs in archives and records management (MS); human-computer interaction (MS); information (PhD); information economics, management and policy (MS); library and information services (MS). One or more master's programs accredited by ALA. Part-time programs available. *Degree requirements:* For master's, variable foreign language requirement, thesis not required; for doctorate, 1 foreign language, dissertation, oral defense of dissertation, preliminary exam. *Entrance requirements:* GRE General Test. Application fee: $55. *Financial aid:* Fellowships, research assistantships, teaching assistantships, Federal Work-Study, and career-related internships or fieldwork available. Aid available to part-time students. • Dr. Daniel E. Atkins III, Dean, 734-763-2285. Application contact: Departmental Office, 734-763-2285. Fax: 734-764-2475. E-mail: si.admissions@umich.edu.

See in-depth description on page 1655.

University of Missouri–Columbia, College of Education, School of Information Science and Learning Technologies, Columbia, MO 65211. Offers program in library science (MA). One or more master's programs accredited by ALA. Part-time and evening/weekend programs available. Faculty: 9 full-time (3 women), 1 (woman) part-time. Students: 58 full-time (37 women), 71 part-time (54 women); includes 9 minority (all African Americans), 2 international. In 1997, 66 degrees awarded. *Entrance requirements:* GRE or MAT, minimum GPA of 3.0. Application deadline: 7/1 (priority date; rolling processing). Application fee: $25 ($50 for international students). *Expenses:* Tuition $3240 per year full-time, $180 per credit hour part-time for state residents; $9108 per year full-time, $506 per credit hour part-time for nonresidents. Fees $55 per year full-time. *Financial aid:* Fellowships, teaching assistantships, Federal Work-Study available. Aid available to part-time students. • Dr. John Wedman, Director of Graduate Studies, 573-882-3828.

The University of North Carolina at Chapel Hill, School of Information and Library Science, Chapel Hill, NC 27599. Awards MSIS, MSLS, PhD, CAS. One or more master's programs accredited by ALA. Part-time programs available. Faculty: 15 full-time (8 women), 23 part-time (13 women). Students: 166 full-time (117 women), 70 part-time (36 women); includes 18 minority (9 African Americans, 4 Asian Americans, 4 Hispanics, 1 Native American), 23 international. Average age 31. 213 applicants, 70% accepted. In 1997, 97 master's awarded; 1 doctorate awarded (100% entered university research/teaching); 4 CASs awarded. *Degree requirements:* For master's, paper, project required, foreign language and thesis not required; for doctorate, dissertation required, foreign language not required. *Entrance requirements:* For master's and doctorate, GRE General Test. Application deadline: 1/1 (priority date; rolling processing; 10/1 for spring admission). Application fee: $55. Electronic applications accepted. *Expenses:* Tuition $1428 per year full-time, $357 per semester (minimum) part-time for state residents; $10,414 per year full-time, $2604 per semester (minimum) part-time for nonresidents. Fees $782 per year full-time, $332 per semester (minimum) part-time. *Financial aid:* In 1997–98, 23 fellowships (16 to first-year students) totaling $76,000, 4 teaching assistantships averaging $1,000 per month and totaling $16,000, 58 assistantships (42 to first-year students) totaling $424,000 were awarded; research assistantships, Federal Work-Study, institutionally sponsored loans, and career-related internships or fieldwork also available. Financial aid application deadline: 1/1; applicants required to submit FAFSA. *Faculty research:* Information retrieval, digital libraries, multimedia networking, management of information resources, special librarianship. • Dr. Barbara B. Moran, Dean, 919-962-8366. E-mail: info@ils.unc.edu. Application contact: Betty Kompst, Student Services Manager, 919-962-8366. Fax: 919-962-8071. E-mail: info@ils.unc.edu.

University of North Carolina at Greensboro, School of Education, Department of Library and Information Studies, Greensboro, NC 27412-0001. Awards MLIS. One or more master's programs accredited by ALA. Part-time programs available. Faculty: 6 full-time (4 women), 12 part-time (6 women), 10 FTE. Students: 35 full-time (28 women), 152 part-time (130 women). Average age 30. 30 applicants, 83% accepted. In 1997, 77 degrees awarded. *Degree requirements:* Thesis, comprehensive exam required, foreign language not required. *Average time to degree:* master's–1.5 years full-time, 3.5 years part-time. *Entrance requirements:* GRE General Test (minimum combined score of 1000), TOEFL (minimum score 550). Application deadline: 7/1 (priority date; rolling processing; 11/1 for spring admission). Application fee: $35. *Expenses:* Tuition $1842 per year full-time, $370 per semester (minimum) part-time for state residents; $10,296 per year full-time, $2484 per semester (minimum) part-time for nonresidents. Fees $806 per year full-time, $111 per semester (minimum) part-time. *Financial aid:* Fellowships, research assistantships, teaching assistantships, graduate assistantships, institutionally sponsored loans, and career-related internships or fieldwork available. Financial aid application deadline: 3/1. *Faculty research:* School library expenditures, summer reading programs, human relations and public libraries, library history, gender studies. • Kieth C. Wright, Chair, 334-334-3477. Fax: 334-334-5060.

University of North Texas, School of Library and Information Sciences, Denton, TX 76203-6737. Offers programs in information science (MS, PhD), library science (MS). One or more master's programs accredited by ALA. Part-time and evening/weekend programs available. Faculty: 13 full-time (7 women), 9 part-time (5 women). Students: 45 full-time (33 women), 157 part-time (129 women); includes 21 minority (7 African Americans, 5 Asian Americans, 9 Hispanics), 4 international. Average age 37. In 1997, 111 master's, 3 doctorates awarded. *Degree requirements:* For master's, computer language, comprehensive exam required, thesis not required; for doctorate, 1 foreign language, computer language, dissertation, comprehensive exam. *Entrance requirements:* For master's, GRE General Test (minimum score 400 on each section, 1000 combined); for doctorate, GRE General Test (minimum combined score of 1100). Application deadline: 7/17 (rolling processing; 11/30 for spring admission). Application fee: $25 ($50 for international students). *Tuition:* $2063 per year full-time, $815 per year part-time for state residents; $5897 per year full-time, $2100 per year part-time for nonresidents. *Financial aid:* In 1997–98, fellowships averaging $671 per month and totaling $185,200, research assistantships averaging $547 per month and totaling $2,756, teaching assistantships averaging $400 per month and totaling $27,440, library assistantships averaging $520 per month and totaling $50,000 were awarded; Federal Work-Study, institutionally sponsored loans, and career-related internships or fieldwork also available. Financial aid application deadline: 4/1. *Faculty research:* Information resources and services, information management and retrieval, computer-based information systems. • Dr. Philip M. Turner, Dean, 940-565-2445.

University of Oklahoma, College of Arts and Sciences, School of Library and Information Studies, Norman, OK 73019-0390. Awards MALIS, MLIS, Certificate, MBA/MLIS, M Ed/MLIS. One or more master's programs accredited by ALA. Part-time and evening/weekend programs available. Faculty: 10 full-time (7 women), 2 part-time (0 women). Students: 28 full-time (25 women), 51 part-time (42 women); includes 12 minority (5 African Americans, 7 Native Americans), 1 international. Average age 37. 121 applicants, 65% accepted. In 1997, 52 master's awarded. *Degree requirements:* For master's, comprehensive exam (MLIS), thesis (MALIS) required, foreign language not required. *Entrance requirements:* For master's, GRE, TOEFL (minimum score 550), minimum GPA of 3.2 in last 60 hours or 3.0 overall. Application deadline: rolling. Application fee: $25. *Expenses:* Tuition $1920 per year full-time, $80 per credit hour part-time for state residents; $6108 per year full-time, $255 per credit hour part-time for nonresidents. Fees $468 per year full-time, $12 per semester (minimum) part-time. *Financial aid:* In 1997–98, 1 research assistantship, 6 teaching assistantships were awarded; fellowships, partial tuition waivers, Federal Work-Study, and career-related internships or fieldwork also available. Aid available to part-time students. *Faculty research:* Management, library history, library science education, school media center administration, bibliometrics. • June Lester, Director, 405-325-3921.

University of Pittsburgh, School of Information Sciences, Department of Library and Information Science, Pittsburgh, PA 15260. Awards MLIS, PhD, Certificate. One or more master's programs accredited by ALA. Part-time programs available. Faculty: 13 full-time (10 women), 2 part-time (both women). Students: 119 full-time (83 women), 123 part-time (100 women); includes 20 minority (16 African Americans, 3 Asian Americans, 1 Native American), 22 international. 187 applicants, 93% accepted. In 1997, 71 master's, 5 doctorates awarded. *Degree requirements:* For master's, thesis optional, foreign language not required; for doctorate, variable foreign language requirement, dissertation. *Average time to degree:* master's–1 year full-time, 2 years part-time; doctorate–3 years full-time, 6 years part-time. *Entrance requirements:* For master's and doctorate, GRE General Test, minimum QPA of 3.0. Application deadline: 7/31 (priority date; rolling processing; 11/30 for spring admission). Application fee: $30 ($40 for international students). *Expenses:* Tuition $8432 per year full-time, $348 per credit part-time for state residents; $17,360 per year full-time, $720 per credit part-time for nonresidents. Fees $480 per year full-time, $180 per year part-time. *Financial aid:* In 1997–98, 48 students received aid, including 3 fellowships (1 to a first-year student) averaging $1,001 per month, 5 research assistantships (1 to a first-year student) averaging $654 per month, 5 teaching assistantships (1 to a first-year student) averaging $937 per month, 35 assistantships, scholarships (27 to first-year students) averaging $422 per month; full and partial tuition waivers, Federal Work-Study, institutionally sponsored loans, and career-related internships or fieldwork also available. Aid available to part-time students. Financial aid application deadline: 2/15; applicants required to submit FAFSA. *Faculty research:* Archives, electronic records and preservation, children's resources and services, medical informatics, management. • Dr. Edie Rasmussen, Chair, 412-624-9435. Fax: 412-648-7001. E-mail: erasmus@sis.pitt.edu. Application contact: Ninette Kay, Admissions Coordinator, 412-624-5146. Fax: 412-624-5231. E-mail: nk@sis.pitt.edu.

See in-depth description on page 1657.

University of Rhode Island, Graduate Library School, Kingston, RI 02881. Awards MLIS. One or more master's programs accredited by ALA. *Application deadline:* 4/15 (priority date; rolling processing). *Application fee:* $35. *Expenses:* Tuition $3446 per year full-time, $191 per credit part-time for state residents; $9850 per year full-time, $547 per credit part-time for nonresidents. Fees $1276 per year full-time, $135 per semester (minimum) part-time.

University of South Carolina, Graduate School, College of Library and Information Science, Columbia, SC 29208. Awards MLIS, Certificate, Specialist, MLIS/MA. One or more master's programs accredited by ALA. Part-time programs available. Postbaccalaureate distance learning degree programs offered. Faculty: 13 full-time (7 women), 7 part-time (all women), 16.5 FTE. Students: 110 full-time (89 women), 230 part-time (201 women); includes 34 minority (25 African Americans, 6 Asian Americans, 1 Hispanic, 2 Native Americans), 8 international. Average age 35. 95 applicants, 91% accepted. In 1997, 233 master's, 4 other advanced degrees awarded. *Entrance requirements:* For master's, GRE General Test (minimum combined score of 950) or MAT (minimum score 50), TOEFL (minimum score 550). Application deadline: 5/1 (priority date; rolling processing; 10/1 for spring admission). Application fee: $35. Electronic applications accepted. *Expenses:* Tuition $3894 per year full-time, $193 per credit hour part-time for state residents; $8114 per year full-time, $404 per credit hour part-time for nonresidents. Fees $125 per year full-time, $37 per semester (minimum) part-time. *Financial aid:* In 1997–98, 11 fellowships (3 to first-year students) totaling $79,750, 30 research assistantships (14 to first-year students) totaling $66,990 were awarded; career-related internships or fieldwork also available. Aid available to part-time students. *Faculty research:* Information technology management, distance education, library services for children and young adults, special libraries. • Dr. Fred W. Roper, Dean, 803-777-3858. Application contact: Nancy Beitz, Admissions Coordinator, 803-777-3887. Fax: 803-777-0457. E-mail: n.beitz@sc.edu.

University of South Florida, College of Arts and Sciences, School of Library and Information Science, Tampa, FL 33620-9951. Offers programs in library and information sciences (MA), school library media (MA). One or more master's programs accredited by ALA. Part-time and evening/weekend programs available. Postbaccalaureate distance learning degree programs offered (minimal on-campus study). Faculty: 6 full-time (5 women). Students: 55 full-time (37 women), 191 part-time (160 women); includes 25 minority (7 African Americans, 2 Asian Americans, 16 Hispanics), 2 international. Average age 38. 108 applicants, 91% accepted. In 1997, 139 degrees awarded. *Entrance requirements:* GRE General Test (minimum combined score of 1000), minimum GPA of 3.0 in last 60 hours. Application deadline: 6/1 (10/15 for spring admission). Application fee: $20. Electronic applications accepted. *Tuition:* $142 per credit hour for state residents; $486 per credit hour for nonresidents. *Financial aid:* In 1997–98, 86 students received aid, including 2 fellowships averaging $720 per month and totaling $13,300, 10 research assistantships averaging $366 per month and totaling $33,000, 2 teaching assistantships averaging $300 per month and totaling $5,400; Federal Work-Study, institutionally sponsored loans, and career-related internships or fieldwork also available. Aid available to part-time students. Financial aid applicants required to submit FAFSA. • Kathleen de la Pena McCook, Director, 813-974-3520. E-mail: kmccook@chuma.cas.usf.edu. Application contact: Sonia Ramirez Wohlmuth, Assistant Director, 813-974-6837. Fax: 813-974-6840. E-mail: swohlmut@chuma.cas.usf.edu.

University of Tennessee, Knoxville, School of Information Sciences, Knoxville, TN 37996. Awards MS. One or more master's programs accredited by ALA. Part-time programs available. Postbaccalaureate distance learning degree programs offered (no on-campus study). Faculty: 11 full-time (6 women), 1 part-time (0 women). Students: 54 full-time (42 women), 138 part-time (110 women); includes 5 minority (4 African Americans, 1 Asian American), 9 international. 60 applicants, 53% accepted. In 1997, 52 degrees awarded. *Degree requirements:* Thesis or alternative required, foreign language not required. *Entrance requirements:* GRE General Test, TOEFL (minimum score 550), minimum GPA of 2.7. Application deadline: 2/1 (priority date; rolling processing). Application fee: $35. Electronic applications accepted. *Tuition:* $3354 per year full-time, $181 per semester hour part-time for state residents; $8410 per year full-time, $462 per semester hour part-time for nonresidents. *Financial aid:* In 1997–98, 12 teaching assistantships were awarded; fellowships, research assistantships, graduate assistantships, Federal Work-Study, institutionally sponsored loans also available. Financial aid application deadline: 2/1. • Dr. C. W. Minkel, Acting Head, 423-974-2148. Fax: 423-974-4967. E-mail: cminkel@utk.edu.

See in-depth description on page 1659.

The University of Texas at Austin, Graduate School, Graduate School of Library and Information Science, Austin, TX 78712. Awards MLIS, PhD. One or more master's programs accredited by ALA. Part-time programs available. Faculty: 14 full-time, 14 part-time. Students: 405 (313 women); includes 47 minority (4 African Americans, 5 Asian Americans, 37 Hispanics, 1 Native American), 24 international. 239 applicants, 54% accepted. In 1997, 165 master's, 2 doctorates awarded. *Degree requirements:* For doctorate, 2 foreign languages (computer language can substitute for one), dissertation. *Entrance requirements:* For master's, GRE General Test (minimum combined score of 1050); for doctorate, GRE General Test. Application deadline: 3/1 (priority date; rolling processing; 10/1 for spring admission). Application fee: $50 ($75 for international students). Electronic applications accepted. *Expenses:* Tuition $2592 per year full-time, $324 per semester (minimum) part-time for state residents; $7704 per year full-time, $963 per semester (minimum) part-time for nonresidents. Fees $778 per year full-time, $161 per semester (minimum) part-time. *Financial aid:* Fellowships, research assistantships, teaching assistantships, partial tuition waivers, Federal Work-Study, and career-related internships or fieldwork available. Aid available to part-time students. Financial aid application deadline: 2/1. *Faculty research:* Information retrieval and artificial intelligence, library history and administration, classification and cataloguing. • Glynn Harmon, Interim Dean, 512-471-3828. Application contact: Dr. Ronald E. Wyllys, Graduate Adviser, 512-471-3969.

University of Toronto, School of Graduate Studies, Social Sciences Division, Faculty of Information Studies, Toronto, ON M5S 1A1, Canada. Awards MIS, MI St, MLS, PhD. One or more master's programs accredited by ALA. MIS and MLS being phased out; applicants no longer accepted. Part-time programs available. Faculty: 27. Students: 149 full-time (108 women), 123 part-time (81 women); includes 9 international. 307 applicants, 60% accepted. In 1997, 98 master's, 4 doctorates awarded. *Degree requirements:* For doctorate, dissertation. *Application fee:* $75. *Expenses:* Tuition $4070 per year for Canadian residents; $7870 per year for nonresidents. Fees $628 per year. • L. C. Howarth, Dean, 416-978-3202. Application contact: Secretary, 416-978-7121. Fax: 416-978-5762. E-mail: dodd@fis.utoronto.ca.

The University of Western Ontario, Social Sciences Division, Faculty of Information and Media Studies, Programs in Library and Information Science, London, ON N6G 1H1, Canada. Awards MLIS, PhD. One or more master's programs accredited by ALA. Program conducted on a trimester basis; admission deadlines: April 1st, October 1st, and February 15th. Part-time and evening/weekend programs available. Faculty: 16 full-time (8 women), 15 part-time (9 women). Students: 134 full-time (86 women), 65 part-time (42 women). In 1997, 109 master's, 3 doctorates awarded. *Degree requirements:* For doctorate, dissertation, comprehensive exam required, foreign language not required. *Average time to degree:* master's–1 year full-time, 8 years part-time; doctorate–5 years full-time. *Entrance requirements:* For master's, TOEFL (minimum score 580), honors degree, minimum B average during previous 2 years; for doctorate, GRE General Test, TOEFL (minimum score 600), MLIS or equivalent, minimum A average. Application fee: $50. *Financial aid:* Research assistantships, teaching assistantships, institutionally sponsored loans, and career-related internships or fieldwork available. *Faculty research:* Information needs and uses, information systems, information policy. • Application contact: C. Morrison, Student Services Graduate Assistant, 519-679-2111 Ext. 8484. Fax: 519-661-3506. E-mail: morrison@julian.uwo.ca.

See in-depth description on page 1661.

University of Wisconsin–Madison, College of Letters and Science, School of Library and Information Studies, Madison, WI 53706-1380. Awards MA, PhD, Certificate. One or more

Directories: Information Studies; Library Science

University of Wisconsin–Madison (continued)
master's programs accredited by ALA. Part-time programs available. Faculty: 8 full-time (4 women), 16 part-time (10 women), 12 FTE. Students: 136 full-time (109 women), 73 part-time (56 women); includes 12 minority (3 African Americans, 6 Asian Americans, 1 Hispanic, 2 Native Americans), 9 international. 168 applicants, 60% accepted. In 1997, 65 master's, 2 doctorates, 1 Certificate awarded. *Degree requirements:* For doctorate, dissertation. *Application deadline:* 1/15. *Application fee:* $45. *Tuition:* $4928 per year full-time, $926 per semester (minimum) part-time for state residents; $15,190 per year full-time, $2849 per semester (minimum) part-time for nonresidents. *Financial aid:* In 1997–98, 26 students received aid, including 2 teaching assistantships averaging $753 per month and totaling $13,554, 3 project assistantships averaging $849 per month and totaling $30,564; Federal Work-Study and career-related internships or fieldwork also available. *Faculty research:* Intellectual freedom, children's literature, print culture history, information systems design and evaluation, school library media centers. • Louise S. Robbins, Director, 608-263-2908. E-mail: lrobbins@macc.wisc.edu. Application contact: Barbara Arnold, Admissions and Placement Adviser, 608-263-2909. Fax: 608-263-4849. E-mail: bjarnold@facstaff.wisc.edu.

University of Wisconsin–Milwaukee, School of Library and Information Science, Milwaukee, WI 53201-0413. Awards MLIS, CAS, MLIS/MA, MLIS/MM, MLIS/MS. One or more master's programs accredited by ALA. Part-time programs available. Faculty: 9 full-time (3 women). Students: 63 full-time (46 women), 160 part-time (131 women); includes 9 minority (5 African Americans, 1 Asian American, 3 Hispanics), 15 international. 116 applicants, 60% accepted. In 1997, 94 master's awarded. *Entrance requirements:* For master's, GRE General Test or MAT. Application deadline: 1/1 (priority date; rolling processing; 9/1 for spring admission). Application fee: $45 ($75 for international students). *Tuition:* $4996 per year full-time, $1030 per semester (minimum) part-time for state residents; $15,216 per year full-time, $2947 per semester (minimum) part-time for nonresidents. *Financial aid:* In 1997–98, 4 fellowships, 2 teaching assistantships, 1 project assistantship were awarded; research assistantships, Federal Work-Study, and career-related internships or fieldwork also available. Aid available to part-time students. Financial aid application deadline: 4/15. • Dr. Mohammed Aman, Dean, 414-229-4709. Application contact: Wilfred Fong, Assistant Dean, 414-229-5421.

Wayne State University, Library and Information Science Program, Detroit, MI 48202. Offers archives administration (Certificate), library and information science (MLIS, Spec). One or more master's programs accredited by ALA. Part-time and evening/weekend programs available. Faculty: 42. Students: 84 full-time (62 women), 366 part-time (310 women); includes 38 minority (29 African Americans, 4 Asian Americans, 4 Hispanics, 1 Native American). 154 applicants, 80% accepted. In 1997, 146 master's, 10 other advanced degrees awarded. *Application deadline:* 7/1 (rolling processing). *Application fee:* $20 ($30 for international students). *Expenses:* Tuition $163 per credit hour for state residents; $355 per credit hour for nonresidents. Fees $498 per year full-time, $114 per semester (minimum) part-time. *Financial aid:* In 1997–98, 4 research assistantships, 15 scholarships were awarded; Federal Work-Study, institutionally sponsored loans, and career-related internships or fieldwork also available. Aid available to part-time students. Financial aid application deadline: 5/15. *Faculty research:* Management, infometrics, imaging processes, library history, bibliographic control. • Dr. Robert P. Holley, Director, 313-577-1825.

Library Science

Appalachian State University, College of Education, Department of Leadership and Educational Studies, Program in Library Science, Boone, NC 28608. Awards MA, MLS, Ed S. Faculty: 10 full-time, 2 part-time. Students: 11 full-time (7 women), 51 part-time (49 women); includes 2 minority (both African Americans), 1 international. 50 applicants, 88% accepted. In 1997, 4 master's awarded. *Degree requirements:* For master's, thesis or alternative, comprehensive exams required, foreign language not required; for Ed S, comprehensive exams required, thesis optional, foreign language not required. *Entrance requirements:* For master's, GRE General Test or MAT; for Ed S, GRE General Test. Application deadline: 7/31 (priority date). Application fee: $35. *Tuition:* $1811 per year full-time, $354 per semester (minimum) part-time for state residents; $9081 per year full-time, $2171 per semester (minimum) part-time for nonresidents. *Financial aid:* Fellowships, research assistantships, teaching assistantships, and career-related internships or fieldwork available. Aid available to part-time students. • Dr. Ralph Hall, Acting Chairperson, 704-262-6041. Application contact: Dr. Carol Truett, Adviser, 704-262-3115.

The Catholic University of America, School of Library and Information Science, Washington, DC 20064. Awards MSLS, JD/MSLS, MSLS/MA, MSLS/MS. One or more master's programs accredited by ALA. MSLS/MA jointly administered by the Departments of English, Greek and Latin, History, and the Schools of Music and Religious Studies; MSLS/MS jointly administered by the Department of Biology; JD/MSLS jointly administered with Columbia School of Law. Part-time and evening/weekend programs available. Postbaccalaureate distance learning degree programs offered (minimal on-campus study). Faculty: 8 (all women). Students: 38 full-time (31 women), 253 part-time (201 women); includes 44 minority (31 African Americans, 10 Asian Americans, 1 Hispanic, 2 Native Americans), 17 international. Average age 35. 136 applicants, 79% accepted. In 1997, 161 degrees awarded. *Degree requirements:* Comprehensive exam required, foreign language and thesis not required. *Entrance requirements:* GRE General Test. Application deadline: 7/1 (priority date; rolling processing; 11/1 for spring admission). Application fee: $50. *Expenses:* Tuition $17,326 per year full-time, $668 per credit hour part-time. Fees $680 per year full-time, $180 per semester part-time. *Financial aid:* Fellowships, research assistantships, project assistantships, full and partial tuition waivers, Federal Work-Study, institutionally sponsored loans, and career-related internships or fieldwork available. Aid available to part-time students. Financial aid application deadline: 2/1. *Faculty research:* Information transfer, archives and manuscripts, legal libraries, information seeking, information storage and retrieval, special collections, information systems. Total annual research expenditures: $3000. • Dr. Elizabeth Aversa, Dean, 202-319-5085. Application contact: Dr. Jean L. Preer, Chair, Admissions Committee, 202-319-5085.

See in-depth description on page 1631.

Central Missouri State University, Department of Library Science and Information Services, Warrensburg, MO 64093. Offers programs in human services/learning resources (Ed S), library science and information services (MS). Part-time programs available. Faculty: 2 full-time. Students: 5 full-time (4 women), 31 part-time (28 women). In 1997, 9 master's awarded. *Degree requirements:* Thesis or alternative. *Entrance requirements:* For master's, minimum GPA of 2.75, interview, 2 years of teaching experience; for Ed S, minimum GPA of 3.25, master's degree. Application deadline: 6/30 (priority date; rolling processing). Application fee: $25 ($50 for international students). *Tuition:* $3288 per year full-time, $137 per credit hour part-time for state residents; $5928 per year full-time, $274 per credit hour part-time for nonresidents. *Financial aid:* In 1997–98, 1 teaching assistantship, 1 administrative and laboratory assistantship were awarded; Federal Work-Study also available. Aid available to part-time students. Financial aid application deadline: 3/1; applicants required to submit FAFSA. • Dr. Larry Dorrell, Chair, 660-543-8633. Fax: 660-543-8001.

Chicago State University, College of Education, Department of Library Science and Communications Media, Chicago, IL 60628. Awards MS Ed. *Entrance requirements:* Minimum GPA of 2.75. Application deadline: 7/1 (11/10 for spring admission). *Tuition:* $2268 per year full-time, $95 per credit hour part-time for state residents; $6804 per year full-time, $284 per credit hour part-time for nonresidents.

Clarion University of Pennsylvania, College of Education and Human Services, Department of Library Science, Clarion, PA 16214. Awards MSLS. One or more master's programs accredited by ALA. Part-time programs available. Faculty: 7 full-time (2 women). Students: 32 full-time (25 women), 64 part-time (57 women); includes 4 minority (2 African Americans, 1 Asian American, 1 Native American), 3 international. 58 applicants, 81% accepted. In 1997, 55 degrees awarded. *Degree requirements:* Thesis or alternative required, foreign language not required. *Entrance requirements:* Minimum QPA of 3.0. Application deadline: 8/1 (priority date; rolling processing). Application fee: $25. *Expenses:* Tuition $3468 per year full-time, $193 per credit hour part-time for state residents; $6236 per year full-time, $346 per credit hour part-time for nonresidents. Fees $921 per year full-time, $90 per credit hour part-time for state residents; $921 per year full-time, $89 per credit hour part-time for nonresidents. *Financial aid:* In 1997–98, 14 research assistantships (13 to first-year students) averaging $267 per month were awarded. Financial aid application deadline: 5/1. • Dr. James Maccaferri, Chairman, 814-226-2271.

Clark Atlanta University, School of Library and Information Studies, Atlanta, GA 30314. Awards MSLS, SLS. One or more master's programs accredited by ALA. Part-time and evening/weekend programs available. Faculty: 7 full-time (1 woman), 3 part-time (1 woman). Students: 39 full-time (29 women), 43 part-time (31 women); includes 52 minority (45 African Americans, 4 Asian Americans, 3 Hispanics). Average age 34. In 1997, 39 master's awarded. *Degree requirements:* For master's, 1 foreign language required, thesis optional; for SLS, 1 foreign language, thesis. *Entrance requirements:* For master's, GRE, TOEFL. Application deadline: rolling. Application fee: $40. *Expenses:* Tuition $9672 per year full-time, $403 per credit hour part-time. Fees $200 per year. *Financial aid:* In 1997–98, 47 students received aid, including 41 fellowships totaling $133,920, 4 tutorial assistantships totaling $13,500; full and partial tuition waivers, Federal Work-Study, institutionally sponsored loans, and career-related internships or fieldwork also available. Aid available to part-time students. Financial aid application deadline: 6/1. *Faculty research:* International research, public libraries, library history, school media, African-American history. • Dr. Arthur C. Gunn, Acting Dean, 404-880-8698. Fax: 404-880-8977. E-mail: agunn@cau.edu.

College of St. Catherine, Graduate Program, Program in Library and Information Science, St. Paul, MN 55105-1789. Awards MA. Offered in cooperation with Dominican University. Part-time and evening/weekend programs available. Faculty: 16 part-time (8 women). Students: 46 full-time (40 women), 36 part-time (30 women); includes 6 minority (2 African Americans, 1 Asian American, 2 Hispanics, 1 Native American). Average age 36. 72 applicants, 83% accepted. *Degree requirements:* Minimum of 12 credits completed in residence at Rosary College required, foreign language and thesis not required. *Entrance requirements:* Michigan English Language Assessment Battery (minimum score 90) or TOEFL (minimum score 600), minimum GPA of 3.2. Application deadline: 2/15. Application fee: $25. *Expenses:* Tuition $460 per credit hour. Fees $60 per year. *Financial aid:* 39 students received aid; institutionally sponsored loans available. Aid available to part-time students. Financial aid application deadline: 4/1; applicants required to submit FAFSA. • Mary Wagner, Director, 612-690-6802. Application contact: Office of Admission, 612-690-6505.

Concordia University, Faculty of Arts and Science, Department of Library Studies, Montréal, PQ H3G 1M8, Canada. Awards Diploma. Admissions temporarily suspended. Students: 2 full-time (1 woman), 18 part-time (12 women); includes 1 international. In 1997, 19 degrees awarded. *Degree requirements:* Comprehensive exam, internship. *Expenses:* Tuition $56 per credit (minimum) for Canadian residents; $249 per credit (minimum) for nonresidents. Fees $158 per year full-time, $117 per year (minimum) part-time. • M. Giguere, Director, 514-848-2526.

Dalhousie University, Faculty of Management, School of Library and Information Studies, Halifax, NS B3H 3J5, Canada. Awards MLIS, LL B/MLIS. One or more master's programs accredited by ALA. Faculty: 4 full-time, 5 part-time. Students: 65 full-time (49 women), 10 part-time (9 women). 69 applicants, 49% accepted. In 1997, 26 degrees awarded. *Degree requirements:* 1 foreign language required, thesis optional. *Entrance requirements:* TOEFL (minimum score 580). Application deadline: 6/1 (rolling processing). Application fee: $55. *Financial aid:* In 1997–98, 20 students received aid, including 14 fellowships (7 to first-year students) totaling $58,000, 6 scholarships (3 to first-year students) totaling $8,350; career-related internships or fieldwork also available. Financial aid application deadline: 3/31. *Faculty research:* Information-seeking behavior, electronic text design, browsing in digital environments, information diffusion among scientists. Total annual research expenditures: $65,000. • Dr. B. H. MacDonald, Director, 902-494-3656. Application contact: Judy Dunn, Graduate Coordinator, 902-494-3656.

Dominican University, Graduate School of Library and Information Science, River Forest, IL 60305-1099. Awards MLIS, MSMIS, CSS, MBA/MLIS, MLIS/MA, MLIS/M Div, MLIS/MM. One or more master's programs accredited by ALA. MLIS/M Div offered jointly with McCormick Theological Seminary; MLIS/MA (public history) offered jointly with Loyola University Chicago; MLIS/MM (music history) offered jointly with Northwestern University. Part-time and evening/weekend programs available. Postbaccalaureate distance learning degree programs offered (minimal on-campus study). Faculty: 9 full-time (2 women), 26 part-time (10 women), 14 FTE. Students: 382; includes 17 minority (7 African Americans, 5 Asian Americans, 5 Hispanics), 8 international. Average age 33. *Degree requirements:* For master's, computer language required, foreign language and thesis not required. *Entrance requirements:* For master's, TOEFL (minimum score 600), minimum GPA of 3.0 or GRE General Test (minimum score 550 required on 2 out of 3 sections). Application deadline: 8/15 (priority date; rolling processing; 12/15 for spring admission). Application fee: $25. *Financial aid:* Fellowships, research assistantships, scholarships, partial tuition waivers, Federal Work-Study, and career-related internships or fieldwork available. Aid available to part-time students. Financial aid application deadline: 4/15. *Faculty research:* Productivity and the information environment, bibliometrics, library history, subject access, library materials and services for children. • Prudence Dalrymple, Dean, 708-524-6472. Fax: 708-524-6657.

Announcement: The Master of Library and Information Science (MLIS) degree at Dominican University is a 36-semester-hour program accredited by the American Library Association. Other programs include a collaborative program at the College of St. Catherine, St. Paul, Minnesota; 1 joint-degree (MS/MIS) and 4 combined-degree programs; and certificates of special studies in 3 fields.

See in-depth description on page 1633.

Drexel University, College of Information Science and Technology, 3141 Chestnut Street, Philadelphia, PA 19104-2875. Offers programs in information studies (PhD, CAS), information systems (MSIS), library and information science (MS). One or more master's programs accredited by ALA. Part-time and evening/weekend programs available. Faculty: 17 full-time (7 women), 17 part-time (6 women), 22.7 FTE. Students: 76 full-time (51 women), 477 part-time

(245 women); includes 59 minority (29 African Americans, 23 Asian Americans, 5 Hispanics, 2 Native Americans), 81 international. Average age 37. 252 applicants, 58% accepted. In 1997, 126 master's, 3 doctorates awarded. *Degree requirements:* For doctorate, dissertation required, foreign language not required. *Entrance requirements:* For master's, GRE General Test, TOEFL (minimum score 600); for doctorate, GRE General Test, TOEFL (minimum score 600), master's degree. Application deadline: 8/21 (rolling processing). Application fee: $35. *Expenses:* Tuition $437 per credit hour. Fees $121 per quarter full-time, $65 per quarter part-time. *Financial aid:* In 1997–98, 2 research assistantships, 5 teaching assistantships, 8 graduate assistantships were awarded; partial tuition waivers, Federal Work-Study, institutionally sponsored loans, and career-related internships or fieldwork also available. Aid available to part-time students. Financial aid application deadline: 2/1. *Faculty research:* Bibliometric analysis, information management, scientific communication, expert systems, man-machine interfaces in information transfer. • Dr. Richard Lytle, Dean, 215-895-2475. Application contact: Anne B. Tanner, Associate Dean, 215-895-2474.

See in-depth description on page 1635.

East Carolina University, School of Education, Department of Library Studies and Educational Technology, Greenville, NC 27858-4353. Offers programs in instruction technology specialist (MA Ed), library science (MLS, CAS). Part-time and evening/weekend programs available. Faculty: 6 full-time (4 women). Students: 4 full-time (all women), 41 part-time (40 women); includes 1 minority (African American). Average age 39. 21 applicants, 95% accepted. In 1997, 20 master's awarded. *Degree requirements:* For master's, comprehensive exams required, thesis optional, foreign language not required. *Entrance requirements:* For master's, GRE General Test or MAT, TOEFL. Application deadline: 6/1 (priority date; rolling processing). Application fee: $40. *Tuition:* $1886 per year full-time, $472 per semester (minimum) part-time for state residents; $9156 per year full-time, $2289 per semester (minimum) part-time for nonresidents. *Financial aid:* Research assistantships, teaching assistantships, Federal Work-Study available. Aid available to part-time students. Financial aid application deadline: 6/1. • Dr. Gene D. Lanier, Director of Graduate Studies, 252-328-6621. Fax: 252-328-4368. E-mail: lanierg@mail.ecu.edu. Application contact: Dr. Paul D. Tschetter, Associate Dean, 252-328-6012. Fax: 252-328-6071. E-mail: grad@mail.ecu.edu.

Emporia State University, School of Graduate Studies, School of Library and Information Management, Emporia, KS 66801-5087. Awards MLS, PhD. One or more master's programs accredited by ALA. Part-time programs available. Faculty: 13 full-time (7 women), 47 part-time (28 women). Students: 53 full-time (41 women), 155 part-time (129 women); includes 9 minority (5 African Americans, 3 Asian Americans, 1 Hispanic), 2 international. 39 applicants, 100% accepted. In 1997, 124 master's, 1 doctorate awarded. *Degree requirements:* For master's, comprehensive exam or thesis required, foreign language not required. *Entrance requirements:* For master's, GRE General Test, TOEFL (minimum score 550); for doctorate, GRE General Test (minimum combined score of 1100), TOEFL (minimum score 650), interview, minimum graduate GPA of 3.5. Application deadline: 8/15 (priority date; rolling processing). Application fee: $30 ($75 for international students). Electronic applications accepted. *Tuition:* $2300 per year full-time, $103 per credit hour part-time for state residents; $6012 per year full-time, $258 per credit hour part-time for nonresidents. *Financial aid:* In 1997–98, 11 research assistantships averaging $558 per month, 7 teaching assistantships averaging $522 per month were awarded; Federal Work-Study, institutionally sponsored loans, and career-related internships or fieldwork also available. Financial aid application deadline: 3/15; applicants required to submit FAFSA. *Faculty research:* Information management in corporate environment. • Dr. Faye N. Vowell, Dean, 316-341-5203. E-mail: vowellfa@emporia.edu.

Florida State University, School of Information Studies, Tallahassee, FL 32306. Offers programs in information studies (Adv M, PhD), library and information studies (MS, PhD). One or more master's programs accredited by ALA. Part-time and evening/weekend programs available. Postbaccalaureate distance learning degree programs offered (minimal on-campus study). Faculty: 14 full-time (6 women), 7 part-time (4 women), 15.75 FTE. Students: 73 full-time (56 women), 368 part-time (261 women); includes 53 minority (30 African Americans, 9 Asian Americans, 13 Hispanics, 1 Native American), 21 international. Average age 38. 190 applicants, 82% accepted. In 1997, 145 master's awarded; 6 doctorates awarded (100% found work related to degree). *Degree requirements:* For doctorate, dissertation required, foreign language not required. *Entrance requirements:* For master's, GRE General Test (minimum combined score of 1000), minimum GPA of 3.0; for doctorate, GRE General Test (minimum combined score of 1000), minimum graduate GPA of 3.5. Application fee: $20. *Tuition:* $139 per credit hour for state residents; $482 per credit hour for nonresidents. *Financial aid:* In 1997–98, 57 students received aid, including 3 fellowships (2 to first-year students) averaging $1,179 per month and totaling $28,304, 21 research assistantships (12 to first-year students) averaging $325 per month and totaling $43,060, 3 teaching assistantships averaging $488 per month and totaling $8,200, 30 assistantships (23 to first-year students) averaging $319 per month and totaling $51,950; Federal Work-Study also available. Financial aid application deadline: 4/1. *Faculty research:* Community information service, needs assessment, disaster preparedness, information policy, usability analysis. • Dr. Jane B. Robbins, Dean, 850-644-5775. Application contact: Marion Davis, Program Assistant, 850-644-8103. Fax: 850-644-9763. E-mail: mdavis@mailer.lis.fsu.edu.

See in-depth description on page 1637.

Gratz College, Program in Judaica Librarianship, Old York Road and Melrose Avenue, Melrose Park, PA 19027. Awards Certificate, MIS/Certificate. MIS/Certificate offered jointly with Drexel University. Part-time programs available. Faculty: 8 full-time (3 women), 11 part-time (7 women). *Degree requirements:* 1 foreign language required, thesis not required. *Application deadline:* rolling. *Application fee:* $50. *Tuition:* $8500 per year full-time, $395 per credit part-time. *Financial aid:* Application deadline 4/1. • Rebecca Landau, Coordinator, 215-635-7300. Application contact: Evelyn Klein, Director of Admissions, 215-635-7300. Fax: 215-635-7320. E-mail: gratzinfo@aol.com.

Indiana University Bloomington, School of Library and Information Science, Bloomington, IN 47405. Awards MIS, MLS, PhD, Spec, DBA/MIS, JD/MLS, MLS/MA, MPA/MLS, PhD/MIS. One or more master's programs accredited by ALA. MLS/MA offered jointly through the School of Fine Arts, School of Journalism, School of Music, Department of Comparative Literature, Department of History, and Department of History and Philosophy of Science. PhD offered through the University Graduate School. Part-time programs available. Faculty: 17 full-time (7 women). Students: 151 full-time (98 women), 147 part-time (109 women); includes 14 minority (2 African Americans, 6 Asian Americans, 4 Hispanics, 2 Native Americans), 20 international. In 1997, 179 master's, 2 doctorates awarded. *Degree requirements:* For doctorate, 1 foreign language (computer language can substitute), dissertation. *Entrance requirements:* For master's, minimum GPA of 3.0; for doctorate, GRE General Test, minimum GPA of 3.5. Application fee: $35. *Expenses:* Tuition $153 per credit hour for state residents; $446 per credit hour for nonresidents. Fees $343 per year. *Financial aid:* Fellowships, partial tuition waivers, and career-related internships or fieldwork available. Aid available to part-time students. *Faculty research:* Scholarly communication, interface design, public library policy, computer-mediated communication, information retrieval. • Dr. Blaise Cronin, Dean, 812-855-2018. Application contact: Rhonda Spencer, Admissions Coordinator, 812-855-2666. Fax: 812-855-6166.

See in-depth description on page 1639.

Inter American University of Puerto Rico, San Germán Campus, Department of Education, Program in Library Science, San Germán, PR 00683-5008. Awards MA. Part-time and evening/weekend programs available. Faculty: 2 full-time (0 women), 2 part-time (1 woman). In 1997, 16 degrees awarded. *Degree requirements:* Comprehensive exam required, foreign language and thesis not required. *Entrance requirements:* Minimum GPA of 3.0, GRE General Test, or PAEG. Application deadline: 4/30 (priority date; rolling processing; 11/15 for spring admission). Application fee: $31. *Expenses:* Tuition $150 per credit. Fees $177 per semester. *Financial aid:* Teaching assistantships available. • Application contact: Mildred Camacho, Admissions Director, 787-892-3090. Fax: 787-892-6350.

Kent State University, College of Fine and Professional Arts, School of Library and Information Science, Kent, OH 44242-0001. Awards MLS. One or more master's programs accredited by ALA. Faculty: 14 full-time. Students: 121 full-time (90 women), 390 part-time (328 women); includes 20 minority (16 African Americans, 3 Asian Americans, 1 Native American), 11 international. 262 applicants, 94% accepted. In 1997, 156 degrees awarded. *Degree requirements:* Thesis optional, foreign language not required. *Entrance requirements:* GRE General Test, minimum GPA of 2.75. Application deadline: 7/12 (rolling processing; 11/29 for spring admission). Application fee: $30. *Tuition:* $4752 per year full-time, $216 per credit hour part-time for state residents; $9213 per year full-time, $419 per credit hour part-time for nonresidents. *Financial aid:* Research assistantships, teaching assistantships, full tuition waivers, Federal Work-Study available. Financial aid application deadline: 2/1. • Dr. Danny P. Wallace, Director, 330-672-2782. Fax: 330-672-7965.

Kutztown University of Pennsylvania, Graduate School, College of Education, Program in Library Science, Kutztown, PA 19530. Awards MLS. Part-time and evening/weekend programs available. Faculty: 3 full-time (2 women). Students: 11 full-time (8 women), 42 part-time (34 women); includes 1 minority (Asian American). Average age 33. In 1997, 26 degrees awarded. *Entrance requirements:* GRE General Test, TOEFL, TSE, interview. Application deadline: 3/1 (8/1 for spring admission). Application fee: $25. *Tuition:* $4111 per year full-time, $225 per credit hour part-time for state residents; $6879 per year full-time, $393 per credit hour part-time for nonresidents. *Financial aid:* Graduate assistantships, partial tuition waivers, Federal Work-Study, and career-related internships or fieldwork available. Financial aid application deadline: 3/15; applicants required to submit FAFSA. • Dr. M. Kathryn Holland, Chairperson, 610-683-4300.

Long Island University, C.W. Post Campus, Palmer School of Library and Information Science, Brookville, NY 11548-1300. Offers programs in archives (Certificate), information studies (PhD), library and information science (MS), records management (Certificate). One or more master's programs accredited by ALA. Part-time and evening/weekend programs available. Postbaccalaureate distance learning degree programs offered (minimal on-campus study). Faculty: 12 full-time (5 women), 30 part-time (18 women). Students: 61 full-time (50 women), 343 part-time (296 women). 179 applicants, 83% accepted. In 1997, 130 master's awarded. *Degree requirements:* For master's, thesis optional, foreign language not required; for doctorate, dissertation required, foreign language not required. *Entrance requirements:* For master's, GRE or MAT, minimum undergraduate GPA of 3.0. Application fee: $30. Electronic applications accepted. *Expenses:* Tuition $480 per credit. Fees $316 per year full-time, $71 per semester (minimum) part-time. *Financial aid:* Fellowships, research assistantships, partial tuition waivers, Federal Work-Study, institutionally sponsored loans, and career-related internships or fieldwork available. Aid available to part-time students. Financial aid application deadline: 5/15; applicants required to submit FAFSA. *Faculty research:* Managing information technology, bibliographic control, organizational culture, scholarly communication. • Anne Woodsworth, Dean, 516-299-2855. E-mail: woodswor@titan.liunet.edu. Application contact: Graduate Admissions, 516-299-2866. Fax: 516-299-4168. E-mail: palmer@titan.liunet.edu.

Announcement: Students can learn to manage the world of information at the Palmer School of Library and Information Science—the school with vision and a focus on the future. The Palmer School offers a BS in information transfer and a PhD in information studies at Long Island University's C.W. Post Campus on Long Island. An MS in library and information science is offered at the C.W. Post Campus and in Manhattan. Selected master's courses are offered at the University's Westchester Campus in Dobbs Ferry. For information, write to the Palmer School of Library and Information Science, Long Island University, Brookville, NY 11548-1300. Telephone: 516-299-2866 or 212-998-2680, fax: 516-299-4168, e-mail: palmer@titan.liunet.edu, World Wide Web: http://www.liunet.edu/palmer

Louisiana State University and Agricultural and Mechanical College, School of Library and Information Science, Baton Rouge, LA 70803. Awards MLIS, CLIS. One or more master's programs accredited by ALA. Evening/weekend programs available. Faculty: 6 full-time (4 women). Students: 93 full-time (66 women), 84 part-time (71 women); includes 30 minority (24 African Americans, 2 Asian Americans, 4 Hispanics), 16 international. Average age 34. 74 applicants, 82% accepted. In 1997, 80 master's, 2 CLISs awarded. *Degree requirements:* For master's, comprehensive exam required, thesis optional, foreign language not required. *Entrance requirements:* For master's, GRE General Test (minimum combined score of 1000), minimum GPA of 3.0. Application deadline: 1/25 (priority date; rolling processing). Application fee: $25. *Tuition:* $2736 per year full-time, $285 per semester (minimum) part-time for state residents; $6636 per year full-time, $460 per semester (minimum) part-time for nonresidents. *Financial aid:* In 1997–98, 4 fellowships, 19 research assistantships (7 to first-year students), 20 service assistantships (5 to first-year students) were awarded; teaching assistantships and career-related internships or fieldwork also available. Aid available to part-time students. *Faculty research:* Information retrieval, management, collection development, public libraries. Total annual research expenditures: $200,000. • Dr. Bert R. Boyce, Dean, 504-388-3158. Application contact: Shirley Watson, Admissions Secretary, 504-388-1481.

McGill University, Faculty of Graduate Studies and Research, Faculty of Education, Graduate School of Library and Information Studies, Montréal, PQ H3A 2T5, Canada. Awards MLIS, PhD, Diploma. One or more master's programs accredited by ALA. Diploma and PhD new for fall 1998. Faculty: 8 full-time (4 women), 12 part-time (4 women). Students: 93 full-time (68 women), 7 part-time (6 women). Average age 32. In 1997, 59 master's awarded. *Degree requirements:* For doctorate, dissertation. *Entrance requirements:* For master's, TOEFL (minimum score 550), minimum GPA of 3.0. Application deadline: 3/1 (rolling processing). Application fee: $60. *Expenses:* Tuition $1668 per year for Canadian residents; $8268 per year for nonresidents. Fees $828 per year for Canadian residents; $1216 per year for nonresidents. *Faculty research:* Thesaurus construction, interface design, bilingual multimedia, organizational structures, bibliographic control. • Jamshid Behesti, Director, 514-398-4204. Fax: 514-398-7193.

North Carolina Central University, Division of Academic Affairs, School of Library and Information Sciences, Durham, NC 27707-3129. Awards MIS, MLS, JD/MLS. One or more master's programs accredited by ALA. Part-time and evening/weekend programs available. Faculty: 9 full-time (4 women), 5 part-time (4 women). Students: 26 full-time (22 women), 150 part-time (125 women); includes 63 minority (51 African Americans, 8 Asian Americans, 2 Hispanics, 2 Native Americans). Average age 37. 38 applicants, 100% accepted. In 1997, 82 degrees awarded. *Degree requirements:* 1 foreign language (computer language can substitute), alternate thesis or research paper. *Entrance requirements:* 90 hours in liberal arts, minimum B average. Application deadline: 8/1. Application fee: $30. *Tuition:* $2027 per year full-time, $508 per semester (minimum) part-time for state residents; $9155 per year full-time, $2290 per semester (minimum) part-time for nonresidents. *Financial aid:* Fellowships, research assistantships, state grants, institutionally sponsored loans, and career-related internships or fieldwork available. Aid available to part-time students. Financial aid application deadline: 5/1. *Faculty research:* African-American resources, planning and evaluation, analysis of economic and physical resources, geography of information, artificial intelligence. • Dr. Benjamin F. Speller Jr., Dean, 919-560-6485.

Pratt Institute, School of Information and Library Science, Program in Library and Information Science, Brooklyn, NY 11205-3899. Awards MS, Adv C, JD/MS, MS/MS. One or more master's programs accredited by ALA. JD/MS offered jointly with the Brooklyn Law School; MS/MS offered jointly with the Program in Art History. Part-time and evening/weekend programs available. *Degree requirements:* For master's, thesis required, foreign language not required. *Average time to degree:* master's–2 years full-time. *Entrance requirements:* For master's, TOEFL (minimum score 550). Application deadline: 3/1 (priority date; rolling processing). Application fee: $35 ($80 for international students). *Expenses:* Tuition $14,520 per year

Directory: Library Science

Pratt Institute (continued)
full-time, $605 per credit part-time. Fees $480 per year. *Faculty research:* Law and medical librarianship, library computer software, confidentiality.

See in-depth description on page 1641.

Queens College of the City University of New York, Social Science Division, Graduate School of Library and Information Studies, 65-30 Kissena Boulevard, Flushing, NY 11367-1597. Awards MLS, AC. One or more master's programs accredited by ALA. Part-time and evening/weekend programs available. Students: 13 full-time (9 women), 358 part-time (261 women); includes 47 minority (20 African Americans, 10 Asian Americans, 17 Hispanics), 2 international. 163 applicants, 87% accepted. In 1997, 95 master's awarded. *Degree requirements:* For master's, thesis required, foreign language not required; for AC, thesis optional, foreign language not required. *Entrance requirements:* For master's, TOEFL, minimum GPA of 3.0; for AC, TOEFL, master's degree or equivalent. Application deadline: 4/1 (rolling processing; 11/1 for spring admission). Application fee: $40. *Expenses:* Tuition $4350 per year full-time, $185 per credit part-time for state residents; $7600 per year full-time, $320 per credit part-time for nonresidents. Fees $104 per year. *Financial aid:* Partial tuition waivers, Federal Work-Study, institutionally sponsored loans, and career-related internships or fieldwork available. Aid available to part-time students. Financial aid application deadline: 4/1; applicants required to submit FAFSA. *Faculty research:* Multimedia and video studies, ethnicity and librarianship, information science and computer applications. • Dr. Marianne Cooper, Director and Chair, 718-997-3790. Application contact: Dr. Karen Smith, Graduate Adviser, 718-997-3790.

Rutgers, The State University of New Jersey, New Brunswick, Program in Communication, Information and Library Studies, New Brunswick, NJ 08903. Awards PhD. Offered in conjunction with the School of Communication, Information and Library Studies. Part-time programs available. Faculty: 46 full-time (17 women), 1 (woman) part-time. Students: 29 full-time (15 women), 72 part-time (42 women); includes 9 minority (8 African Americans, 1 Hispanic), 19 international. Average age 35. 53 applicants, 58% accepted. In 1997, 6 doctorates awarded. Terminal master's awarded for partial completion of doctoral program. *Degree requirements:* For doctorate, dissertation, qualifying exams required, foreign language not required. *Entrance requirements:* For doctorate, GRE General Test. Application deadline: 5/1. Application fee: $40. Electronic applications accepted. *Expenses:* Tuition $6492 per year full-time, $268 per credit part-time for state residents; $9520 per year full-time, $395 per credit part-time for nonresidents. Fees $208 per year (minimum). *Financial aid:* In 1997–98, 3 fellowships, 7 research assistantships (1 to a first-year student), 17 teaching assistantships (5 to first-year students) were awarded; institutionally sponsored loans also available. Financial aid application deadline: 2/1. *Faculty research:* Information science, information policy, communication media studies, library studies. • Lea P. Stewart, Director, 732-932-7447.

Rutgers, The State University of New Jersey, New Brunswick, School of Communication, Information and Library Studies, Department of Library and Information Studies, New Brunswick, NJ 08903. Awards MLS. One or more master's programs accredited by ALA. Part-time programs available. Faculty: 15 full-time (6 women), 11 part-time (6 women). Students: 97 full-time (74 women), 199 part-time (160 women); includes 25 minority (7 African Americans, 10 Asian Americans, 7 Hispanics, 1 Native American), 7 international. Average age 34. 198 applicants, 84% accepted. In 1997, 158 degrees awarded. *Entrance requirements:* GRE General Test (minimum combined score of 1000; average 1140), TOEFL (minimum score 600). Application deadline: 5/1 (rolling processing; 11/1 for spring admission). Application fee: $40. *Expenses:* Tuition $6492 per year full-time, $268 per credit part-time for state residents; $9520 per year full-time, $395 per credit part-time for nonresidents. Fees $208 per year (minimum). *Financial aid:* In 1997–98, 5 scholarships (3 to first-year students) totaling $10,843 were awarded; Federal Work-Study, institutionally sponsored loans, and career-related internships or fieldwork also available. Aid available to part-time students. Financial aid application deadline: 3/1; applicants required to submit FAFSA. *Faculty research:* Information science, library services, management of information services. • Dr. David Carr, Director, 732-932-7917. Fax: 732-932-2644. E-mail: dcarr@scils.rutgers.edu.

St. John's University, Graduate School of Arts and Sciences, Division of Library and Information Science, Jamaica, NY 11439. Offers programs in drug information specialist (MS/MLS), government information specialist (MA/MLS), library and information science (MLS, Adv C). One or more master's programs accredited by ALA. Part-time and evening/weekend programs available. Faculty: 9 full-time (7 women), 2 part-time (0 women). Students: 13 full-time (9 women), 87 part-time (65 women); includes 25 minority (17 African Americans, 2 Asian Americans, 6 Hispanics), 3 international. Average age 35. 65 applicants, 78% accepted. In 1997, 34 master's awarded. *Entrance requirements:* For master's, minimum GPA of 3.0. Application deadline: rolling. Application fee: $40. *Expenses:* Tuition $600 per credit. Fees $150 per year. *Financial aid:* In 1997–98, 3 research assistantships averaging $667 per month were awarded; graduate assistantships, Federal Work-Study, and career-related internships or fieldwork also available. Aid available to part-time students. Financial aid application deadline: 3/1; applicants required to submit FAFSA. *Faculty research:* On-line database management, public library patronage, medieval monastic libraries and archives, children's literature, indexing. • Dr. James Benson, Director, 718-990-6200. Application contact: Shamus J. McGrenra, TOR, Associate Director, Graduate Admissions, 718-990-6107. Fax: 718-990-5736. E-mail: mcgrenrs@stjohns.edu.

Sam Houston State University, College of Education and Applied Science, Department of Library Science, Huntsville, TX 77341. Awards MLS. Part-time and evening/weekend programs available. Students: 3 full-time (all women), 103 part-time (99 women); includes 29 minority (all Hispanics). Average age 41. In 1997, 39 degrees awarded (100% found work related to degree). *Entrance requirements:* GRE General Test (minimum combined score of 800), minimum GPA of 2.8. Application deadline: rolling. Application fee: $15. *Tuition:* $1810 per year full-time, $297 per semester (minimum) part-time for state residents; $6922 per year full-time, $924 per semester (minimum) part-time for nonresidents. *Financial aid:* Teaching assistantships, Federal Work-Study, and career-related internships or fieldwork available. Aid available to part-time students. Financial aid application deadline: 3/1. • Dr. Mary Berry, Chair, 409-294-1150. Fax: 409-294-1153. E-mail: lis_mab@shsu.edu.

San Jose State University, Graduate Studies Program, School of Library and Information Science, San Jose, CA 95192-0001. Awards MLIS. One or more master's programs accredited by ALA. Part-time and evening/weekend programs available. Faculty: 6 full-time (3 women), 4 part-time (3 women). Students: 96 full-time (70 women), 157 part-time (119 women); includes 47 minority (10 African Americans, 25 Asian Americans, 10 Hispanics, 2 Native Americans), 5 international. Average age 36. 250 applicants, 82% accepted. In 1997, 173 degrees awarded. *Degree requirements:* Comprehensive exam required, thesis not required. *Entrance requirements:* Minimum GPA of 3.0. Application deadline: 6/1 (rolling processing). Application fee: $59. *Expenses:* Tuition $0 for state residents; $246 per unit for nonresidents. Fees $2017 per year full-time, $1351 per year part-time. *Financial aid:* In 1997–98, 4 fellowships (all to first-year students), 4 teaching assistantships (all to first-year students) were awarded; Federal Work-Study, institutionally sponsored loans, and career-related internships or fieldwork also available. Aid available to part-time students. Financial aid application deadline: 8/20. *Faculty research:* Evaluation of information services on-line, search strategy, organizational behavior. • Dr. Blanche Woolls, Director, 408-924-2491.

Simmons College, Graduate School of Library and Information Science, Boston, MA 02115. Awards MS, DA, MS Ed/MS, MS/MA. One or more master's programs accredited by ALA. MS Ed/MS offered jointly with the Department of Education; MS/MA offered jointly with the Program in Archives Management. Part-time and evening/weekend programs available. Faculty: 13 full-time, 9 part-time, 17 FTE. Students: 82 full-time (66 women), 392 part-time (320 women); includes 15 minority (7 African Americans, 5 Asian Americans, 3 Hispanics), 13 international. Average age 33. 287 applicants, 90% accepted. In 1997, 192 master's awarded. *Degree requirements:* For master's, technology competency required, foreign language and thesis not required. *Entrance requirements:* For master's, MAT or GRE General Test; for doctorate, interview. Application deadline: 7/1 (priority date; rolling processing; 11/1 for spring admission). Application fee: $25. *Expenses:* Tuition $587 per credit hour. Fees $20 per year. *Financial aid:* 176 students received aid; full and partial tuition waivers, Federal Work-Study, institutionally sponsored loans, and career-related internships or fieldwork available. Aid available to part-time students. Financial aid application deadline: 3/1; applicants required to submit FAFSA. *Faculty research:* Optical technology, visual communications, database management, information policy. • Dr. James Matarazzo, Dean, 617-521-2806. E-mail: jmatarazzo@simmons.edu. Application contact: Judith J. Beals, Director of Admissions, 617-521-2801. Fax: 617-521-3192. E-mail: jbeals@simmons.edu.

See in-depth description on page 1643.

Southern Connecticut State University, School of Communication, Information and Library Science, New Haven, CT 06515-1355. Awards MLS, MS, Diploma, JD/MLS, MLS/MA, MLS/MS. Programs in instructional technology (MS), library science (MLS), library/information studies (Diploma). One or more master's programs accredited by ALA. JD/MLS offered jointly with the University of Connecticut Law School. MLS/MA offered jointly with the Department of History. MLS/MS offered jointly with the Departments of Chemistry, English, and Foreign Languages. Students: 45 full-time (27 women), 184 part-time (145 women); includes 8 minority (5 African Americans, 2 Asian Americans, 1 Hispanic), 2 international. 311 applicants, 22% accepted. In 1997, 86 master's, 1 Diploma awarded. *Degree requirements:* For master's, computer language, thesis or alternative; for Diploma, thesis or alternative. *Entrance requirements:* For master's, GRE General Test (minimum combined score of 1000), interview, minimum QPA of 2.7; for Diploma, master's degree. Application deadline: 7/15 (priority date; rolling processing). Application fee: $40. *Expenses:* Tuition $2632 per year full-time, $188 per credit part-time for state residents; $7200 per year full-time, $188 per credit part-time for nonresidents. Fees $1806 per year full-time, $45 per semester part-time for state residents; $2703 per year full-time, $45 per semester part-time for nonresidents. *Financial aid:* Research assistantships available. • Dr. Nancy Disbrow, Chairperson, 203-392-5781.

See in-depth description on page 1645.

Spalding University, School of Education, Program in School Library and Information Centers, Louisville, KY 40203-2188. Offers school media librarianship (MAML). Part-time and evening/weekend programs available. Faculty: 2 full-time (both women), 3 part-time (2 women). Students: 1 (woman) full-time, 14 part-time (12 women); includes 3 minority (1 African American, 1 Hispanic, 1 Native American). Average age 32. 2 applicants, 100% accepted. *Degree requirements:* Comprehensive exams required, foreign language and thesis not required. *Entrance requirements:* GRE General Test, portfolio. Application deadline: 8/15 (priority date; rolling processing). Application fee: $30. *Expenses:* Tuition $350 per credit hour (minimum). Fees $48 per year full-time, $4 per credit hour part-time. *Financial aid:* In 1997–98, 12 students received aid, including 7 grants, scholarships totaling $9,210; research assistantships, Federal Work-Study, and career-related internships or fieldwork also available. Aid available to part-time students. Financial aid application deadline: 3/15; applicants required to submit FAFSA. • Director, 502-585-7123. Application contact: Jeanne Anderson, Assistant to the Provost and Director of Graduate Office, 502-585-7105. Fax: 502-585-7158. E-mail: gradoffc@spalding6.win.net.

State University of New York at Albany, Nelson A. Rockefeller College of Public Affairs and Policy, School of Information Science and Policy, Albany, NY 12222-0001. Awards MLS, CAS, MLS/MA. One or more master's programs accredited by ALA. Part-time and evening/weekend programs available. Faculty: 10 full-time (3 women), 1 part-time (0 women). Students: 104 full-time (67 women), 143 part-time (106 women); includes 5 minority (4 African Americans, 1 Asian American), 10 international. 115 applicants, 89% accepted. In 1997, 116 master's, 1 CAS awarded. *Application fee:* $50. *Expenses:* Tuition $5100 per year full-time, $213 per credit hour part-time for state residents; $8416 per year full-time, $351 per credit hour part-time for nonresidents. Fees $705 per year full-time, $26.85 per credit hour part-time. *Financial aid:* Fellowships, Federal Work-Study available. • Philip Eppard, Interim Dean, 518-442-5115. Application contact: Gerald Parker, Assistant Provost, 518-442-5200.

State University of New York at Buffalo, Graduate School, School of Information and Library Studies, Buffalo, NY 14260. Awards MLS, Certificate. One or more master's programs accredited by ALA. Part-time and evening/weekend programs available. Faculty: 8 full-time (5 women), 1 part-time (0 women). Students: 103 full-time (74 women), 135 part-time (110 women); includes 11 African Americans, 4 Asian Americans, 1 Hispanic, 5 international. Average age 34. 158 applicants, 67% accepted. In 1997, 105 master's awarded. *Degree requirements:* For master's, thesis optional, foreign language not required; for Certificate, thesis required, foreign language not required. *Entrance requirements:* For master's, minimum GPA of 3.0. Application deadline: 4/1 (priority date; 10/15 for spring admission). Application fee: $35. *Tuition:* $5970 per year full-time, $288 per credit hour part-time for state residents; $9286 per year full-time, $426 per credit hour part-time for nonresidents. *Financial aid:* In 1997–98, 2 fellowships (both to first-year students), 9 graduate assistantships (all to first-year students) were awarded; research assistantships, teaching assistantships, full and partial tuition waivers, Federal Work-Study, institutionally sponsored loans, and career-related internships or fieldwork also available. Aid available to part-time students. Financial aid application deadline: 3/1. *Faculty research:* Information user behavior, storage and information retrieval, digital libraries, information management services to information users. Total annual research expenditures: $13,500. • Dr. George S. Bobinski, Dean, 716-645-2412. Fax: 716-645-3775. E-mail: sils@acsu.buffalo.edu.

Syracuse University, School of Information Studies, Information and Library Science Program, Syracuse, NY 13244-0003. Awards MLS, CAS, JD/MLS. One or more master's programs accredited by ALA. Faculty: 29. Students: 36 full-time (31 women), 114 part-time (88 women); includes 3 minority (2 Asian Americans, 1 Native American), 11 international. 67 applicants, 96% accepted. In 1997, 32 master's awarded. *Degree requirements:* For master's, fieldwork or research paper required, foreign language and thesis not required. *Entrance requirements:* For master's, GRE General Test (minimum combined score of 1000); for CAS, MLS or related degree, 2 years of work experience. Application deadline: rolling. Application fee: $40. *Tuition:* $13,320 per year full-time, $555 per credit hour part-time. *Financial aid:* Application deadline 3/1. • Stewart Sutton, Director. Application contact: Barbara Settel, Assistant Dean, 315-443-2911.

See in-depth description on page 1647.

Texas Woman's University, School of Library and Information Studies, Denton, TX 76204. Awards MA, MLS, PhD. One or more master's programs accredited by ALA. Part-time and evening/weekend programs available. Faculty: 11 full-time (9 women), 8 part-time (all women). Students: 41 full-time (38 women), 240 part-time (227 women); includes 19 minority (11 African Americans, 4 Asian Americans, 3 Hispanics, 1 Native American), 3 international. Average age 40. 79 applicants, 94% accepted. In 1997, 58 master's, 4 doctorates awarded. *Degree requirements:* For master's, thesis; for doctorate, variable foreign language requirement, dissertation. *Average time to degree:* master's–1 year full-time; doctorate–3 years full-time. *Entrance requirements:* For master's, GRE General Test (minimum score 500 on verbal section, 400 on quantitative, 450 on analytical), minimum GPA of 3.0; for doctorate, GRE General Test (minimum combined score of 1000), minimum GPA of 3.0. Application fee: $25. *Financial aid:* In 1997–98, 43 students received aid, including 5 fellowships (1 to a first-year student), 16 teaching assistantships (4 to first-year students), 11 scholarships (5 to first-year students); research assistantships, Federal Work-Study, institutionally sponsored loans, and career-related internships or fieldwork also available. Aid available to part-time students. Financial aid application deadline: 4/1; applicants required to submit FAFSA. *Faculty research:* Information use studies, children's literature, cognitive aspects of information. • Dr. Keith Swigger, Dean, 940-898-2602. Fax: 940-898-2611. E-mail: slis@twu.edu.

See in-depth description on page 1649.

Directory: Library Science

Université de Montréal, Faculty of Arts and Sciences, School of Information and Library Science, Montréal, PQ H3C 3J7, Canada. Offers programs in information and library science (MBSI); information science (PhD), including information systems and resources, information transfer. One or more master's programs accredited by ALA. Faculty: 13 full-time (6 women). Students: 108 full-time (75 women), 8 part-time (6 women). 122 applicants, 59% accepted. In 1997, 53 master's awarded. *Degree requirements:* For master's, computer language required, thesis optional. *Entrance requirements:* For master's, master's degree in library and information science or equivalent, interview. Application deadline: 3/28. Application fee: $30. *Financial aid:* Fellowships available. • Gilles Deschatelets, Director, 514-343-7400. Application contact: Diane Mayar, Assistante á la gestion des dossiers des étudiants, 514-343-6044. Fax: 514-343-5753. E-mail: mayardi@ere.umontreal.ca.

The University of Alabama, College of Communication, School of Library and Information Studies, Tuscaloosa, AL 35487. Offers programs in book arts (MFA), library and information studies (MLIS, Ed S). Faculty: 11 full-time (6 women). Students: 52 full-time (33 women), 92 part-time (78 women); includes 21 minority (13 African Americans, 6 Asian Americans, 2 Native Americans), 7 international. Average age 28. 62 applicants, 92% accepted. In 1997, 81 master's, 3 Ed Ss awarded. *Entrance requirements:* For master's, GRE General Test (minimum combined score of 1500 on three sections) or MAT (minimum score 50), minimum GPA of 3.0. Application deadline: 2/15 (priority date; rolling processing; 11/1 for spring admission). Application fee: $25. Electronic applications accepted. *Tuition:* $2684 per year full-time, $594 per semester (minimum) part-time for state residents; $7216 per year full-time, $1248 per semester (minimum) part-time for nonresidents. *Financial aid:* In 1997–98, 67 students received aid, including 41 fellowships totaling $206,899, 9 research assistantships totaling $41,010, 17 teaching assistantships totaling $67,105; Federal Work-Study and career-related internships or fieldwork also available. Financial aid application deadline: 2/15. *Faculty research:* Instructional design, information equity, youth services, rural information services. • Dr. Joan Atkinson, Director, 205-348-1522. Fax: 205-348-3746. E-mail: jatkinso@slism.slis.ua.edu.

University of Alberta, Faculty of Graduate Studies and Research, School of Library and Information Studies, Edmonton, AB T6G 2E1, Canada. Awards MLIS. One or more master's programs accredited by ALA. Faculty: 6 full-time (4 women), 8 part-time (6 women). Students: 67 full-time (54 women), 26 part-time (22 women). 84 applicants, 56% accepted. In 1997, 29 degrees awarded. *Average time to degree:* master's–2 years full-time, 4 years part-time. *Entrance requirements:* GRE General Test (minimum combined score of 1725 on three sections, 600 on verbal, 525 on quantitative, 600 on analytical). Application deadline: 7/1 (rolling processing). Application fee: $60. *Expenses:* Tuition $390 per course for Canadian residents; $781 per course for nonresidents. Fees $500 per year full-time, $184 per year part-time. *Financial aid:* In 1997–98, 39 students received aid, including 5 tuition scholarships; career-related internships or fieldwork also available. Aid available to part-time students. Financial aid application deadline: 7/1. *Faculty research:* Intellectual freedom, materials for children and young adults, teacher-librarianship, cataloging. • Dr. Alvin Schrader, Director, 403-492-4578. Application contact: Susan Scullion, Student Admissions, 403-492-4578. Fax: 403-492-2430. E-mail: office@slis.ualberta.ca.

The University of Arizona, College of Social and Behavioral Sciences, School of Library Science, Tucson, AZ 85721. Awards MA, PhD. One or more master's programs accredited by ALA. Part-time programs available. *Degree requirements:* For master's, computer language, proficiency in disk operating system (DOS) required, foreign language and thesis not required; for doctorate, dissertation. *Entrance requirements:* For master's, GRE, TOEFL (minimum score 550), minimum GPA of 3.0; for doctorate, GRE General Test, TOEFL (minimum score 550). Application deadline: 2/1 (rolling processing). Application fee: $35. *Tuition:* $2162 per year full-time, $337 per semester (minimum) part-time for state residents; $6860 per year full-time, $1138 per semester (minimum) part-time for nonresidents. *Faculty research:* Microcomputer applications; quantitative methods systems; information transfer, planning, evaluation, and technology.

University of British Columbia, Faculties of Arts and Graduate Studies, School of Library, Archival and Information Studies, Vancouver, BC V6T 1Z2, Canada. Offers programs in archival studies (MAS, CAS), librarianship (MLIS), library and information studies (CAS). One or more master's programs accredited by ALA. Part-time programs available. Faculty: 9 full-time (5 women), 17 part-time (9 women). Students: 66 full-time (51 women), 21 part-time (15 women). Average age 30. 125 applicants, 38% accepted. In 1997, 56 master's awarded. *Degree requirements:* Thesis optional. *Average time to degree:* master's–2 years full-time. *Entrance requirements:* For master's, TOEFL (minimum score 600), interview; for CAS, TOEFL (minimum score 600). Application deadline: 2/1 (priority date). Application fee: $60. *Financial aid:* In 1997–98, 2 fellowships, 3 academic assistantships (1 to a first-year student) were awarded; Federal Work-Study and career-related internships or fieldwork also available. *Faculty research:* Computer systems/database design, library and archival management, archival description and organization, censorship and intellectual freedom, children's literature and youth services. • Dr. Ken Haycock, Director, 604-822-2404. E-mail: ken.haycock@ubc.ca. Application contact: Lynne Lighthall, Graduate Admissions, 604-822-2404. Fax: 604-822-6006. E-mail: admit@slais.ubc.ca.

University of California, Los Angeles, Graduate School of Education and Information Studies, Department of Library and Information Science, Los Angeles, CA 90095. Awards MLIS, PhD, Certificate, MBA/MLIS. Programs in archive and preservation management (MLIS), information access (MLIS), information organization (MLIS), information policy and management (MLIS), information systems (MLIS), library and information science (PhD, Certificate). One or more master's programs accredited by ALA. Part-time programs available. Faculty: 11 full-time (9 women), 13 part-time (9 women). Students: 121 full-time (84 women), 28 part-time (22 women); includes 29 minority (5 African Americans, 13 Asian Americans, 8 Hispanics, 3 Native Americans), 14 international. Average age 33. 164 applicants, 68% accepted. In 1997, 42 master's, 2 doctorates awarded. Terminal master's awarded for partial completion of doctoral program. *Degree requirements:* For master's, 1 foreign language, professional portfolio required, thesis not required; for doctorate, 1 foreign language, dissertation, oral and written qualifying exams, professional portfolio. *Average time to degree:* master's–2 years full-time, 3 years part-time. *Entrance requirements:* For master's, GRE General Test, TOEFL, TWE, previous course work in computer programming and statistics, proficiency in 1 foreign language; for doctorate, GRE General Test (minimum combined score of 1200), TOEFL, TWE, previous course work in computer programming and statistics, 2 samples of research writing in English. Application deadline: 12/15 (priority date; rolling processing). Application fee: $40. Electronic applications accepted. *Expenses:* Tuition $0 for state residents; $9384 per year for nonresidents. Fees $4551 per year. *Financial aid:* In 1997–98, 119 students received aid, including 23 fellowships totaling $116,471, research assistantships totaling $197,997, teaching assistantships totaling $20,122, federal fellowships and scholarships totaling $41,448; full and partial tuition waivers, Federal Work-Study, institutionally sponsored loans, and career-related internships or fieldwork also available. Aid available to part-time students. Financial aid application deadline: 3/1; applicants required to submit FAFSA. *Faculty research:* Multimedia, digital libraries, archives and electronic records, interface design, information technology and policy, preservation, access. • Dr. Michele V. Cloonan, Chair, 310-825-8799. Fax: 310-206-3076. E-mail: mcloonan@ucla.edu. Application contact: Susan S. Abler, Student Affairs Officer, 310-825-5269. Fax: 310-206-4460. E-mail: abler@gseis.ucla.edu.

University of Central Arkansas, College of Education, Department of Applied Academic Technologies, Program in Education Media and Library Science, Conway, AR 72035-0001. Awards MS. Students: 8 full-time (5 women), 58 part-time (52 women); includes 5 minority (all African Americans), 2 international. 24 applicants, 100% accepted. In 1997, 26 degrees awarded. *Degree requirements:* Comprehensive exam required, foreign language and thesis not required. *Entrance requirements:* GRE General Test, minimum GPA of 2.7. Application deadline: 3/1 (priority date; rolling processing; 10/1 for spring admission). Application fee: $15 ($40 for international students). *Expenses:* Tuition $161 per credit hour for state residents; $298 per credit hour for nonresidents. Fees $50 per year full-time, $30 per year part-time. • Dr. Selvin Royal, Interim Chair, Department of Applied Academic Technologies, 501-450-5463. Fax: 501-450-5680. E-mail: selvinr@mail.uca.edu.

University of Denver, University College, Denver, CO 80208. Offerings include library and information services (MLIS). *Average time to degree:* master's–1.5 years full-time, 2.7 years part-time. *Application deadline:* 8/10 (rolling processing; 2/22 for spring admission). *Application fee:* $25. *Expenses:* Tuition $245 per quarter hour for state residents; $310 per quarter hour for nonresidents. Fees $165 per quarter hour (minimum).

University of Hawaii at Manoa, School of Library and Information Studies, Honolulu, HI 96822. Awards MLIS, PhD, Certificate, JD/MLIS, MLIS/MA, MLIS/MS. Programs in advanced library and information studies (Certificate), communication and information science (PhD), library and information studies (MLIS). One or more master's programs accredited by ALA. Part-time programs available. *Degree requirements:* For master's, oral comprehensive exam required, thesis optional, foreign language not required. *Entrance requirements:* For master's, GRE General Test (minimum combined score of 1100), TOEFL (minimum score 600). Application deadline: 3/1 (rolling processing; 9/1 for spring admission). Application fee: $0. *Tuition:* $4029 per year full-time, $214 per credit hour part-time for state residents; $9957 per year full-time, $461 per credit hour part-time for nonresidents. *Faculty research:* Electronic information, retrieval telecommunications, information policy, information needs, database design.

University of Illinois at Urbana–Champaign, Graduate School of Library and Information Science, 501 East Daniel Street, Champaign, IL 61820-6212. Awards MS, PhD, CAS. One or more master's programs accredited by ALA. Faculty: 14 full-time (8 women), 6 part-time (4 women). Students: 234 full-time (158 women); includes 27 minority (10 African Americans, 12 Asian Americans, 5 Hispanics), 34 international. Average age 31. 292 applicants, 61% accepted. In 1997, 123 master's, 4 doctorates awarded. *Degree requirements:* For doctorate, dissertation; for CAS, project. *Entrance requirements:* For master's, GRE General Test, minimum GPA of 4.0 on a 5.0 scale. Application deadline: 6/1 (priority date; rolling processing; 10/1 for spring admission). Application fee: $40 ($50 for international students). *Financial aid:* In 1997–98, 10 fellowships, 140 research assistantships, 11 teaching assistantships were awarded; full and partial tuition waivers also available. Financial aid application deadline: 2/1. • Dr. Leigh S. Estabrook, Dean, 217-333-3280. Application contact: Curt McKay, Assistant Dean, 217-333-3280. Fax: 217-244-3302.

See in-depth description on page 1651.

The University of Iowa, College of Liberal Arts, School of Library and Information Science, Iowa City, IA 52242-1316. Awards MA, JD/MA, MBA/MA. One or more master's programs accredited by ALA. Faculty: 7 full-time, 1 part-time. Students: 53 full-time (40 women), 42 part-time (30 women); includes 2 minority (both Asian Americans), 5 international. 47 applicants, 53% accepted. In 1997, 42 degrees awarded. *Degree requirements:* Thesis optional. *Entrance requirements:* GRE General Test. Application fee: $30 ($50 for international students). *Expenses:* Tuition $3166 per year full-time, $176 per semester hour part-time for state residents; $10,202 per year full-time, $176 per semester hour part-time for nonresidents. Fees $202 per year full-time, $52 per year (minimum) part-time. *Financial aid:* In 1997–98, 12 research assistantships, 4 teaching assistantships were awarded; fellowships also available. Financial aid applicants required to submit FAFSA. • Padmini Srinivasan, Director, 319-335-5707.

University of Kentucky, College of Communications and Information Studies, Program in Library and Information Science, Lexington, KY 40506-0032. Offers library science (MA, MSLS). One or more master's programs accredited by ALA. Part-time programs available. Faculty: 6 full-time (2 women), 3 part-time (0 women). Students: 67 full-time (42 women), 131 part-time (108 women); includes 5 minority (2 African Americans, 1 Asian American, 2 Hispanics), 1 international. 135 applicants, 74% accepted. In 1997, 87 degrees awarded. *Degree requirements:* Variable foreign language requirement, comprehensive exam. *Entrance requirements:* GRE General Test (minimum combined score of 900), minimum undergraduate GPA of 2.75. Application deadline: 7/15 (rolling processing; 11/1 for spring admission). Application fee: $30 ($35 for international students). *Financial aid:* In 1997–98, 3 fellowships, 19 graduate assistantships were awarded; research assistantships, Federal Work-Study, and career-related internships or fieldwork also available. Financial aid application deadline: 4/1. *Faculty research:* Information retrieval systems, information-seeking behavior, organizational behavior, computer cataloging, library resource sharing. Total annual research expenditures: $24,000. • Dr. Timothy Sineath, Director of Graduate Studies, 606-257-8100. Application contact: Dr. Constance L. Wood, Associate Dean, 606-257-4613. Fax: 606-323-1928.

University of Maryland, College Park, College of Library and Information Services, College Park, MD 20742-5045. Awards MA, MLS, MS, PhD, MA/MLS. One or more master's programs accredited by ALA. Part-time and evening/weekend programs available. Faculty: 11 full-time (5 women), 14 part-time (6 women). Students: 95 full-time (72 women), 145 part-time (119 women); includes 20 minority (10 African Americans, 6 Asian Americans, 3 Hispanics, 1 Native American), 9 international. 214 applicants, 61% accepted. In 1997, 113 master's, 1 doctorate awarded. Terminal master's awarded for partial completion of doctoral program. *Degree requirements:* For doctorate, dissertation required, foreign language not required. *Entrance requirements:* For master's, GRE General Test, minimum GPA of 3.0; for doctorate, GRE General Test. Application deadline: 8/15 (rolling processing). Application fee: $50 ($70 for international students). *Expenses:* Tuition $272 per credit hour for state residents; $400 per credit hour for nonresidents. Fees $564 per year full-time, $342 per year part-time. *Financial aid:* In 1997–98, 8 fellowships, 20 teaching assistantships were awarded; research assistantships, full and partial tuition waivers, Federal Work-Study, and career-related internships or fieldwork also available. Financial aid application deadline: 2/1. • Dr. Ann E. Prentice, Dean, 301-405-2033. Fax: 301-314-9145. Application contact: John Mollish, Director, Graduate Admissions and Records, 301-405-4198. Fax: 301-314-9305.

See in-depth description on page 1653.

University of Maryland, College Park, College of Library and Information Services and Department of Geography, Program in Geography, Library, and Information Services, College Park, MD 20742-5045. Awards MA/MLS. Students: 3 full-time (1 woman), 1 part-time (0 women). 1 applicant, 0% accepted. *Application deadline:* 8/15 (rolling processing). *Application fee:* $50 ($70 for international students). *Expenses:* Tuition $272 per credit hour for state residents; $400 per credit hour for nonresidents. Fees $564 per year full-time, $342 per year part-time. *Financial aid:* Fellowships, research assistantships, teaching assistantships available. Financial aid application deadline: 2/1. • Dr. Diane Barlow, Contact Person, 301-405-2038. Application contact: John Mollish, Director, Graduate Admissions and Records, 301-405-4198. Fax: 301-314-9305.

See in-depth description on page 1653.

University of Maryland, College Park, College of Library and Information Services and Department of History, Program in History, Library, and Information Services, College Park, MD 20742-5045. Awards MA/MLS. Students: 10 full-time (5 women), 3 part-time (2 women). 18 applicants, 44% accepted. *Application deadline:* 8/15 (rolling processing). *Application fee:* $50 ($70 for international students). *Expenses:* Tuition $272 per credit hour for state residents; $400 per credit hour for nonresidents. Fees $564 per year full-time, $342 per year part-time. *Financial aid:* In 1997–98, 2 fellowships were awarded; teaching assistantships also available. • Dr. Diane Barlow, Director, 301-405-2038. Fax: 301-314-9145. Application contact: John Mollish, Director, Graduate Admissions and Records, 301-405-4198. Fax: 301-314-9305.

See in-depth description on page 1653.

University of Michigan, School of Information, Ann Arbor, MI 48109. Offers programs in archives and records management (MS); human-computer interaction (MS); information (PhD); information economics, management and policy (MS); library and information services (MS). One or more master's programs accredited by ALA. Part-time programs available. *Degree requirements:* For master's, variable foreign language requirement, thesis not required; for

Directory: Library Science

University of Michigan (continued)

doctorate, 1 foreign language, dissertation, oral defense of dissertation, preliminary exam. *Entrance requirements:* GRE General Test. Application fee: $55. *Financial aid:* Fellowships, research assistantships, teaching assistantships, Federal Work-Study, and career-related internships or fieldwork available. Aid available to part-time students. • Dr. Daniel E. Atkins III, Dean, 734-763-2285. Application contact: Departmental Office, 734-763-2285. Fax: 734-764-2475. E-mail: si.admissions@umich.edu.

See in-depth description on page 1655.

University of Missouri–Columbia, College of Education, School of Information Science and Learning Technologies, Columbia, MO 65211. Offers program in library science (MA). One or more master's programs accredited by ALA. Part-time and evening/weekend programs available. Faculty: 9 full-time (3 women), 1 (woman) part-time. Students: 58 full-time (37 women), 71 part-time (54 women); includes 9 minority (all African Americans), 2 international. In 1997, 66 degrees awarded. *Entrance requirements:* GRE or MAT, minimum GPA of 3.0. Application deadline: 7/1 (priority date; rolling processing). Application fee: $25 ($50 for international students). *Expenses:* Tuition $3240 per year full-time, $180 per credit hour part-time for state residents; $9108 per year full-time, $506 per credit hour part-time for nonresidents. Fees $55 per year full-time. *Financial aid:* Fellowships, teaching assistantships, Federal Work-Study available. Aid available to part-time students. • Dr. John Wedman, Director of Graduate Studies, 573-882-3828.

The University of North Carolina at Chapel Hill, School of Information and Library Science, Chapel Hill, NC 27599. Awards MSIS, MSLS, PhD, CAS. One or more master's programs accredited by ALA. Part-time programs available. Faculty: 15 full-time (8 women), 23 part-time (13 women). Students: 166 full-time (117 women), 70 part-time (36 women); includes 18 minority (9 African Americans, 4 Asian Americans, 4 Hispanics, 1 Native American), 23 international. Average age 31. 213 applicants, 70% accepted. In 1997, 97 master's awarded; 1 doctorate awarded (100% entered university research/teaching); 4 CASs awarded. *Degree requirements:* For master's, paper, project required, foreign language and thesis not required; for doctorate, dissertation required, foreign language not required. *Entrance requirements:* For master's and doctorate, GRE General Test. Application deadline: 1/1 (priority date; rolling processing; 10/1 for spring admission). Application fee: $55. Electronic applications accepted. *Expenses:* Tuition $1428 per year full-time, $357 per semester (minimum) part-time for state residents; $10,414 per year full-time, $2604 per semester (minimum) part-time for nonresidents. Fees $782 per year full-time, $332 per semester (minimum) part-time. *Financial aid:* In 1997–98, 23 fellowships (16 to first-year students) totaling $76,000, 4 teaching assistantships averaging $1,000 per month and totaling $16,000, 58 assistantships (42 to first-year students) totaling $424,000 were awarded; research assistantships, Federal Work-Study, institutionally sponsored loans, and career-related internships or fieldwork also available. Financial aid application deadline: 1/1; applicants required to submit FAFSA. *Faculty research:* Information retrieval, digital libraries, multimedia networking, management of information resources, special librarianship. • Dr. Barbara B. Moran, Dean, 919-962-8366. E-mail: info@ils.unc.edu. Application contact: Betty Kompst, Student Services Manager, 919-962-8366. Fax: 919-962-8071. E-mail: info@ils.unc.edu.

University of North Carolina at Greensboro, School of Education, Department of Library and Information Studies, Greensboro, NC 27412-0001. Awards MLIS. One or more master's programs accredited by ALA. Part-time programs available. Faculty: 6 full-time (4 women), 12 part-time (6 women), 10 FTE. Students: 35 full-time (28 women), 152 part-time (130 women). Average age 30. 30 applicants, 83% accepted. In 1997, 77 degrees awarded. *Degree requirements:* Thesis, comprehensive exam required, foreign language not required. *Average time to degree:* master's–1.5 years full-time, 3.5 years part-time. *Entrance requirements:* GRE General Test (minimum combined score of 1000), TOEFL (minimum score 550). Application deadline: 7/1 (priority date; rolling processing; 11/1 for spring admission). Application fee: $35. *Expenses:* Tuition $1842 per year full-time, $370 per semester (minimum) part-time for state residents; $10,296 per year full-time, $2484 per semester (minimum) part-time for nonresidents. Fees $806 per year full-time, $111 per semester (minimum) part-time. *Financial aid:* Fellowships, research assistantships, teaching assistantships, graduate assistantships, institutionally sponsored loans, and career-related internships or fieldwork available. Financial aid application deadline: 3/1. *Faculty research:* School library expenditures, summer reading programs, human relations and public libraries, library history, gender studies. • Keith C. Wright, Chair, 334-334-3477. Fax: 334-334-5060.

University of North Texas, School of Library and Information Sciences, Denton, TX 76203-6737. Offers programs in information science (MS, PhD), library science (MS). One or more master's programs accredited by ALA. Part-time and evening/weekend programs available. Faculty: 13 full-time (7 women), 9 part-time (5 women). Students: 45 full-time (33 women), 157 part-time (129 women); includes 21 minority (7 African Americans, 5 Asian Americans, 9 Hispanics), 4 international. Average age 37. In 1997, 111 master's, 3 doctorates awarded. *Degree requirements:* For master's, computer language, comprehensive exam required, thesis not required; for doctorate, 1 foreign language, computer language, dissertation, comprehensive exam. *Entrance requirements:* For master's, GRE General Test (minimum score 400 on each section, 1000 combined); for doctorate, GRE General Test (minimum combined score of 1100). Application deadline: 7/17 (rolling processing; 11/30 for spring admission). Application fee: $25 ($50 for international students). *Tuition:* $2063 per year full-time, $815 per year part-time for state residents; $5897 per year full-time, $2100 per year part-time for nonresidents. *Financial aid:* In 1997–98, fellowships averaging $671 per month and totaling $185,200, research assistantships averaging $547 per month and totaling $2,756, teaching assistantships averaging $400 per month and totaling $27,440, library assistantships averaging $520 per month and totaling $50,000 were awarded; Federal Work-Study, institutionally sponsored loans, and career-related internships or fieldwork also available. Financial aid application deadline: 4/1. *Faculty research:* Information resources and services, information management and retrieval, computer-based information systems. • Dr. Philip M. Turner, Dean, 940-565-2445.

University of Oklahoma, College of Arts and Sciences, School of Library and Information Studies, Norman, OK 73019-0390. Awards MALIS, MLIS, Certificate, MBA/MLIS, M Ed/MLIS. One or more master's programs accredited by ALA. Part-time and evening/weekend programs available. Faculty: 10 full-time (7 women), 2 part-time (0 women). Students: 28 full-time (25 women), 51 part-time (42 women); includes 12 minority (5 African Americans, 7 Native Americans), 1 international. Average age 37. 121 applicants, 65% accepted. In 1997, 52 master's awarded. *Degree requirements:* For master's, comprehensive exam (MLIS), thesis (MALIS) required, foreign language not required. *Entrance requirements:* For master's, GRE, TOEFL (minimum score 550), minimum GPA of 3.2 in last 60 hours or 3.0 overall. Application deadline: rolling. Application fee: $25. *Expenses:* Tuition $1920 per year full-time, $80 per credit hour part-time for state residents; $6108 per year full-time, $255 per credit hour part-time for nonresidents. Fees $468 per year full-time, $12 per semester (minimum) part-time. *Financial aid:* In 1997–98, 1 research assistantship, 6 teaching assistantships were awarded; fellowships, partial tuition waivers, Federal Work-Study, and career-related internships or fieldwork also available. Aid available to part-time students. *Faculty research:* Management, library history, library science education, school media center administration, bibliometrics. • June Lester, Director, 405-325-3921.

University of Pittsburgh, School of Information Sciences, Department of Library and Information Science, Pittsburgh, PA 15260. Awards MLIS, PhD, Certificate. One or more master's programs accredited by ALA. Part-time programs available. Faculty: 13 full-time (10 women), 2 part-time (both women). Students: 119 full-time (83 women), 123 part-time (100 women); includes 20 minority (16 African Americans, 3 Asian Americans, 1 Native American), 22 international. 187 applicants, 93% accepted. In 1997, 71 master's, 5 doctorates awarded. *Degree requirements:* For master's, thesis optional, foreign language not required; for doctorate, variable foreign language requirement, dissertation. *Average time to degree:* master's–1 year full-time, 2 years part-time; doctorate–3 years full-time, 6 years part-time. *Entrance requirements:* For master's and doctorate, GRE General Test, minimum QPA of 3.0. Application deadline: 7/31 (priority date; rolling processing; 11/30 for spring admission). Application fee: $30 ($40 for international students). *Expenses:* Tuition $8432 per year full-time, $348 per credit part-time for state residents; $17,360 per year full-time, $720 per credit part-time for nonresidents. Fees $480 per year full-time, $180 per year part-time. *Financial aid:* In 1997–98, 48 students received aid, including 3 fellowships (1 to a first-year student) averaging $1,001 per month, 5 research assistantships (1 to a first-year student) averaging $654 per month, 5 teaching assistantships (1 to a first-year student) averaging $937 per month, 35 assistantships, scholarships (27 to first-year students) averaging $422 per month; full and partial tuition waivers, Federal Work-Study, institutionally sponsored loans, and career-related internships or fieldwork also available. Aid available to part-time students. Financial aid application deadline: 2/15; applicants required to submit FAFSA. *Faculty research:* Archives, electronic records and preservation, children's resources and services, medical informatics, management. • Dr. Edie Rasmussen, Chair, 412-624-9435. Fax: 412-648-7001. E-mail: erasmus@sis.pitt.edu. Application contact: Ninette Kay, Admissions Coordinator, 412-624-5146. Fax: 412-624-5231. E-mail: nk@sis.pitt.edu.

See in-depth description on page 1657.

University of Puerto Rico, Río Piedras, Graduate School of Librarianship, San Juan, PR 00931. Awards M Bibl. Part-time and evening/weekend programs available. *Degree requirements:* Thesis, comprehensive exam required, foreign language not required. *Entrance requirements:* PAEG, interview, minimum GPA of 3.0. Application deadline: 2/21. Application fee: $17. *Faculty research:* Convertibility of OCLC.

University of Rhode Island, Graduate Library School, Kingston, RI 02881. Awards MLIS. One or more master's programs accredited by ALA. *Application deadline:* 4/15 (priority date; rolling processing). *Application fee:* $35. *Expenses:* Tuition $3446 per year full-time, $191 per credit part-time for state residents; $9850 per year full-time, $547 per credit part-time for nonresidents. Fees $1276 per year full-time, $135 per semester (minimum) part-time.

University of South Carolina, Graduate School, College of Library and Information Science, Columbia, SC 29208. Awards MLIS, Certificate, Specialist, MLIS/MA. One or more master's programs accredited by ALA. Part-time programs available. Postbaccalaureate distance learning degree programs offered. Faculty: 13 full-time (7 women), 7 part-time (all women), 16.5 FTE. Students: 110 full-time (89 women), 230 part-time (201 women); includes 34 minority (25 African Americans, 6 Asian Americans, 1 Hispanic, 2 Native Americans), 8 international. Average age 35. 95 applicants, 91% accepted. In 1997, 233 master's, 4 other advanced degrees awarded. *Entrance requirements:* For master's, GRE General Test (minimum combined score of 950) or MAT (minimum score 50), TOEFL (minimum score 550). Application deadline: 5/1 (priority date; rolling processing; 10/1 for spring admission). Application fee: $35. Electronic applications accepted. *Expenses:* Tuition $3894 per year full-time, $193 per credit hour part-time for state residents; $8114 per year full-time, $404 per credit hour part-time for nonresidents. Fees $125 per year full-time, $37 per semester (minimum) part-time. *Financial aid:* In 1997–98, 11 fellowships (3 to first-year students) totaling $79,750, 30 research assistantships (14 to first-year students) totaling $66,990 were awarded; career-related internships or fieldwork also available. Aid available to part-time students. *Faculty research:* Information technology management, distance education, library services for children and young adults, special libraries. • Dr. Fred W. Roper, Dean, 803-777-3858. Application contact: Nancy Beitz, Admissions Coordinator, 803-777-3887. Fax: 803-777-0457. E-mail: n.beitz@sc.edu.

University of Southern Mississippi, College of Liberal Arts, School of Library Science, Hattiesburg, MS 39406-5167. Awards MLS, SLS. One or more master's programs accredited by ALA. Part-time and evening/weekend programs available. Faculty: 6 full-time (4 women). Students: 46 full-time (32 women), 37 part-time (32 women); includes 8 minority (4 African Americans, 3 Asian Americans, 1 Hispanic), 2 international. Average age 36. 65 applicants, 82% accepted. In 1997, 45 master's awarded. *Degree requirements:* For master's, thesis or alternative, research project required, foreign language not required. *Entrance requirements:* For master's, GRE General Test, minimum GPA of 3.0. Application deadline: 8/9 (priority date; rolling processing). Application fee: $0 ($25 for international students). *Tuition:* $2870 per year full-time, $137 per credit hour part-time for state residents; $5972 per year full-time, $172 per credit hour part-time for nonresidents. *Financial aid:* Fellowships, research assistantships, assistantships, scholarships, full and partial tuition waivers, Federal Work-Study, institutionally sponsored loans, and career-related internships or fieldwork available. Financial aid application deadline: 3/15. *Faculty research:* Printing, library history, children's literature, telecommunications, management. • Joy Greiner, Director, 601-266-4228.

University of South Florida, College of Arts and Sciences, School of Library and Information Science, Tampa, FL 33620-9951. Offers programs in library and information sciences (MA), school library media (MA). One or more master's programs accredited by ALA. Part-time and evening/weekend programs available. Postbaccalaureate distance learning degree programs offered (minimal on-campus study). Faculty: 6 full-time (5 women). Students: 55 full-time (37 women), 191 part-time (160 women); includes 25 minority (7 African Americans, 2 Asian Americans, 16 Hispanics), 2 international. Average age 38. 108 applicants, 91% accepted. In 1997, 139 degrees awarded. *Entrance requirements:* GRE General Test (minimum combined score of 1000), minimum GPA of 3.0 in last 60 hours. Application deadline: 6/1 (10/15 for spring admission). Application fee: $20. Electronic applications accepted. *Tuition:* $142 per credit hour for state residents; $486 per credit hour for nonresidents. *Financial aid:* In 1997–98, 86 students received aid, including 2 fellowships averaging $720 per month and totaling $13,300, 10 research assistantships averaging $366 per month and totaling $33,000, 2 teaching assistantships averaging $300 per month and totaling $5,400; Federal Work-Study, institutionally sponsored loans, and career-related internships or fieldwork also available. Aid available to part-time students. Financial aid applicants required to submit FAFSA. • Kathleen de la Pena McCook, Director, 813-974-3520. E-mail: kmccook@chuma.cas.usf.edu. Application contact: Sonia Ramirez Wohlmuth, Assistant Director, 813-974-6837. Fax: 813-974-6840. E-mail: swohlmut@chuma.cas.usf.edu.

University of Tennessee, Knoxville, School of Information Sciences, Knoxville, TN 37996. Awards MS. One or more master's programs accredited by ALA. Part-time programs available. Postbaccalaureate distance learning degree programs offered (no on-campus study). Faculty: 11 full-time (6 women), 1 part-time (0 women). Students: 54 full-time (42 women), 138 part-time (110 women); includes 5 minority (4 African Americans, 1 Asian American), 9 international. 60 applicants, 53% accepted. In 1997, 52 degrees awarded. *Degree requirements:* Thesis or alternative required, foreign language not required. *Entrance requirements:* GRE General Test, TOEFL (minimum score 550), minimum GPA of 2.7. Application deadline: 2/1 (priority date; rolling processing). Application fee: $35. Electronic applications accepted. *Tuition:* $3354 per year full-time, $181 per semester hour part-time for state residents; $8410 per year full-time, $462 per semester hour part-time for nonresidents. *Financial aid:* In 1997–98, 12 teaching assistantships were awarded; fellowships, research assistantships, graduate assistantships, Federal Work-Study, institutionally sponsored loans also available. Financial aid application deadline: 2/1. • Dr. C. W. Minkel, Acting Head, 423-974-2148. Fax: 423-974-4967. E-mail: cminkel@utk.edu.

See in-depth description on page 1659.

The University of Texas at Austin, Graduate School, Graduate School of Library and Information Science, Austin, TX 78712. Awards MLIS, PhD. One or more master's programs accredited by ALA. Part-time programs available. Faculty: 14 full-time, 14 part-time. Students: 405 (313 women); includes 47 minority (4 African Americans, 5 Asian Americans, 37 Hispanics, 1 Native American), 24 international. 239 applicants, 54% accepted. In 1997, 165 master's, 2 doctorates awarded. *Degree requirements:* For doctorate, 2 foreign languages (computer language can substitute for one), dissertation. *Entrance requirements:* For master's, GRE General Test (minimum combined score of 1050); for doctorate, GRE General Test. Application deadline: 3/1 (priority date; rolling processing; 10/1 for spring admission). Application fee: $50 ($75 for international students). Electronic applications accepted. *Expenses:* Tuition $2592 per year full-time, $324 per semester (minimum) part-time for state residents; $7704 per year full-time, $963 per semester (minimum) part-time for nonresidents. Fees $778 per year full-time, $161 per semester (minimum) part-time. *Financial aid:* Fellowships, research assistantships, teaching assistantships, partial tuition waivers, Federal Work-Study, and career-related internships or fieldwork available. Aid available to part-time students. Financial aid application deadline: 2/1. *Faculty research:* Information retrieval and artificial intelligence, library history and administration, classification and cataloguing. • Glynn Harmon, Interim Dean, 512-471-3828. Application contact: Dr. Ronald E. Wyllys, Graduate Adviser, 512-471-3969.

University of Toronto, School of Graduate Studies, Social Sciences Division, Faculty of Information Studies, Toronto, ON M5S 1A1, Canada. Awards MIS, MI St, MLS, PhD. One or more master's programs accredited by ALA. MIS and MLS being phased out; applicants no longer accepted. Part-time programs available. Faculty: 27. Students: 149 full-time (108 women), 123 part-time (81 women); includes 9 international. 307 applicants, 60% accepted. In 1997, 98 master's, 4 doctorates awarded. *Degree requirements:* For doctorate, dissertation. *Application fee:* $75. *Expenses:* Tuition $4070 per year for Canadian residents; $7870 per year for nonresidents. Fees $628 per year. • L. C. Howarth, Dean, 416-978-3202. Application contact: Secretary, 416-978-7121. Fax: 416-978-5762. E-mail: dodd@fis.utoronto.ca.

University of Washington, Graduate School of Library and Information Science, Seattle, WA 98195. Awards MLIS. One or more master's programs accredited by ALA. Part-time and evening/weekend programs available. Faculty: 11 full-time (5 women), 2 part-time (both women). Students: 158 full-time (129 women), 46 part-time (39 women); includes 21 minority (7 African Americans, 9 Asian Americans, 3 Hispanics, 2 Native Americans), 3 international. Average age 32. 243 applicants, 76% accepted. In 1997, 79 degrees awarded. *Degree requirements:* Thesis optional, foreign language not required. *Average time to degree:* master's–2 years full-time. *Entrance requirements:* GRE General Test, TOEFL, minimum GPA of 3.0. Application deadline: 3/15 (rolling processing; 2/1 for spring admission). Application fee: $45. *Tuition:* $5433 per year full-time, $775 per quarter (minimum) part-time for state residents; $13,479 per year full-time, $1925 per quarter (minimum) part-time for nonresidents. *Financial aid:* In 1997–98, 24 students received aid, including 21 fellowships (13 to first-year students) totaling $750,162, 1 research assistantship totaling $14,475, 1 staff assistantship totaling $9,054; Federal Work-Study, institutionally sponsored loans, and career-related internships or fieldwork also available. Financial aid application deadline: 2/28; applicants required to submit FAFSA. *Faculty research:* Relational database design, extracting knowledge for intermediary expert systems, children's services in public libraries. • Betty G. Bengtson, Acting Director, 206-543-1794. E-mail: bbengt@u.washington.edu. Application contact: Dolores Potter, Program Coordinator, 206-543-1794. Fax: 206-616-3152. E-mail: dpotter@u.washington.edu.

The University of Western Ontario, Social Sciences Division, Faculty of Information and Media Studies, Programs in Library and Information Science, London, ON N6G 1H1, Canada. Awards MLIS, PhD. One or more master's programs accredited by ALA. Program conducted on a trimester basis; admission deadlines: April 1st, October 1st, and February 15th. Part-time and evening/weekend programs available. Faculty: 16 full-time (8 women), 15 part-time (9 women). Students: 134 full-time (86 women), 65 part-time (42 women). In 1997, 109 master's, 3 doctorates awarded. *Degree requirements:* For doctorate, dissertation, comprehensive exam required, foreign language not required. *Average time to degree:* master's–1 year full-time, 8 years part-time; doctorate–5 years full-time. *Entrance requirements:* For master's, TOEFL (minimum score 580), honors degree, minimum B average during previous 2 years; for doctorate, GRE General Test, TOEFL (minimum score 600), MLIS or equivalent, minimum A average. Application fee: $50. *Financial aid:* Research assistantships, teaching assistantships, institutionally sponsored loans, and career-related internships or fieldwork available. *Faculty research:* Information needs and uses, information systems, information policy. • Application contact: C. Morrison, Student Services Graduate Assistant, 519-679-2111 Ext. 8484. Fax: 519-661-3506. E-mail: morrison@julian.uwo.ca.

See in-depth description on page 1661.

University of Wisconsin–Madison, College of Letters and Science, School of Library and Information Studies, Madison, WI 53706-1380. Awards MA, PhD, Certificate. One or more master's programs accredited by ALA. Part-time programs available. Faculty: 8 full-time (4 women), 16 part-time (10 women), 12 FTE. Students: 136 full-time (109 women), 73 part-time (56 women); includes 12 minority (3 African Americans, 6 Asian Americans, 1 Hispanic, 2 Native Americans), 9 international. 168 applicants, 60% accepted. In 1997, 65 master's, 2 doctorates, 1 Certificate awarded. *Degree requirements:* For doctorate, dissertation. *Application deadline:* 1/15. *Application fee:* $45. *Tuition:* $4928 per year full-time, $926 per semester (minimum) part-time for state residents; $15,190 per year full-time, $2849 per semester (minimum) part-time for nonresidents. *Financial aid:* In 1997–98, 26 students received aid, including 2 teaching assistantships averaging $753 per month and totaling $13,554, 3 project assistantships averaging $849 per month and totaling $30,564; Federal Work-Study and career-related internships or fieldwork also available. *Faculty research:* Intellectual freedom, children's literature, print culture history, information systems design and evaluation, school library media centers. • Louise S. Robbins, Director, 608-263-2908. E-mail: lrobbins@macc.wisc.edu. Application contact: Barbara Arnold, Admissions and Placement Adviser, 608-263-2909. Fax: 608-263-4849. E-mail: bjarnold@facstaff.wisc.edu.

University of Wisconsin–Milwaukee, School of Library and Information Science, Milwaukee, WI 53201-0413. Awards MLIS, CAS, MLIS/MA, MLIS/MM, MLIS/MS. One or more master's programs accredited by ALA. Part-time programs available. Faculty: 9 full-time (3 women). Students: 63 full-time (46 women), 160 part-time (131 women); includes 9 minority (5 African Americans, 1 Asian American, 3 Hispanics), 15 international. 116 applicants, 60% accepted. In 1997, 94 master's awarded. *Entrance requirements:* For master's, GRE General Test or MAT. Application deadline: 1/1 (priority date; rolling processing; 9/1 for spring admission). Application fee: $45 ($75 for international students). *Tuition:* $4996 per year full-time, $1030 per semester (minimum) part-time for state residents; $15,216 per year full-time, $2947 per semester (minimum) part-time for nonresidents. *Financial aid:* In 1997–98, 4 fellowships, 2 teaching assistantships, 1 project assistantship were awarded; research assistantships, Federal Work-Study, and career-related internships or fieldwork also available. Aid available to part-time students. Financial aid application deadline: 4/15. • Dr. Mohammed Aman, Dean, 414-229-4709. Application contact: Wilfred Fong, Assistant Dean, 414-229-5421.

Wayne State University, Library and Information Science Program, Detroit, MI 48202. Offers archives administration (Certificate), library and information science (MLIS, Spec). One or more master's programs accredited by ALA. Part-time and evening/weekend programs available. Faculty: 42. Students: 84 full-time (62 women), 366 part-time (310 women); includes 38 minority (29 African Americans, 4 Asian Americans, 4 Hispanics, 1 Native American). 154 applicants, 80% accepted. In 1997, 146 master's, 10 other advanced degrees awarded. *Application deadline:* 7/1 (rolling processing). *Application fee:* $20 ($30 for international students). *Expenses:* Tuition $163 per credit hour for state residents; $355 per credit hour for nonresidents. Fees $498 per year full-time, $114 per semester (minimum) part-time. *Financial aid:* In 1997–98, 4 research assistantships, 15 scholarships were awarded; Federal Work-Study, institutionally sponsored loans, and career-related internships or fieldwork also available. Aid available to part-time students. Financial aid application deadline: 5/15. *Faculty research:* Management, infometrics, imaging processes, library history, bibliographic control. • Dr. Robert P. Holley, Director, 313-577-1825.

Western Maryland College, Department of Education, Program in Media/Library Science, Westminster, MD 21157-4390. Awards MS. Part-time and evening/weekend programs available. Faculty: 1 (woman) full-time, 3 part-time (all women). Students: 10 full-time (8 women), 145 part-time (141 women). In 1997, 13 degrees awarded. *Degree requirements:* Thesis optional, foreign language not required. *Entrance requirements:* GRE General Test, MAT, or NTE. Application deadline: rolling. Application fee: $35. *Expenses:* Tuition $210 per credit hour. Fees $30 per semester. *Financial aid:* Career-related internships or fieldwork available. Financial aid application deadline: 3/1. • Dr. Ramona Kerby, Coordinator, 410-857-2500. Application contact: Jeanette Witt, Coordinator of Graduate Records, 410-857-2513. Fax: 410-857-2515. E-mail: jwitt@wmdc.edu.

THE CATHOLIC UNIVERSITY OF AMERICA

School of Library and Information Science

Programs of Study

The School of Library and Information Science offers a master's degree program that prepares graduates to provide high-quality services and to assume leadership roles in a variety of libraries, archives, and other information agencies. The program is accredited by the American Library Association. A post-master's certificate in library and information science is also offered.

The M.S.L.S. degree normally requires 36 semester credit hours and may be completed on a full- or part-time basis. The student is required to take four core courses. The remainder of the program may be tailored to the student's career goals or to an area of specialization. These areas include archives and records management, music librarianship, special collections, legal information systems, design of information storage and retrieval systems, information resources management, book arts, school library media services, children's and young adult services, and biomedical information. Students who have the M.S.L.S. degree may earn a post-master's certificate in one of several specializations by taking 24 graduate semester credit hours.

Several joint-degree programs are available and include the M.S.L.S./M.S., jointly administered with the Department of Biology, and the M.S.L.S./M.A., jointly administered with the Departments of English, Greek and Latin, and History and the Schools of Music and Religious Studies. The joint-degree programs all permit a student to earn two degrees concurrently with fewer credit hours than each would require alone.

An evening and weekend program is offered at various sites in Virginia, including Norfolk, Richmond, and Fairfax, and is available only to Virginia residents. Selected courses are offered at the Library of Congress for Library of Congress employees.

Research Facilities

The Information Technology Laboratory provides hands-on experience in such library applications as OCLC, online searching of major databases incorporating CD-ROM technology, multiple microcomputer applications, Internet access, and database construction. The School maintains an audiovisual laboratory with materials for work in various media.

The Library and Information Science Library, containing 13,000 volumes, is a branch of the University library and is located in the same building as the School. Other library branches are music, engineering/architecture, humanities, nursing, chemistry, physics, and theology/philosophy. The Law Library and Oliveira Lima Collection of rare books are also located on campus. Altogether, the system's holdings contain more than 1.2 million volumes. Through the Washington Research Library Consortium, students have access to the libraries of other institutions.

In addition, federal facilities such as the Library of Congress, the National Library of Medicine, the National Agricultural Library, and the Smithsonian Institution libraries are available to students as both research resources and practicum sites.

Financial Aid

The University awards half tuition and full tuition graduate scholarships each year on a competitive basis. In addition, the School offers a number of other scholarships to full-time students. Positions as Graduate Library Preprofessionals are available; these provide full-time salaried employment within the University library system, employee benefits, and tuition for two courses each semester. The School also provides students with up-to-date information about local part-time and full-time jobs.

Cost of Study

Tuition for the 1998–99 academic year is $663 per semester credit hour for part-time students and $8663 per semester for full-time students. Off-campus part-time courses are $459 per semester credit hour. Summer session tuition is $505 per semester credit hour in 1999.

Living and Housing Costs

Information about off-campus housing may be obtained from the Dean of Students, University Center East. Housing costs vary widely but are comparable to those in other large urban areas. Campus housing is available for graduate students.

Student Group

About 290 full- and part-time students with a variety of arts and sciences backgrounds attend the School in a typical semester. More than 30 percent have earned at least one graduate degree. The average age is 34. Many part-time students work in local libraries and information centers in the Greater Washington metropolitan area.

Location

The Catholic University of America (CUA) is located in a residential area 3 miles directly north of the Capitol, in northeast Washington, D.C. An important part of library and information science education at CUA is access to the rich information and cultural resources of the Washington area. A trip downtown by subway from the Brookland/CUA Metro rapid transit station takes less than 15 minutes.

The University

The Catholic University of America was established in 1887 in the District of Columbia as a national Catholic graduate institution. Undergraduate programs were subsequently added. Currently, there are 5,850 students at the University, of whom 3,600 are graduate students. The 187-acre campus contains many turn-of-the-century buildings of historic interest and is undergoing a planned development that will provide additional academic buildings, housing, and parking. The University recently inaugurated expanded sports and recreational facilities for students.

Applying

Students may enter the program in the fall, spring, or either of two summer sessions. Transcripts, GRE General Test scores, letters of recommendation, and application forms, including a personal statement, are usually required; the GRE is not required if the applicant has earned a graduate degree in another area. To be considered for merit scholarships, students must be accepted by February 1 for entry in the subsequent fall semester and must submit GRE scores. Decisions on admission to academic programs and the awarding of fellowships, scholarships, and other aid at the University are made without regard to the student's sex, race, religious belief, ethnic origin, age, or physical handicap.

Correspondence and Information

Dr. Jean L. Preer, Associate Dean
School of Library and Information Science
The Catholic University of America
Washington, D.C. 20064
Telephone: 202-319-5085

The Catholic University of America

THE FACULTY

In addition to 8 full-time faculty members, the department has more than 30 adjunct faculty members who are distinguished practitioners from the Washington, D.C., area and offer elective courses in their areas of special knowledge.

The campus Metro stop provides convenient access.

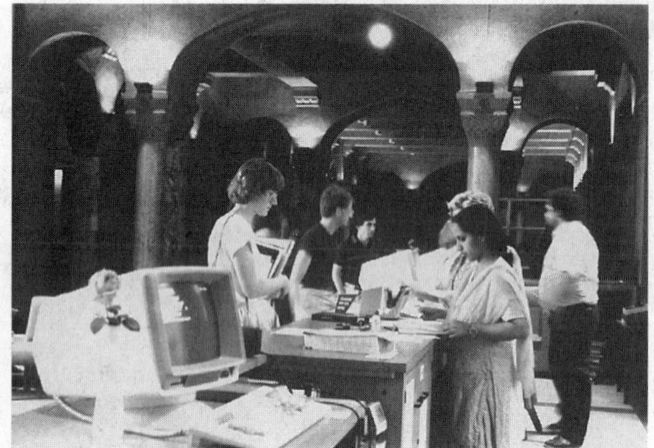

Catholic University library.

Graduate students at the School of Library and Information Science.

DOMINICAN UNIVERSITY

Graduate School of Library and Information Science

Programs of Study

The principal program of the Graduate School of Library and Information Science leads to the Master of Library and Information Science (M.L.I.S.). It is accredited by the American Library Association. The School also offers a joint degree program leading to an M.S. in Management Information Systems (M.S./M.I.S.) and a combined degree program leading to the M.L.I.S./M.B.A., both in cooperation with the Dominican University Graduate School of Business; a combined degree program leading to an M.L.I.S./M.M. in music history in cooperation with Northwestern University School of Music; a combined degree program leading to an M.L.I.S./M.A. in public history in cooperation with Loyola University Graduate School of Arts and Sciences; a combined degree program leading to an M.L.I.S./M.Div. in cooperation with McCormick Theological Seminary; Certificates of Special Studies in law librarianship, library administration, or technical services; Illinois state certification in media; and several concentrations and focus areas.

The Master of Library and Information Science requires 36 semester hours of graduate credit (twelve courses) with a minimum grade point average of 3.0 on a 4.0 scale. Students are required to prove microcomputer competencies in word processing, Windows, and the Internet.

The School has a collaborative program with the College of St. Catherine in St. Paul, Minnesota, whereby students may earn 24 of the 36 semester hours of the program at the College of St. Catherine, with 12 semester hours in residence at Dominican to secure the Dominican University ALA-accredited M.L.I.S. degree.

The three programs that lead to the Certificates of Special Studies (law librarianship, library administration, and technical services) may be earned through 15 semester hours of study beyond the master's degree in library science (depending on the course work completed). Students also have the option of pursuing a joint M.L.I.S. degree and certificate program, which requires a total of 48 semester hours of study.

The joint degree program (M.S. in management information systems) offered by GSLIS and the Graduate School of Business requires 51 semester hours (seventeen courses) and is administered by a faculty committee from both schools. Its unique feature is the integration and convergence of both the business data processing/management information systems/database management systems tradition of information management and the textual information retrieval tradition of information management.

Research Facilities

Dominican University's library and information science collection includes more than 28,000 monograph volumes, more than 27,000 juvenile volumes, and approximately 300 current periodical titles. The general collection includes 180,000 monographs and 35,000 periodical volumes. There are 100,000 government documents that make up the collection in the Federal Documents Depository. The library holdings exceed 200,000 volumes, approximately 1,000 periodical titles in paper, and almost 700 full-text electronic periodicals. The juvenile materials include fiction and nonfiction from preschool through high school levels and an extensive sampling of textbooks on most subjects and levels. Enhancing these resources is the extensive resource-sharing program through the ILLINET and ILCSO networks.

Three microcomputer laboratories, a media laboratory for the production of instructional materials, a book arts laboratory, and an extensive variety of library and information management applications software are available for faculty members and students.

Financial Aid

Financial assistance is awarded annually to students who give evidence of professional promise and scholastic achievement. The amount of financial aid varies. Graduate assistantships are available, with tuition remission. Part-time work study is available. In addition, there are extensive part-time professional and paraprofessional work opportunities available in the Chicago and St. Paul/Minneapolis areas.

Cost of Study

Tuition in 1998–99 is $1380 for each course (3 credit hours).

Living and Housing Costs

The cost of on-campus room and board ranges from $4880 to $5580 for the 1998–99 academic year. Graduate students also live off campus.

Student Group

Almost 400 students from throughout the United States and from various countries are enrolled at the School. Students participate in the American Library Association, the American Society for Information Science, and the Special Libraries Association. The Library and Information Science Student Association (LISSA) includes all students.

Location

Dominican University is in River Forest, a residential suburb of Chicago that can be reached by car (there is ample parking), bus, and train. The River Forest/Oak Park community is famous for its concentration of Frank Lloyd Wright architecture and its literary heritage. It is noted for its quiet tree-lined charm within easy striking distance of downtown Chicago and its numerous cultural attractions.

The University and The School

Dominican University traces its origins to the charter granted in 1848 by the state of Wisconsin to St. Clara Academy. The academy was formally incorporated as St. Clara College in 1901. The College subsequently moved to River Forest, where it was incorporated as Rosary College in 1918. The Department of Library Science was established in 1930. The graduate curriculum leading to the Master of Arts in Library Science degree was inaugurated in 1949. In 1981 the department was renamed the Graduate School of Library and Information Science. The title of the master's degree was changed to the Master of Library and Information Science in 1993, and the institution was renamed Dominican University in May 1997.

Applying

The basic courses in the M.L.I.S. and Certificate of Special Studies programs are offered in the summer, fall, and spring terms. Students may be admitted in any term. The deadlines for submitting applications for financial aid are November 15 and March 15 every year. Applications for admission are accepted on an ongoing basis.

Correspondence and Information

Dr. Prudence Dalrymple, Dean
Graduate School of Library and Information Science
Dominican University
7900 West Division Street
River Forest, Illinois 60305

Telephone: 708-524-6845
Fax: 708-524-6657
E-mail:gslis@dom.edu

Dominican University

THE FACULTY

Prudence Dalrymple, Associate Professor and Dean; Ph.D., Wisconsin–Madison.
William Brace, Professor; Ph.D., Case Western Reserve.
Ann D. Carlson, Associate Professor; M.L.S., Florida State; D.L.S., Columbia.
Bill Crowley, Assistant Professor; M.S.L.S., Columbia; Ph.D., Ohio.
Barbara Herrin, Associate Professor; M.L.S., Emporia; Ph.D., Kansas State.
Michael E. D. Koenig, Professor; M.B.A., Chicago; Ph.D., Drexel.
Gertrude Soonja L. Koh, Professor; M.L.S., C.A.S., Ph.D., Pittsburgh.
Tze-Chung Li, Professor; M.S., Columbia; LL.M., Harvard; Ph.D., New School.
Theodore Spahn, Professor Emeritus; M.A.L.S., Rosary; Ph.D., Michigan.
T. (Kanti) Srikantaiah, Associate Professor; Ph.D., Southern California.
Curt M. White, Associate Professor; Ph.D., Wayne State.
Patrick Williams, Professor Emeritus; M.A.L.S., Rosary.

Senior Fellows

Dawn Heller, M.A.L.S., Rosary.
William Vernon Jackson, A.M., Ph.D., Harvard.

AFFILIATED FACULTY

College of St. Catherine, St. Paul, Minnesota

Helen Humeston, Assistant Professor; Ph.D., Minnesota.
Geraldine B. King, Associate Professor; Ph.D., Minnesota.
Mary M. Wagner, Associate Professor; M.L.S., Washington (Seattle).

ADJUNCT FACULTY

William Baker, Adjunct Professor; M.L.S., Loughborough (England); Ph.D., London. Professor, Northern Illinois University.
Mary Beall, Adjunct Instructor; M.S.L.S., Wayne State. Assistant Documents Librarian, University of Illinois at Chicago.
Kenneth Black, Lecturer; M.A.L.S., Rosary. Assistant Librarian, Dominican University.
Maidel Cason, Adjunct Assistant Professor; M.A., Southern Methodist; M.A., London. Former Academic Library Administrator.
Anders Dahlgren, Adjunct Instructor; M.L.S., Illinois. President, Library Planning Associates, Inc.
Lloyd Davidson, Adjunct Associate Professor; M.L.I.S., Indiana; Ph.D., Berkeley. Head, Access Services, Seeley G. Mudd Library for Science and Engineering, Northwestern.
Annamarie Erickson, Lecturer; M.L.I.S., Rosary. Membership Services Liaison/Automation Technology Specialist, Chicago Library System.
Sally Estes, Adjunct Assistant Professor; M.A.L.S., Rosary. Editor, Books for Youth, *Booklist.*
Norman Frankel, Adjunct Assistant Professor; M.L.S., SUNY at Buffalo. Director of Licensing, Copyright and Permissions, American Medical Association.
Carla Funk, Lecturer; M.L.S., Indiana; M.B.A., Chicago. Executive Director, Medical Library Association.
Jim Goodridge, Adjunct Assistant Professor; M.A.L.S., Rosary. Legal Research Specialist, DePaul University Library.
Margarete Gross, Adjunct Instructor; M.A.L.S., Rosary. Head of the Picture Library and of the Chicago Artist's Archives Visual Performing Arts Division, Chicago Public Library.
Hjordis Halvorson, Adjunct Instructor; M.L.S., Berkeley. Director of Reader Services, Newberry Library.
Elizabeth Huntoon, Adjunct Instructor; M.S., Illinois Urbana-Champaign. Director, Children's Services, Chicago Public Library.
Julie M. Hurd, Adjunct Associate Professor; Ph.D., Chicago. Science Librarian and Associate Professor, University of Illinois at Chicago.
Mary Klatt, Adjunct Instructor; M.A.L.S., Rosary. Coordinator of Searching Services, Loyola University of Chicago, Medical Center Library.
Michael Leonard, Lecturer; M.L.S., Indiana. Head, Northtown Branch, Chicago Public Library.
Alan Leopold, Lecturer; M.A., Chicago; M.A.L.S., Rosary. Rare Book and Manuscript Cataloger, The Newberry Library.
Marilyn A. Lester, Adjunct Associate Professor; Ph.D., Illinois Urbana-Champaign. Former Dean and University Librarian, National-Louis.
Peter A. Lind, Lecturer; Illinois licensed architect and President, LIND Associates.
Logan Ludwig, Adjunct Professor; Ph.D., Saint Louis. Director of the Medical Center Library, Loyola University.
Michael J. Madden, Adjunct Assistant Professor; M.A., Loyola of Chicago; M.A., Chicago. Director, Schaumburg Public Library.
James R. Mouw, Lecturer; M.S.L.S., Western Michigan. Head, Serials Department, University of Chicago.
Patrick Quinn, Adjunct Assistant Professor; B.S., Wisconsin. Archivist, Northwestern University.
Inez Ringland, Adjunct Associate Professor; Ph.D., DePaul. Associate Dean of Information Services and Director, Dominican University Library.
Don L. Roberts, Lecturer; A.M.L.S., Michigan. Head, Music Library, Northwestern University.
Richard A. Stewart, Lecturer; M.A., Chicago; M.A., Northwestern. Head Cataloger, Chicago Public Library.
Penny Swartz, Lecturer; M.A.L.S., Rosary. Librarian/Information Specialist, Niles West High School, Skokie, Illinois.
Jeanne Triner, Adjunct Assistant Professor; J.D., Illinois Urbana-Champaign; M.A.L.S., Rosary; M.S., DePaul. Head library media specialist, Morton West High School.
Nancy Tuohy, Adjunct Assistant Professor; M.A.L.S., Rosary. Library Director, Clausen Miller, P. C.
Joyce Voss, Adjunct Instructor; M.A.L.S., Rosary. Manager of Community Services, Arlington Heights Memorial Library.
R. Conrad Winke, Adjunct Instructor; M.A.L.S., Rosary. Monographic cataloger, Northwestern University.
George Yanos, Adjunct Instructor; B.S., Ohio. Research Programmer at the Institute for Math and Science Education, University of Illinois at Chicago.
Therese Zimm, Adjunct Instructor; M.A., DePaul. ESL Instructor, Winona Public Schools.

DREXEL UNIVERSITY

College of Information Science and Technology

Programs of Study

Drexel University's College of Information Science and Technology prepares practitioners and researchers for the information professions. Three graduate degrees are awarded: Master of Science, Library and Information Science (M.S.); Master of Science in Information Systems (M.S.I.S.); and Ph.D. The Certificate of Advanced Study (C.A.S.) program enrolls professionals who already hold a master's in library science, information systems, or a related field. The master's normally requires 60 credits and may be completed on a full- or part-time basis. The University calendar includes four terms per calendar year; most information studies courses have 4 credits.

In the M.S. program, students complete required courses (32 credits) and then pursue an individual program of study. The curriculum is accredited by the American Library Association.

A student's individual program may include preparation for a professional specialization. For example, the College offers a Pennsylvania Department of Education–approved curriculum leading to school library media certification. The College provides course work needed by students who wish to prepare for certification as a medical information specialist by the Medical Library Association. Through a joint program with Gratz College in Philadelphia, students may obtain certification in Judaica librarianship. Course work is also offered that relates to library and information work in legal, scientific, and business settings, as well as studies in computerized library information systems.

The Ph.D. program comprises an approved plan of study, candidacy examinations, and a dissertation. Three consecutive terms of full-time residence are required; otherwise, doctoral students may pursue studies on either a full- or part-time basis. The doctoral program offers two tracks of study: computer information systems and information and library science. One track must be chosen for program planning and examinations. The Ph.D. normally requires 60 credits beyond the master's, or 90 credits beyond the bachelor's if no applicable master's is held.

The C.A.S. requires 32 credits and offers specialization beyond the master's. This program is regarded as continuing professional education.

Research Facilities

The College's Computing Resource Center supports students and faculty with such features as microcomputer hardware and software, access to the University's mainframes, a networked computer training room, online and CD-ROM information resources, a collection of reference books and sixty periodicals, and audio and video equipment. The College is also home to the Alfred P. Sloan Center for Asynchronous Learning and Training, which conducts research and development for Internet-based distance learning.

The University's library holds extensive collections of materials for all major fields in library and information science and information systems.

Financial Aid

A number of library, graduate, research, and teaching assistantships are awarded each year to incoming students, as are partial tuition scholarships. Assistants receive tuition remission and stipends in return for fulfilling specific work requirements in the College or the University's library. Teaching assistantships are available only for Ph.D. or advanced master's students. Enrolled students may also borrow limited funds through a College-administered loan program. Information on federal and state loan programs is available from Drexel's Graduate Financial Aid Office (Room 241, Randell Hall). No financial aid is available for international students.

Cost of Study

In 1998–99, tuition is $437 per credit. Each term, students are also charged a general University fee based on full-time ($121) or part-time ($65) status.

Living and Housing Costs

Accommodations for single students are available in University residence halls. Ample housing is also available in the neighborhood bordering campus. For the nine-month academic year, books, room and board, and health insurance (if purchased through the University) for a single student are estimated at $9050.

Student Group

The College's graduate students represent diverse academic and professional backgrounds and have varied career expectations. About 75 percent of the 550 graduate students come from the mid-Atlantic region; other regions and countries are also represented. The age range is wide because many students have professional work experience or have pursued graduate studies in other disciplines. The College also enrolls undergraduates pursuing a B.S. in information systems.

The College of Information Science and Technology maintains its own placement office with a full-time director. The director helps students find preprofessional positions and internships and assists graduates in locating professional employment. The placement rate for graduates is high. While many graduates seek jobs in libraries and information centers, about one quarter find positions in other types of organizations, including those focused on computer-based systems technologies. This number of nontraditional placements is increasing.

Location

The campus is located in the University City section of Philadelphia. As one of the nation's oldest and largest cities, Philadelphia is rich in cultural, historical, and academic institutions and is a leading center for business, industry, and government. These resources provide ample opportunities for information science and technology students to pursue preprofessional employment, internships, and permanent employment.

The University

Drexel is a private institution with an approximate enrollment of 2,500 graduate students and 7,500 undergraduate students. In addition to the information science and technology curricula, degree programs are offered in the arts and sciences, business and administration, design arts, and engineering. These varied programs feature a strong professional orientation.

With College approval, graduate students may include courses from other Drexel departments in their program of study. Related curricula include computer science, management and other business specializations, neuropsychology, and technical and science communication.

Applying

Graduate students may apply for admission in any term. Those seeking assistantships and scholarships should apply by February 1 for admission in the following September. An application and fee, transcripts, letters of recommendation, and a personal statement are required. Scores for the GRE General Test are required for some master's and all Ph.D. applicants. GRE scores are required for all applicants seeking assistantships.

Correspondence and Information

Anne B. Tanner, Associate Dean
College of Information Science and Technology–P
Drexel University
Philadelphia, Pennsylvania 19104
Telephone: 215-895-2474
World Wide Web: http://www.cis.drexel.edu

Drexel University

THE FACULTY AND THEIR RESEARCH

Kathleen Bishop, Instructor; M.S., Pennsylvania. Software engineering as applied to speech science, natural language processing.

Thomas Childers, Alice B. Kroeger Professor and Interim Dean; Ph.D., Rutgers. Management and evaluation of information organizations and services, foundations of information work, quality of information services, effectiveness of information organizations.

M. Carl Drott, Associate Professor; Ph.D., Michigan. Computer programming for information processing, search strategy techniques for information retrieval and dissemination, use of systems analysis techniques for dealing with problems in large organizations such as libraries.

Lee Scott Ehrhart, Research Associate Professor; Ph.D., George Mason. Information and software systems engineering; cognitive and behavioral sciences; management and organizational theory; multidisciplinary approaches to system life cycle engineering activities, including requirements identification and modeling, design, and evaluation; human-computer interaction; planning and decision making; multimedia information systems.

Abby Goodrum, Assistant Professor; Ph.D., North Texas. Visual information retrieval, electronic publishing and digital libraries, social impact of information technology and new media.

Belver Griffith, Research Professor and Professor Emeritus; Ph.D., Connecticut. Research methods; design, planning, and evaluation of information services and products; functions of information in technical and scientific work; communications.

John Hall, Associate Professor; Ph.D., Florida State. Academic library service, library administration, organization of materials, technical processes, social aspects of information systems, academic library management information systems and their relation to management decision making, academic library services and use, collective bargaining, cooperation among libraries, application of simulation and gaming techniques to library education.

Lewis Hassell, Visiting Professor; Ph.D., Drexel. Systems analysis techniques, database management systems, computer-supported cooperative work (CSCW), use of computers to support collaboration, applications of linguistics to CSCW, object-oriented analysis and design.

Gregory W. Hislop, Assistant Professor and Associate Dean; Ph.D., Drexel. Software development and modification, software evaluation and reuse, organizing and staffing information systems groups, systems management, software product development, technology support for large organizations.

Maxwell Hughes, Research Professor; Ph.D., Cambridge. Management of information systems, generally in large organizations, specifically in the health-care industry.

Xia Lin, Assistant Professor; Ph.D., Maryland. Information seeking in digital environments, digital libraries, information visualization, information technologies, human-computer interactions, visual interface design.

Cynthia Lopata, Instructor; Ph.D., Drexel. Technology and organizational change processes, technology impact assessment, qualitative research methodologies.

Jacqueline C. Mancall, Professor; Ph.D., Drexel. Collection development, management, delivery of information services to children and adolescents, instructional role of the information specialist, design of library collections and services for user groups based on their communication behavior, application of survey methodology and statistical analysis to collection planning and management.

Katherine W. McCain, Professor; Ph.D., Drexel. Resources in science and technology, serial literature, abstracting and indexing, bibliometric studies of scholarly literatures, information transfer in the biomedical sciences.

Carol Hansen Montgomery, Professor; Ph.D., Drexel. Library automation, evaluation of information systems, user interface design, medical informatics.

Scott Overmyer, Associate Professor; Ph.D., George Mason. System and software requirements analysis, rapid prototyping, human-computer interaction.

Il-Yeol Song, Associate Professor; Ph.D., LSU. Database management systems and systems analysis and design, database modeling and design, object-oriented analysis and design, object-oriented database systems, client-server systems, data warehousing, digital libraries.

June M. Verner, Professor; Ph.D., Massey (New Zealand). Software project management, software metrics, software process improvement, software development tools and techniques.

Howard D. White, Professor; Ph.D., Berkeley. Issues surrounding information work with well-defined clienteles concentrating on services that involve resources of the social sciences, improvement of statistics for use by library management, foundations of information work, expert systems in reference service, library collection evaluation, co-citation mapping of subject specialties, and American attitudes toward censorship.

Associate Professor John Hall chats with prospective students during the College's annual Open House.

Students at work in the College's Computing Resource Center.

FLORIDA STATE UNIVERSITY

School of Information Studies

Programs of Study

The School of Information Studies at Florida State University (FSU) has offered one of the top-ranked programs in the nation for many years. The program maintains a respect for tradition while it continues to explore new ways to educate information professionals.

The master's degree, a Master of Science (M.S.), has been offered since 1947, with majors in library and information studies and school library media specialist certification. The degree requires 42 semester hours and is a course-type master's designed for a graduate student without previous library or information studies courses. User behavior and its interaction with information products, services, and organizations is the primary focus of the library and information studies program. Additional areas of concentration include creation and marketing of information products, analysis of information content, information policy and management, and information systems. The master's program is also available throughout the state of Florida via World Wide Web conferencing.

The specialist degree program has been offered since 1969. It addresses the need for information professionals to become aware of new areas within information studies and to improve skills and/or develop additional competencies in their fields of professional interest. This degree may be completed "summers only" or during regular academic terms and requires 30 semester hours of graduate credit.

The goals of the Doctor of Philosophy (Ph.D.) program are to prepare graduates to demonstrate competence in major aspects of information studies, as evidenced by the successful completion of a preliminary examination, and to prepare candidates to demonstrate mastery of an area of specialization in research methodologies by successful completion of a dissertation. Requirements include a minimum of 12 semester hours of graduate credit per semester, for a minimum of two consecutive semesters.

Research Facilities

The Louis Shores Building provides 2½ floors for laboratories, offices, and other space needed to conduct the School's programs. Access to a variety of online services is provided to students enrolled in specific courses. A vast array of equipment, ranging from computers, networks, and video equipment to still cameras, microphones, and LCD panels, is available for student use. The Harold Goldstein Library includes professional and reference materials, a book collection of 85,000 volumes, access to electronic databases, and a serials and journals subscription list of more than 400 titles and provides excellent support for curricula. The School also maintains a Usability Center for the testing of a variety of information products and services.

Financial Aid

In addition to providing funds on the basis of demonstrated financial need in the form of grants, work awards, and loans, the University offers scholarships to recognize and reward talent, academic achievement, and meritorious performance. Graduate students may apply for long-term loans and college work-study. Graduate fellowships and assistantships are handled through the Office of Graduate Studies and the respective academic departments. The School offers the opportunity for competitive assistantships. Those interested should write to Florida State University, Office of Financial Aid, 2474 University Center, Tallahassee, Florida 32306-1023 for financial aid information.

Cost of Study

In 1997–98, tuition charges were $118.29 per graduate tuition hour for in-state students and $389.03 per graduate tuition hour for out-of-state students.

Living and Housing Costs

The cost of housing is comparable to other Southeastern mid-sized cities. Housing is available on and near campus so that students can get along without a car. University facilities on the main campus include an apartment facility, Rogers Hall, which has one-bedroom double occupancy (twin beds) and apartments reserved for single graduate students. Graduate students are also eligible for housing in a complex 1½ miles from campus. For more housing information, students should contact the Director of University Housing, 104 Cawthon Hall.

Student Group

In fall 1997, there were 73 full-time graduate students enrolled, 17 men and 56 women. Of the 368 part-time graduate students, 107 were men and 261 were women. Degrees conferred in 1996–97 included 145 master's degrees and six Ph.D. degrees.

Student Outcomes

The field represented by information studies includes a diverse set of professional opportunities, including positions in educational, corporate, and public libraries or information centers and the building and use of computer-based information systems for a wide variety of disciplines and businesses. Within its fifty-year history, the School has had graduates occupy positions of leadership that blend concern for human needs for information with involvement in up-to-date and cutting-edge technology.

Location

Located in the center of Tallahassee, the state capital, Florida State University is well known for its beauty. Familiarly known in its beginning years as the "College of Pines," it still retains its unique mixture of Southern ease with Florida exotic. Collegiate Gothic structures are combined with modern architecture in a landscape of rolling hills with live oaks draped in Spanish moss, pines, palms, and dogwoods. The Gulf of Mexico provides opportunities for fishing and boating within an hour's drive, and the capital city attracts traveling Broadway shows, nationally known entertainers, theater, art, and many other cultural events either free or at low cost to students.

The School

Florida State University was established in 1851, and the School of Library and Information Studies (now the School of Information Studies) was established in 1947 as a professional school. The goals of the School are derived from the mission of the University, which is "to serve as a center for advanced graduate and professional studies while emphasizing extensive research and providing excellence in undergraduate programs." The historical strengths of the institution are maintained, while new curricula and research that meets the dynamic environmental needs of tomorrow's information age are designed and developed. Priority is attached to fostering a blending of faculty and student teaching and research, and grants are regularly sought. The melding of teaching and research receives priority in faculty evaluation, merit salary determinations, and in promotion of faculty.

Applying

Application forms and information about graduate programs can be obtained from the School of Information Studies, Florida State University, Tallahassee, Florida 32306-2100. All applicants to any program must meet the University's and the School's standards for admission and acceptance. Admission is selective and is based upon review of academic records, performance on the GRE, quality and quantity of previous work, references of 3 persons, a personal interview by the Dean or representative thereof, and a personal written statement giving career and research objectives. Official test scores on the Graduate Record Examinations (GRE) and two copies of official transcripts of all academic work are to be sent to FSU Graduate Admissions.

Correspondence and Information

Elisabeth Logan
Associate Dean
School of Information Studies
Florida State University
Tallahassee, FL 32306-2100

Telephone: 850-644-5775
E-mail: logan@lis.fsu.edu
World Wide Web: http://www.fsu.edu/~lis

Florida State University

THE FACULTY AND THEIR RESEARCH

Pamela P. Barron. Services and materials for children and young adults.
Ronald D. Blazek. Reference work, research methods, information services in libraries, library history.
Kathleen Burnett. Organization of information, information technologies, the history of information design, rare books and art librarianship.
Charles Wm. Conaway. Reference (social science and Internet resources), information science, archives.
John N. DePew. Collection management, academic library management, conservation and preservation and library technical services.
Eliza T. Dresang. Information-seeking behavior, multimedia information systems, telecommunications, networked information, school library media and information services and sources for children and young adults.
Myke Gluck. Usability analysis and its application in multimedia and spatial information system design.
Thomas L. Hart. AV management, advanced graphics, foundations, young adult media, school library media management.
Elisabeth Logan. Electronic information, user behavior in online environments, bibliometrics.
Alice Robbin. Information policy, resource management, communication and information behavior, research methods.
Jane Robbins. Research and evaluation methodologies, management, education of information professionals.
Gene T. Sherron. Management, networking, telecommunications and information systems.
William Summers. Public libraries and library administration.
Lixin Yu. Computerized information retrieval, the Internet, research methods, statistics and Geographic Information Systems (GIS).

INDIANA UNIVERSITY BLOOMINGTON

School of Library and Information Science

Programs of Study

At the Indiana University Bloomington School of Library and Information Science (SLIS), students can choose from among several degree options, selecting the track that best meets individual needs and career objectives.

The Master of Information Science (M.I.S.), a 42-credit-hour program, prepares students for careers in such areas as information management, on-line searching and information brokerage, competitive intelligence and research analysis, World Wide Web design, and database development and marketing. The program places emphasis on the social and behavioral dimensions of information technology. The Master of Library Science (M.L.S.), accredited by the American Library Association, is a 36-credit-hour program. Students learn the role of both print-based and electronic libraries in society. They become familiar with policy issues and technological trends, and how these impact libraries and information centers. Students learn how to manage and evaluate collections, respond to patrons' information needs, and use technology to improve access to information. Students emerge from the program prepared for careers in library administration, technical services, reference, and collection development at public, school, academic, and special libraries. The Ph.D. program prepares students for higher levels of research and/or teaching positions in library and information science. The program's purpose is to develop a broad understanding of the content, methods, research, and theories of librarianship and information science, and of their relation to other fields of knowledge.

The specialist program, a means of updating knowledge in a given area or of repositioning oneself in the labor market, allows the student to focus on a subject of particular interest. SLIS also offers a unique range of dual master's degree programs in ten disciplines, as well as specializations in music librarianship, African studies, and chemical information.

Research Facilities

SLIS Library's collection includes hundreds of journals and an extensive range of on-line databases and networked CD-ROM resources. OCLC workstations and digital scanning technology are available, as is unrestricted access to electronic information resources on the Internet and World Wide Web. The Clayton Shepherd Computer Laboratory features sixteen networked microcomputers and laser printers. Students have access to a variety of platforms and an array of applications software, including groupware, Internet browsers, and electronic mail. The Center for Information Technology Experimentation and Development (CITED) is a cluster of eleven workstations connected to a Novell server, campus network, Internet, and a CD-ROM server, CITED was designed to encourage experimentation, collaborative project work, and prototype development. The Usability Laboratory was created for the study of human-computer interaction. The lab is equipped with specialized video observation and analysis equipment to facilitate research in information systems use as well as benchmarking of library software. Students can develop and exhibit Internet-based projects on the school's World Wide Web server, allowing them to hone their skills and raise their profiles. Students can also draw upon the magnificent heritage and resources of Indiana University, including IU Libraries, ranked fourteenth in North America in terms of holdings; University Computing Services, which operates one of the world's largest distributed computer networks; and Lilly Library, one of the preeminent rare book collections in the nation.

Financial Aid

Scholarships, graduate assistantships, fellowships, guaranteed hourly positions, and professional organization awards are available. The number of applications far exceeds the number of available awards, however. To be eligible for financial aid from SLIS, a student must be admitted to a graduate degree program. Additional information is available from the Office of Student Financial Assistance at IU Bloomington.

Cost of Study

Tuition rates on the Bloomington campus for 1997–98 were $144.30 per credit hour for Indiana residents and $416.30 per credit hour for non-Indiana residents. Activity, technology, and health service fees of approximately $100 per semester also applied. Students should consult the current schedule of classes for updated information.

Living and Housing Costs

IU Bloomington offers graduate housing for both single and married students. University apartments cost approximately $450 per month; dormitory rooms with variable meal plans are also offered. Off-campus apartments and other housing options, at monthly rents of approximately $400 and up per person, are available as well.

Student Group

SLIS has a full-time equivalent enrollment of 430 students. Students come from many states and twenty countries around the world. Their major areas of undergraduate study vary widely. Most students have prior work experience in business, education, or libraries.

Student Outcomes

Career prospects for SLIS graduates in librarianship and other information professions are excellent. More than 90 percent of graduates landed professional positions within six months of graduation, according to a recent survey. These individuals accepted employment as webmasters, consulting firm analysts, database designers, information brokers, strategic intelligence managers, and librarians in public, academic, school, and special settings.

Location

IU Bloomington, with more than 35,000 students, is the primary residential campus of Indiana University. Known for its physical beauty, the 1,860-acre campus is set in the rolling hills of southern Indiana. Cultural and social activities flourish; there are hundreds of student organizations and nearly 1,000 musical events each year. Students can enjoy Big Ten sports events and participate in an outstanding recreational sports program.

The University and the School

SLIS at Indiana University Bloomington has long been considered one of the top programs of its kind in the nation. With a large faculty, a diverse student body, and state-of-the-art computing facilities, SLIS has the expertise and resources to ensure a first-rate education and solid career preparation. The SLIS faculty, one of the largest and most productive in the nation, provides instruction and career and research guidance. With backgrounds ranging from information science, librarianship, psychology, and law to sociology, computer science, cultural anthropology, and educational technology, faculty members provide students with multiple perspectives on a complex and dynamic field.

Applying

Admission decisions are based on scholastic achievement, reference letters, and a professional goals statement. Applicants must hold a bachelor's degree and an undergraduate minimum grade point average of 3.0 (on a 4.0 scale). GRE test scores are required for applicants with GPAs of less than 3.0. Deadlines are May 15 for matriculation in the fall; November 1 for spring; and March 15 for second summer session. Financial aid application deadlines are earlier. An application fee of $40 is required for all applicants.

Correspondence and Information

Mary Krutulis
Assistant Dean and Director of Admissions
School of Library and Information Science
Indiana University Bloomington
Main Library 011
Bloomington, Indiana 47405-1801

Telephone: 812-855-2018
E-mail: krutulis@indiana.edu
World Wide Web: http://www.slis.indiana.edu

Indiana University Bloomington

THE FACULTY AND THEIR RESEARCH

Johanna Bradley, Assistant Professor; Ph.D., Illinois at Urbana-Champaign, 1991. Networked health information resources, health information professions, collaborative development of health information resources.
Daniel J. Callison, Associate Professor and Director of School Media Education; Ed.D., Indiana, 1982. Information literacy and inquiry, collection development, management of school media programs.
Kenneth D. Crews, Associate Professor and Director, Copyright Management Center on the Indiana University-Purdue University Indianapolis (IUPUI) campus; Ph.D., UCLA, 1990; J.D., Washington (St. Louis), 1980. Copyright and higher education, intellectual property and information access.
Blaise Cronin, Professor and Dean; Ph.D., Queen's (Belfast), 1983. Scholarly communication, social networks, evaluative bibliometrics, information marketing, strategic intelligence management, education for information professionals.
Andrew P. Dillon, Associate Professor and Assistant Director, Institute for the Study of Human Capabilities; Ph.D., Loughborough Tech, 1991. Human-computer interaction, cognition and information spaces, sociocognitive systems design.
Shirley A. Fitzgibbons, Associate Professor; Ph.D., Rutgers, 1976. Motivational factors in reading for grades 4–8, issues in children's literature.
Stephen P. Harter, Professor; Ph.D., Chicago, 1974. Information retrieval, bibliometrics, scholarly communication.
Carol A. Hert, Assistant Professor; Ph.D., Syracuse, 1995. Information retrieval, user behavior on information systems.
Elin K. Jacob, Assistant Professor; Ph.D., North Carolina, Chapel Hill, 1994. Categorization and the cognitive organization of information, development and evaluating of indexing systems.
Rob Kling, Professor; Ph.D., Stanford, 1971. Social impacts of computerization, organizational information systems in context, digital libraries and electronic publishing in professional communication systems, information technologies and changing work organization.
Javed Mostafa, Assistant Professor; Ph.D., Texas at Austin, 1994. Intelligent interfaces, information filtering, automated document representation techniques.
Thomas E. Nisonger, Associate Professor; Ph.D., Columbia, 1976. Collection management and evaluation, bibliometrics, serials.
Uta Priss, Assistant Professor; Ph.D., Darmstadt, 1996. Conceptual knowledge systems, mathematical modeling of lexical databases, thesauri and classification systems, computational linguistics.
Verna L. Pungitore, Associate Professor; Ph.D., Pittsburgh, 1983. Public libraries, planning and evaluation of library services, diffusion of innovation.
Howard Rosenbaum, Assistant Professor; Ph.D., Syracuse, 1996. Computer-mediated communication, managers and information in organizations, information policy and electronic networking, the intersection of sociological and library and information science theories.
Debora Shaw, Associate Professor and Associate Dean; Ph.D., Indiana, 1983. Information seeking and use by humanities scholars and other specialized user groups, design and impact of electronic information sources.
Martha M. Smith, Assistant Professor; Ph.D., Duke, 1980. Information ethics and public policy, philosophy of information technology.
Herbert W. Snyder, Assistant Professor; Ph.D., Syracuse, 1994. Federal information policy, chaos and information systems, financial management for information centers.
Joyce G. Taylor, Lecturer; Ph.D., Indiana, 1993. History of the Studio Museum in Harlem, the black visual artist, archival libraries, art museums.
Bob Travica, Assistant Professor; Ph.D., Syracuse, 1995. Communication systems, group support systems, systems evaluation and design, informational aspects of nontraditional (organic) organizations, macrosocietal effects of computer networks.
Jean Umiker-Sebeok, Associate Professor; Ph.D., Indiana, 1976. Hypertext usability, virtual communities, museum informatics, consumer needs and behavior, semiotics.

Emeritus Faculty

Marian L. Armstrong, Assistant Professor, A.M., Indiana, 1958.
David Kaser, Distinguished Professor, Ph.D., Michigan, 1956.
Marcy Murphy, Associate Professor, Ph.D., Pittsburgh, 1977.
Margaret I. Rufsvold, Professor, A.M., Vanderbilt (Peabody), 1933; H.D.L., Mundelein College, 1969.
Judith Serebnick, Associate Professor, Ph.D., Rutgers, 1978.
George Whitbeck, Associate Professor, Ph.D., Rutgers, 1970.
Herbert S. White, Distinguished Professor, M.S.L.S., Syracuse, 1950.

Senior Fellow

Charles H. Davis, Ph.D., Indiana, 1969.

Visiting Scholars

Sándor Darányi, Ph.D., Eötvös Loránd (Budapest), 1994.
Elisabeth R. Davenport, Ph.D., Strathclyde (Glasgow), 1994.

PRATT INSTITUTE

School of Information and Library Science

Program of Study

The School of Information and Library Science prepares students for leadership positions in the traditional areas of librarianship and also educates men and women for a broad range of opportunities in information-related careers in nonlibrary environments. The program combines a traditional core curriculum (information sources, organization of information, administration of libraries and information centers, collection development, storage and dissemination of recorded information in all formats) with specialized courses emphasizing the latest developments in information access and information handling technologies.

The program offers a Master of Science (M.S.) degree in library and information science and an Advanced Certificate in Library and Information Studies. The 36-credit master's program may be completed in as little as two semesters and one summer and must be completed within four years of enrollment. Courses are also offered on Saturday and Sunday during the spring and fall semesters. Students may concentrate in law, medical, business, records management, or school media.

The School also offers a joint M.S./J.D. degree program with Brooklyn Law School, and M.S. (library information science)/M.S. (art history) with Pratt's School of Art and Design.

Research Facilities

The graduate program is reinforced by highly sophisticated computer equipment. The Department of Academic Computing operates computer labs containing Apple, Macintosh, IBM, and IBM-compatible PC facilities; VAXstations; and Silicon Graphics, Sun, and IRIS workstations, providing ready access and availability to students. The Information and Library Science School has additional computing facilities. Two dedicated InfoNet Centers with more than fifty Pentium computer workstations, scanners, and laser printers are available for students and faculty use at both the Pratt Manhattan Center and at the Information Science Center in Brooklyn. The centers, open seven days per week, are designed to provide access to hundreds of databases and to Internet resources. The CD-ROM laboratory was established to provide for research and production of multimedia works. The Pratt Institute Library has grown with the Institute to house an excellent collection of information and library science, engineering, science, art, and architecture materials.

Financial Aid

Financial aid is available through a variety of programs funded by institutions, New York State, and the federal government. These include the Federal Perkins Loan and Federal Work-Study programs, the Tuition Assistance Program of New York State, and Pratt grants, loans, and student aid. Continuing students in all departments may apply for fellowships and assistantships on a competitive basis. Special alumni-sponsored fellowships are also available.

Cost of Study

In 1998–99, tuition is $21,780 per year ($605 per credit) for the M.S. degree, and student fees are $474 per year. The cost of books and supplies varies widely among the different programs.

Living and Housing Costs

Housing is available for single students. The cost averages $5030 per year. The Office of Residential Life maintains listings of off-campus housing to help students find suitable accommodations.

Student Group

Graduate students at Pratt are drawn from all parts of the United States (forty-seven states) and sixty other countries. The average age is 25 years, and about 10 percent are married. The employment outlook for Pratt graduates is bright. At present, more than 95 percent of the graduates are placed in business and industry, and the growth potential of the job market is seemingly unlimited. Job opportunities have been increasing for graduates of the information and library science program.

Location

Pratt Institute is located in the Clinton Hill section of Brooklyn. It offers information and library science courses at the site of resource support important to various areas of concentration: Brooklyn Law School for law librarianship, the Brooklyn Public Library for urban librarianship, Cornell Medical Center for the medical specialization, and the New York Public Library/mid-Manhattan Branch for major reference resources. Graduate courses are offered at Pratt Manhattan, 295 Lafayette Street. A campus in the heart of New York City can offer special opportunities to its students. New York is the world center for most of the fields that Pratt students study, and the available professional experience and expertise constitute an invaluable resource. A vast variety of cultural and recreational activities are available in the neighborhood, in Brooklyn, in the city, and in the region. Pratt has a parklike campus in a quiet neighborhood of Victorian buildings set in the midst of one of the most vibrant cities in the world.

The Institute

A private, nonsectarian institute of higher education, Pratt was founded in 1887 by industrialist and philanthropist Charles Pratt. Changing with the requirements of the professions for which it educates, Pratt today prepares a student body of 3,800 undergraduate and graduate students for a wide range of careers in design and fine arts, architecture and planning, and information science.

Applying

Applications should be submitted by March 1 for anticipated entrance in the fall semester and by November 15 for anticipated entrance in the spring semester. Applications received after these deadlines are considered only if there are vacancies. Information and application forms may be obtained from the Graduate Admissions Office. It is recommended that applicants visit the campus and the department to which they are applying.

Correspondence and Information

Graduate Admissions Office
Pratt Institute
200 Willoughby Avenue
Brooklyn, New York 11205
Telephone: 718-636-3669
800-331-0834 (toll-free)
Fax: 718-636-3670
World Wide Web: http://www.pratt.edu

Pratt Institute

THE FACULTY

Seoud M. Matta, Professor and Dean; D.L.S., Columbia.
Inez L. Sperr Brisfjord, Associate Professor and Director of Continuing Education; D.S.W., Columbia.
Michael Adams, Visiting Assistant Professor; M.L.S., Syracuse; Ph.D. (English), South Carolina. (Associate Professor, CUNY Graduate Center)
Patricia Anderson, Visiting Instructor; M.L.S., Simmons. (Director, New Rochelle Public Library)
Donna Barkman, Visiting Instructor; M.A. (communications), Columbia Teachers College; M.A. (library science), Wisconsin–Madison. (Adjunct Librarian/Professor, Westchester Community College)
Glen Bencivengo, Associate Professor; M.L.S., J.D., Rutgers.
John Berry III, Visiting Associate Professor; M.S.L.S., Simmons. (Editor-in-Chief, Library Journal)
Mary Biggs, Visiting Associate Professor; Ph.D., Chicago. (Dean of Library, The College of New Jersey)
Jerry Bornstein, Visiting Assistant Professor; M.S.L.I.S., Pratt; M.A., CUNY, Hunter. (Reference/Graduate Services—Baruch College)
Larry Brandwein, Visiting Associate Professor; M.L.S., Columbia. (Former Director, Brooklyn Public Library)
Robert M. Braude, Visiting Associate Professor; M.A. (psychology), M.L.S., UCLA; Ph.D. (education), Nebraska. (Frances and John L. Loeb Librarian/Assistant Dean for Information Resources, Samuel J. Wood Library, Cornell University Medical College)
Kay Ann Cassell, Visiting Instructor; M.L.S., Rutgers. (Associate Director for Programs and Services, New York Public Library)
F. William Chickering, Visiting Associate Professor and Dean of Libraries; M.Ln., Emory; Certificate of Advanced Librarianship, Columbia.
Geraldine Clark, Visiting Associate Professor; M.A. (economics), NYU; M.L.S., Columbia. (Former Director, School Library Services, New York City Board of Education)
Anthony M. Cucchiara, Visiting Assistant Professor; M.S. (library and information science), Pratt; M.B.A. (finance), LIU. (Librarian, Special Collections)
Julie Cummins, Visiting Instructor; M.S.L.S., Syracuse. (Coordinator, Children's Services, New York Public Library)
Ernest DiMattia, Visiting Associate Professor; M.B.A., Connecticut; M.S.L.S., Simmons. (President, Ferguson Library, Stamford, Connecticut)
Susan S. DiMattia, Visiting Associate Professor; M.L.S., Simmons; M.B.A. (marketing), Connecticut. (Business Information Consultant)
Trudy Downs, Visiting Assistant Professor; M.B.A., M.S.I.S., Pittsburgh.
Marilee Foglesong, Visiting Instructor; M.L.S., Illinois. (Coordinator, Young Adult Services, New York Public Library)
Maurice J. Freedman, Visiting Associate Professor; Ph.D. (library and information science), Rutgers. (Director, Westchester Library System)
James Humphry III, Visiting Professor; M.S.L.S., Columbia. (President, H. W. Wilson Foundation)
William V. Jackson, Visiting Associate Professor; M.S. (library science), Illinois; Ph.D., Harvard. (Professor, Texas at Austin)
Cynthia A. Johnson, Visiting Instructor; M.S.L.S., Columbia. (Librarian, Barnard College)
Anne Kelly, Associate Professor; M.L.S., Columbia.
Linda Kruger, Visiting Associate Professor; Ph.D., Columbia.
William D. Mathews, Visiting Instructor; A.B., Boston College. (Vice President, Electronic Technology, Derwint, Inc.)
Elizabeth O'Keefe, M.S.L.I.S., Pratt. (Director, Information Services—Pierpont Morgan Library)
Irene M. Percelli, Visiting Assistant Professor; M.L.S. Rutgers. (Technology Training Coordinator, The New York Public Library—Research Libraries)
Ellen H. Poisson, Associate Professor; D.L.S., Columbia.
Marie Radford, Associate Professor; Ph.D. (communications), Rutgers.
Ann K. Randall, Associate Professor; D.L.S., Columbia.
Carolyn Anne Reid, Visiting Associate Professor; M.A., Missouri–Columbia. (Associate Director and Associate Librarian, Samuel J. Wood Library, Cornell University Medical College)
Sara Robbins, Visiting Associate Professor; M.S. (library and information science), Pratt; J.D., Ohio State. (Law Librarian and Professor of Law, Brooklyn Law School)
Charles P. Rubenstein, Professor and Academic Coordinator; M.S. (library and information science), Pratt; Ph.D. (electrical engineering), Polytechnic of New York.
Ellen Rudley, Visiting Instructor; M.S. (art education), NYU. (Director of Development, Brooklyn Public Library)
Patricia Glass Schuman, Visiting Associate Professor; M.L.S., Columbia. (President, Neal-Schuman Publishers, Inc.)
Nasser Sharify, Visiting Professor; D.L.S., Columbia.
Laurence L. Sherrill, Visiting Associate Professor; Ph.D. (library science), Wisconsin–Madison. (Library Consultant)
Caryl Masyr Smith, Visiting Instructor; M.L.S., Pratt. (Information Management Consultant)
Peggy Teich, Visiting Associate Professor; M.S. (library and information science), Pratt.
Alan R. Thomas, Visiting Associate Professor; M.A. (counseling and guidance), Reading (England); M.A. (library and information studies), Queens (Belfast). (Senior Lecturer, Thames Valley, England)
Bor-sheng Tsai, Associate Professor; Ph.D. (information science), Case Western Reserve.
David L. Weisbrod, Assistant Professor; M.S. (systems analysis), Rutgers.
Judith W. Wild, Visiting Assistant Professor; M.S. (education), Ed.S. (educational technology), Indiana; M.L.S, Columbia. (Librarian, Brooklyn)

SIMMONS COLLEGE

Graduate School of Library and Information Science

Programs of Study

The Master of Science program, accredited by the American Library Association, qualifies graduates for positions in public, college, university, school, and special libraries, as well as in the information-related professions, including systems analysis and design. Special course sequences are provided for concentrations in archives management, records management, and the design of online databases. The School's Unified Media Specialist program, the Supervisor/Director Certificate program, and the joint master's degree program with the education department of the College have been approved by the Massachusetts State Board of Education, thus carrying state, ICC, and NASDTEC program approval. The GSLIS and the Simmons College History Department offer a 56-semester-hour, dual-degree program in archives management, leading to a Master of Science in library and information science and a Master of Arts in history. The master's program may be completed in one calendar year; students may take up to six years on a part-time basis. The M.S. degree is awarded upon successful completion of 36 semester hours.

The Doctor of Arts program provides experienced librarians with intensive, advanced preparation for management careers in libraries and media and information centers. It is designed to provide an individualized program of systematic study that is interdisciplinary in character and centers on applying sound principles of modern management to library administrative problems. Sixty credit hours of graduate work are required to complete the program. For those with two master's degrees, up to 24 hours of that graduate work may be applied toward the 60 hours for the D.A. degree at the discretion of the doctoral committee. For applicants with a master's degree in another subject area, the School has designed a double-degree program that consists of a Master of Science degree, which requires 28 semester hours from the master's-level curriculum, and a Doctor of Arts degree, which requires an additional 32 semester hours of doctoral-level requirements.

Alumni and graduates of other ALA-accredited schools may apply as unclassified or nondegree students to take courses for credit in any regular semester or summer session. Prevailing tuition rates apply. Alumni may audit courses on a space-available basis for one half the current tuition. The School offers a wide range of continuing education opportunities in all areas of library and information services and operations.

Research Facilities

The Simmons libraries include an extensive professional collection—the largest of its kind in the New England region—containing approximately 35,000 books, journals, and documents on library and information science, bibliography, and related fields; a laboratory collection of children's literature, including early juvenile books; and a representative collection of other media to support specialized courses.

Facilities of the Fenway Consortium, including ten libraries in the area, are available through a cooperative arrangement, as are many special collections in academic, public, and special libraries.

Computer facilities in the College's own center, as well as online services provided by major cataloging and reference database vendors, are accessible to students and faculty via terminals located throughout the campus. These include five terminals in the School's own Technology Laboratory.

Financial Aid

Financial aid is given on the basis of need to students who have been admitted to the Master of Science program. Forms of aid include grants, fellowships and scholarships, Perkins and Stafford loans, and employment through the College Work-Study Program. Many Boston-area libraries provide tuition assistance to their full-time employees and, in some cases, grant them time off to take courses. Numerous preprofessional positions are always available to students who wish to work full- or part-time in order to offset tuition costs and gain valuable work experience.

Cost of Study

Tuition for the 1998–99 academic year is $587 per credit hour. Tuition and fees for a 36-credit program are $21,165.

Living and Housing Costs

Accommodations in residence halls are available for men and women on a space-available basis. Charges are $4232 each semester in 1998–99, including room and board. Charges for the six-week summer session were $840 in 1998.

Student Group

There are about 475 students enrolled during the fall and spring semesters and 300 during the summer session. Twenty percent are men, and the average age is 33. Approximately twenty-five states and fifteen countries are represented. In 1997, 185 Master of Science degrees were conferred. Fifty-three Doctor of Arts degrees have been awarded since the inception of the program in 1973.

Location

Simmons College is located in historic Boston, which is recognized worldwide as a great educational, cultural, and bibliographical center. The fine museums, academic and medical institutions, and libraries provide a rich context for both course work and leisure activities. Boston's setting on the Charles River, with mountains to the north and Cape Cod to the south, has a relaxed and natural charm.

The College and The School

The Graduate School of Library and Information Science is a coeducational graduate school of Simmons College, a private, nonsectarian, four-year institution devoted to the career education of women. The School, established in 1902 as one of the original units of Simmons College, is administered by its dean and faculty within the structure of the College. Other graduate schools are the Graduate School of Social Work, the Graduate School of Management, and the Graduate School of Health Studies.

Applying

Application deadlines for the Master of Science program are July 1 for fall, November 1 for spring, and April 1 for the summer session. Applicants must hold a bachelor's degree from an accredited institution and must have achieved a B (3.0) average or better in their overall undergraduate program. Applicants with less than a B (3.0) average will be considered if they submit a score of at least 1000 (verbal and quantitative) on the Graduate Record Examinations or hold a strong advanced degree. Bachelor's degree candidates may file credentials after the first half of their senior year.

Applicants for the Doctor of Arts program must hold a bachelor's degree from an accredited institution, having taken the requisite distribution of liberal arts courses. In addition, they must hold a master's degree from an ALA-accredited program in library and/or information science or a master's in educational media from an accredited institution. They must also submit scores from the GRE General Test or the MAT.

Applicants whose native language is not English must achieve a satisfactory score on the TOEFL or the English Proficiency Test administered by the University of Michigan.

Correspondence and Information

Judith J. Beals, Director of Admissions
Graduate School of Library and Information Science
Simmons College
300 The Fenway
Boston, Massachusetts 02115

Telephone: 617-521-2800
Fax: 617-521-3192
E-mail: gslis@simmons.edu
World Wide Web: http://www.simmons.edu/graduate/gslis

Simmons College

THE FACULTY

James M. Matarazzo, Professor and Dean; Ph.D., Pittsburgh.

A. J. Anderson, Professor; D.Ed., Boston University.
James Baughman, Professor; Ph.D., Case Western Reserve.
Margaret A. Bush, Associate Professor; M.S., Berkeley.
Ching-chih Chen, Professor; Ph.D., Case Western Reserve.
Peter Hernon, Professor; Ph.D., Indiana.
Sheila S. Intner, Professor; D.L.S., Columbia.
Gerald P. Miller, Associate Professor; Ph.D., Michigan.
Patricia G. Oyler, Professor; Ph.D., Pittsburgh.
Robin P. Peek, Assistant Professor; Ph.D., Syracuse.
Carolyn S. Schwartz, Associate Professor; Ph.D., Syracuse.
Allen Smith, Associate Professor; Ph.D., Leeds (England).
Megan Sniffin-Marinoff, Assistant Professor; M.A., NYU.

Visiting Lecturers

Nancy S. Allen, M.L.S., M.A., Lecturer in Art Documentation; Director, Museum of Fine Arts Library, Boston.
Carol E. Chamberlain, M.L.S., Lecturer in Collection Development and Management; Associate Dean, Technical Services and Systems Development, Northeastern University Libraries.
David A. Cobb, M.L.S., Lecturer in Map Librarianship; Head, Harvard Map Collection, Harvard University.
Bernard G. Colo, M.Ed., Lecturer in Design and Production of Instructional Materials; Associate Director of Libraries/Media and Technology, Simmons College.
Ernest DiMattia Jr., M.B.A., M.S., Lecturer in Principles of Management; President, Ferguson Library, Stamford, Connecticut.
Elizabeth K. Eaton, Ph.D., Lecturer in Medical Librarianship; Director, Health Sciences Library, Tufts University.
Alberto M. Hernandez, D.Ed., Lecturer in Literature of the Humanities; Reference Librarian/Bibliographer, Thomas O'Neill Library, Boston College.
Barbara J. Jacobs, M.S. (L.S.), Lecturer in Marketing the Library; Principal and President, Jacobs Plus, Chicago, Illinois.
Inga Karetnikova, Ph.D., Lecturer in Film in Communication; Visiting Associate Professor, Boston University, College of Communications.
Marshall T. Keys, Ph.D., Lecturer in OCLC Systems and Services; Executive Director, NELINET, Inc.
Amy Lucker, M.A., M.S., Lecturer in Art Documentation; Librarian, School of the Museum of Fine Arts.
Jay K. Lucker, M.S., (L.S.), Lecturer in Literature of Science and Technology; Director of Libraries, Massachusetts Institute of Technology, Emeritus.
Martha R. Mahard, D.A., Lecturer in History of Visual Communication and Photographic Archives and Visual Information; Curator of Visual Collections, Fine Arts Library, Fogg Museum, Harvard College Library.
Jean A. Morrow, Ph.D. candidate, Lecturer in Music Librarianship; Director of Libraries, New England Conservatory of Music.
Raymond C. Niro, M.Ed., M.S., Lecturer in Online and Optical Information Services; System Consultant, Knight-Ridder Information, Inc.
Stephen Paling, M.S., Lecturer in Online Information Services; Technical Services Librarian, Cardinal Cushing Library, Emmanuel College.
Laurence Prusak, M.S., Lecturer in Management of Information in Large Organizations; Principal, Ernst & Young Center for Business Innovation.
Shelley Quezada, M.S. (L.S.), Lecturer in Literacy: The Issues and the Library's Response; Program Consultant, Library Services to the Unserved, Commonwealth of Massachusetts Board of Library Commissioners.
Ann Russell, Ph.D., Lecturer in Preservation Management; Executive Director, Northeast Document Conservation Center.
Anita Silvey, M.A., Lecturer in Modern Publishing and Librarianship; Director, Children's Books, Houghton Mifflin Publishing Co.
Harvey D. Varnet, D.A., Lecturer in Principles of Management and the Role of Research; Director of Libraries, Simmons College.
Jim Walsh, M.S.L., Lecturer in U.S. Government Information Policies, Resources, and Services; Head of Reference Services, Wessell Library, Tufts University.
Alice Sizer Warner, M.S. (L.S.), Lecturer in Information Entrepreneurship and Fiscal Management of Library and Information Systems; Proprietor, Information Guild.
Virginia Wise, J.D., Lecturer in Legal Information Sources; Lecturer on Legal Research, Harvard Law School.

Judy Beals, Director of Admissions (standing), and assistants Sharon Wilson (left) and Stephanie Knowles.

Students offer assistance at the GSLIS reserve desk.

The Graduate School of Library and Information Science at Simmons College.

SOUTHERN CONNECTICUT STATE UNIVERSITY

School of Communication, Information and Library Science
Department of Library Science and Instructional Technology

Programs of Study

The department's offerings include the Master of Library Science (M.L.S.) degree program, the M.S. in instructional technology degree program, and a sixth-year diploma program in library/information studies. The department also offers several joint-degree programs.

The Master of Library Science program, integrating library science, information science, and instructional technology, offers preparation for careers in all types of libraries and in a range of alternative information occupations. The program normally requires 36 semester hours of course work, which may be taken on a full- or part-time basis. Connecticut certification as a School Library Media Specialist may be obtained through this program.

The Master of Science in instructional technology program offers concentrations in television production, media production, and the design of systems for teaching and learning. Students normally prepare for careers in business or education. Programs of 36 semester hours are elected. Courses may be taken on a full- or part-time basis.

The Professional Diploma in Library/Information Studies provides for the formal continuing education or specialization needs of information professionals. A master's degree in library or information science is necessary for admission. The program requires 30 semester hours of course work, which may be taken on a full- or part-time basis.

Joint-degree programs enable students to study in two programs concurrently and earn two degrees. The number of credits is reduced and the time for completion shortened. In addition to several campus-based joint master's degree programs, a joint program in library science and law is offered in cooperation with the University of Connecticut School of Law.

Research Facilities

The Hilton C. Buley Library, a five-level modern facility, is the center for research at Southern Connecticut State University. In addition to notable general collections, Buley Library houses a curriculum materials center, a comprehensive audiovisual media center, and a computer resource center. The Department of Library Science and Instructional Technology occupies the fifth level of Buley Library. Facilities include administrative and faculty offices, classrooms, and laboratories for media production and computer-related activities. Television studios are located in Engleman and Earl halls.

Financial Aid

There are a limited number of assistantships offered for service within the department. Other assistantships are offered in Buley Library and other areas of the University. The chief source of aid consists of Federal Stafford Student Loans.

Cost of Study

In 1997–98, tuition for full-time study was $2013 per semester for state residents and $4740 per semester for out-of-state residents. Costs for part-time study were $173 per credit hour plus a $43.50 fee each semester and a $5-per-credit information technology fee. Southern is a member of the New England Regional Student Program, which permits qualified applicants to study library science with in-state tuition and admission privileges.

Living and Housing Costs

On-campus housing is limited for graduate students, but off-campus accommodations are readily available close to the campus at a range of prices. The University Housing Office assists students in locating suitable quarters.

Student Group

The University had 11,395 students enrolled in fall 1997, of whom 3,828 were full- or part-time graduate students. The department had 411 students in its degree programs.

Location

New Haven, Connecticut's third-largest city, is home to three universities, three colleges, and several private schools. The area has many social and cultural attractions and serves as the gateway to New England; New York and Boston are both accessible.

The University and The Department

Southern Connecticut State University, located on a 148-acre campus overlooking New Haven, is one of four institutions of the Connecticut State University System. The department traces its beginning to 1940, when courses were first offered by the State Colleges of Connecticut at Yale University. Authorization to offer degrees in library education was first granted in 1946. Programs of the department are accredited by various authorities, including the American Library Association, New England Association of Schools and Colleges, Connecticut State Department of Education, and Connecticut Commission for Higher Education.

Applying

The department operates on a year-round basis; students may be admitted for the fall, spring, or summer session. Since admission requirements vary for different degree programs, interested applicants should write or call for application forms and a catalog.

Correspondence and Information

Nancy Disbrow, Chairperson
Department of Library Science and Instructional Technology
Southern Connecticut State University
501 Crescent Street
New Haven, Connecticut 06515
Telephone: 203-392-5781
Fax: 203-392-5780
E-mail: libscienceit@scsu.ctstateu.edu

Southern Connecticut State University

THE FACULTY

Edward Harris, Dean; Ph.D., Yale.

Arlene Bielefield, Assistant Professor; J.D., Connecticut.
Mary E. Brown, Assistant Professor; Ph.D., Drexel.
Nancy Disbrow, Associate Professor and Chairperson; Professional Diploma, Fairfield.
James Kusack, Professor; Ph.D., Indiana.
Nolan Lushington, Associate Professor; M.A., M.L.S., Columbia.
James Mullins, Assistant Professor; M.L.S., Texas; M.B.A., Houston.
Gwendolyn Nowlan, Professor; Ed.D., Boston University.
Elsie G. Okobi, Assistant Professor; M.L.S., M.S., Pittsburgh.
Josephine Yu Sche, Associate Professor; Ph.D., Florida State.
William Sugar, Assistant Professor; M.S., Simmons.
Victor A. Triolo, Associate Professor; Ph.D., Wisconsin.

The Hilton C. Buley Library, center for research at Southern Connecticut State University. The Department of Library Science and Instructional Technology occupies the top floor.

SYRACUSE UNIVERSITY

School of Information Studies

Programs of Study

The School of Information Studies offers several graduate degree programs. The School has an interdisciplinary faculty who teach and conduct research in areas such as information resources management, information policy, expert systems, telecommunications, behavior of information users, evaluation and planning of library services, and online retrieval systems. The Ph.D. in information transfer emphasizes three primary areas: information systems, behavioral science, and research methods. The program prepares researchers, educators, systems designers, and managers of exceptional ability to deal with the representation, storage, transfer, retrieval, and use of information. To earn the Ph.D., 78 hours of course work (including 18 dissertation hours), oral defense of a dissertation proposal, and a completed dissertation are required. Three years in residence are usually necessary. The M.L.S. degree program, accredited by the American Library Association, requires the completion of 36 hours of credit. M.L.S. students, working with faculty advisers, set up their programs of study, which sometimes include course work in other academic areas. Approximately 70 percent of the graduates work in library settings. The remainder hold professional positions in such organizations as corporations, museums, utility companies, government agencies, and universities. The M.L.S. may be taken in a distance learning format, requiring brief residencies in Syracuse and completed predominantly through home study with the use of the Internet. The School also offers an M.S. in information resources management, which encompasses courses in management approaches and strategies, user information needs, and technological infrastructures. This program is also offered in a distance learning format. The M.S. in telecommunications and network management program prepares students for a growing number of careers dealing with the management, provision, and use of telecommunication technologies, including design and operation of voice and data networks. This program is also offered in a distance learning format. Students may visit the University's home page or see the specific program descriptions for more detailed information.

Research Facilities

Access to computer facilities at Syracuse University and within the School is excellent. All students have access to data networks connecting the University's mainframe computers (an IBM 3090 and a Sun 6/670) and a client-service environment. Students have access to more than 150 terminals and 160 microcomputers in public clusters throughout the University. All students are provided with free computer accounts and unlimited access to the Internet. The School is located in the Center for Science and Technology, the University's most sophisticated facility for teaching and research in the areas of information science, computing, and information technology. Faculty members and students work with two research centers in the building: the Center for Advanced Technology in Computer Applications and Software Engineering (CASE) and the Northeast Parallel Architectures Center. Through the ERIC Clearinghouse on Information and Technology, jointly operated by the School of Information Studies and the School of Education, students have the opportunity to see an indexing and abstracting service in operation. Students work with faculty members on a variety of research projects. The University library system ranks in the top 2 percent of university libraries in the nation. It contains more than 5 million books, periodicals, and pieces of microform information.

Financial Aid

Fellowships, scholarships, and assistantships are available to full-time students. Most prestigious and competitive are Syracuse University graduate fellowships, which include a 30-credit scholarship and a stipend of $10,894 for the 1998–99 academic year. University scholarships provide 24 hours of tuition, and graduate assistantships provide tuition and a stipend of $8000 per academic year. Tuition scholarships funded by the Gaylord Trust endowment and other small scholarships are available to part-time students. About 20 percent of the School's students receive some sort of merit award while enrolled.

Loans are available through the Financial Aid Office, 200 Archbold. For college work-study contracts, students should contact the University Student Employment Office. These kinds of assistance are awarded according to federal financial-need guidelines.

Cost of Study

Tuition for 1998–99 is $556 per graduate credit hour or $1668 per 3-credit course. Fees are approximately $350 for one year of full-time study.

Living and Housing Costs

Academic-year living expenses are about $8000 for single students. The University has residence hall rooms and on-campus apartments for single and married graduate students. Many also live off campus.

Student Group

Of the School's 450 or so matriculated graduate students, half attend part-time. Ten percent are from other countries; the remainder come from twenty-nine states. The students have diverse backgrounds with undergraduate majors in many different fields. Ninety-five percent of the School's graduates are professionally employed within three months of graduation.

Location

Syracuse, a city of 500,000 people, is set at the transportation crossroads of central New York State and is the commercial, industrial, medical, and cultural center for a wide area. Downtown Syracuse is only a 20-minute walk from the University, yet the campus is spacious and attractive. Winters are snowy; summers are pleasant. Lake Ontario, the Finger Lakes, and the Adirondack and Catskill mountains are nearby.

The University and The School

Syracuse University opened in 1870. It is private and residential and has about 15,000 students, of whom 30 percent are pursuing graduate degrees. The School of Information Studies was originally founded in 1896 as the Library School, when it was one of five such schools in the country. In 1974 its name was changed to the School of Information Studies to reflect its breadth of interests and programs, which include a unique undergraduate degree program in information management and technology.

Applying

Students are encouraged to apply for the fall semester, although admission is possible in either the fall, spring, or summer semester. Students applying for a master's-level program must have a bachelor's degree from an accredited undergraduate institution and an academic record satisfactory for admission to the graduate school, must supply three letters of recommendation and an essay on academic plans and professional goals, and must earn a combined score of at least 1000 on the verbal and quantitative sections of the GRE General Test. Whenever possible, an interview is recommended. International students should plan to take the TOEFL; a score of 550 is expected. Ph.D. applicants must achieve a score of at least 600 each on both the verbal and quantitative sections of the GRE. Students interested in University fellowships must apply by January 10. Other financial aid applicants must submit all materials by March 15.

Correspondence and Information

School of Information Studies
4-206 Center for Science and Technology
Syracuse University
Syracuse, New York 13244-4100

Telephone: 315-443-2911
E-mail: ist@syr.edu
World Wide Web: http://istweb.syr.edu

Syracuse University

THE FACULTY AND THEIR RESEARCH

Robert Benjamin, Professor; B.S. (economics), Pennsylvania (Wharton), 1948. Strategic applications of information technology, managing information technology–enabled change.

Susan Bonzi, Associate Professor; Ph.D. (library and information science), Illinois, 1983. Image retrieval systems. Received the first Information Science Doctoral Dissertation award from American Society for Information Science (ASIS), 1982.

Kevin Crowston, Assistant Professor; Ph.D. (information technologies), MIT, 1991. Organizational implications of technology, coordination-intensive processes in human organizations.

Marta Dosa, Professor Emerita; Ph.D. (library science), Michigan, 1971. Environmental and health information, information planning in developing countries, international information policies. Funded research includes: Health Information Sharing Project (National Institutes of Health/National Library of Medicine), International Clearinghouse on Information Education (UNECLO), and International Federation for Documentation (FID). Received 1986 American Society for Information Science (ASIS) Outstanding Information Science Teacher Award.

Michael B. Eisenberg, Professor; Ph.D. (information transfer), Syracuse, 1986. Information and technology literacy, development and management of Internet services and resources. Director, Information Institute of Syracuse, including the ERIC Clearinghouse on Information and Technology, AskERIC. Coauthor, *Helping with Homework: A Parent's Guide to Information Problem-Solving; Curriculum Initiative;* and *Information Problem-Solving*. Dissertation received national awards from the American Society for Information Science (ASIS) and Association for Library and Information Science Education (ALISE), 1986.

Robert Heckman, Assistant Professor; Ph.D. (information systems), Pittsburgh, 1993. Vendor-provided information systems, user satisfaction, end-user computing.

Jeffrey Katzer, Professor; Ph.D. (communication), Michigan State, 1970. The information environment of managers; information behavior; organizational, economic, and social implications of the information age. Funded research has included: representation of overlaps in computerized information retrieval systems (National Science Foundation), impact of anaphoric resolution in retrieval performance (National Science Foundation). Author and coauthor of *Free Association Behavior and Human Language Processing, Evaluating Information.*

Barbara Kwasnik, Associate Professor; Ph.D. (library and information studies), Rutgers, 1989. Classification research, knowledge representation and organization, research methods. Dissertation received 1989 best dissertation awards from the American Society for Information Science (ASIS) and from the Association for Library and Information Science Education (ALISE). Fulbright Visiting Scholar grantee (Royal School of Librarianship), Copenhagen, Denmark, 1996.

Antje B. Lemke, Professor Emerita; M.S.L.S., Syracuse, 1956. Study of the development of European libraries from the Age of Enlightenment to World War II; biography of Jacob and Wilhelm Grimm, with special emphasis on their contributions to librarianship and bibliography. Translator, *Out of My Life and Thought: An Autobiography of Albert Schweitzer.* Funded research: the Church and universities in Germany in the years of national socialism (Deutsche Forschungsgemeinschaft, Bonn). Awarded Syracuse University's Chancellor's Citation for Exceptional Academic Achievement, 1981.

Elizabeth Liddy, Professor; Ph.D. (information transfer), Syracuse, 1988. Indexing, data-mining, natural-language processing, information retrieval. Received ASIS Doctoral Dissertation Award and ALISE Doctoral Dissertation Award, 1988. Funded research: document retrieval using linguistic knowledge (DARPA) for development of DR-LINK.

Thomas H. Martin, Associate Professor; Ph.D. (communications), Stanford, 1974. Information policy, system design, human interaction with computers, human information processing, organizational communication and the foundations of information science. Assisted in the design of the Stanford Public Information Retrieval System (SPIRES).

Charles McClure, Distinguished Professor; Ph.D. (library and information studies), Rutgers, 1977. Management, planning, and evaluation of information services, federal information policy. Associate Editor, *Government Information Quarterly,* and coauthor, *Federal Information Policies in the 1990s.* Funded research: impacts and uses of national and statewide networks, electronic records management, access to U.S. federal information.

Milton L. Mueller, Associate Professor; Ph.D. (telecommunication), Pennsylvania, 1989. Telecommunication policy and deregulation, universal service.

Michael Nilan, Associate Professor; Ph.D. (communication research), Washington (Seattle), 1985. Employing user behaviors for the design of collaborative work environments in a global electronic network environment, user-based system design.

Steve Sawyer, Assistant Professor; D.B.A. (management information systems), Boston University, 1995. Work group performance and work group use of information technology, social and behavioral aspects of information technology, software development and software development management.

Barbara Settel, Associate Dean; M.L.S., Syracuse, 1976. Design and use of online retrieval systems, training end users, augmenting subject access to books in online catalogs.

Ruth V. Small, Associate Professor; Ph.D. (instructional design, development, and evaluation), Syracuse, 1986. Motivational aspects of information literacy, design and use of information and information technologies in education.

Stuart Sutton, Associate Professor; Ph.D. (library and information studies), Berkeley, 1991. Organization of information and database systems; information retrieval theory; interactive media, including information design, the structuring of interaction, and presentation design; intellectual property issues.

Zixiang (Alex) Tan, Assistant Professor; Ph.D. (telecommunications management and policy), Rutgers, 1996. Telecommunications policy and regulations, economic and social impacts of new technology, standardization policy, telecommunications in Asia.

Robert S. Taylor, Professor Emeritus; M.S. (library science), Columbia, 1950. Descriptions of organizational information environments and information-seeking behavior, definition of the information profession. Funded research: value-added processes in the information life cycle (National Science Foundation). Author, *Value Added Processes in Information Systems.*

Murali Venkatesh, Associate Professor; Ph.D. (management), Indiana, 1991. Group-based decision support systems, human-computer interaction, telecommunications.

Raymond F. von Dran, Professor and Dean; Ph.D. (library and information science), Wisconsin, 1976. Leadership and change in the management of communication and information technology; technology convergence and organizational change; competencies, curriculum, and organization structures in information education; effectiveness of modes of delivery in information education.

Rolf T. Wigand, Professor; Ph.D. (communication), Michigan State, 1975. Electronic commerce, information management, organizational communication, telecommunications policy, technology transfer. Author, *Organizations and Information Management,* Associate Editor, *The Information Society,* and Editor, *Communications.*

Ping Zhang, Assistant Professor; Ph.D. (information systems), Texas at Austin, 1995. Computer technology, information visualization for decision making, human-computer interaction.

Cooperating Adjunct Faculty

Robert Berkowitz, Coordinator for Library and Information Programs, Wayne Central Schools, Wayne, New York. School media management.

Sari Feldman, Director of Community Services, Cleveland Public Library, Ohio.

Jan Fleckenstein, Senior Assistant Librarian, Law Library, Syracuse University. Legal information resources and services.

Kaye Lindauer, Associate for Children's Literature and School Media Specialist, Syracuse University. Children's literature, storytelling.

Carol-Ann Page, President, Human Resources Development Group, Vancouver, British Columbia, Canada. Leadership and change in libraries.

Lesley Pease, Online Services Coordinator, Syracuse University Bird Library, Syracuse, New York. Information resources/services.

Eileen Schroeder, Assistant Professor and Coordinator of Technology Classroom, College of Education, University of Wisconsin–Whitewater. Library media and technology.

John Shuler, Head, Documents, University of Illinois at Chicago, Chicago, Illinois. Government information resources.

Wendy Tarby, Director of Library Services, Crouse Irving Memorial Hospital, Syracuse, New York. Biomedical information resources and services.

TEXAS WOMAN'S UNIVERSITY

School of Library and Information Studies

Programs of Study

The School of Library and Information Studies prepares students for leadership roles in the information professions, including careers in academic, public, special, and school libraries, and for a variety of roles in both private and public agencies as information specialists. Master's degrees in library science are accredited by the American Library Association. The goals for the graduate programs in librarianship and information studies are to develop knowledge that reflects not only an appropriate balance between theory and practice but also the ability to meet the changing information needs of society; to improve library and information service through research, publication, and public service; and to enhance the quality of library and information services through continuing education opportunities. The School offers programs leading to the Master of Arts in Library Science (M.A.L.S.), Master of Library Science (M.L.S.), and Doctor of Philosophy. The Learning Resources Endorsement program meets all requirements of the Texas Education Agency for library certification in public schools in Texas. The M.A.L.S. degree requires 39 hours and is designed to prepare library and information professionals to conduct research. The M.L.S. degree requires 36 hours and is designed to prepare professionals to work in academic, public, school, corporate, and other special libraries as well as other types of environments. The Doctor of Philosophy degree program consists of a minimum of 90 hours beyond the bachelor's degree.

Research Facilities

The School of Library and Information Studies is on the University's main campus in Denton, Texas. In the labs or through the Internet, students have access to a host of online information services such as Dialog, OCLC, and LEXIS-NEXIS. Students use the computers in the Information Retrieval Lab to learn online bibliographic searching, database management, and a variety of other computer applications. A unique resource is the Library Automation Laboratory, which provides students with access to an integrated library automation system and a half-dozen microcomputer-based automation systems. A multimedia lab is available for faculty and student use. Classrooms are equipped for computer system demonstrations. The School also houses a library for children and youth. This library serves as a learning laboratory for TWU students, providing a range of materials for studying children's literature and collection development as well as a training ground for children's programming such as storytelling, puppetry, and book talking. The beautiful Blagg-Huey Library contains more than 1 million items, including books, periodicals, and software, and provides access to online bibliographic search services. It maintains long runs of research journals and monograph series in the field of library and information studies and also houses a special women's collection. Campus collections in the health sciences librarianship program are located in Denton, Dallas, and Houston. Students also have access to print and electronic resources in academic libraries throughout Texas through the TXSHARE consortium.

The School maintains STORYTELL, an Internet listserver for people interested in storytelling as an art and as an enterprise. The School offers unique courses and workshops in the art of storytelling and cosponsors the annual Texas Storytelling Festival.

The Center for Consulting and Planning presents special opportunities for students to learn actively about consulting as a professional activity and about management policy and issues through courses, internships, and action research. The mission of the Center is to enhance the quality of information and library services and to expand knowledge and expertise relating to consulting as a professional activity.

Financial Aid

The School of Library and Information Studies and Texas Woman's University offer scholarships to qualified graduate students. All applications for scholarships must be addressed to the Dean, School of Library and Information Studies, P.O. Box 425438, Denton, Texas 76204-5438. Additional financial aid programs, such as grants, loans, and part-time employment on campus, are administered by the Director of Financial Aid, P.O. Box 425408.

Cost of Study

Tuition and fees per semester credit hour vary according to the number of hours taken. A Texas resident enrolled for 9 hours pays approximately $900 per semester. Nonresidents of Texas who receive a competitive award of $1000 or more are eligible to pay in-state tuition while the scholarship is in effect.

Living and Housing Costs

The six residence halls on the Denton campus provide a wide range of student living styles, including apartments for couples and students with children. Meal service contracts are available on several plans. For more information, students should write to the Department of University Housing, P.O. Box 425379.

Student Group

The School's 1997 enrollment consisted of 299 full- and part-time students. Of these, 89 percent were women and 11 percent were men. About 89 percent were Texas residents, 9 percent out-of-state, and 2 percent international. Seventy-four percent attended as part-time students through flexible scheduling and distance learning. Student chapters of the American Library Association, the Special Library Association, and the Texas Library Association are active in the School.

Location

The School of Library and Information Studies is on the University's 270-acre main campus in Denton, Texas, a community of about 70,000 residents located 35 miles north of Dallas–Fort Worth. Complete programs of study are also offered in Dallas and Fort Worth, Texas. The School offers a complete M.L.S. degree via interactive video at Canyon, Abilene, Edinburg, Texarkana, and Wichita Falls, Texas.

The University and The School

Texas Woman's University is a comprehensive public university, primarily for women, established in 1901. Now in its tenth decade, the University has grown from a small college to a major university with four campuses, more than 500 faculty members, and approximately 10,000 students. The University is fully accredited by the appropriate state, regional, and national agencies.

Texas Woman's University first offered a 2-semester-hour course in library methods in 1916–17. In 1928–29 the program was expanded to include a four-year program offering a major in library science. The master's degree program was initiated in 1949, and the doctoral program began in 1970. Since 1938, the programs for the professional degrees have been continuously accredited by the American Library Association.

Applying

Students should submit to the Office of Graduate Admissions the Application for Graduate Admission, official transcripts from all institutions of higher education previously attended, and GRE scores. Minimum scores of 500 on the verbal, 400 on the quantitative, and 450 on the analytical portions of the GRE are expected. In addition, applicants should send the completed Application for Admission to the School of Library and Information Studies and submit three letters of recommendation. For the doctoral program, applicants must also complete the Application for Admission to the Doctoral Program for the School of Library and Information Studies and interview with the Doctoral Program Committee.

The Learning Resources Endorsement applicants should follow the procedures for the master's program, with the exception that the GRE is not required. Students applying for the all-level certification program are expected to have a bachelor's degree and a valid Texas teacher's certificate.

Correspondence and Information

School of Library and Information Studies
Texas Woman's University
P.O. Box 425438
Denton, Texas 76204-5438

Telephone: 940-898-2602
Fax: 940-898-2611
E-mail: slis@twu.edu
World Wide Web: http://www.twu.edu/slis/lishome/

Texas Woman's University

THE FACULTY AND AREAS OF SCHOLARSHIP AND TEACHING

Keith Swigger, Professor and Dean; Ph.D., Iowa, 1973. Information policy, information needs and uses, research methodologies, strategic planning, libraries as social and cultural agencies, academic culture.

Betty Carter, Professor; Ed.D., Houston, 1987. History and evaluation of literature for children and young adults, the role of literature in the reading lives of young people, nature of scholarly communication and professional writing, nonfiction, reviewing as a literary and scholarly art.

Frances Dowd, Associate Professor; Ph.D., North Texas, 1978. Library management, library materials for children, literacy programs in public libraries.

Viki Ash Geisler, Assistant Professor; Ph.D., Texas at Austin, 1996. Library materials and services for children, public libraries, reference services, outreach services in libraries, naturalistic inquiry as a mode of understanding library services for children and their caregivers.

April Bohannan, Assistant Professor; Ph.D., North Carolina, 1995. Organization of knowledge, technical services in libraries, librarianship as a profession, cataloging and classification, organization and delivery of electronic information.

Evelyn Curry, Assistant Professor; Ph.D., Illinois, 1981. Reference services, special libraries, information storage and retrieval systems, multicultural librarianship, comparative librarianship with focus on development of libraries in Africa.

John D'Angelo, Assistant Professor; Ph.D., North Texas, 1991. Library automation, systems analysis, multimedia equipment and applications, instructional design, information design for effectiveness and useability, including documents, Internet applications, and multimedia presentations.

Jeffrey Huber, Assistant Professor; Ph.D., Pittsburgh, 1991. Health informatics, patterns of information dissemination, organization of knowledge, information seeking and information use among health professionals, outreach information services in health care.

Joy McGregor, Assistant Professor; Ph.D., Florida State, 1993. Foundations of librarianship, librarianship as a profession, methods of research, school libraries and the partnerships between librarians and teachers, information seeking patterns among young people.

Ketty Rodriguez, Assistant Professor; Ph.D., Indiana, 1991. Information storage and retrieval, electronic information resources, technical services in libraries, comparative librarianship with focus on library development in Latin America.

Lynn Westbrook, Assistant Professor; Ph.D., Michigan, 1995. Information needs; electronic information retrieval and management; academic librarianship; information needs and information seeking experiences and behaviors; information seeking strategies in interdisciplinary studies and women's studies; reference and public services in libraries.

Lynn Akin, Visiting Assistant Professor; Ph.D., Texas Woman's, 1996. Librarianship as a profession; information storage and retrieval; public libraries, including services to special populations; information flow among and within disciplines; information dissemination and use.

BRADSHAW PROFESSOR

Each year the endowment for the Lillian Bradshaw Visiting Scholar enables the School to bring an outstanding librarian or library educator to present the Bradshaw Lecture and to conduct a seminar. The 1998 Bradshaw Professor is Amy Spaulding (D.L.S., Columbia, 1983), who lectures and teaches on myth in the age of information.

RESEARCH PROFESSORS

These distinguished professional librarians serve as advisors and occasional teachers:
Naomi Broering, Director of the Jesse Jones Library, Texas Medical Center, Houston.
Richard Waters, Principal Consultant, PROVIDENCE Associates, Inc., Denton.

In addition to full-time faculty members, distinguished professionals serve as adjunct faculty members who teach elective courses in areas of their specialized knowledge and experience.

ADVISORY COMMITTEE

Naomi Broering, Executive Director, Texas Medical Center Library, Houston Academy of Medicine.
Michael Cart, Author, Chico, California.
Donna Duncan, District Libraries Coordinator, Mesquite (Texas) Independent School District.
Susan Elam, Information Consultant, LEXIS/NEXIS, Dallas.
Michael Gorman, Dean of Libraries, California State University, Fresno.
Robert S. Martin, Director and Librarian, Texas State Library and Archives, Austin.
Ramiro Salazar, Director, Dallas (Texas) Public Library.
Mary Kay Snell, Director, Amarillo (Texas) Public Library.
Julie Walker, Executive Director, American Association of School Libraries and Young Adult Library Association, Chicago.
Richard Werking, Director, Nimitz Library, U.S. Naval Academy, Annapolis.

UNIVERSITY OF ILLINOIS AT URBANA–CHAMPAIGN

Graduate School of Library and Information Science

Programs of Study

The University of Illinois at Urbana-Champaign Graduate School of Library and Information Science (GSLIS) is recognized as a premier institution that is able to provide the training and education necessary for professional excellence in the ever-changing information landscape. For more than 100 years, GSLIS has prepared students for careers as leaders in information professions and research. As one of the oldest LIS schools in the country, Illinois helped establish and develop the methods used in the fields of library and information science today. Graduates are adept at using the latest technology and methods for cataloging, research, information gathering, and other professional tasks. The field is necessarily interdisciplinary, and the School recruits individuals with strong theoretical and methodological foundations who understand libraries and the broader context of information systems and services. Students may pursue Ph.D. and M.S. degrees and a certificate of advanced study (CAS). Many master's students and recent graduates cite the opportunity to design their own programs of study as a major advantage at Illinois; examples of specializations include automation, community information systems, information systems architecture, and services for children and young adults. A master's degree candidate with a full-time load can complete the ten-unit program in two semesters and one summer, though many students choose to continue in the program for an additional semester or two. Students have three interchangeable scheduling options for M.S. degree course work: a regular on-campus schedule, the Friday's Only option, and the LEEP3 distance education option. Friday's Only scheduling allows commuting students to complete the M.S. degree in two years by enrolling in on-campus courses offered on Fridays. The LEEP3 distance education option brings students to campus only for brief periods of study; remaining course work is completed remotely, using varied formats that include Internet-based courses with real-time audio and visuals.

Research Facilities

Students work with professors on projects that range from community use of information systems to the impact of story on children's development to the Digital Library Initiative project. (The faculty listing has additional research topics.) Infrastructure includes two labs, which provide twenty-one networked PC stations and advanced workstations for systems research. Research is supported by additional Graduate School resources: the Library Research Center, which conducts research on all types of libraries and information centers; Information Researchers, an information analysis service; the Center for Children's Books, home of an examination collection of more than 14,000 books for and about children and publisher of *The Bulletin of the Center for Children's Books*; the Publications Office, which produces the quarterly journal *Library Trends* and other LIS related materials; and Prairienet, the East-Central Illinois free-net and community information network. UIUC has the third-largest research library in the U.S., which includes a separate Library and Information Science Library. The University hosts the National Center for Supercomputing Applications. All of these resources provide research opportunities as well as student employment.

Financial Aid

Financial aid awards take the form of fellowships, graduate assistantships, and student loans. All fellowships and assistantships include both a stipend and a tuition and service fee waiver of at least the in-state cost. Graduate assistantships comprise the primary source of financial aid and are awarded by the Graduate School, the University Library, and a variety of other campus units. More than 90 percent of all GSLIS on-campus students received support in 1997–98. Graduate assistantships are normally available only to regular on-campus students. All students may be eligible for student loans.

Cost of Study

In 1998–99, the tuition and fees per semester for full-time students are $2758 for Illinois residents and $6196 for nonresidents.

Living and Housing Costs

On-campus housing for graduate students is available through the University; costs are $2500 per semester; meal contracts are also available. Students also live in a variety of off-campus locations, including University-operated family housing.

Student Group

Total enrollment in degree programs at the Graduate School in fall 1997 was 288 (30 percent men, 70 percent women), of whom 178 were from the state of Illinois, 86 were from out-of-state, and 24 were from outside the U.S. There are several active student organizations that sponsor social and educational activities throughout the year, including such job search assistance workshops as resume preparation, interview preparation, and salary negotiation.

Student Outcomes

Recent master's graduates have accepted positions in all types of libraries and in a variety of other organizations, including consulting firms, library vendors, and technology companies. Employers include Yale University Library, Microsoft, Chicago Public Libraries, Ameritech, NASA, DRA, Arthur Andersen, and Illinois Wesleyan University. Almost all Ph.D. graduates assume academic faculty positions.

Location

Champaign-Urbana has a population of about 100,000 and is situated about 140 miles south of Chicago, 120 miles west of Indianapolis, and 170 miles northeast of St. Louis. The Krannert Center for the Performing Arts provides a wide array of entertainment, as do local music venues and theater and dance groups. The Champaign-Urbana area is also adjacent to a number of parks and other natural recreational areas.

The University and The School

The University of Illinois at Urbana-Champaign was founded in 1867. With 36,500 students, of whom 9,800 are graduate students, it is consistently ranked as one of the top universities in the U.S. Graduate education alone is available in more than 100 disciplines, bringing together a student body that varies as widely in its ethnicity as in its interests. Consistently ranked as one of the top three library and information science programs in the U.S., the Graduate School of Library and Information Science, founded in 1893 at the Armour Institute in Chicago, maintains a reputation of excellence and quality.

Applying

Applicants for graduate programs must hold a bachelor's degree, have a minimum grade point average of 3.0 on a 4.0 scale for the junior and senior years of the bachelor's degree or the last 60 semester hours, and submit GRE scores from within the past five years, an essay, and three letters of recommendation. Doctoral applicants must also complete an interview with the School's Advanced Studies Committee after the initial application has been received and reviewed. Admissions are made on a rolling basis for students beginning the program in the fall, spring, or summer semesters. Applicants for the Certificate of Advanced Study programs must hold a master's degree in library and information science or a closely related field, have a minimum grade point average of 3.0 on a 4.0 scale in library and information science course work, have a minimum grade point average of 3.0 on a 4.0 scale in the last 60 semester hours of undergraduate course work, and submit three letters of recommendation.

Correspondence and Information

Dr. Leigh S. Estabrook
Graduate School of Library and Information Science
University of Illinois at Urbana-Champaign
501 East Daniel Street
Champaign, Illinois 61820
Telephone: 217-333-7197 (Admissions)
Fax: 217-244-3302
E-mail: gslis@alexia.lis.uiuc.edu
World Wide Web: http://alexia.lis.uiuc.edu

University of Illinois at Urbana-Champaign

THE FACULTY AND THEIR RESEARCH

Ann P. Bishop, Assistant Professor; Ph.D., Syracuse. Use and impact of computer-based information systems, social equity in access to information, human-centered approaches to designing and evaluating information systems.

Geoffrey C. Bowker, Associate Professor; Ph.D., Melbourne. Themes of organizational memory; social and organizational aspects of the development of large-scale classification systems, particularly in scientific and medical arenas.

J. Stephen Downie, Assistant Professor; Ph.D., Western Ontario. Design and evaluation of IR systems, including multimedia music information retrieval; the political economy of Internet-worked communication systems; database design; Web-based technologies.

David S. Dubin, Assistant Professor; Ph.D., Pittsburgh. Information retrieval, classification and clustering, data visualization, text and document processing.

Leigh S. Estabrook, Professor and Dean; Ph.D., Boston University. Municipal official and librarian assessments of the public library in the political process, the way in which small businesses use information to solve problems, marketing information services.

Les Gasser, Associate Professor; Ph.D., California, Irvine. Coordination of information, coordination theory/tools, multi-agent systems, manufacturing research, intensive industry liaison, R&D project management, multi-agent systems.

Caroline Haythornthwaite, Assistant Professor; Ph.D., Toronto. Organizations and information technology, adoption and diffusion of innovations, computer-mediated communication supporting informal information change, organization theory, social network analysis.

Elizabeth (Betsy) G. Hearne, Associate Professor; Ph.D., Chicago. Literary and artistic analysis of children's books, elements of folklore and mythology that survive in children's literature, publishing history of juvenile literature in the nineteenth and twentieth centuries, cultural and social trends reflected in children's books, developmental role of literature and storytelling from birth to adolescence, impact of story on children's psychological adjustment and reading motivation.

P. Bryan Heidorn, Assistant Professor; Ph.D., Pittsburgh. Image database design; shape and spatial semantics; natural language processing, particularly as related to images.

Christine A. Jenkins, Assistant Professor; Ph.D., Wisconsin–Madison. History of youth services librarianship as women's history, censorship and intellectual freedom issues, representations of minority-status groups in children's and young adult literature, reading engagement, reader-response research and the reader-text interaction.

Robert Alun Jones, Professor; Ph.D., Pennsylvania. Durkheim and his intellectual context, the methodology of the history of ideas, the scholarly use of electronic documents and networked information systems.

Cynthia (Cindy) A. Kehoe, Assistant Professor; Ph.D., Texas at Austin. Metrics for R&D and technology transfer, the professional socialization of graduate students.

Edward Lomax, Assistant Professor; Ph.D., Pittsburgh. Information need and information-seeking behavior in medical oncology, information seeking in multimedia clinical information systems.

Cheryl Knott Malone, Assistant Professor; Ph.D., Texas at Austin. Gender, race, and class in the information professions; LIS history; impact of philanthropy and volunteerism on educational institutions; collection management, particulary academic and research libraries.

Carole L. Palmer, Assistant Professor; Ph.D., Illinois. Information use in the research process, development of cross-disciplinary information services, boundary-crossing practices of interdisciplinary researchers, scholarly and professional communication, synthesis of research results and integration of knowledge, social and cultural contexts of information in research organization, problem-centered information tools.

Deborah L. Rhodes, Visiting Assistant Professor; Ph.D., Pittsburgh. Cost-effectiveness of public library systems in metropolitan areas, resource development in libraries of independent African-American schools, electronic record-keeping systems.

Karen Ruhleder, Assistant Professor; Ph.D., California, Irvine. Ethnography of information systems, analysis of infrastructures to support geographically distributed collaborative work.

Bruce R. Schatz, Professor; Ph.D., Arizona. Network information systems, national information infrastructure; digital libraries, semantic retrieval, electronic communities.

Linda C. Smith, Professor; Ph.D., Syracuse. Information system design, education for library and information science, impact of new technologies on reference and information services.

Susan Leigh Star, Professor; Ph.D., California, San Francisco. Social and organizational aspects of large information systems, most recently in the area of digital libraries and medical classification.

Robert Wedgeworth, Professor and University Librarian; M.S., Illinois. International librarianship.

Terry L. Weech, Associate Professor; Ph.D., Illinois. Collection management, evaluation of library services, library education, library cooperation and networking.

Martha E. Williams, Research Professor; M.A., Loyola Chicago. Information storage and retrieval, online retrieval; systems and techniques to improve/facilitate retrieval; databases; information policy.

Emeritus Faculty

Walter C. Allen, Associate Professor Emeritus; M.S., Columbia.
Pauline Atherton Cochrane, Professor Emeritus; M.A., Rosary College.
James L. Divilbiss, Associate Professor Emeritus; Ph.D., Illinois.
Herbert Goldhor, Professor Emeritus; Ph.D., Chicago.
Kathryn Luther Henderson, Professor Emerita; M.S., Illinois.
Donald W. Krummel, Professor Emeritus; Ph.D., Michigan.
F. W. Lancaster, Professor Emeritus; Fellow, Library Association of Great Britain.
Selma K. Richardson, Professor Emerita; Ph.D., Michigan.

UNIVERSITY OF MARYLAND, COLLEGE PARK

College of Library and Information Services

Programs of Study

The curriculum of the College of Library and Information Services (CLIS) concentrates on areas central to research and practice in librarianship and information science and provides a comprehensive foundation for professional careers in agencies engaged in information activities.

CLIS awards a Master of Library Science degree (accredited by the American Library Association) upon successful completion of 36 credit hours with a minimum average of B within three years from the first registration (five years for the HiLS and GeLS programs below). Four core courses are required for all students; the remaining credits are chosen to fulfill the student's goals. A full-time student can complete the program within one calendar year, although one additional semester is recommended.

The HiLS program, offered cooperatively with the history department, is a course of study (54 credit hours) leading to the M.A. in history and the M.L.S. The GeLS program is offered cooperatively with the geography department; upon completion of 54 credit hours, students earn the M.A. in geography and the M.L.S. The school library media program is accredited or approved by all appropriate national and state agencies.

The interdisciplinary doctoral program prepares students for careers in teaching and research and in information systems design and administration. Two areas, communication and information transfer, and information storage and retrieval, are required of all doctoral students. Three other areas are selected from among such areas as linguistics, psychology, and mass communication. The program requires 60 credits of course work and successful defense of a dissertation. One year of full-time residency is required. Admission to the program is limited so that each student may get the faculty attention a theory-based program requires.

Research Facilities

CLIS maintains its own library to support its academic and research program. Students have access to other libraries in the University of Maryland System, including specialized branches, such as art and computer science. Microcomputer facilities are maintained by CLIS and by UMCP. All students have access to campus mainframe computer resources, such as electronic mail and library catalogs, and to the resources available on the Internet. The Instructional Development and Support Center is a nonprint media facility with equipment, materials, instruction, and individual assistance in all areas of audiovisual production.

CLIS students enrich their programs through use of other resources close at hand. UMCP is home to Archives II, an expansion facility of the National Archives. Three national libraries (Library of Congress, National Agricultural Library, and National Library of Medicine) and hundreds of special libraries extend study opportunities for CLIS students.

Financial Aid

Opportunities include fellowships, assistantships, and scholarships. Awards range from stipends of $10,100 and tuition remission for nine months to one-time awards of $1800. Financial assistance is rarely available to international students. Many employment opportunities in libraries on campus and in the Washington-Baltimore area, such as the National Agricultural Library and National Archives, are available.

Cost of Study

In 1998–99, tuition and mandatory fees for the academic year (fall and spring semesters) for full-time students are $7092 for Maryland residents and $10,164 for nonresidents. The tuition per credit is $272 for residents and $400 for nonresidents.

Living and Housing Costs

On-campus living costs for the nine-month 1998–99 academic year are about $3500 for housing with telephone (dorms or apartments) and approximately $2400 for dining (Department of Resident Life, 301-314-2100). Off-campus living in group rentals costs approximately $375 for rent and utilities and $225 for food per month. The Off-Campus Housing Program maintains a housing location office (301-314-3645).

Student Group

Enrollment in the program was 250 students for spring 1998; 75 percent of the students are women; 65 percent are part-time; 82 percent are from Maryland, the District of Columbia, and Virginia; 63 percent are between the ages of 25 and 39 years; and 4 percent are international. The Student Services Office and active student chapters of professional organizations (ASIS, SLA, SAA) provide social and educational programs. Graduates find professional positions in academic, special, public, and government libraries and in nontraditional settings as information specialists.

Location

College Park is located in the center of the Washington, D.C.–Baltimore, Maryland, metropolitan area, a cosmopolitan center of cultural and intellectual activity and political power. CLIS students have opportunities for experience with agencies such as NASA, the Smithsonian Institute, the National Archives and Maryland State Archives, the Library of Congress, the National Library of Medicine, and the National Agricultural Library. The Maryland countryside offers settings for a variety of leisure activities, from the mountains in the west to the Atlantic beaches on the Eastern Shore.

The University and the College

The College Park campus is the flagship campus of the University of Maryland System, with more than 8,000 graduate students. UMCP is committed to fostering academic excellence through diversity in its faculty, staff, and students. The College has been a leader in preparing information professionals since its inception in 1965. Today CLIS is forging new connections with other academic disciplines to facilitate the exploration of vital questions about information policy and services in the twenty-first century. Students interested in joining faculty members and other students in this challenge are invited to seek further information.

Applying

Requirements for admission to the M.L.S. program include a bachelor's degree, an undergraduate GPA of at least 3.0 on a 4.0 scale, and GRE scores of least 1000 on the verbal and quantitative sections combined. A statement of purpose and three recommendation letters must be submitted. Applications for the M.L.S. and GeLS programs are accepted for the summer and fall semesters only; deadlines are May 1 and June 1, respectively. HiLS applications are accepted for the fall semester; the deadline is January 15. The deadline for applying for financial aid is February 1. International applicants must apply by February 1. Applicants to the doctoral program must submit transcripts, three letters of recommendation, GRE scores, and a statement of research interests. Admission decisions are preceded by an interview. Applications for the fall semester must be made by February 1 and for the spring semester by June 1.

Information about CLIS is available on the Internet at www.clis.umd.edu and at www.umd.edu.

Correspondence and Information

Student Services Office
College of Library and Information Services
University of Maryland
College Park, Maryland 20742-4345

Telephone: 301-405-2038
TTD: 301-405-2040
E-mail: clisumcp@umdacc.umd.edu

University of Maryland, College Park

THE FACULTY AND THEIR RESEARCH

Eileen G. Abels, Associate Professor; Ph.D., UCLA. Reference, online searching, electronic communications, special libraries.
Robert B. Allen, Visiting Professor; Ph.D., California, San Diego. Multimedia information, human-computer interaction, information retrieval.
Diane L. Barlow, Assistant Dean and Lecturer; Ph.D., Maryland. Communication and information transfer.
Bruce W. Dearstyne, Associate Professor; Ph.D., Syracuse. Archives, records management.
Rebecca Green, Associate Professor; Ph.D., Maryland. Information storage and retrieval, classification theory, database design, cognitive linguistics.
Christopher J. Halonen, Instructor; M.L.S., Toronto. Archives, information system management, organizational information management.
Charles B. Lowry, Professor and Dean of Libraries; Ph.D., Florida. Information technology, management, academic libraries.
Anne S. MacLeod, Professor; Ph.D., Maryland. Children's literature in its historical context, storytelling.
M. Delia Neuman, Associate Professor; Ph.D., Ohio State. Computer-based education, instructional systems design, special education, qualitative research, writing and editing.
Douglas W. Oard, Assistant Professor; Ph.D., Maryland. Information technology, computer applications, text filtering, information retrieval.
Ann E. Prentice, Professor and Dean; D.L.S., Columbia. Management of information environments, governance, planning, financial administration, political considerations, community analysis, research methodology, education for the information professions, outcome assessment.
Dagobert Soergel, Professor; D.Phil. Freiburg (Germany). Information storage and retrieval, development of indexing languages, computer applications.
Claude E. Walston, Professor; Ph.D., Ohio State. Computer applications, systems analysis, software management.
Marilyn D. White, Associate Professor; Ph.D., Illinois. Reference and bibliography, online searching, social sciences bibliography, special library, academic library, communication.

Emeritus Faculty

Frank G. Burke, Professor; Ph.D., Chicago. Archives, records management, manuscript and collection administration, archival automation, documentary editing.
Jerry S. Kidd, Professor Emeritus; Ph.D., Northwestern. Systems analysis, research methods, science communication including popularization, user needs.
James W. Liesener, Professor Emeritus; Ph.D., Michigan. School library media services, young adult services, management.
Paul Wasserman, Professor; Ph.D., Michigan. Administration, bibliography, publishing, comparative librarianship.
Hans H. Wellisch, Professor Emeritus; Ph.D., Maryland. Indexing and abstracting, classification.

Adjunct Faculty

Laurie A. Baty, M.A., George Washington. Visual and sound materials.
Diane L. Boehr, M.L.S., Maryland. Advanced cataloging.
William D. Cunningham, M.L.S., Texas. Reference, public library.
Betty Day, Ph.D., Maryland. Humanities reference, electronic services.
Maralita Freeny, M.L.S., Catholic University. Children's materials, children's services in public libraries.
Trudi B. Hahn, Ph.D., Drexel. Research methods, information environments.
Donald Hausrath, M.L.S., Berkeley. International librarianship.
Carla Hayden, Ph.D., Chicago. Library administration, public library.
Neal K. Kaske, Ph.D., Oklahoma. Networks, effectiveness of information services.
Michael J. Kurtz, Ph.D., Georgetown. Archives, records management.
Eric Lindquist, Ph.D., Harvard. Humanities reference.
Michael L. Miller, Ph.D., Ohio State. Archives, electronic records.
Michael S. Miller, M.L.S., Pittsburgh. Legal information.
Thomas C. Phelps, M.L.S., Oregon. Library administration.
Marietta Plank, M.A.L.S., Michigan. Technical services.
Jack Robertson, M.A., Michigan. Fine arts librarianship.
Lawrence Rudner, Ph.D., Catholic University. Research methods, evaluation.
Anne L. Sheldon, M.L.S., Maryland. Storytelling, children's literature.
Karen Sinkule, A.M.L.S., Michigan. Preservation of materials.
Fred W. Weingarten, Ph.D., Oregon State. Information policy.
William G. Wilson, A.M.L.S., Michigan. Reference, public library, academic library.

UNIVERSITY OF MICHIGAN

School of Information

Programs of Study

This is a time of challenge and opportunity. Traditional ways of collecting, maintaining, and accessing information are in transition. Schools and universities are filled with computers. Organizational work structures are shifting. Whole industries are being transformed. Clearly, there is a growing demand for new kinds of information professionals who have broad competencies, a holistic view of information systems, and the skills to solve problems that are beyond anyone's imagining at this moment in time. The School of Information (SI) is educating information professionals who possess all these qualities. Upon graduation, alumni become Webmasters, chief information officers, communications information network coordinators, librarians, digital preservationists, entrepreneurs, consultants, software engineers, and more.

The School of Information offers a 48-credit-hour master's degree program that introduces students to the foundations of the information disciplines in a new and exciting integrated way, offers a variety of advanced courses that prepare students for existing or newly formed specializations, and gives the students venues in which to exercise their knowledge in several practical engagements. Four specializations are formed: library and information services, archives and records management, human-computer interaction, and information economics, management, and policy. Students may choose from one of these or devise a program of their own in consultation with faculty members to prepare them for a new, emerging profession. All students must take five 3-credit foundations courses that introduce students to the fundamentals of library and information science, computer science, psychology, and economics. At least 18 credit hours of advanced courses and 6–15 credit hours of practical-engagement activities are required.

Research Facilities

The University of Michigan (UM) provides access to technologically advanced thriving research and computing environments. Students at the School of Information have access to a robust networking environment, including computers, telecommunications, and video; the Media Union, which houses interdisciplinary projects that explore the use of leading-edge information technology; and libraries that contain more than 6 million volumes and 70,000 serial titles, accessible through online card catalogs and digital libraries. In addition, the Information Technology Services Office at the School of Information maintains a state-of-the-art computing infrastructure and two computing facilities dedicated to SI students. The Advanced Projects Laboratory provides equipment, software, and services related to media integration (digitization, multimedia authoring, and video editing) as well as state-of-the-art equipment that is used by advanced research projects. The Digital Information Access and Dissemination Laboratory, which is available exclusively to SI faculty and staff members, students, and University Library professional staff members, provides a general computing and teaching facility.

Financial Aid

The School of Information offers research assistantships and full and half scholarships to both incoming and continuing students. Approximately 54 percent of the fall 1997 incoming class received financial assistance from the School. Awards are merit based. In addition, the University of Michigan offers several competitive scholarships and fellowships. Minority students may be eligible for tuition assistance as part of UM's commitment to provide higher education to a diversified student body. There are numerous opportunities for employment on campus and in local communities.

Cost of Study

In 1997–98, the tuition per term (four months) for full-time students was $4816 for Michigan residents and $9769 for out-of-state residents.

Living and Housing Costs

Housing and utilities for a single student are approximately $2800 for one 4-month term. The University offers graduate housing for both single and married students. A wide variety of housing options are available off campus; the University Housing Office offers some assistance in locating them.

Student Group

Students join the program from a wide variety of academic and professional backgrounds. Total enrollment at the School is about 250. The average undergraduate GPA of the current class is 3.35, and the average GRE score is 1870. Approximately 70 percent of the student body are women and 30 percent are men. Thirty percent attend the program part-time; many of these students are employed full-time and participate in evening classes.

Student Outcomes

Approximately 74 percent of graduates are employed within three months of graduation. Graduates find challenging work throughout the world in many settings, including libraries, corporations, consulting firms, schools, nonprofit organizations, and universities. Recent graduates have found positions as project managers, researchers, directors, faculty members, Webmasters, digital librarians, consultants, archivists, programmers, and media specialists.

Location

Situated 40 miles west of Detroit, Ann Arbor is a city of about 107,000 well served by interstate expressways and Detroit Metropolitan Airport. Ann Arbor is recognized internationally as a cultural center. Concert series, theatrical and dance productions, classic film series, and conventional movie theaters provide plenty of entertainment.

The University and The School

The University of Michigan, known internationally for fine higher education, has a strong commitment to providing diversity in its academic programs, faculty, and staff. There are about 34,000 students on the Ann Arbor Campus, of whom 13,000 are graduate students. Ranked as one of the top professional schools, the School has a respected reputation in the profession for the education of future library and information leaders, and its master's degree program has been accredited by the American Library Association since 1928.

Applying

Applicants for the master's degree program must hold a bachelor's degree and have an undergraduate grade point average of at least 3.0 on a 4.0 scale. GRE scores earned in the past five years are required. Three letters of recommendation and three essays must be submitted. Applicants wishing to be considered for scholarships from the School are advised to submit a resume. Application deadlines are March 1 for fall enrollment and November 1 for winter enrollment. Applicants not seeking financial aid may apply until August 1 for fall and December 1 for winter. The doctoral degree application deadline is January 15.

It is recommended, but not required, that applicants for the doctoral program hold a master's degree (ideally in an information field relevant to the student's proposed area of research). Students without a master's degree may need to adjust their required course work. Other requirements include a superior academic record, scores from the GRE taken within the past five years, and TOEFL scores from the past three years (international applicants only).

Correspondence and Information

School of Information
University of Michigan
550 East University
Ann Arbor, Michigan 48109-1092

Telephone: 313-763-2285
Fax: 313-764-2475
E-mail: SI.admissions@umich.edu
World Wide Web: http://www.si.umich.edu

University of Michigan

THE FACULTY AND THEIR RESEARCH

Daniel E. Atkins, Professor and Dean; Ph.D., Illinois. Advanced information and collaborative systems and services, digital library architecture.
C. Olivia Frost, Professor and Associate Dean for Professional Programs; Ph.D., Chicago. Providing intellectual access to information, information searching behavior in a networked environment, organization and retrieval of networked and digital information, use of classification to facilitate browsing and visual images in digital libraries, intellectual access to nontextual information in print and digital formats.
Gary M. Olson, Professor (also in Psychology) and Associate Dean for Research and Doctoral Programs; Ph.D., Stanford. Applied cognitive science, human-computer interaction, computer-supported cooperative work, design and evaluation of collaboratories to support distributed science and engineering.
William P. Birmingham, Associate Professor (also in Electrical Engineering and Computer Science); Ph.D., Carnegie Mellon. Concurrent engineering, electronic commerce, knowledge systems, knowledge acquisition, expert systems.
Francis X. Blouin, Professor and Director, Bentley Historical Library; Ph.D., Minnesota. Archival administration, international archival affairs.
Michael D. Cohen, Professor (also in Public Policy and Political Science); Ph.D., California, Irvine. Organizational decision making, processes of learning and adaptation within organizations, organizational effects of information technology.
Lisa Covi, Research Fellow; Ph.D., California, Irvine. Digital libraries, computer-supported cooperative work, social informatics, information retrieval.
Karen Drabenstott, Associate Professor; Ph.D., Syracuse. Subject searching in online catalogs, subject access to visual resources collections, subject authority control, and enhancing bibliographic databases using a library classification, online database coverage, overlap, and redesign; patron searching of online catalogs and digital libraries; subject access to library cataloging records; descriptions of subject contents of visual materials.
Edmund Durfee, Associate Professor (also in Electrical Engineering and Computer Science); Ph.D., Massachusetts. Distributed artificial intelligence, planning, cooperative robotics, real-time problem solving, research methodology, fundamental issues in computation.
Joan C. Durrance, Professor; Ph.D., Michigan. Public libraries, community information networking, access issues, information needs, professional practice.
Thomas Finholt, Assistant Research Scientist and Adjunct Assistant Professor in Psychology; Ph.D., Carnegie Mellon. Impact of collaboratories on their user communities, impact of computer communication technology on information processing in organizations, occupational diseases associated with computer use, distance learning, the design of collaborative computing environments, participatory management.
George Furnas, Professor (also in Electrical Engineering and Computer Science and Psychology); Ph.D., Stanford. Information access and visualization, multivariate statistics, graphical reasoning, adaptive indexing, latent semantic indexing, generalized fish-eye views, purely graphical deduction systems, prosection, social filtering, multitrees, space-scale diagrams, information navigation.
José-Marie Griffiths, Professor, University Chief Information Officer, and Director of the University Information Technology Division; Ph.D., London. Digital libraries, access to heterogeneous distributed databases.
Margaret Hedstrom, Associate Professor; Ph.D., Wisconsin. Management and preservation of electronic records, digital preservation strategies, impact of electronic communications on organizational memory and documentation, remote access to archival materials, cultural preservation and outreach in developing countries.
Maurita P. Holland, Associate Professor and Assistant to the Dean for Academic Outreach; A.M.L.S., Michigan. Special libraries and information centers, knowledge management, distance-independent learning, technology-assisted community networks and programs, professional continuous education.
Jeffrey K. MacKie-Mason, Associate Professor (also in Public Policy and Economics); Ph.D., MIT. Economics of information technology and content, telecommunications, industrial organization, public finance, finance.
Judy S. Olson, Professor (also in Business Administration and Psychology); Ph.D., Michigan. Human-computer interaction, design and evaluation of software for human problem solving in business.
Karen Pettigrew, Research Fellow; Ph.D., Western Ontario. Community networking, public libraries, special libraries, information retrieval, modeling for information seeking.
Paul Resnick, Associate Professor; Ph.D., MIT. Application design space analysis, user-interface evaluation, protocol design, economic game theory, recommender systems.
Elena Rocco, Visiting Research Investigator; M.A., Venice. Computer-supported cooperative work.
Victor Rosenberg, Associate Professor; Ph.D., Chicago. Information retrieval, information policy, technology in the humanities, software development, entrepreneurship.
Thomas P. Slavens, Professor; Ph.D., Michigan. Sources of general information, sources of information in the humanities, sources of information in the social sciences, history of books and printing, history of libraries.
Elliot Soloway, Professor (also in Electrical Engineering and Computer Science and Education); Ph.D., Massachusetts. Use of technology in education, developing software that takes into consideration the unique needs of learners.
Margaret T. Taylor, Adjunct Lecturer; Ph.D., Michigan. Literature for children and young adults, library use and user studies, collection development, patterns of scholarly communication, publishing.
Stephanie Teasley, Assistant Research Scientist; Ph.D., Pittsburgh. Social and cognitive processes in collaboration, technology use to support key aspects of collaboration for both colocated groups and distributed groups.
Spencer Thomas, Assistant Research Scientist; Ph.D., Utah. Use of visualization to aid in the understanding, exploration, and interpretation of raw and derived data and information.
Marshall W. Van Alstyne, Assistant Professor; Ph.D., MIT. Information economics, measurement and management of information capital, pricing strategies for information goods.
Douglas E. Van Houweling, Professor; Ph.D., Indiana. Information systems planning and management, strategic planning, simulation models of political and public policy processes, economic models of politics, technology assessment. (On leave)
David Wallace, Assistant Professor; Ph.D., Pittsburgh. Investigations into computerization of government records and the impact on federal record keeping and access statutes; strategies for preserving electronic records of collaborative processes; creation, implementation, and evaluation of electronic mail policies within organizations; U.S. government information secrecy and classification/declassification policies; policy issues associated with the National Information Infrastructure; history of record keeping in modern and premodern states.
Amy J. Warner, Associate Professor; Ph.D., Illinois. Information retrieval, theory and development of indexing language, natural-language processing applications in online retrieval system design.
Terry Weymouth, Associate Research Scientist (also in Electrical Engineering and Computer Science); Ph.D., Massachusetts. Knowledge-based sensor-guided robot navigation, collaboration technology for the support of medical diagnosis and for the support of distributed remote scientific experimentation.

Part-Time and Adjunct Faculty

Leila Avrin, Adjunct Lecturer; Ph.D., Michigan.
Sandra Bartlett, Adjunct Assistant Professor; Ph.D., Michigan.
Gail Beaver, Adjunct Lecturer; A.M.L.S., Michigan.
Clare Canham-Eaton, Adjunct Lecturer; A.M.L.S., Michigan.
Bonnie A. Dede, Adjunct Lecturer; A.M.L.S., Michigan.
Elaine K. Didier, Adjunct Associate Professor; Ph.D., Michigan.
Calvin Elliker, Adjunct Lecturer; Ph.D., Illinois.
Jonathan A. Franklin, Adjunct Lecturer; J.D., Stanford.
Joseph Janes, Librarian and Director, Internet Public Library; Ph.D., Syracuse.
Barbara MacAdam, Adjunct Lecturer; A.M.L.S., Michigan.
Pamela J. Mackintosh, Adjunct Lecturer; M.Libr., Washington (Seattle).
Michael D. Miller, Adjunct Lecturer; M.P.S., NYU.
Thomas E. Powers, Adjunct Professor; A.M.L.S., Michigan.
Patricia Redman, Adjunct Lecturer; M.S.L.S., Catholic University.
Mark Sandler, Adjunct Lecturer; Ph.D., Michigan State.
Harold Tuckett, Adjunct Lecturer; A.M.L.S., Michigan.

Emeritus Faculty

Russell E. Bidlack, Ph.D., Michigan.
Gwendolyn S. Cruzat, Ph.D., Wayne State.
Richard M. Dougherty, Ph.D., Rutgers.
David W. Hessler, Ph.D., Michigan State.
Anthony Kruzas, Ph.D., Michigan.
Raymond L. Kilgour, Ph.D., Harvard.
Constance Rinehart, A.M.L.S., Michigan.
Helen L. Snoke, Ph.D., Oklahoma.
Rose Vainstein, M.L.S., Illinois.
Robert M. Warner, Ph.D., Michigan.

UNIVERSITY OF PITTSBURGH

School of Information Sciences
Department of Library and Information Science

Programs of Study

The School of Information Sciences of the University of Pittsburgh offers an integrated program of studies to prepare individuals for a broad range of positions in the library, telecommunications, and information sciences. Through its departments, the School offers six degree programs, a strong and flexible program of continuing education, institutes, and workshops. The Department of Library and Information Science has a Master of Library and Information Science program—accredited by the American Library Association—that requires completion of 36 credits of postbaccalaureate study. The Doctor of Philosophy program prepares students for advanced work in research, teaching, and administration. Continuing education needs are met by the program for the Certificate of Advanced Study, which enables recent graduates to continue work in an area of special interest and practicing librarians to keep abreast of current developments. Carefully tailored by the students and their advisers to meet individual needs, this program requires completion of 24 credit hours of study. A series of 2½-day courses is offered in the summer to support the continuing education needs of library and information science professionals.

The program is responsive to the information marketplace by offering programs targeted toward librarianship for academic, public (including children's literature), school, corporate, law, medical, and special libraries and information centers. Specializations in archives and records management, health information management, preservation management, and information systems and technology are also offered. For those wishing to serve as school library media specialists in the commonwealth of Pennsylvania, the department offers the School Library Teacher Certification program in conjunction with the M.L.I.S. program. This curriculum, developed jointly by the School of Information Sciences and the University of Pittsburgh's School of Education, requires completion of 39 credits in a specified plan of course work. The School supports a strong program of internships and practicums, particularly in the master's programs.

Research Facilities

Students have access to rich resources in the Pittsburgh area: the School's professional library of 91,852 volumes; the 4-million-volume collection of the University libraries; the 2.5-million-volume collection of the Carnegie Library of Pittsburgh, adjacent to the campus; and the collections of six additional institutions of higher education, each with special strengths.

Financial Aid

Scholarships, graduate assistantships, teaching fellowships, and loan funds are available. Some part-time employment in libraries is available to students who can demonstrate need and/or meet other requirements. Financial aid is available only to students with U.S. citizenship or permanent resident status.

Cost of Study

In 1997–98, tuition rates were $335 per credit or $4054 per term for full-time study for Pennsylvania residents and $693 per credit or $8347 per term for full-time study for nonresident students.

Living and Housing Costs

Housing for men and women graduate students, both single and married, is available in private and commercial facilities near the campus. The Off-Campus Housing Bureau maintains a listing of available housing. Rents for apartments range upward from $350 per month.

Student Group

Approximately 300 students are enrolled in the Department of Library and Information Science; some attend full-time and some part-time. The student body is international and ethnically and racially diverse. The School encourages applications from members of racial and ethnic minority groups.

Location

Pittsburgh has urban amenities and a neighborhood orientation, making it a very livable city. It is the heart of a large industrial complex and headquarters for many of the nation's largest corporations. The University occupies more than fifty buildings in the Oakland area, approximately 2 miles from the central business district. Cultural and recreational opportunities are unusually rich and easily accessible. Students are within walking distance or a few minutes' ride from the Pittsburgh Symphony and chamber music concerts; opera productions; the galleries, museums, and libraries of the Carnegie Institute and of other organizations; football and baseball games; and theaters where plays, jazz, ballet, and films are presented. Students have use of University facilities for swimming, tennis, and squash.

The School

The School of Information Sciences represents a continuous ninety-five-year tradition of education for the library and information professions in the city of Pittsburgh. The School is the direct continuation of the Carnegie Library School founded in 1901 and was established in 1962 at the University of Pittsburgh. That same year, the School introduced the first information science program in the United States. The School is headquartered on the eight floors of the Information Sciences Building. The facilities include faculty and administrative offices, classrooms, conference rooms, computing laboratories for research and instruction, and the library. The School of Information Sciences is one of the largest schools of its kind: there are more than 700 students and 65 faculty members, and nearly 140 courses are offered each year. It is consistently ranked among the top five schools that prepare students for careers in the information and library professions, and it maintains an international reputation for excellence. The faculty is noted for attaining excellence in teaching, consulting, and research, and the reputation of the alumni is distinguished in the field. Graduates are prepared to enter key positions within the information professions, including systems design and analysis; telecommunications network management; academic, special, and public librarianship; administration; and education.

Applying

Applications are regularly accepted for admission at the beginning of the fall and spring terms. Applicants should consult the School's current *Bulletin* for admission requirements for each of the programs. An application fee of $30 is required for U.S. students, $40 for international students.

Correspondence and Information

Coordinator of Admissions
School of Information Sciences
University of Pittsburgh
Pittsburgh, Pennsylvania 15260
Telephone: 412-624-5146

University of Pittsburgh

THE FACULTY AND THEIR RESEARCH

Toni Carbo, Professor and Dean; Ph.D., Drexel.
Mary Kay Biagini, Associate Professor and Associate Dean; Ph.D., Pittsburgh.
R. Stephen Almagno, Professor; M.L.S., Pittsburgh.
Sally Buchanan, Associate Professor; M.L.S., San Jose State.
Richard J. Cox, Associate Professor; Ph.D., Pittsburgh.
Ellen Gay Detlefsen, Associate Professor; D.L.S., Columbia.
Sara Fine, Professor; Ph.D., Pittsburgh.
Charles P. Friedman, Professor and Director of the Center for Biomedical Informatics; Ph.D., North Carolina at Chapel Hill.
Margaret Hodges, Professor Emerita; M.L.S., Carnegie Tech.
E. J. Josey, Professor Emeritus; M.S.L.S., SUNY at Albany.
Margaret Kimmel, Professor; Ph.D., Pittsburgh.
Richard Krzys, Professor; Ph.D., Case Western Reserve. (On leave)
Rush G. Miller, Professor and Director University Library System; Ph.D., Mississippi State.
William Nasri, Associate Professor Emeritus; Ph.D., Pittsburgh.
Edie Rasmussen, Associate Professor; Ph.D., Sheffield.
Louise Su, Assistant Professor; Ph.D., Rutgers.
Arlene Taylor, Associate Professor; Ph.D., North Carolina at Chapel Hill.
Christinger Tomer, Associate Professor; Ph.D., Case Western Reserve.
James G. Williams, Professor; Ph.D., Pittsburgh.
E. Blanche Woolls, Professor; Ph.D., Indiana. (On leave)
Wendell L. Wray, Professor Emeritus; M.L.S., Carnegie Tech.
Hong Xu, Assistant Professor; Ph.D., Illinois at Urbana-Champaign.
Elizabeth Yakel, Assistant Professor; Ph.D., Michigan.

Adjunct Faculty

Susan Webreck Alman, Ph.D., Pittsburgh.
James Bobick, M.S., Duquesne.
Fern E. Brody, M.L.S., Denver.
Susan K. Broms, M.L.S., Pittsburgh.
Susan Hoehl, M.L.S., Pittsburgh.
Marilyn Jenkins, M.S.L.S., Kentucky.
Amy E. Knapp, M.L.S., Pittsburgh.
Elizabeth Mahoney, M.L.S., SUNY at Albany.
Nancy B. Olson, M.S., Ed.Sp., Mankato State.
George H. Pike, M.L., Washington (Seattle).
Angela Pollis, M.L.S., Pittsburgh.
Marc B. Silverman, M.L.S., Pittsburgh.
Barbara Spielgelman, M.L.S., Pittsburgh.
Mary Vasilakis, M.E.L.S., Duquesne.
Thomas B. Wall, Ph.D., Pittsburgh.

Recent Books and Publications

Almagno, R. S. *Cardinal John J. Wright, Resonare Christum, Volume III: 1969–1979 the Rome Years,* ed. R. S. Almagno. San Francisco: Ignatius Press, 1995.
Biagini, M. K., ed. *School Library Media Quarterly.*
Buchanan, S. A. Disaster preparedness. In *Preservation for Libraries and Archives.* Chicago: American Library Association, 1993. Administering the library conservation program. In *Preservation in Libraries: A Reader.* London and New York: Bowker-Saur, 1993.
Cox, R. J. *Documenting Localities: A Practical Model for American Archivists and Manuscript Curators.* Lanhan, Md.: Scarecrow Press, 1996.
Detlefsen, E. G., B. A. Epstein, P. Mickelson, and T. Detre. Transforming the present—discovering the future: The University of Pittsburgh's NLM Grant on Education and Training of Health Sciences Librarians. *Bull. Med. Libr. Assoc.* 84(4):524–33, 1996.
Fine, S., and P. H. Glasser. *The First Helping Interview: A Critical Time.* Thousand Oaks, Calif.: Sage Publications, 1996.
Josey, E. J. The American Library Association: Then and now. In *Proceedings of the Black Caucus National Conference.* Chicago: American Library Association, 1992.
Collins, M., and **M. M. Kimmel,** *Mister Rogers' Neighborhood: Children, Television and Fred Rogers.* eds. M. Collins and **M. M. Kimmel.** Pittsburgh: University of Pittsburgh Press, 1996.
Kimmel, M. M., and E. Segel. *For Reading Out Loud: A Guide to Sharing Literature with Children.* New York: Dell, 1991.
Nasri, W. Z. Copyright current status and issues. In *ALA World Encyclopedia.* Chicago: American Library Association, 1993.
Allen, R. B., and **E. Rasmussen,** eds. *ACM Digital Libraries '97: Proceedings of the 2nd ACM International Conference on Digital Libraries, Philadelphia, Pennsylvania, July 23–26, 1997.* New York: Association for Computing Machinery, 1997.
Su, L. T. Value of search results as a whole as a measure of information retrieval performance. In *Proceedings of the 59th Annual Meeting of the American Society for Information Science,* vol. 33, Baltimore, Maryland, October 21–24, 1996.
Tomer, C. Technical standards for libraries. In *Encyclopedia of Library and Information Science,* vol. 5. New York: Marcel Dekker, 1994.
Woolls, B. *The School Library Media Manager.* Englewood, Colo.: Libraries Unlimited, 1994.
Woolls, B. *Ideas for School Library Media Centers: Focus on Curriculum,* 2nd ed., in press.

Research Activities

Archives and records management, archival administration and electronic records in North America, interdisciplinary foundations of archival knowledge and practice.
Bibliographic control; subject analysis, technical services; authority control.
Collection management, collections of children's literature in the academic library setting.
Continuing education, education for library and information science.
Human information behavior, information interaction, organizational information behavior and decision making in academic libraries, health information–seeking behavior.
Indexing systems and software, free-text and controlled vocabulary searching.
Information and retrieval in laboratory and operational environments.
Information behavior in biomedicine and health care, educational programs for health information specialists, biomedical informatics.
Information ethics, intellectual freedom and censorship, legal issues in librarianship.
Library media center management, evaluation of school library media centers, adult and young adult materials and reading interests.
Library service to children and young adults, early intervention literacy programs, children's books for a technological society, children in electronic environments.
Library service to special groups, library service to cultural minorities, outreach programs.
Managing libraries and information centers, public libraries and the political environment.
Multimedia databases and retrieval.
Networking issues for library and information services, defining the role of public access computing systems in a national network environment.
Preservation, disaster preparedness and recovery, mass deacidification for library and archival collections, preservation of electronic records.
Special libraries and information centers.
Testing and evaluation of information systems/services.

UNIVERSITY OF TENNESSEE, KNOXVILLE

School of Information Sciences

Program of Study

The School of Information Sciences (SIS) offers a program of study leading to the M.S. degree. The program, which is accredited by the American Library Association, is designed to prepare graduates to function effectively in libraries and other information agencies. This is achieved through a graduate-level program that emphasizes the effective management of information resources in a multiplicity of settings.

The program, which prepares students for beginning-level positions in all types of libraries and information agencies, consists of 43 semester hours, of which 16 semester hours are required courses. Independent study courses, in which the student can develop and carry out specialized projects, as well as supervised practicum experiences in many types of information agencies, provide the student with the opportunity to develop, in consultation with an adviser, a program tailored to individual needs and interests. The student is required to write a thesis or to take the written comprehensive examination prepared by the School.

A Ph.D. program in communications with a primary concentration in information sciences is available through the College of Communications and the School of Information Sciences. The program is interdisciplinary, consisting of a required core curriculum and recommended courses outside the College of Communications in the related social and behavioral sciences. The program is flexible and accommodates a wide variety of career goals.

Research Facilities

The University's libraries own approximately 2 million volumes, 3.5 million manuscripts, 3 million microforms, 30,000 audio and video recordings, and subscriptions to more than 10,000 periodicals and serials. The Online Library Information System provides access to a wide range of information resources available via the Internet. The SIS facilities for instruction include state-of-the-art computer laboratories, available to students and faculty. A variety of equipment supports both course-related activities and individual research. SIS owns a variety of microcomputers that are able to interface with campuswide systems and with regional, national, and international databases. The Center for Information Studies is an interdisciplinary research organization in the School of Information Sciences that serves as a focal point for research related to information systems and services. The Center has completed research for the federal, state, and local government; business; and industry. Projects have included strategic planning efforts, information system and service evaluations, and modeling of scientific and technical communication. Current research is focused on the intersection of information technology, knowledge-based systems, and user behavior.

Financial Aid

A number of fellowships, assistantships, and work opportunities are available to students each year. Fellowships are offered through the University of Tennessee Graduate School. Information may be obtained from the fellowship assistant, UT Graduate Office. Twelve assistantships offered by SIS carry tuition remission and a stipend. Application forms are available through SIS. Numerous part-time job opportunities are available under SIS subcontracts with area information agencies, as well as in libraries and information centers.

Cost of Study

The 1998–99 tuition and fees for full-time study are $150 per semester hour for Tennessee and Common Market State residents and $408 per semester hour for all others.

Living and Housing Costs

Most single graduate students live in off-campus housing. However, single students may be assigned to the University's residence halls or to apartments for single students. Housing on special graduate floors is available on request. Additional information pertaining to single-student housing may be obtained from the Office of Residence Halls at the University.

The University provides modern apartment facilities in several locations for married students. Information and applications for these facilities may be secured from the Office of Rental Properties at the University.

Student Group

The enrollment of the School is approximately 250, including both full- and part-time students. Students come from throughout the United States and from other countries.

Student Outcomes

Recent graduates of the School of Information Sciences have found interesting careers in academic, public, medical, corporate, and school libraries as well as in government information centers. Several work for Internet providers, database producers, and electronic publishers or multimedia developers. Some SIS graduates have established information brokering businesses. As the field of information sciences grows, so do the opportunities for graduates.

Location

Situated only a short distance from the Great Smoky Mountains National Park and surrounded by five major Tennessee Valley Authority lakes, Knoxville is fast gaining the reputation of being in the recreation center of eastern America. It has a metropolitan population of 475,000. The spring Dogwood Arts Festival attracts visitors from many areas. Knoxville's Civic Auditorium and the refurbished Tennessee Theater and Bijou Theater offer such events as road company performances of Broadway plays, performances by the Knoxville Symphony, ballets, presentations by visiting artists, and sporting events. A wide variety of other cultural opportunities are also associated with the Knoxville area.

The University

The Knoxville campus of the University of Tennessee has an enrollment of 25,000. The School of Information Sciences is in the heart of the Knoxville campus. Other facilities on campus, such as the University library, the University computing center, and the student center, are conveniently located nearby, and the downtown area is only a few minutes' walk away.

Applying

General prerequisites for admission are a bachelor's degree and an acceptable college record. The General Test of the Graduate Record Examinations is required of all applicants unless they have earned a graduate degree. The Graduate School requires an official college transcript, and SIS requires a Personal Data form and three recommendations. Further application information and forms are available from the School of Information Sciences. The application deadline is February 15 for fellowships and assistantships.

Correspondence and Information

School of Information Sciences
University of Tennessee, Knoxville
804 Volunteer Boulevard
Knoxville, Tennessee 37996-4330

Telephone: 423-974-2148
Fax: 423-974-4967
E-mail: littlejo@utk.edu
World Wide Web: http://www.sis.utk.edu

University of Tennessee, Knoxville

THE FACULTY AND THEIR RESEARCH

C.W. Minkel, Associate Vice Chancellor for Academic Affairs, Dean of the Graduate School, and Interim Director; Ph. D., Syracuse.

Dania Bilal, Assistant Professor; Ph.D., Florida State. Information seeking, information retrieval, automation.
Patricia L. Fisher, Associate Professor; Ph.D., Florida State. Applied statistics and research methodology.
J. Michael Pemberton, Associate Professor; Ph.D., Tennessee. Academic libraries, records management, archives and manuscripts.
W. David Penniman, Professor and Director of the Center for Information Studies; Ph.D., Ohio State. Information service strategies, reengineering, cost-benefit analysis.
Richard Pollard, Associate Professor; Ph.D., Brunel (England). Automation of library processes, information technologies.
Douglas Raber, Assistant Professor; Ph.D., Indiana. Public libraries, information policy analysis, nature of information culture.
William C. Robinson, Associate Professor; Ph.D., Illinois at Urbana-Champaign. Collection development, contemporary publishing, serial publications, history of the book, special libraries.
George M. Sinkankas, Associate Professor; Ph.D., Pittsburgh. Technical services, indexing and abstracting, nonprint media.
Carol Tenopir, Professor; Ph.D., Illinois at Urbana-Champaign. Information sources and services, information science.
Peiling Wang, Assistant Professor; Ph.D., Maryland. Information organization and access, database management, cognitive science, quantitative research.
Jinx Watson, Assistant Professor; Ed.D., Vanderbilt. Children's literature, library service for children and young people.
Gretchen Whitney, Assistant Professor; Ph.D., Michigan. Information science and services.

UNIVERSITY OF WESTERN ONTARIO

Faculty of Information and Media Studies

Programs of Study

The University of Western Ontario's Faculty of Information and Media Studies has as its mandate the study of the role of information, media, communications, and information technologies in the lives of individuals and in society. To achieve this mandate, the Faculty offers three graduate programs: the professional course-based Master of Arts (M.A.) in journalism and Master of Library and Information Science (M.L.I.S.) programs and a research-based Doctor of Philosophy (Ph.D.) in library and information science program.

The M.A. in journalism is a one-year, full-time program requiring the completion of five courses per term for a total of fifteen courses. Required courses prepare students in the intellectual foundations of journalism, the different media of contemporary journalism, and the different journalistic and media-related work settings. A thesis option, taken in conjunction with course work in the final term, is also available. Students can also complete a four-week noncredit internship in print or electronic media, in public relations, or in other information sectors at the completion of their course of study.

The M.L.I.S. degree is earned by completing fifteen half courses. The five required courses are designed to provide a solid foundation in the knowledge, skills, and values of library and information science. The remaining ten courses are electives chosen from a broad range of options. The M.L.I.S. program can be completed in as little as one year or on an extended part-time basis. Students also have the unique opportunity of participating in the Cooperative Work/Study Program, which allows them to alternate classroom learning with competitively paid work experience.

The Ph.D. in library and information science provides opportunities to conduct research in three areas of specialization: information systems, information needs and uses, and information policy. Advising and teaching faculty members come from a broad spectrum of disciplinary backgrounds, including law, geography, and engineering, and an equally wide range of professional environments.

Research Facilities

An extensive array of computer software, hardware, and other equipment support both qualitative and quantitative research, with assistance from information resource and technology staff. The Faculty's in-house Graduate Library facilities include multimedia computers, video and audio editing studios, and computer-mediated–learning production facilities. The Graduate Library's computer laboratories contain forty networked PC stations featuring a wide array of software applications. Ph.D. students have separate dedicated office space and computer resources. In addition to the Graduate Library, Western has six major campus libraries, making it the sixth-largest academic library system in Canada. The University also has supercomputing facilities, a high-speed fiber-optic network, and Internet access.

Financial Aid

Some scholarships and fellowships are available, including Social Sciences and Humanities Research Council of Canada (SSHRCC) doctoral fellowships and Ontario Graduate Scholarships (OGS), of which some current students are recipients. Graduate teaching assistantships are also available from the University of Western Ontario for doctoral students and some master's students. At the Ph.D. level, students granted a teaching assistantship on admission are granted four years of support. Opportunities exist for Ph.D. students to teach courses in the master's program in library and information science and the undergraduate program in media, information, and technoculture.

Cost of Study

For the 1998–99 academic year, tuition for the M.L.I.S. program is $2000 per term for full-time study. A co-op fee of $550 is payable during each M.L.I.S. co-op term. Tuition for the M.A. in journalism program is $6000 per year. Tuition for the Ph.D. program is $1500 per term for full-time study.

Living and Housing Costs

London has a wide variety of affordable rental accommodations available. The University's Off-Campus Housing Service provides extensive current listings on vacancies and rentals across the city. Shared accommodations begin at Can$300 per month, with one-bedroom apartments at Can$375. Family housing and on-campus residence accommodations are also available through the University.

Student Group

The M.A. in journalism and the M.L.I.S. programs have respective enrollments of approximately 45 full-time students and 170 full-time and part-time students from a variety of educational, professional, and experiential backgrounds. The Ph.D. program has 15 students at various stages of the program, with growth indicated in these numbers in the next few years. The Masters Students Council organizes a number of social and fund-raising events every semester and, together with the Doctoral Students Association, are active participants in Faculty governance committees and Western's Society of Graduate Students.

Location

Home to 325,000 people, London, Ontario, is Canada's tenth-largest city. London combines the facilities of big-city living with the comforts of a smaller community. Known for its unsurpassed beauty, London has miles of pathways for walking, cycling, and in-line skating in the many tree-lined parks that contribute to its "Forest City" reputation.

The University and The Faculty

The University of Western Ontario, founded in 1878, is home to more than 23,000 undergraduate and graduate students and more than 1,300 faculty members. The University offers one of the most picturesque campuses in North America. The Faculty of Information and Media Studies includes the Graduate Programs in Library and Information Science and Journalism in addition to a Bachelor of Arts in Media, Information, and Technoculture. The Faculty has new facilities in the recently renovated Middlesex College, one of Western's landmark buildings. The Graduate Program in Library and Information Science is ranked among the top ten programs in North America, while Western's journalism program is also recognized as one of the best in Canada.

Applying

The M.A. in journalism program accepts about 45 students each May. The M.L.I.S. program accepts approximately 160 applicants throughout the year for start in January, May, or September. All master's degree applicants must have a four-year undergraduate degree or equivalent from a recognized university with a minimum B standing (3.0 GPA). Applicants must supply a resume and two letters of recommendation; journalism applicants must also submit a 1,000-word autobiographical sketch. Ph.D. applicants must hold a master's degree in library and information science or a graduate degree in an allied field with additional relevant course work. Doctoral applicants must submit two letters of reference, a short account of research intent, and recent results of the Graduate Records Examinations (GRE) and complete an interview after initial application review. Students who do not have English as a first language must take the Test of English as a Foreign Language (TOEFL). An application fee of Can$50 is required for all applicants. Students should contact the Faculty for application deadlines and further details.

Correspondence and Information

Graduate Programs Office
Faculty of Information and Media Studies
Room 255, Middlesex College
University of Western Ontario
London, Ontario N6A 5B7
Canada

Telephone: 519-661-4017
Fax: 519-661-3506
E-mail: journalism@julian.uwo.ca (M.A. in journalism program)
mlisinfo@julian.uwo.ca (M.L.I.S. program)
phdinfo@julian.uwo.ca (Ph.D. program)
World Wide Web: http://www.fims.uwo.ca

University of Western Ontario

THE FACULTY AND THEIR RESEARCH

Majunath Pendakur, Professor and Dean; Ph.D., Simon Fraser.
Dale Bent, Lecturer; Ph.D., Stanford.
Tim Blackmore, Assistant Professor; Ph.D., York.
Jacqueline Burkell, Assistant Professor; Ph.D., Western Ontario.
Grant Campbell, Assistant Professor; Ph.D., Queen's.
Tim Craven, Professor; Ph.D., McMaster.
Patricia Dewdney, Associate Professor; Ph.D., Western Ontario.
M. Elizabeth Dolan, Assistant Professor; D.L.S., Columbia.
Mary Doyle, Assistant Professor; M.A., Western Ontario.
Nick Dyer-Witheford, Assistant Professor; Ph.D., Simon Fraser.
Carole Farber, Assistant Professor; Ph.D., British Columbia.
Bernd Frohmann, Associate Professor; Ph.D., Toronto.
Candace Gibson, Associate Professor; Ph.D., MIT.
Roma Harris, Professor, Vice-Provost, and Registrar; Ph.D., Western Ontario.
Ian Kerr, Assistant Professor; Ph.D., Western Ontario.
Judith Knelman, Associate Professor; Ph.D., Toronto.
Gloria Leckie, Associate Professor; Ph.D., Western Ontario.
Lynne McKechnie, Assistant Professor; Ph.D., Western Ontario.
B. Gillian Michell, Associate Professor; Ph.D., USC.
Michael Nelson, Associate Professor; Ph.D., Western Ontario.
Kirsti Nilsen, Lecturer; Ph.D., Toronto.
Michael Nolan, Associate Professor; Ph.D., Western Ontario.
Andrew Osler, Associate Professor; M.A., Toronto.
Yuri Quintana, Assistant Professor; Ph.D., Waterloo.
Steven Reinke, Assistant Professor; M.F.A., Nova Scotia.
Catherine Ross, Professor; Ph.D., Western Ontario.
Romayne Smith-Fullerton, Lecturer; Ph.D., Western Ontario.
David Spencer, Associate Professor; Ph.D., Toronto.
Liwen Vaughan, Associate Professor; Ph.D., Western Ontario.
Margaret Ann Wilkinson, Associate Professor; Ph.D., Toronto.

Emeritus Faculty

F. T. Dolan, Professor Emeritus; Ed.D., Toronto.
J. H. Fyfe, Professor Emeritus; Ph.D., Guelph.
A. J. Jamieson, Professor Emeritus; Ph.D., Maryland.
R. E. Lee, Professor Emeritus; Ph.D., Chicago.
B. M. McCamus, Professor Emeritus; M.L.S., M.B.A., Western Ontario.
G. R. Pendrill, Professor Emeritus; M.A., Cantab.
R. G. Prodick, Professor Emeritus; M.A., Toronto, M.S., Columbia.
H. G. Schulte-Albert, Professor Emeritus; Ph.D., Case Western Reserve.
J. H. White, Professor Emeritus; M.S., Columbia.

RECENT BOOKS AND PUBLICATIONS

Blackmore, T. Krazy as a fool: Erasmus of Rotterdam's Praise of Folly and Herriman of Coconino's Krazy Kat. *J. Popular Cult.,* in press.

Craven, T. C. Human creation of abstracts with selected computer assistance tools. *Information Res.* 3(4):47, 1998.

Hassard Wilkins, J., and **G. J. Leckie.** University professional and managerial staff: Information needs and seeking. *Coll. Res. Libraries* 59(6):561–75, 1997.

Kerr, I. Mind your metaphors: An examination of the Inefficiency Argument as a reason against regulating on-line conduct. In *The Ethics of Electronic Information in the 21st Century,* ed. Lester Pourciau. West Lafayette, Ind.: Purdue University Press, 1998.

Knelman, J. *Twisting in the Wind: The Murderess and the English Press.* Toronto: University of Toronto Press, 1998.

McKechnie, L. (E. F.). Vygotsky's zone of proximal development: A useful theoretical approach for research concerning children, libraries and information. *J. Youth Services Libraries* 11:66–70, 1997.

Nelson, M. J. A prefix trie index for inverted files. *Information Processing Management* 33(6):739–44, 1997.

Vaughan, L. Q., and J. Tague-Sutcliffe. Measuring the impact of information on development: A LISREL-based study of small business in Shanghai. *J. Am. Soc. Information Sci.* 48(10):917–31, 1997.

Wilkinson, M. A. Perceptual differences in approaches to censorship: Information intermediaries and the implementation of law. *Information Soc.* 13(2):185–93, 1997.

RESEARCH ACTIVITIES

Bibliographic instruction in academic libraries.
Crime coverage in nineteenth-century newspapers.
Development and testing of computer tools to assist writers of abstracts and other brief summaries.
Electronic commerce and other legal and ethical issues in multimedia.
Information policy, including copyright and censorship.
Information seeking behaviour of children and young adults.
Information seeking behaviour of lawyers.
Modelling and evaluation of information systems.
Public library services for children and young adults.
Role of the library as a public institution.
Role of science fiction in reflecting, objecting to, and revivifying war in American culture.
Scholarly communication channels and methods.
Statistical evaluation of information retrieval systems.
Work and role of academic librarians.

Academic and Professional Programs in the Medical Professions and Sciences

This part of Book 6 consists of seven sections covering chiropractic, dentistry and dental sciences, medicine, optometry and vision sciences, oriental medicine and acupuncture, pharmacy and pharmaceutical sciences, and veterinary medicine and sciences. This section has a table of contents (listing the program directories, announcements, and in-depth descriptions); program directories, which consist of brief profiles of programs in the relevant fields (and that include 50-word or 100-word announcements following the profiles, if programs have chosen to include them); Cross-Discipline Announcements, if any programs have chosen to submit such entries; and in-depth descriptions, which are more individualized statements included, if programs have chosen to submit them.

Academic and Professional Programs in the Medical Professions and Sciences

[illegible]

Section 33
Chiropractic

This section contains a directory of institutions offering professional programs in chiropractic, followed by in-depth entries submitted by institutions that chose to prepare detailed program descriptions. Additional information about programs listed in the directory but not augmented by an in-depth entry may be obtained by writing directly to the dean of a college at the address given in the directory.

CONTENTS

Program Directory

Announcements

Cross-Discipline Announcements

In-Depth Descriptions

Chiropractic

Anglo-European College of Chiropractic, Program in Chiropractic, Bournemouth, Dorset BH52DF, United Kingdom. Awards M Sc. Postbaccalaureate distance learning degree programs offered.

Canadian Memorial Chiropractic College, Professional Program, Toronto, ON M4G 3E6, Canada. Awards DC. Accredited by CCE. Faculty: 56 full-time (13 women), 44 part-time (12 women). Students: 609 full-time (258 women), 7 part-time (1 woman). In 1997, 149 degrees awarded. *Average time to degree:* first professional–4 years full-time. *Entrance requirements:* 3 full years of University, 15 full courses or 90 hours. Application deadline: 11/30. Application fee: $75. *Tuition:* $11,961 per year for Canadian residents; $14,781 per year for nonresidents. *Financial aid:* Awards and career-related internships or fieldwork available. *Faculty research:* Theories and concepts of chiropractic, sciences related to chiropractic, assessment of the efficacy and efficiency of chiropractic. • Dr. John Mrozek, Dean of Undergraduate Studies, 416-482-2340. Fax: 416-488-0476. Application contact: Dr. Stefan Palister, Director of Admissions, 416-482-2340. Fax: 416-482-9745.

Canadian Memorial Chiropractic College, Certificate Programs, Toronto, ON M4G 3E6, Canada. Offerings in chiropractic clinical sciences (Certificate), chiropractic radiology (Certificate), chiropractic sports sciences (Certificate). Faculty: 16 part-time (2 women). Students: 7 full-time (2 women). Average age 27. In 1997, 1 degree awarded. *Degree requirements:* Thesis. *Average time to degree:* other advanced degree–2.5 years full-time. *Entrance requirements:* DC, board certification. Application deadline: 1/31 (rolling processing). *Tuition:* $11,961 per year for Canadian residents; $14,781 per year for nonresidents. *Financial aid:* Career-related internships or fieldwork available. *Faculty research:* Theories and concepts of chiropractic, sciences related to chiropractic, assessments of the efficacy and efficiency of chiropractic. • Dr. Igor Steiman, Director, 416-482-2340. Fax: 416-482-9745.

Cleveland Chiropractic College of Kansas City, Kansas City, MO 64131-1181. Awards DC. Accredited by CCE. Faculty: 32 full-time (11 women), 12 part-time (2 women). Students: 546 full-time (155 women), 19 part-time (9 women); includes 63 minority (17 African Americans, 21 Asian Americans, 13 Hispanics, 12 Native Americans), 26 international. Average age 29. 246 applicants, 54% accepted. In 1997, 140 degrees awarded. *Degree requirements:* Field experience or internship. *Average time to degree:* first professional–3.5 years full-time. *Entrance requirements:* Minimum GPA of 2.5, 2 years of preprofessional study. Application fee: $50. *Expenses:* Tuition $165 per hour. Fees $102 per trimester. *Financial aid:* 550 students received aid; Federal Work-Study and career-related internships or fieldwork available. Aid available to part-time students. Financial aid applicants required to submit FAFSA. *Faculty research:* Chiropractic clinical science, biomechanics of spine and muscle, somatovisceral effects, biochemical/physiological effects. • Dr. Dwight F. Gerred, Executive Vice President, 816-333-8230. Application contact: Brenda Holland, Director of Admissions, 816-333-8230. Fax: 816-333-4749.

See in-depth description on page 1669.

Cleveland Chiropractic College of Los Angeles, 590 North Vermont Avenue, Los Angeles, CA 90004-2196. Awards DC. Accredited by CCE. Faculty: 32 full-time (9 women), 26 part-time (6 women). Students: 511 full-time (164 women), 19 part-time (4 women); includes 180 minority (15 African Americans, 130 Asian Americans, 33 Hispanics, 2 Native Americans), 50 international. Average age 30. 176 applicants, 71% accepted. In 1997, 125 degrees awarded. *Degree requirements:* Internship required, foreign language and thesis not required. *Entrance requirements:* 60 semester units of course work in liberal arts; 2 semesters of biology, general chemistry, organic chemistry, and general physics. Application deadline: 7/1 (priority date; rolling processing; 12/1 for spring admission). Application fee: $50. *Financial aid:* Federal Work-Study and career-related internships or fieldwork available. Financial aid applicants required to submit FAFSA. *Faculty research:* Biomechanics, spinal x-rays, clinical outcomes, cardiac risk, instructional effectiveness. • Dr. Matthew Givrad, Executive Vice President, 213-660-6166. Fax: 213-660-5387. Application contact: Paul Forgetta, Director of Admissions, 800-466-CCLA. Fax: 213-660-4195. E-mail: ccclaadm@aol.com.

See in-depth description on page 1669.

Institute Francais de Chiropractie, Professional Program, Paris 75018, France. Awards DC. Accredited by CCE.

Life Chiropractic College West, San Lorenzo, CA 94580-1315. Awards DC. Accredited by CCE. Faculty: 40 full-time (15 women), 38 part-time (11 women). Students: 762 full-time (254 women), 30 part-time (13 women). Average age 28. 180 applicants, 66% accepted. In 1997, 217 degrees awarded. *Entrance requirements:* Minimum GPA of 2.25. Application deadline: 8/1 (priority date; rolling processing). Application fee: $45. *Financial aid:* In 1997–98, 750 students received aid, including 2 research assistantships, 15 teaching assistantships; Federal Work-Study and career-related internships or fieldwork also available. Aid available to part-time students. Financial aid applicants required to submit FAFSA. *Faculty research:* Human vertebral column, biomechanics, scoliosis, vertebral artery in stroke, spinal range of motion. Total annual research expenditures: $200,000. • Dr. Gerard W. Clum, President, 510-276-9013. Application contact: Jeffrey D. Cook, Director of Admissions, 800-788-4476. Fax: 510-276-4893. E-mail: admissions@lifewest.edu.

See in-depth description on page 1671.

Life University, Program in Chiropractic, 1269 Barclay Circle, Marietta, GA 30060-2903. Awards DC. Accredited by CCE. Faculty: 175 full-time (47 women), 8 part-time (3 women). Students: 3,498. *Entrance requirements:* Minimum 2 years of college, previous course work in biology, chemistry, English, humanities, physics, and psychology. Application deadline: 9/14 (rolling processing). Application fee: $50. *Tuition:* $13,600 per year full-time, $162 per quarter hour part-time. *Financial aid:* Research assistantships, full tuition waivers, Federal Work-Study, institutionally sponsored loans, and career-related internships or fieldwork available. Aid available to part-time students. • Dr. Ron Kirk, Dean, 770-426-2757. Application contact: Dr. Ronald Roland, Director of Admission Services, 800-543-3202. Fax: 770-428-9886.

See in-depth description on page 1673.

Logan College of Chiropractic, Division of Chiropractic and Clinical Sciences, Chesterfield, MO 63006-1065. Awards DC. Accredited by CCE. Faculty: 43 full-time (13 women), 41 part-time (11 women). Students: 1,095 full-time (294 women); includes 87 minority (24 African Americans, 39 Asian Americans, 19 Hispanics, 5 Native Americans), 114 international. Average age 28. 533 applicants, 84% accepted. In 1997, 241 degrees awarded (1% entered university research/teaching, 99% found other work related to degree). *Degree requirements:* Internship required, foreign language and thesis not required. *Average time to degree:* first professional–3.2 years full-time. *Entrance requirements:* 60 hours of pre-chiropractic including biology, physics, and social sciences. Application deadline: 7/15 (rolling processing). Application fee: $35. *Expenses:* Tuition $13,965 per year. Fees $180 per year. *Financial aid:* 640 students received aid; fellowships, research assistantships, teaching assistantships, Federal Work-Study available. *Faculty research:* Chiropractic clinical trials, ergonomics, physiological correlates of chiropractic treatment, clinical biomechanics. • Dr. William L. Ramsey, Vice President of Academic Affairs, 314-227-2100. Application contact: Melvin Reynolds, Dean of Admissions, 314-227-2100. Fax: 314-227-9338. E-mail: loganadm@logan.edu.

See in-depth description on page 1675.

Los Angeles College of Chiropractic, Professional Program, 16200 E Amber Valley Dr, Box 1166, Whittier, CA 90604-4051. Awards DC. Accredited by CCE. Faculty: 42 full-time (9 women), 39 part-time (17 women). Students: 807 full-time (229 women), 5 part-time (0 women); includes 385 minority (17 African Americans, 302 Asian Americans, 63 Hispanics, 3 Native Americans), 6 international. Average age 28. 457 applicants, 57% accepted. In 1997, 183 degrees awarded. *Degree requirements:* Thesis (for some programs), clinical internship required, foreign language not required. *Application fee:* $50. *Financial aid:* 718 students received aid; fellowships, research assistantships, teaching assistantships, Federal Work-Study, and career-related internships or fieldwork available. Financial aid applicants required to submit FAFSA. *Faculty research:* X-rays, motion palpation. Total annual research expenditures: $428,617. • Dr. John Beckman, Senior Vice President, 562-947-8755 Ext. 325. Application contact: Dr. Charlene Frontiera, Director of Admissions, 562-947-8755 Ext. 321. Fax: 562-947-5724. E-mail: charlene@deltanet.com.

See in-depth description on page 1677.

The National College of Chiropractic, Lombard, IL 60148-4583. Awards DC. Accredited by CCE. Faculty: 54 full-time, 23 part-time. Students: 892; includes 82 minority (19 African Americans, 51 Asian Americans, 12 Hispanics), 202 international. Average age 26. *Entrance requirements:* Minimum 90 hours at an accredited college, 24 hours in science, 6 hours in English, 18 hours in humanities and social sciences (including basic psychology), minimum GPA of 2.5. Application deadline: rolling. Application fee: $55. *Tuition:* $214 per credit hour. *Financial aid:* Fellowships, research assistantships, teaching assistantships, Federal Work-Study available. Aid available to part-time students. Financial aid applicants required to submit FAFSA. *Faculty research:* Biomechanics, immunology. • Dr. James F. Winterstein, President, 800-826-6285. Fax: 630-889-6604. Application contact: Julie Talarico, Director of Admissions, 800-826-6285. Fax: 630-889-6572.

See in-depth description on page 1679.

New York Chiropractic College, Seneca Falls, NY 13148-0800. Awards DC. Accredited by CCE. Faculty: 49 full-time (16 women), 49 part-time (22 women), 65 FTE. Students: 935 full-time (273 women), 1 (woman) part-time; includes 70 minority (9 African Americans, 33 Asian Americans, 26 Hispanics, 2 Native Americans), 101 international. Average age 26. 402 applicants, 32% accepted. In 1997, 257 degrees awarded. *Degree requirements:* Internship required, foreign language and thesis not required. *Average time to degree:* first professional–3.3 years full-time. *Entrance requirements:* Minimum GPA of 2.5. Application deadline: 6/1 (priority date; rolling processing; 11/1 for spring admission). Application fee: $60. *Expenses:* Tuition $15,450 per year. Fees $360 per year. *Financial aid:* 814 students received aid; Federal Work-Study, institutionally sponsored loans available. Financial aid application deadline: 4/15; applicants required to submit FAFSA. *Faculty research:* Physiological responses to spinal adjusting, sacroiliac joint pathology, meridian therapy and stress, sports chiropractic, automatic systems. Total annual research expenditures: $65,000. • John Pecchia, Vice President of Business Affairs, 315-568-3078. Fax: 315-568-3012. Application contact: Barbara Giannesch, Dean of Enrollment Management, 315-568-3040. Fax: 315-568-3015.

See in-depth description on page 1681.

Northwestern College of Chiropractic, Professional Program, Bloomington, MN 55431-1599. Awards DC. Accredited by CCE. Faculty: 48 full-time (14 women), 20 part-time (6 women). Students: 728 full-time (206 women), 68 part-time (16 women); includes 46 minority (7 African Americans, 31 Asian Americans, 5 Hispanics, 3 Native Americans), 121 international. Average age 26. 324 applicants, 86% accepted. In 1997, 206 degrees awarded. *Entrance requirements:* Minimum GPA of 2.5. Application deadline: 5/1 (priority date; rolling processing; 1/1 for spring admission). Application fee: $50. *Expenses:* Tuition $5165 per trimester. Fees $300 per trimester. *Financial aid:* Federal Work-Study and career-related internships or fieldwork available. *Faculty research:* Headache, carpal tunnel syndrome, low back pain, neck pain. Total annual research expenditures: $521,000. • Dr. David A. Gabrielson, Vice President of Academic Affairs, 612-888-4777. Application contact: Lynn Heieie, Associate Director of Admissions, 612-888-4777. Fax: 612-888-6713.

Announcement: Northwestern College of Chiropractic is a regionally and professionally accredited institution offering the Doctor of Chiropractic degree. The 10-trimester curriculum emphasizes physical diagnosis and treatment, prevention, sports health, physical rehabilitation, and neuromusculoskeletal problems. The College maintains 1 student clinic and 4 public clinics within the Twin Cities metro area.

See in-depth description on page 1683.

Palmer College of Chiropractic, Davenport, IA 52803-5287. Awards DC. Accredited by CCE. Part-time programs available. Students: 1,764 (489 women); includes 101 minority (21 African Americans, 45 Asian Americans, 25 Hispanics, 10 Native Americans), 151 international. Average age 27. 342 applicants, 52% accepted. In 1997, 576 degrees awarded. *Entrance requirements:* Previous course work in chiropractic. Application deadline: 10/28 (priority date; rolling processing). Application fee: $50. *Expenses:* Tuition $14,970 per year full-time, $192 per credit part-time. Fees $60 per year. *Financial aid:* Research assistantships, teaching assistantships, full and partial tuition waivers, Federal Work-Study, institutionally sponsored loans, and career-related internships or fieldwork available. Aid available to part-time students. Financial aid applicants required to submit FAFSA. *Faculty research:* Studies to advance the understanding of chiropractic. • Dr. Donald Betz, Provost and Vice President for Academic Affairs, 319-326-9676. Fax: 319-327-0181. Application contact: Gary Mohr, Director of Institutional Advancement, 319-326-9626. Fax: 319-326-8414. E-mail: pcadmit@palmer.edu.

See in-depth description on page 1685.

Palmer College of Chiropractic West, San Jose, CA 95134-1617. Awards DC. Accredited by CCE. Part-time programs available. Postbaccalaureate distance learning degree programs offered (minimal on-campus study). Faculty: 34 full-time (9 women), 34 part-time (10 women). Students: 724; includes 194 minority (6 African Americans, 151 Asian Americans, 31 Hispanics, 6 Native Americans), 128 international. Average age 26. 162 applicants, 50% accepted. In 1997, 172 degrees awarded. *Degree requirements:* Clinical internship required, foreign language and thesis not required. *Entrance requirements:* Minimum GPA of 2.5. Application fee: $50. Electronic applications accepted. *Tuition:* $4195 per quarter. *Financial aid:* Federal Work-Study and career-related internships or fieldwork available. Aid available to part-time students. Financial aid applicants required to submit FAFSA. *Faculty research:* Low back pain complaints, spinal manipulation therapy, cervical biomechanics, clinical trials, practice guidelines. • Application contact: Karin Butters, Director of Enrollment Services and Development, 408-944-6024. Fax: 408-944-6032. E-mail: fukui_k@palmer.edu.

Announcement: Located in San Jose, approximately 50 miles south of San Francisco, where high-tech companies are interspersed among colorful orchards that recall Santa Clara County's agricultural past, Palmer West offers a 13-quarter program (4 academic years) leading to the Doctor of Chiropractic degree. The student body benefits from moderate class size, flexible scheduling, and a distinguished faculty of leading contributors to the growing body of chiropractic research.

See in-depth description on page 1687.

Parker College of Chiropractic, First Professional Degree Program, Dallas, TX 75229-5668. Awards DC. Accredited by CCE. Part-time programs available. *Average time to degree:* first professional–3 years full-time, 5 years part-time. *Entrance requirements:* Minimum GPA of 2.5. Application deadline: 7/15 (priority date; rolling processing). Application fee: $35. Electronic applications accepted. *Tuition:* $15,360 per year full-time, $275 per credit hour part-time. *Faculty research:* Arterial tonometry, bioenergetics, outcome assessment for clinical care.

See in-depth description on page 1689.

Sherman College of Straight Chiropractic, Spartanburg, SC 29304-1452. Awards DC. Accredited by CCE. Faculty: 22 full-time (9 women), 21 part-time (11 women), 29 FTE. Students: 372 full-time (126 women), 26 part-time (12 women); includes 31 minority (9 African Americans, 12 Asian Americans, 10 Hispanics), 10 international. Average age 28. 118 applicants, 47% accepted. In 1997, 64 degrees awarded. *Average time to degree:* first professional–3.5 years full-time. *Entrance requirements:* Minimum GPA of 2.25. Application deadline: 10/5 (priority date; rolling processing; 4/8 for spring admission). Application fee: $35. Electronic applications accepted. *Tuition:* $15,160 per year. *Financial aid:* 321 students received aid; Federal Work-Study, institutionally sponsored loans, and career-related internships or fieldwork available. Aid available to part-time students. Financial aid applicants required to submit FAFSA. *Faculty research:* Chiropractic effect of immune response, biomechanics, videofluoroscopy, dynamic motion. • Application contact: Susan Newlin, Vice President for Enrollment Management, 864-578-8770 Ext. 1223. Fax: 864-599-4860. E-mail: admissions@sherman.edu.

Announcement: Sherman College offers an exceptional program in the philosophy, science, and art of chiropractic, leading to a Doctor of Chiropractic degree. Specialized approach, limited enrollment, spacious campus, modern facilities, low student-faculty ratio. Students selected for motivation as well as academic ability. Accredited by the Commission on Accreditation of the Council on Chiropractic Education to award the Doctor of Chiropractic degree.

See in-depth description on page 1691.

Texas Chiropractic College, Pasadena, TX 77505-1699. Awards DC. Accredited by CCE. Part-time programs available. Faculty: 32 full-time (11 women), 15 part-time (5 women), 35.3 FTE. Students: 492 full-time (123 women), 9 part-time (4 women); includes 171 minority (35 African Americans, 99 Asian Americans, 36 Hispanics, 1 Native American), 7 international. Average age 30. 182 applicants, 59% accepted. In 1997, 130 degrees awarded. *Degree requirements:* Clinical internship required, foreign language and thesis not required. *Average time to degree:* first professional–3.3 years full-time. *Entrance requirements:* TOEFL, 2 years of college. Application deadline: 9/1 (priority date; rolling processing; 12/1 for spring admission). Application fee: $50. *Expenses:* Tuition $13,800 per year full-time, $385 per hour part-time. Fees $225 per year. *Financial aid:* Federal Work-Study, institutionally sponsored loans, and career-related internships or fieldwork available. Aid available to part-time students. Financial aid application deadline: 4/15; applicants required to submit FAFSA. *Total annual research expenditures:* $96,600. • Dr. Shelby Elliott, President, 281-487-1170. Fax: 281-487-0329. Application contact: Robert Cooper, Admissions Director, 281-998-6016. Fax: 281-487-2009.

See in-depth description on page 1693.

University of Bridgeport, College of Chiropractic, 380 University Avenue, Bridgeport, CT 06601. Awards DC. Accredited by CCE. Faculty: 12 full-time (3 women), 23 part-time (7 women), 20 FTE. Students: 218 full-time (77 women), 1 part-time (0 women); includes 34 minority (13 African Americans, 12 Asian Americans, 8 Hispanics, 1 Native American), 9 international. 111 applicants, 86% accepted. In 1997, 34 degrees awarded. *Application deadline:* 3/1 (priority date; rolling processing; 7/1 for spring admission). *Application fee:* $75. *Expenses:* Tuition $12,400 per year. Fees $590 per year full-time, $75 per year part-time. *Financial aid:* 216 students received aid; Federal Work-Study, institutionally sponsored loans available. Aid available to part-time students. Financial aid application deadline: 6/1; applicants required to submit FAFSA. • Dr. Francis A. Zolli, Dean, 203-576-4279. Application contact: Laura Arthur, Admissions Coordinator, 203-576-4352.

See in-depth description on page 1695.

Western States Chiropractic College, Portland, OR 97230-3099. Awards DC. Accredited by CCE. Faculty: 37 full-time (24 women), 50 part-time (31 women), 55 FTE. Students: 489 full-time (141 women); includes 27 minority (2 African Americans, 18 Asian Americans, 4 Hispanics, 3 Native Americans), 191 international. Average age 26. 349 applicants, 48% accepted. In 1997, 160 degrees awarded (100% found work related to degree). *Degree requirements:* Comprehensive exams, internship required, foreign language and thesis not required. *Average time to degree:* first professional–4 years full-time. *Entrance requirements:* 2 years of pre-chiropractic study, minimum GPA of 3.0. Application deadline: rolling. Application fee: $50. *Expenses:* Tuition $13,500 per year. Fees $510 per year. *Financial aid:* In 1997–98, 317 students received aid, including 9 scholarships (4 to first-year students) totaling $35,500; Federal Work-Study and career-related internships or fieldwork also available. Aid available to part-time students. Financial aid applicants required to submit FAFSA. • Randall Hand, Dean of Enrollment Management, 800-641-5641. Fax: 503-251-5723.

See in-depth description on page 1697.

Cross-Discipline Announcements

Bastyr University, Program in Naturopathic Medicine, 14500 Juanita Drive, NE, Bothell, WA 98011.

The 4-year naturopathic medicine program provides training for generalist physicians prepared to use natural therapies in the treatment and prevention of human illness. Licensed in 11 states, naturopathic physicians are increasingly being recognized as primary-care providers. A Certificate of Midwifery is offered for those who wish to practice obstetrics.

National College of Naturopathic Medicine, Professional Program, Portland, OR 97201.

Intensive, accredited 4-year graduate program qualifies graduates to sit for board licensure examination and for family practice as a naturopathic physician (ND). The course of study combines standard medical sciences with naturally based holistic therapeutics. Naturopathic medicine recognizes the integrity of the whole patient and seeks to restore health through facilitating the patient's inherent healing capacity.

CLEVELAND CHIROPRACTIC COLLEGES OF KANSAS CITY AND LOS ANGELES

Program of Study

Cleveland Chiropractic College maintains campuses in Kansas City, Missouri, and Los Angeles, California. Both offer a Doctor of Chiropractic (D.C.) degree program and a Bachelor of Science (B.S.) degree program in human biology, which includes accelerated prerequisite courses for the D.C. degree program. A student may pursue the B.S. and D.C. degree programs concurrently.

The D.C. degree program allows students to select a twelve-trimester (forty-eight month) or an accelerated nine-trimester (thirty-six month) course of study. Course work is offered in the basic sciences (anatomy, physiology, chemistry, microbiology, public health, pathology), clinical sciences (diagnosis, radiology), chiropractic sciences (chiropractic principles techniques, practice management), and practicums (clinical experience). The final trimesters of the program are devoted primarily to clinical practice under the supervision of licensed Doctors of Chiropractic. Both campuses maintain public clinics for this practical experience.

Research Facilities

Both campuses are involved in clinical and basic science research. Students often assist in research in cooperation with faculty and, in certain instances, may receive financial assistance for research.

Financial Aid

Qualified students at each of the campuses are eligible for federally guaranteed loans. Both campuses of Cleveland Chiropractic College participate in the following federal family educational student financial aid programs: Federal Pell Grant, Federal Work-Study, Federal Perkins Loan, Federal Supplemental Educational Opportunity Grant, Federal Stafford Student Loan, and Parent Loan for Undergraduate Students. In addition, there are private loan programs available including Teri Loans, Professional Education Program Loan, Grad Excel, Canadian Chiro, and ChiroLoan. Students may also be eligible for private grants and scholarships.

Cost of Study

For 1998–99, the tuition at Cleveland-KC is $165 per credit for the D.C. degree program and $131 per credit for the B.S. degree program. The tuition at Cleveland-LA is $180 per credit for the D.C. degree program and $125 per credit for the B.S. degree program. These figures are based on full-time enrollment. Special arrangements may be made for a student who enrolls for less than a full trimester load. The campuses do not charge additional out-of-state, laboratory, or graduation fees.

Living and Housing Costs

Monthly rents in the greater Kansas City area start at approximately $400 for a small or shared apartment, and housing is readily available close to campus. In Los Angeles, many apartments are located in the immediate neighborhood of the College. Monthly rent ranges from $400 to $600 for studios and singles.

Student Group

Cleveland-KC currently enrolls 615 students, with 29 percent of these being women. Cleveland-LA's current enrollment is 550, with 32 percent women. Both campuses include students from most states and from many other countries, and each campus subscribes to a nondiscriminatory equal opportunity policy for admission of qualified students.

Location

Noted for its fountains and parks, greater Kansas City has many opportunities for cultural events, education, recreation, and spectator sports. Highlights include the Kansas City Chiefs and Royals, Worlds of Fun, the Nelson Art Gallery, the Kansas City Museum, and the world-famous Country Club Plaza shopping district.

Greater Los Angeles abounds in cultural opportunities and landmarks such as Disneyland, Universal Studios, Beverly Hills, Hollywood, Mann's Chinese Theater, the Getty Museum, and Will Rogers State Park. One of the entertainment capitals of the world, Los Angeles offers numerous sports activities for the spectator (Dodgers, Angels, Kings, Lakers, Clippers) or the participant (from surfing in the Pacific to snowskiing at nearby areas such as Big Bear).

The College

Cleveland Chiropractic College is a multicampus system, with campuses in Kansas City, Missouri, and Los Angeles, California. The College is a private, coeducational, not-for-profit institution of higher education. The primary focus is the preparation of students for the D.C. degree.

The mission of the College lies in the areas of education, scholarship, and service. The educational mission consists of the preparation of competent, entry-level Doctors of Chiropractic who offer the focused, nonduplicated specialty in the detection of the vertebral subluxation complex and its management, primarily through the use of chiropractic spinal adjustments; the preparation of Doctors of Chiropractic as portal-of-entry, primary health-care providers within the health-care delivery system, who are well educated to diagnose, care for the human body, understand and relate fundamental scientific information, and consult with and/or refer to other health-care providers when it is in the best interest of the patient; the continuing education of Doctors of Chiropractic; and the presentation of undergraduate education that leads to a baccalaureate degree. The scholarship mission consists of conducting research and scholarly activities that will further chiropractic education and health-care and scholarly collaboration with other institutions of higher education or health-care providers. The service mission consists of clinical service to the community, services to alumni and other professionals, involvement with community health and professional issues, and patient education.

The College is regionally accredited, and the D.C. program on each campus is professionally accredited. The College attracts students from all parts of the world and has graduates practicing in all fifty states and internationally.

Applying

Applications may be obtained by writing or calling either campus (information given below). Applicants must submit the completed application form, official copies of all transcripts, completed recommendations, and a statement of motivation for becoming a chiropractor. Both campuses require a $50 nonrefundable application fee. Preprofessional requirements for both campuses include 6 semester hours each of the following science courses with lab: biology (excluding botany), inorganic chemistry, organic chemistry, and physics; 6 semester hours of English composition, 3 semester hours of psychology, and 15 semester hours of humanities and/or social sciences. The minimum cumulative GPA is 2.25, with no science grade below C. The international equivalency for courses may be accepted. Applicants must have a minimum of 60 preprofessional credit hours to be admitted. Classes matriculate in September, January, and May.

Correspondence and Information

Director of Admissions
Cleveland Chiropractic College, Kansas City Campus
6401 Rockhill Road
Kansas City, Missouri 64131-1181
Telephone: 816-333-8230
800-467-CCKC (toll-free)
Fax: 816-333-4749
WWW: http://www.clevelandchiropractic.edu

Director of Admissions
Cleveland Chiropractic College, Los Angeles Campus
590 North Vermont Avenue
Los Angeles, California 90004-2196
Telephone: 213-660-6166
800-466-CCLA (toll-free)
Fax: 213-660-5387
WWW: http://www.clevelandchiropractic.edu

Cleveland Chiropractic Colleges of Kansas City and Los Angeles

THE FACULTY AND THEIR RESEARCH

Kansas City Campus

Shaheen Ahmed, Adjunct Faculty; M.D., Nagpur Medical College, 1972: pathology. Paul B. Barlett, Associate Professor; Ph.D., Ohio State, 1984: anatomy. David Clark Beckley, Assistant Professor; D.C., Cleveland Chiropractic (Kansas City), 1975: chiropractic principles and practice. Lawrence D. Beem, Assistant Professor; D.C., Cleveland Chiropractic (Kansas City), 1970: clinic. Andrew S. Bonci, Assistant Professor; D.C., Cleveland Chiropractic (Kansas City), 1989: diagnosis. Michele Bonci, Assistant Professor; D.C., Cleveland Chiropractic (Kansas City), 1989: clinic. Joseph Bowles, Assistant Professor; D.C., Cleveland Chiropractic (Kansas City), 1977: clinic. Ashley E. Cleveland, Adjunct Faculty; D.C., Cleveland Chiropractic (Kansas City), 1995: research. Carl S. Cleveland III, President; D.C., Cleveland Chiropractic (Kansas City), 1975: chiropractic principles and practice. Ray N. Conley, Professor; D.C., Cleveland Chiropractic (Kansas City), 1972: radiology. Jill M. Davis, ; M.A., Kansas, 1992: anatomy. Charles F. Dorlac, Adjunct Faculty; Ph.D., Missouri–Kansas City, 1981: diagnosis. Kenneth L. Elkins, Associate Professor; M.S., Oklahoma, 1968: pathology and microbiology. Thomas E. Forbach, Adjunct Faculty; D.C., Logan Chiropractic, 1976: chiropractic principles and practice. Hugo V. Gibson, Instructor; D.C., Palmer Chiropractic, 1972: chiropractic principles and practice. Mark Howard Gilgus, Adjunct Faculty; J.D., Missouri–Kansas City, 1978: chiropractic principles and practice. Clinton Gowan III, Teaching Fellow; D.C., Cleveland Chiropractic, 1995: clinic. Ned U. Heese, Assistant Professor; D.C., Logan Chiropractic, 1974: chiropractic principles and practice. Lawrence J. Hurd, Assistant Professor; D.C., Palmer Chiropractic, 1978: chiropractic principles and practice. Stephen P. Larsen, Professor; Ph.D., North Texas State, 1972: anatomy. Catherine Leduc, Clinician; D.C., Cleveland Chiropractic, 1993: clinic. J. Alan Lovejoy, Assistant Professor; D.C., Palmer Chiropractic, 1978: clinic. Aleksandr Makarov, Instructor; M.D., Odessa, 1994: anatomy. Michael D. Moore, Instructor; D.C., Palmer Chiropractic, 1982: chiropractic principles and practice. Anwar H. Mujawar, Assistant Professor; M.D., Jawaharlal Nehru Medical College, 1986: pathology. Fred Needles, Instructor; M.S., Missouri–Kansas City, 1992: physics. Thomas K. Nichols, Instructor; D.C., Palmer Chiropractic, 1977: diagnosis. Doran L. Nicholson, Professor; D.C., Cleveland Chiropractic (Kansas City), 1980: radiology. Sandra Norton-Cothran, Resident; D.C., Cleveland Chiropractic, 1996: radiology. Gazala Parvin, Assistant Professor; M.B.B.S., VSS Medical College, Sambalpur University, 1991: physiology. Debra Pentz, Adjunct Faculty; M.B.A., York, 1995: algebra. Muriel Perillat, Professor; D.C., Cleveland Chiropractic (Kansas City), 1979: chiropractic principles and practice. Mark Pfefer, Instructor; D.C., 1988: research. Andrei A. Pikalov, Adjunct Faculty; Ph.D., Institute of Aviation and Space Medicine, Moscow, 1992: research. Ruth Sandefur, Professor; D.C., Cleveland Chiropractic (Kansas City), 1967: diagnosis. Timothy Schoof, Assistant Professor; M.S., Missouri, 1990; M.B.A., Rockhurst, 1994: chemistry. David W. Stewart, Assistant Professor; Ph.D., Texas A&M, 1986: physiology and chemistry. Marcia Thomas, Associate Professor; M.A., Missouri–Kansas City, 1975: library. Rickard J. Thomas, Professor; D.C., Cleveland Chiropractic (Kansas City), 1977: chiropractic principles and practice. William E. Tuttle, Assistant Professor; D.C., Cleveland Chiropractic (Kansas City), 1980: chiropractic principles and practice. Stephen W. Vaitl, Assistant Professor; D.C., Cleveland Chiropractic (Kansas City), 1982: clinic. G. Michael Whitehead, Associate Professor; D.C., Logan Chiropractic, 1979: diagnosis. Ralph R. Wilkinson, Associate Professor; Ph.D., Oregon, 1962: biochemistry. Brad S. Willits, Adjunct Faculty; D.C., Cleveland Chiropractic (Kansas City), 1988: diagnosis. John P. Willits, Adjunct Faculty; D.C., Cleveland Chiropractic (Kansas City), 1965: chiropractic principles and practice.

Los Angeles Campus

Assibi Z. Abudu, Associate Professor; M.D., USC, 1975: diagnosis. Cecilia L. Anderson, Professor; D.C., Cleveland Chiropractic (Los Angeles), 1979: diagnosis and chiropractic science. Constance J. Anderson, Instructor; D.C., Cleveland Chiropractic (Los Angeles), 1992: diagnosis and chiropractic science. Harold Roy Azuma, Assistant Professor; D.C., Cleveland Chiropractic (Los Angeles), 1984: clinic. Lydia Baghdaseriani, Teaching Assistant; D.C., Cleveland Chiropractic (Los Angeles), 1996: chiropractic science. John Bergman, Graduate Teaching Assistant; D.C., Cleveland Chiropractic (Los Angeles), 1997: chiropractic science. Michael Birozy, Associate Professor; D.C., Los Angeles Chiropractic, 1976: clinic. Lily Cabellon, Associate Professor, M.D., Manila Central (Philippines), 1973: basic science. Lucila T. Calimag, Associate Professor; M.D., Far Eastern (Manila), 1966: diagnosis and basic science. Thomas L. Carpenter, Associate Professor and Coordinator of Research; D.C., Los Angeles Chiropractic, 1973: chiropractic science. Francisco Chavez-Almanza, Professor; D.C., Cleveland Chiropractic (Los Angeles), 1988: diagnosis and basic science. Carol A. Claus, Associate Professor and Department Head; D.C., Cleveland Chiropractic (Los Angeles), 1988: chiropractic science. Carl S. Cleveland III, President; D.C., Cleveland Chiropractic (Kansas City), 1975. Edmund A. Cohen, Assistant Professor and Counselor; Ph.D., California School of Professional Psychology, 1978: diagnosis. Maria D. Dell, Associate Professor; Ph.D., Oklahoma, 1986: basic science. Geordie Duckler, Assistant Professor; Ph.D., UCLA, 1997: chiropractic science. Ruth E. Ebeling, Associate Professor; M.S., California State, Long Beach, 1982: basic science. Patricia Ebert, Instructor; D.C., Cleveland Chiropractic (Los Angeles), 1993: chiropractic science and diagnosis. James S. Factor, Assistant Professor and Clinician; D.C., Cleveland Chiropractic (Los Angeles), 1992: chiropractic science. Bradley Fafekas, Instructor; D.C., Cleveland Chiropractic (Los Angeles), 1995: chiropractic science. Clarence E. Franklin, Associate Professor and Counselor; D.C., Los Angeles Chiropractic, 1963: chiropractic science. Howard Friedman, Instuctor; D.C., Cleveland Chiropractic (Los Angeles), 1989: chiropractic science. David F. Gendreau, Assistant Professor; D.C., Los Angeles Chiropractic, 1989: diagnosis. Antonio J. Gonsalves Jr., Assistant Professor; D.C., Cleveland Chiropractic (Los Angeles), 1991: chiropractic science. Neil Hersh, Associate Professor; M.D., Chicago, 1985: diagnosis and basic science. Edward G. Horowitz, Associate Professor and Clinician; D.C., Cleveland Chiropractic (Los Angeles), 1980. Leila L. Iler, Assistant Dean of Instruction and Associate Professor; Ed.D., California State, Northridge, 1994: basic science. William W. Jacobson, Professor and Clinician; D.C., Cleveland Chiropractic (Los Angeles), 1955: chiropractic science. Muffit Jensen, Assistant Professor and Clinician; D.C., Cleveland Chiropractic (Los Angeles), 1990: chiropractic science. Gary Johnson, Associate Professor; D.C., Cleveland Chiropractic (Los Angeles), 1986: diagnosis. Glenn Johnson, Associate Professor; D.C., Cleveland Chiropractic (Los Angeles), 1985: chiropractic science. Mariam Kahan, Associate Professor and Dean of Instruction; Ph.D., UCLA, 1992. Raymond Kato, Assistant Professor; M.S., USC, 1958: basic science. Gyaneshwar Khare, Professor; Ph.D., Kansas State, 1966: basic sciences. Jason Kim, Assistant Professor; Ph.D., USC, 1996: basic science. Fernando Lugo, Assistant Professor; D.C., Cleveland Chiropractic (Los Angeles), 1988: chiropractic science. Thomas Ly, Graduate Teaching Assistant; D.C., Cleveland Chiropractic (Los Angeles), 1997: chiropractic science. Vincent Maples, Associate Professor and Department Head; D.C., Cleveland Chiropractic (Los Angeles), 1978: diagnosis science. Ted E. Marcus, Assistant Professor; Ph.D., California, Santa Barbara, 1982: basic science. Laura Margolis, Instructor; D.C., Cleveland Chiropractic (Los Angeles), 1994: basic science. James Marion, Instructor; D.C., Cleveland Chiropractic (Los Angeles), 1995: chiropractic science. Stephen N. Mayer, Associate Professor and Clinician; D.C., Cleveland Chiropractic (Los Angeles), 1986: diagnosis. Denise Michele, Assistant Professor; D.C., Cleveland Chiropractic (Los Angeles), 1991: chiropractic science. Allen Miller, Assistant Professor and Clinician; D.C., Cleveland Chiropractic (Los Angeles), 1987. Anita Mork, Associate Professor and Department Head, Basic Sciences; M.S., UCLA, 1980: basic science. Richard Morris, Associate Professor; D.C., Cleveland Chiropractic (Los Angeles), 1986: chiropractic science. Charles C. Neault, Associate Professor; D.C., Cleveland Chiropractic (Los Angeles), 1977: chiropractic science. Nancy Obena, Instructor; M.D., Far Eastern (Philippines), 1988: basic science. Bradley Ping, Instructor; D.C., Palmer Chiropractic, 1983: chiropractic science. John M. Raithel III, Assistant Professor and Clinician; D.C., Cleveland Chiropractic (Los Angeles), 1986: chiropractic science. Nels Rinden, Instructor; M.S., California State, Los Angeles, 1980: basic science. Michele Simmons, Instructor; D.C., Cleveland Chiropractic (Los Angeles), 1990: chiropractic science. Ben Solkamans, Instructor and Clinician; D.C., Cleveland Chiropractic (Los Angeles), 1963. Shawn Steel, Assistant Professor; J.D., Northrop, 1978: chiropractic science. William Strickland, Instructor; D.C., Cleveland Chiropractic (Los Angeles), 1994: diagnosis. Victor Tong, Radiologist, Assistant Professor; D.C., Logan Chiropractic, 1979: diagnosis. Gary R. Vitullo, Instructor; D.C., Cleveland Chiropractic (Los Angeles), 1988: chiropractic science. Peter Whiteley, Graduate Teaching Assistant; D.C., Los Angeles Chiropractic, 1997: chiropractic science. Rodney W. Zambrows, Assistant Professor; D.C., Cleveland Chiropractic (Los Angeles), 1989: chiropractic science.

LIFE CHIROPRACTIC COLLEGE WEST

Program of Study

Located in the heart of the San Francisco Bay area, Life Chiropractic College West offers the Doctor of Chiropractic degree. Life West provides a solid academic and clinical experience featuring an integrated emphasis on chiropractic philosophy and technique. Students may complete the program in as few as twelve quarters, with extended academic programs of up to fifteen quarters available.

The chiropractic profession has experienced strong growth in the past few years as public demand for drug-free, noninvasive, preventative health care has increased. Equipped with a strong background in the sciences, a deep understanding of chiropractic philosophy, and training in twelve leading techniques, students complete their classroom and clinic experience well prepared for a career in chiropractic health care.

Chiropractic concerns itself with the relationship between structure (primarily the spine) and function (primarily coordinated by the nervous system) as that relationship may affect the restoration and preservation of health. Chiropractic focuses on the innate ability of the body to heal itself without the use of drugs or surgery.

The purpose of chiropractic professional education is to provide the doctoral candidate with a core of knowledge in the basic and clinical sciences and related health subjects sufficient for the Doctor of Chiropractic to perform the professional obligations of a primary-care clinician.

Life West is accredited by the Council on Chiropractic Education, the agency recognized by the U.S. Department of Education to accredit chiropractic colleges.

Research Facilities

Life West's research department is known for high-quality, provocative research that involves both the faculty and students. Past studies include work in scoliosis, range of motion, and multidisciplinary projects involving collaboration with medical, osteopathic, and podiatric doctors.

Life West's library complements students' research opportunities. It houses the collections, reference and study areas, audiovisual production and viewing facilities, a computer laboratory, and a radiology room.

Three full-time librarians guide students in becoming proficient researchers using both print sources and databases, including extensive health science resources via the Internet. Through contacts and exchanges with chiropractic colleges nationally and with regional academic and health science libraries, the students have access to literally millions of volumes and journal articles.

The networked computer laboratory provides students with access to word processing, printing, Internet Web–browsing, and e-mail. Computer stations also feature software such as Medical Terminology, a National Board review program, and A.D.A.M. Interactive (Animated Dissection for Anatomy in Medicine).

Financial Aid

The College administers a comprehensive financial aid program so that qualified students are not denied a chiropractic education because of financial need.

Grant programs include the Federal Pell Grant, Federal Supplemental Education Opportunity Grant (FSEOG), Bureau of Indian Affairs Grant, and Cal Grant A. Loan programs include Federal Subsidized and Unsubsidized Stafford Loans, Federal PLUS Program, and the Chiroloan. Employment programs include both the Federal Work-Study Program (including the reading tutor program and other community service jobs) and an institutional work-study program. A number of scholarships are also available, as are veterans' educational benefits.

Cost of Study

Tuition for the 1998–99 academic year is $4100 per quarter. For students who choose an extended schedule, there are reduced tuition rates for the extra quarters of study. International students may choose between a 25 percent tuition grant and a 50 percent deferred tuition payment plan.

Living and Housing Costs

Most Life West students choose to live in shared housing near the campus. In this type of arrangement, most students pay no more than $400 per month in rent. Other living expenses vary. For students who choose to live in areas such as San Francisco, rent and other expenses are usually higher.

Student Group

Life West is a diverse community of almost 800 students, approximately 35 percent of whom are women. The average age is 28. More than 20 percent of Life West's students come from outside the United States, representing about thirty countries.

Location

Life West's location allows easy access to San Francisco, San Jose, Oakland, and Berkeley. The Bay Area is home to a rich cultural community and an ideal climate. There are many concerts, theaters, comedy and night clubs, dance companies, and science and art museums. Students can also enjoy outdoor activities year-round as well as a variety of professional sporting events.

The College

Life Chiropractic College West was founded in 1976 as Pacific States Chiropractic College. In 1981, an agreement was reached between Pacific States and Life Chiropractic College in Georgia (now Life University), and the institution was renamed Life Chiropractic College West.

Life West is a traditional chiropractic college, known for its integrated emphasis on chiropractic philosophy and technique.

Applying

Applications for admission are accepted up to two years prior to a student's intended term of entry. In order to be considered by the admissions committee, applicants must have completed, or be working toward, at least 60 semester units of college-level work divided among the basic sciences (biology, general chemistry, organic chemistry, and physics), social sciences/humanities, English/communication skills, and psychology. There is also a minimum GPA requirement. Students should contact the Office of Admissions for detailed information on prerequisites and required application materials.

Correspondence and Information

Office of Admissions
Life Chiropractic College West
2005 Via Barrett
San Lorenzo, California 94580
Telephone: 510-276-9013 (outside the U.S. and Canada)
800-788-4476 (toll-free, U.S. and Canada only)
Fax: 510-276-4893
E-mail: admissions@lifewest.edu
World Wide Web: http://www.lifewest.edu

Life Chiropractic College West

THE FACULTY

John Ammon, D.C.
Jeff Anderson, D.C.
Kris Andrues, D.C.
Richard Asturias, D.C.
Sergio F. Azzolino, D.C.; DACNB
Douglas Bell, D.C.
Ulyss Bidkaram, D.C.
Charles Bixby, D.C.
Griselda Blazey, Ph.D.
John Boss, Ph.D.
David Browning, D.C.
James Carter, D.C.; DACBR
George Casey, D.C.
Gerard W. Clum, D.C.; HCD
Ronald Crawford, D.C.
Candi Cross, D.C.
Steve Dain, M.A., D.C.
Paul DiLeo, M.A., D.C.
David Donaldson, D.C.
Scott Donaldson, D.C.
Naomi Downey, D.C.
Kathy Doyle, D.C.
Kerri Duggins, D.C.
Dean Falltrick, D.C.
Sergio T. Fernando, D.C.
Karen S. Franklin, M.A., D.C.
Bryan Gatterman, D.C.; DACBR
W. Michael Gazdar, D.C.; CCSP
Warren L. Gee, D.C.
Robert Goble, M.B.A., D.C.
Linda Goldman, D.C.
Robert K. Gray, M.M., D.C.
James Hawkins, M.A.; HCD
Colleen J. Hewes, M.S.N., D.C.
Michael Hickey, D.C.
Jerry Hightower, D.C.
Patricia Hospy, D.C.
Stephen James, D.C.
Robert Katona, D.C.
Heidi Keller, M.S., D.C.
Donald Kessler, D.C.; DACAN
Shakati S. Khalsa, D.C.
Kathleen King, D.C.
Kathleen Kinney, D.C.
James Konlande, Ph.D.
Charles A. Lantz, Ph.D., D.C.
Kenneth Lawver, D.C.
Clement Leung, D.C.
Deborah Lindemann, D.C.; RN
Bruce Lipton, Ph.D.
Joe Martin, D.C.
John Martin, D.C.
Adrienne Miller, M.A., J.D.
Jamie Miller, D.C.
George Neukam, D.C.
Gloria Niles, D.C.; DACAN
Lawrence Nordhoff, D.C.
Kenneth Norman, D.C.
Annette Osenga, M.L.S.
Peggie Phillips, M.A.
Carree Picker, M.A., D.C.
Gregory Plaugher, D.C.
Ray Pursell, D.C.
Eric Raines, D.C.
Suzanne Ray, M.S.
Michelle Reddel, M.A., D.C.
Richard Robertshaw, D.C.
Charles Rollis, D.C.
Mitch Roth, D.C.
Michael J. Schmidt, D.C.
Beverly Scott, D.C.
Malik Slosberg, M.A., D.C.
Thomas Sneed, M.S., D.C.
Alan B. Solinger, Ph.D.
Joan Sowers, M.S.
David Spear, Ph.D.
David Straub, M.S.
Norman B. Strutin, D.C.
Marcus S. Strutz, D.C.
Aine Sweeney, B.S.W., M.M., D.C.
Larry Thill, D.C.
Mary Thomas-Weiss, D.C.
Christine Thompson, D.C., DACNB
Pete Tsiglieris, D.C.
Kweli Tutashinda, D.C.
Dorothy Voigt, M.S.
Paul Walton, D.C.; CCSP, CCEP
Paulina Warren, Ph.D.
S. Randall Waters, D.C.
Susan West, D.C.
Jule Wilferd, D.C.

LIFE UNIVERSITY

Program in Chiropractic

Program of Study

Life University offers a comprehensive curriculum leading to the Doctor of Chiropractic degree. The program requires fourteen academic quarters of study and includes courses in basic and clinical sciences and other health-related subjects, as well as an internship at one of three outpatient clinics. Patient care begins as soon as seventh quarter, which is earlier than most other chiropractic colleges. Special emphasis is placed on the relationship between structural and neurological aspects of the body in health and disease. Graduates are eligible for licensure as chiropractors in forty-nine states and many other countries. Faculty and students engage in research that is designed to provide data about chiropractic phenomena, develop the students' natural talents, and encourage students to accept responsibility for health-care leadership.

Research Facilities

Life University has the entire complement of resources required for the training of doctors of chiropractic. Classrooms range in size from tutorial rooms accommodating 20 students to a lecture hall with seating for more than 500. A $14-million modernization of the campus in 1989, followed by a $37-million expansion begun in 1996, provides the University with state-of-the-art learning facilities. These facilities include a functional cadaver laboratory, biochemistry and bacteriological laboratories, and equipment for standard hematological and urinalysis procedures. The Nell K. Williams Learning Resource Center has a collection of 70,000 books, periodicals, and audiovisual aids. The library maintains memberships in the chiropractic library consortium, the National Library of Medicine Regional Program, and the Medical Library Association. Among the library's facilities are an audiovisual room with videocassette machines, a large chart area, a slide projector, and X-ray viewboxes. Computers connected to the Internet are also available.

Financial Aid

Life participates in the Federal Work-Study, Federal Perkins Loan, Federal Subsidized and Unsubsidized Stafford Student Loan, Life University Foreign Student Loan, numerous scholarships, and various state loan programs.

Cost of Study

The 1998–99 tuition charge averages $3400 per quarter. Tuition may vary depending on the course load selected. Laboratory fees vary by course. The application fee is $50; the graduation fee, $75; and the parking fee, $20. An advance payment of $350 on tuition is due at the time of acceptance and is deducted from the tuition due for the first quarter when the student matriculates.

Living and Housing Costs

Limited housing is available on campus. The University provides assistance in locating reasonably priced furnished and unfurnished apartments nearby. A typical unfurnished one-bedroom unit rents for about $475 per month. For lists of available housing, students should contact the Student Affairs Office.

Student Group

Life has more than 4,200 students, of whom approximately 27.5 percent are women. The average age is 27, and about 20 percent are married. More than 42 percent hold a baccalaureate degree or have completed work toward a master's degree when they matriculate. The University offers equal educational opportunities to all without regard to race, color, creed, religion, national origin, sex, disability, marital status, or status with regard to public assistance.

Location

Just 15 minutes from the heart of Atlanta, the beautifully wooded campus is located in suburban Marietta. Cultural and recreational facilities in the area include the state capitol, Fox Theater, Atlanta Symphony, High Museum of Art, Atlanta Zoo, Cyclorama, Six Flags over Georgia, White Water Recreation Facility, Stone Mountain Park, World Congress Center, M. L. King National Historic District, Omni Colosseum, Olympic Stadium, and the Georgia Dome. Among the colleges and universities in metro Atlanta are Georgia State, Georgia Tech, Emory, Clark Atlanta, Mercer, Oglethorpe, Spelman, and Morehouse.

The University

Life University, founded in 1974 by Dr. Sid E. Williams, opened in 1975 with 22 students. Since then, enrollment has increased to more than 4,200, making Life the largest chiropractic institution in the world. Life is situated on a campus of more than 125 acres with approximately 378,264 square feet of instructional, research, and administrative facilities with parking for more than 2,000. It is a completely autonomous institution, fulfilling its purpose as dictated by its charter, honoring its symbol, the Tree of Life, and expressing its belief that "All Things Exist in Mutual Relationship to One Another." Life University is accredited by the Commission on Accreditation of the Southern Association of Colleges and Schools (SACS) to award the Doctor of Chiropractic, Master of Science, Bachelor of Science, and Bachelor of Business Administration degrees. The B.S. degree in nutrition for the chiropractic sciences offers a clinical emphasis oriented toward the practicing health professional. The University was recently approved to offer a B.S. for dietetics, enabling students to become registered dietitians. Life is approved by the Department of Immigration and Naturalization. Since its first commencement, Life has granted more than 7,000 degrees. Life University School of Chiropractic is accredited by the Commission on Accreditation of the Council of Chiropractic Education (CCE).

Applying

The study of the science, art, and philosophy of chiropractic is comprehensive, challenging, and demanding. The Admissions Office investigates carefully what an applicant can bring to the profession, to the University, and eventually to the public. The applicant must have a preprofessional background of not fewer than 60 semester hours (90 quarter hours), including 6 semester hours of writing-based English or communication skills, 3 semester hours of psychology, 15 semester hours of social sciences or humanities, 6 semester hours of biological sciences, 6 semester hours of general or inorganic chemistry, 6 semester hours of organic chemistry, and 6 semester hours of physics. The remaining required hours are electives and include 12 semester hours, totaling 60 semester hours. All science prerequisite courses must contain a laboratory component, have been completed in two or more academic terms, and each passed with a grade of C or better (2.0 on a 4.0 scale). A grade of C- (less than a 2.0 on a 4.0 scale) will not be acceptable in basic science lectures or labs. No introductory courses in chemistry and/or physics are accepted. Biology requirements may be met with courses such as general biology, zoology, anatomy, physiology, and microbiology. Botany or ecology will not be accepted to meet this requirement. Two letters of recommendation from practicing chiropractors must be sent to the Director of Admission Services. In the event the student does not know two chiropractors, letters from someone in a professional field (former teachers, employers, clergy, etc.) will be accepted as long as they are non-relatives. Official transcripts from all institutions at which preprofessional work was completed must reflect a GPA of 2.25 or higher on a 4.0 scale (minimum 2.5 beginning fall 1999). All transcripts from abroad should be sent to World Education Services, Inc., P. O. Box 745, Old Chelsea Station, New York, New York 10011. An additional fee of $125 is required for this mandatory evaluation. For international students, the accepted foreign equivalent of the courses required above is allowed.

Applications for admission may be obtained by writing to the Admissions Services Director or by telephoning. Applications are considered in the order received because class sizes are limited. Consideration of an application received too late for a given quarter is automatically deferred to the next quarter.

Correspondence and Information

Director of Admissions
Life University
1269 Barclay Circle
Marietta, Georgia 30060

Telephone: 770-426-2884
800-543-3202 (toll-free)
World Wide Web: http://www.life.edu

Life University

ADMINISTRATION

Office of Academic Affairs
Keith Asplin, Ph.D., Vice President for Academic Affairs and Academic Dean.
Donald L. Gutstein, D.C., Associate Academic Dean.
Ronald Roland, Ph.D., Director of Admissions and Director of the KT Center.
Danielle L. Martin, Administrative Assistant to the Vice President for Academic Affairs.
Mamie B. Ware, Ph.D., Dean of the School of Undergraduate Studies.
Ronald Kirk, D.C., Dean of the School of Chiropractic (Acting).
Deborah Lancaster, Administrative Assistant to the Dean of the School of Undergraduate Studies.

Cynthia Harrison, M.Ed., Department Head, Developmental Studies.
David Li, Ph.D., Department Head, Management.
Jaleh Dehpahlvan, M.S., Department Head, Nutrition.
Raj Pradhan, M.S., Department Head, Natural Sciences, and Associate Dean of the School of Undergraduate Studies.
Frank Ruechel, M.Ed., Ph.D., Department Head, General Education.

Samuel Demons, Ph.D., Chair, Basic Sciences Division.
Kenneth Heairlston, D.C., Chair, Chiropractic Technique and Analysis Division.
Phillip Sanders, D.C., Chair, Chiropractic Sciences Division.
Matt E. Williams, M.Ed., D.C., Chair, Clinical Sciences.
Rick Sherkel, D.C., Chair, Diagnostic Imaging and Alignment Division.

Judith Peters, B.V.A., Director of the Chiropractic Technician Program.
Bobby Braile, D.C., Director of Postgraduate Education.
Jeffrey Lander, Ph.D., Director of Sport Health Science.
Amanda Timberlake, M.S., Director of Wellness.
Nancy R. Hill, M.S.L.S., Dean and Director of the Nell K. Williams Learning Resources Center.
Michael Hoefer, Ph.D., Director of Scheduling, Advising, and Faculty Development.
Ann Drake, Ph.D., Director of the Academic Assistance Center.

John D. Hopkins, D.C., Resources Coordinator.
Denise L. Gordon, Admissions Coordinator.
Pam Reynolds, B.S., Registrar.
Brian Sheres, D.C., Associate Registrar.

Office of Clinics
D. D. Humber, D.C., Senior Vice President for Clinics.
Daniel L. Michel, D.C., Director of the Main Campus Clinic.
Robert S. Mellette, D.C., Director of the Student Clinic.
Steven J. Mirtschink, D.C., Director of the North Marietta Clinic.
Deborah Pogrelis, D.C., Director of the Luckie Street Clinic.
Michael Boston, M.S.W., D.C., Assistant Director of the Main Campus Clinic.
Edgar Miller, D.C., Assistant Director of the North Marietta Clinic.
Janice Willhite, D.C., Assistant Director of the Main Campus Clinic.
Edie Dahlhauser, Clinics Administrator.

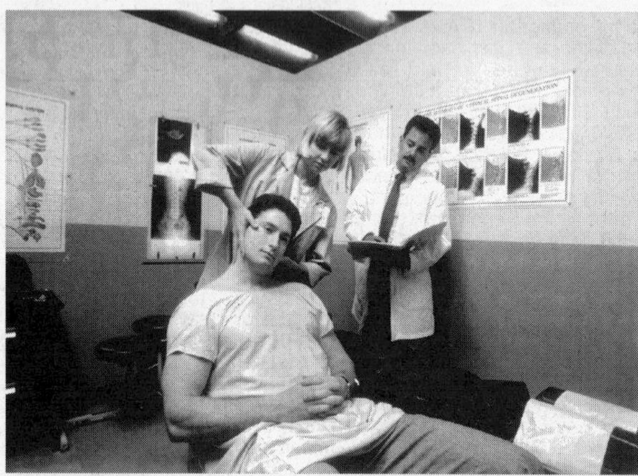

Students receive supervised clinical experience.

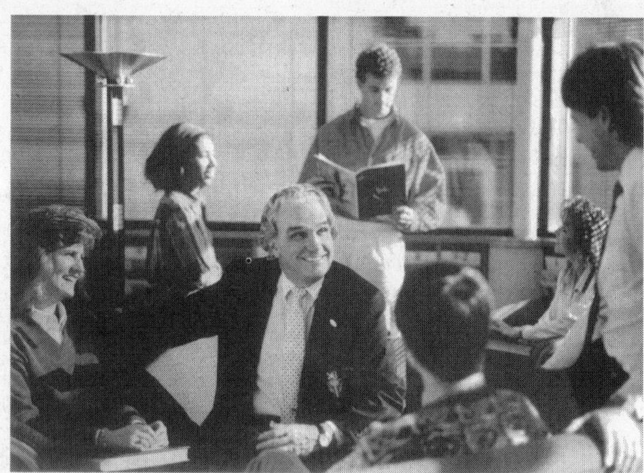

Life University, under the direction of founder and president Dr. Sid E. Williams, has grown to become a leading school of chiropractic.

LOGAN COLLEGE OF CHIROPRACTIC

Graduate School
Division of Chiropractic and Clinical Sciences

Program of Study

Logan College of Chiropractic is a professional health-care institution that prepares students for careers in primary health care and is accredited by the Commission on Accreditation of the Council on Chiropractic Education and the Commission on Institutions of Higher Education of the North Central Association of Colleges and Schools. The graduate program leads to the degree of Doctor of Chiropractic. The curriculum provides courses in chiropractic techniques that include not only the Logan system of body mechanics but other specialized techniques as well. Adjunctive procedures, including physical therapy, office procedures and patient management, and diagnostic and case management, plus specialized courses in chiropractic general studies, round out the curriculum. All students are required to prepare and complete a research project under the direction of the Research Department. There is a special on-campus competitive residency program in roentgenology, which requires specific research. The full course of studies leading to the Doctor of Chiropractic degree is ten trimesters or five academic years. A minimum of three trimesters is spent in outpatient health center work either at the College itself or at the satellite health centers. The last trimester in residence includes an Intern Associate program that is open to all qualified students in residence.

The Postdoctoral and Related Education Department offers special programs for continuing education credit at the license-renewal level.

At the undergraduate level, following four trimesters in basic sciences, a Bachelor of Science degree in human biology may be earned.

Research Facilities

The College's newest construction is a $3.1-million science and research building. Laboratories equipped with state-of-the-art facilities are open to students and faculty members. Also, the outpatient health center participates in the clinical research program, using its patient population, treatment rooms, clinical lab, and computer facility. Laboratories are equipped for work in microbiology (incubators, an autoclave), physiology (physiographs, oscilloscopes), biochemistry (ultracentrifuges, a still, gel electrophoresis equipment, a densitometer), histology (a microtome, cryostat, and teknitron), biomechanics and radiology (X-ray units and developer, an anatomical lab), and peripheral vascular evaluation (equipment for diagnostic Doppler ultrasound and photo plethysomography). Computers are available for data processing and literature searches. Logan College participates in an interlibrary loan program with the University of Missouri, Saint Louis University, and Washington University.

Financial Aid

Financial aid is available in the form of scholarships, grants, loans, and employment. Scholarships and grants are provided by alumni and friends and do not need to be repaid. Loans must be repaid with interest. Employment permits students to earn money while pursuing their course of studies. Special stipends are available for students participating in the residency programs. Information about financial aid is sent to prospective students. Logan College is an eligible institution under the Federal Pell Grant, Federal Supplemental Educational Opportunity Grant, Missouri Grant, Federal Work-Study, PLUS loan, Health Education Assistance Loan, Federal Stafford Student Loan, and Federal Perkins Loan programs.

Cost of Study

Tuition and fees in 1997–98 are $8870 for eight months, and books are approximately $945. These figures are increased, if necessary, according to the cost of living.

Living and Housing Costs

Although there are no on-campus residence facilities, the Admissions Office maintains complete information on accommodations in the area of the campus. In addition, a current student roommate list is supplied. Students are responsible for making their own arrangements. The average cost of room and board is $6344; transportation, $1768; and personal expenses, $2720.

Student Group

The current enrollment at Logan is 1,109 students. Approximately 72 percent are men. Students come from more than forty-five states; about 10 percent of the students are from other countries. The average age of students attending the College is 28 years; about 30 percent are married. Students come from every walk of life and profession and include teachers, nurses, businesspeople, and other health professionals. Approximately 85 percent receive financial aid. Graduates set up their own private practice, join in practice with established chiropractors, or seek teaching positions in other professional schools.

Student Outcomes

More than 93 percent of entering students graduate within four years. A full-time Placement Office assists in setting up preceptorships, associateships, and practice purchases.

Location

Logan College, in Chesterfield, Missouri, a thriving and growing suburb of St. Louis, is a 20-minute drive from the downtown area. St. Louis traces its roots to the French, Spanish, and English explorers, and much of its tradition has been maintained. The Arch—the famous Gateway to the West on the bank of the Mississippi, designed by Saarinen—dominates the city and contains an outstanding museum of the history of western expansion. A full complement of performing arts facilities is found in the city and its suburbs, along with the famous Art Museum and St. Louis Zoo located in Forest Park. St. Louis is the home of the Cardinals baseball, Blues hockey, Rams football, and Ambush soccer teams.

The College

Logan College of Chiropractic was founded by Dr. Hugh B. Logan in 1935 to provide the profession with a not-for-profit institution offering a year-round, ten-trimester program of academic and chiropractic education. The College moved to its present 103-acre campus, abounding in gracious wooded areas, open lawns, flowering orchards, and athletic fields, in 1973. The educational program includes a clinical system that allows students to obtain firsthand experience in caring for the sick and provides service to the community at large. The Dale C. Montgomery Health Center, a state-of-the-art chiropractic health center, opened in 1982 and provides the College and the community with the most comprehensive diagnostic center in the country.

Applying

Logan College admits a new class three times a year, in January, May, and September. Two academic years of study in a liberal arts college are required for admission, including laboratory courses in biology, inorganic chemistry, organic chemistry, physics, English, psychology, and social sciences/humanities. Application should be made six months in advance of the date of anticipated admission. Requests for financial aid should be made to the Financial Aid Office. Transcripts from colleges and universities previously attended must be submitted along with recommendations to the Director of Admissions. Applications will be reviewed upon receipt. All qualified applicants must complete a structured interview. There is an application fee of $35.

Correspondence and Information

Dean of Enrollment
Logan College of Chiropractic
Box 1065
Chesterfield, Missouri 63006-1065
Telephone: 314-227-2100
800-533-9210 (toll-free in the United States and Canada)
Fax: 314-207-2425

Logan College of Chiropractic

THE FACULTY AND AREAS OF RESEARCH

Vinod K. Anand, Professor and Chairperson, Basic Science Division; Ph.D., Punjab (India).
David L. Ayres, Instructor; D.C., Logan Chiropractic; M.D., American (Mexico).
Ralph Barrale, Assistant Professor; D.C., Logan Chiropractic.
Deanna K. Bates, Assistant Professor and Health Center Clinician; D.C., Northwestern Chiropractic.
Thiema W. Baumann, Professor; Ph.D., Saint Louis.
Doris L. Bell, Associate Professor and Director of Multicultural Affairs; D.C., Logan Chiropractic.
Ivy Benjamin, Associate Professor; M.D., Christian Medical College, Vellore (India).
Richard L. Berman, Instructor and Health Center Clinician; D.C., Northwestern Chiropractic.
William Billotti, Instructor and Health Center Clinician; D.C., Logan Chiropractic.
Ruth Birch, Assistant Professor; Ph.D., Illinois at Chicago.
Jason Blumenfeld, Instructor; D.C., Logan Chiropractic.
Robin E. Bozark, Assistant Professor; D.C., Logan Chiropractic.
Kelly Brinkman, Instructor and Health Center Clinician; D.C., Logan Chiropractic.
Glenn A. Bub, Instructor; D.C., Logan Chiropractic.
Rosemary E. Buhr, Associate Professor and Director of Learning Resources; M.A., Webster.
Jerry A. Carpenter, Instructor; D.C., Logan Chiropractic.
Michael P. Casey, Assistant Professor; J.D., Washington (St. Louis).
Gary P. Casper, Instructor and Chairperson, Chiropractic Science Division; D.C., Palmer Chiropractic.
Donald F. Christy, Associate Professor and Dean of Student Services; D.C., Logan Chiropractic, Ed.D., Southern Illinois.
Catherine A. Conway, Associate Professor; D.C., Logan Chiropractic.
Richard W. Cranwell, Professor and Chairperson, Clinical Science Division; D.C., Logan Chiropractic.
Robert Dana, Instructor; D.C., Logan Chiropractic.
Guy A. Dauphin, Associate Professor; M.S., Saint Mary's (Minnesota).
Fawn R. Dunphy, Instructor and Health Center Clinician; D.C., Logan Chiropractic.
J. Paul Ellis, Assistant Professor; M.S., Saint Louis.
Ralph M. Filson, Professor; D.C., Logan Chiropractic.
Thomas Forrester, Consultant, Basic Science Division; Ph.D., Glasgow.
John L. Golden, Radiology Resident; D.C., Logan Chiropractic.
George A. Goodman, Professor; D.C., Logan Chiropractic.
Ronald H. Grant, Associate Professor; D.C., National Chiropractic.
Gary M. Guebert, Assistant Professor; D.C., Logan Chiropractic.
John L. Gutweiler, Professor; Ph.D., Saint Louis.
Scott F. Hainz, Instructor; D.C., Logan Chiropractic.
Bert I. Hanicke, Professor; D.C., Logan Chiropractic.
Roy J. Hillgartner, Instructor; D.C., Logan Chiropractic.
Lynell L. Hinden, Instructor; D.C., Logan Chiropractic.
Larry G. Hutti, Associate Professor; D.C., Logan Chiropractic.
Francis L. Juhan, Instructor; D.C., Logan Chiropractic.
Rita D. Kennedy, Instructor; D.C., Palmer Chiropractic.
Norman W. Kettner, Associate Professor and Chairperson, Department of Radiology; D.C., D.A.C.B.R., Logan Chiropractic.
Joseph M. Kinsella, Instructor and Health Center Clinician; D.C., Logan Chiropractic.
Adam S. Klotzek, Instructor and Health Center Clinician; D.C., Logan Chiropractic.
Mark G. Kram, Instructor; D.C., Logan Chiropractic.
Jennifer W. Krupp, Instructor; D.C., Logan Chiropractic.
Donald R. Kuhn, Instructor; D.C., Logan Chiropractic.
M. Kathleen Kuhn, Instructor; D.C., Logan Chiropractic.
Lois A. Ladd, Instructor; D.C., Logan Chiropractic.
Ted Lane, Instructor; Ph.D., Purdue.
William F. Madosky, Instructor; D.C., Logan Chiropractic.
Donna M. Mannello, Instructor and Assistant Chairperson, Research Division and Ergonomics; D.C., Logan Chiropractic.
Duane J. Marquart, Assistant Professor; D.C., Logan Chiropractic; D.A.C.B.R., National Chiropractic.
Gregory J. Mathews, Instructor; D.C., Logan Chiropractic.
Michael Novak, Instructor; D.C., Logan Chiropractic.
Kathleen O'Brien, Instructor and Health Center Director; D.C., Logan Chiropractic.
Allen Parry, Instructor and Dean of Postdoctoral and Related Education; D.C., Logan Chiropractic.
Eileen J. Powers-Pate, Instructor and Health Center Clinician; D.C., Palmer Chiropractic.
Richard Reinhardt, Instructor; D.C., Logan Chiropractic.
Margaret Rissman, Counselor; Ph.D., Illinois at Urbana-Champaign.
Jean Rose, Instructor; M.A.L.S., Missouri–Columbia.
Gary L. Rovin, Instructor and Health Center Clinician; D.C., Logan Chiropractic.
Phyllis S. Russo, Instructor and Health Center Clinician; D.C., Logan Chiropractic.
Todd A. Ryan, Radiology Resident; D.C., Logan Chiropractic.
Gary E. Sanders, Assistant Professor and Director of Research; Ph.D., Saint Louis.
Peter M. Schoeb, Instructor; D.C., Logan Chiropractic.
Suzanne A. Seekins-Grasse, Instructor; D.C., Logan Chiropractic.
Brian J. Snyder, Assistant Professor; D.C., Logan Chiropractic.
Robert E. Snyders, Assistant Professor; M.A., Northern Illinois.
Stephen Stohler, Instructor; D.C., Logan Chiropractic.
Christopher M. Standring, Instructor; D.C., Logan Chiropractic.
Rodger E. Tepe, Associate Professor and Counselor; Ph.D., Saint Louis.
Joseph F. Unger Jr., Instructor; D.C., Logan Chiropractic.
Rudolf P. Vrugtman, Instructor; M.B.A., Washington (St. Louis).
Robyn Wilkerson, Associate Professor and Associate Dean of Student Services; D.C., Logan Chiropractic.
Michael J. Wittmer, Instructor; D.C., Logan Chiropractic.
Martin A. Wolchansky, Instructor; D.C., Logan Chiropractic.
Max Zebelman, Associate Professor; D.C., Logan Chiropractic; Ph.D., Saint Louis.

FACULTY RESEARCH

Clinical Studies. Effects of chiropractic treatment on spinal structure; neurological responses to chiropractic procedures; peripheral vascular changes in response to chiropractic treatment.
Conservative Approaches to Pain Management. Endorphin levels and pain relief induced by chiropractic adjusting; efficiency of chiropractic adjusting for headache; epidemiology of low back pain and comparison of treatment procedures.
Ergonomics Research. Biomechanical causes of cumulative trauma injuries in several industrial employment settings and comparisons among several types of seating to determine their measured comfort levels.
Spinal Biomechanics. Evaluation of X-ray marking systems and correction factors—projectional and positional artifacts; studies of the sacroiliac joint end and pelvic biomechanics; correlational studies of leg length, bilateral weight bearing, and spinal alignment.
Toftness Research. An investigation into the source, physical characteristics, and physiological mechanics of the Toftness signal and its clinical significance; improvement of instrument design for signal detection.

LOS ANGELES COLLEGE OF CHIROPRACTIC

Programs of Study

Los Angeles College of Chiropractic (LACC) offers a comprehensive curriculum leading to the Doctor of Chiropractic (D.C.) degree. The D.C. degree program has been redesigned to meet the needs of patients in a new age of health care. It is known as the ADVANTAGE program and includes classroom and laboratory instruction in the basic natural sciences, the diagnostic sciences, chiropractic techniques, and a clinical internship in modern chiropractic clinics. The program, which consists of ten trimesters (five academic years), can be completed in 3⅓ calendar years. The faculty is dedicated to preparing each student as a highly skilled and learned practitioner. Faculty members have excellent qualifications in their field of specialization. LACC has a highly trained and readily available staff of counselors to advise students on academic and other requirements. A tutorial program is available to students who need special attention. Upon completion of the program of studies and clinical experience at LACC, graduates are prepared for national and state board licensure examinations and for the practice of chiropractic as primary health-care providers. Other options available to graduates include two 3-year residency programs, in radiology and in clinical chiropractic, offered at the College and careers in teaching and research. A large postgraduate division offers extensive programs, on and off campus, for continuing chiropractic education, license renewal, and advanced education for professional certification and/or eligibility for specialty board examinations. A visiting scholar program brings to the campus the most outstanding scientific contributors to chiropractic knowledge from various countries and backgrounds.

Research Facilities

The research laboratory, the basic science laboratories, the Learning Resource Center, and the College clinics are sites of various research projects. All projects are monitored by a committee. A central computer and a number of personal computers are available to faculty, staff, and students. A newly developed Student Computing Lab offers the latest in instructional technology and literature searching. LACC is an active member of the Consortium for Chiropractic Research, which plans and coordinates the various projects of member chiropractic colleges. Collaborative research is being conducted with several universities and health science research centers.

Financial Aid

Financial aid is available in the form of scholarships, grants, loans, and employment on campus for either pay or tuition credit. A comprehensive packet provides detailed information on all of the financial aid programs. In addition, an adviser who specializes in financial aid is always available for consultation and advice. Most students take advantage of financial aid in one form or another. The Mindlin Honors at Entrance program has been established to recognize needy students of exceptional caliber and promise.

Cost of Study

Tuition and fees totaled $5384 per trimester for the academic year 1997–98. The major additional costs that students incur during their enrollment in the program are for books, a microscope, a spine model, diagnostic instruments, and supplies.

Living and Housing Costs

The College does not provide on-campus residence facilities. It does offer well-informed and efficient hosting and housing services to help students settle promptly in their new environment and find a convenient place to live. Sharing accommodations with other students is a popular option. A great variety of apartments and houses are available near the College; costs are typical of southern California rental fees. If students share expenses for a two- or three-bedroom apartment, they can expect to pay $500–$700 monthly.

Student Group

LACC's current enrollment is about 800 students. The Associated Student Body elects its officers, facilitates campus communications, coordinates projects to benefit the College, and actively represents the students in state and national organizations. Students' extracurricular activities include participation in the many service clubs and organizations on campus and work in various College offices especially the Admissions Office. A sample of active student organizations is Delta Tau Alpha, Sigma Chi Psi, the Yoga and Martial Arts Club, the Sports Injury Council, and various chiropractic techniques groups. Many other campus organizations cater to the specific interests and needs of students.

Student Outcomes

In spring 1995, Los Angeles College of Chiropractic surveyed alumni who graduated since 1956. The randomized sample of alumni produced the following results: currently, 96 percent of alumni practice full-time as chiropractors. While 65 percent are in a solo practice, one in three is in group practice. An additional 1 percent teach or present seminars. LACC alumni are affiliated with other chiropractors (33 percent) and various other health-care specialists. They are also affiliated with health-care organizations, including PPOs (55 percent), insurance companies (32 percent), HMOs (30 percent), and IPOs (24 percent). The majority of alumni reported receiving referrals from other health-care providers (89 percent).

Location

The College is located in Whittier, a quiet and safe residential community. Sports, commercial, and cultural facilities are conveniently located within a short distance of the campus. Less than an hour away are the sandy beaches of the Pacific and the southernmost ridges of the Sierra Nevada. With a temperate climate year-round, Whittier enjoys the best of both coastal breezes and sunny inland skies.

The College

Los Angeles College of Chiropractic was chartered in 1911. The present site in Whittier was acquired in 1981. In addition to the Whittier Clinic on campus, the College owns and operates two large clinics in Glendale and Pasadena and staffs several public service clinics, all in California.

The College has full accreditation with the Council on Chiropractic Education and with the Western Association of Schools and Colleges. LACC is a nonprofit institution, governed by a Board of Regents, with an administrative staff and faculty of some 200 full-time and part-time members.

The 38-acre campus provides a weight and exercise room, an indoor basketball court and sand volleyball court, ten tennis courts, and a field for ball games and track. The campus has many pleasant shady areas for informal gatherings and studying. The College welcomes visitors to the campus and the clinics and recommends a visit, whenever possible, to those who are considering a career in chiropractic.

Applying

LACC admits a new class of 130 students twice a year, in September and January. Students are advised to apply early in order to receive needed preadmission counseling before their requested class is closed. Equal opportunity is extended to all applicants, without regard to race, color, creed, sex, national or ethnic origin, or disability. The minimum academic requirements for admission are 80 semester units toward a B.A. or B.S. degree. However, the typical LACC student has completed more college units. Course work must include one academic year (a minimum of 6 semester units) in each of the following subjects: biological sciences, general chemistry, organic chemistry, physics, and English/communications. A 3-unit course in psychology and 15 semester units in social sciences or humanities are also required. Complete information about matriculating at LACC is available from the Admissions Office.

Correspondence and Information

Dr. Charlene Frontiera, Director of Admissions
Los Angeles College of Chiropractic
16200 East Amber Valley Drive
Whittier, California 90609

Telephone: 562-947-8755 Ext. 321
800-221-5222 (toll-free)

Los Angeles College of Chiropractic

THE FACULTY

Diplomates of the following national chiropractic boards are abbreviated as such: American Board of Chiropractic Orthopedists (DABCO), American Chiropractic Academy of Neurology (DACAN), American Chiropractic Board of Nutrition (DACBN), American Chiropractic Board of Sports Physicians (DACBSP), and American Chiropractic Board of Radiology (DACBR). Certified Chiropractic Sports Physicians are abbreviated as CCSP. An asterisk (*) indicates faculty members also associated with the Division of Postgraduate Education.

Faculty of the College

*Alan Adams, D.C.; DACBN.
Jeffrey Ameen, D.C.
Glenn Anderson, D.C.
Maureen Aoys, D.C.
Samuel Auyong, M.A., D.C.
Sameh Awad, M.D.
Samir Ayad, M.D.
Rand Baird, M.P.H., D.C.
*Marie Bochniak, D.C.
Lorrane Bonnano, D.C.
*Jacqueline Bougie, D.C.; DABCO.
Beverly Bryant, M.A.
Rona Brynin, D.C., CCSP.
Gary Bustin, D.C.; DACBR.
Jonathan Carlos, M.D.
Bruce Carr, Ph.D., D.C.
Jim Chang, Ph.D.
Rocky Comberiati, D.C.
*Mary Connolly, D.C., CCSP.
*Jeffrey Cooley, D.C.; DACBR.
Ian Coulter, Ph.D.
Darryl Curl, D.D.S., D.C.
Jeffrey Devore, D.C.
Thomas Doss, M.D.
Kimray Farrar, D.C., CCSP.
Bertrand Faucret, D.C.
Frank Foderaro, D.C., CCSP.
Vaughn Given, M.A., D.C.
Debra Goldsmith, D.C.
Emile Goubran, Ph.D., M.D.
*Nancy Gour, RN.
Cheri Graybill, M.A.
Tim Hall, D.C.; DACBR.
John Harryson, D.C.
*Phillip Harvey, Ph.D.
*Paul Hooper, D.C.
Joseph Howe, D.C.; DACBR.
John Hsieh, M.S., D.C.
Eric Hurwitz, D.C., Ph.D.
Brian Huth, D.C.
Rod Kaufman, D.C.; DABCO.
Leslie Kay, M.S.
Joseph Keating Jr., Ph.D.
Stephen Lau, Ph.D.
David Lin, Ph.D.
Philip McCormick, D.C.
Betty McInturff, D.C.
Carol Moeller, M.S.
*Paige Morgenthal, D.C.
Chun Fu Peng, Ph.D.
Charles Peterson, D.C.
*Reed Phillips, M.S.C.M., Ph.D., D.C.; DACBR.
Glynna Rangel, D.C.; DACBR.
Debra Reed, D.C.
*Curtis Rigney, D.C.
*Patricia Rogers, D.C.
Kevin Rose, D.C., CCSP; DABCO.
*Michael Sackett, M.S., D.C.; DABCO.
Evelyn Sawires, D.C.
*John Scaringe, D.C., CCSP; DACBSP.
*Gary Schultz, D.C.; DACBR.
Wolfgang Shane, D.C.
David Sikorski, D.C.
Michael Sladich, D.C.; DACBR.
*Dorrie Talmage, D.C.; DABCO.
*Gene Tobias, Ph.D.
Riaz Toufigh, D.C.
*Alfred Traina, D.C.; DABCO.
Steven Weiner, D.C.; DACBR.
*Keith Wells, D.C.
Kathleen Yang, M.P.H., D.C.
*Curtis Yomtob, D.C.; DACBR.
Ashraf Youssef, M.D.

Faculty of the Division of Postgraduate Education

Donald D. Aspegren, D.C.
Michael S. Barry, D.C.; DACBR.
Cynthia Ann Baum, D.C.; DACBR.
Thomas F. Bergmann, D.C.
Leo Bronston, D.C., CCSP; DABCO, DACAN.
Joel P. Carmichael, D.C.; DACBSP.
James Carter, D.C.; DACBR.
David Chao, M.D.
Scott Chapman, D.C.; DABCO.
Joseph Cimino, D.C.
R. Ernest Cohn, D.C.; DABCO.
Donald Corenman, D.C., M.D.; DABCO.
Alan R. Cowen, D.C.
James Cox, D.C.; DACBR.
Gregory Cramer, D.C., Ph.D.
Neil Craton, M.D.
Arthur Croft, D.C.; DABCO.
William D. Defoyd, M.A., D.C.; DABCO.
Carol DeFranca, D.C.; DABCO.
George deFranca, D.C.
Richard E. Erhard, P.T., D.C.
Keith Feder, M.D.
Michael Feuerstein, Ph.D.
Ted Forcum III, D.C., CCSP.
Peter Gale, D.C., CCSP.
James A. Gerber, D.C.; DABCO.
Natalie Gluck, D.C.
Susan Green, D.C.
Gary Greenstein, D.C.
Martin Gruder, D.C.; DABCO, DACAN.
Nicholas Grumbine, D.P.M.
James Haas, M.D.
John Hannon, D.C.; DACBSP, DABCO.
Daniel T. Hansen, D.C.; DABCO.
Bruce Hoffman, D.C.
Joseph Horrigan, D.C.; DACBSP.
Jerry Hyman, D.C.
Gary Jacob, D.C.
Vladimir Janda, M.D.
Kathie Kingett, D.C.
Andrew S. Klein, D.C.; DACBSP.
Matthew Kowalski, D.C.; DABCO.
Robert Lardner, P.T.
Joanne Larricq, D.C., P.T.
Ron LeFebvre, D.C.
David Lemberg, D.C., CCSP; DABCO.
Craig Liebenson, D.C.
Gary Lindquist, D.C.; DACBR.
Michael Lubrani, J.D.
Robert M. Martinez, D.C.; DABCO.
Stuart McGill, Ph.D.
Thomas McKnight, M.P.H., D.O.
William Meeker, M.P.H., D.C.
Michael Mestan, D.C.; DACBR.
Debra L. Mitchell, C.A.
Robert Mootz, D.C.; DABCO.
Rick Morris, D.C., CCSP.
Donald Murphy, D.C.; DACAN.
Daniel Nelson, D.C.; DABCO.
Hang Nguyen, D.C.
Andy Paulin, B.S.
Kelli Pearson, D.C.; DABCO.
Michael Reed, D.C.; DACBSP.
Richard Roth, D.C.; DABCO.
Stephen Rothman, M.D.
Clive Segil, M.D.
Margaret Seron, D.C.; DABCO, DACBR.
Clayton Skaggs, D.C., CCRD.
Malik Slosberg, D.C.
Jeffrey Spencer, D.C., CCSP.
Egilius Spierings, M.D., Ph.D.
Anita Staubach, P.T., A.T.C.
Alan Strizak, M.D.
David Stude, D.C.
Rand Swenson, D.C., Ph.D., M.D.
Gary Tanner, D.C.
Gary A. Tarola, D.C.; DABCO.
John Taylor, D.C.; DACBR.
Janet Thornton, C.A.
John Triano, D.C.
Howard Vernon, D.C., FCCS.
Julian Vickers, D.C.; DABCO, DACAN.
Nick Warner, D.C.
Bruce Weary, D.C.
Henry West Jr., D.C.; DABCO.
Steve Yeomans, D.C.; DABCO.
Terry R. Yochum, D.C.; DACBR.
Ross Ziegler, M.D.
James P. Zurawski, J.D.

NATIONAL COLLEGE OF CHIROPRACTIC

Program of Study

The National College of Chiropractic (NCC) offers a broad-based, comprehensive program that leads to the Doctor of Chiropractic (D.C.) degree and allows the student the option of earning a Bachelor of Science in human biology as well. The curriculum includes didactic, problem-based, and practical instruction in the basic and clinical sciences, as well as an intensive clinical internship in one of seven College-operated modern health-care facilities. The ten-trimester program, which lasts 5 academic years, can be completed in 3⅓ calendar years. The total number of credit hours for the chiropractic course of study is approximately 240. The average number of credit hours taken per trimester is 25 (for a total of ten trimesters). National College faculty members are recognized for their knowledge, commitment, and dedication to students; their contributions to the profession through research and scholarly work are exemplary. NCC provides academic counseling for all students through a specialized advising program, and student tutoring is available and coordinated through the Student Council.

The National College program is designed to train students to meet the requirements of state licensing boards and to sit for numerous international board examinations. National graduates leave NCC capable of making immediate contributions to the growth of the profession; this is demonstrated by the fact that graduates of National College hold a much greater percentage of professional leadership positions than those of any other chiropractic college. The College offers five training residencies in clinical practice, clinical research, family practice, radiology and diagnostic imaging, and orthopedics.

The College offers a heavy schedule of continuing education classes through its postgraduate and continuing education division; these classes are held throughout the United States and in many other countries.

Research Facilities

The College has one of the most prestigious research facilities among chiropractic colleges. Equipment available in the Spinal Ergonomics and Joint Research Laboratory includes a computer-interfaced B-200 IsoStation low-back unit, a specially constructed test frame for Acceptable Maximum Effort static muscle tests, a treatment table equipped with a force plate, and computer-assisted electrodiagnostic apparatus. A complete rehabilitation and conditioning program for patients is also in place. Equipment in the three laboratories is dedicated to cellular, anatomical, physiological, and neurological studies. Access to equipment at local and regional universities and one of the national laboratories is available to investigators and their students who are conducting collaborative projects with scientists at these facilities.

The College is the only chiropractic college to be equipped with a Training and Assessment Center (TAC) and a Magnetic Resonance Imaging (MRI) facility. The TAC offers a unique learning atmosphere for the chiropractic student. The fourteen-room facility allows instructors to observe students, utilizing one-way mirrors, audiovisual monitoring equipment, and an intercom system in ten of the rooms. Some of the advantages of the TAC include remote observation and recording of student-patient interactions utilizing standardized patients, small-group discussion using the problem-based learning process, review of videotaped patient encounters, training in interpersonal skills, faculty development, and performance-based clinical competence assessment. The College's MRI facility, National MRI Center, is equipped with the Hitachi MRP-5000. This scanner offers the latest technological hardware and software advances for high-quality imaging and patient ease and comfort. On-site MRI greatly enhances the College's patient care and research capabilities.

Financial Aid

The College's Financial Aid Office helps students finance their chiropractic education through grants, loans, scholarships, and employment on campus. Federal funds for higher education become available when there is a gap between educational costs and the ability of the student to pay. The principal responsibility for educational costs rests with the student; if the student is financially dependent, the student's parents share this responsibility. The majority of the College's students take advantage of financial aid in one form or another. A comprehensive packet of information on all financial aid programs is available.

Cost of Study

Starting with the fall 1998 trimester, tuition is $216 per credit hour. The major additional costs that students incur during their study are for books, diagnostic instruments, and supplies.

Living and Housing Costs

On-campus residence facilities, which ranged from $1235 per trimester for a dorm room for a single student to $2657 per trimester for a two-bedroom apartment on campus in 1997–98, are available. Private apartments and houses are also available nearby. The typical cost of a one-bedroom apartment is $585 per month.

Student Group

The average enrollment is approximately 875; 30 percent of the student body are women, 3 percent are members of minority groups, and 22 percent are married students. Most students receive some form of financial aid and augment their income with employment. Free health service is available to the student together with an academic advising program that can include tutorial service.

Location

The College is just 23 miles from Chicago, a cultural and industrial hub and home to some of the nation's finest museums, entertainment and sports centers, zoos, restaurants, stores, beaches, and other recreation areas. Located in Lombard, the College benefits from its quiet suburban surroundings, which are characterized by a broad-based economy and moderate cost-of-living level, excellent public and private schools, diverse employment opportunities, and a variety of recreational outlets.

The College

Established in 1906, the College continues to be a leader in progressive chiropractic education. It is accredited by the Council on Chiropractic Education and the North Central Association of Colleges and Schools and is registered by the State Educational Department of the State of New York. It is recognized by all fifty states and every international regulatory agency that controls licensure. Its seven teaching clinics include the National College Chiropractic Center on campus; a clinic in downtown Chicago; a clinic west of campus in Aurora, Illinois; a clinic south of campus in Woodbridge, Illinois; two Salvation Army clinics; and the Student Clinic. The 30-acre campus has a Student Center, a Learning Resource Center, a cafeteria, lecture halls, and laboratories. More than thirty clubs are active under the auspices of the Student Council, ranging from sports clubs to religious organizations and fraternities.

Applying

NCC admits new classes in January, May, and September. Students are encouraged to apply one year in advance. Applicants must have completed 90 semester hours of credit with a minimum GPA of 3.0 on a 4.0 scale or must hold an undergraduate degree and have earned a minimum GPA of 2.5 on a 4.0 scale in order to meet the academic admission requirements. Six semester hours each of biology, general chemistry, organic chemistry, physics, and English are required. A 3-semester-hour psychology class and 15 semester hours of social science/humanities are also required for admission.

Correspondence and Information

Office of Admissions
National College of Chiropractic
200 East Roosevelt Road
Lombard, Illinois 60148-4583
Telephone: 630-629-2000
800-826-NATL (toll-free)

National College of Chiropractic

THE FACULTY

Faculty of the College
Kristine Aikenhead, D.C. William E. Bachop, Ph.D. Jerrilyn Backman, D.C. James A. Baker, D.C. Jane A. Baker, B.A.; RT(R). Barclay W. Bakkum, D.C., Ph.D. Mary Lou Bareither, Ph.D. Elizabeth Beadle, D.C. Robert Beck, D.C. Ronald P. Beideman, D.C. Edward J. Bifulco, D.C. William Bogar, D.C.; Diplomate, American Chiropractic Board of Radiology. Patricia Brennan, Ph.D. Amerigo Carnazzolla, Ph.D. Scott Chapman, D.C. James A. Christiansen, Ph.D. Ezra Cohen, D.C. Gregory D. Cramer, Ph.D. Malford Cullum, Ph.D. Susan A. Darby, Ph.D. Edel Diaz, D.C. Daniel R. Driscoll, D.C. Mary Ellen Druyan, Ph.D. Manuel A. Duarte, D.C. Terry Elder, D.C. Hany Elewa, Ph.D. Leonard E. Fay, D.C. Neil Fried, D.C. Thomas E. Fritz, D.V.M. Robert Frysztak, Ph.D. David A. Gidcumb, D.C. Emory Giles, Ph.D. Richard Gilmore, Ph.D. George E. Goetschel, D.C. Safe Guo, Ph.D. candidate. Maruti Ram Gudavalli, Ph.D. Larry L. Hill, D.C. William J. Hogan, D.C. Maria Hondras, D.C. Cynthia Hsieh, M.L.L.E.S. Frederick Hult, D.C. C. Robert Humphreys, D.C. Grant C. Iannelli, D.C. Russell A. Iwami, M.S.L.S. Gayle Jasinski, D.C. James Jedlicka, D.C. Bian Jiang, Ph.D. Theodore Johnson Jr., D.C. Clifford J. Kaltinger, D.C. Arthur Kaminsky, D.C. Michael Kiely, Ph.D. Steven Kirstukas, Ph.D. Charles J. Kuehner, D.C. Robert Lardner, B.S. Dana J. Lawrence, D.C. Stephen Lee, M.S. Gerald Leerssen, D.C. Daniel Lehoux, D.C. Albert Ockerse, M.D. Jeffrey A. Papp, M.H.S. Jane P. Plass, O.D. Michael B. Poierier, D.C. Mary Powers, D.C. Chih-Wei Rei, D.C. Tari Reinke, D.C. Delilah Renegar, D.C. Daniel Richardson, Ph.D. Chae-Song Ro, M.D. Terry Sandman, D.C.; Diplomate, American Chiropractic Board of Radiology. Nagwa Shenouda, Ph.D. Robert C. Shiel, Ph.D. Grace Shramek, Ph.D. Victoria Sisco, Ph.D. Dennis R. Skogsbergh, D.C.; Diplomate, American Board of Chiropractic Orthopedists and American Chiropractic Board of Radiology. Jonathan Soltys, D.C. Peter C. Stathopoulos, D.C. Sheela Surlekar, M.S. Randy L. Swenson, D.C. Charles C. Tasharski, D.C. Vrajlal H. Vyas, M.D. William E. Waln, D.C. David W. Ward, D.C. Alan Wood Weller, D.C. Joyce E. Whitehead, M.A.L.S. David J. Wickes, D.C. Ronald Williams, D.C. James F. Winterstein, D.C.; Diplomate, American Chiropractic Board of Radiology. Shiwei Yu, M.D.

National-Lincoln School of Postgraduate Education
William R. Aimers, D.C.; Diplomate, American Board of Chiropractic Orthopedists. Leanne Apfelbeck, D.C. Lee E. Arnold, D.C. Donald D. Aspegren, D.C. Jane Baker,* B.A., RT(R). Barclay W. Bakkum,* D.C., Ph.D. Ray W. Bayley II, D.C; Diplomate, American Chiropractic Board of Nutrition. Robert J. Beck,* Ph.D. Ronald P. Beideman,* D.C. John L. Black, D.C., Certified Chiropractic Sports Physician; Diplomate, American Board of Chiropractic Orthopedists. Edward J. Bifulco,* D.C. Kelly Brinkman, D.C. Patricia Brennan,* Ph.D. Michael T. Buehler, D.C.; Diplomate, American Chiropractic Board of Radiology. Jeffrey W. Buncher, D.C.; Diplomate, American Chiropractic Board of Thermography. Scott A. Chapman, D.C.; Diplomate, American Board of Chiropractic Orthopedists. James A. Christiansen,* Ph.D. James M. Cox, D.C.; Diplomate, American Chiropractic Board of Radiology. Jeffrey Cram, Ph.D. Gregory D. Cramer,* Ph.D., D.C. Malford Cullum,* Ph.D. Stanley Daniels, D.C., Certified Chiropractic Sports Physician; Diplomate, American Board of Chiropractic Orthopedists and American Chiropractic Board of Sports Physicians. Susan A. Darby,* Ph.D. Angelo S. Delliquadri, D.C. Manuel A. Duarte,* D.C, Certified Chiropractic Sports Physician; Diplomate, American Board of Chiropractic Orthopedists and American Chiropractic Board of Sports Physicians. Thomas M. Goodrich, D.C.; Diplomate, American Chiropractic Board of Radiology. Robert Gordon, D.C. Jacob Green, M.D. Randolph C. Harding, D.C.; Diplomate, American Board of Chiropractic Orthopedists. Phillip Harvey, Ph.D., RD, FACN. Larry L. Hill,* D.C. Jay M. Holder, D.C. Maria Hondras,* D.C., M.P.H. Robert Humphreys,* D.C. Rebecca Hunter, D.C. Grant Iannelli,* D.C. Gayle Jasinski,* D.C.; Diplomate, American Board of Chiropractic Orthopedists. James Jedlicka,* D.C. Bryan Justice, D.C.; Diplomate, American Board of Chiropractic Orthopedists. Leo Kenney, D.C. David D. Kessler, D.C.; Diplomate, American Board of Chiropractic Orthopedists. Susan Kovach, C.A. Matthew Kowalski, D.C.; Diplomate, American Board of Chiropractic Orthopedists. Jacob Ladenheim, J.D. Dana J. Lawrence,* D.C. Robert Leach, D.C. Carlos Leon-Barth, M.D. Richard A. Leverone, D.C.; Diplomate, American Chiropractic Board of Radiology. Vincent P. Lucido, D.C.; Diplomate, American Board of Chiropractic Orthopedists. Jeffrey C. Mackey, D.C.; Diplomate, American Board of Chiropractic Orthopedists. Edward L. Maurer, D.C.; Diplomate, American Chiropractic Board of Radiology. Brian McCaskey, AT. John Merrick, D.C., RPT. Robert F. Metcalf,* D.C. Charles Neault, D.C. Anne Oestreich,* D.C.; Diplomate, American Chiropractic Board of Radiology. John C. Pammer, D.C.; Diplomate, American Chiropractic Board of Radiology. David B. Parish, D.C., Certified Chiropractic Sports Physician. Michael B. Poierier,* D.C.; Diplomate, American Board of Chiropractic Internists. Terry D. Sandman, D.C.; Diplomate, American Chiropractic Board of Radiology. Robert Sherman, J.D. Robert C. Shiel,* Ph.D. Jeffrey Shurr, D.C. Dennis R. Skogsbergh,* D.C.; Diplomate, American Board of Chiropractic Orthopedists and American Chiropractic Board of Radiology. Louis Sportelli, D.C. Jon Sunderlage, D.C. Rand S. Swenson, D.C, M.D., Ph.D. Randy L. Swenson,* D.C. Gail Tanzer, M.A. Gary A. Tarola, D.C.; Diplomate, American Board of Chiropractic Orthopedists. Charles C. Tasharski,* D.C. William Toth, D.C. John J. Triano,* D.C. John Ventura, D.C.; Diplomate, American Board of Chiropractic Orthopedists. William E. Wain,* D.C. David Wickes, D.C.; Diplomate, American Board of Chiropractic Internists. James F. Winterstein,* D.C.; Diplomate, American Chiropractic Board of Radiology. Steven Yeomans, D.C.; Diplomate, American Board of Chiropractic Orthopedists. Shi Wei Yu, M.D.

**Also on the faculty of the College.*

The National College of Chiropractic.

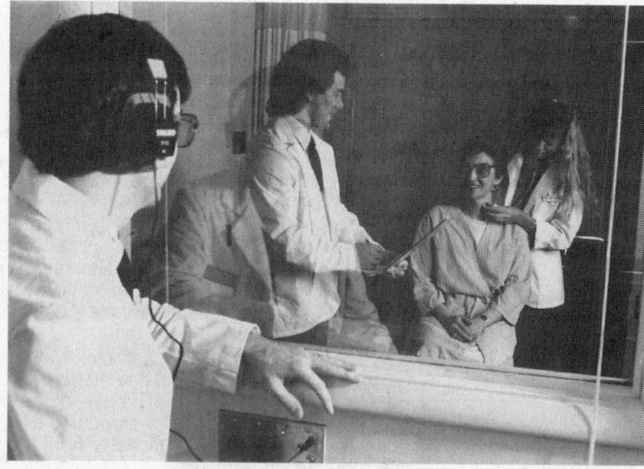

NCC is the only chiropractic college equipped with a Training and Assessment Center.

NEW YORK CHIROPRACTIC COLLEGE

Program of Study

New York Chiropractic College offers a rigorous but highly rewarding program leading to the degree of Doctor of Chiropractic (D.C.) and prepares students for a professional career in chiropractic health care as well as in related research and teaching. The five-year academic program is ten trimesters in length. New York Chiropractic College offers classes the year round, and students generally complete the program in forty months of continuous study. The program is open only to full-time students. It includes two trimesters of internship at one of the College's three health centers.

The College also maintains a number of articulation agreements with institutions in New York and other states that offer prechiropractic programs. Several of these are 3+1 B.S./D.C. programs, which enable the student to save a year in the completion of the two degrees. NYCC's Postgraduate Division offers continuing education for chiropractors to further their professional development and to satisfy the license renewal requirements of various states.

Research Facilities

NYCC's research department encompasses a wide variety of research interests. Current faculty research projects include exercise physiology, biomechanics, nutrition, and cerebral ischemic mechanisms. The on-campus facilities include a human performance laboratory and a state-of-the-art anatomy laboratory. Collaboration with regional universities' research departments provides for extensive research opportunities.

Financial Aid

Financial aid is generally available on the basis of need, as evidenced by information supplied on the FAFSA as well as an institutional application. Federal sources of aid include Federal Perkins Loans, Federal Work-Study, and veterans' benefits to eligible students. Limited grants are available under New York State's Tuition Assistance Program (TAP). Students may obtain Federal Stafford Student Loans and may compete for scholarships offered by chiropractic associations, private foundations, and NYCC.

Cost of Study

Only full-time students are admitted into the doctoral program. For 1998–99, tuition is $5150 per trimester; tuition and fees for the calendar year (three trimesters) from September 1998 through summer 1999 are estimated at $15,810. The estimated cost of textbooks, equipment, and supplies is an additional $700 per trimester.

Living and Housing Costs

NYCC offers excellent on-campus housing in eight residence halls. The cost of a single room is $1595; a double room is $800; suites for married students are $1850 to $1950 (these are trimester rates). Meal plans are additional and range from $225 to $950 per trimester. Off-campus housing is available and comparatively priced. The cost of living in the area is substantially lower than that of urban areas.

Student Group

New York Chiropractic College's 950 students (including senior interns) come from more than twenty states and several other countries. The majority are residents of the Northeast. Students range in age from 21 to over 55, with the largest age group consisting of those in their mid-20s. Thirty percent of the students are women, and 65 percent of all students hold a baccalaureate or higher degree. Many students participate in intramural sports and student government as well as in the more than thirty student organizations that pursue such special interests as nutrition, sports injuries, publications, and research. Numerous technique clubs (e.g., Applied Kinesiology, Gonstead) are active on campus.

Location

New York Chiropractic College is located in Seneca Falls, New York, in the scenic wine-growing region of the Finger Lakes, a popular vacation spot less than a 45-minute drive from Syracuse, Rochester, and Ithaca. Outpatient clinics are located in Buffalo, Syracuse, and Levittown (Long Island). The 286-acre campus has 250 feet of frontage property on Cayuga Lake, the largest of the Finger Lakes. The College borders a state park and has a nine-hole, par 3 golf course on the campus.

The College

Established in 1919 in New York City as Columbia Institute of Chiropractic, the College is the oldest chiropractic institution in the Northeast. In 1976, it moved to Nassau County on suburban Long Island and moved again to a larger campus in upstate New York in 1991. The College is accredited by the Middle States Association of Colleges and Schools and by the Council on Chiropractic Education. It holds an Absolute Charter from the Board of Regents of the University of the State of New York.

Applying

Information and application forms may be obtained by writing to the Admissions Office or by calling 800-234-6922 (toll-free). Admission is a continuous process; there are entering classes in September, January, and May of each year. Approximately 300 students are admitted for each year, and applicants are encouraged to apply ten to twelve months in advance of their desired entrance date. Reference forms are supplied upon receipt of an application.

Correspondence and Information

Admissions Office
New York Chiropractic College
2360 Route 89
Seneca Falls, New York 13148-0800
Telephone: 315-568-3040
800-234-6922 (toll-free)

New York Chiropractic College

THE FACULTY

Anatomy
M. Elizabeth Bedford, Ph.D., Kent State, 1994.
J. Donald Dishman, D.C., Life Chiropractic, 1986.
Susanne S. Firkins, M.S., SUNY Health Science Center at Syracuse, 1992.
Thomas M. Greiner, Ph.D., SUNY at Binghamton, 1994.
Michael L. Lentini, D.C., National Chiropractic, 1991.
Raj J. Philomin, Ph.D., Madras Medical College (India), 1986.
Ronald M. Schassburger, Ph.D., Cornell, 1978.
Maria Thomadaki, D.C., New York Chiropractic, 1994.
Brigitte Tremblay, D.C., New York Chiropractic, 1994.
Narayan Vijayashankar, M.D., Kerala (India), 1960.
Robert A. Walker, Ph.D., Kent State, 1989.

Physiopathology
David S. Aberant, M.S., LIU, C.W. Post, 1970.
Deborah A. Barr, Sc.D., Boston University, 1988.
Scott Coon, D.C., New York Chiropractic, 1994.
Steven Glasser, Ph.D., Rochester, 1978.
Nabil S. Hanna, Ph.D., Laval, 1975.
Chithambaram S. Philomin, M.B.B.S., Stanley Medical College, 1989.
Carolyn M. Pover, Ph.D., Bristol, 1986.
Veronica M. Sciotti, Ph.D., SUNY at Buffalo, 1988.
Lee C. VanDusen, D.C., National Chiropractic, 1985.
Roger O. Walter, Ph.D., SUNY Downstate Medical Center, 1975.

Diagnosis and Clinical Practice
Lisa K. Bloom, D.C., New York Chiropractic, 1990.
Susan E. Conley, D.C., New York Chiropractic, 1995.
Christine M. Cunningham, M.S., SUNY at Stony Brook, 1988.
Stacy R. Davidoff, D.C., New York Chiropractic, 1993.
Gregory A. DeMaille, D.C., New York Chiropractic, 1992.
Pamela Downing, D.C., Cleveland Chiropractic, 1993.
Patrick J. Farrell, D.C., National Chiropractic, 1994.
Margaret M. Finn, D.C., New York Chiropractic, 1992.
Joanne T. Gjelsten, D.C., New York Chiropractic, 1995.
Fiona Jarrett-Thelwell, D.C., New York Chiropractic, 1994.
Stephen J. Mesiti, D.C., New York Chiropractic, 1997.
Michael J. O'Connor, D.C., New York Chiropractic, 1982.
Julie A. Plezbert, D.C., National Chiropractic, 1986.
Patricia A. Ronsvalle, M.S.W., Syracuse, 1996.
Robert Ruddy, D.C., New York Chiropractic, 1996.
Fred L. SanFilipo, D.C., New York Chiropractic, 1982.
Judy M. Silvestrone, D.C., Palmer Chiropractic, 1984.

Technique and Principles
Yusef C. Barnes, D.C., New York Chiropractic, 1997.
Karen A. Bobak, D.C., National Chiropractic, 1986.
Jeffrey Byrne, D.C., New York Chiropractic, 1996.
Brian M. Cunningham, D.C., New York Chiropractic, 1986.
John L. DeCicco, D.C., New York Chiropractic, 1982.
Lisa A. DiMarco, D.C., New York Chiropractic, 1990.
James R. Ebbets, D.C., New York Chiropractic, 1992.
Christopher J. Good, D.C., Palmer Chiropractic, 1982.
Sandra Hartwell-Ford, D.C., New York Chiropractic, 1996.
Adam J. Henby, D.C., National Chiropractic, 1993.
Lloyd E. Henby, D.C., National Chiropractic, 1952.
Michael E. Howard, D.C., Life Chiropractic, 1981.
James M. Inzerillo, D.C., New York Chiropractic, 1990.
Leslie W. Lange, D.C., Palmer Chiropractic West, 1988.
Stacey A. Lenisa, D.C., National Chiropractic, 1995.
Thomas McCloughan, D.C., New York Chiropractic, 1993.
Joseph A. Miller, D.C., National Chiropractic, 1991.
Hunter A. Mollin, D.C., New York Chiropractic, 1980.
David F. Petters, D.C., New York Chiropractic, 1986.
Angela M. Rapposelli, D.C., New York Chiropractic, 1996.
Christopher P. Ryan, D.C., New York Chiropractic, 1987.
Paul W. Ryan, D.C., New York Chiropractic, 1989.
Eileen C. Santipadri, D.C., Palmer Chiropractic, 1981.
Robert T. Story, D.C., National Chiropractic, 1979.
Edward J. Sullivan, D.C., Northwestern Chiropractic, 1991.
Michael S. Young, D.C., New York Chiropractic, 1996.

Research
Ronald Bulbulian, Ph.D., USC, 1980.

Cheektowaga Health Center
Margaret M. Anticola, D.C., Life Chiropractic, 1986.
Matthew C. Coté, D.C., New York Chiropractic, 1980.
Charles D. Coyle, D.C., National Chiropractic, 1988.
Mark A. Dux, D.C., Western States Chiropractic, 1980.
Sherri L. LaShomb, D.C., Palmer Chiropractic, 1988.
David L. Ribakove, D.C., New York Chiropractic, 1992.
Amy L. Schleicher, D.C., National Chiropractic, 1990.
Mark D. Sokolowski, D.C., Palmer Chiropractic, 1985.
Mercedes M. Trzcinski, D.C., Palmer Chiropractic, 1981.

Levittown Health Center
Charles R. Bianculli, D.C., New York Chiropractic, 1980.
Janet A. Gerard, D.C., New York Chiropractic, 1981.
Charles A. Hemsey, D.C., Life Chiropractic, 1981.
Frank S. Lizzio, D.C., New York Chiropractic, 1980.
Serge Nerli, D.C., New York Chiropractic, 1983.
Peter M. Ouzounian, D.C., New York Chiropractic, 1988.
Anthony J. Perrotto, D.C., New York Chiropractic, 1980.
Joseph E. Pfeifer, D.C., New York Chiropractic, 1984.
Karyn M. Phillips, D.C., New York Chiropractic, 1989.
Veronica A. Wicks, D.C., New York Chiropractic, 1988.

Seneca Falls Health Center
Kellie A. Arruda, D.C., New York Chiropractic, 1997.
Catherine R. Bruckner, D.C., New York Chiropractic, 1993.
Dale J. Büchberger, D.C., National Chiropractic, 1988.
Steven Feldman, D.C., New York Chiropractic, 1981.
Dennis M. Homack, D.C., New York Chiropractic, 1997.
William H. Sherwood, D.C., National Chiropractic, 1990.

Syracuse Health Center
Donna D. Coty, D.C., New York Chiropractic, 1995.
Randall H. Corey, D.C., National Chiropractic, 1987.
Daniel A. Dischiavo, D.C., New York Chiropractic, 1989.
Philip T. Dontino Jr., D.C., New York Chiropractic, 1991.
Vincent F. Loia, D.C., New York Chiropractic, 1981.
Daniel D. Patriarco, D.C., National Chiropractic, 1987.

Academic and Administrative Center in Seneca Falls as seen from the library.

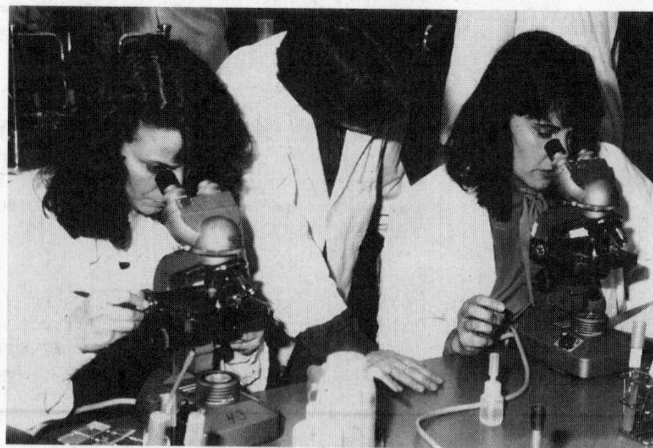

Instructor and students in the Microbiology Laboratory.

NORTHWESTERN COLLEGE OF CHIROPRACTIC

Program of Study

Northwestern College of Chiropractic (NWCC) offers a ten-trimester (three terms per year) program leading to the Doctor of Chiropractic (D.C.) degree. A Bachelor of Science degree in human biology is available for students interested in pursuing both degrees concurrently. The chiropractic curriculum is divided into the following three parts: basic sciences, clinical sciences (including diagnosis, radiology, and chiropractic principles and integrated methods), and clinical (intern) experience in one of the four clinics. NWCC prepares students to be primary-care physicians able to diagnose, treat, and maintain a person's health.

The Chiropractic Physician's Associate Program provides in-depth clinical experience by allowing students to spend their last academic term as associates in private practices of participating doctors of chiropractic throughout the United States.

Research Facilities

At the College's research facility, the Wolfe-Harris Center for Clinical Studies, primary research is conducted in the area of outcomes of chiropractic versus nonchiropractic care. Students are strongly encouraged to become involved in research. Current studies include chiropractic treatment of asthma, hypertension, and headache.

The library maintains all necessary volumes germane to the profession and subscribes to recognized journals in chiropractic and in the basic medical sciences.

Financial Aid

Financial aid is available through programs that include Federal Pell Grants, Federal Supplemental Educational Opportunity Grants, Minnesota State Grants, Federal Perkins Loans, Federal Stafford Student Loans, and Supplemental Loans for Students, as well as Federal Work-Study and institutional work programs. Many state and private scholarships are awarded to the College's students each year on a competitive basis.

Cost of Study

Tuition for the 1998–99 year is approximately $5000 per trimester. The academic program is ten trimesters in length. Laboratory fees is $50 per lab. Eight laboratory experiences are required. The health fee is $10 per academic year, and graduation and national board fees are about $350. The student activity fee is $40 per trimester. Books and supplies for the entire academic period cost approximately $3600.

Living and Housing Costs

The College maintains no on-campus housing, but the admissions department offers information about housing for both new and continuing students. Adequate accommodations are readily available near the campus and throughout the Twin Cities area. Generally, single, independent students can expect costs of $450 per month for room and $225 per month for board; corresponding figures for married students are $470 and $375.

Student Group

Northwestern admits about 225 students per year to maintain a total enrollment of about 700 students. Approximately 30 percent are Minnesota residents, and about 35 percent are women. The average age of the students is 27, and 25 percent are married. The average grade point average of incoming students is 3.0. Student organizations on campus include the Student Senate, Student American Chiropractic Association, Chi Omega Phi fraternity, Legislative Information Network of Chiropractic Colleges, and Student Council of Women Chiropractors of the American Chiropractic Association. The College does not discriminate on the basis of race, color, creed, religion, national origin, sex, marital status, status with regard to public assistance, or disability.

Student Outcomes

More than 95 percent of all Northwestern graduates are successfully practicing chiropractic throughout the United States, Canada, Europe, Asia, and Australia.

Location

The Minneapolis–St. Paul metropolitan area has a population of 2.5 million. The area is noted for its many parks, lakes, and rivers. Many cultural and recreational facilities are located within or near the metropolitan area, including the Guthrie Theatre, the Minneapolis Institute of Art, two zoos, and three professional sports teams. Educational facilities are also quite diverse; they include the University of Minnesota, eleven other private colleges, and eight junior and community colleges, all located within the Twin Cities. The climate presents four distinct seasons.

The College

Northwestern, founded in 1941, has prospered because of its rigorous academic program and modern pedagogical methods. The College campus is located in Bloomington, a suburb of the Twin Cities. The campus consists of 25 acres. The building complex is complete with laboratories, lecture halls, classrooms, a library, an auditorium, a cafeteria, a gymnasium, an indoor swimming pool, and a fitness center. The College maintains five public clinics in addition to the student health services.

Northwestern is accredited by the Council on Chiropractic Education and the North Central Association of Colleges and Schools.

Applying

Students should write to the director of admissions for application materials. Applicants must have a minimum grade point average of 2.5 and 60 semester credits (or 90 quarter credits) of undergraduate studies in a science or health-care preprofessional major. Students should write to the College for a preadmission requirements brochure. Applications are accepted for each academic term: September, January, and April.

Correspondence and Information

Admissions Office
Northwestern College of Chiropractic
2501 West 84th Street
Bloomington, Minnesota 55431
Telephone: 612-888-4777
800-888-4777 (toll-free)
Fax: 612-888-6713
E-mail: admit@nwchiro.edu
World Wide Web: http://www.nwchiro.edu

Northwestern College of Chiropractic

DEPARTMENT CHAIRPERSONS AND DIRECTORS

ACADEMIC AFFAIRS

Charles E. Sawyer, Vice President for Academic Affairs and Research Affairs; D.C., Northwestern Chiropractic, 1977.

Basic Science: Jane E. Wittich, Dean; Ph.D., Minnesota, 1981.
Business and Practice Management: James E. McDonald, Chairperson; M.B.A., St. Thomas (Minnesota), 1989.
Chiropractic Principles and Integrated Methods: Kevin Bartol, Chairperson; D.C., National Chiropractic, 1975.
Clinical Science: William C. Elkington, Dean; D.C., Northwestern Chiropractic, 1984.
Diagnosis: Linda J. Bowers, Chairperson; D.C., Northwestern Chiropractic, 1981.
Radiology: Timothy J. Mick, Chairperson; D.C., Northwestern Chiropractic, 1986.
Research: Charles E. Sawyer, Vice President; D.C., Northwestern Chiropractic, 1977.

CLINIC AFFAIRS

Joyce E. Miller, Dean of Clinics; D.C., Northwestern Chiropractic, 1985.

Community Based Education: Michael B. Porter, Director; M.S.E., Kentucky, 1979.
Burnsville Clinic: Terry A. Erickson, Director; D.C., Palmer Chiropractic, 1988.
Minneapolis Clinic: Steven P. Dandrea, Director; D.C., Northwestern Chiropractic, 1991.
St. Paul Clinic: Jeffrey A. Ewald, Director; D.C., Northwestern Chiropractic, 1981.
Student Health Services: Donald L. Eggebrecht, Director; D.C., Northwestern Chiropractic, 1986.
Wolfe-Harris Center for Clinical Studies—Bloomington Clinic: Zachary J. Zachman, Director; D.C., Northwestern Chiropractic, 1985.
Maternal and Child Health: Ann Packard-Spicer, D.C., Northwestern Chiropractic, 1991.
Occupational Health Services: P. Thomas Davis, D.C., Palmer Chiropractic, 1977.
Radiology Services: Timothy J. Mick, D.C., Northwestern Chiropractic, 1986.
Rehabilitation: Richard Hills, D.C., Northwestern Chiropractic, 1993.

RESEARCH

Wolfe-Harris Center for Clinical Studies—Research and Clinical Trials: Charles E. Sawyer, Vice President for Academic Affairs and Research Affairs; D.C., Northwestern Chiropractic, 1977.

Patient care and outcomes-based research are focal points of the Wolfe-Harris Center for Clinical Studies.

PALMER COLLEGE OF CHIROPRACTIC

Doctor of Chiropractic Program

Programs of Study

Palmer College of Chiropractic offers a program of professional study leading to the Doctor of Chiropractic (D.C.) degree. The College was established to provide students with a sound education in the fundamental principles and practice of the science of chiropractic while they work toward the advancement of chiropractic knowledge through an integration of formal scientific and clinical research programs. The principal characteristic of the graduate programs is the pursuit of new knowledge through research. Palmer College strongly encourages and supports faculty research activity as well as involvement in research by students. This commitment ensures that the College's graduates are familiar with the most recent developments in the field of chiropractic.

The College is currently on the trimester system. The ten-trimester Doctor of Chiropractic program can be completed in three years and four months if the student enrolls in three terms each year. Trimesters begin in October, February, and July. Course work at Palmer College of Chiropractic is divided generally into three areas. Basic science courses include anatomy, physiology, pathology, and chemistry relevant to the study of the healing arts. Preclinical subjects cover the X-ray, diagnosis, and chiropractic technique necessary for understanding the clinical application of the principles of health care and chiropractic. Clinical training in a practical real-life setting rounds out the professional education of the student at Palmer. A persistent theme throughout the program is an emphasis on the philosophy of chiropractic. This important aspect of Palmer's education provides the unifying link between all components of the curriculum.

Palmer College also offers a Bachelor of Science degree in general science. The degree is conferred independently of but in conjunction with the Doctor of Chiropractic degree.

Research Facilities

Palmer College is the dominant contributor in the field of chiropractic research. Its facilities are continually being improved and enlarged. Opened in 1985, the Palmer Center for Chiropractic Research has been a tremendous success. Facilities house individual biochemistry and physiology research laboratories as well as the Research Clinic, laboratories for the transmission electron microscope, scanning electron microscope, and image-intensified X-ray unit. A computerized videofluoroscopy imaging center, an engineering workstation (modeling and graphics), and a three-dimensional goniometer are also housed at the Institute.

The largest chiropractic college library in the world, the Palmer College of Chiropractic library has extensive clinical and basic science holdings as well as the largest collection of chiropractic publications.

Financial Aid

Palmer College offers students assistance in financing the cost of their education through its Office of Financial Planning. Financial assistance may be obtained in the form of Federal Pell Grants, Federal Unsubsidized or Subsidized Stafford Student Loans, Federal Perkins Loans, Federal Parent Loans for Undergraduate Students, Federal Work-Study awards, Educational Assistance for Veterans, Federal Supplemental Educational Opportunity Grants, Iowa Tuition Grants and Iowa Forgivable Loans (Iowa residents only), Palmer College scholarships, and a variety of scholarships offered at the state or association level.

Cost of Study

The tuition is $4860 per trimester for the 1998–99 academic year. The total cost for the three-trimester calendar year for tuition, fees, books, and supplies is $16,490.

Living and Housing Costs

The cost of living in the Quad Cities metropolitan area is well below the national average, varying according to individual lifestyle. Students should expect to spend an average of $500 per month for a two-bedroom apartment (including utilities) in a clean, quiet Quad City neighborhood.

Student Group

The typical student enters Palmer College with more than 100 undergraduate semester hours and a B average. The College's 1,797 students represent all fifty states; about 10 percent of the students are from twenty-six other countries. The average age of students is 27, and approximately 28 percent are women.

A variety of extracurricular activities are offered. There are four professional fraternities and two sororities. Student chapters of the International Chiropractors Association and the American Chiropractic Association have on-campus offices. In addition to the student council, there are a number of student clubs and organizations. The Palmer rugby team has won many national championships. Other interscholastic sports include soccer, hockey, and golf. Basketball, softball, and volleyball are played intramurally, and there are several sports clubs.

Student Outcomes

Palmer alumni practice in approximately thirty nations; one third of all practicing chiropractors throughout the world are Palmer graduates.

Seventy-four percent of Palmer alumni are employed in a solo practice, 24 percent are employed in a group practice, and 2 percent hold other positions, such as college administrator and researcher.

Location

Palmer College is located in Davenport, Iowa, the largest of the municipalities known collectively as the Quad Cities, clustered on the Mississippi River. With a population of approximately 400,000, the greater Quad Cities area constitutes the largest metropolitan area between Chicago and Des Moines.

The College

Palmer College of Chiropractic was founded in Davenport, Iowa, shortly after Daniel David (D. D.) Palmer performed the first recorded chiropractic adjustment in 1895. As knowledge of D. D. Palmer's findings spread, he began to instruct others. The first classes were held in his ample professional office, a few blocks from the present site of the College. Expansion became necessary in 1904, and property was acquired that became the nucleus of the Palmer campus of today. The first and the largest accredited chiropractic college in the world, Palmer College is an educational institution of strength, stature, and tradition with a continuing commitment to energetic achievement. The College is accredited by both the Council on Chiropractic Education and the North Central Association of Colleges and Schools and is recognized by both the International Chiropractors Association and the American Chiropractic Association. In 1991, the Palmer Chiropractic University System was formed, joining Palmer College of Chiropractic and Palmer College of Chiropractic West in San José, California.

Applying

Applications should be submitted as early as possible, up to one year in advance of the trimester of desired entrance. Interested students should contact the Office of Admissions for further information.

Correspondence and Information

Office of Admissions
Palmer College of Chiropractic
1000 Brady Street
Davenport, Iowa 52803
Telephone: 319-326-9656
800-722-3648 (toll-free in the U.S. and Canada)
E-mail: pcadmit@palmer.edu
World Wide Web: http://www.palmer.edu

Palmer College of Chiropractic

THE FACULTY

The College currently employs 138 full-time faculty members and is organized into three divisions: Basic Science, Clinical Science, and Chiropractic Philosophy. Approximately three quarters of the faculty members possess a D.C. degree; 35 percent have master's degrees, and 18 percent a Ph.D. The Palmer Center for Chiropractic Research currently has 8 full-time Research Fellows who carry out their own programs of research and oversee student-based research projects.

Students working in the David D. Palmer Memorial Library and Osteological Museum.

The Heritage Endowment Wall, symbolic of the firm foundation of chiropractic, sits atop Brady Hill on campus. The wall is crowned by busts of the four Palmers who discovered, developed, and perpetuated the chiropractic profession.

West Hall, housing classrooms, an amphitheater, and faculty offices.

PALMER COLLEGE OF CHIROPRACTIC WEST

Program of Study

Palmer College of Chiropractic West is an accredited college that offers a program of study leading to the Doctor of Chiropractic (D.C.) degree. The goals of the College are to graduate Doctors of Chiropractic of the highest caliber who are clinically competent primary health-care providers with concern and compassion for the public, to encourage and conduct research to provide an information base for the profession, and to advance the science, art, and philosophy of chiropractic. The four-year program consists of thirteen quarters. Strong emphasis is placed on the basic sciences in the first half of the program, followed by a corresponding focus on the clinical sciences in the last half of the program. Study of chiropractic principles and procedures is followed throughout the curriculum. The Department of Life Sciences comprises the disciplines of anatomy, chemistry, physics, and physiology. The Department of Diagnosis comprises the disciplines of geriatrics, laboratory diagnosis, microbiology, obstetrics, pathology, pediatrics, physical diagnosis, and roentgenology. The Department of Practice comprises clinical practice, principles and philosophy, and therapeutic procedures. In addition, an elective program of various chiropractic procedures and related subjects is offered. Students spend their ninth to twelfth quarters of study treating patients in the Palmer West Community Clinics, which include the College's campus-based facility on Tasman Drive and two satellite clinics elsewhere within San Jose and Santa Clara. The College's thirteenth quarter, the Practice Development Quarter (PDQ), has been designed to facilitate a smooth and successful transition into practice. The practical aspects of the PDQ provide each Palmer West student the opportunity to gain real-world experience in a field office setting through the College's pregraduate preceptorship program. In addition to the practical aspects, the PDQ program also includes a state board review course and seminars on patient and practice management that feature presentations by Palmer West faculty and special guest lecturers, many of whom are nationally recognized as specialists in their respective areas of expertise. In the students' clinical experience, particular attention is given to the relationship of the structural and neurologic aspects of the body in health and disease. Research by students and faculty is highly encouraged, and students are required to complete two research courses.

Research Facilities

The College maintains several laboratories dedicated to research in biomechanics, physiology, and biochemistry. Specialized equipment relevant to each discipline is constantly being added. The campus teaching clinic provides facilities and subjects for epidemiological investigations, clinical outcome research, and evaluations of physician-practice-based disciplines such as radiography, spinal manipulation, and health education. The library maintains extensive holdings relevant to chiropractic and related professions. Palmer West maintains a VAX 6330 minicomputer that communicates directly with Palmer College in Davenport through a T-1 lease line. Palmer West's VAX and personal computer users are also linked to the Novell Network, which provides access to a variety of other computer networks and databases. Palmer West also maintains a computer lab of twenty-four networked PCs in the College library. Here students may utilize self-tutorials on a variety of basic and clinical science subjects or research health-care issues via the Medline CD-ROM Index Medicus. A radiology laser disk system allows students to review case studies with computer-generated X-rays of the spine and extremities.

The College, through its membership in the Consortium for Chiropractic Research (CCR), is also able to draw on the facilities and expertise of other CCR member institutions in many collaborative projects.

Financial Aid

Students are assisted in maximizing their own resources and those available through federal, state, and private sources. A limited number of students are considered for Federal Pell Grants and Federal Supplemental Educational Opportunity Grants. Students may also qualify for Federal Perkins Loans, Federal Stafford Student Loans, and Federal Unsubsidized Stafford Loans for Students. Student employment opportunities exist for students who qualify for the Federal Work-Study Program and for the institutional Student Work Program. The College also certifies eligibility for veterans' benefits and provides information on a variety of state and private donor scholarships.

Cost of Study

Tuition (subject to change) for the 1998–99 year is $4195 per quarter. No special fees are charged. Book costs average $450 per quarter. Equipment purchases for the entire course of study average $600.

Living and Housing Costs

The College now offers a Housing Service, which offers Housing Days that help students locate housing and roommates. The Student Services Office maintains a roommate-referral service and assists new and continuing students in finding housing. In 1998–99, single students can expect to spend $500 per month for rent (assuming housing is shared) and $250 for board. Married students can expect to spend $900 per month for rent and $350 for board.

Student Group

Palmer West's 740 students come from throughout the United States and other countries, with the largest group coming from California and other western states. A significant number of students come from the Northeast. International students make up nearly 15 percent of the student body. Thirty percent of Palmer West's students are women, and 20 percent are married. The average age of the students is 26. The entering class size is 50–75 students each quarter.

Location

Palmer West is located in San Jose, California at the southern end of the San Francisco Bay Area. This area is known for its rapidly growing computer industry and for providing a strong base for employment and clinical practice.

The College

Palmer West, founded in 1980, joined Palmer College of Chiropractic, the fountainhead of chiropractic education, in 1991 to form the Palmer Chiropractic University System. The Palmer West Campus offers a modern, two-story structure comprising 96,000 square feet with state-of-the-art classrooms and laboratories. The College is accredited by the Council on Chiropractic Education.

Applying

Applications are accepted for entry four times a year—January, April, July, and October. Specific prerequisites are biology, general and organic chemistry, physics, psychology, social sciences/humanities, and English. Interested students should contact the Admissions Office for complete entrance requirements and application procedures.

Correspondence and Information

Admissions Office
Palmer College of Chiropractic West
90 East Tasman Drive
San Jose, California 95134

Telephone: 408-944-6024
800-442-4476 (toll-free)
Fax: 408-944-6032

Palmer College of Chiropractic West

THE FACULTY

Department of Clinics
Dominick Scuderi, Chair; D.C., Palmer Chiropractic, 1981.
Julia Bickerton, D.C., Palmer Chiropractic–West, 1985.
Robert Cook, D.C., Palmer Chiropractic–West, 1988.
Joan Davis, D.C., Western States Chiropractic, 1980; DACBR.
Richard Gardner, D.C., Palmer Chiropractic–West, 1986.
Edward Klein, D.C., Palmer Chiropractic–West, 1990.
Arden Lawson, D.C., Palmer Chiropractic–West, 1986.
Eric Lundberg, D.C., Palmer Chiropractic–West, 1984.
Kevin McCarthy, D.C., Los Angeles Chiropractic, 1980; DABCO.
Sharon Mellott, D.C., Palmer Chiropractic–West, 1982.
John Spencer, D.C., Palmer Chiropractic, 1978; DACR.
Mark Szlazak, D.C., Life Chiropractic West, 1990.

Department of Diagnosis
Thomas Souza, Chair; D.C., Cleveland Chiropractic (Los Angeles), 1983.
Richard Brown, D.P.M., California College of Podiatric Medicine, 1972.
Dorothy Cohen, Ph.D., Illinois, 1977; D.C., Life Chiropractic West, 1988.
Robert Cooperstein, D.C., Life Chiropractic West, 1984.
Joan Davis, D.C., Western States Chiropractic, 1980; DACBR.
Daniel Dugan, M.S., Brigham Young, 1976.
William DuMonthier, D.C., Palmer Chiropractic, 1979.
Peter Fysh, D.C., Philip Institute (Australia), 1980.
Richard Gardner, D.C., Palmer Chiropractic–West, 1986.
Andy Kondrath, M.S., Drake, 1980.
Kevin McCarthy, D.C., Los Angeles Chiropractic, 1980; DABCO.
John McDaniel, D.C., Palmer Chiropractic–West, 1986.
Thomas Milus, D.C., Palmer Chiropractic, 1982; DABCO.
Dale Nansel, Ph.D., Virginia Commonwealth, 1977.
Greg Plaugher, D.C., Los Angeles Chiropractic, 1986.
Susan St. Claire, D.C., Palmer Chiropractic–West, 1984; M.S., Bridgeport, 1992.
Shahinaz Soliman, M.D., Ain Shams (Egypt), 1992.
John Spencer, D.C., Palmer Chiropractic, 1978; DACR.
Mark Szlazak, D.C., Life Chiropractic–West, 1990.

Department of Practice
Peter Fysh, Chair; D.C., Philip Institute (Australia), 1980.
Dematour Betoushana, D.V.M., Tehran (Iran), 1980; D.C., Palmer Chiropractic–West, 1992.
Julia Bickerton, D.C., Palmer Chiropractic–West, 1985.
Rick Chaeff, D.C., Palmer Chiropractic–West, 1988.
Robert Cooperstein, D.C., Life Chiropractic West, 1984.
Kimberlee Davis, D.C., Palmer Chiropractic–West, 1988.
Richard DeSarbo, D.C., Palmer Chiropractic, 1988.
Gerry deWet, D.C., Palmer Chiropractic, 1966.
Ed Feinberg, D.C., Palmer Chiropractic–West, 1984.
Mary Ann Furda, D.C., Palmer Chiropractic–West, 1990.
Virginia Handly, D.C., Palmer Chiropractic, 1986.
Robert Jansen, Ph.D., California, Santa Cruz, 1979.
Edward Klein, D.C., Palmer Chiropractic–West, 1986.
Eric Lundberg, D.C., Palmer Chiropractic–West, 1984.
Joanne Marie Lyon, D.C., Life Chiropractic West, 1988.
Peter Martin, D.C., Palmer Chiropractic, 1968.
John McDaniel, D.C., Palmer Chiropractic–West, 1986.
William Meeker, D.C., Palmer Chiropractic–West, 1982; M.P.H., San Jose State, 1988.
Thomas Milus, D.C., Palmer Chiropractic, 1982; DABCO.
Mehdi Moosavi, D.C., Palmer Chiropractic–West, 1992.
Greg Plaugher, D.C., Los Angeles Chiropractic, 1986.
John Quitoriano, D.C., Palmer Chiropractic–West, 1983.
Susan St. Claire, D.C., Palmer Chiropractic–West, 1984; M.S., Bridgeport, 1992.
Peggy Sherman, D.C., Palmer Chiropractic, 1977.
Gerald Waagen, Ph.D., Utah State, 1979; D.C., Palmer Chiropractic, 1986.

Department of Life Sciences
Susan St. Claire, Chair; D.C., Palmer Chiropractic–West, 1984; M.S., Bridgeport, 1992.
Julia Bickerton, D.C., Palmer Chiropractic–West, 1985.
Richard Brown, D.P.M., California College of Podiatric Medicine, 1972.
May Cheung, D.C., Palmer Chiropractic–West, 1991.
Kenneth Courtney, Ph.D., Washington (Seattle), 1974.
Ilyas Dhami, Ph.D., Surrey (England), 1985.
Daniel Dugan, M.S., Brigham Young, 1976.
Mary Ann Furda, D.C., Palmer Chiropractic–West, 1990.
Thomas Gregory, D.C., Palmer Chiropractic, 1978; Ph.D., Brigham Young, 1991.
Robert Jansen, Ph.D., California, Santa Cruz, 1979.
Andy Kondrath, M.S., Drake, 1980.
Arlene Luckock, Ph.D., Berkeley, 1974.
Mohan Menon, Ph.D., West Indies (Jamaica), 1981.
Mehdi Moosavi, D.C., Palmer Chiropractic–West, 1992.
David Mullen, D.C., Palmer Chiropractic–West, 1990.
Mark Szlazak, D.C., Life Chiropractic West, 1990.
Gerald Waagen, Ph.D., Utah State, 1979; D.C., Palmer Chiropractic, 1986.
Henry Yoshihara, Ph.D., Minnesota, 1966; D.C., Pasadena Chiropractic, 1978.
Hong Zhang, D.C., Palmer Chiropractic, 1992.

PARKER COLLEGE OF CHIROPRACTIC

Programs of Study

Demonstrating the high standards of academic and clinical excellence at Parker College, students consistently rank among top performers on state and national board exams and go on to maintain successful practices. Together with training in the science, philosophy, and art of chiropractic, the program offers course work leading to the Doctor of Chiropractic (D.C.) degree that covers the basic and clinical sciences as well as jurisprudence, office procedure, and business management. Parker College students are exposed to a selection of successful techniques larger and more liberal than those offered by older, more traditional programs. One of the most distinctive features of the curriculum is the influence of the College's world-renowned founder, Dr. James W. Parker. For more than forty-five years, Dr. Parker, through the Seminars of the Parker School for Professional Success (PSPS), taught his success principles to thousands of people in the chiropractic profession. These seminars are included in Parker students' education, and the highly beneficial *Parker Success* textbook is included. The Preparation for Practice inclusion is a major benefit of attending Parker. A concurrent B.S. in anatomy is also offered. Parker College is accredited by the Council on Chiropractic Education (C.C.E.) and by the Commission on Colleges of the Southern Association of Colleges and Schools. The course of study is a four-year academic program condensed into three calendar years of nine trimesters.

Research Facilities

The Parker College Research Program focuses on assessing clinical outcomes; gathering data through automated means in ordinary clinical settings; gathering comprehensive data sets covering all aspects of structure, function, history, symptomology, and treatment; analyzing these comprehensive data sets to reveal the presence of stable, underlying, global patterns; analyzing these patterns longitudinally to reveal how they change over time, particularly in response to treatment; linking individual clinical settings to a centralized computer where data may be stored, analyzed, and redistributed; developing tools that practicing physicians can use to query these comprehensive databases for answers to questions regarding their individual patients; using the comprehensive databases to serve the three major goals of an institution of higher learning—science, service, and education; and publishing results for the scientific community at large. Within the limitations of the College's resources, prototype systems are being developed to achieve these goals, particularly within campus clinics.

Financial Aid

Eligible students have access to the entire selection of standard federal, state, and private loan, grant, and scholarship programs, which enable recipients to receive up to $24,118 every two trimesters. Parker College also participates in the ChiroLoan program, available specifically to chiropractic students, and offers work-study. Private scholarships and supplemental grants are available periodically.

Cost of Study

The College strives to maintain minimal increases in tuition and fees and continues to be one of the lowest in overall cost and the lowest in net tuition among chiropractic colleges. For the trimester beginning May 1998, tuition was $4700 per trimester. Books and lab fees average an additional $618 per trimester.

Living and Housing Costs

The overall cost of living in Dallas is comparable to or lower than that at many other chiropractic college locations. Figures used by the Financial Aid Office indicate that a $6076-per-trimester allowance for off-campus housing, transportation, and personal expenses is about average. A large selection of apartment complexes and condominiums surround the College; many offer special discounts to Parker College students.

Student Group

In keeping with Parker's worldwide mission of international growth and expansion, especially in countries where chiropractic is not yet established, nearly 1,300 full-time students (about 30 percent women) attend; students, nearly 2,000 alumni, and applicants now represent more than 100 countries. Men and women from diverse backgrounds and cultures learn the foundations of chiropractic and natural healing at Parker College. More than twenty-five active on-campus clubs and associations (including a fraternity and a sorority) provide opportunities for socializing and outside interests. A variety of organized sports, such as aerobics, basketball, bicycling, bowling, flag football, golf, Ping-Pong, soccer, softball, tennis, and volleyball, promote healthy recreation. A fully equipped weight room offers state-of-the-art physical fitness training and workouts.

Location

Central to one of the world's largest and busiest airports, the Metroplex is home to more than 4.2 million people. Thus, senior interns at the Parker Public Clinics should experience no shortage of patients for student practices. Distinguished by its warm climate and Western charm, the Dallas area is also a leader in the arts, business, sports, and commerce. Students may take prerequisite courses at community and other colleges near the campus. The Dallas campus, where all classes are held, is ideally situated just off Interstate 35, is conveniently accessible to anywhere in the Metroplex, and is minutes from major restaurants, shopping, hotels, and entertainment. A 109-foot-high revolving lighted globe is a campus landmark seen for miles.

The College

As the youngest, fastest-growing, and third-largest institution in chiropractic, Parker College totals more than 90 acres and spans three campuses. The original ALPHA campus in Irving, where the College opened in 1982, houses one of two remodeled Public Clinics and part of the Research Center. The BETA (Best Educational Thrust Anywhere) main campus, in Dallas, which opened in 1989, is known for its architecture and state-of-the-art facilities showcased in an artistic setting with trees, fountains, canals, and waterfalls. A recent addition is the gymnasium/auditorium, which is fully equipped with the latest acoustics and lighting, a regulation hardwood court, TV, game rooms, and saunas, with a capacity of 2,000. A 30,000-square-foot public clinic on the Dallas campus opened in 1993; and an adjacent 30,000-square-foot student clinic houses the new Rehabilitation Center.

Applying

Students may begin course work in January, May, or September for the spring, summer, or fall trimesters, respectively. Applications should be received at least three months prior to the date of registration. However, applying early, even as much as two or more years, for the chosen trimester, is recommended, as seats are reserved on a first-come, first-served basis. Equal opportunity for enrollment is extended to all eligible students without regard to race, creed, sex, national origin, or disability. Prerequisite requirements for the D.C. degree include 60 credit hours of college work in biology, organic and inorganic chemistry, physics, English or communications skills, psychology, humanities and social science, and electives, with a minimum grade of C in any science course and an overall GPA of 2.5. To be eligible for the B.S. degree, applicants must have completed 8 hours of each required science and 6 hours of math; math courses may be taken at the same time as D.C. courses. Inquiring students will be sent a 20-minute video, a catalog, and other application and informational materials.

Correspondence and Information

Reba S. Sexton, Director of Admissions
Parker College of Chiropractic
2500 Walnut Hill Lane
Dallas, Texas 75229-5668
Telephone: 972-438-6932
800-GET-MY-DC (toll-free)
World Wide Web: http://www.parkercc.edu

Parker College of Chiropractic

THE FACULTY AND ADMINISTRATION

Administration
W. Karl Parker, D.C.; President, FICC, FACC.
Neil Stern, D.C., D.Sc. (honorus), H.H.D. (honorus), Executive Vice President for Academic and Administrative Affairs; FICC, FACC.
Tony Boudreau, B.B.A., Chief Fiscal Officer; CPA.
Walter Brake, M.Ed., Ph.D., Dean of Student Affairs.
Paul A. Jaskoviak, D.C., Dean, School for Advanced and Related Studies; DACAN, CCSP, FICC.
John H. Moltz, Ph.D., Director of Research.
James McChesney, M.Ed., Institutional Research and Analysis.
Linda S. Rhodes, D.C., Director of Development and Alumni Relations.
Thadelua J. Moore, M.L.S., Director, Learning Resources.

Basic Sciences
Venita Allison, Ph.D., Assistant Professor.
Kay Brashear, M.A., Associate Professor.
Alan Campbell, Ph.D., Associate Professor.
James E. Carnes, Ph.D., Associate Professor.
Elizabeth Doller, Ph.D., Professor.
Karen Farmer, Ph.D., Assistant Professor.
Geraldine Gaik, Ph.D., Associate Professor.
Gene Giggleman, D.V.M., Professor.
Marty Hall, D.C., Assistant Professor; DACNB.
Steve Kirk, D.D.S., Associate Professor.
Farshid Marzban, Ph.D., Associate Professor.
John Moltz, Ph.D., Professor.
Robert Mullins, D.C., Assistant Professor.
Mabel Obuseh, D.C., Associate Professor; DLD-RCS.
James B. Parker, Ph.D., Assistant Professor.
Georgina Pearson, M.B., Associate Professor.
J. Michael Perryman, M.D., Associate Professor.
Matt Quintero, M.S., Assistant Professor.
Nuggehalli Srinivasan, Ph.D., Professor.
J. Robyn Strader, Ph.D., Assistant Professor.
Robert Vaupel, Ph.D., Professor.
Ricky Waybright, D.C., Assistant Professor.
Audris Zidermanis, Ph.D., Professor.

Chiropractic Sciences
William Arnold, J.D., Assistant Professor.
Deanne Baker, D.C., Assistant Professor.
Leon Coelho, D.C., Professor.
Larry Eckhardt, D.C., Assistant Professor.
James Fuller, D.C., Assistant Professor.
Jesse Green, J.D., Assistant Professor.
Ray Green, J.D., Assistant Professor.
Cindy Hart, D.C., Assistant Professor.
Robin Hyman, D.C., Professor.
Terry Jetton, D.C., Assistant Professor.
Sue Kelton, D.C., Assistant Professor.
Stephanie Kerr, M.A., Instructor.
Lonnie Knight, D.C., Assistant Professor.
Tom Redenbaugh, D.C., Assistant Professor.
Paula Robinson, M.A., Assistant Professor.
Lee Shaffer, D.C., Professor.
Alfred States, D.C., Professor; DABCO.
Joe Todd, D.C., Assistant Professor.
Charlotte Watts, D.C., Associate Professor; DACNB.
Ronald Wells, D.C., Assistant Professor.
Troy Wierman, D.C., Associate Professor.

Clinical Sciences
Dennis Adams, M.H.A., D.C., Associate Professor.
Lovonne Beaird, D.C., Associate Professor.
Heby Behbahani, M.A., Instructor.
Daniel Diaz, D.C., Assistant Professor.
Norbert Dombrowsky, D.C., Associate Professor; DACBR.
Gary Drew, D.C., Associate Professor.
James Guest, D.C., Assistant Professor; CCN, DACBN.
Kenneth Hansen, D.C., Assistant Professor (radiology resident).
Robert Honigsberg, M.Ed., D.C., Associate Professor; DABCC, DABCO, DABQAURP.
Garland Hunter, D.C., Assistant Professor.
Steven Kleinfeld, D.C., Associate Professor; DABCO.
Kenneth Lustik, D.C., Associate Professor; DACBR.
John Mazion, D.C., Professor; DABCO.
Tom Moore, D.C., Assistant Professor.
Thomas Pfiffner, D.C., Assistant Professor.
Janet Pitts, D.C., Assistant Professor (radiology resident).
Steven Robillard, D.C., Assistant Professor.
Jeff Rockwell, D.C., Assistant Professor.
Douglas Sanford, D.C., Assistant Professor.
Bena Tomlinson, D.C., Assistant Professor.
Kenneth Thomas, D.C., Dean of Clinics.
Gene F. Giggleman, D.V.M., Dean of the Center for Basic Sciences.
Lonnie Knight, D.C., Dean of the Center for Chiropractic Sciences.
Robert Honigsfeld, M.Ed., D.C., Dean of the Center for Clinical Sciences; DABCC, DABCO, DABQAURP.
Ellen Brown, A.A., Registrar.
Reba Sexton, A.A., Director of Admissions.
Jacqueline Bozeman, Director of Financial Aid.
Ruth Barrett, Director of Personnel.
Michael Richardson, M.Ed., Student Activities Director.
Richard Paterik, Ph.D., Director of Student Services.
Dustin Cobb, D.C., Director of Student Development.
Mai Tran, D.C., Associate Professor.
Tamara Uptigrove, D.C., Assistant Professor (radiology resident).

Clinics
David Alcorn, M.S., Instructor.
Daniel Armstrong, D.C., Associate Professor; DACNB, CCSP.
Sheri Bailey, Instructor; RT.
Judith Bast, D.C., Associate Professor; DACBR.
Nancy Bayer, D.C., Assistant Professor.
Agnes Biro, Instructor; RT.
Gary Bohman, D.C., Professor.
Stephen Boyles, D.C., Assistant Professor.
Harold Brinkley, D.C., Assistant Professor.
Wade Browne, D.C., Assistant Professor; RN.
Ralph Burton, D.C., Assistant Professor.
Peggie Chiles, Instructor; RMT.
John Coats, D.C., Assistant Professor; RCRD.
Don Deaton, D.C., Associate Professor.
Janette Doty, D.C., Assistant Professor.
David Enoch, D.C., Assistant Professor.
Hill Flora, D.C., Assistant Professor.
Richard Fuchs, B.S., Instructor; RT.
Pamela Goll, D.C., Assistant Professor.
Joseph Goodman, D.C., Assistant Professor.
Paul Hilyard, D.C., Assistant Professor.
Janet Hoefar, Instructor; RT.
Denise Holtzman, D.C., Assistant Professor.
Dale Johns, D.C., Assistant Professor.
Ali Kamyab, D.C., Assistant Professor.
Adele Kestner, D.C., Assistant Professor.
Brian Kirk, Instructor; RT.
Dan Kurth, D.C., Assistant Professor.
Robert Langford, D.C., Assistant Professor.
Arthur Locke, Instructor; RT.
M. Stan McConnell, D.C., Associate Professor.
Billy Don McCuan, Instructor; RT.
Jack Nunn, D.C., Assistant Professor.
Edward Nutick, Instructor; RT.
Stephen Orwig, D.C., Assistant Professor.
Joseph Parrish, D.C., Associate Professor.
Dorothy Post, D.C., Assistant Professor.
Charles M. Raper, D.C., Associate Professor; DABCO.
Glenn Robinson, D.C., Assistant Professor.
Rena Sawyers, D.C., Assistant Professor.
Paula Schaff, D.C., Assistant Professor.
Nicholas Stratso, D.C., Associate Professor.
Peggie Tesdall, Instructor; RMT.
Kenneth Thomas, D.C., Professor.
Virginia Thompson, D.C., Assistant Professor.
Andy Ullman, D.C., Assistant Professor.
David Walters, D.C., Assistant Professor.
Richard Williams, D.C., Assistant Professor.
Jeffrey Wilson, D.C., Associate Professor.
Frances Wisbauer, D.C., Assistant Professor.

Library and Resource Center
Vaughn Burkholder, M.A., M.S.L.S., Assistant Professor.
Thadelua J. Moore, M.L.S., Assistant Professor.
Becky Sullivan, M.L.S., Instructor.

Research Center
John Moltz, Ph.D., Professor.

Student Affairs—Counseling
Pamela Bell, Ed.D., Assistant Professor.
Walter Brake, Ph.D., Professor.
Jacquelyn Elbel, Ph.D., Professor.
Richard Paterick, Ph.D., Assistant Professor.
Steven Sliwinski, M.A., Instructor.
David Terpstra, M.Div., M.Ed., Instructor

SHERMAN COLLEGE OF STRAIGHT CHIROPRACTIC

Program of Study

Sherman College of Straight Chiropractic offers an intellectually challenging and stimulating chiropractic program leading to the Doctor of Chiropractic degree. Sherman College's goal is to prepare students to become primary-health-care providers capable of locating, analyzing, and correcting vertebral subluxations.

The thirteen-quarter program, which may be completed in thirty-nine months, offers courses that relate to broad areas of the biological sciences, but most courses are concerned directly with the art and philosophy of chiropractic. Electives in the curriculum provide students with exposure to a variety of techniques and additional areas of particular interest. Students serve an internship in the College's health center, where they further develop their chiropractic skills by extensive practical experience under close faculty supervision by licensed Doctors of Chiropractic. The intern experience encompasses an outpatient practice and covers every aspect of postgraduate practice, such as taking case histories and spinographic X rays, conducting spinal examinations, and delivering the chiropractic adjustment. The senior thirteenth-quarter student may also complete an externship with a member of the Sherman College extern faculty in the United States or abroad. The normal course load at Sherman College consists of 360 class hours or laboratory hours per quarter.

Research Facilities

Sherman College engages in and encourages chiropractic research. The research facility is located in the Taylor Building on the College's campus. In part, the research department at the College gathers and classifies data relating to patient profiles, tests the validity of specific instruments and procedures, and encourages verification of the efficacy of the chiropractic adjustment.

Financial Aid

Sherman College administers federal student financial aid funds for the Federal Perkins Loan, Federal Supplemental Educational Opportunity Grant, and Federal Work-Study programs. In addition, Sherman College is an eligible institution for students receiving funds under the provisions of the Federal Stafford Student Loan Program, the Chiroloan Program, the Veterans Administration, the Bureau of Indian Affairs, Vocational Rehabilitation, and Social Security. In addition, a wide variety of College-based scholarships and loans are available to eligible students, including scholarships for international and minority students. The job placement office offers a referral service that lists jobs in the community for students who desire employment.

Cost of Study

Tuition is paid on a quarter basis; there is a minimum of thirteen quarters of study, consisting of three months each. In fall 1998, tuition per quarter is $3790; fees vary from $20 to $50 per quarter. Books and supplies cost approximately $300 per quarter. There is a nonrefundable tuition deposit of $150, which is required to reserve a place in the class the applicant wishes to enter.

Living and Housing Costs

There are moderately priced houses and apartments for rent in the area. One- to three-bedroom apartment rents range from $350 to $650 per month. Students are responsible for their own arrangements, but the Office of Student Services will assist by supplying a list of houses and apartments for rent and information about houses for sale. Personal, recreational, and entertainment expenses vary depending on marital status and family size but generally range from $400 to $600 per quarter.

Student Group

Sherman College has approximately 400 students, representing thirty-eight states and thirteen other countries; 32 percent of students enrolled are women. Most come from the northeastern states. Students range in age from the early 20s to the 50s; the largest group falls in the 21 to 25 age group. Thirty-five percent of Sherman College students have bachelor's degrees, 95 percent receive some type of financial assistance, and 27 percent are married. Because of the immediate need for chiropractors both in the United States and abroad, graduates are very successful in establishing private practices, joining in associateships with other chiropractors, or joining the educational field of chiropractic within a short time after graduation.

Location

Spartanburg is a growing community that retains the charm of the Old South. It is home to Sherman College as well as to three 4-year liberal arts colleges and several 2-year colleges. The area offers an excellent public school system and provides many cultural and entertainment opportunities through art and service organizations such as the YMCA, Spartanburg Symphony, Theatre Spartanburg, and Spartanburg Arts Center. The area is noted for outlet shopping centers, and more than fifty international firms and plants are established there.

The College

Sherman College of Straight Chiropractic was founded in 1973 by Dr. Thomas A. Gelardi. It has the distinction of being the first chiropractic college established in the Southeast. The South Carolina Commission on Higher Education recognizes the College as an institution granting the Doctor of Chiropractic degree. The College is accredited by the Commission on Accreditation of the Council on Chiropractic Education to award the Doctor of Chiropractic degree. At Sherman College, the student finds a highly qualified faculty and staff dedicated to the pursuit of chiropractic academic excellence and the goal of preparing students to be the best straight chiropractic health-care professionals possible.

Applying

The Admission Office highly recommends that all prospective students visit the campus for an interview and tour prior to enrollment. The prerequisite program must include 1 academic year of English; 1 academic year each of general (inorganic) chemistry, organic chemistry, biology, and general physics, each with a laboratory every semester; half an academic year of psychology; and 15 semester hours of social science or humanities. Admission applications are processed on a rolling basis. There is a nonrefundable $35 application fee.

Correspondence and Information

Vice President for Enrollment Services
Sherman College of Straight Chiropractic
P.O. Box 1452
Spartanburg, South Carolina 29304

Telephone: 864-578-8770 Ext. 1221, 1222
800-849-8771 (toll-free)
Fax: 864-599-4860
E-mail: admissions@shermancsc.org
World Wide Web: http://www.shermancsc.org

Sherman College of Straight Chiropractic

THE FACULTY

Kurt Brendstrup, Assistant Professor; D.C., Los Angeles Chiropractic, 1988.
Kelly Bryant-Miller, Instructor; D.C., Sherman Straight Chiropractic, 1988.
Laura Chadwick-Weeks, Instructor and Dean of Chiropractic Health Services; D.C., Sherman Straight Chiropractic, 1990.
Sheldon P. Clayton, Professor; Ph.D., West Virginia, 1977.
William Decken, Assistant Professor; D.C., Sherman Straight Chiropractic, 1986.
Joseph Donofrio, Instructor; D.C., Sherman Straight Chiropractic, 1994.
Anthony C. Duke, Professor and Director of Basic Sciences; Ph.D., Michigan State, 1977.
William Fehl, Assistant Professor; D.C., Sherman Straight Chiropractic, 1983.
Janice Fordree, Instructor; D.C., Sherman Straight Chiropractic, 1989.
William Garren, Instructor; D.C., Sherman Straight Chiropractic, 1977.
Joy A. Gaylor, Instructor; M.M., Converse, 1994.
Cynthia Gibbon, Assistant Professor; D.C., Sherman Straight Chiropractic, 1991.
Timothy Guest, Assistant Professor and Instructor; D.C., Sherman Straight Chiropractic, 1986.
Chrys J. Harris, Instructor; Ph.D., Purdue, 1988.
John F. Hart, Assistant Professor; D.C., Palmer Chiropractic, 1981.
Alan D. Hartley, Assistant Professor; Ph.D., Kent (United Kingdom), 1992.
David B. Koch, Professor and President; D.C., Sherman Straight Chiropractic, 1980.
Patricia Kuhta, Instructor; D.C., Sherman Straight Chiropractic, 1994.
Tyler Mason, Instructor; D.C., Palmer College, 1989.
Fredric McCain, Instructor; D.C., Sherman Straight Chiropractic, 1994.
Leroy G. Moore, Instructor and Senior Vice President; D.C., Sherman Straight Chiropractic, 1976.
Mercy Navis, Assistant Professor; M.S., Madras Medical (India), 1973.
Lynnette Orell-Stewart, Instructor; D.C., Sherman Straight Chiropractic, 1987.
Valerie Pennachio, Assistant Professor; D.C., Sherman Straight Chiropractic, 1990.
John H. Porter, Assistant Professor; D.C., Sherman Straight Chiropractic, 1977.
Beth A. Roraback, Instructor; D.C., Sherman Straight Chiropractic, 1990.
Perry O. Rush, Assistant Professor; D.C., Sherman Straight Chiropractic, 1976.
Claudia Seay, Instructor; D.C., Sherman Straight Chiropractic, 1980.
Rebecca Tummons, Assistant Professor; M.D., Medical University of South Carolina, 1987.
James G. Vidrine, Professor; Ph.D., Iowa State, 1969.
Michael Westbrook, Instructor; D.C., Logan Chiropractic, 1974.
Leslie M. Wise, Professor; D.C., Palmer Chiropractic, 1974.
Qinggen Zhang, Assistant Professor and Director of Research; M.D., Hawaii, 1992.

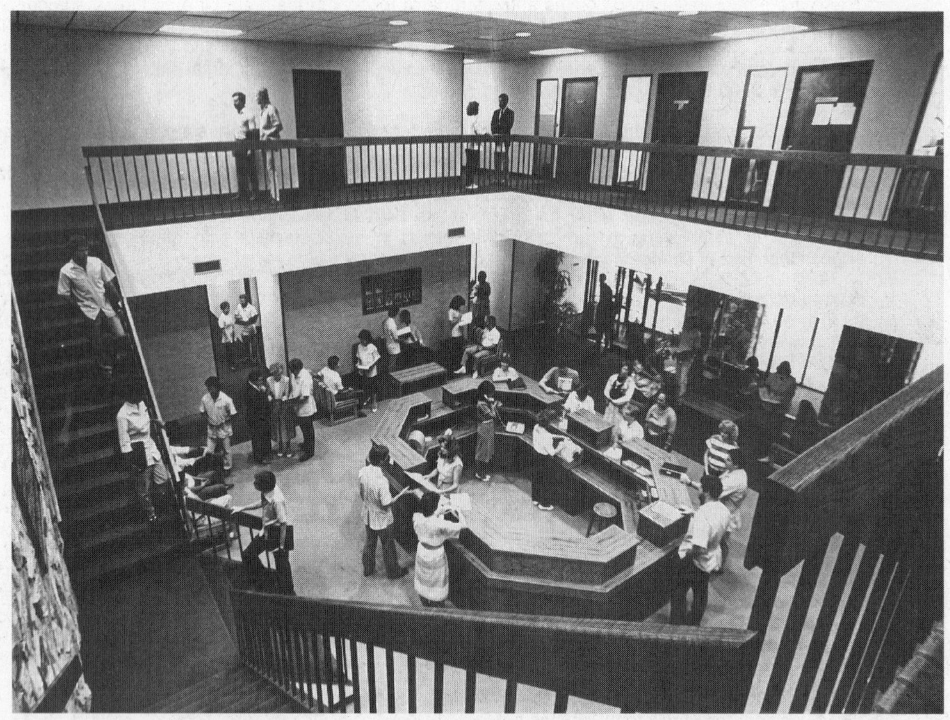

Sherman interns with patients at the Sherman College Health Center.

TEXAS CHIROPRACTIC COLLEGE

Graduate Program

Program of Study

Texas Chiropractic College (TCC) offers the Doctor of Chiropractic (D.C.) degree. The D.C. program consists of ten trimesters that take 3⅓ years to complete. It consists of basic and clinical sciences and a unique internship (trimesters eight, nine, and ten) that includes practice in the TCC clinic and offers hospital rotations, preceptorships, and externships. Hospital rotations place interns with medical doctors and osteopaths for interdisciplinary learning experiences in the Texas Medical Center, the world's largest health-care complex. Preceptorships place interns in chiropractic clinics where they observe the treatment of patients and office procedures. Externships also take place in chiropractic clinics but are true mentor relationships focused on hands-on patient care.

Research Facilities

Basic and clinical science faculty members are involved in research, and students participate whenever possible.

Financial Aid

Financial aid includes grants, scholarships, loans, and the work-study program. The College participates in the following grant programs: Federal Pell Grant, Federal Supplemental Educational Opportunity Grant, Tuition Equalization Grant, and State Student Incentive Grant. A number of scholarships are available. Loan programs include the Federal Subsidized Stafford Loan, Chiro Loan, and Alternative Loans. The College is approved for participation in the Veterans Administration educational benefits programs.

Cost of Study

For the 1998–99 academic year, tuition and fees total $4600 per trimester for the ten-trimester curriculum.

Living and Housing Costs

There are several apartment communities within minutes of the College campus. Monthly rent ranges from approximately $400 to $600.

Student Group

The College currently enrolls approximately 450 students, with 25 percent women. Students come from most states and several other countries.

Location

The College is located in the city of Pasadena (population 126,000), which is within the Houston metropolitan area. Downtown Houston is approximately a 30-minute drive west of the campus, and the Gulf of Mexico a 45-minute drive southeast.

The College

Texas Chiropractic College was founded in 1908 in San Antonio, Texas, and was relocated to Pasadena in 1965. It is accredited professionally by the Council on Chiropractic Education and regionally by the Southern Association of Colleges and Schools.

Applying

Applications may be requested from the Office of Admissions. Applicants must submit the completed application form, $50 fee, official high school and college transcripts, two recommendations, immunization records, and an essay. An interview is required. Results of the TOEFL are required for non-native English speakers. Preprofessional requirements include two semesters each of biology with labs, general physics with labs, general chemistry with labs, and organic chemistry with labs. Also required are two semesters of English, one semester of psychology, and five semesters of social science/humanities electives. A minimum 2.5 overall grade point average and at least 60 semester hours of credit are required.

Correspondence and Information

Office of Admissions
Texas Chiropractic College
5912 Spencer Highway
Pasadena, Texas 77505
Telephone: 281-487-1170
800-468-6839 (toll-free)
Fax: 281-487-2009
World Wide Web: http://www.txchiro.edu

Texas Chiropractic College

THE FACULTY

DIVISION OF BASIC SCIENCES
Department of Physiology and Chemistry
Virginia Wolfenberger, Ph.D., Head.

Department of Pathology and Microbiology
D. D. Malik, D.V.M., Ph.D., Head.

DIVISION OF CLINICAL SCIENCES
Robert D. Davison, D.C., C.C.S.P., Dean.

Department of Chiropractic Principles, Technique and Biokinetics
Lawrence Wald, D.C., D.A.A.P.M., Head.

Department of Clinical Practices
Ronald Grabowski, R.D., D.C., Head.

DIVISION OF CLINICS
Department of Clinical Series
Stephen A. Foster, D.C., Head and Clinic Chief of Staff.

RESIDENT FACULTY

G. Brian Batenchuk, Associate Professor, Clinical Practices; D.C., Palmer Chiropractic, 1979; Diplomate, American Chiropractic Board of Radiology, 1993.
Jesse T. Coats, Instructor, Physiology; D.C., Texas Chiropractic, 1993.
Robert D. Davison, Assistant Professor, Clinical Sciences and Dean, Division of Clinical Sciences; D.C., Texas Chiropractic, 1991.
Robert B. Devinney, Professor, Clinical Practices; Ph.D., Berkeley, 1978.
Edward C. Fritsch Jr., Assistant Professor, Clinical Practices; D.C., Texas Chiropractic, 1989.
Ronald J. Grabowski, Assistant Professor, Clinical Practices and Head, Department of Clinical Practices; R.D., The New York Hospital, 1982; D.C., Texas Chiropractic, 1989.
Susan M. Grigsby, Associate Professor, Department of Physiology and Director of Research; Ph.D., Berkeley, 1985.
Theresa Hocking, Instructor, Library and Public Services Librarian; M.L.S., Arizona, 1979; M.A., Santa Monica, 1990.
Philip C. Lening, Assistant Professor, Clinical Practices; D.C., Texas Chiropractic, 1984.
Marion MacGregor, Associate Professor, Clinical Practices; D.C., Canadian Memorial Chiropractic, 1980.
Dharam Dev Malik, Professor, Pathology and Microbiology and Head, Department of Pathology and Microbiology; D.V.M., College of Veterinary Medicine (India), 1956; Ph.D., Texas A&M, 1964.
Rebecca McKay, Instructor, Library; M.A., Kentucky, 1988; M.L.I.S., LSU, 1992.
Darlene L. Mastrosimone, Assistant Professor, Clinics and Attending Physician, Clinics; D.C., Texas Chiropractic, 1989.
Bruce E. Pendergrass, Assistant Professor, Clinics and Attending Physician, Clinics; D.C., Texas Chiropractic, 1975.
Darrel D. Prouse, Professor, Clinical Practices; D.C., Texas Chiropractic, 1958.
Thomas D. Schultea, Associate Professor, Anatomy; Ph.D., Texas A&M, 1980.
Hasnaa Shafik, Associate Professor, Pathology and Microbiology; M.D., Ainshams, 1974; Ph.D., Texas Medical Branch, 1987.
Sungwoo A. Suh, Assistant Professor, Principles, Techniques; D.C., Texas Chiropractic, 1995.
Jeffrey R. Thompson, Associate Professor; D.C., Palmer Chiropractic, 1980; Diplomate, American Chiropractic Board of Radiology, 1985.
Kenneth K. Tyer Jr., Assistant Professor, Clinical Practices; D.C., Texas Chiropractic, 1987.
Lawrence Wald, Professor, Principles, Technique and Biokinetics and Head, Department of Principles, Technique and Biokinetics; D.C., Texas Chiropractic, 1982.
Raymond L. Warner, Associate Professor, Anatomy; Ph.D., California, Davis, 1970.
Carol Lynn Webb, Instructor, Library and Assistant Director/Technical Services Librarian; M.A., Houston–Clear Lake, 1985; M.L.I.S., Texas, 1991.
Karlene Wise, Assistant Professor, Clinics Rehabilitation Supervisor; D.C., Texas Chiropractic, 1989.
Virginia A. Wolfenberger, Professor, Physiology and Chemistry and Head, Department of Physiology and Chemistry; Ph.D., Texas A&M, 1981.
Lawrence H. Wyatt Jr., Associate Professor; D.C., Logan Chiropractic, 1984; Diplomate, American Chiropractic Board of Radiology, 1988.

UNIVERSITY OF BRIDGEPORT

College of Chiropractic

Program of Study

The University of Bridgeport College of Chiropractic is the singular college of chiropractic in New England. The program is a full-time course of study of four academic years (eight semesters), including a clinical internship, that leads to the Doctor of Chiropractic (D.C.) degree.

[F6]The curriculum presented by the faculty of the College includes course offerings in anatomy, biochemistry, pathology, physiology, microbiology, radiology, diagnosis, orthopedics, neurology, and nutrition. Specialized course offerings include biomechanics, chiropractic technique procedures, physiotherapy and rehabilitation, and chiropractic principles and practice. The curriculum emphasizes the fact that the body is an integrated unit and that the neuromusculoskeletal system can affect the functioning of other systems and these systems can affect the neuromusculoskeletal system. The program of study emphasizes a strong basic and clinical science curriculum.

[F6]It is the purpose of the College to provide a comprehensive, full-time education to qualified students and to produce graduates who will be competent to practice as primary-care doctors of chiropractic.

Research Facilities

Medical research at the College is facilitated by the use of audiovisual formats, MEDLINE, and LEXIS-NEXIS and is complemented by institutionally integrated library holdings of basic and clinical science texts, periodicals, and microfiche collections. Computer-assisted research terminals, available to faculty members and students, are located in the chiropractic building. A newly constructed research lab features state-of-the-art equipment.

An outpatient chiropractic clinic is located on campus. It is equipped with modern mechanical tables, an X-ray laboratory, and ultrasound and interferential therapy units.

Financial Aid

The Office of Financial Aid provides access to fiscal resources for students enrolled in programs offered by the University of Bridgeport. Financial aid for students enrolled in the College of Chiropractic is available in the form of Federal Stafford Student Loans, residence hall directorships, and assistant hall directorships. Financial aid is also available in the form of ChiroLoans for qualified students in the College of Chiropractic. Additional information pertaining to financial aid can be obtained by calling 203-576-4568.

Cost of Study

In academic year 1998–99, tuition is $6200 per semester. The estimated cost of textbooks, equipment, and fees is approximately $500 per semester. The program is offered only on a full-time basis, two semesters per year (August through December and January through May).

Living and Housing Costs

Graduate students may reside in University on-campus residence halls. Off-campus housing in the surrounding area is also available. Information pertaining to housing can be obtained from the Office of Residence Life at 203-576-4395.

Student Group

Currently, there are approximately 250 students enrolled in the College of Chiropractic, 30 percent of whom are women. The College has a Student Government Association, as well as student associations for national chiropractic and local state organizations. The student-faculty ratio is 5:1. Laboratory sections are limited to 20 students. Class size is currently limited to 60 students.

Location

The University of Bridgeport is located in an urban setting in Fairfield County, Connecticut, approximately 55 miles from New York City. Bridgeport, the state's largest city, borders the 86-acre campus to the north. The southern border of the campus is adjacent to Seaside Park on Long Island Sound.

The University

Founded in 1927, the University of Bridgeport is a private, nonsectarian, coeducational, comprehensive, urban university. The University's campus is composed of ninety-one buildings of diverse architectural styles. The Bernard Arts and Humanities Center is a cultural hub, and the Wheeler Recreation Center is a complete recreation and physical fitness facility.

Applying

Students applying to the College of Chiropractic should submit a completed application, application fee, and official transcripts of undergraduate course work to the College of Chiropractic Office of Admissions. Admission requirements include a minimum of 90 hours of undergraduate course work with a minimum cumulative GPA of 2.5. A bachelor's degree and a cumulative GPA of at least 3.0 are preferred. The following courses must be included: 6 hours of communication/language skills, 3 hours of psychology, 3 hours of social science, 3 hours of humanities, 9 hours of electives in social sciences and/or humanities, 6 hours of general biology or zoology or anatomy and physiology, 6 hours of general chemistry, 6 hours of organic chemistry, and 6 hours of physics. Each of the science courses must include a laboratory and must be passed with a grade of "C" or better and must be a course offered for science majors. A minimum grade point average of 2.25 is required in the science prerequisites. A minimum GPA of 3.0 in science courses is preferred.

Correspondence and Information

Office of Admissions
University of Bridgeport
126 Park Avenue
Bridgeport, Connecticut 06601
Telephone: 203-576-4552
World Wide Web: http://www.bridgeport.edu

Office of Admissions
College of Chiropractic
University of Bridgeport
75 Linden Avenue
Bridgeport, Connecticut 06601
Telephone: 203-576-4352
888-UB-CHIRO (toll-free)
WWW: http://www.bridgeport.edu/ubpage/chiro

University of Bridgeport

THE FACULTY AND THEIR RESEARCH

Basic Science Faculty

Rose Galiger, Professor; Ph.D., Rutgers, 1971. Systems physiology, microbiology, immunology, histology.
Ahmed Kahn, Assistant Professor; M.B.B.S., Karachi (Pakistan), 1969. Pathology, anatomy, orthopedics.
Jeddeo Paul, Professor; Ph.D., Birmingham (England), 1958. Biochemistry, clinical nutrition, toxicology.
Nuggehali Raghuvir, Professor; Ph.D., Utah, 1962. Anatomy dissection, physiology.
Michael Reife, Assistant Professor; D.C., National Chiropractic, 1985; Board Certification: Chiropractic Neurology. Spinal anatomy, neurology.
Jinnque Rho, Professor; Ph.D., Massachusetts, 1972. Microbiology, infectious diseases, public health.
Anthony Ross, Assistant Professor; Ph.D., SUNY at Stony Brook, 1987. Neurosciences.
Sharon Sawitzke, Assistant Professor; Ph.D., CUNY, Hunter, 1994. Anatomy.

Clinical Science Faculty

Susan Birge, Adjunct Assistant Professor; Ed.D., Bridgeport, 1996. Psychology.
David Brady, Assistant Professor; D.C., Texas Chiropractic, 1991; Board Certification: Chiropractic Nutrition. Lab diagnosis, physical examination procedures.
Gina Carucci, Adjunct Assistant Professor; D.C., Bridgeport, 1994. Rehabilitation.
Carol Chiovoloni-Grant, Assistant Professor; D.C., National Chiropractic, 1985. Neurology.
Janis Davis, Adjunct Assistant Professor; D.C., New York Chiropractic, 1988; Clinician.
George DeFranca, Assistant Professor; D.C., National Chiropractic, 1982. Technique procedures.
David Dube, Adjunct Associate Professor; D.C., Bridgeport, 1995.
Gary Greenstein, Assistant Professor; D.C., Los Angeles Chiropractic, 1982. Orthopedics.
Emmett Hughes, Adjunct Assistant Professor; D.C., Bridgeport, 1996.
Richard Kane, Adjunct Assistant Professor; D.C., New York Chiropractic, 1985. Case management, clinical diagnosis.
Jonathan Lavelle, Assistant Professor; D.C., Northwestern Chiropractic, 1990; Clinician. Technique procedures.
Richard Marsillo, Adjunct Assistant Professor; D.C., New York Chiropractic, 1991; Board Certification: Neurology. Chiropractic principles.
Anthony Onorato, Associate Professor; D.C., National Chiropractic, 1983. Diagnosis.
Keith Overland, Adjunct Assistant Professor; D.C., New York Chiropractic, 1981. Sports injuries.
Nicholas Palmieri, Assistant Professor; D.C., Los Angeles Chiropractic, 1989. Diagnosis.
Mikell Parsons, Assistant Professor; D.C., Los Angeles Chiropractic, 1991; Board Certification: Nutrition. Clinical diagnosis.
Donna Marie Peano, Adjunct Assistant Professor; D.C., New York Chiropractic, 1994. Technique procedures.
Michael Perillo, Adjunct Assistant Professor; D.C., National Chiropractic, 1978; M.P.H., Columbia, 1994; Board Certification: Orthopedics. Public health.
Stephen Perle, Assistant Professor; D.C., Texas Chiropractic, 1983; Certification: Sports Injury. Technique procedures, ethics, research methods.
Terence Perrault, Assistant Professor; D.C., Western States Chiropractic, 1986; Board Certification: Chiropractic Radiology. Diagnostic imaging.
Sheryl Pressman, Adjunct Assistant Professor; D.C., Los Angeles Chiropractic, 1993; Board Certification: Chiropractic Radiology. Diagnostic imaging.
Barbara Rassow, Assistant Professor; D.C., Western States Chiropractic, 1983. Gynecology/obstetrics.
Lloyd Reiter, Adjunct Assistant Professor; D.C., Los Angeles Chiropractic, 1980. Technique procedures.
Robert Richeson, Adjunct Assistant Professor; D.C., National Chiropractic, 1996. Technique procedures.
Richard Saporito, Adjunct Assistant Professor; D.C., New York Chiropractic, 1980. Technique procedures, case management.
Karen Scotti, Assistant Professor; D.C., New York Chiropractic, 1981; Clinician. Orthopedics.
Karen Shields, Adjunct Assistant Professor; D.C., New York Chiropractic, 1980. Practice management.
Rudolph Sommer, Assistant Professor; J.D., Brooklyn Law, 1953. Jurisprudence.
Behjat Syed, Adjunct Assistant Professor; D.C., Bridgeport, 1994. Technique.
Megan Tabor, Adjunct Assistant Professor; D.C., Bridgeport, 1995; Board Certification: Chiropractic Nutrition. Nutrition, physiotherapy.
Diane Terlaga, Instructor; RT, Naugatuck Valley Community Technical, 1996. Radiology technician, X-ray positioning.
Frank Tortora, Adjunct Assistant Professor; D.C., Chiropractic Institute of New York, 1964. Technique procedures.
Pamela Tunnell, Adjunct Assistant Professor; D.C., New York Chiropractic, 1991. Rehabilitation.
Peter Zilahy, Assistant Professor; D.C., Palmer Chiropractic, 1976; Board Certification: Chiropractic Orthopedics, 1983. Clinical orthopedics.
Frank Zolli, Professor; D.C., New York Chiropractic, 1979. Case management, chiropractic philosophy and history.

WESTERN STATES CHIROPRACTIC COLLEGE

Programs of Study

Western States Chiropractic College's educational goal is to graduate holistic chiropractic physicians who are competent in diagnosis, adjusting, physiological therapeutics, rehabilitation, nutrition, and lifestyle management and who are ready to deliver quality care within the integrated managed-care system.

WSCC offers an innovative program leading to the Doctor of Chiropractic (D.C.) degree and allows students to earn a Bachelor of Science (B.S.) degree in human biology concurrently. The four-year (or three-year accelerated) D.C. program is designed to keep pace with the new era in health-care delivery and managed-health-care networks.

WSCC offers a unique approach to chiropractic education, combining the best in chiropractic and medical primary care. At WSCC, students are assured the best in academic preparation, with a real-world approach to patient care based on validated standards. Students master the core element of chiropractic care, the chiropractic adjustment, and receive instruction in adjustive techniques within every quarter of the WSCC curriculum while working with licensed chiropractic physicians in classes, technique labs, and campus clinics. In addition, WSCC interns experience an integrated practice setting where chiropractic and medical physicians collaborate to offer comprehensive care. This experience prepares WSCC interns to meet the challenges of health-care delivery in a managed-care setting and to acquire greater skills in treating a wider variety of conditions.

The advantages of the WSCC approach to integrated health-care delivery are many. Because chiropractic and medical providers practice in the same environment, they can collaborate on a patient's treatment plan and devote more time to follow-up and individualized care. As interns, students have the opportunity to work with both chiropractic and medical physicians and develop the best possible care for their patients.

Research Facilities

The central focus for research activities is the faculty. Research is coordinated by a research director and is under advisement of the Research Committee of basic science, clinical science, and chiropractic faculty. Students are exposed to the principles of research in research methods classes. Didactic instruction in the requirements of research is supplemented with practical application of these principles by means of a clinical research practicum in the last year. The College is actively involved in collaborative projects with other health professionals, academic institutions, and health-care organizations. Current efforts are focused on a multidisciplinary research network, which is capable of undertaking research in a community setting and providing data on patient outcome and practice patterns. In 1994, the College became the first chiropractic college ever awarded a federal grant for research. The grant from the Department of Health and Human Services funds a collaborative study with Oregon Health Sciences University's Department of Family Medicine.

Financial Aid

The primary responsibility of financing a student's education rests with the student. Students find, however, that they are able to supplement their resources by using aid programs sponsored or supported by the federal government. These funds usually are in the form of loans that require repayment. The financial aid office generally has loan applications and information available for provincial and national Canadian loan programs. Student employment opportunities on campus also are available. A financial aid adviser is available for consultation. The financial aid office helps students put together a workable package for their individual situation.

Cost of Study

Tuition for the 1998–99 year is $4750 per quarter. Tuition is subject to change. The academic program is twelve quarters in length. Fees, books, and supplies cost approximately $536 per quarter. The average amount borrowed by students using financial aid is $18,500 per academic year (three quarters).

Living and Housing Costs

The College does not maintain on-campus housing, but students have a wide variety of off-campus housing opportunities within easy commuting distance of the College. The Student Activities Office helps students with their search for apartments. The estimated monthly cost for room, board, personal expenses, and transportation is $1344. This estimate is based upon an average derived from a survey of what students report they actually spend.

Student Group

The 496 students at Western States Chiropractic College come from throughout the United States and Canada. Approximately 33 percent are women. About 30 percent of students are from the northwestern region of the U.S. and about 33 percent are Canadian. The average age of entering students is 26 years. About one third have earned a bachelor's degree prior to entering WSCC. About 85 percent of all entering students complete the entire Doctor of Chiropractic degree.

Location

The Portland, Oregon, metropolitan area, with a population of approximately 1.5 million, is located approximately 1 hour from the Pacific Ocean and Mt. Hood. The campus is in a pleasant residential neighborhood 10 miles northeast of downtown Portland, near the western end of the Columbia River Gorge.

The College

Western States Chiropractic College was chartered in 1904. The College moved to the current site in northeast Portland in 1973. With a 22-acre campus at their disposal, students study and relax in an academic setting nestled among expansive lawns and the Northwest's flowering and evergreen trees. The College campus is a smoke-free environment.

The College is accredited by the Northwest Association of Schools and Colleges and the Council on Chiropractic Education. WSCC has pioneered many aspects of chiropractic education.

Applying

Western States admits a new class twice a year, in September and January. Students are encouraged to begin the formal application process up to twelve months in advance of their anticipated entry date. Students can request information, unofficial evaluations of previous work, or advice on appropriate course selection at any time. Transcripts from colleges and universities previously attended must be submitted along with other required application information to the Admissions Department. There is an application fee of $50.

Correspondence and Information

Admissions
Western States Chiropractic College
2900 NE 132nd Avenue
Portland, Oregon 97230

Telephone: 503-256-5723
800-641-5641 (toll-free)
Fax: 503-251-5723
E-mail: admissions@wschiro.edu
World Wide Web: http://www.wschiro.edu

Western States Chiropractic College

THE ADMINISTRATION AND THE FACULTY

EXECUTIVE

William H. Dallas, President; D.C., Palmer Chiropractic, 1958.
Ronald G. Sellner, Vice President for Academic Affairs; Ph.D., Penn State, 1971.
Kathryn E. Shay, Chief Fiscal Officer; M.S., Denver, 1991.
Elaine Erdman, Dean of Clinics; D.C., Western States Chiropractic, 1977.
Lester Lamm, Dean of Continuing Education and Postgraduate Studies; D.C., Western States Chiropractic, 1980.
Randall Hand, Dean of Enrollment Management; Ed.D., UCLA, 1980.
Jennifer Boyd, Executive Assistant to the President and Director, Bachelor's Degree Program; Ph.D., Tulsa, 1990.

FACULTY

Laura Baffes, Assistant Professor and Staff Clinician; D.C., National Chiropractic, 1992.
Pamela Bjork, Assistant Professor and Audiovisual Librarian; M.L.S., Washington (Seattle), 1972.
Robert Boal, Professor of Basic Sciences and Chemistry; Ph.D., Boston University, 1976.
William Borman, Assistant Professor of Anatomy; Ph.D., Medical College of Wisconsin, 1994.
Michael Carnes, Associate Professor of Chiropractic Science and Anatomy; D.C., Western States Chiropractic, 1985.
James Carollo, Associate Professor of Basic Sciences; M.S., Oregon Health Sciences, 1980.
Fredrick Colley, Professor of Microbiology and Public Health; Ph.D., Arizona State, 1965.
Catherine Cummins, Assistant Professor of Chiropractic Science; D.C., National Chiropractic, 1992.
Daniel DeLapp, Assistant Professor and Staff Clinician; D.C., Los Angeles Chiropractic, 1986.
Ruth Ann Ehrlich, Instructor, Department of Radiology; RT, St. Elizabeth's School of X-Ray Technology, 1961.
James Gerber, Associate Professor of Clinical Science; D.C., Western States Chiropractic, 1981.
Richard Gillette, Associate Professor of Basic Science; Ph.D., Oregon Health Sciences, 1993.
Lorraine Ginter, Assistant Professor and Staff Clinician; D.C., Western States Chiropractic, 1988.
Mitchell Haas, Associate Professor of Chiropractic Science; D.C., Western States Chiropractic, 1986.
Beverly Harger, Assistant Professor of Radiology; D.C., Western States Chiropractic, 1987.
Janet Harris, Associate Professor of Anatomy; Ph.D., Illinois, 1971.
Henry Hirsh, Technician, Department of Radiology; RTR, Illinois Masonic Medical Center, 1976.
Lisa Hoffman, Assistant Professor of Radiology; D.C., Western States Chiropractic, 1994.
Dennis Hoyer, Associate Professor of Clinical Sciences; D.C., National Chiropractic, 1981.
Mark Kaminski, Associate Professor of Basic Science and Physiology; M.S., Northwestern, 1979.
Barry K. Kop, Assistant Professor of Chiropractic Science; D.C., Western States Chiropractic, 1989.
Nancy Korb, Instructor, Department of Radiology; RTR, Emanuel Hospital, 1969.
Ted A. Laurer, Assistant Professor of Chiropractic Science; D.C., Western States Chiropractic, 1989.
Wayne M. Lemler, Radiological Technician; M.B.A., City (Bellevue), 1989.
Owen Lynch, Assistant Professor and Staff Clinician; D.C., Western States Chiropractic, 1986.
Linda Malone, Basic Science Technician; B.S., Portland, 1971.
Bruce Marks, Assistant Professor and Staff Clinician; D.C., Cleveland Chiropractic, 1986.
Lee McCaffrey, Associate Professor of Chiropractic Sciences; D.C., Western States Chiropractic, 1977.
Charles Novak, Assistant Professor and Staff Clinician; D.C., Western States Chiropractic, 1975.
Joanne Nyiendo, Professor of Microbiology and Director of Research; Ph.D., Oregon State, 1975.
Steven Oliver, Professor and Staff Clinician; D.C., Western States Chiropractic, 1975.
Elizabeth Olsen, Associate Professor of Clinical Sciences; D.C., Western States Chiropractic, 1979.
David Peterson, Professor of Chiropractic Sciences; D.C., Western States Chiropractic, 1979.
Karen Petzing, Assistant Professor and Staff Clinician; D.C., National Chiropractic, 1980.
Michael Price, Associate Professor of Anatomy; Ph.D., Harvard, 1974.
Ravid Raphael, Associate Professor and Staff Clinician; D.C., Western States Chiropractic, 1978.
Lisa Revell, Assistant Professor and Staff Clinician; D.C., Western States Chiropractic, 1981.
Anita Roberts, Assistant Professor; D.C., Palmer Chiropractic, 1980.
Paul Shervey, Associate Professor of Anatomy; Ph.D., North Dakota, 1966.
Peter Shull, Associate Professor of Clinical Science; D.C., Palmer Chiropractic, 1982.
John Taylor, Associate Professor of Radiology; D.C., Canadian Memorial Chiropractic, 1979.
Patricia Turrentine, Technician, Instructional Media Center; B.S., Montana State, 1984.

ADJUNCT FACULTY

Joel Agresta, Clinical Sciences; D.C., Western States Chiropractic, 1983.
Patricia Canfield, Primary Care Provider; D.O., Michigan State University of Osteopathic Medicine, 1985.
Thomas Harris, Primary Care Provider; D.O., College of Osteopathic Medicine of the Pacific, 1991.
David Panzer, Chiropractic Sciences; D.C., Western States Chiropractic, 1983.
Lester Partna, Chiropractic and Clinical Sciences; D.C., Western States Chiropractic, 1989.
Mark Sepulveda, Chiropractic Sciences; D.C., Western States Chiropractic, 1991.

Section 34
Dentistry and Dental Sciences

This section contains directories of institutions offering professional programs in dentistry and graduate studies in oral and dental sciences, followed by in-depth entries submitted by institutions that chose to prepare detailed program descriptions. Additional information about programs listed in the directories but not augmented by an in-depth entry may be obtained by writing directly to the dean of a college or graduate school or chair of a department at the address given in the directory.

For programs offering related work, see also in this book Allied Health; and in Book 3, Anatomy; Biological and Biomedical Sciences; Cell, Molecular, and Structural Biology; Microbiological Sciences; and Pathology.

CONTENTS

Program Directories

In-Depth Descriptions

Dentistry

Baylor College of Dentistry, Professional Program in Dentistry, Dallas, TX 75266-0677. Awards DDS. Approved by ADA. Students: 354 full-time (161 women); includes 131 minority (15 African Americans, 83 Asian Americans, 30 Hispanics, 3 Native Americans). Average age 24. 1,587 applicants, 10% accepted. In 1997, 83 degrees awarded. *Entrance requirements:* DAT. Application deadline: 8/30 (priority date; rolling processing). Application fee: $35. *Financial aid:* Fellowships, research assistantships, teaching assistantships, institutionally sponsored loans available. Aid available to part-time students. Financial aid application deadline: 2/23; applicants required to submit FAFSA. *Faculty research:* Bleaching, implants, craniofacial growth, oral oncology, pulp biology. • Dr. Richard N. Buchanan, Dean, 214-828-8200. Fax: 214-828-8496. E-mail: rbuchanan@tambcd.edu. Application contact: Dr. Jack L. Long, Director of Admissions, 214-828-8230. Fax: 214-828-8396. E-mail: jlong@tambcd.edu.

Boston University, Henry M. Goldman School of Dental Medicine, Professional Program in Dentistry, Boston, MA 02215. Awards DMD. Approved by ADA. Faculty: 83 full-time (23 women), 214 part-time (26 women). Students: 436 full-time (182 women); includes 200 minority (11 African Americans, 167 Asian Americans, 22 Hispanics). Average age 27. 3,108 applicants, 19% accepted. In 1997, 130 degrees awarded. *Average time to degree:* first professional–4 years full-time. *Entrance requirements:* DAT (minimum score 19; average 19), minimum GPA of 3.0. Application deadline: 3/1 (priority date; rolling processing). Application fee: $50. *Financial aid:* 247 students received aid; institutionally sponsored loans and career-related internships or fieldwork available. Aid available to part-time students. Financial aid application deadline: 4/15. • Application contact: Office of Admissions and Student Services, 617-638-4787. Fax: 617-638-4798.

See in-depth description on page 1709.

Case Western Reserve University, School of Dentistry, Professional Program in Dentistry, Cleveland, OH 44106. Awards DDS. Approved by ADA. Faculty: 28 full-time, 236 part-time. Students: 260 full-time (81 women); includes 78 minority (2 African Americans, 73 Asian Americans, 3 Hispanics). Average age 25. 2,430 applicants, 9% accepted. In 1997, 60 degrees awarded. *Entrance requirements:* DAT (minimum score 15; average 18). Application deadline: 2/1 (priority date; rolling processing). Application fee: $35. *Expenses:* Tuition $25,700 per year. Fees $800 per year. *Financial aid:* 159 students received aid; Federal Work-Study, institutionally sponsored loans available. Financial aid application deadline: 4/20; applicants required to submit FAFSA. • Application contact: David A. Dalsky, Director of Admissions, 216-368-2460. Fax: 216-368-3204. E-mail: dad4po.cwru.edu.

Columbia University, School of Dental and Oral Surgery, Professional Program in Dental and Oral Surgery, New York, NY 10032. Awards DDS, DDS/MBA, DDS/MPH, DDS/MS. Approved by ADA. Students: 281 full-time (107 women). Average age 26. 2,045 applicants, 8% accepted. In 1997, 73 degrees awarded. *Average time to degree:* first professional–4 years full-time. *Entrance requirements:* DAT (minimum score 18; average 21), previous course work in biology, organic chemistry, inorganic chemistry, physics, English. Application deadline: 2/15 (rolling processing). Application fee: $50 ($95 for international students). *Tuition:* $27,640 per year. *Financial aid:* Fellowships, research assistantships, teaching assistantships, grants, scholarships, Federal Work-Study, institutionally sponsored loans, and career-related internships or fieldwork available. Financial aid application deadline: 3/15; applicants required to submit FAFSA. • Dr. Martin J. Davis, Assistant Dean, Admissions and Student Affairs, 212-305-3478. Application contact: Ellen M. Watts, Director of Admissions, 212-305-3478.

Creighton University, School of Dentistry, 2500 California Plaza, Omaha, NE 68178-0001. Awards DDS. Approved by ADA. Faculty: 49 full-time (10 women), 69 part-time (7 women), 54 FTE. Students: 331 full-time (100 women); includes 50 minority (7 African Americans, 34 Asian Americans, 6 Hispanics, 3 Native Americans), 3 international. Average age 24. 2,415 applicants, 7% accepted. In 1997, 82 degrees awarded. *Average time to degree:* first professional–4 years full-time. *Entrance requirements:* DAT. Application deadline: 3/1 (priority date; rolling processing). Application fee: $35. *Expenses:* Tuition $21,432 per year. Fees $536 per year. *Financial aid:* Institutionally sponsored loans available. Financial aid application deadline: 5/1; applicants required to submit FAFSA. *Faculty research:* Dental implants, bone calcification, dental materials, laser usage in dentistry. Total annual research expenditures: $62,387. • Dr. Wayne W. Barkmeier, Dean, 402-280-5060. Application contact: Dr. Frank J. Ayers, Chairman, Admissions, 402-280-2881. Fax: 402-280-5094.

Dalhousie University, Faculty of Dentistry, Professional Program in Dentistry, Halifax, NS B3H 3J5, Canada. Awards DDS. Approved by ADA. 224 applicants, 16% accepted. In 1997, 29 degrees awarded. *Entrance requirements:* DAT, TOEFL (minimum score 500). Application deadline: 12/1 (rolling processing). Application fee: $55. • Application contact: Nancy Webb, Coordinator of Admissions, 902-424-2274.

Harvard University, School of Dental Medicine, Professional Program in Dental Medicine, 188 Longwood Avenue, Boston, MA 02115. Awards DMD. Approved by ADA. Students: 140 full-time. In 1997, 22 degrees awarded. *Financial aid:* Federal Work-Study available. Financial aid applicants required to submit CSS PROFILE or FAFSA. • Application contact: Dr. Ellen M. Libert, Associate Dean for Students, 617-432-1443. Fax: 617-432-3881. E-mail: elibert@warren.med.harvard.edu.

Howard University, College of Dentistry, 2400 Sixth Street, NW, Washington, DC 20059-0002. Awards DDS, Certificate. One or more programs approved by ADA. Students: 329 full-time (186 women); includes 251 minority (183 African Americans, 48 Asian Americans, 17 Hispanics, 3 Native Americans), 21 international. Average age 25. 1,607 applicants, 5% accepted. In 1997, 53 DDSs awarded. *Average time to degree:* first professional–4 years full-time. *Entrance requirements:* For DDS, DAT (average 15), 8 semester hours each in biology, physics, organic and general chemistry. Application deadline: 3/1 (rolling processing). Application fee: $45. *Financial aid:* 257 students received aid; Federal Work-Study, institutionally sponsored loans, and career-related internships or fieldwork available. Financial aid application deadline: 4/1; applicants required to submit FAFSA. *Faculty research:* Genetic and molecular biology related growth and development, neoplasias. Total annual research expenditures: $180,000. • Dr. Charles F. Sanders Jr., Dean, 202-806-0440. Fax: 202-806-0354. Application contact: Doris Williams, Director of Admissions, 202-806-0400.

Indiana University–Purdue University Indianapolis, School of Dentistry, Professional Program in Dentistry, Indianapolis, IN 46202. Awards DDS. Approved by ADA. Faculty: 112 full-time (20 women), 113 part-time (5 women). Students: 364 full-time (121 women); includes 66 minority (7 African Americans, 51 Asian Americans, 7 Hispanics, 1 Native American), 8 international. Average age 24. 1,550 applicants. In 1997, 94 degrees awarded. *Average time to degree:* first professional–4 years full-time. *Entrance requirements:* DAT, TOEFL. Application deadline: 7/1 (rolling processing). Application fee: $30 ($50 for international students). *Financial aid:* Federal Work-Study, institutionally sponsored loans available. Financial aid application deadline: 3/1; applicants required to submit FAFSA. *Faculty research:* Preventive dentistry, dental materials, bone metabolism, enzyme metabolism. • Application contact: Carole A. Kacius, Director of Admissions, 317-274-8173.

Loma Linda University, School of Dentistry, Professional Program in Dentistry, Loma Linda, CA 92350. Awards DDS, DDS/MS, DDS/PhD. Approved by ADA. Faculty: 79 full-time (11 women), 159 part-time (20 women). Students: 408 full-time (117 women), 1 part-time (0 women); includes 205 minority (9 African Americans, 178 Asian Americans, 16 Hispanics, 2 Native Americans), 33 international. 1,305 applicants, 9% accepted. In 1997, 94 degrees awarded. *Average time to degree:* first professional–4 years full-time. *Entrance requirements:* DAT. Application deadline: rolling. *Financial aid:* Fellowships, Federal Work-Study, institutionally sponsored loans, and career-related internships or fieldwork available. • Dr. Charles Goodacre, Dean, School of Dentistry, 909-824-4683. Fax: 909-824-4211.

Louisiana State University Medical Center, School of Dentistry, New Orleans, LA 70119. Awards DDS. Approved by ADA. Faculty: 73 full-time (4 women), 63 part-time (5 women). Students: 176 full-time (67 women). Average age 23. 161 applicants, 34% accepted. In 1997, 52 degrees awarded. *Entrance requirements:* DAT, interview. Application deadline: 2/28 (rolling processing). Application fee: $50. *Faculty research:* AIDS, implants, metallurgy, lipids, DNA. • Dr. Eric J. Hovland, Dean, 504-619-8500. E-mail: ehovla@lsusd.lsumc.edu. Application contact: Dr. Jim C. Weir, Assistant Dean for Admissions, 504-619-8579. E-mail: jweir@lsusd.lsumc.edu.

Marquette University, School of Dentistry, Professional Program in Dentistry, Milwaukee, WI 53201-1881. Awards DDS. Approved by ADA. *Entrance requirements:* DAT, 1 year each of biology, inorganic chemistry, organic chemistry, physics, and English. Application deadline: rolling. Application fee: $40. *Tuition:* $17,170 per year for state residents; $28,840 per year for nonresidents. • Application contact: Brian Trecek, Assistant to the Dean and Director of Admissions, 414-288-3532. Fax: 414-288-3586.

McGill University, Professional Program in Dentistry, Montréal, PQ H3A 2T5, Canada. Awards DDS. Approved by ADA. *Expenses:* Tuition $1668 per year for Canadian residents; $8268 per year for nonresidents. Fees $828 per year for Canadian residents; $1216 per year for nonresidents.

Medical College of Georgia, School of Dentistry, Augusta, GA 30912-1003. Awards DMD, DMD/PhD, DMD/MS. Approved by ADA. DMD/MS and DMD/PhD offered jointly with the School of Graduate Studies. Faculty: 75 full-time (10 women), 19 part-time (5 women). Students: 218 full-time (70 women); includes 35 minority (16 African Americans, 18 Asian Americans, 1 Native American). Average age 25. 171 applicants, 33% accepted. In 1997, 48 degrees awarded. *Average time to degree:* first professional–4 years full-time. *Entrance requirements:* DAT (average 18), 50 quarter hours of sciences in biology, chemistry, and physics. Application deadline: 11/1 (rolling processing). Application fee: $0. *Expenses:* Tuition $4862 per year for state residents; $19,448 per year for nonresidents. Fees $1617 per year. *Financial aid:* 187 students received aid; Federal Work-Study, institutionally sponsored loans available. Financial aid application deadline: 5/1; applicants required to submit FAFSA. *Faculty research:* Dental materials biocompatibility, fluoride metabolism, periodontal research, dentin dynamics. Total annual research expenditures: $480,000. • Dr. David R. Myers, Dean, 706-721-2117. Application contact: Dr. Michael H. Miller, Director of Student Admissions and Academic Support, 706-721-3587. Fax: 706-721-6276. E-mail: osaas@mail.mcg.edu.

Medical University of South Carolina, College of Dental Medicine, Charleston, SC 29425-0002. Awards DMD, DMD/PhD. Approved by ADA. Faculty: 51 full-time (6 women), 20 part-time (5 women), 54 FTE. Students: 196 full-time (43 women), 1 part-time (0 women); includes 19 minority (8 African Americans, 10 Asian Americans, 1 Native American), 1 international. Average age 27. 721 applicants, 10% accepted. In 1997, 43 degrees awarded. *Average time to degree:* first professional–4 years full-time. *Entrance requirements:* DAT, interview, 52 hours of specific pre-dental course work. Application deadline: 12/1. Application fee: $55. *Expenses:* Tuition $5324 per year for state residents; $15,266 per year for nonresidents. Fees $80 per year (minimum). *Financial aid:* 3 students received aid; Federal Work-Study available. Aid available to part-time students. Financial aid application deadline: 4/1; applicants required to submit FAFSA. *Faculty research:* Dental implants, dental materials, salivary research, guided tissue regeneration, craniofacial anomalies. • Dr. Richard W. DeChamplain, Dean, 843-792-3811. Application contact: Wanda Taylor, Director of Admissions, 843-792-3281.

Meharry Medical College, School of Dentistry, Nashville, TN 37208-9989. Awards DDS. Approved by ADA. Faculty: 39 full-time (10 women), 16 part-time (5 women), 43.75 FTE. Students: 210 full-time (103 women); includes 188 minority (161 African Americans, 22 Asian Americans, 3 Hispanics, 2 Native Americans), 9 international. Average age 26. 1,464 applicants, 6% accepted. In 1997, 51 degrees awarded. *Entrance requirements:* DAT. Application deadline: 4/1. Application fee: $45. *Expenses:* Tuition $20,785 per year. Fees $1812 per year. *Financial aid:* Federal Work-Study, institutionally sponsored loans, and career-related internships or fieldwork available. Financial aid application deadline: 4/15. • Dr. Kenneth B. Chance, Dean, 615-327-6207. Fax: 615-327-6213. E-mail: chance16@ccvax.mmc.edu. Application contact: Allen D. Mosley, Director of Admissions and Records, 615-327-6223. Fax: 615-327-6228.

New York University, College of Dentistry, Professional Program in Dentistry, New York, NY 10012-1019. Awards DDS. Approved by ADA. Students: 1,179 full-time, 12 part-time; includes 320 minority (25 African Americans, 270 Asian Americans, 24 Hispanics, 1 Native American), 55 international. Average age 24. 2,612 applicants, 25% accepted. In 1997, 195 degrees awarded. *Average time to degree:* first professional–4 years full-time. *Entrance requirements:* DAT. Application deadline: 4/1 (priority date; rolling processing). Application fee: $35. *Financial aid:* 1,050 students received aid; Federal Work-Study, institutionally sponsored loans available. Financial aid application deadline: 3/1. • Application contact: Stephen F. Muller, Associate Dean for Enrollment Services, 212-998-9818.

Nova Southeastern University, Health Professions Division, College of Dental Medicine, Fort Lauderdale, FL 33314-7721. Awards DMD. Eligible for accreditation by ADA. Students: 130 full-time (49 women); includes 48 minority (3 African Americans, 25 Asian Americans, 19 Hispanics, 1 Native American). Average age 25. *Application deadline:* rolling. *Application fee:* $50. *Tuition:* $25,500 per year. • Dr. Seymour Oliet, Dean, 954-262-1108.

The Ohio State University, College of Dentistry, Professional Program in Dentistry, Columbus, OH 43210. Awards DDS, DDS/MS, DDS/PhD. Approved by ADA. Faculty: 96 full-time (23 women), 76 part-time (10 women). Students: 381 full-time (111 women); includes 66 minority (6 African Americans, 56 Asian Americans, 4 Hispanics). Average age 25. 1,242 applicants, 8% accepted. In 1997, 83 degrees awarded. *Average time to degree:* first professional–4 years full-time. *Entrance requirements:* DAT. Application deadline: 1/1 (priority date; rolling processing). Application fee: $30 ($40 for international students). *Expenses:* Tuition $9840 per year for state residents; $27,711 per year for nonresidents. Fees $2184 per year. *Financial aid:* In 1997–98, 1 fellowship (to a first-year student) was awarded; teaching assistantships, Federal Work-Study, institutionally sponsored loans also available. Financial aid application deadline: 3/1; applicants required to submit FAFSA. • Application contact: Michael Rowland, Admission and Recruitment Officer, 614-292-3361. Fax: 614-292-7619.

Oregon Health Sciences University, School of Dentistry, Professional Program in Dentistry, 3181 SW Sam Jackson Park Road, Portland, OR 97201-3098. Awards DMD, MD/DMD. Approved by ADA. Faculty: 72 full-time, 91 part-time. Students: 273 full-time; includes 45 minority (2 African Americans, 37 Asian Americans, 5 Hispanics, 1 Native American). Average age 25. 737 applicants, 10% accepted. In 1997, 69 degrees awarded. *Entrance requirements:* DAT. Application deadline: 11/1. Application fee: $165. *Financial aid:* Research assistantships, Federal Work-Study, institutionally sponsored loans, and career-related internships or fieldwork available. Financial aid application deadline: 3/1. *Faculty research:* Dentin permeability, tooth sensations, fluoride metabolism, immunology of periodontal disease, craniofacial growth. • Application contact: Nora L. Cromley, Assistant Dean of Admissions and Student Affairs, 503-494-5274. Fax: 503-494-4666. E-mail: cromleyn@ohsu.edu.

Southern Illinois University at Edwardsville, School of Dental Medicine, Edwardsville, IL 62026-0001. Awards DMD. Approved by ADA. Faculty: 43 full-time, 39 part-time. Students: 219 full-time (60 women); includes 30 minority (10 African Americans, 14 Asian Americans, 3 Hispanics, 3 Native Americans). Average age 23. 725 applicants, 19% accepted. In 1997, 36 degrees awarded. *Entrance requirements:* DAT. Application deadline: 3/1 (priority date). Application fee: $25. • Dr. Patrick Ferrillo, Dean, 618-474-7120.

State University of New York at Buffalo, Graduate School, School of Dental Medicine, Professional Program in Dental Medicine, Buffalo, NY 14214. Awards DDS. Approved by ADA.

Faculty: 43 full-time (7 women), 101 part-time (30 women). Students: 342 full-time (95 women). 786 applicants, 11% accepted. In 1997, 82 degrees awarded. *Entrance requirements:* DAT (average 18). Application deadline: 3/1. Application fee: $50. *Tuition:* $11,725 per year full-time, $535 per credit hour part-time for state residents; $22,825 per year full-time, $998 per credit hour part-time for nonresidents. *Financial aid:* 320 students received aid; full and partial tuition waivers, Federal Work-Study, institutionally sponsored loans available. Financial aid application deadline: 2/28; applicants required to submit FAFSA. • Application contact: Dr. Robert Joynt, Director of Admissions, 716-829-2839. Fax: 716-833-3517. E-mail: robert_joynt@sdm.buffalo.edu.

State University of New York at Stony Brook, Health Sciences Center, School of Dental Medicine, Professional Program in Dental Medicine, Stony Brook, NY 11794. Offers dental medicine (DDS), orthodontics (Certificate), periodontics (Certificate). One or more programs approved by ADA. Faculty: 72. Students: 146 full-time (71 women); includes 35 minority (1 African American, 28 Asian Americans, 6 Hispanics), 2 international. 894 applicants, 7% accepted. In 1997, 33 DDSs awarded. *Entrance requirements:* For DDS, DAT. Application deadline: 1/15. Application fee: $75. *Financial aid:* Fellowships, Federal Work-Study available. *Total annual research expenditures:* $168,946. • Application contact: Kim M. Lambiase Hammer, Director of Admissions, 516-632-8980.

Temple University, Health Sciences Center, School of Dentistry, Professional Program in Dentistry, Philadelphia, PA 19140. Awards DMD, DMD/MBA. Approved by ADA. Faculty: 59 full-time (10 women), 72 part-time (12 women). Students: 445 full-time (145 women); includes 160 minority (16 African Americans, 119 Asian Americans, 23 Hispanics, 2 Native Americans), 22 international. Average age 25. 2,742 applicants, 4% accepted. In 1997, 103 degrees awarded. *Entrance requirements:* DAT, 6 credits each of biology, chemistry, organic chemistry, physics, and English. Application deadline: 4/1 (rolling processing). Application fee: $30. *Financial aid:* 422 students received aid; institutionally sponsored loans available. Financial aid application deadline: 3/31; applicants required to submit FAFSA. • Application contact: Dr. Lisa P. Deem, Assistant Dean for Admissions and Student Affairs, 215-707-2801. Fax: 215-707-5461.

Tufts University, School of Dental Medicine, International Student Program in Dental Medicine, Medford, MA 02155. Awards DMD. Approved by ADA. Faculty: 29 full-time (7 women), 365 part-time. *Entrance requirements:* National Dental Hygiene Board Exam Part I (minimum score 88; average 91), TOEFL (minimum score 575; average 600), BDS, DDS, or equivalent. Application deadline: 1/15 (rolling processing). Application fee: $75. *Financial aid:* Federal Work-Study, institutionally sponsored loans available. Financial aid application deadline: 5/1; applicants required to submit CSS PROFILE or FAFSA. • Dr. Robert Doherty, Director, 617-636-6787. Application contact: Mark Gonthier, Assistant Dean for Admissions and Student Affairs, 617-636-6539. Fax: 617-636-0309. E-mail: mgonthier@infonet.tufts.edu.

Tufts University, School of Dental Medicine, Professional Program in Dental Medicine, Boston, MA 02111. Awards DMD, DMD/PhD. Approved by ADA. DMD/PhD offered jointly with the Sackler School of Graduate Biomedical Sciences. Faculty: 29 full-time (7 women), 365 part-time. Students: 613 full-time (235 women). Average age 26. 2,648 applicants, 18% accepted. *Entrance requirements:* DAT (minimum score 14; average 18). Application deadline: 3/1 (rolling processing). Application fee: $50. *Financial aid:* 416 students received aid; Federal Work-Study, institutionally sponsored loans available. Financial aid application deadline: 5/1; applicants required to submit CSS PROFILE or FAFSA. • Dr. Nancy Arbree, Assistant Dean for Academic Affairs, 617-636-6522. Application contact: Mark Gonthier, Assistant Dean for Admissions and Student Affairs, 617-636-6539. Fax: 617-636-0309. E-mail: mgonthier@infonet.tufts.edu.

Université de Montréal, Faculty of Dentistry, Professional Program in Dentistry, Montréal, PQ H3C 3J7, Canada. Awards DMD. Approved by ADA. Open only to Canadian residents. Students: 333 full-time (189 women), 1 (woman) part-time. 469 applicants, 19% accepted. In 1997, 82 degrees awarded. *Degree requirements:* 1 foreign language required, thesis not required. *Entrance requirements:* DAT. Application fee: $30. • Dr. Jean Turgeon, Dean, Faculty of Dentistry, 514-343-6005. Application contact: Dr. Gilles Lavigne, Associate Dean for Research, 514-343-2134.

Université Laval, Faculty of Dentistry, Professional Program in Dentistry, Sainte-Foy, PQ G1K 7P4, Canada. Awards DMD. Approved by ADA. Students: 187 full-time (99 women), 2 part-time (0 women). Average age 23. 352 applicants, 20% accepted. In 1997, 44 degrees awarded. *Degree requirements:* 1 foreign language. *Application deadline:* 3/1. *Application fee:* $30. *Expenses:* Tuition $1334 per year (minimum) full-time, $56 per credit (minimum) part-time for Canadian residents; $5966 per year (minimum) full-time, $249 per credit (minimum) part-time for nonresidents. Fees $150 per year full-time, $6.25 per credit part-time. • Robert Denis, Director, 418-656-2131 Ext. 2095. Fax: 418-656-2720. E-mail: fmd@fmd.ulaval.ca.

The University of Alabama at Birmingham, School of Dentistry, Birmingham, AL 35294. Awards DMD, MPH, MS, MSBMS, PhD, DMD/PhD, DMD/MS. One or more programs approved by ADA. Students: 227 full-time (71 women); includes 28 minority (7 African Americans, 16 Asian Americans, 3 Hispanics, 2 Native Americans). Average age 26. 646 applicants, 9% accepted. In 1997, 54 DMDs awarded. *Entrance requirements:* For DMD, DAT. Application deadline: 4/1. Application fee: $25. Electronic applications accepted. *Expenses:* Tuition $7963 per year for state residents; $19,345 per year for nonresidents. Fees $5573 per year. *Financial aid:* Fellowships, Federal Work-Study available. *Faculty research:* Etiology and pathogenesis of dental diseases, dental biomaterials, therapy of dental diseases. • Dr. Mary Lynne Capilouto, Interim Dean, 205-934-4720.

University of Alberta, Faculty of Medicine and Oral Health Sciences, Department of Oral Health Sciences, Professional Program in Dentistry, Edmonton, AB T6G 2E1, Canada. Awards DDS. Approved by ADA. Faculty: 22 full-time (5 women), 130 part-time. Students: 127 full-time (39 women). 370 applicants, 9% accepted. In 1997, 31 degrees awarded. *Entrance requirements:* Interview, DAT (Canadian version). Application deadline: 11/1. Application fee: $60. *Faculty research:* Oral biology, biochemistry of connective tissues, preventive dentistry, applied clinical orthodontics, biomaterials. • Application contact: E. McIsaac, Admissions Officer, 403-492-1319. Fax: 403-492-9531.

University of British Columbia, Faculty of Dentistry, Professional Program in Dentistry, Vancouver, BC V6T 1Z3, Canada. Awards DMD. Approved by ADA. Faculty: 32 full-time (7 women), 130 part-time. Students: 157. 237 applicants, 17% accepted. In 1997, 39 degrees awarded. *Average time to degree:* first professional–4 years full-time. *Entrance requirements:* DAT, interview. Application deadline: 12/1. Application fee: $100 ($200 for international students). • Application contact: B. Farmer, Admissions Coordinator, 604-822-3416. Fax: 604-822-4532. E-mail: fodadms@unixg.ubc.ca.

University of California, Los Angeles, School of Dentistry, Professional Program in Dentistry, Los Angeles, CA 90095. Awards DDS, Certificate, DDS/MS, DDS/PhD, MS/Certificate, PhD/Certificate. One or more programs approved by ADA. Students: 336 full-time (137 women); includes 192 minority (2 African Americans, 171 Asian Americans, 19 Hispanics), 2 international. 93 applicants, 98% accepted. *Entrance requirements:* For DDS, DAT. Application deadline: 1/15. Application fee: $40. *Financial aid:* In 1997–98, 299 students received aid, including teaching assistantships totaling $10,044; full and partial tuition waivers, Federal Work-Study, institutionally sponsored loans also available. Financial aid application deadline: 3/1. • Application contact: School of Dentistry Admissions, 310-825-7354.

University of California, San Francisco, School of Dentistry, San Francisco, CA 94143. Awards DDS. Approved by ADA. *Entrance requirements:* DAT. Application deadline: 1/1 (rolling processing). Application fee: $40. *Expenses:* Tuition $0 for state residents; $9384 per year for nonresidents. Fees $14,837 per year.

University of Colorado Health Sciences Center, School of Dentistry, Denver, CO 80202. Awards DDS. Approved by ADA. Faculty: 52 full-time. Students: 146 full-time (40 women); includes 31 minority (1 African American, 18 Asian Americans, 11 Hispanics, 1 Native American), 1 international. Average age 29. 976 applicants, 5% accepted. In 1997, 31 degrees awarded. *Entrance requirements:* DAT, 1 semester of English composition; 2 semesters each of chemistry, organic chemistry, biology, physics, mathematics, and English literature. Application deadline: 3/15. Application fee: $35. *Financial aid:* Federal Work-Study, institutionally sponsored loans available. Financial aid application deadline: 3/15. *Faculty research:* Pain control, materials research, geriatric dentistry, restorative dentistry, periodontics. • Dr. Robert E. Averbach, Dean, 303-315-8773. Application contact: Dr. Denise K. Kassebaum, Associate Dean for Academic and Student Affairs, 303-315-8891.

University of Connecticut Health Center, School of Dental Medicine, Professional Program in Dental Medicine, Farmington, CT 06030. Awards DMD. Approved by ADA. Faculty: 35 full-time (5 women). Students: 164 full-time (65 women), 2 part-time (both women); includes 23 minority (4 African Americans, 13 Asian Americans, 6 Hispanics), 5 international. Average age 25. 1,163 applicants, 12% accepted. In 1997, 35 degrees awarded. *Average time to degree:* first professional–4 years full-time. *Entrance requirements:* DAT. Application deadline: 2/1 (rolling processing). Application fee: $60. *Expenses:* Tuition $7900 per year for state residents; $20,250 per year for nonresidents. Fees $3725 per year. *Financial aid:* Institutionally sponsored loans available. Financial aid application deadline: 4/1; applicants required to submit FAFSA. *Faculty research:* Neurobiology, cell and molecular biology. • Application contact: Dr. Edward J. Kollar, Associate Dean for Academic and Student Affairs, 860-679-3212. Fax: 860-679-1899. E-mail: kollar@nso.uchc.edu.

University of Detroit Mercy, School of Dentistry, Professional Program in Dentistry, Detroit, MI 48219-0900. Awards DDS. Approved by ADA. *Entrance requirements:* DAT. Application deadline: 1/15. Application fee: $25. *Faculty research:* Peer evaluation in teaching, evaluation of restorative materials, HIV and periodontal disease.

University of Detroit Mercy, School of Dentistry, Professional Program in General Practice Residency, Detroit, MI 48219-0900. Awards MS, Certificate. *Degree requirements:* For master's, computer language, thesis required, foreign language not required; for Certificate, computer language required, foreign language and thesis not required. *Entrance requirements:* For master's, DDS or DMD; for Certificate, DHAT, DDS or DMD. Application fee: $25. *Faculty research:* Implant placement/selection, microbiology and soft tissue associated with dental implants.

University of Florida, College of Dentistry, Professional Programs in Dentistry, Gainesville, FL 32611. Awards DMD. Approved by ADA. Students: 313 full-time (103 women); includes 91 minority (12 African Americans, 37 Asian Americans, 41 Hispanics, 1 Native American), 31 international. Average age 26. 861 applicants, 12% accepted. In 1997, 70 degrees awarded. *Average time to degree:* first professional–4 years full-time. *Entrance requirements:* DAT (minimum score 15; average 18), TOEFL (minimum score 550), interview. Application deadline: 10/15. Application fee: $20. *Expenses:* Tuition $9184 per year for state residents; $24,532 per year for nonresidents. Fees $9173 (one-time charge). *Financial aid:* Federal Work-Study, institutionally sponsored loans available. Financial aid application deadline: 4/15; applicants required to submit FAFSA. • Dr. Carroll Bennett, Associate Dean for Admissions and Student Affairs, 352-392-7206. Fax: 352-392-3070. E-mail: bennett@dental.ufl.edu.

University of Illinois at Chicago, College of Dentistry, Professional Program in Dentistry, Chicago, IL 60607-7128. Awards DDS, DDS/MPH, DDS/MS, DDS/PhD. Approved by ADA. Students: 302 full-time (104 women), 1 part-time (0 women); includes 83 minority (4 African Americans, 64 Asian Americans, 14 Hispanics, 1 Native American), 14 international. 1,541 applicants, 6% accepted. In 1997, 71 degrees awarded. *Entrance requirements:* DAT. Application deadline: 12/31. Application fee: $40 ($50 for international students). *Financial aid:* Fellowships, research assistantships, teaching assistantships available. • Allen Anderson, Dean, College of Dentistry, 312-996-1040.

The University of Iowa, College of Dentistry, Professional Program in Dentistry, Iowa City, IA 52242-1316. Awards DDS. Approved by ADA. Faculty: 79 full-time, 98 part-time. Students: 285 full-time (98 women); includes 45 minority (11 African Americans, 14 Asian Americans, 15 Hispanics, 5 Native Americans), 4 international. Average age 24. 1,146 applicants, 7% accepted. In 1997, 68 degrees awarded. *Average time to degree:* first professional–4 years full-time. *Entrance requirements:* DAT, minimum of 94 semester hours with a minimum GPA of 2.5. Application deadline: 11/1 (rolling processing). Application fee: $30 ($50 for international students). *Financial aid:* 281 students received aid; research assistantships, teaching assistantships available. • Application contact: Dr. Yvonne M. Chalkley, Assistant Dean for Student Affairs, 319-335-7157. Fax: 319-335-7155.

University of Kentucky, College of Dentistry, Lexington, KY 40536-0084. Awards DMD, MS. One or more programs approved by ADA. Faculty: 67 full-time (9 women), 68 part-time (13 women). Students: 236 full-time (89 women); includes 29 minority (9 African Americans, 16 Asian Americans, 2 Hispanics, 2 Native Americans), 5 international. Average age 24. 1,196 applicants, 5% accepted. In 1997, 50 DMDs awarded (60% found work related to degree, 40% continued full-time study); 4 master's awarded (100% found work related to degree). *Degree requirements:* For master's, thesis, comprehensive exam required, foreign language not required. *Average time to degree:* master's–3 years full-time; first professional–4 years full-time. *Entrance requirements:* For DMD, DAT, minimum undergraduate GPA of 3.0; for master's, GRE General Test, minimum undergraduate GPA of 3.0. Application deadline: 11/1 (priority date; rolling processing). Application fee: $25. *Financial aid:* In 1997–98, 176 students received aid, including 6 research assistantships totaling $6,000; teaching assistantships, Federal Work-Study, institutionally sponsored loans, and career-related internships or fieldwork also available. Aid available to part-time students. Financial aid application deadline: 4/1. *Faculty research:* Dental amalgams and mercury, Alzheimer's and aging in oral health. Total annual research expenditures: $750,000. • Leon A. Assael, Dean, 606-323-5786. Application contact: Daniel Seaver, Director of Academic and Student Affairs, 606-323-6071. Fax: 606-323-1042. E-mail: seaver@pop.uky.edu.

University of Louisville, School of Dentistry, Professional Programs in Dentistry, Louisville, KY 40201. Awards DMD. Approved by ADA. Faculty: 50 full-time (12 women), 62 part-time (8 women), 70.46 FTE. Students: 277 full-time (92 women); includes 26 minority (10 African Americans, 12 Asian Americans, 2 Hispanics, 2 Native Americans), 4 international. Average age 26. In 1997, 60 degrees awarded. *Average time to degree:* first professional–4 years full-time. *Application fee:* $10. • Dr. Rowland A. Hutchinson Jr., Dean, School of Dentistry, 502-852-5293.

University of Manitoba, Faculty of Dentistry, Professional Program in Dentistry, Winnipeg, MB R3T 2N2, Canada. Awards DMD. Approved by ADA. Faculty: 46 full-time (6 women), 84 part-time (5 women). Students: 97 full-time (34 women). Average age 23. 270 applicants, 9% accepted. In 1997, 24 degrees awarded (100% found work related to degree). *Entrance requirements:* DAT, interview. Application deadline: 2/25. Application fee: $45. *Financial aid:* Institutionally sponsored loans and career-related internships or fieldwork available. Financial aid application deadline: 6/30. *Faculty research:* Oral physiology, microbiology, and biochemistry of the oral cavity in health and disease; application of clinical research. • Dr. R. C. Baker, Acting Dean, Faculty of Dentistry, 204-789-3631. Fax: 204-888-4113.

University of Maryland, Baltimore, Professional Program in Dentistry, Baltimore, MD 21201-1627. Awards DDS, DDS/PhD. DDS/PhD offered jointly with the Graduate Programs in Dentistry. Faculty: 114 full-time (22 women), 79 part-time (18 women). Students: 391 full-time (164 women). Average age 24. 1,963 applicants, 8% accepted. In 1997, 96 degrees awarded. *Average time to degree:* first professional–4 years full-time. *Entrance requirements:* DAT (minimum score 18). Application deadline: 1/1 (rolling processing). Application fee: $50. *Financial aid:* Research assistantships, Federal Work-Study, institutionally sponsored loans, and career-

Directory: Dentistry

University of Maryland, Baltimore (continued)
related internships or fieldwork available. Financial aid application deadline: 2/15; applicants required to submit FAFSA. *Faculty research:* Neuroscience, cell and molecular biology, infectious diseases and immune function. Total annual research expenditures: $29.9 million. • Dr. Richard R. Ranney, Dean, 410-706-7461. Application contact: Dr. Margaret Wilson, Assistant Dean for Admissions and Student Affairs, 410-706-7472. Fax: 410-706-0945.

University of Medicine and Dentistry of New Jersey, New Jersey Dental School, Newark, NJ 07107-3001. Awards DMD, Certificate, DMD/PhD. One or more programs approved by ADA. Faculty: 99 full-time (24 women), 95 part-time (19 women), 128.7 FTE. Students: 342 full-time (149 women). 1,087 applicants, 18% accepted. In 1997, 75 DMDs, 22 Certificates awarded. *Entrance requirements:* For DMD, DAT (minimum score 13; average 16). Application deadline: 3/15 (priority date; rolling processing). Application fee: $125. *Financial aid:* Fellowships, research assistantships, teaching assistantships, Federal Work-Study, institutionally sponsored loans available. • Dr. Robert A. Saporito, Acting Dean, 973-972-4633. Application contact: Dr. Zia Shey, Associate Dean, Student Affairs and Graduate Dental Education, 973-972-5064. Fax: 973-972-3689.

University of Michigan, School of Dentistry, Professional Program in Dentistry, Ann Arbor, MI 48109. Awards DDS. Approved by ADA. *Entrance requirements:* DAT. Application deadline: 2/1 (rolling processing). Application fee: $50. Electronic applications accepted. *Financial aid:* Fellowships, research assistantships, teaching assistantships available. Financial aid applicants required to submit FAFSA. • William E. Kotowicz, Dean, School of Dentistry, 734-763-3311. Application contact: Marilyn W. Woolfolk, Assistant Dean, 734-763-3316.

University of Minnesota, Twin Cities Campus, School of Dentistry, Professional Program in Dentistry, Minneapolis, MN 55455-0213. Awards DDS. Approved by ADA. Students: 287 full-time (99 women), 3 part-time (1 woman); includes 26 minority (1 African American, 24 Asian Americans, 1 Hispanic), 9 international. 881 applicants, 10% accepted. *Entrance requirements:* DAT (average 16). Application deadline: 1/1 (rolling processing). Application fee: $55. • Gale L. Shea, Director of Enrollment Management, 612-625-7149. E-mail: sheax001@maroon.tc.umn.edu. Application contact: Laura J. Roland, Recruitment Coordinator, 612-624-6960. Fax: 612-626-2654. E-mail: bolan005@maroon.tc.umn.edu.

University of Mississippi Medical Center, School of Dentistry, Jackson, MS 39216-4505. Awards DMD. Approved by ADA. Faculty: 40 full-time (5 women), 45 part-time (8 women), 48.1 FTE. Students: 120 full-time (40 women); includes 14 minority (11 African Americans, 2 Asian Americans, 1 Native American). Average age 25. 145 applicants, 21% accepted. In 1997, 27 degrees awarded. *Entrance requirements:* DAT. Application deadline: 12/1 (rolling processing). Application fee: $25. *Expenses:* Tuition $4400 per year for state residents; $10,400 per year for nonresidents. Fees $998 per year. *Financial aid:* In 1997–98, 8 scholarships (2 to first-year students) were awarded; Federal Work-Study, institutionally sponsored loans also available. Financial aid application deadline: 4/1. *Faculty research:* Bone growth factors, salivary markers of disease, biomaterial synthesis and evaluation, metabolic bone disease, periodontal disease. Total annual research expenditures: $854,157. • Dr. J. Perry McGinnis Jr., Dean, 601-984-6000. Fax: 601-984-6014. E-mail: trip@fiona.umcmed.edu. Application contact: Dr. Billy M. Bishop, Director, Student Services and Records, 601-984-1080. Fax: 601-984-1079. E-mail: bmb@fiona.umsmed.edu.

University of Missouri–Kansas City, School of Dentistry, Professional Program in Dentistry, Kansas City, MO 64110-2499. Awards DDS. Approved by ADA. Faculty: 107 full-time (28 women), 71 part-time (15 women), 119.1 FTE. Students: 311 full-time (111 women). Average age 25. 867 applicants, 11% accepted. In 1997, 74 degrees awarded. *Entrance requirements:* DAT (minimum score 16). Application deadline: 1/1. Application fee: $25. *Expenses:* Tuition $12,915 per year for state residents; $25,974 per year for nonresidents. Fees $326 per year. *Financial aid:* Federal Work-Study, institutionally sponsored loans available. Aid available to part-time students. Financial aid application deadline: 3/15; applicants required to submit FAFSA. *Faculty research:* Aesthetic crowns (microleakage), ultrasonic versus manual filing of root canal, effect of wash times/techniques on enamel/composite bond strengths, analgesic efficacy and postoperative dental pain. • Application contact: Dianne D. Beard, Coordinator, Office of Student Programs, 816-235-2080.

University of Nebraska Medical Center, College of Dentistry, Professional Program in Dentistry, Omaha, NE 68198-0001. Awards DDS. Approved by ADA. Faculty: 58 full-time (11 women), 45 part-time (8 women). Students: 171 full-time (48 women), 1 (woman) part-time; includes 5 minority (1 Asian American, 3 Hispanics, 1 Native American), 2 international. Average age 26. 784 applicants, 7% accepted. In 1997, 44 degrees awarded. *Entrance requirements:* DAT. Application deadline: 3/1 (priority date). Application fee: $25. *Financial aid:* 166 students received aid; Federal Work-Study, institutionally sponsored loans available. Aid available to part-time students. Financial aid application deadline: 3/1; applicants required to submit FAFSA. • Application contact: Glenda Canfield, Admissions Secretary, 402-472-1363.

University of Nebraska Medical Center, College of Dentistry, Program in Dentistry, Omaha, NE 68198-0001. Awards Certificate. Faculty: 39 full-time (6 women). Students: 23 full-time (2 women). Average age 31. 196 applicants, 6% accepted. *Degree requirements:* Thesis or alternative required, foreign language not required. *Entrance requirements:* GRE or National Board Dental Exam, DDS or DMD. Application deadline: 2/1. Application fee: $25. *Financial aid:* Institutionally sponsored loans and career-related internships or fieldwork available. Aid available to part-time students. Financial aid application deadline: 3/1. • Dr. Jeffrey Payne, Chair, 402-472-1318. Application contact: Teresa Powell, Admissions Secretary, 402-472-1366.

The University of North Carolina at Chapel Hill, School of Dentistry, Professional Program in Dentistry, Chapel Hill, NC 27599. Awards DDS. Approved by ADA. Students: 304 full-time (133 women); includes 57 minority (24 African Americans, 22 Asian Americans, 8 Hispanics, 3 Native Americans), 3 international. Average age 24. 999 applicants, 11% accepted. In 1997, 65 degrees awarded. *Entrance requirements:* DAT, interview. Application deadline: 11/1 (rolling processing). Application fee: $60. *Expenses:* Tuition $2502 per year full-time, $626 per semester (minimum) part-time for state residents; $20,340 per year full-time, $5085 per semester (minimum) part-time for nonresidents. Fees $1041 per year full-time, $461 per semester (minimum) part-time. *Financial aid:* Grants, Federal Work-Study, institutionally sponsored loans available. Financial aid application deadline: 3/1. • Dr. Ronald Hunt, Associate Dean for Academic Affairs, 919-966-4451. Application contact: Dr. David Brunson, Director of Admissions and Student Services, 919-966-4565. Fax: 919-966-7007.

University of Oklahoma Health Sciences Center, College of Dentistry, Professional Program in Dentistry, Oklahoma City, OK 73190. Awards DDS. Approved by ADA. Students: 217 full-time (67 women); includes 49 minority (3 African Americans, 14 Asian Americans, 4 Hispanics, 28 Native Americans), 6 international. Average age 26. 654 applicants, 8% accepted. In 1997, 46 degrees awarded (67% found work related to degree, 33% continued full-time study). *Average time to degree:* first professional–4 years full-time. *Entrance requirements:* DAT, TOEFL (minimum score 550), minimum GPA of 2.0. Application deadline: 12/1 (rolling processing). Application fee: $50 ($75 for international students). *Financial aid:* Institutionally sponsored loans available. *Faculty research:* Dental caries, microwave sterilization, dental care delivery systems, dental materials, oral health of Native Americans. • Application contact: Dr. Kevin T. Avery, Assistant Dean for Student Affairs, 405-271-3530.

University of Pennsylvania, School of Dental Medicine, Philadelphia, PA 19104. Awards DMD, DMD/MS Ed. Approved by ADA. DMD/MS Ed offered jointly with the Graduate School of Education. Faculty: 71 full-time (12 women), 169 part-time (28 women). Students: 429 full-time (180 women), 1 (woman) part-time; includes 137 minority (10 African Americans, 111 Asian Americans, 16 Hispanics), 60 international. 1,992 applicants, 14% accepted. In 1997, 123 degrees awarded. *Average time to degree:* first professional–4 years full-time. *Entrance requirements:* DAT. Application deadline: 2/1 (rolling processing). Application fee: $45. *Expenses:* Tuition $33,340 per year. Fees $1178 per year. *Financial aid:* Federal Work-Study, institutionally sponsored loans available. Financial aid application deadline: 6/1; applicants required to submit FAFSA. *Faculty research:* Infectious disease, bone and mineralization, connective tissue, molecular biology, oral pathogens. • Dr. Raymond Fonseca, Dean, 215-898-8941. Application contact: Corky Cacas, Director of Admissions, 215-898-8943. Fax: 215-898-5243.

University of Pittsburgh, School of Dental Medicine, Professional Program in Dental Medicine, Pittsburgh, PA 15260. Awards DMD. Approved by ADA. Faculty: 85 full-time (23 women), 69 part-time (15 women). Students: 340 full-time (123 women); includes 68 minority (13 African Americans, 49 Asian Americans, 5 Hispanics, 1 Native American), 22 international. In 1997, 86 degrees awarded. *Entrance requirements:* DAT (minimum score 16; average 19), TOEFL (minimum score 650). Application fee: $35. *Financial aid:* Federal Work-Study, institutionally sponsored loans available. Financial aid applicants required to submit FAFSA. • Application contact: Dr. Albert Whitehead, Director for Student Services, 412-648-8422. Fax: 412-648-9571. E-mail: aww1+@pitt.edu.

University of Puerto Rico, Medical Sciences Campus, School of Dentistry, Professional Program in Dentistry, San Juan, PR 00936-5067. Awards DMD. Approved by ADA. Students: 161 full-time (88 women). Average age 23. 270 applicants, 17% accepted. In 1997, 45 degrees awarded. *Degree requirements:* 1 foreign language required, thesis not required. *Entrance requirements:* DAT (minimum score 12; average 16), interview. Application deadline: 12/15. Application fee: $15. *Financial aid:* In 1997–98, 40 research assistantships, 2 teaching assistantships were awarded; partial tuition waivers, Federal Work-Study, institutionally sponsored loans also available. Financial aid application deadline: 5/12. • Dr. Antonio Soto Singala, Assistant Dean, 787-758-2525 Ext. 1113. Fax: 787-751-0990.

University of Saskatchewan, College of Dentistry, Saskatoon, SK S7N 5E5, Canada. Awards DMD. Approved by ADA. Faculty: 20 full-time, 55 part-time. Students: 104 full-time (56 women). 800 applicants, 3% accepted. In 1997, 19 degrees awarded. *Application deadline:* 1/31. *Application fee:* $40. *Financial aid:* Career-related internships or fieldwork available. • R. E. McDermott, Dean, 306-966-5122. Application contact: R. Kluge, Admission Secretary, 306-966-5117. Fax: 306-966-5126.

University of Southern California, School of Dentistry, Professional Program in Dentistry, Los Angeles, CA 90089. Awards DDS, Certificate, DDS/MBA, DDS/MS. One or more programs approved by ADA. Students: 596 full-time (202 women); includes 300 minority (9 African Americans, 275 Asian Americans, 12 Hispanics, 4 Native Americans), 12 international. Average age 30. In 1997, 139 DDSs awarded. *Entrance requirements:* For DDS, DAT. Application fee: $55. *Financial aid:* In 1997–98, 67 fellowships, 9 scholarships were awarded; research assistantships, teaching assistantships, Federal Work-Study, institutionally sponsored loans also available. Aid available to part-time students. Financial aid application deadline: 2/15; applicants required to submit FAFSA. • Dr. Howard Landesman, Dean, School of Dentistry, 213-740-2811.

University of Tennessee, Memphis, College of Dentistry, Memphis, TN 38163-0002. Awards DDS, MS. One or more programs approved by ADA. *Degree requirements:* For master's, thesis. *Entrance requirements:* For DDS, DAT, interview, preprofessional evaluation. Application deadline: 2/28 (rolling processing). Application fee: $25.

The University of Texas Health Science Center at San Antonio, Dental School, San Antonio, TX 78229. Awards DDS, MS, Certificate. One or more programs approved by ADA. Faculty: 129 full-time, 84 part-time. Students: 351 full-time (138 women); includes 121 minority (7 African Americans, 63 Asian Americans, 48 Hispanics, 3 Native Americans). Average age 24. 932 applicants, 12% accepted. In 1997, 86 DDSs, 15 master's, 17 Certificates awarded. *Degree requirements:* For master's, thesis required, foreign language not required. *Average time to degree:* master's–3 years full-time; first professional–4 years full-time; other advanced degree–2.5 years full-time. *Entrance requirements:* For DDS, DAT; for master's, GRE General Test (minimum combined score of 1000), DDS; for Certificate, DDS. *Financial aid:* 340 students received aid; teaching assistantships, institutionally sponsored loans available. Financial aid application deadline: 3/1; applicants required to submit FAFSA. *Faculty research:* Nutrition and oral health, periodontal disease, biomaterials, bone mineralization, caries prevention. • Dr. Joseph M. Berrong, Interim Associate Dean, 210-567-3752. Fax: 210-567-6721. E-mail: berrong@uthscsa.edu. Application contact: Lisa Serna, Office of Admissions and Student Services, 210-567-2674. E-mail: serna@uthscsa.edu.

The University of Texas–Houston Health Science Center, Dental Branch, Houston, TX 77025. Awards DDS. Approved by ADA. Students: 248 full-time (107 women). 1,117 applicants, 6% accepted. In 1997, 65 degrees awarded. *Entrance requirements:* DAT. Application deadline: 11/1. Application fee: $80. • Dr. Ronald Johnson, Dean, 713-500-4021. Application contact: Dr. H. Philip Pierpont, Assistant Dean for Student Affairs, 713-500-4151. Fax: 713-500-4425. E-mail: studentaffairs@bite.db.uth.tmc.edu.

University of the Pacific, School of Dentistry, International Dental Studies Program, San Francisco, CA 94115. Awards DDS. Approved by ADA. Faculty: 28 full-time (1 woman). Students: 30 full-time (22 women); includes 10 minority (all Asian Americans), 6 international. Average age 32. 110 applicants, 15% accepted. In 1997, 12 degrees awarded. *Average time to degree:* first professional–2 years full-time. *Entrance requirements:* National Board Dental Exam I (minimum score 75), TOEFL (minimum score 575), foreign dental degree. Application deadline: 3/1 (rolling processing). Application fee: $60. *Expenses:* Tuition $42,300 per year. Fees $3141 per year. *Financial aid:* Institutionally sponsored loans available. Financial aid application deadline: 2/1; applicants required to submit FAFSA. *Faculty research:* Temporomandibular joint, facial pain, cell kinetics, cell membrane transport, virus/cell fusion. • Dr. David B. Nielsen, Associate Dean, Postgraduate and Community Programs, 415-929-6486. Application contact: Patricia King, Director, 415-929-6688.

University of the Pacific, School of Dentistry, Professional Program in Dentistry, San Francisco, CA 94115. Awards DDS. Approved by ADA. Students: 401 full-time (142 women); includes 148 minority (2 African Americans, 141 Asian Americans, 5 Hispanics). Average age 26. 2,251 applicants, 10% accepted. In 1997, 129 degrees awarded. *Average time to degree:* first professional–3 years full-time. *Entrance requirements:* DAT. Application deadline: 3/1 (priority date). Application fee: $75. *Expenses:* Tuition $31,517 per year. Fees $12,605 per year. *Financial aid:* In 1997–98, 324 students received aid, including 5 fellowships (1 to a first-year student) totaling $8,653; institutionally sponsored loans also available. Aid available to part-time students. Financial aid application deadline: 3/2; applicants required to submit FAFSA. *Faculty research:* Cell kinetics, cell membrane transport, virus/cell fusion, implants, bioenergy transduction. • Application contact: Dr. Craig Yarborough, Assistant Dean for Student Services, 415-929-6491.

University of Toronto, Faculty of Dentistry, Professional Program in Dentistry, Toronto, ON M5G 1G6, Canada. Awards DDS, DDS/PhD. Approved by ADA. Students: 291 full-time (122 women). 685 applicants, 13% accepted. In 1997, 64 degrees awarded. *Entrance requirements:* Canadian Dental Aptitude Test. Application deadline: 12/1. Application fee: $120. • Application contact: Alexandra Haldane, Admissions Officer, 416-979-4901 Ext. 4374. Fax: 416-979-4936. E-mail: ahaldane@dental.utoronto.ca.

University of Washington, School of Dentistry, Professional Program in Dentistry, Seattle, WA 98195. Awards DDS, DDS/MS. Approved by ADA. Faculty: 73 full-time (15 women), 46 part-time (12 women). Students: 210 full-time (75 women); includes 86 minority (5 African Americans, 71 Asian Americans, 7 Hispanics, 3 Native Americans). Average age 25. 1,150 applicants, 5% accepted. In 1997, 45 degrees awarded. *Entrance requirements:* DAT (minimum score 20). Application deadline: 12/1 (rolling processing). Application fee: $35. *Tuition:* $8823 per year for state residents; $22,251 per year for nonresidents. *Financial aid:* Full and partial tuition waivers, Federal Work-Study, institutionally sponsored loans available. Aid available to part-time students. Financial aid application deadline: 2/28; applicants required to submit FAFSA. • Application contact: Kathleen Craig, Admissions Assistant, 206-543-5840.

The University of Western Ontario, Faculty of Medicine and Dentistry, School of Dentistry, Professional Program in Dentistry, London, ON N6A 5C1, Canada. Awards DDS. Approved by ADA. Faculty: 115. Students: 160. In 1997, 40 degrees awarded. *Entrance requirements:* DAT (Canadian version), minimum B average. Application deadline: 12/1. Application fee: $0. *Financial aid:* Federal Work-Study, institutionally sponsored loans available. • Application contact: Dr. D. W. Banting, Associate Dean (Academic), 519-661-3330.

Virginia Commonwealth University, Medical College of Virginia-Professional Programs, School of Dentistry, Richmond, VA 23284-9005. Awards DDS, DDS/MS, DDS/PhD. Approved by ADA. DDS/MS and DDS/PhD offered jointly with the School of Graduate Studies. Students: 314 full-time (102 women). Average age 28. In 1997, 78 degrees awarded. *Entrance requirements:* DAT, TOEFL. Application deadline: 2/1 (rolling processing). *Financial aid:* Fellowships available. • Dr. Lindsay M. Hunt, Dean, 804-828-9183. Fax: 804-828-4913. E-mail: lmhunt@gems.vcu.edu. Application contact: Dr. Marshall Brownstein, Assistant Dean, Student Affairs and Admissions, 804-828-9196. Fax: 804-828-5288. E-mail: mbrownstein@gems.vcu.edu.

West Virginia University, School of Dentistry, Professional Program in Dentistry, Morgantown, WV 26506. Awards DDS. Approved by ADA. Students: 156 full-time (37 women); includes 21 minority (4 African Americans, 15 Asian Americans, 2 Hispanics), 1 international. Average age 25. 1,125 applicants, 4% accepted. In 1997, 26 degrees awarded (100% found work related to degree). *Average time to degree:* first professional–4 years full-time. *Entrance requirements:* DAT, TOEFL (minimum score 550). Application deadline: 3/1 (rolling processing). Application fee: $100. *Tuition:* $5374 per year for state residents; $14,058 per year for nonresidents. *Financial aid:* Federal Work-Study, institutionally sponsored loans available. Financial aid application deadline: 3/1; applicants required to submit FAFSA. • Dr. William R. McCutcheon, Associate Dean, 304-293-3549. Application contact: Loreen Hurley, Student Records Assistant, 304-293-6133. Fax: 304-293-8561.

Oral and Dental Sciences

Baylor College of Dentistry, Department of Biomaterials Science, Dallas, TX 75266-0677. Awards MS. Part-time programs available. Faculty: 3 full-time (2 women). Students: 0. 0 applicants. *Degree requirements:* Thesis required, foreign language not required. *Entrance requirements:* GRE General Test, National Board Dental Examination, TOEFL, DDS or DMD. Application fee: $35. *Expenses:* Tuition $48 per quarter hour for state residents; $166 per quarter hour for nonresidents. Fees $24 per quarter hour. *Financial aid:* Fellowships, research assistantships, teaching assistantships, institutionally sponsored loans available. Aid available to part-time students. Financial aid application deadline: 2/23; applicants required to submit FAFSA. *Faculty research:* Titanium casting for dental applications, mercury release, dental amalgams, impression materials. • Dr. Toru Okabe, Chair, 214-828-8190. Fax: 214-828-8458. E-mail: tokabe@tambcd.edu.

Baylor College of Dentistry, Department of Oral and Maxillofacial Surgery, Dallas, TX 75266-0677. Awards MD, Certificate. MD offered jointly with Texas Tech University. Faculty: 7 full-time (0 women), 6 part-time (1 woman). Students: 13 full-time (4 women); includes 1 minority (Hispanic), 1 international. Average age 27. 125 applicants, 2% accepted. In 1997, 3 Certificates awarded. *Degree requirements:* For Certificate, thesis required, foreign language not required. *Average time to degree:* first professional–4 years full-time; other advanced degree–4 years full-time. *Entrance requirements:* For MD, DAT, MCAT; for Certificate, GRE General Test, National Board Dental Examination, TOEFL, DDS or DMD. Application deadline: 10/15. Application fee: $35. *Expenses:* Tuition $48 per quarter hour for state residents; $166 per quarter hour for nonresidents. Fees $24 per quarter hour. *Financial aid:* 4 students received aid; fellowships, research assistantships, teaching assistantships, institutionally sponsored loans available. Aid available to part-time students. Financial aid application deadline: 2/23; applicants required to submit FAFSA. *Faculty research:* Dental implants, temporomandibular joint, recombinant BMP-2. • Dr. Sterling R. Schow, Program Director, 214-828-8104. Fax: 214-828-8382.

Baylor College of Dentistry, Department of Orthodontics, Dallas, TX 75266-0677. Awards MS, Certificate. Faculty: 4 full-time (0 women), 23 part-time (0 women). Students: 10 full-time (4 women); includes 1 minority (Hispanic), 1 international. Average age 29. 171 applicants, 3% accepted. *Degree requirements:* Thesis required, foreign language not required. *Average time to degree:* master's–2 years full-time; other advanced degree–2 years full-time. *Entrance requirements:* GRE General Test, National Board Dental Examination, TOEFL, DDS or DMD. Application deadline: 9/15. Application fee: $35. *Expenses:* Tuition $48 per quarter hour for state residents; $166 per quarter hour for nonresidents. Fees $24 per quarter hour. *Financial aid:* 10 students received aid; fellowships, research assistantships, institutionally sponsored loans available. Aid available to part-time students. Financial aid application deadline: 2/23; applicants required to submit FAFSA. *Faculty research:* Craniofacial biology, distraction osteogenesis, clinical orthodontics, function and shape memory alloys. • Dr. Rolf G. Behrents, Chair, 214-828-8120. Fax: 214-828-8159.

Baylor College of Dentistry, Department of Pediatric Dentistry, Dallas, TX 75266-0677. Awards MS, Certificate. Part-time programs available. Faculty: 8 full-time (4 women), 8 part-time (3 women). Students: 14 full-time (11 women), 1 part-time (0 women); includes 1 minority (Hispanic). Average age 28. 59 applicants, 8% accepted. *Degree requirements:* Thesis required, foreign language not required. *Entrance requirements:* GRE General Test, National Board Dental Examination, TOEFL, DDS or DMD. Application deadline: 11/1. Application fee: $35. *Expenses:* Tuition $48 per quarter hour for state residents; $166 per quarter hour for nonresidents. Fees $24 per quarter hour. *Financial aid:* 10 students received aid; fellowships, research assistantships, teaching assistantships, institutionally sponsored loans available. Aid available to part-time students. Financial aid application deadline: 2/23; applicants required to submit FAFSA. *Faculty research:* Pulp biology, pharmacologic methods of behavior management. • Dr. N. S. Seale, Chair, 214-828-8131. Fax: 214-828-8132.

Baylor College of Dentistry, Department of Periodontics, Dallas, TX 75266-0677. Awards MS, Certificate. Part-time programs available. Faculty: 6 full-time (2 women), 10 part-time (1 woman). Students: 10 full-time (2 women); includes 8 minority (3 Asian Americans, 5 Hispanics). Average age 30. 20 applicants, 15% accepted. *Degree requirements:* Thesis required, foreign language not required. *Average time to degree:* master's–3 years full-time; other advanced degree–3 years full-time. *Entrance requirements:* GRE General Test, National Board Dental Examination, TOEFL, DDS or DMD. Application deadline: 10/1. Application fee: $35. *Expenses:* Tuition $48 per quarter hour for state residents; $166 per quarter hour for nonresidents. Fees $24 per quarter hour. *Financial aid:* Fellowships, research assistantships, teaching assistantships, institutionally sponsored loans available. Aid available to part-time students. Financial aid application deadline: 2/23; applicants required to submit FAFSA. *Faculty research:* Dental implants, quantification of *candida albicans* in adult periodontitis: a survey, smoking, wound healing, stomatology. • Dr. William W. Hallmon, Program Director, 214-828-8140.

Baylor College of Dentistry, Department of Restorative Sciences, Field of Endodontics, Dallas, TX 75266-0677. Awards MS, PhD, Certificate. Faculty: 2 full-time (0 women), 1 part-time (0 women). Students: 12 full-time (4 women); includes 6 international. Average age 32. 84 applicants, 5% accepted. In 1997, 3 master's, 3 Certificates awarded. *Degree requirements:* For master's and doctorate, thesis/dissertation required, foreign language not required. *Entrance requirements:* For master's and Certificate, GRE General Test, National Board Dental Examination, TOEFL, DDS or DMD; for doctorate, GRE General Test, TOEFL, DDS or DMD. Application deadline: 10/1. Application fee: $35. *Expenses:* Tuition $48 per quarter hour for state residents; $166 per quarter hour for nonresidents. Fees $24 per quarter hour. *Financial aid:* Fellowships, research assistantships, teaching assistantships, institutionally sponsored loans available. Aid available to part-time students. Financial aid application deadline: 2/23; applicants required to submit FAFSA. *Faculty research:* Periradicular healing in response to a biologically inductive root-end filling material. • Dr. James L. Gutmann, Director, 214-828-8361. E-mail: jgutmann@tambcd.edu. Application contact: Aglae McCoy, Department Secretary, 214-828-8365. Fax: 214-828-8209. E-mail: amccoy@tambcd.edu.

Baylor College of Dentistry, Department of Restorative Sciences, Field of Prosthodontics, Dallas, TX 75266-0677. Awards MS, Certificate. Part-time programs available. Faculty: 1 full-time (0 women), 12 part-time (2 women). Students: 9 full-time (2 women), 4 part-time (1 woman); includes 3 minority (2 Asian Americans, 1 Hispanic), 2 international. Average age 30. 19 applicants, 16% accepted. In 1997, 2 master's, 3 Certificates awarded. *Degree requirements:* For master's, thesis required, foreign language not required. *Entrance requirements:* GRE General Test, National Board Dental Examination, TOEFL, DDS or DMD. Application deadline: 11/1. Application fee: $35. *Expenses:* Tuition $48 per quarter hour for state residents; $166 per quarter hour for nonresidents. Fees $24 per quarter hour. *Financial aid:* Fellowships, research assistantships, teaching assistantships, institutionally sponsored loans available. Aid available to part-time students. Financial aid application deadline: 2/23; applicants required to submit FAFSA. *Faculty research:* Biomaterials, implants. • Dr. Ronald D. Woody, Director, 214-828-8376. Fax: 214-874-4544. E-mail: rwoody@tambcd.edu.

Boston University, Henry M. Goldman School of Dental Medicine, Graduate Programs in Dentistry, Boston, MA 02215. Offerings in advanced general dentistry (CAGS), dental public health (MS, MSD, D Sc D, CAGS), dentistry (D Sc D), endodontics (MSD, D Sc D, CAGS), nutritional science (MS, D Sc, D Sc D), operative dentistry (MSD, D Sc D, CAGS), oral and maxillofacial surgery (MSD, D Sc D, CAGS), oral biology (MSD, D Sc, D Sc D), orthodontics (MSD, D Sc D, CAGS), pediatric dentistry (MSD, D Sc D, CAGS), periodontology (MSD, D Sc D, CAGS), prosthodontics (MSD, D Sc D, CAGS). Faculty: 83 full-time (23 women), 214 part-time (26 women). Students: 186 full-time (60 women); includes 17 minority (1 African American, 9 Asian Americans, 7 Hispanics), 89 international. Average age 30. 717 applicants, 15% accepted. In 1997, 9 master's, 7 doctorates, 65 CAGSs awarded. *Degree requirements:* For master's and doctorate, thesis/dissertation; for CAGS, thesis (for some programs). *Average time to degree:* master's–1 year full-time; doctorate–2 years full-time; other advanced degree–2.5 years full-time. *Entrance requirements:* For CAGS, dental degree. Application fee: $50. *Expenses:* Tuition $22,830 per year full-time, $713 per credit part-time. Fees $218 per year full-time, $40 per semester part-time. *Financial aid:* 30 students received aid; institutionally sponsored loans and career-related internships or fieldwork available. Aid available to part-time students. Financial aid application deadline: 4/15; applicants required to submit FAFSA. • Application contact: Postdoctoral Admissions, 617-638-4708.

See in-depth description on page 1709.

Case Western Reserve University, Schools of Dentistry and Graduate Studies, Graduate Programs in Dentistry, Cleveland, OH 44106. Offerings in advanced general dentistry (Certificate), endodontics (MSD), oral surgery (Certificate), orthodontics (MSD), pedodontics (Certificate), periodontics (MSD). Faculty: 12 full-time (1 woman), 83 part-time (8 women), 26 FTE. Students: 28 full-time (5 women); includes 9 minority (1 African American, 7 Asian Americans, 1 Hispanic). Average age 32. 400 applicants, 4% accepted. In 1997, 15 master's awarded (100% found work related to degree). *Degree requirements:* For master's, thesis required, foreign language not required. *Average time to degree:* master's–2 years full-time. *Entrance requirements:* For master's, TOEFL (minimum score 550), DDS, minimum GPA of 3.0; for Certificate, DDS. Application deadline: 10/1 (rolling processing). Application fee: $50. *Expenses:* Tuition $25,700 per year. Fees $800 per year. *Financial aid:* 12 students received aid; Federal Work-Study, institutionally sponsored loans available. Financial aid application deadline: 4/20; applicants required to submit FAFSA. • Dr. Stanley Hirsch, Associate Dean for Graduate Studies, 216-368-6731. Fax: 216-368-3204. E-mail: cxk42@po.cwru.edu.

Columbia University, School of Dental and Oral Surgery and Graduate School of Arts and Sciences, Graduate Program in Dental and Oral Surgery, New York, NY 10027. Offers clinical specialty (MA). Faculty: 18 full-time (2 women), 2 part-time (0 women). *Degree requirements:* Thesis, presentation of seminar. *Entrance requirements:* GRE General Test, DDS or equivalent. Application fee: $50 ($95 for international students). *Tuition:* $27,640 per year. *Financial aid:* Fellowships, research assistantships, teaching assistantships, full and partial tuition waivers, institutionally sponsored loans available. *Faculty research:* Analysis of growth/form, pulpal microcirculation, implants, microbiology of oral environment, calcified tissues. • Application contact: Dr. L. Moss-Salentijn, Assistant Dean, 212-305-2425.

Dalhousie University, Faculties of Graduate Studies and Dentistry, Graduate Programs in Dentistry, Department of Oral and Maxillofacial Sciences, Halifax, NS B3H 3J5, Canada. Awards MD/M Sc. Offered jointly with the Faculty of Dentistry and the Faculty of Medicine. Faculty: 11. Students: 5 full-time (0 women). *Application deadline:* 6/1 (rolling processing). *Application fee:* $55. *Financial aid:* Career-related internships or fieldwork available. *Faculty research:* Cleft lip/palate, jaw biomechanics. • Dr. D. S. Precious, Chair, 902-494-1679. Fax: 902-494-2527. Application contact: Doris Mahoney, Secretary, 902-494-1679.

Emory University, School of Medicine, Department of Surgery, Atlanta, GA 30322-1100. Offers programs in general practice (Certificate), oral maxillofacial surgery (Certificate), oral pathology (Certificate). Faculty: 15. Students: 15. *Entrance requirements:* DAT, DDS or MD. *Expenses:* Tuition $25,770 per year. Fees $400 per year. • Dr. Thomas J. Lawley, Dean, School of Medicine, 404-727-5650. Application contact: Dr. John Stone, Associate Dean and Director of Admissions, 404-727-5660. Fax: 404-727-0045. E-mail: medschadmiss@medadm.emory.edu.

Harvard University, School of Dental Medicine, Postdoctoral Programs in Dentistry, 188 Longwood Avenue, Boston, MA 02115. Offerings in advanced general dentistry (Certificate), general practice residency (Certificate), oral biology (M Med Sc, D Med Sc), oral surgery (Certificate), pediatric dentistry (Certificate). Faculty: 90 full-time. Students: 130. In 1997, 14 master's, 9 doctorates awarded. • John DaSilva, Director, 617-432-1376. Application contact: Dr. Ellen M. Libert, Associate Dean for Students, 617-432-1443. Fax: 617-432-3881. E-mail: elibert@warren.med.harvard.edu.

Indiana University–Purdue University Indianapolis, School of Dentistry, Graduate Programs in Dentistry, Indianapolis, IN 46202. Offerings in dental materials (MS, MSD), dental sciences (PhD), diagnostic sciences (MS, MSD), oral biology (PhD), orthodontics (MS, MSD), pediatric dentistry (MSD), periodontics (MSD), preventive and community dentistry (PhD), preventive dentistry (MS, MSD), prosthodontics (MSD). Faculty: 66 full-time (8 women), 23 part-time (1

Directory: Oral and Dental Sciences

Indiana University–Purdue University Indianapolis (continued)

woman). Students: 89 full-time (28 women), 24 part-time (6 women); includes 8 minority (1 African American, 5 Asian Americans, 2 Hispanics), 45 international. Average age 29. 550 applicants, 6% accepted. In 1997, 29 master's, 2 doctorates awarded. *Degree requirements:* Thesis/dissertation, qualifying exam required, foreign language not required. *Average time to degree:* master's–2.5 years full-time; doctorate–4 years full-time. *Entrance requirements:* TOEFL (minimum score 570; average 580), DDS or DMD. Application deadline: 10/1. Application fee: $35 ($55 for international students). *Financial aid:* Research assistantships, teaching assistantships, institutionally sponsored loans available. Financial aid application deadline: 3/1; applicants required to submit FAFSA. *Faculty research:* Histopathology, microbiology, bone physiology, cell differentiation, metabolic/mechanical interactions. • Application contact: Dr. Chris Miller, Director, 317-274-8173. Fax: 317-274-2419.

Loma Linda University, Graduate School, Graduate Programs in Dentistry, Program in Endodontics, Loma Linda, CA 92350. Awards MS, Certificate, MS/Certificate. *Degree requirements:* For master's, thesis required, foreign language not required. *Entrance requirements:* For master's, GRE General Test (minimum score 500 on each section), DDS or DMD, minimum GPA of 3.0. Application fee: $40. *Tuition:* $380 per unit. • Dr. Mahmoud Torabinejad, Coordinator, 909-824-4681.

Loma Linda University, Graduate School, Graduate Programs in Dentistry, Program in Implant Dentistry, Loma Linda, CA 92350. Awards MS, Certificate, MS/Certificate. *Degree requirements:* For master's, thesis required, foreign language not required. *Entrance requirements:* For master's, GRE General Test (minimum score 500 on each section), DDS or DMD, minimum GPA of 3.0. Application fee: $40. *Tuition:* $380 per unit. • Dr. Jaime Lozada, Coordinator.

Loma Linda University, Graduate School, Graduate Programs in Dentistry, Program in Oral and Maxillofacial Surgery, Loma Linda, CA 92350. Awards MS, Certificate, MS/Certificate. *Degree requirements:* For master's, thesis required, foreign language not required. *Entrance requirements:* For master's, GRE General Test (minimum score 500 on each section), DDS or DMD, minimum GPA of 3.0. Application fee: $40. *Tuition:* $380 per unit. • Dr. Keith Hoffmann, Coordinator.

Loma Linda University, Graduate School, Graduate Programs in Dentistry, Program in Orthodontics, Loma Linda, CA 92350. Awards MS, Certificate, MS/Certificate. *Degree requirements:* For master's, thesis required, foreign language not required. *Entrance requirements:* For master's, GRE General Test (minimum score 500 on each section), DDS or DMD, minimum GPA of 3.0. Application fee: $40. *Tuition:* $380 per unit. • Dr. M. Toufic Jeiroudi, Coordinator.

Loma Linda University, Graduate School, Graduate Programs in Dentistry, Program in Periodontics, Loma Linda, CA 92350. Awards MS. *Degree requirements:* Thesis required, foreign language not required. *Entrance requirements:* GRE General Test (minimum score 500 on each section), DDS or DMD, minimum GPA of 3.0. Application fee: $40. *Tuition:* $380 per unit. • Dr. Max Crigger, Coordinator.

Marquette University, School of Dentistry and Graduate School, Graduate Programs in Dentistry, Program in Advanced Education in General Dentistry, Milwaukee, WI 53201-1881. Awards MS. *Degree requirements:* Thesis required, foreign language not required. *Entrance requirements:* TOEFL (minimum score 550), DDS or equivalent. Application deadline: rolling. Application fee: $40. *Expenses:* Tuition $12,060 per year full-time, $670 per credit part-time. Fees $6025 per year. *Financial aid:* Application deadline 10/1. • Dr. Ann Weber, Director, 414-288-6577. Application contact: Dr. Ordean J. Oyen, Dean of Graduate Studies, 414-288-5670. Fax: 414-288-3586.

Marquette University, School of Dentistry and Graduate School, Graduate Programs in Dentistry, Program in Dental Biomaterials, Milwaukee, WI 53201-1881. Awards MS. Part-time programs available. Faculty: 1 full-time (0 women), 1 part-time (0 women). Students: 3 full-time (1 woman); includes 3 international. Average age 26. 8 applicants, 13% accepted. In 1997, 2 degrees awarded (50% entered university research/teaching, 50% found other work related to degree). *Degree requirements:* Thesis required, foreign language not required. *Average time to degree:* master's–2 years full-time. *Entrance requirements:* TOEFL (minimum score 550). Application deadline: 3/1 (rolling processing). Application fee: $40. *Expenses:* Tuition $12,060 per year full-time, $670 per credit part-time. Fees $6025 per year. *Financial aid:* In 1997–98, 2 students received aid, including 2 teaching assistantships averaging $300 per month and totaling $7,200; career-related internships or fieldwork also available. Financial aid application deadline: 10/1. *Faculty research:* Composite resins, dentin bonding agents. • Dr. Virendra Dhuru, Director, 414-288-7152. E-mail: dhuruv@vms.csd.mu.edu. Application contact: Dr. Ordean J. Oyen, Dean of Graduate Studies, 414-288-5670. Fax: 414-288-3586.

Marquette University, School of Dentistry and Graduate School, Graduate Programs in Dentistry, Program in Endodontics, Milwaukee, WI 53201-1881. Awards MS. Faculty: 2 full-time (0 women), 3 part-time (0 women). Students: 4 full-time (0 women); includes 2 international. Average age 28. 87 applicants, 2% accepted. In 1997, 3 degrees awarded (100% found work related to degree). *Degree requirements:* Thesis required, foreign language not required. *Average time to degree:* master's–2 years full-time. *Entrance requirements:* TOEFL (minimum score 550), DDS or equivalent. Application deadline: 10/1 (rolling processing; 6/1 for spring admission). Application fee: $40. *Expenses:* Tuition $12,060 per year full-time, $670 per credit part-time. Fees $6025 per year. *Financial aid:* In 1997–98, 4 students received aid, including 2 teaching assistantships averaging $200 per month and totaling $4,800. Financial aid application deadline: 10/1. *Faculty research:* Mechanical properties of endodontic files, use of lasers in endodontics. • Director, 414-288-7047. Application contact: Dr. Ordean J. Oyen, Dean of Graduate Studies, 414-288-6577. Fax: 414-288-3586.

Marquette University, School of Dentistry and Graduate School, Graduate Programs in Dentistry, Program in Orthodontics, Milwaukee, WI 53201-1881. Awards MS. Faculty: 1 full-time (0 women), 16 part-time (2 women). Students: 10 full-time (4 women); includes 2 international. Average age 26. 150 applicants, 3% accepted. In 1997, 5 degrees awarded (100% found work related to degree). *Degree requirements:* Thesis required, foreign language not required. *Average time to degree:* master's–2 years full-time. *Entrance requirements:* TOEFL (minimum score 550), DDS or equivalent. Application deadline: 10/1 (rolling processing; 6/9 for spring admission). Application fee: $40. *Expenses:* Tuition $12,060 per year full-time, $670 per credit part-time. Fees $6025 per year. *Financial aid:* In 1997–98, 10 students received aid, including 5 teaching assistantships totaling $6,000. Financial aid application deadline: 10/1. • Dr. William L. Lobb, Acting Director, 414-288-7473. Application contact: Dr. Ordean J. Oyen, Dean of Graduate Studies, 414-288-5670. Fax: 414-288-3586.

Marquette University, School of Dentistry and Graduate School, Graduate Programs in Dentistry, Program in Prosthodontics, Milwaukee, WI 53201-1881. Awards MS. *Degree requirements:* Thesis required, foreign language not required. *Entrance requirements:* TOEFL (minimum score 550), DDS or equivalent. Application deadline: rolling. Application fee: $40. *Expenses:* Tuition $12,060 per year full-time, $670 per credit part-time. Fees $6025 per year. *Financial aid:* Application deadline 10/1. • Dr. William W. Nagy, Director, 414-288-6578. Application contact: Dr. Ordean J. Oyen, Dean of Graduate Studies, 414-288-5670. Fax: 414-288-3586.

McGill University, Faculty of Graduate Studies and Research, Faculty of Dentistry, Graduate Program in Oral and Maxillofacial Surgery, Montréal, PQ H3A 2T5, Canada. Awards M Sc, PhD. Faculty: 2 full-time (0 women), 10 part-time (0 women). Students: 10 full-time (6 women), 3 part-time (0 women). Average age 29. 32 applicants, 3% accepted. In 1997, 3 master's awarded (100% found work related to degree). *Degree requirements:* For master's, thesis required, foreign language not required; for doctorate, computer language, dissertation required, foreign language not required. *Entrance requirements:* For master's, Canadian National Dental Examinations, minimum GPA of 3.0, DDS or equivalent. Application deadline: 3/1 (rolling processing). Application fee: $60. *Expenses:* Tuition $1668 per year for Canadian residents; $8268 per year for nonresidents. Fees $828 per year for Canadian residents; $1216 per year for nonresidents. *Financial aid:* Paid residencies available. *Faculty research:* TMJ disorders, implant surgery, laser therapy, pain control studies, antibiotic studies. • Application contact: Lili Saran, Graduate Secretary, 514-937-6011 Ext. 2465.

Medical College of Georgia, Department of Oral Biology, Augusta, GA 30904. Awards MS, PhD. Part-time programs available. Faculty: 27 full-time (4 women). Students: 5 full-time (2 women), 23 part-time (5 women); includes 4 minority (2 African Americans, 2 Asian Americans), 4 international. Average age 33. 10 applicants, 90% accepted. In 1997, 11 master's, 2 doctorates awarded. *Degree requirements:* Thesis/dissertation required, foreign language not required. *Entrance requirements:* For master's, DAT or GRE General Test, TOEFL (minimum score 600), DDS, DMD, equivalent degree, or dental student; for doctorate, DAT or GRE General Test, TOEFL (minimum score 600). Application deadline: 6/30 (priority date; rolling processing). Application fee: $0. *Expenses:* Tuition $2670 per year full-time, $111 per credit part-time for state residents; $10,680 per year full-time, $445 per credit part-time for nonresidents. Fees $286 per year. *Financial aid:* In 1997–98, 2 research assistantships averaging $1,208 per month were awarded; teaching assistantships, Federal Work-Study, institutionally sponsored loans also available. Financial aid application deadline: 5/1. *Faculty research:* Fluoride, microbiology, biochemistry, dental materials, temporomandibular joint. • Dr. George S. Schuster, Chairman, 706-721-2991. Fax: 706-721-3392. E-mail: gschuste@mail.mcg.edu. Application contact: Dr. Gary C. Bond, Associate Dean, 706-721-3278. Fax: 706-721-6829. E-mail: gradstud@mail.mcg.edu.

Medical College of Ohio, Department of Oral Biology, Toledo, OH 43699-0008. Awards MS. Part-time programs available. Faculty: 4 full-time (1 woman), 1 part-time (0 women). Students: 1 full-time (0 women); includes 1 international. Average age 29. 3 applicants, 33% accepted. In 1997, 2 degrees awarded (100% found work related to degree). *Degree requirements:* Thesis, qualifying exam required, foreign language not required. *Average time to degree:* master's–2 years full-time. *Entrance requirements:* GRE General Test, minimum undergraduate GPA of 3.0. Application fee: $30. *Expenses:* Tuition $5939 per year full-time, $189 per credit hour part-time for state residents; $13,699 per year full-time, $428 per credit hour part-time for nonresidents. Fees $519 per year full-time, $356 per year part-time. *Financial aid:* Federal Work-Study, institutionally sponsored loans available. Financial aid applicants required to submit FAFSA. *Faculty research:* Oral biology–tissue cultures. Total annual research expenditures: $4000. • Dr. William Davis, Chairman, 419-383-4117. E-mail: mcogradschool@mco.edu. Application contact: Joann Braatz, Clerk, 419-383-4117. Fax: 419-383-6140. E-mail: mcogradschool@mco.edu.

Medical University of South Carolina, College of Health Professions, Program in Health Sciences, Charleston, SC 29425-0002. Offerings include periodontics (MHS). Postbaccalaureate distance learning degree programs offered (minimal on-campus study). Program faculty: 12 (7 women). *Entrance requirements:* GRE General Test, interview, minimum GPA of 3.0. Application deadline: rolling. Application fee: $55. *Expenses:* Tuition $4072 per year full-time, $221 per semester hour part-time for state residents; $7064 per year full-time, $387 per semester hour part-time for nonresidents. Fees $150 per year (minimum). • Dr. Valerie T. West, Associate Dean, 843-792-3326. E-mail: westvt@musc.edu. Application contact: Fran Clement, Student Services, 843-792-3326. Fax: 843-792-4024. E-mail: clementf@musc.edu.

New York University, College of Dentistry, Postgraduate Programs in Dentistry, New York, NY 10012-1019. Offerings in endodontics (Certificate), implantology (Certificate), oral and maxillofacial surgery (Certificate), orthodontics (Certificate), pediatric dentistry (Certificate), periodontics (Certificate), prosthodontics (Certificate). Students: 149 full-time, 6 part-time; includes 16 minority (6 African Americans, 4 Asian Americans, 6 Hispanics), 71 international. Average age 30. 540 applicants, 21% accepted. In 1997, 99 degrees awarded. *Average time to degree:* other advanced degree–3 years full-time. *Entrance requirements:* DDS. Application deadline: 4/1. Application fee: $35. *Financial aid:* 68 students received aid. Financial aid application deadline: 3/1. • Application contact: Stephen F. Muller, Associate Dean for Enrollment Services, 212-998-9818.

New York University, Graduate School of Arts and Science, Department of Biology, New York, NY 10012-1019. Offerings include oral biology (MS). Department faculty: 22 full-time (6 women), 10 part-time. *Degree requirements:* Thesis or alternative, qualifying paper required, foreign language not required. *Entrance requirements:* GRE General Test, TOEFL. Application deadline: 1/4 (priority date). Application fee: $60. *Expenses:* Tuition $715 per credit. Fees $1048 per year full-time, $229 per semester (minimum) part-time. • Philip Furmanski, Chairman, 212-998-8200. Application contact: Gloria Coruzzi, Director of Graduate Studies, 212-998-8200. Fax: 212-995-4557. E-mail: biology@nyu.edu.

New York University, Graduate School of Arts and Science and College of Dentistry, Department of Dental Materials Science, New York, NY 10012-1019. Awards MS. Faculty: 5 full-time (2 women). Students: 5 full-time (0 women), 2 part-time (both women); includes 5 international. Average age 32. 10 applicants, 100% accepted. In 1997, 6 degrees awarded. *Degree requirements:* Thesis required, foreign language not required. *Entrance requirements:* DDS or DMD. Application deadline: 5/15 (priority date). Application fee: $60. *Expenses:* Tuition $715 per credit. Fees $1048 per year full-time, $229 per semester (minimum) part-time. *Financial aid:* Full and partial tuition waivers, Federal Work-Study available. Financial aid application deadline: 1/4; applicants required to submit FAFSA. *Faculty research:* Calcium phosphate, composite restoratives, surfactants, dental metallurgy, impression materials. • Dr. Allan Schulman, Chairman, 212-998-9630. Fax: 212-995-4557. E-mail: gsas.admissions@nyu.edu.

The Ohio State University, College of Dentistry and Graduate School, Graduate Programs in Dentistry, Columbus, OH 43210. Awards MS, PhD, DDS/MS, DDS/PhD. Offerings include dentistry (MS), oral biology (PhD). Faculty: 78 full-time (12 women). Students: 92 full-time (29 women); includes 5 minority (3 Asian Americans, 2 Hispanics), 26 international. Average age 28. 628 applicants, 6% accepted. In 1997, 24 master's awarded. *Degree requirements:* Thesis/dissertation required, foreign language not required. *Entrance requirements:* GRE, TOEFL. Application deadline: 9/1. Application fee: $30 ($40 for international students). *Tuition:* $5472 per year for state residents; $14,172 per year for nonresidents. *Financial aid:* In 1997–98, 3 fellowships, 82 teaching assistantships (38 to first-year students) were awarded; research assistantships, Federal Work-Study, institutionally sponsored loans also available. Financial aid application deadline: 3/1. *Total annual research expenditures:* $2.7 million. • Application contact: Michael Rowland, Admission and Recruitment Officer, 614-292-3361. Fax: 614-292-7619.

Oregon Health Sciences University, School of Dentistry, Graduate Programs in Dentistry, 3181 SW Sam Jackson Park Road, Portland, OR 97201-3098. Offerings in anatomy (MS), dental materials (MS), endodontology (MS, Certificate), microbiology (MS), oral pathology (MS, Certificate), orthodontics (MS, Certificate), pediatric dentistry (Certificate), peridontology (Certificate). Faculty: 72 full-time, 91 part-time. Students: 28 full-time; includes 4 minority (all Asian Americans). Average age 28. 250 applicants, 5% accepted. In 1997, 14 Certificates awarded (100% found work related to degree). *Degree requirements:* For master's, thesis required, foreign language not required. *Entrance requirements:* GRE General Test, TOEFL, DMD/DDS. Application deadline: 11/1. Application fee: $40. *Financial aid:* Federal Work-Study, institutionally sponsored loans available. Financial aid application deadline: 3/1. • Application contact: Nora L. Cromley, Assistant Dean of Admissions and Student Affairs, 503-494-5274. Fax: 503-494-4666. E-mail: cromleyn@ohsu.edu.

Saint Louis University, Program in Endodontics, St. Louis, MO 63103-2097. Offers dentistry (MS). Faculty: 4 full-time (0 women), 20 part-time (2 women). Students: 5 full-time (1 woman); includes 1 international. 12 applicants, 25% accepted. In 1997, 1 degree awarded. *Degree requirements:* Thesis, comprehensive oral exam required, foreign language not required. *Entrance requirements:* GRE General Test, DDS or DMD, interview. Application deadline:

10/1. Application fee: $40. *Tuition:* $542 per credit hour. *Financial aid:* Federal Work-Study, institutionally sponsored loans available. Aid available to part-time students. Financial aid application deadline: 4/1. *Faculty research:* Nickel-titanium-alloy instrumentation, dentin hypersensitivity, root-end filling materials, biocompatability. • Dr. John Hatton, Director, 314-577-8186. Application contact: Dr. Marcia Buresch, Assistant Dean of the Graduate School, 314-977-2240. Fax: 314-977-3943.

Saint Louis University, Program in Orthodontics, St. Louis, MO 63103-2097. Offers dentistry (MS). Faculty: 4 full-time (0 women), 40 part-time (4 women). Students: 44 full-time (17 women), 1 (woman) part-time; includes 3 minority (1 Asian American, 2 Hispanics), 17 international. 189 applicants, 8% accepted. In 1997, 16 degrees awarded. *Degree requirements:* Thesis, comprehensive oral exam required, foreign language not required. *Entrance requirements:* GRE General Test, DDS or DMD, interview. Application deadline: 10/1. Application fee: $40. *Tuition:* $542 per credit hour. *Financial aid:* In 1997–98, 3 assistantships were awarded. Financial aid application deadline: 4/1. *Faculty research:* Appliance design, orthognathic surgery, apical root shortening, orthodontic-treatment side effects. • Dr. Dennis Killiany, Director, 314-577-8186. Application contact: Dr. Marcia Buresch, Assistant Dean of the Graduate School, 314-977-2240. Fax: 314-977-3943.

Saint Louis University, Program in Periodontics, St. Louis, MO 63103-2097. Offers dentistry (MS). *Degree requirements:* Thesis, comprehensive oral exam required, foreign language not required. *Entrance requirements:* GRE General Test, DDS or DMD, interview. Application fee: $40. *Tuition:* $542 per credit hour. • Dr. D. Douglas Miley, Director, 314-777-8186. Application contact: Dr. Marcia Buresch, Assistant Dean of the Graduate School, 314-977-2240. Fax: 314-977-3943.

State University of New York at Buffalo, Graduate School, School of Dental Medicine, Graduate Programs in Dental Medicine, Department of Oral Biology, Buffalo, NY 14214. Awards PhD. Faculty: 11 full-time (2 women). Students: 6 full-time (3 women), 6 part-time (2 women); includes 1 minority (Hispanic), 4 international. Average age 27. 10 applicants, 30% accepted. In 1997, 2 degrees awarded (100% entered university research/teaching). *Degree requirements:* Dissertation required, foreign language not required. *Entrance requirements:* GRE General Test, TOEFL (minimum score 550), GRE Subject Test (biology) or DDS. Application deadline: 11/1 (priority date). Application fee: $35. *Tuition:* $5970 per year full-time, $288 per credit hour part-time for state residents; $9286 per year full-time, $426 per credit hour part-time for nonresidents. *Financial aid:* Fellowships, research assistantships, Federal Work-Study, institutionally sponsored loans available. Financial aid application deadline: 2/28. *Faculty research:* Oral immunology and microbiology, bone physiology, biochemistry, molecular genetics, neutrophil biology. • Dr. Robert Genco, Chairman, 716-829-2854. Application contact: Dr. Frank Scannapieco, Graduate Director, 716-829-2013.

State University of New York at Buffalo, Graduate School, School of Dental Medicine, Graduate Programs in Dental Medicine, Department of Orthodontics, Buffalo, NY 14214. Awards MS, Certificate. Faculty: 2 full-time (0 women), 5 part-time (2 women). Students: 2 full-time (0 women), 1 (woman) part-time; includes 2 international. Average age 26. In 1997, 3 master's awarded. *Degree requirements:* For master's, thesis required, foreign language not required. *Entrance requirements:* For master's, TOEFL (minimum score 550), DDS, DMD, or equivalent foreign degree. Application deadline: 10/1. Application fee: $35. *Tuition:* $5970 per year full-time, $288 per credit hour part-time for state residents; $9286 per year full-time, $426 per credit hour part-time for nonresidents. *Financial aid:* Federal Work-Study, institutionally sponsored loans available. Financial aid application deadline: 2/28. *Faculty research:* Psychosocial perception of malocclusion, VLC plastics, positioners. • Dr. C. Brian Preston, Chairman, 716-829-2845. Fax: 716-829-2572.

State University of New York at Buffalo, Graduate School, School of Dental Medicine, Graduate Programs in Dental Medicine, Program in Oral Sciences, Buffalo, NY 14214. Awards MS. Part-time programs available. Faculty: 24 full-time (5 women), 12 part-time (3 women). Students: 26 full-time (10 women); includes 2 minority (1 African American, 1 Hispanic), 7 international. Average age 31. In 1997, 8 degrees awarded. *Degree requirements:* Thesis required, foreign language not required. *Entrance requirements:* TOEFL (minimum score 550), DDS, DMD, or equivalent foreign degree. Application deadline: 5/1 (priority date; rolling processing). Application fee: $35. *Tuition:* $5970 per year full-time, $288 per credit hour part-time for state residents; $9286 per year full-time, $426 per credit hour part-time for nonresidents. *Financial aid:* In 1997–98, 11 students received aid, including 5 research assistantships, 2 teaching assistantships; full and partial tuition waivers also available. Financial aid application deadline: 2/28. *Faculty research:* Oral biology and pathology, behavioral sciences, neuromuscular physiology, facial pain, oral microbiology. • Dr. Ernesto DeNardin, Director, 716-829-3518. Fax: 716-833-3517.

State University of New York at Stony Brook, School of Dental Medicine and Graduate School, Department of Oral Biology and Pathology, Stony Brook, NY 11790. Awards PhD. Faculty: 11. Students: 6 full-time (2 women), 1 part-time (0 women); includes 1 minority (Asian American), 2 international. Average age 27. 4 applicants, 25% accepted. In 1997, 2 degrees awarded. *Entrance requirements:* GRE General Test, TOEFL. Application deadline: 1/15. Application fee: $50. *Expenses:* Tuition $5100 per year full-time, $213 per credit hour part-time for state residents; $8416 per year full-time, $351 per credit hour part-time for nonresidents. Fees $529 per year full-time, $77 per semester (minimum) part-time. *Financial aid:* In 1997–98, 6 research assistantships were awarded; fellowships, teaching assistantships, Federal Work-Study also available. Financial aid application deadline: 3/15. *Faculty research:* Collagen metabolism, periodontal disease and diabetes, salivary antimicrobial proteins, dental plaque metabolism and dental caries. Total annual research expenditures: $1.8 million. • Dr. Israel Kleinberg, Chair, 516-632-8923. E-mail: ikleinbe@epo.hsc.sunysb.edu. Application contact: Dr. Bill Kaufman, Director, 516-632-8923. Fax: 516-632-9704.

State University of New York at Stony Brook, Health Sciences Center, School of Dental Medicine, Professional Program in Dental Medicine, Stony Brook, NY 11794. Offerings include orthodontics (Certificate), periodontics (Certificate). Program faculty: 72. *Application deadline:* 1/15. *Application fee:* $75. • Application contact: Kim M. Lambiase Hammer, Director of Admissions, 516-632-8980.

Temple University, School of Dentistry and Graduate School, Graduate Programs in Dentistry, Philadelphia, PA 19140. Offerings in advanced education in general dentistry (Certificate), endodontology (Certificate), oral and maxillofacial surgery (Certificate), oral biology (MS), orthodontics (Certificate), periodontology (Certificate), prosthodontics (Certificate). Faculty: 25 full-time (3 women). Students: 55 full-time (20 women); includes 12 minority (2 African Americans, 8 Asian Americans, 2 Hispanics), 10 international. Average age 30. 287 applicants, 9% accepted. In 1997, 7 master's, 26 Certificates awarded. *Degree requirements:* For master's, thesis. *Entrance requirements:* For master's, GRE General Test (combined average 1000), TOEFL (average 600); for Certificate, TOEFL, DMD or DDS. Application deadline: 10/1. Application fee: $40. *Expenses:* Tuition $323 per semester hour for state residents; $444 per semester hour for nonresidents. Fees $170 per year full-time, $28 per semester (minimum) part-time. *Financial aid:* Fellowships, Federal Work-Study, institutionally sponsored loans, and career-related internships or fieldwork available. *Faculty research:* Saliva and salivary glands, implantology, material science, periodontal disease, geriatric dentistry. Total annual research expenditures: $600,000. • Robert Braun, Associate Dean for Advanced Education, 215-707-2876. Fax: 215-707-4290. E-mail: rbraun@hal.temple.denial.edu.

Tufts University, School of Dental Medicine, Advanced Education Programs in Dental Medicine, Medford, MA 02155. Offering in dentistry (Certificate). Students: 87 full-time (34 women); includes 7 minority (6 Asian Americans, 1 Hispanic), 48 international. Average age 28. In 1997, 49 degrees awarded. *Average time to degree:* other advanced degree–2.5 years full-time. *Entrance requirements:* TOEFL (minimum score 550; average 580). Application deadline: 11/1. Application fee: $50. *Financial aid:* 21 students received aid; Federal Work-Study, institutionally sponsored loans available. Financial aid application deadline: 5/1; applicants required to submit FAFSA. • Dr. Russi Gheewalla, Director, 617-636-6887. Application contact: Mark Gonthier, Assistant Dean for Admissions and Student Affairs, 617-636-6539. Fax: 617-636-0309. E-mail: mgonthier@infonet.tufts.edu.

Tufts University, School of Dental Medicine, Graduate Programs in Dental Medicine, Boston, MA 02111. Awards MS. Faculty: 29 full-time (7 women), 5 part-time (1 woman). Students: 24 full-time (6 women); includes 21 international. In 1997, 13 degrees awarded. *Degree requirements:* Thesis required, foreign language not required. *Average time to degree:* master's–3 years full-time. *Entrance requirements:* TOEFL (minimum score 550; average 575), DDS, DMD, or equivalent; minimum B average. Application deadline: 5/1 (priority date; rolling processing). Application fee: $50. *Financial aid:* Application deadline 5/1; applicants required to submit FAFSA. *Faculty research:* Periodontal research, dental materials, salivary research, epidemiology. • Dr. Catherine Hayes, Director of Graduate Studies, 617-636-0339. Fax: 617-636-6834. E-mail: chayes@infonet.tufts.edu. Application contact: Mark Gonthier, Assistant Dean for Admissions and Student Affairs, 617-636-6539. Fax: 617-636-0309. E-mail: mgonthier@infonet.tufts.edu.

Université de Montréal, Faculties of Dentistry and Graduate Studies, Graduate Programs in Dentistry, Professional Program in Pediatric Dentistry, Montréal, PQ H3C 3J7, Canada. Awards Certificate. Students: 4 full-time (2 women). 8 applicants, 25% accepted. In 1997, 2 degrees awarded. *Application deadline:* 2/1. *Application fee:* $30. • Dr. Leonardo Abelardo, Head, 514-345-4669. Application contact: Dr. Gilles Lavigne, Associate Dean for Research, 514-343-2134.

Université de Montréal, Faculties of Dentistry and Graduate Studies, Graduate Programs in Dentistry, Program in Dental Biology, Montréal, PQ H3C 3J7, Canada. Awards M Sc. Faculty: 16 full-time (5 women), 1 part-time (0 women). Students: 0. 3 applicants, 0% accepted. In 1997, 1 degree awarded. *Application deadline:* 11/1. *Application fee:* $30. • Application contact: Dr. Gilles Lavigne, Associate Dean for Research, 514-343-2134.

Université de Montréal, Faculties of Dentistry and Graduate Studies, Graduate Programs in Dentistry, Program in Multidisciplinary Residency, Montréal, PQ H3C 3J7, Canada. Awards Certificate. Students: 6 full-time (2 women). 32 applicants, 19% accepted. In 1997, 6 degrees awarded. *Application deadline:* 11/1. *Application fee:* $30. • Dr. Remy Dupuis, Head, 514-343-6815. Application contact: Dr. Gilles Lavigne, Associate Dean for Research, 514-343-2134.

Université de Montréal, Faculties of Dentistry and Graduate Studies, Graduate Programs in Dentistry, Program in Orthodontics, Montréal, PQ H3C 3J7, Canada. Awards M Sc, Certificate. Students: 8 full-time (4 women). 39 applicants, 10% accepted. In 1997, 4 Certificates awarded. *Application deadline:* 11/1. *Application fee:* $30. • Claude Remise, Head, 514-343-7133. Application contact: Dr. Gilles Lavigne, Associate Dean for Research, 514-343-2134.

Université de Montréal, Faculties of Dentistry and Graduate Studies, Graduate Programs in Dentistry, Program in Prosthodontics Rehabilitation, Montréal, PQ H3C 3J7, Canada. Awards Certificate. Students: 4 full-time (0 women). 4 applicants, 50% accepted. In 1997, 2 degrees awarded. *Application fee:* $30. • Richard Tache, Head, 514-343-6053. Application contact: Dr. Gilles Lavigne, Associate Dean for Research, 514-343-2134.

Université Laval, Faculty of Dentistry, Graduate Programs in Dentistry, Sainte-Foy, PQ G1K 7P4, Canada. Awards M Sc, Diploma. Students: 14 full-time (4 women). Average age 28. 355 applicants, 21% accepted. *Application deadline:* 3/1. *Application fee:* $30. *Expenses:* Tuition $1334 per year (minimum) full-time, $56 per credit (minimum) part-time for Canadian residents; $5966 per year (minimum) full-time, $249 per credit (minimum) part-time for nonresidents. Fees $150 per year full-time, $6.25 per credit part-time. • Pierre Gagnon, Director, 418-656-2131 Ext. 7214. Fax: 418-656-2720. E-mail: pierre.gagnon@fmd.ulaval.ca.

The University of Alabama at Birmingham, Graduate School and School of Dentistry, Graduate Programs in Dentistry, Birmingham, AL 35294. Awards MPH, MS, DMD/MS. Offerings include dental public health (MPH), dentistry (MS), oral biology (MS). Students: 5 full-time (2 women); includes 4 minority (all Asian Americans). Average age 26. 8 applicants, 100% accepted. In 1997, 14 degrees awarded. *Application deadline:* rolling. *Application fee:* $30 ($60 for international students). Electronic applications accepted. *Expenses:* Tuition $99 per credit hour for state residents; $198 per credit hour for nonresidents. Fees $516 per year (minimum) full-time, $73 per quarter (minimum) part-time for state residents; $516 per year (minimum) full-time, $73 per unit (minimum) part-time for nonresidents. • Dr. Firoz Rahemtulla, Director, 205-934-5426.

University of Alberta, Faculty of Medicine and Oral Health Sciences, Department of Oral Health Sciences, Division of Orthodontics, Edmonton, AB T6G 2E1, Canada. Awards M Sc. Faculty: 2 full-time (0 women), 7 part-time (1 woman), 3.5 FTE. Students: 9 full-time (3 women); includes 1 Native American. Average age 35. 65 applicants, 5% accepted. In 1997, 2 degrees awarded. *Degree requirements:* Thesis. *Average time to degree:* master's–2.6 years full-time. *Entrance requirements:* TOEFL (minimum score 580). Application deadline: 10/1. Application fee: $60. *Financial aid:* Institutionally sponsored loans available. • Dr. K. Glover, Head, 403-492-4469. Fax: 403-492-1624. E-mail: ken.glover@ualberta.ca.

University of Alberta, Faculty of Medicine and Oral Health Sciences, Department of Oral Health Sciences, Graduate Programs in Dental Sciences, Edmonton, AB T6G 2E1, Canada. Awards M Sc, PhD, Postgraduate Diploma. Faculty: 7 full-time (1 woman), 1 part-time (0 women). Students: 4 full-time (0 women). 75 applicants, 4% accepted. In 1997, 2 master's, 2 doctorates awarded. *Degree requirements:* For master's and doctorate, thesis/dissertation; for Postgraduate Diploma, thesis required, foreign language not required. *Average time to degree:* master's–3 years full-time; doctorate–5 years full-time. *Entrance requirements:* For Postgraduate Diploma, DDS. Application fee: $65. *Financial aid:* In 1997–98, 2 students received aid, including 1 research assistantship (to a first-year student), 1 teaching assistantship (to a first-year student); fellowships also available. *Faculty research:* Oral biology, growth and development, preventive dentistry, applied clinical orthodontics, clinical trials. • Dr. Nadine Milos, Director, Graduate Studies and Research, 403-492-4958. Application contact: Pat LaPointe, Secretary, 403-492-8041. Fax: 403-492-1624. E-mail: plapoint@gpu.srv.ualberta.ca.

University of British Columbia, Faculties of Dentistry and Graduate Studies, Graduate Programs in Dentistry, Vancouver, BC V6T 1Z3, Canada. Offerings in dental science (M Sc), oral biology (PhD), periodontics (Diploma). Faculty: 32 full-time (7 women), 3 part-time (1 woman). Students: 20 full-time (13 women), 3 part-time (2 women). 40 applicants, 13% accepted. In 1997, 4 master's, 2 doctorates awarded. *Degree requirements:* For master's, thesis required, foreign language not required; for doctorate, dissertation, comprehensive exam required, foreign language not required. *Average time to degree:* master's–3 years full-time; doctorate–4.5 years full-time. *Entrance requirements:* For master's and doctorate, TOEFL (minimum score 570). Application deadline: rolling. Application fee: $50. *Financial aid:* In 1997–98, 5 fellowships (1 to a first-year student) totaling $79,365, 7 research assistantships (2 to first-year students) averaging $1,175 per month and totaling $57,517, 5 teaching assistantships (1 to a first-year student) averaging $1,714 per month and totaling $42,845 were awarded. Financial aid application deadline: 11/30. *Faculty research:* Cell biology, oral physiology, microbiology, immunology, biomaterials, developmental biology. Total annual research expenditures: $1.8 million. • D. M. Brunette, Associate Dean, Research and Graduate Training, 604-822-4486. E-mail: brunette@unixg.ubc.ca. Application contact: Vicky Koulouris, Secretary, 604-822-4486. Fax: 604-822-6698.

University of California, Los Angeles, School of Dentistry and Graduate Division, Graduate Programs in Dentistry, Program in Oral Biology, Los Angeles, CA 90095. Awards MS, PhD, DDS/MS, DDS/PhD, MD/PhD, MS/Certificate, PhD/Certificate. Students: 23 full-time (9 women); includes 15 minority (all Asian Americans), 3 international. 29 applicants, 59% accepted. *Degree requirements:* For master's, computer language, thesis required, foreign language not required; for doctorate, dissertation, oral and written qualifying exams required, foreign language

Directory: Oral and Dental Sciences

University of California, Los Angeles (continued)
not required. *Entrance requirements:* For master's, DAT or GRE General Test. Application deadline: 1/15. Application fee: $40. *Financial aid:* In 1997–98, 22 students received aid, including fellowships totaling $76,602; research assistantships, teaching assistantships, full and partial tuition waivers, Federal Work-Study, institutionally sponsored loans also available. Financial aid application deadline: 3/1. *Faculty research:* Neurophysiology, immunology of periodontal disease. • Dr. George Bernard, Director, 310-825-1955. Application contact: Departmental Office, 310-825-1955. E-mail: jasonp@dent.ucla.edu.

University of California, San Francisco, Program in Oral Biology, San Francisco, CA 94143. Awards MS, PhD. Faculty: 32 full-time. In 1997, 7 master's, 5 doctorates awarded. Terminal master's awarded for partial completion of doctoral program. *Degree requirements:* Thesis/dissertation. *Entrance requirements:* GRE General Test. Application fee: $40. *Expenses:* Tuition $0 for state residents; $9384 per year for nonresidents. Fees $4488 per year. *Financial aid:* Application deadline 1/10. • Caroline Damsky, Director, 415-476-2944. Application contact: Paul Riofsky, Program Assistant, 415-476-2944.

University of Connecticut, Field of Dental Science, Storrs, CT 06269. Awards M Dent Sc. Faculty: 34. Students: 9 full-time (4 women), 17 part-time (10 women); includes 3 minority (2 Asian Americans, 1 Hispanic), 10 international. Average age 29. 9 applicants, 100% accepted. In 1997, 6 degrees awarded. *Entrance requirements:* GRE General Test. Application deadline: 10/1 (priority date; rolling processing; 11/1 for spring admission). Application fee: $40 ($45 for international students). *Expenses:* Tuition $5272 per year full-time, $293 per credit part-time for state residents; $13,696 per year full-time, $761 per credit part-time for nonresidents. Fees $948 per year full-time, $640 per year part-time. *Financial aid:* Research assistantships available. • Edward J. Kollar, Director, 860-674-3210.

University of Connecticut Health Center, School of Dental Medicine and Graduate School, Graduate Programs in Dental Medicine, Farmington, CT 06030. Offerings in dental medicine (PhD), dental science (MDS). Faculty: 35 full-time (5 women). Students: 48 full-time (13 women); includes 18 minority (17 Asian Americans, 1 Hispanic), 12 international. Average age 27. 213 applicants, 5% accepted. In 1997, 4 master's awarded (50% entered university research/teaching, 50% found other work related to degree). *Degree requirements:* For master's, thesis required, foreign language not required; for doctorate, 1 foreign language (computer language can substitute), dissertation. *Average time to degree:* master's–3 years full-time; doctorate–6 years full-time. *Entrance requirements:* For master's, National Board Dental Examinations I/II; for doctorate, National Board Dental Examinations I/II or GRE General Test. Application fee: $60. *Financial aid:* Fellowships, teaching assistantships, institutionally sponsored loans available. Financial aid applicants required to submit FAFSA. *Faculty research:* Cell and molecular biology, immunology, neurobiology, epidemiology, developmental biology. • Gerald Maywell, Head, 860-679-2550. Application contact: Dr. Edward J. Kollar, Associate Dean for Academic and Student Affairs, 860-679-2207. Fax: 860-679-1899. E-mail: kollar@nso.uchc.edu.

University of Connecticut Health Center, School of Dental Medicine, Program in Oral Biology, Farmington, CT 06030. Awards DMD/PhD. Faculty: 35 full-time (5 women). Students: 3 full-time (all women). Average age 25. 2 applicants, 100% accepted. *Application deadline:* rolling. *Application fee:* $60. *Expenses:* Tuition $7900 per year for state residents; $20,250 per year for nonresidents. Fees $3725 per year. *Financial aid:* Fellowships available. • Dr. William Upholt, Director, 860-679-3388.

University of Connecticut Health Center, Programs in Biomedical Sciences, Program in Oral Biology, Farmington, CT 06030. Awards PhD. *Degree requirements:* Dissertation required, foreign language not required. *Entrance requirements:* GRE General Test, TOEFL. Application deadline: 3/1 (priority date; rolling processing). Application fee: $35. *Faculty research:* Developmental biology, muscle physiology, biology of mineralized tissues.

University of Detroit Mercy, School of Dentistry, Department of Endodontics, Detroit, MI 48219-0900. Awards MS, Certificate. *Degree requirements:* For master's, computer language, thesis required, foreign language not required; for Certificate, computer language required, foreign language and thesis not required. *Entrance requirements:* For master's, DDS or DMD; for Certificate, DHAT, DDS or DMD. Application fee: $25. *Faculty research:* Roof and filling materials, cavity preparations, pulp biology.

University of Detroit Mercy, School of Dentistry, Department of Orthodontics, Detroit, MI 48219-0900. Awards MS, Certificate. *Degree requirements:* For master's, computer language, thesis required, foreign language not required; for Certificate, computer language required, foreign language and thesis not required. *Entrance requirements:* For master's, DDS or DMD; for Certificate, DHAT, DDS or DMD. Application fee: $25. *Faculty research:* Changes in oral flora due to fixed orthodontic appliances, cranioskeletal osteogenesis.

University of Florida, College of Dentistry and Graduate School, Graduate Programs in Dentistry, Department of Endodontics, Gainesville, FL 32611. Awards MS. Faculty: 1 full-time (0 women). Students: 9 full-time (2 women); includes 1 minority (Hispanic). Average age 33. 39 applicants, 8% accepted. In 1997, 2 degrees awarded. *Degree requirements:* Thesis, National Dental Boards I and II. *Entrance requirements:* GRE General Test (minimum combined score of 1000), TOEFL (minimum score 550), minimum GPA of 3.0. Application deadline: 10/1. Application fee: $20. *Tuition:* $3355 per year for state residents; $11,295 per year for nonresidents. *Financial aid:* In 1997–98, 1 fellowship was awarded. *Faculty research:* Sealability of obturation materials, pulp response to restorative materials, cytotoxicity of endodontic materials. Total annual research expenditures: $6000. • Dr. F. J. Vertucci, Chair, 352-392-4301. E-mail: vertucci@dental.ufl.edu. Application contact: Dr. Carroll Bennett, Director of Admissions and Student Affairs, 352-392-7206. Fax: 352-392-3070.

University of Florida, College of Dentistry and Graduate School, Graduate Programs in Dentistry, Department of Orthodontics, Gainesville, FL 32611. Awards MS. Faculty: Students: 9 full-time (4 women); includes 3 minority (1 African American, 2 Hispanics). Average age 33. 49 applicants, 6% accepted. In 1997, 2 degrees awarded. *Degree requirements:* Thesis, National Dental Boards I and II. *Average time to degree:* master's–3 years full-time. *Entrance requirements:* GRE General Test (minimum combined score of 1000), TOEFL (minimum score 550), minimum GPA of 3.0. Application deadline: 10/1. Application fee: $20. *Tuition:* $3355 per year for state residents; $11,295 per year for nonresidents. *Financial aid:* In 1997–98, 2 students received aid, including 1 fellowship (to a first-year student). *Faculty research:* Class II treatment, orthodontic tooth movement, orthognathic surgery, craniofacial development, outcomes assessment of orthodontic treatment. Total annual research expenditures: $444,746. • Dr. Timothy T. Wheeler, Chair, 352-392-4135. E-mail: twheeler@dental.ufl.edu. Application contact: Dr. Carroll Bennett, Director of Admissions and Student Affairs, 352-392-7206. Fax: 352-392-3070.

University of Florida, College of Dentistry and Graduate School, Graduate Programs in Dentistry, Department of Periodontics, Gainesville, FL 32611. Awards MS. Faculty: Students: 6 full-time (1 woman); includes 1 minority (Hispanic). Average age 35. 10 applicants, 20% accepted. *Degree requirements:* Thesis, National Dental Boards I and II required, foreign language not required. *Average time to degree:* master's–3 years full-time. *Entrance requirements:* GRE General Test (minimum combined score of 1000), TOEFL (minimum score 550), minimum GPA of 3.0. Application deadline: 10/1. Application fee: $20. *Tuition:* $3355 per year for state residents; $11,295 per year for nonresidents. *Faculty research:* Effect of hormones on pain in periodontal therapies, periondontal regeneration with alloplast, selective repopulation of periodontal pockets. Total annual research expenditures: $6679. • Dr. Robert Bates, Acting Chair, 352-392-4305. Application contact: Dr. Carroll Bennett, Director of Admissions and Student Affairs, 352-392-7206. Fax: 352-392-3070.

University of Florida, College of Dentistry and Graduate School, Graduate Programs in Dentistry, Department of Prosthodontics, Gainesville, FL 32611. Awards MS. Students: 5 full-time (2 women); includes 2 minority (1 Asian American, 1 Hispanic), 2 international. Average age 38. 8 applicants, 38% accepted. In 1997, 1 degree awarded. *Degree requirements:* Thesis, National Dental Boards I and II required, foreign language not required. *Average time to degree:* master's–3 years full-time. *Entrance requirements:* GRE General Test (minimum combined score of 1000), TOEFL (minimum score 550), minimum GPA of 3.0. Application deadline: 10/1. Application fee: $20. *Tuition:* $3355 per year for state residents; $11,295 per year for nonresidents. *Financial aid:* Fellowships available. • Dr. Dean Morton, Director, 352-392-4231. E-mail: dmorton@dental.ufl.edu. Application contact: Dr. Carroll Bennett, Director of Admissions and Student Affairs, 352-392-7206. Fax: 352-392-3070.

University of Florida, College of Medicine and Graduate School, Interdisciplinary Program in Biomedical Sciences, Department of Oral Biology, Gainesville, FL 32610. Awards PhD. Faculty: 20 full-time (2 women). Students: 7 full-time (3 women); includes 1 minority (African American), 2 international. Average age 29. Terminal master's awarded for partial completion of doctoral program. *Degree requirements:* For doctorate, dissertation required, foreign language not required. *Entrance requirements:* For doctorate, GRE General Test (minimum combined score of 1200), TOEFL (minimum score 600), minimum GPA of 3.0. Application deadline: 2/1 (rolling processing). Application fee: $20. Electronic applications accepted. *Tuition:* $138 per credit hour for state residents; $481 per credit hour for nonresidents. *Financial aid:* In 1997–98, 6 students received aid, including 1 research assistantship averaging $1,319 per month, 5 traineeships averaging $2,200 per month; fellowships also available. *Faculty research:* Bacterial genetics, cell adhesion, salivary glands, cell proliferation. Total annual research expenditures: $1.04 million. • Dr. William P. McArthur, Graduate Coordinator, 352-846-0778. Fax: 352-392-3070. E-mail: mcarthur@dental.ufl.edu.

University of Illinois at Chicago, College of Dentistry and Graduate College, Graduate Programs in Dentistry, Chicago, IL 60607-7128. Awards MS, DDS/MS. Offerings include oral sciences (MS). Students: 6 full-time (4 women), 1 part-time (0 women); includes 1 minority (Asian American), 5 international. Average age 29. 12 applicants, 83% accepted. In 1997, 8 degrees awarded. *Degree requirements:* Thesis. *Entrance requirements:* GRE General Test, TOEFL (minimum score 550), DDS, DVM, or MD. Application deadline: 7/3 (11/8 for spring admission). Application fee: $40 ($50 for international students). *Financial aid:* In 1997–98, 3 fellowships were awarded; research assistantships, teaching assistantships also available. • Allen Anderson, Dean, College of Dentistry, 312-996-1040.

The University of Iowa, College of Dentistry and Graduate College, Graduate Programs in Dentistry, Department of Endodontics, Iowa City, IA 52242-1316. Awards MS, Certificate. Faculty: 4 full-time (1 woman), 5 part-time (0 women). Students: 7 full-time (4 women); includes 2 minority (both African Americans). In 1997, 2 master's awarded. *Degree requirements:* For master's, thesis. *Entrance requirements:* For master's, GRE, TOEFL, DDS. Application deadline: 9/15. Application fee: $30 ($50 for international students). *Expenses:* Tuition $3166 per year full-time, $176 per semester hour part-time for state residents; $10,202 per year full-time, $176 per semester hour part-time for nonresidents. Fees $202 per year full-time, $52 per year (minimum) part-time. • Dr. Eric Rivera, Head, 319-335-7471. Fax: 319-335-7155.

The University of Iowa, College of Dentistry and Graduate College, Graduate Programs in Dentistry, Department of Operative Dentistry, Iowa City, IA 52242-1316. Awards MS, Certificate. Faculty: 9 full-time (1 woman), 7 part-time (0 women). Students: 8 full-time (3 women); includes 1 minority (African American), 4 international. In 1997, 4 master's awarded. *Degree requirements:* For master's, thesis. *Entrance requirements:* For master's, GRE, TOEFL, DDS. Application fee: $30 ($50 for international students). *Expenses:* Tuition $3166 per year full-time, $176 per semester hour part-time for state residents; $10,202 per year full-time, $176 per semester hour part-time for nonresidents. Fees $202 per year full-time, $52 per year (minimum) part-time. • Dr. John Reinhardt, Head, 319-335-7207. Application contact: Dr. Gerald Denehy, 319-335-7207. Fax: 319-355-7155.

The University of Iowa, College of Dentistry and Graduate College, Graduate Programs in Dentistry, Department of Oral Pathology, Radiology and Medicine, Iowa City, IA 52242-1316. Offers program in stomatology (MS, Certificate). Faculty: 10 full-time (3 women), 2 part-time (1 woman). Students: 6 full-time (2 women); includes 1 minority (African American), 1 international. In 1997, 1 master's awarded. *Degree requirements:* For master's, thesis. *Entrance requirements:* For master's, GRE, TOEFL, DDS with a minimum GPA of 2.7. Application deadline: 10/1. Application fee: $30 ($50 for international students). *Expenses:* Tuition $3166 per year full-time, $176 per semester hour part-time for state residents; $10,202 per year full-time, $176 per semester hour part-time for nonresidents. Fees $202 per year full-time, $52 per year (minimum) part-time. • Dr. Gilbert Lilly, Head, 319-335-9656. Application contact: Dr. Steven Vincent, Director, 319-335-9656. Fax: 319-335-7155.

The University of Iowa, College of Dentistry and Graduate College, Graduate Programs in Dentistry, Department of Oral Science, Iowa City, IA 52242-1316. Awards MS, PhD. Faculty: 9 full-time (0 women). Students: 6 full-time (3 women); includes 5 international. In 1997, 1 master's, 1 doctorate awarded. *Degree requirements:* Thesis/dissertation. *Entrance requirements:* For master's, GRE, TOEFL, DDS. Application fee: $30 ($50 for international students). *Expenses:* Tuition $3166 per year full-time, $176 per semester hour part-time for state residents; $10,202 per year full-time, $176 per semester hour part-time for nonresidents. Fees $202 per year full-time, $52 per year (minimum) part-time. • Dr. Christopher Squier, Associate Dean for Research and Graduate Studies, 319-335-7388. Fax: 319-335-7155.

The University of Iowa, College of Dentistry and Graduate College, Graduate Programs in Dentistry, Department of Oral and Maxillofacial Surgery, Iowa City, IA 52242-1316. Awards MS. Faculty: 5 full-time (1 woman), 4 part-time (0 women). Students: 10 full-time (1 woman); includes 1 international. In 1997, 1 degree awarded. *Degree requirements:* Thesis. *Entrance requirements:* GRE, TOEFL, DDS. Application deadline: 10/1. Application fee: $30 ($50 for international students). *Expenses:* Tuition $3166 per year full-time, $176 per semester hour part-time for state residents; $10,202 per year full-time, $176 per semester hour part-time for nonresidents. Fees $202 per year full-time, $52 per year (minimum) part-time. • Dr. Daniel Lew, Head, 319-335-7456. Fax: 319-355-7155. Application contact: Dr. Kirk Fridrich, 319-356-1981.

The University of Iowa, College of Dentistry and Graduate College, Graduate Programs in Dentistry, Department of Orthodontics, Iowa City, IA 52242-1316. Awards MS, Certificate. Faculty: 5 full-time (1 woman), 5 part-time (0 women). Students: 10 full-time (3 women); includes 2 international. In 1997, 5 master's awarded. *Degree requirements:* For master's, thesis. *Entrance requirements:* For master's, GRE, TOEFL, DDS. Application deadline: 9/1. Application fee: $30 ($50 for international students). *Expenses:* Tuition $3166 per year full-time, $176 per semester hour part-time for state residents; $10,202 per year full-time, $176 per semester hour part-time for nonresidents. Fees $202 per year full-time, $52 per year (minimum) part-time. • Dr. John Casko, Head, 319-335-7308. Application contact: Dr. Thomas Southard, Graduate Program Director, 319-335-7288. Fax: 319-335-7155.

The University of Iowa, College of Dentistry and Graduate College, Graduate Programs in Dentistry, Department of Pediatric Dentistry, Iowa City, IA 52242-1316. Awards MS, Certificate. Faculty: 5 full-time (0 women), 7 part-time (2 women). Students: 7 full-time (3 women); includes 1 minority (Hispanic), 1 international. In 1997, 2 master's awarded. *Degree requirements:* For master's, thesis. *Entrance requirements:* For master's, GRE, TOEFL, DDS. Application deadline: 9/30. Application fee: $30 ($50 for international students). *Expenses:* Tuition $3166 per year full-time, $176 per semester hour part-time for state residents; $10,202 per year full-time, $176 per semester hour part-time for nonresidents. Fees $202 per year full-time, $52 per year (minimum) part-time. • Dr. Jimmy Pinkham, Head, 319-335-7478. Application contact: Dr. Arthur Nowak, Graduate Program Director, 319-335-7479. Fax: 319-335-7155.

The University of Iowa, College of Dentistry and Graduate College, Graduate Programs in Dentistry, Department of Periodontics, Iowa City, IA 52242-1316. Awards MS, Certificate.

Faculty: 8 full-time (3 women), 4 part-time (0 women). Students: 8 full-time (2 women); includes 3 minority (1 African American, 1 Asian American, 1 Hispanic), 2 international. In 1997, 3 master's awarded. *Degree requirements:* For master's, thesis. *Entrance requirements:* For master's, GRE, TOEFL, DDS. Application deadline: 10/1. Application fee: $30 ($50 for international students). *Expenses:* Tuition $3166 per year full-time, $176 per semester hour part-time for state residents; $10,202 per year full-time, $176 per semester hour part-time for nonresidents. Fees $202 per year full-time, $52 per year (minimum) part-time. • Dr. Georgia Johnson, Head, 319-335-7238. Fax: 319-335-7155.

The University of Iowa, College of Dentistry and Graduate College, Graduate Programs in Dentistry, Department of Preventive and Community Dentistry, Iowa City, IA 52242-1316. Offers program in dental public health (MS). Faculty: 8 full-time (4 women), 26 part-time (10 women). Students: 6 full-time (4 women), 3 part-time (all women); includes 4 international. In 1997, 2 degrees awarded. *Degree requirements:* Thesis. *Entrance requirements:* GRE, TOEFL, DDS. Application deadline: 7/1. Application fee: $30 ($50 for international students). *Expenses:* Tuition $3166 per year full-time, $176 per semester hour part-time for state residents; $10,202 per year full-time, $176 per semester hour part-time for nonresidents. Fees $202 per year full-time, $52 per year (minimum) part-time. • Dr. Henrietta Logan, Interim Head, 319-335-7184. Application contact: Dr. Steven Levy, Graduate Program Director, 319-335-7185. Fax: 319-335-7155.

The University of Iowa, College of Dentistry and Graduate College, Graduate Programs in Dentistry, Department of Prosthodontics, Iowa City, IA 52242-1316. Awards MS, Certificate. Faculty: 8 full-time (2 women), 8 part-time (1 woman). Students: 9 full-time (1 woman); includes 7 international. In 1997, 1 master's awarded. *Degree requirements:* For master's, thesis. *Entrance requirements:* For master's, GRE, TOEFL, DDS. Application deadline: 11/1. Application fee: $30 ($50 for international students). *Expenses:* Tuition $3166 per year full-time, $176 per semester hour part-time for state residents; $10,202 per year full-time, $176 per semester hour part-time for nonresidents. Fees $202 per year full-time, $52 per year (minimum) part-time. • Dr. Forrest Scandrett, Head, 319-335-7258. Application contact: Dr. Steven Aquilino, Director, 319-335-7258. Fax: 319-335-7155.

University of Kentucky, Graduate School and College of Dentistry, Graduate Program in Dentistry, Lexington, KY 40506-0032. Awards MS. Faculty: 21 full-time (2 women), 3 part-time (0 women). Students: 7 full-time (2 women), 2 part-time (0 women); includes 1 international. 8 applicants, 13% accepted. In 1997, 5 degrees awarded. *Degree requirements:* Thesis, comprehensive exam required, foreign language not required. *Entrance requirements:* GRE General Test, minimum undergraduate GPA of 2.5. Application deadline: 7/19 (rolling processing; 12/15 for spring admission). Application fee: $30 ($35 for international students). *Financial aid:* In 1997–98, 4 teaching assistantships were awarded; fellowships, research assistantships, Federal Work-Study, institutionally sponsored loans also available. Aid available to part-time students. Financial aid application deadline: 6/1. • Dr. Thomas Lillich, Director of Graduate Studies, 606-257-5656. E-mail: lillich@pop.uky.edu. Application contact: Dr. Constance L. Wood, Associate Dean, 606-257-4613. Fax: 606-323-1928.

University of Louisville, School of Dentistry and Graduate School, Graduate Programs in Dentistry, Program of Oral Biology, Louisville, KY 40292-0001. Awards MS. Students: 9 full-time (4 women), 7 part-time (1 woman); includes 3 minority (2 African Americans, 1 Asian American), 1 international. Average age 30. In 1997, 10 degrees awarded. *Degree requirements:* Thesis. *Average time to degree:* master's–1 year full-time, 2 years part-time. *Entrance requirements:* DAT or GRE General Test (minimum combined score of 1000), minimum GPA of 2.75. Application fee: $10. *Faculty research:* Secretory immunity, oral microbiology, calcium and bone metabolism. • Dr. Ronald J. Doyle, Director, 502-852-6928.

University of Manitoba, Faculties of Dentistry and Graduate Studies, Graduate Programs in Dentistry, Winnipeg, MB R3T 2N2, Canada. Offerings include dental diagnostic and surgical sciences (M Sc, Diploma), with options in oral and maxillofacial surgery (Diploma), orthodontics (M Sc), periodontology (Diploma); oral biology (M Sc, PhD); restorative dentistry (M Sc), with option in dental materials. Faculty: 15 full-time, 3 part-time. *Degree requirements:* For master's and doctorate, thesis/dissertation required, foreign language not required. *Application fee:* $50. • Dr. C. Dawes, Associate Dean (Research), 204-789-3512. Fax: 204-888-4113.

University of Maryland, Baltimore, Graduate School, Graduate Programs in Dentistry, Department of Oral Pathology, Baltimore, MD 21201-1627. Awards MS, PhD. Faculty: 7 (0 women). Students: 3 part-time (2 women); includes 1 minority (African American). 2 applicants, 50% accepted. *Degree requirements:* For master's, thesis or alternative required, foreign language not required; for doctorate, dissertation required, foreign language not required. *Entrance requirements:* GRE General Test, TOEFL, DDS, DMD. Application deadline: 7/1. Application fee: $42. *Financial aid:* Fellowships, research assistantships, teaching assistantships available. Aid available to part-time students. Financial aid application deadline: 2/15. *Faculty research:* Histopathology, epidemiology of oral lesions, embryology. • Dr. John J. Sauk, Chairman, 410-706-7936. Application contact: Dr. Bernard A. Levy, Director, 410-706-7936.

University of Maryland, Baltimore, Graduate School, Graduate Programs in Dentistry, Department of Oral and Craniofacial Biological Sciences, Baltimore, MD 21201-1627. Awards MS, PhD, DDS/PhD. Students: 7 full-time (4 women), 2 part-time (1 woman); includes 1 minority (African American), 4 international. 7 applicants, 71% accepted. *Degree requirements:* For doctorate, dissertation required, foreign language not required. *Entrance requirements:* GRE General Test, TOEFL. Application deadline: 7/1. Application fee: $42. *Financial aid:* Application deadline 2/15. • Dr. Ronald Dubner, Chair, 410-706-0860. Application contact: Dr. Norman Capra, Program Director, 410-706-4219.

University of Maryland, Baltimore, Graduate School, Graduate Programs in Dentistry, Program in Oral Biology, Baltimore, MD 21201-1627. Awards MS. Faculty: 65 (9 women). Students: 1 (woman) full-time, 3 part-time (2 women); includes 1 minority (African American). 15 applicants, 47% accepted. In 1997, 7 degrees awarded. *Entrance requirements:* GRE General Test, TOEFL, minimum GPA of 3.0. Application deadline: 7/1. Application fee: $42. *Financial aid:* Fellowships, research assistantships, teaching assistantships available. Financial aid application deadline: 2/15. • Dr. Glenn Minah, Director, 410-706-7539. Fax: 410-706-0193.

University of Medicine and Dentistry of New Jersey, Graduate School of Biomedical Sciences, Graduate Programs in Biomedical Sciences, Department of Oral Biology, Newark, NJ 07107-3001. Awards MS. *Degree requirements:* Thesis. *Entrance requirements:* GRE General Test, TOEFL, DDS or DMD. Application deadline: 2/1 (priority date; 10/1 for spring admission). Application fee: $40. *Financial aid:* Fellowships, Federal Work-Study, institutionally sponsored loans available. Financial aid application deadline: 5/1. *Faculty research:* Clinical pain, dental materials, periodontal disease. • Dr. Zia Shey, Chairperson, 973-972-5064. Application contact: Dr. Willie Mae Coram, Assistant Dean, 973-972-4511. Fax: 973-972-7148.

University of Michigan, School of Dentistry and Horace H. Rackham School of Graduate Studies, Graduate Programs in Dentistry, Ann Arbor, MI 48109. Awards MS, PhD, Certificate. *Degree requirements:* For master's, thesis; for doctorate, oral defense of dissertation, preliminary exam. *Entrance requirements:* For doctorate, GRE. Application fee: $55. *Financial aid:* Fellowships, research assistantships, teaching assistantships available. • Graduate Chair, 734-763-1068. Application contact: Karen Cole, Coordinator, 734-763-1068. E-mail: joice@umich.edu.

University of Minnesota, Twin Cities Campus, School of Dentistry and Graduate School, Graduate Programs in Dentistry, Division of Endodontics, Minneapolis, MN 55455-0213. Awards MS. *Degree requirements:* Thesis required, foreign language not required. • Dr. Walter Bowles, Director, 612-624-9613.

University of Minnesota, Twin Cities Campus, School of Dentistry and Graduate School, Graduate Programs in Dentistry, Division of Oral Biology, Minneapolis, MN 55455-0213. Awards MS, PhD. *Degree requirements:* For master's, thesis required, foreign language not required. • Robert Ophaug, Director, 612-625-5198.

University of Minnesota, Twin Cities Campus, School of Dentistry and Graduate School, Graduate Programs in Dentistry, Division of Orthodontics, Minneapolis, MN 55455-0213. Awards MS. *Degree requirements:* Thesis required, foreign language not required. • Dr. Michael Speidel, Director, 612-625-5678.

University of Minnesota, Twin Cities Campus, School of Dentistry and Graduate School, Graduate Programs in Dentistry, Division of Pediatric Dentistry, Minneapolis, MN 55455-0213. Awards MS. *Degree requirements:* Thesis required, foreign language not required. • Dr. Jacob Lee, Director, 612-625-0694.

University of Minnesota, Twin Cities Campus, School of Dentistry and Graduate School, Graduate Programs in Dentistry, Division of Periodontology, Minneapolis, MN 55455-0213. Awards MS. *Degree requirements:* Thesis required, foreign language not required. • Dr. James Hinrichs, Director, 612-625-9107.

University of Minnesota, Twin Cities Campus, School of Dentistry and Graduate School, Graduate Programs in Dentistry, Division of Prosthodontics, Minneapolis, MN 55455-0213. Awards MS. *Degree requirements:* Thesis required, foreign language not required. • Dr. James Hotlan, Director, 612-625-5650.

University of Minnesota, Twin Cities Campus, School of Dentistry and Graduate School, Graduate Programs in Dentistry, Program in Oral Health Services for Older Adults, Minneapolis, MN 55455-0213. Awards MS. *Degree requirements:* Thesis required, foreign language not required. • Dr. Stephen Shuman, Director, Graduate Programs in Dentistry, 612-625-1191.

University of Minnesota, Twin Cities Campus, School of Dentistry and Graduate School, Graduate Programs in Dentistry, Program in Temporal Mandibular Joint, Minneapolis, MN 55455-0213. Awards MS. *Degree requirements:* Thesis required, foreign language not required. • Dr. James Fricton, Director, 612-624-2411.

University of Missouri–Kansas City, School of Dentistry, Graduate Programs in Dentistry, Program in Oral Biology, Kansas City, MO 64108. Awards MS, PhD. PhD offered through the School of Graduate Studies. Faculty: 6 full-time (3 women). Students: 4 part-time (0 women); includes 1 minority (Asian American). Average age 38. In 1997, 1 master's awarded. *Degree requirements:* For master's, thesis required, foreign language not required; for doctorate, dissertation. *Application deadline:* 10/1. *Application fee:* $25. *Expenses:* Tuition $182 per credit hour for state residents; $508 per credit hour for nonresidents. Fees $60 per year. *Financial aid:* Research assistantships, full and partial tuition waivers, Federal Work-Study, institutionally sponsored loans available. Aid available to part-time students. Financial aid application deadline: 3/13. *Faculty research:* Dentin adhesive systems, adverse gastrointestinal effects of erythromycin products. • Dr. J. David Eick, Chairperson, 816-235-2067. Application contact: Dr. Paulette Spencer, Director, Graduate Studies and Research, 816-235-2071. Fax: 816-235-2157.

University of Missouri–Kansas City, School of Dentistry, Graduate Programs in Dentistry, Programs in Dental Specialties, Kansas City, MO 64110-2499. Offerings in advanced education in dentistry (Graduate Dental Certificate), diagnostic sciences (Graduate Dental Certificate), oral and maxillofacial surgery (Graduate Dental Certificate), orthodontics and dentofacial orthopedics (Graduate Dental Certificate), pediatric dentistry (Graduate Dental Certificate), periodontics (Graduate Dental Certificate), prosthodontics (Graduate Dental Certificate). Faculty: 9 full-time (7 women). Students: 5 full-time (0 women), 50 part-time (12 women); includes 6 minority (1 African American, 3 Asian Americans, 2 Hispanics), 11 international. Average age 30. In 1997, 5 degrees awarded. *Entrance requirements:* DDS. Application deadline: 10/1. Application fee: $25. *Tuition:* $13,947 per year for state residents; $28,045 per year for nonresidents. *Financial aid:* Partial tuition waivers, Federal Work-Study, institutionally sponsored loans, and career-related internships or fieldwork available. Aid available to part-time students. Financial aid application deadline: 3/15. • Robert D. Cowan, Chairperson, Advanced Education Programs, 816-235-2164. Fax: 816-235-2157.

University of Nebraska Medical Center, Graduate Program in Dentistry, Omaha, NE 68198-0001. Awards MS. Part-time programs available. Faculty: 36. Students: 2 full-time (0 women), 5 part-time (2 women); includes 1 international. Average age 29. 69 applicants, 7% accepted. In 1997, 4 degrees awarded. *Degree requirements:* Thesis required, foreign language not required. *Entrance requirements:* GRE General Test or National Board Dental Exam. Application fee: $25. *Financial aid:* In 1997–98, 5 research assistantships, 7 graduate assistantships (5 to first-year students) were awarded; fellowships, teaching assistantships, institutionally sponsored loans also available. Aid available to part-time students. Financial aid application deadline: 3/1. *Faculty research:* Oral microbiology and immunology, dental materials, periodontal therapy, neurophysiology, pharmacology. • Dr. Jeffrey Payne, Graduate Committee Chair, 402-472-1318. Application contact: Jo Wagner, Associate Director of Admissions, 402-559-4206.

The University of North Carolina at Chapel Hill, School of Dentistry and Graduate School, Graduate Programs in Dentistry, Chapel Hill, NC 27599. Offerings in dental hygiene education (MS), dentistry (MS), oral biology (MS, PhD), oral epidemiology (PhD). Faculty: 82 full-time (15 women). Students: 73 full-time (41 women); includes 29 minority (3 African Americans, 22 Asian Americans, 4 Hispanics). Average age 28. 639 applicants, 7% accepted. In 1997, 21 master's awarded. *Degree requirements:* Thesis/dissertation required, foreign language not required. *Average time to degree:* master's–3 years full-time. *Entrance requirements:* For master's, dental degree; for doctorate, GRE General Test. Application deadline: 10/1. Application fee: $55. Electronic applications accepted. *Expenses:* Tuition $2502 per year full-time, $626 per semester (minimum) part-time for state residents; $12,764 per year full-time, $3191 per semester (minimum) part-time for nonresidents. Fees $1041 per year full-time, $461 per semester (minimum) part-time. *Financial aid:* In 1997–98, 49 teaching assistantships (27 to first-year students) were awarded; fellowships, research assistantships also available. Financial aid application deadline: 3/1; applicants required to submit FAFSA. *Faculty research:* Biomaterials, clinical trials, neurobiology, oral epidemiology. • Dr. Ronald Hunt, Associate Dean for Academic Affairs, 919-966-4451. Fax: 919-966-7007. Application contact: Kim Miller, Admissions Office, School of Dentistry, 919-966-4451.

See in-depth description on page 1711.

University of Oklahoma Health Sciences Center, College of Dentistry and Graduate College, Graduate Programs in Dentistry, Department of Orthodontics, Oklahoma City, OK 73190. Awards MS. Faculty: 3 full-time (0 women), 9 part-time (0 women). Students: 9 full-time (1 woman); includes 3 minority (2 Asian Americans, 1 Hispanic), 1 international. Average age 29. 150 applicants, 3% accepted. In 1997, 5 degrees awarded (40% entered university research/teaching, 60% found other work related to degree). *Degree requirements:* Thesis required, foreign language not required. *Average time to degree:* master's–2 years full-time. *Entrance requirements:* TOEFL (minimum score 550), minimum GPA of 3.0, DDS/DMD. Application deadline: 10/1 (priority date). Application fee: $25 ($50 for international students). *Financial aid:* 9 students received aid; institutionally sponsored loans available. Financial aid application deadline: 3/1; applicants required to submit FAFSA. *Faculty research:* Craniofacial growth and development, biomechanical principles in orthodontics. • Dr. Ram S. Nanda, Chairperson, 405-271-6087. Application contact: Charlene Eddy, Staff Secretary, 405-271-4271. Fax: 405-271-1178.

University of Oklahoma Health Sciences Center, College of Dentistry and Graduate College, Graduate Programs in Dentistry, Department of Periodontics, Oklahoma City, OK 73190. Awards MS. Faculty: 3 full-time (0 women), 6 part-time (1 woman). Students: 6 full-time (1 woman); includes 2 minority (both Asian Americans). Average age 32. 11 applicants, 18% accepted. In 1997, 2 degrees awarded (100% found work related to degree). *Degree requirements:* Thesis required, foreign language not required. *Average time to degree:* master's–3 years full-time. *Entrance requirements:* GRE General Test (minimum combined score of 1000), TOEFL (minimum score 500), minimum GPA of 3.0, DDS/DMD. Application

Directory: Oral and Dental Sciences

University of Oklahoma Health Sciences Center (continued)

deadline: 11/1 (rolling processing). Application fee: $25 ($50 for international students). *Financial aid:* Institutionally sponsored loans available. *Faculty research:* Wound healing and periodontal regeneration, clinical research in periodontal diagnoses and treatment. • Dr. John J. Dmytryk, Director, 405-271-6531. Application contact: Office of Admissions and Records, 405-271-2347.

University of Pittsburgh, School of Dental Medicine, Graduate Programs in Dental Medicine, Pittsburgh, PA 15260. Offerings in anesthesiology (Certificate), endodontics (MDS, Certificate), maxillofacial prosthodontics (Certificate), orthodontics (Certificate), pediatric dentistry (MDS, Certificate), periodontics (MDS, Certificate), prosthodontics (MDS, Certificate). Students: 44 full-time (12 women), 1 part-time (0 women); includes 5 minority (1 African American, 3 Asian Americans, 1 Hispanic), 14 international. In 1997, 4 master's awarded. *Application fee:* $40 ($50 for international students). Electronic applications accepted. *Expenses:* Tuition $9402 per year full-time, $388 per credit part-time for state residents; $19,372 per year full-time, $799 per credit part-time for nonresidents. Fees $480 per year full-time, $180 per year part-time. *Financial aid:* Clinical fellowships, graduate assistantships, Federal Work-Study, institutionally sponsored loans available. Financial aid applicants required to submit FAFSA. *Faculty research:* Immunology of periodontal disease, craniofacial development. • Application contact: Dr. Albert Whitehead, Director for Student Services, 412-648-8422. Fax: 412-648-9571. E-mail: aww1+@pitt.edu.

University of Puerto Rico, Medical Sciences Campus, School of Dentistry, Graduate Programs in Dentistry, San Juan, PR 00936-5067. Offerings in dentistry (Certificate), general dentistry (MSD), oral and maxillofacial surgery (MSD), orthodontics (MSD), pediatric dentistry (MSD), prosthodontics (MSD). Faculty: 8 full-time (1 woman), 20 part-time (5 women). Students: 31 full-time (14 women). Average age 27. 68 applicants, 18% accepted. In 1997, 17 Certificates awarded. *Degree requirements:* For master's, 1 foreign language required, thesis not required. *Entrance requirements:* For master's, DDS or DMD. Application deadline: 10/15. Application fee: $15. *Financial aid:* Stipends available. *Faculty research:* Analgesic drugs, anti-inflammatory drugs, saliva cytoanalysis, dental materials, oral health conditions of school-age population. • Application contact: Dr. Antonio Soto Singala, Assistant Dean, 787-758-2525 Ext. 1113. Fax: 787-751-0990.

University of Rochester, School of Medicine and Dentistry, Graduate Programs in Medicine and Dentistry, Center for Oral Biology, Rochester, NY 14642. Awards MS. Faculty: 6 full-time. Students: 4 full-time (2 women), 2 part-time (0 women); includes 3 minority (2 African Americans, 1 Hispanic), 1 international. 6 applicants, 17% accepted. In 1997, 2 degrees awarded. *Degree requirements:* Thesis required, foreign language not required. *Entrance requirements:* GRE General Test, DDS or equivalent. Application deadline: 2/1. Application fee: $25. *Expenses:* Tuition $21,485 per year full-time, $672 per credit hour part-time. Fees $336 per year. *Financial aid:* Fellowships, research assistantships, teaching assistantships, full and partial tuition waivers available. Financial aid application deadline: 2/1. • Dr. Lawrence Tabak, Director, 716-275-3441. Application contact: Pat Noonan, Graduate Program Secretary, 716-275-3265.

University of Southern California, School of Dentistry and Graduate School, Program in Craniofacial Biology, Los Angeles, CA 90089. Awards MS, PhD. Students: 51 full-time (22 women), 4 part-time (1 woman); includes 15 minority (3 African Americans, 9 Asian Americans, 3 Hispanics), 28 international. Average age 31. 25 applicants, 60% accepted. In 1997, 7 master's, 1 doctorate awarded. *Degree requirements:* Thesis/dissertation. *Entrance requirements:* GRE General Test. Application deadline: 6/1 (priority date; 10/15 for spring admission). Application fee: $55. *Expenses:* Tuition $706 per unit. Fees $414 per year full-time, $32 per year part-time. *Financial aid:* In 1997–98, 38 fellowships, 2 research assistantships, 3 scholarships were awarded; teaching assistantships, Federal Work-Study, institutionally sponsored loans also available. Aid available to part-time students. Financial aid application deadline: 2/15; applicants required to submit FAFSA. • Dr. Charles Schuler, Director, 213-740-6799.

The University of Texas Health Science Center at San Antonio, Dental School and Graduate School of Biomedical Sciences, Graduate Program in Dentistry, San Antonio, TX 78284-6200. Awards MS, Certificate. Students: 71 full-time (20 women); includes 9 minority (1 African American, 5 Asian Americans, 3 Hispanics), 9 international. 463 applicants, 6% accepted. In 1997, 15 master's, 17 Certificates awarded. *Degree requirements:* For master's, thesis required, foreign language not required. *Average time to degree:* master's–3 years full-time; other advanced degree–2.5 years full-time. *Entrance requirements:* For master's, GRE General Test (minimum combined score of 1000), DDS; for Certificate, DDS. Application deadline: 10/15. Application fee: $0. *Financial aid:* 10 students received aid; institutionally sponsored loans available. Financial aid application deadline: 3/1; applicants required to submit FAFSA. • Dr. Spencer Redding, Associate Dean, 210-567-3798. Fax: 210-567-6721. E-mail: redding@uthscsa.edu.

The University of Texas–Houston Health Science Center, Graduate School of Biomedical Sciences, Program in Oral Biomaterials, Houston, TX 77225-0036. Awards MS. Faculty: 5 full-time (1 woman). Students: 0. 6 applicants, 67% accepted. In 1997, 1 degree awarded. *Degree requirements:* Thesis required, foreign language not required. *Entrance requirements:* GRE General Test, TOEFL (minimum score 550), TWE (minimum score 4). Application deadline: 1/15 (priority date; rolling processing; 11/1 for spring admission). Application fee: $10. Electronic applications accepted. *Financial aid:* Fellowships available. Financial aid application deadline: 1/15. *Faculty research:* Dental materials, adhesion, optical properties, mechanical properties. Total annual research expenditures: $80,000. • Dr. John Powers, Director, 713-500-4470. Fax: 713-500-4500. E-mail: jpowers@mail.db.uth.tmc.edu. Application contact: Anne Baronitis, Director of Admissions, 713-500-9860. Fax: 713-500-9877. E-mail: abaron@gsbs.gs.uth.tmc.edu.

University of the Pacific, School of Dentistry, Graduate Orthodontics Program, San Francisco, CA 94115. Awards MSD. Faculty: 4 full-time (0 women), 19 part-time (4 women), 6 FTE. Students: 12 full-time (3 women); includes 3 minority (all Asian Americans), 3 international. Average age 31. 122 applicants, 5% accepted. In 1997, 5 degrees awarded. *Degree requirements:* Thesis required, foreign language not required. *Average time to degree:* master's–2 years full-time. *Entrance requirements:* GRE General Test, TOEFL, DDS. Application deadline: 10/1. Application fee: $40. *Tuition:* $34,400 per year. *Financial aid:* 8 students received aid; institutionally sponsored loans available. Financial aid application deadline: 2/1. *Faculty research:* Osteoblast cell studies, digitized orthodontic records, periodontal orthodontic relationships, orthotreatment outcomes. • Dr. Robert Boyd, Chairperson, 415-929-6555.

University of Toronto, Faculty of Dentistry, Diploma Specialty Programs, Toronto, ON M5S 1A1, Canada. Offerings in dental anesthesia (Diploma), dental public health (Diploma), endodontics (Diploma), oral and maxillofacial surgery and anesthesia (Diploma), oral pathology (Diploma), oral radiology (Diploma), orthodontics (Diploma), prosthodontics (Diploma). Faculty: 47 full-time (7 women). Students: 49 full-time (21 women), 1 part-time (0 women); includes 2 international. Average age 28. 153 applicants, 12% accepted. In 1997, 17 degrees awarded. *Degree requirements:* Thesis, essay required, foreign language not required. *Application deadline:* 4/1. *Application fee:* $100. *Expenses:* Tuition $4070 per year for Canadian residents; $7870 per year for nonresidents. Fees $628 per year. *Financial aid:* In 1997–98, 4 students received aid, including 4 fellowships averaging $900 per month and totaling $10,800; bursaries and career-related internships or fieldwork also available. Financial aid application deadline: 9/30. *Faculty research:* Plaque and periodontal biology, biomaterials/dental implants, community dentistry, growth development, neurophysiology. • Application contact: Alexandra Haldane, Admissions Officer, 416-979-4901 Ext. 4373. Fax: 416-979-4936. E-mail: ahaldane@dental.utoronto.ca.

University of Toronto, Faculty of Dentistry, Graduate Programs in Dentistry, Toronto, ON M5G 1G6, Canada. Awards M Sc, PhD. Part-time programs available. Faculty: 44 part-time. Students: 41 full-time (20 women), 17 part-time (6 women); includes 10 international. 35 applicants, 49% accepted. In 1997, 7 master's, 4 doctorates awarded. *Degree requirements:* Thesis/dissertation required, foreign language not required. *Average time to degree:* master's–2 years full-time, 4 years part-time; doctorate–4 years full-time. *Application fee:* $75. *Expenses:* Tuition $4070 per year for Canadian residents; $7870 per year for nonresidents. Fees $628 per year. *Financial aid:* Fellowships, research assistantships, teaching assistantships, bursaries available. • Dr. A. R. Ten Cate, Director, 416-979-4901 Ext. 4481. Application contact: Coordinator, 416-979-4901 Ext. 4482. Fax: 416-979-4936. E-mail: lmockler@dental.utoronto.ca.

University of Washington, School of Dentistry and Graduate School, Graduate Programs in Dentistry, Seattle, WA 98195. Awards MS, MSD, PhD, MSD/PhD. Faculty: 73 full-time (15 women), 46 part-time (12 women). Students: 64 full-time (25 women); includes 14 minority (12 Asian Americans, 2 Hispanics), 15 international. 540 applicants, 5% accepted. In 1997, 23 master's awarded. *Degree requirements:* For master's, thesis optional, foreign language not required. *Application deadline:* 10/1. *Application fee:* $35. *Tuition:* $5433 per year full-time, $775 per quarter (minimum) part-time for state residents; $13,479 per year full-time, $1925 per quarter (minimum) part-time for nonresidents. *Financial aid:* 21 students received aid. Financial aid application deadline: 2/28. • Application contact: Admissions, 206-543-5982.

The University of Western Ontario, Faculty of Medicine and Dentistry, School of Dentistry, Division of Orthodontics, London, ON N6A 5C1, Canada. Awards M Cl D. Faculty: Students: 9. Average age 30. 60 applicants, 5% accepted. In 1997, 3 degrees awarded. *Degree requirements:* Thesis required, foreign language not required. *Entrance requirements:* Minimum B average, 1 year of general practice preferred. Application deadline: 10/1. Application fee: $100. *Financial aid:* Career-related internships or fieldwork available. • Dr. G. Z. Wright, Chair, 519-661-3558.

West Virginia University, School of Dentistry, Graduate Programs in Dentistry, Morgantown, WV 26506. Offering in dental specialities (MS). Students: 17 full-time (4 women); includes 1 minority (Asian American), 3 international. Average age 30. 128 applicants, 5% accepted. In 1997, 6 degrees awarded (100% found work related to degree). *Degree requirements:* Thesis required, foreign language not required. *Entrance requirements:* TOEFL, National Dental Hygiene Board Exam, DDS/DMD from accredited North American school. Application deadline: 9/15 (rolling processing). Application fee: $45 ($100 for international students). *Financial aid:* In 1997–98, 7 teaching assistantships were awarded; Federal Work-Study, institutionally sponsored loans also available. Financial aid application deadline: 3/1; applicants required to submit FAFSA. *Faculty research:* Growth and development, cephalographics, endodontic interpretation and therapy. Total annual research expenditures: $2000. • Dr. William R. McCutcheon, Associate Dean, 304-293-3549. Application contact: Marilyn Powley, Graduate School Admissions Officer, 304-293-3549. Fax: 304-293-8561.

West Virginia University, School of Dentistry, Program in Dental Hygiene, Morgantown, WV 26506. Awards MS. Part-time programs available. Faculty: 3 full-time (all women). Students: 3 full-time (all women), 3 part-time (all women); includes 1 minority (Asian American). Average age 30. 4 applicants, 75% accepted. In 1997, 2 degrees awarded. *Degree requirements:* Thesis required, foreign language not required. *Average time to degree:* master's–2.5 years full-time, 4 years part-time. *Entrance requirements:* GRE, MAT, TOEFL, BS in dental hygiene, minimum GPA of 2.5. Application deadline: 7/1 (rolling processing). Application fee: $45. *Tuition:* $5374 per year for state residents; $14,058 per year for nonresidents. *Financial aid:* Federal Work-Study, institutionally sponsored loans available. Financial aid application deadline: 3/1; applicants required to submit FAFSA. *Faculty research:* Educational administration and innovation in dentistry. • Dr. Christina DeBiase, Coordinator, 304-293-8729. Application contact: Dr. William R. McCutcheon, Associate Dean, 304-293-3549. Fax: 304-293-8561.

BOSTON UNIVERSITY

Goldman School of Dental Medicine

Programs of Study

The Goldman School of Dental Medicine provides predoctoral education leading to the D.M.D. degree and postdoctoral education in the following specialties: oral and maxillofacial surgery, orthodontics, periodontology, endodontics, pediatric dentistry, prosthodontics, and dental public health. The School has also instituted advanced education programs in operative dentistry and oral biology.

The D.M.D. program prepares students for the practice of dental medicine with an emphasis on prevention and early detection of dental disease. The School sees as its primary goal the education of dentists who are well grounded in the basic medical sciences, skilled in the exercise of clinical care, and sensitive to the needs of their patients and community. To this end, the curriculum combines a didactic program, a team approach to clinical care, and a series of planned practical learning experiences in dental offices outside the dental school. These off-site experiences are the core of the APEX (Applied Professional EXperience) Program, in which students serve as dental interns and receive a salary enabling them to help defray their educational expenses.

The D.M.D. program requires four years of didactic and clinical study. The first year begins with a preparatory program in oral radiology, dental assisting techniques, and preventive dentistry. The basic science courses are introduced in the first year and taught jointly by the faculties of the Schools of Medicine and Dental Medicine. This foundation year includes preclinical dental sciences and rotations in private dental offices as dental interns. During the second year, the focus begins to shift from the basic sciences to the clinical dental sciences, with increased opportunity for the student to treat patients in the School's clinic as a member of a dental team. This team is composed of students from each of the four classes, together with faculty members who oversee and coordinate the clinical activities. Team meetings stimulate learning and deal with the problems and questions that arise in any dental practice. Sophomore students assist other team members in providing comprehensive care to patients. The third and fourth years of study emphasize clinical dental practice, with increasing exposure to the specialty areas of dentistry. Students provide dental care for children with special needs, carry out dental procedures requiring general anesthesia, and manage patients with systemic diseases. Students spend the majority of their time in diagnosis, treatment planning, and patient care. Through seminars and a computer laboratory, students learn to organize and administer a dental practice, including the application of data management systems. Fourth-year students have a six-week externship in which they practice clinical dentistry at one of more than twenty sites from Boston to Hawaii.

Research Facilities

Research is an important component of the program offered at the dental school, complementing classroom learning and clinical experience. The School has scientific investigators studying important aspects of oral health, including defense mechanisms, bone-cell regulation, protein biochemistry, and molecular biology. Research is also directed toward the development of new restorative materials and improving methods to determine biocompatibility of implants and other dental materials. Many projects are supported by grants and offer opportunities for students in all programs to participate in research. Through the years, the School has earned a position of international prominence in basic and applied research. More recently, the School's commitment to research has resulted in the ongoing expansion of laboratory space and facilities, the addition of faculty members, and increases in private and federal funding for important research endeavors, including new initiatives in clinical epidemiology, health policy, and health services research.

Financial Aid

There are several sources of financial assistance available to dental students entering Boston University. A booklet, *Financial Assistance—Goldman School of Dental Medicine,* is available from the Boston University Medical Center, Office of Student Financial Management, 715 Albany Street, Boston, Massachusetts 02118 (617-638-5130). Funding varies from year to year, but the Loans and Scholarship Committee usually responds quickly to applications.

Cost of Study

Full-time tuition figures for the 1998–99 academic year are as follows: the predoctoral program costs $32,246, and the postdoctoral program costs $31,186. Students in the D.M.D. program are required to purchase two instrument kits from the University during enrollment in the program. The approximate cost for the two kits is $8000. For students enrolled in clinical postdoctoral programs, estimated costs for instruments range from $400 to $9800.

Living and Housing Costs

The cost of living in Boston is as high as in any other major city in the United States. For those who are interested in living in dormitories or University-owned apartments, the Office of Housing aids students on a first-come, first-served basis. Monthly rent for one-bedroom apartments ranged from $700 to $900 in 1997–98. Roommate referral services are available to help defray the cost of housing.

Student Group

The School is coeducational and nonsectarian, with approximately 625 full-time students enrolled in the various dental programs. Students come from all over the United States and many other countries.

Location

Because of its compact size, Boston is a perfect city for walking, and many attractions are easy to reach. Theaters, Red Sox games at Fenway Park, sailing on the Charles, Boston Pops concerts at Symphony Hall, sight-seeing on Cape Cod, and camping in the Berkshires all provide pleasant diversions. Home to approximately sixty colleges and universities, Boston is an unrivaled center for learning.

The University and The School

The Goldman School of Dental Medicine was established as part of Boston University Medical Center in 1963. Boston University Medical Center, located in Boston's South End, forms a semiautonomous but integral part of the University. It consolidates the resources and activities of the Goldman School of Dental Medicine, the School of Medicine, the School of Public Health, and Boston Medical Center.

Applying

The D.M.D. program of the Goldman School is a participant in the American Association of Dental Schools Application Service (AADSAS). All applications must be processed through this service. Applicants must obtain copies of application materials prepared by the AADSAS and return them to that service. Once their accuracy has been verified, applicants make all subsequent communications regarding admission directly with the dental school. Applications for fall semester admission must be filed before March 1. A nonrefundable $50 application fee is required. The Dental Admission Test is required and should be taken no later than October of the year prior to admission. In addition, students are asked to attend a personal interview and provide three letters of recommendation.

Correspondence and Information

Office of Admissions and Student Services
Goldman School of Dental Medicine
Boston University
100 East Newton Street, Room 305
Boston, Massachusetts 02118

Telephone: 617-638-4787
Fax: 617-638-4798

Boston University

THE FACULTY

Salomon Amar, Associate Professor of Periodontology and Oral Biology; D.D.S., Ph.D., Louis Pasteur (France).
Thomas Armstrong, Associate Clinical Professor of Restorative Sciences/ Biomaterials; D.D.S., Howard.
Nargess Ashayeri, Associate Clinical Professor of Restorative Sciences/Biomaterials; D.M.D., Boston University.
Fayez Badlissi, Clinical Instructor of Periodontology and Oral Biology; D.M.D., Boston University.
Neal Bellanti, Professor of Restorative Sciences/Biomaterials and Associate Dean for Academic Affairs; D.D.S., Missouri.
Joseph Boffa, Associate Professor of Health Policy and Health Services Research; D.D.S., SUNY at Buffalo.
Aljernon Bolden, Associate Professor of Health Policy and Health Services Research; D.M.D., Tufts.
Donald Booth, Professor and Chairman of Oral and Maxillofacial Surgery and Associate Dean for Hospital Affairs; D.M.D., Harvard.
Nancy Bouchard, Clinical Instructor of Diagnostic Sciences and Patient Services; M.H.P., Northeastern.
Mahdi Bouhmadouche, Assistant Clinical Professor of Diagnostic Sciences and Patient Services; D.M.D., Boston University.
William Bourassa, Professor of Pediatric Dentistry; D.M.D., Louisville.
Fred Bourgeois, Assistant Clinical Professor of Diagnostic Sciences and Patient Services; D.M.D., Boston University.
Joseph Calabrese, Assistant Professor of Restorative Sciences/ Biomaterials; D.M.D., Boston University.
Santo Cataudella, Associate Professor of Oral and Maxillofacial Surgery; D.M.D., Tufts.
Catherine Champagne, Assistant Research Professor of Periodontology and Oral Biology; Ph.D., Université des Sciences et Techniques (France).
Pelly Chang, Assistant Clinical Professor of Restorative Sciences/ Biomaterials; D.M.D., Boston University.
Laisheng Chou, Associate Professor of Restorative Sciences/Biomaterials; D.M.D., Shanghai Medical (China).
David Cottrell, Assistant Professor of Oral and Maxillofacial Surgery; D.M.D., Pennsylvania.
Serge Dibart, Assistant Professor of Periodontology and Oral Biology; D.M.D., Boston University.
Stephen DuLong, Associate Professor of Restorative Sciences/Biomaterials and Assistant Dean for Clinical Services; D.M.D., Boston University.
Jean Emerling, Professor of Restorative Sciences/Biomaterials; D.D.S., SUNY at Buffalo.
Paul Farsai, Assistant Professor of Restorative Sciences/Biomaterials; D.M.D., Boston University.
Karl Flanzer, Assistant Clinical Professor of Restorative Sciences/Biomaterials; D.M.D., Tufts.
Deborah Fournier, Assistant Professor of Diagnostic Sciences and Patient Services; Ph.D., Syracuse.
Catherine Frankl, Assistant Professor of Health Policy and Health Services Research; J.D., Boston University.
Spencer N. Frankl, Professor of Pediatric Dentistry and Dean of the School; D.D.S., Temple.
Paula Friedman, Professor of Diagnostic Sciences and Patient Services and Associate Dean for Administration; D.D.S., Columbia.
Raul I. Garcia, Professor and Chairman of Health Policy and Health Services Research; D.M.D., Harvard.
Anthony Gianelly, Professor and Chairman of Orthodontics; D.M.D., Harvard.
Russell A. Giordano II, Assistant Professor of Restorative Sciences/Biomaterials; D.M.D., Harvard.
Dana Graves, Professor of Periodontology and Oral Biology; D.D.S., Columbia.
Michelle Henshaw, Assistant Professor of Health Policy and Health Services Research; D.D.S., California, San Francisco.
Christopher Hughes, Associate Professor and Chairman of Pediatric Dentistry; D.M.D., Pennsylvania.
Jeffrey Hutter, Associate Professor of Endodontics; D.M.D., Pennsylvania.
John Ictech-Cassis, Assistant Clinical Professor of Restorative Sciences/Biomaterials; D.D.S., Universita Tecnologica de Mexico.
Zhimon Jacobson, Clinical Professor of Restorative Sciences/Biomaterials; D.D.S., National University of Iran.
Spyros Karatzas, Assistant Professor of Periodontology and Oral Biology; D.D.S., Athens (Greece).
Thomas Kilgore, Professor of Oral and Maxillofacial Surgery and Associate Dean for Advanced Education; D.M.D., Pennsylvania.
Celeste Kong, Associate Professor of Restorative Sciences/Biomaterials; D.M.D., Philippines.
Elizabeth Krall, Associate Professor of Health Policy and Health Services Research; Ph.D., Pittsburgh.
Maria Kukuruzinska, Associate Professor of Periodontology and Oral Biology; Ph.D., Johns Hopkins.
Mark Lamkin, Assistant Research Professor of Periodontology and Oral Biology; Ph.D., Boston University.
Urs Lendenmann, Assistant Research Professor of Periodontology and Oral Biology; Ph.D., Swiss Federal Institute of Technology.
Robert Lincoln, Assistant Clinical Professor of Oral and Maxillofacial Surgery; D.M.D., Tufts.
Weldon Lloyd, Associate Research Professor of Periodontology and Oral Biology; D.Sc., Boston University.
Christine Lo, Assistant Clinical Professor of Restorative Sciences/Biomaterials; D.M.D., Boston University.
Philip Maloney, Professor of Oral and Maxillofacial Surgery; D.M.D., Tufts.
Madalyn Mann, Associate Professor of Diagnostic Sciences and Patient Services; M.S., Boston University.
John McManama, Professor of Restorative Sciences/Biomaterials; D.D.S., Loyola of Chicago.
Steven Morgano, Associate Clinical Professor of Restorative Sciences/Biomaterials; D.M.D., Tufts.
Emrey Moskowitz, Clinical Instructor of Diagnostic Sciences and Patient Services; D.D.S., California, San Francisco.
Dan Nathanson, Professor and Chairman of Restorative Sciences/Biomaterials and Assistant Dean for Continuing Education and External Affairs; D.M.D., Hebrew (Jerusalem).
Thomas Ollerhead, Assistant Clinical Professor of Endodontics; L.D.S., Royal College of Surgeons (England).
Frank Oppenheim, Professor and Chairman of Periodontology and Oral Biology; D.D.S., Zurich (Switzerland).
Maxine Peck, Assistant Professor of Diagnostic Sciences and Patient Services; M.S., Boston University.
A. Stephen Polins, Professor of Periodontology and Oral Biology; D.D.S., Howard.
John Richardson, Professor of Diagnostic Sciences and Patient Services; D.D.S., Temple.
Steven Roberts, Clinical Instructor of Restorative Sciences/Biomaterials; D.M.D., Boston University.
Bruce Robinson, Assistant Clinical Professor of Diagnostic Sciences and Patient Services; D.M.D., Georgetown.
Lynda Rose, Instructor of Health Policy and Health Services Research; B.A., Emmanuel.
Leila Joy Rosenthal, Assistant Clinical Professor of Restorative Sciences/Biomaterials; M.F.A., Boston University.
Carlos Sabrosa, Clinical Instructor of Restorative Sciences/Biomaterials; D.D.S., Universidade do Estado do Rio de Janiero.
Parviz Sadooghi, Associate Clinical Professor; Restorative Sciences/Biomaterials; D.M.D., Boston University.
Herbert Schilder, Professor and Chairman of Endodontics; D.D.S., NYU.
M. Reza Setayesh, Associate Professor of Periodontology and Oral Biology; D.M.D., Boston University.
Sydell Shaw, Assistant Clinical Professor of Diagnostic Sciences and Patient Services and Associate Dean for Admissions and Student Services; D.D.S., NYU.
Hyman Smukler, Professor of Periodontology and Oral Biology; D.M.D., Boston University.
Dmitri Svirsky, Assistant Clinical Professor of Restorative Sciences/Biomaterials; D.M.D., Boston University.
Philip Trackman, Assistant Professor of Periodontology and Oral Biology; Ph.D., Boston University.
Thomas Van Dyke, Professor of Periodontology and Oral Biology; D.D.S., Case Western Reserve.
Robert Dale Welch, Assistant Research Professor of Health Policy and Health Services Research; D.D.S., Maryland.
Dawn West, Assistant Clinical Professor of Oral and Maxillofacial Surgery; D.M.D., Boston University.
Benjamin Wu, Assistant Professor of Restorative Sciences/Biomaterials; Ph.D., MIT.
Elie Zebouni, Assistant Clinical Professor of Restorative Sciences/Biomaterials; D.M.D., Boston University.
Lawrence Zoller, Associate Professor of Oral and Maxillofacial Surgery; Ph.D., Rutgers.

UNIVERSITY OF NORTH CAROLINA AT CHAPEL HILL

School of Dentistry
Ph.D. Program in Oral Biology

Program of Study

Oral biology encompasses the study of the structure and function of normal and abnormal tissues of the oral cavity and related areas, as well as the study of disease and healing mechanisms specific to various oral conditions. The discipline of oral biology applies and extends the concepts of immunology, embryology, physiology, cellular and molecular biology, pharmacology, microbiology, and biochemistry to understanding the growth and development and pathologies associated with the oral cavity. Attention in dental research and practice is now focusing on the dynamics of oral disease and on prevention and treatment at the earliest stages of development, including research on risk factors for disease as well as the cellular and molecular events in disease pathogenesis. Molecular approaches for oral disease analysis and the complexity of disease elements require advanced training in the discipline of oral biology. Modern biomedical research is also identifying systemic relationships between oral conditions, health status, and diseases such as atherosclerosis, HIV, and cancer. The oral cavity also offers an ideal model for the study of biological structures and cellular mechanisms that are important throughout the body and in immune response.

The UNC oral biology Ph.D. program has three primary areas of emphasis: orofacial neurobiology, cellular and molecular biology of host-pathogens interactions, and the biology of extracellular matrices. These areas represent central concepts for study at advanced levels in the discipline of oral biology. Expertise and authority in these particular concepts are well represented within the strongest research and training qualifications of program faculty members. Curricular requirements are based on training areas, with common core requirements for all students. Students begin with emphasis on basic sciences courses (cell biology and anatomy, microbiology, biochemistry) followed by the examination of specific biological applications. Research interests and qualifications such as the D.D.S. or M.D. will also determine course requirements. Participation in research in progress is a key element of the program, and students start laboratory rotations in their first semester to allow maximum time for research involvement. Program participants are involved early in their academic careers with certain key research areas targeted by the National Institutes of Health for national scientific focus. In addition, UNC's proximity and access to the Research Triangle's unique blend of universities, private industry, and national scientific organizations offer a wealth of resources for scientific study, collaboration, and research development.

Research Facilities

The oral biology Ph.D. program is based at the University of North Carolina School of Dentistry, recognized internationally as one of the strongest research-oriented dental schools. Peer recognition of the scientific merit of current research is constant, through invitations for presentations, funded grant proposals, and frequent peer-reviewed publications in the scientific literature. The oral biology Ph.D. program is located in the Dental Research Center, the central base for much of the research in the five-building School of Dentistry, with access to SEM/TEM microscopy, tissue culture facilities, anaerobic microbiology support, ALAC-accredited animal facilities, a P-3 level isolation facility, atomic absorption spectrophotometry, computers and software for image analyses/enhancement and finite element analyses, and a Clinical Research Unit including an 8-patient operatory. Also available are biostatistical assistance, medical illustration, photography, radiology, and grants management. Additional scientific resources are available through program faculty laboratories located in the Dental Research Center, the School of Medicine, the Carolinas Medical Center, and Research Triangle Park.

Financial Aid

Graduate research assistantships are awarded competitively for students accepted into the oral biology Ph.D. program. Support is provided through program resources during the first two years at the rate of $14,000 annually with health insurance and may include a special tuition rate for out-of-state students. Support for dissertation research (beginning in the third year) is made available by faculty mentors.

Cost of Study

For North Carolina residents, tuition and fees effective in 1998 are $1110 per semester (full-time students); for out-of-state students, rates were $5603 per semester.

Cost of Living

Space in University residences is available for single students and some married students. In 1997–98 dormitory costs were $1130 per semester for double accommodations and $1560 to $1780 for single accommodations. Apartments for married students rented for $330 (one bedroom) or $375 (two bedrooms) per month. Students may apply for this housing prior to marriage and prior to acceptance into a graduate program. Housing possibilities also include many apartment complexes and rental houses off campus with convenient campus access through an extensive local bus service.

Student Group

The University has a current enrollment of approximately 23,000 men and women, of whom about 6,200 are graduate students. The School of Dentistry annually has approximately 215 D.D.S. candidates, 65 graduate students in clinical specialty programs, and 40 in other advanced training programs (oral biology, oral epidemiology).

Student Outcomes

The program's objective is to train individuals for careers in research and teaching in areas related to oral biology; Ph.D. graduates have the qualifications and research expertise to become productive faculty members at leading universities and senior scientists in various academic institutions or industrial settings.

Location

The Research Triangle, formed by the proximity and shared resources of the University of North Carolina at Chapel Hill, Duke University, and North Carolina State University, provides an exciting, stimulating environment offering intellectual challenge, scientific and biomedical expertise, and a wide array of cultural events and artistic forums. The adjacent Research Triangle Park is the second-largest research and development park in the United States and includes firms known as world leaders in the fields of medical research, pharmaceutics, scientific equipment and research, and information technology. Raleigh-Durham International Airport is conveniently located in the center of the Research Triangle, about 20 miles from the UNC-CH campus. The mild climate and nearby mountains and beaches add to the reputation of the Chapel Hill area as an ideal place to live.

The University

The University of North Carolina was established in Chapel Hill in 1795. The Division of Health Affairs has the Schools of Medicine, Dentistry, Public Health, Pharmacy, and Nursing. Numerous other professional schools, including those of law and business, are located here, and the University's College of Arts and Sciences is ranked by *U.S. News & World Report* and other surveys as among the very best of the nation's public universities for undergraduate education.

Applying

Individuals with a significant background in biological sciences, dentistry, and/or medicine who have an interest in developing research skills and focus and studying current issues in oral biology are encouraged to apply. Preference is given to students who wish to study for the Ph.D. degree. Research experience is an asset, and a statement of research interests and goals is desirable. Applications are generally accepted for admission to the fall semester, preferably by January 31. Application requirements include the GRE (and the TOEFL for international applicants), documentation of previous scientific or medical studies, and transcripts for all undergraduate and graduate education. Selection of candidates will be made on a competitive basis by faculty members of the oral biology program who serve on a selection committee; candidates' research interests, research qualifications, and appropriate opportunities are significant factors in selection.

Correspondence and Information

Graduate Program Coordinator
Oral Biology Ph.D. Program, School of Dentistry
101 Dental Research Center, Campus Box #7455
University of North Carolina at Chapel Hill
Chapel Hill, North Carolina 27599-7455

Telephone: 919-966-1538
Fax: 919-966-3683
E-mail: frances_hess@dentistry.unc.edu

University of North Carolina at Chapel Hill

THE FACULTY AND THEIR RESEARCH

Orofacial Neurobiology

Greg Essick, Associate Professor, Prosthodontics; D.D.S., 1979, Ph.D., 1983, North Carolina at Chapel Hill. Somatosensory and motor research, neural mechanisms: tactile psychophysics with emphasis on motion processing and perception.

Mark Hollins, Professor, Psychology; Ph.D., Brown, 1971. Somatosensory and motor research, sensation and perception: tactile perception of objects and events, psychophysical analysis of pain and analgesia.

Edward F. Kelly, Research Associate Professor, Diagnostic Sciences; Ph.D., Harvard, 1970. Neural mechanisms, electrophysiological measurement, noninvasive imaging of human brain function.

Martin Kendal-Reed, Research Assistant Professor, Dental Ecology; Ph.D., Warwick (United Kingdom), 1991. Biological psychology, human psychophysiology, human olfaction and chemosensation, olfactory development, methodology in human psychophysiology and brain imaging, cognitive aspects of olfaction.

Alan Light, Professor, Physiology; Ph.D., SUNY Health Science Center at Syracuse, 1977. Somatosensory and motor research, pain sensation: descending modulation of pain pathways, ascending nociceptive pathways and neurobiolgical modulation of neural transmission, synaptic activation and gene expression of c-fos.

William Maixner, Associate Professor, Endodontics and Pharmacology; Ph.D., 1982, D.D.S., 1983, Iowa. Neural coding of nociceptive information, pain perception.

Glenn Matsushima, Assistant Professor, Microbiology and Immunology and Research Scientist, UNC Neuroscience Center; Ph.D., USC, 1988. Neuroimmunology and inflammation in the central nervous system using molecular and cellular approaches to study the regulation of macrophages.

Gerry S. Oxford, Professor, Physiology; Ph.D., Emory, 1974. Neural mechanisms: relationships of neurotransmitters and modulatory peptides and receptors for those with ion channels in neuronal and endocrine cell membranes; electrophysiology of neural mechanisms: modulation of ion channels, functional characterization of ion channel activity in the cellular process of hormone and neurotransmitter secretion.

Aldo Rustioni, Professor, Cell Biology and Anatomy; M.D., Milan (Italy), 1965. Neuroanatomy, neurocytology, neurohistochemistry, electron microscopy, neurophysiology, somatosensory system, neurotransmitters and modulation of somatosensation.

Donald W. Warren, Kenan Professor, Dental Ecology and Surgery; D.D.S., North Carolina at Chapel Hill, 1959; Ph.D., Pennsylvania, 1963. Craniofacial development, cleft palate, speech aerodynamics, respiration, olfaction.

John Zuniga, Associate Professor, Oral and Maxillofacial Surgery; D.M.D., Tufts, 1978; Ph.D., Rochester, 1986. Oral and maxillofacial surgery, nerve injury and regeneration, orofacial pain and sensation.

Biology of Host-Pathogens Interactions

Roland R. Arnold, Professor, Diagnostic Sciences and Periodontics; Ph.D., LSU, 1975. Host-pathogen interactions in periodontal diseases, lactoferrin, neutrophil function, secretory immunity, host-microbial biology, specific and innate host defense factors.

Patrick M. Flood, Associate Professor of Periodontics and of Microbiology and Immunology; Ph.D., Chicago, 1980. Host-microbial biology, cellular immunology, immune response, virology, antigen processing and presentation, mechanisms of T-cell activation.

Robert E. Johnston, Professor, Microbiology and Immunology; Ph.D., Texas at Austin, 1973. Virology, viral pathogenesis, genetic analysis and strategies for immune modulation: molecular genetics of alphavirus pathogenesis, design of alphavirus vaccines, and development of vaccine vectors based on alphavirus vaccines.

Thomas Kawula, Assistant Professor, Microbiology and Immunology; Ph.D., North Carolina at Chapel Hill, 1987. Molecular basis for bacterial pathogenesis, genetic analysis, and approaches for study of certain pathogens and infectivity mechanisms.

Glenn Matsushima, Assistant Professor, Microbiology and Immunology and Research Scientist, UNC Neuroscience Center; Ph.D., USC, 1988. Neuroimmunology and inflammation in the central nervous system using molecular and cellular approaches to study the regulation of macrophages.

Steven Offenbacher, Professor, Periodontics; D.D.S., 1976, Ph.D., 1977, Virginia Commonwealth; M.M.Sc., Harvard, 1980. Inflammatory mediators, host response, periodontal diseases, smokeless tobacco, oral and enteric endotoxins, relationships of inflammatory mediators and periodontal diseases to low birth weights and risks in pregnancy outcomes and as risk factors in cardiovascular diseases.

Nancy Raab-Traub, Professor, Microbiology and Immunology; Ph.D., Chicago, 1980. Pathogenesis of Epstein-Barr virus, EBV gene expression and structural analyses, EBV-associated lymphomas.

Diane Shugars, Assistant Professor, Dental Ecology and Microbiology and Immunology; D.D.S., 1983; M.P.H., 1988; Ph.D., 1993, North Carolina at Chapel Hill. Human immunodeficiency viruses and AIDS—pathogenesis, molecular biology, and immunology; infectious diseases and antiviral agents, virus-host cell interactions.

Gerald Sonnenfeld, Adjunct Professor, Diagnostic Sciences and Director, Division of Research Immunology, Carolinas Medical Center, Charlotte, North Carolina; Ph.D., Pittsburgh. Immune system, regulatory role of interferon in immune response, response of immune system to space flight, cell-mediated immunity, immunotoxicology.

Christina Teng, Adjunct Associate Professor, Periodontics, and Research Biologist and Supervisor, Laboratory of Reproductive and Developmental Toxicology, NIEHS, Research Triangle Park; Ph.D., Texas at Austin, 1969. Effect of environmental estrogen on the regulation of lactoferrin gene expression in a variety of cell types, molecular analysis of lactoferrin gene structure, interactions of regulatory elements and trans-acting cellular factors, human lactoferrin structure and function relationship.

Jenny Ting, Alumni Distinguished Professor, Microbiology and Immunology; Ph.D., Northwestern, 1979. Molecular immunology, tumor immunology, neuroimmunology, transplantation biology, and transcriptional regulation, including regulation of major histocompatibility (MHC) genes by cytokines such as interferons and tumor necrosis factors, MHC function in neurodegenerative diseases.

Roland Tisch, Assistant Professor, Microbiology and Immunology; Ph.D., Toronto, 1990. Immunology, inflammation, diabetes, T-cell biology, molecular mechanisms in development of insulin-dependent diabetes mellitus, therapeutic intervention in autoimmunity.

Biology of Extracellular Matrices

Ikramudden Aukhil, Professor, Periodontics; B.D.S./M.S., Michigan, 1981. Tissue regeneration, structure/function of extracellular matrix proteins tenascin and fibronectin, wound healing.

James W. Bawden, Alumni Distinguished Professor, Pediatric Dentistry; D.D.S., 1954, Ph.D., 1961, Iowa. Enamel mineralization, mechanisms of fluoride action, clinical effects of topical fluorides, signal transduction.

Lyndon Cooper, Associate Professor of Prosthodontics and of Biochemistry and Biophysics; D.D.S., NYU, 1983, Ph.D., Rochester, 1990. Stress determinants in osteoblast physiology, molecular determinants of osseointegration in dental implants.

Miles Crenshaw, Professor, Pediatric Dentistry, Ph.D., Duke, 1964. Biomineralization, matrix control of mineral induction and postnucleation growth.

Philip Hirsch, Professor Emeritus, Pharmacology; Ph.D., Berkeley, 1954. Hormonal regulation of calcium metabolism.

Malcolm Johnston, Professor Emeritus of Orthodontics and of Cell Biology and Anatomy; M.Sc.D., Toronto, 1956; Ph.D., Rochester, 1965. Craniofacial development.

Gayle Lester, Research Associate Professor, Surgery (Division of Orthopaedic Surgery) and Pharmacology; Ph.D., Virginia Commonwealth, 1977. Bone physiology and osteoinduction focusing on biochemistry of extracellular matrix; vitamin D metabolism, calcium homeostasis, and markers of bone turnover; osteoporosis; osteosarcoma and mechanisms of drug resistance; ligament healing and cellular modulation of collagen synthesis.

Lola Reid, Professor, Physiology; Ph.D., North Carolina at Chapel Hill, 1974. Regulation of synthesis and abundance of tissue-specific mRNAs by cooperative effects of hormones and extracullular matrix, especially heparin proteoglycans; identification, isolation, and regulation of growth and differentiation of liver stem cells and related precursor cell populations.

Svein Toverud, Professor Emeritus, Pharmacology; D.M.D., Harvard, 1954; Ph.D., Oslo, 1964. Hormonal regulation of bone and calcium metabolism, particularly in pregnancy and lactation; regulation of secretion of parathyroid hormone and calcitriol; regulation of intestinal calcium absorption.

John Timothy Wright, Professor, Pediatric Dentistry; D.D.S., West Virginia, 1978; M.S., Alabama at Birmingham, 1983. Development, fluoride, hereditary conditions affecting human enamel: epidermolysis bullosa, amelogenesis imperfecta.

Mitsuo Yamauchi, Professor, Periodontics; D.D.S., 1976, Ph.D., 1983, Tokyo. Collagen biochemistry, physiology and metabolism of bone, characterization of collagens in various connective tissue.

Section 35
Medicine

This section contains directories of institutions offering professional programs and graduate work in allopathic medicine, bioethics, naturopathic medicine, osteopathic medicine, and podiatric medicine, followed by in-depth entries submitted by institutions that chose to prepare detailed program descriptions. Additional information about programs listed in the directories but not augmented by an in-depth entry may be obtained by writing directly to the dean of a medical school or college at the address given in the directory.

CONTENTS

Program Directories

Announcements

Cross-Discipline Announcement

In-Depth Descriptions

Allopathic Medicine

Albany Medical College, Professional Program, Albany, NY 12208-3479. Awards MD. Accredited by LCME. *Entrance requirements:* MCAT. Application deadline: 11/15 (rolling processing). Application fee: $70.

Allegheny University of the Health Sciences, School of Medicine, Professional Program in Medicine, Philadelphia, PA 19102-1192. Awards MD, MD/MS, MD/PhD. Accredited by LCME. Faculty: 1,096 full-time (312 women), 131 part-time (57 women). Students: 1,067 full-time (498 women), 1 part-time (0 women); includes 366 minority (133 African Americans, 173 Asian Americans, 57 Hispanics, 3 Native Americans), 23 international. Average age 25. 10,857 applicants, 6% accepted. In 1997, 312 degrees awarded. *Degree requirements:* National Board Exam Parts I and II required, foreign language and thesis not required. *Entrance requirements:* MCAT. Application deadline: 12/1. Application fee: $55. *Expenses:* Tuition $25,725 per year. Fees $525 per year. *Financial aid:* Federal Work-Study, institutionally sponsored loans available. Financial aid application deadline: 5/1; applicants required to submit FAFSA. • Application contact: Dr. Sue Zarro, Associate Dean for Student Affairs and Admissions, 215-762-3063.

Baylor College of Medicine, Medical School, Professional Program in Medicine, Houston, TX 77030-3498. Awards MD, MD/PhD. Accredited by LCME. Students: 687 full-time (281 women); includes 304 minority (49 African Americans, 188 Asian Americans, 61 Hispanics, 6 Native Americans), 7 international. Average age 25. 3,234 applicants, 9% accepted. In 1997, 158 degrees awarded. *Average time to degree:* first professional–4 years full-time. *Entrance requirements:* MCAT, 90 hours of pre-med course work. Application deadline: 11/1 (rolling processing). Application fee: $35. *Expenses:* Tuition $6550 per year for state residents; $19,650 per year for nonresidents. Fees $717 per year (minimum). *Financial aid:* 494 students received aid; Federal Work-Study, institutionally sponsored loans available. Financial aid application deadline: 5/8; applicants required to submit FAFSA. • Dr. W. Bradshaw, Dean of Education, 713-798-8878. Fax: 713-798-3096. Application contact: Dr. L. Leighton Hill, Assistant Dean, 713-798-4842.

Boston University, School of Medicine, Professional Program in Medicine, Boston, MA 02118. Awards MD, MD/MPH, MD/PhD, MD/MA. Accredited by LCME. Part-time programs available. Students: 601 full-time (230 women), 27 part-time (13 women); includes 215 minority (26 African Americans, 167 Asian Americans, 19 Hispanics, 3 Native Americans), 21 international. Average age 25. In 1997, 156 degrees awarded. *Application deadline:* 11/1. *Application fee:* $95. *Financial aid:* Fellowships, Federal Work-Study available. Aid available to part-time students. • Application contact: Dr. John F. O'Connor, Associate Dean for Admissions, 617-638-4630.

Brown University, Program in Medicine, Providence, RI 02912. Awards MD, MD/PhD. Accredited by LCME. Faculty: 296 full-time, 672 part-time. Students: 263 full-time (113 women), 1 part-time (0 women); includes 56 minority (19 African Americans, 25 Asian Americans, 11 Hispanics, 1 Native American). In 1997, 79 degrees awarded. *Application deadline:* 11/1. *Application fee:* $60. *Expenses:* Tuition $26,896 per year. Fees $1202 per year. *Financial aid:* Fellowships, Federal Work-Study available. • Donald Marsh, Dean, 401-863-3330.

Case Western Reserve University, School of Medicine, Professional Program in Medicine, Cleveland, OH 44106. Awards MD, MD/MS, MD/PhD. Accredited by LCME. Faculty: 1,362 full-time (373 women), 1,920 part-time (543 women). Students: 560 full-time (250 women); includes 195 minority (66 African Americans, 113 Asian Americans, 16 Hispanics). Average age 23. 7,318 applicants, 4% accepted. In 1997, 150 degrees awarded. *Entrance requirements:* MCAT, interview. Application deadline: 10/15 (rolling processing). Application fee: $60. • C. Kent Smith, Vice Dean, 216-368-2822. Application contact: Albert C. Kirby, Associate Dean, Admissions and Student Affairs, 216-368-3450.

Charles R. Drew University of Medicine and Science, Professional Program in Medicine, Los Angeles, CA 90059. Awards MD. Faculty: 228. Students: 102; includes 91 minority (44 African Americans, 8 Asian Americans, 36 Hispanics, 3 Native Americans). *Entrance requirements:* MCAT. Application deadline: 11/15. Application fee: $50. *Tuition:* $9993 per year for state residents; $19,377 per year for nonresidents. • Dr. M. Roy Wilson, Dean of the College of Medicine, 213-563-4928. Application contact: American Medical College Admission Service, 202-828-0635.

Columbia University, College of Physicians and Surgeons, Professional Program in Medicine, New York, NY 10032. Awards MD, MD/MPH, MD/MS, MD/PhD, MD/DDS. Accredited by LCME. Part-time programs available. Students: 624 full-time (264 women); includes 176 minority (30 African Americans, 120 Asian Americans, 25 Hispanics, 1 Native American), 19 international. Average age 23. 4,141 applicants, 7% accepted. In 1997, 150 degrees awarded. *Average time to degree:* first professional–4 years full-time. *Entrance requirements:* MCAT. Application deadline: 10/15. Application fee: $75. *Tuition:* $28,008 per year. *Financial aid:* Fellowships, research assistantships, teaching assistantships, scholarships, traineeships, full tuition waivers, Federal Work-Study, and career-related internships or fieldwork available. Aid available to part-time students. • Application contact: Chairman, Committee on Admissions, 212-305-3595. Fax: 212-305-3545. E-mail: pt8@columbia.edu.

Cornell University Medical College, Medical College, Professional Program in Medicine, New York, NY 10021-4896. Awards MD. Accredited by LCME.

Creighton University, School of Medicine, Professional Program in Medicine, Omaha, NE 68178-0001. Awards MD, MD/PhD. Accredited by LCME. Students: 462 full-time (161 women); includes 78 minority (8 African Americans, 37 Asian Americans, 31 Hispanics, 2 Native Americans), 5 international. Average age 24. 6,237 applicants, 2% accepted. In 1997, 110 degrees awarded (100% continued full-time study). *Average time to degree:* first professional–4 years full-time. *Entrance requirements:* MCAT (average 9). Application deadline: 12/1 (rolling processing). Application fee: $65. *Expenses:* Tuition $26,550 per year. Fees $536 per year. *Financial aid:* 398 students received aid; institutionally sponsored loans available. Aid available to part-time students. Financial aid application deadline: 4/1; applicants required to submit FAFSA. *Faculty research:* Hereditary cancer, osteoporosis, diabetes. Total annual research expenditures: $11.13 million. • Dr. Henry Nipper, Assistant Dean of Medical Admissions, 402-280-2799. Application contact: James L. Glass, Director of Medical Admissions, 402-280-2798. Fax: 402-280-1241. E-mail: medschadm@creighton.edu.

Dalhousie University, Faculty of Medicine, Professional Program in Medicine, Halifax, NS B3H 3J5, Canada. Awards MD, MD/PhD, MD/M Sc. Accredited by LCME. MD/PhD offered jointly with the Departments of Biochemistry, Microbiology and Immunology, Pharmacology, and Physiology and Biophysics. Students: 380. *Entrance requirements:* MCAT. Application deadline: rolling. Application fee: $55. • Dr. John Ruedy, Dean, Faculty of Medicine, 902-494-1846. Application contact: Brenda L. Detienne, Admissions Coordinator, 902-494-1874.

Dartmouth College, Dartmouth Medical School, Hanover, NH 03755. Awards MD, MD/PhD, MD/MBA. Accredited by LCME. Faculty: 146 full-time, 716 part-time. Students: 308 full-time (141 women); includes 55 minority (8 African Americans, 25 Asian Americans, 15 Hispanics, 7 Native Americans), 12 international. 7,136 applicants, 3% accepted. In 1997, 59 degrees awarded. *Entrance requirements:* MCAT, 1 year each of general biology, general chemistry, organic chemistry, and physics; half a semester of calculus. Application deadline: 11/1 (rolling processing). Application fee: $60. *Expenses:* Tuition $24,860 per year. Fees $4230 per year. *Financial aid:* In 1997–98, 251 students received aid, including 126 scholarships (29 to first-year students) totaling $1.445 million; fellowships, research assistantships, teaching assistantships, Federal Work-Study, institutionally sponsored loans, and career-related internships or fieldwork also available. Financial aid applicants required to submit CSS PROFILE or FAFSA. • Dr. John C. Baldwin, Dean, 603-650-1471. Application contact: Andrew G. Welch, Director of Admissions, 603-650-1505. Fax: 603-650-1614.

Duke University, School of Medicine, Professional Program in Medicine, Durham, NC 27708-0586. Awards MD, MD/MPH, MD/PhD, MD/AM, MD/JD, MD/MBA. Accredited by LCME. MD/MPH offered in cooperation with the University of North Carolina at Chapel Hill. In 1997, 99 degrees awarded. *Entrance requirements:* MCAT. Application deadline: 10/15. Application fee: $65. *Expenses:* Tuition $26,700 per year. Fees $3164 per year. *Financial aid:* Merit scholarships available. Financial aid application deadline: 5/1. • Application contact: Dr. Brenda Armstrong, Director of Admissions, 919-684-2985.

East Carolina University, School of Medicine, Professional Program in Medicine, Greenville, NC 27858-4353. Awards MD, MD/PhD. Accredited by LCME. Faculty: 24 full-time (4 women). Students: 297 full-time (146 women); includes 82 minority (52 African Americans, 17 Asian Americans, 6 Hispanics, 7 Native Americans). Average age 27. In 1997, 73 degrees awarded. *Entrance requirements:* MCAT. Application deadline: 6/1. Application fee: $40. *Tuition:* $1886 per year full-time, $472 per semester (minimum) part-time for state residents; $9156 per year full-time, $2289 per semester (minimum) part-time for nonresidents. *Financial aid:* Application deadline 6/1. • Dr. James A. Hallock, Dean, School of Medicine, 252-816-2201. Application contact: Dr. Sam Pennington, Associate Dean for Research and Graduate Studies, 252-816-2827. Fax: 252-816-3260. E-mail: snpennington@brody.med.ecu.edu.

Eastern Virginia Medical School, Professional Program in Medicine, Norfolk, VA 23501-1980. Awards MD, MD/PhD. Accredited by LCME. MD/PhD offered jointly with Old Dominion University. Students: 405 full-time (177 women); includes 99 minority (26 African Americans, 63 Asian Americans, 8 Hispanics, 2 Native Americans), 1 international. 5,655 applicants, 5% accepted. In 1997, 104 degrees awarded. *Average time to degree:* first professional–4 years full-time. *Entrance requirements:* MCAT, bachelor's degree or equivalent, previous course work in sciences. Application deadline: 11/15 (priority date; rolling processing). Application fee: $80. *Expenses:* Tuition $14,500 per year for state residents; $26,000 per year for nonresidents. Fees $1448 per year. *Financial aid:* 345 students received aid; Federal Work-Study, institutionally sponsored loans available. Financial aid application deadline: 3/15; applicants required to submit CSS PROFILE or FAFSA. • Dr. Donald Lewis, Associate Dean for Admissions, 757-446-5812. Application contact: Susan Castora, Director of Admissions, 757-446-5812. Fax: 757-446-5896.

East Tennessee State University, James H. Quillen College of Medicine, Professional Programs in Medicine, Johnson City, TN 37614-0734. Awards MD. Accredited by LCME. Faculty: 90 full-time (19 women), 17 part-time (1 woman). Students: 243 full-time (101 women), 6 part-time (1 woman); includes 41 minority (24 African Americans, 13 Asian Americans, 3 Hispanics, 1 Native American), 1 international. Average age 28. 2,090 applicants, 3% accepted. In 1997, 61 degrees awarded. *Entrance requirements:* MCAT. Application deadline: 12/1 (rolling processing). Application fee: $25. *Tuition:* $10,310 per year for state residents; $19,258 per year for nonresidents. *Financial aid:* Grants, Federal Work-Study, institutionally sponsored loans, and career-related internships or fieldwork available. Financial aid application deadline: 5/10. • Application contact: Edwin D. Taylor, Assistant Dean for Admissions and Records, 423-439-6221.

Emory University, School of Medicine, Professional Program in Medicine, Atlanta, GA 30322-4510. Awards MD, MD/MPH, MD/PhD. Accredited by LCME. Faculty: 1,153 full-time, 54 part-time. Students: 452 full-time (188 women); includes 135 minority (54 African Americans, 74 Asian Americans, 6 Hispanics, 1 Native American), 8 international. Average age 22. 7,765 applicants, 3% accepted. In 1997, 107 degrees awarded. *Entrance requirements:* MCAT. Application deadline: 10/15 (rolling processing). Application fee: $60. *Expenses:* Tuition $25,770 per year. Fees $400 per year. *Financial aid:* Fellowships, research assistantships, teaching assistantships, Federal Work-Study, institutionally sponsored loans, and career-related internships or fieldwork available. Financial aid application deadline: 2/15; applicants required to submit FAFSA. *Total annual research expenditures:* $77.65 million. • Dr. Jonas A. Shulman, Executive Associate Dean, 404-727-5655. Application contact: Dr. John Stone, Associate Dean and Director of Admissions, 404-727-5660. Fax: 404-727-0045. E-mail: medschadmiss@medadm.emory.edu.

Finch University of Health Sciences/The Chicago Medical School, School of Medicine, North Chicago, IL 60064-3095. Awards MD, MD/MS, MD/PhD. Accredited by LCME. Faculty: 303 full-time, 50 part-time. Students: 758 full-time (297 women); includes 326 minority (74 African Americans, 238 Asian Americans, 14 Hispanics), 11 international. Average age 25. 11,211 applicants, 2% accepted. In 1997, 171 degrees awarded (100% found work related to degree). *Degree requirements:* Clerkship required, foreign language and thesis not required. *Entrance requirements:* MCAT. Application deadline: 12/15 (rolling processing). Application fee: $65. *Tuition:* $32,270 per year. *Financial aid:* Institutionally sponsored loans available. Financial aid application deadline: 1/29; applicants required to submit FAFSA. *Faculty research:* Immunology, critical care, cognitive function, neuroscience, cellular and molecular biology. • Herman Finch, Chief Executive Officer, 847-578-3000. Application contact: Kristine Jones, Director of Admissions and Records, 847-578-3204.

Georgetown University, School of Medicine, Washington, DC 20057. Awards MD, MD/PhD, MD/MBA. Accredited by LCME. *Entrance requirements:* MCAT (average 10.1 on three sections), greater than 90 credit hours with 1 year of course work in biology, organic chemistry, inorganic chemistry, physics, mathematics, and English. Application deadline: 11/1 (rolling processing). Application fee: $55. *Expenses:* Tuition $28,650 per year. Fees $142 (one-time charge).

The George Washington University, School of Medicine and Health Sciences, Professional Program in Medicine, Washington, DC 20052. Awards MD, MD/MPH, MD/PhD. Accredited by LCME. Faculty: 696 full-time (252 women), 1,902 part-time (445 women). Students: 627 full-time (320 women), 1 (woman) part-time; includes 195 minority (45 African Americans, 121 Asian Americans, 25 Hispanics, 4 Native Americans), 14 international. Average age 26. 11,428 applicants, 3% accepted. In 1997, 153 degrees awarded. *Entrance requirements:* MCAT, minimum 90 undergraduate semester hours. Application deadline: 12/1 (rolling processing). Application fee: $55. *Financial aid:* Federal Work-Study, institutionally sponsored loans, and career-related internships or fieldwork available. • Dr. John F. Williams, Associate Dean for Admissions, 202-994-3506. Application contact: Diane P. McQuail, Director of Admissions, 202-994-3506.

Harvard University, Medical School, Professional Program in Medicine, Boston, MA 02115. Awards MD, MD/MPH, MD/PhD, MD/MPP. Accredited by LCME. Students: 721 full-time (348 women); includes 318 minority (76 African Americans, 181 Asian Americans, 55 Hispanics, 6 Native Americans), 40 international. Average age 24. 3,708 applicants, 7% accepted. In 1997, 188 degrees awarded. *Average time to degree:* first professional–4 years full-time. *Entrance requirements:* MCAT, previous course work in biology, chemistry, physics, calculus, and expository writing. Application deadline: 10/15. Application fee: $75. *Expenses:* Tuition $26,000 per year. Fees $1624 per year. *Financial aid:* 500 students received aid; fellowships, research assistantships, teaching assistantships, partial tuition waivers, Federal Work-Study, institutionally sponsored loans, and career-related internships or fieldwork available. Financial aid application deadline: 3/31; applicants required to submit CSS PROFILE or FAFSA. • Dr. Daniel D. Federman, Dean for Medical Education, 617-432-1550. Application contact: Dr. Gerald Foster, Associate Dean for Admissions, 617-432-1550. Fax: 617-432-3307. E-mail: hmsadm@warren.med.harvard.edu.

Harvard University, Medical School and Graduate School of Arts and Sciences, Division of Health Sciences and Technology, Program in Medical Sciences, Cambridge, MA 02138. Awards MD, MD/MM Sc. Accredited by LCME. Offered jointly with Massachusetts Institute of Technology. Students: 188 full-time (44 women); includes 103 minority (6 African Americans, 90 Asian Americans, 7 Hispanics), 20 international. 451 applicants, 9% accepted. In 1997, 29 degrees awarded. *Application deadline:* 10/15 (rolling processing). *Application fee:* $70. *Expenses:* Tuition $26,000 per year. Fees $1316 per year. • Application contact: Dr. Daniel C. Shannon, Director of MD Admissions, HST Division, 617-726-5576.

Howard University, College of Medicine, Professional Program in Medicine, 2400 Sixth Street, NW, Washington, DC 20059-0002. Awards MD, MD/PhD. Accredited by LCME. In 1997, 114 degrees awarded. *Degree requirements:* U.S. Medical Licensing Exam Steps I and II required, foreign language and thesis not required. *Entrance requirements:* MCAT, previous course work in biology, English, general and organic chemistry, mathematics, and physics. Application deadline: 12/15 (rolling processing). Application fee: $45. *Financial aid:* Application deadline 4/1. *Faculty research:* Cancer, diabetes, hypertension, sickle cell anemia, human genome. • Dr. Floyd J. Malveaux, Interim Vice President for Health Affairs and Dean, College of Medicine, 202-806-6270. Application contact: Ann Finney, Admissions Officer, 202-806-6270.

Indiana University–Purdue University Indianapolis, School of Medicine, Professional Program in Medicine, Indianapolis, IN 46202-2896. Awards MD, MD/MS, MD/PhD. Accredited by LCME. Students: 1,110 full-time (427 women); includes 170 minority (43 African Americans, 109 Asian Americans, 15 Hispanics, 3 Native Americans), 5 international. Average age 25. 2,604 applicants. In 1997, 252 degrees awarded. *Entrance requirements:* MCAT. Application deadline: 12/15. Application fee: $35. *Financial aid:* Fellowships, Federal Work-Study available. • Application contact: Robert M. Stump Jr., Director of Admissions, 317-274-3772.

Johns Hopkins University, School of Medicine, Professional Program in Medicine, Baltimore, MD 21205. Awards MD, MD/PhD. Accredited by LCME. Faculty: 1,793 full-time (570 women), 1,304 part-time (315 women). Students: 475 full-time (216 women); includes 130 minority (9 African Americans, 112 Asian Americans, 9 Hispanics), 6 international. Average age 24. 3,941 applicants, 3% accepted. In 1997, 114 degrees awarded. *Application deadline:* 11/1. *Application fee:* $60. *Financial aid:* Fellowships, research assistantships, teaching assistantships available. • Dr. Edward D. Miller, Dean of Medical Faculty and Chief Executive Officer, School of Medicine, 410-955-3180. Application contact: Dr. Leon Gordis, Associate Dean of Admissions, 410-955-3182.

Loma Linda University, School of Medicine, Professional Program in Medicine, Loma Linda, CA 92350. Awards MD, MD/MS, MD/PhD. Accredited by LCME. Faculty: 665 full-time (148 women), 36 part-time (14 women). Students: 662 full-time (272 women); includes 202 minority (31 African Americans, 148 Asian Americans, 21 Hispanics, 2 Native Americans), 68 international. 4,284 applicants, 5% accepted. In 1997, 148 degrees awarded. *Average time to degree:* first professional–4 years full-time. *Entrance requirements:* MCAT, 1 year of biology, chemistry, organic chemistry, and physics. Application deadline: 11/15. Application fee: $100. *Financial aid:* Fellowships, research assistantships, teaching assistantships, full and partial tuition waivers, Federal Work-Study, institutionally sponsored loans, and career-related internships or fieldwork available. Aid available to part-time students. • Dr. Leonard Werner, Associate Dean for Educational Affairs, 909-824-4255. Fax: 909-824-4146.

Louisiana State University Medical Center, School of Medicine in New Orleans, 433 Bolivar Street, New Orleans, LA 70112-2223. Awards MD, MD/PhD. Accredited by LCME. Open only to residents of Louisiana. Faculty: 450. Students: 712 full-time (294 women); includes 206 minority (94 African Americans, 89 Asian Americans, 18 Hispanics, 5 Native Americans). Average age 24. 1,226 applicants, 13% accepted. *Entrance requirements:* MCAT. Application deadline: 11/15 (priority date; rolling processing). Application fee: $50. Electronic applications accepted. *Faculty research:* Medical and basic sciences. • Dr. Robert L. Marier, Dean, 504-568-4007. Fax: 504-568-4008. E-mail: rmarier@lsumc.edu. Application contact: Dr. S. McClugage, Assistant Dean for Admissions, 504-568-6262. Fax: 504-568-7701. E-mail: ms-admissions@lsumc.edu.

Louisiana State University Medical Center, School of Medicine in Shreveport, Shreveport, LA 71130-3932. Awards MD. Accredited by LCME. *Entrance requirements:* MCAT. Application deadline: 12/15 (priority date; rolling processing). Application fee: $50. *Faculty research:* Biomedical science, molecular biology, cardiovascular science.

Loyola University Chicago, Stritch School of Medicine, Maywood, IL 60153. Awards MD, MD/PhD. Accredited by LCME. Faculty: 589 full-time (169 women), 791 part-time (170 women). Students: 519 full-time (234 women); includes 74 minority (15 African Americans, 42 Asian Americans, 16 Hispanics, 1 Native American). Average age 25. 9,114 applicants, 3% accepted. In 1997, 125 degrees awarded (100% continued full-time study). *Average time to degree:* first professional–4 years full-time. *Entrance requirements:* MCAT. Application deadline: 11/15 (rolling processing). Application fee: $50. *Financial aid:* Application deadline 3/1. *Faculty research:* Neuroscience, oncology, cardiovascular disease, burns and shock trauma. Total annual research expenditures: $17.89 million. • Dr. Daniel H. Winship, Dean, 708-216-3223. Fax: 708-216-4305. Application contact: LaDonna E. Norstrom, Assistant Dean for Admissions, 708-216-3229.

Marshall University, School of Medicine, Professional Program in Medicine, Huntington, WV 25755-2020. Awards MD. Accredited by LCME. Faculty: 152 full-time (43 women), 16 part-time (8 women). Students: 201 full-time (67 women); includes 30 minority (3 African Americans, 22 Asian Americans, 2 Hispanics, 3 Native Americans). Average age 26. 1,047 applicants, 5% accepted. In 1997, 48 degrees awarded (100% continued full-time study). *Entrance requirements:* MCAT, 1 year of course work in biology, physics, chemistry, and organic chemistry. Application deadline: 11/15 (rolling processing). *Financial aid:* 185 students received aid; Federal Work-Study, institutionally sponsored loans, and career-related internships or fieldwork available. Aid available to part-time students. Financial aid applicants required to submit FAFSA. • Application contact: Cynthia A. Warren, Director of Admissions, 304-696-7312. Fax: 304-696-7272. E-mail: cindy@musom01.mu.wvnet.edu.

Mayo Medical School, Rochester, MN 55905. Awards MD, MD/PhD, MD/Certificate. Accredited by LCME. MD offered through the Mayo Foundation's Division of Education; MD/Certificate and MD/PhD offered jointly with the Mayo Graduate School. Faculty: 1,200. Students: 167 full-time (85 women); includes 31 minority (19 African Americans, 9 Hispanics, 3 Native Americans). Average age 24. 3,621 applicants, 1% accepted. In 1997, 38 degrees awarded (100% continued full-time study). *Average time to degree:* first professional–4 years full-time. *Entrance requirements:* MCAT, previous undergraduate course work in biology, chemistry, physics, and biochemistry. Application deadline: 11/1 (rolling processing). Application fee: $60. *Financial aid:* 160 students received aid; institutionally sponsored loans and career-related internships or fieldwork available. Financial aid application deadline: 5/1. • Dr. Burton A. Sandok, Dean. Application contact: Marion K. Kelly, Assistant Dean, 507-284-2316. Fax: 507-284-2634.

McGill University, Professional Program in Medicine, Montréal, PQ H3A 2T5, Canada. Awards MD, MD/PhD, MD/MBA. Accredited by LCME. *Expenses:* Tuition $1668 per year for Canadian residents; $8268 per year for nonresidents. Fees $828 per year for Canadian residents; $1216 per year for nonresidents.

McMaster University, Faculty of Health Sciences, Professional Program in Health Sciences, Hamilton, ON L8S 4M2, Canada. Awards MD. Accredited by LCME. *Application fee:* $0. *Tuition:* $7199 per year for Canadian residents; $32,954 per year for nonresidents. • Dr. Russell Joffe, Acting Dean/Vice President, Faculty of Health Sciences, 905-525-9140 Ext. 22100. Fax: 905-546-0800. Application contact: Dr. R. Haslam, Chair, Graduate Programs in Health Sciences, 905-525-9140 Ext. 22983. Fax: 905-546-1129.

Medical College of Georgia, School of Medicine, Augusta, GA 30912-1003. Awards MD, MD/PhD. Accredited by LCME. MD/PhD offered jointly with the School of Graduate Studies. Faculty: 531 full-time (97 women), 47 part-time (23 women). Students: 717 full-time (224 women); includes 108 minority (36 African Americans, 56 Asian Americans, 14 Hispanics, 2 Native Americans), 1 international. Average age 24. 1,664 applicants, 15% accepted. In 1997, 179 degrees awarded (100% continued full-time study). *Average time to degree:* first professional–4 years full-time. *Entrance requirements:* MCAT (average 10.2). Application deadline: 11/1 (rolling processing). Application fee: $0. *Expenses:* Tuition $4862 per year for state residents; $19,448 per year for nonresidents. Fees $423 per year. *Financial aid:* In 1997–98, 578 students received aid, including 10 fellowships (6 to first-year students) averaging $919 per month, 5 research assistantships averaging $919 per month; Federal Work-Study, institutionally sponsored loans, and career-related internships or fieldwork also available. Aid available to part-time students. Financial aid application deadline: 2/15; applicants required to submit FAFSA. *Faculty research:* Aging, birth defects, cancer, cardiovascular diseases, diabetes. Total annual research expenditures: $8.2 million. • Dr. Darrell G. Kirch, Dean, 706-721-2231. Fax: 706-721-7035. Application contact: Dr. Mary Ella Logan, Associate Dean for Admissions, 706-721-3186. Fax: 706-721-0959.

Medical College of Ohio, School of Medicine, Toledo, OH 43699-0008. Awards MD, MD/MPH, MD/MS, MD/PhD. Accredited by LCME. MD/MS, MD/PhD, and MD/MPH offered jointly with the Graduate School. Students: 540 full-time (211 women), 27 part-time (13 women). *Degree requirements:* Computer language required, foreign language and thesis not required. *Entrance requirements:* MCAT, interview. Application deadline: 11/1 (rolling processing). Application fee: $30. *Financial aid:* Fellowships, Federal Work-Study, institutionally sponsored loans, and career-related internships or fieldwork available. Financial aid application deadline: 6/1; applicants required to submit FAFSA. *Faculty research:* Hypertension, cancer, peptide synthesis, carcinogenic agents, drug effects. • Dr. Almira F. Gohara, Dean, 419-383-4356.

Medical College of Wisconsin, Medical School, Professional Program in Medicine, Milwaukee, WI 53226-0509. Awards MD, MD/MS, MD/PhD, MD/MA. Accredited by LCME. Students: 814 full-time (288 women); includes 213 minority (26 African Americans, 130 Asian Americans, 50 Hispanics, 7 Native Americans), 10 international. 6,521 applicants, 6% accepted. In 1997, 193 degrees awarded (100% continued full-time study). *Average time to degree:* first professional–4 years full-time. *Entrance requirements:* MCAT, interview, minimum 4 years of college. Application deadline: 11/1 (rolling processing). Application fee: $60. *Tuition:* $16,264 per year for state residents; $26,355 per year for nonresidents. *Financial aid:* 712 students received aid; fellowships available. • Application contact: Lesley A. Mack, Registrar, 414-456-8733.

Medical University of South Carolina, College of Medicine, Charleston, SC 29425-0002. Awards MD, MD/PhD. Accredited by LCME. Faculty: 435 full-time (37 women). Students: 545 full-time (222 women), 4 part-time (1 woman); includes 125 minority (77 African Americans, 39 Asian Americans, 6 Hispanics, 3 Native Americans), 3 international. Average age 27. 3,185 applicants, 6% accepted. In 1997, 126 degrees awarded. *Average time to degree:* first professional–4 years full-time. *Entrance requirements:* MCAT (average 27), interview. Application deadline: 12/1. Application fee: $55. *Expenses:* Tuition $8180 per year for state residents; $23,504 per year for nonresidents. Fees $80 per year (minimum). *Financial aid:* 16 students received aid; partial tuition waivers, Federal Work-Study available. Financial aid application deadline: 4/1; applicants required to submit FAFSA. • Dr. Layton McCurdy Jr., Dean, 843-792-2081. Application contact: Wanda Taylor, Director of Admissions, 843-792-2055.

Meharry Medical College, School of Medicine, Nashville, TN 37208-9989. Awards MD. Accredited by LCME. Faculty: 234 full-time (59 women), 30 part-time (6 women), 246.3 FTE. Students: 384 full-time (186 women). Average age 26. 4,908 applicants, 3% accepted. In 1997, 64 degrees awarded. *Entrance requirements:* MCAT. Application deadline: 12/15 (rolling processing). Application fee: $45. *Expenses:* Tuition $20,785 per year. Fees $1812 per year. *Financial aid:* Partial tuition waivers, Federal Work-Study, institutionally sponsored loans available. Financial aid application deadline: 4/15. *Faculty research:* Signal transduction, membrane biology, neurophysiology, tropical medicine. • Dr. A. Cherrie Epps, Dean, 615-327-6204. Fax: 615-327-6568. E-mail: meharrysom@ccvax.edu. Application contact: Allen D. Mosley, Director of Admissions and Records, 615-327-6223. Fax: 615-327-6228.

Memorial University of Newfoundland, Faculty of Medicine, Professional Program in Medicine, St. John's, NF A1C 5S7, Canada. Awards MD. Accredited by LCME. Students: 239 full-time (119 women); includes 42 international. Average age 23. 745 applicants, 8% accepted. In 1997, 54 degrees awarded. *Entrance requirements:* MCAT, B Sc, previous course work in English. Application deadline: 11/14. Application fee: $50. *Expenses:* Tuition $1896 per year (minimum). Fees $60 per year for Canadian residents; $621 per year for nonresidents. • Dr. Alan Goodridge, Assistant Dean, 709-737-6669. Application contact: Dr. Wanda Parsons, Assistant Dean of Admissions, 709-737-6615.

Mercer University, School of Medicine, 1400 Coleman Avenue, Macon, GA 31207-0003. Awards MD, MFS. One or more programs accredited by LCME. *Entrance requirements:* For MD, MCAT. Application deadline: 12/1 (rolling processing). Application fee: $25. *Faculty research:* Anatomy, biochemistry/nutrition, genetics, microbiology/immunology, neuroscience.

Michigan State University, College of Human Medicine, Professional Program in Human Medicine, East Lansing, MI 48824-1020. Awards MD. Accredited by LCME. Part-time programs available. Students: 452 (237 women); includes 156 minority (61 African Americans, 52 Asian Americans, 40 Hispanics, 3 Native Americans). In 1997, 140 degrees awarded. *Entrance requirements:* MCAT. Application deadline: 12/1 (rolling processing). Application fee: $30 ($40 for international students). *Expenses:* Tuition $10,587 per year for state residents; $22,531 per year for nonresidents. Fees $303 per year. *Financial aid:* Fellowships, research assistantships, teaching assistantships, Federal Work-Study, institutionally sponsored loans, and career-related internships or fieldwork available. Aid available to part-time students. Financial aid application deadline: 4/1. • Dr. Ruth Hoppe, Associate Dean, Academic Programs, 517-353-5440. Application contact: Jane Moxley-Smith, Director of Admissions, 517-353-9620.

Morehouse School of Medicine, Professional Program, Atlanta, GA 30310-1495. Awards MD, MD/MPH, MD/PhD. Accredited by LCME. Faculty: 115 full-time (43 women), 46 part-time (16 women). Students: 145 full-time (86 women); includes 145 minority (135 African Americans, 9 Asian Americans, 1 Hispanic). Average age 27. 2,928 applicants, 1% accepted. In 1997, 29 degrees awarded. *Degree requirements:* U.S. Medical Licensing Exam Steps I and II required, foreign language and thesis not required. *Average time to degree:* first professional–4 years full-time. *Entrance requirements:* MCAT. Application deadline: 12/1 (rolling processing). Application fee: $45. *Expenses:* Tuition $18,200 per year. Fees $2454 per year. *Financial aid:* Federal Work-Study, institutionally sponsored loans, and career-related internships or fieldwork available. Financial aid application deadline: 4/30. *Faculty research:* Endocrinology, metabolism, cell biology, muscle physiology, cardiology. Total annual research expenditures: $5.6 million. • Dr. E. Nigel Harris, Dean, 404-752-1720. Fax: 404-752-1594. Application contact: Karen Lewis, Assistant Director of Admissions, 404-752-1650. Fax: 404-752-1512. E-mail: karen@link.msm.edu.

Mount Sinai School of Medicine of the City University of New York, School of Medicine, New York, NY 10029-6504. Awards MD, MD/PhD. Accredited by LCME. Faculty: 1,029 full-time, 252 part-time. Students: 476 full-time (234 women); includes 208 minority (46 African Americans, 128 Asian Americans, 31 Hispanics, 3 Native Americans), 3 international. Average age 26. 5,273 applicants, 2% accepted. In 1997, 120 degrees awarded. *Average time to degree:* first professional–4 years full-time. *Entrance requirements:* MCAT, 3 years of college pre-medical course work. Application deadline: 11/1 (rolling processing). Application fee: $100. *Expenses:* Tuition $22,050 per year. Fees $1075 per year. *Financial aid:* 360 students received aid; Federal Work-Study, institutionally sponsored loans available. Financial aid applicants required to submit FAFSA. *Total annual research expenditures:* $68 million. • Dr. Arthur Rubenstein, Dean, 212-241-7335. Fax: 212-410-6111. Application contact: Jay A. Cohen, Assistant Dean, Admissions and Student Affairs, 212-241-6696. Fax: 212-828-4135.

New York Medical College, Professional Program, Valhalla, NY 10595-1691. Awards MD, MD/PhD. Accredited by LCME. Faculty: 1,192 full-time (377 women), 135 part-time (39 women). Students: 780 full-time (313 women); includes 368 minority (32 African Americans, 307 Asian Americans, 29 Hispanics), 11 international. Average age 26. 10,985 applicants, 5% accepted.

Directory: Allopathic Medicine

New York Medical College (continued)

In 1997, 190 degrees awarded. *Average time to degree:* first professional–4 years full-time. *Entrance requirements:* MCAT (average 31). Application deadline: 12/1 (rolling processing). Application fee: $100. *Tuition:* $28,735 per year for state residents; $28,835 per year for nonresidents. *Financial aid:* 135 students received aid; Federal Work-Study, institutionally sponsored loans available. Aid available to part-time students. Financial aid application deadline: 4/20; applicants required to submit FAFSA. *Faculty research:* Vascular function, hormonal regulation of blood pressure, melanoma immunotherapy, physiological and molecular control of heart failure. Total annual research expenditures: $18.7 million. • Dr. Ralph A. O'Connell, Provost and Dean, School of Medicine, 914-594-4900. Fax: 914-594-4145. Application contact: Dr. Fern Juster, Admissions Office, 914-594-4507. Fax: 914-594-4613.

New York University, School of Medicine, Professional Program in Medicine, New York, NY 10012-1019. Awards MD, MD/PhD, MD/MA, MD/MPA. Accredited by LCME. Faculty: 848 full-time, 48 part-time. Students: 692 full-time (274 women); includes 297 minority (36 African Americans, 240 Asian Americans, 21 Hispanics), 7 international. Average age 24. 4,506 applicants, 9% accepted. In 1997, 139 degrees awarded. *Average time to degree:* first professional–4 years full-time. *Entrance requirements:* MCAT. Application deadline: 8/15 (rolling processing). Application fee: $75. *Expenses:* Tuition $21,945 per year. Fees $4070 per year. *Faculty research:* AIDS, cancer, neuroscience, molecular biology. Total annual research expenditures: $100 million. • Application contact: Raymond Brienza, Assistant Dean, Admissions, 212-263-5290. Fax: 212-725-2140.

Northeastern Ohio Universities College of Medicine, Professional Program, Rootstown, OH 44272-0095. Awards MD, MD/PhD. Accredited by LCME. MD/PhD offered jointly with Kent State University. Faculty: 467 full-time (75 women), 1,250 part-time (201 women). Students: 422 full-time (185 women); includes 201 minority (18 African Americans, 182 Asian Americans, 1 Native American). Average age 23. 1,183 applicants, 1% accepted. In 1997, 92 degrees awarded (100% found work related to degree). *Average time to degree:* first professional–4 years full-time. *Entrance requirements:* MCAT, 1 year of organic chemistry and physics. Application deadline: 11/1 (rolling processing). Application fee: $30. *Expenses:* Tuition $3991 per trimester for state residents; $7739 per trimester for nonresidents. Fees $345 per year. *Financial aid:* Fellowships, Federal Work-Study, institutionally sponsored loans available. Aid available to part-time students. Financial aid application deadline: 4/15; applicants required to submit FAFSA. *Faculty research:* Lipid metabolism, osteolytic and metabolic bone diseases, virology, clinical outcomes, auditory system. • Dr. Terriann Crisp, Director of Graduate Studies, 330-325-6506. Application contact: Karen Berger, Associate Director of Admissions, 330-325-6270. Fax: 330-325-8372. E-mail: admission@neoucom.edu.

Northwestern University, Medical School, Professional Program in Medicine, 303 East Chicago Avenue, Chicago, IL 60611-3008. Awards MD, MD/MPH, MD/PhD, MD/MM. Accredited by LCME. MD/MM offered jointly with J. L. Kellogg Graduate School of Management; MD/MPH, MD/PhD offered jointly with the Graduate School. *Average time to degree:* first professional–4 years full-time. *Entrance requirements:* MCAT (average 10.2 verbal reasoning, 10.8 physical sciences, 10.4 biological sciences). Application deadline: 10/15 (rolling processing). Application fee: $50.

Northwestern University, Division of Interdepartmental Programs, Combined MD/PhD Medical Scientist Training Program, Evanston, IL 60208. Awards MD/PhD. Accredited by LCME. Application must be made to both The Graduate School and the Medical School. Students: 5 full-time (all women); includes 4 minority (1 Asian American, 3 Hispanics). 6 applicants, 100% accepted. *Application deadline:* 1/15. *Application fee:* $50 ($55 for international students). *Tuition:* $20,430 per year full-time, $2424 per course part-time. *Financial aid:* In 1997–98, fellowships averaging $1,256 per month were awarded. *Faculty research:* Cardiovascular epidemiology, cancer epidemiology, nutritional interventions for the prevention of cardiovascular disease and cancer, women's health, outcomes research. • David Engman, Co-Director, 847-503-1288. E-mail: d-engman@nwu.edu. Application contact: Sharon McBride, Assistant, 847-503-5232. E-mail: mstp@nwu.edu.

The Ohio State University, Medical Sciences Training Program, Columbus, OH 43210. Awards MD/PhD. Faculty: 9 full-time (3 women), 160 part-time (31 women). Students: 44 full-time (12 women); includes 4 minority (1 African American, 3 Asian Americans). Average age 25. 61 applicants, 11% accepted. *Application deadline:* 12/13 (priority date; rolling processing). *Application fee:* $40. *Tuition:* $5472 per year full-time, $554 per quarter (minimum) part-time for state residents; $14,172 per year full-time, $1424 per quarter (minimum) part-time for nonresidents. *Financial aid:* In 1997–98, 4 fellowships (all to first-year students) averaging $1,000 per month, 10 research assistantships (2 to first-year students) averaging $1,000 per month were awarded; Federal Work-Study, institutionally sponsored loans also available. • Dr. M. Sue O'Dorisio, Director, 614-722-2775. Fax: 614-722-2716. E-mail: odorisim@pediatrics.ohio-state.edu. Application contact: Catherine Kelly, Program Coordinator, 614-292-7790. Fax: 614-292-4021. E-mail: ckelly@smtp.med.ohio-state.edu.

The Ohio State University, College of Medicine and Public Health, Professional Program in Medicine, Columbus, OH 43210. Awards MD, MD/MPH, MD/MS, MD/PhD, MD/MHA. Accredited by LCME. Faculty: 575 full-time, 40 part-time. Students: 867 full-time (327 women); includes 219 minority (49 African Americans, 143 Asian Americans, 25 Hispanics, 2 Native Americans), 14 international. Average age 23. 3,946 applicants, 5% accepted. In 1997, 201 degrees awarded (100% found work related to degree). *Average time to degree:* first professional–4 years full-time. *Entrance requirements:* MCAT (minimum score 10 on verbal, physical science, and biological science sections; P on writing sample). Application deadline: 11/1 (rolling processing). Application fee: $30 ($40 for international students). *Tuition:* $11,574 per year for state residents; $31,650 per year for nonresidents. *Financial aid:* 725 students received aid; Federal Work-Study, institutionally sponsored loans available. Aid available to part-time students. Financial aid application deadline: 3/1; applicants required to submit FAFSA. *Faculty research:* AIDS, molecular biology, protein engineering, arthritis and geriatrics, cardiomyopathy. • Application contact: Dr. Mark Notestine, Director of Admissions, 614-292-7137. Fax: 614-292-1544. E-mail: admiss.med@osu.edu.

Oregon Health Sciences University, School of Medicine, Professional Program in Medicine, 3181 SW Sam Jackson Park Road, Portland, OR 97201-3098. Awards MD, MD/MPH, MD/PhD, MD/DMD. Accredited by LCME. Faculty: 200. Students: 389 full-time (179 women); includes 68 minority (10 African Americans, 37 Asian Americans, 19 Hispanics, 2 Native Americans). Average age 26. 2,113 applicants, 5% accepted. In 1997, 92 degrees awarded (100% found work related to degree). *Degree requirements:* National Board Exam Parts I and II required, foreign language and thesis not required. *Entrance requirements:* MCAT, 1 year of course work in biology and physics, 2 years of course work in chemistry and genetics, 6 undergraduate hours in psychology. Application deadline: 9/4 (rolling processing). Application fee: $60. • Dr. Edward Keenan, Associate Dean, 503-494-5100. Application contact: Vicki Fields, 503-494-2998. Fax: 503-494-3400.

Pennsylvania State University Milton S. Hershey Medical Center, College of Medicine, Hershey, PA 17033-2360. Awards MD, MD/PhD. Accredited by LCME. Students: 435 full-time (194 women). Average age 25. In 1997, 108 degrees awarded. *Entrance requirements:* MCAT. Application deadline: 12/1. Application fee: $40. *Financial aid:* Fellowships available. • Dr. C. McCollister Evarts, Senior Vice President and Dean, 717-531-8323.

Ponce School of Medicine, PO Box 7004, Ponce, PR 00732-7004. Awards MD. *Degree requirements:* 1 foreign language required, thesis not required. *Entrance requirements:* MCAT. Application deadline: 12/15 (priority date; rolling processing). Application fee: $50.

Queen's University at Kingston, Faculty of Medicine, Professional Program in Medicine, Kingston, ON K7L 3N6, Canada. Awards MD. Accredited by LCME. Faculty: 336 full-time, 234 part-time. *Entrance requirements:* MCAT. Application deadline: 10/15 (priority date). Application fee: $75. *Tuition:* $3803 per year (minimum) full-time, $1901 per year (minimum) part-time for Canadian residents; $7330 per year (minimum) for nonresidents. • Application contact: Dr. R. V. Birtwhistle, Associate Dean, 613-545-2542. Fax: 613-545-6884.

Rush University, Rush Medical College, Chicago, IL 60612-3832. Awards MD, MD/PhD. Accredited by LCME. Faculty: 538 full-time, 215 part-time. Students: 494 full-time (215 women); includes 176 minority (39 African Americans, 123 Asian Americans, 13 Hispanics, 1 Native American). Average age 24. 5,216 applicants, 5% accepted. In 1997, 110 degrees awarded (100% found work related to degree). *Average time to degree:* first professional–4 years full-time. *Entrance requirements:* MCAT, interview. Application deadline: 11/15 (rolling processing). Application fee: $50. *Financial aid:* Federal Work-Study, institutionally sponsored loans available. Aid available to part-time students. Financial aid application deadline: 5/15; applicants required to submit FAFSA. • Dr. Erich E. Brueschke, Dean, 312-942-3237. Fax: 312-942-2828. Application contact: Jan L. Schmidt, Director of Admissions, 312-942-6913. Fax: 312-942-2333.

Saint Louis University, School of Medicine, Professional Program in Medicine, St. Louis, MO 63103-2097. Awards MD, MD/PhD. Accredited by LCME. Faculty: 512 full-time (133 women), 1,127 part-time (226 women). Students: 606 full-time (239 women); includes 147 minority (26 African Americans, 109 Asian Americans, 10 Hispanics, 2 Native Americans), 7 international. 4,884 applicants, 7% accepted. In 1997, 139 degrees awarded. *Degree requirements:* U.S. Medical Licensing Exam Steps I and II required, foreign language not required. *Average time to degree:* first professional–4 years full-time. *Entrance requirements:* MCAT (average 30). Application deadline: 12/15 (rolling processing). Application fee: $100. *Expenses:* Tuition $28,500 per year. Fees $1150 per year. *Financial aid:* 515 students received aid; fellowships, research assistantships, teaching assistantships, Federal Work-Study, institutionally sponsored loans, and career-related internships or fieldwork available. Aid available to part-time students. Financial aid application deadline: 4/15; applicants required to submit FAFSA. *Faculty research:* Development of an AIDS vaccine, several surgical methods of treating coronary artery disease, medical coronary angioplasty, hormonal signaling mechanisms, fetal pulmonary development. • Application contact: Dr. William C. Mootz, Interim Dean of Admissions, 314-577-8205. Fax: 314-577-8214.

Southern Illinois University at Carbondale, School of Medicine, Professional Programs in Medicine, Carbondale, IL 62901-6806. Awards MD, JD/MD. Accredited by LCME. *Expenses:* Tuition $9116 per year for state residents; $27,348 per year for nonresidents. Fees $1034 per year. • Dr. Carl J. Getto, Dean and Provost, School of Medicine, 217-782-3318.

Stanford University, School of Medicine, Professional Program in Medicine, Stanford, CA 94305-9991. Awards MD. Accredited by LCME. Faculty: 502 full-time (101 women). Students: 336 full-time (156 women), 119 part-time (48 women); includes 182 minority (20 African Americans, 108 Asian Americans, 46 Hispanics, 8 Native Americans), 7 international. Average age 27. 6,391 applicants, 3% accepted. In 1997, 84 degrees awarded. *Entrance requirements:* MCAT. Application deadline: 11/1. Application fee: $65 ($75 for international students). *Financial aid:* Research assistantships, teaching assistantships, institutionally sponsored loans available. Financial aid application deadline: 11/1. • Harry B. Greenberg, Associate Chair, 650-493-5000. Fax: 650-723-5488. E-mail: hbgreen@leland.stanford.edu. Application contact: Medical School Admissions Office, 650-723-6861.

State University of New York at Buffalo, Graduate School, School of Medicine, Professional Program in Medicine, Buffalo, NY 14214. Awards MD, MD/PhD. Accredited by LCME. Faculty: 677 full-time (172 women), 4 part-time (1 woman). Students: 563 full-time (259 women); includes 113 minority (25 African Americans, 76 Asian Americans, 12 Hispanics). Average age 23. 3,000 applicants, 5% accepted. In 1997, 150 degrees awarded. *Entrance requirements:* MCAT (average 30), interview. Application deadline: 12/1 (rolling processing). Application fee: $50. *Tuition:* $11,805 per year full-time, $575 per credit hour part-time for state residents; $22,905 per year full-time, $1038 per credit hour part-time for nonresidents. *Financial aid:* 551 students received aid; fellowships, research assistantships, teaching assistantships, full and partial tuition waivers, Federal Work-Study, institutionally sponsored loans, and career-related internships or fieldwork available. Financial aid application deadline: 2/21. *Faculty research:* Microbial pathogenesis, neuronal plasticity, structural biology of ion channels, structural development, cell biology of development. Total annual research expenditures: $58 million. • Dr. Dennis Nadler, Associate Dean, 716-829-2803. E-mail: dnadler@ubmedc.buffalo.edu. Application contact: Dr. Thomas Guttuso, Director of Admissions, 716-829-3466. Fax: 716-829-2798.

State University of New York at Stony Brook, Health Sciences Center, School of Medicine, Medical Scientist Training Program, Stony Brook, NY 11794. Awards MD/PhD. *Application deadline:* 1/15. *Financial aid:* Full tuition waivers available. • Dr. Norman H. Edelman, Dean of the School of Medicine, Health Sciences Center, 516-444-2080. Fax: 516-444-6032.

State University of New York at Stony Brook, Health Sciences Center, School of Medicine, Professional Program in Medicine, Stony Brook, NY 11794. Awards MD, MD/PhD. Accredited by LCME. Faculty: 495. Students: 418 full-time (185 women); includes 162 minority (24 African Americans, 112 Asian Americans, 22 Hispanics, 4 Native Americans). 3,338 applicants, 8% accepted. In 1997, 104 degrees awarded. *Entrance requirements:* MCAT, interview. Application deadline: 1/15. Application fee: $75. *Financial aid:* Fellowships available. *Total annual research expenditures:* $24.5 million. • Application contact: Dr. Jack Fuhrer, Interim Associate Dean for Admissions, 516-444-2113. Fax: 516-444-6032. E-mail: admissions@dean.som.sunysb.edu.

State University of New York Health Science Center at Brooklyn, College of Medicine, 450 Clarkson Avenue, Brooklyn, NY 11203-2098. Awards MD, MD/PhD. Accredited by LCME. Students: 771 full-time (329 women); includes 324 minority (81 African Americans, 209 Asian Americans, 34 Hispanics). Average age 23. 4,070 applicants, 9% accepted. In 1997, 176 degrees awarded (100% found work related to degree). *Average time to degree:* first professional–4 years full-time. *Entrance requirements:* MCAT. Application deadline: 12/15 (rolling processing). Application fee: $65. *Expenses:* Tuition $10,840 per year for state residents; $21,940 per year for nonresidents. Fees $220 per year. *Financial aid:* Full and partial tuition waivers, Federal Work-Study, and career-related internships or fieldwork available. Aid available to part-time students. Financial aid application deadline: 5/1; applicants required to submit FAFSA. *Faculty research:* AIDS epidemiology, virus/host interaction, molecular genetics, developmental neurobiology, prostate cancer. • Dr. Eugene B. Feigelson, Dean, 718-270-3776. Application contact: Liliana Montano, Director of Admissions, 718-270-3013.

State University of New York Health Science Center at Syracuse, College of Medicine, Syracuse, NY 13210-2334. Awards MD, MD/PhD. Accredited by LCME. Faculty: 324. Students: 622 full-time (283 women); includes 194 minority (40 African Americans, 134 Asian Americans, 19 Hispanics, 1 Native American), 3 international. 3,222 applicants, 5% accepted. In 1997, 141 degrees awarded. *Average time to degree:* first professional–4 years full-time. *Entrance requirements:* MCAT. Application deadline: 12/1 (rolling processing). Application fee: $60. *Expenses:* Tuition $10,840 per year for state residents; $21,940 per year for nonresidents. Fees $475 per year. *Financial aid:* 543 students received aid; full and partial tuition waivers, Federal Work-Study, institutionally sponsored loans, and career-related internships or fieldwork available. Aid available to part-time students. Financial aid application deadline: 4/1. • Dr. Gregory Eastwood, Dean, 315-464-4515. Application contact: Ronald W. Wolk, Associate Dean, 315-464-4570. Fax: 315-464-8823.

Temple University, Health Sciences Center, School of Medicine, Professional Program in Medicine, Philadelphia, PA 19140. Awards MD, MD/PhD. Accredited by LCME. Faculty: 435 full-time (118 women), 47 part-time (15 women). Students: 739 full-time (284 women); includes 318 minority (99 African Americans, 175 Asian Americans, 42 Hispanics, 2 Native Americans). Average age 25. 8,278 applicants, 6% accepted. In 1997, 169 degrees awarded. *Average time to degree:* first professional–4 years full-time. *Entrance requirements:* MCAT (average 10). Application deadline: 1/15 (rolling processing). Application fee: $55. *Financial aid:* 641 students received aid; alumni scholarships, Federal Work-Study, institutionally sponsored loans available. Financial aid application deadline: 3/31; applicants required to submit FAFSA. *Faculty research:*

Homeostasis, molecular biology and immunology of cancer, prevention of sudden cardiac death, *in utero* diagnosis and treatment. Total annual research expenditures: $2.04 million. • Application contact: Dr. Audrey Uknis, Assistant Dean for Admissions, 215-707-3656.

Texas A&M University, College of Medicine, Professional Program in Medicine, College Station, TX 77843. Awards MD, MD/PhD. Accredited by LCME. Faculty: 55 (4 women). Students: 192 full-time (73 women). Average age 25. 1,261 applicants, 4% accepted. In 1997, 47 degrees awarded. *Entrance requirements:* MCAT. Application deadline: 11/1 (rolling processing). Application fee: $35 ($75 for international students). • Application contact: Filomeno Maldonado, Director of Admissions, 409-845-7743.

Texas Tech University Health Sciences Center, School of Medicine, Lubbock, TX 79430-0002. Awards MD, MD/PhD, MD/MBA. Accredited by LCME. Open only to residents of Texas, eastern New Mexico, and southwestern Oklahoma. MD/MBA offered jointly with Texas Tech University. Faculty: 74. Students: 480. In 1997, 113 degrees awarded (100% found work related to degree). *Average time to degree:* first professional–4 years full-time. *Entrance requirements:* MCAT (average 29). Application deadline: 11/1 (rolling processing). Application fee: $40. *Financial aid:* Institutionally sponsored loans and career-related internships or fieldwork available. • Dr. Joel Kuppersmith, Dean, 806-743-3000. Application contact: Barbara Ewalt, Director of Admissions, 806-743-2297.

Thomas Jefferson University, Jefferson Medical College, Philadelphia, PA 19107. Awards MD, MD/PhD, MD/MBA, MD/MHA. Accredited by LCME. MD/MBA and MD/MHA offered jointly with Widener University. Faculty: 689 full-time (167 women), 42 part-time (11 women). Students: 901 full-time (331 women); includes 207 minority (20 African Americans, 160 Asian Americans, 22 Hispanics, 5 Native Americans), 10 international. 9,979 applicants, 4% accepted. In 1997, 212 degrees awarded. *Entrance requirements:* MCAT. Application deadline: 11/15 (priority date). Application fee: $65. *Tuition:* $26,770 per year. *Financial aid:* 680 students received aid; Federal Work-Study, institutionally sponsored loans available. Financial aid application deadline: 3/1; applicants required to submit FAFSA. • Dr. Joseph S. Gonnella, Senior Vice President and Dean for Academic Affairs, 215-955-6980. Application contact: Dr. Benjamin Bacharach, Associate Dean for Admissions, 215-955-6983. Fax: 215-923-6939.

Thomas Jefferson University, MD/PhD Program, Philadelphia, PA 19107. Awards MD/PhD. Accredited by LCME. Students: 12 full-time (5 women); includes 5 minority (all Asian Americans). 154 applicants, 6% accepted. *Application deadline:* 11/15. *Application fee:* $30. *Tuition:* $12,300 per year (minimum). *Financial aid:* Fellowships, research assistantships, Federal Work-Study, institutionally sponsored loans available. Financial aid application deadline: 5/1; applicants required to submit FAFSA. • Dr. Scott Waldman, Academic Director, 215-955-6608. Fax: 215-955-5681. E-mail: scott.waldman@mail.tju.edu. Application contact: Jessie F. Pervall, Director of Admissions, 215-503-4400. Fax: 215-503-3433. E-mail: cgs-info@mail.tju.edu.

Tufts University, School of Medicine, Professional Program in Medicine, Medford, MA 02155. Awards MD, MD/MPH, MD/PhD. Accredited by LCME. MD/PhD offered jointly with the Sackler School of Graduate Biomedical Sciences. *Entrance requirements:* MCAT. Application deadline: 2/1. Application fee: $65.

Tulane University, School of Medicine, Professional Programs in Medicine, New Orleans, LA 70112. Awards MD, MD/MPH, MD/PhD, MD/MPHTM, MD/MSPH. Accredited by LCME. *Average time to degree:* first professional–4 years full-time. *Entrance requirements:* MCAT (minimum score 7). Application deadline: 12/31. Application fee: $95.

Tulane University, School of Public Health and Tropical Medicine, Department of Tropical Medicine, New Orleans, LA 70118-5669. Awards MPHTM, MSPH, Sc D, Diploma, MD/MPHTM. Part-time programs available. Students: 38 full-time (15 women), 8 part-time (4 women); includes 9 minority (3 African Americans, 3 Asian Americans, 2 Hispanics, 1 Native American), 12 international. Average age 37. Terminal master's awarded for partial completion of doctoral program. *Degree requirements:* For master's, 1 foreign language required, thesis not required; for doctorate, 1 foreign language, dissertation. *Entrance requirements:* For master's, GRE General Test (minimum combined score of 1000; average 1100), TOEFL (minimum score 525). Application deadline: 4/15 (priority date; rolling processing; 10/15 for spring admission). Application fee: $40. *Financial aid:* Federal Work-Study available. Financial aid application deadline: 2/1. *Faculty research:* Malaria immunology, entomology. • Dr. Donald Krogstad, Chair, 504-587-7313. E-mail: tropmed@mailhost.tcs.tulane.edu. Application contact: Karen Rachal, Senior Program Coordinator, 504-584-3558. Fax: 504-589-7313. E-mail: krachal@mailhost.tcs.tulane.edu.

Uniformed Services University of the Health Sciences, School of Medicine, Professional Program in Medicine, Bethesda, MD 20814-4799. Awards MD. Accredited by LCME. Faculty: 129 full-time (31 women), 233 part-time (56 women). Students: 666 full-time (178 women); includes 139 minority (19 African Americans, 89 Asian Americans, 26 Hispanics, 5 Native Americans). Average age 23. 3,205 applicants, 8% accepted. In 1997, 156 degrees awarded (100% found work related to degree). *Entrance requirements:* MCAT, average GPA of 3.5, U.S. citizenship. Application deadline: 11/1 (rolling processing). Application fee: $0. *Tuition:* $0. *Financial aid:* Career-related internships or fieldwork available. • Dr. Val Hemming, Dean, 301-295-3016. Application contact: Joan Stearman, Director of Admissions, 301-295-3101. Fax: 301-295-3545.

Universidad Central del Caribe, Escuela de Medicina, Professional Program, Bayamon, PR 00960-6032. Awards MD, MA/MS. Faculty: 126 full-time (43 women), 56 part-time (21 women). Students: 278 full-time (134 women), 5 part-time (4 women); includes 272 minority (1 African American, 7 Asian Americans, 263 Hispanics, 1 Native American). Average age 22. 1,044 applicants, 10% accepted. In 1997, 63 degrees awarded (100% found work related to degree). *Degree requirements:* 1 foreign language required, thesis not required. *Entrance requirements:* MCAT, minimum GPA of 2.5. Application deadline: 12/15. Application fee: $50. *Financial aid:* 230 students received aid; career-related internships or fieldwork available. Financial aid application deadline: 6/30. *Faculty research:* Membrane neurotransmitter receptors, brain neurotransmission, cocaine toxicology, membrane transport, antimetabolite pharmacology. • Dr. Julia Bonilla, Dean of Medicine, 787-798-3001. Application contact: Irma Cordero, Admissions Director, 787-740-1611. Fax: 787-269-7550.

Université de Montréal, Faculty of Medicine, Professional Program in Medicine, Montréal, PQ H3C 3J7, Canada. Awards MD. Accredited by LCME. Open only to Canadian residents. Students: 746 full-time (460 women), 13 part-time (11 women). 1,576 applicants, 7% accepted. In 1997, 159 degrees awarded. *Entrance requirements:* Proficiency in French. Application deadline: 3/1. Application fee: $30. • Patrick Vinay, Dean, Faculty of Medicine, 514-343-6351. Application contact: Dr. Jean-Luc Malo, Graduate Chair, 514-343-6300.

Université de Montréal, Faculties of Medicine and Graduate Studies, Graduate Programs in Medicine, Program in Specialized Studies, Montréal, PQ H3C 3J7, Canada. Offerings include family medicine (DES), family medicine and emergency (DES), medicine (DES), surgery (DES). Program faculty: 204 full-time (32 women), 36 part-time (1 woman). *Application deadline:* 10/1. *Application fee:* $30. • Dr. Jean-Paul Perreault, Vice Dean, 514-343-7798.

Université de Sherbrooke, Faculty of Medicine, Professional Program in Medicine, Sherbrooke, PQ J1K 2R1, Canada. Awards MD. Accredited by LCME. *Application deadline:* 3/1. *Application fee:* $30. Electronic applications accepted.

Université Laval, Faculty of Medicine, Professional Program in Medicine, Sainte-Foy, PQ G1K 7P4, Canada. Awards MD. Accredited by LCME. Students: 549 full-time (348 women), 40 part-time (20 women); includes 5 international. Average age 24. 1,429 applicants, 15% accepted. In 1997, 121 degrees awarded. *Entrance requirements:* Interview, proficiency in French. Application deadline: 3/1. Application fee: $30. *Expenses:* Tuition $1334 per year (minimum) full-time, $56 per credit (minimum) part-time for Canadian residents; $5966 per year (minimum) full-time, $249 per credit (minimum) part-time for nonresidents. Fees $150 per year full-time, $6.25 per credit part-time. • Pierre Bigonesse, Director, 418-656-2131 Ext. 4576. Fax: 418-656-3442. E-mail: pierre.bigonesse@med.ulaval.ca.

The University of Alabama at Birmingham, School of Medicine, Birmingham, AL 35233. Awards MD, MS, MSBMS, PhD, MD/PhD. One or more programs accredited by LCME. Students: 605 full-time (221 women); includes 132 minority (62 African Americans, 58 Asian Americans, 5 Hispanics, 7 Native Americans), 5 international. Average age 26. 1,984 applicants, 12% accepted. In 1997, 164 MDs awarded. *Entrance requirements:* For doctorate, MCAT, interview. Application deadline: 11/1. Application fee: $50. Electronic applications accepted. *Tuition:* $9128 per year for state residents; $22,722 per year for nonresidents. *Financial aid:* Fellowships and career-related internships or fieldwork available. • Dr. William B. Deal Jr., Interim Dean, 205-934-1111.

University of Alberta, Faculty of Medicine and Oral Health Sciences, Professional Program in Medicine, Edmonton, AB T6G 2E1, Canada. Awards MD. Accredited by LCME. Open only to Canadian residents. Faculty: 375 full-time, 320 part-time. Students: 444 full-time. Average age 24. 1,000 applicants. In 1997, 113 degrees awarded. *Entrance requirements:* MCAT, interview. Application deadline: 11/1. Application fee: $60. • Application contact: Dr. C. Baker, Acting Assistant Dean, Admissions, 403-492-6350.

The University of Arizona, College of Medicine, Professional Programs in Medicine, Tucson, AZ 85721. Awards MD, MD/PhD. Accredited by LCME. MD program open only to state residents. *Entrance requirements:* MCAT, previous course work in general chemistry, organic chemistry, biology/zoology, physics, and English. Application fee: $0. *Tuition:* $8434 per year. *Faculty research:* Developmental biology, cellular structure and function, immunology, clinical cancer research, heart and respiratory disease.

University of Arkansas for Medical Sciences, College of Medicine, Professional Program in Medicine, 4301 West Markham, Little Rock, AR 72205-7199. Awards MD, MD/PhD. Accredited by LCME. Students: 569 full-time (198 women); includes 87 minority (43 African Americans, 30 Asian Americans, 7 Hispanics, 7 Native Americans). In 1997, 123 degrees awarded. *Entrance requirements:* MCAT. *Expenses:* Tuition $8502 per year for state residents; $17,006 per year for nonresidents. Fees $1400 per year. *Financial aid:* Research assistantships available. • Application contact: Tom South, Director of Student Admissions, 501-686-5354.

University of British Columbia, Faculty of Medicine, Professional Program in Medicine, Vancouver, BC V6T 1Z2, Canada. Awards MD, MD/PhD. Accredited by LCME. *Entrance requirements:* MCAT (average 10.41). Application deadline: 12/15. Application fee: $105 ($155 for international students).

University of British Columbia, Faculties of Medicine and Graduate Studies, Graduate Programs in Medicine, Department of Surgery, Vancouver, BC V6T 1W5, Canada. Awards M Sc. *Degree requirements:* Thesis required, foreign language not required. *Average time to degree:* master's–2 years full-time. *Entrance requirements:* TOEFL (minimum score 550). Application deadline: 4/30. Application fee: $60. *Faculty research:* Photodynamic therapy, transplantation immunobiology, isolated cell culture, neurophysiology.

The University of Calgary, Faculty of Medicine, Professional Program in Medicine, Calgary, AB T2N 1N4, Canada. Awards MD. Accredited by LCME. Students: 218 full-time (113 women). 1,180 applicants, 6% accepted. In 1997, 58 degrees awarded (100% found work related to degree). *Average time to degree:* first professional–3 years full-time. *Entrance requirements:* MCAT. Application deadline: 11/30 (rolling processing). Application fee: $65. *Tuition:* $6110 per year for Canadian residents; $30,000 per year for nonresidents. *Financial aid:* Career-related internships or fieldwork available. • Dr. A. Jones, Associate Dean (Medical Education), 403-220-3843. E-mail: meyers@med.ucalgary.ca. Application contact: Adéle Meyers, Coordinator, Admissions and Student Affairs, 403-220-6849. Fax: 403-270-2681. E-mail: meyers@med.ucalgary.ca.

University of California, Davis, School of Medicine, Davis, CA 95616. Awards MD, MD/MPH, MD/PhD, MD/MBA. Accredited by LCME. MD/MPH offered jointly with the University of California, Berkeley. Faculty: 425 full-time (95 women), 46 part-time (13 women). Students: 415 full-time (176 women); includes 189 minority (22 African Americans, 129 Asian Americans, 36 Hispanics, 2 Native Americans). Average age 24. 5,401 applicants, 4% accepted. In 1997, 91 degrees awarded. *Average time to degree:* first professional–4 years full-time. *Entrance requirements:* MCAT. Application deadline: 11/1 (rolling processing). Application fee: $40. *Financial aid:* 332 students received aid; Federal Work-Study, institutionally sponsored loans available. Financial aid application deadline: 3/2; applicants required to submit FAFSA. *Faculty research:* Genetics, cardiovascular physiology, cancer biology, women's health, environmental health, cell and molecular biology, neuroscience, infectious diseases, wound healing, nutrition, health services. Total annual research expenditures: $42 million. • Dr. Joseph Silva Jr., Dean, 530-752-0321. Application contact: Edward D. Dagang, Director of Admissions, 530-752-2717. E-mail: medadmsinfo@ucdavis.edu.

University of California, Irvine, College of Medicine, Professional Program in Medicine, Irvine, CA 92697. Awards MD, MD/PhD. Accredited by LCME. Students: 392 full-time (165 women); includes 195 minority (9 African Americans, 150 Asian Americans, 36 Hispanics). 4,266 applicants, 5% accepted. In 1997, 86 degrees awarded. *Entrance requirements:* MCAT, pre-medical course work. Application deadline: 11/1. Application fee: $40. Electronic applications accepted. *Expenses:* Tuition $0 for state residents; $9384 per year for nonresidents. Fees $10,450 per year. *Financial aid:* Fellowships, institutionally sponsored loans available. Financial aid application deadline: 3/2; applicants required to submit FAFSA. • Application contact: Peggy Harvey-Lee, Director of Admissions, 949-824-5388.

University of California, Los Angeles, School of Medicine, Professional Program in Medicine, Los Angeles, CA 90095. Awards MD, MD/PhD, MD/MBA. Accredited by LCME. Students: 544 full-time (222 women); includes 261 minority (50 African Americans, 123 Asian Americans, 86 Hispanics, 2 Native Americans), 1 international. 5,269 applicants, 5% accepted. *Entrance requirements:* MCAT. Application fee: $40. *Expenses:* Tuition $0 for state residents; $9384 per year for nonresidents. Fees $4551 per year. *Financial aid:* Fellowships, research assistantships, teaching assistantships, scholarships, full and partial tuition waivers, Federal Work-Study, institutionally sponsored loans available. Financial aid application deadline: 3/1. • Application contact: School of Medicine Admissions, 310-825-6081.

University of California, San Diego, School of Medicine, Professional Program in Medicine, 9500 Gilman Drive, La Jolla, CA 92093-5003. Awards MD, MD/PhD. Accredited by LCME. Faculty: 700. *Degree requirements:* Thesis required, foreign language not required. *Entrance requirements:* MCAT. Application deadline: 11/1 (rolling processing). Application fee: $40. *Expenses:* Tuition $0 for state residents; $9384 per year full-time, $4692 per year part-time for nonresidents. Fees $4887 per year full-time, $3344 per year part-time. • Application contact: Office of Admissions, 619-534-3880.

University of California, San Francisco, School of Medicine, San Francisco, CA 94143. Awards MD, PhD, MD/MPH, MD/MS, MD/PhD. One or more programs accredited by LCME. Students: 612 full-time (340 women); includes 339 minority (55 African Americans, 189 Asian Americans, 84 Hispanics, 11 Native Americans). Average age 24. 5,508 applicants, 4% accepted. In 1997, 170 MDs awarded. Terminal master's awarded for partial completion of doctoral program. *Degree requirements:* For doctorate, dissertation required, foreign language not required. *Entrance requirements:* For MD, MCAT (average 12), interview; for doctorate, GRE General Test, GRE Subject Test, TOEFL (minimum score 550). Application deadline: 11/1 (rolling processing). Application fee: $40. *Expenses:* Tuition $0 for state residents; $9384 per year for nonresidents. Fees $9943 per year. *Financial aid:* 532 students received aid; partial tuition waivers, Federal Work-Study, institutionally sponsored loans available. Financial aid application deadline: 2/1; applicants required to submit FAFSA. *Total annual research expenditures:* $206 million. • Dr. Haile T. Debas, Dean, 415-476-2342. Fax: 415-476-0689.

Directory: Allopathic Medicine

University of California, San Francisco (continued)
E-mail: hdebas@medsch.ucsf.edu. Application contact: Kathleen Ryan, Admissions Officer, 415-476-4044. Fax: 415-476-5490. E-mail: kryan@medsch.ucsf.edu.

University of Chicago, Pritzker School of Medicine, Chicago, IL 60637-1513. Awards MD, MD/PhD, MD/MBA. Accredited by LCME. Faculty: 654 full-time. Students: 423 full-time (201 women); includes 134 minority (37 African Americans, 85 Asian Americans, 11 Hispanics, 1 Native American), 12 international. Average age 24. 8,220 applicants, 3% accepted. In 1997, 104 degrees awarded. *Entrance requirements:* MCAT. Application deadline: 11/15 (rolling processing). Application fee: $55. *Financial aid:* In 1997–98, 75 teaching assistantships (3 to first-year students), 388 scholarships, training grants (77 to first-year students) were awarded; Federal Work-Study, institutionally sponsored loans, and career-related internships or fieldwork also available. Financial aid application deadline: 4/1; applicants required to submit FAFSA. *Faculty research:* Human genetics, diabetes, developmental biology, structural biology, ecology and evolution. Total annual research expenditures: $69.25 million. • Dr. Glenn D. Steele Jr., Dean, 773-702-9000. Application contact: Dr. Norma Wagoner, Dean of Students, 773-702-1939. Fax: 773-702-2598.

University of Cincinnati, College of Medicine, Physician Scientist Training Program, Cincinnati, OH 45267. Awards MD/PhD. Accredited by LCME. 66 applicants, 9% accepted. *Application deadline:* 2/1 (rolling processing). *Application fee:* $30. *Financial aid:* Graduate assistantships available. Financial aid application deadline: 5/1. • Dr. John Hutton, Dean, College of Medicine, 513-558-7334. E-mail: john.hutton@uc.edu. Application contact: Linda Moeller, Director, Graduate Affairs, 513-558-7343. E-mail: linda.moeller@uc.edu.

University of Cincinnati, College of Medicine, Professional Program in Medicine, Cincinnati, OH 45267. Awards MD. Accredited by LCME. *Entrance requirements:* MCAT (average 9.7 biological science, 9.5 physical science, 9.3 verbal reasoning). Application deadline: 11/15 (rolling processing). Application fee: $30. *Financial aid:* Application deadline 5/1. *Faculty research:* Molecular genetics, environmental health, neuroscience and cell biology, cardiovascular science, developmental biology. • Dr. J. Robert Suriano, Associate Dean, 513-558-5575. E-mail: robert.suriano@uc.edu. Application contact: Clarice Fooks, Assistant Dean for Admissions, 513-558-7314. Fax: 513-558-1165.

University of Colorado Health Sciences Center, School of Medicine, Denver, CO 80262. Awards MD, MD/PhD, MD/MBA. Accredited by LCME. MD/PhD offered jointly with Graduate School; MD/MBA offered jointly with University of Colorado at Denver. Faculty: 923 full-time. Students: 525 full-time (242 women), 14 part-time (4 women); includes 111 minority (12 African Americans, 37 Asian Americans, 57 Hispanics, 5 Native Americans). Average age 28. 2,454 applicants, 8% accepted. In 1997, 127 degrees awarded. *Entrance requirements:* MCAT. Application fee: $50. *Financial aid:* Fellowships, research assistantships, teaching assistantships, Federal Work-Study, institutionally sponsored loans, and career-related internships or fieldwork available. Aid available to part-time students. • Dr. Richard Krugman, Dean, 303-315-7565.

University of Connecticut Health Center, School of Medicine, Farmington, CT 06030. Awards MD, MD/MPH, MD/PhD, MD/MBA. Accredited by LCME. Students: 336 full-time (167 women), 1 (woman) part-time; includes 68 minority (25 African Americans, 32 Asian Americans, 10 Hispanics, 1 Native American), 3 international. Average age 24. In 1997, 81 degrees awarded. *Entrance requirements:* MCAT. Application deadline: 12/15 (rolling processing). Application fee: $60. *Expenses:* Tuition is $9,100 per year for residents, $20,700 per year for nonresidents, and $13,650 per year for students residing in Maine, New Hampshire, and Rhode Island. There are additional mandatory fees of $3,725 per year. *Financial aid:* 275 students received aid; partial tuition waivers, institutionally sponsored loans available. Financial aid applicants required to submit FAFSA. • Dr. Peter J. Deckers, Dean, 860-679-2413. Fax: 860-679-1282. Application contact: Keat Sanford, Assistant Dean and Director, 860-679-3874. E-mail: sanford@nso1.uchc.edu.

University of Connecticut Health Center, Programs in Biomedical Sciences, Combined Degree Program, Farmington, CT 06030. Awards MD/PhD. Offered jointly with the School of Medicine. *Application deadline:* 3/1 (priority date; rolling processing). *Application fee:* $35.

University of Florida, College of Medicine, Professional Program in Medicine, Gainesville, FL 32610. Awards MD, MD/PhD. Accredited by LCME. Faculty: 590 full-time (121 women), 36 part-time (23 women). Students: 472 full-time (218 women); includes 144 minority (35 African Americans, 81 Asian Americans, 25 Hispanics, 3 Native Americans). 2,270 applicants, 5% accepted. In 1997, 116 degrees awarded (100% found work related to degree). *Entrance requirements:* MCAT (average 30). Application deadline: 12/1 (rolling processing). Application fee: $20. *Tuition:* $10,447 per year for state residents; $28,098 per year for nonresidents. *Financial aid:* Institutionally sponsored loans available. *Faculty research:* Neurobiology, gene therapy and genetic imaging technologies, diabetes and autoimmune diseases, transplantation. Total annual research expenditures: $55,000. • Dr. Hugh M. Hill, Associate Dean for Student Affairs, 352-392-3071. Application contact: Dr. Robert Hatch, Chair, Admissions Committee, 352-392-4569.

University of Hawaii at Manoa, John A. Burns School of Medicine, Professional Programs in Medicine, Honolulu, HI 96822. Awards MD. Accredited by LCME. Students: 229 full-time (112 women); includes 193 minority (1 African American, 159 Asian Americans, 2 Hispanics, 31 Native Americans). Average age 23. 1,631 applicants, 3% accepted. In 1997, 55 degrees awarded. *Entrance requirements:* MCAT. Application deadline: 12/1. Application fee: $0. *Financial aid:* Fellowships, research assistantships, teaching assistantships available. Financial aid application deadline: 3/1; applicants required to submit FAFSA. • Dr. Gwen S. Naguwa, Associate Dean for Students, 808-956-8300. E-mail: naguwag@jabsom.biomed.hawaii.edu.

University of Illinois at Chicago, College of Medicine, Professional Program in Medicine, Chicago, IL 60607-7128. Awards MD, MD/MS, MD/PhD. Part-time programs available. Faculty: 825 full-time, 2,650 part-time. Students: 756 (277 women); includes 579 minority (174 African Americans, 269 Asian Americans, 129 Hispanics, 7 Native Americans). 6,405 applicants, 5% accepted. In 1997, 297 degrees awarded. *Entrance requirements:* MCAT. Application deadline: 12/15. Application fee: $40 ($50 for international students). *Financial aid:* Fellowships, research assistantships, teaching assistantships available. *Faculty research:* Biomedical and clinical sciences. • Gerald S. Moss, Dean, College of Medicine, 312-996-3500.

University of Illinois at Urbana–Champaign, Medical Scholars Program, Urbana, IL 61801. Awards MD/PhD, MD/JD, MD/MBA. Offered jointly with the University of Illinois at Chicago College of Medicine. Students: 170 full-time (41 women); includes 49 minority (11 African Americans, 30 Asian Americans, 8 Hispanics). 186 applicants, 24% accepted. *Application deadline:* 12/1. *Application fee:* $0. *Financial aid:* Fellowships, research assistantships, teaching assistantships, institutionally sponsored loans available. • Dr. Diane Gottheil, Acting Director, 217-333-8146. E-mail: gottheil@uiuc.edu. Application contact: Dr. Jennifer Bloom, Coordinator, 217-333-8146. Fax: 217-244-7078. E-mail: mspo@uiuc.edu.

The University of Iowa, College of Medicine and Graduate College, Medical Scientist Training Program, Iowa City, IA 52242-1316. Awards MD/PhD. Faculty: 60 full-time (20 women), 40 part-time (10 women). Students: 45 full-time (13 women); includes 11 minority (3 African Americans, 6 Asian Americans, 2 Hispanics). Average age 25. 22 applicants, 14% accepted. *Application deadline:* 11/15 (priority date; rolling processing). *Application fee:* $50. *Financial aid:* In 1997–98, 45 students received aid, including 5 research assistantships averaging $1,356 per month; institutionally sponsored loans also available. *Total annual research expenditures:* $450,000. • Dr. Gary Koretzky, Director, 319-335-6844. Fax: 319-335-6887. E-mail: gary-koretzky@uiowa.edu.

The University of Iowa, College of Medicine, Professional Program in Medicine, Iowa City, IA 52242-1316. Awards MD, MD/PhD. Accredited by LCME. Faculty: 732 full-time (111 women), 42 part-time (19 women). Students: 689 (302 women); includes 102 minority (22 African Americans, 53 Asian Americans, 26 Hispanics, 1 Native American). Average age 22. 2,400 applicants, 7% accepted. In 1997, 169 degrees awarded (100% found work related to degree). *Average time to degree:* first professional–4 years full-time. *Entrance requirements:* MCAT, previous course work in biology, chemistry, physics, and mathematics. Application deadline: 11/1 (rolling processing). Application fee: $30. *Financial aid:* Federal Work-Study, institutionally sponsored loans available. Financial aid applicants required to submit FAFSA. • Dr. Robert P. Kelch, Dean, 319-335-8064. Fax: 319-335-8318. Application contact: Thomas C. Taylor, Director of Admissions, 319-335-6703. Fax: 319-335-8049. E-mail: thomas_taylor@uiowa.edu.

University of Kansas, School of Medicine, Kansas City, KS 66160. Awards MD, MD/MS, MD/PhD. Accredited by LCME. Faculty: 302 full-time (78 women), 86 part-time (25 women). Students: 694 full-time (276 women), 9 part-time (4 women); includes 164 minority (47 African Americans, 79 Asian Americans, 35 Hispanics, 3 Native Americans). Average age 27. 1,570 applicants, 14% accepted. In 1997, 166 degrees awarded. *Entrance requirements:* MCAT, interview. Application deadline: 10/15. *Financial aid:* 646 students received aid; Federal Work-Study, institutionally sponsored loans, and career-related internships or fieldwork available. Aid available to part-time students. Financial aid application deadline: 4/3; applicants required to submit FAFSA. • Dr. Deborah Powell, Executive Dean, 913-588-5287. Application contact: Peggy Heinen, Admissions Coordinator, 913-588-5283. Fax: 913-588-5259.

University of Kentucky, College of Medicine, Professional Program in Medicine, Lexington, KY 40506-0032. Awards MD, MD/PhD. Accredited by LCME. Faculty: 545 full-time (132 women), 64 part-time (25 women). Students: 391 full-time (151 women); includes 66 minority (28 African Americans, 36 Asian Americans, 2 Hispanics), 3 international. Average age 24. 1,540 applicants, 9% accepted. In 1997, 89 degrees awarded. *Entrance requirements:* MCAT. Application deadline: 11/1 (rolling processing). Application fee: $30. *Financial aid:* Application deadline 4/1; applicants required to submit FAFSA. • Dr. Carol Elam, Assistant Dean for Admissions, College of Medicine, 606-323-6161. Fax: 606-323-2076.

University of Louisville, School of Medicine, Professional Programs in Medicine, Louisville, KY 40292-0001. Awards MD, MD/MS, MD/PhD. Accredited by LCME. Faculty: 433 full-time (109 women), 55 part-time (34 women), 451 FTE. Students: 559 full-time (259 women); includes 91 minority (39 African Americans, 43 Asian Americans, 3 Hispanics, 6 Native Americans). Average age 26. In 1997, 140 degrees awarded. *Entrance requirements:* MCAT. Application deadline: 1/15. Application fee: $15. • Dr. Donald R. Kmetz, Dean, School of Medicine, 502-852-5184.

University of Maryland, Baltimore, Professional Program in Medicine, Baltimore, MD 21201-1627. Awards MD, MD/PhD. Accredited by LCME. MD/PhD offered jointly with the Graduate Programs in Medicine and the University of Maryland, Baltimore County. *Entrance requirements:* MCAT. Application deadline: 11/1 (rolling processing). Application fee: $40. *Faculty research:* Vaccine development, AIDS, hypertension, reproduction, genetics.

University of Massachusetts Medical Center at Worcester, Medical School, Worcester, MA 01655-0115. Awards MD, MD/PhD. Accredited by LCME. Faculty: 176 full-time (33 women). Students: 422 full-time (218 women); includes 57 minority (20 African Americans, 30 Asian Americans, 5 Hispanics, 2 Native Americans). Average age 27. 958 applicants, 10% accepted. In 1997, 98 degrees awarded. *Entrance requirements:* MCAT, state residency. Application deadline: 11/1. Application fee: $50. • Dr. Aaron Lazare, Dean, 508-856-0011. Application contact: Dr. Jane Cronin, Director of Admissions, 508-856-2323. Fax: 508-856-3629.

University of Medicine and Dentistry of New Jersey, New Jersey Medical School, Newark, NJ 07107-3001. Awards MD, MD/PhD. Accredited by LCME. Faculty: 635 full-time (200 women), 70 part-time (26 women), 659.5 FTE. Students: 699 full-time (246 women); includes 366 minority (58 African Americans, 236 Asian Americans, 71 Hispanics, 1 Native American). 3,570 applicants, 12% accepted. In 1997, 168 degrees awarded. *Entrance requirements:* MCAT. Application deadline: 12/1 (rolling processing). Application fee: $125. *Financial aid:* Fellowships, research assistantships, teaching assistantships, Federal Work-Study, institutionally sponsored loans available. Financial aid application deadline: 5/1. *Faculty research:* Molecular genetics, neurosciences, membranes, cancer, hypertension. Total annual research expenditures: $26.5 million. • Dr. Ruy V. Lourenço, Dean, 973-972-4538. Fax: 973-972-7104. Application contact: Betty Taylor, Director of Admissions, 973-972-4631. Fax: 973-972-7986. E-mail: btaylor@umdnj.edu.

University of Medicine and Dentistry of New Jersey, Robert Wood Johnson Medical School, Professional Program in Medicine, Piscataway, NJ 08854. Awards MD, MD/MPH, MD/PhD. Accredited by LCME. MD/MPH and MD/PhD offered jointly with Rutgers, The State University of New Jersey, New Brunswick. Faculty: 737 full-time (219 women), 114 part-time (59 women), 797 FTE. Students: 625 full-time (264 women); includes 309 minority (91 African Americans, 170 Asian Americans, 47 Hispanics, 1 Native American). 3,322 applicants, 11% accepted. In 1997, 150 degrees awarded. *Entrance requirements:* MCAT. Application deadline: 2/15. Application fee: $125. *Financial aid:* Fellowships, research assistantships, teaching assistantships, Federal Work-Study, institutionally sponsored loans, and career-related internships or fieldwork available. Aid available to part-time students. Financial aid application deadline: 5/1; applicants required to submit FAFSA. • Application contact: Dr. David Seiden, Associate Dean for Admissions and Student Affairs, 732-235-4576. Fax: 732-235-5078. E-mail: seiden@umdnj.edu.

University of Miami, School of Medicine, Professional Program in Medicine, Coral Gables, FL 33124. Awards MD, MD/PhD. Accredited by LCME. Faculty: 1,025 full-time, 1,926 part-time. Students: 603 full-time (281 women); includes 257 minority (47 African Americans, 113 Asian Americans, 97 Hispanics). Average age 22. 2,503 applicants, 9% accepted. In 1997, 153 degrees awarded (100% found work related to degree). *Entrance requirements:* MCAT (average 30), 90 pre-med semester hours. Application deadline: 12/15 (rolling processing). Application fee: $50. *Expenses:* Tuition $24,920 per year for state residents; $30,070 per year for nonresidents. Fees $120 per year. *Financial aid:* 482 students received aid; Federal Work-Study, institutionally sponsored loans, and career-related internships or fieldwork available. Financial aid application deadline: 4/1; applicants required to submit CSS PROFILE or FAFSA. *Faculty research:* AIDS, cancer, diabetes, neuroscience, reproductive science. Total annual research expenditures: $105 million. • Application contact: Dr. Robert Hinkley, Associate Dean for Admissions, 305-243-6791. Fax: 305-243-6548. E-mail: miami-md@mednet.med.miami.edu.

University of Michigan, Medical School, Professional Program in Medicine, Ann Arbor, MI 48109. Awards MD, MD/MPH, MD/PhD. Accredited by LCME. *Entrance requirements:* MCAT. • Dr. Giles G. Bole Jr., Dean, Medical School, 734-763-9600. Application contact: Cheryl J. Grostic, Staff Assistant, 734-936-1508. Fax: 734-763-4936. E-mail: cgrostic@umich.edu.

University of Michigan, Medical School and Horace H. Rackham School of Graduate Studies, Graduate Programs in Medicine, Medical Scientist Training Program, Ann Arbor, MI 48109. Awards MD/PhD. Students: 58 full-time (14 women); includes 20 minority (3 African Americans, 15 Asian Americans, 2 Hispanics). Average age 25. 127 applicants, 7% accepted. *Application deadline:* 12/1. *Application fee:* $55. Electronic applications accepted. *Financial aid:* 58 students received aid; fellowships, research assistantships, teaching assistantships, institutionally sponsored loans available. Financial aid applicants required to submit FAFSA. • Ronald J. Koenig, Director, 734-764-6176. E-mail: rkoenig@umich.edu. Application contact: Carol Kruise, Program Secretary, 734-764-6176. Fax: 734-764-8180. E-mail: ckruise@umich.edu.

University of Minnesota, Duluth, School of Medicine, Professional Program in Medicine, Duluth, MN 55812-2496. Awards MD. Accredited by LCME. Offered in cooperation with the University of Minnesota, Twin Cities Campus. Students: 103 full-time (51 women), 6 part-time (2 women). 1,142 applicants, 6% accepted. *Entrance requirements:* MCAT. Application deadline:

9/2 (rolling processing). Application fee: $50. • Application contact: Lillian A. Repesh, Associate Dean for Admissions and Student Affairs, 218-726-8511. Fax: 218-726-6235.

University of Minnesota, Twin Cities Campus, Medical School, Professional Program in Medicine, Minneapolis, MN 55455-0213. Awards MD. Accredited by LCME. *Application deadline:* 11/15 (rolling processing). *Application fee:* $50.

University of Mississippi Medical Center, School of Medicine, Jackson, MS 39216-4505. Awards MD, MD/PhD. Accredited by LCME. Faculty: 373 full-time (99 women), 51 part-time (19 women). Students: 389 full-time (121 women), 1 (woman) part-time; includes 57 minority (35 African Americans, 19 Asian Americans, 3 Hispanics). Average age 24. 607 applicants, 20% accepted. In 1997, 90 degrees awarded (100% continued full-time study). *Entrance requirements:* MCAT. Application deadline: 11/1 (rolling processing). *Tuition:* $6838 per year for state residents; $13,198 per year for nonresidents. *Financial aid:* In 1997–98, 386 students received aid, including 227 scholarships (52 to first-year students); Federal Work-Study, institutionally sponsored loans also available. Aid available to part-time students. Financial aid application deadline: 4/1. *Faculty research:* Cardiovascular physiology (computer simulation), transplant immunology, reproductive endocrinology, protein structure, neurotransmitter vesicle structure. • Dr. A. Wallace Conerly, Dean, 601-984-1010. Application contact: Dr. Billy M. Bishop, Director, Student Services and Records, 601-984-1080. Fax: 601-984-1079. E-mail: bmb@fiona.umsmed.edu.

University of Missouri–Columbia, School of Medicine, Professional Program in Medicine, Columbia, MO 65211. Awards MD, MD/MS, MD/PhD. Accredited by LCME. Faculty: 425 full-time (115 women), 49 part-time (17 women). Students: 377 full-time (166 women); includes 62 minority (14 African Americans, 40 Asian Americans, 5 Hispanics, 3 Native Americans). Average age 26. 988 applicants, 13% accepted. In 1997, 94 degrees awarded (100% continued full-time study). *Average time to degree:* first professional–4 years full-time. *Entrance requirements:* MCAT (average 29), specified pre-med courses. Application deadline: 11/1 (rolling processing). Application fee: $0. *Expenses:* Tuition $14,036 per year for state residents; $28,224 per year for nonresidents. Fees $682 per year. *Financial aid:* 370 students received aid; Federal Work-Study, institutionally sponsored loans, and career-related internships or fieldwork available. Financial aid application deadline: 8/15; applicants required to submit FAFSA. *Faculty research:* Basic and clinical biomedical sciences. • Dr. Lester R. Bryant, Dean, 573-882-1566. Application contact: Dr. Shari L. Swindell, Coordinator, Admissions and Records, 573-882-2923. Fax: 573-884-4808. E-mail: shari_l._swindell@muccmail.missouri.edu.

University of Missouri–Kansas City, School of Medicine, Kansas City, MO 64110-2499. Awards MD, MD/PhD. Accredited by LCME. Students: 356 full-time (194 women); includes 143 minority (12 African Americans, 122 Asian Americans, 8 Hispanics, 1 Native American). Average age 22. In 1997, 82 degrees awarded. *Degree requirements:* 1 foreign language required, thesis not required. *Entrance requirements:* ACT. Application deadline: 1/1. Application fee: $25. *Expenses:* Tuition $15,494 per year full-time, $16,494 per year part-time for state residents; $31,395 per year for nonresidents. Fees $326 per year. *Financial aid:* Full and partial tuition waivers, Federal Work-Study, institutionally sponsored loans, and career-related internships or fieldwork available. Aid available to part-time students. *Faculty research:* Gastritis, rat cancer, cholecystitis in dogs, pulmonary venocclusive disease, etiology of hemoptysis. • Dr. Marjorie Sirridge, Interim Dean, 816-235-1808.

University of Nebraska Medical Center, College of Medicine, Omaha, NE 68198-0001. Awards MD. Accredited by LCME. Faculty: 357 full-time, 47 part-time. Students: 486 full-time (216 women); includes 44 minority (6 African Americans, 25 Asian Americans, 8 Hispanics, 5 Native Americans). Average age 22. In 1997, 125 degrees awarded. *Entrance requirements:* MCAT. Application deadline: 11/1 (rolling processing). Application fee: $25. *Financial aid:* 445 students received aid; full tuition waivers, Federal Work-Study, institutionally sponsored loans, and career-related internships or fieldwork available. Aid available to part-time students. Financial aid application deadline: 2/1; applicants required to submit FAFSA. • Dr. Harold Maurer, Dean, 402-559-4204. Application contact: Cheryl E. Scruggs, Director of Admissions, 402-559-2259. Fax: 402-559-4148. E-mail: cscruggs@unmc.edu.

University of Nevada, Reno, School of Medicine, Professional Programs in Medicine, Reno, NV 89557. Awards MD, MD/PhD. Accredited by LCME. Students: 208; includes 10 minority (7 Asian Americans, 2 Hispanics, 1 Native American). Average age 23. *Degree requirements:* National Medical Board Exam Parts I and II required, foreign language and thesis not required. *Entrance requirements:* MCAT. Application deadline: rolling. *Financial aid:* Research assistantships, teaching assistantships, Federal Work-Study, institutionally sponsored loans available. Aid available to part-time students. Financial aid application deadline: 3/1. • Gale H. Starich, Director, 702-784-4631. E-mail: gale@physio.unr.edu.

University of New Mexico, School of Medicine, Albuquerque, NM 87131-2039. Awards MD. Accredited by LCME. *Entrance requirements:* MCAT, previous course work in biology, general chemistry, organic chemistry, and physics. Application deadline: 11/15. Application fee: $25. *Tuition:* $6478 per year for state residents; $18,572 per year for nonresidents.

The University of North Carolina at Chapel Hill, School of Medicine, Professional Program in Medicine, Chapel Hill, NC 27599. Awards MD, MD/MPH, MD/PhD. Accredited by LCME. Faculty: 597 full-time. Students: 665 full-time. 3,035 applicants, 5% accepted. In 1997, 157 degrees awarded. *Entrance requirements:* MCAT. Application deadline: 11/15 (rolling processing). Application fee: $55. *Expenses:* Tuition $2502 per year for state residents; $22,984 per year for nonresidents. Fees $791 per year. • Dr. Elizabeth S. Mann, Associate Dean, 919-962-8331.

University of North Dakota, School of Medicine, Professional Program in Medicine, Grand Forks, ND 58202. Awards MD, MD/PhD. Accredited by LCME. Faculty: 121 full-time (18 women), 91 part-time. Students: 233 full-time (101 women); includes 39 minority (9 Asian Americans, 30 Native Americans). Average age 26. 339 applicants, 25% accepted. In 1997, 60 degrees awarded. *Average time to degree:* first professional–4 years full-time. *Entrance requirements:* MCAT, minimum GPA of 3.0. Application deadline: 11/1. Application fee: $35. *Financial aid:* Full and partial tuition waivers, institutionally sponsored loans available. Aid available to part-time students. Financial aid application deadline: 4/15; applicants required to submit FAFSA. • Application contact: Marilyn Martin, 701-777-2840.

University of Oklahoma Health Sciences Center, College of Medicine, Professional Program in Medicine, Oklahoma City, OK 73190. Awards MD, MD/PhD. Accredited by LCME. Students: 587 full-time (238 women); includes 116 minority (16 African Americans, 44 Asian Americans, 17 Hispanics, 39 Native Americans), 14 international. Average age 25. In 1997, 144 degrees awarded. *Entrance requirements:* MCAT. Application deadline: 10/31. Application fee: $25 ($50 for international students). *Financial aid:* Fellowships available. *Faculty research:* Behavior and drugs, structure and function of endothelium, genetics and behavior, gene structure and function, action of antibiotics. • Application contact: Dr. Nancy Hall, Associate Dean, 405-271-2339.

University of Ottawa, Faculty of Medicine, Ottawa, ON K1N 6N5, Canada. Awards M Sc, PhD. Accredited by LCME. Faculty: 138 full-time, 29 part-time. Students: 183 full-time (94 women), 27 part-time (12 women); includes 6 international. Average age 31. In 1997, 21 master's, 18 doctorates awarded. *Degree requirements:* Thesis/dissertation required, foreign language not required. *Entrance requirements:* For master's, honors degree or equivalent, minimum B average; for doctorate, master's degree, minimum B+ average. Application fee: $35. *Expenses:* Tuition $4677 per year for Canadian residents; $9900 per year for nonresidents. Fees $230 per year. *Financial aid:* Fellowships, research assistantships, teaching assistantships, and career-related internships or fieldwork available. • Dr. Peter Walker, Dean, 613-562-5800 Ext. 8113. Application contact: Yvonne Lefebvre, Vice Dean of Research, 613-562-5800 Ext. 8116. Fax: 613-562-5457.

University of Pennsylvania, School of Medicine, Professional Program in Medicine, Philadelphia, PA 19104. Awards MD, MD/MS, MD/PhD, MD/JD, MD/MBA. Accredited by LCME. Faculty: 1,173 full-time (275 women), 1,347 part-time (398 women). Students: 689 full-time (300 women); includes 277 minority (70 African Americans, 155 Asian Americans, 47 Hispanics, 5 Native Americans), 11 international. Average age 23. 7,950 applicants, 4% accepted. In 1997, 142 degrees awarded. *Entrance requirements:* MCAT. Application deadline: 11/1. Application fee: $55. *Expenses:* Tuition $28,470 per year. Fees $1170 per year. *Financial aid:* 549 students received aid; fellowships, research assistantships, teaching assistantships, Federal Work-Study, institutionally sponsored loans, and career-related internships or fieldwork available. Financial aid application deadline: 5/1; applicants required to submit FAFSA. • Application contact: Gaye Sheffer, Director of Admissions and Financial Aid, 215-898-8001.

University of Pittsburgh, School of Medicine, Professional Program in Medicine, Pittsburgh, PA 15260. Awards MD, MD/MA. Accredited by LCME. Faculty: 1,357 full-time (365 women), 60 part-time (34 women). Students: 562 full-time (268 women); includes 153 minority (41 African Americans, 98 Asian Americans, 13 Hispanics, 1 Native American). 5,275 applicants, 8% accepted. In 1997, 151 degrees awarded. *Average time to degree:* first professional–4 years full-time. *Entrance requirements:* MCAT, TOEFL, 1 year of biology, chemistry, English, inorganic chemistry, organic chemistry, and physics. Application deadline: 11/1 (rolling processing). Application fee: $50. Electronic applications accepted. *Expenses:* Tuition $20,534 per year for state residents; $27,724 per year for nonresidents. Fees $444 per year. *Financial aid:* 440 students received aid; scholarships, Federal Work-Study, institutionally sponsored loans available. Financial aid application deadline: 4/1; applicants required to submit FAFSA. • Dr. Edward Curtiss, Associate Dean of Admissions, 412-648-9891. E-mail: admissions@fs1.dean-med.pitt.edu. Application contact: Linda Berardi-Demo, Admissions Director, 412-648-9891. Fax: 412-648-8768. E-mail: admissions@fsl.dean-med.pitt.edu.

University of Puerto Rico, Medical Sciences Campus, School of Medicine, Professional Program in Medicine, San Juan, PR 00936-5067. Awards MD. Accredited by LCME. *Degree requirements:* 1 foreign language. *Entrance requirements:* MCAT, interview. Application deadline: 12/1. Application fee: $15.

University of Rochester, School of Medicine and Dentistry, Professional Program in Medicine, Rochester, NY 14627-0001. Awards MD, MD/MPH, MD/MS, MD/PhD. Accredited by LCME. Faculty: 409 full-time. Students: 422 full-time (186 women); includes 138 minority (45 African Americans, 76 Asian Americans, 15 Hispanics, 2 Native Americans), 7 international. 3,914 applicants, 7% accepted. In 1997, 91 degrees awarded. *Entrance requirements:* MCAT. Application deadline: 10/15. Application fee: $70. *Expenses:* Tuition $21,485 per year full-time, $672 per credit hour part-time. Fees $336 per year. *Financial aid:* Fellowships, research assistantships, teaching assistantships, full and partial tuition waivers, Federal Work-Study available. Aid available to part-time students. Financial aid application deadline: 11/1. • Dr. Edward Hundert, Senior Associate Dean, 716-275-4656. Application contact: Barbara Mittiga, Administrative Assistant, 716-275-4539.

University of Saskatchewan, College of Medicine, Professional Program in Medicine, Saskatoon, SK S7N 5A2, Canada. Awards MD. Accredited by LCME. Students: 231 full-time. In 1997, 55 degrees awarded. *Application deadline:* 7/1 (priority date). *Application fee:* $25. *Financial aid:* Application deadline 1/31. • Dr. D. R. Popkin, Dean, College of Medicine, 306-966-6149. Fax: 306-966-6164.

University of South Alabama, College of Medicine, Professional Program in Medicine, Mobile, AL 36688-0002. Awards MD. Accredited by LCME. Faculty: 169 full-time (39 women), 22 part-time (5 women). Students: 254 full-time (97 women); includes 41 minority (20 African Americans, 18 Asian Americans, 1 Hispanic, 2 Native Americans). In 1997, 65 degrees awarded. *Entrance requirements:* MCAT. Application fee: $25. • Dr. William A. Gardner Jr., Interim Dean, College of Medicine, 334-460-7189.

University of South Carolina, School of Medicine, Professional Program in Medicine, Columbia, SC 29208. Awards MD. Accredited by LCME. Faculty: 162 full-time, 15 part-time. Students: 282 full-time (115 women); includes 47 minority (14 African Americans, 26 Asian Americans, 7 Hispanics). Average age 26. In 1997, 73 degrees awarded (100% continued full-time study). *Entrance requirements:* MCAT. Application deadline: 12/1 (priority date; rolling processing). Application fee: $45. Electronic applications accepted. *Expenses:* Tuition $8134 per year for state residents; $22,550 per year for nonresidents. Fees $125 per year. *Financial aid:* 235 students received aid; institutionally sponsored loans available. Financial aid application deadline: 7/1. • Application contact: Dr. Robert F. Sabalis, Associate Dean for Medical Education and Academic Affairs, 803-733-3325.

University of South Dakota, School of Medicine, Professional Program in Medicine, Sioux Falls, SD 57105. Awards MD. Accredited by LCME. Faculty: 153 full-time, 258 part-time. Students: 204 full-time (97 women); includes 13 minority (4 Asian Americans, 1 Hispanic, 8 Native Americans), 1 international. Average age 24. 992 applicants, 6% accepted. In 1997, 50 degrees awarded (100% found work related to degree). *Average time to degree:* first professional–4 years full-time. *Entrance requirements:* MCAT. Application deadline: 11/15 (priority date; rolling processing). Application fee: $15. *Faculty research:* Hypertension, endocrinology. • Dr. Robert Talley, Vice President, Health Affairs/Dean, School of Medicine, 605-357-1300. Application contact: Dr. Harry E. Settles, Interim Dean, Student Affairs, 605-677-5233.

University of Southern California, School of Medicine, Professional Program in Medicine, Los Angeles, CA 90089. Awards MD, MD/PhD. Accredited by LCME. Students: 637 full-time (271 women); includes 318 minority (32 African Americans, 197 Asian Americans, 83 Hispanics, 6 Native Americans), 13 international. Average age 24. In 1997, 160 degrees awarded (100% found work related to degree). *Entrance requirements:* MCAT. Application deadline: 11/1 (rolling processing). Application fee: $70. *Expenses:* Tuition $30,468 per year. Fees $1029 per year. *Financial aid:* Career-related internships or fieldwork available. Financial aid application deadline: 2/1. • Application contact: Dr. Arleen Marx, Assistant Dean for Admissions, 213-342-2552. Fax: 213-342-2663.

University of South Florida, College of Medicine, Professional Program in Medicine, Tampa, FL 33620-9951. Awards MD. Accredited by LCME. Faculty: 316 full-time (75 women). Students: 385 full-time (134 women); includes 111 minority (25 African Americans, 46 Asian Americans, 34 Hispanics, 6 Native Americans). Average age 29. In 1997, 86 degrees awarded. *Application fee:* $20. *Tuition:* $10,458 per year for state residents; $28,109 per year for nonresidents. *Financial aid:* Fellowships, research assistantships, Federal Work-Study, institutionally sponsored loans available. Aid available to part-time students. Financial aid applicants required to submit FAFSA. • Dr. R. Manning, Associate Dean of Student Affairs, 813-974-2068. E-mail: rmanning@com1.med.usf.edu. Application contact: J. Layman, Director of Admissions, 813-974-2229. Fax: 813-974-3886. E-mail: jlayman@com1.med.usf.edu.

University of Tennessee, Memphis, College of Medicine, Memphis, TN 38163-0002. Awards MD, MD/PhD. Accredited by LCME. *Entrance requirements:* MCAT, interview, preprofessional evaluation. Application deadline: 11/15 (rolling processing). Application fee: $25.

The University of Texas Health Science Center at San Antonio, Medical School, San Antonio, TX 28284-7790. Awards MD. Accredited by LCME. Faculty: 835 full-time (249 women), 125 part-time (62 women), 860 FTE. Students: 814 full-time (340 women); includes 298 minority (21 African Americans, 161 Asian Americans, 109 Hispanics, 7 Native Americans), 1 international. Average age 25. 3,159 applicants, 7% accepted. In 1997, 210 degrees awarded (98% continued full-time study). *Average time to degree:* first professional–4 years full-time. *Entrance requirements:* MCAT. Application deadline: 10/15 (rolling processing). Application fee: $45 ($80 for international students). *Financial aid:* 682 students received aid; full and partial tuition waivers, institutionally sponsored loans available. Financial aid applicants required to submit FAFSA. *Faculty research:* Geriatrics, molecular medicine, diabetes, genetics, anticancer

Directory: Allopathic Medicine

The University of Texas Health Science Center at San Antonio (continued)
agents, AIDS and children, obesity. Total annual research expenditures: $68.9 million. • James J. Young, Dean, 210-567-4420. Fax: 210-567-6962. Application contact: Dr. David J. Jones, Director of Admissions, 210-567-4515. Fax: 210-567-6135. E-mail: jonesd@uthscsa.edu.

The University of Texas–Houston Health Science Center, Medical School, Houston, TX 77225-0036. Awards MD, MD/MPH, MD/PhD. Accredited by LCME. Faculty: 650. Students: 836 full-time (375 women); includes 316 minority (34 African Americans, 105 Asian Americans, 172 Hispanics, 5 Native Americans), 2 international. Average age 22. 3,253 applicants, 8% accepted. In 1997, 198 degrees awarded (100% continued full-time study). *Entrance requirements:* MCAT (average 27.2). Application deadline: 10/15 (rolling processing). Application fee: $45. • Dr. L. Maximilian Buja, Dean, 713-500-5010. Application contact: Dr. Albert E. Gunn, Associate Dean for Admissions, 713-500-5118. Fax: 713-500-0604.

The University of Texas Medical Branch at Galveston, School of Medicine, Galveston, TX 77555. Awards MD, MD/PhD. Accredited by LCME. *Entrance requirements:* MCAT. Application deadline: 10/15. Application fee: $45. *Faculty research:* Neuroscience, immunology, virology, genetics, cell biology.

The University of Texas Southwestern Medical Center at Dallas, Southwestern Medical School, Dallas, TX 75235. Awards MD, MD/PhD. Accredited by LCME. Students: 809 full-time (270 women); includes 278 minority (19 African Americans, 194 Asian Americans, 57 Hispanics, 8 Native Americans). Average age 25. 3,174 applicants, 12% accepted. In 1997, 208 degrees awarded. *Entrance requirements:* MCAT (average 32.8). Application deadline: 10/15. Application fee: $45. *Financial aid:* 700 students received aid; Federal Work-Study, institutionally sponsored loans available. Financial aid application deadline: 3/15; applicants required to submit FAFSA. *Faculty research:* Endocrinology, molecular biology, immunology, cancer biology, neuroscience. Total annual research expenditures: $140.5 million. • Dr. William B. Neaves, Dean, 214-648-2509. Application contact: Scott Wright, Administrative Director of Admission Committee, 214-648-2670. Fax: 214-648-3289. E-mail: admissions@mednet.swmed.edu.

University of Toronto, Faculty of Medicine, Toronto, ON M5S 1A1, Canada. Awards MD, MD/PhD. Accredited by LCME. Faculty: 1,860 full-time, 2,498 part-time. Students: 703 full-time (286 women); includes 2 international. Average age 24. 1,629 applicants, 11% accepted. In 1997, 174 degrees awarded. *Average time to degree:* first professional–4 years full-time. *Entrance requirements:* MCAT. Application deadline: 10/15. Application fee: $250. *Financial aid:* In 1997–98, 537 scholarships were awarded; research assistantships also available. • Arnold Aberman, Dean, 416-978-6585. Application contact: Judith Irvine, Coordinator Admissions Awards, and Registrarial Affairs, 416-978-2717. Fax: 416-971-2163. E-mail: judy.irvine@utoronto.ca.

University of Utah, School of Medicine, Professional Program in Medicine, Salt Lake City, UT 84132. Awards MD, MD/MPH, MD/PhD. Accredited by LCME. MD/MPH new for fall 1998. Faculty: 638 full-time (123 women), 14 part-time (10 women). Students: 397 full-time (129 women); includes 65 minority (5 African Americans, 27 Asian Americans, 18 Hispanics, 15 Native Americans), 8 international. Average age 24. 1,257 applicants, 13% accepted. In 1997, 99 degrees awarded. *Entrance requirements:* MCAT, 2 years of course work in chemistry, 1 year of course work in physics, 1 year of course work in English composition or speech. Application deadline: 10/15 (rolling processing). Application fee: $50. *Tuition:* $7421 per year for state residents; $15,771 per year for nonresidents. *Faculty research:* Molecular biology, genetics, immunology, cardiology. • Dr. Victoria E. Judd, Assistant Dean, 801-581-7498. E-mail: victoria.judd@hsc.utah.edu. Application contact: Kathy Z. Doulis, Office of Admissions, 801-581-7498. Fax: 801-585-3300. E-mail: kathy.doulis@hsc.utah.edu.

University of Vermont, College of Medicine, Professional Program in Medicine, Burlington, VT 05405-0160. Awards MD, MD/MS, MD/PhD. Accredited by LCME. Students: 383; includes 67 minority (2 African Americans, 55 Asian Americans, 8 Hispanics, 2 Native Americans). 7,071 applicants, 2% accepted. In 1997, 91 degrees awarded. *Entrance requirements:* MCAT. Application deadline: 11/1 (priority date; rolling processing). Application fee: $75. *Expenses:* Tuition $18,150 per year for state residents; $31,770 per year for nonresidents. Fees $681 per year. • Dr. Marga S. Sproul, Associate Dean for Admissions, 802-656-2154. Application contact: Bonnie Schneck, 802-656-2154.

University of Virginia, School of Medicine, Charlottesville, VA 22908. Awards MD, MD/PhD. Accredited by LCME. Faculty: 701 full-time (167 women), 34 part-time (20 women), 718 FTE. Students: 553 full-time (242 women); includes 166 minority (61 African Americans, 92 Asian Americans, 9 Hispanics, 4 Native Americans), 4 international. Average age 25. 4,474 applicants, 7% accepted. In 1997, 140 degrees awarded. *Application deadline:* 11/15. *Application fee:* $50. *Tuition:* $11,642 per year for state residents; $23,952 per year for nonresidents. *Financial aid:* Fellowships available. • Robert M. Carey, Dean, 804-924-8418. Application contact: Beth A. Bailey, Director, Admissions Office, 804-924-5571. E-mail: bab7g@virginia.edu.

University of Virginia, Graduate School of Arts and Sciences, Department of Surgery, Charlottesville, VA 22903. Awards MS. Faculty: 32 full-time (3 women), 1 part-time (0 women). Students: 3 full-time (0 women). Average age 28. 1 applicant, 100% accepted. In 1997, 1 degree awarded. *Application deadline:* 7/15 (rolling processing; 12/1 for spring admission). *Application fee:* $40. *Tuition:* $4870 per year full-time, $941 per semester (minimum) part-time for state residents; $15,818 per year full-time, $2745 per semester (minimum) part-time for nonresidents. *Financial aid:* Application deadline 2/1. • R. Scott Jones, Chairman, 804-924-2150. Application contact: Duane J. Osheim, Associate Dean, 804-924-7184.

University of Washington, School of Medicine, Professional Program in Medicine, Seattle, WA 98195. Awards MD, MD/MPH, MD/PhD, MD/MA. Accredited by LCME. Students: 738 full-time (350 women); includes 168 minority (18 African Americans, 96 Asian Americans, 27 Hispanics, 27 Native Americans). Average age 27. 3,188 applicants, 7% accepted. In 1997, 148 degrees awarded. *Entrance requirements:* MCAT or GRE, minimum 3 years of college. Application deadline: 11/1 (rolling processing). Application fee: $35. *Tuition:* $8823 per year for state residents; $22,251 per year for nonresidents. *Financial aid:* Partial tuition waivers, institutionally sponsored loans available. Aid available to part-time students. Financial aid application deadline: 2/28; applicants required to submit FAFSA. • Application contact: Pat Fero, Office of Admissions, 206-543-7212. E-mail: askuwsom@u.washington.edu.

The University of Western Ontario, Faculty of Medicine and Dentistry, Professional Program in Medicine, London, ON N6A 5B8, Canada. Awards MD. Accredited by LCME. • Dr. L. S. Valberg, Dean, Faculty of Medicine and Dentistry, 519-661-3459.

The University of Western Ontario, Biosciences Division, Department of Family Medicine, London, ON N6A 5B8, Canada. Awards M Cl Sc. Part-time programs available. *Entrance requirements:* Medical degree, minimum B average. *Faculty research:* Family medicine education, dietary counselling, alcohol problems, palliative care support, multicultural health care.

University of Wisconsin–Madison, Medical School, Professional Program in Medicine, Madison, WI 53706-1380. Awards MD. Accredited by LCME. *Tuition:* $15,512 per year for state residents; $22,826 per year for nonresidents. • Dr. Phillip M. Farrell, Dean, Medical School, 608-263-4910. Fax: 608-265-3286. E-mail: philip.farrell@mail.admin.wisc.edu.

Vanderbilt University, School of Medicine, Nashville, TN 37232. Awards MD, MPH, MD/PhD. One or more programs accredited by LCME. MD/PhD offered jointly with the Graduate School. Faculty: 1,022 full-time (265 women), 851 part-time (195 women). Students: 413 full-time (136 women); includes 83 minority (8 African Americans, 61 Asian Americans, 10 Hispanics, 4 Native Americans), 3 international. Average age 22. 5,838 applicants, 6% accepted. In 1997, 100 MDs awarded (100% found work related to degree). *Average time to degree:* first professional–4 years full-time. *Entrance requirements:* For MD, MCAT, interview, previous course work in English, physics, chemistry, and biology. Application deadline: 10/15 (rolling processing). Application fee: $50. *Financial aid:* 334 students received aid; institutionally sponsored loans available. Financial aid application deadline: 3/1; applicants required to submit FAFSA. *Total annual research expenditures:* $120 million. • Dr. John E. Chapman, Dean, 615-322-2164. Application contact: Dr. John N. Lukens, Chairman, Committee on Admissions, 615-322-2145. Fax: 615-343-8397.

Virginia Commonwealth University, Medical College of Virginia-Professional Programs, School of Medicine, Professional Program in Medicine, Richmond, VA 23284-9005. Awards MD, MD/MS, MD/PhD. Accredited by LCME. Students: 668 full-time (268 women); includes 206 minority (57 African Americans, 133 Asian Americans, 13 Hispanics, 3 Native Americans), 3 international. Average age 26. In 1997, 170 degrees awarded. *Entrance requirements:* MCAT (average 9.6). Application deadline: 11/15 (rolling processing). *Financial aid:* Fellowships, research assistantships, teaching assistantships, full and partial tuition waivers, Federal Work-Study, and career-related internships or fieldwork available. • James M. Messmer, Associate Dean, 804-828-9790. Fax: 804-828-3832. Application contact: Cynthia Heldberg, Assistant Dean, Admissions, 804-828-9629. Fax: 804-828-7628. E-mail: cmheldbe@vcu.edu.

Wake Forest University, School of Medicine, Professional Program in Medicine, Winston-Salem, NC 27103. Awards MD, MD/MS, MD/PhD, MD/MBA. Accredited by LCME. Faculty: 731 full-time, 550 part-time. Students: 452 full-time (182 women); includes 97 minority (42 African Americans, 45 Asian Americans, 8 Hispanics, 2 Native Americans), 6 international. Average age 23. 6,564 applicants, 3% accepted. In 1997, 106 degrees awarded (100% continued full-time study). *Average time to degree:* first professional–4 years full-time. *Entrance requirements:* MCAT, 32 hours of course work in science. Application deadline: 11/1 (rolling processing). Application fee: $55. Electronic applications accepted. *Tuition:* $26,500 per year. *Financial aid:* 350 students received aid; full and partial tuition waivers, institutionally sponsored loans, and career-related internships or fieldwork available. Financial aid application deadline: 4/1; applicants required to submit CSS PROFILE or FAFSA. *Faculty research:* Cancer, stroke, infectious diseases, membrane biology, nutrition. • Application contact: Dr. Lewis Nelson, Associate Dean for Student Services and Admissions, 336-716-2883. Fax: 336-716-5807.

Washington University in St. Louis, School of Medicine, Professional Program in Medicine, St. Louis, MO 63130-4899. Awards MD, MD/PhD, MD/MA, MD/MHA. Accredited by LCME. Faculty: 1,285 full-time, 1,172 part-time. Students: 563 full-time (260 women); includes 213 minority (41 African Americans, 161 Asian Americans, 8 Hispanics, 3 Native Americans), 14 international. Average age 23. 5,823 applicants, 5% accepted. In 1997, 125 degrees awarded. *Entrance requirements:* MCAT. Application deadline: 12/31 (rolling processing). Application fee: $50. *Tuition:* $29,670 per year. *Financial aid:* Institutionally sponsored loans and career-related internships or fieldwork available. • Application contact: Dr. W. Edwin Dodson, Associate Dean, 314-362-6848. Fax: 314-362-4658. E-mail: wumscoa@msnotes.wustl.edu.

Wayne State University, School of Medicine, Professional Program in Medicine, Detroit, MI 48201. Awards MD, MD/PhD. Accredited by LCME. Part-time programs available. Students: 1,027 full-time (405 women), 11 part-time (3 women). 3,655 applicants, 7% accepted. In 1997, 262 degrees awarded. *Entrance requirements:* MCAT. Application deadline: 12/15. Application fee: $20. *Expenses:* Tuition $10,739 per year for state residents; $21,812 per year for nonresidents. Fees $360 per year. *Financial aid:* Fellowships available. • Dr. Charles F. Whitten, Associate Dean, 313-577-1546. Application contact: Dr. James Collins, Assistant Dean, 313-577-1546.

West Virginia University, School of Medicine, Professional Program in Medicine, Morgantown, WV 26506. Awards MD, MD/PhD. Accredited by LCME. Students: 358 full-time (149 women); includes 55 minority (7 African Americans, 46 Asian Americans, 2 Hispanics). Average age 25. 1,128 applicants, 10% accepted. In 1997, 80 degrees awarded (100% found work related to degree). *Average time to degree:* first professional–4 years full-time. *Entrance requirements:* MCAT. Application deadline: 11/15 (rolling processing). Application fee: $45. *Tuition:* $9204 per year for state residents; $22,704 per year for nonresidents. *Financial aid:* In 1997–98, 13 research assistantships (2 to first-year students) averaging $1,027 per month were awarded; full and partial tuition waivers, institutionally sponsored loans also available. Financial aid application deadline: 2/1; applicants required to submit FAFSA. • Dr. John W. Traubert, Associate Dean, 304-293-2408.

Wright State University, School of Medicine, Professional Program in Medicine, Dayton, OH 45435. Awards MD. Accredited by LCME. Faculty: 135 full-time (34 women), 17 part-time (1 woman). Students: 372 full-time (206 women); includes 101 minority (72 African Americans, 20 Asian Americans, 5 Hispanics, 4 Native Americans). Average age 24. In 1997, 88 degrees awarded (100% found work related to degree). *Entrance requirements:* MCAT. Application deadline: 11/15. Application fee: $50. *Tuition:* $13,988 per year for state residents; $19,488 per year for nonresidents. *Financial aid:* In 1997–98, 1 research assistantship, 1 teaching assistantship were awarded. Financial aid applicants required to submit FAFSA. • Dr. Paul Carlson, Associate Dean for Student Affairs and Admissions, 937-775-2934. Fax: 937-775-3322.

Yale University, School of Medicine, Professional Program in Medicine, New Haven, CT 06520. Awards MD. Accredited by LCME. Students: 484 full-time (240 women); includes 191 minority (46 African Americans, 107 Asian Americans, 32 Hispanics, 6 Native Americans), 13 international. Average age 24. 3,511 applicants, 6% accepted. In 1997, 90 degrees awarded. *Degree requirements:* Thesis. *Average time to degree:* first professional–4 years full-time. *Entrance requirements:* MCAT. Application deadline: 10/15 (rolling processing). Application fee: $60. Electronic applications accepted. *Financial aid:* In 1997–98, 290 students received aid, including 290 scholarships (76 to first-year students); institutionally sponsored loans also available. Aid available to part-time students. Financial aid application deadline: 4/1; applicants required to submit FAFSA. • Dr. Robert Gifford, Associate Dean, 203-785-2644. Fax: 203-737-5495. E-mail: medicalschool.admissions@quickmail.yale.edu. Application contact: M. Lynne Wootton, Director of Admissions, 203-785-2643. E-mail: medicalschool.admissions@quickmail.yale.edu.

Yeshiva University, Albert Einstein College of Medicine, Professional Program in Medicine, Bronx, NY 10461. Awards MD, MD/PhD. Accredited by LCME. *Degree requirements:* Independent scholars project required, foreign language and thesis not required. *Entrance requirements:* MCAT, interview. Application deadline: 3/15 (rolling processing). Application fee: $70. *Expenses:* Tuition $27,650 per year. Fees $1600 per year. *Faculty research:* Cancer, diabetes mellitus, liver disease, infectious disease, neuroscience.

Bioethics

Case Western Reserve University, Frances Payne Bolton School of Nursing, Nursing/Bioethics Program, Cleveland, OH 44106. Awards MSN/MA. Offered jointly with the Program in Bioethics. Students: 0. *Application fee:* $75. *Tuition:* $18,400 per year full-time, $767 per credit hour part-time. *Financial aid:* Fellowships, research assistantships, teaching assistantships available. Financial aid application deadline: 6/30. • Application contact: Molly Blank, Admission Counselor, 216-368-2529. Fax: 216-368-3542. E-mail: mab44@po.cwru.edu.

Case Western Reserve University, Schools of Graduate Studies and Medicine, Program in Bioethics, Cleveland, OH 44106. Awards MA, JD/MA, MSN/MA. JD/MA new for fall 1998. Part-time programs available. Faculty: 3 full-time (0 women), 13 part-time (6 women). Students: 6 full-time (3 women), 16 part-time (14 women); includes 2 minority (both Asian Americans), 2 international. Average age 37. 28 applicants, 50% accepted. In 1997, 14 degrees awarded. *Degree requirements:* Comprehensive exam required, thesis not required. *Entrance requirements:* GRE General Test (minimum combined score of 1500 on three sections; average 1700), TOEFL (minimum score 550). Application deadline: 3/1 (priority date). Application fee: $25. *Tuition:* $18,400 per year full-time, $767 per credit hour part-time. *Financial aid:* 7 students received aid; full and partial tuition waivers, institutionally sponsored loans available. Aid available to part-time students. Financial aid application deadline: 3/1. *Faculty research:* Ethical issues in genetics, conflicts of interest, organ donation, end-of-life decision making, clinical ethics consultation. • Thomas H. Murray, Director, 216-368-6196. E-mail: thm2@po.cwru.edu. Application contact: Deidre Gruning, Coordinator of Graduate Programs, 216-368-8718. Fax: 216-368-8713. E-mail: dxc38@po.cwru.edu.

Drew University, Program in Medical Humanities, Madison, NJ 07940-1493. Awards MMH, CMH. Part-time and evening/weekend programs available. Faculty: 2 full-time (1 woman), 6 part-time (2 women). Students: 2 full-time (both women), 26 part-time (22 women); includes 3 minority (all African Americans). Average age 37. 26 applicants, 77% accepted. In 1997, 11 CMHs awarded. *Degree requirements:* For master's, thesis required, foreign language not required. *Application deadline:* rolling. *Application fee:* $35. *Expenses:* Tuition $20,960 per year full-time, $1164 per credit part-time. Fees $530 per year (minimum). *Financial aid:* In 1997–98, 3 scholarships were awarded; full and partial tuition waivers also available. Financial aid application deadline: 2/15; applicants required to submit FAFSA. *Faculty research:* Biomedical ethics, medical narrative, history of medicine, medicine and the arts. • Dr. Thomas Magnell, Area Convener, 973-408-3843. Fax: 973-408-3040. E-mail: tmagnell@drew.edu.

Duquesne University, Graduate School of Liberal Arts, Program in Health Care Ethics, Pittsburgh, PA 15282-0001. Awards MA, DHCE, PhD. Part-time programs available. Faculty: 2 full-time. Students: 7 full-time (4 women), 16 part-time (7 women); includes 1 international. 18 applicants, 83% accepted. In 1997, 2 master's awarded. Terminal master's awarded for partial completion of doctoral program. *Degree requirements:* For master's, thesis (PhD) required, foreign language not required. *Entrance requirements:* For master's, GRE General Test, TOEFL; for doctorate, master's degree in health care ethics. Application deadline: 8/15 (rolling processing). Application fee: $40. *Expenses:* Tuition $481 per credit. Fees $39 per credit. *Financial aid:* Federal Work-Study available. Aid available to part-time students. Financial aid application deadline: 5/1. • Dr. David Kelly, Director, 412-396-6532.

Loma Linda University, Graduate School, Program in Biomedical and Clinical Ethics, Loma Linda, CA 92350. Awards MA. *Entrance requirements:* GRE General Test. Application fee: $40. *Tuition:* $380 per unit. • Dr. Gerald Winslow, Coordinator, 909-824-4536.

McGill University, Faculty of Graduate Studies and Research, Faculty of Medicine, Program in Experimental Medicine, Montréal, PQ H3A 2T5, Canada. Offerings include bioethics (M Sc). Program faculty: 68 full-time (14 women), 25 part-time (8 women). *Degree requirements:* Thesis. *Entrance requirements:* TOEFL (minimum score 550). Application deadline: 3/1 (rolling processing). Application fee: $60. *Expenses:* Tuition $1668 per year for Canadian residents; $8268 per year for nonresidents. Fees $828 per year for Canadian residents; $1216 per year for nonresidents. • Dr. Gerald B. Price, Director, 514-398-3466. E-mail: divexmed@medcor.mcgill.ca. Application contact: Dominique Besso, Student Affairs Coordinator, 514-398-3466. Fax: 514-398-3425. E-mail: divexmed@medcor.mcgill.ca.

Medical College of Wisconsin, Program in Bioethics, Milwaukee, WI 53226-0509. Awards MA, MD/MA. Part-time programs available. Faculty: 6 full-time (1 woman), 4 part-time (1 woman). Students: 7 full-time (5 women), 16 part-time (14 women). Average age 43. 12 applicants, 83% accepted. In 1997, 4 degrees awarded (75% found work related to degree, 25% continued full-time study). *Degree requirements:* Thesis required, foreign language not required. *Average time to degree:* master's–2 years full-time, 4 years part-time. *Entrance requirements:* GRE General Test, TOEFL (minimum score 580). Application deadline: 2/15 (priority date; rolling processing). Application fee: $40. *Expenses:* Tuition $9135 per year full-time, $509 per credit part-time. Fees $115 per year. *Financial aid:* Available to part-time students. Financial aid application deadline: 2/15; applicants required to submit FAFSA. *Faculty research:* Ethics committees and consultation, ethics of managed care, discussion of code status by physicians. • Dr. Mark Kuczewski, Director, 414-456-8498. Fax: 414-266-8654. E-mail: markk@mcw.edu.

Rush University, College of Health Sciences, Program in Healthcare Ethics, Chicago, IL 60612-3832. Awards MA. *Entrance requirements:* GRE General Test. Application fee: $40. *Tuition:* $8160 per year full-time, $370 per credit hour part-time. *Financial aid:* Application deadline 4/15. • Dr. John E. Trufant, Dean, College of Health Sciences, 312-942-7120. Fax: 312-942-2100. E-mail: jtrufant@rushu.rush.edu. Application contact: Hicela Castruita, Director, College Admissions Services, 312-942-7100. Fax: 312-942-2219.

See in-depth description on page 1739.

Saint Louis University, Center for Health Care Ethics, St. Louis, MO 63103-2097. Awards PhD. Faculty: 4 full-time (0 women), 7 part-time (4 women). Students: 11 full-time (3 women), 5 part-time (3 women); includes 1 minority (Asian American), 2 international. 21 applicants, 76% accepted. *Degree requirements:* 2 foreign languages, dissertation. *Entrance requirements:* GRE General Test, master's degree in ethics or a health field. Application fee: $40. *Tuition:* $542 per credit hour. *Financial aid:* In 1997–98, 1 fellowship, 1 research assistantship, 6 assistantships were awarded. Financial aid application deadline: 4/1. *Faculty research:* Theory/methods in health care ethics; clinical ethics; ethics of transplantation; human embryo research/treatment; managing HIV/AIDS. • Dr. Gerard Magill, Department Chairman, 314-577-8195. Application contact: Dr. Marcia Buresch, Assistant Dean of the Graduate School, 314-977-2240. Fax: 314-977-3943.

Trinity International University, Trinity Evangelical Divinity School, Deerfield, IL 60015-1284. Offerings include Christian thought (MA), with options in bioethics, Christianity and contemporary culture, church history, systematic theology. *Tuition:* $9230 per year full-time, $462 per hour part-time. • Dr. W. Bingham Hunter, Dean, 847-317-8002. Fax: 847-317-8014. Application contact: Ken Botton, Director of Admissions, 800-345-8337. Fax: 847-317-8097. E-mail: kbotton@tiu.edu.

Trinity International University, Program in Bioethics, Deerfield, IL 60015-1284. Awards MA. *Entrance requirements:* GRE General Test or MAT. Application deadline: 9/1 (priority date; rolling processing). Application fee: $25. *Tuition:* $9230 per year full-time, $462 per hour part-time. *Financial aid:* Application deadline 4/1. • Application contact: Ken Botton, Director of Admissions, 800-533-0975. Fax: 847-317-8097. E-mail: kbotton@tiu.edu.

Université de Montréal, Programs in Bioethics, Montréal, PQ H3C 3J7, Canada. Awards DESS. 19 applicants, 74% accepted. In 1997, 13 degrees awarded. *Application fee:* $30. • Hubert Doucet, Director, 514-343-5848.

University of Maryland, Baltimore, Graduate School, Graduate Programs in Medicine, Program in Applied Professional Ethics-Medicine, Baltimore, MD 21201-1627. Awards MA. Students: 0. *Entrance requirements:* GRE General Test, TOEFL, minimum GPA of 3.0. Application deadline: 7/1. Application fee: $42. *Expenses:* Tuition $253 per credit hour for state residents; $454 per credit hour for nonresidents. Fees $317 per year. *Financial aid:* Application deadline 2/15. • Dr. Henry Silverman, Director, 410-706-6250.

University of Pittsburgh, Faculty of Arts and Sciences, Department of History and Philosophy of Science, Program in Medical Ethics, Pittsburgh, PA 15260. Awards MA, JD/MA, MD/MA. *Entrance requirements:* GRE General Test. Application deadline: 2/1. Application fee: $30 ($40 for international students). *Expenses:* Tuition $8018 per year full-time, $329 per credit part-time for state residents; $16,508 per year full-time, $680 per credit part-time for nonresidents. Fees $480 per year full-time, $180 per year part-time. *Financial aid:* Application deadline 2/1. • Dr. Merrilee H. Salmon, Chairman, Department of History and Philosophy of Science, 412-624-5896. E-mail: mhsalmon@vms.cis.pitt.edu. Application contact: Lynn Pingel, Graduate Admissions Secretary, 412-624-5896. Fax: 412-624-6825. E-mail: mlpingel@vms.cis.pitt.edu.

University of Tennessee, Knoxville, College of Arts and Sciences, Department of Philosophy, Knoxville, TN 37996. Offerings include medical ethics (MA, PhD). Department faculty: 15 full-time (4 women), 2 part-time (1 woman). *Degree requirements:* For master's, thesis or alternative required, foreign language not required; for doctorate, 1 foreign language, dissertation. *Entrance requirements:* GRE General Test, TOEFL (minimum score 550), minimum GPA of 2.7. Application deadline: 2/1 (priority date; rolling processing). Application fee: $35. Electronic applications accepted. *Tuition:* $3354 per year full-time, $181 per semester hour part-time for state residents; $8410 per year full-time, $462 per semester hour part-time for nonresidents. • Dr. Kathleen Bohstedt, Head, 423-974-3255. Fax: 423-974-3509. E-mail: kbohsted@utk.edu. Application contact: Dr. John Nolt, Graduate Representative, 423-974-7210. E-mail: nolt@utk.edu.

University of Toronto, School of Graduate Studies, Life Sciences Division, Collaborative Program in Bioethics, Toronto, ON M5S 1A1, Canada. Awards LL M, MA, MH Sc, M Sc, PhD, SJD. *Degree requirements:* For master's, thesis (for some programs); for doctorate, dissertation. *Application fee:* $75. *Expenses:* Tuition $4070 per year for Canadian residents; $7870 per year for nonresidents. Fees $628 per year. • W. R. C. Harvey, Director, 416-978-3962. Fax: 416-978-1911.

University of Virginia, Graduate School of Arts and Sciences, Program in Clinical Ethics, Charlottesville, VA 22903. Awards MA. Students: 1 (woman) part-time. Average age 57. 0 applicants. *Application fee:* $40. *Tuition:* $4870 per year full-time, $941 per semester (minimum) part-time for state residents; $15,818 per year full-time, $2745 per semester (minimum) part-time for nonresidents. • John C. Fletcher, Director, Center for Biomedical Ethics, 804-924-5974.

University of Washington, College of Arts and Sciences, Department of Philosophy, Seattle, WA 98195. Offerings include medical ethics (PhD). Terminal master's awarded for partial completion of doctoral program. Department faculty: 14 full-time (3 women), 5 part-time (2 women). *Degree requirements:* Dissertation required, foreign language not required. *Entrance requirements:* GRE, TOEFL (minimum score 580), minimum GPA of 3.0. Application deadline: 1/15. Application fee: $45. *Tuition:* $5433 per year full-time, $775 per quarter (minimum) part-time for state residents; $13,479 per year full-time, $1925 per quarter (minimum) part-time for nonresidents. • Kenneth Clatterbaugh, Chairman, 206-543-5086. Fax: 206-685-8740. E-mail: clatter@u.washington.edu. Application contact: Departmental Office, 206-543-5855. E-mail: philinfo@u.washington.edu.

University of Washington, School of Medicine and Graduate School, Graduate Programs in Medicine, Department of Medical History and Ethics, Seattle, WA 98195. Offers program in medical/health care ethics (MA). Faculty: 5 full-time (1 woman), 6 part-time (2 women). Students: 7 full-time (3 women). Average age 40. *Degree requirements:* Project required, foreign language and thesis not required. *Entrance requirements:* Minimum GPA of 3.0. Application deadline: 3/1. Application fee: $45. *Financial aid:* Federal Work-Study, institutionally sponsored loans available. Financial aid application deadline: 2/28; applicants required to submit FAFSA. *Faculty research:* History of eighteenth- to twentieth-century medicine, history of biological sciences, philosophy of medicine, allocation of resources, bioethics, clinical medical ethics. • Dr. Albert R. Jonsen, Chairman, 206-543-5145. Application contact: Nancy Hoffman, Program Assistant, 206-543-5145. Fax: 206-685-7515. E-mail: mheinfo@u.washington.edu.

Naturopathic Medicine

Bastyr University, Program in Naturopathic Medicine, 14500 Juanita Drive, NE, Bothell, WA 98011. Awards ND. Accredited by CNME. Part-time programs available. Students: 385 full-time (276 women), 28 part-time (19 women). Average age 28. 382 applicants, 58% accepted. In 1997, 32 degrees awarded. *Average time to degree:* doctorate–4 years full-time, 5 years part-time. *Entrance requirements:* 3 years of undergraduate course work with 1 year of course work in biology, chemistry, and organic chemistry. Application deadline: 2/1 (priority date; rolling processing). Application fee: $60. *Expenses:* Tuition $180 per credit hour. Fees $15 per credit hour. *Financial aid:* Federal Work-Study and career-related internships or fieldwork available. Aid available to part-time students. Financial aid application deadline: 4/15; applicants required to submit FAFSA. • Dr. Sally Ringdahl, Dean, 425-823-1300. Application contact: Stephen Bangs, Director of Admissions, 425-602-3100. Fax: 425-823-6222.

See in-depth description on page 1729.

Canadian College of Naturopathic Medicine, Program in Naturopathic Medicine, Toronto, ON M4P 1E4, Canada. Awards ND. Candidate for accreditation by CNME. Students: 332 full-time (263 women). *Entrance requirements:* 1 year of course work in general biology, general chemistry, general psychology; 1 semester of course work in organic chemistry and

Directories: Naturopathic Medicine; Osteopathic Medicine

Canadian College of Naturopathic Medicine (continued)
biochemistry. Application deadline: 1/31 (7/31 for spring admission). • Chris Pilgrim, Vice President, Learner Services, 416-486-8584 Ext. 222. Application contact: Helen Papathanides, Admissions and Recruitment Officer, 416-486-8584 Ext. 241. Fax: 416-484-6821. E-mail: helenp@ccnm.edu.

National College of Naturopathic Medicine, Professional Program, Portland, OR 97201. Offers program in naturopathic medicine (ND). Accredited by CNME. Faculty: 47. Students: 390 full-time (288 women); includes 47 minority (2 African Americans, 30 Asian Americans, 11 Hispanics, 4 Native Americans), 29 international. Average age 29. 307 applicants, 39% accepted. In 1997, 50 degrees awarded. *Average time to degree:* doctorate–4 years full-time. *Entrance requirements:* Bachelor's degree. Application deadline: 2/1 (priority date; rolling processing; 1/15 for spring admission). Application fee: $60. *Financial aid:* Federal Work-Study, institutionally sponsored loans, and career-related internships or fieldwork available. Aid available to part-time students. Financial aid applicants required to submit CSS PROFILE or FAFSA. • Dr. Guru Khalsa, Dean of Academic Affairs, 503-499-4343 Ext. 108. Fax: 503-499-0022. Application contact: Glenn Young, Assistant Director of Admissions, 503-499-4343. Fax: 503-499-0027. E-mail: admissions@ncnm.edu.

Announcement: Intensive, accredited 4-year graduate program qualifies graduates to sit for board licensure examination and for family practice as a naturopathic physician (ND). The course of study combines standard medical sciences with naturally based holistic therapeutics. Naturopathic medicine recognizes the integrity of the whole patient and seeks to restore health through facilitating the patient's inherent healing capacity.

See in-depth description on page 1733.

Southwest College of Naturopathic Medicine and Health Sciences, Program in Naturopathic Medicine, Tempe, AZ 85282. Awards ND, ND/Certificate. Candidate for accreditation by CNME. Faculty: 13 full-time (4 women), 50 part-time (16 women). Students: 219 full-time (138 women), 8 part-time (6 women); includes 15 minority (4 African Americans, 6 Asian Americans, 3 Hispanics, 2 Native Americans), 9 international. Average age 33. 150 applicants, 60% accepted. In 1997, 38 degrees awarded. *Average time to degree:* doctorate–4 years full-time. *Entrance requirements:* Bachelor's degree. Application deadline: 7/1 (priority date; rolling processing; 2/1 for spring admission). Application fee: $65 ($90 for international students). *Financial aid:* 198 students received aid. Aid available to part-time students. Financial aid applicants required to submit FAFSA. • Dr. Kareen O'Brien, Dean, 602-990-7424. Application contact: Melissa Frownfelter, Assistant Dean of Students, 602-858-9100. Fax: 602-858-9116.

See in-depth description on page 1741.

University of Bridgeport, College of Naturopathic Medicine, 380 University Avenue, Bridgeport, CT 06601. Awards ND. Faculty: 2 full-time (0 women). Students: 15 full-time (9 women); includes 5 minority (3 African Americans, 2 Asian Americans). 33 applicants, 85% accepted. *Entrance requirements:* Minimum GPA of 2.5. Application deadline: 8/1 (priority date; rolling processing; 12/1 for spring admission). Application fee: $40 ($50 for international students). Electronic applications accepted. *Expenses:* Tuition $12,800 per year. Fees $590 per year full-time, $75 per year part-time. *Financial aid:* 13 students received aid. • Dr. Edward V. O'Connor, Dean, 203-576-4110.

See in-depth description on page 1743.

Osteopathic Medicine

Kirksville College of Osteopathic Medicine, Arizona School of Health Sciences, PO Box 11037, Phoenix, AZ 85061-1037. Offers programs in occupational therapy (MS), physical therapy (MS), physician assistant (MS), sports health care (MS). Faculty: 30 full-time (18 women), 14 part-time (8 women). Students: 343 full-time (215 women); includes 26 minority (2 African Americans, 13 Asian Americans, 8 Hispanics, 3 Native Americans). Average age 29. 702 applicants, 20% accepted. In 1997, 41 degrees awarded (100% found work related to degree). *Degree requirements:* Thesis required, foreign language not required. *Average time to degree:* master's–2 years full-time. *Entrance requirements:* GRE General Test (combined average 1639 on three sections), MCAT (average 25 for physician assistant). Application deadline: 2/1 (rolling processing). Application fee: $50. *Tuition:* $15,990 per year. *Financial aid:* 302 students received aid; Federal Work-Study and career-related internships or fieldwork available. Financial aid application deadline: 6/1; applicants required to submit FAFSA. • Dr. James Dearing, Associate Dean, 602-841-4077. Fax: 602-841-4092. Application contact: Stephanie Seyer, Assistant Director of Admissions, 660-626-2237. Fax: 660-626-2815.

Kirksville College of Osteopathic Medicine, Kirksville, MO 63501. Awards DO. Accredited by AOA. Faculty: 73 full-time (9 women), 48 part-time (7 women). Students: 577 full-time (158 women); includes 129 minority (3 African Americans, 120 Asian Americans, 6 Hispanics), 2 international. Average age 26. 4,157 applicants, 4% accepted. In 1997, 131 degrees awarded. *Entrance requirements:* MCAT, minimum 3 years of college, minimum GPA of 2.5. Application deadline: 2/1 (rolling processing). Application fee: $50. *Tuition:* $23,500 per year. *Financial aid:* In 1997–98, 506 students received aid, including 5 fellowships; Federal Work-Study and career-related internships or fieldwork also available. Aid available to part-time students. Financial aid application deadline: 5/1; applicants required to submit FAFSA. *Faculty research:* Basis of hypocholesterolemic drug-induced cataracts; radiation mutagenesis in bacteria; diabetes, exercise, and coronary microcirculation; regulation of cardiovascular system; metabolic changes in heart during ischemia. Total annual research expenditures: $3.335 million. • Dr. James J. McGovern, President, 816-626-2391. Fax: 816-626-2672. Application contact: Lori Haxton, Director of Admissions, 816-626-2237. Fax: 816-626-2483.

Announcement: KCOM is the founding school of osteopathic medicine and is distinguished by education firmly based on holistic care, wellness, and academic excellence and has a reputation for training general practitioners while providing a strong clinical and basic-science education for specialization. Interested applicants are encouraged to complete a premedical curriculum and the Medical College Admissions Test. Applications to KCOM are processed by the American Association of Colleges of Osteopathic Medicine Application Service starting June 1. Admission to KCOM is very competitive, so an early application is encouraged. As the national college of osteopathic medicine, KCOM is a private institution and admits students from across the nation.

Lake Erie College of Osteopathic Medicine, Professional Program, Erie, PA 16509. Awards DO. Accredited by AOA. Faculty: 37 full-time (5 women), 179 part-time (37 women). Students: 409; includes 53 minority (6 African Americans, 41 Asian Americans, 2 Hispanics, 4 Native Americans). Average age 25. 3,781 applicants, 6% accepted. In 1997, 37 degrees awarded. *Degree requirements:* National Osteopathic Medical Licensing Exam, Levels 1 and 2 required, foreign language and thesis not required. *Average time to degree:* first professional–4 years full-time. *Entrance requirements:* MCAT (minimum score 7; average 8), minimum GPA of 3.2. Application deadline: 2/1 (rolling processing). Application fee: $50. *Expenses:* Tuition $20,500 per year. Fees $925 per year. *Financial aid:* 394 students received aid; institutionally sponsored loans available. Financial aid application deadline: 6/30; applicants required to submit FAFSA. • Dr. Silvia M. Ferretti, Dean and Vice President of Academic Affairs, 814-866-6641. Application contact: Elaine Morse, Admissions Coordinator, 814-866-6641. Fax: 814-866-8123.

Michigan State University, College of Osteopathic Medicine, Osteopathic Medicine—Dual Degree Medical Scientist Training Program, East Lansing, MI 48824-1020. Awards DO/PhD. Accredited by AOA. Students: 9 full-time (4 women); includes 2 minority (both Asian Americans), 2 international. Average age 26. *Financial aid:* Fellowships, research assistantships available. Financial aid application deadline: 12/1. • Dr. Veronica H. Maher, Associate Dean for Graduate Studies, 517-353-7785. Fax: 517-353-9004.

Michigan State University, College of Osteopathic Medicine, Professional Program in Osteopathic Medicine, East Lansing, MI 48824-1020. Awards DO. Accredited by AOA. Faculty: 56 full-time (7 women), 1 part-time (0 women). Students: 500 full-time (202 women), 7 part-time (4 women); includes 116 minority (30 African Americans, 48 Asian Americans, 32 Hispanics, 6 Native Americans), 1 international. Average age 26. 1,450 applicants, 8% accepted. In 1997, 104 degrees awarded (100% found work related to degree). *Entrance requirements:* MCAT, minimum GPA of 2.5; previous course work in biology, chemistry, physics. *Expenses:* Tuition $10,587 per year full-time, $15,087 per year part-time for state residents; $22,531 per year for nonresidents. Fees $303 per year. *Financial aid:* 467 students received aid; fellowships, partial tuition waivers, Federal Work-Study, institutionally sponsored loans, and career-related internships or fieldwork available. Aid available to part-time students. Financial aid application deadline: 4/2; applicants required to submit FAFSA. • Dr. Philip Greenman, Associate Dean, Academic Affairs, 517-353-8640. Application contact: Dr. Katherine E. White, Assistant Dean, Student Affairs, 517-353-7741.

Midwestern University, College of Osteopathic Medicine, Downers Grove, IL 60515-1235. Awards DO. Accredited by AOA. Faculty: 174 full-time (38 women), 68 part-time (19 women). Students: 630 full-time (253 women); includes 178 minority (22 African Americans, 128 Asian Americans, 28 Hispanics). Average age 27. In 1997, 154 degrees awarded (100% continued full-time study). *Entrance requirements:* MCAT, 1 year each of organic chemistry, general chemistry, biology, physics, and English. Application deadline: 2/1 (rolling processing). Application fee: $40. *Expenses:* Tuition $20,892 per year for state residents; $25,377 per year for nonresidents. Fees $280 per year. *Financial aid:* Fellowships, full and partial tuition waivers, Federal Work-Study, institutionally sponsored loans, and career-related internships or fieldwork available. Financial aid application deadline: 6/1; applicants required to submit FAFSA. *Faculty research:* Cadmium toxicity, amino acid transport, metabolic actions of vanadium, diabetes and obesity. • Dr. John Fernandes, Dean, 630-515-6059. Application contact: Julie Rosenthall, Director of Admissions, 800-458-6253. Fax: 630-971-6086. E-mail: mwuinfo@mwu.edu.

See in-depth description on page 1731.

New York Institute of Technology, New York College of Osteopathic Medicine, Old Westbury, NY 11568-8000. Awards DO, DO/MBA, DO/MS. Accredited by AOA. Faculty: 44 full-time (17 women), 317 part-time (107 women). Students: 937 full-time (417 women), 22 part-time (11 women); includes 286 minority (105 African Americans, 123 Asian Americans, 58 Hispanics), 2 international. Average age 27. 4,400 applicants, 8% accepted. In 1997, 197 degrees awarded (100% continued full-time study). *Average time to degree:* first professional–4 years full-time. *Entrance requirements:* MCAT, 6 hours of biology, English, general chemistry, organic chemistry, and physics; minimum GPA of 2.75. Application deadline: 2/1 (rolling processing). Application fee: $60. *Tuition:* $22,000 per year. *Financial aid:* Fellowships, full and partial tuition waivers available. Financial aid application deadline: 4/1. *Faculty research:* Regulation of hemoglobin synthesis, repair of central nervous system following damage, effects of exercise on platelet function, educational technology. • Dr. Stanley Schiowitz, Dean, 516-626-6922. Fax: 516-686-3830. E-mail: sschiowi@iris.nyit.edu. Application contact: Michael J. Schaefer, Director of Admissions, 516-626-6947. Fax: 516-686-3831. E-mail: mschaefer@iris.nyit.edu.

See in-depth description on page 1737.

Nova Southeastern University, Health Professions Division, College of Osteopathic Medicine, Fort Lauderdale, FL 33314-7721. Awards DO. Accredited by AOA. Students: 582 full-time (212 women), 3 part-time (2 women); includes 158 minority (26 African Americans, 75 Asian Americans, 52 Hispanics, 5 Native Americans), 11 international. Average age 27. In 1997, 117 degrees awarded. *Average time to degree:* first professional–4 years full-time. *Entrance requirements:* MCAT (average 8). Application deadline: 3/1 (rolling processing). Application fee: $50. *Tuition:* $19,240 per year for state residents; $22,620 per year for nonresidents. *Financial aid:* Fellowships, scholarships, Federal Work-Study, institutionally sponsored loans, and career-related internships or fieldwork available. Aid available to part-time students. Financial aid application deadline: 4/1. *Faculty research:* Teaching strategies, simulated patient use, HIV-AIDS education, minority health issues, managed care education. Total annual research expenditures: $593,000. • Dr. Cyril Blavo, Interim Dean, 954-262-1807. Application contact: Marc Weiner, Admissions Counselor, 954-262-1113.

Ohio University, College of Osteopathic Medicine, Athens, OH 45701-2979. Awards DO, DO/PhD. Accredited by AOA. Faculty: 78 full-time (14 women), 16 part-time (6 women), 83.73 FTE. Students: 420 full-time (181 women); includes 92 minority (38 African Americans, 32 Asian Americans, 20 Hispanics, 2 Native Americans). Average age 25. 3,127 applicants, 5% accepted. In 1997, 96 degrees awarded (100% found work related to degree). *Degree requirements:* National Board Exam Parts I and II (DO); comprehensive exams, dissertation (DO/PhD). *Average time to degree:* first professional–4 years full-time. *Entrance requirements:* GRE (DO/PhD), MCAT (DO) (average score 9), interview. Application deadline: 1/2 (rolling processing). Application fee: $25. *Tuition:* $11,316 per year for state residents; $16,035 per year for nonresidents. *Financial aid:* In 1997–98, 391 students received aid, including 8 fellowships averaging $550 per month, 12 research assistantships (all to first-year students); Federal Work-Study, institutionally sponsored loans, and career-related internships or fieldwork also available. Aid available to part-time students. Financial aid application deadline: 4/1; applicants required to submit FAFSA. *Faculty research:* Primary care, aging. Total annual research expenditures: $2.1 million. • Dr. Barbara Ross-Lee, Dean, 740-593-2178. Fax: 740-593-0761. Application contact: Dr. James Artis, Director of Admissions, 740-593-4313. Fax: 740-593-2256.

Oklahoma State University College of Osteopathic Medicine, Tulsa, OK 74107-1898. Awards DO, DO/PhD. Accredited by AOA. Faculty: 48 full-time (10 women), 203 part-time (51 women). Students: 348 full-time (117 women). Average age 27. 2,107 applicants, 4% accepted. In 1997, 86 degrees awarded. *Entrance requirements:* MCAT (minimum score 8.7), interview, minimum 3 years of college, minimum GPA of 3.0. Application deadline: 11/1 (priority date; rolling processing). Application fee: $25. *Expenses:* Tuition $8684 per year for state residents; $21,460 per year for nonresidents. Fees $631 per year. *Financial aid:* In 1997–98, 315 students received aid, including 3 fellowships totaling $9,000; grants, full and partial tuition waivers, Federal Work-Study, institutionally sponsored loans also available. Financial aid application deadline: 6/1; applicants required to submit FAFSA. *Faculty research:* Opioid analgesia, renal physiology, physiology, venom factors, parasitology, virology. Total annual research expenditures: $2.5 million. • Dr. Thomas Wesley Allen, Provost and Dean, 918-582-1972 Ext. 8201. Fax: 918-561-8413. Application contact: Dr. Daniel Overack, Assistant Dean for Admissions, 918-582-1972. Fax: 918-561-8412.

Philadelphia College of Osteopathic Medicine, Program in Osteopathic Medicine, Philadelphia, PA 19131. Awards DO, DO/MBA, DO/MPH. Accredited by AOA. DO/MBA offered jointly with Saint Joseph's University; DO/MPH offered jointly with Temple University. Students: 982 (387 women). *Entrance requirements:* MCAT, minimum GPA of 3.1. Application deadline: 3/1 (priority date; rolling processing). Application fee: $50. *Tuition:* $21,925 per year. • Application contact: Carol A. Fox, Associate Dean for Admission and Enrollment Management, 215-871-6700. Fax: 215-871-6719.

Pikeville College, School of Osteopathic Medicine, Pikeville, KY 41501. Awards DO. Accredited by AOA. Faculty: 17 full-time (5 women), 117 part-time (18 women). Students: 60 full-time (14 women); includes 7 Asian Americans, 1 international. 450 applicants, 13% accepted. *Entrance requirements:* MCAT. Application deadline: 2/1 (rolling processing). Application fee: $75. *Tuition:* $22,000 per year. *Financial aid:* 54 students received aid. Financial aid application deadline: 8/1; applicants required to submit FAFSA. *Faculty research:* Primary care in medically underserved areas. • Dr. John A. Strosnider, Dean, 606-432-9617. Application contact: Stephen M. Payson, Associate Dean for Student Affairs, 606-432-9640. Fax: 606-432-9328. E-mail: spayson@pc.edu.

University of Health Sciences, College of Osteopathic Medicine, Kansas City, MO 64106-1453. Awards DO. Accredited by AOA. Faculty: 37 full-time (8 women), 70 part-time (10 women). Students: 787 full-time (208 women), 1 part-time (0 women); includes 81 minority (3 African Americans, 69 Asian Americans, 9 Hispanics), 9 international. Average age 27. 4,465 applicants, 8% accepted. In 1997, 131 degrees awarded (100% continued full-time study). *Degree requirements:* National Board Exam required, foreign language not required. *Average time to degree:* first professional–4 years full-time. *Entrance requirements:* MCAT (average 8.5), interview. Application deadline: 2/1 (rolling processing). Application fee: $35. *Expenses:* Tuition $24,710 per year. Fees $50 per year. *Financial aid:* In 1997–98, 725 students received aid, including 1 fellowship totaling $23,310; institutionally sponsored loans and career-related internships or fieldwork also available. Financial aid application deadline: 4/1; applicants required to submit FAFSA. *Faculty research:* Clinical pharmacology, metabolic diseases. Total annual research expenditures: $50,000. • Dr. Anthony J. Silvagni, Vice President for Academic Affairs/Dean, 816-283-2300. Application contact: Minnie Marrs, Admissions Director, 816-283-2350. Fax: 816-283-2349.

See in-depth description on page 1745.

University of Medicine and Dentistry of New Jersey, School of Osteopathic Medicine, Newark, NJ 07107-3001. Awards DO, DO/PhD. Accredited by AOA. Faculty: 149 full-time (55 women), 21 part-time (10 women), 160 FTE. Students: 302 full-time (148 women); includes 107 minority (28 African Americans, 54 Asian Americans, 22 Hispanics, 3 Native Americans). 3,106 applicants, 4% accepted. In 1997, 62 degrees awarded. *Entrance requirements:* MCAT. Application deadline: 2/1 (rolling processing). Application fee: $125. *Financial aid:* Fellowships, research assistantships, teaching assistantships, Federal Work-Study, institutionally sponsored loans, and career-related internships or fieldwork available. Financial aid application deadline: 5/1. • Dr. Frederick J. Humphrey II, Dean, 609-566-6998. Fax: 609-566-6865. Application contact: Dr. Warren Wallace, Director of Admissions/Recruitment, 609-566-7052. Fax: 609-566-6895.

University of New England, College of Osteopathic Medicine, Biddeford, ME 04005-9526. Awards DO. Accredited by AOA. Faculty: 18 full-time (5 women), 20 part-time. Students: 396 full-time (171 women); includes 33 minority (27 Asian Americans, 4 Hispanics, 2 Native Americans), 2 international. Average age 27. 2,976 applicants, 6% accepted. In 1997, 79 degrees awarded. *Entrance requirements:* MCAT, interview. Application deadline: 3/1. Application fee: $55. *Expenses:* Tuition $23,850 per year. Fees $260 per year. *Financial aid:* Fellowships, partial tuition waivers, institutionally sponsored loans available. Aid available to part-time students. Financial aid application deadline: 5/1; applicants required to submit FAFSA. • Dr. Stephen Shannon, Dean, 207-283-0171 Ext. 2340. Fax: 207-283-3249. Application contact: Patricia T. Cribby, Dean of Admissions and Enrollment Management, 207-283-0171 Ext. 2297. Fax: 207-286-3678. E-mail: jshea@mailbox.une.edu.

University of North Texas Health Science Center at Fort Worth, Professional Program, Fort Worth, TX 76107-2699. Awards DO, DO/MPH, DO/MS, DO/PhD. Accredited by AOA. DO/MPH offered jointly with the University of North Texas. Faculty: 203 full-time (44 women), 22 part-time (6 women), 210.8 FTE. Students: 454 full-time (187 women). Average age 26. 2,194 applicants, 9% accepted. In 1997, 91 degrees awarded. *Entrance requirements:* MCAT. Application deadline: 12/1 (priority date; rolling processing). Application fee: $0. *Tuition:* $1482 per year full-time, $297 per semester (minimum) part-time for state residents; $5316 per year full-time, $936 per semester (minimum) part-time for nonresidents. *Financial aid:* In 1997–98, 374 students received aid, including 6 teaching assistantships totaling $74,000; Federal Work-Study, institutionally sponsored loans also available. Financial aid application deadline: 5/1; applicants required to submit FAFSA. *Faculty research:* Tuberculosis, aging, cardiovascular disease, cancer. Total annual research expenditures: $7.26 million. • Dr. Benjamin Cohen, Vice President and Executive Dean for Health Affairs, 817-735-2506. Fax: 817-735-2486. Application contact: Dr. T. John Leppi, Associate Dean of Admissions, 817-735-2204. Fax: 817-735-2225.

University of Osteopathic Medicine and Health Sciences, College of Osteopathic Medicine and Surgery, Des Moines, IA 50312-4104. Awards DO. Accredited by AOA. Faculty: 59 full-time (20 women). Students: 795 full-time (255 women), 7 part-time (0 women); includes 94 minority (11 African Americans, 72 Asian Americans, 7 Hispanics, 4 Native Americans), 2 international. Average age 24. 4,100 applicants, 8% accepted. *Entrance requirements:* MCAT, minimum GPA of 3.0. Application deadline: 2/1 (rolling processing). Application fee: $50. *Expenses:* Tuition $22,150 per year. Fees $75 per year. *Financial aid:* 780 students received aid; Federal Work-Study, institutionally sponsored loans available. Aid available to part-time students. Financial aid application deadline: 4/1; applicants required to submit FAFSA. • Dr. Kendall Reed, Interim Dean, 515-271-1573. Application contact: Dr. Dennis L. Bates, Director of Admissions, 515-271-1450. Fax: 515-271-1578.

Western University of Health Sciences, College of Osteopathic Medicine, Pomona, CA 91766-1854. Awards DO. Accredited by AOA. Faculty: 1,278. Students: 694. Average age 29. 4,007 applicants, 4% accepted. In 1997, 140 degrees awarded (100% found work related to degree). *Entrance requirements:* MCAT, minimum 3 years of college. Application deadline: 1/15. Application fee: $60. *Financial aid:* In 1997–98, 12 fellowships were awarded; full tuition waivers, Federal Work-Study, institutionally sponsored loans, and career-related internships or fieldwork also available. • Dr. Mitchell Kasovac, Dean, 909-469-5200. Application contact: Susan M. Hanson, Director of Admissions, 909-469-5335.

West Virginia School of Osteopathic Medicine, Professional Program, Lewisburg, WV 24901-1128. Awards DO. Accredited by AOA. Faculty: 39 full-time (11 women), 4 part-time (2 women), 40.75 FTE. Students: 261 full-time (106 women); includes 19 minority (6 African Americans, 12 Asian Americans, 1 Hispanic). Average age 28. 2,119 applicants, 3% accepted. In 1997, 64 degrees awarded. *Entrance requirements:* MCAT, minimum GPA of 2.5 in science. Application deadline: 1/2 (rolling processing). Application fee: $50. *Financial aid:* In 1997–98, 249 students received aid, including 10 teaching assistantships averaging $888 per month; full tuition waivers, Federal Work-Study also available. Financial aid application deadline: 4/1; applicants required to submit FAFSA. *Faculty research:* Hepatotoxicity, enzymes and reperfusion, human development, myclination. • James R. Stookey, Academic Dean, 304-645-6270. Application contact: John N. Gorby, Director of Admissions and Registrar, 304-645-6270 Ext. 373. Fax: 304-645-4859.

Podiatric Medicine

Barry University, School of Graduate Medical Sciences, Program in Podiatric Medicine, Miami Shores, FL 33161-6695. Awards DPM. Accredited by APMA. Faculty: 13 full-time (3 women), 19 part-time (6 women). Students: 243 full-time (78 women), 8 part-time (2 women); includes 65 minority (9 African Americans, 27 Asian Americans, 27 Hispanics, 2 Native Americans), 10 international. Average age 29. 470 applicants, 15% accepted. In 1997, 62 degrees awarded. *Entrance requirements:* MCAT, previous course work in science and English. Application deadline: 6/1 (rolling processing). Application fee: $50. Electronic applications accepted. *Tuition:* $18,400 per year full-time, $575 per credit part-time. *Financial aid:* Career-related internships or fieldwork available. Aid available to part-time students. Financial aid applicants required to submit FAFSA. • Application contact: Alex Collins, Director of Graduate Medical Sciences, 305-899-3130. Fax: 305-899-3253. E-mail: collins@jeanne.barry.edu.

See in-depth description on page 1727.

California College of Podiatric Medicine, 1210 Scott Street, San Francisco, CA 94115. Awards DPM, MS. Accredited by APMA. Faculty: 59 full-time (29 women), 31 part-time (13 women). Students: 400 full-time (145 women); includes 100 minority (4 African Americans, 85 Asian Americans, 10 Hispanics, 1 Native American), 2 international. Average age 25. 500 applicants, 37% accepted. In 1997, 100 DPMs, 20 master's awarded. *Degree requirements:* For master's, thesis required, foreign language not required. *Entrance requirements:* For DPM, MCAT, 90 hours of undergraduate course work; 1 year of course work in organic chemistry, inorganic chemistry, and physics; 2 years of course work in biological sciences; for master's, DPM. Application deadline: 4/1 (priority date; rolling processing). Application fee: $95. *Expenses:* Tuition $18,850 per year. Fees $2025 per year. *Financial aid:* In 1997–98, 112 fellowships (all to first-year students) totaling $3.7 million were awarded; Federal Work-Study, institutionally sponsored loans also available. Financial aid application deadline: 6/1; applicants required to submit FAFSA. *Faculty research:* Biomechanics, surgery, diabetics, sports medicine. • Dr. Jeff Page, Senior Vice President and Executive Dean, 415-292-0481. Application contact: Frank L. Jimenez, Director of Admissions, 800-334-2276. Fax: 415-292-0439.

Dr. William M. Scholl College of Podiatric Medicine, 1001 North Dearborn Street, Chicago, IL 60610-2856. Awards DPM. Accredited by APMA. Faculty: 17 full-time (4 women), 15 part-time (4 women). Students: 400 full-time (112 women); includes 86 minority (16 African Americans, 55 Asian Americans, 11 Hispanics, 4 Native Americans), 12 international. Average age 26. 685 applicants. In 1997, 100 degrees awarded (100% found work related to degree). *Degree requirements:* National Podiatric Board Exam Parts I and II required, foreign language and thesis not required. *Average time to degree:* first professional–4 years full-time. *Entrance requirements:* MCAT. Application deadline: 6/1 (rolling processing). Application fee: $90. *Expenses:* Tuition $19,800 per year for state residents; $20,450 per year for nonresidents. Fees $125 per year. *Financial aid:* Federal Work-Study available. Aid available to part-time students. Financial aid application deadline: 5/1; applicants required to submit FAFSA. • Dr. Terence Albright, President, 312-280-2910. Application contact: Cassandra Flambouras, Director, Student Recruitment, 312-280-2995.

New York College of Podiatric Medicine, New York, NY 10035-1815. Awards DPM, DPM/MS. Accredited by APMA. DPM/MS (community health) offered jointly with New York Medical College. Faculty: 115. Students: 485; includes 20 international. Average age 27. In 1997, 108 degrees awarded. *Degree requirements:* Comprehensive exam required, foreign language and thesis not required. *Entrance requirements:* MCAT, 1 year of biology, physics, general and organic chemistry; 90 credits of college-level courses. Application deadline: 7/20 (rolling processing). Application fee: $50. *Expenses:* Tuition $18,800 per year. Fees $666 per year. *Financial aid:* In 1997–98, 90 students received aid, including 52 scholarships (all to first-year students); Federal Work-Study also available. Financial aid application deadline: 4/15. • Dr. Louis Levine, President and Chief Executive Officer, 212-410-8024. Application contact: Steve Broder, Director of Admissions, 800-526-6966. Fax: 212-722-4918.

See in-depth description on page 1735.

Ohio College of Podiatric Medicine, Cleveland, OH 44106-3082. Awards DPM. Accredited by APMA. Faculty: 18 full-time (3 women), 13 part-time (8 women). Students: 447 full-time. *Entrance requirements:* MCAT, previous course work in biology, chemistry, and physics. Application deadline: 6/1 (priority date; rolling processing). Application fee: $95. *Expenses:* Tuition $16,500 per year. Fees $1805 per year. *Financial aid:* Federal Work-Study, institutionally sponsored loans, and career-related internships or fieldwork available. Financial aid application deadline: 5/30. *Faculty research:* Drug interactions using perfused liver and isolated hepatocytes, effects of diabetes mellitus on bone marrow lymphocytes, microcircuitry of the spinal cord in relation to posture and locomotion. • John E. Andrews, Dean of Student Affairs, 216-231-3300 Ext. 341. Fax: 216-231-1005.

Temple University, Health Sciences Center, School of Podiatric Medicine, Philadelphia, PA 19122-6096. Awards DPM, DPM/PhD. DPM/PhD offered jointly with Drexel University and the University of Pennsylvania. Faculty: 36 full-time (7 women), 53 part-time (5 women). Students: 393 full-time (155 women). Average age 26. In 1997, 103 degrees awarded. *Degree requirements:* National Board Exam required, foreign language and thesis not required. *Entrance requirements:* MCAT (average 20), interview. Application deadline: 6/1 (rolling processing). Application fee: $0. *Expenses:* Tuition $323 per semester hour for state residents; $444 per semester hour for nonresidents. Fees $170 per year full-time, $28 per semester (minimum) part-time. *Financial aid:* Federal Work-Study, institutionally sponsored loans, and career-related internships or fieldwork available. Financial aid application deadline: 6/30; applicants required to submit FAFSA. *Faculty research:* Gait analysis, infectious diseases, diabetic neuropathy, peripheral vascular disease. • Dr. Richard M. Englert, Acting Chief Administrative Officer. Application contact: David Martin, Interim Director of Admissions, 215-625-5448.

University of Osteopathic Medicine and Health Sciences, College of Podiatric Medicine and Surgery, Des Moines, IA 50312-4104. Awards DPM. Accredited by APMA. Faculty: 59 full-time (18 women). Students: 278 full-time (83 women); includes 39 minority (11 African Americans, 21 Asian Americans, 5 Hispanics, 2 Native Americans), 6 international. Average age 24. 404 applicants, 45% accepted. *Entrance requirements:* MCAT, interview; minimum GPA of 2.5; 1 year of organic chemistry, inorganic chemistry, physics, biology, and English. Application deadline: 4/15 (priority date; rolling processing). *Expenses:* Tuition $19,760 per year. Fees $75 per year. *Financial aid:* 265 students received aid; Federal Work-Study, institutionally sponsored loans available. Financial aid application deadline: 7/15; applicants required to submit FAFSA. *Faculty research:* Physics of Equinus, gait analysis. • Dr. Robert Yoho, Dean, 515-271-1488. Application contact: Dr. Dennis L. Bates, Director of Admissions, 515-271-1450. Fax: 515-271-1578.

See in-depth description on page 1747.

Cross-Discipline Announcement

Duke University, Graduate School, Department of Pathology, Durham, NC 27708-0586.

Graduate study in the Department of Pathology at Duke University trains students in the molecular aspects of disease in preparation for a career of investigation in molecular medicine. Broad areas of current research within the department include inflammation, tumor biology, and vascular biology. For more information, see Section 15 in *Peterson's Guide to Graduate Programs in the Biological Sciences* or go on line (http://pathology.mc.duke.edu).

BARRY UNIVERSITY

School of Graduate Medical Sciences Podiatric Medicine and Surgery Program

Program of Study

The Barry University School of Graduate Medical Sciences offers an accredited professional program leading to the degree of Doctor of Podiatric Medicine (D.P.M.). Barry University has the only podiatric medical program in the nation that is fully integrated into a comprehensive university offering a variety of undergraduate and graduate degrees.

In the first year of study, students obtain an understanding of the structure and function of the human body. Courses include bacteriology, histology, biochemistry, gross and lower anatomy, and physiology. The second year of the program covers pathology, pharmacology, orthopedics, and podiatric surgery. The third year is a blend of clinical experience and advanced-level instruction, which introduces the treatment of human pathologies. The fourth year is primarily a clinical learning experience with advanced seminars and electives, enabling the student to attain further proficiency in diagnosing and treating the podiatric patient.

Current interests include microcirculatory and muscle physiology, as well as biomedical and gait analysis.

Research Facilities

Barry University's Podiatric Medicine and Surgery Program maintains modern state-of-the-art laboratory facilities, with neurodiagnostic and rehabilitative equipment that includes a Sorvall MT-2B ultramicrotome, an LKB7800 knifemaker, a Lipshaw Model 2500 tissue processor, a laminar flow fume hood, a Napco Model 5831 vacuum oven, and an Olympus BH-2 intravital microscope.

Financial Aid

Most financial aid is awarded through the Health Education Assistance and Federal Stafford Student Loan programs. Scholarships valued at $2500, $5000, and half tuition are also available for highly qualified applicants. Scholarships are renewable for all four years, provided the student maintains the required minimum GPA. No formal application is required for the scholarships. Further information and applications for the loans are available from the Barry University Office of Financial Aid.

Cost of Study

Tuition and fees for the 1997–98 academic year were $18,300.

Living and Housing Costs

The cost of living in Miami is quite reasonable when compared to that in other major cities. The average apartment rents for $550.

Student Group

The Podiatric Medicine and Surgery Program has an enrollment of approximately 250 students, representing thirty-nine states, the District of Columbia, Canada, Puerto Rico, and the U.S. Virgin Islands.

Location

Miami Shores is only minutes from the urban centers of Miami and Fort Lauderdale, and all the recreational facilities and cultural opportunities of Florida's Gold Coast area are easily accessible. Golf, tennis, swimming, soccer, skin and scuba diving, waterskiing, sailing, and horseback riding are available all year long, and the fall season is particularly exciting for fans of the Miami Dolphins. The Florida Grand Opera and the Miami City Ballet provide a full season of highly acclaimed performances, as does the Coconut Grove Playhouse. Among the numerous recreational and ecological features of the Miami area are the Florida Keys, the Everglades, national parks, and marine and state parks.

The University

Barry University is an independent, Catholic, coeducational institution of higher learning with a tradition of academic excellence. Founded in 1940, the University has grown steadily in size and diversity while maintaining a very low student-faculty ratio.

As part of the podiatric medicine curriculum, the Barry podiatric medical program offers a Master of Science degree in biomedical sciences. A bachelor's degree option is available for early admission students.

Applying

Barry University's podiatric medical program participates in the American Association of Colleges of Podiatric Medicine Application Service (AACPMAS). Application forms are available by contacting the American Association of Colleges of Podiatric Medicine, 1350 Piccard Drive, Suite 322, Rockville, Maryland 20850 (telephone: 800-922-9266).

Admission requirements include a minimum of 90 undergraduate semester hours, which must include 6 credits in English, 8 credits in general chemistry, 8 credits in organic chemistry, 8 credits in biology, and 8 credits in physics. Official transcripts are required from each college or university previously attended. All applicants must take the Medical College Admission Test (MCAT). In addition, three letters of recommendation must be submitted to the School. One of the recommendation letters must be from a podiatrist stating that the applicant has visited a D.P.M.'s office.

Correspondence and Information

Office of Graduate Medical Sciences Admissions
Barry University
11300 Northeast 2nd Avenue
Miami Shores, Florida 33161
Telephone: 305-899-3130
800-695-2279 (toll-free)
Fax: 305-899-3253

Barry University

THE FACULTY

John E. Accola, D.P.M.
Kip Amazon, M.D.
Herbert Applebaum, M.D.
Irving Block, D.P.M.
Alexander Bonner, D.P.M.
Jackie Buchman, D.P.M.
James Cochran, M.D.
Avriel Cohen, D.P.M.
Malcolm Cohen, D.P.M.
Michael Cohen, D.P.M.
Gerald Conover, Ph.D.
Stephanie Drabin, M.D.
Chester A. Evans, D.P.M.
Andrew Gutterman, M.D.
Nick Hall, Ph.D.
Elizabeth T. Hays, Ph.D.
Michael Kambour, M.D.
Keith Kashuk, D.P.M.
Steven Kringold, D.P.M.
Andrew Leve, D.P.M.
Richard Levin, D.P.M.
James M. Losito, D.P.M.
Thomas Mark, M.D.
Thomas J. Merrill, D.P.M.
Morton Morris, D.O.
Frank Moya, M.D.
John P. Nelson, D.P.M.
John Niven, M.D.
John A. Prior, D.P.M.
Leslie Rosen, M.D.
Sheldon Ross, D.P.M.
John Sause, Ph.D.
Larry Semer, D.P.M.
Stephen Sinkoe, D.P.M.
David J. Skliar, D.P.M.
Allen Smith, Ph.D.
Charles C. Southerland Jr., D.P.M.
Steven Spinner, D.P.M.
Bobbie J. Stewart, Ph.D.
Alan Streigold, D.P.M.

BASTYR UNIVERSITY

School of Naturopathic Medicine

Program of Study

Bastyr University offers a four-year program of professional education leading to the Doctor of Naturopathic Medicine (N.D.) degree. The naturopathic medical profession and the University are dedicated to being effective leaders in the promotion of the health and well-being of the human community. Naturopathic physicians are licensed to practice independently as primary health-care providers in eleven states and several Canadian provinces. The goal of the program is to educate individuals who practice humanistically oriented family medicine as naturopathic physicians. The curriculum is founded on the traditional concepts of naturopathic medicine: prevention of disease, encouragement of the body's inherent healing abilities, treatment of the whole person, responsibility for one's own health, and education of patients in health-promoting lifestyles. During the first two years of the program, students receive a thorough foundation in the basic medical sciences along with instruction in naturopathic medicine, clinical and laboratory diagnosis, nutrition, and counseling. The second two years focus on clinical diagnosis and therapeutics, including clinical studies in nutrition, botanical medicine, homeopathy, manipulation, physiotherapy, hydrotherapy, obstetrics, pediatrics, geriatrics, and other specialty areas. Students also receive clinical training through supervised practice at the Bastyr Natural Health Clinic and through externships in the offices of practicing physicians. The University offers a Certificate in Midwifery for naturopathic medical students and graduates, which meets the requirements for becoming a licensed midwife in Washington as well as those for certification by the American College of Naturopathic Obstetrics.

Research Facilities

The University helps pursue research on the use of nutrition and natural therapies in the management and treatment of health-care problems and in the prevention of chronic disease. Original research is conducted regularly and a research fellowship has been funded. The University has established an AIDS Research Center with funding from the NIH Office of Complementary and Alternative Medicine. Students are engaged in primary clinical research at the Natural Health Clinic. The University maintains a library with current journals; special collections in alternative medicine, acupuncture, nutrition, midwifery, and naturopathic medicine; Dialog (a medical computer research service); and audiovisual aids. Students also have access to the nearby University of Washington Health Sciences Library.

Financial Aid

Students are eligible to participate in federal financial aid programs, including the Federal Stafford Student Loan, Federal Perkins Loan, Federal Supplemental Loans for Students, and Federal Work-Study programs. Applicants seeking financial aid must submit the Free Application for Federal Student Aid (FAFSA) by April 15 for maximum consideration. Students who wish to provide health care in an underserved area as a naturopathic physician and/or a midwife are eligible for the Washington State Health Professional Loan Repayment and Scholarship Program. A limited number of professional scholarships are available. Complete financial aid information is provided on request.

Cost of Study

Tuition for 1998–99 is $180 per credit; tuition for the clinical portion of the program is $206 per credit. Fees are approximately $135 per quarter. Total tuition and fees for a full-time student average $15,400 per year. Books and supplies cost approximately $1500 per year.

Living and Housing Costs

The University provides limited on-campus housing. Most students share off-campus housing averaging $380 a month per person. Student Services provides information on both on-campus and off-campus housing. The Washington Association of Student Financial Aid Administrators estimates that living expenses, including transportation and personal expenses, average $880 per month.

Student Group

The University's total enrollment in 1997–98 was 680, of whom 557 were graduate and professional students. More than 413 students were enrolled in the naturopathic medicine program. Approximately 70 percent of the students are women. The average age of the 1998 entering class in naturopathic medicine is 28. Bastyr students come from all over the United States and Canada and from a number of other countries; 25 percent are residents of Washington.

Location

The academic and administrative campus is on a 40-acre site adjoining St. Edward's State Park in Juanita, Washington, about 15 miles northeast of Seattle. Several hiking trails to Lake Washington begin at the edge of the campus; abundant opportunities for outdoor activities exist nearby in the Puget Sound area. The clinical campus is located in a Seattle neighborhood. The city offers a full range of activities and facilities, including museums, theaters, fine restaurants of many cuisines, a major opera and symphony orchestra, and major-league sports.

The University

Bastyr University was founded as a naturopathic medical college in 1978 to meet the growing need for scientifically trained naturopathic physicians, brought about by increased consumer interest in, and demand for, health-oriented care and preventive medicine. Since 1984, as a part of its mission to provide comprehensive education in the natural health sciences, the University has added graduate and undergraduate programs in nutrition, Oriental medicine, acupuncture, and applied behavioral sciences. Bastyr University is accredited by the Northwest Association of Schools and Colleges, and the naturopathic medicine program is accredited by the Council on Naturopathic Medical Education.

The cafeteria serves a buffet of vegetarian food as well as healthy snacks and beverages. The University operates the Natural Health Clinic. Students receive reduced rates for naturopathic health care.

Applying

Admission is based on academic achievement, personal and social development, relevant experience, financial planning, and demonstrated humanistic qualities. Credentials to be submitted are all official transcripts, two letters of recommendation, a completed application form, and a $60 application fee. Minimum prerequisites are completion of three years of undergraduate education (135 quarter credits or 90 semester credits, no less than one third of which must be upper division). In recent years, more than 90 percent of entrants have held a bachelor's degree. Required courses include 8 quarter hours of math (including algebra and statistics), 18 quarter hours of chemistry (including a two-term sequence of organic), 12 quarter hours of biology (must include work in cell biology and genetics), 5 quarter hours of physics, 8 quarter hours of psychology, and 18 quarter hours of English and humanities. Courses are not accepted unless the grade earned is a C (2.0) or better, and the courses must have been taken within seven years of matriculation. Waivers are granted in exceptional cases. All applicants who meet the basic admission standards are interviewed by the Admissions Committee. For priority consideration, applications should be received by the University by February 1 for admission the following fall, although late applications are considered if space is available.

Correspondence and Information

Admissions Office
Bastyr University
14500 Juanita Drive, NE
Bothell, Washington 98011

Telephone: 425-823-1300
Fax: 425-823-6222
World Wide Web: http://www.bastyr.edu

Bastyr University

THE FACULTY AND THEIR RESEARCH

Sally Ringdahl, Dean of Naturopathic Medicine; N.D., Bastyr; M.Ed., British Columbia.
Pamela Snider, Assistant Dean of Naturopathic Medicine; N.D., Bastyr.
Jane Guiltinan, Chief Medical Officer; N.D., Bastyr.
Lise Auschuler, Chair of Botanical Medicine; N.D., Bastyr.
Carlo Calabrese, Chair of Research Department; N.D., National College of Naturopathic Medicine; M.P.H., Washington (Seattle).
Chair of Physical Medicine (vacant).
Terry Courtney, Chair of Oriental Medicine; M.P.H., Boston University; L.Ac., New England School of Acupuncture.
Ellen Goldman, Chair of Homeopathic Medicine; N.D., Bastyr.
Mark Kestin, Chair of Nutrition; Ph.D., Flinders (Australia); M.P.H., Harvard.
Morgan Martin, Chair of Midwifery; N.D., Bastyr; LM.
Sheryl Miller, Chair of Basic Sciences; Ph.D., Wayne State.
Mark Nolting, Chair of Oriental Medicine; N.D., Bastyr; C.A., Northwest Institute of Acupuncture and Oriental Medicine.
William Roedel, Chair of Psychology; Ph.D., Loyola (Baltimore); M.Div., Catholic University.
Leanna Standish, Director of Research; Ph.D., Massachusetts; N.D., M.S., Bastyr.

Core Academic and Clinical Faculty

Debra Brammer, N.D., Bastyr.
Qiang Cao, O.M.D., Shanghai College of Traditional Chinese Medicine; N.D., Bastyr.
Rich Frederickson, Ph.D., North Dakota.
Alan Gaby, M.D., Maryland.
John Hibbs, N.D., Bastyr.
Nancy Holmes, Psy.D., Northern Colorado.
Chongyun Liu, O.M.D., Chengdu College of Traditional Chinese Medicine.
Wendy Nelson, Ph.D., Berkeley.
Jeffrey Novack, Ph.D., Washington (Seattle).
Lucy Smith, N.D., Bastyr.
Aleyamma P. Thomas, Ph.D., Manitoba.

Clinical Residents

Jill Fresonke, N.D., Bastyr.
Marleen Haverty, N.D., Bastyr.
Stephanie Hoener, N.D., Bastyr.
Kathleen Jannel, N.D., Bastyr.
Susan Stratton, N.D., Bastyr.
Kameron Wells, N.D., Bastyr.
Catherine Youngblood, N.D., Bastyr.

Adjunct Faculty

Lizbeth Adams, Ph.D., Washington (Seattle).
Kristen Anderson, M.D., Texas-Houston Health Science Center.
Robert Anderson, M.D., Washington (Seattle).
David Bove, N.D., M.S., Bastyr.
Don Brown, N.D., Bastyr.
Timothy Callahan, M.A., Washington (Seattle).
William Caradonna, B.S., Northeastern; R.Ph.
George Cody, J.D., Willamette.
Walter Crinnion, N.D., Bastyr.
Lauren Cullen, N.D., Bastyr.
Michael Culp, N.D., Bastyr.
Robin diPasquale, N.D., Bastyr.
Colleen Donovan, N.D., Bastyr.
Linda Dyson, N.D., Bastyr.
Deborah Frances, N.D., National College of Naturopathic Medicine.
Susan Heideke, N.D., Bastyr.
Angela Hein, N.D., Bastyr.
Dirk Hein, M.A., College of Traditional Chinese Acupuncture (U.K.).
Krista Heron, N.D., National College of Naturopathic Medicine.
Ron Hobbs, N.D., Bastyr.
Henry Hochberg, M.D., Yeshiva (Einstein).
Greg Hovander, B.S., Washington (Seattle); R.Ph.
David Kailin, M.P.H., Washington (Seattle).
Paul Karsten, Ph.D., Samra.
Mark Lamden, N.D., Bastyr.
Davis Lamson, N.D., Bastyr; M.S., Arizona.
Christy Lee-Engel, N.D., Bastyr.
Buck Levin, Ph.D., North Carolina; RD.
Doug Lewis, N.D., Bastyr.
Brad Lichtenstein, N.D., Bastyr.
Jay Little, N.D., Bastyr.
Richard Mann, N.D., Bastyr.
Lisa Meserole, N.D., Bastyr; M.S., Washington (Seattle); RD.
John Miller, D.C., Western States Chiropractic.
Bruce Milliman, N.D., Bastyr.
William Mitchell, N.D., National College of Naturopathic Medicine.
Harold Modell, Ph.D., Mississippi Medical Center.
Michael Murray, N.D., Bastyr.
David Musnik, M.D., California, San Francisco; M.P.H., Berkeley.
Jana Nalbandian, N.D., Bastyr.
Ian Nesbit, N.D., Bastyr.
Jody Noe, M.S., Old Dominion.
Diane Pelletier, Ph.D., Arizona.
Cindy Phillips, N.D., Bastyr.
Joseph Pizzorno, N.D., National College of Naturopathic Medicine.
Dirk Powell, N.D., Bastyr.
Cathy Rogers, N.D., National College of Naturopathic Medicine.
Steven Sandburg-Lewis, N.D., National College of Naturopathic Medicine.
Marian Small, N.D., Bastyr; C.A., Northwest Institute of Acupuncture and Oriental Medicine.
Dianne Spicer, D.N., Chicago National College of Naprapathy.
Perry Jo Wise, N.D., Bastyr.
Jared Zeff, N.D., National College of Naturopathic Medicine.

Current Research Projects

Demographic and clinical characteristics of naturopathic patients: A study of patients treated at the Canadian College of Naturopathic Medicine. T. Jaeger, J. Waalen, and C. Calabrese.
A comparison of health outcomes in alternative medicine users vs. nonusers among HIV+ men from the MACS database. L. Standish, and N. Kass.
Echinacea in the prevention and amelioration of respiratory infections. C. Calabrese, S. Marra, and D. Brown.
In vitro studies of Bercedin, an anti-infective of plant origin. G. Bermudez Cedeno, C. Calabrese, and L. Meserole.
Alternative medical care outcomes in AIDS: An observational, longitudinal study of HIV positive patients using alternative therapies. L. Standish, C. Calabrese. (Part of a cooperating grant from NIH, OCAM, and NIAID)
The influence of *Echinacea* on phagocytosis in human neutrophils and monocytes. C. Calabrese, C. Holzer. (Sponsored by Madaus AG)
In vitro study of high dilutions of Taxol on breast cancer cells. L. Adams, G. Sivan, L. Standish.
Double blind crossover trial of a homeopathic medication for tinnitus. L. Standish, M. Culp

MIDWESTERN UNIVERSITY

Chicago College of Osteopathic Medicine
Arizona College of Osteopathic Medicine

Program of Study

Midwestern University (MWU) offers a four-year program leading to the Doctor of Osteopathic Medicine (D.O.) degree at two colleges on two campuses: the Chicago College of Osteopathic Medicine (CCOM), located in Downers Grove, Illinois, and the Arizona College of Osteopathic Medicine (AZCOM), located in Glendale, Arizona. As scientists and practitioners of the healing arts, osteopathic physicians subscribe to a philosophy that regards the body as an integrated whole, with structures and functions working interdependently. As an extension of this philosophy, osteopathic physicians treat their patients as unique persons with biological, psychological, and sociological needs—an approach that underscores the osteopathic commitment to patient-oriented versus disease-oriented health care. In recognition of this approach, MWU's colleges of osteopathic medicine have developed and continue to refine curricula that educate students in the biopsychosocial approach to patient care, as well as the basic medical arts and sciences. Within this curricular format, CCOM and AZCOM medical students spend their first two years both completing a rigorous basic science curriculum and preparing for their clinical studies. During their third and fourth years, students rotate through a variety of clinical departments at both ambulatory and hospital sites. Required rotations include family medicine, internal medicine, surgery, pediatrics, psychiatry, community medicine, obstetrics/gynecology, and emergency medicine.

By stimulating intellectual curiosity and teaching problem-solving skills, the CCOM and AZCOM curricula encourage students to regard learning as a lifelong process. Midwestern University is accredited by the Commission on Institutions of Higher Education of the North Central Association (NCA) of Colleges and Schools.

Research Facilities

Midwestern University faculty members are engaged in extramurally funded research programs in the Chicago College of Osteopathic Medicine and the Arizona College of Osteopathic Medicine. The Downers Grove campus has 24,000 square feet of laboratory space, an AAALAC-accredited animal resource facility with 9,000 square feet of space, and a well-equipped library designated as a Resource Library by the National Library of Medicine. The Glendale campus has state-of-the-art laboratories and a modern library with computer resources. The University also supports basic biomedical research using the resources of a specialized Magnetic Resonance Laboratory that includes 300- and 500-MHz NB spectrometers capable of measuring most of the nucleides of the periodic table. Research conducted by the faculty members is supported by the University and through agencies such as the National Institutes of Health, the National Oceanic and Atmospheric Administration, the American Heart Association, the American Diabetes Association, and the Arthritis Foundation. Research expenditures have averaged $2 million in each of the last few years.

Financial Aid

The Office of Financial Aid provides students with information about federal, state, and private sources of financial assistance; helps students coordinate the financial aid application and renewal processes; and assists students in making informed decisions about the financing of their education. All students seeking financial aid must meet general eligibility requirements regarding citizenship, financial need, and satisfactory academic progress. The office helps coordinate three types of financial aid: scholarships and grants, employment programs, and loans. The office automatically mails a financial aid packet to accepted students who return a signed matriculation agreement and submit their initial deposit.

Cost of Study

Tuition for CCOM for the 1998–99 academic year is $20,892 for in-state students and $25,377 for out-of-state students, with a $280 activity fee. Tuition for AZCOM for the 1998–99 academic year is $24,045, with a $150 activity fee.

Living and Housing Costs

The University provides on-campus student housing opportunities at both campuses. Off-campus housing is also available in both the Downers Grove and Glendale communities. On-campus housing costs range from $6000 to $8000 annually, with approximate food costs of approximately $2500 per year.

Student Group

The total osteopathic medical student population of Midwestern University for the 1997–98 academic year was approximately 835 full-time students, which included a first-year class of 162 for CCOM and 107 for AZCOM. Students come from nearly every state and several other countries. Nearly 40 percent of the students are women. The student body is diverse in terms of age, ethnicity, and background.

Student Outcomes

From 1990 to 1996, approximately 72 percent of CCOM graduates selected an American Osteopathic Association–approved internship for their first year of postdoctoral training. More than 50 percent of CCOM's recent graduates have entered primary-care disciplines of family medicine, pediatrics, and internal medicine. CCOM's alumni have served and continue to serve in hospitals, medical schools, private practices, and government facilities throughout the nation.

Location

Midwestern University operates two campuses. The Downers Grove, Illinois, campus—a 105-acre campus with innovative facilities—is nestled serenely in a wooded setting 25 miles west of downtown Chicago. The Glendale, Arizona, campus—a 124-acre campus that includes state-of-the-art facilities in a peaceful setting—is 15 miles northwest of downtown Phoenix. Both campuses offer suburban environments, with proximity to metropolitan communities and major transportation routes.

The University

Midwestern University is committed to educating the health-care team of the next century. The University's flagship school, the Chicago College of Osteopathic Medicine, was founded in 1900. Midwestern has since encompassed the Chicago College of Pharmacy (1991), the College of Allied Health Professions (1992), the Arizona College of Osteopathic Medicine (1995), and the College of Pharmacy–Glendale (1998). With two outstanding campuses, hundreds of caring faculty members, and thousands of top-notch graduates, Midwestern University is changing the face of health professions education.

Applying

Interested students should apply directly to the American Association of Colleges of Osteopathic Medicine Application Services (AACOMAS) at 6110 Executive Boulevard, Suite 405, Rockville, Maryland 20852-3991 (telephone: 301-968-4190). AACOMAS applications are available by June 1. MWU uses a rolling admissions process in which applications are reviewed and interview decisions are made at regular intervals during the admissions cycle. Applicants are notified of their selection status within two to four weeks of their interview date. To be competitive, candidates should apply early.

Correspondence and Information

Office of Admissions
Midwestern University
555 31st Street
Downers Grove, Illinois 60515

Telephone: 630-515-6171
800-458-6253 (toll-free)
E-mail: admiss@midwestern.edu
World Wide Web: http://www.midwestern.edu

Midwestern University

THE FACULTY AND THEIR RESEARCH

R. Kosinski, Professor; Ph.D., Loyola (Chicago). The dorsal root ganglion (funded by the American Osteopathic Association).
S. Lynch, Assistant Professor; Ph.D., Ulster (Ireland). Metal ion-dependent LDL oxidation by thiols (funded by the American Health Assistance Foundation).
D. Mann, Professor; Ph.D., Michigan State. Amino acid transport system Xc and Aag in mouse (funded by the NIH).
A. Mayer, Associate Professor; Ph.D., Buenos Aires. Neuroinflammation, microglia and marine natural products (funded by the Sea Grant Program of the NOAA); effect of selective cyclooxygenase-2 inhibitors on eicosanoid generation (funded by the Arthritis Foundation).
K. O'Hagan, Associate Professor; Ph.D., Rutgers. Arterial baroreflex in a model of pre-eclampsia in rabbits (funded by the NIH).
D. Paulson, Professor; Ph.D., Texas Tech. Cardiac consequences of secondary carnitine deficiency (funded by the NIH).
J. Peuler, Associate Professor; Ph.D., Penn State. Autonomic neural effects of dietary calcium; insulin and sex steroids in hypertension (funded by the NIH); insulin and sex steroids in hypertension (funded by the American Heart Association of Metropolitan Chicago).
B. Plotkin, Associate Professor; Ph.D., Tennessee. Relevance of OMT in depression (funded by the American Osteopathic Association).
W. Prozialeck, Professor; Ph.D., Thomas Jefferson. Mechanisms of cadium toxicity in epithelial cells (funded by the NIH).
K. Ramsey, Associate Professor; Ph.D., Arkansas. Immunity and persistence in chlamydial infections, role of nitric oxide in chlamydial infection of mice (funded by the NIH), nitric oxide in Reiter's arthritis (funded by the Arthritis Foundation).
M. Schaenboen, Associate Professor; D. O., Iowa College of Osteopathic Medicine and Surgery. Stroke prevention in the African-American community (funded by the NIH).
B. Shakoor, Assistant Professor; Ph.D., Illinois. Improving hypertension control in the inner city (funded by the NIH).
J. Smith, Associate Professor; Ph.D., Michigan. Nitric oxide suppression of diabetic heart contraction (funded by the NIH).
P. Standley, Assistant Professor; Ph.D., Wayne State. Regulation of vascular insulin-like growth factor 1 (funded by the American Heart Association).
B. Suprenant, Assistant Professor; D.O., Chicago College of Osteopathic Medicine. Mode selection trial in sinus node dysfunction (funded by the NIH).
G. Wahler, Associate Professor; Ph.D., Minnesota. Subcellular mechanisms for dysfunction in myocytes (funded by the American Heart Association), electrophysiological effects of phospholipid metabolites (funded by the American Diabetes Association and the NIH).

NATIONAL COLLEGE OF NATUROPATHIC MEDICINE

Doctoral Program in Naturopathic Medicine
Master of Science in Oriental Medicine

Programs of Study

National College of Naturopathic Medicine offers a Doctor of Naturopathic Medicine (N.D.) degree and a Master of Science in Oriental Medicine (M.S.O.M.) degree. With the College's academic emphasis in holistic, preventative medical education, both degree programs focus not only on technical excellence, but also on patient-centered care. The N.D. degree program is a fully accredited, intensive four-year graduate program that prepares students to become naturopathic general practitioners. Naturopathic medicine is a science-based, vitalistic philosophy and practice rooted in the principle of *vis medicatrix naturae,* the healing power of nature. Approaching health and healing from the basis of wellness rather than disease, N.D.'s work with patients to restore health by stimulating the body's innate healing capacity through natural therapeutics. The first two years of study are focused on the standard medical sciences (anatomy and physiology; biochemistry; clinical, physical, and laboratory diagnosis; embryology; histology; immunology; microbiology; neurosciences; pathology; pharmacognosy; pharmacology; and psychology) as well as the philosophy of naturopathic medicine. During the last two years, students receive clinical training in diagnosis and treatment through externships under licensed physicians at the College's clinics and in private practice. Upper-division course work and training include such areas as botanical medicine, cardiovascular diseases, classical Chinese medicine, clinical nutrition, counseling, dermatology, endocrinology, gastroenterology, geriatrics, gynecology, homeopathy, minor surgery, natural childbirth, neurology, obstetrics, oncology, orthopedics, pediatrics, and physical medicine (manipulation, exercise therapy, and hydrotherapy). N.D. students may also apply to pursue certificates in homeopathy, naturopathic obstetrics, qigong, or classical Chinese herbal medicine. Graduates are qualified to sit for the N.P.I.E.X., a board licensing examination.

The M.S.O.M. degree program is a three-year graduate program that explores Chinese medicine as explained by the classics. A candidate for accreditation, the M.S.O.M. delves beyond conventional studies in acupuncture to investigate the encompassing nature of classical Chinese medicine as a philosophy, art, practice, and way of life. Designed primarily for individuals who already have advanced medical degrees, the M.S.O.M. is an intensive, experiential program. The program examines many aspects of health and health care, from acupuncture to qigong to herbal medicine. M.S.O.M. students study classical Chinese medicine through a unique fusion of ancient mentor-apprenticeship and contemporary didactic methods. Second-year students of the College's N.D. program may apply to the M.S.O.M. program for a six-year dual-degree program. Graduates of the M.S.O.M. program are qualified to sit for licensing as acupuncturists in the state of Oregon.

Research Facilities

The College has an active research program administered by the Dean of Research and an Institutional Review Board. Research projects evaluate efficacy of therapeutics in the treatment of acute and chronic diseases. Students involved in research have full access to the College library's extensive collection of naturopathic literature as well as to the libraries of Oregon Health Sciences University, Western States Chiropractic College, and Oregon College of Oriental Medicine. The College also has computer hardware and software designed to facilitate data acquisition and analysis and full clinical facilities, including a state-licensed lab and the largest natural products dispensary in the Northwest.

Financial Aid

Financial aid is available to N.D. students and dual-degree students through the Federal Stafford Student Loan and Federal Work-Study programs and to veterans through Title 38.

Cost of Study

Tuition for the 1998–99 academic year is $14,352. Books and supplies are estimated to cost an additional $1100 to $2000 per year.

Living and Housing Costs

There is no on-campus housing, but the College is located in an area with ample rental housing at reasonable and varied costs. The Student Services Office (telephone: 503-499-4343, Ext. 172) maintains a shared housing network. Total living expenses (food, housing, transportation, and entertainment) are estimated at $1190 per month.

Student Group

The student body of 400 is a diverse mix of students from all over the continent and the world.

Student Outcomes

Most graduates enter private practice as naturopathic family physicians or acupuncturists and Chinese medicine practitioners.

Location

National College's campus and administrative offices are located near the city center of Portland. The main teaching clinic is located in southeast suburban Portland, 7 miles from the city center, in a quiet neighborhood that is surrounded by grass and trees. The Greater Portland area is a progressive metropolis with 1.5 million inhabitants. A moderate climate, a light-rail mass transit system, more parks per capita than any city in the country, the annual Rose Festival, a professional symphony orchestra, several professional ballet companies, an active theater program, a world-class zoo, art museums, and an NBA basketball franchise have earned Portland the billing of America's "most liveable city." Year-round skiing, hiking, and fishing are possible within an hour's drive of the city. The Pacific coast is 1½ hours away, and the Columbia River Gorge is at the city's doorstep.

The College

Founded in 1956, National College of Naturopathic Medicine is the oldest accredited naturopathic medical college in North America. As such, it has been the heart of the profession, preserving and extending the legacy of naturopathic medicine and helping the public to broaden its understanding of health care. National College of Naturopathic Medicine integrates natural healing methods from around the world with solid foundations in Western sciences. As part of a supportive, close-knit community, students pursue a vitalistically grounded and academically rigorous clinical, patient-centered program. Both the N.D. program and the M.S.O.M. program offer a holistic approach to health and well-being. The community of faculty members, students, and administrative staff members is drawn together by the College's mission to provide whole-person health care that emphasizes prevention, demonstrates an appreciation for quality of life, and honors the natural recuperative ability of the human body. The learning environment is dynamic and supportive. The College is authorized to grant the N.D. and M.S.O.M. degrees by the state of Oregon through the Office of Degree Authorization. The College is accredited by the Council on Naturopathic Medical Education, a specialized accreditor recognized by the U.S. Secretary of Education. In addition, the Council of Education of the Canadian Naturopathic Association recognizes the College, as do all state and provincial boards of naturopathic examiners.

Applying

Admission to the College is competitive, and, in addition to completion of the prerequisites, candidates must demonstrate outstanding moral character, individual maturity, and academic promise. All applicants must have completed a bachelor's degree. Specific requirements for each program may be obtained from the Office of Admissions. Students who competitively meet admission requirements are invited to a required on-campus interview.

Correspondence and Information

Office of Admissions
National College of Naturopathic Medicine
049 Southwest Porter Street
Portland, Oregon 97201

Telephone: 503-499-4343, Ext. 0
E-mail: admissions@ncnm.edu
World Wide Web: http://www.ncnm.edu

National College of Naturopathic Medicine

THE FACULTY AND ADMINISTRATION

Satya Ambrose, Instructor (clinical education); N.D., National College of Naturopathic Medicine.
Sharleen Andrews-Miller, Instructor (Northwest herbs); B.S., Portland State.
Laura Baffes, Instructor (naturopathic manipulative therapeutics); D.C., National Chiropractic.
Deah Baird, Instructor (endocrinology); N.D., Bastyr.
Diipali Barrett, Instructor (clinical correlate, gynecology lab, hydrotherapy lab); N.D., National College of Naturopathic Medicine.
Richard Barrett, Associate Professor (EENT, clinical/physical diagnosis lab, and clinical education and case presentation); N.D., National College of Naturopathic Medicine.
Marlane Bassett, Instructor (clinical education, gynecology lab); N.D., National College of Naturopathic Medicine.
Rita Bettenburg, Associate Professor (clinical education and case presentation, clinical/physical diagnosis, pediatrics); N.D., National College of Naturopathic Medicine.
Ann Blair, Instructor (pharmacology); Ph.D., Oregon State.
Bill Borman, Assistant Professor (embryology, histology lab); Ph.D., Medical College of Wisconsin.
John Brons, Assistant Professor (anatomy, physiology, clinical correlate); M.Ac.O.M., Oregon College of Oriental Medicine.
Dan Carter, Assistant Professor (clinical education, lab diagnosis, public health); N.D., National College of Naturopathic Medicine.
Laurent Chaix, Instructor (clinical education); N.D., National College of Naturopathic Medicine.
Michael C. C. Chung, Instructor (theory, herbs, clinic observation, case presentation); M.T.C.M., Tianjin College of Traditional Chinese Medicine (China).
James Cleaver, Chinese Medicine Clinic Coordinator; Dipl.Ac. (NCCA), Five Branches Institute, College of Traditional Chinese Medicine.
Frederick Colley, Professor (microbiology); Ph.D., Arizona State; M.P.H., Berkeley.
Elizabeth Collins, Instructor (clinical correlates, palpation lab); N.D., National College of Naturopathic Medicine.
John Collins, Associate Professor (clinical education, homeopathy); N.D., National College of Naturopathic Medicine.
L. Vicky Crouse, Instructor (geriatrics, urology, clinical/physical diagnosis lab); N.D., National College of Naturopathic Medicine.
Catherine Cummins, Instructor (naturopathic manipulative therapeutics); D.C., Western States Chiropractic.
Bracey R. Dangerfield, Instructor (biochemistry, immunology, organic chemistry, research and statistics); Ph.D., Maharishi International.
Jack Daugherty, Associate Professor (clinical education); D.C., Western States Chiropractic; N.D., National College of Naturopathic Medicine.
Daniel De Lapp, Instructor (dermatology); D.C., Los Angeles Chiropractic; M.Ac.O.M., Oregon College of Oriental Medicine; N.D., National College of Naturopathic Medicine.
Prem Dev, Instructor (clinical education, homeopathy); N.D., National College of Naturopathic Medicine.
Bruce Dickson, Instructor (clinical education, homeopathy); N.D., National College of Naturopathic Medicine.
Trish Egan, Laboratory Coordinator (clinical education); M.F.A., Portland State.
Durr Elmore, Associate Professor (homeopathy); D.C., Western States Chiropractic; N.D., National College of Naturopathic Medicine.
Karen Frangos, Instructor (exercise therapeutics); N.D., National College of Naturopathic Medicine.
William Frazier, Instructor (clinical theater, traditional mentorship); L.Ac.
Adolfo Freinquel, Teaching Assistant (homeopathy); B.A., Buenos Aires (Argentina).
David Frierman, Instructor (clinic internship); B.A., Berkeley.
Heiner Fruehauf, Associate Professor and Classical Chinese Medicine Department Chair (classical Chinese medicine theory); Ph.D., Chicago.
Jennifer Gaddy, Instructor (clinical education); N.D., National College of Naturopathic Medicine.
Gregory Garcia, Instructor (clinical education, doctor/patient relations, medical ethics); N.D., National College of Naturopathic Medicine.
Steve Gardner, Assistant Professor (proctology); D.C., Western States Chiropractic; N.D., National College of Naturopathic Medicine.
Elliot Geller, Instructor (communication skills); M.S.W., Portland State.
Mary Grabowska, Instructor (obstetrics); N.D., National College of Naturopathic Medicine; M.Ac.O.M., Oregon College of Oriental Medicine.
Donna Guthrie, Instructor (clinical education); N.D., National College of Naturopathic Medicine.
Rick Hovgaard, Instructor (physiotherapy); N.D., National College of Naturopathic Medicine.
Victoria Hudson, Professor (gynecology, oncology); N.D., National College of Naturopathic Medicine.
Clyde B. Jensen, Professor (pharmacology) and President; Ph.D., North Dakota.
Mark Kaminski, Assistant Professor (histology, genetics); M.S., Northwestern.
Judith Kessler, Instructor (stress management, psychological assessment); Psy.D., Yeshiva.
G. S. S. Khalsa, Professor (endocrinology, chronic viral disease) and Dean of Academic Affairs; N.D., National College of Naturopathic Medicine.
Robert King, Instructor (counseling techniques); M.S.W., Washington (Seattle).
Janina Kneeland, Instructor (histology lab); N.D., National College of Naturopathic Medicine; M.Ac.O.M., Oregon College of Oriental Medicine.
Mengke Kou, Instructor (traditional mentorship, research, clinic observation, clinic internship, clinical theater, clinical case presentation); M.M., Chengdu University of Traditional Chinese Medicine (China).
Rihui Long, Instructor (theory, traditional mentorship, classical case studies, research, clinic observation, clinic internship, clinical theater); M.M., Chengdu University of Traditional Chinese Medicine (China).
Anna MacIntosh, Professor (physiology, nutrition) and Dean of Research; Ph.D., California, Irvine; N.D., National College of Naturopathic Medicine.
Louise Marshall, Assistant Professor (bodywork/massage); N.D., National College of Naturopathic Medicine.
Elsbeth Martindale, Instructor (psychology); Psy.D., Biola.
Russell Marz, Assistant Professor (nutrition); N.D., National College of Naturopathic Medicine; M.Ac.O.M., Oregon College of Oriental Medicine.
Susan Gaia Mather, Instructor (colonics); N.D., National College of Naturopathic Medicine.
Jennifer Means, Instructor (clinical education); M.Ac.O.M., Oregon College of Oriental Medicine; N.D., National College of Naturopathic Medicine.
Chris D. Meletis, Assistant Professor (natural pharmacology, nutrition) and Dean of Clinical Affairs; N.D., National College of Naturopathic Medicine.
Stephen Messer, Instructor (homeopathy); M.S.Ed., CUNY, City College; N.D., National College of Naturopathic Medicine.
Martin Milner, Associate Professor (cardiology); N.D., National College of Naturopathic Medicine.
Judy Peabody, Instructor (clinical education, clinical case presentation); N.D., National College of Naturopathic Medicine.
Stacey Raffety, Instructor (IV therapy); M.Ac.O.M., Oregon College of Oriental Medicine; N.D., National College of Naturopathic Medicine.
Steven Sandberg-Lewis, Associate Professor (pathology, gastroenterology, environmental medicine, clinical education, advanced clinical case presentation, jurisprudence); N.D., National College of Naturopathic Medicine.
Timothy Sellers, Instructor (clinical education); D.C., Western States Chiropractic.
Jill Stansbury, Assistant Professor (botanical materia medica, naturopathic medical philosophy and therapeutics); N.D., National College of Naturopathic Medicine.
Sonja Straub, Instructor (counseling techniques); Ph.D., Union (Ohio).
Eric Stroud, Instructor (business practice); D.C., Western States Chiropractic.
Ellen Sudak, Instructor (points, techniques); M.Ac.O.M., Oregon College of Oriental Medicine.
Nora Tallman, Assistant Professor (obstetrics); N.D., National College of Naturopathic Medicine.
Dickson Thom, Assistant Professor (clinical sciences, neurology, clinical/physical diagnosis, clinical education); D.D.S., Toronto; N.D., National College of Naturopathic Medicine.
Edythe Vickers, Instructor (clinic observation); N.D., National College of Naturopathic Medicine.
Qingyu Wang, Instructor (qigong); B.A., Sichuan (China). Lineage holder, Jinjing Qigong (China).
Brent Warner, Instructor (naturopathic manipulative therapeutics, office orthopedics, palpation lab); D.C., Western States Chiropractic.
Tyrone Wei, Associate Professor (diagnostic imaging); D.C., Western States Chiropractic.
Robert Wilson, Instructor (emergency medicine, minor surgery, somatic reeducation, clinical education); N.D., National College of Naturopathic Medicine.
Kimberley Windstar, Instructor (gynecology lab, clinical education); M.Ed., California State; N.D., National College of Naturopathic Medicine.
Haosheng Zhang, Instructor (herbs, theory, research, Oriental dietetics, clinical theater, clinic observation, clinic internship); M.M., Chengdu University of Traditional Chinese Medicine (China).
Katherine Zieman, Instructor (obstetrics); N.D., National College of Naturopathic Medicine.

NEW YORK COLLEGE OF PODIATRIC MEDICINE

Program of Study

The New York College of Podiatric Medicine (NYCPM), the first and largest college of podiatric medicine, established in 1911, is an independent, nonprofit institution located in New York City. It shares its Manhattan location with the Foot Clinics of New York, the largest foot-care center in the world.

The Doctor of Podiatric Medicine degree is awarded. After an intensive two-year program of basic science training identical to that of an allopathic institution, students enter an extensive two-year program of clinical training. The curriculum is arranged so that courses in anatomy and physiology, bacteriology, biochemistry, biomechanics, histology, neurology, pathology, and pharmacology move from the study of normal structure and function in the human body to an admixture of basic and clinical science training.

The clinical opportunities in the Foot Clinics of New York are unsurpassed in regard to the number of patients seen and the variety of podiatric treatment given. Annually, 62,000 patients receive podiatric care in the seven clinical divisions (Podiatric Medicine, Surgery, General Podiatry, Orthopedics, Pediatrics, Radiology, and Sports Medicine). First-year students are introduced to the clinics through observation of patients and their treatment. Second-year students are assigned to the general clinics, where they become familiar with the diagnosis and treatment of various podiatric lesions. The third year is a blend of clinical experience and instruction, and the student begins to learn the treatment of human pathologies. The fourth year is primarily a clinical learning experience, with advanced seminars and a large array of clinical externship opportunities.

Three fourth-year externships of six weeks in length are available at the more than fifty health-care institutions affiliated with the College. One-, two-, and three-year residencies in surgery, medicine, orthopedics, pediatrics, and general podiatry are available at the College and these same institutions.

Research Facilities

The College's research facilities are centered on two separate libraries. The print library contains more than 10,000 books and 300 periodicals. Access to additional print sources is obtained through MEDLINE and consortium agreements with Medical Library Center of New York, New York–New Jersey chapter/MLA, Manhattan/Bronx Small Health Sciences Library Group, and METRO. The audiovisual library contains an extensive collection of videotapes, slide presentations, and computer software packages to support the curriculum, research, and clinical needs of students, faculty, and the profession.

Financial Aid

The NYCPM's financial aid office helps students participate in the most favorable combination of aid programs available to them. GSL, HEAL, and work-study are a few of the financial aid options. College-sponsored academic and need-based scholarships and loans are available. Ninety-five percent of the student body receives financial aid.

Cost of Study

Tuition and fees for the 1997–98 academic year were $20,266; additional costs include books, supplies, and instruments.

Living and Housing Costs

Living expenses vary greatly in the New York metropolitan area. Utilities, rent, telephone, food, transportation, and personal expenses are included in the NYCPM's estimated $9340 cost of living. The Student Affairs Office assists students with housing, and maintains affiliation with several dormitory and apartment-type residences that cater to medical students.

Student Group

The New York College is proud of its student diversity, having a student population that represents most American states. International students represent Canada, the United Kingdom, the Philippines, Spain, and the former Soviet Union. The average student population from year to year is 460 students.

Location

As a truly international city, New York plays host to activities that support every possible interest: music, from classical to the intricate alternative scene; clubs; Broadway and off-Broadway productions; museums beyond number; the green Adirondack Mountains and the beautiful beaches of Long Island and New Jersey, both only a short ride away. Every major professional sport is represented, many by two teams.

The College

From its inception by a small group of medical pioneers in 1911, the College has dedicated itself to providing a professional medical education, serving as a catalyst in the fields of research and advancement, and making available superior health care. The New York College commits itself to serving the needs of its students and its graduates, involving itself nationally and internationally to provide the most excellent postgraduate opportunities available in the field. To this end, strong basic science and clinical programs are enhanced by extensive externship, residency, and continuing education programs.

Applying

Applicants to the New York College of Podiatric Medicine should contact the admissions office directly for information.

Prospective applicants are required to have at least 90 undergraduate credit hours. A bachelor's degree is recommended, with at least 8 credits each in biology, general chemistry, organic chemistry, and physics, with an additional 6 credits in English. Applicants are strongly urged to take a broad selection of course work beyond the science curriculum that prepares them for entrance. In addition to premed majors, graduates from unrelated majors (science or nonscience) are also welcome to apply so long as the minimum requirements previously stated have been completed. Students must submit an official transcript from every undergraduate and graduate institution they have attended. The MCAT is required, but is not used strictly in the admissions process, where academics and personal experience have been found to be the prime indicators of success. Three letters of recommendation and an interview are also mandatory.

Correspondence and Information

Steve Broder
Assistant Vice President
Recruitment, Admissions, and Alumni Affairs
New York College of Podiatric Medicine
1800 Park Avenue
New York, New York 10035
Telephone: 800-526-6966 (toll-free)
Fax: 212-722-4918
E-mail: sbroder@nycpm.edu
World Wide Web: http://www.nycpm.edu

New York College of Podiatric Medicine

THE FACULTY

BASIC SCIENCE
Kenneth Astrin, Ph.D.
Judith Binstock, Ph.D.
Robert Bressler, Assistant Dean, Basic Sciences; Ph.D.
Eileen Chusid, Ph.D.
Gus Constantouris, D.P.M.
A. DiLandro, Ed.D.
Daria Dykyj, Ph.D.
Rosalinda Guce, M.D.
Clark Lambert, M.D., Ph.D. (Adjunct)
Zev Leifer, Ph.D.
Allan Levine, D.C.
Dionysios Liveris, Ph.D.
Sushama Rich, M.D.
Anastasia Stavroupoulus, Ph.D.
Patricia Wade, Ph.D.

COMMUNITY HEALTH
Barry Block, D.P.M., J.D. (Adjunct)
Neil Kornfeld, J.D.
Mary Lou McGanney, Associate Dean; Ph.D.
Simon Nzuzi, Vice President, Community and Minority Affairs, and Chair, Community Health; D.P.M.
James Provenzano, M.L.S. (Library service)
Ephraim Sturm, M.A. (Adjunct)
Barry Taub, J.D.

MEDICINE
Donna Marie Alfieri, D.P.M.
Glenroy Aska, D.P.M.
Jerry Ballentine, D.O. (Adjunct)
Hugh Bryant, D.P.M.
Hugh Butts, M.D. (Adjunct)
Nancy Clark, D.P.M.
Randy Cohen, Director, Radiology; D.P.M.
Elizabeth Cruz, D.P.M.; PA.
Linda D'Auria, Clinic Administrator; D.P.M.
Michael DellaCorte, D.P.M. (Adjunct)
Lawrence Diamond, Medical Director; M.D.
Nabil Fahim, D.P.M.
Bruce Frankel, Assistant Dean, Clinical Sciences; D.P.M.
Theodore Gaeta, D.O. (Adjunct)
Deborah Gaines, D.P.M.
David George, Assistant Dean, Graduate Medical Education; D.P.M.
Emilio Goez, D.P.M.
Patrick Grisafi, D.P.M. (Adjunct)
Melvyn Grovit, Chair; D.P.M.
Carl Harris, D.P.M.
Maureen Jennings, Assistant Dean, Institutional Research; D.P.M.
Faiz Kashan, M.D.
Mark Kosinski, D.P.M.
Mark Lebwohl, M.D. (Adjunct)
Thomas Leecost, D.P.M.
Amira Mantoura, D.P.M.
Andrew Manzo, D.P.M.
Bryan Markinson, D.P.M.
Patrick Nowak, D.P.M.
Stuart Oster, M.D.
Gene Potter, D.P.M., Ph.D.
E. Ramsey-Parker, D.P.M.
Donald Rudikoff, M.D.
Denise Sampson, D.P.M.; PA.
David Simpson, M.D. (Adjunct)
Theodore Spevack, D.O. (Adjunct)
Frank Spinosa, D.P.M. (Adjunct)
Arthur Steinhart, D.P.M.
Mark Swartz, M.D. (Adjunct)
Freida Trainor, Ph.D.
Monte Tuckman, D.P.M.
Demi Turner, D.P.M.
Katherine Ward, D.P.M.
David Westring, M.D. (Adjunct)
Fay Woomer, D.P.M.

ORTHOPEDICS
Robert Biller, D.P.M. (Adjunct)
Mark Caselli, Chair; D.P.M.
Joseph D'Amico, D.P.M. (Visiting)
Jonathan DeLand, M.D. (Visiting)
Aaron Glockenberg, D.P.M.
Lauren Jones, D.P.M.
Steven Levitz, D.P.M.
Loretta Logan, D.P.M.
Lewis Maharan, M.D. (Visiting)
Barney Martin, D.P.M. (Visiting)
Stephen McIlveen, M.D. (Visiting)
John McNerney, D.P.M. (Visiting)
Paul Milone, D.P.M. (Visiting)
Thomas Novella, D.P.M. (Visiting)
Stephen Perle, D.C. (Visiting)
John Rainieri, D.P.M. (Visiting)
Elliott Rosensweet, D.P.M.
Edward Rzonca, D.P.M. (Visiting)
Robert Schwartz, C.Ped. (Visiting)
Ellen Sobel, D.P.M., Ph.D.

PEDIATRICS
John Connors, D.P.M.
Douglas David, D.P.M.
Jeffrey Falcone, D.P.M.
Laurence Lowy, D.P.M.
Barbara Resseque, D.P.M.
Marianne Surasi, D.P.M.
Russell Volpe, Chair; D.P.M.
Elissa Wernick, D.P.M.
Justin Wernick, D.P.M.

SURGERY
Tzvi Bar-David, D.P.M. (Adjunct)
Raymond Cavaliere, D.P.M. (Adjunct)
Thomas DeLauro, D.P.M.
Howard Friedman, D.P.M.
Clifford Gevirtz, M.D., M.P.H. (Adjunct)
Renato Giorgini, D.P.M. (Adjunct)
Gerald Gorecki, D.P.M. (Adjunct)
Jonathan Haber, D.P.M.
Anthony Hernandez, Director, International Program; D.P.M.
Joseph Hogan, D.P.M. (Adjunct)
Tanya Jackson, D.P.M.
Kevin Jules, Chair; D.P.M.
Stanley Kalish, D.P.M. (Adjunct)
Guido LaPorta, D.P.M. (Adjunct)
Charles Lombardi, D.P.M. (Adjunct)
Francis Lynch, D.P.M. (Visiting)
David Novicki, D.P.M. (Adjunct)
Philip Organ, D.P.M. (Adjunct)
Martin Pressman, D.P.M. (Adjunct)
John Prignano, D.P.M.
Susan Rice, D.P.M.
Richard Schachter, D.P.M. (Adjunct)
Rocco Sellitto, D.P.M. (Adjunct)
Keith Springer, D.P.M.
Michael Trepal, Vice President, Academic Affairs, and Dean; D.P.M.
Edwin Wolf, D.P.M.

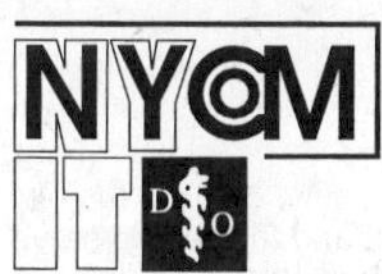

NEW YORK COLLEGE OF OSTEOPATHIC MEDICINE OF NEW YORK INSTITUTE OF TECHNOLOGY

Program of Study

New York College of Osteopathic Medicine (NYCOM), the first school of osteopathic medicine in New York State, is dedicated to the predoctoral and postdoctoral education of osteopathic physicians, the fostering of careers in family medicine, and research on human health and disease, with a focus on the roles of the neuromuscular and musculoskeletal systems. The curriculum emphasizes needs and opportunities in primary health care and community health services, particularly health-care problems of the inner city and smaller communities.

NYCOM's educational goals are pursued during a four-year program leading to the degree of Doctor of Osteopathic Medicine. Courses in the biomedical sciences are offered at NYCOM, while training in the clinical sciences takes place at NYCOM, its affiliated hospitals, cooperating physicians' offices, and NYCOM-operated health-care centers. In addition, sixteen affiliated hospitals, in association with NYCOM, offer the largest internship program in the osteopathic profession, annually training more than 150 D.O.'s in their first postdoctoral year. Residency programs in family practice, surgery, emergency medicine, internal medicine, radiology, osteopathic manipulative medicine, psychiatry, pediatrics, and dermatology have also been established.

The two-year on-campus portion of the program consists primarily of didactic instruction in the basic sciences and clinical sciences. The curriculum becomes progressively more clinical with the study of the cardiovascular, respiratory, gastrointestinal, endocrine, renal, hematogenous, and nervous systems, including the biochemistry, microbiology, pathology, pharmacology, and physiology of each system. Other courses include community medicine, dermatology, differential diagnosis, emergency medicine, family practice, gerontology, obstetrics/gynecology, pediatrics, radiology, rehabilitation medicine, and surgery. Intensive course work in osteopathic principles and practice is given during the first two years of the program. Continuous clinical rotations in all disciplines, with a program focusing on family practice and preventive health care, constitute the last two years. A Rural Preceptorship Program permits third-year students to complete their rotations in a rural environment. In 1992 NYCOM introduced a three-year Accelerated Program to Educate Emigre Physicians in Osteopathic Medicine (APEP). Combined D.O./M.B.A. and D.O./M.S. in clinical nutrition programs are also available.

Research Facilities

NYCOM is housed in two buildings. The award-winning Nelson A. Rockefeller Academic Center houses a multilevel library with an extensive collection of texts, journals, and audiovisual aids; a media office; study rooms; and laboratories for student instruction and faculty research. The second building, the Academic Health Care Center, houses a family health-care center for research and evaluation in patient care, the W. Kenneth Riland Institute of Neuro-Musculoskeletal Disorders, a spacious anatomy laboratory for student instruction, faculty and administrative offices, classrooms, a student lounge, and an auditorium.

Financial Aid

Students can apply for scholarships and loans provided by government and private sources. Aid programs administered by the College require that the student meet three criteria: good standing with the College, satisfactory academic progress, and demonstrated financial need. Need is calculated by subtracting all available resources reported on the Graduate and Professional School Financial Aid Service (GAPSFAS) form from the College-determined student budget. The Financial Aid Office then attempts to meet the remaining need. Institutional guidelines and federal and state regulations determine how aid is administered.

Cost of Study

Tuition for the academic year 1998–99 is $22,000. Fixed expenses in addition to tuition include fees, books, supplies, health insurance, and uniforms; these average $5469 in the first year of study.

Living and Housing Costs

Housing is available in the surrounding communities. Estimated living expenses (rent, food, utilities, transportation, and miscellaneous personal expenses) range from $7385 (ten-month cost for students living with parents) to $16,450 (twelve-month cost for students not living with parents).

Student Group

The 1998–99 enrollment of the College is 980 and includes a first-year class of 220 students. Women constitute approximately 40 percent. The student body is a diverse one with respect to age, ethnicity, and background. NYCOM offers a seven-week Basic Science Summer Program (BSSP) for traditionally underrepresented minorities, who constitute 17 percent of the student body.

Student Outcomes

One hundred percent of NYCOM graduates are accepted into postgraduate internship or residency programs. Of the 211 graduates in the class of 1998, 70 percent are pursuing osteopathic internships (64 percent in NYCOM-college coordinated program). Approximately 60 percent of NYCOM graduates enter primary care.

Location

NYCOM is located on the scenic 750-acre campus of the New York Institute of Technology some 22 miles east of New York City in the suburban community of Old Westbury on the North Shore of Long Island. The nearby New York metropolitan area is unparalleled in its cultural and recreational offerings. The area is one of the major health-care centers in the country, and it is an excellent resource for NYCOM's medical program. Leading medical practitioners and researchers lecture at the College during the academic year.

The College and The Institute

Founded in 1977, the New York College of Osteopathic Medicine is the osteopathic medical college of the New York Institute of Technology. A multicampus institution of higher learning, New York Institute of Technology offers varied curricula leading to associate, baccalaureate, and master's degrees in such areas as architecture, fine arts, business, computer science, media, labor relations, and several health-related fields. The Institute and the College offer a combined seven-year B.S./D.O. program.

Applying

NYCOM participates in the American Association of Colleges of Osteopathic Medicine Application Service (AACOMAS). Application forms may be obtained by writing to AACOMAS, Suite 310, 5550 Friendship Boulevard, Chevy Chase, Maryland 20815-7231. Applications must be submitted no later than February 1 of the year in which admission is sought. Selected applicants are invited for a personal interview, at which time a supplemental application must be completed and a $60 fee remitted. Careful consideration is given to applicants' academic records, MCAT scores (required), letters of reference (an osteopathic physician's recommendation is strongly suggested), and extracurricular and health-related activities. Required courses include 8 hours of biology, 8 hours of inorganic chemistry, 8 hours of organic chemistry, 8 hours of physics, and 6 hours of English, with no grade below C. A bachelor's degree and a personal interview are required. Acceptances are issued on a rolling basis. NYCOM provides equal opportunity in admission and student aid, regardless of sex, race, handicap, color, or national or ethnic origin.

Correspondence and Information

Michael J. Schaefer
Director of Admissions
New York College of Osteopathic Medicine
of New York Institute of Technology
Old Westbury, New York 11568

Telephone: 516-686-3747
World Wide Web: http://www.nyit.edu/nycom/nycom

New York College of Osteopathic Medicine of New York Institute of Technology

THE FACULTY

The NYCOM faculty numbers approximately 325 full- and part-time members, all of whom possess either the D.O., M.D., or Ph.D. degree. Faculty members include those who teach the basic and clinical sciences in the classroom and at affiliated and cooperating hospitals and those who serve as instructors and role models in an extensive preceptorship program required of all students. Additional faculty members are employed at NYCOM's three Family Health Care Centers.

RESEARCH PROGRAMS IN PROGRESS

Mark A. W. Andrews, Assistant Professor of Physiology; Ph.D., Medical College of Georgia. Osteopathic treatment of muscle with compromised innervation; biophysics of crossbridge interactions in skeletal, cardiac, and smooth muscle; exercise physiology and mechanisms of fatigue.

Dennis J. Dowling, Associate Professor and Chairman of Osteopathic Manipulative Medicine; D.O., NYCOM. Investigation of immunological responses to osteopathic manipulative techniques (lymphatic pump).

Brian H. Hallas, Associate Professor, Chairman, and Course Director of Neuroscience; Ph.D., Purdue. Recovery of function by using embryonic brainstem transplants in the damaged mammalian brainstem.

Cynthia Harris, Assistant Professor of Pharmacology; Ph.D., Illinois. Behavioral pharmacology of drugs of abuse, using operant conditioning and drug discrimination technology.

John Hunter, Assistant Professor of Anatomy; Ph.D., Brown. Molar tooth diversity, disparity, and ecology in genozoic ungulate radiations.

Christine Hutak, Assistant Professor of Pharmacology; Ph.D., St. John's (New York). In vitro evaluation of primary irritation.

Marie E. Kavanagh, Associate Professor of Pathology; M.D., Faculté de Medecine d'Haiti. Effect of anoxia on thiamine esters in the neonatal rat, recovery of function using embryonic brainstem transplants in the mammalian brainstem.

Chellappa Kumar, Assistant Professor and Course Director of Biochemistry; Ph.D., Indian Institute of Technology. Enzymology of oxygen, spectroscopy and structure of metalloproteins, noninvasive methods of monitoring organ function and pathology.

W. Desmond Maxwell, Assistant Professor of Neuroscience; Ph.D., Queen's (Belfast). Early Cretaceous neonate and juvenile dinosaurs; cloverly formations, U.S.A.; vertebrate paleontology of the lower Cretaceous Holly Creek formation, southeastern Oklahoma.

Baruch May, Assistant Professor of Microbiology; Ph.D., Pittsburgh. Biochemical genetics in nitrogen metabolism: diagnosis and treatment of urea cycle and purine nucleotide enzyme deficiencies.

Claudia McCarty, Assistant Professor of Osteopathic Medicine; D.O., NYCOM. Osteopathic manipulative therapy in the treatment of Parkinson's disease.

Charles Pavia, Associate Professor and Course Director of Microbiology; Ph.D., North Carolina. Nicotine's effects on bacteria, infectious etiology of Crohn's disease.

J. Michael Plavcan, Assistant Professor of Anatomical Sciences; Ph.D., Duke. Evolution of sexual dimorphism in primates and humans, human craniofacial development, vertebrate paleontology.

Scott D. Sampson, Assistant Professor of Anatomical Sciences; Ph.D., Toronto. Unusual narial structures in dinosaurs and other vertebrates: a case study in the functional interpretation of anatomical novelty in the fossil record.

Thomas A. Scandalis, Associate Professor and Course Director of Family Practice; D.O., NYCOM. The effects of OMT on range of motion in the arthritic knee.

Donna Shanies, Assistant Professor of Biochemistry; Ph.D., NYU. Regulation of hemoglobin synthesis.

Nikos Solounias, Associate Professor and Chairman of Anatomy; Ph.D., Colorado. Paleoecology of fossil horses (family Equidae) over the past 55 million years.

Larry R. Stepp, Assistant Professor of Physiology; Ph.D., Vanderbilt. Physiological mechanisms for the regulation of enzymatic activity.

John Strauss, Assistant Professor of Physiology; Ph.D., Cincinnati. Smooth muscle physiology.

Michael Wells, Associate Professor of Neuroscience; Ph.D., Florida. Rehabilitation of patients with Parkinson's disease.

David Yens, Associate Professor and Director of Educational Development Resource Unit; Ph.D., Penn State. Efficacy of education technologies, especially computers, for undergraduate and graduate medical education.

Steven J. Youmans, Assistant Professor of Physiology; Ph.D., Indiana. Membrane transport and its regulation.

The Academic Health Care Center. The Nelson A. Rockefeller Academic Center is shown in the background.

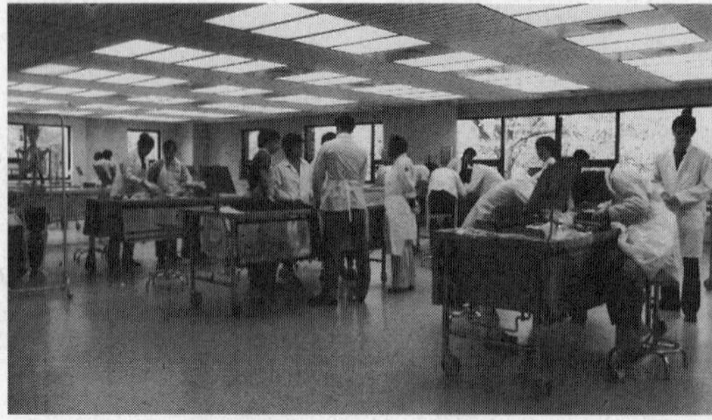

The Anatomy Laboratory.

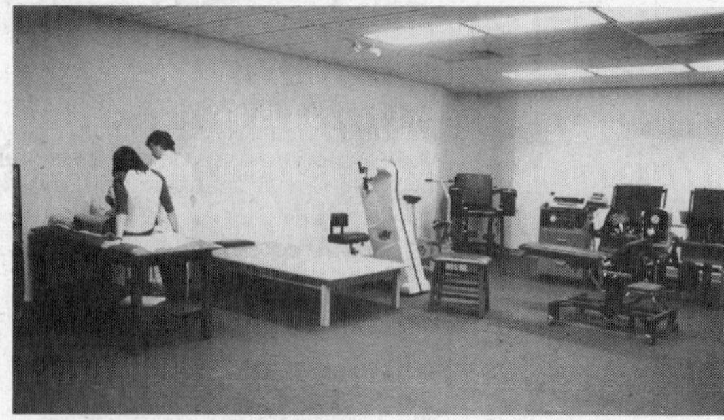

The sports and rehabilitation medicine treatment facility, located in the Academic Health Care Center.

RUSH UNIVERSITY

College of Health Sciences
Graduate Program in Healthcare Ethics

Program of Study

The Department of Religion, Health, and Human Values offers a program leading to the Master of Arts degree. The program is designed so that people from a variety of backgrounds can broaden their skills, expand their roles in order to serve on ethics committees or in ethics consultation services, teach ethics in their institutions, and provide informed comment about health-care ethics issues of the day.

The program's interdisciplinary emphasis complements the education and practice of students who are in health-care professions and orients non-health-care professionals to the many roles and interactions of those who work in the healing professions.

Because health-care ethics have to be understood in context, the program features courses in medical sociology, medical economics, and health-care organizations in addition to traditional courses that focus on fundamental concepts, tools, and skills of ethical analysis. Employing Rush University's distinctive practitioner-teacher model and focusing on cases from the beginning, the program always keeps the relationship between theory and practice central to the curriculum.

The program can be completed in one year of full-time study or on a part-time basis. It equips graduates to provide ethical analysis of cases; recommend appropriate clinical or administrative interventions; develop or revise policies; educate staff members, patients, and families about ethical issues; provide informed public comment about current health-care issues; and identify and pursue issues that require formal research.

Students may enter the program concurrently with or after completing M.D., J.D., nursing, ministry, allied health, or non-health-care degrees.

Research Facilities

Facilities for research in health-care ethics include the Rush-Presbyterian–St. Luke's Medical Center's inpatient, outpatient, and home-care units and pertinent units of the Rush System for Health. Research opportunities include patient autonomy and advance directives, administrative ethics and administrative structures that foster the ethical responsibility of all people who care for patients, issues related to specific diagnoses, and genetics.

Financial Aid

Financial need is met through student and family resources, as well as loans and employment. A limited amount of scholarship assistance is available. The Student Financial Aid Office provides assistance for all admitted students in need so that Rush University can be a viable choice for all who desire to attend.

Cost of Study

In 1997–98, the tuition for the Program in Healthcare Ethics was $3960 per quarter for 12 or more quarter hours.

Living and Housing Costs

The student living on campus spends about $1020 per month for rent, food, transportation, and personal expenses. The student living off campus has expenses of $1300 per month. In addition, the estimated cost of books and supplies is $220 quarterly.

Student Group

Rush University enrolls about 500 graduate students. Fifty percent are full-time students; 5 percent are international students. Approximately 6 students are admitted each academic year in Healthcare Ethics.

Location

Rush University is located at Rush-Presbyterian–St. Luke's Medical Center on Chicago's Near West Side. Facilities on campus include the Presbyterian-St. Luke's Hospital, the Marshall Field outpatient mental health facility, a cancer center, research buildings, academic buildings, professional office buildings, apartment buildings, the Laurance Armour Day School, and the Johnston R. Bowman Health Center for the Elderly. The Medical Center, the University of Illinois at Chicago Health Sciences Center, Cook County Hospital, and Westside Veterans Administration Hospital constitute one of the largest medical center complexes in the world. Easily accessible are the Loop (downtown Chicago) and the western suburbs, both 15 minutes away. Lake Michigan, sports, and numerous cultural activities are available in the exciting Chicago area.

The University and The College

Rush University comprises the College of Nursing, the College of Health Sciences, the Graduate College, and Rush Medical College. Because the University believes that education of health professionals is best achieved in an institution committed to both education and service, all faculty members are practitioner-teachers. Rush University is part of a cooperative health-care delivery system that serves approximately 1.5 million people through its resources and those of affiliated health-care and academic institutions. Basic research and clinical investigation are an integral responsibility of each practitioner-teacher. Consequently, research in both traditional disciplines and multidisciplinary fields is emphasized.

Rush University College of Health Sciences was established in 1975. Its current elements are the Departments of Clinical Nutrition, Communicative Disorders and Sciences, Health Systems Management, Medical Physics, Medical Technology, Occupational Therapy, and Healthcare Ethics.

Applying

Each applicant must provide the admissions office with the following: a completed application, a $40 application fee, three recommendations, official transcripts of all undergraduate and graduate work, and results of the General Test of the Graduate Record Examinations.

Correspondence and Information

College Admission Services
Rush University
600 South Paulina, Suite 440
Chicago, Illinois 60612
Telephone: 312-942-7100
Fax: 312-942-2219

Rush University

THE FACULTY AND THEIR RESEARCH

Russell Burck, Ph.D. Advance directives, ethical issues in transplantation, withholding medical nutrition and hydration.
Laurel Arthur Burton, Ph.D. Narrative ethics; spirituality, health and ethics; organizational/business ethics.
Marcia Bosek, D.N.Sc. Ethical decision making, ethical issues in genetics, qualitative methods.
Christine Kennelly, M.S. Pediatric ethics.
Kristin Nelson, Ph.D. candidate. Virtue ethics, principalism.
Anthony J. Perry, M.D. Relationship between the physician's ethical norms and the physician's practice.
Mark Sheldon, Ph.D. Ethical issues in pediatrics, Jehovah's Witnesses and blood transfusion, physician-patient relationship, physician-assisted death.
Susan Zinner, M.B.A. Pediatric ethics, informed consent; consent/assent in children.

SOUTHWEST COLLEGE OF NATUROPATHIC MEDICINE AND HEALTH SCIENCES

Graduate Programs

Programs of Study

Southwest College offers two academic programs: a Doctor of Naturopathic Medicine (N.D.) program and an acupuncture program. The Doctor of Naturopathic Medicine program is a four-year graduate medical degree program that is taken in sixteen quarters. Upon completion of the graduation requirements, the student is awarded a Doctor of Naturopathic Medicine degree. Students are trained to become primary care physicians with a specialized focus in preventive medicine and natural therapeutics. Southwest College also offers an Evening N.D. Program for D.O.'s, M.D.'s, and D.C.'s.

Naturopathic medicine is a distinct system of medical health care: the art, science, and practice of diagnosing and treating people and preventing disease. Naturopathic physicians seek to restore and maintain optimal health. They can practice independently or with provider groups and may also become educators, authors, and researchers. Naturopathic medicine honors patients as unique human beings, enabling them to take responsibility for their own health. Naturopathic physicians are health coaches, providing evaluations and recommendations for patients who are committed to becoming healthier. They educate patients to optimize their lifestyles, to increase their immune function, and to decrease illness.

Research Facilities

The Southwest College Research Institute plays a vital role in the College's academic environment. The mission of the Institute is to serve the public by conducting and promoting research on natural therapies and natural medicines and by advancing knowledge of issues surrounding research in natural medicine. The Institute provides a full range of research and informational services to support experimental, developmental, and outcome research. The Institute provides assistance to students and faculty members in their research endeavors. Students may participate in studies that offer them opportunities to gain experience in testing protocols and practices and to fulfill required research competencies.

Financial Aid

Financial aid is available to students through Federal Stafford Student Loans and alternative loans, which help cover the cost of attendance. Students must complete the Free Application for Federal Student Aid (FAFSA) to have the School determine their eligibility. Alternative loans are based upon credit with a variable interest rate. A complete packet of financial aid information and forms is available in the Office of Financial Aid.

Cost of Study

Tuition for the N.D. program for the 1998–99 academic year is $16.15 per didactic contact hour and $170 per clinic shift. Total tuition and fees for a full-time student in the N.D. program average $14,500 per year. Books and supplies cost approximately $1200 per year.

Living and Housing Costs

Southwest College does not provide student housing. The Department of Recruitment and Admissions maintains a housing information board that is located in the main hall of campus. Students may also place ads for housing in the *Vital Force* (the college newspaper) or in the *Admissions Buzz* (the newsletter of the Department of Recruitment and Admissions). Information about available housing in the Tempe, Mesa, and Scottsdale areas may be obtained by contacting the Department of Recruitment and Admissions. Living expenses, including food, housing, and transportation, are estimated at $800 per month.

Student Group

Southwest College has an eclectic group of students who come from around the United States as well as international locations. Sixty-five percent of the students are women. The average age is 33. Southwest College currently has a student body of 265.

Location

The College is located in the health-oriented Southwest, which is ideally suited to exposing students to a wide variety of health-care alternatives. Southwest College is located only 5 miles from Arizona State University, the fifth-largest university in the nation. Known for its highly educated populace, Tempe is a sophisticated city and center for learning, culture, and technology. The academic and administrative campus is on a 7.6-acre site in Tempe, and the College medical center is located 5 miles north of campus in Scottsdale. Known as the "Valley of the Sun," the Phoenix area enjoys a multitude of sunshine year-round. The temperature in the winter months (November through February) averages 70°F; the average temperature is 87°F in the spring and fall. The summer months (June through August) tend to be warmer, with temperatures averaging 105°F.

Recreational activities include hiking, mountain biking, walking, golfing, skydiving, and tubing on the Salt River. Tempe residents are within 2 hours of the beautiful San Francisco Peaks of Flagstaff, Arizona, for those who desire skiing, winter sports, camping in the cool pines, or just the sight of snow. Arizona has its share of lakes and rivers, including Saguaro Lake, Roosevelt Lake, Lake Powell, and the Salt River.

The College

Southwest College was founded in 1993. The College's mission is to serve the public by providing education, health-care services, and research in the art and sciences of natural medicine based upon the principles and practices of naturopathic medicine. The vision of Southwest College is to be recognized as a leader in natural medicine through excellence and innovation in preparing successful naturopathic physicians and acupuncturists through quality health-care delivery, clinical research, publications for the health-care providers and the general public, and intense commitment to advancing natural medicine and health sciences. The College is a candidate for accreditation with the Council on Naturopathic Medical Education (CNME), a specialized accreditor recognized by the United States Department of Education.

Application

Applicants are considered on the basis of academic performance, occupational history, professional potential, level of maturity, concern for others, and previous experience with and knowledge of natural medicine. Accepted students should possess communication skills, an ability to establish positive relationships, and maturity and integrity and must demonstrate a commitment to naturopathic or Oriental medicine. Prospective students must complete and submit an application, a $65 nonrefundable application fee, three letters of recommendation (academic, occupational, and health care/personal), official transcripts from each postsecondary institution attended, and a demographic survey. Academically, applicants must have completed a bachelor's degree at an accredited or candidate college or university with a minimum GPA of 2.5 in all postsecondary work, including the following prerequisite courses with a minimum GPA of 3.0: 6 semester credits of English, 6 semester credits of humanities, 6 semester credits of psychology, 8 semester credits of general biology, 4 semester credits of anatomy and physiology, 3 semester credits of botany, 8 semester credits of general chemistry, and 4 semester credits of organic chemistry. Southwest College accepts applications on a rolling basis. Applications are accepted as early as March for spring admission the following year and September for fall admission the following year. Deadlines for application are February 1 for the March class and July 1 for the fall class.

Correspondence and Information

Department of Recruitment and Admissions
Southwest College of Naturopathic Medicine and Health Sciences
2140 East Broadway Road
Tempe, Arizona 85282

Telephone: 602-858-9100
World Wide Web: http://www.scnm.edu

Southwest College of Naturopathic Medicine and Health Sciences

THE FACULTY

Larry Abel, Associate Professor and Supervising Physician; N.D., National College of Naturopathic Medicine, 1986.
Ruth Bar-Shalom, Instructor; N.D., National College of Naturopathic Medicine, 1987.
Ian D. Bier, Assistant Professor; Dean, School of Acupuncture; Chair, Department of Acupuncture and Oriental Medicine; and Supervising Physician; N.D., Bastyr, 1995.
Francis Brinker, Instructor; N.D., National College of Naturopathic Medicine, 1981.
Sherry Briskey, Instructor and Supervising Physician; N.D., National College of Naturopathic Medicine, 1994.
Nick Buratovich, Associate Professor and Chair, Physical Medicine Department; N.D., National College of Naturopathic Medicine, 1981.
Tim Callahan, Instructor; M.A., Washington (Seattle), 1993.
Alan Christianson, Instructor; N.D., Southwest College of Naturopathic Medicine and Health Sciences, 1996.
Michael Cohn, Instructor; Ed.D., Ball State, 1979.
Walter Crinnion, Instructor; N.D., Bastyr, 1982.
Yong Deng, Endowed Chair (Gero-Vita); M.D., Chengdu University of TCM (China), 1983.
Gary Dreger, Instructor and Supervising Physician; N.D., National College of Naturopathic Medicine, 1986; M.Ac.O.M., Oregon College of Oriental Medicine, 1995.
John Dye, Associate Professor; N.D., National College of Naturopathic Medicine, 1979.
Janis Gruska, Assistant Professor; N.D., National College of Naturopathic Medicine, 1991.
Myra Harris, Instructor; J.D., Arizona State, 1996.
Meizhen Hou, Instructor; Certificate of Acupuncture and Moxibusition, Tianjim College of Traditional Medicine, 1991.
Susan Hua Luo, Instructor; bachelor's degree, Beijing University of Traditional Chinese Medical Sciences, 1979.
Paul Karsten, Instructor; Ph.D., Samra University of Oriental Medicine, 1985.
Dana Keaton, Chair, Nutrition Department; N.D., National College of Naturopathic Medicine, 1989.
Richard Laherty, Associate Professor; Ph.D., Berkeley, 1978.
Kathryn Leyva, Assistant Professor; Ph.D., Northern Arizona, 1996.
Cesar Linan, Assistant Professor; M.D., San Marcos (Peru), 1996.
Claudio Lind, Instructor; M.D., Vienna, 1986.
Heather Luper, Instructor and Supervising Acupuncturist; L.Ac., Oregon College of Oriental Medicine, 1993.
Scott Luper, Associate Professor, Supervising Physician, and Chair, Department of Diagnostics; N.D., National College of Naturopathic Medicine, 1994.
Bill Mitchell, Instructor; N.D., National College of Naturopathic Medicine, 1976.
Paul Mittman, Chair, Homeopathy Department; N.D., National College of Naturopathic Medicine, 1985.
Robert Myers, Instructor; N.D., National College of Naturopathic Medicine, 1971.
Kareen O'Brien, Instructor and Dean of the School of Naturopathic Medicine; N.D., Bastyr, 1993.
Terry Oleson, Instructor; Ph.D., California, Irvine, 1973.
Kenneth Proefrock, Instructor; N.D., Southwest College of Naturopathic Medicine and Health Sciences, 1996.
Thomas Reece, Medical Director and Supervising Physician; D.O., Kirksville College of Osteopathic Medicine, 1990.
Michael S. Reed, Instructor; D.C., Columbia University of Chiropractic, 1971; FACC, FICC.
Bruce Sadilek, Instructor; N.D., Southwest College of Naturopathic Medicine and Health Sciences, 1997.
Andre Saine, Instructor; N.D., National College of Naturopathic Medicine, 1982; diplomate of the Homeopathic Academy of Naturopathic Physicians, 1988.
Chad Schroer, Instructor; N.D., National College of Naturopathic Medicine, 1993.
James Sensenig, Instructor; N.D., National College of Naturopathic Medicine, 1979.
Farra Swan, Instructor; N.D., Bastyr, 1982.
Alda Vicente, Assistant Instructor; M.D., Rio de Janeiro, 1977; FTE.
Robert Waters, Associate Professor and Chair, Research Department; Ph.D., Montana State, 1975.

CURRENT RESEARCH THROUGH THE SOUTHWEST COLLEGE RESEARCH INSTITUTE

The Effect of L-Carnitine on Weight, BMI and Body Fat Percentage
A Controlled Trial of Pregnenolone for Premenstrual Syndrome (data currently being analyzed)
Acupuncture in Smoking Cessation: A Randomized Placebo-Controlled Trial (three-year study in second year)
A Protocol for the Investigation of the Effect of a Thymic Extract on the Course of Infections with HIV-1 (data currently being analyzed)
A Controlled Trial of the Effects of Vitamin-Mineral Supplementation on the Intelligence, Academic Performance and Behavior of American School Children (paper submitted for publication)
Demographic and Clinical Outcomes of Naturopathic Patients: A Study of Patients Treated at the Southwest Naturopathic Medical Center
The Tolerability and Efficacy of Echinaguard Juice on Children with Recurring Upper-Respiratory Infections

UNIVERSITY OF BRIDGEPORT

College of Naturopathic Medicine

Program of Study

The University of Bridgeport College of Naturopathic Medicine offers an intensive program of professional education leading to the Doctor of Naturopathic Medicine (N.D.) degree. Naturopathic medicine is grounded in the vitalistic tradition of medicine, which emphasizes wellness and the treatment of disease through the restoration of health. The program is a full-time course of study of four academic years (eight semesters), including clinical training.

During the first two years, studies include the foundation medical sciences such as anatomy, embryology, histology, microbiology, immunology, public health, biochemistry, pathology, and laboratory and clinical diagnosis. The second two years are devoted to the clinical sciences such as botanical medicine, therapeutic nutrition, homeopathy, physical medicine, cardiology, gynecology, pediatrics, gastroenterology, and therapeutic exercise. During these two years, students receive clinical training under the supervision of licensed naturopathic physicians in the College's teaching facilities. In addition to the traditional didactic and clinical training in naturopathic medicine, a thesis is required for graduation.

The goal of the College is to provide the education and clinical training necessary to produce highly qualified, competent, and caring doctors of natural medicine.

This is a new program at the University, licensed by the state in December 1996. The inaugural class began the degree program in the fall 1997 semester. Subsequent classes will be admitted for each spring and fall semester thereafter.

Research Facilities

Medical research at the College is facilitated by the use of audiovisual formats, MEDLINE, and LEXIS-NEXIS and is complemented by institutionally integrated library holdings of basic and clinical science texts, periodicals, and microfiche collections. Computer-assisted research terminals, available to faculty members and students, are located in the College and the University library.

Financial Aid

The Office of Financial Aid provides financial assistance to students enrolled in programs offered by the University of Bridgeport. Financial aid for students enrolled in the College of Naturopathic Medicine is available in the form of student loans, work-study, and payment plans. Additional information pertaining to financial aid can be obtained by calling 203-576-4568.

Cost of Study

In academic year 1998–99, tuition is $6400 per semester. The estimated cost of textbooks, equipment, and fees is approximately $1200 per semester. The program is offered only on a full-time basis, two semesters per year (August through December and January through May).

Living and Housing Costs

Graduate students may reside in University on-campus residence halls. Off-campus housing in the surrounding area is also available. Information pertaining to housing can be obtained from the Office of Residence Life at 203-576-4395.

Student Group

The 1997–98 academic year marked the inauguration of the N.D. degree program at the University of Bridgeport. Class size for both the fall and spring semesters is between 20 and 30 students. Typical of naturopathic programs is a class consisting of slightly more women than men, with a mean age in the low thirties.

Student Outcomes

Doctors of naturopathic medicine are typically involved in general private practice. Increasing opportunities are available in teaching, research, writing, and publishing.

Location

The University of Bridgeport is located in an urban setting in Fairfield County, Connecticut, 1 hour from New York City and 3 hours from Boston. Bridgeport, the state's largest city, borders the 86-acre campus to the north. The southern border of the campus is adjacent to Seaside Park on Long Island Sound.

The University

Founded in 1927, the University of Bridgeport is a private, nonsectarian, coeducational, comprehensive, urban university. The University's campus is composed of buildings of diverse architectural styles. The Arnold Bernhard Arts and Humanities Center is a cultural hub, and the Wheeler Recreation Center is a complete recreation and physical fitness facility.

Applying

Students applying to the College of Naturopathic Medicine should submit a completed application, application fee, and official transcripts of undergraduate course work to the Office of Admissions. Admission requirements include a bachelor's degree with a minimum cumulative GPA of 2.5. The following courses must be included: 6 hours of communication/language skills; 3 hours of psychology; 3 hours of social science; 3 hours of humanities; 9 hours of electives in social sciences and/or humanities; 6 hours of general biology, zoology, or anatomy and physiology; 6 hours of general chemistry; 6 hours of organic chemistry; and 6 hours of physics. Each of the science courses must include a laboratory, must be passed with a grade of C or better, and must be a course offered for science majors. A minimum grade point average of 2.5 is required in the science prerequisites. A minimum GPA of 3.0 in science courses is preferred.

Correspondence and Information

University of Bridgeport
College of Naturopathic Medicine
221 University Avenue
Bridgeport, Connecticut 06601
Telephone: 203-576-4109
800-EXCEL-UB (392-3582) (toll-free)
Fax: 203-576-4107
E-mail: natmed@bridgeport.edu
World Wide Web: http://www.bridgeport.edu

University of Bridgeport

THE FACULTY

A partial listing of appointed faculty members is as follows.

Ron Hobbs, Dean; N.D., Bastyr, 1984.

Paul Epstein, Adjunct Associate Professor; N.D., National College of Naturopathic Medicine, 1984. Mind-body medicine.
Rose Galiger, Professor; Ph.D., Rutgers, 1971. Histology, immunology.
Peter Galton, Professor; Ph.D., 1967, D.Sc., 1983, London. Anatomy, anatomy dissection.
Leena Guptha, Adjunct Assistant Professor; N.D., D.O., 1990, Lic.Ac., 1992, British College of Naturopathy and Osteopathy. Physical medicine.
Ahmed Kahn, Assistant Professor; M.B.B.S., Karachi (Pakistan), 1969. Pathology.
Edward O'Connor, Assistant Professor; Ph.D., Albany Medical College, 1992. Physiology and research.
Jeddeo Paul, Professor; Ph.D., Birmingham (England), 1958. Biochemistry.
Donna Marie Peano, Adjunct Professor; D.C., New York Chiropractic, 1994. Palpation, biomechanics.
Stephen Perle, Assistant Professor; D.C., Texas Chiropractic, 1983. Research methodology.
Nuggehali Raghuvir, Professor; Ph.D., Utah, 1962. Embryology.
Jinnque Rho, Professor; Ph.D., Massachusetts, 1972. Microbiology, public health.
Anthony Ross Jr., Adjunct Professor; Ph.D., SUNY at Stony Brook, 1987. Embryology.
Sharon Sawitzke, Assistant Professor; Ph.D., CUNY, Hunter, 1994. Embryology.
James S. Sensenig, Professor; N.D., National College of Naturopathic Medicine, 1978. History, philosophy.
Karen Shields, Adjunct Professor; D.C., New York Chiropractic, 1980. Communication skills.

UNIVERSITY OF HEALTH SCIENCES

College of Osteopathic Medicine

Program of Study

The four-year medical program at the University of Health Sciences College of Osteopathic Medicine (UHS-COM) leads to the Doctor of Osteopathic Medicine (D.O.) degree. Students spend the first two years in classroom and lab studies and the second two years in clinical rotations in hospitals and clinics across the country. Years one and two include gross anatomy, biochemistry, histology, physiology, neuroanatomy, immunology, radiology, physical diagnosis, medical ethics, sports medicine, medical jurisprudence, human sexuality, microbiology, pharmacology, pathology, psychiatry, obstetrics, gynecology, pediatrics, osteopathic diagnosis and treatment, family medicine, internal medicine, cardiovascular medicine, gerontology, neurology, oncology, emergency medicine, surgery, ophthalmology, otorhinolaryngology, anesthesiology, and a primary care practicum. Years three and four include twenty-two clinical rotations, three months of which are required to be in an ambulatory care, rural clinic setting.

Research Facilities

Alumni Hall houses sixty-one networked state-of-the-art computer study rooms and three computer-supported audiovisual rooms. The library, basic science labs, and research facilities moved to newly constructed areas in a 96,000-square-foot Educational Pavilion in 1996. The library, with 3 professional medical librarians and 4 support staff members, subscribes to 230 periodicals and 185 serial titles and has a collection of nearly 54,000 book volumes and 24,000 bound periodicals. Its media services support the autotutorial curriculum approach and CME/GME with a collection of more than 7,400 titles. There is worldwide access to collections of libraries that catalog via the On-line Computer Library Center. DATA TREK On-Line Cataloging System and the CD-ROM Literature Search System are networked across campus. CD-ROM literature searches can access bibliographic and full-text databases. Biomedical information is searched and retrieved from more than 500 online databases through the National Library of Medicine, Dialog, and BRS. Databases include MEDLINE, ERIC, CANCERLIT, TOXLINE, HEALTHLINE, AVLINE, and others.

Financial Aid

Detailed information on financial aid in the form of loans, scholarships, grants, and fellowships is available from the Office of Financial Aid. There are certain special loan programs available for UHS-COM medical students. The primary sources are the Subsidized Stafford and Unsubsidized Stafford Loan programs.

Cost of Study

For 1997–98, tuition was $23,310. Books, instruments, and fees totaled $2550. Approximate living expenses totaled $12,300.

Living and Housing Costs

Kansas City enjoys a moderate cost of living. Affordable housing and employment opportunities for spouses and significant others are more easily found in Kansas City than in most U.S. cities its size. A UHS-COM student budget for each year has been established at the following levels: first year, $38,160; second year, $40,170; third year, $34,320; and fourth year, $39,800. These figures include living and educational expenses.

Student Group

There are approximately 800 full-time osteopathic medical students enrolled at UHS-COM. They come from nearly every state and several other countries. Women comprise nearly 30 percent of the student body. Members of minority groups make up 4 percent of the student body.

Student Outcomes

Traditionally, two thirds of the graduates enter the field of primary care.

Location

UHS-COM is located approximately 1 mile northeast of downtown Kansas City, Missouri, in a historic section of the city that is undergoing revitalization. It is easily accessible by interstate highways that also connect the campus to the suburbs of the metropolitan area.

The University and The College

Major renovations and new construction projects have recently been completed on campus. A 96,000-square-foot Educational Pavilion was finished in 1996. It houses the campus library, a 225-seat theater-style classroom, basic science labs, faculty offices, osteopathic treatment labs, research facilities, a sports medicine complex, meeting rooms, and the campus cafeteria.

The UHS College of Osteopathic Medicine is accredited by the Bureau of Professional Education of the American Osteopathic Association (AOA). The AOA is the only accrediting agency for osteopathic medicine approved by the United States Department of Education and by the Council of Post-Secondary Accreditation. UHS-COM also is approved by the Board of Education of the State of Missouri as an educational institution offering education and training to veterans.

Applying

From June 1 to February 1, UHS-COM participates in a centralized application processing service known as the American Association of Colleges of Osteopathic Medicine Application Service (AACOMAS). AACOMAS gathers all the necessary material on each applicant and transmits the information in a standardized format to the college(s) that the applicant chooses. Applicants may either obtain application request cards directly from UHS-COM or obtain an application directly from AACOMAS (5550 Friendship Boulevard, Suite 310, Chevy Chase, Maryland 20815-7231; telephone: 301-968-4100). The AACOMAS deadline is February 1. UHS-COM accepts supplemental applications until the class is considered full.

The University gives consideration to all applicants for admission and for financial aid without respect to sex, race, handicap, color, creed, or ethnic origin. University policies are nondiscriminatory. Applicants to the college are considered on their intellectual ability, scholastic achievement, commitment, and suitability to succeed in the study of osteopathic medicine. Minimum academic requirements for admission to the first-year class include a baccalaureate degree or commendable completion of at least three fourths (90 semester hours or 135 term credit hours) of the required credits for a baccalaureate degree from a regionally accredited college or university, Medical College Admissions Test (MCAT) scores, and satisfactory completion of the following college courses, including laboratory work: English composition and literature (6 semester hours), general chemistry (8 semester hours), organic chemistry (8 semester hours, 4 semester hours of which may be biochemistry), physics (8 semester hours), and biological sciences (12 semester hours). The ability to use a personal or network computer has become an integral part of the UHS-COM curriculum and is becoming a clinical necessity. Therefore, it is strongly recommended that each entering student have a good working knowledge of common PC use and applications. Applicants are strongly advised to provide evidence of a solid foundation and to demonstrate proficiency in the biological and physical sciences. They are expected to have studied comparative vertebrate anatomy, genetics, bacteriology, and mathematics. Furthermore, they are encouraged to have taken courses in sociology, philosophy, and psychology.

Correspondence and Information

College of Osteopathic Medicine
University of Health Sciences
1750 Independence Boulevard
Kansas City, Missouri 64106-1453

Telephone: 816-283-2000
800-234-4UHS (toll-free)

University of Health Sciences

THE FACULTY

Professors

J. Lewis Alderman, Ph.D., Professor of Physiology and of Pharmacology.
Robert E. Arnold, D.O., Professor of Surgery.
Mary L. Butterworth, D.O., Professor of Anesthesiology.
Anthony Dekker, D.O., Professor of Family Medicine.
Donald L. McCandless, Ph.D., Professor of Pharmacology.
Michael M. Patterson, Ph.D., Professor of Osteopathic Principles and Practice and of Physiology.
James W. Phillips, Ph.D., Professor of Biochemistry.
Douglas R. Rushing, Ph.D., Professor of Biochemistry.
Anthony J. Silvagni, Pharm.D., D.O., Professor of Clinical Pharmacology and of Family Medicine.
Robert E. Stephens, Ph.D., Professor of Anatomy.
Warren W. Tuttle, Ph.D., Professor of Pharmacology.

Associate Professors

Gary O. Ballam, Ph.D., Associate Professor of Physiology.
William G. Brooks, D.O., Associate Professor of Osteopathic Principles and Practice.
Bonnie Buxton, Ph.D., Associate Professor of Microbiology.
Nehad I. El-Sawi, Ph.D., Associate Professor of Microbiology.
Janice D. Grebe, Ph.D., Associate Professor of Anatomy.
Edward R. Friedlander, M.D., Associate Professor of Pathology.
Lauritz A. Jensen, D.A., Associate Professor of Microbiology.
Callis G. Morrill, Ph.D., Associate Professor of Physiology.
Larry W. Segars, Pharm.D., Associate Professor of Pharmacology.
Norbert W. Seidler, Ph.D., Associate Professor of Biochemistry.
Kenneth J. Steier, D.O., Associate Professor of Internal Medicine.
Pamela Thomas, Ph.D., Associate Professor of Anatomy.
Elaine M. Wallace, D.O., Associate Professor of Osteopathic Principles and Practice and of Family Medicine.

Assistant Professors

Lori Boyajian, D.O., Assistant Professor of Family Medicine.
James M. Carl, D.O., Assistant Professor of Pediatrics.
Maria Cole, Ph.D., Assistant Professor of Anatomy.
V. James Guillory, D.O., Assistant Professor of Preventive Medicine.
Dale Pratt Harrington, D.O., Assistant Professor of Family Medicine.
John G. Horton, D.O., Assistant Professor of Family Medicine.
Diane R. Karius, Ph.D., Assistant Professor of Physiology.
David McWhorter, Ph.D., Assistant Professor of Anatomy.
Bruce B. Peters, D.O., Assistant Professor of Pediatrics.
Kevin D. Treffer, D.O., Assistant Professor of Osteopathic Principles and Practice.

Instructor

Donald L. Weaver, M.A., Instructor of Family Medicine.

UNIVERSITY OF OSTEOPATHIC MEDICINE AND HEALTH SCIENCES

College of Podiatric Medicine and Surgery

Program of Study

The College of Podiatric Medicine and Surgery was established in 1981 and offers a four-year curriculum of podiatric medical education leading to the Doctor of Podiatric Medicine (D.P.M.) degree. The fully accredited program is in the only school of podiatric medicine in the nation that is part of a health sciences university. The University offers an unusual opportunity for the podiatric medical profession and students to focus on the delivery of podiatric medical services as one phase of total health care.

Students complete an innovative core of basic science instruction followed by full-time modules studying each organ system in the second year. This reflects the interrelationship and interdependence of body structure and function. Clinical correlations relate each organ system to medical and podiatric practice.

Problem-based learning is provided in the third year with groups of 6–8 students assigned for six-week periods to full-time faculty throughout the year. Clinical experiences are integrated in each of these several time periods directed by these faculty. Developing patient-management skills is emphasized in hospitals, rural and urban ambulatory clinics, long-term-care facilities, and community practice. First-year students also receive physical diagnosis training in the Standardized Patient Assessment Laboratory, which uses live, scripted patients to assess students. In the fourth year, students are assigned to affiliated major medical centers throughout the nation for core hospital rotations of at least four months.

Research Facilities

The University maintains well-equipped research laboratories. Current research is conducted in gait analysis and sports medicine. A ten-story multispecialty interdisciplinary medical clinic houses outpatient surgery, a 1,500-seat continuing education center, and additional clinical facilities on campus.

Financial Aid

The University of Osteopathic Medicine and Health Sciences maintains an Office of Financial Aid to assist students with financial needs through employment programs, scholarships, and loans. The office also offers financial counseling. Students who seek financial aid must complete the Financial Aid Form from the University Office of Financial Aid. A number of scholarships also are available for academically superior students.

Cost of Study

Tuition for the 1998–99 academic year is $19,760. Books, supplies, and the estimated cost of instruments total $3600.

Living and Housing Costs

Estimated living expenses for a first-year student for the 1997–98 year were $11,790. This estimate covers rent ($480 per month), utilities, telephone, food, personal expenses, clothing, transportation (car payments, operation, insurance), and life, health, and renter's insurance. Married students with no dependents should expect to pay an additional $175 for living expenses. Most of the University's students live close enough to walk to campus.

Student Group

The College has approximately 240 full-time students. In 1997–98, students enrolled from twenty-seven states. The University has approximately 1,300 students.

Student Outcomes

More than 90 percent of graduates go on to postgraduate training in the areas of surgery, primary care, or biomechanics.

Location

Metropolitan Des Moines features more than 2,600 acres of public parks and lakes for hiking, fishing, and water and cross-country skiing. City life is enhanced by a botanical center; an art museum; a center for science and industry; a civic center; Living History Farms; superb restaurants; and Big Eight, Big Ten, Missouri Valley Conference sporting events, and Triple A baseball. Iowans are proud of their reputation for having the finest educational system and one of the highest literacy rates in the nation.

The College

The history of the College of Podiatric Medicine and Surgery reflects a commitment to teaching, learning, and serving. Its goals are to provide education that will ensure development of competent doctors of podiatric medicine, to contribute to the accumulation of knowledge and the development of podiatric medicine through research, to create opportunities for podiatrists as teachers and investigators, and to provide podiatric care coordinated with total, holistic care delivery. An emphasis on serving the podiatric health needs of rural America is provided.

Applying

The College participates in the American Association of Colleges of Podiatric Medicine Application Service (AACPMAS) and considers applicants who apply through that service from July 1 to June 1. Requests for application materials should be directed to AACPMAS, 1350 Piccard Drive, Suite 322, Rockville, Maryland 20850-4307. Admission decisions are based on educational background, as reflected in official transcripts; performance on the Medical College Admission Test (required); letters of recommendation; and a personal interview.

Entering students must have completed 90 semester hours (135 quarter hours) of accredited undergraduate study. Most applicants hold a bachelor's degree. Preprofessional college credits must include 6 semester (9 quarter) hours of English or language arts, 8 semester (12 quarter) hours of general biology or zoology, 8 semester (12 quarter) hours of general chemistry, 8 semester (12 quarter) hours of organic chemistry, and 8 semester (12 quarter) hours of physics. Science prerequisites must include laboratory work where applicable. Nonscience majors are encouraged to apply if they meet the prerequisites.

Correspondence and Information

College of Podiatric Medicine and Surgery
University of Osteopathic Medicine
and Health Sciences
3200 Grand Avenue
Des Moines, Iowa 50312
Telephone: 515-271-1488
800-240-CPMS (toll-free outside Iowa)

University of Osteopathic Medicine and Health Sciences

THE FACULTY

Anatomy
Craig Canby, Ph.D.; William J. Dyche, Ph.D.; Makhdoom Ali Khan, Ph.D.; Frank M. Kneussl, Ph.D.; Priti S. Lacy, Ph.D.; D. Matz, Ph.D.; Gerald D. Meetz, Ph.D.; Maria Patestas, Ph.D.; Ann Valder, Ph.D.

Behavioral Science
David Drake, D.O.; Rebecca Monsma, M.S.W., LSW.

Biochemistry
Thomas Breithaupt, Ph.D.; Edward Burt, Ph.D.; Diane C. Hills, Ph.D.; Joan M. Mahoney, Ph.D.; Thomas Mueller, Ph.D.; David Spreadbury, Ph.D.

Family Practice
Eric A. Ravitz, D.O.; Karin Ravitz, D.O.; Fred W. Strickland Jr., M.A., D.O.

Internal Medicine
Gary Hoff, D.O.; Victor Kaylarian, D.O.

Microbiology
James C. Johnson, Ph.D.; Bryan Larsen, Ph.D; Thomas Mueller, Ph.D.; Terry F. Simpson, M.S.; Musau WaKabongo, Ph.D.

Ophthalmology
George B. Clavenna, D.O.

Osteopathic Manipulative Medicine
David R. Boesler, D.O.

Pathology
Roche P. Ramos, M.D., FCAP; Karuna Sayeed, M.D.

Pediatrics
William Salow, D.O.

Physical Therapy
Susan Bravard, PT; Terri Casey, PT; M. Susan Cigelman, Ed.D., PT; Steven R. Clark, PT; Susan J. Robel, PT; Katherine L. Mercuris, M.A., PT; Teri Stumbo, M.H.A., PT; Joseph Weir, PT; Tim Zipple, PT.

Physician Assistant Program
Jodi L. Cahalan, PA-C; William Case, PA-C; Dan Chambers, PA-C; Pam Chambers, PA-C; Barry Fish, PA-C; Gregory Kolbinger, PA-C.

Physiology/Pharmacology
Daniel R. Deavers, Ph.D.; Edward P. Finnerty, Ph.D.; Mearl A. Kilmore, Ph.D.; Adeeb B. Makar, Ph.D.; J. Matz, Ph.D.; Richard McCabe, Ph.D.; L. Mortensen, Ph.D.; Nancy A. O'Connell, Ph.D.; Wayne H. Terry, Ph.D.

Podiatric Medicine
Denise Freeman, D.P.M.; David Jenkins, D.P.M.; Ronald E. Johnson, D.P.M.; Elizabeth Loverso, D.P.M.; Kathleen Satterfield, D.P.M.; Jeffrey Siegel, D.P.M.; Robert Yoho, D.P.M.

Radiology
John Agnew, D.O.

Surgery
Kendall Reed, D.O., FACOS; Mehrunnisa Sultan, M.D.

Other Disciplines
Larry Marquardt, M.Ed., M.L.S., Librarian; Walter Milne, M.S.Ed., Audiovisual Services; Mary Pat Wohlford-Wessels, M.S., RRA, Health Care Administration Program.

Students in the College of Podiatric Medicine and Surgery receive part of their clinical training at the on-campus Tower Medical Clinic.

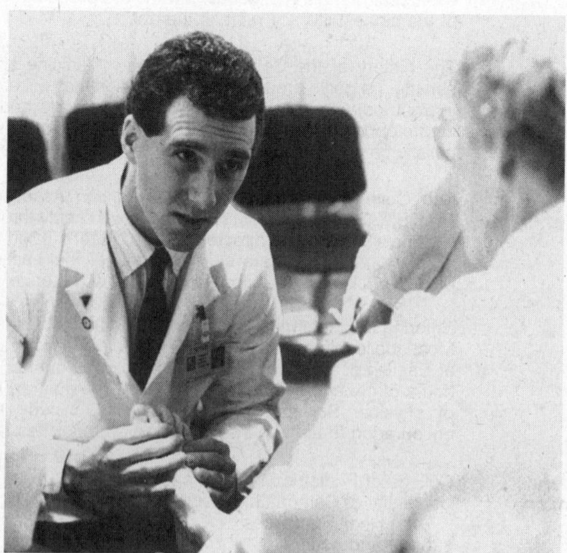

Podiatric doctors are trained to care for foot problems common to older adults.

Section 36
Optometry and Vision Sciences

This section contains directories of institutions offering professional programs in optometry and graduate studies in vision sciences, followed by in-depth entries submitted by institutions that chose to prepare detailed program descriptions. Additional information about programs listed in the directories but not augmented by an in-depth entry may be obtained by writing directly to the dean of a school or chair of a department at the address given in the directory.

For programs offering related work, see in Book 2 Psychology and Counseling; in Book 3, Biological and Biomedical Sciences, Biophysics, Neuroscience, and Physiology; in Book 4, Physics; and in Book 5, Bioengineering, Biomedical Engineering, and Biotechnology.

CONTENTS

Program Directories

Announcements

Cross-Discipline Announcement

In-Depth Descriptions

Optometry

Ferris State University, College of Optometry, Big Rapids, MI 49307-2742. Awards OD. Accredited by AOA. Faculty: 20 full-time, 16 part-time. Students: 126 full-time (75 women); includes 6 minority (5 Asian Americans, 1 Hispanic), 17 international. Average age 23. 242 applicants, 13% accepted. In 1997, 33 degrees awarded. *Entrance requirements:* OAT. Application deadline: 2/1 (rolling processing). Application fee: $20. *Expenses:* Tuition $220 per credit hour for state residents; $450 per credit hour for nonresidents. Fees $100 per year. *Financial aid:* Federal Work-Study and career-related internships or fieldwork available. Financial aid application deadline: 4/1. • Dr. Alan Lewis, Dean, 616-592-3706. Application contact: Dr. Thomas R. Colladay, Associate Dean, 616-592-3703.

Illinois College of Optometry, Chicago, IL 60616-3816. Awards OD, OD/PhD. Programs in biological sciences (OD/PhD), vision sciences (OD/PhD). Accredited by AOA. OD/PhD (biological sciences) offered jointly with Boston University. OD/PhD offered jointly with the University of Chicago. OD/PhD (vision sciences) new for fall 1998. Faculty: 56 full-time (26 women), 28 part-time (7 women). Students: 621 full-time (291 women); includes 136 minority (6 African Americans, 118 Asian Americans, 11 Hispanics, 1 Native American), 36 international. Average age 24. 855 applicants, 34% accepted. In 1997, 137 degrees awarded. *Average time to degree:* first professional–4 years full-time. *Entrance requirements:* OAT. Application deadline: 4/15 (priority date). Application fee: $50. *Financial aid:* In 1997–98, 545 students received aid, including 28 scholarships (5 to first-year students) totaling $241,000; Federal Work-Study and career-related internships or fieldwork also available. Aid available to part-time students. Financial aid application deadline: 3/15; applicants required to submit FAFSA. *Faculty research:* Eye disease treatment, binocular vision, geriatric care, sports vision, pediatric vision. • Dr. Charles Mullen, President, 312-949-7701. Application contact: Dr. Mark Colip, Dean for Student Affairs, 312-949-7680.

Indiana University Bloomington, School of Optometry, Professional Programs in Optometry, Bloomington, IN 47405. Awards OD. Accredited by AOA. Students: 237 full-time (118 women), 53 part-time (28 women); includes 20 minority (4 African Americans, 12 Asian Americans, 3 Hispanics, 1 Native American), 26 international. In 1997, 67 degrees awarded. *Entrance requirements:* OAT. Application deadline: 1/1 (priority date; rolling processing). Application fee: $30 ($35 for international students). *Expenses:* Tuition $186 per credit hour for state residents; $515 per credit hour for nonresidents. Fees $343 per year. *Financial aid:* Fellowships, research assistantships, teaching assistantships, scholarships, Federal Work-Study available. Aid available to part-time students. Financial aid application deadline: 3/1. *Faculty research:* Glaucoma, myopia, corneal physiology and pathology, epidemiology of vision disorders. Total annual research expenditures: $362,783. • Application contact: Jacqueline S. Olson, Coordinator of Students Affairs, 812-855-1917. Fax: 812-855-8664. E-mail: iubopt@indiana.edu.

Inter American University of Puerto Rico, Metropolitan Campus, School of Optometry, San Juan, PR 00936. Awards OD. Accredited by AOA. Faculty: 15 full-time (5 women), 29 part-time (13 women). Students: 137 full-time (91 women), 11 part-time (5 women); includes 142 minority (2 Asian Americans, 134 Hispanics, 6 Native Americans), 6 international. Average age 22. 90 applicants, 44% accepted. In 1997, 28 degrees awarded. *Degree requirements:* Thesis. *Entrance requirements:* OAT, interview. Application fee: $25. *Financial aid:* In 1997–98, 1 fellowship was awarded. • Dr. Hector Santiago, Dean. Application contact: Antonia Sanchez, Director of Student Services, 787-765-1915. Fax: 787-767-3920. E-mail: anrviera@ns.inter.edu.

New England College of Optometry, Boston, MA 02115-1100. Awards OD. Accredited by AOA. Faculty: 29 full-time (7 women), 55 part-time (12 women). Students: 414 full-time (238 women); includes 128 minority (19 African Americans, 93 Asian Americans, 15 Hispanics, 1 Native American), 69 international. Average age 25. 864 applicants, 22% accepted. In 1997, 102 degrees awarded. *Entrance requirements:* OAT, minimum GPA of 2.5. Application deadline: 3/31. Application fee: $75. *Expenses:* Tuition $21,600 per year. Fees $400 per year. *Financial aid:* In 1997–98, 2 fellowships were awarded; Federal Work-Study, institutionally sponsored loans, and career-related internships or fieldwork also available. Financial aid application deadline: 4/1. • Application contact: Lawrence Shattuck, Director of Admissions, 617-236-6210.

Announcement: The New England College of Optometry offers 3 programs of study leading to the Doctor of Optometry degree. The standard 4-year program is for applicants who hold a baccalaureate degree or who have completed a minimum of 3 years of specific undergraduate course work. There are an accelerated 27-month program for applicants holding a doctoral degree in science and an advanced-placement International Program for those who have earned a degree in optometry from a recognized international school of optometry. The College also offers postgraduate residency and fellowship programs in specialized areas of optometry.

Northeastern State University, College of Optometry, Tahlequah, OK 74464-2399. Awards OD. Accredited by AOA. Applicants must be residents of Oklahoma, Arkansas, Kansas, Colorado, or New Mexico. Faculty: 18 full-time (4 women), 8 part-time (4 women). Students: 94 full-time (44 women); includes 13 minority (1 African American, 2 Asian Americans, 3 Hispanics, 7 Native Americans). Average age 26. 102 applicants, 24% accepted. In 1997, 21 degrees awarded (96% found work related to degree, 4% continued full-time study). *Degree requirements:* Research project required, foreign language and thesis not required. *Entrance requirements:* OAT. Application deadline: 2/1. Application fee: $15. *Expenses:* Tuition $4682 per year for state residents; $11,110 per year for nonresidents. Fees $400 per year. *Financial aid:* In 1997–98, 5 residencies were awarded; full and partial tuition waivers, Federal Work-Study, institutionally sponsored loans also available. Financial aid application deadline: 3/1. *Faculty research:* Extended-wear and bifocal contact lenses, methods of vision therapy, glaucoma, low vision, diabetes. • Dr. Bill Monaco, Dean, 918-456-5511 Ext. 4000. Application contact: Mary Stratton, Director of Admissions, 918-456-5511 Ext. 4000.

Nova Southeastern University, Health Professions Division, College of Optometry, Fort Lauderdale, FL 33314-7721. Awards OD. Accredited by AOA. Students: 406 full-time (184 women); includes 155 minority (11 African Americans, 106 Asian Americans, 37 Hispanics, 1 Native American), 20 international. Average age 26. In 1997, 83 degrees awarded. *Average time to degree:* first professional–4 years full-time. *Entrance requirements:* OAT, minimum GPA of 2.5. Application deadline: 4/1 (rolling processing). Application fee: $50. *Expenses:* Tuition $14,900 per year for state residents; $18,900 per year for nonresidents. Fees $100 per year. *Financial aid:* Scholarships, Federal Work-Study, institutionally sponsored loans available. Aid available to part-time students. Financial aid application deadline: 4/1. • Dr. David S. Loshin, Dean, 954-262-1402. Application contact: Adriana Stella, Admissions Counselor, 954-262-1101.

The Ohio State University, College of Optometry, Professional Program in Optometry, Columbus, OH 43210. Awards OD, OD/MS. Accredited by AOA. Students: 247 full-time (125 women); includes 41 minority (3 African Americans, 34 Asian Americans, 4 Hispanics). 446 applicants, 14% accepted. In 1997, 63 degrees awarded. *Average time to degree:* first professional–4 years full-time. *Application deadline:* 2/15. *Application fee:* $25. *Tuition:* $5928 per year for state residents; $26,853 per year for nonresidents. *Financial aid:* Federal Work-Study, institutionally sponsored loans available. Financial aid application deadline: 2/1; applicants required to submit FAFSA. • Dr. John Schoessler, Dean, College of Optometry, 614-292-3246. Fax: 614-292-7493.

Pacific University, College of Optometry, Professional Program in Optometry, Forest Grove, OR 97116-1797. Awards OD. Accredited by AOA. *Degree requirements:* Thesis required, foreign language not required. *Entrance requirements:* OAT, minimum 2 years of college. Application deadline: 3/31 (rolling processing). Application fee: $50.

Pennsylvania College of Optometry, Philadelphia, PA 19141-3323. Awards OD, OD/MS. Accredited by AOA. Faculty: 41 full-time (17 women), 25 part-time (13 women), 54.10 FTE. Students: 611 full-time (332 women); includes 159 minority (29 African Americans, 113 Asian Americans, 17 Hispanics), 22 international. Average age 23. 910 applicants, 30% accepted. In 1997, 132 degrees awarded. *Entrance requirements:* OAT, interview. Application deadline: 3/31 (priority date; rolling processing). Application fee: $50. *Financial aid:* Federal Work-Study, institutionally sponsored loans, and career-related internships or fieldwork available. Financial aid application deadline: 4/15; applicants required to submit FAFSA. *Faculty research:* Contact lenses, diabetes, retinal disease, vision rehabilitation. • Dr. Thomas Lewis, President, 215-276-6210. E-mail: tom@pco.edu. Application contact: Robert E. Horne, Director of Admissions, 215-276-6262. Fax: 215-276-6081. E-mail: rhorne@pco.edu.

Southern California College of Optometry, Fullerton, CA 92831-1615. Awards OD. Accredited by AOA. Faculty: 40 full-time (12 women), 44 part-time (13 women), 50.34 FTE. Students: 380 full-time (247 women); includes 235 minority (5 African Americans, 210 Asian Americans, 19 Hispanics, 1 Native American), 4 international. Average age 25. 614 applicants, 24% accepted. In 1997, 94 degrees awarded (100% found work related to degree). *Degree requirements:* Thesis required, foreign language not required. *Entrance requirements:* OAT. Application deadline: 3/15 (priority date; rolling processing). Application fee: $50. *Expenses:* Tuition $17,850 per year. Fees $90 per year. *Financial aid:* Teaching assistantships, Federal Work-Study, institutionally sponsored loans, and career-related internships or fieldwork available. Financial aid application deadline: 6/1. *Faculty research:* Structure and function of the human visual system. • Dr. Morris S. Berman, Dean, Academic Affairs, 714-449-7455. E-mail: mberman@scco.edu. Application contact: Dr. Lorraine I. Voorhees, Dean of Student Affairs, 714-449-7445. Fax: 714-992-7878. E-mail: lvoorhees@scco.edu.

Southern College of Optometry, Memphis, TN 38104-2222. Awards OD. Accredited by AOA. Faculty: 43 full-time (10 women), 3 part-time (0 women). Students: 481 full-time (212 women); includes 51 minority (8 African Americans, 31 Asian Americans, 10 Hispanics, 2 Native Americans), 10 international. Average age 26. 1,012 applicants, 20% accepted. In 1997, 94 degrees awarded. *Degree requirements:* Clinical experience required, foreign language and thesis not required. *Entrance requirements:* OAT, 3 years of undergraduate pre-optometry course work. Application deadline: 3/1 (priority date; rolling processing). Application fee: $50. *Expenses:* Tuition $9872 per year for state residents; $14,872 per year for nonresidents. Fees $440 per year. *Financial aid:* 400 students received aid; Federal Work-Study, institutionally sponsored loans, and career-related internships or fieldwork available. Aid available to part-time students. Financial aid application deadline: 4/1; applicants required to submit FAFSA. • Joseph H. Hauser, Director of Records and Admissions, 901-722-3228. Fax: 901-722-3279.

State University of New York College of Optometry, Professional Program, New York, NY 10010-3610. Awards OD, OD/MPH, OD/MS, OD/PhD. Accredited by AOA. OD/MPH offered jointly with University at Albany, State University of New York. Faculty: 45 full-time (10 women), 102 part-time (28 women). Students: 278 full-time (175 women); includes 106 minority (9 African Americans, 88 Asian Americans, 9 Hispanics), 21 international. Average age 24. 493 applicants, 22% accepted. In 1997, 58 degrees awarded. *Average time to degree:* first professional–4 years full-time. *Entrance requirements:* OAT (minimum score 320 preferred; average 345). Application deadline: 2/15 (priority date; rolling processing). Application fee: $75. *Expenses:* Tuition $10,840 per year for state residents; $21,940 per year for nonresidents. Fees $122 per year. *Financial aid:* In 1997–98, 215 students received aid, including 16 minority fellowships (4 to first-year students); full and partial tuition waivers, Federal Work-Study, and career-related internships or fieldwork also available. Financial aid application deadline: 4/15. *Faculty research:* Vision research. • Dr. Edward Johnston, Vice President for Student Affairs, 212-780-5100. Fax: 212-780-5104. E-mail: admissions@sunyopt.edu.

Université de Montréal, School of Optometry, Professional Program in Optometry, Montréal, PQ H3C 3J7, Canada. Awards OD. Accredited by AOA. Open only to Canadian residents. Students: 159 full-time (112 women). 377 applicants, 11% accepted. In 1997, 40 degrees awarded. *Degree requirements:* Thesis. *Application deadline:* 3/1. *Application fee:* $30. • Application contact: Dr. Pierre Simonet, Director, 514-343-6471.

The University of Alabama at Birmingham, School of Optometry, Birmingham, AL 35294. Awards OD, MS, PhD, OD/MPH, OD/MS. One or more programs accredited by AOA. Part-time programs available. Faculty: 34 full-time, 5 part-time. Students: 155 full-time (71 women); includes 21 minority (8 African Americans, 13 Asian Americans), 2 international. Average age 26. 340 applicants, 17% accepted. In 1997, 38 ODs awarded. *Entrance requirements:* For OD, OAT, interview. Application deadline: 3/1. Application fee: $25. *Tuition:* $6732 per year for state residents; $16,056 per year for nonresidents. *Financial aid:* In 1997–98, 12 fellowships were awarded; Federal Work-Study and career-related internships or fieldwork also available. Aid available to part-time students. • Dr. Arol Augsburger, Dean, 205-934-4488.

University of California, Berkeley, School of Optometry, Berkeley, CA 94720-1500. Awards OD. Accredited by AOA. Faculty: 24 full-time (3 women), 93 part-time (20 women), 44 FTE. Students: 246 full-time; includes 148 minority (2 African Americans, 130 Asian Americans, 14 Hispanics, 2 Native Americans), 15 international. Average age 24. 340 applicants, 18% accepted. In 1997, 63 degrees awarded. *Degree requirements:* Thesis required, foreign language not required. *Entrance requirements:* OAT (average 360). Application deadline: 12/31. Application fee: $40. *Expenses:* Tuition $0 for state residents; $9384 per year for nonresidents. Fees $4409 per year. *Financial aid:* Scholarships, Federal Work-Study, and career-related internships or fieldwork available. Financial aid application deadline: 3/1; applicants required to submit FAFSA. • Dr. Anthony J. Adams, Dean, 510-642-3414. Application contact: Sandy Jaeger, Student Affairs Officer, 510-642-9537. Fax: 510-643-5109. E-mail: ucbso@spectacle.berkeley.edu.

University of Houston, College of Optometry, Professional Program in Optometry, 4800 Calhoun, Houston, TX 77204-2163. Awards OD. Accredited by AOA. Faculty: 47 full-time (15 women), 30 part-time (14 women), 53 FTE. In 1997, 97 degrees awarded. *Entrance requirements:* OAT (minimum score 330 on each section), minimum GPA of 3.0. Application deadline: 2/1 (rolling processing). Application fee: $50 ($75 for international students). *Expenses:* Tuition $4104 per year full-time, $120 per semester (minimum) part-time for state residents; $13,300 per year full-time, $350 per credit hour part-time for nonresidents. Fees $1697 per year full-time, $119 per semester (minimum) part-time. *Financial aid:* Teaching assistantships available. Financial aid application deadline: 4/1. *Faculty research:* Refractive error development, corneal physiology, low vision, binocular vision. • Dr. Roger Boltz, Associate Dean, 713-743-1883. E-mail: boltz@uh.edu. Application contact: Dr. Kathryn Peek, Director, Student Affairs and Admissions, 713-743-2040. Fax: 713-743-0965. E-mail: kpeek@uh.edu.

See in-depth description on page 1755.

University of Missouri–St. Louis, School of Optometry, Professional Program in Optometry, St. Louis, MO 63121-4499. Awards OD. Accredited by AOA. Students: 161 full-time; includes 22 minority (5 African Americans, 12 Asian Americans, 1 Hispanic, 4 Native Americans). 416 applicants, 11% accepted. In 1997, 36 degrees awarded. *Average time to degree:* first professional–4 years full-time. *Entrance requirements:* OAT (average 310), 90 hours of undergraduate course work. Application deadline: 3/15 (rolling processing). Application fee: $50. *Expenses:* Tuition $14,349 per year for state residents; $27,540 per year for nonresidents. Fees $399 per year. *Financial aid:* In 1997–98, 145 students received aid, including research assistantships totaling $12,000; teaching assistantships also available. Financial aid application deadline: 4/1. • Application contact: Sharon L. Davis, Coordinator, 314-516-6263. Fax: 314-516-6708. E-mail: ssldavi@umslvma.umsl.edu.

University of Waterloo, Faculty of Science, School of Optometry, Professional Programs in Optometry, Waterloo, ON N2L 3G1, Canada. Awards OD. Accredited by AOA. Students: 241 full-time (139 women). 286 applicants, 21% accepted. In 1997, 58 degrees awarded. *Entrance requirements:* OAT (minimum score 350). Application deadline: 1/30. Application fee: $75. *Tuition:* $3220 per year. *Financial aid:* Fellowships available. *Faculty research:* Physiological optics, fundamental and clinical vision sciences. • Application contact: Marie Amodeo, Administrative Assistant, 519-885-4567 Ext. 2782. Fax: 519-725-0784. E-mail: mamodeo@sciborg.uwaterloo.ca.

Vision Sciences

Emory University, School of Medicine, Programs in Allied Health Professions, Program in Ophthalmic Technology, Atlanta, GA 30322-1100. Awards MM Sc. Faculty: 3 full-time (all women). Students: 10 full-time (7 women); includes 1 minority (Hispanic). Average age 27. 6 applicants, 33% accepted. In 1997, 4 degrees awarded (100% found work related to degree). *Entrance requirements:* GRE General Test (minimum combined score of 1500 on three sections). Application deadline: 5/1 (priority date; rolling processing). Application fee: $50. *Financial aid:* Federal Work-Study, institutionally sponsored loans available. Financial aid application deadline: 3/15; applicants required to submit CSS PROFILE or FAFSA. • Mary Gemmill, Director, 404-778-4305. E-mail: mgemmill@emory.edu.

Indiana University Bloomington, School of Optometry and Graduate School, Graduate Program in Visual Sciences and Physiological Optics, Bloomington, IN 47405. Awards MS, PhD. PhD offered through the University Graduate School. Students: 4 full-time (2 women), 3 part-time (1 woman); includes 4 international. In 1997, 1 doctorate awarded. Terminal master's awarded for partial completion of doctoral program. *Degree requirements:* Thesis/dissertation required, foreign language not required. *Entrance requirements:* GRE. Application deadline: 2/15 (priority date). Application fee: $30 ($35 for international students). *Expenses:* Tuition $186 per credit hour for state residents; $515 per credit hour for nonresidents. Fees $343 per year. *Financial aid:* Fellowships, research assistantships, teaching assistantships, scholarships available. Financial aid application deadline: 3/1. *Faculty research:* Visual psychophysics, neurophysiology of visual systems, anatomy of visual system, biochemistry of visual system, corneal pathophysiology. Total annual research expenditures: $362,783. • P. Sarita Soni, Associate Dean, 812-855-4475. Fax: 812-855-7045. E-mail: sonip@indiana.edu. Application contact: Jacqueline S. Olson, Coordinator of Student Affairs, 812-855-1917. Fax: 812-855-8664. E-mail: iubopt@indiana.edu.

See in-depth description on page 1753.

Pacific University, College of Optometry, Graduate Programs in Optometry, Forest Grove, OR 97116-1797. Offerings in clinical optometry (MS), visual function in learning (M Ed). *Degree requirements:* Thesis required, foreign language not required. *Entrance requirements:* GRE General Test. Application deadline: 3/31 (rolling processing). Application fee: $50.

Pennsylvania College of Optometry, Department of Vision Impairment, 8360 Old York Road, Elkins Park, PA 19027. Awards M Ed, MS, OD/MS. Programs in education of children and youth with visual and multiple impairments (M Ed), low vision rehabilitation (MS), orientation and mobility therapy (MS), rehabilitation teaching (MS). Part-time programs available. Faculty: 5 full-time (all women), 10 part-time (8 women). Students: 1 (woman) full-time, 19 part-time (15 women). 21 applicants, 100% accepted. In 1997, 12 degrees awarded. *Average time to degree:* master's–1 year full-time, 2.5 years part-time. *Entrance requirements:* GRE or MAT. Application deadline: 6/16 (rolling processing). Application fee: $50. *Financial aid:* Scholarships, Federal Work-Study, institutionally sponsored loans, and career-related internships or fieldwork available. Financial aid applicants required to submit FAFSA. *Faculty research:* Low vision, knowledge utilization, technology transfer. • Dr. Kathleen M. Huebner, Assistant Dean, 215-276-6093. Fax: 215-276-6292. E-mail: kathyh@pco.edu. Application contact: Diane Wormsley, Recruitment Committee Chair, 215-780-1366. Fax: 215-780-1357. E-mail: lwormsley@pco.edu.

Announcement: Four programs are offered: education of children and youth with visual and multiple disabilities, orientation and mobility (O&M), rehabilitation teaching, and low-vision rehabilitation. Master's degrees and/or certificates are earned on a part-time basis, with most course work taught during evening or Saturday classes. O&M also has full-time and summers-only programs. Some programs are available through distance education. Scholarships are available for most programs. Course work is enhanced through close contact with the Eye Clinic, the Feinbloom Center (a low-vision rehabilitation clinic), and through guest lectures by optometry faculty members. For more information, visit the Web site at http://www.pco.edu

State University of New York College of Optometry, Graduate Programs, New York, NY 10010-3610. Awards MS, PhD, OD/MS, OD/PhD. Part-time programs available. Faculty: 23 full-time (1 woman), 3 part-time (all women). Students: 8 full-time (5 women), 14 part-time (8 women); includes 6 minority (all Asian Americans), 6 international. In 1997, 2 doctorates awarded. Terminal master's awarded for partial completion of doctoral program. *Degree requirements:* For master's, thesis, comprehensive exam required, foreign language not required; for doctorate, dissertation required, foreign language not required. *Entrance requirements:* GRE General Test. Application deadline: 3/1 (priority date; rolling processing). Application fee: $50. *Expenses:* Tuition $5100 per year for state residents; $8416 per year for nonresidents. Fees $81 per year. *Financial aid:* In 1997–98, 6 graduate assistantships averaging $1,000 per month were awarded; fellowships, research assistantships, teaching assistantships, full and partial tuition waivers, Federal Work-Study also available. Financial aid application deadline: 3/1. *Faculty research:* Oculomotor systems, perception, physiological optics, ocular biochemistry, accommodation, color and motion. • Dr. Jerry Feldman, Associate Dean, 212-780-5140. E-mail: jfeldman@sunyopt.edu. Application contact: Debra Berger, Assistant to Associate Dean, 212-780-5044. Fax: 212-780-5094. E-mail: berger@sunyopt.edu.

Université de Montréal, School of Optometry, Graduate Programs in Optometry, Montréal, PQ H3C 3J7, Canada. Offering in physiological optics (M Sc). Offered jointly with the Faculty of Graduate Studies. Part-time programs available. Faculty: 12 full-time (2 women), 4 part-time (1 woman). Students: 5 full-time (2 women), 2 part-time (both women). 3 applicants, 33% accepted. In 1997, 1 degree awarded. *Degree requirements:* Thesis required, foreign language not required. *Entrance requirements:* OD or appropriate bachelor's degree, minimum GPA of 2.7. Application deadline: 3/1. Application fee: $30. *Financial aid:* Research assistantships, teaching assistantships, and career-related internships or fieldwork available. Aid available to part-time students. *Faculty research:* Binocular vision, visual electrophysiology, eye movements, corneal metabolism, glare sensitivity. • Application contact: Dr. Jocelyn Faubert, Graduate Officer, 514-343-7719.

The University of Alabama at Birmingham, Graduate School and School of Optometry, Graduate Program in Vision Science, Birmingham, AL 35294. Awards MS, PhD, OD/MS. Students: 14 full-time (4 women); includes 6 minority (1 African American, 5 Asian Americans). 12 applicants, 100% accepted. In 1997, 3 master's, 2 doctorates awarded. Terminal master's awarded for partial completion of doctoral program. *Degree requirements:* Thesis/dissertation required, foreign language not required. *Entrance requirements:* For master's, GRE General Test (minimum combined score of 1000), OAT, interview; for doctorate, GRE General Test (minimum combined score of 1100), OAT, interview. Application deadline: rolling. Application fee: $30 ($60 for international students). Electronic applications accepted. *Expenses:* Tuition $99 per credit hour for state residents; $198 per credit hour for nonresidents. Fees $516 per year (minimum) full-time, $73 per quarter (minimum) part-time for state residents; $516 per year (minimum) full-time, $73 per unit (minimum) part-time for nonresidents. • Dr. Lawrence E. Mays, Department Chair, Physiological Optics, 205-934-6743.

The University of Alabama in Huntsville, College of Engineering, Department of Electrical and Computer Engineering, Huntsville, AL 35899. Offerings include optical science and engineering (PhD). Department faculty: 23 full-time (1 woman), 2 part-time (0 women), 23.5 FTE. *Degree requirements:* Dissertation, oral and written exams required, foreign language not required. *Entrance requirements:* GRE General Test (minimum combined score of 1500 on three sections), minimum GPA of 3.0. Application deadline: 7/24 (priority date; rolling processing; 11/15 for spring admission). Application fee: $20. Electronic applications accepted. *Tuition:* $2886 per year full-time, $540 per semester (minimum) part-time for state residents; $5298 per year full-time, $1098 per semester (minimum) part-time for nonresidents. • Dr. Reza Adhami, Chair, 205-890-6316. Fax: 205-890-6803. E-mail: adhami@ebs330.eb.uah.edu.

University of Alberta, Faculties of Medicine and Oral Health Sciences and Graduate Studies and Research, Graduate Programs in Medicine, Department of Ophthalmology, Edmonton, AB T6G 2E1, Canada. Offers program in medical sciences/opthalmology (M Sc, PhD). Part-time programs available. Faculty: 1 full-time (0 women), 1 part-time (0 women). Students: 6 full-time (2 women). Average age 28. 10 applicants, 0% accepted. Terminal master's awarded for partial completion of doctoral program. *Degree requirements:* For doctorate, dissertation required, foreign language not required. *Application deadline:* 4/1 (priority date; rolling processing). *Application fee:* $60. *Financial aid:* 1 student received aid. *Faculty research:* Heritable ocular disorders. Total annual research expenditures: $240,500. • Dr. I. M. MacDonald, Head, 403-477-4924. E-mail: macdonal@gpu.srv.ualberta.ca. Application contact: Dr. Michael Walter, Associate Professor, 403-492-9805. Fax: 403-492-6934. E-mail: mwalter@gpu.srv.ualberta.ca.

University of California, Berkeley, Group in Vision Science, Berkeley, CA 94720-1500. Awards MS, PhD. Faculty: 24 full-time (3 women), 5 part-time (0 women). Students: 34 full-time (11 women); includes 6 minority (5 Asian Americans, 1 Hispanic), 3 international. Average age 27. 30 applicants, 30% accepted. In 1997, 1 master's, 2 doctorates awarded. *Degree requirements:* Thesis/dissertation required, foreign language not required. *Entrance requirements:* GRE General Test, minimum GPA of 3.0. Application deadline: 2/10. Application fee: $40. *Expenses:* Tuition $0 for state residents; $9384 per year for nonresidents. Fees $4409 per year. *Financial aid:* 33 students received aid; fellowships, research assistantships, teaching assistantships, partial tuition waivers, Federal Work-Study, institutionally sponsored loans available. Financial aid application deadline: 1/5; applicants required to submit FAFSA. *Faculty research:* Visual neuroscience, bioengineering, computational vision, molecular cell biology, basic and clinical psychophysics. • Martin S. Banks, Chair, 510-642-9341. Application contact: Fran Stone, Student Affairs Officer, 510-642-9804. Fax: 510-643-5109. E-mail: fstone@spectacle.berkeley.edu.

University of Chicago, Division of the Biological Sciences, Department of Ophthalmology and Visual Science, Chicago, IL 60637-1513. Awards SM, PhD. Faculty: 12 full-time (5 women). Students: 2 full-time (1 woman); includes 2 international. Average age 29. 12 applicants, 0% accepted. Terminal master's awarded for partial completion of doctoral program. *Degree requirements:* For doctorate, dissertation. *Entrance requirements:* For doctorate, GRE General Test, TOEFL. Application deadline: 1/5 (priority date). Application fee: $55. *Expenses:* Tuition $23,616 per year full-time, $3258 per course part-time. Fees $378 per year. *Financial aid:* 2 students received aid; research assistantships, institutionally sponsored loans available. Financial aid application deadline: 6/1. *Faculty research:* Visual psychophysics, visual molecular biology, immunology, transplantation, infections, disease. • Dr. J. T. Ernest, Chairman, 773-702-8888. Fax: 773-702-8094. E-mail: jernest@midway.uchicago.edu. Application contact: Fran Lietz, Student Affairs Secretary, 773-702-1985. Fax: 773-834-0714. E-mail: flietz@midway.uchicago.edu.

University of Guelph, Ontario Veterinary College and Faculty of Graduate Studies, Graduate Programs in Veterinary Sciences, Department of Clinical Studies, Guelph, ON N1G 2W1, Canada. Offerings include ophthalmology (M Sc, DV Sc). Department faculty: 22 full-time (6 women), 3 part-time (1 woman). *Degree requirements:* Thesis/dissertation. *Average time to degree:* doctorate–3 years full-time; other advanced degree–1.5 years full-time. *Application deadline:* 2/1 (rolling processing). *Application fee:* $60. *Expenses:* Tuition $4725 per year full-time, $3165 per year part-time for Canadian residents; $6999 per year for nonresidents. Fees $612 per year full-time, $38 per year (minimum) part-time for Canadian residents; $612 per year for nonresidents. • Dr. S. Kruth, Chair, 519-823-8800 Ext. 4012. Application contact: Dr. M. Hurtig, Graduate Coordinator, 519-823-8800 Ext. 4028. Fax: 519-767-0311. E-mail: mhurtig@ovcnet.uoguelph.ca.

University of Houston, College of Optometry, Program in Physiological Optics/Vision Science, 4800 Calhoun, Houston, TX 77204-2163. Awards MS Phys Op, PhD. Faculty: 22 full-time (3 women), 1 part-time (0 women). 46 applicants, 20% accepted. In 1997, 1 master's, 3 doctorates awarded. *Degree requirements:* For master's, thesis required, foreign language not required; for doctorate, 1 foreign language (computer language can substitute), dissertation, oral or written qualifying exam. *Average time to degree:* master's–3 years full-time; doctorate–5 years full-time. *Entrance requirements:* GRE General Test (minimum combined score of 1150), minimum GPA of 3.0. Application deadline: 1/31 (rolling processing). Application fee: $0 ($25 for international students). *Expenses:* Tuition $4104 per year full-time, $120 per semester (minimum) part-time for state residents; $13,300 per year full-time, $350 per credit hour part-time for nonresidents. Fees $1697 per year full-time, $119 per semester (minimum) part-time. *Financial aid:* In 1997–98, research assistantships averaging $1,100 per month, teaching assistantships averaging $1,100 per month were awarded; fellowships, institutionally sponsored loans, and career-related internships or fieldwork also available. Financial aid application deadline: 1/31. *Faculty research:* Space perception, amblyopia, binocular vision, development of visual skills, strabismus, visual cell biology, refractive error. • Dennis M. Levi, Associate Dean, Graduate Studies/Research, 713-743-1885. E-mail: dlevi@uh.edu. Application contact: D'Anna Harrison, Graduate Coordinator, 713-743-1885. Fax: 713-743-1888. E-mail: dharrison@uh.edu.

See in-depth descriptions on pages 1755 and 1757.

University of Louisville, School of Medicine and Graduate School, Graduate Programs in Medicine, Department of Ophthalmology and Visual Sciences, Louisville, KY 40292-0001. Awards PhD. Faculty: 19 full-time (3 women), 3 part-time (1 woman), 20 FTE. Students: 9 full-time (7 women); includes 6 international. Average age 30. *Degree requirements:* Dissertation. *Entrance requirements:* GRE General Test. Application deadline: 1/15. Application fee: $15. • Thom J. Zimmerman, Chair, 502-852-5477. Application contact: Nicholas Delamere, Director, 502-852-5461.

Directory: Vision Sciences; Cross-Discipline Announcement

University of Missouri–St. Louis, School of Optometry and Graduate School, Program in Physiological Optics, St. Louis, MO 63121-4499. Awards MS, PhD. Students: 5 full-time (3 women), 2 part-time (1 woman); includes 5 minority (all Asian Americans). 10 applicants, 60% accepted. In 1997, 1 master's awarded (100% found work related to degree). *Degree requirements:* Thesis/dissertation. *Average time to degree:* master's–1.8 years full-time. *Entrance requirements:* For master's, GRE General Test (combined average 1000), TOEFL (minimum score 600); for doctorate, GRE General Test (combined average 1100), TOEFL (minimum score 600). Application deadline: 3/15 (rolling processing). Application fee: $25 ($40 for international students). *Expenses:* Tuition $3903 per year full-time, $167 per credit hour part-time for state residents; $11,745 per year full-time, $489 per credit hour part-time for nonresidents. Fees $816 per year full-time, $34 per credit hour part-time. *Financial aid:* In 1997–98, 1 fellowship averaging $1,000 per month, 1 research assistantship averaging $1,000 per month, 4 teaching assistantships averaging $1,000 per month were awarded; Federal Work-Study, institutionally sponsored loans also available. Financial aid application deadline: 3/15. • Dr. Carol Peck, Director of Graduate Studies, 314-516-5812. Fax: 314-516-5150. E-mail: scpeck@umslvma.umsl.edu.

University of Waterloo, Faculty of Science, School of Optometry, Graduate Programs in Optometry, Waterloo, ON N2L 3G1, Canada. Awards M Sc, PhD. Part-time programs available. Faculty: 25 full-time (9 women), 9 part-time (3 women). Students: 13 full-time (5 women), 6 part-time (5 women). 25 applicants, 2% accepted. In 1997, 1 master's, 1 doctorate awarded. *Degree requirements:* For master's, thesis required, foreign language not required; for doctorate, dissertation. *Entrance requirements:* For master's, TOEFL (minimum score 575), honors degree, minimum B average; for doctorate, TOEFL (minimum score 575), master's degree. Application deadline: 8/1 (priority date; rolling processing). Application fee: $50. *Tuition:* $3220 per year. *Financial aid:* In 1997–98, 9 research assistantships (2 to first-year students), 16 teaching assistantships (2 to first-year students) were awarded; fellowships, institutionally sponsored loans, and career-related internships or fieldwork also available. *Faculty research:* Fundamental and clinical vision science, optics, psychophysics, perception. Total annual research expenditures: $1.967 million. • Dr. J. Flanagan, Graduate Officer, 519-888-4567 Ext. 3176. E-mail: jgflanag@sciborg.uwaterloo.ca. Application contact: S. Dahmer, Graduate Secretary, 519-888-4567 Ext. 5039. Fax: 519-725-0784. E-mail: sdahmer@sciborg.uwaterloo.ca.

Cross-Discipline Announcement

Cornell University, Graduate School of Medical Sciences, Graduate Program in Neuroscience, New York, NY 10021.

Students with an interest in the visual system will find many research opportunities within the vision community of the Graduate Program in Neuroscience at Cornell University Medical College. An in-depth description can be found in the Neuroscience section of Book 3 in this series.

INDIANA UNIVERSITY

School of Optometry
Graduate Program in Visual Sciences and Physiological Optics

Program of Study

The School of Optometry and the Indiana University Graduate School offer a graduate program in visual sciences and physiological optics leading to the M.S. and Ph.D. degrees. Admission requirements are flexible to accommodate students with varying backgrounds such as optometry, psychology, physics, medicine, biological sciences, chemistry, neurosciences, computer science, optics, and many other areas. A bachelor's degree or the equivalent is necessary, and an optometric degree is desirable though not required. Ordinarily, to earn either the M.S. or the Ph.D. degree students must demonstrate intermediate-level competence in visual anatomy, visual optics, physiology and biochemistry of vision, monocular visual function, and ocular motility and binocular visual function. Competence in these areas is assumed for those who have recent optometric degrees from recognized programs. Others may demonstrate competence by successful completion of relevant courses offered by the graduate program or the School of Optometry and approved by the Associate Dean for Graduate Programs. Students who wish to pursue highly interdisciplinary programs may petition to reduce the number of areas of competence required to a minimum of three. Students commence their research training by joining an ongoing faculty-directed research project during their first few weeks in residence. The research topic may or may not be in the student's specific field of interest or in the field in which the student intends to do dissertation research. For the M.S. degree, a thesis research proposal must be submitted and approved by the end of the first year of study. For the Ph.D. degree, written research reports are required annually until advancement to candidacy. Nomination to candidacy will normally occur only after completion of 30 credit hours of didactic course work, two annual research reports, and successful completion of written and oral qualifying examinations specified by the student's advisory committee.

Research Facilities

The visual science laboratories in the School of Optometry are equipped for research investigations into monocular and binocular visual functions, photoreceptors, electrophysiology, psychophysics, optics, and perception. The individual faculty members' laboratories all have computer workstations, linked through a local network and also to the University's UNIX system of computers. Shared research facilities include histological laboratories for preparation and study of tissues and specimens; an electron microscope; an electronics shop, machine shop, and carpentry shop with full-time technical personnel; and photography and darkroom facilities. The Borish Center for Ophthalmic Research and the clinics of the School are available for research in corneal topography, contact lenses, binocular vision, low vision, adaptation, strabismus, and contrast sensitivity.

Financial Aid

The School hopes to support all full-time graduate students. Students who do not have other means of support may be awarded fellowship/assistantship appointments up to $10,000 per academic year plus fee scholarships covering registration fees for 24 credit hours per year. It is expected that summer support for students holding academic-year appointments will be provided from faculty research grants. Students may obtain additional support through teaching or research assistantships requiring additional work. Other scholarships and fellowships are available through the University and from outside sources such as the American Optometric Foundation, the National Institutes of Health, and other agencies.

Cost of Study

Graduate fees for 1997–98 were $428 per credit hour for nonresidents and $147 for Indiana residents. A normal course load is 9 to 12 credit hours per semester. Students holding fee scholarships pay only $21.95 per credit hour. There is a nonrefundable application fee of $40.

Living and Housing Costs

For a single student the twelve-month living expense, exclusive of tuition and fees, is estimated at $12,370. This consists of $8370 for room and board plus approximately $4000 for miscellaneous expenses exclusive of clothing or travel. Married students should add $8500 for a spouse plus $3500 for each additional dependent. Health and accident insurance ($600) is required for all international students and their dependents.

Student Group

The graduate program in visual sciences and physiological optics usually has 10 to 15 full-time students working toward the M.S. and Ph.D. degrees. These students have a wide variety of backgrounds, including optometry, psychology, medicine, biology, physics, and engineering. The program has an international flavor, with at least 2 or 3 of the students coming from other countries. There are usually also 3 or 4 postdoctoral fellows and research associates working with individual faculty members. The School of Optometry also has some 290 professional students pursuing the Doctor of Optometry degree.

Location

Bloomington is located in the hills of southern Indiana, 50 miles from Indianapolis. Approximately 35,000 students, one fourth of whom are graduate students and 2,000 of whom are international students, attend the scenic woodland campus. Bloomington, with a population of 61,000, exclusive of IU students, is the cultural and recreational center of southern Indiana. State parks in the surrounding area provide camping, hiking, riding, and cycling facilities, and nearby Lake Monroe offers fishing, boating, and water sports.

The University and The Program

Indiana University, founded at Bloomington in 1820, is one of the oldest and largest state-supported universities in the United States. Its eight campuses serve more than 80,000 students from all fifty states and more than 100 other countries. The residential campus at Bloomington and the urban center campus at Indianapolis form its core. The Graduate Program in Physiological Optics began in 1953. Designed as an interdisciplinary program, which continues to utilize faculty from the Schools of Optometry, Education, and Medicine; the Medical Sciences Program; the Departments of Psychology, Neural Sciences, Physiology, Physics, Biology, and Mathematics; and other academic units, the program develops and guides its students and their research.

Applying

Applicants must have a bachelor's degree or the equivalent and must submit a completed application form, official transcripts of all college work, official GRE General Test scores, a statement of their interests in visual science and their plans and aspirations for career development, and three letters of recommendation from persons familiar with the applicant's academic and research potential. International students must also supply official TOEFL scores of 630 or higher, an application fee of $40, and evidence of financial support. Applications should be submitted at least six months prior to the desired admittance date.

Correspondence and Information

P. Sarita Soni
Associate Dean for Research and Graduate Programs
School of Optometry
Indiana University
Bloomington, Indiana 47405-3680
Telephone: 812-855-4475
Fax: 812-855-7045
E-mail: sonip@indiana.edu

For a bulletin or an application:
Office of Student Affairs
Indiana University
Bloomington, Indiana 47405-3680
Telephone: 812-855-1917
Fax: 812-855-4389
E-mail: iubopt@indiana.edu
World Wide Web: http://www.opt.indiana.edu

Indiana University

THE FACULTY AND THEIR RESEARCH

Merrill J. Allen, Professor Emeritus; O.D., 1941, Ph.D., 1949, Ohio State. Vision and highway safety, amblyopia, strabismus, learning disabilities and macular degeneration. (e-mail: allen@indiana.edu)

Carolyn G. Begley, Associate Professor of Optometry and Visual Sciences; O.D., Indiana, 1983. Cellular biology of the corneal epithelium, corneal physiology, microbiology and toxicity of contact lens solutions, ocular immunology. (e-mail: cbegley@indiana.edu)
Effect of lens care systems on corneal fluorescein staining and subjective comfort in hydrogel lens wearers. *ICLC* 21(1–2):7–13, 1994. With Edrington and Chalmer.
The effects of soft contact lens disinfection solutions on rabbit corneal epithelium. *CLAO* 2(1):52–58, 1994. With Waggoner, Jani, and Meetz.

Arthur Bradley, Associate Professor of Optometry and Visual Sciences; Ph.D., Berkeley, 1983. Optical and neural factors that limit normal and pathological visual performance, application of noninvasive techniques for diagnosis and monitoring of ocular disease. (e-mail: bradley@indiana.edu)
Psychophysical determination of the size and shape of the human foveal avascular zone. *Ophthal. Physiol. Opt.* 12:18–23, 1992. With Applegate, Zeffren, and van Heuven.
Effects of target distance and pupil size on letter contrast sensitivity with simultaneous vision bifocal contact lenses. *Optom. Vis. Sci.* 70:476–81, 1993. With Rahman, Soni, and Zhang.

Susana T. L. Chung, Assistant Professor of Optometry and Visual Sciences; Ph.D., Houston, 1995. Low vision rehabilitation, spatial vision in normal and abnormal visual systems. (e-mail: chung@indiana.edu)
Vernier in motion: What accounts for the threshold elevation? *Vision Res.* 36:2395–410, 1996. With Levi and Bedell.
Moving Vernier in amblyopic and peripheral vision: Greater tolerance to motion blur. *Vision Res.* 37:2527–33, 1997. With Levi.

Shaban Demirel, Assistant Professor of Optometry and Visual Sciences; Ph.D., Melbourne, 1995. Effect of patient factors on clinical visual field testing, structural and functional changes occurring in the optic nerve and retina early in the glaucomatous and diabetic disease processes, modeling of normal and abnormal visual processes. (e-mail: sdemirel@indiana.edu)
Eye movements during perimetry and the effect that fixational instability has on perimetric outcomes. *J. Glaucoma* 3:28–35, 1994. With Vingrys.
The slope of frequency-of-seeing curves in normal, amblyopic, and pathological vision. In *Vision Sciences and Its Applications,* vol. 1, *OSA Technical Digest Series,* pp. 244–7. Washington, D.C.: Optical Society of America, 1997. With Johnson, Fendrich, and Vingrys.

Robert D. DeVoe, Professor of Optometry and Visual Sciences; Ph.D., Rockefeller, 1961. Pharmacology and intracellular recording and identification of motion-detecting neurons in the vertebrate (turtle) retina, ultraviolet sensitivities of photoreceptor and other cells in the turtle retina. (e-mail: devoe@indiana.edu)
Not by ganglion cells alone: Directional selectivity is widespread in identified cells of the turtle retina. In *Neurobiology of the Inner Retina,* pp. 235–46, ed. R. Weiler and N. N. Osborne. Berlin: Springer-Verlag, 1989. With Carras, Criswell, and Guy.

Ronald W. Everson, Associate Professor Emeritus; O.D., Indiana, 1954. Aniseikonia, anisometropia, optics of the eye. (e-mail: everson@indiana.edu)

David A. Goss, Professor of Optometry; O.D., Pacific, 1974; Ph.D., Indiana, 1980. Myopia, ocular accommodation, clinical analysis of vergence function, optics of ocular refractive anomalies, optometric history. (e-mail: dgoss@indiana.edu)
Cross-sectional study of changes in the ocular components in school children. *Appl. Opt.* 32:4169–74, 1993. With Jackson.
Retinal-image mediated ocular growth as a mechanism for juvenile-onset myopia and for emmetropization: A literature review. *Doc. Ophthalmol.* 90:341–75, 1995. With Wickham.
Clinical findings before the onset of myopia in youth: 3. heterophoria. *Optom. Vis. Sci.* 73:269–78, 1996. With Jackson.

S. Lee Guth, Professor Emeritus; Ph.D., Illinois, 1963. Visual psychophysics. (e-mail: guth@indiana.edu)
Model for color vision and light adaptation. *J. Opt. Soc. Am.*, vol. A, pp. 976–93, 1991.

Gary S. Hafner, Professor of Optometry and Adjunct Associate Professor of Anatomy; Ph.D., Indiana, 1972. Invertebrate photoreceptor anatomy, membrane dynamics. (e-mail: hafner@indiana.edu)

Gordon G. Heath, Professor Emeritus and Dean Emeritus; O.D., Los Angeles College of Optometry, 1951; Ph.D., Berkeley, 1960. Directional sensitivity of the retina and photoreceptors, color blindness, corneal topography. (e-mail: heath@indiana.edu)

Sally L. Hegeman, Associate Professor of Optometry and Adjunct Associate Professor of Pharmacology and Toxicology; Ph.D., California, San Francisco, 1969. Ocular pharmacology, hormonal control mechanisms in diabetes. (e-mail: hegemans@indiana.edu)

Douglas G. Horner, Assistant Professor of Optometry and Visual Sciences; O.D., Pacific University, 1974; Ph.D., Houston, 1987. Eye movements. (e-mail: hornerdg@indiana.edu)
Selective nonconjugate binocular adaptation of vertical saccades and pursuits. *Vision Res.* 30(11):1827–44, 1990. With Schor and Gleason.
Measures of corneal topography, chapter alignment of videokeratoscopes. In *An Atlas of Corneal Topography,* ed. D. D. R. Sanders and D. D. Koch. Thorofare, N.J.: Sack, Inc., 1992. With Mandell.

Gerald E. Lowther, Professor of Optometry and Visual Sciences; O.D., 1967, Ph.D., 1972, Ohio State. Contact lens materials, design, fitting, aftercare problems, and care systems; keratoconus; dry eye; interactive multimedia education. (e-mail: glowther@indiana.edu)
Comparison of hydrogel contact lens patients with and without the symptom of drying. *ICLC* 20:9–10, 1993.
Comparison of simulated K's as measured by computerized videokeratographers to keratometer measurements. *ICLC* 21: 180–4, 1994. With Pole.

Edwin C. Marshall, Professor of Optometry; O.D., Indiana, 1971; M.P.H., North Carolina, 1982. Health policy and administration, health-care delivery systems, health manpower, epidemiology of vision disorders, health professions education. (e-mail: marshall@indiana.edu)
Epidemiology of tumors affecting the visual system. *Optometry Clinics,* 1993.
Rationing the public's health and the optometric agenda. *J. Am. Opt. Assoc.,* 1994.

Donald T. Miller, Assistant Professor of Optometry and Visual Sciences; Ph.D., Rochester. High-resolution fundus imaging, assessment and correction of ocular aberrations, ophthalmic optics, application of advanced optical techniques to vision-related problems.
Images of cone photoreceptors in the living human eye. *Vision Res.* 36:1067–79, 1996.
Supernormal vision and high-resolution retinal imaging through adaptive optics. *J. Opt. Soc. Am.* 14:2884–92, 1997.

Paul A. Pietsch, Professor Emeritus; Ph.D., Pennsylvania, 1960. Developmental biology: regeneration; neurobiology: memory. (e-mail: pietsch@indiana.edu)

P. Sarita Soni, Professor of Optometry and Visual Sciences; O.D., Indiana, 1976. Ocular physiology and pathology in general; corneal and ocular response to drugs; contact lens design, fitting, compliance, and lens-care systems; myopia reduction with contact lenses and/or laser. (e-mail: sonip@indiana.edu)
Effects of oral contraceptive steroids on human corneal thickness. *Am. J. Optom. Physiol. Optics* 57(11): 825–34, 1980.
Orthokeratology. In *Clinical Contact Lens Practice,* ed. Bennett and Weissman. Philadelphia: Lippincott Co., 1993. With Horner.

Larry N. Thibos, Professor of Optometry and Visual Sciences; Ph.D., Berkeley, 1975. Effects of optical aberrations of the eye on visual performance, limits to spatial vision imposed by retinal architecture, characterization of vision in the peripheral field. (e-mail: thibos@indiana.edu)
Characterization of spatial aliasing and contrast sensitivity in peripheral vision. *Vision Res.* 36:249–58, 1996. With Still and Bradley.
Effects of refractive error on detection acuity and resolution acuity in peripheral vision. *Invest. Ophthalmol. Vis. Sci.* 38:2134–43, 1997. With Wang and Bradley

UNIVERSITY OF HOUSTON

College of Optometry

Programs of Study

The College of Optometry offers a Doctor of Optometry degree, residency certification in four areas of postgraduate clinical training, and a combined master's degree/residency program in conjunction with the College's Graduate Program in Physiological Optics/Vision Science. In addition, the College offers a Bachelor of Science in Optometry degree to those students who matriculate with the required course prerequisites but without a bachelor's degree.

The Doctor of Optometry, a postbaccalaureate degree, is awarded to students who successfully complete the professional curriculum, which is four years (including two summer sessions) in length. The first three semesters provide a basic physiological and biomedical science education (e.g., optics, anatomy, physiology, vision science) through lectures and laboratories and prepares students to begin patient care. During the fourth semester, students begin directed patient care in the University Eye Institute while continuing their didactic and laboratory education in clinically-related subjects, including ocular disease and pharmacology, pediatrics, contact lenses, ophthalmic optics, vision perception, lasers and refractive surgery, geriatrics and low vision, environmental optometry, and practice management. Following the spring semester of the second professional year, students spend an intense seven-week assignment providing patient care in a variety of clinical areas, including Family Practice (with adult and pediatric patients), the Cornea and Contact Lens Service, and learning advanced diagnostic techniques in the Ocular Diagnostic and Medical Eye Service. During the remaining two semesters of the third professional year, students continue their clinical experience at the University Eye Institute with similar rotations. The fourth professional year is divided into advanced clinical experiences in the University Eye Institute (one semester) and two semesters at affiliated, multidisciplinary, educational clinical settings for concentrated experiences providing care to diverse patient populations.

The College also offers advanced clinical training as one-calendar-year residency programs in cornea and contact lenses, pediatrics, low vision, and family practice. A joint M.S./residency program, in which a graduate obtains the M.S. degree in physiological optics/vision science and completes a residency in two calendar years, is also available.

Research Facilities

The physical facilities and associated resources of the College are exceptional. The College facility contains two large amphitheater-style classrooms and numerous seminar rooms and teaching laboratories, including a complete anatomy lab for teaching gross and ocular human anatomy. The University Eye Institute houses nearly seventy fully equipped examination/treatment operatories, as well as specialized areas containing computerized corneal topographers, lasers (argon, YAG, and excimer), a scanning laser ophthalmoscope, computerized visual field instruments, and imaging and ultrasound equipment. An extensive optometry/vision science library, which contains a large, modern computer laboratory for student use, is also on site. Research facilities include an electron microscope, computing, electronics, and machine shop support, as well as a number of world-class individual faculty laboratories. The total research expenditure for 1997–98 was approximately $3 million for the College.

Financial Aid

The University and College provide a variety of financial aid programs for eligible students who need financial resources. This effort is assisted by an in-house financial aid counselor. A number of student loans, including Health Professional Student Loans, Federal Stafford Student Loans, Federal Unsubsidized Stafford Loans, and Perkins Loans are available, as are a number of scholarships and awards. Additional information may be obtained through the Office of Student Affairs. Postdoctoral residents are paid an annual stipend of $22,500 plus medical benefits.

Cost of Study

In 1998–99, tuition for Texas residents is $108 per semester credit hour (SCH) and $350 per semester credit hour for nonresident and international students. The normal academic load is about 20 SCH each semester, with the exception of the third-year summer session. Fees and facility charges are approximately $450 each semester. In addition, approximately $4000 in clinical equipment is required during the four years.

Living and Housing Costs

Annual costs for housing, food, transportation, and moderate entertainment are about $8000 for a single student and $12,000 for a married student without children. The University has housing facilities on or near campus for single men and women, with room and board costs at about $3900 for the 1998–99 academic year. Married student housing is available, ranging from efficiencies to three-bedroom apartments. A varied choice of housing is available off campus; rent for a one-bedroom apartment begins at about $350 per month.

Student Group

In 1997, 104 students entered the first-year class, coming from ten different states, although 80 percent of the students are from Texas. Enrollment is approximately evenly divided between women and men, with minority representation making up about 50 percent. The average matriculating first-professional-year student is 24 years old with an overall GPA of 3.41 and an average OAT score of 335.

Student Outcomes

University of Houston students taking the National Board of Examiners in Optometry examinations had pass rates that were above the national average for a recent Basic Science section (76 percent vs. 64 percent) and Clinical Science section (94 percent vs. 93 percent).

Location

Houston, a large and growing area with a population of about 2.5 million, is a center for business, the petrochemical industry, and health care. The city provides a wide range of cultural activities, sports, and other warm-weather recreational activities. It is the home of one of the largest medical complexes in the world, NASA, and a number of technology-related businesses.

The University and The College

The University of Houston is a state-assisted institution composed of fourteen colleges. The 525-acre campus is located 3 miles southeast of Houston's downtown area.

The College of Optometry was founded in 1952 and has been located in its present building since 1976. Since then, the physical facilities have undergone many renovations and upgrades to provide the most modern environment possible.

Applying

Students applying for admission to the College of Optometry should have a bachelor's degree or higher, or should have completed a minimum of 90 semester hours of specified undergraduate courses. Of these, at least 60 semester hours of specific prerequisite math/science courses must be completed satisfactorily prior to admission. Starting in 2000, all applicants will be required to have a bachelor's degree or higher. Applicants are also required to take the Optometric Admissions Test. Applications are accepted between September 1 and February 1. Competitive applicants are invited to visit the College for an interview. Applications may be obtained from the address below.

Correspondence and Information

Dr. Kathryn Peek
Director, Office of Student Affairs
College of Optometry
University of Houston
Houston, Texas 77204-6052

Telephone: 713-743-2040
800-282-8426 (toll-free)
E-mail: osa@mail-gw.opt.uh.edu

University of Houston

THE FACULTY AND THEIR RESEARCH

Norman Bailey, Optometrist; M.A., Vanderbilt (Peabody), 1985; O.D., Indiana, 1969. Primary care.
Harold Bedell, Professor; Ph.D., Florida, 1978. Normal and abnormal eye movements and space perception, peripheral vision, amblyopia, strabismus, nystagmus.
Jan Bergmanson, Professor; Ph.D., The City University (London), 1975; O.D., Pennsylvania College of Optometry, 1982; Diplomate in Cornea and Contact Lenses. Corneal response to contact lens wear, ultrastructural analysis of radiation effects on ocular tissue, corneal laser procedures.
Rudolph Black, Visiting Assistant Professor; O.D., Houston, 1975. Primary care, adult vision.
Roger Boltz, Associate Professor and Associate Dean; O.D., 1972, Ph.D., 1978, Houston. Contact lenses, primary care, corneal pathology.
Yuzo Chino, Professor; Ph.D., Syracuse, 1973. Neural plasticity, effects of abnormal visual experience on the psychophysical and neurophysiological aspects of visual system development, neuroanatomy and neurophysiology.
Kia Eldred, Visiting Assistant Professor; O.D., Houston, 1987. Vision rehabilitation, adult vision, gerontology.
Karen Fern, Associate Professor and Director of Pediatric and Binocular Vision Service; O.D., Pacific University, 1981. Pediatrics, binocular vision, vision development, preschool vision screenings, assessing visual functions in preschool children.
Merton Flom, Professor; O.D., 1951, Ph.D., 1957, Berkeley. Binocular vision, space perception, acuity, strabismus, amblyopia.
Donald Fox, Professor; Ph.D., Cincinnati, 1977. Apoptosis, effects of drugs and chemicals on the developing and mature retina, cell and molecular biology, biochemistry, neurophysiology and morphology.
Laura Frishman, Professor; Ph.D., Pittsburgh, 1979. Visual physiology in the retina and brain, concentration on intraretinal analysis of the components of the electroretinogram (ERG) and study of the time course, spatial organization and retinal circuitry of post-receptoral adaptation mechanisms in rod-dominated vision.
Nancy George, Visiting Associate Professor; O.D., Houston, 1981. Primary care, ocular disease, retinal blood flow.
Ronald Harwerth, Professor; O.D., Houston, 1964; Ph.D., Texas at Houston, 1971. Psychophysics of vision, animal psychophysics, binocular vision in monkey and man, experimental glaucoma in monkey.
Ralph Herring, Optometrist and Director of Business and Finance Administration for the University Eye Institute; O.D., Houston, 1982. Primary care, adult vision, gerontology, sports vision, ocular effects of HIV, health-care administration.
Nicky Holdeman, Associate Professor, Director of the University Eye Institute, and Chief of Medical Services; O.D., Houston, 1976; M.D., Texas Tech, 1987. Medical management of ocular disease, ocular manifestations of systemic disease, ocular trauma.
Bai-Chuan Jiang, Research Assistant Professor; Ph.D., Shanghai Institute of Physiology, Academia Sinica, 1986. Accommodation, convergence, and myopia; phychophysics of vision; optics.
Randall Jose, Associate Professor; O.D., Berkeley, 1969. Low vision patient care, design of optical systems for the partially-sighted.
Penelope Kegel-Flom, Associate Professor; Ph.D., Berkeley, 1970. Patient communication, evaluations, admissions, educational research, women's health, leadership.
Robin Kralich, Visiting Assistant Professor; O.D., Southern College of Optometry, 1995. Clinical science.
Kimberly Lambreghts, Visiting Assistant Professor; O.D., SUNY College of Optometry, 1993.
Norman Leach, Optometrist and Director of the Cornea and Contact Lens Service; O.D., 1970, M.S., 1972, Houston. Primary care, contact lenses.
Dennis Levi, Professor and Associate Dean; O.D., 1971, Ph.D., 1977, Houston. Spatial vision, amblyopia and binocular anomalies.
Ruth Manny, Associate Professor and Chair, Clinical Sciences Department; O.D., 1975, Ph.D., 1981, Houston. Pediatrics, binocular vision, development of normal and abnormal vision in human infants.
Danica Marrelli, Visiting Assistant Professor; O.D., Houston, 1992. Ocular disease diagnosis and management, primary care.
Stephen Morse, Associate Professor; O.D., Illinois College of Optometry, 1977; M.P.H., Texas, 1984; Ph.D., Houston, 1991. Accommodation, myopia development, primary care, public health.
Anastas Pass, Associate Professor; O.D., Illinois College of Optometry, 1979; M.S., Houston, 1981. Clinical visual psychophysics and electrophysiology, ocular and/or visual manifestations of ocular and systemic neurological disorders, glaucoma.
Paul Pease, Associate Professor; O.D., Pennsylvania College of Optometry, 1967; Ph.D., Berkeley, 1975. Normal and abnormal color vision, macular pigment, chromatic aberration, environmental optometry.
David Perrigin, Associate Professor; O.D., Houston, 1969. Primary care, epidemiology of refractive errors, ocular photo-documentation.
Judy Perrigin, Associate Professor; O.D., Houston, 1977. Contact lenses, primary care, medical laboratory analysis, ocular microbiology, epidemiology of refractive errors.
Marcus Piccolo, Associate Professor; O.D., Pennsylvania College of Optometry, 1978. Ocular disease, ocular pharmacology, contact lenses and primary care.
Sam Quintero, Associate Professor; O.D., Houston, 1972. Primary care, diagnostic procedures.
Nelson Reber, Professor; O.D., Houston, 1963. Primary care.
Lewis Reich, Research Assistant Professor; M.S., Pennsylvania College of Optometry; O.D., Berkeley, 1988; Vision rehabilitation, spatial vision, optics of low vision devices.
John Robson, Adjunct Professor; Ph.D., St. John's, 1961. Vision science.
Jerome Rosner, Professor; O.D., Pennsylvania College of Optometry, 1944. Primary care, pediatrics, visually-related learning disorders.
Gary Savage, Associate Professor; O.D., 1973, Ph.D., 1988, Berkeley. Vision at low light levels, effects of aging on the eye-visual performance.
Pat Segu, Optometrist; O.D., Houston, 1992. Primary care, HIV-related eye disease.
David M. Sherry, Assistant Professor; Ph.D., Florida, 1989. Synapse formation and regeneration by retinal neurons, neuroanantomy of retinal neurotransmitter circuitry.
Earl Smith III, Greeman-Petty Professor of Vision Development and Chair, Basic Sciences Department; O.D., 1972, Ph.D., 1978, Houston. Psychophysical and neurophysiological aspects of amblyopia and strabismus, emmetropization, refractive anomalies.
Gregory Stephens, Associate Professor; O.D./Ph.D., Ohio State, 1979. Ophthalmic optics, ophthalmic materials testing, binocular vision.
Scott Stevenson, Assistant Professor; Ph.D., Brown, 1987. Visual information processing, depth perception, voluntary and involuntary eye movements, eye alignment.
Jerald Strickland, Professor and Dean; O.D., 1959, Ph.D., 1976, Indiana. Primary care, adult vision, environmental vision, health-care administration.
Diane Suarez, Visiting Assistant Professor; O.D., SUNY, 1994. Primary care.
Mark Swan, Assistant Professor; O.D., Ferris State, 1988; M.Ed., Berkeley, 1991. Reading dysfunction, pediatrics, binocular vision, VDT workstations.
James Walters, Associate Professor and Director of the OD/Medical Clinic; Ph.D., Michigan State, 1969; O.D., New England College of Optometry, 1974. Ocular pathology, retinal pathology, clinical electrophysiology.
Elizabeth Westin, Assistant Professor; O.D., Illinois College of Optometry, 1981. Contact lenses, primary care, corneal pathology.
Bruce Wick, Associate Professor; O.D., Berkeley, 1972; Ph.D., Houston, 1991. Primary care, binocular vision.
William Woessner, Associate Professor; O.D., Southern College of Optometry, 1968. Age-related changes in visual function, corneal development, pupillography.
Stanley Woo, Visiting Assistant Professor; O.D., Berkeley, 1994. Low vision patient care, clinical and functional outcomes, measures and psychophysics of low vision.

UNIVERSITY OF HOUSTON

College of Optometry
Graduate Program in Physiological Optics / Vision Science

Program of Study

The Graduate Program in Physiological Optics/Vision Science prepares the student to earn the M.S. and/or Ph.D. degree and thereby embark on a career in teaching and/or research in the basic science of vision. Students are accepted into the program with a B.S. degree (or the equivalent) from a variety of fields such as optometry, physiological optics, medicine, ophthalmology, anatomy, physiology, psychology, bioengineering, and biophysics.

The need for new knowledge in the vision sciences is great, and teaching and research opportunities are numerous in a spectrum of academic, industrial, and professional settings. Although the program has sufficient structure to provide a broad base of scientific knowledge about vision systems, it is at the same time appropriately flexible to permit students to develop expertise in areas of special interest, such as visual psychophysics; form and space perception; neurophysiology of vision; pharmacology, toxicology, and pathology of the visual system; physiology of the eye; eye-movement control systems; color mechanisms; and the development of vision.

The M.S. track requires about two years of study, including 30 semester hours of courses, teaching experience, and a research project with a thesis.

The Ph.D. track normally requires about four years of study, including 60 semester hours of courses, preliminary examinations, teaching experience, a foreign language or research skill, a qualifying examination, and research with a dissertation. Beginning fall 1998, a combined O.D./Ph.D. program, which requires six to seven years of study will be offered.

Research Facilities

The facilities and resources for the program are exceptional. The research laboratories all have workstations, linked through a local network and to the Internet. Shared facilities include histological laboratories, a scanning laser ophthalmoscope, eye-trackers, an electron microscope, animal quarters, an electronics shop and machine shop with full-time technical personnel, and complete audiovisual facilities. A large optometry clinic is available for patient-based research.

Financial Aid

The College's policy is to assist full-time students who are working toward the M.S. or Ph.D. degree to obtain financial support whenever they need it. College funds make available half-time teaching assistantships (starting at $9000 for nine months) and half-time clinical postdoctoral appointments (starting at $15,600 for twelve months), which are available to qualified optometrists and physicians. Research assistantships, funded by grants to faculty members, are also available at the same levels as teaching assistantships and clinical appointments. Predoctoral fellowships (paying $10,008) and post-O.D. or post-M.D. fellowships (paying $19,608–$32,300) may be available to U.S. citizens on a competitive basis through National Institutes of Health training grants to the College. Support levels are based on student qualifications and experience. Students who hold appointments at least half-time receive an out-of-state tuition waiver; postdoctoral appointments also include a waiver of general fees. Other scholarships and fellowships are available through the University and from outside agencies such as the National Institutes of Health, the American Optometric Foundation, and the Auxiliary to the American Optometric Association.

Cost of Study

The tuition and fees for students who are Texas residents are about $1260 per semester in 1998–99 (for a course load of 12 hours); for nonresident students, these costs are about $3500 per semester.

Living and Housing Costs

Annual costs for housing, food, and moderate entertainment amount to about $6000 for a single student and about $11,000 for a married student without children. The University has housing facilities on or near the campus; costs are about $3800 for room and board for the academic year in 1998–99. A varied choice of housing is available off campus; one-bedroom-apartment rents average about $350 per month.

Student Group

Enrollment in the program is usually about 25 students, a majority of whom proceed to the Ph.D. degree. Enrollment in the College is about 425; university enrollment is about 31,000. Most students in the program are nonresidents about 30 years old; one half are women. The program's students come from such fields as biology, chemistry, biophysics, engineering, medicine, optometry, and psychology.

Student Outcomes

Some recent Ph.D. graduates hold postdoctoral research positions at the Wilmer Eye Institute at Johns Hopkins, Harvard, Cambridge, and Berkeley. Others hold faculty and research positions at the Universities of Waterloo, Indiana, Aston, Virginia, San Diego, Melbourne, and Houston. Recent M.S. graduates are now Ph.D. candidates, hold faculty positions (e.g., the Universities of Houston and Nigeria and Southern California College of Optometry), or are in private practice and industry, including the C. Everett Koop Institute.

Location

Houston, a fast-developing and growing metropolis, is a center for business, health care, and science that offers many opportunities for the young scientist. The dynamic atmosphere affects every level of life and is especially invigorating to the educational community. The city provides a wide range of cultural amenities (museums, symphony, ballet, opera, and theater), sports facilities (spectator as well as participant), and recreational opportunities (beaches, the space center, and interesting day trips to surrounding areas).

The University and The College

The University of Houston is a state-supported university composed of fourteen colleges and schools. The 525-acre campus is 3 miles south of Houston's central business district.

The College of Optometry, opened in 1952, offers a professional program leading to the O.D. degree in addition to the Graduate Program in Physiological Optics/Vision Science. In 1976, to provide for expansion, the College moved to its present building—one of the most modern optometric facilities in the country. The research laboratories, teaching clinics, and extensive library are complemented by a dedicated faculty of renowned vision scientists.

Applying

Students applying for admittance to the Graduate Program in Physiological Optics/Vision Science should submit a completed application, official transcripts of all college work, official GRE General Test scores, three letters of recommendation from teachers or others familiar with the applicant's scholarship and research potential, a curriculum vitae, and a statement of research interests and academic goals. International students must supply official TOEFL scores (550 or higher required) and official TSE scores. The application deadline is January 31 to be considered for fall semester admittance.

Correspondence and Information

Dennis M. Levi, Associate Dean
Graduate Studies/Research
College of Optometry
University of Houston
Houston, Texas 77204-6052

Telephone: 713-743-1885
Fax: 713-743-1888
E-mail: dharrison@uh.edu

University of Houston

RESEARCH SUPERVISORS AND THEIR INTERESTS

Harold E. Bedell, Professor; Ph.D., Florida. Normal and abnormal space perception, control of eye movements, peripheral vision, clinical applications of visual psychophysics, nystagmus.
Jan P. G. Bergmanson, Professor; Ph.D., City University (London); O.D., Pennsylvania College of Optometry. Anatomy and pathology of cornea, corneal response to contact lenses, corneal wound healing and laser effects on ocular tissues.
Yuzo M. Chino, Professor; Ph.D., Syracuse. Neural plasticity, binocular vision, amblyopia, development.
Karen D. Fern, Associate Professor; O.D., Pacific University. Vision development, assessing visual functions in preschool children, preschool vision screening.
Merton C. Flom, Professor; M.Optom., Ph.D., Berkeley. Binocular vision, space perception, acuity, strabismus, amblyopia.
Donald A. Fox, Professor; Ph.D., Cincinnati. Retinal cellular and molecular biology; effects of lead and drugs on cellular biochemistry, physiology, and morphology of developing and mature retina; mechanisms of apoptotic cell death.
Laura J. Frishman, Professor; M.S., Ph.D., Pittsburgh. Retinal physiology, retinal origins and cellular mechanisms of the electroretinogram (ERG).
Ronald S. Harwerth, Professor; O.D., Houston; Ph.D., Texas Health Science Center at Houston. Psychophysics of vision, animal psychophysics, binocular vision, visual field defects from glaucoma.
Bai-chuan Jiang, Research Associate Professor; Ph.D., Chinese Academy of Sciences. Oculomotor systems, myopia, spatial vision, image quality and optics.
Norman Leach, Associate Professor and Director of the Cornea and Contact Lens Service; O.D., M.S., Houston. Primary care, contact lenses.
Dennis M. Levi, Professor; O.D., Ph.D., Houston. Spatial vision, amblyopia and binocular anomalies.
Ruth E. Manny, Associate Professor; O.D., Ph.D., Houston. Development of normal and abnormal vision in human infants, preschool vision screening, refractive error development.
Stephen Morse, Associate Professor; O.D., Illinois College of Optometry; M.P.H., Texas; Ph.D., Houston. Binocular vision, oculomotor system, refractive error development, vision issues in public health.
Anastas F. Pass, Associate Professor; O.D., Illinois College of Optometry; M.S., Houston. Assessment of ocular and visual manifestations of (CNS) neurological disorders, ocular disease, imaging, telemedicine.
Paul L. Pease, Associate Professor; O.D., Pennsylvania College of Optometry; Ph.D., Berkeley. Normal color vision and color vision deficiencies, color vision testing, human factors in lighting.
Marcus Piccolo, Associate Professor; O.D., Pennsylvania College of Optometry. Ocular disease, ocular pharmacology, contact lenses and primary care.
John Robson, Senior Research Professor; M.A., Ph.D., Cambridge. Retinal electrophysiology, visual neurophysiology, light adaptation, contrast sensitivity, normal lens pigmentation.
Gary L. Savage, Associate Professor; O.D., Ph.D., Berkeley. Vision at low light levels, effects of aging on the eye/visual performance.
David M. Sherry, Assistant Professor; Ph.D., Florida. Synapse formation and regeneration by retinal neurons, neuroanatomy of retinal neurotransmitter circuitry.
Earl L. Smith III, Professor; O.D., Ph.D., Houston. Myopia, amblyopia, binocular vision, effects of visual experience on visual system development.
Gregory L. Stephens, Associate Professor; O.D., Ph.D., Ohio State. Ophthalmic optics, lens design, binocular vision.
Scott Stevenson, Assistant Professor; Ph.D., Brown. Vergence eye movements and binocular coordination, stereoscopic depth perception, modeling of binocular image matching processes.
Bruce Wick, Associate Professor; O.D., Berkeley; Ph.D., Houston. Binocular vision, interactions between accommodation and vergence, strabismus, amblyopia, nystagmus.

The College of Optometry building at the University of Houston.

A student in Dr. David Sherry's lab examines immunolabeled retinal photoreceptors for analysis of regenerative growth and synapse formation.

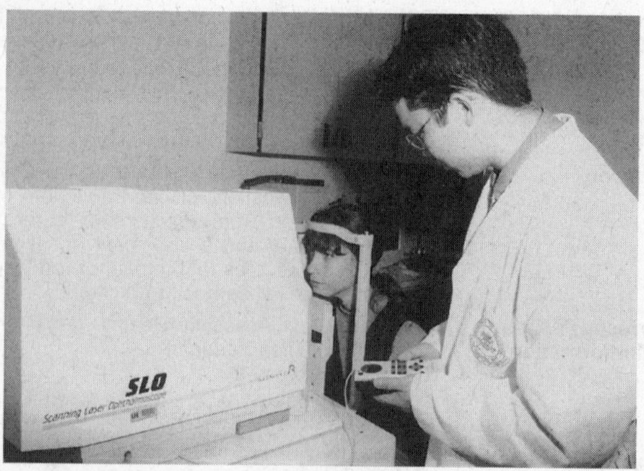

Dr. Stanley Woo evaluates a retina using the Scanning Laser Ophthalmoscope.

Section 37
Oriental Medicine and Acupuncture

This section contains a directory of institutions offering graduate work in Oriental medicine and acupuncture, followed by in-depth entries submitted by institutions that chose to prepare detailed program descriptions. Additional information about programs listed in the directory but not augmented by an in-depth entry may be obtained by writing directly to the dean of a school or chair of a department at the address given in the directory.

CONTENTS

Program Directory

Announcements

In-Depth Descriptions

See also:

Oriental Medicine and Acupuncture

Academy of Chinese Culture and Health Sciences, Program in Traditional Chinese Medicine, Oakland, CA 94612. Awards MS. Accredited by NACSCAOM. Part-time and evening/weekend programs available. Faculty: 6 full-time (3 women), 28 part-time (15 women). Students: 161 (93 women); includes 82 minority (3 African Americans, 76 Asian Americans, 3 Hispanics), 16 international. Average age 40. 41 applicants, 95% accepted. In 1997, 19 degrees awarded. *Degree requirements:* Thesis required, foreign language not required. *Average time to degree:* master's–3 years full-time, 5 years part-time. *Entrance requirements:* TOEFL (minimum score 500). Application deadline: 9/8 (priority date; rolling processing; 1/8 for spring admission). Application fee: $50 ($100 for international students). *Faculty research:* Herbs, acupuncture. • Jane Zhang, Director of Administration, 510-763-7787. E-mail: jane@acchs.edu. Application contact: Y. Chun Hsieh, Admissions Administrator, 510-763-7787. Fax: 510-834-8646. E-mail: ychun@acchs.edu.

Announcement: The Academy is a regionally and nationally accredited graduate studies program that prepares individuals to become licensed physicians of Chinese medicine and acupuncture. This 3-year curriculum, given in English and Chinese, covers the fundamental principles of a 5,000-year-old philosophy of healing the mind and body, continued by the founding President, a Chinese Taoist. The Master of Science degree, awarded in traditional Chinese medicine, provides the eligibility for individuals to take a state licensing exam to become fully certified licensed acupuncturists. Centrally located in Oakland and the California Bay area, the Academy is easily accessible via BART.

American College of Traditional Chinese Medicine, Graduate Program, San Francisco, CA 94107. Offers program in traditional Chinese medicine (MS). Accredited by NACSCAOM. Part-time programs available. Faculty: 8 full-time (2 women), 25 part-time (14 women), 18 FTE. Students: 138 full-time (89 women), 58 part-time (39 women); includes 72 minority (3 African Americans, 66 Asian Americans, 3 Hispanics). Average age 35. 73 applicants, 60% accepted. In 1997, 16 degrees awarded (100% found work related to degree). *Degree requirements:* 1 foreign language required, thesis not required. *Average time to degree:* master's–3.5 years full-time, 6 years part-time. *Application deadline:* 8/15 (priority date; rolling processing; 3/15 for spring admission). *Application fee:* $100 ($125 for international students). *Tuition:* $134 per credit (minimum). *Financial aid:* In 1997–98, 80 students received aid, including 18 teaching assistantships averaging $188 per month; Federal Work-Study and career-related internships or fieldwork also available. Aid available to part-time students. Financial aid applicants required to submit FAFSA. • Li Xin Huang, President, 415-282-7600 Ext. 12. E-mail: lhuang@actcm.org. Application contact: Lori Long, Admissions Officer, 415-282-7600 Ext. 14. Fax: 415-282-0856. E-mail: lhuang@actcm.org.

Bastyr University, Acupuncture and Oriental Medicine Program, 14500 Juanita Drive, NE, Bothell, WA 98011. Awards MS. Accredited by NACSCAOM. Part-time programs available. Students: 58 full-time (50 women), 36 part-time (27 women). Average age 31. 65 applicants, 80% accepted. In 1997, 21 degrees awarded. *Average time to degree:* master's–3 years full-time, 4 years part-time. *Entrance requirements:* BS degree with 1 year of course work in biochemistry, anatomy, physiology, and traditional Chinese medicine. Application deadline: 4/1 (priority date; rolling processing). Application fee: $60. *Expenses:* Tuition $180 per credit hour. Fees $15 per credit hour. *Financial aid:* Federal Work-Study and career-related internships or fieldwork available. Aid available to part-time students. Financial aid application deadline: 4/15; applicants required to submit FAFSA. • Dr. Mark Nolting, Chair, 425-823-1300. Application contact: Stephen Bangs, Director of Admissions, 425-602-3100. Fax: 425-823-6222.

See in-depth description on page 1763.

Dongguk–Royal University, Program in Oriental Medicine, Los Angeles, CA 90017. Awards MS. Accredited by NACSCAOM. Faculty: 50. Students: 300. *Application deadline:* rolling. *Application fee:* $100 ($200 for international students). *Tuition:* $100 per unit. • Samuel Kim, Dean of Academics, 213-482-6646. Application contact: Xianze Zhao, Dean of Admission, 213-482-6646.

Emperor's College of Traditional Oriental Medicine, Program in Chinese Medicine and Acupuncture, Santa Monica, CA 90403. Awards MTOM. Accredited by NACSCAOM. Faculty: 50. Students: 387. *Application fee:* $150. *Tuition:* $108 per unit. • Academic Dean, 310-453-8300. Application contact: Catherine Allen, Director of Development, 310-453-8300.

Five Branches Institute: College of Traditional Chinese Medicine, Program in Traditional Chinese Medicine, Santa Cruz, CA 95062. Awards MTCM. Accredited by NACSCAOM. Faculty: 27 part-time (13 women), 10 FTE. Students: 100 full-time (60 women); includes 10 minority (6 Asian Americans, 2 Hispanics, 2 Native Americans), 5 international. Average age 35. 50 applicants, 50% accepted. In 1997, 21 degrees awarded (100% found work related to degree). *Degree requirements:* Comprehensive exam required, foreign language and thesis not required. *Average time to degree:* master's–4 years full-time. *Entrance requirements:* 6 units in anatomy and physiology, 9 units in basic sciences. Application deadline: rolling. Application fee: $30. *Tuition:* $6550 per year. *Financial aid:* Scholarships and career-related internships or fieldwork available. • Rich Callahan, Chief Administrative Officer, 408-476-9424. E-mail: tcm@fivebranches.com. Application contact: Meredith Bigley, Admissions Director, 408-476-9424. Fax: 408-476-8928. E-mail: tcm@fivebranches.com.

International Institute of Chinese Medicine, Program in Oriental Bodywork, Santa Fe, NM 87502. Awards Certificate. Part-time and evening/weekend programs available. Faculty: 1 (woman) full-time, 4 part-time (2 women). Students: 2 full-time (0 women); includes 1 minority (Hispanic). Average age 25. 4 applicants, 50% accepted. In 1997, 2 degrees awarded (100% found work related to degree). *Average time to degree:* other advanced degree–1 year full-time. *Application deadline:* 7/1 (priority date; rolling processing; 11/1 for spring admission). *Application fee:* $50. *Expenses:* Tuition $150 per credit full-time, $165 per credit part-time. Fees $170 per semester. *Financial aid:* Federal Work-Study available. • Dr. Michael Zeng, Director, 505-473-5233. E-mail: 102152.3463@compuserve.com. Application contact: Dr. Eric Winkel, Administrator, 505-473-5233. Fax: 505-473-9279. E-mail: 102152.3463@compuserve.com.

See in-depth description on page 1765.

International Institute of Chinese Medicine, Program in Oriental Medicine, Santa Fe, NM 87502. Awards MOM. Accredited by NACSCAOM. Part-time programs available. Faculty: 10 full-time (5 women), 21 part-time (10 women). Students: 143 full-time (94 women), 6 part-time (3 women); includes 13 minority (4 African Americans, 5 Asian Americans, 3 Hispanics, 1 Native American), 6 international. Average age 36. 70 applicants, 51% accepted. In 1997, 29 degrees awarded. *Average time to degree:* master's–3 years full-time, 6 years part-time. *Application deadline:* 7/1 (priority date; rolling processing; 11/1 for spring admission). *Application fee:* $50. *Expenses:* Tuition $150 per credit full-time, $165 per credit part-time. Fees $170 per semester. *Financial aid:* 99 students received aid; partial tuition waivers and career-related internships or fieldwork available. Aid available to part-time students. Financial aid applicants required to submit FAFSA. *Faculty research:* Use of oriental medicine in treating drug addiction. • Dr. Michael Zeng, Director, 505-473-5233. E-mail: 102152.3463@compuserve.com. Application contact: Dr. Eric Winkel, Administrator, 505-478-5233. Fax: 505-473-9279. E-mail: 102152.3463@compuserve.com.

See in-depth description on page 1765.

Kyung San University USA, School of Oriental Medicine, Garden Grove, CA 92644. Awards MSOM. Candidate for accreditation by NACSCAOM. Part-time programs available. Faculty: 13. Students: 80. *Degree requirements:* Thesis, clinical internship required, foreign language not required. *Application deadline:* 9/6 (priority date; rolling processing; 3/10 for spring admission). *Application fee:* $100. *Expenses:* Tuition $5000 per year. Fees $105 per year. *Financial aid:* Full and partial tuition waivers, institutionally sponsored loans, and career-related internships or fieldwork available. *Faculty research:* Lipidemia and herbal medicine, OB/GYN and acupuncture. • P. S. Jeong, Academic Dean, 714-636-0337. E-mail: admin@kyungsan.edu. Application contact: E. S. Lee, Registrar, 714-636-0337. Fax: 714-636-8459. E-mail: admin@kyungsan@edu.

Meiji College of Oriental Medicine, Program in Oriental Medicine, San Francisco, CA 94115. Awards MS. Accredited by NACSCAOM. Faculty: 5 full-time (2 women), 12 part-time (3 women). Students: 68 full-time (51 women), 6 part-time (5 women); includes 12 minority (10 Asian Americans, 2 Hispanics), 2 international. Average age 35. 44 applicants, 75% accepted. In 1997, 10 degrees awarded (100% found work related to degree). *Average time to degree:* master's–3 years full-time, 5 years part-time. *Entrance requirements:* Interview, minimum GPA of 2.5. Application deadline: 7/31 (rolling processing). Application fee: $50. *Expenses:* Tuition $7000 per year. Fees $33 per year. *Financial aid:* 34 students received aid; institutionally sponsored loans available. Financial aid application deadline: 7/31. *Faculty research:* Stimulus therapy, oxygen hemoglobin and acupuncture needling. • Hirohisa Oda, President, 415-771-1019. Application contact: Teresa Voelker, Admissions Officer, 415-771-1019. Fax: 415-771-1036.

See in-depth description on page 1767.

Mercy College, Department of Acupuncture and Oriental Medicine, Dobbs Ferry, NY 10522-1189. Awards MPS. Candidate for accreditation by NACSCAOM. Faculty: 3. Students: 13 (6 women). *Degree requirements:* Thesis required, foreign language not required. *Entrance requirements:* Minimum undergraduate GPA of 3.0. Application deadline: 2/1. Application fee: $60. *Tuition:* $12,600 per year. • William G. Prensky, Director, 914-674-7384. Application contact: Admissions Office, 800-MERCY-NY. Fax: 914-674-7382. E-mail: admission@merlin.mercynet.edu.

National College of Naturopathic Medicine, Program in Chinese Medicine, Portland, OR 97201. Offers Oriental medicine (MS). Candidate for accreditation by NACSCAOM. Program new for fall 1998. *Entrance requirements:* MD, ND, DO, DC, or Nurse Practitioner. Application deadline: 2/1 (1/15 for spring admission). Application fee: $60. • Dr. Heiner Fruehauf, Chair. Application contact: Andrea Smith, Assistant Dean of Academic Affairs.

See in-depth description on page 1733.

New England School of Acupuncture, Program in Acupuncture, Watertown, MA 02472. Awards M Ac, Certificate. One or more programs accredited by NACSCAOM. Certificate being phased out; applicants no longer accepted. Part-time programs available. Faculty: 60 part-time (35 women). Students: 179 full-time (122 women), 28 part-time (26 women). *Average time to degree:* master's–3 years full-time; other advanced degree–3 years full-time. *Application deadline:* rolling. *Application fee:* $50. *Expenses:* Tuition $8775 per year full-time, $240 per credit part-time. Fees $240 per year. *Financial aid:* Available to part-time students. Financial aid application deadline: 6/1; applicants required to submit FAFSA. • Evelyn Fowler, Academic Dean, 617-926-1788 Ext. 120. Application contact: Cindy Rosenbaum, Dean of Students and Admissions, 617-926-1788 Ext. 119. Fax: 617-924-4167.

See in-depth description on page 1769.

Northwest Institute of Acupuncture and Oriental Medicine, Program in Acupuncture, Seattle, WA 98103. Offers acupuncture (M Ac), advanced herbal studies (Certificate), traditional Chinese medicine (MTCM). One or more programs accredited by NACSCAOM. MTCM new for fall 1998. Faculty: 9 full-time (5 women), 34 part-time (18 women). Students: 183 full-time (129 women), 18 part-time (12 women); includes 23 minority (20 Asian Americans, 3 Hispanics), 13 international. Average age 37. In 1997, 34 master's awarded. *Average time to degree:* master's–3 years full-time, 4 years part-time. *Entrance requirements:* For master's, minimum 3 years of college, previous course work in general biology and psychology. Application deadline: 5/1 (priority date; rolling processing). Application fee: $50. *Expenses:* Tuition $8308 per year full-time, $145 per credit hour part-time. Fees $25 per year. *Financial aid:* 113 students received aid. Financial aid application deadline: 8/31; applicants required to submit FAFSA. *Faculty research:* Outcomes research on acupuncture efficacy, pilot clinical trials. • Frederick O. Lanphear, President, 206-633-2419. E-mail: flanphear@niaom.org. Application contact: Mary McGhee, Dean of Students/Admissions Adviser, 206-633-2419. Fax: 206-633-5578. E-mail: mmcghee@niaom.org.

See in-depth description on page 1771.

Oregon College of Oriental Medicine, Graduate Program in Acupuncture and Oriental Medicine, Portland, OR 97216. Awards M Ac OM. Accredited by NACSCAOM. Part-time programs available. Faculty: 7 full-time (4 women), 23 part-time (12 women). Students: 146 full-time (94 women), 24 part-time (17 women); includes 13 minority (2 African Americans, 9 Asian Americans, 2 Hispanics), 2 international. Average age 34. 109 applicants, 84% accepted. In 1997, 39 degrees awarded. *Average time to degree:* master's–3 years full-time, 4.5 years part-time. *Entrance requirements:* Minimum 3 years of college, previous course work in chemistry, biology, and psychology. Application deadline: 7/1 (priority date; rolling processing). Application fee: $50. *Expenses:* Tuition $8516 per year full-time, $5072 per year part-time. Fees $30 per year. *Financial aid:* 138 students received aid; Federal Work-Study available. Aid available to part-time students. Financial aid applicants required to submit FAFSA. • Dr. Elizabeth A. Goldblatt, President, 503-253-3443. Application contact: James Eddy, Dean of Institutional Affairs, 503-253-3443. Fax: 503-253-2701. E-mail: 103226.164@compuserve.com.

See in-depth description on page 1773.

Pacific College of Oriental Medicine, Master's Program in Traditional Oriental Medicine, 7445 Mission Valley Road, Suite 105, San Diego, CA 92108. Awards MTOM. Accredited by NACSCAOM. Part-time and evening/weekend programs available. Faculty: 8 full-time (4 women), 40 part-time (20 women). Students: 330. *Application deadline:* 9/8 (rolling processing). *Application fee:* $50 ($100 for international students). *Expenses:* Tuition $160 per unit. Fees $20 per semester. *Financial aid:* Career-related internships or fieldwork available. Aid available to part-time students. Financial aid applicants required to submit FAFSA. *Faculty research:* PMS, acupuncture, herbs. • Jack Miller, President, 619-574-6909. E-mail: 76545.2617.compuserve.com. Application contact: Reine S. Deming, Director of Admissions, 800-729-0941. Fax: 619-574-6641. E-mail: rdeming@ormed.edu.

See in-depth description on page 1775.

Pacific College of Oriental Medicine, Pacific Institute of Oriental Medicine, Program in Acupuncture, 915 Broadway, 3rd Floor, New York, NY 10010. Awards Diploma. Accredited by NACSCAOM. Students: 80 part-time. *Entrance requirements:* Associate's degree. Application deadline: 7/7 (priority date; rolling processing; 3/21 for spring admission). Application fee: $50 ($100 for international students). • Application contact: Jennifer Parks, Admissions Counselor, 212-982-3456. Fax: 212-982-6514.

See in-depth description on page 1775.

Pacific College of Oriental Medicine, Pacific Institute of Oriental Medicine, Program in Traditional Oriental Medicine, 915 Broadway, 3rd Floor, New York, NY 10010. Awards Diploma. Accredited by NACSCAOM. Students: 240. *Application deadline:* 7/7 (priority date; rolling processing; 3/21 for spring admission). *Application fee:* $50 ($100 for international students). • Application contact: Jennifer Parks, Admissions Counselor, 212-982-3456. Fax: 212-982-6514.

See in-depth description on page 1775.

Directory: Oriental Medicine and Acupuncture

Samra University of Oriental Medicine, Program in Oriental Medicine, Los Angeles, CA 90034-2014. Awards MS. Accredited by NACSCAOM. Part-time and evening/weekend programs available. Faculty: 80. Students: 322 full-time, 138 part-time. *Degree requirements:* Comprehensive exam required, foreign language and thesis not required. *Average time to degree:* master's–4 years full-time, 6 years part-time. *Application deadline:* rolling. *Application fee:* $75 ($100 for international students). *Tuition:* $95 per unit. *Financial aid:* Available to part-time students. *Faculty research:* Herbal therapy; alleviation of AIDS symptoms, cancer, colds, flu. • Dr. Kathryn P. White, Academic Dean, 310-202-6444 Ext. 113. Fax: 310-202-6004. E-mail: academicdean@samra.edu. Application contact: Dr. Aaron Sui, Admissions Director, 310-202-6444 Ext. 102. Fax: 310-202-6007. E-mail: admissions@samra.edu.

See in-depth description on page 1777.

Santa Barbara College of Oriental Medicine, Program in Acupuncture and Oriental Medicine, Santa Barbara, CA 93101. Awards M Ac OM. Accredited by NACSCAOM. Faculty: 18. Students: 96. *Entrance requirements:* Minimum 2 years of college. Application deadline: 5/31 (priority date; rolling processing). Application fee: $50 ($100 for international students). *Expenses:* Tuition $142 per unit. Fees $25 per trimester. • JoAnn Hickey, President, 805-682-9594. Application contact: Allegra Heidelinde, Registrar, 805-898-1180. Fax: 805-682-1864.

South Baylo University, Program in Acupuncture and Oriental Medicine, Anaheim, CA 92801-1701. Awards MS. Accredited by NACSCAOM. Part-time and evening/weekend programs available. Faculty: 52. Students: 220 full-time, 330 part-time. *Degree requirements:* Thesis, clinical internship required, foreign language not required. *Application fee:* $100. *Expenses:* Tuition $4500 per year full-time, $800 per quarter (minimum) part-time. Fees $165 per year. *Financial aid:* In 1997–98, 6 fellowships were awarded; research assistantships, teaching assistantships also available. • Dr. Wen-Shu Wu, Dean, 714-533-1495. Application contact: Ronald Sokolsky, Director, 714-533-1495.

Southwest Acupuncture College, Program in Oriental Medicine, Santa Fe, NM 87505. Awards MS. Accredited by NACSCAOM. Part-time and evening/weekend programs available. Faculty: 6 full-time (4 women), 14 part-time (10 women). Students: 143 full-time (104 women), 13 part-time (8 women); includes 7 minority (3 African Americans, 2 Asian Americans, 2 Hispanics), 1 international. Average age 31. 92 applicants, 82% accepted. In 1997, 15 degrees awarded. *Average time to degree:* master's–3 years full-time, 4 years part-time. *Application deadline:* rolling. *Application fee:* $50. *Tuition:* $10,000 per year. *Financial aid:* 129 students received aid. Financial aid application deadline: 5/31; applicants required to submit FAFSA. • Skya Gardner Abbate, Chairman, 505-438-8884. Fax: 505-438-8883.

Southwest College of Naturopathic Medicine and Health Sciences, Program in Acupuncture, Tempe, AZ 85282. Awards Certificate, ND/Certificate. Students: 48 full-time (29 women), 2 part-time (1 woman); includes 5 minority (4 Asian Americans, 1 Hispanic). Average age 34. 60 applicants, 97% accepted. In 1997, 6 degrees awarded. *Average time to degree:* other advanced degree–2 years full-time. *Entrance requirements:* Minimum GPA of 2.5. Application deadline: 7/1 (priority date; rolling processing). Application fee: $65 ($90 for international students). • Dr. Ian Bier, Dean, 602-858-9100.

Announcement: Southwest College offers a master's-level Certificate in Acupuncture. Upon completion of the 3-academic–year program, students are awarded a Certificate in Acupuncture. Through this course of study, students are prepared to take the National Commission for the Certification of Acupuncturists National Board Examination.

See in-depth description on page 1741.

Tai Hsuan Foundation: College of Acupuncture and Herbal Medicine, Program in Acupuncture and Oriental Medicine, Honolulu, HI 96826. Awards M Ac OM. Accredited by NACSCAOM. Part-time programs available. Faculty: 16 part-time (7 women). Students: 30 full-time (15 women), 4 part-time (0 women); includes 12 minority (8 Asian Americans, 4 Hispanics). Average age 26. 28 applicants, 100% accepted. In 1997, 7 degrees awarded. *Average time to degree:* master's–3 years full-time. *Entrance requirements:* Minimum 60 college credits. Application deadline: 9/1 (rolling processing; 12/30 for spring admission). Application fee: $50. *Financial aid:* 5 students received aid. Financial aid application deadline: 9/1; applicants required to submit FAFSA. • Eric Ono, Vice President of Academic Affairs, 808-947-4788. Application contact: Lili Chen, Vice President of Admissions, 808-947-4788. Fax: 808-947-1152.

Traditional Acupuncture Institute, Program in Acupuncture, Columbia, MD 21044-3422. Awards M Ac. Accredited by NACSCAOM. Faculty: 70 part-time (50 women). Students: 197 full-time (147 women); includes 15 minority (2 African Americans, 11 Asian Americans, 1 Hispanic, 1 Native American), 4 international. Average age 30. 70 applicants, 57% accepted. In 1997, 47 degrees awarded. *Average time to degree:* master's–3 years full-time. *Application deadline:* rolling. *Application fee:* $65. *Tuition:* $11,530 per year (minimum). *Financial aid:* Partial tuition waivers, institutionally sponsored loans available. Financial aid applicants required to submit FAFSA. • Barbara Ellrich, Vice President, 410-997-4888. Application contact: Vicki Rapoport, Admissions Coordinator, 410-997-4888 Ext. 647.

Yo San University of Traditional Chinese Medicine, Program in Acupuncture and Traditional Chinese Medicine, Santa Monica, CA 90401. Awards MATCM. Accredited by NACSCAOM. Part-time programs available. Faculty: 2 full-time (1 woman), 36 part-time (22 women). Students: 140. Average age 32. 69 applicants, 91% accepted. In 1997, 8 degrees awarded. *Degree requirements:* Observation and practice internships, exam required, foreign language and thesis not required. *Average time to degree:* master's–4 years full-time, 6 years part-time. *Entrance requirements:* Minimum 2 years of college, interview, minimum GPA of 2.5. Application deadline: 8/7 (rolling processing). Application fee: $50 ($100 for international students). *Expenses:* Tuition $7500 per year full-time, $160 per unit part-time. Fees $75 per year. *Financial aid:* 90 students received aid. Aid available to part-time students. Financial aid applicants required to submit FAFSA. • David Boyd, Academic Dean, 310-917-2202 Ext. 15. Application contact: Doris Johnson, Admissions Counselor, 310-917-2202 Ext. 13. Fax: 310-917-2203.

BASTYR UNIVERSITY

Department of Acupuncture and Oriental Medicine

Programs of Study

Bastyr University, a small private university featuring a strong sense of community that fosters both academic and personal growth, offers two Master of Science degree programs in the field of acupuncture and Oriental medicine. The curriculum is based on traditional Chinese medicine (TCM) and is enhanced by contemporary Japanese, European, and American acupuncture. The 3½-year Master of Science in Acupuncture and Oriental Medicine (M.S.A.O.M.) is the model comprehensive program and encompasses Chinese herbal medicine and Chinese medical language in addition to the core theory, TCM diagnosis, TCM pathology, TCM techniques, acupuncture therapeutics, and clinical training required in the Master of Science in Acupuncture (M.S.A.). The shorter three-year quarter-credit M.S.A. is a viable choice for medical professionals who desire advanced comprehensive training in acupuncture. Students may study in day or evening programs. Clinical training takes place at the Bastyr Natural Health Clinic, a comprehensive, multidisciplinary clinic that provides training for students in all of the University's programs. The clinic includes a fully stocked Chinese herbal dispensary. Students also have the opportunity to train at external clinic sites with diverse populations from the community. Students in good academic standing may apply to complete clinical internship credits at the Chengdu University of Traditional Chinese Medicine. Graduates of the M.S. programs are eligible to apply for licensure in Washington State as well as in most other states that offer similar licensure. Currently, acupuncture is legal to practice in thirty-four states and several provinces. The M.S.A. and M.S.A.O.M. degree programs at Bastyr University are accredited by the Accreditation Commission for Acupuncture and Oriental Medicine (ACAOM).

Research Facilities

The University's mission includes the pursuit of scientific research on nonallopathic therapies in the management and treatment of health-care problems and in the prevention of chronic disease. Current research includes an NIH grant for the nationwide study on the use of alternative medicine for the treatment of HIV/AIDS. The University maintains a medical library with current journals; special collections in the areas of Oriental medicine, nutrition, and naturopathic medicine; and audiovisual equipment and materials. The library provides students with access to Dialog, a computer research service. Students also have access to the University of Washington Health Sciences Library.

Financial Aid

Students are eligible to participate in state and federal financial aid programs, including the Washington State Need Grant, Washington State Education Opportunity Grant, Federal Pell Grant, Federal Supplemental Educational Opportunity Grant (FSEOG), Federal Stafford Student Loan, Federal Perkins Loan, and Federal Work-Study. Complete financial aid information is provided by the University on request.

Cost of Study

Tuition for 1998–99 is $180 per credit; tuition for clinical courses is $206 per credit. Fees are approximately $100 per quarter. Total tuition and fees for a full-time student in the first year are $13,300. Books and supplies cost approximately $1100.

Living and Housing Costs

The University provides limited dormitory housing. Many students live in shared housing facilities off campus; the average rent per person is approximately $340 per month. The Student Services Office can direct students to listings of available housing. The Washington Association of Student Financial Aid Administrators estimates that living expenses, including transportation and personal expenses, average $850 per month.

Student Group

The University's total enrollment in 1997–98 was 680; of the 557 graduate and professional students who attended the University, 94 were graduate students in the Department of Acupuncture and Oriental Medicine. Seventy percent of the students were women. The average age was 32. Twenty-five percent were Washington residents; thirty-two other states were represented. Eighteen percent of the students were from other countries.

Location

The academic and administrative campus is on a 40-acre site adjoining St. Edward's State Park in Bothell, Washington, about 15 miles northeast of Seattle. Several hiking trails to Lake Washington begin at the edge of the campus; abundant opportunities for outdoor activities exist nearby in the Puget Sound area. The clinical campus is located in a Seattle neighborhood. The city offers a full range of activities and facilities, including museums, theaters, ethnic restaurants, a major opera and symphony orchestra, major-league sports, and outdoor activities. The Puget Sound area has a large number of academic institutions, including five universities and many colleges, community colleges, and professional schools.

The University

Bastyr University was founded as a naturopathic medical college in 1978. The University's mission includes serving as an effective leader in the improvement of the health and well-being of the human community. Since 1984, as a part of its mission to provide comprehensive education in the natural health sciences, the University has added graduate and undergraduate programs in Oriental medicine and nutrition as well as B.S. and M.A. programs in applied behavioral sciences through the Leadership Institute of Seattle (LIOS). Bastyr University is accredited by the Northwest Association of Schools and Colleges.

Applying

Admission is based on academic achievement, personal and social development, relevant experience, and demonstrated humanistic qualities. Credentials to be submitted are all official transcripts, two letters of recommendation, a completed application form, and a $60 application fee. Minimum prerequisites are a baccalaureate degree with a C or better in one course of college-level algebra or precalculus, one course of general psychology, one course of general biology with lab, and courses of general chemistry with lab science (major level). Specific information is available from the Admissions Office or by viewing the catalog on the University's Web site. Applicants who meet the basic admissions standards may be asked for an interview. An interview is required for admission to the M.S.A. program. Applications should be received by the University by April 1 for admission the following fall, although late applications are considered if space is available. Applicants who seek financial aid should complete the application process by June 1.

Correspondence and Information

Admissions Office
Bastyr University
14500 Juanita Drive, NE
Bothell, Washington 98011

Telephone: 425-602-3100
Fax: 425-823-6222
World Wide Web: http://www.bastyr.edu

Bastyr University

THE FACULTY

Boonchai Apirakchai, M.D., Jinan (China).
Qiang Cao, O.M.D., Shanghai University of Traditional Chinese Medicine; N.D., Bastyr; L.Ac.
Terry Courtney, M.P.H., Boston University; L.Ac., New England School of Acupuncture.
Carl Dahlgren, L.Ac., College of Traditional Chinese Acupuncture (U.K.).
Weiyi Ding, O.M.D., Shanghai University of Traditional Chinese Medicine.
Matthew Ferguson, M.S., Bastyr; L.Ac.
Xiaoming (Helen) Han, M.A., Oklahoma State, Jilin University (China).
Dirk Hein, M.A., College of Traditional Chinese Acupuncture (U.K.); L.Ac.
Jianxin Huang, O.M.D., Nanjing University of Traditional Chinese Medicine (China); L.Ac.
Eric Jones, N.D., Bastyr.
David Kailin, M.P.H., Washington (Seattle); L.Ac.
Paul Karsten, L.Ac., Samra.
Tai Lahans, M.Ac., Northwest Institute of Acupuncture and Oriental Medicine; L.Ac.
Zhi Sheng Ling, M.D., State Medical Institute, Kishinev (Moldova).
Chongyun Liu, O.M.D., Chengdu University of Traditional Chinese Medicine (China).
Sheryl Miller, Ph.D., Wayne State.
Barbara Mitchell, J.D., Florida State; L.Ac., Northwest Institute of Acupuncture and Oriental Medicine.
Wendy Nelson, Ph.D., Berkeley.
Mark Nolting, N.D., Bastyr; L.Ac., Northwest Institute of Acupuncture and Oriental Medicine and Chongqing Institute of Traditional Chinese Medicine.
Jeffrey Novack, Ph.D., Washington (Seattle).
Mark Reinhard, L.Ac., Northwest Institute of Acupuncture and Oriental Medicine.
Naomi Rhoads, L.Ac., Northwest Institute of Acupuncture and Oriental Medicine.
Marian Small, N.D., Bastyr; L.Ac., Northwest Institute of Acupuncture and Oriental Medicine.
Aleyamma Thomas, Ph.D., Manitoba.
Yajuan Wang, M.D., Qinghai Medical College (China); L.Ac.
Ying Wang, O.M.D., Harbin University of Traditional Chinese Medicine (China); L.Ac.
Jason Wright, M.S., Bastyr; L.Ac.
Katherine Yonkers, M.S.A., Bastyr.

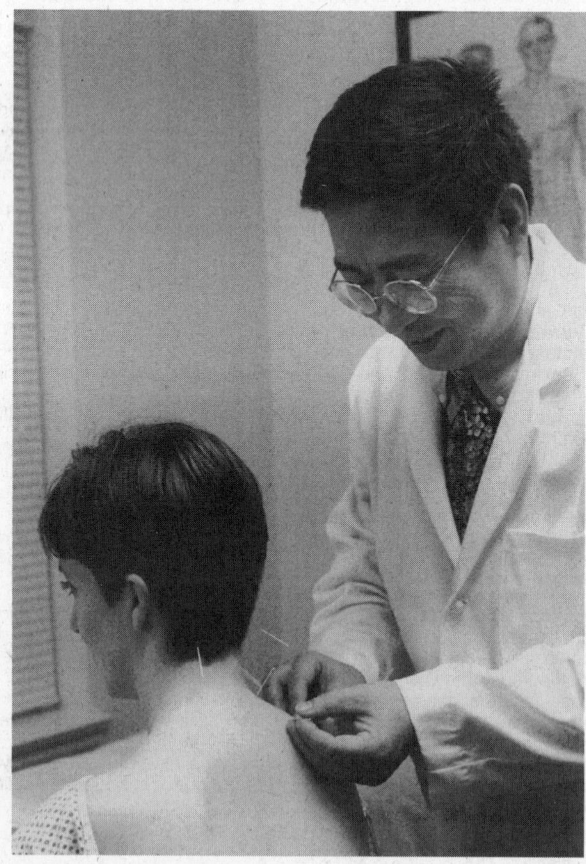

Dr. Qiang Cao with patient.

INTERNATIONAL INSTITUTE OF CHINESE MEDICINE

Oriental Medicine

Program of Study

The International Institute of Chinese Medicine (IICM) offers a four-year accredited program with a focus on comprehensive Oriental medicine training that leads to the Master of Oriental Medicine degree. In addition to acupuncture and Chinese herbal medicine, the program also offers Oriental medicine bodywork, nutrition, and physical and mental exercise and breathing therapy. The total curriculum of 2,520 hours (131 credits) includes more than 945 practice hours spent in observation, hands-on experience, and actual treatment. This program satisfies the legal requirements to qualify graduates to take the licensing examinations for the states of New Mexico and California, as well as other states, and the diplomate exam of the National Commission for the Certification of Acupuncture and Oriental Medicine (NCCAOM). IICM also offers a Continuing Education Certificate Program that is designed for those who seek to supplement their Oriental medicine training and to develop their expertise. The Albuquerque campus offers an 815-hour tui na (Oriental bodywork) certificate, with advanced training and clinical experience in tui na.

Research Facilities

The Santa Fe and Albuquerque campuses have Advanced Student Clinics that see hundreds of patients each month. Each of the herbal pharmacies is stocked with more than 300 herbs and many patent medicines. The main campus runs a drug detox program that is highly successful and offers full acupuncture treatments, herbology, qi gong, and counseling.

Financial Aid

IICM is certified to participate in the Title IV Federal Financial Aid Program, which includes Federal Stafford Subsidized and Unsubsidized Student Loans. To apply for a Federal Stafford Student Loan, a student must complete the Free Application for Federal Student Aid (FAFSA). FAFSA forms may be obtained at the financial aid office of IICM, and the application process takes approximately six weeks to complete. The FAFSA application generates a Student Aid Report, which should be submitted to the Financial Aid Director at IICM to determine eligibility. Students who require assistance or have questions should contact the Financial Aid Office.

Cost of Study

IICM is a nonprofit, tax-exempt institution. Tuition is $150 per course hour for full-time students and $165 per course hour for part-time students. A typical semester course load is 21 course hours. Tuition for a typical semester is $3150. Fees are approximately $50 per semester, and books and supplies cost approximately $200 per semester.

Living and Housing Costs

Most students find housemates and pay about $350 per month plus utilities. There are many apartments that rent for $450 to $550 per month. Santa Fe's living costs are slightly higher than Albuquerque's.

Student Group

Student activities are organized by the Student Council, which also produces the *Panda Press* newsletter.

Location

The Santa Fe campus is situated on 2.2 acres adjacent to the Agua Fria Village and just to the south of the city, with views of the Jemez and Sangre de Cristo Mountains. Albuquerque's campus is located at 4600 Montgomery Boulevard, across from St. Joseph's Hospital. There is also a Denver campus, which is located at 1385 South Colorado Boulevard, Empire Park Building A. All campuses are located close to Interstate 25.

The Institute

The International Institute of Chinese Medicine was founded in 1984 by Dr. Michael Zeng, who came to the United States from the People's Republic of China and brought extensive knowledge of acupuncture and traditional Chinese medicine. Dr. Zeng and his wife, Dr. Nancy Zeng, are former faculty members of Chengdu University of Traditional Chinese Medicine, and both have more than thirty-seven years of experience as acupuncturists, herbalists, and Oriental and Western medical doctors.

Applying

IICM accepts applicants who demonstrate strong motivation and a firm commitment to the study of traditional Chinese medicine. Documentation that shows the student has earned 60 credit hours or 90 quarter credits of general education that led to an associate degree or to a baccalaureate degree from an accredited institution is required for admission into the master's degree program. English-language proficiency is also required for entry into the program. Special requirements for admission into the Continuing Education Program are listed with that program's description. The Tui Na Certificate Program is open to graduates of high school who are 18 years of age or older. Materials to be submitted are official transcripts, two letters of recommendation, a letter from a licensed health-care practitioner concerning the student's physical and emotional ability to undertake a demanding course of study, an autobiographical sketch, the completed application form, and a $50 application fee. Students are accepted three times each year (fall, spring, and summer).

Correspondence and Information

Admissions Office
International Institute of Chinese Medicine
P.O. Box 29988
Sante Fe, New Mexico 87592-9988
Telephone: 800-377-4561 (toll-free)
Fax: 505-473-9279
World Wide Web: http://www.thuntek.net/iicm

International Institute of Chinese Medicine

THE FACULTY

Michael Zeng, President and Academic Dean; M.D., D.O.M., Dipl.Ac. (NCCAOM), Dipl.C.H. (NCCAOM), Chengdu University of Traditional Chinese Medicine (China).

Nancy P. Zeng, Vice President and Dean of Faculty; M.D., D.O.M., Dipl.Ac. (NCCAOM), Dipl.C.H. (NCCAOM), Chengdu University of Traditional Chinese Medicine (China).

Ying Chun Chi, D.O.M., Zhejiang College of Traditional Chinese Medicine (China).
Jamie Cobb, D.C., National Chiropractic; D.O.M., Midwest Center for the Study of Oriental Medicine.
Michael Crawford, D.C., Los Angeles Chiropractic.
Xu Hou, D.O.M., M.Med., Shanxi College of Traditional Chinese Medicine (China).
Tantan Huang, O.M.D., Chengdu University of Traditional Chinese Medicine (China).
Cynthia Knudson, M.D., Colorado.
Bin Lin, M.D., D.O.M., Dipl.Ac. (NCCAOM), Dipl.C.H. (NCCAOM), Henan Province Traditional Chinese Medicine Hospital (China).
Zhi Qiao, M.D., Fourth Military Medical University (China).
Cynthia Stephen, D.O.M., Dipl.Ac. (NCCAOM), Midwest Center for the Study of Oriental Medicine.
Stephen Swart, D.O.M., M.Ac., Dipl.Ac. (NCCAOM), Southwest Acupuncture.
Dehui Wang, M.Med., O.M.D., Jiangxi Institute of Traditional Chinese Medicine (China).
Kezhuang Zhao, D.O.M., Chengdu University of Traditional Chinese Medicine (China).
Jiaxin Zhuang, O.M.D., Jiangxi Institute of Traditional Chinese Medicine (China).

MEIJI COLLEGE OF ORIENTAL MEDICINE

Program of Study

Meiji College of Oriental Medicine offers the Master of Science degree in Oriental medicine. The majority of the courses are devoted to the theory and practice of acupuncture and Oriental herbology, with the remainder of the program focused on Oriental and Western clinical sciences. While the curriculum is based on Traditional Chinese Medicine (TCM), the program is complemented by instruction in the Japanese and Korean traditions of Oriental medicine, such as Japanese needling techniques, abdominal palpation, and electrical acupuncture. The curriculum is designed so that the courses in TCM theory, acupuncture, Oriental herbology, and Western clinical sciences are taken simultaneously in order to provide a comprehensive understanding of Oriental medicine.

The academic program consists of 2,455 hours of lecture and clinical courses. Individuals are instructed in the clinical practice of Oriental medicine while developing a working knowledge of the basic diagnostic and treatment procedures of Western medicine. Meiji College provides one of the most extensive Oriental medical clinical programs in the country, offering more than 1,000 hours of training in its clinic and herbal dispensary. Clinical practice hours are dispersed throughout the program, with the greatest concentration in the third year.

The three-year course of study at Meiji College is equivalent to four academic years. The College operates year-round on a quarterly basis, with most students enrolled full-time. Lecture classes are held on Tuesdays, Thursdays, and Saturdays from 9 a.m. to 5 p.m. The curriculum provides graduates with the necessary background in acupuncture and Oriental herbology to sit for the California State Acupuncture Licensing Exam and the NCCAOM Certification Exam.

Research Facilities

The Meiji College library is home to a comprehensive general collection of roughly 1,800 titles on Oriental medicine, Oriental and Western herbology, acupuncture, Western medicine, alternative medicine, general science, general reference, and medical reference. A large collection of classical and contemporary medical and scientific texts in Japanese and Chinese is also available, as is a growing video collection. To keep students and faculty members informed of the constantly changing medical field, the library subscribes to twenty-two medical journals from Japan, China, the U.S., and England, spanning Western medicine, Oriental medicine, and herbology. The College provides access to the National Library of Medicine's Database Network (MEDLARS) and the University of California's library system (MELVYL).

Financial Aid

The College currently has two types of loan programs available for qualified applicants. Private in-house loans from Meiji College may be awarded to full-time students following review and assessment of student merit and need. These loans are limited in number and are provided in the form of a tuition credit. Awards are made on a yearly basis prior to the commencement of the academic year. Both full- and part-time students may apply for the Nellie Mae EXCEL loan. This loan is based on debt-to-income ratio, and those eligible may borrow from $2000 up to the cost of attendance.

Cost of Study

Tuition is assessed quarterly and is due before the start of each quarter. Tuition for the 1998–99 academic year is $1750 per quarter ($7000 annually) for full-time students. Part-time tuition is $10 per hour of instruction. The cost of books, physical and diagnostic supplies, and fees amounts to approximately $500–$700 for the first year, $300–$500 for the second year, and $100–$200 for the third year.

Living and Housing Costs

The College does not provide student housing. There is a wide range of housing available in San Francisco and the surrounding areas, and costs of living in the Bay Area vary greatly. Applicants with specific questions on housing are welcome to call the Admissions Office.

Student Group

Total student enrollment for the 1997–98 school year was 80. Approximately 90 percent of the students are full-time, and 70 percent are women. Students range in age from 25–55. Meiji's student body comes from a wide variety of ethnic, educational, and occupational backgrounds. While some students come to Meiji straight from undergraduate programs, many students come to the College from prior professions in the fields of health services, law, business, and the arts. The College anticipates 90 students for the 1998–99 year.

Student Outcomes

Acupuncture and Oriental herbal medicine are rapidly gaining recognition across the United States as effective, low-cost, medical treatments that work in harmony with the body's natural healing ability. In California, acupuncture practitioners are primary health-care providers licensed by the Acupuncture Committee of the California Medical Board. The majority of Meiji graduates are practicing acupuncture in northern California in private practices, joint practices, or clinic settings. Meiji College has an average passing rate of 87 percent on the California licensing exam.

Location

The College is moving its entire campus from its San Francisco location to Berkeley by the end of 1998. Its new 14,000-square-foot floor plan offers four spacious classrooms, clinical facilities, administrative offices, and a student lounge area. The clinic is the most modern acupuncture college clinic in the Bay Area. The new campus is just blocks from the University of California, Berkeley, campus and is easily accessible by an excellent public transportation system. The surrounding neighborhoods offer affordable housing and a variety of restaurants, movie theaters, and supermarkets for students' convenience.

The College

Meiji College was established in 1991 by Meiji Institute of Oriental Medicine in Kyoto and Osaka, the largest school of Oriental medicine in Japan. The Japanese origins of Meiji College bring a special perspective to the teaching of Oriental medicine. The curriculum reflects the importance placed on Western scientific knowledge in traditional Oriental medical education. Meiji College is approved by the Bureau for Private Post-secondary and Vocational Education, as well as the Acupuncture Committee of the California Medical Board. Meiji College is a candidate for accreditation with the Accreditation Commission for Acupuncture and Oriental Medicine (ACAOM).

Applying

New students are enrolled every fall. The application deadline for the fall quarter is July 31. Prospective applicants are encouraged to apply for admission well in advance due to the limited class size. Admission requirements include a bachelor's degree and a minimum cumulative GPA of 2.5. Candidates must submit a completed application form, official transcripts, two letters of recommendation, an essay, a resume, a health certificate, and a $50 application fee. Upon receipt of all materials, qualified applicants are contacted for a personal interview.

Correspondence and Information

Admissions Office
Meiji College of Oriental Medicine
1426 Fillmore Street, Suite 301
San Francisco, California 94115

Telephone: 415-771-1019
Fax: 415-771-1036

After December 31, 1998:

Admissions Office
Meiji College of Oriental Medicine
2550 Shattuck Avenue
Berkeley, California 94704

Meiji College of Oriental Medicine

THE FACULTY AND THEIR RESEARCH

Hirohisa Oda, President and Dean of Research; D.Med., Tottori National University School of Medicine (Japan); L. Pharm., L. Hygiene Tech., L.Ac. (Japan).
Shinichiro Yamada, Dean of Faculty; B.A., Meijo (Japan); L.Ac. (Japan and California).
Jason Su, Dean of Clinic; B.Med., Zhejiang College of Traditional Chinese Medicine (China); L.Ac.
Margaret Oda, Associate Dean of Faculty; B.A., California, Santa Barbara; L.Ac. (Japan and California).
Emmie Zhu, Instructor; D.Med., Shanghai First Medical (China); L.Ac.
Brian Barlay, Instructor; M.S., American College of Traditional Chinese Medicine; L.Ac.
Denise Daniel, Instructor; M.S., American College of Traditional Chinese Medicine; L.Ac.
Wladislaw Ellis, Instructor; M.D., UCLA; L.Ac.
Samuel Ferguson, Instructor; Ph.D., Pennsylvania.
Mary LeVesque, Instructor; M.S., American College of Traditional Chinese Medicine; L.Ac.
Glenn Oberman, Instructor; M.A., California, Santa Barbara; O.M.D., L.Ac.
Gary Ross, Instructor; M.D., George Washington.
Gary Wedemayer, Instructor; Ph.D., Berkeley.
John Yeh, Instructor; M.D., Shanghai Medical (China).
Zhi-Bin Zhang, Instructor; M.S., Guang Zhou College of Traditional Chinese Medicine (China); L.Ac.

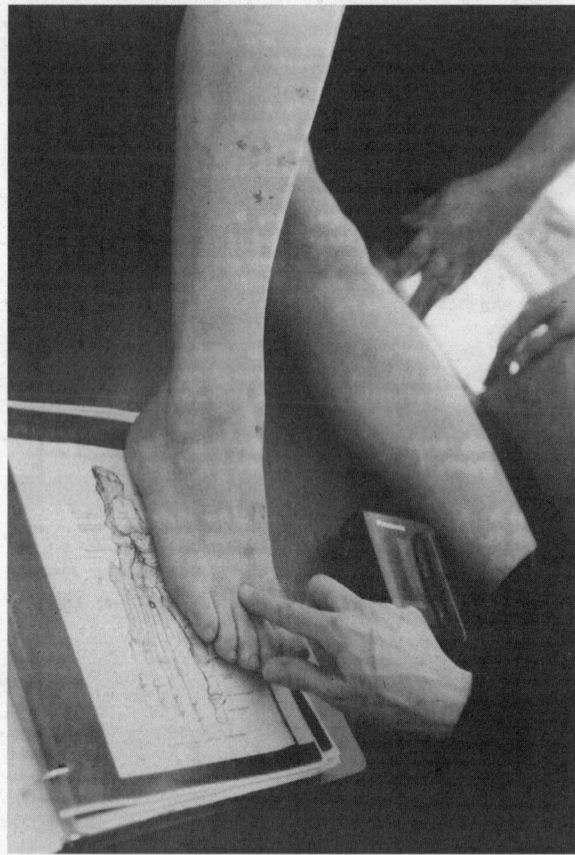
Practicing point location.

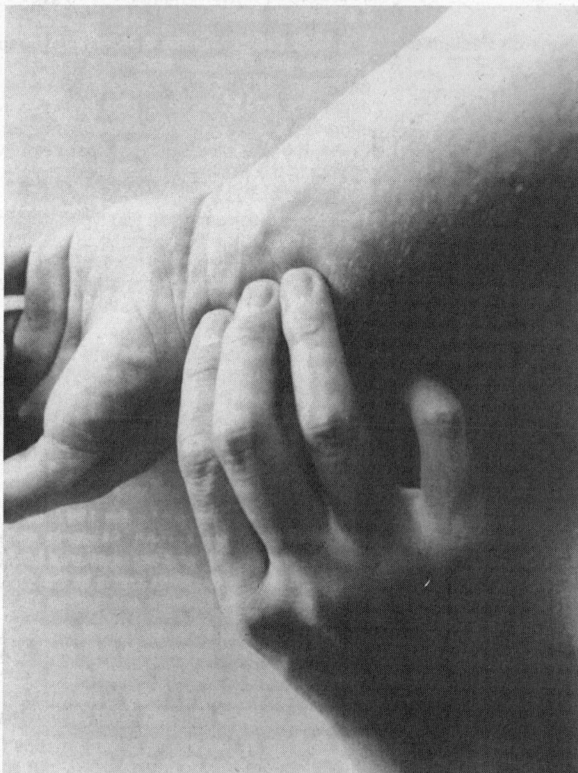
Traditional pulse diagnosis.

NESA 氣

NEW ENGLAND SCHOOL OF ACUPUNCTURE

Graduate Program in Acupuncture and Oriental Medicine

Program of Study

The New England School of Acupuncture (NESA) is the oldest college of Oriental medicine in the United States. NESA's three-year master's degree program—taught by an expert and experienced faculty that includes a number of well-known scholars and clinicians—includes more than 1,000 hours of hands-on clinical instruction as well as a full year of clinical internship in acupuncture and herbal medicine. The program gives students the tools they need to become skilled and caring practitioners of Oriental medicine and the credentials necessary for licensure in Massachusetts and many other states.

From the start of the master's program, students learn essential clinical skills as the theoretical foundation is being laid. The program covers the major aspects of Oriental medicine, with the focus on acupuncture and Chinese herbal medicine. Opportunities to learn diverse acupuncture techniques—such as Japanese styles and Five Element and other approaches—exist through electives that match a student's professional interests. In addition, students gain a solid grounding in Western science and medicine, nutrition, tui na, and qi gong.

During the clinical experience, students progress from observing and assisting acupuncture practitioners to treating other students to treating patients under the supervision of experienced clinical faculty members during a yearlong internship. NESA students enjoy exciting opportunities for assistantships and internships in the NESA Clinic and at such off-campus clinical sties as the Boston Regional Medical Center (a full-service hospital), the AIDS Care Project (a Boston-area clinic), and other facilities. The rich clinical experience prepares students to treat diverse patients and conditions and to practice in a variety of settings.

Research Facilities

Students and faculty members at NESA are involved in a variety of research projects on and off campus, coordinated by NESA's Research Department.

Financial Aid

NESA participates in the Federal Family Education Loan (FFEL) program, which includes subsidized and unsubsidized Federal Stafford Student Loans, and the Educational Resources Institute (TERI) loan program.

Cost of Study

Full-time annual tuition (three semesters) will be $9225 for the 1999–2000 academic year. Tuition may vary depending on the actual number of credits taken. There is an additional tuition charge of approximately $1600 for the Chinese herbal medicine elective track in the second and third years. Books and supplies are estimated at $1000 for the three years of study.

Living and Housing Costs

NESA students are able to find housing in the numerous communities in and around Watertown and Boston. The College Scholarship Service estimates that the cost of housing, food, and other living expenses for the Boston metropolitan area is between $13,000 and $14,000 per academic year.

Student Group

NESA attracts a well-educated and highly motivated group of students that range in age from early 20s to mid-60s. NESA students reflect many different educational and cultural backgrounds, careers, and life experiences, yet they share a deep commitment to the study and practice of acupuncture and Oriental medicine. Approximately 250 students attend NESA.

Student Outcomes

More than 600 practitioners have graduated from NESA, many of whom have made significant contributions to the field. NESA alumni have founded colleges of Oriental medicine; authored well-known texts; established acupuncture clinics in hospitals, community health centers, and extended-care facilities; established the Boston-based AIDS Care Project; initiated groundbreaking research on acupuncture treatment for post-stroke patients and carpal tunnel syndrome; and engaged in other clinical research projects.

Location

Close to Boston and Cambridge's Harvard Square, NESA's location makes it convenient for students to pursue enriching opportunities outside of the classroom. Some of the most internationally known, well-respected medical centers and educational institutions are within easy reach and offer lectures, workshops, and other activities to expand knowledge and skills. For fun and relaxation, the metropolitan area is rich in history, culture, and entertainment, and the natural beauty of New England is just a short day trip away.

The School

The New England School of Acupuncture—the oldest college of acupuncture and Oriental medicine in the United States—was founded in 1975 by master acupuncturist James Tin Yau So. NESA's mission is to be a leader in the development of traditional and Oriental medicine as a medical art and science by offering an outstanding professional program. NESA is accredited by the Accreditation Commission for Acupuncture and Oriental Medicine and approved by the Massachusetts Board of Higher Education to grant Master of Acupuncture degrees.

Applying

Prospective students are strongly encouraged to visit the School and observe classes before applying. Interested students should call ahead to arrange a visit. Applicants to the program must have a bachelor's degree from an accredited institution. In addition, all applicants must have an admission interview. New students are admitted to the program at the beginning of the fall semester only. Prospective students who have completed the application process, including the admission interview, before the end of December receive early acceptance decisions by the end of January. The deadline for applications is May 1. Applications received after the May 1 deadline are considered on a space-available basis.

Correspondence and Information

Office of Admissions
New England School of Acupuncture
30 Common Street
Watertown, Massachusetts 02172
Telephone: 617-926-1788
Fax: 617-924-4167
E-mail: info@nesa.edu
World Wide Web: http://www.nesa.edu

New England School of Acupuncture

THE FACULTY AND THEIR RESEARCH

Elizabeth Angus, M.Ed. General physics.
Robert Ayres, M.S. Anatomy and physiology.
Pamela Bemis, Lic.Ac. Clinical skills, point location, clinical internship education.
Stephen Birch, Guest Lecturer; Lic.Ac. Palpatory diagnosis and treatment studies.
Loocie Brown, M.Ed.; Lic.Ac. Clinical skills of traditional Chinese medicine.
Yili Cao, Lic.Ac. Materials and methods of traditional Chinese medicine, clinical supervision.
Pak-Kui Chan, Lic.Ac. Tui na.
Song Nian Chen, M.D.; Lic.Ac. Clinical supervision, traditional Chinese medicine etiology and pathology of disease.
Xiaoming Cheng, Lic.Ac. Traditional Chinese medicine etiology and pathology of disease, clinical supervision.
Agatha Colbert, M.D. Western pathophysiology and pharmacology.
Patrick Cunningham, Chair, Related Studies Department; Lic.Ac. Clinical anatomy and structural analysis.
David Euler, Lic.Ac. Kiiko Matsumoto–style acupuncture, clinical supervision.
Geffin Falken, N.D.; LPN. East and West nutrition, microbiology.
Alison Feeley, M.S.W.; Lic.S.W. Psychological issues of clinical practice.
Martin Feldman, Chair, Japanese Acupuncture Department; Lic.Ac. Palpatory diagnosis and treatment studies, clinical supervision.
Barbara Ferro, M.Ed., M.Ac.; RN, Lic.Ac. Point location.
Andrew Gamble, Guest Lecturer; Lic.Ac. Herbal medicine.
Merry Gerard, Lic.Ac. Specialized approaches to acupuncture, Five Element acupuncture.
Richard Glickman-Simon, Chair, Western Medicine Department; M.D. Western pathophysiology and pharmacology.
Thomas Harrigan, Lic.S.W. Psychological issues of clinical practice.
Ellen Highfield, Lic.Ac. Microsystems of acupuncture treatment.
Dan T. Hom, Guest Lecturer; M.S.C.M.; Lic.Ac. Advanced adjunctive modalities.
Stephen Howard, Lic.Ac. Actions and effects of points and channels, case presentation, clinical supervision, special topics in traditional Chinese medicine.
Amy Hull, Lic.Ac. Point location, actions and effects of points and channels, clinical skills, clinical internship education, clinical supervision.
Diane Iuliano, Lic.Ac. Clinical skills, traditional Chinese medicine etiology and pathology of disease, clinical supervision, palpatory diagnosis studies, microsystems of acupuncture treatment.
Eliha Jacobe, Lic.Ac. Kiiko Matsumoto–style acupuncture, clinical supervision.
Yan Ping Jin, Lic.Ac. Herbal formulas, clinical supervision.
Joseph Kay, Lic.Ac. Palpatory diagnosis and treatment, clinical supervision, traditional Chinese medical theory.
Joseph Kelliher, Lic.Ac. Materials and methods of traditional Chinese medicine, clinical internship education.
Mary Kinneavy, Lic.Ac. Palpatory diagnosis and treatment studies, clinical supervision.
Takayuki (Kouei) Kuwahara, Lic.Ac. Palpatory diagnosis and treatment studies.
Mitchell Levine, M.D. Western pathophysiology and pharmacology.
Zhiping Li, M.A.; Lic.Ac. Clinical education, clinical supervision, tui na.
Linda Loney, M.D. Western pathophysiology and pharmacology.
Weidong Lu, Chair, Herbal Medicine Department; Lic.Ac. Herbal pharmacopoeia, diagnostic skills, special topics in traditional Chinese medicine, herbal medicine, clinical supervision.
Kiiko Matsumoto, Lic.Ac. Kiiko Matsumoto–style acupuncture, clinical supervision.
Mary Moore, M.S.N., M.Div. Western pathophysiology and pharmacology.
William Mueller, Lic.Ac. Specialized approaches to acupuncture, Five Element acupuncture.
Eileen Murray, Lic.Ac. Materials and methods of traditional Chinese medicine, clinical internship education, clinical supervision.
Margaret Naeser, Guest Lecturer; Ph.D. Microsystems of acupuncture treatment.
Eileen Power, M.Ed.; Lic.Ac. Practice development and management.
Dana Quinn, Lic.Ac. Clinical internship education, diagnostic skills.
Christopher Ryan, M.D. Western pathophysiology and pharmacology.
Kathy Seltzer, Lic.Ac. Materials and methods of traditional Chinese medicine, clinical internship education.
Elizabeth Sommers, M.P.H.; Lic.Ac. Research design and evaluation.
Kristina Stinson, Ph.D. General biology.
Kuen-Shii Tsay, Lic.Ac. Advanced needle techniques of traditional Chinese medicine, actions and effects of points and channels.
Peter Valaskatgis, Chair, Traditional Chinese Medicine Department; Lic.Ac. Traditional Chinese medical theory, traditional Chinese medicine etiology and pathology of disease, clinical supervision.
Paulina Watson, Lic.Ac. Clinical supervision.
Peter Wayne, Ph.D. Qi gong.
Liying Wu, Lic.Ac. Herbal internal medicine, clinical supervision.
Ping Yao, Lic.Ac. Clinical supervision.
Dongyan Yu, Lic.Ac. Herbal internal medicine.
Yao Zhang, M.Sc.; Lic.Ac. Herbal internal medicine, women's health.
Yue Zhang, Lic.Ac. Clinical supervision.
Zhen-zhen Zhang, Lic.Ac. Clinical skills, clinical internship education, clinical supervision, traditional Chinese medicine etiology and pathology.
Min Zhu, Lic.Ac. Clinical supervision, clinical education, clinical skills, special topics of traditional Chinese medicine.
Chunhan Zu, Lic.Ac. Herbal internal medicine, pediatrics.

New England School of Acupuncture herbal pharmacy.

NORTHWEST INSTITUTE OF ACUPUNCTURE & ORIENTAL MEDICINE

NORTHWEST INSTITUTE OF ACUPUNCTURE AND ORIENTAL MEDICINE

Graduate Programs

Programs of Study

The Northwest Institute of Acupuncture and Oriental Medicine is dedicated to fostering wellness in individuals and in the community. The Master of Acupuncture (M.Ac.) and the Master of Traditional Chinese Medicine (M.T.C.M.) degrees are fully accredited and offer the highest quality of traditional Chinese medicine training. These programs are designed to comprehensively train students in the diagnostic, communication, and treatment skills required to practice acupuncture independently. The major emphasis in the degree programs is on clinical training. Sufficient hands-on and practical experience in the development of a diagnosis and the practice of acupuncture and herbal knowledge (for the M.T.C.M. degree) is considered crucial to developing an effective practitioner.

Both programs consist of approximately 45 quarter credits of Western science in addition to Oriental medical science. The three-year M.Ac. degree also includes two years of clinical science and supervised clinical practice, while the four-year M.T.C.M. degree combines the study of acupuncture and Chinese herbology. M.T.C.M. students also take specialized courses in herbal studies foundations, therapeutics, and clinical problem-solving. An optional China Internship Program, following the academic studies, is available for both degree programs. These graduate programs are accredited by the Accreditation Commission for Acupuncture and Oriental Medicine (ACAOM) and qualify graduates to sit for the national certification exams.

In addition, the Institute offers a variety of continuing education workshops and seminars for students and graduates to pursue special interest/specialty topics. Advanced certificate programs include TCM pediatric acupuncture, Japanese acupuncture, Toyo Hari, and community and public health (residency).

Throughout their training, students are provided with unique and diversified opportunities to learn in a wide variety of clinical settings. An active in-house community clinic, with patients totaling more than 12,000 per year, provides training in general practice acupuncture, as well as specialized training in gynecology, obstetrics, maternity care, acute injury and neuromusculoskeletal (NMS) problems, Tuina, and Japanese acupuncture.

The Institute's commitment to community service and partnerships is reflected in its extensive network of satellite clinics. Students have the opportunity to provide acupuncture and Oriental medicine within Western-oriented medical hospitals, community health clinics, area nursing homes, and the criminal justice system, while treating populations of elderly, refugees, homeless youth, and patients with HIV or chronic fatigue. Students learn to become integral members of the larger health-care team. The community-based satellite clinics treat more than 13,000 patients annually.

Research Facilities

The Institute has recently added research to its institutional mission. Current endeavors include the development of a computerized clinic database. A community practitioners' network is being developed to gather information about specific conditions treated by acupuncture, and a safety monitoring system has already been implemented. The Institute is collaborating with local health-care facilities on several larger studies and is pursuing funding on additional pilot studies.

Financial Aid

Federal financial aid is available through the Federal Stafford Student Loan Program and veterans' benefits. The Institute has also been designated as a Canada Student Loan school.

Cost of Study

Tuition costs in 1998–99 average $25,338 for the three-year M.Ac. program and $30,344 for the four-year M.T.C.M. program. Books and medical supplies cost an additional $400–$500 per academic year.

Living and Housing Costs

The Institute is located in a residential area, with rentals available at reasonable rates. For financial aid purposes, living expenses for nine months are estimated at approximately $8420. Many students share housing, with monthly rent costs as low as $250–$350 a month. Students often post room availability on the bulletin board located in the student lounge.

Student Group

The Institute serves a diverse body of more than 200 students from across the United States, Canada, Mexico, Asia, Europe, Central and South America, and Africa. The average age is 37, and 67 percent of the students are women. Many students are embarking on a major change from diverse careers in Western health-care practices, psychology, software engineering, the arts, and more. A majority of the students attend on a full-time basis.

Location

The Northwest Institute of Acupuncture and Oriental Medicine's academic and administrative campus and teaching clinic are located in the Wallingford district of Seattle, Washington. Convenient to restaurants, theaters, and shopping, the Institute is easily accessible by major bus lines. Seattle, consistently voted among the best places to live in the U.S., offers an abundance of outdoor recreational opportunities, from boating on Puget Sound or in the San Juan Islands to hiking or skiing in the Olympic and Cascade Mountains. The city is also home to world-class performing arts, professional sports, and cultural events.

The Institute

The Northwest Institute of Acupuncture and Oriental Medicine was founded in 1981 as a nonprofit educational institution. The Institute seeks to create a supportive learning community through collaboration and consensus in the classrooms, clinics, and institutional governance. With a mission of providing the highest quality education for practitioners of acupuncture and Oriental medicine, the Institute works to foster more effective forms of health care in the U.S.

Applying

Applicants are accepted throughout the year for enrollment. Programs begin each fall quarter. As space availability is limited, prospective students are encouraged to submit applications as soon as possible. Prerequisites include three years of accredited college or university study (135 quarter or 90 semester credits), although a bachelor's degree is recommended. Applicants must have also completed one course each in biology and psychology. Credentials to be submitted include all official transcripts, two letters of recommendation, an essay, TOEFL scores for students with English as a second language, and a completed application form with the $50 application fee. An in-person interview is required of all qualified applicants.

Correspondence and Information

Admissions Office
Northwest Institute of Acupuncture and Oriental Medicine
1307 North 45th Street, Suite 306
Seattle, Washington 98103

Telephone: 206-633-2419
Fax: 206-633-5578
E-mail: mmcghee@niaom.org
World Wide Web: http://www.halcyon.com/niaom

Northwest Institute of Acupuncture and Oriental Medicine

THE FACULTY

Teresa Barlow, B.Sc., B.Ac., International College of Oriental Medicine (England).
Sara Bayer, M.A., L.Ac., California Acupuncture College (San Diego) and International Acupuncture Training Institute (Beijing).
Patrick Bufi, N.D., Bastyr.
Donna Carey, M.S., L.Ac., Academy of Chinese Culture and Health Sciences (Oakland).
Wimsey Cherrington, L.M.T., C.T.P.
Chu-Lan Chiong, M.Ac., L.Ac., Northwest Institute of Acupuncture and Oriental Medicine.
Sunny Chu, M.D., O.M.D., Medical Sciences University (Canton).
Neil Conaty, L.Ac., Northwest Institute of Acupuncture and Oriental Medicine.
John Cook, M.B. Ch.B. (II), Sheffield-Hallam Medical School (England).
Lesli Dalaba, M.Ac., L.Ac., Northwest Institute of Acupuncture and Oriental Medicine.
Marjorie de Muynck, L.M.P., Shiatsu instructor.
John Fenoli, M.S.E., M.Ac., L.Ac., Florida Tech and Northwest Institute of Acupuncture and Oriental Medicine.
Richard Grady, M.D., Michigan.
Carolyn Grissom, M.Ac., L.Ac., Northwest Institute of Acupuncture and Oriental Medicine.
Mette Hanson, M.S., Oregon State.
Alex Holland, M.Ac., L.Ac., Northwest Institute of Acupuncture and Oriental Medicine and Chongqing Research Institute of Traditional Chinese Medicine (China).
Yi Jiao Hong, B.A., Zhejiang Normal University (China) and Zhejiang College of Traditional Chinese Medicine (China).
John Hostetler, M.Ac., L.Ac., Ohio Wesleyan and Northwest Institute of Acupuncture and Oriental Medicine.
Jianxin Huang, M.T.C.M., L.Ac., Nanjing College of Traditional Chinese Medicine (China).
Angela Hughes, Dipl.Ac., London School of Acupuncture and Traditional Chinese Medicine.
Stephen Hunt, M.D., Oklahoma.
Kayo King, M.Ac., L.Ac., Northwest Institute of Acupuncture and Oriental Medicine.
Lori King, M.Ac., L.Ac., Northwest Institute of Acupuncture and Oriental Medicine.
Fred Lanphear, Ph.D., Penn State.
Anne Lindblad, L.Ac., B.S., Georgetown, Taipei Institute of Traditional Chinese Medicine, and Northwest Institute of Acupuncture and Oriental Medicine.
Brenda Loew, M.Ac., L.Ac., Northwest Institute of Acupuncture and Oriental Medicine and Zhejiang College of Traditional Chinese Medicine (China).
Shou Chun Ma, M.T.C.M., L.Ac., Chengdu (China).
Xin Dong Ma, M.T.C.M., Heilongjiang College of Traditional Chinese Medicine.
Heather McFarlane, M.Ac., L.Ac., L.M.P., Northwest Institute of Acupuncture and Oriental Medicine.
Cindy Micleu, M.Ac., L.Ac., Northwest Institute of Acupuncture and Oriental Medicine and Chongqing Research Institute of Traditional Chinese Medicine (China).
Harrison Moretz, Director and Chief Instructor of Taoist Studies Institute (Seattle).
Yasuo Mori, L.M.P., Kagochima Kaizai University.
Diane Pelletier, Ph.D., Arizona.
Paul Ponton, M.Ac., L.Ac., Northwest Institute of Acupuncture and Oriental Medicine.
Shad Reinstein, M.Ac., L.Ac., B.A., Case Western Reserve and Northwest Institute of Acupuncture and Oriental Medicine.
Leslie Schear, M.A., L.M., Seattle Midwifery School.
Julian Scott, B.Ac., Ph.D., International College of Oriental Medicine (England).
Karen Sherman, Ph.D., Cornell, M.P.H., Washington (Seattle).
Dan Tennenbaum, L.Ac., Cambridge School of Acupuncture and Shenghui University of Acupuncture.
Michelle Thoreson, L.Ac., Northwest Institute of Acupuncture and Oriental Medicine.
Cathy Travis, M.Ac., L.Ac., Northwest Institute of Acupuncture and Oriental Medicine.
XueZhong (Lincoln) Wang, M.T.C.M., L.Ac., Beijing College of Traditional Chinese Medicine.
Christopher Woon, M.Ac., L.Ac., Emperor's College of Traditional Oriental Medicine.
Jian-Feng Yang, M.T.C.M., L.Ac., Chengdu (China).
Julie Zinkus, L.Ac., New England School of Acupuncture.
Daniel Zizza, L.Ac., Northwest Institute of Acupuncture and Oriental Medicine.

OREGON COLLEGE OF ORIENTAL MEDICINE

Program in Acupuncture and Oriental Medicine

Program of Study

Candidates who complete this three-calendar–year (four-academic–year) graduate program are awarded the Master of Acupuncture and Oriental Medicine (M.Ac.O.M.) degree, are qualified to sit for the national certification exams, and are prepared to enter into independent health-care practice as regulated by each individual state. The academic program presents course work and training in all aspects of traditional Oriental medicine, including the theory and practice of acupuncture, herbal medicine, traditional Chinese physiotherapy, exercise, and qi-cultivation; adjunctive courses in Western biomedicine, including anatomy, physiology, pathology, pharmacology, and clinical diagnosis; and relevant course work in public and community health, clinical research, practice management, and practitioner/patient dynamics. At the heart of the academic program is the college clinic, whose mission is to provide high-quality, affordable health care to the public and to support the development of Oriental medicine as a vital healing methodology complementary to Western medicine. Acupuncture and Oriental medical services are provided in the clinic by student interns who practice under the direct supervision of experienced acupuncturists, many from China, who are licensed in the state of Oregon. Students complete 860 hours of supervised clinical training and as third-year interns treat more than 400 patients in supervised clinical settings. All students complete an internship rotation in a community health clinic, underscoring the College's commitment to practitioner training in public health. A specialized certificate program in teacher training is additionally available to advanced students of qigong.

Research Facilities

The College has incorporated clinical research into the core curriculum by providing both the didactic course Topics in Clinical Research as well as the project-oriented research practicum experience. The College Clinic supports student research projects through the organization and accessibility of patient demographics and outcomes data. Students, faculty members, and alumni involved in research have full access to the College's outstanding library and computerized online search services as well as Internet access. By virtue of their enrollment, students have library privileges at the Oregon Health Sciences University and the nearby National College of Naturopathic Medicine and Western States Chiropractic College.

Financial Aid

Federal financial aid is available through the Federal Stafford Loan Program, veteran's benefits, and the Federal College Work-Study Program. A college payment plan is also available.

Cost of Study

Tuition costs in 1998–99 total $8500 for nine months (three quarters) of enrollment. Books and medical supplies cost an additional $500–600 per academic year.

Living and Housing Costs

The College is located in a residential area, with rentals available at reasonable rates. Many students share housing with monthly costs as low as $250–$300. Students can often find housing by utilizing the bulletin board maintained for this purpose in the student lounge. For financial aid purposes, living expenses for nine months are estimated at approximately $7000.

Student Group

A diverse student body of 170 individuals (67 percent women) from across the United States, Canada, Mexico, Asia, and Europe bring impressive knowledge and experience to the study of Oriental medicine. Many students are engaged in a major career change from such fields as law, computer science, research, and teaching, as well as from the medical fields of nursing, physical therapy, and therapeutic massage. Increasingly, younger students pursue this educational path as their first professional degree program. The academic environment encourages cooperative study among students, who form supportive practice and study groups in support of their learning process.

Student Outcomes

The majority of the College's graduates enter into private practice or group practice with complementary health-care providers. Several pursue careers in public health settings and have accepted positions with public agencies that provide services to clients with HIV/AIDS, chemical dependency, and mental illness. These treatment settings include homeless shelters, residential treatment facilities, jails and prisons, and outpatient drop-in clinics.

Location

The College is situated on a 1-acre campus 10 miles east of downtown Portland. Portland, Oregon, a city of 481,000, is heralded by many observers as one of America's most liveable cities. Surrounded by the exhilarating beauty of the Pacific Northwest, Portland is blessed with lively commerce, a burgeoning performing arts scene, a symphony orchestra, an NBA franchise, an award-winning school district, and a beautiful urban parks system. Mount Hood and the Columbia Gorge offer some of the best hiking, skiing, fishing, boating, and windsurfing in the country. Eighty miles to the west is the rugged Oregon coastline, a favorite weekend retreat for city dwellers.

The College

The Oregon College of Oriental Medicine was established as a nonprofit educational institution in 1983 in response to the growing need for comprehensive professional training in traditional Oriental medicine. The College has grown significantly in recent years and now includes nearly 200 individuals—students, faculty, staff, and board of trustees—who learn, practice, and support traditional medicine within the school's own campus and facilities. Through the efforts of this community, the College has emerged as an important contributor to national and regional health care and education. In addition to academic excellence, the College mission includes a commitment to public health as evidenced by its relationships with numerous clinics offering affordable community health care. The learning environment is supportive and conducive to the development of academic and clinical competencies requisite for success in independent health-care practice. The four-academic–year professional master's degree program in acupuncture and Oriental medicine is accredited by the Accreditation Commission for Acupuncture and Oriental Medicine (ACAOM), a specialized accrediting agency recognized by the U.S. Department of Education. Approval to grant the degree of Master of Acupuncture and Oriental Medicine has been conferred by the state of Oregon Office of Educational Policy and Planning.

Applying

Candidates for admission must demonstrate the potential to become caring, dedicated, and skilled practitioners of traditional Oriental medicine and evidence the maturity and preparation necessary to undertake the challenging academic program. Minimum requirements for admission include the successful completion of at least three years of college at a federally accredited institution, although it is recommended that incoming students have completed a four-year college degree. As part of the required undergraduate education, or in addition to it, applicants must also have completed college-level courses in general biology, general chemistry, and psychology. The application process includes a completed application form and $50 fee as well as complete and official academic transcripts, two admission essays, and two formal letters of recommendation. An on-campus interview is required of all qualified applicants. Applicants are accepted beginning in September for enrollment in the following year's entering class, and admission decisions are made on a rolling basis.

Correspondence and Information

Office of Admissions
Oregon College of Oriental Medicine
10525 Southeast Cherry Blossom Drive
Portland, Oregon 97216
Telephone: 503-253-3443
Fax: 503-253-2701
E-mail: 103226.164@compuserve.com
World Wide Web: http://www.infinite.org/oregon.acupuncture

Oregon College of Oriental Medicine

THE FACULTY AND THEIR RESEARCH

Harry Affley, B.S., Multnomah School of the Bible, 1993. Taiji quan.
Satya Ambrose, Clinical Supervisor; N.D., National College of Naturopathic Medicine, 1989; L.Ac. Clinical seminar, case observation and demonstration.
Cindy Anderson, M.Ac.O.M., Oregon College of Oriental Medicine, 1994. Point location, observation skills.
Paul Anderson, N.D., National College of Naturopathic Medicine, 1996. Anatomy and physiology.
Natalie Arndt, Cert.Ac., California Acupuncture College, 1986; L.Ac. Traditional Chinese herbal medicine.
Hui-Xian Chen, B.A., Institute of Foreign Languages (Beijing), 1954. Qigong.
Joseph J. Coletto, N.D., National College of Naturopathic Medicine, 1983; L.Ac. Point location, living anatomy, Western clinical diagnosis, acupuncture techniques, clinical skills.
Daniel DeLapp, D.C., Los Angeles Chiropractic, 1986; L.Ac. Structural diagnosis.
David C. Eisen, Clinical Supervisor; Dip.Ac., New England School of Acupuncture, 1982; L.Ac. Public health, community health and chemical dependency, auricular acupuncture.
Lindy Ferrigno, L.M.T., Shiatsu Education Center of America, 1972. Shiatsu.
Marnie Freeman, M.Ac.O.M., Oregon College of Oriental Medicine, 1994. Chinese herbal medicine.
Lucinda Friedman, B.A., Illinois, 1971; L.M.T. Jin Shin Do; dynamics of illness.
Sally Green, D.C., Western States Chiropractic, 1981; L.Ac. Structural diagnosis, meridian therapy.
Hong Jin, Clinical Supervisor; B.M., Nanjing College of Traditional Chinese Medicine (China), 1985; L.Ac. Pathology and therapeutics, point actions and indications.
Robert Kaneko, Clinic Director and Clinical Supervisor; B.S.Ac., SAMRA University of Oriental Medicine, 1985; L.Ac. Case observation and demonstration, clinical seminar section.
Regina Lellman, N.D., National College of Naturopathic Medicine, 1995. Western medical pathology, pharmacology.
Wei Li, Clinical Supervisor; M.S., Anhui Provincial Medical University (China), 1988; L.Ac. Chinese herbal medicine.
Guohui Liu, Clinical Supervisor; M.S., Chengdu College of Traditional Chinese Medicine (China), 1985; L.Ac. Chinese herbal medicine.
Roger Lore, Clinical Supervisor; Dip.Ac., Southwest Acupuncture College, 1987; L.Ac. Auricular acupuncture, acupuncture techniques.
Yan Lu, Clinical Supervisor; B.M. Heilongjiang College of Traditional Chinese Medicine (China), 1990; L.Ac. Tuina.
Hong Luo, Clinical Supervisor; B.S., Guangzhou College of Traditional Medicine (China), 1986; L.Ac. Case observation and demonstration, Chinese herbal medicine.
Russell Marz, N.D., National College of Naturopathic Medicine, 1983; L.Ac. Diet and nutrition.
Mitchell Bebel Stargrove, N.D., National College of Naturopathic Medicine, 1988; L.Ac. Medical history East and West.
Eric F. Stephens, Dip.Ac., Hong Kong Acupuncture College, 1979; L.Ac. Case observation and demonstration.
Brooke Winter, Dip.Ac., Oregon College of Oriental Medicine, 1989; L.Ac. Traditional Chinese medical theory.
Shizeng Yang, B.A., Beijing Institute of Physical Education (China), 1982; L.M.T. Tuina, qigong.

PACIFIC COLLEGE OF ORIENTAL MEDICINE
PACIFIC INSTITUTE OF ORIENTAL MEDICINE

Graduate Programs in Oriental Medicine and Acupuncture

Programs of Study

Pacific College of Oriental Medicine and its New York branch, Pacific Institute of Oriental Medicine, offer accredited master's-level degree (Master of Traditional Oriental Medicine) and diploma programs in Oriental medicine (Diploma of Traditional Oriental Medicine) and acupuncture (Diploma of Acupuncture). Graduates are eligible for New York and California state licensure and national certification as acupuncturists.

The educational process at Pacific College of Oriental Medicine is as complete as it is fascinating. The fundamentals of all aspects of traditional Oriental medicine are introduced in the first academic year with an emphasis on practicality. Acupuncture, herbal medicine, anatomy, body therapy, biosciences, and therapeutic exercise form a curriculum of immediate interest and usefulness. Students learn to view health and disease from both Western and traditional Asian holistic perspectives. Pacific's mission is to instruct students in the most valuable aspects of both systems.

The academic work of the first year prepares the student for the clinical assistantship experience. As a clinical assistant, the student works as part of a team of assistants, interns, and licensed acupuncturists in the College's busy community clinic. The second-year classroom experience leads to more in-depth understanding of the practice of acupuncture and Oriental medicine, including advanced needling techniques and advanced herbal prescriptions. The second year's clinical experience prepares students for the responsibility of accepting their own patients as interns in the third year.

The third- and fourth-year academic courses and clinical internship are exciting and inspiring. Much classroom time is spent discussing clinical cases. Medical understanding deepens and the student embodies and assimilates, as well as memorizes, the fine points of their art. Students directly experience the result of their studies when their patients' conditions improve.

The demographics of the United States promise a rewarding career in this holistic, complementary medical profession. The aging of the baby boom generation ensures a large population of patients who are interested in holistic medicine.

Research

Pacific College of Oriental Medicine was one of the few recipients of the NIH Office of Alternative Medicine's original research grants. The College is currently researching the effects of Oriental medicine on premenstrual syndrome. It has conducted pilot studies of acupuncture's effect on tinnitus and body therapy's effect on the side effects of chemotherapy.

Financial Aid

Pell Grants and Stafford Loans are available to eligible students.

Cost of Study

In 1997–98, the total cost per unit of instruction at the San Diego campus was $155. In New York, the cost per unit was $175. Total tuition for the Master's of Traditional Oriental Medicine program offered in San Diego was $30,535. The tuition for the equivalent program offered in New York, the Diploma of Traditional Oriental Medicine, was $34,470. The tuition for the Diploma of Acupuncture, offered only in New York, was $28,345. Books add approximately $2000 to the overall cost of attendance.

Living and Housing Costs

The cost of a student living in San Diego is slightly less than other large California cities. Students find it easy to find affordable apartments in the lovely neighborhoods near the college. As might be expected, the cost of living in New York is higher than in San Diego. Students relocated to New York can call the Pacific Institute for advice on nearby housing.

Student Group

In 1998–99, there are more than 300 master's-level students at each campus. In San Diego, there are an additional 50 nondegree body therapy students.

Student Outcomes

All master's-level programs lead to primary health-care competence in the field of Oriental medicine. Pacific's record of students passing state and national examinations is among the best in the nation. Graduates typically build a private practice as associates in established clinics. Others are hired by multidisciplinary clinics and work alongside medical doctors, chiropractors, and others.

Location

Acceptance to Pacific College allows students to study in one of the United States' most beautiful cities, San Diego, or in one of its most exciting, New York. Pacific College of Oriental Medicine is located conveniently in the heart of San Diego in Mission Valley. The school is minutes from beaches, shopping centers, and affordable housing. San Diego's nickname, "America's Finest City," is earned by its sunshine, beaches, mountains, and small-town atmosphere within a growing metropolis. Pacific Institute of Oriental Medicine is located in the historic Flatiron District, which was named for the unmistakable Flatiron Building. The Institute is surrounded by fine restaurants, convenient markets, trendy boutiques, and local theaters. The neighborhood's Romanesque facades have been restored, preserving the beauty of the buildings, the last of the preskyscraper era. The area is lively at all times during the day and evening and even the most innocent "out-of-towner" should feel safe and comfortable exploring the area.

The College

Pacific College was founded in 1986 with the mission of training primary health-care providers in the field of Oriental medicine. Pacific provides technical medical training while encouraging compassion for and understanding of patients' deepest needs. All executive board members of the College's Board of Directors are acupuncturists who lend direct, professional experience to the governance and direction of the institution.

Applying

Candidates are accepted for entry each tri-semester, which begins in January, April, or September of each year. As space availability is limited, prospective students are encouraged to submit applications as soon as possible.

Applicants must have satisfactorily completed an associate's degree or its equivalent, which is defined as at least 60 semester credits/90 quarter credits, the majority of which are of substantial academic content. The institution also considers credits from a professional medical program that requires at least the equivalent training of a registered nurse or a physician's assistant if they are earned from an institution accredited by an agency recognized by the U.S. Secretary of Education. Up to 30 semester units may be recognized by passing standardized tests or by military training equivalency.

Correspondence and Information

Pacific College of Oriental Medicine
7445 Mission Valley Road
San Diego, California 92108
Telephone: 619-574-6909
800-729-0941 (toll-free)
Fax: 619-574-6641
E-mail: 76545.2617@compuserve.com
jmiller@ormed.edu
World Wide Web: http://www.ormed.edu

Pacific Institute of Oriental Medicine
915 Broadway, 3rd Floor
New York, New York 10010
Telephone: 212-982-3456
800-729-3468 (toll-free)
Fax: 212-982-6514
World Wide Web: http://www.ormed.edu

Pacific College of Oriental Medicine/Pacific Institute of Oriental Medicine

THE FACULTY

San Diego Faculty
Alan Gregory Bantick, L.Ac. Needle technique, Taoism.
Matthew Callison, L.Ac., M.T.O.M. Applied kinesiology.
Maria Carrera, M.A. Alexander technique.
Barbara Clark, H.H.P. Jin Shin.
Robert B. Damon, L.Ac., M.S. Herbal medicine.
Allen Duerrstein, L.Ac., M.T.O.M. Spirituality in acupuncture.
Jeanann Eckert, L.Ac.
Carol Elliot, L.Ac., M.T.O.M. Homeopathy.
Jian Min Fan, L.Ac., M.S. Kidney Qi.
Kovida Fisher, L.Ac., M.D. Internal medicine.
Richard M. Gold, L.Ac., Ph.D. Body therapy.
David Hallisey, M.A. Taoism.
Bill Helm, B.S. Internal Qi Gong.
Ted Kardash, Ph.D. Taoism.
Ted Kaptchuk, L.Ac., O.M.D.
Clifford Lara, D.C. Orthopedic-neurological evaluation.
Steve Levitt, L.Ac., O.M.D.
Mimi Miller, L.Ac., M.T.O.M.
Walter Muryasz, B.S.
Toni Narins, L.Ac., M.T.O.M. Nutrition.
Charlene Penner, M.D. Trager psychophysical integration.
Erin Raskin, L.Ac., M.S. Ayurvedic medicine.
Z'ev Rosenberg, L.Ac., M.T.O.M. Herbal medicine.
Alex Tiberi, L.Ac. Style of acupuncture.
Colleen Timmons, L.Ac., M.T.O.M.
James Tsai, L.Ac., M.D.
Ana de Vedia, L.Ac., M.T.O.M.
Mei-fang Wei, L.Ac., M.D.
James Williams, L.Ac., O.M.D.

New York Faculty
Zhaoyang Chen, M.A. Psychology.
Jonathan Daniel, M.S., D.C., L.Ac. Chiropractic.
Kevin Ergil, M.A., M.S., L.Ac., F.A.A.P.M. Asian medicine.
Marnae Ergil, M.A. Traditional Chinese medicine.
Ann Fenichel, M.A., Ed.M. Counseling psychology.
Katharina Fennemann, Dipl. Ac., M.T.O.M., N.D. Naturopathy.
Elizabeth Harper, M.S. Exercise science.
Peter Kadar, L.Ac.
Darien Lamb, L.Ac.
Bruce Lipton, M.A., Tai Ji.
Caroline Radice, L.Ac., M.S. AIDS awareness.
Vittoria Repetto, D.C. Chiropractic.
Elaine Stern, L.Ac. Herbal medicine.
Chunyan Teng, M.B./B.S., L.Ac. Qi Gong.
Vasilios Theofanopoulos, M.S., Ph.D. candidate.
Christopher Trahan, L.Ac. Western herbology.
MaryAnne Travaglione, L.Ac., M.T.O.M.
Jennifer Weiss, L.Ac.
Wu Yan, M.B./B.S., M.S.
Hongwei Zhang, L.Ac. Scalp acupuncture.

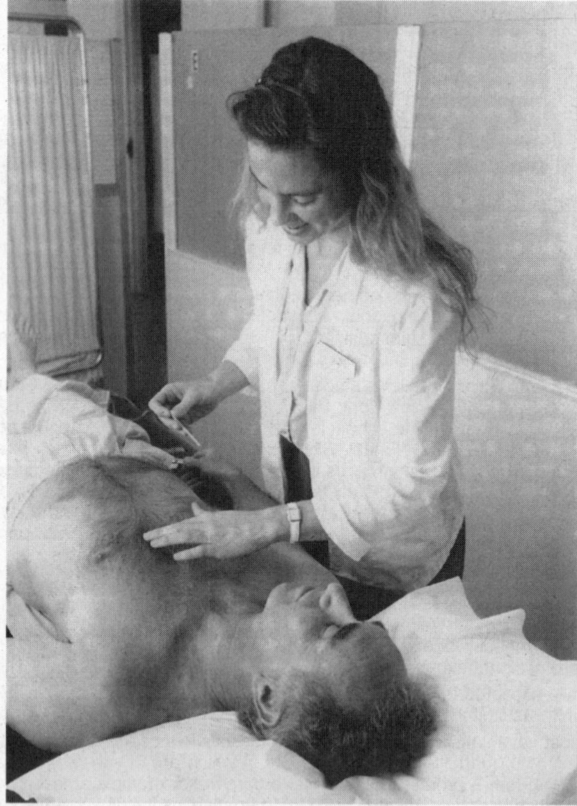

Clinical acupuncture at Pacific College of Oriental Medicine.

SAMRA UNIVERSITY OF ORIENTAL MEDICINE

Program in Acupuncture and Oriental Medicine

Programs of Study

A private, nonprofit corporation, Samra University of Oriental Medicine is known internationally as a premier teaching institution. The University's reputation draws students from throughout the world. To accommodate students' varying backgrounds, classes are taught separately in three languages: English, Mandarin Chinese, and Korean. Samra offers a four-academic–year course of study, which can be completed in thirty-six consecutive months of full-time study, leading to the degree of Master of Science in Oriental Medicine. Classes include subject matter in four departments: Oriental medical theory, acupuncture, Chinese herbology, and Western clinical sciences plus an 800-hour clinical internship experience. A compete listing of required and elective courses is available in the current catalog. After completion of the master's degree, students are prepared to sit for the California State Licensing Examination as well as the acupuncture and Chinese herbology examinations given by the National Certification Commission for Acupuncture and Oriental Medicine (NCCAOM), which are used as a basis for licensure in most states, including California.

Samra University has developed a cooperative working relationship with Beijing University of Chinese Medicine in Beijing, China, in which students may elect to complete part of their pre-master's internship and/or continue their studies after graduation. In the United States, the profession is currently developing an advanced program of study leading to the granting of the degree of Doctor of Oriental Medicine. Samra will offer that program as soon as it is approved.

Research Facilities

Samra University Research Institute, founded in 1997, is working with local hospitals and other agencies in conducting a variety of research studies. Students may elect to take introductory courses in acupuncture and Oriental medical research as part of their course work, and selected students may become actively involved in research projects. Current projects include a study of the use of acupuncture for postoperative cardiac bypass patients and the use of acupuncture in treating low back pain.

Financial Aid

Federal Pell Grants and Federal Stafford Student Loans are available to eligible students.

Cost of Study

The cost of study at Samra University of Oriental Medicine is $105 per quarter unit (effective spring 1999). Total tuition for the Master of Science degree is $25,520. Books and medical supplies add approximately $2100 to the overall cost of attendance.

Living and Housing Costs

The cost of a student living in west Los Angeles and the surrounding areas is about the same as that of other large California cities. A number of affordable apartments are available in neighborhoods close to the University.

Student Group

Samra University of Oriental Medicine has approximately 500 master's degree students in its three language programs. More than half are studying in the English language section, with the remaining half studying in the Mandarin or Korean language sections.

Student Outcomes

Samra University's record of graduates passing state and national examinations is among the best in the nation. Graduates may build private practices as associates in established clinics, start their own clinics, or be hired by multidisciplinary clinics and hospitals, working alongside physicians, chiropractors, psychologists, and other health-care providers.

Today the use of Oriental medicine in all its aspects is widely accepted throughout the United States, with many insurance companies, hospitals, and health centers incorporating the medicine into their delivery of clinical services. Oriental medicine satisfies the growing need for safe, effective, holistic, and relatively low-cost health care.

Location

Samra University is located conveniently in the heart of west Los Angeles, close to Beverly Hills, Century City, Culver City, and Santa Monica. The school is minutes from Los Angeles's Chinatown, Little Tokyo, and Koreatown and is convenient by freeway from the Asian-dominated city of Monterey Park. Samra University also is minutes from the Santa Monica beach. The Los Angeles area has beautiful terrain, with mountains overlooking the city and seashore, and a variety of ski, lake, desert, and seashore resort areas are within a 2-hour drive.

The University

Samra University of Oriental Medicine is the oldest, largest, and one of the most distinguished universities of traditional Chinese medicine in the United States. Founded in 1969 by a Chinese physician, Homer Cheng, M.D., as the Sino-American Medical Rehabilitation Association (SAMRA), Samra's initial mission was to train medical missionaries working in Third World areas in the principles and techniques of acupuncture and traditional Chinese medicine.

Samra originally delivered its education program through branch training centers in Kowloon, Malaysia, England, Hong Kong, and Philadelphia as well as in Los Angeles. As the University evolved, the activities centered chiefly in Los Angeles, California, and the other branches were closed. In 1979, Samra University of Oriental Medicine was the first Chinese medical school approved by the California Medical Board to educate and train persons who qualify to sit for the acupuncture licensing examinations. It also was the first university authorized by the California Department of Education to offer certificates of study and to grant degrees in Chinese medicine. Samra University of Oriental Medicine is accredited by the national Accreditation Commission for Acupuncture and Oriental Medicine.

Applying

Candidates are accepted for admission each quarter, beginning in January, April, July, and October. As space availability is limited, prospective students are encouraged to submit applications as soon as possible.

While most students possess bachelor's, master's, or doctoral degrees in other fields, the minimum qualification for admission is an Associate of Arts degree or its equivalent, which is defined as at least 60 semester credits or 90 quarter credits, the majority of which must be of a substantial academic content and acceptable for transfer to state universities. Admission is based upon academic achievement, personal and social development, and demonstrated humanistic qualities. Required credentials to be submitted include an application with a nonrefundable $75 fee, official transcripts of all academic work beyond the high school degree, and a short essay. Specific information is available from the Admissions Office. Applicants are encouraged to come for an interview and tour of the campus.

Correspondence and Information

Samra University of Oriental Medicine
3000 South Robertson Boulevard, 4th Floor
Los Angeles, California 90034
Telephone: 310-202-6444
Fax: 310-202-6007
E-mail: admissions@samra.edu

Samra University of Oriental Medicine

THE FACULTY

Marilyn F. Allen, M.S. Clinic management.
Allen Arnette, D.C., L.Ac. Acupuncture anatomy.
Susan Caldwell, M.S. Nutrition.
David Chan, Ph.D., O.M.D., L.Ac. Chinese medical philosophy.
Bao He Chen, M.S.O.M., L.Ac. Clinic Supervisor.
Cheng Su Chen, L.Ac. Clinic Supervisor.
Jirui Chen, B.Med., B.S. Western medicine.
Qing Chen, M.Med., L.Ac. Herbal prescription.
Chin Sok Chong, L.Ac. Associate Dean of Korean Section.
Ki Myeong Chung, M.S., L.Ac. Chinese internal medicine.
Marsha A. Connor, D.O.M., B.S.N., L.Ac.; RN.
Roc Doo, M.S.O.M., L.Ac. Clinic Supervisor.
Cormac Ferguson, M.T.O.M., L.Ac., Dipl.Ac. Herbology.
Lillian Garnier, B.A. Facial diagnosis and Feng Shui.
Steven Given, L.Ac. Clinic Supervisor.
Irina Guershman, L.Ac., Dipl.Ac. Oriental medical theory.
Hua Gu, Ph.D., L.Ac. Acupuncture orthopedics.
Soo Ihl Ha, M.S.O.M., L.Ac. Clinic Supervisor.
Kil Ye Han, M.S.O.M., L.Ac. Herbal prescription.
Karen E. Hentoff, M.A., M.S.O.M., L.Ac. Fundamental theory.
Dae Sun Hong, M.B.A., M.S.O.M., L.Ac. Chinese medical diagnosis.
Liqun Hu, Ph.D. candidate. Psychology of patient care.
Tianyu Huang, Ph.D., L.Ac. Pharmacology.
Xing Jiang, L.Ac. Chinese internal medicine.
Yeung Hwa Kwon, L.Ac. Acupuncture.
Han Joo Lee, M.S.O.M., L.Ac. Herbology.
Heiwon Lee, L.Ac. Acupuncture.
Katherine E. Lee, M.D. Western medicine.
Kyong Won Lee, L.Ac. Clinical observation.
Lance Lee, M.S.O.M., D.C., L.Ac. Topographical anatomy.
Peter Lee, L.Ac. Herbology.
Seung Jae Lee, L.Ac. Chinese nutrition.
Soo Rok Lee, L.Ac. Herbology.
David DaDe Li, M.S.O.M., L.Ac. Pathology.
Jian Feng Li, O.M.D., L.Ac. Clinic Supervisor.
Ming-Dong Li, O.M.D., M.S.O.M., L.Ac. Associate Dean of Chinese Section.
Rui-Quan Li, L.Ac. Traditional Chinese medicine ophthalmology.
Weiguo Li, M.D., Ph.D. Western medicine.
Youfu Li, M.S. Tai Qi.
Yu-Tian Li, B.Med., L.Ac. Clinic Supervisor.
David Lin, Ph.D. Nutrition.
Chung-Qing Liu, M.S.O.M., L.Ac.
Biao Lu, M.Med., L.Ac. Acupuncture techniques.
Kyung Chon Moon, L.Ac. Fundamental theory.
Yuguo Ni, B.Med., L.Ac. Western medicine and herbal prescription.
Frederick Obey, L.Ac. Herbal prescription.
Terrence Oleson, Ph.D. Auricular therapy.
Cyndee Overland, L.Ac. Fundamental theory.
Soo Hoon Owh, L.Ac. Oriental medical theory.
Irit Potter, M.S.O.M., L.Ac. Japanese meridian therapy.
Yu Qin Qi, B.Med., L.Ac. Oriental medical theory.
Tan Quach, M.S.O.M., L.Ac. Tai Qi and acupuncture.
Michael Redmond, Ph.D. candidate; RN. Western sciences.
Sharon Shao, L.Ac. Oriental medical theory.
Dae Su Shin, M.S.O.M., L.Ac. Clinic Supervisor.
Dong Kil Shin, M.S.O.M., L.Ac. Herbal prescription.
Soon Shik Shin, M.A., L.Ac. Acupuncture.
Aaron Sui, L.Ac. Dean of Admissions.
L. Cass Terry, M.B.A., M.D., Ph.D., Pharm.D. Western medicine.
Tuan A. Tran, Ph.D., D.C. Western medicine.
Harold C. Valery, M.D. Western medicine.
Tammy C. Venters, M.S.O.M., L.Ac. Associate Academic Dean.
Boris Wang, Ph.D.
Kathryn White, Ph.D., D.H.M., L.Ac. Academic Dean.
Lorraine Wilcox, M.S.O.M., L.Ac. Clinical observation.
Pei Lin Wu, B.Med., L.Ac. Traditional Chinese medicine gynecology.
Xiao-Ming Xu, B.Med., L.Ac. Chinese internal medicine.
Yu You, Ph.D., L.Ac. Chinese internal medicine.
Man Li Yu, B.Med., L.Ac. Oriental medical theory and herbology.
Amir Zagross, M.T.O.M., L.Ac. Acupuncture.
Dafang Zeng, O.M.D., L.Ac. Traditional Chinese medicine dermatology and orthopedics.
Ji Zhang, B.Med., L.Ac. Clinical Supervisor. Five element theory.
Li Guo Zhao, L.Ac. Anatomy and physiology.
Yong Ji Zhao, B.Med. Western medicine.
Rong Zhou, O.M.D., L.Ac. Chinese internal medicine.

The campus and clinic.

Intern preparing herbal formula.

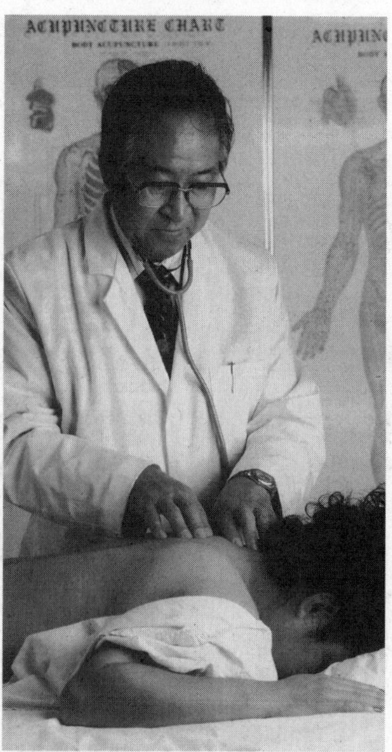

Doctor examining the patient.

Section 38
Pharmacy and Pharmaceutical Sciences

This section contains directories of institutions offering professional programs in pharmacy and graduate studies in pharmaceutical sciences, followed by in-depth entries submitted by institutions that chose to prepare detailed program descriptions. Additional information about programs listed in the directories but not augmented by an in-depth entry may be obtained by writing directly to the dean of a school or chair of a department at the address given in the directory.

For programs offering related work, see also in this book Allied Health; in Book 3, Biochemistry, Biological and Biomedical Sciences, Nutrition, Pharmacology and Toxicology, and Physiology; in Book 4, Chemistry; and in Book 5, Bioengineering, Biomedical Engineering, and Biotechnology; and Chemical Engineering.

CONTENTS

Pharmaceutical Sciences

Auburn University, School of Pharmacy and Graduate School, Graduate Program in Pharmacy, Auburn University, AL 36849-0001. Awards MS, PhD. Part-time programs available. Faculty: 32 full-time (8 women). Students: 13 full-time (7 women), 16 part-time (8 women); includes 2 minority (both African Americans), 15 international. 27 applicants, 30% accepted. In 1997, 3 master's, 4 doctorates awarded. *Degree requirements:* Thesis/dissertation required, foreign language not required. *Entrance requirements:* GRE General Test. Application deadline: 9/1 (rolling processing; 3/1 for spring admission). Application fee: $25 ($50 for international students). *Expenses:* Tuition $2760 per year full-time, $76 per credit hour part-time for state residents; $8280 per year full-time, $228 per credit hour part-time for nonresidents. Fees $30 per year full-time, $160 per quarter part-time for state residents; $30 per year full-time, $480 per quarter part-time for nonresidents. *Financial aid:* Fellowships, research assistantships, teaching assistantships available. *Faculty research:* Pharmaceutical sciences, communications, facilities design, substance abuse. Total annual research expenditures: $600,000. • Application contact: Dr. John F. Pritchett, Dean of the Graduate School, 334-844-4700.

Butler University, College of Pharmacy, Indianapolis, IN 46208-3485. Offers program in pharmaceutical science (Pharm D, MS). Part-time and evening/weekend programs available. Faculty: 6 full-time (0 women), 2 part-time (1 woman), 6.5 FTE. Students: 61 full-time (48 women), 11 part-time (7 women); includes 4 minority (all Asian Americans), 8 international. Average age 26. 47 applicants, 98% accepted. In 1997, 21 Pharm Ds, 3 master's awarded. *Degree requirements:* For master's, research paper or thesis required, foreign language not required. *Application deadline:* 8/1 (priority date; rolling processing; 12/15 for spring admission). *Application fee:* $25. *Tuition:* $310 per credit hour. *Financial aid:* 1 student received aid. *Faculty research:* Chemical and physical stability of drugs and drug products, pharmacology of central acting and antiseizure drugs, pharmacokinetics and disposition of xenobiotics *in vivo*, protein binding studies, synthesis of bis-hydantoins. • Dr. Robert A. Sandmann, Dean, 317-940-9322. Fax: 317-940-6172. Application contact: Dr. Beverly Sandmann, Principal Graduate Adviser, 317-940-9553.

Creighton University, Graduate Programs in Medicine and College of Arts and Sciences, Department of Pharmacology, Omaha, NE 68178-0001. Offerings include pharmaceutical sciences (MS). Department faculty: 5 full-time (1 woman), 15 part-time (2 women). *Degree requirements:* Thesis. *Average time to degree:* doctorate–5 years full-time. *Application deadline:* 4/1 (priority date; rolling processing). *Application fee:* $25. *Expenses:* Tuition $402 per credit hour. Fees $536 per year full-time, $28 per semester part-time. • Dr. Frank J. Dowd, Director, 402-280-2726. Application contact: Dr. Barbara J. Braden, Dean, Graduate School, 402-280-2870. Fax: 402-280-5762.

Dalhousie University, Faculty of Health Professions, College of Pharmacy, Halifax, NS B3H 3J5, Canada. Awards M Sc, PhD. Admissions temporarily suspended. Faculty: 7 full-time (2 women), 1 part-time (0 women). Students: 2 full-time (1 woman). *Degree requirements:* For master's, thesis; for doctorate, 1 foreign language (computer language can substitute), dissertation. *Financial aid:* Fellowships available. • Dr. R. F. Chandler, Director, 902-494-2097.

Duquesne University, School of Pharmacy, Graduate School of Pharmaceutical Sciences, Program in Medicinal Chemistry, Pittsburgh, PA 15282-0001. Awards MS, PhD. Faculty: 3 full-time (0 women). Students: 7 full-time (1 woman), 8 part-time (2 women); includes 1 minority (African American), 14 international. 43 applicants, 19% accepted. In 1997, 2 master's awarded (50% found work related to degree, 50% continued full-time study); 1 doctorate awarded (100% entered university research/teaching). *Degree requirements:* For master's, thesis required, foreign language not required; for doctorate, 1 foreign language, computer language, dissertation. *Entrance requirements:* GRE General Test, TOEFL, TSE. Application deadline: 3/1 (priority date; rolling processing). Application fee: $40. *Expenses:* Tuition $530 per credit. Fees $39 per credit. *Financial aid:* In 1997–98, 6 research assistantships, 10 teaching assistantships were awarded; fellowships also available. *Faculty research:* Synthetic medicinal chemistry, antitumor agents, drug design, estrone sulfatase/aromatase inhibitors, anti-opportunistic infection agents. • Dr. Aleem Gangjee, Director, Graduate School of Pharmaceutical Sciences, 412-396-5662.

See in-depth description on page 1791.

Duquesne University, School of Pharmacy, Graduate School of Pharmaceutical Sciences, Program in Pharmaceutics, Pittsburgh, PA 15282-0001. Awards MS, PhD, MBA/MS. Offerings include pharmaceutical chemistry (MS, PhD), pharmaceutics (MS, PhD). Part-time programs available. Faculty: 5 full-time (1 woman), 1 part-time (0 women). Students: 7 full-time (6 women), 17 part-time (4 women); includes 20 international. 64 applicants, 11% accepted. In 1997, 2 master's awarded (50% found work related to degree, 50% continued full-time study); 2 doctorates awarded (100% found work related to degree). *Degree requirements:* For master's, thesis required, foreign language not required; for doctorate, 1 foreign language, computer language, dissertation. *Entrance requirements:* GRE General Test, TOEFL, TSE. Application deadline: 3/1 (priority date; rolling processing). Application fee: $40. *Expenses:* Tuition $530 per credit. Fees $39 per credit. *Financial aid:* In 1997–98, 15 teaching assistantships were awarded; fellowships, research assistantships, and career-related internships or fieldwork also available. *Faculty research:* Integration of analytical, physiochemical, and pharmacokinetic aspects of drug and cosmetic delivery system development. • Dr. Lawrence H. Block, Head, 412-396-6362.

See in-depth description on page 1791.

Florida Agricultural and Mechanical University, Division of Graduate Studies, Research, and Continuing Education, College of Pharmacy and Pharmaceutical Sciences, Graduate Programs in Pharmaceutical Sciences, Tallahassee, FL 32307-3200. Offerings in environmental toxicology (PhD), medicinal chemistry (MS, PhD), pharmacology/toxicology (MS, PhD). Students: 35 (19 women); includes 23 minority (21 African Americans, 2 Asian Americans). *Degree requirements:* Thesis/dissertation, publishable paper required, foreign language not required. *Entrance requirements:* GRE General Test (minimum combined score of 1000), minimum GPA of 3.0 in last 60 hours. Application fee: $20. *Expenses:* Tuition $140 per credit hour for state residents; $484 per credit hour for nonresidents. Fees $130 per year. *Financial aid:* Fellowships, research assistantships, grants, Federal Work-Study available. *Faculty research:* Anticancer agents, anti-inflammatory drugs, chronopharmacology, neuroendocrinology, microbiology. • Application contact: Dr. Thomas J. Fitzgerald, Chairman, Graduate Committee, 850-599-3301.

See in-depth description on page 1793.

Idaho State University, College of Pharmacy, Department of Pharmaceutical Sciences, Pocatello, ID 83209. Offers programs in pharmaceutic science (PhD), pharmaceutical chemistry (MS), pharmaceutics (MS), pharmacognosy (MS), pharmacology (MS, PhD). Faculty: 10 full-time (2 women), 1 (woman) part-time. Students: 7 full-time (5 women), 2 part-time (1 woman); includes 1 minority (Asian American), 2 international. Average age 31. In 1997, 2 master's, 2 doctorates awarded. *Degree requirements:* For master's, 1 foreign language, thesis. *Entrance requirements:* GRE General Test. Application deadline: 8/1 (priority date). Application fee: $30. *Faculty research:* Metabolic toxicity of heavy metals, neuroendicine pharmacology, cardiovascular pharmacology, cancer biology, immunopharmacology. Total annual research expenditures: $320,000. • Dr. Christopher Daniels, Interim Chair, 208-236-2682.

Long Island University, Brooklyn Campus, Arnold and Marie Schwartz College of Pharmacy and Health Sciences, Graduate Programs in Pharmacy, Division of Pharmaceutics and Industrial Pharmacy, Brooklyn, NY 11201-8423. Offers programs in cosmetic science (MS), industrial pharmacy (MS), pharmaceutics (PhD). Part-time and evening/weekend programs available. Faculty: 14 full-time (1 woman), 1 (woman) part-time. Students: 47 full-time (10 women), 38 part-time (13 women); includes 28 minority (7 African Americans, 17 Asian Americans, 4 Hispanics), 53 international. Average age 24. In 1997, 17 master's awarded. Terminal master's awarded for partial completion of doctoral program. *Degree requirements:* For master's, thesis optional, foreign language not required; for doctorate, dissertation, candidacy exam required, foreign language not required. *Average time to degree:* master's–2 years full-time, 5 years part-time; doctorate–5 years part-time. *Entrance requirements:* Minimum GPA of 3.0. Application deadline: rolling. Application fee: $30. *Expenses:* Tuition $480 per credit. Fees $415 per year full-time, $73 per semester (minimum) part-time. *Financial aid:* In 1997–98, 14 students received aid, including 5 fellowships, 9 teaching assistantships. • Dr. Fotios Plakogiannis, Director, 718-488-1101. Application contact: Bernard W. Sullivan, Associate Director of Admissions, 718-488-1011.

Long Island University, Brooklyn Campus, Arnold and Marie Schwartz College of Pharmacy and Health Sciences, Graduate Programs in Pharmacy, Division of Pharmacology/Toxicology/Medicinal Chemistry, Brooklyn, NY 11201-8423. Offers programs in pharmacology/toxicology (MS), pharmacotherapeutics (MS). Part-time and evening/weekend programs available. Faculty: 12 full-time (3 women). Students: 5 full-time (2 women), 48 part-time (29 women); includes 28 minority (11 African Americans, 13 Asian Americans, 4 Hispanics), 5 international. Average age 24. In 1997, 11 degrees awarded. *Degree requirements:* Thesis optional, foreign language not required. *Average time to degree:* master's–2 years full-time, 5 years part-time. *Entrance requirements:* Minimum GPA of 3.0. Application deadline: rolling. Application fee: $30. *Expenses:* Tuition $480 per credit. Fees $415 per year full-time, $73 per semester (minimum) part-time. *Financial aid:* In 1997–98, 3 students received aid, including 3 teaching assistantships. • Dr. R. R. Raje, Director, 718-488-1062. Application contact: Bernard W. Sullivan, Associate Director of Admissions, 718-488-1011.

Long Island University, Brooklyn Campus, Arnold and Marie Schwartz College of Pharmacy and Health Sciences, Graduate Programs in Pharmacy, Division of Pharmacy Administration, Brooklyn, NY 11201-8423. Offers programs in drug regulatory affairs (MS), hospital pharmacy administration (MS), pharmaceutical and health care marketing administration (MS). Part-time and evening/weekend programs available. Faculty: 7 full-time (1 woman), 8 part-time (1 woman). Students: 5 full-time (4 women), 25 part-time (13 women); includes 12 minority (5 African Americans, 7 Asian Americans), 7 international. Average age 28. In 1997, 4 degrees awarded. *Degree requirements:* Thesis optional, foreign language not required. *Average time to degree:* master's–2 years full-time, 5 years part-time. *Entrance requirements:* Minimum GPA of 3.0. Application deadline: rolling. Application fee: $30. *Expenses:* Tuition $480 per credit. Fees $415 per year full-time, $73 per semester (minimum) part-time. *Financial aid:* In 1997–98, 4 students received aid, including 4 teaching assistantships averaging $350 per month. • Dr. Steven Strauss, Director, 718-488-1105. Application contact: Bernard W. Sullivan, Associate Director of Admissions, 718-488-1011.

Long Island University, Brooklyn Campus, Arnold and Marie Schwartz College of Pharmacy and Health Sciences, Graduate Programs in Pharmacy, Division of Pharmacy Practice, Brooklyn, NY 11201-8423. Offers program in drug information and communication (MS). Part-time and evening/weekend programs available. Faculty: 19 full-time (10 women), 3 part-time (all women). Students: 1 (woman) full-time, 9 part-time (6 women); includes 3 minority (1 African American, 2 Asian Americans). Average age 24. In 1997, 4 degrees awarded. *Degree requirements:* Thesis optional, foreign language not required. *Average time to degree:* master's–2 years full-time, 5 years part-time. *Entrance requirements:* Minimum GPA of 3.0. Application deadline: rolling. Application fee: $30. *Expenses:* Tuition $480 per credit. Fees $415 per year full-time, $73 per semester (minimum) part-time. *Financial aid:* In 1997–98, 6 students received aid, including 6 teaching assistantships averaging $350 per month. • Prof. Stanley Feifer, Director, 718-488-1064. Application contact: Bernard W. Sullivan, Associate Director of Admissions, 718-488-1011.

Long Island University, C.W. Post Campus, School of Health Professions, Department of Health Sciences, Program in Medical Biology, Brookville, NY 11548-1300. Offerings include medical chemistry (MS). Program faculty: 4 full-time (1 woman), 12 part-time (6 women), 7 FTE. *Degree requirements:* Computer language, thesis required, foreign language not required. *Average time to degree:* master's–2 years full-time, 4 years part-time. *Entrance requirements:* TOEFL (minimum score 500), minimum GPA of 2.75 in major. Application deadline: rolling. Application fee: $30. Electronic applications accepted. *Expenses:* Tuition $480 per credit. Fees $316 per year full-time, $71 per semester (minimum) part-time. • Dr. Ronald R. Modesto, Co-Chair, 516-299-2762. E-mail: rmodesto@eagle.liunet.edu. Application contact: Robin Steadman, Graduate Adviser, 516-299-2337.

Massachusetts College of Pharmacy and Allied Health Sciences, Graduate Program in Pharmaceutics/Industrial Pharmacy, 179 Longwood Avenue, Boston, MA 02115-5896. Awards MS, PhD. Faculty: 4 full-time (0 women), 2 part-time (0 women). Students: 14 full-time (10 women), 4 part-time (3 women). Average age 25. 38 applicants, 39% accepted. In 1997, 2 doctorates awarded (100% found work related to degree). Terminal master's awarded for partial completion of doctoral program. *Degree requirements:* For master's, thesis, oral defense of thesis required, foreign language not required; for doctorate, 1 foreign language (computer language can substitute), dissertation, oral defense of dissertation, qualifying exam. *Average time to degree:* master's–3 years full-time; doctorate–5 years full-time. *Entrance requirements:* GRE General Test (minimum combined score of 1650 on three sections), TOEFL (minimum score 550), minimum QPA of 3.0. Application deadline: 2/1 (priority date). Application fee: $60. *Expenses:* Tuition $528 per credit. Fees $200 per semester. *Financial aid:* In 1997–98, 12 students received aid, including 2 fellowships (both to first-year students) totaling $8,000, 1 research assistantship averaging $1,200 per month, 6 teaching assistantships averaging $1,200 per month and totaling $63,000, 1 library assistantship averaging $1,200 per month and totaling $10,500. Financial aid application deadline: 2/1. *Faculty research:* Tablet technology, excipient development, process development, physical pharmacy, biopharmaceutics, transdermal and novel drug delivery. Total annual research expenditures: $50,000. • Dr. Timothy Maher, Director, Division of Pharmaceutical Sciences, 617-732-2940. Fax: 617-732-2963. Application contact: Lovie Condrick, Coordinator of Graduate Admissions, 617-732-2986. Fax: 617-732-2801. E-mail: admissions@mcp.edu.

See in-depth description on page 1795.

Medical University of South Carolina, Department of Pharmaceutical Sciences, Charleston, SC 29425-0002. Offers programs in manufacturing pharmacy (PhD), natural products/pharmaceutical chemistry (PhD), pharmaceutics/biopharmaceutics (PhD), pharmacokinetics (PhD). Offered jointly with the University of South Carolina. Faculty: 15 part-time (3 women). Students: 14 full-time (5 women); includes 1 minority (African American), 1 international. Average age 31. 16 applicants, 50% accepted. In 1997, 4 degrees awarded. *Degree requirements:* Computer language, dissertation, teaching and research seminar, oral and written exams required, foreign language not required. *Entrance requirements:* GRE General Test (minimum combined score of 1650 on three sections), GRE Subject Test (international applicants), TOEFL, background in pharmacy, mathematics, or other science area; interview. Application deadline: rolling. Application fee: $55. Electronic applications accepted. *Expenses:* Tuition $3212 per year (minimum) full-time, $1515 per year (minimum) part-time for state residents; $4112 per year (minimum) full-time, $2015 per year (minimum) part-time for nonresidents. Fees $80 per year (minimum). *Financial aid:* In 1997–98, 5 fellowships (2 to first-year students) averaging $1,250 per month were awarded; research assistantships, teaching assistantships, partial tuition waivers, Federal Work-Study also available. Financial aid application deadline: 4/1; applicants required to submit FAFSA. *Faculty research:* New anticancer agents and antiarthritic agents, stereoselectivity and dynamics of drug disposition, chemical mechanisms of drug decomposition, design and formulation of innovative drug delivery systems. • Dr. K. S. Patrick, Chairman, 843-792-3111. Application contact: Julie Johnston, Director of Admissions, 843-792-8710.

Directory: Pharmaceutical Sciences

Memorial University of Newfoundland, School of Graduate Studies, School of Pharmacy, St. John's, NF A1C 5S7, Canada. Awards M Sc. Students: 5 full-time (1 woman); includes 4 international. 29 applicants, 3% accepted. In 1997, 4 degrees awarded. *Degree requirements:* Thesis. *Entrance requirements:* B Sc in pharmacy or related area. Application fee: $40. *Expenses:* Tuition $1896 per year (minimum). Fees $60 per year for Canadian residents; $621 per year for nonresidents. *Financial aid:* Fellowships, research assistantships available. *Faculty research:* Pharmaceutics, medicinal chemistry, physical pharmacy, pharmacology, toxicology. • Dr. Christopher W. Loomis, Acting Director, 709-737-7903. E-mail: cwloomis@morgan.ucs.mun.ca.

Mercer University, Cecil B. Day Campus, Southern School of Pharmacy, Graduate Programs in Pharmacy, Athens, GA 30602. Offering in pharmaceutical sciences (PhD). *Degree requirements:* Dissertation. *Entrance requirements:* GRE, Pharm D or BS in pharmacy, minimum GPA of 3.0. Application deadline: 1/31 (rolling processing). Application fee: $25. *Tuition:* $463 per semester hour. *Financial aid:* Teaching assistantships, Federal Work-Study, institutionally sponsored loans, and career-related internships or fieldwork available. Aid available to part-time students. Financial aid application deadline: 5/1. • Application contact: Dr. James Bartling, Associate Dean for Student Affairs and Admissions, 770-986-3232. Fax: 770-986-3063. E-mail: bartling_jw@mercer.edu.

North Dakota State University, College of Pharmacy, Department of Pharmaceutical Sciences, Fargo, ND 58105. Offers programs in pharmaceutical sciences (PhD), pharmacology/toxicology (MS). Faculty: 6 full-time (0 women), 1 part-time (0 women). Students: 11 full-time (3 women); includes 9 international. Average age 30. 34 applicants, 15% accepted. In 1997, 3 master's awarded (100% found work related to degree); 1 doctorate awarded (100% found work related to degree). Terminal master's awarded for partial completion of doctoral program. *Degree requirements:* Computer language, thesis/dissertation required, foreign language not required. *Average time to degree:* master's–2 years full-time; doctorate–4 years full-time. *Entrance requirements:* GRE General Test, TOEFL (minimum score 600). Application deadline: 4/1 (rolling processing). Application fee: $25. *Tuition:* $2572 per year full-time, $107 per credit part-time for state residents; $6868 per year full-time, $286 per credit part-time for nonresidents. *Financial aid:* In 1997–98, 11 research assistantships (3 to first-year students) averaging $700 per month were awarded; teaching assistantships, institutionally sponsored loans also available. Financial aid application deadline: 4/15. • Application contact: Dr. William Shelver, Chair, 701-231-7661.

Northeastern University, Bouvé College of Pharmacy and Health Sciences Graduate School, Program in Medicinal Chemistry, Boston, MA 02115-5096. Awards MS. Part-time and evening/weekend programs available. Students: 2 part-time (1 woman). Average age 30. In 1997, 1 degree awarded. *Degree requirements:* Comprehensive exam required, thesis optional, foreign language not required. *Entrance requirements:* Minimum GPA of 3.0, bachelor's degree in science. Application deadline: rolling. Application fee: $50. *Expenses:* Tuition $440 per credit hour. Fees $55 per quarter full-time, $13.25 per quarter part-time. *Financial aid:* Federal Work-Study available. Aid available to part-time students. Financial aid application deadline: 3/1; applicants required to submit FAFSA. *Faculty research:* Novel receptor probes, synthesis of steroids, phosphorous-containing antiinfections, natural products, radiopharmaceuticals. • Dr. Robert N. Hanson, Program Director, 617-373-3313. Application contact: Bill Purnell, Director of Graduate Admissions, 617-373-2708. Fax: 617-373-4701. E-mail: w.purnell@nunet.neu.edu.

See in-depth description on page 1797.

Northeastern University, Bouvé College of Pharmacy and Health Sciences Graduate School, Programs in Biomedical Sciences, Boston, MA 02115-5096. Offerings include medicinal chemistry (PhD), pharmaceutics (PhD). Terminal master's awarded for partial completion of doctoral program. Faculty: 14 full-time (1 woman), 14 part-time (5 women). *Degree requirements:* Dissertation, qualifying exam required, foreign language not required. *Entrance requirements:* GRE General Test, TOEFL. Application deadline: 2/15. Application fee: $50. *Expenses:* Tuition $440 per credit hour. Fees $55 per quarter full-time, $13.25 per quarter part-time. • Dr. Medhi Boroujerdi, Associate Dean, 617-373-3380. Fax: 617-266-6756. Application contact: Bill Purnell, Director of Graduate Admissions, 617-373-2708. Fax: 617-373-4701. E-mail: w.purnell@nunet.neu.edu.

Northeast Louisiana University, College of Pharmacy and Health Sciences, School of Pharmacy, Program in Pharmaceutical Sciences, Monroe, LA 71209-0001. Awards MS. *Entrance requirements:* GRE General Test (minimum combined score of 1000) or GMAT (minimum score 455), minimum GPA of 2.5. Application deadline: 5/1 (priority date; rolling processing; 11/1 for spring admission). Application fee: $15 ($25 for international students). *Tuition:* $2028 per year full-time, $240 per semester (minimum) part-time for state residents; $6852 per year full-time, $240 per semester (minimum) part-time for nonresidents.

Northeast Louisiana University, College of Pharmacy and Health Sciences, School of Pharmacy, Program in Pharmacy, Monroe, LA 71209-0001. Awards PhD. *Degree requirements:* Dissertation required, foreign language not required. *Entrance requirements:* GRE General Test (minimum combined score of 1000) or GMAT (minimum score 455). Application deadline: 5/1 (priority date; rolling processing). Application fee: $15 ($25 for international students). *Tuition:* $2028 per year full-time, $240 per semester (minimum) part-time for state residents; $6852 per year full-time, $240 per semester (minimum) part-time for nonresidents.

The Ohio State University, College of Pharmacy and Graduate School, Graduate Programs in Pharmacy, Division of Medicinal Chemistry and Pharmacognosy, Columbus, OH 43210. Offers program in pharmacy (MS, PhD). Faculty: 9 full-time (1 woman). Students: 20 full-time (7 women); includes 9 international. Average age 25. 106 applicants, 15% accepted. In 1997, 1 master's awarded (100% found work related to degree); 4 doctorates awarded (25% entered university research/teaching, 75% found other work related to degree). *Degree requirements:* Thesis/dissertation required, foreign language not required. *Average time to degree:* master's–2 years full-time; doctorate–5 years full-time. *Entrance requirements:* For master's, GRE General Test, TOEFL (minimum score 550), TSE (minimum score 60); for doctorate, GRE General Test, TOEFL (minimum score 550), TSE (minimum score 60), minimum GPA of 3.0. Application deadline: 1/15 (priority date; 1/1 for spring admission). Application fee: $30 ($40 for international students). *Tuition:* $5472 per year full-time, $554 per quarter (minimum) part-time for state residents; $14,172 per year full-time, $1424 per quarter (minimum) part-time for nonresidents. *Financial aid:* In 1997–98, 17 students received aid, including 1 fellowship averaging $1,334 per month, 2 research assistantships averaging $1,175 per month, 12 teaching assistantships (3 to first-year students) averaging $1,175 per month, traineeships averaging $1,175 per month. Financial aid application deadline: 1/15. *Faculty research:* Drug design, natural products, synthesis of enzyme inhibitors, drug metabolism and anticancer agents. • Dr. Robert Curley, Coordinator, 614-292-7628. Fax: 614-292-2435. E-mail: curley.1@osu.edu.

See in-depth description on page 1799.

The Ohio State University, College of Pharmacy and Graduate School, Graduate Programs in Pharmacy, Division of Pharmaceutics and Pharmaceutical Chemistry, Columbus, OH 43210. Offers program in pharmacy (MS, PhD). Faculty: 10 full-time (1 woman). Students: 36 full-time (17 women), 1 (woman) part-time; includes 3 minority (all Asian Americans), 25 international. Average age 25. 135 applicants, 10% accepted. In 1997, 4 master's awarded (100% found work related to degree); 6 doctorates awarded (33% entered university research/teaching, 67% found other work related to degree). *Degree requirements:* For doctorate, dissertation required, foreign language not required. *Average time to degree:* master's–2 years full-time; doctorate–5 years full-time. *Entrance requirements:* For master's, GRE General Test, TOEFL (minimum score 550), TSE (minimum score 60); for doctorate, GRE General Test, TOEFL (minimum score 550), TSE (minimum score 60), minimum GPA of 3.0. Application deadline: 1/15 (priority date; 1/1 for spring admission). Application fee: $30 ($40 for international students). *Tuition:* $5472 per year full-time, $554 per quarter (minimum) part-time for state residents; $14,172 per year full-time, $1424 per quarter (minimum) part-time for nonresidents. *Financial aid:* In 1997–98, 34 students received aid, including 2 fellowships averaging $1,175 per month, 20 research assistantships averaging $1,175 per month, 12 teaching assistantships (4 to first-year students) averaging $1,175 per month. Financial aid application deadline: 1/15. *Faculty research:* Absorption, metabolism, and elimination of drugs; drug release from emulsions, liposomes, and liquid crystals; clinical and forensic research application. • Dr. Peter W. Swann, Coordinator, 614-688-5609. Fax: 614-292-7766. E-mail: swann.1@osu.edu.

See in-depth description on page 1799.

Oregon State University, Graduate School, College of Pharmacy, Corvallis, OR 97331. Awards Pharm D, MAIS, MS, PhD. Part-time programs available. Faculty: 21 full-time (2 women). Students: 21 full-time, 3 part-time; includes 1 minority (Asian American), 12 international. Average age 30. 43 applicants, 7% accepted. In 1997, 6 Pharm Ds, 4 master's awarded. Terminal master's awarded for partial completion of doctoral program. *Degree requirements:* For master's, thesis, minimum GPA of 3.0 required, foreign language not required; for doctorate, variable foreign language requirement, dissertation, minimum GPA of 3.0. *Entrance requirements:* For master's and doctorate, GRE General Test, TOEFL (minimum score 550), minimum GPA of 3.0 in last 90 hours. Application deadline: 3/1 (rolling processing). Application fee: $50. *Tuition:* $6207 per year full-time, $810 per quarter (minimum) part-time for state residents; $10,551 per year full-time, $1293 per quarter (minimum) part-time for nonresidents. *Financial aid:* In 1997–98, 3 fellowships, 8 research assistantships (1 to a first-year student), 7 teaching assistantships were awarded; Federal Work-Study, institutionally sponsored loans, and career-related internships or fieldwork also available. Aid available to part-time students. Financial aid application deadline: 2/1. *Faculty research:* Pharmacology/toxicology, pharmacokinetics, biopharmaceutics, neuroscience, natural products. • Dr. Richard A. Ohvall, Dean, 541-737-3424. Application contact: Office Specialist, 541-737-5784. Fax: 541-737-3999.

Purdue University, School of Pharmacy and Pharmacal Sciences and Graduate School, Graduate Programs in Pharmacy and Pharmacal Sciences, Department of Industrial and Physical Pharmacy, West Lafayette, IN 47907. Awards PhD. Faculty: 7 full-time (0 women). Students: 31 full-time (11 women); includes 3 minority (2 African Americans, 1 Asian American), 22 international. Average age 30. 45 applicants, 11% accepted. In 1997, 10 doctorates awarded. Terminal master's awarded for partial completion of doctoral program. *Degree requirements:* For doctorate, computer language, dissertation required, foreign language not required. *Entrance requirements:* For doctorate, GRE General Test, TOEFL, minimum B average; BS in biology, chemistry, or pharmacy. Application deadline: rolling. Application fee: $30. Electronic applications accepted. *Tuition:* $3500 per year full-time, $126 per credit hour part-time for state residents; $11,720 per year full-time, $387 per credit hour part-time for nonresidents. *Financial aid:* In 1997–98, 30 students received aid, including 8 fellowships averaging $1,059 per month and totaling $101,664, 16 research assistantships averaging $1,015 per month and totaling $194,880, 6 teaching assistantships averaging $920 per month; traineeships also available. Aid available to part-time students. Financial aid applicants required to submit FAFSA. *Faculty research:* Controlled drug delivery systems, liposomes, antacids, coating technology. • Dr. S. R. Byrn, Head of the Graduate Program, 765-494-1460. Application contact: Dr. G. E. Peck, Graduate Committee Chair, 765-494-1400.

See in-depth description on page 1801.

Purdue University, School of Pharmacy and Pharmacal Sciences and Graduate School, Graduate Programs in Pharmacy and Pharmacal Sciences, Department of Medicinal Chemistry and Molecular Pharmacology, West Lafayette, IN 47907. Awards MS, PhD, MS/PhD. Programs in analytical medicinal chemistry (PhD), computational and biophysical medicinal chemistry (PhD), medicinal and bioorganic chemistry (PhD), medicinal biochemistry and molecular biology (PhD), molecular pharmacology and toxicology (PhD), natural products and pharmacognosy (PhD), nuclear pharmacy (MS), radiopharmaceutical chemistry and nuclear pharmacy (PhD). Faculty: 26 full-time (2 women). Students: 64 full-time (29 women), 5 part-time (2 women); includes 3 minority (all Asian Americans), 30 international. Average age 29. 157 applicants, 22% accepted. In 1997, 4 master's, 18 doctorates awarded. Terminal master's awarded for partial completion of doctoral program. *Degree requirements:* Thesis/dissertation required, foreign language not required. *Entrance requirements:* For master's, GRE General Test, TOEFL, minimum B average; BS in biology, chemistry, or pharmacy; for doctorate, GRE General Test, TOEFL, minimum B average; BS in biology, chemistry, or pharmacology. Application deadline: rolling. Application fee: $30. Electronic applications accepted. *Tuition:* $3500 per year full-time, $126 per credit hour part-time for state residents; $11,720 per year full-time, $387 per credit hour part-time for nonresidents. *Financial aid:* In 1997–98, 7 fellowships averaging $1,057 per month and totaling $88,788, 35 research assistantships (10 to first-year students) averaging $1,100 per month, 21 teaching assistantships averaging $1,108 per month and totaling $279,216, 8 traineeships (1 to a first-year student) averaging $834 per month were awarded. Aid available to part-time students. Financial aid applicants required to submit FAFSA. *Faculty research:* Drug design and development, cancer research, drug synthesis and analysis, chemical pharmacology, environmental toxicology. • Dr. R. F. Borch, Head of the Graduate Program, 765-494-1403. Application contact: Dr. D. E. Bergstrom, Graduate Committee, 765-494-6275.

See in-depth description on page 1801.

Purdue University, School of Pharmacy and Pharmacal Sciences and Graduate School, Graduate Programs in Pharmacy and Pharmacal Sciences, Department of Pharmacy Practice, West Lafayette, IN 47907. Offers programs in clinical pharmacy (MS, PhD), pharmacy administration (MS, PhD). Faculty: 20 full-time (4 women). Students: 14 full-time (9 women), 7 part-time (4 women); includes 4 minority (3 African Americans, 1 Asian American), 6 international. Average age 32. 29 applicants, 7% accepted. In 1997, 1 master's, 2 doctorates awarded. Terminal master's awarded for partial completion of doctoral program. *Degree requirements:* For master's, thesis optional, foreign language not required; for doctorate, dissertation required, foreign language not required. *Entrance requirements:* GRE General Test, TOEFL, minimum B average, BS in pharmacy or Pharm D. Application deadline: rolling. Application fee: $30. Electronic applications accepted. *Tuition:* $3500 per year full-time, $126 per credit hour part-time for state residents; $11,720 per year full-time, $387 per credit hour part-time for nonresidents. *Financial aid:* In 1997–98, 18 students received aid, including 6 fellowships averaging $985 per month and totaling $70,920, 3 research assistantships averaging $1,050 per month and totaling $37,800, 9 teaching assistantships averaging $960 per month and totaling $103,680; traineeships and career-related internships or fieldwork also available. Aid available to part-time students. Financial aid applicants required to submit FAFSA. *Faculty research:* Clinical drug studies, pharmacy education advancement, administrative studies. • Dr. S. R. Abel, Head of the Graduate Program, 317-494-5966. Application contact: Dr. H. L. Mason, Graduate Committee Chair, 765-494-1469.

See in-depth description on page 1801.

Rutgers, The State University of New Jersey, New Brunswick, Program in Pharmaceutical Science, New Brunswick, NJ 08903. Offers industrial pharmacy (MS, PhD), medicinal chemistry (MS, PhD), pharmaceutical chemistry (MS, PhD), pharmaceutics (MS, PhD). Part-time programs available. Faculty: 10 full-time (0 women). Students: 41 full-time (17 women), 20 part-time (9 women); includes 7 minority (6 Asian Americans, 1 Hispanic), 14 international. Average age 24. 121 applicants, 17% accepted. In 1997, 1 master's awarded (100% found work related to degree); 6 doctorates awarded (100% found work related to degree). Terminal master's awarded for partial completion of doctoral program. *Degree requirements:* For master's, thesis or alternative required, foreign language not required; for doctorate, dissertation required, foreign language not required. *Entrance requirements:* GRE General Test. Application deadline: 6/1 (rolling processing). Application fee: $40. *Expenses:* Tuition $6492 per year full-time, $268 per credit part-time for state residents; $9520 per year full-time, $395 per credit part-time for nonresidents. Fees $208 per year (minimum). *Financial aid:* In 1997–98, 17 fellowships (5 to first-year students), 8 research assistantships (1 to a first-year student), 9 teaching assistant-

Directory: Pharmaceutical Sciences

Rutgers, The State University of New Jersey, New Brunswick (continued)
ships (5 to first-year students) were awarded. Financial aid application deadline: 4/1. • Dr. Edmund La Voie, Director, 732-932-2674. Fax: 732-932-5767.

St. John's University, College of Pharmacy and Allied Health Professions, Graduate Programs in Pharmacy, Program in Pharmaceutical Sciences, Jamaica, NY 11439. Offers clinical pharmacy (MS), cosmetic sciences (MS), industrial pharmacy (MS, PhD), medical chemistry (MS, PhD), pharmacology (MS), pharmacology/toxicology (PhD), pharmacotherapeutics (MS). Part-time and evening/weekend programs available. Students: 74 full-time (33 women), 77 part-time (39 women); includes 33 minority (7 African Americans, 17 Asian Americans, 9 Hispanics), 60 international. Average age 31. 100 applicants, 53% accepted. In 1997, 29 master's, 3 doctorates awarded. Terminal master's awarded for partial completion of doctoral program. *Degree requirements:* For master's, comprehensive exam required, thesis optional, foreign language not required; for doctorate, 1 foreign language (computer language can substitute), dissertation, comprehensive and qualifying exams. *Entrance requirements:* For master's, minimum GPA of 3.0; for doctorate, GRE General Test (minimum combined score of 1000), minimum GPA of 3.5 (undergraduate), 3.0 (graduate). Application deadline: 6/1 (priority date; rolling processing; 10/1 for spring admission). Application fee: $40. *Expenses:* Tuition $675 per credit. Fees $150 per year. *Financial aid:* Fellowships, teaching assistantships, Federal Work-Study, and career-related internships or fieldwork available. Aid available to part-time students. Financial aid application deadline: 3/1; applicants required to submit FAFSA. *Faculty research:* Neurotoxicology, biochemical toxicology, molecular pharmacology, neuropharmacology, intermediary metabolism. • Dr. S. William Zito, Chair, 718-990-6678. Application contact: Shamus J. McGrenra, TOR, Associate Director, Graduate Admissions, 718-990-6107. Fax: 718-990-5736. E-mail: mcgrenrs@stjohns.edu.

St. Louis College of Pharmacy, Program in Pharmacy Administration, St. Louis, MO 63110-1088. Offers managed care pharmacy (MS), pharmacy administration (MS). Part-time and evening/weekend programs available. Faculty: 3 full-time (1 woman), 4 part-time (0 women). Students: 20 part-time (6 women). Average age 35. 2 applicants, 0% accepted. In 1997, 1 degree awarded (100% found work related to degree). *Degree requirements:* Thesis or alternative required, foreign language not required. *Average time to degree:* master's–4 years part-time. *Entrance requirements:* GMAT (average 506). Application deadline: 8/1 (priority date; rolling processing). Application fee: $35. *Tuition:* $300 per credit hour. *Faculty research:* Geriatric pharmacy, health economics, pharmacoeconomics, job satisfaction, managed care and insurance. • Dr. Kenneth Schafermeyer, Director of Graduate Studies, 314-367-8700 Ext. 1743. Fax: 314-367-8132. E-mail: kschafermeyer@slcop.stlcop.edu.

South Dakota State University, College of Pharmacy, Department of Pharmaceutical Sciences, Brookings, SD 57007. Awards MS. Faculty: 7 full-time (1 woman). Students: 2 full-time (1 woman), 1 part-time (0 women); includes 3 international. In 1997, 2 degrees awarded. *Degree requirements:* Thesis, oral exam required, foreign language not required. *Entrance requirements:* GRE General Test, TOEFL (minimum score 550). Application deadline: 3/1 (rolling processing). Application fee: $15. *Expenses:* Tuition $82 per credit hour for state residents; $242 per credit hour for nonresidents. Fees $37 per credit hour. *Financial aid:* In 1997–98, 2 research assistantships were awarded; teaching assistantships, Federal Work-Study also available. Financial aid application deadline: 3/1; applicants required to submit FAFSA. *Faculty research:* Drugs of abuse, anti-cancer drugs, neuromuscular transmission, sustained drug delivery, drug metabolism. • Dr. Gary Chappell, Head, 605-688-6197.

State University of New York at Buffalo, Graduate School, School of Pharmacy, Department of Medicinal Chemistry, Buffalo, NY 14260. Awards MS, PhD. Faculty: 6 full-time (0 women). Students: 20 full-time (12 women), 8 part-time (5 women); includes 5 minority (all Asian Americans), 11 international. Average age 25. 56 applicants, 11% accepted. In 1997, 1 master's, 2 doctorates awarded. Terminal master's awarded for partial completion of doctoral program. *Degree requirements:* For master's, 1 foreign language (computer language can substitute), thesis or alternative; for doctorate, 1 foreign language (computer language can substitute), dissertation. *Entrance requirements:* For master's, TOEFL (minimum score 550), BS in biology, chemistry, or pharmacology; for doctorate, TOEFL (minimum score 550), BS or MS in chemistry, pharmacology, or biochemistry. Application deadline: 5/1 (rolling processing; 10/15 for spring admission). Application fee: $35. *Tuition:* $5970 per year full-time, $288 per credit hour part-time for state residents; $9286 per year full-time, $426 per credit hour part-time for nonresidents. *Financial aid:* In 1997–98, 16 students received aid, including 4 fellowships (2 to first-year students) averaging $920 per month and totaling $43,200, 1 research assistantship averaging $820 per month, 13 graduate assistantships (4 to first-year students) averaging $820 per month and totaling $127,920; teaching assistantships, full and partial tuition waivers, Federal Work-Study, institutionally sponsored loans also available. Financial aid application deadline: 2/28. *Faculty research:* Design and synthesis of anti-cancer drugs, enzyme inhibitors, antimicrobials, anti-inflammatories, design and synthesis of anti-AIDS compounds. Total annual research expenditures: $666,460. • Dr. Robert A. Coburn, Interim Chairman, 716-645-6367. Application contact: Dr. Michael R. Detty, Director of Graduate Studies, 716-645-6369. Fax: 716-645-2393.

State University of New York at Buffalo, Graduate School, School of Pharmacy, Department of Pharmaceutics, Buffalo, NY 14260. Awards MS, PhD. Faculty: 8 full-time (2 women), 1 part-time (0 women). Students: 9 full-time (5 women), 15 part-time (4 women); includes 1 minority (Asian American), 14 international. Average age 25. 66 applicants, 12% accepted. In 1997, 1 master's awarded. Terminal master's awarded for partial completion of doctoral program. *Degree requirements:* For doctorate, dissertation required, foreign language not required. *Entrance requirements:* TOEFL (minimum score 550). Application deadline: 3/1 (rolling processing). Application fee: $35. *Tuition:* $5970 per year full-time, $288 per credit hour part-time for state residents; $9286 per year full-time, $426 per credit hour part-time for nonresidents. *Financial aid:* In 1997–98, 3 fellowships averaging $908 per month, 7 research assistantships averaging $826 per month, 9 graduate assistantships (4 to first-year students) averaging $826 per month and totaling $89,382 were awarded; institutionally sponsored loans also available. Financial aid application deadline: 2/28. *Faculty research:* Pharmacokinetics, biopharmaceutics, drug delivery systems, physical pharmacy, drug metabolism and analysis. • Dr. Ho-Leung Fung, Chair, 716-645-2842 Ext. 222. E-mail: hlfung@acsu.buffalo.edu. Application contact: Dr. Marilyn Morris, Director, 716-645-2842 Ext. 230. Fax: 716-645-3693. E-mail: memorris@acsu.buffalo.edu.

Temple University, Health Sciences Center, School of Pharmacy, Department of Pharmaceutical Sciences, Program in Medicinal and Pharmaceutical Chemistry, Philadelphia, PA 19140. Awards MS, PhD. Students: 5 (3 women); includes 4 international. 41 applicants, 12% accepted. In 1997, 1 master's, 1 doctorate awarded. *Degree requirements:* For master's, thesis required, foreign language not required; for doctorate, 2 foreign languages, dissertation. *Entrance requirements:* For master's, GRE General Test (minimum combined score of 1000), TOEFL (minimum score 575), minimum undergraduate GPA of 3.0; for doctorate, GRE General Test (minimum combined score of 1000), TOEFL (minimum score 575). Application deadline: 6/1. Application fee: $40. *Financial aid:* Application deadline 6/1. • Application contact: Dr. Reza Fassihi, Director of Graduate Studies, 215-707-4948. Fax: 215-707-3678.

See in-depth description on page 1803.

Temple University, Health Sciences Center, School of Pharmacy, Department of Pharmaceutical Sciences, Program in Pharmaceutics, Philadelphia, PA 19140. Awards MS, PhD. Students: 21 (7 women); includes 5 minority (2 African Americans, 3 Asian Americans), 9 international. In 1997, 2 master's, 1 doctorate awarded. *Degree requirements:* For master's, thesis required, foreign language not required; for doctorate, 2 foreign languages, dissertation. *Entrance requirements:* For master's, GRE General Test (minimum combined score of 1000), TOEFL (minimum score 575), minimum undergraduate GPA of 3.0; for doctorate, GRE General Test (minimum combined score of 1000), TOEFL (minimum score 575), minimum GPA of 3.0. Application deadline: 6/1. Application fee: $40. *Financial aid:* Application deadline 6/1. • Application contact: Dr. Reza Fassihi, Director of Graduate Studies, 215-707-4948. Fax: 215-707-3678.

See in-depth description on page 1803.

Temple University, Health Sciences Center, School of Pharmacy, Department of Pharmaceutical Sciences, Program in Quality Assurance/Regulatory Affairs, Philadelphia, PA 19140. Awards MS. Students: 101 (62 women); includes 13 minority (4 African Americans, 7 Asian Americans, 2 Native Americans), 1 international. 54 applicants, 85% accepted. In 1997, 36 degrees awarded. *Degree requirements:* Thesis required, foreign language not required. *Entrance requirements:* GRE General Test (minimum combined score of 1000), TOEFL (minimum score 575), minimum undergraduate GPA of 3.0. Application deadline: 6/1. Application fee: $40. *Financial aid:* Application deadline 6/1. • Application contact: Dr. Reza Fassihi, Director of Graduate Studies, 215-707-4948. Fax: 215-707-3678.

See in-depth description on page 1803.

Université de Montréal, Faculty of Pharmacy, Montréal, PQ H3C 3J7, Canada. Offers programs in hospital pharmacy (M Sc), pharmacy (M Sc, PhD). Part-time programs available. Faculty: 30 full-time (12 women), 12 part-time (all women). Students: 69 full-time (43 women), 11 part-time (6 women). 48 applicants, 33% accepted. In 1997, 37 master's, 5 doctorates awarded. Terminal master's awarded for partial completion of doctoral program. *Degree requirements:* Thesis/dissertation required, foreign language not required. *Entrance requirements:* Proficiency in French. Application deadline: 2/1. Application fee: $30. *Financial aid:* Fellowships, teaching assistantships, Federal Work-Study, institutionally sponsored loans, and career-related internships or fieldwork available. *Faculty research:* Novel drug delivery systems, immunoassay development, medicinal chemistry of CNS compounds, pharmacokinetics and biopharmaceutic compounds. • Robert Goyer, Dean, 514-343-6440. Application contact: Huy Ong, Vice Dean, 514-343-6467.

Université Laval, Faculty of Pharmacy, Sainte-Foy, PQ G1K 7P4, Canada. Awards M Sc, PhD, Diploma. Students: 48 full-time (29 women), 77 part-time (57 women); includes 8 international. Average age 31. 61 applicants, 79% accepted. In 1997, 30 master's awarded. *Application deadline:* 3/1. *Application fee:* $30. *Expenses:* Tuition $1334 per year (minimum) full-time, $56 per credit (minimum) part-time for Canadian residents; $5966 per year (minimum) full-time, $249 per credit (minimum) part-time for nonresidents. Fees $150 per year full-time, $6.25 per credit part-time. • Gilles Barbeau, Acting Dean, 418-656-2131 Ext. 5639. Fax: 418-656-2305. E-mail: gilles.barbeau@pha.ulaval.ca.

University of Alberta, Faculty of Pharmacy and Pharmaceutical Sciences, Edmonton, AB T6G 2N8, Canada. Awards M Pharm, M Sc, PhD. Terminal master's awarded for partial completion of doctoral program. *Degree requirements:* Thesis/dissertation. *Average time to degree:* master's–3 years full-time; doctorate–5 years full-time. *Entrance requirements:* TOEFL (minimum score 550). Application deadline: 5/1. Application fee: $45. *Expenses:* Tuition $390 per course for Canadian residents; $781 per course for nonresidents. Fees $500 per year full-time, $184 per year part-time. *Faculty research:* Medicinal chemistry, radiopharmacy and pharmaceutics, pharmacokinetics, pharmacology, pharmaceutical biotechnology.

The University of Arizona, College of Pharmacy, Program in Pharmaceutical Sciences, Tucson, AZ 85721. Awards MS, PhD. *Degree requirements:* For master's, thesis required, foreign language not required; for doctorate, 1 foreign language (computer language can substitute), dissertation. *Entrance requirements:* GRE General Test, TOEFL (minimum score 550), minimum GPA of 3.0. Application deadline: 3/1 (rolling processing). Application fee: $35. *Tuition:* $2162 per year full-time, $337 per semester (minimum) part-time for state residents; $6860 per year full-time, $1138 per semester (minimum) part-time for nonresidents. *Faculty research:* Drug design, natural products isolation, biological applications of NMR and mass spectrometry, drug formulation and delivery, pharmacokinetics.

University of Arkansas for Medical Sciences, College of Pharmacy, 4301 West Markham, Little Rock, AR 72205-7199. Awards Pharm D, MS. Faculty: 24 full-time (5 women). Students: 305 full-time (189 women), 7 part-time (4 women); includes 24 minority (16 African Americans, 6 Asian Americans, 1 Hispanic, 1 Native American), 3 international. In 1997, 93 Pharm Ds, 2 master's awarded. *Degree requirements:* For master's, thesis required, foreign language not required. *Application fee:* $0. *Tuition:* $3860 per year full-time, $193 per credit hour part-time for state residents; $7720 per year full-time, $386 per credit hour part-time for nonresidents. *Financial aid:* In 1997–98, 5 research assistantships were awarded. Aid available to part-time students. • Dr. L. D. Milne, Dean, 501-686-5557. Application contact: Dr. Kim Light, 501-686-5557.

University of British Columbia, Faculty of Pharmaceutical Sciences, Program in Pharmaceutical Sciences, Vancouver, BC V6T 1Z2, Canada. Awards M Sc, PhD. *Degree requirements:* For master's, thesis; for doctorate, dissertation, comprehensive exam. *Entrance requirements:* TOEFL. Application deadline: 4/15 (priority date; rolling processing). Application fee: $60.

University of California, San Francisco, School of Pharmacy and Graduate Division, Department of Pharmaceutical Chemistry, San Francisco, CA 94143. Awards PhD, Pharm D/PhD. Faculty: 18 full-time (1 woman), 68 part-time (15 women). Students: 64 full-time (34 women). 158 applicants, 20% accepted. In 1997, 9 doctorates awarded (55% entered university research/teaching, 45% found other work related to degree). Terminal master's awarded for partial completion of doctoral program. *Degree requirements:* For doctorate, dissertation required, foreign language not required. *Average time to degree:* doctorate–5.5 years full-time. *Entrance requirements:* For doctorate, GRE General Test, TOEFL, minimum GPA of 3.0. Application deadline: 1/15. Application fee: $40. *Expenses:* Tuition $0 for state residents; $9384 per year for nonresidents. Fees $7512 per year. *Financial aid:* In 1997–98, 17 fellowships (4 to first-year students) averaging $1,200 per month, 24 research assistantships (4 to first-year students) averaging $1,417 per month, 8 teaching assistantships averaging $1,417 per month, 19 training grants (4 to first-year students) averaging $958 per month were awarded; full tuition waivers, institutionally sponsored loans, and career-related internships or fieldwork also available. Financial aid application deadline: 1/10. *Faculty research:* Drug delivery, drug metabolism and chemical toxicology, macromolecular structure, molecular parasitology, pharmacokinetics. • Thomas L. James, Chairman, 415-476-1914. Fax: 415-476-0688. E-mail: pcgradpg@cgl.ucsf.edu.

See in-depth description on page 1805.

University of Cincinnati, College of Pharmacy, Division of Pharmaceutical Sciences, Cincinnati, OH 45221. Awards MS, PhD. Faculty: 15 full-time (2 women). Students: 36 full-time (18 women), 28 part-time (12 women); includes 9 minority (all Asian Americans), 24 international. In 1997, 3 master's, 5 doctorates awarded. *Degree requirements:* Thesis/dissertation required, foreign language not required. *Entrance requirements:* GRE General Test (minimum combined score of 1600 on three sections), TOEFL (minimum score 600), minimum GPA of 3.0. Application deadline: 2/1 (priority date; rolling processing). Application fee: $30. *Tuition:* $7228 per year full-time, $185 per credit hour part-time for state residents; $13,812 per year full-time, $352 per credit hour part-time for nonresidents. *Financial aid:* Fellowships, graduate assistantships, full tuition waivers available. Aid available to part-time students. Financial aid application deadline: 2/1. • Dr. William Cacini, Head, 513-558-0740. Application contact: Marcie Sedam, Assistant to the Director, 513-558-3784.

See in-depth description on page 1807.

University of Colorado Health Sciences Center, School of Pharmacy, Programs in Pharmacy, Denver, CO 80262. Offerings in pharmaceutical sciences (MS, PhD), toxicology (PhD). Offered through Graduate School. Students: 23 full-time (13 women), 2 part-time (both women); includes 4 minority (1 African American, 1 Asian American, 1 Hispanic, 1 Native American). In 1997, 3 doctorates awarded. *Degree requirements:* For doctorate, dissertation required, foreign language not required. *Entrance requirements:* GRE General Test, minimum GPA of 2.75. Application fee: $30. *Financial aid:* Federal Work-Study, institutionally sponsored loans, and career-related internships or fieldwork available. Aid available to part-time students. Financial aid application deadline: 3/15. • Dr. Mark Manning, Co-Director, 303-315-5592.

See in-depth description on page 1809.

University of Connecticut, School of Pharmacy, Department of Pharmaceutical Sciences, Storrs, CT 06269. Offers programs in medicinal chemistry (MS, PhD), natural products chemistry (MS, PhD), pharmaceutics (MS, PhD). Students: 35. Terminal master's awarded for partial completion of doctoral program. *Degree requirements:* Thesis/dissertation. *Entrance requirements:* GRE General Test, TOEFL. Application deadline: 6/1 (priority date; rolling processing; 11/1 for spring admission). Application fee: $40 ($45 for international students). *Expenses:* Tuition $5272 per year full-time, $293 per credit part-time for state residents; $13,696 per year full-time, $761 per credit part-time for nonresidents. Fees $948 per year full-time, $640 per year part-time. *Financial aid:* Fellowships, research assistantships, teaching assistantships, Federal Work-Study, and career-related internships or fieldwork available. Financial aid application deadline: 3/15. • Application contact: Graduate Admissions Committee, 860-486-4066. Fax: 860-486-4998. E-mail: bogner@uconnvm.uconn.edu.

See in-depth description on page 1811.

University of Florida, College of Pharmacy and Graduate School, Graduate Programs in Pharmacy, Gainesville, FL 32611. Awards MS, MSP, PhD, Pharm D/PhD. Offerings include medicinal chemistry (PhD); pharmaceutics (MSP, PhD), including pharmaceutics, pharmacy; pharmacodynamics (MSP, PhD); pharmacy health care administration (MS, PhD). Part-time programs available. Faculty: 37 full-time (8 women). Students: 51 full-time (19 women), 15 part-time (7 women); includes 9 minority (3 African Americans, 3 Asian Americans, 3 Hispanics), 27 international. Average age 29. 104 applicants, 22% accepted. In 1997, 3 master's, 6 doctorates awarded. Terminal master's awarded for partial completion of doctoral program. *Degree requirements:* Thesis/dissertation. *Entrance requirements:* GRE General Test (minimum combined score of 1000; average 1171), TOEFL (minimum score 550), minimum GPA of 3.0. Application deadline: 6/5 (rolling processing; 10/1 for spring admission). Application fee: $20. Electronic applications accepted. *Tuition:* $138 per credit hour for state residents; $481 per credit hour for nonresidents. *Financial aid:* In 1997–98, 53 students received aid, including 5 fellowships averaging $2,050 per month, 29 research assistantships averaging $908 per month, 18 teaching assistantships averaging $864 per month, 1 graduate assistantship averaging $888 per month; full tuition waivers, institutionally sponsored loans also available. Aid available to part-time students. *Faculty research:* Drug discovery, outcomes research, toxicology, drug design, pharmacokynetic and pharmacodynamic modeling. • Dr. William J. Millard, Associate Dean for Research and Graduate Studies, 352-392-8622. E-mail: millard@cop.health.ufl.edu. Application contact: Marlene Hughes, Program Assistant, 352-392-8626. Fax: 352-392-4583. E-mail: marlene@cop.health.ufl.edu.

University of Georgia, College of Pharmacy, Department of Clinical and Administrative Sciences, Athens, GA 30602. Offers programs in experimental therapeutics (PhD), experimental therapeutics (MS), pharmacy care administration (MS, PhD). *Degree requirements:* For master's, thesis required, foreign language not required; for doctorate, 1 foreign language (computer language can substitute), dissertation. *Entrance requirements:* GRE General Test, minimum GPA of 3.0. Application fee: $30. *Financial aid:* Application deadline 2/15. • Dr. Joseph T. DiPiro, Head. Application contact: Dr. Randall L. Tackett, Graduate Coordinator, 706-542-7400.

See in-depth description on page 1813.

University of Georgia, College of Pharmacy, Department of Pharmaceutical and Biomedical Sciences, Athens, GA 30602. Offers programs in medicinal chemistry (MS, PhD), pharmaceutics (MS, PhD), pharmacology (MS, PhD), toxicology (MS, PhD). Faculty: 35 full-time (6 women). Students: 61 full-time (29 women), 4 part-time (1 woman); includes 6 minority (4 African Americans, 2 Asian Americans), 39 international. 204 applicants, 11% accepted. In 1997, 2 master's, 16 doctorates awarded. Terminal master's awarded for partial completion of doctoral program. *Degree requirements:* For master's, thesis required, foreign language not required; for doctorate, 1 foreign language (computer language can substitute), dissertation. *Entrance requirements:* GRE General Test, minimum GPA of 3.0. Application fee: $30. *Financial aid:* Fellowships, research assistantships, teaching assistantships, assistantships, partial tuition waivers, Federal Work-Study, institutionally sponsored loans, and career-related internships or fieldwork available. Aid available to part-time students. Financial aid application deadline: 2/15. • Dr. F. Douglas Boudinot, Head. Application contact: Dr. Anthony C. Capomacchia, Graduate Coordinator, 706-542-5339.

See in-depth description on page 1813.

University of Houston, College of Pharmacy, Department of Pharmacological and Pharmaceutical Sciences, 4800 Calhoun, Houston, TX 77204-2163. Offers programs in medical chemistry and pharmacology (MS), pharmaceutics (MS, PhD), pharmacology (MS, PhD). Faculty: 15 full-time (4 women). Students: 14 full-time (10 women); includes 1 minority (African American), 9 international. Average age 24. 65 applicants, 8% accepted. In 1997, 2 master's awarded. Terminal master's awarded for partial completion of doctoral program. *Degree requirements:* Thesis/dissertation required, foreign language not required. *Entrance requirements:* GRE General Test (minimum combined score of 1200), TOEFL (minimum score 550). Application deadline: 3/1 (priority date; 10/1 for spring admission). Application fee: $25 ($100 for international students). *Expenses:* Tuition $1152 per year full-time, $120 per semester (minimum) part-time for state residents; $4482 per year full-time, $249 per credit hour part-time for nonresidents. Fees $977 per year full-time, $119 per semester (minimum) part-time. *Financial aid:* Research assistantships, teaching assistantships, institutionally sponsored loans available. Aid available to part-time students. Financial aid application deadline: 4/1. *Faculty research:* Cardiovascular and renal pharmacology, cellular pharmacology, signal transduction, aging, drug delivery systems. • Dr. Douglas Eikenburg, Chair, 713-743-1217. E-mail: deikenburg@uh.edu. Application contact: Shaki Commisariat, Graduate Programs Office Manager, 713-743-1227. Fax: 713-743-1229. E-mail: shaki@uh.edu.

University of Illinois at Chicago, College of Pharmacy and Graduate College, Graduate Programs in Pharmacy, Chicago, IL 60607-7128. Offerings in forensic science (MS), medicinal chemistry (MS, PhD), pharmaceutics (MS, PhD), pharmacodynamics (MS, PhD), pharmacognosy (MS, PhD), pharmacokinetics (MS, PhD), pharmacy administration (MS, PhD). Faculty: 42 full-time (4 women). Students: 93 full-time (47 women), 35 part-time (22 women); includes 15 minority (5 African Americans, 7 Asian Americans, 3 Hispanics), 71 international. Average age 29. 161 applicants, 30% accepted. In 1997, 7 master's, 11 doctorates awarded. Terminal master's awarded for partial completion of doctoral program. *Degree requirements:* Variable foreign language requirement, thesis/dissertation. *Entrance requirements:* GRE General Test, TOEFL. Application deadline: 7/3 (11/8 for spring admission). Application fee: $40 ($50 for international students). *Financial aid:* In 1997–98, 5 fellowships, 32 research assistantships, 33 teaching assistantships were awarded; full tuition waivers, institutionally sponsored loans, and career-related internships or fieldwork also available. • Dr. Michael E. Johnson, Associate Dean, Research and Graduate Education, 312-996-0796.

The University of Iowa, College of Pharmacy and Graduate College, Graduate Programs in Pharmacy, Iowa City, IA 52242-1316. Awards MS, PhD. Faculty: 33 full-time. Students: 55 full-time (29 women), 22 part-time (11 women); includes 6 minority (1 African American, 5 Asian Americans), 52 international. 144 applicants, 29% accepted. In 1997, 4 master's, 18 doctorates awarded. *Degree requirements:* For doctorate, dissertation, comprehensive exam. *Entrance requirements:* GRE General Test. Application deadline: rolling. Application fee: $20 ($30 for international students). *Expenses:* Tuition $3166 per year full-time, $176 per semester hour part-time for state residents; $10,202 per year full-time, $176 per semester hour part-time for nonresidents. Fees $202 per year full-time, $52 per year (minimum) part-time. *Financial aid:* In 1997–98, 8 fellowships, 40 research assistantships (9 to first-year students), 20 teaching assistantships (3 to first-year students) were awarded. • Michael Duffel, Assistant Dean, 319-335-8840.

University of Kansas, School of Pharmacy, Department of Medicinal Chemistry, Lawrence, KS 66045. Awards MS, PhD. Faculty: 7 full-time (1 woman). Students: 17 full-time (7 women), 5 part-time (3 women); includes 1 minority (African American), 6 international. 73 applicants, 10% accepted. In 1997, 4 master's, 5 doctorates awarded. *Degree requirements:* For doctorate, dissertation. *Entrance requirements:* GRE General Test, TOEFL (minimum score 570). Application fee: $20. *Expenses:* Tuition $2400 per year full-time, $100 per credit hour part-time for state residents; $7890 per year full-time, $329 per credit hour part-time for nonresidents. Fees $428 per year full-time, $31 per credit hour part-time. *Financial aid:* In 1997–98, 6 fellowships (1 to a first-year student), 8 research assistantships (6 to first-year students), 1 teaching assistantship were awarded. *Faculty research:* Synthetic and medicinal organic chemistry, metabolism and enzyme mechanism, natural products isolation, biological properties, protein structure and folding. Total annual research expenditures: $3 million. • Gary Grunewald, Chair, 785-864-4495. Application contact: Dr. Gunda Georg, Admissions Coordinator, 785-864-4498. E-mail: ggeorge@rx.pharm.ukans.edu.

University of Kansas, School of Pharmacy, Department of Pharmaceutical Chemistry, Lawrence, KS 66045. Awards MS, PhD. Faculty: 6 full-time. Students: 35 full-time (16 women), 7 part-time (4 women); includes 5 minority (1 African American, 4 Asian Americans), 15 international. In 1997, 7 master's, 10 doctorates awarded. *Degree requirements:* Thesis/dissertation, qualifying exam. *Entrance requirements:* For master's, GRE General Test, TOEFL (minimum score 570), bachelor's degree in biological sciences, chemical engineering, chemistry, or pharmacy; for doctorate, GRE General Test, TOEFL (minimum score 570). Application fee: $20. *Expenses:* Tuition $2400 per year full-time, $100 per credit hour part-time for state residents; $7890 per year full-time, $329 per credit hour part-time for nonresidents. Fees $428 per year full-time, $31 per credit hour part-time. *Financial aid:* Fellowships, research assistantships, teaching assistantships, training grants available. • Ronald T. Borchardt, Chair, 785-864-4820. Application contact: John Stobaugh, Graduate Director.

Announcement: Objective of the graduate program in pharmaceutical chemistry is to provide graduates at MS and PhD levels with expertise in the area broadly defined as pharmaceutics, with emphases in physical pharmacy, preformulation, formulation, physical biochemistry, pharmaceutical analysis. Students with BS degrees in biological sciences, pharmacy, chemistry, chemical engineering are eligible to apply. Graduates compete successfully for positions in the biotechnology and pharmaceutical industries and in academia. In industry, most graduates hold positions of responsibility in the areas of preformulation (physicochemical characterization), drug delivery, and analysis. Financial assistance in the form of teaching/research assistantships, training grants, and fellowships is available. The current annual stipend level is approximately $16,000. Students with University appointments are eligible for reduced in-state tuition rates.

University of Kansas, School of Pharmacy, Department of Pharmacy Practice, Lawrence, KS 66045. Awards MS. Faculty: 15 full-time. Students: 3 full-time (2 women), 3 part-time (1 woman). In 1997, 6 degrees awarded. *Degree requirements:* Thesis required, foreign language not required. *Entrance requirements:* GRE General Test, TOEFL (minimum score 570), bachelor's degree in pharmacy. Application fee: $20. *Expenses:* Tuition $2400 per year full-time, $100 per credit hour part-time for state residents; $7890 per year full-time, $329 per credit hour part-time for nonresidents. Fees $428 per year full-time, $31 per credit hour part-time. *Financial aid:* Research assistantships available. *Faculty research:* Drug trials, drug stability, pharmacoeconomics, education. Total annual research expenditures: $80,000. • Harold N. Godwin, Chair, 785-864-4881.

University of Kentucky, College of Pharmacy and Graduate School, Graduate Programs in Pharmaceutical Sciences, Lexington, KY 40536-0082. Awards MS, PhD. Faculty: 47 full-time (7 women). Students: 65 full-time (27 women); includes 3 minority (all Asian Americans), 26 international. Average age 24. 122 applicants, 14% accepted. In 1997, 1 master's, 10 doctorates awarded. Terminal master's awarded for partial completion of doctoral program. *Degree requirements:* For master's, thesis optional, foreign language not required; for doctorate, dissertation, comprehensive exam required, foreign language not required. *Entrance requirements:* For master's, GRE General Test, minimum undergraduate GPA of 2.5; for doctorate, GRE General Test, minimum graduate GPA of 3.0. Application deadline: 7/19 (rolling processing). Application fee: $30 ($35 for international students). *Financial aid:* In 1997–98, 65 students received aid, including 8 fellowships, 28 research assistantships, 29 teaching assistantships; institutionally sponsored loans also available. Aid available to part-time students. Financial aid application deadline: 4/15. *Faculty research:* Drug development, biotechnology, cardiology, pharmacokinetics, CNS pharmacology, clinical pharmacology. Total annual research expenditures: $4 million. • Dr. Robert Blouin, Director of Research and Graduate Studies, 606-257-1998. Fax: 606-257-7564.

University of Manitoba, Faculty of Pharmacy, Winnipeg, MB R3T 2N2, Canada. Awards M Sc, PhD. *Degree requirements:* For master's, 1 foreign language, thesis.

University of Maryland, Baltimore, Graduate School, Graduate Programs in Pharmacy, Department of Pharmacy Practice and Science, Baltimore, MD 21201-1627. Awards PhD, Pharm D/PhD. Program in pharmacy administration (PhD). Part-time programs available. Faculty: 10 full-time (2 women). Students: 16 full-time (8 women); includes 11 minority (4 African Americans, 7 Asian Americans). Average age 25. 17 applicants, 18% accepted. In 1997, 1 master's, 3 doctorates awarded. Terminal master's awarded for partial completion of doctoral program. *Degree requirements:* For doctorate, dissertation required, foreign language not required. *Average time to degree:* doctorate–3 years full-time. *Entrance requirements:* For doctorate, GRE General Test, minimum GPA of 3.0. Application deadline: 4/1 (priority date; rolling processing). Application fee: $45. *Expenses:* Tuition $253 per credit hour for state residents; $454 per credit hour for nonresidents. Fees $317 per year. *Financial aid:* Fellowships, research assistantships, teaching assistantships available. Aid available to part-time students. Financial aid application deadline: 2/15. *Faculty research:* Drug use review, drug policy, pharmacoeconomics, pharmacoepidemiology. • Dr. Gary Smith, Chair, 410-706-2963. Application contact: Dr. Julie Zito, Director, Graduate Programs, 410-706-0524. Fax: 410-706-4725. E-mail: jzito@pharmacy.ab.umd.edu.

University of Maryland, Baltimore, Graduate School, Graduate Programs in Pharmacy, Department of Pharmaceutical Sciences, Program in Biomedicinal Chemistry, Baltimore, MD 21201-1627. Awards MS, PhD. Terminal master's awarded for partial completion of doctoral program. *Degree requirements:* Thesis/dissertation required, foreign language not required. *Entrance requirements:* GRE General Test, TOEFL (minimum score 600), minimum GPA of 3.0. Application deadline: 4/1 (priority date; rolling processing). Application fee: $42. *Expenses:* Tuition $253 per credit hour for state residents; $454 per credit hour for nonresidents. Fees $317 per year. *Financial aid:* Fellowships, research assistantships, teaching assistantships available. Aid available to part-time students. Financial aid application deadline: 2/15. *Faculty research:* Biomedical mass spectometry, pesticide biotransformation and biosynthesis, regulation and formation of secondary metabolites. • Dr. Russell Digate, Interim Chair, Department of Pharmaceutical Sciences, 410-706-2422. E-mail: digate@pharmacy.ab.umd.edu. Application contact: Dana Sample, Graduate Program Administrator, 410-706-0549. Fax: 410-706-0346. E-mail: dsample@pharmacy.ab.umd.edu.

University of Maryland, Baltimore, Graduate School, Graduate Programs in Pharmacy, Department of Pharmaceutical Sciences, Program in Pharmaceutics, Baltimore, MD 21201-1627. Awards MS, PhD. Part-time programs available. *Degree requirements:* For master's, thesis required, foreign language not required; for doctorate, dissertation, qualifying exam required, foreign language not required. *Entrance requirements:* GRE General Test, TOEFL (minimum score 600), minimum GPA of 3.0. Application deadline: 4/1 (priority date; rolling

Directory: Pharmaceutical Sciences

University of Maryland, Baltimore (continued)

processing). Application fee: $42. *Expenses:* Tuition $253 per credit hour for state residents; $454 per credit hour for nonresidents. Fees $317 per year. *Financial aid:* Fellowships, research assistantships, teaching assistantships available. Aid available to part-time students. Financial aid application deadline: 2/15. *Faculty research:* Behavioral pharmacology, biochemical pharmacology, drug metabolism, neurotoxicology, psychopharmacology. • Dr. Russell Digate, Interim Chair, Department of Pharmaceutical Sciences, 410-706-2422. E-mail: digate@pharmacy.ab.umd.edu. Application contact: Dana Sample, Graduate Program Administrator, 410-706-0549. Fax: 410-706-0346. E-mail: dsample@pharmacy.ab.umd.edu.

University of Michigan, College of Pharmacy and Horace H. Rackham School of Graduate Studies, Graduate Programs in Pharmaceutical Sciences, Interdepartmental Program in Medicinal Chemistry, Ann Arbor, MI 48109. Awards MS, PhD. Offered through the Horace H. Rackham School of Graduate Studies. Students: 20 full-time (8 women); includes 4 minority (2 African Americans, 1 Asian American, 1 Hispanic), 5 international. 34 applicants, 32% accepted. In 1997, 3 doctorates awarded. Terminal master's awarded for partial completion of doctoral program. *Degree requirements:* For doctorate, dissertation, oral defense of dissertation required, foreign language not required. *Average time to degree:* doctorate–5 years full-time. *Entrance requirements:* For master's, GRE General Test, TOEFL (miminum score of 560); for doctorate, GRE General Test. Application deadline: rolling. Application fee: $55. *Financial aid:* Fellowships, research assistantships, teaching assistantships available. Financial aid application deadline: 3/15. *Faculty research:* Enzymology, organic synthesis, molecular biology, virology. Total annual research expenditures: $3 million. • James K. Coward, Director, 734-647-8429. E-mail: jkcoward@umich.edu. Application contact: Kathleen Johnston, Administrative Assistant, 734-647-8429. Fax: 734-647-8430. E-mail: kmjohn@umich.edu.

University of Michigan, College of Pharmacy and Horace H. Rackham School of Graduate Studies, Graduate Programs in Pharmaceutical Sciences, Program in Pharmaceutical Chemistry (Computational), Ann Arbor, MI 48109. Awards MS, PhD. *Degree requirements:* For doctorate, dissertation, oral defense of dissertation, preliminary exam required, foreign language not required. *Entrance requirements:* For master's, GRE General Test, TOEFL (miminum score of 560); for doctorate, GRE General Test. Application deadline: rolling. Application fee: $55. Electronic applications accepted. *Financial aid:* Fellowships, research assistantships, teaching assistantships available. • Application contact: Denise Smith, Administrative Assistant, 734-764-7312. Fax: 734-763-2022.

University of Michigan, College of Pharmacy and Horace H. Rackham School of Graduate Studies, Graduate Programs in Pharmaceutical Sciences, Program in Pharmaceutics, Ann Arbor, MI 48109. Awards MS, PhD. *Degree requirements:* For doctorate, dissertation, oral defense of dissertation, preliminary exam required, foreign language not required. *Entrance requirements:* For master's, GRE General Test, TOEFL (miminum score of 560); for doctorate, GRE General Test. Application deadline: rolling. Application fee: $55. Electronic applications accepted. *Financial aid:* Fellowships, research assistantships, teaching assistantships available. • Application contact: Denise Smith, Administrative Assistant, 734-764-7312. Fax: 734-763-2022.

University of Minnesota, Twin Cities Campus, College of Pharmacy and Graduate School, Graduate Programs in Pharmacy, Graduate Program in Hospital Pharmacy, Minneapolis, MN 55455-0213. Awards MS. Part-time programs available. Faculty: 13 full-time (3 women), 5 part-time (2 women). Students: 2 full-time (1 woman), 2 part-time (both women). 5 applicants, 20% accepted. In 1997, 1 degree awarded. *Degree requirements:* Computer language, thesis (for some programs) required, foreign language not required. *Average time to degree:* master's–2.2 years full-time. *Entrance requirements:* GRE General Test, TOEFL (minimum score 580). Application deadline: 2/1 (priority date; rolling processing; 12/15 for spring admission). Application fee: $50. *Financial aid:* In 1997–98, 1 student received aid, including 1 teaching assistantship totaling $10,500; fellowships, research assistantships, institutionally sponsored loans, and career-related internships or fieldwork also available. *Faculty research:* Experimental pharmacotherapeutics, clinical pharmacy research. • Nina Graves, Director of Graduate Studies, 612-624-9493. E-mail: grave001@maroon.tc.umn.edu. Application contact: Randi Tesdahl, Executive Secretary, 612-624-2973. Fax: 612-625-9931. E-mail: tesda001@maroon.tc.umn.edu.

University of Minnesota, Twin Cities Campus, College of Pharmacy and Graduate School, Graduate Programs in Pharmacy, Graduate Program in Medicinal Chemistry, Minneapolis, MN 55455-0213. Awards MS, PhD. Faculty: 10 full-time (1 woman), 7 part-time (0 women). Students: 17 full-time (9 women); includes 6 international. 70 applicants, 33% accepted. In 1997, 3 doctorates awarded. Terminal master's awarded for partial completion of doctoral program. *Degree requirements:* Thesis/dissertation required, foreign language not required. *Average time to degree:* master's–2.5 years full-time; doctorate–5 years full-time. *Entrance requirements:* GRE General Test, TOEFL (minimum score 580), BS in biology, chemistry, or pharmacy. Application deadline: 1/15 (priority date; rolling processing). Application fee: $50. *Financial aid:* In 1997–98, fellowships totaling $12,000, teaching assistantships totaling $10,500 were awarded; research assistantships also available. *Faculty research:* Drug metabolism, drug design and synthesis, molecular modeling, drug-macromolecule interactions, chemical mechanisms of carcinogenicity and toxicity. • Rodney L. Johnson, Director of Graduate Studies, 612-624-7997. Fax: 612-624-0139. E-mail: johns002@tc.umn.edu. Application contact: Candice Mcdermott, Executive Secretary, 612-624-5153. Fax: 612-626-2125. E-mail: mcder002@tc.umn.edu.

University of Minnesota, Twin Cities Campus, College of Pharmacy and Graduate School, Graduate Programs in Pharmacy, Graduate Program in Pharmaceutics, Minneapolis, MN 55455-0213. Awards MS, PhD. Faculty: 6 full-time (2 women), 7 part-time (0 women). Students: 28 full-time (15 women), 1 part-time (0 women); includes 2 minority (both Asian Americans), 26 international. 62 applicants, 10% accepted. In 1997, 2 master's, 5 doctorates awarded. Terminal master's awarded for partial completion of doctoral program. *Degree requirements:* Thesis/dissertation required, foreign language not required. *Average time to degree:* master's–2.5 years full-time; doctorate–5 years full-time. *Entrance requirements:* For master's, GRE General Test (score in 70th percentile or higher on analytical and quantitative sections), TOEFL (minimum score 580), BS in science; for doctorate, GRE General Test (score in 70th percentile or higher on analytical and quantitative secitons), TOEFL (minimum score 580), BS in biology, biomedical engineering, chemical engineering, chemistry, pharmacy, or other science. Application deadline: 12/31 (priority date; rolling processing). Application fee: $50. *Financial aid:* In 1997–98, 2 fellowships totaling $12,000, 13 research assistantships, 6 teaching assistantships totaling $10,500 were awarded; Federal Work-Study, institutionally sponsored loans, and career-related internships or fieldwork also available. Aid available to part-time students. Financial aid application deadline: 12/31. *Faculty research:* Biopharmaceutics, pharmacokinetics, drug delivery, physical pharmacy. • Timothy S. Wiedman, Director of Graduate Studies, 612-624-5459. Fax: 612-625-2125. E-mail: wiede001@tc.umn.edu. Application contact: Candice McDermott, Executive Secretary, 612-624-5153. Fax: 612-626-2125. E-mail: mcder002@tc.umn.edu.

University of Minnesota, Twin Cities Campus, College of Pharmacy and Graduate School, Graduate Programs in Pharmacy, Graduate Program in Social and Administrative Pharmacy, Minneapolis, MN 55455-0213. Awards MS, PhD. Faculty: 20 full-time (5 women), 9 part-time (2 women). Students: 15 full-time (9 women), 7 part-time (4 women); includes 1 minority (Native American), 9 international. 12 applicants, 33% accepted. In 1997, 1 master's, 3 doctorates awarded. *Degree requirements:* For master's, thesis required (for some programs), foreign language not required; for doctorate, dissertation required, foreign language not required. *Average time to degree:* master's–2 years full-time; doctorate–5 years full-time. *Entrance requirements:* For master's, GRE General Test, TOEFL (minimum score 580), BS in science; for doctorate, GRE General Test, TOEFL (minimum score 580). Application deadline: 2/1 (priority date; rolling processing; 12/15 for spring admission). Application fee: $50. *Financial aid:* In 1997–98, 9 students received aid, including fellowships totaling $12,000, 9 teaching assistantships (3 to first-year students) totaling $10,500; research assistantships and career-related internships or fieldwork also available. *Faculty research:* Pharmacy in managed care, pharmaceutical economics, pharmacy practice management, international pharmacy, pharmaceutical policy. • Ronald S. Hadsall, Director of Graduate Studies, 612-624-2487. E-mail: hadsa001@maroon.tc.umn.edu. Application contact: Randi Tesdahl, Executive Secretary, 612-624-2973. Fax: 612-625-9931. E-mail: tesda001@maroon.tc.umn.edu.

University of Mississippi, Graduate School, School of Pharmacy, Department of Medicinal Chemistry, University, MS 38677-9702. Awards MS, PhD. Faculty: 6 full-time (0 women). Students: 13 full-time (6 women), 1 part-time (0 women); includes 1 minority (African American), 5 international. *Degree requirements:* Thesis/dissertation required, foreign language not required. *Entrance requirements:* For master's, GRE General Test, TOEFL, minimum GPA of 3.0; for doctorate, GRE General Test, TOEFL. Application deadline: 8/1 (rolling processing). Application fee: $0 ($25 for international students). *Financial aid:* Application deadline 3/1. • Dr. Robert D. Sindelar, Chairman, 601-232-7101.

University of Mississippi, Graduate School, School of Pharmacy, Department of Pharmaceutics, University, MS 38677-9702. Awards MS, PhD. Faculty: 6 full-time (2 women). Students: 16 full-time (3 women); includes 14 international. In 1997, 1 doctorate awarded. *Degree requirements:* Thesis/dissertation required, foreign language not required. *Entrance requirements:* For master's, GRE General Test, TOEFL, minimum GPA of 3.0; for doctorate, GRE General Test, TOEFL. Application deadline: 8/1 (rolling processing). Application fee: $0 ($25 for international students). *Financial aid:* Application deadline 3/1. • Dr. Alan Jones, Chairman, 601-232-7341.

University of Mississippi, Graduate School, School of Pharmacy, Department of Pharmacognosy, University, MS 38677-9702. Awards MS, PhD. Faculty: 3 full-time (0 women). Students: 12 full-time (3 women), 1 (woman) part-time; includes 2 minority (1 African American, 1 Hispanic), 3 international. *Degree requirements:* Thesis/dissertation required, foreign language not required. *Entrance requirements:* For master's, GRE General Test, TOEFL, minimum GPA of 3.0; for doctorate, GRE General Test, TOEFL. Application deadline: 8/1 (rolling processing). Application fee: $0 ($25 for international students). *Financial aid:* Application deadline 3/1. • Dr. Charles Hufford, Chairman, 601-232-7032.

University of Mississippi, Graduate School, School of Pharmacy, Department of Pharmacy Administration, University, MS 38677-9702. Awards MS, PhD. Faculty: 5 full-time (1 woman). Students: 9 full-time (2 women); includes 3 international. In 1997, 1 doctorate awarded. *Degree requirements:* Thesis/dissertation required, foreign language not required. *Entrance requirements:* For master's, GRE General Test, TOEFL, minimum GPA of 3.0; for doctorate, GRE General Test, TOEFL. Application deadline: 8/1 (rolling processing). Application fee: $0 ($25 for international students). *Financial aid:* Application deadline 3/1. • Dr. Dewey Garner, Chairman, 601-232-5104.

University of Missouri–Kansas City, School of Pharmacy, Graduate Programs in Pharmaceutical Sciences, Kansas City, MO 64110-2499. Awards MS. Students: 14 full-time (7 women), 5 part-time (1 woman); includes 14 international. Average age 30. In 1997, 1 degree awarded. *Degree requirements:* Thesis required, foreign language not required. *Entrance requirements:* GRE General Test, minimum GPA of 3.0 (undergraduate), 3.5 (graduate). Application deadline: 3/1 (10/1 for spring admission). Application fee: $25. *Expenses:* Tuition $220 per credit hour for state residents; $508 per credit hour for nonresidents. Fees $362 per year. *Financial aid:* Fellowships, research assistantships, teaching assistantships, full and partial tuition waivers, Federal Work-Study, institutionally sponsored loans, and career-related internships or fieldwork available. Financial aid application deadline: 3/15. • Application contact: Shelly M. Janasz, Manager, Student Services, 816-235-1613. Fax: 816-235-5190. E-mail: sjanasz@cctr.umkc.edu.

The University of Montana–Missoula, School of Pharmacy and Allied Health Sciences, Programs in Pharmaceutical Sciences, Missoula, MT 59812-0002. Offerings in pharmaceutical sciences (MS), pharmacology (PhD). Faculty: 11 full-time (1 woman). Students: 11 full-time (3 women); includes 3 minority (2 Asian Americans, 1 Hispanic). Average age 25. In 1997, 2 master's awarded (100% continued full-time study). *Degree requirements:* For master's, oral defense of thesis required, foreign language not required; for doctorate, research dissertation defense required, foreign language not required. *Average time to degree:* master's–2 years full-time. *Entrance requirements:* GRE General Test (minimum combined score of 1500 on three sections; average 2000), TOEFL. Application deadline: 9/1 (rolling processing). Application fee: $30. *Tuition:* $2499 per year (minimum) full-time, $376 per semester (minimum) part-time for state residents; $6528 per year (minimum) full-time, $1048 per semester (minimum) part-time for nonresidents. *Financial aid:* In 1997–98, 4 teaching assistantships were awarded; grants, full and partial tuition waivers, Federal Work-Study also available. Financial aid application deadline: 3/1. *Faculty research:* Neuroendocrinology, neuropharmacology, molecular biochemistry, cardiovascular pharmacology, pharmacognosy. Total annual research expenditures: $166,595. • Dr. Vernon Grund, Chair, 406-243-4765. E-mail: grund@selway.umt.edu. Application contact: Dr. Diana Lurie, Associate Professor, 406-243-2103. Fax: 406-243-4353. E-mail: lurie@selway.umt.edu.

See in-depth description on page 1815.

University of Nebraska Medical Center, Program in Pharmaceutical Sciences, Omaha, NE 68198-0001. Awards MS, PhD. Faculty: 31. Students: 16 full-time (9 women), 8 part-time (2 women); includes 2 minority (1 African American, 1 Asian American), 14 international. Average age 27. 54 applicants, 4% accepted. In 1997, 1 doctorate awarded. Terminal master's awarded for partial completion of doctoral program. *Degree requirements:* Thesis/dissertation required, foreign language not required. *Entrance requirements:* For master's, GRE General Test (minimum combined score of 1500 on three sections; average 1700); for doctorate, GRE. Application deadline: 3/1 (rolling processing). Application fee: $25. *Financial aid:* In 1997–98, 4 fellowships (1 to a first-year student) averaging $1,000 per month, 8 research assistantships (2 to first-year students) averaging $1,000 per month, 9 teaching assistantships (3 to first-year students) averaging $833 per month were awarded; institutionally sponsored loans also available. Aid available to part-time students. Financial aid application deadline: 3/1. *Faculty research:* Pharmaceutics, medicinal chemistry, toxicology, chemical carcinogenesis, pharmacokinetics. • Dr. Donald Miller, Chair, 402-559-6575. Application contact: Jo Wagner, Associate Director of Admissions, 402-559-4206.

University of New Mexico, College of Pharmacy, Graduate Programs in Pharmaceutical Sciences, Albuquerque, NM 87131-2039. Offerings in pharmaceutical sciences (MS, PhD), including hospital pharmacy (MS), radiopharmacy (MS), toxicology (MS, PhD); pharmacy administration (MS, PhD). Part-time programs available. Faculty: 29 full-time (9 women), 3 part-time (0 women), 30.11 FTE. Students: 5 full-time (2 women), 11 part-time (5 women); includes 1 international. Average age 35. 30 applicants, 47% accepted. In 1997, 2 master's, 2 doctorates awarded. Terminal master's awarded for partial completion of doctoral program. *Degree requirements:* For master's, computer language, thesis (for some programs) required, foreign language not required; for doctorate, 2 foreign languages (computer language can substitute for one), dissertation. *Entrance requirements:* For master's, GRE General Test, Pharm D (hospital pharmacy or radiopharmacy), BS in biology or chemistry (toxicology); for doctorate, GRE General Test. Application deadline: 8/1. Application fee: $25. *Expenses:* Tuition $2442 per year full-time, $103 per credit hour part-time for state residents; $8691 per year full-time, $103 per credit hour (minimum) part-time for nonresidents. Fees $32 per year. *Financial aid:* Fellowships, research assistantships, teaching assistantships, residencies, Federal Work-Study, and career-related internships or fieldwork available. Aid available to part-time students. Financial aid application deadline: 6/1. *Faculty research:* Radio imaging, immunology, hospital pharmacy practice. Total annual research expenditures: $289,929. • Dr. Scott Burchiel, Associate Dean of Graduate Studies, 505-272-0920. E-mail: burchiel@unm.edu. Application contact: Irma Montano, Graduate Committee, Administrative Assistant to the Dean, 505-272-3241. Fax: 505-272-6749. E-mail: toxinfo@unm.edu.

The University of North Carolina at Chapel Hill, School of Pharmacy and Graduate School, Research Graduate Programs in Pharmacy, Chapel Hill, NC 27599. Awards MS, PhD. Part-time programs available. Postbaccalaureate distance learning degree programs offered (minimal on-campus study). Faculty: 42 full-time (14 women), 13 part-time (5 women). Students: 75 full-time (37 women), 3 part-time (all women); includes 45 minority (4 African Americans, 40 Asian Americans, 1 Hispanic). Average age 30. 105 applicants, 9% accepted. In 1997, 6 master's, 5 doctorates awarded. Terminal master's awarded for partial completion of doctoral program. *Degree requirements:* For master's, thesis, comprehensive exam required, foreign language not required; for doctorate, dissertation, comprehensive exam. *Average time to degree:* master's–2 years full-time, 4 years part-time; doctorate–5 years full-time. *Entrance requirements:* For master's, GRE General Test (minimum combined score of 1000; average 1150), minimum GPA of 3.0; for doctorate, GRE General Test (minimum combined score of 1000; average 1280), minimum GPA of 3.0. Application deadline: 5/1 (rolling processing; 10/31 for spring admission). Application fee: $55. *Expenses:* Tuition $1428 per year full-time, $357 per semester (minimum) part-time for state residents; $10,414 per year full-time, $2604 per semester (minimum) part-time for nonresidents. Fees $782 per year full-time, $332 per semester (minimum) part-time. *Financial aid:* In 1997–98, 51 students received aid, including 3 fellowships (1 to a first-year student) averaging $917 per month and totaling $33,000, 16 research assistantships (2 to first-year students) averaging $1,125 per month and totaling $216,000, 32 teaching assistantships (4 to first-year students) averaging $1,125 per month and totaling $432,000; Federal Work-Study, institutionally sponsored loans also available. Financial aid application deadline: 3/1; applicants required to submit CSS PROFILE. *Faculty research:* Structure-activity relationships; design, fabrication, evaluation, and use of drug delivery systems; social and management science privileges as they apply to the practice of pharmacy; drug development laboratory. • Dr. Kim R. Brouwer, Acting Chair, 919-962-7030. Fax: 919-966-6919. E-mail: kbrouwer.pharm@mhs.unc.edu.

Announcement: The School of Pharmacy offers graduate degrees in medicinal chemistry and natural products (e.g., structure-based drug design, molecular modeling), pharmaceutics (e.g., drug delivery, pharmacokinetics/pharmacodynamics, macromolecular therapeutics), and pharmaceutical policy and evaluative sciences (e.g., outcomes research, pharmacoeconomics, pharmacoepidemiology). Opportunities in preclinical and clinical research are available in many therapeutic areas, including AIDS, cancer, and cardiovascular and degenerative diseases, as well as in aging and toxicokinetics. Other schools, institutes, and centers at UNC and the pharmaceutical companies (e.g., Glaxo Wellcome) and institutes (e.g., EPA, NIEHS, CIIT, NC Biotechnology Center) located in Research Triangle Park offer a rich environment for scientific collaboration. World Wide Web: http://sunsite.unc.edu/pharmacy/pharmacy.html

University of Oklahoma Health Sciences Center, College of Pharmacy and Graduate College, Graduate Programs in Pharmacy, Oklahoma City, OK 73190. Awards MS, PhD, MS/MBA. MS/MBA offered jointly with Oklahoma State University and the University of Oklahoma. Faculty: 23 full-time (3 women), 6 part-time (1 woman). Students: 3 full-time (1 woman), 13 part-time (6 women); includes 4 minority (1 African American, 3 Asian Americans), 7 international. Average age 30. 68 applicants, 9% accepted. In 1997, 3 doctorates awarded. Terminal master's awarded for partial completion of doctoral program. *Degree requirements:* For master's, thesis, comprehensive exam required, foreign language not required; for doctorate, dissertation, oral and written comprehensive exam required, foreign language not required. *Entrance requirements:* GRE General Test (minimum combined score of 1000), TOEFL (minimum score 550). Application deadline: 4/1 (priority date). Application fee: $25 ($50 for international students). *Financial aid:* Fellowships, research assistantships, teaching assistantships, institutionally sponsored loans, and career-related internships or fieldwork available. *Faculty research:* Medicinal chemistry, pharmacokinetics/biopharmaceutics, nuclear pharmacy, pharmacy administration, pharmacodynamics and toxicology. • Dr. Victor Yanchick, Dean, 405-271-6484. Application contact: Dr. Robert Magarian, Chair, Graduate Affairs Committee, 405-271-6484.

University of Pittsburgh, School of Pharmacy, Graduate Programs in Pharmacy, Department of Pharmaceutical Sciences, Pittsburgh, PA 15260. Awards MS, PhD. Postbaccalaureate distance learning degree programs offered (no on-campus study). Faculty: 52 full-time (23 women), 4 part-time (1 woman). Students: 16 full-time (4 women), 3 part-time (1 woman); includes 2 minority (both Asian Americans), 12 international. 50 applicants, 8% accepted. In 1997, 1 master's, 1 doctorate awarded. *Degree requirements:* Thesis/dissertation required, foreign language not required. *Average time to degree:* master's–2 years full-time; doctorate–5 years full-time. *Entrance requirements:* GRE General Test, TOEFL. Application deadline: 3/1 (priority date; rolling processing). Application fee: $30 ($40 for international students). *Expenses:* Tuition $9402 per year full-time, $388 per credit part-time for state residents; $19,372 per year full-time, $799 per credit part-time for nonresidents. Fees $480 per year full-time, $180 per year part-time. *Financial aid:* In 1997–98, 12 teaching assistantships (3 to first-year students) totaling $286,000 were awarded; Federal Work-Study, institutionally sponsored loans also available. *Faculty research:* Drug delivery, gene therapy, pharmacodynamics, drug metabolism, cardiovascular pharmacology. Total annual research expenditures: $910,000. • Dr. Regis Vollmer, Chairman, 412-648-8565. E-mail: vollm+@pitt.edu. Application contact: Andrea M. Farrell, Graduate Secretary, 412-648-1014. Fax: 412-648-1086. E-mail: farrellam@msx.upmc.edu.

University of Rhode Island, College of Pharmacy, Graduate Programs in Pharmacy, Department of Medicinal Chemistry, Kingston, RI 02881. Awards MS, PhD. *Degree requirements:* Thesis/dissertation. *Application deadline:* 4/15. *Application fee:* $35. *Expenses:* Tuition $3446 per year full-time, $191 per credit part-time for state residents; $9850 per year full-time, $547 per credit part-time for nonresidents. Fees $1276 per year full-time, $135 per semester (minimum) part-time.

University of Rhode Island, College of Pharmacy, Graduate Programs in Pharmacy, Department of Pharmaceutics, Kingston, RI 02881. Awards MS, PhD. *Application deadline:* 4/15. *Application fee:* $35. *Expenses:* Tuition $3446 per year full-time, $191 per credit part-time for state residents; $9850 per year full-time, $547 per credit part-time for nonresidents. Fees $1276 per year full-time, $135 per semester (minimum) part-time.

University of Rhode Island, College of Pharmacy, Graduate Programs in Pharmacy, Department of Pharmacognosy, Kingston, RI 02881. Awards MS, PhD. Terminal master's awarded for partial completion of doctoral program. *Application deadline:* 4/15. *Application fee:* $35. *Expenses:* Tuition $3446 per year full-time, $191 per credit part-time for state residents; $9850 per year full-time, $547 per credit part-time for nonresidents. Fees $1276 per year full-time, $135 per semester (minimum) part-time.

University of Rhode Island, College of Pharmacy, Graduate Programs in Pharmacy, Department of Pharmacy Administration, Kingston, RI 02881. Awards MS. *Degree requirements:* Thesis. *Entrance requirements:* GRE or MAT, Pharm D. Application deadline: 4/15. Application fee: $35. *Expenses:* Tuition $3446 per year full-time, $191 per credit part-time for state residents; $9850 per year full-time, $547 per credit part-time for nonresidents. Fees $1276 per year full-time, $135 per semester (minimum) part-time.

University of Saskatchewan, College of Pharmacy and Nutrition, Saskatoon, SK S7N 5A2, Canada. Awards M Sc, PhD. *Degree requirements:* Thesis/dissertation. *Entrance requirements:* For master's, CANTEST (minimum score 4.5) or International English Language Testing System (minimum score 6) or Michigan English Language Assessment Battery (minimum score 80), or TOEFL (minimum score 550; average 560); for doctorate, TOEFL. Application deadline: 7/1 (priority date; rolling processing). Application fee: $0.

University of South Carolina, College of Pharmacy and Graduate School, Department of Basic Pharmaceutical Sciences, Columbia, SC 29208. Awards MS, PhD. PhD offered jointly with the Medical University of South Carolina. Part-time programs available. Faculty: 16 full-time (2 women). Students: 18 full-time (8 women), 13 part-time (5 women); includes 7 minority (6 African Americans, 1 Asian American), 8 international. Average age 28. In 1997, 2 master's, 4 doctorates awarded. *Degree requirements:* For master's, 1 foreign language (computer language can substitute), thesis, written comprehensive exam; for doctorate, 1 foreign language (computer language can substitute), dissertation, oral and written comprehensive exams. *Entrance requirements:* For master's, GRE General Test (minimum combined score of 1000), TOEFL (minimum score 500), BS in biology, chemistry, pharmacy, or related field; for doctorate, GRE General Test (minimum combined score of 1000), TOEFL (minimum score 500). Application deadline: 8/1. Application fee: $35. Electronic applications accepted. *Expenses:* Tuition $4482 per year full-time, $221 per credit hour part-time for state residents; $11,676 per year full-time, $556 per credit hour part-time for nonresidents. Fees $525 per year full-time, $237 per semester (minimum) part-time. *Financial aid:* Teaching assistantships, Federal Work-Study, institutionally sponsored loans available. Financial aid application deadline: 8/1. *Faculty research:* Synthesis of heterocyclic compounds, pharmacokinetics, neuropharmacology. • Application contact: Dr. J. Walter Sowell, Interim Graduate Director, 803-777-7916. Fax: 803-777-2775.

University of Southern California, School of Pharmacy and Graduate School, Graduate Programs in Pharmacy, Graduate Program in Pharmaceutical Sciences, Los Angeles, CA 90033. Awards MS, PhD, Pharm D/PhD. Faculty: 10 full-time, 1 part-time. Students: 23 full-time (12 women), 4 part-time (3 women); includes 10 minority (1 African American, 8 Asian Americans, 1 Hispanic), 14 international. Average age 31. 95 applicants, 7% accepted. In 1997, 1 master's, 4 doctorates awarded. *Degree requirements:* Thesis/dissertation. *Entrance requirements:* GRE General Test. Application deadline: 2/1 (priority date; 10/15 for spring admission). Application fee: $55. *Expenses:* Tuition $16,944 per year full-time, $706 per unit part-time. Fees $414 per year full-time, $32 per year part-time. *Financial aid:* In 1997–98, 8 fellowships, 15 research assistantships, 8 teaching assistantships, 3 scholarships were awarded; Federal Work-Study, institutionally sponsored loans also available. Aid available to part-time students. Financial aid application deadline: 2/15; applicants required to submit FAFSA. • Dr. Vincent Lee, Director, 213-342-1368. Application contact: Graduate Affairs Office, 213-342-1474.

See in-depth description on page 1817.

University of Southern California, School of Pharmacy and Graduate School, Graduate Programs in Pharmacy, Program in Pharmaceutical Economics and Policy, Los Angeles, CA 90089. Awards MS, PhD. Faculty: 6 full-time, 5 part-time. Students: 7 full-time (2 women), 1 part-time (0 women); includes 1 minority (Asian American), 6 international. Average age 28. 5 applicants, 0% accepted. *Degree requirements:* Thesis/dissertation. *Entrance requirements:* GRE General Test. Application deadline: 3/1 (priority date; 9/1 for spring admission). Application fee: $55. *Expenses:* Tuition $16,944 per year full-time, $706 per unit part-time. Fees $414 per year full-time, $32 per year part-time. *Financial aid:* In 1997–98, 4 research assistantships, 4 teaching assistantships were awarded; fellowships, scholarships, Federal Work-Study, institutionally sponsored loans also available. Aid available to part-time students. Financial aid application deadline: 2/15; applicants required to submit FAFSA. • Dr. Michael B. Nichol, Director, 213-342-3296. Application contact: Graduate Afffairs Office, 213-342-1474.

See in-depth description on page 1817.

University of Tennessee, Memphis, Colleges of Graduate Health Sciences and Pharmacy, Department of Pharmaceutical Sciences, Memphis, TN 38163-0002. Awards MS, PhD, Pharm D/PhD. *Degree requirements:* For master's, computer language, thesis, oral and written comprehensive exams required, foreign language not required; for doctorate, computer language, dissertation, oral and written preliminary and comprehensive exams required, foreign language not required. *Entrance requirements:* GRE General Test (minimum combined score of 1500), TOEFL (minimum score 525), minimum GPA of 3.0. Application fee: $0.

The University of Texas at Austin, College of Pharmacy, Graduate Programs in Pharmacy, Austin, TX 78712. Awards MS Phr, PhD. Students: 89 full-time (46 women), 18 part-time (11 women); includes 16 minority (3 African Americans, 9 Asian Americans, 4 Hispanics), 38 international. 182 applicants, 19% accepted. In 1997, 7 master's, 10 doctorates awarded. *Degree requirements:* Thesis/dissertation required, foreign language not required. *Average time to degree:* master's–2 years full-time, 3 years part-time; doctorate–5 years full-time. *Entrance requirements:* GRE General Test (minimum combined score of 1000; average 1250). Application deadline: 3/1 (priority date; rolling processing; 10/1 for spring admission). Application fee: $50 ($75 for international students). Electronic applications accepted. *Expenses:* Tuition $2592 per year full-time, $324 per semester (minimum) part-time for state residents; $7704 per year full-time, $963 per semester (minimum) part-time for nonresidents. Fees $778 per year full-time, $161 per semester (minimum) part-time. *Financial aid:* In 1997–98, 78 students received aid, including fellowships averaging $1,000 per month, research assistantships averaging $820 per month, 40 teaching assistantships averaging $820 per month; Federal Work-Study also available. Financial aid application deadline: 2/1; applicants required to submit FAFSA. *Faculty research:* Synthetic medical chemistry, synthetic molecular biology, bioorganic chemistry, pharmacoeconomics, pharmacy practice, pharmacotherapy. • Application contact: Mickie Sheppard, Graduate Coordinator, 512-471-6590. E-mail: mickies@mail.utexas.edu.

University of the Pacific, School of Pharmacy and Graduate School, Graduate Programs in Pharmaceutical Sciences, Department of Pharmaceutics and Medicinal Chemistry, Stockton, CA 95211-0197. Offers programs in biopharmaceutics/pharmacokinetics (MS, PhD), industrial pharmacy (MS, PhD), medicinal chemistry (MS, PhD), nuclear pharmacy (MS, PhD). Faculty: 5 full-time (1 woman). Students: 4 full-time (2 women), 4 part-time (2 women); includes 5 international. Terminal master's awarded for partial completion of doctoral program. *Degree requirements:* For master's, thesis required, foreign language not required; for doctorate, dissertation, qualifying exam. *Entrance requirements:* GRE General Test, TOEFL, BS in chemistry or pharmacy. Application deadline: 3/1 (10/15 for spring admission). Application fee: $50. *Expenses:* Tuition $28,500 per year full-time, $594 per unit part-time. Fees $30 per year (minimum). *Financial aid:* Teaching assistantships, full and partial tuition waivers, institutionally sponsored loans available. Financial aid application deadline: 3/1. *Faculty research:* Synthesis of medicinals, development of drug delivery systems, percutaneous absorption. • Dr. Donald G. Floriddia, Chairman, 209-946-2420. E-mail: dfloriddia@uop.edu. Application contact: Dr. Ravindra C. Vasavada, Director of Graduate Studies, 209-946-2339. Fax: 209-946-2410. E-mail: rvasarada@uop.edu.

See in-depth description on page 1819.

University of the Pacific, School of Pharmacy and Graduate School, Graduate Programs in Pharmaceutical Sciences, Department of Pharmacy Practice, Stockton, CA 95211-0197. Offers program in clinical pharmacy (MS, PhD). Faculty: 5 full-time (0 women). Students: 1 (woman) full-time, 2 part-time (1 woman); includes 3 international. Terminal master's awarded for partial completion of doctoral program. *Degree requirements:* For master's, thesis required, foreign language not required; for doctorate, dissertation, qualifying exam. *Entrance requirements:* GRE General Test, TOEFL. Application deadline: 3/1 (10/15 for spring admission). Application fee: $50. *Expenses:* Tuition $28,500 per year full-time, $594 per unit part-time. Fees $30 per year (minimum). *Financial aid:* Teaching assistantships, full and partial tuition waivers, Federal Work-Study, institutionally sponsored loans available. Aid available to part-time students. Financial aid application deadline: 3/1. *Faculty research:* Health care delivery systems, statistical techniques in pharmacokinetic analysis, pediatric clinical pharmacokinetics. • Patrick N. Catania, Chairman, 209-946-3144. Fax: 209-946-2410. E-mail: pcatania@uop.edu. Application contact: Dr. Ravindra C. Vasavada, Director of Graduate Studies, 209-946-2339. Fax: 206-946-2410. E-mail: rvasada@uop.edu.

See in-depth description on page 1819.

University of the Sciences in Philadelphia, Program in Medicinal Chemistry and Pharmacognosy, Philadelphia, PA 19104-4495. Awards MS, PhD. Part-time programs available. Faculty: 10 full-time (0 women). Students: 5 full-time (3 women), 13 part-time (6 women); includes 1 minority (Asian American), 8 international. Average age 30. 20 applicants, 45% accepted. In

Directory: Pharmaceutical Sciences

University of the Sciences in Philadelphia (continued)
1997, 1 master's, 1 doctorate awarded. Terminal master's awarded for partial completion of doctoral program. *Degree requirements:* Thesis/dissertation required, foreign language not required. *Entrance requirements:* For master's, GRE General Test, GRE Subject Test (biology or chemistry), TOEFL; for doctorate, GRE General Test, TOEFL. Application deadline: 5/1 (rolling processing; 10/1 for spring admission). Application fee: $30. *Financial aid:* In 1997–98, 15 students received aid, including 11 teaching assistantships; fellowships, full tuition waivers, institutionally sponsored loans also available. *Faculty research:* Analytical, organic, and physical chemistry; biochemistry; pharmacognosy; biotechnology; natural product synthesis. Total annual research expenditures: $341,700. • Dr. Rodney Wigent, Director, 215-596-8974. E-mail: r.wigent@pcps.edu. Application contact: Dr. Charles W. Gibley Jr., Dean, 215-596-8937. Fax: 215-596-8764. E-mail: graduate@pcps.edu.

See in-depth description on page 1821.

University of the Sciences in Philadelphia, Program in Pharmaceutical Sciences, Philadelphia, PA 19104-4495. Awards MS, PhD. Part-time and evening/weekend programs available. Faculty: 6 full-time (0 women), 1 part-time (0 women), 6.1 FTE. Students: 18 full-time (10 women), 14 part-time (6 women); includes 15 minority (3 African Americans, 12 Asian Americans), 13 international. Average age 33. 20 applicants, 50% accepted. In 1997, 2 master's, 2 doctorates awarded. Terminal master's awarded for partial completion of doctoral program. *Degree requirements:* For master's, thesis required (for some programs), foreign language not required; for doctorate, dissertation required, foreign language not required. *Entrance requirements:* GRE General Test, TOEFL (minimum score 550). Application deadline: 5/1 (rolling processing; 11/1 for spring admission). Application fee: $30. *Financial aid:* In 1997–98, 22 students received aid, including 3 fellowships, 3 research assistantships averaging $1,080 per month and totaling $32,500, 8 teaching assistantships (2 to first-year students) averaging $1,060 per month and totaling $95,125; full and partial tuition waivers, institutionally sponsored loans also available. *Faculty research:* Specialized systemic delivery of drugs, pharmacokinetics, pharmacodynamics, physics of tablet compression, controlled release of drugs. Total annual research expenditures: $311,329. • Dr. Edwin Sugita, Director, 215-596-8944. E-mail: e.sugita@pcps.edu. Application contact: Dr. Charles W. Gibley Jr., Dean, 215-596-8937. Fax: 215-596-8764. E-mail: graduate@pcps.edu.

See in-depth description on page 1821.

University of Toledo, College of Pharmacy, Graduate Programs in Pharmacy, Program in Medicinal and Biological Chemistry, Toledo, OH 43606-3398. Awards MS, PhD. Faculty: 8 full-time (2 women). Students: 18 full-time (10 women); includes 17 international. Average age 30. 119 applicants, 5% accepted. In 1997, 1 master's, 1 doctorate awarded. Terminal master's awarded for partial completion of doctoral program. *Degree requirements:* Thesis/dissertation required, foreign language not required. *Average time to degree:* master's–2 years full-time; doctorate–5 years full-time. *Entrance requirements:* GRE General Test, TOEFL. Application deadline: 9/8 (priority date). Application fee: $30. Electronic applications accepted. *Tuition:* $5907 per year full-time, $246 per hour part-time for state residents; $11,835 per year full-time, $493 per hour part-time for nonresidents. *Financial aid:* In 1997–98, teaching assistantships averaging $1,583 per month were awarded; research assistantships, full tuition waivers also available. *Faculty research:* Neuroscience, molecular modeling, immunotoxicology, organic synthesis, peptide biochemistry. • Dr. Richard Hudson, Chairman, 419-530-1979. Application contact: Dr. William Messer, Coordinator, 419-530-1958. Fax: 419-530-7946.

University of Toledo, College of Pharmacy, Graduate Programs in Pharmacy, Program in Pharmaceutical Science, Toledo, OH 43606-3398. Offers administrative pharmacy (MSPS), industrial pharmacy (MSPS), pharmacology (MSPS). Faculty: 11 full-time (3 women). Students: 23 full-time (13 women); includes 22 international. Average age 25. 71 applicants, 17% accepted. In 1997, 11 degrees awarded. *Degree requirements:* Thesis required, foreign language not required. *Average time to degree:* master's–2 years full-time. *Entrance requirements:* GRE General Test, TOEFL. Application deadline: 9/8 (priority date). Application fee: $30. Electronic applications accepted. *Tuition:* $5907 per year full-time, $246 per hour part-time for state residents; $11,835 per year full-time, $493 per hour part-time for nonresidents. *Financial aid:* In 1997–98, 14 students received aid, including teaching assistantships averaging $781 per month and totaling $9,375; full tuition waivers also available. *Faculty research:* Drug disposition, neuropharmacology, pharmacokinetics, product stability, pharmacy and health care administration. • Dr. Kenneth A. Bachmann, Director of Graduate Studies, 419-530-1912. Fax: 419-530-1909. E-mail: kbachma@utnet.utoledo.edu.

University of Toronto, School of Graduate Studies, Life Sciences Division, Department of Pharmaceutical Sciences, Toronto, ON M5S 1A1, Canada. Awards M Sc, PhD. Part-time programs available. Faculty: 41. Students: 50 full-time (27 women), 10 part-time (8 women); includes 4 international. 35 applicants, 46% accepted. In 1997, 7 master's, 1 doctorate awarded. *Degree requirements:* Thesis/dissertation. *Application fee:* $75. *Expenses:* Tuition $4070 per year for Canadian residents; $7870 per year for nonresidents. Fees $628 per year. • P. J. O'Brien, Chair, 416-978-2716. Application contact: Secretary, 416-978-2179. Fax: 416-978-8511. E-mail: pharmacy.grad@utoronto.ca.

University of Utah, College of Pharmacy and Graduate School, Graduate Programs in Pharmacy, Medicinal Chemistry Program, Salt Lake City, UT 84112-1107. Awards MS, PhD. Terminal master's awarded for partial completion of doctoral program. *Degree requirements:* For doctorate, dissertation required, foreign language not required. *Entrance requirements:* For doctorate, minimum GPA of 3.0. Application deadline: rolling. Application fee: $30 ($50 for international students). *Tuition:* $2045 per year full-time, $562 per semester (minimum) part-time for state residents; $6129 per year full-time, $1607 per semester (minimum) part-time for nonresidents. *Faculty research:* Cancer chemotherapy, NMR spectroscopy, mass spectrometry, chemotherapeutic agents, antimetabolites.

University of Utah, College of Pharmacy and Graduate School, Graduate Programs in Pharmacy, Pharmaceutics and Pharmaceutical Chemistry Program, 301 Skaggs Hall, Salt Lake City, UT 84112. Awards MS, PhD. Terminal master's awarded for partial completion of doctoral program. *Degree requirements:* Thesis/dissertation required, foreign language not required. *Entrance requirements:* GRE and TOEFL (international students), curriculum vitae. Application deadline: rolling. Application fee: $30 ($50 for international students). *Tuition:* $2045 per year full-time, $562 per semester (minimum) part-time for state residents; $6129 per year full-time, $1607 per semester (minimum) part-time for nonresidents. *Faculty research:* Drug delivery, transdermal delivery, pharmacokinetics, polymer science.

University of Washington, School of Pharmacy and Graduate School, Graduate Programs in Pharmacy, Department of Medicinal Chemistry, Seattle, WA 98195. Awards PhD. Faculty: 12 (2 women). Terminal master's awarded for partial completion of doctoral program. *Degree requirements:* For doctorate, dissertation required, foreign language not required. *Entrance requirements:* For doctorate, GRE General Test, TOEFL, minimum GPA of 3.0. Application deadline: 2/15. Application fee: $45. *Tuition:* $5433 per year full-time, $775 per quarter (minimum) part-time for state residents; $13,479 per year full-time, $1925 per quarter (minimum) part-time for nonresidents. *Financial aid:* Fellowships, research assistantships, Federal Work-Study, institutionally sponsored loans available. *Faculty research:* Chemical and molecular aspects of drug action, metabolism and drug toxicity, theoretical studies on protein folding, NMR of macromolecules and biomedical mass spectrometry. • Wendel L. Nelson, Chairman, 206-543-2209. Application contact: Meg Running, Graduate Program Assistant, 206-543-2224. E-mail: medchem@u.washington.edu.

University of Washington, School of Pharmacy and Graduate School, Graduate Programs in Pharmacy, Department of Pharmaceutics, Seattle, WA 98195. Awards MS, PhD. Part-time and evening/weekend programs available. Faculty: 8 full-time (0 women), 1 (woman) part-time, 8.25 FTE. Students: 22 full-time (15 women); includes 3 minority (1 African American, 2 Asian Americans), 6 international. Average age 31. 131 applicants, 4% accepted. In 1997, 3 doctorates awarded (100% found work related to degree). *Degree requirements:* For master's, thesis; for doctorate, 1 foreign language (computer language can substitute), dissertation. *Average time to degree:* doctorate–8 years full-time. *Entrance requirements:* GRE General Test, TOEFL. Application deadline: 3/1. Application fee: $45. *Tuition:* $5433 per year full-time, $775 per quarter (minimum) part-time for state residents; $13,479 per year full-time, $1925 per quarter (minimum) part-time for nonresidents. *Financial aid:* In 1997–98, 19 students received aid, including 1 fellowship averaging $1,088 per month and totaling $3,264, 12 research assistantships (2 to first-year students) totaling $182,784, 4 grants averaging $1,088 per month and totaling $52,224; full tuition waivers, institutionally sponsored loans also available. Financial aid application deadline: 3/1. *Faculty research:* Pharmacokinetics/pharmacodynamics, drug metabolism. • Rene H. Levy, Chair, 206-543-9434. E-mail: rhlevy@u.washington.edu. Application contact: Cathy Johnson, Administrative Assistant, 206-543-9434. Fax: 206-543-3204. E-mail: pceut@u.washington.edu.

See in-depth description on page 1823.

University of Wisconsin–Madison, School of Pharmacy and Graduate School, Graduate Programs in Pharmacy, Department of Pharmaceutical Biochemistry, Madison, WI 53706-1380. Awards PhD. *Degree requirements:* Dissertation. *Application fee:* $38.

See in-depth description on page 1825.

University of Wisconsin–Madison, School of Pharmacy and Graduate School, Graduate Programs in Pharmacy, Department of Pharmaceutical Chemistry, Madison, WI 53706-1380. Awards PhD. *Degree requirements:* Dissertation. *Application fee:* $38.

See in-depth description on page 1825.

University of Wisconsin–Madison, School of Pharmacy and Graduate School, Graduate Programs in Pharmacy, Department of Pharmaceutics, Madison, WI 53706-1380. Awards PhD. *Degree requirements:* Dissertation. *Application fee:* $38.

See in-depth description on page 1825.

University of Wisconsin–Madison, School of Pharmacy and Graduate School, Graduate Programs in Pharmacy, Department of Pharmacology-Pharmacy, Madison, WI 53706-1380. Awards PhD. *Degree requirements:* Dissertation. *Application fee:* $38.

See in-depth description on page 1825.

University of Wisconsin–Madison, School of Pharmacy and Graduate School, Graduate Programs in Pharmacy, Department of Social and Administrative Sciences in Pharmacy, Madison, WI 53706-1380. Awards PhD. *Degree requirements:* Dissertation. *Application fee:* $38.

See in-depth description on page 1825.

Virginia Commonwealth University, Schools of Graduate Studies and Pharmacy, School of Pharmacy Graduate Programs, Department of Pharmacy and Pharmaceutics, Richmond, VA 23284-9005. Awards MS, PhD, Pharm D/PhD. Average age 29. Terminal master's awarded for partial completion of doctoral program. *Degree requirements:* Computer language, thesis/dissertation required, foreign language not required. *Entrance requirements:* GRE General Test, TOEFL (minimum score 600). Application fee: $30 ($0 for international students). *Tuition:* $4960 per year full-time, $257 per credit part-time for state residents; $12,652 per year full-time, $684 per credit part-time for nonresidents. *Financial aid:* Research assistantships, teaching assistantships available. *Faculty research:* Drug delivery systems, drug development. • Dr. William H. Barr, Chair, 804-828-8334. E-mail: whbarr@gems.vcu.edu. Application contact: Dr. Wesley J. Poynor, Director, Graduate Program, 804-828-6348. Fax: 804-828-8359. E-mail: poynor@pha1.pha.vcu.edu.

Announcement: The department is proud of its PhD track in pharmacotherapy that involves the student in the intensive ongoing human clinical research program in collaboration with nationally recognized clinical scientists. Applicants should have had a moderate exposure to clinical therapeutics. Other tracks offered include pharmacokinetics, pharmacodynamics, pharmaceutical analysis, pharmaceutics (especially aerosol delivery), and pharmacy administration. There is also a combined Pharm D/PhD degree program.

Wayne State University, College of Pharmacy and Allied Health Professions, Faculty of Pharmacy, Department of Pharmaceutical Sciences, Detroit, MI 48202. Awards MS, PhD. Faculty: 11 full-time (0 women), 1 part-time (0 women). Students: 16 full-time (5 women), 11 part-time (8 women); includes 8 international. 134 applicants, 3% accepted. In 1997, 4 master's awarded (100% found work related to degree); 2 doctorates awarded (100% entered university research/teaching). Terminal master's awarded for partial completion of doctoral program. *Degree requirements:* Thesis/dissertation required, foreign language not required. *Entrance requirements:* For master's, GRE General Test, minimum GPA of 2.6; for doctorate, GRE General Test, minimum GPA of 3.0. Application deadline: 1/31 (priority date; rolling processing). Application fee: $20 ($30 for international students). *Expenses:* Tuition $163 per credit hour for state residents; $355 per credit hour for nonresidents. Fees $498 per year full-time, $114 per semester (minimum) part-time. *Financial aid:* In 1997–98, 16 students received aid, including 1 fellowship (to a first-year student), 7 research assistantships (1 to a first-year student); scholarships also available. Aid available to part-time students. *Faculty research:* Neuroelectrophysiology of dopamine neurons, mechanisms for drug effects on behavior, syntheses and mechanistic studies of famesylation, molecular mechanisms of apostosis, drug metabolism in HIV patients. • Dr. George B. Corcoran, Chairman, 313-577-1737. Fax: 313-577-2033.

See in-depth description on page 1827.

West Virginia University, School of Pharmacy, Program in Pharmaceutical Sciences, Morgantown, WV 26506. Awards MS, PhD. Average age 27. Terminal master's awarded for partial completion of doctoral program. *Degree requirements:* For master's, thesis required, foreign language not required; for doctorate, 1 foreign language (computer language can substitute), dissertation, written and oral comprehensive exams. *Entrance requirements:* GRE General Test, TOEFL (minimum score 550), minimum GPA of 2.75. Application deadline: 3/1 (priority date). Application fee: $45. *Tuition:* $3808 per year for state residents; $10,848 per year for nonresidents. *Financial aid:* Full and partial tuition waivers, Federal Work-Study, institutionally sponsored loans, and career-related internships or fieldwork available. Financial aid application deadline: 2/1; applicants required to submit FAFSA. *Faculty research:* Pharmaceutics, medicinal chemistry, behavioral and administration pharmacy, medical informatics, biopharmaceutics/pharmacokinetics. • Application contact: Dr. Patrick S. Callery, Assistant Dean for Research and Graduate Programs, 304-293-1482. Fax: 304-293-5483. E-mail: pcallery@hsc.wvu.edu.

Pharmacy

Albany College of Pharmacy of Union University, Program in Pharmacy, Albany, NY 12208-3425. Awards Pharm D. Accredited by ACPE. Part-time programs available. Postbaccalaureate distance learning degree programs offered (minimal on-campus study). Faculty: 13 full-time (3 women), 11 part-time (6 women). Students: 28 full-time (21 women), 4 part-time (2 women); includes 6 minority (all Asian Americans), 2 international. Average age 27. 44 applicants, 84% accepted. *Average time to degree:* first professional–2 years full-time, 5 years part-time. *Application deadline:* 2/1 (rolling processing). *Application fee:* $50. *Expenses:* Tuition $12,250 per year full-time, $408 per credit hour part-time. Fees $217 per year. *Financial aid:* Available to part-time students. *Faculty research:* Therapeutic use of drugs, pharmacokinetics, pharmaceutical care. • Dr. Margaret Malone, Director, 518-445-7275. Application contact: Jacqueline Harris, Assistant Registrar, 518-445-7221. Fax: 518-445-7202.

Auburn University, School of Pharmacy, Professional Program in Pharmacy, Auburn University, AL 36849-0001. Awards Pharm D. Accredited by ACPE. Part-time programs available. Faculty: 32 full-time (8 women). Students: 144 full-time (97 women); includes 12 minority (8 African Americans, 3 Asian Americans, 1 Native American). 27 applicants, 30% accepted. In 1997, 11 degrees awarded. *Application deadline:* 9/1 (rolling processing; 3/1 for spring admission). *Application fee:* $25. *Financial aid:* Federal Work-Study available. Aid available to part-time students. Financial aid application deadline: 3/15. • Robert E. Smith, Head, 334-844-4033.

Butler University, College of Pharmacy, Indianapolis, IN 46208-3485. Offers program in pharmaceutical science (Pharm D, MS). One or more programs accredited by ACPE. Part-time and evening/weekend programs available. Faculty: 6 full-time (0 women), 2 part-time (1 woman), 6.5 FTE. Students: 61 full-time (48 women), 11 part-time (7 women); includes 4 minority (all Asian Americans), 8 international. Average age 26. 47 applicants, 98% accepted. In 1997, 21 Pharm Ds, 3 master's awarded. *Degree requirements:* For master's, research paper or thesis required, foreign language not required. *Application deadline:* 8/1 (priority date; rolling processing; 12/15 for spring admission). *Application fee:* $25. *Tuition:* $310 per credit hour. *Financial aid:* 1 student received aid. *Faculty research:* Chemical and physical stability of drugs and drug products, pharmacology of central acting and antiseizure drugs, pharmacokinetics and disposition of xenobiotics *in vivo*, protein binding studies, synthesis of bis-hydantoins. • Dr. Robert A. Sandmann, Dean, 317-940-9322. Fax: 317-940-6172. Application contact: Dr. Beverly Sandmann, Principal Graduate Adviser, 317-940-9553.

Campbell University, School of Pharmacy, Buies Creek, NC 27506. Awards Pharm D. Accredited by ACPE. Faculty: 36 full-time (12 women), 5 part-time (3 women). Students: 338 full-time (220 women); includes 28 minority (9 African Americans, 13 Asian Americans, 2 Hispanics, 4 Native Americans). Average age 24. 513 applicants, 16% accepted. In 1997, 83 degrees awarded. *Degree requirements:* Computer language required, foreign language and thesis not required. *Entrance requirements:* PCAT. Application deadline: 2/15 (priority date; rolling processing). Application fee: $50. *Expenses:* Tuition $12,680 per year. Fees $88 per year. *Financial aid:* Federal Work-Study, institutionally sponsored loans, and career-related internships or fieldwork available. Financial aid applicants required to submit FAFSA. *Faculty research:* Immunology, medicinal chemistry, pharmaceutics, applied pharmacology. Total annual research expenditures: $75,000. • Dr. Ronald Maddox, Dean, 910-893-1200 Ext. 1685. Fax: 910-893-1697. E-mail: pharmacy@camel.campbell.edu. Application contact: Dr. Daniel Teat, Assistant Dean for Admissions, 910-893-1200 Ext. 1690. Fax: 910-893-1937. E-mail: pharmacy@camel.campbell.edu.

Creighton University, School of Pharmacy and Allied Health Professions, Professional Program in Pharmacy, Omaha, NE 68178-0001. Awards Pharm D. Accredited by ACPE. Postbaccalaureate distance learning degree programs offered (no on-campus study). Faculty: 42 full-time (19 women), 2 part-time. Students: 371 full-time (231 women); includes 107 minority (11 African Americans, 84 Asian Americans, 12 Hispanics), 19 international. Average age 26. 803 applicants, 12% accepted. In 1997, 80 degrees awarded. *Average time to degree:* first professional–6 years full-time. *Application deadline:* 5/31 (priority date; rolling processing). *Application fee:* $50. *Expenses:* Tuition $6772 per year. Fees $268 per year. *Financial aid:* Federal Work-Study, institutionally sponsored loans, and career-related internships or fieldwork available. *Faculty research:* Drug synthesis, Phase II drug studies, molecular mechanism of toxicity, pharmaceutics, pharmacology of the eye. • Application contact: John J. Flemming, Director of Admissions, 402-280-2662. Fax: 402-280-5739. E-mail: spahp_admin8@creighton.edu.

Drake University, College of Pharmacy and Health Sciences, Program in Pharmacy, Des Moines, IA 50311-4516. Awards Pharm D, JD/Pharm D, Pharm D/MBA. Accredited by ACPE. Pharm D/MBA offered jointly with the College of Business and Public Administration; JD/Pharm D offered jointly with the Law School. Faculty: 23 full-time (8 women), 9 part-time (5 women), 27.5 FTE. Students: 37 full-time (26 women); includes 7 minority (1 African American, 3 Asian Americans, 3 Hispanics). Average age 25. 70 applicants, 99% accepted. In 1997, 26 degrees awarded. *Entrance requirements:* Interview. Application deadline: 12/1 (priority date). Application fee: $25. Electronic applications accepted. *Tuition:* $16,950 per year full-time, $550 per hour part-time. *Financial aid:* In 1997–98, 10 teaching assistantships averaging $300 per month were awarded; Federal Work-Study, institutionally sponsored loans, and career-related internships or fieldwork also available. Aid available to part-time students. Financial aid application deadline: 3/1; applicants required to submit FAFSA. *Faculty research:* Health policy and services, pharmaceutical care outcomes, cardiovascular pharmacology, pharmacokinetics of chiral drugs, drug delivery systems. • Application contact: Renae Chesnut, Director of Student Services, 800-44-DRAKE Ext. 3018. Fax: 515-271-4171. E-mail: renae.chestnut@drake.edu.

Duquesne University, School of Pharmacy, Professional Program in Pharmacy, Pittsburgh, PA 15282-0001. Awards Pharm D. Accredited by ACPE. Students enter program as first year undergraduates. Faculty: 16 full-time, 42 part-time. Students: 695. *Average time to degree:* first professional–6 years full-time. *Entrance requirements:* PCAT (transfer students into second or third year). *Expenses:* Tuition $530 per credit. Fees $39 per credit. • Dr. P. Randall L. Vanderveen, Dean, School of Pharmacy, 412-396-6380.

Ferris State University, College of Pharmacy, Big Rapids, MI 49307-2742. Awards Pharm D. Accredited by ACPE. Faculty: 10 full-time (3 women), 36 part-time (19 women). Students: 8 full-time (4 women), 9 part-time (5 women); includes 1 minority (Native American). *Entrance requirements:* PCAT. Application deadline: 1/31. Application fee: $20. *Expenses:* Tuition $220 per credit hour for state residents; $450 per credit hour for nonresidents. Fees $100 per year. • Ian Mathison, Dean, 616-592-2254. Application contact: Dr. Edmund Hengesh, Acting Assistant Dean, 616-592-3780. Fax: 616-592-3829.

Florida Agricultural and Mechanical University, Division of Graduate Studies, Research, and Continuing Education, College of Pharmacy and Pharmaceutical Sciences, Professional Program in Pharmacy and Pharmaceutical Sciences, Tallahassee, FL 32307-3200. Awards Pharm D. Accredited by ACPE. Students: 638 (449 women); includes 569 minority (512 African Americans, 51 Asian Americans, 4 Hispanics, 2 Native Americans). *Entrance requirements:* Minimum GPA of 2.5. Application deadline: 3/1. Application fee: $20. *Expenses:* Tuition $140 per credit hour for state residents; $484 per credit hour for nonresidents. Fees $130 per year. • Application contact: Carlton Bailey, Director, 850-599-3039. Fax: 850-599-3347.

Howard University, College of Pharmacy, Nursing and Allied Health Sciences, Division of Pharmacy, 2400 Sixth Street, NW, Washington, DC 20059-0002. Awards Pharm D. Accredited by ACPE. Faculty: 26 full-time (7 women), 127 part-time (44 women). Students: 300 full-time (203 women), 2 part-time (0 women); includes 276 minority (217 African Americans, 57 Asian Americans, 2 Hispanics), 14 international. Average age 25. 352 applicants, 23% accepted. In 1997, 23 degrees awarded. *Average time to degree:* first professional–4 years full-time. *Entrance requirements:* PCAT (score in 40th percentile or higher). Application deadline: 2/1. Application fee: $45. Electronic applications accepted. *Expenses:* Tuition $10,840 per year. Fees $575 per year. *Financial aid:* In 1997–98, 8 research assistantships totaling $8,800 were awarded; Federal Work-Study, institutionally sponsored loans, and career-related internships or fieldwork also available. Aid available to part-time students. Financial aid application deadline: 2/15; applicants required to submit FAFSA. *Faculty research:* Kinetics of drug absorption, stealth liposomes, synthesis, opiate analgesics. • Dr. Vafant G. Telang, Associate Dean, 202-806-6530. E-mail: vtelang@fac.howard.edu. Application contact: Dr. Bertram A. Nicholas Jr., Assistant Dean for Student Services, 202-806-6551. Fax: 202-806-4636. E-mail: bnicholas@fac.howard.edu.

Idaho State University, College of Pharmacy, Department of Pharmacy Practice and Administrative Sciences, Pocatello, ID 83209. Offers programs in pharmacy (Pharm D), pharmacy administration (MS, PhD). One or more programs accredited by ACPE. Faculty: 20 full-time (10 women), 1 (woman) part-time. Students: 209 full-time (101 women), 37 part-time (23 women); includes 29 minority (2 African Americans, 20 Asian Americans, 4 Hispanics, 3 Native Americans), 7 international. Average age 29. In 1997, 73 Pharm Ds awarded. *Degree requirements:* For master's, 1 foreign language, thesis. *Entrance requirements:* For Pharm D, minimum GPA of 2.5, 2 years of pre-pharmacy; for master's and doctorate, GRE General Test. Application deadline: 8/1 (priority date). Application fee: $30. *Faculty research:* Pharmaceutical care outcomes, drug use review, pharmacoeconomics. Total annual research expenditures: $350,500. • Dr. Vaughn Culbertson, Chairman, 208-236-2586.

Long Island University, Brooklyn Campus, Arnold and Marie Schwartz College of Pharmacy and Health Sciences, Professional Program in Pharmacy, Brooklyn, NY 11201-8423. Awards Pharm D. Candidate for accreditation by ACPE. Part-time programs available. Faculty: 19 full-time (10 women), 3 part-time (all women). Students: 7 full-time (6 women), 7 part-time (5 women); includes 3 minority (1 African American, 2 Hispanics), 2 international. In 1997, 4 degrees awarded. *Degree requirements:* Thesis, research project required, foreign language not required. *Average time to degree:* first professional–2 years full-time, 5 years part-time. *Expenses:* Tuition $480 per credit. Fees $415 per year full-time, $73 per semester (minimum) part-time. *Financial aid:* In 1997–98, 6 teaching assistantships were awarded. • Dr. Stephen M. Gross, Dean, Arnold and Marie Schwartz College of Pharmacy and Health Sciences, 718-488-1004. Application contact: Bernard W. Sullivan, Associate Director of Admissions, 718-488-1011.

Medical University of South Carolina, College of Pharmacy, Charleston, SC 29425-0002. Awards Pharm D. Accredited by ACPE. Faculty: 14 full-time (5 women). Students: 37 full-time (29 women), 2 part-time (both women); includes 3 minority (2 African Americans, 1 Asian American), 2 international. Average age 28. 50 applicants, 58% accepted. In 1997, 16 degrees awarded. *Degree requirements:* Project required, foreign language and thesis not required. *Entrance requirements:* Interview, minimum GPA of 2.5. Application deadline: 12/31. Application fee: $55. *Expenses:* Tuition $4132 per year full-time, $207 per semester hour part-time for state residents; $11,632 per year full-time, $491 per semester hour part-time for nonresidents. Fees $580 per year (minimum). *Financial aid:* Partial tuition waivers, Federal Work-Study available. Aid available to part-time students. Financial aid application deadline: 4/1; applicants required to submit FAFSA. *Faculty research:* Industrial pharmacy, medicinal chemistry, pharmaceutics, pharmacokinetics, bioavailability. • Dr. John L. Early, Dean, 843-792-8450. Application contact: Wanda Taylor, Director of Admissions, 843-792-3281.

Mercer University, Cecil B. Day Campus, Southern School of Pharmacy, Professional Program in Pharmacy, Athens, GA 30602. Awards Pharm D, MBA/Pharm D, Pharm D/PhD. Accredited by ACPE. In 1997, 124 degrees awarded. *Entrance requirements:* Minimum GPA of 2.5. Application deadline: 1/31 (rolling processing). Application fee: $25. *Tuition:* $15,058 per year. *Financial aid:* Teaching assistantships, Federal Work-Study, institutionally sponsored loans, and career-related internships or fieldwork available. Aid available to part-time students. Financial aid application deadline: 5/1. • Application contact: Dr. James Bartling, Associate Dean for Student Affairs and Admissions, 770-986-3232. Fax: 770-986-3063. E-mail: bartling_jw@mercer.edu.

Midwestern University, College of Pharmacy, Downers Grove, IL 60515-1235. Awards Pharm D. Accredited by ACPE. Faculty: 32 full-time (23 women), 8 part-time (3 women). Students: 63 full-time (44 women), 37 part-time (16 women); includes 34 minority (6 African Americans, 22 Asian Americans, 6 Hispanics). Average age 26. In 1997, 34 degrees awarded. *Entrance requirements:* PCAT. Application deadline: 2/28. Application fee: $30. *Expenses:* Tuition $13,770 per year for state residents; $15,438 per year for nonresidents. Fees $280 per year. *Financial aid:* Federal Work-Study, institutionally sponsored loans available. Aid available to part-time students. Financial aid applicants required to submit FAFSA. • Dr. Mary Lee, Acting Dean, 630-971-6417. Application contact: Julie Rosenthall, Director of Admissions, 800-458-6253. Fax: 630-971-6086. E-mail: mwuinfo@mwu.edu.

Announcement: Midwestern University is committed to educating the health-care team of the next century. The University administers the Chicago College of Osteopathic Medicine, the Chicago College of Pharmacy, the College of Allied Health Professions, the Arizona College of Osteopathic Medicine, and the College of Pharmacy–Glendale. The University operates campuses in Downers Grove, Illinois, and in Glendale, Arizona. The Chicago College of Pharmacy offers both Bachelor of Science (BS) and Doctor of Pharmacy (Pharm D) degrees. As students complete the curriculum, they work closely with a small group of students and a faculty adviser, completing assignments and focusing on problem-solving skills. This small group approach gives a sense of the team-oriented health-care structure in which students will play an essential role after graduation. Contact the Office of Admissions, Midwestern University, 555 31st Street, Downers Grove, IL 60515; 800-458-6253; e-mail: admiss@midwestern.edu; WWW: http://www.midwestern.edu

Northeastern University, Bouvé College of Pharmacy and Health Sciences Graduate School, Professional Program in Pharmacy, Boston, MA 02115-5096. Awards Pharm D. Accredited by ACPE. Students enter program as undergraduates. *Entrance requirements:* Prior admission to undergraduate pharmacy program. *Expenses:* Tuition $440 per credit hour. Fees $55 per quarter full-time, $13.25 per quarter part-time. • Application contact: Office of Undergraduate Admissions, 617-373-2200. Fax: 617-373-8780. E-mail: admissions@neu.edu.

See in-depth description on page 1797.

Nova Southeastern University, Health Professions Division, College of Pharmacy, Fort Lauderdale, FL 33314-7721. Awards Pharm D. Accredited by ACPE. Students: 436 full-time (267 women), 81 part-time (45 women); includes 196 minority (28 African Americans, 73 Asian Americans, 91 Hispanics, 4 Native Americans), 19 international. Average age 27. In 1997, 48 degrees awarded. *Average time to degree:* first professional–4 years full-time. *Entrance requirements:* PCAT (score in 70th percentile or higher). Application deadline: 4/15 (rolling processing). Application fee: $50. *Expenses:* Tuition $12,940 per year for state residents; $15,600 per year for nonresidents. Fees $100 per year. *Financial aid:* Scholarships, Federal Work-Study, institutionally sponsored loans, and career-related internships or fieldwork available. Aid available to part-time students. Financial aid application deadline: 4/1. *Faculty research:* Computer-aided instruction, pharmoeconomics, cell structure and drug receptors, toxicology, gerontology. Total annual research expenditures: $75,000. • Dr. William Hardigan, Dean, 954-262-1300. Fax: 954-916-2278. E-mail: hardigan@hpd.nova.edu. Application contact: Carol Tolefsen, Admissions Counselor, 954-262-1111. Fax: 954-916-2282. E-mail: carol@hpd.nova.edu.

The Ohio State University, College of Pharmacy, Professional Program in Pharmacy, Columbus, OH 43210. Awards Pharm D. Accredited by ACPE. Faculty: 48 full-time (7 women), 22 part-time (3 women). *Entrance requirements:* PCAT, TOEFL (minimum score 575), minimum GPA of 3.0. Application deadline: 1/1 (priority date). Application fee: $30 ($40 for international students). *Tuition:* $6456 per year for state residents; $15,702 per year for nonresidents.

Directory: Pharmacy

The Ohio State University (continued)

Financial aid: Federal Work-Study, institutionally sponsored loans, and career-related internships or fieldwork available. Aid available to part-time students. Financial aid application deadline: 2/1. *Faculty research:* Clinical pharmacokinetics, drug metabolism, critical care therapeutics, drug interactions, stereoselective drug dispositions. • Application contact: Katherine Kelley, Admissions Counselor, 614-292-2266. Fax: 614-292-2588. E-mail: kelley.168@osu.edu.

See in-depth description on page 1799.

Purdue University, School of Pharmacy and Pharmacal Sciences, Professional Program in Pharmacy and Pharmacal Sciences, West Lafayette, IN 47907. Awards Pharm D. Accredited by ACPE. Faculty: 15 full-time (5 women), 37 part-time (20 women). Students: 330 full-time (233 women), 9 part-time (7 women); includes 42 minority (8 African Americans, 29 Asian Americans, 3 Hispanics, 2 Native Americans), 10 international. Average age 25. 56 applicants, 80% accepted. In 1997, 12 degrees awarded. *Average time to degree:* first professional–2 years full-time, 6 years part-time. *Entrance requirements:* BS in pharmacy from an ACPE-accredited college of pharmacy. Application deadline: 1/2 (priority date; rolling processing). Application fee: $30. *Financial aid:* Scholarships and career-related internships or fieldwork available. Aid available to part-time students. Financial aid applicants required to submit FAFSA. • Dr. H. L. Mason, Associate Dean, 765-494-1469. Fax: 765-494-7880.

Rutgers, The State University of New Jersey, New Brunswick, College of Pharmacy, New Brunswick, NJ 08903. Awards Pharm D. Accredited by ACPE. Part-time programs available. Faculty: 14 full-time (7 women), 9 part-time (5 women). Students: 84 full-time (56 women), 32 part-time (19 women); includes 9 minority (1 African American, 8 Asian Americans). Average age 24. 127 applicants, 69% accepted. In 1997, 13 degrees awarded. *Degree requirements:* Thesis. *Entrance requirements:* GRE General Test. Application deadline: 3/1 (priority date; rolling processing; 12/1 for spring admission). Application fee: $40. *Expenses:* Tuition $6492 per year full-time, $268 per credit part-time for state residents; $9520 per year full-time, $395 per credit part-time for nonresidents. Fees $208 per year (minimum). *Financial aid:* In 1997–98, 3 teaching assistantships (all to first-year students) were awarded; scholarships, partial tuition waivers, and career-related internships or fieldwork also available. Financial aid application deadline: 3/1. *Faculty research:* Pharmacokinetics, infectious diseases, cardiology, neurology, pharmacodynamics. Total annual research expenditures: $1.032 million. • Dr. Joseph Barone, Director, 732-445-3285.

St. John's University, College of Pharmacy and Allied Health Professions, Professional Program in Pharmacy, Jamaica, NY 11439. Awards Pharm D. Accredited by ACPE. Students: 9 full-time (6 women), 9 part-time (7 women); includes 3 minority (1 African American, 1 Asian American, 1 Hispanic). Average age 29. 49 applicants, 27% accepted. In 1997, 3 degrees awarded. *Entrance requirements:* Bachelor's degree from an ACPE-accredited program, interview. Application deadline: 2/15 (rolling processing; 10/1 for spring admission). Application fee: $40. *Expenses:* Tuition $675 per credit. Fees $150 per year. *Financial aid:* In 1997–98, 9 clinical assistantships (3 to first-year students) averaging $556 per month were awarded; Federal Work-Study and career-related internships or fieldwork also available. Aid available to part-time students. Financial aid application deadline: 3/1; applicants required to submit FAFSA. *Faculty research:* Patient outcomes, drug-drug-infections, pharmacolcinetics, pharmcodynamics. • Dr. Joseph Brocavich, Chair, 718-990-5345. Application contact: Shamus J. McGrenra, TOR, Associate Director, Graduate Admissions, 718-990-6107. Fax: 718-990-5736. E-mail: mcgrenrs@stjohns.edu.

St. Louis College of Pharmacy, Professional Program in Pharmacy, St. Louis, MO 63110-1088. Awards Pharm D. Accredited by ACPE. Faculty: 21 full-time (12 women), 14 part-time (7 women). Students: 31 full-time (17 women), 3 part-time (2 women); includes 11 minority (all Asian Americans), 1 international. Average age 24. 44 applicants, 77% accepted. In 1997, 34 degrees awarded. *Average time to degree:* first professional–6 years full-time, 8 years part-time. *Entrance requirements:* Postbaccalaureate course work from an accredited college of pharmacy. Application deadline: 4/30 (priority date). Application fee: $35. *Expenses:* Tuition $14,000 per year full-time, $610 per credit hour part-time. Fees $120 per year. *Faculty research:* Geriatrics, cardiology, psychobiology, infectious diseases. • Dr. Michael Maddux, Assistant Dean, 314-367-8700 Ext. 1719. Fax: 314-367-2784.

Samford University, McWhorter School of Pharmacy, Birmingham, AL 35229-0002. Awards Pharm D. Accredited by ACPE. Postbaccalaureate distance learning degree programs offered (minimal on-campus study). Faculty: 36 full-time (15 women), 1 part-time (0 women). Students: 410 full-time (305 women), 25 part-time (13 women); includes 45 minority (19 African Americans, 23 Asian Americans, 1 Hispanic, 2 Native Americans). Average age 25. 451 applicants, 86% accepted. In 1997, 73 degrees awarded. *Entrance requirements:* Minimum GPA of 2.5. Application deadline: 4/1 (rolling processing). Application fee: $25. *Tuition:* $13,356 per year full-time, $472 per credit hour part-time. *Financial aid:* Federal Work-Study, institutionally sponsored loans, and career-related internships or fieldwork available. Financial aid application deadline: 5/2; applicants required to submit FAFSA. *Faculty research:* Managed care, clinical drug studies, pharmacoeconomics, natural drug products, pharmacy administration. • Dr. Joe Dean, Dean, 205-870-2820. E-mail: jodean@samford.edu. Application contact: Susan Alverson, Assistant Dean for Student/Alumni Affairs, 205-870-2053. Fax: 205-870-2759. E-mail: cbfoster@samford.edu.

Shenandoah University, School of Pharmacy, 1460 University Drive, Winchester, VA 22601-5195. Awards Pharm D. Candidate for accreditation by ACPE. Postbaccalaureate distance learning degree programs offered (minimal on-campus study). Faculty: 13 full-time (4 women), 2 part-time (1 woman). Students: 137 full-time (87 women); includes 40 minority (5 African Americans, 31 Asian Americans, 3 Hispanics, 1 Native American), 5 international. Average age 25. 200 applicants, 75% accepted. *Entrance requirements:* PCAT, interview. Application deadline: 3/15. Application fee: $30. Electronic applications accepted. *Tuition:* $15,600 per year. *Faculty research:* Informatics, medical information systems, biotechnology, clinical practice, managed care, ambulatory care. • Dr. Alan McKay, Dean, 540-665-1280. Fax: 540-665-1283. E-mail: amckay@su.edu. Application contact: Michael Carpenter, Director of Admissions, 540-665-4581. Fax: 540-665-4627. E-mail: admit@su.edu.

South Dakota State University, College of Pharmacy, Professional Program in Pharmacy, Brookings, SD 57007. Awards Pharm D. Accredited by ACPE. Students: 102 full-time (62 women); includes 2 Asian Americans. 47 applicants, 100% accepted. In 1997, 2 degrees awarded. *Entrance requirements:* Bachelor's degree in pharmacy. Application deadline: 3/1 (rolling processing). Application fee: $15. *Expenses:* Tuition $82 per credit hour for state residents; $242 per credit hour for nonresidents. Fees $37 per credit hour. *Financial aid:* Application deadline 3/1. • Dr. Danny Lattin, Dean, College of Pharmacy, 605-688-6197. Fax: 605-688-6232. Application contact: Dr. Chandradhar Dwivedi, Coordinator of Graduate Studies, 605-688-4247.

State University of New York at Buffalo, Graduate School, School of Pharmacy, Professional Program in Pharmacy, Buffalo, NY 14260. Awards Pharm D. Accredited by ACPE. Faculty: 8 full-time (2 women), 14 part-time (8 women). Students: 26 full-time (16 women), 4 part-time (3 women); includes 7 minority (6 Asian Americans, 1 Hispanic), 2 international. Average age 26. 57 applicants, 25% accepted. In 1997, 7 degrees awarded. *Degree requirements:* Project required, thesis not required. *Entrance requirements:* BS in pharmacy. Application deadline: 2/15 (priority date; rolling processing). Application fee: $35. *Tuition:* $7685 per year full-time, $321 per credit hour part-time for state residents; $13,135 per year full-time, $548 per credit hour part-time for nonresidents. *Financial aid:* In 1997–98, 4 students received aid, including 4 teaching assistantships (all to first-year students); graduate assistantships, Federal Work-Study also available. Financial aid application deadline: 2/28. *Faculty research:* Pharmacokinetics, pharmacoepidemiology, AIDS, renal transplant. • Dr. Gene Morse, Chairman, 716-645-2828. Fax: 716-645-2886. Application contact: Dr. Jerome J. Schentag, Director, 716-645-2828. Fax: 716-695-2886.

Temple University, Health Sciences Center, School of Pharmacy, Professional Program in Pharmacy, Philadelphia, PA 19140. Awards Pharm D. Accredited by ACPE. *Application deadline:* 6/1. *Application fee:* $40. *Financial aid:* Application deadline 6/1. • Dr. Peter Doukas, Dean, School of Pharmacy, 215-707-4990. Application contact: Dr. Reza Fassihi, Director of Graduate Studies, 215-707-4948. Fax: 215-707-3678.

Texas Southern University, College of Pharmacy and Health Sciences, Houston, TX 77004-4584. Awards Pharm D. Accredited by ACPE. Faculty: 7 full-time (2 women). Students: 15 full-time (7 women), 29 part-time (7 women); includes 24 minority (19 African Americans, 2 Asian Americans, 3 Hispanics), 7 international. Average age 26. 48 applicants, 54% accepted. In 1997, 15 degrees awarded. *Average time to degree:* first professional–2 years full-time. *Entrance requirements:* GRE General Test. Application deadline: 1/31. Application fee: $35 ($75 for international students). *Financial aid:* Fellowships, teaching assistantships, partial tuition waivers, Federal Work-Study, institutionally sponsored loans, and career-related internships or fieldwork available. *Faculty research:* Basic and clinical pharmacokinetics, metabolism studies, diabetes, hypertension, sickle cell. • Dr. Pedro Lecca, Acting Dean, 713-313-7164.

The University of Arizona, College of Pharmacy, Department of Pharmacy Practice and Science, Tucson, AZ 85721. Offers program in pharmacy (Pharm D, MS, PhD). One or more programs accredited by ACPE. Part-time programs available. Terminal master's awarded for partial completion of doctoral program. *Degree requirements:* For master's and doctorate, thesis/dissertation required, foreign language not required. *Entrance requirements:* For master's and doctorate, GRE General Test, TOEFL (minimum score 575), minimum GPA of 3.0. Application fee: $35. *Tuition:* $2162 per year full-time, $337 per semester (minimum) part-time for state residents; $6860 per year full-time, $1138 per semester (minimum) part-time for nonresidents. *Faculty research:* Health/service administrative pharmacy education, geriatric pharmacy, social and behavioral pharmacy management and economics.

University of Arkansas for Medical Sciences, College of Pharmacy, 4301 West Markham, Little Rock, AR 72205-7199. Awards Pharm D, MS. One or more programs accredited by ACPE. Faculty: 24 full-time (5 women). Students: 305 full-time (189 women), 7 part-time (4 women); includes 24 minority (16 African Americans, 6 Asian Americans, 1 Hispanic, 1 Native American), 3 international. In 1997, 93 Pharm Ds, 2 master's awarded. *Degree requirements:* For master's, thesis required, foreign language not required. *Application fee:* $0. *Tuition:* $3860 per year full-time, $193 per credit hour part-time for state residents; $7720 per year full-time, $386 per credit hour part-time for nonresidents. *Financial aid:* In 1997–98, 5 research assistantships were awarded. Aid available to part-time students. • Dr. L. D. Milne, Dean, 501-686-5557. Application contact: Dr. Kim Light, 501-686-5557.

University of British Columbia, Faculty of Pharmaceutical Sciences, Program in Pharmacy, Vancouver, BC V6T 1Z2, Canada. Awards Pharm D. *Application deadline:* 4/15 (priority date; rolling processing). *Application fee:* $60.

University of California, San Francisco, School of Pharmacy, Program in Pharmacy, San Francisco, CA 94143. Awards Pharm D. Accredited by ACPE. Faculty: 79 full-time (29 women), 6 part-time (1 woman), 81.75 FTE. Students: 458 full-time (118 women); includes 333 minority (13 African Americans, 294 Asian Americans, 25 Hispanics, 1 Native American), 2 international. Average age 24. 874 applicants, 17% accepted. In 1997, 118 degrees awarded. *Average time to degree:* first professional–4 years full-time. *Application deadline:* 11/1. *Application fee:* $40. *Expenses:* Tuition $0 for state residents; $9384 per year for nonresidents. Fees $7512 per year. *Financial aid:* Fellowships, research assistantships, teaching assistantships, training grants, full tuition waivers, Federal Work-Study, institutionally sponsored loans, and career-related internships or fieldwork available. *Faculty research:* Drug delivery, drug metabolism and chemical toxicology, macromolecular structure, molecular parasitology, pharmacokinetics. • Application contact: Rez O'Sullivan, Admissions Adviser, 415-476-2732. Fax: 415-476-6805. E-mail: rez@ista.ucsf.edu.

See in-depth description on page 1805.

University of Cincinnati, College of Pharmacy, Division of Pharmacy Practice, Cincinnati, OH 45221. Awards Pharm D. Accredited by ACPE. Students: 28 full-time (17 women); includes 5 minority (2 African Americans, 2 Asian Americans, 1 Hispanic). In 1997, 11 degrees awarded. *Entrance requirements:* GRE General Test, TOEFL, BS in pharmacy or equivalent, minimum GPA of 3.0. Application deadline: 1/1 (priority date; rolling processing). Application fee: $30. *Tuition:* $7228 per year full-time, $185 per credit hour part-time for state residents; $13,812 per year full-time, $352 per credit hour part-time for nonresidents. *Financial aid:* 28 students received aid; fellowships, full and partial tuition waivers, and career-related internships or fieldwork available. Financial aid application deadline: 1/1. • Dr. William Fant, Head, 513-558-0717. Application contact: Marcie Sedam, Assistant to the Director, 513-558-3784.

See in-depth description on page 1807.

University of Colorado Health Sciences Center, School of Pharmacy, Professional Program in Pharmacy, Denver, CO 80262. Awards Pharm D. Accredited by ACPE. Faculty: 39 full-time. Students: 32 full-time (26 women); includes 6 minority (1 African American, 4 Asian Americans, 1 Hispanic), 2 international. Average age 26. 44 applicants, 32% accepted. In 1997, 14 degrees awarded. *Application deadline:* 3/1. *Application fee:* $50. • Application contact: Dr. Carol Balmer, Director, 303-315-6077.

University of Florida, College of Pharmacy, Professional Program in Pharmacy, Gainesville, FL 32611. Awards Pharm D, MBA/Pharm D, Pharm D/PhD, Pharm D/MPAS. Accredited by ACPE. Part-time programs available. Postbaccalaureate distance learning degree programs offered (no on-campus study). Students: 15. 616 applicants, 19% accepted. *Entrance requirements:* PCAT, minimum GPA of 2.5. Application deadline: 1/15 (rolling processing). Application fee: $20. *Tuition:* $138 per credit hour for state residents; $481 per credit hour for nonresidents. *Financial aid:* Fellowships, Federal Work-Study, institutionally sponsored loans available. Aid available to part-time students. Financial aid applicants required to submit FAFSA. *Faculty research:* Drug discovery, drug delivery, pharmacodynamics, socioeconomics of pharmacy, neurobiology of aging. • Dr. Michael McKenzie, Associate Dean for Academic and Student Affairs, 352-392-3405. Fax: 352-392-0021. E-mail: frontdsk@cop.health.ufl.edu.

University of Georgia, College of Pharmacy, Professional Program in Pharmacy, Athens, GA 30602. Awards Pharm D. Accredited by ACPE. Students: 375. • Application contact: Dr. George E. Francisco, Associate Dean, 706-542-1911.

University of Houston, College of Pharmacy, Department of Clinical Sciences and Administration, 4800 Calhoun, Houston, TX 77204-2163. Offerings include hospital pharmacy (MSPHR). Department faculty: 5 full-time (1 woman). *Degree requirements:* Thesis required, foreign language not required. *Entrance requirements:* GRE General Test, TOEFL (minimum score 550), bachelor's degree in pharmacy. Application deadline: 5/1 (priority date). Application fee: $25 ($100 for international students). *Expenses:* Tuition $1152 per year full-time, $120 per semester (minimum) part-time for state residents; $4482 per year full-time, $249 per credit hour part-time for nonresidents. Fees $977 per year full-time, $119 per semester (minimum) part-time. • Dr. Mark Stratton, Chair, 713-795-8387. Application contact: Dr. William McCormick, 713-795-8367. Fax: 713-795-8383.

University of Houston, College of Pharmacy, Professional Program in Pharmacy, 4800 Calhoun, Houston, TX 77204-2163. Awards Pharm D. Candidate for accreditation by ACPE. *Application fee:* $25 ($100 for international students). *Expenses:* Tuition $1152 per year full-time, $120 per semester (minimum) part-time for state residents; $4482 per year full-time, $249 per credit hour part-time for nonresidents. Fees $977 per year full-time, $119 per semester (minimum) part-time. *Financial aid:* Research assistantships, teaching assistantships, institutionally sponsored loans available. Aid available to part-time students. Financial aid application deadline: 4/1. • Thomas L. Lemke, Associate Dean, 713-743-1256.

University of Illinois at Chicago, College of Pharmacy, Professional Program in Pharmacy, Chicago, IL 60607-7128. Awards Pharm D. Accredited by ACPE. Faculty: 51. Students: 628 full-time (418 women), 132 part-time (71 women); includes 328 minority (37 African Americans, 269 Asian Americans, 20 Hispanics, 2 Native Americans), 21 international. In 1997, 164 degrees awarded. *Entrance requirements:* PCAT. Application fee: $40 ($50 for international students). *Financial aid:* Fellowships available. • Rosalie Sagraves, Dean, College of Pharmacy, 312-996-7240. Application contact: Dr. John C. Russell, Associate Dean for Student Affairs, 312-996-7242.

The University of Iowa, College of Pharmacy, Professional Program in Pharmacy, Iowa City, IA 52242-1316. Awards Pharm D. Accredited by ACPE. *Expenses:* Tuition $3166 per year full-time, $176 per semester hour part-time for state residents; $10,202 per year full-time, $176 per semester hour part-time for nonresidents. Fees $202 per year full-time, $52 per year (minimum) part-time. • Associate Dean, 319-335-8795.

University of Kentucky, College of Pharmacy, Professional Program in Pharmacy, Lexington, KY 40506-0032. Awards Pharm D. Accredited by ACPE. Part-time programs available. Postbaccalaureate distance learning degree programs offered (minimal on-campus study). Students: 240 full-time (169 women), 141 part-time (73 women); includes 29 minority (6 African Americans, 23 Asian Americans), 6 international. Average age 24. 235 applicants, 57% accepted. In 1997, 70 degrees awarded (10% entered university research/teaching, 75% found other work related to degree, 15% continued full-time study). *Average time to degree:* first professional–4 years full-time, 5 years part-time. *Entrance requirements:* PCAT, interview, minimum GPA of 2.5. Application deadline: 2/1. Application fee: $75 ($80 for international students). *Financial aid:* 200 students received aid; fellowships, Federal Work-Study, institutionally sponsored loans, and career-related internships or fieldwork available. Financial aid application deadline: 1/15; applicants required to submit FAFSA. *Faculty research:* Cardiology, pharmacokinetics, pediatrics, critical care, nutrition. Total annual research expenditures: $3.5 million. • Dr. William Lubawy, Head, 606-257-5304. Application contact: College of Pharmacy Admissions, 606-323-6163. Fax: 606-257-7297.

University of Maryland, Baltimore, Professional Program in Pharmacy, Baltimore, MD 21201-1627. Awards Pharm D, Pharm D/PhD, Pharm D/MBA. Accredited by ACPE. Pharm D/PhD offered jointly with the Graduate Programs in Pharmacy. Pharm D/MBA offered jointly with the University of Baltimore. Faculty: 400. In 1997, 98 degrees awarded. *Entrance requirements:* PCAT, 63 hours in pre-pharmacy course work. Application deadline: 2/1. Application fee: $45. *Expenses:* Tuition $253 per credit hour for state residents; $454 per credit hour for nonresidents. Fees $317 per year. *Financial aid:* Application deadline 2/15. • Dr. Robert S. Beardsley, Associate Dean for Student Affairs, 410-706-7650. Application contact: Brenda Conrad, Recruitment Coordinator, 410-706-7653.

University of Maryland, Baltimore, Graduate School, Graduate Programs in Pharmacy, Baltimore, MD 21201-1627. Awards MS, PhD, Pharm D/PhD. Offerings include pharmaceutical sciences (MS, PhD), including biomedicinal chemistry, pharmaceutics, pharmacology and toxicology; pharmacy practice and science (PhD), including pharmacy administration. One or more programs accredited by ACPE. Part-time programs available. Faculty: 33 full-time (8 women), 5 part-time (0 women). Students: 98 full-time (48 women). 98 applicants, 32% accepted. In 1997, 2 master's, 14 doctorates awarded. Terminal master's awarded for partial completion of doctoral program. *Degree requirements:* Thesis/dissertation required, foreign language not required. *Entrance requirements:* GRE General Test, minimum GPA of 3.0. Application deadline: 4/1 (priority date; rolling processing). *Expenses:* Tuition $253 per credit hour for state residents; $454 per credit hour for nonresidents. Fees $317 per year. *Financial aid:* Fellowships, research assistantships, teaching assistantships, Federal Work-Study, institutionally sponsored loans, and career-related internships or fieldwork available. Aid available to part-time students. Financial aid application deadline: 2/15. *Faculty research:* Drug delivery, drug metabolism and pharmacokinetics, drug design, dosage formulation, pharmacoepidemiology, pharmacoeconomics. • Dr. David Knapp Jr., Dean, 410-706-7651. E-mail: knapp@pharmacy.ab.umd.edu. Application contact: Dr. Myron Weiner, Associate Dean for Academic Affairs, 410-706-2970. Fax: 410-706-4012. E-mail: weiner@pharmacy.ab.umd.edu.

University of Michigan, College of Pharmacy, Professional Program in Pharmacy, Ann Arbor, MI 48109. Awards Pharm D, Pharm D/PhD. Accredited by ACPE. Students: 223 full-time (156 women). In 1997, 55 degrees awarded. *Average time to degree:* first professional–4 years full-time. *Application deadline:* 2/1 (priority date). *Application fee:* $40 ($55 for international students). • Application contact: Rosemary Laczko, Student Services Associate, 734-764-7364. E-mail: rlaczko@umich.edu.

University of Minnesota, Twin Cities Campus, College of Pharmacy, Professional Program in Pharmacy, Minneapolis, MN 55455-0213. Awards Pharm D. Accredited by ACPE. Faculty: 48 full-time (15 women), 43 part-time (10 women), 52.3 FTE. Students: 109 full-time (34 women), 5 part-time (2 women). Average age 26. 261 applicants, 42% accepted. In 1997, 47 degrees awarded. *Degree requirements:* Oral exam required, foreign language and thesis not required. *Average time to degree:* first professional–4 years full-time. *Entrance requirements:* 2 years of pharmacy-related course work. Application deadline: 2/1. Application fee: $50. *Financial aid:* Federal Work-Study, institutionally sponsored loans, and career-related internships or fieldwork available. Aid available to part-time students. Financial aid applicants required to submit FAFSA. • Wendy L. St. Peter, Associate Dean, 612-624-1900. Fax: 612-624-2974. E-mail: pharosaa@tc.umm.edu.

University of Mississippi, Graduate School, School of Pharmacy, Professional Program in Pharmacy, University, MS 38677-9702. Awards Pharm D. Accredited by ACPE. Faculty: 18 full-time (6 women). Students: 120 full-time (67 women), 1 (woman) part-time; includes 9 minority (4 African Americans, 5 Asian Americans). In 1997, 27 degrees awarded. *Application deadline:* 8/1 (rolling processing). *Application fee:* $0 ($25 for international students). *Financial aid:* Application deadline 3/1. • Dr. Kenneth Roberts, Dean, School of Pharmacy, 601-232-7265.

University of Missouri–Kansas City, School of Pharmacy, Professional Program in Pharmacy, Kansas City, MO 64110-2499. Awards Pharm D. Accredited by ACPE. Students: 56 full-time (36 women); includes 10 minority (2 African Americans, 8 Asian Americans). Average age 26. In 1997, 16 degrees awarded. *Entrance requirements:* PCAT, interview, minimum GPA of 2.5. Application deadline: 3/1 (10/1 for spring admission). Application fee: $25. *Expenses:* Tuition $7998 per year for state residents; $17,823 per year for nonresidents. Fees $362 per year. *Financial aid:* Application deadline 3/15. • Application contact: Shelly M. Janasz, Manager, Student Services, 816-235-1613. Fax: 816-235-5190. E-mail: sjanasz@cctr.umkc.edu.

University of Nebraska Medical Center, College of Pharmacy, Omaha, NE 68198-0001. Awards Pharm D, Pharm D/MS. Accredited by ACPE. Faculty: 23 full-time (3 women). Students: 254 full-time (175 women), 2 part-time (1 woman); includes 15 minority (5 African Americans, 8 Asian Americans, 2 Hispanics). Average age 23. 320 applicants, 22% accepted. In 1997, 60 degrees awarded. *Entrance requirements:* 2 years (60 semester hours) of pre-pharmacy work. Application deadline: 2/1 (priority date; rolling processing). Application fee: $25. *Financial aid:* Federal Work-Study, institutionally sponsored loans, and career-related internships or fieldwork available. Aid available to part-time students. Financial aid application deadline: 3/1; applicants required to submit FAFSA. *Faculty research:* Biopharmaceutics, chemical carcinogenesis, drug design, pharmaceutics, pharmacokinetics. • Dr. Clarence T. Ueda, Dean, 402-559-4333. Application contact: Dr. Edward B. Roche, Associate Dean, 402-559-4334. Fax: 402-559-5060.

University of New Mexico, College of Pharmacy, Professional Program in Pharmacy, Albuquerque, NM 87131-2039. Awards Pharm D. Accredited by ACPE. Students: 155 full-time (89 women), 36 part-time (21 women); includes 95 minority (4 African Americans, 43 Asian Americans, 43 Hispanics, 5 Native Americans), 1 international. Average age 29. 149 applicants, 59% accepted. In 1997, 5 degrees awarded. *Entrance requirements:* Interview. Application deadline: 3/1. Application fee: $25. *Expenses:* Tuition $2442 per year full-time, $103 per credit hour part-time for state residents; $8691 per year full-time, $103 per credit hour (minimum) part-time for nonresidents. Fees $32 per year. • Reynaldo Sqenz, Associate Dean, 505-272-9625. Application contact: Mitzie Hermanson, Student Adviser, 505-272-0912. Fax: 505-272-6749.

University of Oklahoma Health Sciences Center, College of Pharmacy, Professional Program in Pharmacy, Oklahoma City, OK 73190. Awards Pharm D. Accredited by ACPE. Students: 56 full-time (35 women); includes 14 minority (2 African Americans, 6 Asian Americans, 2 Hispanics, 4 Native Americans), 2 international. In 1997, 144 degrees awarded. *Application fee:* $25 ($50 for international students). • Application contact: Parke Largent, Director of Student Services, 405-271-6595.

University of Pittsburgh, School of Pharmacy, Professional Program in Pharmacy, Pittsburgh, PA 15260. Awards Pharm D. Accredited by ACPE. Faculty: 52 full-time (23 women), 4 part-time (1 woman). Students: 60 full-time (45 women); includes 9 minority (8 Asian Americans, 1 Hispanic), 1 international. In 1997, 9 degrees awarded. *Average time to degree:* first professional–2 years full-time. *Entrance requirements:* BS in pharmacy. Application deadline: 3/1. Application fee: $30 ($40 for international students). *Expenses:* Tuition $9974 per year for state residents; $13,936 per year for nonresidents. Fees $444 per year. • Dr. Denise Howrie, Director, 412-624-3330. Application contact: Anna Schmotzer, Secretary, 412-624-3330. Fax: 412-648-1850.

University of Puerto Rico, Medical Sciences Campus, School of Pharmacy, San Juan, PR 00936-5067. Awards MS. Part-time and evening/weekend programs available. *Degree requirements:* Thesis required, foreign language not required. *Average time to degree:* master's–2.5 years full-time, 4.5 years part-time. *Entrance requirements:* GRE, interview. Application deadline: 4/15. Application fee: $15. *Faculty research:* Controlled release, solid dosage form, screening of anti-HIV drugs, pharmacokinetic/pharmacodynamic of drugs.

University of Rhode Island, College of Pharmacy, Professional Program in Pharmacy, Kingston, RI 02881. Awards Pharm D. Accredited by ACPE. *Application deadline:* 4/15. *Application fee:* $35. *Expenses:* Tuition $3446 per year full-time, $191 per credit part-time for state residents; $9850 per year full-time, $547 per credit part-time for nonresidents. Fees $1276 per year full-time, $135 per semester (minimum) part-time.

University of South Carolina, College of Pharmacy, Professional Program in Pharmacy, Columbia, SC 29208. Awards Pharm D. Accredited by ACPE. Faculty: 16 full-time (2 women). Students: 100 full-time (74 women), 11 part-time (6 women); includes 18 minority (8 African Americans, 8 Asian Americans, 2 Hispanics). Average age 26. In 1997, 55 degrees awarded (100% found work related to degree). *Degree requirements:* 1 foreign language required (computer language can substitute), thesis not required. *Application deadline:* 3/15. *Application fee:* $35. Electronic applications accepted. *Expenses:* Tuition $4482 per year full-time, $221 per credit hour part-time for state residents; $11,676 per year full-time, $556 per credit hour part-time for nonresidents. Fees $525 per year full-time, $237 per semester (minimum) part-time. *Financial aid:* Federal Work-Study and career-related internships or fieldwork available. Financial aid application deadline: 3/15. *Faculty research:* Cancer, heterocyclic chemistry, neuropharmacology. • Vicki Young, Assistant Dean, 803-777-4151. Fax: 803-777-2775.

University of Southern California, School of Pharmacy, Professional Program in Pharmacy, Los Angeles, CA 90033. Awards Pharm D, Pharm D/PhD, Pharm D/MBA. Accredited by ACPE. Students: 665 full-time (484 women); includes 485 minority (7 African Americans, 462 Asian Americans, 15 Hispanics, 1 Native American), 20 international. Average age 25. 802 applicants, 26% accepted. In 1997, 155 degrees awarded. *Application fee:* $55. *Expenses:* Tuition $21,532 per year. Fees $760 per year. *Financial aid:* In 1997–98, 171 fellowships, 52 scholarships were awarded; research assistantships, teaching assistantships, Federal Work-Study, institutionally sponsored loans also available. Aid available to part-time students. Financial aid application deadline: 2/15; applicants required to submit FAFSA. • Dr. Timothy M. Chan, Dean, School of Pharmacy, 213-342-1369.

University of Tennessee, Memphis, College of Pharmacy, Memphis, TN 38163-0002. Awards Pharm D, MS, PhD, Pharm D/PhD. One or more programs accredited by ACPE. MS and PhD offered jointly with the College of Graduate Health Sciences. *Degree requirements:* For Pharm D, computer language required, foreign language and thesis not required; for master's and doctorate, computer language, thesis/dissertation required, foreign language not required. *Entrance requirements:* For Pharm D, PCAT; for master's and doctorate, GRE General Test (minimum combined score of 1500), TOEFL (minimum score 525), minimum GPA of 3.0. Application fee: $0.

The University of Texas at Austin, College of Pharmacy, Professional Program in Pharmacy, San Antonio, TX 78284. Awards Pharm D. Accredited by ACPE. Jointly administered with the University of Texas Health Science Center at San Antonio. *Entrance requirements:* GRE General Test. Application deadline: 1/15. Application fee: $50 ($75 for international students). *Expenses:* Tuition $2592 per year full-time, $324 per semester (minimum) part-time for state residents; $7704 per year full-time, $963 per semester (minimum) part-time for nonresidents. Fees $778 per year full-time, $161 per semester (minimum) part-time.

University of the Pacific, School of Pharmacy, Professional Program in Pharmacy, Stockton, CA 95211-0197. Awards Pharm D, Pharm D/PhD. Accredited by ACPE. Students: 619 full-time (383 women); includes 10 African Americans, 6 international. Average age 24. In 1997, 189 degrees awarded. *Application deadline:* 2/1. *Expenses:* Tuition $28,500 per year full-time, $594 per unit part-time. Fees $30 per year (minimum). *Financial aid:* Partial tuition waivers, Federal Work-Study, institutionally sponsored loans, and career-related internships or fieldwork available. Aid available to part-time students. • Dr. Philip Oppenheimer, Dean, School of Pharmacy, 209-946-2561. Fax: 209-946-2410.

See in-depth description on page 1819.

University of the Sciences in Philadelphia, Philadelphia College of Pharmacy, Professional Program in Pharmacy Practice, Philadelphia, PA 19104-4495. Awards Pharm D. Accredited by ACPE. Faculty: 19 full-time (10 women), 17 part-time (9 women), 22 FTE. Students: 150; includes 13 minority (3 African Americans, 10 Asian Americans). 35 applicants, 69% accepted. *Entrance requirements:* BS in pharmacy from an ACPE-accredited program, license to practice pharmacy in the U.S.. Application deadline: 4/15 (10/24 for spring admission). Application fee: $50. *Financial aid:* Career-related internships or fieldwork available. Aid available to part-time students. Financial aid application deadline: 4/15; applicants required to submit FAFSA. *Faculty research:* Pharmacokinetics, oncology, critical care, pediatrics, cardiology. • Dr. John Connors, Director, 215-596-8973. Fax: 215-895-1185. E-mail: j.connors@pcps.edu. Application contact: Andrea Bagden, Secretary, 215-596-8492.

University of Toledo, College of Pharmacy, Program in Pharmacy, Toledo, OH 43606-3398. Awards Pharm D. Accredited by ACPE. Students: 25 full-time (20 women); includes 1 minority (Asian American), 1 international. Average age 27. 27 applicants, 52% accepted. In 1997, 5 degrees awarded. *Average time to degree:* first professional–2 years full-time. *Entrance requirements:* TOEFL, GRE General Test or minimum GPA of 2.7. Application deadline: 1/15 (priority date). Application fee: $30. Electronic applications accepted. *Tuition:* $5907 per year full-time, $246 per hour part-time for state residents; $11,835 per year full-time, $493 per hour part-time for nonresidents. *Financial aid:* In 1997–98, 15 students received aid, including 13 teaching assistantships (all to first-year students). • Charles Hicks, Chairman, 419-530-1951. E-mail: chicks@utnet.utoledo.edu. Application contact: Kathy Hagmeyer, 419-530-1924. Fax: 419-530-1950. E-mail: khagmey@utnet.utoledo.edu.

University of Utah, College of Pharmacy and Graduate School, Department of Pharmacy Practice, Salt Lake City, UT 84112-1107. Awards MS. *Degree requirements:* Thesis optional.

Directory: Pharmacy; Cross-Discipline Announcements

University of Utah (continued)

Entrance requirements: GRE, undergraduate degree in pharmacy. *Tuition:* $2045 per year full-time, $562 per semester (minimum) part-time for state residents; $6129 per year full-time, $1607 per semester (minimum) part-time for nonresidents.

University of Utah, College of Pharmacy, Professional Program in Pharmacy, Salt Lake City, UT 84112-1107. Awards Pharm D. Accredited by ACPE. *Entrance requirements:* BS in pharmacy. Application deadline: rolling. Application fee: $30 ($50 for international students). *Tuition:* $2045 per year full-time, $562 per semester (minimum) part-time for state residents; $6129 per year full-time, $1607 per semester (minimum) part-time for nonresidents. *Faculty research:* Pain management, pharmacokinetic aspects of antiarrhythmics and anticoagulants, patient compliance.

University of Washington, School of Pharmacy, External Pharmacy Program, Seattle, WA 98195. Awards Pharm D. Accredited by ACPE. Part-time and evening/weekend programs available. Postbaccalaureate distance learning degree programs offered (no on-campus study). Faculty: 13 part-time (6 women), 1 FTE. Students: 253 part-time (166 women). 146 applicants, 99% accepted. *Degree requirements:* Thesis. *Entrance requirements:* Pharmacy license. Application deadline: 3/31 (priority date; 3/31 for spring admission). Application fee: $40. *Tuition:* $5433 per year full-time, $775 per quarter (minimum) part-time for state residents; $13,479 per year full-time, $1925 per quarter (minimum) part-time for nonresidents. • Stanley S. Weber, Director, 206-616-8762. Fax: 206-685-9297. E-mail: weberst@u.washington.edu.

University of Washington, School of Pharmacy, Professional Program in Pharmacy, Seattle, WA 98195. Awards Pharm D. Accredited by ACPE. Students: 213 full-time (156 women); includes 90 minority (6 African Americans, 71 Asian Americans, 9 Hispanics, 4 Native Americans). 504 applicants, 14% accepted. In 1997, 13 degrees awarded. *Degree requirements:* Thesis required, foreign language not required. *Entrance requirements:* PCAT. Application deadline: 2/13. Application fee: $45. *Tuition:* $5433 per year full-time, $775 per quarter (minimum) part-time for state residents; $13,479 per year full-time, $1925 per quarter (minimum) part-time for nonresidents. *Financial aid:* 159 students received aid; partial tuition waivers and career-related internships or fieldwork available. Financial aid application deadline: 2/28; applicants required to submit FAFSA. • Nanci Murphy, Director, Academic and Student Programs, 206-685-2715. E-mail: pharminf@u.washington.edu. Application contact: Office Assistant III, 206-543-2453. Fax: 206-616-2740. E-mail: pharminf@u.washington.edu.

University of Wisconsin–Madison, School of Pharmacy, Professional Program in Pharmacy, Madison, WI 53706-1380. Awards Pharm D. Accredited by ACPE. *Application fee:* $38.

See in-depth description on page 1825.

University of Wisconsin–Madison, School of Pharmacy and Graduate School, Graduate Programs in Pharmacy, Department of Continuing Education in Pharmacy, Madison, WI 53706-1380. Awards PhD. *Degree requirements:* Dissertation. *Application fee:* $38.

See in-depth description on page 1825.

University of Wisconsin–Madison, School of Pharmacy and Graduate School, Graduate Programs in Pharmacy, Department of Hospital Pharmacy, Madison, WI 53706-1380. Awards MS. *Application fee:* $38.

See in-depth description on page 1825.

Virginia Commonwealth University, Medical College of Virginia-Professional Programs, School of Pharmacy, Professional Program in Pharmacy, Richmond, VA 23284-9005. Awards Pharm D, Pharm D/PhD. Accredited by ACPE. Part-time programs available. Students: 323 full-time (251 women), 3 part-time (2 women); includes 106 minority (19 African Americans, 86 Asian Americans, 1 Native American), 2 international. Average age 25. In 1997, 3 degrees awarded. *Degree requirements:* Computer language, research project required, foreign language and thesis not required. *Entrance requirements:* GRE General Test, BS in pharmacy. Application deadline: 2/15 (priority date; rolling processing). *Financial aid:* Institutionally sponsored loans available. Financial aid application deadline: 3/1. *Faculty research:* Oncology, cardiology, infectious diseases, epilepsy, connective tissue. • Application contact: Thomas P. Reinders, Associate Dean, Student Affairs, 804-828-3002. Fax: 804-828-7436. E-mail: tpreinde@vcu.edu.

Washington State University, College of Pharmacy, Department of Pharmaceutical Science, Pullman, WA 99164-1610. Awards Pharm D. Accredited by ACPE. *Application deadline:* 3/1 (rolling processing). *Application fee:* $35. *Tuition:* $5334 per year full-time, $267 per credit hour part-time for state residents; $13,380 per year full-time, $677 per credit hour part-time for nonresidents. *Financial aid:* Application deadline 4/1. • Dr. Richard Okita, Chair.

Wayne State University, College of Pharmacy and Allied Health Professions, Faculty of Pharmacy, Department of Pharmacy Practice, Detroit, MI 48202. Awards Pharm D, MS. One or more programs accredited by ACPE. Part-time programs available. Faculty: 19 full-time (11 women), 7 part-time (1 woman). Students: 17 full-time (8 women), 5 part-time (4 women). 34 applicants, 38% accepted. In 1997, 8 Pharm Ds awarded. *Degree requirements:* For master's, thesis optional, foreign language not required. *Entrance requirements:* For Pharm D, bachelor's degree in pharmacy; for master's, GRE General Test, bachelor's degree in pharmacy. Application fee: $20 ($30 for international students). *Expenses:* Tuition $163 per credit hour for state residents; $355 per credit hour for nonresidents. Fees $498 per year full-time, $114 per semester (minimum) part-time. *Financial aid:* Fellowships, scholarships, and career-related internships or fieldwork available. Aid available to part-time students. • Richard Slaughter, Chairperson, 313-577-0824. Fax: 313-577-5369.

Western University of Health Sciences, College of Pharmacy, Pomona, CA 91766-1854. Awards Pharm D. Candidate for accreditation by ACPE. Faculty: 12. Students: 95. *Application deadline:* 2/1 (priority date; rolling processing). *Application fee:* $60. *Tuition:* $21,570 per year. • Dr. Harry Rosenberg, Dean, 909-469-5549. Application contact: Susan M. Hanson, Director of Admissions, 909-469-5335.

West Virginia University, School of Pharmacy, Professional Program in Pharmacy, Morgantown, WV 26506. Awards Pharm D. Students enter program as undergraduates. Average age 23. *Application deadline:* 3/1 (priority date). *Application fee:* $45. *Tuition:* $4672 per year for state residents; $13,390 per year for nonresidents. • Application contact: Jennifer Clutter, Academic Adviser, 304-293-1552. Fax: 304-293-5483.

Wilkes University, School of Pharmacy, Wilkes-Barre, PA 18766-0002. Awards Pharm D. Candidate for accreditation by ACPE. Faculty: 11 full-time, 1 part-time. Students: 127 full-time (84 women). *Application deadline:* rolling. • Dr. Bernard Graham, Dean, 717-408-4280.

Xavier University of Louisiana, College of Pharmacy, New Orleans, LA 70125-1098. Awards Pharm D. Accredited by ACPE. Part-time and evening/weekend programs available. Postbaccalaureate distance learning degree programs offered (minimal on-campus study). Faculty: 21 full-time (7 women). Students: 3 full-time (all women), 30 part-time (19 women); includes 17 minority (14 African Americans, 3 Asian Americans), 1 international. Average age 33. 16 applicants, 100% accepted. In 1997, 20 degrees awarded. *Average time to degree:* first professional–1 year full-time, 2 years part-time. *Entrance requirements:* BS in pharmacy. Application deadline: 5/15 (priority date; 11/15 for spring admission). Application fee: $25. *Financial aid:* In 1997–98, teaching assistantships averaging $500 per month, 10 grants averaging $500 per month and totaling $20,000 were awarded; institutionally sponsored loans and career-related internships or fieldwork also available. Aid available to part-time students. Financial aid application deadline: 4/1. • Dr. Marcellus Grace, Dean, 504-483-7421. Application contact: Dr. Carlen McLin, Coordinator, 504-483-7425.

Announcement: A center for excellence in pharmaceutical education, Xavier University of Louisiana College of Pharmacy continues to lead the nation in producing African-American pharmacists who are highly trained professionals and leaders in pharmacy. The College offers entry-level and postbaccalaureate Doctor of Pharmacy (PharmD) degrees as its only academic programs. The postbaccalaureate PharmD program is designed for mature, motivated practitioners who wish to update their BS degree to the PharmD. The College is committed to training pharmacists to meet the expanding demand for pharmaceutical care. Xavier's program provides students with new competencies and skills for clinical practice and research.

Cross-Discipline Announcements

University of California, Irvine, College of Medicine and Office of Research and Graduate Studies, Graduate Programs in Medicine, Department of Pharmacology, Irvine, CA 92697.

The PhD program in pharmacology covers most aspects of pharmacology, from the discovery of molecules to their involvement in behavior. The program emphasizes studies on ligand-receptor interactions and offers research in molecular and cellular pharmacology, neuropharmacology, and cardiovascular pharmacology. For more information, see the in-depth description in the pharmacology section of Book 3 of this series.

University of Wisconsin–Madison, Training Program in Biotechnology, Madison, WI 53706-1380.

The University of Wisconsin–Madison offers a predoctoral training program in biotechnology. Trainees receive PhDs in their major field (for example, pharmacy) while receiving extensive cross-disciplinary training through the minor degree. Trainees participate in industrial internships and a weekly student seminar series with other program participants. These experiences reinforce the cross-disciplinary nature of the program. Students choose a major and a minor professor from a list of more than 150 faculty members in 40 different departments who do research related to biotechnology. See in-depth description in the Biochemical Engineering, Bioengineering, and Biotechnology section of the Engineering and Applied Sciences volume of this series.

DUQUESNE UNIVERSITY

Graduate School of Pharmaceutical Sciences

Programs of Study

The Graduate School of Pharmaceutical Sciences offers the Ph.D. and M.S. degrees in pharmaceutics, pharmaceutical chemistry, medicinal chemistry, and pharmacology-toxicology. In conjunction with the Graduate School of Business Administration, the department offers an M.B.A./M.S. in industrial pharmacy, an 81-credit, nonthesis program, requiring concurrent graduate-level enrollment in both business administration and the pharmaceutical sciences. Fifty-six credits in core business administration course work and 25 credits of course work in the pharmaceutical sciences are required. M.S. programs require a minimum of 30 postbaccalaureate semester hours; 24 credits are for course work, including 2 credits of seminar, and an additional 6 credits are for thesis research. Ph.D. programs require a minimum of 60 postbaccalaureate semester hours; 54 credits are for course work, including 4 credits of seminar, and an additional 6 credits are for dissertation research. Each Ph.D. candidate must demonstrate the ability to read technical literature in an approved foreign language by passing examinations as required.

Research Facilities

The Graduate School of Pharmaceutical Sciences is located in the Richard King Mellon Hall of Science. Laboratory instrumentation includes nuclear magnetic resonance spectrometers, infrared spectrometers, near-infrared spectrometers, ultraviolet-visible spectrophotometers, atomic absorption spectrophotometers, gas chromatographs, high-pressure liquid chromatographs, rheometers, dissolution and disintegration testing equipment. Recent additions are a benchtop quadrupole GC-mass spectrometer with electron impact and positive ion chemical ionizations; liquid chromatograph with UV diode array and refractive index detectors; capillary electrophoresis with UV diode array detector; and Evans and Sutherland PS360, Silicon Graphics Indigo^2 Extreme graphics, and Power Macintosh and Pentium Pro systems, with appropriate peripherals, software for molecular and macromolecular three-dimensional modeling, and protein crystal structure databases. Mellon Hall facilities include a fully equipped manufacturing laboratory/pilot plant with slant cone and high shear mixers, a microfluidizer, fluid bed and spray dryers, coaters, a capsule filling machine, and fully computer controlled/monitored 38-station Hata tablet press. Modern animal facilities in adjacent Bayer Hall provide the opportunity for physiological, pharmacological, and toxicologic evaluations of drugs and chemicals. The Gumberg Library at Duquesne houses a state-of-the-art integrated, online library system complete with a computerized card catalog, advanced computer disk (CD-ROM) system, online networked databases, and array of technical support functions. The system enables students to access extensive local, national, and international databases and library catalogs around the world. Students have direct access to other university and research libraries in the Pittsburgh area.

Financial Aid

Teaching and research assistantships, which may include full remission of tuition and fees, are available.

Cost of Study

In 1998–99, tuition is $507 per credit, plus a University fee of $37 per credit.

Living and Housing Costs

For 1998–99, room and board at University dormitories cost $5978 per student per academic year for double occupancy. Food and clothing costs are similar to those in other cities of comparable size. The University offers a Student Health Care program, required for all international students.

Student Group

The University enrolls 9,500 students; typically, 45–50 students, representing a mix of U.S. (32 percent) and international (68 percent), are enrolled in graduate programs in the Graduate School of Pharmaceutical Sciences.

Student Outcomes

Most recent M.S. graduates have continued studies at the doctoral level or are employed in a variety of research laboratory settings. Graduates of Ph.D. programs are employed in research and administrative positions in industry and in research and teaching in academia.

Location

Allegheny County has a population in excess of 1 million; one third live in the city of Pittsburgh. Downtown is headquarters for many major corporations and the hub of cultural and recreational activities. Pittsburgh fields professional teams in football, baseball, and hockey. Perhaps the most engaging quality is the "hometown" flavor of the many neighborhoods that comprise Pittsburgh.

The University

Duquesne is a private, Catholic, coeducational university and has been listed as one of the top ten national Catholic universities in the country. The 43-acre campus overlooks the Monongahela River. Students and 397 full-time faculty members are organized into the College and Graduate School of Liberal Arts; and Schools of Pharmacy, Nursing, Law, Business Administration, Education, Music, Health Sciences, and Natural and Environmental Sciences. All campus facilities have been refurbished, with recent additions of current computer labs, a multipurpose athletic complex, and a student living-learning center. The University supports many intercollegiate and intramural athletics programs. The Tamburitzans and the Red Masquers are well established ethnic dance and theatrical groups.

Applying

Students are admitted for the fall or spring semester. Assistantships are normally awarded in spring for the following academic year. Applicants should have earned a baccalaureate degree in chemistry, biology, or pharmacy, depending on the proposed field of study. Any deficiencies in undergraduate course work must be resolved. Challenge examinations are not accepted for graduate credit. The completed application and supporting documents (official transcripts of all undergraduate and graduate course work, a brief statement of purpose and intent with regard to the specific area of graduate study chosen, three letters of recommendation from persons acquainted with the academic abilities of the applicant, and results of the GRE General Test) must be sent to the director. Applicants whose native language or principal language of instruction is not English are required to submit TOEFL scores to the Graduate School and to sit for on-campus English language testing. International students who are applying for a teaching assistantship are required to submit TSE scores.

Correspondence and Information

Director
Graduate School of Pharmaceutical Sciences
School of Pharmacy
Duquesne University
Pittsburgh, Pennsylvania 15282
Telephone: 412-396-5662

Duquesne University

THE FACULTY AND THEIR RESEARCH

Medicinal Chemistry

Aleem Gangjee, Professor of Medicinal Chemistry; Ph.D., Iowa. Synthetic medicinal chemistry, computer-assisted drug design, inhibitors of folate metabolizing enzymes, antitumor agents related to folates, antiopportunistic infection agents, nucleosides, heterocyclic chemistry and stereochemistry.

Marc W. Harrold, Associate Professor of Medicinal Chemistry; Ph.D., Ohio State. Synthetic medicinal chemistry, myoinositol 1–phosphatase inhibitors, drug design, development of computer-based educational tools.

Pui-Kai Li, Associate Professor of Medicinal Chemistry; Ph.D., Ohio State. Estrone sulfatase inhibitors, synthesis and biological testing of aromatase inhibitors, male antifertility agents.

Pharmaceutical Chemistry and Pharmaceutics

Christianah M. Adeyeye, Associate Professor of Pharmaceutics; Ph.D., Georgia. Preformulation, development, stability, and bioavailability evaluation of sustained released liquid, semisolid, and solid dosage forms, excipient characterization, biopharmaceutical technology, and unit process optimization.

Lawrence H. Block, Professor of Pharmaceutics; Ph.D., Maryland. Theoretical aspects of pharmacokinetics and pharmacodynamics, controlled and modified release, drug and cosmetic delivery system development, biopolymer modifications for delivery system optimization, hydrogels for electrically modulated drug delivery, multiphase emulsions.

Riccardo L. Boni, Assistant Professor of Pharmaceutical Chemistry; Ph.D., Manitoba. Development and application of analytical methods used in pharmaceutical analysis, with emphasis on GC/MS and LC/MS.

Charles C. Collins, Associate Professor of Pharmaceutics; Ph.D., West Virginia. Pharmacokinetics, dissolution technology development and evaluation, solid dosage form development and excipient evaluation, controlled release technology, biopharmaceutics, bioadhesive evaluation, drug delivery system quality control, in vivo/in vitro correlations.

James K. Drennen III, Associate Professor of Pharmaceutics; Ph.D., Kentucky. Pharmaceutical and medical applications of near-infrared spectroscopy.

Pharmacology and Toxicology

J. Douglas Bricker, Associate Professor of Pharmacology and Toxicology; Ph.D., Duquesne. Effects of drugs, chemicals, and disease states on the regulation of calcium uptake mechanisms, development and screening of antidotal agents for clinical use, and in vitro toxicity testing methods.

Frederick W. Fochtman, Associate Professor of Pharmacology and Toxicology; Ph.D., Duquesne. Analytical toxicology, clinical and forensic toxicology, forensic urine drug testing.

David A. Johnson, Associate Professor of Pharmacology and Toxicology; Ph.D., Massachusetts College of Pharmacy. Drugs that enhance the function of neuronal pathways involved with learning and memory, neuropathology and treatment of eating disorders.

Scott F. Long, Assistant Professor of Pharmacology and Toxicology; Ph.D., Mississippi. Behavioral pharmacology and metabolic disposition of drugs of abuse with emphasis on cocaine and anabolic-androgenic steroids, cardiovascular pharmacology and toxicology of anabolic-androgenic steroids, toxicology of agricultural chemicals.

Charles L. Winek, Professor of Toxicology; Ph.D., Ohio State. Forensic toxicology, medical-legal aspects of toxicological problems, drug concentrations in bone marrow, factors affecting blood alcohol concentrations.

Paula A. Witt-Enderby, Assistant Professor of Pharmacology and Toxicology; Ph.D., Arizona. Molecular pharmacology of melatonin receptors with emphasis on the regulation of receptors, second messengers, and gene regulation

FLORIDA AGRICULTURAL AND MECHANICAL UNIVERSITY

College of Pharmacy and Pharmaceutical Sciences Graduate Programs in Pharmaceutical Sciences and Public Health

Program of Study

The College of Pharmacy and Pharmaceutical Sciences offers a comprehensive program of course work and research leading to the Master of Public Health (M.P.H.) degree and the Ph.D. and M.S. degrees in pharmaceutical sciences with concentrations in pharmacology/toxicology, medicinal chemistry, environmental toxicology (Ph.D. only), and pharmaceutics. The course of study is designed to give students a strong background in modern principles of their chosen area of specialization and in a variety of research subspecialties. Theoretical principles are presented, and application of these principles in research is emphasized. Students may pursue research in any of the areas of specialization of the faculty members listed on the reverse of this page. The student selects a research adviser and, in conjunction with that adviser, proposes a program of study, presents a tentative thesis/dissertation subject and outline, and selects a committee that oversees his or her progress in research. At least 3 faculty members sit on an M.S. advisory committee and at least 5 on a Ph.D. committee. After completion of course work, the student takes a comprehensive written exam; doctoral students must also take a comprehensive oral exam. During the course of their research, students are required to make presentations at national meetings. Students seeking the M.S. are required to complete at least one paper for publication in a refereed scientific journal; students seeking the Ph.D. are required to complete at least two. Final degree requirements include completion of a thesis (M.S. candidates) or dissertation (Ph.D. candidates) on research conducted by the student and a public oral defense of the work. Students seeking the M.P.H. degree must do so through the Institute of Public Health. They must select an adviser and complete a special project in public health.

The College provides research internships at pharmaceutical research laboratories, as well as federal research laboratories. Graduate students are encouraged to gain research experience in these laboratories.

Research Facilities

The College is housed in the Dyson Pharmacy Building, and most of the research laboratories are housed in the new state-of-the-art Science Research Facility. This building also houses an animal facility, a biomedical research library, and all the infrastructure needed for research. Major laboratory equipment includes a mass spectrometer, a scintillation counter, an ultracentrifuge (L8-80M), environmental chambers, gas and liquid chromatographs, a spectrofluorometer, and a variety of physiographs. Recent additions include a computer-assisted Perkin-Elmer 1480 spectrophotometer, an EM360 NMR spectrometer, a Perkin-Elmer 3030 atomic absorption spectrometer, and a Beckman DU-65 UV-VIS spectrophotometer. The College also maintains two off-campus facilities in Miami and Tampa, Florida. Clinical research and student training are conducted at these campuses.

Financial Aid

Stipends paying from $14,200 to $16,200 per year are available in the form of research assistantships, work-study funds, and fellowships for qualified students. Tuition waivers may also be available. Students in need of financial assistance should indicate this in a letter accompanying their application for admission.

Cost of Study

In 1998–99, graduate tuition is $140 per semester credit hour for in-state students and $484 per semester credit hour for out-of-state students. These fees are subject to change.

Living and Housing Costs

Dormitory rooms rent for $995 to $1755 per semester in 1998–99. Apartments are available in University-owned married student housing. Off-campus housing is available at a wide range of prices in locations throughout the city.

Student Group

Total enrollment in the College of Pharmacy and Pharmaceutical Sciences is approximately 700 graduate and undergraduate students. While the academic backgrounds of the graduate students are varied, they include undergraduate degrees in scientific fields such as pharmacy, biology, chemistry, and microbiology.

Location

Tallahassee has a population of approximately 268,000. It is the capital of Florida and the home of two state universities and a community college. These institutions support a wide variety of cultural, social, and recreational activities. In addition, the Civic Center makes the city a regional entertainment center. The beaches of the north Florida coasts are easily reached from Tallahassee.

The University and The College

Florida A&M University was founded in 1887 and currently comprises eleven schools and colleges and a School of Graduate Studies, Research, and Continuing Education. The University was named College of the Year in 1997 by *Time Magazine Princeton Review.* The College of Pharmacy and Pharmaceutical Sciences has achieved national and international prominence in various areas of research and each year sponsors a highly successful clinical pharmacy symposium that addresses clinical research aspects in areas of current interest in medicine, pharmacy, and the pharmaceutical sciences. The College is one of the top schools of pharmacy in the nation in attracting National Institutes of Health research funds.

Applying

Applications are accepted for the fall semester only. Applications should be received on or before the end of April. All applicants must have a bachelor's degree from an accredited college or university. A minimum cumulative grade point average of 3.0 in the last 60 semester hours while working for a baccalaureate degree or a minimum combined score of 1000 on the quantitative and verbal sections of the General Test of the Graduate Record Examinations is required for admission to the M.S. and M.P.H. programs. Applicants to the Ph.D. program must have both a GPA of at least 3.0 and a combined GRE General Test score of 1000 or must have an M.S. degree from an accredited institution. Regardless of their GPA, all students must take the GRE and have their scores on record as part of the admission process. While the GPA and the GRE scores are important, the Graduate Committee considers other factors such as the availability of space and letters of recommendation.

Correspondence and Information

Dean, College of Pharmacy and Pharmaceutical Sciences
Florida Agricultural and Mechanical University
Tallahassee, Florida 32307-3800
Telephone: 850-599-3301

Florida Agricultural and Mechanical University

THE FACULTY AND THEIR RESEARCH

Medicinal Chemistry

Seth Y. Ablordeppey, Associate Professor; Ph.D., Mississippi, 1990. Molecular modeling, drug design and synthesis.
James L. Day, Professor; Ph.D., Ohio State, 1966. Pharmacokinetics of anticancer drugs.
Surendar S. Lamba, Professor; Ph.D., Colorado, 1966. Pharmacognosy and antisickling drugs.
Henry Lee, Professor; Ph.D., Oklahoma State, 1971. Biochemistry, synthesis of medicinal compounds and anti-inflammatory steroids.
R. Renee Reams Brown, Assistant Professor; Ph.D., Brigham Young, 1984. Protein chemistry and biological calorimetry.
K. Ken Redda, Professor; Ph.D., Alberta, 1978. Synthesis of anticancer compounds, drug metabolism.

Pharmaceutics

Ahmed F. Asker, Professor; Ph.D., Florida, 1964. Industrial pharmaceutics and product development.
Godfried Owusu-Ababio, Associate Professor; Ph.D., Alberta, 1994. Pharmaceutics and biopharmaceutics, controlled release, polymeric drug-delivery systems.
Mandip S. Sachdeva, Assistant Professor; Ph.D., Dalhousie, 1989. Formulation and in vivo evaluation of targeted drug-delivery systems.
Saber Samaan, Associate Professor; Ph.D., London, 1981. Drug pharmacokinetics and chronopharmacology.
Lambros Tterlikkis, Professor; Ph.D., California, Riverside, 1968. Biopharmaceutics and pharmacokinetics of anticancer drugs.

Pharmacology/Toxicology/Environmental Toxicology

Karam F. Soliman, Distinguished Professor and Assistant Dean for Research; Ph.D., Georgia, 1972. Neuroendocrine pharmacology, adrenal pharmacology, neuropharmacology of drug abuse.
Clivel Charlton, Professor; Ph.D., Howard, 1983. Neuropharmacology, neurodegenerative disorders, the methylation process in aging and Parkinson's disease.
Thomas J. Fitzgerald, Professor; Ph.D., Ohio State, 1965. Molecular pharmacology, microtubules, antimitotic agents.
Carl B. Goodman, Assistant Professor; Ph.D., Florida A&M, 1992. Drugs of abuse, neurotoxicology/neuropharmacology.
Ann S. Heiman, Professor; Ph.D., Florida, 1984. Immunopharmacology, pharmacologic modulation of activation-coupling events.
Maurice S. Holder, Associate Professor; Ph.D., Howard, 1978. Cardiovascular physiology, angiotensin, antihypertensive drugs, calcium channel blockers.
Malak G. Kolta, Professor; Ph.D., Auburn, 1982. Neuropharmacology/neurotoxicology, drugs of abuse, diabetes.
Ebenezer T. Oriaku, Associate Professor; Ph.D., Florida A&M, 1991. Neuropharmacology/gastrointestinal pharmacology, biochemical pharmacology.
Donald Palm, Assistant Professor; Ph.D., Penn State, 1991. Neuropharmacology, stroke and cardiovascular research, neurodegenerative diseases.
Magdi R. I. Soliman, Professor; Ph.D., Georgia, 1972. Neuropharmacology, chronopharmacology and chronobiotic research.
Farid K. R. Stino, Professor; Ph.D., Georgia, 1971. Pharmacogenetics, experimental design and biostatistics.
Ronald Thomas, Assistant Professor; Ph.D., Alabama, 1995. Environmental/estrogen-induced carcinogenesis.

Public Health

Cynthia M. Harris, Associate Professor and Director; Ph.D., Meharry, 1985; DABT. Nutritional biochemistry, environmental toxicology, risk assessment, risk communication.
C. Perry Brown, Associate Professor; Dr.Ph.H., UCLA, 1982. Chronic disease prevention, HIV epidemiology and prevention.
Adrienne L. Hollis, Assistant Professor; Ph.D., Meharry, 1988. Nutritional biochemistry, environmental health science, inhalation toxicology.

MASSACHUSETTS COLLEGE OF PHARMACY AND ALLIED HEALTH SCIENCES

Graduate Studies

Programs of Study

The College's small size encourages close relationships between students and faculty members. Through an integrated curriculum, programs of graduate study in the pharmaceutical sciences are designed on an individual basis, depending on the academic background and research interests of the student. Course work at other institutions is encouraged. Students may select their own research advisers and projects, and interdisciplinary studies may be arranged.

The College offers graduate programs leading to the M.S. and Ph.D. degrees in organic/medicinal, analytical medicinal, and bioorganic chemistry, pharmaceutics/industrial pharmacy, and pharmacology.

Organic/medicinal, analytical medicinal, and bioorganic chemistry offers a challenging interdisciplinary approach to study the effects of modifying the chemical structure of a drug on its biological activity, to develop a method for the analysis of drugs in pharmaceutical and biological systems, or to study the isolation of natural substances from plant material for potential therapeutic use.

Specialization in pharmaceutics or industrial pharmacy offers a crafted balance between theoretical foundations and practical applications to study the approaches for the development of drug delivery systems, formulation development, product development and evaluation, and the pharmacokinetics of a drug and its formulation.

Pharmacology is the medical science that involves all facets of the effects drugs and environmental chemicals have on biological systems and their constituent parts. It includes everything from the intermolecular reactions of chemical compounds within a cell to the evaluation of the effectiveness of a drug in the prevention, diagnosis, and treatment of human disease.

The M.S. degree requires a minimum of 30 semester hours of credit, a thesis based on original research, and a final oral examination. The Ph.D. degree requires 50 hours of course and research credit, one skill, major and minor qualifying examinations, a dissertation based on original research, and a final oral examination.

Research Facilities

The research facilities are well equipped for each of the areas of specialization. In addition, there are such specialized facilities as a suite for radioisotope research and a product development laboratory equipped for tableting, coating, encapsulation, and the manufacture of liquids, ointments, and sterile products. Instruments available include infrared, ultraviolet, and nuclear magnetic resonance spectrometers, gas chromatographs, and high-pressure liquid chromatographs. Computer and animal facilities are also available. In addition, research instrument facilities are available at other institutions in the Greater Boston/Cambridge area. The Sheppard Library contains approximately 70,000 volumes and receives more than 700 periodicals. Graduate students and faculty may also use the facilities of other nearby university libraries.

Financial Aid

Graduate students receive financial assistance from the College in the form of graduate assistantships, Bradbury-White tuition scholarships or faculty research grants and contracts. Personal sources or other non-College sources may also be available. In 1997–98, stipends for teaching and research assistantships ranged from $10,000 to $11,000 for nine months, depending on experience. Summer assistantships are also available. Tuition is remitted for teaching assistants; Bradbury-White partial-tuition scholarships are available for those students without teaching assistantships and are awarded on a competitive basis according to merit. Research assistantships, when available, are awarded on an individual basis. Applications for assistantships should be addressed to the Dean for Graduate Studies. New students are expected to support themselves during their first year of study.

Cost of Study

In 1997–98, tuition for graduate students was $506 per semester hour with a total average course load of 12–15 semester hours for first-year students. A health plan is also available at a cost to the student.

Living and Housing Costs

College housing is not available, but apartments and rooms are available in the metropolitan Boston area and in the immediate Longwood Medical Area. The large number of students in the area makes sharing apartments feasible, at costs that are affordable for graduate students. The estimated cost of food, housing, books and supplies, personal expenses, and transportation for a single student is $11,000 for twelve months.

Student Group

The College has an enrollment of approximately 1,700 students, 35 of whom are in the pharmaceutical sciences graduate program. The average number of students in chemistry is 8; in pharmacology, 12; and in pharmaceutics/industrial pharmacy, 15.

Student Outcomes

Over the past three years, 80 percent of the graduates of the program have entered the pharmaceutical industry as research scientists in their respective disciplines. The remainder have gone on to medical school, postdoctorate study, government research laboratories, or academia.

Location

Boston, a center of internationally renowned teaching hospitals, research centers, and universities and colleges, is an invigorating and stimulating environment in which to live and learn. Boston is a home of the arts and provides numerous cultural and social opportunities, including classical and jazz concerts, opera, ballet, museums, theaters, and professional sports; outdoor activities are abundant.

The College

The Massachusetts College of Pharmacy was founded in 1823. It is a private, coeducational institution located in the Longwood Medical Area, which offers an educational, professional, and cultural environment and a unique opportunity for graduate study. The George Robert White building was constructed on the present site during 1917–18 and serves both undergraduate and graduate students. The T. Iorio Science Building provides new facilities for research and graduate instruction.

Applying

Application forms, available on request, should be received before February 1 for September admission. Students are usually matriculated in September. Candidates for graduate degrees must hold a bachelor's degree in biology, chemistry, pharmacy, or another field acceptable to the Graduate Council. Applicants must submit a letter of intent outlining the goals of their education and their career objectives. Scores from the GRE General Test must be submitted. Students from countries in which English has not been the primary educational language must submit TSE scores. Detailed information can be obtained by contacting the address below.

Correspondence and Information

Coordinator of Graduate Admissions
Massachusetts College of Pharmacy and Allied Health Sciences
179 Longwood Avenue
Boston, Massachusetts 02115

Telephone: 617-732-2850
Fax: 617-732-2801
E-mail: admissions@mcp.edu
World Wide Web: http://www.mcp.edu/gs/gs.htm

Massachusetts College of Pharmacy and Allied Health Sciences

THE FACULTY AND THEIR RESEARCH

A. A. Belmonte, Professor of Pharmaceutics, Provost, and Dean of the College; Ph.D., Connecticut.
D. A. Williams, Professor of Chemistry and Dean for Graduate Studies; Ph.D., Minnesota. Organic and analytical medicinal chemistry, methods development and photochemical stability.

Organic/Medicinal Chemistry and Analytical Medicinal Chemistry Research Faculty

Current research activity includes the organic synthesis of biologically active molecules, mechanistic enzymology, the analysis and stability of drugs in pharmaceuticals, the synthesis of laser dyes for the life sciences, and the isolation and characterization of plant substances.

W. O. Foye, Emeritus Professor of Pharmaceutical Sciences; Ph.D., Indiana. Organic chemistry and biochemistry, sulfur-containing compounds, metal-binding agents, anticancer agents.
L. M. Gracz, Assistant Professor of Chemistry; Ph.D., California, Santa Barbara. Biochemical pharmacology.
C. J. Kelley, Associate Professor of Chemistry; Ph.D., Indiana. Organic synthesis and natural products structure identification.
S. G. Kerr, Assistant Professor of Medicinal Chemistry; Ph.D., SUNY at Buffalo. Nucleoside chemistry and mechanistic enzymology of DNA polymerases.
A. S. Mehanna, Assistant Professor of Chemistry; Ph.D., Pittsburgh. Design and synthesis of cardiovascular and blood-substitute agents.

Industrial Pharmacy/Pharmaceutics Research Faculty

Typical research activities include formulation development, novel drug delivery systems, transdermal delivery systems, process technology improvement, product development and evaluation, and pharmacokinetics.

H. N. Bhargava, Professor of Industrial Pharmacy; Ph.D., North Dakota State. Product formulation and process development of pharmaceutical and cosmetic products.
T. Ghosh, Associate Professor of Pharmaceutics; Ph.D., Northeast Louisiana. Transdermal and novel drug delivery systems.
S. S. Jambhekar, Associate Professor of Industrial Pharmacy; Ph.D., Nebraska. Sustained release, dissolution, product stability, complexation.

Pharmacology Research Faculty

Current departmental research includes central nervous system neurotransmitter pharmacology, behavioral and neuropharmacology, nutritional pharmacology, cardiovascular pharmacology, pulmonary physiology and drug metabolism.

I. Acworth, Adjunct Assistant Professor of Pharmacology; D.Phil., Oxford. Neurochemistry.
D. W. James, Associate Professor of Pharmacology; Ph.D., University of the Pacific. Cardiovascular physiology, general pharmacology.
L. J. Kelly, Associate Professor of Physiology; Ph.D., Johns Hopkins. Cardiovascular and pulmonary physiology.
D. C. Kosegarten, Associate Professor of Pharmacology; Ph.D., Rhode Island. Cardiovascular pharmacology, isolated-organ preparations, experimental hypertension.
B. LeDuc, Assistant Professor of Pharmacology; Ph.D., Tufts. Drug metabolism.
K. W. Locke, Adjunct Associate Professor of Pharmacology; Ph.D., Emory. Behavioral and neuropharmacology.
T. J. Maher, Sawyer Professor of Pharmaceutical Sciences and Director, Division of Pharmaceutical Sciences; Ph.D., Massachusetts College of Pharmacy. Central nervous system transmitter pharmacology.
M. Zdanowicz, Assistant Professor of Pharmacology; Ph.D., St. John's. Role of growth factors in musculoskeletal diseases.

Additional Graduate Faculty

J. M. DeMott, Assistant Professor of Chemistry; Ph.D., Lowell. Analytical and electroanalytical chemistry.
A. R. Garafalo, Professor of Chemistry; Ph.D., Northeastern. Teaching methodology.
E. Krupat, Professor of Psychology; Ph.D., Michigan. Environmental and social psychology.
V. Wootten, Assistant Professor of Biology; Ph.D., Purdue. Neurotoxicology.
R. Zackroff, Assistant Professor of Biology; Ph.D., Temple. Cell biology.

NORTHEASTERN UNIVERSITY

Bouvé College of Pharmacy and Health Sciences

Programs of Study

Bouvé College of Pharmacy and Health Sciences offers graduate programs in the biomedical sciences; in speech language pathology and audiology; in the cardiopulmonary sciences; in counseling, rehabilitation, and special education; and in health professions. The College offers the following graduate programs: Doctor of Philosophy (Ph.D.) in biomedical science, with specializations in medical laboratory science, medicinal chemistry, interdisciplinary pharmaceutics, pharmacology, and toxicology, and Doctor of Philosophy (Ph.D.) in school and counseling psychology. The Certificate of Advanced Graduate Study (C.A.G.S.) is available in counseling psychology, school psychology, and rehabilitation counseling. The Master of Science (M.S.) degree is offered in applied behavior analysis, applied educational psychology with specialties in school counseling and school psychology, clinical exercise physiology, college student development and counseling, counseling psychology, rehabilitation counseling, speech-language pathology, audiology, perfusion technology, general biomedical sciences, medical laboratory science, medicinal chemistry, and pharmacology. The Master of Science in Education (M.S.Ed.) is offered in special needs and intensive special needs. The Master of Health Professions (M.H.P.) is offered with the following options: general, health policy, physician assistant, and regulatory toxicology. Also offered are nondegree programs in special education, school counseling, and school psychology.

Research Facilities

Research at Bouvé College of Pharmacy and Health Sciences is broad in range and diverse in approach. The Department of Speech-Language Pathology and Audiology maintains laboratory facilities that provide the space and equipment needed to complete research projects. These facilities have state-of-the-art signal-generation equipment with computer-assisted data management and analysis. The College maintains the Cardiovascular Health and Exercise Center. This professional clinic serves the University and the Boston community, developing individualized fitness and cardiopulmonary risk education programs. Mugar Life Science Building houses modern, well-equipped laboratories as well as the animal-care facilities, molecular modeling center, Center for Drug Targeting, the Barnett Institute of Chemical Analysis and Materials Science, and the laboratories of the Departments of Biology and Pharmacy. University libraries contain more than 808,000 volumes, 1.8 million microforms, 170,000 government documents, 8,900 serial subscriptions, and 16,000 audio, video, and software titles. A central library contains online technologically sophisticated services, a gateway to external networked information resources, and a network of CD-ROM optical disc databases. Students also have access to research collections through the Boston Library Consortium.

Financial Aid

Northeastern University awards need-based financial aid to graduate students through the Federal Perkins Loan, Federal Work-Study, and Federal Stafford Student Loan programs and also offers a limited number of minority fellowships and Martin Luther King Jr. Scholarships. Need-based financial aid is available only to U.S. citizens or permanent residents of the United States; all applicants must file a Free Application for Federal Student Aid (FAFSA), a Northeastern University financial aid application, and a financial aid transcript from their undergraduate institution.

Bouvé College of Pharmacy and Health Sciences provides financial assistance through a limited number of teaching, research, and administrative assistantship awards that include tuition remission and a stipend typically ranging from $9750 to $12,075. These assistantships require a maximum of 20 hours of work per week. Also available are a number of tuition assistantships that provide partial or full tuition remission and require a maximum of 10 hours of work per week.

Cost of Study

The cost of tuition for the 1998–99 academic year in the Bouvé College of Pharmacy and Health Sciences is $440 per quarter hour of credit. Where applicable, special tuition charges are made for thesis, dissertation, teaching, practicums, or fieldwork. A booklet listing all fees and tuition costs is available upon request from the address below.

Living and Housing Costs

For 1998–99, quarterly on-campus room rates for a single bedroom range from $1340 to $1715. A single efficiency apartment is $2040 to $2325. A shared bedroom in an apartment ranges from $1630 to $1775 per quarter. While there are several board options available, graduate students typically pay approximately $1085 per quarter for a 10-meal-per-week plan. Off-campus living accommodations also exist in the vicinity of the University.

Student Group

Approximately 19,690 undergraduate and 4,634 graduate students were enrolled at Northeastern University in fall 1997, representing a wide variety of academic, professional, geographic, and cultural backgrounds. Bouvé College of Pharmacy and Health Sciences graduate programs enroll 677 students; 474 attend on a full-time basis.

Location

Boston, the capital of Massachusetts, offers students many academic, cultural, and recreational opportunities. In addition to the abundant resources available within Northeastern University, students have access to the resources of the other educational and cultural institutions of the Greater Boston area. The city is home to people of every intellectual, political, economic, racial, ethnic, and religious background. Boston is a mixture of Colonial tradition and modern technology. It is a place where the past is appreciated, the present enjoyed, and the future anticipated.

The University and The College

Founded in 1898, Northeastern University is a privately endowed nonsectarian institution of higher learning and is among the largest private universities in the country. Today, Northeastern has seven colleges, nine graduate and professional schools, two part-time undergraduate divisions, a number of continuing and special education programs and institutes, several suburban campuses, and an extensive research division. The College offers many exciting clinical and research programs and opportunity for interdisciplinary learning.

Applying

Admission to some programs is granted on a rolling basis. Applicants must have the appropriate educational and professional background and must complete all admissions procedures for the selected programs of study. Test requirements vary by program and degree. TOEFL scores (minimum score of 600) are required of those applicants whose native language is not English. Interested students should contact the address below for information regarding testing requirements. All Ph.D. programs have application deadlines as well as speech language pathology and audiology and counseling psychology. Please refer to program information. Application materials for other master's programs must be submitted at least one month prior to registration.

Correspondence and Information

William Purnell, Director of Graduate Admissions
Bouvé College of Pharmacy and Health Sciences
203 Mugar Life Science Building
Northeastern University–P9
Boston, Massachusetts 02115

Telephone: 617-373-2708
E-mail: w.purnell@nunet.neu.edu

Northeastern University

THE FACULTY

Department of Cardiopulmonary Sciences
Mary E. Watson, Associate Professor and Chairperson; Ed.D., Boston University.

Thomas A. Barnes, Associate Professor; Ed.D., Nova.
Marilyn A. Cairns, Associate Professor; Sc.D., Boston University.
William Jay Gillespie, Associate Professor; Ed.D., Boston University.
Patrick F. Plunkett, Associate Professor; Ed.D., Northeastern.

Department of Counseling Psychology, Rehabilitation, and Special Education
Emanuel J. Mason, Professor and Chairperson; Ph.D., Temple.

Carmen Armengol, Assistant Professor; Ph.D., Penn State.
Mary B. Ballou, Associate Professor; Ph.D., Kent State.
Patricia M. Fetter, Associate Professor; Ph.D., Syracuse.
Deborah Greenwald, Associate Professor; Ph.D., Michigan.
Thomas F. Harrington, Professor; Ph.D., Purdue.
Louis J. Kruger, Assistant Professor; Psy.D., Rutgers.
Louise LaFontaine, Associate Professor; Ed.D., Boston University.
Chieh Li, Assistant Professor; Ed.D., Massachusetts at Amherst.
Karin Lifter, Associate Professor; Ph.D., Columbia.
Lawrence Litwack, Professor; Ed.D., Boston University.
Barbara F. Okun, Professor; Ph.D., Northwestern.
William G. Quill, Associate Professor; Ed.D., Massachusetts at Amherst.
William Sanchez, Assistant Professor; Ph.D., Boston University.
James F. Scorzelli, Professor; Ph.D., Wisconsin.
Ena Vazquez-Nuttall, Professor; Ed.D., Boston University.

Department of Health Professionals
Jean Ellis, Lecturer; M.P.H., Yale.
Suzanne B. Greenberg, Program Director; M.S., Simmons.
Frances Grodstein, Lecturer; Sc.D., Harvard.
Rosann M. Ippolito, Senior Clinical Specialist; M.P.H., PA-C, Northeastern.
James McKensy, Lecturer; M.S., Yale.
Susan Moore, Lecturer; M.H.P., Georgia Tech.
Robert Schatz, Associate Professor; Ph.D., Michigan.
Thomas J. Williams, Associate Clinical Specialist; M.P.H., Northeastern.

Department of Medical Laboratory Science
Britta L. Karlson, Associate Professor; M.S., Northeastern.

Department of Pharmaceutical Sciences
Mehdi Boroujerdi, Professor and Acting Chairperson; Ph.D., North Carolina.

Abdul B. Abou-Samra, Adjunct Associate Professor of Pharmacology; M.D., Aleppo; D.Sc., Lyons.
Mansoor M. Amiji, Assistant Professor; Ph.D., Purdue.
Norman R. Boisse, Associate Professor; Ph.D., Cornell.
Richard C. Deth, Professor; Ph.D., Miami (Florida).
Jonathan E. Freedman, Assistant Professor; Ph.D., Johns Hopkins.
Roger W. Giese, Professor; Ph.D., MIT.
James J. Gozzo, Adjunct Professor; Ph.D., Boston College.
Robert N. Hanson, Professor; Ph.D., Berkeley.
Ban-An Khaw, Professor; Ph.D., Boston College.
Ralph H. Loring, Clinical Associate Professor; Ph.D., Cornell.
Eric J. Mack, Assistant Professor; Ph.D., Utah.
Robert A. Schatz, Associate Professor; Ph.D., Rhode Island.
Barbara L. Waszczak, Associate Professor; Michigan.
Keith J. Watling, Adjunct Associate Professor of Pharmacology; Ph.D., Southampton.

Department of Pharmacy Practice
Samuel J. Matthews, Associate Professor and Interim Chairperson; Pharm.D., Minnesota.

Judith Barr, Associate Professor; Sc.D., Harvard.
Todd Brown, Clinical Assistant Specialist; B.S., Northeastern.
Robert J. Cersosimo, Associate Professor; Pharm.D., Utah.
Deb Copeland, Lecturer; Pharm.D., Rhode Island.
Jeanne Lucich, Lecturer; Pharm.D., California, San Francisco.
Kristin Oberg, Assistant Professor; Pharm.D., USC.
Gerald E. Schumacher, Professor; Ph.D., Wayne State.
Shirley Tsinoder, Lecturer; Pharm.D., California, San Francisco.

Department of Speech-Language Pathology and Audiology
Kevin P. Kearns, Chairperson; Ph.D., Kansas.

Helen Anis, Clinical Supervisor and Clinical Assistant Professor; M.A., Connecticut.
Linda Ferrier, Associate Professor; Ph.D., Boston University.
Mary Florentine, Associate Professor; Ph.D., Northeastern.
Mary Beth Lannon, Clinical Supervisor and Clinical Instructor; Ed.D., Northeastern.
Gregory Lof, Assistant Professor; Ph.D., Wisconsin.
Christine Rankovic, Senior Research Scientist; Ph.D., Minnesota.
Robert B. Redden, Associate Professor; Ed.D., Boston University.

THE OHIO STATE UNIVERSITY

College of Pharmacy

Programs of Study

The College of Pharmacy offers programs leading to the degrees of Master of Science, Doctor of Philosophy, and Doctor of Pharmacy. M.S. and Ph.D. degree programs are offered in four areas of specialization. The pharmaceutical administration discipline focuses on issues related to the pharmaceutical care delivery system, pharmacoeconomics, drug distribution and public policy, strategic planning for pharmaceutical organizations, and drug-use behavior and evaluation. The medicinal chemistry and pharmacognosy discipline focuses on the interdisciplinary application of chemical, biochemical, and molecular principles to the identification and development of therapeutic agents. The pharmaceutics area focuses on pharmacodynamics and pharmacokinetics, with a special emphasis on drug delivery and targeting systems. The pharmacology area focuses on determination of biochemical and physiological mechanisms by which drugs exert their effects. Graduates of these programs are prepared for careers that exploit research skills and independent thinking in pharmaceutical sciences. The M.S. in hospital pharmacy educates to conceptualize, plan, coordinate, and evaluate pharmaceutical care in organized health-care settings. The Doctor of Pharmacy (Pharm.D.) program is a two-year postbaccalaureate professional doctoral degree program that provides a combination of academic and clinical experience for selected pharmacy graduates.

Research Facilities

Ample laboratory space to provide an excellent research environment for all students working on laboratory-based projects is found in modern laboratories in the newly built Riffe Building and in laboratories in Parks Hall. An outstanding Pharmacy and Bioscience Library subscribes to approximately 1,500 journals and contains more than 150,000 books. Modern equipment necessary for sophisticated research in chemistry, biochemistry, molecular biology, and biotechnology is available in the College. This includes such items as NMR and ESR spectrometers, radioisotope equipment, gas chromatographs, liquid chromatographs, and physiological recording systems. Cell culture facilities and an animal vivarium provide additional capabilities.

Financial Aid

Financial support is granted on a competitive basis. Graduate associates are normally appointed on a twelve-month basis. In 1997–98, stipends for graduate associateships ranged from $13,296 to $15,000 per year. In addition, tuition and fees are waived for all graduate associates. A limited number of government and industrial fellowships, University fellowships, and research associateships are also available.

Cost of Study

In 1998–99, tuition and fees for graduate students enrolled in any quarter for 10 or more credit hours are $1738 for Ohio residents and $4500 for nonresidents. Health insurance is optional for most students, but it is required of all international students. The cost of student health insurance is $191 each quarter.

Living and Housing Costs

University housing is available for single students, married students, or single parents with dependent children. The University provides information on available apartments and rooming houses in the community as well as counseling for students who have questions concerning rental procedures.

Student Group

The Ohio State University includes more than 10,000 graduate students in its total annual enrollment of more than 50,000 students. The graduate programs in the College of Pharmacy enroll approximately 100 U.S. and international students who come from a wide geographic distribution and represent a variety of undergraduate academic disciplines and institutions.

Student Outcomes

Nearly half of the graduates find positions in the pharmaceutical industry, nearly half enter academia, and a small number switch to a career outside of the pharmaceutical sciences. Those entering academic careers are nearly evenly distributed between institutions in which teaching is the major expected job function and those in which a high level of research is expected along with teaching.

Location

The state's capital and largest city, Columbus is the only city in the northeast quadrant of the country that grew in population during the last census period. Currently, the city has a metropolitan population of just over a million. Columbus is primarily a service-industry community, although there is some light manufacturing. The city has all the amenities of a major metropolitan area—a thriving downtown complete with excellent restaurants, a symphony, a ballet company, theaters, museums, and art galleries. Whether weekend athletes, amateur musicians, or fine arts buffs, students will find a wealth of recreational and cultural pursuits to complement their life in the laboratory, library, or classroom at the Ohio State University and in Columbus.

The University and The College

The Ohio State University, established in 1870, is the premier graduate degree–granting university in Ohio and is among the most prominent institutions of higher education in the world. The University offers 114 fields of specialization with 128 programs leading to the master's degree and 93 leading to the Ph.D.

Although pharmacy was first studied at the Ohio State University in the Department of Chemistry, a School of Pharmacy was founded in 1885 and the College of Pharmacy was established in 1895. Today, the College is internationally recognized as a major teaching and research institute in the field of pharmacy.

Applying

Applicants should have a bachelor's degree in pharmacy or in another appropriate field, depending on the area of study selected. Applications are accepted throughout the year, but students seeking financial assistance should apply before January 15. International students whose native language is not English must submit proof of proficiency in English to be considered for admission. The Division of Pharmaceutical Administration requires a minimum TOEFL score of 600. TSE scores are required for graduate teaching associateships. GRE General Test scores must be submitted by all applicants.

Correspondence and Information

For further information, students should contact:

Office of Graduate Studies and Research
College of Pharmacy
The Ohio State University
500 West 12th Avenue
Columbus, Ohio 43210-1291

Telephone: 614-292-2266
Fax: 614-292-2588
E-mail: gadmbrks@dendrite.pharmacy.ohio-state.edu
World Wide Web: http://www.pharmacy.ohio-state.edu

The Ohio State University

THE FACULTY AND THEIR RESEARCH

Division of Medicinal Chemistry and Pharmacognosy

Stephen C. Bergmeier, Ph.D., Assistant Professor. Development of novel synthetic methods for the synthesis of biologically interesting molecules.

Robert W. Brueggemeier, Ph.D., Professor. Aromatase inhibitors, steroid biochemistry, hormones and cancer, radiochemicals.

John M. Cassady, Ph.D., Professor and Dean. Chemistry of natural cancer chemotherapeutic and chemopreventive agents, synthesis of inhibitors of posttranslational processing of tyrosine protein kinase, synthesis of dopamine autoreceptor agonists.

Robert W. Curley, Ph.D., Professor. Vitamin A and its retinoid analogues, stereoselective syntheses of stable isotope-labeled amino acids, NMR studies of drug-receptor interactions.

Jennifer V. Hines, Ph.D., Assistant Professor. Studying ligand-macromolecular receptor interactions in order to ascertain the key structural features required for ligand binding.

Jogikal M. Jagadeesh, Ph.D., Associate Professor. Analytical instrumentation, image processing, pattern recognition, biological and machine vision systems.

Carter L. Olson, Ph.D., Professor. New methods for measuring the transport of drugs across membranes, fluorescence kinetic measurements to study drug binding, lab computer automation.

Nigel D. Priestley, Ph.D., Assistant Professor. Multidisciplinary approach to the study of polyketide biosynthesis in streptomyces.

Larry W. Robertson, Ph.D., Professor. Fermentation and microbial products, microbiological transformations of drugs, antibiotics, drug metabolism, metabolism and biological activities of cannabinoids.

Division of Pharmaceutics and Pharmaceutical Chemistry

Jessie L.-S. Au, Pharm.D., Ph.D., Dorothy M. Davis Professor. Pharmacodynamics of anticancer and anti-AIDS drugs in cultured cells, tissues, animals, and patients; treatment of bladder, head and neck, prostate, breast, and ovarian cancers.

Kenneth K. Chan, Ph.D., Professor. Application of stable isotopes in pharmacokinetics, metabolism and mechanism of action; alkylating agents; cancer chemotherapy and drug development; liposome drug formulation; analytical method development; mass spectrometry.

Sylvan G. Frank, Ph.D., Professor. Design and evaluation of drug delivery systems; emulsions, liposomes, and liquid crystals; micelle stability and solubilization; small-particle formation and microencapsulation; iontophoresis; percolation theory; fractal geometry.

Ram Ganapathi, Ph.D., Associate Professor. Molecular pharmacology of anti-tumor drug resistance.

William L. Hayton, Ph.D., Professor. Pharmacokinetics and metabolism in aquatic species, scaling for body size and environmental factors, aquaculture drug development.

Robert J. Lee, Ph.D., Assistant Professor. Receptors mediated targeted drug delivery systems.

Steven P. Schwendeman, Ph.D., Assistant Professor. Controlled drug delivery.

Alfred E. Staubus, Pharm.D., Ph.D., Associate Professor. Clinical and forensic applications of biopharmaceutics and pharmacokinetics.

Peter W. Swaan, Ph.D., Assistant Professor. Optimization of oral drug delivery; oral vaccination.

M. Guillaume Wientjes, Ph.D., Assistant Professor. Pharmacokinetics and pharmacodynamics of drugs for bladder and prostate cancer in patients, animals, and cell culture; use of regional and targeted drug delivery.

Division of Pharmacology

John A. Bauer, Ph.D., Assistant Professor. Signal transduction; physiological and pathological roles of nitric oxide; congestive heart failure.

Dale G. Hoyt, Ph.D., Assistant Professor. Apotosis caused by DNA-damaging agents, DNA repair; genotoxic stress.

Dennis B. McKay, Ph.D., Associate Professor. Cellular and molecular pharmacology, neurosecretory mechanisms, receptor mechanisms involved with adrenal catecholamine secretion.

Popat N. Patil, Ph.D., Professor. Autonomic nervous system pharmacology with the emphasis on steric aspects of drug receptor interactions, desensitization, morphology of sensory and synaptic receptors, ocular pharmacology, and drug melanin interactions.

Ralf G. Rahwan, Ph.D., Professor. Toxicology and cardiovascular, gastrointestinal, and endocrine pharmacology; mechanisms of action of calcium antagonists.

Norman J. Uretsky, Ph.D., Professor. Neuropharmacology, neurotransmitter release in animal behavior and neurological diseases.

David Van Wagner, Ph.D., Assistant Professor. Cardiac electrophysiology.

Lane J. Wallace, Ph.D., Professor. Excitatory amino acid neurobiology, mechanisms of drug addiction; diabetes and urinary bladder function.

Anthony P. Young, Ph.D., Associate Professor. Molecular and cellular pharmacology, regulation of glutamine synthetase gene expression during retinal development, and glucocorticoid-mediated muscle atrophy; nitric oxide synthase gene expression.

Division of Pharmacy Practice and Administration

Robert A. Buerki, Ph.D., Associate Professor. Ethics and pharmacy practice, history of pharmacy, pharmacy communications.

James D. Coyle, Pharm.D., Assistant Professor. Cardiovascular pharmacotherapeutics emphasizing antiarrhythmic drug therapy, individual and population-based pharmacokinetics and pharmacodynamics.

Joseph F. Dasta, M.S., Professor. Critical care, pharmacy and pharmacokinetics.

George Hinkle, M.S., Clinical Assistant Professor. Nuclear pharmacy, medical use of radionuclides, radiolabeled antibodies.

Daren L. Knoell, Pharm.D., Assistant Professor. Nonviral gene delivery.

James M. McAuley, Ph.D., Assistant Professor. Pharmacokinetics and pharmacodynamics of centrally acting drugs, influence of gender and hormones on drug response.

Alicia S. Miller, M.S., Assistant Director, Department of Hospital Pharmacy. Productivity and ergonomic design, computer and information management, financial analysis.

Milap C. Nahata, Pharm.D., Professor. Pediatric and antimicrobial pharmacokinetics and therapy.

Dev S. Pathak, D.B.A., Merrell-Dow Professor. Pharmacoeconomics, marketing of pharmaceutical and health-care programs, public policy and drug distribution, strategic planning, and pharmaceutical organizations.

Craig A. Pedersen, Ph.D., Assistant Professor. Pharmacoeconomics and health-care outcomes.

Richard H. Reuning, Ph.D., Professor. Pharmacokinetics and metabolism of digitalis glycosides, enterohepatic cycling.

Philip J. Schneider, M.S., Clinical Associate Professor. Parenteral nutrition, hospital pharmacy administration.

Jon C. Schommer, Ph.D., Associate Professor. Application of consumer behavior theories to research problems in pharmacy practice, such as pharmacist-patient communications.

Sheryl L. Szeinbach, Ph.D., Professor. Distribution of pharmaceutical products and services; service delivery decision-making processes that involve utility analysis (pharmacoeconomics) and risk assessment; organizational structure, automation, and information technology.

James A. Visconti, Ph.D., Professor. Drug information, infectious disease therapeutics.

PURDUE UNIVERSITY

School of Pharmacy and Pharmacal Sciences

Programs of Study

The School of Pharmacy and Pharmacal Sciences offers programs of study and research leading to the degree of Doctor of Philosophy in analytical medicinal chemistry, biochemistry, biopharmaceutics, cancer research, clinical pharmacy, industrial and physical pharmacy, medicinal chemistry, molecular pharmacology, pharmacodynamics, pharmacognosy, pharmacy administration, and radiopharmaceutical chemistry. The degree of Master of Science or Doctor of Philosophy is offered in nuclear pharmacy. The programs are administered by the faculty of the three departments of the School: Industrial and Physical Pharmacy, Medicinal Chemistry and Molecular Pharmacology, and Pharmacy Practice. The various graduate degree programs differ in their specific requirements, but all emphasize a solid foundation of basic skills and understanding, a rich diversity of knowledge related to the area of research specialization, and individual training in a specific area of research.

Research and graduate education in pharmacy and pharmacal sciences are highly interdisciplinary, involving interaction and study with faculty in many traditional disciplines. Included are biochemistry, biology, chemistry, computer science, education, engineering, math, medicine, pathology, physics, physiology, and statistics. While the research programs of the School of Pharmacy and Pharmacal Sciences are constantly evolving, they are nevertheless well established and internationally respected.

Research Facilities

Equipment necessary for modern pharmaceutical research in all of the School's departments is available either within the School or as part of interdisciplinary facilities. Major equipment includes NMR spectrometers for both solutions (from 300 to 600 MHz) and solids work, mass spectrometers, facilities for both crystal and powder X-ray diffraction, animal facilities, DNA and peptide synthesis and analysis facilities, and dedicated systems for molecular graphics. Purdue University Computing Center maintains several high-performance computing systems for research, including clusters of IBM RS 6000 workstations as well as large-scale parallel systems of an IBM SP2 and a 140-node Intel Paragon. The excellent campus library system includes the Pharmacy, Nursing, and Health Sciences Library, which contains more than 40,000 volumes.

Financial Aid

Nearly all graduate students admitted to the School receive twelve-month appointments as teaching or research assistants. Salaries for these appointments ranged from $11,000 to $17,000 per year in 1997–98. In addition, all tuition and fees except for $294 per semester and $147 per summer session are remitted. Many students are supported by graduate fellowships. Graduate counselorships that pay for room and board and remission of all tuition and fees, except for $294 per semester and $147 for the summer session, are available as well.

Cost of Study

Tuition and fees for nonresidents and residents of Indiana for 1997–98 were about $13,960 and $4170, respectively, for two semesters and the summer. These costs are waived for graduate students receiving assistantship support (further information is given in Financial Aid, above).

Living and Housing Costs

Housing is exceptionally affordable in the Lafayette area. A ten-story graduate house provides rooms (no board) for single students; a twelve-story graduate house has cafeteria facilities. Room rents ranged from $270 to $484 per month for 1997–98. Married students can rent one of 1,244 University-owned one- and two-bedroom apartments. Rents, including all utilities except telephone, ranged from $398 to $488 per month. Ample off-campus housing is also available.

Student Group

In 1997, the University enrolled 6,157 graduate and professional students of a total number of 35,715 students on the West Lafayette campus. The graduate programs of the School of Pharmacy and Pharmacal Sciences enrolled 160 students, the largest full-time graduate enrollment of any school of pharmacy in the United States. These students come from a wide variety of undergraduate academic disciplines and institutions, with representation from fourteen countries and twenty-two states. In 1997, the graduate enrollment of the School was 56 percent men and 44 percent women.

Student Outcomes

Recent graduates of the School's programs hold positions in research or pharmaceutical marketing in the pharmaceutical industry and as faculty in both pharmacy schools and basic-science departments of academic institutions.

Location

Greater Lafayette is conveniently located 60 miles northwest of Indianapolis and 125 miles southeast of Chicago, and the cultural offerings of those cities are readily accessible. Purdue's main campus is located in West Lafayette across the Wabash River from Lafayette. The population of the twin cities is about 100,000.

The Lafayette area is comfortable and safe. It has daily and weekly newspapers, an art gallery, a historical museum, a symphony orchestra, a choral society, civic and University theater groups, a public radio station, and 240 acres of public parks, which contribute to the community's recreational and cultural life. Opportunities for sports enthusiasts abound, ranging from Big Ten football and basketball to intramural sports and individual sports such as fishing, golf, canoeing, hiking, bicycling, and spelunking.

The University and The School

Purdue University was founded in 1869 as a land-grant university and has grown to be twentieth in size (by enrollment) of all colleges and universities in the United States. The West Lafayette campus includes 2,204 faculty members in sixty-one academic departments. The 1,579-acre main campus provides ample space for its 144 principal buildings. Long recognized for the high quality of its educational programs, Purdue University's research effort has been expanding steadily. It is internationally recognized for its engineering, agriculture, science, and pharmacy programs. The distinguished faculty includes one Nobel laureate and numerous members of the National Academy of Sciences and the National Academy of Engineering.

The School of Pharmacy was founded in 1884 and includes 56 faculty members. The faculty and graduate students conduct research and teach in a wide variety of traditional as well as interdisciplinary fields related to pharmacy and human health. More than 6,485 baccalaureate, 363 Pharm.D., and 790 Ph.D. degrees have been awarded by the School.

Applying

Students may apply at any time for admission to the August, January, or June session. Scores on the General Test of the Graduate Record Examinations are required of all students. International students must also submit scores on the Test of English as a Foreign Language (TOEFL) to be considered for admission. Purdue is an equal access/equal opportunity university.

Correspondence and Information

Chair, Graduate Admissions Committee
School of Pharmacy and Pharmacal Sciences
Purdue University
West Lafayette, Indiana 47907
Telephone: 765-494-1362

Purdue University

THE FACULTY AND THEIR RESEARCH

Faculty members in nuclear pharmacy hold appointments in the Department of Medicinal Chemistry and Molecular Pharmacology, and those in pharmacy administration hold appointments in the Department of Pharmacy Practice.

Department of Industrial and Physical Pharmacy

Stephen R. Byrn, Ph.D.; Charles B. Jordan Professor and Head. Solid-state chemistry of drugs; pharmaceutical manufacturing.
Raymond E. Galinsky, Pharm.D., Professor. Pharmacokinetics, biopharmaceutics, and drug metabolism in animal models of human disease.
Stanley L. Hem, Ph.D., Professor. Stability of pharmaceuticals, characterization of amorphous systems, particle interactions.
Dane O. Kildsig, Ph.D., Professor. Surface chemistry of solids; liposome systems; solubility phenomena.
Kenneth R. Morris, Ph.D., Associate Professor. Pharmaceutical materials science.
Steven L. Nail, Ph.D., Associate Professor. Physical chemistry of freeze-drying, stability of drugs in solid state.
Kinam Park, Ph.D., Professor. Controlled drug delivery using hydrogels; tissue engineering; biomaterials.
Garnet E. Peck, Ph.D., Professor and Director, Industrial Pharmacy Laboratory. Dosage form design; controlled-drug delivery; drug-excipient interactions; coating technology; roller compaction.

Department of Medicinal Chemistry and Molecular Pharmacology

Richard F. Borch, M.D., Ph.D., Lilly Distinguished Professor and Head. Anticancer drug design; design and synthesis of mechanism-based anticancer drugs.
Donald E. Bergstrom, Ph.D., Walther Professor and Associate Head. Nucleic acid chemistry.
Curtis L. Ashendel, Ph.D., Associate Professor. Biochemistry of carcinogenesis and cell signal transduction; protein kinase C; raf/ras oncogenes.
Eric L. Barker, Ph.D., Assistant Professor. Structure of antidepressant- and cocaine-sensitive serotonin transporters; mechanisms of endogenous cannabinoid transport.
Douglas J. Beussman, Ph.D., Assistant Professor. Mass spectrometry; analysis and structure elucidation of biomolecules; combinatorial library analysis.
Joseph L. Borowitz, Ph.D., Professor. Biochemical pharmacology; mechanisms of cyanide neurotoxicity.
Ching-jer Chang, Ph.D., Professor. Isolation of bioactive agents from plants; bioorganic chemistry of enzyme modeling; molecular toxicology and DNA modification; biomedical application of spectroscopy.
Mark Cushman, Ph.D., Professor. Design and synthesis of antibiotics; antiviral agents and anticancer agents.
V. Jo Davisson, Ph.D., Associate Professor. Bioorganic chemistry; enzyme inhibition; directed evolution and biotechnology.
H. Patrick Fletcher, Ph.D., Associate Professor. Clinical pharmacology; effects of drugs and toxins on endocrine systems.
Robert L. Geahlen, Ph.D., Professor. Protein phosphorylation; protein-tyrosine kinases; protein myristoylation.
Mark A. Green, Ph.D., Professor. Positron emission tomography (PET); synthesis of radiopharmaceuticals with labeled metal nuclides.
Marietta L. Harrison, Ph.D., Associate Professor. Signal transduction; protein phosphorylation; cell transformation.
Peter Heinstein, Ph.D., Professor. Transmembrane signaling and regulatory mechanisms in secondary product metabolism.
Gregory H. Hockerman, Ph.D., Assistant Professor. Molecular pharmacology of L-type calcium channels.
Gary E. Isom, Ph.D., Professor. Biochemical mechanisms of neurotoxicity; excitotoxic neurotransmitters in xenobiotic neurotoxicity.
G. Marc Loudon, Ph.D., Gustav E. Cwalina Distinguished Professor and Associate Dean. Bioorganic and peptide chemistry.
Roger P. Maickel, Ph.D., Professor. Biochemical, behavioral, and environmental pharmacology.
Jerry L. McLaughlin, Ph.D., Professor of Pharmacognosy. Isolation of medicinal constituents of plants.
D. James Morré, Ph.D., Dow Distinguished Professor of Medicinal Chemistry. Cancer research; membrane organization; biogenesis and function.
David E. Nichols, Ph.D., Professor. Structure-activity relationships of centrally active drugs; hallucinogens; antiparkinson drugs; effects of drugs on brain monoamine systems.
Charles Pidgeon, Ph.D., Professor. Lipid chemistry; liposomes; peptide/lipid interactions.
Carol B. Post, Ph.D., Associate Professor. Studies of protein structure, protein-ligand interactions, and enzymatic catalysis using experimental NMR and molecular dynamics.
David J. Riese II, Ph.D., Assistant Professor. Hormone-receptor interactions; receptor kinase signal transduction; tumor cell biology.
Stanley M. Shaw, Ph.D., Professor and Head, Division of Nuclear Pharmacy. Radiopharmaceuticals; radiation biology; nuclear pharmacy.
Val J. Watts, Ph.D., Assistant Professor. Molecular signaling of dopamine receptors; second messenger pathways and receptor modulation.

Department of Pharmacy Practice

Steven R. Abel, Pharm.D., Professor and Head. Ocular pharmacology; practice advancement and assessment.
Robert W. Bennett, M.S., Associate Professor. Educational outcomes in ambulatory pharmaceutical care; practice advancement.
Charles H. Brown, M.S., Associate Professor. Drug therapy monitoring: cardiopulmonary; anticoagulation pharmacotherapy in the elderly.
Bruce C. Carlstedt, Ph.D., Professor. Computer applications of pharmacokinetics; pharmacy education; pharmacy practice.
Robert K. Chalmers, Ph.D., Bucke Professor. Assessment of educational outcomes; service learning strategies.
Julie A. Everett, Pharm.D., Assistant Professor. Pediatrics; sedation; neuromuscular blockade; pain management.
Claudine Fenton, Pharm.D., Assistant Professor. Drug information; pharmacokinetics; AIDS research.
Deanna S. Kania, Pharm.D., Clinical Assistant Professor. Ambulatory care; diabetes management; anticoagulation; HIV/AIDS.
Mary M. Losey, M.S., Associate Professor. Career counseling.
Holly L. Mason, Ph.D., Professor and Associate Dean for Professional Programs. Career path research; assessing educational outcomes.
Bruce A. Mueller, Pharm.D., Associate Professor. Kidney disease; hemodialysis and pharmacokinetics.
Matthew M. Murawski, Ph.D., Assistant Professor. Health-related quality of life and patient outcomes.
Michael D. Murray, Pharm.D., M.P.H., Associate Professor. Pharmacoepidemiology; drug therapy in the elderly; clinical pharmacology of NSAIDs.
Gail D. Newton, Ph.D., Associate Professor. Educational outcomes; innovative teaching methodologies.
Nicholas G. Popovich, Ph.D., Professor and Associate Head. Educational outcomes; innovative teaching methodologies.
Michael T. Rupp, Ph.D., Professor. Pharmacoeconomics; evaluation of pharmacy services; public policy in health care.
Theresa A. Salazar, Pharm.D., Assistant Professor. Ambulatory care; service documentation; geriatrics.
Meri K. Scott, Ph.D., Assistant Professor. Kidney disease; hemodialysis.
Steven A. Scott, Pharm.D., Associate Professor. Oncologic therapeutics; outcome-based education assessment.
Kevin M. Sowinski, Pharm.D., Assistant Professor. Cardiovascular therapeutics; pharmacokinetics and pharmacodynamics.
Joseph Thomas III, Ph.D., Associate Professor. Health outcomes; pharmaceutical economics.
Ronnie A. Weatherman, Pharm.D., Assistant Professor. Anticoagulation; ambulatory care; standardized patients; drug diversion.
Craig D. Williams, Pharm.D., Clinical Assistant Professor. Ambulatory care; practice advancement in the ambulatory setting.

TEMPLE UNIVERSITY

of the Commonwealth System of Higher Education

School of Pharmacy
Programs in the Pharmaceutical Sciences

Programs of Study

Doctor of Philosophy and Master of Science programs in pharmaceutics and medicinal/pharmaceutical chemistry and Master of Science programs in quality assurance/regulatory affairs are offered by the Graduate Faculty in the School of Pharmacy. The pharmacology program is now offered through the School of Medicine, and interested students should direct their inquiries to the school's graduate department.

The School of Pharmacy programs are interdepartmental and provide for specialization in the areas described. They are designed to give the superior student an opportunity for the extension of demonstrated talent for the acquisition and application of basic knowledge. The requirements are those of the Graduate School of Temple University: demonstration of scholarship by performance in appropriate course work, satisfactory performance in comprehensive examinations, selection and prosecution of a significant research problem, and preparation and defense of a scholarly thesis.

Research Facilities

The laboratories are located in the Pharmacy and Allied Health Building at the Health Sciences Center. Special equipment for research with radioisotopes and analytical instrumentation are available for student research problems.

Financial Aid

Fellowships that provide various stipends per month and the waiver of tuition and fees are provided for some students accepted into the M.S. programs. Doctoral fellowships are also available from the University. In 1997–98, graduate assistantships were available at $10,000 each plus remission of tuition.

Cost of Study

Temple University is a state-related university. The annual tuition in 1998–99 is $308 per semester hour for residents of Pennsylvania and $427 per semester hour for nonresidents. Minimal fees are charged for various services, such as microfilming. (Costs are subject to change.)

Living and Housing Costs

Graduate students usually live in apartments or rooms in various sections of the city. Costs vary considerably, but 1 or 2 students often occupy an apartment renting for an average of $375 per month.

Student Group

More than 400 graduate students are enrolled at the Health Sciences Center as part of a student population of almost 2,500, which includes professional students. The School of Pharmacy has 145 graduate students enrolled in its various programs.

Student Outcomes

The majority of the graduates from the Doctor of Philosophy and the Master of Science degree programs have secured positions with the surrounding pharmaceutical industry. Other Ph.D. graduates have found employment in universities and industry settings throughout the country. The graduates are currently engaged in research and development, pharmaceutical production, and analytical laboratory work as well as quality assurance/regulatory affairs.

Location

The historic city of Philadelphia has much to offer in art, music, and cultural pursuits. Most of the seminars, colloquia, and similar events sponsored by other educational and research institutions in the city are open to all graduate students.

The University

Temple University is a state-affiliated institution founded in 1884 and is now one of the largest universities in the country. The Health Sciences Center houses the Schools of Medicine, Dentistry, and Pharmacy; the College of Allied Health Professions; and the Temple University Hospital. It is located on Broad Street five blocks from the North Philadelphia Station of Amtrak and some 1½ miles north of the Broad and Montgomery Avenue campus of Temple University.

Applying

Applicants should have a bachelor's degree in pharmacy or a related field, depending on the area of study selected. International students whose native language is not English must submit proof of proficiency in English (minimum TOEFL score of 575 required) to be considered for admission.

Applications—including all transcripts of college work, two letters of recommendation, and GRE General Test scores—should be submitted before June 1. Students are encouraged to apply early. Personal interviews may be recommended. Notification of admission is given as soon as possible.

Students may apply at any time but are admitted to begin work in September or January. A complete graduate bulletin is sent on request.

Correspondence and Information

Director of Graduate Studies
School of Pharmacy
Temple University
3307 North Broad Street
Philadelphia, Pennsylvania 19140
Telephone: 215-707-4948

Temple University

THE FACULTY AND THEIR RESEARCH

Michael R. Borenstein, Ph.D., Associate Professor and Chairman of Pharmaceutical Sciences. Synthesis and evaluation of novel pharmacologic agents especially with regard to the structural prerequisites for anticonvulsant and CNS activity; development of analytical methodologies (GC/MS and HPLC) for therapeutic drug monitoring, pharmacokinetics, drug metabolism, and dosage forms.

Daniel J. Canney, Ph.D., Assistant Professor of Medicinal Chemistry. Synthesis, characterization, and biological evaluation (structure-activity studies) of novel muscarinic and nicotinic ligands, mechanism-based inhibitors of aromatic amino acid decarboxylase (AADC), and amino/amido-lactone derivatives and potential anticonvulsant agents; development of synthetic strategies for the synthesis of organotin precursors of radioiodinated compounds for use in radioligand binding, autoradiography, and/or SPECT imaging studies.

Peter H. Doukas, Ph.D., Dean. Compounds affecting the disposition of acetylcholine; nicotinic agonists and antagonists; proconvulsants and anticonvulsants; inhibitors of platelet aggregation.

Reza A. Fassihi, Ph.D., Professor of Biopharmaceutics and Industrial Pharmacy. Drug product design, formulation and development of conventional and modified drug dosage forms, intrinsic permeability of the intestinal wall and drug transport, biopharmaceutical aspects of medicine, in vitro and in vivo evaluation of pharmaceuticals.

Cherng Ju Kim, Ph.D., Assistant Professor of Pharmaceutics and Director of Graduate Studies. Novel polymeric drug delivery systems, kinetics of drug release, osmotic pump delivery.

Chana R. Kowarski, Ph.D., Professor of Pharmacy. Nasal insulin products: preparation and in vivo evaluation with the continuous glucose monitor; sustained-release products: development and evaluation in vitro and in vivo (coating and microencapsulation); drug stability problems; pharmacokinetic comparison of continuous- with intermittent-withdrawal methodology.

Robert B. Raffa, Ph.D., Associate Professor of Pharmacology. In vivo evaluation of opioid and nonopioid peptide and nonpeptide analgesics, mechanisms, tolerance, and dependence; isolated tissue preparations; theoretical pharmacology; synergistic drug interactions; thermodynamics of the drug-receptor interaction.

Tully J. Speaker, Ph.D., Professor of Pharmacy and Toxicology. Analytical toxicology, drug metabolism, chromatography theory, percutaneous absorption, microencapsulation.

Salvatore J. Turco, Pharm.D., Professor of Pharmacy. Particulate matter in parenteral solutions, drug distribution systems and drug packaging.

Tsang-Bin Tzeng, Ph.D., Assistant Professor of Pharmaceutics. Pharmacokinetics, pharmacodynamics, drug metabolism bioanalysis, population pharmacokinetics.

UNIVERSITY OF CALIFORNIA, SAN FRANCISCO

Graduate Program in Pharmaceutical Chemistry

Program of Study

The Ph.D. degree program in pharmaceutical chemistry offers an opportunity for students to apply physical, chemical, biological, pharmacological, and toxicological principles to the design, delivery, and application of drugs and biomolecules leading to novel therapies. In pursuing these goals, students may choose one of three major directions of study: the Medicinal Chemistry Pathway, the Pharmaceutics Pathway, or the Toxicology Pathway.

Students in the Medicinal Chemistry Pathway apply physical, organic, and theoretical chemistry toward understanding the mechanisms of action of molecules of biological importance and drug design. Students in the Pharmaceutics Pathway undertake fundamental research in experimental therapeutics, with a focus on the areas of drug delivery, pharmacokinetics/pharmacodynamics, mechanisms of drug action, drug metabolism, and clinical pharmacology. Students in the Toxicology Pathway study the biochemical and molecular bases of the toxic effects caused by drugs and other xenobiotics.

Basic program requirements, in addition to course requirements, entail gaining experience as a teaching assistant for three quarters, passing the oral qualifying examination, and, finally, submitting the doctoral dissertation. In addition, students in the Pharmaceutics and Toxicology Pathways must develop proficiency in biostatistics.

Research Facilities

The Departments of Pharmaceutical Chemistry and Biopharmaceutical Sciences maintain several specialized research facilities featuring state-of-the-art equipment. The Mass Spectrometry Facility is equipped with several state-of-the-art instruments required for research on biomacromolecules, including matrix laser time-of-flight, electrospray quadrupole, and multisource magnetic sector ion optical systems; these are also used in various tandem versions for collision-induced dissociation. Microbore and capillary HPLC-ES MS are available for analysis of complex mixtures as well. The Computer Graphics Laboratory includes a high-performance departmental server used for storage and searches of sequence and structure databases and for performing theoretical studies on protein and nucleic acid structure and function. High-performance workstations are used for generating three-dimensional interactive molecular models. All systems are interconnected via a high-speed network and are capable of distributed computations. Color hard copy (slides and prints) and high-quality video are used for disseminating results. The Nuclear Magnetic Resonance Laboratory has a 500-MHz NMR spectrometer and two 600-MHz spectrometers. These spectrometers are equipped with pulsed-field gradients and triple resonance probes of various sizes on which all modern 2-D, 3-D, and 4-D NMR spectroscopic experiments on samples in solution can be carried out. The lab is equipped with a large number of Silicon Graphics and Sun computers for data processing and associated structure calculations using locally written (but globally distributed) software as well as commercial software. The lab is linked via Ethernet to other local computers and national supercomputer laboratories. The lab also has a routine 300-MHz NMR spectrometer. Several computer facilities are available, including a cluster of Hewlett-Packard 735s, several Silicon Graphics computers, and numerous workstations. The Confocal Microscope Facility has two Bio-Rad laser-scanning confocal microscopes, an MRC-600 mounted on an upright stand, and an MRC-1024 on an inverted microscope. Each is equipped with Krypton/Argon and HeNe lasers, and the MRC-600 has hardware for compensated reflection imaging and software for time-course/ratiometric measurements.

Financial Aid

Most doctoral candidates received funding as teaching assistants, research assistants, fellows, or trainees at the standardized level of $17,000 in 1997–98.

Cost of Study

The graduate program covers annual fees for most of its students. Annual fees for full-time graduate study are estimated at $4485 for 1998–99. An additional $8984 in nonresident tuition is required for students who are not residents of California; nonresident tuition drops to $2246 for students once they have advanced to candidacy. Some nonresident tuition scholarships are available for students with distinguished academic records from a U.S. institution.

Living and Housing Costs

The University is located in a residential area with a large selection of rooms and apartments. In 1997–98, University apartments for student families, located near the campus, rented for $591 per month for a one-bedroom unit and $716 per month for a two-bedroom unit. The University Residence Program has housing, which ranged in price from $367 to $482 per month for singles and from $267 to $316 per month for shares. The University also has apartments (Turk Boulevard Housing), which rented for $367 to $413 per month.

Student Group

About 75 full-time graduate students are in the program and come from the United States and several other countries. They are members of the departmental Graduate Student Organization (GSO) and the campuswide Graduate Student Association (GSA). Social, recreational, and professional programs are planned by these groups as well as by the Guy S. Millberry Student Union.

Student Outcomes

Of the alumni who graduated in the last five years (1992–97), 46 percent are currently employed as postdoctoral scholars, 23 percent are in industrial positions, 16 percent are in academia, and 8 percent are in government or other fields related to pharmaceutical chemistry. Of the alumni who graduated between 1987 and 1992, 48 percent are in industrial positions, 23 percent are in academia, and 9 percent are in government or related fields. Another 10 percent are unknown.

Location

The University of California, San Francisco (UCSF), surrounded by the Pacific Ocean, the Golden Gate Bridge, and San Francisco Bay, is located in the center of San Francisco and commands an impressive view of the city. The campus community enjoys all the social and cultural advantages of a cosmopolitan, metropolitan area as well as easy access to the beaches and redwood groves of Marin County and San Mateo County (only 30 minutes by car from the campus) and the ski slopes of the Sierra (a 3- or 4-hour drive from the campus).

The University

The University of California, San Francisco, is one of nine campuses of a statewide university system. The Medical Sciences and Health Sciences Buildings at UCSF house the graduate and professional programs in pharmacy, medicine, dentistry, nursing, and the basic health sciences. The campus also includes three hospitals and the Millberry Student Union, which is the cultural, social, and recreational center of the campus.

Applying

A formal application is required of all persons seeking admission to the Graduate Division. Application forms may be obtained from the chairman of the department. Scores on the General Test of the Graduate Record Examinations (GRE), letters of recommendation, and complete official transcripts of previous college work are required. Completed forms must be submitted by January 15. Students are admitted for the fall quarter only.

Correspondence and Information

Thomas L. James, Ph.D., Chairman
Department of Pharmaceutical Chemistry
University of California, San Francisco
San Francisco, California 94143-0446

Telephone: 415-476-1914
E-mail: pcgradpg@cgl.ucsf.edu

University of California, San Francisco

THE FACULTY AND THEIR RESEARCH

Patricia C. Babbitt, Assistant Professor of Biopharmaceutical Sciences and Pharmaceutical Chemistry; Ph.D., California, San Francisco. Protein structure mediation function through comparative studies on protein superfamilies.

Leslie Z. Benet, Professor of Biopharmaceutical Sciences and Pharmaceutical Chemistry; Ph.D., California, San Francisco. Pharmacokinetics and biopharmaceutics, immunopharmacology, drug metabolism, effect of disease states on drug kinetics and dynamics.

Frances M. Brodsky, Professor of Biopharmaceutical Sciences, Pharmaceutical Chemistry, and Microbiology and Immunology; D.Phil., Oxford. Endocytosis and drug delivery, role of intracellular membrane traffic in the immune response, antibodies as biological probes.

Alma L. Burlingame, Professor of Chemistry and Pharmaceutical Chemistry; Ph.D., MIT. Protein biology, carbohydrate structure determination, elucidation of posttranslational modifications and xenobiotic-macromolecule adducts, mass spectrometry.

Charles S. Craik, Professor of Pharmaceutical Chemistry, Molecular and Cellular Pharmacology, and Biochemistry and Biophysics; Ph.D., Columbia. Protein design and engineering, enzyme mechanism and inhibitor design, role of proteolysis in infectious disease and cancer.

Christopher Cullander, Assistant Professor of Biopharmaceutical Sciences and Pharmaceutical Chemistry; Ph.D., Berkeley. Transport of drugs and toxics into and across external epithelia, noninvasive skin sampling, electrochemical phenomena at implant/tissue interfaces.

Ken A. Dill, Professor of Pharmaceutical Chemistry and Biopharmaceutical Sciences; Ph.D., California, San Diego. Protein folding, theory of structure and function in membranes and proteins, statistical mechanics, biopolymer physical chemistry.

Thomas E. Ferrin, Professor of Pharmaceutical Chemistry; Ph.D., California, San Francisco. Macromolecular structure and function through use of computational algorithms and interactive three-dimensional computer graphics.

Kathleen M. Giacomini, Professor of Biopharmaceutical Sciences, Pharmaceutical Chemistry, and Pharmacology; Ph.D., SUNY at Buffalo. Molecular mechanisms of epithelial transporters relevant to drug targeting, nucleosides and nucleoside analogs, organic cations.

Bradford W. Gibson, Professor of Chemistry and Pharmaceutical Chemistry; Ph.D., MIT. Structural biology and mass spectroscopy, mechanisms of bacterial pathogenesis, vaccine/drug design, tyrosine kinase inhibitors.

Susan P. Hawkes, Associate Professor of Biopharmaceutical Sciences and Pharmaceutical Chemistry; Ph.D., London. Carcinogenesis, extracellular matrix remodeling in normal and disease processes, metalloproteinases and their inhibitors.

Betty-ann Hoener, Professor of Biopharmaceutical Sciences and Pharmaceutical Chemistry; Ph.D., Ohio State. Drug metabolism and disposition, classroom research.

C. Anthony Hunt, Associate Professor of Biopharmaceutical Sciences and Pharmaceutical Chemistry; Ph.D., Florida. Gene regulating and therapeutic oligonucleotides, selective tissue delivery of drugs, bioinformatics, decision support systems for drug development.

Thomas L. James, Professor of Chemistry, Pharmaceutical Chemistry, and Radiology; Ph.D., Wisconsin. NMR, structure and dynamics in nucleic acids, proteins, nucleic acid–protein and drug-receptor interactions.

Stephen B. Kahl, Professor of Chemistry and Pharmaceutical Chemistry; Ph.D., Indiana. Bioorganic chemistry of boron clusters, neutron capture therapy and photodynamic therapy using boron compounds, drug and imaging agent delivery systems.

George L. Kenyon, Professor of Chemistry and Pharmaceutical Chemistry and Dean of the School of Pharmacy; Ph.D., Harvard. Enzyme mechanisms, rational design of enzyme inhibitors and drugs.

Peter A. Kollman, Professor of Chemistry and Pharmaceutical Chemistry; Ph.D., Princeton. Theoretical studies of molecules of organic and biological interest using molecular mechanics/dynamics, free energy calculations, and quantum mechanical calculations.

Deanna L. Kroetz, Assistant Professor of Biopharmaceutical Sciences and Pharmaceutical Chemistry; Ph.D., Washington (Seattle). Molecular mechanisms of CYP4A regulation, cytochrome P450 eicosanoids in the regulation of renal function and blood pressure, fatty acid metabolism by CYP4A enzymes, nuclear receptors in the regulation of P450 enzymes.

Irwin D. Kuntz, Professor of Chemistry and Pharmaceutical Chemistry; Ph.D., Berkeley. Drug design, protein-ligand interactions, NMR, protein hydration, protein folding, protein structure.

Emil T. Lin, Professor of Biopharmaceutical Sciences and Pharmaceutical Chemistry; Ph.D., Purdue. Bioanalytical methodology development, stereospecific inversion of phenylpropionic acids and drug metabolism.

Susan M. Miller, Assistant Professor of Pharmaceutical Chemistry; Ph.D., Berkeley. Enzyme mechanisms emphasizing redox systems, protein-protein interactions and structure-function relationships pertaining to mechanisms of regulation and catalysis.

Svein Oie, Professor of Biopharmaceutical Sciences and Pharmaceutical Chemistry; Ph.D., SUNY at Buffalo. Molecular and biochemical factors influencing drug disposition, pharmacokinetics, absorption, and transport.

Norman J. Oppenheimer, Professor of Chemistry and Pharmaceutical Chemistry; Ph.D., California, San Diego. Enzymology and function of dehydrogenases and glycosidases, chemistry and biochemistry of pyridine nucleotides.

Paul R. Ortiz de Montellano, Professor of Chemistry, Pharmaceutical Chemistry, and Pharmacology; Ph.D., Harvard. Enzyme structure and mechanism, inhibitor design, protein engineering, cytochrome P450, nitric oxide synthases, peroxidases, AIDS chemotherapy.

Wolfgang Sadee, Professor of Biopharmaceutical Sciences and Pharmaceutical Chemistry; Ph.D., Free University of Berlin. Molecular biology of neurotransmitter receptors, receptor regulation, molecular mechanisms of drug addiction.

Daniel V. Santi, Professor of Biochemistry and Pharmaceutical Chemistry; Ph.D., SUNY at Buffalo; M.D., California, San Francisco. Enzyme mechanisms, mutagenesis, interaction of small molecules with proteins, inhibitor design, protozoan biochemistry.

Thomas S. Scanlan, Associate Professor of Chemistry, Pharmaceutical Chemistry, and Molecular and Cellular Pharmacology; Ph.D., Stanford. Bioorganic chemistry, synthetic organic chemistry, enzyme structure and mechanism, receptor-mediated cellular signaling.

Richard H. Shafer, Professor of Chemistry and Pharmaceutical Chemistry; Ph.D., Harvard. Physical chemistry of nucleic acids and nucleic acid–drug complexes, unusual DNA conformations.

Martin D. Shetlar, Professor of Chemistry and Pharmaceutical Chemistry; Ph.D., Berkeley. Structure, photochemistry, and photobiology of DNA and DNA-protein complexes; heavy metal–induced DNA damage, including DNA-protein cross-linking.

Ronald A. Siegel, Associate Professor of Biopharmaceutical Sciences and Pharmaceutical Chemistry; Sc.D., MIT. Drug delivery, polymer science, modeling of transport in complex systems, pharmacodynamics of tolerance, cardiovascular time series.

Francis C. Szoka, Professor of Biopharmaceutical Sciences and Pharmaceutical Chemistry; Ph.D., SUNY at Buffalo. Targeted drug delivery in liposomes, peptide-bilayer interactions, gene therapy.

Robert A. Upton, Associate Professor of Biopharmaceutical Sciences and Pharmaceutical Chemistry; Ph.D., Sydney. Biopharmaceutics, pharmacokinetics, pharmacodynamics, drug metabolism, drug analysis in biological fluids.

Davide Verotta, Assistant Professor of Biopharmaceutical Sciences, Pharmaceutical Chemistry, and Biostatistics; Ph.D., Berkeley. Parametric and nonparametric mathematical and statistical modeling, data analysis, pharmacokinetics, pharmacodynamics, cancer therapy.

Ching Chung Wang, Professor of Chemistry and Pharmaceutical Chemistry; Ph.D., Berkeley. Design of antiparasitic drugs through molecular and structural biological studies on the potential targets in parasites.

UNIVERSITY OF CINCINNATI

College of Pharmacy

Programs of Study

The University of Cincinnati College of Pharmacy offers a comprehensive series of advanced-degree programs covering the major areas within the broad heading of the pharmaceutical sciences for students with a background in biology, business, chemistry, engineering, or pharmacy. The goal of these programs is to develop the experimental and professional skills required to pursue careers in the academic, industrial, governmental, and practice environments of the profession.

The Master of Science and Doctor of Philosophy degrees are offered through the Division of Pharmaceutical Sciences. Areas of specialization include biopharmaceutics, cosmetic science, industrial pharmacy, medicinal chemistry, pharmaceutical analysis, pharmacokinetics, pharmacology, pharmacy administration, and physical pharmacy. The Doctor of Pharmacy degree is offered through the Division of Pharmacy Practice. Each program is designed to provide a well-rounded educational experience through advanced course work, seminars, independent study, and supervised scientific or practice-oriented research.

Although a student's program will vary according to his or her goals and interests, it typically will involve two years for the Master of Science degree and four years for the Doctor of Philosophy degree. A B.S.Pharm. degree is not required for these programs. The Doctor of Pharmacy curriculum is designed for completion over two years. Students must have a B.S.Pharm. degree to enter this program. A thesis, dissertation, or clinical investigation study is required along with an oral defense of the research presented. The Ph.D. degree requires a written and oral comprehensive examination for admission to candidacy.

Of special interest are a number of academic-industrial cooperative research programs, through which students have the opportunity to receive some of their training at national and international industrial locations.

Research Facilities

The College of Pharmacy is located in the University of Cincinnati Medical Center complex. All offices and laboratories are air conditioned and equipped for customary and specialized research. The College maintains an especially well equipped computer resource center. The Health Sciences Library is across the street from the College and, in addition to having an outstanding collection, provides a variety of online resources.

Financial Aid

The College offers a limited number of graduate teaching assistantships with stipends of $13,104 over nine months and a complete waiver of tuition and fees. University Graduate Scholarships that waive tuition cost but not fees are also available. A limited number of other awards are available in the form of research assistantships and fellowships. In some areas, a twelve-month appointment is available with a supplemental stipend.

Cost of Study

For the 1998–99 academic year, tuition for full-time study is $1807 per quarter for Ohio residents and $3453 per quarter for nonresidents. This includes the general fee of $185 per quarter.

Living and Housing Costs

The University maintains furnished apartments for single and married students that range from approximately $380 to $565 per month. Rent includes utilities and telephone. Many students prefer to live in rooms or apartments nearer the Medical Center. Rents for these vary considerably, but in general the cost of living in the Cincinnati area is very reasonable. Estimated room and board costs for a calendar year are $6500.

Student Group

The total graduate student population is about 5,000 students, of whom 1,000 are enrolled in the medical school and in graduate programs of the Medical Center complex. In the College of Pharmacy, there are 64 full-time and 28 part-time students, representing a mixture of U.S. (72 percent) and other (28 percent) students and equal numbers of men and women.

Location

The city of Cincinnati is located in southwestern Ohio on the famous Seven Hills overlooking the beautiful Ohio River valley. The city and the University provide many opportunities for cultural, social, and sporting events and activities, all of which support diverse interests and life-styles. Although Cincinnati is a cosmopolitan city with a population of more than a million, there are numerous wooded parks within the city that contribute to one of the country's nicest urban landscapes.

The University

The University of Cincinnati traces its origin to 1819, the year of the founding of the Cincinnati College and the Medical College of Ohio. In 1870, the city of Cincinnati established the University of Cincinnati, which later absorbed these colleges. For many years, the country's oldest and second-largest municipal university, the University of Cincinnati became a state university in 1977. With its various components located on several campuses, the University consists of eighteen colleges and divisions, providing a comprehensive range of undergraduate, graduate, and professional programs. These comprise the complex of learning, research, and public service that give the University national and international renown.

Applying

Students are usually admitted in the fall quarter of the academic year and are strongly encouraged to apply on or before April 15 of the year in which they desire admission, although applications continue to be processed if openings still exist. All programs require an undergraduate average of B or better for admission consideration, although consideration is also given to an applicant's professional accomplishments. Candidates must submit completed application forms, official transcripts from all colleges and universities attended, letters of evaluation from individuals able to assess their academic and professional abilities and potential, and scores of a minimum of 1600 on the General Test of the Graduate Record Examinations. International students must submit a minimum score of 600 on the Test of English as a Foreign Language (TOEFL). Prospective students are encouraged to contact individual faculty members whose interests (indicated on the reverse of this page) may coincide with their own.

Correspondence and Information

Director of Graduate Studies
College of Pharmacy
136 Health Professions Building
University of Cincinnati
3223 Eden Avenue
Cincinnati, Ohio 45267-0004

Telephone: 513-558-3784
E-mail: marcia.sedam@uc.edu
World Wide Web: http://129.137.232.101/inpharmatics.html

University of Cincinnati

THE FACULTY AND THEIR RESEARCH

Division of Pharmaceutical Sciences

Daniel Acosta Jr., Professor of Pharmacology and Toxicology and Dean; Ph.D., Kansas. Cellular toxicology; in vitro models of cardiotoxicity, nephrotoxicity, hepatotoxicity, ocular toxicity, and dermatotoxicity.
Arthur R. Buckley, Associate Professor; Ph.D., Arizona. Molecular genetic regulation of hormone/cytokine-stimulated cell proliferation and survival, immune cell signaling, genetic dysregulation of tumor progression.
William Cacini, Professor and Division Chairman; Ph.D., Minnesota. Diabetic nephropathy, renal pharmacology and toxicology, tubular transport mechanisms.
Carol A. Caperelli, Professor; Ph.D., Johns Hopkins. Bioorganic chemistry, mechanistic enzymology of purine biosynthesis and folate metabolism, protein-protein and protein–nucleic acid interactions, enzyme structure/function.
Pankaj B. Desai, Associate Professor; Ph.D., South Carolina. Pharmacokinetics and pharmacodynamics of anticancer drugs, inter-individual and inter-species variation in drug metabolism, drug delivery systems.
Gary A. Gudelsky, Associate Professor; Ph.D., Michigan State. Neuropharmacology, psychostimulant-induced neurotransmitter release and toxicity, mechanisms of antipsychotic drug action.
Raymond Jang, Professor; Ph.D., Ohio State. Evaluation of the performance of pharmacists in traditional and newer drug-related roles; cost benefit/cost-effectiveness of innovative pharmaceutical services; examination of the economic, social, and psychological factors that enhance or inhibit role development, with particular interest in the attitudinal and value components of self-image and success orientation; relationship of psychological characteristics and academic and career achievement.
James J. Knittel, Associate Professor; Ph.D., Connecticut. Structure-activity relationships of neuropeptides, computer-assisted drug design, design and synthesis of conformationally restricted peptides.
Alex C. Lin, Assistant Professor; Ph.D., Auburn. Improvement of medication distribution systems; innovative pharmacy facility planning and design; computer applications in pharmacy, with emphasis on the use of computer simulation in pharmaceutical care systems.
Giovanni M. Pauletti, Assistant Professor; Ph.D., Swiss Federal Institute of Technology. Biopharmaceutics, pharmacokinetics, oral drug delivery systems to the brain, membrane transport of drugs.
Adel Sakr, Professor and Director of Industrial Pharmacy Graduate Program; Ph.D., Strathclyde (Scotland). Pharmaceutical technology, pharmaceutical product development, formulation and bioavailability of oral solid dosage form: tablets and capsules, fluid-bed technology, roller compactor technology, high-shear mixing compression technology, formulation and manufacturing factors that affect dosage form, cosmetic technology, sustained-release and controlled-release design and formulation, novel drug-delivery systems, colonic drug delivery, target drug delivery systems, in vitro/in vivo evaluation of per–oral dosage forms.
Latif S. Shenouda, Professor; Ph.D., Michigan. Preformulation (physicochemical) and formulation factors that affect performance of dosage forms, both in vitro and in vivo; thermal methods of analysis; polymorphic characterization and kinetics of solid-state reversion; micromeritics; physical and chemical stability of pharmaceuticals; dissolution and pH-solubility profiles; formulation and development of conventional solid and liquid dosage forms; formulation, development, and evaluation of new controlled-release delivery systems.
Theresa I. Shireman, Assistant Professor; Ph.D., Wisconsin. Pharmacoeconomics, health economics, health services research, drug utilization review, health policy, health outcomes and quality of life, pharmacoepidemiology.
Kenneth A. Skau, Associate Professor; Ph.D., Ohio State. Neuropathologies and myopathies, muscular dystrophy, axonal transport, acetylcholinesterase pharmacology, diabetic neuropathy.
Victor D. Warner, Professor; Ph.D., Kansas. Systematic study of antibacterial agents involving the synthesis of analogs to determine the effect of functional groups and their location on activity.
R. Randall Wickett, Associate Professor; Ph.D., Oregon State. Preformulation, formulation, and in vitro and in vivo development and evaluation of cosmetic products.

Division of Pharmacy Practice

Jerry A. Bennett, Associate Professor; Pharm.D., Tennessee. Psychopharmacology; Phase I, II, and III studies.
Michael B. Bottorff, Professor; Pharm.D., Kentucky. Clinical pharmacokinetics and pharmacodynamics of cardiovascular drugs, concentration-effect modeling, clinical pharmacology of beta blockers and antiarrhythmics, polymorphic drug metabolism, hepatic enzyme induction and inhibition, informatics.
Kristina Capó, Assistant Professor; Pharm.D., Florida A&M. Ambulatory medicine practice, development and maintenance of ambulatory pharmacy practice in retail settings that support the delivery of pharmaceutical care.
Robert J. Cluxton, Associate Professor; Pharm.D., Cincinnati. Drug literature evaluation, geriatrics, Alzheimer's disease, depression, postmarketing drug surveillance.
Wayne Conrad, Professor; Pharm.D., Kentucky. Hospital pharmacy practice, drug utilization review, quality assurance, evaluation of innovative approaches to education or training, evaluation of expanded pharmacy roles or services.
William K. Fant, Associate Professor and Division Chairman; Pharm.D., Cincinnati. Development of multimedia programs designed to enhance learning and problem-solving skills; evaluation of communication tools, including the Internet, in health sciences research, teaching, and practice settings; infectious diseases; medical informatics; quality assurance.
Daniel P. Healy, Associate Professor; Pharm.D., Kentucky. Preclinical pharmacology and experimental therapeutics of antimicrobials and immunomodulators in bacterial sepsis.
Phillip Jennings, Assistant Professor; Pharm.D., Tennessee. Ambulatory medicine practice, development and maintenance of ambulatory pharmacy practice in institutional settings that support the delivery of pharmaceutical care.
Jill Martin, Research Assistant Professor; Pharm.D., Kentucky. Transplantation and pharmacoeconomics, cost-effective use of drug therapy in solid organ transplant patients.
Steven A. Myre, Associate Professor; Pharm.D., Minnesota. Phase I, II, and III human studies; clinical pharmacokinetics; renal drug therapy; transplantation pharmacotherapy.
J. Richard Wuest, Professor; Pharm.D., Cincinnati. Community pharmacy practice, socioeconomics and pharmacy, continuing education for practicing pharmacists, computerized drug information for community pharmacy practice.
Peter Yurkowski, Associate Professor; Pharm.D., Maryland. Internal medicine practice, development and maintenance of adult internal medicine practice in support of the delivery of pharmaceutical care

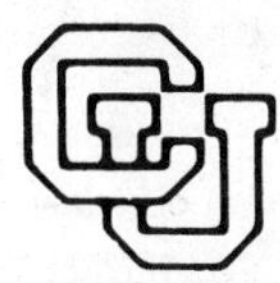

UNIVERSITY OF COLORADO HEALTH SCIENCES CENTER

School of Pharmacy

Programs of Study

The School of Pharmacy offers graduate programs leading to the Ph.D. degree in pharmaceutical sciences and in toxicology. Basic and advanced courses are available in the areas of pharmacology, toxicology, neuropharmacology, medicinal chemistry, pharmacokinetics, and pharmaceutics.

Graduate students currently enrolled have bachelor's degrees in the areas of pharmacy, chemistry, biology, biochemistry, and molecular biology. The diverse backgrounds of the graduate students reflect the broad research interests of the faculty. These include the mechanisms of toxicity of drugs and environmental chemicals, cancer research, drug addiction research, neuropharmacology, pharmacokinetics, medicinal chemistry, and the design of novel drug delivery systems.

Research Facilities

The School of Pharmacy has excellent facilities in a building on the Health Sciences Center Campus. These include 27,000 square feet of research laboratory space, 6,250 square feet of office space, 4,000 square feet of conference rooms and administrative offices, 7,000 square feet of classroom space, and 3,000 square feet of reading room/lounge/group study rooms. The research space is equipped with modern instrumentation, including liquid chromatograph/mass spectrometer and gas chromatograph/mass spectrometer/computer systems and apparatus for high-performance liquid chromatography, gas chromatography, nuclear magnetic resonance spectroscopy, liquid and gamma scintillation counting, DNA and amino acid sequencing, tissue culture, electrophoresis and differential centrifugation equipment, rodent breeding, and behavior-testing facilities.

Financial Aid

Financial assistance is available in the form of graduate teaching and research assistantships and University doctoral fellowships. In 1998–99, monthly stipends are approximately $1250. For students seeking fellowship support, early application (before February 1) is recommended.

Cost of Study

The proposed tuition for graduate students in 1998–99 is $119 per quarter hour for residents of Colorado and $415 per quarter hour for nonresidents. Financial assistance in the form of tuition waivers is available for research and teaching assistants. Insurance and activity fees for all graduate students amount to $2243 annually.

Living and Housing Costs

At present, no University housing is available. Students generally have little difficulty, however, finding suitable inexpensive housing close to campus. The cost of incidentals (rent, food, travel, etc.) is estimated by the Office of Financial Aid at $12,720 a year.

Student Group

Currently, 90 professional students are pursuing Pharm.D. degrees in a four-year program in the School of Pharmacy, and 25 graduate students (16 women, 9 men) are seeking Ph.D. degrees. There are also many postdoctoral fellows and professional research assistants in the School of Pharmacy.

Location

The University of Colorado Health Sciences Center Campus is located in a quiet residential area of east Denver. A modern city of approximately 1.5 million, Denver has a wide variety of cultural and recreational facilities. The climate in Denver and its environs is exceptionally pleasant with mild, sunny winters and warm, dry summers, which allows residents to partake of the many recreational opportunities afforded by the Rocky Mountains.

The University

What began in 1883 as a medical school with 2 students has evolved into the largest comprehensive health facility in the region and has gained both national and international recognition for accomplishments in biomedical research and patient care. The Center has undergone considerable expansion in the past decade, and current facilities include the enlarged and modernized Denison Library; the Schools of Medicine, Nursing, Dentistry, and Pharmacy; and a 400-bed teaching hospital. An eight-story biomedical research building was completed in 1991.

Applying

Applications for graduate admission can be obtained by calling or writing to the School of Pharmacy. The application packet contains specific instructions regarding the completion of forms, the forwarding of academic transcripts, and letters of recommendation. The Graduate Committee should receive all material before February 1, and admission is normally granted only for the fall quarter.

Correspondence and Information

Graduate Admissions
Department of Pharmaceutical Sciences
School of Pharmacy
University of Colorado Health Sciences Center
Box C238
4200 East Ninth Avenue
Denver, Colorado 80262
Telephone: 303-315-7732

University of Colorado Health Sciences Center

THE FACULTY AND THEIR RESEARCH

Ralph J. Altiere, Professor; Ph.D., New York Medical College, 1979. Pulmonary physiology and pharmacology, neural regulation of airway function, pulmonary vascular pharmacology.
John F. Carpenter, Associate Professor; Ph.D., Southwestern Louisiana, 1985. Cellular physiology and pathophysiology, metabolic regulation, protein structure and function, protein preservation and formulation.
Carlos E. Catalano, Associate Professor; Pharm.D., 1983, Ph.D., 1987, California, San Francisco. Mechanisms of viral assembly, molecular mechanisms of genotoxicity.
Louis Diamond, Professor and Dean; Ph.D., Maryland, 1967. Pulmonary physiology, pharmacology, and toxicology.
V. Gene Erwin, Professor; Ph.D., Colorado, 1965. Pharmacogenetic approaches to studies of the neurochemistry and neuropharmacology of alcohol and cocaine.
Richard D. Irons, Professor; Ph.D., Rochester, 1974. Molecular mechanisms of leukemogenesis.
Gary R. Krieger, Assistant Professor Adjoint; M.D., Johns Hopkins, 1981. Occupational health, environmental risk assessment.
David J. Kroll, Assistant Professor; Ph.D., Florida, 1989. Molecular pharmacology and transcriptional regulation of DNA topoisomerase II.
Alvin M. Malkinson, Professor; Ph.D., Johns Hopkins, 1968. Genetic, biochemical, and histologic aspects of mouse lung tumor development; protein phosphorylation; signal transduction.
Mark C. Manning, Associate Professor and Director of Pharmaceutical Sciences Graduate Program; Ph.D., Northwestern, 1983. Stability and transport of polypeptide drugs.
Lawrence K. Ng, Assistant Professor; Ph.D., Wisconsin–Madison, 1991. Design and development of strategy to enhance membrane flux of peptide and protein drugs (drug-targeting and transport across the blood-brain barrier).
Lori Dwyer Nield, Assistant Research Professor; Ph.D., Kentucky, 1991. Involvement of protein kinase C signal transduction in lung tumorigenesis.
Susan M. Paulsen, Assistant Professor and Coordinator and Director of Professional Pharmacy Skills Course; Pharm.D., Colorado, 1997. Evaluating the utilization of clinical pharmacy services in the ambulatory care setting.
Dennis R. Petersen, Professor and Director of Molecular Toxicology and Environmental Health Sciences Program; Ph.D., Wyoming, 1974. Pharmacogenetics and toxicological aspects of hepatic aldehyde metabolism.
David Ross, Professor and Department Chairman; Ph.D., Aston in Birmingham (England), 1982. Relationship of metabolism to toxicity, mechanisms of bone marrow toxicity of myelotoxins and leukemogens, mechanisms of selective toxicity of cancer chemotherapeutic agents to human tumor cells.
James A. Ruth, Professor; Ph.D., Northwestern, 1974. Toxic mechanisms in drugs of abuse, metabolism of α-β-unsaturated aldehydes and butadiene.
Robert I. Scheinman, Assistant Professor; Ph.D., Washington (Seattle), 1990. Regulation of gene expression focusing on NF-kB and steroid hormone receptors, mechanism of immunosuppression and growth regulation.
David C. Thompson, Assistant Research Professor; Ph.D., Melbourne, 1985. Airway pharmacology and physiology.
John A. Thompson, Professor; Ph.D., UCLA, 1969. Chemical and biochemical aspects of the metabolism and toxicity of drugs and environmental chemicals.
Vasilis K. Vasiliou, Assistant Professor; Ph.D., Ioannina School of Medicine (Greece), 1988. Cellular responses to oxidative stress, pharmacogenetics of alcohol drinking preference and toxicity.

CURRENT RESEARCH

Research in the School is supported by a variety of federal and nonfederal agencies. Federal agencies include NIEHS, NCI, NHLBI, NIAAA, NIDA, NSF, NASA, and ONR. Current research support exceeds $3 million annually.

Biochemistry and Cellular Biology. Areas of study include mechanistic enzymology and molecular mechanisms of carcinogenesis and tumor promotion. Catalysis at the molecular level is of interest and is investigated in two general research areas: the biochemistry of virus assembly and the molecular mechanisms of genotoxicity. The interactions of compounds that can damage DNA directly or interfere with the proteins that regulate DNA behavior (replication, repair, transcription) are studied. Biochemical, biophysical, and molecular biological methods are extensively utilized to obtain a detailed picture of the processes involved in enzymatic catalysis.

Medicinal Chemistry. The focus of this interdisciplinary program provides students with the foundation necessary for applying chemical theory and techniques to studies of pharmacological and toxicological problems. Course work involves advanced training in organic, biological, and analytical chemistry, together with courses in pharmacology and toxicology. Students participate in an ongoing research program in one of several areas, including neurochemistry, drug metabolism, enzyme mechanisms, and chemical carcinogenesis.

Pharmaceutics. This field is concerned with the stability, the delivery, and the analysis of known drug compounds. Research projects include the design of delivery systems and stable formulations for recombinant protein drugs, mechanistic studies on physical and chemical stabilization of proteins and peptides, drug delivery across the blood-brain barrier, lyophilization technology, and advanced spectroscopic structural studies.

Pharmacology. Areas of study include autonomic, cardiovascular, pulmonary, and endocrine pharmacology. Neuropharmacology is an additional focus of research, and elucidation of neurochemical pathways underlying alcohol addiction is a major research area.

Toxicology and Carcinogenesis. Areas of study are centered on elucidation of mechanisms of toxicity of drugs and environmental pollutants. Major research areas include studies of bone marrow toxicity and leukemogenesis, drug- and toxin-induced hepatic and lung injury, and mechanisms of DNA damage and tumor induction by environmental toxins. The role of metabolic mechanisms in toxicity is a central theme, and the elucidation of pathways of selective toxicity to human tumor cells is an additional focus of research in this area.

UNIVERSITY OF CONNECTICUT

Department of Pharmaceutical Sciences
Graduate Programs in Pharmaceutics and Medicinal and Natural Products Chemistry

Programs of Study

Programs are offered leading to the M.S. and Ph.D. degrees in pharmaceutics, medicinal chemistry, and natural products chemistry.

Research is a key component of the graduate program. Pharmaceutics research covers the areas of novel film coatings, reactive polymer dissolution, iontophoresis, microencapsulation, interfacial rheology of biopolymers, protein stability and delivery, mechanisms of protein aggregation, protein hydrolysis, carrier proteins, drug transport across cell cultured membranes, liposomes, biophysics of transmembrane transport, drug delivery to the lung, pharmacokinetics, pharmacodynamics, pharmacometrics, isolated perfused kidney studies to characterize mechanisms of drug interactions, antibiotic therapy, and the postantibiotic effect. Medicinal chemistry involves contemporary methods for the design, synthesis, and evaluation of novel therapeutic agents using solid-phase synthesis and HTS. In addition, studies of the molecular mechanisms of drug action use biophysical methods such as NMS, DSC, X-ray diffraction, and MS. Other projects include modifying drug structures to facilitate transport and targeting and studying these processes using modern physicochemical methods. The natural products chemists deal with isolation, structural elucidation, and synthesis of those molecules in nature that possess pharmacological activity.

Research Facilities

Extensive laboratory facilities are available for research in modern synthetic chemistry, physical chemistry, and biophysics within the School of Pharmacy. Major equipment within the School includes a high-field multinuclear NMR spectrometer, differential scanning calorimeter, spectrofluorometer, particle sizing equipment, Fourier transform infrared spectrometer, high-pressure liquid chromatographs, spectrophotometers, multi-channel iontophoresis power source, and a surface rheometer. In addition, equipment is available at the University's Institute of Material Science and Biotechnology Center. This includes excellent high-field solution and solid-state NMR spectrometers, electron microscopes, analytical ultracentrifuges, and protein sequencers, as well as equipment for single-crystal and small-angle X-ray diffraction analysis.

Financial Aid

A limited number of teaching and research assistantships are offered through the School and are awarded on a competitive basis to qualified applicants. Stipends range from $13,610 to $15,915 for full-time appointments for the academic year. Appointments carry health benefits and a waiver of tuition. A limited number of special fellowships are also available to exceptionally qualified students.

Cost of Study

Tuition fees for full-time students carrying 9 or more credits are $3115 per semester for in-state students and $7327 for out-of-state students.

Living and Housing Costs

Housing is available in a limited number of on-campus graduate dormitories at a cost of approximately $4400 per year. Off-campus housing is also available with rents ranging from $300 to $700 per month, depending on size, location, and sharing of accommodations.

Student Group

Of a total University population of approximately 26,000 students, about 2,500 are working toward doctoral degrees. Within the School of Pharmacy, there are 50 graduate students, with 25 in the area of pharmaceutics and 10 in the areas of medicinal and natural products chemistry.

Location

The University is housed on a 3,100-acre rural campus in Storrs in pastoral northeastern Connecticut. Its proximity to Hartford (30 miles), Boston (80 miles) and New York City (130 miles) provides for cultural, recreational, and sporting attractions. Storrs is also near the beaches of southern New England and the mountains of northern New England.

The University and The Department

Founded in 1881 as the Storrs Agricultural College, the University has grown into a major northeastern public university while retaining a rural New England atmosphere. More than 120 buildings are housed on 3,100 acres in and around Storrs. A faculty of more than 1,200 serves the needs of the University's 26,000 students. The Department of Pharmaceutical Sciences is located in the School of Pharmacy in the heart of the Storrs campus within walking distance of graduate dormitories, the University Library, the chemistry department, and the computer center.

Applying

Applicants should hold, or expect to receive, a B.S. or B.A. degree in pharmacy, biology, chemistry, chemical engineering, or a related area. At least a B average or equivalent is required to be competitive. GRE General Test scores, TOEFL scores (for international applicants), and three letters of reference are also required. Applicants are accepted throughout the year for admission in September or January. Requests for financial aid should be received early in the cycle.

Correspondence and Information

Graduate Admissions Committee
University of Connecticut
372 Fairfield Road
P.O. Box U-92P
Storrs, Connecticut 06269-2092
Telephone: 860-486-4066
Fax: 860-486-4998
E-mail: phrmacy8@uconnvm.uconn.edu

University of Connecticut

THE FACULTY AND THEIR RESEARCH

PHARMACEUTICS

Robin H. Bogner, Associate Professor; Ph.D., Rutgers. Development of novel tablet film coatings, the characterization of the microenvironment near the surface of dissolving polymer films, stabilization of proteins during lyophilization, iontophoresis of charged macromolecules.

Diane J. Burgess, Associate Professor; Ph.D., London. Surface and colloid chemistry, with emphasis in the areas of microencapsulation and emulsion technology for targeted- and controlled-release delivery of traditional and biotechnology drugs.

Moses S. S. Chow, Professor of Clinical Pharmacy; Pharm.D., California, San Francisco. Cardiovascular pharmacology, pharmacokinetics, pharmacoeconomics and drug usage evaluations.

Donna J. Fournier, Associate Professor; Ph.D., Connecticut. Transport phenomena, renal function and nephrotoxicity, reproductive endocrinology and drug delivery.

Devendra S. Kalonia, Associate Professor; Ph.D., Connecticut. Stability, aggregation and solution behavior of proteins, kinetics and mechanisms of peptide hydrolysis, solubility and dissolution of peptides, drug delivery of biotechnology drugs and the use of biodegradable polymers in drug delivery.

Paul A. Kramer, Professor; Ph.D., Wisconsin. Pulmonary absorption of macromolecules, pharmacokinetics and dynamics of drugs used in dental therapeutics.

Charles H. Nightingale, Research Professor; Ph.D., SUNY at Buffalo. Pharmacokinetics, antibiotics and infectious diseases.

Michael J. Pikal, Professor; Ph.D., Iowa State. Lyophilization of proteins and other pharmaceuticals—process, formulation, and stability.

Kevin R. Sweeney, Associate Professor; Ph.D., Connecticut. Pharmacokinetics, pharmacodynamics and pharmacometrics, characterization and modeling of concentration versus time profiles, mechanisms of renal elimination and drug response.

Adjunct and Associated Faculty

Michael Beatrice, Adjunct Professor; M.S., Oklahoma. Regulatory aspects of the development of drugs and biologics.

Dennis Chapron, Associate Professor of Clinical Pharmacy; M.S., North Carolina. Drug disposition and response in the elderly, drug-drug and drug-disease interactions and clinical outcomes, use of prescription databases for pharmacoepidemiological studies, renal drug excretion mechanisms.

Marc R. Gastonguay, Adjunct Assistant Professor; Ph.D., Georgetown. Pharmacokinetic and pharmacodynamic modeling.

Daniel P. McNamara, Adjunct Associate Professor; Ph.D., Michigan. Effects of buffers on the dissolution of acidic and basic compounds, metered dose inhaler formulation.

MEDICINAL AND NATURAL PRODUCTS CHEMISTRY

Marlene Bouvier, Assistant Professor; Ph.D., McGill. Biochemical and structural approaches to the study of folding and assembly of class 1 MHC molecules, X-ray crystallography, design and synthesis of antigenic peptides, molecular biology.

James G. Henkel, Associate Professor; Ph.D., Brown. Antineoplastic agents, physicochemical aspects of drug action, chemistry of bridged polycyclic systems, central nervous system active substances.

Alexandros Makriyannis, Professor; Ph.D., Kansas. Drug design, drug-receptor and drug-membrane interactions, nuclear magnetic resonance spectroscopy.

Karl A. Nieforth, Professor; Ph.D., Purdue. Synthesis and evaluation of drug antagonists, in particular narcotic and hallucinogenic antagonists.

David G. Rhodes, Associate Professor; Ph.D., Connecticut. Physical studies of drug-membrane interactions, structure and function of membranes and drug-membrane complexes, cellular uptake of antisense oligonucleotides, liposomal drug delivery.

Sandra C. Vigil-Cruz, Assistant Professor; Ph.D., Oregon State. Peptide drug design, solid-phase and combinatorial synthesis of pharmacological probes and potential therapeutic agents targeting AIDS and breast cancer.

Zbigniew J. Witczak, Assistant Professor; Ph.D., Lódz. Synthesis of natural products from carbohydrates, levoglucosenone, carbohydrate mimetics, and chemistry of thio- and phosphorosugars as potential cytotoxic, antitumor, and antiviral agents; insulin-mimetic oligosaccharide synthesis, C-glycosides and C-disaccharides; molecular modeling of carbohydrates.

Adjunct and Associated Faculty

Alireza Banijamali, Adjunct Professor; Ph.D., Connecticut. Drug metabolism.

John Devlin, Adjunct Professor; Ph.D., Sheffield. High throughput screening and synthesis.

Xiang-Qun Xie, Adjunct Assistant Professor; Ph.D., Connecticut. Nuclear magnetic resonance and drug design.

UNIVERSITY OF GEORGIA

College of Pharmacy

Programs of Study

The College of Pharmacy offers programs of study and research that lead to the Master of Science or Doctor of Philosophy degree in experimental therapeutics, medicinal chemistry, pharmaceutics, pharmacology, pharmacy care administration, and toxicology. The programs are administered by the faculty of the two departments of the College: Clinical and Administrative Sciences and Pharmaceutical and Biomedical Sciences. The various graduate degree programs differ in the specific requirements, but all emphasize a solid foundation of basic skills and understanding, a broad background of knowledge in the area of research specialization, and individual training in a specific area of research. Specific information about the programs can be found on the College's Web site (address below).

Clinical and administrative sciences include the general areas of pharmacy care administration and experimental therapeutics. Pharmacy care administration is the study of the economic, social, behavioral, and political aspects of pharmaceutical services and disease state management; it is an interdisciplinary program that may contain elective concentration of courses in business administration, psychology, statistics, political science, and other disciplines that affect ethical drug issues. The program prepares the student to address the complex sociopolitical problems that relate to ethical drug consumption, manufacturing, distribution, and payment mechanisms. Experimental therapeutics is a multidisciplinary program that involves the investigation of disease processes and the efficacy and toxicity of therapeutic regimens.

Pharmaceutical and biomedical sciences include the disciplines of medicinal chemistry, pharmaceutics, and pharmacology and toxicology. Areas of concentration within these disciplines include biochemical pharmacology, computational chemistry and computational molecular biology, drug discovery and synthesis, drug-dosage formulation and delivery, pharmacokinetics and drug metabolism, pharmaceutical and biomedical analysis, and interdisciplinary toxicology.

Research Facilities

Research laboratories and equipment that are necessary for modern pharmaceutical and biomedical research are available on both the University of Georgia and Medical College of Georgia campuses. Modern equipment that is necessary for sophisticated research is available in the College. This includes such items as NMR and mass spectrometers, radioisotope equipment, gas chromatographs, liquid chromatographs, and physiological recording systems. Cell-culture facilities and an animal care unit provide additional capabilities. Computer systems, both within the College and the University, support the research enterprise.

Financial Aid

Teaching assistantships are available, and tuition is waived for those students who receive assistantships.

Cost of Study

Tuition for 1998–99 is $111 per semester hour for in-state residents and $445 per semester hour for out-of-state residents. These fees are waived for students who are granted teaching assistantships. Semester fees are currently $310 and represent the only fees that are required of students with assistantships.

Living and Housing Costs

Subsidized housing is available for married students. Single students may stay in dormitories. Housing also exists throughout Athens and the surrounding community. More detailed information is available from the campus Housing Office (World Wide Web: http://www.uga.edu).

Student Group

Approximately 70 graduate students are enrolled in the College's graduate programs. The graduate student body is diverse and consists of students from throughout the United States and other countries.

Student Outcomes

Students usually take positions with major research universities, drug company research divisions, and the government. A number of students take postdoctoral positions. There has been an increase in the demand for pharmaceutical scientists who are trained in an interdisciplinary institution. Virtually all graduates are successful in obtaining positions.

Location

The University of Georgia is located in Athens, a city that is 70 miles northeast of Atlanta. The metropolitan population of Athens exceeds 100,000, although the atmosphere is that of an active college town. Athens is also a well-known music and cultural center. The city is located in the foothills of the Smoky Mountains. A moderate climate allows for a wide range of outdoor activities year-round. Water and mountain sports are available within a 1- to 2-hour drive, while Atlantic and Gulf Coast beaches are within about 6 hours.

The University

The University of Georgia, established in 1785, is the oldest state-chartered university in the nation. The University campus covers 3,500 acres and has its own transit system that serves all academic buildings, dormitories, and married student housing.

Applying

Individuals should contact the Graduate Coordinator of the program of interest for more information. Application for admission may be made electronically as well as via paper application to the Graduate School. Applicants who wish to apply electronically may use the following Web address for access to the system: http://www.gradsch.uga.edu. The current cost is $30 per application. Applications and supporting credentials must be submitted by the July 1 deadline for fall semester matriculation. The entering class may be filled before the deadline, so it is strongly recommended that applications be submitted by February 15. Performance on the General and Subject Tests of the Graduate Record Examinations is considered together with transcripts, letters of recommendation, other degrees, and previous work experience. Members of minority groups are strongly urged to apply. Requests for applications, the Graduate School Bulletin, and other information may be made to the addresses below.

Correspondence and Information

Clinical and administrative sciences:
Dr. Randall L. Tackett
Graduate Coordinator
Department of Clinical and Administrative Sciences
College of Pharmacy
University of Georgia
Athens, Georgia 30602-2354
Telephone: 706-542-7400
Fax: 706-542-5228
E-mail: rtackett@rx.uga.edu
World Wide Web: http://www.rx.uga.edu

Pharmaceutical and biomedical sciences:
Dr. A. C. Capomacchia
Graduate Coordinator
Department of Pharmaceutical and Biomedical Sciences
College of Pharmacy
University of Georgia
Athens, Georgia 30602-2352
Telephone: 706-542-5339
Fax: 706-542-5358
E-mail: tcapomac@rx.uga.edu
World Wide Web: http://www.rx.uga.edu

University of Georgia

THE FACULTY AND THEIR RESEARCH

Department of Clinical and Administrative Sciences

Marie A. Chisholm, Pharm.D., Assistant Professor. Outcomes associated with pharmaceutical care services, educational predictors of success in pharmacy school.

James W. Cooper, Ph.D., Professor. Geriatric drug therapy outcomes, long-term care, pharmacoepidemiology, pharmacoeconomics, adverse drug reactions, pharmacist's effect on drug-related problems at all levels of care.

Joseph T. DiPiro, Pharm.D., Professor and Head. Surgical infectious diseases and immunopharmacology.

Jeffrey A. Kotzan, Ph.D., Professor. Health-systems research, including outcomes and policy, with a special emphasis on large databases, such as Medicaid and other managed-care systems.

Bradley C. Martin, Pharm.D., Ph.D., Associate Professor. Pharmacoeconomics/technology assessment and health-policy analysis, burden of illness studies, cost effectiveness modeling, quality of life instrument validation, and prescription cost containment analyses, with specific expertise in disorders affecting the CNS.

Allison W. Miller, Pharm.D., Assistant Professor. Mechanisms linking insulin resistance to vascular dysfunction, physiologic and pathophysiologic significance of endothelial-mediated vasodilators.

Gloria J. Nichols-English, Ph.D., Assistant Professor. Theoretical framework and concepts of multicultural patient care, pharmaceutical care, practice outcomes research, evaluation program effectiveness, quality of life, pharmacoeconomic and humanistic health outcomes in minority and women's health.

Matthew Perri III, Ph.D., Professor and Associate Head. How patients process and act on information provided by health-care professionals or the media, direct-to-consumer advertising, generic substitution, medication compliance, patient counseling.

Sylvie Poirier, Ph.D., Assistant Professor. Pharmacist compensation for pharmacy care services, evaluation of pharmacy services, pharmacoepidemiology, instructional research.

Randall L. Tackett, Ph.D., Professor and Graduate Coordinator. Racial and gender differences in cardiovascular disease and drug responses, endothelial dysfunction, free radicals, substances of abuse.

Alvin V. Terry, Ph.D., Assistant Professor. Central cholinergic function in memory disorders and neurodegenerative diseases.

Michael R. Ujhelyi, Pharm.D., Associate Professor. Assessing ion channel conductance and electropharmacology during ventricular fibrillation and defibrillation to determine electrophysiologic regulators and mechanisms of these processes.

William E. Wade, Pharm.D., Associate Professor. Outcomes research conducted through a network of independent community pharmacists, drug therapy in renal transplant recipients.

Department of Pharmaceutical and Biomedical Sciences

Michael Bartlett, Ph.D., Assistant Professor. Application of mass spectroscopy to the study of biological problems.

J. Warren Beach, Ph.D., Associate Professor. Use of carbohydrates as templates for the stereoselective synthesis of novel nucleoside analogues as antiprotozoal and antiviral agents.

F. Douglas Boudinot, Ph.D., Professor and Department Head. Biopharmaceutics, pharmacokinetics, pharmacodynamics, drug analysis and drug metabolism.

James V. Bruckner, Ph.D., Professor. Pharmacokinetics and toxicology of solvents, risk assessment of potentially hazardous chemicals, environmental toxicology.

O. Rebecca Bunce, Ph.D., Associate Professor. Tissue inhibitors of metalloproteinases (TIMP) and their influence on their expression on tumor angiogenesis and metastasis.

Anthony C. Capomacchia, Ph.D., Associate Professor and Graduate Coordinator. Chemiluminescence analysis in body matrices through CL analysis of the reactive oxygen species superoxide, hydrogen peroxide, and lipid hydroperoxides using stopped-flow, flow injection, and HPLC; CL instrument and detector development with stopped-flow, flow injection, and HPLC.

Chung K. Chu, Ph.D., Professor. Design and synthesis of antiviral agents against human immunodeficiency virus and hepatitis B virus, anticancer agents.

Cham E. Dallas, Ph.D, Associate Professor. Validate risk-based approaches for evaluating and responding to hazards due to exposure to environmental contaminants.

Stuart Feldman, Ph.D., Professor and Dean. Biopharmaceutics and pharmacokinetics of medicinal agents in pediatrics, pregnancy, and zero gravity.

Phillip Greenspan, Ph.D., Associate Professor. Low-density lipoprotein (LDL) and cholesterol metabolism, oxidation of LDL, lipid histochemistry, phospholipid metabolism.

Diane K. Hartle, Ph.D., Associate Professor. Neurobiology of essential hypertension and testing of potential antihypertensive drugs.

W. Ben Iturrian, Ph.D., Associate Professor. Genetic animal model for epilepsy or dystonia, ultrasounds as neuroprotectant, novel neurosteroids, screening natural products for neurological effects.

H. Won Jun, Ph.D., Professor. Formulation studies of controlled-release drug delivery systems for oral, transdermal, and parenteral use.

D. Robert Lu, Ph.D., Associate Professor. Boron neutron capture therapy, targeting drug delivery systems to cancer cells.

James C. Price, Ph.D., Professor. Development of colloidal dosage forms for poorly soluble drugs, development of methods of manufacture of controlled-release microcapsule/microsphere dosage forms that minimize the use of volatile solvents.

Thomas G. Reigle, Ph.D., Associate Professor. Brain biogenic amines and their involvement in drug action.

Peter C. Ruenitz, Ph.D., Professor. Molecular mechanisms of action of triarylethylene estrogens and antiestrogens.

James C. Stewart, Ph.D., Professor. Applications of analytical chemistry to the study of the pharmaceutical sciences.

E. Will Taylor, Ph.D., Associate Professor. Computational chemistry and biology as applied to nucleic acid and protein structure; problems in antiviral, CNS, and cardiovascular research; molecular modeling and computer-assisted drug design; cloning and characterization of novel viral genes; antiviral and anticancer effects of selenium.

Catherine A. White, Ph.D., Associate Professor. Targeting of antibiotics to the reticuloendothelial system and the lungs for the treatment of opportunistic and/or facultative infections.

THE UNIVERSITY OF MONTANA–MISSOULA

School of Pharmacy
Graduate Programs in Pharmacology / Pharmaceutical Sciences

Programs of Study

The department maintains a comprehensive research program with focus areas in neurosciences, cardiovascular sciences, and endocrinology. Research collaborations occur with nearby pharmaceutical industry. Research training experiences are in place for both undergraduate and graduate students. Degree opportunities include a Ph.D. in pharmacology/pharmaceutical sciences and the M.S. in pharmaceutical sciences. The Ph.D. program emphasizes training in pharmacology and toxicology with additional emphasis available in pharmaceutics-pharmacokinetics, medicinal chemistry, pharmacognosy, and the biological sciences. Courses in biochemistry and statistics are required, and elective courses in molecular biology, microbiology, immunology, molecular genetics, and advanced biochemistry are integrated into the plan of study according to the student's focus. In general, degree training consists of two years of course work and two years of research leading to the completion and defense of a Ph.D. dissertation. The M.S. degree requires one year of course work and the completion of a thesis.

Research Facilities

The School of Pharmacy and Allied Health Sciences is one of the newer buildings on The University of Montana campus. Laboratories are designed for modern research and are well-equipped. Other collaborating entities include Ribi ImmunoChem Research Inc., The McLaughlin Research Institute, Rocky Mountain National Laboratories, Western Montana Clinic, the State of Montana Crime Laboratories, the Community Hospital Medical Center, and St. Patrick Hospital.

Financial Aid

Teaching assistantships, research assistantships, and summer employment opportunities are available to highly qualified graduate program applicants, and tuition waivers are granted to most students. Current academic year stipends and summer employment total up to $14,000.

Cost of Study

An average annual tuition cost for nonresidents is $7565 and for residents is $2908. In most cases, tuition costs are waived; however, some incidental fees (including health insurance) must be paid directly by the student.

Living and Housing Costs

The University maintains nine residence halls on a space-available basis. Families may apply to live in one of 518 apartments located on the south campus. There are new housing units under construction. These apartments, ranging from studio to four-bedroom sizes, rent for $197 to $443 per month and are within walking distance of the main campus.

Student Group

Montana's 12,000 students, of whom about 1,600 are enrolled in graduate studies, represent nearly every state and fifty-seven nations. The University of Montana is accredited by the Northwest Association of Schools and Colleges, and the Graduate School is a member of the Council of Graduate Schools.

Location

The University of Montana is located in Missoula, a city of 60,000 situated midway between Yellowstone and Glacier national parks in the mountains and forests of Western Montana. Because of its popular setting, mountain streams, and ski slopes, Missoula remains a major center of tourism and is easily reached by interstate highway and airlines. The average high temperature is 21 degrees in January and 84 degrees in July.

The University

The University of Montana is one of two major universities in the state. The Missoula campus has seven professional schools (business administration, education, fine arts, forestry, journalism, law, and pharmacy and allied health sciences) as well as a College of Arts and Sciences, a College of Technology, and a Graduate School. The University competes in NCAA Division I in basketball and was the 1995 national champion in Division I-A football.

Applying

Students are usually admitted in the fall semester of the academic year and are strongly encouraged to apply on or before March 1 of the year in which they desire admission, although applications continue to be processed if openings still exist. All graduate programs require a minimum undergraduate and/or master's GPA of 3.0; a combined (quantitative, verbal, and analytical) score of 1500 is required (1200 for the M.S. program) on the Graduate Record Examinations (GRE). International students whose native language is not English must show a score of 540 or above on the Test of English as a Foreign Language (TOEFL).

Correspondence and Information

Graduate Program Coordinator
The University of Montana
School of Pharmacy
Department of Pharmaceutical Sciences, PhP 140
Missoula, Montana 59812-1075
Telephone: 406-243-4765
E-mail: bbrooks@selway.umt.edu

The University of Montana–Missoula

THE FACULTY AND THEIR RESEARCH

Howard D. Beall, Assistant Professor; Ph.D. (medicinal chemistry), Florida. Metabolic mechanisms of activation of antitumor quinones in human tumor cells.
Role of NAD(P)H:quinone oxidoreductase (DT-0diaphorase) in cytotoxicity and induction of DNA damage by streptonigrin. *Biochem. Pharmacol.* 51:645–52, 1996. With Liu et al.

Richard J. Bridges, Associate Professor; Ph.D. (biochemistry), Cornell. Neuropharmacology and neurotoxicology of exitatory amino acid neurotransmitters (e.g., glutamate, aspartate).
Methylation of the NMDA receptor agonist L-*trans*-2,3-pyrrolidine-dicarboxylate: Enhanced excitotoxic potency and selectivity. *Toxicol. Appl. Pharmacol.*, in press. With Willis et al.

Todd G. Cochran, Associate Professor; Ph.D. (pharmaceutical sciences), Washington (Seattle). Cytochrome P_{450} and pharmacokinetics.
Evolution of a neonatal gentamicin dosing protocol in a small community hospital. *Perinatology* 12:346–53, 1992. With Rivey, North, Harper, and Simmerman.

Carlos M. G. Duran, Professor and Endowed Chair; M.D., Ph.D., Oxford. Ischemic heart valve disease, development of innovative techniques for heart valve transplantation or repair, examination of methods for visualization of repaired aortic and mitral valves.
The sheep as an animal model for heart valve research. *J. Cardiovasc. Surg.* 4:543–9, 1996. With Ali, Kumar, and Bjornstad.

A. Craig Eddy, Associate Professor; M.D., Cincinnati. Traumatic injury to the heart and great vessels, endocarditis and cardiac valve repair.
Traumatic injury to the heart and great vessels, current opinion in *Critical Care,* 1995. With Rice.

Charles L. Eyer, Professor; Ph.D. (pharmacology), Washington State. Oxidative damage, metal neurotoxicity, cellular responses to stress.
Role of protein kinase C in trimetyltin-mediated neurotoxicity. *J. Neurochem.* 65(5):2238–43, 1995. With Pavlakovic, Kane, Kanthasamy, and Isom.

David S. Freeman, Associate Professor; Ph.D. (pharmaceutical sciences), Washington (Seattle). Effects of pharmaceutical agents on serum lipoprotein patterns.
Effect of prazosin and beta-blocker monotherapy on serum lipids: A cross-over, placebo controlled study. *J. Clin. Pharmacol.* 27:756–61, 1987. With Magarian, Dietz, and Carlson.

Vernon R. Grund, Professor and Chairman; Ph.D. (pharmacology), Minnesota. Cardiovascular pharmacology.
Fatty acid uptake in diabetic rat adipocytes. *Mol. Cell. Biochem.* 167:51–60, 1997. With Fraser, Woodford, Colles, and Schroeder.

Craig A. Johnston, Associate Professor; Ph.D. (pharmacology and toxicology and neurosciences), Michigan State. Neuroendocrine pharmacology and neurochemistry.
Oxytocin receptor mRNA expression in the ventromedial hypothalamus during the estrous cycle. *J. Neurosci.* 15(7):5058–64, 1995. With Bale and Dorsa.

Diana I. Lurie, Assistant Professor; Ph.D. (neuroscience), Pennsylvania. Development and regeneration of the nervous system, identification of cellular changes in neurons and glia.
Development of Cat-301 immunoreactivity in auditory brainstem nuclei of the gerbil. *J. Comp. Neurol.*, in press. With Pasic, Hockfield, and Rubel.

Rustem S. Medora, Professor; Ph.D. (pharmaceutical sciences), Rhode Island. Ethnopharmacology of Central and South American psychoactive plants.
Comparative pharmacology of parthenolide at serotonin receptors. *Am. Soc. Pharmacog.* 37:P123, 1996. With Colson et al.

Keith K. Parker, Associate Professor; Ph.D. (pharmacology), California, San Francisco. Neurochemistry and molecular neuropharmacology, particularly the development of new anti-migraine drugs and drug effects on gene control elements of the developing nervous system.
Rabbit cerebral cortex 5HT1a receptors. *Comp. Biochem. Physiol.*, in press. With Weber, Hayataka, and O'Connor.

Jerry R. Smith, Associate Professor; Ph.D. (pharmacology), Mississippi. Cardiovascular pharmacology, drug metabolism and toxicology; development and application of ischemic-reperfusion-injured rat heart models for studying anti-ischemic agents.
Myocardial ischemia/reperfusion protection using monophosphoryl lipid a is abrogated by the ATP-sensitive potassium channel blocker, glibenclamide. *Cardiovasc. Res.* 32:1071–80, 1996. With Elliott et al.

Affiliated Faculty Research

George A. Carlson, Ph.D., Director and Senior Scientist, McLaughlin Research Institute. Investigation of nervous system disorders, the genetics of CNS disorders, skeletal muscle disorders in transgenic mouse models.

Howard Chandler, Assistant Professor; M.D., Wake Forest. Comparative neuroanatomy and cell biology of glial cells and glial tumors. Rat posterior parietal cortex: Topography of cortico-cortical and thalamic connections.

David Cheung, Ph.D., Director of Tissue Engineering Laboratory, The International Heart Institute of Montana. Cardiovascular biology and tissue engineering methodologies used in the study of structural and functional relationships in normal and pathological connective tissues of the mammalian cardiovascular system.

Douglas Coffin, Ph.D., Scientist, McLaughlin Research Institute. Use of transgenic mouse models for studies on vascular morphogenesis, cardiac disorders, and abnormal bone growth.

William R. Crain, Ph.D., Senior Scientist, McLaughlin Research Institute. Targeted point mutations of genes in mice.

Gary T. Elliott, Ph.D., Vice President, Pharmaceutical Development, Ribi ImmunoChem Research, Inc. Pathogenesis of septic (endotoxin) shock and ischemia-reperfusion injury (role of cytokines, free radicals, neutrophils, and adenosine metabolism) and the application of immune modulators as therapeutic agents
thereof.

Claude F. Garon, Ph.D., Chief, Microscopy Branch, NIH-Rocky Mountain Laboratories. Application of recombinant DNA technology and electron microscopy to relate gene structure with function in the study of microbial infection.

James D. Hutchison Jr., M.S., Forensic Toxicologist, Montana Department of Justice. Development of analytical techniques to detect therapeutic and subtherapeutic blood levels of the new, more efficacious benzodiazepines.

Glen D. Leesman, Ph.D., Director of Computer Simulations, NaviCyte Corp. Pharmaceutics and pharmacokinetic modeling, assessment of formulation variables for the optimization of physiochemical and biological properties.

John A. Mercer, Ph.D., Research Scientist, McLaughlin Research Institute. Molecular genetics, selective gene expression in the failing heart, molecular cloning of mouse myosin expression in brain.

Jack H. Nunberg, Ph.D., Director, Biotechnology Center, The University of Montana. Research in virology and molecular biology of human immunodeficiency virus (HIV) towards the development of vaccines and antiviral agents.

John L. Portis, M.D., Senior Investigator, Laboratory of Persistent Viral Diseases, NIH-Rocky Mountain Laboratories. Application of recombinant DNA technology and electron microscopy to relate gene structure with function in the study of microbial infection.

Susan A. Queen, Ph.D., Assistant Professor of Physical Therapy, The University of Montana. Neurotoxicity of cyclosporin-like immunosuppressants in cortical astrocyte cultures.

Ethan B. Russo, M.D., Staff Neurologist, Western Montana Clinic. Neuropharmacology and ethnopharmacology, clinical pharmacology of neurological drugs.

Bryan L. Spangelo, Ph.D., Associate Professor of Chemistry, University of Nevada, Las Vegas. Production of cytokines by the central nervous system: regulation of the secretion of glial-derived interleukin-6 by other cytokines and thymic peptides.

Charles M. Thompson, Ph.D., Associate Professor of Chemistry, University of Montana. Synthesis and biochemical evaluation of pharmacologically active molecules.

Edwin B. Walker, Ph.D., Senior Scientist II, Director, Flow Cytometry Lab-Ribi Immunochem Research, Inc. Mechanism of pathogenesis of septic shock using in vitro human and murine monocyte macrophage culture and human endothelial culture systems.

Patricia A. Weber, Ph.D., Research Scientist, Cardiovascular Pharmacology, Ribi ImmunoChem Research Inc. Role of monophosphoryl lipid-A in the prevention of myocardial ischemia and reperfusion injury.

UNIVERSITY OF SOUTHERN CALIFORNIA

School of Pharmacy

Programs of Study

The School of Pharmacy at the University of Southern California (USC) offers graduate programs in pharmaceutical economics and policy, pharmaceutical sciences, and molecular pharmacology and toxicology.

The programs that lead to the Master of Science (M.S.) and Doctor of Philosophy (Ph.D.) degrees in pharmaceutical economics and policy focus on economics and outcomes assessment of pharmaceuticals, pharmacy services, and medical technology. The programs also include research into the finance and delivery of pharmaceuticals and pharmacy services. Graduates have the capability to conduct research and provide training and expertise in assisting health-care organizations to make decisions regarding the costs and benefits of alternative therapeutic strategies.

The programs that lead to the M.S. and Ph.D. degrees in pharmaceutical sciences have an emphasis on cancer pharmacology, cell biology, computational drug design, drug targeting and delivery, medicinal chemistry, membrane biophysics, molecular pharmacology, and pharmacokinetics. The pharmaceutical sciences program provides highly interdisciplinary educational opportunities. Utilizing a broad spectrum of state-of-the-art techniques, faculty members are engaged in research directed toward understanding the mechanisms of drug interactions at transport barriers and target sites and developing new strategies in the design, functional analysis, delivery, and optimization of therapeutic agents.

The programs that lead to the M.S. and Ph.D. degrees in molecular pharmacology and toxicology have an emphasis on molecular pharmacology, gene regulation, neuropharmacology, free-radical biochemistry, toxicology, and neurotoxicology. The molecular pharmacology and toxicology program offers superb interdisciplinary educational opportunities. Faculty members are engaged in research directed toward understanding the mechanisms of drug action, gene regulation, neurobiology of behavior, learning and memory, neurobiology of drug tolerance, and the induction and regulation of signal transduction systems. A major focus of research of the toxicology faculty is the role of free-radical mechanisms in metabolic regulation, carcinogenesis, and membrane-associated disorders. All areas of research emphasize the potential for development of therapeutic agents.

Research Facilities

The graduate programs of the School of Pharmacy are housed in the seven-story Pharmaceutical Sciences Center and the three-story Center for Health Professionals on the University's Health Science Campus. There are collaborative research programs with the USC Comprehensive Cancer Center, the Doheny Eye Institute and Hospital, and the L.A. County–USC Medical Center, all of which are adjacent to the School of Pharmacy; with the science, public administration, and economics departments on the University Park Campus; and with a number of other prestigious clinical research facilities in the Los Angeles area. The School has the full range of equipment found in any modern research facility. The Norris Medical Library, located on the Health Science Campus, supports computerized searches through Ovid Online. With the University Park Campus libraries, the number of volumes exceeds 1.5 million.

Financial Aid

Fellowships, teaching assistantships, and research assistantships are awarded on a competitive basis to qualified individuals. The annual stipends for these awards range up to $16,515 and $8208, respectively, for half-time and quarter-time appointments for the 1998–99 fiscal year. Half-time fellows and assistants receive full tuition remission (up to 12 units per semester), while quarter-time positions receive up to 8 units of tuition remission per semester.

Cost of Study

Tuition fees are approximately $720 per semester unit in 1998–99. Fellows and assistants receive tuition remission, as outlined in the Financial Aid section above.

Living and Housing Costs

A limited number of double rooms are available in Seaver Hall, located next to the School. Rents range from $355 to $495 per month. Off-campus housing is also available. Rents range from $400 to $1000 a month, depending on size, location, and whether or not accommodations are shared. Total living expenses, including transportation, average $1200 per month.

Student Group

Of a total University population of 27,353 full-time and part-time students, almost 12,000 are pursuing graduate or professional degrees. Within the School of Pharmacy there are approximately 60 graduate students. Approximately 95 percent of the students receive some form of financial assistance. The demand from the pharmaceutical industry, academia, and government for graduates in selected areas is high.

Location

The health sciences campus is 5 miles from downtown Los Angeles and is easily accessible from all parts of greater Los Angeles. The ocean, mountains, and deserts are all close by. Recreational and sporting facilities are excellent. Cultural and entertainment attractions are numerous, including the Los Angeles Philharmonic, the Los Angeles Chamber Orchestra, the Hollywood Bowl, numerous theaters, and the Music Center. Los Angeles supports professional basketball, hockey, soccer, and baseball teams, and numerous college sporting events are held throughout the year. The southern California climate, with mild winters and warm, dry summers, is renowned.

The University

Founded in 1880, the University is the oldest major independent, coeducational, nonsectarian university in the West. The modern health sciences campus, 7 miles from the main campus and adjacent to the L.A. County–USC Medical Center, houses not only the School of Pharmacy but also the School of Medicine, the Doheny Eye Institute and Hospital, and the USC Comprehensive Cancer Center, all of which have active research programs. There are excellent opportunities for collaborative work.

Applying

Applicants must have, or expect to receive, a bachelor's or higher-level degree in an appropriate field prior to beginning graduate studies (students should contact the respective department for details). A GPA of at least 3.0 and qualifying verbal and quantitative GRE test scores are required. International applicants must also submit a TOEFL score. Applicants who meet graduate admission standards are notified of acceptance by April 1. Fellowships and teaching assistantships are offered to top applicants who have expressed the desire for financial aid. The application deadline for some of the fellowships is February 1.

Correspondence and Information

For more information or applications, students should contact the specific department of interest.

Department of Pharmaceutical Economics and Policy
Telephone: 213-342-1460

Department of Pharmaceutical Sciences
Telephone: 213-342-1451
Fax: 213-342-1390
E-mail: josefina@hsc.usc.edu

Department of Molecular Pharmacology and Toxicology
Telephone: 213-342-1406

Graduate Affairs Office
School of Pharmacy
University of Southern California
1985 Zonal Avenue
Los Angeles, California 90033
Telephone: 213-342-1474
Fax: 213-342-2258
E-mail: pharmgrd@hsc.usc.edu

University of Southern California

THE FACULTY AND THEIR RESEARCH

Pharmaceutical Economics and Policy

Richard L. Ernst, Assistant Research Professor of Pharmaceutical Economics and Policy; Ph.D., Berkeley, 1970. Theoretical foundations of cost-effective analysis for the planning of pharmaceutical formularies, provision of health care in general.

Joel W. Hay, Associate Professor of Pharmaceutical Economics and Policy; Ph.D., Yale, 1980. Health economics, pharmaceutical economics, HIV/AIDS medical costs and epidemiology, health insurance reform, economic assessment of medical technology, medical interventions.

Kathleen A. Johnson, Assistant Professor of Pharmaceutical Economics and Policy and of Clinical Pharmacy; Ph.D., UCLA, 1991. Health services research, clinical pharmacy, pharmaceutical economics, health economics, OTC nonprescription drugs, women's health issues.

Gordon G. Liu, Assistant Professor of Pharmaceutical Economics and Policy; Ph.D., CUNY Graduate Center, 1991. Health economics, pharmaceutical economics, health-care system simulation, Chinese health-care financing, demography.

Jeffrey S. McCombs, Associate Professor of Pharmaceutical Economics and Policy; Ph.D., California, San Diego, 1982. Health economics, pharmaceutical economics, capitated medical systems, noncompliance with drug therapies and with drug formularies.

Michael B. Nichol, Associate Professor and Chairman of Pharmaceutical Economics and Policy; Ph.D., USC, 1987. State health policy, pharmaceutical economics, pharmacy counseling and patient behavior, occupational licensure, application of ethical principles of pharmacy.

Pharmaceutical Sciences

M. B. Bolger, Associate Professor of Pharmaceutical Sciences; Ph.D., California, San Francisco, 1978. Molecular mechanisms of drug and hormone action; biophysical, biochemical, and computational study of ligand-receptor interaction.

S. F. Hamm-Alvarez, Assistant Professor of Pharmaceutical Sciences; Ph.D., Duke, 1990. Role of kinesin and cytoplasmic dynein in vesicle transport along microtubules, regulation of microtubule-dependent vesicle transport in intact cells.

I. S. Haworth, Assistant Professor of Pharmaceutical Sciences; Ph.D., Liverpool, 1989. Computational drug design, NMR spectroscopy, structure and dynamics of DNA and DNA-ligand complexes, molecular modeling, molecular dynamics.

R. T. Koda, Professor of Pharmaceutical Sciences; Pharm.D., Ph.D., USC, 1961. Dosage form development, pharmacokinetics and drug disposition.

V. H. L. Lee, Professor and Chairman of Pharmaceutical Sciences; Ph.D., Wisconsin–Madison, 1979. Peptide and protein drug delivery, ocular drug delivery, oral drug delivery, pulmonary drug delivery, controlled drug delivery, drug transport mechanisms.

E. J. Lien, Professor of Pharmaceutical Sciences; Ph.D., California, San Francisco, 1966. Quantitative structure-activity correlation of chemotherapeutic agents, centrally acting drugs and natural products, design synthesis and testing of new antiviral and antitumor agents, isolation and testing of immunostimulating polysaccharides from plants, especially Chinese medicinal plants.

C. T. Okamoto, Assistant Professor of Pharmaceutical Sciences; Ph.D., Berkeley, 1989. Protein sorting in epithelial cells.

W. C. Shen, Professor and Vice Chair of Pharmaceutical Sciences; Ph.D., Boston University, 1972. Endocytosis and transcytosis of proteins in epithelial cells.

H. Von Grafenstein, Assistant Professor of Pharmaceutical Sciences; M.D., Munich, 1983; Ph.D., Max Planck Institute for Biochemistry (Munich), 1983. Regulation and function of vesicles undergoing regulated or constitutive cycles of exocytosis and endocytosis, antigen processing, interaction of the secretory apparatus of β-cells in the pancreas with the immune system.

W. Wolf, Professor of Pharmaceutical Sciences; Ph.D., Paris, 1956. Pharmacokinetic imaging, noninvasive studies of drug biodistribution, targeting and metabolism using NMRS and nuclear medicine imaging (including PET) techniques, pharmacokinetics of antitumor agents, synthesis and mechanism of action of radiopharmaceuticals.

Molecular Pharmacology and Toxicology

J. D. Adams Jr., Associate Professor of Molecular Pharmacology and Toxicology; Ph.D., California, San Francisco, 1981. Bioactivation of drugs and toxins in Parkinson's disease and other diseases.

R. L. Alkana, Professor of Molecular Pharmacology and Toxicology and Assistant Dean, Interdisciplinary Programs; Pharm.D., USC, 1970; Ph.D., California, Irvine, 1975. Mechanisms of psychoactive drug action, neuropharmacology and behavioral pharmacology/toxicology, pharmacogenetics, allosteric signal transduction.

D. K. Ann, Associate Professor and Interim Chairman of Molecular Pharmacology and Toxicology; Ph.D., Purdue, 1984. Molecular mechanism(s) governing tissue-specific and inducible gene expression and signal transduction.

R. E. Brinton, Associate Professor of Molecular Pharmacology and Toxicology and of Neurosciences; Ph.D., Arizona, 1984. Neurobiology of learning and memory; peptide and steroid induction of morphological, biochemical, and genomic plasticity in cultured nerve cells.

E. Cadenas, Professor of Molecular Pharmacology and Toxicology and of Biochemistry and Molecular Biology; Ph.D., Buenos Aires, 1977. Free-radical chemistry and biology, cell-cycle regulation by oxidants and antioxidants.

T. M. Chan, Professor and Dean; Ph.D., California, Davis, 1972. Metabolic toxicology, metabolic and hormonal abnormalities in obesity and diabetes, perturbation of cell growth and intermediary metabolism by free radicals and related oxidants.

R. F. Duncan, Associate Professor of Molecular Pharmacology and Toxicology and of Microbiology; Ph.D., Hawaii, 1978. Function of stress proteins in cell regulation and cell survival during stress, molecular mechanisms that regulate the rate of protein synthesis.

H. J. Forman, Professor of Molecular Pharmacology and Toxicology, Pathology, and Pediatrics; Ph.D., Columbia, 1971. Molecular and cellular aspects of the role of oxidants in signal transduction and the mechanism of adaptation to oxidative stress.

D. Johnson, Associate Professor of Molecular Pharmacology and Toxicology and of Biochemistry and Molecular Biology; Ph.D., Georgetown, 1980. Regulation of gene expression by viral proteins and by the activation of signal transduction pathways.

A. Sevanian, Professor of Molecular Pharmacology and Toxicology and of Pathology; Ph.D., UCLA, 1977. Mechanisms of lipid peroxidation in biological membranes and lipoproteins, lipoprotein oxidation and atherosclerosis, effect of lipid oxidation products on vascular cell signaling.

J. C. Shih, Professor of Molecular Pharmacology and Toxicology; Ph.D., California, Riverside, 1968. Biochemistry and molecular biology of serotonin receptors and enzymes related to catecholamine metabolism, molecular basis of mental disorders, neurodegeneration and aggressive behavior.

UNIVERSITY OF THE PACIFIC

School of Pharmacy

Programs of Study

Master's and doctoral programs are offered in five areas of specialization: clinical pharmacy, medicinal chemistry, pharmaceutics, pharmacology, and physiology. In addition, combined Pharm.D./Ph.D. and Pharm.D./M.S. degree programs are also offered. The requirements for the master's degree include, among others, completion of a minimum of twenty-six semester units of course work plus four units of thesis and two semesters of full-time residence following the baccalaureate degree.

Because of academic area interrelationships, all doctoral students declare a major in one of the five areas of specialization and a minor in either another area or another University department. Doctoral requirements are formulated on an individual basis by the candidate and his or her adviser. Students are required to spend at least six semesters of residence wholly devoted to graduate study and investigation; at least 30 units, in addition to the dissertation, must be completed at this University. Students may be admitted to doctoral candidacy after completing 45 units beyond the B.S. degree, meeting the skill requirements (two research skills, one of which may be a foreign language), and successfully passing the qualifying examination.

The combined Pharm.D./Ph.D. and Pharm.D./M.S. degree programs are intended for students who are interested in careers in research and teaching but who wish to also possess a professional degree in pharmacy. The entrance requirements include all prepharmacy Pharm.D. requirements, a baccalaureate degree with a minimum GPA of 3.0, and certain other standards. Students in the Pharm.D./Ph.D. program are eligible for financial support beginning with the third year of the program.

Interdisciplinary programs involve mechanisms of drug absorption and bioavailability; controlled drug delivery; clinical pharmacokinetics; evaluation of alternative health-care systems; molecular mechanisms of drug action; drug metabolism; protein chemistry; regulation of protein synthesis at the transcriptional and translational levels; cardiac physiology/pharmacology; nuclear cardiology; epidemiology and the solution of problems of clinical importance by means of clinical studies in acute-care, home-care, and long-term-care facilities; biomedical engineering; electrophysiology-pharmacology; multidimensional drug screening and evaluation; biometrics; and cytoculture and tissue culture. The overall goal of the graduate program is to provide the student with a multidisciplinary perspective on drug therapy and the multidisciplinary tools for solving basic problems in individual and community health.

Research Facilities

The School of Pharmacy complex has standardized research laboratories for each of the areas of specialization, as well as the following specialized facilities: a radioisotope suite; an explosion-proof area for distillation and hydrogenation procedures; tissue culture laboratories with walk-in incubators and sterile rooms; a specially shielded electrophysiology complex; polygraphic laboratories; a manufacturing pharmacy laboratory; a machine shop; an electronics laboratory; rooms for ultrasonic, chromatographic, electrophoretic, spectrophotometric, ultracentrifugation, and preparative gas chromatographic processes; and a large-scale crude-drug extraction area. The University's science library is located in the same building. The School is affiliated with several acute- and long-term-care facilities where clinical studies are conducted.

Financial Aid

Graduate assistantships pay full tuition plus a cash stipend of $11,330. Graduate fellowships remit full or partial tuition for the academic year. Applications for assistantships and fellowships should be addressed to the dean of the Graduate School. Interested residents may apply for state of California fellowships (tuition costs) by writing directly to the State Scholarship and Loan Commission, Fellowship Section, 714 P Street, Sacramento, California 95814.

Cost of Study

In 1998–99, the tuition cost per unit is $594 for up to 15½ units per semester. The School of Pharmacy operates on a trimester plan. There is a student health fee of $345 per year. Additional student fees range from $500 to $700.

Living and Housing Costs

On-campus living expenses are $8988 for three semesters of residence in 1998–99. Private housing is also available.

Student Group

The number of students on the Stockton campus is approximately 4,000. In the School of Pharmacy, there are approximately 500 students in the professional degree program and 30 students in the graduate programs.

Student Outcomes

Upon graduation a majority of the students find attractive employment opportunities in pharmaceutical or biotechnology companies throughout the United States; others are employed by academic institutions or government agencies, such as the Food and Drug Administration.

Location

Stockton is located in the Central Valley of California and has a population of 225,000. It is an inland deepwater seaport, serving as the agricultural, industrial, and transportational hub of the valley. The Mother Lode country, the Sierra Nevada, Lake Tahoe, Squaw Valley, and Yosemite Park are all within easy driving distance, as are San Francisco and the Bay Area.

The University

The University of the Pacific is California's first institution of higher learning, chartered in 1851. The functional divisions of the University are now the Graduate School, College of the Pacific, the Conservatory of Music, and the Schools of Pharmacy, Dentistry (San Francisco), Law (Sacramento), Education, Engineering, International Studies, and Business/Public Administration. The School of Pharmacy was organized in 1955, and the first programs were approved in 1968.

Applying

Official application forms, accompanied by a $50 application fee, should be filed with the dean of the Graduate School. The applicant must ask each college or university previously attended to forward an official transcript to the Graduate School. Fellowship applications should be filed by March 1. Scores on the Graduate Record Examinations General Test are required. Any applicant whose native language is not English must have TOEFL results forwarded to the Graduate School.

Correspondence and Information

Dean, the Graduate School
University of the Pacific
Stockton, California 95211
World Wide Web: http://www.petersons.com/sites/832260si.html

University of the Pacific

THE FACULTY AND THEIR RESEARCH

Department of Pharmaceutics and Medicinal Chemistry

William K. Chan, Assistant Professor of Medicinal Chemistry, Pharm.D./Ph.D., California, San Francisco. Molecular pharmacology and biological chemistry, human drug metabolism.

Madhukar G. Chaubal, Professor of Medicinal Chemistry; Ph.D., Rhode Island. Radioisotope technology, chemistry of medicinal plants, biogenesis of natural medicinal principles.

Donald G. Floriddia, Professor of Pharmaceutics; Ph.D., University of the Pacific. Clinical pharmacokinetics, computer-based pharmacokinetics, parenteral dosage forms, nuclear pharmacy, and pharmaceutical home health care.

David S. Fries, Professor of Medicinal Chemistry; Ph.D., Medical College of Virginia; postdoctoral study at Minnesota. Enzyme inhibitor design and synthesis, analgetic antagonists, CNS-active agents, drug metabolism, toxicology.

G. Craig Hill, Assistant Professor of Medicinal Chemistry; Ph.D., Arizona; postdoctoral study at Texas. Molecular modeling, high-field NMR, molecular biology, template-directed design and synthesis of DNA-binding antitumor antibiotics.

Xiaoling Li, Assistant Professor of Pharmaceutics; Ph.D., Utah. Controlled-release drug delivery systems, delivery systems for antisense oligonucleotides, novel polymers for biomedical and pharmaceutical application.

Alice Jean Matuszak, Professor of Medicinal Chemistry; Ph.D., Kansas. Structure-activity relationships of drug molecules, drug metabolism and testing of heterocyclic compounds, pharmacy history.

Donald L. Sorby, Professor Emeritus of Medicinal Chemistry; Ph.D., Washington (Seattle). Absorbent effects on drug absorption, mechanism of drug-protein interactions, drug release from dosage forms.

Ravindra C. Vasavada, Professor of Pharmaceutics; Ph.D., Rhode Island. Design, development, and evaluation of controlled-release drug delivery systems; bioavailability of oral and topical products.

Joel Wagner, Assistant Clinical Professor of Pharmaceutics; Pharm.D., USC. Parenteral dosage forms; pharmaceutical-care practices, clinical pharmacokinetics.

Department of Pharmacy Practice

Richard R. Abood, Professor of Pharmacy Administration; J.D., Nebraska–Lincoln. Health-care law, medicaid reimbursement.

Patrick N. Catania, Professor of Clinical Pharmacy; Ph.D., University of the Pacific. Geriatric practice in long-term care, home health care, programmed drug delivery.

Sian Carr-Lopez, Associate Professor of Clinical Pharmacy; Pharm.D., University of the Pacific. Geriatrics.

Mary Ferrill, Associate Professor of Pharmacy Practice; Pharm.D., Nebraska. Drug information.

Jeffrey A. Goad, Assistant Professor of Pharmacy Practice; Pharm.D., USC. Infectious disease, pediatrics.

Berit Gundersen, Associate Professor of Clinical Pharmacy; Pharm.D., University of the Pacific. Geriatrics, ambulatory care.

Arthur F. Harralson, Professor of Clinical Pharmacy; Pharm.D., California, San Francisco. Pharmacokinetics; perinatal pharmacology, toxicology, and drug screening; biomedical computer applications.

Matthew K. Ito, Associate Professor of Clinical Pharmacy; Pharm.D., USC. Clinical pharmacokinetics, infectious disease, cardiology.

S. Lena Kang, Assistant Professor of Pharmacy Practice; Pharm.D., California, San Francisco. Infectious disease and pharmacotherapy.

Sonja Kaubisch, Assistant Professor of Pharmacy Practice; Pharm.D., California, San Francisco. Therapeutic outcomes.

William A. Kehoe, Professor of Clinical Pharmacy; Pharm.D., California, San Francisco. Clinical pharmacokinetics, psychotherapeutics.

Audrey J. Lee, Assistant Professor of Pharmacy Practice; Pharm.D., California, San Francisco. Ambulatory care and pharmacotherapy.

Bertram L. Lum, Professor of Clinical Pharmacy; Pharm.D., University of the Pacific. Oncology clinical trials, genitourinary neoplasms, platinum analogues, anthracycline analogues, cytokines, chemoprevention, anthracycline cardiotoxicity.

Linda L. Norton, Assistant Professor of Pharmacy Practice; Pharm.D., University of the Pacific. Biomedical informatics, patient outcomes.

Ome Ogbru, Assistant Professor of Pharmacy Practice; Pharm.D., University of the Pacific. General pharmacotherapy.

Darwin Sarnoff, Professor of Health Care Practices; Ph.D., Purdue. Health-care economics, computer technology.

Sharette Sterné, Assistant Professor of Pharmacy Practice; Pharm.D., University of the Pacific. Ambulatory care.

Robert B. Supernaw, Professor of Pharmacy Practice; Pharm.D., University of the Pacific. Pain management, long-term care, clinical pharmacy.

Paul J. Williams, Professor of Clinical Pharmacy; Pharm.D., North Carolina. Therapeutic drug monitoring, clinical pharmacokinetics, cardiovascular pharmacotherapy.

Department of Physiology and Pharmacology

James W. Blankenship, Professor of Pharmacology and Toxicology; Ph.D., Utah. Biochemical pharmacology, polyamine metabolism, nuclear regulation and function.

Katherine K. Knapp, Professor of Physiology; Ph.D., California, Davis. Tumor biology, fibrin-tumor relationships, pharmacy manpower research.

John C. Livesey, Assistant Professor of Pharmacology and Toxicology; Ph.D., Minnesota. Cataract-inhibitory drugs, tumor cell biology, DNA damage and repair.

Denis J. Meerdink, Associate Professor of Physiology; Ph.D., Iowa State. Cardiac metabolism, physiology, and pharmacology; myocardial ischemia and blood flow; mathematical modeling of capillary-tissue exchange; myocardial perfusion imaging agents; nuclear medicine.

Howell I. Runion, Professor of Physiology; Ph.D., Glasgow. Neuromuscular physiology, pathophysiology of peripheral nerve injury, neurophysiology, electroencephalography, electronic instrumentation and design.

Timothy J. Smith, Assistant Professor of Pharmacology and Toxicology; Ph.D., Minnesota. Chemical bioactivation and drug delivery, comparative pharmacology and toxicology.

UNIVERSITY OF THE SCIENCES IN PHILADELPHIA

Division of Graduate Studies

Programs of Study

University of the Sciences in Philadelphia (USP) offers Doctor of Philosophy degrees with research specializations in chemistry, pharmaceutics, pharmacognosy, pharmacology, and toxicology. Master of Science degrees with research specializations are offered in biotechnology, cell biology, chemistry, pharmaceutics, pharmacognosy, pharmacology, and toxicology. M.S. (nonthesis) degrees are offered in biomedical writing, biotechnology, cell biology, health psychology, pharmaceutics, and pharmacy administration. Each is administered by the appropriate department, with general supervision by the graduate faculty. Interdisciplinary studies involving two or more departments are encouraged.

A minimum of 20 semester hours of didactic credits has been established for either the M.S. or the Ph.D. degree and 30 semester hours for the M.S. (nonthesis) degree. In order to receive an M.S. thesis degree, a student must satisfactorily complete a minimum of 24 research credits at USP. Each doctoral student must complete at least 48 research credits at USP to receive a Ph.D. degree.

Research Facilities

The McNeil Research Center includes well-equipped laboratories and an experimental greenhouse for graduate study and research in pharmaceutics, medicinal chemistry, and pharmacognosy. The pharmaceutical development and manufacturing laboratory in Griffith Hall is among the most complete of any college of pharmaceutical sciences. The Pharmacology/Toxicology Center provides modern laboratories and AAALAC-accredited animal-care facilities for instruction and research in pharmacology and toxicology. Throughout the campus there are special laboratories equipped with instrumentation for cell biology, fluorescence DNA sequencing, receptor binding, high-pressure liquid chromatography, spectrometry, capillary electrophoresis, kinetics, rheology, radioisotope methodology, and nuclear magnetic resonance studies (proton, fluorine, and phosphorus, and other commonly used techniques).

The USP Institute for Pharmaceutical Economics (IPE) was founded to provide national and international leadership in the application of the economic, social, and administrative sciences to health-care and pharmaceutical research, education, and service. The pharmacy administration graduate program works with the IPE on various activities and projects.

The Joseph W. England Library at USP provides an outstanding collection in the areas of pharmaceutics, pharmacology and toxicology, medicinal chemistry, and pharmacognosy. In addition to its 70,000 volumes, 770 print periodical subscriptions, and 1,100 electronic subscriptions, the library provides access to the world's literature in health sciences through its indexes and computer databases.

Financial Aid

Graduate students in the University may be supported by fellowships funded directly through the American Foundation for Pharmaceutical Education, other national associations such as the Society of Toxicology, the federal government (such as NIH), and the pharmaceutical industry (such as SmithKline Beecham). Information on these fellowships is available from the program directors. In addition, the University awards tuition scholarships, fellowships, and teaching assistantships. Employment for spouses is available in the city.

Cost of Study

Tuition for full-time students, including all fees, was $19,410 for the 1997–98 academic year. Tuition for part-time students was $539 per credit.

Living and Housing Costs

Costs in Philadelphia are comparable to those in other urban areas of the eastern United States. Apartments and furnished rooms are available nearby. For a single student, the cost of living, excluding tuition and fees, for nine months is approximately $10,800; for married couples, it is approximately $13,050.

Student Group

Of a total student body of 2,198, 24 are full-time graduate students and 53 are part-time graduate students. In the graduate population, several countries (Asian, European, Middle Eastern, South American) are always represented. The average age of the graduate students is 32; 36 percent of the students are married. Ninety-two percent of the full-time graduate students receive financial aid from USP.

Student Outcomes

Graduates have served postdoctoral positions at Harvard, the University of North Carolina, Jefferson University, the University of Florida, and the Medical College of Pennsylvania and have accepted employment in the pharmaceutical industry at Merck, Parke Davis, Zeneca, FMC Corporation, Cephalon, Pharmavene, Rhone-Poulenc Rorer, Robert Wood Johnson Pharmaceutical Research Institute, and Bayer Corporation.

Location

Metropolitan Philadelphia is the home of forty universities, colleges, and seminaries; a world-renowned orchestra; famous museums; and numerous historic landmarks. Growth and community development have greatly improved the city; its suburban environs are unexcelled. As a founder-member of the West Philadelphia Corporation, the University City Science Center, and Campus Philadelphia, USP participates actively in community development and improvement. Within a 12-minute streetcar ride to the center of the city are fine shops, restaurants, theaters, and places of cultural and historical interest. High-speed Metroliners reach New York City in less than 1½ hours and Washington, D.C., in less than 2 hours.

The University

Founded in 1821 as America's first college of pharmacy, USP has expanded its programs to include preparation, at the undergraduate level, for professional careers in biochemistry, biology, chemistry, medical technology, microbiology, occupational therapy, pharmaceutical chemistry, pharmacology and toxicology, pharmacy, physical therapy, physician assistant studies, premed, and science teacher certification.

USP is located on a 10-acre site in a part of Philadelphia known as University City, an area providing a fine academic environment. Three of the fifteen buildings of the University, including residence halls, a student activities center, and the Physical Therapy Building, have been built recently.

The gymnasium provides facilities for exercise and physical education. Archery, basketball, baseball, volleyball, riflery, softball, golf, and tennis are popular intramural and varsity sports. Twelve professional and social fraternities, five honor societies, and ten national scientific societies are represented at USP. AGAPE, the Hillel Foundation, and the Newman Club are the student religious groups on campus. Music, drama, photography, radio, volunteerism, three college publications, and fourteen student organizations are other areas of student extracurricular activity.

Applying

Requests for application forms should be addressed to the Dean of the Graduate School. International applicants must request and complete a Certification of Finances form, which verifies that they have sufficient funds to provide subsistence for at least one year, before an application can be mailed to them. Applications for fall admission must be completed by May 1; the deadline for spring admission is October 1; and for summer it is March 1. Because appointments are limited, early application is encouraged. Applicants seeking financial aid should state that they wish assistance in a letter to the Program Director of their proposed major. All students are required to submit recent official GRE General Test scores, and international students must also submit official TOEFL scores. Students who are not U.S. citizens must be accepted for admission and pay the required deposit before the University sends the form required for a student visa.

Correspondence and Information

Charles W. Gibley Jr., Ph.D.
Dean of the School of Graduate Studies
University of the Sciences in Philadelphia
600 South Forty-third Street
Philadelphia, Pennsylvania 19104

Telephone: 215-596-8937
Fax: 215-596-8764
E-mail: graduate@usip.edu
World Wide Web: http://www.usip.edu

University of the Sciences in Philadelphia

THE FACULTY

P. Angiolillo, Ph.D., Pennsylvania.
E. Birnbaum, Ph.D., Illinois.
S. Barker, M.S., Temple.
B. Bourbon, Ph.D., Pennsylvania.
L. Chiarello, Ph.D., Hahnemann Medical College.
K. Cody, Ph.D., NYU.
A. DerMarderosian, Ph.D., Rhode Island.
A. D'mello, Ph.D., Pittsburgh.
J. Eshraghi, Ph.D., Temple.
P. Gupta, Ph.D., Wisconsin.
P. Harvison, Ph.D., Yeshiva (Einstein).
R. Hock, Ph.D., Yeshiva (Einstein).
M. Kasschau, Ph.D., South Carolina.
J. Kauffman, Ph.D., MIT.
W. McGhan, Ph.D., Minnesota.
C. Moore, Ed.D., Temple.
D. Morel, Ph.D., Case Western Reserve.
S. Murphy, Ph.D., Hahnemann Medical College.
J. Nikelly, Ph.D., Cornell.
C. Ofner, Ph.D., Temple.
R. Orzechowski, Ph.D., Temple.
J. Pierce, Ph.D., Temple.
J. Porter, Ph.D., Montana.
D. Sabapathi, Ph.D., Temple.
D. Scheerhorn, Ph.D., Iowa.
R. Schemm, Ed.D., Temple.
R. Schnaare, Ph.D., Purdue.
J. Schwartz, Ph.D., Michigan.
J. Snow, Ph.D., California, Santa Barbara.
E. Stanek, Pharm.D., Illinois.
E. Sugita, Ph.D., Purdue.
J. Tarloff, Ph.D., Medical College of Ohio.
R. Tchao, Ph.D., Nottingham (England).
S. Tejani-Butt, Ph.D., Virginia Commonwealth.
C. Thoman, Ph.D., Massachusetts Amherst.
K. Thomulka, Ph.D., Hahnemann Medical College.
M. Weis, Ph.D., Medical University of South Carolina.
R. Wigent, Ph.D., Michigan Tech.
M. Zanger, Ph.D., Kansas.

CURRENT RESEARCH

Cell Biology and Biotechnology. This master's degree program is designed to give a theoretical and practical background in biotechnological techniques and applications, functions of cells at the molecular and cellular levels, methods for studying cell systems, and study of the genetics of cell systems. The major research emphasis includes studies of cell adhesion, plant-microbe interactions, cell-signal transduction, oncogene function, studies of the genetics of prokaryotes and eukaryotes, bacterial metabolism and bioluminescence, and novel approaches to medicinal natural products.

Medicinal Chemistry and Pharmacognosy. The Department of Chemistry offers graduate programs in chemistry (specialties in analytical, medicinal, organic, or physical chemistry and biochemistry) and pharmacognosy (specialties in analytical pharmacognosy, biotechnology and cell culture, and natural product synthesis).

Pharmaceutics. Pharmaceutics applies the theories and techniques of the mathematical, chemical, biological, and pharmaceutical sciences to develop and evaluate drug delivery systems and to test their in vivo performance. Major areas of research are the specialized systemic delivery of drugs, receptor binding of drugs, applications of spheronized granules, rheological properties of pharmaceutical systems, physics of tablet compression, suspension and emulsion technology, controlled release of drugs, pharmacokinetics, pharmacodynamics, cross linking in proteins, membrane characterization, and utilization of physical models.

Pharmacology and Toxicology. The Pharmacology and Toxicology Program has these areas of research: autonomic, cardiovascular and neuropsychopharmacology, cancer biology, drug metabolism, and toxicology. (For further information, see Peterson's Guides to Graduate Study, Volume 3, *Graduate Programs in the Biological Sciences,* Section 16: Pharmacology and Toxicology.)

Pharmacy Administration. Major areas of study and research in the Pharmacy Administration Program include pharmaceutical economics, cost effectiveness analysis, pharmaceutical care, marketing research, health communications, and management sciences. Additional areas of research include technology assessment and decision analysis as well as patient education and compliance. The University is strategically located near several major health science centers, business schools, and international pharmaceutical firms and has collaborative arrangements for learning and research.

UNIVERSITY OF WASHINGTON

Department of Pharmaceutics

Program of Study

The Department of Pharmaceutics offers a graduate program that leads to the M.S. and Ph.D. degrees. The program provides research training in the fundamental aspects of drug disposition, drug delivery, and drug action in animals and man. Drug disposition includes the phenomena of absorption, distribution, and elimination. Pharmacokinetics is the study of the time course of these processes and the time course of pharmacological effects. Drug delivery includes targeting of drugs to tissues or specific cells to improve their therapeutic effect. These areas of research have a wide range of applications, particularly in the pharmacological characterization of new drug molecules in pharmaceutical development. Graduates of this program possess expertise in a variety of analytical techniques and in the elaboration of mathematical models to describe drug disposition and pharmacological processes.

During the first two years of study, students take courses in medicinal chemistry, pharmacology, physiology, biochemistry, mathematics, computer science, biostatistics, and pharmacokinetics. Students join the program with backgrounds in chemistry, pharmacy, or biological sciences. Students with basic science degrees complete additional course work in pharmacology, medicinal chemistry, and basic pharmacokinetics. Students with a pharmacy degree usually need to strengthen their background in the physical sciences. Beyond the department requirements for course work in the areas mentioned, the program is designed to be flexible and can easily be adapted to meet the interests and needs of the individual student. From the second year on, each student engages in thesis research under the direction of a dissertation adviser and a committee of faculty members.

The research program of the department includes six NIH-funded laboratories addressing a variety of fundamental and clinical problems pertaining to drug transport, metabolism, and toxicity associated with several diseases (AIDS, cystic fibrosis, leukemia, epilepsy, pain management, transplantation). Most projects involve collaborative arrangements with investigators from other departments in the University or at the Fred Hutchinson Cancer Research Center. The collaborative relationship of Pharmaceutics faculty with colleagues in the Department of Medicinal Chemistry in the field of drug metabolism has received worldwide recognition.

Thesis research can involve experimental animal work, in vitro studies, clinical investigations, or a combination of approaches. Graduate students are given the opportunity to participate in interdisciplinary research, which provides an added dimension to their training.

The Department of Pharmaceutics sponsors an active program of research meetings and seminars, in which current developments in pharmaceutical sciences are discussed by the faculty, students, and visiting scholars from other universities and research institutes. This program continually exposes students to new ideas and innovations in pharmaceutical research.

A wide range of career paths are available to graduates of this program. Opportunities include research in the pharmaceutical industry; research in hospitals, institutes, and foundations; teaching and research in academic institutions; and positions with government regulatory agencies.

Research Facilities

The Department of Pharmaceutics is located in the H-Wing of the Health Sciences Center adjoining the University Medical Center Hospital, where all the other health-related basic science and clinical departments are located. The laboratories are state-of-the-art and are equipped with modern analytical instrumentation and biological containment facilities. Areas for the housing and care of experimental animals are situated on the same floor as the research laboratories. The department has direct access to the mass spectrometry facility operated by the Department of Medicinal Chemistry within the School of Pharmacy. Several microcomputers and a network linkage to the mainframes on campus are also available.

Financial Aid

All students accepted into the program receive stipend support throughout their graduate training. In 1998–99, stipends are $15,372 a year. In addition, students are granted tuition and fee waivers in the amount of $8046. The net cost of tuition to the individual is $650 per year. Funds for stipends come from a variety of sources, including an NIH predoctoral training grant and NIH research grants of faculty members.

Cost of Study

As described above, tuition and fee waivers cover all but $650 of annual costs.

Living and Housing Costs

The approximate costs of room and board (three-meals-per-day plan) in a residence hall on campus range from $1100 to $1400 per quarter for a single room and from $3790 to $4685 for a double room per year (three quarters). In University-owned apartments near campus, rates range from $300 to $600 per month for single occupancy. Privately owned housing in the community is also available at a variety of rates.

Student Group

There are 22 graduate students enrolled in the pharmaceutics graduate program. Students come from every state of the Union and many foreign nations. Most students enter the program immediately after completing their baccalaureate (or master's) degree in pharmacy, chemistry, or biological sciences. A close relationship exists between the graduate students in this program and those in the Department of Medicinal Chemistry.

Location

Seattle offers the educational and cultural advantages of a major metropolitan center, and its setting on Puget Sound provides superb recreational opportunities.

The University

The campus is located in a residential area of Seattle on the shores of Lake Washington and Lake Union. The University is a major resource center for health science education and research in the Northwest. The School of Pharmacy is consistently rated among the top professional institutions in the country.

Applying

Students who have a baccalaureate degree in pharmacy, chemistry, biology, or a related discipline are invited to apply. Application forms for graduate admission may be obtained by telephoning or writing to the Department of Pharmaceutics. The application packet contains detailed instructions regarding the completion of forms and the forwarding of transcripts, letters of recommendation, and GRE General Test scores. Complete applications must be received by March 1 for admission at the beginning of the autumn quarter. All competitive applicants are invited to visit and interview with the faculty members at the department's expense (about 10 applicants per year).

Correspondence and Information

René H. Levy, Ph.D., Chair
Department of Pharmaceutics
Box 357610
University of Washington
Seattle, Washington 98195-7610

Telephone: 206-543-9434
800-543-9434 (toll-free)
Fax: 206-543-3204
World Wide Web: http://weber.u.washington.edu/~pceut/

University of Washington

THE FACULTY AND THEIR RESEARCH

T. Andrew Bowdle, Adjunct Assistant Professor and Associate Professor of Anesthesiology; M.D., Ph.D., Washington (Seattle), 1980. Pharmacokinetics and pharmacology of regional anesthetics used in disease and aging.
William E. Bradley, Affiliate Professor; M.D., Minnesota, 1957. Neurology, urology.
Milo Gibaldi, Professor and Dean of the School of Pharmacy; Ph.D., Columbia, 1963. Theoretical and clinical pharmacokinetics. (206-543-2451)
Rodney J. Y. Ho, Associate Professor; Ph.D., Tennessee, 1987. Drug, protein, cytokine, and gene delivery, disposition, and targeting. (206-685-3914)
Shiu-Lok Hu, Professor; Ph.D., Berkeley, 1978. AIDS. (206-221-4939)
René H. Levy, Professor and Chair of the Department; Ph.D., California, San Francisco, 1970. Mechanism of metabolic interactions among antiepileptic drugs, toxic interactions between cytokines and drugs. (206-543-9434)
Danny D. Shen, Professor; Ph.D., SUNY at Buffalo, 1975. Hepatic drug metabolism in uremia, CNS pharmacokinetics of anticonvulsants, pharmacodynamics of opioid analgesic. (206-685-2920)
John T. Slattery, Professor; Ph.D., SUNY at Buffalo, 1978. Bone marrow transplantation, malignancies of solid organs and blood, genetic diseases. (206-543-7736)
Kenneth Thummel, Associate Professor; Ph.D., Washington (Seattle), 1987. Regulation of drug metabolizing systems, drug interactions, altered hepatic drug metabolism and cytochrome P-450 expression by diabetes and morbid obesity. (206-543-0819)
Jashvant D. Unadkat, Professor; Ph.D., Manchester (England), 1982. AIDS, cystic fibrosis. (206-685-2869)

UNIVERSITY OF WISCONSIN–MADISON

School of Pharmacy

Programs of Study

The School of Pharmacy's graduate program areas include pharmaceutical sciences, social and administrative sciences in pharmacy, and pharmacy. The graduate pharmacy program, which differs from the professional doctoral (Pharm.D.) program, is a two-year curriculum leading to the M.S. degree program, which runs concurrently with an American Society of Health-System Pharmacists (ASHP) residency program in hospital pharmacy. The other programs award the M.S. and Ph.D. degrees.

The characteristic feature of graduate study and research in the pharmaceutical sciences at the University of Wisconsin (UW) is a fundamental approach at the chemistry/biology interface, with emphasis on underlying mechanisms at the molecular level and their quantitative description. The pharmaceutical sciences provide an interdisciplinary training program and research directed toward understanding fundamental aspects of drug delivery and targeting, developing new strategies in drug discovery and design, and elucidating mechanisms of drug action and toxicities.

The objective of the graduate program in social and administrative sciences in pharmacy is to prepare students for independent, theory-based research leading to new knowledge and understanding of drug use, patient and provider communication and behaviors, health outcomes, pharmacy practice, patient care systems, and the pharmacy profession. This goal is accomplished by integrating theories and concepts from basic disciplines such as economics, sociology, psychology, management sciences, education, epidemiology, history, and law into pharmacy and pharmaceuticals.

Research Facilities

The School of Pharmacy is located in the heart of the Madison campus, with easy access to a variety of campus resources, including branch libraries, the Biotechnology Center, the Integrated Microscopic Facility, and the Clinical Sciences Center. The School of Pharmacy also houses the campus Molecular Modeling Laboratory, the Sonderegger Research Center, the F. B. Power Pharmaceutical Library, and an animal vivarium that can house all common animal species.

The modern equipment necessary to conduct sophisticated research in the pharmaceutical sciences is available, including NMR and mass spectrometers. The Sonderegger Research Center provides a support facility for interdisciplinary faculty members to conduct both basic and applied research that helps policy makers, the profession, and citizens to promote health and improve the health-care system.

In fall 2000, the School of Pharmacy's undergraduate, professional, and graduate programs will be housed in a new building. Rennebohm Hall will be a seven-story, state-of-the-art teaching and research facility with approximately 130,000 assigned square feet.

Financial Aid

Financial aid is available through the School of Pharmacy, the University, and national and international agencies. Most graduate students are supported as project, research, or teaching assistants. The University has several fellowships and scholarships available to support new and continuing graduate students, including fellowships to assist economically disadvantaged applicants and applicants who are members of minority groups.

Cost of Study

The 1997–98 tuition rate per semester for full-time graduate enrollment (8 to 12 credits) was $2346 for Wisconsin residents and $7198 for nonresidents. Tuition is waived for all graduate students with appointments of at least ⅓-time as University fellows, project assistants, research assistants, and teaching assistants.

Living and Housing Costs

Rental property is abundant in Madison. A reasonable amount to budget for a shared apartment is $300 to $350 per month. Some University housing is available for single and married graduate students; there is a waiting list and applications should be submitted at the earliest possible date. For a nonresident graduate student without a University appointment, 1998–99 estimated expenses for nine months total $24,995 (including tuition).

Student Group

In September 1998, 64 graduate students enrolled in the School's programs; 10 are first-year students. Forty-one students are in pharmaceutical sciences, 17 are in social and administrative sciences in pharmacy, and 6 are in the M.S. in pharmacy program.

Student Outcomes

Recent Ph.D. graduates have received postdoctoral appointments (Harvard and Duke) or positions in industry (Parke Davis and Alcon Laboratories), education (the University of Texas and Ohio State University), and government agencies (FDA and NIH).

Location

Madison, situated in the rolling hills of southern Wisconsin, is surrounded by four lakes. It is cosmopolitan yet compact and offers a variety of cultural and recreational activities through its Civic Center, fourteen beaches, and numerous parks. Assorted athletic and entertainment events and facilities are available locally or within a 20-minute drive. Biking, sailing, fishing, golf, tennis, and hiking are popular warm-weather activities, while skiing (both downhill and cross-country), ice-skating, ice fishing, sledding, and snowmobiling are enjoyed in the winter. Temperatures range from 0° and below in winter to 80° to 90° in summer. The spectrum of activities, people, and climate make Madison a delightful place to be all year round.

The University and The School

The University of Wisconsin–Madison, founded in 1849, offers more than 150 graduate programs. Undergraduate, nondegree, and continuing education programs also are available. The campus is 1 mile from the state capitol building. The University has a 1,200-acre arboretum, an art museum, theaters, and sports and recreational facilities. The School of Pharmacy celebrated 100 years of providing education in 1983. From a single laboratory and 28 students, it has grown to about 75 faculty and administrative staff members and an enrollment of 65 graduate and 470 undergraduate (pharmacology/toxicology) and professional students.

Applying

Applications for the entire academic year (fall, spring, and summer) must be received by the January 15 deadline. Application materials are sent to both the School of Pharmacy and the UW Graduate School. The School requires the application, a statement of reasons for graduate study, official college transcripts, three recommendations (two must be academic), the department financial aid form, and GRE General Test scores. The UW Graduate School requires the application, a $45 application fee, official college transcripts, and, from international applicants, a financial support statement and English test scores. Applicants whose required materials have been received and reviewed by the deadline are given priority for financial aid available through the School of Pharmacy.

Correspondence and Information

Ms. Linda R. Frei
Graduate Program Coordinator
School of Pharmacy
University of Wisconsin–Madison
425 North Charter Street
Madison, Wisconsin 53706-1515

Telephone: 608-262-1200
Fax: 608-262-3397
E-mail: lrfrei@pharmacy.wisc.edu
World Wide Web: http://www.wisc.edu/pharmacy/

University of Wisconsin–Madison

THE FACULTY AND THEIR RESEARCH

Pharmacy

Pamela A. Ploetz, Clinical Associate Professor; B.S. (pharmacy), Wisconsin, 1968. Development of pharmacy practice models and relationships to education and research, drug utilization review, quality improvement and clinical economics. (telephone: 608-263-1295)

Thomas S. Thielke, Clinical Professor; M.S. (pharmacy), Wisconsin, 1969. Pharmacy computer systems, health system pharmacy consulting, financial management, health-care delivery systems, integration of clinical and distributive pharmacy services, drug-use process reengineering, automation, integrated pharmacy systems. (telephone: 608-263-1287)

Lee C. Vermeulen, Clinical Assistant Professor and Director, Center for Drug Policy and Clinical Economics; M.S. (pharmacy), Wisconsin, 1992. Drug policy development and assessment, technology assessment, clinical economics and outcomes research. (telephone: 608-262-7537)

Pharmaceutical Sciences

Ralph Albrecht, Professor; Ph.D. (bacteriology), Wisconsin–Madison, 1976. Structure-function relationships in biological and biological-biomaterial interactions using high-resolution labeling in conjunction with correlative light microscopy and electron microscopy, including receptor-ligand-cytoskeleton interactions, biomaterial biocompatibility, microvascular development, and immmunotoxicology. (telephone: 608-263-4162)

Paul Bass, Professor; Ph.D. (pharmacology), McGill, 1957. Gastrointestinal tract pharmacology, including drug absorption; motility. (telephone: 608-262-5753)

Ronald R. Burnette, Associate Professor; Ph.D. (pharmaceutical chemistry), California, San Francisco, 1982. Physical chemical characterization (primarily by NMR) of microemulsions, micelles, and emulsions; development of a molecular-level mechanistic understanding of the delivery and stability of encapsulated drugs. (telephone: 608-262-3814)

Margaret Clagett-Dame, Associate Professor; Ph.D. (biochemistry), Wisconsin, 1985. Retinoid receptor structure-function relationships; retinoids and neural development. (telephone: 608-262-3450)

Timothy D. Heath, Associate Professor; Ph.D. (biochemistry), London, 1976. Design and fabrication of macromolecular drug delivery systems. (telephone: 608-263-3986)

Warren Heideman, Associate Professor; Ph.D. (pharmacology), Washington (Seattle), 1983. Signal transduction across biological membranes. (telephone: 608-262-1795)

Ulfert Hornemann, Professor; Ph.D. (organic chemistry-biochemistry), Munich Technical, 1967. Structure and function of tRNA anticodon arm-related heptazoop hairpins; streptomyces DNA amplification. (telephone: 608-263-1447)

C. Richard Hutchinson, Professor; Ph.D. (organic chemistry), Minnesota, 1970. Genetics and biochemistry of antibiotic formation by bacteria. (telephone: 608-262-7582)

Guilherme Indig, Assistant Professor; Ph.D. (physical chemistry), São Paulo, 1988. Host-guest complexes of dyes and biopolymer polyelectrolytes, molecular recognition, and photoinduced therapy. (telephone: 608-265-6664)

W. John Kao, Assistant Professor; Ph.D. (macromolecular science), Case Western Reserve, 1996. Mechanisms of cell adhesion and activation on biomaterials, biomaterial biocompatibility and biodegradation, novel materials for tissue engineering. (telephone: 608-262-1416)

Glen S. Kwon, Assistant Professor; Ph.D. (pharmaceutics), Utah, 1991. Polymeric biomaterials as anticancer drug and antigen delivery systems. (telephone: 608-265-5183)

Charles T. Lauhon, Assistant Professor; Ph.D. (organic chemistry), Berkeley, 1992. Bioorganic chemistry of RNA, biochemistry of RNA-modifying enzymes; nucleotide-based drug design. (telephone: 608-262-3083)

William S. Mellon, Professor; Ph.D. (pharmacology), Ohio State, 1976. Biochemical pharmacology of hormones, including receptor structure, hormonal control of cellular differentiation, and mechanism of action of immunosuppressive agents. (telephone: 608-262-3196)

Dexter B. Northrop, Professor; Ph.D. (biochemistry), Case Western Reserve, 1969. Enzymology, with an emphasis on kinetics and reaction mechanisms. (telephone: 608-263-2519)

Richard E. Peterson, Professor; Ph.D. (pharmacology), Marquette, 1972. Reproductive and developmental toxicology of dioxins, PCBs, and other endocrine disruptors. (telephone: 608-263-5453)

Daniel H. Rich, Professor; Ph.D. (organic chemistry), Cornell, 1968. Synthesis and conformational analysis of cyclic peptides, design and synthesis of transition-state analog inhibitors of therapeutically important enzymes. (telephone: 608-263-2499)

Joseph R. Robinson, Professor; Ph.D. (pharmacy), Wisconsin, 1966. Ocular drug disposition, oral drug administration, controlled drug delivery. (telephone: 608-262-7968)

Thomas A. Rudy, Professor; Ph.D. (pharmacology), Ohio State, 1970. Central nervous system pharmacology, with emphasis on the effects of drugs on neural mechanisms controlling body temperature and the pathophysiology and treatment of fever. (telephone: 608-262-4424)

Charles J. Sih, Professor; Ph.D. (microbiology), Wisconsin, 1958. Enzymatic oxidative coupling, mechanism of thyroxine formation. (telephone: 608-262-3031)

George Zografi, Professor; Ph.D. (pharmaceutics), Michigan, 1960. Interfacial phenomena, including monolayers and bilayered vesicles as membrane models, polymer surface activity, water vapor sorption, and relaxation behavior of amorphous solids. (telephone: 608-262-2991)

Social and Administrative Sciences in Pharmacy

Betty A. Chewning, Assistant Professor; Ph.D. (educational psychology), Wisconsin, 1973. Measurement of health quality of life outcomes, client medication and self-care decisions, contraceptive behavior, computer-aided health education, the pharmacist-client relationship. (telephone: 608-263-4878)

James E. DeMuth, Professor; Ph.D. (continuing education in pharmacy), Wisconsin, 1974. Evaluation of adult education offerings, computer applications to education, educational delivery systems. (telephone: 608-262-2422)

Alan L. Hanson, Professor; Ph.D. (continuing education in pharmacy), Wisconsin, 1978. Pharmacists' and pharmacy students' attitudes toward continuing education, impact of continuing education on pharmacists' professional practice, preparing pharmacy students to become lifelong learners. (telephone: 608-262-2099)

David H. Kreling, Associate Professor; Ph.D. (pharmacy administration), Texas at Austin, 1984. Pharmacy and health-care economics and policy; third-party drug programs and reimbursement; development, marketing, and utilization of pharmacy goods and services. (telephone: 608-262-3454)

David A. Mott, Assistant Professor; Ph.D. (pharmacy administration), Wisconsin–Madison, 1995. Pharmacy labor economics; insurance effects on financing, selection, and use of prescription goods and services; health-care and pharmacy public policy. (telephone: 608-265-9268)

Jeanine K. Mount, Associate Professor; Ph.D. (sociology), Purdue, 1985. Quality assurance and improvement systems, pharmacy practice development, health-care organizations, organization of pharmacy practice and health-care delivery. (telephone: 608-262-8678)

John Scarborough, Professor; Ph.D. (Greek and Roman history; history of medicine), Illinois, 1967. Medicine and pharmacy in Greco-Roman antiquity. (telephone: 608-262-8195)

Bonnie L. Svarstad, Professor; Ph.D. (sociology), Wisconsin, 1974. Professional-patient communication, patient compliance, epidemiology of drug use, psychotropic drug use in nursing homes. (telephone: 608-265-2128)

Melvin H. Weinswig, Professor; Ph.D. (pharmaceutical chemistry), Illinois, 1961. Innovative educational delivery systems, attitudinal changes in participants toward continuing education. (telephone: 608-262-1414)

Joseph B. Wiederholt, Professor; Ph.D. (pharmacy administration), Georgia, 1981. Patient risk assessment/management of drug and alternative therapies, consumer behavior related to drug products and pharmacists' services, structure of the pharmaceutical channels of distribution. (telephone: 608-262-0452)

WAYNE STATE UNIVERSITY

College of Pharmacy and Allied Health Professions
Department of Pharmaceutical Sciences

Programs of Study

The Department of Pharmaceutical Sciences offers graduate programs of study leading to Master of Science and Doctor of Philosophy degrees. The objective of each program is to prepare scholar scientists for careers in medicinal chemistry, pharmaceutics, pharmacokinetics, pharmacology, or toxicology.

Graduate study committees aid in the planning and implementation of each student's program. An annual review is conducted to evaluate student performance in course work, seminars, and research. The M.S. degree requires 24 credits in course work and 8 credits of research toward a thesis. Successful completion of written and oral comprehensive examinations is required prior to the student's admission to candidacy for the Ph.D. degree. The Ph.D. candidate is required to successfully defend a dissertation based on independent research.

Research Facilities

The research facilities of the Faculty of Pharmacy are located in Shapero Hall. The College of Pharmacy and Allied Health Professions is generously equipped for research in each of the major pharmaceutical disciplines. Students and faculty members have access to all support facilities of the University complex, including a computer center and five libraries containing more than 2 million books as well as bound journals, microforms, films, maps, and audio and visual recordings.

Wayne State University operates one of the largest academic computer centers in the country, supporting graphics, statistical analysis, and word processing at more than 3,000 terminals, many of which are located in Shapero Hall.

Financial Aid

Graduate assistantships cover tuition for up to 10 graduate credit hours per semester and provide a stipend and medical insurance. Graduate fellowships are also available.

Cost of Study

Graduate fees for the fall 1997 semester (10 credit hours) were $1659 for state residents and $3479 for nonresidents.

Living and Housing Costs

The estimated cost of living for single students is $5000–$6000 per year. Private apartments and residence hall housing are available on campus. The city and surrounding communities also offer a variety of housing arrangements, from renovated town houses to ultramodern apartments in and near the downtown area.

Student Group

Approximately 34,000 students—representing a wide range of ages, occupations, and nationalities—are enrolled in graduate, professional, and undergraduate programs on the WSU campus. The department has 18 graduate students.

Location

Wayne State University is an integral part of Detroit's cultural center. Immediately adjacent to the campus are the Detroit Public Library, the Detroit Historical Museum, the Center for Creative Studies, the International Institute, and the Detroit Institute of Arts. Additional cultural and leisure-time offerings are available within a 5- to 10-minute drive. The Civic Center is the scene of conventions; fairs, shows, and festivals take place in Cobo Hall, Hart Plaza, and the Renaissance Center; and sports events are held in Joe Louis Arena and Tiger Stadium. Orchestra Hall, the home of the Detroit Symphony, is near the world-famous Fox and Fisher theaters. Attractive suburban communities are within a half-hour drive via an extensive network of freeways.

The University

Wayne State University, now in its second century of service, has developed over the past 100 years into one of the largest institutions of higher learning in the United States. The University's history dates back to 1868, when five Detroit physicians formed the Detroit Medical College. The college became a publicly controlled medical school in 1918 and was later joined with the Detroit Teachers College and the College of the City of Detroit to form the nucleus of what was to become a state university in 1956. Once confined to a single building, Old Main, WSU now occupies 180 acres, which includes a medical campus in the Detroit Medical Center as well as the main campus. The University comprises twelve colleges and schools—the College of Liberal Arts; the School of Medicine; the School of Social Work; the School of Business Administration; the College of Nursing; the College of Engineering; the College of Education; the School of Law; the College of Pharmacy and Allied Health Professions; the College of Lifelong Learning; the College of Urban, Labor, and Metropolitan Affairs; and the College of Fine, Performing and Communication Arts.

Applying

A completed application for graduate admission form, a $20 graduate application fee, and an official transcript from each college or university attended are required before any student can be considered for admission to graduate study. Candidates for admission should possess a strong background in chemistry, biology, mathematics, and pharmaceutical sciences or have had other preparation appropriate to the graduate major area. Applicants are expected to provide letters of recommendation from faculty members with whom they have studied and to take any entrance examinations that may be specified by the Department of Pharmaceutical Sciences. The application deadline for fall semester is January 30.

Correspondence and Information

Chairman, Graduate Program Committee
Department of Pharmaceutical Sciences
528 Shapero Hall
College of Pharmacy and Allied Health Professions
Wayne State University
Detroit, Michigan 48202

Wayne State University

THE FACULTY AND THEIR RESEARCH

Hanley N. Abramson, Associate Dean for Academic Affairs (Medicinal Chemistry); Ph.D., Michigan, 1968. Synthesis of natural products and their analogues, synthesis of quinone-type antitumor agents and determination of their pharmacological mechanisms.

David J. P. Bassett, Adjunct Professor (Occupational and Environmental Health Sciences); Ph.D., London, 1978. Pulmonary and inhalation toxicology, cellular and biochemical mechanisms of lung injury.

Randall L. Commissaris, Associate Professor (Pharmacology); Ph.D., Michigan State, 1981. Behavioral pharmacology, neuropharmacology: mechanism(s) for drug effects on behavior, with particular emphasis on drugs of abuse and drugs used in psychiatry.

George B. Corcoran, Professor and Chair (Pharmacology and Toxicology); Ph.D., George Washington, 1980. Molecular mechanisms of cell death, liver damage by drugs and chemicals, drug biotransformation, apoptosis and necrosis.

Merlin E. Ekstrom, Adjunct Associate Professor (Pharmacy and Pharmaceutics); D.V.M., Oklahoma State, 1967; Diplomate, American College of Veterinary Pathologists, 1974. Comparative pathology and laboratory animal science and medicine: laboratory animal model selection.

Peter D. Frade, Adjunct Associate Professor (Analytical Chemistry); Ph.D., Wayne State, 1978. Neurochemistry: analytical studies of neurotransmitters, neurotoxins, and neurohormones (panacrines) at ultra-trace levels in biological materials; lipoxidation reactions involving higher-order fatty acids.

George C. Fuller, Dean (Pharmacology); Ph.D., Purdue, 1967. Biochemical pharmacology: pharmacological control of allergy and inflammation, disease-induced alteration in collagen metabolism.

Richard A. Gibbs, Assistant Professor (Medicinal Chemistry); Ph.D., California, Riverside, 1988. Bioorganic chemistry: mechanistic and inhibitory studies of protein prenylation and related posttranslational modifications, design and synthesis of haptens for the induction of catalytic antibodies.

Aiko Hirata, Adjunct Instructor (Pharmacology); B.S., Tokyo Medical and Dental, 1963. Isolation and characterization of messenger proteins for anti-inflammatory action of glucocorticoids.

Fusao Hirata, Professor (Pharmacology and Toxicology); M.D., Tokyo Medical and Dental, 1967; Ph.D., Kyoto, 1972. Molecular mechanism of action of steroids and related xenobiotics, molecular pathogenesis and therapeutics of hyperreactive airways, characterization of genes for physiological cell death (apoptosis).

Eun W. Lee, Adjunct Associate Professor (Toxicology); Ph.D., Thomas Jefferson, 1970. Biochemical toxicology: mechanisms of chemical toxicity in the induction of neoplastic, neurologic, and hematopoietic disorders.

Robert A. Levine, Adjunct Professor (Pharmacology); Ph.D., George Washington, 1982. Role of regulation of biogenic amine neurotransmitters synthesis and related neurological diseases.

William J. Lindblad, Associate Professor (Pharmacology); Ph.D., Rhode Island, 1980. Biochemical pharmacology: cellular and biochemical responses to tissue injury, mechanisms of hepatic fibrosis, pharmacologic control of collagen metabolism.

Robert T. Louis-Ferdinand, Professor (Pharmacology and Toxicology); Ph.D., Rhode Island, 1970. Biochemical mechanisms of drug tolerance, biochemical basis for the toxicity of environmental pollutants and their interactions with drug effects.

Michael J. McCabe Jr., Adjunct Assistant Professor (Research, Chemical Toxicology); Ph.D., Albany Medical College, 1990. Cellular and molecular mechanisms of immunomodulation by toxic metals; signal transduction associated with programmed cell death (apoptosis).

Howard J. Normile, Adjunct Associate Professor; Ph.D., Wayne State, 1983. Neurophysiology and behavioral pharmacology; focus on functional interactions between neural substrates, using as model systems: learning/memory and cognitive disorders, locomotor activity, and ingestive behavior.

David K. Pitts, Assistant Professor (Pharmacology); Ph.D., Wayne State, 1985. Neuropharmacology: electrophysiology of central monoamine-containing neurons, developmental neuropharmacology, central autonomic pharmacology.

Joel G. Pounds, Associate Professor (Toxicology); Ph.D., Wisconsin, 1977. Cellular and molecular mechanisms of trace-element toxicity, interaction between metals and the calcium messenger system.

Edward T. Roginsky, Adjunct Instructor (Analytical Chemistry); Ph.D., Wayne State, 1983. Development of test kits for drugs of abuse in urine, saliva, and blood.

Steven E. Rose, Adjunct Assistant Professor (Pharmaceutics); Ph.D., Michigan, 1990. Assay development, solid-dosage form development, pharmacokinetics.

Roh-Yu Shen, Assistant Professor (Research, Pharmacology); Ph.D., Michigan, 1989. Neurophysiology, neuropharmacology, cellular basis for alcohol addiction and fetal alcohol syndrome.

J. Christopher States, Adjunct Associate Professor (Toxicology); Ph.D., Albany Medical College, 1980. DNA damage by metabolically activated chemicals, human DNA repair genes, role of DNA repair in chemoresistance.

Craig K. Svensson, Associate Professor (Pharmaceutics); Pharm.D., Maryland, 1981; Ph.D., SUNY at Buffalo, 1984. Pharmacokinetics: effect of immunomodulators on drug metabolism, factors altering drug acetylation.

Bonita G. Taffe, Adjunct Assistant Professor (Occupational and Environmental Health Sciences); M.P.H., Columbia, 1981; Ph.D., Johns Hopkins, 1988. Molecular toxicology: characterization and comparison of oxidative DNA damage; repair mechanisms and mutational analysis in oxidant sensitive and resistant model systems.

Henry C. Wormser, Professor (Medicinal Chemistry); Ph.D., Wisconsin, 1965. Synthesis of natural products, their analogues, and potentially active pharmacological agents.

Patrick M. Woster, Associate Professor (Medicinal Chemistry); Ph.D., Nebraska, 1986. Synthesis and biological evaluation of rigid analog and transition-state analog enzyme inhibitors as potential therapeutic agents.

Alice M. Young, Adjunct Associate Professor (Pharmacology); Ph.D., Minnesota, 1976. Behavioral pharmacology and neuropharmacology: mechanism(s) for the effects of drugs of abuse on behavior, with particular emphasis on drug tolerance and dependence with behavioral stimulants.

Section 39
Veterinary Medicine and Sciences

This section contains directories of institutions offering professional programs in veterinary medicine and graduate studies in veterinary sciences, followed by in-depth entries submitted by institutions that chose to prepare detailed program descriptions. Additional information about programs listed in the directories but not augmented by an in-depth entry may be obtained by writing directly to the dean of a school or chair of a department at the address given in the directory.

For programs offering related work, see in Book 2 Economics (Agricultural Economics and Agribusiness); in Book 3, Biological and Biomedical Sciences and Zoology; in Book 4, Agricultural and Food Sciences, Marine Sciences and Oceanography, and Natural Resources; and in Book 5, Bioengineering, Biomedical Engineering, and Biotechnology.

CONTENTS

Veterinary Medicine

Auburn University, College of Veterinary Medicine, Professional Program in Veterinary Medicine, Auburn University, AL 36849-0001. Awards DVM, DVM/MS. Limited accreditation by AVMA. Faculty: 87 full-time (21 women). Students: 360 full-time (217 women). In 1997, 85 degrees awarded. *Degree requirements:* Preceptorship required, foreign language and thesis not required. *Application deadline:* 9/1 (rolling processing). *Application fee:* $25. *Financial aid:* Fellowships available. Financial aid application deadline: 3/15. • Application contact: John Fletcher, Director of Admissions, 334-844-4080.

Colorado State University, College of Veterinary Medicine and Biomedical Sciences, Professional Program in Veterinary Medicine, Fort Collins, CO 80523-0015. Awards DVM. Accredited by AVMA. Faculty: 151 full-time (23 women). Students: 532 full-time (388 women); includes 66 minority (2 African Americans, 22 Asian Americans, 34 Hispanics, 8 Native Americans), 1 international. Average age 26. 746 applicants, 18% accepted. In 1997, 128 degrees awarded. *Entrance requirements:* GRE General Test, residency in a member state of the Western Interstate Commission for Higher Education. Application deadline: 10/1. Application fee: $40. Electronic applications accepted. *Tuition:* $8630 per year for state residents; $28,530 per year for nonresidents. *Financial aid:* Fellowships, research assistantships, teaching assistantships, traineeships available. *Faculty research:* Oncology, equine medicine, environmental toxicology, animal reproduction, infectious diseases. Total annual research expenditures: $25 million. • Application contact: Dr. Sherry McConnell, Assistant Dean of Admissions and Advising, 970-491-7052. Fax: 970-491-2250. E-mail: smconnell@vines.colostate.edu.

Cornell University, Professional School of Veterinary Medicine, Ithaca, NY 14853-0001. Awards DVM. Accredited by AVMA. Faculty: 123 full-time (20 women), 3 part-time (1 woman). Students: 319 full-time (230 women); includes 40 minority (7 African Americans, 13 Asian Americans, 19 Hispanics, 1 Native American), 1 international. Average age 25. 1,179 applicants, 7% accepted. In 1997, 75 degrees awarded. *Average time to degree:* first professional–4 years full-time. *Entrance requirements:* GRE General Test (average 600 verbal, 720 quantitative). Application deadline: 10/1. Application fee: $40. *Financial aid:* 270 students received aid; Federal Work-Study, institutionally sponsored loans available. Financial aid application deadline: 2/1; applicants required to submit CSS PROFILE or FAFSA. *Total annual research expenditures:* $16.66 million. • Donald F. Smith, Dean, 607-253-3771. Application contact: Joseph M. Piekunka, Director of Admissions, 607-253-3700 Ext. 1.

Iowa State University of Science and Technology, College of Veterinary Medicine, Professional Program in Veterinary Medicine, Ames, IA 50011. Awards DVM. Accredited by AVMA. Students: 399 full-time (236 women), 8 part-time (6 women); includes 8 minority (1 African American, 1 Asian American, 6 Hispanics), 1 international. In 1997, 91 degrees awarded. *Expenses:* Tuition $6082 per year full-time, $253 per credit part-time for state residents; $16,582 per year full-time, $253 per credit part-time for nonresidents. Fees $200 per year. *Financial aid:* Federal Work-Study available. • Dr. Richard F. Ross, Dean, College of Veterinary Medicine, 515-294-1250. E-mail: rfross@iastate.edu.

Kansas State University, College of Veterinary Medicine, Professional Program in Veterinary Medicine, Manhattan, KS 66506. Awards DVM. Accredited by AVMA. Faculty: 78 full-time (11 women). Students: 374 full-time (169 women); includes 14 minority (1 Asian American, 10 Hispanics, 3 Native Americans). Average age 24. 295 applicants, 36% accepted. In 1997, 94 degrees awarded. *Entrance requirements:* GRE General Test, 70 hours of preprofessional requirements. Application deadline: 10/15 (rolling processing). Application fee: $50. *Tuition:* $5299 per year for state residents; $17,305 per year for nonresidents. *Financial aid:* Federal Work-Study, institutionally sponsored loans available. Financial aid application deadline: 3/15. *Faculty research:* Surgery and medicine, laboratory medicine, electron microscopy, respiratory studies, therapeutic drug response. • Application contact: Dr. Jody E. Johnson, Assistant Dean, 785-532-4335. Fax: 785-532-5884. E-mail: admit@vet.ksu.edu.

Louisiana State University and Agricultural and Mechanical College, School of Veterinary Medicine, Baton Rouge, LA 70803. Awards DVM, MS, PhD. One or more programs accredited by AVMA. DVM available to state and contract students and limited number of highly qualified out-of-state applicants. Faculty: 64 full-time (13 women), 4 part-time (1 woman). Students: 41 full-time (19 women), 21 part-time (5 women). Average age 34. 23 applicants, 65% accepted. In 1997, 14 master's, 4 doctorates awarded. Terminal master's awarded for partial completion of doctoral program. *Degree requirements:* For master's and doctorate, thesis/dissertation required, foreign language not required. *Entrance requirements:* For DVM, GRE General Test (minimum combined score of 1000) or MCAT, TOEFL (minimum score 550); for master's, GRE General Test (minimum combined score of 1000); for doctorate, GRE General Test (minimum combined score of 1000), TOEFL (minimum score 550). *Financial aid:* In 1997–98, 6 fellowships (1 to a first-year student), 27 research assistantships (3 to first-year students), 2 teaching assistantships (1 to a first-year student), 1 service assistantship were awarded; Federal Work-Study, institutionally sponsored loans, and career-related internships or fieldwork also available. *Faculty research:* Veterinary microbiology, immunology, pathology, anatomy, epidemiology, parasitology, toxicology, physiology, pharmacology. Total annual research expenditures: $5 million. • Dr. David L. Huxsoll, Dean, 504-346-3151. Fax: 504-346-3295.

Michigan State University, College of Veterinary Medicine, Professional Program in Veterinary Medicine, East Lansing, MI 48824-1020. Awards DVM. Accredited by AVMA. Students: 395 full-time (314 women); includes 24 minority (6 African Americans, 5 Asian Americans, 10 Hispanics, 3 Native Americans). 1,218 applicants, 8% accepted. In 1997, 94 degrees awarded. *Entrance requirements:* GRE, MCAT. Application deadline: 10/1. Application fee: $130. *Expenses:* Tuition $10,789 per year for state residents; $22,239 per year for nonresidents. Fees $303 per year. • Dr. Janver Krehbiel, Associate Dean for Academic and Student Affairs, 517-355-7624. Fax: 517-432-1037. E-mail: krehbiel@cvm.msu.edu. Application contact: Hilda Mejia Abreu, Coordinator of Admissions, 517-353-9793. Fax: 517-432-2391. E-mail: abreu@cvm.msu.edu.

Mississippi State University, College of Veterinary Medicine, Professional Program in Veterinary Medicine, Mississippi State, MS 39762. Awards DVM. Accredited by AVMA. Faculty: 67 full-time (19 women), 30 part-time (4 women). Students: 188 full-time (110 women); includes 4 minority (2 African Americans, 1 Asian American, 1 Native American), 2 international. Average age 24. 320 applicants, 15% accepted. In 1997, 46 degrees awarded. *Average time to degree:* first professional–8 years full-time. *Entrance requirements:* VCAT (average 190), minimum GPA of 3.0. Application deadline: 10/1. Application fee: $25. *Financial aid:* Federal Work-Study available. Financial aid application deadline: 4/1; applicants required to submit FAFSA. • Dr. Philip Bushby, Academic Director, 601-325-1271. Application contact: Dr. P. Mikell Davis, Student Affairs Coordinator, 601-325-1129. Fax: 601-325-8714. E-mail: davis@cvm.msstate.edu.

North Carolina State University, College of Veterinary Medicine, Professional Program in Veterinary Medicine, Raleigh, NC 27695. Awards DVM. Accredited by AVMA. *Average time to degree:* first professional–4 years full-time. *Entrance requirements:* GRE. Application deadline: 11/1 (rolling processing). Application fee: $130. *Tuition:* $3460 per year for state residents; $21,190 per year for nonresidents.

The Ohio State University, College of Veterinary Medicine, Professional Program in Veterinary Medicine, Columbus, OH 43210. Awards DVM, DVM/MS, DVM/PhD. Limited accreditation by AVMA. *Entrance requirements:* GRE General Test, MCAT, or VAT, 96 hours of pre-veterinary course work. Application deadline: 11/1. Application fee: $20.

Oklahoma State University, College of Veterinary Medicine, Professional Program in Veterinary Medicine, Stillwater, OK 74078. Awards DVM. Accredited by AVMA. Faculty: 56 full-time (7 women), 2 part-time (0 women). Students: 287 full-time (167 women), 4 part-time (3 women); includes 28 minority (6 African Americans, 3 Asian Americans, 2 Hispanics, 17 Native Americans), 1 international. Average age 26. In 1997, 67 degrees awarded. *Entrance requirements:* GRE General Test, GRE Subject Test (biology). Application deadline: 10/1. Application fee: $0. *Financial aid:* Partial tuition waivers, Federal Work-Study, and career-related internships or fieldwork available. Aid available to part-time students. Financial aid application deadline: 3/1. *Faculty research:* Infectious diseases, physiology, toxicology, biomedical lasers, clinical studies. Total annual research expenditures: $1.3 million. • Michael Lorenz, Associate for Academic Affairs, 405-744-6651. Application contact: Pat Stormont, 405-744-6653. Fax: 405-744-6633. E-mail: vmadmps@okway.okstate.edu.

Oregon State University, College of Veterinary Medicine, Professional Program in Veterinary Medicine, Corvallis, OR 97331. Awards DVM. Accredited by AVMA. DVM admissions open only to residents of Oregon and other states participating in the Western Interstate Commission for Higher Education (WICHE). Faculty: 28 full-time (6 women), 2 part-time (1 woman). In 1997, 36 degrees awarded. *Entrance requirements:* VCAT and/or GRE, minimum GPA of 3.3 during previous 2 years, 3.2 overall. Application deadline: 11/1. Application fee: $50. *Financial aid:* Scholarships, Federal Work-Study, institutionally sponsored loans available. Aid available to part-time students. Financial aid application deadline: 2/1. • Application contact: Associate Dean, 541-737-2098. Fax: 541-737-4245.

Purdue University, School of Veterinary Medicine, Professional Program in Veterinary Medicine, West Lafayette, IN 47907. Awards DVM, DVM/MS, DVM/PhD. Accredited by AVMA. Faculty: 76 full-time (13 women), 1 part-time (0 women). Students: 261 full-time (186 women); includes 14 minority (1 African American, 5 Asian Americans, 8 Hispanics), 4 international. Average age 24. 1,006 applicants, 10% accepted. In 1997, 60 degrees awarded. *Entrance requirements:* GRE General Test, TOEFL (minimum score 600). Application deadline: 10/1. Application fee: $0. *Financial aid:* Partial tuition waivers, Federal Work-Study, institutionally sponsored loans available. Aid available to part-time students. Financial aid application deadline: 3/1; applicants required to submit FAFSA. • J. F. Van Vleet, Associate Dean, 765-494-9185. Application contact: Denise A. Ottinger, Director, Student Services, 765-494-7893. Fax: 765-496-2891. E-mail: admissions@vet.purdue.edu.

Texas A&M University, College of Veterinary Medicine, Professional Programs in Veterinary Medicine, College Station, TX 77843. Awards DVM, DVM/PhD. Accredited by AVMA. Faculty: 134 full-time (22 women). Students: 476 full-time (268 women); includes 32 minority (2 African Americans, 4 Asian Americans, 23 Hispanics, 3 Native Americans). 320 applicants, 40% accepted. In 1997, 114 degrees awarded. *Entrance requirements:* GRE, MCAT. Application deadline: 10/1. Application fee: $35 ($75 for international students). *Faculty research:* Reproductive biology, theriogenology, genetics, endrocrinology, animal behavior. • Application contact: Tammi Caskey, Coordinator of Admissions, 409-845-5038. Fax: 409-845-5088.

Tufts University, School of Veterinary Medicine, Professional Program in Veterinary Medicine, Medford, MA 02155. Awards DVM, DVM/MA, DVM/MS, DVM/PhD. Accredited by AVMA. DVM/MA offered jointly with Fletcher School of Law and Diplomacy; DVM/PhD offered jointly with both the Sackler School of Graduate Biomedical Sciences and the University of Massachusetts Medical Center at Worcester. Students: 295 full-time. In 1997, 75 degrees awarded. *Degree requirements:* Thesis optional, foreign language not required. *Entrance requirements:* GRE General Test. Application deadline: 12/1. Application fee: $60. *Financial aid:* Institutional aid awards, Federal Work-Study, institutionally sponsored loans, and career-related internships or fieldwork available. Financial aid application deadline: 3/15. • Application contact: Rebecca Russo, Director of Admissions, 508-839-7920. Fax: 508-839-2953.

Tuskegee University, College of Veterinary Medicine and Allied Health, Professional Program in Veterinary Medicine, Tuskegee, AL 36088. Awards DVM. Accredited by AVMA. Faculty: 62 full-time (6 women). Students: 231 full-time (142 women); includes 176 minority (142 African Americans, 7 Asian Americans, 27 Hispanics). Average age 25. In 1997, 57 degrees awarded. *Entrance requirements:* VCAT. Application deadline: 7/15 (rolling processing). Application fee: $35. *Financial aid:* Application deadline 4/15. • Dr. Albert W. Dade, Dean, College of Veterinary Medicine and Allied Health, 334-727-8174.

Université de Montréal, Faculty of Veterinary Medicine, Professional Program in Veterinary Medicine, Montréal, PQ H3C 3J7, Canada. Awards DVM. Accredited by AVMA. Open only to Canadian residents. Part-time programs available. Students: 294 full-time (211 women). 597 applicants, 12% accepted. In 1997, 77 degrees awarded. *Entrance requirements:* Minimum A average. Application deadline: 3/1. Application fee: $30. *Financial aid:* Teaching assistantships and career-related internships or fieldwork available. *Faculty research:* Animal reproduction, infectious diseases of swine, physiology of exercise in horses, viral diseases of cattle, health management and epidemiology. • Application contact: André Dallaire, Associate Dean of Graduate Studies, 514-773-8218.

University of California, Davis, School of Veterinary Medicine, Professional Program in Veterinary Medicine, Davis, CA 95616. Awards DVM, DVM/MPVM, DVM/PhD. Accredited by AVMA. Faculty: 225. Students: 430 full-time (296 women). Average age 25. 1,130 applicants, 11% accepted. In 1997, 104 degrees awarded. *Average time to degree:* first professional–4 years full-time. *Entrance requirements:* GRE General Test (combined average 2011 on three sections). Application deadline: 10/1. *Expenses:* Tuition $0 for state residents; $8984 per year for nonresidents. Fees $8447 per year. *Financial aid:* Fellowships, teaching assistantships, training grants, Federal Work-Study, institutionally sponsored loans available. Aid available to part-time students. Financial aid application deadline: 3/2; applicants required to submit FAFSA. • Dr. Robert Hansen, Associate Dean, Student Programs, 530-752-1383. Application contact: Yasmin Williams, Director of Admissions, 530-752-1383. Fax: 530-752-2801.

University of Florida, College of Veterinary Medicine, Professional Program in Veterinary Medicine, Gainesville, FL 32611. Awards DVM. Accredited by AVMA. Faculty: 88. Students: 314 full-time (216 women); includes 50 minority (11 African Americans, 8 Asian Americans, 29 Hispanics, 2 Native Americans). Average age 25. 763 applicants, 10% accepted. In 1997, 75 degrees awarded. *Entrance requirements:* GRE General Test. Application deadline: 10/1. Application fee: $155. *Tuition:* $7836 per year for state residents; $20,729 per year for nonresidents. *Financial aid:* In 1997–98, 86 scholarships totaling $85,741 were awarded; Federal Work-Study, institutionally sponsored loans, and career-related internships or fieldwork also available. Financial aid application deadline: 7/1; applicants required to submit FAFSA. • Dr. James P. Thompson, Associate Dean, 352-392-4700 Ext. 5300. Fax: 352-846-2744. E-mail: jthompson.vetmed3@mail.health.ufl.edu.

University of Georgia, College of Veterinary Medicine, Professional Program in Veterinary Medicine, Athens, GA 30602. Awards DVM. Accredited by AVMA. Faculty: 109 full-time (31 women), 24 part-time (10 women). Students: 303 full-time (189 women). Average age 27. 680 applicants, 12% accepted. In 1997, 75 degrees awarded. *Average time to degree:* first professional–8 years full-time. *Entrance requirements:* GRE General Test, VCAT. Application deadline: 10/1. Application fee: $30. *Financial aid:* 80 students received aid; Federal Work-Study available. Financial aid application deadline: 2/15. *Total annual research expenditures:* $10 million. • Sheila W. Allen, Associate Dean for Academic Affairs, 706-542-5728. Fax: 706-542-1004. E-mail: sallen@calc.vet.uga.edu.

University of Guelph, Ontario Veterinary College and Faculty of Graduate Studies, Graduate Programs in Veterinary Sciences, Department of Clinical Studies, Guelph, ON N1G 2W1, Canada. Offerings include medicine (M Sc, DV Sc), surgery (M Sc, DV Sc). Department faculty: 22 full-time (6 women), 3 part-time (1 woman). *Degree requirements:* Thesis/dissertation. *Average time to degree:* doctorate–3 years full-time; other advanced degree–1.5 years full-time. *Application deadline:* 2/1 (rolling processing). *Application fee:* $60. *Expenses:* Tuition $4725 per year full-time, $3165 per year part-time for Canadian residents; $6999 per year for nonresidents. Fees $612 per year full-time, $38 per year (minimum) part-time for Canadian residents; $612 per year for nonresidents. • Dr. S. Kruth, Chair, 519-823-8800 Ext. 4012.

Application contact: Dr. M. Hurtig, Graduate Coordinator, 519-823-8800 Ext. 4028. Fax: 519-767-0311. E-mail: mhurtig@ovcnet.uoguelph.ca.

University of Illinois at Urbana–Champaign, College of Veterinary Medicine, Professional Program in Veterinary Medicine, Urbana, IL 61801. Awards DVM. Accredited by AVMA. Students: 343 full-time (237 women); includes 22 minority (4 African Americans, 8 Asian Americans, 9 Hispanics, 1 Native American). 379 applicants, 31% accepted. In 1997, 87 degrees awarded. *Entrance requirements:* VCAT. Application deadline: 11/1. Application fee: $40 ($50 for international students). *Financial aid:* In 1997–98, 90 research assistantships were awarded; full tuition waivers, Federal Work-Study, and career-related internships or fieldwork also available. Financial aid application deadline: 3/15. *Total annual research expenditures:* $4.1 million. • Application contact: Dr. Gay Y. Miller, Associate Dean for Academic/Student Affairs, 217-333-1192.

University of Minnesota, Twin Cities Campus, College of Veterinary Medicine, Professional Program in Veterinary Medicine, St. Paul, MN 55108. Awards DVM. Accredited by AVMA. Faculty: 85 full-time (15 women). Students: 296 full-time (209 women); includes 12 minority (3 African Americans, 7 Asian Americans, 1 Hispanic, 1 Native American), 4 international. Average age 25. 1,174 applicants, 6% accepted. In 1997, 71 degrees awarded. *Average time to degree:* first professional–4 years full-time. *Entrance requirements:* GRE General Test (combined average 1890 on three sections). Application deadline: 11/1. Application fee: $50. *Financial aid:* Federal Work-Study and career-related internships or fieldwork available. Financial aid application deadline: 4/1; applicants required to submit FAFSA. *Faculty research:* Infectious toxic diseases of animals, zoonotic animal models of human disease, epidemiologic and preventive medicine. • Dr. A. Trent, Associate Dean, 612-624-4747. Application contact: Larry Bjorklund, Director, Student Affairs and Admissions, 612-624-4747.

University of Missouri–Columbia, College of Veterinary Medicine, Professional Program in Veterinary Medicine, Columbia, MO 65211. Awards DVM. Accredited by AVMA. Faculty: 93 full-time (17 women), 18 part-time (3 women). Students: 248 full-time (168 women); includes 7 minority (2 Asian Americans, 4 Hispanics, 1 Native American). Average age 23. 232 applicants, 28% accepted. In 1997, 66 degrees awarded. *Entrance requirements:* VCAT, minimum GPA of 2.5 for in-state residents, 3.0 for out-of-state residents. Application deadline: 11/1. Application fee: $50. Electronic applications accepted. *Financial aid:* In 1997–98, 58 students received aid, including 2 fellowships averaging $1,417 per month and totaling $34,000, 28 research assistantships (5 to first-year students) averaging $1,167 per month; research associateships, full tuition waivers, Federal Work-Study, institutionally sponsored loans, and career-related internships or fieldwork also available. *Faculty research:* Cardiovascular physiology, food safety, infectious diseases, laboratory animal medicine, opthalmology. Total annual research expenditures: $4 million. • Application contact: Dr. C. B. Chastain, Associate Dean for Academic Affairs, 573-884-6774. Fax: 573-884-5044.

University of Pennsylvania, School of Veterinary Medicine, Philadelphia, PA 19104. Awards VMD, VMD/PhD, VMD/MBA. Accredited by AVMA. Faculty: 230 full-time, 5 part-time. Students: 416 full-time (308 women); includes 17 minority (1 African American, 10 Asian Americans, 6 Hispanics), 9 international. Average age 25. 1,203 applicants, 16% accepted. In 1997, 117 degrees awarded. *Entrance requirements:* GRE. Application deadline: 10/1. Application fee: $0. *Expenses:* Tuition $21,722 per year for state residents; $26,048 per year for nonresidents. Fees $1178 per year. *Financial aid:* Federal Work-Study, institutionally sponsored loans, and career-related internships or fieldwork available. *Total annual research expenditures:* $12 million. • Dr. Alan M. Kelly, Dean. Application contact: Malcolm Keiter, Director of Admissions, 215-898-5434. Fax: 215-573-8819.

University of Prince Edward Island, Atlantic Veterinary College, Professional Program in Veterinary Medicine, Charlottetown, PE C1A 4P3, Canada. Awards DVM. Accredited by AVMA. Faculty: 99 full-time (29 women). Students: 460 full-time (341 women), 7 part-time (3 women). In 1997, 52 degrees awarded. *Average time to degree:* first professional–4 years full-time. *Application deadline:* 12/1. *Application fee:* $35. *Expenses:* Tuition $4970 per year. Fees $433 per year for Canadian residents; $14,803 per year for nonresidents. *Financial aid:* Research assistantships available. *Faculty research:* Shellfish toxicology, animal nutrition, fish health, toxicology, animal health management. • Dr. Jeanne Lofstedt, Associate Dean of Academic Affairs, 902-566-0928. Fax: 902-566-0958. Application contact: John R. DeGrace, Registrar, 902-566-0608.

University of Saskatchewan, Western College of Veterinary Medicine, Professional Program in Veterinary Medicine, Saskatoon, SK S7N 5A2, Canada. Awards DVM. Accredited by AVMA. Students: 280 full-time. In 1997, 70 degrees awarded. *Degree requirements:* Thesis. *Application deadline:* 7/1 (priority date). *Application fee:* $50. *Financial aid:* Fellowships, teaching assistantships available. Financial aid application deadline: 1/31. • Dr. A. Livingston, Dean, Western College of Veterinary Medicine, 306-966-7448. Fax: 306-966-8747.

University of Tennessee, Knoxville, College of Veterinary Medicine, Knoxville, TN 37996. Awards DVM. Accredited by AVMA. Faculty: 83 full-time (19 women). Students: 249 full-time (169 women), 1 part-time (0 women); includes 18 minority (4 African Americans, 3 Asian Americans, 6 Hispanics, 5 Native Americans), 1 international. 506 applicants, 14% accepted. In 1997, 66 degrees awarded. *Entrance requirements:* VCAT, TOEFL (minimum score 550), interview, minimum GPA of 2.7. Application deadline: 11/1. Application fee: $25. *Financial aid:* In 1997–98, 1 fellowship, 7 teaching assistantships were awarded; research assistantships, graduate assistantships, institutionally sponsored loans, and career-related internships or fieldwork also available. Financial aid application deadline: 2/1. • Dr. G. M. H. Shires, Dean, 423-974-7262. Fax: 423-974-4773. Application contact: Dr. James Brace, Associate Dean.

University of Wisconsin–Madison, School of Veterinary Medicine, Professional Program in Veterinary Medicine, Madison, WI 53706-1380. Awards DVM. Accredited by AVMA. Faculty: 75 full-time. Students: 311 full-time (211 women), 4 part-time (all women); includes 9 minority (1 African American, 2 Asian Americans, 4 Hispanics, 2 Native Americans), 2 international. Average age 24. 594 applicants, 13% accepted. *Entrance requirements:* GRE General Test. Application deadline: 10/1. Application fee: $45. *Tuition:* $11,362 per year for state residents; $16,666 per year for nonresidents. *Financial aid:* 315 students received aid; research assistantships, teaching assistantships, Federal Work-Study, institutionally sponsored loans available. Aid available to part-time students. Financial aid application deadline: 3/1. • Application contact: Dr. Susan J. Hyland, Associate Dean of Academic Affairs, 608-263-2525.

Virginia Polytechnic Institute and State University, Virginia-Maryland Regional College of Veterinary Medicine, Professional Programs in Veterinary Medicine, Blacksburg, VA 24061. Awards DVM. Accredited by AVMA. Offered jointly with the University of Maryland, College Park. Students: 337 full-time (244 women), 1 (woman) part-time; includes 1 international. Average age 25. 725 applicants, 13% accepted. In 1997, 80 degrees awarded. *Entrance requirements:* GRE Subject Test (biology), TOEFL. Application deadline: 11/15 (priority date). Application fee: $30. *Tuition:* $8653 per year for state residents; $21,493 per year for nonresidents. • Dr. Blair Meldrum, Associate Dean, 540-231-7666.

Washington State University, College of Veterinary Medicine, Professional Program in Veterinary Medicine, Pullman, WA 99164-1610. Awards DVM, DVM/MS, DVM/PhD. Limited accreditation by AVMA. Offered jointly with Oregon State University and the University of Idaho. Students: 273 full-time (179 women); includes 11 minority (5 African Americans, 6 Asian Americans). Average age 25. 1,173 applicants, 6% accepted. In 1997, 63 degrees awarded. *Entrance requirements:* GRE. Application deadline: 8/1 (priority date; rolling processing). Application fee: $30. *Financial aid:* Research assistantships, teaching assistantships available. *Faculty research:* Biotechnology, immunology, pathology, neurosciences, clinical sciences. • Dr. Kenneth Myers, Associate Dean, 509-335-1531. Fax: 509-335-3063. Application contact: Dr. Kathleen Potter, Director of Admissions, 509-335-4456. Fax: 509-335-6094. E-mail: admissions@vetmed.wsu.edu.

Veterinary Sciences

Allegheny University of the Health Sciences, School of Medicine, Biomedical Graduate Programs, Program in Laboratory Animal Science, Philadelphia, PA 19102-1192. Awards MLAS. Part-time programs available. Faculty: 4 full-time (0 women), 7 part-time (2 women). Students: 17 full-time (12 women), 2 part-time (both women). Average age 24. 12 applicants, 58% accepted. In 1997, 7 degrees awarded. *Degree requirements:* Comprehensive exam required, foreign language and thesis not required. *Entrance requirements:* GRE General Test (minimum combined score of 1410 on three sections), TOEFL, minimum GPA of 2.75. Application deadline: 4/1 (rolling processing). Application fee: $50. *Expenses:* Tuition $10,950 per year. Fees $60 per year. *Financial aid:* Federal Work-Study, institutionally sponsored loans, and career-related internships or fieldwork available. Aid available to part-time students. Financial aid application deadline: 5/1; applicants required to submit FAFSA. *Faculty research:* Laboratory animal medicine, experimental surgery, development of animal models for human diseases. • Dr. Jerald Silverman, Director, 215-762-7970. Application contact: Meghna Mudé, Academic Coordinator, 215-762-7967.

Auburn University, College of Veterinary Medicine and Graduate School, Graduate Program in Veterinary Medicine, Auburn University, AL 36849-0001. Awards MS, PhD, DVM/MS. Offerings include anatomy, physiology and pharmacology (MS), including anatomy and histology, physiology and pharmacology; biomedical sciences (PhD); large animal surgery and medicine (MS); pathobiology (MS); radiology (MS); small animal surgery and medicine (MS). Part-time programs available. Students: 12 full-time (5 women), 37 part-time (16 women); includes 3 minority (all African Americans), 16 international. 31 applicants, 26% accepted. In 1997, 8 master's, 5 doctorates awarded. *Degree requirements:* For doctorate, dissertation. *Entrance requirements:* For master's, GRE General Test; for doctorate, GRE General Test, GRE Subject Test. Application deadline: 9/1 (rolling processing; 3/1 for spring admission). Application fee: $25 ($50 for international students). *Expenses:* Tuition $2760 per year full-time, $76 per credit hour part-time for state residents; $8280 per year full-time, $228 per credit hour part-time for nonresidents. Fees $30 per year full-time, $160 per quarter part-time for state residents; $30 per year full-time, $480 per quarter part-time for nonresidents. *Financial aid:* Research assistantships, teaching assistantships, Federal Work-Study available. Aid available to part-time students. Financial aid application deadline: 3/15. • Application contact: Dr. John F. Pritchett, Dean of the Graduate School, 334-844-4700.

Colorado State University, College of Veterinary Medicine and Biomedical Sciences and Graduate School, Graduate Programs in Veterinary Medicine and Biomedical Sciences, Department of Clinical Sciences, Fort Collins, CO 80523-0015. Awards MS, PhD. Part-time programs available. Faculty: 45 full-time (6 women). Students: 25 full-time (12 women), 5 part-time (2 women); includes 2 minority (1 Asian American, 1 Hispanic), 6 international. Average age 32. 8 applicants, 75% accepted. In 1997, 8 master's, 1 doctorate awarded. Terminal master's awarded for partial completion of doctoral program. *Degree requirements:* For doctorate, dissertation required, foreign language not required. *Entrance requirements:* GRE General Test, TOEFL, DVM, minimum GPA of 3.0. Application deadline: 2/1 (priority date; rolling processing). Application fee: $30. Electronic applications accepted. *Expenses:* Tuition $2632 per year full-time, $109 per credit hour part-time for state residents; $10,216 per year full-time, $425 per credit hour part-time for nonresidents. Fees $708 per year full-time, $32 per semester (minimum) part-time. *Financial aid:* In 1997–98, 3 research assistantships were awarded; fellowships, teaching assistantships, traineeships, Federal Work-Study, institutionally sponsored loans also available. *Faculty research:* Bone densitometry, orthopedics, oncology, epidemiology, food quality assurance, canine nephrology. Total annual research expenditures: $1.4 million. • A. P. Knight, Head, 970-491-1274. Fax: 970-491-1275. E-mail: aknight@ugus.vth.colostate.edu.

Cornell University, Graduate Fields of Veterinary Medicine, Field of Veterinary Medicine, Ithaca, NY 14853-0001. Offers programs in anatomy (MS, PhD), cancer biology (MS, PhD), clinical sciences (MS, PhD), infectious diseases (MS, PhD), pathology (MS, PhD), pharmacology (MS, PhD), veterinary physiology (MS, PhD), virology (MS, PhD). Faculty: 84 full-time. Students: 37 full-time (21 women); includes 1 minority (Asian American), 19 international. 37 applicants, 19% accepted. In 1997, 4 master's, 4 doctorates awarded. *Degree requirements:* Thesis/dissertation required, foreign language not required. *Entrance requirements:* GRE General Test, TOEFL. Application deadline: 1/15 (priority date). Application fee: $65. *Financial aid:* In 1997–98, 29 students received aid, including 10 fellowships (3 to first-year students), 19 research assistantships (2 to first-year students); teaching assistantships, full and partial tuition waivers, institutionally sponsored loans also available. Financial aid applicants required to submit FAFSA. *Faculty research:* Receptors and signal transduction, viral and bacterial infectious diseases, tumor metastasis, clinical sciences/nutritional disease, development/neurologic disorders. • Director of Graduate Studies, 607-253-3276. Application contact: Graduate Field Assistant, 607-253-3276. Fax: 607-253-3756. E-mail: vetgradpgms@cornell.edu.

Iowa State University of Science and Technology, College of Veterinary Medicine and Graduate College, Graduate Programs in Veterinary Medicine, Ames, IA 50011. Offerings in biomedical engineering (MS, PhD); biomedical sciences (MS, PhD), including veterinary anatomy, veterinary physiology; microbiology, immunology, and preventive medicine (MS, PhD); veterinary clinical sciences (MS); veterinary pathology (MS, PhD). Part-time programs available. Faculty: 101 full-time, 12 part-time. Students: 52 full-time (28 women), 46 part-time (18 women); includes 4 minority (1 African American, 1 Asian American, 2 Hispanics), 35 international. 124 applicants, 17% accepted. In 1997, 12 master's, 11 doctorates awarded. Terminal master's awarded for partial completion of doctoral program. *Degree requirements:* For doctorate, dissertation. *Entrance requirements:* TOEFL. *Expenses:* Tuition $3166 per year full-time, $176 per credit part-time for state residents; $9324 per year full-time, $518 per credit part-time for nonresidents. Fees $200 per year. *Financial aid:* In 1997–98, 37 research assistantships (5 to first-year students), 5 teaching assistantships, 4 scholarships (1 to a first-year student) were awarded; fellowships, institutionally sponsored loans, and career-related internships or fieldwork also available. • Dr. Richard F. Ross, Dean, College of Veterinary Medicine, 515-294-1250. E-mail: rfross@iastate.edu.

Kansas State University, College of Veterinary Medicine and Graduate School, Graduate Programs in Veterinary Medicine, Department of Clinical Sciences, Manhattan, KS 66506. Offers program in veterinary medicine and surgery (MS). Faculty: 22 full-time (7 women), 3 part-time (2 women). Students: 1 (woman) full-time, 10 part-time (6 women); includes 3 international. 11 applicants, 100% accepted. In 1997, 3 degrees awarded (100% found work related to degree). *Degree requirements:* Thesis required, foreign language not required.

Directory: Veterinary Sciences

Kansas State University (continued)
Average time to degree: master's–1 year full-time, 3 years part-time. *Entrance requirements:* DVM. *Tuition:* $2218 per year full-time, $401 per semester (minimum) part-time for state residents; $6336 per year full-time, $1087 per semester (minimum) part-time for nonresidents. *Financial aid:* Institutionally sponsored loans available. *Faculty research:* Clinical orthopedics, hematologic disorders, endocrine function, gastrointestinal function. • Richard M. DeBowes, Head, 785-532-5708. Application contact: Susan Kraft, Graduate Coordinator, 785-532-5690.

Louisiana State University and Agricultural and Mechanical College, School of Veterinary Medicine, Baton Rouge, LA 70803. Awards DVM, MS, PhD. DVM available to state and contract students and limited number of highly qualified out-of-state applicants. Faculty: 64 full-time (13 women), 4 part-time (1 woman). Students: 41 full-time (19 women), 21 part-time (5 women). Average age 34. 23 applicants, 65% accepted. In 1997, 14 master's, 4 doctorates awarded. Terminal master's awarded for partial completion of doctoral program. *Degree requirements:* For master's and doctorate, thesis/dissertation required, foreign language not required. *Entrance requirements:* For DVM, GRE General Test (minimum combined score of 1000) or MCAT, TOEFL (minimum score 550); for master's, GRE General Test (minimum combined score of 1000); for doctorate, GRE General Test (minimum combined score of 1000), TOEFL (minimum score 550). *Financial aid:* In 1997–98, 6 fellowships (1 to a first-year student), 27 research assistantships (3 to first-year students), 2 teaching assistantships (1 to a first-year student), 1 service assistantship were awarded; Federal Work-Study, institutionally sponsored loans, and career-related internships or fieldwork also available. *Faculty research:* Veterinary microbiology, immunology, pathology, anatomy, epidemiology, parasitology, toxicology, physiology, pharmacology. Total annual research expenditures: $5 million. • Dr. David L. Huxsoll, Dean, 504-346-3151. Fax: 504-346-3295.

Michigan State University, College of Veterinary Medicine and Graduate School, Graduate Programs in Veterinary Medicine, East Lansing, MI 48824-1020. Offerings in anatomy (MS, PhD); large animal clinical sciences (MS, PhD); microbiology (MS, PhD); pathology (MS, PhD); pharmacology/toxicology (MS, PhD), including pharmacology; small animal clinical sciences (MS). Students: 36 full-time (20 women); includes 7 minority (4 African Americans, 2 Asian Americans, 1 Hispanic), 9 international. Average age 33. In 1997, 2 master's, 8 doctorates awarded. *Degree requirements:* For master's, thesis or alternative required, foreign language not required; for doctorate, dissertation required, foreign language not required. *Application fee:* $30 ($40 for international students). *Expenses:* Tuition $4609 per year full-time, $223 per credit hour part-time for state residents; $8704 per year full-time, $450 per credit hour part-time for nonresidents. Fees $576 per year full-time, $476 per year part-time. *Financial aid:* Fellowships, research assistantships available. *Faculty research:* Molecular genetics, food safety/toxicology, comparative orthopedics, airway disease, population medicine. • Dr. Charles D. Mackenzie, Associate Dean for Research and Graduate Studies, 517-432-2388. E-mail: mackenzie@cvm.msu.edu. Application contact: Victoria Hoelzer-Maddox, Administrative Assistant, 517-353-3118. Fax: 517-432-1037. E-mail: hoelzer-maddox@cvm.msu.edu.

See in-depth description on page 1835.

Mississippi State University, College of Veterinary Medicine and Graduate School, Graduate Programs in Veterinary Medicine, Mississippi State, MS 39762. Awards MS, PhD. Faculty: 38 full-time (7 women), 4 part-time (0 women). Students: 23 full-time (8 women), 4 part-time (3 women); includes 4 minority (3 African Americans, 1 Hispanic), 11 international. Average age 30. 15 applicants, 40% accepted. In 1997, 3 master's awarded (100% entered university research/teaching); 3 doctorates awarded (100% entered university research/teaching). Terminal master's awarded for partial completion of doctoral program. *Degree requirements:* For master's, thesis (for some programs); for doctorate, dissertation. *Average time to degree:* master's–4 years full-time; doctorate–4 years full-time. *Application deadline:* 3/1 (priority date; rolling processing; 9/1 for spring admission). *Application fee:* $25. *Tuition:* $3017 per year full-time, $168 per credit hour part-time for state residents; $6119 per year full-time, $340 per credit hour part-time for nonresidents. *Financial aid:* In 1997–98, 23 students received aid, including 19 research assistantships (4 to first-year students); career-related internships or fieldwork also available. Financial aid application deadline: 4/1. *Faculty research:* Food animal health (poultry and warm-water aquaculture) using immunology, microbiology, molecular biology, parasitology, pathology, pharmacology, and environmental toxicology. • Dr. A. Jerald Ainsworth, Coordinator, 601-325-1195. E-mail: ainsworth@cvm.msstate.edu. Application contact: Cathy Sims, Executive Secretary, 601-325-1417. Fax: 601-325-1031. E-mail: sims@cvm.msstate.edu.

North Carolina State University, College of Veterinary Medicine and Graduate School, Graduate Programs in Comparative Biomedical Sciences, Raleigh, NC 27695. Awards MS, PhD, DVM/PhD. Offerings include cell biology and morphology (MS, PhD), epidemiology and population medicine (MS, PhD), immunology (MS, PhD), microbiology and immunology (MS, PhD), pathology (MS, PhD), pharmacology (MS, PhD), specialized veterinary medicine (MS). Part-time programs available. Faculty: 116 full-time (27 women), 51 part-time (7 women). Students: 35 full-time (18 women), 17 part-time (14 women); includes 8 minority (6 African Americans, 2 Asian Americans), 12 international. Average age 34. 40 applicants, 28% accepted. In 1997, 4 master's, 7 doctorates awarded. *Degree requirements:* Thesis/dissertation. *Entrance requirements:* GRE General Test (minimum combined score of 1100). Application deadline: 6/25 (rolling processing; 11/25 for spring admission). Application fee: $45. *Tuition:* $2370 per year full-time, $517 per semester (minimum) part-time for state residents; $11,536 per year full-time, $2809 per semester (minimum) part-time for nonresidents. *Financial aid:* In 1997–98, research assistantships averaging $1,279 per month and totaling $2 were awarded; fellowships, teaching assistantships also available. Financial aid application deadline: 2/15. *Faculty research:* Infectious diseases, immunology and virology, tumor biology, toxicological pathology, food safety. • Dr. Jack H. Britt, Associate Dean, 919-829-4213. Fax: 919-829-4222. E-mail: jack_britt@ncsu.edu.

North Dakota State University, College of Agriculture, Department of Veterinary and Microbiological Sciences, Fargo, ND 58105. Offers programs in cellular and molecular biology (PhD), microbiology (MS), natural resource management (MS), veterinary sciences (MS). MS (natural resource management) offered in cooperation with the Interdisciplinary Program in Natural Resource Management. PhD offered in cooperation with the Cellular and Molecular Biology Program. Part-time programs available. Faculty: 10 full-time (2 women). Students: 9 full-time (7 women), 3 part-time (all women); includes 2 minority (1 Asian American, 1 Native American), 1 international. Average age 25. 15 applicants, 27% accepted. In 1997, 2 master's awarded (100% found work related to degree). *Degree requirements:* For master's, thesis required, foreign language not required; for doctorate, dissertation, oral and written preliminary exams required, foreign language not required. *Average time to degree:* master's–2 years full-time. *Entrance requirements:* For master's, GRE, TOEFL (minimum score 525); for doctorate, GRE, TOEFL. Application deadline: 3/15 (priority date; rolling processing). Application fee: $25. *Tuition:* $2572 per year full-time, $107 per credit part-time for state residents; $6868 per year full-time, $286 per credit part-time for nonresidents. *Financial aid:* In 1997–98, 4 research assistantships (1 to a first-year student) averaging $600 per month, 5 teaching assistantships (2 to first-year students) averaging $600 per month were awarded; Federal Work-Study, institutionally sponsored loans also available. Financial aid application deadline: 4/15. *Faculty research:* Bacterial gene regulation, antibiotic resistance, molecular virology, mechanisms of bacterial pathogenesis, immunology of animals. • Dr. D. L. Berryhill, Interim Chair, 701-231-7511. Application contact: Dr. E. S. Berry, Graduate Program Director, 701-231-7520. Fax: 701-231-7514.

The Ohio State University, College of Veterinary Medicine and Graduate School, Graduate Programs in Veterinary Medicine, Department of Veterinary Biosciences, Columbus, OH 43210. Offers programs in anatomy and cellular biology (MS, PhD), pathobiology (MS, PhD), pharmacology (MS, PhD), toxicology (MS, PhD), veterinary physiology (MS, PhD). *Degree requirements:* Thesis/dissertation, final exam. *Entrance requirements:* For master's, GRE General Test; for doctorate, GRE General Test, master's degree. Application fee: $25. *Tuition:* $5472 per year full-time, $554 per quarter (minimum) part-time for state residents; $14,172 per year full-time, $1424 per quarter (minimum) part-time for nonresidents. *Faculty research:* Microvasculature, muscle biology, neonatal lung and bone development.

The Ohio State University, College of Veterinary Medicine and Graduate School, Graduate Programs in Veterinary Medicine, Department of Veterinary Clinical Sciences, Columbus, OH 43210. Awards MS, PhD. *Degree requirements:* For master's, thesis, internship required, foreign language not required; for doctorate, dissertation. *Entrance requirements:* GRE General Test, DVM. Application deadline: 1/2. Application fee: $25 ($50 for international students). *Tuition:* $5472 per year full-time, $554 per quarter (minimum) part-time for state residents; $14,172 per year full-time, $1424 per quarter (minimum) part-time for nonresidents. *Faculty research:* Equine exercise physiology, orthopedic surgery, oncology.

The Ohio State University, College of Veterinary Medicine and Graduate School, Graduate Programs in Veterinary Medicine, Department of Veterinary Preventive Medicine, Columbus, OH 43210. Awards MS, PhD. *Degree requirements:* Thesis/dissertation. *Entrance requirements:* GRE General Test, minimum undergraduate GPA of 2.7, DVM. Application fee: $25. *Tuition:* $5472 per year full-time, $554 per quarter (minimum) part-time for state residents; $14,172 per year full-time, $1424 per quarter (minimum) part-time for nonresidents. *Faculty research:* Epidemiology; herd health; environmental health; animal health research pertaining to diagnosis, prevention, and control.

Oklahoma State University, College of Veterinary Medicine and Graduate College, Graduate Program in Veterinary Biomedical Sciences, Stillwater, OK 74078. Awards MS, PhD. Postbaccalaureate distance learning degree programs offered (minimal on-campus study). Students: 12 full-time (5 women), 17 part-time (11 women); includes 3 minority (1 African American, 1 Asian American, 1 Hispanic), 10 international. Average age 34. In 1997, 2 master's awarded. Terminal master's awarded for partial completion of doctoral program. *Degree requirements:* Thesis/dissertation required, foreign language not required. *Entrance requirements:* GRE General Test, GRE Subject Test, TOEFL (minimum score 550). Application deadline: 7/1 (priority date; rolling processing; 10/1 for spring admission). Application fee: $25. *Financial aid:* Partial tuition waivers, Federal Work-Study, and career-related internships or fieldwork available. Aid available to part-time students. Financial aid application deadline: 3/1; applicants required to submit FAFSA. *Faculty research:* Infectious diseases, physiology, toxicology, biomedical lasers, clinical studies. • Charles W. Qualls, Graduate Coordinator, 405-744-4465. Fax: 405-744-5275. E-mail: pathcwq@okway.okstate.edu. Application contact: Diana Moffeit, Assistant to Graduate Coordinator, 405-744-6750. Fax: 405-744-8263. E-mail: coldmtn@okway.okstate.edu.

Oregon State University, College of Veterinary Medicine, Program in Comparative Veterinary Medicine, Corvallis, OR 97331. Awards PhD. Faculty: 7 full-time (2 women). *Degree requirements:* 1 foreign language, dissertation. *Entrance requirements:* TOEFL (minimum score 550), minimum GPA of 3.0 in last 90 hours. Application deadline: 11/1. Application fee: $50. *Financial aid:* In 1997–98, 2 students received aid, including 1 fellowship, 1 research assistantship; Federal Work-Study, institutionally sponsored loans also available. Aid available to part-time students. Financial aid application deadline: 2/1. *Faculty research:* Microbiology, virology, toxicology. • Associate Dean, 541-737-2098. Fax: 541-737-4245.

Oregon State University, College of Veterinary Medicine, Program in Veterinary Sciences, Corvallis, OR 97331. Offers microbiology (MS), pathology (MS), toxicology (MS). Part-time programs available. Faculty: 4 full-time (0 women). In 1997, 3 degrees awarded (100% found work related to degree). *Degree requirements:* Thesis required, foreign language not required. *Entrance requirements:* TOEFL (minimum score 550), minimum GPA of 3.0 in last 90 hours. Application deadline: 11/1. Application fee: $50. *Tuition:* $6207 per year full-time, $810 per quarter (minimum) part-time for state residents; $10,551 per year full-time, $1293 per quarter (minimum) part-time for nonresidents. *Financial aid:* In 1997–98, 2 students received aid, including 2 research assistantships (1 to a first-year student); scholarships, Federal Work-Study, institutionally sponsored loans also available. Aid available to part-time students. Financial aid application deadline: 2/1. *Faculty research:* Calf diseases, bovine foot rot, caliciviruses, effects of toxic agents on immune systems. • Associate Dean, 541-737-2098. Fax: 541-737-4245.

Pennsylvania State University Milton S. Hershey Medical Center, Department of Comparative Medicine, Program in Laboratory Animal Medicine, Hershey, PA 17033-2360. Awards MS. Students: 3 full-time (1 woman). Average age 27. *Degree requirements:* Thesis required, foreign language not required. *Entrance requirements:* TOEFL (minimum score 550). Application deadline: 7/26. Application fee: $40. • Dr. C. Max Lang, Chairman, Department of Comparative Medicine, 717-531-8460.

Pennsylvania State University University Park Campus, College of Agricultural Sciences, Department of Veterinary Science, Program in Pathobiology, University Park, PA 16802-1503. Awards MS, PhD. Students: 8 full-time (5 women). *Entrance requirements:* GRE General Test, TOEFL (minimum score 550). Application deadline: 2/1. Application fee: $40. *Expenses:* Tuition $6534 per year full-time, $276 per credit part-time for state residents; $13,460 per year full-time, $561 per credit part-time for nonresidents. Fees $252 per year (minimum) full-time, $43 per semester (minimum) part-time. • Dr. Sam Sordillo, Chair, 814-865-7696.

See in-depth description on page 1837.

Purdue University, School of Veterinary Medicine and Graduate School, Graduate Programs in Veterinary Medicine, Department of Basic Medical Sciences, West Lafayette, IN 47907. Offers programs in anatomy (MS, PhD), pharmacology (MS, PhD), physiology (MS, PhD). Part-time programs available. Faculty: 18 full-time (3 women), 1 part-time (0 women). Students: 24 full-time (11 women); includes 4 minority (all Asian Americans), 4 international. Average age 27. 27 applicants, 11% accepted. In 1997, 1 master's awarded. Terminal master's awarded for partial completion of doctoral program. *Degree requirements:* Thesis/dissertation required, foreign language not required. *Average time to degree:* master's–3 years full-time. *Entrance requirements:* GRE General Test, TOEFL (minimum score 550). Application deadline: 7/1 (priority date; 12/1 for spring admission). Application fee: $30. Electronic applications accepted. *Financial aid:* In 1997–98, 2 fellowships averaging $1,157 per month, 15 research assistantships (4 to first-year students) averaging $956 per month, 2 teaching assistantships averaging $956 per month were awarded. Financial aid application deadline: 3/1; applicants required to submit FAFSA. *Faculty research:* Development and regeneration, tissue injury and shock, biomedical engineering, ovarian function, bone and cartilage biology, cell and molecular biology. Total annual research expenditures: $885,961. • Dr. Gordon L. Coppoc, Head, 765-494-8632. E-mail: coppoc@vet.purdue.edu. Application contact: Dr. Ronald Hullinger, Chairman, Graduate Committee, 765-494-8580. Fax: 765-494-0781. E-mail: bmsgrad@vet.purdue.edu.

Purdue University, School of Veterinary Medicine and Graduate School, Graduate Programs in Veterinary Medicine, Department of Veterinary Clinical Sciences, West Lafayette, IN 47907. Awards MS, PhD. Faculty: 32 full-time (7 women). Students: 12 full-time (4 women); includes 2 minority (both Hispanics), 4 international. Terminal master's awarded for partial completion of doctoral program. *Degree requirements:* Thesis/dissertation required, foreign language not required. *Average time to degree:* master's–3 years full-time; doctorate–5 years full-time. *Entrance requirements:* For master's, DVM. Application deadline: 2/1 (8/1 for spring admission). Application fee: $30. *Financial aid:* In 1997–98, 5 fellowships, 4 teaching assistantships were awarded; full tuition waivers, institutionally sponsored loans also available. Financial aid application deadline: 3/1; applicants required to submit FAFSA. *Faculty research:* Flow cytometry, chemotherapy, biologic response modifiers, broncho-alveolar lavage. • Ralph C. Richardson, Head, 765-494-1103. Fax: 765-496-1108. E-mail: rcr@vet.purdue.edu.

Purdue University, School of Veterinary Medicine and Graduate School, Graduate Programs in Veterinary Medicine, Department of Veterinary Pathobiology, West Lafayette, IN 47907. Offers programs in bacteriology (MS, PhD), epidemiology (MS, PhD), immunology (MS, PhD), parasitology (MS, PhD), pathology (MS, PhD), toxicology (MS, PhD), virology (MS, PhD). Faculty: 26 full-time (3 women). Students: 36 full-time (16 women), 2 part-time (both women); includes 8 minority (2 African Americans, 3 Asian Americans, 3 Hispanics), 13 international. In 1997, 7 master's awarded; 4 doctorates awarded (100% found work related to degree). Terminal master's awarded for partial completion of doctoral program. *Degree requirements:* For master's, thesis required (for some programs), foreign language not required; for doctorate, dissertation required, foreign language not required. *Entrance requirements:* GRE General Test, TOEFL (minimum score 575). Application fee: $30. *Financial aid:* Fellowships, research assistantships, teaching assistantships available. Financial aid application deadline: 3/1; applicants required to submit FAFSA. • Dr. H. L. Thacker, Interim Head, 765-494-7543.

Texas A&M University, College of Veterinary Medicine and Office of Graduate Studies, Graduate Programs in Veterinary Medicine, College Station, TX 77843. Awards MS, PhD, DVM/PhD. Offerings include veterinary anatomy and public health (MS, PhD), including anatomy (MS, PhD), epidemiology (MS), genetics (PhD), toxicology (PhD), veterinary public health (MS); veterinary large animal medicine and surgery (MS); veterinary pathobiology (MS, PhD), including genetics, pathology, toxicology, veterinary microbiology; veterinary physiology and pharmacology (MS, PhD), including physiology, toxicology; veterinary small animal medicine and surgery (MS). Part-time programs available. Students: 184 (93 women); includes 7 minority (2 African Americans, 2 Asian Americans, 3 Hispanics). In 1997, 8 master's, 6 doctorates awarded. Terminal master's awarded for partial completion of doctoral program. *Entrance requirements:* GRE General Test, TOEFL. Application fee: $35 ($75 for international students). *Financial aid:* Fellowships, research assistantships, teaching assistantships, partial tuition waivers, Federal Work-Study, institutionally sponsored loans, and career-related internships or fieldwork available. Aid available to part-time students. *Faculty research:* Physiology, pharmacology, anatomy, public health, small and large animal medicine and surgery. • Dr. Duane C. Kraemer, Associate Dean, Research and Graduate Programs, 409-845-5092. E-mail: dkraemer@cvm.tamu.edu. Application contact: Kathie Henning, Administrative Secretary, 409-845-5092. Fax: 409-845-5088. E-mail: khenning@cvm.tamu.edu.

Announcement: The graduate faculty in the College of Veterinary Medicine at Texas A&M University consists of 130 members in 5 departments. MS and/or PhD degree programs are offered in veterinary anatomy, veterinary microbiology, veterinary pathology (DVM required), and veterinary physiology. MS degree programs are available in epidemiology, veterinary medicine and surgery (DVM required), veterinary public health, veterinary parasitology, and veterinary medical sciences. Some programs are interdisciplinary and cross departmental and college lines, such as those in genetics, toxicology, and nutrition. Participating departments in these programs may have joint admissions policies. For further information, contact the Associate Dean for Research and Graduate Programs, College of Veterinary Medicine, 409-845-5092.

See in-depth description on page 1839.

Tufts University, School of Veterinary Medicine, Program in Animals and Public Policy, Medford, MA 02155. Awards MS, DVM/MS. Faculty: 25 part-time. Students: 10 full-time (9 women). 23 applicants, 43% accepted. In 1997, 8 degrees awarded. *Degree requirements:* Thesis required, foreign language not required. *Entrance requirements:* GRE General Test. Application deadline: 4/1. Application fee: $60. *Financial aid:* Application deadline 3/15. *Faculty research:* Veterinary ethics, veterinary jurisprudence, companion animal demographics and control, human/animal relationships, wildlife policy issues, animal research ethics. • Application contact: Rebecca Russo, Director of Admissions, 508-839-7920. Fax: 508-839-2953.

Tuskegee University, College of Veterinary Medicine and Allied Health, Programs in Veterinary Medicine, Tuskegee, AL 36088. Awards MS. Faculty: 62 full-time (6 women). Students: 5 full-time (0 women); includes 5 minority (2 African Americans, 3 Asian Americans). Average age 25. In 1997, 5 degrees awarded. *Degree requirements:* Thesis required, foreign language not required. *Entrance requirements:* GRE General Test. Application deadline: 7/15 (rolling processing). Application fee: $35. *Financial aid:* Application deadline 4/15. • Dr. Albert W. Dade, Dean, College of Veterinary Medicine and Allied Health, 334-727-8174.

Université de Montréal, Faculties of Veterinary Medicine and Graduate Studies, Graduate Programs in Veterinary Medicine, Montréal, PQ H3C 3J7, Canada. Awards M Sc, PhD, Certificate, DES. Part-time programs available. Faculty: 74 full-time (15 women). Students: 67 full-time (37 women), 1 (woman) part-time. 41 applicants, 17% accepted. In 1997, 12 master's, 19 other advanced degrees awarded. *Degree requirements:* For master's, 1 foreign language required, thesis optional. *Application deadline:* 2/1. *Application fee:* $30. *Financial aid:* Research assistantships, teaching assistantships, and career-related internships or fieldwork available. *Faculty research:* Animal reproduction, infectious diseases of swine, physiology of exercise in horses, viral diseases of cattle, health management and epidemiology. • Application contact: André Dallaire, Associate Dean of Graduate Studies, 514-773-8218.

The University of Arizona, College of Agriculture, Department of Veterinary Science, Tucson, AZ 85721. Offers program in pathobiology (MS, PhD). *Degree requirements:* For doctorate, dissertation. *Entrance requirements:* TOEFL (minimum score 550). Application fee: $35. *Tuition:* $2162 per year full-time, $337 per semester (minimum) part-time for state residents; $6860 per year full-time, $1138 per semester (minimum) part-time for nonresidents.

University of California, Davis, School of Veterinary Medicine and Graduate Studies, Graduate Professional Programs in Veterinary Medicine, Davis, CA 95616. Awards MPVM, DVM/MPVM. Faculty: 15 full-time, 10 part-time. Students: 16 full-time; includes 5 international. 24 applicants, 83% accepted. In 1997, 13 degrees awarded. *Degree requirements:* Thesis. *Average time to degree:* master's–1 year full-time. *Entrance requirements:* TOEFL, DVM or equivalent. Application deadline: 8/5 (rolling processing). Application fee: $40. *Expenses:* Tuition $0 for state residents; $8984 per year for nonresidents. Fees $8447 per year. *Financial aid:* Fellowships, student employeeships, training grants, Federal Work-Study, institutionally sponsored loans available. Aid available to part-time students. Financial aid application deadline: 3/2; applicants required to submit FAFSA. • Dr. Bruno Chomel, Director, 530-752-1383. Application contact: Yasmin Williams, Director of Admissions, 530-752-1383. Fax: 530-752-2801.

University of California, Davis, School of Veterinary Medicine, Resident Certification Program, Davis, CA 95616. Awards Certificate. Faculty: 80 full-time. Students: 75 full-time (47 women). 220 applicants, 11% accepted. In 1997, 25 degrees awarded. *Degree requirements:* Thesis or alternative. *Average time to degree:* other advanced degree–3 years full-time. *Entrance requirements:* DVM or equivalent, 1 year of related experience. Application fee: $0. *Expenses:* Tuition $0 for state residents; $8984 per year for nonresidents. Fees $8447 per year. *Faculty research:* Small animal and large animal medicine, surgery, infectious diseases, pathology. • Dr. Bradford Smith, Director, 530-752-2957. Application contact: Esther Finn, Coordinator, 530-752-2957. Fax: 530-752-9620.

University of Florida, College of Veterinary Medicine and Interdisciplinary Program in Biomedical Sciences, Graduate Program in Veterinary Medical Sciences, Gainesville, FL 32611. Offers veterinary medical science (MS, PhD). Faculty: 100. Students: 62. 33 applicants, 27% accepted. In 1997, 3 master's, 6 doctorates awarded. Terminal master's awarded for partial completion of doctoral program. *Degree requirements:* Thesis/dissertation required, foreign language not required. *Entrance requirements:* GRE General Test (minimum combined score of 1000), minimum GPA of 3.0. Application deadline: 6/9 (priority date; rolling processing; 10/1 for spring admission). Application fee: $20. *Tuition:* $138 per credit hour for state residents; $481 per credit hour for nonresidents. *Financial aid:* In 1997–98, 34 students received aid, including 20 research assistantships averaging $889 per month, 13 teaching assistantships; fellowships, institutionally sponsored loans also available. *Faculty research:* Infectious diseases, pathology, physiology, toxicology, clinical sciences. Total annual research expenditures: $4.279 million. • Dr. Charles H. Courtney, Associate Dean for Research and Graduate Studies, 352-392-4700 Ext. 5100. E-mail: chc@vetmed1.vetmed.ufl.edu. Application contact: Sally O'Connell, Program Assistant, 352-392-4700 Ext. 5100. Fax: 352-392-8351. E-mail: sao@vetmed1.vetmed.ufl.edu.

University of Georgia, College of Veterinary Medicine and Graduate School, Graduate Programs in Veterinary Medicine, Athens, GA 30602. Offerings in avian medicine (MAM); medical microbiology and parasitology (MS, PhD), including medical microbiology, parasitology; pathology (MS, PhD); physiology and pharmacology (MS, PhD), including pharmacology, physiology, toxicology; veterinary anatomy and radiology (MS), including veterinary anatomy. Faculty: 78 full-time (21 women). Students: 54 full-time, 14 part-time; includes 7 minority (2 African Americans, 3 Asian Americans, 2 Hispanics), 21 international. 75 applicants, 32% accepted. In 1997, 20 master's, 11 doctorates awarded. *Degree requirements:* For master's, thesis (MS) required, foreign language not required; for doctorate, 1 foreign language (computer language can substitute), dissertation. *Entrance requirements:* GRE General Test. Application deadline: 7/1 (priority date; 11/15 for spring admission). Application fee: $30. Electronic applications accepted. *Tuition:* $3290 per year for state residents; $11,300 per year for nonresidents. *Financial aid:* Fellowships, research assistantships, teaching assistantships, assistantships available. • Dr. Keith W. Prasse, Dean, College of Veterinary Medicine, 706-542-3461. Fax: 706-542-8254. E-mail: prassek@cale.vet.uga.edu.

University of Guelph, Ontario Veterinary College and Faculty of Graduate Studies, Graduate Programs in Veterinary Sciences, Guelph, ON N1G 2W1, Canada. Offerings in biomedical sciences (M Sc, DV Sc, PhD), including morphology, pharmacology, physiology, toxicology; clinical studies (M Sc, DV Sc, Diploma), including anesthesiology (M Sc, DV Sc), clinical studies (Diploma), medicine (M Sc, DV Sc), neurology (M Sc, DV Sc), ophthalmology (M Sc, DV Sc), radiology (M Sc, DV Sc), surgery (M Sc, DV Sc); pathobiology (M Sc, DV Sc, PhD, Diploma), including anatomic pathology (DV Sc, Diploma), clinical pathology (Diploma), comparative pathology (M Sc, PhD), immunology (M Sc, PhD), laboratory animal science (DV Sc), pathology (M Sc, PhD, Diploma), veterinary infectious diseases (M Sc, PhD), zoo animal/wildlife medicine (DV Sc); population medicine (M Sc, DV Sc, PhD, Diploma), including epidemiology (M Sc, DV Sc, PhD), population medicine (Diploma), preventive medicine (M Sc, DV Sc), theriogenology (M Sc, DV Sc). Faculty: 112. Students: 101 full-time (43 women), 9 part-time (3 women); includes 29 international. *Degree requirements:* For master's and doctorate, thesis/dissertation. *Application deadline:* 2/1 (rolling processing). *Application fee:* $60. *Expenses:* Tuition $4725 per year full-time, $3165 per year part-time for Canadian residents; $6999 per year for nonresidents. Fees $612 per year full-time, $38 per year (minimum) part-time for Canadian residents; $612 per year for nonresidents. *Financial aid:* Fellowships, research assistantships, teaching assistantships, and career-related internships or fieldwork available. • Application contact: Dr. W. McDonell, Associate Dean, 519-823-8800 Ext. 4095.

University of Idaho, College of Graduate Studies, College of Agriculture, Department of Animal and Veterinary Science, Moscow, ID 83844-4140. Offers programs in animal physiology (PhD), veterinary science (MS). Faculty: 11 full-time (1 woman). Students: 18 full-time (6 women), 4 part-time (all women); includes 5 international. In 1997, 4 master's awarded. *Degree requirements:* For doctorate, dissertation. *Entrance requirements:* For master's, GRE General Test, minimum GPA of 2.8; for doctorate, minimum undergraduate GPA of 2.8, 3.0 graduate. Application deadline: 8/1 (12/15 for spring admission). Application fee: $35 ($45 for international students). *Expenses:* Tuition $0 for state residents; $6000 per year full-time, $95 per credit part-time for nonresidents. Fees $2676 per year full-time, $134 per credit part-time. *Financial aid:* In 1997–98, 11 research assistantships (4 to first-year students) averaging $1,168 per month and totaling $115,670, 1 teaching assistantship averaging $1,056 per month and totaling $9,500 were awarded. Financial aid application deadline: 2/15. *Faculty research:* Agribusiness, range-livestock management. • Dr. Richard A. Battaglia, Head, 208-885-6345.

University of Illinois at Urbana–Champaign, College of Veterinary Medicine and Graduate College, Graduate Programs in Veterinary Medicine, Department of Veterinary Biosciences, Urbana, IL 61801. Awards MS, PhD. Faculty: 22 full-time (1 woman), 5 part-time (2 women). Students: 30 full-time (12 women); includes 2 minority (1 African American, 1 Asian American), 13 international. 9 applicants, 22% accepted. In 1997, 4 master's, 2 doctorates awarded. *Degree requirements:* Thesis/dissertation. *Entrance requirements:* Minimum GPA of 4.0 on a 5.0 scale. Application deadline: rolling. Application fee: $40 ($50 for international students). *Financial aid:* In 1997–98, 21 students received aid, including 1 fellowship, 19 research assistantships, 1 teaching assistantship; full and partial tuition waivers also available. • Dr. David R. Gross, Head, 217-333-2506. Fax: 217-244-1652. Application contact: Dr. Kenneth Holmes, Director of Graduate Studies.

See in-depth description on page 1841.

University of Illinois at Urbana–Champaign, College of Veterinary Medicine and Graduate College, Graduate Programs in Veterinary Medicine, Department of Veterinary Clinical Medicine, Urbana, IL 61801. Awards MS, PhD. Faculty: 28 full-time (5 women). Students: 19 full-time (10 women); includes 1 minority (Asian American), 2 international. 6 applicants, 100% accepted. In 1997, 4 master's awarded. *Degree requirements:* For master's, thesis required, foreign language not required; for doctorate, 1 foreign language, dissertation. *Entrance requirements:* Minimum GPA of 4.0 on a 5.0 scale. Application deadline: rolling. Application fee: $40 ($50 for international students). *Financial aid:* In 1997–98, 1 research assistantship was awarded; fellowships, teaching assistantships, full and partial tuition waivers, and career-related internships or fieldwork also available. • H. Fred Troutt, Head, 217-333-5310.

University of Illinois at Urbana–Champaign, College of Veterinary Medicine and Graduate College, Graduate Programs in Veterinary Medicine, Department of Veterinary Pathobiology, Urbana, IL 61801. Awards MS, PhD. Part-time programs available. Postbaccalaureate distance learning degree programs offered (minimal on-campus study). Faculty: 35 full-time (8 women). Students: 34 full-time (14 women); includes 2 minority (1 Asian American, 1 Hispanic), 7 international. Average age 26. 21 applicants, 38% accepted. In 1997, 2 master's, 5 doctorates awarded. Terminal master's awarded for partial completion of doctoral program. *Degree requirements:* For master's, thesis required, foreign language not required; for doctorate, computer language, dissertation required, foreign language not required. *Entrance requirements:* Minimum GPA of 4.0 on a 5.0 scale. Application deadline: rolling. Application fee: $40 ($50 for international students). *Financial aid:* In 1997–98, 27 students received aid, including 1 fellowship, 5 research assistantships (2 to first-year students), 3 teaching assistantships; full and partial tuition waivers also available. *Faculty research:* Epidemiology, immunology, microbiology, parasitology, clinical pathology. • Wanda M. Haschek-Hock, Head, 217-333-2449. Fax: 217-244-7421.

University of Kentucky, Graduate School Programs from the College of Agriculture, Department of Veterinary Science, Lexington, KY 40506-0032. Awards MS, PhD. Faculty: 26 full-time (5 women), 1 part-time (0 women). Students: 24 full-time (12 women), 6 part-time (1 woman); includes 10 international. 20 applicants, 30% accepted. In 1997, 3 master's, 2 doctorates awarded. *Degree requirements:* Thesis/dissertation, comprehensive exam required, foreign language not required. *Entrance requirements:* For master's, GRE General Test, minimum undergraduate GPA of 2.5; for doctorate, GRE General Test, minimum graduate GPA of 3.0. Application deadline: 7/19 (rolling processing). Application fee: $30 ($35 for international students). *Financial aid:* In 1997–98, 2 fellowships, 22 research assistantships (2 to first-year students) were awarded; Federal Work-Study, institutionally sponsored loans also available. Aid available to part-time students. *Faculty research:* Microbiology, reproductive physiology, genetics, pharmacology/toxicology, parasitology. • Dr. Ernest Bailey, Director of Graduate Studies, 606-257-1145. E-mail: vsc003@ukcc.uky.edu. Application contact: Dr. Constance L. Wood, Associate Dean, 606-257-4613. Fax: 606-323-1928.

See in-depth description on page 1843.

University of Massachusetts Amherst, College of Food and Natural Resources, Department of Veterinary and Animal Sciences, Amherst, MA 01003-0001. Offers program in mammalian and avian biology (MS, PhD). Part-time programs available. Faculty: 15 full-time (4 women). Students: 11 full-time (6 women), 16 part-time (8 women); includes 1 minority (African American),

Directory: Veterinary Sciences; Cross-Discipline Announcement

University of Massachusetts Amherst (continued)

13 international. Average age 31. 27 applicants, 52% accepted. In 1997, 2 master's, 2 doctorates awarded. Terminal master's awarded for partial completion of doctoral program. *Degree requirements:* Thesis/dissertation required, foreign language not required. *Entrance requirements:* GRE General Test. Application deadline: 3/1 (priority date; rolling processing; 10/1 for spring admission). Application fee: $40. *Expenses:* Tuition $2640 per year full-time, $110 per credit part-time for state residents; $3690 per year (minimum) full-time, $165 per credit (minimum) part-time for nonresidents. Fees $2856 per year full-time, $422 per semester part-time for state residents; $3204 per year full-time, $480 per semester part-time for nonresidents. *Financial aid:* In 1997–98, 1 fellowship, 19 research assistantships, 5 teaching assistantships were awarded; Federal Work-Study also available. Aid available to part-time students. Financial aid application deadline: 3/1. • Dr. Robert Duby, Director, 413-545-2312. Fax: 413-545-6326. E-mail: duby@vasci.umass.edu.

University of Minnesota, Twin Cities Campus, College of Veterinary Medicine and Graduate School, Graduate Programs in Veterinary Medicine, Program in Molecular Veterinary Biosciences, Minneapolis, MN 55455-0213. Awards MS, PhD. Part-time programs available. Students: 18 full-time (10 women), 5 part-time (1 woman); includes 10 minority (1 African American, 9 Asian Americans), 1 international. 27 applicants, 15% accepted. *Degree requirements:* Thesis/dissertation required, foreign language not required. *Entrance requirements:* TOEFL (minimum score 550). Application deadline: 7/15 (rolling processing; 12/15 for spring admission). Application fee: $40 ($50 for international students). Electronic applications accepted. *Financial aid:* In 1997–98, 22 students received aid, including 2 fellowships (both to first-year students) totaling $22,300, 16 research assistantships (1 to a first-year student) totaling $224,000, 3 teaching assistantships totaling $42,000. Financial aid application deadline: 7/1. *Faculty research:* Molecular regulation of immune responses to infection; molecular mechanisms of bacterial, viral, and parasite pathogenesis; identification of genes affecting animal health/performance; genome characterization; cellular and molecular biology. • Mitchell Abrahamsen, Director, 612-624-2700.

University of Minnesota, Twin Cities Campus, College of Veterinary Medicine and Graduate School, Graduate Programs in Veterinary Medicine, Program in Veterinary Medicine, Minneapolis, MN 55455-0213. Awards MS, PhD. Part-time programs available. Students: 35 full-time (10 women), 31 part-time (8 women); includes 14 minority (10 Asian Americans, 4 Hispanics), 12 international. In 1997, 4 master's, 6 doctorates awarded. *Degree requirements:* Thesis/dissertation required, foreign language not required. *Entrance requirements:* TOEFL (minimum score 550). Application deadline: 7/15 (rolling processing; 12/15 for spring admission). Application fee: $40 ($50 for international students). *Financial aid:* In 1997–98, 17 students received aid, including 7 research assistantships, 10 teaching assistantships. Financial aid application deadline: 7/1. *Faculty research:* Infectious diseases, internal medicine, population medicine, surgery/radiology/anesthesiology, theriogenology. • Carlos Pijoan, Director, 612-625-8781.

University of Missouri–Columbia, College of Veterinary Medicine and Graduate School, Graduate Programs in Veterinary Medicine, Columbia, MO 65211. Offerings in pathobiology (MS, PhD), including laboratory animal medicine (MS), pathobiology (PhD), pathology (MS); veterinary biomedical sciences (MS, PhD), including physiology (PhD), veterinary biomedical sciences (MS); veterinary medicine and surgery (MS). Faculty: 96 full-time (17 women). Students: 20 full-time (9 women), 26 part-time (14 women); includes 3 minority (all Asian Americans), 13 international. In 1997, 6 master's, 2 doctorates awarded. *Degree requirements:* For master's, thesis; for doctorate, 2 foreign languages, dissertation. *Entrance requirements:* GRE General Test, minimum GPA of 3.0. Application fee: $25 ($50 for international students). *Tuition:* $3240 per year full-time, $180 per credit hour part-time for state residents; $9108 per year full-time, $506 per credit hour part-time for nonresidents. • Dr. H. Richard Adams, Dean, College of Veterinary Medicine, 573-882-3768. Fax: 573-884-5044.

University of Nebraska–Lincoln, College of Agricultural Sciences and Natural Resources, Department of Veterinary and Biomedical Sciences, Lincoln, NE 68588. Awards MS, PhD. Faculty: 22 full-time (2 women). Students: 5 full-time (4 women), 6 part-time (1 woman); includes 1 minority (African American), 4 international. Average age 31. 7 applicants, 14% accepted. In 1997, 11 master's awarded. *Degree requirements:* For master's, thesis optional, foreign language not required; for doctorate, dissertation, comprehensive exams. *Entrance requirements:* For master's, GRE General Test, TOEFL (minimum score 550); for doctorate, GRE General Test, MCAT, or VAT; TOEFL (minimum score 550). Application deadline: 3/1 (priority date; rolling processing). Application fee: $35. Electronic applications accepted. *Expenses:* Tuition $110 per credit hour for state residents; $270 per credit hour for nonresidents. Fees $480 per year full-time, $110 per semester part-time. *Financial aid:* In 1997–98, 3 fellowships totaling $4,000, research assistantships totaling $299,959 were awarded; teaching assistantships, Federal Work-Study also available. Aid available to part-time students. Financial aid application deadline: 2/15. *Faculty research:* Virology, immunobiology, molecular biology, bacteriology, gene regulation. Total annual research expenditures: $1.1 million. • Dr. John A. Schmitz, Head, 402-472-2952.

University of Prince Edward Island, Atlantic Veterinary College, Graduate Program in Veterinary Medicine, Charlottetown, PE C1A 4P3, Canada. Awards M Sc, PhD. Faculty: 99 full-time (29 women). Students: 36 full-time (22 women), 4 part-time (1 woman). In 1997, 7 master's awarded. *Degree requirements:* Thesis/dissertation required, foreign language not required. *Entrance requirements:* For master's, DVM or B Sc honors degree; for doctorate, M Sc. Application fee: $35. *Expenses:* Tuition $4350 per year full-time, $438 per course part-time for Canadian residents; $4350 per year for nonresidents. Fees $369 per year full-time, $5 per course part-time for Canadian residents; $4264 per year for nonresidents. *Financial aid:* Research assistantships and career-related internships or fieldwork available. *Faculty research:* Animal health management, animal nutrition, infectious diseases, fin fish and shellfish health, pharmacology, basic biomedical disciplines. • Dr. Ian Dohoo, Associate Dean of Graduate Studies and Research, 902-566-0640. Fax: 902-566-0846. E-mail: dohoo@upei.ca. Application contact: John R. DeGrace, Registrar, 902-566-0608.

University of Saskatchewan, Western College of Veterinary Medicine and College of Graduate Studies and Research, Graduate Programs in Veterinary Medicine, Saskatoon, SK S7N 5A2, Canada. Offerings in herd medicine and theriogenology (M Sc, M Vet Sc, PhD); toxicology (M Sc, PhD, Diploma); veterinary anatomy (M Sc, M Vet Sc, PhD); veterinary anesthesiology, radiology, and surgery (M Sc, M Vet Sc, PhD); veterinary internal medicine (M Sc, M Vet Sc, PhD); veterinary medicine (M Sc, PhD); veterinary microbiology (M Sc, M Vet Sc, PhD); veterinary pathology (M Sc, M Vet Sc, PhD); veterinary physiology (M Sc, M Vet Sc, PhD). Faculty: 52 full-time. *Degree requirements:* For doctorate, dissertation. *Entrance requirements:* International English Language Testing System (minimum score 6) or Michigan English Language Assessment Battery (minimum score 80) or TOEFL (minimum score 550). Application deadline: 7/1 (priority date). Application fee: $50. *Financial aid:* Fellowships, teaching assistantships available. Financial aid application deadline: 1/31. • Dr. A. Livingston, Dean, Western College of Veterinary Medicine, 306-966-7448. Fax: 306-966-8747.

University of Wisconsin–Madison, School of Veterinary Medicine, Graduate Program in Veterinary Medicine, Madison, WI 53706-1380. Awards MS, PhD. Terminal master's awarded for partial completion of doctoral program. *Degree requirements:* Thesis/dissertation required, foreign language not required. *Application fee:* $45. *Tuition:* $11,362 per year for state residents; $16,666 per year for nonresidents. *Financial aid:* Application deadline 3/1. • Application contact: Dr. Norman J. Wilsman, Associate Dean of Research, 608-263-1008.

Utah State University, College of Agriculture, Department of Animal, Dairy and Veterinary Sciences, Logan, UT 84322. Offers programs in animal science (MA, MS, PhD), bioveterinary science (MA, MS), dairy science (MA, MS), molecular biology (MS, PhD). Part-time programs available. Faculty: 20 full-time (2 women). Students: 11 full-time (4 women), 5 part-time (2 women). Average age 26. 20 applicants, 35% accepted. In 1997, 2 master's, 2 doctorates awarded. *Degree requirements:* For master's, thesis required (for some programs), foreign language not required; for doctorate, dissertation required, foreign language not required. *Entrance requirements:* GRE General Test (score in 40th percentile or higher), TOEFL (minimum score 550), minimum GPA of 3.0. Application deadline: 5/15 (priority date; rolling processing; 10/15 for spring admission). Application fee: $40. *Expenses:* Tuition $1448 per year full-time, $624 per year part-time for state residents; $5082 per year full-time, $2192 per year part-time for nonresidents. Fees $421 per year full-time, $165 per year part-time. *Financial aid:* Fellowships, research assistantships, scholarships, partial tuition waivers, Federal Work-Study, institutionally sponsored loans, and career-related internships or fieldwork available. Financial aid application deadline: 4/1. *Faculty research:* Monoclonal antibodies, antiviral chemotherapy, management systems, biotechnology, rumen fermentation manipulation. • Robert C. Lamb, Head, 435-797-2162. Fax: 435-797-2118. Application contact: Jeffrey L. Walters, Graduate Program Coordinator, 435-797-2161.

Virginia Polytechnic Institute and State University, Virginia-Maryland Regional College of Veterinary Medicine and Graduate School, Graduate Programs in Veterinary Medical Sciences, Blacksburg, VA 24061. Awards MS, PhD. Part-time and evening/weekend programs available. Students: 34 full-time (16 women), 22 part-time (10 women); includes 4 minority (1 African American, 1 Asian American, 2 Native Americans), 19 international. 23 applicants, 43% accepted. In 1997, 10 master's, 3 doctorates awarded. *Degree requirements:* Thesis/dissertation. *Entrance requirements:* TOEFL (minimum score 575). Application deadline: 12/1 (priority date; rolling processing). Application fee: $25. *Tuition:* $4927 per year full-time, $792 per semester (minimum) part-time for state residents; $7537 per year full-time, $1227 per semester (minimum) part-time for nonresidents. *Financial aid:* Fellowships available. • Dr. John C. Lee, Associate Dean, 540-231-4807. Application contact: Linda Price, Office of Research and Graduate Studies, 540-231-4992.

Washington State University, College of Veterinary Medicine and Graduate School, Graduate Programs in Veterinary Medicine, Department of Veterinary Clinical Sciences, Pullman, WA 99164-1610. Awards MS, PhD. *Degree requirements:* Thesis/dissertation, oral exam. *Entrance requirements:* GRE General Test, minimum GPA of 3.0. Application deadline: 1/31 (priority date). Application fee: $35. *Tuition:* $5334 per year full-time, $267 per credit hour part-time for state residents; $13,380 per year full-time, $667 per credit hour part-time for nonresidents. • Dee Madison, Chair, 509-335-0763. Fax: 509-335-0880. E-mail: madisond@vetmed.wsu.edu.

Washington State University, College of Veterinary Medicine and Graduate School, Graduate Programs in Veterinary Medicine, Department of Veterinary Comparative Anatomy, Pharmacology, and Physiology, Pullman, WA 99164-1610. Offers programs in neuroscience (MS, PhD), veterinary science (MS, PhD). Part-time programs available. Terminal master's awarded for partial completion of doctoral program. *Degree requirements:* Thesis/dissertation, oral exam. *Entrance requirements:* GRE General Test, minimum GPA of 3.0. Application deadline: 1/31 (priority date). Application fee: $35. *Tuition:* $5334 per year full-time, $267 per credit hour part-time for state residents; $13,380 per year full-time, $667 per credit hour part-time for nonresidents. *Financial aid:* Research assistantships, teaching assistantships, Federal Work-Study, institutionally sponsored loans, and career-related internships or fieldwork available. • Pam Colbert, Chair, 509-335-0986. Fax: 509-335-4650. E-mail: colbertp@vetmed.wsu.edu.

West Virginia University, College of Agriculture, Forestry and Consumer Sciences, Division of Animal and Veterinary Sciences, Program in Animal and Veterinary Sciences, Morgantown, WV 26506. Awards MS. Part-time programs available. Students: 15 full-time (4 women), 1 (woman) part-time; includes 7 international. Average age 29. In 1997, 4 degrees awarded. *Degree requirements:* Thesis, oral and written exams required, foreign language not required. *Entrance requirements:* TOEFL (minimum score 550), minimum GPA of 2.5. Application fee: $45. *Tuition:* $2820 per year full-time, $149 per credit hour part-time for state residents; $8104 per year full-time, $443 per credit hour part-time for nonresidents. *Financial aid:* In 1997–98, 10 research assistantships (4 to first-year students) were awarded; full and partial tuition waivers, Federal Work-Study, institutionally sponsored loans also available. Financial aid application deadline: 2/1; applicants required to submit FAFSA. *Faculty research:* Animal nutrition, reproductive physiology, food science. • Dr. Hillar Klandorf, Coordinator, 304-293-2406.

Cross-Discipline Announcement

Iowa State University of Science and Technology, Graduate Programs in Veterinary Medicine and College of Agriculture, Department of Microbiology, Immunology, and Preventive Medicine, Ames, IA 50011.

The Department of Microbiology, Immunology and Preventive Medicine offers students in the veterinary curriculum instruction in the areas of bacteriology, mycology, virology, immunology, epidemiology, and public health. Microbiology, immunology, and regulatory and preventive medicine aspects of infectious diseases of animals are emphasized. Please see in-depth description in Book 3, Section 11, Microbiological Sciences.

MICHIGAN STATE UNIVERSITY

College of Veterinary Medicine

Programs of Study

The College of Veterinary Medicine is organized into seven departments: anatomy, large animal clinical sciences, microbiology, pathology, pharmacology and toxicology, physiology, and small animal clinical sciences. The basic science departments are shared with the Colleges of Human Medicine, Osteopathic Medicine, Natural Science, and Agriculture and Natural Resources and therefore have large numbers of faculty, diverse research programs, and particularly strong opportunities for graduate education. The seven academic departments offer the Master of Science degree, and all departments except small animal clinical sciences offer the Doctor of Philosophy degree. These programs provide basic education in subdisciplines of each department and intensive training in specialty areas related to the student's interest. They are designed to prepare candidates for positions in teaching or research. Particularly strong research and graduate training programs exist in environmental toxicology, neurosciences, toxicology, microbial genetics, cardiovascular and respiratory physiology and pathophysiology, population medicine, and orthopedics.

Research Facilities

Research and training programs are supported by well-equipped modern laboratory facilities devoted to both basic and clinical research. Central facilities are also available for electron microscopy, macromolecular structure, and laboratory animal care. The Veterinary Teaching Hospital and Animal Health Diagnostic Laboratory also offer extensive facilities for clinical research in surgery, radiology, endocrinology, and other specialties. The campus libraries house more than 400,000 biomedical volumes.

Financial Aid

The College of Veterinary Medicine offers competitive fellowships to veterinarians wishing to pursue the Ph.D. degree. The fellowships, which provide a postdoctoral stipend, tuition, and health insurance, are awarded after acceptance into the graduate program of one of the departments. Applicants must possess the D.V.M. or an equivalent degree. Preference is given to U.S. citizens or nationals.

The Department of Small Animal Clinical Sciences offers thirteen-month rotating internships designed to provide general clinical training and a basis for further education in a specialty area. Residencies designed to meet the training requirement for board certification are offered in a variety of clinical specialties by the Departments of Large Animal Clinical Sciences, Pathology, and Small Animal Clinical Sciences. Concurrent work toward an advanced degree is possible.

A limited number of fellowships and assistantships are available through departments.

Cost of Study

The spring semester 1998 costs for graduate study were in-state tuition and fees of $3185.50 and out-of-state tuition of $5837.50; books and supplies were approximately $996 per year; and thesis costs were variable typing costs plus $78 for the Ph.D. or $68 for the M.S. for graduate school processing of thesis.

Living and Housing Costs

Married housing on campus ranges from $381 to $410 per month for a one-bedroom apartment and from $422 to $454 per month for a two-bedroom apartment; a single-student apartment ranges from $381 to $454 per month. A single room in the graduate dormitory with meal service is $1873 per semester and a double room is $1602 per semester; both include a $280 meal credit. Off-campus housing is available in houses and apartments.

Student Group

As of fall 1997, the University had 32,591 undergraduate, 6,559 graduate, and 1,362 graduate-professional students. The College of Veterinary Medicine had 36 graduate students enrolled, with thirteen from other countries.

Student Outcomes

Graduates of the program find employment in academia, state and federal departments of agriculture, the chemical and pharmaceutical industries, and regulatory and extension agencies. Others may continue their education in postdoctoral positions.

Location

The Michigan State University campus, occupying more than 5,000 acres of developed and natural areas, is located in East Lansing (a small, residential city with a population of 50,000), adjacent to Lansing, the state capital. The natural beauty of the campus is enhanced by the Red Cedar River and the diversity of trees, shrubs, and flowers. Several natural areas, where development is kept to a minimum, and botanical and horticultural gardens contribute to the relaxing and picturesque atmosphere. Outdoor campus recreational opportunities include bicycling, tennis, walking, and canoeing. Lansing offers several museums and theaters and a large civic arena. Michigan is well known for its numerous and beautiful lakes, which offer a wide range of water sports opportunities.

The University and The College

Michigan State University was founded in 1855 as one of the first land-grant universities in the United States, with a strong emphasis in agriculture. The College of Veterinary Medicine, established in 1910, reflects the University's commitment to research and public service. It has strong ties to the medical, natural science, and agriculture colleges on campus. Intercollege collaborations provide the student with a wide range of educational opportunities. The University is situated on more than 2,100 acres of beautifully landscaped campus adjacent to the extensive University farms. Cultural opportunities and sports facilities are readily available.

Applying

The application deadline is approximately sixty days before the beginning of the term. Applicants are notified approximately four to six weeks after receipt of the application form. A bachelor's degree is required for admission to graduate study. Admission is made through the University Office of Admissions and Scholarships, with approval made by the department in which the applicant proposes to work. Scholastic record, experience, personal qualifications, and area of subject-matter interest are taken into consideration. In the departments of pathology, large animal clinical sciences, and small animal clinical sciences, a professional medical degree is also required. Although an interview is not necessary for admission, contact with the appropriate department before submission of the application form may be helpful.

Correspondence and Information

The departmental chairpersons should be contacted for information about specific departmental programs.

For information about the M.S./Ph.D. program:

Office of Research and Graduate Studies
College of Veterinary Medicine
G-100 Veterinary Medical Center
Michigan State University
East Lansing, Michigan 48824-1314
E-mail: hoelzer-maddox@cvm.msu.edu
World Wide Web: http://cvm.msu.edu/programs/graduat0

For information about the D.V.M. program:

Office of Admissions
College of Veterinary Medicine
A-126 E. Fee Hall
Michigan State University
East Lansing, Michigan 48824-1316
Telephone: 517-353-9793
E-mail: admiss@cvm.msu.edu
World Wide Web: http://cvm.msu.edu/programs/profess0

Michigan State University

THE FACULTY AND THEIR RESEARCH

Department of Anatomy

Joseph Vorro, Chair. Neuroanatomical tracing techniques; basal ganglia structure and function; immunohistochemistry; motor control circuitry; electromyography; neurotoxic effects of organophosphates; transplacental carcinogenesis; synaptic growth, function, and degeneration.

Department of Large Animal Clinical Sciences

Frederik J. Derksen, Chair. Anesthesiology, endocrinology, epidemiology, medicine, nutrition, parasitology, physiology, production medicine, radiology, surgery, theriogenology, veterinary economics.

Department of Microbiology

Jerry B. Dodgson, Chair. General microbiology; physiology; microbial biochemistry; immunology; genetics; ecology; pathogenesis; bacteriology; virology; parasitology; mycology; developmental, cell, and molecular biology.

Department of Pathology

Willie M. Reed, Interim Chair. Immunopathology and neuropathology; toxicologic, reproductive, cardiovascular, and ophthalmic pathology; oncology; hematology; pathology of infectious diseases; tropical pathology; pathology of animal models for human disease.

Department of Pharmacology and Toxicology

Kenneth E. Moore, Chair. Biochemical and pulmonary pharmacology and toxicology; cardiovascular, gastrointestinal, and neuroendocrine pharmacology; neuropharmacology; parasite chemotherapy; environmental toxicology; immunotoxicology.

Department of Physiology

William S. Spielman, Chair. Systemic, cell, and molecular physiology; neurophysiology and cardiovascular, endocrine, exercise, gastrointestinal, renal, reproductive, and respiratory physiology; breast cancer; diabetes; bone and muscle metabolism.

Department of Small Animal Clinical Sciences

Curtis W. Probst, Chair. Small animal anesthesiology, radiology, medicine, surgery, ophthalmology, dermatology, cardiology.

PENNSYLVANIA STATE UNIVERSITY

Department of Veterinary Science
Graduate Program in Pathobiology

Programs of Study

The Graduate Program in Pathobiology offers both the M.S. and the Ph.D. degrees. It is designed to provide flexibility in graduate work while offering opportunities to study in the areas of animal nutrition, biochemistry, immunology, microbiology, physiology, or toxicology. Applicants should have either a baccalaureate degree in an appropriate field of biological science, a degree as a graduate veterinarian, or their equivalents. Undergraduate preparation should include biology, biostatistics and biochemistry (preferred), chemistry, mathematics through calculus, and physics.

Graduate instruction is under the direction of graduate faculty members from the Department of Veterinary Science and related departments or areas that include animal nutrition, biochemistry, biology, biophysics, dairy and animal science, immunology, microbiology, physiology, zoology, and others. The Ph.D. program is designed for completion in three to four academic years. Doctoral candidates usually complete certain required courses and obtain laboratory experience before selecting an area of specialization and completing an original research problem, which includes the defense of the Ph.D. dissertation. A committee appointed for each student, with the approval of the department head, determines specific requirements for courses and research and administers the comprehensive examination and thesis defense.

Research Facilities

Facilities for departmental research activities include laboratories in the Henning Building, the Agricultural Sciences and Industries Building, the Animal Diagnostic Laboratory, the Centralized Biological Laboratory, and the Environmental Resources Research Institute. Opportunities to utilize research equipment such as electron microscopes, a DNA synthesizer, and a protein sequencer exist in the Biotechnology Institute and the Intercollege Research Program. The University has an extensive modern library that has cooperative arrangements with other regional resource libraries. A University computer center is also available.

Financial Aid

Financial support is available on a competitive basis to qualified applicants. A determined effort is made to provide all students who are placed in the departmental program with a stipend that covers tuition and living expenses.

Cost of Study

For the 1997–98 academic year, full-time tuition (9–13 credits without a graduate assistantship, 8–11 credits with an assistantship) cost $3184 per semester for Pennsylvania residents and $6624 per semester for out-of-state students. Tuition rates are subject to change for the 1998–99 academic year.

Living and Housing Costs

For the 1997–98 academic year, housing at the University Park Campus for married graduate students included one- and two-bedroom apartments at costs that ranged from $437 to $516 per month. Apartments for single students cost between $1434 and $1523 per semester. Residence hall housing is available for unmarried graduate students at University Park. In 1997–98, these costs ranged from $1110 to $1519 per semester, excluding meals. Rates at University Park are subject to change for the 1998–99 year.

The University offers some on-campus housing. For those who prefer off-campus housing, private homes and apartment complexes in town and in nearby communities offer a choice of accommodations at a wide range of prices.

Student Group

The pathobiology program has approximately 10–15 students enrolled. Related activities in immunology, microbiology, nutrition, and physiology in other departments or interdepartmental units increase the opportunities for graduate student interaction.

Location

Pennsylvania State University is located in University Park, Pennsylvania, which is surrounded by the community of State College, Pennsylvania. The town of State College retains a collegiate atmosphere that is enhanced by many small shops, restaurants, cinemas, and bookstores. The rural agricultural area around State College provides outstanding skiing, hiking, boating, and swimming.

The University and The Department

The Graduate School at Penn State University was formally established in 1922. Today, the University Park Campus enrolls approximately 7,000 graduate students who may choose from 150 approved fields of study. The Penn State College of Agricultural Sciences now is the sixth-largest agricultural college in the nation. The Department of Veterinary Science was established as part of the College in 1953. After twenty-four years in existence as the Veterinary Science Graduate Program, the name of the program was changed to pathobiology in 1992.

Applying

Applications are accepted throughout the year, but most are reviewed in January and February. Offers of admission are made as early as possible (typically by March) for the following summer or fall semester. A completed application should include an undergraduate transcript, scores from the GRE General Test (with a minimum combined verbal and quantitative score of 1200), three letters of recommendation, and the applicant's written statement of purpose, which details his or her background and plans for graduate study. In addition, international students must take the TOEFL and earn a minimum score of 550. These materials should reach the pathobiology graduate program office no later than March 1. Inquiries about the application process should be directed to the address below. Students should also feel free to contact individual faculty members in their areas of interest.

Correspondence and Information

Director, Pathobiology Graduate Program
115 W. L. Henning Building
Department of Veterinary Science
College of Agricultural Sciences
Pennsylvania State University
University Park, Pennsylvania 16802
Telephone: 814-863-5786
Fax: 814-863-6140
E-mail: pathobiology@psu.edu
World Wide Web: http://www.cas.psu.edu/docs/CASDEPT/VET/pathobiology.htm

Pennsylvania State University

THE FACULTY AND THEIR RESEARCH

Department of Veterinary Science

Pamela H. Correll, Ph.D., Assistant Professor. Role of the STK receptor tyrosine kinase in cell-mediated immunity and in the regulation of hematopoiesis.
Mary Lou Eskew, Ph.D., Research Assistant. Phagocytic cell function, immunology, and inflammation; role of prostaglandins and leukotrienes in immune function.
Frederick G. Ferguson, D.V.M., Ph.D., Professor. Immunology, biotechnology, animal disease.
Lester C. Griel Jr., D.V.M., Professor. Clinical medicine, experimental surgery and anesthesia.
Arthur L. Hattel, D.V.M., Research Associate. Diagnostic pathology, diseases of the GI system.
Andrew J. Henderson, Ph.D., Assistant Professor. Transcriptional regulation of HIV and molecular events regulating hematopoiesis.
Lawrence J. Hutchinson, D.V.M., Professor and Extension Veterinarian. Disease control in food-producing animals, Johne's disease in cattle, reproductive health problems in cattle, mastitis.
Carol Maddox, Ph.D., Research Associate and Diagnostic Veterinary Microbiologist. Bacterial gastroenteritis.
V. Reddy Padala, Ph.D., Senior Research Associate. Biochemistry, mechanisms of inhibition of lipid peroxidation in subcellular membranes.
Gary H. Perdew, Ph.D., Professor. Molecular toxicology, role of the Ah receptor in dioxin toxicity, heat shock protein biochemistry.
C. Channa Reddy, Ph.D., Distinguished Professor. Prostaglandins and leukotrienes, molecular biology of antioxidant enzymes.
A. Catharine Ross, Ph.D., Professor and Head. Vitamin A (retinoid) actions in the immune system and liver.
Richard W. Scholz, Ph.D., Professor. Antioxidants (Se, vitamin E) and host defense mechanisms.
Lorraine M. Sordillo, Ph.D., Associate Professor. Cytokine biology, immunology, bovine mastitis.
Jack Vanden Heuvel, Ph.D., Assistant Professor. Molecular mechanisms of gene regulation by tumor promoters.
Daniel Weinstock, D.V.M., Ph.D., Senior Research Associate. Antiviral cell-mediated immune function in the avian species.
Richard A. Wilson, Ph.D., Professor. Molecular and genetic studies of infection and immunity.
Don M. Wojchowski, Ph.D., Associate Professor. Mammalian cell growth and differentiation, especially hematopoiesis and cytokine receptor activation, including the erythropoietin receptor system.

Department of Microbiology and Cell Biology

Andrea M. Mastro, Ph.D., Professor. Immunology, immune-endocrine interactions, mammalian cell biology.

TEXAS A&M UNIVERSITY

Texas Veterinary Medical Center
College of Veterinary Medicine

Programs of Study

The various component parts of the Texas Veterinary Medical Center offer a wide range of graduate programs leading to the M.S. and Ph.D. degrees. Degree programs are available through the five academic departments in the College of Veterinary Medicine. M.S. and/or Ph.D. degree programs are offered in veterinary anatomy, veterinary microbiology, veterinary pathology (D.V.M. required), and veterinary physiology. M.S. degree programs are available in epidemiology, veterinary medical sciences, veterinary medicine and surgery (D.V.M. required), veterinary public health, and veterinary parasitology. Some of the programs are interdisciplinary and cross departmental and College lines (i.e., programs in genetics, toxicology, and nutrition). Participating departments in these programs may have joint admissions policies.

Research Facilities

Research and graduate education programs are supported by numerous individual laboratories operated by dedicated scientists who have as their first priority the acquisition and transfer of knowledge. Modern equipment is available, and state-of-the-art technology is constantly being introduced. Centralized facilities include the Veterinary Medical Park for care and use of large animals, a Laboratory Animals Resources and Research facility, an Image Analysis Laboratory, a Flow Cytometry Laboratory, and a Biomedical Media Resources Center with computer laboratories. In addition, resources of the Veterinary Teaching Hospital and the Diagnostic Laboratory are available to support research projects. A building construction program, recently completed, provides new and modern research laboratory space sufficient to meet needs extending into the twenty-first century. The Texas Veterinary Medical Center shares the Medical Sciences Library facility with the Texas A&M University College of Medicine, located across the street. Easy, all-weather access to both the library and colleagues in the College of Medicine is provided by a tunnel. The Medical Sciences Library currently houses more than 120,000 volumes, including more than 1,800 serial titles. Full library services are available, including computerized literature searches, interlibrary loans, and a dedicated professional staff.

Financial Aid

Research and teaching assistantships are awarded on a competitive basis by the College as well as by interdisciplinary programs and departments. Many investigators have research grants that provide graduate research assistantships. Stipends are on a twelve-month basis, are at levels competitive with those available nationally, and usually include a waiver of out-of-state tuition.

Cost of Study

Tuition during the 1998–99 academic year varies per semester credit hour for Texas residents and nonresident and international students. Additional fees also vary depending upon the number of credit hours and number of courses. Other services, such as the Student Center and the Health Center, cost approximately $70 per semester. Resident fees for 9 credit hours average $1210; nonresident fees average $3137. Resident fees for 12 credit hours average $1574; for nonresidents, $4142. All fees are subject to change without notice.

Living and Housing Costs

On-campus housing is not available for graduate students except during the summer months. Married student housing is available on a limited basis. A wide range of off-campus rental housing is available, with prices starting from about $360 per month for an efficiency apartment and $470 for a two-bedroom, one-bath apartment. Many opportunities to share expenses are also available. An off-campus housing office can efficiently aid in the matching process. A shuttle-bus service to the campus is convenient to most off-campus housing locations.

Student Group

Texas A&M University has a total enrollment of approximately 43,000 students, about 6,500 of whom are enrolled in graduate programs. All of the fifty states and many countries are represented on campus.

Location

College Station and the adjoining city of Bryan have a population of 120,000 and are located within 100 miles of both Austin and Houston and within 180 miles of Dallas, San Antonio, and the Gulf Coast. Waterskiing, fishing, hunting, boating, and horseback riding are all popular sports in the area. The Sunbelt location provides ample opportunity to participate in these activities. The community offers good school systems, numerous licensed day-care facilities, a regional shopping mall, and a range of cultural activities. The two cities maintain forty parks, six swimming pools, four golf courses, and numerous tennis courts. Both country and city living are available within a few miles of the University.

The University

Texas A&M University, the state's oldest public institution of higher learning, was founded in 1876 as a land-grant college. It is also one of the sixteen sea-grant universities in the nation and was recently designated as a space-grant university. Texas A&M has the state's largest and the nation's sixth-largest research budget; funded research amounted to about $360 million in 1996–97. The main campus is situated on 5,200 acres. Its recreational facilities include an eighteen-hole golf course, tennis courts, indoor and outdoor swimming pools, and a polo field. The Memorial Student Center and Rudder Conference Center provide numerous opportunities in all academic areas. Two major concert series offer a choice of popular and classical events during the year. Texas A&M University is a member of the Big Twelve, and campus athletic events are frequent.

Applying

Applicants interested in a career in one of the disciplines offered are invited to apply. Those applying must have a bachelor's degree or its equivalent. Satisfactory scores on the verbal and quantitative portions of the Graduate Record Examinations are required as well as a strong course work foundation in the sciences. International students must score at least 550 on the TOEFL.

Correspondence and Information

Office of the Associate Dean for Research and Graduate Programs
College of Veterinary Medicine
Texas A&M University
College Station, Texas 77843-4461
Telephone: 409-845-5092
Fax: 409-845-5088
World Wide Web: http://www.tamu.edu

Texas A&M University

THE FACULTY AND THEIR RESEARCH

The graduate faculty consists of approximately 130 members located in five departments. Current research in each department is listed below, together with the name of each departmental Graduate Advisor.

Veterinary Anatomy and Public Health
Graduate Advisor: Dr. D. L. Busbee, Telephone: 409-845-3519, Fax: 409-847-8981, E-mail: chanks@cvm.tamu.edu

Cell biology; molecular biology; genetics; molecular genetics, including transgenesis and gene targeting; embryology/developmental biology; histology and cellular ultrastructure; cellular imaging; macroscopic anatomy; reproductive biology; neuroscience; toxicology; aquatic/marine toxicology; food safety; food science and technology; epidemiology.

Veterinary Large Animal Medicine and Surgery
Graduate Advisor: Dr. N. Cohen, Telephone: 409-845-9127, Fax: 409-847-8863.

Infectious and acquired diseases of large animals; orthopedic surgery; internal medicine; theriogenology; radiology; general surgery. Applicants must have D.V.M. degree or equivalent.

Veterinary Pathobiology
Graduate Advisor: Dr. G. G. Wagner, Telephone: 409-845-5941, Fax: 409-845-9231.

Bacteriology; mycology; virology; molecular and cellular immunology; protozoology; helminthology; entomology; comparative pathology; transgenic mice and gene targeting; molecular genetics; avian diseases; aquatic animal medicine; mechanisms for host responses to pathogens; molecular basis of cellular interactions with microbial pathogens; general molecular biology of viruses, bacteria, and parasites; comparative molecular genetics; infectious diseases; noninfectious diseases; clinical pathology; neoplastic diseases; neuropathology; diseases of laboratory animals; mechanisms of metabolic disease.

Veterinary Physiology and Pharmacology
Graduate Advisor: Dr. J. S. Wasser, Telephone: 409-845-7261, Fax: 409-845-6544.

Cardiovascular physiology; gamete and embryo physiology; endocrinology; comparative oncology; equine laminitis; cellular and molecular biology; clinical pharmacology; veterinary, plant, and environmental toxicology.

Veterinary Small Animal Medicine and Surgery
Graduate Advisor: Dr. S. M. Hartsfield, Telephone: 409-845-2351, Fax: 409-845-6978, E-mail: shartsfield@cvm.tamu.edu

Dermatology; anesthesiology; nephrology and urology; cardiology; nutrition; behavior; gastroenterology; orthopedic surgery; general surgery; oncology; ophthalmology; radiology; neurology. Applicants must have D.V.M. degree or equivalent. Most graduate students are selected through the AAVC Internship/Residency Matching Program. Details can be found in the *Directory of Internships and Residencies*, available from American Association of Veterinary Clinicians, 1024 Dublin Road, Columbus, Ohio 43215.

UNIVERSITY OF ILLINOIS AT URBANA–CHAMPAIGN

College of Veterinary Medicine
Department of Veterinary Biosciences

Programs of Study

Members of the Department of Veterinary Biosciences direct graduate programs leading to the M.S. and Ph.D. degrees in morphology, pharmacology, physiology, toxicology, and nuclear medicine. Graduate programs in veterinary biosciences provide broad training in biological science and other relevant disciplines. Students are required to take relatively few core courses, providing the opportunity for in-depth study in areas of special interest. Interdisciplinary research programs are encouraged.

Master of Science candidates are expected to complete a minimum of 8 units (1 unit equals 4 semester credits), including thesis work, and participate in departmental and interdepartmental seminar programs. Doctor of Philosophy candidates are expected to complete an M.S. program or the equivalent and an additional 16 units of course and thesis work. Students are expected to develop a plan of study with their research adviser during the first year they are enrolled in a degree program. This study plan must be approved by the student's advisory committee and the Departmental Graduate Studies Committee.

Individuals holding the D.V.M. or equivalent degree are eligible for residency programs providing advanced training in clinical pharmacology and clinical toxicology.

Research Facilities

The Department of Veterinary Biosciences has ample space and equipment for research in many areas. Complete animal-care facilities, including a 75-acre farm, a fully equipped companion- and food-animal hospital, and confinement and conditioning quarters, are readily available. Expansion programs for food-animal and equine research are being pursued. The department's research laboratories are equipped to handle standard and specialized analytical procedures in endocrinology, toxicology, and pharmacology. Analytical instrumentation, including liquid scintillation and gamma counters, gas and high-pressure liquid chromatographs, and a multichannel analyzer, is available for a variety of projects in pharmacokinetics, physiology, and toxicology. Tissue and organ culture laboratories, a transmission electron microscope, scanning electron microscope support equipment, well-equipped histology laboratories for routine and special procedures, and complete College and departmental photographic services are integral parts of the graduate program, providing support for projects in anatomy, embryology, and biomechanics. A gamma camera and image processing and display equipment are available through the nuclear medicine program.

A network of PCs are used for certain online and analytical procedures. In addition, most laboratories and offices are equipped with PCs. Some are connected to the central Computing Services Office, which contains mainframe systems including IBM, CONVEX, Pyramid, and DEC machines.

The library system on the Urbana-Champaign campus is the third-largest university library in the United States, with more than 6 million volumes available. The College of Veterinary Medicine has its own library, featuring 600 specialty serial titles and 20,000 reference volumes.

Financial Aid

Students are eligible for financial aid of various types including fellowships; teaching and research assistantships, which include a tuition and fee waiver; and tuition scholarships. If awarded, the amount of aid varies with the source, the type of support, and the progress of the student.

Cost of Study

Tuition in 1998–99 is $1942 per semester for state residents and $5380 per semester for nonresidents of Illinois. Other fees amount to $627 per semester. Books and supplies cost about $600 per year.

Living and Housing Costs

For 1998–99, the cost of rooms for single students in graduate dormitories ranges from $2324 to $2892 per academic year. A twenty-meal-per-week plan costs an additional $3238 per year. Information concerning privately owned apartments and University-owned housing for married students ($406–$750 per month, plus utilities in 1998–99) is available from the campus housing office. Students should write to the Housing Director, 200 Clark Hall, University of Illinois, Champaign, Illinois 61820.

Student Group

There are approximately 26,000 undergraduate and 9,000 graduate students, representing all of the United States and many other countries, at the University. Graduate enrollment in the Department of Veterinary Biosciences is currently 34, including 24 doctoral students. In addition, about 350 students are enrolled in the professional curriculum.

Location

The College is located 120 miles south of Chicago, 120 miles west of Indianapolis, and 165 miles northeast of St. Louis in the twin cities of Urbana and Champaign (with a population of 100,000). Excellent city and county parks and conservation areas provide outdoor activities all year. Nearby Clinton Lake provides sailing, waterskiing, and camping opportunities. Cross-country skiing, biking, swimming, tennis, and golf facilities are plentiful.

The College and The Department

The Department of Veterinary Biosciences is one of three departments in the College of Veterinary Medicine, founded in the mid-1940's. Facilities include a 56,500-square-foot Companion Animal Hospital and Clinic and a 71,700-square-foot Food Animal Hospital. A 158,000-square-foot Basic Sciences Building was completed in 1982.

Applying

Completed applications, with fees of $40 domestic and $50 international, can be sent at any time. The department requires applicants to submit a GRE score. Research assistantship offers are made as the applications are processed. Domestic applications must be received by March 1 to be eligible for departmental teaching assistantships. Applications, scores, and letters of reference should be sent to one of the addresses listed below.

Correspondence and Information

Assistant Head and Director
of Graduate Training Program
Department of Veterinary Biosciences, Room 3516-P
College of Veterinary Medicine
University of Illinois
2001 South Lincoln Avenue
Urbana, Illinois 61801
Telephone: 217-333-2506

Graduate College
330 Administration Building
University of Illinois
Urbana, Illinois 61801

University of Illinois at Urbana-Champaign

THE FACULTY AND THEIR RESEARCH

Val R. Beasley, Professor; D.V.M., Purdue, 1972; Ph.D., Illinois, 1983. Toxicology: domestic animal, environmental, wildlife, and ecological toxicology. Current research: fate and effects of mycotoxins and phytotoxins, amphibian declines.
David Bunick, Associate Professor; Ph.D., Pennsylvania, 1982. Molecular biology and physiology of male reproduction. Current research: regulation of testis gene expression with special interest in temperature effects, the regulation of aromatase expression and the role of estrogen production in male reproductive tissues, and the role of calnexin-t in germ-cell development.
Paul S. Cooke, Associate Professor; Ph.D., Berkeley, 1983. Anatomy: endocrinology and developmental biology. Current research: role of steroid hormones in the differentiation, growth, and morphogenesis of male and female reproductive organs.
Mrinal K. Dewanjee, Professor; Ph.D., McGill, 1967. Noninvasive nuclear imaging of thrombus on cardiovascular diseases and prostheses, evaluation of drugs in animal models and patients for inhibition of thrombus and inflammation, in vivo hybridization of gamma-emitting oligonucleotide probes with amplified mRNA tagets of oncogenes in cancer.
Jo Ann C. Eurell, Associate Professor; D.V.M., Purdue, 1974; Ph.D., Texas A&M, 1979. Anatomy: bone and joint pathobiology, with special emphasis on the vertebral column.
Thomas E. Eurell, Associate Professor; Ph.D., Texas A&M, 1981; D.V.M., Florida, 1983. Toxicology: acute-phase reactive proteins, immunopathogenesis of infectious and noninfectious diseases, soluble mediators in the immune response in vitro models in toxicology.
David R. Gross, Professor and Head of Department; D.V.M., Colorado State, 1960; Ph.D., Ohio State, 1974. Physiology: cardiovascular function and hemodynamics. Current research: role of neuropeptides in vascular control, vascular and cardiac muscle dynamics and mechanical properties, artificial cardiovascular devices.
Larry G. Hansen, Professor; Ph.D., North Carolina State, 1970. Toxicology: xenobiotic metabolism, residue analysis. Current research: endocrine disruption by PCBs, bioassay of environmental residues.
Aslam S. Hassan, Associate Professor; Ph.D., Oregon, 1979. Physiology: gastrointestinal system, liver function. Current research: regulation of cholesterol metabolism.
Rex A. Hess, Associate Professor; Ph.D., Clemson, 1983. Physiology/morphology: male reproductive biology, endocrinology, and toxicology, emphasizing spermatogenesis, testicular development, and epididymal structure and function. Current research: mechanisms of toxicant-induced testicular atrophy and the role of Sertoli cells; sperm as a source of estrogen for epididymal function.
James E. Hixon, Professor; Ph.D., California, Davis, 1968. Physiology: fertility in domestic animals, endocrinology of reproduction. Current research: control of corpus luteum function in pregnant and nonpregnant food animals.
Kenneth R. Holmes, Associate Professor and Assistant Head; Ph.D., Michigan State, 1972. Morphology and physiology, bioengineering: mammalian temperature regulation, bioheat transfer, microvascular angioarchitecture. Current research: development of a pulse-heated thermistor microprobe for the measurement of normal and tumor tissue blood perfusion.
Gary A. Iwamoto, Professor; Ph.D., California, Davis, 1978. Anatomy and physiology: neural control of the cardiovascular system, cardiovascular and exercise physiology. Current research: electrophysiological and nueroanatomical properties of central nervous system pathways that mediate somatosympathetic reflexes and neuroendocrine function.
Gary L. Jackson, Professor; Ph.D., Illinois, 1967. Physiology (neuroendocrinology): neuroendocrine regulation of luteinizing hormone and prolactin secretion. Current research: neural pathways and neurochemical mechanisms by which environmental factors and gonadal steroids alter gonadotropin secretion.
Gary D. Koritz, Professor; D.V.M., 1968, Ph.D., 1975, Illinois. Pharmacology: comparative pharmacokinetics of drugs, toxins, and environmental contaminants in animals. Current research: pharmacokinetics and pharmacodynamics of antibacterial drugs.
Murli Manohar, Professor; B.V.Sc., Punjab Agricultural University, 1968; Ph.D., Wisconsin, 1978. Physiology: cardiopulmonary physiology, including myocardial perfusion and ventricular function. Current research: coronary circulation and respiratory function in large animals, equine exercise physiology, exercise-induced pulmonary hemorrhage.
Gerald J. Pijanowski, Associate Professor; D.V.M., Cornell, 1972; Ph.D., Purdue, 1978. Anatomy: biomechanics of the musculoskeletal system, interaction between the mechanical environment of the musculoskeletal system and the biological structure. Current research: analysis and modeling of external skeletal fixator frames, simulation of locomotion.
David J. Schaeffer, Associate Professor; Ph.D., NYU, 1969. Environmental toxicology: stress effects on ecosystems, sampling methods, modeling, and statistical analysis; ecosystem health; applied statistics, including design and analysis of biomedical studies; photoinduced toxicity, including effects of ultraviolet co-exposure on toxicity and mutagenicity of metals, organic compounds, and PCBs.
Susan L. Schantz, Associate Professor; Ph.D., Wisconsin, 1985. Environmental toxicology: developmental and neurotoxicology. Current research: long-term effects of prenatal and lactational exposure to environmental contaminants on nervous system function; role of exposure to environmental contaminants on nervous system decline in aging.
Mark R. Simon, Associate Professor; Ph.D., CUNY Graduate Center, 1974. Anatomy: cartilage growth, mechanical and endocrine factors in cartilage development. Current research: effects of increased, intermittent compressive forces and the role of TGFβ in physical growth.
Mike E. Tumbleson, Professor; Ph.D., Minnesota, 1964. Biochemistry: malnutrition, alcoholism and drug interactions, mammalian metabolism.
A. Robert Twardock, Professor; D.V.M., Illinois, 1956; Ph.D., Cornell, 1961. Nuclear medicine: mineral metabolism; applications of radioisotopes in biological and medical research and diagnosis; use of nuclear medicine imaging techniques in animal disease diagnosis, with emphasis on skeletal, renal, and respiratory systems.
Ted Whittem, Assistant Professor; B.V.Sc., Melbourne, 1980; Ph.D., Georgia, 1991. Diplomate A.C.U.C.P. 1994, F.A.C.U.Sc. 1995. Clinical pharmacology, endocrinology, pharmacokinetics. Current research: pharmacokinetics of intramuscular injections, clinical efficacy of surgical antimicrobial prophylaxis.

Affiliated Faculty from the Department of Veterinary Clinical Medicine (members indicated by *) and the Institute for Environmental Studies (members indicated by †)

*Gordon J. Baker, Professor; B.V.Sc., M.R.C.V.S., Bristol (England), 1962; Ph.D., Glasgow (Scotland), 1979; Diplomate, A.C.V.S., 1983. Equine surgery. Current research: equine dental disease, endodontics, respiratory surgery, expansion of imaging modalities.
*G. John Benson, Professor; D.V.M., Illinois, 1971; M.S., Illinois, 1978. Pharmacology: anesthetics and anesthetic adjuncts. Current research: perioperative stress response and analgesics.
*Robert B. Clarkson, Associate Professor; Ph.D., Princeton, 1969. Physical chemistry: magnetic resonance of living systems, biosensors, in vivo electron magnetic resonance, free radicals, molecular structure in disordered systems, MRI.
†Bettina M. Francis, Associate Professor; Ph.D., Michigan, 1971. Toxicology: developmental; irreversible effects of pesticide exposure; neurotoxicology. Current research: effects of xenobiotics on gene expression during organogenesis, developmental toxicity of diphenyl ethers, interactions of genotype and environment in the etiology of birth defects.
†Elizabeth H. Jeffery, Associate Professor; Ph.D., London, 1973. Toxicology: xenobiotic metabolism and bioactivation of toxins. Current research: mechanism of action of cytochrome P450, aluminum toxicology, diet and cancer.
*Theodore F. Lock, Professor; D.V.M., Missouri, 1971. Theriogenology: equine reproduction. Current research: early embryonic death and ovarian function in mares, distribution of antibiotics in mare reproductive tract.
*Randall S. Ott, Professor; D.V.M., Georgia, 1968. Theriogenology: bovine reproduction. Current research: infertility associated with testicular hypoplasia in bulls, effects of zeranol implants on reproduction of beef cattle.
*Alan J. Parker, Professor; B.V.Sc., Bristol (England), 1968; Ph.D., Illinois, 1976. Neurology. Current research: electroencephalography—computer evaluation in food and companion animals, stroke and drug studies in companion animals.

UNIVERSITY OF KENTUCKY

College of Agriculture
Department of Veterinary Science

Programs of Study

The faculty of the Department of Veterinary Science offers graduate training leading to the M.S. and Ph.D. degrees in the areas of virology, bacteriology, parasitology, reproductive physiology, immunology, genetics, pharmacology, toxicology, and veterinary pathology. The goal of this program is to provide students with the skills and knowledge necessary for highly competitive research careers in these disciplines. A unique aspect of this program is that the research focuses on the health of the horse. The program of study combines basic biomedical education and basic research with the opportunity to investigate problems of direct concern to the horse industry and develop strategies for resolving those problems. Students completing this program find careers in research, service, and teaching in public and private educational institutions, government agencies, and industry.

Students with baccalaureate degrees or professional degrees (i.e., D.V.M. or M.D.) may enroll in either the M.S. or Ph.D. program. The M.S. program involves completion of 24 units of course work, completion of a research project, and preparation of a thesis under the supervision of a faculty adviser. The Ph.D. program involves completion of course work recommended by an advisory committee, successful completion of a qualifying examination, design and completion of a significant research project, and preparation and defense of a dissertation. The M.S. program may be completed in two years and the Ph.D. program completed in three to four years, depending upon the preparation and abilities of the student.

Research Facilities

The Department of Veterinary Science comprises three units: the M. H. Gluck Equine Research Center, the Equine Blood Typing and Research Laboratory, and the Livestock Disease Diagnostic Center. The Gluck Equine Research Center is primarily a research and graduate training facility with spacious, well-equipped laboratories for conducting molecular, cellular, biochemical, and physiological studies. It houses the main research arm of the Department of Veterinary Science. The Equine Blood Typing and Research Laboratory, housed in a separate facility adjacent to the Medical Center, is primarily a service laboratory providing parentage testing and analysis under contract to more than thirty horse registries in North and South America. The Livestock Disease Diagnostic Center, located off campus to the north of Lexington, is a full-service laboratory providing necropsy and other diagnostic services for the livestock and companion animal industries in Kentucky. The department also maintains a farm with more than 400 horses for use in research and an animal facility for the care and maintenance of laboratory animals. In addition, the department also uses core research facilities for protein and nucleic acid analysis, transgenic mouse research, and flow sorting in collaboration with research programs in the College of Medicine, the School of Biology, the College of Pharmacy, other departments in the College of Agriculture, and other biomedical research programs on campus.

Financial Aid

Most graduate students are supported through research assistantships funded by grants or donations to the Department of Veterinary Science. Highly qualified applicants are considered for the Geoffrey C. Hughes Fellowships, the Maxwell and Muriel Gluck Fellowships, and the Mellon Fellowship. Other fellowships and assistantships are provided through faculty research grants, the Graduate School, and the University of Kentucky Equine Research Foundation.

Cost of Study

For the 1998–99 academic year, in-state graduate tuition is $2976. Tuition for out-of-state students is $8256. Students holding University fellowships or research assistantships are treated as in-state students for tuition purposes.

Living and Housing Costs

Most students live in private apartments off campus. Housing costs range from $350 to $550 per month for an apartment.

Student Group

There are approximately 24,000 students at the University of Kentucky, including approximately 5,000 graduate students. The Department of Veterinary Science included 31 students in 1997–98, of whom 19 were pursuing Ph.D. degrees. Successful applicants have been those highly motivated to pursue a career in animal health research.

Student Outcomes

The majority of graduates are employed in faculty positions at research and teaching institutions, including Purdue University, the University of Wisconsin, the University of California, the University of Missouri, Utah State University, and Australian National University; graduates are also employed in the biomedical and pharmaceutical industries and in regulatory and extension agencies.

Location

The University of Kentucky is located in Lexington, Kentucky, a beautiful bluegrass region of rolling hills and horse farms. The county has approximately 220,000 residents, many of whom are employed by the University of Kentucky, local horse and other agricultural industries, IBM, Lexmark, Toyota Manufacturing, and regional headquarters for banking, insurance, and other industries. By car, Lexington is approximately 80 minutes from Cincinnati and Louisville; 6 hours from Chicago and Atlanta; 10 hours from Washington, D.C.; and 12 hours from New York City.

The University and The Department

The University of Kentucky is a land-grant institution founded in 1865. The University has been listed for the last several years as a Category I Research University by the Carnegie Foundation; only fifty-nine public universities are classified in this highest ranking. Regarded as the flagship university of the state, it offers a wide range of educational opportunities. The College of Agriculture has eleven departments that provide education and award bachelor's, master's, and doctoral degrees in areas ranging from economics to engineering to agricultural biotechnology.

Applying

Applications can be submitted at any time. An application includes completed application and fellowship forms; GRE scores for the verbal, quantitative, and analytic sections; TOEFL scores for nonnative English speakers; college transcripts showing class performance and completion of degree programs; and an application fee of $30 to be sent to the Graduate School. In addition, the applicant should provide a short (one-page) written statement of interest and goals and arrange to have three letters of recommendation sent to the Department of Veterinary Science graduate program. Applicants should have a minimum undergraduate GPA of 3.0 on a 4.0 scale, a minimum combined score of 1100 (verbal and quantitative) on the GRE, and minimum TOEFL scores of 550 (if appropriate). Applicants with lesser qualifications may be admitted on the recommendation of a faculty member who commits to serving as adviser. Potential students are strongly encouraged to review the research activities of the faculty and contact potential advisers early to discuss their application.

Correspondence and Information

Director of Graduate Studies
Department of Veterinary Science
M. H. Gluck Equine Research Center
University of Kentucky
Lexington, Kentucky 40546-0099

Fax: 606-257-8542
E-mail: ebailey@ca.uky.edu
World Wide Web: http://www.uky.edu/Agriculture/VetScience/gluck1.htm

University of Kentucky

THE FACULTY AND THEIR RESEARCH

GLUCK EQUINE RESEARCH CENTER

George P. Allen, Professor; Ph.D., Kentucky, 1975. Pathogenesis, molecular biology, and immunological control of herpesvirus-related respiratory and abortigenic diseases of the horse; current emphasis on identification, characterization, and development of vaccinal immunogens of equine herpesvirus-1 (EHV-1) proteins that elicit protective immune responses in the horse. (e-mail: gallen@ca.uky.edu)

Ernest Bailey, Professor; Ph.D., California, Davis, 1980. Immunology and genetics of the horse, especially molecular genetics, cytogenetics, gene mapping, and major histocompatibility research related to health and performance of horses as well as phylogenetics of the Equidae. (e-mail: ebailey@ca.uky.edu)

Thomas M. Chambers, Associate Professor; Ph.D., Notre Dame, 1982. Molecular biology of negative-strand RNA viruses, with emphasis on functional, genetic, and antigenic characteristics of equine influenza virus; vectors for presentation of influenza viral antigens to the equine immune system; structure-function analysis of influenza viral proteins. (e-mail: tcham1@ukcc.uky.edu)

Roberta M. Dwyer, Assistant Professor; D.V.M., Iowa State, 1985; Diplomate, American College of Veterinary Preventive Medicine. Epidemiology of equine infectious diseases, especially rotavirus, salmonellosis, rabies, and zoonotic pathogens; equine disease prevention and control. (e-mail: rmdwye1@ukcc.uky.edu)

Barry P. Fitzgerald, Associate Professor; Ph.D., Reading (England), 1979. Investigation of the neuroendocrine mechanisms governing seasonal reproduction in domestic species, with specialization in the mare. (e-mail: bfitz@pop.uky.edu)

Charles J. Issel, Professor; D.V.M., California, Davis, 1969; Ph.D., Wisconsin–Madison, 1973; Diplomate, American College of Veterinary Microbiologists. Infectious diseases of the horse, with emphasis on the epizootiology, diagnosis, and control of equine infectious anemia (caused by lentivirus); mechanisms of virus persistence, vector transmission, vaccine development. (e-mail: cissel@pop.uky.edu)

Eugene T. Lyons, Professor; Ph.D., Colorado State, 1963. Internal parasites of domestic animals, particularly horses but also sheep, cattle, and mammalian wildlife species. (e-mail: elyons1@pop.uky.edu)

William H. McCollum, Professor; Ph.D., Wisconsin, 1954. Infectious diseases of the horse, especially equine viral arteritis and equine rhinovirus infections. (e-mail: whmcco2@ukcc.uky.edu)

Karen J. McDowell, Associate Professor; Ph.D., Florida, 1986. Embryonic/uterine physiology and causes of embryonic loss in the mare; synthesis and secretion of proteins by the embryo, oviduct, and uterus of the mare and accessory sex glands of the stallion; embryonic/uterine interactions and communication; early embryonic development. (e-mail: kmcd@ukcc.uky.edu)

David G. Powell, Extension Professor; B.V.Sc., 1965, F.R.C.V.S., Bristol (England). Epidemiologic studies on equine diseases. (e-mail: dkpowe00@ukcc.uky.edu)

John F. Timoney, Professor; M.V.B., M.R.C.V.S., 1965, Ph.D., 1969, D.Sc., 1983, Ireland. Streptococcal infections of the horse, with special reference to the molecular biology and pathogenesis of *Streptococcus equi* and *S. zooepidemicus* infections and the mechanisms involved in stimulation of mucosal immunity; characterization of horse complement components that interact with the bacterial cell wall. (e-mail: jtimoney@ukcc.uky.edu)

Peter J. Timoney, Professor and Chairperson; M.V.B., Ireland, 1964; Ph.D., Dublin, 1974; F.R.C.V.S., Royal College of Veterinary Surgeons, 1978. Pathogenesis and epidemiology of equine infectious diseases; molecular biology and epidemiology of equine arteritis virus, with emphasis on the mode of virus persistence in the stallion; development of an in vitro model of virus persistence; development of improved diagnostic procedures for equine arteritis virus infection. (e-mail: ptimoney@ca.uky.edu)

Thomas Tobin, Professor; M.V.B., Ireland, 1964; Ph.D., Toronto, 1969; Diplomate, American Board of Toxicology. Studies on the detection, actions, uses, and effects of drugs and especially drugs in the performance horse; development of improved analytical procedures for the detection of drugs abused in racing horses, with special reference to the value of ELISA tests; aspects of basic and forensic toxicology, with an emphasis on immunochemical aspects of drug detection. (e-mail: ttobin@ca.uky.edu)

EQUINE BLOOD TYPING AND RESEARCH LABORATORY

E. Gus Cothran, Research Associate Professor and Director; Ph.D., Oklahoma, 1982. Biochemical genetic relationships and evolution of the Equidae, population structure and the maintenance of genetic variation in horse breeds, genetic relationship of domestic horse breeds, genetics of wild horse populations, conservation genetics of rare breeds, evolution of the protease inhibitor system in equids, and relationships among genetic variation and reproductive characteristics in horses; gene mapping in the horse. (e-mail: gcothran@mik.uky.edu)

Kathryn Trembicki Graves, Research Assistant Professor; Ph.D., Cornell, 1985. Gene mapping in the horse using horse-mouse somatic cell hybrids, identification of lymphocyte differentiation markers in the horse using monoclonal and polyclonal antibodies and studying their role in disease resistance. (e-mail: ktgraves@mik.uky.edu)

LIVESTOCK DISEASE DIAGNOSTIC CENTER

J. Michael Donahue, Clinical Professor; Ph.D., Missouri, 1971. Bacterial and mycotic infections of the horse, with special reference to the pathogenesis, epidemiology, and significance of equine leptospirosis. (e-mail: mdonahue@ca.uky.edu)

Ralph C. Giles, Clinical Professor; D.V.M., Auburn, 1970. Veterinary pathology. (e-mail: rgiles@ca.uky.edu)

Lenn R. Harrison, Clinical Professor and Director; V.M.D., Pennsylvania, 1967. Pathogenesis of respiratory diseases, especially viral infections likely to cause pulmonary lesions; diagnostic investigation of disease problems of all domestic species. (e-mail: lharriso@ca.uky.edu)

C. B. Hong, Clinical Professor; Ph.D., Cornell, 1972. Diagnostic pathology, oncology, reproductive pathology, toxicologic pathology, immunopathology, and viral diseases. (e-mail: chong@ca.uky.edu)

K. B. Poonacha, Clinical Professor; D.V.M., Madras (India), 1963; Ph.D., Wisconsin, 1972; Diplomate, American College of Veterinary Pathologists. Pathology and epidemiology of leptospirosis in the horse population in central Kentucky and of the significance of leptospires as a cause of abortion in mares and icterus in neonatal foals. (e-mail: kpoonach@ca.uky.edu)

Patricia B. Scharko, Associate Extension Professor; D.V.M., Georgia, 1983; M.P.H., North Carolina at Chapel Hill, 1989; Diplomate, American College of Veterinary Preventive Medicine. Ruminants. (e-mail: psharko@ca.uky.edu)

Roy A. Smith, Associate Clinical Professor; Ph.D., Alberta, 1974. Development of diagnostic tests; poisonous plants, with particular interest in chemotaxonomy; diketopiperazine mycotoxins; detection of poisonous plants in ingesta by chemical analysis; use of livestock and wildlife as sentinels of environmental contamination. (e-mail: rasmith@ca.uky.edu)

Thomas W. Swerczek, Professor; D.V.M., Kansas State, 1964; Ph.D., Connecticut, 1972. Pathogenesis of equine fetal diseases and diseases of foals, interrelationship between endogenous metabolites of steroids and bacterial diseases of suckling foals, pathogenesis of dietary-enhanced bacterial diseases.

Robert R. Tramontin, Associate Clinical Professor; D.V.M., Auburn, 1965. Pathology, morphometrics of the equine heart. (e-mail: rtramont@ca.uky.edu)

Mary Lynne Vickers, Associate Clinical Professor; Ph.D., Wisconsin, 1981. Development of rapid diagnostic tests for viral diseases, viral agents causing respiratory disease, and epidemiology of bovine viral diarrhea virus. (e-mail: mvickers@ca.uky.edu)

Neil M. Williams, Assistant Clinical Professor; D.V.M., Mississippi State, 1982; Ph.D., Kentucky, 1992. Equine pathology, pathogenesis of equine infectious diseases, intracellular pathogens and macrophage function. (e-mail: nmwillia@ca.uky.edu)

Academic and Professional Programs in Physical Education, Sports, and Recreation

This part of Book 6 consists of three sections covering physical education, sports, and recreation. Each section has a table of contents (listing the program directories, announcements, and in-depth descriptions); program directories, which consist of brief profiles of programs in the relevant fields (and that include 50-word or 100-word announcements following the profiles, if programs have chosen to include them); Cross-Discipline Announcements, if any programs have chosen to submit such entries; and in-depth descriptions, which are more individualized statements included, if programs have chosen to submit them.

Section 40
Leisure Studies and Recreation

This section contains directories of institutions offering graduate work in leisure studies and recreation and park management, followed by in-depth entries provided by institutions that chose to prepare detailed program descriptions. Additional information about programs listed in the directories but not augmented by an in-depth entry may be obtained by writing directly to the dean of a school or chair of a department at the address given in the directory.

For programs offering related work, in Book 2, see Performing Arts and in Book 4, see Natural Resources.

CONTENTS

Program Directories

In-Depth Descriptions

See also:

Leisure Studies

Aurora University, George Williams College, School of Recreation Administration, Aurora, IL 60506-4892. Offers programs in administration of leisure services (MS), outdoor pursuits recreation administration (MS), outdoor therapeutic recreation administration (MS), therapeutic recreation administration (MS). Part-time and evening/weekend programs available. Faculty: 4 full-time (3 women), 3 part-time (2 women). Students: 22 full-time (15 women), 16 part-time (9 women). 14 applicants, 86% accepted. In 1997, 21 degrees awarded. *Degree requirements:* Thesis optional, foreign language not required. *Entrance requirements:* Minimum GPA of 2.75. Application deadline: 9/1 (priority date; rolling processing). Application fee: $25. *Tuition:* $408 per semester hour. *Financial aid:* In 1997–98, 2 fellowships (both to first-year students), 3 teaching assistantships (all to first-year students) were awarded; partial tuition waivers, institutionally sponsored loans, and career-related internships or fieldwork also available. Aid available to part-time students. • Dr. Rita Yerkes, Dean, 630-844-5406. Application contact: Office of Admissions, 630-844-5533. Fax: 630-844-5463.

Boston University, School of Education, Department of Developmental Studies and Counseling, Program in Leisure Education, Boston, MA 02215. Awards Ed M, CAGS. Students: 2 full-time (both women), 1 part-time (0 women); includes 1 minority (Asian American). Average age 24. In 1997, 1 master's awarded. *Degree requirements:* For CAGS, comprehensive exam required, foreign language and thesis not required. *Entrance requirements:* GRE or MAT, TOEFL. Application deadline: 2/15 (priority date; rolling processing). Application fee: $50. *Expenses:* Tuition $22,830 per year full-time, $713 per credit part-time. Fees $218 per year full-time, $40 per semester part-time. *Financial aid:* Application deadline 3/30. *Faculty research:* Therapeutic recreation, computer networking, professional ethics, environmental recreation. • Dr. Gerald Fain, Coordinator, 617-353-4478. E-mail: fain@bu.edu.

Bowling Green State University, College of Education and Allied Professions, School of Human Movement, Sport, and Leisure Studies, Bowling Green, OH 43403. Offers programs in development kinesiology (M Ed), recreation and leisure (M Ed), sport administration (M Ed). Part-time programs available. Faculty: 18 full-time (11 women), 1 (woman) part-time. Students: 36 full-time (22 women), 18 part-time (12 women); includes 5 minority (4 African Americans, 1 Hispanic), 3 international. 68 applicants, 60% accepted. In 1997, 29 degrees awarded. *Degree requirements:* Thesis or alternative required, foreign language not required. *Entrance requirements:* GRE General Test, TOEFL (minimum score 565), minimum GPA of 2.6. Application deadline: 4/1 (rolling processing). Application fee: $30. Electronic applications accepted. *Tuition:* $6070 per year full-time, $284 per credit hour part-time for state residents; $11,358 per year full-time, $536 per credit hour part-time for nonresidents. *Financial aid:* In 1997–98, 40 assistantships were awarded; Federal Work-Study and career-related internships or fieldwork also available. Financial aid application deadline: 2/15; applicants required to submit FAFSA. *Faculty research:* Teacher-learning process, travel and tourism, sport marketing and management, exercise physiology and sport psychology, life-span motor development. • Dr. Mary Ann Roberton, Director, 419-372-7234. Application contact: Dr. Janet Parks, Graduate Coordinator, 419-372-2878.

California State University, Long Beach, College of Health and Human Services, Department of Recreation and Leisure Studies, Long Beach, CA 90840-4903. Awards MS. Faculty: 4 full-time (2 women), 3 part-time (1 woman). Students: 4 full-time (2 women), 9 part-time (5 women); includes 4 minority (2 African Americans, 2 Hispanics), 3 international. Average age 31. 9 applicants, 22% accepted. In 1997, 2 degrees awarded. *Degree requirements:* Comprehensive exam or thesis required, foreign language not required. *Entrance requirements:* GRE General Test. Application deadline: 8/1 (rolling processing; 12/1 for spring admission). Application fee: $55. *Expenses:* Tuition $0 for state residents; $246 per unit for nonresidents. Fees $1846 per year full-time, $1180 per year part-time. *Financial aid:* Application deadline 3/2. • Dr. Michael A. Blazey, Chair, 562-985-4071. E-mail: mblazey@csulb.edu. Application contact: Dr. Kathleen J. Halberg, Graduate Coordinator, 562-985-8075. Fax: 562-985-8154. E-mail: halbergk@csulb.edu.

California State University, Northridge, College of Health and Human Development, Department of Leisure Studies and Recreation, Northridge, CA 91330. Awards MS. Faculty: 9 full-time, 1 part-time. Students: 3 full-time (0 women), 13 part-time (5 women); includes 5 minority (1 African American, 2 Asian Americans, 1 Hispanic, 1 Native American), 1 international. Average age 34. 10 applicants, 90% accepted. *Degree requirements:* Thesis required (for some programs), foreign language not required. *Entrance requirements:* GRE, TOEFL. Application deadline: 11/30. Application fee: $55. *Expenses:* Tuition $0 for state residents; $246 per unit for nonresidents. Fees $1970 per year full-time, $1304 per year part-time. *Financial aid:* Application deadline 3/1. • Dr. Robert Winslow, Chair, 818-677-3202.

Central Michigan University, College of Education and Human Services, Department of Recreation, Parks, and Leisure Studies Administration, Mount Pleasant, MI 48859. Awards MA, MS, MSA. Faculty: 16 full-time (6 women). Students: 12 full-time (9 women), 7 part-time (4 women); includes 1 minority (African American), 1 international. Average age 29. In 1997, 6 degrees awarded. *Degree requirements:* Thesis or alternative required, foreign language not required. *Application deadline:* 3/1 (priority date). *Application fee:* $30. *Expenses:* Tuition $139 per credit hour (minimum) for state residents; $276 per credit hour (minimum) for nonresidents. Fees $260 per year full-time, $150 per semester part-time. *Financial aid:* In 1997–98, 3 research assistantships (2 to first-year students) were awarded; fellowships, teaching assistantships, Federal Work-Study, and career-related internships or fieldwork also available. Financial aid application deadline: 3/7. *Faculty research:* Study of ethics in parks and recreation professionals in Michigan, computer touch-tone information services at visitor centers, creative play spaces for children. • Roger Coles, Chairperson, 517-774-3858. Fax: 517-774-4374. E-mail: 3443755@cmich.edu.

Dalhousie University, Faculty of Health Professions, School of Health and Human Performance, Division of Leisure Studies, Halifax, NS B3H 3J5, Canada. Awards MA. Part-time programs available. Faculty: 7 full-time (3 women). Students: 13 full-time (9 women), 6 part-time (5 women); includes 2 minority (1 African American, 1 Asian American). 20 applicants, 95% accepted. In 1997, 4 degrees awarded (25% entered university research/teaching, 75% found other work related to degree). *Degree requirements:* Thesis required, foreign language not required. *Average time to degree:* master's–4 years full-time. *Entrance requirements:* TOEFL (minimum score 580). Application deadline: 6/1 (rolling processing). Application fee: $55. *Financial aid:* 6 students received aid; research assistantships, teaching assistantships available. Financial aid application deadline: 3/1. *Faculty research:* Leisure and lifestyles of social groups, historical analysis of leisure, sport and leisure administration. • Dr. C. Putnam, Associate Director, School of Health and Human Performance, 902-494-1167. Fax: 902-494-5120. E-mail: putnam@ac.dal.ca.

Howard University, Graduate School of Arts and Sciences, Department of Physical Education, Recreation, and Health Education, 2400 Sixth Street, NW, Washington, DC 20059-0002. Offerings include recreation and leisure studies (MS). Department faculty: 8 full-time (4 women). *Degree requirements:* Thesis, comprehensive exam. *Average time to degree:* master's–2 years full-time, 3 years part-time. *Entrance requirements:* GRE General Test, minimum GPA of 3.0. Application deadline: 4/1 (11/1 for spring admission). Application fee: $45. *Expenses:* Tuition $10,200 per year full-time, $567 per credit hour part-time. Fees $405 per year. • Dr. Marshall Banks, Chair, 202-806-7142.

Indiana University Bloomington, School of Health, Physical Education and Recreation, Program in Recreation and Park Administration, Bloomington, IN 47405. Offerings include leisure behavior (PhD). PhD offered through the University Graduate School. Terminal master's awarded for partial completion of doctoral program. Program faculty: 14 full-time (6 women). *Application deadline:* rolling. *Application fee:* $35. *Expenses:* Tuition $153 per credit hour for state residents; $446 per credit hour for nonresidents. Fees $343 per year. • Dr. Joel Meier, Chairperson, 812-855-4711. Application contact: Program Office, 812-855-4711. Fax: 812-855-3998. E-mail: recpark@indiana.edu.

New York University, School of Education, Department of Health Studies, Program in Recreation and Leisure Studies, New York, NY 10012-1019. Awards MA, PhD, CAS. Part-time and evening/weekend programs available. Faculty: 3 full-time (2 women), 7 part-time. Students: 19 full-time, 29 part-time. 9 applicants, 67% accepted. In 1997, 1 master's, 1 doctorate awarded. Terminal master's awarded for partial completion of doctoral program. *Degree requirements:* For master's, thesis required (for some programs), foreign language not required; for doctorate, dissertation. *Entrance requirements:* For master's, TOEFL; for doctorate, GRE General Test, TOEFL, interview; for CAS, TOEFL, master's degree. Application deadline: 2/1 (priority date; rolling processing; 12/1 for spring admission). Application fee: $40 ($60 for international students). *Financial aid:* Partial tuition waivers, Federal Work-Study, institutionally sponsored loans available. Aid available to part-time students. Financial aid application deadline: 3/1; applicants required to submit FAFSA. *Faculty research:* Therapeutic recreation, child development and play, personnel management in recreation and leisure services. • Claudette B. Lefebvre, Director, 212-998-5600. Application contact: Office of Graduate Admissions, 212-998-5030. Fax: 212-995-4328.

Oklahoma State University, College of Education, School of Health, Physical Education, and Leisure, Stillwater, OK 74078. Offers programs in health (MS, Ed D), leisure sciences (MS, Ed D), physical education (MS, Ed D), physical education and leisure sciences (Ed D). Faculty: 13 full-time (5 women). Students: 29 full-time (17 women), 45 part-time (26 women); includes 6 minority (3 African Americans, 2 Hispanics, 1 Native American), 2 international. Average age 32. In 1997, 9 master's, 1 doctorate awarded. *Degree requirements:* For doctorate, dissertation. *Entrance requirements:* TOEFL (minimum score 550). Application deadline: 7/1 (priority date). Application fee: $25. *Financial aid:* In 1997–98, 10 students received aid, including 10 teaching assistantships (2 to first-year students) averaging $1,008 per month and totaling $90,750; partial tuition waivers, Federal Work-Study, and career-related internships or fieldwork also available. Aid available to part-time students. Financial aid application deadline: 3/1. • Dr. Lowell Caneday, Director, 405-744-5493.

Pennsylvania State University University Park Campus, College of Health and Human Development, School of Hotel, Restaurant, and Recreation Management, Program in Leisure Studies, University Park, PA 16802-1503. Awards M Ed, MS, PhD. Students: 29 full-time (16 women), 23 part-time (13 women). In 1997, 17 master's, 5 doctorates awarded. *Entrance requirements:* GRE General Test. Application fee: $40. *Expenses:* Tuition $6534 per year full-time, $276 per credit part-time for state residents; $13,460 per year full-time, $561 per credit part-time for nonresidents. Fees $252 per year (minimum) full-time, $43 per semester (minimum) part-time. • Dr. Alan R. Graefe, Professor in Charge, 814-863-8986.

See in-depth description on page 1317.

Radford University, Graduate College, College of Nursing and Health Services, Department of Leisure Services, Radford, VA 24142. Awards MS. Program being phased out; applicants no longer accepted. Part-time programs available. Postbaccalaureate distance learning degree programs offered (minimal on-campus study). Faculty: 5 full-time (1 woman). Students: 1 (woman) part-time. Average age 43. In 1997, 6 degrees awarded. *Degree requirements:* Thesis or alternative, comprehensive exam required, foreign language not required. *Expenses:* Tuition $2302 per year full-time, $147 per credit hour part-time for state residents; $5672 per year full-time, $287 per credit hour part-time for nonresidents. Fees $1222 per year full-time. *Financial aid:* Fellowships, scholarships/grants, Federal Work-Study, institutionally sponsored loans, and career-related internships or fieldwork available. Financial aid applicants required to submit FAFSA. • Dr. Gary C. Nussbaum, Chairperson, 540-831-5221. Fax: 540-831-6314. E-mail: gnussbau@runet.edu.

San Francisco State University, College of Health and Human Services, Department of Recreation and Leisure Studies, San Francisco, CA 94132-1722. Awards MS. Part-time programs available. *Entrance requirements:* Minimum GPA of 2.5 in last 60 units. Application deadline: 11/30 (priority date; rolling processing). Application fee: $55. *Expenses:* Tuition $0 for state residents; $246 per unit for nonresidents. Fees $1982 per year full-time, $1316 per year part-time. *Faculty research:* Leisure systems, leisure education, play theory and leadership, ethnic and cultural diversity, commercial recreation and tourism.

San Jose State University, College of Applied Arts and Sciences, Department of Recreation and Leisure Studies, San Jose, CA 95192-0001. Awards MS. Faculty: 3 full-time (0 women). Students: 6 full-time (all women), 10 part-time (8 women); includes 6 minority (2 Asian Americans, 3 Hispanics, 1 Native American), 1 international. Average age 30. 17 applicants, 71% accepted. In 1997, 1 degree awarded. *Application deadline:* 6/1 (rolling processing). *Application fee:* $59. *Expenses:* Tuition $0 for state residents; $246 per unit for nonresidents. Fees $2017 per year full-time, $1351 per year part-time. • Dr. Paul Brown, Chair, 408-924-3000.

Southern Connecticut State University, School of Professional Studies, Department of Recreation and Leisure Studies, New Haven, CT 06515-1355. Awards MS. Faculty: 2 full-time. Students: 2 full-time (0 women), 23 part-time (15 women); includes 4 minority (1 African American, 1 Asian American, 2 Hispanics). 41 applicants, 17% accepted. In 1997, 2 degrees awarded. *Entrance requirements:* Minimum undergraduate QPA of 3.0 in graduate major field or 2.5 overall; interview. Application deadline: 7/15 (priority date; rolling processing). Application fee: $40. *Expenses:* Tuition $2632 per year full-time, $188 per credit part-time for state residents; $7200 per year full-time, $188 per credit part-time for nonresidents. Fees $1806 per year full-time, $45 per semester part-time for state residents; $2703 per year full-time, $45 per semester part-time for nonresidents. *Financial aid:* In 1997–98, 1 teaching assistantship was awarded; career-related internships or fieldwork also available. • Dr. William Faraclas, Chairperson, 203-392-6950. Application contact: Dr. Bruce Shattuck, Graduate Coordinator, 203-392-6388.

State University of New York College at Brockport, School of Professions, Department of Recreation and Leisure Studies, Brockport, NY 14420-2997. Awards MS. Faculty: 3 full-time (2 women), 2 part-time (1 woman), 3.4 FTE. Students: 4 full-time (2 women), 5 part-time (4 women); includes 3 minority (1 African American, 1 Asian American, 1 Hispanic). Average age 31. 10 applicants, 70% accepted. In 1997, 1 degree awarded (100% found work related to degree). *Degree requirements:* Thesis optional, foreign language not required. *Average time to degree:* master's–2 years full-time, 3.5 years part-time. *Entrance requirements:* Minimum GPA of 3.0, sample of written work. Application deadline: rolling. Application fee: $50. *Expenses:* Tuition $5100 per year full-time, $213 per credit hour part-time for state residents; $8416 per year full-time, $351 per credit hour part-time for nonresidents. Fees $440 per year full-time, $22.60 per credit hour part-time. *Financial aid:* In 1997–98, 1 scholarship (to a first-year student) totaling $535 was awarded; Federal Work-Study and career-related internships or fieldwork also available. Aid available to part-time students. Financial aid application deadline: 4/1; applicants required to submit FAFSA. *Faculty research:* Leisure behavior, leisure service delivery systems, therapeutic recreation, international issues in recreation and leisure. • Dr. David L. Jewell, Chair, 716-395-2643. Fax: 716-395-5246.

Temple University, School of Tourism and Hospitality, Department of Sport Management and Leisure Studies, Program in Sport and Recreation Administration, Philadelphia, PA 19122-6096. Awards Ed M. Part-time and evening/weekend programs available. Students: 90 (40 women); includes 22 minority (21 African Americans, 1 Asian American), 3 international. 78 applicants, 63% accepted. In 1997, 39 degrees awarded. *Degree requirements:* Computer language required, foreign language and thesis not required. *Entrance requirements:* GRE General Test or MAT, minimum undergraduate GPA of 2.8. Application deadline: 6/1 (priority date; 10/1 for spring admission). Application fee: $40. *Expenses:* Tuition $323 per semester hour for state residents; $444 per semester hour for nonresidents. Fees $170 per year full-time, $28 per semester (minimum) part-time. *Financial aid:* Teaching assistantships available. • Application contact: Dr. Elizabeth Barber, Graduate Coordinator, 215-204-8706. Fax: 215-204-1455. E-mail: betsyb@astro.temple.edu.

See in-depth description on page 1903.

Université du Québec à Trois-Rivières, Program in Leisure Sciences, Trois-Rivières, PQ G9A 5H7, Canada. Awards MA. Part-time programs available. Students: 11 full-time (8 women), 1 (woman) part-time. 18 applicants, 94% accepted. *Degree requirements:* Thesis optional. *Entrance requirements:* Appropriate bachelor's degree, proficiency in French. Application deadline: 2/1. Application fee: $30. *Financial aid:* Fellowships, research assistantships, teaching assistantships available. • Michel Bellefleur, Director, 819-376-5132. Fax: 819-376-5092. E-mail: michel_bellefleur@uqtr.uquebec.ca. Application contact: Suzanne Camirand, Admissions Officer, 819-376-5045 Ext. 2591. Fax: 819-376-5210. E-mail: suzanne_camirand@uqtr.uquebec.ca.

University of Connecticut, School of Education, Field of Sport and Leisure Sciences, Division of Leisure Science, Storrs, CT 06269. Awards MA, PhD. Faculty: 1. Students: 4 part-time (2 women); includes 2 minority (1 African American, 1 Asian American). Average age 37. 2 applicants, 100% accepted. In 1997, 2 master's awarded. Terminal master's awarded for partial completion of doctoral program. *Degree requirements:* For master's, thesis or alternative; for doctorate, dissertation. *Entrance requirements:* For doctorate, GRE General Test. Application deadline: 3/15 (priority date; rolling processing; 12/1 for spring admission). Application fee: $40 ($45 for international students). *Expenses:* Tuition $5272 per year full-time, $293 per credit part-time for state residents; $13,696 per year full-time, $761 per credit part-time for nonresidents. Fees $948 per year full-time, $640 per year part-time. *Financial aid:* In 1997–98, 1 fellowship totaling $637, 1 research assistantship totaling $12,825 were awarded; teaching assistantships also available. Financial aid application deadline: 2/15. • William M. Servedio, Head, 860-486-3623.

University of Georgia, College of Education, School of Health and Human Performance, Department of Recreation and Leisure Studies, Athens, GA 30602. Awards MA, M Ed, Ed D. Faculty: 5 full-time (1 woman). Students: 20 full-time (11 women), 4 part-time (3 women); includes 2 minority (1 Asian American, 1 Native American), 6 international. 30 applicants, 40% accepted. In 1997, 8 master's, 1 doctorate awarded. *Degree requirements:* For master's, thesis (MA) required, foreign language not required; for doctorate, dissertation required, foreign language not required. *Entrance requirements:* For master's, GRE General Test or MAT; for doctorate, GRE General Test. Application deadline: 7/1 (priority date; 11/15 for spring admission). Application fee: $30. Electronic applications accepted. *Tuition:* $3290 per year full-time, $643 per semester (minimum) part-time for state residents; $11,300 per year full-time, $1645 per semester (minimum) part-time for nonresidents. *Financial aid:* Fellowships, research assistantships, teaching assistantships, assistantships available. • Dr. Diane M. Samdahl, Graduate Coordinator, 706-542-4334. Fax: 706-542-7917. E-mail: dsamdahl@coe.uga.edu.

University of Illinois at Urbana–Champaign, College of Applied Life Studies, Department of Leisure Studies, Urbana, IL 61801. Awards MS, PhD. Faculty: 13 full-time (3 women). Students: 51 full-time (23 women); includes 3 minority (2 African Americans, 1 Asian American), 10 international. 42 applicants, 52% accepted. In 1997, 10 master's, 6 doctorates awarded. *Degree requirements:* For doctorate, 2 foreign languages, dissertation. *Entrance requirements:* For master's, GRE General Test, minimum GPA of 4.0 on a 5.0 scale. Application deadline: rolling. Application fee: $40 ($50 for international students). *Financial aid:* In 1997–98, 22 research assistantships, 9 teaching assistantships were awarded; fellowships, full and partial tuition waivers also available. Financial aid application deadline: 2/15. • William R. McKinney, Head, 217-333-4410.

The University of Iowa, College of Liberal Arts, Department of Sport, Health, Leisure and Physical Studies, Iowa City, IA 52242-1316. Offerings include leisure studies (MA). Department faculty: 14 full-time. *Degree requirements:* Thesis optional. *Application deadline:* 4/15 (rolling processing). *Application fee:* $30 ($50 for international students). *Expenses:* Tuition $3166 per year full-time, $176 per semester hour part-time for state residents; $10,202 per year full-time, $176 per semester hour part-time for nonresidents. Fees $202 per year full-time, $52 per year (minimum) part-time. • Yvonne Slatton, Chair, 319-335-9335.

The University of Memphis, College of Education, Department of Human Movement Sciences and Education, Memphis, TN 38152. Offerings include sport and leisure commerce (MS). Department faculty: 16 full-time (4 women), 6 part-time (0 women). *Degree requirements:* Thesis, comprehensive exam required, foreign language not required. *Entrance requirements:* GRE General Test (minimum combined score of 750) or MAT (minimum score 33). Application deadline: 5/1 (priority date; rolling processing; 11/1 for spring admission). Application fee: $25 ($50 for international students). *Tuition:* $2862 per year full-time, $166 per credit hour part-time for state residents; $6696 per year full-time, $379 per credit hour part-time for nonresidents. • Dr. Ralph C. Wilcox, Chairman, 901-678-2324. Application contact: Dr. Mary D. Fry, Coordinator of Graduate Studies in Health, 901-678-4986.

University of Minnesota, Twin Cities Campus, College of Education and Human Development, School of Kinesiology and Leisure Studies, Division of Recreation, Park, and Leisure Studies, Minneapolis, MN 55455-0213. Awards MA, M Ed, PhD. Part-time programs available. Terminal master's awarded for partial completion of doctoral program. *Degree requirements:* For master's, thesis (for some programs), final oral exam; for doctorate, dissertation, preliminary written/oral exam, final oral exam. *Entrance requirements:* For master's, GRE or MAT, minimum GPA of 3.0; for doctorate, GRE or MAT, minimum GPA of 3.0, sample of written work. Application deadline: 7/15 (rolling processing; 12/15 for spring admission). Application fee: $30. *Financial aid:* Fellowships, research assistantships, teaching assistantships, full and partial tuition waivers, Federal Work-Study, institutionally sponsored loans, and career-related internships or fieldwork available. Aid available to part-time students. *Faculty research:* Therapeutic recreation, outdoor recreation, leisure services management. • Dr. Stuart J. Schleien, Head, 612-625-5300. Application contact: Pam Bridson, Senior Secretary, 612-625-5300. Fax: 612-626-7700. E-mail: brids001@maroon.tc.umn.edu.

University of Mississippi, Graduate School, School of Education, Department of Exercise Science and Leisure Management, University, MS 38677-9702. Offers programs in exercise science (MA, MS), exercise science and leisure management (PhD), leisure management (MA), wellness (MS). Faculty: 9 full-time (1 woman). Students: 29 full-time (12 women), 12 part-time (8 women); includes 7 minority (4 African Americans, 2 Hispanics, 1 Native American), 2 international. In 1997, 14 master's, 3 doctorates awarded. *Degree requirements:* For master's, thesis required (for some programs), foreign language not required; for doctorate, dissertation. *Entrance requirements:* For master's, GRE General Test, TOEFL, minimum GPA of 3.0; for doctorate, GRE General Test, TOEFL. Application deadline: 8/1 (rolling processing). Application fee: $0 ($25 for international students). *Financial aid:* Application deadline 3/1. • Dr. Eugene R. Anderson, Chairman, 601-232-5520.

University of Nevada, Las Vegas, William F. Harrah College of Hotel Administration, Department of Leisure Studies, Las Vegas, NV 89154-9900. Awards MS. Part-time programs available. Faculty: 3 full-time (2 women). Students: 19 full-time (11 women), 9 part-time (4 women); includes 2 international. 22 applicants, 77% accepted. In 1997, 1 degree awarded. *Degree requirements:* Comprehensive exam required, thesis optional, foreign language not required. *Entrance requirements:* GRE General Test, minimum GPA of 3.0 during previous 2 years, 2.75 overall. Application deadline: 6/15 (priority date; rolling processing; 11/15 for spring admission). Application fee: $40 ($95 for international students). *Expenses:* Tuition $93 per credit for state residents; $93 per credit full-time, $190 per credit part-time for nonresidents. Fees $5570 per year full-time for nonresidents. *Financial aid:* In 1997–98, 5 research assistantships were awarded; teaching assistantships also available. Financial aid application deadline: 3/1. • Cynthia Carruthers, Interim Chair, 702-895-1188.

See in-depth description on page 483.

The University of North Carolina at Chapel Hill, College of Arts and Sciences, Curriculum in Leisure Studies and Recreation Administration, Chapel Hill, NC 27599. Awards MSRA. Faculty: 4 full-time. Students: 17 full-time (11 women); includes 1 minority (African American), 1 international. 29 applicants, 62% accepted. In 1997, 8 degrees awarded. *Degree requirements:* Comprehensive exam required, foreign language not required. *Entrance requirements:* GRE General Test (minimum combined score of 1000), minimum GPA of 3.0. Application deadline: 1/1 (priority date; rolling processing). Application fee: $55. *Expenses:* Tuition $1428 per year full-time, $357 per semester (minimum) part-time for state residents; $10,414 per year full-time, $2604 per semester (minimum) part-time for nonresidents. Fees $782 per year full-time, $332 per semester (minimum) part-time. *Financial aid:* In 1997–98, 9 research assistantships, 2 teaching assistantships, 4 graduate assistantships were awarded; fellowships and career-related internships or fieldwork also available. Financial aid application deadline: 3/1. • Dr. Karla Henderson, Chairman, 919-962-0534.

University of Northern Iowa, College of Education, School of Health, Physical Education, and Leisure Services, Program in Leisure Services, Cedar Falls, IA 50614. Offers youth agency administration (MA). Students: 10 full-time (5 women), 11 part-time (8 women); includes 7 minority (4 African Americans, 3 Asian Americans), 2 international. Average age 33. 12 applicants, 92% accepted. In 1997, 8 degrees awarded. *Degree requirements:* Thesis or alternative required, foreign language not required. *Entrance requirements:* Minimum GPA of 3.5, 3 years of educational experience. Application fee: $20 ($30 for international students). *Expenses:* Tuition $3166 per year full-time, $176 per hour part-time for state residents; $7805 per year full-time, $176 per hour part-time for nonresidents. Fees $194 per year full-time, $12.50 per semester (minimum) part-time. *Financial aid:* Assistantships, full tuition waivers, Federal Work-Study, institutionally sponsored loans, and career-related internships or fieldwork available. Financial aid application deadline: 3/1. • Robert Long, Director, 319-273-2293.

University of North Texas, College of Education, Department of Kinesiology, Health Promotion, and Recreation, Program in Recreation and Leisure Studies, Denton, TX 76203-6737. Awards MS, Certificate. Part-time programs available. *Degree requirements:* For master's, thesis required (for some programs), foreign language not required. *Entrance requirements:* For master's, GRE General Test (minimum score 375 on each section; 800 combined). Application deadline: 7/17. Application fee: $25 ($50 for international students). *Tuition:* $2063 per year full-time, $815 per year part-time for state residents; $5897 per year full-time, $2100 per year part-time for nonresidents. *Financial aid:* Teaching assistantships, Federal Work-Study, institutionally sponsored loans, and career-related internships or fieldwork available. Financial aid application deadline: 4/1. • Application contact: Barbara Wilhite, Adviser, 940-565-2651.

University of South Alabama, College of Education, Department of Health, Physical Education and Leisure Services, Mobile, AL 36688-0002. Offers programs in exercise technology (MS), health education (M Ed), leisure services (MS), physical education (M Ed), therapeutic recreation (MS). Part-time programs available. Faculty: 10 full-time (2 women). Students: 28 full-time (17 women), 17 part-time (11 women); includes 7 minority (6 African Americans, 1 Hispanic), 2 international. 22 applicants, 91% accepted. In 1997, 17 degrees awarded. *Degree requirements:* Comprehensive exam required, foreign language and thesis not required. *Entrance requirements:* GRE General Test (minimum combined score of 1000) or MAT (minimum score 37). Application deadline: 9/1 (priority date; rolling processing). Application fee: $25. *Financial aid:* In 1997–98, 10 teaching assistantships were awarded; career-related internships or fieldwork also available. Aid available to part-time students. Financial aid application deadline: 4/1. • Dr. Frederick Scaffidi, Chairman, 334-460-7131.

University of Toledo, College of Education and Allied Professions, Department of Health Promotion and Human Performance, Toledo, OH 43606-3398. Offerings include recreation and leisure education (M Ed). Department faculty: 17 full-time (5 women). *Application deadline:* 8/1 (priority date; rolling processing). *Application fee:* $30. Electronic applications accepted. *Tuition:* $5907 per year full-time, $246 per hour part-time for state residents; $11,835 per year full-time, $493 per hour part-time for nonresidents. • Dr. Carol Plimpton, Chair, 419-530-2747. Fax: 419-530-4759. E-mail: cplimpt@utnet.utoledo.edu.

University of Utah, College of Health, Department of Recreation and Leisure, Salt Lake City, UT 84112-1107. Awards M Phil, MS, Ed D, PhD. Faculty: 8 full-time (3 women), 12 part-time (2 women). Students: 30 full-time (14 women), 13 part-time (7 women); includes 2 minority (1 African American, 1 Asian American), 3 international. Average age 32. In 1997, 11 master's, 1 doctorate awarded. *Degree requirements:* For master's, thesis or alternative, oral and written comprehensive exams required, foreign language not required; for doctorate, dissertation required, foreign language not required. *Entrance requirements:* For master's, TOEFL (minimum score 500), minimum GPA of 3.0; for doctorate, GRE or MAT, TOEFL (minimum score 500), minimum GPA of 3.2. Application deadline: 7/1. Application fee: $30 ($50 for international students). *Tuition:* $2045 per year full-time, $562 per semester (minimum) part-time for state residents; $6129 per year full-time, $1607 per semester (minimum) part-time for nonresidents. *Financial aid:* In 1997–98, 7 teaching assistantships were awarded; career-related internships or fieldwork also available. *Faculty research:* Commercial, therapeutic, community, and outdoor recreation; tourism. • Dr. Gary D. Ellis, Chair, 801-581-8547. Fax: 801-581-5580. Application contact: Dr. Cathryn Morris, Director of Graduate Studies, 801-581-8542.

University of Victoria, Faculty of Education, School of Physical Education, Victoria, BC V8W 2Y2, Canada. Offerings include leisure service administration (MA). School faculty: 14 full-time (5 women), 5 part-time (0 women). *Average time to degree:* master's–2.9 years full-time. *Application deadline:* 4/30 (rolling processing). *Application fee:* $50. *Tuition:* $2080 per year full-time, $557 per semester part-time. • Dr. D. Docherty, Director, 250-721-8375. E-mail: docherty@uvic.ca. Application contact: Gladys Whittal, Graduate Secretary, 250-721-8373. Fax: 250-721-6601. E-mail: gwhittal@uvic.ca/.

University of Waterloo, Faculty of Applied Health Sciences, Department of Recreation and Leisure Studies, Waterloo, ON N2L 3G1, Canada. Awards MA, PhD. Part-time programs available. Faculty: 13 full-time (4 women), 2 part-time (1 woman). Students: 27 full-time (21 women), 2 part-time (both women). 31 applicants, 29% accepted. In 1997, 3 master's, 1 doctorate awarded. *Degree requirements:* Computer language, thesis/dissertation. *Entrance requirements:* For master's, TOEFL (minimum score 600), honors degree, minimum B average; for doctorate, GRE, TOEFL (minimum score 600), master's degree. Application deadline: 1/15. Application fee: $50. *Tuition:* $3220 per year. *Financial aid:* In 1997–98, 4 research assistantships (3 to first-year students), 16 teaching assistantships (8 to first-year students) were awarded; scholarships, Federal Work-Study, and career-related internships or fieldwork also available. *Faculty research:* Tourism, leisure behavior, special populations, leisure service management, outdoor resources. • Dr. R. Johnson, Chair, 519-888-4567 Ext. 2519. E-mail: johnson@healthy.uwaterloo.ca. Application contact: Dr. S. Shaw, Associate Chair of Graduate Studies, 519-888-4567 Ext. 5019. Fax: 519-746-6776. E-mail: sshaw@healthy.uwaterloo.ca.

University of West Florida, College of Arts and Social Sciences, Department of Health, Leisure, and Sports, Pensacola, FL 32514-5750. Offers programs in health (MS); health, leisure, and sports (MS); physical education (MS). Part-time and evening/weekend programs available. Students: 23 full-time (17 women), 31 part-time (25 women); includes 7 minority (5 African Americans, 1 Asian American, 1 Native American), 1 international. Average age 35. 25 applicants, 100% accepted. In 1997, 20 degrees awarded. *Degree requirements:* Thesis or alternative. *Entrance requirements:* GRE General Test (minimum combined score of 1000), minimum GPA of 3.0. Application deadline: 7/1 (rolling processing; 11/1 for spring admission). Application fee: $20. *Tuition:* $131 per credit hour (minimum) for state residents; $436 per

Directories: Leisure Studies; Recreation and Park Management

University of West Florida (continued)
credit hour (minimum) for nonresidents. *Financial aid:* Teaching assistantships available. • Dr. C. B. Williamson, Chairperson, 850-474-2592.

Washington State University, College of Education, Department of Kinesiology and Leisure Studies, Pullman, WA 99164-1610. Offers programs in kinesiology (M Ed, MS), recreation and leisure studies (M Ed, MS). Faculty: 10 full-time (3 women). Students: 11 full-time (6 women), 1 part-time (0 women); includes 1 international. In 1997, 2 degrees awarded. *Degree requirements:* Oral exam required, foreign language not required. *Average time to degree:* master's–1.5 years full-time. *Entrance requirements:* GRE General Test, minimum GPA of 3.0. Application deadline: 3/1 (priority date; rolling processing). Application fee: $35. *Tuition:* $5334 per year full-time, $267 per credit hour part-time for state residents; $13,380 per year full-time, $677 per credit hour part-time for nonresidents. *Financial aid:* Research assistantships, teaching assistantships, teaching associateships, partial tuition waivers, Federal Work-Study, institutionally sponsored loans, and career-related internships or fieldwork available. Financial aid application deadline: 4/1; applicants required to submit FAFSA. *Total annual research expenditures:* $93,361. • Dr. Edward Udd, Chair, 509-335-4593.

Recreation and Park Management

Adams State College, School of Education and Graduate Studies, Department of Health, Physical Education, and Recreation, Alamosa, CO 81102. Awards MA. Part-time programs available. In 1997, 11 degrees awarded. *Degree requirements:* Comprehensive exam required, foreign language and thesis not required. *Entrance requirements:* GRE General Test or MAT, minimum undergraduate GPA of 2.75. Application deadline: 5/15 (priority date; rolling processing; 10/15 for spring admission). Application fee: $25. *Tuition:* $2164 per year full-time, $111 per credit part-time for state residents; $7284 per year full-time, $377 per credit part-time for nonresidents. *Financial aid:* In 1997–98, 8 coaching assistantships (6 to first-year students) averaging $500 per month and totaling $32,000 were awarded; Federal Work-Study, institutionally sponsored loans, and career-related internships or fieldwork also available. Aid available to part-time students. Financial aid application deadline: 4/15; applicants required to submit FAFSA. • Dr. Jeff Geiser, Head, 719-587-7402.

Arizona State University, College of Public Programs, Department of Recreation Management and Tourism, Tempe, AZ 85287. Offers program in recreation (MS). Faculty: 12 full-time (5 women). Students: 24 full-time (18 women), 16 part-time (11 women); includes 4 minority (1 African American, 1 Asian American, 1 Hispanic, 1 Native American), 5 international. Average age 30. 31 applicants, 81% accepted. In 1997, 11 degrees awarded. *Degree requirements:* Thesis or alternative. *Application fee:* $45. *Expenses:* Tuition $2088 per year full-time, $110 per hour part-time for state residents; $9040 per year full-time, $377 per hour part-time for nonresidents. Fees $72 per year full-time, $18 per semester (minimum) part-time. *Faculty research:* International travel, philosophy of leisure, recreation resource policy, sociology of play, urban recreation administration. • Dr. Carlton Yoshioka, Chair, 602-965-7291.

Aurora University, George Williams College, School of Recreation Administration, Aurora, IL 60506-4892. Offerings include outdoor therapeutic recreation administration (MS), therapeutic recreation administration (MS). School faculty: 4 full-time (3 women), 3 part-time (2 women). *Degree requirements:* Thesis optional, foreign language not required. *Entrance requirements:* Minimum GPA of 2.75. Application deadline: 9/1 (priority date; rolling processing). Application fee: $25. *Tuition:* $408 per semester hour. • Dr. Rita Yerkes, Dean, 630-844-5406. Application contact: Office of Admissions, 630-844-5533. Fax: 630-844-5463.

Baker College Center for Graduate Studies, Programs in Business, Flint, MI 48507. Offerings include health and recreation services management (MBA). MBA (health and recreation services management) enrollment limited to international students. Faculty: 8 full-time, 73 part-time. *Application deadline:* rolling. *Application fee:* $25. *Tuition:* $215 per quarter hour. • Dr. Michael Heberling, President, 800-469-3165. Application contact: Chuck Gurden, Director of Admissions, 800-469-3165. Fax: 810-766-4399.

Baylor University, School of Education, Department of Health, Human Performance and Recreation, Waco, TX 76798. Awards MS Ed. Part-time programs available. Faculty: 13 full-time (5 women), 3 part-time (1 woman). Students: 34 full-time (17 women), 18 part-time (6 women); includes 2 minority (1 African American, 1 Asian American), 2 international. 30 applicants, 87% accepted. In 1997, 20 degrees awarded. *Degree requirements:* Thesis optional, foreign language not required. *Average time to degree:* master's–2 years full-time, 2.5 years part-time. *Entrance requirements:* GRE General Test. Application deadline: 4/1 (priority date; rolling processing; 10/1 for spring admission). Application fee: $25. Electronic applications accepted. *Expenses:* Tuition $7392 per year full-time, $308 per semester hour part-time. Fees $1024 per year. *Financial aid:* In 1997–98, 35 students received aid, including 22 teaching assistantships averaging $800 per month; recreation supplements, partial tuition waivers, Federal Work-Study, institutionally sponsored loans, and career-related internships or fieldwork also available. *Faculty research:* Behavior change theory, pedagogy, nutrition and enzyme therapy, exercise testing, health planning, ethics. • Dr. Nancy Goodloe, Director of Graduate Studies, 254-710-3505. E-mail: nancy_goodloe@baylor.edu.

Bowling Green State University, College of Education and Allied Professions, School of Human Movement, Sport, and Leisure Studies, Bowling Green, OH 43403. Offerings include recreation and leisure (M Ed). School faculty: 18 full-time (11 women), 1 (woman) part-time. *Degree requirements:* Thesis or alternative required, foreign language not required. *Entrance requirements:* GRE General Test, TOEFL (minimum score 565), minimum GPA of 2.6. Application deadline: 4/1 (rolling processing). Application fee: $30. Electronic applications accepted. *Tuition:* $6070 per year full-time, $284 per credit hour part-time for state residents; $11,358 per year full-time, $536 per credit hour part-time for nonresidents. • Dr. Mary Ann Roberton, Director, 419-372-7234. Application contact: Dr. Janet Parks, Graduate Coordinator, 419-372-2878.

Brigham Young University, College of Physical Education, Department of Recreation Management and Youth Leadership, Provo, UT 84602-1001. Awards MS. Faculty: 9 full-time (0 women). Students: 5 full-time (3 women), 7 part-time (4 women); includes 1 international. Average age 30. 0 applicants. In 1997, 13 degrees awarded. *Degree requirements:* Oral exam required, thesis optional, foreign language not required. *Average time to degree:* master's–2 years full-time, 4 years part-time. *Entrance requirements:* GRE General Test (minimum combined score of 1380 on three sections), minimum GPA of 3.0 in last 60 hours. Application deadline: 2/1 (rolling processing). Application fee: $30. *Tuition:* $3200 per year full-time, $178 per credit hour part-time for state residents; $4800 per year full-time, $266 per credit hour part-time for nonresidents. *Financial aid:* In 1997–98, 6 research assistantships, 2 administrative aides were awarded; fellowships, full and partial tuition waivers, institutionally sponsored loans, and career-related internships or fieldwork also available. Aid available to part-time students. Financial aid application deadline: 3/1. *Faculty research:* Decision-making and problem-solving among youth. • Dr. S. Harold Smith, Chair, 801-378-4369. Application contact: Dr. Joyce M. Harrison, Associate Dean, 801-378-4271. Fax: 801-378-6585. E-mail: harrisonj@byu.edu.

California State University, Chico, College of Communication and Education, Department of Recreation Parks Management, Chico, CA 95929-0722. Offers program in recreation administration (MA). Faculty: 15 full-time (2 women), 7 part-time (3 women). Students: 15 full-time (11 women), 8 part-time (5 women); includes 3 minority (2 Hispanics, 1 Native American). Average age 28. In 1997, 5 degrees awarded. *Degree requirements:* Thesis or alternative required, foreign language not required. *Entrance requirements:* GRE General Test. Application deadline: 4/1 (rolling processing). Application fee: $55. *Expenses:* Tuition $0 for state residents; $246 per unit for nonresidents. Fees $2108 per year full-time, $1442 per year part-time. *Financial aid:* Fellowships, stipends, and career-related internships or fieldwork available. • Dr. James E. Fletcher, Chair, 530-898-6408. Application contact: Dr. David Simcox, Graduate Coordinator, 530-898-4052.

California State University, Long Beach, College of Health and Human Services, Department of Recreation and Leisure Studies, Long Beach, CA 90840-4903. Awards MS. Faculty: 4 full-time (2 women), 3 part-time (1 woman). Students: 4 full-time (2 women), 9 part-time (5 women); includes 4 minority (2 African Americans, 2 Hispanics), 3 international. Average age 31. 9 applicants, 22% accepted. In 1997, 2 degrees awarded. *Degree requirements:* Comprehensive exam or thesis required, foreign language not required. *Entrance requirements:* GRE General Test. Application deadline: 8/1 (rolling processing; 12/1 for spring admission). Application fee: $55. *Expenses:* Tuition $0 for state residents; $246 per unit for nonresidents. Fees $1846 per year full-time, $1180 per year part-time. *Financial aid:* Application deadline 3/2. • Dr. Michael A. Blazey, Chair, 562-985-4071. E-mail: mblazey@csulb.edu. Application contact: Dr. Kathleen J. Halberg, Graduate Coordinator, 562-985-8075. Fax: 562-985-8154. E-mail: halbergk@csulb.edu.

California State University, Northridge, College of Health and Human Development, Department of Leisure Studies and Recreation, Northridge, CA 91330. Awards MS. Faculty: 9 full-time, 1 part-time. Students: 3 full-time (0 women), 13 part-time (5 women); includes 5 minority (1 African American, 2 Asian Americans, 1 Hispanic, 1 Native American), 1 international. Average age 34. 10 applicants, 90% accepted. *Degree requirements:* Thesis required (for some programs), foreign language not required. *Entrance requirements:* GRE, TOEFL. Application deadline: 11/30. Application fee: $55. *Expenses:* Tuition $0 for state residents; $246 per unit for nonresidents. Fees $1970 per year full-time, $1304 per year part-time. *Financial aid:* Application deadline 3/1. • Dr. Robert Winslow, Chair, 818-677-3202.

California State University, Sacramento, School of Health and Human Services, Department of Recreation and Leisure Studies, Sacramento, CA 95819-6048. Offers program in recreation administration (MS). Part-time programs available. *Degree requirements:* Thesis or alternative, writing proficiency exam. *Entrance requirements:* TOEFL (minimum score 550). Application deadline: 4/15 (11/1 for spring admission). Application fee: $55. *Expenses:* Tuition $0 for state residents; $246 per unit for nonresidents. Fees $2012 per year full-time, $1346 per year part-time. *Financial aid:* Research assistantships, teaching assistantships, Federal Work-Study, and career-related internships or fieldwork available. Aid available to part-time students. Financial aid application deadline: 3/1. • Dr. Steven Walker, Chairman, 916-278-6752. Application contact: Dr. Eddie Cajucom, Coordinator, 916-278-6429.

Central Michigan University, College of Education and Human Services, Department of Recreation, Parks, and Leisure Studies Administration, Mount Pleasant, MI 48859. Awards MA, MS, MSA. Faculty: 16 full-time (6 women). Students: 12 full-time (9 women), 7 part-time (4 women); includes 1 minority (African American), 1 international. Average age 29. In 1997, 6 degrees awarded. *Degree requirements:* Thesis or alternative required, foreign language not required. *Application deadline:* 3/1 (priority date). *Application fee:* $30. *Expenses:* Tuition $139 per credit hour (minimum) for state residents; $276 per credit hour (minimum) for nonresidents. Fees $260 per year full-time, $150 per semester part-time. *Financial aid:* In 1997–98, 3 research assistantships (2 to first-year students) were awarded; fellowships, teaching assistantships, Federal Work-Study, and career-related internships or fieldwork also available. Financial aid application deadline: 3/7. *Faculty research:* Study of ethics in parks and recreation professionals in Michigan, computer touch-tone information services at visitor centers, creative play spaces for children. • Roger Coles, Chairperson, 517-774-3858. Fax: 517-774-4374. E-mail: 3443755@cmich.edu.

Central Washington University, College of Education and Professional Studies, Department of Physical Education, Health Education and Leisure Services, Ellensburg, WA 98926. Offers program in health, physical education and recreation (MS). Part-time programs available. Faculty: 16 full-time (5 women). Students: 12 full-time (9 women), 4 part-time (2 women); includes 1 minority (Hispanic). 24 applicants, 50% accepted. In 1997, 7 degrees awarded. *Degree requirements:* Thesis or alternative required, foreign language not required. *Entrance requirements:* Minimum GPA of 3.0. Application deadline: 4/1 (priority date; rolling processing; 1/1 for spring admission). Application fee: $35. *Expenses:* Tuition $4200 per year full-time, $140 per credit hour part-time for state residents; $12,780 per year full-time, $426 per credit hour part-time for nonresidents. Fees $240 per year. *Financial aid:* In 1997–98, 10 teaching assistantships (7 to first-year students) averaging $1,108 per month and totaling $99,720 were awarded; research assistantships, Federal Work-Study also available. Financial aid application deadline: 2/15. • Dr. John Gregor, Chairman, 509-963-1911. Application contact: Christie A. Fevergeon, Program Coordinator, Graduate Studies and Research, 509-963-3103. Fax: 509-963-1799. E-mail: masters@cwu.edu.

Clemson University, College of Health, Education, and Human Development, Department of Parks, Recreation, and Tourism Management, Clemson, SC 29634. Awards MPRTM, MS, PhD. Part-time programs available. Students: 33 full-time (17 women), 25 part-time (16 women); includes 3 minority (1 African American, 2 Hispanics), 10 international. Average age 25. 49 applicants, 49% accepted. In 1997, 5 master's, 4 doctorates awarded. *Degree requirements:* For master's, thesis required (for some programs), foreign language not required; for doctorate, dissertation required, foreign language not required. *Entrance requirements:* For master's, GRE General Test, TOEFL, minimum undergraduate GPA of 3.0; for doctorate, GRE General Test, TOEFL, minimum graduate GPA of 3.0. Application deadline: 5/1 (priority date; 10/1 for spring admission). Application fee: $35. *Expenses:* Tuition $3154 per year full-time, $130 per credit hour part-time for state residents; $6452 per year full-time, $264 per credit hour part-time for nonresidents. Fees $190 per year. *Financial aid:* Fellowships, research assistantships, teaching assistantships, assistantships, partial tuition waivers, and career-related internships or fieldwork available. Financial aid application deadline: 4/15. *Faculty research:* Recreation resource management, leisure behavior, therapeutic recreation, community leisure services. • Dr. Ann James, Chair, 864-656-3400. E-mail: ajms@clemson.edu. Application contact: Dr. Fran McGuire, Graduate Coordinator, 864-656-2183. Fax: 864-656-2226. E-mail: lefty@clemson.edu.

Cleveland State University, College of Education, Department of Health, Physical Education, Recreation and Dance, Cleveland, OH 44115-2440. Offers programs in community health (M Ed), exercise science (M Ed), health education (M Ed), human performance (M Ed), pedagogy (M Ed), recreation (M Ed), sport education (M Ed), sport management (M Ed), sport management/exercise science (M Ed). Part-time programs available. Faculty: 11 full-time (6 women). Students: 7 full-time (4 women), 10 part-time (3 women); includes 2 minority (both African Americans). Average age 26. 18 applicants, 61% accepted. In 1997, 31 degrees awarded. *Degree requirements:* Thesis optional, foreign language not required. *Entrance requirements:* GRE General Test or MAT (score in 50th percentile or higher), minimum undergraduate GPA of 2.75. Application deadline: 9/1 (priority date; rolling processing). Application fee: $25. *Expenses:* Tuition $5252 per year full-time, $202 per credit hour part-time for state residents; $10,504 per year full-time, $404 per credit hour part-time for nonresidents. Fees $2.25 per credit hour (minimum). *Financial aid:* In 1997–98, 4 teaching assistantships were awarded; career-related internships or fieldwork also available. Financial aid application deadline: 3/31. *Faculty research:* Mental imagery in motor learning, biomechanical analysis of motor skill, improvement of speed in running, instructional design. • Dr. Vincent Melograno, Chairman, 216-687-4878. Fax: 216-687-5410. E-mail: v.melograno@popmail.csuohio.edu.

Colorado State University, College of Natural Resources, Department of Natural Resource Recreation and Tourism, Fort Collins, CO 80523-0015. Offers programs in commercial recreation and tourism (MS), human dimensions in natural resources (PhD), recreation resource management (MS, PhD), resource interpretation (MS). Faculty: 7 full-time (2 women). Students: 21 full-time (11 women), 24 part-time (11 women); includes 3 minority (2 Asian Americans, 1 Hispanic), 2 international. Average age 35. 68 applicants, 21% accepted. In 1997, 10 master's, 3 doctorates awarded. *Degree requirements:* For master's, thesis or alternative required, foreign language not required; for doctorate, dissertation. *Entrance requirements:* For master's, GRE General Test (minimum combined score of 1000), TOEFL (minimum score 550), minimum GPA of 3.0; for doctorate, GRE General Test (minimum combined score of 1000), TOEFL, minimum GPA of 3.0. Application deadline: 2/1 (priority date; rolling processing). Application fee: $30. Electronic applications accepted. *Expenses:* Tuition $2632 per year full-time, $109 per credit hour part-time for state residents; $10,216 per year full-time, $425 per credit hour part-time for nonresidents. Fees $708 per year full-time, $32 per semester (minimum) part-time. *Financial aid:* In 1997–98, 2 research assistantships (1 to a first-year student) averaging $921 per month, 4 teaching assistantships (2 to first-year students) averaging $921 per month, 1 traineeship were awarded; fellowships, Federal Work-Study, and career-related internships or fieldwork also available. Aid available to part-time students. Financial aid application deadline: 2/1; applicants required to submit FAFSA. *Faculty research:* International tourism, wilderness preservation, resource interpretation, human dimensions in natural resources, protected areas management. Total annual research expenditures: $600,000. • Michael J. Manfredo, Interim Chair, 970-491-6591. Application contact: Maureen Donnelly, Graduate Program Administrator, 970-491-2023. Fax: 970-491-2255. E-mail: maureend@cnr.colostate.edu.

Delta State University, School of Education, Division of Health, Physical Education and Recreation, Cleveland, MS 38733-0001. Offers program in physical education and recreation (M Ed). Part-time and evening/weekend programs available. Faculty: 4 full-time (0 women), 2 part-time (0 women), 5 FTE. Students: 27 full-time (5 women), 3 part-time (0 women); includes 7 minority (all African Americans). Average age 27. 15 applicants, 100% accepted. In 1997, 7 degrees awarded. *Degree requirements:* Thesis optional, foreign language not required. *Entrance requirements:* GRE General Test (minimum combined score of 800) or MAT (minimum score 34), Class A teaching certificate. Application deadline: 8/1 (priority date; rolling processing). Application fee: $0. *Tuition:* $2596 per year full-time, $121 per semester hour part-time for state residents; $5546 per year full-time, $285 per semester hour part-time for nonresidents. *Financial aid:* Research assistantships, Federal Work-Study, institutionally sponsored loans, and career-related internships or fieldwork available. Aid available to part-time students. Financial aid application deadline: 6/1. *Faculty research:* Blood pressure, body fat, power and reaction time, learning disorders for athletes, effects of walking. • Dr. Milton R. Wilder Jr., Chairperson, 601-846-4555. E-mail: mwilder@dsu.deltast.edu. Application contact: Dr. John Thornell, Dean of Graduate Studies and Continuing Education, 601-846-4310. Fax: 601-846-4016.

Eastern Kentucky University, College of Health, Physical Education, Recreation and Athletics, Department of Recreation and Park Administration, Richmond, KY 40475-3101. Awards MS. Part-time programs available. Students: 5. In 1997, 4 degrees awarded. *Entrance requirements:* GRE General Test, minimum GPA of 2.5. Application fee: $0. *Tuition:* $2390 per year full-time, $133 per credit hour part-time for state residents; $6630 per year full-time, $365 per credit hour part-time for nonresidents. *Financial aid:* Research assistantships, teaching assistantships, Federal Work-Study available. Aid available to part-time students. • Dr. Larry Belknap, Chair, 606-622-1833.

Florida Agricultural and Mechanical University, Division of Graduate Studies, Research, and Continuing Education, College of Education, Department of Health, Physical Education, and Recreation, Tallahassee, FL 32307-3200. Awards M Ed, MS Ed. Part-time and evening/weekend programs available. Students: 12 (3 women); includes 10 minority (all African Americans). Average age 23. In 1997, 5 degrees awarded. *Degree requirements:* Thesis optional, foreign language not required. *Entrance requirements:* GRE General Test (minimum combined score of 1000), minimum GPA of 3.0. Application deadline: 5/13. Application fee: $20. *Expenses:* Tuition $140 per credit hour for state residents; $484 per credit hour for nonresidents. Fees $130 per year. *Financial aid:* Teaching assistantships, Federal Work-Study, institutionally sponsored loans available. *Faculty research:* Administration/curriculum, work behavior, psychology. • Dr. Barbara Thompson, Chairperson, 850-599-3135.

Florida International University, College of Education, Department of Health, Physical Education, and Recreation, Program in Parks and Recreation Administration, Miami, FL 33199. Awards MS. Part-time and evening/weekend programs available. Students: 5 full-time (all women), 5 part-time (3 women); includes 6 minority (2 African Americans, 4 Hispanics). Average age 29. 3 applicants, 67% accepted. In 1997, 4 degrees awarded. *Degree requirements:* Thesis optional, foreign language not required. *Entrance requirements:* GRE General Test (minimum combined score of 1000) or minimum GPA of 3.0 in last 60 credits of baccalaureate. Application deadline: 4/1 (priority date; rolling processing; 10/1 for spring admission). Application fee: $20. *Expenses:* Tuition $138 per credit hour for state residents; $482 per credit hour for nonresidents. Fees $46 per semester. *Financial aid:* Research assistantships available. • Dr. Robert Wolff, Chairperson, Department of Health, Physical Education, and Recreation, 305-348-3486. Fax: 305-348-3571. E-mail: wolffr@fiu.edu.

Florida State University, College of Education, Department of Human Services and Studies, Program in Recreation and Leisure Services Administration, Tallahassee, FL 32306. Awards MS. Part-time programs available. Faculty: 5 full-time (4 women), 1 (woman) part-time. Students: 10 full-time (7 women); includes 3 minority (1 African American, 2 Hispanics). 10 applicants, 100% accepted. In 1997, 5 degrees awarded. *Degree requirements:* Comprehensive exam required, thesis optional. *Entrance requirements:* GRE General Test (minimum combined score of 1000), minimum GPA of 3.0. Application deadline: 7/1 (priority date; rolling processing; 11/1 for spring admission). Application fee: $20. *Tuition:* $139 per credit hour for state residents; $482 per credit hour for nonresidents. *Financial aid:* Fellowships, research assistantships, teaching assistantships, and career-related internships or fieldwork available. • Dr. Cheryl Beeler, Chair, Department of Human Services and Studies, 850-644-3854. E-mail: beeler@mail.coe.fsu.edu. Application contact: Admissions Secretary, 850-644-3854. Fax: 850-644-4335.

Fort Hays State University, College of Health and Life Sciences, Department of Health and Human Performance, Hays, KS 67601-4099. Offers program in health, physical education, and recreation (MS). Part-time programs available. Faculty: 4 full-time (0 women). Students: 22 full-time (7 women), 17 part-time (6 women); includes 1 minority (Hispanic). Average age 29. 17 applicants, 82% accepted. In 1997, 20 degrees awarded. *Entrance requirements:* GRE General Test or MAT. Application deadline: 7/1 (priority date; rolling processing). Application fee: $25 ($35 for international students). *Tuition:* $94 per credit hour for state residents; $249 per credit hour for nonresidents. *Financial aid:* Research assistantships, teaching assistantships available. *Faculty research:* Isoproterenol hydrochloride and exercise, dehydrogenase and high-density lipoprotein levels in athletics, venous blood parameters to adipose fat. • Dr. Don Fuertges, Chairman, 785-628-4352.

Frostburg State University, School of Education, Program in Parks and Recreational Management, Frostburg, MD 21532-1099. Awards MS.

Georgia Southern University, College of Health and Professional Studies, Department of Recreation and Sport Management, Program in Recreation Administration, Statesboro, GA 30460-8126. Awards MS. Students: 12 full-time (8 women); includes 3 minority (2 African Americans, 1 Hispanic), 1 international. 10 applicants, 60% accepted. In 1997, 4 degrees awarded. *Entrance requirements:* GMAT, GRE General Test (minimum score 450 on each section), or MAT (minimum score 44), minimum GPA of 2.5 (MRA), minimum GPA of 2.75, interview (MS). Application deadline: 7/15 (priority date; rolling processing; 11/15 for spring admission). Application fee: $0. Electronic applications accepted. *Tuition:* $2619 per year full-time, $287 per semester (minimum) part-time for state residents; $8619 per year full-time, $1037 per semester (minimum) part-time for nonresidents. *Financial aid:* Application deadline 4/15. • Application contact: Dr. John R. Diebolt, Associate Graduate Dean, 912-681-5384. Fax: 912-681-0740. E-mail: gradschool@gsvms2.cc.gasou.edu.

Hardin–Simmons University, Irvin School of Education, Department of Physical Education, Program in Sports and Recreation Management, Abilene, TX 79698-0001. Awards M Ed. Part-time programs available. Faculty: 3 full-time (0 women). Students: 23 part-time (7 women); includes 3 minority (1 African American, 2 Hispanics). Average age 28. In 1997, 3 degrees awarded. *Degree requirements:* Internship, project required, thesis optional, foreign language not required. *Application deadline:* 8/15 (priority date; rolling processing; 1/5 for spring admission). *Application fee:* $25. *Expenses:* Tuition $280 per semester hour. Fees $630 per year full-time. *Financial aid:* In 1997–98, 5 fellowships (2 to first-year students) averaging $250 per month and totaling $4,500, 8 recreation assistantships (6 to first-year students) averaging $380 per month and totaling $28,000 were awarded; full and partial tuition waivers, Federal Work-Study, and career-related internships or fieldwork also available. Aid available to part-time students. Financial aid application deadline: 3/15; applicants required to submit FAFSA. *Faculty research:* Sports psychology, coaching education, sport sociology, corporate fitness, recreation programming. • Dr. Warren Simpson, Director, 915-670-1220. Fax: 915-670-1572. Application contact: Dr. J. Paul Sorrels, Dean of Graduate Studies, 915-670-1298. Fax: 915-670-1564.

Howard University, Graduate School of Arts and Sciences, Department of Physical Education, Recreation, and Health Education, 2400 Sixth Street, NW, Washington, DC 20059-0002. Offers programs in exercise physiology (MS), recreation and leisure studies (MS), school and community health education (MS). Part-time programs available. Faculty: 8 full-time (4 women). Students: 19 full-time (10 women); includes 19 minority (all African Americans). In 1997, 3 degrees awarded. *Degree requirements:* Thesis, comprehensive exam. *Average time to degree:* master's–2 years full-time, 3 years part-time. *Entrance requirements:* GRE General Test, minimum GPA of 3.0. Application deadline: 4/1 (11/1 for spring admission). Application fee: $45. *Expenses:* Tuition $10,200 per year full-time, $567 per credit hour part-time. Fees $405 per year. *Financial aid:* Research assistantships, teaching assistantships, grants, institutionally sponsored loans, and career-related internships or fieldwork available. Financial aid application deadline: 4/1. *Faculty research:* Women's health, work and health, AIDS, men's health, hypertension, sports nutrition, social science, urban recreation, therapeutic recreation, commercial recreation. • Dr. Marshall Banks, Chair, 202-806-7142.

Indiana University Bloomington, School of Health, Physical Education and Recreation, Program in Recreation and Park Administration, Bloomington, IN 47405. Offers administration (MS), leisure behavior (PhD), outdoor recreation resources (MS), recreation (Re D, Re Dir), recreational sports administration (MS), therapeutic recreation (MS). PhD offered through the University Graduate School. Faculty: 14 full-time (6 women). Students: 35 full-time (17 women), 26 part-time (9 women); includes 8 minority (2 African Americans, 1 Asian American, 4 Hispanics, 1 Native American), 8 international. In 1997, 38 master's awarded. Terminal master's awarded for partial completion of doctoral program. *Degree requirements:* For master's, computer language required, foreign language and thesis not required; for doctorate, computer language, dissertation required, foreign language not required; for Re Dir, computer language required, thesis optional, foreign language not required. *Entrance requirements:* For master's, GRE or minimum GPA of 2.8; for doctorate and Re Dir, GRE. Application deadline: rolling. Application fee: $35. *Expenses:* Tuition $153 per credit hour for state residents; $446 per credit hour for nonresidents. Fees $343 per year. *Financial aid:* Fellowships, teaching assistantships, fee scholarships, fee remissions, partial tuition waivers, Federal Work-Study, institutionally sponsored loans, and career-related internships or fieldwork available. Financial aid application deadline: 3/1. *Faculty research:* Leisure counseling, gerontology, special populations, planning and development. • Dr. Joel Meier, Chairperson, 812-855-4711. Application contact: Program Office, 812-855-4711. Fax: 812-855-3998. E-mail: recpark@indiana.edu.

Lehman College of the City University of New York, Division of Natural and Social Sciences, Department of Health Services, Program in Recreation, 250 Bedford Park Boulevard West, Bronx, NY 10468-1589. Offers recreation education (MA, MS Ed). Part-time and evening/weekend programs available. Faculty: 2 full-time (both women), 6 part-time (2 women). Students: 51 part-time (35 women). Average age 28. *Degree requirements:* Thesis or alternative, comprehensive exam. *Entrance requirements:* Minimum GPA of 2.7. Application deadline: 4/1 (priority date; rolling processing; 11/1 for spring admission). Application fee: $40. *Expenses:* Tuition $4350 per year full-time, $185 per credit part-time for state residents; $7600 per year full-time, $320 per credit part-time for nonresidents. Fees $120 per year full-time, $80 per year part-time. *Financial aid:* Partial tuition waivers, Federal Work-Study, and career-related internships or fieldwork available. Aid available to part-time students. Financial aid application deadline: 5/15; applicants required to submit FAFSA. *Faculty research:* Therapeutic recreation philosophy, curriculum, current approaches to treatment, impact of societal trends, ethical issues. • Robin Kunstler, Adviser, 718-960-8775.

Michigan State University, College of Agriculture and Natural Resources, Department of Park, Recreation and Tourism Resources, East Lansing, MI 48824-1020. Offers program in park, recreation and tourism resources (MS, PhD). Part-time and evening/weekend programs available. Faculty: 11 (2 women). Students: 64 (27 women); includes 5 minority (2 African Americans, 2 Asian Americans, 1 Hispanic), 26 international. In 1997, 9 master's, 1 doctorate awarded. *Degree requirements:* For master's, thesis or alternative, final exam; for doctorate, dissertation, qualifying exam. *Entrance requirements:* GRE General Test (minimum combined score of 1000; average 1100). Application deadline: 1/15 (priority date; rolling processing). Application fee: $30 ($40 for international students). *Expenses:* Tuition $4609 per year full-time, $223 per credit hour (minimum) part-time for state residents; $8704 per year full-time, $450 per credit hour (minimum) part-time for nonresidents. Fees $576 per year full-time, $476 per year part-time. *Financial aid:* In 1997–98, 25 students received aid, including 5 fellowships, 16 research assistantships, 4 teaching assistantships; Federal Work-Study also available. *Faculty research:* Tourism behavior and economics, economic inputs of recreation and tourism, park and recreation policy management, visitor management, input/output modeling. • Dr. Joseph D. Fridgen, Chairperson, 517-353-5190. Fax: 517-432-3597. E-mail: jfridgen@pilot.msu.edu.

Middle Tennessee State University, College of Education, Department of Health, Physical Education, Recreation and Safety, Murfreesboro, TN 37132. Awards MS, DA. Faculty: 17 full-time (6 women). Students: 50 full-time (28 women), 70 part-time (39 women); includes 21 minority (17 African Americans, 1 Asian American, 3 Hispanics), 1 international. Average age 30. 80 applicants, 66% accepted. In 1997, 31 master's, 1 doctorate awarded. *Degree requirements:* For master's, comprehensive exams required, foreign language and thesis not required; for doctorate, dissertation, comprehensive exams required, foreign language not required. *Entrance requirements:* For master's, Cooperative English Test, MAT; for doctorate, GRE or MAT. Application deadline: 8/1 (priority date). Application fee: $5. *Expenses:* Tuition $2560 per year full-time, $129 per semester hour part-time for state residents; $7386 per year full-time, $340 per semester hour part-time for nonresidents. Fees $486 per year full-time, $17 per semester (minimum) part-time. *Financial aid:* Teaching assistantships, institutionally sponsored loans, and career-related internships or fieldwork available. Aid available to part-time students. Financial aid application deadline: 5/1; applicants required to submit FAFSA. • Dr. Martha Whaley, Chair, 615-898-2811. Fax: 615-898-5020. E-mail: mwhaley@mtsu.edu.

Directory: Recreation and Park Management

Morehead State University, College of Education and Behavioral Sciences, Department of Health, Physical Education and Recreation, Morehead, KY 40351. Offers programs in health, physical education and recreation (MA, Ed D); sports administration (MS). MS offered jointly with Eastern Kentucky University. Part-time and evening/weekend programs available. Faculty: 9 full-time (4 women), 6 part-time (3 women). Students: 15 full-time (7 women), 4 part-time (1 woman); includes 1 minority (African American), 1 international. Average age 25. 14 applicants, 100% accepted. In 1997, 17 master's awarded. *Degree requirements:* For master's, oral exam, written core exam required, thesis optional, foreign language not required. *Entrance requirements:* For master's, GRE General Test (minimum combined score of 1000), minimum GPA of 2.5; major/minor in health, physical education, or recreation. Application deadline: 8/1 (priority date; rolling processing; 12/1 for spring admission). Application fee: $0. *Tuition:* $2470 per year full-time, $138 per semester hour part-time for state residents; $6710 per year full-time, $373 per semester hour part-time for nonresidents. *Financial aid:* In 1997–98, 2 teaching assistantships (1 to a first-year student) averaging $471 per month and totaling $8,000 were awarded; research assistantships, Federal Work-Study also available. Financial aid application deadline: 4/1; applicants required to submit FAFSA. *Faculty research:* Child growth and performance, instructional strategies, outdoor leadership qualities, exercise science, athletic training. • Dr. Jack Sheltmire, Chair, 606-783-2180. Fax: 606-783-5058. E-mail: j.sheltmire@morehead-st.edu. Application contact: Betty Cowsert, Graduate Admissions Officer, 606-783-2039. Fax: 606-783-5061.

New York University, School of Education, Department of Health Studies, Program in Recreation and Leisure Studies, New York, NY 10012-1019. Awards MA, PhD, CAS. Part-time and evening/weekend programs available. Faculty: 3 full-time (2 women), 7 part-time. Students: 19 full-time, 29 part-time. 9 applicants, 67% accepted. In 1997, 1 master's, 1 doctorate awarded. Terminal master's awarded for partial completion of doctoral program. *Degree requirements:* For master's, thesis required (for some programs), foreign language not required; for doctorate, dissertation. *Entrance requirements:* For master's, TOEFL; for doctorate, GRE General Test, TOEFL, interview; for CAS, TOEFL, master's degree. Application deadline: 2/1 (priority date; rolling processing; 12/1 for spring admission). Application fee: $40 ($60 for international students). *Financial aid:* Partial tuition waivers, Federal Work-Study, institutionally sponsored loans available. Aid available to part-time students. Financial aid application deadline: 3/1; applicants required to submit FAFSA. *Faculty research:* Therapeutic recreation, child development and play, personnel management in recreation and leisure services. • Claudette B. Lefebvre, Director, 212-998-5600. Application contact: Office of Graduate Admissions, 212-998-5030. Fax: 212-995-4328.

North Carolina Central University, Division of Academic Affairs, College of Arts and Sciences, Department of Physical Education and Recreation, Durham, NC 27707-3129. Offers programs in general physical education (MS), recreation administration (MS), special physical education (MS), therapeutic recreation (MS). Part-time and evening/weekend programs available. Faculty: 18 full-time (9 women), 2 part-time (0 women). Students: 10 full-time (7 women), 26 part-time (13 women); includes 30 minority (all African Americans). Average age 30. 10 applicants, 90% accepted. In 1997, 3 degrees awarded. *Degree requirements:* 1 foreign language (computer language can substitute), thesis, comprehensive exam. *Entrance requirements:* Minimum GPA of 3.0 in major, 2.5 overall. Application deadline: 8/1. Application fee: $30. *Tuition:* $2027 per year full-time, $508 per semester (minimum) part-time for state residents; $9155 per year full-time, $2290 per semester (minimum) part-time for nonresidents. *Financial aid:* Federal Work-Study, institutionally sponsored loans, and career-related internships or fieldwork available. Aid available to part-time students. Financial aid application deadline: 5/1. *Faculty research:* Physical activity patterns of children with disabilities, physical fitness test of North Carolina school children, exercise physiology, motor learning/development. • Dr. Virginia Politino, Chairperson, 919-560-6186. Application contact: Dr. Bernice D. Johnson, Interim Dean, College of Arts and Sciences, 919-560-6368.

North Carolina State University, College of Forest Resources, Department of Parks, Recreation and Tourism Management, Raleigh, NC 27695. Offers programs in geographic information systems (MS), maintenance management (MRRA, MS), recreation planning (MRRA, MS), recreation resources administration/public administration (MRRA), recreation/park management (MRRA, MS), sports management (MRRA, MS), travel and tourism management (MS). Faculty: 15 full-time (5 women), 7 part-time (0 women). Students: 29 full-time (15 women), 33 part-time (15 women); includes 6 minority (3 African Americans, 2 Asian Americans, 1 Hispanic), 2 international. Average age 29. 42 applicants, 45% accepted. In 1997, 23 degrees awarded. *Degree requirements:* Thesis required (for some programs), foreign language not required. *Entrance requirements:* GRE General Test, TOEFL (minimum score 550). Application deadline: 6/25 (11/25 for spring admission). Application fee: $45. *Tuition:* $2370 per year full-time, $517 per semester (minimum) part-time for state residents; $11,536 per year full-time, $2809 per semester (minimum) part-time for nonresidents. *Financial aid:* In 1997–98, 21 research assistantships (3 to first-year students) averaging $654 per month and totaling $61,815, 6 teaching assistantships totaling $18,099 were awarded; fellowships, institutionally sponsored loans, and career-related internships or fieldwork also available. Financial aid application deadline: 4/1. *Faculty research:* Park and recreation management, tourism policy and development, spatial information systems, natural resource recreation management, recreational sports management. Total annual research expenditures: $740,100. • Dr. Philip S. Rea, Head, 919-515-3675. E-mail: phil_rea@ncsu.edu. Application contact: Dr. Beth E. Wilson, Director of Graduate Programs, 919-515-3665. Fax: 919-515-3687. E-mail: beth_wilson@ncsu.edu.

The Ohio State University, College of Education, School of Physical Activity and Educational Services, Program in Health, Physical Education, and Recreation, Columbus, OH 43210. Awards MA, M Ed, PhD. Part-time programs available. Faculty: 44. Students: 114 full-time (56 women), 38 part-time (26 women); includes 27 minority (18 African Americans, 6 Asian Americans, 2 Hispanics, 1 Native American), 20 international. 241 applicants, 34% accepted. In 1997, 46 master's, 11 doctorates awarded. *Degree requirements:* For master's, thesis optional, foreign language not required; for doctorate, dissertation required, foreign language not required. *Entrance requirements:* GRE. Application deadline: 8/15 (rolling processing). Application fee: $30 ($40 for international students). *Tuition:* $5472 per year full-time, $554 per quarter (minimum) part-time for state residents; $14,172 per year full-time, $1424 per quarter (minimum) part-time for nonresidents. *Financial aid:* Fellowships, research assistantships, teaching assistantships, administrative assistantships, Federal Work-Study, institutionally sponsored loans available. Aid available to part-time students. • Dr. W. Michael Sherman, Director, School of Physical Activity and Educational Services, 614-292-5679. Fax: 614-688-4613. E-mail: sherman.4@osu.edu.

Old Dominion University, Darden College of Education, Department of Exercise Science, Physical Education, and Recreation, Norfolk, VA 23529. Offerings include physical education (MS Ed), with options in administration, athletic training, curriculum and instruction, exercise science and wellness, recreation administration, sports management. Department faculty: 8 full-time (3 women), 4 part-time (2 women), 9.3 FTE. *Degree requirements:* Comprehensive exams, internship, research project required, foreign language and thesis not required. *Entrance requirements:* GRE General Test (minimum combined score of 900), minimum GPA of 2.5. Application deadline: 7/1 (rolling processing; 11/1 for spring admission). Application fee: $30. *Expenses:* Tuition $180 per credit hour for state residents; $477 per credit hour for nonresidents. Fees $140 per year full-time, $32 per semester part-time. • Dr. Patrick Tow, Chair, 757-683-3351. E-mail: ptow@odu.edu. Application contact: Dr. Elizabeth Dowling, Graduate Program Director, 757-683-4514. Fax: 757-683-4270. E-mail: ldowling@odu.edu.

San Francisco State University, College of Health and Human Services, Department of Recreation and Leisure Studies, San Francisco, CA 94132-1722. Awards MS. Part-time programs available. *Entrance requirements:* Minimum GPA of 2.5 in last 60 units. Application deadline: 11/30 (priority date; rolling processing). Application fee: $55. *Expenses:* Tuition $0 for state residents; $246 per unit for nonresidents. Fees $1982 per year full-time, $1316 per year part-time. *Faculty research:* Leisure systems, leisure education, play theory and leadership, ethnic and cultural diversity, commercial recreation and tourism.

San Jose State University, College of Applied Arts and Sciences, Department of Recreation and Leisure Studies, San Jose, CA 95192-0001. Awards MS. Faculty: 3 full-time (0 women). Students: 6 full-time (all women), 10 part-time (8 women); includes 6 minority (2 Asian Americans, 3 Hispanics, 1 Native American), 1 international. Average age 30. 17 applicants, 71% accepted. In 1997, 1 degree awarded. *Application deadline:* 6/1 (rolling processing). *Application fee:* $59. *Expenses:* Tuition $0 for state residents; $246 per unit for nonresidents. Fees $2017 per year full-time, $1351 per year part-time. • Dr. Paul Brown, Chair, 408-924-3000.

Slippery Rock University of Pennsylvania, College of Human Service Professions, Department of Parks, Recreation, and Environmental Education, Slippery Rock, PA 16057. Offerings include recreation programming (MS), therapeutic recreation (MS). *Application deadline:* 7/1 (priority date; rolling processing; 11/1 for spring admission). *Application fee:* $25. *Tuition:* $4484 per year full-time, $247 per credit part-time for state residents; $7667 per year full-time, $423 per credit part-time for nonresidents.

South Dakota State University, College of Arts and Science, Department of Health, Physical Education and Recreation, Brookings, SD 57007. Awards MS. Faculty: 3 full-time (1 woman). Students: 13 full-time (5 women), 12 part-time (2 women); includes 1 minority (African American). 19 applicants, 100% accepted. In 1997, 9 degrees awarded. *Degree requirements:* Thesis, oral and written exams required, foreign language not required. *Average time to degree:* master's–2 years full-time, 4 years part-time. *Entrance requirements:* GRE, TOEFL (minimum score 525). Application deadline: 10/15 (priority date; rolling processing; 3/15 for spring admission). Application fee: $15. *Expenses:* Tuition $82 per credit hour for state residents; $242 per credit hour for nonresidents. Fees $37 per credit hour. *Financial aid:* In 1997–98, 7 teaching assistantships (6 to first-year students), 1 administrative assistantship (to a first-year student) were awarded; Federal Work-Study and career-related internships or fieldwork also available. *Faculty research:* Reaction time in the elderly wellness center facilities and programming, effective teaching behaviors in physical education, assessment of human fitness. • Dr. Patty Hacker, Acting Head, 605-688-5625. Fax: 605-688-5999.

Southern Connecticut State University, School of Professional Studies, Department of Recreation and Leisure Studies, New Haven, CT 06515-1355. Awards MS. Faculty: 2 full-time. Students: 2 full-time (0 women), 23 part-time (15 women); includes 4 minority (1 African American, 1 Asian American, 2 Hispanics). 41 applicants, 17% accepted. In 1997, 2 degrees awarded. *Entrance requirements:* Minimum undergraduate QPA of 3.0 in graduate major field or 2.5 overall; interview. Application deadline: 7/15 (priority date; rolling processing). Application fee: $40. *Expenses:* Tuition $2632 per year full-time, $188 per credit part-time for state residents; $7200 per year full-time, $188 per credit part-time for nonresidents. Fees $1806 per year full-time, $45 per semester part-time for state residents; $2703 per year full-time, $45 per semester part-time for nonresidents. *Financial aid:* In 1997–98, 1 teaching assistantship was awarded; career-related internships or fieldwork also available. • Dr. William Faraclas, Chairperson, 203-392-6950. Application contact: Dr. Bruce Shattuck, Graduate Coordinator, 203-392-6388.

Southern Illinois University at Carbondale, College of Education, Department of Health Education and Recreation, Program in Recreation, Carbondale, IL 62901-6806. Awards MS Ed. Part-time programs available. Faculty: 6 full-time (3 women), 1 (woman) part-time. Students: 25 full-time (15 women); includes 3 minority (2 African Americans, 1 Hispanic), 3 international. Average age 26. 17 applicants, 88% accepted. In 1997, 19 degrees awarded. *Degree requirements:* Thesis required, foreign language not required. *Entrance requirements:* TOEFL (minimum score 550), minimum GPA of 2.7. Application deadline: rolling. Application fee: $20. *Expenses:* Tuition $2964 per year full-time, $99 per semester hour part-time for state residents; $8892 per year full-time, $270 per semester hour part-time for nonresidents. Fees $1034 per year full-time, $298 per semester (minimum) part-time. *Financial aid:* In 1997–98, 4 research assistantships (3 to first-year students) averaging $922 per month, 4 teaching assistantships (3 to first-year students) were awarded; fellowships, full tuition waivers, Federal Work-Study, institutionally sponsored loans, and career-related internships or fieldwork also available. Aid available to part-time students. Financial aid application deadline: 2/1. *Faculty research:* Leisure across the life span, outdoor recreation, recreation therapy, leisure service administration. • Dr. Regina Glover, Chair, Department of Health Education and Recreation, 618-453-2777. E-mail: rbglover@siu.edu. Application contact: Phyllis McCowen, Administrative Assistant, 618-453-2582. Fax: 618-453-1829. E-mail: mccowen@siu.edu.

Southern Illinois University at Edwardsville, School of Education, Department of Health, Recreation, and Physical Education, Edwardsville, IL 62026-0001. Awards MS Ed. Part-time programs available. Students: 37 full-time (12 women), 19 part-time (7 women); includes 4 minority (2 African Americans, 1 Asian American, 1 Hispanic), 4 international. 35 applicants, 80% accepted. In 1997, 10 degrees awarded. *Degree requirements:* Thesis or alternative, final exam required, foreign language not required. *Application deadline:* 7/24. *Application fee:* $25. *Expenses:* Tuition $1716 per year full-time, $95 per credit hour part-time for state residents; $5149 per year full-time, $286 per credit hour part-time for nonresidents. Fees $463 per year full-time, $433 per year part-time. *Financial aid:* In 1997–98, 6 teaching assistantships, 13 assistantships were awarded; fellowships, research assistantships, Federal Work-Study, institutionally sponsored loans also available. Aid available to part-time students. • Dr. John Baker, Chairperson, 618-692-3028. Application contact: Kay Covington, Graduate Program Director, 618-692-3226.

Southern University and Agricultural and Mechanical College, College of Education, Program in Leisure and Recreation Studies, Baton Rouge, LA 70813. Offers therapeutic recreation (MS). Faculty: 2 full-time (both women). Students: 11 full-time (8 women), 27 part-time (17 women); includes 23 minority (all African Americans). Average age 27. 18 applicants, 72% accepted. In 1997, 24 degrees awarded. *Degree requirements:* Thesis optional. *Entrance requirements:* GMAT or GRE General Test, TOEFL. Application deadline: 6/1 (priority date; rolling processing; 11/1 for spring admission). Application fee: $5. *Tuition:* $2226 per year full-time, $267 per semester (minimum) part-time for state residents; $6262 per year full-time, $267 per semester (minimum) part-time for nonresidents. *Financial aid:* Application deadline 4/15. • Dr. Patricia Melson, Chairman, 504-771-2951.

Southwestern Oklahoma State University, School of Education, Program in Health, Physical Education and Recreation, Weatherford, OK 73096-3098. Awards M Ed. M Ed distance learning degree program offered to Oklahoma residents only. Part-time programs available. Postbaccalaureate distance learning degree programs offered. Students: 3 full-time (2 women), 1 part-time (0 women); includes 2 minority (1 African American, 1 Asian American). 1 applicant, 100% accepted. In 1997, 1 degree awarded. *Degree requirements:* Exam required, foreign language and thesis not required. *Entrance requirements:* GRE General Test, TOEFL (minimum score 550), minimum GPA of 2.5. Application deadline: rolling. Application fee: $15. *Expenses:* Tuition $60 per credit hour (minimum) for state residents; $147 per credit hour (minimum) for nonresidents. Fees $109 per year full-time, $24 per semester (minimum) part-time. *Financial aid:* Research assistantships, teaching assistantships, partial tuition waivers, Federal Work-Study, institutionally sponsored loans, and career-related internships or fieldwork available. Aid available to part-time students. Financial aid application deadline: 3/1; applicants required to submit FAFSA. • Dr. Ken Rose, Chair, 580-774-3254.

Springfield College, Programs in Recreation and Leisure Services, Springfield, MA 01109-3797. Offerings in outdoor recreational management (M Ed, MS), recreational management (M Ed, MS), therapeutic recreational management (M Ed, MS). Part-time and evening/weekend programs available. Faculty: 5 full-time (1 woman), 4 part-time (all women), 6 FTE. Students: 23 full-time (14 women), 3 part-time (1 woman); includes 2 international. Average age 26. 25 applicants, 80% accepted. In 1997, 17 degrees awarded. *Degree requirements:* Comprehensive exam required, foreign language and thesis not required. *Entrance requirements:* Interview. Application deadline: (12/1 for spring admission). Application fee: $40. *Expenses:* Tuition $474 per credit. Fees $25 per year. *Financial aid:* In 1997–98, 2 teaching assistantships (both to first-year students) were awarded; fellowships, full and partial tuition waivers,

Federal Work-Study, and career-related internships or fieldwork also available. Financial aid application deadline: 3/1. • Dr. Donald R. Snyder, Director, 413-748-3269. Application contact: Donald J. Shaw Jr., Director of Graduate Admissions, 413-748-3225. Fax: 413-748-3694. E-mail: dshaw@spfldcol.edu.

State University of New York College at Brockport, School of Professions, Department of Recreation and Leisure Studies, Brockport, NY 14420-2997. Awards MS. Faculty: 3 full-time (2 women), 2 part-time (1 woman), 3.4 FTE. Students: 4 full-time (2 women), 5 part-time (4 women); includes 3 minority (1 African American, 1 Asian American, 1 Hispanic). Average age 31. 10 applicants, 70% accepted. In 1997, 1 degree awarded (100% found work related to degree). *Degree requirements:* Thesis optional, foreign language not required. *Average time to degree:* master's–2 years full-time, 3.5 years part-time. *Entrance requirements:* Minimum GPA of 3.0, sample of written work. Application deadline: rolling. Application fee: $50. *Expenses:* Tuition $5100 per year full-time, $213 per credit hour part-time for state residents; $8416 per year full-time, $351 per credit hour part-time for nonresidents. Fees $440 per year full-time, $22.60 per credit hour part-time. *Financial aid:* In 1997–98, 1 scholarship (to a first-year student) totaling $535 was awarded; Federal Work-Study and career-related internships or fieldwork also available. Aid available to part-time students. Financial aid application deadline: 4/1; applicants required to submit FAFSA. *Faculty research:* Leisure behavior, leisure service delivery systems, therapeutic recreation, international issues in recreation and leisure. • Dr. David L. Jewell, Chair, 716-395-2643. Fax: 716-395-5246.

State University of New York College at Cortland, Division of Professional Studies, Department of Recreation Education, Cortland, NY 13045. Awards MS, MS Ed. Part-time and evening/weekend programs available. In 1997, 17 degrees awarded. *Degree requirements:* Thesis (for some programs), comprehensive exam. *Application deadline:* rolling. *Application fee:* $50. *Expenses:* Tuition $5100 per year full-time, $213 per credit hour part-time for state residents; $8416 per year full-time, $351 per credit hour part-time for nonresidents. Fees $644 per year full-time, $79 per semester (minimum) part-time. • Dr. Anderson Young, Chair, 607-753-4941. Application contact: Jeanne M. Bechtel, Director of Admissions, 607-753-4711. Fax: 607-753-5998.

Temple University, School of Social Administration, Department of Health Studies, Program in Health Studies, Philadelphia, PA 19122-6096. Offerings include therapeutic recreation (Ed M). Program faculty: 11 full-time (8 women). *Application deadline:* 2/1 (10/15 for spring admission). *Application fee:* $40. *Expenses:* Tuition $323 per semester hour for state residents; $444 per semester hour for nonresidents. Fees $170 per year full-time, $28 per semester (minimum) part-time. • Application contact: Dr. Sheryl B. Ruzek, Graduate Coordinator, 215-204-5110. Fax: 215-204-1455.

See in-depth description on page 1517.

Temple University, School of Tourism and Hospitality, Department of Sport Management and Leisure Studies, Program in Sport and Recreation Administration, Philadelphia, PA 19122-6096. Awards Ed M. Part-time and evening/weekend programs available. Students: 90 (40 women); includes 22 minority (21 African Americans, 1 Asian American), 3 international. 78 applicants, 63% accepted. In 1997, 39 degrees awarded. *Degree requirements:* Computer language required, foreign language and thesis not required. *Entrance requirements:* GRE General Test or MAT, minimum undergraduate GPA of 2.8. Application deadline: 6/1 (priority date; 10/1 for spring admission). Application fee: $40. *Expenses:* Tuition $323 per semester hour for state residents; $444 per semester hour for nonresidents. Fees $170 per year full-time, $28 per semester (minimum) part-time. *Financial aid:* Teaching assistantships available. • Application contact: Dr. Elizabeth Barber, Graduate Coordinator, 215-204-8706. Fax: 215-204-1455. E-mail: betsyb@astro.temple.edu.

See in-depth description on page 1903.

Tennessee State University, College of Education, Department of Health, Physical Education and Recreation, Nashville, TN 37209-1561. Awards MA Ed. Part-time and evening/weekend programs available. Faculty: 6 full-time (2 women). Students: 5 full-time (1 woman), 3 part-time (1 woman); includes 8 minority (all African Americans). Average age 28. 15 applicants, 80% accepted. In 1997, 6 degrees awarded. *Degree requirements:* Thesis required, foreign language not required. *Average time to degree:* master's–1.5 years full-time, 2 years part-time. *Entrance requirements:* GRE General Test or MAT, minimum GPA of 2.5. Application deadline: rolling. Application fee: $15. *Tuition:* $2962 per year full-time, $182 per credit hour part-time for state residents; $7788 per year full-time, $393 per credit hour part-time for nonresidents. *Financial aid:* In 1997–98, 2 teaching assistantships (1 to a first-year student) averaging $550 per month and totaling $7,500 were awarded; fellowships also available. Aid available to part-time students. Financial aid application deadline: 5/1. *Faculty research:* Speed and strength, agility assessment, physical fitness testing, athletes' attitudes toward school. • Dr. Kim Freeland, Head, 615-963-7486. Fax: 615-963-5594. Application contact: Dr. Clinton M. Lipsey, Dean of the Graduate School, 615-963-5901. Fax: 615-963-5963. E-mail: clipsey@picard.tnstate.edu.

Texas A&M University, College of Agriculture and Life Sciences, Department of Recreation, Park and Tourism Sciences, College Station, TX 77843. Offers programs in natural resources development (M Agr), recreation and resources development (M Agr, MS, PhD). Faculty: 15 full-time (1 woman), 3 part-time (1 woman), 15.9 FTE. Students: 7 full-time (3 women), 7 part-time (0 women); includes 6 minority (1 African American, 2 Asian Americans, 3 Hispanics), 7 international. Average age 31. 32 applicants, 53% accepted. In 1997, 7 master's, 5 doctorates awarded. *Degree requirements:* Thesis/dissertation required, foreign language not required. *Entrance requirements:* GRE General Test (minimum score 400 on verbal section, 1100 combined), TOEFL (minimum score 550). Application deadline: 4/15 (priority date; rolling processing; 10/15 for spring admission). Application fee: $35 ($75 for international students). *Financial aid:* In 1997–98, 1 fellowship (to a first-year student), 14 research assistantships (1 to a first-year student), 13 teaching assistantships (5 to first-year students) were awarded; institutionally sponsored loans and career-related internships or fieldwork also available. Financial aid application deadline: 4/15. *Faculty research:* Administration and tourism, outdoor recreation, commercial recreation, environmental law, system planning. • Peter A. Witt, Head, 409-845-7324. E-mail: pwitt@rpts.tamu.edu. Application contact: Marguerite Van Dyke, Graduate Recruitment Coordinator, 409-845-5412. Fax: 409-845-0446. E-mail: mvandyke@rpts.tamu.edu.

University of Alberta, Faculty of Graduate Studies and Research, Faculty of Physical Education and Recreation, Edmonton, AB T6G 2E1, Canada. Offerings include recreation (MA, M Sc, PhD). *Degree requirements:* For master's, thesis (for some programs); for doctorate, dissertation. *Entrance requirements:* For master's, TOEFL (minimum score 550; average 580), bachelor's in related field; for doctorate, TOEFL (minimum score 550; average 580), master's degree in related field with thesis. Application deadline: 2/1 (priority date; rolling processing). Application fee: $60. *Expenses:* Tuition $390 per course for Canadian residents; $781 per course for nonresidents. Fees $500 per year full-time, $184 per year part-time. • Dr. H. A. Quinney, Dean, 403-492-3198. Application contact: Anne Jordan, Department Office, 403-492-3198. Fax: 403-492-2364. E-mail: ajordan@per.ualberta.ca.

University of Arkansas, College of Education, Department of Health Science, Kinesiology, Recreation and Dance, Program in Recreation, Fayetteville, AR 72701-1201. Awards M Ed. Students: 15 full-time (6 women), 4 part-time (3 women); includes 3 minority (2 African Americans, 1 Hispanic). 20 applicants, 85% accepted. In 1997, 3 degrees awarded. *Degree requirements:* Thesis optional, foreign language not required. *Application fee:* $25 ($35 for international students). *Tuition:* $3144 per year full-time, $173 per credit hour part-time for state residents; $7140 per year full-time, $395 per credit hour part-time for nonresidents. *Financial aid:* Research assistantships, teaching assistantships, Federal Work-Study, and career-related internships or fieldwork available. Aid available to part-time students. Financial aid application deadline: 4/1; applicants required to submit FAFSA. • Dr. Dean Gorman, Coordinator, 501-575-2890.

University of Florida, College of Health and Human Performance, Department of Recreation, Parks and Tourism, Gainesville, FL 32611. Offers programs in recreation (MSRS); recreation, parks and tourism (PhD). Faculty: 11. Students: 13 full-time (10 women), 8 part-time (7 women); includes 1 minority (Asian American). Average age 33. 12 applicants, 92% accepted. In 1997, 12 master's awarded. *Entrance requirements:* For master's, GRE General Test, minimum GPA of 3.0. Application deadline: 6/5 (priority date; rolling processing). Application fee: $20. *Tuition:* $138 per credit hour for state residents; $481 per credit hour for nonresidents. *Financial aid:* In 1997–98, 13 students received aid, including 3 fellowships averaging $542 per month, 4 research assistantships averaging $372 per month, 4 teaching assistantships averaging $624 per month, 2 graduate assistantships averaging $978 per month; Federal Work-Study and career-related internships or fieldwork also available. *Faculty research:* Recreation resource planning, commercial recreation, campus recreation, therapeutic recreation. • Stephen Anderson, Chair, 352-392-4042. Application contact: Dr. Anthony Fedler, Graduate Coordinator, 352-392-4048. Fax: 352-392-7588.

University of Georgia, College of Education, School of Health and Human Performance, Department of Recreation and Leisure Studies, Athens, GA 30602. Awards MA, M Ed, Ed D. Faculty: 5 full-time (1 woman). Students: 20 full-time (11 women), 4 part-time (3 women); includes 2 minority (1 Asian American, 1 Native American), 6 international. 30 applicants, 40% accepted. In 1997, 8 master's, 1 doctorate awarded. *Degree requirements:* For master's, thesis (MA) required, foreign language not required; for doctorate, dissertation required, foreign language not required. *Entrance requirements:* For master's, GRE General Test or MAT; for doctorate, GRE General Test. Application deadline: 7/1 (priority date; 11/15 for spring admission). Application fee: $30. Electronic applications accepted. *Tuition:* $3290 per year full-time, $643 per semester (minimum) part-time for state residents; $11,300 per year full-time, $1645 per semester (minimum) part-time for nonresidents. *Financial aid:* Fellowships, research assistantships, teaching assistantships, assistantships available. • Dr. Diane M. Samdahl, Graduate Coordinator, 706-542-4334. Fax: 706-542-7917. E-mail: dsamdahl@coe.uga.edu.

University of Idaho, College of Graduate Studies, College of Education, Division of Health, Physical Education, Recreation, and Dance, Programs in Recreation, Moscow, ID 83844-4140. Awards MS. Students: 8 full-time (2 women); includes 1 minority (African American). *Entrance requirements:* Minimum GPA of 2.8. Application deadline: 8/1 (12/15 for spring admission). Application fee: $35 ($45 for international students). *Expenses:* Tuition $0 for state residents; $6000 per year full-time, $95 per credit part-time for nonresidents. Fees $2676 per year full-time, $134 per credit part-time. *Financial aid:* Research assistantships available. Financial aid application deadline: 2/15. • Dr. Calvin Lathen, Director, Division of Health, Physical Education, Recreation, and Dance, 208-885-7921.

University of Manitoba, Faculty of Physical Education and Recreation Studies, Winnipeg, MB R3T 2N2, Canada. Awards M Sc.

University of Maryland, College Park, College of Health and Human Performance, Program in Recreation, College Park, MD 20742-5045. Awards MA, Ed D, PhD. Program being phased out; applicants no longer accepted. Students: 1 (woman) full-time, 4 part-time (1 woman); includes 2 minority (both African Americans). In 1997, 1 master's awarded. *Expenses:* Tuition $272 per credit hour for state residents; $400 per credit hour for nonresidents. Fees $564 per year full-time, $342 per year part-time. *Financial aid:* Fellowships, research assistantships, teaching assistantships, and career-related internships or fieldwork available. • Dr. John Burt, Dean, College of Health and Human Performance, 301-405-1362. Fax: 301-314-9167. Application contact: John Mollish, Director, Graduate Admissions and Records, 301-405-4198. Fax: 301-314-9305.

University of Minnesota, Twin Cities Campus, College of Education and Human Development, School of Kinesiology and Leisure Studies, Division of Recreation, Park, and Leisure Studies, Minneapolis, MN 55455-0213. Awards MA, M Ed, PhD. Part-time programs available. Terminal master's awarded for partial completion of doctoral program. *Degree requirements:* For master's, thesis (for some programs), final oral exam; for doctorate, dissertation, preliminary written/oral exam, final oral exam. *Entrance requirements:* For master's, GRE or MAT, minimum GPA of 3.0; for doctorate, GRE or MAT, minimum GPA of 3.0, sample of written work. Application deadline: 7/15 (rolling processing; 12/15 for spring admission). Application fee: $30. *Financial aid:* Fellowships, research assistantships, teaching assistantships, full and partial tuition waivers, Federal Work-Study, institutionally sponsored loans, and career-related internships or fieldwork available. Aid available to part-time students. *Faculty research:* Therapeutic recreation, outdoor recreation, leisure services management. • Dr. Stuart J. Schleien, Head, 612-625-5300. Application contact: Pam Bridson, Senior Secretary, 612-625-5300. Fax: 612-626-7700. E-mail: brids001@maroon.tc.umn.edu.

University of Missouri–Columbia, School of Natural Resources, Program in Parks, Recreation and Tourism, Columbia, MO 65211. Awards MS. Students: 9 full-time (3 women), 4 part-time (2 women); includes 5 international. In 1997, 9 degrees awarded. *Entrance requirements:* GRE General Test, minimum GPA of 3.0. Application deadline: 5/1 (priority date; rolling processing). Application fee: $25 ($50 for international students). *Expenses:* Tuition $3240 per year full-time, $180 per credit hour part-time for state residents; $9108 per year full-time, $506 per credit hour part-time for nonresidents. Fees $55 per year full-time. • Dr. Randy Vessell, Director of Graduate Studies, 573-882-9515.

The University of Montana–Missoula, School of Forestry, Program in Recreation Management, Missoula, MT 59812-0002. Awards MS. Students: 2 full-time (both women). Average age 25. 4 applicants, 25% accepted. *Degree requirements:* Thesis optional, foreign language not required. *Entrance requirements:* GRE General Test (minimum combined score of 1540 on three sections). Application deadline: 1/31. Application fee: $30. *Tuition:* $2499 per year (minimum) full-time, $376 per semester (minimum) part-time for state residents; $6528 per year (minimum) full-time, $1048 per semester (minimum) part-time for nonresidents. *Financial aid:* Research assistantships, teaching assistantships, Federal Work-Study available. Financial aid application deadline: 3/1. • Dr. Don Potts, Associate Dean, 406-243-5521.

University of Montevallo, College of Education, Department of Health, Physical Education, and Recreation, Montevallo, AL 35115. Awards M Ed, Ed S. Part-time and evening/weekend programs available. *Entrance requirements:* For master's, GRE General Test (minimum combined score of 850), MAT (minimum score 35), minimum undergraduate GPA of 2.75 in last 60 hours or 2.5 overall. Application deadline: 7/15 (11/15 for spring admission). Application fee: $10.

University of Nebraska at Omaha, College of Education, School of Health, Physical Education and Recreation, Omaha, NE 68182. Awards MA, MS. Part-time programs available. Faculty: 9 full-time (1 woman). Students: 28 full-time (14 women), 111 part-time (76 women); includes 5 minority (all African Americans), 6 international. Average age 34. 75 applicants, 81% accepted. In 1997, 27 degrees awarded. *Degree requirements:* Thesis (for some programs), comprehensive exam required, foreign language not required. *Entrance requirements:* Minimum GPA of 3.0. Application deadline: 7/1 (priority date; rolling processing; 12/1 for spring admission). Application fee: $35. *Expenses:* Tuition $1670 per year full-time, $94 per credit hour part-time for state residents; $4082 per year full-time, $227 per credit hour part-time for nonresidents. Fees $302 per year full-time, $108 per semester (minimum) part-time. *Financial aid:* In 1997–98, 67 students received aid, including 8 research assistantships; fellowships, full tuition waivers, Federal Work-Study, institutionally sponsored loans also available. Aid available to part-time students. Financial aid application deadline: 3/1; applicants required to submit FAFSA. • Dr. Dan Blanke, Director, 402-554-2670.

University of Nebraska–Lincoln, Teachers College, School of Health and Human Performance, Lincoln, NE 68588. Offerings include health, physical education, and recreation (M Ed, MPE). School faculty: 12 full-time (2 women). *Degree requirements:* Thesis required (for some programs), foreign language not required. *Entrance requirements:* GRE General Test or MAT,

Directory: Recreation and Park Management

University of Nebraska–Lincoln (continued)
TOEFL (minimum score 500). Application deadline: 3/1 (priority date; rolling processing). Application fee: $35. Electronic applications accepted. *Expenses:* Tuition $110 per credit hour for state residents; $270 per credit hour for nonresidents. Fees $480 per year full-time, $110 per semester part-time. • William Murphy, Chair, 402-472-3882. E-mail: wmurphy@unlinfo.unl.edu.

University of New Brunswick, Faculty of Physical Education and Recreation, Fredericton, NB E3B 5A3, Canada. Awards MPE. Part-time programs available. *Entrance requirements:* TOEFL, TWE. Application deadline: 3/1 (priority date; rolling processing). Application fee: $25.

University of New Mexico, College of Education, Program in Health, Physical Education and Recreation, Albuquerque, NM 87131-2039. Awards Ed D, PhD. Part-time programs available. Faculty: 15 full-time (7 women), 14 part-time (4 women), 18.55 FTE. Students: 56 full-time (30 women), 53 part-time (29 women); includes 23 minority (5 African Americans, 2 Asian Americans, 11 Hispanics, 5 Native Americans), 18 international. Average age 39. 33 applicants, 67% accepted. In 1997, 21 doctorates awarded. Terminal master's awarded for partial completion of doctoral program. *Degree requirements:* For doctorate, dissertation required, foreign language not required. *Application fee:* $25. *Expenses:* Tuition $2442 per year full-time, $103 per credit hour part-time for state residents; $8691 per year full-time, $103 per credit hour (minimum) part-time for nonresidents. Fees $32 per year. *Financial aid:* In 1997–98, 17 students received aid, including 3 research assistantships (1 to a first-year student) averaging $770 per month and totaling $23,100, 14 teaching assistantships (6 to first-year students) averaging $770 per month and totaling $107,800; fellowships, Federal Work-Study, institutionally sponsored loans, and career-related internships or fieldwork also available. Aid available to part-time students. *Faculty research:* Physical education pedagogy, sports psychology, sports administration, cardic rehabilitation, sports physiology, physical fitness assessment, exercise prescription. Total annual research expenditures: $17,132. • Dr. Mary Jo Campbell, Graduate Coordinator, 505-277-5151. Application contact: Sally Renfro, Division Administrator, 505-277-5151. Fax: 505-277-6227.

University of New Mexico, College of Education, Program in Parks and Recreation, Albuquerque, NM 87131-2039. Offers parks and recreation (MA), recreation (Ed S). Part-time programs available. Students: 11 full-time (4 women), 6 part-time (2 women); includes 7 minority (1 African American, 4 Hispanics, 2 Native Americans), 2 international. Average age 33. 5 applicants, 60% accepted. In 1997, 8 master's awarded. *Degree requirements:* For master's, comprehensive exam or thesis required, foreign language not required. *Application deadline:* 6/17 (11/17 for spring admission). *Application fee:* $25. *Expenses:* Tuition $2442 per year full-time, $103 per credit hour part-time for state residents; $8691 per year full-time, $103 per credit hour (minimum) part-time for nonresidents. Fees $32 per year. *Financial aid:* Federal Work-Study, institutionally sponsored loans, and career-related internships or fieldwork available. Aid available to part-time students. Financial aid application deadline: 4/17. *Faculty research:* Environemntal education, gerontology, international education. • Dr. Paul Miko, Graduate Adviser, 505-277-5151. E-mail: pmiko@unm.edu. Application contact: Sally Renfro, Division Administrator, 505-277-5151. Fax: 505-277-6227. E-mail: srenfro@unm.edu.

The University of North Carolina at Chapel Hill, College of Arts and Sciences, Curriculum in Leisure Studies and Recreation Administration, Chapel Hill, NC 27599. Awards MSRA. Faculty: 4 full-time. Students: 17 full-time (11 women); includes 1 minority (African American), 1 international. 29 applicants, 62% accepted. In 1997, 8 degrees awarded. *Degree requirements:* Comprehensive exam required, foreign language not required. *Entrance requirements:* GRE General Test (minimum combined score of 1000), minimum GPA of 3.0. Application deadline: 1/1 (priority date; rolling processing). Application fee: $55. *Expenses:* Tuition $1428 per year full-time, $357 per semester (minimum) part-time for state residents; $10,414 per year full-time, $2604 per semester (minimum) part-time for nonresidents. Fees $782 per year full-time, $332 per semester (minimum) part-time. *Financial aid:* In 1997–98, 9 research assistantships, 2 teaching assistantships, 4 graduate assistantships were awarded; fellowships and career-related internships or fieldwork also available. Financial aid application deadline: 3/1. • Dr. Karla Henderson, Chairman, 919-962-0534.

University of North Carolina at Greensboro, School of Health and Human Performance, Department of Recreation, Parks and Tourism, Greensboro, NC 27412-0001. Offers program in parks and recreation management (MS). Faculty: 6 full-time (3 women). Students: 5 full-time (all women), 3 part-time (0 women). 8 applicants, 63% accepted. *Degree requirements:* Thesis required, foreign language not required. *Entrance requirements:* GRE General Test. Application deadline: 7/1 (priority date; rolling processing; 11/1 for spring admission). Application fee: $35. *Expenses:* Tuition $1842 per year full-time, $370 per semester (minimum) part-time for state residents; $10,296 per year full-time, $2484 per semester (minimum) part-time for nonresidents. Fees $806 per year full-time, $111 per semester (minimum) part-time. *Financial aid:* In 1997–98, 5 research assistantships totaling $22,080 were awarded; fellowships, teaching assistantships also available. • Stuart Schleien, Head, 336-334-5327.

University of North Texas, College of Education, Department of Kinesiology, Health Promotion, and Recreation, Program in Recreation and Leisure Studies, Denton, TX 76203-6737. Awards MS, Certificate. Part-time programs available. *Degree requirements:* For master's, thesis required (for some programs), foreign language not required. *Entrance requirements:* For master's, GRE General Test (minimum score 375 on each section; 800 combined). Application deadline: 7/17. Application fee: $25 ($50 for international students). *Tuition:* $2063 per year full-time, $815 per year part-time for state residents; $5897 per year full-time, $2100 per year part-time for nonresidents. *Financial aid:* Teaching assistantships, Federal Work-Study, institutionally sponsored loans, and career-related internships or fieldwork available. Financial aid application deadline: 4/1. • Application contact: Barbara Wilhite, Adviser, 940-565-2651.

University of Rhode Island, College of Human Science and Services, Department of Physical Education, Health and Recreation, Kingston, RI 02881. Offers programs in health (MS), physical education (MS), recreation (MS). *Entrance requirements:* MAT or GRE. Application deadline: 4/15 (priority date; rolling processing; 11/15 for spring admission). Application fee: $35. *Expenses:* Tuition $3446 per year full-time, $191 per credit part-time for state residents; $9850 per year full-time, $547 per credit part-time for nonresidents. Fees $1276 per year full-time, $135 per semester (minimum) part-time.

University of South Alabama, College of Education, Department of Health, Physical Education and Leisure Services, Mobile, AL 36688-0002. Offerings include therapeutic recreation (MS). Department faculty: 10 full-time (2 women). *Application deadline:* 9/1 (priority date; rolling processing). *Application fee:* $25. • Dr. Frederick Scaffidi, Chairman, 334-460-7131.

University of Southern Mississippi, College of Health and Human Sciences, School of Human Performance and Recreation, Hattiesburg, MS 39406-5167. Offers programs in human performance (Ed D, PhD), physical education (MS), recreation (MS). Part-time programs available. Faculty: 18 full-time (3 women), 1 part-time (0 women). Students: 67 full-time (24 women), 26 part-time (13 women); includes 4 minority (2 African Americans, 2 Asian Americans), 2 international. Average age 29. 63 applicants, 79% accepted. In 1997, 36 master's, 3 doctorates awarded. *Degree requirements:* For master's, thesis optional, foreign language not required. *Entrance requirements:* For master's, GRE General Test, minimum GPA of 2.75; for doctorate, GRE General Test, minimum GPA of 2.75 in last 60 hours. Application deadline: 8/9 (priority date; rolling processing). Application fee: $0 ($25 for international students). *Tuition:* $2870 per year full-time, $137 per credit hour part-time for state residents; $5972 per year full-time, $172 per credit hour part-time for nonresidents. *Financial aid:* Fellowships, research assistantships, teaching assistantships, partial tuition waivers, Federal Work-Study, institutionally sponsored loans, and career-related internships or fieldwork available. Financial aid application deadline: 3/15. *Faculty research:* Exercise physiology, health behaviors, resource management, activity interaction, site development. • Dr. Sandra Gangstead, Director, 601-266-5386.

University of Tennessee, Knoxville, College of Human Ecology, Department of Consumer and Industry Services Management, Program in Recreation, Tourism, and Hospitality Management, Knoxville, TN 37996. Offers hospitality management (MS), recreation administration (MS), therapeutic recreation (MS), tourism (MS). Part-time programs available. Students: 11 full-time (6 women), 11 part-time (10 women); includes 1 minority (Asian American), 1 international. Average age 24. 13 applicants, 85% accepted. In 1997, 16 degrees awarded. *Degree requirements:* Thesis or alternative required, foreign language not required. *Entrance requirements:* TOEFL (minimum score 550), GRE General Test, minimum GPA of 2.7. Application deadline: 2/1 (priority date; rolling processing). Application fee: $35. Electronic applications accepted. *Tuition:* $3354 per year full-time, $181 per semester hour part-time for state residents; $8410 per year full-time, $462 per semester hour part-time for nonresidents. *Financial aid:* Career-related internships or fieldwork available. Financial aid application deadline: 2/1. • Dr. Nancy B. Fair, Head, Department of Consumer and Industry Services Management, 423-974-2141. Fax: 423-974-5236. E-mail: nbfair@utk.edu.

See in-depth description on page 1857.

University of Toledo, College of Education and Allied Professions, Department of Health Promotion and Human Performance, Toledo, OH 43606-3398. Offerings include recreation and leisure education (M Ed). Department faculty: 17 full-time (5 women). *Application deadline:* 8/1 (priority date; rolling processing). *Application fee:* $30. Electronic applications accepted. *Tuition:* $5907 per year full-time, $246 per hour part-time for state residents; $11,835 per year full-time, $493 per hour part-time for nonresidents. • Dr. Carol Plimpton, Chair, 419-530-2747. Fax: 419-530-4759. E-mail: cplimpt@utnet.utoledo.edu.

University of Utah, College of Health, Department of Recreation and Leisure, Salt Lake City, UT 84112-1107. Awards M Phil, MS, Ed D, PhD. Faculty: 8 full-time (3 women), 12 part-time (2 women). Students: 30 full-time (14 women), 13 part-time (7 women); includes 2 minority (1 African American, 1 Asian American), 3 international. Average age 32. In 1997, 11 master's, 1 doctorate awarded. *Degree requirements:* For master's, thesis or alternative, oral and written comprehensive exams required, foreign language not required; for doctorate, dissertation required, foreign language not required. *Entrance requirements:* For master's, TOEFL (minimum score 500), minimum GPA of 3.0; for doctorate, GRE or MAT, TOEFL (minimum score 500), minimum GPA of 3.2. Application deadline: 7/1. Application fee: $30 ($50 for international students). *Tuition:* $2045 per year full-time, $562 per semester (minimum) part-time for state residents; $6129 per year full-time, $1607 per semester (minimum) part-time for nonresidents. *Financial aid:* In 1997–98, 7 teaching assistantships were awarded; career-related internships or fieldwork also available. *Faculty research:* Commercial, therapeutic, community, and outdoor recreation; tourism. • Dr. Gary D. Ellis, Chair, 801-581-8547. Fax: 801-581-5580. Application contact: Dr. Cathryn Morris, Director of Graduate Studies, 801-581-8542.

University of Waterloo, Faculty of Applied Health Sciences, Department of Recreation and Leisure Studies, Waterloo, ON N2L 3G1, Canada. Awards MA, PhD. Part-time programs available. Faculty: 13 full-time (4 women), 2 part-time (1 woman). Students: 27 full-time (21 women), 2 part-time (both women). 31 applicants, 29% accepted. In 1997, 3 master's, 1 doctorate awarded. *Degree requirements:* Computer language, thesis/dissertation. *Entrance requirements:* For master's, TOEFL (minimum score 600), honors degree, minimum B average; for doctorate, GRE, TOEFL (minimum score 600), master's degree. Application deadline: 1/15. Application fee: $50. *Tuition:* $3220 per year. *Financial aid:* In 1997–98, 4 research assistantships (3 to first-year students), 16 teaching assistantships (8 to first-year students) were awarded; scholarships, Federal Work-Study, and career-related internships or fieldwork also available. *Faculty research:* Tourism, leisure behavior, special populations, leisure service management, outdoor resources. • Dr. R. Johnson, Chair, 519-888-4567 Ext. 2519. E-mail: johnson@healthy.uwaterloo.ca. Application contact: Dr. S. Shaw, Associate Chair of Graduate Studies, 519-888-4567 Ext. 5019. Fax: 519-746-6776. E-mail: sshaw@healthy.uwaterloo.ca.

University of Wisconsin–La Crosse, College of Health, Physical Education and Recreation, Department of Recreation Management and Therapeutic Recreation, La Crosse, WI 54601-3742. Offers program in recreation (MS), including recreation administration, therapeutic recreation. Part-time programs available. Faculty: 8 full-time (2 women). Students: 12 full-time (7 women), 4 part-time (3 women); includes 1 minority (African American), 1 international. Average age 27. 22 applicants, 91% accepted. In 1997, 8 degrees awarded (88% found work related to degree, 12% continued full-time study). *Degree requirements:* Thesis optional, foreign language not required. *Entrance requirements:* Minimum GPA of 3.0 during previous 2 years, 2.85 overall. Application deadline: 3/15 (rolling processing). Application fee: $38. *Tuition:* $3737 per year full-time, $208 per credit part-time for state residents; $11,921 per year full-time, $633 per credit part-time for nonresidents. *Financial aid:* In 1997–98, 7 students received aid, including 2 research assistantships (both to first-year students) averaging $546 per month and totaling $9,828, 5 assistantships (all to first-year students) averaging $546 per month and totaling $24,570; Federal Work-Study and career-related internships or fieldwork also available. Aid available to part-time students. Financial aid application deadline: 3/15; applicants required to submit FAFSA. *Faculty research:* Economic and market analysis, risk management, leisure education, counseling attitudinal behavior, tourism. • Dr. Jearold W. Holland, Director, 608-785-8207. Fax: 608-785-8206. E-mail: holland@mail.uwlax.edu. Application contact: Tim Lewis, Director of Admissions, 608-785-8939. Fax: 608-785-6695. E-mail: admissions@mail.uwlax.edu.

University of Wyoming, College of Arts and Sciences, Department of Geography, Laramie, WY 82071. Offerings include recreation and park administration (MS). Department faculty: 10 full-time (2 women), 1 (woman) part-time. *Application deadline:* 3/1 (priority date; rolling processing). *Application fee:* $40. *Expenses:* Tuition $2430 per year full-time, $135 per credit hour part-time for state residents; $7518 per year full-time, $418 per credit hour part-time for nonresidents. Fees $386 per year full-time, $9.25 per credit hour part-time. • Dr. Ronald Beiswenger, Head, 307-766-3311.

Utah State University, College of Natural Resources, Department of Forest Resources, Logan, UT 84322. Offerings include recreation resources management (MS, PhD). Terminal master's awarded for partial completion of doctoral program. Department faculty: 16 full-time (4 women). *Degree requirements:* For doctorate, 1 foreign language, computer language, dissertation. *Entrance requirements:* For doctorate, GRE General Test (score in 40th percentile or higher), TOEFL (minimum score 550), minimum GPA of 3.0. Application deadline: 6/15 (priority date; rolling processing; 10/15 for spring admission). Application fee: $40. *Expenses:* Tuition $1448 per year full-time, $624 per year part-time for state residents; $5082 per year full-time, $2192 per year part-time for nonresidents. Fees $421 per year full-time, $165 per year part-time. • Dr. Terry L. Sharik, Head, 435-797-3219. Fax: 435-797-4040. E-mail: forestry@cc.usu.edu.

Virginia Commonwealth University, School of Education, Program in Recreation, Parks and Tourism, Richmond, VA 23284-9005. Awards MS. Faculty: 5 full-time (1 woman). Students: 5 full-time (4 women), 4 part-time (2 women); includes 2 minority (1 African American, 1 Native American). Average age 28. 4 applicants, 50% accepted. In 1997, 9 degrees awarded. *Degree requirements:* Thesis or alternative. *Entrance requirements:* GRE General Test or MAT. Application deadline: 7/1 (rolling processing; 11/15 for spring admission). Application fee: $30 ($0 for international students). *Tuition:* $4960 per year full-time, $257 per credit part-time for state residents; $12,652 per year full-time, $684 per credit part-time for nonresidents. *Financial aid:* Full and partial tuition waivers available. Financial aid application deadline: 3/1. • Dr. Michael S. Wise, Chair, 804-828-1130. Fax: 804-828-1307. Application contact: Dr. Michael D. Davis, Interim Director, Graduate Studies, 804-828-6530. Fax: 804-828-1323. E-mail: mddavis@vcu.edu.

Directory: Recreation and Park Management

Virginia Polytechnic Institute and State University, College of Forestry and Wildlife Resources, Department of Forestry, Mail Code 0324, Blacksburg, VA 24061. Offerings include outdoor recreation (MF, MS, PhD). Department faculty: 25 (1 woman). *Degree requirements:* For master's, degree paper (MF), thesis (MS) required, foreign language not required; for doctorate, dissertation, oral defense, preliminary exam, qualifying exam, competency in statistics required, foreign language not required. *Entrance requirements:* GRE General Test, TOEFL, minimum GPA of 3.0. Application deadline: 12/1 (priority date; rolling processing). Application fee: $25. *Expenses:* Tuition $4122 per year for state residents; $6732 per year for nonresidents. Fees $806 per year. • Dr. Harold E. Burkhart, Head, 540-231-6952. Fax: 540-231-3698. E-mail: burkhart@vt.edu.

Washington State University, College of Education, Department of Kinesiology and Leisure Studies, Pullman, WA 99164-1610. Offerings include recreation and leisure studies (M Ed, MS). Department faculty: 10 full-time (3 women). *Degree requirements:* Oral exam required, foreign language not required. *Average time to degree:* master's–1.5 years full-time. *Entrance requirements:* GRE General Test, minimum GPA of 3.0. Application deadline: 3/1 (priority date; rolling processing). Application fee: $35. *Tuition:* $5334 per year full-time, $267 per credit hour part-time for state residents; $13,380 per year full-time, $677 per credit hour part-time for nonresidents. • Dr. Edward Udd, Chair, 509-335-4593.

Wayne State University, College of Education, Division of Health and Physical Education, Detroit, MI 48202. Offerings include recreation and park services (MA). Division faculty: 34. *Application deadline:* 7/1. *Application fee:* $20 ($30 for international students). *Expenses:* Tuition $163 per credit hour for state residents; $355 per credit hour for nonresidents. Fees $498 per year full-time, $114 per semester (minimum) part-time. • Dr. Sarah Erbaugh, Assistant Dean, 313-577-4265. Application contact: John Wirth, Graduate Program Coordinator, 313-577-5896. Fax: 313-577-5999.

Western Illinois University, College of Education and Human Services, Department of Recreation, Park, and Tourism Administration, Macomb, IL 61455-1390. Awards MS. Part-time programs available. Faculty: 12 full-time (2 women). Students: 28 full-time (11 women), 5 part-time (1 woman); includes 2 minority (1 African American, 1 Native American), 6 international. Average age 28. 28 applicants, 64% accepted. In 1997, 21 degrees awarded. *Degree requirements:* Thesis or alternative required, foreign language not required. *Application deadline:* rolling. *Application fee:* $0 ($25 for international students). *Expenses:* Tuition $2304 per year full-time, $96 per semester hour part-time for state residents; $6912 per year full-time, $288 per semester hour part-time for nonresidents. Fees $944 per year full-time, $33 per semester hour part-time. *Financial aid:* In 1997–98, 23 students received aid, including 23 research assistantships averaging $610 per month; full tuition waivers and career-related internships or fieldwork also available. Financial aid applicants required to submit FAFSA. *Faculty research:* Park district services, disability rehabilitation. • Dr. B. Nicholas DiGrino, Chairperson, 309-298-1967. Application contact: Barbara Baily, Director of Graduate Studies, 309-298-1806. Fax: 309-298-2245. E-mail: barb_baily@ccmail.wiu.edu.

Western Kentucky University, College of Education, Department of Physical Education and Recreation, Program in Recreation, Bowling Green, KY 42101-3576. Awards MS. Part-time programs available. Faculty: 3 full-time (0 women). Students: 15 full-time (9 women), 10 part-time (5 women). Average age 27. 8 applicants, 100% accepted. In 1997, 11 degrees awarded. *Degree requirements:* Thesis or alternative required, foreign language not required. *Entrance requirements:* GRE General Test (minimum combined score of 1150 on three sections; average 1590), minimum GPA of 2.75. Application deadline: 8/1 (priority date; rolling processing; 12/1 for spring admission). Application fee: $20. *Tuition:* $2460 per year full-time, $133 per credit hour part-time for state residents; $6700 per year full-time, $369 per credit hour part-time for nonresidents. *Financial aid:* Teaching assistantships, Federal Work-Study, institutionally sponsored loans available. Aid available to part-time students. Financial aid application deadline: 4/1; applicants required to submit FAFSA. • Dr. William Kummer, Coordinator, 502-745-6021.

West Virginia University, College of Agriculture, Forestry and Consumer Sciences, Division of Forestry, Program in Recreation and Parks Management, Morgantown, WV 26506. Awards MS. Part-time programs available. Students: 8 full-time (6 women), 1 part-time (0 women); includes 1 minority (Asian American), 2 international. Average age 31. 6 applicants, 50% accepted. In 1997, 4 degrees awarded (100% found work related to degree). *Degree requirements:* Thesis required (for some programs), foreign language not required. *Entrance requirements:* GRE, TOEFL (minimum score 550), minimum GPA of 3.0. Application deadline: rolling. Application fee: $45. *Tuition:* $2820 per year full-time, $149 per credit hour part-time for state residents; $8104 per year full-time, $443 per credit hour part-time for nonresidents. *Financial aid:* In 1997–98, 1 research assistantship, 1 graduate administrative assistantship were awarded; full and partial tuition waivers, Federal Work-Study, institutionally sponsored loans also available. Financial aid application deadline: 2/1; applicants required to submit FAFSA. *Faculty research:* Attitudes, use patterns and impacts of outdoor recreation in West Virginia. • Dr. Steve Hollenhorst, Head, 304-293-2941. Fax: 304-293-2441. E-mail: shollenh@wvu.edu.

Wright State University, College of Education and Human Services, Department of Health, Physical Education, and Recreation, Dayton, OH 45435. Awards MA, M Ed. Students: 3 full-time (2 women), 2 part-time (1 woman). Average age 30. 2 applicants, 50% accepted. *Degree requirements:* Thesis (for some programs), comprehensive exam required, foreign language not required. *Entrance requirements:* GRE General Test, MAT, TOEFL (minimum score 550). Application fee: $25. *Tuition:* $5109 per year full-time, $161 per credit hour part-time for state residents; $9039 per year full-time, $282 per credit hour part-time for nonresidents. *Financial aid:* Available to part-time students. Financial aid applicants required to submit FAFSA. *Faculty research:* Motor learning, motor development, exercise physiology, adapted physical education. • Dr. G. William Gayle, Chair, 937-775-3223. Fax: 937-775-3301. Application contact: Gerald C. Malicki, Assistant Dean and Director of Graduate Admissions and Records, 937-775-2976. Fax: 937-775-2357. E-mail: wsugrad@wright.edu.

UNIVERSITY OF TENNESSEE, KNOXVILLE

College of Human Ecology
Department of Consumer and Industry Services Management
Recreation, Tourism and Hospitality Management Program

Programs of Study

The Department of Consumer and Industry Services Management offers a Master of Science degree in recreation, tourism and hospitality management with concentrations in either therapeutic recreation, recreation administration, tourism, or hospitality management. The M.S. degree with thesis requires 33 semester hours of course work and research. The nonthesis M.S. requires a comprehensive examination at the end of completing 36 semester hours of course work.

The recreation administration concentration focuses on administration and management of recreation and leisure industry facilities and programs.

The therapeutic recreation concentration is designed to provide graduate-level preparation as a therapeutic recreation specialist. The concentration requirements are consistent with the standards published by the National Council for Therapeutic Recreation Certification.

Students specializing in the tourism management concentration focus on the entrepreneurial nature of tourism development and the economy.

Students who wish to specialize in the hospitality management concentration enter a program with emphasis on management issues concerning the efficient and effective use of resources in food service and lodging organizations. Students pursuing this major take courses in food service and lodging administration, marketing, human resource management, finance, and research methods. Collateral study may include systems design and equipment, experimental food production, law, and business. Departmental faculty members in this program maintain active involvement in the food service and lodging industries and facilitate access to industry for student research and development. The Nutrition Department offers an ADA-approved dietetic internship (D.I.) leading to dietetic registration (RD) eligibility. This program requires a separate application and is intended to be taken in conjunction with any departmental graduate program.

Research Facilities

The Institute for Tourism and Leisure Industries serves as a center of expertise for supporting five distinct missions: research, tourism, leisure industries, economic development, and training. This is done through feasibility studies, technical assistance, research projects, and training programs designed to develop and focus on strategies that address how tourism and leisure industries improve the economic climate and quality of life in east Tennessee.

Financial Aid

Graduate teaching assistantships are provided for some students each year. Funds are provided by the University and from grants from the federal government, private foundations, and industry. Some students who do not receive assistantships are given $600 per semester in exchange for faculty assistance. A limited number of graduate research assistantships are available to students applying for the recreation and tourism concentrations. All half-time assistantships range in value from $7000 to $9600, depending upon the source, and include a remission of tuition and fees.

Cost of Study

All fees, except a $140 per semester program and services fee, are waived for those with graduate assistantships. For those not supported by assistantships, there is an additional maintenance fee of $1232 per semester for in-state students and $3400 per semester for out-of-state students.

Living and Housing Costs

Modern University apartments are available for both single graduate students and married graduate students with or without families. Privately owned apartments across a wide price range are also available in the campus area.

Student Group

Approximately 19,500 undergraduate and 7,000 graduate students are registered on campus. There are approximately 60 graduate students in the Department of Consumer and Industry Services Management; approximately 30 percent are international students.

Student Outcomes

Students specializing in recreation administration are prepared to effectively manage leisure services in a variety of settings, including youth agencies, sport programs, corporate recreation, military recreation, and publicly sponsored recreation programs. Therapeutic recreation students are prepared for positions in clinical and community-based programs focusing on treatment, education, and community inclusion. Tourism management students are prepared for tourism industry positions with such employers as visitor and convention bureaus, tourism development organizations, resorts, theme parks, and other tourism-based leisure ventures. The hospitality management concentration provides the necessary training to find management positions in the hospitality industry for those with undergraduate degrees in other disciplines. Those already in management positions find increased upward mobility in the industry.

Location

The University is located along the Tennessee River in the foothills of the Smoky Mountains, approximately 30 minutes from the Great Smoky Mountain National Park. The Knoxville metropolitan area has a population of about 400,000. The area offers an exceptionally high quality of life, a mild climate year-round, low-cost housing, and easy access to all major cities in the Southeast and on the Atlantic seaboard.

The University

The University of Tennessee, founded in 1794, is a comprehensive state research university with a strong commitment to graduate research and training. The University has several campuses across the state. The main campus, the agricultural campus, the College of Veterinary Medicine, and a graduate medical campus are located in Knoxville; the medical school is located in Memphis.

Applying

Applications are considered twice per year: March 1 for fall and summer semesters and November 1 for the spring semester. Applications must be complete with the College of Human Ecology application form, three recommendations, and GRE scores by these dates to be considered for the subsequent semester. Applicants who are not applying for financial assistantships are welcome to submit application materials after the deadline. Files are reviewed based on availability of space in the program.

Correspondence and Information

Dr. Nancy Fair, Ph.D.
Department of Consumer and Industry Services Management
University of Tennessee, Knoxville
1215 West Cumberland Avenue, Room 230
Knoxville, Tennessee 37996-1900

Telephone: 423-974-4357
Fax: 423-974-5236
E-mail: smithgb@utk.edu

University of Tennessee, Knoxville

THE FACULTY AND THEIR RESEARCH

Youssri Allam, Ph.D., Associate Professor. Hospitality management and marketing, hospitality education.

Mary Dale Blanton, Re.D., Associate Professor. Recreation, sport, and tourism planning; programming.

Carol A. Costello, Ph.D., Associate Professor. Food service management and casino gaming; impact of Native American casinos in the gaming industry.
Evaluating the effectiveness of two instructional techniques for teaching food safety principles to quick service employees. *J. Foodservice Sys.*, 1997.

Gene A. Hayes, Ph.D., Professor. Inclusion of disabled children in community programs; attitudes toward disabled individuals; outdoor education for disabled persons; therapeutic recreation, self-esteem, and wellness.

Francis T. Hendrick, Ph.D., Assistant Professor. Social-psychological nature of leisure decision making, tourism, and the long-term stability of leisure perceptions among middle-aged adults.

Ken L. Krick, Re.D., Associate Professor. Management of leisure, sport, and tourism facilities and services.

Mark McGrath, Ed.D., Assistant Professor. Examining questions related to the people connected to the hospitality industry—employees, suppliers, and customers.
Environmental attributes: An intergroup comparison of preference in restaurant environments. Presented at the Proceedings of the 27th Annual Conference of the Environmental Design Research Association, 1996. With Gupta and Andriani.

Katherine A. Young, J.D., Assistant Professor. Legal trends and regulatory changes affecting the hospitality industry.
Environmental tobacco smoke and employees: Hospitality-industry operators face legal liability. *Cornell Hotel Restaurant Administration Q.*, 1997.

Recent Dissertations and Theses

Melissa Edwards, M.S. An analysis of the differential impact the Camp Koinonia experience had on University of Tennessee students who served as camp counselors and activity staff: 1995–1997.

Fredrick Brown, M.S. The relationship of activity implementation to camper outcomes as a function of activity programming for children with varying degrees of disability severity.

Sharon Cunningham, M.S. The effects of a therapeutic recreation program on community transition: A case study.

Tom Gaddis, Ph.D. Evaluating the effectiveness of two instructional techniques for teaching food safety principles to food service employees.

Mohamed Abdul-Ghani, Ph.D. Comparison of the effect of instructional versus industry-specific computer simulation of students learning in a front office management course.

Katrina Frances Heuberger, M.S. The concept of wellness in therapeutic recreation programs.

Carmen T. Munoz, Ph.D. Development of an assessment instrument to evaluate process layout of food service facilities and evaluation of managers' knowledge of layout and design.

Heather Hayes Terry, M.S. An exploratory study of perceived freedom in leisure among HIV-positive individuals and persons with AIDS.

Lisa Modenos, M.S. Status of play therapy programs across the State of Tennessee that service children with special needs.

Ellen D. Oliver, M.S. Defining excellent head counselors: A review of cabin counselor evaluations and personal demographics.

Carl Pfaffenberg, Ph.D. Indian and riverboat casino patrons: An analytical description of demographic characteristics, expectations, and items of importance.

Stephanie Taylor, M.S. State anxiety and self-confidence differences between a stressful period prior to sport performance of Division I track and field athletics.

Leigh Ann Wooley, M.S. An integrated adventure recreation program: The effects on attitudes toward persons with disabilities.

Heewon Yang, M.S. Establishing the reliability of the smiley face assessment scale: Test-retest.

Anne Burnett Young, M.S. Emotional and cognitive reactions to memory laden music in chemically dependent adolescent females.

Section 41
Physical Education and Kinesiology

This section contains directories of institutions offering graduate work in exercise and sports science, kinesiology and movement studies, and physical education, followed by in-depth entries submitted by institutions that chose to prepare detailed program descriptions. Additional information about programs listed in the directories but not augmented by an in-depth entry may be obtained by writing directly to the dean of a graduate school or chair of a department at the address given in the directory.

For programs offering related work, see also in this book Business Administration and Management and Education; and in Book 2, Performing Arts.

CONTENTS

Program Directories

Announcements

Cross-Discipline Announcements

In-Depth Descriptions

See also:

Exercise and Sports Science

Adelphi University, School of Education, Department of Physical Education, Recreation, and Human Performance Science, Garden City, NY 11530. Offerings include exercise physiology (Certificate). *Application deadline:* rolling. *Application fee:* $50. *Expenses:* Tuition $16,000 per year full-time, $485 per credit part-time. Fees $500 per year full-time, $150 per semester part-time. • Dr. Ronald Feingold, Chairperson, 516-877-4260.

American University, College of Arts and Sciences, Department of Health and Fitness, Washington, DC 20016-8001. Offers program in health fitness management (MS). Part-time and evening/weekend programs available. Faculty: 8 full-time (2 women). Students: 21 full-time (18 women), 18 part-time (17 women); includes 7 minority (3 African Americans, 3 Asian Americans, 1 Hispanic), 7 international. 29 applicants, 86% accepted. In 1997, 13 degrees awarded. *Degree requirements:* Comprehensive exam required, foreign language and thesis not required. *Entrance requirements:* GMAT or GRE, previous undergraduate course work in anatomy, physiology, and exercise physiology. Application deadline: 2/1 (10/1 for spring admission). Application fee: $50. *Expenses:* Tuition $687 per credit hour. Fees $180 per year full-time, $110 per year part-time. *Financial aid:* Fellowships, research assistantships, teaching assistantships, Federal Work-Study, institutionally sponsored loans, and career-related internships or fieldwork available. Aid available to part-time students. Financial aid application deadline: 2/1. *Faculty research:* Cost/benefit analyses of fitness worksite programs, physical fitness testing, spiritual well-being. • Dr. Robert Karch, Chair, 202-885-3020. Fax: 202-885-3090. Application contact: Monica Riggi, Graduate Admissions Coordinator, 202-885-6279. Fax: 202-885-6288.

See in-depth description on page 1885.

Appalachian State University, College of Fine and Applied Arts, Department of Health, Leisure, and Exercise Science, Program in Exercise Science, Boone, NC 28608. Awards MS. Students: 15 full-time (12 women), 1 part-time (0 women); includes 1 international. 34 applicants, 65% accepted. In 1997, 6 degrees awarded. *Degree requirements:* Comprehensive exams required, thesis optional. *Entrance requirements:* GRE General Test. Application deadline: 7/31 (priority date). Application fee: $35. *Tuition:* $1811 per year full-time, $354 per semester (minimum) part-time for state residents; $9081 per year full-time, $2171 per semester (minimum) part-time for nonresidents. • Application contact: Dr. Alan Utter, Coordinator, 704-262-3140.

Arizona State University, Interdisciplinary Program in Exercise Science, Tempe, AZ 85287. Awards PhD. 28 applicants, 25% accepted. *Degree requirements:* Dissertation. *Entrance requirements:* GRE. Application fee: $45. *Expenses:* Tuition $2088 per year full-time, $110 per hour part-time for state residents; $9040 per year full-time, $377 per hour part-time for nonresidents. Fees $72 per year full-time, $18 per semester (minimum) part-time. *Faculty research:* Biomechanics, physiology of exercise, motor behavior/sport psychology. • Dr. Daniel M. Landers, Executive Director, 602-965-7664.

Arizona State University, College of Liberal Arts and Sciences, Department of Exercise Science and Physical Education, Tempe, AZ 85287. Awards MPE, MS. Faculty: 24 full-time (6 women), 1 (woman) part-time. Students: 47 full-time (20 women), 15 part-time (8 women); includes 7 minority (3 Asian Americans, 3 Hispanics, 1 Native American), 8 international. Average age 30. 104 applicants, 38% accepted. In 1997, 16 degrees awarded. *Degree requirements:* Thesis or alternative. *Entrance requirements:* GRE. Application fee: $45. *Expenses:* Tuition $2088 per year full-time, $110 per hour part-time for state residents; $9040 per year full-time, $377 per hour part-time for nonresidents. Fees $72 per year full-time, $18 per semester (minimum) part-time. *Faculty research:* Biomechanics, motor behavior/sport psychology, physiology of exercise, exercise and wellness. • Dr. William J. Stone, Chair, 602-965-3875. Application contact: Graduate Secretary, 602-965-3591.

Ashland University, College of Education, Graduate Studies in Teacher Education, Program in Sports Science, Ashland, OH 44805-3702. Awards M Ed. Part-time and evening/weekend programs available. Faculty: 5 full-time (1 woman), 11 part-time (3 women). In 1997, 27 degrees awarded. *Degree requirements:* Practicum or thesis. *Entrance requirements:* GRE General Test or MAT, teaching certificate. Application deadline: rolling. Application fee: $15. *Tuition:* $275 per credit hour. *Financial aid:* Coaching scholarships available. • Frank Pettigrew, Chair, 419-289-5450. E-mail: fpettig@ashland.edu. Application contact: Dr. Joe Bailey, Director, 419-289-5377. Fax: 419-289-5097. E-mail: jbailey@ashland.edu.

Ball State University, College of Applied Science and Technology, Interdepartmental Program in Human Bioenergetics, 2000 University Avenue, Muncie, IN 47306-1099. Awards PhD. *Degree requirements:* Dissertation required, foreign language not required. *Entrance requirements:* GRE General Test (minimum combined score of 1000), minimum graduate GPA of 3.2. Application fee: $15 ($25 for international students). *Expenses:* Tuition $3454 per year full-time, $518 per semester (minimum) part-time for state residents; $9316 per year full-time, $1221 per semester (minimum) part-time for nonresidents. Fees $242 per year full-time, $18 per semester (minimum) part-time. • Dr. Donald Smith, Dean, College of Applied Science and Technology, 765-285-5818.

Barry University, School of Human Performance and Leisure Sciences, Program in Athletic Training, Miami Shores, FL 33161-6695. Awards MS. Part-time and evening/weekend programs available. Faculty: 4 full-time (2 women). Students: 4 full-time (3 women), 1 (woman) part-time; includes 2 minority (both Hispanics), 1 international. Average age 34. 5 applicants, 40% accepted. *Degree requirements:* Thesis or alternative, project or thesis, written comprehensive exam required, foreign language not required. *Entrance requirements:* GRE General Test (minimum combined score of 1000), minimum GPA of 3.0. Application deadline: rolling. Application fee: $30. Electronic applications accepted. *Tuition:* $450 per credit (minimum). *Financial aid:* 3 students received aid; career-related internships or fieldwork available. Aid available to part-time students. Financial aid application deadline: 5/1; applicants required to submit FAFSA. *Faculty research:* Over-the-counter, nonsteroidal anti-inflammatory drugs; pain management; prevention and injury analysis. • Dr. Carl Cramer, Coordinator, 305-899-3497. E-mail: cramer@bu4090.barry.edu. Application contact: Desh Sherman-Moeller, Administrative Assistant, 305-899-3490. Fax: 305-899-3556. E-mail: sherman@bu4090.barry.edu.

Benedictine University, Department of Exercise Physiology, Lisle, IL 60532-0900. Offers programs in exercise physiology (MS), fitness management (MS). Faculty: 2 full-time (1 woman), 15 part-time (10 women). Students: 42 (30 women). *Degree requirements:* Thesis (for some programs), oral comprehensive exam required, foreign language not required. *Entrance requirements:* MAT. Application fee: $30. • Dr. Peter Healey, Director, 630-829-6232. Fax: 630-960-1126. E-mail: phealey@ben.edu.

See in-depth description on page 1887.

Bloomsburg University of Pennsylvania, School of Graduate Studies, College of Arts and Sciences, Department of Health, Physical Education and Athletics, Program in Exercise Science and Adult Fitness, Bloomsburg, PA 17815-1905. Awards MS. Faculty: 3 full-time (1 woman). Students: 14 full-time (9 women), 7 part-time (4 women); includes 2 minority (1 Asian American, 1 Hispanic), 1 international. Average age 24. 8 applicants, 100% accepted. In 1997, 3 degrees awarded. *Degree requirements:* Thesis, practical clinical experience required, foreign language not required. *Entrance requirements:* GRE General Test or MAT, minimum QPA of 2.5. Application deadline: rolling. Application fee: $25. *Expenses:* Tuition $3468 per year full-time, $193 per credit part-time for state residents; $6236 per year full-time, $346 per credit part-time for nonresidents. Fees $748 per year full-time, $166 per semester (minimum) part-time. *Faculty research:* Energy and lipid metabolism, exercise electrocardiography, cardiac rehabilitation, coronary risks, cardiovascular adaptations in heart disease. • Dr. Leon Szmedra, Coordinator, 717-389-4581. Fax: 717-389-2099. E-mail: lszmedra@husky.bloomu.edu.

Boise State University, College of Education, Department of Health, Physical Education, and Recreation, Program in Exercise and Sport Studies, Boise, ID 83725-0399. Awards MS. Part-time programs available. Faculty: 12 full-time (3 women), 1 (woman) part-time. Students: 22 full-time (7 women), 30 part-time (8 women); includes 3 international. Average age 32. 43 applicants, 91% accepted. In 1997, 8 degrees awarded. *Degree requirements:* Thesis. *Entrance requirements:* Minimum GPA of 3.0. Application deadline: 7/26 (priority date; rolling processing; 11/29 for spring admission). Application fee: $20 ($30 for international students). Electronic applications accepted. *Tuition:* $3020 per year full-time, $135 per credit part-time for state residents; $8900 per year full-time, $135 per credit part-time for nonresidents. *Financial aid:* In 1997–98, 10 students received aid, including 10 graduate assistantships; Federal Work-Study, institutionally sponsored loans, and career-related internships or fieldwork also available. Aid available to part-time students. Financial aid application deadline: 3/1. • Dr. Ron Pfeiffer, Director, 208-385-3709.

Brigham Young University, College of Physical Education, Department of Physical Education, Provo, UT 84602-1001. Offerings include athletic training (MS), exercise physiology (M Ed, MS), exercise science/wellness (PhD). M Ed and PhD (corrective physical education) being phased out; applicants no longer accepted. Department faculty: 23 full-time (8 women). *Degree requirements:* For doctorate, dissertation, written comprehensive and oral exams required, foreign language not required. *Entrance requirements:* For doctorate, GRE General Test (minimum combined score of 1530 on three sections), minimum GPA of 3.5 in last 60 hours. Application deadline: 2/1 (rolling processing). Application fee: $30. *Tuition:* $3200 per year full-time, $178 per credit hour part-time for state residents; $4800 per year full-time, $266 per credit hour part-time for nonresidents. • Dr. Earlene Durrant, Chair, 801-378-2547. Application contact: A. Garth Fisher, Graduate Coordinator, 801-378-3981. Fax: 801-378-8389.

Brooklyn College of the City University of New York, Department of Physical Education, 2900 Bedford Avenue, Brooklyn, NY 11210-2889. Offerings include exercise science and rehabilitation (MS), with options in psychosocial aspects of physical activity, sports management. Department faculty: 16 full-time, 4 part-time, 18 FTE. *Average time to degree:* master's–3 years part-time. *Application deadline:* 3/1 (11/1 for spring admission). *Application fee:* $40. *Expenses:* Tuition $4350 per year full-time, $185 per credit part-time for state residents; $7600 per year full-time, $320 per credit part-time for nonresidents. Fees $500 per year for state residents; $806 per year for nonresidents. • Dr. Charles Tobey, Chairperson, 718-951-5514. Application contact: Michael Hipscher, Graduate Deputy, 718-951-5514.

California Baptist College, Graduate Program in Education, Riverside, CA 92504-3206. Offerings include sport leadership (MS Ed). Program faculty: 8 full-time (7 women), 4 part-time (2 women). *Application deadline:* rolling. *Application fee:* $40. *Expenses:* Tuition $275 per unit. Fees $100 per year. • Dr. Marsha Savage, Chair, 909-689-5771. Application contact: Gail Ronveaux, Director of Graduate Services, 909-343-4249. Fax: 909-351-1808. E-mail: gradser@cal.baptist.edu.

California State University, Fresno, Division of Graduate Studies, School of Health and Social Work, Department of Kinesiology, 5241 North Maple Avenue, Fresno, CA 93740. Offerings include exercise science (MA). Department faculty: 9 full-time (4 women). *Degree requirements:* Thesis or alternative required, foreign language not required. *Average time to degree:* master's–3.5 years full-time. *Entrance requirements:* GRE General Test, TOEFL (minimum score 550), minimum GPA of 2.5. Application deadline: 8/1 (priority date; rolling processing; 12/1 for spring admission). Application fee: $55. Electronic applications accepted. *Expenses:* Tuition $0 for state residents; $246 per unit for nonresidents. Fees $1872 per year full-time, $1206 per year part-time. • Catherine Jackson, Chair, 209-278-2016. E-mail: catherine_jackson@csufresno.edu. Application contact: Rose Lyon, Coordinator, 209-278-2005. Fax: 209-278-7010. E-mail: rose_lyon@csufresno.edu.

California University of Pennsylvania, School of Education, Department of Athletic Training, 250 University Avenue, California, PA 15419-1394. Awards MS. Summer admission only. Faculty: 4 full-time (1 woman). Students: 17 full-time (11 women). In 1997, 16 degrees awarded. *Degree requirements:* Thesis, comprehensive exam required, foreign language not required. *Entrance requirements:* TOEFL (minimum score 550), minimum GPA of 3.0. Application deadline: rolling. Application fee: $25. *Expenses:* Tuition $3468 per year full-time, $193 per credit part-time for state residents; $6236 per year full-time, $346 per credit part-time for nonresidents. Fees $886 per year full-time, $153 per semester (minimum) part-time. *Financial aid:* Graduate assistantships available. • William Biddington, Coordinator, 724-938-4562.

Central Connecticut State University, School of Education and Professional Studies, Department of Physical Education and Health Fitness Studies, New Britain, CT 06050-4010. Awards MS. Part-time and evening/weekend programs available. Faculty: 10 full-time (4 women), 9 part-time (3 women), 13.7 FTE. Students: 20 full-time (13 women), 26 part-time (11 women); includes 1 international. Average age 29. 32 applicants, 63% accepted. In 1997, 9 degrees awarded. *Degree requirements:* Thesis or alternative, comprehensive exam required, foreign language not required. *Entrance requirements:* TOEFL (minimum score 550), minimum GPA of 2.7, bachelor's degree in physical education (preferred). Application deadline: 6/1 (priority date; rolling processing; 12/1 for spring admission). Application fee: $40. *Expenses:* Tuition $4458 per year full-time, $175 per credit hour part-time for state residents; $9943 per year full-time, $175 per credit hour part-time for nonresidents. Fees $45 per semester. *Financial aid:* In 1997–98, 1 research assistantship was awarded; Federal Work-Study and career-related internships or fieldwork also available. Financial aid application deadline: 3/15; applicants required to submit FAFSA. *Faculty research:* Exercise science, athletic training, preparation of physical education for schools. • Dr. Jack Olcott, Chair, 860-832-2155.

Central Michigan University, College of Education and Human Services, Department of Physical Education and Sport, Mount Pleasant, MI 48859. Offers programs in athletic administration (MA), athletic coaching (Certificate), coaching (MA), exercise science (MA), sports administration (MSA), teaching (MA). Faculty: 15 full-time (3 women). Students: 37 full-time (15 women), 58 part-time (20 women); includes 9 minority (6 African Americans, 3 Hispanics), 5 international. Average age 27. In 1997, 18 master's awarded. *Degree requirements:* For master's, thesis or alternative required, foreign language not required. *Entrance requirements:* For master's, minimum GPA of 2.5 in last 20 hours. Application deadline: 3/1 (priority date). Application fee: $30. *Expenses:* Tuition $139 per credit hour (minimum) for state residents; $276 per credit hour (minimum) for nonresidents. Fees $260 per year full-time, $150 per semester part-time. *Financial aid:* In 1997–98, 2 fellowships, 12 teaching assistantships (10 to first-year students) were awarded; Federal Work-Study and career-related internships or fieldwork also available. Financial aid application deadline: 3/7. *Faculty research:* Biomechanical analysis of sports skills, sociological studies, psychological studies. • Dr. James E. Hornak, Chairperson, 517-774-6658. Fax: 517-774-4374. E-mail: 34naewv@cmich.edu.

Central Missouri State University, College of Education and Human Services, Department of Physical Education, Warrensburg, MO 64093. Offerings include physical education/exercise and sports science (MS). Department faculty: 13 full-time. *Application deadline:* 6/30 (priority date; rolling processing). *Application fee:* $25 ($50 for international students). *Tuition:* $3288 per year full-time, $137 per credit hour part-time for state residents; $5928 per year full-time, $274 per credit hour part-time for nonresidents. • Dr. James Conn, Chair, 660-543-4256. Fax: 660-543-4167. E-mail: jhc4126@cmsu2.cmsu.edu.

Cleveland State University, College of Education, Department of Health, Physical Education, Recreation and Dance, Cleveland, OH 44115-2440. Offerings include exercise science (M Ed), sport education (M Ed), sport management/exercise science (M Ed). Department faculty: 11 full-time (6 women). *Degree requirements:* Thesis optional, foreign language not required. *Entrance requirements:* GRE General Test or MAT (score in 50th percentile or higher), minimum undergraduate GPA of 2.75. Application deadline: 9/1 (priority date; rolling processing). Application fee: $25. *Expenses:* Tuition $5252 per year full-time, $202 per credit hour part-time for state residents; $10,504 per year full-time, $404 per credit hour part-time for nonresidents. Fees $2.25 per credit hour (minimum). • Dr. Vincent Melograno, Chairman, 216-687-4878. Fax: 216-687-5410. E-mail: v.melograno@popmail.csuohio.edu.

College of St. Scholastica, Program in Exercise Physiology, Duluth, MN 55811-4199. Awards MA. Part-time programs available. Faculty: 3 full-time (0 women). Students: 14 full-time (8 women), 1 (woman) part-time. Average age 25. 14 applicants, 100% accepted. In 1997, 6 degrees awarded. *Degree requirements:* Thesis. *Entrance requirements:* GRE General Test. Application deadline: 7/1 (priority date). Application fee: $50. *Tuition:* $7968 per year full-time, $332 per credit part-time. *Financial aid:* 15 students received aid. Aid available to part-time students. Financial aid applicants required to submit FAFSA. • Dr. Tommy Boone, Director, 218-723-6297. E-mail: tboone2@css.edu. Application contact: Debra Bekkering, Graduate Administrative Assistant, 218-723-6285. Fax: 218-723-6796. E-mail: dbekkeri@ess.edu.

Colorado State University, College of Applied Human Sciences, Department of Exercise and Sport Science, Fort Collins, CO 80523-0015. Offers programs in exercise science (MS), wellness management (MS). Faculty: 15 full-time (6 women). Students: 24 full-time (13 women), 4 part-time (2 women); includes 4 minority (1 African American, 2 Asian Americans, 1 Hispanic), 5 international. Average age 24. 81 applicants, 37% accepted. In 1997, 16 degrees awarded. *Degree requirements:* Thesis required, foreign language not required. *Entrance requirements:* GRE General Test, TOEFL, minimum GPA of 3.0. Application deadline: 2/1 (priority date; rolling processing). Application fee: $30. Electronic applications accepted. *Expenses:* Tuition $2632 per year full-time, $109 per credit hour part-time for state residents; $10,216 per year full-time, $425 per credit hour part-time for nonresidents. Fees $708 per year full-time, $32 per semester (minimum) part-time. *Financial aid:* In 1997–98, 1 fellowship, 22 teaching assistantships were awarded; research assistantships, traineeships, full and partial tuition waivers, Federal Work-Study, institutionally sponsored loans, and career-related internships or fieldwork also available. Aid available to part-time students. *Faculty research:* Metabolism and metabolic disease; obesity, diabetes, hypertension; physical activity and health across the lifespan; wellness; sports biomechanics. • Richard Gay Israel, Head, 970-491-7161. Application contact: Dolores Price, Senior Secretary, 970-491-1504. Fax: 970-491-0216. E-mail: price@cahs.colostate.edu.

East Carolina University, School of Health and Human Performance, Department of Exercise and Sports Science, Greenville, NC 27858-4353. Awards MA, MA Ed. Faculty: 7 full-time (2 women). Students: 36 full-time (14 women), 21 part-time (6 women); includes 3 minority (all African Americans). Average age 26. 67 applicants, 52% accepted. In 1997, 28 degrees awarded. *Degree requirements:* Comprehensive exams required, thesis optional, foreign language not required. *Entrance requirements:* GRE General Test or MAT, TOEFL. Application deadline: 6/1 (priority date; rolling processing). Application fee: $40. *Tuition:* $1886 per year full-time, $472 per semester (minimum) part-time for state residents; $9156 per year full-time, $2289 per semester (minimum) part-time for nonresidents. *Financial aid:* Research assistantships, teaching assistantships available. Aid available to part-time students. Financial aid application deadline: 6/1. • James Decker, Coordinator of Graduate Studies, 252-328-0001. Fax: 252-328-4634. E-mail: deckerj@mail.ecu.edu.

East Stroudsburg University of Pennsylvania, School of Health Sciences and Human Performance, Department of Movement Studies and Exercise Science, East Stroudsburg, PA 18301-2999. Offerings include cardiac rehabilitation and exercise science (MS). *Application deadline:* 7/31 (priority date; rolling processing; 11/30 for spring admission). *Application fee:* $15 ($25 for international students). *Expenses:* Tuition $3468 per year full-time, $193 per credit part-time for state residents; $6236 per year full-time, $346 per credit part-time for nonresidents. Fees $700 per year full-time, $39 per credit part-time.

Florida Atlantic University, College of Education, Department of Health Sciences, Program in Exercise Science/Wellness, Boca Raton, FL 33431-0991. Awards MS. Faculty: 6 full-time (3 women). Students: 12 full-time (8 women), 18 part-time (10 women); includes 3 minority (all Hispanics). Average age 29. 35 applicants, 63% accepted. In 1997, 4 degrees awarded. *Entrance requirements:* GRE General Test (minimum combined score of 1000), minimum GPA of 3.0 during last 60 hours. Application deadline: rolling. Application fee: $20. *Expenses:* Tuition $2520 per year full-time, $140 per credit hour part-time for state residents; $8712 per year full-time, $484 per credit hour part-time for nonresidents. Fees $5 per year (minimum). *Financial aid:* Career-related internships or fieldwork available. *Faculty research:* AIDS, aging, genetic determinants of endurance exercise. Total annual research expenditures: $30,000. • Dr. Ray Welsh, Coordinator, 954-236-1262.

Florida State University, College of Human Sciences, Department of Nutrition, Food, and Movement Sciences, Tallahassee, FL 32306. Offerings include human science (MS), with options in clinical nutrition, food science, nutrition and sport, nutrition science, nutrition, education and health promotion. Department faculty: 13 full-time (9 women). *Degree requirements:* Thesis optional, foreign language not required. *Entrance requirements:* GRE General Test (minimum combined score of 1000), minimum GPA of 3.0. Application fee: $20. *Tuition:* $139 per credit hour for state residents; $482 per credit hour for nonresidents. • Dr. Robert Moffatt, Chair, 850-644-1828. E-mail: rmoffatt@mailer.fsu.edu. Application contact: Dr. Cathy Levenson, Graduate Coordinator, 850-644-4800. Fax: 850-644-0700.

Furman University, Department of Health and Exercise Science, Greenville, SC 29613. Awards MA. Students: 19 full-time (11 women), 34 part-time (18 women). *Application deadline:* rolling. *Application fee:* $25. *Tuition:* $185 per credit hour. • Dr. William Pierce, Chairman.

George Mason University, Graduate School of Education, Program in Health Science, Fairfax, VA 22030-4444. Offers exercise science and health (MS). Faculty: 11 full-time (3 women), 12 part-time (7 women), 14.28 FTE. Students: 7 full-time (5 women), 16 part-time (9 women); includes 4 minority (1 African American, 3 Hispanics), 1 international. Average age 30. 15 applicants, 80% accepted. In 1997, 9 degrees awarded. *Degree requirements:* Computer language, comprehensive written exams required, thesis optional, foreign language not required. *Entrance requirements:* Minimum GPA of 3.0 in last 60 hours. Application deadline: 5/1 (11/1 for spring admission). Application fee: $30. Electronic applications accepted. *Tuition:* $4344 per year full-time, $181 per credit hour part-time for state residents; $12,504 per year full-time, $521 per credit hour part-time for nonresidents. *Financial aid:* Available to part-time students. Financial aid application deadline: 3/1; applicants required to submit FAFSA. • Application contact: Dr. Brett Wright, Chairman, 703-993-2064.

The George Washington University, School of Public Health and Health Services, Program in Exercise Science, Washington, DC 20052. Awards MS. Faculty: 3 full-time (all women), 1 (woman) part-time. Students: 16 full-time (12 women), 25 part-time (19 women); includes 6 minority (3 African Americans, 2 Asian Americans, 1 Native American). Average age 28. 33 applicants, 100% accepted. In 1997, 3 degrees awarded. *Degree requirements:* Thesis, comprehensive exam required, foreign language not required. *Entrance requirements:* GRE General Test or MAT. Application deadline: 5/15 (priority date; rolling processing; 11/15 for spring admission). Application fee: $50. *Expenses:* Tuition $680 per semester hour. Fees $35 per semester hour. *Faculty research:* Fitness and cardiac rehabilitation, exercise testing, women in exercise. • Dr. Bo Fernhall, Faculty Coordinator, 202-994-7246. Fax: 202-994-1420. Application contact: Michelle Sparacino, Director of Recruitment, 202-994-2160. Fax: 202-994-3773. E-mail: sphhs-info@gwumc.edu.

Announcement: The George Washington University School of Public Health and Health Services offers the MS degree in exercise science. Graduates specialize in clinical exercise physiology or exercise, nutrition, and eating behavior. Practical and clinical research opportunities are available. Visit the Web site (http://gwumc.edu/sphhs).

See in-depth description on page 1495.

Georgia State University, College of Education, Department of Kinesiology and Health, Program in Exercise Science, Atlanta, GA 30303-3083. Awards MS. Students: 23 full-time (14 women), 11 part-time (9 women); includes 4 minority (all African Americans), 1 international. Average age 28. 31 applicants, 81% accepted. In 1997, 19 degrees awarded. *Degree requirements:* Comprehensive exam. *Entrance requirements:* GRE General Test (minimum combined score of 900) or MAT (minimum score 50), minimum GPA of 2.7. Application deadline: 7/15 (1/15 for spring admission). Application fee: $25. *Expenses:* Tuition $2673 per year full-time, $99 per semester hour part-time for state residents; $10,692 per year full-time, $396 per semester hour part-time for nonresidents. Fees $228 per year. *Financial aid:* Research assistantships available. *Faculty research:* Body composition, blood lactates, exercise psychology. • Dr. Jeff C. Rupp, Chair, Department of Kinesiology and Health, 404-651-2536.

Georgia State University, College of Education, Department of Kinesiology and Health, Program in Sport Science, Atlanta, GA 30303-3083. Awards PhD. Students: 4 full-time (0 women), 3 part-time (1 woman); includes 2 minority (both Asian Americans), 2 international. Average age 35. 2 applicants, 50% accepted. *Degree requirements:* Dissertation, comprehensive exam. *Entrance requirements:* GRE General Test (minimum score 500 on verbal section, 500 on either quantitative or analytical sections) or MAT (minimum score 53), minimum GPA of 3.3. Application deadline: 4/1 (10/1 for spring admission). Application fee: $25. *Expenses:* Tuition $2673 per year full-time, $99 per semester hour part-time for state residents; $10,692 per year full-time, $396 per semester hour part-time for nonresidents. Fees $228 per year. *Financial aid:* Research assistantships, teaching assistantships available. • Dr. Jeff C. Rupp, Chair, Department of Kinesiology and Health, 404-651-2536.

Georgia State University, College of Education, Department of Kinesiology and Health, Program in Sports Medicine, Atlanta, GA 30303-3083. Awards MS. Students: 12 full-time (5 women); includes 1 minority (Asian American), 1 international. Average age 25. 9 applicants, 44% accepted. In 1997, 6 degrees awarded. *Degree requirements:* Comprehensive exam. *Entrance requirements:* GRE General Test (minimum combined score of 900) or MAT (minimum score 50), minimum GPA of 2.7. Application deadline: 7/15 (1/15 for spring admission). Application fee: $25. *Expenses:* Tuition $2673 per year full-time, $99 per semester hour part-time for state residents; $10,692 per year full-time, $396 per semester hour part-time for nonresidents. Fees $228 per year. *Financial aid:* Research assistantships available. *Faculty research:* Movement analysis. • Dr. Jeff C. Rupp, Chair, Department of Kinesiology and Health, 404-651-2536.

Howard University, Graduate School of Arts and Sciences, Department of Physical Education, Recreation, and Health Education, 2400 Sixth Street, NW, Washington, DC 20059-0002. Offerings include exercise physiology (MS). Department faculty: 8 full-time (4 women). *Degree requirements:* Thesis, comprehensive exam. *Average time to degree:* master's–2 years full-time, 3 years part-time. *Entrance requirements:* GRE General Test, minimum GPA of 3.0. Application deadline: 4/1 (11/1 for spring admission). Application fee: $45. *Expenses:* Tuition $10,200 per year full-time, $567 per credit hour part-time. Fees $405 per year. • Dr. Marshall Banks, Chair, 202-806-7142.

Indiana State University, School of Health and Human Performance, Department of Athletic Training, Terre Haute, IN 47809-1401. Awards MA, MS. Faculty: 6 full-time (3 women). Students: 22 full-time (7 women), 6 part-time (4 women); includes 1 minority (African American), 6 international. Average age 26. 18 applicants, 28% accepted. In 1997, 20 degrees awarded. *Application deadline:* rolling. *Application fee:* $20. *Tuition:* $143 per credit hour for state residents; $325 per credit hour for nonresidents. *Financial aid:* In 1997–98, 11 research assistantships (all to first-year students), 7 teaching assistantships (all to first-year students) were awarded. Financial aid application deadline: 3/1. • Dr. Christopher Engersoll, Chairperson, 812-237-8232.

Indiana University Bloomington, School of Health, Physical Education and Recreation, Program in Kinesiology, Bloomington, IN 47405. Offerings include applied sport science (MS), biomechanics (MS), clinical exercise physiology (MS), exercise physiology (MS), human performance (PhD), motor control (MS), motor development (MS), motor learning (MS), social science of sport (MS). PhD offered through the University Graduate School. Terminal master's awarded for partial completion of doctoral program. Program faculty: 12 full-time (2 women). *Degree requirements:* For master's, thesis optional, foreign language not required. *Entrance requirements:* For master's, GRE. Application deadline: rolling. Application fee: $35. *Expenses:* Tuition $153 per credit hour for state residents; $446 per credit hour for nonresidents. Fees $343 per year. • Dr. Harold Morris, Chairperson, 812-855-3114. Application contact: Program Office, 812-855-5523. Fax: 812-855-9417. E-mail: kines@indiana.edu.

Indiana University of Pennsylvania, College of Health and Human Services, Department of Health and Physical Education, Indiana, PA 15705-1087. Offerings include sports studies (MS). *Degree requirements:* Thesis optional, foreign language not required. *Entrance requirements:* TOEFL (minimum score 500). Application deadline: 7/1 (priority date; rolling processing; 11/1 for spring admission). Application fee: $30. *Expenses:* Tuition $3468 per year full-time, $193 per credit part-time for state residents; $6236 per year full-time, $346 per credit part-time for nonresidents. Fees $313 per year (minimum) full-time, $84 per year part-time. • Dr. James Mill, Chairperson and Graduate Coordinator, 724-357-2770. E-mail: jimmill@grove.iup.edu.

Ithaca College, School of Health Sciences and Human Performance, Program in Exercise and Sport Sciences, Ithaca, NY 14850-7020. Awards MS. Part-time and evening/weekend programs available. Faculty: 14 full-time (5 women). Students: 22 full-time (10 women), 2 part-time (both women). Average age 25. 31 applicants, 97% accepted. In 1997, 10 degrees awarded. *Degree requirements:* Comprehensive exams required, thesis optional, foreign language not required. *Entrance requirements:* GRE General Test, TOEFL (minimum score 550). Application deadline: 3/1 (priority date; rolling processing; 12/1 for spring admission). Application fee: $30. *Tuition:* $552 per credit hour. *Financial aid:* In 1997–98, 22 students received aid, including 15 graduate assistantships (10 to first-year students) totaling $147,312; career-related internships or fieldwork also available. Financial aid application deadline: 3/1; applicants required to submit FAFSA. *Faculty research:* Analysis of teaching and coaching behavior, exercise physiology and aging, optimizing exercise performance, physiological and psychological factors that affect human performance, sport and exercise psychology. • Dr. Gary A. Sforzo, Chairperson, 607-274-3359. E-mail: sforzo@ithaca.edu.

Kent State University, College of Fine and Professional Arts, School of Exercise, Leisure and Sport, Kent, OH 44242-0001. Offers programs in exercise physiology (PhD), physical education (MA). Faculty: 19 full-time. Students: 53 full-time (24 women), 22 part-time (9 women); includes 4 minority (3 African Americans, 1 Hispanic), 1 international. 57 applicants, 74% accepted. In 1997, 33 master's, 1 doctorate awarded. *Degree requirements:* For master's, thesis optional, foreign language not required; for doctorate, dissertation required, foreign language not required. *Entrance requirements:* For master's, minimum GPA of 2.75; for doctorate, minimum GPA of 3.0. Application deadline: 7/12 (rolling processing; 11/29 for spring admission). Application fee: $30. *Tuition:* $4752 per year full-time, $216 per credit hour part-time for state residents; $9213 per year full-time, $419 per credit hour part-time for nonresidents. *Financial aid:* Fellowships, research assistantships, teaching assistantships, full tuition waivers, Federal Work-Study, institutionally sponsored loans, and career-related internships or fieldwork available. Financial aid application deadline: 2/1. • Director, 330-672-2012.

Kirksville College of Osteopathic Medicine, Arizona School of Health Sciences, PO Box 11037, Phoenix, AZ 85061-1037. Offerings include sports health care (MS). School faculty: 30 full-time (18 women), 14 part-time (8 women). *Degree requirements:* Thesis required, foreign language not required. *Average time to degree:* master's–2 years full-time. *Entrance requirements:* GRE General Test (combined average 1639 on three sections), MCAT (average 25 for physician assistant). Application deadline: 2/1 (rolling processing). Application fee: $50. *Tuition:* $15,990 per year. • Dr. James Dearing, Associate Dean, 602-841-4077. Fax: 602-841-

Directory: Exercise and Sports Science

Kirksville College of Osteopathic Medicine (continued)
4092. Application contact: Stephanie Seyer, Assistant Director of Admissions, 660-626-2237. Fax: 660-626-2815.

Lakehead University, Faculty of Arts and Science, School of Kinesiology, Thunder Bay, ON P7B 5E1, Canada. Offers program in applied sport science and coaching (MA, M Sc). Part-time programs available. *Degree requirements:* Thesis required, foreign language not required. *Entrance requirements:* TOEFL (minimum score 550), minimum B average. Application deadline: 2/1 (priority date; rolling processing). Application fee: $0. *Faculty research:* Social psychology and physical education, sport history, sports medicine, exercise physiology, gerontology.

Life University, Program in Sport Health Science, 1269 Barclay Circle, Marietta, GA 30060-2903. Offers chiropractic sport science (MS), exercise and sport science (MS), sport coaching (MS), sport injury management (MS). Part-time programs available. Faculty: 5 full-time (1 woman), 1 part-time (0 women). Students: 45 full-time (25 women), 40 part-time (15 women); includes 20 minority (17 African Americans, 3 Hispanics). Average age 26. 41 applicants, 100% accepted. In 1997, 13 degrees awarded. *Application deadline:* rolling. *Application fee:* $50. *Tuition:* $13,600 per year full-time, $162 per quarter hour part-time. *Financial aid:* Full and partial tuition waivers, Federal Work-Study, and career-related internships or fieldwork available. Aid available to part-time students. Financial aid applicants required to submit FAFSA. *Faculty research:* Cryotherapy, neuromuscular adaptations, ergogenic aids, resistance training, biomechanics. • Dr. Jeffrey Lander, Director, 770-426-2771. Fax: 770-426-2861. E-mail: jlander@life.edu. Application contact: Denise Gordon, Admissions Coordinator, 800-543-3202. Fax: 770-428-9886. E-mail: dgordon@life.edu.

Long Island University, Brooklyn Campus, School of Health Professions, Division of Sports Sciences, Brooklyn, NY 11201-8423. Offers programs in adapted physical education (MS), athletic training and sports sciences (MS), exercise physiology (MS), health sciences (MS). Part-time and evening/weekend programs available. Faculty: 3 full-time (0 women), 9 part-time (1 woman). Students: 29 full-time (13 women), 24 part-time (9 women); includes 15 minority (8 African Americans, 1 Asian American, 6 Hispanics). 62 applicants, 82% accepted. In 1997, 18 degrees awarded. *Application deadline:* rolling. *Application fee:* $30. Electronic applications accepted. *Expenses:* Tuition $480 per credit. Fees $415 per year full-time, $73 per semester (minimum) part-time. *Financial aid:* In 1997–98, 3 students received aid, including 3 assistantships; career-related internships or fieldwork also available. • Dr. Milorad Stricevic, Associate Dean, 718-488-1026. Application contact: Bernard W. Sullivan, Associate Director of Admissions, 718-488-1011.

Malone College, Graduate School, Program in Education, Canton, OH 44709-3897. Offerings include physical education and sport (MA). Program faculty: 10 full-time (6 women), 11 part-time (5 women), 12.68 FTE. *Degree requirements:* Research practicum required, foreign language and thesis not required. *Entrance requirements:* Minimum GPA of 3.0, teaching license. Application deadline: 9/6 (rolling processing; 1/2 for spring admission). Application fee: $20. *Tuition:* $300 per credit hour. • Dr. Marietta Daulton, Director, 330-471-8447. Fax: 330-471-8478. E-mail: mdaulton@malone.edu. Application contact: Dan Depasquale, Director of Graduate Student Services, 800-257-4723. Fax: 330-471-8343. E-mail: depasquale@malone.edu.

Marshall University, College of Education, Division of Health, Physical Education and Recreation, Program in Exercise Science, Huntington, WV 25755-2020. Awards MS. Faculty: 2 (0 women). Students: 25 full-time (10 women), 8 part-time (4 women); includes 1 minority (Native American). In 1997, 11 degrees awarded. *Degree requirements:* Thesis optional. *Entrance requirements:* GRE General Test (minimum combined score of 1200). *Tuition:* $2364 per year full-time, $132 per hour part-time for state residents; $6894 per year full-time, $383 per hour part-time for nonresidents. • Dr. William Marley, Coordinator, 304-696-2936. Application contact: Dr. James Harless, Director of Admissions, 304-696-3160.

Marshall University, College of Education, Division of Health, Physical Education and Recreation, Program in Health and Physical Education, Huntington, WV 25755-2020. Offerings include athletic training (MS). Program faculty: 6 (1 woman). *Degree requirements:* Thesis optional. *Entrance requirements:* GRE General Test (minimum combined score of 1200). *Tuition:* $2364 per year full-time, $132 per hour part-time for state residents; $6894 per year full-time, $383 per hour part-time for nonresidents. • Application contact: Dr. James Harless, Director of Admissions, 304-696-3160.

Miami University, School of Education and Allied Professions, Department of Physical Education, Health, and Sports Studies, Oxford, OH 45056. Offers programs in exercise science (MS), sports studies (MS). Part-time programs available. Faculty: 24. Students: 45 full-time (21 women), 14 part-time (6 women); includes 5 minority (4 African Americans, 1 Hispanic), 5 international. 97 applicants, 63% accepted. In 1997, 26 degrees awarded. *Entrance requirements:* Minimum undergraduate GPA of 3.0 during previous 2 years or 2.75 overall. Application deadline: 3/1 (priority date; rolling processing; 12/1 for spring admission). Application fee: $35. *Tuition:* $5932 per year full-time, $255 per credit hour part-time for state residents; $12,392 per year full-time, $524 per credit hour part-time for nonresidents. *Financial aid:* Research assistantships, teaching assistantships, full tuition waivers, Federal Work-Study available. Financial aid application deadline: 3/1. • Dr. Thelma Horn, Director of Graduate Study, 513-529-2700.

Michigan State University, College of Education, Department of Kinesiology, East Lansing, MI 48824-1020. Offers program in physical education and exercise science-urban studies (MS, PhD). Faculty: 15 (8 women). Students: 93 (40 women); includes 14 minority (7 African Americans, 3 Asian Americans, 4 Hispanics), 20 international. In 1997, 18 master's, 5 doctorates awarded. *Degree requirements:* For master's, thesis optional, foreign language not required; for doctorate, dissertation required, foreign language not required. *Entrance requirements:* GRE General Test. Application deadline: rolling. Application fee: $30 ($40 for international students). *Expenses:* Tuition $4609 per year full-time, $223 per credit hour (minimum) part-time for state residents; $8704 per year full-time, $450 per credit hour (minimum) part-time for nonresidents. Fees $576 per year full-time, $476 per year part-time. *Financial aid:* In 1997–98, 15 fellowships, 16 research assistantships, 24 teaching assistantships were awarded; Federal Work-Study, institutionally sponsored loans, and career-related internships or fieldwork also available. Aid available to part-time students. Financial aid application deadline: 6/30; applicants required to submit FAFSA. *Faculty research:* Exercise physiology, psychosocial aspects of sport and exercise, motor behavior, biomechanics. • Dr. Deborah Feltz, Chairperson, 517-355-4732.

Mississippi State University, College of Education, Department of Physical Health, Education, Recreation, and Sports, Mississippi State, MS 39762. Offerings include physical education (MS), with options in exercise science, health education/health promotion, sport administration, teaching/coaching. Department faculty: 9 full-time (2 women), 1 part-time (0 women). *Degree requirements:* Comprehensive oral or written exam required, thesis optional, foreign language not required. *Entrance requirements:* Minimum QPA of 2.75 in last 2 years. Application deadline: 7/26 (priority date; rolling processing; 11/10 for spring admission). Application fee: $0 ($25 for international students). *Tuition:* $3017 per year full-time, $168 per credit hour part-time for state residents; $6119 per year full-time, $340 per credit hour part-time for nonresidents. • Dr. Robert Boling, Head, 601-325-2963. Fax: 601-325-4525. E-mail: rbb4@ra.msstate.edu.

Montclair State University, College of Education and Human Services, Department of Health Professions, Physical Education, Recreation, and Leisure Studies, Program in Physical Education, Upper Montclair, NJ 07043-1624. Offerings include exercise science (MA). Program faculty: 10 full-time. *Degree requirements:* Comprehensive exam, research project required, foreign language and thesis not required. *Entrance requirements:* GRE, appropriate bachelor's degree. Application deadline: 4/1 (rolling processing; 11/1 for spring admission). Application fee: $40. *Expenses:* Tuition $201 per credit for state residents; $257 per credit for nonresidents. Fees $22.05 per credit. • Dr. Ree K. Arnold, Adviser, 973-655-7091.

New Mexico Highlands University, School of Education, Las Vegas, NM 87701. Offerings include human performance and sport (MA). School faculty: 32 full-time (14 women). *Degree requirements:* Thesis or alternative required, foreign language not required. *Entrance requirements:* Minimum undergraduate GPA of 3.0. Application deadline: 8/1 (priority date; rolling processing). Application fee: $15. *Expenses:* Tuition $1816 per year full-time, $227 per hour part-time for state residents; $7468 per year full-time, $227 per hour part-time for nonresidents. Fees $10 per year. • Dr. James Abreu, Dean, 505-454-3357. Application contact: Dr. Glen W. Davidson, Academic Vice President, 505-454-3311. Fax: 505-454-3558. E-mail: glendavidson@venus.nmhu.edu.

Northeastern Illinois University, College of Arts and Sciences, Department of Biology, Program in Exercise Science and Cardiac Rehabilitation, Chicago, IL 60625-4699. Awards MS. Part-time and evening/weekend programs available. Faculty: 3 full-time (1 woman), 1 part-time (0 women). Students: 11 full-time (7 women), 49 part-time (40 women); includes 5 minority (4 Asian Americans, 1 Hispanic), 3 international. Average age 35. 44 applicants, 100% accepted. In 1997, 20 degrees awarded. *Degree requirements:* Internship required, thesis optional, foreign language not required. *Entrance requirements:* 21 hours of undergraduate course work in sciences, previous field experience, minimum GPA of 2.75. Application deadline: 3/18 (priority date; rolling processing; 9/30 for spring admission). Application fee: $0. *Expenses:* Tuition $2226 per year full-time, $93 per credit hour part-time for state residents; $6678 per year full-time, $278 per credit hour part-time for nonresidents. Fees $358 per year full-time, $14.90 per credit hour part-time. *Financial aid:* In 1997–98, 18 students received aid, including 8 research assistantships averaging $450 per month; full and partial tuition waivers, Federal Work-Study, institutionally sponsored loans, and career-related internships or fieldwork also available. Aid available to part-time students. *Faculty research:* Behavioral medicine, health care cost containment, clinical cardiology, industrial medicine, muscle inflammation. • Dr. George Lesmes, Coordinator, 773-792-2888. Application contact: Dr. Mohan K. Sood, Dean of Graduate College, 773-583-4050 Ext. 6143. Fax: 773-794-6670.

Northeastern University, Bouvé College of Pharmacy and Health Sciences Graduate School, Department of Cardiopulmonary Sciences, Program in Clinical Exercise Physiology, Boston, MA 02115-5096. Awards MS. Part-time and evening/weekend programs available. Students: 26 full-time (17 women), 10 part-time (7 women). 48 applicants, 77% accepted. In 1997, 17 degrees awarded. *Degree requirements:* Comprehensive exam required, thesis optional, foreign language not required. *Entrance requirements:* GRE General Test or MAT. Application deadline: rolling. Application fee: $50. *Expenses:* Tuition $440 per credit hour. Fees $55 per quarter full-time, $13.25 per quarter part-time. *Financial aid:* Research assistantships, teaching assistantships, administrative assistantships, Federal Work-Study, and career-related internships or fieldwork available. Aid available to part-time students. Financial aid application deadline: 3/1; applicants required to submit FAFSA. *Faculty research:* Exercise in cardiovascular pulmonary and metabolic diseases, mechanisms related to lactate and ventilation threshold, body composition assessment techniques. • Dr. William Gillispie, Director, 617-373-5695. Application contact: Bill Purnell, Director of Graduate Admissions, 617-373-2708. Fax: 617-373-4701. E-mail: w.purnell@nunet.neu.edu.

See in-depth description on page 1889.

Northern Michigan University, College of Behavioral Sciences and Human Services, Department of Health, Physical Education and Recreation, Marquette, MI 49855-5301. Offers program in exercise science (MS). Part-time programs available. Faculty: 10 full-time (2 women). Students: 13 full-time (7 women), 9 part-time (4 women). 9 applicants, 100% accepted. In 1997, 10 degrees awarded. *Degree requirements:* Thesis or alternative required, foreign language not required. *Entrance requirements:* GRE General Test, minimum GPA of 3.0 in major, 2.75 overall; 9 hours of course work in human anatomy, physiology, kinesiology. Application deadline: 7/1 (priority date; rolling processing; 11/1 for spring admission). Application fee: $25. *Expenses:* Tuition $135 per credit hour for state residents; $215 per credit hour for nonresidents. Fees $183 per year full-time, $94 per year (minimum) part-time. *Financial aid:* In 1997–98, 8 graduate assistantships averaging $770 per month were awarded; full tuition waivers, Federal Work-Study, institutionally sponsored loans, and career-related internships or fieldwork also available. Aid available to part-time students. Financial aid application deadline: 3/1. • Dr. M. Cameron Howes, Head, 906-227-2528. Application contact: Dr. Phil Watts, Coordinator, 906-227-2130.

Oakland University, School of Health Sciences, Program in Exercise Science, Rochester, MI 48309-4401. Awards MS. Faculty: 3 full-time. Students: 18 full-time (10 women), 32 part-time (22 women); includes 4 minority (1 African American, 2 Asian Americans, 1 Hispanic). Average age 28. 23 applicants, 78% accepted. In 1997, 15 degrees awarded. *Entrance requirements:* Minimum GPA of 3.0 for unconditional admission. Application deadline: 7/15 (3/15 for spring admission). Application fee: $30. *Expenses:* Tuition $3852 per year full-time, $214 per credit hour part-time for state residents; $8532 per year full-time, $474 per credit hour part-time for nonresidents. Fees $420 per year. *Financial aid:* Full tuition waivers, Federal Work-Study, institutionally sponsored loans available. Financial aid application deadline: 3/1; applicants required to submit FAFSA. • Dr. Stafford Rorke, Director, 248-370-4038.

Ohio University, Graduate Studies, College of Health and Human Services, School of Recreation and Sport Sciences, Program in Exercise Physiology, Athens, OH 45701-2979. Awards MSP Ex. Students: 1 full-time (0 women). 14 applicants, 29% accepted. *Degree requirements:* Thesis or alternative required, foreign language not required. *Entrance requirements:* GRE General Test or MAT. Application fee: $30. *Tuition:* $5430 per year full-time, $216 per quarter hour part-time for state residents; $10,431 per year full-time, $423 per quarter hour part-time for nonresidents. *Financial aid:* Federal Work-Study, institutionally sponsored loans available. Financial aid application deadline: 3/15. • Dr. Keith Ernce, Director, School of Recreation and Sport Sciences, 740-593-0284.

Oregon State University, Graduate School, College of Health and Human Performance, Department of Exercise and Sport Science, Program in Human Performance, Corvallis, OR 97331. Awards MAIS, MS, PhD. Faculty: 17 full-time (6 women). Students: 46 full-time, 9 part-time; includes 5 minority (2 Asian Americans, 2 Hispanics, 1 Native American), 12 international. Average age 30. In 1997, 7 master's awarded; 7 doctorates awarded (50% entered university research/teaching, 50% found other work related to degree). Terminal master's awarded for partial completion of doctoral program. *Degree requirements:* For master's, thesis, minimum GPA of 3.0 required, foreign language not required; for doctorate, dissertation, 2 languages (may include foreign, statistical, computer, braille, or sign), minimum GPA of 3.0. *Entrance requirements:* TOEFL (minimum score 550), minimum GPA of 3.0 in last 90 hours. Application deadline: 2/1 (priority date). Application fee: $50. *Tuition:* $6207 per year full-time, $810 per quarter (minimum) part-time for state residents; $10,551 per year full-time, $1293 per quarter (minimum) part-time for nonresidents. *Financial aid:* In 1997–98, 2 research assistantships, 20 teaching assistantships (5 to first-year students) were awarded; Federal Work-Study, institutionally sponsored loans, and career-related internships or fieldwork also available. Aid available to part-time students. Financial aid application deadline: 2/1. *Faculty research:* Exercise metabolism, biomechanics of sport, bone metabolism, sport psychology, teacher behavior. Total annual research expenditures: $15,000. • Application contact: Graduate Coordinator, 541-737-3718. Fax: 541-737-4230.

Purdue University, School of Liberal Arts, Department of Health, Kinesiology and Leisure Studies, West Lafayette, IN 47907. Offers programs in exercise physiology (PhD), health and fitness (MS), health promotion (MS, PhD), history/philosophy of sport (PhD), motor control (PhD), motor development (PhD), movement and sport science (MS), sport biomechanics (PhD), sport pedagogy (PhD), sport psychology (PhD), teaching and learning (MS). Part-time programs available. Faculty: 18 full-time (5 women), 2 part-time (1 woman). Students: 42 full-time (24 women), 19 part-time (11 women); includes 2 minority (1 African American, 1

Asian American), 12 international. 65 applicants, 48% accepted. In 1997, 7 master's, 4 doctorates awarded. *Degree requirements:* For master's, thesis required (for some programs), foreign language not required; for doctorate, dissertation required, foreign language not required. *Entrance requirements:* GRE General Test, TOEFL (minimum score 550). Application deadline: 2/15 (priority date; rolling processing). Application fee: $30. Electronic applications accepted. *Tuition:* $3500 per year full-time, $126 per credit hour part-time for state residents; $11,720 per year full-time, $387 per credit hour part-time for nonresidents. *Financial aid:* In 1997–98, 24 students received aid, including 3 research assistantships, 21 teaching assistantships (5 to first-year students) averaging $960 per month; fellowships also available. Aid available to part-time students. Financial aid applicants required to submit FAFSA. *Faculty research:* Wellness, motivation, teaching effectiveness, learning and development. Total annual research expenditures: $100,000. • Dr. T. J. Templin, Head, 765-494-3178. Application contact: W. A. Harper, Graduate Committee Chair, 765-494-1518. Fax: 765-496-1239. E-mail: wharper@purdue.edu.

Queens College of the City University of New York, Mathematics and Natural Sciences Division, Department of Family, Nutrition and Exercise Sciences, Program in Physical Education and Exercise Sciences, 65-30 Kissena Boulevard, Flushing, NY 11367-1597. Awards MS Ed. Degree awarded through the School of Education. Part-time and evening/weekend programs available. Students: 7 full-time (4 women), 65 part-time (25 women); includes 5 minority (1 African American, 4 Hispanics), 2 international. 41 applicants, 76% accepted. In 1997, 23 degrees awarded. *Degree requirements:* Research project required, thesis optional, foreign language not required. *Entrance requirements:* TOEFL (minimum score 600), minimum GPA of 3.0. Application deadline: 4/1 (rolling processing; 11/1 for spring admission). Application fee: $40. *Expenses:* Tuition $4350 per year full-time, $185 per credit part-time for state residents; $7600 per year full-time, $320 per credit part-time for nonresidents. Fees $104 per year. *Financial aid:* Partial tuition waivers, Federal Work-Study, institutionally sponsored loans, and career-related internships or fieldwork available. Aid available to part-time students. Financial aid application deadline: 4/1; applicants required to submit FAFSA. • Dr. Michael Toner, Graduate Adviser, 718-997-4150. Application contact: Mario Caruso, Director of Graduate Admissions, 718-997-5200. Fax: 718-997-5193. E-mail: graduate%queens.bitnet@cunyvm.cuny.edu.

Queen's University at Kingston, School of Physical and Health Education, Kingston, ON K7L 3N6, Canada. Offers programs in biomechanics (MA, M Sc), exercise physiology (MA, M Sc), exercise science (PhD), social psychology of sport and exercise rehabilitation (MA, M Sc), sociology of sport (MA, M Sc, PhD). Part-time programs available. Students: 24 full-time (8 women), 7 part-time (6 women). In 1997, 11 master's awarded. *Degree requirements:* For master's, thesis optional, foreign language not required; for doctorate, dissertation, comprehensive exam. *Entrance requirements:* For master's, TOEFL (minimum score 600); for doctorate, TOEFL. Application deadline: 2/28 (priority date). Application fee: $60. Electronic applications accepted. *Tuition:* $3803 per year (minimum) full-time, $1901 per year (minimum) part-time for Canadian residents; $7330 per year (minimum) for nonresidents. *Financial aid:* Fellowships, research assistantships, teaching assistantships, institutionally sponsored loans available. Financial aid application deadline: 3/1. • Dr. J. M. Stevenson, Director, 613-545-2666. Application contact: Dr. L. A. Wolfe, Graduate Coordinator, 613-545-4693.

St. Cloud State University, College of Education, Department of Health, Physical Education, Recreation and Sport Science, St. Cloud, MN 56301-4498. Offers programs in exercise science (MS), physical education (MS), sports management (MS). Faculty: 15 full-time (5 women), 6 part-time (2 women). Students: 17 full-time (3 women), 7 part-time (1 woman). In 1997, 10 degrees awarded. *Degree requirements:* Thesis or alternative required, foreign language not required. *Entrance requirements:* GRE General Test, minimum GPA of 2.75. Application fee: $20 ($100 for international students). *Expenses:* Tuition $128 per credit for state residents; $203 per credit for nonresidents. Fees $16.32 per credit. *Financial aid:* In 1997–98, 10 graduate assistantships were awarded; Federal Work-Study also available. Financial aid application deadline: 3/1. • Dr. Rodney Dobey, Chairperson, 320-255-4251. Application contact: Ann Anderson, Graduate Studies Office, 320-255-2113. Fax: 320-654-5371. E-mail: anna@grad.stcloud.msus.edu.

San Diego State University, College of Professional Studies and Fine Arts, Department of Exercise and Nutritional Sciences, Program in Exercise Science, San Diego, CA 92182. Awards MA. Students: 23 full-time (12 women), 72 part-time (38 women); includes 11 minority (3 African Americans, 5 Asian Americans, 3 Hispanics), 1 international. 61 applicants, 82% accepted. In 1997, 12 degrees awarded. *Entrance requirements:* GRE General Test (minimum combined score of 950), TOEFL (minimum score 550). Application deadline: 6/1 (priority date; rolling processing; 10/1 for spring admission). Application fee: $55. *Expenses:* Tuition $0 for state residents; $246 per unit for nonresidents. Fees $1932 per year full-time, $1266 per year part-time. • Application contact: Patricia Patterson, Graduate Adviser, 619-594-5979. Fax: 619-594-6553. E-mail: ensgrad@mail.sdsu.edu.

Smith College, Department of Exercise and Sport Studies, Northampton, MA 01063. Awards MSESS. Part-time programs available. Faculty: 4 full-time (2 women). Students: 16 full-time (15 women), 1 (woman) part-time; includes 2 minority (1 African American, 1 Asian American). Average age 22. 29 applicants, 41% accepted. In 1997, 5 degrees awarded. *Degree requirements:* Thesis. *Average time to degree:* master's–2 years full-time, 4 years part-time. *Entrance requirements:* GRE General Test. Application deadline: 4/15 (12/1 for spring admission). Application fee: $50. *Tuition:* $21,680 per year full-time, $2720 per course part-time. *Financial aid:* In 1997–98, 8 teaching assistantships (4 to first-year students) totaling $73,360, 7 scholarships (3 to first-year students) totaling $49,444 were awarded; institutionally sponsored loans and career-related internships or fieldwork also available. Aid available to part-time students. Financial aid application deadline: 1/15; applicants required to submit CSS PROFILE or FAFSA. • James Johnson, Chair, 413-585-3975. E-mail: jjohnson@science.smith.edu. Application contact: Donald Siegel, Graduate Adviser, 413-585-3977. E-mail: dsiegel@sophia.smith.edu.

Springfield College, Programs in Movement Science, Springfield, MA 01109-3797. Offerings include exercise physiology (M Ed, MPE, MS), with options in clinical exercise physiology, science and research. Faculty: 2 full-time (0 women), 6 part-time (1 woman), 4 FTE. *Degree requirements:* Thesis required, foreign language not required. *Application deadline:* (12/1 for spring admission). *Application fee:* $40. *Expenses:* Tuition $474 per credit. Fees $25 per year. • Charles J. Redmond, Director, 413-748-3231. Application contact: Donald J. Shaw Jr., Director of Graduate Admissions, 413-748-3225. Fax: 413-748-3694. E-mail: dshaw@spfldcol.edu.

Springfield College, Programs in Physical Education, Springfield, MA 01109-3797. Offerings include sport studies (M Ed, MPE, MS, CAS). Faculty: 25 full-time (13 women), 2 part-time (0 women), 26 FTE. *Degree requirements:* For master's, comprehensive exam, research project required, foreign language and thesis not required; for CAS, comprehensive exam required, foreign language and thesis not required. *Application deadline:* 2/1 (priority date; rolling processing; 12/1 for spring admission). *Application fee:* $40. *Expenses:* Tuition $474 per credit. Fees $25 per year. • Dr. Betty L. Mann, Director, 413-748-3125. Application contact: Donald J. Shaw Jr., Director of Graduate Admissions, 413-748-3225. Fax: 413-748-3694. E-mail: dshaw@spfldcol.edu.

State University of New York at Buffalo, Graduate School, School of Health Related Professions, Department of Physical Therapy, Exercise and Nutrition Sciences, Buffalo, NY 14260. Offers program in exercise science (MS, PhD). Part-time programs available. Faculty: 11 full-time (4 women), 1 part-time (0 women). Students: 11 full-time (7 women), 12 part-time (9 women). Average age 23. 24 applicants, 46% accepted. In 1997, 1 master's awarded. *Degree requirements:* For master's, thesis or alternative, comprehensive exam required, foreign language not required; for doctorate, dissertation, comprehensive exam required, foreign language not required. *Entrance requirements:* For master's, TOEFL (minimum score 550), minimum GPA of 2.8; for doctorate, GRE General Test, TOEFL (minimum score 550), minimum GPA of 2.8. Application deadline: rolling. Application fee: $35. *Tuition:* $5970 per year full-time, $288 per credit hour part-time for state residents; $9286 per year full-time, $426 per credit hour part-time for nonresidents. *Financial aid:* In 1997–98, 7 teaching assistantships (3 to first-year students) averaging $900 per month, 1 stipend averaging $900 per month and totaling $9,000 were awarded; research assistantships, full and partial tuition waivers, Federal Work-Study, institutionally sponsored loans, and career-related internships or fieldwork also available. Financial aid application deadline: 4/15; applicants required to submit FAFSA. *Faculty research:* Biomechanics and gait, exercise-induced muscle injury, respiratory muscle function, respiratory control. Total annual research expenditures: $180,275. • Dr. Frank Cerny, Chair, 716-829-2941 Ext. 208. Fax: 716-829-2034. E-mail: cerny@acsu.buffalo.edu. Application contact: Dr. Peter Horvath, Director of Graduate Studies, 716-829-3680 Ext. 235. Fax: 716-829-3700. E-mail: phorvath@acsu.buffalo.edu.

Syracuse University, School of Education, Health and Physical Education Program, Syracuse, NY 13244-0003. Offerings include health and physical education (MS, CAS), with option in exercise science. Program faculty: 5 full-time (2 women), 3 part-time (1 woman). *Degree requirements:* For master's, thesis or alternative; for CAS, thesis. *Entrance requirements:* GRE. Application deadline: rolling. Application fee: $40. *Tuition:* $13,320 per year full-time, $555 per credit hour part-time. • Dr. Jay Graves, Chair, 315-443-9696.

Texas Tech University, Graduate School, College of Arts and Sciences, Department of Health, Physical Education and Recreation, Lubbock, TX 79409. Offerings include sports health (MS). Department faculty: 18 full-time (10 women). *Entrance requirements:* GRE General Test (combined average 948). Application deadline: 4/15 (priority date; rolling processing; 11/1 for spring admission). Application fee: $25 ($50 for international students). Electronic applications accepted. *Expenses:* Tuition $864 per year full-time, $120 per semester (minimum) part-time for state residents; $5976 per year full-time, $747 per semester (minimum) part-time for nonresidents. Fees $1961 per year full-time, $257 per semester (minimum) part-time. • Dr. Elizabeth B. Hall, Chair, 806-742-3371. Fax: 806-742-1688.

Texas Woman's University, College of Health Sciences, Department of Kinesiology, Denton, TX 76204. Offerings include exercise and sports nutrition (MS, PhD), exercise physiology (MS, PhD). Terminal master's awarded for partial completion of doctoral program. Department faculty: 10 full-time (6 women), 9 part-time (8 women), 11 FTE. *Degree requirements:* For master's, thesis or alternative required, foreign language not required; for doctorate, dissertation, qualifying exam required, foreign language not required. *Average time to degree:* master's–2 years full-time, 5 years part-time; doctorate–4 years full-time, 8 years part-time. *Entrance requirements:* For master's, GRE General Test (minimum combined score of 850); for doctorate, GRE General Test (minimum combined score of 850), minimum GPA of 3.0. Application fee: $25. • Dr. Jerry Wilkerson, Interim Chair, 940-898-2576. Application contact: Dr. Harry Meeuwsen, Graduate Coordinator, 940-898-2594.

United States Sports Academy, Graduate Programs, Department of Sport Fitness Management, Daphne, AL 36526-7055. Awards MSS. Part-time programs available. Postbaccalaureate distance learning degree programs offered (minimal on-campus study). *Degree requirements:* Comprehensive exam required, thesis optional, foreign language not required. *Entrance requirements:* GRE General Test (minimum combined score of 800), MAT (minimum score 27), minimum GPA of 2.75. Application deadline: 8/15 (priority date; rolling processing). Application fee: $25 ($125 for international students). *Expenses:* Tuition $300 per semester hour (minimum) for state residents; $350 per semester hour (minimum) for nonresidents. Fees $100 (one-time charge). *Faculty research:* Human performance.

See in-depth description on page 1893.

United States Sports Academy, Graduate Programs, Department of Sports Medicine, Daphne, AL 36526-7055. Awards MSS. Part-time programs available. Postbaccalaureate distance learning degree programs offered (minimal on-campus study). *Degree requirements:* Comprehensive exam required, thesis optional, foreign language not required. *Entrance requirements:* GRE General Test (minimum combined score of 800), MAT (minimum score 27), minimum GPA of 2.75. Application deadline: 8/15 (priority date; rolling processing). Application fee: $25 ($125 for international students). *Expenses:* Tuition $300 per semester hour (minimum) for state residents; $350 per semester hour (minimum) for nonresidents. Fees $100 (one-time charge). *Faculty research:* Psychiatric aspects of injury rehabilitation, geriatric exercises and mobility.

See in-depth description on page 1893.

The University of Akron, College of Education, Department of Physical Education and Health Education, Program in Athletic Training/Sports Medicine, Akron, OH 44325-0001. Awards MA, MS. Students: 3 full-time (all women), 3 part-time (2 women). Average age 28. In 1997, 1 degree awarded. *Degree requirements:* Thesis or alternative, written comprehensive exam required, foreign language not required. *Entrance requirements:* GRE or MAT, minimum GPA of 2.75. Application deadline: 8/15 (rolling processing). Application fee: $25 ($50 for international students). *Expenses:* Tuition $178 per credit hour for state residents; $333 per credit hour for nonresidents. Fees $145 per year full-time, $32 per semester (minimum) part-time. • Phillip Buckenmeyer, Director of Graduate Programs in Physical Education and Health Education, 330-972-7471.

The University of Akron, College of Education, Department of Physical Education and Health Education, Program in Exercise Physiology/Adult Fitness, Akron, OH 44325-0001. Awards MA, MS. Students: 14 full-time (9 women), 7 part-time (4 women); includes 1 minority (Native American), 1 international. Average age 29. In 1997, 2 degrees awarded. *Degree requirements:* Thesis or alternative, written comprehensive exam required, foreign language not required. *Entrance requirements:* GRE or MAT, minimum GPA of 2.75. Application deadline: 8/15 (rolling processing). Application fee: $25 ($50 for international students). *Expenses:* Tuition $178 per credit hour for state residents; $333 per credit hour for nonresidents. Fees $145 per year full-time, $32 per semester (minimum) part-time. • Phillip Buckenmeyer, Director of Graduate Programs in Physical Education and Health Education, 330-972-7474.

University of Alberta, Faculty of Graduate Studies and Research, Faculty of Physical Education and Recreation, Edmonton, AB T6G 2E1, Canada. Offers program in recreation (MA, M Sc, PhD). Part-time programs available. Students: 60 full-time (34 women), 55 part-time (28 women); includes 10 international. 90 applicants, 47% accepted. *Degree requirements:* For master's, thesis (for some programs); for doctorate, dissertation. *Entrance requirements:* For master's, TOEFL (minimum score 550; average 580), bachelor's in related field; for doctorate, TOEFL (minimum score 550; average 580), master's degree in related field with thesis. Application deadline: 2/1 (priority date; rolling processing). Application fee: $60. *Expenses:* Tuition $390 per course for Canadian residents; $781 per course for nonresidents. Fees $500 per year full-time, $184 per year part-time. *Financial aid:* In 1997–98, 63 students received aid, including 28 research assistantships averaging $513 per month, 35 teaching assistantships averaging $573 per month, 12 tuition scholarships; career-related internships or fieldwork also available. Aid available to part-time students. *Faculty research:* Motivation and adherence to physical ability, performance enhancement, adapted physical activity, exercise physiology, sport administration, tourism. • Dr. H. A. Quinney, Dean, 403-492-3198. Application contact: Anne Jordan, Department Office, 403-492-3198. Fax: 403-492-2364. E-mail: ajordan@per.ualberta.ca.

The University of Arizona, School of Health Related Professions, Department of Exercise and Sport Science, Tucson, AZ 85721. Awards MA, MS. *Entrance requirements:* TOEFL (minimum score 550), minimum GPA of 2.5. Application deadline: 8/1 (rolling processing). Application fee: $35. *Tuition:* $2162 per year full-time, $337 per semester (minimum) part-time for state residents; $6860 per year full-time, $1138 per semester (minimum) part-time for nonresidents.

Directory: Exercise and Sports Science

University of California, Davis, Programs in the Biological Sciences, Program in Exercise Science, Davis, CA 95616. Awards MS. Program being phased out; applicants no longer accepted. Students: 16. *Degree requirements:* Thesis. *Expenses:* Tuition $0 for state residents; $9384 per year for nonresidents. Fees $4466 per year full-time, $2923 per year part-time. • Christina González, Dean, Graduate Studies, 530-752-0650. Application contact: Rosemarie H. Kraft, Associate Dean, 530-752-0655. Fax: 530-752-6222.

University of Connecticut, School of Education, Field of Sport and Leisure Sciences, Division of Sport Science, Storrs, CT 06269. Awards MA, PhD. Faculty: 1. Students: 5 full-time (2 women), 1 (woman) part-time. Average age 26. 9 applicants, 78% accepted. Terminal master's awarded for partial completion of doctoral program. *Degree requirements:* For master's, thesis or alternative; for doctorate, dissertation. *Entrance requirements:* For doctorate, GRE General Test. Application deadline: 3/15 (priority date; rolling processing; 12/1 for spring admission). Application fee: $40 ($45 for international students). *Expenses:* Tuition $5272 per year full-time, $293 per credit part-time for state residents; $13,696 per year full-time, $761 per credit part-time for nonresidents. Fees $948 per year full-time, $640 per year part-time. *Financial aid:* In 1997–98, research assistantships totaling $9,619 were awarded. Financial aid application deadline: 2/15. • William M. Servedio, Head, 860-486-3623.

University of Delaware, College of Health and Nursing Sciences, Department of Health and Exercise Scien ces, Newark, DE 19716. Offers programs in biomechanics (MS), cardiac rehabilitation (MS), exercise physiology (MS), health promotion (MS), professional development (MA). Part-time and evening/weekend programs available. Faculty: 12 full-time (3 women). Students: 19 full-time (9 women), 28 part-time (16 women); includes 5 minority (3 African Americans, 1 Asian American, 1 Hispanic). Average age 25. 38 applicants, 50% accepted. In 1997, 11 degrees awarded. *Degree requirements:* Thesis required (for some programs), foreign language not required. *Average time to degree:* master's–2.5 years full-time, 4.5 years part-time. *Entrance requirements:* GRE General Test (combined average 1150), interview. Application deadline: 7/1 (priority date; rolling processing; 12/1 for spring admission). Application fee: $45. *Expenses:* Tuition $4250 per year full-time, $236 per credit hour part-time for state residents; $12,250 per year full-time, $681 per credit hour part-time for nonresidents. Fees $466 per year full-time, $15 per semester (minimum) part-time. *Financial aid:* In 1997–98, 16 students received aid, including 3 fellowships (1 to a first-year student), 1 research assistantship, 6 teaching assistantships (4 to first-year students), 6 assistantships, tuition scholarships (3 to first-year students); full and partial tuition waivers, Federal Work-Study, and career-related internships or fieldwork also available. Aid available to part-time students. Financial aid application deadline: 4/15. *Faculty research:* Sport biomechanics, rehabilitation biomechanics, exercise physiology. Total annual research expenditures: $100,000. • Application contact: Gail E. Manogue, Administrative Assistant, 302-831-8370.

University of Florida, College of Health and Human Performance, Department of Exercise and Sport Science, Gainesville, FL 32611. Awards MESS, MSESS, PhD, JD/MESS, MBA/MESS. Faculty: 31. Students: 75 full-time (25 women), 52 part-time (25 women); includes 11 minority (3 African Americans, 2 Asian Americans, 6 Hispanics), 5 international. 197 applicants, 48% accepted. In 1997, 59 master's awarded. *Degree requirements:* For master's, thesis required (for some programs), foreign language not required; for doctorate, dissertation required, foreign language not required. *Entrance requirements:* For master's, GRE General Test (minimum combined score of 1000), minimum GPA of 3.0; for doctorate, GRE General Test (minimum combined score of 1000). Application deadline: 6/5 (priority date; rolling processing; 11/1 for spring admission). Application fee: $20. *Tuition:* $138 per credit hour for state residents; $481 per credit hour for nonresidents. *Financial aid:* In 1997–98, 58 students received aid, including 12 fellowships averaging $454 per month, 3 research assistantships averaging $440 per month, 43 teaching assistantships averaging $714 per month, 11 graduate assistantships averaging $896 per month; career-related internships or fieldwork also available. Financial aid application deadline: 2/28. *Faculty research:* Fitness/rehabilitation, achievement motivation, cognitive processes in motor learning, respiratory/metabolic adaptations to exercise, exercise prescription. • Dr. Robert N. Singer, Chair, 352-392-0584. Application contact: Dr. Sue Whiddon, Graduate Coordinator, 352-392-0584. Fax: 352-392-5262. E-mail: swhiddon@hhp.ufl.edu.

University of Georgia, College of Education, School of Health and Human Performance, Department of Exercise Science, Athens, GA 30602. Awards M Ed, Ed D, PhD. Faculty: 7 full-time (1 woman). Students: 45 full-time, 3 part-time (2 women); includes 4 minority (2 African Americans, 1 Asian American, 1 Hispanic), 7 international. 101 applicants, 31% accepted. In 1997, 14 master's, 5 doctorates awarded. *Degree requirements:* For doctorate, dissertation required, foreign language not required. *Entrance requirements:* For master's, GRE General Test or MAT; for doctorate, GRE General Test. Application deadline: 7/1 (priority date; 11/15 for spring admission). Application fee: $30. Electronic applications accepted. *Tuition:* $3290 per year full-time, $643 per semester (minimum) part-time for state residents; $11,300 per year full-time, $1645 per semester (minimum) part-time for nonresidents. • Dr. Ted A. Baumgartner, Graduate Coordinator, 706-542-4424. Fax: 706-542-3148.

University of Georgia, College of Education, School of Health and Human Performance, Department of Physical Education and Sport Studies, Athens, GA 30602. Awards MA, M Ed, Ed D, PhD, Ed S. Faculty: 7 full-time (3 women). Students: 48 full-time (14 women), 18 part-time (5 women); includes 5 minority (4 African Americans, 1 Hispanic), 4 international. 72 applicants, 57% accepted. In 1997, 21 master's, 1 doctorate, 1 Ed S awarded. *Degree requirements:* For master's, thesis (MA) required, foreign language not required; for doctorate, dissertation required, foreign language not required. *Entrance requirements:* For master's and Ed S, GRE General Test or MAT; for doctorate, GRE General Test. Application deadline: 7/1 (priority date; 11/15 for spring admission). Application fee: $30. Electronic applications accepted. *Tuition:* $3290 per year full-time, $643 per semester (minimum) part-time for state residents; $11,300 per year full-time, $1645 per semester (minimum) part-time for nonresidents. *Financial aid:* Fellowships, research assistantships, teaching assistantships, assistantships available. • Dr. Paul G. Schempp, Graduate Coordinator, 706-542-4462. Fax: 706-542-3417.

University of Houston, College of Education, Department of Health and Human Performance, 4800 Calhoun, Houston, TX 77204-2163. Offerings include exercise science (MS). Department faculty: 10 full-time (3 women), 9 part-time (5 women). *Application deadline:* 7/3. *Application fee:* $35 ($75 for international students). *Expenses:* Tuition $1152 per year full-time, $120 per semester (minimum) part-time for state residents; $4482 per year full-time, $249 per credit hour part-time for nonresidents. Fees $977 per year full-time, $119 per semester (minimum) part-time. • Dr. Dennis Smith, Chairperson, 713-743-9853. Fax: 713-743-9860.

University of Houston–Clear Lake, School of Human Sciences and Humanities, Programs in Human Sciences, Houston, TX 77058-1098. Offerings include fitness and human performance (MA). Faculty: 27. *Application deadline:* rolling. *Application fee:* $30 ($60 for international students). *Tuition:* $207 per credit hour for state residents; $336 per credit hour for nonresidents. • Dr. Hilary Karp, Division Co-Chair, 281-283-3383.

The University of Iowa, College of Liberal Arts, Department of Exercise Science, Iowa City, IA 52242-1316. Offers programs in exercise science (MS, PhD), physical education (PhD). Faculty: 7 full-time, 2 part-time. Students: 15 full-time (5 women), 14 part-time (7 women); includes 1 minority (Asian American), 7 international. 61 applicants, 20% accepted. In 1997, 3 master's, 3 doctorates awarded. *Degree requirements:* For master's, thesis optional; for doctorate, dissertation, comprehensive exam. *Entrance requirements:* GRE General Test. Application deadline: rolling. Application fee: $30 ($50 for international students). *Expenses:* Tuition $3166 per year full-time, $176 per semester hour part-time for state residents; $10,202 per year full-time, $176 per semester hour part-time for nonresidents. Fees $202 per year full-time, $52 per year (minimum) part-time. *Financial aid:* In 1997–98, 6 fellowships, 9 research assistantships (2 to first-year students), 14 teaching assistantships (7 to first-year students) were awarded. Financial aid applicants required to submit FAFSA. • Jerry Maynard, Chair, 319-335-9497. Fax: 319-335-6966.

The University of Iowa, College of Liberal Arts, Department of Sport, Health, Leisure and Physical Studies, Iowa City, IA 52242-1316. Offers programs in leisure studies (MA), physical education and sports studies (MA, PhD). Faculty: 14 full-time. Students: 40 full-time (26 women), 21 part-time (10 women); includes 4 minority (3 African Americans, 1 Hispanic), 4 international. 64 applicants, 34% accepted. In 1997, 14 master's, 4 doctorates awarded. *Degree requirements:* For master's, thesis optional; for doctorate, dissertation, comprehensive exam. *Application deadline:* 4/15 (rolling processing). *Application fee:* $30 ($50 for international students). *Expenses:* Tuition $3166 per year full-time, $176 per semester hour part-time for state residents; $10,202 per year full-time, $176 per semester hour part-time for nonresidents. Fees $202 per year full-time, $52 per year (minimum) part-time. *Financial aid:* In 1997–98, 9 research assistantships (2 to first-year students), 31 teaching assistantships (14 to first-year students) were awarded; fellowships also available. Financial aid applicants required to submit FAFSA. • Yvonne Slatton, Chair, 319-335-9335.

University of Louisville, School of Education, Department of Health Promotion, Physical Education and Sport Studies, Program in Exercise Physiology, Louisville, KY 40292-0001. Awards MS. Students: 14 full-time (6 women), 11 part-time (6 women); includes 3 minority (1 Asian American, 2 Hispanics). Average age 27. In 1997, 11 degrees awarded. *Degree requirements:* Thesis optional, foreign language not required. *Entrance requirements:* GRE General Test. Application deadline: rolling. Application fee: $25. • Dr. Bryant A. Stamford, Director, 502-852-6649.

University of Massachusetts Amherst, College of Food and Natural Resources, Department of Sport Studies, Amherst, MA 01003-0001. Awards MS, PhD. Part-time programs available. Faculty: 10 full-time (3 women). Students: 27 full-time (13 women), 21 part-time (6 women); includes 6 minority (4 African Americans, 1 Asian American, 1 Hispanic), 2 international. Average age 27. 113 applicants, 34% accepted. In 1997, 35 master's, 1 doctorate awarded. *Degree requirements:* For doctorate, dissertation required, foreign language not required. *Entrance requirements:* GMAT or GRE General Test. Application deadline: 3/1 (priority date; rolling processing). Application fee: $40. *Expenses:* Tuition $2640 per year full-time, $110 per credit part-time for state residents; $3690 per year (minimum) full-time, $165 per credit (minimum) part-time for nonresidents. Fees $2856 per year full-time, $422 per semester part-time for state residents; $3204 per year full-time, $480 per semester part-time for nonresidents. *Financial aid:* In 1997–98, 6 fellowships, 4 research assistantships, 13 teaching assistantships were awarded; Federal Work-Study also available. Aid available to part-time students. Financial aid application deadline: 3/1. • Dr. Glenn M. Wong, Director, 413-545-0471. Fax: 413-545-2425. E-mail: gwong@sporstudy.umass.edu.

University of Massachusetts Amherst, School of Public Health and Health Sciences, Department of Exercise Science, Amherst, MA 01003-0001. Awards MS, PhD. Part-time programs available. Faculty: 8 full-time (2 women). Students: 32 full-time (11 women), 29 part-time (11 women); includes 2 minority (1 Asian American, 1 Hispanic), 4 international. Average age 27. 100 applicants, 38% accepted. In 1997, 3 master's, 3 doctorates awarded. Terminal master's awarded for partial completion of doctoral program. *Degree requirements:* For master's, thesis optional, foreign language not required; for doctorate, dissertation required, foreign language not required. *Entrance requirements:* GRE General Test. Application deadline: 3/1 (priority date; rolling processing; 10/1 for spring admission). Application fee: $40. *Expenses:* Tuition $2640 per year full-time, $110 per credit part-time for state residents; $3690 per year (minimum) full-time, $165 per credit (minimum) part-time for nonresidents. Fees $2856 per year full-time, $422 per semester part-time for state residents; $3204 per year full-time, $480 per semester part-time for nonresidents. *Financial aid:* In 1997–98, 12 fellowships, 24 research assistantships, 29 teaching assistantships were awarded; Federal Work-Study also available. Aid available to part-time students. Financial aid application deadline: 3/1. • Dr. Joseph Hamill, Director, 413-545-1337. Fax: 413-545-2906. E-mail: jhamill@excsci.umass.edu.

The University of Memphis, College of Education, Department of Human Movement Sciences and Education, Memphis, TN 38152. Offers programs in exercise and sport science (MS), health promotion (MS), sport and leisure commerce (MS). Part-time and evening/weekend programs available. Faculty: 16 full-time (4 women), 6 part-time (0 women). Students: 41 full-time (17 women), 22 part-time (9 women); includes 8 minority (5 African Americans, 1 Asian American, 2 Hispanics), 6 international. Average age 27. 64 applicants, 69% accepted. In 1997, 12 degrees awarded. *Degree requirements:* Thesis, comprehensive exam required, foreign language not required. *Entrance requirements:* GRE General Test (minimum combined score of 750) or MAT (minimum score 33). Application deadline: 5/1 (priority date; rolling processing; 11/1 for spring admission). Application fee: $25 ($50 for international students). *Tuition:* $2862 per year full-time, $166 per credit hour part-time for state residents; $6696 per year full-time, $379 per credit hour part-time for nonresidents. *Financial aid:* In 1997–98, 12 research assistantships totaling $30,000, 1 teaching assistantship totaling $2,500 were awarded; partial tuition waivers and career-related internships or fieldwork also available. *Faculty research:* Sport marketing and consumer analysis, urban wellness and health promotion, applied muscle physiology, sport nutrition, sport psychology and motor learning. • Dr. Ralph C. Wilcox, Chairman, 901-678-2324. Application contact: Dr. Mary D. Fry, Coordinator of Graduate Studies in Health, 901-678-4986.

University of Miami, School of Education, Department of Educational and Psychological Studies, Program in Educational Research/Exercise Physiology, Coral Gables, FL 33124. Awards PhD. *Degree requirements:* Dissertation required, foreign language not required. *Entrance requirements:* GRE General Test, GRE Subject Test, TOEFL (minimum score 550). Application deadline: rolling. Application fee: $35. *Expenses:* Tuition $815 per credit hour. Fees $174 per year. *Financial aid:* Application deadline 3/1. • Dr. James D. McKinney, Coordinator of Educational Research, 305-284-3388.

University of Miami, School of Education, Department of Exercise and Sport Sciences, Program in Exercise Physiology, Coral Gables, FL 33124. Offers educational research/exercise physiology (PhD), exercise physiology (MS Ed). Part-time programs available. Faculty: 6 full-time (2 women), 3 part-time (1 woman). Students: 6 full-time (1 woman), 1 (woman) part-time; includes 2 minority (1 African American, 1 Hispanic). Average age 27. 25 applicants, 40% accepted. In 1997, 4 degrees awarded. *Degree requirements:* Computer language, comprehensive exam, thesis, internship required, foreign language and thesis not required. *Entrance requirements:* GRE General Test (minimum combined score of 1000), GRE Subject Test, TOEFL (minimum score 550). Application deadline: rolling. Application fee: $35. *Expenses:* Tuition $815 per credit hour. Fees $174 per year. *Financial aid:* 6 students received aid; graduate assistantships and career-related internships or fieldwork available. Financial aid application deadline: 3/1. *Faculty research:* Sports nutrition, obesity, strength, aging, electromyography. Total annual research expenditures: $76,820. • Dr. Arlette Perry, Director, Human Performance Laboratory, 305-284-3024. Fax: 305-284-3003.

Announcement: The University of Miami offers the MS and PhD degrees in exercise physiology and sports medicine. Emphasis is placed on scientific research and clinical fieldwork, with interdisciplinary opportunities in the Medical School, athletic training facility, and Sports Medicine Clinic. Graduate assistantships in research and fitness evaluation are also available.

University of Miami, School of Education, Department of Exercise and Sport Sciences, Program in Sports Medicine, Coral Gables, FL 33124. Awards MS Ed, PhD. Faculty: 5 full-time (1 woman), 3 part-time (1 woman). Students: 6 full-time (5 women), 6 part-time (2 women); includes 7 minority (4 African Americans, 1 Asian American, 2 Hispanics). Average age 22. 27 applicants, 59% accepted. In 1997, 5 degrees awarded. *Degree requirements:* Comprehensive exam, thesis, internship required, thesis optional, foreign language not required. *Entrance requirements:* GRE General Test (minimum combined score of 1000), GRE Subject Test, TOEFL (minimum score 550). Application deadline: rolling. Application fee: $35. *Expenses:* Tuition $815 per credit hour. Fees $174 per year. *Financial aid:* 1 student received aid; graduate assistantships, full and partial tuition waivers, Federal Work-Study, institutionally sponsored loans, and career-related internships or fieldwork available. Financial aid application deadline: 3/1. • Dr. Bobby Robertson, Coordinator, 305-284-3289. Fax: 305-284-3003.

Announcement: The University of Miami offers the MS degree program in sports medicine. The program is designed to prepare students in the field of sports medicine by providing a curriculum that includes kinesiology and human anatomy (direction). Emphasis is on injury assessment, management, and rehabilitation of injuries. Clinical experiences are included in athletic training facilities, sports medicine clinic, and others. Graduate assistantships are available.

University of Mississippi, Graduate School, School of Education, Department of Exercise Science and Leisure Management, University, MS 38677-9702. Offers programs in exercise science (MA, MS), exercise science and leisure management (PhD), leisure management (MA), wellness (MS). Faculty: 9 full-time (1 woman). Students: 29 full-time (12 women), 12 part-time (8 women); includes 7 minority (4 African Americans, 2 Hispanics, 1 Native American), 2 international. In 1997, 14 master's, 3 doctorates awarded. *Degree requirements:* For master's, thesis required (for some programs), foreign language not required; for doctorate, dissertation. *Entrance requirements:* For master's, GRE General Test, TOEFL, minimum GPA of 3.0; for doctorate, GRE General Test, TOEFL. Application deadline: 8/1 (rolling processing). Application fee: $0 ($25 for international students). *Financial aid:* Application deadline 3/1. • Dr. Eugene R. Anderson, Chairman, 601-232-5520.

University of Missouri–Columbia, College of Human Environmental Science, Department of Human Nutrition, Foods, and Food System Management, Columbia, MO 65211. Offerings include exercise science (MA). Offered jointly with the Department of Food Science. Department faculty: 11 full-time (5 women). *Application deadline:* rolling. *Application fee:* $25 ($50 for international students). *Expenses:* Tuition $3240 per year full-time, $180 per credit hour part-time for state residents; $9108 per year full-time, $506 per credit hour part-time for nonresidents. Fees $55 per year full-time. • Dr. Richard Dowdy, Director of Graduate Studies, 573-882-7014.

University of Missouri–Columbia, College of Human Environmental Science, Program in Exercise Physiology, Columbia, MO 65211. Awards PhD. Part-time programs available. Students: 7 full-time (3 women), 6 part-time (3 women); includes 2 international. In 1997, 5 master's awarded. Terminal master's awarded for partial completion of doctoral program. *Degree requirements:* For doctorate, dissertation. *Expenses:* Tuition $3240 per year full-time, $180 per credit hour part-time for state residents; $9108 per year full-time, $506 per credit hour part-time for nonresidents. Fees $55 per year full-time. • Tom Thomas, Graduate Adviser, 573-882-0062.

University of Nebraska at Kearney, College of Education, Department of Health, Physical Education, Recreation, and Leisure Studies, Kearney, NE 68849-0001. Offerings include exercise science (MA Ed). Department faculty: 5 full-time (0 women). *Degree requirements:* Thesis optional. *Entrance requirements:* GRE General Test. Application deadline: 8/1 (priority date; rolling processing; 12/15 for spring admission). Application fee: $35. *Expenses:* Tuition $1494 per year full-time, $83 per credit hour part-time for state residents; $2826 per year full-time, $157 per credit hour part-time for nonresidents. Fees $229 per year full-time, $11.25 per semester (minimum) part-time. • Dr. Don Lackey, Chair, 308-865-8331.

University of Nevada, Las Vegas, College of Health Sciences, Department of Kinesiology, Las Vegas, NV 89154-9900. Offerings include exercise physiology (MS). Department faculty: 9 full-time (1 woman). *Degree requirements:* Comprehensive exam required, thesis optional, foreign language not required. *Entrance requirements:* GRE General Test (minimum combined score of 1000), minimum GPA of 3.0 during previous 2 years, 2.75 overall. Application deadline: 6/15 (priority date; rolling processing; 11/15 for spring admission). Application fee: $40 ($95 for international students). *Expenses:* Tuition $93 per credit for state residents; $93 per credit full-time, $190 per credit part-time for nonresidents. Fees $5570 per year full-time for nonresidents. • Dr. John Young, Co-Chair, 702-895-3766. Application contact: Graduate College Admissions Evaluator, 702-895-3320.

University of New Orleans, College of Education, Department of Health and Physical Education, New Orleans, LA 70148. Offerings include exercise physiology (MA). Department faculty: 9 full-time (5 women). *Application deadline:* 7/1 (priority date; rolling processing). *Application fee:* $20. *Expenses:* Tuition $2362 per year full-time, $373 per semester (minimum) part-time for state residents; $7888 per year full-time, $1423 per semester (minimum) part-time for nonresidents. Fees $170 per year full-time, $25 per semester (minimum) part-time. • Dr. Robert Eason, Chairperson, 504-280-6420. E-mail: blehp@uno.edu. Application contact: Dr. Mark Loftin, Graduate Coordinator, 504-280-6417. Fax: 504-280-6018. E-mail: mxlhp@uno.edu.

The University of North Carolina at Chapel Hill, College of Arts and Sciences, Department of Physical Education, Exercise and Sport Science, Chapel Hill, NC 27599. Offers programs in athletic training (MA), exercise physiology (MA), sports administration (MA), sports psychology (MA). Faculty: 12 full-time, 5 part-time. Students: 41 full-time (20 women), 12 part-time (6 women); includes 5 minority (3 Asian Americans, 2 Hispanics), 1 international. 166 applicants, 18% accepted. In 1997, 27 degrees awarded. *Degree requirements:* Thesis (for some programs), comprehensive exam required, foreign language not required. *Entrance requirements:* GRE General Test, NTE, minimum GPA of 3.0. Application deadline: 1/1 (priority date; rolling processing). Application fee: $55. *Expenses:* Tuition $1428 per year full-time, $357 per semester (minimum) part-time for state residents; $10,414 per year full-time, $2604 per semester (minimum) part-time for nonresidents. Fees $782 per year full-time, $332 per semester (minimum) part-time. *Financial aid:* In 1997–98, 1 research assistantship, 46 teaching assistantships were awarded; graduate assistantships also available. Financial aid application deadline: 3/1. • Dr. Frederick O. Mueller, Chairman, 919-962-0017. Application contact: Dr. Pamela Robinson, Director of Graduate Studies, 919-962-5173.

University of North Carolina at Greensboro, School of Health and Human Performance, Department of Exercise and Sports Science, Greensboro, NC 27412-0001. Awards M Ed, MS, PhD. Faculty: 16 full-time (8 women), 2 part-time (1 woman). Students: 49 full-time (22 women), 12 part-time (6 women); includes 2 minority (both African Americans), 6 international. 146 applicants, 31% accepted. In 1997, 21 master's, 7 doctorates awarded. *Degree requirements:* Thesis/dissertation required, foreign language not required. *Entrance requirements:* GRE General Test. Application deadline: 2/15 (priority date; rolling processing; 11/1 for spring admission). Application fee: $35. *Expenses:* Tuition $1842 per year full-time, $370 per semester (minimum) part-time for state residents; $10,296 per year full-time, $2484 per semester (minimum) part-time for nonresidents. Fees $806 per year full-time, $111 per semester (minimum) part-time. *Financial aid:* In 1997–98, 26 assistantships totaling $213,060 were awarded; fellowships, research assistantships, teaching assistantships also available. • Dr. Diane Gill, Head, 336-334-5308.

University of North Florida, College of Health, Jacksonville, FL 32224-2645. Offerings include human performance (MS). MSN new for fall 1998. College faculty: 14 full-time (9 women). *Application deadline:* rolling. *Application fee:* $20. *Tuition:* $3388 per year full-time, $141 per credit hour part-time for state residents; $11,634 per year full-time, $485 per credit hour part-time for nonresidents. • Dr. Joan Farrell, Dean, 904-646-2840.

University of Oklahoma, College of Arts and Sciences, Department of Health and Sports Sciences, Norman, OK 73019-0390. Offers programs in health and exercise science (MS), sport management and behavior (MS). Part-time and evening/weekend programs available. Faculty: 7 full-time (2 women), 2 part-time (1 woman). Students: 13 full-time (5 women), 22 part-time (10 women); includes 1 minority (Native American), 1 international. 24 applicants, 54% accepted. In 1997, 11 degrees awarded. *Degree requirements:* Thesis or alternative, comprehensive exam. *Entrance requirements:* GRE General Test (minimum score 500 on each section), TOEFL (minimum score 550), minimum GPA of 3.0. Application deadline: 6/1 (priority date; rolling processing). Application fee: $25. *Expenses:* Tuition $1920 per year full-time, $80 per credit hour part-time for state residents; $6108 per year full-time, $255 per credit hour part-time for nonresidents. Fees $468 per year full-time, $12 per semester (minimum) part-time. *Financial aid:* In 1997–98, 13 students received aid, including 3 research assistantships, 10 teaching assistantships; partial tuition waivers, Federal Work-Study, institutionally sponsored loans, and career-related internships or fieldwork also available. *Faculty research:* Cardiovascular risk prevention, stress management, sport psychology. • Dr. E. Laurette Taylor, Chairperson, 405-325-5211. Fax: 405-325-1365.

University of Oregon, Graduate School, College of Arts and Sciences, Department of Exercise and Movement Science, Eugene, OR 97403. Awards MS, PhD. Faculty: 4 full-time (1 woman), 1 (woman) part-time, 4.5 FTE. Students: 60 full-time (26 women), 8 part-time (4 women); includes 6 minority (3 Asian Americans, 3 Hispanics), 15 international. 115 applicants, 41% accepted. In 1997, 26 master's, 8 doctorates awarded. *Degree requirements:* For master's, thesis optional; for doctorate, 1 foreign language (computer language can substitute), dissertation. *Entrance requirements:* For master's, GRE General Test (minimum score 470 on verbal section, 500 on quantitative), TOEFL (minimum score 550), minimum GPA of 2.75 in undergraduate course work; for doctorate, GRE General Test (minimum score 520 on verbal section, 560 on quantitative). Application deadline: 7/18. Application fee: $50. *Tuition:* $6429 per year full-time, $873 per quarter (minimum) part-time for state residents; $10,857 per year full-time, $1360 per quarter (minimum) part-time for nonresidents. *Financial aid:* In 1997–98, 44 teaching assistantships (10 to first-year students) were awarded; Federal Work-Study also available. *Faculty research:* Balance control, muscle fatigue, lower extremity function, knee control. • Dr. Marjorie Woollacott, Head, 541-346-4107. Application contact: Carol Budweg, Graduate Secretary, 541-346-5430. E-mail: cbudweg@oregon.uoregon.edu.

University of Pittsburgh, School of Education, Department of Health, Physical, and Recreation Education, Pittsburgh, PA 15260. Offerings include movement science (MHPE, MS, PhD), with options in developmental movement (MS, PhD), exercise physiology (MS, PhD), health promotion and education (MHPE), sports medicine (MS, PhD). Department faculty: 10 full-time (6 women). *Degree requirements:* For doctorate, dissertation. *Average time to degree:* master's–2 years full-time, 4 years part-time; doctorate–4 years full-time, 6 years part-time. *Entrance requirements:* For doctorate, GRE General Test, TOEFL (minimum score 650). Application deadline: 2/1. Application fee: $30 ($40 for international students). *Expenses:* Tuition $8018 per year full-time, $329 per credit part-time for state residents; $16,508 per year full-time, $680 per credit part-time for nonresidents. Fees $480 per year full-time, $180 per year part-time. • Dr. Louis A. Pingel, Associate Dean, 412-648-1775. E-mail: pingel1+@pitt.edu. Application contact: Jackie Harden, Manager, 412-648-7060. Fax: 412-648-1899. E-mail: jackie@sched.fsl.pitt.edu.

University of South Alabama, College of Education, Department of Health, Physical Education and Leisure Services, Mobile, AL 36688-0002. Offerings include exercise technology (MS). Department faculty: 10 full-time (2 women). *Application deadline:* 9/1 (priority date; rolling processing). *Application fee:* $25. • Dr. Frederick Scaffidi, Chairman, 334-460-7131.

University of South Carolina, Graduate School, School of Public Health, Department of Exercise Science, Columbia, SC 29208. Awards MS, DPT, PhD. Part-time programs available. Faculty: 8 full-time (3 women). Students: 68 full-time (39 women), 14 part-time (10 women); includes 4 minority (2 African Americans, 1 Asian American, 1 Hispanic), 2 international. Average age 26. 48 applicants, 52% accepted. In 1997, 17 master's awarded. *Degree requirements:* For master's, project. *Entrance requirements:* GRE. Application fee: $35. Electronic applications accepted. *Expenses:* Tuition $4480 per year full-time, $220 per credit hour part-time for state residents; $9338 per year full-time, $457 per credit hour part-time for nonresidents. Fees $125 per year full-time, $37 per semester (minimum) part-time. *Faculty research:* Effects of acute and chronic exercise on human function and health, motor control. • Dr. Russell Pate, Chair, 803-777-2456.

University of Southern California, Graduate School, College of Letters, Arts and Sciences, Department of Exercise Science, Los Angeles, CA 90089. Awards MA, MS, PhD. Students: 13 full-time (4 women), 4 part-time (1 woman); includes 5 minority (1 African American, 4 Asian Americans), 1 international. Average age 30. 21 applicants, 24% accepted. In 1997, 3 doctorates awarded. *Degree requirements:* For doctorate, dissertation. *Entrance requirements:* GRE General Test. Application deadline: 7/1 (priority date; 12/1 for spring admission). Application fee: $55. *Expenses:* Tuition $16,944 per year full-time, $706 per unit part-time. Fees $414 per year full-time, $32 per year part-time. *Financial aid:* In 1997–98, 1 research assistantship, 11 teaching assistantships, 5 scholarships were awarded; fellowships, Federal Work-Study, institutionally sponsored loans also available. Aid available to part-time students. Financial aid application deadline: 2/15; applicants required to submit FAFSA. • Dr. Casey Donovan, Chairman, 213-740-2478.

University of Tennessee, Knoxville, College of Education, Program in Education I, Knoxville, TN 37996. Offerings include exercise science (PhD). *Degree requirements:* 1 foreign language (computer language can substitute), dissertation. *Entrance requirements:* GRE General Test, TOEFL (minimum score 550), minimum GPA of 2.7. Application deadline: 2/1 (priority date; rolling processing). Application fee: $35. Electronic applications accepted. *Tuition:* $3354 per year full-time, $181 per semester hour part-time for state residents; $8410 per year full-time, $462 per semester hour part-time for nonresidents. • Dr. Tom George, Associate Dean, 423-974-0907. Fax: 423-974-8718. E-mail: tgeorge1@utk.edu.

University of Tennessee, Knoxville, College of Education, Program in Human Performance and Sport Studies, Knoxville, TN 37996. Offers exercise science (MS), sport management (MS). Part-time and evening/weekend programs available. Students: 86 full-time (31 women), 41 part-time (18 women); includes 9 minority (5 African Americans, 2 Asian Americans, 2 Hispanics), 7 international. 216 applicants, 56% accepted. In 1997, 58 degrees awarded. *Degree requirements:* Thesis optional, foreign language not required. *Entrance requirements:* TOEFL (minimum score 550), minimum GPA of 2.7. Application deadline: 2/1 (priority date; rolling processing). Application fee: $35. Electronic applications accepted. *Tuition:* $3354 per year full-time, $181 per semester hour part-time for state residents; $8410 per year full-time, $462 per semester hour part-time for nonresidents. *Financial aid:* Graduate assistantships, Federal Work-Study, institutionally sponsored loans, and career-related internships or fieldwork available. Financial aid application deadline: 2/1. • Dr. Tom George, Associate Dean, 423-974-0907. Fax: 423-974-8718. E-mail: tgeorge1@utk.edu.

The University of Texas at El Paso, College of Nursing and Health Science, Program in Kinesiology and Sports Studies, 500 West University Avenue, El Paso, TX 79968-0001. Awards MS. *Degree requirements:* Thesis required, foreign language not required. *Entrance requirements:* GRE General Test, TOEFL (minimum score 550), course work in statistics. Application deadline: 7/1 (priority date; rolling processing; 11/1 for spring admission). Application fee: $15 ($65 for international students). *Tuition:* $2063 per year full-time, $284 per credit hour part-time for state residents; $5753 per year full-time, $425 per credit hour part-time for nonresidents.

The University of Texas at Tyler, School of Education and Psychology, Department of Health and Kinesiology, Tyler, TX 75799-0001. Offerings include clinical exercise physiology (MS). Department faculty: 4 full-time (2 women), 6 part-time (3 women). *Application fee:* $0 ($50 for international students). *Tuition:* $2144 per year full-time, $337 per semester (minimum) part-time for state residents; $7256 per year full-time, $964 per semester (minimum) part-time for nonresidents. • Dr. James Schwane, Chairperson, 903-566-7031. Fax: 903-566-7065. E-mail: jschwane@mail.uttyl.edu. Application contact: Martha D. Wheat, Director of Admissions and Student Records, 903-566-7201. Fax: 903-566-7068.

University of the Pacific, Department of Sport Sciences, Stockton, CA 95211-0197. Awards MA. Faculty: 8 full-time (4 women), 3 part-time (1 woman). Students: 10 full-time (6 women), 3 part-time (0 women); includes 2 international. In 1997, 7 degrees awarded. *Degree requirements:*

Directories: Exercise and Sports Science; Kinesiology and Movement Studies

University of the Pacific (continued)

Thesis required, foreign language not required. *Entrance requirements:* GRE General Test. Application deadline: 3/1 (priority date; rolling processing; 10/15 for spring admission). Application fee: $50. *Expenses:* Tuition $19,000 per year full-time, $594 per unit part-time. Fees $30 per year (minimum). *Financial aid:* In 1997–98, 7 teaching assistantships (5 to first-year students) were awarded; institutionally sponsored loans also available. Aid available to part-time students. Financial aid application deadline: 3/1. • Dr. Thomas Stubbs, Chairperson, 209-946-2232.

University of Toledo, College of Education and Allied Professions, Department of Health Promotion and Human Performance, Toledo, OH 43606-3398. Offerings include exercise science (MS). Department faculty: 17 full-time (5 women). *Application deadline:* 8/1 (priority date; rolling processing). *Application fee:* $30. Electronic applications accepted. *Tuition:* $5907 per year full-time, $246 per hour part-time for state residents; $11,835 per year full-time, $493 per hour part-time for nonresidents. • Dr. Carol Plimpton, Chair, 419-530-2747. Fax: 419-530-4759. E-mail: cplimpt@utnet.utoledo.edu.

University of Utah, College of Health, Department of Exercise and Sport Science, Salt Lake City, UT 84112-1107. Awards M Phil, MS, Ed D, PhD. Faculty: 13 full-time (6 women), 18 part-time (6 women). Students: 49 full-time (15 women), 10 part-time (6 women); includes 4 minority (2 African Americans, 2 Asian Americans), 1 international. Average age 30. In 1997, 22 master's, 2 doctorates awarded. Terminal master's awarded for partial completion of doctoral program. *Degree requirements:* For master's, thesis, comprehensive exam required, foreign language not required; for doctorate, computer language, dissertation, research project required, foreign language not required. *Entrance requirements:* For master's, TOEFL (minimum score 500), minimum GPA of 3.0, undergraduate major or minor in physical education; for doctorate, GRE General Test or MAT, TOEFL (minimum score 500), minimum GPA of 3.3. Application deadline: 3/1. Application fee: $30 ($50 for international students). *Tuition:* $2045 per year full-time, $562 per semester (minimum) part-time for state residents; $6129 per year full-time, $1607 per semester (minimum) part-time for nonresidents. *Financial aid:* In 1997–98, 12 teaching assistantships were awarded; institutionally sponsored loans and career-related internships or fieldwork also available. *Faculty research:* Exercise physiology, psychosocial aspects of sports and physical education, special physical education, elementary/secondary physical education, administration. • Sandy K. Beveridge, Chair, 801-585-3992. Fax: 801-581-5580. Application contact: Barry B. Shultz, Director of Graduate Studies, 801-581-4440. E-mail: barry.shultz@health.utah.edu.

University of Victoria, Faculty of Education, School of Physical Education, Victoria, BC V8W 2Y2, Canada. Offerings include sports and exercise science (MA, M Sc). School faculty: 14 full-time (5 women), 5 part-time (0 women). *Average time to degree:* master's–2.9 years full-time. *Application deadline:* 4/30 (rolling processing). *Application fee:* $50. *Tuition:* $2080 per year full-time, $557 per semester part-time. • Dr. D. Docherty, Director, 250-721-8375. E-mail: docherty@uvic.ca. Application contact: Gladys Whittal, Graduate Secretary, 250-721-8373. Fax: 250-721-6601. E-mail: gwhittal@uvic.ca/.

University of Wisconsin–La Crosse, College of Health, Physical Education and Recreation, Department of Exercise and Sport Science, Program in Adult Fitness/Cardiac Rehabilitation, La Crosse, WI 54601-3742. Awards MS. Faculty: 3 full-time (1 woman), 14 part-time (4 women), 4.5 FTE. Students: 13 full-time (5 women), 1 (woman) part-time; includes 1 minority (Asian American). Average age 24. 58 applicants, 26% accepted. In 1997, 15 degrees awarded (93% found work related to degree). *Degree requirements:* Thesis required, foreign language not required. *Entrance requirements:* Minimum GPA of 3.0. Application deadline: 2/1. Application fee: $38. *Tuition:* $3737 per year full-time, $208 per credit part-time for state residents; $11,921 per year full-time, $633 per credit part-time for nonresidents. *Financial aid:* In 1997–98, 9 students received aid, including 4 teaching assistantships (all to first-year students) averaging $546 per month and totaling $19,656; Federal Work-Study, institutionally sponsored loans, and career-related internships or fieldwork also available. Financial aid application deadline: 3/15; applicants required to submit FAFSA. *Faculty research:* Cardiovascular physiology, ECG, wellness, risk factors. • Dr. John Porcari, Coordinator, 608-785-8684. E-mail: porcari@mail.uwlax.edu. Application contact: Tim Lewis, Director of Admissions, 608-785-8939. Fax: 608-785-6695. E-mail: admissions@mail.uwlax.edu.

University of Wisconsin–La Crosse, College of Health, Physical Education and Recreation, Department of Exercise and Sport Science, Program in Human Performance, La Crosse, WI 54601-3742. Awards MS. Part-time and evening/weekend programs available. Faculty: 14 full-time (5 women), 6 part-time (2 women), 17.16 FTE. Students: 30 full-time (10 women), 12 part-time (2 women); includes 2 minority (both Hispanics), 1 international. Average age 25. 60 applicants, 83% accepted. In 1997, 20 degrees awarded (88% found work related to degree). *Degree requirements:* Thesis optional, foreign language not required. *Average time to degree:* master's–1 year full-time, 2 years part-time. *Entrance requirements:* Minimum GPA of 3.0 during previous 2 years, 2.85 overall. Application deadline: 3/1 (priority date; rolling processing). Application fee: $38. *Tuition:* $3737 per year full-time, $208 per credit part-time for state residents; $11,921 per year full-time, $633 per credit part-time for nonresidents. *Financial aid:* In 1997–98, 8 students received aid, including 7 teaching assistantships (all to first-year students) averaging $546 per month and totaling $34,398; full and partial tuition waivers, Federal Work-Study, institutionally sponsored loans, and career-related internships or fieldwork also available. Aid available to part-time students. Financial aid application deadline: 3/15; applicants required to submit FAFSA. *Faculty research:* Energy metabolism, muscle training, biomechanics-motor learning, exercise physiology, sport psychology. • Dr. Marilyn K. Miller, Coordinator, 608-785-6527. Fax: 608-785-6520. E-mail: mille_mk@mail.uwlax.edu. Application contact: Tim Lewis, Director of Admissions, 608-785-8067.

Virginia Polytechnic Institute and State University, College of Human Resources and Education, Department of Human Nutrition, Foods and Exercise, Blacksburg, VA 24061. Offerings include clinical exercise physiology (MS, PhD). Department faculty: 16 full-time (12 women). *Degree requirements:* Thesis/dissertation. *Entrance requirements:* GRE, TOEFL. Application deadline: 12/1 (priority date; rolling processing). Application fee: $25. *Tuition:* $4927 per year full-time, $792 per semester (minimum) part-time for state residents; $7537 per year full-time, $1227 per semester (minimum) part-time for nonresidents. • Dr. Eleanor D. Schlenker, Head, 540-231-4672.

Wake Forest University, Department of Health and Exercise Science, Winston-Salem, NC 27109. Awards MS. Faculty: 7 full-time (1 woman). Students: 14 full-time (8 women). Average age 24. 45 applicants, 18% accepted. In 1997, 8 degrees awarded (100% found work related to degree). *Degree requirements:* 1 foreign language (computer language can substitute), thesis. *Entrance requirements:* GRE General Test. Application deadline: 2/15. Application fee: $25. *Tuition:* $17,150 per year full-time, $550 per hour part-time. *Financial aid:* In 1997–98, 14 students received aid, including 7 fellowships (all to first-year students) totaling $114,100, 7 teaching assistantships totaling $114,100; scholarships also available. Aid available to part-time students. Financial aid application deadline: 2/15; applicants required to submit FAFSA. *Faculty research:* Cardiac rehabilitation, biomechanics, health psychology, exercise physiology. • Dr. Tony Marsh, Director, 336-758-5391. E-mail: marshap@wfu.edu.

West Chester University of Pennsylvania, School of Health Sciences, Department of Kinesiology, West Chester, PA 19383. Offerings include exercise and sport physiology (MS), general exercise science (MS). Department faculty: 1 full-time, 9 part-time. *Application deadline:* 4/15 (priority date; rolling processing; 10/15 for spring admission). *Application fee:* $25. *Expenses:* Tuition $3468 per year full-time, $193 per credit part-time for state residents; $6236 per year full-time, $346 per credit part-time for nonresidents. Fees $660 per year full-time, $38 per credit part-time. • Dr. Monita Lank, Chair, 610-436-2260. Application contact: Dr. John G. Williams, Graduate Coordinator, 610-436-3119.

Western Michigan University, College of Education, Department of Health, Physical Education and Recreation, Kalamazoo, MI 49008. Offerings include athletic training (MA), coaching and sports studies (MA), exercise science (MA). *Application deadline:* 2/15 (priority date; rolling processing). *Application fee:* $25. *Expenses:* Tuition $154 per credit hour for state residents; $372 per credit hour for nonresidents. Fees $602 per year full-time, $132 per semester part-time. • Dr. Debra Berkey, Chair, 616-387-2705. Application contact: Paula J. Boodt, Coordinator, Graduate Admissions and Recruitment, 616-387-2000. E-mail: paulaboodt@wmich.edu.

West Texas A&M University, College of Education and Social Sciences, Department of Sports and Exercise Science, Canyon, TX 79016-0001. Awards MS. Part-time and evening/weekend programs available. Faculty: 3 full-time (1 woman), 3 part-time (0 women). Students: 9 full-time (4 women), 16 part-time (7 women); includes 4 minority (2 Asian Americans, 2 Hispanics), 2 international. Average age 34. 13 applicants, 8% accepted. In 1997, 2 degrees awarded. *Degree requirements:* Thesis or alternative, comprehensive exam required, foreign language not required. *Average time to degree:* master's–3 years full-time, 6 years part-time. *Entrance requirements:* GRE General Test (combined average 964). Application deadline: rolling. Application fee: $0 ($50 for international students). Electronic applications accepted. *Expenses:* Tuition $46 per semester hour for state residents; $259 per semester hour for nonresidents. Fees $156 per semester (minimum). *Financial aid:* Teaching assistantships, Federal Work-Study, institutionally sponsored loans, and career-related internships or fieldwork available. Aid available to part-time students. Financial aid applicants required to submit FAFSA. • Dr. Rick Lambson, Head, 806-651-2370. E-mail: rlambson@wtamu.edu.

West Virginia University, School of Medicine, Graduate Programs in Human Performance and Applied Exercise Science, Exercise Physiology Program, Morgantown, WV 26506. Awards MS. Students: 18 full-time (9 women), 1 (woman) part-time; includes 1 minority (African American). Average age 24. 60 applicants, 27% accepted. In 1997, 16 degrees awarded. *Degree requirements:* Clinical rotation required, thesis optional, foreign language not required. *Average time to degree:* master's–1.5 years full-time. *Application deadline:* 3/15. *Application fee:* $45. *Tuition:* $9204 per year for state residents; $22,704 per year for nonresidents. *Financial aid:* 9 students received aid. Financial aid application deadline: 2/1; applicants required to submit FAFSA. *Faculty research:* Diabetes and exercise, exercise and immune function, strength training in children, effects of sports drinks, effects of nitric oxide on cardiovascular system. Total annual research expenditures: $124,300. • Dr. Rachel Yeater, Director, 304-293-7693. Fax: 304-293-4146.

Wichita State University, College of Education, Department of Health and Physical Education, Wichita, KS 67260. Offerings include physical education (M Ed), with option in exercise science and wellness; sports administration (M Ed), with option in exercise science and wellness. Department faculty: 5 full-time (3 women), 17 part-time (9 women). *Degree requirements:* Comprehensive exam required, thesis optional, foreign language not required. *Entrance requirements:* TOEFL (minimum score 550), minimum GPA of 2.75. Application deadline: 7/1 (priority date; rolling processing; 1/1 for spring admission). Application fee: $25 ($40 for international students). Electronic applications accepted. *Expenses:* Tuition $2303 per year full-time, $96 per credit hour part-time for state residents; $7691 per year full-time, $321 per credit hour part-time for nonresidents. Fees $490 per year full-time, $75 per semester (minimum) part-time. • Dr. Susan K. Kovar, Chairperson, 316-978-3340. E-mail: kovar@wsuhub.uc.twsu.edu. Application contact: Dr. Lori Miller, Graduate Coordinator, 316-978-3340. Fax: 316-978-3302. E-mail: lmiller@wsuhub.uc.twsu.edu.

York University, Faculty of Arts, Program in Exercise and Health Science, Toronto, ON M3J 1P3, Canada. Awards MA, M Sc. Part-time programs available. *Degree requirements:* Thesis required, foreign language not required. *Application deadline:* 3/15. *Application fee:* $60.

Kinesiology and Movement Studies

Angelo State University, College of Sciences, Department of Kinesiology, San Angelo, TX 76909. Offers programs in kinesiology (MS), physical education (MAT). Part-time and evening/weekend programs available. Faculty: 3 full-time (2 women). Students: 5 full-time (1 woman), 4 part-time (3 women). Average age 27. 11 applicants, 82% accepted. In 1997, 5 degrees awarded. *Degree requirements:* Thesis, comprehensive exam required, foreign language not required. *Entrance requirements:* GRE General Test, minimum GPA of 2.5. Application deadline: 8/7 (priority date; rolling processing; 1/2 for spring admission). Application fee: $25 ($50 for international students). *Expenses:* Tuition $1022 per year full-time, $36 per semester hour part-time for state residents; $7382 per year full-time, $246 per semester hour part-time for nonresidents. Fees $1140 per year full-time, $165 per semester (minimum) part-time. *Financial aid:* In 1997–98, 2 fellowships, 1 teaching assistantship, 1 graduate assistantship were awarded; partial tuition waivers, Federal Work-Study, and career-related internships or fieldwork also available. Aid available to part-time students. Financial aid application deadline: 8/1. • Dr. Melanie A. Croy, Head, 915-942-2174.

Boston University, Sargent College of Health and Rehabilitation Sciences, Department of Physical Therapy, Boston, MA 02215. Offerings include applied kinesiology (D Sc). Department faculty: 14 full-time (11 women), 5 part-time (1 woman). *Degree requirements:* Computer language, dissertation required, foreign language not required. *Entrance requirements:* GRE General Test (minimum combined score of 1000; average 1350), master's degree. Application deadline: 2/1 (rolling processing). Application fee: $50. *Expenses:* Tuition $22,830 per year full-time, $713 per credit part-time. Fees $218 per year full-time, $40 per semester part-time. • Dr. Catherine Certo, Chairman, 617-353-2720.

See in-depth description on page 1235.

Boston University, School of Education, Department of Curriculum and Teaching, Program in Human Movement, Boston, MA 02215. Awards Ed M, Ed D, CAGS. Students: 6 full-time (1 woman), 16 part-time (8 women); includes 1 minority (African American), 1 international. Average age 27. In 1997, 17 master's, 2 CAGSs awarded. *Degree requirements:* For doctorate, dissertation, comprehensive exam required, foreign language not required; for CAGS, comprehensive exam required, foreign language and thesis not required. *Entrance requirements:* For master's and CAGS, GRE or MAT, TOEFL; for doctorate, GRE General Test or MAT, TOEFL. Application deadline: 2/15 (priority date; rolling processing). Application fee: $50. *Expenses:* Tuition $22,830 per year full-time, $713 per credit part-time. Fees $218 per year full-time, $40 per semester part-time. *Financial aid:* Application deadline 3/30. *Faculty research:*

Sports theory, biofeedback, exercise. • Dr. John Cheffers, Coordinator, 617-353-3302. E-mail: cheffers@bu.edu.

Bowling Green State University, College of Education and Allied Professions, School of Human Movement, Sport, and Leisure Studies, Bowling Green, OH 43403. Offers programs in development kinesiology (M Ed), recreation and leisure (M Ed), sport administration (M Ed). Part-time programs available. Faculty: 18 full-time (11 women), 1 (woman) part-time. Students: 36 full-time (22 women), 18 part-time (12 women); includes 5 minority (4 African Americans, 1 Hispanic), 3 international. 68 applicants, 60% accepted. In 1997, 29 degrees awarded. *Degree requirements:* Thesis or alternative required, foreign language not required. *Entrance requirements:* GRE General Test, TOEFL (minimum score 565), minimum GPA of 2.6. Application deadline: 4/1 (rolling processing). Application fee: $30. Electronic applications accepted. *Tuition:* $6070 per year full-time, $284 per credit hour part-time for state residents; $11,358 per year full-time, $536 per credit hour part-time for nonresidents. *Financial aid:* In 1997–98, 40 assistantships were awarded; Federal Work-Study and career-related internships or fieldwork also available. Financial aid application deadline: 2/15; applicants required to submit FAFSA. *Faculty research:* Teacher-learning process, travel and tourism, sport marketing and management, exercise physiology and sport psychology, life-span motor development. • Dr. Mary Ann Roberton, Director, 419-372-7234. Application contact: Dr. Janet Parks, Graduate Coordinator, 419-372-2878.

California Polytechnic State University, San Luis Obispo, College of Science and Mathematics, Department of Physical Education and Kinesiology, San Luis Obispo, CA 93407. Awards MS. Faculty: 16 full-time, 5 part-time. Students: 20 full-time, 10 part-time. 36 applicants, 75% accepted. In 1997, 6 degrees awarded. *Degree requirements:* Thesis optional. *Entrance requirements:* Minimum GPA of 2.75. Application deadline: 7/1 (3/1 for spring admission). Application fee: $55. *Expenses:* Tuition $0 for state residents; $164 per unit for nonresidents. Fees $2102 per year full-time, $1632 per year part-time. *Financial aid:* Federal Work-Study and career-related internships or fieldwork available. Aid available to part-time students. • Dwayne Head, Head, 805-756-2545.

California State Polytechnic University, Pomona, College of Letters, Arts, and Social Sciences, Program in Kinesiology, Pomona, CA 91768-2557. Awards MS. Part-time programs available. Students: 29 part-time (16 women); includes 7 minority (3 Asian Americans, 4 Hispanics). 5 applicants, 80% accepted. In 1997, 3 degrees awarded. *Degree requirements:* Thesis or alternative. *Application deadline:* rolling. *Application fee:* $55. *Expenses:* Tuition $0 for state residents; $164 per unit for nonresidents. Fees $1953 per year full-time, $1287 per year part-time. *Financial aid:* 10 students received aid; Federal Work-Study, institutionally sponsored loans available. Aid available to part-time students. Financial aid application deadline: 3/2; applicants required to submit FAFSA. • Dr. Wanda J. Rainbolt, Coordinator, 909-869-2788. E-mail: wjrainbolt@csupomona.edu.

California State University, Fresno, Division of Graduate Studies, School of Health and Social Work, Department of Kinesiology, 5241 North Maple Avenue, Fresno, CA 93740. Offers program in exercise science (MA). Part-time and evening/weekend programs available. Faculty: 9 full-time (4 women). Students: 10 full-time (2 women), 17 part-time (7 women); includes 7 minority (1 African American, 3 Asian Americans, 3 Hispanics). Average age 31. 16 applicants, 94% accepted. In 1997, 9 degrees awarded. *Degree requirements:* Thesis or alternative required, foreign language not required. *Average time to degree:* master's–3.5 years full-time. *Entrance requirements:* GRE General Test, TOEFL (minimum score 550), minimum GPA of 2.5. Application deadline: 8/1 (priority date; rolling processing; 12/1 for spring admission). Application fee: $55. Electronic applications accepted. *Expenses:* Tuition $0 for state residents; $246 per unit for nonresidents. Fees $1872 per year full-time, $1206 per year part-time. *Financial aid:* In 1997–98, 5 teaching assistantships totaling $26,841, 9 scholarships totaling $4,316 were awarded; Federal Work-Study and career-related internships or fieldwork also available. Financial aid application deadline: 3/1; applicants required to submit FAFSA. *Faculty research:* Refugee education, homeless, geriatrics, fitness. • Catherine Jackson, Chair, 209-278-2016. E-mail: catherine_jackson@csufresno.edu. Application contact: Rose Lyon, Coordinator, 209-278-2005. Fax: 209-278-7010. E-mail: rose_lyon@csufresno.edu.

California State University, Long Beach, College of Health and Human Services, Department of Kinesiology and Physical Education, Long Beach, CA 90840-4901. Awards MA. Faculty: 20 full-time. Students: 40 full-time (21 women), 47 part-time (29 women); includes 18 minority (5 African Americans, 6 Asian Americans, 6 Hispanics, 1 Native American), 4 international. Average age 30. 86 applicants, 80% accepted. In 1997, 19 degrees awarded. *Degree requirements:* Oral and written comprehensive exams or thesis required, foreign language not required. *Entrance requirements:* GRE General Test (minimum combined score of 1350 on three sections), minimum GPA of 2.75 during previous 2 years. Application deadline: 8/1 (rolling processing; 12/1 for spring admission). Application fee: $55. *Expenses:* Tuition $0 for state residents; $246 per unit for nonresidents. Fees $1846 per year full-time, $1180 per year part-time. *Financial aid:* Application deadline 3/2. *Faculty research:* Pulmonary functioning, feedback and practice structure, strength training, history and politics of sports, special population research issues. • Dr. Dixie Grimmett, Chair, 562-985-4051. E-mail: dgrimmet@csulb.edu. Application contact: Dr. Michael LaCourse, Graduate Coordinator, 562-985-4558. Fax: 562-985-8067. E-mail: mlacour@csulb.edu.

California State University, Northridge, College of Health and Human Development, Department of Kinesiology, Northridge, CA 91330. Awards MA. Part-time and evening/weekend programs available. Faculty: 23 full-time, 12 part-time. Students: 25 full-time (12 women), 27 part-time (11 women); includes 11 minority (8 Asian Americans, 3 Hispanics), 3 international. Average age 28. 35 applicants, 97% accepted. *Degree requirements:* Thesis or alternative required, foreign language not required. *Entrance requirements:* TOEFL, GRE General Test (score in 50th percentile or higher) or minimum GPA of 3.0. Application deadline: 11/30. Application fee: $55. *Expenses:* Tuition $0 for state residents; $246 per unit for nonresidents. Fees $1970 per year full-time, $1304 per year part-time. *Financial aid:* Teaching assistantships available. Financial aid application deadline: 3/1. • Dr. William Vincent, Chair, 818-677-3205. Application contact: Graduate Coordinator, 818-677-2585 Ext. 3207.

Dalhousie University, Faculty of Health Professions, School of Health and Human Performance, Division of Kinesiology, Halifax, NS B3H 3J5, Canada. Awards M Sc. Part-time programs available. Faculty: 7 full-time (2 women), 1 (woman) part-time. Students: 13 full-time (7 women), 8 part-time (4 women); includes 3 minority (1 African American, 2 Asian Americans). 13 applicants, 54% accepted. In 1997, 4 degrees awarded (75% found work related to degree, 25% continued full-time study). *Degree requirements:* Thesis required, foreign language not required. *Average time to degree:* master's–3 years full-time, 7 years part-time. *Entrance requirements:* TOEFL (minimum score 580). Application deadline: 6/1 (rolling processing). Application fee: $55. *Financial aid:* 10 students received aid; research assistantships, teaching assistantships, institutionally sponsored loans available. *Faculty research:* Sport science, fitness, neuromuscular physiology, biomechanics, ergonomics, sport psychology. • Dr. C. Putnam, Associate Director, School of Health and Human Performance, 902-494-1167. Fax: 902-494-5120. E-mail: putnam@ac.dal.ca.

Florida State University, College of Human Sciences, Department of Nutrition, Food, and Movement Sciences, Tallahassee, FL 32306. Offers programs in human science (MS), including clinical nutrition, food science, nutrition and sport, nutrition science, nutrition, education and health promotion; movement science (MS, PhD), including exercise physiology, motor learning and control; nutrition and food science (PhD). Faculty: 13 full-time (9 women). Students: 43 full-time (27 women), 16 part-time (7 women); includes 7 minority (1 African American, 4 Asian Americans, 2 Hispanics), 13 international. 224 applicants, 52% accepted. In 1997, 17 master's awarded (100% found work related to degree); 1 doctorate awarded. *Degree requirements:* For master's, thesis optional, foreign language not required; for doctorate, dissertation. *Entrance requirements:* GRE General Test (minimum combined score of 1000), minimum GPA of 3.0. Application fee: $20. *Tuition:* $139 per credit hour for state residents; $482 per credit hour for nonresidents. *Financial aid:* In 1997–98, 2 fellowships (1 to a first-year student), 15 teaching assistantships (4 to first-year students), 9 graduate assistantships (4 to first-year students) were awarded; research assistantships, Federal Work-Study also available. *Faculty research:* Nutrition and exercise, vitamin A deficiency, protein biochemistry, cardiovascular responses to exercises, physiological effects of cigarette smoking related to health and wellness. • Dr. Robert Moffatt, Chair, 850-644-1828. E-mail: rmoffatt@mailer.fsu.edu. Application contact: Dr. Cathy Levenson, Graduate Coordinator, 850-644-4800. Fax: 850-644-0700.

Georgia Southern University, College of Health and Professional Studies, Department of Kinesiology and Health, Program in Kinesiology, Statesboro, GA 30460-8126. Awards MS. Part-time programs available. Students: 24 full-time (13 women), 4 part-time (2 women); includes 1 minority (Asian American), 1 international. Average age 26. 12 applicants, 92% accepted. In 1997, 8 degrees awarded. *Degree requirements:* Terminal exam required, thesis optional, foreign language not required. *Entrance requirements:* GRE General Test (minimum score 450 on each section), MAT (minimum score 48), minimum GPA of 2.75. Application deadline: 7/15 (priority date; rolling processing; 11/15 for spring admission). Application fee: $0. Electronic applications accepted. *Tuition:* $2619 per year full-time, $287 per semester (minimum) part-time for state residents; $8619 per year full-time, $1037 per semester (minimum) part-time for nonresidents. *Financial aid:* Research assistantships, teaching assistantships, Federal Work-Study, and career-related internships or fieldwork available. Aid available to part-time students. Financial aid application deadline: 4/15. *Faculty research:* Exercise and children, resistance training, team dynamics, energetics and movement, pain management. • Dr. James L. McMillan, Graduate Program Director, 912-681-0200. Fax: 912-681-0381. E-mail: mcmillan@gsvms2.cc.gasou.edu. Application contact: Dr. John R. Diebolt, Associate Graduate Dean, 912-681-5384. Fax: 912-681-0740. E-mail: gradschool@gsvms2.cc.gasou.edu.

Indiana University Bloomington, School of Health, Physical Education and Recreation, Program in Kinesiology, Bloomington, IN 47405. Offers adapted physical education (MS), administration (MS), applied sport science (MS), athletic administration/sport management (MS), athletic training (MS), biomechanics (MS), clinical exercise physiology (MS), exercise physiology (MS), human performance (PhD), motor control (MS), motor development (MS), motor learning (MS), physical education (PED, PE Dir), social science of sport (MS), sport management (MS). PhD offered through the University Graduate School. Part-time programs available. Faculty: 12 full-time (2 women). Students: 87 full-time (42 women), 28 part-time (14 women); includes 2 African Americans, 1 Asian American, 10 international. In 1997, 71 master's, 2 doctorates awarded. Terminal master's awarded for partial completion of doctoral program. *Degree requirements:* For master's and PE Dir, thesis optional, foreign language not required; for doctorate, dissertation required, foreign language not required. *Entrance requirements:* GRE. Application deadline: rolling. Application fee: $35. *Expenses:* Tuition $153 per credit hour for state residents; $446 per credit hour for nonresidents. Fees $343 per year. *Financial aid:* Fellowships, research assistantships, teaching assistantships, fee scholarships, fee remissions, partial tuition waivers, Federal Work-Study, institutionally sponsored loans, and career-related internships or fieldwork available. Financial aid application deadline: 3/1. *Faculty research:* Exercise physiology and biochemistry, sports biomechanics, human motor control, adaption of fitness and exercise to special populations. • Dr. Harold Morris, Chairperson, 812-855-3114. Application contact: Program Office, 812-855-5523. Fax: 812-855-9417. E-mail: kines@indiana.edu.

Inter American University of Puerto Rico, San Germán Campus, Department of Education, Program in Physical Education and Scientific Analysis of Human Body Movement, San Germán, PR 00683-5008. Awards MA Ed. Part-time and evening/weekend programs available. Faculty: 2 full-time (1 woman). In 1997, 9 degrees awarded. *Degree requirements:* Comprehensive exam required, foreign language and thesis not required. *Entrance requirements:* Minimum GPA of 3.0, GRE General Test, or PAEG. Application deadline: 4/30 (priority date; rolling processing; 11/15 for spring admission). Application fee: $31. *Expenses:* Tuition $150 per credit. Fees $177 per semester. *Financial aid:* Teaching assistantships available. • Application contact: Mildred Camacho, Admissions Director, 787-892-3090. Fax: 787-892-6350.

James Madison University, College of Education and Psychology, Department of Kinesiology, Harrisonburg, VA 22807. Awards MS. Part-time programs available. Faculty: 4 full-time (3 women). Students: 23 full-time (10 women), 11 part-time (6 women); includes 2 minority (1 Asian American, 1 Hispanic). Average age 30. In 1997, 12 degrees awarded. *Degree requirements:* Thesis or alternative required, foreign language not required. *Entrance requirements:* GRE General Test. Application deadline: 7/1 (priority date; rolling processing). Application fee: $50. *Tuition:* $134 per credit hour for state residents; $404 per credit hour for nonresidents. *Financial aid:* In 1997–98, 4 teaching assistantships totaling $39,483, 15 assistantships totaling $144,302 were awarded; fellowships, Federal Work-Study also available. Financial aid application deadline: 2/15; applicants required to submit FAFSA. • Dr. Michael Goldberger, Head, 540-568-6145.

Kansas State University, College of Arts and Sciences, Department of Kinesiology, Manhattan, KS 66506. Awards MS. Part-time programs available. Faculty: 8 full-time (2 women). Students: 21 full-time (10 women), 4 part-time (1 woman); includes 1 minority (African American), 2 international. Average age 24. 26 applicants, 65% accepted. In 1997, 11 degrees awarded. *Degree requirements:* Thesis optional, foreign language not required. *Average time to degree:* master's–2 years full-time. *Entrance requirements:* GRE General Test (minimum combined score of 1500 on three sections). Application deadline: 3/15 (priority date; rolling processing). *Tuition:* $2218 per year full-time, $401 per semester (minimum) part-time for state residents; $6336 per year full-time, $1087 per semester (minimum) part-time for nonresidents. *Financial aid:* In 1997–98, research assistantships averaging $780 per month, teaching assistantships averaging $780 per month were awarded; fellowships, full tuition waivers, Federal Work-Study, institutionally sponsored loans, and career-related internships or fieldwork also available. *Faculty research:* Exercise physiology, vascular function, cardiorespiratory disease, exercise psychology, exercise adherence and compliance. Total annual research expenditures: $300,000. • David Dzewaltowski, Head, 785-532-6765. Fax: 785-532-6486. E-mail: kines@ksu.edu.

Lamar University, College of Education and Human Development, Division of Health, Kinesiology, and Dance, Beaumont, TX 77710. Awards MS. Faculty: 6 full-time (1 woman). Students: 1 (woman) full-time, 1 part-time (0 women). Average age 24. In 1997, 2 degrees awarded (100% found work related to degree). *Degree requirements:* Thesis optional, foreign language not required. *Average time to degree:* master's–2 years full-time, 4 years part-time. *Entrance requirements:* GRE General Test (minimum score 450 on each section), TOEFL (minimum score 500), minimum GPA of 2.5. Application deadline: 8/1 (rolling processing; 12/1 for spring admission). Application fee: $0. *Expenses:* Tuition $1296 per year full-time, $360 per year part-time for state residents; $6432 per year full-time, $1608 per year part-time for nonresidents. Fees $238 per year full-time, $103 per year part-time. *Financial aid:* In 1997–98, 2 teaching assistantships were awarded. Financial aid application deadline: 4/1. *Faculty research:* Motor learning, exercise physiology. • Dr. Harold Blackwell, Chair, 409-880-8724.

Louisiana State University and Agricultural and Mechanical College, College of Education, Department of Kinesiology, Baton Rouge, LA 70803. Awards MS, PhD. Faculty: 14 full-time (4 women), 1 part-time (0 women). Students: 70 full-time (36 women), 25 part-time (14 women); includes 12 minority (9 African Americans, 1 Asian American, 2 Hispanics), 8 international. Average age 27. 67 applicants, 69% accepted. In 1997, 24 master's, 5 doctorates awarded. Terminal master's awarded for partial completion of doctoral program. *Degree requirements:* For master's, thesis required (for some programs), foreign language not required; for doctorate, 1 foreign language (computer language can substitute), dissertation, residency. *Entrance requirements:* For master's, GRE General Test (minimum combined score of 1000; average 1080), minimum GPA of 3.0; for doctorate, GRE General Test (minimum combined score of 1000; average 1100), minimum GPA of 3.0. Application deadline: 1/25 (priority date; rolling processing). Application fee: $25. *Tuition:* $2736 per year full-time, $285 per semester (minimum) part-time for state residents; $6636 per year full-time, $460 per semester (minimum)

Directory: Kinesiology and Movement Studies

Louisiana State University and Agricultural and Mechanical College (continued)

part-time for nonresidents. *Financial aid:* In 1997–98, 3 fellowships (1 to a first-year student), 1 research assistantship, 16 teaching assistantships (6 to first-year students), 6 service assistantships (2 to first-year students) were awarded; Federal Work-Study and career-related internships or fieldwork also available. *Faculty research:* Exercise physiology, motor learning and control, pedagogy, adult fitness and cardiac rehabilitation, biomechanics. • Dr. B. Don Franks, Chair, 504-388-2036. Application contact: Dr. Richard A. Magill, Coordinator of Graduate Studies, 504-388-3548.

McMaster University, Faculty of Social Sciences, Department of Kinesiology, Hamilton, ON L8S 4M2, Canada. Offers programs in human biodynamics (PhD), kinesiology (M Sc). Faculty: 10 full-time (3 women), 4 part-time (0 women). Students: 19 full-time (8 women), 7 part-time (3 women); includes 1 minority (Asian American), 3 international. Average age 24. 43 applicants, 21% accepted. In 1997, 3 master's awarded. *Degree requirements:* For master's, thesis required, foreign language not required. *Average time to degree:* master's–2 years full-time. *Entrance requirements:* For master's, minimum B+ average in undergraduate course work. Application deadline: 3/1 (priority date; rolling processing). Application fee: $50. *Expenses:* Tuition $4422 per year full-time, $1590 per year part-time for Canadian residents; $12,000 per year full-time, $6165 per year part-time for nonresidents. Fees $257 per year full-time, $188 per year part-time. *Financial aid:* 19 students received aid; research assistantships, teaching assistantships available. Financial aid application deadline: 3/1. *Faculty research:* Physiology, exercise rehabilitation, motor control, motor learning, motor development, biomechanics, psychomotor behavior, cardiac rehabilitation. Total annual research expenditures: $176,479. • Dr. Janet Starkes, Chair, 905-525-9140 Ext. 23578. Application contact: Nick Cipriano, Graduate Coordinator, 905-525-9140 Ext. 23579. Fax: 905-523-6011. E-mail: cipriano@mcmail.cis.mcmaster.ca.

New York University, School of Education, Department of Physical Therapy, New York, NY 10012-1019. Offerings include pathokinesiology (MA). Department faculty: 8 full-time (6 women), 11 part-time. *Degree requirements:* Thesis required (for some programs), foreign language not required. *Entrance requirements:* TOEFL, physical therapy certificate. Application deadline: 2/1 (priority date; rolling processing; 12/1 for spring admission). Application fee: $40 ($60 for international students). • Wen K. Ling, Chairperson, 212-998-9408. Fax: 212-995-4190. Application contact: Office of Graduate Admissions, 212-998-5030. Fax: 212-995-4328.

Oregon State University, Graduate School, College of Health and Human Performance, Department of Exercise and Sport Science, Program in Movement Studies for the Disabled, Corvallis, OR 97331. Awards MAIS, MS. Faculty: 16 full-time (7 women). Students: 3 full-time. Average age 28. 2 applicants, 0% accepted. In 1997, 1 degree awarded (100% found work related to degree). *Degree requirements:* Thesis, minimum GPA of 3.0 required, foreign language not required. *Entrance requirements:* TOEFL (minimum score 550), minimum GPA of 3.0 in last 90 hours. Application deadline: 3/1 (rolling processing). Application fee: $50. *Tuition:* $6207 per year full-time, $810 per quarter (minimum) part-time for state residents; $10,551 per year full-time, $1293 per quarter (minimum) part-time for nonresidents. *Financial aid:* Research assistantships, teaching assistantships, Federal Work-Study, institutionally sponsored loans, and career-related internships or fieldwork available. Aid available to part-time students. Financial aid application deadline: 2/1. *Faculty research:* Fitness testing of disabled, biomechanics of disabled, assessment of disabled athletes, biomechanics of wheeling, energy cost of wheeling. Total annual research expenditures: $5000. • Dr. Jeffery A. McCubbin, Director, 541-737-5921. Fax: 541-737-4230.

Pennsylvania State University University Park Campus, College of Health and Human Development, Department of Kinesiology, University Park, PA 16802-1503. Awards M Ed, MS, D Ed, PhD. Students: 40 full-time (11 women), 12 part-time (3 women). *Degree requirements:* Thesis/dissertation. *Entrance requirements:* GRE General Test. Application fee: $40. *Expenses:* Tuition $6534 per year full-time, $276 per credit part-time for state residents; $13,460 per year full-time, $561 per credit part-time for nonresidents. Fees $252 per year (minimum) full-time, $43 per semester (minimum) part-time. • Dr. Karl M. Newell, Head, 814-863-1163. Application contact: Dr. Robert B. Eckhardt, Chair, 814-863-0847.

See in-depth description on page 1317.

Sam Houston State University, College of Education and Applied Science, Division of Health and Kinesiology, Department of Kinesiology, Huntsville, TX 77341. Awards MA, M Ed. Part-time and evening/weekend programs available. Students: 1 (woman) full-time, 18 part-time (6 women); includes 1 minority (African American). Average age 30. In 1997, 9 degrees awarded. *Entrance requirements:* GRE, MAT. Application fee: $15. *Tuition:* $1810 per year full-time, $297 per semester (minimum) part-time for state residents; $6922 per year full-time, $924 per semester (minimum) part-time for nonresidents. *Financial aid:* Teaching assistantships, institutionally sponsored loans available. *Faculty research:* Adult fitness, mainstreaming, coaching technologies, sport psychology. • Application contact: Dr. Gary Oden, Coordinator, 409-294-1211.

Simon Fraser University, Faculty of Applied Science, School of Kinesiology, Burnaby, BC V5A 1S6, Canada. Awards M Sc, PhD. Faculty: 18 full-time (5 women). Students: 51 full-time (20 women), 1 part-time (0 women). Average age 31. In 1997, 2 master's, 6 doctorates awarded. *Degree requirements:* For master's, thesis; for doctorate, dissertation, comprehensive exams. *Entrance requirements:* For master's, TOEFL (minimum score 570), TWE (minimum score 5), or International English Language Test (minimum score 7.5), minimum GPA of 3.0; for doctorate, TOEFL (minimum score 570), TWE (minimum score 5), or International English Language Test (minimum score 7.5), minimum GPA of 3.5. Application fee: $55. *Expenses:* Tuition $768 per trimester. Fees $207 per year full-time, $61 per trimester part-time. *Financial aid:* In 1997–98, 15 fellowships were awarded; research assistantships, teaching assistantships also available. *Faculty research:* Biomechanics, bioengineering, environmental physiology, sports medicine. • J. Hoffer, Director, 604-291-3573. Application contact: Graduate Secretary, 604-291-4061. Fax: 604-291-3040.

Sonoma State University, School of Natural Sciences, Department of Kinesiology, Rohnert Park, CA 94928-3609. Awards MA. Part-time programs available. Faculty: 10 full-time (5 women), 8 part-time (6 women). Students: 2 full-time (both women), 17 part-time (10 women); includes 3 minority (1 Asian American, 1 Hispanic, 1 Native American). Average age 33. 13 applicants, 54% accepted. In 1997, 3 degrees awarded. *Degree requirements:* Thesis, oral exam. *Entrance requirements:* Minimum GPA of 2.8. Application deadline: 11/30 (rolling processing; 9/1 for spring admission). Application fee: $55. *Expenses:* Tuition $0 for state residents; $246 per unit for nonresidents. Fees $2130 per year full-time, $1464 per year part-time. *Financial aid:* Career-related internships or fieldwork available. Financial aid application deadline: 3/2. *Faculty research:* Exercise physiology, adult fitness, prosocial behavior, moral development, sport psychology. • Dr. Martha Yates, Chair, 707-664-2357. E-mail: martha.yates@sonoma.edu. Application contact: Dr. Ellen Carlton, 707-664-3918. E-mail: ellen.carlton@sonoma.edu.

Southeastern Louisiana University, College of Education, Department of Kinesiology and Health Studies, Hammond, LA 70402. Offers programs in health studies (MA), kinesiology (MA). Part-time programs available. Faculty: 11 full-time, 2 part-time. Students: 3 full-time (1 woman), 10 part-time (8 women); includes 1 international. Average age 30. In 1997, 12 degrees awarded. *Degree requirements:* Thesis optional, foreign language not required. *Entrance requirements:* GRE General Test (minimum combined score of 800), minimum GPA of 2.5, 30 hours of physical education. Application deadline: 7/15 (priority date; rolling processing; 12/15 for spring admission). Application fee: $10 ($25 for international students). Electronic applications accepted. *Expenses:* Tuition $2010 per year full-time, $287 per semester (minimum) part-time for state residents; $5232 per year full-time, $287 per semester (minimum) part-time for nonresidents. Fees $5 per year. *Financial aid:* Research assistantships, teaching assistantships, Federal Work-Study, and career-related internships or fieldwork available. Aid available to part-time students. Financial aid application deadline: 5/1; applicants required to submit FAFSA. *Faculty research:* Endocrine response/adaption to exercise, hemispheric function and the teaching of motor skills, teacher knowledge and elementary physical education analysis of HARE self-esteem scale with elementary students. Total annual research expenditures: $12,000. • Dr. Parris R. Watts, Head, 504-549-2129. Fax: 504-549-5119. E-mail: pwatts@selu.edu.

Southern Arkansas University–Magnolia, Graduate Program in Education, Program in Secondary Education, Magnolia, AR 71753. Offerings include health, kinesiology and recreation (M Ed). *Degree requirements:* Thesis or alternative, comprehensive exam required, foreign language not required. *Average time to degree:* master's–2 years full-time. *Entrance requirements:* GRE, minimum GPA of 2.5. Application deadline: 8/15. Application fee: $0. *Expenses:* Tuition $95 per hour for state residents; $138 per hour for nonresidents. Fees $2 per hour. • Dr. Danield L. Bernard, Dean, Graduate Studies, Graduate Program in Education, 870-235-4055. Fax: 870-235-5035. E-mail: dlbernard@mail.saumag.edu.

Springfield College, Programs in Movement Science, Springfield, MA 01109-3797. Offerings in biomechanics (M Ed, MPE, MS); exercise physiology (M Ed, MPE, MS), including clinical exercise physiology, science and research; interdisciplinary studies (M Ed, MPE, MS). Part-time programs available. Faculty: 2 full-time (0 women), 6 part-time (1 woman), 4 FTE. Students: 21 full-time, 5 part-time; includes 4 international. Average age 25. 25 applicants, 64% accepted. In 1997, 6 degrees awarded. *Degree requirements:* Thesis required, foreign language not required. *Application deadline:* (12/1 for spring admission). *Application fee:* $40. *Expenses:* Tuition $474 per credit. Fees $25 per year. *Financial aid:* Fellowships, teaching assistantships, full and partial tuition waivers, Federal Work-Study, and career-related internships or fieldwork available. Financial aid application deadline: 3/1. • Charles J. Redmond, Director, 413-748-3231. Application contact: Donald J. Shaw Jr., Director of Graduate Admissions, 413-748-3225. Fax: 413-748-3694. E-mail: dshaw@spfldcol.edu.

Teachers College, Columbia University, Graduate Faculty of Education, Department of Biobehavioral Studies, Program in Motor Learning, 525 West 120th Street, New York, NY 10027-6696. Awards Ed M, MA, Ed D. Part-time and evening/weekend programs available. Faculty: 2 full-time (1 woman), 2 part-time (1 woman), 2.6 FTE. Students: 2 full-time (1 woman), 42 part-time (31 women); includes 10 minority (3 African Americans, 5 Asian Americans, 2 Hispanics), 6 international. Average age 37. 8 applicants, 88% accepted. In 1997, 4 master's awarded. Terminal master's awarded for partial completion of doctoral program. *Degree requirements:* For master's, integrative paper required, foreign language not required; for doctorate, dissertation. *Entrance requirements:* For doctorate, GRE General Test (minimum combined score of 880). Application deadline: 5/15 (12/1 for spring admission). Application fee: $50. *Expenses:* Tuition $640 per credit. Fees $120 per semester. *Financial aid:* Teaching assistantships, clinical traineeships, full and partial tuition waivers, Federal Work-Study, institutionally sponsored loans, and career-related internships or fieldwork available. Aid available to part-time students. Financial aid application deadline: 2/1. *Faculty research:* Motor control, analysis of tasks, biomechanical aspect of learning, skill acquisition, recovery of motor behavior. • Application contact: Victor Singletary, Office of Admissions, 212-678-3710. Fax: 212-678-4171.

Temple University, College of Education, Department of Physical Education, Philadelphia, PA 19122-6096. Offerings include kinesiology (PhD), with options in behavioral science, somatic science. Terminal master's awarded for partial completion of doctoral program. Department faculty: 11 full-time (5 women). *Degree requirements:* Dissertation required, foreign language not required. *Entrance requirements:* GRE General Test, minimum undergraduate GPA of 2.8, 3.0 during previous 2 years. Application deadline: 2/1 (10/1 for spring admission). Application fee: $40. *Expenses:* Tuition $323 per semester hour for state residents; $444 per semester hour for nonresidents. Fees $170 per year full-time, $28 per semester (minimum) part-time. • Dr. Michael R. Sitler, Chair, 215-204-1950. Fax: 215-204-8705. E-mail: sitler@astro.temple.edu. Application contact: Dr. Michael L. Sachs, Admissions Chair, 215-204-1950.

See in-depth description on page 1891.

Texas A&M University, College of Education, Department of Health and Kinesiology, Program in Kinesiology, College Station, TX 77843. Offers kinesiology (MS, PhD), physical education (M Ed, Ed D). Students: 42 full-time (4 women), 22 part-time (20 women); includes 5 minority (1 African American, 2 Asian Americans, 2 Hispanics), 2 international. Average age 28. 81 applicants, 56% accepted. In 1997, 13 master's, 7 doctorates awarded. *Degree requirements:* For master's, thesis required (for some programs), foreign language not required; for doctorate, dissertation required, foreign language not required. *Entrance requirements:* GRE General Test, TOEFL. Application deadline: rolling. Application fee: $35 ($75 for international students). *Financial aid:* In 1997–98, 5 fellowships (4 to first-year students) averaging $1,000 per month, 29 teaching assistantships averaging $675 per month and totaling $225,000 were awarded; research assistantships, institutionally sponsored loans, and career-related internships or fieldwork also available. Financial aid application deadline: 4/15. *Faculty research:* Bone physiology, muscle injury, motor learning, motor development, sports pedagogy. • Application contact: Susan Lanier, Graduate Secretary, 409-845-4530. Fax: 409-847-8987.

Texas A&M University–Kingsville, College of Education, Department of Health and Kinesiology, Kingsville, TX 78363. Awards MA, MS. Part-time programs available. Faculty: 6 part-time (3 women). Students: 6 full-time (3 women), 15 part-time (6 women); includes 12 minority (all Hispanics). Average age 24. *Degree requirements:* Thesis or alternative, comprehensive exam required, foreign language not required. *Entrance requirements:* GRE General Test (minimum combined score of 1000), minimum GPA of 3.0. Application deadline: 6/1 (rolling processing; 11/15 for spring admission). Application fee: $15 ($25 for international students). *Tuition:* $1822 per year full-time, $281 per semester (minimum) part-time for state residents; $6934 per year full-time, $908 per semester (minimum) part-time for nonresidents. *Financial aid:* Teaching assistantships, partial tuition waivers, Federal Work-Study, institutionally sponsored loans available. Financial aid application deadline: 5/15. *Faculty research:* Body composition, electromyography. • Randy Hughes, Chairman, 512-593-2301.

Texas Christian University, School of Education, Department of Kinesiology and Physical Education, Fort Worth, TX 76129-0002. Awards MS. Part-time and evening/weekend programs available. Students: 19 (8 women). 17 applicants, 71% accepted. In 1997, 8 degrees awarded. *Degree requirements:* Thesis optional, foreign language not required. *Entrance requirements:* GRE General Test (minimum combined score of 1000), TOEFL (minimum score 550). Application deadline: 3/1 (rolling processing; 12/1 for spring admission). Application fee: $0. *Expenses:* Tuition $10,350 per year full-time, $345 per credit hour part-time. Fees $1240 per year full-time, $50 per credit hour part-time. *Financial aid:* Graduate assistantships available. Financial aid application deadline: 3/1. • Dr. Joel Mitchell, Chairperson, 817-257-7665.

Texas Woman's University, College of Health Sciences, Department of Kinesiology, Denton, TX 76204. Offers programs in adapted physical education (MS, PhD), administration (MS, PhD), biomechanics (MS, PhD), exercise and sports nutrition (MS, PhD), exercise physiology (MS, PhD), motor behavior (MS, PhD), pedagogy (MS, PhD). Part-time and evening/weekend programs available. Faculty: 10 full-time (6 women), 9 part-time (8 women), 11 FTE. Students: 49 full-time (36 women), 48 part-time (32 women); includes 6 minority (2 African Americans, 4 Hispanics), 5 international. Average age 31. 40 applicants, 58% accepted. In 1997, 3 master's awarded (100% found work related to degree); 6 doctorates awarded (80% entered university research/teaching, 20% found other work related to degree). Terminal master's awarded for partial completion of doctoral program. *Degree requirements:* For master's, thesis or alternative required, foreign language not required; for doctorate, dissertation, qualifying exam required, foreign language not required. *Average time to degree:* master's–2 years full-time, 5 years part-time; doctorate–4 years full-time, 8 years part-time. *Entrance requirements:* For master's, GRE General Test (minimum combined score of 850); for doctorate, GRE General Test (minimum combined score of 850), minimum GPA of 3.0. Application fee: $25. *Financial aid:* In 1997–98, 32 students received aid, including 17 fellowships (1 to a first-year student) averaging $745 per month and totaling $49,738, 2 research assistantships (1 to a first-year student) averaging $824 per month, 13 teaching assistantships (1 to a first-year student) totaling $49,188; grants, partial tuition waivers, Federal Work-Study, institutionally sponsored loans, and career-related internships or fieldwork also available. Aid available to part-time students. Financial aid application deadline: 4/1. *Faculty research:* Learning complex motor skills, gait analysis, vestibular function, bone density, attention deficit hyperactive disorder. Total annual research expenditures: $105,699. • Dr. Jerry Wilkerson, Interim Chair, 940-898-2576. Application contact: Dr. Harry Meeuwsen, Graduate Coordinator, 940-898-2594.

Université de Montréal, Department of Physical Education, Montréal, PQ H3C 3J7, Canada. Offerings include human movement sciences (M Sc, PhD). Department faculty: 23 full-time (7 women). *Degree requirements:* For master's, 1 foreign language, thesis (for some programs); for doctorate, 1 foreign language, dissertation, general exam. *Application deadline:* 2/1. *Application fee:* $30. • Claude Alain, Chairman, 514-343-6166.

Université de Sherbrooke, Faculty of Physical Education, Program in Physical Education, Sherbrooke, PQ J1K 2R1, Canada. Offerings include kinanthropology (M Sc). *Degree requirements:* Thesis required, foreign language not required. *Entrance requirements:* Minimum GPA of 2.7. Application deadline: 7/31 (priority date; rolling processing). Application fee: $15.

Université du Québec à Montréal, Program in Human Movement Studies, Montréal, PQ H3C 3P8, Canada. Awards M Sc. Part-time programs available. *Degree requirements:* Thesis optional. *Entrance requirements:* Appropriate bachelor's degree or equivalent and proficiency in French. Application deadline: 3/1. Application fee: $50.

University of Arkansas, College of Education, Department of Health Science, Kinesiology, Recreation and Dance, Program in Kinesiology, Fayetteville, AR 72701-1201. Awards MS, PhD. Students: 38 full-time (17 women), 10 part-time (9 women); includes 5 minority (1 Asian American, 1 Hispanic, 3 Native Americans), 2 international. 24 applicants, 79% accepted. In 1997, 7 master's, 2 doctorates awarded. *Degree requirements:* For doctorate, dissertation. *Application fee:* $25 ($35 for international students). *Tuition:* $3144 per year full-time, $173 per credit hour part-time for state residents; $7140 per year full-time, $395 per credit hour part-time for nonresidents. *Financial aid:* Teaching assistantships, Federal Work-Study, and career-related internships or fieldwork available. Aid available to part-time students. Financial aid application deadline: 4/1; applicants required to submit FAFSA. • Dr. Dean Gorman, Coordinator, 501-575-2890.

University of British Columbia, Faculty of Education, School of Human Kinetics, Vancouver, BC V6T 1Z2, Canada. Awards MA, MHK, M Sc, PhD. Part-time programs available. *Degree requirements:* For master's, thesis required (for some programs), foreign language not required; for doctorate, dissertation required, foreign language not required. *Entrance requirements:* For master's, TOEFL (minimum score 550); for doctorate, TOEFL. Application deadline: 4/30 (priority date; rolling processing; 2/1 for spring admission). Application fee: $60. *Faculty research:* Exercise physiology, biomechanics, motor learning.

The University of Calgary, Faculty of Kinesiology, Calgary, AB T2N 1N4, Canada. Awards M Kin, M Sc. Faculty: 17 full-time (6 women), 2 part-time (0 women). Students: 23 full-time (8 women), 5 part-time (3 women); includes 2 minority (1 Asian American, 1 Native American), 2 international. Average age 26. 37 applicants, 22% accepted. In 1997, 13 degrees awarded. *Degree requirements:* Thesis (for some programs), thesis (M Sc) required, foreign language not required. *Average time to degree:* master's–2 years full-time, 2.5 years part-time. *Entrance requirements:* TOEFL (minimum score 550). Application deadline: 3/31. Application fee: $60. *Expenses:* Tuition $5448 per year full-time, $908 per course part-time for Canadian residents; $10,896 per year full-time, $1816 per course part-time for nonresidents. Fees $285 per year full-time, $119 per semester (minimum) part-time. *Financial aid:* In 1997–98, 3 research assistantships averaging $980 per month and totaling $10,000, 18 teaching assistantships (2 to first-year students) averaging $900 per month and totaling $100,000 were awarded; career-related internships or fieldwork also available. Financial aid application deadline: 3/31. *Faculty research:* Load acting on the human body, muscle mechanics and physiology, optimizing high performance athlete performance, eye movement in sports, analysis of body composition. Total annual research expenditures: $1.2 million. • Dr. Preston Wiley, Associate Dean, 403-220-3421. Application contact: Marion Benaschak, Graduate Secretary, 403-220-5183. Fax: 403-220-0546.

University of Central Arkansas, College of Health and Applied Sciences, Department of Kinesiology, Conway, AR 72035-0001. Awards MS. Faculty: 7 full-time (2 women), 1 (woman) part-time, 7.33 FTE. Students: 7 full-time (3 women), 6 part-time (4 women); includes 2 minority (1 African American, 1 Native American), 1 international. 1 applicant, 100% accepted. In 1997, 8 degrees awarded. *Degree requirements:* Comprehensive exam required, thesis optional. *Entrance requirements:* GRE General Test, minimum GPA of 2.7. Application deadline: 3/1 (priority date; rolling processing; 10/1 for spring admission). Application fee: $15 ($40 for international students). *Expenses:* Tuition $161 per credit hour for state residents; $298 per credit hour for nonresidents. Fees $50 per year full-time, $30 per year part-time. *Financial aid:* In 1997–98, 10 assistantships were awarded. Financial aid application deadline: 2/15. • Dr. Deborah Howell-Cresswell, Chairperson, 501-450-3148. Fax: 501-450-5503. E-mail: debbieh@mail.uca.edu.

University of Colorado at Boulder, College of Arts and Sciences, Department of Kinesiology, Boulder, CO 80309. Offers programs in kinesiology (PhD), physical education (MS). Faculty: 9 full-time (1 woman). Students: 54 full-time (23 women), 7 part-time (1 woman); includes 6 minority (1 African American, 5 Asian Americans), 2 international. Average age 27. 82 applicants, 66% accepted. In 1997, 16 master's awarded. *Degree requirements:* For master's, thesis or alternative, comprehensive exam required, foreign language not required; for doctorate, dissertation. *Entrance requirements:* For master's, GRE General Test. Application deadline: 3/1 (priority date; rolling processing). Application fee: $40 ($60 for international students). *Expenses:* Tuition $3170 per year full-time, $531 per semester (minimum) part-time for state residents; $14,652 per year full-time, $2442 per semester (minimum) part-time for nonresidents. Fees $667 per year full-time, $130 per semester (minimum) part-time. *Financial aid:* Research assistantships, teaching assistantships available. Financial aid application deadline: 3/1. *Total annual research expenditures:* $2.2 million. • Dr. Russell Moore, Chair, 303-492-1093. E-mail: rmoore@spot.colorado.edu. Application contact: Melanie Evans, Graduate Program Administrator, 303-492-3122. Fax: 303-492-4009. E-mail: melanie.evans@colorado.edu.

University of Delaware, College of Health and Nursing Sciences, Interdisciplinary Program in Biomechanics and Movement Science, Newark, DE 19716. Awards MS, PhD. *Entrance requirements:* For master's, GRE General Test. Application deadline: 7/1. Application fee: $45. *Expenses:* Tuition $4250 per year full-time, $236 per credit hour part-time for state residents; $12,250 per year full-time, $681 per credit hour part-time for nonresidents. Fees $466 per year full-time, $15 per semester (minimum) part-time. • James Richards, Director, 302-831-6796.

University of Illinois at Chicago, College of Associated Health Professions, School of Kinesiology, Chicago, IL 60607-7128. Awards MS. Part-time programs available. Faculty: 16 full-time (1 woman). Students: 5 full-time (3 women), 63 part-time (38 women); includes 8 minority (3 African Americans, 2 Asian Americans, 2 Hispanics, 1 Native American), 2 international. Average age 28. 49 applicants, 82% accepted. In 1997, 21 degrees awarded. *Degree requirements:* Thesis required, foreign language not required. *Entrance requirements:* GRE General Test, TOEFL (minimum score 550), minimum GPA of 3.75 on a 5.0 scale. Application deadline: 7/3 (11/8 for spring admission). Application fee: $40 ($50 for international students). *Financial aid:* In 1997–98, 11 research assistantships, 3 teaching assistantships were awarded; fellowships, full tuition waivers, and career-related internships or fieldwork also available. *Faculty research:* Mitochondrial biogenesis, glucocorticoid lipid metabolism, at-risk youth, motor control. • Lawrence Oscai, Interim Director, 312-996-2757. Application contact: Dr. Warren Palmer, Director of Graduate Studies, 312-996-4810.

University of Illinois at Urbana–Champaign, College of Applied Life Studies, Department of Kinesiology, Urbana, IL 61801. Awards MS, MST, PhD. PhD offered jointly with the University of Illinois at Chicago. Faculty: 26 full-time (7 women). Students: 70 full-time (28 women); includes 3 minority (all African Americans), 14 international. 66 applicants, 44% accepted. In 1997, 23 master's, 7 doctorates awarded. *Degree requirements:* For doctorate, dissertation. *Entrance requirements:* For master's, GRE General Test, TOEFL, minimum GPA of 4.0 on a 5.0 scale; for doctorate, GRE, TOEFL, minimum graduate GPA of 4.5 on a 5.0 scale. Application deadline: 3/1 (priority date; rolling processing). Application fee: $40 ($50 for international students). *Financial aid:* In 1997–98, 2 fellowships, 18 research assistantships, 34 teaching assistantships were awarded; full and partial tuition waivers also available. Financial aid application deadline: 2/15. • James E. Misner, Head, 217-244-0823. Application contact: Graduate Program Office, 217-333-1083.

Announcement: Major areas of specialization at the master's and doctoral levels include biodynamics of physical activity (exercise physiology, work output, energy, and movement efficiency); coordination, control, and skill (biomechanics, mechanisms, and processes involved in the action of human movement); pedagogical kinesiology (human movement concepts and theories central to educational aspects of kinesiology); and social science of physical activity (sport and exercise psychology and social, cultural, and historical aspects of physical activity). Master's degree only: physical activity management (corporate fitness and wellness) and therapeutic kinesiology (sports medicine, athletic training—prior NATA certification required).

University of Kentucky, Graduate School Programs from the College of Education, Program in Kinesiology and Health Promotion, Lexington, KY 40506-0032. Awards MS, Ed D. Faculty: 12 full-time (3 women), 2 part-time (0 women). Students: 59 full-time (26 women), 26 part-time (12 women); includes 4 minority (3 African Americans, 1 Hispanic), 6 international. 69 applicants, 77% accepted. In 1997, 30 master's, 1 doctorate awarded. Terminal master's awarded for partial completion of doctoral program. *Degree requirements:* For master's, comprehensive exam required, thesis optional, foreign language not required; for doctorate, dissertation, comprehensive exam required, foreign language not required. *Entrance requirements:* For master's, GRE General Test, minimum undergraduate GPA of 2.5; for doctorate, GRE General Test, minimum graduate GPA of 3.0. Application deadline: 7/19 (rolling processing). Application fee: $30 ($35 for international students). *Financial aid:* In 1997–98, 3 fellowships, 1 research assistantship, 8 teaching assistantships, 8 graduate assistantships were awarded; Federal Work-Study, institutionally sponsored loans, and career-related internships or fieldwork also available. Aid available to part-time students. • Dr. Richard Riggs, Director of Graduate Studies, 606-257-3645. E-mail: rsrigg01@ukcc.uky.edu. Application contact: Dr. Constance L. Wood, Associate Dean, 606-257-4613. Fax: 606-323-1928.

University of Maine, College of Education and Human Development, Program in Kinesiology and Physical Education, Orono, ME 04469. Awards MAT, M Ed, MS, CAS. Part-time and evening/weekend programs available. *Degree requirements:* For master's, thesis or alternative required, foreign language not required. *Entrance requirements:* For master's, MAT, TOEFL (minimum score 550); for CAS, MA, M Ed, or MS. Application deadline: 2/1 (priority date; rolling processing; 10/15 for spring admission). Application fee: $50. *Expenses:* Tuition $194 per credit hour for state residents; $548 per credit hour for nonresidents. Fees $378 per year full-time, $33 per semester (minimum) part-time. *Financial aid:* Career-related internships or fieldwork available. Aid available to part-time students. Financial aid application deadline: 3/1. • Application contact: Scott Delcourt, Director of the Graduate School, 207-581-3218. Fax: 207-581-3232. E-mail: graduate@maine.edu.

University of Maryland, College Park, College of Health and Human Performance, Department of Kinesiology, College Park, MD 20742-5045. Awards MA, PhD. Faculty: 23 full-time (9 women), 4 part-time (1 woman). Students: 61 full-time (27 women), 45 part-time (26 women); includes 8 minority (1 African American, 5 Asian Americans, 1 Hispanic, 1 Native American), 9 international. 97 applicants, 40% accepted. In 1997, 9 master's, 7 doctorates awarded. *Degree requirements:* For master's, thesis optional, foreign language not required; for doctorate, dissertation required, foreign language not required. *Entrance requirements:* For master's, GRE General Test, minimum GPA of 3.0; for doctorate, GRE General Test, minimum GPA of 3.5. Application deadline: rolling. Application fee: $50 ($70 for international students). *Expenses:* Tuition $272 per credit hour for state residents; $400 per credit hour for nonresidents. Fees $564 per year full-time, $342 per year part-time. *Financial aid:* In 1997–98, 1 fellowship, 2 research assistantships, 35 teaching assistantships were awarded; career-related internships or fieldwork also available. *Faculty research:* Sports, biophysical and professional studies. • Dr. David H. Clarke, Chairman, 301-405-2453. Fax: 301-314-9167. Application contact: John Mollish, Director, Graduate Admissions and Records, 301-405-4198. Fax: 301-314-9305.

University of Michigan, Programs in Kinesiology, Ann Arbor, MI 48109. Awards AM, MS, PhD, Certificate. Faculty: 18. Students: 38 full-time (19 women); includes 2 minority (both African Americans), 5 international. 45 applicants, 49% accepted. Terminal master's awarded for partial completion of doctoral program. *Degree requirements:* For master's, thesis; for doctorate, dissertation, oral defense of dissertation, preliminary exam. *Entrance requirements:* For master's, GRE General Test; for doctorate, GRE General Test, master's degree. Application deadline: 3/1 (rolling processing). Application fee: $55. *Financial aid:* In 1997–98, 4 fellowships totaling $22,500 were awarded; graduate assistantships also available. Financial aid application deadline: 3/1. • Dr. Dee W. Edington, Director, 734-764-1343. Application contact: Beverly Ballard, Graduate Secretary, 734-764-1343. Fax: 734-936-1925. E-mail: bballard@umich.edu.

See in-depth description on page 1895.

University of Minnesota, Twin Cities Campus, College of Education and Human Development, School of Kinesiology and Leisure Studies, Division of Kinesiology, Minneapolis, MN 55455-0213. Awards MA, M Ed, PhD. Part-time programs available. Terminal master's awarded for partial completion of doctoral program. *Degree requirements:* For master's, thesis (for some programs), final oral exam; for doctorate, dissertation, preliminary written/oral exam, final oral exam. *Entrance requirements:* For master's, GRE or MAT, minimum GPA of 3.0; for doctorate, GRE or MAT, minimum GPA of 3.0, sample of written work. Application deadline: 7/15 (rolling processing; 12/15 for spring admission). Application fee: $30. *Financial aid:* Fellowships, research assistantships, teaching assistantships, full and partial tuition waivers, Federal Work-Study, institutionally sponsored loans, and career-related internships or fieldwork available. Aid available to part-time students. *Faculty research:* Biomechanics, biodynamics, sport psychology, exercise physiology, motor development, human factors, adapted physical education. • Dr. Robert C. Serfass, Head, 612-625-1007. Application contact: Allen Burton, Director of Gradaute Studies, 612-625-0531. Fax: 612-626-7700.

University of Nevada, Las Vegas, College of Health Sciences, Department of Kinesiology, Las Vegas, NV 89154-9900. Offers programs in exercise physiology (MS), kinesiology (MS). Faculty: 9 full-time (1 woman). Students: 27 full-time (7 women), 16 part-time (6 women); includes 10 minority (1 African American, 5 Asian Americans, 4 Hispanics), 2 international. 31 applicants, 87% accepted. In 1997, 16 degrees awarded. *Degree requirements:* Comprehensive exam required, thesis optional, foreign language not required. *Entrance requirements:* GRE General Test (minimum combined score of 1000), minimum GPA of 3.0 during previous 2 years, 2.75 overall. Application deadline: 6/15 (priority date; rolling processing; 11/15 for spring admission). Application fee: $40 ($95 for international students). *Expenses:* Tuition $93 per credit for state residents; $93 per credit full-time, $190 per credit part-time for nonresidents. Fees $5570 per year full-time for nonresidents. *Financial aid:* In 1997–98, 10 teaching assistantships were awarded; research assistantships also available. Financial aid application deadline: 3/1. • Dr. John Young, Co-Chair, 702-895-3766. Application contact: Graduate College Admissions Evaluator, 702-895-3320.

University of New Hampshire, School of Health and Human Services, Department of Kinesiology, Durham, NH 03824. Awards MS. Faculty: 11 full-time. Students: 16 full-time (8

Directory: Kinesiology and Movement Studies

University of New Hampshire (continued)

women), 9 part-time (5 women). Average age 27. 27 applicants, 59% accepted. In 1997, 5 degrees awarded. *Degree requirements:* Thesis or alternative required, foreign language not required. *Entrance requirements:* GRE General Test. Application deadline: 7/1 (priority date; rolling processing). Application fee: $50. *Expenses:* Tuition $5440 per year full-time, $302 per credit hour part-time for state residents; $8160 per year (minimum) full-time, $453 per credit hour (minimum) part-time for nonresidents. Fees $868 per year full-time, $15 per year part-time. *Financial aid:* In 1997–98, 2 research assistantships (both to first-year students), 9 teaching assistantships (3 to first-year students), 1 scholarship (to a first-year student) were awarded; full and partial tuition waivers, Federal Work-Study, and career-related internships or fieldwork also available. Aid available to part-time students. Financial aid application deadline: 2/15. *Faculty research:* Exercise specialist, sports studies, special physical education, pediatric exercises and motor behavior. • Dr. Ronald Croce, Chairperson, 603-862-2080. Application contact: Dr. Timothy Quinn, Graduate Coordinator, 603-862-1830.

The University of North Carolina at Chapel Hill, School of Medicine and Graduate School, Graduate Programs in Medicine, Department of Medical Allied Health Professions, Division of Physical Therapy, Program in Human Movement Science, Chapel Hill, NC 27599. Awards MS. Faculty: 16 full-time (13 women). Students: 15 full-time (11 women); includes 3 international. 23 applicants, 57% accepted. In 1997, 4 degrees awarded. *Degree requirements:* Comprehensive exam, oral defense of thesis required, foreign language not required. *Entrance requirements:* GRE General Test (minimum combined score of 1000), minimum GPA of 3.0. Application deadline: 1/1 (priority date; rolling processing). Application fee: $55. Electronic applications accepted. *Expenses:* Tuition $1428 per year for state residents; $10,414 per year for nonresidents. Fees $782 per year. *Financial aid:* In 1997–98, 3 fellowships (1 to a first-year student) averaging $532 per month and totaling $5,244, 3 graduate assistantships, traineeships (2 to first-year students) averaging $375 per month and totaling $4,500 were awarded; Federal Work-Study, institutionally sponsored loans also available. Financial aid application deadline: 1/1. *Faculty research:* Motor development, motor control; treatment of sports/orthopaedic patient problems; movement in older adults; postural control across the lifespan; research in clinical practice; fetal, preterm, infant movement; functional assessment acress the lifespan. • Dr. Darlene K. Sekerak, Director, Division of Physical Therapy, 919-966-4708. E-mail: dsekerak@css.unc.edu.

University of North Dakota, College of Education and Human Development, Department of Health, Physical Education, and Recreation, Grand Forks, ND 58202. Offers program in kinesiology (MS). Part-time programs available. Faculty: 9 full-time (3 women). Students: 10 full-time (3 women), 20 part-time (6 women). 16 applicants, 88% accepted. In 1997, 5 degrees awarded. *Degree requirements:* Thesis or alternative required, foreign language not required. *Entrance requirements:* TOEFL (minimum score 550), GRE General Test, minimum GPA of 3.0. Application deadline: 3/1 (priority date; rolling processing). Application fee: $20. *Financial aid:* In 1997–98, 9 students received aid, including 3 fellowships totaling $7,200, 6 teaching assistantships totaling $19,937; research assistantships, assistantships, full and partial tuition waivers, Federal Work-Study, institutionally sponsored loans also available. Financial aid application deadline: 3/15. • Dr. Tom Steen, Director, 701-777-4324. Fax: 701-777-3619. E-mail: steen@badlands.nodak.edu.

University of Northern Colorado, College of Health and Human Sciences, School of Kinesiology and Physical Education, Greeley, CO 80639. Awards MA, Ed D. Faculty: 13 full-time (7 women), 1 (woman) part-time. Students: 125 full-time (47 women), 27 part-time (8 women); includes 17 minority (4 African Americans, 5 Asian Americans, 8 Hispanics), 9 international. Average age 30. 162 applicants, 77% accepted. In 1997, 67 master's, 8 doctorates awarded. *Degree requirements:* For master's, comprehensive exams required, thesis not required; for doctorate, dissertation, comprehensive exams. *Entrance requirements:* For doctorate, GRE General Test. Application deadline: rolling. Application fee: $35. *Expenses:* Tuition $2327 per year full-time, $129 per credit hour part-time for state residents; $9578 per year full-time, $532 per credit hour part-time for nonresidents. Fees $752 per year full-time, $184 per semester (minimum) part-time. *Financial aid:* In 1997–98, 96 students received aid, including 10 fellowships (6 to first-year students) totaling $17,450, 16 teaching assistantships (5 to first-year students) totaling $97,595, 9 graduate assistantships (4 to first-year students) totaling $60,043. Financial aid application deadline: 3/1. • Dr. Jim Stiehl, Director, 970-351-2535.

University of North Texas, College of Education, Department of Kinesiology, Health Promotion, and Recreation, Program in Kinesiology, Denton, TX 76203-6737. Awards MS. Part-time programs available. *Degree requirements:* Thesis required (for some programs), foreign language not required. *Entrance requirements:* GRE General Test (minimum score 375 on each section; 800 combined). Application deadline: 7/17. Application fee: $25 ($50 for international students). *Tuition:* $2063 per year full-time, $815 per year part-time for state residents; $5897 per year full-time, $2100 per year part-time for nonresidents. *Financial aid:* Teaching assistantships, Federal Work-Study, institutionally sponsored loans, and career-related internships or fieldwork available. Financial aid application deadline: 4/1. • Application contact: Noreen Goggin, Adviser, 940-565-2651.

University of Oregon, Graduate School, College of Arts and Sciences, Department of Exercise and Movement Science, Eugene, OR 97403. Awards MS, PhD. Faculty: 4 full-time (1 woman), 1 (woman) part-time, 4.5 FTE. Students: 60 full-time (26 women), 8 part-time (4 women); includes 6 minority (3 Asian Americans, 3 Hispanics), 15 international. 115 applicants, 41% accepted. In 1997, 26 master's, 8 doctorates awarded. *Degree requirements:* For master's, thesis optional; for doctorate, 1 foreign language (computer language can substitute), dissertation. *Entrance requirements:* For master's, GRE General Test (minimum score 470 on verbal section, 500 on quantitative), TOEFL (minimum score 550), minimum GPA of 2.75 in undergraduate course work; for doctorate, GRE General Test (minimum score 520 on verbal section, 560 on quantitative). Application deadline: 7/18. Application fee: $50. *Tuition:* $6429 per year full-time, $873 per quarter (minimum) part-time for state residents; $10,857 per year full-time, $1360 per quarter (minimum) part-time for nonresidents. *Financial aid:* In 1997–98, 44 teaching assistantships (10 to first-year students) were awarded; Federal Work-Study also available. *Faculty research:* Balance control, muscle fatigue, lower extremity function, knee control. • Dr. Marjorie Woollacott, Head, 541-346-4107. Application contact: Carol Budweg, Graduate Secretary, 541-346-5430. E-mail: cbudweg@oregon.uoregon.edu.

University of Ottawa, Faculty of Health Sciences, School of Human Kinetics, Ottawa, ON K1N 6N5, Canada. Awards MA. Faculty: 18 full-time. Students: 49 full-time (26 women), 4 part-time (2 women); includes 3 international. Average age 28. In 1997, 36 degrees awarded. *Degree requirements:* Thesis required, foreign language not required. *Entrance requirements:* Honors degree or equivalent, minimum B average. Application deadline: 7/1 (rolling processing). Application fee: $35. *Expenses:* Tuition $4677 per year for Canadian residents; $9900 per year for nonresidents. Fees $230 per year. *Financial aid:* Fellowships, research assistantships, teaching assistantships, Federal Work-Study, and career-related internships or fieldwork available. Financial aid application deadline: 10/1. *Faculty research:* Sports marketing, politics in sports, intervention/consultation in sports, aging and performance, sports administration. • Roger Gauthier, Director and Associate Dean, 613-562-5851. Application contact: Hal Hansen, Assistant Director, 613-562-5800 Ext. 4227. Fax: 613-562-5149.

University of Pittsburgh, School of Education, Department of Health, Physical, and Recreation Education, Pittsburgh, PA 15260. Offers program in movement science (MHPE, MS, PhD), including developmental movement (MS, PhD), exercise physiology (MS, PhD), health promotion and education (MHPE), sports medicine (MS, PhD). MHPE offered jointly with the Graduate School of Public Health. Part-time and evening/weekend programs available. Faculty: 10 full-time (6 women). Students: 69 full-time (24 women), 36 part-time (20 women); includes 7 minority (4 African Americans, 2 Hispanics, 1 Native American), 7 international. 20 applicants, 75% accepted. In 1997, 29 master's, 6 doctorates awarded. *Degree requirements:* Thesis/dissertation. *Average time to degree:* master's–2 years full-time, 4 years part-time; doctorate–4 years full-time, 6 years part-time. *Entrance requirements:* GRE General Test, TOEFL (minimum score 650). Application deadline: 2/1. Application fee: $30 ($40 for international students). *Expenses:* Tuition $8018 per year full-time, $329 per credit part-time for state residents; $16,508 per year full-time, $680 per credit part-time for nonresidents. Fees $480 per year full-time, $180 per year part-time. *Financial aid:* In 1997–98, 10 assistantships averaging $1,150 per month were awarded; partial tuition waivers, Federal Work-Study, institutionally sponsored loans also available. Aid available to part-time students. Financial aid application deadline: 5/1; applicants required to submit FAFSA. • Dr. Louis A. Pingel, Associate Dean, 412-648-1775. E-mail: pingel1+@pitt.edu. Application contact: Jackie Harden, Manager, 412-648-7060. Fax: 412-648-1899. E-mail: jackie@sched.fsl.pitt.edu.

University of Southern California, Graduate School, School of Health Affairs, Department of Biokinesiology and Physical Therapy, Program in Biokinesiology, Los Angeles, CA 90089. Awards MS, PhD. Students: 11 full-time (9 women), 6 part-time (4 women); includes 1 minority (Hispanic), 5 international. Average age 32. 12 applicants, 42% accepted. In 1997, 4 master's awarded. *Degree requirements:* For doctorate, dissertation required, foreign language not required. *Entrance requirements:* GRE General Test. Application deadline: 2/1 (priority date). Application fee: $55. *Financial aid:* In 1997–98, 7 teaching assistantships were awarded; fellowships, research assistantships, Federal Work-Study, institutionally sponsored loans also available. Aid available to part-time students. Financial aid application deadline: 2/15; applicants required to submit FAFSA. • Dr. Sandra Howell, Interim Chair, Department of Biokinesiology and Physical Therapy, 213-342-2900.

The University of Texas at Austin, Graduate School, College of Education, Department of Kinesiology and Health Education, Austin, TX 78712. Offers programs in health education (MA, M Ed, Ed D, PhD), kinesiology (MA, M Ed, Ed D, PhD). Part-time programs available. Faculty: 19 full-time (9 women). Students: 97 full-time (55 women), 29 part-time (19 women); includes 23 minority (8 African Americans, 1 Asian American, 12 Hispanics, 2 Native Americans), 12 international. 135 applicants, 51% accepted. In 1997, 40 master's, 3 doctorates awarded. Terminal master's awarded for partial completion of doctoral program. *Degree requirements:* For master's, thesis (for some programs); for doctorate, dissertation. *Entrance requirements:* GRE General Test (minimum combined score of 1000; average 1100). Application deadline: 2/1 (priority date; rolling processing; 5/1 for spring admission). Application fee: $50 ($75 for international students). Electronic applications accepted. *Expenses:* Tuition $2592 per year full-time, $324 per semester (minimum) part-time for state residents; $7704 per year full-time, $963 per semester (minimum) part-time for nonresidents. Fees $778 per year full-time, $161 per semester (minimum) part-time. *Financial aid:* In 1997–98, 2 fellowships, 20 research assistantships, 30 teaching assistantships were awarded; Federal Work-Study and career-related internships or fieldwork also available. Financial aid application deadline: 2/1; applicants required to submit FAFSA. *Faculty research:* Health promotion, human performance, exercise biochemistry, motor behavior, sports administration. • Dr. Dorothy Lovett, Chairperson, 512-471-1273. E-mail: dot.lovett@utxvm.cc.utexas.edu. Application contact: Ann M. Scarborough, Graduate Adviser, 512-471-1273. Fax: 512-471-8914. E-mail: a.scarborough@utexas.edu.

The University of Texas at El Paso, College of Nursing and Health Science, Program in Kinesiology and Sports Studies, 500 West University Avenue, El Paso, TX 79968-0001. Awards MS. *Degree requirements:* Thesis required, foreign language not required. *Entrance requirements:* GRE General Test, TOEFL (minimum score 550), course work in statistics. Application deadline: 7/1 (priority date; rolling processing; 11/1 for spring admission). Application fee: $15 ($65 for international students). *Tuition:* $2063 per year full-time, $284 per credit hour part-time for state residents; $5753 per year full-time, $425 per credit hour part-time for nonresidents.

The University of Texas at Tyler, School of Education and Psychology, Department of Health and Kinesiology, Tyler, TX 75799-0001. Offers programs in allied health/interdisciplinary studies (MS), clinical exercise physiology (MS), health and kinesiology (M Ed), kinesiology (MS), kinesiology/interdisciplinary studies (MS). Part-time programs available. Faculty: 4 full-time (2 women), 6 part-time (3 women). In 1997, 10 degrees awarded. *Degree requirements:* Thesis (for some programs), comprehensive exam required, foreign language not required. *Application fee:* $0 ($50 for international students). *Tuition:* $2144 per year full-time, $337 per semester (minimum) part-time for state residents; $7256 per year full-time, $964 per semester (minimum) part-time for nonresidents. *Financial aid:* Laboratory technicianships available. Financial aid application deadline: 7/1. *Faculty research:* Osteoporosis, muscle soreness, economy of locomotion, adoption of rehabilitation programs. • Dr. James Schwane, Chairperson, 903-566-7031. Fax: 903-566-7065. E-mail: jschwane@mail.uttyl.edu. Application contact: Martha D. Wheat, Director of Admissions and Student Records, 903-566-7201. Fax: 903-566-7068.

The University of Texas–Pan American, College of Education, Department of Health and Kinesiology, Edinburg, TX 78539-2999. Offers program in kinesiology (M Ed). Part-time and evening/weekend programs available. *Degree requirements:* Thesis optional. *Entrance requirements:* GRE General Test. Application deadline: 7/17 (11/16 for spring admission). Application fee: $0. *Tuition:* $2156 per year full-time, $283 per semester (minimum) part-time for state residents; $6788 per year full-time, $862 per semester (minimum) part-time for nonresidents. *Faculty research:* History, physiology of exercise, fitness levels, Mexican-American children, winter tourist profiles, sports psychology.

University of Waterloo, Faculty of Applied Health Sciences, Department of Kinesiology, Waterloo, ON N2L 3G1, Canada. Awards M Sc, PhD. Part-time programs available. Faculty: 17 full-time (3 women), 19 part-time (3 women). Students: 36 full-time (15 women), 15 part-time (9 women). 80 applicants, 23% accepted. In 1997, 11 master's, 4 doctorates awarded. *Degree requirements:* Computer language, thesis/dissertation. *Entrance requirements:* For master's, TOEFL (minimum score 550), honors degree, minimum B average; for doctorate, GRE, TOEFL (minimum score 550), master's degree. Application deadline: 2/1. Application fee: $50. *Tuition:* $3220 per year. *Financial aid:* In 1997–98, 2 research assistantships, 34 teaching assistantships (16 to first-year students) were awarded. *Faculty research:* Work physiology, biomechanics and neural control of human movement, psychomotor learning and performance, sociology of sport. • Dr. J. Frank, Chair, 519-888-4567 Ext. 3668. Application contact: Dr. L. Brawley, Associate Chair for Graduate Studies, 519-888-4567 Ext. 3153. Fax: 519-746-6776. E-mail: lrbrawley@healthy.uwaterloo.ca.

The University of Western Ontario, Biosciences Division, Faculty of Kinesiology, London, ON N6A 5B8, Canada. Awards MA, M Sc, PhD. Faculty: 30 (8 women). Students: 59 (30 women). Average age 25. 47 applicants, 100% accepted. In 1997, 8 master's, 2 doctorates awarded. *Degree requirements:* For master's, thesis optional; for doctorate, dissertation, comprehensive exam. *Average time to degree:* master's–2 years full-time; doctorate–4 years full-time. *Entrance requirements:* For doctorate, MA degree in physical education. Application fee: $35. *Financial aid:* Teaching assistantships available. Financial aid application deadline: 4/1. *Faculty research:* Exercise physiology/biochemistry, sports injuries, sport psychology, sport history, sport philosophy, motor learning. • Dr. R. C. Watson, Acting Director, 519-661-3075. Application contact: Dr. G. D. Marsh, Graduate Chair, 519-661-3075.

University of Windsor, Faculty of Human Kinetics, Windsor, ON N9B 3P4, Canada. Awards MHK. Part-time programs available. *Degree requirements:* Thesis optional. *Entrance requirements:* TOEFL (minimum score 600), minimum B average. Application deadline: 7/1 (priority date; rolling processing). Application fee: $50. *Expenses:* Tuition $4370 per year (minimum) full-time, $345 per course (minimum) part-time for Canadian residents; $8453 per year (minimum) full-time, $915 per course (minimum) part-time for nonresidents. Fees $462 per year (minimum) full-time, $141 per year (minimum) part-time. *Faculty research:* Movement sciences, sport and lifestyle management, historical and sociological studies of sport.

University of Wisconsin–Madison, School of Education, Department of Kinesiology, Madison, WI 53706-1380. Offers programs in kinesiology (MS, PhD), therapeutic science (MS). *Degree requirements:* For doctorate, dissertation. *Entrance requirements:* GRE General Test. Application fee: $38. *Tuition:* $4928 per year full-time, $926 per semester (minimum) part-time for state residents; $15,190 per year full-time, $2849 per semester (minimum) part-time for nonresidents.

University of Wisconsin–Milwaukee, School of Allied Health Professions, Program in Human Kinetics, Milwaukee, WI 53201-0413. Awards MS. Part-time programs available. Faculty: 8 full-time (6 women). Students: 5 full-time (3 women), 15 part-time (9 women). 18 applicants, 72% accepted. In 1997, 3 degrees awarded. *Entrance requirements:* GRE General Test. Application deadline: 1/1 (priority date; rolling processing; 9/1 for spring admission). Application fee: $45 ($75 for international students). *Tuition:* $4996 per year full-time, $1030 per semester (minimum) part-time for state residents; $15,216 per year full-time, $2947 per semester (minimum) part-time for nonresidents. *Financial aid:* In 1997–98, 4 teaching assistantships were awarded; fellowships, research assistantships, project assistantships, and career-related internships or fieldwork also available. Aid available to part-time students. Financial aid application deadline: 4/15. • Ann Snyder, Chair, 414-229-6080.

Virginia Polytechnic Institute and State University, College of Human Resources and Education, Department of Human Nutrition, Foods and Exercise, Blacksburg, VA 24061. Offerings include muscle physiology and biochemistry (MS, PhD). Department faculty: 16 full-time (12 women). *Degree requirements:* Thesis/dissertation. *Entrance requirements:* GRE, TOEFL. Application deadline: 12/1 (priority date; rolling processing). Application fee: $25. *Tuition:* $4927 per year full-time, $792 per semester (minimum) part-time for state residents; $7537 per year full-time, $1227 per semester (minimum) part-time for nonresidents. • Dr. Eleanor D. Schlenker, Head, 540-231-4672.

Washington State University, College of Education, Department of Kinesiology and Leisure Studies, Pullman, WA 99164-1610. Offers programs in kinesiology (M Ed, MS), recreation and leisure studies (M Ed, MS). Faculty: 10 full-time (3 women). Students: 11 full-time (6 women), 1 part-time (0 women); includes 1 international. In 1997, 2 degrees awarded. *Degree requirements:* Oral exam required, foreign language not required. *Average time to degree:* master's–1.5 years full-time. *Entrance requirements:* GRE General Test, minimum GPA of 3.0. Application deadline: 3/1 (priority date; rolling processing). Application fee: $35. *Tuition:* $5334 per year full-time, $267 per credit hour part-time for state residents; $13,380 per year full-time, $677 per credit hour part-time for nonresidents. *Financial aid:* Research assistantships, teaching assistantships, teaching associateships, partial tuition waivers, Federal Work-Study, institutionally sponsored loans, and career-related internships or fieldwork available. Financial aid application deadline: 4/1; applicants required to submit FAFSA. *Total annual research expenditures:* $93,361. • Dr. Edward Udd, Chair, 509-335-4593.

Washington University in St. Louis, Graduate School of Arts and Sciences, Interdisciplinary Program in Movement Science, St. Louis, MO 63130-4899. Awards PhD. Students: 8 full-time (5 women). 6 applicants, 33% accepted. *Degree requirements:* Dissertation. *Entrance requirements:* GRE General Test. Application deadline: rolling. Application fee: $35. *Tuition:* $22,200 per year full-time, $925 per credit hour part-time. *Financial aid:* Fellowships, research assistantships available. • Dr. Shirley Sahrmann, Chairperson, 314-286-1411.

West Chester University of Pennsylvania, School of Health Sciences, Department of Kinesiology, West Chester, PA 19383. Offers programs in coaching (Certificate), driver education (Certificate), exercise and sport physiology (MS), general exercise science (MS), physical education (MS), safety (Certificate), sport and athletic administration (MSA). Faculty: 1 full-time, 9 part-time. Students: 14 full-time (6 women), 34 part-time (15 women); includes 3 minority (2 African Americans, 1 Asian American), 1 international. Average age 28. 35 applicants, 86% accepted. In 1997, 11 master's awarded. *Degree requirements:* For master's, comprehensive exam required, foreign language and thesis not required. *Entrance requirements:* For master's, GRE, interview. Application deadline: 4/15 (priority date; rolling processing; 10/15 for spring admission). Application fee: $25. *Expenses:* Tuition $3468 per year full-time, $193 per credit part-time for state residents; $6236 per year full-time, $346 per credit part-time for nonresidents. Fees $660 per year full-time, $38 per credit part-time. *Financial aid:* In 1997–98, 4 research assistantships were awarded. Financial aid application deadline: 2/15. • Dr. Monita Lank, Chair, 610-436-2260. Application contact: Dr. John G. Williams, Graduate Coordinator, 610-436-3119.

Physical Education

Adams State College, School of Education and Graduate Studies, Department of Health, Physical Education, and Recreation, Alamosa, CO 81102. Awards MA. Part-time programs available. In 1997, 11 degrees awarded. *Degree requirements:* Comprehensive exam required, foreign language and thesis not required. *Entrance requirements:* GRE General Test or MAT, minimum undergraduate GPA of 2.75. Application deadline: 5/15 (priority date; rolling processing; 10/15 for spring admission). Application fee: $25. *Tuition:* $2164 per year full-time, $111 per credit part-time for state residents; $7284 per year full-time, $377 per credit part-time for nonresidents. *Financial aid:* In 1997–98, 8 coaching assistantships (6 to first-year students) averaging $500 per month and totaling $32,000 were awarded; Federal Work-Study, institutionally sponsored loans, and career-related internships or fieldwork also available. Aid available to part-time students. Financial aid application deadline: 4/15; applicants required to submit FAFSA. • Dr. Jeff Geiser, Head, 719-587-7402.

Adelphi University, School of Education, Department of Physical Education, Recreation, and Human Performance Science, Garden City, NY 11530. Offers programs in coaching (advanced) (Certificate), exercise physiology (Certificate), physical education (MA), special physical education (Certificate), sports management (Certificate). Part-time and evening/weekend programs available. Students: 23 full-time (9 women), 129 part-time (52 women); includes 15 minority (10 African Americans, 2 Asian Americans, 3 Hispanics), 6 international. Average age 29. In 1997, 51 master's awarded. *Degree requirements:* For master's, internship required, foreign language and thesis not required. *Application deadline:* rolling. *Application fee:* $50. *Expenses:* Tuition $16,000 per year full-time, $485 per credit part-time. Fees $500 per year full-time, $150 per semester part-time. *Financial aid:* Research assistantships, teaching assistantships, and career-related internships or fieldwork available. Financial aid application deadline: 3/1. *Faculty research:* Physical education for the handicapped, sport sociology, sport pedagogy. • Dr. Ronald Feingold, Chairperson, 516-877-4260.

Alabama Agricultural and Mechanical University, School of Education, Department of Curriculum and Instruction, Area in Health and Physical Education, PO Box 1357, Normal, AL 35762-1357. Offers program in physical education (M Ed, MS). Part-time and evening/weekend programs available. Faculty: 2 full-time (1 woman). *Degree requirements:* Comprehensive exam required, foreign language not required. *Entrance requirements:* GRE General Test. Application deadline: 5/1. Application fee: $15 ($20 for international students). *Expenses:* Tuition $2782 per year full-time, $565 per semester (minimum) part-time for state residents; $5164 per year full-time, $1015 per semester (minimum) part-time for nonresidents. Fees $560 per year full-time, $390 per year part-time. *Financial aid:* Fellowships and career-related internships or fieldwork available. Financial aid application deadline: 4/1. *Faculty research:* Cardiorespiratory assessment. • Dr. Earnest Dees, Chair, Department of Curriculum and Instruction, 205-851-5520. Fax: 205-851-5526.

Alabama State University, School of Graduate Studies, College of Education, Division of Health, Physical Education, Recreation, and Safety, Department of Health and Physical Education, Montgomery, AL 36101-0271. Offers program in physical education (M Ed, Ed S). Faculty: 1 full-time (0 women). Students: 5 full-time (3 women), 25 part-time (10 women); includes 16 minority (all African Americans). In 1997, 6 master's, 1 Ed S awarded. *Degree requirements:* For master's, comprehensive exam required, thesis optional; for Ed S, thesis. *Entrance requirements:* For master's, GRE General Test, MAT or NTE. Application deadline: 7/15 (rolling processing; 12/15 for spring admission). Application fee: $10. *Expenses:* Tuition $85 per credit hour for state residents; $170 per credit hour for nonresidents. Fees $486 per year. • Application contact: Dr. Fred Dauser, Dean of Graduate Studies, 334-229-4276. Fax: 334-229-4928.

Albany State University, School of Education, Program in Health and Physical Education, Albany, GA 31705-2717. Awards M Ed. Faculty: 4 part-time (0 women). Students: 14 full-time (4 women). Average age 30. 3 applicants, 100% accepted. In 1997, 3 degrees awarded. *Degree requirements:* Comprehensive exam. *Entrance requirements:* GRE General Test (minimum combined score of 800), MAT (minimum score 44) or NTE (minimum score 550 required. Application deadline: 9/1. Application fee: $10. *Financial aid:* Federal Work-Study and career-related internships or fieldwork available. Aid available to part-time students. Financial aid application deadline: 4/1. *Faculty research:* Strength training, sport psychology. • Dr. Wilburn Campbell, Chairman, 912-430-4762. Fax: 912-430-3020. E-mail: wilburnc@fld94.alsnet.peachnet.edu.

Albany State University, School of Education, Program in Physical Education, Albany, GA 31705-2717. Awards M Ed. *Degree requirements:* Comprehensive exam. *Entrance requirements:* GRE General Test (minimum combined score of 800), MAT (minimum score 44) or NTE (minimum score 550). Application deadline: 9/1. Application fee: $10. *Financial aid:* Application deadline 4/1. • Dr. Claude Perkins, Dean, School of Education, 912-430-4715. Fax: 912-430-4993. E-mail: cperkins@fld94.alsnet.peachnet.edu.

Alcorn State University, School of Psychology and Education, Lorman, MS 39096-9402. Offerings include secondary education (MS Ed), with option in health and physical education. *Degree requirements:* Thesis optional, foreign language not required. *Application deadline:* 7/1 (priority date; rolling processing; 12/1 for spring admission). *Application fee:* $10. *Tuition:* $2470 per year full-time, $378 per semester (minimum) part-time for state residents; $5331 per year full-time, $855 per semester (minimum) part-time for nonresidents.

Angelo State University, College of Sciences, Department of Kinesiology, San Angelo, TX 76909. Offerings include physical education (MAT). Department faculty: 3 full-time (2 women). *Application deadline:* 8/7 (priority date; rolling processing; 1/2 for spring admission). *Application fee:* $25 ($50 for international students). *Expenses:* Tuition $1022 per year full-time, $36 per semester hour part-time for state residents; $7382 per year full-time, $246 per semester hour part-time for nonresidents. Fees $1140 per year full-time, $165 per semester (minimum) part-time. • Dr. Melanie A. Croy, Head, 915-942-2174.

Appalachian State University, College of Fine and Applied Arts, Department of Health, Leisure, and Exercise Science, Program in Health and Physical Education, Boone, NC 28608. Offers master teacher (MA), sports management (MA). Students: 9 full-time (0 women), 1 part-time (0 women); includes 1 minority (African American). 6 applicants, 50% accepted. In 1997, 1 degree awarded. *Degree requirements:* Thesis or alternative, comprehensive exams required, foreign language not required. *Entrance requirements:* GRE General Test. Application deadline: 7/31 (priority date). Application fee: $35. *Tuition:* $1811 per year full-time, $354 per semester (minimum) part-time for state residents; $9081 per year full-time, $2171 per semester (minimum) part-time for nonresidents. *Financial aid:* Fellowships, research assistantships, teaching assistantships available. • Application contact: Dr. Alan Utter, Coordinator, 704-262-3140.

Arizona State University, College of Liberal Arts and Sciences, Department of Exercise Science and Physical Education, Tempe, AZ 85287. Awards MPE, MS. Faculty: 24 full-time (6 women), 1 (woman) part-time. Students: 47 full-time (20 women), 15 part-time (8 women); includes 7 minority (3 Asian Americans, 3 Hispanics, 1 Native American), 8 international. Average age 30. 104 applicants, 38% accepted. In 1997, 16 degrees awarded. *Degree requirements:* Thesis or alternative. *Entrance requirements:* GRE. Application fee: $45. *Expenses:* Tuition $2088 per year full-time, $110 per hour part-time for state residents; $9040 per year full-time, $377 per hour part-time for nonresidents. Fees $72 per year full-time, $18 per semester (minimum) part-time. *Faculty research:* Biomechanics, motor behavior/sport psychology, physiology of exercise, exercise and wellness. • Dr. William J. Stone, Chair, 602-965-3875. Application contact: Graduate Secretary, 602-965-3591.

Arkansas State University, College of Education, Department of Health, Physical Education, and Recreation, State University, AR 72467. Offers program in physical education (MS, MSE, SCCT). Part-time programs available. Faculty: 11 full-time (2 women). Students: 12 full-time (8 women), 21 part-time (6 women); includes 4 minority (3 African Americans, 1 Native American). Average age 29. In 1997, 12 master's awarded. *Degree requirements:* For master's, thesis or alternative, comprehensive exam required, foreign language not required; for SCCT, comprehensive exam required, foreign language and thesis not required. *Entrance requirements:* For master's, GRE General Test or MAT, appropriate bachelor's degree; for SCCT, GRE General Test or MAT, master's degree. Application deadline: 7/1 (priority date; rolling processing; 11/15 for spring admission). Application fee: $15 ($25 for international students). *Expenses:* Tuition $2760 per year full-time, $115 per credit hour part-time for state residents; $6936 per year full-time, $289 per credit hour part-time for nonresidents. Fees $506 per year full-time, $44 per semester (minimum) part-time. *Financial aid:* Teaching assistantships available. Aid available to part-time students. Financial aid application deadline: 7/1; applicants required to submit FAFSA. • Dr. Jim Stillwell, Chair, 870-972-3066. Fax: 870-972-3828. E-mail: jstillwel@tunica.astate.edu.

Arkansas Tech University, School of Education, Department of Health and Physical Education, Russellville, AR 72801-2222. Awards M Ed, PhD. *Degree requirements:* For master's, action research project, comprehensive exam required, thesis optional. *Entrance requirements:* For master's, GRE General Test. Application deadline: rolling. Application fee: $0 ($30 for international students). *Expenses:* Tuition $98 per credit hour for state residents; $196 per credit hour for nonresidents. Fees $30 per semester. *Financial aid:* Application deadline 4/15. • Dr. Annette Holeyfield, Head, 501-968-0344.

Auburn University, College of Education, Department of Health and Human Performance, Auburn University, AL 36849-0001. Awards M Ed, MS, Ed D, PhD, Ed S. Part-time programs available. Faculty: 14 full-time (3 women). Students: 56 full-time (23 women), 31 part-time (11 women); includes 6 minority (3 African Americans, 3 Hispanics), 6 international. 84 applicants, 37% accepted. In 1997, 27 master's, 1 doctorate awarded. *Degree requirements:* For master's, thesis (MS) required, foreign language not required; for doctorate, dissertation required, foreign language not required; for Ed S, exam, field project required, foreign language and thesis not required. *Entrance requirements:* For master's, GRE General Test; for doctorate, GRE General Test (minimum score 400 on each section), interview, master's degree; for Ed S, GRE General Test, interview, master's degree. Application deadline: 9/1 (rolling processing; 3/1 for spring admission). Application fee: $25 ($50 for international students). *Expenses:*

Directory: Physical Education

Auburn University (continued)

Tuition $2760 per year full-time, $76 per credit hour part-time for state residents; $8280 per year full-time, $228 per credit hour part-time for nonresidents. Fees $30 per year full-time, $160 per quarter part-time for state residents; $30 per year full-time, $480 per quarter part-time for nonresidents. *Financial aid:* Research assistantships, teaching assistantships, Federal Work-Study available. Aid available to part-time students. Financial aid application deadline: 3/15. *Faculty research:* Biomechanics, exercise physiology, motor skill learning, school health, curriculum development. • Dr. Dennis G. Wilson, Head, 334-844-4483. Application contact: Dr. John F. Pritchett, Dean of the Graduate School, 334-844-4700.

Auburn University Montgomery, School of Education, Department of Foundations, Secondary, and Physical Education, Montgomery, AL 36124-4023. Offers programs in physical education (M Ed), secondary education (M Ed, Ed S). Part-time and evening/weekend programs available. Students: 64 full-time (36 women), 34 part-time (22 women); includes 26 minority (25 African Americans, 1 Native American). Average age 31. In 1997, 73 master's, 12 Ed Ss awarded. *Degree requirements:* Comprehensive exam required, thesis optional, foreign language not required. *Entrance requirements:* For master's, GRE General Test or MAT, certification, BS in teaching; for Ed S, GRE General Test or MAT, certification. Application deadline: 9/1 (priority date; rolling processing; 3/28 for spring admission). Application fee: $25. Electronic applications accepted. *Tuition:* $2664 per year full-time, $85 per quarter hour part-time for state residents; $7080 per year full-time, $255 per quarter hour part-time for nonresidents. *Financial aid:* In 1997–98, 3 teaching assistantships were awarded. • Dr. Jennifer Brown, Head, 334-244-3545.

Austin Peay State University, Department of Health and Human Performance, Clarksville, TN 37044-0001. Awards MA Ed, MS. Part-time and evening/weekend programs available. Students: 31 full-time (19 women), 21 part-time (13 women); includes 11 minority (all African Americans), 1 international. In 1997, 17 degrees awarded. *Entrance requirements:* GRE General Test. Application deadline: 7/31 (priority date; rolling processing; 12/4 for spring admission). Application fee: $15. *Expenses:* Tuition $2438 per year full-time, $123 per semester hour part-time for state residents; $7034 per year full-time, $324 per semester hour part-time for nonresidents. Fees $484 per year (minimum) full-time, $154 per semester (minimum) part-time. *Financial aid:* Graduate assistantships, Federal Work-Study, institutionally sponsored loans, and career-related internships or fieldwork available. Aid available to part-time students. Financial aid application deadline: 4/1; applicants required to submit FAFSA. *Faculty research:* Aging, aging and physical activity. • Rebecca Glass, Chair, 931-648-6111. Fax: 931-648-7040. E-mail: glassr@apsu.edu.

Azusa Pacific University, School of Education and Behavioral Studies, Department of Education, Program in Physical Education, Azusa, CA 91702-7000. Awards M Ed. Evening/weekend programs available. Faculty: 10 full-time (3 women), 16 part-time (3 women). Students: 32. *Degree requirements:* Core exams, oral exam, oral presentation required, foreign language and thesis not required. *Entrance requirements:* BA in physical education or 12 units of previous course work in education, minimum GPA of 3.0. Application fee: $45 ($65 for international students). *Expenses:* Tuition $350 per unit. Fees $57 per year. • Dr. Donald Lawrence, Chair, 626-969-3408.

Ball State University, College of Applied Science and Technology, School of Physical Education, 2000 University Avenue, Muncie, IN 47306-1099. Awards MA, MAE, PhD. Faculty: 32. Students: 48 full-time (22 women), 50 part-time (18 women); includes 3 minority (all African Americans), 16 international. Average age 24. 110 applicants, 50% accepted. In 1997, 35 master's, 2 doctorates awarded. *Degree requirements:* For doctorate, dissertation required, foreign language not required. *Entrance requirements:* For doctorate, GRE General Test (minimum combined score of 1000), minimum graduate GPA of 3.2. Application fee: $15 ($25 for international students). *Expenses:* Tuition $3454 per year full-time, $518 per semester (minimum) part-time for state residents; $9316 per year full-time, $1221 per semester (minimum) part-time for nonresidents. Fees $242 per year full-time, $18 per semester (minimum) part-time. *Financial aid:* Teaching assistantships available. • Dr. John Reno, Director, 765-285-1748.

Baylor University, School of Education, Department of Health, Human Performance and Recreation, Waco, TX 76798. Awards MS Ed. Part-time programs available. Faculty: 13 full-time (5 women), 3 part-time (1 woman). Students: 34 full-time (17 women), 18 part-time (6 women); includes 2 minority (1 African American, 1 Asian American), 2 international. 30 applicants, 87% accepted. In 1997, 20 degrees awarded. *Degree requirements:* Thesis optional, foreign language not required. *Average time to degree:* master's–2 years full-time, 2.5 years part-time. *Entrance requirements:* GRE General Test. Application deadline: 4/1 (priority date; rolling processing; 10/1 for spring admission). Application fee: $25. Electronic applications accepted. *Expenses:* Tuition $7392 per year full-time, $308 per semester hour part-time. Fees $1024 per year. *Financial aid:* In 1997–98, 35 students received aid, including 22 teaching assistantships averaging $800 per month; recreation supplements, partial tuition waivers, Federal Work-Study, institutionally sponsored loans, and career-related internships or fieldwork also available. *Faculty research:* Behavior change theory, pedagogy, nutrition and enzyme therapy, exercise testing, health planning, ethics. • Dr. Nancy Goodloe, Director of Graduate Studies, 254-710-3505. E-mail: nancy_goodloe@baylor.edu.

Bemidji State University, Division of Professional Studies, Field of Physical Education, Bemidji, MN 56601-2699. Awards MS Ed. Part-time programs available. Students: 6 full-time (0 women), 10 part-time (5 women). Average age 34. *Degree requirements:* Thesis, departmental qualifying exam required, foreign language not required. *Application deadline:* 5/1. *Application fee:* $20. *Expenses:* Tuition $128 per credit for state residents; $134 per credit (minimum) for nonresidents. Fees $517 per year full-time, $35 per credit (minimum) part-time. *Financial aid:* Teaching assistantships, Federal Work-Study, and career-related internships or fieldwork available. Aid available to part-time students. Financial aid application deadline: 5/1. • Dr. Karl Salscheider, Chair, 218-755-2770.

Boston University, School of Education, Department of Curriculum and Teaching, Program in Human Movement, Boston, MA 02215. Awards Ed M, Ed D, CAGS. Students: 6 full-time (1 woman), 16 part-time (8 women); includes 1 minority (African American), 1 international. Average age 27. In 1997, 17 master's, 2 CAGSs awarded. *Degree requirements:* For doctorate, dissertation, comprehensive exam required, foreign language not required; for CAGS, comprehensive exam required, foreign language and thesis not required. *Entrance requirements:* For master's and CAGS, GRE or MAT, TOEFL; for doctorate, GRE General Test or MAT, TOEFL. Application deadline: 2/15 (priority date; rolling processing). Application fee: $50. *Expenses:* Tuition $22,830 per year full-time, $713 per credit part-time. Fees $218 per year full-time, $40 per semester part-time. *Financial aid:* Application deadline 3/30. *Faculty research:* Sports theory, biofeedback, exercise. • Dr. John Cheffers, Coordinator, 617-353-3302. E-mail: cheffers@bu.edu.

Bridgewater State College, School of Education, Department of Movement Arts, Health Promotion, and Leisure Studies, Program in Physical Education, Bridgewater, MA 02325-0001. Awards MS. Evening/weekend programs available. *Degree requirements:* Thesis or alternative required, foreign language not required. *Entrance requirements:* GRE General Test. Application deadline: 4/1 (10/1 for spring admission). Application fee: $25. *Expenses:* Tuition $1675 per year full-time, $70 per credit part-time for state residents; $6450 per year full-time, $269 per credit part-time for nonresidents. Fees $1588 per year full-time, $66 per credit hour part-time for state residents; $1588 per year full-time, $66 per credit part-time for nonresidents. *Financial aid:* Career-related internships or fieldwork available. • Application contact: Graduate School, 508-697-1300.

Brigham Young University, College of Physical Education, Department of Physical Education, Provo, UT 84602-1001. Offers programs in athletic training (MS), corrective physical education (PhD), curriculum and instruction (PhD), exercise physiology (M Ed, MS), exercise science/wellness (PhD), health promotion (M Ed, MS), physical education (M Ed, MS). M Ed and PhD (corrective physical education) being phased out; applicants no longer accepted. Faculty: 23 full-time (8 women). Students: 37 full-time (17 women); includes 2 minority (both Asian Americans), 3 international. Average age 24. 60 applicants, 50% accepted. In 1997, 13 master's, 1 doctorate awarded. *Degree requirements:* For master's, thesis (for some programs), oral exam required, foreign language not required; for doctorate, dissertation, written comprehensive and oral exams required, foreign language not required. *Entrance requirements:* For master's, GRE General Test (minimum combined score of 1380 on three sections), minimum GPA of 3.0 in last 60 hours; for doctorate, GRE General Test (minimum combined score of 1530 on three sections), minimum GPA of 3.5 in last 60 hours. Application deadline: 2/1 (rolling processing). Application fee: $30. *Tuition:* $3200 per year full-time, $178 per credit hour part-time for state residents; $4800 per year full-time, $266 per credit hour part-time for nonresidents. *Financial aid:* In 1997–98, 15 research assistantships (10 to first-year students), 35 teaching assistantships (30 to first-year students), 6 scholarships were awarded; fellowships, partial tuition waivers, institutionally sponsored loans, and career-related internships or fieldwork also available. Aid available to part-time students. Financial aid application deadline: 3/1. *Faculty research:* Substrate metabolism, sports traumatology, mastery learning, obesity and metabolism. Total annual research expenditures: $130,000. • Dr. Earlene Durrant, Chair, 801-378-2547. Application contact: A. Garth Fisher, Graduate Coordinator, 801-378-3981. Fax: 801-378-8389.

Brooklyn College of the City University of New York, Department of Physical Education, 2900 Bedford Avenue, Brooklyn, NY 11210-2889. Offers programs in exercise science and rehabilitation (MS), including psychosocial aspects of physical activity, sports management; physical education (MS, MS Ed). Part-time programs available. Faculty: 16 full-time, 4 part-time, 18 FTE. Students: 3 full-time (2 women), 43 part-time (13 women); includes 15 minority (8 African Americans, 2 Asian Americans, 5 Hispanics), 4 international. Average age 25. In 1997, 15 degrees awarded (100% found work related to degree). *Degree requirements:* Comprehensive exam or thesis required, foreign language not required. *Average time to degree:* master's–3 years part-time. *Entrance requirements:* GRE, TOEFL (minimum score 500), previous course work in physical education and education, minimum GPA of 3.0. Application deadline: 3/1 (11/1 for spring admission). Application fee: $40. *Expenses:* Tuition $4350 per year full-time, $185 per credit part-time for state residents; $7600 per year full-time, $320 per credit part-time for nonresidents. Fees $500 per year for state residents; $806 per year for nonresidents. *Financial aid:* Partial tuition waivers, Federal Work-Study, institutionally sponsored loans and career-related internships or fieldwork available. Financial aid application deadline: 4/15; applicants required to submit FAFSA. *Faculty research:* Exercise physiology, motor learning, sports psychology, women in athletics. Total annual research expenditures: $9231. • Dr. Charles Tobey, Chairperson, 718-951-5514. Application contact: Michael Hipscher, Graduate Deputy, 718-951-5514.

California Polytechnic State University, San Luis Obispo, College of Science and Mathematics, Department of Physical Education and Kinesiology, San Luis Obispo, CA 93407. Awards MS. Faculty: 16 full-time, 5 part-time. Students: 20 full-time, 10 part-time. 36 applicants, 75% accepted. In 1997, 6 degrees awarded. *Degree requirements:* Thesis optional. *Entrance requirements:* Minimum GPA of 2.75. Application deadline: 7/1 (3/1 for spring admission). Application fee: $55. *Expenses:* Tuition $0 for state residents; $164 per unit for nonresidents. Fees $2102 per year full-time, $1632 per year part-time. *Financial aid:* Federal Work-Study and career-related internships or fieldwork available. Aid available to part-time students. • Dwayne Head, Head, 805-756-2545.

California State University, Chico, College of Communication and Education, Department of Physical Education, Chico, CA 95929-0722. Awards MA. Faculty: 35 full-time (14 women), 14 part-time (2 women). Students: 30 full-time (14 women), 19 part-time (11 women); includes 11 minority (4 African Americans, 1 Asian American, 5 Hispanics, 1 Native American). Average age 27. In 1997, 17 degrees awarded. *Degree requirements:* Thesis or alternative, oral exam required, foreign language not required. *Entrance requirements:* GRE General Test. Application deadline: 4/1 (rolling processing). Application fee: $55. *Expenses:* Tuition $0 for state residents; $246 per unit for nonresidents. Fees $2108 per year full-time, $1442 per year part-time. *Financial aid:* Fellowships, teaching assistantships available. • Dick Trimmer, Chair, 530-898-6373. Application contact: Dr. C. Don Scott, Graduate Coordinator, 530-898-6248.

California State University, Dominguez Hills, School of Education, Department of Graduate Education, Program in Physical Education, Carson, CA 90747-0001. Awards MA. *Entrance requirements:* Minimum GPA of 2.75. Application deadline: 6/1. Application fee: $55. *Expenses:* Tuition $0 for state residents; $246 per unit for nonresidents. Fees $1896 per year full-time, $1230 per year part-time. • Application contact: Admissions Office, 310-243-3600.

California State University, Fullerton, School of Human Development and Community Service, Department of Kinesiology and Health Promotion, PO Box 34080, Fullerton, CA 92834-9480. Offers program in physical education (MS). Part-time programs available. Faculty: 16 full-time (7 women), 61 part-time, 26.3 FTE. Students: 10 full-time (5 women), 85 part-time (45 women); includes 16 minority (3 African Americans, 9 Asian Americans, 4 Hispanics), 3 international. Average age 28. 48 applicants, 83% accepted. In 1997, 14 degrees awarded. *Degree requirements:* Project or thesis required, foreign language not required. *Entrance requirements:* Minimum GPA of 3.0 in field, 2.5 overall. Application fee: $55. *Expenses:* Tuition $0 for state residents; $246 per unit for nonresidents. Fees $1947 per year full-time, $1281 per year part-time. *Financial aid:* Teaching assistantships, state grants, Federal Work-Study, institutionally sponsored loans, and career-related internships or fieldwork available. Aid available to part-time students. Financial aid application deadline: 3/1. • Dr. Roberta Rikli, Chair, 714-278-3316. Application contact: Dr. William Beam, Adviser, 714-278-3316.

California State University, Hayward, School of Education, Department of Kinesiology and Physical Education, Hayward, CA 94542-3000. Offers program in physical education (MS). Faculty: 11 full-time (4 women). Students: 22 full-time (10 women), 43 part-time (23 women); includes 12 minority (3 African Americans, 3 Asian Americans, 5 Hispanics, 1 Native American). 19 applicants, 79% accepted. In 1997, 15 degrees awarded. *Degree requirements:* Comprehensive exam, project, or thesis required, foreign language not required. *Entrance requirements:* Minimum GPA of 3.0. Application deadline: 4/19 (priority date; rolling processing; 1/5 for spring admission). Application fee: $55. *Expenses:* Tuition $0 for state residents; $164 per unit for nonresidents. Fees $1827 per year full-time, $1161 per year part-time. *Financial aid:* Federal Work-Study, institutionally sponsored loans available. Aid available to part-time students. Financial aid application deadline: 3/1. • Dr. Richard S. Rivenes, Chair, 510-885-3061. Application contact: Dr. Maria De Anda-Ramos, Executive Director, Admissions and Outreach, 510-885-2624.

California State University, Long Beach, College of Health and Human Services, Department of Kinesiology and Physical Education, Long Beach, CA 90840-4901. Awards MA. Faculty: 20 full-time. Students: 40 full-time (21 women), 47 part-time (29 women); includes 18 minority (5 African Americans, 6 Asian Americans, 6 Hispanics, 1 Native American), 4 international. Average age 30. 86 applicants, 80% accepted. In 1997, 19 degrees awarded. *Degree requirements:* Oral and written comprehensive exams or thesis required, foreign language not required. *Entrance requirements:* GRE General Test (minimum combined score of 1350 on three sections), minimum GPA of 2.75 during previous 2 years. Application deadline: 8/1 (rolling processing; 12/1 for spring admission). Application fee: $55. *Expenses:* Tuition $0 for state residents; $246 per unit for nonresidents. Fees $1846 per year full-time, $1180 per year part-time. *Financial aid:* Application deadline 3/2. *Faculty research:* Pulmonary functioning, feedback and practice structure, strength training, history and politics of sports, special population research issues. • Dr. Dixie Grimmett, Chair, 562-985-4051. E-mail: dgrimmet@csulb.edu. Application contact: Dr. Michael LaCourse, Graduate Coordinator, 562-985-4558. Fax: 562-985-8067. E-mail: mlacour@csulb.edu.

California State University, Los Angeles, School of Health and Human Services, Department of Physical Education and Recreation/Leisure Studies, Los Angeles, CA 90032-8530.

Offers program in physical education (MA). Part-time and evening/weekend programs available. Faculty: 11 full-time, 12 part-time. Students: 8 full-time (2 women), 22 part-time (11 women); includes 20 minority (4 African Americans, 2 Asian Americans, 14 Hispanics). *Degree requirements:* Comprehensive exam, project, or thesis required, foreign language not required. *Entrance requirements:* TOEFL (minimum score 550), minimum GPA of 2.75. Application deadline: 6/30 (rolling processing; 2/1 for spring admission). Application fee: $55. *Expenses:* Tuition $0 for state residents; $164 per unit for nonresidents. Fees $1763 per year full-time, $1097 per year part-time. *Financial aid:* 4 students received aid; Federal Work-Study available. Aid available to part-time students. Financial aid application deadline: 3/1. • Dr. Melva Irvin, Chair, 213-343-4650.

California State University, Sacramento, School of Health and Human Services, Department of Health and Physical Education, Sacramento, CA 95819-6048. Offers program in physical education (MS). Part-time programs available. *Degree requirements:* Thesis or alternative, writing proficiency exam. *Entrance requirements:* TOEFL (minimum score 550). Application deadline: 4/15 (11/1 for spring admission). Application fee: $55. *Expenses:* Tuition $0 for state residents; $246 per unit for nonresidents. Fees $2012 per year full-time, $1346 per year part-time. *Financial aid:* Research assistantships, teaching assistantships, Federal Work-Study, and career-related internships or fieldwork available. Aid available to part-time students. Financial aid application deadline: 3/1. • Dr. Pamela Milchrist, Chair, 916-278-6389. Application contact: Dr. Karen Scarborough, Coordinator, 916-278-7309.

California State University, Stanislaus, School of Education, Department of Physical Education, Concentration in Physical Education, Turlock, CA 95382. Awards MA Ed. Faculty: 5 full-time (1 woman). Students: 0. 0 applicants. In 1997, 2 degrees awarded. *Degree requirements:* Thesis required, foreign language not required. *Entrance requirements:* MAT. Application fee: $55. *Expenses:* Tuition $0 for state residents; $246 per unit for nonresidents. Fees $1779 per year full-time, $1113 per year part-time. *Financial aid:* Application deadline 3/2; applicants required to submit FAFSA. *Faculty research:* Cardiac rehabilitation and exercise. • Dr. William Morris, Coordinator, 209-667-3325.

Campbell University, School of Education, Buies Creek, NC 27506. Offerings include physical education (M Ed). School faculty: 8 full-time (6 women), 6 part-time (0 women). *Application deadline:* 8/1 (priority date; rolling processing; 1/2 for spring admission). *Application fee:* $25. *Tuition:* $168 per credit hour (minimum). • Dr. Margaret Giesbrecht, Dean, 910-893-1630. Fax: 910-893-1999. E-mail: giesbrec@mailcenter.campbell.edu. Application contact: James S. Farthing, Director of Graduate Admissions, 910-893-1200 Ext. 1318. Fax: 910-893-1288.

Canisius College, School of Education and Human Services, Program in Physical Education, Buffalo, NY 14208-1098. Awards MS. Part-time and evening/weekend programs available. Faculty: 6 full-time (1 woman), 1 part-time (0 women). Students: 9 full-time (4 women), 34 part-time (18 women). 31 applicants, 84% accepted. *Degree requirements:* Research project or thesis required, foreign language not required. *Entrance requirements:* GRE General Test, minimum GPA of 2.5. Application deadline: 8/1 (priority date; rolling processing). Application fee: $20. *Expenses:* Tuition $415 per credit hour. Fees $15 per credit hour. *Financial aid:* Graduate assistantships, partial tuition waivers, and career-related internships or fieldwork available. Financial aid application deadline: 7/1. *Faculty research:* Instructional methodology for adapted physical education, competitive anxiety, obsessiveness in sport. • Dr. Gregory Reeds, Chairman, 716-888-2952. Application contact: Kevin Smith, Graduate Recruitment and Admissions, 716-888-2544. Fax: 716-888-3290.

Central Connecticut State University, School of Education and Professional Studies, Department of Physical Education and Health Fitness Studies, New Britain, CT 06050-4010. Awards MS. Part-time and evening/weekend programs available. Faculty: 10 full-time (4 women), 9 part-time (3 women), 13.7 FTE. Students: 20 full-time (13 women), 26 part-time (11 women); includes 1 international. Average age 29. 32 applicants, 63% accepted. In 1997, 9 degrees awarded. *Degree requirements:* Thesis or alternative, comprehensive exam required, foreign language not required. *Entrance requirements:* TOEFL (minimum score 550), minimum GPA of 2.7, bachelor's degree in physical education (preferred). Application deadline: 6/1 (priority date; rolling processing; 12/1 for spring admission). Application fee: $40. *Expenses:* Tuition $4458 per year full-time, $175 per credit hour part-time for state residents; $9943 per year full-time, $175 per credit hour part-time for nonresidents. Fees $45 per semester. *Financial aid:* In 1997–98, 1 research assistantship was awarded; Federal Work-Study and career-related internships or fieldwork also available. Financial aid application deadline: 3/15; applicants required to submit FAFSA. *Faculty research:* Exercise science, athletic training, preparation of physical education for schools. • Dr. Jack Olcott, Chair, 860-832-2155.

Central Michigan University, College of Education and Human Services, Department of Physical Education and Sport, Mount Pleasant, MI 48859. Offers programs in athletic administration (MA), athletic coaching (Certificate), coaching (MA), exercise science (MA), sports administration (MSA), teaching (MA). Faculty: 15 full-time (3 women). Students: 37 full-time (15 women), 58 part-time (20 women); includes 9 minority (6 African Americans, 3 Hispanics), 5 international. Average age 27. In 1997, 18 master's awarded. *Degree requirements:* For master's, thesis or alternative required, foreign language not required. *Entrance requirements:* For master's, minimum GPA of 2.5 in last 20 hours. Application deadline: 3/1 (priority date). Application fee: $30. *Expenses:* Tuition $139 per credit hour (minimum) for state residents; $276 per credit hour (minimum) for nonresidents. Fees $260 per year full-time, $150 per semester part-time. *Financial aid:* In 1997–98, 2 fellowships, 12 teaching assistantships (10 to first-year students) were awarded; Federal Work-Study and career-related internships or fieldwork also available. Financial aid application deadline: 3/7. *Faculty research:* Biomechanical analysis of sports skills, sociological studies, psychological studies. • Dr. James E. Hornak, Chairperson, 517-774-6658. Fax: 517-774-4374. E-mail: 34naewv@cmich.edu.

Central Missouri State University, College of Education and Human Services, Department of Physical Education, Warrensburg, MO 64093. Offers programs in elementary education (MSE), K–12 education (MSE), physical education (Ed S), physical education/exercise and sports science (MS), secondary education (MSE). Part-time programs available. Faculty: 13 full-time. Students: 17 full-time (6 women), 31 part-time (12 women). In 1997, 17 master's awarded. *Degree requirements:* For master's, comprehensive exam, research project, or thesis (MS); comprehensive exam or thesis (MSE). *Entrance requirements:* For master's, GRE General Test (MSE), minimum GPA of 2.5, bachelor's degree in physical education (MS); minimum GPA of 2.75, teaching certificate (MSE). Application deadline: 6/30 (priority date; rolling processing). Application fee: $25 ($50 for international students). *Tuition:* $3288 per year full-time, $137 per credit hour part-time for state residents; $5928 per year full-time, $274 per credit hour part-time for nonresidents. *Financial aid:* In 1997–98, 3 teaching assistantships, 8 administrative and laboratory assistantships were awarded; Federal Work-Study also available. Aid available to part-time students. Financial aid application deadline: 3/1; applicants required to submit FAFSA. • Dr. James Conn, Chair, 660-543-4256. Fax: 660-543-4167. E-mail: jhc4126@cmsu2.cmsu.edu.

Central Washington University, College of Education and Professional Studies, Department of Physical Education, Health Education and Leisure Services, Ellensburg, WA 98926. Offers program in health, physical education and recreation (MS). Part-time programs available. Faculty: 16 full-time (5 women). Students: 12 full-time (9 women), 4 part-time (2 women); includes 1 minority (Hispanic). 24 applicants, 50% accepted. In 1997, 7 degrees awarded. *Degree requirements:* Thesis or alternative required, foreign language not required. *Entrance requirements:* Minimum GPA of 3.0. Application deadline: 4/1 (priority date; rolling processing; 1/1 for spring admission). Application fee: $35. *Expenses:* Tuition $4200 per year full-time, $140 per credit hour part-time for state residents; $12,780 per year full-time, $426 per credit hour part-time for nonresidents. Fees $240 per year. *Financial aid:* In 1997–98, 10 teaching assistantships (7 to first-year students) averaging $1,108 per month and totaling $99,720 were awarded; research assistantships, Federal Work-Study also available. Financial aid application deadline: 2/15. • Dr. John Gregor, Chairman, 509-963-1911. Application contact: Christie A. Fevergeon, Program Coordinator, Graduate Studies and Research, 509-963-3103. Fax: 509-963-1799. E-mail: masters@cwu.edu.

Chicago State University, College of Education, Department of Health, Physical Education and Recreation-Athletics, Chicago, IL 60628. Offers program in physical education (MS Ed). *Degree requirements:* Thesis optional, foreign language not required. *Entrance requirements:* Minimum GPA of 2.75. Application deadline: 7/1 (11/10 for spring admission). *Tuition:* $2268 per year full-time, $95 per credit hour part-time for state residents; $6804 per year full-time, $284 per credit hour part-time for nonresidents.

The Citadel, The Military College of South Carolina, Department of Health and Physical Education, Charleston, SC 29409. Awards M Ed. Faculty: 3 full-time (0 women), 1 part-time (0 women). Students: 3 full-time (2 women), 24 part-time (7 women); includes 4 minority (all African Americans). In 1997, 2 degrees awarded. *Entrance requirements:* GRE, MAT, or 12 hours of graduate course work with a minimum GPA of 3.0. Application deadline: rolling. Application fee: $25. *Expenses:* Tuition $130 per credit hour for state residents; $260 per credit hour for nonresidents. Fees $30 per semester. • Dr. Gary Wilson, Head, 803-953-5060.

Cleveland State University, College of Education, Department of Health, Physical Education, Recreation and Dance, Cleveland, OH 44115-2440. Offers programs in community health (M Ed), exercise science (M Ed), health education (M Ed), human performance (M Ed), pedagogy (M Ed), recreation (M Ed), sport education (M Ed), sport management (M Ed), sport management/exercise science (M Ed). Part-time programs available. Faculty: 11 full-time (6 women). Students: 7 full-time (4 women), 10 part-time (3 women); includes 2 minority (both African Americans). Average age 26. 18 applicants, 61% accepted. In 1997, 31 degrees awarded. *Degree requirements:* Thesis optional, foreign language not required. *Entrance requirements:* GRE General Test or MAT (score in 50th percentile or higher), minimum undergraduate GPA of 2.75. Application deadline: 9/1 (priority date; rolling processing). Application fee: $25. *Expenses:* Tuition $5252 per year full-time, $202 per credit hour part-time for state residents; $10,504 per year full-time, $404 per credit hour part-time for nonresidents. Fees $2.25 per credit hour (minimum). *Financial aid:* In 1997–98, 4 teaching assistantships were awarded; career-related internships or fieldwork also available. Financial aid application deadline: 3/31. *Faculty research:* Mental imagery in motor learning, biomechanical analysis of motor skill, improvement of speed in running, instructional design. • Dr. Vincent Melograno, Chairman, 216-687-4878. Fax: 216-687-5410. E-mail: v.melograno@popmail.csuohio.edu.

The College of New Jersey, Graduate Division, School of Education, Department of Health and Physical Education, Program in Health Education, Ewing, NJ 08628. Offerings include physical education (M Ed). *Average time to degree:* master's–2 years full-time. *Application deadline:* 4/15 (10/15 for spring admission). *Application fee:* $50. *Expenses:* Tuition $6892 per year full-time, $287 per credit hour part-time for state residents; $9602 per year full-time, $402 per credit hour part-time for nonresidents. Fees $799 per year full-time, $33 per credit hour part-time. • Dr. Aristomen Chilakos, Coordinator, 609-771-3160. Fax: 609-637-5153.

The College of New Jersey, Graduate Division, School of Education, Department of Health and Physical Education, Programs in Health and Physical Education, Ewing, NJ 08628. Awards M Ed. Part-time and evening/weekend programs available. Students: 1 full-time (0 women), 17 part-time (9 women); includes 2 minority (1 Hispanic, 1 Native American). Average age 28. In 1997, 8 degrees awarded. *Degree requirements:* Comprehensive exam required, foreign language and thesis not required. *Average time to degree:* master's–2 years full-time. *Entrance requirements:* MAT, minimum GPA of 2.75 overall or 3.0 in field. Application deadline: 4/15 (10/15 for spring admission). Application fee: $50. *Expenses:* Tuition $6892 per year full-time, $287 per credit hour part-time for state residents; $9602 per year full-time, $402 per credit hour part-time for nonresidents. Fees $799 per year full-time, $33 per credit hour part-time. *Financial aid:* Graduate assistantships available. Financial aid application deadline: 5/1; applicants required to submit FAFSA. • Dr. Aristomen Chilakos, Coordinator, 609-771-3160. Fax: 609-637-5153.

Columbus State University, College of Education, Department of Physical Education and Leisure Management, Columbus, GA 31907-5645. Offers program in physical education (M Ed). *Degree requirements:* Exit exam required, foreign language and thesis not required. *Entrance requirements:* GRE General Test (minimum combined score of 800), MAT (minimum score 44). Application deadline: 7/10 (priority date; rolling processing; 10/23 for spring admission). Application fee: $20. *Tuition:* $1718 per year full-time, $151 per semester hour part-time for state residents; $6218 per year full-time, $401 per semester hour part-time for nonresidents. *Financial aid:* Research assistantships, teaching assistantships, full tuition waivers, Federal Work-Study, institutionally sponsored loans, and career-related internships or fieldwork available. Aid available to part-time students. Financial aid application deadline: 7/15; applicants required to submit FAFSA. • Dr. Tom Ford, Chair, 706-568-2046. Fax: 706-569-2634. E-mail: ford_tom@colstate.edu. Application contact: Katie Thornton, Graduate Admissions, 706-568-2279. Fax: 706-568-2462. E-mail: thornton_katie@colstate.edu.

Delta State University, School of Education, Division of Health, Physical Education and Recreation, Cleveland, MS 38733-0001. Offers program in physical education and recreation (M Ed). Part-time and evening/weekend programs available. Faculty: 4 full-time (0 women), 2 part-time (0 women), 5 FTE. Students: 27 full-time (5 women), 3 part-time (0 women); includes 7 minority (all African Americans). Average age 27. 15 applicants, 100% accepted. In 1997, 7 degrees awarded. *Degree requirements:* Thesis optional, foreign language not required. *Entrance requirements:* GRE General Test (minimum combined score of 800) or MAT (minimum score 34), Class A teaching certificate. Application deadline: 8/1 (priority date; rolling processing). Application fee: $0. *Tuition:* $2596 per year full-time, $121 per semester hour part-time for state residents; $5546 per year full-time, $285 per semester hour part-time for nonresidents. *Financial aid:* Research assistantships, Federal Work-Study, institutionally sponsored loans, and career-related internships or fieldwork available. Aid available to part-time students. Financial aid application deadline: 6/1. *Faculty research:* Blood pressure, body fat, power and reaction time, learning disorders for athletes, effects of walking. • Dr. Milton R. Wilder Jr., Chairperson, 601-846-4555. E-mail: mwilder@dsu.deltast.edu. Application contact: Dr. John Thornell, Dean of Graduate Studies and Continuing Education, 601-846-4310. Fax: 601-846-4016.

DePaul University, School of Education, Program in Educational Leadership, Chicago, IL 60604-2287. Offerings include physical education (MA, M Ed). Program faculty: 2 full-time (1 woman), 2 part-time (0 women). *Degree requirements:* Oral exam or thesis required, foreign language not required. *Entrance requirements:* Interview, minimum GPA of 2.75, work experience. Application deadline: rolling. Application fee: $25. *Expenses:* Tuition $320 per credit hour. Fees $30 per year. • Dr. Barbara Sizemore, Dean, School of Education, 312-325-7000 Ext. 1666. Fax: 312-325-7748. Application contact: Director of Graduate Admissions, 312-325-7000 Ext. 1666. E-mail: mmurphy@wppost.depaul.edu.

Drury College, Graduate Programs in Education, Program in Physical Education, Springfield, MO 65802-3791. Awards M Ed. Part-time and evening/weekend programs available. Faculty: 7 full-time (6 women), 1 part-time (0 women). Students: 25. 14 applicants, 86% accepted. *Degree requirements:* Thesis required, foreign language not required. *Entrance requirements:* MAT (minimum score 35), minimum GPA of 2.75. Application fee: $15. *Tuition:* $170 per credit hour. • Dr. Bruce Harger, Director of Athletics and Exercise Sport Science, 417-873-7271.

Eastern Illinois University, College of Education and Professional Studies, Department of Physical Education, 600 Lincoln Avenue, Charleston, IL 61920-3099. Awards MS. Part-time programs available. Faculty: 15 full-time (3 women). Students: 40 full-time (17 women), 15 part-time (7 women). In 1997, 36 degrees awarded. *Application deadline:* 7/31 (priority date; rolling processing). *Application fee:* $25. *Expenses:* Tuition $3459 per year full-time, $96 per semester hour part-time for state residents; $10,377 per year full-time, $288 per semester hour part-time for nonresidents. Fees $1566 per year full-time, $37 per semester hour part-time. *Financial aid:* In 1997–98, 9 teaching assistantships were awarded; Federal Work-Study

Directory: Physical Education

Eastern Illinois University (continued)

also available. Aid available to part-time students. • Dr. Phoebe Church, Chairperson, 217-581-2215. E-mail: cfplc@eiu.edu. Application contact: Dr. Scott Crawford, Coordinator, 217-581-6363. E-mail: cfscc@eiu.edu.

Eastern Kentucky University, College of Health, Physical Education, Recreation and Athletics, Department of Physical Education, Richmond, KY 40475-3101. Offers programs in physical education (MS), sports administration (MS). Part-time programs available. Faculty: 4 full-time (2 women). Students: 33 full-time (18 women), 8 part-time (3 women); includes 3 minority (2 African Americans, 1 Asian American). In 1997, 12 degrees awarded. *Average time to degree:* master's–1 year full-time, 3 years part-time. *Entrance requirements:* GRE General Test, minimum GPA of 2.5. Application deadline: 8/15. Application fee: $0. *Tuition:* $2390 per year full-time, $133 per credit hour part-time for state residents; $6630 per year full-time, $365 per credit hour part-time for nonresidents. *Financial aid:* Research assistantships, teaching assistantships, Federal Work-Study available. Aid available to part-time students. *Faculty research:* Nutrition and exercise. • Lonnie Davis, Chair, 606-622-1887. Fax: 606-622-1254. E-mail: phedavis@acs.eku.edu.

Eastern Kentucky University, College of Education, Department of Curriculum and Instruction, Program in Secondary and Higher Education, Richmond, KY 40475-3101. Offerings include physical education (MA Ed). *Entrance requirements:* GRE General Test, minimum GPA of 2.5. Application fee: $0. *Tuition:* $2390 per year full-time, $133 per credit hour part-time for state residents; $6630 per year full-time, $365 per credit hour part-time for nonresidents. • Dr. Imogene Ramsey, Chair, Department of Curriculum and Instruction, 606-622-2154.

Eastern Michigan University, College of Education, Department of Health, Physical Education, Recreation and Dance, Program in Physical Education, Ypsilanti, MI 48197. Awards MS. In 1997, 10 degrees awarded. *Average time to degree:* master's–2 years full-time, 5 years part-time. *Entrance requirements:* GRE, TOEFL. Application deadline: 5/15 (3/15 for spring admission). Application fee: $30. *Expenses:* Tuition $2691 per year full-time, $150 per credit hour part-time for state residents; $6300 per year full-time, $350 per credit hour part-time for nonresidents. Fees $368 per year full-time, $88 per semester (minimum) part-time. *Financial aid:* Application deadline 3/15. • Dr. Jonathan Ehrman, Coordinator, 734-487-0380.

Eastern Nazarene College, Graduate Studies, Division of Education, Quincy, MA 02170-2999. Offerings include physical education (M Ed, Certificate). M Ed and Certificate also available through weekend program for administration, special needs, and reading only. Division faculty: 9 full-time (5 women), 11 part-time (5 women). *Entrance requirements:* For master's, TOEFL (minimum score 500). Application deadline: rolling. Application fee: $35. *Expenses:* Tuition $350 per credit. Fees $125 per semester full-time, $15 per semester part-time. • Dr. Lorne Ranstrom, Chair, 617-745-3528. Application contact: Cleo P. Cakridas, Graduate Enrollment Counselor, 617-745-3870. Fax: 617-745-3907. E-mail: cakridac@enc.edu.

Eastern New Mexico University, College of Education and Technology, School of Health and Physical Education, Portales, NM 88130. Offers program in physical education (MS). Part-time programs available. Faculty: 3 full-time (2 women). Students: 6 full-time (1 woman), 9 part-time (5 women); includes 3 minority (1 Asian American, 2 Hispanics). 4 applicants, 50% accepted. In 1997, 9 degrees awarded. *Degree requirements:* Thesis optional, foreign language not required. *Entrance requirements:* Minimum GPA of 2.5. Application deadline: rolling. Application fee: $10. *Tuition:* $1956 per year full-time, $82 per credit hour part-time for state residents; $6702 per year full-time, $280 per credit hour part-time for nonresidents. *Financial aid:* In 1997–98, 1 fellowship, 1 research assistantship, 8 teaching assistantships (4 to first-year students) were awarded; Federal Work-Study also available. Aid available to part-time students. Financial aid application deadline: 4/1. • Dr. Mary Drabbs, Graduate Coordinator, 505-562-2236.

Eastern Washington University, College of Education and Human Development, Department of Physical Education, Health and Recreation, Cheney, WA 99004-2431. Offers programs in college instruction in physical education (MS), physical education (MS). Faculty: 11 full-time (1 woman). Students: 15 full-time (7 women), 5 part-time (2 women); includes 2 minority (1 African American, 1 Hispanic). 20 applicants, 80% accepted. In 1997, 2 degrees awarded. *Degree requirements:* Thesis or alternative, comprehensive exam. *Entrance requirements:* Minimum GPA of 3.0. Application deadline: 4/1 (priority date; rolling processing; 1/15 for spring admission). Application fee: $35. *Tuition:* $4200 per year full-time, $140 per credit part-time for state residents; $12,780 per year full-time, $415 per credit part-time for nonresidents. *Financial aid:* Teaching assistantships, Federal Work-Study, institutionally sponsored loans, and career-related internships or fieldwork available. Financial aid application deadline: 2/1. • Dr. Howard Uibel, Chairman, 509-359-2341. Application contact: Dr. Alan Coelho, Director, 509-359-2342.

East Stroudsburg University of Pennsylvania, School of Health Sciences and Human Performance, Department of Movement Studies and Exercise Science, East Stroudsburg, PA 18301-2999. Offers programs in cardiac rehabilitation and exercise science (MS); health and physical education (M Ed), including sports management; physical education (MS). Part-time and evening/weekend programs available. *Degree requirements:* Thesis (for some programs), comprehensive exam required, foreign language not required. *Application deadline:* 7/31 (priority date; rolling processing; 11/30 for spring admission). *Application fee:* $15 ($25 for international students). *Expenses:* Tuition $3468 per year full-time, $193 per credit part-time for state residents; $6236 per year full-time, $346 per credit part-time for nonresidents. Fees $700 per year full-time, $39 per credit part-time.

East Tennessee State University, College of Education, Department of Physical Education, Exercise and Sport Sciences, Johnson City, TN 37614-0734. Offers program in physical education (MA, M Ed). Part-time and evening/weekend programs available. Faculty: 8 full-time (3 women). Students: 40 full-time (25 women), 19 part-time (9 women); includes 5 minority (4 African Americans, 1 Native American), 3 international. Average age 25. 35 applicants, 94% accepted. In 1997, 15 degrees awarded. *Degree requirements:* Comprehensive exam (M Ed), oral and written comprehensive exams, thesis (MA) required, foreign language not required. *Entrance requirements:* GRE General Test, TOEFL (minimum score 550), major or minor in physical education or equivalent, interview, minimum GPA of 2.7. Application deadline: 7/15 (priority date; rolling processing; 11/1 for spring admission). Application fee: $25 ($35 for international students). *Tuition:* $2944 per year full-time, $158 per credit hour part-time for state residents; $7770 per year full-time, $369 per credit hour part-time for nonresidents. *Financial aid:* In 1997–98, 14 research assistantships (7 to first-year students), 5 teaching assistantships (1 to a first-year student), 8 assistantships (5 to first-year students) were awarded; Federal Work-Study, institutionally sponsored loans, and career-related internships or fieldwork also available. *Faculty research:* Physiology of exercise, corporate wellness, teacher preparation, assessing change in motor skills, legal liabilities. • Dr. Whitfield B. East, Chair, 423-439-5257. Application contact: Dr. Judith Johnston, Graduate Coordinator, 423-439-5796. Fax: 423-439-5383.

Edinboro University of Pennsylvania, School of Education, Department of Health and Physical Education, Edinboro, PA 16444. Awards Certificate. Students: 1 part-time (0 women). Average age 37. *Degree requirements:* Thesis required, foreign language not required. *Entrance requirements:* GRE or MAT (score in 30th percentile or higher). Application deadline: rolling. Application fee: $25. *Expenses:* Tuition $3468 per year full-time, $193 per credit part-time for state residents; $6236 per year full-time, $346 per credit part-time for nonresidents. Fees $898 per year full-time, $50 per semester (minimum) part-time. • Dr. Kenneth Felker, Chair, 814-732-2777. Application contact: Dr. Philip Kerstetter, Dean of Graduate Studies, 814-732-2856. Fax: 814-732-2611. E-mail: kerstetter@edinboro.edu.

Emporia State University, School of Graduate Studies, The Teachers College, Division of Health, Physical Education and Recreation, Emporia, KS 66801-5087. Offers program in physical education (MS). Postbaccalaureate distance learning degree programs offered (minimal on-campus study). Faculty: 7 full-time (3 women). Students: 13 full-time (3 women), 5 part-time (4 women). 8 applicants, 100% accepted. In 1997, 5 degrees awarded. *Degree requirements:* Comprehensive exam or thesis required, foreign language not required. *Entrance requirements:* GRE General Test or MAT, TOEFL (minimum score 550). Application deadline: 8/15 (priority date; rolling processing). Application fee: $30 ($75 for international students). Electronic applications accepted. *Tuition:* $2300 per year full-time, $103 per credit hour part-time for state residents; $6012 per year full-time, $258 per credit hour part-time for nonresidents. *Financial aid:* In 1997–98, 1 research assistantship averaging $558 per month, 14 teaching assistantships averaging $522 per month were awarded; fellowships, Federal Work-Study, institutionally sponsored loans, and career-related internships or fieldwork also available. Financial aid application deadline: 3/15; applicants required to submit FAFSA. • Dr. Joella H. Mehrhof, Chair, 316-341-5946. E-mail: mehrhofj@emporia.edu.

Fairleigh Dickinson University, Teaneck–Hackensack Campus, University College: Arts, Sciences, and Professional Studies, Peter Sammartino School of Education, Program in Physical Science Education, 1000 River Road, Teaneck, NJ 07666-1914. Offers physical education (MAT), science education (MAT). Faculty: 11 full-time (8 women), 27 part-time (10 women). *Degree requirements:* Research project required, thesis not required. *Application deadline:* rolling. *Application fee:* $35. *Expenses:* Tuition $522 per credit. Fees $302 per year full-time, $138 per year part-time. *Faculty research:* Mathematics for students with learning disabilities, gender issues in education, social problem-solving and conflict resolution in the classroom, multicultural education in the elementary classroom, problems encountered by international students in college programs. • Dr. Eloise Forster, Interim Director, Peter Sammartino School of Education, 201-692-2834. Fax: 201-692-2603.

Florida Agricultural and Mechanical University, Division of Graduate Studies, Research, and Continuing Education, College of Education, Department of Health, Physical Education, and Recreation, Tallahassee, FL 32307-3200. Awards M Ed, MS Ed. Part-time and evening/weekend programs available. Students: 12 (3 women); includes 10 minority (all African Americans). Average age 23. In 1997, 5 degrees awarded. *Degree requirements:* Thesis optional, foreign language not required. *Entrance requirements:* GRE General Test (minimum combined score of 1000), minimum GPA of 3.0. Application deadline: 5/13. Application fee: $20. *Expenses:* Tuition $140 per credit hour for state residents; $484 per credit hour for nonresidents. Fees $130 per year. *Financial aid:* Teaching assistantships, Federal Work-Study, institutionally sponsored loans available. *Faculty research:* Administration/curriculum, work behavior, psychology. • Dr. Barbara Thompson, Chairperson, 850-599-3135.

Florida International University, College of Education, Department of Health, Physical Education, and Recreation, Program in Physical Education, Miami, FL 33199. Awards MS. Part-time and evening/weekend programs available. Students: 4 full-time (2 women), 16 part-time (10 women); includes 12 minority (3 African Americans, 1 Asian American, 8 Hispanics). Average age 30. 15 applicants, 73% accepted. In 1997, 5 degrees awarded. *Entrance requirements:* GRE General Test (minimum combined score of 1000) or minimum GPA of 3.0, teaching certificate in physical education. Application deadline: 4/1 (priority date; rolling processing; 10/1 for spring admission). Application fee: $20. *Expenses:* Tuition $138 per credit hour for state residents; $482 per credit hour for nonresidents. Fees $46 per semester. *Faculty research:* Psychology, medicine, sociology of sports, movement education, exercise physiology. • Dr. Robert Wolff, Chairperson, Department of Health, Physical Education, and Recreation, 305-348-3486. Fax: 305-348-3571. E-mail: wolffr@fiu.edu.

Florida State University, College of Education, Department of Physical Education, Tallahassee, FL 32306. Offers programs in adapted physical education (MS), sports administration (MS, Ed D, PhD, Ed S), teacher education (MS, Ed D, PhD, Ed S). Faculty: 6 full-time (3 women), 6 part-time (0 women). Students: 80 full-time (24 women), 41 part-time (16 women); includes 21 minority (15 African Americans, 4 Asian Americans, 2 Hispanics). 115 applicants, 57% accepted. In 1997, 39 master's, 6 doctorates awarded. *Degree requirements:* For master's and Ed S, comprehensive exam required, thesis optional; for doctorate, dissertation, comprehensive exam. *Entrance requirements:* GRE General Test (minimum combined score of 1000), minimum GPA of 3.0. Application deadline: 7/1 (priority date; rolling processing; 11/1 for spring admission). Application fee: $20. *Tuition:* $139 per credit hour for state residents; $482 per credit hour for nonresidents. *Financial aid:* Fellowships, research assistantships, teaching assistantships, and career-related internships or fieldwork available. • Dr. Dewayne Johnson, Chair, 850-644-4813. E-mail: djohnson@mail.coe.fsu.edu. Application contact: Admission Secretary, 850-644-4813. Fax: 850-644-0975.

Fort Hays State University, College of Health and Life Sciences, Department of Health and Human Performance, Hays, KS 67601-4099. Offers program in health, physical education, and recreation (MS). Part-time programs available. Faculty: 4 full-time (0 women). Students: 22 full-time (7 women), 17 part-time (6 women); includes 1 minority (Hispanic). Average age 29. 17 applicants, 82% accepted. In 1997, 20 degrees awarded. *Entrance requirements:* GRE General Test or MAT. Application deadline: 7/1 (priority date; rolling processing). Application fee: $25 ($35 for international students). *Tuition:* $94 per credit hour for state residents; $249 per credit hour for nonresidents. *Financial aid:* Research assistantships, teaching assistantships available. *Faculty research:* Isoproterenol hydrochloride and exercise, dehydrogenase and high-density lipoprotein levels in athletics, venous blood parameters to adipose fat. • Dr. Don Fuertges, Chairman, 785-628-4352.

Frostburg State University, School of Education, Department of Educational Professions, Program in Health and Physical Education, Frostburg, MD 21532-1099. Awards M Ed. Part-time and evening/weekend programs available. *Application deadline:* 7/15 (rolling processing). *Application fee:* $30.

Frostburg State University, School of Education, Department of Educational Professions, Program in Human Performance, Frostburg, MD 21532-1099. Awards MS. *Application deadline:* 7/15 (rolling processing). *Application fee:* $30.

Gardner–Webb University, Department of Physical Education, Boiling Springs, NC 28017. Awards MA. Part-time and evening/weekend programs available. Faculty: 4 full-time (1 woman). Students: 22 part-time (12 women); includes 1 minority (African American). Average age 26. 22 applicants, 91% accepted. In 1997, 5 degrees awarded. *Degree requirements:* Comprehensive exam required, foreign language and thesis not required. *Entrance requirements:* GRE General Test (minimum combined score of 900), MAT (minimum score 35), or NTE, minimum GPA of 2.5. Application deadline: 8/1. Application fee: $25. *Tuition:* $178 per semester hour full-time, $220 per semester hour part-time. *Financial aid:* In 1997–98, 3 assistantships (all to first-year students) were awarded. • Dr. Jeffrey Tubbs, Chair, 704-434-4427. Fax: 704-434-4739. E-mail: jtubbs@gardner-webb.edu.

Georgia College and State University, School of Health Sciences, Department of Health, Physical Education, and Recreation, Milledgeville, GA 31061. Offers program in health and physical education (M Ed, Ed S). Students: 32 full-time (20 women), 18 part-time (11 women); includes 4 minority (all African Americans), 4 international. Average age 32. In 1997, 12 master's, 2 Ed Ss awarded. *Degree requirements:* For master's, computer language required, foreign language and thesis not required; for Ed S, computer language, oral exam, research project required, foreign language and thesis not required. *Entrance requirements:* For master's, GRE General Test (minimum combined score of 800) or NTE (minimum score 550 on each core battery test), minimum GPA of 2.5, NT-4 certificate; for Ed S, GRE General Test (minimum combined score of 900) or NTE (minimum score 575 on each core battery test), master's degree, minimum graduate GPA of 3.25, NT-5 certificate, 2 years of teaching experience. Application deadline: 7/31 (priority date; rolling processing). Application fee: $10. *Financial aid:* Assistantships, Federal Work-Study, and career-related internships or fieldwork available. Aid available to part-time students. Financial aid application deadline: 4/15. • Dr. James Lidstone, Chair, 912-445-4072.

Directory: Physical Education

Georgia Southern University, College of Education, Department of Middle Grades and Secondary Education, Program in Health and Physical Education, Statesboro, GA 30460-8126. Awards M Ed, Ed S. Part-time programs available. Students: 4 full-time (1 woman), 8 part-time (4 women). Average age 30. 2 applicants, 50% accepted. In 1997, 6 master's awarded. *Degree requirements:* For master's, exams required, foreign language and thesis not required; for Ed S, exams required, thesis not required. *Entrance requirements:* For master's, GRE General Test (minimum score 450 on each section) or MAT (minimum score 44), minimum GPA of 2.5; for Ed S, GRE General Test (minimum score 450 on each section) or MAT (minimum score 49), minimum graduate GPA of 3.25. Application deadline: 7/15 (priority date; rolling processing; 11/15 for spring admission). Application fee: $0. Electronic applications accepted. *Tuition:* $2619 per year full-time, $287 per semester (minimum) part-time for state residents; $8619 per year full-time, $1037 per semester (minimum) part-time for nonresidents. *Financial aid:* Federal Work-Study and career-related internships or fieldwork available. Aid available to part-time students. Financial aid application deadline: 4/15. • Application contact: Dr. John R. Diebolt, Associate Graduate Dean, 912-681-5384. Fax: 912-681-0740. E-mail: gradschool@gsvms2.cc.gasou.edu.

Georgia Southwestern State University, School of Education, Americus, GA 31709-4693. Offerings include health and physical education (M Ed). *Entrance requirements:* GRE General Test (minimum score 400 on each section) or MAT (minimum score 44), minimum GPA of 2.5. Application deadline: 9/1 (rolling processing; 3/15 for spring admission). Application fee: $10. • Dr. Kurt Myers, Chair, 912-931-2145. Application contact: Chris Laney, Graduate Admissions Specialist, 912-931-2027. Fax: 912-931-2059. E-mail: claney@gsw1500.gsw.peachnet.edu.

Georgia State University, College of Education, Department of Kinesiology and Health, Program in Health and Physical Education, Atlanta, GA 30303-3083. Awards M Ed, Ed S. Part-time and evening/weekend programs available. Students: 7 full-time (3 women), 3 part-time (1 woman). Average age 31. 5 applicants, 100% accepted. In 1997, 4 master's, 1 Ed S awarded. *Degree requirements:* For master's, comprehensive exam. *Entrance requirements:* For master's, GRE General Test (minimum combined score of 800) or MAT (minimum score 44), minimum GPA of 2.5. Application deadline: 7/15 (1/15 for spring admission). Application fee: $25. *Expenses:* Tuition $2673 per year full-time, $99 per semester hour part-time for state residents; $10,692 per year full-time, $396 per semester hour part-time for nonresidents. Fees $228 per year. *Financial aid:* Teaching assistantships and career-related internships or fieldwork available. *Faculty research:* Exercise science, teacher behavior. • Dr. Jeff C. Rupp, Chair, Department of Kinesiology and Health, 404-651-2536.

Hardin–Simmons University, Irvin School of Education, Department of Physical Education, Program in Secondary Physical Education, Abilene, TX 79698-0001. Awards M Ed. Part-time programs available. Faculty: 3 full-time (0 women). Students: 4 full-time (2 women), 3 part-time (2 women); includes 1 minority (African American). Average age 30. In 1997, 4 degrees awarded. *Degree requirements:* Project required, foreign language and thesis not required. *Application deadline:* 8/15 (priority date; rolling processing; 1/5 for spring admission). *Application fee:* $25. *Expenses:* Tuition $280 per semester hour. Fees $630 per year full-time. *Financial aid:* In 1997–98, 7 students received aid, including 1 fellowship averaging $250 per month and totaling $1,000, coaching assistantships averaging $250 per month and totaling $13,000; full and partial tuition waivers, Federal Work-Study, and career-related internships or fieldwork also available. Aid available to part-time students. Financial aid application deadline: 3/15; applicants required to submit FAFSA. *Faculty research:* Exercise physiology, kinesiology. • Dr. Tony Grice, Director, 915-670-1470. Fax: 915-670-1572. Application contact: Dr. J. Paul Sorrels, Dean of Graduate Studies, 915-670-1298. Fax: 915-670-1564.

Henderson State University, School of Education, Department of Secondary Education, Arkadelphia, AR 71999-0001. Offerings include physical education (MSE). Postbaccalaureate distance learning degree programs offered (minimal on-campus study). *Degree requirements:* Thesis optional, foreign language not required. *Entrance requirements:* GRE General Test or MAT, minimum GPA of 2.7, teacher certification. Application deadline: 7/31 (priority date; rolling processing). Application fee: $15. Electronic applications accepted. *Expenses:* Tuition $120 per credit hour for state residents; $240 per credit hour for nonresidents. Fees $105 per semester (minimum) full-time, $52 per semester (minimum) part-time. • Dr. Charles Weiner, Chairperson, 870-230-5163. Fax: 870-230-5455. E-mail: weinerc@holly.hsu.edu.

Hofstra University, School of Education and Allied Human Services, Department of Health, Physical Education and Recreation, Program in Physical Education, Hempstead, NY 11549. Awards MS. Part-time and evening/weekend programs available. Faculty: 7 full-time (5 women), 5 part-time (3 women). Students: 34 full-time (9 women), 69 part-time (19 women). Average age 27. 48 applicants, 92% accepted. In 1997, 18 degrees awarded. *Degree requirements:* Departmental qualifying exam, final essay. *Entrance requirements:* GRE General Test, interview, minimum GPA of 2.5. Application deadline: rolling. Application fee: $40 ($75 for international students). *Expenses:* Tuition $10,968 per year full-time, $457 per credit hour part-time. Fees $670 per year full-time, $112 per semester (minimum) part-time. *Financial aid:* In 1997–98, 20 students received aid, including 2 teaching assistantships (both to first-year students); full and partial tuition waivers, Federal Work-Study, institutionally sponsored loans, and career-related internships or fieldwork also available. Aid available to part-time students. Financial aid applicants required to submit FAFSA. *Faculty research:* Pedagogy, sociocultural research, curriculum comparative studies, instructional strategies. Total annual research expenditures: $22,000. • Dr. Rhonda Clements, Coordinator, 516-463-5176. E-mail: hprrlc@hofstra.edu. Application contact: Mary Beth Carey, Dean of Admissions, 516-463-6700. Fax: 516-560-7660. E-mail: hofstra@hofstra.edu.

Humboldt State University, College of Professional Studies, Department of Physical Education, Arcata, CA 95521-8299. Awards MA. Faculty: 30 full-time (9 women), 13 part-time (8 women). Students: 16 full-time (6 women), 13 part-time (3 women); includes 3 minority (1 Asian American, 2 Hispanics). Average age 28. 20 applicants, 100% accepted. In 1997, 7 degrees awarded. *Degree requirements:* Thesis or alternative required, foreign language not required. *Entrance requirements:* GMAT, TOEFL (minimum score 550), minimum GPA of 2.5. Application deadline: rolling. Application fee: $55. *Expenses:* Tuition $0 for state residents; $246 per unit for nonresidents. Fees $1996 per year full-time, $1330 per year part-time. *Financial aid:* Teaching assistantships, Federal Work-Study, institutionally sponsored loans, and career-related internships or fieldwork available. Financial aid application deadline: 3/1. *Faculty research:* Human performance, adapted physical education, physical therapy. • Dr. Scott Nelson, Coordinator, 707-826-4336.

Illinois State University, College of Applied Science and Technology, Department of Health, Physical Education and Recreation, Normal, IL 61790-2200. Offers programs in health education (MA, MS), physical education (MA, MS). Faculty: 12 full-time (6 women). Students: 74 full-time (35 women), 38 part-time (18 women); includes 11 minority (6 African Americans, 1 Asian American, 4 Hispanics), 3 international. 64 applicants, 95% accepted. In 1997, 38 degrees awarded. *Degree requirements:* Thesis or alternative. *Entrance requirements:* GRE General Test (minimum combined score of 1000), minimum GPA of 2.6 in last 60 hours. Application deadline: rolling. Application fee: $0. *Expenses:* Tuition $2454 per year full-time, $102 per hour part-time for state residents; $7362 per year full-time, $307 per hour part-time for nonresidents. Fees $1048 per year full-time, $44 per hour part-time. *Financial aid:* In 1997–98, 1 teaching assistantship, 50 assistantships averaging $453 per month were awarded; research assistantships, full and partial tuition waivers, Federal Work-Study, and career-related internships or fieldwork also available. Financial aid application deadline: 4/1. *Total annual research expenditures:* $38,761. • Dr. Marlene Mawson, Chairperson, 309-438-8661.

Indiana State University, School of Health and Human Performance, Department of Physical Education, Terre Haute, IN 47809-1401. Awards MA, MS. Faculty: 11 full-time (4 women), 1 part-time (0 women). Students: 17 full-time (6 women), 10 part-time (5 women); includes 2 minority (1 African American, 1 Hispanic), 4 international. Average age 30. 17 applicants, 76% accepted. In 1997, 14 degrees awarded. *Entrance requirements:* Minor in physical education. Application deadline: rolling. Application fee: $20. *Tuition:* $143 per credit hour for state residents; $325 per credit hour for nonresidents. *Financial aid:* In 1997–98, 8 teaching assistantships (5 to first-year students) were awarded; research assistantships also available. Financial aid application deadline: 3/1. *Faculty research:* Exercise science. • Dr. Alan Lacy, Chairperson, 812-237-4048.

Indiana University Bloomington, School of Health, Physical Education and Recreation, Program in Kinesiology, Bloomington, IN 47405. Offers adapted physical education (MS), administration (MS), applied sport science (MS), athletic administration/sport management (MS), athletic training (MS), biomechanics (MS), clinical exercise physiology (MS), exercise physiology (MS), human performance (PhD), motor control (MS), motor development (MS), motor learning (MS), physical education (PED, PE Dir), social science of sport (MS), sport management (MS). PhD offered through the University Graduate School. Part-time programs available. Faculty: 12 full-time (2 women). Students: 87 full-time (42 women), 28 part-time (14 women); includes 2 African Americans, 1 Asian American, 10 international. In 1997, 71 master's, 2 doctorates awarded. Terminal master's awarded for partial completion of doctoral program. *Degree requirements:* For master's and PE Dir, thesis optional, foreign language not required; for doctorate, dissertation required, foreign language not required. *Entrance requirements:* GRE. Application deadline: rolling. Application fee: $35. *Expenses:* Tuition $153 per credit hour for state residents; $446 per credit hour for nonresidents. Fees $343 per year. *Financial aid:* Fellowships, research assistantships, teaching assistantships, fee scholarships, fee remissions, partial tuition waivers, Federal Work-Study, institutionally sponsored loans, and career-related internships or fieldwork available. Financial aid application deadline: 3/1. *Faculty research:* Exercise physiology and biochemistry, sports biomechanics, human motor control, adaption of fitness and exercise to special populations. • Dr. Harold Morris, Chairperson, 812-855-3114. Application contact: Program Office, 812-855-5523. Fax: 812-855-9417. E-mail: kines@indiana.edu.

Indiana University of Pennsylvania, College of Health and Human Services, Department of Health and Physical Education, Indiana, PA 15705-1087. Offers programs in aquatics administration and facilities management (MS), sport broadcast journalism (MS), sport management (MS), sports studies (MS). Part-time programs available. Students: 8 full-time (2 women), 5 part-time (1 woman); includes 2 minority (both African Americans). Average age 27. 12 applicants, 75% accepted. In 1997, 9 degrees awarded. *Degree requirements:* Thesis optional, foreign language not required. *Entrance requirements:* TOEFL (minimum score 500). Application deadline: 7/1 (priority date; rolling processing; 11/1 for spring admission). Application fee: $30. *Expenses:* Tuition $3468 per year full-time, $193 per credit part-time for state residents; $6236 per year full-time, $346 per credit part-time for nonresidents. Fees $313 per year (minimum) full-time, $84 per year part-time. *Financial aid:* Application deadline 3/15. • Dr. James Mill, Chairperson and Graduate Coordinator, 724-357-2770. E-mail: jimmill@grove.iup.edu.

Inter American University of Puerto Rico, Metropolitan Campus, Division of Education, Program in Health and Physical Education, San Juan, PR 00919-1293. Awards MA. Students: 13 part-time (4 women); includes 13 minority (all Hispanics). In 1997, 9 degrees awarded. *Degree requirements:* Comprehensive exam required, foreign language and thesis not required. *Entrance requirements:* GRE or PAEG, interview. Application deadline: 5/15 (priority date; rolling processing; 11/15 for spring admission). Application fee: $31. Electronic applications accepted. *Expenses:* Tuition $3272 per year full-time, $1740 per year part-time. Fees $328 per year full-time, $176 per year part-time. *Financial aid:* Federal Work-Study available. Aid available to part-time students. • Dr. Amalia Charneco, Director, Division of Education, 787-758-5652. Application contact: Jenny Maldonado, Administrative Assistant, 787-250-1912 Ext. 2393. Fax: 787-250-1197.

Inter American University of Puerto Rico, San Germán Campus, Department of Education, Program in Physical Education and Scientific Analysis of Human Body Movement, San Germán, PR 00683-5008. Awards MA Ed. Part-time and evening/weekend programs available. Faculty: 2 full-time (1 woman). In 1997, 9 degrees awarded. *Degree requirements:* Comprehensive exam required, foreign language and thesis not required. *Entrance requirements:* Minimum GPA of 3.0, GRE General Test, or PAEG. Application deadline: 4/30 (priority date; rolling processing; 11/15 for spring admission). Application fee: $31. *Expenses:* Tuition $150 per credit. Fees $177 per semester. *Financial aid:* Teaching assistantships available. • Application contact: Mildred Camacho, Admissions Director, 787-892-3090. Fax: 787-892-6350.

Iowa State University of Science and Technology, College of Education, Department of Health and Human Performance, Ames, IA 50011. Awards MS. Faculty: 18 full-time, 1 part-time. Students: 32 full-time (13 women), 29 part-time (15 women); includes 5 minority (2 African Americans, 3 Hispanics), 2 international. 65 applicants, 77% accepted. In 1997, 14 degrees awarded. *Degree requirements:* Thesis or alternative. *Entrance requirements:* GRE General Test, TOEFL. Application deadline: 3/1 (priority date). Application fee: $20 ($30 for international students). *Expenses:* Tuition $3166 per year full-time, $176 per credit part-time for state residents; $9324 per year full-time, $518 per credit part-time for nonresidents. Fees $200 per year. *Financial aid:* In 1997–98, 14 research assistantships (7 to first-year students), 18 teaching assistantships (4 to first-year students), 2 scholarships (1 to a first-year student) were awarded; fellowships and career-related internships or fieldwork also available. • Dr. Shirley Wood, Interim Chair, 515-294-6459. E-mail: sjwood@iastate.edu. Application contact: Richard Engelhorn, 515-294-8131. E-mail: hhpgrad@iastate.edu.

Jackson State University, School of Education, Department of Health, Physical Education and Recreation, Jackson, MS 39217. Awards MS Ed. Part-time and evening/weekend programs available. Faculty: 5 full-time (0 women). Students: 5 full-time (1 woman), 13 part-time (2 women); includes 17 minority (all African Americans). 6 applicants, 67% accepted. In 1997, 6 degrees awarded. *Degree requirements:* Thesis or alternative, comprehensive exam. *Entrance requirements:* GRE General Test (minimum combined score of 1000), TOEFL (minimum score 550). Application deadline: 3/1 (priority date; rolling processing; 10/1 for spring admission). Application fee: $20. *Tuition:* $2688 per year (minimum) full-time, $150 per semester hour part-time for state residents; $5546 per year (minimum) full-time, $309 per semester hour part-time for nonresidents. *Financial aid:* Application deadline 3/1. • Dr. Melvin Evans, Chair, 601-968-2373. Fax: 601-968-2374. Application contact: Mae Robinson, Admissions Coordinator, 601-968-2455. Fax: 601-968-8246. E-mail: mrobinson@ccaix.jsums.edu.

Jacksonville State University, College of Education, Program in Health and Physical Education, Jacksonville, AL 36265-9982. Awards MS Ed. Part-time and evening/weekend programs available. Faculty: 7 full-time (2 women). Students: 4 full-time (3 women), 32 part-time (10 women); includes 4 minority (all African Americans). In 1997, 23 degrees awarded. *Degree requirements:* Thesis optional. *Entrance requirements:* GRE General Test or MAT. Application deadline: rolling. Application fee: $20. *Expenses:* Tuition $2140 per year full-time, $107 per semester hour part-time for state residents; $4280 per year full-time, $214 per semester hour part-time for nonresidents. Fees $30 per semester. *Financial aid:* Available to part-time students. Financial aid application deadline: 4/1. • Application contact: College of Graduate Studies and Continuing Education, 205-782-5329.

Kent State University, College of Fine and Professional Arts, School of Exercise, Leisure and Sport, Kent, OH 44242-0001. Offers programs in exercise physiology (PhD), physical education (MA). Faculty: 19 full-time. Students: 53 full-time (24 women), 22 part-time (9 women); includes 4 minority (3 African Americans, 1 Hispanic), 1 international. 57 applicants, 74% accepted. In 1997, 33 master's, 1 doctorate awarded. *Degree requirements:* For master's, thesis optional, foreign language not required; for doctorate, dissertation required, foreign language not required. *Entrance requirements:* For master's, minimum GPA of 2.75; for doctorate, minimum GPA of 3.0. Application deadline: 7/12 (rolling processing; 11/29 for spring admission). Application fee: $30. *Tuition:* $4752 per year full-time, $216 per credit hour part-time for state residents; $9213 per year full-time, $419 per credit hour part-time for nonresidents. *Financial aid:* Fellowships, research assistantships, teaching assistantships, full tuition waivers, Federal Work-Study, institutionally sponsored loans, and career-related internships or fieldwork available. Financial aid application deadline: 2/1. • Director, 330-672-2012.

Directory: Physical Education

Lakehead University, Faculty of Arts and Science, School of Kinesiology, Thunder Bay, ON P7B 5E1, Canada. Offers program in applied sport science and coaching (MA, M Sc). Part-time programs available. *Degree requirements:* Thesis required, foreign language not required. *Entrance requirements:* TOEFL (minimum score 550), minimum B average. Application deadline: 2/1 (priority date; rolling processing). Application fee: $0. *Faculty research:* Social psychology and physical education, sport history, sports medicine, exercise physiology, gerontology.

Long Island University, Brooklyn Campus, School of Health Professions, Division of Sports Sciences, Brooklyn, NY 11201-8423. Offerings include adapted physical education (MS). Division faculty: 3 full-time (0 women), 9 part-time (1 woman). *Application deadline:* rolling. *Application fee:* $30. Electronic applications accepted. *Expenses:* Tuition $480 per credit. Fees $415 per year full-time, $73 per semester (minimum) part-time. • Dr. Milorad Stricevic, Associate Dean, 718-488-1026. Application contact: Bernard W. Sullivan, Associate Director of Admissions, 718-488-1011.

Longwood College, Department of Education, Farmville, VA 23909-1800. Offerings include curriculum and instruction specialist-elementary (MS), with options in English (MS), mild disabilities (MS), modern language (MS), physical education (MS), speech and drama (MS). Department faculty: 34 part-time. *Degree requirements:* Thesis (for some programs), comprehensive exam. *Entrance requirements:* Minimum GPA of 2.5. Application deadline: 5/1 (priority date; rolling processing; 10/15 for spring admission). Application fee: $25. *Expenses:* Tuition $3048 per year full-time, $127 per credit hour part-time for state residents; $8160 per year full-time, $340 per credit hour part-time for nonresidents. Fees $920 per year full-time, $31 per credit hour part-time. • Dr. Frank Howe, Chair, 804-395-2324. Application contact: Admissions Office, 804-395-2060.

Loras College, Department of Physical Education, Dubuque, IA 52004-0178. Awards MA. Faculty: 2. Students: 5. *Application deadline:* rolling. *Application fee:* $25. *Tuition:* $320 per credit. • Robert Tucker, Chair, 319-588-7196. Application contact: Office of Admissions, 319-588-7236. Fax: 319-588-7964.

Louisiana Tech University, College of Education, Department of Curriculum, Instruction and Leadership, Ruston, LA 71272. Offerings include secondary education (M Ed), with options in business education, English education, foreign language education, health and physical education, mathematics education, science education, social studies education, speech education. Department faculty: 16 full-time (11 women). *Application deadline:* 7/29 (2/3 for spring admission). *Application fee:* $20 ($30 for international students). *Tuition:* $2382 per year full-time, $223 per quarter (minimum) part-time for state residents; $5307 per year full-time, $223 per quarter (minimum) part-time for nonresidents. • Dr. Samuel V. Dauzat, Head, 318-257-4609.

Louisiana Tech University, College of Education, Department of Health and Physical Education, Ruston, LA 71272. Awards MS. Part-time programs available. Faculty: 9 full-time (3 women). Students: 13 full-time (8 women), 2 part-time (1 woman); includes 1 minority (African American), 10 international. Average age 27. In 1997, 14 degrees awarded. *Degree requirements:* Computer language, thesis or alternative required, foreign language not required. *Entrance requirements:* GRE General Test. Application deadline: 7/29 (2/3 for spring admission). Application fee: $20 ($30 for international students). *Tuition:* $2382 per year full-time, $223 per quarter (minimum) part-time for state residents; $5307 per year full-time, $223 per quarter (minimum) part-time for nonresidents. *Financial aid:* Fellowships, research assistantships available. Financial aid application deadline: 2/1. • Dr. Billy Jack Talton, Head, 318-257-4432.

Lynchburg College, School of Education and Human Development, Lynchburg, VA 24501-3199. Offerings include adapted physical education (M Ed), physical education (M Ed). M Ed (adapted physical education, physical education) admissions temporarily suspended. *Entrance requirements:* Minimum GPA of 3.0 (undergraduate). Application fee: $20.

Malone College, Graduate School, Program in Education, Canton, OH 44709-3897. Offerings include physical education and sport (MA). Program faculty: 10 full-time (6 women), 11 part-time (5 women), 12.68 FTE. *Degree requirements:* Research practicum required, foreign language and thesis not required. *Entrance requirements:* Minimum GPA of 3.0, teaching license. Application deadline: 9/6 (rolling processing; 1/2 for spring admission). Application fee: $20. *Tuition:* $300 per credit hour. • Dr. Marietta Daulton, Director, 330-471-8447. Fax: 330-471-8478. E-mail: mdaulton@malone.edu. Application contact: Dan Depasquale, Director of Graduate Student Services, 800-257-4723. Fax: 330-471-8343. E-mail: depasquale@malone.edu.

Mankato State University, College of Allied Health and Nursing, Department of Human Performance, South Rd and Ellis Ave, PO Box 8400, Mankato, MN 56002-8400. Awards MA, MS, MT, SP. Part-time programs available. Faculty: 10 full-time (4 women). Students: 60 full-time (26 women), 19 part-time (4 women); includes 2 minority (1 African American, 1 Asian American), 2 international. Average age 28. 56 applicants, 86% accepted. In 1997, 14 master's awarded. *Degree requirements:* For master's, thesis, comprehensive exam required, foreign language not required; for SP, thesis required, foreign language not required. *Entrance requirements:* For master's, GRE General Test, minimum GPA of 3.0 during previous 2 years; for SP, GRE General Test, minimum GPA of 3.0. Application deadline: 7/10 (priority date; rolling processing; 10/30 for spring admission). Application fee: $20. *Tuition:* $126 per credit (minimum) for state residents; $200 per credit for nonresidents. *Financial aid:* Research assistantships, teaching assistantships, Federal Work-Study, institutionally sponsored loans, and career-related internships or fieldwork available. Aid available to part-time students. Financial aid application deadline: 3/15; applicants required to submit FAFSA. *Faculty research:* Exercise physiology. • Dr. Harry Krampf, Chairperson, 507-389-1917. Application contact: Joni Roberts, Admissions Coordinator, 507-389-2321. Fax: 507-389-5974. E-mail: grad@mankato.msus.edu.

Marshall University, College of Education, Division of Health, Physical Education and Recreation, Program in Health and Physical Education, Huntington, WV 25755-2020. Offers athletic training (MS), health and physical education (MS). Faculty: 6 (1 woman). Students: 41 full-time (14 women), 8 part-time (2 women); includes 4 minority (all African Americans), 2 international. In 1997, 15 degrees awarded. *Degree requirements:* Thesis optional. *Entrance requirements:* GRE General Test (minimum combined score of 1200). *Tuition:* $2364 per year full-time, $132 per hour part-time for state residents; $6894 per year full-time, $383 per hour part-time for nonresidents. • Application contact: Dr. James Harless, Director of Admissions, 304-696-3160.

McGill University, Faculty of Graduate Studies and Research, Faculty of Education, Department of Physical Education, Montréal, PQ H3A 2T5, Canada. Awards MA. Part-time programs available. Faculty: 10 full-time (2 women). Students: 29 full-time (17 women), 14 part-time (8 women); includes 3 international. 15 applicants, 33% accepted. *Degree requirements:* Thesis required, foreign language not required. *Entrance requirements:* TOEFL (minimum score 550), minimum GPA of 3.0. Application deadline: 3/1 (rolling processing). Application fee: $60. *Expenses:* Tuition $1668 per year for Canadian residents; $8268 per year for nonresidents. Fees $828 per year for Canadian residents; $1216 per year for nonresidents. *Financial aid:* Fellowships, teaching assistantships available. *Faculty research:* Biomechanics, exercise physiology, adapted physical education, psychology of motor behavior, pedagogy. • Dr. Greg Reid, Director, 514-398-4184 Ext. 0477. Fax: 514-398-4186. E-mail: reid@education.mcgill.ca.

McNeese State University, College of Education, Department of Health and Human Performance, Lake Charles, LA 70609-2495. Offers program in health and physical education (M Ed). Evening/weekend programs available. Faculty: 7 full-time (2 women). Students: 1 (woman) full-time, 3 part-time (2 women). In 1997, 9 degrees awarded. *Entrance requirements:* GRE General Test, teaching certificate, 18 hours in professional education. Application deadline: 7/15 (priority date; rolling processing). Application fee: $10 ($25 for international students). *Tuition:* $2118 per year full-time, $344 per semester (minimum) part-time for state residents; $7308 per year full-time, $344 per semester (minimum) part-time for nonresidents. *Financial aid:* Application deadline 5/1. • Dr. Hans Leis Jr., Head, 318-475-5374.

Memorial University of Newfoundland, School of Graduate Studies, School of Physical Education and Athletics, St. John's, NF A1C 5S7, Canada. Awards MPE. Students: 8 full-time (5 women), 2 part-time (both women). Average age 25. 6 applicants, 67% accepted. In 1997, 4 degrees awarded. *Degree requirements:* Computer language required, foreign language and thesis not required. *Entrance requirements:* BPE with minimum B average. Application deadline: 2/15 (rolling processing). Application fee: $40. *Expenses:* Tuition $1896 per year (minimum). Fees $60 per year for Canadian residents; $621 per year for nonresidents. *Financial aid:* 6 students received aid; fellowships, research assistantships, teaching assistantships available. Financial aid application deadline: 2/15. *Faculty research:* Administration, sociology of sports, kinesiology, physiology/recreation. Total annual research expenditures: $10,000. • Dr. Colin Higgs, Director, 709-737-8129. E-mail: chiggs@morgan.ucs.mun.ca. Application contact: Dr. Basil Kavanagh, Graduate Officer, 709-737-8676. E-mail: basilk@morgan.ucs.mun.ca.

Michigan State University, College of Education, Department of Kinesiology, East Lansing, MI 48824-1020. Offers program in physical education and exercise science-urban studies (MS, PhD). Faculty: 15 (8 women). Students: 93 (40 women); includes 14 minority (7 African Americans, 3 Asian Americans, 4 Hispanics), 20 international. In 1997, 18 master's, 5 doctorates awarded. *Degree requirements:* For master's, thesis optional, foreign language not required; for doctorate, dissertation required, foreign language not required. *Entrance requirements:* GRE General Test. Application deadline: rolling. Application fee: $30 ($40 for international students). *Expenses:* Tuition $4609 per year full-time, $223 per credit hour (minimum) part-time for state residents; $8704 per year full-time, $450 per credit hour (minimum) part-time for nonresidents. Fees $576 per year full-time, $476 per year part-time. *Financial aid:* In 1997–98, 15 fellowships, 16 research assistantships, 24 teaching assistantships were awarded; Federal Work-Study, institutionally sponsored loans, and career-related internships or fieldwork also available. Aid available to part-time students. Financial aid application deadline: 6/30; applicants required to submit FAFSA. *Faculty research:* Exercise physiology, psychosocial aspects of sport and exercise, motor behavior, biomechanics. • Dr. Deborah Feltz, Chairperson, 517-355-4732.

Middle Tennessee State University, College of Education, Department of Health, Physical Education, Recreation and Safety, Murfreesboro, TN 37132. Awards MS, DA. Faculty: 17 full-time (6 women). Students: 50 full-time (28 women), 70 part-time (39 women); includes 21 minority (17 African Americans, 1 Asian American, 3 Hispanics), 1 international. Average age 30. 80 applicants, 66% accepted. In 1997, 31 master's, 1 doctorate awarded. *Degree requirements:* For master's, comprehensive exams required, foreign language and thesis not required; for doctorate, dissertation, comprehensive exams required, foreign language not required. *Entrance requirements:* For master's, Cooperative English Test, MAT; for doctorate, GRE or MAT. Application deadline: 8/1 (priority date). Application fee: $5. *Expenses:* Tuition $2560 per year full-time, $129 per semester hour part-time for state residents; $7386 per year full-time, $340 per semester hour part-time for nonresidents. Fees $486 per year full-time, $17 per semester (minimum) part-time. *Financial aid:* Teaching assistantships, institutionally sponsored loans, and career-related internships or fieldwork available. Aid available to part-time students. Financial aid application deadline: 5/1; applicants required to submit FAFSA. • Dr. Martha Whaley, Chair, 615-898-2811. Fax: 615-898-5020. E-mail: mwhaley@mtsu.edu.

Midwestern State University, Division of Education, Program in Physical Education, Wichita Falls, TX 76308-2096. Awards MSK. Part-time and evening/weekend programs available. Faculty: 2 full-time (1 woman). Students: 17. Average age 35. In 1997, 4 degrees awarded. *Degree requirements:* Thesis required (for some programs), foreign language not required. *Entrance requirements:* GRE General Test, MAT (average 46), TOEFL (minimum score 550). Application deadline: 8/7 (12/15 for spring admission). Application fee: $0 ($50 for international students). *Expenses:* Tuition $44 per hour for state residents; $259 per hour for nonresidents. Fees $90 per year (minimum) full-time, $9 per semester (minimum) part-time. *Financial aid:* In 1997–98, 12 teaching assistantships were awarded; assistantships, partial tuition waivers, Federal Work-Study, institutionally sponsored loans, and career-related internships or fieldwork also available. Aid available to part-time students. • Dr. Clarence Darter, Coordinator, 817-689-4232.

Mississippi State University, College of Education, Department of Physical Health, Education, Recreation, and Sports, Mississippi State, MS 39762. Offers program in physical education (MS), including exercise science, health education/health promotion, sport administration, teaching/coaching. Part-time programs available. Faculty: 9 full-time (2 women), 1 part-time (0 women). Students: 39 full-time (16 women), 27 part-time (13 women); includes 10 minority (all African Americans), 2 international. Average age 27. In 1997, 41 degrees awarded. *Degree requirements:* Comprehensive oral or written exam required, thesis optional, foreign language not required. *Entrance requirements:* Minimum QPA of 2.75 in last 2 years. Application deadline: 7/26 (priority date; rolling processing; 11/10 for spring admission). Application fee: $0 ($25 for international students). *Tuition:* $3017 per year full-time, $168 per credit hour part-time for state residents; $6119 per year full-time, $340 per credit hour part-time for nonresidents. *Financial aid:* In 1997–98, 6 students received aid, including 6 teaching assistantships averaging $652 per month; Federal Work-Study and career-related internships or fieldwork also available. Aid available to part-time students. Financial aid application deadline: 4/1. *Faculty research:* Perceived/actual fitness level, exercise and aging, risk factors and fitness. • Dr. Robert Boling, Head, 601-325-2963. Fax: 601-325-4525. E-mail: rbb4@ra.msstate.edu.

Montclair State University, College of Education and Human Services, Department of Health Professions, Physical Education, Recreation, and Leisure Studies, Program in Physical Education, Upper Montclair, NJ 07043-1624. Offers coaching and sports administration (MA), exercise science (MA), teaching and administration of physical education (MA). Part-time and evening/weekend programs available. Faculty: 10 full-time. Students: 13 full-time (4 women), 56 part-time (26 women); includes 5 minority (2 African Americans, 1 Asian American, 2 Hispanics). In 1997, 18 degrees awarded. *Degree requirements:* Comprehensive exam, research project required, foreign language and thesis not required. *Entrance requirements:* GRE, appropriate bachelor's degree. Application deadline: 4/1 (rolling processing; 11/1 for spring admission). Application fee: $40. *Expenses:* Tuition $201 per credit for state residents; $257 per credit for nonresidents. Fees $22.05 per credit. *Financial aid:* Research assistantships available. Financial aid application deadline: 3/1; applicants required to submit FAFSA. • Dr. Ree K. Arnold, Adviser, 973-655-7091.

Morehead State University, College of Education and Behavioral Sciences, Department of Health, Physical Education and Recreation, Morehead, KY 40351. Offers programs in health, physical education and recreation (MA, Ed D); sports administration (MS). MS offered jointly with Eastern Kentucky University. Part-time and evening/weekend programs available. Faculty: 9 full-time (4 women), 6 part-time (3 women). Students: 15 full-time (7 women), 4 part-time (1 woman); includes 1 minority (African American), 1 international. Average age 25. 14 applicants, 100% accepted. In 1997, 17 master's awarded. *Degree requirements:* For master's, oral exam, written core exam required, thesis optional, foreign language not required. *Entrance requirements:* For master's, GRE General Test (minimum combined score of 1000), minimum GPA of 2.5; major/minor in health, physical education, or recreation. Application deadline: 8/1 (priority date; rolling processing; 12/1 for spring admission). Application fee: $0. *Tuition:* $2470 per year full-time, $138 per semester hour part-time for state residents; $6710 per year full-time, $373 per semester hour part-time for nonresidents. *Financial aid:* In 1997–98, 2 teaching assistantships (1 to a first-year student) averaging $471 per month and totaling $8,000 were awarded; research assistantships, Federal Work-Study also available. Financial aid application deadline: 4/1; applicants required to submit FAFSA. *Faculty research:* Child growth and performance, instructional strategies, outdoor leadership qualities, exercise science, athletic training. • Dr. Jack Sheltmire, Chair, 606-783-2180. Fax: 606-783-5058. E-mail: j.sheltmire@morehead-st.edu. Application contact: Betty Cowsert, Graduate Admissions Officer, 606-783-2039. Fax: 606-783-5061.

Murray State University, College of Education, Department of Health, Physical Education, and Recreation, Murray, KY 42071-0009. Offers program in physical education (MA). Part-time programs available. Faculty: 9 full-time (5 women). Students: 9 full-time (1 woman), 24 part-time (8 women); includes 3 minority (all African Americans), 1 international. 10 applicants, 100% accepted. In 1997, 5 degrees awarded. *Entrance requirements:* GRE General Test, TOEFL (minimum score 500). Application deadline: rolling. Application fee: $20. *Expenses:* Tuition $2500 per year full-time, $124 per hour part-time for state residents; $6740 per year full-time, $357 per hour part-time for nonresidents. Fees $360 per year full-time, $180 per year part-time. *Financial aid:* Research assistantships, teaching assistantships, Federal Work-Study available. Financial aid application deadline: 4/1. • Dr. Yvonne Stephens, Director, 502-762-6279. Fax: 502-762-6125.

New Mexico Highlands University, School of Education, Las Vegas, NM 87701. Offerings include human performance and sport (MA). School faculty: 32 full-time (14 women). *Degree requirements:* Thesis or alternative required, foreign language not required. *Entrance requirements:* Minimum undergraduate GPA of 3.0. Application deadline: 8/1 (priority date; rolling processing). Application fee: $15. *Expenses:* Tuition $1816 per year full-time, $227 per hour part-time for state residents; $7468 per year full-time, $227 per hour part-time for nonresidents. Fees $10 per year. • Dr. James Abreu, Dean, 505-454-3357. Application contact: Dr. Glen W. Davidson, Academic Vice President, 505-454-3311. Fax: 505-454-3558. E-mail: glendavidson@venus.nmhu.edu.

North Carolina Agricultural and Technical State University, Graduate School, School of Education, Department of Health and Physical Education, Greensboro, NC 27411. Awards MS. Part-time and evening/weekend programs available. Faculty: 6 full-time (1 woman). Students: 6 full-time (2 women), 14 part-time (8 women); includes 8 minority (all African Americans). Average age 32. 16 applicants, 56% accepted. In 1997, 5 degrees awarded. *Degree requirements:* Thesis or alternative, comprehensive exam, qualifying exam required, foreign language not required. *Entrance requirements:* GRE General Test, minimum GPA of 3.0. Application deadline: 6/1 (priority date; rolling processing; 12/1 for spring admission). Application fee: $35. *Tuition:* $1662 per year full-time, $272 per semester (minimum) part-time for state residents; $8790 per year full-time, $2054 per semester (minimum) part-time for nonresidents. *Financial aid:* Research assistantships, teaching assistantships, graduate assistantships available. Financial aid application deadline: 6/1. • Dr. Deborah Callaway, Chairperson, 336-334-7719. Fax: 336-334-7258.

North Carolina Central University, Division of Academic Affairs, College of Arts and Sciences, Department of Physical Education and Recreation, Durham, NC 27707-3129. Offers programs in general physical education (MS), recreation administration (MS), special physical education (MS), therapeutic recreation (MS). Part-time and evening/weekend programs available. Faculty: 18 full-time (9 women), 2 part-time (0 women). Students: 10 full-time (7 women), 26 part-time (13 women); includes 30 minority (all African Americans). Average age 30. 10 applicants, 90% accepted. In 1997, 3 degrees awarded. *Degree requirements:* 1 foreign language (computer language can substitute), thesis, comprehensive exam. *Entrance requirements:* Minimum GPA of 3.0 in major, 2.5 overall. Application deadline: 8/1. Application fee: $30. *Tuition:* $2027 per year full-time, $508 per semester (minimum) part-time for state residents; $9155 per year full-time, $2290 per semester (minimum) part-time for nonresidents. *Financial aid:* Federal Work-Study, institutionally sponsored loans, and career-related internships or fieldwork available. Aid available to part-time students. Financial aid application deadline: 5/1. *Faculty research:* Physical activity patterns of children with disabilities, physical fitness test of North Carolina school children, exercise physiology, motor learning/development. • Dr. Virginia Politino, Chairperson, 919-560-6186. Application contact: Dr. Bernice D. Johnson, Interim Dean, College of Arts and Sciences, 919-560-6368.

North Dakota State University, College of Human Development and Education, School of Education, Program in Pedagogy, Fargo, ND 58105. Offers pedagogy (M Ed, MS), physical education and athletic administration (M Ed, MS). Faculty: 6 full-time (2 women). Students: 9 full-time (5 women), 8 part-time (3 women). Average age 27. 17 applicants, 100% accepted. In 1997, 2 degrees awarded (100% found work related to degree). *Degree requirements:* Thesis required (for some programs), foreign language not required. *Entrance requirements:* Cooperative English Test, GRE, MAT, TOEFL (minimum score 525). Application deadline: 5/1 (rolling processing). Application fee: $25. *Tuition:* $2572 per year full-time, $107 per credit part-time for state residents; $6868 per year full-time, $286 per credit part-time for nonresidents. *Financial aid:* Teaching assistantships, full tuition waivers, Federal Work-Study, institutionally sponsored loans, and career-related internships or fieldwork available. Financial aid application deadline: 4/15. • Dr. Roman Horejsi, Coordinator, 701-231-8682. Fax: 701-231-8872. E-mail: horejsi@plains.nodak.edu.

Northeast Louisiana University, College of Education, Department of Health and Human Performance, Monroe, LA 71209-0001. Awards M Ed. Part-time and evening/weekend programs available. *Degree requirements:* Thesis optional, foreign language not required. *Entrance requirements:* GRE General Test. Application deadline: 6/1 (priority date; rolling processing; 11/1 for spring admission). Application fee: $15 ($25 for international students). *Tuition:* $2028 per year full-time, $240 per semester (minimum) part-time for state residents; $6852 per year full-time, $240 per semester (minimum) part-time for nonresidents. *Faculty research:* Cardiovascular disease risk factors; exercise and immunological system; attitude, exercise, and the aged.

Northern Arizona University, College of Health Professions, Department of Health, Physical Education, Exercise Science, and Nutrition, Flagstaff, AZ 86011. Offers programs in physical education (MA); public health (MPH), including health education and health promotion. Part-time programs available. Faculty: 11 full-time (3 women). Students: 14 full-time (7 women), 2 part-time (1 woman); includes 2 minority (both Hispanics), 2 international. 19 applicants, 63% accepted. In 1997, 13 degrees awarded. *Degree requirements:* Thesis or alternative required, foreign language not required. *Entrance requirements:* GRE General Test, minimum GPA of 3.0. Application deadline: 3/15 (priority date; rolling processing). Application fee: $45. *Expenses:* Tuition $2088 per year full-time, $330 per semester (minimum) part-time for state residents; $8004 per year full-time, $1002 per semester (minimum) part-time for nonresidents. Fees $72 per year full-time, $18 per semester (minimum) part-time. *Financial aid:* In 1997–98, 13 teaching assistantships were awarded; partial tuition waivers, Federal Work-Study, institutionally sponsored loans, and career-related internships or fieldwork also available. *Faculty research:* Muscle fiber type conversions, small animal locomotive study, electromyographic patterns. • Dr. Paul Brynteson, Chairperson, 520-523-4122. Application contact: Richard Coast, Graduate Coordinator, 520-523-4122.

Northern Illinois University, College of Education, Department of Physical Education, De Kalb, IL 60115-2854. Awards MS Ed. Part-time and evening/weekend programs available. Faculty: 25 full-time (12 women). Students: 38 full-time (25 women), 49 part-time (25 women); includes 6 minority (2 African Americans, 2 Asian Americans, 1 Hispanic, 1 Native American), 4 international. Average age 27. 81 applicants, 77% accepted. In 1997, 17 degrees awarded. *Degree requirements:* Comprehensive exam required, thesis optional, foreign language not required. *Entrance requirements:* GRE General Test, TOEFL (minimum score 550), minimum GPA of 2.75, undergraduate major in related area. Application deadline: 6/1 (rolling processing; 11/1 for spring admission). Application fee: $30. *Tuition:* $3984 per year full-time, $154 per credit hour part-time for state residents; $8160 per year full-time, $328 per credit hour part-time for nonresidents. *Financial aid:* In 1997–98, 34 teaching assistantships, 3 staff assistantships were awarded; fellowships, research assistantships, full tuition waivers, Federal Work-Study, and career-related internships or fieldwork also available. Aid available to part-time students. • Dr. Judith Bischoff, Chair, 815-753-1407. Application contact: Dr. Keith Lambrecht, Director, Graduate Studies, 815-753-3907.

Northern State University, Division of Graduate Studies in Education, Program in Teaching and Learning, Aberdeen, SD 57401-7198. Offerings include health, physical education, and coaching (MS Ed). Offered jointly with Huron University, Jamestown College, and the University of Mary. Program faculty: 98 full-time (28 women). *Degree requirements:* Thesis required, foreign language not required. *Average time to degree:* master's–1.5 years full-time. *Entrance requirements:* Minimum GPA of 2.75. Application deadline: 8/15 (priority date; rolling processing; 12/15 for spring admission). Application fee: $15. *Expenses:* Tuition $1999 per year full-time, $83 per credit hour part-time for state residents; $6034 per year full-time, $251 per credit hour part-time for nonresidents. Fees $954 per year full-time, $40 per credit hour part-time. • Dr. Paul Deputy, Head, 605-626-2415. Application contact: Dr. Sharon Tebben, Director of Graduate Studies, 605-626-2558. Fax: 605-626-2542.

North Georgia College & State University, Graduate School, Program in Education, Dahlonega, GA 30597-1001. Offerings include secondary education (M Ed), with options in art education, biology education, chemistry education, English education, mathematics education, modern languages education, physical education, science education, social science education. Program faculty: 57 full-time (15 women), 7 part-time (4 women). *Degree requirements:* Comprehensive exam required, thesis optional, foreign language not required. *Entrance requirements:* GRE General Test (minimum combined score of 800) or MAT (minimum score 44), minimum GPA of 2.75. Application deadline: 9/1 (priority date; rolling processing). Application fee: $25. • Dr. Bob Michael, Dean, School of Education, 706-864-1533. Application contact: Mai-Lan Ledbetter, Coordinator of Graduate Admissions, 706-864-1543. Fax: 706-864-1668. E-mail: mledbetter@nugget.ngc.peachnet.edu.

Northwest Missouri State University, College of Education and Human Services, Department of Health, Physical Education, Recreation and Dance, 800 University Drive, Maryville, MO 64468-6001. Offers program in health and physical education (MS Ed). Part-time programs available. Faculty: 13 full-time (4 women). Students: 24 full-time (6 women), 12 part-time (2 women); includes 1 minority (African American). 21 applicants, 100% accepted. In 1997, 21 degrees awarded. *Degree requirements:* Comprehensive exam required, foreign language and thesis not required. *Entrance requirements:* GRE General Test (minimum combined score of 700), TOEFL (minimum score 550), minimum undergraduate GPA of 2.75, teaching certificate, writing sample. Application deadline: rolling. Application fee: $0 ($50 for international students). *Expenses:* Tuition $113 per credit hour for state residents; $197 per credit hour for nonresidents. Fees $3 per credit hour. *Financial aid:* In 1997–98, 11 research assistantships averaging $585 per month, 16 teaching assistantships averaging $585 per month, 4 administrative assistantships averaging $585 per month were awarded. Financial aid application deadline: 3/1. • Dr. Terry Barmann, Program Director, 816-562-1706. Application contact: Dr. Frances Shipley, Dean of Graduate School, 816-562-1145. E-mail: gradsch@acad.nwmissouri.edu.

The Ohio State University, College of Education, School of Physical Activity and Educational Services, Program in Health, Physical Education, and Recreation, Columbus, OH 43210. Awards MA, M Ed, PhD. Part-time programs available. Faculty: 44. Students: 114 full-time (56 women), 38 part-time (26 women); includes 27 minority (18 African Americans, 6 Asian Americans, 2 Hispanics, 1 Native American), 20 international. 241 applicants, 34% accepted. In 1997, 46 master's, 11 doctorates awarded. *Degree requirements:* For master's, thesis optional, foreign language not required; for doctorate, dissertation required, foreign language not required. *Entrance requirements:* GRE. Application deadline: 8/15 (rolling processing). Application fee: $30 ($40 for international students). *Tuition:* $5472 per year full-time, $554 per quarter (minimum) part-time for state residents; $14,172 per year full-time, $1424 per quarter (minimum) part-time for nonresidents. *Financial aid:* Fellowships, research assistantships, teaching assistantships, administrative assistantships, Federal Work-Study, institutionally sponsored loans available. Aid available to part-time students. • Dr. W. Michael Sherman, Director, School of Physical Activity and Educational Services, 614-292-5679. Fax: 614-688-4613. E-mail: sherman.4@osu.edu.

Ohio University, Graduate Studies, College of Health and Human Services, School of Recreation and Sport Sciences, Programs in Physical Education, Athens, OH 45701-2979. Awards MSPE. Students: 87 full-time (34 women), 4 part-time (1 woman); includes 4 minority (3 African Americans, 1 Asian American), 4 international. 106 applicants, 63% accepted. *Degree requirements:* Thesis or alternative required, foreign language not required. *Entrance requirements:* GRE General Test or MAT. Application fee: $30. *Tuition:* $5430 per year full-time, $216 per quarter hour part-time for state residents; $10,431 per year full-time, $423 per quarter hour part-time for nonresidents. *Financial aid:* Federal Work-Study available. Financial aid application deadline: 3/15. • Dr. Keith Ernce, Director, School of Recreation and Sport Sciences, 740-593-0284.

Oklahoma State University, College of Education, School of Health, Physical Education, and Leisure, Stillwater, OK 74078. Offers programs in health (MS, Ed D), leisure sciences (MS, Ed D), physical education (MS, Ed D), physical education and leisure sciences (Ed D). Faculty: 13 full-time (5 women). Students: 29 full-time (17 women), 45 part-time (26 women); includes 6 minority (3 African Americans, 2 Hispanics, 1 Native American), 2 international. Average age 32. In 1997, 9 master's, 1 doctorate awarded. *Degree requirements:* For doctorate, dissertation. *Entrance requirements:* TOEFL (minimum score 550). Application deadline: 7/1 (priority date). Application fee: $25. *Financial aid:* In 1997–98, 10 students received aid, including 10 teaching assistantships (2 to first-year students) averaging $1,008 per month and totaling $90,750; partial tuition waivers, Federal Work-Study, and career-related internships or fieldwork also available. Aid available to part-time students. Financial aid application deadline: 3/1. • Dr. Lowell Caneday, Director, 405-744-5493.

Old Dominion University, Darden College of Education, Department of Exercise Science, Physical Education, and Recreation, Norfolk, VA 23529. Offers program in physical education (MS Ed), including administration, athletic training, curriculum and instruction, exercise science and wellness, recreation administration, sports management. Part-time and evening/weekend programs available. Faculty: 8 full-time (3 women), 4 part-time (2 women), 9.3 FTE. Students: 42 full-time (19 women), 30 part-time (14 women); includes 14 minority (10 African Americans, 2 Asian Americans, 2 Hispanics), 2 international. Average age 28. In 1997, 24 degrees awarded. *Degree requirements:* Comprehensive exams, internship, research project required, foreign language and thesis not required. *Entrance requirements:* GRE General Test (minimum combined score of 900), minimum GPA of 2.5. Application deadline: 7/1 (rolling processing; 11/1 for spring admission). Application fee: $30. *Expenses:* Tuition $180 per credit hour for state residents; $477 per credit hour for nonresidents. Fees $140 per year full-time, $32 per semester part-time. *Financial aid:* In 1997–98, 50 students received aid, including 1 fellowship totaling $500, 28 research assistantships (12 to first-year students) totaling $201,012, 4 teaching assistantships totaling $18,128; tuition grants, partial tuition waivers, and career-related internships or fieldwork also available. Financial aid application deadline: 2/15; applicants required to submit FAFSA. *Faculty research:* Exercise physiology, nutrition and sports, sports psychology, pedagogy. Total annual research expenditures: $84,638. • Dr. Patrick Tow, Chair, 757-683-3351. E-mail: ptow@odu.edu. Application contact: Dr. Elizabeth Dowling, Graduate Program Director, 757-683-4514. Fax: 757-683-4270. E-mail: ldowling@odu.edu.

Oregon State University, Graduate School, College of Health and Human Performance, Program in Physical Education, Corvallis, OR 97331. Awards MAT. Students: 0. Average age 30. 10 applicants, 70% accepted. In 1997, 7 degrees awarded. *Degree requirements:* Minimum GPA of 3.0 required, foreign language not required. *Entrance requirements:* GRE General Test, NTE, California Basic Educational Skills Test, TOEFL (minimum score 550), minimum GPA of 3.0 in last 90 hours. Application deadline: 1/15. Application fee: $50. *Tuition:* $6207 per year full-time, $810 per quarter (minimum) part-time for state residents; $10,551 per year full-time, $1293 per quarter (minimum) part-time for nonresidents. *Financial aid:* Fellowships, Federal Work-Study, institutionally sponsored loans, and career-related internships or fieldwork available. Financial aid application deadline: 2/1. • Dr. Barbara Cusimano, Coordinator, 541-737-5925.

Pittsburg State University, School of Education, Department of Health, Physical Education and Recreation, Pittsburg, KS 66762-5880. Offers program in physical education (MS). Students: 12 full-time (4 women), 36 part-time (20 women); includes 2 minority (1 Hispanic, 1 Native American). In 1997, 12 degrees awarded. *Degree requirements:* Thesis or alternative required, foreign language not required. *Application fee:* $40. *Tuition:* $2418 per year full-time, $103 per credit hour part-time for state residents; $6130 per year full-time, $258 per credit hour part-

Directory: Physical Education

Pittsburg State University (continued)
time for nonresidents. *Financial aid:* Teaching assistantships, Federal Work-Study, and career-related internships or fieldwork available. *Faculty research:* Personality of athletes, fitness activities for children, aerobic conditioning, fitness evaluation. • Dr. Robert Hefley, Chairman, 316-235-4665.

Prairie View A&M University, College of Education, Department of Health and Human Performance, Prairie View, TX 77446-0188. Offers programs in health education (MA Ed, MS Ed), physical education (MA Ed, MS Ed). Faculty: 2 full-time (1 woman). Students: 6 full-time (1 woman), 3 part-time (2 women); includes 9 minority (8 African Americans, 1 Hispanic). Average age 31. In 1997, 7 degrees awarded (100% found work related to degree). *Degree requirements:* Thesis optional, foreign language not required. *Average time to degree:* master's–2.5 years full-time, 4 years part-time. *Entrance requirements:* GRE General Test. Application deadline: 7/1 (priority date; rolling processing; 11/1 for spring admission). Application fee: $10. *Tuition:* $2202 per year full-time, $336 per semester (minimum) part-time for state residents; $6000 per year full-time, $963 per semester (minimum) part-time for nonresidents. *Financial aid:* Career-related internships or fieldwork available. Financial aid application deadline: 6/31. • Dr. Mary V. White, Head, 409-857-4210. Fax: 409-857-2911.

Purdue University, School of Liberal Arts, Department of Health, Kinesiology and Leisure Studies, West Lafayette, IN 47907. Offerings include teaching and learning (MS). Department faculty: 18 full-time (5 women), 2 part-time (1 woman). *Degree requirements:* Thesis required (for some programs), foreign language not required. *Entrance requirements:* GRE General Test, TOEFL (minimum score 550). Application deadline: 2/15 (priority date; rolling processing). Application fee: $30. Electronic applications accepted. *Tuition:* $3500 per year full-time, $126 per credit hour part-time for state residents; $11,720 per year full-time, $387 per credit hour part-time for nonresidents. • Dr. T. J. Templin, Head, 765-494-3178. Application contact: W. A. Harper, Graduate Committee Chair, 765-494-1518. Fax: 765-496-1239. E-mail: wharper@purdue.edu.

Queens College of the City University of New York, Mathematics and Natural Sciences Division, Department of Family, Nutrition and Exercise Sciences, Program in Physical Education and Exercise Sciences, 65-30 Kissena Boulevard, Flushing, NY 11367-1597. Awards MS Ed. Degree awarded through the School of Education. Part-time and evening/weekend programs available. Students: 7 full-time (4 women), 65 part-time (25 women); includes 5 minority (1 African American, 4 Hispanics), 2 international. 41 applicants, 76% accepted. In 1997, 23 degrees awarded. *Degree requirements:* Research project required, thesis optional, foreign language not required. *Entrance requirements:* TOEFL (minimum score 600), minimum GPA of 3.0. Application deadline: 4/1 (rolling processing; 11/1 for spring admission). Application fee: $40. *Expenses:* Tuition $4350 per year full-time, $185 per credit part-time for state residents; $7600 per year full-time, $320 per credit part-time for nonresidents. Fees $104 per year. *Financial aid:* Partial tuition waivers, Federal Work-Study, institutionally sponsored loans, and career-related internships or fieldwork available. Aid available to part-time students. Financial aid application deadline: 4/1; applicants required to submit FAFSA. • Dr. Michael Toner, Graduate Adviser, 718-997-4150. Application contact: Mario Caruso, Director of Graduate Admissions, 718-997-5200. Fax: 718-997-5193. E-mail: graduate%queens.bitnet@cunyvm.cuny.edu.

Radford University, Graduate College, College of Education and Human Development, Department of Physical and Health Education, Radford, VA 24142. Offers program in physical education (MS). Part-time programs available. Postbaccalaureate distance learning degree programs offered (minimal on-campus study). Faculty: 8 full-time (1 woman). Students: 4 full-time (2 women), 10 part-time (6 women). Average age 26. 14 applicants, 57% accepted. In 1997, 2 degrees awarded. *Degree requirements:* Comprehensive exam required, foreign language and thesis not required. *Entrance requirements:* GMAT, GRE General Test, MAT, or NTE; TOEFL (minimum score 550), minimum GPA of 2.7. Application deadline: 2/1 (priority date; rolling processing; 10/1 for spring admission). Application fee: $25. Electronic applications accepted. *Expenses:* Tuition $2302 per year full-time, $147 per credit hour part-time for state residents; $5672 per year full-time, $287 per credit hour part-time for nonresidents. Fees $1222 per year full-time. *Financial aid:* In 1997–98, 7 students received aid, including 2 fellowships totaling $4,844, 3 research assistantships totaling $13,872, 7 teaching assistantships totaling $29,604, scholarships/grants totaling $37,641; Federal Work-Study, institutionally sponsored loans, and career-related internships or fieldwork also available. Financial aid application deadline: 2/1; applicants required to submit FAFSA. • Dr. Carl A. Stockton, Chairperson, 540-831-5305. Fax: 540-831-6053. E-mail: cstockto@runet.edu.

Rowan University, College of Education, Department of Health and Exercise Science, Glassboro, NJ 08028-1701. Offers programs in administration and supervision in health and physical education or athletics (MA), health and exercise science (Certificate). Part-time and evening/weekend programs available. Students: 20 (18 women); includes 1 minority (African American). 24 applicants, 88% accepted. *Application deadline:* 11/1 (priority date; rolling processing; 4/1 for spring admission). *Application fee:* $50. *Tuition:* $5728 per year full-time, $258 per credit hour part-time for state residents; $8968 per year full-time, $393 per credit hour part-time for nonresidents. • Dr. James Burd, Adviser, 609-256-4783.

St. Cloud State University, College of Education, Department of Health, Physical Education, Recreation and Sport Science, St. Cloud, MN 56301-4498. Offers programs in exercise science (MS), physical education (MS), sports management (MS). Faculty: 15 full-time (5 women), 6 part-time (2 women). Students: 17 full-time (3 women), 7 part-time (1 woman). In 1997, 10 degrees awarded. *Degree requirements:* Thesis or alternative required, foreign language not required. *Entrance requirements:* GRE General Test, minimum GPA of 2.75. Application fee: $20 ($100 for international students). *Expenses:* Tuition $128 per credit for state residents; $203 per credit for nonresidents. Fees $16.32 per credit. *Financial aid:* In 1997–98, 10 graduate assistantships were awarded; Federal Work-Study also available. Financial aid application deadline: 3/1. • Dr. Rodney Dobey, Chairperson, 320-255-4251. Application contact: Ann Anderson, Graduate Studies Office, 320-255-2113. Fax: 320-654-5371. E-mail: anna@grad.stcloud.msus.edu.

Saint Mary's College of California, School of Liberal Arts, Program in Health, Physical Education, and Recreation, Moraga, CA 94575. Awards MA. Part-time programs available. Faculty: 6 part-time (1 woman). Students: 71 full-time (18 women), 15 part-time (5 women); includes 15 minority (8 African Americans, 3 Asian Americans, 4 Hispanics). Average age 26. 65 applicants, 45% accepted. In 1997, 18 degrees awarded. *Degree requirements:* Comprehensive exams or thesis required, foreign language not required. *Average time to degree:* master's–3 years full-time. *Entrance requirements:* Minimum GPA of 2.75, BA in physical education, field experience. Application deadline: 8/1 (priority date; rolling processing; 12/15 for spring admission). Application fee: $20. *Tuition:* $1319 per course. *Financial aid:* In 1997–98, 6 teaching assistantships were awarded; fellowships, institutionally sponsored loans, and career-related internships or fieldwork also available. Aid available to part-time students. Financial aid applicants required to submit FAFSA. *Faculty research:* Administrative aspects of physical education and athletics. • Dr. Craig Johnson, Chair, 925-631-4377. Fax: 925-376-0829.

San Francisco State University, College of Health and Human Services, Department of Kinesiology, San Francisco, CA 94132-1722. Offers program in physical education (MA). *Degree requirements:* Thesis, exam, project required, foreign language not required. *Entrance requirements:* Minimum GPA of 2.75. Application deadline: 11/30 (priority date; rolling processing). Application fee: $55. *Expenses:* Tuition $0 for state residents; $246 per unit for nonresidents. Fees $1982 per year full-time, $1316 per year part-time. *Faculty research:* Metabolism, movement analysis, nutrition, ventilation, skill development.

San Jose State University, College of Applied Arts and Sciences, Department of Human Performance, San Jose, CA 95192-0001. Offers program in physical education (MA). Faculty: 25 full-time (7 women), 8 part-time (2 women). Students: 23 full-time (14 women), 65 part-time (30 women); includes 18 minority (3 African Americans, 9 Asian Americans, 5 Hispanics, 1 Native American), 3 international. Average age 30. 74 applicants, 76% accepted. In 1997, 15 degrees awarded. *Degree requirements:* Comprehensive exams. *Entrance requirements:* Bachelor's degree in physical education. Application deadline: 6/1 (rolling processing). Application fee: $59. *Expenses:* Tuition $0 for state residents; $246 per unit for nonresidents. Fees $2017 per year full-time, $1351 per year part-time. • Dr. James Bryant, Chair, 408-924-3010. Application contact: Dr. Craig Cisar, Graduate Adviser, 408-924-3018.

Slippery Rock University of Pennsylvania, College of Human Service Professions, Department of Physical Education, Slippery Rock, PA 16057. Awards M Ed, MS. Part-time and evening/weekend programs available. *Degree requirements:* Comprehensive exams required, thesis optional. *Entrance requirements:* GRE, minimum GPA of 2.75. Application deadline: 7/1 (priority date; rolling processing; 11/1 for spring admission). Application fee: $25. *Tuition:* $4484 per year full-time, $247 per credit part-time for state residents; $7667 per year full-time, $423 per credit part-time for nonresidents.

South Dakota State University, College of Arts and Science, Department of Health, Physical Education and Recreation, Brookings, SD 57007. Awards MS. Faculty: 3 full-time (1 woman). Students: 13 full-time (5 women), 12 part-time (2 women); includes 1 minority (African American). 19 applicants, 100% accepted. In 1997, 9 degrees awarded. *Degree requirements:* Thesis, oral and written exams required, foreign language not required. *Average time to degree:* master's–2 years full-time, 4 years part-time. *Entrance requirements:* GRE, TOEFL (minimum score 525). Application deadline: 10/15 (priority date; rolling processing; 3/15 for spring admission). Application fee: $15. *Expenses:* Tuition $82 per credit hour for state residents; $242 per credit hour for nonresidents. Fees $37 per credit hour. *Financial aid:* In 1997–98, 7 teaching assistantships (6 to first-year students), 1 administrative assistantship (to a first-year student) were awarded; Federal Work-Study and career-related internships or fieldwork also available. *Faculty research:* Reaction time in the elderly wellness center facilities and programming, effective teaching behaviors in physical education, assessment of human fitness. • Dr. Patty Hacker, Acting Head, 605-688-5625. Fax: 605-688-5999.

Southeast Missouri State University, Department of Secondary Education, Cape Girardeau, MO 63701-4799. Offerings include physical education (MA). *Degree requirements:* Thesis or alternative required, foreign language not required. *Entrance requirements:* GRE General Test (score in 50th percentile or higher), minimum GPA of 2.75. Application deadline: 4/1 (priority date; rolling processing; 11/21 for spring admission). Application fee: $20 ($100 for international students). *Tuition:* $2034 per year full-time, $113 per credit hour part-time for state residents; $3672 per year full-time, $204 per credit hour part-time for nonresidents. • Dalton Curtis, Chairperson, 573-651-5965. Application contact: Office of Graduate Studies, 573-651-2192.

Southern Connecticut State University, School of Education, Department of Exercise Science, New Haven, CT 06515-1355. Offers programs in physical education (MS Ed), physical education and recreation for the handicapped (MS Ed). Faculty: 7 full-time, 1 part-time. Students: 15 full-time (8 women), 53 part-time (33 women); includes 2 minority (both Hispanics). 94 applicants, 34% accepted. In 1997, 10 degrees awarded. *Degree requirements:* Thesis or alternative required, foreign language not required. *Entrance requirements:* Interview. Application deadline: 7/15 (priority date; rolling processing). Application fee: $40. *Expenses:* Tuition $2632 per year full-time, $188 per credit part-time for state residents; $7200 per year full-time, $188 per credit part-time for nonresidents. Fees $1806 per year full-time, $45 per semester part-time for state residents; $2703 per year full-time, $45 per semester part-time for nonresidents. *Financial aid:* In 1997–98, 8 teaching assistantships were awarded. • Dr. Joan Barbarich, Chair, 203-392-6088. Application contact: Dr. Robert Axtell, Coordinator, 203-392-6037.

Southern Illinois University at Carbondale, College of Education, Department of Physical Education, Carbondale, IL 62901-6806. Awards MS Ed. Part-time programs available. Faculty: 15 full-time (7 women). Students: 21 full-time (11 women), 2 part-time (1 woman); includes 3 minority (2 African Americans, 1 Asian American). Average age 25. 21 applicants, 48% accepted. In 1997, 9 degrees awarded. *Degree requirements:* Thesis required, foreign language not required. *Entrance requirements:* GRE, TOEFL (minimum score 550), minimum GPA of 2.7. Application deadline: rolling. Application fee: $20. *Expenses:* Tuition $2964 per year full-time, $99 per semester hour part-time for state residents; $8892 per year full-time, $270 per semester hour part-time for nonresidents. Fees $1034 per year full-time, $298 per semester (minimum) part-time. *Financial aid:* In 1997–98, 10 teaching assistantships were awarded; fellowships, research assistantships, full tuition waivers, Federal Work-Study, institutionally sponsored loans, and career-related internships or fieldwork also available. Aid available to part-time students. *Faculty research:* Caffeine and exercise effects, ground reaction forces in walking and running, social psychology of sports. • Dr. Ronald Knowlton, Chair, 618-536-2431.

Southern Illinois University at Edwardsville, School of Education, Department of Health, Recreation, and Physical Education, Edwardsville, IL 62026-0001. Awards MS Ed. Part-time programs available. Students: 37 full-time (12 women), 19 part-time (7 women); includes 4 minority (2 African Americans, 1 Asian American, 1 Hispanic), 4 international. 35 applicants, 80% accepted. In 1997, 10 degrees awarded. *Degree requirements:* Thesis or alternative, final exam required, foreign language not required. *Application deadline:* 7/24. *Application fee:* $25. *Expenses:* Tuition $1716 per year full-time, $95 per credit hour part-time for state residents; $5149 per year full-time, $286 per credit hour part-time for nonresidents. Fees $463 per year full-time, $433 per year part-time. *Financial aid:* In 1997–98, 6 teaching assistantships, 13 assistantships were awarded; fellowships, research assistantships, Federal Work-Study, institutionally sponsored loans also available. Aid available to part-time students. • Dr. John Baker, Chairperson, 618-692-3028. Application contact: Kay Covington, Graduate Program Director, 618-692-3226.

Southwestern Oklahoma State University, School of Education, Program in Health, Physical Education and Recreation, Weatherford, OK 73096-3098. Awards M Ed. M Ed distance learning degree program offered to Oklahoma residents only. Part-time programs available. Postbaccalaureate distance learning degree programs offered. Students: 3 full-time (2 women), 1 part-time (0 women); includes 2 minority (1 African American, 1 Asian American). 1 applicant, 100% accepted. In 1997, 1 degree awarded. *Degree requirements:* Exam required, foreign language and thesis not required. *Entrance requirements:* GRE General Test, TOEFL (minimum score 550), minimum GPA of 2.5. Application deadline: rolling. Application fee: $15. *Expenses:* Tuition $60 per credit hour (minimum) for state residents; $147 per credit hour (minimum) for nonresidents. Fees $109 per year full-time, $24 per semester (minimum) part-time. *Financial aid:* Research assistantships, teaching assistantships, partial tuition waivers, Federal Work-Study, institutionally sponsored loans, and career-related internships or fieldwork available. Aid available to part-time students. Financial aid application deadline: 3/1; applicants required to submit FAFSA. • Dr. Ken Rose, Chair, 580-774-3254.

Southwest Texas State University, School of Education, Department of Health, Physical Education, and Recreation, Program in Health and Physical Education, San Marcos, TX 78666. Awards MA. Part-time and evening/weekend programs available. Students: 0. *Degree requirements:* Thesis, comprehensive exam required, foreign language not required. *Entrance requirements:* GRE General Test (minimum combined score of 900), TOEFL (minimum score 550), minimum GPA of 2.75 in last 60 hours. Application deadline: 7/15 (priority date; rolling processing; 11/15 for spring admission). Application fee: $25 ($50 for international students). *Expenses:* Tuition $648 per year full-time, $120 per semester (minimum) part-time for state residents; $4500 per year full-time, $750 per semester (minimum) part-time for nonresidents. Fees $1264 per year full-time, $314 per semester (minimum) part-time. *Financial aid:* Teaching assistantships, Federal Work-Study, institutionally sponsored loans, and career-related internships or fieldwork available. Financial aid application deadline: 4/1; applicants required to submit FAFSA. *Faculty research:* HIV/AIDS, youth fitness, leisure behavior, leisure program services and management evaluation. • Dr. Robert Patton, Graduate Adviser, 512-245-2938. Fax: 512-245-8678. E-mail: rp03@swt.edu.

Southwest Texas State University, School of Education, Department of Health, Physical Education, and Recreation, Program in Physical Education, San Marcos, TX 78666. Awards M Ed. Part-time and evening/weekend programs available. Students: 21 full-time (11 women), 30 part-time (14 women); includes 9 minority (2 African Americans, 7 Hispanics). Average age 28. In 1997, 24 degrees awarded. *Degree requirements:* Comprehensive exam required, foreign language and thesis not required. *Entrance requirements:* GRE General Test (minimum combined score of 900), TOEFL (minimum score 550), minimum GPA of 2.75 in last 60 hours. Application deadline: 7/15 (priority date; rolling processing; 11/15 for spring admission). Application fee: $25 ($50 for international students). *Expenses:* Tuition $648 per year full-time, $120 per semester (minimum) part-time for state residents; $4500 per year full-time, $750 per semester (minimum) part-time for nonresidents. Fees $1264 per year full-time, $314 per semester (minimum) part-time. *Financial aid:* Teaching assistantships, Federal Work-Study, institutionally sponsored loans, and career-related internships or fieldwork available. Aid available to part-time students. Financial aid application deadline: 4/1; applicants required to submit FAFSA. *Faculty research:* AIDS education, employee wellness, isometric strength evaluation. • Dr. Robert Patton, Graduate Adviser, 512-245-2938. Fax: 512-245-8678. E-mail: rp03@swt.edu.

Springfield College, Programs in Physical Education, Springfield, MA 01109-3797. Offerings in adapted physical education (M Ed, MPE, MS, CAS), advanced level coaching (M Ed, MPE, MS, CAS), athletic administration (M Ed, MPE, MS, CAS), community physical education (M Ed, MPE, MS, CAS), general physical education (DPE), sport management (M Ed, MPE, MS, CAS), sport psychology (M Ed, MPE, MS, DPE, CAS), sport studies (M Ed, MPE, MS, CAS), teaching and administration (M Ed, MPE, MS, CAS). Part-time and evening/weekend programs available. Faculty: 25 full-time (13 women), 2 part-time (0 women), 26 FTE. Students: 101 full-time, 19 part-time; includes 12 international. Average age 26. 147 applicants, 75% accepted. In 1997, 48 master's, 3 doctorates awarded. Terminal master's awarded for partial completion of doctoral program. *Degree requirements:* For master's, comprehensive exam, research project required, foreign language and thesis not required; for doctorate, dissertation required, foreign language not required; for CAS, comprehensive exam required, foreign language and thesis not required. *Entrance requirements:* For doctorate, GRE General Test, interview. Application deadline: 2/1 (priority date; rolling processing; 12/1 for spring admission). Application fee: $40. *Expenses:* Tuition $474 per credit. Fees $25 per year. *Financial aid:* Fellowships, teaching assistantships, full and partial tuition waivers, Federal Work-Study, and career-related internships or fieldwork available. Financial aid application deadline: 3/1. • Dr. Betty L. Mann, Director, 413-748-3125. Application contact: Donald J. Shaw Jr., Director of Graduate Admissions, 413-748-3225. Fax: 413-748-3694. E-mail: dshaw@spfldcol.edu.

State University of New York at Stony Brook, School of Professional Development and Continuing Studies, Stony Brook, NY 11794. Offerings include coaching (Certificate). School faculty: 1 full-time, 101 part-time. *Application deadline:* 1/15. *Application fee:* $50. *Expenses:* Tuition $5100 per year full-time, $213 per credit hour part-time for state residents; $8416 per year full-time, $351 per credit hour part-time for nonresidents. Fees $529 per year full-time, $77 per semester (minimum) part-time. • Dr. Paul J. Edelson, Dean, 516-632-7052. E-mail: paul.edelson@sunysb.edu. Application contact: Sandra Romansky, Director of Admissions and Advisement, 516-632-7050. Fax: 516-632-9046. E-mail: sandra.romansky@sunysb.edu.

State University of New York College at Brockport, School of Arts and Performance, Department of Physical Education, Brockport, NY 14420-2997. Awards MS Ed. Part-time and evening/weekend programs available. Faculty: 11 full-time (5 women). Students: 10 full-time (6 women), 44 part-time (13 women); includes 2 minority (1 African American, 1 Asian American), 1 international. Average age 31. In 1997, 26 degrees awarded. *Degree requirements:* Thesis or alternative required, foreign language not required. *Application deadline:* rolling. *Application fee:* $50. *Expenses:* Tuition $5100 per year full-time, $213 per credit hour part-time for state residents; $8416 per year full-time, $351 per credit hour part-time for nonresidents. Fees $440 per year full-time, $22.60 per credit hour part-time. *Financial aid:* In 1997–98, 5 teaching assistantships (3 to first-year students) were awarded; Federal Work-Study and career-related internships or fieldwork also available. Aid available to part-time students. Financial aid application deadline: 4/1; applicants required to submit FAFSA. *Faculty research:* Interscholastic programs, curriculum design, athletic administration, adapted physical education. • Dr. Frank Short, Chairperson, 716-395-2229.

State University of New York College at Cortland, Division of Professional Studies, Department of Physical Education, Cortland, NY 13045. Awards MS Ed. Part-time and evening/weekend programs available. In 1997, 27 degrees awarded. *Entrance requirements:* Provisional certification. Application deadline: rolling. Application fee: $50. *Expenses:* Tuition $5100 per year full-time, $213 per credit hour part-time for state residents; $8416 per year full-time, $351 per credit hour part-time for nonresidents. Fees $644 per year full-time, $79 per semester (minimum) part-time. *Financial aid:* Partial tuition waivers, Federal Work-Study, and career-related internships or fieldwork available. Aid available to part-time students. Financial aid applicants required to submit CSS PROFILE or FAFSA. • Dr. John Cottone, Chair, 607-753-4955. Application contact: Jeanne M. Bechtel, Director of Admissions, 607-753-4711. Fax: 607-753-5998.

State University of West Georgia, College of Education, Department of Physical Education and Recreation, Carrollton, GA 30118. Offers program in physical education (M Ed, Ed S). Part-time and evening/weekend programs available. Faculty: 4 full-time (3 women). Students: 10 full-time (3 women), 16 part-time (9 women); includes 1 minority (African American), 1 international. Average age 31. In 1997, 12 master's awarded. *Degree requirements:* For Ed S, research project required, foreign language and thesis not required. *Entrance requirements:* For master's, GRE General Test (minimum combined score of 800), minimum GPA of 2.5; for Ed S, GRE General Test (minimum combined score of 800), master's degree, minimum graduate GPA of 3.25. Application deadline: 8/30 (rolling processing). Application fee: $15. *Expenses:* Tuition $2428 per year full-time, $83 per semester hour part-time for state residents; $8428 per year full-time, $250 per semester hour part-time for nonresidents. Fees $428 per year. *Financial aid:* Research assistantships, assistantships, and career-related internships or fieldwork available. Aid available to part-time students. Financial aid applicants required to submit FAFSA. • Dr. Lynn P. Gaskin, Chair, 770-836-6530. Application contact: Dr. Jack O. Jenkins, Dean, Graduate School, 770-836-6419. Fax: 770-836-2301. E-mail: jjenkins@cob.as.westga.edu.

Stephen F. Austin State University, College of Education, Department of Kinesiology and Health Science, Nacogdoches, TX 75962. Offers programs in health education (M Ed), physical education (M Ed). Faculty: 9 full-time (4 women), 1 part-time (0 women). Students: 9 full-time (2 women), 9 part-time (7 women); includes 4 minority (3 African Americans, 1 Hispanic). 12 applicants, 75% accepted. In 1997, 16 degrees awarded. *Degree requirements:* Comprehensive exam required, foreign language and thesis not required. *Entrance requirements:* GRE General Test (minimum combined score of 1000). Application deadline: 8/1 (priority date; rolling processing; 12/15 for spring admission). Application fee: $0 ($25 for international students). *Tuition:* $1465 per year full-time, $263 per semester (minimum) part-time for state residents; $5299 per year full-time, $890 per semester (minimum) part-time for nonresidents. *Financial aid:* Teaching assistantships available. Financial aid application deadline: 3/1. • Dr. Mel Finkenberg, Chair, 409-468-3503.

Sul Ross State University, Department of Physical Education, Alpine, TX 79832. Awards M Ed. Part-time programs available. Faculty: 3 full-time (0 women). Students: 9 full-time (3 women), 4 part-time (2 women); includes 9 minority (1 African American, 8 Hispanics). Average age 29. In 1997, 6 degrees awarded. *Entrance requirements:* GMAT (minimum score 400) or GRE General Test (minimum combined score of 850), minimum GPA of 2.5 in last 60 hours of undergraduate work. Application deadline: rolling. Application fee: $0 ($50 for international students). *Expenses:* Tuition $864 per year full-time, $120 per semester (minimum) part-time for state residents; $5976 per year full-time, $747 per semester (minimum) part-time for nonresidents. Fees $754 per year full-time, $105 per semester (minimum) part-time. *Financial aid:* Teaching assistantships, Federal Work-Study, institutionally sponsored loans, and career-related internships or fieldwork available. Aid available to part-time students. Financial aid application deadline: 5/1; applicants required to submit FAFSA. • Dr. Roger Grant, Chairman, 915-837-8226. Fax: 915-837-8046.

Syracuse University, School of Education, Health and Physical Education Program, Syracuse, NY 13244-0003. Offers health and physical education (MS, CAS), including exercise science. Faculty: 5 full-time (2 women), 3 part-time (1 woman). Students: 35 full-time (18 women), 13 part-time (9 women); includes 5 minority (2 African Americans, 1 Asian American, 2 Hispanics), 1 international. 32 applicants, 84% accepted. In 1997, 11 master's awarded. *Degree requirements:* For master's, thesis or alternative; for CAS, thesis. *Entrance requirements:* GRE. Application deadline: rolling. Application fee: $40. *Tuition:* $13,320 per year full-time, $555 per credit hour part-time. *Financial aid:* Fellowships, research assistantships, teaching assistantships, administrative assistantships, Federal Work-Study, and career-related internships or fieldwork available. Aid available to part-time students. Financial aid application deadline: 3/1. *Faculty research:* Bone density, obesity in females, cardiovascular functioning, attitudes toward physical eduation, sports management and psychology. • Dr. Jay Graves, Chair, 315-443-9696.

Tarleton State University, College of Education, Department of Health and Physical Education, Stephenville, TX 76402. Awards M Ed, Certificate. Part-time and evening/weekend programs available. Faculty: 4 full-time (0 women). Students: 21 full-time (7 women), 26 part-time (9 women); includes 5 minority (3 African Americans, 2 Hispanics). In 1997, 15 master's awarded. *Degree requirements:* For master's, comprehensive exam required, foreign language and thesis not required. *Entrance requirements:* For master's, GRE General Test, minimum GPA of 2.9 during last 60 hours. Application deadline: 8/5 (priority date; rolling processing; 12/1 for spring admission). Application fee: $25 ($100 for international students). *Expenses:* Tuition $46 per hour for state residents; $249 per hour for nonresidents. Fees $49 per hour. *Financial aid:* Teaching assistantships, Federal Work-Study, institutionally sponsored loans, and career-related internships or fieldwork available. Aid available to part-time students. Financial aid application deadline: 5/1; applicants required to submit FAFSA. • Dr. Ron Newsome, Head, 254-968-9186.

Teachers College, Columbia University, Graduate Faculty of Education, Department of Health and Behavior Studies, Program in Curriculum and Teaching in Physical Education, 525 West 120th Street, New York, NY 10027-6696. Awards Ed M, MA, Ed D. Part-time and evening/weekend programs available. Faculty: 1 full-time (0 women). Students: 2 full-time (1 woman), 42 part-time (16 women); includes 11 minority (3 African Americans, 6 Hispanics, 2 Native Americans), 3 international. Average age 35. 11 applicants, 100% accepted. In 1997, 9 master's awarded. Terminal master's awarded for partial completion of doctoral program. *Degree requirements:* For master's, integrative paper required, foreign language not required; for doctorate, dissertation. *Entrance requirements:* For doctorate, GRE General Test (minimum combined score of 880). Application deadline: 5/15 (12/1 for spring admission). Application fee: $50. *Expenses:* Tuition $640 per credit. Fees $120 per semester. *Financial aid:* Full and partial tuition waivers, Federal Work-Study, institutionally sponsored loans, and career-related internships or fieldwork available. Aid available to part-time students. Financial aid application deadline: 2/1. *Faculty research:* Analysis of teaching, teacher performance, program development, data bank project in physical education. • Application contact: Ursula Felton, Office of Admissions, 212-678-3710. Fax: 212-678-4171.

Temple University, College of Education, Department of Physical Education, Philadelphia, PA 19122-6096. Offers programs in kinesiology (PhD), including behavioral science, somatic science; physical education (Ed M), including behavioral science, somatic science. Part-time programs available. Faculty: 11 full-time (5 women). Students: 122 (65 women); includes 12 minority (11 African Americans, 1 Hispanic), 4 international. 120 applicants, 29% accepted. In 1997, 13 master's, 10 doctorates awarded. Terminal master's awarded for partial completion of doctoral program. *Degree requirements:* Thesis/dissertation required, foreign language not required. *Entrance requirements:* For master's, GRE General Test or MAT, minimum undergraduate GPA of 2.8, 3.0 during previous 2 years; for doctorate, GRE General Test, minimum undergraduate GPA of 2.8, 3.0 during previous 2 years. Application deadline: 2/1 (10/1 for spring admission). Application fee: $40. *Expenses:* Tuition $323 per semester hour for state residents; $444 per semester hour for nonresidents. Fees $170 per year full-time, $28 per semester (minimum) part-time. *Financial aid:* 55 students received aid; fellowships, research assistantships, teaching assistantships, Federal Work-Study, and career-related internships or fieldwork available. • Dr. Michael R. Sitler, Chair, 215-204-1950. Fax: 215-204-8705. E-mail: sitler@astro.temple.edu. Application contact: Dr. Michael L. Sachs, Admissions Chair, 215-204-1950.

See in-depth description on page 1891.

Tennessee State University, College of Education, Department of Health, Physical Education and Recreation, Nashville, TN 37209-1561. Awards MA Ed. Part-time and evening/weekend programs available. Faculty: 6 full-time (2 women). Students: 5 full-time (1 woman), 3 part-time (1 woman); includes 8 minority (all African Americans). Average age 28. 15 applicants, 80% accepted. In 1997, 6 degrees awarded. *Degree requirements:* Thesis required, foreign language not required. *Average time to degree:* master's–1.5 years full-time, 2 years part-time. *Entrance requirements:* GRE General Test or MAT, minimum GPA of 2.5. Application deadline: rolling. Application fee: $15. *Tuition:* $2962 per year full-time, $182 per credit hour part-time for state residents; $7788 per year full-time, $393 per credit hour part-time for nonresidents. *Financial aid:* In 1997–98, 2 teaching assistantships (1 to a first-year student) averaging $550 per month and totaling $7,500 were awarded; fellowships also available. Aid available to part-time students. Financial aid application deadline: 5/1. *Faculty research:* Speed and strength, agility assessment, physical fitness testing, athletes' attitudes toward school. • Dr. Kim Freeland, Head, 615-963-7486. Fax: 615-963-5594. Application contact: Dr. Clinton M. Lipsey, Dean of the Graduate School, 615-963-5901. Fax: 615-963-5963. E-mail: clipsey@picard.tnstate.edu.

Tennessee Technological University, College of Education, Department of Health and Physical Education, Cookeville, TN 38505. Awards MA. Part-time programs available. Faculty: 7 full-time (0 women). Students: 11 full-time (3 women), 4 part-time (0 women); includes 1 minority (African American). Average age 27. 6 applicants, 100% accepted. In 1997, 13 degrees awarded. *Entrance requirements:* MAT, TOEFL (minimum score 525). Application deadline: 3/1 (priority date; 8/1 for spring admission). Application fee: $25 ($30 for international students). *Tuition:* $2960 per year full-time, $147 per semester hour part-time for state residents; $7786 per year full-time, $358 per semester hour part-time for nonresidents. *Financial aid:* In 1997–98, 13 students received aid, including 2 research assistantships, 11 teaching assistantships (7 to first-year students); fellowships and career-related internships or fieldwork also available. Financial aid application deadline: 4/1. • Dr. Bower L. Johnston, Interim Chairperson, 615-372-3467. Fax: 615-372-6319. E-mail: bjohnston@tntech.edu. Application contact: Dr. Rebecca F. Quattlebaum, Dean of the Graduate School, 615-372-3233. Fax: 615-372-3497. E-mail: rquattlebaum@tntech.edu.

Texas A&M University, College of Education, Department of Health and Kinesiology, Program in Kinesiology, College Station, TX 77843. Offerings include physical education (M Ed, Ed D). *Application deadline:* rolling. *Application fee:* $35 ($75 for international students). • Application contact: Susan Lanier, Graduate Secretary, 409-845-4530. Fax: 409-847-8987.

Texas A&M University–Commerce, College of Education, Department of Health and Physical Education, Commerce, TX 75429-3011. Awards M Ed, MS. Faculty: 7 full-time (3 women), 2 part-time (1 woman). Students: 18 full-time (5 women), 25 part-time (10 women); includes 6 minority (3 African Americans, 2 Hispanics, 1 Native American). In 1997, 20 degrees awarded. *Degree requirements:* Thesis (for some programs), comprehensive exam required, foreign language not required. *Entrance requirements:* GRE General Test. Application deadline: rolling. Application fee: $0 ($25 for international students). *Tuition:* $2382 per year full-time, $343 per semester (minimum) part-time for state residents; $7518 per year full-time, $343 per semester

Directory: Physical Education

Texas A&M University–Commerce (continued)
(minimum) part-time for nonresidents. *Financial aid:* Research assistantships, teaching assistantships, Federal Work-Study, institutionally sponsored loans available. • Dr. Margaret Harbison, Head, 903-886-5549. Application contact: Pam Hammonds, Graduate Admissions Adviser, 903-886-5167. Fax: 903-886-5165.

Texas Christian University, School of Education, Department of Kinesiology and Physical Education, Fort Worth, TX 76129-0002. Awards MS. Part-time and evening/weekend programs available. Students: 19 (8 women). 17 applicants, 71% accepted. In 1997, 8 degrees awarded. *Degree requirements:* Thesis optional, foreign language not required. *Entrance requirements:* GRE General Test (minimum combined score of 1000), TOEFL (minimum score 550). Application deadline: 3/1 (rolling processing; 12/1 for spring admission). Application fee: $0. *Expenses:* Tuition $10,350 per year full-time, $345 per credit hour part-time. Fees $1240 per year full-time, $50 per credit hour part-time. *Financial aid:* Graduate assistantships available. Financial aid application deadline: 3/1. • Dr. Joel Mitchell, Chairperson, 817-257-7665.

Texas Southern University, College of Education, Department of Health, Physical Education and Recreation, Houston, TX 77004-4584. Offers programs in health education (MS), physical education (MS). Part-time and evening/weekend programs available. Faculty: 3 full-time (1 woman). Students: 5 full-time (4 women), 8 part-time (2 women); includes 2 international. Average age 26. 12 applicants, 50% accepted. In 1997, 1 degree awarded. *Degree requirements:* Comprehensive exam required, thesis optional, foreign language not required. *Entrance requirements:* GRE General Test, TOEFL, minimum GPA of 2.5. Application deadline: 7/15 (priority date; rolling processing). Application fee: $35 ($75 for international students). • Dr. T. Robinson, Head, 713-313-7087.

Texas Tech University, Graduate School, College of Arts and Sciences, Department of Health, Physical Education and Recreation, Lubbock, TX 79409. Offers programs in physical education (MS), sports health (MS). Part-time programs available. Faculty: 18 full-time (10 women). Students: 31 full-time (14 women), 15 part-time (4 women); includes 2 minority (1 African American, 1 Hispanic), 1 international. Average age 27. 46 applicants, 52% accepted. In 1997, 15 degrees awarded. *Entrance requirements:* GRE General Test (combined average 948). Application deadline: 4/15 (priority date; rolling processing; 11/1 for spring admission). Application fee: $25 ($50 for international students). Electronic applications accepted. *Expenses:* Tuition $864 per year full-time, $120 per semester (minimum) part-time for state residents; $5976 per year full-time, $747 per semester (minimum) part-time for nonresidents. Fees $1961 per year full-time, $257 per semester (minimum) part-time. *Financial aid:* In 1997–98, 18 students received aid, including 2 research assistantships (1 to a first-year student) averaging $733 per month and totaling $13,200, 12 teaching assistantships (2 to first-year students) averaging $744 per month and totaling $80,399; fellowships, Federal Work-Study, institutionally sponsored loans also available. Aid available to part-time students. Financial aid application deadline: 5/15; applicants required to submit FAFSA. *Faculty research:* Adaptive physical education (disabled students), tobacco use and lifestyle, information processing capabilities within human performance. Total annual research expenditures: $4349. • Dr. Elizabeth B. Hall, Chair, 806-742-3371. Fax: 806-742-1688.

Announcement: The MS degree in physical education offers tracks in adapted physical activity, biomechanics, leisure services administration, motor behavior, physical education, scientific bases of exercise, and sport and fitness management. The program requires 30 hours (thesis) or 36 hours (nonthesis). The MS degree in sports health is an interdisciplinary program offered with the medical school. Students may specialize in preventive and rehabilitative sports health or clinical exercise physiology. The program requires 36 hours (thesis) or 42 hours (nonthesis). Students should inquire about specific prerequisites. For more information, contact 806-742-3371, e-mail: unjas@ttacs.ttu.edu, World Wide Web: http://www.ttu.edu/~hper/grad

Texas Tech University, Graduate School, College of Education, Division of Curriculum and Instruction, Lubbock, TX 79409. Offerings include physical education (Certificate). Division faculty: 23 full-time (12 women). *Application deadline:* 4/15 (priority date; rolling processing; 11/1 for spring admission). *Application fee:* $25 ($50 for international students). Electronic applications accepted. *Expenses:* Tuition $864 per year full-time, $120 per semester (minimum) part-time for state residents; $5976 per year full-time, $747 per semester (minimum) part-time for nonresidents. Fees $2321 per year full-time, $302 per semester (minimum) part-time. • Dr. William E. Sparkman, Chair, 805-742-2371.

Texas Woman's University, College of Health Sciences, Department of Kinesiology, Denton, TX 76204. Offerings include adapted physical education (MS, PhD), pedagogy (MS, PhD). Terminal master's awarded for partial completion of doctoral program. Department faculty: 10 full-time (6 women), 9 part-time (8 women), 11 FTE. *Degree requirements:* For master's, thesis or alternative required, foreign language not required; for doctorate, dissertation, qualifying exam required, foreign language not required. *Average time to degree:* master's–2 years full-time, 5 years part-time; doctorate–4 years full-time, 8 years part-time. *Entrance requirements:* For master's, GRE General Test (minimum combined score of 850); for doctorate, GRE General Test (minimum combined score of 850), minimum GPA of 3.0. Application fee: $25. • Dr. Jerry Wilkerson, Interim Chair, 940-898-2576. Application contact: Dr. Harry Meeuwsen, Graduate Coordinator, 940-898-2594.

United States Sports Academy, Graduate Programs, Department of Sport Coaching, Daphne, AL 36526-7055. Awards MSS. Part-time programs available. Postbaccalaureate distance learning degree programs offered (minimal on-campus study). *Degree requirements:* Comprehensive exam required, thesis optional, foreign language not required. *Entrance requirements:* GRE General Test (minimum combined score of 800), MAT (minimum score 27), minimum GPA of 2.75. Application deadline: 8/15 (priority date; rolling processing). Application fee: $25 ($125 for international students). *Expenses:* Tuition $300 per semester hour (minimum) for state residents; $350 per semester hour (minimum) for nonresidents. Fees $100 (one-time charge). *Faculty research:* Effect of attentional skill on sports performance, survey of coaching qualifications, coaching certification.

See in-depth description on page 1893.

Université de Montréal, Department of Physical Education, Montréal, PQ H3C 3J7, Canada. Offers programs in human movement sciences (M Sc, PhD), sport and fitness management (M Sc). Faculty: 23 full-time (7 women). 58 applicants, 36% accepted. In 1997, 1 master's awarded. *Degree requirements:* For master's, 1 foreign language, thesis (for some programs); for doctorate, 1 foreign language, dissertation, general exam. *Application deadline:* 2/1. *Application fee:* $30. *Faculty research:* Physiology of exercise, psychology of sports, biomechanics, dance, sociology of sports. • Claude Alain, Chairman, 514-343-6166.

Université de Sherbrooke, Faculty of Physical Education, Program in Physical Education, Sherbrooke, PQ J1K 2R1, Canada. Offers kinanthropology (M Sc), physical activity (Diploma). *Degree requirements:* For master's, thesis required, foreign language not required. *Entrance requirements:* For master's, minimum GPA of 2.7; for Diploma, bachelor's degree in physical education. Application deadline: 7/31 (priority date; rolling processing). Application fee: $15. *Faculty research:* Physical fitness, nutrition, human factors, sociology, teaching.

Université du Québec à Trois-Rivières, Program in Physical Education, Trois-Rivières, PQ G9A 5H7, Canada. Awards M Sc. Part-time programs available. Students: 7 full-time (3 women), 1 (woman) part-time. 14 applicants, 71% accepted. *Degree requirements:* Thesis. *Entrance requirements:* Appropriate bachelor's degree, proficiency in French. Application deadline: 2/1. Application fee: $30. *Financial aid:* Fellowships, research assistantships, teaching assistantships available. • Claude Dugas, Director, 819-376-5128 Ext. 3783. Fax: 819-376-5012. E-mail: claude_dugas@uqtr.uquebec.ca. Application contact: Suzanne Camirand, Admissions Officer, 819-376-5045 Ext. 2591. Fax: 819-376-5210. E-mail: suzanne_camirand@uqtr.uquebec.ca.

Université Laval, Faculty of Education, Department of Physical Education, Sainte-Foy, PQ G1K 7P4, Canada. Awards M Sc, PhD. Students: 47 full-time (21 women), 29 part-time (16 women). 31 applicants, 94% accepted. In 1997, 12 master's, 8 doctorates awarded. *Application deadline:* 3/1. *Application fee:* $30. *Expenses:* Tuition $1334 per year (minimum) full-time, $56 per credit (minimum) part-time for Canadian residents; $5966 per year (minimum) full-time, $249 per credit (minimum) part-time for nonresidents. Fees $150 per year full-time, $6.25 per credit part-time. • Rene Larouche, Acting Director, 418-656-2131 Ext. 7754. Fax: 418-656-3020.

The University of Akron, College of Education, Department of Physical Education and Health Education, Program in Adapted Physical Education, Akron, OH 44325-0001. Awards MA, MS. Students: 5 part-time (4 women). Average age 37. *Degree requirements:* Thesis or alternative, written comprehensive exam required, foreign language not required. *Entrance requirements:* GRE or MAT, minimum GPA of 2.75. Application deadline: 8/15 (rolling processing). Application fee: $25 ($50 for international students). *Expenses:* Tuition $178 per credit hour for state residents; $333 per credit hour for nonresidents. Fees $145 per year full-time, $32 per semester (minimum) part-time. • Phillip Buckenmeyer, Director of Graduate Programs in Physical Education and Health Education, 330-972-7474.

The University of Akron, College of Education, Department of Physical Education and Health Education, Program in Outdoor Education, Akron, OH 44325-0001. Awards MA, MS. Students: 6 full-time (4 women), 37 part-time (22 women); includes 1 minority (African American). Average age 35. In 1997, 11 degrees awarded. *Degree requirements:* Thesis or alternative, written comprehensive exam required, foreign language not required. *Entrance requirements:* GRE or MAT, minimum GPA of 2.75. Application deadline: 8/15 (rolling processing). Application fee: $25 ($50 for international students). *Expenses:* Tuition $178 per credit hour for state residents; $333 per credit hour for nonresidents. Fees $145 per year full-time, $32 per semester (minimum) part-time. • Phillip Buckenmeyer, Director of Graduate Programs in Physical Education and Health Education, 330-972-7474.

The University of Alabama at Birmingham, Graduate School, School of Education, Department of Human Studies, Program in Physical Education, Birmingham, AL 35294. Awards MA Ed, Ed S. Evening/weekend programs available. Students: 16 full-time (7 women), 10 part-time (7 women); includes 3 minority (all African Americans). 25 applicants, 84% accepted. In 1997, 15 master's awarded. *Degree requirements:* For master's, thesis optional, foreign language not required; for Ed S, comprehensive exam. *Entrance requirements:* For master's, GRE General Test, MAT, or NTE, minimum GPA of 3.0. Application deadline: rolling. Application fee: $30 ($60 for international students). Electronic applications accepted. *Expenses:* Tuition $99 per credit hour for state residents; $198 per credit hour for nonresidents. Fees $516 per year (minimum) full-time, $73 per quarter (minimum) part-time for state residents; $516 per year (minimum) full-time, $73 per unit (minimum) part-time for nonresidents. • Dr. David M. Macrina, Chairperson, Department of Human Studies, 205-934-2446.

University of Alberta, Faculty of Graduate Studies and Research, Faculty of Physical Education and Recreation, Edmonton, AB T6G 2E1, Canada. Offers program in recreation (MA, M Sc, PhD). Part-time programs available. Students: 60 full-time (34 women), 55 part-time (28 women); includes 10 international. 90 applicants, 47% accepted. *Degree requirements:* For master's, thesis (for some programs); for doctorate, dissertation. *Entrance requirements:* For master's, TOEFL (minimum score 550; average 580), bachelor's in related field; for doctorate, TOEFL (minimum score 550; average 580), master's degree in related field with thesis. Application deadline: 2/1 (priority date; rolling processing). Application fee: $60. *Expenses:* Tuition $390 per course for Canadian residents; $781 per course for nonresidents. Fees $500 per year full-time, $184 per year part-time. *Financial aid:* In 1997–98, 63 students received aid, including 28 research assistantships averaging $513 per month, 35 teaching assistantships averaging $573 per month, 12 tuition scholarships; career-related internships or fieldwork also available. Aid available to part-time students. *Faculty research:* Motivation and adherence to physical ability, performance enhancement, adapted physical activity, exercise physiology, sport administration, tourism. • Dr. H. A. Quinney, Dean, 403-492-3198. Application contact: Anne Jordan, Department Office, 403-492-3198. Fax: 403-492-2364. E-mail: ajordan@per.ualberta.ca.

University of Arkansas, College of Education, Department of Health Science, Kinesiology, Recreation and Dance, Program in Physical Education, Fayetteville, AR 72701-1201. Awards MAT, M Ed. Students: 11 full-time (1 woman). 7 applicants, 100% accepted. In 1997, 6 degrees awarded. *Degree requirements:* Thesis optional, foreign language not required. *Application fee:* $25 ($35 for international students). *Tuition:* $3144 per year full-time, $173 per credit hour part-time for state residents; $7140 per year full-time, $395 per credit hour part-time for nonresidents. *Financial aid:* Research assistantships, teaching assistantships, Federal Work-Study, and career-related internships or fieldwork available. Aid available to part-time students. Financial aid application deadline: 4/1; applicants required to submit FAFSA. • Dr. Dean Gorman, Coordinator, 501-575-2890.

University of Arkansas at Pine Bluff, Program in Education, Pine Bluff, AR 71601-2799. Offerings include secondary education (M Ed), with options in aquaculture, English, general science, mathematics, physical education, social studies. Program faculty: 51. *Entrance requirements:* GRE, minimum GPA of 2.75; NTE or Standard Arkansas Teaching Certificate. Application deadline: rolling. Application fee: $0. *Expenses:* Tuition $82 per credit hour for state residents; $192 per credit hour for nonresidents. Fees $25 per year. • Dr. Calvin Johnson, Dean, 870-543-8256.

University of Central Florida, College of Education, Department of Exceptional and Physical Education, Program in Physical Education, Orlando, FL 32816. Awards MA, M Ed. Part-time and evening/weekend programs available. Students: 38 full-time (24 women), 16 part-time (12 women); includes 6 minority (2 African Americans, 1 Asian American, 3 Hispanics), 1 international. Average age 32. 26 applicants, 65% accepted. In 1997, 26 degrees awarded. *Degree requirements:* Thesis or alternative required, foreign language not required. *Entrance requirements:* GRE General Test (minimum combined score of 840). Application deadline: 7/15 (12/15 for spring admission). Application fee: $20. *Expenses:* Tuition $3288 per year full-time, $137 per credit hour part-time for state residents; $11,520 per year full-time, $480 per credit hour part-time for nonresidents. Fees $105 per year. *Financial aid:* Teaching assistantships, Federal Work-Study, institutionally sponsored loans, and career-related internships or fieldwork available. Aid available to part-time students. • Application contact: Dr. Patricia Higginbothan, Coordinator, 407-823-2050.

University of Colorado at Boulder, College of Arts and Sciences, Department of Kinesiology, Boulder, CO 80309. Offerings include physical education (MS). Department faculty: 9 full-time (1 woman). *Degree requirements:* Thesis or alternative, comprehensive exam required, foreign language not required. *Entrance requirements:* GRE General Test. Application deadline: 3/1 (priority date; rolling processing). Application fee: $40 ($60 for international students). *Expenses:* Tuition $3170 per year full-time, $531 per semester (minimum) part-time for state residents; $14,652 per year full-time, $2442 per semester (minimum) part-time for nonresidents. Fees $667 per year full-time, $130 per semester (minimum) part-time. • Dr. Russell Moore, Chair, 303-492-1093. E-mail: rmoore@spot.colorado.edu. Application contact: Melanie Evans, Graduate Program Administrator, 303-492-3122. Fax: 303-492-4009. E-mail: melanie.evans@colorado.edu.

University of Dayton, School of Education, Department of Health and Sport Science, Dayton, OH 45469-1611. Offers program in physical education (MS Ed). Evening/weekend programs available. Faculty: 8 full-time (3 women). Students: 6 full-time (4 women), 20 part-time (15 women); includes 5 minority (2 African Americans, 2 Asian Americans, 1 Hispanic). Average age 30. 4 applicants, 100% accepted. In 1997, 5 degrees awarded. *Degree requirements:* Comprehensive exam required, foreign language and thesis not required. *Entrance requirements:* GRE General Test (minimum score 430 on verbal section, 490 on analytical), MAT, minimum GPA of 2.75. Application deadline: 8/1 (priority date; rolling processing). Application fee: $30.

Financial aid: In 1997–98, 4 teaching assistantships (3 to first-year students) were awarded. *Faculty research:* Exercise science, sport management. • Lloyd Laubach, Chairperson, 937-229-4225.

University of Delaware, College of Health and Nursing Sciences, Department of Health and Exercise Scien ces, Newark, DE 19716. Offerings include professional development (MA). Department faculty: 12 full-time (3 women). *Average time to degree:* master's–2.5 years full-time, 4.5 years part-time. *Application deadline:* 7/1 (priority date; rolling processing; 12/1 for spring admission). *Application fee:* $45. *Expenses:* Tuition $4250 per year full-time, $236 per credit hour part-time for state residents; $12,250 per year full-time, $681 per credit hour part-time for nonresidents. Fees $466 per year full-time, $15 per semester (minimum) part-time. • Application contact: Gail E. Manogue, Administrative Assistant, 302-831-8370.

University of Florida, College of Health and Human Performance, Program in Health and Human Performance, Gainesville, FL 32611. Awards PhD. Students: 26 full-time (12 women), 16 part-time (7 women); includes 6 minority (4 African Americans, 2 Hispanics), 9 international. 41 applicants, 29% accepted. In 1997, 5 degrees awarded. *Degree requirements:* Dissertation. *Entrance requirements:* GRE General Test. Application deadline: 6/5 (priority date; rolling processing). Application fee: $20. *Tuition:* $138 per credit hour for state residents; $481 per credit hour for nonresidents. *Financial aid:* In 1997–98, 28 students received aid, including 6 fellowships averaging $1,064 per month, 1 research assistantship averaging $422 per month, 20 teaching assistantships averaging $700 per month, 1 graduate assistantship averaging $1,000 per month. • Dr. Patrick J. Bird, Dean, College of Health and Human Performance, 357-392-0578 Ext. 225. Fax: 352-392-3186. E-mail: pbird@hhp.ufl.edu.

University of Georgia, College of Education, School of Health and Human Performance, Department of Physical Education and Sport Studies, Athens, GA 30602. Awards MA, M Ed, Ed D, PhD, Ed S. Faculty: 7 full-time (3 women). Students: 48 full-time (14 women), 18 part-time (5 women); includes 5 minority (4 African Americans, 1 Hispanic), 4 international. 72 applicants, 57% accepted. In 1997, 21 master's, 1 doctorate, 1 Ed S awarded. *Degree requirements:* For master's, thesis (MA) required, foreign language not required; for doctorate, dissertation required, foreign language not required. *Entrance requirements:* For master's and Ed S, GRE General Test or MAT; for doctorate, GRE General Test. Application deadline: 7/1 (priority date; 11/15 for spring admission). Application fee: $30. Electronic applications accepted. *Tuition:* $3290 per year full-time, $643 per semester (minimum) part-time for state residents; $11,300 per year full-time, $1645 per semester (minimum) part-time for nonresidents. *Financial aid:* Fellowships, research assistantships, teaching assistantships, assistantships available. • Dr. Paul G. Schempp, Graduate Coordinator, 706-542-4462. Fax: 706-542-3417.

University of Houston, College of Education, Department of Health and Human Performance, 4800 Calhoun, Houston, TX 77204-2163. Offers programs in allied health (M Ed, Ed D), exercise science (MS), health education (M Ed), physical education (M Ed, Ed D). Ed D (allied health) offered jointly with Baylor College of Medicine. Part-time and evening/weekend programs available. Faculty: 10 full-time (3 women), 9 part-time (5 women). Students: 48 full-time (27 women), 61 part-time (42 women); includes 33 minority (17 African Americans, 4 Asian Americans, 11 Hispanics, 1 Native American), 8 international. Average age 35. In 1997, 21 master's, 2 doctorates awarded. *Degree requirements:* For master's, comprehensive exam or thesis required, foreign language not required; for doctorate, dissertation, comprehensive exam required, foreign language not required. *Entrance requirements:* For master's, GRE General Test or MAT; for doctorate, GRE General Test, interview. Application deadline: 7/3. Application fee: $35 ($75 for international students). *Expenses:* Tuition $1152 per year full-time, $120 per semester (minimum) part-time for state residents; $4482 per year full-time, $249 per credit hour part-time for nonresidents. Fees $977 per year full-time, $119 per semester (minimum) part-time. *Financial aid:* In 1997–98, 26 teaching assistantships averaging $700 per month were awarded; research assistantships, Federal Work-Study, and career-related internships or fieldwork also available. *Faculty research:* Motor development, physical fitness, comprehensive school health, leadership, sports law. • Dr. Dennis Smith, Chairperson, 713-743-9853. Fax: 713-743-9860.

University of Idaho, College of Graduate Studies, College of Education, Division of Health, Physical Education, Recreation, and Dance, Program in Physical Education, Moscow, ID 83844-4140. Awards M Ed, MS, PhD. Students: 23 full-time (14 women), 10 part-time (7 women); includes 3 minority (1 African American, 1 Asian American, 1 Native American), 3 international. *Degree requirements:* For doctorate, dissertation. *Entrance requirements:* For master's, minimum GPA of 2.8; for doctorate, minimum undergraduate GPA of 2.8, 3.0 graduate. Application deadline: 8/1 (12/15 for spring admission). Application fee: $35 ($45 for international students). *Expenses:* Tuition $0 for state residents; $6000 per year full-time, $95 per credit part-time for nonresidents. Fees $2676 per year full-time, $134 per credit part-time. *Financial aid:* Research assistantships, teaching assistantships available. Financial aid application deadline: 2/15. • Dr. Calvin Lathen, Director, Division of Health, Physical Education, Recreation, and Dance, 208-885-7921.

The University of Iowa, College of Liberal Arts, Department of Exercise Science, Iowa City, IA 52242-1316. Offerings include physical education (PhD). Department faculty: 7 full-time, 2 part-time. *Degree requirements:* Dissertation, comprehensive exam. *Entrance requirements:* GRE General Test. Application deadline: rolling. Application fee: $30 ($50 for international students). *Expenses:* Tuition $3166 per year full-time, $176 per semester hour part-time for state residents; $10,202 per year full-time, $176 per semester hour part-time for nonresidents. Fees $202 per year full-time, $52 per year (minimum) part-time. • Jerry Maynard, Chair, 319-335-9497. Fax: 319-335-6966.

The University of Iowa, College of Liberal Arts, Department of Sport, Health, Leisure and Physical Studies, Iowa City, IA 52242-1316. Offers programs in leisure studies (MA), physical education and sports studies (MA, PhD). Faculty: 14 full-time. Students: 40 full-time (26 women), 21 part-time (10 women); includes 4 minority (3 African Americans, 1 Hispanic), 4 international. 64 applicants, 34% accepted. In 1997, 14 master's, 4 doctorates awarded. *Degree requirements:* For master's, thesis optional; for doctorate, dissertation, comprehensive exam. *Application deadline:* 4/15 (rolling processing). *Application fee:* $30 ($50 for international students). *Expenses:* Tuition $3166 per year full-time, $176 per semester hour part-time for state residents; $10,202 per year full-time, $176 per semester hour part-time for nonresidents. Fees $202 per year full-time, $52 per year (minimum) part-time. *Financial aid:* In 1997–98, 9 research assistantships (2 to first-year students), 31 teaching assistantships (14 to first-year students) were awarded; fellowships also available. Financial aid applicants required to submit FAFSA. • Yvonne Slatton, Chair, 319-335-9335.

University of Kansas, School of Education, Department of Health, Sport, and Exercise Sciences, Lawrence, KS 66045. Offers programs in health education (MS Ed), physical education (MS Ed, Ed D, PhD). Faculty: 10 full-time. Students: 64 full-time (28 women), 141 part-time (72 women); includes 10 minority (4 African Americans, 2 Asian Americans, 1 Hispanic, 3 Native Americans), 7 international. In 1997, 54 master's, 7 doctorates awarded. *Degree requirements:* For doctorate, variable foreign language requirement, dissertation. *Entrance requirements:* For master's, minimum GPA of 3.0; for doctorate, GRE General Test (minimum combined score of 1000), minimum graduate GPA of 3.5. Application deadline: 7/1. Application fee: $25. *Expenses:* Tuition $2400 per year full-time, $100 per credit hour part-time for state residents; $7890 per year full-time, $329 per credit hour part-time for nonresidents. Fees $428 per year full-time, $31 per credit hour part-time. *Financial aid:* Fellowships, research assistantships, teaching assistantships available. • Joseph Donnelly, Chair, 785-864-3371. Application contact: Dr. James D. LaPoint, Graduate Coordinator, 785-864-0785. Fax: 785-864-3343. E-mail: jdl@falcon.cc.ukans.edu.

University of Louisville, School of Education, Department of Health Promotion, Physical Education and Sport Studies, Program in Physical Education, Louisville, KY 40292-0001. Awards MAT, M Ed. Students: 36 full-time (21 women), 18 part-time (8 women); includes 9 minority (7 African Americans, 1 Asian American, 1 Hispanic). Average age 28. In 1997, 28 degrees awarded. *Entrance requirements:* GRE General Test. Application deadline: rolling. Application fee: $25. • Dr. Richard Fee, Chair, Department of Health Promotion, Physical Education and Sport Studies, 502-852-6645.

University of Maine, College of Education and Human Development, Program in Kinesiology and Physical Education, Orono, ME 04469. Awards MAT, M Ed, MS, CAS. Part-time and evening/weekend programs available. *Degree requirements:* For master's, thesis or alternative required, foreign language not required. *Entrance requirements:* For master's, MAT, TOEFL (minimum score 550); for CAS, MA, M Ed, or MS. Application deadline: 2/1 (priority date; rolling processing; 10/15 for spring admission). Application fee: $50. *Expenses:* Tuition $194 per credit hour for state residents; $548 per credit hour for nonresidents. Fees $378 per year full-time, $33 per semester (minimum) part-time. *Financial aid:* Career-related internships or fieldwork available. Aid available to part-time students. Financial aid application deadline: 3/1. • Application contact: Scott Delcourt, Director of the Graduate School, 207-581-3218. Fax: 207-581-3232. E-mail: graduate@maine.edu.

University of Manitoba, Faculty of Physical Education and Recreation Studies, Winnipeg, MB R3T 2N2, Canada. Awards M Sc.

University of Manitoba, Faculty of Education, Department of Curriculum: Mathematics and Natural Sciences, Winnipeg, MB R3T 2N2, Canada. Offerings include physical education (M Ed). *Degree requirements:* Thesis or alternative required, foreign language not required.

University of Massachusetts Amherst, School of Education, Program in Education, Amherst, MA 01003-0001. Offerings include physical education teacher education (M Ed, Ed D, CAGS). *Degree requirements:* For doctorate, dissertation required, foreign language not required. *Entrance requirements:* For master's and doctorate, GRE General Test. Application deadline: 3/1 (rolling processing; 10/1 for spring admission). Application fee: $40. *Expenses:* Tuition $2640 per year full-time, $110 per credit part-time for state residents; $3690 per year (minimum) full-time, $165 per credit (minimum) part-time for nonresidents. Fees $2856 per year full-time, $422 per semester part-time for state residents; $3204 per year full-time, $480 per semester part-time for nonresidents. • John C. Carey, Director, 413-545-0236.

The University of Montana–Missoula, School of Education, Department of Health and Human Performance, Missoula, MT 59812-0002. Awards MS. Part-time programs available. Faculty: 10 full-time (3 women). Students: 18 full-time (16 women). Average age 30. 28 applicants, 61% accepted. In 1997, 8 degrees awarded. *Degree requirements:* Thesis or alternative required, foreign language not required. *Average time to degree:* master's–2 years full-time. *Entrance requirements:* GRE General Test (minimum score 450 on each section), minimum GPA of 3.0. Application deadline: 3/15. Application fee: $30. *Tuition:* $2499 per year (minimum) full-time, $376 per semester (minimum) part-time for state residents; $6528 per year (minimum) full-time, $1048 per semester (minimum) part-time for nonresidents. *Financial aid:* In 1997–98, 4 students received aid, including 4 teaching assistantships; Federal Work-Study also available. Financial aid application deadline: 3/1. *Faculty research:* Exercise physiology, performance psychology, nutrition, pre-employment physical screening, program evaluation, ethics. • Dr. Sharon Uhlig, Chair, 406-243-4211.

University of Montevallo, College of Education, Department of Health, Physical Education, and Recreation, Montevallo, AL 35115. Awards M Ed, Ed S. Part-time and evening/weekend programs available. *Entrance requirements:* For master's, GRE General Test (minimum combined score of 850), MAT (minimum score 35), minimum undergraduate GPA of 2.75 in last 60 hours or 2.5 overall. Application deadline: 7/15 (11/15 for spring admission). Application fee: $10.

University of Nebraska at Kearney, College of Education, Department of Health, Physical Education, Recreation, and Leisure Studies, Kearney, NE 68849-0001. Offers programs in adapted physical education (MA Ed), exercise science (MA Ed), master teacher (MA Ed). Part-time and evening/weekend programs available. Faculty: 5 full-time (0 women). Students: 10 full-time (3 women), 21 part-time (9 women); includes 1 minority (African American), 1 international. In 1997, 14 degrees awarded. *Degree requirements:* Thesis optional. *Entrance requirements:* GRE General Test. Application deadline: 8/1 (priority date; rolling processing; 12/15 for spring admission). Application fee: $35. *Expenses:* Tuition $1494 per year full-time, $83 per credit hour part-time for state residents; $2826 per year full-time, $157 per credit hour part-time for nonresidents. Fees $229 per year full-time, $11.25 per semester (minimum) part-time. *Financial aid:* In 1997–98, 6 research assistantships, 2 teaching assistantships, 9 graduate assistantships were awarded; career-related internships or fieldwork also available. Aid available to part-time students. Financial aid application deadline: 3/1; applicants required to submit FAFSA. • Dr. Don Lackey, Chair, 308-865-8331.

University of Nebraska at Omaha, College of Education, School of Health, Physical Education and Recreation, Omaha, NE 68182. Awards MA, MS. Part-time programs available. Faculty: 9 full-time (1 woman). Students: 28 full-time (14 women), 111 part-time (76 women); includes 5 minority (all African Americans), 6 international. Average age 34. 75 applicants, 81% accepted. In 1997, 27 degrees awarded. *Degree requirements:* Thesis (for some programs), comprehensive exam required, foreign language not required. *Entrance requirements:* Minimum GPA of 3.0. Application deadline: 7/1 (priority date; rolling processing; 12/1 for spring admission). Application fee: $35. *Expenses:* Tuition $1670 per year full-time, $94 per credit hour part-time for state residents; $4082 per year full-time, $227 per credit hour part-time for nonresidents. Fees $302 per year full-time, $108 per semester (minimum) part-time. *Financial aid:* In 1997–98, 67 students received aid, including 8 research assistantships; fellowships, full tuition waivers, Federal Work-Study, institutionally sponsored loans also available. Aid available to part-time students. Financial aid application deadline: 3/1; applicants required to submit FAFSA. • Dr. Dan Blanke, Director, 402-554-2670.

University of Nebraska–Lincoln, Teachers College, School of Health and Human Performance, Lincoln, NE 68588. Offers program in health, physical education, and recreation (M Ed, MPE). Faculty: 12 full-time (2 women). Students: 21 full-time (8 women), 14 part-time (10 women); includes 1 minority (Asian American), 6 international. Average age 29. 27 applicants, 74% accepted. In 1997, 19 degrees awarded. *Degree requirements:* Thesis required (for some programs), foreign language not required. *Entrance requirements:* GRE General Test or MAT, TOEFL (minimum score 500). Application deadline: 3/1 (priority date; rolling processing). Application fee: $35. Electronic applications accepted. *Expenses:* Tuition $110 per credit hour for state residents; $270 per credit hour for nonresidents. Fees $480 per year full-time, $110 per semester part-time. *Financial aid:* In 1997–98, 1 fellowship totaling $700, 11 research assistantships totaling $74,250 were awarded; teaching assistantships, Federal Work-Study also available. Aid available to part-time students. Financial aid application deadline: 2/15. *Faculty research:* Exercise science, health behaviors, fitness, teacher effectiveness. Total annual research expenditures: $18,167. • William Murphy, Chair, 402-472-3882. E-mail: wmurphy@unlinfo.unl.edu.

University of Nevada, Reno, College of Human and Community Sciences, Department of Health Ecology, Reno, NV 89557. Offers program in physical education (MS). Faculty: 9 (4 women). Students: 6 full-time (2 women), 16 part-time (4 women); includes 2 minority (both Hispanics), 1 international. Average age 31. 5 applicants, 20% accepted. In 1997, 6 degrees awarded. *Degree requirements:* Thesis optional, foreign language not required. *Entrance requirements:* TOEFL (minimum score 500), minimum GPA of 2.75. Application deadline: 3/1 (priority date; rolling processing). Application fee: $40. *Expenses:* Tuition $0 for state residents; $5770 per year full-time, $200 per credit part-time for nonresidents. Fees $93 per credit. *Financial aid:* Research assistantships, teaching assistantships, Federal Work-Study, institutionally sponsored loans available. Financial aid application deadline: 3/1. *Faculty research:* Biomechanics and basic fundamentals of skiing, social psychology in sports and recreation, fitness and aging, elementary physical education, body fat evaluation. • Dr. Charles Bullock, Chair, 702-784-4041. Application contact: Dr. Olena Plummer, Graduate Director, 702-784-4041. E-mail: olenap@scs.unr.edu.

Directory: Physical Education

University of New Brunswick, Faculty of Physical Education and Recreation, Fredericton, NB E3B 5A3, Canada. Awards MPE. Part-time programs available. *Entrance requirements:* TOEFL, TWE. Application deadline: 3/1 (priority date; rolling processing). Application fee: $25.

University of New Mexico, College of Education, Program in Health, Physical Education and Recreation, Albuquerque, NM 87131-2039. Awards Ed D, PhD. Part-time programs available. Faculty: 15 full-time (7 women), 14 part-time (4 women), 18.55 FTE. Students: 56 full-time (30 women), 53 part-time (29 women); includes 23 minority (5 African Americans, 2 Asian Americans, 11 Hispanics, 5 Native Americans), 18 international. Average age 39. 33 applicants, 67% accepted. In 1997, 21 doctorates awarded. Terminal master's awarded for partial completion of doctoral program. *Degree requirements:* For doctorate, dissertation required, foreign language not required. *Application fee:* $25. *Expenses:* Tuition $2442 per year full-time, $103 per credit hour part-time for state residents; $8691 per year full-time, $103 per credit hour (minimum) part-time for nonresidents. Fees $32 per year. *Financial aid:* In 1997–98, 17 students received aid, including 3 research assistantships (1 to a first-year student) averaging $770 per month and totaling $23,100, 14 teaching assistantships (6 to first-year students) averaging $770 per month and totaling $107,800; fellowships, Federal Work-Study, institutionally sponsored loans, and career-related internships or fieldwork also available. Aid available to part-time students. *Faculty research:* Physical education pedagogy, sports psychology, sports administration, cardic rehabilitation, sports physiology, physical fitness assessment, exercise prescription. Total annual research expenditures: $17,132. • Dr. Mary Jo Campbell, Graduate Coordinator, 505-277-5151. Application contact: Sally Renfro, Division Administrator, 505-277-5151. Fax: 505-277-6227.

University of New Mexico, College of Education, Program in Physical Education, Albuquerque, NM 87131-2039. Awards MS, Certificate, Ed S. Part-time programs available. Faculty: 15 full-time (7 women), 14 part-time (4 women), 18.55 FTE. Students: 21 full-time (7 women), 24 part-time (11 women); includes 9 minority (1 Asian American, 7 Hispanics, 1 Native American), 1 international. Average age 30. 24 applicants, 71% accepted. In 1997, 30 master's awarded. *Degree requirements:* For master's, comprehensive exams or thesis required, foreign language not required. *Application deadline:* 6/1 (10/1 for spring admission). *Application fee:* $25. *Expenses:* Tuition $2442 per year full-time, $103 per credit hour part-time for state residents; $8691 per year full-time, $103 per credit hour (minimum) part-time for nonresidents. Fees $32 per year. *Financial aid:* In 1997–98, 3 teaching assistantships (all to first-year students) averaging $770 per month were awarded; fellowships, research assistantships, Federal Work-Study, institutionally sponsored loans also available. Aid available to part-time students. *Faculty research:* Physical education pedagogy, exercise prescription, sports psychology, sports administration, cardiac rehabilitation, sports physiology, exercise testing, fitness assessment. • Dr. Mary Jo Campbell, Graduate Adviser, 505-277-5151. E-mail: njcampbe@unm.edu. Application contact: Sally Renfro, Division Administrator, 505-277-5151. Fax: 505-277-6227. E-mail: srenfro@unm.edu.

University of New Orleans, College of Education, Department of Health and Physical Education, New Orleans, LA 70148. Offers programs in adapted physical education (MA); exercise physiology (MA); gerontology (Certificate); health and physical education (Certificate); physical education (M Ed); science, pedagogy and coaching sport management (MA). Evening/weekend programs available. Faculty: 9 full-time (5 women). Students: 31 full-time (14 women), 40 part-time (24 women); includes 15 minority (14 African Americans, 1 Hispanic), 18 international. Average age 32. 27 applicants, 100% accepted. In 1997, 52 master's awarded. *Entrance requirements:* For master's, GRE General Test. Application deadline: 7/1 (priority date; rolling processing). Application fee: $20. *Expenses:* Tuition $2362 per year full-time, $373 per semester (minimum) part-time for state residents; $7888 per year full-time, $1423 per semester (minimum) part-time for nonresidents. Fees $170 per year full-time, $25 per semester (minimum) part-time. *Financial aid:* Teaching assistantships, grants, partial tuition waivers available. *Faculty research:* Motor control, health science, biomechanics. Total annual research expenditures: $71,902. • Dr. Robert Eason, Chairperson, 504-280-6420. E-mail: blehp@uno.edu. Application contact: Dr. Mark Loftin, Graduate Coordinator, 504-280-6417. Fax: 504-280-6018. E-mail: mxlhp@uno.edu.

The University of North Carolina at Chapel Hill, College of Arts and Sciences, Department of Physical Education, Exercise and Sport Science, Chapel Hill, NC 27599. Offers programs in athletic training (MA), exercise physiology (MA), sports administration (MA), sports psychology (MA). Faculty: 12 full-time, 5 part-time. Students: 41 full-time (20 women), 12 part-time (6 women); includes 5 minority (3 Asian Americans, 2 Hispanics), 1 international. 166 applicants, 18% accepted. In 1997, 27 degrees awarded. *Degree requirements:* Thesis (for some programs), comprehensive exam required, foreign language not required. *Entrance requirements:* GRE General Test, NTE, minimum GPA of 3.0. Application deadline: 1/1 (priority date; rolling processing). Application fee: $55. *Expenses:* Tuition $1428 per year full-time, $357 per semester (minimum) part-time for state residents; $10,414 per year full-time, $2604 per semester (minimum) part-time for nonresidents. Fees $782 per year full-time, $332 per semester (minimum) part-time. *Financial aid:* In 1997–98, 1 research assistantship, 46 teaching assistantships were awarded; graduate assistantships also available. Financial aid application deadline: 3/1. • Dr. Frederick O. Mueller, Chairman, 919-962-0017. Application contact: Dr. Pamela Robinson, Director of Graduate Studies, 919-962-5173.

University of Northern Colorado, College of Health and Human Sciences, School of Kinesiology and Physical Education, Greeley, CO 80639. Awards MA, Ed D. Faculty: 13 full-time (7 women), 1 (woman) part-time. Students: 125 full-time (47 women), 27 part-time (8 women); includes 17 minority (4 African Americans, 5 Asian Americans, 8 Hispanics), 9 international. Average age 30. 162 applicants, 77% accepted. In 1997, 67 master's, 8 doctorates awarded. *Degree requirements:* For master's, comprehensive exams required, thesis not required; for doctorate, dissertation, comprehensive exams. *Entrance requirements:* For doctorate, GRE General Test. Application deadline: rolling. Application fee: $35. *Expenses:* Tuition $2327 per year full-time, $129 per credit hour part-time for state residents; $9578 per year full-time, $532 per credit hour part-time for nonresidents. Fees $752 per year full-time, $184 per semester (minimum) part-time. *Financial aid:* In 1997–98, 96 students received aid, including 10 fellowships (6 to first-year students) totaling $17,450, 16 teaching assistantships (5 to first-year students) totaling $97,595, 9 graduate assistantships (4 to first-year students) totaling $60,043. Financial aid application deadline: 3/1. • Dr. Jim Stiehl, Director, 970-351-2535.

University of Northern Iowa, College of Education, School of Health, Physical Education, and Leisure Services, Program in Physical Education, Cedar Falls, IA 50614. Awards MA. Part-time and evening/weekend programs available. Students: 13 full-time (6 women), 7 part-time (2 women); includes 1 minority (African American), 3 international. Average age 33. 18 applicants, 89% accepted. In 1997, 6 degrees awarded. *Degree requirements:* Thesis or alternative required, foreign language not required. *Entrance requirements:* Minimum GPA of 3.5, 3 years of educational experience. Application deadline: 8/1 (priority date; rolling processing). Application fee: $20 ($30 for international students). *Expenses:* Tuition $3166 per year full-time, $176 per hour part-time for state residents; $7805 per year full-time, $176 per hour part-time for nonresidents. Fees $194 per year full-time, $12.50 per semester (minimum) part-time. *Financial aid:* Full and partial tuition waivers, Federal Work-Study, and career-related internships or fieldwork available. Aid available to part-time students. Financial aid application deadline: 3/1. • Dr. Sharon Huddleston, Head, 319-273-2730.

University of Regina, Faculty of Graduate Studies and Research, Special Case Programs, Program in Physical Activity Studies, Regina, SK S4S 0A2, Canada. Awards MPAS. Faculty: 10 full-time (2 women), 1 part-time. Students: 2 full-time, 10 part-time. 9 applicants, 22% accepted. *Degree requirements:* Thesis required, foreign language not required. *Entrance requirements:* TOEFL (minimum score 580). Application deadline: rolling. Application fee: $0. *Tuition:* $1875 per year full-time, $187 per credit part-time for Canadian residents; $2812 per year full-time, $374 per credit part-time for nonresidents. *Financial aid:* In 1997–98, fellowships averaging $1,142 per month, research assistantships averaging $1,014 per month, 2 teaching assistantships averaging $888 per month, 2 scholarships averaging $750 per month were awarded. Financial aid application deadline: 6/15. *Faculty research:* Adapted physical activity, recreation administration, sport administration, fitness and lifestyle. • Dr. E. Nicholls, Dean, 306-585-4797. Fax: 306-585-4854. E-mail: ernie.nicholls@uregina.ca. Application contact: Dr. G. W. Maslany, Associate Dean, 306-585-4161. Fax: 306-585-4893. E-mail: maslany@max.cc.uregina.ca.

University of Rhode Island, College of Human Science and Services, Department of Physical Education, Health and Recreation, Kingston, RI 02881. Offers programs in health (MS), physical education (MS), recreation (MS). *Entrance requirements:* MAT or GRE. Application deadline: 4/15 (priority date; rolling processing; 11/15 for spring admission). Application fee: $35. *Expenses:* Tuition $3446 per year full-time, $191 per credit part-time for state residents; $9850 per year full-time, $547 per credit part-time for nonresidents. Fees $1276 per year full-time, $135 per semester (minimum) part-time.

University of Saskatchewan, College of Physical Education, Saskatoon, SK S7N 5A2, Canada. Awards M Sc, PhD. *Degree requirements:* Thesis/dissertation. *Entrance requirements:* For master's, CANTEST (minimum score 4.5) or International English Language Testing System (minimum score 6) or Michigan English Language Assessment Battery (minimum score 80), or TOEFL (minimum score 550; average 560). Application deadline: 7/1 (priority date; rolling processing). Application fee: $0.

University of South Alabama, College of Education, Department of Health, Physical Education and Leisure Services, Mobile, AL 36688-0002. Offers programs in exercise technology (MS), health education (M Ed), leisure services (MS), physical education (M Ed), therapeutic recreation (MS). Part-time programs available. Faculty: 10 full-time (2 women). Students: 28 full-time (17 women), 17 part-time (11 women); includes 7 minority (6 African Americans, 1 Hispanic), 2 international. 22 applicants, 91% accepted. In 1997, 17 degrees awarded. *Degree requirements:* Comprehensive exam required, foreign language and thesis not required. *Entrance requirements:* GRE General Test (minimum combined score of 1000) or MAT (minimum score 37). Application deadline: 9/1 (priority date; rolling processing). Application fee: $25. *Financial aid:* In 1997–98, 10 teaching assistantships were awarded; career-related internships or fieldwork also available. Aid available to part-time students. Financial aid application deadline: 4/1. • Dr. Frederick Scaffidi, Chairman, 334-460-7131.

University of South Alabama, College of Education, Department of Interdepartmental Education, Mobile, AL 36688-0002. Offerings include physical education (Ed S). *Application deadline:* 9/1 (priority date; rolling processing). *Application fee:* $25. • George E. Uhlig, Dean, College of Education, 334-460-6205.

University of South Carolina, Graduate School, College of Education, Department of Physical Education, Columbia, SC 29208. Awards IMA, MAT, MS, PhD. Part-time programs available. Faculty: 6 full-time (3 women). Students: 23 full-time (10 women), 20 part-time (6 women); includes 3 minority (2 African Americans, 1 Asian American). Average age 34. In 1997, 6 master's, 3 doctorates awarded. *Degree requirements:* For master's, thesis (for some programs); for doctorate, 1 foreign language, computer language, dissertation, comprehensive exam. *Entrance requirements:* For master's, GRE General Test or MAT (minimum score 35); for doctorate, GRE General Test (combined average 1000). Application deadline: rolling. Application fee: $35. Electronic applications accepted. *Expenses:* Tuition $3894 per year full-time, $193 per credit hour part-time for state residents; $8114 per year full-time, $404 per credit hour part-time for nonresidents. Fees $125 per year full-time, $37 per semester (minimum) part-time. *Financial aid:* Research assistantships, teaching assistantships, and career-related internships or fieldwork available. *Faculty research:* Teaching/learning processes, anthropometric measurement, growth and development, motor development. Total annual research expenditures: $1.526 million. • Judith Rink, Chair, 803-777-3172. Application contact: John Spurgeon, Graduate Director, 803-777-3172.

University of South Dakota, School of Education, Division of Health, Physical Education and Recreation, Vermillion, SD 57069-2390. Awards MA. Part-time programs available. Faculty: 5 full-time (2 women), 1 (woman) part-time. Students: 20 full-time (6 women), 7 part-time (2 women). 20 applicants, 45% accepted. In 1997, 9 degrees awarded. *Degree requirements:* Thesis required (for some programs), foreign language not required. *Entrance requirements:* GRE General Test, MAT. Application deadline: rolling. Application fee: $15. *Expenses:* Tuition $1530 per year full-time, $85 per credit hour part-time for state residents; $4518 per year full-time, $251 per credit hour part-time for nonresidents. Fees $792 per year full-time, $44 per credit hour part-time. *Financial aid:* Teaching assistantships available. • Dr. Gale Weidow, Chair, 605-677-5336.

University of Southern Mississippi, College of Health and Human Sciences, School of Human Performance and Recreation, Hattiesburg, MS 39406-5167. Offers programs in human performance (Ed D, PhD), physical education (MS), recreation (MS). Part-time programs available. Faculty: 18 full-time (3 women), 1 part-time (0 women). Students: 67 full-time (24 women), 26 part-time (13 women); includes 4 minority (2 African Americans, 2 Asian Americans), 2 international. Average age 29. 63 applicants, 79% accepted. In 1997, 36 master's, 3 doctorates awarded. *Degree requirements:* For master's, thesis optional, foreign language not required. *Entrance requirements:* For master's, GRE General Test, minimum GPA of 2.75; for doctorate, GRE General Test, minimum GPA of 2.75 in last 60 hours. Application deadline: 8/9 (priority date; rolling processing). Application fee: $0 ($25 for international students). *Tuition:* $2870 per year full-time, $137 per credit hour part-time for state residents; $5972 per year full-time, $172 per credit hour part-time for nonresidents. *Financial aid:* Fellowships, research assistantships, teaching assistantships, partial tuition waivers, Federal Work-Study, institutionally sponsored loans, and career-related internships or fieldwork available. Financial aid application deadline: 3/15. *Faculty research:* Exercise physiology, health behaviors, resource management, activity interaction, site development. • Dr. Sandra Gangstead, Director, 601-266-5386.

University of South Florida, College of Education, School of Physical Education, Wellness, and Sport Studies, Tampa, FL 33620-9951. Offers program in physical education (MA). Part-time and evening/weekend programs available. Faculty: 10 full-time (3 women). Students: 14 part-time (5 women); includes 3 minority (1 Asian American, 2 Hispanics). Average age 31. 8 applicants, 50% accepted. In 1997, 7 degrees awarded. *Entrance requirements:* GRE General Test (minimum combined score of 1000), minimum GPA of 3.5 in last 60 hours. Application deadline: 6/1 (10/15 for spring admission). Application fee: $20. Electronic applications accepted. *Tuition:* $142 per credit hour for state residents; $486 per credit hour for nonresidents. *Financial aid:* Federal Work-Study, institutionally sponsored loans available. Aid available to part-time students. Financial aid applicants required to submit FAFSA. • Louis Bowers, Director, 813-974-3443. Fax: 813-974-4979. E-mail: bowers@tempest.coedu.usf.edu.

University of Tennessee at Chattanooga, School of Education, Department of Exercise Science, Health, and Leisure Studies, Chattanooga, TN 37403-2598. Offers program in athletic training (MS). Program new for fall 1998. *Entrance requirements:* GRE General Test or MAT. Application deadline: rolling. Application fee: $25. *Tuition:* $2864 per year full-time, $160 per credit hour part-time for state residents; $6806 per year full-time, $379 per credit hour part-time for nonresidents. *Financial aid:* Application deadline 4/1. • Dr. Mary Tanner, Dean, School of Education, 423-755-4249. Fax: 423-755-4044. E-mail: mtanner@utcvm.utc.edu. Application contact: Dr. Deborah Arfken, Assistant Provost for Graduate Studies, 423-755-4667. Fax: 423-755-4478. E-mail: darfken@utcvm.utc.edu.

The University of Texas of the Permian Basin, Graduate School, College of Arts and Sciences, Department of Behavioral Science, Program in Physical Education, Odessa, TX 79762-0001. Awards MA. Part-time and evening/weekend programs available. *Degree requirements:* Thesis required, foreign language not required. *Entrance requirements:* GRE General Test (minimum combined score of 1200), minimum GPA of 3.0. *Expenses:* Tuition $1314 per year full-time, $73 per hour part-time for state residents; $4896 per year full-time,

$272 per hour part-time for nonresidents. Fees $383 per year full-time, $111 per semester (minimum) part-time.

University of the Incarnate Word, School of Graduate Studies, College of Professional Studies, Programs in Education, Program in Physical Education, San Antonio, TX 78209-6397. Awards MA, M Ed. *Entrance requirements:* GRE, MAT, TOEFL (minimum score 550). Application deadline: 8/15 (priority date; rolling processing; 12/31 for spring admission). Application fee: $20. *Expenses:* Tuition $350 per semester hour. Fees $180 per year full-time, $111 per semester (minimum) part-time. • Application contact: Brian F. Dalton, Dean of Enrollment Services, 210-829-6005. Fax: 210-829-3921.

University of Toledo, College of Education and Allied Professions, Department of Health Promotion and Human Performance, Toledo, OH 43606-3398. Offerings include physical education (M Ed, Ed D, PhD). Department faculty: 17 full-time (5 women). *Degree requirements:* For doctorate, dissertation, comprehensive exams required, foreign language not required. *Entrance requirements:* For doctorate, GRE, minimum GPA of 2.7 (undergraduate), 3.0 (graduate). Application deadline: 8/1 (priority date; rolling processing). Application fee: $30. Electronic applications accepted. *Tuition:* $5907 per year full-time, $246 per hour part-time for state residents; $11,835 per year full-time, $493 per hour part-time for nonresidents. • Dr. Carol Plimpton, Chair, 419-530-2747. Fax: 419-530-4759. E-mail: cplimpt@utnet.utoledo.edu.

University of Victoria, Faculty of Education, School of Physical Education, Victoria, BC V8W 2Y2, Canada. Offers programs in coaching studies (M Ed), curriculum and instruction (MA), leisure service administration (MA), sports and exercise science (MA, M Sc). Part-time programs available. Faculty: 14 full-time (5 women), 5 part-time (0 women). Students: 85 full-time (39 women), 6 part-time (3 women); includes 5 international. Average age 30. 26 applicants, 58% accepted. In 1997, 11 degrees awarded. *Degree requirements:* Thesis required (for some programs), foreign language not required. *Average time to degree:* master's–2.9 years full-time. *Application deadline:* 4/30 (rolling processing). *Application fee:* $50. *Tuition:* $2080 per year full-time, $557 per semester part-time. *Financial aid:* In 1997–98, 1 fellowship (to a first-year student) averaging $1,500 per month and totaling $12,000, 2 research assistantships (both to first-year students) averaging $1,000 per month and totaling $18,000, 6 teaching assistantships (3 to first-year students) averaging $1,000 per month and totaling $40,000, 9 awards (6 to first-year students) totaling $70,000 were awarded; institutionally sponsored loans and career-related internships or fieldwork also available. Financial aid application deadline: 2/15. *Faculty research:* Motor control, physical training and performance, children and exercise, mental skills in sport, teaching effectiveness. Total annual research expenditures: $60,000. • Dr. D. Docherty, Director, 250-721-8375. E-mail: docherty@uvic.ca. Application contact: Gladys Whittal, Graduate Secretary, 250-721-8373. Fax: 250-721-6601. E-mail: gwhittal@uvic.ca/.

University of Virginia, Curry School of Education, Department of Human Services, Program in Health and Physical Education, Charlottesville, VA 22903. Awards M Ed, Ed D. Faculty: 36 full-time (12 women), 2 part-time (1 woman), 37 FTE. Students: 42 full-time (23 women), 5 part-time (all women); includes 5 minority (3 African Americans, 2 Hispanics). Average age 27. 109 applicants, 31% accepted. In 1997, 39 master's, 4 doctorates awarded. *Degree requirements:* For doctorate, dissertation required, foreign language not required. *Entrance requirements:* GRE General Test. Application deadline: 3/1 (11/15 for spring admission). Application fee: $40. *Tuition:* $4876 per year full-time, $944 per semester (minimum) part-time for state residents; $15,824 per year full-time, $2748 per semester (minimum) part-time for nonresidents. • Application contact: Linda Berry, Student Enrollment Coordinator, 804-924-0738. E-mail: lrb8e@virginia.edu.

The University of West Alabama, College of Education, Department of Physical Education and Athletic Training, Livingston, AL 35470. Offers program in physical education (MAT, M Ed). Part-time programs available. *Average time to degree:* master's–1 year full-time, 2 years part-time. *Entrance requirements:* GRE General Test, MAT, minimum GPA of 2.75. Application deadline: 9/10 (priority date; rolling processing; 3/24 for spring admission). Application fee: $15. *Tuition:* $70 per quarter hour.

University of West Florida, College of Arts and Social Sciences, Department of Health, Leisure, and Sports, Pensacola, FL 32514-5750. Offerings include physical education (MS). *Degree requirements:* Thesis or alternative. *Entrance requirements:* GRE General Test (minimum combined score of 1000), minimum GPA of 3.0. Application deadline: 7/1 (rolling processing; 11/1 for spring admission). Application fee: $20. *Tuition:* $131 per credit hour (minimum) for state residents; $436 per credit hour (minimum) for nonresidents. • Dr. C. B. Williamson, Chairperson, 850-474-2592.

University of Wisconsin–La Crosse, College of Health, Physical Education and Recreation, Department of Exercise and Sport Science, Program in General Pedagogy, La Crosse, WI 54601-3742. Awards MS. Faculty: 14 full-time (5 women), 6 part-time (2 women), 17.16 FTE. Students: 1 full-time (0 women), 6 part-time (0 women). Average age 27. 10 applicants, 50% accepted. In 1997, 1 degree awarded (100% found work related to degree). *Degree requirements:* Thesis optional, foreign language not required. *Entrance requirements:* Minimum GPA of 3.0 during previous 2 years, 2.85 overall. Application deadline: 3/1 (priority date; rolling processing). Application fee: $38. *Tuition:* $3737 per year full-time, $208 per credit part-time for state residents; $11,921 per year full-time, $633 per credit part-time for nonresidents. *Financial aid:* In 1997–98, teaching assistantships averaging $546 per month were awarded; Federal Work-Study, institutionally sponsored loans, and career-related internships or fieldwork also available. Financial aid application deadline: 3/15; applicants required to submit FAFSA. *Faculty research:* Teaching methodology, curriculum, fitness, sport administration, adventure education. • Dr. Jeffrey Steffen, Graduate Program Coordinator, 608-785-6535. E-mail: steffan@mail.uwlax.edu. Application contact: Tim Lewis, Director of Admissions, 608-785-8939. Fax: 608-785-6695. E-mail: admissions@mail.uwlax.edu.

University of Wisconsin–La Crosse, College of Health, Physical Education and Recreation, Department of Exercise and Sport Science, Program in Special Adaptive Physical Education, La Crosse, WI 54601-3742. Awards MS. Part-time programs available. Faculty: 3 full-time (0 women). Students: 4 full-time (2 women); includes 1 minority (Asian American). Average age 24. 15 applicants, 80% accepted. In 1997, 5 degrees awarded (80% found work related to degree, 20% continued full-time study). *Degree requirements:* Critical analysis project or thesis required, foreign language not required. *Average time to degree:* master's–1.2 years full-time, 4.5 years part-time. *Entrance requirements:* Minimum GPA of 3.0 during previous 2 years, 2.85 overall. Application deadline: 7/1 (priority date; rolling processing). Application fee: $38. *Tuition:* $3737 per year full-time, $208 per credit part-time for state residents; $11,921 per year full-time, $633 per credit part-time for nonresidents. *Financial aid:* In 1997–98, 3 students received aid, including 3 federal training stipends averaging $772 per month and totaling $23,160; partial tuition waivers, Federal Work-Study, institutionally sponsored loans, and career-related internships or fieldwork also available. Aid available to part-time students. Financial aid application deadline: 3/15; applicants required to submit FAFSA. *Faculty research:* Physical fitness of the physically disabled, teacher preparation in adapted physical education, motor development of the disabled. • Dr. Patrick DiRocco, Coordinator, 608-785-8695. Fax: 608-785-8206. E-mail: dirocco@mail.uwlax.edu. Application contact: Tim Lewis, Director of Admissions, 608-785-8939. Fax: 608-785-6695. E-mail: admissions@mail.uwlax.edu.

University of Wyoming, College of Health Sciences, Department of Physical and Health Education, Laramie, WY 82071. Awards MS. Part-time programs available. Faculty: 8 full-time (3 women). Students: 11 full-time (7 women), 13 part-time (5 women). Average age 26. 21 applicants, 43% accepted. In 1997, 13 degrees awarded (38% found work related to degree, 62% continued full-time study). *Degree requirements:* Thesis optional, foreign language not required. *Average time to degree:* master's–2 years full-time, 4 years part-time. *Entrance requirements:* GRE General Test (minimum combined score of 900), minimum GPA of 3.0. Application deadline: 6/1 (priority date; rolling processing; 11/1 for spring admission). Application fee: $40. *Expenses:* Tuition $2430 per year full-time, $135 per credit hour part-time for state residents; $7518 per year full-time, $418 per credit hour part-time for nonresidents. Fees $386 per year full-time, $9.25 per credit hour part-time. *Financial aid:* In 1997–98, 18 students received aid, including 7 graduate assistantships (4 to first-year students) averaging $470 per month; career-related internships or fieldwork also available. Financial aid application deadline: 3/1. *Faculty research:* Teacher effectiveness, effects of exercising on heart function, physiological responses of overtraining, psychological benefits of physical activity, instruction assessment and supervision of effective teaching in physical education, physical activity of children. Total annual research expenditures: $25,000. • Dr. Paul Thomas, Associate Dean, 307-766-5285. Application contact: Dr. Mark Byra, Graduate Coordinator, 307-766-5227. Fax: 307-766-4098. E-mail: byra@uwyo.edu.

Utah State University, College of Education, Department of Health, Physical Education and Recreation, Logan, UT 84322. Offers programs in health education (MS), physical education (M Ed, MS). Faculty: 12 full-time (5 women). Students: 46 full-time (17 women), 14 part-time (7 women). Average age 34. 21 applicants, 76% accepted. In 1997, 12 degrees awarded. *Entrance requirements:* GRE General Test (score in 40th percentile or higher) or MAT, TOEFL (minimum score 550), minimum GPA of 3.0. Application deadline: 6/15 (priority date; rolling processing; 10/15 for spring admission). Application fee: $40. *Expenses:* Tuition $1448 per year full-time, $624 per year part-time for state residents; $5082 per year full-time, $2192 per year part-time for nonresidents. Fees $421 per year full-time, $165 per year part-time. *Financial aid:* Teaching assistantships, full tuition waivers, Federal Work-Study, institutionally sponsored loans, and career-related internships or fieldwork available. Financial aid application deadline: 2/10. *Faculty research:* Sport psychology intervention, motor learning biomechanics, pedagogy, physiology. • Dr. Art Jones, Head, 435-797-1499. E-mail: ajonz@fsl.ed.usu.edu. Application contact: Dr. Richard Gordin, Graduate Program Chair, 435-797-1506. Fax: 435-797-3759. E-mail: gordin@cc.usu.edu.

Valdosta State University, College of Education, Department of Health and Physical Education, Valdosta, GA 31698. Awards M Ed. Faculty: 3 full-time (0 women). Students: 13 full-time (4 women), 4 part-time (0 women); includes 1 minority (Asian American), 1 international. 10 applicants, 70% accepted. In 1997, 12 degrees awarded. *Entrance requirements:* GRE General Test (minimum combined score of 800). Application deadline: 8/1 (rolling processing). Application fee: $10. *Expenses:* Tuition $2472 per year full-time, $83 per semester hour part-time for state residents; $8472 per year full-time, $333 per semester hour part-time for nonresidents. Fees $236 per year full-time. *Financial aid:* Teaching assistantships available. • Dr. Stan Andrews, Head, 912-333-7161. E-mail: sandrews@grits.valdosta.peachnet.edu. Application contact: Coordinator, 912-333-7161. Fax: 912-333-5972.

Virginia Commonwealth University, School of Education, Program in Physical Education, Richmond, VA 23284-9005. Awards MS. Faculty: 7 full-time (2 women). Students: 8 full-time (4 women), 14 part-time (11 women); includes 2 minority (both African Americans). Average age 29. 18 applicants, 89% accepted. In 1997, 8 degrees awarded. *Entrance requirements:* GRE General Test or MAT. Application deadline: 7/1 (rolling processing; 11/15 for spring admission). Application fee: $30 ($0 for international students). *Tuition:* $4960 per year full-time, $257 per credit part-time for state residents; $12,652 per year full-time, $684 per credit part-time for nonresidents. *Financial aid:* Federal Work-Study, institutionally sponsored loans, and career-related internships or fieldwork available. Aid available to part-time students. Financial aid application deadline: 3/1. • Dr. Jack H. Schiltz, Head, 804-828-1284. Fax: 804-828-1946. Application contact: Dr. Michael D. Davis, Interim Director, Graduate Studies, 804-828-6530. Fax: 804-828-1323. E-mail: mddavis@vcu.edu.

Virginia Polytechnic Institute and State University, College of Human Resources and Education, Department of Teaching and Learning, Blacksburg, VA 24061. Offerings include health and physical education (MS Ed). *Application deadline:* 12/1 (priority date; rolling processing). *Application fee:* $25. *Tuition:* $4927 per year full-time, $792 per semester (minimum) part-time for state residents; $7537 per year full-time, $1227 per semester (minimum) part-time for nonresidents. • Dr. John Burton, Head, 540-231-5347. E-mail: teach@vt.edu.

Wayne State College, Division of Physical Education, Wayne, NE 68787. Awards MSE. Faculty: 3 part-time (0 women). Students: 16 full-time (6 women), 10 part-time (2 women); includes 5 minority (4 African Americans, 1 Hispanic). Average age 28. In 1997, 13 degrees awarded. *Degree requirements:* Comprehensive exam, research paper required, thesis optional, foreign language not required. *Entrance requirements:* GRE General Test, minimum GPA of 2.8. Application deadline: rolling. Application fee: $10. *Expenses:* Tuition $1788 per year full-time, $75 per credit hour part-time for state residents; $3576 per year full-time, $149 per credit hour part-time for nonresidents. Fees $360 per year full-time, $15 per credit hour part-time. *Financial aid:* In 1997–98, 5 teaching assistantships (3 to first-year students) were awarded; career-related internships or fieldwork also available. Financial aid application deadline: 5/1; applicants required to submit FAFSA. *Faculty research:* Aerobic fitness for school-age children, life-style adjustment programs for senior citizens, computerized evaluation of student athletes, wellness education. • Dr. Ralph Barclay, Head, 402-375-7301.

Wayne State College, Division of Education, Program in Curriculum and Instruction, Wayne, NE 68787. Offerings include health and physical education/health (MSE), health and physical education/pedagogy (MSE). *Degree requirements:* Comprehensive exam, research paper required, foreign language not required. *Entrance requirements:* GRE General Test. Application deadline: rolling. Application fee: $10. *Expenses:* Tuition $1788 per year full-time, $75 per credit hour part-time for state residents; $3576 per year full-time, $149 per credit hour part-time for nonresidents. Fees $360 per year full-time, $15 per credit hour part-time. • Dr. Diane Alexander, Head, Division of Education, 402-375-7389.

Wayne State University, College of Education, Division of Health and Physical Education, Detroit, MI 48202. Offers programs in health education (M Ed), physical education (M Ed), recreation and park services (MA), sports administration (MA). Faculty: 34. Students: 30 full-time (14 women), 144 part-time (73 women). 79 applicants, 75% accepted. In 1997, 48 degrees awarded. *Degree requirements:* Thesis required (for some programs), foreign language not required. *Entrance requirements:* GRE General Test. Application deadline: 7/1. Application fee: $20 ($30 for international students). *Expenses:* Tuition $163 per credit hour for state residents; $355 per credit hour for nonresidents. Fees $498 per year full-time, $114 per semester (minimum) part-time. *Financial aid:* In 1997–98, 5 teaching assistantships (2 to first-year students) averaging $800 per month and totaling $40,000 were awarded; career-related internships or fieldwork also available. *Faculty research:* Fitness in urban children, motor development of crack babies, effects of caffeine on metabolism/exercise, body composition of elite youth sports participants, systematic observation of teaching. • Dr. Sarah Erbaugh, Assistant Dean, 313-577-4265. Application contact: John Wirth, Graduate Program Coordinator, 313-577-5896. Fax: 313-577-5999.

West Chester University of Pennsylvania, School of Health Sciences, Department of Kinesiology, West Chester, PA 19383. Offers programs in coaching (Certificate), driver education (Certificate), exercise and sport physiology (MS), general exercise science (MS), physical education (MS), safety (Certificate), sport and athletic administration (MSA). Faculty: 1 full-time, 9 part-time. Students: 14 full-time (6 women), 34 part-time (15 women); includes 3 minority (2 African Americans, 1 Asian American), 1 international. Average age 28. 35 applicants, 86% accepted. In 1997, 11 master's awarded. *Degree requirements:* For master's, comprehensive exam required, foreign language and thesis not required. *Entrance requirements:* For master's, GRE, interview. Application deadline: 4/15 (priority date; rolling processing; 10/15 for spring admission). Application fee: $25. *Expenses:* Tuition $3468 per year full-time, $193 per credit part-time for state residents; $6236 per year full-time, $346 per credit part-time for nonresidents. Fees $660 per year full-time, $38 per credit part-time. *Financial aid:* In 1997–98, 4 research assistantships were awarded. Financial aid application deadline: 2/15. • Dr. Monita Lank, Chair, 610-436-2260. Application contact: Dr. John G. Williams, Graduate Coordinator, 610-436-3119.

Directory: Physical Education; Cross-Discipline Announcements

Western Carolina University, College of Education and Allied Professions, Department of Health and Human Performance, Cullowhee, NC 28723. Offers program in physical education (MA Ed, MAT). Part-time and evening/weekend programs available. Faculty: 7 (3 women). Students: 6 full-time (2 women), 3 part-time (1 woman); includes 1 minority (African American). 4 applicants, 75% accepted. In 1997, 6 degrees awarded. *Degree requirements:* Comprehensive exam required, thesis optional, foreign language not required. *Entrance requirements:* GRE General Test. Application deadline: rolling. Application fee: $35. *Tuition:* $1799 per year full-time, $144 per credit hour (minimum) part-time for state residents; $9069 per year full-time, $1053 per credit hour (minimum) part-time for nonresidents. *Financial aid:* In 1997–98, 8 students received aid, including 8 teaching assistantships (3 to first-year students) totaling $30,000; fellowships, research assistantships, Federal Work-Study, institutionally sponsored loans also available. Financial aid application deadline: 3/15. • Dr. David Claxton, Head, 828-227-7332. Application contact: Kathleen Owen, Assistant to the Dean, 828-227-7398. Fax: 828-227-7480.

Western Carolina University, College of Education and Allied Professions, Department of Administration, Curriculum and Instruction, Programs in Secondary Education, Cullowhee, NC 28723. Offerings include physical education (MAT). *Degree requirements:* Comprehensive exam required, foreign language and thesis not required. *Entrance requirements:* GRE General Test. Application deadline: rolling. Application fee: $35. *Tuition:* $1799 per year full-time, $144 per credit hour (minimum) part-time for state residents; $9069 per year full-time, $1053 per credit hour (minimum) part-time for nonresidents. • Application contact: Kathleen Owen, Assistant to the Dean, 828-227-7398. Fax: 828-227-7480.

Western Illinois University, College of Education and Human Services, Department of Physical Education, Macomb, IL 61455-1390. Offers programs in physical education (MS), sport management (MS). Part-time programs available. Faculty: 18 full-time (12 women). Students: 59 full-time (22 women), 33 part-time (10 women); includes 3 minority (1 African American, 1 Hispanic, 1 Native American), 7 international. Average age 28. 60 applicants, 75% accepted. In 1997, 50 degrees awarded. *Degree requirements:* Thesis or alternative required, foreign language not required. *Entrance requirements:* Minimum GPA of 3.0. Application deadline: rolling. Application fee: $0 ($25 for international students). *Expenses:* Tuition $2304 per year full-time, $96 per semester hour part-time for state residents; $6912 per year full-time, $288 per semester hour part-time for nonresidents. Fees $944 per year full-time, $33 per semester hour part-time. *Financial aid:* In 1997–98, 37 students received aid, including 37 research assistantships averaging $610 per month; full tuition waivers also available. Financial aid applicants required to submit FAFSA. *Faculty research:* Steroid metabolism, health education. • Dr. Donna Phillips, Chairperson, 309-298-1981. Application contact: Barbara Baily, Director of Graduate Studies, 309-298-1806. Fax: 309-298-2245. E-mail: barb_baily@ccmail.wiu.edu.

Western Kentucky University, College of Education, Department of Physical Education and Recreation, Program in Physical Education, Bowling Green, KY 42101-3576. Awards MA Ed, MS. Part-time and evening/weekend programs available. Faculty: 6 full-time (1 woman). Students: 5 part-time (1 woman). Average age 26. 7 applicants, 71% accepted. In 1997, 3 degrees awarded. *Degree requirements:* Thesis optional, foreign language not required. *Entrance requirements:* GRE General Test. Application deadline: 8/1 (priority date; rolling processing; 12/1 for spring admission). Application fee: $20. *Tuition:* $2460 per year full-time, $133 per credit hour part-time for state residents; $6700 per year full-time, $369 per credit hour part-time for nonresidents. *Financial aid:* Teaching assistantships, Federal Work-Study, institutionally sponsored loans available. Aid available to part-time students. Financial aid application deadline: 4/1; applicants required to submit FAFSA. • Dr. Thaddeus Crews, Coordinator, 502-745-3347.

Western Maryland College, Department of Education, Program in Physical Education, Westminster, MD 21157-4390. Awards MS. Part-time and evening/weekend programs available. Faculty: 1 full-time (0 women), 4 part-time (1 woman). Students: 6 full-time (1 woman), 134 part-time (112 women). In 1997, 8 degrees awarded. *Degree requirements:* Thesis optional, foreign language not required. *Entrance requirements:* GRE General Test, MAT, or NTE. Application deadline: rolling. Application fee: $35. *Expenses:* Tuition $210 per credit hour. Fees $30 per semester. *Financial aid:* Application deadline 3/1. • Dr. Samuel Case, Chairman, 410-857-2570. Application contact: Jeanette Witt, Coordinator of Graduate Records, 410-857-2513. Fax: 410-857-2515. E-mail: jwitt@wmdc.edu.

Western Michigan University, College of Education, Department of Health, Physical Education and Recreation, Kalamazoo, MI 49008. Offers programs in administration (MA), athletic training (MA), coaching and sports studies (MA), exercise science (MA), motor development (MA), physical education (MA), special education for handicapped children (MA). Students: 7 full-time (3 women), 91 part-time (45 women); includes 6 minority (2 African Americans, 3 Asian Americans, 1 Hispanic), 6 international. 88 applicants, 82% accepted. In 1997, 45 degrees awarded. *Application deadline:* 2/15 (priority date; rolling processing). *Application fee:* $25. *Expenses:* Tuition $154 per credit hour for state residents; $372 per credit hour for nonresidents. Fees $602 per year full-time, $132 per semester part-time. *Financial aid:* Fellowships, research assistantships, teaching assistantships, Federal Work-Study available. Financial aid application deadline: 2/15; applicants required to submit FAFSA. • Dr. Debra Berkey, Chair, 616-387-2705. Application contact: Paula J. Boodt, Coordinator, Graduate Admissions and Recruitment, 616-387-2000. E-mail: paulaboodt@wmich.edu.

Western Washington University, College of Arts and Sciences, Department of Physical Education and Health, Bellingham, WA 98225-5996. Offers program in physical education (M Ed). Part-time programs available. Faculty: 6 (4 women). Students: 19 full-time (13 women), 3 part-time (1 woman). 21 applicants, 81% accepted. In 1997, 3 degrees awarded. *Degree requirements:* Thesis required, foreign language not required. *Entrance requirements:* GRE General Test, TOEFL (average 567), minimum GPA of 3.0 in last 60 semester hours or last 90 quarter hours. Application deadline: 6/1 (rolling processing; 2/1 for spring admission). Application fee: $35. *Expenses:* Tuition $4200 per year full-time, $140 per credit part-time for state residents; $12,780 per year full-time, $426 per credit part-time for nonresidents. Fees $249 per year full-time, $83 per quarter part-time. *Financial aid:* Teaching assistantships, partial tuition waivers, Federal Work-Study, institutionally sponsored loans available. Aid available to part-time students. Financial aid application deadline: 3/31. • Dr. Kathy Knutzen, Chair, 360-650-3055. Application contact: Dr. Lorraine Brilla, Graduate Adviser, 360-650-3056.

West Virginia University, School of Physical Education, Morgantown, WV 26506. Awards MS, Ed D. Faculty: 25 full-time (7 women), 6 part-time (1 woman). Students: 95 full-time (32 women), 31 part-time (12 women); includes 7 minority (6 African Americans, 1 Asian American), 6 international. Average age 27. 140 applicants, 71% accepted. In 1997, 38 master's, 5 doctorates awarded. *Degree requirements:* For doctorate, dissertation, comprehensive exam, oral exam required, foreign language not required. *Entrance requirements:* For master's, GRE or MAT, TOEFL (minimum score 550), minimum GPA of 3.0; for doctorate, GRE General Test or MAT, TOEFL (minimum score 550), minimum GPA of 3.5. Application deadline: 3/1 (priority date). Application fee: $45. *Tuition:* $2820 per year full-time, $149 per credit hour part-time for state residents; $8104 per year full-time, $443 per credit hour part-time for nonresidents. *Financial aid:* In 1997–98, 1 research assistantship, 3 teaching assistantships averaging $589 per month, 3 graduate administrative assistantships (1 to a first-year student) were awarded; full and partial tuition waivers, Federal Work-Study, institutionally sponsored loans, and career-related internships or fieldwork also available. Aid available to part-time students. Financial aid application deadline: 2/1; applicants required to submit FAFSA. *Faculty research:* Sport psychosociology, teacher education, exercise psychology, counseling. • Dr. Lynn Housner, Assistant Dean, 304-293-3295 Ext. 287. Application contact: Carol Straight, Student Records Assistant, 304-293-3295 Ext. 265. Fax: 304-293-4641. E-mail: u7460@wvnvm.wvnet.edu.

Whitworth College, Graduate Studies in Education, Program in Physical Education and Sport Administration, Spokane, WA 99251-0001. Awards MA. *Degree requirements:* Comprehensive exams, internship, practicum, research project, or thesis required, foreign language not required. *Entrance requirements:* GRE General Test. Application deadline: 9/1 (priority date; rolling processing; 2/1 for spring admission). Application fee: $25.

Wichita State University, College of Education, Department of Health and Physical Education, Wichita, KS 67260. Offers programs in physical education (M Ed), including exercise science and wellness; sports administration (M Ed), including exercise science and wellness. Part-time programs available. Faculty: 5 full-time (3 women), 17 part-time (9 women). Students: 23 full-time (9 women), 69 part-time (30 women); includes 8 minority (2 African Americans, 3 Asian Americans, 2 Hispanics, 1 Native American), 1 international. Average age 29. 72 applicants, 54% accepted. In 1997, 29 degrees awarded. *Degree requirements:* Comprehensive exam required, thesis optional, foreign language not required. *Entrance requirements:* TOEFL (minimum score 550), minimum GPA of 2.75. Application deadline: 7/1 (priority date; rolling processing; 1/1 for spring admission). Application fee: $25 ($40 for international students). Electronic applications accepted. *Expenses:* Tuition $2303 per year full-time, $96 per credit hour part-time for state residents; $7691 per year full-time, $321 per credit hour part-time for nonresidents. Fees $490 per year full-time, $75 per semester (minimum) part-time. *Financial aid:* In 1997–98, 11 teaching assistantships averaging $638 per month and totaling $56,000, 17 graduate assistantships averaging $679 per month and totaling $91,951 were awarded; research assistantships, Federal Work-Study, institutionally sponsored loans, and career-related internships or fieldwork also available. Financial aid application deadline: 4/1. • Dr. Susan K. Kovar, Chairperson, 316-978-3340. E-mail: kovar@wsuhub.uc.twsu.edu. Application contact: Dr. Lori Miller, Graduate Coordinator, 316-978-3340. Fax: 316-978-3302. E-mail: lmiller@wsuhub.uc.twsu.edu.

Winona State University, Graduate Studies, College of Education, Education Program, Winona, MN 55987-5838. Offerings include physical education (MS). *Entrance requirements:* GRE General Test. Application deadline: 8/8 (priority date; rolling processing; 2/17 for spring admission). Application fee: $20. • Dr. Robert Clay, Chairperson, 507-457-5353. E-mail: rclay@vax2.winona.msus.edu.

Winthrop University, College of Education, Program in Physical Education, Rock Hill, SC 29733. Awards MS. Part-time programs available. Students: 2 full-time (1 woman), 2 part-time (1 woman). Average age 33. In 1997, 1 degree awarded. *Degree requirements:* Comprehensive exam required, thesis optional, foreign language not required. *Entrance requirements:* GRE General Test (minimum combined score of 800) or NTE, minimum GPA of 3.0. Application deadline: 7/15 (priority date; rolling processing; 12/1 for spring admission). Application fee: $35. *Tuition:* $3928 per year full-time, $164 per credit hour part-time for state residents; $7060 per year full-time, $294 per credit hour part-time for nonresidents. *Financial aid:* Graduate assistantships, graduate scholarships, Federal Work-Study, and career-related internships or fieldwork available. Aid available to part-time students. Financial aid application deadline: 2/1; applicants required to submit FAFSA. • Dr. Mickey Taylor, Chairman, 803-323-2123. Fax: 803-323-2124. E-mail: taylorm@winthrop.edu. Application contact: Sharon Johnson, Director of Graduate Studies, 803-323-2204. Fax: 803-323-2292. E-mail: johnsons@winthrop.edu.

Wright State University, College of Education and Human Services, Department of Health, Physical Education, and Recreation, Dayton, OH 45435. Awards MA, M Ed. Students: 3 full-time (2 women), 2 part-time (1 woman). Average age 30. 2 applicants, 50% accepted. *Degree requirements:* Thesis (for some programs), comprehensive exam required, foreign language not required. *Entrance requirements:* GRE General Test, MAT, TOEFL (minimum score 550). Application fee: $25. *Tuition:* $5109 per year full-time, $161 per credit hour part-time for state residents; $9039 per year full-time, $282 per credit hour part-time for nonresidents. *Financial aid:* Available to part-time students. Financial aid applicants required to submit FAFSA. *Faculty research:* Motor learning, motor development, exercise physiology, adapted physical education. • Dr. G. William Gayle, Chair, 937-775-3223. Fax: 937-775-3301. Application contact: Gerald C. Malicki, Assistant Dean and Director of Graduate Admissions and Records, 937-775-2976. Fax: 937-775-2357. E-mail: wsugrad@wright.edu.

Cross-Discipline Announcements

Ohio University, Graduate Studies, College of Arts and Sciences, Department of Biological Sciences, Athens, OH 45701-2979.

The Department of Biological Sciences offers master's and doctoral degrees in biological sciences. Graduate education is conducted in 5 research focus groups. The exercise physiology and muscle biology group focuses on effects of exercise, nutrition, gender, and aging on human performance, muscle histology, muscle physiology, and reproductive endocrinology.

State University of New York at Albany, School of Public Health, Executive Park South, Albany, NY 12203-3727.

The MS in health policy, management, and behavior and the MPH with concentrations in health administration and behavioral science combine the teaching of theory with contemporary public health practice. The participation of the NYS Department of Health provides outstanding training for careers in health policy analysis and program development and evaluation. MS students can select from 3 tracks: health systems, management, and social behavior and community health. See the in-depth description of the School of Public Health.

AMERICAN UNIVERSITY

Department of Health and Fitness
Health Fitness Management Program

Program of Study

In response to the recognized need for the development of professional health fitness leaders for business, community, industry, and federal, state, and local government, American University instituted a Master of Science degree program in health fitness management in 1980. Offered through the Department of Health and Fitness, the program integrates managerial and leadership skills with scientific and clinical knowledge of exercise physiology, human physiological chemistry, behavioral psychology, and nutrition. The primary objective of this program is to provide a competency-based, multidisciplinary academic track for individuals interested in assuming leadership and managerial positions within the health and fitness industry. The program requires completion of 42 semester hours of graduate study. Students have an option of completing in-service training or a master's thesis. Up to 6 semester hours of graduate study may be transferred at the time an applicant is admitted to the program. Applicants who have the necessary educational and/or professional background may apply for a waiver of specific courses (up to 9 semester hours).

Research Facilities

The Health Fitness Management Program is an integral part of the University's National Center for Health Fitness (NCHF). The central purpose of the NCHF is to provide leadership for the nation in the area of health risk identification and lifestyle improvement. Within the 6,000-square-foot space occupied by the NCHF is a human performance laboratory with state-of-the-art diagnostic equipment for assessment of cardiovascular fitness and pulmonary function; there are also a modern hydrostatic weighing facility, a recording studio for production of health fitness promotion materials, and equipment used to facilitate student learning. A computer communication system is also an integral part of the NCHF system. In addition to the main center on campus, the NCHF operates several off-campus facilities, two of which are work-site health and fitness centers.

The Bender Library and Learning Resources Center houses more than 600,000 volumes and 3,000 periodical titles as well as extensive microform collections and a nonprint media center. Graduate students have unlimited borrowing privileges at six other college and university libraries in the Washington Research Library Consortium, all accessible through the online catalog. Microcomputer resources are extensive and can be used 24 hours a day at various campus locations.

Financial Aid

Fellowships, scholarships, and graduate assistantships are available to full-time students. Special opportunity grants for minority group members parallel the regular honor awards and take the form of assistantships and scholarships. Research and teaching fellowships provide stipends plus tuition. Graduate assistantships provide up to 18 credit hours of tuition remission per year.

Cost of Study

For the 1998–99 academic year, tuition is $687 per credit hour. Special fees are charged for applied human physiology and human physiological chemistry labs.

Living and Housing Costs

Although many graduate students live off campus, the University provides graduate dormitory rooms and apartments. The Off-Campus Housing Office maintains a referral file of rooms and apartments. Housing costs in Washington, D.C., are comparable to those in other major metropolitan areas.

Student Group

Approximately 45 students are enrolled in the M.S. program. Students of all ages come from educational backgrounds in health, education, business, psychology, communications, and other disciplines.

Student Outcomes

Students who graduate from American University with a master's degree in health fitness management find employment in a variety of positions in the health field. The majority of graduates work in corporate or commercial fitness centers. Other areas and sites of employment include health education, hospital-based wellness programs, nonprofit organizations, government agencies, private consulting, pharmaceuticals, research, the managed care industry, and many others.

Location

Opportunities for research, internships, cooperative educational placements, and part-time jobs exist in every discipline. Local bus and rail transportation from the campus provides easy access to sites such as the President's Council on Physical Fitness and various corporations in the greater metropolitan area.

The University

American University was founded as a Methodist institution, chartered by Congress in 1893, and intended originally for graduate study only. The University is located on an 84-acre site in a residential area of northwest Washington. As a member of the Consortium of Universities of the Washington Metropolitan Area, American University can offer its degree candidates the option of taking courses at other consortium universities for residence credit.

Applying

The department requires completion of a supplemental application form, a Statement of Health Fitness Philosophy, and a resume. A personal interview is encouraged. Course work in undergraduate human anatomy and physiology and exercise physiology are program prerequisites. There is a $50 application fee.

Correspondence and Information

To contact faculty members and for specific program information:

Dr. Robert C. Karch, Program Director
Health Fitness Management Program
College of Arts and Sciences
American University
National Center for Health Fitness
Nebraska Hall-Lower Level
4400 Massachusetts Avenue, NW
Washington, D.C. 20016-8037

Telephone: 202-885-6275
Fax: 202-885-6288
E-mail: nchfms@american.edu
World Wide Web: http://www.healthy.american.edu

For an application and University catalog:

Graduate Admissions Office
American University
4400 Massachusetts Avenue, NW
Washington, D.C. 20016-8001

Telephone: 202-885-6000
E-mail: afa@american.edu

American University

THE FACULTY AND THEIR RESEARCH

Elmore R. Alexander III, Professor and Associate Dean of Academic Affairs; Ph.D., Georgia.
Judith Barlow, Assistant Professor of Computer Science and Information Systems; Ph.D., Colorado.
Mark Bergel, Adjunct Faculty and Deputy Director of NCHF; Ph.D., American. Stress management, mind-body-spirit, alternative medicine.
Frederick W. Carson, Associate Professor of Chemistry; Ph.D., Chicago. Human biochemistry.
Carlos J. Crespo, Assistant Professor of Health and Fitness; Dr.P.H., Loma Linda. Applied physiology and research methods.
Robert C. Karch, Professor of Health and Fitness and Chair/Program Director; Ed.D., American. Strategic planning and critical issues in health promotion.
David C. Martin, Professor and Director of Human Resource Management Program; Ph.D., Maryland. Organizational behavior and human resource management.
Marc Schaeffer, Research Faculty of Health and Fitness; Ph.D., Uniformed Services Health Sciences. Health promotion evaluation.
Morley Segal, Professor of Public Administration; Ph.D., Claremont. Organizational management.
Anastasia Snelling, Assistant Professor of Health and Fitness; Ph.D., American. Nutrition and health communications.
Brian T. Yates, Associate Professor of Psychology; Ph.D., Stanford. Behavioral medicine.

Selected Master's Theses

"Health Promotion Activities: Differences Between Most and Least Admired Companies," Jennifer Posa (1997).
"The Prevalence of Health Promotion Programs in Health Maintenance Organizations," Holly Morganti (1997).
"Certification in the Fitness Industry: The Exam Development for ACE and ACSM from 1975–1994," Tiffiny Marinelli (1995).
"A Study Comparing Maryland State Legislators' Health Behaviors to Those of Their Constituents," Tiffin Bumpass (1992).
"The Correlation Between Physical Activity and Perceived Health Status of People Over Fifty Years of Age," Sharon Jessup (1992).
"The Relationship Between Nutrition Knowledge, Dietary Habits, Human Performance, and HDL-Levels Among Army Special Forces Soldiers," Ann Philopena (1991).
"The Effect of a Five-Week Aerobic Exercise Program in the Body Image of Adolescent Girls," Patricia Scanlon (1991).
"Job Satisfaction and Turnover of Aerobic Dance Instructors," Kelly Eitel (1989).
"The Relationship Between Estimated Risk Age and Perceived Stress," Mary Laedtke (1989).

BENEDICTINE UNIVERSITY

Department of Exercise Physiology

Programs of Study

Benedictine University offers two exercise-related programs, both of which lead to the Master of Science degree. Both programs may be completed on a part-time or full-time basis. The exercise physiology program, with a specialization in preventive and rehabilitative cardiovascular health (PARCH), requires 90 quarter hours of credit and is designed for those who wish to work in both the prevention of cardiovascular disease and the rehabilitation of those who have experienced cardiovascular problems. The program is designed in accordance with the policies of the American College of Sports Medicine (ACSM). The PARCH program requires course work in the biological bases of cardiovascular disease and four internships that must include both preventive and rehabilitative sites.

The Master of Science in Fitness Management (MFM) requires 78 quarter hours of credit and is designed for the person who plans to work more as a manager than as an exercise physiologist but still needs to have a basic understanding of exercise physiology in order to effectively supervise and manage personnel in a cardiovascular fitness setting. Required courses come from the graduate departments of exercise physiology, management, and public health.

Both programs require the passing of a comprehensive oral examination in physiology.

Internships are an important part of the program. They provide the student with hands-on experience under the guidance of a practicing professional. There are two types of internships: preventive and rehabilitative. Sites available for preventive internships include YMCAs, corporate settings, and fitness programs. Sites for rehabilitative internships are primarily located in hospitals.

Research Facilities

The University has modern, well-equipped laboratories for physical fitness and cardiovascular health programs. Equipment includes cycle ergometers, computerized treadmills, a Sensormedics MMC, an electrocardiograph, and anthropometric measurement devices, including a hydrostatic weighing tank. The Theodore Lownik Library is the central depository on campus for all media research materials. The collection contains more than 165,000 cataloged items, approximately 30,000 federal government documents, and a variety of audiovisual educational items. The library receives nearly 1,000 periodical and newspaper titles regularly. The DIALOG computer research service makes available on line more than 200 scholarly and commercial databases. Through participation in the OCLC network, the library has interlibrary loan access to all libraries in the United States and Canada. The library also receives direct truck delivery of books through its membership in ILLINET.

Financial Aid

The only form of financial aid generally available to graduate students at Benedictine University is a Federal Stafford Student Loan. Graduate students may borrow up to $18,500 a year (a minimum of $10,000 must be in unsubsidized Stafford Loans). These low-interest loans may be used for tuition, fees, books, living expenses, and other college-related costs. Loan applicants are required to submit the Free Application for Federal Student Aid (FAFSA). Federal regulations require demonstration of financial need to qualify for the Federal Stafford Student Loan Program.

Cost of Study

The 1997–98 tuition was $295 per quarter credit hour.

Living and Housing Costs

The University provides no housing or assistance in securing off-campus housing. Accommodations in surrounding communities range from moderate to expensive.

Student Group

The programs mainly attract students with backgrounds in physical education, biology, nursing, and physical therapy. Approximately 80 percent of the students are female; the average age is 25. Graduates enter positions in the fields of cardiac rehabilitation and preventive medicine (mainly in the area of corporate fitness) in approximately equal numbers; however, the number of positions in corporate fitness is increasing rapidly. Graduates are very successful in obtaining employment in the field of exercise physiology.

Location

Benedictine University is located near the village of Lisle, about 1 mile west of Route 53. It is about 25 miles from downtown Chicago and a 5-minute drive from the Route 53 exit of the East-West Tollway (Interstate 88). From the east and west, it is easily accessible from Ogden Avenue (Route 34). The North-South Tollway's Maple Avenue exit is 2 miles east of the campus. Students take advantage of the many cultural and recreational facilities located in Chicago and the surrounding area.

The University

Benedictine University is an independent, coeducational University founded in 1887 by the Benedictine monks of St. Procopius Abbey. The University, which has an operating budget that exceeds $14 million, has demonstrated financial stability. Benedictine University is a comprehensive, multifaceted university oriented by Christian values and affiliated with the Benedictine Order of the Catholic Church.

Applying

Requirements for admission include a bachelor's degree with a GPA of at least 2.75 (on a 4.0 scale) and previous course work in general anatomy and physiology, general chemistry (may be taken concurrently with a graduate program), and mathematics through college algebra. Additional information can be obtained from the Office of Graduate Admissions.

Correspondence and Information

Department of Exercise Physiology
Benedictine University
5700 College Road
Lisle, Illinois 60532
Telephone: 630-829-6227

Benedictine University

THE FACULTY

Peter Healey, Professor of Physiology and Director; Ph.D., University of Health Sciences (Chicago).
Jane Schluter, Ph.D., Marquette.

Support Faculty
Dorothy Hines, M.S., Illinois Benedictine.
Catherine Matis, M.S., Rush; RD.
Peter Sorensen, Professor of Management; Ph.D., IIT.
Jon Colby Swanson, Professor of Public Health; Ph.D., Illinois.
Edward M. Winkler, Ph.D., Kansas State.

Part-Time Faculty
Chuck Barnard, B.S., SUNY College at Cortland; PTC.
Ann Gavic-Ott, M.S., Wisconsin–La Crosse.
Ming Hwang, M.D., Kaohsiung Medical (Taiwan).
John Joyce, M.S., George Williams.
Michael Kett, M.S., George Williams; RPT.
Sally Ranft, M.S., Illinois Benedictine.
Cindy Smith, M.S., Illinois Benedictine.
Jack Stanko, M.D., Loyola of Chicago.
Linda Ugo, M.S., Illinois Benedictine.

NORTHEASTERN UNIVERSITY

Bouvé College of Pharmacy and Health Sciences
Programs in Clinical Exercise Physiology and Perfusion Technology

Programs of Study

The Master of Science degree programs in the Department of Cardiopulmonary Sciences gives students the opportunity to concentrate in clinical exercise physiology or perfusion technology. The curriculum includes course and lab work, as well as clinical practice in Boston's finest hospitals and health-care facilities.

The clinical exercise physiology program offers a choice between a rehabilitative emphasis (secondary prevention) and a preventive emphasis (primary prevention). This M.S. degree program gives students the opportunity to develop advanced knowledge and competencies in clinical exercise physiology. Clinical exercise physiologists practice in clinical settings, especially hospitals and clinics, as part of a health-care team that administers tests and develops primary and secondary prevention programs of exercise, counseling, and education for patients with cardiopulmonary, metabolic, and muscular diseases. Clinical exercise physiologists may also practice in health-promotion programs with populations that are apparently healthy or high-risk.

The Perfusion Technology program was designed to educate a cadre of practitioners at the graduate level who will fill leadership and research roles in the profession.

A perfusion technologist is a person qualified by academic and clinical education to provide cardiopulmonary support during any medical or surgical situation where it is necessary to temporarily replace the patient cardiac and/or respiratory functions. The perfusionist utilizes technology such as heart/lung machines, ventricular assist devices, and artificial hearts, as well as pharmacological interventions to maintain the patient during the period of circulatory support. The profession developed as a result of the introduction of coronary bypass surgery in the late 1960s and experienced dramatic growth during the 1980s. There are approximately 2,500 certified clinical perfusionists practicing in the United States today.

Research Facilities

Northeastern offers state-of-the-art academic facilities and laboratories. Bouvé College has modern laboratories for teaching and biomedical research. The cardiopulmonary sciences laboratories house high-tech equipment that supplements classroom learning.

University libraries contain more than 808,000 volumes, 1.8 million microforms, 170,000 government documents, 8,900 serial subscriptions, and 16,000 audio, video, and software titles. A central library contains online technologically sophisticated services, a gateway to external networked information resources, and a network of CD-ROM optical disk databases. Students also have access to research collections through the Boston Library Consortium. A high-speed data network links users and facilities on the central campus and on the three satellite campuses. The campus network is also connected via the global Internet to computing resources around the world. Students have access to DEC VAX systems, public access microcomputer labs (PC and Macintosh), a computer and conferencing system, a multimedia lab, and specialized computing equipment.

Financial Aid

Northeastern awards need-based financial aid through the Federal Perkins Loan, Federal Work-Study, and Federal Stafford Student Loan programs and also offers minority fellowships and Martin Luther King, Jr. Scholarships. Need-based aid is available only to U.S. citizens or permanent U.S. residents; all applicants must file the Free Application for Federal Student Aid, a Northeastern University financial aid application, and a financial aid transcript from their undergraduate institution. The graduate school offers full-time students limited aid through teaching assistantships that include tuition remission and a stipend of $10,600 per academic year. These assistantships require a maximum of 20 hours of work per week. Limited tuition assistantships that provide partial funding of tuition remission and require 10 hours of work per week are also offered.

Cost of Study

Tuition for the 1998–99 academic year in the College is $440 per quarter hour of credit. There are special tuition charges for theses and dissertations. A list of fees and tuition costs is available upon request.

Living and Housing Costs

For 1998–99, quarterly on-campus room rates for a single bedroom range from $1340 to $1715. A single efficiency apartment is $2040 to $2325. A shared bedroom in an apartment ranges from $1630 to $1775 per quarter. While there are several board options available, graduate students typically pay approximately $1085 per quarter for ten meals per week. Off-campus living accommodations are also available in the vicinity of the University.

Student Group

In fall 1997, 19,691 undergraduate and 4,634 graduate students were enrolled at Northeastern University, representing a wide variety of academic, professional, geographic, and cultural backgrounds. Bouvé College of Pharmacy and Health Sciences graduate programs enroll 677 students; 474 attend on a full-time basis.

Location

Boston, the capital of Massachusetts, offers many academic, cultural, and recreational opportunities. In addition to the abundant resources available within Northeastern University, students have access to the resources of the other educational and cultural institutions of the greater Boston area. The city is home to people of every intellectual, political, economic, racial, ethnic, and religious background. Boston is a mixture of Colonial tradition and modern technology. It is a place where the past is appreciated, the present enjoyed, and the future anticipated.

The University and The College

Founded in 1898, Northeastern University is a privately endowed nonsectarian institution of higher learning and is among the largest private universities in the country. Today, Northeastern has seven colleges, nine graduate and professional schools, two part-time undergraduate divisions, a number of continuing and special education programs and institutes, several suburban campuses, and an extensive research division. The College offers many exciting clinical and research programs and opportunity for interdisciplinary learning.

Applying

Fall entrance is preferred. Admission is granted on a rolling basis. Applicants must have the appropriate educational and professional background and must complete all admissions procedures for the selected programs of study. Test requirements include the GRE, MAT, or MCAT. TOEFL scores (minimum score of 600) are required of those applicants whose native language is not English.

Correspondence and Information

Bill Purnell, Director of Graduate Admissions
Bouvé College of Pharmacy and Health Sciences
203 Mugar Life Sciences Building
Northeastern University-P9
Boston, Massachusetts 02115
Telephone: 617-373-3211
E-mail: w.purnell@nunet.neu.edu

Department of Cardiopulmonary Sciences
100 Dockser Hall
Northeastern University
Boston, Massachusetts 02115

Northeastern University

THE FACULTY AND THEIR RESEARCH

Thomas A. Barnes, Associate Professor of Cardiopulmonary Sciences and Director, Cardiovascular Technology and Respiratory Therapy Programs; Ed.D., Nova; RRT. Respiratory therapy, performance and safety testing of resuscitation and emergency medical devices.

Marilyn A. Cairns, Associate Professor of Cardiopulmonary Sciences; Sc.D., Boston University. Applied anatomy and biomechanics.

Joseph A. Curro, Assistant Clinical Professor of Cardiopulmonary Sciences and Director, Clinical Education; M.B.A., Western New England; RRT. Respiratory therapy, development and evaluation of exercise physiology internship sites.

Fred G. Davis, Chairman, Department of Anesthesia, Lahey-Hitchcock Clinic, Burlington, Massachusetts; Associate Professor of Anesthesia, Tufts University School of Medicine; and Medical Director, Perfusion Technology; M.D., Hahnemann Medical College.

Daniel Fitzgerald, Director of Perfusion Services, Brigham and Women's Hospital and Technical Coordinator, Perfusion Program; CCP. Design and evaluation of extracorporeal devices.

Ernest V. Gervino, Adjunct Associate Professor of Cardiopulmonary Sciences; Sc.D., Boston University. Clinical exercise physiology, new modalities of clinical exercise testing for surgical risk stratification and detection of ischemic heart disease.

William J. Gillespie, Associate Professor of Cardiopulmonary Sciences and Director, Clinical Exercise Physiology Program; Ed.D., Boston University. Clinical exercise physiology, therapeutic aspects of exercise for individuals with cardiovascular, pulmonary, or metabolic disorders.

Richard B. Morrison, Associate Professor of Health, Sport, and Leisure Studies; Ed.D., Boston University. Research design, market research, and strategic management in the sport and fitness industries.

Eric P. Pepin, Clinical Assistant Professor of Cardiopulmonary Sciences; Ed.D., Northern Colorado. Perfusion technology, exercise physiology, physical activity and chronic disease, pathophysiology of cardiopulmonary bypass.

Patrick F. Plunkett, Associate Professor of Cardiopulmonary Sciences and Director, Perfusion Technology Program; Ed.D., Northeastern. Perfusion technology, compliment activation of extra corporeal circuits, application of neural networks to outcomes prediction.

Mary E. Watson, Chairperson and Associate Professor of Cardiopulmonary Sciences; Ed.D., Boston University; RRT. Respiratory therapy, curriculum development related to health education and exercise compliance for both the healthy and pulmonary patient populations.

Bruce Weiner, Adjunct Assistant Professor of Pharmacy; M.S., R.Ph., Florida. Clinical pharmacology, clinical research in cardiovascular pharmacology with applications to geriatric populations.

TEMPLE UNIVERSITY

Department of Physical Education

Programs of Study

The Department of Physical Education at Temple University offers graduate programs leading to the Ed.M. in physical education and the Ph.D. in kinesiology. The focus of the discipline is on the study of movement in and of the human organism and on the factors that affect and are affected by both the functional and aesthetic qualities of movement. One of the missions of the graduate program is the development of scholars to carry forth the search for and dissemination of knowledge in the discipline of kinesiology. The two primary areas within the Ph.D. program are somatic science (athletic training and exercise physiology) and behavioral science (curriculum and instruction and psychosocial interactions).

The Ed.M. degree consists of course work and either a thesis or project option. The thesis option requires the completion of a minimum of 30 semester hours, which include the writing of a thesis (6 semester hours). The project option requires the completion of a minimum of 33 semester hours of course work and the writing of a project (3 semester hours). The Ph.D. program of study is based upon the baccalaureate degree in physical education (kinesiology) and consists of four primary areas: basic core courses in the discipline of kinesiology (15 semester hours), a research component (24 semester hours), elective courses in somatic science or behavioral science (33 semester hours), and a preliminary examination/dissertation proposal defense (10 semester hours).

Research Facilities

The Biokinetics Research Laboratory serves as the research center for the College of Health, Physical Education, Recreation and Dance (HPERD). Its facilities and equipment are extensive and available to all graduate faculty and students within the College.

Temple University Hospital and Sports Medicine Centers also serve as important venues in which graduate faculty and students in the department conduct research. Cross-disciplinary research initiatives have been established with physicians and researchers in the Departments of Cardiology, Physiology, and Orthopedics and Sports Medicine. Collaborative research with these medical specialists and researchers serves to advance knowledge in the basic sciences and in clinical and applied practices.

Temple University facilities also include the Paley Library and the Medical Library at the Medical School. The Computer Science Center and associated services provide additional support to the graduate program.

Financial Aid

A variety of financial aid is available to full-time graduate students in physical education. University-funded support is available on a competitive basis for teaching assistantships, research assistantships, and University fellowships. An application for a department teaching or research assistantship may be obtained from Dr. Michael Sitler, Chair, Department of Physical Education, 114 Pearson Hall, Temple University, Philadelphia, Pennsylvania 19122; telephone: 215-204-1950; fax: 215-204-8705; e-mail: sitler@astro.temple.edu

Applications and supporting materials for teaching or research assistantship positions are due February 15, although materials submitted later may be considered. Recipients of positions with instructional responsibilities will be required to attend an orientation and training workshop in late August.

Cost of Study

Graduate tuition for 1997–98 was $308 per credit hour for Pennsylvania residents and $429 per credit hour for nonresidents; a $50 computer fee, a $25 activity fee, and a $35 health fee were also required.

Living and Housing Costs

There is limited on-campus housing available for graduate students. Rooms, apartments, and houses are available for graduate students in the surrounding city and suburbs.

Student Group

Temple University has an enrollment of approximately 28,000 students. The Department of Physical Education has approximately 750 students enrolled in its undergraduate and graduate programs.

Student Outcomes

A review of recent doctoral graduates reveals that approximately 60 percent have obtained faculty positions in higher education and 5 percent hold other types of positions in higher education. Twelve percent are employed in allied health–related institutions, such as hospitals and clinics. Another 12 percent are employed in public school positions, where they use their degree to enhance their teaching abilities and provide leadership within their school districts. The remaining 10 percent are self-employed.

Location

Philadelphia is the nation's tenth-largest city. Having been the preeminent city of Colonial America, Philadelphia contains many historic sites, including Independence Hall, the birthplace of liberty. A center of culture, Philadelphia has many museums, concert halls, and libraries. Temple University is located minutes from downtown Philadelphia, and its location within the city allows for the use of all of Philadelphia as its campus.

The University and The Department

Temple University is composed of fourteen schools and colleges, including the College of Health, Physical Education, Recreation and Dance. With its main campus located on Broad Street and Montgomery Avenue in Philadelphia, Temple is one of the city's major universities. The Department of Physical Education functions as a part of Temple University by teaching the concepts of the discipline of kinesiology concerned with the social, behavioral, physical, and aesthetic aspects of human movement.

Applying

Applicants must have a bachelor's degree or its equivalent from an accredited institution of higher learning and an overall grade point average of at least 2.8 (on a 4.0 scale) or at least 3.0 during the last two years. Two copies of official transcripts are required from each institution of higher education attended. Applicants to the master's program are required to take the Graduate Record Examinations (GRE) or Miller Analogies Test (MAT); Ph.D. applicants must take the GRE. Applicants must also submit a written statement of their career goals (150 words), submit a current vita, and be interviewed. Doctoral applicants must demonstrate writing competency during the interview and are required to submit three letters of recommendation. Master's applicants are required to submit the names and telephone numbers of three references. Application deadlines are October 1, February 1, April 1. and June 1, with admissions decision deadlines within one month of the application deadline.

Correspondence and Information

Dr. Michael Sachs, Graduate Coordinator
Department of Physical Education
Temple University
Philadelphia, Pennsylvania 19122
Telephone: 215-204-8718
Fax: 215-204-8705
E-mail: msachs@vm.temple.edu

Temple University

THE FACULTY AND THEIR RESEARCH

Weiyun Chen, Assistant Professor; Ph.D., Alabama. Professor Chen's research includes the developmental process of becoming expert teachers, pre-service teachers' construction of pedagogical content knowledge of teaching physical and health education, and using constructivist teaching techniques to facilitate students' critical thinking skills and cooperative abilities. (125 Pearson Hall; telephone: 215-204-1954; e-mail: wchen001@nimbbus.temple.edu)

Zebulon Kendrick, Professor; Ph.D., Temple. Professor Kendrick is a member of the board of directors of the American Aging Association and an editor on the Scientific Advisory Board for the Annals of Sports Medicine. He publishes extensively in medical and professional journals. His research includes the cellular, biochemical, and physiological adaptations of exercise physiology. (18 Pearson Hall; telephone: 215-204-8790; e-mail: zkendric@nimbus.temple.edu)

Carl G. Mattacola, Assistant Professor; Ph.D., Virginia; ATC. Professor Mattacola contributes regularly in athletic training/sports medicine journals. His research includes the evaluation of postural stability following exercise, training, and injury. (123 Pearson Hall; telephone: 215-204-9555; e-mail: mcarl@nimbus.temple.edu)

Carole A. Oglesby, Professor; Ph.D., Purdue. Professor Oglesby is a recipient of the R. Tait McKenzie Award, one of the highest honors accorded members of the physical education profession, and is the first in the discipline to receive the Billie Jean King Award from the Women's Sports Foundation. She is past president of the National Association for Girls and Women in Sport, has been president of the National Association for Sport and Physical Education's Sport Psychology Foundation, and has served as a representative for other groups to the United States Olympic Committee. Her research includes gender identity and sport and psychological development through sport. (122 Pearson Hall; telephone: 215-204-1948; e-mail: reds@astro.temple.edu)

Albert M. Paolone, Professor; Ed.D, Temple; FACSM. Professor Paolone is a founder and past chair of the Mid-Atlantic Regional Chapter of the American College of Sports Medicine. He is the 1995 Peter V. Karpovich Distinguished Lecturer in Exercise Physiology at Springfield College. His research includes human physiological responses to environmental stressors and exercise stress testing. (22 Pearson Hall; telephone: 215-204-1957; e-mail: apaolone@nimbus.temple.edu)

Marcella V. Ridenhour, Professor; Ph.D., Purdue. Professor Ridenhour is the chairperson of the Motor Development Academy of AAHPERD. Her research investigates the design of "age-appropriate" motor skills and environments for infants and young children. Her published research studies have investigated the design of toys, sleds, cribs, playgrounds, child-proofing, infant walkers, strollers, and high chairs. (124 Pearson Hall; telephone: 215-204-1960; e-mail: marrid@home.com)

Michael L. Sachs, Associate Professor; Ph.D., Florida State. Professor Sachs is past president of the Association for the Advancement of Applied Sport Psychology. He is a reviewer for the Division of Exercise and Sports Psychology of the American Psychological Association and has written numerous professional articles and book chapters. His research includes exercise and sport psychology, particularly the use of exercise as therapy; addiction to exercise; and cognitive strategies used during exercise. (132 Pearson Hall; telephone: 215-204-8718; e-mail: msachs@vm.temple.edu)

Mayra C. Santiago, Associate Professor; Ph.D., Minnesota. Professor Santiago's research includes exercise physiology in the applied areas of health promotion and disease prevention via exercise and physical activity in populations of individuals at risk; at-risk populations of middle-age sedentary women, adults with physical disabilities, and obese women; adults with physical disabilities, directed toward affecting both physical and mental health improvements. (126 Pearson Hall; telephone: 215-204-8719; e-mail; msantiag@nimbus.temple.edu)

Michael R. Sitler, Associate Professor; Ed.D, NYU; ATC. Professor Sitler has received several awards for his research, including the American Academy of Orthopaedic Surgeons' O'Donaghue Award in 1989 for outstanding research. He is an editorial board member of the *Journal of Sport Rehabilitation* and a 1997 recipient of the Lindback Foundation Award for distinguished teaching. His research includes the identification of factors associated with sports injuries and their prevention and functional efficacy of prophylactic bracing as well as postsurgical clinical outcomes. (114 Pearson Hall; telephone: 215-204-1950; e-mail: sitler@astro.temple.edu)

Ricky Swalm, Associate Professor; Ph.D., Temple. Professor Swalm has organized and conducted the computer and pedagogy sessions for National Association for Sport and Physical Education at the annual meetings of the American Alliance for Health, Physical Education, Recreation, and Dance. His research includes computer technology and multimedia in physical education and investigating predominant learning styles of physical education students and identifying congruent styles between teaching and learning in order to enhance development. (140 Pearson Hall; telephone: 215-204-8713; e-mail: rswalm@thunder.temple.edu)

Marianne Torbert, Professor; Ph.D., USC. Professor Torbert serves on the editorial board of *Teaching Elementary Physical Education.* Her research includes the development of the "needs approach" for gross motor activity involving young children. (121 Pearson Hall; telephone: 215-204-6287; e-mail: mtorbert@vm.temple.edu)

UNITED STATES SPORTS ACADEMY

Graduate School

Programs of Study

The United States Sports Academy is a sport-specific institution that offers a Master of Sport Science degree in the areas of sport coaching, sport fitness management, sport management, and sports medicine. A Doctor of Education degree in sport management is also offered. The Academy offers a flexible program consisting of both practical and classroom experience. The practical experience, or mentorship program, is an important facet of the Academy. It enables the student to gain valuable hands-on experience in the areas of coaching, cardiac rehabilitation, corporate wellness, fitness-center management, athletics administration, clinical and institutional sports medicine, and research.

Research Facilities

The Human Performance Lab has the capability of assessing the metabolic parameters of human performance, including oxygen uptake, carbon dioxide production, pulmonary function testing, and body composition.

The Biomechanics Laboratory has the capability of performing two- and three-dimensional video analysis, force plate analysis, electromyographic analysis, and lifting and gait analysis. The lab is used for analyzing athletic performance, the progress in rehabilitation, the physical potential of athletes, and the diagnosis of weaknesses and faults in performance.

The Sports Medicine Lab is equipped with a range of rehabilitative equipment, including ultrasound, electrical modalities, isokinetic rehabilitation equipment, and hydrotherapy modalities. Students learn to use evaluation devices such as Ariel CES systems.

The Academy maintains a library learning center and computer laboratory for student research. The library collection includes reference materials, books, periodicals, journals, films, and audiocassettes and videocassettes on sport-related subjects. The library also participates in on-line computerized data search programs, allowing students access to citations in sport and sport-related areas. Students also have access to the Internet through the library's computer lab. In addition, interlibrary loans are processed through OCLC. The Academy is a member of the Network of Alabama Academic Libraries.

Financial Aid

A variety of financial aid programs are available to qualified students. Federal programs include Federal Stafford Student Loans, Federal Perkins Loans, Federal Work-Study, and veterans' benefits. Campus programs include several service scholarships that pay up to full tuition. Recipients are determined by consideration of academic performance, prior work experience, and students' ability to benefit from graduate study. Students interested in any of these programs should check with the Office of Financial Aid to determine their eligibility.

Cost of Study

The Master of Sport Science degree requires a minimum of 33 semester hours of credit. The resident tuition in 1998–99 is $250 per credit hour. The distance learning tuition in 1998–99 is $300 per credit hour. The Doctor of Education degree is a 60-semester-hour program and tuition is $350 per credit hour. Because the Academy is a private institution, there is no difference between in-state and out-of-state tuition.

Living and Housing Costs

The Academy is surrounded by a range of high-quality, low-cost apartments with both long-term and short-term leases that meet the needs of single and married students. The estimated cost of room, board, transportation, and miscellaneous living expenses is $9500 per year. This cost may vary according to the student's life style.

Student Group

The United States Sports Academy enrolls more than 300 new students per year from all over the United States and from several countries. The diversity of ethnic and economic backgrounds enables students to increase their knowledge and awareness of trends and concepts in the world of sport.

Location

The United States Sports Academy is located in Daphne, Alabama, on the beautiful eastern shore of historic Mobile Bay just off Interstate 10. The Gulf Coast is famous for its boating, fishing, and white sand beaches. The area enjoys semitropical weather most of the year, with an average temperature that ranges from the 50s in January to the 80s in July. In addition to Mobile, several large urban communities, such as New Orleans, Atlanta, and Pensacola, are within driving distance.

The Academy

The United States Sports Academy is a freestanding graduate school of sport dedicated to the pursuit of sport excellence. The Academy is accredited by the Commission on Colleges of the Southern Association of Colleges and Schools (1866 Southern Lane, Decatur, Georgia 30033-4097; telephone: 404-679-4501) to award the Master of Sport Science degree and the Doctor of Education degree. The United States Sports Academy accepts graduate students regardless of race, religion, gender, age, disability, or national origin.

The Alabama State Board of Education (ASBE) has approved the Academy's programs to prepare students as trainers, coaches, and coach-trainers at the master's degree (Class A) certification level. A student who satisfactorily completes the ASBE requirements will be eligible for Class A or master's-level certification in Alabama and in other states that have signed the National Association of State Directors of Teacher's Education and Certification (NASDTEC) reciprocity agreement, provided the state in which the student seeks such reciprocity has such certification programs. Requirements for certification for coaches, trainers, and coach-trainers are listed under the State Department of Education Administrative Code.

Applying

Minimum requirements for admission into the master's degree program include a baccalaureate degree from an accredited four-year institution. An application with three letters of recommendation or the name, address, and phone number of three references is required. Admission to full standing requires a minimum 2.75 undergraduate average (on a 4.0 scale) and a minimum GRE score of 800 (combining verbal and quantitative scores) or a MAT score of 27 or a GMAT score of 400. Students with a GPA below 2.75 and/or test scores below these standards are subject to provisional admission. International students are required to submit a TOEFL score of at least 550. A student who chooses the distance learning delivery system may begin the program any time after acceptance. Residential students begin at the beginning of any semester. Admission requirements for the doctoral degree are available upon request.

Correspondence and Information

Office of Student Services
United States Sports Academy
One Academy Drive
Daphne, Alabama 36526

Telephone: 334-626-3303
800-223-2668 (toll-free)
Fax: 334-626-1149
E-mail: academy@ussa-sport.ussa.edu
World Wide Web: http://www.ussa.sport.edu

United States Sports Academy

DIVISION OF ACADEMIC AFFAIRS

The Master of Sport Science degree program consists of majors offered by the following departments.

DEPARTMENT OF SPORT COACHING

Those interested in sport coaching should have a background in sport as a player or coach. Generally, undergraduate majors in health, physical education, recreation, or sport training are most suitable.

The graduate program in sport coaching is designed to prepare a student for leadership in the dynamic career of sport coaching. Program objectives are established to prepare each student for the multiplicity of demands involved in the control and operation of individual and team sports.

DEPARTMENT OF SPORT FITNESS MANAGEMENT

Those interested in sport fitness management generally have undergraduate majors in exercise physiology, pre-physical therapy, physical education, nursing, medical technology, biology, psychology, or recreation. Those with strong backgrounds in the natural sciences are also encouraged to apply. Anatomical kinesiology and basic exercise physiology are prerequisites for certain courses required to complete this major.

The graduate curriculum in sport fitness management is designed to prepare each student for a career in such areas as cardiac rehabilitation, wellness, preventive medicine, corporate fitness programs, health club management, individualized training, YMCAs, and other civic organizations. Program objectives prepare a student for a variety of demands involved in the evaluation and prescription for preventive and rehabilitative programs.

DEPARTMENT OF SPORT MANAGEMENT

Those interested in sport management generally have undergraduate majors associated with business administration, management, finance, marketing, human relations, physical education, communications, or sport.

The graduate curriculum in sport management is designed to prepare each student for the increasing number of career leadership opportunities in the field of sport and recreational management. Students in sport management may pursue additional courses in sports facilities, sport journalism, or sport travel and tourism. Program objectives prepare the student for a multiplicity of demand involved in the operation of sport programs at various levels. Sport management students will be prepared for careers as sports facility managers, sport information directors, sport front office administrators, or sport community relations directors.

DEPARTMENT OF SPORTS MEDICINE

Those interested in sports medicine may be accepted from a variety of backgrounds. Generally they have undergraduate majors in health, physical education, nursing, physical therapy, or athletic training. Those with strong backgrounds in the natural sciences—such as biology, physiology, or biochemistry—are encouraged to apply. Anatomical kinesiology and basic exercise physiology are prerequisites for certain courses required to complete this major.

The graduate curriculum in sports medicine is designed to prepare students for many opportunities, including experience in athletic training at the high school, collegiate, or professional level. Some of these experiences may be applied toward the required number of contact hours necessary for National Athletic Trainers Association certification. Program objectives prepare the student for the prevention, management, evaluation, and rehabilitation of athletic injuries, along with the multiplicity of demand involved in the successful operation of sports medicine programs at various levels.

MASTER STUDY OPTIONS

The degree program is personalized, high-quality instruction delivered through the following study options:

Resident Study

Under the guidance of on-campus faculty, a student focuses on traditional classroom and laboratory experiences. Resident study allows a student to select courses from a flexible curriculum designed to meet individual needs. Two 6-week summer sessions are offered. During summer one, a residential student can complete core courses; during the fall and spring, a student completes an approved mentorship in the community; and during summer two, a residential student completes major courses and takes the comprehensive examination.

Distance Learning

Distance Learning offers the student the opportunity to earn the master's degree through a combination of independent and practical activities. Students selecting this delivery system may be able to complete their degree with a minimum of travel away from their home and place of work. Students work with a faculty member who delivers the class using a course syllabus, required text readings, and teaching technologies, such as computers. Distance Learning may also take place through telecourses produced on video, site-to-site teaching by video, and interactive video discs.

Mentorship/Thesis

All master degree students must complete either a field experience or a thesis as part of their degree requirement. Mentorship provides many opportunities for practical learning experiences because the student can select, within established guidelines, both the site and the type of experience desired. All mentorships are subject to review and approval by the Vice President of Academic Affairs.

Thesis work provides capable students with the opportunity to be intellectually challenged through planning and conducting independent research under the guidance of a thesis chair and committee. Thesis hours must be approved by the Vice President of Academic Affairs. The thesis proposal defense and the final thesis defense are conducted in a public committee meeting format on the Daphne campus only.

DOCTOR OF EDUCATION DEGREE PROGRAM

The Doctor of Education degree in sport management, like the master's degree, is designed for the working professional. The 60 semester hours required for completing the degree may be earned through a combination of on-campus study, mentorship, and directed individualized study. The degree normally requires 3 to 3½ years to complete. Financial aid is available for doctoral students.

UNIVERSITY OF MICHIGAN

Division of Kinesiology
Programs in Kinesiology

Programs of Study The Division of Kinesiology offers a Ph.D. program in kinesiology and two types of programs at the master's degree level: the M.A. and M.S. degrees and the Certificate of Graduate Study (C.G.S.). The M.A. and M.S. degrees require 30 credits of course work or 24 credits of courses plus a 6-credit thesis. Students select one of three options: the comprehensive track, which allows for flexible in-depth study of human movement; the Ph.D. preparation track, intended for students who plan to pursue a doctoral degree; and the specialist track in either facility management or corporate worksite wellness. The specialist track requires additional courses that qualify students for the C.G.S. The C.G.S. requires 19 credits of study. It may be taken in combination with the specialist track or pursued by itself to enhance professional skills. Students who take a majority of courses in the social sciences (management, telecommunications, law, and psychology) receive the M.A. degree. Those who take a majority of credits in science-based course work (exercise physiology, biomechanics, and motor control) receive the M.S. degree.

The doctoral program in kinesiology provides for the study of movement at an advanced level. The program emphasizes scholarly and teaching competence and research activity and culminates in a doctoral dissertation. Graduates assume careers as scholars, teachers, researchers, and professionals in kinesiology or allied fields. Ph.D. students choose from a set of core courses in kinesiology as well as cognate courses from other units and complete a minimum of 30 credits beyond the master's level. All Ph.D. students work closely with a faculty adviser from the beginning of their degree programs. Two qualifying examinations are taken prior to candidacy, after which the student completes an original doctoral dissertation.

Research Facilities The Division of Kinesiology offers students research opportunities in several areas, including human motor research, exercise physiology, sport marketing, facility management, worksite wellness, and psychological aspects of sport and fitness. The Center for Human Motor Research combines the Motor Behavior, Biomechanics, and Sensorimotor Integration Laboratories. The Motor Behavior Lab has movement-tracking and electromyography systems and accelerometers, plus custom devices to study reaching and aiming. In the Biomechanics Lab, whole-body motion is studied using a video-based 3-D motion analysis system with analog data acquisition and three force platforms. The Sensorimotor Integration Laboratory is equipped for assessment of arm-movement kinematics, eye monitoring, and electromyography measures of muscle activity. The Applied Physiology Lab has a complete setup for analysis of energy expenditure during exercise and rest, both in the lab and in the field; it is also equipped to measure ECG, lactate and other blood indices, all pulmonary function parameters, and strength. The Behnke Body Composition Lab has a climatically controlled walk-in tank and segmental volume tanks for underwater weighing. The Exercise Endocrinology Lab contains gamma and beta counters, a spectrophotometer, and refrigerated high- and low-speed centrifuges. In the Sports Facility Research Laboratory, students conduct feasibility studies and gain experience in the management, marketing, and daily operations of multipurpose arenas. The Health Management Research Center (HMRC), which maintains a data bank of 2 million employee health surveys, has forty high-volume capacity networked client service workstations and peripherals, remote accesses, and SAS and SPSS statistical packages. Other research labs focus on sport marketing, advertising, exercise adherence, telecommunications, and youth fitness. The Division of Kinesiology has equipped its classrooms with computer projection systems, scanners, visualizers, laser disks, and other advanced teaching technology.

Financial Aid The Division of Kinesiology offers several stipends to first-year graduate students; they range from $4000 to $7500 and are based on student quality indices, especially GPA and GRE scores. The Division also offers a limited number of research and teaching assistantships.

Cost of Study Full-term graduate tuition in the Division of Kinesiology is $5236 for residents and $10,682 for nonresidents. Tuition is subject to change without notice by the University Regents.

Living and Housing Costs Ann Arbor offers a variety of single and shared living options in the campus area, from modern apartments to Victorian houses to student-run co-ops. Family units are also available through University housing. Room, board, and personal expenses for two terms are estimated at $6500.

Student Group The Division enrolls approximately 50 master's degree students, 15 doctoral students, and 650 undergraduates.

Student Outcomes Recent master's degree program alumni and alumnae are employed in worksite wellness programs and research, sports facility management, athletic and recreation administration, athletic training, and sport marketing. Many have continued studies in Ph.D. programs, physical therapy units, and medical schools.

Location With its eclectic blend of tree-lined neighborhoods, industrial parks, shopping areas, theaters, and restaurants, Ann Arbor (population 112,000) combines small-town accessibility with the advantages of a large metropolitan area. Cultural offerings include visiting scholars, internationally acclaimed orchestras and soloists, the Summer Festival, the Art Fair, and other special events. The Arboretum and an extensive park system provide a wide range of outdoor recreational opportunities. It is an ethnically diverse community with a four-season climate.

The University Founded in 1817, the University of Michigan is widely regarded as a world leader in research and scholarship. The Division of Kinesiology is one of eighteen schools and colleges enrolling some 36,000 students on the Ann Arbor campus. The University's library system, among the best in the nation, exceeds 6.6 million volumes and 70,000 serial titles. With its numerous parks and museums, computing centers, and theaters and concert halls, the University offers an infinite variety of learning opportunities.

Applying The Division of Kinesiology welcomes applications from students of all academic disciplines who are interested in the study of human movement. Admission decisions are made by June 1, and early applications are encouraged. Students begin in the fall semester. Applicants should submit scores on the General Test of the Graduate Record Examinations (GRE), official transcripts of academic work, three letters of recommendation, and a statement of purpose indicating goals, previous experience, and choice of track. Applications for financial support should be received by March 1.

Correspondence and Information
Graduate Secretary, Kinesiology
401 Washtenaw Avenue
University of Michigan
Ann Arbor, Michigan 48109-2214

Telephone: 734-764-1343
Fax: 734-936-1925
E-mail: kin.gradsec@umich.edu (application questions)
gradcomm@umich.edu (program content questions)
World Wide Web: http://www.edu/~divkines/kinweb/

University of Michigan

THE FACULTY AND THEIR RESEARCH

Kinesiology faculty members are involved in a variety of research projects and offer graduate students an opportunity to explore many interest areas and design individualized programs of course work. Many students participate in joint research between kinesiology faculty members and their colleagues in public health, engineering, business, law and at the Medical School and various departments, centers, and institutes. Kinesiology faculty members who are associated with the graduate program are listed below.

Rosa Angulo-Kinzler, Assistant Professor; Ph.D., Indiana. Motor development and neural sciences.
Marvin Boluyt, Visiting Assistant Professor; Ph.D., Michigan. Anatomy, physiology, cardiovascular fitness, and aging.
Katarina Borer, Professor; Ph.D., Pennsylvania. Growth, nutrition and exercise.
Christine Brooks, Associate Professor; Ed.D., North Carolina at Greensboro. Sport marketing.
Susan Brown, Assistant Professor; Ph.D., Western Ontario. Motor control in disabled and other populations.
Dee W. Edington, Professor; Ph.D., Michigan State. Worksite wellness, health-care cost containment, health promotion.
Merle Foss, Professor; Ph.D., Iowa. Wellness and exercise, strength training.
Anne Garcia, Assistant Professor; Ph.D., California, San Francisco. Health psychology, exercise adherence.
Tom George, Visiting Assistant Professor; Ph.D., Michigan State. Sports psychology, performance enhancement.
Melissa Gross, Assistant Professor; Ph.D., UCLA. Biomechanics, neuromotor control.
C. Keith Harrison, Assistant Professor; Ed.D., USC. Race, culture, and sport.
Victor Katch, Professor; Ed.D., Berkeley. Exercise physiology, nutrition, body composition, weight control.
Charles Kuntzleman, Adjunct Associate Professor; Ed.D., Temple. Physical education, youth fitness.
B. Pat Maloy, Associate Professor; J.D., Notre Dame. Legal aspects of sport, recreation and facility management.
David Moore, Associate Professor; Ph.D., Indiana. Consumer responses to marketing of sports participation and health and fitness programs.
Bruce Watkins, Associate Professor; Ph.D., Kansas. Sports and the media, telecommunications, developmental psychology.

Section 42
Sports Administration

This section contains a directory of institutions offering graduate work in sports administration, followed by in-depth entries submitted by institutions that chose to prepare detailed program descriptions. Additional information about programs listed in the directory but not augmented by an in-depth entry may be obtained by writing directly to the dean of a college at the address given in the directory.

For programs offering related work, see also in this book Business Administration and Management, Education, and Physical Education.

CONTENTS

Program Directory

Announcements

In-Depth Descriptions

See also:

Sports Administration

Adelphi University, School of Education, Department of Physical Education, Recreation, and Human Performance Science, Garden City, NY 11530. Offerings include sports management (Certificate). *Application deadline:* rolling. *Application fee:* $50. *Expenses:* Tuition $16,000 per year full-time, $485 per credit part-time. Fees $500 per year full-time, $150 per semester part-time. • Dr. Ronald Feingold, Chairperson, 516-877-4260.

Appalachian State University, College of Fine and Applied Arts, Department of Health, Leisure, and Exercise Science, Program in Health and Physical Education, Boone, NC 28608. Offerings include sports management (MA). *Degree requirements:* Thesis or alternative, comprehensive exams required, foreign language not required. *Entrance requirements:* GRE General Test. Application deadline: 7/31 (priority date). Application fee: $35. *Tuition:* $1811 per year full-time, $354 per semester (minimum) part-time for state residents; $9081 per year full-time, $2171 per semester (minimum) part-time for nonresidents. • Application contact: Dr. Alan Utter, Coordinator, 704-262-3140.

Barry University, School of Human Performance and Leisure Sciences, Program in Sport Management, Miami Shores, FL 33161-6695. Awards MS. Part-time and evening/weekend programs available. Faculty: 4 full-time (3 women), 1 part-time (0 women), 4.25 FTE. Students: 1 (woman) full-time, 8 part-time (1 woman); includes 1 minority (Hispanic). Average age 28. 14 applicants, 43% accepted. *Degree requirements:* Thesis or alternative, project or thesis, written comprehensive exam required, foreign language not required. *Entrance requirements:* GMAT (minimum score 450) or GRE General Test (minimum combined score of 1000), minimum GPA of 3.0. Application deadline: rolling. Application fee: $30. Electronic applications accepted. *Tuition:* $450 per credit (minimum). *Financial aid:* Career-related internships or fieldwork available. Aid available to part-time students. Financial aid application deadline: 5/1; applicants required to submit FAFSA. *Faculty research:* Economic impact of professional sports. • Dr. Hal Walker, Coordinator, 305-899-3493. E-mail: hjwalker@bu4090.barry.edu. Application contact: Desh Sherman-Moeller, Administrative Assistant, 305-899-3490. Fax: 305-899-3556. E-mail: sherman@bu4090.barry.edu.

Barry University, Schools of Human Performance and Leisure Sciences and Business, Program in Sport Management and Business Administration, Miami Shores, FL 33161-6695. Awards MBA/MS. Part-time and evening/weekend programs available. Faculty: 4 full-time (3 women), 1 part-time (0 women), 4.25 FTE. Students: 3 full-time (0 women), 7 part-time (0 women); includes 4 minority (2 African Americans, 1 Asian American, 1 Hispanic). Average age 28. 6 applicants, 50% accepted. *Application deadline:* rolling. *Application fee:* $30. Electronic applications accepted. *Tuition:* $450 per credit (minimum). *Financial aid:* 9 students received aid; career-related internships or fieldwork available. Aid available to part-time students. Financial aid application deadline: 5/1; applicants required to submit FAFSA. *Faculty research:* Economic impact of professional sports. • Dr. Hal Walker, Coordinator, 305-899-3493. E-mail: hjwalker@bu4090.barry.edu. Application contact: Desh Sherman-Moeller, Administrative Assistant, 305-899-3490. Fax: 305-899-3556. E-mail: sherman@bu4090.barry.edu.

Boise State University, College of Education, Department of Health, Physical Education, and Recreation, Program in Physical Education, Boise, ID 83725-0399. Offers athletic administration (MPE). Offered jointly with Idaho State University. Part-time programs available. Students: 11 part-time (6 women). Average age 32. 4 applicants, 100% accepted. *Degree requirements:* Thesis. *Entrance requirements:* Minimum GPA of 3.0. Application deadline: 7/26 (priority date; rolling processing; 11/29 for spring admission). Application fee: $20 ($30 for international students). Electronic applications accepted. *Tuition:* $3020 per year full-time, $135 per credit part-time for state residents; $8900 per year full-time, $135 per credit part-time for nonresidents. *Financial aid:* Graduate assistantships, Federal Work-Study, institutionally sponsored loans, and career-related internships or fieldwork available. Aid available to part-time students. Financial aid application deadline: 3/1. • Dr. Ron Pfeiffer, Director, 208-385-3709.

Bowling Green State University, College of Education and Allied Professions, School of Human Movement, Sport, and Leisure Studies, Bowling Green, OH 43403. Offerings include sport administration (M Ed). School faculty: 18 full-time (11 women), 1 (woman) part-time. *Degree requirements:* Thesis or alternative required, foreign language not required. *Entrance requirements:* GRE General Test, TOEFL (minimum score 565), minimum GPA of 2.6. Application deadline: 4/1 (rolling processing). Application fee: $30. Electronic applications accepted. *Tuition:* $6070 per year full-time, $284 per credit hour part-time for state residents; $11,358 per year full-time, $536 per credit hour part-time for nonresidents. • Dr. Mary Ann Roberton, Director, 419-372-7234. Application contact: Dr. Janet Parks, Graduate Coordinator, 419-372-2878.

Brooklyn College of the City University of New York, Department of Physical Education, 2900 Bedford Avenue, Brooklyn, NY 11210-2889. Offerings include exercise science and rehabilitation (MS), with options in psychosocial aspects of physical activity, sports management. Department faculty: 16 full-time, 4 part-time, 18 FTE. *Average time to degree:* master's–3 years part-time. *Application deadline:* 3/1 (11/1 for spring admission). *Application fee:* $40. *Expenses:* Tuition $4350 per year full-time, $185 per credit part-time for state residents; $7600 per year full-time, $320 per credit part-time for nonresidents. Fees $500 per year for state residents; $806 per year for nonresidents. • Dr. Charles Tobey, Chairperson, 718-951-5514. Application contact: Michael Hipscher, Graduate Deputy, 718-951-5514.

Canisius College, School of Education and Human Services, Program in Sport Administration, Buffalo, NY 14208-1098. Awards MS. Faculty: 3 full-time (1 woman), 6 part-time (2 women). *Degree requirements:* Research project required, foreign language not required. *Entrance requirements:* GRE General Test. Application deadline: rolling. Application fee: $20. *Expenses:* Tuition $415 per credit hour. Fees $15 per credit hour. • James Riordan, Director, 716-888-3179. Application contact: Kevin Smith, Graduate Recruitment and Admissions, 716-888-2544. Fax: 716-888-3290.

Central Michigan University, College of Education and Human Services, Department of Physical Education and Sport, Mount Pleasant, MI 48859. Offerings include athletic administration (MA), sports administration (MSA). Department faculty: 15 full-time (3 women). *Degree requirements:* Thesis or alternative required, foreign language not required. *Entrance requirements:* Minimum GPA of 2.5 in last 20 hours. Application deadline: 3/1 (priority date). Application fee: $30. *Expenses:* Tuition $139 per credit hour (minimum) for state residents; $276 per credit hour (minimum) for nonresidents. Fees $260 per year full-time, $150 per semester part-time. • Dr. James E. Hornak, Chairperson, 517-774-6658. Fax: 517-774-4374. E-mail: 34naewv@cmich.edu.

Cleveland State University, College of Education, Department of Health, Physical Education, Recreation and Dance, Cleveland, OH 44115-2440. Offerings include sport management (M Ed), sport management/exercise science (M Ed). Department faculty: 11 full-time (6 women). *Degree requirements:* Thesis optional, foreign language not required. *Entrance requirements:* GRE General Test or MAT (score in 50th percentile or higher), minimum undergraduate GPA of 2.75. Application deadline: 9/1 (priority date; rolling processing). Application fee: $25. *Expenses:* Tuition $5252 per year full-time, $202 per credit hour part-time for state residents; $10,504 per year full-time, $404 per credit hour part-time for nonresidents. Fees $2.25 per credit hour (minimum). • Dr. Vincent Melograno, Chairman, 216-687-4878. Fax: 216-687-5410. E-mail: v.melograno@popmail.csuohio.edu.

Concordia University, Faculty of Commerce and Administration, Montréal, PQ H3G 1M8, Canada. Offerings include accounting (Diploma), with options in institutional administration, sports administration. *Application fee:* $30. *Expenses:* Tuition $56 per credit (minimum) for Canadian residents; $249 per credit (minimum) for nonresidents. Fees $152 per year full-time, $111 per year (minimum) part-time. • Dr. M. Anvari, Dean, 514-848-2700. Fax: 514-848-4502. Application contact: Dale Doreen, Director, 514-848-2958. Fax: 514-848-4208.

Eastern Kentucky University, College of Health, Physical Education, Recreation and Athletics, Department of Physical Education, Richmond, KY 40475-3101. Offerings include sports administration (MS). Department faculty: 4 full-time (2 women). *Average time to degree:* master's–1 year full-time, 3 years part-time. *Entrance requirements:* GRE General Test, minimum GPA of 2.5. Application deadline: 8/15. Application fee: $0. *Tuition:* $2390 per year full-time, $133 per credit hour part-time for state residents; $6630 per year full-time, $365 per credit hour part-time for nonresidents. • Lonnie Davis, Chair, 606-622-1887. Fax: 606-622-1254. E-mail: phedavis@acs.eku.edu.

East Stroudsburg University of Pennsylvania, School of Health Sciences and Human Performance, Department of Movement Studies and Exercise Science, East Stroudsburg, PA 18301-2999. Offerings include health and physical education (M Ed), with option in sports management. *Application deadline:* 7/31 (priority date; rolling processing; 11/30 for spring admission). *Application fee:* $15 ($25 for international students). *Expenses:* Tuition $3468 per year full-time, $193 per credit part-time for state residents; $6236 per year full-time, $346 per credit part-time for nonresidents. Fees $700 per year full-time, $39 per credit part-time.

Florida State University, College of Education, Department of Physical Education, Tallahassee, FL 32306. Offerings include sports administration (MS, Ed D, PhD, Ed S). Department faculty: 6 full-time (3 women), 6 part-time (0 women). *Degree requirements:* For master's and Ed S, comprehensive exam required, thesis optional; for doctorate, dissertation, comprehensive exam. *Entrance requirements:* GRE General Test (minimum combined score of 1000), minimum GPA of 3.0. Application deadline: 7/1 (priority date; rolling processing; 11/1 for spring admission). Application fee: $20. *Tuition:* $139 per credit hour for state residents; $482 per credit hour for nonresidents. • Dr. Dewayne Johnson, Chair, 850-644-4813. E-mail: djohnson@mail.coe.fsu.edu. Application contact: Admission Secretary, 850-644-4813. Fax: 850-644-0975.

The George Washington University, School of Business and Public Management, Department of Tourism Studies, Washington, DC 20052. Offerings include sport management (MTA). Department faculty: 1 full-time (0 women), 3 part-time (2 women), 2 FTE. *Application deadline:* 4/1 (priority date; rolling processing; 10/1 for spring admission). *Application fee:* $50. *Expenses:* Tuition $680 per semester hour. Fees $35 per semester hour. • Dr. Douglas Frechtling, Program Director, 202-994-6280. Fax: 202-994-1420.

Georgia Southern University, College of Health and Professional Studies, Department of Recreation and Sport Management, Program in Sport Management, Statesboro, GA 30460-8126. Awards MS. Part-time programs available. Students: 22 full-time (9 women), 3 part-time (all women); includes 2 minority (both African Americans), 1 international. Average age 27. 38 applicants, 29% accepted. In 1997, 18 degrees awarded. *Degree requirements:* Internship, terminal exam required, thesis optional, foreign language not required. *Average time to degree:* master's–2 years full-time, 4 years part-time. *Entrance requirements:* GRE General Test (minimum score 450 on each section), MAT (minimum score 44), minimum GPA of 2.75. Application deadline: 7/15 (priority date; rolling processing; 11/15 for spring admission). Application fee: $0. Electronic applications accepted. *Tuition:* $2619 per year full-time, $287 per semester (minimum) part-time for state residents; $8619 per year full-time, $1037 per semester (minimum) part-time for nonresidents. *Financial aid:* Research assistantships, teaching assistantships, Federal Work-Study, and career-related internships or fieldwork available. Aid available to part-time students. Financial aid application deadline: 4/15. *Faculty research:* Sport marketing, sport sociology, sport law. • Application contact: Dr. John R. Diebolt, Associate Graduate Dean, 912-681-5384. Fax: 912-681-0740. E-mail: gradschool@gsvms2.cc.gasou.edu.

Georgia State University, College of Education, Department of Kinesiology and Health, Program in Sports Administration, Atlanta, GA 30303-3083. Awards MS. Students: 44 full-time (20 women), 10 part-time (3 women); includes 11 minority (10 African Americans, 1 Asian American), 4 international. Average age 26. 45 applicants, 69% accepted. In 1997, 30 degrees awarded. *Degree requirements:* Comprehensive exam. *Entrance requirements:* GRE General Test (minimum combined score of 900) or MAT (minimum score 50), minimum GPA of 2.7. Application deadline: 7/15 (1/15 for spring admission). Application fee: $25. *Expenses:* Tuition $2673 per year full-time, $99 per semester hour part-time for state residents; $10,692 per year full-time, $396 per semester hour part-time for nonresidents. Fees $228 per year. *Financial aid:* Research assistantships available. • Dr. Jeff C. Rupp, Chair, Department of Kinesiology and Health, 404-651-2536.

Gonzaga University, Graduate School, School of Education, Program in Sports and Athletic Administration, Spokane, WA 99258-0001. Awards MASPAA. *Degree requirements:* Comprehensive exam required, foreign language and thesis not required. *Entrance requirements:* TOEFL (minimum score 550). Application fee: $40. *Tuition:* $7380 per year (minimum) full-time, $410 per credit (minimum) part-time. • Dr. John Sunderland, Chairperson.

Grambling State University, College of Education, Program in Sports Administration, Grambling, LA 71245. Awards MS. Part-time programs available. Faculty: 5 full-time (2 women), 2 part-time (0 women). Students: 16 full-time (8 women), 4 part-time (0 women); includes 20 minority (all African Americans). Average age 25. 12 applicants, 100% accepted. In 1997, 10 degrees awarded. *Average time to degree:* master's–1.5 years full-time, 2.5 years part-time. *Entrance requirements:* GRE General Test (combined average 800). Application deadline: 8/24 (priority date; rolling processing; 1/12 for spring admission). Application fee: $15. *Tuition:* $1960 per year full-time, $297 per semester (minimum) part-time for state residents; $7110 per year full-time, $297 per semester (minimum) part-time for nonresidents. *Financial aid:* In 1997–98, 4 teaching assistantships (all to first-year students) averaging $500 per month and totaling $18,000 were awarded; institutionally sponsored loans and career-related internships or fieldwork also available. Financial aid application deadline: 5/31. *Faculty research:* Sports psychology and sport history. • Dr. Willie Daniel, Head, 318-274-2294. Fax: 318-274-6053.

Hardin–Simmons University, Irvin School of Education, Department of Physical Education, Program in Sports and Recreation Management, Abilene, TX 79698-0001. Awards M Ed. Part-time programs available. Faculty: 3 full-time (0 women). Students: 23 part-time (7 women); includes 3 minority (1 African American, 2 Hispanics). Average age 28. In 1997, 3 degrees awarded. *Degree requirements:* Internship, project required, thesis optional, foreign language not required. *Application deadline:* 8/15 (priority date; rolling processing; 1/5 for spring admission). *Application fee:* $25. *Expenses:* Tuition $280 per semester hour. Fees $630 per year full-time. *Financial aid:* In 1997–98, 5 fellowships (2 to first-year students) averaging $250 per month and totaling $4,500, 8 recreation assistantships (6 to first-year students) averaging $380 per month and totaling $28,000 were awarded; full and partial tuition waivers, Federal Work-Study, and career-related internships or fieldwork also available. Aid available to part-time students. Financial aid application deadline: 3/15; applicants required to submit FAFSA. *Faculty research:* Sports psychology, coaching education, sport sociology, corporate fitness, recreation programming. • Dr. Warren Simpson, Director, 915-670-1220. Fax: 915-670-1572. Application contact: Dr. J. Paul Sorrels, Dean of Graduate Studies, 915-670-1298. Fax: 915-670-1564.

Idaho State University, College of Education, Division II, Pocatello, ID 83209. Offerings include athletic administration (MPE). MPE offered jointly with Boise State University. Postbaccalaureate distance learning degree programs offered (no on-campus study). Division faculty: 11 full-time (2 women). *Average time to degree:* master's–2 years full-time, 4 years part-time; other advanced degree–1 year full-time, 2 years part-time. *Application deadline:* 7/1 (priority date; rolling processing; 12/1 for spring admission). *Application fee:* $30. *Tuition:* $3130 per year full-time, $136 per credit hour part-time for state residents; $9370 per year full-time, $226 per credit hour part-time for nonresidents. • Dr. T. C. Mattocks, Director. E-mail: mattheo@isu.edu. Application contact: Dr. Stephanie Salzman, Director, Office of Standards and Assessment, 208-236-3114. Fax: 208-236-4697. E-mail: salzstep@isu.edu.

Indiana University Bloomington, School of Health, Physical Education and Recreation, Program in Kinesiology, Bloomington, IN 47405. Offerings include administration (MS), athletic administration/sport management (MS), sport management (MS). Program faculty: 12 full-time (2 women). *Degree requirements:* Thesis optional, foreign language not required. *Entrance requirements:* GRE. Application deadline: rolling. Application fee: $35. *Expenses:* Tuition $153 per credit hour for state residents; $446 per credit hour for nonresidents. Fees $343 per year. • Dr. Harold Morris, Chairperson, 812-855-3114. Application contact: Program Office, 812-855-5523. Fax: 812-855-9417. E-mail: kines@indiana.edu.

Indiana University Bloomington, School of Health, Physical Education and Recreation, Program in Recreation and Park Administration, Bloomington, IN 47405. Offerings include recreational sports administration (MS). Program faculty: 14 full-time (6 women). *Degree requirements:* Computer language required, foreign language and thesis not required. *Entrance requirements:* GRE or minimum GPA of 2.8. Application deadline: rolling. Application fee: $35. *Expenses:* Tuition $153 per credit hour for state residents; $446 per credit hour for nonresidents. Fees $343 per year. • Dr. Joel Meier, Chairperson, 812-855-4711. Application contact: Program Office, 812-855-4711. Fax: 812-855-3998. E-mail: recpark@indiana.edu.

Indiana University of Pennsylvania, College of Health and Human Services, Department of Health and Physical Education, Indiana, PA 15705-1087. Offerings include aquatics administration and facilities management (MS), sport management (MS). *Degree requirements:* Thesis optional, foreign language not required. *Entrance requirements:* TOEFL (minimum score 500). Application deadline: 7/1 (priority date; rolling processing; 11/1 for spring admission). Application fee: $30. *Expenses:* Tuition $3468 per year full-time, $193 per credit part-time for state residents; $6236 per year full-time, $346 per credit part-time for nonresidents. Fees $313 per year (minimum) full-time, $84 per year part-time. • Dr. James Mill, Chairperson and Graduate Coordinator, 724-357-2770. E-mail: jimmill@grove.iup.edu.

Lynn University, School of Graduate Studies, School of Hospitality Administration, Boca Raton, FL 33431-5598. Offerings include sports and athletics administration (MS). School faculty: 5 full-time (1 woman), 2 part-time (1 woman). *Degree requirements:* Computer language, project required, foreign language not required. *Average time to degree:* master's–1.6 years full-time, 3.6 years part-time. *Entrance requirements:* GMAT, minimum undergraduate GPA of 3.0. Application deadline: rolling. Application fee: $50. Electronic applications accepted. *Expenses:* Tuition $375 per credit hour. Fees $60 per year. • Dr. Linsley DeVeau, Dean, 561-994-0770 Ext. 260. Fax: 561-997-9541. E-mail: admission@lynn.edu. Application contact: Peter Gallo, Graduate Admissions Counselor, 800-544-8035. Fax: 561-241-3552. E-mail: admission@lynn.edu.

Mississippi State University, College of Education, Department of Physical Health, Education, Recreation, and Sports, Mississippi State, MS 39762. Offerings include physical education (MS), with options in exercise science, health education/health promotion, sport administration, teaching/coaching. Department faculty: 9 full-time (2 women), 1 part-time (0 women). *Degree requirements:* Comprehensive oral or written exam required, thesis optional, foreign language not required. *Entrance requirements:* Minimum QPA of 2.75 in last 2 years. Application deadline: 7/26 (priority date; rolling processing; 11/10 for spring admission). Application fee: $0 ($25 for international students). *Tuition:* $3017 per year full-time, $168 per credit hour part-time for state residents; $6119 per year full-time, $340 per credit hour part-time for nonresidents. • Dr. Robert Boling, Head, 601-325-2963. Fax: 601-325-4525. E-mail: rbb4@ra.msstate.edu.

Montclair State University, College of Education and Human Services, Department of Health Professions, Physical Education, Recreation, and Leisure Studies, Program in Physical Education, Upper Montclair, NJ 07043-1624. Offerings include coaching and sports administration (MA). Program faculty: 10 full-time. *Degree requirements:* Comprehensive exam, research project required, foreign language and thesis not required. *Entrance requirements:* GRE, appropriate bachelor's degree. Application deadline: 4/1 (rolling processing; 11/1 for spring admission). Application fee: $40. *Expenses:* Tuition $201 per credit for state residents; $257 per credit for nonresidents. Fees $22.05 per credit. • Dr. Ree K. Arnold, Adviser, 973-655-7091.

Morehead State University, College of Education and Behavioral Sciences, Department of Health, Physical Education and Recreation, Morehead, KY 40351. Offerings include sports administration (MS). MS offered jointly with Eastern Kentucky University. Department faculty: 9 full-time (4 women), 6 part-time (3 women). *Application deadline:* 8/1 (priority date; rolling processing; 12/1 for spring admission). *Application fee:* $0. *Tuition:* $2470 per year full-time, $138 per semester hour part-time for state residents; $6710 per year full-time, $373 per semester hour part-time for nonresidents. • Dr. Jack Sheltmire, Chair, 606-783-2180. Fax: 606-783-5058. E-mail: j.sheltmire@morehead-st.edu. Application contact: Betty Cowsert, Graduate Admissions Officer, 606-783-2039. Fax: 606-783-5061.

North Carolina State University, College of Forest Resources, Department of Parks, Recreation and Tourism Management, Raleigh, NC 27695. Offerings include sports management (MRRA, MS). Department faculty: 15 full-time (5 women), 7 part-time (0 women). *Degree requirements:* Thesis required (for some programs), foreign language not required. *Entrance requirements:* GRE General Test, TOEFL (minimum score 550). Application deadline: 6/25 (11/25 for spring admission). Application fee: $45. *Tuition:* $2370 per year full-time, $517 per semester (minimum) part-time for state residents; $11,536 per year full-time, $2809 per semester (minimum) part-time for nonresidents. • Dr. Philip S. Rea, Head, 919-515-3675. E-mail: phil_rea@ncsu.edu. Application contact: Dr. Beth E. Wilson, Director of Graduate Programs, 919-515-3665. Fax: 919-515-3687. E-mail: beth_wilson@ncsu.edu.

North Dakota State University, College of Human Development and Education, School of Education, Program in Pedagogy, Fargo, ND 58105. Offers pedagogy (M Ed, MS), physical education and athletic administration (M Ed, MS). Faculty: 6 full-time (2 women). Students: 9 full-time (5 women), 8 part-time (3 women). Average age 27. 17 applicants, 100% accepted. In 1997, 2 degrees awarded (100% found work related to degree). *Degree requirements:* Thesis required (for some programs), foreign language not required. *Entrance requirements:* Cooperative English Test, GRE, MAT, TOEFL (minimum score 525). Application deadline: 5/1 (rolling processing). Application fee: $25. *Tuition:* $2572 per year full-time, $107 per credit part-time for state residents; $6868 per year full-time, $286 per credit part-time for nonresidents. *Financial aid:* Teaching assistantships, full tuition waivers, Federal Work-Study, institutionally sponsored loans, and career-related internships or fieldwork available. Financial aid application deadline: 4/15. • Dr. Roman Horejsi, Coordinator, 701-231-8682. Fax: 701-231-8872. E-mail: horejsi@plains.nodak.edu.

Northwestern State University of Louisiana, Department of Health and Human Performance, Program in Sport Administration, Natchitoches, LA 71497. Awards M Ed. *Degree requirements:* Thesis or alternative required, foreign language not required. *Entrance requirements:* GRE General Test (minimum combined score of 800), minimum undergraduate GPA of 2.5. Application deadline: 8/1 (priority date; rolling processing; 1/10 for spring admission). Application fee: $15 ($25 for international students). *Tuition:* $2147 per year full-time, $336 per semester (minimum) part-time for state residents; $6437 per year full-time, $336 per semester (minimum) part-time for nonresidents. *Financial aid:* Career-related internships or fieldwork available. Financial aid application deadline: 7/15. • Application contact: Dr. Tom Hanson, Dean, Graduate Studies and Research, 318-357-5851. Fax: 318-357-5019.

Announcement: Northwestern State University of Louisiana offers 33-hour MEd degrees in sport administration and health promotion. Faculty members develop mentoring relationships with students, which may result in professional publications and presentations. An internship experience culminates the degree and often provides employment opportunities for new graduates. Located in the picturesque part of northwest Louisiana, Northwestern is a reasonably priced university of approximately 9,000 students. Through graduate assistantships, qualified students may become involved in an array of University experiences, including athletics, teaching, and research. For information, students may contact Dr. Susan Molstad (telephone: 318-357-5103; e-mail: molstad@alpha.nsula.edu).

Ohio University, Graduate Studies, College of Health and Human Services, School of Recreation and Sport Sciences, Program in Sports Administration, Athens, OH 45701-2979. Awards MSA. Students: 41 full-time (10 women), 8 part-time (3 women); includes 7 minority (5 African Americans, 2 Hispanics), 15 international. 139 applicants, 20% accepted. *Degree requirements:* Thesis or alternative, 11 week internship required, foreign language not required. *Entrance requirements:* GRE General Test or MAT, interview. Application fee: $30. *Tuition:* $5430 per year full-time, $216 per quarter hour part-time for state residents; $10,431 per year full-time, $423 per quarter hour part-time for nonresidents. *Financial aid:* Federal Work-Study, institutionally sponsored loans available. Financial aid application deadline: 3/15. • Dr. Keith Ernce, Director, School of Recreation and Sport Sciences, 740-593-0284.

Old Dominion University, Darden College of Education, Department of Exercise Science, Physical Education, and Recreation, Norfolk, VA 23529. Offerings include physical education (MS Ed), with options in administration, athletic training, curriculum and instruction, exercise science and wellness, recreation administration, sports management. Department faculty: 8 full-time (3 women), 4 part-time (2 women), 9.3 FTE. *Degree requirements:* Comprehensive exams, internship, research project required, foreign language and thesis not required. *Entrance requirements:* GRE General Test (minimum combined score of 900), minimum GPA of 2.5. Application deadline: 7/1 (rolling processing; 11/1 for spring admission). Application fee: $30. *Expenses:* Tuition $180 per credit hour for state residents; $477 per credit hour for nonresidents. Fees $140 per year full-time, $32 per semester part-time. • Dr. Patrick Tow, Chair, 757-683-3351. E-mail: ptow@odu.edu. Application contact: Dr. Elizabeth Dowling, Graduate Program Director, 757-683-4514. Fax: 757-683-4270. E-mail: ldowling@odu.edu.

Robert Morris College, Program in Business Administration, 881 Narrows Run Road, Moon Township, PA 15108-1189. Offerings include sport management (MBA, MS). Only part-time programs offered. Program faculty: 35 full-time (6 women), 35 part-time (5 women). *Entrance requirements:* GMAT (minimum score 450), minimum GPA of 2.5. Application deadline: 8/1 (priority date; rolling processing; 11/30 for spring admission). Application fee: $25 ($35 for international students). *Expenses:* Tuition $328 per credit. Fees $15 per credit. • Dr. Joseph F. Constable, Dean, School of Management, 412-262-8451. Fax: 412-262-8494. E-mail: constabl@robert-morris.edu. Application contact: Vincent J. Kane, Recruiting Coordinator, 412-262-8535. Fax: 412-299-2425.

St. Cloud State University, College of Education, Department of Health, Physical Education, Recreation and Sport Science, St. Cloud, MN 56301-4498. Offerings include sports management (MS). Department faculty: 15 full-time (5 women), 6 part-time (2 women). *Degree requirements:* Thesis or alternative required, foreign language not required. *Entrance requirements:* GRE General Test, minimum GPA of 2.75. Application fee: $20 ($100 for international students). *Expenses:* Tuition $128 per credit for state residents; $203 per credit for nonresidents. Fees $16.32 per credit. • Dr. Rodney Dobey, Chairperson, 320-255-4251. Application contact: Ann Anderson, Graduate Studies Office, 320-255-2113. Fax: 320-654-5371. E-mail: anna@grad.stcloud.msus.edu.

St. Thomas University, School of Graduate Studies, Department of Professional Management, Department of Sports Administration, Miami, FL 33054-6459. Awards MBA. Part-time and evening/weekend programs available. *Degree requirements:* Comprehensive exam required, foreign language and thesis not required. *Average time to degree:* master's–1 year full-time. *Entrance requirements:* TOEFL (minimum score 550), interview, minimum GPA of 3.0 or GMAT. Application deadline: 5/1 (rolling processing; 10/1 for spring admission). Application fee: $30. *Tuition:* $410 per credit.

Seton Hall University, W. Paul Stillman School of Business, Center for Sports Management, South Orange, NJ 07079-2692. Awards MBA. Part-time and evening/weekend programs available. *Entrance requirements:* GMAT (minimum score 500), TOEFL (minimum score 550). Application deadline: 6/1 (priority date; rolling processing). Application fee: $50. *Expenses:* Tuition $538 per credit. Fees $185 per semester. *Financial aid:* Research assistantships and career-related internships or fieldwork available. Aid available to part-time students. Financial aid applicants required to submit FAFSA. • Dr. Ann Mayo, Director, 973-761-9707. Application contact: Student Information Office, 973-761-9222. Fax: 973-761-9217. E-mail: busgrad@shu.edu.

Springfield College, Programs in Health Science, Springfield, MA 01109-3797. Offerings include sports injury prevention and management (M Ed, MPE, MS). Faculty: 5 full-time (2 women), 6 part-time (1 woman), 7 FTE. *Degree requirements:* Thesis (for some programs), comprehensive exam required, foreign language not required. *Application deadline:* (12/1 for spring admission). *Application fee:* $40. *Expenses:* Tuition $474 per credit. Fees $25 per year. • Charles J. Redmond, Director, 413-748-3231. Application contact: Donald J. Shaw Jr., Director of Graduate Admissions, 413-748-3225. Fax: 413-748-3694. E-mail: dshaw@spfldcol.edu.

Springfield College, Programs in Physical Education, Springfield, MA 01109-3797. Offerings include athletic administration (M Ed, MPE, MS, CAS), sport management (M Ed, MPE, MS, CAS), teaching and administration (M Ed, MPE, MS, CAS). Faculty: 25 full-time (13 women), 2 part-time (0 women), 26 FTE. *Degree requirements:* For master's, comprehensive exam, research project required, foreign language and thesis not required; for CAS, comprehensive exam required, foreign language and thesis not required. *Application deadline:* 2/1 (priority date; rolling processing; 12/1 for spring admission). *Application fee:* $40. *Expenses:* Tuition $474 per credit. Fees $25 per year. • Dr. Betty L. Mann, Director, 413-748-3125. Application contact: Donald J. Shaw Jr., Director of Graduate Admissions, 413-748-3225. Fax: 413-748-3694. E-mail: dshaw@spfldcol.edu.

Temple University, School of Tourism and Hospitality, Department of Sport Management and Leisure Studies, Program in Sport and Recreation Administration, Philadelphia, PA 19122-6096. Awards Ed M. Part-time and evening/weekend programs available. Students: 90 (40 women); includes 22 minority (21 African Americans, 1 Asian American), 3 international. 78 applicants, 63% accepted. In 1997, 39 degrees awarded. *Degree requirements:* Computer language required, foreign language and thesis not required. *Entrance requirements:* GRE General Test or MAT, minimum undergraduate GPA of 2.8. Application deadline: 6/1 (priority date; 10/1 for spring admission). Application fee: $40. *Expenses:* Tuition $323 per semester hour for state residents; $444 per semester hour for nonresidents. Fees $170 per year full-time, $28 per semester (minimum) part-time. *Financial aid:* Teaching assistantships available. • Application contact: Dr. Elizabeth Barber, Graduate Coordinator, 215-204-8706. Fax: 215-204-1455. E-mail: betsyb@astro.temple.edu.

See in-depth description on page 1903.

Directory: Sports Administration

United States Sports Academy, Graduate Programs, Department of Sport Management, Daphne, AL 36526-7055. Awards MSS, Ed D. Part-time programs available. Postbaccalaureate distance learning degree programs offered (minimal on-campus study). *Degree requirements:* For master's, comprehensive exam required, thesis optional, foreign language not required; for doctorate, dissertation, oral and written exams required, foreign language not required. *Entrance requirements:* For master's, GRE General Test (minimum combined score of 800), MAT (minimum score 27), minimum GPA of 2.75; for doctorate, GRE General Test (minimum combined score of 950), master's degree. Application deadline: 8/15 (priority date; rolling processing). Application fee: $25 ($125 for international students). *Expenses:* Tuition $300 per semester hour (minimum) for state residents; $350 per semester hour (minimum) for nonresidents. Fees $100 (one-time charge). *Faculty research:* Computers in sport management, leadership behavior, personnel evaluation, tourism.

See in-depth description on page 1893.

Université de Montréal, Department of Physical Education, Montréal, PQ H3C 3J7, Canada. Offerings include sport and fitness management (M Sc). Department faculty: 23 full-time (7 women). *Degree requirements:* 1 foreign language, thesis (for some programs). *Application deadline:* 2/1. *Application fee:* $30. • Claude Alain, Chairman, 514-343-6166.

University of Alberta, Faculty of Graduate Studies and Research, Program in Business Administration, Edmonton, AB T6G 2E1, Canada. Offerings include leisure and sport management (MBA). *Degree requirements:* Thesis or alternative required, foreign language not required. *Entrance requirements:* GMAT, TOEFL. Application deadline: 5/31 (priority date; rolling processing). Application fee: $60. *Expenses:* Tuition $390 per course for Canadian residents; $781 per course for nonresidents. Fees $500 per year full-time, $184 per year part-time. • Dr. Kay Devine, Associate Dean, 403-492-3946. E-mail: kay.devine@ualberta.ca. Application contact: Darren Bondar, Assistant Director, 403-492-3946. Fax: 403-492-7825. E-mail: darren.bondar@ualberta.ca.

University of Denver, Daniels College of Business, General Business Administration Program, Denver, CO 80208. Offerings include sports management (MSM). MSMGEN offered jointly with the Department of Engineering; MSMC new for fall 1998. Program faculty: 76 full-time (15 women). *Application deadline:* 5/1 (priority date; rolling processing; 1/1 for spring admission). *Application fee:* $50. *Expenses:* Tuition $18,216 per year full-time, $506 per credit hour part-time. Fees $159 per year. • Dr. Tom Howard, Director, 303-871-4402. Application contact: Jan Johnson, Executive Director, Student Services, 303-871-3416. Fax: 303-871-4466. E-mail: dcb@du.edu.

University of Miami, School of Education, Department of Educational and Psychological Studies, Program in Higher Education, Coral Gables, FL 33124. Offerings include higher education/sports administration (Ed D, PhD). Program being phased out; applicants no longer accepted. Program faculty: 2 full-time (1 woman), 4 part-time (3 women). *Degree requirements:* Dissertation required, foreign language not required. *Average time to degree:* master's–2.5 years part-time; doctorate–5 years part-time. *Expenses:* Tuition $815 per credit hour. Fees $174 per year. • Dr. Thomas Angelo, Coordinator, 305-284-2968. Fax: 305-284-3003. E-mail: tangelo@umiami.ir.miami.edu.

University of Miami, School of Education, Department of Exercise and Sport Sciences, Program in Sports Administration, Coral Gables, FL 33124. Offers higher education/sports administration (Ed D, PhD), sports administration (MS Ed). Ed D and PhD offered jointly with Program in Higher Education. Part-time programs available. Faculty: 4 full-time (1 woman), 7 part-time (4 women). Students: 10 full-time (2 women), 10 part-time (3 women); includes 6 minority (4 African Americans, 1 Asian American, 1 Hispanic). Average age 26. 39 applicants, 56% accepted. In 1997, 9 master's awarded. *Degree requirements:* For master's, comprehensive exam or thesis, internship required, thesis optional, foreign language not required; for doctorate, computer language, dissertation required, foreign language not required. *Entrance requirements:* For master's, GRE General Test (minimum combined score of 1000), GRE Subject Test, TOEFL (minimum score 550); for doctorate, GRE General Test, GRE Subject Test, TOEFL (minimum score 550). Application deadline: rolling. Application fee: $35. *Expenses:* Tuition $815 per credit hour. Fees $174 per year. *Financial aid:* 10 students received aid; graduate assistantships, full and partial tuition waivers, Federal Work-Study, institutionally sponsored loans, and career-related internships or fieldwork available. Financial aid application deadline: 3/1. *Faculty research:* Constitutional procedural due process, legal liability, tort law, leadership, ethics. • Dr. Harry C. Mallios, Chairman, Department of Exercise and Sport Sciences, 305-284-3011. Fax: 305-284-3003.

Announcement: The University of Miami offers the MS and PhD degrees in sports administration. The program prepares students for careers in organizations both public and private, amateur and professional, according to personal and professional interests and goals. An additional dimension is provided by field experience at a sponsor organization. Graduate assistantships are available.

University of New Orleans, College of Education, Department of Health and Physical Education, New Orleans, LA 70148. Offerings include science, pedagogy and coaching sport management (MA). Department faculty: 9 full-time (5 women). *Application deadline:* 7/1 (priority date; rolling processing). *Application fee:* $20. *Expenses:* Tuition $2362 per year full-time, $373 per semester (minimum) part-time for state residents; $7888 per year full-time, $1423 per semester (minimum) part-time for nonresidents. Fees $170 per year full-time, $25 per semester (minimum) part-time. • Dr. Robert Eason, Chairperson, 504-280-6420. E-mail: blehp@uno.edu. Application contact: Dr. Mark Loftin, Graduate Coordinator, 504-280-6417. Fax: 504-280-6018. E-mail: mxlhp@uno.edu.

The University of North Carolina at Chapel Hill, College of Arts and Sciences, Department of Physical Education, Exercise and Sport Science, Chapel Hill, NC 27599. Offerings include sports administration (MA). Department faculty: 12 full-time, 5 part-time. *Degree requirements:* Thesis (for some programs), comprehensive exam required, foreign language not required. *Entrance requirements:* GRE General Test, NTE, minimum GPA of 3.0. Application deadline: 1/1 (priority date; rolling processing). Application fee: $55. *Expenses:* Tuition $1428 per year full-time, $357 per semester (minimum) part-time for state residents; $10,414 per year full-time, $2604 per semester (minimum) part-time for nonresidents. Fees $782 per year full-time, $332 per semester (minimum) part-time. • Dr. Frederick O. Mueller, Chairman, 919-962-0017. Application contact: Dr. Pamela Robinson, Director of Graduate Studies, 919-962-5173.

University of Oklahoma, College of Arts and Sciences, Department of Health and Sports Sciences, Norman, OK 73019-0390. Offerings include sport management and behavior (MS). Department faculty: 7 full-time (2 women), 2 part-time (1 woman). *Degree requirements:* Thesis or alternative, comprehensive exam. *Entrance requirements:* GRE General Test (minimum score 500 on each section), TOEFL (minimum score 550), minimum GPA of 3.0. Application deadline: 6/1 (priority date; rolling processing). Application fee: $25. *Expenses:* Tuition $1920 per year full-time, $80 per credit hour part-time for state residents; $6108 per year full-time, $255 per credit hour part-time for nonresidents. Fees $468 per year full-time, $12 per semester (minimum) part-time. • Dr. E. Laurette Taylor, Chairperson, 405-325-5211. Fax: 405-325-1365.

University of Rhode Island, College of Business Administration, Kingston, RI 02881. Offerings include international sports management (MBA). *Application deadline:* 4/15 (priority date; rolling processing). *Application fee:* $35. *Expenses:* Tuition $3446 per year full-time, $191 per credit part-time for state residents; $9850 per year full-time, $547 per credit part-time for nonresidents. Fees $1276 per year full-time, $135 per semester (minimum) part-time.

University of St. Thomas, Graduate School of Business, Day MBA Program, St. Paul, MN 55105-1096. Offerings include sports and entertainment management (MBA). Program faculty: 13 part-time. *Degree requirements:* Computer language required, foreign language and thesis not required. *Entrance requirements:* GMAT (score in 50th percentile or higher). Application deadline: 5/1 (priority date; rolling processing). Application fee: $30. *Tuition:* $473 per credit hour. • Application contact: Jim O'Connor, Student Adviser, 612-962-4233. Fax: 612-962-4260.

University of St. Thomas, Graduate School of Business, Evening MBA Program, St. Paul, MN 55105-1096. Offerings include sports and entertainment management (MBA). Program faculty: 16 full-time (2 women), 89 part-time (17 women). *Degree requirements:* Computer language required, foreign language and thesis not required. *Entrance requirements:* GMAT (score in 50th percentile or higher). Application deadline: 8/1 (priority date; rolling processing; 12/1 for spring admission). Application fee: $30. *Tuition:* $416 per credit hour. • Dr. Stanford Nyquist, MBA Director, 612-962-4242. Application contact: Martha Ballard, Director of Student Services, 612-962-4226. Fax: 612-962-4260.

University of San Francisco, College of Arts and Sciences, Program in Sports and Fitness Management, San Francisco, CA 94117-1080. Awards MA. Evening/weekend programs available. Faculty: 2 full-time (1 woman), 6 part-time (2 women). Students: 64 full-time (28 women); includes 7 minority (4 African Americans, 2 Asian Americans, 1 Hispanic), 5 international. Average age 27. 89 applicants, 74% accepted. In 1997, 23 degrees awarded. *Degree requirements:* Thesis or alternative required, foreign language not required. *Average time to degree:* master's–2 years full-time. *Entrance requirements:* Interview, minimum GPA of 2.75. Application deadline: 3/31 (priority date; rolling processing). Application fee: $40 ($50 for international students). *Tuition:* $658 per unit (minimum). *Financial aid:* 39 students received aid; Federal Work-Study, institutionally sponsored loans, and career-related internships or fieldwork available. Financial aid application deadline: 3/2. *Faculty research:* Media and sports, sports marketing, sports law, management and organization. • Lawrence A. Wenner, Graduate Program Director, 415-422-2678. Fax: 415-422-6267. E-mail: wenner@usfca.edu.

University of Tennessee, Knoxville, College of Education, Program in Human Performance and Sport Studies, Knoxville, TN 37996. Offerings include sport management (MS). *Degree requirements:* Thesis optional, foreign language not required. *Entrance requirements:* TOEFL (minimum score 550), minimum GPA of 2.7. Application deadline: 2/1 (priority date; rolling processing). Application fee: $35. Electronic applications accepted. *Tuition:* $3354 per year full-time, $181 per semester hour part-time for state residents; $8410 per year full-time, $462 per semester hour part-time for nonresidents. • Dr. Tom George, Associate Dean, 423-974-0907. Fax: 423-974-8718. E-mail: tgeorge1@utk.edu.

University of the Incarnate Word, School of Graduate Studies, College of Professional Studies, Programs in Administration, San Antonio, TX 78209-6397. Offerings include sports management (MAA). *Entrance requirements:* GMAT, GRE, MAT, TOEFL (minimum score 550). Application deadline: 8/15 (priority date; rolling processing; 12/31 for spring admission). Application fee: $20. *Expenses:* Tuition $350 per semester hour. Fees $180 per year full-time, $111 per semester (minimum) part-time. • Victor Prosper, Coordinator, 210-829-3185. Fax: 210-829-3169. Application contact: Brian F. Dalton, Dean of Enrollment Services, 210-829-6005. Fax: 210-829-3921. E-mail: briand@the-college.iwctx.edu.

University of Wisconsin–La Crosse, College of Health, Physical Education and Recreation, Department of Exercise and Sport Science, Program in General Sports Administration, La Crosse, WI 54601-3742. Awards MS. Part-time programs available. Faculty: 14 full-time (5 women), 6 part-time (2 women), 17.16 FTE. Students: 17 full-time (9 women), 14 part-time (6 women); includes 1 minority (African American), 2 international. Average age 27. 70 applicants, 71% accepted. In 1997, 9 degrees awarded. *Degree requirements:* Thesis optional, foreign language not required. *Entrance requirements:* Minimum GPA of 3.0 during previous 2 years, 2.85 overall. Application deadline: 3/1 (priority date; rolling processing). Application fee: $38. *Tuition:* $3737 per year full-time, $208 per credit part-time for state residents; $11,921 per year full-time, $633 per credit part-time for nonresidents. *Financial aid:* In 1997–98, 4 students received aid, including 4 assistantships averaging $546 per month and totaling $19,656; Federal Work-Study, institutionally sponsored loans, and career-related internships or fieldwork also available. Financial aid application deadline: 3/15; applicants required to submit FAFSA. • Dr. Jane Meyer, Coordinator, 608-785-8194. E-mail: meyer_jc@mail.uwlax.edu. Application contact: Tim Lewis, Director of Admissions, 608-785-8939. Fax: 608-785-6695. E-mail: admissions@mail.uwlax.edu.

Wayne State University, College of Education, Division of Health and Physical Education, Detroit, MI 48202. Offerings include sports administration (MA). Division faculty: 34. *Application deadline:* 7/1. *Application fee:* $20 ($30 for international students). *Expenses:* Tuition $163 per credit hour for state residents; $355 per credit hour for nonresidents. Fees $498 per year full-time, $114 per semester (minimum) part-time. • Dr. Sarah Erbaugh, Assistant Dean, 313-577-4265. Application contact: John Wirth, Graduate Program Coordinator, 313-577-5896. Fax: 313-577-5999.

West Chester University of Pennsylvania, School of Business and Public Affairs, Program in Sport and Athletic Administration, West Chester, PA 19383. Awards MSA. *Degree requirements:* Comprehensive exam required, thesis optional, foreign language not required. *Entrance requirements:* GMAT, GRE, or MAT, interview, minimum GPA of 3.0. Application deadline: 4/15 (priority date; rolling processing; 10/15 for spring admission). Application fee: $25. *Expenses:* Tuition $3468 per year full-time, $193 per credit part-time for state residents; $6236 per year full-time, $346 per credit part-time for nonresidents. Fees $660 per year full-time, $38 per credit part-time. *Financial aid:* Application deadline 2/15. • Dick Yoder, Graduate Coordinator, 610-436-3356.

West Chester University of Pennsylvania, School of Health Sciences, Department of Kinesiology, West Chester, PA 19383. Offerings include sport and athletic administration (MSA). Department faculty: 1 full-time, 9 part-time. *Application deadline:* 4/15 (priority date; rolling processing; 10/15 for spring admission). *Application fee:* $25. *Expenses:* Tuition $3468 per year full-time, $193 per credit part-time for state residents; $6236 per year full-time, $346 per credit part-time for nonresidents. Fees $660 per year full-time, $38 per credit part-time. • Dr. Monita Lank, Chair, 610-436-2260. Application contact: Dr. John G. Williams, Graduate Coordinator, 610-436-3119.

Western Illinois University, College of Education and Human Services, Department of Physical Education, Macomb, IL 61455-1390. Offerings include sport management (MS). Department faculty: 18 full-time (12 women). *Degree requirements:* Thesis or alternative required, foreign language not required. *Entrance requirements:* Minimum GPA of 3.0. Application deadline: rolling. Application fee: $0 ($25 for international students). *Expenses:* Tuition $2304 per year full-time, $96 per semester hour part-time for state residents; $6912 per year full-time, $288 per semester hour part-time for nonresidents. Fees $944 per year full-time, $33 per semester hour part-time. • Dr. Donna Phillips, Chairperson, 309-298-1981. Application contact: Barbara Baily, Director of Graduate Studies, 309-298-1806. Fax: 309-298-2245. E-mail: barb_baily@ccmail.wiu.edu.

Western Michigan University, College of Education, Department of Health, Physical Education and Recreation, Kalamazoo, MI 49008. Offerings include administration (MA). *Application deadline:* 2/15 (priority date; rolling processing). *Application fee:* $25. *Expenses:* Tuition $154 per credit hour for state residents; $372 per credit hour for nonresidents. Fees $602 per year full-time, $132 per semester part-time. • Dr. Debra Berkey, Chair, 616-387-2705. Application contact: Paula J. Boodt, Coordinator, Graduate Admissions and Recruitment, 616-387-2000. E-mail: paulaboodt@wmich.edu.

Whitworth College, Graduate Studies in Education, Program in Physical Education and Sport Administration, Spokane, WA 99251-0001. Awards MA. *Degree requirements:* Comprehensive exams, internship, practicum, research project, or thesis required, foreign language not required. *Entrance requirements:* GRE General Test. Application deadline: 9/1 (priority date; rolling processing; 2/1 for spring admission). Application fee: $25.

Wichita State University, College of Education, Department of Health and Physical Education, Wichita, KS 67260. Offerings include sports administration (M Ed), with option in exercise science and wellness. Department faculty: 5 full-time (3 women), 17 part-time (9 women). *Degree requirements:* Comprehensive exam required, thesis optional, foreign language not required. *Entrance requirements:* TOEFL (minimum score 550), minimum GPA of 2.75. Application deadline: 7/1 (priority date; rolling processing; 1/1 for spring admission). Application fee: $25 ($40 for international students). Electronic applications accepted. *Expenses:* Tuition $2303 per year full-time, $96 per credit hour part-time for state residents; $7691 per year full-time, $321 per credit hour part-time for nonresidents. Fees $490 per year full-time, $75 per semester (minimum) part-time. • Dr. Susan K. Kovar, Chairperson, 316-978-3340. E-mail: kovar@wsuhub.uc.twsu.edu. Application contact: Dr. Lori Miller, Graduate Coordinator, 316-978-3340. Fax: 316-978-3302. E-mail: lmiller@wsuhub.uc.twsu.edu.

Xavier University, College of Social Sciences, Department of Education, Program in Sport Administration, Cincinnati, OH 45207-2111. Awards M Ed. Part-time and evening/weekend programs available. Faculty: 1 full-time (0 women), 4 part-time (1 woman), 2 FTE. Students: 16 full-time (4 women), 43 part-time (14 women); includes 8 minority (7 African Americans, 1 Hispanic). Average age 30. 43 applicants, 72% accepted. In 1997, 26 degrees awarded. *Degree requirements:* Internship required, foreign language and thesis not required. *Entrance requirements:* GRE or MAT (minimum score 35), minimum GPA of 2.8. Application deadline: rolling. Application fee: $25. *Financial aid:* In 1997–98, 19 students received aid, including 19 scholarships (9 to first-year students); career-related internships or fieldwork also available. Aid available to part-time students. *Faculty research:* Sport management, youth sport, coaching education, sport medicine. • Dr. Ron Quinn, Director of Health and Sport Studies, 513-745-3653. Fax: 513-745-4291. E-mail: xugrad@admin.xu.edu. Application contact: Sheila Speth, Director of Graduate Services, 513-745-3360. Fax: 513-745-1048. E-mail: xugrad@admin.xu.edu.

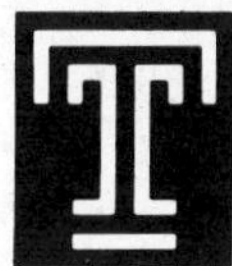

TEMPLE UNIVERSITY

Department of Sport Management and Leisure Studies

Program of Study

The Department of Sport Management and Leisure Studies offers a program leading to the Master of Education (Ed.M.) in sport and recreation administration. The master's degree program is designed to meet the growing demand for supervisors and administrators in the areas of sport management, sport administration, arena management, college athletics, sports governing bodies, marketing, ticketing, fund-raising, professional sports, amateur sports, intramurals, campus recreation, commercial recreation, public recreation and parks, resort management, voluntary agencies, private agencies, and leisure services. The curriculum includes courses in administration, philosophy and ethics, legal aspects, finance and fund-raising, athletic governance, facility management, sports marketing, and research methods. The strength of the program lies in its internship opportunities based on a nationwide network. Students work closely with their advisers, internship coordinators, and faculty mentors. The master's degree can be completed in one calendar year by full-time students or in two years by part-time students. The master's program offers four specialty options (thesis, project, comprehensive exam, and practicum) with requirements ranging from 30 to 39 semester hours.

Research Facilities

The Department of Sport Management and Leisure Studies is housed in Vivacqua Hall on Broad Street, where faculty offices and classrooms are located. The College of Health, Physical Education, Recreation and Dance has its own computer laboratory and research laboratory. Because professionals in this field should have an education that enables them to be expert managers, marketers, and planners in the public, private, and commercial sectors, the primary research and learning facilities for the department are located within the community. Examples of internship sites for graduate students are college athletics, professional sports, sports governing bodies, arenas, stadiums, recreation agencies, convention centers, and resorts. The program is based not only on the theoretical foundation that defines the profession but also on the practical application of management techniques in a real-life setting.

Financial Aid

The University offers financial aid through grants, loans, and work-study programs based on need as calculated by Student Financial Services. The Department of Sport Management and Leisure Studies offers graduate assistantships, which include a stipend plus a tuition scholarship. As a state-related university, Temple extends special benefits to students who are residents of Pennsylvania, while for out-of-state students, it works to keep tuition as low as resources and the demands of quality education permit.

Cost of Study

Graduate tuition for 1997–98 was $308 per credit hour for Pennsylvania residents and $429 per credit hour for nonresidents; a $50 computer fee, a $25 activity fee, and a $35 health fee were also required.

Living and Housing Costs

Costs for student housing are estimated to be approximately $12,000. There is limited on-campus housing available for graduate students. Rooms, apartments, and houses are available for graduate students in the surrounding city and suburbs.

Student Group

The Department of Sport Management and Leisure Studies enrolls approximately 80 graduate students each year, about 50 percent of whom are women. Approximately half of the students are full-time and half are part-time. Generally, 10 percent are international students.

Student Outcomes

The rapid growth of sport and leisure has created a demand for qualified sport and recreation administrators who can plan, organize, and direct recreation and sport programs and facilities. The strength of the program lies in its internship opportunities and professional placements. The master's program places approximately 90 percent of its graduates directly in their field of study. Placements of recent graduate students range from college athletics, professional teams, and arena management to campus recreation, municipal recreation, and convention and tourism bureaus.

Location

Philadelphia is listed among the country's most livable cities. A culturally diverse city, Philadelphia has many art museums, a symphony orchestra, and America's oldest zoo. There are professional sports teams in hockey, basketball, football, and baseball, as well as many college sports. Temple University's location provides access to outstanding internship sites and potential job placements in the region.

The University and The Department

Temple University is one of the nation's senior comprehensive research institutions and enrolls more than 28,000 students in fifteen schools and colleges. Graduate students enjoy studying at Temple because it offers culturally diverse campus life within an urban/metropolitan setting that is rich in vitality. Educators in the Department of Sport Management and Leisure Studies have been given the direct charge from recreation and industry leaders to prepare students who will possess a wide variety of skills, including excellent human and conceptual skills, and flexibility.

Applying

Students should apply by June 1 for the fall semester and by October 1 for the spring semester. Applicants must have a minimum undergraduate grade point average of 2.8 and must submit three letters of recommendation, transcripts from all accredited institutions previously attended, Graduate Record Examinations (GRE) or Miller Analogies Test (MAT) scores, a 350–500-word statement of goals addressing the candidate's academic and professional objectives as well as strengths and weaknesses, and a resume detailing previous educational and work experience. Each of the admission criteria will be weighted equally in reaching a final decision.

Correspondence and Information

Dr. Elizabeth Barber, Graduate Coordinator
316-F Vivacqua Hall
Temple University
Philadelphia, Pennsylvania 19122
Telephone: 215-204-8706
Fax: 215-204-1455
E-mail: betsyb@astro.temple.edu

Temple University

THE FACULTY AND THEIR RESEARCH

Elizabeth H. Barber, Associate Professor; Ph.D., Iowa. Travel and tourism, professional preparation in sport and recreation.
Michael Jackson, Professor; H.S.D., Indiana. Facility management, administration of sport.
Richard Kraus, Professor Emeritus; Ed.D., Columbia Teachers College. Philosophy of recreation and leisure.
Bonnie Parkhouse, Professor; Ph.D., Minnesota. Sport management, fund-raising, gender equity, marketing of sport and recreation.
Ira Shapiro, Professor and Chairperson; Ph.D., North Carolina at Chapel Hill. Philosophy, ethics, professional preparation in sport and recreation.
Ted Tedrick, Professor; Ph.D., Maryland. Leisure and aging, sport and recreation administration.

Academic and Professional Programs in Social Work

This part of Book 6 consists of one section covering social work. This section has a table of contents (listing the program directory, announcements, and in-depth descriptions); program directory, which consists of brief profiles of programs in the relevant fields (and that include 50-word or 100-word announcements following the profiles, if programs have chosen to include them); Cross-Discipline Announcements, if any programs have chosen to submit such entries; and in-depth descriptions, which are more individualized statements included, if programs have chosen to submit them.

Section 43
Social Work

This section contains directories of institutions offering graduate programs in human services and social work, followed by in-depth entries submitted by institutions that chose to prepare detailed program descriptions. Additional information about programs listed in the directories but not augmented by an in-depth entry may be obtained by writing directly to the dean of a graduate school or chair of a department at the address given in the directory.

For programs offering related work, see also in this book Allied Health and Education. In Book 2, see Criminology and Forensics, Home Economics and Family Studies, Psychology and Counseling, and Sociology, Anthropology, and Archaeology.

CONTENTS

Program Directories

Announcements

Cross-Discipline Announcements

In-Depth Descriptions

See also:

Human Services

Abilene Christian University, College of Arts and Sciences, Department of Sociology and Social Work, Abilene, TX 79699-9100. Offers program in social services administration (MS). Part-time programs available. Faculty: 4 part-time (0 women). Students: 2 full-time (1 woman), 3 part-time (all women); includes 1 minority (Native American), 1 international. 6 applicants, 83% accepted. *Degree requirements:* Comprehensive exam required, foreign language and thesis not required. *Entrance requirements:* GRE General Test or MAT. Application deadline: 4/1 (priority date; rolling processing; 11/1 for spring admission). Application fee: $25 ($45 for international students). *Expenses:* Tuition $308 per credit hour. Fees $430 per year full-time, $85 per semester (minimum) part-time. *Financial aid:* Federal Work-Study and career-related internships or fieldwork available. Aid available to part-time students. Financial aid application deadline: 4/1. • Dr. Tom Winter, Director of Social Work, 915-674-2306. Application contact: Dr. Carley Dodd, Graduate Dean, 915-674-2354. Fax: 915-674-6717. E-mail: gradinfo@nicanor.acu.edu.

Antioch New England Graduate School, Graduate School, Department of Organization and Management, Program in Human Services Administration, 40 Avon Street, Keene, NH 03431-3516. Awards MHSA, MHSA/Psy D. Faculty: 1 (woman) full-time, 18 part-time (9 women). Students: 9 full-time (7 women), 8 part-time (7 women). Average age 40. In 1997, 13 degrees awarded. *Degree requirements:* Practicum required, foreign language and thesis not required. *Application deadline:* 8/1 (rolling processing; 12/1 for spring admission). *Application fee:* $40. *Expenses:* Tuition $12,700 per year full-time, $330 per credit part-time. Fees $165 per year. *Financial aid:* 9 students received aid; Federal Work-Study and career-related internships or fieldwork available. Financial aid applicants required to submit FAFSA. *Faculty research:* Leadership training for elected/nonelected municipal leaders, focus group research to determine community needs, work force stress related to aging. • Application contact: Carolyn S. Bassett, Co-Director of Admissions, 603-357-6265 Ext. 287. Fax: 603-357-0718. E-mail: cbassett@antiochne.edu.

Baylor University, College of Arts and Sciences, Department of Sociology, Anthropology, Social Work, and Gerontology, Program in Sociology, Waco, TX 76798. Offerings include social work (MA). *Entrance requirements:* GRE General Test. Application deadline: 8/1 (rolling processing). Application fee: $25. *Expenses:* Tuition $7392 per year full-time, $308 per semester hour part-time. Fees $1024 per year. • Dr. Lawrence Felice, Director of Graduate Studies, Department of Sociology, Anthropology, Social Work, and Gerontology, 254-710-1165.

Bellevue University, Graduate School, Bellevue, NE 68005-3098. Offerings include human services (MS). Postbaccalaureate distance learning degree programs offered (no on-campus study). School faculty: 22 full-time (9 women), 13 part-time (5 women). *Average time to degree:* master's–2 years full-time, 3 years part-time. *Application deadline:* 7/15 (priority date; rolling processing; 11/15 for spring admission). *Application fee:* $50. • Dr. Douglas Frost, Dean, 402-293-2025. E-mail: frostd@scholars.bellevue.edu. Application contact: Elizabeth Wall, Director of Marketing and Enrollment, 402-293-3702. Fax: 402-293-3730. E-mail: eaw@scholars.bellevue.edu.

Boricua College, Program in Human Services, New York, NY 10032-1560. Awards MS. Students: 19. *Application deadline:* rolling. *Application fee:* $100. *Tuition:* $7300 per year. • Application contact: Miriam Pfeiffer, Director of Student Services, 718-782-2200.

Brandeis University, The Heller Graduate School, Program in Management, Waltham, MA 02454-2728. Offerings include child, youth, and family services (MBA, MM); human services (MBA, MM). *Average time to degree:* master's–1 year full-time, 3 years part-time. *Entrance requirements:* GRE General Test or GMAT (MM), GRE General Test (MBA). Application fee: $50. *Expenses:* Tuition $22,390 per year full-time, $1940 per course part-time. Fees $45 per year (minimum). • Application contact: Karen Cooney, Admissions Officer, 781-736-3820. Fax: 781-736-3881. E-mail: cooney@binah.cc.brandeis.edu.

California State University, Sacramento, School of Health and Human Services, Division of Social Work, Sacramento, CA 95819-6048. Offerings include family and children's services (MSW). *Degree requirements:* Thesis or alternative, writing proficiency exam required, foreign language not required. *Entrance requirements:* TOEFL (minimum score 550), minimum GPA of 2.5 during previous 2 years. Application deadline: 4/15 (11/1 for spring admission). Application fee: $55. *Expenses:* Tuition $0 for state residents; $246 per unit for nonresidents. Fees $2012 per year full-time, $1346 per year part-time. • Dr. Juan Hernandez, Chair, 916-278-6943.

Concordia University, Program in Human Services, River Forest, IL 60305-1499. Awards MA, CAS. Part-time and evening/weekend programs available. Faculty: 11 full-time (4 women), 8 part-time (3 women). Students: 18 (14 women); includes 3 minority (all African Americans), 3 international. In 1997, 12 master's awarded. *Degree requirements:* For master's, thesis, comprehensive exams required, foreign language not required; for CAS, thesis, final project required, foreign language not required. *Entrance requirements:* For master's, minimum GPA of 2.9; for CAS, master's degree. Application deadline: rolling. Application fee: $0. *Tuition:* $372 per semester hour. *Financial aid:* Research assistantships, institutionally sponsored loans available. Aid available to part-time students. • Dr. Richard Marrs, Coordinator, 708-209-3147. Application contact: Mary Betancourt, Admissions Secretary, 708-209-4093. Fax: 708-209-3454. E-mail: crfdngrad@curf.edu.

Cornell University, Graduate Fields of Human Ecology, Field of Human Service Studies, Ithaca, NY 14853-0001. Offers programs in health services administration (MHA), human service administration (MPS, MS, PhD), program evaluation and planning (MPS, MS, PhD). Faculty: 28 full-time. Students: 54 full-time (37 women); includes 17 minority (6 African Americans, 9 Asian Americans, 1 Hispanic, 1 Native American), 9 international. 87 applicants, 59% accepted. In 1997, 24 master's, 5 doctorates awarded. Terminal master's awarded for partial completion of doctoral program. *Degree requirements:* For master's, thesis (MS) required, foreign language not required; for doctorate, dissertation required, foreign language not required. *Entrance requirements:* GMAT, GRE General Test, or MAT; TOEFL. Application deadline: 3/15. Application fee: $65. Electronic applications accepted. *Financial aid:* In 1997–98, 22 students received aid, including 7 fellowships (2 to first-year students), 5 research assistantships, 10 teaching assistantships (3 to first-year students); full and partial tuition waivers, institutionally sponsored loans also available. Financial aid applicants required to submit FAFSA. *Faculty research:* Empowerment and family support; evaluation/research design, methodology, and analysis; health policy, financing, and management; human service needs, programs, and agencies. • Director of Graduate Studies, 607-255-7772. Application contact: Graduate Field Assistant, 607-255-7772. Fax: 607-255-4071. E-mail: hss_grad@cornell.edu.

DePaul University, School of Education, Program in Human Services and Counseling, Chicago, IL 60604-2287. Offers agencies, family concerns, and higher education (MA, M Ed); elementary schools (MA, M Ed); human services management (MA, M Ed); secondary schools (MA, M Ed). Faculty: 3 full-time (1 woman). Students: 49 full-time (42 women), 52 part-time (42 women); includes 32 minority (22 African Americans, 3 Asian Americans, 6 Hispanics, 1 Native American), 3 international. Average age 32. 47 applicants, 83% accepted. In 1997, 16 degrees awarded. *Degree requirements:* Oral exam or thesis required, foreign language not required. *Entrance requirements:* Interview, minimum GPA of 2.75, work experience. Application deadline: rolling. Application fee: $25. *Expenses:* Tuition $320 per credit hour. Fees $30 per year. *Financial aid:* Career-related internships or fieldwork available. • Dr. Barbara Sizemore, Dean, School of Education, 312-325-7000 Ext. 1666. Fax: 312-325-7748. Application contact: Director of Graduate Admissions, 312-325-7000 Ext. 1666. E-mail: mmurphy@wppost.depaul.edu.

Drury College, Graduate Programs in Education, Program in Human Services, Springfield, MO 65802-3791. Awards M Ed. Part-time and evening/weekend programs available. Students: 30; includes 3 minority (1 African American, 1 Asian American, 1 Hispanic). 12 applicants, 100% accepted. In 1997, 11 degrees awarded. *Degree requirements:* Thesis required, foreign language not required. *Entrance requirements:* MAT (minimum score 35), minimum GPA of 2.75. Application fee: $15. *Tuition:* $170 per credit hour. *Financial aid:* Career-related internships or fieldwork available. • Dr. Daniel R. Beach, Director, Graduate Programs in Education, 417-873-7271. Fax: 417-873-7432. E-mail: dbeach@lib.drury.edu.

Fielding Institute, Programs in Human and Organization Development, Santa Barbara, CA 93105-3538. Offerings include human services (MA, DHS). Terminal master's awarded for partial completion of doctoral program. Faculty: 28 full-time (13 women), 4 part-time (1 woman). *Average time to degree:* master's–3.2 years full-time; doctorate–5.8 years full-time. *Application deadline:* 6/1 (3/1 for spring admission). *Application fee:* $60. *Tuition:* $12,250 per year. • Dr. Barbara Mink, Dean, 805-687-1099 Ext. 2930. Fax: 805-687-4590. Application contact: Judy Brown, Admissions Counselor, 805-687-1099 Ext. 4020. Fax: 805-687-9793. E-mail: jsbrown@fielding.edu.

Florida State University, College of Education, Department of Human Services and Studies, Tallahassee, FL 32306. Offers programs in counseling and human systems (MS, Ed S), counseling psychology (PhD), recreation and leisure services administration (MS), rehabilitation services (MS, Ed D, PhD, Ed S), school psychology (MS, Ed S). Part-time programs available. Faculty: 12 full-time (6 women), 2 part-time (1 woman). Students: 105 full-time (80 women), 41 part-time (26 women); includes 33 minority (20 African Americans, 5 Asian Americans, 7 Hispanics, 1 Native American). 207 applicants, 51% accepted. In 1997, 63 master's, 4 doctorates awarded. *Degree requirements:* For master's and Ed S, comprehensive exam required, thesis optional; for doctorate, dissertation, comprehensive exam. *Entrance requirements:* GRE General Test (minimum combined score of 1000), minimum GPA of 3.0. Application deadline: 7/1 (priority date; rolling processing; 11/1 for spring admission). Application fee: $20. *Tuition:* $139 per credit hour for state residents; $482 per credit hour for nonresidents. *Financial aid:* Fellowships, research assistantships, teaching assistantships, and career-related internships or fieldwork available. *Total annual research expenditures:* $284,071. • Dr. Cheryl Beeler, Chair, 850-644-3854. E-mail: beeler@mail.coe.fsu.edu. Application contact: Admissions Secretary, 850-644-3854. Fax: 850-644-4335.

Franklin University, Department of Human Services Management, Columbus, OH 43215-5399. Awards MS. Program new for fall 1998. *Application deadline:* 7/15 (priority date; rolling processing). *Application fee:* $30 ($40 for international students). *Expenses:* Tuition $280 per credit hour. Fees $25 per trimester. *Financial aid:* Application deadline 6/30. • Application contact: MBA Associate, 614-341-6387. Fax: 614-221-7723.

The Graduate School of America, Graduate School, Human Services Field, Minneapolis, MN 55401. Awards MS, PhD. Part-time and evening/weekend programs available. Postbaccalaureate distance learning degree programs offered (minimal on-campus study). Faculty: 4 full-time (0 women), 9 part-time (4 women). Students: 116 full-time (64 women); includes 24 minority (17 African Americans, 2 Asian Americans, 3 Hispanics, 2 Native Americans), 1 international. Average age 45. In 1997, 5 master's, 3 doctorates awarded. Terminal master's awarded for partial completion of doctoral program. *Degree requirements:* For master's, project required, thesis optional, foreign language not required; for doctorate, dissertation required, foreign language not required. *Entrance requirements:* For master's, TOEFL (minimum score 550), minimum GPA of 2.7; for doctorate, TOEFL (minimum score 550), minimum GPA of 3.0. Application deadline: rolling. Application fee: $50. Electronic applications accepted. *Expenses:* Tuition $7160 per year (minimum). Fees $795 per year (minimum). *Financial aid:* 39 students received aid; institutionally sponsored loans available. *Faculty research:* Compulsive and addictive behaviors, marriage and family therapy, psychology, substance abuse. • Dr. Robert Ford, Chair, 612-339-8650. E-mail: bford0680@aol.com. Application contact: Associate Director of Admissions, 800-987-1133. Fax: 612-337-5396. E-mail: tgsainfo@tgsa.edu.

Indiana University Northwest, Division of Public and Environmental Affairs, Gary, IN 46408-1197. Offerings include human services administration (MPA). Division faculty: 7 full-time (2 women), 5 part-time (2 women), 8.25 FTE. *Entrance requirements:* GRE General Test. Application deadline: 8/15 (priority date; rolling processing). Application fee: $25. • Joseph M. Pellicciotti, Director, 219-980-6695. E-mail: jpelli@iunhaw1.iun.indiana.edu. Application contact: Suzanne Green, Recorder, 219-980-6695. Fax: 219-980-6737. E-mail: sgreen@iunhaw1.iun.indiana.edu.

Kansas State University, College of Human Ecology, School of Family Studies and Human Services, Manhattan, KS 66506. Offers programs in family studies and human services (MS), human ecology (PhD). Faculty: 21 full-time (10 women). Students: 104 (78 women); includes 20 minority (9 African Americans, 7 Asian Americans, 1 Hispanic, 3 Native Americans), 7 international. 192 applicants, 30% accepted. In 1997, 44 master's awarded. *Degree requirements:* For master's, thesis or alternative required, foreign language not required. *Tuition:* $2218 per year full-time, $401 per semester (minimum) part-time for state residents; $6336 per year full-time, $1087 per semester (minimum) part-time for nonresidents. *Financial aid:* In 1997–98, 13 research assistantships (6 to first-year students) averaging $800 per month and totaling $90,000, 22 teaching assistantships (6 to first-year students) averaging $800 per month and totaling $150,000, 15 graduate assistantships (3 to first-year students) averaging $900 per month and totaling $162,000 were awarded. *Faculty research:* Infancy, gerontology, family therapy, speech and language, family systems. Total annual research expenditures: $430,000. • John P. Murray, Director, 785-532-5510. Application contact: Robert Poresky, Graduate Coordinator, 785-532-5510.

Lehigh University, College of Education, Department of Education and Human Services, Program in Counseling Psychology, Bethlehem, PA 18015-3094. Offerings include counseling and human services (M Ed). Program faculty: 4 full-time (2 women), 5 part-time (4 women). *Entrance requirements:* GRE General Test or MAT, TOEFL, minimum GPA of 2.75. Application deadline: 2/1. Application fee: $40. Electronic applications accepted. *Expenses:* Tuition $470 per credit. Fees $12 per semester full-time, $6 per semester part-time. • Dr. April E. Metzler, Coordinator, 610-758-6093. Fax: 610-758-6223. E-mail: aem3@lehigh.edu.

Lesley College, Graduate School of Arts and Social Sciences, Cambridge, MA 02138-2790. Offerings include intercultural relations (MA, CAGS), with options in development project administration (MA), individually designed (MA), intercultural conflict resolution (MA), intercultural health and human services (MA), intercultural training and consulting (MA), international education exchange (MA), international student advising (MA), managing culturally diverse human resources (MA), multicultural education (MA). Postbaccalaureate distance learning degree programs offered (minimal on-campus study). School faculty: 24 full-time (14 women), 344 part-time (225 women). *Application deadline:* rolling. *Application fee:* $45. *Tuition:* $425 per credit. • Dr. Martha B. McKenna, Dean, 617-349-8467. Application contact: Graduate Admissions, 617-349-8300. Fax: 617-349-8366.

Lincoln University, Graduate Program in Human Services, Lincoln University, PA 19352. Awards M Hum Svcs. Evening/weekend programs available. Faculty: 6 full-time, 15 part-time. Students: 512 full-time. *Degree requirements:* Thesis required, foreign language not required. *Entrance requirements:* 5 years of work experience in human services. Application deadline: 6/1 (priority date; rolling processing). Application fee: $25. *Tuition:* $5175 per year for state residents; $7790 per year for nonresidents. *Financial aid:* Application deadline 8/1. *Faculty research:* Gerontology/minority aging, computers in composition instruction. • Dr. Szabi Ishtai-Zee, Acting Director, 610-932-8300 Ext. 3360. Application contact: Jernice Lea, Director of Field and Recruitment, 610-932-8300 Ext. 3362.

Lindenwood University, Programs in Individualized Education, St. Charles, MO 63301-1695. Offerings include human service agency management (MS). Faculty: 10 full-time (7 women), 23 part-time (6 women). *Application deadline:* 6/30 (priority date; rolling processing; 12/1 for spring admission). *Application fee:* $25. *Tuition:* $5880 per year full-time, $245 per credit hour part-time. • Dr. Dan Kemper, Dean, 314-916-9125. Application contact: John Guffey, Director of Graduate Admissions, 314-949-4933. Fax: 314-949-4910.

Lindsey Wilson College, Department of Human Services, Columbia, KY 42728-1298. Offers program in counseling and human development (M Ed). Faculty: 4 full-time (2 women), 1 part-time (0 women). Students: 43 full-time (40 women). *Application deadline:* rolling. *Application fee:* $30. *Tuition:* $8640 per year full-time, $480 per hour part-time. • Dr. John Rigney, Chair, 800-264-0138. Fax: 502-384-8200.

Mankato State University, College of Social and Behavioral Sciences, Department of Sociology (Corrections), South Rd and Ellis Ave, PO Box 8400, Mankato, MN 56002-8400. Offerings include sociology (MA, MT), with option in human services planning and administration (MA). Department faculty: 17 full-time (4 women). *Application deadline:* 7/10 (priority date; rolling processing; 10/30 for spring admission). *Application fee:* $20. *Tuition:* $126 per credit (minimum) for state residents; $200 per credit for nonresidents. • Dr. Joe Davis, Chairperson, 507-389-1561. Application contact: Joni Roberts, Admissions Coordinator, 507-389-2321. Fax: 507-389-5974. E-mail: grad@mankato.msus.edu.

Moorhead State University, Department of Public and Human Services Administration, Moorhead, MN 56563-0002. Awards MS. Part-time and evening/weekend programs available. Faculty: 1 full-time (0 women), 5 part-time (3 women). Students: 2 full-time (1 woman), 6 part-time (4 women). 7 applicants, 100% accepted. *Degree requirements:* Final oral exam, final project paper or thesis required, foreign language not required. *Entrance requirements:* GRE General Test, TOEFL (minimum score 550), minimum GPA of 2.75. Application deadline: 5/1 (priority date; rolling processing; 9/1 for spring admission). Application fee: $20 ($35 for international students). Electronic applications accepted. *Tuition:* $145 per credit hour for state residents; $220 per credit hour for nonresidents. *Financial aid:* In 1997–98, 2 administrative assistantships were awarded; Federal Work-Study and career-related internships or fieldwork also available. Financial aid application deadline: 7/15; applicants required to submit FAFSA. • Dr. James Danielson, Chair, Political Science, 218-236-4021.

Murray State University, College of Education, Department of Educational Leadership and Counseling, Program in Human Services, Murray, KY 42071-0009. Awards MS. Part-time programs available. Students: 17 full-time (11 women), 49 part-time (37 women); includes 11 minority (10 African Americans, 1 Hispanic), 12 international. 28 applicants, 100% accepted. In 1997, 35 degrees awarded. *Entrance requirements:* GRE General Test or MAT, TOEFL (minimum score 500). Application deadline: rolling. Application fee: $20. *Expenses:* Tuition $2500 per year full-time, $124 per hour part-time for state residents; $6740 per year full-time, $357 per hour part-time for nonresidents. Fees $360 per year full-time, $180 per year part-time. *Financial aid:* Research assistantships, teaching assistantships, Federal Work-Study available. Financial aid application deadline: 4/1. • Dr. Thomas Holcomb, Director, 502-762-2797. Fax: 502-762-3799.

National–Louis University, College of Arts and Sciences, Program in Human Services, 2840 Sheridan Road, Evanston, IL 60201-1730. Offers addictions counseling (MS, Certificate), addictions treatment (Certificate), career counseling and development studies (Certificate), community wellness and prevention (MS, Certificate), counseling (MS, Certificate), eating disorders counseling (Certificate), employee assistance programs (MS, Certificate), gerontology administration (Certificate), gerontology counseling (MS, Certificate), human services administration (MS, Certificate), long-term care administration (Certificate). Part-time programs available. Students: 30 full-time (21 women), 224 part-time (189 women); includes 52 minority (40 African Americans, 6 Asian Americans, 6 Hispanics). Average age 39. In 1997, 40 master's, 6 Certificates awarded. *Degree requirements:* For master's, internship required, thesis optional, foreign language not required. *Entrance requirements:* For master's, MAT or Watson-Glaser Critical Thinking Appraisal (minimum score 48), interview, minimum GPA of 3.0. Application deadline: rolling. Application fee: $25. *Tuition:* $411 per semester hour. *Financial aid:* Available to part-time students. Financial aid applicants required to submit FAFSA. *Faculty research:* Religion and aging, drug abuse prevention, hunger, homelessness, multicultural diversity. • Dr. Sue Nesbitt, Coordinator, 847-475-1100 Ext. 3454. Application contact: Dr. David McCulloch, Vice President for University Services, 800-443-5522 Ext. 5127. Fax: 847-465-0593. E-mail: dmcc@wheeling1.nl.edu.

National University, School of Education and Human Services, Department of Human Services, La Jolla, CA 92037-1011. Offers programs in career development and community counseling (MCDCC), human services (MHS). Students: 12 full-time (9 women), 11 part-time (9 women); includes 8 minority (5 African Americans, 1 Asian American, 2 Hispanics). Average age 39. *Entrance requirements:* Interview, minimum GPA of 2.5. Application deadline: rolling. Application fee: $60 ($100 for international students). *Tuition:* $7830 per year full-time, $870 per course part-time. *Financial aid:* Application deadline 5/1. • Dr. Jacqueline Caesar, Chair, 619-642-8350.

New England College, Program in Organizational Management, 7 Main Street, Henniker, NH 03242-3293. Offerings include human services (MS). College faculty: 7 full-time, 13 part-time. *Degree requirements:* Independent research project required, foreign language not required. *Application deadline:* rolling. *Application fee:* $25. *Expenses:* Tuition $175 per credit. Fees $20 per semester. • Dr. Patricia Prinz, Director of Graduate and Continuing Studies, 603-428-2252. Fax: 603-428-2266. Application contact: Robert Godard, Associate Director, 603-428-2483.

Rider University, School of Graduate Education and Human Services, Program in Human Services Administration, Lawrenceville, NJ 08648-3001. Awards MA. Part-time and evening/weekend programs available. Faculty: 2 full-time (1 woman), 4 part-time (0 women). Students: 14 full-time, 106 part-time. 35 applicants, 80% accepted. In 1997, 25 degrees awarded. *Degree requirements:* Comprehensive exams, research project required, foreign language and thesis not required. *Entrance requirements:* Interview, minimum GPA of 2.5. Application deadline: 8/15 (priority date; rolling processing; 12/15 for spring admission). Application fee: $35. *Tuition:* $329 per credit hour. *Financial aid:* Career-related internships or fieldwork available. Aid available to part-time students. *Faculty research:* Development of administrators in public, health/human services, and nonprofit areas. • Dr. Marcia Steinhauer, Coordinator, 609-896-5357. Application contact: Dr. John Carpenter, Dean, Continuing Studies, 609-896-5036. Fax: 609-896-5261.

Roberts Wesleyan College, Division of Social Work and Social Sciences, Rochester, NY 14624-1997. Offerings include physical and mental health services (MSW). Division faculty: 8 full-time (2 women), 4 part-time (2 women). *Degree requirements:* Computer language required, foreign language and thesis not required. *Average time to degree:* master's–2 years full-time. *Entrance requirements:* Minimum GPA of 2.75. Application deadline: 4/1 (priority date; rolling processing). Application fee: $35. *Tuition:* $340 per credit hour. • Dr. William Descoteaux, Chair, 716-594-6490. Fax: 716-594-6480. Application contact: Kathy Merz, Admissions Secretary, 716-594-6600. Fax: 716-594-6585.

Rosemont College, College of Graduate Studies, Program in Counseling Psychology, Rosemont, PA 19010-1699. Offerings include human services (MA). Program faculty: 4 full-time (2 women), 5 part-time (2 women). *Degree requirements:* Thesis or alternative required, foreign language not required. *Entrance requirements:* GRE or MAT. Application deadline: rolling. Application fee: $50. *Tuition:* $425 per credit. • Edward Samulewicz, Director, 610-527-0200 Ext. 2359. Application contact: Stan Rostkowski, Enrollment Coordinator, 610-527-0200 Ext. 2187. Fax: 610-526-2964. E-mail: roscolgrad@rosemont.edu.

Sage Graduate School, Graduate School, Division of Management Studies, Program in Public Administration, Troy, NY 12180-4115. Offerings include human services administration (MS). Program faculty: 3 full-time (1 woman), 1 part-time (0 women). *Entrance requirements:* Minimum GPA of 2.75. Application deadline: 8/1 (rolling processing; 12/15 for spring admission). Application fee: $25. *Expenses:* Tuition $360 per credit hour. Fees $50 per semester. • Application contact: Melissa Robertson, Associate Director of Admissions, 518-244-6878. Fax: 518-244-6880. E-mail: sgsadm@sage.edu.

St. Edward's University, School of Education, Austin, TX 78704-6489. Offers program in human services (MA). Part-time and evening/weekend programs available. Faculty: 7 full-time (0 women), 12 part-time (6 women). Students: 37 full-time (32 women), 137 part-time (106 women); includes 30 minority (10 African Americans, 20 Hispanics), 3 international. Average age 36. 88 applicants, 84% accepted. In 1997, 39 degrees awarded. *Average time to degree:* master's–1.5 years full-time, 2.7 years part-time. *Entrance requirements:* GRE General Test (minimum combined score of 1400 on three sections), TOEFL (minimum score 500), minimum GPA of 2.75. Application deadline: 8/1 (priority date; rolling processing; 12/1 for spring admission). Application fee: $25. *Financial aid:* Scholarships, institutionally sponsored loans, and career-related internships or fieldwork available. Aid available to part-time students. Financial aid application deadline: 3/1; applicants required to submit FAFSA. *Faculty research:* Utilization of statistics for managerial decision making, budget and analysis. • Dr. J. Frank Smith, Dean, 512-448-8555. Application contact: Tom Evans, Director of Graduate Admissions, 512-448-8600. Fax: 512-448-8492. E-mail: seu.grad@admin.stedwards.edu.

Announcement: The Master of Arts in Human Services program is specifically designed for the working adult student. Classes are offered in the evening to accommodate most work schedules. Concentrations are available in administration, social and psychological services, counseling, conflict resolution, and sports management.

St. Mary's University of San Antonio, Department of Counseling and Human Services, San Antonio, TX 78228-8507. Offers programs in counseling (PhD, Sp C), marriage and family relations (Certificate), marriage and family therapy (MA), mental health (MA), mental health and substance abuse counseling (Certificate), substance abuse (MA). *Degree requirements:* For master's, internship required, foreign language and thesis not required; for doctorate, dissertation, internship required, foreign language not required. *Entrance requirements:* For master's, GRE General Test, MAT; for doctorate, GRE General Test. Application deadline: 8/1. Application fee: $15. *Expenses:* Tuition $383 per credit hour (minimum). Fees $217 per year full-time, $58 per semester part-time.

Spertus Institute of Jewish Studies, Judaica Studies Graduate Programs Institute of Advanced Judaica, Program in Human Services Administration, 618 South Michigan Avenue, Chicago, IL 60605-1901. Awards MSHSA, MAJCS/MSHSA. Evening/weekend programs available. Faculty: 2 full-time (1 woman), 24 part-time (11 women). Students: 108 full-time; includes 88 minority (84 African Americans, 2 Asian Americans, 2 Hispanics), 1 international. Average age 32. In 1997, 70 degrees awarded. *Degree requirements:* 1 foreign language, thesis. *Entrance requirements:* Interview, minimum GPA of 2.75. Application deadline: rolling. Application fee: $50. *Expenses:* Tuition $8000 per year full-time, $165 per quarter hour part-time. Fees $75 per year. *Financial aid:* 85 students received aid. Financial aid applicants required to submit FAFSA. • Peter Levine, Associate Dean, 312-922-9012. Application contact: Lisa Burnstein, Director of Student Services, 312-922-9012. Fax: 312-922-6406. E-mail: college@spertus.edu.

Spertus Institute of Jewish Studies, Judaica Studies Graduate Programs Institute of Advanced Judaica, Program in Jewish Communal Studies, 618 South Michigan Avenue, Chicago, IL 60605-1901. Awards MAJCS, MAJCS/MSHSA. Faculty: 12 part-time. Students: 0. *Degree requirements:* 1 foreign language, thesis. *Entrance requirements:* Interview, minimum GPA of 3.0. Application deadline: rolling. Application fee: $50. *Expenses:* Tuition $8000 per year full-time, $165 per quarter hour part-time. Fees $75 per year. *Financial aid:* Scholarships available. Aid available to part-time students. Financial aid applicants required to submit FAFSA. • Application contact: Lisa Burnstein, Director of Student Services, 312-922-9012. Fax: 312-922-6406. E-mail: college@spertus.edu.

Springfield College, Program in Human Services, Springfield, MA 01109-3797. Awards MS. Part-time and evening/weekend programs available. Faculty: 25 full-time (12 women), 46 part-time (27 women). Students: 139 full-time (105 women), 53 part-time (42 women); includes 3 international. Average age 35. 209 applicants, 75% accepted. In 1997, 120 degrees awarded. *Degree requirements:* Project required, foreign language and thesis not required. *Application deadline:* (12/1 for spring admission). *Application fee:* $40. *Financial aid:* Fellowships, Federal Work-Study, and career-related internships or fieldwork available. Financial aid application deadline: 3/1. • Dr. Daniel Nussbaum, Dean, 413-788-2441. Application contact: Donald J. Shaw Jr., Director of Graduate Admissions, 413-748-3225. Fax: 413-748-3694. E-mail: dshaw@spfldcol.edu.

State University of New York at Oswego, School of Education, Department of Counseling and Psychological Services, Program in Human Services/Counseling, Oswego, NY 13126. Awards MS. Students: 15 full-time (13 women), 30 part-time (19 women); includes 3 minority (2 African Americans, 1 Hispanic). Average age 31. 33 applicants, 85% accepted. In 1997, 15 degrees awarded. *Degree requirements:* Comprehensive exams. *Entrance requirements:* GRE General Test, GRE Subject Test, interview, minimum GPA of 3.0. Application deadline: 7/1. Application fee: $50. *Expenses:* Tuition $5100 per year full-time, $213 per credit hour part-time for state residents; $8416 per year full-time, $351 per credit hour part-time for nonresidents. Fees $135 per year (minimum). *Financial aid:* Partial tuition waivers, Federal Work-Study, institutionally sponsored loans, and career-related internships or fieldwork available. Financial aid application deadline: 3/1. • Dr. Thomas Cushman, Chair, Department of Counseling and Psychological Services, 315-341-4051.

Syracuse University, School of Social Work, Syracuse, NY 13244-0003. Offerings include family mental health (MSW). School faculty: 15. *Entrance requirements:* GRE General Test. Application deadline: rolling. Application fee: $40. *Tuition:* $13,320 per year full-time, $555 per credit hour part-time. • William Pollard, Dean, 315-443-5582. Application contact: Linda Littlejohn, Director of Admissions, 315-443-5555.

Universidad del Turabo, Programs in Public Affairs, Program in Human Services Administration, Gurabo, PR 00778-3030. Awards MPA. *Entrance requirements:* GRE, PAEG, interview. Application deadline: 8/5. Application fee: $25.

Université de Montréal, Programs in Applied Human Sciences, Montréal, PQ H3C 3J7, Canada. Awards PhD. 37 applicants, 35% accepted. In 1997, 4 degrees awarded. *Degree requirements:* Dissertation, general exam. *Application fee:* $30. • Deena White, Director, 514-343-7165.

University of Bridgeport, College of Graduate and Undergraduate Studies, School of Education and Human Resources, Division of Counseling and Human Resources, 380 University Avenue, Bridgeport, CT 06601. Offers programs in community agency counseling (MS), human resource development and counseling (MS). MS (human resource development and counseling) offered jointly with the School of Business. Part-time and evening/weekend programs available. Faculty: 3 full-time (1 woman), 9 part-time (4 women), 6 FTE. Students: 11 full-time (9 women), 82 part-time (62 women); includes 19 minority (13 African Americans, 6 Hispanics), 6 international. Average age 49. 80 applicants, 46% accepted. In 1997, 26 degrees awarded. *Application deadline:* rolling. *Application fee:* $35 ($50 for international students). *Tuition:* $340 per credit. *Financial aid:* In 1997–98, 46 students received aid, including 8 teaching assistantships; fellowships, research assistantships, Federal Work-Study, institutionally sponsored loans, and career-related internships or fieldwork also available. Aid available to part-time students. Financial aid application deadline: 6/1; applicants required to submit FAFSA. *Faculty research:* Corporate elder care programs. • Dr. Joseph E. Nechasek, Director, 203-576-4175.

See in-depth description on page 501.

University of Colorado at Colorado Springs, School of Education, Colorado Springs, CO 80933-7150. Offerings include counseling and human services (MA). School faculty: 13 full-time (6 women). *Degree requirements:* Thesis or alternative, comprehensive exams, microcomputer proficiency required, foreign language not required. *Entrance requirements:*

Directories: Human Services; Social Work

University of Colorado at Colorado Springs (continued)
GRE General Test, MAT. Application deadline: rolling. Application fee: $40 ($50 for international students). *Expenses:* Tuition $2760 per year full-time, $115 per credit hour part-time for state residents; $9960 per year full-time, $415 per credit hour part-time for nonresidents. Fees $399 per year (minimum) full-time, $106 per year (minimum) part-time. • Dr. Greg R. Weisenstein, Dean, 719-262-4103. E-mail: gweisens@mail.uccs.edu. Application contact: Connie Wroten, Academic Adviser, 719-262-3268. Fax: 719-262-3554. E-mail: cwroten@mail.uccs.edu.

University of Massachusetts Boston, College of Public and Community Service, Program in Human Services, Boston, MA 02125-3393. Awards MS. Students: 60 full-time (40 women), 13 part-time (10 women); includes 28 minority (21 African Americans, 7 Hispanics), 2 international. 50 applicants, 68% accepted. In 1997, 19 degrees awarded. *Entrance requirements:* MAT, minimum GPA of 2.75. Application deadline: 3/1 (priority date; 11/1 for spring admission). Application fee: $25 ($35 for international students). *Expenses:* Tuition $2640 per year full-time, $110 per credit part-time for state residents; $8930 per year full-time, $373 per credit part-time for nonresidents. Fees $2650 per year full-time, $420 per semester (minimum) part-time for state residents; $2736 per year full-time, $420 per semester (minimum) part-time for nonresidents. *Financial aid:* In 1997–98, 3 research assistantships (1 to a first-year student) averaging $225 per month and totaling $8,000, 3 teaching assistantships (1 to a first-year student) averaging $225 per month and totaling $8,000 were awarded; administrative assistantships also available. Financial aid application deadline: 3/1; applicants required to submit FAFSA. • Dr. Anna Madison, Director, 617-287-7225. Application contact: Lisa Lavely, Director of Graduate Admissions and Records, 617-287-6400. Fax: 617-287-6236.

University of Oklahoma, College of Arts and Sciences, Department of Human Relations, Norman, OK 73019-0390. Awards MHR. Part-time and evening/weekend programs available. Faculty: 12 full-time (6 women), 3 part-time (1 woman). Students: 67 full-time (45 women), 144 part-time (115 women); includes 59 minority (40 African Americans, 1 Asian American, 5 Hispanics, 13 Native Americans), 6 international. Average age 36. In 1997, 346 degrees awarded. *Degree requirements:* Thesis optional. *Entrance requirements:* TOEFL (minimum score 550). Application deadline: 6/1 (priority date; rolling processing). Application fee: $25. *Expenses:* Tuition $1920 per year full-time, $80 per credit hour part-time for state residents; $6108 per year full-time, $255 per credit hour part-time for nonresidents. Fees $468 per year full-time, $12 per semester (minimum) part-time. *Financial aid:* In 1997–98, 1 research assistantship was awarded; teaching assistantships, partial tuition waivers, Federal Work-Study, institutionally sponsored loans, and career-related internships or fieldwork also available. *Faculty research:* Chemical dependency, organizational change and development, nonverbal communication, women's studies, race relations. • Dr. Barbara Hillyer, Chair, 405-325-1756.

University of Sarasota, College of Behavioral Sciences, Program in Human Services/Administration, Sarasota, FL 34235-8246. Awards MA, Ed D. Part-time and evening/weekend programs available. Postbaccalaureate distance learning degree programs offered (minimal on-campus study). Faculty: 2 full-time (0 women), 3 part-time (1 woman). Students: 53 full-time (28 women), 64 part-time (28 women). Terminal master's awarded for partial completion of doctoral program. *Degree requirements:* For master's, thesis optional; for doctorate, dissertation, comprehensive exam required, foreign language not required. *Average time to degree:* master's–2 years full-time, 3 years part-time; doctorate–3 years full-time, 4 years part-time. *Entrance requirements:* For master's, TOEFL (minimum score 550); for doctorate, TOEFL (minimum score 550), minimum undergraduate GPA of 3.0. Application deadline: rolling. Application fee: $50. *Financial aid:* Available to part-time students. Financial aid applicants required to submit FAFSA. • Dr. J. Maxwell Jackson, Director, 800-331-5995. Fax: 941-379-9464. E-mail: maxwell_jackson@embanet.com. Application contact: Kathy Ketterer, Admissions Representative, 800-331-5995. Fax: 941-371-8910. E-mail: kathy_ketterer@embanet.com.

Valdosta State University, College of Arts and Sciences, Department of Sociology, Program in Social Services, Valdosta, GA 31698. Awards MS. Evening/weekend programs available. *Degree requirements:* Thesis or alternative required, foreign language not required. *Entrance requirements:* GRE General Test (minimum combined score of 800). Application deadline: 8/1 (rolling processing; 11/15 for spring admission). Application fee: $10. *Expenses:* Tuition $2472 per year full-time, $83 per semester hour part-time for state residents; $8472 per year full-time, $333 per semester hour part-time for nonresidents. Fees $236 per year full-time. • Dr. J. Michael Brooks, Head, Department of Sociology, 912-333-5943. E-mail: mbrooks@grits.valdosta.peachnet.edu.

Villanova University, Graduate School of Liberal Arts and Sciences, Program in Human Organization Science, Human Services Administration Option, Villanova, PA 19085-1699. Awards MS. Part-time and evening/weekend programs available. Students: 2 full-time (1 woman), 6 part-time (all women); includes 1 minority (Hispanic). Average age 28. 5 applicants, 100% accepted. *Degree requirements:* Comprehensive exam required, foreign language and thesis not required. *Entrance requirements:* GRE General Test, minimum GPA of 3.0. Application deadline: 8/1 (priority date; 12/1 for spring admission). Application fee: $40. *Expenses:* Tuition $400 per credit. Fees $60 per year. *Financial aid:* Federal Work-Study and career-related internships or fieldwork available. Financial aid application deadline: 4/1. • Steve Jacobs, Coordinator, 610-519-4786.

Walden University, Graduate Programs, Program in Human Services, 155 Fifth Avenue South, Minneapolis, MN 55401. Awards PhD. Part-time and evening/weekend programs available. Postbaccalaureate distance learning degree programs offered. *Degree requirements:* Dissertation, brief dispersed residency sessions required, foreign language not required. *Entrance requirements:* 3 years of professional experience. Application deadline: rolling. Application fee: $50. *Tuition:* $3125 per quarter.

Wayne State University, Interdisciplinary Program in Developmental Disabilities, Detroit, MI 48202. Awards Certificate. Students: 3 part-time (all women). 0 applicants. In 1997, 2 degrees awarded. *Entrance requirements:* Master's degree. Application deadline: rolling. Application fee: $0. *Expenses:* Tuition $163 per credit hour for state residents; $355 per credit hour for nonresidents. Fees $498 per year full-time, $114 per semester (minimum) part-time. • Dr. Barbara Leroy, Director. Application contact: Susan St. Peter, Educational Director, 313-577-2654.

Youngstown State University, College of Health and Human Services, Department of Health Professions, Youngstown, OH 44555-0002. Offers program in health and human services (MHHS). Part-time and evening/weekend programs available. Faculty: 2 full-time (1 woman). Students: 8 full-time (6 women), 12 part-time (10 women). 21 applicants, 100% accepted. *Degree requirements:* Thesis optional, foreign language not required. *Entrance requirements:* GRE General Test, TOEFL (minimum score 550), minimum GPA of 3.0. Application deadline: 8/15 (priority date; rolling processing; 2/15 for spring admission). Application fee: $30 ($75 for international students). *Expenses:* Tuition $90 per credit hour for state residents; $144 per credit hour (minimum) for nonresidents. Fees $528 per year full-time, $244 per year (minimum) part-time. *Financial aid:* In 1997–98, 2 students received aid, including 2 scholarships totaling $2,580; Federal Work-Study, institutionally sponsored loans also available. Aid available to part-time students. Financial aid application deadline: 3/1. *Faculty research:* Drug prevention, multiskilling in health care, organizational behavior, health care management, health behaviors, research management. • Joseph J. Mistovich, Chair, 330-742-3327. Application contact: Dr. Peter J. Kasvinsky, Dean of Graduate Studies, 330-742-3091. Fax: 330-742-1580. E-mail: amgrad03@ysub.ysu.edu.

Social Work

Adelphi University, School of Social Work, Garden City, NY 11530. Offers programs in clinical practice (Certificate), social welfare (DSW), social work (MSW). One or more programs accredited by CSWE. Part-time and evening/weekend programs available. Students: 267 full-time (214 women), 489 part-time (409 women); includes 153 minority (98 African Americans, 9 Asian Americans, 46 Hispanics), 2 international. Average age 35. In 1997, 283 master's, 6 doctorates awarded. *Degree requirements:* For doctorate, dissertation required, foreign language not required. *Entrance requirements:* For master's, minimum undergraduate GPA of 3.0. Application deadline: rolling. Application fee: $50. *Expenses:* Tuition $16,000 per year full-time, $485 per credit part-time. Fees $500 per year full-time, $150 per semester part-time. *Financial aid:* Research assistantships, assistantships, full and partial tuition waivers, Federal Work-Study, and career-related internships or fieldwork available. Financial aid application deadline: 3/1. *Faculty research:* Services for rape victims, refugees, child welfare, international feminization of poverty, public welfare. • Dr. Roger Levin, Associate Dean, 516-877-4341. Application contact: Muriel Levin, Admissions Coordinator, 516-877-4384.

See in-depth description on page 1925.

Alabama Agricultural and Mechanical University, School of Arts and Sciences, Department of Behavioral Sciences, PO Box 1357, Normal, AL 35762-1357. Offers program in social work (MSW). Accredited by CSWE. Faculty: 6 full-time (2 women), 2 part-time (1 woman). In 1997, 21 degrees awarded. *Degree requirements:* Thesis required, foreign language not required. *Entrance requirements:* GRE General Test. Application deadline: 5/1 (priority date; rolling processing). Application fee: $15 ($20 for international students). *Expenses:* Tuition $2782 per year full-time, $565 per semester (minimum) part-time for state residents; $5164 per year full-time, $1015 per semester (minimum) part-time for nonresidents. Fees $560 per year full-time, $390 per year part-time. *Financial aid:* Application deadline 4/1. • Dr. Melbourne Henry, Chair, 205-851-5478. Fax: 205-851-5970.

Andrews University, School of Graduate Studies, College of Arts and Sciences, Department of Social Work, Berrien Springs, MI 49104. Awards MSW. Candidate for accreditation by CSWE. *Application deadline:* rolling. *Application fee:* $30. *Expenses:* Tuition $290 per quarter hour (minimum). Fees $75 per quarter. • Dr. Sharon W. Pittman, Chair, 616-471-6196. Fax: 616-471-3868. Application contact: Eileen Lesher, 616-471-3490.

Arizona State University, School of Social Work, Tempe, AZ 85287. Awards MSW, PhD. One or more programs accredited by CSWE. Faculty: 31 full-time (18 women), 1 part-time (0 women). Students: 444 full-time (378 women), 99 part-time (81 women); includes 102 minority (20 African Americans, 12 Asian Americans, 49 Hispanics, 21 Native Americans), 8 international. Average age 33. 361 applicants, 79% accepted. In 1997, 154 master's, 4 doctorates awarded. *Degree requirements:* For doctorate, dissertation. *Entrance requirements:* For master's, GRE or MAT. Application fee: $45. *Expenses:* Tuition $2088 per year full-time, $110 per hour part-time for state residents; $9040 per year full-time, $377 per hour part-time for nonresidents. Fees $72 per year full-time, $18 per semester (minimum) part-time. *Faculty research:* Management methods in social services, evaluation of day-care service delivery, evaluation of minority community mental health training. • Dr. Emilia E. Martinez-Brawley, Dean, 602-965-2795. Application contact: Graduate Secretary, 602-965-3304.

Augsburg College, Program in Social Work, Minneapolis, MN 55454-1351. Awards MSW. Accredited by CSWE. Part-time and evening/weekend programs available. *Degree requirements:* Thesis required, foreign language not required. *Entrance requirements:* Previous course work in human biology and statistics. Application deadline: 1/15 (1/15 for spring admission). Application fee: $25.

Aurora University, George Williams College, School of Social Work, Aurora, IL 60506-4892. Awards MSW. Accredited by CSWE. Part-time and evening/weekend programs available. Faculty: 19 full-time (14 women), 6 part-time (3 women). Students: 211 full-time (170 women), 77 part-time (71 women). 172 applicants, 66% accepted. In 1997, 101 degrees awarded. *Degree requirements:* Thesis optional, foreign language not required. *Entrance requirements:* Minimum GPA of 2.8. Application deadline: 2/1 (priority date; rolling processing). Application fee: $25. *Tuition:* $408 per semester hour. *Financial aid:* Career-related internships or fieldwork available. • Dr. Sandra Alcorn, Dean, 630-844-5420. Application contact: Office of Admissions, 630-844-5533. Fax: 630-844-5463.

Barry University, School of Social Work, Doctoral Program in Social Work, Miami Shores, FL 33161-6695. Awards PhD. Part-time and evening/weekend programs available. Faculty: 31 full-time (19 women), 17 part-time (12 women), 34 FTE. Students: 9 full-time (5 women), 42 part-time (33 women); includes 14 minority (6 African Americans, 8 Hispanics), 1 international. Average age 41. 20 applicants, 60% accepted. In 1997, 8 degrees awarded. *Degree requirements:* Dissertation required, foreign language not required. *Entrance requirements:* MSW from an accredited school of social work, 2 years of professional experience. Application deadline: rolling. Application fee: $30. Electronic applications accepted. *Tuition:* $450 per credit (minimum). *Financial aid:* Full tuition waivers and career-related internships or fieldwork available. Aid available to part-time students. Financial aid application deadline: 5/15; applicants required to submit FAFSA. *Faculty research:* Family and children services, homelessness, gerontology, school social work. • Dr. Elaine Nuehring, Director, 305-899-3900. E-mail: nuehring@aquinas.barry.edu. Application contact: Philip Mack, Director of Admissions, 305-899-3900. Fax: 305-899-3934. E-mail: sswadm@aquinas.barry.edu.

Barry University, School of Social Work, Master's Program in Social Work, Miami Shores, FL 33161-6695. Awards MSW. Accredited by CSWE. Part-time and evening/weekend programs available. Faculty: 31 full-time (19 women), 17 part-time (12 women), 34 FTE. Students: 215 full-time (175 women), 184 part-time (150 women); includes 162 minority (81 African Americans, 2 Asian Americans, 79 Hispanics), 5 international. Average age 35. 326 applicants, 78% accepted. In 1997, 146 degrees awarded. *Degree requirements:* Fieldwork required, foreign language and thesis not required. *Entrance requirements:* Minimum GPA of 3.0. Application deadline: rolling. Application fee: $30. Electronic applications accepted. *Tuition:* $450 per credit (minimum). *Financial aid:* Full tuition waivers and career-related internships or fieldwork available. Aid available to part-time students. Financial aid application deadline: 5/15; applicants required to submit FAFSA. *Faculty research:* Family and children services, homelessness, gerontology, school social work. • Application contact: Philip Mack, Director of Admissions, 305-899-3900. Fax: 305-899-3934. E-mail: sswadm@aquinas.barry.edu.

Boise State University, College of Social Science and Public Affairs, School of Social Work, Boise, ID 83725-0399. Awards MSW. Accredited by CSWE. Part-time programs available. Faculty: 10 full-time (6 women), 1 part-time (0 women). Students: 38 full-time (27 women); includes 2 minority (1 African American, 1 Native American). Average age 32. 58 applicants, 47% accepted. In 1997, 17 degrees awarded. *Application deadline:* 7/26 (priority date; rolling processing; 11/29 for spring admission). *Application fee:* $20 ($30 for international students). Electronic applications accepted. *Tuition:* $3020 per year full-time, $135 per credit part-time for state residents; $8900 per year full-time, $135 per credit part-time for nonresidents. *Financial aid:* In 1997–98, 4 students received aid, including 3 graduate assistantships; Federal Work-Study, institutionally sponsored loans, and career-related internships or fieldwork also available. Aid available to part-time students. Financial aid application deadline: 3/1. • Dr. Martha Wilson, Coordinator, 208-385-3147. Fax: 208-385-4291.

Boston College, Graduate School of Social Work, Chestnut Hill, MA 02167-9991. Awards MSW, PhD, JD/MSW, MA/MSW, MSW/MBA. One or more programs accredited by CSWE. Part-time programs available. Faculty: 22 full-time (13 women), 27 part-time (15 women). Students: 510; includes 10 international. 960 applicants, 42% accepted. In 1997, 190 master's, 3 doctorates awarded. *Degree requirements:* For master's, 2 internships required, foreign language and thesis not required; for doctorate, dissertation required, foreign language not required. *Entrance requirements:* For doctorate, GRE or MAT, MSW. Application deadline: 3/1. Application fee: $40. *Expenses:* Tuition $18,460 per year full-time, $504 per credit hour (minimum) part-time. Fees $80 per year (minimum) full-time, $30 per semester part-time. *Financial aid:* Teaching assistantships, partial tuition waivers, Federal Work-Study, institutionally sponsored loans, and career-related internships or fieldwork available. Aid available to part-time students. Financial aid applicants required to submit FAFSA. *Faculty research:* Social Security utilization, women and employment, cross-cultural practice, gerontology, AIDS. • Dr. June Gary Hopps, Dean, 617-552-4020. Application contact: Dr. William C. Howard, Director of Admissions, 617-552-4024.

See in-depth description on page 1927.

Boston University, School of Social Work, Boston, MA 02215. Awards MSW, PhD, M Div/MSW, MSW/Ed D, MSW/Ed M, MSW/MPH, MSW/MTS. Programs in clinical practice with groups (MSW), clinical practice with individuals and families (MSW), macro social work practice (MSW), social work and sociology (PhD), special education and social work (MSW/Ed D, MSW/Ed M). One or more programs accredited by CSWE. Part-time programs available. Faculty: 26 full-time (18 women), 93 part-time (74 women), 50.8 FTE. Students: 308 full-time (266 women), 287 part-time (244 women); includes 82 minority (36 African Americans, 26 Asian Americans, 19 Hispanics, 1 Native American), 3 international. Average age 26. 858 applicants, 66% accepted. In 1997, 273 master's awarded. *Degree requirements:* For doctorate, 1 foreign language, dissertation, critical essay. *Average time to degree:* master's–2 years full-time, 3 years part-time. *Entrance requirements:* For master's, GRE General Test (combined average 1580 on three sections) or MAT (average 53), minimum GPA of 3.0; for doctorate, GRE General Test (combined average 1629 on three sections) or MAT (average 81), sample of written work. Application deadline: 3/2. Application fee: $50. *Expenses:* Tuition $18,024 per year full-time, $563 per credit part-time. Fees $218 per year full-time, $40 per semester part-time. *Financial aid:* 171 students received aid; Federal Work-Study, institutionally sponsored loans, and career-related internships or fieldwork available. Aid available to part-time students. Financial aid application deadline: 3/12; applicants required to submit FAFSA. *Faculty research:* Health and aging, child and adolescent substance abuse, mental health. Total annual research expenditures: $1.3 million. • Wilma Peebles-Wilkins, Dean, 617-353-3760. Application contact: Philip S. Mack, Director of Admissions, 617-353-3765. Fax: 617-353-5612. E-mail: busswad@bu.edu.

Boston University, School of Education, Dual Degree Program in Administration, Training, and Policy Studies and Social Work, Boston, MA 02215. Awards MSW/Ed M. Students: 0. Average age 37. *Expenses:* Tuition $22,830 per year full-time, $713 per credit part-time. Fees $218 per year full-time, $40 per semester part-time. • Dr. Vivian Johnson, Coordinator, 617-353-3832. E-mail: vjohnson@bu.edu. Application contact: Office of Graduate Admissions, 617-353-4237. E-mail: sedgrad@bu.edu.

Boston University, School of Social Work and Department of Special Education, Dual Degree Program in Special Education and Social Work, Boston, MA 02215. Awards MSW/Ed D, MSW/Ed M. Students: 2 full-time (both women). Average age 24. *Application fee:* $50. *Expenses:* Tuition $18,024 per year full-time, $563 per credit part-time. Fees $218 per year full-time, $40 per semester part-time. • Dr. Gerald Fain, Coordinator, 617-353-4478. E-mail: fain@bu.edu.

Boston University, Department of Sociology and School of Social Work, Interdisciplinary Doctoral Program in Social Work and Sociology, Boston, MA 02215. Awards PhD. Faculty: 20 full-time (6 women), 3 part-time (0 women). Students: 13 full-time (11 women), 11 part-time (7 women); includes 4 minority (2 African Americans, 1 Asian American, 1 Hispanic), 1 international. Average age 42. 18 applicants, 67% accepted. Terminal master's awarded for partial completion of doctoral program. *Degree requirements:* For doctorate, 1 foreign language, dissertation, critical essay. *Entrance requirements:* For doctorate, GRE General Test or MAT, TOEFL (minimum score 550), sample of written work. Application deadline: 1/15 (rolling processing). Application fee: $50. *Expenses:* Tuition $22,830 per year full-time, $713 per credit part-time. Fees $218 per year full-time, $40 per semester part-time. *Financial aid:* In 1997–98, 6 scholarships were awarded; fellowships, research assistantships, Federal Work-Study, and career-related internships or fieldwork also available. Aid available to part-time students. Financial aid application deadline: 1/15; applicants required to submit FAFSA. *Faculty research:* Social welfare policy, social work research, social work practice. • Catherine Kohler Riessman, Director, 617-353-3757.

Brigham Young University, College of Family, Home, and Social Sciences, School of Social Work, Provo, UT 84602-1001. Awards MSW. Accredited by CSWE. Faculty: 11 full-time (4 women), 11 part-time (5 women). Students: 70 full-time (39 women); includes 8 minority (1 African American, 5 Asian Americans, 1 Hispanic, 1 Native American), 9 international. Average age 29. 155 applicants, 30% accepted. In 1997, 31 degrees awarded. *Average time to degree:* master's–2 years full-time. *Application deadline:* 2/1. *Application fee:* $30. *Tuition:* $3200 per year full-time, $178 per credit hour part-time for state residents; $4800 per year full-time, $266 per credit hour part-time for nonresidents. *Financial aid:* In 1997–98, 70 students received aid, including 14 research assistantships (13 to first-year students) averaging $220 per month, 4 teaching assistantships (3 to first-year students) averaging $440 per month, 30 administrative aides, paid field practicums; partial tuition waivers and career-related internships or fieldwork also available. *Faculty research:* Family violence and abuse, women, depression, gerontology, civil defense. • Dr. Kyle L. Pehrson, Director, 801-378-3282. Application contact: Lisa Willey, Graduate Secretary, 801-378-5681. E-mail: lisa_willey@byu.edu.

Bryn Mawr College, Graduate School of Social Work and Social Research, Bryn Mawr, PA 19010-2899. Awards MLSP, MSS, PhD. One or more programs accredited by CSWE. Part-time programs available. Faculty: 17 full-time (10 women), 29 part-time (26 women), 29.3 FTE. Students: 232 full-time (207 women), 61 part-time (55 women); includes 51 minority (38 African Americans, 8 Asian Americans, 5 Hispanics), 6 international. Average age 34. 299 applicants, 58% accepted. In 1997, 120 master's awarded; 4 doctorates awarded (50% entered university research/teaching, 50% found other work related to degree). *Degree requirements:* For master's, fieldwork; for doctorate, 2 foreign languages (computer language can substitute for one), dissertation. *Average time to degree:* master's–2 years full-time, 3 years part-time; doctorate–5 years full-time, 6.5 years part-time. *Entrance requirements:* For master's, TOEFL (minimum score 620; average 640); for doctorate, GRE General Test, TOEFL (minimum score 620; average 640). Application deadline: 3/1 (priority date; rolling processing). Application fee: $40. *Expenses:* Tuition $19,177 per year full-time, $2215 per course (minimum) part-time. Fees $80 per year. *Financial aid:* In 1997–98, 234 students received aid, including 8 fellowships (5 to first-year students) averaging $556 per month and totaling $40,000, 3 research assistantships averaging $967 per month and totaling $26,100, 4 teaching assistantships averaging $967 per month and totaling $34,800, 1 award averaging $556 per month and totaling $5,000; Federal Work-Study, institutionally sponsored loans, and career-related internships or fieldwork also available. Aid available to part-time students. Financial aid application deadline: 3/1; applicants required to submit FAFSA. *Faculty research:* Aging, substance abuse, child and public welfare, occupational health and safety, children and adolescents. Total annual research expenditures: $1.5 million. • Ruth W. Mayden, Dean, 610-520-2600. Application contact: Nancy Kirby, Assistant Dean and Director of Admissions, 610-520-2601.

See in-depth description on page 1929.

California State University, Bakersfield, School of Arts and Sciences, Program in Social Work, 9001 Stockdale Highway, Bakersfield, CA 93311-1099. Awards MSW. Program new for fall 1998. Offered jointly with California State University, Long Beach. *Application deadline:* rolling. *Application fee:* $55. *Expenses:* Tuition $0 for state residents; $246 per unit full-time, $164 per unit part-time for nonresidents. Fees $1584 per year full-time, $918 per year part-time. • Dr. Ken Nyberg, Director, 805-664-2368.

California State University, Fresno, Division of Graduate Studies, School of Health and Social Work, Department of Social Work Education, 5241 North Maple Avenue, Fresno, CA 93740. Awards MSW. Accredited by CSWE. Part-time and evening/weekend programs available. Faculty: 14 full-time (3 women). Students: 124 full-time (95 women), 19 part-time (15 women); includes 78 minority (13 African Americans, 18 Asian Americans, 45 Hispanics, 2 Native Americans), 1 international. Average age 31. 86 applicants, 81% accepted. In 1997, 52 degrees awarded. *Degree requirements:* Thesis or alternative required, foreign language not required. *Average time to degree:* master's–3.5 years full-time. *Entrance requirements:* GRE General Test, TOEFL (minimum score 550), minimum GPA of 2.5. Application deadline: 2/3 (priority date; rolling processing). Application fee: $55. Electronic applications accepted. *Expenses:* Tuition $0 for state residents; $246 per unit for nonresidents. Fees $1872 per year full-time, $1206 per year part-time. *Financial aid:* In 1997–98, 110 scholarships totaling $660,851 were awarded; fellowships, Federal Work-Study, and career-related internships or fieldwork also available. Financial aid application deadline: 3/1; applicants required to submit FAFSA. *Faculty research:* Children at risk, international cooperation, child welfare training. • Dr. G. Visweswaran, Chair, 209-278-3992. Fax: 209-278-7191. E-mail: vishu_visweswaran@csufresno.edu.

California State University, Long Beach, College of Health and Human Services, Department of Social Work, Long Beach, CA 90840-0902. Awards MSW. Accredited by CSWE. Part-time programs available. Students: 138 full-time (113 women), 427 part-time (356 women); includes 202 minority (42 African Americans, 53 Asian Americans, 102 Hispanics, 5 Native Americans), 6 international. Average age 33. 319 applicants, 77% accepted. In 1997, 178 degrees awarded. *Degree requirements:* Thesis required, foreign language not required. *Application deadline:* 8/1 (rolling processing). *Application fee:* $55. *Expenses:* Tuition $0 for state residents; $246 per unit for nonresidents. Fees $1846 per year full-time, $1180 per year part-time. *Financial aid:* Application deadline 3/2. • Dr. Janet Black, Acting Director, 562-985-4615. E-mail: jblack@csulb.edu. Application contact: Dr. Ginger Wilson, Graduate Coordinator, 562-985-4615. Fax: 562-985-5514. E-mail: gkwilson@csulb.edu.

California State University, Los Angeles, School of Health and Human Services, Department of Social Work, Los Angeles, CA 90032-8530. Awards MSW. Candidate for accreditation by CSWE. Faculty: 9 full-time, 8 part-time. Students: 25 full-time (21 women); includes 16 minority (1 African American, 4 Asian Americans, 11 Hispanics). *Entrance requirements:* TOEFL (minimum score 550). Application deadline: 6/30 (rolling processing; 2/1 for spring admission). Application fee: $55. *Expenses:* Tuition $0 for state residents; $164 per unit for nonresidents. Fees $1763 per year full-time, $1097 per year part-time. *Financial aid:* Application deadline 3/1. • Neil Cohen, Head, 213-343-4680.

California State University, Sacramento, School of Health and Human Services, Division of Social Work, Sacramento, CA 95819-6048. Offers programs in family and children's services (MSW), health care (MSW), mental health (MSW), social justice and corrections (MSW). Accredited by CSWE. *Degree requirements:* Thesis or alternative, writing proficiency exam required, foreign language not required. *Entrance requirements:* TOEFL (minimum score 550), minimum GPA of 2.5 during previous 2 years. Application deadline: 4/15 (11/1 for spring admission). Application fee: $55. *Expenses:* Tuition $0 for state residents; $246 per unit for nonresidents. Fees $2012 per year full-time, $1346 per year part-time. *Financial aid:* Federal Work-Study and career-related internships or fieldwork available. Aid available to part-time students. Financial aid application deadline: 3/1. • Dr. Juan Hernandez, Chair, 916-278-6943.

California State University, San Bernardino, Graduate Studies, School of Social and Behavioral Sciences, Department of Social Work, San Bernardino, CA 92407-2397. Awards MSW. Accredited by CSWE. Part-time and evening/weekend programs available. Faculty: 7 full-time (5 women), 2 part-time (1 woman). Students: 115 full-time (87 women), 23 part-time (18 women); includes 62 minority (27 African Americans, 3 Asian Americans, 30 Hispanics, 2 Native Americans). 174 applicants, 47% accepted. In 1997, 44 degrees awarded. *Degree requirements:* Field practicum, research project required, foreign language and thesis not required. *Entrance requirements:* Minimum GPA of 2.75 in last 2 years, liberal arts background. Application deadline: 8/31 (priority date). Application fee: $55. *Expenses:* Tuition $0 for state residents; $164 per unit for nonresidents. Fees $1922 per year full-time, $1256 per year part-time. *Financial aid:* Fellowships, research assistantships, stipends for practicum, Federal Work-Study, institutionally sponsored loans, and career-related internships or fieldwork available. Aid available to part-time students. Financial aid application deadline: 5/1. *Faculty research:* Addiction, computers in social work practice, minority issues, gerontology. • Dr. Rosemary McCaslin, Director, 909-880-5501. Application contact: Dr. Nancy Mary, Coordinator of Admissions, 909-880-5560.

California State University, Stanislaus, College of Arts, Letters, and Sciences, Program in Social Work, Turlock, CA 95382. Awards MSW. Accredited by CSWE. Students: 87 (72 women); includes 30 minority (4 African Americans, 7 Asian Americans, 19 Hispanics). 87 applicants, 57% accepted. In 1997, 23 degrees awarded. *Degree requirements:* Thesis. *Entrance requirements:* GRE General Test, GRE Subject Test. Application fee: $55. *Expenses:* Tuition $0 for state residents; $246 per unit for nonresidents. Fees $1779 per year full-time, $1113 per year part-time. *Financial aid:* Federal Work-Study and career-related internships or fieldwork available. Financial aid application deadline: 3/2; applicants required to submit FAFSA. • Dr. Ellen Dunbar, Coordinator, 209-667-3091.

California University of Pennsylvania, School of Education, Department of Social Work and Gerontology, 250 University Avenue, California, PA 15419-1394. Offers program in social work (MSW). Program new for fall 1998. *Degree requirements:* Comprehensive exam required, foreign language not required. *Entrance requirements:* TOEFL. Application fee: $25. *Expenses:* Tuition $3468 per year full-time, $193 per credit part-time for state residents; $6236 per year full-time, $346 per credit part-time for nonresidents. Fees $886 per year full-time, $153 per semester (minimum) part-time. • Dr. Virginia Majewski, Head, 724-938-5910. Application contact: Coordinator, 724-938-5910.

Carleton University, Faculty of Social Sciences, School of Social Work, Ottawa, ON K1S 5B6, Canada. Awards MSW. Part-time programs available. *Degree requirements:* Thesis optional. *Entrance requirements:* TOEFL (minimum score 550), basic research methods course. Application deadline: 10/15 (priority date; rolling processing). Application fee: $35. *Faculty research:* Social administration, program evaluation, history of Canadian social welfare, women's issues, education in social work.

Case Western Reserve University, Mandel School of Applied Social Sciences, Cleveland, OH 44106. Awards MNO, MSSA, PhD, CNM, JD/MSSA, MSSA/MBA, MSSA/MNO, MSSA/PhD. Programs in nonprofit organizations (MNO, CNM), social administration (MSSA), social welfare (PhD). One or more programs accredited by CSWE. Evening/weekend programs available. Students: 454 full-time (387 women), 28 part-time (27 women); includes 103 minority (86 African Americans, 5 Asian Americans, 10 Hispanics, 2 Native Americans), 11 international. Average age 33. 406 applicants, 90% accepted. In 1997, 189 master's awarded. *Degree requirements:* For master's, fieldwork required, foreign language and thesis not required; for doctorate, dissertation required, foreign language not required. *Average time to degree:* master's–2 years full-time, 3 years part-time. *Entrance requirements:* For master's, GRE

Directory: Social Work

Case Western Reserve University (continued)

General Test, MAT, or minimum GPA of 2.7; for doctorate, GRE General Test or MAT, minimum GPA of 2.7. Application deadline: 3/31. Application fee: $25. *Tuition:* $19,003 per year full-time, $613 per credit hour part-time. *Financial aid:* 386 students received aid; partial tuition waivers, Federal Work-Study, institutionally sponsored loans, and career-related internships or fieldwork available. Aid available to part-time students. Financial aid application deadline: 4/27; applicants required to submit FAFSA. *Faculty research:* Models of social work practice, improved delivery in health and social services, evaluating community-based initiatives. • Dr. Darlyne Bailey, Dean, 216-368-2256. E-mail: dxb5@po.cwru.edu. Application contact: Ann Toomey, Director, Recruitment and Admissions, 800-863-6772. Fax: 216-368-5065. E-mail: aet2@po.cwru.edu.

Announcement: The Mandel School of Applied Social Sciences awards a master's degree in social work and a PhD in social welfare for students with an undergraduate degree in psychology and related mental health majors. Social work career options include mental health counseling and research in private, nonprofit, and government mental health agencies. Contact MSASS at 10900 Euclid Avenue, Cleveland, OH 44106-7164, 800-944-2290 Ext. 2280 (toll-free).

See in-depth description on page 1931.

The Catholic University of America, National Catholic School of Social Service, Washington, DC 20064. Awards MSW, PhD, MSW/JD. One or more programs accredited by CSWE. Part-time programs available. Faculty: 19 full-time (16 women), 24 part-time (20 women), 27 FTE. Students: 180 full-time (157 women), 115 part-time (100 women); includes 42 minority (23 African Americans, 10 Asian Americans, 9 Hispanics), 4 international. Average age 31. 230 applicants, 75% accepted. In 1997, 144 master's, 4 doctorates awarded. *Degree requirements:* For master's, graduation paper or thesis; for doctorate, 1 foreign language, dissertation, comprehensive exam. *Average time to degree:* master's–2 years full-time, 4 years part-time. *Entrance requirements:* For master's, GRE or MAT; for doctorate, GRE, MSW. Application fee: $50. *Expenses:* Tuition $17,325 per year full-time, $668 per credit hour part-time. Fees $680 per year full-time, $360 per year part-time. *Financial aid:* 100 students received aid; fellowships, small grants, Federal Work-Study, institutionally sponsored loans, and career-related internships or fieldwork available. Aid available to part-time students. Financial aid applicants required to submit FAFSA. *Faculty research:* Family and child services, social policy, health and mental health, ethics, spirituality and social work practice. • Dr. Ann Patrick Conrad, Dean, 202-319-5454. Application contact: Loretta V. Saks, Director of Admissions and Financial Aid, 202-319-5496. Fax: 202-319-5093. E-mail: cua-ncsss@cua.edu.

See in-depth description on page 1933.

Central Michigan University, College of Humanities and Social and Behavioral Sciences, Department of Sociology, Anthropology and Social Work, Mount Pleasant, MI 48859. Offers programs in social and criminal justice (MA), social work administration (MSA), sociology (MA). Faculty: 22 full-time (5 women). Students: 18 full-time (10 women), 19 part-time (13 women); includes 6 minority (4 African Americans, 2 Native Americans), 1 international. Average age 30. In 1997, 12 degrees awarded. *Degree requirements:* Thesis or alternative required, foreign language not required. *Entrance requirements:* Minimum GPA of 3.0 in last 20 hours. Application deadline: 3/1 (priority date; rolling processing). Application fee: $30. *Expenses:* Tuition $139 per credit hour (minimum) for state residents; $276 per credit hour (minimum) for nonresidents. Fees $260 per year full-time, $150 per semester part-time. *Financial aid:* In 1997–98, 2 fellowships, 6 teaching assistantships (all to first-year students) were awarded; research assistantships, Federal Work-Study also available. Financial aid application deadline: 3/7. *Faculty research:* Sociological theory, race concept, environmental justice, cultural anthropology. • Dr. Robert Newby, Chairperson, 517-774-3160. Fax: 517-774-7106. E-mail: robert.newby@cmich.edu.

Clark Atlanta University, School of Social Work, Atlanta, GA 30314. Awards MSW, PhD. One or more programs accredited by CSWE. Part-time programs available. Students: 109 full-time (92 women), 32 part-time (25 women); includes 137 minority (all African Americans), 1 international. In 1997, 64 master's awarded. Terminal master's awarded for partial completion of doctoral program. *Degree requirements:* For master's, computer language, thesis required, foreign language not required; for doctorate, 1 foreign language, dissertation. *Application deadline:* 4/1 (rolling processing; 11/1 for spring admission). *Application fee:* $40. *Expenses:* Tuition $9672 per year full-time, $403 per credit hour part-time. Fees $200 per year. *Financial aid:* Fellowships, scholarships, Federal Work-Study, and career-related internships or fieldwork available. Aid available to part-time students. Financial aid application deadline: 4/30. • Dr. Dorcas Bowles, Dean, 404-880-8555. Application contact: Michelle Clark-Davis, Graduate Program Assistant, 404-880-8709.

Cleveland State University, College of Arts and Sciences, Department of Social Work, Cleveland, OH 44115-2440. Awards MSW. Candidate for accreditation by CSWE. Faculty: 14 full-time (6 women). Students: 36 full-time (28 women), 1 part-time (0 women); includes 14 minority (9 African Americans, 4 Hispanics, 1 Native American). Average age 35. 83 applicants, 22% accepted. In 1997, 9 degrees awarded. *Application deadline:* 7/15 (12/1 for spring admission). *Application fee:* $25. *Expenses:* Tuition $5252 per year full-time, $202 per credit hour part-time for state residents; $10,504 per year full-time, $404 per credit hour part-time for nonresidents. Fees $2.25 per credit hour (minimum). • Dr. Maggie Jackson, Chairperson, 216-487-4599. Fax: 216-687-5590. E-mail: mag.jackson@csuohio.edu.

College of St. Catherine, Graduate Program, Program in Social Work, St. Paul, MN 55105-1789. Awards MSW. Accredited by CSWE. Offered jointly with the University of St. Thomas. Part-time and evening/weekend programs available. Faculty: 10 full-time (9 women), 10 part-time (7 women). Students: 89 (69 women); includes 4 minority (2 African Americans, 1 Asian American, 1 Hispanic). Average age 35. 182 applicants, 56% accepted. *Degree requirements:* Clinical research paper required, foreign language and thesis not required. *Entrance requirements:* Michigan English Language Assessment Battery (minimum score 90) or TOEFL (minimum score 600), minimum GPA of 3.0. Application deadline: 2/1. Application fee: $25. *Expenses:* Tuition $398 per credit hour. Fees $60 per year. *Financial aid:* Institutionally sponsored loans and career-related internships or fieldwork available. Aid available to part-time students. Financial aid application deadline: 4/1; applicants required to submit FAFSA. • Barbara W. Shank, Department Chair, 612-647-4416. Application contact: Office of Admission, 612-690-6505.

Colorado State University, College of Applied Human Sciences, Department of Social Work, Fort Collins, CO 80523-0015. Awards MSW. Accredited by CSWE. Faculty: 12 full-time (7 women). Students: 56 full-time (46 women), 6 part-time (4 women); includes 5 minority (2 African Americans, 1 Asian American, 2 Hispanics). Average age 34. 119 applicants, 54% accepted. In 1997, 44 degrees awarded. *Degree requirements:* Research paper required, foreign language not required. *Entrance requirements:* GRE General Test, TOEFL, minimum GPA of 3.0, 18 credits in social or behavioral sciences, previous course work in human biology and statistics or two years experience. Application deadline: 1/31. Application fee: $30. Electronic applications accepted. *Expenses:* Tuition $2632 per year full-time, $109 per credit hour part-time for state residents; $10,216 per year full-time, $425 per credit hour part-time for nonresidents. Fees $708 per year full-time, $32 per semester (minimum) part-time. *Financial aid:* In 1997–98, 1 research assistantship (to a first-year student) averaging $1,000 per month and totaling $12,000, 1 teaching assistantship averaging $921 per month and totaling $8,289 were awarded; fellowships, Federal Work-Study, institutionally sponsored loans, and career-related internships or fieldwork also available. *Faculty research:* Rural social work, school social work, mental health, child welfare, international social work. Total annual research expenditures: $6.5 million. • Ben P. Granger, Head, 970-491-6612. E-mail: granger@cahs.colostate.edu. Application contact: Dawn Carlson, Administrative Assistant, 970-491-2536. Fax: 970-491-7280. E-mail: dcarlson@cahs.colostate.edu.

Columbia University, School of Social Work, New York, NY 10025. Awards MSSW, PhD, JD/MS, MBA/MS, MPA/MS, MPH/MS, MS/MA, MS/M Div, MS/MS, MS/MS Ed. One or more programs accredited by CSWE. MS/M Div offered jointly with Union Theological Seminary; MS/MA with Jewish Theological Seminary of America; MS/MS Ed with Bank Street College of Education. MS/MS offered jointly with the Program in Urban Planning; M Phil and PhD offered through the Graduate School of Arts and Sciences. Students: 672 full-time (588 women), 132 part-time (100 women); includes 232 minority (80 African Americans, 80 Asian Americans, 64 Hispanics, 8 Native Americans). Average age 26. 1,239 applicants, 61% accepted. In 1997, 365 master's awarded. *Degree requirements:* For doctorate, dissertation required, foreign language not required. *Average time to degree:* master's–2 years full-time, 3 years part-time. *Entrance requirements:* For doctorate, GRE General Test. Application deadline: 3/1 (priority date; rolling processing). Application fee: $60. *Tuition:* $19,260 per year full-time, $642 per credit part-time. *Financial aid:* Federal Work-Study, institutionally sponsored loans, and career-related internships or fieldwork available. Financial aid applicants required to submit FAFSA. • Dr. Ronald A. Feldman, Dean. Application contact: Office of Admissions, 212-854-2856. Fax: 212-854-2975. E-mail: cussw-admit@columbia.edu.

See in-depth description on page 1935.

Dalhousie University, Faculty of Health Professions, The Maritime School of Social Work, Halifax, NS B3H 3J5, Canada. Awards MSW. Part-time programs available. Postbaccalaureate distance learning degree programs offered (no on-campus study). Faculty: 15 full-time, 1 part-time. Students: 19 full-time (14 women), 36 part-time (27 women); includes 7 minority (4 African Americans, 3 Native Americans). In 1997, 24 degrees awarded. *Degree requirements:* Thesis optional, foreign language not required. *Average time to degree:* master's–1.2 years full-time, 3.5 years part-time. *Entrance requirements:* TOEFL (minimum score 580), minimum GPA of 3.0. Application deadline: 2/1. Application fee: $55. *Financial aid:* 8 students received aid; fellowships, teaching assistantships, institutionally sponsored loans, and career-related internships or fieldwork available. Financial aid application deadline: 9/15. • Glenn Drover, Director, 902-494-3760.

Delaware State University, Department of Social Work, Program in Social Work, Dover, DE 19901-2277. Awards MSW. Accredited by CSWE. Evening/weekend programs available. *Degree requirements:* Computer language required, foreign language and thesis not required. *Entrance requirements:* GRE, minimum GPA of 3.0 in major, 2.75 overall. Application deadline: 6/30 (priority date; rolling processing). Application fee: $10. *Faculty research:* Gerontology, human behavior, corrections, child welfare, adolescent behavior policy.

Delta State University, School of Arts and Sciences, Department of Social Work, Cleveland, MS 38733-0001. Awards MSW. Part-time programs available. Faculty: 2 full-time (both women), 1 (woman) part-time, 2.75 FTE. Students: 0. 0 applicants. *Degree requirements:* Thesis or alternative required, foreign language not required. *Application deadline:* 8/1 (priority date; rolling processing). *Application fee:* $0. *Tuition:* $2596 per year full-time, $121 per semester hour part-time for state residents; $5546 per year full-time, $285 per semester hour part-time for nonresidents. *Financial aid:* Research assistantships, Federal Work-Study, institutionally sponsored loans, and career-related internships or fieldwork available. Aid available to part-time students. Financial aid application deadline: 6/1. • Carol Boyd, Chairperson, 601-846-4409. E-mail: cboyd@dsu.deltast.edu. Application contact: Dr. John Thornell, Dean of Graduate Studies and Continuing Education, 601-846-4310. Fax: 601-846-4016.

East Carolina University, School of Social Work, Greenville, NC 27858-4353. Awards MSW. Accredited by CSWE. Faculty: 11 full-time (4 women). Students: 134 full-time (113 women), 35 part-time (29 women); includes 29 minority (25 African Americans, 2 Asian Americans, 2 Hispanics). Average age 32. 268 applicants, 48% accepted. In 1997, 100 degrees awarded. *Degree requirements:* Comprehensive exams required, foreign language and thesis not required. *Entrance requirements:* GRE General Test or MAT, TOEFL. Application deadline: 1/15 (priority date). Application fee: $40. *Tuition:* $1886 per year full-time, $472 per semester (minimum) part-time for state residents; $9156 per year full-time, $2289 per semester (minimum) part-time for nonresidents. *Financial aid:* Research assistantships, teaching assistantships, Federal Work-Study available. Aid available to part-time students. Financial aid application deadline: 6/1. • Dr. Linner Griffin, Director of Graduate Studies, 252-328-4199. Fax: 252-328-4196. E-mail: griffinl@mail.ecu.edu. Application contact: Dr. Paul D. Tschetter, Associate Dean, 252-328-6012. Fax: 252-328-6071. E-mail: grad@mail.ecu.edu.

Eastern Michigan University, College of Health and Human Services, Department of Social Work, Program in Social Work, Ypsilanti, MI 48197. Awards MSW. Accredited by CSWE. In 1997, 66 degrees awarded. *Entrance requirements:* TOEFL (minimum score 500). Application deadline: 5/15 (rolling processing; 3/15 for spring admission). Application fee: $30. *Expenses:* Tuition $2691 per year full-time, $150 per credit hour part-time for state residents; $6300 per year full-time, $350 per credit hour part-time for nonresidents. Fees $368 per year full-time, $88 per semester (minimum) part-time. *Financial aid:* Application deadline 3/15. • Dr. Marti Bombyle, Head, 734-487-0393.

Eastern Washington University, College of Letters and Social Sciences, School of Social Work and Human Services, Cheney, WA 99004-2431. Awards MSW, MPA/MSW. Accredited by CSWE. Part-time programs available. Faculty: 14 full-time (7 women). Students: 112 full-time (88 women), 43 part-time (32 women); includes 19 minority (4 Asian Americans, 8 Hispanics, 7 Native Americans). 150 applicants, 61% accepted. In 1997, 42 degrees awarded. *Degree requirements:* Comprehensive exam required, foreign language and thesis not required. *Entrance requirements:* Minimum GPA of 3.0. Application deadline: 2/15 (rolling processing). Application fee: $35. *Tuition:* $4200 per year full-time, $140 per credit part-time for state residents; $12,780 per year full-time, $415 per credit part-time for nonresidents. *Financial aid:* Research assistantships, Federal Work-Study, institutionally sponsored loans, and career-related internships or fieldwork available. Financial aid application deadline: 2/1. • Dr. Michael Frumkin, Director, 509-359-6482.

Florida Gulf Coast University, College of Professional Studies, School of Public and Social Services, Program in Social Work, Fort Myers, FL 33965-6565. Awards MSW. Part-time and evening/weekend programs available. Students: 20 (17 women); includes 6 minority (1 African American, 1 Asian American, 4 Hispanics). Average age 36. 34 applicants, 62% accepted. *Entrance requirements:* GRE General Test (minimum combined score of 1000), minimum GPA of 3.0. Application fee: $20. Electronic applications accepted. *Financial aid:* In 1997–98, 6 research assistantships were awarded; partial tuition waivers and career-related internships or fieldwork also available. Aid available to part-time students. *Faculty research:* Gerontology, clinical case management. • Patricia Washington, Chair, 941-590-7826. Fax: 941-590-7842. E-mail: pwashing@fgcu.edu. Application contact: Glenn Parker, Counselor/Adviser, 941-590-7760. Fax: 941-590-7758. E-mail: gparker@fgcu.edu.

Florida International University, College of Urban and Public Affairs, School of Social Work, Miami, FL 33199. Awards MSW, PhD. One or more programs accredited by CSWE. Part-time and evening/weekend programs available. Faculty: 11 full-time (3 women), 1 (woman) part-time, 11.75 FTE. Students: 189 full-time (159 women), 104 part-time (75 women); includes 128 minority (52 African Americans, 5 Asian Americans, 71 Hispanics), 2 international. Average age 37. 220 applicants, 50% accepted. In 1997, 161 master's, 4 doctorates awarded. *Degree requirements:* For doctorate, dissertation, comprehensive exams required, foreign language not required. *Entrance requirements:* For master's, GRE General Test (minimum combined score of 1000), minimum GPA of 3.0; for doctorate, GRE General Test (minimum combined score of 1000). Application deadline: 4/1 (priority date; rolling processing; 10/1 for spring admission). Application fee: $20. *Expenses:* Tuition $138 per credit hour for state residents; $482 per credit hour for nonresidents. Fees $46 per semester. • Dr. Max Rothman, Acting Director, 305-919-5880. Fax: 305-919-5313.

Florida State University, School of Social Work, Tallahassee, FL 32306. Awards MSW, PhD, JD/MSW, MPA/MSW. Programs in administrative practice (MSW), clinical social work (MSW), marriage and the family (PhD), social services practice (MSW), social work (PhD). One or more programs accredited by CSWE. MPA/MSW offered jointly with the School of Public Administration and Policy. Part-time and evening/weekend programs available. Postbaccalaureate distance learning degree programs offered (no on-campus study). Faculty: 26 full-time (16 women), 25 part-time (14 women), 33.25 FTE. Students: 169 full-time (136 women), 227 part-time (185 women); includes 80 minority (55 African Americans, 7 Asian Americans, 16 Hispanics, 2 Native Americans). Average age 27. 458 applicants, 75% accepted. In 1997, 231 master's awarded; 4 doctorates awarded (100% entered university research/teaching). *Degree requirements:* For doctorate, dissertation required, foreign language not required. *Average time to degree:* master's–2 years full-time, 3 years part-time; doctorate–2.5 years full-time, 5 years part-time. *Entrance requirements:* GRE General Test (minimum combined score of 1000), minimum GPA of 3.0. Application deadline: 2/15 (priority date; rolling processing; 11/15 for spring admission). *Tuition:* $139 per credit hour for state residents; $482 per credit hour for nonresidents. *Financial aid:* In 1997–98, 81 students received aid, including 2 fellowships (both to first-year students) averaging $375 per month, 45 research assistantships (27 to first-year students) averaging $414 per month, 7 teaching assistantships averaging $510 per month; Federal Work-Study, institutionally sponsored loans, and career-related internships or fieldwork also available. Financial aid application deadline: 4/1. *Faculty research:* Family violence, AIDS, aging, family therapy, trauma. Total annual research expenditures: $1.5 million. • Dr. Dianne H. Montgomery, Dean, 850-644-4752. E-mail: dmontgom@mailer.fsu.edu. Application contact: Sheila Sansom, Coordinator, 850-644-6742. Fax: 850-644-9750. E-mail: ssansom@mailer.fsu.edu.

Fordham University, Graduate School of Social Service, New York, NY 10023. Awards MSW, PhD, JD/MSW. One or more programs accredited by CSWE. Part-time programs available. Faculty: 52 full-time (14 women), 126 part-time (29 women). Students: 904 full-time (763 women), 626 part-time (508 women); includes 435 minority (224 African Americans, 24 Asian Americans, 187 Hispanics), 2 international. 1,983 applicants, 75% accepted. In 1997, 626 master's, 10 doctorates awarded. *Application deadline:* 6/1 (priority date; rolling processing; 12/1 for spring admission). *Application fee:* $40. *Financial aid:* 450 students received aid; fellowships, research assistantships, partial tuition waivers, Federal Work-Study, and career-related internships or fieldwork available. Aid available to part-time students. Financial aid applicants required to submit FAFSA. • Dr. Mary Ann Quaranta, Dean, 212-636-6600. Application contact: Elaine Gerald, Dean of Admissions, 212-636-6600. Fax: 212-636-6613.

Gallaudet University, College of Arts and Sciences, Department of Social Work, Washington, DC 20002-3625. Awards MSW. Accredited by CSWE. Students: 13 full-time (9 women), 4 part-time (3 women); includes 3 minority (2 African Americans, 1 Hispanic), 1 international. *Degree requirements:* Thesis optional. *Entrance requirements:* GRE General Test or MAT. Application deadline: 2/15 (priority date; rolling processing). Application fee: $50. *Expenses:* Tuition $7064 per year full-time, $392 per credit part-time. Fees $50 (one-time charge). *Financial aid:* Application deadline 8/1. • Dr. Janet Pray, Chair, 202-651-5160. Application contact: Deborah DeStefano, Director of Admissions, 202-651-5253. Fax: 202-651-5744. E-mail: adm_destefan@gallua.bitnet.

Governors State University, College of Health Professions, Program in Social Work, University Park, IL 60466. Awards MSW. Students: 54 part-time (46 women). 0 applicants. *Application fee:* $0. *Expenses:* Tuition $1140 per trimester full-time, $95 per credit hour part-time for state residents; $3420 per trimester full-time, $285 per credit hour part-time for nonresidents. Fees $95 per trimester. *Financial aid:* Application deadline 5/1. • Joan Porche, Head, 708-235-2179.

Graduate School and University Center of the City University of New York, Program in Social Welfare, New York, NY 10036-8099. Awards DSW. Faculty: 17 full-time (7 women). Students: 60 full-time (43 women); includes 15 minority (11 African Americans, 1 Asian American, 3 Hispanics). Average age 44. 56 applicants, 34% accepted. In 1997, 9 degrees awarded. *Degree requirements:* Dissertation, project, qualifying exam. *Entrance requirements:* GRE General Test, MSW or equivalent. Application deadline: 3/1. Application fee: $40. *Expenses:* Tuition $4350 per year full-time, $185 per credit (minimum) part-time for state residents; $7600 per year full-time, $320 per credit (minimum) part-time for nonresidents. Fees $69 per year. *Financial aid:* In 1997–98, 16 students received aid, including 15 fellowships (1 to a first-year student); research assistantships, full and partial tuition waivers, Federal Work-Study, institutionally sponsored loans, and career-related internships or fieldwork also available. Financial aid application deadline: 2/1; applicants required to submit FAFSA. • Dr. Harold Weissman, Executive Officer, 212-452-7048.

Grambling State University, School of Social Work, Grambling, LA 71245. Awards MSW. Candidate for accreditation by CSWE. Part-time and evening/weekend programs available. Faculty: 8 full-time (2 women), 4 part-time (2 women), 10 FTE. Students: 26 full-time (25 women), 3 part-time (2 women); includes 29 minority (20 African Americans, 9 Hispanics). Average age 25. 28 applicants, 71% accepted. In 1997, 99 degrees awarded. *Degree requirements:* Thesis or alternative required, foreign language not required. *Average time to degree:* master's–2 years full-time, 3 years part-time. *Entrance requirements:* GRE. Application deadline: 4/15 (priority date). Application fee: $15. *Tuition:* $1960 per year full-time, $297 per semester (minimum) part-time for state residents; $7110 per year full-time, $297 per semester (minimum) part-time for nonresidents. *Financial aid:* Graduate assistantships, Federal Work-Study, institutionally sponsored loans, and career-related internships or fieldwork available. Financial aid application deadline: 5/31. *Faculty research:* Welfare history, social services in Louisiana, stress and child abuse, the black family, rurality. • Dr. Birdex Copeland, Dean, 318-274-3303. Fax: 318-274-3254.

Grand Valley State University, School of Social Work, Allendale, MI 49401-9403. Awards MSW. Accredited by CSWE. Part-time programs available. Faculty: 20 full-time (16 women), 7 part-time (4 women). Students: 141 full-time (117 women), 217 part-time (165 women); includes 37 minority (21 African Americans, 5 Asian Americans, 6 Hispanics, 5 Native Americans), 3 international. Average age 34. 104 applicants, 76% accepted. In 1997, 116 degrees awarded (100% found work related to degree). *Average time to degree:* master's–2 years full-time, 4 years part-time. *Application deadline:* 5/15 (priority date; rolling processing). *Application fee:* $20. *Financial aid:* In 1997–98, 8 research assistantships (4 to first-year students) were awarded; Federal Work-Study, institutionally sponsored loans, and career-related internships or fieldwork also available. *Faculty research:* Alcoholism evaluation research, mental health, public assistance, child welfare. • Dr. Rodney Mulder, Dean, 616-771-6550. Application contact: Dr. Doris Perry, Chair, Admissions, 616-771-6550. Fax: 616-771-6570.

Gratz College, Program in Jewish Communal Studies, Old York Road and Melrose Avenue, Melrose Park, PA 19027. Awards MA, Certificate, MA/Certificate, MSW/Certificate. MSW/Certificate offered jointly with the University of Pennsylvania. Part-time and evening/weekend programs available. Faculty: 8 full-time (3 women), 11 part-time (7 women). *Degree requirements:* For master's, 1 foreign language, internship. *Application deadline:* rolling. *Application fee:* $50. *Tuition:* $8500 per year full-time, $395 per credit part-time. *Financial aid:* Application deadline 4/1. • Dr. Rela M. Geffen, Coordinator, 215-635-7300. Application contact: Evelyn Klein, Director of Admissions, 215-635-7300. Fax: 215-635-7320. E-mail: gratzinfo@aol.com.

Hebrew Union College–Jewish Institute of Religion, Irwin Daniels School of Jewish Communal Services, Los Angeles, CA 90007-3796. Awards MAJCS, Certificate, MAJCS/MA, MAJCS/MAJE, MAJCS/MPA, MAJCS/MSG, MAJCS/MSW. MAJCS/MA (communications management, gerontology), MAJCS/MPA, MAJCS/MSG offered jointly with University of Southern California. MAJCS/MSW offered jointly with University of Pittsburgh, University of Southern California, and Washington University. Faculty: 3 full-time (1 woman), 7 part-time (2 women). Students: 26 full-time (20 women), 1 (woman) part-time; includes 1 international. Average age 27. In 1997, 18 master's awarded. *Degree requirements:* For master's, project or thesis required, foreign language not required. *Average time to degree:* master's–2 years full-time; other advanced degree–1 year full-time. *Entrance requirements:* For master's, GRE General Test. Application deadline: 3/1. Application fee: $55. *Expenses:* Tuition $7500 per year full-time, $315 per unit part-time. Fees $296 per year full-time. *Financial aid:* Institutionally sponsored loans and career-related internships or fieldwork available. Financial aid applicants required to submit FAFSA. • Dr. Steven Windmueller, Director, 213-749-3424. Application contact: Rabbi Sheldon Marder, Associate Dean, 213-749-3424. Fax: 213-747-6128. E-mail: marder@mizar.usc.edu.

Howard University, School of Social Work, Washington, DC 20008. Awards MSW, DSW, PhD. One or more programs accredited by CSWE. DSW being phased out; applicants no longer accepted. Part-time programs available. Students: 21 full-time (14 women), 16 part-time (10 women); includes 29 minority (28 African Americans, 1 Asian American), 1 international. Average age 30. 22 applicants, 50% accepted. In 1997, 3 doctorates awarded. *Degree requirements:* For doctorate, dissertation, comprehensive exam, qualifying exam required, foreign language not required. *Entrance requirements:* For master's, GRE General Test, TOEFL, minimum GPA of 2.5; for doctorate, GRE General Test, TOEFL, minimum GPA of 3.3, MSW or master's in related field. Application deadline: 4/1 (priority date; rolling processing; 10/1 for spring admission). Application fee: $45. *Expenses:* Tuition $10,200 per year full-time, $567 per credit hour part-time. Fees $405 per year. *Financial aid:* Fellowships, research assistantships, teaching assistantships, grants, scholarships, Federal Work-Study, institutionally sponsored loans, and career-related internships or fieldwork available. Financial aid application deadline: 4/1. *Faculty research:* Infant mortality, child and family services, displaced populations, social work practice, domestic violence, black males, mental health. • Dr. Fariyal Ross-Sheriff, Director, PhD Program, 202-806-7306. Application contact: Blanchita P. Porter, Director of Admissions, 202-806-7300. Fax: 202-387-4309.

See in-depth description on page 1937.

Hunter College of the City University of New York, School of Social Work, 695 Park Avenue, New York, NY 10021-5085. Awards MSW, DSW. One or more programs accredited by CSWE. DSW offered jointly with the Graduate School and University Center of the City University of New York. Faculty: 36 full-time, 35 part-time. Students: 449 full-time (366 women), 272 part-time (196 women); includes 351 minority (204 African Americans, 40 Asian Americans, 106 Hispanics, 1 Native American). Average age 34. 1,119 applicants, 41% accepted. In 1997, 236 master's awarded. *Degree requirements:* For master's, major paper required, foreign language and thesis not required; for doctorate, dissertation required, foreign language not required. *Entrance requirements:* For master's, TOEFL (minimum score 550). Application deadline: 2/15 (priority date; rolling processing). Application fee: $40. *Expenses:* Tuition $4350 per year full-time, $185 per credit part-time for state residents; $7600 per year full-time, $320 per credit part-time for nonresidents. Fees $26 per year. *Financial aid:* Fellowships, Federal Work-Study, and career-related internships or fieldwork available. *Faculty research:* Child welfare, AIDS, homeless, aging, mental health, criminal justice, occupational social work. • Bogart R. Leashore, Dean, 212-452-7085. Application contact: Ana Paulino, Director for Admissions, 212-452-7005.

Indiana University Northwest, Program in Social Work, Gary, IN 46408-1197. Awards MSW. Accredited by CSWE. Part-time and evening/weekend programs available. Faculty: 4 full-time (3 women). Students: 81 part-time (71 women); includes 32 minority (23 African Americans, 1 Asian American, 7 Hispanics, 1 Native American). Average age 38. 73 applicants, 77% accepted. *Average time to degree:* master's–4 years part-time. *Entrance requirements:* Minimum GPA of 2.5; previous undergraduate course work in human biology, research methodology, and statistics. Application deadline: 2/2. Application fee: $25. *Financial aid:* In 1997–98, 43 students received aid, including 27 tuition remissions (8 to first-year students) totaling $6,806; partial tuition waivers, Federal Work-Study, and career-related internships or fieldwork also available. Aid available to part-time students. Financial aid application deadline: 6/1; applicants required to submit FAFSA. *Faculty research:* Educational outcomes, generalist practice, homelessness. Total annual research expenditures: $1000. • Dr. Grafton Hull Jr., Director, 219-980-7111. Fax: 219-981-4264. E-mail: ghull@iunhaw1.iun.indiana.edu.

Indiana University–Purdue University Indianapolis, School of Social Work, Doctoral Program in Social Work, Indianapolis, IN 46202-2896. Awards PhD. Part-time programs available. Faculty: 12 full-time (6 women), 1 part-time (0 women), 12.15 FTE. Students: 7 full-time (4 women), 8 part-time (5 women); includes 4 minority (all African Americans). Average age 41. 15 applicants, 20% accepted. Terminal master's awarded for partial completion of doctoral program. *Degree requirements:* For doctorate, computer language, dissertation, residential internship, externship required, foreign language not required. *Entrance requirements:* For doctorate, GRE General Test. Application deadline: 4/1. Application fee: $35 ($55 for international students). *Financial aid:* In 1997–98, 7 students received aid, including 7 fellowships (3 to first-year students) averaging $1,018 per month and totaling $57,000, 4 research assistantships averaging $230 per month and totaling $7,300, 7 teaching assistantships (2 to first-year students) averaging $450 per month; full and partial tuition waivers, Federal Work-Study, institutionally sponsored loans, and career-related internships or fieldwork also available. Aid available to part-time students. Financial aid application deadline: 6/1; applicants required to submit FAFSA. *Faculty research:* Diversity issues, mental health corrections, HIV/AIDS, gerontology. Total annual research expenditures: $120,000. • Dr. Gerald T. Powers, Director, 317-274-6724. E-mail: gpowers@indyvax.iupui.edu. Application contact: Mary Lindop, Program Office, 317-274-4811. Fax: 317-274-8630.

Indiana University–Purdue University Indianapolis, School of Social Work, Master's Program in Social Work, Indianapolis, IN 46202-2896. Awards MSW. Part-time and evening/weekend programs available. Students: 270 full-time (235 women), 202 part-time (178 women); includes 95 minority (69 African Americans, 2 Asian Americans, 21 Hispanics, 3 Native Americans), 2 international. Average age 34. 470 applicants, 72% accepted. In 1997, 200 degrees awarded. *Degree requirements:* Field practicum required, foreign language and thesis not required. *Average time to degree:* master's–2 years full-time, 4 years part-time. *Entrance requirements:* Minimum GPA of 2.5, previous course work in social behavior and statistics. Application deadline: 2/1. Application fee: $35 ($55 for international students). *Financial aid:* Research assistantships, full and partial tuition waivers, Federal Work-Study, institutionally sponsored loans, and career-related internships or fieldwork available. Aid available to part-time students. Financial aid application deadline: 3/1; applicants required to submit FAFSA. • Dr. Paul Sachdev, Director, 317-274-6712. E-mail: psachdev@iussw.iupui.edu. Application contact: Rhonda Brock, Student Services Secretary, 317-274-8364. Fax: 317-274-8630. E-mail: rbrock@iupui.edu.

Indiana University South Bend, Program in Social Work, South Bend, IN 46634-7111. Awards MSW. Accredited by CSWE. Offered jointly with Indiana University–Purdue University Indianapolis. Part-time and evening/weekend programs available. Faculty: 2 full-time (1 woman), 5 part-time (2 women). Students: 23 full-time (19 women), 19 part-time (15 women); includes 9 minority (7 African Americans, 1 Hispanic, 1 Native American). Average age 35. 60 applicants, 42% accepted. *Application deadline:* 2/1. *Application fee:* $35 ($40 for international students). *Expenses:* Tuition $3240 per year full-time, $135 per credit hour part-time for state residents; $7776 per year full-time, $324 per credit hour part-time for nonresidents. Fees $222 per year full-time, $34 per semester (minimum) part-time. *Financial aid:* Federal Work-Study and career-related internships or fieldwork available. Aid available to part-time students. Financial aid application deadline: 3/1. • Director, 219-237-4464. Fax: 219-237-4876. Application contact: Graduate Director, 219-237-4183. Fax: 219-237-6549.

Institute for Clinical Social Work, Graduate Programs, 68 East Wacker Place, #1400, Chicago, IL 60601. Offers program in clinical social work (PhD). Part-time programs available. Faculty: 67 part-time (35 women). Students: 82 full-time (60 women), 16 part-time (14 women); includes 1 international. Average age 38. 23 applicants, 91% accepted. In 1997, 5 degrees awarded. *Degree requirements:* Dissertation, supervised practicum required, foreign language not required. *Average time to degree:* doctorate–7 years full-time. *Entrance requirements:* 2 years of experience, master's degree. Application deadline: 5/1. Application fee: $50. *Tuition:* $9000 per year full-time, $700 per course part-time. *Financial aid:* Research assistantships, teaching assistantships, institutionally sponsored loans available. Financial aid application deadline: 9/1. *Faculty research:* Impact of AIDS on partners, effects of learning disabilities on children and families, clinical social work issues. • Thomas K. Kennemore, President, 312-

Directory: Social Work

Institute for Clinical Social Work (continued)
726-8480. Application contact: Dr. Barbara Berger, Dean of Admissions, 312-726-8480 Ext. 31. Fax: 312-726-7216.

Inter American University of Puerto Rico, Metropolitan Campus, Division of Behavioral Science and Allied Professions, Program in Social Work, San Juan, PR 00919-1293. Awards MA. Candidate for accreditation by CSWE. Evening/weekend programs available. Faculty: 5 full-time (3 women), 20 part-time (15 women). Students: 45 full-time (36 women), 65 part-time (52 women); includes 110 minority (all Hispanics). Average age 30. *Degree requirements:* Comprehensive exam. *Entrance requirements:* GRE or PAEG, interview. Application deadline: 5/15 (priority date; rolling processing; 11/15 for spring admission). Application fee: $31. Electronic applications accepted. *Expenses:* Tuition $3272 per year full-time, $1740 per year part-time. Fees $328 per year full-time, $176 per year part-time. *Financial aid:* Federal Work-Study available. Aid available to part-time students. • Dr. Carmen A. Escoda, Director, 787-250-1912 Ext. 2272. Application contact: Nilda Martínez, Admissions Office, 787-250-1912 Ext. 2101.

Jackson State University, School of Social Work, Jackson, MS 39217. Awards MSW, PhD. One or more programs accredited by CSWE. PhD new for fall 1998. Evening/weekend programs available. Faculty: 5 full-time (4 women). Students: 57 full-time (43 women), 23 part-time (19 women); includes 61 minority (all African Americans), 1 international. 127 applicants, 56% accepted. In 1997, 13 master's awarded. *Degree requirements:* For master's, comprehensive exam; for doctorate, dissertation, comprehensive exam. *Entrance requirements:* For master's, GRE General Test (minimum combined score of 1000), TOEFL (minimum score 550); for doctorate, MAT (minimum score 45). Application deadline: 2/1. Application fee: $20. *Tuition:* $2688 per year (minimum) full-time, $150 per semester hour part-time for state residents; $5546 per year (minimum) full-time, $309 per semester hour part-time for nonresidents. *Financial aid:* 24 students received aid. Financial aid application deadline: 3/1. • Dr. Gwendolyn S. Prater, Dean, 601-987-4388. Fax: 601-364-2396. Application contact: Mae Robinson, Admissions Coordinator, 601-968-2455. Fax: 601-968-8246. E-mail: mrobinson@ccaix.jsums.edu.

Kean University, School of Liberal Arts, Department of Social Work, Union, NJ 07083. Awards MSW. Candidate for accreditation by CSWE. Students: 64 full-time (54 women); includes 20 minority (12 African Americans, 2 Asian Americans, 6 Hispanics). Average age 31. In 1997, 6 degrees awarded. *Application deadline:* 6/15 (11/15 for spring admission). *Application fee:* $35. *Tuition:* $5926 per year full-time, $248 per credit part-time for state residents; $7312 per year full-time, $304 per credit part-time for nonresidents. • Dr. Carol Williams, Coordinator, 908-527-2835. Application contact: Joanne Morris, Director of Graduate Admissions, 908-527-2665. Fax: 908-527-2286. E-mail: grad_adm@turbo.kean.edu.

Lakehead University, Faculty of Arts and Science, Department of Social Work, Thunder Bay, ON P7B 5E1, Canada. Awards MSW. Part-time programs available. *Degree requirements:* Thesis or alternative required, foreign language not required. *Entrance requirements:* TOEFL (minimum score 550), honors degree in social work. Application deadline: 2/1 (priority date; rolling processing). Application fee: $0. *Faculty research:* Clinical psychology, social work and practice theory, long-term care, health care for frail elderly, women's studies.

Laurentian University, École de Service Social, Sudbury, ON P3E 2C6, Canada. Awards MSS. Open only to French-speaking students. Faculty: 9 full-time (2 women), 1 (woman) part-time. Students: 26 part-time (20 women). 12 applicants, 50% accepted. In 1997, 3 degrees awarded. *Degree requirements:* Thesis required, foreign language not required. *Application deadline:* 5/31. *Application fee:* $50. *Expenses:* Tuition $4977 per year full-time, $830 per course part-time for Canadian residents; $9072 per year full-time, $3024 per course part-time for nonresidents. Fees $194 per year full-time, $15 per year part-time. • Dr. Michel-André Beauvolsk, Coordonnateur, 705-675-1151 Ext. 5081. Fax: 705-675-4817. Application contact: Office of Admissions, 705-675-1151 Ext. 3917. Fax: 705-675-4843.

Laurentian University, School of Social Work, Sudbury, ON P3E 2C6, Canada. Awards MSW. Faculty: 11 full-time (4 women), 2 part-time (0 women). Students: 24 part-time (18 women). 18 applicants, 56% accepted. In 1997, 4 degrees awarded. *Application deadline:* 5/31. *Application fee:* $50. *Expenses:* Tuition $4977 per year full-time, $830 per course part-time for Canadian residents; $9072 per year full-time, $3024 per course part-time for nonresidents. Fees $194 per year full-time, $15 per year part-time. *Faculty research:* Combatting discrimination, victims of criminal harassment and those who help them, visible minorities in schools, women in mining, women in the economy. • Dr. Duncan Matheson, Coordinator, 705-675-1151 Ext. 5068. Fax: 705-675-4817. Application contact: Office of Admissions, 705-675-1151 Ext. 3917. Fax: 705-675-4843.

Loma Linda University, Graduate School, Department of Social Work, Loma Linda, CA 92350. Awards MSW. Accredited by CSWE. *Entrance requirements:* GRE General Test. Application fee: $40. *Tuition:* $380 per unit. • Dr. Beverly Buckles, Chair, 909-478-8550.

Louisiana State University and Agricultural and Mechanical College, School of Social Work, Baton Rouge, LA 70803. Awards MSW, PhD. One or more programs accredited by CSWE. Part-time programs available. Faculty: 16 full-time (8 women), 1 part-time (0 women). Students: 173 full-time (144 women), 61 part-time (46 women); includes 31 minority (25 African Americans, 4 Asian Americans, 2 Hispanics), 1 international. Average age 31. 236 applicants, 63% accepted. In 1997, 97 master's awarded. *Degree requirements:* For master's, field instruction required, foreign language and thesis not required. *Entrance requirements:* GRE General Test (minimum combined score of 1000), minimum GPA of 3.0. Application deadline: 3/1. Application fee: $25. *Tuition:* $2736 per year full-time, $285 per semester (minimum) part-time for state residents; $6636 per year full-time, $460 per semester (minimum) part-time for nonresidents. *Financial aid:* In 1997–98, 2 fellowships, 5 research assistantships, 3 teaching assistantships, 14 service assistantships (3 to first-year students) were awarded; career-related internships or fieldwork also available. Aid available to part-time students. *Faculty research:* Methodology, child welfare, aging, social development, corrections, social work history. • Dr. Kenneth A. Millar, Dean, 504-388-1351. Application contact: Admissions Secretary, 504-388-5875.

Loyola University Chicago, School of Social Work, 820 North Michigan Avenue, Chicago, IL 60611-2196. Awards MSW, DSW, JD/MSW, M Div/MSW. One or more programs accredited by CSWE. Part-time programs available. Faculty: 24 full-time (16 women), 50 part-time (30 women). Students: 209 full-time (177 women), 363 part-time (295 women); includes 114 minority (81 African Americans, 13 Asian Americans, 20 Hispanics), 8 international. Average age 28. 593 applicants, 61% accepted. In 1997, 210 master's, 4 doctorates awarded. *Degree requirements:* For master's, 2 clinical practica required, foreign language and thesis not required; for doctorate, dissertation, clinical practicum, comprehensive exam required, foreign language not required. *Average time to degree:* master's–2 years full-time, 3 years part-time; doctorate–6 years full-time. *Entrance requirements:* For master's, minimum GPA of 3.0, work or volunteer experience in social services; for doctorate, MAT, MSW, minimum GPA of 3.0, 3 years of post-MSW clinical experience. Application deadline: rolling. Application fee: $30. *Tuition:* $465 per semester hour. *Financial aid:* In 1997–98, 120 students received aid, including 31 research assistantships (6 to first-year students) averaging $220 per month, 20 partial scholarships; full and partial tuition waivers and career-related internships or fieldwork also available. Aid available to part-time students. Financial aid application deadline: 2/28; applicants required to submit FAFSA. *Faculty research:* Clinical social work, ethics, health care, school social work. • Dr. Joseph A. Walsh, Dean, 312-915-7005. Application contact: Jude Gonzales, Director of Admissions, 312-915-7005. Fax: 312-915-7645. E-mail: socialwork@luc.edu.

Marywood University, Graduate School of Social Work, Scranton, PA 18509-1598. Awards MSW, MPA/MSW. Accredited by CSWE. Part-time and evening/weekend programs available. Faculty: 14 full-time (10 women), 29 part-time (21 women). Students: 219 full-time (180 women), 149 part-time (127 women); includes 20 minority (5 African Americans, 4 Asian Americans, 8 Hispanics, 3 Native Americans). Average age 35. 196 applicants, 62% accepted. In 1997, 149 degrees awarded. *Average time to degree:* master's–2 years full-time, 3 years part-time. *Entrance requirements:* Minimum undergraduate GPA of 3.0. Application deadline: 5/15 (10/15 for spring admission). Application fee: $20. *Expenses:* Tuition $459 per credit hour. Fees $530 per year full-time, $180 per year part-time. *Financial aid:* In 1997–98, 5 research assistantships totaling $39,150, 120 scholarships/tuition reductions totaling $250,000 were awarded; career-related internships or fieldwork also available. Aid available to part-time students. Financial aid application deadline: 5/1; applicants required to submit FAFSA. *Faculty research:* Impaired professionals, ethics, child welfare, communities, professional gatekeeping. • Dr. William Whitaker, Dean, 717-348-6282. Fax: 717-348-1817. Application contact: Virginia Haskett, Director of Admissions, 717-348-6282. Fax: 717-961-4742.

See in-depth description on page 1939.

McGill University, Faculty of Graduate Studies and Research, Faculty of Arts, School of Social Work, Montréal, PQ H3A 2T5, Canada. Awards MSW, PhD, MSW/LL B. PhD offered jointly with the Université de Montréal. PhD new for fall 1998. Part-time programs available. Students: 105. 120 applicants, 53% accepted. In 1997, 93 master's awarded. *Degree requirements:* For master's, thesis or alternative; for doctorate, 1 foreign language, dissertation. *Entrance requirements:* For master's, TOEFL (minimum score 550), BSW, minimum GPA of 3.0; for doctorate, TOEFL (minimum score 550), BSW, MSW, bilingual (English and French), work experience. Application deadline: 2/1 (rolling processing). Application fee: $60. *Expenses:* Tuition $1668 per year for Canadian residents; $8268 per year for nonresidents. Fees $828 per year for Canadian residents; $1216 per year for nonresidents. • Dr. William Rowe, Director, 514-398-7070. Application contact: Lillian Iannone, Admissions Secretary, 514-398-7070. Fax: 514-398-4760.

McMaster University, Faculty of Social Sciences, School of Social Work, Hamilton, ON L8S 4M2, Canada. Offers programs in analysis of social welfare policy (MSW), analysis of social work practice (MSW). Part-time programs available. Faculty: 12 full-time (6 women), 1 part-time (0 women). Students: 8 full-time (6 women), 30 part-time (22 women). 57 applicants, 39% accepted. In 1997, 8 degrees awarded. *Entrance requirements:* Minimum B+ average. Application deadline: 2/15 (priority date; rolling processing). Application fee: $50. *Expenses:* Tuition $4422 per year full-time, $1590 per year part-time for Canadian residents; $12,000 per year full-time, $6165 per year part-time for nonresidents. Fees $257 per year full-time, $188 per year part-time. *Financial aid:* In 1997–98, 6 teaching assistantships were awarded. Financial aid application deadline: 3/1. *Faculty research:* Health policy, income maintenance, child welfare, native issues, immigration policies, racism. Total annual research expenditures: $875,550. • Dr. Ewan Macintyre, Director, 905-525-9140 Ext. 24596. Application contact: Graduate Secretary, 905-525-9140 Ext. 24596. Fax: 905-577-4667. E-mail: socwork@mcmail.cis.mcmaster.ca.

Memorial University of Newfoundland, School of Graduate Studies, School of Social Work, St. John's, NF A1C 5S7, Canada. Awards MSW, PhD. Part-time and evening/weekend programs available. Faculty: 10 full-time (5 women). Students: 38 full-time (32 women), 55 part-time (43 women); includes 1 international. 37 applicants, 51% accepted. In 1997, 13 master's awarded. *Degree requirements:* For doctorate, dissertation. *Entrance requirements:* For doctorate, MAT. Application deadline: 3/15 (priority date; rolling processing). Application fee: $40. *Expenses:* Tuition $1896 per year (minimum). Fees $60 per year for Canadian residents; $621 per year for nonresidents. *Financial aid:* Fellowships and career-related internships or fieldwork available. *Faculty research:* Violence, child abuse, sexual abuse, social policy, diversity. • Dr. Elizabeth Dow, Director, 709-737-8044. Fax: 709-737-2405. E-mail: jpennell@morgan.ucs.mun.ca. Application contact: Dr. Leslie Bella, Graduate Officer, 709-737-4512. Fax: 709-737-4512. E-mail: lbella@morgan.ucs.mun.ca.

Michigan State University, College of Social Science, Interdisciplinary Program, East Lansing, MI 48824-1020. Offerings include social science-social work (PhD). Terminal master's awarded for partial completion of doctoral program. *Degree requirements:* Dissertation. *Application deadline:* rolling. *Application fee:* $30 ($40 for international students). *Expenses:* Tuition $4609 per year full-time, $223 per credit hour (minimum) part-time for state residents; $8704 per year full-time, $450 per credit hour (minimum) part-time for nonresidents. Fees $576 per year full-time, $476 per year part-time. • Dr. Philip Smith, Director, 517-355-9733.

Michigan State University, College of Social Science, School of Social Work, East Lansing, MI 48824-1020. Offers programs in administration and program evaluation (MSW), administration and program evaluation-urban studies (MSW), clinical social work (MSW), clinical social work-urban studies (MSW). Accredited by CSWE. Postbaccalaureate distance learning degree programs offered (minimal on-campus study). Faculty: 14 full-time (7 women). Students: 219 (183 women); includes 28 minority (16 African Americans, 4 Asian Americans, 3 Hispanics, 5 Native Americans), 9 international. Average age 25. 205 applicants, 48% accepted. In 1997, 66 degrees awarded. *Average time to degree:* master's–2 years full-time, 3 years part-time. *Application deadline:* 1/20 (rolling processing). *Application fee:* $30 ($40 for international students). *Expenses:* Tuition $4609 per year full-time, $223 per credit hour (minimum) part-time for state residents; $8704 per year full-time, $450 per credit hour (minimum) part-time for nonresidents. Fees $576 per year full-time, $476 per year part-time. *Financial aid:* In 1997–98, 37 students received aid, including 29 fellowships (15 to first-year students), 2 research assistantships averaging $502 per month and totaling $4,518, 5 teaching assistantships; Federal Work-Study and career-related internships or fieldwork also available. Aid available to part-time students. *Faculty research:* Women at risk, juvenile offenders, infant mental health, poverty, welfare reforms. • Dr. John Herrick, Director, 517-355-7515. E-mail: 224661jmh@msu.edu.

Newman University, School of Social Work, Wichita, KS 67213-2084. Awards MSW. Candidate for accreditation by CSWE. Program new for fall 1998. *Tuition:* $257 per credit hour. • Dr. Vimala Pillari, Director, 316-942-4291 Ext. 324.

New Mexico Highlands University, School of Social Work, Las Vegas, NM 87701. Awards MSW. Accredited by CSWE. Part-time programs available. Faculty: 23 full-time (11 women). Students: 120 full-time (87 women), 20 part-time (18 women); includes 50 minority (5 African Americans, 1 Asian American, 40 Hispanics, 4 Native Americans), 3 international. Average age 39. In 1997, 69 degrees awarded. *Degree requirements:* Thesis or alternative required, foreign language not required. *Entrance requirements:* Minimum undergraduate GPA of 3.0. Application deadline: 8/1 (priority date; rolling processing). Application fee: $15. *Expenses:* Tuition $1816 per year full-time, $227 per hour part-time for state residents; $7468 per year full-time, $227 per hour part-time for nonresidents. Fees $10 per year. *Financial aid:* Federal Work-Study available. Financial aid application deadline: 3/1. • Dr. Alfredo Garcia, Dean, 505-454-3563. Application contact: Dr. Glen W. Davidson, Academic Vice President, 505-454-3311. Fax: 505-454-3558. E-mail: glendavidson@venus.nmhu.edu.

New Mexico State University, College of Health and Social Services, Department of Social Work, Las Cruces, NM 88003-8001. Awards MSW. Accredited by CSWE. Faculty: 9 full-time (6 women). Students: 76 full-time (54 women), 2 part-time (both women); includes 34 minority (4 African Americans, 27 Hispanics, 3 Native Americans). Average age 34. 120 applicants, 43% accepted. In 1997, 38 degrees awarded. *Degree requirements:* Research project required, thesis optional, foreign language not required. *Entrance requirements:* GRE or MAT. Application deadline: 7/1 (priority date; rolling processing; 11/1 for spring admission). Application fee: $15 ($35 for international students). Electronic applications accepted. *Tuition:* $2514 per year full-time, $105 per credit hour part-time for state residents; $7848 per year full-time, $327 per credit hour part-time for nonresidents. *Financial aid:* Fellowships, research assistantships, teaching assistantships, and career-related internships or fieldwork available. Financial aid application deadline: 3/1. *Faculty research:* Family preservation, child abuse and neglect, women's issues, AIDS, multicultural issues. • Dr. Christine Marlow, Head, 505-646-2143. Fax: 505-646-4116. E-mail: cmarlow@nmsu.edu.

New York University, Shirley M. Ehrenkranz School of Social Work, New York, NY 10012-1019. Awards MSW, PhD, JD/MSW, MSW/MS. One or more programs accredited by CSWE.

Faculty: 41 full-time (32 women), 95 part-time (68 women), 70 FTE. Students: 602 full-time (516 women), 437 part-time (372 women); includes 243 minority (109 African Americans, 33 Asian Americans, 99 Hispanics, 2 Native Americans), 7 international. Average age 28. 2,840 applicants, 60% accepted. In 1997, 459 master's, 21 doctorates awarded. *Degree requirements:* For doctorate, dissertation required, foreign language not required. *Average time to degree:* master's–2 years full-time, 3 years part-time. *Application deadline:* 7/1 (rolling processing; 11/15 for spring admission). *Application fee:* $35. *Financial aid:* In 1997–98, 482 grants (150 to first-year students) were awarded; partial tuition waivers, Federal Work-Study, and career-related internships or fieldwork also available. Aid available to part-time students. Financial aid application deadline: 3/1; applicants required to submit FAFSA. *Faculty research:* Social welfare policies, foster care, aging. • Thomas Meenaghan, Dean, 212-998-5959. Fax: 212-995-4172. Application contact: Stuart Gitlin, Director of Admissions, 212-998-5910. Fax: 212-995-4171. E-mail: essw.admissions@nyu.edu.

Norfolk State University, School of Social Work, 2401 Corprew Avenue, Norfolk, VA 23504-3907. Awards MSW, DSW. One or more programs accredited by CSWE. Part-time programs available. Faculty: 21 full-time, 9 part-time. Students: 106 full-time (91 women), 48 part-time (41 women); includes 79 minority (77 African Americans, 2 Asian Americans), 69 international. In 1997, 69 master's awarded. *Application deadline:* 8/1. *Application fee:* $30. *Tuition:* $3718 per year full-time, $198 per credit hour part-time for state residents; $7668 per year full-time, $404 per credit hour part-time for nonresidents. • Dr. Moses Newsome, Dean, 757-683-8668. Application contact: Dr. Margaret Kerekes, Coordinator, 757-683-8793.

North Carolina Agricultural and Technical State University, Graduate School, College of Arts and Sciences, Department of Sociology and Social Work, Greensboro, NC 27411. Awards MSW. Candidate for accreditation by CSWE. Offered jointly with the University of North Carolina at Greensboro. Part-time and evening/weekend programs available. Students: 12 full-time (all women); includes 9 minority (all African Americans). *Degree requirements:* Comprehensive exam, qualifying exam required, foreign language not required. *Entrance requirements:* GRE General Test. Application deadline: 6/1 (priority date; rolling processing; 12/1 for spring admission). Application fee: $35. *Tuition:* $1662 per year full-time, $272 per semester (minimum) part-time for state residents; $8790 per year full-time, $2054 per semester (minimum) part-time for nonresidents. *Financial aid:* Fellowships, research assistantships, teaching assistantships, and career-related internships or fieldwork available. Financial aid application deadline: 6/1. • Dr. Sarah Kirk, Chairperson, 336-334-7894. Fax: 336-334-7194.

The Ohio State University, College of Social Work, Columbus, OH 43210. Awards MSW, PhD. One or more programs accredited by CSWE. Part-time programs available. Faculty: 29. Students: 294 full-time (250 women), 111 part-time (86 women); includes 67 minority (56 African Americans, 5 Asian Americans, 5 Hispanics, 1 Native American), 7 international. 562 applicants, 39% accepted. In 1997, 171 master's, 9 doctorates awarded. *Degree requirements:* For master's, thesis optional, foreign language not required; for doctorate, dissertation required, foreign language not required. *Application deadline:* 8/15 (rolling processing). *Application fee:* $30 ($40 for international students). *Tuition:* $5472 per year full-time, $554 per quarter (minimum) part-time for state residents; $14,172 per year full-time, $1424 per quarter (minimum) part-time for nonresidents. *Financial aid:* Fellowships, research assistantships, teaching assistantships, administrative assistantships, Federal Work-Study, institutionally sponsored loans available. Aid available to part-time students. • Tony Tripodi, Dean, 614-292-6288. Fax: 614-292-6940. E-mail: tripodi.5@osu.edu.

Our Lady of the Lake University of San Antonio, Worden School of Social Service, 411 Southwest 24th Street, San Antonio, TX 78207-4689. Awards MSW. Accredited by CSWE. Part-time programs available. Faculty: 13 full-time (5 women), 6 part-time (4 women), 16 FTE. Students: 135 full-time (111 women), 72 part-time (51 women); includes 97 minority (24 African Americans, 1 Asian American, 71 Hispanics, 1 Native American), 1 international. Average age 34. In 1997, 88 degrees awarded. *Degree requirements:* Computer language, practicum required, thesis optional, foreign language not required. *Average time to degree:* master's–2 years full-time, 4 years part-time. *Entrance requirements:* GRE General Test or MAT. Application deadline: 4/2 (rolling processing; 11/1 for spring admission). Application fee: $15. *Expenses:* Tuition $371 per credit hour. Fees $57 per semester full-time, $32 per semester part-time. *Financial aid:* In 1997–98, 141 students received aid, including 11 research assistantships (5 to first-year students); partial tuition waivers, Federal Work-Study, institutionally sponsored loans, and career-related internships or fieldwork also available. Financial aid application deadline: 4/15. *Faculty research:* Cross-cultural social work practice, mental health, adult literacy, spirituality, maternal health care, experiential learning. • Dr. Santos Hernandez, Dean, 210-431-3969. Fax: 210-431-4028. E-mail: herns@lake.ollusa.edu. Application contact: Debbie Hamilton, Director of Admissions, 210-434-6711 Ext. 314. Fax: 210-436-2314.

Pontifical Catholic University of Puerto Rico, College of Arts and Humanities, Department of Social Work, Ponce, PR 00731-6382. Awards MSW. Part-time and evening/weekend programs available. Faculty: 5 full-time (4 women). Students: 1 (woman) full-time, 53 part-time (45 women); includes 54 minority (all Hispanics). Average age 32. 25 applicants, 100% accepted. *Application deadline:* 4/30 (priority date; rolling processing). *Application fee:* $15. Electronic applications accepted. *Financial aid:* Application deadline 7/15. • Rev. Esteban Santaella, Chairperson, 787-841-2000 Ext. 358. Application contact: Manuel Luciano, Director of Admissions, 787-841-2000 Ext. 426. Fax: 787-840-4295.

Portland State University, Graduate School of Social Work, Portland, OR 97207-0751. Offers programs in social work (MSW), social work and social research (PhD). One or more programs accredited by CSWE. Part-time programs available. Faculty: 35 full-time (24 women), 5 part-time (2 women), 36 FTE. Students: 285 full-time (223 women), 52 part-time (36 women); includes 50 minority (16 African Americans, 10 Asian Americans, 19 Hispanics, 5 Native Americans), 1 international. Average age 35. 645 applicants, 44% accepted. In 1997, 121 master's, 1 doctorate awarded. *Degree requirements:* For doctorate, dissertation. *Entrance requirements:* For master's, TOEFL (minimum score 550), minimum GPA of 3.0 in upper-division course work or 2.75 overall. Application deadline: 3/1. Application fee: $50. *Tuition:* $6101 per year full-time, $689 per semester (minimum) part-time for state residents; $10,445 per year full-time, $689 per semester (minimum) part-time for nonresidents. *Financial aid:* In 1997–98, 6 research assistantships (2 to first-year students) were awarded; teaching assistantships, Federal Work-Study, institutionally sponsored loans, and career-related internships or fieldwork also available. Aid available to part-time students. Financial aid application deadline: 3/1; applicants required to submit FAFSA. *Faculty research:* Child welfare; child mental health; social welfare policies and services; work, family, and dependent care; adult mental health. Total annual research expenditures: $11.6 million. • Dr. James Ward, Dean, 503-725-4712. E-mail: james@ssw.pdx.edu. Application contact: Janet Putnam, 503-725-4712. Fax: 503-725-5545. E-mail: janet@ssw.pdx.edu.

Radford University, Graduate College, College of Nursing and Health Services, School of Social Work, Radford, VA 24142. Awards MSW. Accredited by CSWE. Part-time programs available. Postbaccalaureate distance learning degree programs offered (minimal on-campus study). Faculty: 10 full-time (6 women). Students: 59 full-time (51 women), 75 part-time (63 women); includes 3 minority (2 African Americans, 1 Native American). Average age 32. 129 applicants, 57% accepted. In 1997, 28 degrees awarded. *Degree requirements:* Comprehensive exam required, foreign language and thesis not required. *Entrance requirements:* GMAT, GRE General Test, MAT, or NTE; TOEFL (minimum score 550), minimum GPA of 2.7. Application deadline: 2/1 (priority date; rolling processing; 10/1 for spring admission). Application fee: $25. Electronic applications accepted. *Expenses:* Tuition $2302 per year full-time, $147 per credit hour part-time for state residents; $5672 per year full-time, $287 per credit hour part-time for nonresidents. Fees $1222 per year full-time. *Financial aid:* In 1997–98, 95 students received aid, including 8 fellowships totaling $32,550, 7 research assistantships totaling $23,250, scholarships/grants totaling $732,861; teaching assistantships, Federal Work-Study, institutionally sponsored loans, and career-related internships or fieldwork also available. Financial aid application deadline: 2/1; applicants required to submit FAFSA. • Dr. Kay S. Hoffman, Director, 540-831-5266. Fax: 540-831-6053. E-mail: khoffman@runet.edu.

Rhode Island College, School of Graduate Studies, School of Social Work, Providence, RI 02908-1924. Awards MSW. Accredited by CSWE. Part-time programs available. Faculty: 14 full-time (9 women), 5 part-time (1 woman). Students: 114 full-time (97 women), 62 part-time (47 women); includes 7 minority (2 African Americans, 1 Asian American, 4 Hispanics). In 1997, 52 degrees awarded. *Degree requirements:* Thesis or alternative required, foreign language not required. *Application deadline:* 2/1 (rolling processing). *Application fee:* $25. *Tuition:* $4064 per year full-time, $214 per credit part-time for state residents; $7658 per year full-time, $376 per credit part-time for nonresidents. *Financial aid:* Career-related internships or fieldwork available. Financial aid application deadline: 4/1. • Dr. George Metrey, Dean, 401-456-8043.

Roberts Wesleyan College, Division of Social Work and Social Sciences, Rochester, NY 14624-1997. Offers programs in child and family services (MSW), physical and mental health services (MSW). Accredited by CSWE. Faculty: 8 full-time (2 women), 4 part-time (2 women). Students: 98 full-time (83 women), 2 part-time (1 woman); includes 10 minority (6 African Americans, 1 Hispanic, 3 Native Americans). Average age 35. 99 applicants, 65% accepted. In 1997, 51 degrees awarded. *Degree requirements:* Computer language required, foreign language and thesis not required. *Average time to degree:* master's–2 years full-time. *Entrance requirements:* Minimum GPA of 2.75. Application deadline: 4/1 (priority date; rolling processing). Application fee: $35. *Tuition:* $340 per credit hour. *Financial aid:* 98 students received aid; fellowships, partial tuition waivers, and career-related internships or fieldwork available. Financial aid applicants required to submit FAFSA. *Faculty research:* Religion and social work, family studies, values and ethics. • Dr. William Descoteaux, Chair, 716-594-6490. Fax: 716-594-6480. Application contact: Kathy Merz, Admissions Secretary, 716-594-6600. Fax: 716-594-6585.

Rutgers, The State University of New Jersey, New Brunswick, School of Social Work, New Brunswick, NJ 08903. Awards MSW, PhD, M Div/MSW. One or more programs accredited by CSWE. PhD offered through the Graduate School; M Div/MSW offered jointly with Drew University, New Brunswick Theological Seminary, and Princeton Theological Seminary. Program offered jointly with Rutgers, The State University of New Jersey, Camden and Newark. Part-time programs available. Faculty: 35 full-time (19 women), 45 part-time (31 women). Students: 255 full-time (209 women), 447 part-time (360 women); includes 150 minority (84 African Americans, 10 Asian Americans, 56 Hispanics). Average age 32. 1,052 applicants, 25% accepted. In 1997, 290 master's awarded. *Degree requirements:* For doctorate, dissertation required, foreign language not required. *Average time to degree:* master's–2 years full-time, 4 years part-time. *Entrance requirements:* For master's, social work experience; for doctorate, GRE. Application deadline: 3/1. Application fee: $40. *Expenses:* Tuition $6492 per year full-time, $268 per credit part-time for state residents; $9520 per year full-time, $395 per credit part-time for nonresidents. Fees $208 per year (minimum). *Financial aid:* In 1997–98, 6 fellowships, 11 research assistantships were awarded; scholarships, traineeships, Federal Work-Study, and career-related internships or fieldwork also available. Aid available to part-time students. Financial aid application deadline: 3/1. *Faculty research:* Children and families; alcohol and other drugs; health, mental health, and aging. • Mary E. Davidson, Dean, 732-932-7253. Application contact: Arnold Korotkin, Acting Assistant Dean, 732-932-7126.

Rutgers, The State University of New Jersey, New Brunswick, Program in Social Work, New Brunswick, NJ 08903. Offers direct intervention in interpersonal situations (PhD), social policy analysis and administration (PhD), social work (PhD). Part-time programs available. Faculty: 29 (16 women). Students: 4 full-time (3 women), 47 part-time (34 women); includes 11 minority (5 African Americans, 1 Asian American, 5 Hispanics), 7 international. Average age 36. 24 applicants, 46% accepted. In 1997, 10 degrees awarded (30% entered university research/teaching, 60% found other work related to degree, 10% continued full-time study). *Degree requirements:* Dissertation required, foreign language not required. *Average time to degree:* doctorate–5 years full-time, 7 years part-time. *Entrance requirements:* GRE General Test. Application deadline: 3/31 (priority date; rolling processing). Application fee: $40. *Expenses:* Tuition $6492 per year full-time, $268 per credit part-time for state residents; $9520 per year full-time, $395 per credit part-time for nonresidents. Fees $208 per year (minimum). *Financial aid:* In 1997–98, 5 students received aid, including 2 research assistantships, 3 teaching assistantships (1 to a first-year student); partial tuition waivers, Federal Work-Study, and career-related internships or fieldwork also available. Financial aid application deadline: 3/31; applicants required to submit FAFSA. *Faculty research:* Women, substance abuse, aging, organizational behavior, social service needs assessment. • Dr. Bernard Neugeboren, Director, 732-932-7584. Application contact: Helen Forner, Program Secretary, 732-932-6967. Fax: 732-932-8181.

St. Ambrose University, College of Arts and Sciences, Program in Social Work, Davenport, IA 52803-2898. Awards MSW. Candidate for accreditation by CSWE. Part-time and evening/weekend programs available. *Degree requirements:* Integration projects required, foreign language and thesis not required. *Entrance requirements:* Minimum GPA of 3.0, previous coursework in statistics, bachelor's degree in liberal arts. Application deadline: 8/1 (priority date; rolling processing). Application fee: $25. Electronic applications accepted. *Faculty research:* Social work practice, cults/sects, family therapy, developmental disabilities.

Saint Louis University, School of Social Services, St. Louis, MO 63103-2097. Awards MSW, MPH/MSW. Accredited by CSWE. Part-time and evening/weekend programs available. Faculty: 19 full-time (8 women), 12 part-time (6 women). Students: 148 full-time (124 women), 108 part-time (83 women). 171 applicants, 73% accepted. In 1997, 94 degrees awarded. *Degree requirements:* Comprehensive oral exam required, foreign language and thesis not required. *Application deadline:* 3/1 (priority date; rolling processing; 10/1 for spring admission). *Application fee:* $40. *Tuition:* $507 per credit hour. *Financial aid:* Federal Work-Study and career-related internships or fieldwork available. Aid available to part-time students. Financial aid application deadline: 3/1; applicants required to submit FAFSA. *Faculty research:* Welfare reform, child welfare, homelessness. • Dr. Susan Tebb, Dean, 314-977-2730. Fax: 314-977-2731. Application contact: Gary Behrman, Director of Admissions, 314-977-2752.

Salem State College, Program in Social Work, Salem, MA 01970-5353. Awards MSW. Accredited by CSWE. *Entrance requirements:* GRE General Test or MAT. Application deadline: rolling. Application fee: $25. *Expenses:* Tuition $140 per credit hour for state residents; $230 per credit hour for nonresidents. Fees $20 per credit hour.

San Diego State University, College of Health and Human Services, School of Social Work, San Diego, CA 92182. Awards MSW, JD/MSW, MSW/MPH. Accredited by CSWE. JD/MSW offered jointly with California Western School of Law. Part-time programs available. Students: 227 full-time (194 women), 88 part-time (72 women); includes 98 minority (18 African Americans, 24 Asian Americans, 52 Hispanics, 4 Native Americans), 2 international. Average age 31. In 1997, 121 degrees awarded. *Entrance requirements:* GRE General Test (minimum combined score of 950), TOEFL (minimum score 550). Application deadline: 3/1. Application fee: $55. *Expenses:* Tuition $0 for state residents; $246 per unit for nonresidents. Fees $1932 per year full-time, $1266 per year part-time. *Financial aid:* In 1997–98, 10 research assistantships (7 to first-year students) averaging $300 per month were awarded; fellowships and career-related internships or fieldwork also available. *Faculty research:* Child maltreatment, substance abuse, neighborhood studies, child welfare. Total annual research expenditures: $3 million. • Anita S. Harbert, Director, 619-594-6247. E-mail: aharbert@mail.sdsu.edu. Application contact: Dan Finnegan, Graduate Coordinator, 619-594-6850. Fax: 619-594-5991. E-mail: dfinnegan@mail.sdsu.edu.

San Francisco State University, College of Health and Human Services, School of Social Work Education, San Francisco, CA 94132-1722. Awards MSW. Accredited by CSWE. Part-time programs available. *Degree requirements:* Thesis optional, foreign language not required. *Entrance requirements:* Minimum GPA of 2.5 in last 60 units. Application deadline: 1/31

Directory: Social Work

San Francisco State University (continued)
(priority date; rolling processing). Application fee: $55. *Expenses:* Tuition $0 for state residents; $246 per unit for nonresidents. Fees $1982 per year full-time, $1316 per year part-time. *Faculty research:* U.S. social policy alternatives, aging and health care, mental health in communities of color, community organizing in minority communities, racism and oppression.

San Jose State University, College of Social Work, School of Social Work, San Jose, CA 95192-0001. Awards MSW. Accredited by CSWE. Faculty: 7 full-time (2 women), 5 part-time (3 women). Students: 192 full-time (145 women), 37 part-time (31 women); includes 120 minority (21 African Americans, 35 Asian Americans, 63 Hispanics, 1 Native American). Average age 34. 408 applicants, 43% accepted. In 1997, 97 degrees awarded. *Application deadline:* 6/1 (rolling processing). *Application fee:* $59. *Expenses:* Tuition $0 for state residents; $246 per unit for nonresidents. Fees $2017 per year full-time, $1351 per year part-time. *Financial aid:* Application deadline 5/31. • Dr. Simon Dominguez, Coordinator, 408-924-5837.

Simmons College, School of Social Work, Boston, MA 02115. Offers program in clinical social work (MSW, PhD). One or more programs accredited by CSWE. Part-time programs available. Faculty: 21 full-time, 60 part-time. Students: 183 full-time (153 women), 98 part-time (92 women); includes 40 minority (18 African Americans, 7 Asian Americans, 14 Hispanics, 1 Native American). Average age 27. 474 applicants, 57% accepted. In 1997, 124 master's, 3 doctorates awarded. *Degree requirements:* For master's, thesis or alternative required, foreign language not required; for doctorate, dissertation required, foreign language not required. *Average time to degree:* master's–2 years full-time, 3 years part-time; doctorate–7 years part-time. *Entrance requirements:* For master's, minimum GPA of 3.0 in last 2 years of undergraduate course work; for doctorate, MAT (minimum score 50; average 65), interview, minimum GPA of 3.0 in last 2 years of undergraduate course work. Application deadline: 2/15. Application fee: $45. *Financial aid:* In 1997–98, 151 students received aid, including 8 fellowships (3 to first-year students); full tuition waivers, Federal Work-Study, institutionally sponsored loans, and career-related internships or fieldwork also available. Aid available to part-time students. Financial aid application deadline: 3/1; applicants required to submit FAFSA. *Faculty research:* Adolescence and depression, multicultural social work, competence, domestic violence, narrative theory. • Dr. Joseph M. Regan, Dean, 617-521-3900. Application contact: Deborah Sheehan, Director of Admissions, 617-521-3920. Fax: 617-521-3980. E-mail: ssw@simmons.edu.

See in-depth description on page 1941.

Smith College, School for Social Work, Northampton, MA 01063. Awards MSW, PhD. One or more programs accredited by CSWE. Faculty: 15 full-time, 100 part-time. Students: 416 full-time (370 women); includes 60 minority (28 African Americans, 14 Asian Americans, 15 Hispanics, 3 Native Americans), 4 international. Average age 33. 470 applicants, 84% accepted. In 1997, 112 master's, 8 doctorates awarded. *Degree requirements:* Thesis/dissertation required, foreign language not required. *Entrance requirements:* For doctorate, MAT. Application deadline: 2/15. Application fee: $50. *Expenses:* Tuition $10,418 per year. Fees $145 per year. *Financial aid:* 206 students received aid; institutionally sponsored loans available. Financial aid application deadline: 7/15; applicants required to submit CSS PROFILE or FAFSA. • Anita Lightburn, Dean, 413-585-7950. Application contact: Sandra Austin, Office of Admissions, 413-585-7960.

See in-depth description on page 1943.

Southern Connecticut State University, School of Professional Studies, Department of Social Work, New Haven, CT 06515-1355. Awards MSW. Accredited by CSWE. Faculty: 12 full-time, 5 part-time. Students: 69 full-time (57 women), 93 part-time (74 women); includes 19 minority (11 African Americans, 1 Asian American, 7 Hispanics). 655 applicants, 6% accepted. In 1997, 44 degrees awarded. *Entrance requirements:* Minimum undergraduate QPA of 3.0 in graduate major field or 2.5 overall; interview. Application deadline: 3/1 (12/1 for spring admission). Application fee: $40. *Expenses:* Tuition $2632 per year full-time, $188 per credit part-time for state residents; $7200 per year full-time, $188 per credit part-time for nonresidents. Fees $1806 per year full-time, $45 per semester part-time for state residents; $2703 per year full-time, $45 per semester part-time for nonresidents. *Faculty research:* Social work practice; social service development; services for women, the aging, children, and families in educational and health care systems. • Dr. Elbert Siegel, Chairperson, 203-392-6551. Application contact: Anthony Maltese, Graduate Coordinator, 203-392-6551.

Southern Illinois University at Carbondale, College of Education, School of Social Work, Carbondale, IL 62901-6806. Awards MSW, JD/MSW. Accredited by CSWE. Faculty: 7 full-time (2 women), 2 part-time (both women). Students: 60 full-time (48 women), 21 part-time (15 women); includes 13 minority (11 African Americans, 1 Asian American, 1 Hispanic), 2 international. Average age 30. 46 applicants, 65% accepted. In 1997, 43 degrees awarded. *Entrance requirements:* GRE General Test, TOEFL (minimum score 550), minimum GPA of 2.7. Application deadline: 3/1 (rolling processing). Application fee: $20. *Expenses:* Tuition $2964 per year full-time, $99 per semester hour part-time for state residents; $8892 per year full-time, $270 per semester hour part-time for nonresidents. Fees $1034 per year full-time, $298 per semester (minimum) part-time. *Financial aid:* In 1997–98, 6 research assistantships were awarded; career-related internships or fieldwork also available. Financial aid application deadline: 5/1. *Faculty research:* Service delivery systems, comparative race relations, advocacy research, gerontology, child welfare and health. • Dr. Martin Tracy, Director, 618-453-2243. Application contact: Sandy Schenk, Assistant to Graduate Director, 618-453-1202. Fax: 618-453-1219. E-mail: sandy@siu.edu.

Southern Illinois University at Edwardsville, College of Arts and Sciences, Department of Social Work, Edwardsville, IL 62026-0001. Awards MSW. Candidate for accreditation by CSWE. Students: 39 full-time (32 women); includes 6 minority (4 African Americans, 1 Hispanic, 1 Native American). 79 applicants, 27% accepted. *Degree requirements:* Thesis or alternative, final exam required, foreign language not required. *Application deadline:* 7/24. *Application fee:* $25. *Expenses:* Tuition $1716 per year full-time, $95 per credit hour part-time for state residents; $5149 per year full-time, $286 per credit hour part-time for nonresidents. Fees $463 per year full-time, $433 per year part-time. *Financial aid:* In 1997–98, 9 assistantships were awarded; fellowships, research assistantships, teaching assistantships also available. • Dr. Thomas Regulus, Chair, 618-692-5758.

Southern University at New Orleans, School of Social Work, New Orleans, LA 70126-1009. Awards MSW. Accredited by CSWE. Part-time and evening/weekend programs available. Faculty: 21. Students: 266. Average age 35. *Degree requirements:* Thesis, statistics required, foreign language not required. *Application deadline:* 3/1. *Application fee:* $25. *Expenses:* Tuition $2448 per year full-time, $341 per semester (minimum) part-time for state residents; $4364 per year full-time, $494 per semester (minimum) part-time for nonresidents. Fees $75 per year. *Financial aid:* Fellowships, institutionally sponsored loans, and career-related internships or fieldwork available. *Faculty research:* Service needs of people with AIDS, suicidal rate of people with AIDS. • Mlle M. Charles, Dean, 504-286-5376. Application contact: D. J. Smith, Director of Student Affairs, 504-286-5376. Fax: 504-286-5387.

Southwest Missouri State University, College of Health and Human Services, Department of Social Work, Springfield, MO 65804-0094. Awards MSW. Candidate for accreditation by CSWE. Faculty: 3 full-time (0 women). Students: 24 full-time (19 women), 9 part-time (6 women). *Degree requirements:* Comprehensive exam required, foreign language not required. *Entrance requirements:* GRE, minimum GPA of 3.0. Application deadline: 8/7 (priority date; rolling processing). Application fee: $25. *Expenses:* Tuition $1980 per year full-time, $110 per credit hour part-time for state residents; $3960 per year full-time, $220 per credit hour part-time for nonresidents. Fees $274 per year full-time, $73 per semester part-time. *Financial aid:* In 1997–98, 2 graduate assistantships totaling $5,250 were awarded. • Dr. John Gunther, Head, 417-836-6953. Fax: 417-836-6967.

Southwest Texas State University, School of Health Professions, Department of Social Work, San Marcos, TX 78666. Awards MSW. Candidate for accreditation by CSWE. Faculty: 10 full-time (8 women), 2 part-time (0 women). Students: 55 full-time (44 women), 36 part-time (28 women); includes 15 minority (3 African Americans, 1 Asian American, 11 Hispanics). Average age 33. In 1997, 21 degrees awarded. *Degree requirements:* Comprehensive exam required, foreign language not required. *Entrance requirements:* GRE General Test (minimum combined score of 900), TOEFL (minimum score 550), minimum GPA of 2.75 in last 60 hours. Application deadline: 7/15 (priority date; rolling processing; 11/15 for spring admission). Application fee: $25 ($50 for international students). *Expenses:* Tuition $648 per year full-time, $120 per semester (minimum) part-time for state residents; $4500 per year full-time, $750 per semester (minimum) part-time for nonresidents. Fees $1264 per year full-time, $314 per semester (minimum) part-time. *Financial aid:* Assistantships, Federal Work-Study, institutionally sponsored loans, and career-related internships or fieldwork available. Aid available to part-time students. Financial aid application deadline: 4/1; applicants required to submit FAFSA. *Faculty research:* Domestic or workplace violence, parental participation and school social work, addictions and co-dependency. • Dr. Karen Brown, Chair, 512-245-2592. E-mail: kb01@swt.edu. Application contact: Dr. Michael Smith, Graduate Adviser, 512-245-2592. Fax: 512-245-8097. E-mail: ms17@swt.edu.

Spalding University, School of Professional Psychology and Social Work, Department of Social Work, Louisville, KY 40203-2188. Awards MSW. Candidate for accreditation by CSWE. Evening/weekend programs available. Faculty: 5 full-time (4 women), 3 part-time (1 woman), 6 FTE. Students: 26 full-time (23 women), 4 part-time (3 women); includes 5 minority (all African Americans). Average age 35. 60 applicants, 57% accepted. *Degree requirements:* Thesis or alternative, project presentation required, foreign language not required. *Entrance requirements:* 18 hours of course work in social sciences including methods and statistics, human biology. Application deadline: 4/1. Application fee: $30. *Expenses:* Tuition $350 per credit hour (minimum). Fees $48 per year full-time, $4 per credit hour part-time. *Financial aid:* In 1997–98, 22 students received aid, including 4 research assistantships (all to first-year students) totaling $29,440, 6 scholarships (all to first-year students) totaling $22,050; Federal Work-Study and career-related internships or fieldwork available. Aid available to part-time students. Financial aid application deadline: 3/15; applicants required to submit FAFSA. *Faculty research:* AIDS, drug/alcohol, child welfare, critical thinking, reflective practice. • Dr. Jillian Johnson, Chair, 502-585-7183. Application contact: Jeanne Anderson, Assistant to the Provost and Director of Graduate Office, 502-585-7105. Fax: 502-585-7158. E-mail: gradoffc@spalding6.win.net.

Springfield College, Program in Social Work, Springfield, MA 01109-3797. Awards MSW. Accredited by CSWE. Evening/weekend programs available. Faculty: 8 full-time (4 women), 11 part-time (7 women), 11 FTE. Students: 65 full-time (50 women), 61 part-time (52 women); includes 6 minority (5 African Americans, 1 Hispanic), 1 international. Average age 35. 181 applicants, 51% accepted. In 1997, 64 degrees awarded (100% found work related to degree). *Degree requirements:* Fieldwork required, foreign language and thesis not required. *Entrance requirements:* Minimum GPA of 3.0 during previous 2 years. Application deadline: 2/1 (priority date). Application fee: $40. *Expenses:* Tuition $474 per credit. Fees $25 per year. *Financial aid:* Fellowships, Federal Work-Study, and career-related internships or fieldwork available. Financial aid application deadline: 3/1. *Faculty research:* Community structure and social change, special services and program evaluation, evaluating social work practice. • Dr. Francine Vecchiolla, Dean, 413-788-2401. Application contact: Donald J. Shaw Jr., Director of Graduate Admissions, 413-748-3225. Fax: 413-748-3694. E-mail: dshaw@spfldcol.edu.

State University of New York at Albany, Nelson A. Rockefeller College of Public Affairs and Policy, School of Social Welfare, Albany, NY 12222-0001. Awards MSW, PhD, MSW/MA. One or more programs accredited by CSWE. MSW/MS offered jointly with the State University of New York at New Paltz; MSW/MA offered jointly with the School of Criminal Justice. Part-time and evening/weekend programs available. Faculty: 19 full-time (9 women), 8 part-time (7 women). Students: 294 full-time (247 women), 136 part-time (106 women); includes 53 minority (27 African Americans, 11 Asian Americans, 13 Hispanics, 2 Native Americans), 6 international. 404 applicants, 51% accepted. In 1997, 166 master's, 8 doctorates awarded. *Degree requirements:* For doctorate, computer language, dissertation required, foreign language not required. *Entrance requirements:* For doctorate, GRE General Test. Application fee: $50. *Expenses:* Tuition $5100 per year full-time, $213 per credit hour part-time for state residents; $8416 per year full-time, $351 per credit hour part-time for nonresidents. Fees $705 per year full-time, $26.85 per credit hour part-time. *Financial aid:* Fellowships, Federal Work-Study, and career-related internships or fieldwork available. *Faculty research:* Welfare reform, homelessness, children and families, mental health, substance abuse. • Lynn Videka-Sherman, Dean, 518-442-5324. Application contact: Gerald Parker, Assistant Provost, 518-442-5200.

State University of New York at Buffalo, Graduate School, School of Social Work, Buffalo, NY 14260. Awards MSW, PhD, JD/MSW. One or more programs accredited by CSWE. Faculty: 15 full-time (10 women). Students: 195 full-time (165 women), 99 part-time (80 women); includes 47 minority (36 African Americans, 1 Asian American, 5 Hispanics, 5 Native Americans), 6 international. Average age 32. In 1997, 151 master's awarded. *Degree requirements:* For doctorate, dissertation required, foreign language not required. *Entrance requirements:* For master's, GRE General Test, BS in social work or BA in liberal arts, behavior, or social sciences; for doctorate, GRE General Test, MSW. Application deadline: 4/1. Application fee: $35. *Tuition:* $5970 per year full-time, $288 per credit hour part-time for state residents; $9286 per year full-time, $426 per credit hour part-time for nonresidents. *Financial aid:* In 1997–98, 4 research assistantships averaging $1,000 per month, 4 teaching assistantships averaging $1,000 per month were awarded; fellowships, graduate assistantships, Federal Work-Study, institutionally sponsored loans, and career-related internships or fieldwork also available. Aid available to part-time students. Financial aid application deadline: 2/28. *Faculty research:* Social welfare policy, mental health, child welfare, alcohol and other addictions, community. • Dr. Lawrence Shulman, Dean, 716-645-3381 Ext. 221. Fax: 716-645-3883. Application contact: Ann Still, Coordinator, 716-645-3383.

State University of New York at Stony Brook, Health Sciences Center, School of Social Welfare, Doctoral Program in Social Welfare, Stony Brook, NY 11794. Awards PhD. Faculty: 15 full-time, 13 part-time. Students: 5 full-time (4 women), 2 part-time (1 woman). 9 applicants, 67% accepted. *Degree requirements:* Dissertation. *Average time to degree:* doctorate–3 years full-time, 4 years part-time. *Entrance requirements:* GRE General Test. Application deadline: 2/1. Application fee: $50. *Financial aid:* Fellowships available. Financial aid application deadline: 2/1. • Dr. Joel Blau, Director, 516-444-3149. Fax: 516-444-7565. E-mail: joelb@ssw.hsc.sunysb.edu.

See in-depth description on page 1945.

State University of New York at Stony Brook, Health Sciences Center, School of Social Welfare, Master's Program in Social Work, Stony Brook, NY 11794. Awards MSW. Accredited by CSWE. Students: 276 full-time (233 women), 18 part-time (14 women); includes 75 minority (42 African Americans, 4 Asian Americans, 28 Hispanics, 1 Native American), 3 international. Average age 35. In 1997, 144 degrees awarded. *Degree requirements:* Project or thesis required, foreign language not required. *Entrance requirements:* Interview. Application deadline: 3/1. Application fee: $50. *Financial aid:* Application deadline 3/1. • Application contact: Dr. Michael Lewis, Director, 516-444-3166. Fax: 516-444-7565. E-mail: michaell@ssw.hsc.sunysb.edu.

See in-depth description on page 1945.

Stephen F. Austin State University, College of Applied Arts and Science, School of Social Work, Nacogdoches, TX 75962. Awards MSW. Candidate for accreditation by CSWE. Students: 22 full-time (18 women), 18 part-time (16 women); includes 5 minority (all African Americans). 30 applicants, 40% accepted. *Entrance requirements:* GRE General Test. Application deadline: 7/1 (rolling processing). Application fee: $0 ($25 for international students). *Tuition:* $1465 per year full-time, $263 per semester (minimum) part-time for state residents; $5299 per year full-time, $890 per semester (minimum) part-time for nonresidents. *Financial aid:* In 1997–98, 1 research assistantship totaling $5,600 was awarded; Federal Work-Study, institutionally sponsored loans, and career-related internships or fieldwork also available. Aid available to part-time students. Financial aid application deadline: 3/1. • Dr. Michael Daley, Associate Dean, 409-468-5105.

Syracuse University, School of Social Work, Syracuse, NY 13244-0003. Awards MSW, JD/MSW. Programs in family mental health (MSW), gerontology (MSW), health care (MSW), occupational social work (MSW). Accredited by CSWE. Part-time and evening/weekend programs available. Faculty: 15. Students: 174 full-time (146 women), 184 part-time (148 women); includes 41 minority (27 African Americans, 4 Asian Americans, 5 Hispanics, 5 Native Americans). 207 applicants, 72% accepted. In 1997, 155 degrees awarded. *Entrance requirements:* GRE General Test. Application deadline: rolling. Application fee: $40. *Tuition:* $13,320 per year full-time, $555 per credit hour part-time. *Financial aid:* Fellowships, research assistantships, teaching assistantships, partial tuition waivers, Federal Work-Study, and career-related internships or fieldwork available. Financial aid application deadline: 3/1. • William Pollard, Dean, 315-443-5582. Application contact: Linda Littlejohn, Director of Admissions, 315-443-5555.

Temple University, School of Social Administration, Program in Social Work, Philadelphia, PA 19122-6096. Awards MSW. Accredited by CSWE. Part-time and evening/weekend programs available. Faculty: 23 full-time (13 women). Students: 491 (405 women); includes 133 minority (121 African Americans, 12 Hispanics), 2 international. 629 applicants, 46% accepted. In 1997, 190 degrees awarded. *Entrance requirements:* Minimum GPA of 3.0 during previous 2 years, 2.8 overall. Application deadline: 6/15 (priority date; rolling processing). Application fee: $40. *Expenses:* Tuition $323 per semester hour for state residents; $444 per semester hour for nonresidents. Fees $170 per year full-time, $28 per semester (minimum) part-time. *Financial aid:* Fellowships, research assistantships, teaching assistantships, traineeships, field assistantships, partial tuition waivers, Federal Work-Study, institutionally sponsored loans, and career-related internships or fieldwork available. Financial aid application deadline: 6/15. • Application contact: Donna Chavers, Director of Admissions, 215-204-8621.

Tulane University, School of Social Work, New Orleans, LA 70118-5669. Awards MSW, PhD, Certificate, JD/MSW, MSW/MPH. One or more programs accredited by CSWE. JD/MSW new for fall 1998. Students: 225 full-time (202 women), 13 part-time (11 women); includes 31 minority (25 African Americans, 3 Asian Americans, 3 Hispanics), 1 international. 280 applicants, 77% accepted. In 1997, 120 master's, 7 doctorates awarded. *Degree requirements:* For master's and doctorate, thesis/dissertation. *Average time to degree:* master's–1.3 years full-time. *Entrance requirements:* For master's, TOEFL. Application deadline: 3/31 (11/15 for spring admission). Application fee: $25. *Financial aid:* Fellowships, Federal Work-Study available. Financial aid application deadline: 2/1. • Dr. Suzanne England, Dean, 504-865-5314. Application contact: Gail Brown, Admissions Coordinator, 504-865-5314.

See in-depth description on page 1947.

Université de Moncton, Faculty of Social Sciences, School of Social Work, Moncton, NB E1A 3E9, Canada. Awards MSS. Faculty: 11 full-time (5 women). Students: 10 full-time (7 women). Average age 25. In 1997, 6 degrees awarded. *Degree requirements:* 1 foreign language, major paper. *Entrance requirements:* Minimum GPA of 3.0. Application deadline: 4/30. Application fee: $50. *Financial aid:* Research assistantships, teaching assistantships, and career-related internships or fieldwork available. Financial aid application deadline: 4/30. *Faculty research:* Burnout and education, mental health (institutionalization), unemployment's effect on youth, women and health services. • Marcelle Laforest, Director, 506-858-4181.

Université de Montréal, Programs in Social Administration, Montréal, PQ H3C 3J7, Canada. Awards DESS. 11 applicants, 82% accepted. In 1997, 17 degrees awarded. *Application fee:* $30. • Claude Larivère, Director, 514-343-7025.

Université de Montréal, Faculty of Arts and Sciences, School of Social Service, Montréal, PQ H3C 3J7, Canada. Awards M Sc, PhD. Program in social work (M Sc). Offered jointly with McGill University. Part-time programs available. Faculty: 18 full-time (6 women). Students: 85 full-time (70 women), 32 part-time (30 women). 108 applicants, 41% accepted. In 1997, 27 master's awarded. *Degree requirements:* For master's, 1 foreign language, thesis (for some programs). *Application deadline:* 2/1. *Application fee:* $30. *Financial aid:* Research assistantships, teaching assistantships, institutionally sponsored loans, and career-related internships or fieldwork available. Financial aid application deadline: 9/1. *Faculty research:* Family violence, social policies analysis, community development, gerontology, prevention. • Jean Panet-Raymond, Director, 514-343-6596. Application contact: Ricardo Zuniga, Graduate Director, 514-343-5950.

Université de Sherbrooke, Faculty of Letters and Human Sciences, Department of Social Service, Sherbrooke, PQ J1K 2R1, Canada. Awards MSS. *Application deadline:* 6/1. *Application fee:* $15.

Université du Québec à Montréal, Program in Social Intervention, Montréal, PQ H3C 3P8, Canada. Awards MA. Part-time programs available. *Degree requirements:* Thesis. *Entrance requirements:* Appropriate bachelor's degree or equivalent and proficiency in French. Application deadline: 3/1 (priority date). Application fee: $50.

Université du Québec en Abitibi-Témiscamingue, Program in Psychosocial Intervention, Rouyn-Noranda, PQ J9X 5E4, Canada. Awards Diploma. Part-time programs available. *Entrance requirements:* Appropriate bachelor's degree, proficiency in French. Application deadline: 4/1. Application fee: $30.

Université Laval, Faculty of Social Sciences, School of Social Work, Sainte-Foy, PQ G1K 7P4, Canada. Awards M Serv Soc, PhD. Students: 66 full-time (52 women), 112 part-time (85 women). 106 applicants, 54% accepted. In 1997, 28 master's, 3 doctorates awarded. *Application deadline:* 3/1. *Application fee:* $30. *Expenses:* Tuition $1334 per year (minimum) full-time, $56 per credit (minimum) part-time for Canadian residents; $5966 per year (minimum) full-time, $249 per credit (minimum) part-time for nonresidents. Fees $150 per year full-time, $6.25 per credit part-time. • Lise Tessier, Director, 418-656-2131 Ext. 2371. Fax: 418-656-3567. E-mail: lise.tessier@svs.ulaval.ca.

The University of Akron, College of Fine and Applied Arts, School of Social Work, Akron, OH 44325-0001. Awards MSW. Candidate for accreditation by CSWE. Students: 37 full-time (34 women), 3 part-time (0 women); includes 13 minority (10 African Americans, 2 Hispanics, 1 Native American), 1 international. Average age 35. In 1997, 9 degrees awarded. *Application deadline:* rolling. *Application fee:* $25 ($50 for international students). *Expenses:* Tuition $178 per credit hour for state residents; $333 per credit hour for nonresidents. Fees $145 per year full-time, $32 per semester (minimum) part-time. *Financial aid:* In 1997–98, 31 students received aid, including 9 research assistantships; Federal Work-Study also available. Financial aid application deadline: 3/1. • Dr. Marvin Feit, Director, 330-972-5975. E-mail: marvinfeit@uakron.edu.

The University of Alabama, School of Social Work, Tuscaloosa, AL 35487. Awards MSW, PhD. One or more programs accredited by CSWE. Faculty: 21 full-time (9 women). Students: 168 full-time (136 women), 38 part-time (32 women); includes 30 minority (25 African Americans, 1 Asian American, 3 Hispanics, 1 Native American), 8 international. Average age 32. 316 applicants, 55% accepted. In 1997, 106 master's, 2 doctorates awarded. *Degree requirements:* For doctorate, dissertation. *Average time to degree:* master's–2 years full-time; doctorate–5 years full-time. *Entrance requirements:* For master's, GRE General Test (minimum combined score of 1500 on three sections) or MAT (minimum score 50), minimum GPA of 2.5; for doctorate, GRE General Test (minimum combined score of 1500 on three sections) or MAT (minimum score 50), minimum GPA of 3.0. Application deadline: 2/1 (priority date). Application fee: $25. Electronic applications accepted. *Tuition:* $2684 per year full-time, $594 per semester (minimum) part-time for state residents; $7216 per year full-time, $1248 per semester (minimum) part-time for nonresidents. *Financial aid:* In 1997–98, 128 students received aid, including 26 fellowships, 9 research assistantships, 5 teaching assistantships; partial tuition waivers, Federal Work-Study, and career-related internships or fieldwork also available. Financial aid application deadline: 2/1. *Faculty research:* Social service delivery structures; direct clinical services with individuals, families, and groups; theory and practice development. • Dr. Lucinda L. Roff, Dean, 205-348-3924. Application contact: Dr. Richard T. Crow, Associate Dean, 205-348-3929.

University of Alaska Anchorage, College of Health, Education and Social Welfare, School of Social Welfare, Department of Social Work, Anchorage, AK 99508-8060. Awards MSW. Candidate for accreditation by CSWE. Students: 53 full-time (46 women), 6 part-time (5 women); includes 12 minority (3 African Americans, 1 Hispanic, 8 Native Americans). 69 applicants, 74% accepted. In 1997, 28 degrees awarded. *Degree requirements:* Computer language, thesis or alternative, research project required, foreign language not required. *Entrance requirements:* GRE General Test. Application deadline: 1/15. Application fee: $45. *Tuition:* $7892 per year for state residents; $12,573 per year for nonresidents. *Faculty research:* Community diversity issues, current policy issues, victim-offender mediation, racism program evaluation, gender issues, family therapy, incest. • Application contact: Linda Berg Smith, Associate Vice Chancellor for Enrollment Services, 907-786-1529.

University of Arkansas at Little Rock, College of Professional Studies, School of Social Work, Program in Social Work, Little Rock, AR 72204-1099. Offers clinical social work (MSW), social program administration (MSW). Accredited by CSWE. Students: 120 full-time (96 women), 42 part-time (33 women); includes 25 minority (22 African Americans, 2 Asian Americans, 1 Native American), 2 international. Average age 32. 165 applicants, 60% accepted. In 1997, 86 degrees awarded. *Entrance requirements:* GRE General Test or MAT. Application fee: $25 ($30 for international students). *Expenses:* Tuition $2466 per year full-time, $137 per credit hour part-time for state residents; $5256 per year full-time, $292 per credit hour part-time for nonresidents. Fees $216 per year full-time, $36 per semester (minimum) part-time. *Financial aid:* Graduate assistantships available. • Amy Garland, Coordinator, 501-569-3240.

University of British Columbia, Faculties of Arts and Graduate Studies, School of Social Work, Vancouver, BC V6T 1Z2, Canada. Awards MSW. Part-time programs available. Faculty: 15 full-time (8 women). Students: 29 full-time (26 women), 49 part-time (38 women); includes 17 minority (1 African American, 11 Asian Americans, 5 Native Americans). Average age 32. 90 applicants, 56% accepted. In 1997, 29 degrees awarded. *Degree requirements:* Thesis or essay. *Average time to degree:* master's–1.5 years full-time, 3 years part-time. *Entrance requirements:* BSW. Application deadline: 12/31. Application fee: $52. *Financial aid:* In 1997–98, 1 fellowship (to a first-year student) averaging $1,105 per month and totaling $13,500 was awarded; Federal Work-Study, institutionally sponsored loans, and career-related internships or fieldwork also available. Financial aid application deadline: 6/30. *Faculty research:* Child and family services, services for women, culturally specific services, social and community development. • Elaine Stolar, Director, 604-822-2277. Fax: 604-822-8656. Application contact: Admissions Office, 604-822-2609. E-mail: suzy@socialwork.ubc.ca.

The University of Calgary, Faculty of Social Work, Calgary, AB T2N 1N4, Canada. Awards MSW, PhD. Faculty: 27 full-time (11 women). Students: 52 full-time (45 women), 11 part-time (10 women). Average age 33. 152 applicants, 39% accepted. In 1997, 32 master's, 1 doctorate awarded. *Degree requirements:* For master's, thesis (for some programs); for doctorate, dissertation, candidacy exam. *Average time to degree:* master's–1 year full-time, 3 years part-time. *Entrance requirements:* For master's, BSW, minimum undergraduate GPA of 3.5; for doctorate, minimum graduate GPA of 3.8, MSW. Application deadline: 1/31 (priority date). Application fee: $65. *Expenses:* Tuition $5448 per year full-time, $908 per course part-time for Canadian residents; $10,896 per year full-time, $1816 per course part-time for nonresidents. Fees $285 per year full-time, $119 per semester (minimum) part-time. *Financial aid:* In 1997–98, 26 students received aid, including 16 research assistantships (14 to first-year students) averaging $980 per month and totaling $105,840, 5 teaching assistantships (2 to first-year students) averaging $1,369 per month, 25 fee remissions (6 to first-year students) totaling $3,000; full and partial tuition waivers and career-related internships or fieldwork also available. Financial aid application deadline: 2/1. *Faculty research:* Family violence, direct practice, gerontology, child welfare, community development. Total annual research expenditures: $900,000. • R. J. Thomlison, Dean, 403-220-5945. E-mail: rthomlis@ucalgary.ca. Application contact: M. Buk, Director, Student Services, 403-220-4694. Fax: 403-282-7269. E-mail: mbuk@ucalgary.ca.

University of California, Berkeley, School of Social Welfare, Berkeley, CA 94720-1500. Awards MSW, PhD, JD/MSW, MSW/PhD. One or more programs accredited by CSWE. Faculty: 27 full-time (13 women), 28 part-time (17 women). Students: 234 full-time (176 women); includes 84 minority (26 African Americans, 26 Asian Americans, 24 Hispanics, 8 Native Americans), 3 international. 660 applicants, 23% accepted. In 1997, 94 master's, 5 doctorates awarded. *Degree requirements:* For doctorate, dissertation, qualifying exam. *Entrance requirements:* GRE General Test, minimum GPA of 3.0. Application deadline: rolling. Application fee: $40. *Expenses:* Tuition $0 for state residents; $9384 per year for nonresidents. Fees $4409 per year. *Financial aid:* Fellowships, research assistantships, teaching assistantships available. Financial aid application deadline: 1/5. *Faculty research:* Child welfare, law and social welfare, minority mental health, social welfare policy analysis, health services, psychopathology, gerontology. • Dr. James Midgley, Dean, 510-642-5039. Application contact: Doris J. Britt, Assistant to the Dean for Admission, 510-642-1660. E-mail: djb@uclink2.berkeley.edu.

University of California, Los Angeles, School of Public Policy and Social Research, Program in Social Welfare, Los Angeles, CA 90095. Awards MSW, PhD. One or more programs accredited by CSWE. Faculty: 8 (5 women). Students: 210 full-time (177 women); includes 95 minority (24 African Americans, 27 Asian Americans, 43 Hispanics, 1 Native American), 12 international. 469 applicants, 32% accepted. *Degree requirements:* For master's, comprehensive exam, research project required, foreign language and thesis not required; for doctorate, dissertation, oral and written qualifying exams required, foreign language not required. *Entrance requirements:* For master's, GRE General Test, TOEFL, minimum GPA of 3.0; for doctorate, GRE General Test, TOEFL, minimum undergraduate GPA of 3.0. Application deadline: 2/15. Application fee: $40. Electronic applications accepted. *Expenses:* Tuition $0 for state residents; $9384 per year for nonresidents. Fees $4551 per year. *Financial aid:* In 1997–98, 162 students received aid, including fellowships totaling $336,541, research assistantships totaling $128,025, teaching assistantships totaling $48,811, federal fellowships and scholarships totaling $630,752; full and partial tuition waivers, Federal Work-Study, institutionally sponsored loans also available. Financial aid application deadline: 3/1. • Dr. James Lubben, Dean, 310-825-7737. Application contact: Departmental Office, 310-825-7737. E-mail: swinfo@sppsr.ucla.edu.

University of Central Florida, College of Health and Public Affairs, Department of Social Work, Orlando, FL 32816. Awards MSW. Accredited by CSWE. Faculty: 12. Students: 144 full-time (129 women), 5 part-time (4 women); includes 32 minority (18 African Americans, 1 Asian American, 13 Hispanics), 1 international. Average age 32. 209 applicants, 45% accepted. In 1997, 80 degrees awarded. *Entrance requirements:* GRE General Test. Application deadline: 3/1. Application fee: $20. *Expenses:* Tuition $3288 per year full-time, $137 per credit hour part-time for state residents; $11,520 per year full-time, $480 per credit hour part-time for nonresidents. Fees $105 per year. • Dr. I. Colby, Chair, 407-823-2114. E-mail: pcolby@pegasus.cc.ucf.edu.

University of Chicago, School of Social Service Administration, Chicago, IL 60637-1513. Awards AM, PhD, AM/M Div, MBA/AM. Programs in social service administration (PhD), social work (AM). One or more programs accredited by CSWE. Part-time and evening/weekend programs available. Faculty: 29. Students: 206 full-time (164 women), 118 part-time (83 women); includes 99 minority (64 African Americans, 8 Asian Americans, 26 Hispanics, 1

Directory: Social Work

University of Chicago (continued)

Native American), 8 international. 650 applicants, 27% accepted. In 1997, 169 master's, 9 doctorates awarded. *Degree requirements:* For doctorate, dissertation required, foreign language not required. *Application deadline:* 2/15 (priority date; rolling processing). *Application fee:* $60. *Financial aid:* Fellowships, research assistantships, teaching assistantships, scholarships, Federal Work-Study, institutionally sponsored loans, and career-related internships or fieldwork available. Aid available to part-time students. Financial aid application deadline: 4/15; applicants required to submit FAFSA. *Faculty research:* Family treatment, sex abuse and therapeutic problems, the aged, child welfare, health administration. • Dr. Jeanne C. Marsh, Dean, 773-702-1250. Application contact: Stanley Ramos, Assistant Dean of Enrollment, 773-702-1492. Fax: 773-702-0874. E-mail: ssa.dos@midway.uchicago.edu.

See in-depth description on page 1949.

University of Cincinnati, School of Social Work, Cincinnati, OH 45221. Awards MSW. Accredited by CSWE. Part-time programs available. Faculty: 1 full-time. Students: 140 full-time (110 women), 44 part-time (39 women); includes 35 minority (34 African Americans, 1 Asian American), 1 international. 275 applicants, 34% accepted. In 1997, 75 degrees awarded. *Average time to degree:* master's–2.1 years full-time. *Entrance requirements:* GRE General Test. Application deadline: 2/1. Application fee: $30. *Tuition:* $7228 per year full-time, $185 per credit hour part-time for state residents; $13,812 per year full-time, $352 per credit hour part-time for nonresidents. *Financial aid:* Fellowships, graduate assistantships, full tuition waivers, and career-related internships or fieldwork available. Financial aid application deadline: 5/1. • Dr. Philip Jackson, Director, 513-556-4619. E-mail: philip.jackson@uc.edu. Application contact: Gerald Bostwick, Graduate Program Director, 513-556-4624. Fax: 513-556-2077. E-mail: gerald.bostwick@uc.edu.

University of Connecticut, School of Social Work, Storrs, CT 06269. Awards MSW, JD/MSW, MBA/MSW, MPA/MSW. Accredited by CSWE. Faculty: 22. Students: 370 full-time (287 women); includes 96 minority (56 African Americans, 5 Asian Americans, 33 Hispanics, 2 Native Americans), 1 international. Average age 23. 541 applicants, 35% accepted. In 1997, 168 degrees awarded. *Application deadline:* 4/1 (priority date; rolling processing). *Application fee:* $30. *Expenses:* Tuition $5272 per year full-time, $293 per credit part-time for state residents; $13,696 per year full-time, $761 per credit part-time for nonresidents. Fees $948 per year full-time, $640 per year part-time. *Financial aid:* In 1997–98, 3 research assistantships (1 to a first-year student) were awarded; teaching assistantships, Federal Work-Study also available. • Mark Abrahamson, Dean, 860-241-4727. Application contact: Tilitha Conyers, Director of Admissions, 860-241-4730.

University of Dayton, School of Education, Department of Counselor Education and Human Services, Dayton, OH 45469-1611. Offerings include school social worker (MS Ed). Department faculty: 8 full-time (1 woman), 5 part-time (4 women). *Degree requirements:* Exit exam required, thesis optional, foreign language not required. *Average time to degree:* master's–2 years full-time, 3.5 years part-time. *Entrance requirements:* GRE General Test (minimum score 430 on verbal section, 490 on analytical), minimum GPA of 2.75. Application deadline: 2/15 (priority date; rolling processing). Application fee: $30. • Dr. William Drury, Chairperson, 937-229-3644.

University of Denver, Graduate School of Social Work, Denver, CO 80208. Awards MSW, PhD, JD/MSW, M Div/MSW, MSW/MA. One or more programs accredited by CSWE. MSW/MA offered jointly with the Center for Judaic Studies, Department of Human Communication, and Graduate School of International Studies. M Div/MSW offered jointly with Iliff School of Theology. Part-time and evening/weekend programs available. Faculty: 24 full-time (16 women). Students: 355 full-time (293 women), 32 part-time (27 women); includes 54 minority (15 African Americans, 7 Asian Americans, 23 Hispanics, 9 Native Americans), 4 international. Average age 34. 519 applicants, 80% accepted. In 1997, 210 master's awarded (100% found work related to degree); 5 doctorates awarded (100% entered university research/teaching). *Degree requirements:* For doctorate, dissertation required, foreign language not required. *Entrance requirements:* For doctorate, GRE General Test or MAT, MSW. Application deadline: 5/1 (rolling processing). Application fee: $40 ($45 for international students). *Expenses:* Tuition $18,216 per year full-time, $506 per credit hour part-time. Fees $159 per year. *Financial aid:* In 1997–98, 335 students received aid, including 3 fellowships totaling $5,800, 6 research assistantships averaging $837 per month and totaling $46,287, 5 teaching assistantships averaging $853 per month and totaling $38,400, 31 scholarships totaling $77,431; partial tuition waivers, Federal Work-Study, institutionally sponsored loans, and career-related internships or fieldwork also available. Aid available to part-time students. Financial aid application deadline: 2/1; applicants required to submit FAFSA. *Faculty research:* Children, youth, and families; community mental health; drug dependency; gerontology; health. Total annual research expenditures: $1.739 million. • Dr. Catherine Alter, Dean, 303-871-2886. Application contact: Joan Harwick, Director, Graduate Admissions, 303-871-2841. Fax: 303-871-2845.

See in-depth description on page 1951.

University of Georgia, School of Social Work, Athens, GA 30602. Awards MSW, PhD. One or more programs accredited by CSWE. Faculty: 15 full-time (8 women). Students: 201 full-time, 51 part-time (39 women); includes 32 minority (25 African Americans, 2 Asian Americans, 3 Hispanics, 2 Native Americans), 4 international. 428 applicants, 26% accepted. In 1997, 129 master's, 4 doctorates awarded. *Degree requirements:* For doctorate, 1 foreign language (computer language can substitute), dissertation. *Entrance requirements:* GRE General Test. Application deadline: 7/1 (priority date; 11/15 for spring admission). Application fee: $30. Electronic applications accepted. *Tuition:* $3290 per year full-time, $643 per semester (minimum) part-time for state residents; $11,300 per year full-time, $1645 per semester (minimum) part-time for nonresidents. *Financial aid:* Fellowships, research assistantships, teaching assistantships, assistantships available. • Dr. Bonnie L. Yegidis, Dean, 706-542-5424. Fax: 706-542-3845. Application contact: Dr. Nancy P. Kropf, Graduate Coordinator, 706-542-5422. Fax: 706-542-5282.

See in-depth description on page 1953.

University of Hawaii at Manoa, College of Health Sciences and Social Welfare, School of Social Work, Honolulu, HI 96822. Offers programs in social welfare (PhD), social work (MSW). One or more programs accredited by CSWE. Part-time programs available. Faculty: 22 full-time (11 women), 102 part-time (65 women). Students: 120 full-time (102 women), 123 part-time (92 women); includes 88 minority (5 African Americans, 76 Asian Americans, 5 Hispanics, 2 Native Americans), 5 international. 275 applicants, 60% accepted. In 1997, 107 master's awarded. *Degree requirements:* For doctorate, dissertation required, foreign language not required. *Average time to degree:* master's–2 years full-time, 3 years part-time. *Entrance requirements:* For doctorate, TOEFL (minimum score 560), master's degree (MSW preferred), minimum GPA of 3.0. Application deadline: 3/1 (rolling processing). Application fee: $25. *Tuition:* $4029 per year full-time, $214 per credit hour part-time for state residents; $9957 per year full-time, $461 per credit hour part-time for nonresidents. *Financial aid:* Fellowships, research assistantships, full tuition waivers, Federal Work-Study, institutionally sponsored loans, and career-related internships or fieldwork available. Aid available to part-time students. Financial aid application deadline: 2/1; applicants required to submit FAFSA. *Faculty research:* Health, mental health, AIDS, substance abuse, rural health, community-based research, social policy. • Dr. Patricia Ewalt, Dean, 808-956-3828. Application contact: Toni Hathaway, Admissions Coordinator, 808-956-7182. Fax: 808-956-5964.

University of Houston, Graduate School of Social Work, 4800 Calhoun, Houston, TX 77204-2163. Awards MSW, PhD, MBA/MSW. One or more programs accredited by CSWE. Part-time programs available. Faculty: 22 full-time (14 women), 25 part-time (18 women). Students: 217 full-time (192 women), 172 part-time (137 women); includes 142 minority (78 African Americans, 13 Asian Americans, 50 Hispanics, 1 Native American), 2 international. Average age 33. 361 applicants, 55% accepted. In 1997, 138 master's, 1 doctorate awarded. *Degree requirements:* For master's, field internship required, thesis optional, foreign language not required; for doctorate, dissertation, clinical research internships, written comprehensive exam required, foreign language not required. *Average time to degree:* master's–2 years full-time, 4 years part-time. *Entrance requirements:* For master's, TOEFL (minimum score 550), GRE or minimum GPA of 3.0; for doctorate, TOEFL (minimum score 550). Application deadline: 3/15 (priority date; rolling processing). Application fee: $40 ($115 for international students). *Expenses:* Tuition $1152 per year full-time, $120 per semester (minimum) part-time for state residents; $4482 per year full-time, $249 per credit hour part-time for nonresidents. Fees $977 per year full-time, $119 per semester (minimum) part-time. *Financial aid:* In 1997–98, 10 research assistantships (5 to first-year students) averaging $650 per month and totaling $65,000 were awarded; graduate assistantships, Federal Work-Study, institutionally sponsored loans, and career-related internships or fieldwork also available. Financial aid application deadline: 4/1; applicants required to submit FAFSA. *Faculty research:* Health care, gerontology, political social work, mental health, children and families. • Dr. Karen A. Holmes, Dean, 713-743-8085. Fax: 713-743-3267. E-mail: kaholmes@uh.edu. Application contact: Mimi Lane, Admissions Analyst, 713-743-8078. Fax: 713-743-8149.

University of Illinois at Chicago, Jane Addams College of Social Work, Chicago, IL 60607-7128. Awards MSW, PhD. One or more programs accredited by CSWE. Part-time programs available. Faculty: 28 full-time (15 women). Students: 314 full-time (251 women), 255 part-time (204 women); includes 183 minority (105 African Americans, 22 Asian Americans, 55 Hispanics, 1 Native American), 3 international. 948 applicants, 28% accepted. In 1997, 239 master's, 6 doctorates awarded. *Degree requirements:* For doctorate, dissertation required, foreign language not required. *Entrance requirements:* For master's, GMAT, TOEFL (minimum score 550), minimum GPA of 3.75 on a 5.0 scale; for doctorate, GRE General Test or MAT, TOEFL (minimum score 550), minimum GPA of 3.75 on a 5.0 scale. Application deadline: 2/1. Application fee: $40 ($50 for international students). *Financial aid:* In 1997–98, 4 fellowships, 22 research assistantships, 3 teaching assistantships were awarded. • C. F. Hairston, Dean, 312-996-3219. Application contact: Barbara Bergstrom, Director of Admissions, 312-996-3218.

University of Illinois at Urbana–Champaign, School of Social Work, Urbana, IL 61801. Awards MSW, PhD. One or more programs accredited by CSWE. Faculty: 18 full-time (7 women). Students: 270 full-time (223 women); includes 41 minority (28 African Americans, 8 Asian Americans, 3 Hispanics, 2 Native Americans), 16 international. 385 applicants, 63% accepted. In 1997, 157 master's, 6 doctorates awarded. *Degree requirements:* For doctorate, dissertation required, foreign language not required. *Entrance requirements:* For master's, minimum GPA of 4.0 on a 5.0 scale. Application deadline: rolling. Application fee: $40 ($50 for international students). *Financial aid:* In 1997–98, 11 fellowships, 112 research assistantships, 9 teaching assistantships were awarded; full and partial tuition waivers and career-related internships or fieldwork also available. Financial aid application deadline: 2/15. • Jill D. Kagle, Dean, 217-333-2260. Fax: 217-244-5220.

The University of Iowa, College of Liberal Arts, School of Social Work, Iowa City, IA 52242-1316. Awards MSW, PhD, JD/MSW, MSW/MA, MSW/MS. Accredited by CSWE. MSW/MA and MSW/MS offered jointly with the Program in Urban and Regional Planning. Faculty: 16 full-time, 8 part-time. Students: 148 full-time (125 women), 90 part-time (78 women); includes 23 minority (15 African Americans, 1 Asian American, 6 Hispanics, 1 Native American), 1 international. 225 applicants, 66% accepted. In 1997, 83 master's awarded. *Degree requirements:* For master's, thesis optional; for doctorate, dissertation, comprehensive exam. *Entrance requirements:* GRE General Test. Application deadline: 2/1. Application fee: $30 ($50 for international students). *Expenses:* Tuition $3166 per year full-time, $176 per semester hour part-time for state residents; $10,202 per year full-time, $176 per semester hour part-time for nonresidents. Fees $202 per year full-time, $52 per year (minimum) part-time. *Financial aid:* In 1997–98, 18 fellowships (5 to first-year students), 8 research assistantships (2 to first-year students), 7 teaching assistantships were awarded. Financial aid applicants required to submit FAFSA. • Patricia Kelley, Director, 319-335-1250.

University of Kansas, School of Social Welfare, Doctoral Program in Social Work, Lawrence, KS 66045. Awards PhD. Faculty: 22 full-time. Students: 6 full-time (5 women), 35 part-time (29 women); includes 2 minority (both Hispanics), 1 international. 17 applicants, 35% accepted. In 1997, 4 degrees awarded. *Degree requirements:* Computer language, dissertation required, foreign language not required. *Entrance requirements:* GRE General Test, TOEFL (minimum score 570). Application deadline: 2/28. Application fee: $25. *Expenses:* Tuition $2400 per year full-time, $100 per credit hour part-time for state residents; $7890 per year full-time, $329 per credit hour part-time for nonresidents. Fees $428 per year full-time, $31 per credit hour part-time. *Financial aid:* In 1997–98, 15 research assistantships (4 to first-year students) averaging $1,500 per month, 10 teaching assistantships (2 to first-year students) averaging $1,000 per month were awarded; fellowships, partial tuition waivers, Federal Work-Study also available. Aid available to part-time students. Financial aid application deadline: 5/31. *Faculty research:* Community support and housing for long-term mentally ill, developing wrap-around services for children or youth. Total annual research expenditures: $4 million. • Dennis Saleeby, Chair, 785-864-4720. Application contact: Jan Lewis, Director of Admissions, 785-864-4720. Fax: 785-864-5277. E-mail: janl@sw1.socwel.ukans.edu.

University of Kansas, School of Social Welfare, Master's Program in Social Work, Lawrence, KS 66045. Awards MSW, JD/MSW. Accredited by CSWE. Students: 407 full-time (341 women), 85 part-time (73 women); includes 99 minority (61 African Americans, 3 Asian Americans, 19 Hispanics, 16 Native Americans), 2 international. 398 applicants, 61% accepted. In 1997, 187 degrees awarded. *Average time to degree:* master's–2 years full-time, 3 years part-time. *Entrance requirements:* TOEFL (minimum score 570). Application deadline: 2/15. Application fee: $25. *Expenses:* Tuition $2400 per year full-time, $100 per credit hour part-time for state residents; $7890 per year full-time, $329 per credit hour part-time for nonresidents. Fees $428 per year full-time, $31 per credit hour part-time. *Financial aid:* 213 students received aid. • Application contact: Jan Lewis, Director of Admissions, 785-864-4720. Fax: 785-864-5277. E-mail: janl@sw1.socwel.ukans.edu.

University of Kentucky, College of Social Work, Program in Social Work, Lexington, KY 40506-0032. Awards MSW, PhD. One or more programs accredited by CSWE. Faculty: 24 full-time (12 women), 2 part-time (both women). Students: 202 full-time (169 women), 134 part-time (103 women); includes 31 minority (29 African Americans, 2 Asian Americans), 1 international. 309 applicants, 67% accepted. In 1997, 182 master's awarded. *Degree requirements:* For master's, comprehensive exam required, foreign language and thesis not required. *Entrance requirements:* For master's, GRE General Test, minimum undergraduate GPA of 2.5. Application deadline: 4/15 (rolling processing). Application fee: $30 ($35 for international students). *Financial aid:* In 1997–98, 22 fellowships, 2 research assistantships, 2 graduate assistantships were awarded; teaching assistantships, institutionally sponsored loans, and career-related internships or fieldwork also available. Aid available to part-time students. *Faculty research:* Aging, family and children, domestic violence, delinquency, health and mental health. Total annual research expenditures: $93,993. • Dr. John W. Landon, Director of Graduate Studies, 606-257-4893. Application contact: Dr. Constance L. Wood, Associate Dean, 606-257-4613. Fax: 606-323-1928.

University of Louisville, Raymond A. Kent School of Social Work, Louisville, KY 40292-0001. Awards MSSW, PhD. One or more programs accredited by CSWE. PhD offered jointly with the University of Kentucky. Faculty: 21 full-time (12 women), 12 part-time (9 women), 25 FTE. Students: 318 full-time (256 women), 86 part-time (65 women); includes 41 minority (35 African Americans, 2 Asian Americans, 4 Hispanics), 2 international. Average age 33. In 1997, 120 master's awarded. *Degree requirements:* For doctorate, dissertation. *Entrance requirements:* GRE General Test. Application deadline: rolling. Application fee: $25. • Dr. Terry Singer, Acting Dean, 502-852-3944.

See in-depth description on page 1955.

University of Maine, College of Business, Public Policy and Health, School of Social Work, Orono, ME 04469. Awards MSW. Accredited by CSWE. Faculty: 8 full-time. Students: 44 full-time (30 women), 25 part-time (20 women). 86 applicants, 57% accepted. In 1997, 22 degrees awarded. *Entrance requirements:* GRE General Test, TOEFL (minimum score 550). Application deadline: 2/1 (priority date; rolling processing; 10/15 for spring admission). Application fee: $50. *Expenses:* Tuition $194 per credit hour for state residents; $548 per credit hour for nonresidents. Fees $378 per year full-time, $33 per semester (minimum) part-time. *Financial aid:* Application deadline 3/1. • Dr. Gail Werrbach, Interim Director, 207-581-2387. Fax: 207-581-2396. Application contact: Scott Delcourt, Director of the Graduate School, 207-581-3218. Fax: 207-581-3232. E-mail: graduate@maine.edu.

University of Manitoba, Faculty of Social Work, Winnipeg, MB R3T 2N2, Canada. Awards MSW. *Degree requirements:* Thesis or alternative required, foreign language not required. *Application deadline:* 3/15.

University of Maryland, Baltimore, Graduate School, Graduate Programs in Social Work, Doctoral Program in Social Work, Baltimore, MD 21201-1777. Awards PhD. Students: 35 full-time (27 women), 8 part-time (6 women); includes 3 minority (all African Americans). Average age 40. 20 applicants, 55% accepted. In 1997, 7 degrees awarded. *Degree requirements:* Dissertation. *Entrance requirements:* GRE General Test, minimum GPA of 3.0, MSW. Application deadline: 2/1 (priority date; rolling processing). Application fee: $42. *Expenses:* Tuition $253 per credit hour for state residents; $454 per credit hour for nonresidents. Fees $317 per year. *Financial aid:* Fellowships, research assistantships, teaching assistantships available. • Dr. Carlton Munson, Director, 410-706-3602. E-mail: cmunson@ssw02.ab.umd.edu. Application contact: Tammy Derry, Administrative Assistant, 410-706-7960. Fax: 410-706-0273. E-mail: tderry@ssw02.ab.umd.edu.

See in-depth description on page 1957.

University of Maryland, Baltimore, Graduate School, Graduate Programs in Social Work, Master's Program in Social Work, Baltimore, MD 21201-1627. Awards MSW, JD/MSW, MBA/MSW, MSW/MA. Accredited by CSWE. MBA/MSW offered jointly with the University of Maryland, College Park. MSW/MA offered jointly with Baltimore Hebrew University. Faculty: 42 full-time (17 women), 40 part-time (22 women). Students: 712 full-time (590 women), 245 part-time (203 women); includes 274 minority (224 African Americans, 15 Asian Americans, 29 Hispanics, 6 Native Americans), 5 international. Average age 29. 906 applicants, 70% accepted. In 1997, 367 degrees awarded. *Average time to degree:* master's–2 years full-time, 3 years part-time. *Entrance requirements:* Minimum GPA of 3.0. Application deadline: 2/15. Application fee: $40. *Expenses:* Tuition $253 per credit hour for state residents; $454 per credit hour for nonresidents. Fees $317 per year. *Financial aid:* 255 students received aid; Federal Work-Study and career-related internships or fieldwork available. Aid available to part-time students. Financial aid application deadline: 3/15; applicants required to submit FAFSA. *Faculty research:* Child welfare, occupational social work, homelessness, community organization, multiculturalism. • Dr. Geoffrey Greif, Associate Dean, 410-706-3567. Application contact: Dr. Rivkah Lambert, Assistant Dean for Admissions, 410-706-7922. Fax: 410-706-6046. E-mail: socwork_info@ssw02.ab.umd.edu.

See in-depth description on page 1957.

University of Michigan, School of Social Work, Ann Arbor, MI 48109. Awards MSW, PhD, MSW/MBA, MSW/MPH, MSW/MPP, MSW/MUP. One or more programs accredited by CSWE. PhD offered through the Horace H. Rackham School of Graduate Studies. Terminal master's awarded for partial completion of doctoral program. *Degree requirements:* For doctorate, oral defense of dissertation, preliminary exam. *Entrance requirements:* For doctorate, GRE General Test. Application fee: $50. *Financial aid:* Fellowships, research assistantships, teaching assistantships, full and partial tuition waivers, Federal Work-Study, and career-related internships or fieldwork available. Aid available to part-time students. Financial aid applicants required to submit FAFSA. • Paula Allen-Meares, Dean, 734-764-5347. Fax: 734-764-9954. E-mail: pameares@umich.edu. Application contact: Clarita Mays, Assistant Dean of Student and Multicultural Affairs, 734-764-3309. Fax: 734-936-1961. E-mail: clarita@umich.edu.

See in-depth description on page 1959.

University of Minnesota, Duluth, Graduate School, College of Education and Human Service Professions, Department of Social Work, Duluth, MN 55812-2496. Awards MSW. Accredited by CSWE. Part-time programs available. Faculty: 6 full-time (2 women), 3 part-time (2 women), 7 FTE. Students: 38 full-time (31 women), 37 part-time (28 women); includes 5 minority (1 African American, 4 Native Americans). Average age 35. 80 applicants, 61% accepted. In 1997, 30 degrees awarded. *Entrance requirements:* Minimum GPA of 3.0. Application deadline: 2/2. Application fee: $40 ($50 for international students). *Expenses:* Tuition $5130 per year full-time, $299 per credit part-time for state residents; $10,074 per year full-time, $536 per credit part-time for nonresidents. Fees $612 per year full-time, $76 per quarter part-time. *Financial aid:* In 1997–98, 27 students received aid, including 22 fellowships (10 to first-year students) totaling $35,000, 1 research assistantship totaling $5,200, 4 teaching assistantships (all to first-year students) totaling $26,000; full and partial tuition waivers, Federal Work-Study, institutionally sponsored loans, and career-related internships or fieldwork also available. Aid available to part-time students. Financial aid application deadline: 2/2. *Faculty research:* Domestic abuse, substance abuse, minority health, child welfare. Total annual research expenditures: $63,895. • Dr. Melanie Shepard, Head/Director, 218-726-7245. E-mail: mshepard@d.umn.edu. Application contact: Dr. Joyce Kramer, Director of Graduate Studies, 218-726-8865. Fax: 218-726-7073. E-mail: jkramer@d.umn.edu.

University of Minnesota, Twin Cities Campus, College of Human Ecology, School of Social Work, Minneapolis, MN 55455-0213. Awards MSW, PhD, MSW/MPH, MSW/MPP. One or more programs accredited by CSWE. Part-time and evening/weekend programs available. Postbaccalaureate distance learning degree programs offered. Faculty: 41 full-time (24 women), 12 part-time (8 women). Students: 137 full-time (108 women), 137 part-time (100 women); includes 59 minority (27 African Americans, 17 Asian Americans, 6 Hispanics, 9 Native Americans), 10 international. Average age 34. 350 applicants, 35% accepted. In 1997, 92 master's awarded; 3 doctorates awarded (67% entered university research/teaching, 33% found other work related to degree). *Degree requirements:* For doctorate, dissertation required, foreign language not required. *Average time to degree:* master's–2 years full-time, 4 years part-time; doctorate–4 years full-time, 7 years part-time. *Entrance requirements:* For master's, minimum GPA of 3.0, 1 year of work experience; for doctorate, GRE, minimum GPA of 3.0, MSW. Application deadline: 1/15. Application fee: $40 ($50 for international students). *Financial aid:* In 1997–98, 142 students received aid, including 57 fellowships, 5 research assistantships, 14 teaching assistantships; full and partial tuition waivers, Federal Work-Study, institutionally sponsored loans, and career-related internships or fieldwork also available. Aid available to part-time students. Financial aid applicants required to submit FAFSA. *Faculty research:* Child welfare, child sexual abuse, domestic violence, long-term care, community health. Total annual research expenditures: $2.887 million. • Jean Quam, Director, 612-624-4882. Application contact: Megan Morrissey, Director of Admissions, 612-624-1096. Fax: 612-626-0395. E-mail: mmorri@che2.che.umn.edu.

University of Missouri–Columbia, College of Human Environmental Science, Department of Social Work, Columbia, MO 65211. Awards MSW. Accredited by CSWE. Part-time programs available. Faculty: 15 full-time (8 women). Students: 93 full-time (80 women), 11 part-time (8 women); includes 9 minority (4 African Americans, 1 Asian American, 2 Hispanics, 2 Native Americans). In 1997, 55 degrees awarded. *Entrance requirements:* GRE General Test, minimum GPA of 3.0. Application deadline: 2/1 (priority date; rolling processing). Application fee: $25 ($50 for international students). *Expenses:* Tuition $3240 per year full-time, $180 per credit hour part-time for state residents; $9108 per year full-time, $506 per credit hour part-time for nonresidents. Fees $55 per year full-time. *Financial aid:* Fellowships, Federal Work-Study available. Aid available to part-time students. • Dr. Joseph Chandy, Director of Graduate Studies, 573-882-6208.

University of Missouri–St. Louis, Program in Gerontology, St. Louis, MO 63121-4499. Offerings include gerontological social work (Certificate). Program faculty: 3 (2 women). *Application deadline:* 7/1 (priority date; rolling processing; 12/1 for spring admission). *Application fee:* $0. Electronic applications accepted. *Expenses:* Tuition $3903 per year full-time, $167 per credit hour part-time for state residents; $11,745 per year full-time, $489 per credit hour part-time for nonresidents. Fees $816 per year full-time, $34 per credit hour part-time. • Dr. Robert Calsyn, Director, 314-516-5421. Application contact: Graduate Admissions, 314-516-5458. Fax: 314-516-6759. E-mail: gradadm@umslvma.umsl.edu.

University of Nebraska at Omaha, College of Public Affairs and Community Service, School of Social Work, Omaha, NE 68182. Awards MSW. Accredited by CSWE. Faculty: 7 full-time (5 women), 1 part-time (0 women). Students: 125 full-time (99 women), 70 part-time (61 women); includes 7 minority (4 African Americans, 2 Hispanics, 1 Native American). Average age 34. 137 applicants, 49% accepted. In 1997, 89 degrees awarded. *Degree requirements:* Comprehensive exam required, foreign language and thesis not required. *Entrance requirements:* GRE General Test or MAT, minimum GPA of 3.0. Application deadline: 3/1 (priority date; rolling processing; 10/1 for spring admission). Application fee: $35. *Expenses:* Tuition $1670 per year full-time, $94 per credit hour part-time for state residents; $4082 per year full-time, $227 per credit hour part-time for nonresidents. Fees $302 per year full-time, $108 per semester (minimum) part-time. *Financial aid:* In 1997–98, 110 students received aid, including 4 research assistantships; fellowships, full tuition waivers, Federal Work-Study, institutionally sponsored loans, and career-related internships or fieldwork also available. Aid available to part-time students. Financial aid application deadline: 3/1; applicants required to submit FAFSA. • Dr. Sunny Andrews, Director, 402-554-2791.

University of Nevada, Las Vegas, Greenspun College of Urban Affairs, School of Social Work, Las Vegas, NV 89154-9900. Awards MSW. Accredited by CSWE. Faculty: 11 full-time (3 women). Students: 31 full-time (22 women), 15 part-time (10 women); includes 7 minority (1 African American, 2 Asian Americans, 3 Hispanics, 1 Native American). 103 applicants, 37% accepted. In 1997, 36 degrees awarded. *Degree requirements:* Thesis or alternative, comprehensive exam required, foreign language not required. *Entrance requirements:* GRE General Test, minimum GPA of 3.0 during previous 2 years, 2.75 overall. Application deadline: 2/15. Application fee: $40 ($95 for international students). *Expenses:* Tuition $93 per credit for state residents; $93 per credit full-time, $190 per credit part-time for nonresidents. Fees $5570 per year full-time for nonresidents. *Financial aid:* In 1997–98, 3 teaching assistantships were awarded; research assistantships also available. Financial aid application deadline: 3/1. • Dr. Leroy Pelton, Director, 702-895-3311. Application contact: Graduate Coordinator, 702-895-3311.

University of Nevada, Reno, College of Human and Community Sciences, Department of Social Work, Reno, NV 89557. Awards MSW. Accredited by CSWE. Part-time and evening/weekend programs available. Faculty: 8 (6 women). Students: 28 full-time (21 women), 2 part-time (both women); includes 4 minority (2 African Americans, 1 Asian American, 1 Hispanic). Average age 32. 59 applicants, 44% accepted. In 1997, 20 degrees awarded. *Degree requirements:* Thesis optional, foreign language not required. *Entrance requirements:* GRE General Test, TOEFL (minimum score 500), minimum GPA of 2.75. Application deadline: 2/1 (priority date; rolling processing). Application fee: $40. *Expenses:* Tuition $0 for state residents; $5770 per year full-time, $200 per credit part-time for nonresidents. Fees $93 per credit. *Financial aid:* Research assistantships, teaching assistantships, full tuition waivers, institutionally sponsored loans available. Financial aid application deadline: 3/1. *Faculty research:* Policy practice, poverty, women's issues, race and diversity, vulnerable family. • Dr. Dean Pierce, Chair, 702-784-6542. Application contact: Dr. Susan K. Chandler, Director of Graduate Studies, 702-784-6542. E-mail: chandler@scs.unr.edu.

University of New England, College of Health Professions, Program in Social Work, Biddeford, ME 04005-9526. Awards MSW. Accredited by CSWE. Part-time programs available. Faculty: 12 full-time (7 women). Students: 123 full-time (99 women), 52 part-time (42 women); includes 1 minority (Asian American). Average age 36. 199 applicants, 60% accepted. In 1997, 64 degrees awarded (100% found work related to degree). *Average time to degree:* master's–2 years full-time, 3.5 years part-time. *Application deadline:* 1/15 (rolling processing). *Application fee:* $40. *Expenses:* Tuition $335 per credit. Fees $230 per year. *Financial aid:* Federal Work-Study and career-related internships or fieldwork available. Aid available to part-time students. Financial aid application deadline: 5/1; applicants required to submit FAFSA. *Faculty research:* Domestic violence, solution focused practice, empowerment models. • Dr. Stephen Rose, Director, 207-283-0171 Ext. 2512. Fax: 207-284-7633. Application contact: Patricia T. Cribby, Dean of Admissions and Enrollment Management, 207-283-0171 Ext. 2297. Fax: 207-286-3678. E-mail: jshea@mailbox.une.edu.

See in-depth description on page 1961.

University of New Hampshire, School of Health and Human Services, Department of Social Work, Durham, NH 03824. Awards MSW. Accredited by CSWE. Faculty: 3 full-time. Students: 70 full-time (58 women), 65 part-time (54 women); includes 2 minority (1 African American, 1 Asian American). Average age 37. 142 applicants, 56% accepted. In 1997, 27 degrees awarded. *Application deadline:* 2/1 (rolling processing). *Application fee:* $50. *Expenses:* Tuition $5440 per year full-time, $302 per credit hour part-time for state residents; $8160 per year (minimum) full-time, $453 per credit hour (minimum) part-time for nonresidents. Fees $868 per year full-time, $15 per year part-time. *Financial aid:* In 1997–98, 1 fellowship, 5 teaching assistantships were awarded; research assistantships, scholarships also available. Financial aid application deadline: 2/15. • Dr. Robert Jolley, Chairperson, 603-862-1799.

The University of North Carolina at Chapel Hill, School of Social Work, Chapel Hill, NC 27599. Awards MSW, Certificate, JD/MSW. One or more programs accredited by CSWE. Part-time programs available. Faculty: 42 full-time, 5 part-time. Students: 190 full-time (146 women), 51 part-time (41 women); includes 39 minority (24 African Americans, 7 Asian Americans, 6 Hispanics, 2 Native Americans), 2 international. 501 applicants, 27% accepted. In 1997, 90 master's awarded. *Degree requirements:* For master's, comprehensive exam required, foreign language and thesis not required. *Entrance requirements:* For master's, GRE General Test (minimum combined score of 1000), minimum GPA of 3.0. Application deadline: 1/1 (priority date; rolling processing). Application fee: $55. *Expenses:* Tuition $1428 per year full-time, $357 per semester (minimum) part-time for state residents; $10,414 per year full-time, $2604 per semester (minimum) part-time for nonresidents. Fees $782 per year full-time, $332 per semester (minimum) part-time. *Financial aid:* In 1997–98, 29 research assistantships, 2 teaching assistantships, 8 graduate assistantships were awarded; fellowships also available. Financial aid application deadline: 3/1. • Dr. Richard Edwards, Dean, 919-962-1225.

University of North Carolina at Greensboro, School of Human Environmental Sciences, Department of Social Work, Greensboro, NC 27412-0001. Awards MSW. Offered jointly with North Carolina Agricultural and Technical University. Faculty: 7 full-time (4 women). Students: 18 full-time (16 women); includes 3 minority (all African Americans). 69 applicants, 41% accepted. *Entrance requirements:* GRE General Test. Application fee: $35. *Expenses:* Tuition $1842 per year full-time, $370 per semester (minimum) part-time for state residents; $10,296 per year full-time, $2484 per semester (minimum) part-time for nonresidents. Fees $806 per year full-time, $111 per semester (minimum) part-time. *Financial aid:* In 1997–98, 2 research assistantships totaling $8,000 were awarded; fellowships also available. • Dr. Thomas Scullion, Chair, 336-334-5147.

University of North Dakota, College of Education and Human Development, School of Social Work, Grand Forks, ND 58202. Awards MSW. Accredited by CSWE. Faculty: 10 full-time (5 women). Students: 26 full-time (17 women), 6 part-time (5 women). 39 applicants, 46% accepted. In 1997, 16 degrees awarded. *Degree requirements:* Thesis or alternative required, foreign language not required. *Entrance requirements:* TOEFL (minimum score 550), minimum GPA of 3.0. Application deadline: 2/1. Application fee: $20. *Financial aid:* In 1997–98, 4 students received aid, including 2 fellowships totaling $4,800, 2 teaching assistantships total-

Directory: Social Work

University of North Dakota (continued)

ing $7,250; research assistantships, assistantships, full and partial tuition waivers also available. Financial aid application deadline: 3/15. *Faculty research:* Mental health, gerontology, chemical abuse, children and families. • Dr. Ralph Woehle, Director, 701-777-2669. Fax: 701-777-4257. E-mail: ralph_woehle@mail.und.nodak.edu.

University of Oklahoma, College of Arts and Sciences, School of Social Work, Norman, OK 73019-0390. Awards MSW. Accredited by CSWE. Faculty: 13 full-time (5 women), 7 part-time (4 women). Students: 78 full-time (67 women), 3 part-time (all women); includes 15 minority (8 African Americans, 4 Hispanics, 3 Native Americans), 1 international. Average age 35. 225 applicants, 37% accepted. In 1997, 74 degrees awarded. *Entrance requirements:* GRE, TOEFL (minimum score 550). Application deadline: 3/15. Application fee: $25. *Expenses:* Tuition $1920 per year full-time, $80 per credit hour part-time for state residents; $6108 per year full-time, $255 per credit hour part-time for nonresidents. Fees $468 per year full-time, $12 per semester (minimum) part-time. *Financial aid:* In 1997–98, 1 research assistantship, 3 teaching assistantships were awarded; partial tuition waivers, institutionally sponsored loans, and career-related internships or fieldwork also available. Aid available to part-time students. Financial aid application deadline: 3/1. *Faculty research:* Job effectiveness, practice, child welfare, aging, mental health. Total annual research expenditures: $150,000. • Dr. Julia M. Norlin, Director, 405-325-2821. Application contact: Dr. Wayne Chess, Graduate Coordinator, 405-325-2821.

University of Ottawa, Faculty of Social Sciences, School of Social Work, Ottawa, ON K1N 6N5, Canada. Awards MSW. Program offered in French. Faculty: 4 full-time. Students: 48 full-time (40 women), 12 part-time (all women). Average age 31. In 1997, 12 degrees awarded. *Degree requirements:* Thesis or alternative, internship required, foreign language not required. *Entrance requirements:* Honors degree or equivalent, minimum B average. Application fee: $60. *Expenses:* Tuition $4677 per year for Canadian residents; $9900 per year for nonresidents. Fees $230 per year. *Financial aid:* Teaching assistantships, Federal Work-Study available. • Roland Lecomte, Director, 613-562-5494. Application contact: Suzanne Gauthier, Administrative Assistant, 613-562-5800 Ext. 6384. Fax: 613-562-5495.

University of Pennsylvania, School of Social Work, Graduate Group on Social Welfare, Philadelphia, PA 19104. Awards PhD. Faculty: 29 full-time (12 women). Students: 15 full-time (12 women), 38 part-time (26 women); includes 13 minority (7 African Americans, 4 Asian Americans, 2 Hispanics), 3 international. Average age 31. 44 applicants, 23% accepted. In 1997, 5 doctorates awarded (60% entered university research/teaching, 40% found other work related to degree). Terminal master's awarded for partial completion of doctoral program. *Degree requirements:* For doctorate, dissertation required, foreign language not required. *Average time to degree:* doctorate–4 years full-time. *Entrance requirements:* For doctorate, GRE General Test (minimum combined score of 1000; average 1200), TOEFL (minimum score 600), MSW or master's degree in related field. Application deadline: 1/15 (rolling processing). Application fee: $65. Electronic applications accepted. *Financial aid:* In 1997–98, 18 students received aid, including 3 fellowships (2 to first-year students) averaging $1,400 per month, 18 research assistantships (10 to first-year students) averaging $1,160 per month; teaching assistantships, institutionally sponsored loans, and career-related internships or fieldwork also available. Financial aid application deadline: 3/15; applicants required to submit FAFSA. *Faculty research:* Mental health, child welfare, organizational behavior, urban poverty, comparative social welfare. • Dr. Michael Reisch, Doctoral Chair, 215-898-5550. Application contact: Nicole Gant, Department Receptionist, 215-898-5512. Fax: 215-573-2099. E-mail: admission@caster.ssw.upenn.edu.

Announcement: The interdisciplinary PhD program offers students a way to prepare themselves for a wide range of careers in research on significant social problems. Students are free to develop an individualized study plan that combines courses at the School of Social Work with those taken in the other departments and professional schools of the University.

See in-depth description on page 1963.

University of Pennsylvania, School of Social Work, Program in Social Work, Philadelphia, PA 19104. Awards MSW, JD/MSW, MSW/PhD, MSW/Certificate, MSW/MBA, MSW/MCP, MSW/MS Ed. Accredited by CSWE. MSW/Certificate (Lutheran social ministry) offered jointly with Lutheran Theological Seminary at Philadelphia; MSW/Certificate (Catholic social ministry) offered jointly with St. Charles Borromeo Seminary; MSW/Certificate (Jewish communal services) offered jointly with Gratz College. Students: 340. In 1997, 155 degrees awarded. *Degree requirements:* Fieldwork required, foreign language and thesis not required. *Entrance requirements:* TOEFL. Application deadline: 3/15. Application fee: $65. *Financial aid:* Fellowships, scholarships, Federal Work-Study available. Aid available to part-time students. Financial aid application deadline: 3/15. • Application contact: Orneice Dorsey Leslie, Director of Admissions, 215-898-5521. Fax: 215-573-2099. E-mail: admission@ssw.upenn.edu.

See in-depth description on page 1963.

University of Pittsburgh, School of Social Work, Program in Social Work, Pittsburgh, PA 15260. Awards MSW, PhD, MPA/MSW, MPIA/MSW, MSW/MAJCS, MSW/M Div, MURP/MSW, PhD/MPH. One or more programs accredited by CSWE. MSW/M Div offered jointly with the Pittsburgh Theological Seminary; MSW/MAJCS offered jointly with the Hebrew Union College–Jewish Institute of Religion. Part-time programs available. Postbaccalaureate distance learning degree programs offered (no on-campus study). Faculty: 23 full-time (13 women), 23 part-time (19 women). Students: 217 full-time (176 women), 98 part-time (73 women); includes 46 minority (36 African Americans, 5 Asian Americans, 5 Hispanics), 4 international. 538 applicants, 38% accepted. In 1997, 189 master's, 17 doctorates awarded. *Degree requirements:* For master's, comprehensive exam, practicum required, foreign language and thesis not required; for doctorate, dissertation, comprehensive exam required, foreign language not required. *Average time to degree:* master's–2 years full-time, 3.7 years part-time; doctorate–4 years full-time, 8 years part-time. *Entrance requirements:* For master's, minimum QPA of 3.0, previous course work in descriptive statistics and human biology; for doctorate, MSW or related degree. Application deadline: 3/31 (rolling processing). Application fee: $30 ($40 for international students). *Expenses:* Tuition $8018 per year full-time, $329 per credit part-time for state residents; $16,508 per year full-time, $680 per credit part-time for nonresidents. Fees $480 per year full-time, $180 per year part-time. *Financial aid:* In 1997–98, 124 students received aid, including 1 research assistantship (to a first-year student) averaging $1,286 per month, 10 teaching assistantships averaging $1,286 per month and totaling $42,423, 92 graduate assistantships, scholarships (37 to first-year students) averaging $1,349 per month and totaling $620,649; Federal Work-Study, institutionally sponsored loans, and career-related internships or fieldwork also available. Financial aid application deadline: 6/1; applicants required to submit FAFSA. *Faculty research:* Chronic mental health issues; child abuse and neglect; family preservation; poverty, race relations, and community empowerment; program evaluation. Total annual research expenditures: $3.515 million. • Application contact: Dr. Grady H. Roberts Jr., Assistant Dean of Admissions, 412-624-6346. Fax: 412-624-6323.

University of Puerto Rico, Río Piedras, College of Social Sciences, Beatriz Lassalle Graduate School of Social Work, San Juan, PR 00931. Awards MSW. Accredited by CSWE. *Degree requirements:* Thesis, comprehensive exam required, foreign language not required. *Entrance requirements:* PAEG, interview, minimum GPA of 3.0. Application deadline: 2/21. Application fee: $17. *Faculty research:* Stressful life events, sexual education, self-esteem, aging population, community social work.

University of Regina, Faculty of Graduate Studies and Research, Faculty of Social Work, Regina, SK S4S 0A2, Canada. Awards MSW. Faculty: 18 full-time (7 women), 3 part-time. Students: 17 full-time, 49 part-time; includes 1 international. 71 applicants, 35% accepted. In 1997, 3 degrees awarded. *Degree requirements:* Thesis optional, foreign language not required. *Entrance requirements:* TOEFL (minimum score 580), BSW or equivalent. Application deadline: 2/15. Application fee: $0. *Tuition:* $196 per credit for Canadian residents; $383 per credit for nonresidents. *Financial aid:* In 1997–98, fellowships averaging $1,131 per month, research assistantships averaging $1,000 per month, 5 teaching assistantships averaging $880 per month, 6 scholarships averaging $750 per month were awarded; career-related internships or fieldwork also available. Financial aid application deadline: 6/15. *Faculty research:* Social research, social planning, social policy implementation, policy planning, social administration. • Dr. Sharon McKay, Dean, 306-585-4563. E-mail: swprgrm@max.cc.uregina.ca. Application contact: Dr. Doug Durst, Program Coordinator, 306-585-4577. Fax: 306-585-4872. E-mail: doug.durst@uregina.ca.

University of St. Thomas, Program in Social Work, St. Paul, MN 55105-1096. Awards MSW. Offered jointly with the College of St. Catherine. Part-time and evening/weekend programs available. Faculty: 8 full-time (5 women), 4 part-time (3 women). Students: 105 full-time (86 women), 51 part-time (46 women); includes 6 minority (4 African Americans, 1 Asian American, 1 Hispanic). Average age 33. 178 applicants, 51% accepted. In 1997, 77 degrees awarded. *Degree requirements:* Thesis, fieldwork required, foreign language not required. *Entrance requirements:* Previous course work in developmental psychology, human biology, and research methods. Application deadline: 1/10. Application fee: $30. *Tuition:* $414 per credit hour. *Financial aid:* In 1997–98, 6 research assistantships (all to first-year students) totaling $7,500, 5 grants (4 to first-year students) totaling $8,910 were awarded; fellowships, teaching assistantships, Federal Work-Study, and career-related internships or fieldwork also available. Aid available to part-time students. Financial aid application deadline: 4/1. • Dr. Barbara W. Shank, Dean/Department Chair, 612-962-5801. Application contact: Melanie Guentzel, Coordinator of Student Services, 612-962-5810. Fax: 612-962-5819. E-mail: mjguentzel@stthomas.edu.

University of South Carolina, Graduate School, College of Social Work, Columbia, SC 29208. Awards MSW, PhD, MSW/MPA, MSW/MPH. One or more programs accredited by CSWE. Faculty: 23 full-time (10 women), 26 part-time (17 women). Students: 374 full-time (322 women), 136 part-time (121 women); includes 99 minority (87 African Americans, 5 Asian Americans, 7 Hispanics), 32 international. Average age 33. 841 applicants, 33% accepted. In 1997, 189 master's, 5 doctorates awarded. *Degree requirements:* For master's, computer language required, foreign language and thesis not required; for doctorate, computer language, dissertation required, foreign language not required. *Entrance requirements:* For master's, minimum undergraduate GPA of 3.0. Application deadline: 3/1. Application fee: $35. Electronic applications accepted. *Expenses:* Tuition $4480 per year full-time, $220 per credit hour part-time for state residents; $9338 per year full-time, $457 per credit hour part-time for nonresidents. Fees $125 per year full-time, $37 per semester (minimum) part-time. *Financial aid:* In 1997–98, 191 students received aid, including 3 fellowships (2 to first-year students), 68 research assistantships (30 to first-year students); teaching assistantships, Federal Work-Study, institutionally sponsored loans, and career-related internships or fieldwork also available. Financial aid application deadline: 5/1. *Faculty research:* Child welfare, gerontology, mental health, health. • Dr. Frank B. Raymond III, Dean, 803-777-4886. Application contact: Dr. John T. Gandy, Associate Dean, 803-777-5190. Fax: 803-777-3498.

University of Southern California, Graduate School, School of Social Work, Los Angeles, CA 90089. Awards MSW, PhD, JD/MSW, MPA/MSW, M Pl/MSW, MSW/MAJCS, MSW/MS. One or more programs accredited by CSWE. MSW/MAJCS offered jointly with Hebrew Union College–Jewish Institute of Religion. Students: 381 full-time (334 women), 130 part-time (115 women); includes 171 minority (68 African Americans, 55 Asian Americans, 43 Hispanics, 5 Native Americans), 5 international. Average age 36. 620 applicants, 62% accepted. In 1997, 179 master's, 4 doctorates awarded. *Degree requirements:* For doctorate, dissertation. *Entrance requirements:* For doctorate, GRE General Test. Application deadline: 4/1 (priority date). Application fee: $55. *Expenses:* Tuition $16,944 per year full-time, $706 per unit part-time. Fees $414 per year full-time, $32 per year part-time. *Financial aid:* In 1997–98, 213 fellowships, 3 research assistantships, 4 teaching assistantships, 129 scholarships were awarded; Federal Work-Study, institutionally sponsored loans also available. Aid available to part-time students. Financial aid application deadline: 2/15; applicants required to submit FAFSA. • Dr. Marilyn L. Flynn, Dean, 213-740-8311.

University of Southern Indiana, Graduate Studies, School of Education and Human Services, Department of Social Work, Evansville, IN 47712-3590. Awards MSW. Accredited by CSWE. Part-time and evening/weekend programs available. Faculty: 8 full-time (4 women), 3 part-time (1 woman). Students: 47 full-time (35 women), 39 part-time (31 women); includes 4 minority (2 African Americans, 2 Hispanics). Average age 34. 86 applicants, 67% accepted. In 1997, 38 degrees awarded. *Entrance requirements:* Minimum GPA of 2.8. Application deadline: 3/1. Application fee: $25. *Tuition:* $129 per credit hour for state residents; $260 per credit hour for nonresidents. • David C. Cousert, Director, 812-464-1843. E-mail: dccouser.ucs@smtp.usi.edu.

University of Southern Mississippi, College of Health and Human Sciences, School of Social Work, Hattiesburg, MS 39406-5167. Awards MSW. Accredited by CSWE. Part-time programs available. Faculty: 11 full-time (7 women). Students: 87 full-time (76 women), 27 part-time (24 women); includes 22 minority (19 African Americans, 3 Hispanics). Average age 32. 145 applicants, 52% accepted. In 1997, 56 degrees awarded. *Degree requirements:* Practicum required, foreign language and thesis not required. *Entrance requirements:* GRE General Test, minimum GPA of 2.75. Application deadline: 8/9 (priority date; rolling processing). Application fee: $0 ($25 for international students). *Tuition:* $2870 per year full-time, $137 per credit hour part-time for state residents; $5972 per year full-time, $172 per credit hour part-time for nonresidents. *Financial aid:* Teaching assistantships, scholarships, Federal Work-Study, and career-related internships or fieldwork available. Financial aid application deadline: 3/15. • Dr. Earlie Washington, Director, 601-266-4163. Application contact: Dr. Tim Rehner, Coordinator of Admissions, 601-266-4163.

University of South Florida, College of Arts and Sciences, School of Social Work, Tampa, FL 33620-9951. Awards MSW. Accredited by CSWE. Part-time and evening/weekend programs available. Faculty: 9 full-time (5 women). Students: 109 full-time (95 women), 33 part-time (24 women); includes 20 minority (11 African Americans, 1 Asian American, 8 Hispanics). Average age 37. 117 applicants, 51% accepted. In 1997, 29 degrees awarded. *Degree requirements:* Comprehensive exam required, foreign language and thesis not required. *Entrance requirements:* GRE General Test (minimum combined score of 1000), minimum GPA of 3.0 in last 60 hours, 1 year of work experience in social work and related fields. Application deadline: 1/15 (6/1 for spring admission). Application fee: $20. Electronic applications accepted. *Tuition:* $142 per credit hour for state residents; $486 per credit hour for nonresidents. *Financial aid:* In 1997–98, 82 students received aid, including 3 fellowships averaging $700 per month and totaling $19,000, 15 research assistantships averaging $185 per month and totaling $23,000; Federal Work-Study, institutionally sponsored loans also available. Aid available to part-time students. Financial aid applicants required to submit FAFSA. *Faculty research:* Posttraumatic stress disorder, substance abuse among social work, breast cancer telephone support groups, social service organization change. • Jean Amuso, Director, 813-974-1362. E-mail: amuso@luna.ras.usf.edu. Application contact: Aaron A. Smith, Graduate Chair, 813-974-1372. Fax: 813-974-4675. E-mail: asmith@luna.cas.usf.edu.

University of Tennessee, Knoxville, College of Social Work, Knoxville, TN 37996. Offers programs in clinical social work practice (MSSW), management and community practice (MSSW), social work (PhD). One or more programs accredited by CSWE. Part-time programs available. Faculty: 33 full-time (19 women). Students: 279 full-time (239 women), 119 part-time (94 women); includes 51 minority (44 African Americans, 2 Asian Americans, 3 Hispanics, 2 Native Americans), 2 international. 470 applicants, 38% accepted. In 1997, 168 master's, 4 doctorates awarded. *Degree requirements:* For master's, thesis or alternative required, foreign language not required; for doctorate, dissertation required, foreign language not required. *Entrance requirements:* GRE General Test, TOEFL (minimum score 550), minimum GPA of 2.7. Application deadline: 2/1 (priority date; rolling processing). Application fee: $35. Electronic applications accepted. *Tuition:* $3354 per year full-time, $181 per semester hour part-time for state residents; $8410 per year full-time, $462 per semester hour part-time for nonresidents. *Financial aid:* In 1997–98, 5 fellowships, 2 teaching assistantships, 19 graduate assistantships were awarded; research assistantships, Federal Work-Study, institutionally sponsored loans, and career-related internships or fieldwork also available. Financial aid application deadline: 2/1. • Dr. Karen Sowers-Hoag, Dean, 423-974-3175. Fax: 423-974-4803. E-mail: kmsowers@utk.edu.

The University of Texas at Arlington, School of Social Work, Arlington, TX 76019-0407. Awards MSSW, PhD, MSSW/MA. One or more programs accredited by CSWE. Faculty: 25 full-time (12 women), 1 (woman) part-time. Students: 375 full-time (310 women), 280 part-time (239 women); includes 151 minority (81 African Americans, 18 Asian Americans, 46 Hispanics, 6 Native Americans), 4 international. 442 applicants, 61% accepted. In 1997, 234 master's, 7 doctorates awarded. *Degree requirements:* For master's, thesis or alternative; for doctorate, dissertation required, foreign language not required. *Entrance requirements:* For master's, TOEFL (minimum score 550); for doctorate, TOEFL (minimum score 550), minimum graduate GPA of 3.4. Application fee: $25 ($50 for international students). *Tuition:* $3206 per year full-time, $468 per semester (minimum) part-time for state residents; $8612 per year full-time, $1137 per semester (minimum) part-time for nonresidents. *Financial aid:* Research assistantships, teaching assistantships, Federal Work-Study, institutionally sponsored loans, and career-related internships or fieldwork available. • Dr. Santos Hernandez, Dean, 817-272-3181. Application contact: Marjie Barret, Graduate Adviser, 817-272-3181.

Announcement: The School of Social Work offers BSW, MSSW, and PhD programs. The BSW program prepares generalist practitioners. The MSSW trains clinical, administrative, and community practitioners. Advanced standing may be granted to BSW graduates from accredited schools. The PhD program is research based and offers clinical and administrative specialties.

The University of Texas at Austin, Graduate School, School of Social Work, Austin, TX 78712. Awards MSSW, PhD. One or more programs accredited by CSWE. Students: 275 full-time (234 women), 70 part-time (58 women); includes 49 minority (7 African Americans, 3 Asian Americans, 38 Hispanics, 1 Native American), 9 international. Average age 28. 329 applicants, 61% accepted. In 1997, 104 master's, 6 doctorates awarded. *Degree requirements:* For doctorate, dissertation. *Average time to degree:* master's–2 years full-time, 3 years part-time; doctorate–3 years full-time, 5 years part-time. *Entrance requirements:* GRE General Test (minimum combined score of 1000). Application deadline: 2/1 (priority date; rolling processing; 2/1 for spring admission). Application fee: $50 ($75 for international students). *Expenses:* Tuition $2592 per year full-time, $324 per semester (minimum) part-time for state residents; $7704 per year full-time, $963 per semester (minimum) part-time for nonresidents. Fees $778 per year full-time, $161 per semester (minimum) part-time. *Financial aid:* Fellowships, Federal Work-Study, institutionally sponsored loans, and career-related internships or fieldwork available. Financial aid application deadline: 2/1; applicants required to submit FAFSA. • Dr. Barbara White, Dean, 512-471-1937. Application contact: Dorothy Van Soest, Graduate Adviser, 512-471-9245.

The University of Texas–Pan American, College of Health and Human Services, Department of Social Work, Edinburg, TX 78539-2999. Awards MSSW. Candidate for accreditation by CSWE. Program new for fall 1998. Part-time programs available. *Tuition:* $2156 per year full-time, $283 per semester (minimum) part-time for state residents; $6788 per year full-time, $862 per semester (minimum) part-time for nonresidents. • Dr. J. Patrick Mace, Chair, 956-381-3575. Fax: 956-381-3516. E-mail: jpmace@panam.edu.

University of Toronto, School of Graduate Studies, Social Sciences Division, Faculty of Social Work, Toronto, ON M5S 1A1, Canada. Awards MSW, PhD, LL B/MSW. Part-time programs available. Faculty: 56. Students: 262 full-time (212 women), 38 part-time (29 women); includes 4 international. 559 applicants, 35% accepted. In 1997, 145 master's, 4 doctorates awarded. *Degree requirements:* For doctorate, dissertation. *Application fee:* $75. *Expenses:* Tuition $4070 per year for Canadian residents; $7870 per year for nonresidents. Fees $628 per year. *Financial aid:* Career-related internships or fieldwork available. • W. Shera, Dean, 416-978-3258. Application contact: Secretary, 416-978-3257. Fax: 416-978-7072. E-mail: umbrello@fsw.utoronto.ca.

University of Utah, Graduate School of Social Work, Salt Lake City, UT 84112-1107. Awards MSW, PhD, MPA/PhD. One or more programs accredited by CSWE. Part-time programs available. Faculty: 19 full-time (9 women), 376 part-time (205 women). Students: 234 full-time (149 women), 32 part-time (24 women); includes 42 minority (3 African Americans, 9 Asian Americans, 10 Hispanics, 20 Native Americans), 3 international. Average age 35. In 1997, 79 master's, 5 doctorates awarded. *Degree requirements:* For master's, thesis or alternative required, foreign language not required; for doctorate, dissertation, comprehensive exam required, foreign language not required. *Entrance requirements:* For master's, TOEFL (minimum score 500), GRE General Test, MAT, or minimum GPA of 3.0; for doctorate, GRE, TOEFL (minimum score 500). Application deadline: 3/15. Application fee: $30 ($50 for international students). *Tuition:* $2045 per year full-time, $562 per semester (minimum) part-time for state residents; $6129 per year full-time, $1607 per semester (minimum) part-time for nonresidents. *Financial aid:* In 1997–98, 2 teaching assistantships were awarded; fellowships, Federal Work-Study, institutionally sponsored loans also available. Aid available to part-time students. Financial aid application deadline: 4/1. *Faculty research:* Clinical/direct practice, alcohol and drug abuse, health and mental health, gerontology. • Kay L. Dea, Dean, 801-581-6194. Fax: 801-585-3219. E-mail: kdea@socwk.utah.edu. Application contact: Au-Deane Cowley, Associate Dean, 801-581-8828. E-mail: acowley@socwk.utah.edu.

University of Vermont, College of Education and Social Services, Department of Social Work, Burlington, VT 05405-0160. Awards MSW. Accredited by CSWE. Students: 75; includes 4 minority (1 African American, 2 Asian Americans, 1 Hispanic). 114 applicants, 48% accepted. In 1997, 32 degrees awarded. *Entrance requirements:* GRE General Test, TOEFL (minimum score 550). Application deadline: 4/15 (priority date; rolling processing). Application fee: $25. *Expenses:* Tuition $302 per credit for state residents; $755 per credit for nonresidents. Fees $434 per year full-time, $46 per semester (minimum) part-time. *Financial aid:* Application deadline 3/1. • S. Witkin, Director, 802-656-8800.

University of Victoria, Faculty of Human and Social Development, Programs in Human and Social Development, Human and Social Development Multidisciplinary Program, Victoria, BC V8W 2Y2, Canada. Awards MA, MN, MSW. Part-time programs available. Faculty: 23 full-time (18 women). Students: 86 full-time (64 women), 29 part-time (26 women); includes 1 international. Average age 41. 63 applicants, 40% accepted. In 1997, 10 degrees awarded. *Degree requirements:* Thesis required, foreign language not required. *Average time to degree:* master's–2.1 years full-time. *Application deadline:* 3/15 (rolling processing). *Application fee:* $50. *Tuition:* $2080 per year full-time, $557 per semester part-time. *Financial aid:* In 1997–98, 1 fellowship (to a first-year student) totaling $11,500, 8 research assistantships (4 to first-year students) totaling $16,000 were awarded; institutionally sponsored loans also available. Financial aid application deadline: 2/15. *Faculty research:* Women's issues, public policy formation and implementation, health promotion and education, children, youth and families. • Application contact: Dr. Kathy Teghtsoonian, Graduate Adviser, 250-472-4431. Fax: 250-721-7067. E-mail: ktex@uvic.ca.

University of Washington, School of Social Work, Seattle, WA 98195. Awards MSW, PhD, MPH/MSW. One or more programs accredited by CSWE. Evening/weekend programs available. Faculty: 44 full-time (27 women), 33 part-time (17 women). Students: 245 full-time (190 women), 78 part-time (56 women); includes 91 minority (35 African Americans, 40 Asian Americans, 8 Hispanics, 8 Native Americans), 8 international. Average age 31. 484 applicants, 49% accepted. In 1997, 128 master's, 5 doctorates awarded. *Degree requirements:* For master's, thesis optional, foreign language not required; for doctorate, dissertation required, foreign language not required. *Entrance requirements:* For master's, GRE General Test, TOEFL (minimum score 580), minimum GPA of 3.0; for doctorate, master's degree, sample of scholarly work, minimum GPA of 3.0. Application deadline: 1/16 (rolling processing). Application fee: $45. *Tuition:* $5433 per year full-time, $775 per quarter (minimum) part-time for state residents; $13,479 per year full-time, $1925 per quarter (minimum) part-time for nonresidents. *Financial aid:* 188 students received aid; fellowships, research assistantships, teaching assistantships, Federal Work-Study, institutionally sponsored loans, and career-related internships or fieldwork available. Aid available to part-time students. Financial aid application deadline: 2/15; applicants required to submit FAFSA. *Faculty research:* Health and mental health; children, youth, and families; multicultural issues; social work administration. Total annual research expenditures: $3.9 million. • Nancy R. Hooyman, Dean, 206-685-1662. Application contact: John Armstrong, Director of Admissions, 206-543-5676. Fax: 206-543-1228. E-mail: armstroj@u.washington.edu.

University of Windsor, Faculty of Social Science, School of Social Work, Windsor, ON N9B 3P4, Canada. Awards MSW. Program being phased out; applicants no longer accepted. *Degree requirements:* Thesis optional. *Expenses:* Tuition $4370 per year (minimum) full-time, $345 per course (minimum) part-time for Canadian residents; $8453 per year (minimum) full-time, $915 per course (minimum) part-time for nonresidents. Fees $462 per year (minimum) full-time, $141 per year (minimum) part-time.

University of Wisconsin–La Crosse, Department of Social Work, La Crosse, WI 54601-3742. Awards MSW. MSW offered jointly with the University of Wisconsin–Milwaukee. Postbaccalaureate distance learning degree programs offered (minimal on-campus study). Faculty: 1 (woman) full-time. Students: 0. *Degree requirements:* Thesis optional, foreign language not required. *Entrance requirements:* Minimum GPA of 3.0, 21 undergraduate credits in social sciences, 1 course in human biology. Application deadline: 1/2. *Tuition:* $3737 per year full-time, $208 per credit part-time for state residents; $11,921 per year full-time, $633 per credit part-time for nonresidents. *Financial aid:* Career-related internships or fieldwork available. *Faculty research:* Social welfare, professional ethics, moral development, program evaluation. • Hope Hagar, Chair, 608-785-8479. Fax: 608-785-8486. E-mail: hagar@mail.uwlax.edu.

University of Wisconsin–Madison, College of Letters and Science, School of Social Work, Madison, WI 53706-1380. Offers programs in social welfare (PhD), social work (MSSW). One or more programs accredited by CSWE. Faculty: 25 full-time (13 women), 11 part-time (3 women), 27.97 FTE. Students: 256 full-time (230 women); includes 22 minority (5 African Americans, 10 Asian Americans, 4 Hispanics, 3 Native Americans), 14 international. Average age 29. 395 applicants, 47% accepted. *Degree requirements:* For doctorate, dissertation required, foreign language not required. *Entrance requirements:* For doctorate, GRE General Test. Application deadline: 2/1 (priority date). Application fee: $45. *Tuition:* $4928 per year full-time, $926 per semester (minimum) part-time for state residents; $15,190 per year full-time, $2849 per semester (minimum) part-time for nonresidents. *Financial aid:* Fellowships, research assistantships, teaching assistantships, project assistantships available. *Faculty research:* Poverty, caregiving, child welfare, developmental disabilities, mental health, severe mental illnesses, adolescence, family, social policy, child support. • Dr. Joan Robertson, Director, 608-263-3561. E-mail: jfrobert@facstaff.wisc.edu. Application contact: William A. Heiss, Assistant to the Director, 608-263-3660. Fax: 608-263-3836. E-mail: wmheiss@facstaff.wisc.edu.

University of Wisconsin–Milwaukee, School of Social Welfare, Program in Social Work, Milwaukee, WI 53201-0413. Awards MSW. Accredited by CSWE. Part-time programs available. Students: 194 full-time (168 women), 177 part-time (156 women); includes 41 minority (25 African Americans, 2 Asian Americans, 13 Hispanics, 1 Native American), 1 international. 438 applicants, 46% accepted. In 1997, 143 degrees awarded. *Degree requirements:* Thesis or alternative required, foreign language not required. *Application deadline:* 1/1 (priority date; rolling processing; 9/1 for spring admission). *Application fee:* $45 ($75 for international students). *Tuition:* $4996 per year full-time, $1030 per semester (minimum) part-time for state residents; $15,216 per year full-time, $2947 per semester (minimum) part-time for nonresidents. *Financial aid:* In 1997–98, 4 fellowships, 1 research assistantship, 2 teaching assistantships, 6 project assistantships were awarded; career-related internships or fieldwork also available. Aid available to part-time students. Financial aid application deadline: 4/15. • Joan Jones, Director, 414-229-6036.

University of Wyoming, College of Health Sciences, Department of Social Work, Laramie, WY 82071. Awards MSW. Candidate for accreditation by CSWE. Students: 9 full-time (7 women). 21 applicants, 24% accepted. *Degree requirements:* Thesis or alternative required, foreign language not required. *Entrance requirements:* GRE General Test (minimum combined score of 900), minimum GPA of 3.0. Application deadline: rolling. Application fee: $40. Electronic applications accepted. *Expenses:* Tuition $2430 per year full-time, $135 per credit hour part-time for state residents; $7518 per year full-time, $418 per credit hour part-time for nonresidents. Fees $386 per year full-time, $9.25 per credit hour part-time. *Financial aid:* In 1997–98, 9 students received aid, including 3 research assistantships averaging $933 per month and totaling $8,451; Federal Work-Study, institutionally sponsored loans, and career-related internships or fieldwork also available. Aid available to part-time students. Financial aid application deadline: 3/1. *Faculty research:* Social work education, child welfare, mental health, diversity, school social work, rural social work. • Pat Conway, Chair, 307-766-6113. E-mail: pconway@uwyo.edu. Application contact: Sharon Kopf, Office Associate, 307-766-5422. Fax: 307-766-6839. E-mail: sekopf@uwyo.edu.

Valdosta State University, Program in Social Work, Valdosta, GA 31698. Awards MSW. Accredited by CSWE. Faculty: 4 full-time (3 women). Students: 62 full-time (46 women), 5 part-time (3 women); includes 9 minority (7 African Americans, 1 Hispanic, 1 Native American), 2 international. 76 applicants, 64% accepted. In 1997, 29 degrees awarded. *Degree requirements:* 5 practica required, foreign language and thesis not required. *Entrance requirements:* GRE General Test (minimum combined score of 800), minimum GPA of 3.0 in last 2 years. Application deadline: 3/15 (rolling processing). Application fee: $10. *Expenses:* Tuition $2472 per year full-time, $83 per semester hour part-time for state residents; $8472 per year full-time, $333 per semester hour part-time for nonresidents. Fees $236 per year full-time. *Financial aid:* Assistantships and career-related internships or fieldwork available. • Dr. Peggy Cleveland, Director, 912-249-4864. Fax: 912-245-4341. E-mail: phclevel@grits.valdosta.peachnet.edu.

Virginia Commonwealth University, School of Social Work, Doctoral Program in Social Work, Richmond, VA 23284-9005. Awards PhD. Students: 11 full-time (8 women), 21 part-time (14 women); includes 5 minority (4 African Americans, 1 Asian American), 1 international. Average age 40. 21 applicants, 62% accepted. In 1997, 6 degrees awarded. *Degree requirements:* Computer language, dissertation, comprehensive exam required, foreign language not required. *Entrance requirements:* GRE General Test. Application deadline: 4/15 (priority date). Application fee: $30 ($0 for international students). *Tuition:* $4960 per year full-time, $257 per credit part-time for state residents; $12,652 per year full-time, $684 per credit part-time for nonresidents. *Financial aid:* Fellowships, research assistantships, teaching assistantships, full and partial tuition waivers, Federal Work-Study, institutionally sponsored loans, and career-related internships or fieldwork available. Aid available to part-time students. Financial aid application deadline: 5/1. • Application contact: Dr. Ann M. Nichols-Casebolt, Associate Dean, 804-828-0412. Fax: 804-828-0716.

Virginia Commonwealth University, School of Social Work, Master's Program in Social Work, Richmond, VA 23284-9005. Awards MSW, JD/MSW, MSW/MA. Accredited by CSWE. JD/MSW offered jointly with the University of Richmond; MSW/MA offered jointly with Union Theological Seminary and Presbyterian School of Christian Education. Students: 373 full-time (325 women), 301 part-time (270 women); includes 136 minority (103 African Americans, 6 Asian Americans, 15 Hispanics, 12 Native Americans), 2 international. Average age 31. 662 applicants, 79% accepted. In 1997, 231 degrees awarded. *Application deadline:* 2/1. *Application fee:* $30 ($0 for international students). *Tuition:* $4960 per year full-time, $257 per credit part-time for state residents; $12,652 per year full-time, $684 per credit part-time for nonresidents. *Financial aid:* Fellowships, research assistantships, teaching assistantships, full and partial tuition waivers, Federal Work-Study, institutionally sponsored loans, and career-related internships or fieldwork available. Aid available to part-time students. Financial aid application

Directory: Social Work

Virginia Commonwealth University (continued)
deadline: 3/1. • Application contact: Dr. Jaclyn Miller, Assistant Dean, 804-828-0703. Fax: 804-828-0716. E-mail: jmiller@vcu.edu.

Walla Walla College, Department of Sociology and Social Work, College Place, WA 99324-1198. Awards MSW. Accredited by CSWE. Part-time programs available. Faculty: 15 full-time (10 women), 12 part-time (8 women). Students: 121 full-time (97 women), 26 part-time (18 women); includes 16 minority (5 Asian Americans, 8 Hispanics, 3 Native Americans), 2 international. Average age 34. In 1997, 99 degrees awarded. *Entrance requirements:* Minimum GPA of 2.75. Application deadline: 7/15 (priority date; rolling processing). Application fee: $40. *Tuition:* $346 per quarter hour. *Financial aid:* Federal Work-Study and career-related internships or fieldwork available. Aid available to part-time students. Financial aid application deadline: 4/1; applicants required to submit FAFSA. • Dr. Wilma Hepker, Chair, 509-527-2273. Application contact: Dr. Joe Galusha, Dean of Graduate Studies, 509-527-2421. Fax: 509-527-2253. E-mail: galujo@wwc.edu.

Washington University in St. Louis, George Warren Brown School of Social Work, St. Louis, MO 63130-4899. Awards MSW, PhD, JD/MSW, MAJCS/MSW, M Arch/MSW, MAUD/MSW, MBA/MSW. One or more programs accredited by CSWE. MAJCS/MSW offered jointly with Hebrew Union College–Jewish Institute of Religion (California). Part-time and evening/weekend programs available. Faculty: 38 full-time (18 women), 48 part-time (30 women). Students: 398 full-time (337 women), 72 part-time (60 women); includes 78 minority (50 African Americans, 14 Asian Americans, 4 Hispanics, 10 Native Americans), 34 international. Average age 28. 579 applicants, 83% accepted. In 1997, 217 master's, 5 doctorates awarded. *Degree requirements:* For doctorate, dissertation. *Entrance requirements:* For master's, minimum GPA of 3.0; for doctorate, GRE, MAT. Application deadline: rolling. Application fee: $25 ($0 for international students). *Expenses:* Tuition $604 per credit hour. Fees $10 per year full-time. *Financial aid:* In 1997–98, 380 students received aid, including 143 fellowships (59 to first-year students); research assistantships, teaching assistantships, partial tuition waivers, Federal Work-Study, institutionally sponsored loans, and career-related internships or fieldwork also available. Aid available to part-time students. Financial aid applicants required to submit FAFSA. *Faculty research:* Mental health services, social development, public child welfare, at-risk teens, social development, dietary risks in African-American women. • Dr. Shanti K. Khinduka, Dean, 314-935-6693. E-mail: khinduka@gwbssw.wustl.edu. Application contact: Elizabeth M. George, Assistant Dean of Admissions and Student Resources, 314-935-6676. Fax: 314-935-8511. E-mail: mswadmis@gwbssw.wustl.edu.

See in-depth description on page 1965.

Wayne State University, School of Social Work, Detroit, MI 48202. Offers programs in social work (MSW), social work practice with families and couples (Certificate). One or more programs accredited by CSWE. Part-time and evening/weekend programs available. Faculty: 80. Students: 418 full-time (352 women), 176 part-time (139 women); includes 123 minority (108 African Americans, 6 Asian Americans, 4 Hispanics, 5 Native Americans), 7 international. Average age 34. 244 applicants, 61% accepted. In 1997, 255 master's, 15 Certificates awarded. *Degree requirements:* For master's, thesis optional. *Application deadline:* 3/31 (2/28 for spring admission). *Application fee:* $20 ($30 for international students). *Expenses:* Tuition $163 per credit hour for state residents; $355 per credit hour for nonresidents. Fees $498 per year full-time, $114 per semester (minimum) part-time. *Financial aid:* In 1997–98, 27 scholarships (5 to first-year students) totaling $28,360 were awarded; partial tuition waivers, institutionally sponsored loans, and career-related internships or fieldwork also available. Aid available to part-time students. Financial aid application deadline: 5/1; applicants required to submit FAFSA. *Faculty research:* Child abuse, neglect, foster care, black individual/family development, occupational social work. Total annual research expenditures: $682,366. • Leon Chestang, Dean, 313-577-4400. Fax: 313-577-8770. Application contact: Cecille Y. Dumbrigue, Admissions and Student Services Office, 313-577-4409.

See in-depth description on page 1967.

West Chester University of Pennsylvania, School of Business and Public Affairs, Department of Social Work, West Chester, PA 19383. Awards MSW. Candidate for accreditation by CSWE. Students: 14 full-time (all women), 1 (woman) part-time; includes 2 minority (both African Americans), 1 international. 25 applicants, 76% accepted. *Degree requirements:* Comprehensive exam required, thesis optional, foreign language not required. *Entrance requirements:* GRE, MAT, interview, minimum GPA of 3.0. Application deadline: 4/15 (priority date; rolling processing; 10/15 for spring admission). Application fee: $25. *Expenses:* Tuition $3468 per year full-time, $193 per credit part-time for state residents; $6236 per year full-time, $346 per credit part-time for nonresidents. Fees $660 per year full-time, $38 per credit part-time. *Financial aid:* Application deadline 2/15. • Mildred Joyner, Chair, 610-436-2527. Application contact: Dr. Larry Ortiz, Graduate Coordinator, 610-436-2664. E-mail: lortiz@wcupa.edu.

Western Michigan University, College of Health and Human Services, School of Social Work, Kalamazoo, MI 49008. Awards MSW. Accredited by CSWE. Part-time programs available. Students: 138 full-time (111 women), 130 part-time (107 women); includes 39 minority (30 African Americans, 1 Asian American, 3 Hispanics, 5 Native Americans), 6 international. 262 applicants, 36% accepted. In 1997, 85 degrees awarded. *Application deadline:* 3/1. *Application fee:* $25. *Expenses:* Tuition $154 per credit hour for state residents; $372 per credit hour for nonresidents. Fees $602 per year full-time, $132 per semester part-time. *Financial aid:* Fellowships, research assistantships, teaching assistantships, Federal Work-Study available. Financial aid application deadline: 2/15; applicants required to submit FAFSA. • Dr. Philip Popple, Director, 616-387-3180. Application contact: Paula J. Boodt, Coordinator, Graduate Admissions and Recruitment, 616-387-2000. E-mail: paulaboodt@wmich.edu.

West Virginia University, School of Social Work, Morgantown, WV 26506. Awards MSW, MSW/MPA. Accredited by CSWE. Part-time programs available. Faculty: 11 full-time (7 women), 9 part-time (6 women). Students: 166 full-time (136 women), 66 part-time (56 women); includes 14 minority (11 African Americans, 1 Asian American, 1 Hispanic, 1 Native American), 1 international. Average age 34. 253 applicants, 75% accepted. In 1997, 69 degrees awarded. *Degree requirements:* Fieldwork required, foreign language and thesis not required. *Average time to degree:* master's–2 years full-time, 4 years part-time. *Entrance requirements:* GRE, TOEFL (minimum score 550), minimum GPA of 2.75. Application deadline: 3/1. Application fee: $45. *Tuition:* $2820 per year full-time, $149 per credit hour part-time for state residents; $8104 per year full-time, $443 per credit hour part-time for nonresidents. *Financial aid:* In 1997–98, 35 students received aid, including 6 research assistantships (4 to first-year students) averaging $612 per month and totaling $34,740, 1 teaching assistantship (to a first-year student) averaging $612 per month and totaling $5,508, 9 grants, stipends (4 to first-year students) averaging $260 per month and totaling $21,076; full and partial tuition waivers, Federal Work-Study, institutionally sponsored loans, and career-related internships or fieldwork also available. Financial aid application deadline: 3/1; applicants required to submit FAFSA. *Faculty research:* Rural and small town social work practice, gerontology, child abuse, health and mental health, welfare reform. Total annual research expenditures: $208,000. • Dr. Karen V. Harper, Dean, 304-293-3501. E-mail: kharper@wvu.edu. Application contact: Dr. Barry L. Locke, Assistant Dean, 304-293-3501. Fax: 304-293-5936. E-mail: blocke2@wvu.edu.

Wheelock College, Graduate School, Joint Social Work and Education Program, Boston, MA 02215. Awards MSW/M Ed. *Application deadline:* rolling. *Application fee:* $35 ($40 for international students). Electronic applications accepted. *Tuition:* $525 per credit. *Financial aid:* Application deadline 4/1. • Dr. Patricia Hogan, Dean of Social Work, 617-734-5200 Ext. 170. E-mail: phogan@wheelock.edu. Application contact: Martha Sheehan, Director of Graduate Admissions, 617-734-5200 Ext. 212. Fax: 617-232-7127. E-mail: msheehan@wheelock.edu.

Widener University, School of Human Service Professions, Center for Social Work Education, Chester, PA 19013-5792. Awards MSW. Accredited by CSWE. Part-time programs available. Faculty: 12 full-time (7 women), 7 part-time (6 women). Students: 82 full-time (68 women), 87 part-time (70 women); includes 22 minority (19 African Americans, 1 Asian American, 1 Hispanic, 1 Native American). Average age 35. 400 applicants, 38% accepted. In 1997, 69 degrees awarded. *Degree requirements:* Field practica required, foreign language and thesis not required. *Average time to degree:* master's–2 years full-time, 3 years part-time. *Entrance requirements:* Minimum GPA of 3.0. Application deadline: 3/15 (priority date; rolling processing). Application fee: $25. *Tuition:* $455 per credit. *Financial aid:* In 1997–98, 9 students received aid, including 6 fellowships (3 to first-year students) totaling $5,000, 2 graduate assistantships totaling $12,900; Federal Work-Study, institutionally sponsored loans, and career-related internships or fieldwork also available. Aid available to part-time students. Financial aid applicants required to submit FAFSA. *Faculty research:* Clinical practice, clinical supervision, gerontology, child welfare, self-psychology. occupational/environmental health, women's issues. Total annual research expenditures: $85,000. • Dr. Paula Silver, Acting Associate Dean and Director, 610-499-1153. Fax: 610-499-4617.

Announcement: MSW program prepares clinical social workers for agency-based practice with individuals, families, and small groups. The program provides a multitheoretical approach to working with diverse client populations (including psychodynamic systems, cognitive/behavioral, and others). The program stresses the inherent human strength and potential of clients. The ability to use oneself creatively and differentially to help clients help themselves in ways that respect their unique circumstances and values is seen as a critical component of clinical social work practice. All of the graduate social work classes are seminar-style with limited enrollment, and the field placement process is highly individualized and is based on the student's learning needs, interests, and geographical preferences.

Wilfrid Laurier University, Faculty of Social Work, Waterloo, ON N2L 3C5, Canada. Awards MSW, DSW, M Div/MTS/MSW. M Div/MTS/MSW offered jointly with Waterloo Lutheran Seminary. Part-time programs available. Faculty: 18 full-time, 10 part-time. Students: 201 full-time, 34 part-time. 471 applicants, 29% accepted. In 1997, 111 master's, 5 doctorates awarded. *Degree requirements:* For master's, thesis optional, foreign language not required; for doctorate, dissertation. *Application deadline:* 1/15. *Application fee:* $100. *Financial aid:* Fellowships available. • Dr. Jannah Hurn Mather, Dean, 519-884-1970 Ext. 2205. Application contact: D. Taylor, 519-884-0710 Ext. 2022. E-mail: dtaylor@mach2.wlu.ca.

Yeshiva University, Wurzweiler School of Social Work, New York, NY 10033-3201. Awards MSW, DSW, MSW/Certificate. One or more programs accredited by CSWE. Part-time and evening/weekend programs available. Faculty: 27 full-time (13 women), 35 part-time (25 women). Students: 331 full-time (260 women), 180 part-time (134 women); includes 102 minority (62 African Americans, 5 Asian Americans, 31 Hispanics, 4 Native Americans), 26 international. Average age 32. 602 applicants, 67% accepted. In 1997, 216 master's, 7 doctorates awarded. *Degree requirements:* Thesis/dissertation required, foreign language not required. *Average time to degree:* master's–2 years full-time, 3 years part-time; doctorate–4 years full-time, 6 years part-time. *Entrance requirements:* Interview. Application deadline: 5/1 (priority date; rolling processing; 10/31 for spring admission). Application fee: $35. *Expenses:* Tuition $14,630 per year (minimum) full-time, $555 per credit (minimum) part-time. Fees $170 per year. *Financial aid:* 228 students received aid; institutionally sponsored loans and career-related internships or fieldwork available. Financial aid application deadline: 5/15; applicants required to submit FAFSA. *Faculty research:* Child abuse, AIDS, day care, nonprofits, gerontology, Jewish communal service. • Dr. Sheldon R. Gelman, Dean, 212-960-0820. Application contact: Michele Sarracco, Director of Admissions, 212-960-0811. Fax: 212-960-0822.

York University, Program in Social Work, Toronto, ON M3J 1P3, Canada. Awards MSW. Part-time and evening/weekend programs available. *Degree requirements:* Thesis required, foreign language not required. *Application deadline:* 2/15. *Application fee:* $60.

Cross-Discipline Announcements

Boston College, Wallace E. Carroll Graduate School of Management, Chestnut Hill, MA 02167-9991.

The Boston College MBA/MSW degree is perfect for students interested in using their management skills primarily in the nonprofit or public sectors. In the 3-year program, students get significant real-world experience through MSW field placements and MBA consulting projects. See in-depth descriptions in this volume.

Brandeis University, The Heller Graduate School, Waltham, MA 02454-2728.

The Heller Graduate School at Brandeis University offers a PhD in social policy as well as a Master of Management and a Master of Business Administration in health and human services. Specialization areas: health care; child, youth, and family services; aging; substance abuse; mental health; disabilities; and social change. PhD graduates pursue careers in academia, research, and administration. Master's graduates are leaders in nonprofit, profit, and public human services organizations, having been cross-trained in social policy and cutting-edge management education. See in-depth description for PhD program in Book 2, Public, Regional, and Industrial Affairs section and the in-depth description for the master's programs in Book 6, Business Administration and Management section. See also *Peterson's Guide to MBA Programs.*

University of Chicago, Graduate Program in Health Administration and Policy, 969 East 60th Street, Office 6011, Chicago, IL 60637-1513.

The Graduate Program in Health Administration and Policy is an accredited, certificate-granting program completed through the normal course load required for the MA in social service administration.

University of Southern California, Graduate School, Leonard Davis School of Gerontology, Los Angeles, CA 90089.

Dual-degree programs in gerontology and social work are offered in cooperation with the USC School of Social Work. The MSG/MSW dual degree prepares individuals for work in programs or agencies that deliver services to the elderly and their families. These positions exist in a wide range of social and institutional settings. Program features a strong alumni network and a wide variety of tuition funding sources.

Walden University, Graduate Programs, 155 Fifth Avenue South, Minneapolis, MN 55401.

Nationally recognized faculty members mentor experienced professionals through residency-based and computer-mediated instruction in Walden University's distance learning programs. Degrees are offered in applied management and decision sciences (PhD), education (MS, PhD), health services (PhD), human services (PhD), and psychology (MS, PhD). Accredited by the North Central Association of Colleges and Schools. For more information, see Book 1 of this series.

ADELPHI UNIVERSITY

ADELPHI UNIVERSITY

School of Social Work

Programs of Study

The School of Social Work of Adelphi University offers an accredited curriculum leading to the Master of Social Work degree and the degree of Doctor in Social Welfare. The School's mission and curriculum approach social problems from a multicultural, gender-specific, cross-national perspective. Graduates are prepared to think biologically, psychologically, socially, economically, and politically. Given a social problem, they are trained to intervene with individuals, couples, groups, families, communities, and organizations; to analyze, develop, and advocate for relevant programs and policies; and to conduct appropriate research on the subject.

The M.S.W. degree requires 64 credits, including course work and field internship. To accommodate students with varied needs, the School has established several routes for entry into the program and fulfillment of academic credits: Full-Time, Two Year program; the accelerated sixteen-month program; the one-year Residency Program; the Advanced Standing Program, available to graduates of Adelphi's Bachelor of Science in Social Welfare program and to graduates of other bachelor's programs accredited by the Council on Social Work Education (CSWE); and the Part-Time Matriculated Program, which is intended primarily for students with current employment and family responsibilities and may be completed in up to four years. The first year of the M.S.W. program is also offered at the off-campus Hudson Valley Program in Poughkeepsie, New York, and courses toward the M.S.W. are offered at the Manhattan Center in New York City. Second-year M.S.W. students select a concentration in one of the following two fields of practice: health, mental health, and chemical dependency services or social services to families across the life span. Internships are developed with approximately 1,100 health and social welfare agencies on Long Island and the New York metropolitan area.

The D.S.W. degree is offered. The degree requires a minimum of 48 semester hours of doctoral course credit and the completion of a research project and dissertation. The program is designed to produce a scholar practitioner.

A 16-credit, post-master's certificate program in bilingual social work is offered jointly with the School of Education. This program, intended for bilingual social workers seeking certification in bilingual social work, meets the New York State mandated course requirements for bilingual certification and is registered with the New York State Education Department.

A noncredit, post-master's certificate program is offered. The Post-Master's Certificate in Clinical Practice prepares professionals for advanced practice and is organized over two academic years, including a summer session. Six credits may be transferred toward doctoral requirements.

Research Facilities

Research and educational opportunities are available through Adelphi's Centers for Social Work Services, Policy and Research. Programs include the Refugee Assistance Program, Breast Cancer Support, and the Long Island Coalition for Full Employment. The Practice Research Center, a joint endeavor with the Long Island Jewish/Hillside Medical Center, is designed to stimulate and support practice-based research by faculty and students. Each year, social work students conduct research in small groups as part of their field instruction experience. Swirbul Library contains an extensive collection of social work reference texts, journals, and archival material. It also provides access to databases in a sophisticated network of services. Voice mail is provided at the School of Social Work, enhancing communications.

Financial Aid

Graduate assistantships are awarded on the basis of merit and need. They involve nonteaching assignments and remission of tuition. Several scholarship funds have been established for social work students, with particular attention to the need for ethnic and cultural diversity in the profession. A number of field agency stipends are also available.

Cost of Study

Tuition was $465 per credit in 1997–98.

Living and Housing Costs

The University assists single and married students in finding suitable accommodations whenever possible. The cost of living is dependent upon location and the number of rooms rented.

Student Group

There are approximately 950 students in the social work master's program and 80 students at various stages of study in the doctoral program.

Location

Adelphi University is located in Garden City, Long Island, a small village praised nationally for its high quality of life. Long Island was recently rated by *American Demographics Magazine* as the best place to live in America. Garden City is only 18 miles east of New York City. The School of Social Work also operates programs at the Manhattan Center in New York City and the Hudson Valley Program in Poughkeepsie, New York.

The University and The School

Adelphi has a beautifully landscaped campus of 75 acres in an attractive residential community. In a *USA Today* survey, Adelphi was ranked as the safest campus in the nation. The School also offers a program leading to the Bachelor of Science in Social Welfare. An accelerated continuum provides an opportunity for selected students to earn a baccalaureate and a master's in social work in five years rather than six. The School also offers the ANSWER Program at the Manhattan Center, which helps paraprofessionals upgrade their skills and attain the B.S.S.W. through a work/study arrangement. The School, which was founded in 1949, is fully accredited by CSWE through the year 2002.

Applying

The M.S.W. program is open on a competitive basis to men and women who hold a bachelor's degree from an accredited college or university. The application fee is $50. The D.S.W. program is designed to build upon an M.S.W. degree or, in special cases, another master's degree in a closely related field.

Correspondence and Information

For the M.S.W. program:

Graduate Admissions Office
Adelphi University
1 South Avenue
Garden City, New York 11530
Telephone: 800-ADELPHI (toll-free)
E-mail: admissions@adelphi.edu
World Wide Web: http://www.adelphi.edu

For the D.S.W. program:

Dr. Ellen Rosenberg
Director of Doctoral Division
School of Social Work
Adelphi University
Box 703
Garden City, New York 11530
Telephone: 516-877-4386

Adelphi University

THE FACULTY AND THEIR RESEARCH

Roger Levin, Ph.D., Dean ad Interim.
Louise Skolnik, D.S.W., Associate Dean.

Richard Belson, D.S.W., Associate Professor. Human behavior and social environment, family treatment.
Roni Berger, Ph.D., Assistant Professor. Direct practice and research.
Ellen Bogolub, Ph.D., Assistant Professor. Divorce, children and families.
Carl Buxbaum, M.S.W., Associate Professor. Social policy, administration, community mental health.
Catherine Caicedo, M.S., Assistant Professor. Direct practice, ethnicity.
Gertrude Goldberg, D.S.W., Associate Professor. Social policy, administration, service delivery.
Lawrence Grossman, D.S.W., Professor. Research, policy.
Cecil St. George Henry, Ed.D., Professor. Human behavior and social environment.
Ivory Holmes, Ed.D., Associate Professor. Direct practice.
Gideon Horowitz, Ph.D., Professor. Research.
Rebecca Loew, Ph.D., Assistant Professor. Social policy and research.
J. Julian Rivera, M.S.W., Associate Professor. Direct practice, ethnicity.
Ellen Rosenberg, D.S.W., Associate Professor. Human behavior and social environment, research.
Herbert Schwarz, M.S.W., Assistant Professor. Direct practice.
Brooke Spiro, D.S.W., Associate Professor. Social policy.
Carol Sussal, D.S.W., Associate Professor. Direct practice.
Narayan Viswanathan, D.S.W., Professor. Social policy, administration.
Janice Wood Wetzel, Ph.D., Professor. Depression, international social work.
W. Cody Wilson, Ph.D., Professor and Director of Doctoral Division. Research.

BOSTON COLLEGE

Graduate School of Social Work

Program of Study

The Graduate School of Social Work at Boston College offers programs leading to the Master of Social Work (M.S.W.) and Doctor of Social Work (Ph.D.) degrees. Joint degrees with the Graduate School of Management (M.S.W./M.B.A.), the Law School (M.S.W./J.D.), and the Institute of Pastoral Ministry (M.S.W./M.A.) are also offered. Advanced standing may be applied for by candidates who have graduated from a B.S.W. program accredited by the Council on Social Work Education and by those who have completed one year at another graduate school of social work.

The M.S.W. curriculum consists of foundation requirements common to all students, with methods courses and field practice providing a focus in clinical social work or social planning and administration. Students also have the option of subconcentrating in child welfare, occupational social work, health and medical care, gerontology, or forensic social work.

Studies may be started on either a full-time or a part-time basis. The traditional Full-Time Plan consists of concurrent class and field instruction for two academic years. The Part-Time Plan extends the first half of class work and fieldwork over a two-year span. Foundation courses and practicum placements are also available part-time at sites in Portland, Maine, and Plymouth, Worcester, and Chicopee, Massachusetts. All students are expected to be in full-time status in their final year of enrollment.

Field placements are arranged in public and private social work agencies and occupational settings.

The Ph.D. program is designed to prepare graduates for leadership roles in research and teaching in clinical and social planning areas of practice. An M.S.W. degree, demonstrated success in social work practice, and evidence of ability to successfully complete a research-oriented course of study are prerequisites for admission to the Ph.D. program.

Research Facilities

The Thomas P. O'Neill Jr. Library, which opened in 1984, houses 1 million volumes. Special services include video and media departments, a photocopy center, and a resource room for the visually impaired. The Quest Online Catalog offers access to all holdings. Access to computerized databases is available.

The Social Work Library, located in McGuinn Hall, has been maintained to serve the specific needs of the School and owns a comprehensive collection focusing on all aspects of social work education.

Financial Aid

There is a basic two-tier approach to financial aid. All eligible students are expected to pursue university-administered financial aid in the form of Federal Stafford Student Loans, Federal Perkins Loans, and Federal Work-Study programs. In conjunction with this, all students are eligible to apply for assistantships, scholarships, and agency grants administered by the School.

Every effort is made to match Work-Study–eligible students with practicum sites that qualify for Work-Study. The School-administered funds include VA stipends, stipends for students from minority groups with a subconcentration in child welfare, stipends in forensic social work, graduate assistantships (final year only), and Presidential Scholarships (students from minority groups and international students).

Cost of Study

Tuition in 1998–99 is $18,460 for full-time M.S.W. students, $504 per credit hour for part-time M.S.W. students, and $580 per credit hour for doctoral students.

Living and Housing Costs

The cost of living for a single independent student is approximately $10,805. For a married student, it is $12,000, with approximately $1800 added for each dependent.

There is limited on-campus housing for graduate students. An off-campus housing office assists students in locating individual living accommodations.

Student Group

The total enrollment for the Graduate School of Social Work in the fall of 1997 was 560 students. The student body is diverse, representing many undergraduate colleges and international universities. The School is committed to recruitment of ethnic and racial minority and other underrepresented groups. The involvement of an active alumni association has contributed significantly to the excellent employment prospects available to graduates.

Location

The College is located on the city line with Newton. There is good access by private and public transportation to the city of Boston, its surrounding suburbs, and the countryside of New England.

The College and The School

Boston College is one of the oldest Jesuit-sponsored universities in the United States. It has professional and graduate schools, doctoral programs, research institutes, community service programs, an excellent faculty, and rich resources of libraries, research equipment, computers, and other facilities.

The Graduate School of Social Work was established in 1936 and is fully accredited by the Council on Social Work Education. The Ph.D. degree program was instituted in 1979.

The educational programs focus upon the development of humanitarian values and social work skills to the extent of each student's potential through involvement, in a scholarly and sensitive way, in the learning-teaching process. There is special emphasis on educating value-committed knowledgeable practitioners for work with the disadvantaged and the high-risk groups for social, economic, and political discrimination and deprivation.

Applying

Requirements for admission to the M.S.W. program include a baccalaureate degree from an accredited college or university, a minimum of 20 semester hours in social or behavioral sciences, scores on the TOEFL for ESL students, a grade point average indicative of ability to complete graduate study, and the personal qualifications necessary for professional practice. MAT or GRE scores are required for doctoral applicants.

Early submission of all necessary application materials facilitates decision making on admissions and financial aid.

Correspondence and Information

William C. Howard, Ph.D.
Director of Admissions
Graduate School of Social Work
McGuinn Hall
Boston College
Chestnut Hill, Massachusetts 02167
Telephone: 617-552-4024

Boston College

THE FACULTY AND THEIR RESEARCH

June Gary Hopps, Professor and Dean; Ph.D., Brandeis, 1974. Program evaluation, social welfare policy.
Albert F. Hanwell, Associate Professor and Associate Dean; M.S.W., Boston College, 1951. Child welfare.
Betty Blythe, Professor; Ph.D., Washington (Seattle), 1983. Child welfare, family preservation, practice evaluation.
Ann T. Burns, Field Coordinator; M.S.W., Howard, 1967. Professional gatekeeping.
Robert L. Castagnola, Associate Professor; M.S.W., Boston College, 1958. Homelessness, corrections, hospice.
Pauline Collins, Assistant Dean for Field Education; Ph.D., Michigan, 1990. Mentor: supportive relationships in the human services.
Ann O. Freed, Adjunct Professor; M.S.S., Smith, 1941. Gerontology, cross-national practice, borderline personalities.
William C. Howard, Director of Admissions; Ph.D., Brandeis, 1989. Alcoholism, industrial social work.
Demetrius S. Iatridis, Professor; Ph.D., Bryn Mawr, 1954. Policy analysis, comparative social services.
Hugo Kamya, Assistant Professor; Ph.D., Boston University, 1994. Immigration, families and AIDS.
Karen Kayser, Associate Professor; Ph.D., Michigan, 1988. Marital and family therapy.
Eric R. Kingson, Associate Professor; Ph.D., Brandeis, 1979. Gerontology, Social Security.
Paul Kline, Adjunct Assistant Professor; D.S.W., Boston College, 1990. Child and adolescent treatment.
Vincent J. Lynch, Director of Continuing Education; D.S.W., Boston College, 1987. Managed mental health care, AIDS.
Richard A. Mackey, Professor; D.S.W., Catholic University, 1966. Ego psychology, marriage and family.
Anthony N. Maluccio, Professor; D.S.W., Columbia, 1976. Child welfare, competence-centered social work.
Katherine McInnis-Dittrich, Associate Professor; Ph.D., Wisconsin, 1987. Women and work, rural social work.
Regina O'Grady-Le Shane, Director of Special Projects; Ph.D., Brandeis, 1982. Women and employment, gerontology.
Thomas O'Hare, Associate Professor; Ph.D., Rutgers, 1988. Mental health/substance abuse co-occurrence, clinical evaluation.
Elaine B. Pinderhughes, Professor; M.S.S.W., Columbia, 1948. Cross-cultural social work and clinical practice.
Richard Rowland, Adjunct Associate Professor; Ph.D., Brandeis, 1970. Health and welfare policy, elder issues.
Robbie C. Tourse, Director of Field Placement; Ph.D., Boston College, 1990. Cross-cultural practice.
Thanh VanTran, Professor; Ph.D., Texas at Arlington, 1985. Gerontology, statistics.
Nancy W. Veeder, Associate Professor; Ph.D., Brandeis, 1974; M.B.A., Boston College, 1990. Family planning, human service management.
Dorothy E. Weitzman, Adjunct Assistant Professor; M.S.W., Columbia, 1968. Child welfare, career planning.
Leon F. Williams, Associate Professor; Ph.D., Brandeis, 1980. Cross-cultural social work, gerontology.

BRYN MAWR COLLEGE

Graduate School of Social Work and Social Research

Programs of Study

The Graduate School of Social Work and Social Research offers three degree programs: Master of Social Service (M.S.S.), which prepares graduates for the variety of professional roles in social work practice through concentrations in clinical social work, social service management, and advocacy, planning, and program development; Master of Law and Social Policy (M.L.S.P.), a post-master's degree program for professionals in social work, in other human service professions, in public administration, and in policy analysis related to social welfare; and Doctor of Philosophy (Ph.D.), which prepares individuals for intellectual leadership in the profession as advanced social work researchers and educators. Full-time and part-time programs of study are offered.

Through daylong spring and fall continuing education courses and a weeklong Summer Institute, the School provides professional social workers with challenging educational opportunities designed to meet the needs of practitioners working in a variety of settings.

Social work has reemerged as the profession of choice for the problem solver, the advocate, and the promoter of social justice. Since its inception in 1915 as the Graduate Department of Social Economy and Social Research, the Bryn Mawr program has maintained its commitment to casework, public welfare, and social research. As the scope of social problems has changed and the methods for meeting human needs have become more complex, the School continues its tradition of preparing social workers to serve all persons within the social welfare system and to provide leadership in changing economic, political, and social structures to more effectively meet the needs of individuals, families, and communities.

Master's candidates are assigned to one of more than 200 agencies and organizations. While most field placements are in the five-county Philadelphia metropolitan region, agencies are also used in New Jersey, Delaware, and Washington, D.C. Field instruction and courses are taken concurrently in order to enhance the blend of practice and theory.

Career development services include a Career Development program that encompasses the following three areas: networking, career development skills, and career counseling. Through the career mentors program, graduates serve as mentors to applicants, current students, and fellow alumni. A job bank, an annual jobs fair, a series of programs related to the job search process, a daylong workshop for graduating students, and individual career counseling are components of career development services. These services are also available to the School's alumni.

Research Facilities

The Mariam Coffin Canady Library and the two auxiliary libraries of Bryn Mawr College contain more than 1 million books, documents, and microforms and regularly receive more than 1,800 periodicals as well as many scholarly services.

Eugenia Chase Guild Hall is a computing center that houses the College's academic and computing services. It is also the hub of the campuswide data network, which makes possible access to e-mail, standard campus supportive software (e.g., Microsoft, Office, SPSS), and the on-line library catalog. The School has computers that are available to all its students. The building has a high-speed data network that connects with computers in faculty member offices, classrooms, administrative offices, and computing laboratories.

Financial Aid

Financial assistance is awarded to students who have need based upon information provided on the GAPSFAS and the Bryn Mawr College Financial Aid Forms. Financial assistance is given to all eligible students who apply for aid in a timely fashion. Full-time and part-time funding is available. The total amount of financial aid available each year is usually increased at a rate proportional to tuition increases. Admissions decisions are made independently of financial need.

Cost of Study

Tuition for the 1998–99 academic year for full-time students is $19,180. A one-semester M.S.S. or M.L.S.P. course is $2210; a one-semester Ph.D. course is $3230. The field instruction fee is $80 per year. The graduation fee is $60.

Living and Housing Costs

Graduate housing is available for approximately 40 students at Glenmede, the graduate residence center located a half mile from the main campus and a mile from the School. The 1998–99 charge for residents is $4560 for the academic year.

Student Group

The Graduate School of Social Work and Social Research is coeducational. The enrollment is approximately 325 men and women in the three programs.

Location

Bryn Mawr College is located 11 miles west of central Philadelphia on a campus that features building styles ranging from the first examples of collegiate Gothic in the country to the most modern designs. The School is easily accessible by automobile and by commuter rail service from central Philadelphia.

The College

Founded in 1885, Bryn Mawr was the first women's college to offer both graduate and undergraduate degrees to women, awarding its first Ph.D. in 1888. The Graduate School of Social Work and Social Research was opened at Bryn Mawr College in 1915 as the Carola Woerishoffer Graduate Department of Social Economy and Social Research. It was established as a tribute to Carola Woerishoffer, a Bryn Mawr graduate of the class of 1907 who left $750,000 to the College, the largest gift in Bryn Mawr's history at that time. An ardent social reformer, Carola Woerishoffer was killed in an automobile accident while investigating the conditions in labor camps as an employee of the New York State Bureau of Industries and Immigration. This was the first graduate program of social work education to be offered by a college or university in the United States. Subsequently, the department name was modified from Social Economy and Social Research to Social Work and Social Research. In 1970, it became one of the three schools that comprise Bryn Mawr College.

Applying

Applications must be supported by official transcripts from all undergraduate and graduate work as well as by three letters of recommendation, two of which should be from professors and one from a supervisor of the applicant's social work–related employment, internship, or volunteer work. An essay and a personal interview are required. International applicants to all programs must submit TOEFL results. Applicants to the Ph.D. program must submit scores from the Graduate Record Examinations. There is an application fee of $40. The deadline for application to all the programs and for financial aid is March 1. There is a rolling admissions process, and Admissions Committees begin reviewing completed applications in early January. Students are admitted for fall enrollment only.

Correspondence and Information

Office of Admissions
Graduate School of Social Work and Social Research
Bryn Mawr College
300 Airdale Road
Bryn Mawr, Pennsylvania 19010-1697
Telephone: 610-520-2601
E-mail: swadmiss@brynmawr.edu
World Wide Web: http://www.brynmawr.edu/Adm/grads.html#gsswsr

Bryn Mawr College

THE FACULTY AND THEIR RESEARCH

Ruth W. Mayden, Dean; M.S.S., Bryn Mawr. Social work education and administration, child welfare, mental health, advocacy.

Raymond Albert, M.S.W., J.D., Connecticut. Social work and law, poverty law and poverty policy, poverty dynamics and working class black males, dispute resolution.

Leslie Alexander, Ph.D., Bryn Mawr. Mental health, effectiveness of clinical practice, work and family issues across the life span, the alliance in adult intensive case management with consumers with severe mental illness.

Jeffrey Applegate, D.S.W., Boston College. Clinical social work theory and practice, men as caregivers, life span developmental theory, application of psychodynamic developmental theory to clinical practice.

James Baumohl, D.S.W., Berkeley. History of social welfare and criminal justice, alcohol and drug control policy, urban poverty.

Dana Becker, Ph.D., Bryn Mawr. Clinical social work practice with the severely and chronically mentally ill, addicted persons, antisocial and drug-abusing adolescents.

Cynthia Bisman, Ph.D., Kansas. Development of social work practice theory and research methodologies, family therapy, mental health, clinical practice.

Maria Corwin, Ph.D., Smith. Mental health, managed care, time-limited clinical social work practice, culturally sensitive practice, cross-cultural practice.

Diane Frankel, M.S.S., Bryn Mawr. Clinical social work practice with mental health; individuals, couples, and families.

Lenard W. Kaye, D.S.W., Columbia. Social gerontology, home health care, continuum of independent living programs, gender considerations in use of gerontological services, male caregiving.

Toba Kerson, D.S.W., Ph.D., Pennsylvania. Health, social work practice in relation to health policy and program development, chronic physical illness.

Nancy J. Kirby, M.S.S., Bryn Mawr. Child welfare, maternal and child health, community health services.

Julia Littell, Ph.D., Chicago. Child welfare policy and practice, reform efforts and innovations in services for children and families, evaluation of social programs.

James A. Martin, Ph.D., Pittsburgh. Mental health, stress and social support, traumatic stress, family policy and the military.

Marcia L. Martin, Ph.D., Bryn Mawr. Clinical social work theory and supervision, AIDS, mental health, social work field instruction.

Barbara Matz, Ed.D., West Virginia. Social work regulation, career development in social work, public policy and women's issues.

Carolyn Needleman, Ph.D., Washington (St. Louis). Occupational and environmental health, social work in the workplace, community development.

Sanford Schram, Ph.D., SUNY at Albany. Public policy, politics and public policy, power and democracy, politics of social welfare.

Janet R. Shapiro, Ph.D., Michigan. Child and adolescent development, parenting, role of psychological theory in clinical practice.

Thomas Vartanian, Ph.D., Notre Dame. Economics of welfare, asset depletion and the elderly, long-term-care financing.

CASE WESTERN RESERVE UNIVERSITY

Mandel School of Applied Social Sciences

Programs of Study

Ranked among the top schools of social work in the country, the Mandel School of Applied Social Sciences offers a course of study leading to the Master of Science in Social Administration degree (M.S.S.A.), an advanced program for a Doctor of Philosophy in social welfare (Ph.D.), and several joint degree programs: the Master of Science in Social Administration/Doctor of Jurisprudence (M.S.S.A./J.D.), Master of Science in Social Administration/Doctor of Philosophy (M.S.S.A./Ph.D.), and Master of Science in Social Administration/Master of Nonprofit Organizations (M.S.S.A./M.N.O.). An M.N.O. is offered in conjunction with the Weatherhead School of Management and the School of Law at CWRU.

Master's degree students pursue degrees through a variety of study options, including a traditional two-year course of full-time study, a specialized weekend program for employed social workers, the Senior-Year-In-Absentia Program for undergraduate students of superior ability from approved schools, and extended-degree programs. Ph.D. students pursue their degrees through a full-time or summer-study option program.

Master's degree students pursue their course of study in one of two specializations, with an emphasis on one career track within that specialization. The Direct Practice Specialization includes concentrations in health; mental health; children, youth, and families; alcohol and other drug abuse; and aging. The Macro Practice Specialization includes concentrations in management, community development, and fund-raising. A School Social Worker Certification program is also offered in conjunction with the Division of Education at Baldwin-Wallace College.

Research Facilities

Applied research and evaluation studies are conducted in the community by faculty and students. Projects often involve seeking new ways to apply social science and management science technologies to problems of policy formulation, program design, and coordination and evaluation of human service programs. Applied research, program evaluation, and the development of instruments and techniques for ongoing program feedback and decision making are among the approaches used in solution-oriented collaborative projects that involve current and emerging issues in human service delivery systems.

Financial Aid

Financial aid is granted on the basis of financial need and promise for the field of social work. Scholarship, grant-in-aid, and college work-study funds are available from the University, the MSASS Alumni Association, private groups, individuals, agencies in the community, and federal aid programs. More than 80 percent of the students receive financial assistance. To apply for aid, students must submit the graduate FAF and the School's financial aid form.

Cost of Study

For the 1998–99 academic year, tuition is $613 per credit hour for master's students and $767 per credit hour for Ph.D. students who are enrolled for 13 or more credit hours.

Living and Housing Costs

For the 1998–99 academic year, full-time students at the Mandel School of Applied Social Sciences need approximately $30,000 for tuition and living expenses.

Student Group

The University enrolls over 9,900 students. Approximately 6,200 students are seeking graduate or professional degrees. Although many students are from Ohio, most of the fifty states are represented. Nearly 1,000 international students representing over eighty-five different countries provide a contemporary international perspective. On average, 500 students are enrolled at the Mandel School.

Location

Case Western Reserve University is located in University Circle, a 500-acre parklike concentration of educational, scientific, medical, artistic, musical, and cultural institutions on the eastern edge of the city of Cleveland.

The University

CWRU is a nationally recognized independent university. Established in 1967 by the federation of Case Institute of Technology (founded in 1880) and Western Reserve University (founded in 1826), the University is composed of an institute of science and technology, a liberal arts college, a school of graduate studies, and seven professional schools. Seven of Case Western Reserve's faculty members and alumni have been awarded Nobel prizes, and many others are nationally recognized for their work.

Applying

Students are admitted in the fall and spring semesters. Applications should be filed as early as possible and must be submitted by March 31 with a $25 nonrefundable application fee. Material considered with application forms includes personal statements that are submitted by the applicant, reference letters, official transcripts from each college attended, and evidence of superior personal qualifications.

To be admitted to the Ph.D. program, a candidate should have a master's degree from an accredited school of social work or a master's degree in a related field and should demonstrate a superior record in undergraduate and graduate studies. Practical experience in social welfare is required. Application to the Ph.D. program will be considered from people with master's degrees in allied fields with the recognition that their program will include equivalency requirements related to knowledge of social welfare. The Miller Analogies Test or Graduate Record Examinations is required for application.

Correspondence and Information

Office of Admissions
Mandel School of Applied Social Sciences
Case Western Reserve University
10900 Euclid Avenue
Cleveland, Ohio 44106-7164
Telephone: 216-368-5883
800-863-6772 (toll-free)
Fax: 216-368-5065

Case Western Reserve University

THE FACULTY AND THEIR RESEARCH

Albert J. Abramovitz, Ph.D., Case Western Reserve. Management, governance, community relations, citizen involvement.
Sarah Andrews, M.S.S.A., Case Western Reserve. Family development, women and chronic illness.
Darlyne Bailey, Ph.D., Case Western Reserve. Organizational behavior, nonprofit leadership and governance, workplace diversity, community development, community-based consortia development and evaluation.
David E. Biegel, Ph.D., Maryland. Mental health, social support, aging, caregiving.
Craig Boitel, M.S.S.A., Case Western Reserve. Field education, clinical social work, affective disorders.
Pranab Chatterjee, Ph.D., Chicago. Organizational behavior/small-group behavior, comparative social welfare systems, technology transfer.
Claudia J. Coulton, Ph.D., Case Western Reserve. Research and statistics, poverty, neighborhoods, urban affairs.
Kathleen J. Farkas, Ph.D., Case Western Reserve. Alcohol and other drug abuse, gender issues, aging.
Elizabeth Farmer, Ph.D., Duke. Research methodology, mental health services.
Wallace J. Gingerich, Ph.D., Washington (St. Louis). Practice evaluation, family therapy, computer applications, clinical social work practice.
Ronald K. Green, J.D., Tennessee. Management, training, child welfare.
Victor K. Groza, Ph.D., Oklahoma. Child welfare, special needs adoption, family therapy, gay and lesbian issues.
Merl C. Hokenstad Jr., Ph.D., Brandeis. International social welfare, social work education, health and social services policy and programs for older people.
Deborah Regenbogen Jacobson, D.S.W., Tulane. Practice evaluation.
Alice K. Johnson, Ph.D., Washington (St. Louis). Homelessness (especially homeless families), program evaluation, social welfare policy, international child welfare.
Lenore A. Kola, Ph.D., Boston University. Alcohol and other drug abuse, employee assistance programs.
Baila Miller, Ph.D., Illinois at Chicago. Aging, family caregiving, research and statistical methods.
David Miller, Ph.D., Pittsburgh. African-American males, child maltreatment, violence.
Sharon E. Milligan, Ph.D., Pittsburgh. Social support among women with chronic illness; race, social support, and African-American elderly; race and family caregiving.
Arthur J. Naparstek, Ph.D., Brandeis. Social policy, community planning and development, management.
Regina Nixon, Ph.D., Howard. Poverty/high-risk populations, cultural diversity.
R. Susan Pearlmutter, Ph.D., Kansas. Management, leadership, welfare and poverty, public social service.
Marvin L. Rosenberg, D.S.W., Western Reserve. Social policy, ethics in the professions.
Mark I. Singer, Ph.D., Case Western Reserve. Adolescent mental health, adolescent substance abuse, youth-related violence.
Gerald Strom, M.S.W., Howard. Field education, child abuse, growth development, sexual abuse investigation and treatment.
Ilga B. Svechs, Ph.D., Union. Child development, child abuse, clinical social work practice.
Elizabeth M. Tracy, Ph.D., Washington (Seattle). Family preservation services, child welfare, social support services.
Kathleen Wells, Ph.D., Colorado. Research methods, child mental health, child welfare.
Zoe Breen Wood, M.S.W., Virginia Commonwealth. Child welfare, policy and practice.
John A. Yankey, Ph.D., Pittsburgh. Nonprofit strategic planning and marketing; fund-raising/development; nonprofit mergers, acquisitions, and consolidations.
Dennis R. Young, Ph.D., Stanford. Nonprofit management, economics of nonprofit organizations.

Research Activities

In addition to ongoing independent faculty research, the Mandel School of Applied Social Sciences sponsors academic centers involved in specific research, practice implementation, and dissemination of information.

Center on Urban Poverty and Social Change. The overall mission of this project is to link the University's capacity for social policy and social welfare–related research, analysis, and data management to community-based organizations and groups addressing aspects of urban poverty.
Center for Community Development. The goal of the organization is to implement a comprehensive, coordinated action plan to rebuild inner city neighborhoods.
Mandel Center for Nonprofit Organizations. The mission of the Mandel Center is to foster effective management, leadership, and governance of nonprofit organizations in human services, the arts, education, community development, religion, and other areas through instruction, research, and related academic institutions.
Journal of Applied Social Sciences. Substantively, the journal seeks contributions that underscore the linkages between theory and practice, theoretical content that contributes to practice applications, and applications whose findings confirm, refute, or extend existing theory or point to the development of new theoretical formulations.
Center for Public Sector Leadership. The center provides and integrates education, training, research, and organizational development to shape and influence public policy and enhance public sector agencies' capacities to serve their constituencies.
Cuyahoga County Community Mental Health Research Institute. The Institute implements a well-defined program of research that helps mental health agencies within Cuyahoga County to improve the delivery of services to people with mental disorders.
Joseph and Florence Mandel Alzheimer's Caregiving Insitute. The Institute provides an interdisciplinary approach to research, education, and training about issues affecting caregivers of persons with Alzheimer's disease.

THE CATHOLIC UNIVERSITY OF AMERICA

The National Catholic School of Social Service

Programs of Study

The National Catholic School of Social Service (NCSSS) offers courses of study leading to a Master's in Social Work (M.S.W.) and a doctoral degree (Ph.D.). NCSSS educates students to contribute to the fulfillment of social welfare objectives and to be of service to all people. The 60-credit master's program, fully accredited by CSWE, offers concentrations in clinical social work (with specialized tracks in work with individual adults, children and adolescents, and family practice) and social policy, planning, and administration. The master's program prepares students for careers providing clinical services, working to affect social policy in agencies as well as in political arenas, and serving as administrators of social service organizations in such areas as health and mental health, family and children's services, and gerontology. NCSSS and the University's Columbus School of Law offer a dual-degree M.S.W./J.D. program.

The doctoral program, the third oldest in the country, seeks to educate social workers to participate responsibly in the formulation of social welfare objectives that express the humanistic and religious values of a democratic society. It also seeks to further the development of the profession through scholarly research, theory building, and leadership. Doctoral students focus their studies in theory and research development in clinical practice, social policy development and administration, or in an individualized educational program. They may pursue interdisciplinary study by taking courses within the NCSSS and other University schools or within the Consortium of Universities of the Washington Metropolitan Area.

Research Facilities

The John K. Mullen Library contains over 1 million volumes, including 7,500 serials. In addition, students have access to many of the libraries in the Washington, D.C. area, including the Library of Congress and the National Library of Medicine. Students also have access to the libraries of the Consortium of Universities in the Washington, D.C., metropolitan area.

Financial Aid

The University awards a limited number of graduate scholarships to master's and doctoral students on a competitive basis each year; interested applicants must submit their application portfolios and GRE scores by February 1. Departmental scholarships are awarded to qualified doctoral students; some of these funds support doctoral students from minority groups.

In addition, NCSSS awards several grants to full-time M.S.W. students. Some of these grants require meeting certain requirements set forth by the donors. Financial need is a major consideration in awarding NCSSS grants. All eligible students are expected to pursue University-administered loans. Federal work-study funding may also be awarded for work completed in the field internship.

Cost of Study

Tuition in 1998–99 is $17,325 per academic year for full-time students and $668 per credit hour for part-time students.

Living and Housing Costs

The cost of living is comparable to that of other large east-coast cities. On-campus housing is available for single graduate students. Many students live in adjacent off-campus areas. Additional information about on- and off-campus housing may be obtained from the Office of Resident Life, 106 St. Bonaventure, The Catholic University of America, Washington, D.C. 20064, and the Office of Off-Campus Housing, University Center East, The Catholic University of America, Washington, D.C. 20064.

Student Group

Approximately 6,000 students, 3,600 of whom are graduate students, are enrolled at the University. Of these, about 290 are enrolled at NCSSS. Coming from all over the United States and several other countries, students bring with them diverse work and volunteer experiences, as well as varied cultural, religious, and ethnic backgrounds.

Student Outcomes

Graduates are involved in a range of practice, including counseling, advocacy, community organization, teaching, policy and program development, and administration. M.S.W. graduates are employed in federal agencies, schools, family service and family preservation agencies, hospitals, child welfare agencies, national associations, community development programs, residential treatment centers, hospices, and programs serving the elderly. Doctoral graduates are social work educators in the United States and abroad, clinical researchers, and policy analysts with local, government, and national agencies.

Location

CUA's 144-acre, tree-lined campus in the northeast quadrant of Washington, D.C., provides a picturesque setting for study and reflection, just a few miles away from the nation's capital. Campus activities include a wide range of concerts, theater productions, lecture programs, and film series. Cultural, artistic, and scholarly resources of the Washington, D.C., area, within easy subway access of the campus, include the Smithsonian Institution, Capitol Hill, the John F. Kennedy Center for the Performing Arts, the National Institutes of Health, and the Library of Congress.

The University and The School

Established as a graduate institution in 1889, Catholic University has evolved into a modern university committed to graduate, undergraduate, and professional education and to the cultivation of the arts. A community of scholars, the University is dedicated to scholarship and research as well as service to the larger community.

The National Catholic School of Social Service is grounded in the social justice and charity foundation of Catholic intellectual tradition and Judeo-Christian values and in the tradition of a modern university that welcomes all forms of human inquiry and values.

Applying

Applications to the M.S.W. program are accepted for fall semesters only. Early submission of applications is encouraged, especially for those seeking scholarships or grants. Deadlines for completion of application portfolios are as follows: advanced standing/M.S.W. transfer students, April 1; full-time, May 1; and part-time, May 30. Those seeking University scholarships must submit all admissions materials, including GRE scores, by February 1. Doctoral applications are accepted for fall and spring semesters.

Correspondence and Information

Loretta V. Saks, LCSW-C, Director of Admissions
and Financial Aid
National Catholic School of Social Service
Cardinal Station
The Catholic University of America
Washington, D.C. 20064
Telephone: 202-319-5496
Fax: 202-319-5093
E-mail: cua-ncsss@cua.edu
World Wide Web: http://www.cua.edu/www/sss

The Catholic University of America

THE FACULTY AND THEIR RESEARCH

Frederick L. Ahearn Jr., Professor; D.S.W., Columbia. Refugees, disasters and disaster victims, planning social services, community organization, and international social work.
Sandra Stukes Chipungu, Associate Professor; Ph.D., Michigan. Child welfare services, kinship care, women and substance abuse, high-risk youth programs, African-American families, public policies.
Sr. Ann Patrick Conrad, Dean and Associate Professor; D.S.W., Catholic University. Social justice, religion and social work, organizational research, object relations theory, social work supervision, social work ethics.
Carole Cox, Associate Professor; D.S.W., Maryland. Aging, service utilization by aged, ethnicity and aging, hospice care, home-care services for AIDS patients.
Barbara Early, Associate Professor; D.S.W., Catholic University. Children and families, clinical supervision, family preservation.
Barbara Bailey Etta, Assistant Professor and Director of Field Instruction; D.S.W., Howard. Child welfare, field practicum, AIDS and the African-American community.
Cathleen Gray, Associate Professor; Ph.D., Maryland. Conflict resolution, divorce mediation.
Michele Hawkins, Associate Professor, Assistant Dean, and Co-Chair, M.S.W. Program; Ph.D., Southern Illinois. Policy, health and mental health, violence.
Suzanne Heurtin-Roberts, Assistant Professor; Ph.D., Berkeley. Health and mental health services for African Americans, cultural diversity, women's health, health behavior, cultural and services research, qualitative research methods.
Sr. M. Vincentia Joseph, Professor; D.S.W., Catholic University. Supervision and consultation, role coping, social work ethics, religion and spirituality in social work practice, organizational burnout, and social work education.
John H. Noble Jr., Professor; Ph.D., Brandeis. Health, mental health, disability, and employment policies; theories of organizational and intergovernmental behavior, quantitative and qualitative research methods; advocacy.
Elizabeth M. Plionis, Associate Professor; D.S.W., Maryland. Medical social work, school social work, child and adolescent development, teaching social work.
Marie Raber, Assistant Professor, Assistant Dean, and Chair, Baccalaureate Program; D.S.W., Fordham. Occupational social work; consultant work in employee assistant programs, career management, and human resources development with organizations; influence of workplace issues on the individual and the family.
Juliet Cassuto Rothman, Visiting Assistant Professor; Ph.D., American. Ethical issues in social work, societal oppression and diversity, theory and practice.
Christine Anlauf Sabatino, Assistant Professor; D.S.W., Catholic University. Clinical social work practice; public and private school social work practice and research, particularly in areas of early intervention and special education programs; and child treatment.
Joseph Shields, Associate Professor, Assistant Dean, and Chair, Ph.D. Program; Ph.D., Catholic University. Substance abuse prevention, organizational planning, religion in society.
Elizabeth D. Smith, Associate Professor and Editor, *Social Thought*; D.S.W., Catholic University. Transpersonal and spiritual dimensions of social work with the terminally ill, enhancement of clinical practice through research methods.
Doris J. Snow, Visiting Assistant Professor; D.S.W., Catholic University. Family mental health.
Daniel Thursz, Cardinal O'Boyle Professor; D.S.W., Catholic University. Gerontology, social policy, community organization, volunteerism.
Elizabeth Timberlake, Professor; D.S.W., Catholic University. Clinical social work with children, homeless women and children, school social work, children's coping and adaptation with handicapping conditions, mental health, clinical practice research issues.
Mary Jeanne Verdieck, Associate Professor, Associate Dean, and Co-chair, M.S.W. Program; Ph.D., Catholic University. Research methodology, child welfare.

The International Center on Global Aging

The International Center on Global Aging was established in 1996 to improve the lives of older people throughout the world by advancing the international understanding of the strengths and needs of older people and of policies and programs to serve them. The center provides opportunities for the direct personal exchange of ideas and information; supports comparative studies of aging policies and programs from social, political, economic, and cultural perspectives among countries; and supports international visitors who come to the United States to study aging, conduct seminars on aging issues, and provide training on aging.

COLUMBIA UNIVERSITY

School of Social Work

Programs of Study

The School of Social Work offers a Master of Science degree in social work. Students may select from a variety of degree programs, all of which require combined study in class and fieldwork. Degree programs offered are a two-year full-time program, advanced standing (for B.S.W. graduates), a reduced residency program (for students who are currently employed in social service agencies), an extended program (combination of part- and full-time study over a period of three to four years), and a transfer program (for graduate students transferring from a full-time accredited M.S.W. program).

A student may choose one of the following five social work method areas: clinical, advanced generalist practice and programming (AGPP), social administration, social policy, and social research. Students also choose fields of practice that determine their second-year fieldwork assignment.

Fieldwork represents the central component in each student's professional education. Columbia students benefit from an extensive network of more than 300 public and private agencies and organizations. These include such training settings as medical and psychiatric hospitals, mental-health clinics, family agencies, facilities for the aging, community programs, courts, unions, employee assistance programs, corporations, schools, and planning and coordinating councils.

The School also offers various dual-degree programs for graduate students who seek to combine social work with other professional studies. Dual-degree programs are currently offered in conjunction with the following schools: Bank Street College (special education), Columbia University School of Business, Columbia University School of Architecture (urban planning), Columbia University School of Law, Columbia University School of International and Public Affairs (public policy and public administration), Columbia University School of Public Health, Jewish Theological Seminary, and Union Theological Seminary.

In addition, the School offers the following minor programs to students: business administration, international social welfare, law, and public policy and administration.

Research Facilities

The Whitney M. Young, Jr. Memorial Library of the School of Social Work houses one of the most outstanding collections in the field and is expanded yearly. The library includes more than 75,000 bound volumes and an estimated 20,000 pieces of unbound material. Students also have access to the many other collections in the University library system. A computer laboratory is available to social work students and is located in the School of Social Work.

Financial Aid

Financial aid is awarded through the Office of Student Financial Services at the School of Social Work. Aid is awarded on the basis of need, with consideration given to family contributions, a spouse's income, the applicant's savings, and employment income. Social work students finance their education with funds from various sources including, but not limited to, federal and state loan programs, Federal Stafford Student Loans, Federal Stafford Unsubsidized Loans, and Federal Perkins Loans; school loans, school scholarships, Federal Work-Study funds, and the New York State Tuition Assistance Program (TAP) supplement the various loan funds. Eighty-four percent of the 1997–98 class received some form of financial assistance.

Further information regarding financial aid opportunities may be obtained from the Office of Student Financial Services, 622 West 113th Street, New York, New York 10025 (telephone: 212-854-2867).

Cost of Study

For 1998–99, the cost per point is $641. At 30 points per year, which is the average for full-time matriculation, tuition costs $19,230. Miscellaneous costs, including books, travel, and fees, are estimated at $2836.

Living and Housing Costs

The cost of living (including housing) for the 1998–99 academic year is estimated at $16,297 for a single person, $21,414 for a married couple, and $6303 for a student living at home.

University housing is available to full-time social work students attending the Morningside campus.

Student Group

Forty-two percent of the 1997–98 student population was 25 years old or younger, 28 percent was between 26 and 30, 16 percent was from 31 to 40, and 14 percent was over 40 years of age. Eighty-six percent of the students are women. Asian-American, African-American, and Latino students constitute 35 percent of the class; international students make up 10 percent.

Location

Through its location in the city of New York, the School provides students with a rich and stimulating learning experience of urban living and the problems associated with such a setting. This location allows students to become part of an environment that presents a broad array of social service needs and social work resources. Students also have an opportunity to explore one of the most fascinating urban settings in the country, rich with cultural and ethnic diversity.

The School

The Columbia University School of Social Work, the oldest school of social work in the country, opened in 1898 under the auspices of the Charity Organization Society (now the Community Service Society).

Originally named the New York School of Philanthropy, it was renamed the New York School of Social Work in 1916 and the Columbia University School of Social Work in 1963, culminating a lengthy affiliation with Columbia University.

In 1983, the School opened its educational site on the campus of Purchase College, State University of New York (SUNY) to provide greater accessibility to students who reside in Westchester County, Rockland County, and Connecticut. The spacious classroom and ground facilities are accessible by both public bus service and automobile, with ample parking space available on campus lots. The site is centrally located near several major highways and is 1 mile south of Greenwich, Connecticut, and 3 miles north of White Plains, New York.

Applying

Applicants for admission into the Columbia M.S. degree program must have a bachelor's degree in arts, letters, philosophy, or science from an accredited college or university. The application consists of a personal statement, all official transcripts, and three letters of reference. GRE scores are not required but may be submitted to strengthen the application. It is recommended that applicants submit the necessary materials on or before March 1, particularly if financial aid or housing assistance is being sought. In some cases, the Office of Admissions may request an interview.

Dual-degree applicants must apply to each school separately and meet the admission requirements of both schools.

Correspondence and Information

Admissions Office
School of Social Work
Columbia University
622 West 113th Street
New York, New York 10025
Telephone: 212-854-2856
Fax: 212-854-2975

Columbia University

FULL-TIME FACULTY

Sheila H. Akabas, Professor of Social Work and Director, Center for Social Policy and Practice in the Workplace; Ph.D., NYU. Labor and social policy, equal employment opportunities, employee assistance programs, substance abuse.
Cynthia Bailey-Dempsey, Assistant Professor of Social Work; Ph.D., SUNY at Albany. School social work, homeless youth, developmental research.
Denise Burnette, Associate Professor of Social Work; Ph.D., Berkeley. Teaching research methods, quality of life, qualitative and quantitative research methods.
Grace Christ, Associate Professor of Social Work; D.S.W., Columbia. Psychosocial oncology, hospital social work, AIDS caregivers.
Richard A. Cloward, Professor of Social Work and Founder, HumanSERVE; Ph.D., Columbia. Deviant behavior, politics of social welfare.
Martha Dore, Associate Professor of Social Work; Ph.D., Chicago. Emotionally disturbed youth, family abuse, foster care, program evaluation.
Nabila El-Bassel, Associate Professor; D.S.W., Columbia. Alcoholism, substance abuse, occupational social work, AIDS, international social work.
Ronald A. Feldman, Professor of Social Work and Dean; Ph.D., Michigan. Adolescent mental health.
Irwin Garfinkel, Professor of Social Work; Ph.D., Michigan. Social policy, child support.
Alex Gitterman, Professor of Social Work and Director, Maternal and Child Health Training Project; Ed.D., Columbia. Organizational behavior, school drug prevention, family services.
Neil Guterman, Assistant Professor; Ph.D., Michigan. Preventive intervention in child and family welfare, clinical effectiveness and clinician efficacy.
Idris Andrew Hamid, Assistant Professor; Ph.D., Michigan. Substance abuse among adolescents.
Peg Hess, Associate Professor of Social Work; Ph.D., Illinois at Urbana-Champaign. Child welfare policy, program, and practice.
Andre Ivanoff, Associate Professor of Social Work; Ph.D., Washington (Seattle). Suicidal behavior, homeless women.
Aurora P. Jackson, Assistant Professor of Social Work; Ph.D., Ohio State. Correlates of positive outcomes for mothers and children based on maternal working status among poor single black mothers with preschool-age children.
Helene Jackson, Associate Professor of Social Work; Ph.D., Smith. Adolescent mental health, child sexual abuse, multicultural training.
Sheila B. Kamerman, Professor of Social Work and Co-Director, Cross-National Studies Research Program; D.S.W., Columbia. Income support policies for families with young children, social services, the welfare state.
James P. Kunz, Instructor; Ph.D., Michigan. Social policy, intergenerational effects of welfare and policy, causes and consequences of teen pregnancy, social work and the law.
Ellen Lukens, Assistant Professor of Social Work; Ph.D., Columbia. Families, mental health, siblings and chronic illness, supervision, clinical services research, qualitative and quantitative methods.
Randy Magen, Assistant Professor of Social Work; Ph.D., Wisconsin. Multimethod approach, stress management, family abuse, group dynamics.
Gerald Mallon, Assistant Professor; D.S.W., CUNY, Hunter. Social welfare needs of gay and lesbian adolescents, residential treatment, animal-assisted activity therapy.
Lawrence Martin, Associate Professor; Ph.D., Arizona State. Productivity in government, public-private sector enterprise, public policy.
Mark A. Mattaini, Assistant Professor and Associate Director, Center for the Study of Social Work Practice; D.S.W., Columbia. Assessment, addictive behaviors, behavioral practice.
Brenda G. McGowan, Professor of Social Work; D.S.W., Columbia. Child welfare, case advocacy, children's rights.
Marcia K. Meyers, Assistant Professor of Social Work; Ph.D., Berkeley. Child poverty, child welfare, social policy.
Abraham Monk, Professor of Social Work and Director, Institute on Aging and Adult Human Development; Ph.D., Brandeis. Social gerontology, organizational development, older hospital patients.
Claudia L. Moreno, Assistant Professor of Social Work; Ph.D., Ohio State. Developmental disabilities; health; Hispanics; cross-cultural social work; clinical practice with children, adolescents, and their families.
Ada Chan Yuk-Sim Mui, Associate Professor of Social Work; Ph.D., Washington (St. Louis). Older volunteers, the effectiveness of hospital discharge plans for elderly patients, racial differences in family caregiving.
Edward J. Mullen, Professor of Social Work and Director, Center for the Study of Social Work Practice; D.S.W., Columbia. Expanding research-based knowledge about social work practice.
Howard W. Polsky, Professor of Social Work; Ph.D., Wisconsin. The application of social science theory to social work.
Robert F. Schilling, Associate Professor of Social Work; Ph.D., Wisconsin. Child and substance abuse, families with disabled members.
Steven Schinke, Professor of Social Work and Director, AIDS Prevention Research Center; Ph.D., Wisconsin. Clinical interventions to prevent social, behavioral, and health problems among early adolescents.
Tazuko Shibusawa, Assistant Professor; Ph.D., UCLA. Clinical social work and cross-cultural social work.
Barbara Levy Simon, Associate Professor of Social Work; Ph.D., Bryn Mawr. Administration, organizational culture and behavior, social welfare history and policy, feminization of poverty.
Renee Solomon, Associate Professor of Social Work; D.S.W., CUNY, Hunter. Social work practice with older people and their families.
Mary E. Sormanti, Instructor; Ph.D., Boston College. Practice, pediatric oncology, health care, families and bereavement.
Jane Waldfogel, Assistant Professor; Ph.D., Harvard. Urban studies, econometrics and statistical methods.
Karina L. Walters, Assistant Professor of Social Work; Ph.D., UCLA. Urban American Indian mental health, gay and lesbian group identity, cross-cultural sensitivity training.
Darrell P. Wheeler, Assistant Professor; Ph.D., Pittsburgh. Ethnographic approaches to program evaluation, HIV prevention, mentally ill homeless.
Marianne Yoshioka, Assistant Professor of Social Work; Ph.D., Florida State. Marriage and family, cultural competency in practice, intervention design and development, addictions and HIV prevention.

HOWARD UNIVERSITY

School of Social Work

Programs of Study

The Howard University School of Social Work offers two graduate degrees: the Master of Social Work and the Doctor of Philosophy in Social Work. The mission of the School of Social Work, congruent with the mission of Howard University, is to provide a high-quality social work education for students irrespective of race, creed, gender, or national origin. The School is committed to educating students for professional social work practice and scholarship who will be able to assist in the solution of human, organizational, policy, and social problems, particularly those affecting the African-American and other minority communities and the poor.

The M.S.W. degree (60 credit hours) equips graduates for advanced social work practice in direct services (with individuals, small groups, and families) and community organization and social service management (with large groups, communities, or institutions). Concentrations are offered in special settings, including criminal justice, family and child welfare, social gerontology, social work with displaced populations, social work in health-care settings, and social work in mental health settings, accompanied by field instruction in community agencies and institutions.

The Ph.D. program prepares social workers for leadership positions in the field and as social work researchers and educators. Two concentrations are offered: health systems and family and child service systems. Individual concentrations may be developed.

Research Facilities

The on-site social work library has an outstanding collection of professional books, journals, and microform publications and a computer library search capacity. By virtue of its Washington, D.C., location, students and faculty members have access to unexcelled library resources that include the immense resources of the Library of Congress and the specialized libraries of government agencies such as the National Institutes of Health and the National Institute of Mental Health. The computer facilities in Inabel Burns Lindsay Hall, designed for student instructional and research activities, allow students access to the Howard University mainframe computer. The School's Family Resource and Research Center, located in a nearby inner-city neighborhood, is funded by the William H. Cosby Jr. and Camille O. Hanks Cosby Foundation. This center is designed to provide field instruction and a site for research and demonstration projects on strengthening family life.

Financial Aid

Limited financial aid is available through the University's Office of Financial Aid and Student Employment in the form of tuition scholarships, fellowships, loans, grants, and part-time employment. A limited number of graduate assistantships, based on need and academic performance, are available through the School of Social Work, and a few teaching assistantships are available only to advanced doctoral students. Some agencies that provide field instruction placements to social work students may offer paid field instruction opportunities or work-study arrangements through the Office of Field Instruction.

Cost of Study

Graduate tuition and fees are approximately $5200 per semester. Fees include student activities and on-campus health services and benefits. Approximately $800 to $1000 should be allocated for books and supplies. All costs are subject to change.

Living and Housing Costs

The University provides limited accommodations for graduate students. An Off-Campus Housing Office is available to provide assistance in securing reasonable housing in the greater metropolitan Washington, D.C., area, which includes Washington, D.C., and nearby Virginia and Maryland. An estimated range of $850 to $1500 per month should be allowed for living costs.

Student Group

A total of 418 students were enrolled in the two graduate programs in 1997–98; 380 were in the master's-level program and 38 were in the doctoral program. Of this very diverse group, 20 percent were men, and there were students from nineteen countries around the world. All students are automatically members of the School of Social Work Student Government Association (SGA), which recommends policy to the School, plans activities for the student body, and implements programs of community service. The SGA is a member of the Graduate Student Assembly of Howard University.

Student Outcomes

Graduates of the M.S.W. program are employed in a wide variety of public and private social service settings, such as public welfare departments, courts, hospitals and nursing homes, child development facilities, schools, mental health clinics and hospitals, homeless shelters and refugee centers, federal agencies, and private practice. Most doctoral graduates pursue careers as social work researchers, educators, and administrators.

Location

Howard University is located in one of the most stimulating cities in the world, the nation's capital, internationally recognized for its political power, prestige, and influence. The city's attractions range from its imposing national monuments, museums, zoos, parks, touring Broadway productions, and international cuisine to its unique educational resources and exciting nightlife. As the power center of the world, it gives students an opportunity for firsthand observation and participation in the political process.

The University and The School

Howard University, established in 1867, is a private institution with a tradition of developing and nurturing leadership. It is the most comprehensive historically black university in the world, with seventeen schools and colleges offering approximately 180 areas of study, a number of research institutes, a major teaching hospital, a public television station, a commercial radio station, and a scholarly publishing house. The School of Social Work has contributed significantly to the University's worldwide reputation for its commitment to excellence and positive response to the pressing societal problems that jeopardize the well-being of the nation and underrepresented people worldwide.

Applying

Completed applications for admission to the School of Social Work must be received on or before April 1 for the fall semester and October 1 for the spring semester. A baccalaureate degree (broadly based in the liberal arts) from an accredited undergraduate college or university, with a cumulative GPA of 2.5 or higher, is required for admission to the master's program. A Master of Social Work degree is required for admission to the Doctor of Philosophy in Social Work program.

Correspondence and Information

For the M.S.W. program:
Blanchita P. Porter
Director, Admissions and Financial Aid
School of Social Work
Howard University
Washington, D.C. 20059
Telephone: 202-806-6450
Fax: 202-387-4309

For the Ph.D. program:
Dr. Fayrial Ross-Sheriff
Director, Ph.D. Program
School of Social Work
Howard University
Washington, D.C. 20059
Telephone: 202-806-7305
Fax: 202-387-4309

Howard University

THE FACULTY AND THEIR RESEARCH

Alvis V. Adair, Professor; Ph.D., Michigan. Program evaluation, mental retardation.
Joyce T. Berry, Visiting Professor and Director of the Multidisciplinary Gerontology Center; Ph.D., Fordham; J.D., Georgetown. Gerontology, law, social policy.
Sheryl Brissett-Chapman, Assistant Professor; Ed.D., Harvard. Child welfare, children and families, social welfare policy.
Annie Woodley Brown, Assistant Professor and Assistant Dean of Student Affairs; D.S.W., Howard. Troubled adolescents, children and family services, family violence.
Flora B. Bryant, Assistant Professor; Ph.D., Union (Ohio). Human behavior, clinical practice, psychopathology.
Don E. Clarkson, Assistant Professor; M.S.W., Howard. Group work.
James E. Craigen, Associate Professor and Program Coordinator, Macro Sequence; M.S.W., Atlanta. Community organization, case management, systems theory, information systems and social work.
Sandra Edmonds Crewe, Assistant Professor; Ph.D., Howard. Federal housing programs, welfare reform, worker-client interactions, ethnography.
Richard A. English, Professor and Dean; Ph.D., Michigan. Social policy, displaced populations, black family, human service organizations.
Lawrence E. Gary, Professor; Ph.D., Michigan. Mental health, black males.
Ruby M. Gourdine, Associate Professor and Director of Field Instruction; D.S.W., Howard. Adolescent pregnancy, school social work, developmental disabilities, family violence.
Anthony J. Grasso, Associate Professor; D.S.W., CUNY, Hunter. Administration and social policy, utilization of research information, management information systems for evaluation of human service organizations.
Gladys Walton Hall, Associate Professor and Program Coordinator, Direct Services (Micro) Sequence; Ph.D., Maryland. Mental health, direct services.
Brin D. Hawkins, Associate Professor and Associate Dean of Academic Affairs; Ph.D., Brandeis. Gerontology, social service management, social policy.
Norma S. C. Jones, Associate Professor; D.S.W., Howard. Family therapy, cross-cultural development and research.
Mignonette N. Keller, Assistant Professor; Ph.D., Howard. Family theory and therapy, aging.
Joyce A. Ladner, Professor; Ph.D., Washington (St. Louis). Black adolescent development, family theory and black families.
Maxwell C. Manning, Assistant Professor; Ph.D., NYU. Racial identity, mental health and health, cultural competence, systems development, program evaluation.
Patricia M. O'Mealley, Assistant Professor; M.S.W., Howard. Mental health, clinical practice, staff development.
Dorothy M. Pearson, Professor; Ph.D., Wisconsin. Mental health, black women, social work education.
Nancy E. Randolph, Visiting Professor; Ph.D., Alabama. Social work education, accreditation.
Fayrial Ross-Sheriff, Professor and Director, Ph.D. Program; Ph.D., Michigan. Displaced populations, refugee and immigrant families, Muslim families, family violence.
Philip H. Schervish, Associate Professor and Coordinator of Research; Ph.D., Illinois. Multicriteria decision supports, social welfare economics, information technology applications.
Jacqueline M. Smith, Associate Professor; Ph.D., Michigan. Gerontology, social research, social work technology, black families and religion, practice research.
Cudore L. Snell, Associate Professor and Program Coordinator, Human Behavior and Social Environment Sequence; D.S.W., Howard. Street males, HIV men, AIDS, human diversity, help-seeking behavior.
Odessa D. Thompson, Associate Professor; Ph.D., Harvard. Psychoanalytic theory, learning disabilities, medical social work.
Clarice D. Walker, Associate Professor; M.S., Columbia. Black families, foster care, child and family welfare.
Hulon Willis Jr., Assistant Professor; M.S.W., Howard. Criminal justice, social work management.

RESEARCH AND SPECIAL PROJECTS

The Multidisciplinary Center for Gerontology. The MCG, housed in the School, is funded by the U.S. Administration on Aging. The center's programs encompass career preparation, continuing education and training, research, consultation, and public information dissemination to advance the interests of the American minority aged, particularly the African-American aged.
The Cosby Initiative. A gift from the William H. Cosby Jr. and Camille O. Hanks Cosby Foundation supports the following programs at the School: the Cosby Fellowship Award for an outstanding second-year student interested in practice related to teen pregnancy, family preservation, poverty, and issues of growth and development of African-American children and youth; the Cosby Scholar; a visiting scholar; the Seminar on African-American Families, led by the Cosby Scholar; the Annual Cosby Lecture, given by the Cosby Scholar; and the Baker's Dozen Family Resource and Research Center.
HBCU Policy Analyses Project for At-Risk Youth. This project, funded by the U.S. Department of Health and Human Services, provides short-term studies to the Office of the Assistant Secretary for Planning and Evaluation in policy research.
Healthy Start and Infant Mortality Projects. The Healthy Start Evaluation Project (1993–98), funded by the District of Columbia government, evaluates selected components of the federally initiated Healthy Start Program for reducing the infant mortality rate by 50 percent in five years. The Infant Mortality Review Project, also funded by the District of Columbia government, encompasses an in-depth case review of infant deaths in the District of Columbia. Faculty members are also involved in the National Institutes of Health's five-year, multicenter initiative to study community interventions to reduce infant mortality in Washington, D.C.
Housing and Community Studies Center. The Housing and Community Studies Center, funded primarily by grants and contracts from HUD, focuses on training, technical assistance, and research. Activities include program evaluations, housing research, and training in organizational effectiveness, fair housing, financial management, and board relations.
African-American Male Development Program. This program conducts research on the perceptions of masculinity in African-American and African communities and provides technical assistance to community groups on African-American male development.
Homeless Intervention Project. Two research projects are under way to evaluate the health-care delivery system for the homeless. These projects employ nurses and recruit homeless persons into nursing careers
Mental Health in the Black Community. The focal point of this research has been the social and cultural correlates of depressive symptoms in African-American adults.
Job Training Skills and Development for Public Housing Residents. The goal of the project, funded by the Department of Housing and Urban Development, is to provide skill development training and conduct research in the area of public housing residents.
Howard University Student Training Initiative for Social Work Practice for Victims and Perpetrators of Domestic Violence. This project is funded by the U.S. Department of Health and Human Services, Administration for Children and Families, Office of Community Services Family Violence Prevention and Services. The project provides stipends for students who show promise and demonstrate serious interest and commitment to issues of domestic violence in underserved populations.
Howard University and Prince George's County Welfare Reform Research Project. This project develops customer profiles and identifies issues related to welfare reform.

MARYWOOD UNIVERSITY

School of Social Work

Program of Study

The M.S.W. program consists of 45 credits of classroom courses and 15 credits of practicum education. Concentration is in integrative practice, with specializations in either interpersonal intervention or administration. The foundation content is designed to develop basic knowledge of social welfare policy, problems and issues of human behavior from the psychosocial and sociocultural perspective, the ethical foundations of social work practice, essential characteristics of the scientific method and the process of reviewing and relating research literature to practice, and theory and methods of intervention. The second year facilitates students' development of advanced social work skills. The first semester incorporates course work in both interpersonal intervention and administration with practicum experience in the student's chosen practice specialization. Course work and practicum experience in the specialization continue through the year and, in tandem with electives, support the development of advanced knowledge and skill in the student's chosen area. The full-time program calls for two academic years of study. Summer courses are available for those who prefer a lighter class load in fall or spring. There are two basic part-time plans to complete the program in three or four years. In Scranton, part-time students do classwork on Saturdays; on the Lehigh Valley Campus classes are offered on Monday and Wednesday evenings. Practicum agency placements usually can be developed for students in the region in which they live. Practicum assignments are 16 hours per week, undertaken in the semesters when the student takes theory and practice classes. Advanced standing is available to those who have earned a B.S.W. degree from a CSWE-accredited program within five years of application to Marywood. An M.P.A. may be earned in combination with the M.S.W. under a dual-degree program. Students with a special interest in work with the aging may earn a Certificate of Specialization in Gerontology by taking 12 credit hours through the Gerontology Institute at Marywood, and students can prepare for certification in practicing social work in schools.

Research Facilities

The Learning Resources Center includes the library and media center. The library collection encompasses more than 202,000 volumes, 1,100 periodical titles, and more than 41,000 nonprint items. The library is open, with a professional librarian on duty, 88 hours a week. The library collection is accessible through an online database. CD-ROM databases are available. The media center provides graphic, photographic, television, multi-image, and equipment services. The University has integrated its library and academic computing services. Research and data analysis are supported by a host computer on the campus fiber-optic network. Compilers for several languages and SPSS-X can be accessed from the 22 VT 320 terminals or any remote location via modem link. Graduate students may secure an account for 24-hour remote access.

Financial Aid

Partial tuition scholarships are awarded on the basis of financial need to full- and part-time students. Cultural diversity scholarships are available. A limited number of assistantships are available. Assistantships are approved for 18 credits and include a stipend for 15 to 20 hours of work per week. Applications are available from the School of Social Work. Students enrolled for at least 6 credits per semester can borrow under the Federal Stafford Student Loan.

Cost of Study

Tuition for 1998–99 is $459 per credit ($464 at the Lehigh Valley Center). General fees are $530 per year full-time, $180 per semester part-time. Deferred payment plans are offered.

Living and Housing Costs

On-campus housing is available for graduate students. Arrangements can be made for full-semester use for on-campus housing or for weekly use for a fixed number of days by the semester. The Office of Student Affairs maintains a listing of private off-campus rooms and apartments. Meals can be obtained in the dining center. Full room and board costs on campus begin at $5200. Rents off campus are less than in major metropolitan areas.

Student Group

The total enrollment at Marywood University in 1997–98 was about 2,800, of whom about 1,200 were graduate students. The School of Social Work enrolls approximately 375 students, including 140 at the Lehigh Valley Center. An entering class includes about 40 in each part-time program (Saturday and Lehigh Valley) and about 50 full-time, of whom 15 have advanced standing. About 20 percent receive scholarships. The average age of students is 34 years, and all have related work experience, through volunteer activity, internships, or employment. Class size in all programs is typically 20. The group of students who enter as a class can expect to work together throughout their program. Each course is evaluated by students each semester, and faculty members are regularly rated highly for knowledge, quality of teaching, and accessibility.

Student Outcomes

Degree completion rates are 85 percent or better. Graduates move quickly into professional-level employment. More than 80 percent have prepared for work with individuals, families, and small groups, and accept positions of direct service in varied fields of practice. Mental health and family/children's service settings employ the largest number of graduates. Health-care settings also employ significant numbers, and graduates are found in the full range of social work practice areas.

Location

Marywood University is situated in a suburban section of Scranton, a city of about 80,000. It is located a little more than 100 miles from New York City to the east and from Philadelphia to the south. It is served by the Wilkes-Barre Scranton International Airport and is easily accessible by a network of interstate highways. The Pocono Mountains resort areas and several beautiful lakes can be reached within 45 minutes or less. Montage Mountain ski area is 15 minutes away.

The University and The School

Marywood University, established 1915, is an independent, comprehensive Catholic university, owned and sponsored by the Congregation of Sisters, Servants of the Immaculate Heart of Mary. Graduate studies were inaugurated in 1921. The School of Social Work opened in 1969, and is fully accredited by the Council on Social Work Education. The school prepares students for advanced practice with individuals, families, and groups, or in program planning and social service agency administration.

Applying

Application deadlines are: for fall semester (full- or part-time), May 15; for summer (full-time advanced standing and part-time), February 15; for spring (advanced standing only), October 15; for assistantships, February 15; for scholarships, May 1. Applications must include three references; official transcripts, showing course work in social and behavior sciences, 6 credits minimum, and humanities; and a personal statement. Individual interviews are required; telephone interviews can be arranged.

Correspondence and Information

Director of Admissions
School of Social Work
Marywood University
Scranton, Pennsylvania 18509

Telephone: 717-348-6282
800-548-4898 (toll-free)
Fax: 717-961-4742
E-mail: ssw_adm@ac.marywood.edu
World Wide Web: http://www.marywood.edu

Maryland University

THE FACULTY AND THEIR RESEARCH

Phyllis Black, Professor; D.S.W., Catholic. Professional gatekeeping, practice boundaries and ethics.
Stephen Burke, Associate Professor; Ph.D., M.S.W., Minnesota. Military families in times of deployment, rural service delivery.
Doris Chechotka-McQuade, Assistant Professor; M.S.W., Adelphi; Ph.D., Fordham. Stress management in hospice settings, grief.
Geraldine Dawson, Assistant Professor; M.D., Einstein (Yeshiva); M.S.W., Smith. Psychopharmacology, attention deficit hyperactivity disorder, resiliency in childhood.
John Greggo, Assistant Professor; M.S.W., Marywood. Family-of-origin experiences of counseling professionals, welfare reform.
Joanne Gumpert, Associate Professor; D.S.W., Adelphi. Peer group involvement of military family adolescents, social work professionals' ways of knowing, practice with groups in rural areas.
Elizabeth Hartley, Associate Professor; D.S.W., Pennsylvania. International comparisons of early life experiences that influence career choices for social work.
George Haskett, Associate Professor; D.S.W., Columbia; M.P.A., Virginia Commonwealth. Critical thinking and social policy, child welfare and welfare reform, privatization.
Dorothy Jeffreys, Professor; M.S.W., Ph.D., Michigan. Adolescent development in military families, women aboard ships in the U.S. Navy.
Lloyd Lyter, Assistant Professor; M.S.W., Marywood; M.P.A., Temple; Ph.D., Rutgers. HIV and chemical dependency.
Kathryn Skinner, Assistant Professor; M.S.W., NYU; Ph.D., SUNY at Albany. Hospital ethics committees and social work roles.
Jane Strobino, Associate Professor; D.S.W., Catholic. Student evaluations of teaching, instructional innovations and strategies.
Joanne Whelley, Associate Professor; D.S.W., Fordham. Family preservation, professional gatekeeping.
William Whitaker, Professor and Dean; M.S.W., Atlanta; Ph.D., Brandeis. Hunger and poverty, grassroots social movements and social change, international social welfare.

SIMMONS COLLEGE

School of Social Work

Programs of Study

The M.S.W. program of the School of Social Work (SSW) prepares men and women for direct practice in social work, with particular competence in clinical methods. The program consists of two years of full-time academic and field study. An extended program taking three or four years is available for a small number of students. Master's students have two days of classes and three days of field work each week each year. A yearlong group research project is required in the second year. Most of the curriculum consists of required courses, but there is choice within the requirements. Many electives are offered in the second year. The knowledge and values of all roles in social work are taught; however, emphasis is on the needs of professionals who will work primarily with individuals, families, and small groups. Applicants with a B.S.W. may apply for credit toward the M.S.W. degree.

The Ph.D. program is a continuation of the School's long-standing commitment to excellence in direct practice. Its orientation is to the development of the advanced knowledge required for leadership in a variety of clinical roles. The program is offered on a part-time basis, with classes scheduled on Thursdays. All students must be currently involved in clinical practice. Four to 8 students are admitted to each class. Course work extends over three years. Qualifying examinations and a dissertation are required.

Research Facilities

The School has its own library, staffed by 2 full-time librarians, located on-site. One of three professional libraries within the College Library System, the SSW Library has a specialized collection in the fields of social work practice, human behavior, social work research, social policy, and related subject areas. The collection consists of about 21,000 monographs, more than 200 journal subscriptions, and extensive archival and historical materials. The computerized catalog and information retrieval systems provide access to materials. Students may use all libraries in the College Library System, as well as the member libraries of the Fenway Library Consortium. The School has several available microprinters in its own computer laboratory. This laboratory also provides access to several local mainframe computers.

Financial Aid

The School offers financial aid to both first- and second-year master's students. Since this aid is granted on the basis of need, applicants must complete the Simmons College financial aid form and the Free Application for Federal Student Aid, available from the Office of Financial Aid (telephone: 617-521-2036; e-mail: financialaid@simmons.edu). Aid packages are made up of a combination of College-funded grants and loans, fieldwork-related work-study, and federal loans. A limited number of federal, state, and Veterans Administration traineeships are also available. Students are also encouraged to investigate outside loan programs. A limited amount of aid is available for Ph.D. students.

Cost of Study

The M.S.W. program entails a total of 60 credit hours. The Ph.D. program requires a course load of 45 credit hours. The 1998–99 charge per credit hour is $560. A full-time master's student takes 30 credits a year for an annual tuition total of $16,800. A doctoral student takes 15 credits a year for a yearly tuition of $8400. In addition to tuition charges, master's students are charged $30 and doctoral students $10 in yearly fees.

Living and Housing Costs

College housing is available for social work graduate students. The large student population attending colleges and universities in the Boston area does increase the opportunities for students in cooperative living situations to share housing and food expenses. An excellent public transportation system facilitates easy access to Boston from several nearby communities.

Student Group

The School of Social Work currently has about 270 M.S.W. students and 35 doctoral students. About 11 percent are men, and close to 19 percent are ALANA members (Asian, Latino, African, and Native Americans). More than one third receive some form of financial aid. Students come from diverse backgrounds, and some have advanced degrees in other fields. Graduates find employment throughout New England and the country in public and private family and children's agencies, general hospitals, mental hospitals, health and mental health clinics, schools, courts, and industrial settings. Doctoral students are enrolled on a part-time basis and must be currently involved in clinical practice. They must have had three years of post-M.S.W. work.

Location

The School of Social Work is housed in two town houses on Commonwealth Avenue in Boston's Back Bay. This area is rich in historic sites and is accessible to many cultural and educational institutions. The School is near the Boston Public Garden, the Public Library, and public transportation. Classes are held in both buildings on Commonwealth Avenue as well as at the Main Campus at 300 The Fenway.

The College and The School

Simmons is a private women's college of about 4,000 students, which opened its doors in 1902 with the mission of educating women for work. The School of Social Work was established in 1904, the first such school in the country to be affiliated with an institution of higher learning. From its beginnings, the School educated both women and men. All the College's facilities are available to social work students; the School, however, is located about 2 miles from the main campus. Since opening, the School of Social Work has had ongoing training affiliations with a network of social agencies, hospitals, and clinics in the greater Boston area. It also constantly adds affiliations with new, innovative institutions. The School's atmosphere is scholarly and serious, with a structured program and mostly seminar-size classes.

Applying

Application for the master's program requires the submission of all college and university transcripts, three letters of reference, and a personal statement. The applicant should have maintained a GPA of 3.0 in the last two years of undergraduate study. The doctoral application requires the same material plus a case analysis, resume, and a Miller Analogies Test score. Doctoral applicants are also often seen for a personal interview. Master's applications are due by December 15 for early decision or February 15 for general consideration; doctoral applications are due January 31. The School encourages early application. Financial aid information and forms are available from the College Office of Financial Aid.

Correspondence and Information

Deborah Sheehan, M.S.W., Director of Admissions
School of Social Work
Simmons College
51 Commonwealth Avenue
Boston, Massachusetts 02116

Telephone: 617-521-3920
617-232-9511 (TDDY)
E-mail: sswadmission@simmons.edu
World Wide Web: http://www.simmons.edu

Simmons College

THE FACULTY AND ADMINISTRATION AND THEIR SPECIALIZATIONS

Approximately 40 adjunct professors, not listed here, also offer graduate students the knowledge gained through their rich and diverse practice backgrounds.

Myrna Bocage, Associate Professor; Ph.D., Brandeis. Field education, health care, delivery of medical services.
Carol Elaine Bonner, Associate Professor and Associate Dean; M.S.W., Simmons; M.B.A., Boston University. Field education, clinical services, supervision, organizations and their management, diversity and cross-cultural issues.
Deanna Brooks, Associate Professor; M.S.W., Smith. Field education, human behavior, and theories and psychopathy.
Ruth Grossman Dean, Professor and Director, Doctoral Program; D.S.W., Boston College. Treatment, learning and teaching, supervision.
Ann Fleck-Henderson, Associate Professor; Ph.D., Fielding Institute. Developmental theories, theories and practice of learning and teaching, clinical teaching.
Eileen Freiberg-Dale, Associate Professor; M.S.S.S., Boston University. Field education, clinical practice, research with Social Workers for Peace and Nuclear Disarmament.
Abbie K. Frost, Associate Professor; Ph.D., Case Western Reserve. Research on mental health functioning of children and adolescents, employee assistance programs, substance abuse, program evaluation.
Mary Gilfus, Associate Professor; Ph.D., Brandeis. Multicultural feminist perspectives on social work theory and practice.
Johnnie Hamilton-Mason, Assistant Professor; M.S.W., Simmons. Cross-cultural mental health practice, treatment with adolescents, field education.
Emeline Homonoff, Associate Professor; D.S.W., Boston College. Field education, supervision, organizational theory.
Denise Humm-Delgado, Associate Professor; Ph.D., Brandeis. Social policy, long-term care, services for and practice with Puerto Rican populations.
Stefan Krug, Associate Professor; Ph.D., Simmons. Clinical practice, substance abuse and recovery, cross-cultural mental health.
Michael P. Melendez, Associate Professor; M.S.W., Boston University. Clinical practice, cross-cultural mental health practice, substance abuse and recovery, family treatment.
Kathleen H. Millstein, Associate Professor; D.S.W., Boston College. Research on single-subject design, clinical practice with children and families.
Joseph M. Regan, Professor and Dean; Ph.D., Brandeis. Administration, research on theory and practice of ethics.
Helen Zarsky Reinherz, Professor; Sc.D., Harvard. Mental health of children, adolescents, and young adults; prevention and longitudinal research methods.
Priscilla Mullen Riley, Associate Professor and Director, Field Education; M.S.W., Boston College. Field education, clinical practice, supervision.
Suzanne Sankar, Assistant Professor; M.S.W., Simmons. Field education, community mental health, multicultural practice.
Beverly C. Sealey, Associate Professor; Ph.D., Brandeis. Field education, cultural diversity, child welfare and protective services, forensic social work and social work and the law, social welfare policy and services.
Deborah Sheehan, Director of Admissions; M.S.W., Boston University. Child welfare, administration, social work practice, feminist perspective.
Carol R. Swenson, Professor; D.S.W., Columbia. Clinical practice, social support, qualitative research.

SMITH COLLEGE

School for Social Work

Program of Study

The School for Social Work, open to both men and women, offers a concentration in clinical practice leading to the M.S.W. and Ph.D. degrees. Clinical social work practice is concerned with the interdependence between individuals and their environment and the use of relationships to promote healing, growth, and empowerment. The School also recognizes the pernicious consequences of racism and works to identify and overcome the overt and covert aspects of racism. The program is organized on the Block Plan, designed to integrate theory and practice through a carefully devised sequence of summer academic sessions and intervening winter sessions devoted to clinical internships. The summer sessions provide students with the theoretical framework for practice during the winter months. During the winter, students are placed for eight months in 137 affiliated agencies located in twenty-two geographic areas: Alaska, California, Colorado, Connecticut, the District of Columbia, Georgia, Illinois, Kansas, Maine, Maryland, Massachusetts, New Hampshire, New Jersey, New Mexico, New York, North Carolina, Ohio, Pennsylvania, Rhode Island, Texas, Vermont, and Virginia. The School enters a class once a year, in June.

The M.S.W. program is twenty-seven months in length and comprises three academic ten-week summer sessions and two intervening full-time eight-month field placements in agencies affiliated with the School. The M.S.W. may also be earned through a fifteen-month advanced-standing program (two summers and one winter) that the School offers to graduates of accredited B.S.W. programs who have had twenty months of postbaccalaureate work experience in human services.

The Ph.D. program of twenty-seven months is oriented to the preparation of advanced casework practitioner-scholars, supervisors, and educators. Its residency period consists of two 10-week academic sessions, a final 5-week summer academic session, two intervening clinical internships of three days a week, and a research internship.

Research Facilities

The School utilizes two of Smith College's four libraries—the William Allen Neilson Library (more than 1.1 million volumes, 96,500 microforms, and 2,300 current periodicals and newspapers) and the Science Library (more than 136,000 volumes, 20,000 microfilms, and 700 periodicals)—in addition to the Five College (Amherst College, Hampshire College, Mount Holyoke College, and the University of Massachusetts) interlibrary loan system. The Reference Department offers students extensive bibliographic and research assistance throughout the summer. Students have access to the Academic Computing Center in Seelye Hall and, through that office, to all computer services of the campus. There are computer databases, including Internet access and access to the Five College computer links. The Clinical Research Institute provides small grants for faculty research and is engaged in ongoing agency-based research.

Financial Aid

Financial assistance is available to first- and second-year students in the M.S.W. program and is based on financial need. Every effort is made to assist students in obtaining loan funds under the federally insured loan program.

Cost of Study

For 1998–99, the total tuition cost of the program is $24,840 for twenty-seven months ($10,410 for each full year and $4004 for the final summer). For the B.S.W. advanced standing program, the total tuition is $14,422 for fifteen months; for the Ph.D. program, it is $27,614 for twenty-seven months. Other fees, books, and supplies average approximately $1000 per year. In addition, students should estimate expenses for typing and copying the research project during the final summer.

Living and Housing Costs

On-campus summer housing is available in coed and single-sex dormitories. The cost of room and board for the 1998 summer session is $1800. Off-campus housing is available, and students make their own arrangements. During the field placement period, students must also make their own living arrangements. Expenses include transportation from the School to the agency assignment, rent, food, utilities, medical insurance, and other normal living costs.

Student Group

In 1997–98, there were 416 students (370 women and 46 men ranging in age from 22 to 60) enrolled full-time: 386 in the master's program and 30 in the doctoral program, coming from forty states and four other countries. Students in the master's program have rich and varied backgrounds of work and volunteer experiences in the helping professions; some have made career changes from such fields as education, law, nursing, and business. Graduates are employed as clinical social workers, consultants, directors of agencies, directors of training, supervisors, and administrators, and some are engaged in private practice in conjunction with teaching or agency work and other similar combinations.

Student Outcomes

Job prospects for Smith graduates have proven quite positive. In a survey of recent graduates, more than 75 percent of respondents were able to secure a job within three months of beginning their search. While graduates were hired into a variety of settings, 34 percent found employment in social service agencies, 24 percent in hospitals, and 22 percent in outpatient mental health clinics. Within these settings, 32 percent described their field of practice as mental health, 19 percent as children and youth, and 13 percent as family services or child welfare.

Location

Smith is located in Northampton, Massachusetts. The Five College area is rich in cultural and recreational opportunities during the summer.

The School

The School for Social Work, founded in 1918, continues to demonstrate its commitment to excellence in clinical practice. It pursues its mission through the study of individuals, groups, and families; the interrelated social, cultural, ethnic, and organizational factors that shape the environment in which development occurs; and the service processes through which social workers safeguard and facilitate growth. The School implements its educational mission through the degree-conferring master's and doctoral programs, the Program of Continuing Education, the Clinical Research Institute, the publication of *Smith College Studies in Social Work,* and extension courses for nonmatriculated students.

Applying

The requirements for entry into Plan A of the M.S.W. program include a baccalaureate degree from an accredited college or university and approximately 20 semester hours in the social, biological, and psychological sciences. The advanced-standing program for B.S.W. graduates requires the submission of a case and twenty months postbaccalaureate work experience. The application deadline for the following June is February 15. Applications received by January 1 are given preference in admission and early review of field placement requests. The deadline for application to the Ph.D. program is February 1; an M.S.W. degree is required. Financial aid applications should be filed as soon after January 1 as possible. The nonrefundable application fee for admission is $50.

Correspondence and Information

Office of Admission
School for Social Work
Smith College
Northampton, Massachusetts 01063

Telephone: 413-585-7960
E-mail: sswadmis@smith.edu
World Wide Web: http://www.smith.edu/dept/ssw/sswmsw.html

Smith College

THE FACULTY

Anita L. Lightburn, Professor and Dean; Ed.D., Columbia.
Susan Donner, Associate Professor and Associate Dean; Ph.D., Smith.
Jeane W. Anastas, Professor and Cochair, Doctoral Program; Ph.D., Brandeis.
Joan Berzoff, Professor and Cochair, Doctoral Program; Ed.D., Boston University.

Katherine Basham, Associate Professor, Ph.D., Smith.
James Drisko, Associate Professor; D.S.W., Boston College.
Joyce E. Everett, Associate Professor; Ph.D., Brandeis.
Mary F. Hall, Associate Professor; Ph.D., Simmons.
Carolyn Jacobs, Associate Professor; Ph.D., Brandeis.
Joshua Miller, Associate Professor, Ph.D., Connecticut.
Roger R. Miller, Professor; D.S.W., Western Reserve.
Catherine Nye, Assistant Professor; Ph.D., Chicago.
Caroline Rosenthal, Assistant Professor; M.S.W., Berkeley.
Jerome Sachs, Associate Professor; D.S.W., Adelphi.
Krishna Samantri, Associate Professor; Ph.D., USC.
Gerald Schamess, Professor; M.S.S., Columbia.
Phebe Sessions, Associate Professor; Ph.D., Brandeis.

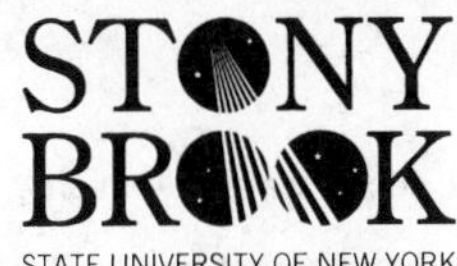

STATE UNIVERSITY OF NEW YORK AT STONY BROOK

School of Social Welfare

Programs of Study

The School of Social Welfare is committed to a society organized around the principles of equality, human dignity, and social justice. In fulfillment of this mission, it offers two graduate programs. The Master of Social Work (M.S.W.) degree prepares students for advanced social work practice. A doctoral program leading to a Ph.D. degree, which emphasizes policy and research in the field of health and mental health, prepares students for careers in social welfare research, teaching, and policy analysis.

The M.S.W. program generally requires two years (64 credits) and combines classroom study with field placements in social welfare agencies. It enables students to concentrate during their second year in either a direct practice sequence emphasizing the provision of services to individuals, families, and groups or a policy, administration, and research sequence that prepares students for administrative, community organizing, and policy-related positions in the social welfare field. The M.S.W. program also offers a modified full-time option that can be completed in 2½ or 3 years, as well as specializations in alcohol and substance abuse, health, and student-community development. Completion of the course work for the Ph.D. program requires three years full-time or four years part-time. A total of 54 course credits are required for the doctorate, including both research and teaching practica under faculty mentorship before the writing and defense of the dissertation.

Research Facilities

The School of Social Welfare is located within the Health Sciences Center, which includes the University Hospital and the Medical School as well as the Schools of Dental Medicine, Nursing, and Health Technology and Management. These facilities offer a unique opportunity for interdisciplinary practice and research experience at both the master's and doctoral levels. The Health Sciences Center Library contains approximately 275,000 volumes in social welfare and the health sciences. Students may also utilize the 1.7 million volumes of the University's Frank Melville, Jr. Memorial Library for related areas of inquiry. In addition, computer labs are located both in the Health Sciences Center and at other sites on campus.

Financial Aid

A variety of financial aid is available. This aid includes the Graduate Tuition Waiver program for former Educational Opportunity Program students, as well as several fellowships for minority students and tuition waivers for New York State residents in the doctoral program. Doctoral students are also eligible for renewable University-wide fellowships paying as much as $14,000 per year.

Cost of Study

For state residents, tuition is $5100 a year for full-time students or $213 per credit hour part-time. It is $8416 per year full-time or $351 per credit hour part-time for nonresidents. Fees are $182 per year full-time or $11.85 per semester (minimum) part-time.

Living and Housing Costs

Campus residences vary in cost. A double room costs $3294. University apartments range from $690 per month for a private one-bedroom to $1060 per month for two bedrooms. Rooms in these and other larger units may also be shared, at rates varying from $244 to $372 per month. Off-campus housing is also available at prices ranging from $300 or $400 per month for shares to $1400 per month for a house. The University meal plan costs $1990 per year. Students who cook their own meals may expect to spend between $45 and $60 a week on food.

Student Group

In the most recent demographic analysis, the M.S.W. program had 277 full-time students, including 210 women, and 52 part-time students, including 40 women. Eighty-eight students, or more than one third of the School, were members of minority groups: 56 African Americans, 3 Asian Americans, 27 Latinos, and 3 Native Americans. The average age of students in the M.S.W. program is 35. The doctoral program admits up to 8 full-time and 4 part-time students each year. Its composition is diverse.

Student Outcomes

Graduates of the M.S.W. program hold a wide variety of positions in social welfare. They are employed as social workers in schools, in hospitals, and in facilities dealing with substance abuse. Graduates do counseling in community agencies for different populations, including young people, victims of domestic violence, and the aged. They also advocate and do policy-related work in all these arenas. The Ph.D. program trains students for positions in the field of social welfare as teachers, researchers, and policy analysts.

Location

One of four university centers in the State University of New York system, SUNY at Stony Brook is located 60 miles east of New York City on Long Island's wooded north shore. The campus consists of 1100 acres, with a total of 105 University buildings. In addition to excellent academic resources, students find diverse cultural and recreational opportunities, including the Staller Center for the Arts, a 26-acre nature preserve, and the nearby beaches of Long Island Sound. The School of Social Welfare is located in the Health Sciences Center on the East Campus.

The University and The Program

The University was founded in 1957 as a small college in Oyster Bay, Long Island, that educated students to become math and science teachers. In 1960, the State Board of Regents mandated the college to become a comprehensive research university. Construction of the new campus at Stony Brook began in 1962. The School of Social Welfare opened in 1971 and has now prepared about 3,000 people for careers in social work.

Applying

The deadline for application and financial aid requests for the M.S.W. programs is March 1. The deadline for the Ph.D. program is February 1. Personal interviews are required for the Ph.D. program but are optional for the M.S.W. program. Applicants to the Ph.D. program are notified by March 15, while M.S.W. applicants are notified by May 1. The Graduate Record Examinations are required only for doctoral applicants.

Correspondence and Information

M.S.W. program inquiries should be directed to:

Dr. Carlos Vidal
Assistant Dean for Offices of Field Instruction Admissions, and Student Services
School of Social Welfare, Health Sciences Center
State University of New York at Stony Brook
Stony Brook, New York 11794-8231
Telephone: 516-444-3141
E-mail: kathya@ssw.hsc.sunysb.edu
World Wide Web: http://uhmc.sunysb.edu/socwelf/adm

Ph.D. program inquiries should be directed to:

Dr. Joel Blau
Director, Ph.D. Program
School of School Welfare, Health Sciences Center
State University of New York at Stony Brook
Stony Brook, New York 11794-8231
Telephone: 516-444-3149
E-mail: joelb@ssw.hsc.sunysb.edu
World Wide Web: http://uhmc.sunysb.edu/socwelf/phd.html

State University of New York at Stony Brook

THE FACULTY AND THEIR RESEARCH

Joel Blau, Associate Professor and Director of the Ph.D. program; D.S.W., Columbia. Social policy, history of social welfare, poverty, homelessness, the political economy of social welfare, comparative social welfare.
Ruth Brandwein, Professor; Ph.D., Brandeis. Family violence, welfare, and poverty; women in administration; organizational and social change; single-parent families; feminist frameworks; history of U.S. social policy; international social welfare.
Frances Brisbane, Professor and Dean; Ph.D., Union Graduate School. Alcoholism, counseling with people of color, complementary medicine.
Angel P. Campos, Associate Professor; Ed.D., Columbia. Hispanics/Latinos in the United States, the Hispanic/Latino family, mental health and the Hispanic/Latino, cross-cultural social work practice, cultural competency in social work practice, social gerontology, social work education.
Paul Colson, Assistant Professor; Ph.D., Chicago. Homelessness, HIV prevention, psychosocial models of tuberculosis and HIV treatment, service delivery in impoverished communities.
Harvey A. Farberman, Associate Professor; Ph.D., Minnesota. Philosophy of social work, public mental health services, research.
Linda E. Francis, Assistant Professor; Ph.D., Indiana. Mental health, health services research, qualitative methods.
Robert Lefferts, Professor; Ph.D., Brandeis. Program evaluation, market research, advocacy research, health and mental health service delivery.
Michael A. Lewis, Assistant Professor; Ph.D., CUNY Graduate Center. Poverty and social policy, the application of sociology, economics, and moral philosophy to the examination of social policy and social programs.
Abraham Lurie, Professor; Ph.D., NYU. Mental health, case management, the aged.
Esther S. Marcus, Professor; Ph.D., NYU. Teen pregnancy, developmental disabilities, adult children of alcoholics, preventive intervention with families.
Kathleen Monahan, Assistant Professor; D.S.W., Adelphi. Siblings and sexual abuse, battered women, domestic violence, disability.
Carolyn Peabody, Lecturer; M.S.W., M.A., SUNY at Stony Brook. Advocacy/empowerment theory and practice, feminist theory and practice, mental health, lesbian and gay issues, development of political issues among oppressed populations, impact of sexual abuse histories among mental health populations.
Charles Robbins, Associate Dean and Director of Social Work, University Hospital; D.S.W., Yeshiva. Violence in intimate relationships and as a public health problem, health-care policy, social work and health care, the use of complementary medicine.
E. Jean Scully, Clinical Assistant Professor; M.S.W., SUNY at Stony Brook. Bereavement counseling, death and dying, critical incident stress debriefing, trauma crisis counseling, intervention with adults and children, care of the caregiver, clinical supervision, grief support groups.
Carlos M. Vidal, Clinical Associate Professor and Assistant Dean; Ph.D., Fordham. Child welfare policy and research methods, Hispanics, empowerment and advocacy, health-care issues among children of color, violence in schools and communities of color.

RESEARCH, SERVICE, AND TRAINING PROJECTS

The Child Welfare Training Program. This program offers training to staff members from public and voluntary child welfare agencies. Funded by the New York State Department of Social Services, it blends instruction in practical skills with a theoretical framework so that child welfare professionals can successfully work toward meeting the needs of clients under their care.
Family Violence Education and Research Center. This center promotes better services to individuals, families, organizations, and communities affected by violence. Its educational component provides training for professionals, organizations, and community members who encounter various forms of family violence. Its research program is designed to increase knowledge and understanding of the nature and extent of violence as well as the effectiveness of various policies, interventions, and treatment modalities.
The Sayville Mental Health Project. This project provides services to mentally ill people who have been discharged from state hospitals. It also works to improve the living conditions of people residing in adult homes by making sure that such homes meet the required standards of care.
The Sudden Infant Death Regional Resource Center. The SIDS center offers services to families whose babies died suddenly. It also provides professional education programs to people such as police, medical examiners, and nurses who have contact with these families.

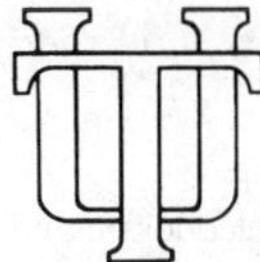

TULANE UNIVERSITY

School of Social Work

Programs of Study

The School of Social Work offers opportunities for full-time and part-time study leading to the degrees of Master of Social Work and Ph.D. in social work.

The four-semester M.S.W. program consists of 60 graduate credit hours taken within a sixteen-month period, which includes one summer semester. Students may also choose to complete the first semester of study on a part-time basis, while continuing to work. Students who have completed an undergraduate major in social work at an accredited school of social work may be granted advanced standing. The curriculum includes required courses in human growth and social environment, family analysis, research, social welfare policy and history, and social work practice as well as a field practicum. A certificate in gerontology is available. The School of Social Work also offers two joint-degree programs: the Master of Social Work/Master of Public Health with the Tulane University School of Public Health and Tropical Medicine and the Master of Social Work/J.D. with the Tulane Law School.

The doctoral program at the Tulane University School of Social Work is dedicated to helping students integrate theory, practice, research, and teaching. The focus is on the scholarship of practice. This advanced graduate study will provide students the training necessary to develop, evaluate, and expand the existing professional practice knowledge base for effective services and policies. Toward accomplishment of this mission, the program is committed to learning and the development of scholars who will: apply critical and innovative thinking in addressing social work practice and problems; advance social work knowledge through research; disseminate social work knowledge through publication and teaching; and provide leadership in social work practice, teaching, and scholarship.

Research Facilities

The University's nine libraries hold a total of 1.8 million volumes and 16,750 periodicals. The University Computer Center provides each graduate student with an individual account for research. The presence of so many disciplines on one campus creates a lively academic atmosphere. The Elizabeth Wisner Social Welfare Research Center for Families and Children provides opportunities for community-based research. The Tulane Center on Aging for Research, Education, and Services is cosponsored by the School of Social Work, and the Porter-Cason Institute supports education for family-centered practice. The Campus Affiliates Program (CAP) Child and Family Development Project involves Tulane and Xavier Universities and residents of the C. J. Peete Housing Development. The Center for Life-long Learning fosters and provides nondegree professional education for lifelong learning. Other research centers include the Institute for Research and Training on HIV Counseling, the Disaster and Volunteerism Research Center, and the Visualization Center.

Financial Aid

Social work students may apply for federally funded loans. The School also has a work-study program through which students may be paid for time spent in the field. Any student certified eligible for aid by the University Office of Financial Aid and who is in a not-for-profit field setting qualifies for this program. In addition, partial tuition scholarships are offered.

The application for aid is processed after a student has been accepted for admission to the School. Application forms are available from the director of admissions at the School of Social Work.

Cost of Study

The tuition and fees for 1998–99 are as follows: for students taking a full program (12 credit hours), tuition is $5680 per semester, the University fee is $250 per semester, and the student activity fee is $292 per semester, for a total of $6222 per semester. For students taking less than a full program, tuition is $474 per credit hour, the University fee is $21 per semester hour, and the student activity fee is $20 per semester.

Living and Housing Costs

University housing for graduate and professional students is limited and is allotted on a first-come, first-served basis. On-campus apartments for graduate students are available in Charles Rosen House and Stadium Place apartments. Monthly rates vary according to the size of the rental unit and the number of occupants. In 1998–99, the range is from $550 to $750. For information on housing, write to the Director of Housing, Office of Housing, Tulane University, 29 McAlister Drive, New Orleans, Louisiana 70118 (telephone: 504-865-5724).

Student Group

The total enrollment for the School of Social Work in the fall of 1997 was 280 students—250 full-time and part-time students in the master's program and 30 full-time and part-time students in the doctoral program. The students come from different cultural, ethnic, and regional backgrounds.

Location

New Orleans defies sharp definition. Tulane students often find that the city—with its numerous educational, cultural, and recreational resources—is as much a place of learning and intellectual challenge as the classroom. New Orleans encourages people to slow down and see and enjoy what is around them. Mardi Gras lasts only two weeks, but its spirit lingers throughout the year.

The University and The School

The Tulane University School of Social Work is located on the University's 100-acre main campus, which is in a residential section of New Orleans. The University consists of eleven academic divisions, and Newcomb College is an integral part of the main campus. Tulane seeks a national and international student body, and students come from all fifty states and sixty countries. Approximately 8,800 students are enrolled—5,350 undergraduates, 3,440 graduate students, and 2,240 part-time students (undergraduate and graduate). The present School of Social Work, the oldest in the South, began in 1914. The School established the Master of Social Work degree program in 1927 and added its doctoral program in 1959.

Applying

Application forms may be obtained from the associate dean and should be returned with a nonrefundable application fee of $25. Full-time master's degree students must begin study in the fall; part-time master's degree students must begin study in the spring. Doctoral students enter in the fall. While most students are admitted for full-time enrollment, some enter on a part-time basis. The School accepts applications from transfer students and international students.

Correspondence and Information

For more information and application forms:

Office of Admissions
School of Social Work
Tulane University
New Orleans, Louisiana 70118-5672

Telephone: 504-865-5314

Tulane University

THE FACULTY AND THEIR RESEARCH

Holly Ackerman, Assistant Professor; Ph.D., Florida. Migration studies, social movements, Cuban studies, history of social work.

Richard D. Ager, Assistant Professor; Ph.D. (joint degree in social work and psychology), Michigan. Family and couple therapy, alcoholism and substance abuse.

Tenolian R. Bell, Assistant Professor; Ph.D., Ohio. Social work practice, mental health, the African-American community, social justice issues, religion and social work, social movements.

Suzanne England, Professor and Dean; Ph.D., Illinois at Chicago. Health, maternal and child health, gerontology.

Valerie Gordon-Garofalo, Assistant Professor; Ph.D., Texas. Social work with groups, field practicums, HIV/AIDS, theories of human behavior.

Robert G. Hayden, Professor; Ph.D. (psychology), Pennsylvania. Social work research methodology, policy.

Jeanette Jennings, Associate Professor; Ph.D. (social work and political science), Michigan. African-American studies, social policy, administration, gerontology.

Sarah Kreutziger, Assistant Professor and Director of the Center for Life-long Learning; Ph.D., Tulane. Continuing education (social work), health-care issues, women's issues, history, spiritual values.

Judith Lewis, Associate Professor and Director of Field Instruction; Ph.D., Maryland. Human behavior, field instruction, group practice, ethnic and minority issues, aging, women's issues.

Marva Lewis, Assistant Professor; Ph.D. (sociocultural psychology), Colorado. Mother/child interactions.

Ronald E. Marks, Associate Professor and Associate Dean; M.P.H., Ph.D. (social work), Pittsburgh. Research, human behavior, gerontology.

Jayashree Nimmagadda, Assistant Professor; M.S.W., Madras (India); Ph.D., Illinois. Addiction and indigenization of practice.

Lynn Pearlmutter, Associate Professor; D.S.W., Tulane. Family and couple therapy, child abuse, group therapy and object relations theory.

Ruth Raines-Eudy, Assistant Professor; Ph.D., Washington (St. Louis). Maternal and child health, health, regional poverty, policy practice.

Elizabeth L. Torre, Associate Professor; M.R.E., Union Theological Seminary (New York); Ph.D. (social work), Tulane. Human behavior, social work practice in industry, family.

Carol T. Tully, Associate Professor; Ph.D. (social work), Virginia Commonwealth. Social work practice, gerontology, lesbian/gay issues, curriculum issues.

Lilia O. Valdez, Associate Professor and Associate Dean for Admissions, Alumni and External Affairs, and International Programs; M.S.W., Tulane. Cross-cultural issues, international programs.

Robert Watkins, Assistant Professor and Associate Dean for Academic Administration and Information Technology; M.S.W., Southern at New Orleans; J.D., Tulane. Gerontology, with emphasis on legal and financial issues in late life; development of care alternative for those afflicted with Alzheimer's disease; social implications of an aging world; impact of information technologies on social work education, training, and its use in the practice setting.

Michael J. Zakour, Associate Professor and Director of the Ph.D. Program; Ph.D., Washington (St. Louis). Social administration and evaluation, planning, policy and research, emergency social services, volunteerism, ethnic and minority issues, health-care system.

UNIVERSITY OF CHICAGO

School of Social Service Administration

Programs of Study

The School of Social Service Administration offers programs of study leading to the Master of Arts and Doctor of Philosophy degrees.

The Master of Arts program, a two-year curriculum of general study and specialization, prepares students for a wide range of career opportunities in the field of social work. In the first two quarters, students take core courses on the policy and programs of social welfare, the practice of social intervention, and research and evaluation. These courses stress the common themes and problems that occur in diverse social work efforts. In the remaining four quarters, students select a faculty-planned concentration in advanced clinical social work practice or social administration. Specialization within a concentration is also available. Classroom and field instruction are integrated throughout the course of the program.

The School also has an extended evening part-time program that enables students to work full-time and complete the degree requirements in three years as well as a planned part-time day program.

The Doctor of Philosophy program prepares students for careers in research and teaching. Specializations are offered in social development (policy, planning, and management), social treatment, and combined social development and social treatment. Programs are tailored to the student's scholarly and research interests. A dissertation is required.

The School of Social Service Administration and the Graduate School of Business offer a joint-degree program, which leads to both the A.M. and the M.B.A. degrees in three academic years. The School also offers a joint-degree program with the Divinity School, which leads to both the A.M. and M.Div. degrees in four academic years. The School of Social Service Administration has developed dual-degree arrangements with several schools from the Chicago Cluster of Theological Schools. The concurrent dual-degree program enables students to receive both the A.M. and M.Div. degrees in one less year than it would if both degree programs were taken sequentially. Interested students must apply to both schools in each of the specific programs.

Research Facilities

The Joseph Regenstein Library is a graduate research library in the social sciences and humanities. It is the center of the University library's collections of approximately 3.5 million volumes and is complemented by the library of the School of Social Service Administration.

Students may participate in the work of various research projects, as well as in the Committee on Public Policy Studies, the Center for Health Administration Studies, the Center for Urban Research and Policy Studies, and the National Opinion Research Center (NORC).

Financial Aid

Assistance is available through scholarships and loans drawn from federal funds and from School and University sources. A number of research and teaching assistantships are also available to doctoral students. More than three fourths of the students receive scholarship aid from the School and from outside sources.

Cost of Study

Tuition for the full-time program is $20,370 for 1998–99. The cost of the part-time program is $14,566 per year in 1998–99.

Living and Housing Costs

The cost of living for a single student for the 1998–99 academic year—including tuition, academic supplies, room, and board—is approximately $33,120; estimated expenses for married students are in excess of $30,000. Housing is available in University dormitories and apartments and in private lodgings off campus.

Student Group

Each year the School admits approximately 150 students to the master's degree program and 10 to the doctoral program. Students come to the School from a wide range of academic disciplines and with a great variety of work experiences in social work and other fields. Students vary widely in age (more than a quarter of the master's degree students are over 30 years old) and by culture, race, and ethnicity. Thirty-one percent of the entering 1997–98 student body were members of minority groups.

Recent SSA graduates are pursuing a variety of careers. They work as clinicians in traditional social work agencies and in such nontraditional settings as corporate headquarters, banks, and industrial plants; as policy analysts with local, state, and federal agencies, as well as with nonprofit advocacy groups; as consultants with management consulting firms; as researchers in academia and agencies; as community planners and organizers working on a wide range of problems; and in a variety of other positions in the private, public, and voluntary sectors.

Location

The University of Chicago is located in Hyde Park, a politically independent and racially integrated neighborhood 15 minutes from the Loop, the heart of downtown Chicago. Students at the School have access to Chicago's outstanding cultural, recreational, and athletic activities. The University is less than a mile from Lake Michigan, which offers picnic areas, beaches, harbors, and miles of walking and bicycle paths. An unusually wide range of cultural and recreational facilities is also available on campus.

The School

The School of Social Service Administration is part of the University of Chicago and shares the University's dedication to excellence in teaching, research, and service. The School was incorporated into the University in 1920, bringing the programs of the Chicago School of Civics and Philanthropy together with programs in other parts of the University. The School has its own building, designed by Ludwig Mies van der Rohe and opened in 1964. The building is located near the Law School, the National Opinion Research Center, and the University of Chicago Hospitals. The *Social Service Review*, an outstanding scholarly journal in the field, has been published continuously by the School since 1927. The School also works closely with the Woodlawn Social Services Center, which houses a variety of social service agencies and is the site of some training and demonstration programs.

Applying

Students enter the A.M. and Ph.D. programs in the autumn quarter only. The application deadline for the master's program and for the Ph.D. program is February 15. Interviews are normally not required, but prospective students are encouraged to visit the School. Applicants for financial assistance must file the Free Application for Federal Student Aid (available from Box 4032, Iowa City, Iowa 52243-4032).

Correspondence and Information

Assistant Dean of Enrollment and Career Services
School of Social Service Administration
University of Chicago
969 East Sixtieth Street
Chicago, Illinois 60637

Telephone: 773-702-1492
Fax: 773-702-0874
E-mail: ssa.dos@midway.uchicago.edu
World Wide Web: http://www.chas.uchicago.edu/ssa

University of Chicago

THE FACULTY

Sharon B. Berlin, Ph.D., Professor.
Evelyn Z. Brodkin, Ph.D., Associate Professor and Lecturer, Law School.
Pastora San Juan Cafferty, Ph.D., Professor; Member, Center for Latin American Studies.
Thomas A. D'Aunno, Ph.D., Associate Professor.
Irene Elkin, Ph.D.; Professor, Department of Psychiatry.
Sarah Gehlert, Ph.D., Assistant Professor.
Kyoung Ja Hyun, Ph.D., Assistant Professor.
Penny Ruff Johnson, A.M., Lecturer.
Waldo Johnson, Ph.D., Assistant Professor.
Susan J. Lambert, Ph.D., Associate Professor.
Edward F. Lawlor, Ph.D., Associate Professor, Harris Graduate School of Public Policy Studies; Director, Graduate Program in Health Administration and Policy; Senior Scholar, Center for Clinical Medical Ethics.
Laurence E. Lynn Jr., Ph.D., Professor, Harris Graduate School of Public Policy Studies; Director, Center for Urban Research and Policy Studies; Director, The Management Institute.
Jeanne C. Marsh, Ph.D., Professor.
Dolores G. Norton, Ph.D., Professor; Faculty Associate, Center for the Study of Urban Inequality.
Cheryl Peek, A.M., Lecturer.
Elsie Pinkston, Ph.D., Professor; Faculty Associate, Center on Aging, Health and Society; Director, Center for Social Work Practice Research.
William Pollak, Ph.D., Associate Professor.
Harold A. Richman, Ph.D., Hermon Dunlap Smith Professor, Social Sciences Collegiate Division; Director, Chapin Hall Center for Children, NORC.
Jeanne B. Robinson, Ph.D., Senior Lecturer.
Melissa Roderick, Ph.D., Assistant Professor.
Tina L. Rzepnicki, Ph.D., Associate Professor; Research Associate, Chapin Hall Center for Children, NORC.
John R. Schuerman, Ph.D., Professor; Research Associate, Chapin Hall Center for Children, NORC.
William Sites, Ph.D., Associate Professor.
Michael Sosin, Ph.D., Professor; Research Associate, Population Studies Center.
Irving Spergel, D.S.W., George Herbert Jones Professor.
Karen Teigiser, A.M., Senior Lecturer.
Mark Testa, Ph.D., Associate Professor; Faculty Associate, Center for the Study of Urban Inequality; Research Associate, Chapin Hall Center for Children, NORC.
Froma Walsh, Ph.D., Professor, Department of Psychiatry; Co-Director, Center for Family Health.
Henry Webber, A.M., Senior Lecturer.
Stephen E. Wong, Ph.D., Assistant Professor.

UNIVERSITY OF DENVER

Graduate School of Social Work

Programs of Study

The University of Denver Graduate School of Social Work offers courses of study leading to a master's degree in social work (M.S.W.), a Ph.D. in social work, and certificates in several areas.

The foundation year of the two-year master's degree program is designed to provide students with a firm base in and understanding of social systems, theories of human development, general practice theory and methodology, and themes of diversity. In the concentration year, students choose an area of specialization from direct or indirect social work practice. Students intensify their knowledge and skills in their concentration with a series of required courses and electives, applied evaluation research, and a field practicum. Special dual-degree programs are offered in international studies, law, human communication, and theology. Under a flexible dual-degree program, students may propose a dual degree that fits their educational and career goals. The period of study may be extended beyond two years for students who deem this necessary. Classes are held during the week, on weekends, and occasionally in the evenings to accommodate students who are employed.

The program leading to the Ph.D. in social work is both theory- and research-oriented to encourage the development of scholarly and professional competence in social work at an advanced level. It includes three components that are individualized to facilitate achievement of each student's career goals: courses offered by the School of Social Work and by other departments within the University, a comprehensive examination, and dissertation research. Students may enroll either full-time or part-time. Course work for full-time students is usually completed during the first year of study. Course work is followed first by the comprehensive examination necessary for advancement to final candidacy and then by dissertation research conducted under the guidance of members of the faculty.

Research Facilities

The Information Technology Center provides computer facilities for students. Students can access the University's mainframe VAX computer from the center or from other computing access and support labs throughout the University.

Financial Aid

A limited number of federal grants and tuition scholarships are available to incoming students. In addition, University scholarship funds, administered by the Graduate School of Social Work, are awarded to students who qualify for them. The University's Office of Student Financial Services can provide information on the Federal Perkins Loan, Federal Stafford Student Loans, and work-study. Filing the Free Application for Federal Student Aid (FAFSA) is required.

Cost of Study

In 1998–99, tuition for full-time study (12 to 18 quarter-hour credits) is $18,216 per year, or $6072 per quarter. Part-time students pay $506 per credit hour. Health insurance is also required.

Living and Housing Costs

The estimated cost of living in 1998–99 for a single student without children is $12,005 per academic year. This estimate is exclusive of tuition costs. Contact the Department of Residence for graduate housing information.

Student Group

The School's total enrollment in the academic year 1997–98 was 383 students, of whom 303 were full-time master's students and 80 were part-time. There were 20 doctoral students. Fifteen students were enrolled in the family therapy certification program. Students came from approximately thirty states and several other countries. The School's ethnic mixture includes African Americans, Chicanos, Native Americans, and Asians.

Location

The Denver metropolitan area has an excellent climate the year round because of its location on a mile-high plateau at the foot of the Rockies. Its 1997 estimated population was 2,186,675. As the capital of Colorado, Denver is the center of regional offices of federal services and state social welfare, education, and health programs. It is rich in both public and voluntarily supported agencies, which provide field-instruction facilities and teaching staff for social work students. Facilities for skiing, skating, camping, and fishing and outstanding cultural programs in music, art, and drama are readily accessible in the area.

The University

The University of Denver, the oldest and one of the largest of the voluntarily supported institutions of higher education in the Rocky Mountain West, was founded in 1864. The charter was secured by Dr. John Evans, second governor of the Colorado Territory, who had earlier founded Northwestern University in Illinois. In 1996 the Graduate School of Social Work completed its sixty-fifth year. University students, about 50 percent of whom are engaged in graduate study, come from all states and many countries. Since the founding, there have been no restrictions regarding race, color, or creed in admissions policies or practices. While the University retains its relationship with the Methodist Church, under whose auspices it was founded, its charter provides that "no test of religious faith shall ever be applied as a condition of admission."

Applying

Applicants for the master's program must have an undergraduate degree from an accredited college or university, should present a broad background in the social sciences. It is recommended that incoming students have some competence in using a personal computer, including word processing and software package access. Admission factors include experience, grade point average, career goals, and references. Applicants are urged to submit all application materials by January 1 of the year in which they are seeking admission. Applications are reviewed on a rolling admissions basis. Official transcripts must be sent directly to the Graduate School of Social Work by the registrars of all colleges and universities previously attended. There is a $40 application fee. Applicants for the doctoral program must hold a master's degree in social work from an accredited school of social work (or, in selected instances, a master's degree in another social science discipline), have a superior academic record, have had preferably at least two years of successful post-master's experience, and show evidence of maturity, scholarly capabilities, and readiness for advanced study. Entrance examinations are not required.

Correspondence and Information

For the master's program:
Director of Admissions
Graduate School of Social Work
University of Denver
2148 South High Street
Denver, Colorado 80208
Telephone: 303-871-2886 or 2841

For the doctoral program:
Doctoral Admissions
Graduate School of Social Work
University of Denver
2148 South High Street
Denver, Colorado 80208
Telephone: 303-871-2841 or 3634

University of Denver

THE FACULTY AND THEIR RESEARCH INTERESTS

Catherine F. Alter, Professor; Ph.D., Maryland. Welfare reform and effectiveness of welfare-to-work programs, applications of network theory and analysis to program evaluation.
Maria Yellow Horse Brave Heart, Assistant Professor; Ph.D., Smith. American Indian/Alaska Native mental health and child welfare, genocide, intergenerational trauma and unresolved grief, psychodynamic theory and practice, substance abuse prevention, minority issues and diversity.
Judith F. Bula, Associate Professor; Ph.D., Bryn Mawr. Practice with families, women's issues, adult learning theories and methods, domestic violence.
Diane B. Byington, Associate Professor; Ph.D., Florida State. Women's issues, health policy, international health care.
Constance L. Calkin, Assistant Professor; Ph.D., Denver. Women's issues, women in social work administration, adolescent health.
William A. Cloud, Associate Professor; Ph.D., Denver. Drug dependency, macro social work practice, macro practice in minority communities.
Enid Opal Cox, Professor; D.S.W., Columbia. Social policy, social services, gerontology, empowerment-oriented practice, mental health prevention, older women, minority issues, long-term-care social work services.
Jean F. East, Assistant Professor; Ph.D., Denver. Welfare reform, women in poverty, community empowerment, postmodernism.
Sue Henry, Professor; D.S.W., Denver. Social work with groups, women's issues, administration, theory building, social work education.
JoKatherine Holliman-Page, Field Coordinator; M.S.W., Howard. Intervention techniques, communication and humanities, marriage and family, sociology of minorities, organizational development and human diversity.
Carole Fee Ivanoff, Assistant Director of Field and Student Services; M.S.W., Illinois at Urbana-Champaign. Gate keeping in social work education, evaluating direct practice skills, factors affecting women's professional success.
Jeffrey M. Jenson, Associate Professor; Ph.D., Washington (Seattle). Etiology, prevention, and treatment of juvenile delinquency and adolescent substance abuse; youth violence; juvenile gangs and juvenile justice; family and child welfare policy.
John F. Jones, Professor; Ph.D., Minnesota. International social development, social policy and administration, mental health, child protective services.
John A. Kayser, Associate Professor; Ph.D., Denver. Direct work with children, youth, and families; children's rights; human growth and development; diversity, narrative research, teaching and curriculum development.
Judy Krysik, Assistant Professor; Ph.D., Arizona. Social policy, research methods, services to children and families, comparative family policy and the welfare state, program evaluation.
Antonio F. Ledesma, Assistant Professor; Ph.D., Denver. Theory and practice of psychotherapy, human communication process, conflict management, and dynamics of human communication in the therapeutic relationship.
Susan S. Manning, Associate Professor; Ph.D., Denver. Ethics, mental health.
Pamela K. Metz, Associate Professor; Ed.D., Colorado. Social work education, transitions, women's issues, loss, grief, recovery.
Christian E. Molidor, Assistant Professor; Ph.D., Illinois at Chicago. Teenage dating violence, gang and juvenile violence, research in youth violence issues.
James R. Moran, Associate Professor; Ph.D., Wisconsin–Madison. American Indian issues, child welfare, poverty, alcohol use and abuse, community approaches to social problems.
Kathleen Ohman, Professor; Ph.D., Illinois at Urbana-Champaign. Child welfare policy and practice, law.
Lynn Parker, Assistant Professor; Ph.D., Denver. Feminist social work practice methods.
Ruth J. Parsons, Professor; Ph.D., Denver. Interventions in the aging field, conflict resolution, mediation social work, mental health of the elderly, integrated methods as a practice framework, empowerment as a base of social work.
Cathryn C. Potter, Assistant Professor; Ph.D., Denver. Child welfare, juvenile justice, children's mental health practice, policy and research, family-based practice in public agency settings.
Howard L. Raiten, Assistant Professor; Ph.D., Bryn Mawr. Critical social work, social development, cross-cultural and international social welfare issues, mental health.
Cathryne L. Schmitz, Assistant Professor; Ph.D., Ohio. Child and family poverty, high-risk children and families, diversity and oppression.
Jose A. Sisneros, Clinical Assistant Professor; M.S.W., Arizona. Mental health, alcohol and drug dependency, domestic violence, mentoring minority students.
Susan A. Taylor, Lecturer; M.S.W., St. Louis. Health and social welfare policy and practice, administration and management of organizations, political and economic development of high-risk communities, housing and homelessness, women's issues, mental retardation and developmental disabilities.

Administration

Catherine Foster Alter, Dean.
Linda K. Clark, Assistant Dean.
Constance Calkin, Director of Field and Student Services.
Joan Harwick, Director of M.S.W. and Ph.D. Admissions and Recruitment.
James R. Moran, Director of Research.
Kathleen Ohman, Director of M.S.W. Program.
Ruth J. Parsons, Director of Ph.D. Program.
Cathryn Potter, Director of Child Welfare Program.
Susan Baak, Registrar.
Tsutae (Tae) Beal, Assistant to the Dean.
Gigi Camas, Bridge Project Administrator.
Judi Choury, Ph.D. and M.S.W. Admissions Assistant.
Marsha J. Dawe, Director of Development.
Michelle DeBaca, Receptionist and Faculty Assistant.
Neysa Folmer, Faculty, Research, and Ph.D. Assistant.
Ruth Griffith, Receptionist and Faculty Assistant.
Lisa Harris, Technology Coordinator.
JoKatherine Holliman-Page, Field Coordinator.
Carole Fee Ivanoff, Assistant Director of Field and Student Services.
Lynette Jones, Assistant to the Director of Development.
Lorie Klumb, Director of Center for Community Enrichment.
Julie Kuhn-Farrar, Field and Student Services Assistant.
Mary Krane, Bridge Project Executive Director.
Jeanne Orrben, Bridge Project Coordinator.
Denise Palma, Bridge Project Program Coordinator.
Pat Sheller, Assistant to the Director of Admissions.

UNIVERSITY OF GEORGIA

School of Social Work

Programs of Study

The School of Social Work offers programs leading to the Master of Social Work and the Doctor of Philosophy in social work.

The M.S.W. program is a two-year (four-semester) program. The curriculum offers a first-year generalist course of study followed by a second year of study in either of two areas of specialization: community empowerment and program development (CEPD) or family-centered social work practice (FCSWP). The CEPD concentration focuses on skills in the areas of program development, community and economic development, proposal writing, human services management, and program design. The FCSWP concentration focuses on skills in working with individuals, families, and small groups, with a special focus on models of family practice.

The doctoral program specializes in the development of knowledge for social work practice research. The three-year program includes advanced study in theory, research methods, assessment and evaluation of practice, internship, and the dissertation. The program prepares students for advanced practice and academic careers involving teaching and research.

Research Facilities

The University of Georgia Library is the largest university library in the state of Georgia and is a member of the Association of Research Libraries, consisting of the largest research libraries in the United States. It contains more than 2 million books, serials, and documents, as well as many other items including manuscripts, drawings, and maps. Other facilities include the University Computer Center and the School of Social Work Research Center. Recent social work research has been done on such topics as mental health, alcohol addiction, aging, and child abuse and neglect.

Financial Aid

A limited number of nonteaching, research, and teaching assistantships are offered through the School of Social Work. In addition, several Veterans Administration traineeships in health and mental health are granted. A few agencies provide stipends to practicum students.

Each year, the Graduate School selects graduate nonteaching assistants and graduate research assistants from a list of students recommended by their major department.

Cost of Study

In 1998–99, residents of Georgia pay a matriculation fee of approximately $1400 at the beginning of each semester. Nonresidents pay $2746 per semester. Inquiries about the doctoral-level program should be directed to the doctoral office at 706-542-5461.

Living and Housing Costs

The estimated cost of living for a Georgia resident is $13,552 for the 1998–99 academic year. This estimate includes tuition and fees, books and supplies, room and board, and personal expenses for two semesters. The additional out-of-state fees assessed all non-Georgia residents increase this estimate to $15,918.

Student Group

The 400 students enrolled in the School represent diverse geographical backgrounds and professional experience. Included are a number of nontraditional students, such as those changing careers. The 35 doctoral students all possess M.S.W.'s and have diverse social work practice experience. The School makes special efforts to recruit students who are members of minority groups.

Location

Athens has a population of about 90,000 and is located 65 miles northeast of Atlanta. Its location makes it easy to visit the mountains of north Georgia; the ski slopes of North Carolina; the beaches of Georgia, Florida, and South Carolina; and numerous state parks. Athens can be reached easily by airplane, automobile, or bus. The town's elevation influences the climate, which is generally moderate the year round.

The University

Incorporated in 1785 and actually established in 1801, the University is a state-supported coeducational institution with more than 29,000 students and nearly 2,300 faculty members. It is the nation's oldest chartered state university. Thirteen schools and colleges, with auxiliary divisions, administer the University's programs of teaching, research, and service. The campus occupies 3,500 acres and has its own transit system.

Applying

Students applying to the M.S.W. and Ph.D. degree programs are admitted in the fall. M.S.W. students who qualify for advanced standing are admitted in the summer, joining the class admitted the preceding fall. Formal applications and supporting credentials, along with a $30 fee, must be received by departmental deadlines. An overall undergraduate GPA of 2.75 or better is required for admission into the M.S.W. program, and the Ph.D. program requires an M.S.W., a graduate GPA of 3.4 or better, and preferably a 3.0 or better undergraduate GPA. All applicants are required to take the General Test of the Graduate Record Examinations. Applicants are expected to show evidence of the capacity to relate meaningfully to others, freedom from prejudice combined with scrupulous self-awareness, sensitivity to the needs of others, and a strong motivation to assist others in problem-solving efforts. Applicants are encouraged to apply early.

Correspondence and Information

School of Social Work
Tucker Hall
University of Georgia
Athens, Georgia 30602-7016
Telephone: 706-542-3364

University of Georgia

THE FACULTY

Bonnie L. Yegidis, Professor and Dean; Ph.D., South Florida.
Paul Ammons, Associate Professor; Ed.D., Oklahoma State.
Chrystal Barranti, Public Service Assistant; Ph.D., Georgia.
David Boyle, Assistant Professor; Ph.D., Georgia.
Maurice Daniels, Associate Professor; Ed.D., Indiana.
Katheryn B. Davis, Assistant Professor; M.S.W., Georgia.
Kevin DeWeaver, Professor; Ph.D., Florida State.
Cheryl D. Dozier, Assistant Professor; D.S.W., CUNY, Hunter.
James Gaudin, Professor; Ph.D., Florida State.
Thomas P. Holland, Professor; Ph.D., Brandeis.
Alicia R. Isaac, Assistant Professor; D.P.A., Georgia.
Geraldine Jackson-White, Assistant Professor; Ed.D., Georgia.
Nancy P. Kropf, Associate Professor; Ph.D., Virginia Commonwealth.
P. David Kurtz, Professor; Ph.D., Michigan.
Tara Larrison, Academic Professional; M.S.W., Boston College.
Lettie L. Lockhart, Professor; Ph.D., Florida State.
Ray MacNair, Associate Professor; Ph.D., Michigan.
Martha J. Markward, Assistant Professor; Ph.D., Illinois.
T. Ray Mills, Assistant Professor; M.S.W., Florida State.
Larry Nackerud, Assistant Professor; Ph.D., Cornell.
James Pippin, Associate Professor; Ed.D., Georgia.
Margaret M. Robinson, Assistant Professor; Ph.D., Virginia Commonwealth.
Letha See, Associate Professor; Ph.D., Bryn Mawr.
Bruce A. Thyer, Research Professor; Ph.D., Michigan.
Mimi Tracey, Academic Professional; M.S.W., Hawaii.

Professors Emeriti

Richard J. Anderson, Professor Emeritus; Ed.D., Illinois State.
S. Kathryn Bigham, Assistant Professor and Assistant Dean Emerita; M.S., Boston University.
Merle M. Foeckler, Associate Professor Emerita; M.S., Columbia.
Allie Kilpatrick, Professor Emerita; Ph.D., Florida State.
David Levine, Professor Emeritus; Ph.D., Minnesota.
Pauline Lide, Professor Emerita; D.S.W., Smith.
Norman Polansky, Regents Professor Emeritus; Ph.D., Michigan.
Myrtle Reul, Professor Emerita; Ed.D., Michigan State.
Charles A. Stewart, Dean Emeritus; Ph.D., Florida State.

UofL

UNIVERSITY OF LOUISVILLE

Raymond A. Kent School of Social Work

Program of Study

The Kent School of Social Work offers a graduate program of study that leads to the Master of Science in Social Work (M.S.S.W.) degree. The School's central mission is to educate highly skilled professional social workers who can respond effectively to personal, interpersonal, and social problems ranging from individual and family distress to social injustice and from ill health and slum housing to child abuse, unemployment, and poverty. Preparation for leadership in advanced professional practice is a vital part of the School's curriculum. The program is fully accredited by the Council on Social Work Education (CSWE).

The M.S.S.W. program is designed to help students achieve their maximum potential through a carefully structured curriculum of foundation and specialized courses. Students without an accredited undergraduate degree in social work, such as the Bachelor of Social Work, are admitted to the Regular Program and may complete their studies in four semesters. Sixty semester hours, composed of foundation courses, method of practice courses, electives, and field instruction, are required.

Graduates of an undergraduate social work program accredited by the Council on Social Work Education are considered for admission to the Advanced Standing Program. Full-time students may complete the 36-semester-hour Advanced Standing Program in three semesters of classroom work, with one semester largely devoted to a block field placement.

The Weekend Program offers an opportunity for working students or commuters from other geographic areas to earn an M.S.S.W. degree by attending classes on Friday and Saturday that duplicate the weekday program. The Weekend Program is offered on the Shelby Campus of the University of Louisville, located on the eastern edge of the city. Part-time students must enroll for a minimum of 6 credit hours each semester. All part-time students enrolled in Kent must complete the program within four years.

Research Facilities

The University has a number of outstanding on-campus research facilities and, as a member of ORAU, provides access to the facilities and educational programs of Oak Ridge National Laboratory. The Kentucky Institute for the Environment and Sustainable Development provides an exciting venue for interdisciplinary research in environmental science, policy, and education. The Urban Studies Institute is in direct contact with the community through public service and research related to problems of urban life, community development, and city planning. The Center for Applied Microcirculatory Research combines physiological, clinical, and engineering expertise in a unique research program dedicated to developing microcirculatory science as a new health-care discipline. The Kentucky Lions Eye Research Institute is a modern 75,000-square-foot facility equipped for molecular biological, biochemical, physicochemical, electrophysiological, morphometric, and transgenic studies of the eye and the visual system. The General Electric Factory Automation Laboratory provides a model factory environment and includes a rapid prototyping center, industrial robots, computer-aided engineering facilities, and space for research and development projects. The University library's holdings total more than 1.3 million volumes and microtexts and nearly 13,000 serials. Students also have access to the collections of six other area institutions.

Financial Aid

A limited number of scholarships and stipends are available for graduate study in social work to qualified full-time students. These awards are based upon financial need and academic merit and vary in amount. Preference is given to minority students. Some awards require a specific commitment by the student to work for an organization for a stated period of time following completion of graduate work. A Free Application for Federal Student Aid (FAFSA) is required for all scholarships, stipends, and training grants administered through the Kent School. The FAFSA is available at any college or university. The priority deadline for filing this form is the April 1 preceding the academic year in which the student enrolls.

Cost of Study

Full-time tuition is $1435 per semester for residents of Kentucky and $4075 per semester for nonresidents. Part-time tuition is $158.50 per credit hour for residents and $452 per credit hour for nonresidents. Tuition is subject to change without notice.

Living and Housing Costs

Limited on-campus housing (dormitories and married student facilities) is available, but most Kent students live off campus. More information is available from the Housing Office, Student Activities Building (telephone: 502-852-6636). Those interested in weekend housing only on the Shelby Campus should call 502-852-0365.

Student Group

The Kent School enrolls approximately 400 M.S.S.W. degree students. A majority of the School's students enter with prior social work experience, although it is not uncommon for students to enroll immediately upon completion of their undergraduate study. The student body is well diversified in ethnic origin and cultural background, and although a majority of students come from Kentucky and Indiana, numerous other states are represented. Graduates work in a variety of roles in public and voluntary agencies as well as in private practice. Many alumni hold leadership positions in public and private agencies throughout the country. The Kent School Student Association (KSSA) is an active student organization that maintains an office within the School.

Location

Louisville, an urban community of nearly 1 million people, combines urban sophistication and small-town friendliness. In addition to the vital industries and businesses, the city's attractions include historic neighborhoods that maintain their identities; bustling night spots, theaters, and restaurants; quiet tree-lined suburbs; and abundant resources for outdoor recreation. Louisville is also a major cultural center. Actors Theater and the Kentucky Center for the Arts present some of the best theater, ballet, opera, and symphonic programs. Performances of jazz, blues, country, rock and roll, and new wave music are also showcased in Louisville.

The University and The School

The University of Louisville enrolls more than 20,000 students and, as Kentucky's urban university, is committed to the highest standards of instruction, research, and community service. The Kent School has offered the master's degree in social work since 1937.

Applying

Applications may be filed at any time during the year; the deadline for fall admission is January 10. All materials must be received by this date. Early application is strongly recommended. A complete application file must include two official transcripts from each college or university attended, a $25 processing fee, three letters of reference, and a 300- to 500-word autobiographical statement. A student must also meet the following requirements: a bachelor's degree from an accredited institution of higher learning, a minimum cumulative grade point average of 2.5 on a 4.0 scale (3.0 or higher preferred) from the school awarding the bachelor's degree, a minimum of 18 credit hours in the social sciences (i.e., psychology, sociology, anthropology, economics, political science, history, geography, and communications), and a minimum of 3 credit hours each in statistics, research methodology, and human biology as prerequisites for admission.

Correspondence and Information

Admissions Office
Kent School of Social Work
University of Louisville
Louisville, Kentucky 40292

Telephone: 502-852-6402
Fax: 502-852-0422
E-mail: kentapp@ulkyvm.louisville.edu

University of Louisville

THE FACULTY AND ADMINISTRATION

Administration
Terry L. Singer, M.Div., M.S.W., Ph.D., Dean.
Sam L. Neal, B.S.C., M.S.S.W., J.D., Associate Dean.
Linda C. Chatmon, M.S.S.W., Director of Admissions and Student Affairs.
Martha A. Fuller, M.S.S.W., Director of Field Instruction.
Suzanne M. Hanna, Ph.D., Director of Family Therapy Program.
Ruth Huber, M.S.W., Ph.D., Director of Doctoral Program.
Theresa Jaggers, M.P.A., Assistant to the Dean.
Elana Nance, B.S.B.A., Unit Business Administrator.

Staff
Cindy Ashbaugh, Program Assistant.
Linda Exton, Program Assistant.
Jane Isert, Clerical Specialist.
L. Kay McCulloch, Administrative Assistant.
Norma Niev, Program Assistant.

Faculty
Alana Atchinson, M.S.W., Ph.D. candidate, Assistant Professor of Social Work.
*Gerard Barber, M.P.H., M.S.W., Ph.D., Professor of Social Work and Program Faculty, Ph.D. Program in Urban and Public Affairs.
*Joseph H. Brown, Ph.D., Professor of Family Therapy.
*Dana M. Christensen, B.F.A., Ph.D., Professor of Family Therapy.
Stanley R. Frager, Ph.D., Associate Professor of Social Work.
Priscilla Gibson, M.S.W., Ph.D., Assistant Professor of Social Work.
*David S. Gochman, Ph.D., Professor of Social Work and Program Faculty, Ph.D. Program in Urban and Public Affairs.
*Suzanne M. Hanna, Ph.D., Associate Professor of Family Therapy.
*Ruth Huber, M.S.W., Ph.D., Associate Professor of Social Work.
*Thomas R. Lawson, Ph.D., Professor of Social Work and Program Faculty, Ph.D. Program in Urban and Public Affairs.
Thomas F. Maher, M.S.W., J.D., Associate Professor of Social Work.
Mary Ann Millet, M.S.S.W., Associate Professor of Social Work.
Sam L. Neal, B.S.C., M.S.S.W., J.D., Associate Professor of Social Work.
*Ruth Paton, M.S.S.W., Ph.D., Associate Professor of Social Work.
Bibhuti K. Sar, M.S.W., Ph.D., Assistant Professor of Social Work.
*Terry L. Singer, M.Div., M.S.W., Ph.D., Professor of Social Work.
*Gale Goldberg Wood, M.S.W., Ed.D., Professor of Social Work.
*Daniel P. Wulff, M.S.W., Ph.D., Assistant Professor of Social Work.

**Graduate Faculty* (marked *)

UNIVERSITY OF MARYLAND, BALTIMORE

School of Social Work

Programs of Study

Since its establishment in 1961, the School of Social Work has derived its mission from the humanistic commitments, values, and goals of the profession of social work, the purposes of the University System of Maryland, and the needs of the communities served by the School. Its primary aim is to educate students for skilled and ethical professional practice and scholarship.

Two method-of-practice concentrations are offered within the M.S.W. program: clinical and management and community organization (MACO). Seven specializations are offered in fields of practice within the M.S.W. program: aging, families and children, health, mental health, employee assistance programs, social and community development, and substance abuse. The School offers three dual-degree programs; the M.S.W./J.D. (Master of Social Work/Juris Doctor) with the University of Maryland School of Law; M.S.W./M.A., offered through the Baltimore Institute for Jewish Communal Service; and M.S.W./M.B.A. with the College of Business and Management, University of Maryland, College Park. The Ph.D. program is designed for professionals who hold the Master of Social Work degree and is committed to educating social workers who, upon completion of their studies, have the advanced intellectual, analytic, research, statistical, computer, and theoretical knowledge and skills to provide leadership, scholarship, teaching, and research that advances social work practice, theory, policy, and research.

Research Facilities

Opened in April 1998, the six-story state-of-the-art library building was designed to support digital information technologies. It houses library services and collections as well as campus computing services. The new library building has three times the space for collections and six times the seating and study space of the old library, 1,500 data connections, 111 study carrels, a café, and comfortable lounge seating. There are three computer classrooms and a 35-workstation Research and Information Commons area with access to a wide variety of databases, the Internet and World Wide Web, and computer software packages. The library cooperates with other University System of Maryland campus libraries through an extensive automated system.

The Computer Center maintains two computer labs—an all-purpose student lab and a training lab for class instruction. The School has a Local Area Network (LAN) with a student and a faculty server. E-mail permits communication both within and outside of the School and a dial-in permits access from outside the School. During 1997–98 the School moved to a Windows environment, and students and faculty members have access to the World Wide Web. The Media Center of the School of Social Work is a state-of-the-art facility that produces educational, informational, and training programs for faculty members, students, other departments, outside nonprofit organizations, and departments of the state of Maryland.

Financial Aid

Fellowships, research and teaching assistantships, Federal Work-Study, and career-related internships or fieldwork are available. Fellowships and assistantships are reserved for doctoral students.

Costs of Study

Tuition for Master of Social Work students who are enrolled for nine or more credit hours per semester in the 1998–99 academic year are $2563 for Maryland residents and $5728.50 for nonresidents. For Master of Social Work students who are enrolled for fewer than nine credit hours per semester, tuition is $253 per credit hour for residents and $457 per credit hour for nonresidents (plus fees). Doctoral students who are Maryland residents pay $231 per credit hour; nonresidents pay $416 per credit hour.

Living and Housing Costs

Rental accommodations are available at reasonable cost in refurnished traditional Baltimore row houses adjacent to campus. On-campus housing is limited.

Student Group

There are about 1,000 master-level and 42 Ph.D. students of rich ethnic diversity in the graduate programs. The alumni association of the School was established in 1972 to meet the professional, educational, and social needs of its graduates.

Location

The University of Maryland, Baltimore, a downtown campus of professional schools, is the focus of urban renewal that reaches to the nationally admired attractions of the nearby Inner Harbor. The Chesapeake Bay and Eastern Shore offer a maritime environment. The District of Columbia is an hour south, and New York City is 4 hours north of the University. The Baltimore-Washington area has much to offer lovers of art, theater, and professional sports.

The School

The School of Social Work celebrated its 35th anniversary in fall 1996. Since 1961, the School has grown to become one of the largest in the United States, with more than 1,300 students enrolled in its three academic programs. In 1983, the School consolidated all of its Baltimore City–based faculty members and students in one building. Louis L. Kaplan Hall, a blocklong complex designed expressly for the School and its programs, was dedicated in 1992. The most recent addition to the School is the Social Work Community Outreach Service. Inaugurated in fall 1992, the Outreach Service is the direct and visible manifestation of the School's commitment to serving the needs of its surrounding community. Within the service's framework, faculty and staff members and students develop and test innovative modalities of social services delivery to needy inner-city residents and their families.

Applying

Students are admitted in the fall semester only. Applications become available after September 1 for admission the following fall. The Office of Admissions operates a self-managed application process, which means that the applicant is responsible for submitting all required documents with the application by the appropriate deadline. Minimum requirements for consideration for admissions to the M.S.W. program are a bachelor's degree from a regionally accredited college or university, a minimum of 24 credit hours in the liberal arts, and a minimum 3.0 grade point average on the last 60 credit hours leading to the award of the baccalaureate degree.

The primary admission requirements for the social work Ph.D. program are an M.S.W. degree from an accredited program, GRE General Test scores, three letters of reference, a personal statement of 5,000 words or more that describes the applicant's desire to advance practice knowledge and skills through research, a sample of writing skills, and an interview with the doctoral program faculty. The deadline for all application materials is January 1.

Correspondence and Information

Marianne Wood, Assistant Dean for Admissions
Louis L. Kaplan Hall
School of Social Work
University of Maryland, Baltimore
525 West Redwood Street
Baltimore, Maryland 21201

Telephone: 410-706-7922 (master's)
410-706-7960 (doctoral)
Fax: 410-706-6046
E-mail: info@ssw.umaryland.edu
World Wide Web: http://ssw.umaryland.edu

University of Maryland, Baltimore

THE FACULTY AND THEIR RESEARCH

Anthony Abbondandolo, School of Social Work Assistant Professor; Ph.D., Maryland College Park. Clinical practice.
Howard Altstein, Professor; Ph.D., Illinois. Transracial and intercountry adoptions.
Mark Battle, Visiting Professor; M.S.S.A., Case Western Reserve. Community planning for HIV prevention, local community mobilization for community empowerment and community-based clinical practice.
John R. Belcher, Professor; Ph.D., Ohio State. Understanding the process of homelessness, particularly as the result of economic dislocation; research with the severely mentally disabled and the development of models of treatment.
James X. Bembry, Assistant Professor; Ph.D., Maryland, Baltimore. Community service, child welfare, child advocacy, social work education, teen parents, mental health, group work, family counseling, social work and the law.
Catherine Born, Research Associate Professor; Ph.D., Maryland, Baltimore. Advocacy, poverty, child support enforcement, dependency and public welfare.
Caroline Long Burry, Assistant Professor; Ph.D., South Carolina. Child welfare, families and children, mental health, social work education.
Enrique Codas, Assistant Professor; M.S.W., Puerto Rico. Research methodology as applied to practice, epistemology of social interventions, social analysis, Latin Americans/Hispanics.
Llewellyn J. Cornelius, Associate Professor and Assistant Dean for Informatics; Ph.D., Chicago. Poverty, health policy, institutional racism, ethnicity, access to medical care for the disadvantaged.
Richard T. Criste, Assistant Professor and Assistant Dean for Undergraduate Field Instruction; Ph.D., Maryland College Park. Addictions, undergraduate social work education, mutual-help groups.
Joseph Crymes, Professor; Ph.D., Cornell. Foster care, adoptions, impact of government policy on family stability, automated agency information systems.
Diane DePanfilis, Assistant Professor; Ph.D., Maryland, Baltimore. Child maltreatment, child welfare, child protective services, measuring outcomes of early interventions with families.
Frederick A. DiBlasio, Professor; Ph.D., Virginia Commonwealth. Clinical use of forgiveness and other clinical practice issues.
Ralph L. Dolgoff, Professor; D.S.W., Columbia. Poverty, social policy, social work profession, supervision, delivery of social services, history of social welfare, social work education, ethical decision making by social workers with groups, ethics.
Harriet Douglas, Clinical Instructor; M.S.W., Catholic University. Domestic violence, adult survivors of child sexual abuse.
Paul E. Ephross, Professor; Ph.D., Chicago. Social work with groups, human sexual behavior, program evaluation, life-cycle issues, ethnicity and intergroup relations.
Donald Fandetti, Associate Professor, D.S.W., Columbia. Social policies and social services for children and families.
Anamarie Goicoechea-Balbona, Assistant Professor; Ph.D., Pittsburgh. Exploring community-based organizations that serve women, developing a curriculum model for AIDS education, interconnection between health and poverty.
Muriel Gray, Associate Professor; Ph.D., Maryland College Park. Substance abuse case management, differential EAP case management, cultural diversity.
Geoffrey L. Greif, Professor and Associate Dean for the Master's Program; D.S.W., Columbia. AIDS and the family, parental abduction, single parents, practice in the Baltimore City schools, group work, African-American families.
David A. Hardcastle, Professor; Ph.D., Case Western Reserve. Poverty, income maintenance, community and human resources development, social administration, policy research, application of research methodologies in practice, professional labor markets and regulations.
Donna Harrington, Assistant Professor; Ph.D., Maryland. Child maltreatment and development; relationship between maternal substance use, parenting, and child development; how maternal illness (HIV infection) influences parenting and child development.
Jesse J. Harris, Dean and Professor; D.S.W., Maryland, Baltimore. History of social work within the armed services, stress of families, psychosocial stress of soldiers and military families.
Aminifu R. Harvey, Associate Professor; D.S.W., Howard. Social work services to African-American youth and their families, role and significance of culture in the delivery of social services and psychotherapy to families and individuals of African descent.
Carolyn Knight, Assistant Professor; Ph.D., Maryland. Field education in social work, group work in social work practice, education treatment issues associated with adult survivor's of child sexual abuse.
Alfred Lucco, Associate Professor; Ph.D., Chicago. Children of separation and divorce, effectiveness of psychotherapy, techniques of psychotherapy, managed mental-health-care delivery systems.
Dale A. Masi, Professor; D.S.W., Catholic University. Human services in industry, particularly employee assistance programs, managed mental health.
Daphne L. McClellan, Assistant Professor; Ph.D., Brandeis. Domestic violence, social policy.
Gust W. Mitchell, Associate Professor, Associate Dean of the Baccalaureate Program, and Chair of the Social Work Department; D.S.W., Catholic University. Children and youth, family, cross-cultural studies.
Carlton E. Munson, Professor and Director of the Doctoral Program; D.S.W., Maryland, Baltimore. Trauma and loss in children, student and practitioner stress reactions, trends in social work education curriculum and enrollment patterns.
Aina O. Nucho, Professor; Ph.D., Bryan Mawr. Art therapy, guided imagery, stress management, child sexual abuse, post-traumatic stress syndrome, psychoneuroimmunology, mental illness.
Julianne S. Oktay, Professor; Ph.D., Michigan. Social work in health care, breast cancer, personal-care services for the elderly and disabled.
Joshua N. Okundaye, Assistant Professor; Ph.D., Maryland. Substance abuse treatment, addictions, and youth.
Malinda B. Orlin, Associate Professor; Ph.D., Pittsburgh. Welfare policy and politics, community development, academic and professional administration.
Howard A. Palley, Professor; Ph.D., Syracuse. Health-care policy, social policies and the elderly, comparative social and health policy, social policy analysis, and social development.
Margarete Parrish, Assistant Professor; Ph.D., Rutgers. Psychosocial adaptation to trauma, adolescence, adolescent females in the juvenile justice system, sexually abused adolescents, violence among adolescents, substance abuse and dependency.
Julia B. Rauch, Professor; Ph.D., Bryn Mawr. Maternal and child health, especially psychosocial aspects of genetic disorders; burden in families with children with affective disorders; social work education in maternal and child health.
Deborah Rejent, Assistant Professor; D.S.W., Columbia. Psychoanalysis, clinical social work education, impact of mental illness in children on parents.
Cyprian Lamar Rowe, Assistant Professor; Ph.D., Howard. Children of the homeless, the elderly, African-American fathers, African-American mental health issues.
Constance Corley Saltz, Professor; Ph.D., Michigan. Aging, long-term care, interdisciplinary teams, rehabilitation, caregiving.
Steven Daniel Soifer, Associate Professor; Ph.D., Brandeis. Community organizing theory and practice, social movements, Jewish issues in social work.
Raju Varghese, Associate Professor; Ed.D., Temple. Group dynamics and organizational theory, social work consultation, intercultural relations and family and individual development.
Thomas V. Vassil, Associate Professor; Ph.D., Chicago. Impact of organizational cultures on individual behavior in residential setting, social work practice with groups, treatment strategies for children and adolescents.
Betsy Vourlekis, Associate Professor; Ph.D., Maryland College Park. Quality assurance technology for psychosocial care in health and mental health care settings, psychosocial needs of nursing home residents and families, case management.
Stanley Wenocur, Professor; Ph.D., Berkeley. Voluntary sector, homelessness, emergency food services, community organization, mental health, philanthropy/federated fundraising and alternative fundraising, political economy of social work and social welfare, organizational and social change.
K. Nancy Wilson, School of Social Work Assistant Professor; M.S.W., Maryland, Baltimore. Policy development and social service delivery system coordination.
Nancy P. Wingfield, Assistant Professor; Ph.D., Virginia Tech. Gerontology, community organization and macroplanning.
Susan Zuravin, Associate Professor; Ph.D., Maryland College Park. Child maltreatment, foster care, child development and mental health, poverty

UNIVERSITY OF MICHIGAN

School of Social Work

Programs of Study

The School offers programs leading to the Master of Social Work and a Doctor of Philosophy in social work and social science. Joint degrees with the School of Public Health (M.S.W./M.P.H.), the Graduate School of Business Administration (M.S.W./M.B.A.), the School of Public Policy Studies (M.S.W./M.P.P.), and the College of Architecture and Urban Planning (M.S.W./M.U.P.) are offered; also offered are certificates in aging, Judaic studies and Jewish communal service, and preparation in school social work.

The M.S.W. has a 60-credit-hour, dual-concentration curriculum that offers opportunities for professional training and field instruction in a choice of practice methods and practice areas. Methods include interpersonal practice, community organization, management of human services, and social policy and evaluation. Practice areas include health, mental health, children and youth in families in society, adults and the elderly in families in society, and community and social systems.

The doctoral program grants a Ph.D. in social work and one of the social sciences disciplines (i.e., anthropology, economics, political science, psychology, or sociology). Students not only gain expertise in knowledge development and research in social work but are also trained as social scientists, thus acquiring broad career options. These include teaching and research positions in schools of social work, social science departments, research institutes, and public and private social planning and social welfare agencies. The specifics of the program vary with the social department and the student's prior preparation. The program is not geared for individuals primarily interested in advanced clinical practice training.

Research Facilities

The School has its own library, which receives more than 400 periodicals and has more than 31,000 volumes. It is an integral part of the University library system, which has a collection of more than 5 million volumes. The School also has its own on-site computer laboratory, which provides easy access to numerous microcomputers that are also connected to the Computer Center, whose hardware, statistical packages, and training centers are rated among the best in the world. Many of the School's full-time faculty members are leading scholars in their field. Several hold joint appointments or collaborative relations with other University of Michigan teaching and research units, including the Departments of Anthropology, Education, Psychology, Sociology, Economics, and Psychiatry; School of Public Health; School of Public Policy Studies; Institute for Social Research; Institute of Gerontology; Institute of Labor and Industrial Relations; Population Studies Center; and the Law School's Child Advocacy Clinic.

Financial Aid

In the M.S.W. program, financial aid through the School of Social Work is awarded on the basis of mission, financial need, and merit. This aid may take the form of grants, scholarships, and memorial awards. The University's Office of Financial Aid administers Federal Stafford Student Loans, Federal Perkins Loans, and college work-study to eligible students. In the doctoral program, various fellowships offered through University, departmental, and federal funds provide stipends and tuition awards for study to outstanding students. Teaching and research assistantships provide stipends and complete tuition waivers and are available in social work and the social science departments. The Michigan Minority Merit Fellowship Program provides stipends and full tuition for up to four years.

Cost of Study

Graduate student tuition per semester is approximately $5400 for state residents and $10,400 for nonresidents in 1998–99. Tuition charges are subject to approval by the Board of Regents.

Living and Housing Costs

Estimated average monthly living expenses are $1200. Rooms, apartments, and houses for single and married students are available for a wide range of rents in Ann Arbor and the surrounding area.

Student Group

In fall 1997, there were 636 students enrolled in the M.S.W. program and 78 active students in the Ph.D. program. Although a majority of the students in the School come from Michigan, the School has a diverse student body with a representation from local, national, and international undergraduate and graduate colleges and universities. In continuing to expand its diversified student body, the School encourages applications from members of ethnic and racial minorities, nonresidents, international students, and other underrepresented groups.

Location

Ann Arbor, with a population of 107,000, is located 40 miles southwest of Detroit. It has the charm of a small city and the excitement of a cosmopolitan center. High-technology industry and research activities are centered in Ann Arbor. The landscape is a blend of parks, office buildings, boutiques, malls, bike paths, and tree-lined streets. Cultural, recreational, and social opportunities are plentiful.

The University and The School

Founded in 1817, the University of Michigan has long been recognized as a leader among institutions of higher education. The University had a fall 1997 student enrollment of 36,964 students; 15,165 were graduate students. The School of Social Work, accredited since 1922, is internationally recognized for its outstanding programs.

Applying

Applicants for the M.S.W. program must have a baccalaureate degree from an accredited college or university with competitive grades; a minimum of 20 semester hours in social sciences; one course in human biology; and personal qualifications considered essential for successful professional practice. Admission to the M.S.W. program is limited to the fall term. Preference is given to applications received by March 1. Decisions will be made by March 1 for applications received by December 1.

Applicants for the Ph.D. program must have scholarly potential and promise for advanced and original work in social work and their elected social science. Graduate Record Examinations results are required. In requesting application materials, individuals should include a brief statement of their academic background, the social science desired for specialization, and career goals. All materials, including GRE scores, must be received by January 2.

Correspondence and Information

For the M.S.W. program:
Office of Admissions and Student Services
School of Social Work
University of Michigan
1080 South University
Ann Arbor, Michigan 48109-1106
Telephone: 734-764-3309

For the Ph.D. program:
Doctoral Program in Social Work and Social Sciences
School of Social Work
University of Michigan
1080 South University
Ann Arbor, Michigan 48109-1106
Telephone: 734-763-5768

University of Michigan

THE FACULTY AND THEIR RESEARCH

Paula Allen-Meares, Professor and Dean; Ph.D., Illinois at Urbana-Champaign. Health care, educational organizations, parenting.
Ron Avi Astor, Assistant Professor; Ph.D., Berkeley. Children's reasoning process, school-based violence prevention.
Oscar Barbarin, Professor; Ph.D., Rutgers. African-American family functioning, stress, coping, major childhood illness.
Candyce Berger, Assistant Dean of Hospital Social Work Services and Associate Professor; Ph.D., USC. Health care.
William Birdsall, Associate Professor; Ph.D., Johns Hopkins. Poverty, income inequality, living arrangements, juvenile justice.
David L. Burton, Assistant Professor; Ph.D., Washington (Seattle). Sexually aggressive children; gay, lesbian, bisexual, transgenderal clients.
Barry Checkoway, Professor; Ph.D., Pennsylvania. Community organization, social planning, neighborhood work.
Mary E. Corcoran, Professor; Ph.D., MIT. Poverty, sex discrimination, social stratification and unemployment.
Tom A. Croxton, Professor; J.D., Michigan. Juvenile justice system, law and social work, ethics, malpractice.
Sandra K. Danziger, Associate Professor; Ph.D., Boston University. Adolescent pregnancy/parenthood, welfare and child support.
Sheldon H. Danziger, Professor; Ph.D., MIT. Poverty, income inequality, social welfare programs and policies.
Ruth E. Dunkle, Professor and Associate Dean; Ph.D., Syracuse. Clinical gerontology, long-term care.
Kathleen M. L. Coulborn Faller, Professor; Ph.D., Michigan. Child welfare, child abuse/neglect, sexual abuse.
Sheila C. Feld, Professor; Ph.D., Michigan. Social motivation, mental health, marital/parental roles, service delivery.
Phillip A. Fellin, Professor; Ph.D., Michigan. Program evaluation, mental health of the elderly, homelessness and illness.
Larry M. Gant, Assistant Professor; Ph.D., Michigan. Program evaluation, African-American populations, HIV/AIDS intervention research.
Charles D. Garvin, Professor; Ph.D., Chicago. Interpersonal practice, gender/ethnicity, group work, long-term mental illness.
Rose Gibson, Professor; Ph.D., Michigan. Aging and the life course, health and aging, sociocultural factors in aging.
Lorraine Gutierrez, Visiting Associate Professor; Ph.D., Michigan. Empowerment-oppressed groups, mental health, Latinos.
Lawrence A. Hirschfeld, Assistant Professor; Ph.D., Columbia. Young children's conceptual and social understandings.
Leslie Doty Hollingsworth, Assistant Professor; Ph.D., Purdue. African-American family preservation, kinship foster care, transracial adoption.
Berit Ingersoll-Dayton, Associate Professor; Ph.D., Michigan. Social support of families in later life, employed caregivers.
Siri D. Jayaratne, Professor; Ph.D., Michigan. Work stress, professional practice, human service prevention programs.
Sherrie A. Kossoudji, Assistant Professor; Ph.D., Michigan. Labor economics, adoption, family decision making, migrant workers.
Armand A. Lauffer, Professor; Ph.D., Brandeis. Community organizing, planning, organizational development, Jewish communal service.
Edith Lewis, Associate Professor; Ph.D., Wisconsin–Madison. Culturally competent empowerment, women and families of color.
Frank F. Maple, Professor; M.S.W., Michigan. School social work, interviewing methods, group and family treatment.
Susan C. McDonough, Assistant Professor; Ph.D., Illinois at Urbana-Champaign. Children's mental health, preventive interventions.
Carol T. Mowbray, Associate Professor; Ph.D., Michigan. Psychosocial rehabilitation, dual diagnosis, women's mental health, homelessness.
Robert M. Ortega, Assistant Professor; Ph.D., Michigan. Child welfare, juvenile justice, serious mental illness.
Thomas J. Powell, Professor; Ph.D., Smith. Mental health policies, self-help and community-based support systems.
Beth Glover Reed, Associate Professor; Ph.D., Cincinnati. Gender/ethnicity in social systems, feminist/multicultural practice, alcohol/drugs.
Lawrence S. Root, Professor; Ph.D., Chicago. Social welfare/employment policy, employee assistance plans, older workers.
Daniel G. Saunders, Associate Professor; Ph.D., Wisconsin–Madison. Family violence, domestic abuse.
Brett A. Seabury, Associate Professor; D.S.W., Columbia. Interpersonal practice, child welfare, indigenous healing systems.
Kristine A. Siefert, Professor; Ph.D., Minnesota. Health of women and children, prevention, health care for the underserved.
Michael Spencer, Assistant Professor; Ph.D., Washington (Seattle). Race, poverty, mental health, children and families.
Robert J. Taylor, Associate Professor; Ph.D., Michigan. Informal social support networks of adult/elderly African-Americans.
Richard Tolman, Associate Professor; Ph.D., Wisconsin–Madison. Group work and family violence, interpersonal practice.
John E. Tropman, Professor; Ph.D., Michigan. Decision-making systems, social/welfare policies, disadvantaged groups.
David Tucker, Professor; Ph.D., Toronto. Organizational ecology, dynamic modeling, knowledge development and production.
Diane Vinokur-Kaplan, Assistant Professor; Ph.D., Michigan. Management, funding and staffing of human service workplaces.
John Wallace, Assistant Professor; Ph.D., Michigan. Mental health of African-American children and youth, poverty, prevention.
Helen R. Weingarten, Associate Professor; Ph.D., Michigan. Family transitions, policy/gender differences, conflict management.
Mieko Yoshihama, Assistant Professor; Ph.D., UCLA. Violence against women/immigrants, race, culture, class, mental health.
Mayer N. Zald, Professor; Ph.D., Michigan. Sociology of social welfare, social movements, accounting/budgeting systems.

UNIVERSITY OF NEW ENGLAND

School of Social Work

Programs of Study

The School of Social Work at the University of New England affirms a commitment to the core social work values of human dignity, individual and cultural diversity, self-determination, and social justice. The School is accredited by the Council on Social Work Education to offer the M.S.W. degree and to prepare graduates for advanced practice in the social work profession.

The School offers a foundation curriculum and two advanced concentrations: clinical social work and integrated social work. The M.S.W. program can be completed in two years of full-time study or three to four years of part-time study. The goals of the School include helping students (1) to understand the potential for individual and collective human development when people live with dignity and social justice, participate in relationships embodying these values, and have adequate material and emotional resources; (2) to comprehend the depth and complexity of oppression, its acute and extended impact on people, and people's strengths in survival and resistance; (3) to identify people's strengths across diverse populations and build upon them in an array of practice settings; (4) to help develop knowledge and skills necessary to carry out multiple social work interventions consistent with the School's mission and the profession's ethics; and (5) to help students empower individuals and groups often denied the dignity and resources required to live stable, contributing lives for themselves, their families, and their communities.

Graduates of the School work in a variety of programs and settings, including direct service roles in child protective services, family services, shelters for battered women and children, poverty programs, medical hospitals and outpatient or primary-care health settings; in services for people with HIV/AIDS, in mental health centers and substance abuse clinics; in special services for gay and lesbian people; and in state and local policy and planning and corrections and courts, among many others. Graduates are prepared to work with individuals, families, groups, neighborhoods, and organizations with diverse populations and in many different types of settings.

Extensive resources are committed to the fieldwork education component. Faculty advisers serve as liaisons to field agencies. Field education faculty members work with each student to create placements throughout Maine, New Hampshire, Massachusetts, and Vermont. Students in field placement take seminars as part of the required curriculum along with practice and theory courses. In addition to their placements and integrating seminars, students are required to choose a field of practice elective where current information is presented about health or mental health, domestic violence, child welfare, aging, or social work in school settings.

Research Facilities

The University library holds many volumes and periodicals for the programs in social work.

Financial Aid

Social work students may apply for federally funded loans, limited University-sponsored scholarship aid, Federal Work-Study, and alternative loan programs.

Cost of Study

The tuition and fees for 1998–99 are $345 per credit hour, and the general service fee is $240.

Living and Housing Costs

Overnight housing for social work students is available on both the University and Westbrook College Campuses. On-campus apartments for graduate students are available in the Housing Park, and students must sign a lease. Rates vary according to the size of the rental unit. For the academic year 1997–98, costs ranged from $4200 to $5300. There are privately owned apartments available in the vicinity of the campus. The monthly rates vary from $400 to $800. For information on housing, students should write to the director of housing at the University address below.

Student Group

Projected enrollment for the School of Social Work in fall 1998 is 192 students. Students come from different cultural, ethnic, and regional backgrounds. A student organization includes all students as members.

Student Outcomes

The Master in Social Work degree at the University offers graduates the opportunity to play active service roles in domestic violence, health and mental health, alcohol and substance abuse, poverty and public welfare, women's and children's services, homelessness, HIV/AIDS, and other emerging areas of service delivery. The program prepares graduates to work directly with individuals, couples, families, organizations, and communities.

Location

The University of New England has two campuses. The 540-acre University Campus is set on the banks of the Saco River and the shore of the Atlantic Ocean in southern Maine. The town of Biddeford is situated between two resort areas, Kennebunkport and Old Orchard Beach, 20 miles south of Portland, Maine's largest city. The 40-acre Westbrook College Campus, located in Portland, is in a quiet residential area just outside the city.

The University and The School

The University of New England's School of Social Work is the only independent school of social work in northern New England. The University has been ranked among the best regional liberal arts colleges in the country and was chosen one of the ten best regional colleges in the North in 1992 and 1993 by *U.S. News & World Report* in its annual "America's Best Colleges" survey. More than 2,500 students are enrolled from throughout the United States and numerous other countries, with a majority from the Northeast region.

Applying

Application forms are available from the Graduate Admissions Office. The deadline for submission of all materials is January 15. The School of Social Work has an advanced standing option for graduates of accredited B.S.W. programs who meet the criteria established by the School.

Correspondence and Information

Graduate Admissions Office
University of New England
Hills Beach Road
Biddeford, Maine 04005
Telephone: 800-477-4UNE (toll-free)

University of New England

THE FACULTY AND THEIR RESEARCH

Nancy Ayer, Instructor; M.S.W., West Virginia. Community organization, disabilities, field education.

Marcia B. Cohen, Associate Professor; Ph.D., Brandeis; M.S.W., Columbia. Homelessness, empowerment-oriented social work practice, self-directed group work.

Robert E. Cummings, Associate Professor, Ph.D. Brandeis; M.S.W., Boston College. Schizoid process in personality development, developmental theory using object relations perspective.

Kathryn A. DeLois, Assistant Professor; Ph.D., Washington (Seattle); M.S.W., Boston College. Feminist research methods, lesbian and gay issues, empowerment practice.

Christine A. Dietz, Assistant Professor; Ph.D. candidate, SUNY at Buffalo; M.S.W., Iowa. Gay and lesbian issues, family violence, direct practice.

Elizabeth A. Gray, Instructor; M.S.W., Connecticut. Social work with the elderly/caregivers, women's issues, field education.

Clay T. Graybeal, Associate Professor; Ph.D., Rutgers; M.S.W., Fordham. Strengths-based practice, solution-focused practice, values and decision making, solution-oriented brief therapy, strengths-based models of social work practice.

Vernon L. Moore, Associate Professor; Ed.D., Vanderbilt; M.S.W., Louisville. Community and organizational development, families.

David C. Prichard, Assistant Professor; Ph.D. candidate, Virginia Commonwealth. Trauma, crisis intervention, managed care, brief solution-focused therapy.

Stephen M. Rose, Professor; Ph.D., Brandeis; M.S.S.A. (M.S.W.), Case Western Reserve. Interpersonal violence, empowerment practice, public sector mental health.

Phyl Rubenstein, Assistant Professor, M.S.W., Georgia. Feminist practice, family violence, field education.

Elizabeth H. Ruff, Associate Professor and Director, Field Education; M.S.W., Connecticut. Social work in political arena, rural social work, field education.

Joanne Thompson, Professor and Program Director; Ph.D., Rutgers; M.S.W., Arkansas. Community practice and management.

UNIVERSITY OF PENNSYLVANIA

School of Social Work

Programs of Study

The School of Social Work at Penn offers opportunities for full-time and part-time study leading to the degrees of Master of Social Work and Doctor of Philosophy in social welfare. In addition, students can combine the M.S.W. with the Master of Business Administration (M.S.W./M.B.A.), the Master of City Planning (M.S.W./M.C.P.), the Master of Education (M.S.W./M.S.Ed.), the Juris Doctor, and the Doctor of Philosophy (M.S.W./Ph.D.) degree program. The School also offers an M.S.W./Certificate in Jewish Communal Studies, an M.S.W./Certificate in Catholic Social Ministry, and an M.S.W./Certificate in Lutheran Social Ministries.

The primary goal of the master's program is to prepare social workers for leadership roles in the development and provision of services to individuals, families, groups, and communities. The curriculum consists of one year of foundation study followed by a year of advanced study. Core requirements include courses in social work practice, research, social policy, individual and social processes, and institutional racism. Students normally spend two days per week in the classroom and three days per week in a field placement in a social agency. The second year is based on the student's selection of one of two methodological concentrations: direct practice or macro practice. Within macro practice, students choose one of two subconcentrations: social and economic development or administration, policy, and planning. Students may focus their course work in a field of practice in one of the following areas: aging, health, behavioral health (which includes mental health and addictions), services to children and youth, and adult/juvenile justice. Students complete required and optional courses focusing on knowledge and skill development in a specific area of interest, utilizing particular modes of social intervention.

The doctoral program prepares students with a master's degree for leadership positions in social work and related fields. The program awards an interdisciplinary Doctor of Philosophy (Ph.D.) degree in social welfare, which prepares students to address a wide range of social problems related to human welfare. Most graduates of the doctoral program pursue leadership positions in public and private human services organizations or careers in postsecondary teaching and research.

Research Facilities

The School operates two research centers: the Center for the Study of Social Work Practice and the Center for Research and Education in the Workplace. In addition, the School maintains a microcomputing laboratory for student use. The University operates a mainframe computer facility and the Social Science Data Center through which students can gain access to the resources of the Inter-University Consortium for Political and Social Research.

Financial Aid

Financial aid is based primarily on need. Students applying for aid must file a GAPSFAS form. More than 60 percent of M.S.W. students receive financial aid. In addition, the School recognizes merit by offering a range of scholarships to those who qualify. The doctoral program provides aid in the form of merit fellowships and graduate assistantships, which enable students to gain teaching experience and to collaborate with members of the faculty on research projects.

Cost of Study

For full-time M.S.W. students in 1998–99, tuition is $22,134 per year, including student fees; for part-time students it is $2761 per course unit. For Ph.D. students, tuition is $24,200 per year.

Living and Housing Costs

Including tuition and fees, the annual cost of living for a single student was about $26,000 for the 1997–98 year and about $29,000 for married students. Living accommodations are available in Graduate Towers, the University's apartment building, or in privately owned off-campus housing.

Student Group

The student body is diverse, representing a wide range of age groups and educational, geographical, and ethnic backgrounds. The School is committed to recruiting racial and ethnic minorities. The following are student organizations within the School: Student Council, Alliance of Black Social Work Students, Hispanos Unidos, and the Feminist Collective.

Location

The campus of the University of Pennsylvania is located near central Philadelphia, a metropolitan area with a population of more than 5 million. The city of Philadelphia and the University both offer a variety of cultural, recreational, and educational opportunities. Excellent rail and bus services connect Philadelphia to the Washington, D.C. (2 hours), and New York (1½ hours) areas. Philadelphia also operates an international airport that serves all parts of the country and most parts of the world with direct airline service.

The University

The University of Pennsylvania is a private, Ivy League university with a long and distinguished history of education in social work.

The University was founded by Benjamin Franklin and is the oldest university in the country. The School of Social Work, one of the oldest in the country, was established in 1909. The University has pioneered in the development of many professional fields of higher education in addition to social work, including city planning, nursing, medicine, law, education, veterinary medicine, dentistry, and business.

Applying

Students are admitted once a year, in the fall, to the School's full-time M.S.W. and Ph.D. programs. Applications for the full-time M.S.W. program are accepted between September 15 and March 15 preceding the fall semester in which the student plans to enroll. Applications for the Ph.D. program are accepted between September 15 and February 1. It is important to file early as enrollment is limited. Part-time students are admitted in all terms: fall, spring, and summer.

Correspondence and Information

Office of Admissions
School of Social Work
University of Pennsylvania
3701 Locust Walk P
Philadelphia, Pennsylvania 19104-6214
Telephone: 215-898-5511
World Wide Web: http://www.ssw.upenn.edu

University of Pennsylvania

THE FACULTY AND THEIR RESEARCH

Howard D. Arnold, Associate Professor and Associate Dean; M.S.W., Pennsylvania, 1963. Social work practice, family dynamics, institutional racism.
Joretha Bourjolly, Assistant Professor; Ph.D., Bryn Mawr, 1996. Effects of chronic illness on individuals and family members as well as the impact of racial and economic factors on the delivery of health care.
Louis Carter, Associate Professor; M.S.W., Pennsylvania, 1962. Criminal and juvenile justice, family systems, social work practice.
Ram A. Cnaan, Associate Professor; Ph.D., Pittsburgh, 1981. Social work research methods, social policy, volunteerism and volunteer action, information technology applications.
Burton Cohen, Adjunct Assistant Professor; Ph.D., Pennsylvania, 1983. Organizational development in public and nonprofit agencies.
Dennis Culhane, Associate Professor; Ph.D., Boston College, 1990. Homelessness.
Richard J. Estes, Professor; D.S.W., Berkeley, 1973. International and comparative social welfare, social indicators, mental health, evaluative research, computer technology.
Richard James Gelles, Professor; Ph.D., New Hampshire, 1973. Child welfare, family violence, child abuse.
Helaine Greenberg, Adjunct Assistant Professor; D.S.W., Pennsylvania, 1989. Bereavement, childhood oncology.
Robert Rehner Iversen, Assistant Professor; Ph.D., Bryn Mawr, 1991. Practice with children and families, research on women and poverty.
Beth Miriam Lewis, Assistant Professor; D.S.W., Hunter, 1993. Occupational health, social work in health care, social work in the work place.
Diane Metzendorf, Lecturer; D.S.W., Pennsylvania, 1992. Women's issues, health care–trauma, computer technology.
Michael Reisch, Professor; Ph.D., SUNY at Binghamton, 1975. Social policy, community organization, public policy analysis, history and philosophy of social welfare, administration of nonprofit organization.
Lauren Rich, Assistant Professor; Ph.D., Michigan, 1993. Child support enforcement, children and intergenerational poverty.
Roberta G. Sands, Associate Professor; Ph.D., Louisville, 1979. Mental health, women's issues, clinical social work practice, interprofessional communications, ethnographic sociolinguistic research.
Ira M. Schwartz, Professor and Dean; M.S.W., Washington (Seattle), 1968. Policy research in the areas of juvenile justice, child welfare, and children's mental health.
Vivian Seltzer, Professor; Ph.D., Bryn Mawr, 1975. Adolescents, psychosocial development, adolescent behavior, adolescent problems, adolescent peer group relations, child development and behavior.
William Silver, Lecturer; D.S.W., Pennsylvania, 1976. Structural family therapy, marriage and family.
Kenwyn K. Smith, Associate Professor; Ph.D., Yale, 1974. Group and intergroup relations, organizational change, organizational politics, conflict management, impact of organizational dynamics on the health of employees.
Phyllis Solomon, Professor; Ph.D., Case Western Reserve, 1978. Social work research methods, mental health policy and service delivery systems, severely mentally disabled persons and their families.
Mark J. Stern, Professor; Ph.D., York (England), 1980. Social welfare policy; social history and social welfare; poverty in the United States, 1900–present.
Peter B. Vaughan, Associate Professor and Associate Dean; Ph.D., Michigan, 1977. Interdisciplinary team practice, mental health, health-care access.
Yin-Ling Irene Wong, Assistant Professor; Ph.D., Wisconsin, 1995. Social policy, homelessness, homelessness prevention and poverty research.

WASHINGTON UNIVERSITY IN ST. LOUIS

George Warren Brown School of Social Work

Programs of Study

The George Warren Brown School of Social Work (GWB) offers a curriculum leading to the degree of Master of Social Work and, in collaboration with the Graduate School of Arts and Sciences, the degree of Doctor of Philosophy in social work. The School is characterized by flexibility in the choice of courses, including the practicum; individually planned curricula; interdisciplinary collaboration; and the combination of experimental and traditional courses. Both the M.S.W. and Ph.D. programs require concentrated academic work. Students with superior academic preparation are encouraged to apply.

The master's degree curriculum prepares students for advanced social work practice in the fields of children, youth, and family; gerontology; health; mental health; and social and economic development. Specializations are available in the areas of family therapy, management, and research. The program involves 60 credit hours for graduation and ordinarily requires two academic years of full-time study or four academic years of part-time study for completion. Students with a B.S.W. from a CSWE-accredited school enroll in an advanced-standing program that permits them to complete the requirements in sixteen months.

The Ph.D. program is highly interdisciplinary and is designed to prepare graduates for teaching and research careers. The average time needed to complete all Ph.D. requirements is three years of full-time study for students with the M.S.W. degree and four to five years for those without it.

A special feature of the School is the availability of programs leading to joint degrees in social work and law (J.D./M.S.W.), architecture (M.S.W./M.Arch.), business administration (M.S.W./M.B.A.), and Jewish communal services (M.S.W./J.C.S.). In addition, students often enroll in courses in other graduate schools of the University.

Research Facilities

GWB is housed in two connecting buildings that were built for teaching and research—Goldfarb Hall, opened in 1998, and Brown Hall, the first academic building dedicated to social work. A wide range of computing equipment and services is available for use by students for classroom instruction and research projects. Library holdings in the social and behavioral sciences and social welfare are strong and up to date. There are ample opportunities for collaborative and interdisciplinary work throughout the University. Most of the faculty members have ongoing research projects in which both M.S.W. and Ph.D. students participate. The School houses the Center for Mental Health Services Research, a joint project of GWB and the National Institute of Mental Health; the Kathryn M. Buder Center for American Indian Studies; and the Center for Social Development.

Financial Aid

More than 100 scholarships, five loan programs, college work-study arrangements, paid practica, and part-time employment assistance are among the various types of financial aid administered by the School of Social Work in conjunction with Washington University's Office of Student Financial Services. The School gives full consideration to all applicants for admission and financial aid without respect to age, color, creed, disability, marital status, national origin, race, or sex. Approximately 80 percent of M.S.W. students receive financial aid.

Cost of Study

The tuition for master's degree students is $604 per credit hour in 1998–99. Tuition for the doctoral program is $22,000 per year. Additional expenses, including the cost of books and supplies, come to about $1000 per year.

Living and Housing Costs

Approximately $750 per month should be budgeted to provide for living costs. Most students prefer to rent an apartment in the vicinity of the School.

Student Group

In fall 1997, there were 397 full-time and 71 part-time students in the M.S.W. program. Forty-seven students were working toward the Ph.D. degree in social work. Students from forty states and thirteen other countries were enrolled in the program.

Location

The St. Louis area offers a variety of musical, cultural, and sports events throughout the academic year. Washington University is contiguous with the city of St. Louis and adjoins its suburbs. There is a delightful potpourri of shops, ethnic restaurants, churches, bookstores, movie theaters, and art museums within a mile of the campus. In addition, St. Louis social agencies offer outstanding practicum opportunities to students.

The University and The School

GWB was ranked the top school of social work in the nation by *U.S. News & World Report* in March 1997. The School of Social Work is one of the eight graduate and professional schools that constitute Washington University—a medium-sized, private, urban institution. GWB profits from all of the University's resources, including an outstanding and internationally recognized faculty, a diverse and talented student body, a superior library, and an overall environment of creative excellence. The School is one of the few social work programs in the country to have its own placement office for graduates. It is fully accredited by the Council on Social Work Education.

Applying

Applicants must have an undergraduate degree or be in the process of obtaining one. No specific undergraduate major is required; however, a minimum of 30 semester hours in the social sciences and liberal arts is recommended. Undergraduate performance should demonstrate intellectual capacity for graduate study, with a B average as the minimum requirement. Applicants are advised to apply as early as possible.

Correspondence and Information

For the M.S.W. program:
Elizabeth M. George
Assistant Dean of Admissions and Student Resources
George Warren Brown School of Social Work
Box 1196, One Brookings Drive
Washington University in St. Louis
St. Louis, Missouri 63130
Telephone: 314-935-6676
314-935-7252 (TTY/TDD)
Fax: 314-935-8511
E-mail: mswadmis@gwbssw.wustl.edu
World Wide Web: http://gwbweb.wustl.edu

For the Ph.D. program:
Dr. Michael W. Sherraden
Chairperson, Ph.D. Program
George Warren Brown School of Social Work
Box 1196, One Brookings Drive
Washington University in St. Louis
St. Louis, Missouri 63130
Telephone: 314-935-6605
314-935-7252 (TTY/TDD)
Fax: 314-935-8511
E-mail: phdsw@gwbssw.wustl.edu
World Wide Web: http://gwbweb.wustl.edu

Washington University in St. Louis

THE FACULTY

Professors

Larry E. Davis, Ph.D., Michigan. Impact of race, gender, and class on professional interactions; male-female relationships; interracial group dynamics.
David F. Gillespie, Ph.D., Washington (Seattle). Disaster preparedness, organizational theory, interorganizational relations.
Shanti K. Khinduka, Ph.D., Brandeis. Social work education, international social development, interethnic relations.
Martha N. Ozawa, Bettie Bofinger Brown Professor of Social Policy; Ph.D., Wisconsin–Madison. Policy analysis of social welfare programs, income support programs, social security, unemployment.
Enola K. Proctor, Frank Bruno Professor for Social Work Research; Ph.D., Washington (St. Louis). Mental health and health services; treatment planning in direct practice; evaluation of clinical social work; race, gender, and socioeconomic status.
Aaron Rosen, Ph.D., Michigan. Direct practice, mental health clinical judgments and decisions, systematic practice.
Michael W. Sherraden, Benjamin E. Youngdahl Professor of Social Development and Chair, Ph.D. Program; Ph.D., Michigan. Social policy and administration, youth policy.
Arlene Stiffman, Ph.D., Washington (St. Louis). Child and adolescent mental health, high-risk behaviors.

Associate Professors

Wendy Auslander, Ph.D., Washington (St. Louis). Minority health and health promotion, family functioning and chronic illness, juvenile diabetes, AIDS prevention in teens.
Letha Chadiha, Ph.D., Michigan. Family relations, home care of African-American elderly, social roles and social functioning.
F. Brett Drake, Ph.D., UCLA. Social stress, substance abuse, child abuse and neglect, burnout of child welfare workers.
David Katz, Ph.D., Michigan. Service for chronically mentally ill, human capital development as a social welfare policy.
Jack A. Kirkland, M.S.W., Syracuse. Community work, group relations, international social development, racism, social planning.
Nancy Morrow-Howell, Ph.D., Berkeley. Gerontology, care for dependent elderly, hospital discharge planning for elderly.
Shanta Pandey, Ph.D., Case Western Reserve. Social policy, poverty, program evaluation.
Robert L. Pierce, Ph.D., Washington (St. Louis). Multicultural training, child maltreatment, child welfare.
Mark Rank, Ph.D., Wisconsin–Madison. Poverty and welfare recipients, social stratification, family, social policy.
Nancy R. Vosler, Ph.D., Virginia Commonwealth. Families and work, family policy, impact of unemployment on families.
Gautam N. Yadama, Ph.D., Case Western Reserve. International community development, rural farming and forestry.

Assistant Professors

Matthew O. Howard, Ph.D., Washington (Seattle). Alcohol and drug abuse, substance abuse in American Indians, clinical issues related to alcoholism.
Melissa Jonson-Reid, Ph.D., Berkeley. Outcomes of children exposed to violence, child welfare and juvenile justice services outcomes, interagency school-based interventions.
J. Curtis McMillen, Ph.D., Maryland at Baltimore. Child welfare, clinical social work practice.
David E. Pollio, Ph.D., Michigan. Homelessness/street people, poverty, psychopathology, group work.
Shirley L. Porterfield, Ph.D., Wisconsin–Madison. Labor markets, social welfare and public policy, economic development.
James Herbert Williams, Ph.D., Washington (Seattle). Correlates and predictors of juvenile delinquency, African-American families.

Visiting Professors

Dan Edwards, D.S.W., Utah. American Indians, policy and practice.
Richard Estes, Ph.D., Berkeley. International and comparative social welfare strategies, long-range planning.
David G. Gil, D.S.W., Pennsylvania. Child welfare, social policy.
Nancy Humphreys, D.S.W., UCLA. Public welfare, administration, women's issues, political social work.
Nazneen Mayadas, D.S.W., Washington (St. Louis). Skills training, mental health.
John Morris, M.S.W., Washington (St. Louis). Mental health policy.
John Robertson, Ph.D., Columbia. Poverty, child welfare policy, community development.
Rosemary Sarri, Ph.D., Michigan. Social policy, children and youth.
Calvin Streeter, Ph.D., Washington (St. Louis). Management and network analysis.

Adjunct Faculty

Robert Benjamin, J.D./M.S.W., Saint Louis. Family law, law and social work, mediation.
William Kahn, M.S.W., Pittsburgh. Management, marketing, resource development.
Vered Slonim-Nevo, D.S.W., UCLA. Family therapy, treatment evaluation, human behavior, research.

Lecturers

Mahasweta Banerjee, Ph.D., Washington (St. Louis). Organizational theory, research and evaluation.
Laura Barrett, M.S.W., Washington (St. Louis). Organizing, lobbying, and housing for low-income families.
Eddie Brown, D.S.W., Utah. Policies and programs for American Indians.
Jeanne Bubb, M.S.W., Washington (St. Louis). Health care.
Sandra Burgess, Pharm.D., Illinois at Chicago. Pharmacology.
Ellen Burkemper, M.S.W., Washington (St. Louis). Family therapy, behavioral theory.
Jean Caine, M.S.W., Washington (St. Louis). Family therapy, women's issues.
David Cronin, Ph.D., Saint Louis. Public child welfare.
Osei Darkwa, Ph.D., Washington (St. Louis). Social policy and research.
Therese Dent, Ph.D., Saint Louis. Program development, policy implementation, field education.
Daniel Frigo, Ph.D., Washington (St. Louis). Mental health.
Jane Geiler, J.D., Saint Louis; M.S.W., North Carolina. Law and social work, sexual abuse.
Linda Griffith, M.S.W., Saint Louis. Mental health.
Michael Harris, Ph.D., US International. Health care and family therapy.
Gary Hirschberg, M.S.W., Washington (St. Louis). Work with HIV-positive individuals and their families.
Stephen Jones, M.S.W., Utah. Family therapy.
Lee Judy, M.S.W., Washington (St. Louis). Crisis intervention.
Sally Kaplan, Ph.D., Washington (St. Louis). Health policy.
Dana Wilson Klar, J.D./M.S.W., Washington (St. Louis). American Indian issues.
Roz Marx, M.S.W., Washington (St. Louis). Gerontology.
Larry McEvoy, M.A., SUNY at Binghamton. Statistical analysis.
Mary Anne Mica, M.S.W., Washington (St. Louis). Child welfare, foster care, adoption.
Pam Moussette, M.S.W., Washington (St. Louis). Women and domestic violence.
Betul Ozmat, M.S.W., Washington (St. Louis). Marketing, community relations.
Deborah Paulsrud, M.S.W., Washington (St. Louis). Child welfare, social work practice.
Barbara Richter, M.S.W., Washington (St. Louis). Management, fiscal management.
Barry Rosenberg, M.S.W., SUNY at Albany. Working with boards and volunteers.
Judith Schechtman, M.S.W., Washington (St. Louis). Human sexuality, child sexual abuse.
Meg Schnabel, M.S.W., Washington (St. Louis). Women and domestic violence.
Suzanne Shepard, Ph.D., Washington (St. Louis). Treatment evaluation and research.
Barbara Silverstein, Ph.D., Saint Louis. Group work.
Donald Sloane, M.S.W., Washington (St. Louis). Behavioral therapy.
Huey Way, Pharm.D., Nebraska. Pharmacology.
Danny Wedding, Ph.D., Hawaii. Mental health practice and policy, psychotherapies.
Lillian Weger, M.S.W., Columbia. Psychosocial methods.
Karl Wilson, Ph.D., Florida. Mental health policy.

WAYNE STATE UNIVERSITY

School of Social Work

Program of Study

The Master of Social Work (M.S.W.) program prepares students for advanced social work practice that includes preparation for the provision of leadership to the profession. The professional School of Social Work, accredited by the Council on Social Work Education, has as its mission the teaching of the knowledge, values, and skills of the social work profession. Graduates of the School are trained to understand the needs of vulnerable populations and those for whom the quality of life is threatened. Through research, the faculty members of the School contribute to the knowledge base of the social work profession, and the faculty members and students serve the community by participating in professional societies, civic and community groups, and human service organizations.

The School is an integral part of Wayne State University, an urban university in a culturally diverse, industrialized, metropolitan area. The School is committed in its teaching, research, and service activities to addressing the problems of people living in this environment. Both in class and in the human service organizations, which are the sites for field education (practica), students learn how to provide effective social services and to influence social policies. The School's activities are intended ultimately to alleviate the condition of those affected by poverty, racism, sexism, homophobia, and unemployment and those with emotional disturbances or physical and/or developmental challenges. Students learn methods of intervention with individuals, families, groups, communities, and organizations. Consistent with its emphasis on serving people in the Detroit metropolitan area, the School shares with the University a commitment to recruiting students of minority ethnic backgrounds.

The School offers full-time and part-time study programs leading to the M.S.W. degree. The full-time degree program consists of four semesters of study (60 credit hours) in which field work is concurrent with class work. Students spend three full days a week in the field and two days in classes for two consecutive years. Required classes in the full-time program may be offered in both day and evening sessions. The part-time program (60 credit hours) permits students to complete degree requirements over a four-year period. Applicants who hold a baccalaureate degree from an undergraduate social work program accredited by the Council on Social Work Education are eligible for advanced standing. If admitted to the M.S.W. Advanced Standing Program, they may complete their degree full-time (three semesters/37 credit hours) or part-time (seven semesters/37 credit hours). For the M.S.W. part-time study programs, experience in the human service field is preferred. Graduate students in the Advanced Standing Program are required to select a field of practice in which to concentrate their studies. The School offers four fields: mental health, health care, family/children and youth, and community practice and social action.

Research Facilities

Wayne State, with three mainframe computers, operates one of the largest computing centers in the Detroit area. Links with MichNet provide users with access to the Internet (NSFNET), SprintNet, AutoNet, and Datapac networks. The University is also linked to the BITNET academic network. The School houses its own computer lab, which is available for student use, and all students are given e-mail access.

Financial Aid

The Office of Scholarships and Financial Aid provides students with information regarding sources of funds and offers both group and individual sessions on planning to finance graduate education. Subsidized and unsubsidized loans are available to cover the cost of tuition, books, fees, and limited living expenses. University graduate and professional scholarships are also offered to both full- and part-time graduate students. The School has several private scholarships and some agency stipends that are available for students.

Cost of Study

Tuition in 1998–99 for Michigan residents is $163 per credit hour. Non-Michigan residents pay $338 per credit hour. A nonrefundable registration fee of $69 is assessed each term. An omnibus fee of $15 per credit hour up to a maximum of 12 credits ($120) is assessed each term.

Living and Housing Costs

The University Housing Office provides information to assist students in locating on-campus housing. Double and single rooms in residence halls as well as efficiency and one- and two-bedroom modern private apartments are available on campus. There are 120 apartments specially equipped for handicapped students. Apartment rental rates for 1998–99 range from $274 to $929 per month.

Student Group

The School of Social Work has approximately 800 full- and part-time students: 200 undergraduate B.S.W. students and 600 M.S.W. graduate students. Approximately 90 percent are from metropolitan Detroit and reflect the rich diversity in races, cultures, and lifestyles of the area. The other 10 percent are from the rest of the state of Michigan, the U.S., Canada, and other countries. Classes in the first year of the M.S.W. program average 28 students. However, in the second-year Advanced Curriculum, class sizes range from 7 to 28 students.

Location

The modern University campus is a distinctive element in Detroit's expansive cultural center, which includes the Fisher Theatre; the Detroit Institute of Arts, Historical Museum, Science Center, and Public Library; and four University theaters. Also near the campus are the Engineering Society of Detroit, The Detroit Medical Center, the Merrill Palmer Institute, and the world headquarters of General Motors.

The University

Tracing its origins to 1868, Wayne State occupies a 185-acre campus that is graced by open courtyards and malls and whose 105 buildings represent a blend of traditional and ultramodern architecture. The University faculty, numbering 2,600, continues to distinguish itself by its dedication to teaching, scholarly activity, and service.

Applying

The regular M.S.W. full- and part-time programs begin only in the fall term, and applicants must apply by February 28 of the year in which they wish to enter the program. The Advanced Standing M.S.W. programs begin in the summer term, and applicants must apply by January 31 of the year in which they plan to enter the program. Applications are accepted as early as one year in advance of the desired entry term.

Correspondence and Information

School of Social Work
Wayne State University
Detroit, Michigan 48202
Telephone: 313-577-4409
Fax: 313-577-4266
World Wide Web: http://www.ssw.wayne.edu

Wayne State University

THE FACULTY AND THEIR RESEARCH

David Allasio, M.S.W. Child abuse/neglect, foster care, protective services, medical social work.
Charlla Allen, Ph.D. candidate. Community social work, family/children/youth services, women and reproductive health.
Ann Rosengrant Alvarez, Ph.D. Community practice, social development, international social work, reproductive health, women's issues, social policy, qualitative research.
Creigs Beverly, Ph.D. African-male resiliency, community development, human underdevelopment, international social work, public health, mental health, social welfare policy, substance abuse, youth/high risk, violence.
Beverly Black, Ph.D. Attitude change, domestic violence, homophobia, sexual assault, volunteerism, women's issues.
Jerrold Brandell, Ph.D. Child and adolescent psychotherapy, process analysis, psychoanalysis and clinical social work.
Margaret Brunhofer, Ph.D. Clinical practice, ethics, grief and loss, mental health.
Leon W. Chestang, Ph.D. Administration/management, African-American families, cultural diversity, family/children/youth services, race.
Donna Cochran, Ph.D. Father-daughter relationships, minority issues in aging.
Pamela DeWeese, Ph.D. Clinical practice, mental health, anthropology.
Cecille Dumbrigue, M.S.W.; ACSW. Administration/management, community practice, social group work, social policy.
Anwar Najor-Durack, M.S.W.; ACSW. Marriage/family therapy, mental health, multicultural practice.
Lois Garriott, M.S.W.; ACSW. Clinical practice, mental health, sexual abuse/incest survivors.
Barbara Goldstein, Ph.D. Clinical practice, mental health.
Pamela Herrington-Shaw, Ph.D. Clinical practice/supervision, marriage/family therapy.
Loren Hoffman, M.S.W.; ACSW. Crisis intervention, field education, marriage/family therapy, mental health, social group work.
Christine Hyduk, Ph.D. Geriatric assessment, gerontology, health care.
Ronald Jirovec, Ph.D. Gerontology, political social work, social welfare policy.
Louise Kerlin, M.S.W.; ACSW. Anxiety/dissociative disorders, child abuse/neglect, domestic violence, mental health.
Paul Koonter, M.S.W.; ACSW. Behavior modification, medical social work, stress management.
Alice Lamont, Ph.D. Cooperative learning, practice methods, research, social group work.
Sally Jo Large, Ed.D. Community organization and development, education, health care, practice methods, research.
Brenda McGadney, Ph.D. Adult day care, African-American family and church supports/frail elders, aging research, clinical practice, health care, HIV/AIDS, mental health primary/secondary/tertiary prevention issues.
Patricia Metz, M.S.W.; ACSW. Attention deficit disorders, parent-child relationships, parents/schools, school social work.
Ernestine Moore, J.D. Child abuse/delinquency/neglect, child welfare, domestic violence, juvenile social policy, welfare reform.
David Moxley, Ph.D. Advocacy, case management, community mental health, community practice.
Durrenda Onolemhemhen, Ph.D. Cultural diversity, health care, international social work, undergraduate professional education and training.
Carol Premo, Ph.D. Clinical practice, mental health.
Carolyn Pryor, Ph.D. International social work, school social work/service delivery, dispute resolution, dropout prevention, family relations, neighborhood development, parent involvement, substance abuse prevention.
Melvyn Raider, Ph.D. Couples and family therapy, marriage therapy, program evaluation, school-based mental health.
Anna Santiago, Ph.D. Domestic violence, research methodology, urban institutions/race/class/ethnicity/gender.
Sandra Schiff, Ph.D. Blended families, chemical dependency, diversity, geriatrics.
Peggy Stern, M.S.W.; ACSW. Child/adolescent mental health, domestic violence, grief/loss, play therapy, trauma, women's issues.
Milton Tambor, Ph.D. Occupational social work, employee assistance, unions/management.
James Tripp, Ph.D. Clinical practice, mental health/outpatient social work services, social work in the black community.
Eileen Trzcinski, Ph.D. Family policy, research.
Phyllis Vroom, Ph.D. Adolescent/family practice with African Americans, aging urban elderly, urban middle school education.
Arlene Weisz, Ph.D. Brief treatment, domestic violence, substance abuse, violence against women.
Susan Whitelaw, Ph.D. Family and child welfare/delivery of services, policy, practice.
Annette Woodroffe, Ph.D. Social work practice methods, spirituality in social work.

Research and Training Opportunities in Business, Education, Health, Information Studies, Law, and Social Work

This part of Book 6 consists of one section covering research and training opportunities in business, education, health, information studies, law, and social work. The section contains a table of contents; a profile directory, which consists of brief profiles of the academic centers and institutes followed by 50-word and 100-word announcements, if centers and institutes have chosen to submit such entries; and in-depth descriptions, which are more individualized statements, if centers and institutes have chosen to submit them.

Section 44
Research and Training Opportunities

Academic Centers and Institutes

The role and importance of academic centers and institutes in the graduate study experience has increased dramatically in recent years. In response to growing requests for information on such centers and institutes, the profiles in this section include the data on academic centers and institutes that were submitted in 1998 by each institution in response to Peterson's Supplemental Survey of Academic Centers and Institutes.

This section provides detailed information on university-owned and university-operated centers and institutes offering graduate students research or study opportunities. To qualify for inclusion in this section, a center or institute must be a formal and integral part of a graduate degree program. Such centers and institutes are separate from, but may sometimes maintain affiliations with, other special research facilities also located on the university's campus, such as laboratory or computer facilities.

Centers and institutes listed are academic in nature and do not include university business, administrative, or operational units or departments. Most have formally dedicated faculty and staff members associated with them and may provide training programs in the early part of a Ph.D. program. Many are interdisciplinary; however, some centers and institutes may focus on a single discipline, a major research project, or a specialized area of study. In some cases, graduate degrees may be awarded by the institute or research unit, although most do not.

Centers and institutes appear alphabetically by institution, followed by in-depth entries submitted by centers or institutes that chose to prepare detailed descriptions. The following items appear for each center or institute profile when available. Readers may contact centers and institutes directly for further information.

Name of Center or Institute. The name of the center or institute appears in boldface type.

Founding Year. The year the center or institute was established.

Academic Areas of Research and Training. Specific areas of graduate research or training listed (e.g., cancer research in molecular and cell biology, epidemiology, and psychology).

Degrees Offered. For those centers and institutes that do award degrees, these may include master's and/or doctoral degrees in specific academic fields or areas.

Number of Graduate Students Served in 1997–1998. Figures are provided separately for the total number of students served in 1997–98 and, for some institutions, how many students were served specifically at the master's, doctoral, and postgraduate levels, respectively.

Faculty. Figures are provided for the total number of faculty members associated with the center or institute and those associated with the center or institute but having their primary affiliation with another unit of the university.

Faculty Affiliations. The names of departments, programs, and other units with which faculty members are affiliated are listed here.

Annual Research Budget. Figures for the center or institute's annual research budget are listed.

Director. The name and title of the center or institute's director is provided, along with his/her address, telephone number, fax number, and e-mail address.

Information Contact. Provides the name and title of the person who should receive inquiries from interested students, with the address, telephone number, fax number, and e-mail address for this individual.

CONTENTS

Profile Directory

Announcement

Research and Training Opportunities

American University, Washington, DC 20016-8001

National Center for Health Fitness (NCHF) Founded in 1980. *Academic areas of research and training:* Educational programs, health promotion programming, research and program evaluation, community service, international health promotion initiatives, youth at risk programs. *Degrees offered:* MS. *Graduate students served 1997–98:* 45: 44 at the master's level; 1 at the doctoral level. *Faculty:* 11: 4 affiliated solely with the center. *Faculty affiliations:* Departments of Chemistry, Computer Science and Information Systems, Health and Fitness, Psychology, Public Administration; Kogod College of Business. *Annual research budget:* $1 million. *Director:* Dr. Robert C. Karch, Executive Director, 202-885-6275, Fax: 202-885-6288, E-mail: nchfms@american.edu.

Arizona State University, Tempe, AZ 85287

Center for Advanced Purchasing Studies (CAPS) Founded in 1986. *Academic areas of research and training:* Strategic purchasing and supply management. *Degrees offered:* None. *Graduate students served 1997–98:* 5 at the master's level; 1 at the doctoral level. *Faculty:* 2 affiliated solely with the center. *Annual research budget:* $1.3 million. *Director:* Dr. Phillip Carter, 602-752-2277, Fax: 602-491-7885, E-mail: pcarter@napm.org.

Center for Services Marketing and Management Founded in 1985. *Academic areas of research and training:* Service quality, customer loyalty, service encounters, customer satisfaction, service recovery, services strategy. *Degrees offered:* None. *Graduate students served 1997–98:* 58: 50 at the master's level; 6 at the doctoral level; 2 at the postgraduate level. *Faculty:* 16: 1 affiliated solely with the center. *Faculty affiliations:* College of Business. *Annual research budget:* $250,000. *Director:* Dr. Stephen W. Brown, 602-965-6201, Fax: 602-965-2180.

Exercise and Sport Research Institute Founded in 1985. *Academic areas of research and training:* Exercise science, biomechanics, exercise physiology, motor behavior, sport psychology. *Degrees offered:* None. *Graduate students served 1997–98:* 30: 15 at the master's level; 15 at the doctoral level. *Faculty:* 11. *Faculty affiliations:* Department of Exercise Science and Physical Education. *Annual research budget:* $20,000. *Director:* Dr. Philip E. Martin, 602-965-1023, Fax: 602-965-8108, E-mail: philip.martin@asu.edu.

Joan and David Lincoln Center for Applied Ethics Founded in 1986. *Academic areas of research and training:* Relationships between ethical practices and financial performance. *Degrees offered:* None. *Graduate students served 1997–98:* 4: 3 at the master's level; 1 at the doctoral level. *Faculty:* 11: 1 affiliated solely with the center. *Faculty affiliations:* College of Business, School of Architecture. *Annual research budget:* $60,000. *Director:* Dr. Marianne Jennings, 602-965-2710, Fax: 602-965-3995, E-mail: marianne.jennings@asu.edu.

Manufacturing Institute Founded in 1997. *Academic areas of research and training:* Virtual manufacturing. *Degrees offered:* None. *Director:* Dr. Ampere Tseng, Co-Director, 602-965-8201, Fax: 602-965-2910, E-mail: ampere.tseng@asu.edu.

Babson College, Babson Park, MA 02157-0310

Center for Entrepreneurial Study Founded in 1978. *Academic areas of research and training:* Entrepreneurship. *Degrees offered:* None. *Graduate students served 1997–98:* 6: 3 at the master's level; 3 at the doctoral level. *Faculty:* 18: 8 affiliated solely with the center. *Faculty affiliations:* Management Division. *Annual research budget:* $30,000. *Director:* Dr. William D. Bygrave, Administrative Director, 781-239-4420, Fax: 781-239-4178, E-mail: bygrave@babson.edu.

Boston College, Chestnut Hill, MA 02167-9991

Center for Child, Family, and Community Partnerships Founded in 1996. *Academic areas of research and training:* Promote positive youth, family, school, and community development. *Degrees offered:* None. *Graduate students served 1997–98:* 20: 10 at the master's level; 10 at the doctoral level. *Faculty:* 40. *Faculty affiliations:* Schools of Education, Law, Nursing, Social Work; Wallace E. Carroll Graduate School of Management. *Annual research budget:* $800,000. *Director:* Dr. Richard Lerner, 617-552-0764, Fax: 617-552-0766, E-mail: lernerr@bc.edu.

Boston University, Boston, MA 02215

Center for International Health Founded in 1980. *Academic areas of research and training:* Health care in developing countries, health care and financing, health care management, population policy and demography, maternal and child heath. *Degrees offered:* None. *Graduate students served 1997–98:* 90 at the master's level. *Faculty:* 45: 8 affiliated solely with the center. *Annual research budget:* $850,000. *Director:* Dr. William J. Bicknell, 617-638-5234, E-mail: wbicknel@bu.edu. *Information contact:* Ms. Lisa Bilgen de Herrera, Director of Marketing and Business Development, 617-414-1450, Fax: 617-638-4476, E-mail: lbilgen@bu.edu.

Center for Law and Technology Founded in 1987. *Academic areas of research and training:* Biological advances: legal issues, computers and law, environmental regulation, intellectual property rights, risk assessment and scientific evidence, internet law and policy, corporate environmental management. *Degrees offered:* None. *Graduate students served 1997–98:* 2 at the doctoral level. *Faculty:* 1 affiliated solely with the center. *Faculty affiliations:* Departments of Biology, Engineering, Philosophy, Public Health; School of Law. *Director:* Prof. Michael Baram, 617-353-5294, Fax: 617-353-3077, E-mail: mbaram@bu.edu.

Center for the Study of Communication and the Deaf Founded in 1982. *Academic areas of research and training:* Role of language in deaf children's thinking, learning of American Sign Language as a second language, American Sign Language/English curriculum, American Sign Language assessment inventory. *Degrees offered:* None. *Graduate students served 1997–98:* 40: 37 at the master's level; 3 at the doctoral level. *Faculty:* 19: 4 affiliated solely with the center. *Faculty affiliations:* Departments of Developmental Studies and Counseling, Psychology; Program in Applied Linguistics. *Annual research budget:* $211,000. *Director:* Dr. Robert Hoffmeister, 617-353-3205, Fax: 617-353-3292, E-mail: rhoff@bu.edu.

Communication Research Center *Academic areas of research and training:* New communication technology, public opinion, surveys, focus groups, customer satisfaction, message impact, influence of television, international impact of television. *Degrees offered:* None. *Graduate students served 1997–98:* 35 at the master's level. *Faculty:* 6: 2 affiliated solely with the center. *Faculty affiliations:* School of Mass Communication and Public Relations. *Director:* Dr. Michael Elasmar, 617-353-5895, Fax: 617-353-3405, E-mail: elasmar@bu.edu.

Human Bioenergetics Laboratory Founded in 1979. *Academic areas of research and training:* Exercise physiology, human performance research. *Degrees offered:* None. *Graduate students served 1997–98:* 3: 2 at the master's level; 1 at the postgraduate level. *Faculty:* 2 affiliated solely with the laboratory. *Faculty affiliations:* Department of Health Sciences. *Director:* Dr. Gary S. Skrinar, 617-353-2719.

Bradley University, Peoria, IL 61625-0002

Center for Business and Economic Research Founded in 1979. *Academic areas of research and training:* Management information systems, survey research, research and development management. *Degrees offered:* None. *Graduate students served 1997–98:* 5 at the master's level. *Faculty:* 3. *Faculty affiliations:* College of Business Administration. *Annual research budget:* $20,000. *Director:* Dr. Bernard Goitein, 309-677-2278, Fax: 309-677-3374, E-mail: bjg@bradley.edu.

Brandeis University, Waltham, MA 02454-2728

The Institute for Health Policy Founded in 1978. *Academic areas of research and training:* Health research and policy, policy and implementation, finance and reimbursement, long-term care, program evaluation, state health policy, substance abuse, vulnerable populations. *Degrees offered:* None. *Graduate students served 1997–98:* 20. *Faculty:* 40 affiliated solely with the institute. *Annual research budget:* $10 million. *Director:* Dr. Stanley Wallack, 781-736-3900, Fax: 781-736-3881.

The Nathan and Toby Starr Center for Mental Retardation Founded in 1985. *Academic areas of research and training:* Disability policy, research. *Degrees offered:* None. *Graduate students served 1997–98:* 5 at the doctoral level. *Faculty:* 5 affiliated solely with the center. *Annual research budget:* $500,000. *Director:* Dr. Marty Krauss, 781-736-3832, Fax: 781-736-3864, E-mail: krauss@binah.cc.brandeis.edu. *Information contact:* Ms. Karen Cooney, Admissions Officer, 781-736-3820, Fax: 781-736-3881, E-mail: cooney@binah.cc.brandeis.edu.

Brigham Young University, Provo, UT 84602-1001

Institute of Marketing Founded in 1976. *Academic areas of research and training:* Retail, sales, services, marketing. *Degrees offered:* None. *Graduate students served 1997–98:* 200. *Faculty:* 24: 12 affiliated solely with the center. *Faculty affiliations:* Marriott School of Management. *Annual research budget:* $30,000. *Director:* Dr. William Price, 801-378-2953, Fax: 801-378-2361, E-mail: marketinginstitute@byu.edu.

Brooklyn College of the City University of New York, Brooklyn, NY 11210-2889

Carleton Washburne Early Childhood Center Founded in 1953. *Academic areas of research and training:* Early childhood education, arts in education, teacher research. *Degrees offered:* None. *Graduate students served 1997–98:* 2 at the master's level. *Faculty:* 1. *Faculty affiliations:* School of Education. *Director:* Dr. Carol Korn-Bursztyn, 718-951-5431, Fax: 718-951-4816, E-mail: ckbbc@cunyvm.cuny.edu.

Brown University, Providence, RI 02912

Center for Gerontology and Health Care Research Founded in 1982. *Academic areas of research and training:* Health services research, chronic disease epidemiology, biostatistics, geriatric pharmaco-epidemiology. *Degrees offered:* None. *Graduate students served 1997–98:* 3 at the postgraduate level. *Faculty:* 32. *Faculty affiliations:* Departments of Community Health, Economics, Sociology; Division of Applied Mathematics; Programs in Family Medicine, Medicine, Population Studies, Psychiatry. *Director:* Dr. Vincent Mor, 401-863-1560, Fax: 401-863-3489, E-mail: vincent_mor@brown.edu.

Institute for International Health Founded in 1988. *Academic areas of research and training:* International health activities. *Degrees offered:* None. *Graduate students served 1997–98:* 12: 5 at the master's level; 7 at the postgraduate level. *Faculty:* 10. *Faculty affiliations:* Brown University AIDS Program, Population Studies and Training Center, Thomas J. Watson Jr. Institute for International Studies. *Annual research budget:* $250,000. *Director:* Dr. Charles Carpenter, 401-331-8500 Ext. 4025, Fax: 401-331-8501, E-mail: charles_carpenter@brown.edu. *Information contact:* Ms. Sharon S. D'Antuono, Coordinator, 401-863-1373, Fax: 401-863-1243, E-mail: sharonnd@brownvm.brown.edu.

California State University, Chico, Chico, CA 95929-0722

Center for Economic Development and Planning Founded in 1986. *Academic areas of research and training:* Economic development, community development, economic analysis, leadership training. *Degrees offered:* None. *Graduate students served 1997–98:* 35: 30 at the master's level; 5 at the doctoral level. *Faculty:* 17: 5 affiliated solely with the center. *Faculty affiliations:* College of Business, Departments of Geography and Planning, Political Science. *Annual research budget:* $400,000. *Director:* Mr. Dan Ripke, 530-898-4598, Fax: 530-898-4734, E-mail: dripke@oavax.csuchico.edu.

California State University, Long Beach, Long Beach, CA 90840-0119

Center for Health Care Innovation Founded in 1986. *Academic areas of research and training:* Health care, long-term health care, managed care, integrated delivery systems, teen health, health promotion. *Degrees offered:* None. *Graduate students served 1997–98:* 7 at the master's level. *Faculty:* 5: 1 affiliated solely with the center. *Faculty affiliations:* Programs in Health Care Administration, Health Education. *Annual research budget:* $100,000. *Director:* Dr. Connie Evashwick, 562-985-5881, Fax: 562-985-5886, E-mail: cevashwk@csulb.edu.

California State University, Los Angeles, Los Angeles, CA 90032-8530

Bureau of Business and Economic Research Founded in 1975. *Academic areas of research and training:* Economic development, small business assistance, community development. *Degrees offered:* None. *Graduate students served 1997–98:* 2 at the master's level. *Faculty:* 10. *Faculty affiliations:* Departments of Economics and Statistics, Management, Marketing. *Director:* Stephen Pollard, 213-343-2933, Fax: 213-343-5462, E-mail: spollar@calstatela.edu.

California University of Pennsylvania, California, PA 15419-1394

Character Education Institute Founded in 1995. *Academic areas of research and training:* Preparation of teachers and administrators for their role as character educators, outreach to school districts seeking to learn about education character. *Degrees offered:* None. *Graduate students served 1997–98:* 112: 110 at the master's level; 2 at the doctoral level. *Faculty:* 46: 1 affiliated solely with the institute. *Faculty affiliations:* School of Education. *Annual research budget:* $100,000. *Director:* Dr. Henry Huffman, 724-938-4500, Fax: 724-938-4156, E-mail: huffman@cup.edu.

Carnegie Mellon University, Pittsburgh, PA 15213-3891

Carnegie Bosch Institute for Applied Studies in International Management Founded in 1990. *Academic areas of research and training:* International management. *Degrees offered:* None. *Graduate students served 1997–98:* 7: 6 at the master's level; 1 at the doctoral level. *Faculty:* 9: 1 affiliated solely with the institute. *Faculty affiliations:* Graduate School of Industrial Administration. *Annual research budget:* $400,000. *Director:* Dr. Michael A. Trick, President, 412-268-3697, Fax: 412-268-7057, E-mail: cbi@andrew.cmu.edu.

Case Western Reserve University, Cleveland, OH 44106

Center for Biomedical Ethics Founded in 1987. *Academic areas of research and training:* Bioethics. *Degrees offered:* MA. *Graduate students served 1997–98:* 31 at the master's level. *Faculty:* 17: 3 affiliated solely with the center. *Faculty affiliations:* Departments of Anthropology, Epidemiology and Biostatistics, Neurology, Pediatrics, Philosophy, Psychiatry; Schools of Law, Medicine, Nursing; Center for Human Genetics, Ireland Cancer Center at University Hospitals. *Annual research budget:* $150,000. *Director:* Dr. Thomas H. Murray, 216-368-6206, E-mail: thm2@po.cwru.edu. *Information contact:* Ms. Deidre J. Gruning, Coordinator of Graduate Programs, 216-368-8718, Fax: 216-368-8713, E-mail: dxc38@po.cwru.edu.

Cuyahoga County Community Mental Health Research Institute Founded in 1994. *Academic areas of research and training:* Mental health services research, research training.

Degrees offered: None. *Graduate students served 1997–98:* 12: 6 at the master's level; 5 at the doctoral level; 1 at the postgraduate level. *Faculty affiliations:* Mandel School of Applied Social Sciences. *Annual research budget:* $250,000. *Director:* Dr. David E. Biegel, Co-Director, 216-368-2308, Fax: 216-368-6121, E-mail: deb@po.cwru.edu.

Central Michigan University, Mount Pleasant, MI 48859

Center for Research on Adult Learning Founded in 1994. *Academic areas of research and training:* Instructional methodology, adult and non-traditional student learning experiences, extended degree programs. *Degrees offered:* None. *Graduate students served 1997–98:* 5: 3 at the master's level; 2 at the doctoral level. *Faculty:* 1. *Faculty affiliations:* College of Extended Learning. *Director:* Dr. Megan P. Goodwin, 517-774-2534, Fax: 517-774-3542, E-mail: megan.goodwin@cmich.edu.

Chapman University, Orange, CA 92866

The A. Gary Anderson Center for Economic Research Founded in 1978. *Academic areas of research and training:* Regional economic forecasting, economic impact studies. *Degrees offered:* None. *Graduate students served 1997–98:* 3 at the master's level. *Faculty:* 5: 1 affiliated solely with the center. *Faculty affiliations:* School of Business and Economics. *Annual research budget:* $130,000. *Director:* Dr. Esmael Adibi, 714-997-6693, Fax: 714-997-6601.

Clemson University, Clemson, SC 29634

The Houston Center for the Study of the Black Experience Affecting Higher Education Founded in 1988. *Academic areas of research and training:* Education, sociology, business, minorities. *Degrees offered:* None. *Graduate students served 1997–98:* 3 at the master's level. *Faculty:* 1 affiliated solely with the center. *Faculty affiliations:* Departments of Agricultural Economics, Business, Economics, Education, Health Sciences, History, Psychology, Sociology. *Annual research budget:* $150,000. *Director:* Dr. Herman G. Green, 864-656-0313, E-mail: gherman@clemson.clemson.edu. *Information contact:* Mrs. Dixie A. Schmittou, Developmental and Public Relations Manager, 864-656-0607, Fax: 864-656-0314, E-mail: dixiean@clemson.edu.

Recreation, Travel, and Tourism Institute Founded in 1985. *Academic areas of research and training:* Recreation, tourism, travel, marketing, leisure behavior. *Degrees offered:* None. *Graduate students served 1997–98:* 5: 3 at the master's level; 2 at the doctoral level. *Faculty:* 5: 1 affiliated solely with the institute. *Faculty affiliations:* Department of Parks, Recreation and Tourism Management. *Annual research budget:* $50,000. *Director:* Dr. William C. Norman, 864-656-2060, Fax: 864-656-2226, E-mail: wnorman@clemson.edu.

Colorado State University, Fort Collins, CO 80523-0015

Colorado Injury Control Research Center (CICRC) Founded in 1995. *Academic areas of research and training:* Rural injury control and prevention, acute care, rehabilitation. *Degrees offered:* None. *Graduate students served 1997–98:* 3 at the master's level. *Faculty:* 10. *Faculty affiliations:* Departments of Environmental Health, Journalism and Technical Communication, Occupational Therapy, Physiology, Preventive Medicine and Biometrics, Psychology, Surgery. *Annual research budget:* $82,870. *Director:* Dr. Lorann Stallones, 970-491-6156, Fax: 970-491-2940, E-mail: loranns@cvmbs.colostate.edu.

High Plains Inter-Mountain Center for Agricultural Health and Safety (HI-CAHS) Founded in 1991. *Academic areas of research and training:* Occupational disease and injury in agriculture. *Degrees offered:* MS; PhD. *Graduate students served 1997–98:* 50: 40 at the master's level; 10 at the doctoral level. *Faculty:* 14: 7 affiliated solely with the center. *Faculty affiliations:* Department of Social Work and Environmental Health, Program in Agricultural Engineering, School of Education. *Annual research budget:* $1 million. *Director:* Dr. Roy M. Buchan, 970-491-6151, Fax: 970-491-7778, E-mail: rbuchan@lamar.colostate.edu.

Human Performance Research Laboratory Founded in 1981. *Academic areas of research and training:* Exercise science, cardiovascular studies, metabolic studies, obesity studies. *Degrees offered:* None. *Graduate students served 1997–98:* 10 at the master's level. *Faculty:* 6: 4 affiliated solely with the laboratory. *Faculty affiliations:* Departments of Exercise and Sport Science, Food Science and Human Nutrition. *Director:* Dr. Matt Hickey, 970-491-5727, Fax: 970-491-0445, E-mail: hickey@cahs.colostate.edu.

Research and Development Center for the Advancement of Student Learning Founded in 1995. *Academic areas of research and training:* Applied, action, or policy research. *Degrees offered:* None. *Graduate students served 1997–98:* 6: 4 at the master's level; 2 at the doctoral level. *Faculty:* 2. *Faculty affiliations:* College of Applied Human Services, School of Education; Poudre School District. *Annual research budget:* $200,000. *Director:* Dr. Brian Cobb, Co-Director, 970-416-3583, E-mail: cobb@cahs.colostate.edu. *Information contact:* Dr. Ann Foster, Co-Director, 970-416-3582, Fax: 970-416-3580, E-mail: annf@psd.k12.co.us.

Veterinary Diagnostic Laboratories Founded in 1965. *Academic areas of research and training:* Veterinary pathology, veterinary microbiology. *Degrees offered:* None. *Graduate students served 1997–98:* 6 at the doctoral level; 6 at the postgraduate level. *Faculty affiliations:* Departments of Microbiology, Pathology. *Director:* Dr. Barbara E. Powers, 970-491-1281, Fax: 970-491-0320, E-mail: bpowers@vth.colostate.edu.

Columbia University, New York, NY 10027

Center for Reproductive Sciences Founded in 1975. *Academic areas of research and training:* Reproductive biology, neuroendocrinology, genetics, chemistry of gonadotropins, perinatology and reproductive oncology. *Degrees offered:* None. *Graduate students served 1997–98:* 5: 2 at the master's level; 2 at the doctoral level; 1 at the postgraduate level. *Faculty:* 30: 6 affiliated solely with the center. *Faculty affiliations:* Departments of Anatomy and Cell Biology, Genetics and Development, Medicine, Obstetrics and Gynecology, Pathology, Physiology. *Annual research budget:* $2.9 million. *Director:* Dr. Rogerio A. Lobo, 212-305-2377, Fax: 212-305-3869.

Herbert Irving Comprehensive Cancer Center Founded in 1972. *Academic areas of research and training:* Cancer research, epidemiology, genetics, radiology, pathology, biochemistry, carcinogenesis, microbiology, urology, dermatology, pediatrics. *Degrees offered:* None. *Faculty:* 262: 2 affiliated solely with the center. *Faculty affiliations:* Programs in Health Sciences. *Annual research budget:* $4 million. *Director:* Dr. Karen Antman, 212-305-8602, Fax: 212-305-3035.

Creighton University, Omaha, NE 68178-0001

Center for Health Policy and Ethics Founded in 1987. *Academic areas of research and training:* Health sciences professional education, health policy and bioethical issues including chronic disease and palliative care. *Degrees offered:* None. *Faculty:* 5: 4 affiliated solely with the center. *Faculty affiliations:* School of Nursing. *Director:* Dr. Ruth B. Purtilo, 402-280-2017.

DePaul University, Chicago, IL 60604-2287

Health Law Institute Founded in 1985. *Academic areas of research and training:* Public and private ethical issues, malpractice issues, health care issues relating to private and public sectors. *Degrees offered:* LL M. *Graduate students served 1997–98:* 53: 9 at the master's level; 44 at the postgraduate level. *Faculty:* 6: 5 affiliated solely with the institute. *Faculty affiliations:* Programs in Public Services. *Director:* Prof. Donald Hermann, 312-362-8383, E-mail: dhermann@wppost.depaul.edu. *Information contact:* Ms. Virginia Knittle, Administrator, 312-362-6836, Fax: 312-362-5280, E-mail: gknittle@wppost.depaul.edu.

Duke University, Durham, NC 27708-0586

Center for Clinical Health Policy Research Founded in 1997. *Academic areas of research and training:* Clinical health policy, cost-effectiveness analyses, cerebrovascular disease. *Degrees offered:* None. *Faculty:* 23: 3 affiliated solely with the center. *Faculty affiliations:* Department of Economics, Program in Biostatistics, School of Medicine. *Annual research budget:* $2 million. *Director:* Dr. David B. Matchair, Associate Professor, 919-286-3399, Fax: 919-286-5601.

École Polytechnique de Montréal, Montréal, PQ H3C 3A7, Canada

Centre for Research and Computational Thermochemistry (CRCT) Founded in 1984. *Academic areas of research and training:* Materials science, metallurgy, chemical thermodynamics. *Degrees offered:* None. *Graduate students served 1997–98:* 6: 2 at the master's level; 4 at the doctoral level. *Faculty:* 3: 2 affiliated solely with the center. *Faculty affiliations:* Department of Metallurgical and Materials Engineering. *Annual research budget:* $300,000. *Director:* Dr. Arthur D. Pelton, Co-Director, E-mail: apelton@mail.polymtl.ca. *Information contact:* Dr. Christopher W. Bale, Co-Director, 514-340-4770, Fax: 514-340-5840, E-mail: crct@mail.polymtl.ca.

Emory University, Atlanta, GA 30322-1100

Center for Injury Control Founded in 1995. *Academic areas of research and training:* Epidemiology, prevention, public policy, emergency medicine, trauma care systems, program evaluation. *Graduate students served 1997–98:* 22: 21 at the master's level; 1 at the postgraduate level. *Faculty:* 11: 3 affiliated solely with the center. *Faculty affiliations:* The Rollins School of Public Health, School of Medicine. *Annual research budget:* $386,000. *Director:* Dr. Arthur Kellerman, 404-727-9977, E-mail: ake1101@sph.emory.edu.

Department of International Health Founded in 1991. *Academic areas of research and training:* International health and development, nutrition, infectious disease, policy and management, population sciences, reproductive health. *Degrees offered:* None. *Graduate students served 1997–98:* 173: 168 at the master's level; 5 at the doctoral level. *Faculty:* 90: 10 affiliated solely with the department. *Faculty affiliations:* The Rollins School of Public Health, School of Medicine, Carter Center. *Annual research budget:* $7.6 million. *Director:* Dr. Reynaldo Martorell, Chair, 404-727-9854, Fax: 404-727-1278, E-mail: rmart77@sph.emory.edu.

Integrated Microscopy and Microanalytical Facility Founded in 1985. *Academic areas of research and training:* Microscopy services for faculty and graduate students in Cancer Center, Cardiology Center and Department of Chemistry. *Degrees offered:* None. *Graduate students served 1997–98:* 7 at the doctoral level. *Faculty:* 41: 1 affiliated solely with the facility. *Faculty affiliations:* Department of Chemistry; Programs in Cardiology, Cell and Developmental Biology, Molecular Medicine. *Director:* Dr. Robert P. Apkarian, 404-727-7766, Fax: 404-727-7760, E-mail: rapkari@emory.edu.

National Institute of Church Finance and Administration Founded in 1975. *Academic areas of research and training:* Church business administration. *Degrees offered:* None. *Graduate students served 1997–98:* 10 at the doctoral level. *Faculty:* 6. *Faculty affiliations:* Candler School of Theology, Robert C. Goizueta Business School. *Director:* Tom Frank, 404-727-6331.

Vascular Surgery Center Founded in 1995. *Academic areas of research and training:* Clinical vascular surgery, basic and clinical research in vascular disorders. *Degrees offered:* None. *Graduate students served 1997–98:* 3 at the postgraduate level. *Faculty:* 14: 10 affiliated solely with the center. *Faculty affiliations:* Departments of Radiology, Surgery. *Director:* Dr. Robert Smith III, 404-727-8145, Fax: 404-727-1734, E-mail: rsmith@surgery.eushc.org.

Emporia State University, Emporia, KS 66801-5087

Center for Business and Economic Development Founded in 1996. *Academic areas of research and training:* Service operations management, services marketing, non-profit management, focus group studies, strategic planning, small business management, older workers. *Degrees offered:* None. *Graduate students served 1997–98:* 2 at the master's level. *Faculty:* 12. *Faculty affiliations:* Division of Management, Marketing, Finance and Economics. *Director:* Dr. William L. Smith, 316-341-5729, Fax: 316-341-6347, E-mail: smithwil@esumail.emporia.edu.

Center for Economic Education Founded in 1984. *Academic areas of research and training:* Economics education for K-12 teachers. *Degrees offered:* None. *Graduate students served 1997–98:* 55: 3 at the master's level; 51 at the postgraduate level. *Faculty:* 3: 1 affiliated solely with the center. *Faculty affiliations:* Division of Management, Marketing, Finance, and Economics. *Director:* Mr. Robert B. Catlett, 316-343-6439, E-mail: catlettr@esumail.emporia.edu.

Fairleigh Dickinson University, Florham–Madison Campus, Madison, NJ 07940-1099

Center for Human Resource Management Studies Founded in 1990. *Academic areas of research and training:* Provides a partnership between education, industry and the community, creating a learning environment committed to the development of knowledge and leadership in the management of human resources. *Degrees offered:* None. *Graduate students served 1997–98:* 100 at the master's level. *Faculty:* 9. *Faculty affiliations:* College of Business Administration. *Annual research budget:* $200,000. *Director:* Dr. Daniel Twomey, 973-443-8577, E-mail: dtwomey@fdusvrl.fdu.edu. *Information contact:* Mr. Gerald Dawson, Executive Director, 973-443-8977, Fax: 973-443-8506, E-mail: gdawson@fdusvrl.fdu.edu.

Florida Institute of Technology, Melbourne, FL 32901-6975

Center for Environmental Education Founded in 1993. *Academic areas of research and training:* Teacher-education/professional development, curriculum development, assessment and evaluation, environmental education, human dimensions. *Degrees offered:* None. *Graduate students served 1997–98:* 8 at the master's level; 4 at the doctoral level. *Faculty:* 8: 1 affiliated solely with the center. *Faculty affiliations:* Departments of Biological Sciences; Science Education; Programs in Environmental Science and Environmental Resource Management, Oceanography. *Annual research budget:* $175,000. *Director:* Dr. Robert Fronk, 407-768-8000 Ext. 8126, E-mail: fronk@fit.edu. *Information contact:* Dr. Thomas Marcinkowski, Associate Professor, 407-768-8000 Ext. 8946, Fax: 407-984-8461, E-mail: marcinko@winnie.fit.edu.

Florida State University, Tallahassee, FL 32306

Center for Performance Technology Founded in 1971. *Academic areas of research and training:* Early education, institutional research, instructional systems, measurement and assessment, electronic performance support systems. *Degrees offered:* None. *Graduate students served 1997–98:* 15: 7 at the master's level; 8 at the doctoral level. *Faculty:* 14: 12 affiliated solely with the center. *Faculty affiliations:* Departments of Educational Administration, Educational Leadership. *Annual research budget:* $1 million. *Director:* Dr. Robert K. Branson, 850-644-4720, Fax: 850-644-5803, E-mail: rbranson@cpt.fsu.edu.

George Mason University, Fairfax, VA 22030-4444

Center for Bilingual/Multicultural/ESL Education Founded in 1978. *Academic areas of research and training:* Bilingual/multicultural/ESL education. *Degrees offered:* MA; PhD. *Graduate students served 1997–98:* 222: 190 at the master's level; 17 at the doctoral level. *Faculty:* 34: 16 affiliated solely with the center. *Faculty affiliations:* Program in Modern and Classical Languages. *Annual research budget:* $15,000. *Director:* Dr. Harold Chu, 703-993-3688, Fax: 703-993-3336, E-mail: hchu@gmu.edu.

Directory: Research and Training Opportunities

Center for Health Policy Founded in 1994. *Academic areas of research and training:* Health care policy, leadership, health professions education/practice, telehealth technology, quality of health care. *Degrees offered:* None. *Graduate students served 1997–98:* 7 at the doctoral level. *Faculty:* 7: 2 affiliated solely with the center. *Faculty affiliations:* College of Nursing and Health Science. *Annual research budget:* $25,000. *Director:* Dr. Mary Wakefield, 703-993-1930, Fax: 703-993-1953, E-mail: mwakefi1@gmu.edu.

Center for Human disAbilities (CHd) Founded in 1988. *Academic areas of research and training:* Training, technical assistance, research, model program development, policy analysis in special education, early childhood special education, severe disabilities, instructional technology, assistive technology, inclusion. *Degrees offered:* None. *Graduate students served 1997–98:* 150: 140 at the master's level; 10 at the doctoral level. *Faculty:* 12: 7 affiliated solely with the center. *Faculty affiliations:* Interdisciplinary Program in Education, Program in Special Education. *Annual research budget:* $75,000. *Director:* Dr. Michael Behrmann, 703-993-3670, Fax: 703-934-7482, E-mail: mbehrman@gmu.edu.

Georgetown University, Washington, DC 20057

Center for Food and Nutrition Policy Founded in 1992. *Academic areas of research and training:* Food and nutrition in health; regulation of food safety, health claims, and trade; new food technologies; public understanding and communication. *Degrees offered:* None. *Graduate students served 1997–98:* 8: 4 at the master's level; 3 at the doctoral level; 1 at the postgraduate level. *Faculty affiliations:* School of Business; The Georgetown Public Policy Institute; North Carolina State University. *Director:* Dr. Lester Crawford, E-mail: ceres@erols.com. *Information contact:* Dr. Robin Woo, Deputy Director, 202-965-6400, Fax: 202-965-6444, E-mail: ceres@erols.com.

Landegger Program in International Business Diplomacy Founded in 1978. *Academic areas of research and training:* International business, business-government relations. *Degrees offered:* None, Certificate. *Graduate students served 1997–98:* 120 at the master's level. *Faculty affiliations:* Edmund A. Walsh School of Foreign Service. *Director:* Dr. John M. Kline, 202-687-5854, Fax: 202-687-6033.

National Center for Education in Maternal and Child Health Founded in 1982. *Academic areas of research and training:* Maternal and child health policy, information services, continuing education. *Degrees offered:* None. *Graduate students served 1997–98:* 5 at the master's level. *Faculty:* 11 affiliated solely with the center. *Director:* Dr. Rochelle Mayer, E-mail: rochelle_mayer@ncemch.org. *Information contact:* Dr. Vince Hutchins, Distinguished Research Professor, 703-524-7802, Fax: 703-524-9335, E-mail: vhutchins@ncemch.org.

The George Washington University, Washington, DC 20052

Biostatistics Center Founded in 1972. *Academic areas of research and training:* Statistics, biostatistics, epidemiology. *Degrees offered:* None. *Graduate students served 1997–98:* 18: 13 at the master's level; 5 at the doctoral level. *Faculty:* 10 affiliated solely with the center. *Faculty affiliations:* Department of Statistics, School of Public Health and Health Services. *Annual research budget:* $14.28 million. *Director:* Dr. John M. Lachin III, 301-881-9260, Fax: 301-881-3742, E-mail: jml@biostat.bsc.gwu.edu.

The Burdetsky Labor-Management Institute Founded in 1982. *Academic areas of research and training:* Labor-management relations, human resources. *Degrees offered:* None. *Graduate students served 1997–98:* 3 at the doctoral level. *Faculty:* 13: 3 affiliated solely with the institute. *Faculty affiliations:* Departments of Health Services Management and Policy, Management Science, Public Administration, Strategic Management and Public Policy, Tourism Studies. *Annual research budget:* $15,000. *Director:* Dr. Ben Burdetsky, 202-994-5504. *Information contact:* Prof. Susan Galloway Goldberg, Associate Director, 202-994-5291, Fax: 202-994-5225.

Center for International Health Founded in 1991. *Academic areas of research and training:* Advancement and illumination of the health and development link to enhance human well-being worldwide. *Degrees offered:* None. *Graduate students served 1997–98:* 75 at the master's level. *Faculty:* 18: 10 affiliated solely with the center. *Faculty affiliations:* Elliott School of International Affairs; Schools of Medicine and Health Sciences, Public Health and Health Services. *Director:* Dr. Rosalia Rodriguez-Garcia. *Information contact:* Mr. Eric Madsen, Administrative Officer, 202-994-5682, Fax: 202-994-0900, E-mail: cih@gwis2.circ.gwu.edu.

Educational Resources Information Center (ERIC) Clearinghouse on Higher Education Founded in 1968. *Academic areas of research and training:* Acquire, abstract and index literature related to higher education; prepare various publications and research reports such as ASHE-ERIC Higher Education Report Series and ERIC Digests. *Degrees offered:* None. *Graduate students served 1997–98:* 10 at the doctoral level. *Faculty:* 4. *Faculty affiliations:* Graduate School of Education and Human Development. *Annual research budget:* $800,000. *Director:* Dr. Jonathan D. Fife, 800-773-3742 Ext. 22, Fax: 202-452-1844, E-mail: jfife@eric-he.edu.

Research Program in Social and Organizational Learning Founded in 1993. *Academic areas of research and training:* Social and organizational learning, cybernetics, systems theory. *Degrees offered:* None. *Graduate students served 1997–98:* 15: 2 at the master's level; 3 at the doctoral level; 10 at the postgraduate level. *Faculty:* 6: 1 affiliated solely with the program. *Faculty affiliations:* Departments of Management Science, Marketing, Strategic Management and Public Policy; Program in Administrative Sciences. *Director:* Stuart A. Umpleby, 202-994-5219, E-mail: umpleby@gwu.edu. *Information contact:* Ms. Wafa Abou-Zaki, Executive Director, 202-994-5203, Fax: 202-994-5225, E-mail: 74563.1454@compuserve.com.

Georgia State University, Atlanta, GA 30303-3083

The Gerontology Center Founded in 1978. *Academic areas of research and training:* Nursing, nutrition, sociology, urban studies, quality of life in long-term care settings. *Degrees offered:* Certificate. *Graduate students served 1997–98:* 53: 45 at the master's level; 7 at the doctoral level; 1 at the postgraduate level. *Faculty:* 30: 1 affiliated solely with the center. *Faculty affiliations:* College of Law; Departments of Anthropology and Geography, Communication, Counseling and Psychological Services, Physical Therapy, Psychology, Sociology; Institute of Health Administration; Programs in Social Work, Urban Studies; Schools of Art and Design, Music, Nursing. *Annual research budget:* $125,500. *Director:* Dr. Frank Whittington, 404-651-1856, E-mail: fwhittington@gsu.edu. *Information contact:* Mary MacKinnon, Assistant to the Director, 404-651-1087, Fax: 404-651-4272, E-mail: mmackinnon@gsu.edu.

Graduate School and University Center of the City University of New York, New York, NY 10036-8099

Howard Samuels State Management and Policy Center Founded in 1988. *Academic areas of research and training:* Political science, sociology, education, higher education, ecodevelopment, welfare, state and city politics and policy. *Degrees offered:* None. *Graduate students served 1997–98:* 15 at the doctoral level. *Faculty affiliations:* Programs in Political Science, Sociology. *Annual research budget:* $1 million. *Director:* Dr. Marilyn Gittell, 212-642-2974, Fax: 212-642-1934, E-mail: mgittell@aol.com.

National Center on Educational Restructuring and Inclusion (NCERI) Founded in 1994. *Academic areas of research and training:* School restructuring, inclusive education. *Degrees offered:* None. *Graduate students served 1997–98:* 5 at the master's level; 10 at the doctoral level; 1 at the postgraduate level. *Faculty:* 11: 1 affiliated solely with the center. *Faculty affiliations:* Programs in Educational Psychology, Psychology, Sociology. *Director:* Dr. Dorothy Kerzner Lipsky, 212-642-2656, Fax: 212-642-1972, E-mail: dkl@aquila.gc.cuny.edu.

Harvard University, Cambridge, MA 02138

Harvard Project on Schooling and Children Founded in 1993. *Academic areas of research and training:* Interdisciplinary research on children's education, learning, and well-being; evaluating children's educational and social programs. *Degrees offered:* None. *Graduate students served 1997–98:* 4 at the postgraduate level. *Faculty:* 100: 50 affiliated solely with the project. *Director:* Dr. Kay Merseth, Executive Director, E-mail: mersetka@hugse1.harvard.edu. *Information contact:* Postdoctoral Coordinator, 617-496-4938, Fax: 617-495-1994, E-mail: hpsc@harvard.edu.

Harvard University offers postdoctoral fellowships in evaluating programs for children. Students develop innovative, interdisciplinary approaches to the theory and practice of evaluating programs in support of children's well-being. Appointment is for 24 months beginning September 1999. Annual stipend: $38,250. Requirements: PhD or equivalent within the past 5 years, strong interest in or experience with interdisciplinary methods, children's social programming, and/or program evaluation. Candidates sought from a wide variety of fields, including but not limited to policy, education, health, social work, and social sciences. Application deadline: February 16, 1999. Contact Postdoctoral Coordinator, Harvard Project on Schooling and Children, 126 Mt. Auburn Street, Cambridge, MA 02138; e-mail: hpsc@harvard.edu

---

Illinois State University, Normal, IL 61790-2200

Center for Higher Education and Educational Finance Founded in 1980. *Academic areas of research and training:* Educational finance, higher education policy, higher education finance. *Degrees offered:* None. *Graduate students served 1997–98:* 4: 2 at the master's level; 2 at the doctoral level. *Faculty:* 9. *Faculty affiliations:* Center for Mathematics, Science and Technology, Department of Educational Administration. *Annual research budget:* $50,000. *Director:* Dr. David A. Strand, 309-438-2143. *Information contact:* Dr. Edward R. Hines, Professor, 309-438-2045, Fax: 309-438-8683, E-mail: erhines@rs6000.cmp.ilstu.edu.

Indiana University Bloomington, Bloomington, IN 47405

Borish Center for Ophthalmic Research Founded in 1995. *Academic areas of research and training:* Cornea and contact lenses, visual function and psychophysics, binocular vision and pediatrics, ocular disease and pharmacology, epidemiology and health policy, advanced instructional technology. *Degrees offered:* None. *Graduate students served 1997–98:* 5 at the master's level; 5 at the doctoral level; 2 at the postgraduate level. *Faculty:* 27. *Faculty affiliations:* Departments of Psychology, Speech and Hearing; Graduate Program in Visual Science and Physiological Optics; School of Optometry; Indiana University–Purdue University Indianapolis School of Medicine. *Director:* Dr. P. Sarita Soni, Co-Director, 812-855-4093, E-mail: sonip@indiana.edu. *Information contact:* Ms. Lee Wagoner, Center Coordinator, 812-855-7659, Fax: 812-855-5417, E-mail: lwagoner@indiana.edu.

Bowen Research Center Founded in 1991. *Academic areas of research and training:* Health care cost containment, preventive medicine, rural health care. *Degrees offered:* None. *Graduate students served 1997–98:* 25: 22 at the master's level; 3 at the doctoral level. *Faculty:* 50: 20 affiliated solely with the center. *Faculty affiliations:* School of Public and Environmental Affairs, Indiana University–Purdue University Indianapolis School of Medicine. *Annual research budget:* $1 million. *Director:* Dr. Deborah A. Freund, Co-Director. *Information contact:* Deborah Allen, Co-Director, 317-278-0300.

Center for Econometric Model Research (CEMR) *Director:* R. Jeffrey Green, Co-Director. *Information contact:* Morton Marcus, Co-Director, 812-855-5507, Fax: 812-855-7763.

Center for Excellence in Education Founded in 1990. *Academic areas of research and training:* Education research, software development, educational technology. *Degrees offered:* None. *Graduate students served 1997–98:* 20: 4 at the master's level; 16 at the doctoral level. *Faculty:* 6. *Faculty affiliations:* Department of Anthropology, School of Education, Indiana University–Purdue University Indianapolis School of Medicine. *Annual research budget:* $750,000. *Director:* Howard D. Mehlinger, 812-856-8201, Fax: 812-856-8245, E-mail: mehlinge@indiana.edu.

Center for Health and Safety Studies Founded in 1965. *Academic areas of research and training:* College student alcohol use, comprehensive school health education, HIV/AIDS education, occupational health and safety consultation and instruction, public health education, smoking and alcohol education. *Degrees offered:* None. *Graduate students served 1997–98:* 63: 49 at the master's level; 14 at the doctoral level. *Faculty:* 5 affiliated solely with the center. *Faculty affiliations:* Department of Applied Health Science. *Annual research budget:* $500,000. *Director:* Dr. James W. Crowe, 812-855-2429, Fax: 812-855-3936, E-mail: crowe@indiana.edu.

Center for Postsecondary Research and Planning Founded in 1994. *Academic areas of research and training:* Questionnaire sales and scoring. *Degrees offered:* None. *Graduate students served 1997–98:* 1 at the doctoral level. *Faculty:* 1. *Faculty affiliations:* School of Education. *Director:* Dr. George Kuh, 812-856-8041, Fax: 812-856-8394, E-mail: cseq@indiana.edu.

Center for Real Estate Studies Founded in 1985. *Academic areas of research and training:* Increase professionalism in and support for the real estate industry. *Degrees offered:* None. *Graduate students served 1997–98:* 5: 4 at the master's level; 1 at the doctoral level. *Faculty:* 3: 1 affiliated solely with the center. *Annual research budget:* $350,000. *Director:* Dr. Jeffrey D. Fisher, E-mail: cres@indiana.edu. *Information contact:* Ms. Cinda Smith, Associate Director, 812-855-7794, Fax: 812-855-9472, E-mail: cres@indiana.edu.

Family Literacy Center (FLC) Founded in 1989. *Academic areas of research and training:* Information and resources to promote family learning. *Degrees offered:* None. *Graduate students served 1997–98:* 13: 8 at the master's level; 5 at the doctoral level. *Faculty:* 1 affiliated solely with the center. *Faculty affiliations:* Department of Language Education. *Annual research budget:* $65,000. *Director:* Dr. Carl B. Smith, 812-855-5847, Fax: 812-855-4220, E-mail: smith2@indiana.edu.

General Clinical Research Center Founded in 1962. *Academic areas of research and training:* Clinical research. *Degrees offered:* None. *Graduate students served 1997–98:* 50: 10 at the master's level; 30 at the doctoral level; 10 at the postgraduate level. *Faculty:* 400: 200 affiliated solely with the center. *Faculty affiliations:* Indiana University–Purdue University Indianapolis School of Medicine. *Annual research budget:* $2 million. *Director:* Munro Peacock, 317-274-4356.

Herman B. Wells Center for Pediatric Research Founded in 1991. *Academic areas of research and training:* Cancer, hematopoietic stem cell biology, pediatric endocrinology, pediatric pulmonology, perinatal metabolism, DNA repair, gene therapy. *Degrees offered:* None. *Graduate students served 1997–98:* 20: 5 at the doctoral level; 15 at the postgraduate level. *Faculty:* 20 affiliated solely with the center. *Faculty affiliations:* Programs in Biochemistry and Molecular Biology, Genetics, Microbiology, Pharmacology, Physiology. *Annual research budget:* $8 million. *Director:* Dr. David A. Williams, 317-274-8960, Fax: 317-274-8679, E-mail: dwilliams@wpo.iupui.edu.

Indiana University of Pennsylvania, Indiana, PA 15705-1087

Small Business Institute Founded in 1984. *Academic areas of research and training:* Free business consulting services in all functional areas for projects that have strategic focus. *Degrees offered:* None. *Graduate students served 1997–98:* 110: 15 at the master's level. *Faculty:* 4. *Faculty affiliations:* Program in Management. *Annual research budget:* $100,000. *Director:* Dr. Stephen Osborne, 724-357-2535, E-mail: osborne@grove.iup.edu. *Information contact:* Dr. Prashanth B. Nagendra, Assistant Director, 724-357-4880, Fax: 724-357-5743, E-mail: nagendra@iup.grove.edu.

Directory: Research and Training Opportunities

Indiana University–Purdue University Indianapolis, Indianapolis, IN 46202-2896

The Center for Law and Health Founded in 1987. *Academic areas of research and training:* Law and health policy. *Degrees offered:* None. *Graduate students served 1997–98:* 200 at the doctoral level. *Faculty:* 2 affiliated solely with the center. *Faculty affiliations:* Schools of Medicine, Public and Environmental Affairs. *Annual research budget:* $70,000. *Director:* Eleanor D. Kinney, Co-Director, 317-274-4091, Fax: 317-274-3955, E-mail: ekinney@iupui.edu. *Information contact:* Ms. Phyllis Bonds, Administrator, 317-274-1912, Fax: 317-274-4994, E-mail: pbonds@iupui.edu.

Iowa State University of Science and Technology, Ames, IA 50011

Business Research Institute *Academic areas of research and training:* Accounting, finance, industrial relations, marketing, management information systems, management, transportation and logistics. *Degrees offered:* None. *Graduate students served 1997–98:* 25 at the master's level. *Faculty:* 57: 2 affiliated solely with the institute. *Faculty affiliations:* College of Business, Program in Transportation. *Annual research budget:* $175,000. *Director:* Dr. Benjamin J. Allen, Dean, 515-294-2422, E-mail: ballen@iastate.edu. *Information contact:* Ms. Barbara Clark, Executive Coordinator, 515-294-3656, Fax: 515-294-6060, E-mail: baclark@iastate.edu.

Industrial Relations Center (IRC) Founded in 1966. *Academic areas of research and training:* Industrial relations, human resource management, labor relations. *Degrees offered:* None. *Graduate students served 1997–98:* 25 at the master's level. *Faculty:* 20. *Faculty affiliations:* Departments of Economics, Management, Political Science, Psychology, Sociology. *Director:* Dr. Paula Morrow, 515-294-8118, Fax: 515-294-2446, E-mail: busgrad@iastate.edu.

James Madison University, Harrisonburg, VA 22807

Center for Direct, Interactive and Retail Marketing Founded in 1989. *Academic areas of research and training:* Retail studies, direct and database marketing, electronic commerce. *Degrees offered:* None. *Faculty:* 15. *Faculty affiliations:* Programs in Hospitality Management, Marketing. *Annual research budget:* $20,000. *Director:* Dr. Claire Bolfing, 540-568-3036, E-mail: bolfincp@jmu.edu. *Information contact:* Dawn Huffman, Operations Director, 540-568-3223, Fax: 540-568-2754.

Johns Hopkins University, Baltimore, MD 21218-2699

Center for Clinical Trials Founded in 1990. *Academic areas of research and training:* Biostatistics, clinical trials, epidemiology, eye disease, AIDS, asthma, emphysema, cancer. *Degrees offered:* None. *Graduate students served 1997–98:* 7: 5 at the doctoral level; 2 at the postgraduate level. *Faculty:* 20. *Faculty affiliations:* Departments of Biostatistics, Epidemiology, International Health; Programs in Oncology, Opthalmology; School of Medicine. *Director:* Dr. Curtis L. Meinert, 410-955-8198, E-mail: cct@phnet.sph.jhu.edu. *Information contact:* Mrs. Susan Tonascia, Research Associate, 410-955-3785, Fax: 410-955-0932.

Center for Communication Programs (CCP) Founded in 1988. *Academic areas of research and training:* Health communication, research methodologies, reproductive health. *Degrees offered:* None. *Graduate students served 1997–98:* 25: 15 at the master's level; 10 at the doctoral level. *Faculty:* 8. *Faculty affiliations:* School of Hygiene and Public Health. *Annual research budget:* $4 million. *Director:* Dr. Phyllis T. Piotrow, 410-659-6399, Fax: 410-659-6266, E-mail: ppiotrow@jhuccp.org.

Center for Hospital Finance and Management *Academic areas of research and training:* Health financing. *Degrees offered:* None. *Faculty:* 22: 7 affiliated solely with the center. *Faculty affiliations:* School of Medicine. *Annual research budget:* $10 million. *Director:* Dr. Gerard F. Anderson, 410-955-3241, E-mail: ganderso@jhsph.edu. *Information contact:* Ms. Karen Diener, Administrative Assistant, 410-955-7310, Fax: 410-955-2301, E-mail: kdiener@jhsph.edu.

Center for Injury Research and Policy Founded in 1987. *Academic areas of research and training:* Injury control, primary prevention, acute care, rehabilitation. *Degrees offered:* None. *Graduate students served 1997–98:* 1,521: 647 at the master's level; 577 at the doctoral level; 297 at the postgraduate level. *Faculty:* 20: 9 affiliated solely with the center. *Faculty affiliations:* Schools of Medicine, Nursing; Bayview Medical Center; Maryland Institute for Emergency Medical Services/Shock Trauma. *Annual research budget:* $654,336. *Director:* Dr. Ellen J. MacKenzie, 410-614-4026, E-mail: emackenz@jhsph.edu. *Information contact:* Ms. Susanne Ogaitis, Assistant Director for External Affairs, 410-955-2636, Fax: 410-614-2797, E-mail: sogaitis@jhsph.edu.

Institute for International Programs Founded in 1985. *Academic areas of research and training:* Health, family planning. *Degrees offered:* None. *Faculty:* 100. *Faculty affiliations:* Departments of International Health, Molecular Microbiology and Immunology, Population Dynamics. *Annual research budget:* $7 million. *Director:* Dr. Robert E. Black, 410-955-3934, Fax: 410-955-7159, E-mail: rblack@phnet.sph.jhu.edu.

Women's and Children's Health Policy Center (WCHPC) Founded in 1991. *Academic areas of research and training:* Attributes of primary care, assessing the status of health systems serving maternal and child health populations, identification of health-care system characteristics, models of health-care services organization and delivery. *Degrees offered:* None. *Graduate students served 1997–98:* 50: 35 at the master's level; 15 at the doctoral level. *Faculty:* 14: 1 affiliated solely with the center. *Faculty affiliations:* Departments of Health Policy and Management, Maternal and Child Health. *Annual research budget:* $900,000. *Director:* Dr. Bernard Guyer, Chair, 410-955-3384, E-mail: bguyer@jhsph.edu. *Information contact:* Holly Allen Grason, Director, 410-502-5443, Fax: 410-955-2303, E-mail: hgrason@jhsph.edu.

Kansas State University, Manhattan, KS 66506

Veterinary Diagnostic Laboratory *Academic areas of research and training:* Infectious diseases of animals, parasitology, pathobiology, epidemiology, toxicology. *Degrees offered:* MS; PhD None. *Graduate students served 1997–98:* 32: 15 at the master's level; 17 at the doctoral level. *Faculty:* 36: 30 affiliated solely with the laboratory. *Faculty affiliations:* Program in Pathobiology. *Director:* Dr. M. M. Chengappa, Interim Head, 785-532-4605, Fax: 785-532-4039, E-mail: chengap@ksu.edu.

Kent State University, Kent, OH 44242-0001

Ohio Employee Ownership Center Founded in 1987. *Academic areas of research and training:* Employee ownership, adult education and training, economic development. *Degrees offered:* None. *Graduate students served 1997–98:* 2: 1 at the master's level; 1 at the doctoral level. *Faculty:* 3: 1 affiliated solely with the center. *Faculty affiliations:* Department of Sociology; Graduate Schools of Education, Management. *Annual research budget:* $40,000. *Director:* Mr. John Logue, E-mail: jlogue@kent.edu. *Information contact:* Mr. Alex J. Teodosio, Program Coordinator, 330-672-3028, Fax: 330-672-4063, E-mail: ateodosi@kent.edu.

Louisiana State University and Agricultural and Mechanical College, Baton Rouge, LA 70803

National Ports and Waterways Institute Founded in 1982. *Academic areas of research and training:* Maritime research, management, economics, finance, international trade, technology, government, operational analysis. *Degrees offered:* None. *Graduate students served 1997–98:* 8: 4 at the master's level; 2 at the doctoral level; 2 at the postgraduate level. *Faculty:* 25: 10 affiliated solely with the institute. *Faculty affiliations:* Departments of Coastal Studies, Engineering, Management; The George Washington University Department of Engineering Management. *Annual research budget:* $1.5 million. *Director:* Dr. Anatoly Hochstein, 703-276-7101, Fax: 703-276-7102, E-mail: npwi@seas.gwu.edu.

Real Estate Research Institute Founded in 1980. *Academic areas of research and training:* Residential and commercial real estate, office markets. *Degrees offered:* None. *Graduate students served 1997–98:* 5: 3 at the master's level; 2 at the doctoral level. *Faculty:* 5: 2 affiliated solely with the institute. *Faculty affiliations:* Departments of Economics, Finance. *Annual research budget:* $30,000. *Director:* R. Kelley Pace, E-mail: kelleypace@compuserve.com. *Information contact:* V. Carlos Slawson Jr., Associate Director, 504-388-6238, Fax: 504-388-6366, E-mail: fislaw@unix1.sncc.lsu.edu.

Massachusetts Institute of Technology, Cambridge, MA 02139-4307

Center for Coordination Science (CCS) *Academic areas of research and training:* Coordination technology and theory, organizational structures. *Degrees offered:* None. *Graduate students served 1997–98:* 6: 2 at the master's level; 4 at the doctoral level. *Faculty affiliations:* Sloan School of Management. *Annual research budget:* $1.4 million. *Director:* Dr. Thomas W. Malone, 617-253-6843, Fax: 617-258-7579, E-mail: malone@mit.edu. *Information contact:* Mr. John Quimby, Research Scientist, 617-258-7376, Fax: 617-253-4424, E-mail: quimby@mit.edu.

Center for Educational Computing Initiatives (CECI) Founded in 1991. *Academic areas of research and training:* Development and use of computation and communications in education. *Degrees offered:* None. *Graduate students served 1997–98:* 11: 7 at the master's level; 3 at the doctoral level; 1 at the postgraduate level. *Faculty:* 10. *Faculty affiliations:* Departments of Civil and Environmental Engineering, Electrical Engineering and Computer Science; Programs in History, Literature. *Annual research budget:* $1 million. *Director:* Prof. Steven R. Lerman, 617-253-4277, E-mail: lerman@mit.edu. *Information contact:* Ms. Pam Homsy, Assistant Director for Administration, 617-253-0113, Fax: 617-253-8632, E-mail: pam@ceci.mit.edu.

Center for Information Systems Research (CISR) Founded in 1974. *Academic areas of research and training:* Management information systems; strategic, managerial, and organizational impacts of information technology. *Degrees offered:* None. *Graduate students served 1997–98:* 10: 7 at the master's level; 3 at the doctoral level. *Faculty:* 9: 1 affiliated solely with the center. *Faculty affiliations:* Sloan School of Management. *Director:* Dr. John F. Rockart, 617-253-2348. *Information contact:* Ms. Christine Foglia, Administrative Officer, 617-253-6657, Fax: 617-253-4424, E-mail: cisr@mit.edu.

Medical College of Georgia, Augusta, GA 30912-1003

Center for the Study of Occupational Therapy Education Founded in 1972. *Academic areas of research and training:* Higher education, occupational therapy assessment and intervention in pediatrics, occupational therapy education and practice. *Degrees offered:* None. *Graduate students served 1997–98:* 5 at the master's level. *Faculty:* 11. *Faculty affiliations:* Department of Occupational Therapy. *Annual research budget:* $111,000. *Director:* Dr. Nancy D. Prendergast, Acting Chair, E-mail: nprender@mail.mcg.edu. *Information contact:* Dr. Carol Endebrock Lee, Curriculum Coordinator, 706-721-3641, Fax: 706-721-9718, E-mail: clee@mail.mcg.edu.

Medical College of Wisconsin, Milwaukee, WI 53226-0509

Cancer Center Founded in 1984. *Academic areas of research and training:* Clinical and basic science opportunities in aspects of cancer research and care. *Degrees offered:* None. *Faculty:* 200. *Faculty affiliations:* Departments of Clinical, Basic Science. *Annual research budget:* $8 million. *Director:* Dr. J. Frank Wilson, 414-257-5635, Fax: 414-257-5033.

Eye Institute Founded in 1975. *Academic areas of research and training:* Ophthalmology. *Degrees offered:* None. *Graduate students served 1997–98:* 22 at the postgraduate level. *Faculty:* 51: 47 affiliated solely with the institute. *Faculty affiliations:* Departments of Cell Biology, Epidemiology, Microbiology; Program in Biophysics. *Director:* Dr. Dale K. Heuer, 414-456-7915, Fax: 414-456-6563, E-mail: dheuer@mcw.edu.

Midwest Children's Cancer Center Founded in 1974. *Academic areas of research and training:* Clinical and laboratory cancer research. *Degrees offered:* None. *Graduate students served 1997–98:* 6: 2 at the doctoral level; 4 at the postgraduate level. *Faculty:* 20. *Faculty affiliations:* Department of Pediatrics. *Annual research budget:* $1.5 million. *Director:* Dr. Bruce M. Camitta, 414-456-4118, Fax: 414-456-6543, E-mail: bcamitta@post.its.mcw.edu.

Michigan State University, East Lansing, MI 48824-1020

Center for Ethics and Humanities in the Life Sciences Founded in 1977. *Academic areas of research and training:* Ethics and humanities resources in health care and science. *Degrees offered:* None. *Graduate students served 1997–98:* 10: 4 at the master's level; 6 at the doctoral level. *Faculty:* 56: 4 affiliated solely with the center. *Faculty affiliations:* Colleges of Arts and Letters, Human Medicine, Natural Science, Nursing, Osteopathic Medicine, Social Science, Veterinary Medicine. *Director:* Howard Brody, 517-355-7550, E-mail: brody@pilot.msu.edu. *Information contact:* Ms. Libby Bogdan-Lovis, Assistant Director, 517-432-5185, Fax: 517-353-3289, E-mail: bogdan10@pilot.msu.edu.

Middle Tennessee State University, Murfreesboro, TN 37132

Center for the Study and Treatment of Dyslexia Founded in 1993. *Academic areas of research and training:* Dyslexic studies: identification and intervention, school psychology, special education, reading, elementary education, speech and language. *Degrees offered:* None. *Graduate students served 1997–98:* 18: 17 at the master's level; 1 at the doctoral level. *Faculty:* 4: 1 affiliated solely with the center. *Faculty affiliations:* Department of Elementary and Special Education, Major in Reading, Program in School Psychology. *Director:* Dr. Diane J. Sawyer, Professor, 615-848-1271, Fax: 615-848-1392, E-mail: dyslexia@frank.mtsu.edu.

Mississippi State University, Mississippi State, MS 39762

The Rehabilitation Research and Training Center on Blindness and Low Vision Founded in 1981. *Academic areas of research and training:* Employment and career development issues affecting persons who are blind or visually impaired. *Degrees offered:* None. *Graduate students served 1997–98:* 100: 45 at the master's level; 5 at the doctoral level; 50 at the postgraduate level. *Faculty:* 6: 3 affiliated solely with the center. *Faculty affiliations:* Departments of Counselor Education and Educational Psychology; Psychology; Sociology, Anthropology, and Social Work. *Director:* Dr. J. Elton Moore, 601-325-2001, Fax: 601-325-8989, E-mail: jemoore@ra.msstate.edu.

T. K. Martin Center for Technology and Disability Founded in 1996. *Academic areas of research and training:* Assistive technology direct service, agricultural and biological engineering, industrial engineering, social work. *Degrees offered:* None. *Graduate students served 1997–98:* 2: 1 at the master's level. *Faculty:* 2 affiliated solely with the center. *Annual research budget:* $800,000. *Director:* Dr. Harry F. Rizer, E-mail: brizer@tkmartin.msstate.edu. *Information contact:* Ms. Judy Duncan, Case Manager, 601-325-1028, Fax: 601-325-0896, E-mail: jduncan@tkmartin.msstate.edu.

Montclair State University, Upper Montclair, NJ 07043-1624

Institute for the Advancement of Philosophy for Children Founded in 1974. *Academic areas of research and training:* Development of curriculum materials for the teaching of philosophy to children; development of appropriate pedagogy and theory; dissemination of the approach to teachers, schools, and countries. *Degrees offered:* None. *Graduate students served 1997–98:* 5 at the master's level. *Faculty:* 5: 2 affiliated solely with the institute. *Faculty affiliations:* College of Education and Human Services. *Annual research budget:* $150,000. *Director:* Dr. Matthew Lipman, Professor, E-mail: lipman@saturn.montclair.edu. *Information contact:* Ms. Joanne Matkowski, Assistant Director, 973-655-4277, Fax: 973-655-5455.

Directory: Research and Training Opportunities

New York Institute of Technology, Old Westbury, NY 11568-8000

Center for Labor and Industrial Relations Founded in 1977. *Academic areas of research and training:* Human resources management, labor relations, labor markets. *Degrees offered:* None. *Graduate students served 1997–98:* 11 at the master's level. *Faculty:* 4: 2 affiliated solely with the center. *Faculty affiliations:* Schools of Education, Management. *Annual research budget:* $50,000. *Director:* Dr. Richard E. Dibble, 516-686-7722, Fax: 516-686-7716.

New York University, New York, NY 10012-1019

Center for Transportation Policy and Management Founded in 1996. *Academic areas of research and training:* Transportation policy and management, urban transportation issues. *Degrees offered:* None. *Graduate students served 1997–98:* 10 at the master's level. *Faculty:* 3: 1 affiliated solely with the center. *Faculty affiliations:* Institute of Public Administration; Polytechnic University. *Annual research budget:* $125,000. *Director:* Mr. Elliot Sander, 212-998-7531, Fax: 212-995-4161.

General Clinical Research Center (GCRC) Founded in 1960. *Academic areas of research and training:* Clinical research in AIDS, TB, cancer (adult and pediatric), obstetrics/gynecology, urology, environmental medicine, PET scan imaging, schizophrenia. *Degrees offered:* None. *Graduate students served 1997–98:* 7 at the postgraduate level. *Faculty:* 254: 127 affiliated solely with the center. *Faculty affiliations:* Departments of Environmental Medicine, Medicine, Neurology, Obstetrics/Gynecology, Pediatrics, Psychiatry, Radiation Oncology, Radiology, Surgery, Urology. *Annual research budget:* $3.071 million. *Director:* Dr. William Rom, 212-263-6479, E-mail: romwl@gcrc.med.nyu.edu. *Information contact:* Ms. Alexandra Stack, Administrator, 212-263-7900, Fax: 212-263-8501, E-mail: stackal@gcrc.med.nyu.edu.

Health Research Program *Academic areas of research and training:* Social, organizational, financial, and managerial concerns related to the delivery of health care and social services. *Degrees offered:* None. *Faculty:* 10: 4 affiliated solely with the program. *Faculty affiliations:* Program in Health Policy and Management. *Annual research budget:* $4 million. *Director:* Mr. John Billings, 212-998-7455, Fax: 212-995-4166, E-mail: billings@is2.nyu.edu.

Institute for Education and Social Policy Founded in 1994. *Academic areas of research and training:* School finance issues, multidisciplinary research and action projects, policy evaluation, urban education, technical assistance to community groups. *Degrees offered:* None. *Graduate students served 1997–98:* 8: 6 at the master's level; 2 at the doctoral level. *Faculty:* 8: 2 affiliated solely with the institute. *Faculty affiliations:* Robert F. Wagner Graduate School of Public Service, School of Education. *Annual research budget:* $1 million. *Director:* Mr. Norm Fruchter, 212-998-5874, Fax: 212-995-4564, E-mail: fruchter@is2.nyu.edu.

Northeastern University, Boston, MA 02115-5096

Center for Community Health Education, Research, and Service (CCHERS) Founded in 1991. *Academic areas of research and training:* Community-based, primary care health professions education. *Degrees offered:* None. *Graduate students served 1997–98:* 30: 10 at the master's level; 20 at the doctoral level. *Faculty:* 50. *Faculty affiliations:* Bouvé College of Pharmacy and Health Sciences, School of Nursing. *Director:* Mr. Elmer Freeman, Executive Director, 617-373-4591, Fax: 617-373-8797, E-mail: efreeman@lynx.dac.neu.edu.

Center for Law and Computer Science Founded in 1987. *Academic areas of research and training:* Artificial intelligence and law, computer-assisted legal research, intelligent text retrieval. *Degrees offered:* None. *Faculty affiliations:* College of Computer Science, School of Law. *Director:* Dr. Carole D. Hafner, Co-Director, E-mail: hafner@ccs.new.edu. *Information contact:* Prof. Donald H. Berman, Co-Director, 617-373-5116, Fax: 617-373-5121.

Center for the Enhancement of Science and Mathematics Education (CESAME) Founded in 1989. *Academic areas of research and training:* K-12 science and mathematics education, implementation of exemplary curricular education reform. *Degrees offered:* None. *Graduate students served 1997–98:* 2 at the master's level. *Faculty:* 4. *Faculty affiliations:* Departments of Biology, Mathematics, Physics; Graduate School of Engineering. *Annual research budget:* $1.5 million. *Director:* Dr. Michael Silevitch, 617-373-3033, Fax: 617-373-8496, E-mail: msilevit@lynx.neu.edu.

Northern Arizona University, Flagstaff, AZ 86011

Bureau of Business and Economic Research *Academic areas of research and training:* Business and economic information services, marketing research, economic impact analysis, economic development. *Degrees offered:* None. *Graduate students served 1997–98:* 2 at the master's level. *Faculty:* 6: 1 affiliated solely with the bureau. *Faculty affiliations:* College of Business Administration. *Director:* Dr. Jerry N. Conover, 520-523-7387, Fax: 520-523-7331, E-mail: jerry.conover@nau.edu.

Institute for Human Development Founded in 1967. *Academic areas of research and training:* Native Americans, early childhood, assistive technology, interdisciplinary models of service delivery, vocational rehabilitation. *Degrees offered:* Certificate. *Graduate students served 1997–98:* 18: 13 at the master's level; 5 at the doctoral level. *Faculty:* 27: 7 affiliated solely with the institute. *Faculty affiliations:* Departments of Educational Psychology; Engineering; Health, Physical Education, and Nutrition; Nursing; Physical Therapy; Psychology; Sociology and Social Work; Speech Pathology; Program in Special Education. *Annual research budget:* $316,000. *Director:* Dr. Richard W. Carroll, 520-523-4791, E-mail: richard.carroll@nau.edu. *Information contact:* Mr. Thomas Uno, Assistant to the Executive Director, 520-523-7032, Fax: 520-523-9127, E-mail: thomas.uno@nau.edu.

Northwestern University, Evanston, IL 60208

Institute for Health Services Research and Policy Studies Founded in 1996. *Academic areas of research and training:* Conduct health services research and policy analysis in the areas of health economics and financing, health policy, organizational behavior, health outcomes and medical decision making, law and medicine, long-term care and aging, mental health services, child health disabilities. *Degrees offered:* None. *Graduate students served 1997–98:* 25: 10 at the master's level; 10 at the doctoral level; 5 at the postgraduate level. *Faculty:* 80: 20 affiliated solely with the institute. *Faculty affiliations:* Department of Economics; Medical School; Program in Health Services Management; Cancer Center; Children's Memorial Hospital; VA Hospital. *Annual research budget:* $2.4 million. *Director:* Dr. Peter Budetti, 847-491-5643, E-mail: p-budetti@nwu.edu. *Information contact:* Mr. Jeffery M. Erdman, Coordinator of Marketing and Research Projects, 847-491-5115, Fax: 847-491-2202, E-mail: jme352@nwu.edu.

The Institute for the Learning Sciences (ILS) Founded in 1989. *Academic areas of research and training:* Human learning processes, development of multimedia educational technology. *Degrees offered:* None. *Graduate students served 1997–98:* 38 at the master's level; 49 at the doctoral level; 1 at the postgraduate level. *Faculty:* 12. *Faculty affiliations:* Departments of Computer Science, Psychology; School of Education and Social Policy. *Annual research budget:* $6.5 million. *Director:* Prof. Roger C. Schank, 847-491-3636, Fax: 847-467-2490, E-mail: schank@ils.nwu.edu. *Information contact:* Ms. Joanne Raleigh, Graduate Programs Coordinator, 847-467-1332, Fax: 847-491-5258, E-mail: raleigh@cs.nwu.edu.

Transportation Center Founded in 1954. *Academic areas of research and training:* Improving the systems of moving materials, people, energy, and information; executive education programs; provides resources and outreach to transportation and logistics studies programs. *Degrees offered:* MS. *Graduate students served 1997–98:* 50: 45 at the master's level; 5 at the doctoral level. *Faculty:* 47: 25 affiliated solely with the center. *Faculty affiliations:* Departments of Civil Engineering, Economics, Industrial Engineering; J. L. Kellogg Graduate School of Management. *Director:* Dr. Aaron J. Gellman, 847-491-7286, E-mail: a-gellman@nwu.edu. *Information contact:* Ms. Judy Robinson, Academic and Placement Manager, 847-491-2276, Fax: 847-491-3090, E-mail: j-robinson@nwu.edu.

Ohio University, Athens, OH 45701-2979

George Hill Center for Counseling and Research Founded in 1991. *Academic areas of research and training:* Counselor training, curriculum development, rural mental health issues. *Degrees offered:* None. *Graduate students served 1997–98:* 100: 70 at the master's level; 30 at the doctoral level. *Faculty:* 8. *Faculty affiliations:* Departments of Counselor Education, Educational Research. *Director:* Dr. Richard J. Hazler, 740-593-4461, Fax: 740-593-0799, E-mail: hazler@ouvaxa.cats.ohiou.edu.

Ohio University Insurance Institute Founded in 1992. *Degrees offered:* None. *Graduate students served 1997–98:* 300. *Faculty:* 12: 5 affiliated solely with the institute. *Faculty affiliations:* College of Business. *Director:* John E. Reynolds, 740-593-2004, Fax: 740-593-9539, E-mail: jreynolds1@ohiou.edu.

Pennsylvania State University University Park Campus, University Park, PA 16802-1503

Center for Health Policy Research Founded in 1989. *Academic areas of research and training:* Health services. *Degrees offered:* None. *Graduate students served 1997–98:* 7 at the doctoral level. *Faculty:* 15: 1 affiliated solely with the center. *Faculty affiliations:* College of Business; Departments of Biobehavioral Health, Health Policy and Administration, Industrial and Management Systems Engineering; The Mary Jean and Frank P. Smeal College of Business Administration; Hershey Medical School; Pennsylvania Office of Rural Health. *Annual research budget:* $1 million. *Director:* Dr. Pamela F. Short, 814-863-8786, Fax: 814-863-0846, E-mail: pxs46@.psu.edu.

Center for Intelligent Transportation Systems (CITranS) Founded in 1994. *Academic areas of research and training:* Business logistics, civil engineering, mechanical engineering, industrial engineering. *Degrees offered:* None. *Graduate students served 1997–98:* 10: 5 at the master's level; 4 at the doctoral level; 1 at the postgraduate level. *Faculty:* 14. *Faculty affiliations:* Departments of Business Law, Business Logistics, Civil Engineering, Mechanical Engineering; Program in Industrial Engineering; Applied Research Laboratory; Gerontology Center. *Annual research budget:* $250,000. *Director:* Dr. Konstadinos Goulias Jr., 814-863-7926, E-mail: kxg2@psu.edu. *Information contact:* Mr. Michael L. Patten, Program Manager, 814-863-0572, Fax: 814-865-3039, E-mail: mlp2@psu.edu.

Center for Locomotion Studies Founded in 1986. *Academic areas of research and training:* Lower extremities biomechanics, the foot in diabetes, locomotion in zero-gravity, geriatric gait issues. *Degrees offered:* None. *Graduate students served 1997–98:* 17: 3 at the master's level; 14 at the doctoral level. *Faculty:* 27: 2 affiliated solely with the center. *Faculty affiliations:* Departments of Biobehavioral Health, Communication Disorders, Kinesiology, Mechanical Engineering, Orthopaedics and Rehabilitation, Statistics. *Director:* Dr. Peter Cavanagh, E-mail: prc@psu.edu. *Information contact:* Dr. Lorraine M. Mulfinger, Program Coordinator, 814-865-1972, Fax: 814-863-4755, E-mail: lxm14@psu.edu.

Institute for Real Estate Studies Founded in 1988. *Academic areas of research and training:* Property investment and valuation, property rights, law and economics. *Degrees offered:* None. *Graduate students served 1997–98:* 2 at the doctoral level. *Faculty affiliations:* Departments of Finance, Insurance, Real Estate. *Annual research budget:* $10,000. *Director:* Dr. Kenneth M. Lusht, 814-865-4172, Fax: 814-865-6284, E-mail: kml@psu.edu.

Institute for the Study of Organizational Effectiveness Founded in 1993. *Academic areas of research and training:* Organizational effectiveness and leadership, global competitiveness. *Degrees offered:* None. *Graduate students served 1997–98:* 2 at the doctoral level. *Faculty:* 18: 9 affiliated solely with the institute. *Faculty affiliations:* Departments of Business Logistics, Management Science and Information Systems; Program in Management and Organization. *Annual research budget:* $30,000. *Director:* Dr. Albert A. Vicere, Managing Director, 814-865-3435, Fax: 814-865-3372, E-mail: al.vicere@psu.edu.

Institute for the Study of Adult Literacy Founded in 1985. *Academic areas of research and training:* Adult education, workplace literacy, family literacy, special needs population. *Degrees offered:* None. *Graduate students served 1997–98:* 2 at the doctoral level. *Faculty:* 7: 2 affiliated solely with the institute. *Faculty affiliations:* Colleges of Agricultural Sciences, Business, Education, Health and Human Development; Milton S. Hershey Medical Center. *Annual research budget:* $939,488. *Director:* Dr. Eunice N. Askov, 814-863-3777, Fax: 814-863-6108, E-mail: ena1@psu.edu.

Institute for the Study of Business Markets (ISBM) Founded in 1983. *Academic areas of research and training:* Business-to-business marketing. *Degrees offered:* None. *Graduate students served 1997–98:* 5: 2 at the master's level; 3 at the doctoral level. *Faculty:* 6: 1 affiliated solely with the institute. *Faculty affiliations:* Department of Marketing. *Annual research budget:* $200,000. *Director:* Dr. Ralph Oliva, Executive Director, E-mail: rao8@psu.edu. *Information contact:* Mr. Gary W. Holler, Business and Services Manager, 814-863-2782, Fax: 814-863-0413, E-mail: gwh3@psu.edu.

Shaver's Creek Environmental Center Founded in 1976. *Academic areas of research and training:* Environmental education, natural history interpretation, cultural history interpretation, adventure education. *Degrees offered:* None. *Graduate students served 1997–98:* 6 at the master's level. *Faculty:* 18: 6 affiliated solely with the center. *Faculty affiliations:* Departments of Forestry, Leisure Studies, Recreation and Parks, Science Education. *Director:* Mr. Gerald R. Potter, 814-863-2000, Fax: 814-865-2706, E-mail: grp2@psu.edu.

Polytechnic University, Brooklyn Campus, Brooklyn, NY 11201-2990

Center for Advanced Technology in Telecommunications (CATT) Founded in 1983. *Academic areas of research and training:* Telecommunications, distributed information systems, ATM and internet, wireless networks, multimedia, imaging, network management. *Degrees offered:* MS. *Graduate students served 1997–98:* 101: 80 at the master's level; 20 at the doctoral level; 1 at the postgraduate level. *Faculty:* 20. *Faculty affiliations:* Departments of Computer Science, Electrical Engineering. *Annual research budget:* $4.3 million. *Director:* Dr. Shiv Panwar, Interim Director, 718-260-3740, Fax: 718-260-3074, E-mail: panwar@kanchi.poly.edu.

Polytechnic Research Institute for Development and Enterprise (PRIDE) Founded in 1995. *Academic areas of research and training:* Distanceless learning, life-long learning, telemedicine, multimedia technologies, information service and internet technology. *Degrees offered:* None. *Graduate students served 1997–98:* 12: 4 at the master's level; 6 at the doctoral level; 2 at the postgraduate level. *Faculty:* 14: 10 affiliated solely with the institute. *Faculty affiliations:* Centers for Advanced Technology in Telecommunications, Applied Large Scale Computing; Polymer Research Institute. *Annual research budget:* $1.5 million. *Director:* Dr. Ifay F. Chang, Executive Director, 914-323-2061, Fax: 914-323-2070, E-mail: ifay@pride-i2.poly.edu. *Information contact:* Ms. Fran Lenkowski, Assistant to the Director, 914-323-2062, Fax: 914-323-2010, E-mail: frank@pride-i2.poly.edu.

Portland State University, Portland, OR 97207-0751

Center for Science Education Founded in 1993. *Academic areas of research and training:* Providing both a leadership and facilitating role for the improvement of science education within the university and the larger community. *Degrees offered:* MS. *Graduate students served 1997–98:* 9: 6 at the master's level; 3 at the doctoral level. *Faculty:* 9: 8 affiliated solely with the center. *Faculty affiliations:* University Honors Program. *Annual research budget:* $650,000. *Director:* Dr. William Becker, 503-725-4266, Fax: 503-725-3884, E-mail: beckerw@pdx.edu.

Regional Research Institute for Human Services Founded in 1972. *Academic areas of research and training:* Child welfare, mental health, program evaluation, public welfare. *Degrees offered:* None. *Graduate students served 1997–98:* 48: 38 at the master's level; 10 at the doctoral level. *Faculty:* 16: 1 affiliated solely with the institute. *Faculty affiliations:* Department of Psychology; Schools of Social Work, Urban and Public Affairs. *Annual research budget:* $3.5 million. *Director:* Nancy M. Koroloff, 503-725-4040, Fax: 503-725-4180, E-mail: nmk@pdx.edu.

Purdue University, West Lafayette, IN 47907

Center for the Human-Animal Bond Founded in 1982. *Academic areas of research and training:* Animal sciences, biology, child development, ethology, philosophy. *Degrees offered:* None. *Graduate students served 1997–98:* 3 at the master's level; 8 at the doctoral level; 2 at the postgraduate level. *Faculty:* 21: 6 affiliated solely with the center. *Faculty affiliations:* Departments of Animal Sciences, Biological Sciences, Child Development and Family Studies, Philosophy, Psychology, Sociology and Anthropology, Veterinary Pathobiology. *Director:* Dr. Alan M. Beck, 765-494-0854, Fax: 765-494-9830, E-mail: abeck@purdue.edu.

Gifted Education Resource Institute Founded in 1980. *Academic areas of research and training:* Gifted education, talent development. *Degrees offered:* None. *Graduate students served 1997–98:* 20: 5 at the master's level; 14 at the doctoral level; 1 at the postgraduate level. *Faculty:* 25: 1 affiliated solely with the institute. *Faculty affiliations:* Departments of Child Development and Family Studies, Curriculum and Instruction, Educational Studies; Schools of Consumer and Family Sciences, Education. *Annual research budget:* $500,000. *Director:* Dr. Sidney Moon, 765-494-7243, Fax: 765-496-1228, E-mail: geri@soe.purdue.edu.

School Mathematics and Science Center (SMSC) Founded in 1985. *Academic areas of research and training:* Biology, chemistry, curriculum and instruction, earth and atmospheric sciences, mathematics, physics, science outreach, educational technology. *Degrees offered:* None. *Graduate students served 1997–98:* 25 at the master's level; 15 at the doctoral level; 2 at the postgraduate level. *Faculty:* 19. *Faculty affiliations:* Departments of Biology, Chemistry, Curriculum and Instruction, Earth and Atmospheric Sciences, Mathematics, Physics. *Annual research budget:* $650,000. *Director:* Dr. Gerald H. Krockover, Interim Director, 765-494-5889, Fax: 765-494-7938, E-mail: hawk1@purdue.edu.

Radford University, Radford, VA 24142

Business Assistance Center *Academic areas of research and training:* Economic development, training and development, entrepreneurship, international trade, internet commerce. *Degrees offered:* None. *Graduate students served 1997–98:* 10 at the master's level. *Faculty:* 5 affiliated solely with the center. *Annual research budget:* $750,000. *Director:* Dr. Jerry Kopf, Executive Director, 540-831-6056, Fax: 540-831-6735, E-mail: jkopf@runct.edu.

Rensselaer Polytechnic Institute, Troy, NY 12180-3590

Center for Services Research and Education Founded in 1990. *Academic areas of research and training:* Service sector, role of technology, information systems management, operation research, statistics. *Degrees offered:* None. *Graduate students served 1997–98:* 25 at the master's level; 4 at the doctoral level. *Faculty:* 40: 20 affiliated solely with the center. *Faculty affiliations:* Departments of Civil Engineering, Decision Sciences and Engineering Systems; Lally School of Management and Technology. *Annual research budget:* $286,000. *Director:* Dr. Dan Berg, 518-276-2895, Fax: 518-276-8227, E-mail: bergd@rpi.edu.

Rush University, Chicago, IL 60612-3832

Center for Health Management Studies Founded in 1979. *Academic areas of research and training:* Organization, financing and delivery of health care, occupational health, cost analysis. *Degrees offered:* None. *Graduate students served 1997–98:* 35 at the master's level. *Faculty:* 5. *Faculty affiliations:* Department of Health System Management. *Director:* Dr. Gerald L. Glandon, Associate Director, 312-942-5402, Fax: 312-942-4957, E-mail: gglandon@hsmsun.tob.rpslmc.edu.

Rutgers, The State University of New Jersey, New Brunswick, New Brunswick, NJ 08903

Center of Alcohol Studies (CAS) Founded in 1940. *Academic areas of research and training:* Acquisition and dissemination of knowledge on psychoactive substance use and related phenomena with primary emphasis on alcohol use and consequences. *Degrees offered:* None. *Graduate students served 1997–98:* 10 at the doctoral level. *Faculty:* 30: 20 affiliated solely with the center. *Faculty affiliations:* Graduate School of Applied and Professional Psychology; School of Social Work; Institute for Health, Health Care Policy, and Aging Research; Rutgers, the State University of New Jersey-Newark School of Criminal Justice. *Annual research budget:* $4.6 million. *Director:* Dr. Robert J. Pandina, 732-445-2518, E-mail: rpandina@rci.rutgers.edu. *Information contact:* Mr. Charles Rouse, Business Administrator, 732-445-2190, Fax: 732-445-3500, E-mail: chrouse@rci.rutgers.edu.

Santa Clara University, Santa Clara, CA 95053-0001

Markkula Center for Applied Ethics *Academic areas of research and training:* Ethics, applied ethics, bioethics, human rights. *Degrees offered:* None. *Graduate students served 1997–98:* 300. *Faculty:* 40: 4 affiliated solely with the center. *Faculty affiliations:* Leavey School of Business and Administration; Programs in Communication, Philosophy; School of Engineering, Law. *Director:* Dr. Thomas Shanks, SJ, Executive Director, 408-554-5319, E-mail: tshanks@scu.edu.

Southern Illinois University at Carbondale, Carbondale, IL 62901-6806

Center for Dewey Studies Founded in 1961. *Academic areas of research and training:* Research and study of the life and work of John Dewey; currently preparing an electronic edition of the complete correspondence prior to a selected letter-press edition. *Degrees offered:* None. *Graduate students served 1997–98:* 35: 5 at the master's level; 17 at the doctoral level; 13 at the postgraduate level. *Faculty:* 1 affiliated solely with the center. *Faculty affiliations:* Departments of Educational Administration, Elementary and Special Education; Program in Philosophy. *Director:* Dr. Larry Hickman, 618-453-2629, Fax: 618-453-1733, E-mail: lhickman@siu.edu.

Southern Methodist University, Dallas, TX 75275

Caruth Institute of Owner-Managed Business Founded in 1970. *Academic areas of research and training:* Quality entrepreneurial education for undergrads, MBAs, EMBAs, and the outside business community; Southwest venture forum; Dallas 100 Awards; Metroplex Growth Capitol Conference; Business-Leader-Spotlight speaker series. *Degrees offered:* None. *Graduate students served 1997–98:* 285 at the master's level. *Faculty:* 4 affiliated solely with the institute. *Director:* Mr. Jerry F. White, 214-768-3689, Fax: 214-768-3604, E-mail: jwhite@mail.cox.smu.edu.

Finance Institute Founded in 1983. *Academic areas of research and training:* Finance, investments, capital markets. *Degrees offered:* None. *Graduate students served 1997–98:* 25 at the master's level. *Faculty:* 32. *Faculty affiliations:* Edwin L. Cox School of Business. *Director:* Dr. Marc Reinganum, 214-768-2260, Fax: 214-768-4099, E-mail: mreingan@mail.cox.smu.edu.

Stanford University, Stanford, CA 94305-9991

Stanford Center for Research in Disease Prevention Founded in 1971. *Academic areas of research and training:* Cardiovascular disease prevention, chronic disease prevention, behavioral medicine, health communication, tobacco control, obesity, physical activity, preventive medicine, health psychology, health policy. *Degrees offered:* None. *Graduate students served 1997–98:* 2 at the master's level; 3 at the doctoral level; 10 at the postgraduate level. *Faculty:* 21: 15 affiliated solely with the center. *Faculty affiliations:* Department of Communication; Graduate Programs in Medicine; Programs in Health Research and Policy, Psychiatry. *Annual research budget:* $5 million. *Director:* Dr. Stephen Fortmann, 650-723-6145, Fax: 650-725-6906, E-mail: fortmann@stanford.edu. *Information contact:* Dr. William Haskell, Deputy Director, 650-725-5012, Fax: 650-723-7018, E-mail: haskell@scrdp.stanford.edu.

Stanford Integrated Manufacturing Association (SIMA) Founded in 1984. *Academic areas of research and training:* Research and teaching in integrated manufacturing technologies. *Degrees offered:* None. *Graduate students served 1997–98:* 80; 60 at the master's level; 20 at the doctoral level. *Faculty:* 40: 20 affiliated solely with the center. *Faculty affiliations:* Graduate School of Business, School of Engineering. *Annual research budget:* $1.2 million. *Director:* Richard Reis, 650-725-0919, E-mail: reis@stanford.edu. *Information contact:* Ms. Susan C. Hansen, Assistant Director, 650-723-9038, Fax: 650-723-5034, E-mail: susan.hansen@stanford.edu.

State University of New York at Albany, Albany, NY 12222-0001

Capital Area School Development Association Founded in 1949. *Academic areas of research and training:* Education. *Degrees offered:* None. *Graduate students served 1997–98:* 5: 1 at the master's level; 4 at the doctoral level. *Faculty:* 2 affiliated solely with the center. *Annual research budget:* $75,000. *Director:* Dr. Richard Bamberger, 518-442-3796, Fax: 518-442-3746, E-mail: casda@cnsvax.albany.edu.

Quality Forum *Academic areas of research and training:* Total quality, TQM, teams and team building, non-profit management, customer service, benchmarking, focus groups. *Degrees offered:* None. *Graduate students served 1997–98:* 5: 4 at the master's level; 1 at the doctoral level. *Faculty:* 6. *Faculty affiliations:* Nelson A. Rockefeller College of Public Affairs and Policy; Schools of Business, Information Science and Policy, Social Welfare. *Director:* Thomas Kinney, 518-442-5705, Fax: 518-442-5771, E-mail: thomas.kinney@albany.edu.

State University of New York at Binghamton, Binghamton, NY 13902-6000

Center for Leadership Studies (CLS) Founded in 1987. *Academic areas of research and training:* Leadership training and research, team and organization leadership, transformational leadership, leadership assessment. *Degrees offered:* None. *Graduate students served 1997–98:* 12: 6 at the master's level; 6 at the doctoral level. *Faculty:* 7: 1 affiliated solely with the center. *Faculty affiliations:* School of Management. *Annual research budget:* $180,000. *Director:* Dr. Bernard Bass, 607-777-4028, Fax: 607-777-4188, E-mail: bbass@binghamton.edu.

Kresge Center for Nursing Research (CNR) Founded in 1987. *Academic areas of research and training:* Alzheimer's Disease, family violence, adolescent health, health promotion for elders, rural health care, AIDS NET. *Degrees offered:* None. *Graduate students served 1997–98:* 10 at the master's level. *Faculty:* 25: 18 affiliated solely with the center. *Faculty affiliations:* Departments of Africana Studies, Geography, Political Science; School of Education and Human Development. *Annual research budget:* $6,000. *Director:* Dr. Gale Spencer, 607-777-4625, Fax: 607-777-4440, E-mail: gspencer@binghamton.edu.

State University of New York at Buffalo, Buffalo, NY 14260

Canada-United States Trade Center Founded in 1988. *Academic areas of research and training:* Advancing basic and applied research on economic interactions and related issues between the United States and Canada; promote the development of graduate and undergraduate courses concerning Canadian and American relations. *Degrees offered:* None. *Graduate students served 1997–98:* 8: 5 at the master's level; 2 at the doctoral level; 1 at the postgraduate level. *Faculty:* 10: 7 affiliated solely with the center. *Faculty affiliations:* Departments of Geography, Marketing, Planning; School of Management. *Director:* Alan D. MacPherson, 716-645-2299 Ext. 20, Fax: 716-645-2329, E-mail: geoadm@ubvms.cc.buffalo.edu.

Center for Advanced Molecular Biology and Immunology Founded in 1985. *Academic areas of research and training:* Biological, biomedical, and life sciences. *Degrees offered:* None. *Graduate students served 1997–98:* 19: 18 at the doctoral level; 1 at the postgraduate level. *Faculty:* 68. *Faculty affiliations:* Departments of Biochemistry at Roswell Park, Biological Sciences, Biophysics at Roswell Park, Microbiology/Immunology at Roswell Park, Oral Biology, Pharmacology and Toxicology; Graduate Programs in Medicine; Program in Biochemical Pharmacology. *Annual research budget:* $220,000. *Director:* Dr. Jeremy Breunn, Co-Director, 716-645-2868, E-mail: cambruen@acsu.buffalo.edu. *Information contact:* Mrs. Xochitl Nicholson, Program Administrator, 716-645-2164, Fax: 716-645-3776, E-mail: xen@acsu.buffalo.edu.

Center for Assistive Technology (CAT) Founded in 1988. *Academic areas of research and training:* Assistive devices, technology for the aging, rehabilitation research. *Degrees offered:* None. *Graduate students served 1997–98:* 17: 15 at the master's level; 2 at the doctoral level. *Faculty:* 18: 2 affiliated solely with the center. *Faculty affiliations:* Departments of Communicative Disorders, Counseling and Educational Psychology, Occupational Therapy, Physical Therapy and Exercise Science, Rehabilitation Medicine; Schools of Architecture and Planning, Engineering and Applied Sciences, Nursing. *Annual research budget:* $3 million. *Director:* Dr. William C. Mann, E-mail: wmann@acsu.buffalo.edu. *Information contact:* Dr. William J. Gavin, Director of Graduate Studies, 716-829-3141, Fax: 716-829-3217, E-mail: gavin@shaman.socsci.buffalo.edu.

Center for Functional Assessment Research *Academic areas of research and training:* Measurement, occupational and physical therapy, rehabilitation, disability. *Degrees offered:* None. *Graduate students served 1997–98:* 5: 4 at the master's level; 1 at the postgraduate level. *Faculty:* 12: 3 affiliated solely with the center. *Faculty affiliations:* Department of Rehabilitation Medicine. *Annual research budget:* $800,000. *Director:* Dr. Carl V. Granger, E-mail: granger@acsu.buffalo.edu. *Information contact:* Mr. James Phillips, Functional Assessment Information Service, 716-829-2076, Fax: 716-829-2080, E-mail: farinfo@ubvms.cc.edu.

Center for Hearing and Deafness Founded in 1994. *Academic areas of research and training:* Audiology, engineering, neurology, otolaryngology, psychology. *Degrees offered:* None. *Graduate students served 1997–98:* 4: 3 at the master's level; 1 at the doctoral level. *Faculty:* 20. *Faculty affiliations:* Departments of Anatomy, Biophysics, Communicative Disorders, Mechanical and Aerospace Engineering, Neurology, Pediatrics, Psychology. *Annual research budget:* $600,000. *Director:* Dr. Donald Henderson, 716-829-2001, Fax: 716-829-2980, E-mail: donaldhe@acsu.buffalo.edu.

Center for Management Development Founded in 1977. *Academic areas of research and training:* General management. *Degrees offered:* None. *Graduate students served 1997–98:* 180: 25 at the master's level; 155 at the postgraduate level. *Faculty:* 50. *Faculty affiliations:* Schools of Engineering and Applied Sciences, Law, Management, Medicine. *Director:* Mr. Ronald J. Krul, Executive Director, 716-645-3200 Ext. 134, Fax: 716-645-3202, E-mail: krul@mgt.buffalo.edu.

The English Language Institute (ELI) Founded in 1971. *Academic areas of research and training:* Teaching English as a second language. *Degrees offered:* None. *Graduate students served 1997–98:* 20: 15 at the master's level; 5 at the doctoral level. *Faculty:* 31: 29 affiliated solely with the institute. *Faculty affiliations:* Graduate School of Education. *Annual research budget:* $80,000. *Director:* Dr. Stephen C. Dunnett, E-mail: elibuffalo@acsu.buffalo.edu. *Information contact:* Ms. Kathy L. Curtis, Associate Director, 716-645-2077, Fax: 716-645-6198, E-mail: curtiskl@acsu.buffalo.edu.

State University of New York Maritime College, Throgs Neck, NY 10465-4198

International Transportation Research Center Founded in 1993. *Academic areas of research and training:* Business, transportation, logistics, international transportation, transportation management. *Degrees offered:* None. *Graduate students served 1997–98:* 5 at the

Directory: Research and Training Opportunities

International Transportation Research Center (continued)

master's level. *Faculty:* 15: 5 affiliated solely with the center. *Faculty affiliations:* Departments of Business Administration and Transportation Management. *Director:* Dr. Shmuel Z. Yahalom, 718-409-7290, E-mail: syahaloms@sunymaritime.edu. *Information contact:* Ms. Pam Dettmer, Assistant Administrator, 718-409-7285, Fax: 718-409-7359.

Syracuse University, Syracuse, NY 13244-0003

Center on Human Policy Founded in 1971. *Academic areas of research and training:* Disability studies, disability policy, services for people with developmental disabilities. *Degrees offered:* None. *Graduate students served 1997–98:* 5: 1 at the master's level; 4 at the doctoral level. *Faculty:* 5: 2 affiliated solely with the center. *Faculty affiliations:* College of Law, Program in Social Sciences, School of Education. *Annual research budget:* $650,000. *Director:* Steven J. Taylor, 315-443-3851, Fax: 315-443-4338, E-mail: thechp@sued.syr.edu.

Educational Resources Information Clearinghouse Founded in 1977. *Academic areas of research and training:* Library and information science, educational technology. *Degrees offered:* None. *Graduate students served 1997–98:* 500 at the master's level; 30 at the doctoral level. *Faculty:* 6: 4 affiliated solely with the center. *Faculty affiliations:* School of Information Studies. *Director:* Michael Eisenberg, 315-443-3460.

Kiebach Center for International Business Studies Founded in 1991. *Academic areas of research and training:* International business. *Degrees offered:* None. *Graduate students served 1997–98:* 100: 80 at the master's level; 20 at the doctoral level. *Faculty:* 6: 4 affiliated solely with the center. *Faculty affiliations:* Programs in Finance, International Business, Marketing, Quantitative Methods. *Annual research budget:* $30,000. *Director:* Peter Koveos, 315-443-1386.

Teachers College, Columbia University, New York, NY 10027-6696

Center for Educational and Psychological Services Founded in 1937. *Academic areas of research and training:* Clinical, counseling, and educational psychology. *Degrees offered:* MA; PhD; M Ed/Ed D. *Graduate students served 1997–98:* 170: 140 at the master's level. *Faculty:* 20. *Faculty affiliations:* Programs in Clinical, Counseling, Educational Psychology. *Director:* Dr. Laurence R. Lewis, 212-678-3262.

Institute on Education and the Economy (IEE) Founded in 1986. *Academic areas of research and training:* Links between education and work, work reform, labor, school-to-work transition, skills standards. *Degrees offered:* None. *Graduate students served 1997–98:* 15: 5 at the master's level; 10 at the doctoral level. *Faculty:* 7. *Faculty affiliations:* Departments of Curriculum and Teaching, Economics, Higher and Adult Education, Minority Education, Psychology, Sociology, Technology and Education. *Annual research budget:* $400,000. *Director:* Dr. Thomas Bailey, E-mail: tb3@columbia.edu. *Information contact:* Jennifer D'Alvia, Administrative Assistant, 212-678-3091, Fax: 212-678-3699, E-mail: iee@columbia.edu.

National Center for Restructuring Education, Schools, and Teaching (NCREST) Founded in 1990. *Academic areas of research and training:* Authentic assessment, case study development, documentation, policy development, school reform, school restructuring, professional development. *Degrees offered:* None. *Graduate students served 1997–98:* 23: 9 at the master's level; 14 at the doctoral level. *Faculty:* 7: 2 affiliated solely with the center. *Faculty affiliations:* Department of Curriculum and Teaching; Programs in Educational Administration, Philosophy of Education. *Annual research budget:* $3 million. *Director:* Dr. Linda Darling-Hammond, Co-Director, 212-678-4142, Fax: 212-678-4039, E-mail: ld70@columbia.edu. *Information contact:* Dr. Gary Griffin, Co-Director, 212-678-3787, Fax: 212-678-4170, E-mail: gag20@columbia.edu.

Tennessee Technological University, Cookeville, TN 38505

Center for Manufacturing Research and Technology Utilization Founded in 1984. *Academic areas of research and training:* Business, engineering, sciences. *Degrees offered:* None. *Graduate students served 1997–98:* 70: 51 at the master's level; 14 at the doctoral level. *Faculty:* 35: 5 affiliated solely with the center. *Faculty affiliations:* Colleges of Business Administration, Education, Engineering. *Annual research budget:* $1.5 million. *Director:* Ted S. Lundy, 931-372-3362, E-mail: tlundy@tntech.edu. *Information contact:* April Olberding, Editor, 931-372-3969, Fax: 931-372-6345, E-mail: april0@tntech.edu.

Texas A&M University, College Station, TX 77843

Center for Business and Economic Analysis Founded in 1990. *Academic areas of research and training:* Economic policy issues, U.S. and Texas economy, industry studies. *Degrees offered:* None. *Graduate students served 1997–98:* 2 at the master's level; 1 at the doctoral level. *Faculty:* 2: 1 affiliated solely with the center. *Faculty affiliations:* Department of Finance. *Annual research budget:* $200,000. *Director:* Dr. Jared E. Hazleton, 409-845-4057, Fax: 409-845-8784, E-mail: j-hazleton@tamu.edu.

Center for International Business Studies Founded in 1985. *Academic areas of research and training:* International competitiveness of American business, accounting and financial policy, marketing and management strategy, production management, corporate restructuring, emerging markets. *Degrees offered:* None. *Graduate students served 1997–98:* 30: 25 at the master's level; 5 at the doctoral level. *Faculty:* 35: 5 affiliated solely with the center. *Faculty affiliations:* Departments of Accounting, Business Analysis and Research, Finance, Management, Marketing. *Annual research budget:* $200,000. *Director:* Dr. Julian Gaspar, 409-845-5234, Fax: 409-845-1710, E-mail: jgaspar@unix.tamu.edu.

Real Estate Center Founded in 1971. *Academic areas of research and training:* Applied research relating to various aspects of residential and commercial real estate, enhancing understanding of real estate industry. *Degrees offered:* None. *Graduate students served 1997–98:* 8 at the master's level. *Faculty:* 11: 7 affiliated solely with the center. *Faculty affiliations:* Departments of Agricultural Economics, Finance, Rural Sociology. *Annual research budget:* $1.5 million. *Director:* Dr. R. Malcolm Richards, 409-845-2076, Fax: 409-845-0460, E-mail: rmalcolm@tamu.edu.

Texas Tech University, Lubbock, TX 79409

Center of Sports Health and Human Performance Founded in 1990. *Academic areas of research and training:* Cardiac rehabilitation, exercise physiology, sports health, motor performance, biomechanics. *Degrees offered:* None. *Graduate students served 1997–98:* 10 at the master's level. *Faculty:* 29: 4 affiliated solely with the center. *Faculty affiliations:* Departments of Cardiology, Family Practice, Food and Nutrition, Health, Physical Education and Recreation, Orthopedics. *Director:* Dr. Jeff A. Stuyt, Associate Professor, E-mail: unjas@ttacs.ttu.edu. *Information contact:* Dr. Lanie Dornier, Associate Chairperson for Graduate Programs, 806-742-3371, Fax: 806-742-1688, E-mail: pllad@ttacs.ttu.edu.

Institute for Banking and Financial Studies Founded in 1983. *Academic areas of research and training:* Banking, corporate finance, financial markets, investments, real estate. *Degrees offered:* None. *Graduate students served 1997–98:* 19: 5 at the master's level; 14 at the doctoral level. *Faculty:* 10. *Faculty affiliations:* Departments of Agricultural Economics, Economics and Geography; Programs in Accounting, Finance, Information Systems and Quantitative Sciences, Management, Marketing. *Annual research budget:* $15,000. *Director:* Dr. R. Stephen Sears, 806-742-3377, Fax: 806-742-2099, E-mail: odrss@coba2.ttu.edu.

Texas Wine Marketing Research Institute Founded in 1989. *Academic areas of research and training:* Agricultural economics, consumer studies, marketing, wine marketing. *Degrees offered:* None. *Graduate students served 1997–98:* 3: 2 at the master's level; 1 at the doctoral level. *Faculty:* 2: 1 affiliated solely with the institute. *Faculty affiliations:* Program in Restaurant, Hotel, and Institutional Management. *Annual research budget:* $100,000. *Director:* Dr. Tim H. Dodd, 806-742-3077, Fax: 806-742-0125, E-mail: tdodd@ttu.edu.

Texas Woman's University, Denton, TX 76204

Center for Research on Women's Health Founded in 1993. *Academic areas of research and training:* Biology, communication sciences and disorders, family sciences, health studies, kinesiology, nursing, nutrition and food sciences, occupational and physical therapy, psychology, women's studies, library sciences. *Degrees offered:* None. *Graduate students served 1997–98:* 10: 4 at the master's level; 6 at the doctoral level. *Faculty:* 94: 4 affiliated solely with the center. *Faculty affiliations:* College of Nursing; Departments of Biology, Communication Sciences and Disorders, Family Sciences, Health Studies, Kinesiology, Library Sciences, Nutrition and Food Sciences, Psychology, Women's Studies; Schools of Occupational and Physical Therapy. *Annual research budget:* $115,401. *Director:* Dr. Charlotte Sanborn, 940-898-2792, Fax: 940-898-2793, E-mail: f_sanborn@twu.edu.

Tulane University, New Orleans, LA 70118-5669

Tulane Cancer Center Founded in 1993. *Academic areas of research and training:* Cancer research, molecular biology, cellular biology, virology, genetics. *Degrees offered:* None. *Graduate students served 1997–98:* 20: 8 at the doctoral level; 12 at the postgraduate level. *Faculty:* 107. *Faculty affiliations:* Department of Cell and Molecular Biology, School of Medicine. *Annual research budget:* $6 million. *Director:* Dr. Roy S. Weiner, 504-585-6060, Fax: 504-585-6077, E-mail: rweiner@tmc.tulane.edu.

Tulane Center for Cardiovascular Health Founded in 1992. *Academic areas of research and training:* Cardiovascular disease intervention and prevention, Health Ahead/Heart Smart health education program for elementary school children (K-6). *Degrees offered:* None. *Graduate students served 1997–98:* 20. *Faculty:* 16: 6 affiliated solely with the center. *Faculty affiliations:* Departments of Biostatistics, Community Health Sciences, Epidemiology. *Director:* Dr. Gerald S. Berenson, 504-585-7197, Fax: 504-585-7194, E-mail: berenson@mailhost.tcs.tulane.edu.

Tulane Regional Primate Research Center Founded in 1964. *Academic areas of research and training:* Behavioral and biomedical research with primates. *Degrees offered:* None. *Graduate students served 1997–98:* 3 at the doctoral level. *Faculty:* 30: 20 affiliated solely with the center. *Faculty affiliations:* Schools of Medicine, Public Health and Tropical Medicine. *Annual research budget:* $10 million. *Director:* Dr. Peter J. Gerone, 504-892-2040, Fax: 504-893-1352, E-mail: gerone@tpc.tulane.edu.

Université de Montréal, Montréal, PQ H3C 3J7, Canada

Public Law Research Centre Founded in 1962. *Academic areas of research and training:* Computer communications law, human rights, legal theory, multidisciplinary health law. *Degrees offered:* None. *Graduate students served 1997–98:* 55: 30 at the master's level; 22 at the doctoral level; 3 at the postgraduate level. *Faculty:* 18: 8 affiliated solely with the center. *Faculty affiliations:* Faculty of Law. *Annual research budget:* $2 million. *Director:* Jacques Frémont, 514-343-6263, Fax: 514-343-7508, E-mail: fremont@droit.umontreal.ca.

The University of Alabama, Tuscaloosa, AL 35487

Human Resource Institute Founded in 1972. *Academic areas of research and training:* Human resources management, industrial relations, organizational behavior. *Degrees offered:* None. *Faculty affiliations:* Department of Marketing and Management. *Director:* Dr. Trevor Bain, 205-348-8939, Fax: 205-348-6695, E-mail: tbain@cba.ua.edu.

The University of Alabama at Birmingham, Birmingham, AL 35294

Center for Aging Founded in 1976. *Academic areas of research and training:* Gerontology, psychology, medical sociology, medicine, dentistry, nursing, public health, optometry, health related professions. *Degrees offered:* None. *Graduate students served 1997–98:* 25: 23 at the master's level; 2 at the doctoral level. *Faculty:* 90. *Faculty affiliations:* Departments of Neurology, Ophthalmology and Psychiatry, Psychology, Sociology; Schools of Dentistry, Health Related Professions, Medicine, Nursing, Optometry, Public Health. *Director:* Dr. Richard M. Allman, 205-934-9261, E-mail: rallman@aging.dom.uab.edu. *Information contact:* Dr. Patricia S. Baker, Director of Gerontology Education Program, 205-934-4399, Fax: 205-934-7354.

Center for Health Promotion Founded in 1993. *Academic areas of research and training:* Health promotion and disease prevention, acute and chronic diseases, underserved populations. *Degrees offered:* None. *Graduate students served 1997–98:* 24 at the master's level; 16 at the doctoral level; 5 at the postgraduate level. *Faculty:* 134: 3 affiliated solely with the center. *Faculty affiliations:* Schools of Dentistry, Education, Engineering, Health Related Professions, Medicine, Optometry, Public Health, Social and Behavioral Sciences. *Annual research budget:* $7 million. *Director:* Dr. James Raczynski, 205-934-6020, Fax: 205-975-6753, E-mail: jraczynski@bmu.dopm.uab.edu.

Lister Hill Center for Health Policy Founded in 1987. *Academic areas of research and training:* Health policy, health care markets, managed care, maternal and child health, strategic planning in health organizations, outcomes research. *Degrees offered:* None. *Faculty:* 32. *Faculty affiliations:* Schools of Business, Health Related Professions, Medicine, Optometry, Public Health, Social and Behavioral Science. *Annual research budget:* $350,000. *Director:* Dr. Michael A. Morrisey, 205-975-8966, E-mail: morrisey@uab.edu. *Information contact:* Mr. Kalai Mugilan, Assistant to the Director, 205-975-9007, Fax: 205-934-3347, E-mail: kmugilan@hcop.soph.uab.edu.

Research Center in Oral Biology Founded in 1987. *Degrees offered:* None. *Graduate students served 1997–98:* 5 at the doctoral level; 3 at the postgraduate level. *Faculty:* 10. *Faculty affiliations:* Departments of Biochemistry and Molecular Genetics, Cell Biology, Microbiology, Oral Biology, Orthodontics; Cancer Center. *Annual research budget:* $1.135 million. *Director:* Dr. Suzanne M. Michalek, Professor, 205-934-3470, Fax: 205-934-1426, E-mail: suemichalek@micro.microbio.uab.edu.

Sparkman Center for International Public Health Education Founded in 1981. *Academic areas of research and training:* International public health, international nutrition, tropical infectious diseases. *Degrees offered:* None. *Graduate students served 1997–98:* 18: 12 at the master's level; 4 at the doctoral level; 2 at the postgraduate level. *Faculty:* 33: 8 affiliated solely with the center. *Faculty affiliations:* Departments of Epidemiology, Health Behavior, International Health, Microbiology; Program in Nutrition Sciences; School of Medicine. *Annual research budget:* $300,000. *Director:* Dr. Charles Stephensen, Acting Director, E-mail: cbs@uab.edu. *Information contact:* Ms. Erin Branigan, Coordinator, 205-934-1732, Fax: 205-975-3329, E-mail: branigan@uab.edu.

Vision Science Research Center (VSRC) Founded in 1978. *Academic areas of research and training:* Vision science, central visual studies/systems, physiology, pharmacology, biochemistry, oculomotor systems/studies, clinical trials, myopia studies, retinal anatomy. *Degrees offered:* None. *Graduate students served 1997–98:* 44. *Faculty:* 43. *Faculty affiliations:* Departments of Biomedical Engineering, Cell Biology, Chemistry, Hematology/Oncology, Ophthalmology, Pharmacology, Physiological Optics, Physiology and Biophysics, Psychology; School of Optometry. *Director:* Dr. Virginia Brooks, Assistant to Director, 205-934-0322, Fax: 205-934-5725, E-mail: pgamlin@vision.vsrc.uab.edu.

The University of Arizona, Tucson, AZ 85721

Arizona Poison and Drug Information Center (APDIC) Founded in 1979. *Academic areas of research and training:* Clinical toxicology, poison control, poison and drug information, environmental toxicology, emergency medicine, clinical pharmacy. *Degrees offered:* None. *Graduate students served 1997–98:* 18: 8 at the master's level; 6 at the doctoral level; 4 at the postgraduate level. *Faculty affiliations:* Colleges of Medicine, Pharmacy. *Director:* Dr. Theodore Tong, 520-626-1587, Fax: 520-626-4063, E-mail: tong@pharmacy.arizona.edu.

Directory: Research and Training Opportunities

University of Arkansas, Fayetteville, AR 72701-1201

Research and Training Center for Persons Who are Deaf or Hard of Hearing Founded in 1981. *Academic areas of research and training:* Rehabilitation, career preparation, entry, and advancement of persons who are deaf or hard of hearing in the workplace. *Degrees offered:* None. *Graduate students served 1997–98:* 14 at the master's level. *Faculty:* 11: 8 affiliated solely with the center. *Faculty affiliations:* Department of Rehabilitation Education and Research. *Annual research budget:* $745,000. *Director:* Dr. Douglas Watson, 501-686-9691, Fax: 501-686-9698, E-mail: dwatson@comp.uark.edu.

Southwest Radiation Calibration Center (SRCC) Founded in 1985. *Academic areas of research and training:* Health physics, nuclear engineering. *Degrees offered:* None. *Graduate students served 1997–98:* 3: 2 at the master's level; 1 at the doctoral level. *Faculty:* 2: 1 affiliated solely with the center. *Faculty affiliations:* Department of Mechanical Engineering. *Director:* Dr. Leon West, Professor, 501-575-3449. *Information contact:* Mr. Tim J. Welty, Manager, 501-575-3440, Fax: 501-575-7318, E-mail: tjw@engr.uark.edu.

University of Arkansas at Little Rock, Little Rock, AR 72204-1099

The Center for Research on Teaching and Learning (CRTL) Founded in 1974. *Academic areas of research and training:* Education and human service, program evaluation, child care policy, educational reform policy. *Degrees offered:* None. *Graduate students served 1997–98:* 10: 6 at the master's level; 4 at the doctoral level. *Faculty:* 15: 10 affiliated solely with the center. *Faculty affiliations:* Department of Educational Leadership. *Annual research budget:* $4 million. *Director:* Dr. Larry R. Dickerson, 501-569-3422, Fax: 501-569-8503, E-mail: lrdickerson@ualr.edu.

University of Bridgeport, Bridgeport, CT 06601

The Ernest C. Trefz Center for Venture Management and Entrepreneurial Studies Founded in 1982. *Academic areas of research and training:* Retention and development of small businesses, international business services and network development, regional socioeconomic issues. *Degrees offered:* None. *Graduate students served 1997–98:* 5 at the master's level. *Faculty:* 20. *Faculty affiliations:* School of Business. *Director:* Dr. Glenn A. Bassett, 203-576-4384, Fax: 203-576-4388.

University of British Columbia, Vancouver, BC V6T 1Z2, Canada

Centre for Applied Ethics Founded in 1993. *Academic areas of research and training:* Bioethics, business ethics, ethics and information, professional ethics, technology and environmental ethics, research ethics. *Degrees offered:* None. *Graduate students served 1997–98:* 9: 6 at the master's level; 3 at the doctoral level. *Faculty:* 33: 3 affiliated solely with the center. *Faculty affiliations:* Departments of Anthropology and Sociology, Civil Engineering, Computer Science, Educational Studies, Geography, Germanic Studies, Health Care Ethics, Philosophy, Political Science; Faculties of Commerceand Business Administration, Dentistry, Forestry, Medicine; School of Nursing. *Annual research budget:* $40,000. *Director:* Dr. Michael McDonald, Professor, 604-822-5139, Fax: 604-822-8627, E-mail: mcdonald@ethics.ubc.ca.

Institute of Health Promotion Research Founded in 1990. *Academic areas of research and training:* Health promotion, health policy. *Degrees offered:* PhD. *Graduate students served 1997–98:* 21: 1 at the master's level; 17 at the doctoral level; 3 at the postgraduate level. *Faculty:* 113: 3 affiliated solely with the institute. *Faculty affiliations:* Departments of Counseling Psychology, Psychology; Faculties of Arts, Commerce and Business Administration, Dentistry, Education, Medicine; School of Nursing. *Annual research budget:* $1.7 million. *Director:* Dr. Lawrence W. Green, 604-822-5776, E-mail: lgreen@unixg.ubc.ca. *Information contact:* Dr. C. James Frankish, Associate Director, 604-822-2258, Fax: 604-822-9210, E-mail: frankish@unixg.ubc.ca.

University of California, Berkeley, Berkeley, CA 94720-1500

Center for Social Services Research Founded in 1994. *Academic areas of research and training:* Child welfare, aging, poverty, mental health, public health. *Degrees offered:* None. *Graduate students served 1997–98:* 33: 20 at the master's level; 13 at the doctoral level. *Faculty:* 7 affiliated solely with the center. *Annual research budget:* $1.5 million. *Director:* Dr. Jill Duerr Berrick, 510-642-1899, Fax: 510-642-1895, E-mail: cssr@uclink2.berkeley.edu.

Earl Warren Legal Institute Founded in 1967. *Academic areas of research and training:* Empirical research in law and legal institutions. *Degrees offered:* None. *Graduate students served 1997–98:* 9 at the doctoral level. *Faculty:* 12. *Faculty affiliations:* Boalt Hall School of Law; Department of History; Schools of Public Health, Social Welfare. *Annual research budget:* $400,000. *Director:* Franklin E. Zimring, 510-642-5125.

University of California, Davis, Davis, CA 95616

California Regional Primate Research Center (CRPRC) Founded in 1962. *Academic areas of research and training:* Behavioral biology and neurobiology, developmental and reproductive biology, virology, immunology, primate medicine, respiratory diseases. *Degrees offered:* None. *Graduate students served 1997–98:* 50: 20 at the doctoral level. *Faculty:* 21. *Faculty affiliations:* Schools of Medicine, Veterinary Medicine. *Annual research budget:* $13 million. *Director:* Dr. Andrew G. Hendrickx, 530-752-0420, Fax: 530-752-8201, E-mail: aghendrickx@ucdavis.edu.

Institute of Toxicology and Environmental Health (ITEH) Founded in 1965. *Academic areas of research and training:* Human toxicology, comparative toxicology and epidemiology, study of health effects on humans and animals of potentially toxic chemicals and radiation in the environment. *Degrees offered:* None. *Graduate students served 1997–98:* 69: 4 at the master's level; 39 at the doctoral level; 26 at the postgraduate level. *Faculty:* 32: 4 affiliated solely with the institute. *Faculty affiliations:* College of Agricultural and Environmental Sciences; Programs in Anatomy, Physiology and Cell Biology; Schools of Medicine, Veterinary Medicine. *Annual research budget:* $8 million. *Director:* Dr. James W. Overstreet, 530-752-1340, E-mail: jwoverstreet@ucdavis.edu. *Information contact:* Ms. Pat Hunter, Assistant Director for Administration, 530-752-7281, Fax: 530-752-5300, E-mail: pahunter@ucdavis.edu.

University of California, Hastings College of the Law, San Francisco, CA 94102-4978

Public Law Research Institute (PLRI) Founded in 1982. *Academic areas of research and training:* Legal issues. *Degrees offered:* None. *Graduate students served 1997–98:* 60 at the doctoral level. *Faculty:* 4: 3 affiliated solely with the institute. *Director:* David J. Jung, 415-565-4639, Fax: 415-565-4865, E-mail: jungd@uchastings.edu. *Information contact:* Katherine Lodato, Public Law Research Fellow, 415-565-4671.

University of California, Los Angeles, Los Angeles, CA 90095

Brain Research Institute (BRI) Founded in 1959. *Academic areas of research and training:* Neuroscience. *Degrees offered:* None. *Graduate students served 1997–98:* 510: 254 at the doctoral level; 256 at the postgraduate level. *Faculty affiliations:* College of Letters and Science; Schools of Dentistry, Engineering and Applied Science, Medicine; Center for the Study of Opioid Receptors and Drugs of Abuse; Crump Institute for Biological Imaging, Jules Stein Eye Institute; Laboratory of Structural Biology and Molecular Medicine; Mental Retardation Research Center. *Annual research budget:* $60 million. *Director:* Dr. Allan Tobin, 310-825-5061, Fax: 310-206-5855, E-mail: atobin@bri.medsch.ucla.edu.

CURE: Digestive Diseases Research Center Founded in 1974. *Academic areas of research and training:* Digestive disease research. *Degrees offered:* None. *Graduate students served 1997–98:* 25: 5 at the doctoral level; 20 at the postgraduate level. *Faculty:* 152: 99 affiliated solely with the center. *Faculty affiliations:* Department of Physiology; Programs in Anesthesiology, Oncology, Psychiatry, Surgery. *Director:* John H. Walsh, 310-312-9284, Fax: 310-268-4963, E-mail: jwalsh@ucla.edu.

Jonsson Comprehensive Cancer Center Founded in 1974. *Academic areas of research and training:* Multidisciplinary research to improve treatment, diagnosis, and prevention of cancer; signal transduction, tumor immunology, viral and chemical carcinogenesis and clinical/translational research in numerous types of cancer. *Degrees offered:* None. *Graduate students served 1997–98:* 46: 11 at the doctoral level; 35 at the postgraduate level. *Faculty:* 298. *Faculty affiliations:* Departments of Biology, Chemistry and Biochemistry; Program in Molecular Biology; Schools of Dentistry, Medicine, Nursing, Public Health. *Annual research budget:* $113 million. *Director:* Dr. Judith C. Gasson, 310-825-5268, Fax: 310-206-5553, E-mail: jgasson@jccc.medsch.ucla.edu.

Jules Stein Eye Institute Founded in 1964. *Academic areas of research and training:* Vision science, retina, cornea, glaucoma, lens, molecular biophysics of membranes. *Degrees offered:* None. *Graduate students served 1997–98:* 39: 19 at the doctoral level; 20 at the postgraduate level. *Faculty:* 37: 34 affiliated solely with the institute. *Faculty affiliations:* Department of Physiological Sciences; Programs in Neurobiology, Pathology and Laboratory Medicine; School of Medicine. *Annual research budget:* $4.8 million. *Director:* Dr. Bartly J. Mondino, 310-825-5053, Fax: 310-206-7488, E-mail: hill@jsei.ucla.edu.

Laboratory of Structural Biology and Molecular Medicine (LSBMM) Founded in 1947. *Academic areas of research and training:* Structural and computational biology, molecular nuclear medicine. *Degrees offered:* None. *Graduate students served 1997–98:* 70: 46 at the doctoral level; 24 at the postgraduate level. *Faculty:* 40. *Faculty affiliations:* Departments of Biological Chemistry, Biomathematics, Chemistry and Biochemistry; Programs in Biobehavioral Sciences, Mathematics and Statistics, Microbiology and Molecular Genetics, Nuclear Medicine, Pharmacology, Psychiatry, Radiological Sciences, Surgery-Neurology; School of Medicine. *Annual research budget:* $12.72 million. *Director:* Dr. David Eisenberg, 310-825-3754, Fax: 310-206-3914.

University of California, Riverside, Riverside, CA 92521-0102

California Educational Research Cooperative (CERC) Founded in 1988. *Academic areas of research and training:* Educational planning and decision-making cooperative made up of county offices and member districts. *Degrees offered:* None. *Graduate students served 1997–98:* 10: 1 at the master's level; 9 at the doctoral level. *Faculty:* 3: 2 affiliated solely with the center. *Faculty affiliations:* School of Education. *Director:* Dr. Douglas E. Mitchell, 909-787-3026, Fax: 909-787-3491, E-mail: mitchell@mail.ucr.edu.

University of California, San Diego, La Jolla, CA 92093-5003

Center for AIDS Research Founded in 1994. *Academic areas of research and training:* Develop vaccines and therapies for HIV and associated infection; translational research. *Degrees offered:* None. *Graduate students served 1997–98:* 25. *Faculty:* 22: 11 affiliated solely with the center. *Faculty affiliations:* Department of Biology; Programs in Infectious Diseases, Pathology; School of Medicine. *Annual research budget:* $1.073 million. *Director:* Dr. Flossie Wong-Staal, 619-534-7957, Fax: 619-534-7743, E-mail: fwongstaal@ucsd.edu. *Information contact:* Dr. Carole Sussman, Administrator, 619-534-5545, Fax: 619-822-1934, E-mail: csussman@ucsd.edu.

University of California, San Francisco, San Francisco, CA 94143

Institute for Health and Aging (IHA) Founded in 1979. *Academic areas of research and training:* Social and behavioral sciences, aging, gender, breast cancer prevention outreach, Alzheimer's disease, aging, long-term care, older women's issues. *Degrees offered:* None. *Graduate students served 1997–98:* 15: 2 at the master's level; 8 at the doctoral level; 5 at the postgraduate level. *Faculty:* 22 affiliated solely with the institute. *Faculty affiliations:* Department of Social and Behavioral Sciences, Program in Medical Anthropology, School of Medicine. *Annual research budget:* $7.1 million. *Director:* Dr. Carroll L. Estes, 415-476-3236, Fax: 415-502-5208, E-mail: cestes@itsa.ucsf.edu.

University of Chicago, Chicago, IL 60637-1513

The Ben May Institute for Cancer Research Founded in 1951. *Degrees offered:* None. *Graduate students served 1997–98:* 35: 10 at the doctoral level; 25 at the postgraduate level. *Faculty affiliations:* Departments of Biochemistry and Molecular Biology, Pharmacological and Physiological Sciences; Pritzker School of Medicine. *Annual research budget:* $3.332 million. *Director:* Jeffery A. Bluestone, 773-702-0401, Fax: 773-702-3701, E-mail: jbluest@flowcity.bsd.uchicago.edu.

MacLean Center for Clinical Medical Ethics Founded in 1984. *Academic areas of research and training:* Medical ethics, doctor-patient relationship, ethics of managed care. *Degrees offered:* Certificate. *Graduate students served 1997–98:* 12 at the postgraduate level. *Faculty:* 9: 3 affiliated solely with the center. *Faculty affiliations:* Pritzker School of Medicine; Programs in Health Services Research, Obstetrics/Gynecology, Pediatrics. *Annual research budget:* $1 million. *Director:* Dr. Mark Siegler, 773-702-1453, Fax: 773-702-0090.

University of Chicago School Mathematics Project Founded in 1983. *Academic areas of research and training:* Mathematics education, kindergarten through grade 12 curriculum development, teacher training. *Degrees offered:* None. *Graduate students served 1997–98:* 9: 3 at the master's level; 5 at the doctoral level; 1 at the postgraduate level. *Faculty:* 6. *Faculty affiliations:* Departments of Education, Mathematics. *Annual research budget:* $400,000. *Director:* Zalman Usiskin, 773-702-1130, Fax: 773-702-0248, E-mail: ucsmp@uchicago.edu.

University of Colorado at Boulder, Boulder, CO 80309

Bueno Center for Multicultural Education Founded in 1975. *Academic areas of research and training:* Bilingual, multicultural, and special education; English as a Second Language. *Degrees offered:* None. *Graduate students served 1997–98:* 65: 48 at the master's level; 17 at the doctoral level. *Faculty:* 5 affiliated solely with the center. *Director:* Leonard Baca, 303-492-5416, Fax: 303-492-2883, E-mail: leonard.baca@colorado.edu.

Center for Lifelong Learning and Design (L3D) Founded in 1994. *Academic areas of research and training:* Lifelong learning, design, knowledge management, human management, human-computer interaction, organizational learning. *Degrees offered:* None. *Graduate students served 1997–98:* 30: 10 at the master's level; 10 at the doctoral level; 10 at the postgraduate level. *Faculty:* 14: 4 affiliated solely with the center. *Faculty affiliations:* Departments of Computer Science Psychology; Programs in Architecture and Planning, Cognitive Science; School of Education. *Annual research budget:* $1.5 million. *Director:* Dr. Gerhard Fischer, 303-492-1502, E-mail: gerhard@cs.colorado.edu.

University of Colorado Health Sciences Center, Denver, CO 80262

Barbara Davis Center for Childhood Diabetes Founded in 1980. *Academic areas of research and training:* Type I diabetes. *Degrees offered:* None. *Graduate students served 1997–98:* 10: 3 at the master's level; 4 at the doctoral level; 3 at the postgraduate level. *Faculty:* 17: 15 affiliated solely with the center. *Faculty affiliations:* Department of Immunology, Program in Surgery. *Annual research budget:* $1 million. *Director:* Dr. H. Peter Chase, Clinical Director, 303-315-8796, Fax: 303-315-4124.

University of Dayton, Dayton, OH 45469-1611

Center for Business and Economic Research Founded in 1985. *Academic areas of research and training:* Marketing, business and economic development, forecasting, public

Directory: Research and Training Opportunities

Center for Business and Economic Research (continued)

finance, useability. *Degrees offered:* None. *Faculty affiliations:* Department of Psychology; Programs in Accounting, Economics, Information Systems Management, Management Science, Marketing. *Director:* Dr. John E. Weiler, 937-229-2453, Fax: 937-229-2371.

University of Delaware, Newark, DE 19716

Center for Disabilities Studies: A University–Affiliated Program Founded in 1993. *Academic areas of research and training:* Disabilities policy, early intervention, disabilities prevention, aging and disabilities, family services and supports, program evaluation. *Degrees offered:* None. *Graduate students served 1997–98:* 12: 5 at the master's level; 7 at the doctoral level. *Faculty:* 18. *Faculty affiliations:* College of Health and Nursing Sciences; Departments of Educational Studies, Individual and Family Studies, Nutrition and Dietetics, Psychology, Sociology and Criminal Justice; Programs in Consumer Studies, Physical Therapy. *Annual research budget:* $1.6 million. *Director:* Dr. Donald L. Peters, 302-831-6974, Fax: 302-831-4690, E-mail: donald.peters@mvs.udel.edu.

University of Georgia, Athens, GA 30602

Institute of Higher Education Founded in 1964. *Academic areas of research and training:* Professional development of administrators, faculty; analysis, interpretation, and evaluation of trends, developments, and critical issues affecting higher education. *Degrees offered:* PhD; Ed D. *Graduate students served 1997–98:* 40 at the doctoral level. *Faculty:* 6 affiliated solely with the institute. *Director:* Dr. Cameron Fincher, 706-542-3464, Fax: 706-542-7588, E-mail: cfincher@arches.uga.edu.

University of Hawaii at Manoa, Honolulu, HI 96822

Curriculum Research and Development Group (CRDG) Founded in 1966. *Academic areas of research and training:* Curriculum design and development in science, educational evaluation, English language education, mathematics, social studies (K-12), teacher professional development of teachers in service. *Degrees offered:* None. *Graduate students served 1997–98:* 62: 31 at the master's level; 22 at the doctoral level. *Faculty:* 21: 20 affiliated solely with the group. *Faculty affiliations:* Departments of Comparative Education, Educational Psychology, Educational Technology, Teacher Education and Curriculum Studies. *Annual research budget:* $1.3 million. *Director:* Dr. Arthur R. King Jr., 808-956-7961, Fax: 808-956-9486, E-mail: aking@hawaii.edu.

University of Houston, Houston, TX 77204-2163

Institute for Health Care Marketing Founded in 1986. *Academic areas of research and training:* Health promotion, impact of managed care, hospital and group practice marketing. *Degrees offered:* None. *Graduate students served 1997–98:* 5: 1 at the master's level; 4 at the doctoral level. *Faculty affiliations:* College of Business Administration. *Director:* Dr. Betsy Gelb, 713-743-4555, Fax: 713-743-4572, E-mail: gelb@uh.edu.

Southwest Center for International Business *Academic areas of research and training:* Coordinate study abroad, faculty exchange, and international alliance programs. *Degrees offered:* None. *Graduate students served 1997–98:* 50: 40 at the master's level. *Faculty:* 4 affiliated solely with the center. *Annual research budget:* $100,000. *Director:* Dr. Tom Duening, 713-743-4600, Fax: 713-743-4022, E-mail: duening@uh.edu.

University of Illinois at Chicago, Chicago, IL 60607-7128

Center for Research in Information Management Founded in 1990. *Academic areas of research and training:* Management of information systems resources. *Degrees offered:* None. *Graduate students served 1997–98:* 2 at the doctoral level. *Faculty:* 7: 2 affiliated solely with the center. *Faculty affiliations:* Departments of Information and Decision Sciences, Marketing; Program in Management. *Annual research budget:* $50,000. *Director:* Dr. Robert Abrams, 312-996-2676, E-mail: rabrams@uic.edu. *Information contact:* Herbert H. Zuegel, Associate Director, 312-996-2679, Fax: 312-413-0385, E-mail: hzuegel@uic.edu.

Center for Research in Law and Justice *Academic areas of research and training:* Provide administrative and technical support to faculty and students engaged in funded research, sponsor presentations and seminars by scholars and practitioners. *Degrees offered:* None. *Graduate students served 1997–98:* 18 at the master's level. *Faculty affiliations:* Department of Criminal Justice. *Director:* Dr. Jess Maghan, Executive Director, 312-413-7691, Fax: 312-996-5755, E-mail: jess.maghan@uic.edu.

Great Lakes Center for Occupational and Environmental Safety and Health Founded in 1978. *Academic areas of research and training:* Occupational and environmental safety and health. *Degrees offered:* None. *Graduate students served 1997–98:* 42: 25 at the master's level; 5 at the doctoral level; 12 at the postgraduate level. *Faculty:* 37: 7 affiliated solely with the center. *Faculty affiliations:* Colleges of Engineering, Nursing; Program in Agriculture; School of Public Health. *Annual research budget:* $2 million. *Director:* Dr. Daniel Hryhorczuk, 312-996-7887, Fax: 312-413-7369.

Health Research and Policy Centers Founded in 1987. *Academic areas of research and training:* Health promotion, disease prevention, health policy, health services research, gerontology. *Degrees offered:* None. *Graduate students served 1997–98:* 27 at the master's level; 18 at the doctoral level; 7 at the postgraduate level. *Faculty:* 36: 1 affiliated solely with the center. *Faculty affiliations:* Colleges of Dentistry, Nursing; Departments of Economics, Marketing, Psychology, Sociology; Programs in African-American Studies, Community Health Sciences, Emergency Medicine, Epidemiology and Biostatistics, Maternal and Child Health, Medical-Surgical Nursing, Obstetrics and Gynecology, Occupational Therapy, Public Health Nursing; Survey Research Laboratory. *Annual research budget:* $4 million. *Director:* Dr. Brian Flay, 312-996-2806, E-mail: bflay@uic.edu. *Information contact:* Dr. William Baldyga, Associate Director, 312-996-0786, Fax: 312-996-2703, E-mail: bbaldyga@uic.edu.

Institute for Tuberculosis Research Founded in 1947. *Academic areas of research and training:* Biotechnology, characterization and isolation of immunostimulants from mycobacteria, formulation studies. *Degrees offered:* None. *Graduate students served 1997–98:* 6: 2 at the master's level; 2 at the doctoral level; 2 at the postgraduate level. *Faculty:* 1 affiliated solely with the institute. *Faculty affiliations:* College of Pharmacy. *Annual research budget:* $400,000. *Director:* Dr. Michael J. Groves, 312-996-3906, Fax: 312-996-4689, E-mail: groves@uic.edu.

Jane Addams Center for Social Policy and Research Founded in 1979. *Academic areas of research and training:* Collaborative research, poor and oppressed urban groups, development of knowledge of social service policies and programs for social justice and social change. *Degrees offered:* None. *Graduate students served 1997–98:* 6: 4 at the master's level; 2 at the doctoral level. *Faculty affiliations:* Jane Addams College of Social Work. *Annual research budget:* $685,000. *Director:* Dr. Creasie Finney Hairston, Dean, 312-996-3219, Fax: 312-996-2770. *Information contact:* Ms. Shonda Wills, Project Coordinator, 312-413-2303, Fax: 312-996-1802, E-mail: polctr@jaddams.csw.uic.edu.

The University of Iowa, Iowa City, IA 52242-1316

Institute for Rural and Environmental Health Founded in 1955. *Academic areas of research and training:* Rural and agricultural health, environmental and occupational health, industrial hygiene, environmental toxicology, injury epidemiology, water quality, international rural and environmental health. *Degrees offered:* MS; PhD. *Graduate students served 1997–98:* 37: 26 at the master's level; 10 at the doctoral level; 1 at the postgraduate level. *Faculty:* 21: 12 affiliated solely with the institute. *Faculty affiliations:* College of Law; Departments of Biomedical Engineering, Civil and Environmental Engineering; Program in Internal Medicine: Hygienic Laboratory, Public Health Laboratory. *Annual research budget:* $5 million. *Director:* Dr. Nancy Sprince, Interim Director, 319-335-4414. *Information contact:* Ms. Barbara Pies, Graduate Program Studies Coordinator, 319-335-4558, Fax: 319-335-4225, E-mail: barbara-pies@uiowa.edu.

University of Kentucky, Lexington, KY 40506-0032

Center for Real Estate Studies Founded in 1987. *Academic areas of research and training:* Real estate market analysis, finance, and investment. *Degrees offered:* None. *Graduate students served 1997–98:* 35 at the master's level. *Faculty:* 2: 1 affiliated solely with the center. *Faculty affiliations:* Program in Finance. *Annual research budget:* $52,000. *Director:* Dr. Steven H. Ott, 606-257-2968, Fax: 606-257-3577, E-mail: shott01@pop.uky.edu.

Graduate Center for Toxicology Founded in 1968. *Academic areas of research and training:* Interdisciplinary program to train scientists to deal with environmental problems and the effects of toxic substances on people. *Degrees offered:* None. *Graduate students served 1997–98:* 48: 4 at the master's level; 40 at the doctoral level; 4 at the postgraduate level. *Faculty:* 58: 4 affiliated solely with the center. *Faculty affiliations:* College of Pharmacy; Department of Microbiology and Immunology; Programs in Anatomy and Neurobiology, Biochemistry, Biological Sciences, Nutrition and Food Sciences, Pathology, Pharmacology. *Annual research budget:* $2 million. *Director:* Dr. Mary Vore, 606-257-3760, Fax: 606-323-1059.

University of Maryland, Baltimore County, Baltimore, MD 21250-5398

Maryland Institute for Policy Analysis and Research (MIPAR) Founded in 1982. *Academic areas of research and training:* Public policy issues, including those related to: education, health, public welfare, housing, emergency health services, information management, growth management, environment. *Degrees offered:* None. *Graduate students served 1997–98:* 13: 3 at the master's level; 10 at the doctoral level. *Faculty:* 16: 1 affiliated solely with the institute. *Faculty affiliations:* Departments of Education, Emergency Health Service. *Annual research budget:* $2.6 million. *Director:* Dr. Donald Norris, 410-455-1080, Fax: 410-455-1184, E-mail: norris@umbc.edu.

University of Maryland, College Park, College Park, MD 20742-5045

Institute for the Study of Exceptional Children and Youth Founded in 1981. *Academic areas of research and training:* Special education policy, education reform. *Degrees offered:* None. *Graduate students served 1997–98:* 6: 1 at the master's level; 5 at the doctoral level. *Faculty:* 1. *Faculty affiliations:* Department of Special Education. *Annual research budget:* $550,000. *Director:* Dr. Philip J. Burke, 301-405-6515, E-mail: pburke@educ.umd.edu. *Information contact:* Dr. Margaret J. McLaughlin, Associate Director, 301-405-6495, Fax: 301-314-9158, E-mail: mm48@umail.umd.edu.

The Maryland Center for Quality and Productivity (MCQP) Founded in 1977. *Academic areas of research and training:* Management. *Degrees offered:* None. *Graduate students served 1997–98:* 5: 3 at the master's level; 2 at the doctoral level. *Faculty:* 1 affiliated solely with the center. *Director:* Dr. Thomas C. Tuttle, 301-405-7099, E-mail: ttuttle@bmgtmail.umd.edu. *Information contact:* June S. Sherer, Business Manager, 301-405-7098, Fax: 301-314-9119, E-mail: jsherer@bmgtmail.umd.edu.

University of Massachusetts Amherst, Amherst, MA 01003-0001

Scientific Reasoning Research Institute (SRRI) Founded in 1987. *Academic areas of research and training:* Cognitive science, physics learning and teaching, probability and statistics. *Degrees offered:* None. *Graduate students served 1997–98:* 4: 1 at the master's level; 3 at the doctoral level. *Faculty:* 7. *Faculty affiliations:* Departments of Biology, Physics and Astronomy, Psychology; School of Education. *Annual research budget:* $300,000. *Director:* William J. Gerace, E-mail: wjgerace@phast.umass.edu. *Information contact:* Dorothy B. Freeman, Staff Assistant, 413-545-0988, Fax: 413-545-1691, E-mail: dfreeman@srri.umass.edu.

University of Massachusetts Lowell, Lowell, MA 01854-2881

The Demonstration School Founded in 1990. *Academic areas of research and training:* Bilingualism and language acquisition, early childhood education, elementary education, language development, leadership and schooling, multicultural education, teacher certification. *Degrees offered:* None. *Graduate students served 1997–98:* 100: 80 at the master's level; 20 at the doctoral level. *Faculty:* 19: 15 affiliated solely with the school. *Faculty affiliations:* Colleges of Education, Health Professions; Departments of Athletics, Music Education, Psychology. *Annual research budget:* $15,000. *Director:* Dr. Ann C. Benjamin, 978-934-4660, Fax: 978-934-4129, E-mail: benjamin_ann@uml.edu.

University of Medicine and Dentistry of New Jersey, Newark, NJ 07107-3001

Environmental and Occupational Health Sciences Institute (EOHSI) Founded in 1986. *Academic areas of research and training:* Environmental and occupational medicine, exposure assessment, public health toxicology. *Degrees offered:* None. *Graduate students served 1997–98:* 250. *Faculty:* 87. *Faculty affiliations:* Robert Wood Johnson Medical School; Rutgers, the State University of New Jersey. *Annual research budget:* $25 million. *Director:* Dr. Bernard D. Goldstein, 732-445-0205, E-mail: bgold@eohsi.rutgers.edu. *Information contact:* Ms. Candace Botnick, Public Affairs Coordinator, 732-445-0206, Fax: 732-445-0131, E-mail: botnick@eohsi.rutgers.edu.

The University of Memphis, Memphis, TN 38152

Bureau of Business and Economic Research Founded in 1963. *Academic areas of research and training:* Applied business and economic research. *Degrees offered:* None. *Graduate students served 1997–98:* 10: 8 at the master's level; 2 at the doctoral level. *Faculty:* 2 affiliated solely with the bureau. *Annual research budget:* $1 million. *Director:* Dr. John E. Gnuschke, 901-678-2281, Fax: 901-678-4086, E-mail: jgnuschk@memphis.edu.

University of Miami, Coral Gables, FL 33124

Bascom Palmer Eye Institute (BPEI) Founded in 1962. *Academic areas of research and training:* Ophthalmic research. *Degrees offered:* None. *Graduate students served 1997–98:* 12: 3 at the doctoral level; 9 at the postgraduate level. *Faculty:* 46: 40 affiliated solely with the institute. *Faculty affiliations:* Departments of Biomedical Engineering, Microbiology and Immunology; Programs in Neurological Surgery, Pathology, Pediatrics, Radiation Oncology. *Director:* Dr. Richard Parrish, Chairman, 305-326-6389.

University of Michigan, Ann Arbor, MI 48109

Center for Neural Communication Technology (CNCT) Founded in 1994. *Academic areas of research and training:* Research, training, and distribution of micromachined nervous system implants. *Degrees offered:* None. *Graduate students served 1997–98:* 4 at the doctoral level. *Faculty:* 6. *Faculty affiliations:* Departments of Biomedical Engineering, Electrical Engineering and Computer Science; Interdepartmental Program in Neuroscience. *Annual research budget:* $300,000. *Director:* Dr. David J. Anderson, 734-763-4367, Fax: 734-763-8041, E-mail: dja@eecs.umich.edu.

University of Mississippi, University, MS 38677-9702

The National Center for the Development of Natural Products (NCDNP) Founded in 1995. *Academic areas of research and training:* Discovery, development, and commercialization of natural product-derived pharmaceuticals and agrichemicals. *Degrees offered:* None. *Graduate students served 1997–98:* 15: 2 at the master's level; 10 at the doctoral level; 3 at the postgraduate level. *Faculty:* 36: 14 affiliated solely with the center. *Faculty affiliations:* Departments of Medicinal Chemistry, Pharmaceutics, Pharmacognosy, Pharmacology. *Annual research budget:* $3 million. *Director:* Dr. Alice M. Clark, 601-232-1005, Fax: 601-232-1006, E-mail: ncdnp@olemiss.edu.

University of Missouri–St. Louis, St. Louis, MO 63121-4499

Center for Business and Industrial Studies Founded in 1985. *Academic areas of research and training:* Sponsored research on managerial problems, development of analytical models. *Degrees offered:* None. *Graduate students served 1997–98:* 8 at the master's level. *Faculty:* 35. *Faculty affiliations:* School of Business Administration. *Annual research budget:* $225,000. *Director:* Dr. L. Douglas Smith, 314-516-6108, Fax: 314-516-6420.

The University of Montana–Missoula, Missoula, MT 59812-0002

Institute for Tourism and Recreation Research (ITRR) Founded in 1987. *Academic areas of research and training:* Tourism, recreation, resource management, environment, visitors' surveys, economic impacts. *Degrees offered:* None. *Graduate students served 1997–98:* 2: 1 at the master's level; 1 at the postgraduate level. *Faculty:* 14: 2 affiliated solely with the institute. *Faculty affiliations:* Department of Sociology; Schools of Business Administration, Forestry. *Annual research budget:* $250,000. *Director:* Dr. Norma Nickerson, 406-243-5686, Fax: 406-243-6656, E-mail: nnickers@forestry.umt.edu.

University of Nebraska–Lincoln, Lincoln, NE 68588

Center for Leadership Development (CLD) Founded in 1988. *Academic areas of research and training:* Leadership and human resource development. *Degrees offered:* None. *Graduate students served 1997–98:* 6: 4 at the master's level; 2 at the doctoral level. *Faculty:* 20: 2 affiliated solely with the center. *Annual research budget:* $1 million. *Director:* Dr. Allen G. Blezek, 402-472-2809, Fax: 402-472-6799, E-mail: aged010@unlvm.unl.edu.

Mid-America Transportation Center (MATC) Founded in 1995. *Academic areas of research and training:* Design and operation of surface transportation facilities and services. *Degrees offered:* None. *Graduate students served 1997–98:* 51: 41 at the master's level; 10 at the doctoral level. *Faculty:* 69: 7 affiliated solely with the center. *Faculty affiliations:* Departments of Chemical Engineering, Civil Engineering, Community and Regional Planning, Computer Science and Engineering, Economics, Electrical Engineering, Industrial and Management Systems Engineering, Mechanical Engineering. *Annual research budget:* $2 million. *Director:* Dr. Patrick T. McCoy, 402-472-5019, E-mail: pmccoy@unlinfo.unl.edu. *Information contact:* Mrs. Barbara Gnirk, Assistant Director, 402-472-4595, Fax: 402-472-0859, E-mail: bgnirk@unlinfo.unl.edu.

University of Nebraska Medical Center, Omaha, NE 68198-0001

Munroe-Meyer Institute for Genetics and Rehabilitation (MMI) Founded in 1958. *Academic areas of research and training:* Interdisciplinary leadership in neurodevelopmental disabilities, medicine, psychology, speech, nutrition, nursing, occupational therapy, physical therapy, public administration. *Degrees offered:* None. *Graduate students served 1997–98:* 198: 18 at the master's level; 30 at the doctoral level; 150 at the postgraduate level. *Faculty:* 38: 26 affiliated solely with the institute. *Faculty affiliations:* University of Nebraska at Omaha, University of Nebraska–Lincoln. *Director:* Dr. J. Michael Leibowitz, Deputy Director, E-mail: mrimedia@unmc.edu.

University of Nevada, Las Vegas, Las Vegas, NV 89154-9900

The Lied Institute for Real Estate Studies Founded in 1989. *Academic areas of research and training:* Economic and real estate research. *Degrees offered:* None. *Faculty:* 11: 3 affiliated solely with the institute. *Faculty affiliations:* College of Architecture, Construction Management and Planning; Departments of Accounting, Economics, Finance, Marketing. *Director:* Debra March, 702-895-4824, Fax: 702-895-4650, E-mail: dmarch@ccmail.nevada.edu.

University of New Hampshire, Durham, NH 03824

Center for Venture Research Founded in 1984. *Academic areas of research and training:* Early stage equity financing of high growth ventures. *Degrees offered:* None. *Graduate students served 1997–98:* 3 at the master's level. *Faculty:* 7: 1 affiliated solely with the center. *Faculty affiliations:* Whittemore School of Business and Economics. *Annual research budget:* $100,000. *Director:* Dr. Jeffrey Sohl, E-mail: jesohl@christa.unh.edu. *Information contact:* Ms. Laura Hill, Administrative Assistant, 603-862-3341, Fax: 603-862-4468, E-mail: lahill@hopper.unh.edu.

University of New Mexico, Albuquerque, NM 87131-2039

Bureau of Business and Economic Research (BBER) Founded in 1945. *Academic areas of research and training:* Provide economic research and public service to New Mexico's private and public sectors in order to promote economic development in the state. *Degrees offered:* None. *Graduate students served 1997–98:* 4: 3 at the master's level; 1 at the doctoral level. *Faculty:* 3 affiliated solely with the bureau. *Annual research budget:* $450,000. *Director:* Dr. M. Brian McDonald, 505-277-2216, Fax: 505-277-7066, E-mail: dbinfo@unm.edu.

University of New Orleans, New Orleans, LA 70148

Center for Economic Development Founded in 1978. *Academic areas of research and training:* Provide technical assistance, research, and strategic planning services to local communities in South Louisiana; economic development, public service, research, training, education, policy. *Degrees offered:* None. *Faculty:* 1. *Faculty affiliations:* Department of Economics and Finance. *Annual research budget:* $350,000. *Director:* Dr. Ivan Miestchovich Jr., 504-280-6663, Fax: 504-280-3952, E-mail: ijmcd@uno.edu.

The University of North Carolina at Chapel Hill, Chapel Hill, NC 27599

Cecil G. Sheps Center for Health Services Research Founded in 1968. *Academic areas of research and training:* Primary health care services and health professions; health care organization; medical practice; mental health services and systems research; aging, disablement, and long-term care; child health services, health care economics and finance, preventitive health services, rural health research, international health services research. *Degrees offered:* None. *Graduate students served 1997–98:* 40: 4 at the master's level; 16 at the doctoral level; 20 at the postgraduate level. *Faculty:* 23: 2 affiliated solely with the center. *Faculty affiliations:* Departments of Epidemiology, Health Policy and Administration, Maternal and Child Health, Sociology; Programs in Dental Ecology, Family Medicine, Pediatrics, Psychiatry; Schools of Medicine, Pharmacy, Social Work. *Annual research budget:* $6.386 million. *Director:* Dr. Gordon H. Defriese, 919-966-7100, Fax: 919-966-5764, E-mail: gordon_defriese@unc.edu.

Center for Cardiovascular Sciences and Medicine Founded in 1996. *Academic areas of research and training:* Molecular cardiology, vascular biology, health care outcomes, clinical trials in cardiovascular disease. *Degrees offered:* None. *Graduate students served 1997–98:* 6 at the postgraduate level. *Faculty:* 40: 30 affiliated solely with the center. *Faculty affiliations:* Departments of Biomedical Engineering, Epidemiology, Pharmacology, Physiology; School of Public Health. *Annual research budget:* $3 million. *Director:* Dr. Sidney C. Smith Jr., 919-966-0732, Fax: 919-966-1743, E-mail: scs@med.unc.edu.

Center for Global Business Research Founded in 1990. *Academic areas of research and training:* International business, privatization, business and the environment, trade and investment, international competitiveness. *Degrees offered:* None. *Graduate students served 1997–98:* 3 at the doctoral level. *Faculty:* 16: 4 affiliated solely with the center. *Faculty affiliations:* Kenan-Flagler Business School. *Director:* Dr. Dennis A. Rondinelli, 919-962-8201, Fax: 919-962-8202.

Center for Pharmaceutical Outcomes Research Founded in 1994. *Academic areas of research and training:* Pharmaceutical outcomes research, pharmacoeconomics and policy, pharmacoepidemiology. *Degrees offered:* None. *Graduate students served 1997–98:* 8 at the master's level; 6 at the doctoral level. *Faculty:* 10: 2 affiliated solely with the center. *Faculty affiliations:* Departments of Epidemiology, Health Policy and Administration; Division of Pharmacy Policy and Evaluative Sciences. *Annual research budget:* $130,000. *Director:* Dr. Abraham G. Hartzema, 919-962-0080, Fax: 919-966-8486, E-mail: bram_hartzema@unc.edu.

The Center for Research on Chronic Illness (CRCI) *Academic areas of research and training:* Prevention or management of chronic illness or diseases in vulnerable people. *Degrees offered:* None. *Graduate students served 1997–98:* 8: 2 at the doctoral level; 6 at the postgraduate level. *Faculty:* 45. *Faculty affiliations:* Department of Psychology; Schools of Medicine, Nursing, Public Health. *Annual research budget:* $1,994. *Director:* Dr. Joanne Harrell, E-mail: jharrell.uncson@mhs.unc.edu. *Information contact:* Ms. Ginny Dudek, Project Manager, 919-966-0453, Fax: 919-966-0456, E-mail: gdudek.uncson@mhs.unc.edu.

Frank Porter Graham Child Development Center Founded in 1966. *Academic areas of research and training:* Research, training, and policy analyses related to young children, their families, and the institutions or programs designed to serve young children. *Degrees offered:* None. *Graduate students served 1997–98:* 70: 20 at the master's level; 50 at the doctoral level. *Faculty:* 52: 37 affiliated solely with the center. *Faculty affiliations:* Department of Psychology; Schools of Education, Medicine, Nursing, Public Health. *Annual research budget:* $17 million. *Director:* Dr. Don Bailey, 919-966-4250, E-mail: don_bailey@unc.edu. *Information contact:* Dr. Virginia Buysse, Assistant Director, 919-966-7171, Fax: 919-966-7532, E-mail: virginia_buysse@unc.edu.

Global Manufacturing Research Center Founded in 1991. *Academic areas of research and training:* International manufacturing. *Degrees offered:* None. *Faculty:* 2. *Faculty affiliations:* Kenan-Flagler Business School. *Director:* Dr. D. Clay Whybark, 919-962-3206, Fax: 919-962-5539, E-mail: clay_whybark@unc.edu.

Lineberger Comprehensive Cancer Center Founded in 1975. *Academic areas of research and training:* Cancer research including basic laboratory science, clinical research, and care; cancer prevention; population science. *Degrees offered:* None. *Faculty affiliations:* College of Arts and Sciences; Schools of Dentistry, Medicine, Nursing, Pharmacy, Public Health. *Director:* Dr. H. Shelton Earp III, 919-966-3036, Fax: 919-966-3015.

University of North Carolina at Charlotte, Charlotte, NC 28223-0001

Center for Banking Studies Founded in 1995. *Academic areas of research and training:* Banking and financial services management, financial research, graduate banking education, financial institution regulation. *Degrees offered:* None. *Graduate students served 1997–98:* 100: 90 at the master's level. *Faculty:* 91: 4 affiliated solely with the center. *Faculty affiliations:* College of Business Administration. *Annual research budget:* $100,000. *Director:* Dr. Tony Plath, 704-547-4413, Fax: 704-547-3123, E-mail: daplath@email.uncc.edu.

University of North Dakota, Grand Forks, ND 58202

The Center for Innovation and Business Development Founded in 1984. *Academic areas of research and training:* Technology entrepreneurship, product innovation, business and market planning. *Degrees offered:* None. *Graduate students served 1997–98:* 7: 6 at the master's level; 1 at the doctoral level. *Faculty:* 22: 12 affiliated solely with the center. *Faculty affiliations:* Departments of Industrial Technology, Mechanical Engineering; Programs in Finance, Management, Marketing. *Director:* Bruce Gjovig, E-mail: gjovig@prairie.nodak.edu. *Information contact:* James Melland, Associate Director, 701-777-3132, Fax: 701-777-2339.

Natural Resource Center on Native American Aging Founded in 1993. *Academic areas of research and training:* Health care, nutrition. *Degrees offered:* None. *Faculty:* 3 affiliated solely with the center. *Faculty affiliations:* School of Social Work, Center for Rural Health. *Director:* Alan Allery, 701-777-3293, Fax: 701-777-3292, E-mail: allery@badlands.nodak.edu.

University of North Texas, Denton, TX 76203-6737

Center for Economic Development and Research Founded in 1989. *Academic areas of research and training:* Public policy, economic development. *Degrees offered:* MS. *Graduate students served 1997–98:* 12 at the master's level. *Faculty:* 6: 4 affiliated solely with the center. *Faculty affiliations:* College of Business Administration, Program in Geography. *Annual research budget:* $200,000. *Director:* Dr. Bernard L. Weinstein, 940-565-4049, Fax: 940-565-4658, E-mail: budw@scs.cmm.unt.edu.

Center for Play Therapy Founded in 1988. *Academic areas of research and training:* Play therapy, supervised play therapy practica and internships, play therapy summer Institute workshops, annual play therapy conference. *Degrees offered:* MA; MS; PhD. *Graduate students served 1997–98:* 7: 1 at the master's level; 5 at the doctoral level; 1 at the postgraduate level. *Faculty:* 1 affiliated solely with the center. *Director:* Dr. Garry Landreth, 940-565-3864, Fax: 940-565-4461, E-mail: cpt@coefs.coe.unt.edu.

Center for Quality and Productivity Founded in 1987. *Academic areas of research and training:* Quality control, productivity. *Degrees offered:* None. *Graduate students served 1997–98:* 3: 2 at the doctoral level; 1 at the postgraduate level. *Faculty:* 7. *Faculty affiliations:* College of Business Administration, School of Library and Information Sciences. *Annual research budget:* $40,000. *Director:* Dr. Victor R. Prybutok, 940-565-3110, Fax: 940-565-4935, E-mail: prybutok@unt.edu.

Counseling and Human Development Center Founded in 1987. *Academic areas of research and training:* Individual and group counseling experiences required of counselor education graduate students. *Degrees offered:* None. *Graduate students served 1997–98:* 76: 64 at the master's level; 12 at the doctoral level. *Faculty:* 13. *Faculty affiliations:* Program in Counselor Education, Counseling and Testing Center. *Director:* Beth Durodoye, 940-565-2970, Fax: 940-565-2905, E-mail: durodoye@coefs.coe.unt.edu.

Institute of Petroleum Accounting Founded in 1982. *Academic areas of research and training:* Petroleum accounting, financial management. *Degrees offered:* None. *Graduate students served 1997–98:* 10 at the doctoral level. *Faculty:* 6: 2 affiliated solely with the institute. *Faculty affiliations:* Departments of Accounting, Economics. *Annual research budget:* $100,000. *Director:* Dr. Teddy L. Coe, 940-565-3170, Fax: 940-369-8839, E-mail: coet@unt.edu.

Speech and Hearing Center Founded in 1966. *Academic areas of research and training:* Diagnosis and management of speech, language, and hearing disorders. *Degrees offered:* None. *Graduate students served 1997–98:* 100 at the master's level. *Faculty:* 14 affiliated solely with the center. *Director:* Ms. Pat Summers, 940-565-2262, Fax: 940-565-4058, E-mail: summers@cas.unt.edu.

University of Notre Dame, Notre Dame, IN 46556

Center for Civil and Human Rights Founded in 1973. *Academic areas of research and training:* International human rights law and domestic civil rights statutes, human rights implementation, regional regimes, accountability, development, and environment. *Degrees offered:* JSD. *Graduate students served 1997–98:* 12: 11 at the master's level; 1 at the doctoral level. *Faculty:* 8: 3 affiliated solely with the center. *Faculty affiliations:* Law School. *Annual research budget:* $198,000. *Director:* David T. Link, Interim Director and Dean of Law

Directory: Research and Training Opportunities

Center for Civil and Human Rights (continued)
School, 219-631-8555. *Information contact:* Mr. Garth Meintjes, Associate Director, 219-631-8544, Fax: 219-631-8702, E-mail: garth.meintjes.1@nd.edu.

University of Pennsylvania, Philadelphia, PA 19104

Center for the Study of the History of Nursing Founded in 1985. *Academic areas of research and training:* History of nursing and health care. *Degrees offered:* None. *Graduate students served 1997–98:* 10 at the doctoral level. *Faculty:* 4. *Faculty affiliations:* School of Nursing. *Director:* Dr. Karen Buhler-Wilkenson. *Information contact:* Ms. Margo Szabunia, Curator, 215-898-4502, Fax: 215-573-2168, E-mail: nhistory@pobox.upenn.edu.

University of Pittsburgh, Pittsburgh, PA 15260

Alzheimer's Disease Research Center Founded in 1985. *Academic areas of research and training:* Alzheimer's Disease research and training. *Degrees offered:* None. *Graduate students served 1997–98:* 24: 12 at the master's level; 12 at the postgraduate level. *Faculty:* 27. *Faculty affiliations:* Graduate School of Public Health, School of Medicine. *Annual research budget:* $1.5 million. *Director:* Dr. Steven DeKosky, 412-624-6889, Fax: 412-692-2710, E-mail: dekosky@vms.cis.pitt.edu.

Center for Medical Ethics Founded in 1986. *Academic areas of research and training:* Bioethics, medical ethics. *Degrees offered:* MA. *Graduate students served 1997–98:* 10 at the master's level. *Faculty:* 24: 12 affiliated solely with the center. *Faculty affiliations:* Faculty of Arts and Sciences; Graduate School of Public and International Affairs; Schools of Law, Medicine, Nursing, Public Health. *Annual research budget:* $200,000. *Director:* Dr. Alan Meisel, Professor of Bioethics and Law, 412-647-5701, Fax: 412-647-5877, E-mail: meisel@med.pitt.edu.

Head Injury Research Center Founded in 1990. *Academic areas of research and training:* Basic and clinical research of traumatic brain injury. *Degrees offered:* None. *Faculty:* 7. *Faculty affiliations:* Programs in Anesthesia/CCM, Neurology, Neurosurgery, Psychiatry; School of Medicine. *Director:* Dr. Donald Marion, Professor, 412-647-0956, Fax: 412-647-7337, E-mail: dmarion@neuronet.pitt.edu.

Health Policy Institute Founded in 1980. *Academic areas of research and training:* Health policy. *Degrees offered:* None. *Graduate students served 1997–98:* 2: 1 at the master's level; 1 at the doctoral level. *Faculty:* 6: 2 affiliated solely with the institute. *Faculty affiliations:* Graduate School of Public Health. *Annual research budget:* $350,000. *Director:* Dr. Beaufort B. Longest Jr., 412-624-6104, Fax: 412-624-7747, E-mail: longest@vms.cis.pitt.edu.

Pittsburgh Poison Center Founded in 1971. *Academic areas of research and training:* Clinical toxicology. *Degrees offered:* None. *Graduate students served 1997–98:* 4: 3 at the doctoral level. *Faculty:* 4: 1 affiliated solely with the center. *Faculty affiliations:* Schools of Medicine, Pharmacy. *Director:* Dr. Edward P. Krenzelok, 412-692-5600, Fax: 412-692-7497.

Protein Research Laboratory Founded in 1964. *Academic areas of research and training:* Biochemical aspects of endocrinology, biochemical focus on cancer, development of artificial liver, cell differentiation. *Degrees offered:* None. *Faculty:* 4: 2 affiliated solely with the laboratory. *Faculty affiliations:* Program in Surgery, School of Medicine. *Annual research budget:* $500,000. *Director:* Dr. Frances M. Finn, 412-648-9632, Fax: 412-648-2117, E-mail: fmf+@pitt.edu.

University of Regina, Regina, SK S4S 0A2, Canada

Social Policy Research Unit (SPR) Founded in 1972. *Academic areas of research and training:* Child welfare, family violence, international work, social policy and the economy, status of women issues. *Degrees offered:* None. *Graduate students served 1997–98:* 50 at the master's level. *Faculty:* 15 affiliated solely with the unit. *Annual research budget:* $80,000. *Director:* Dr. Dave Broad, 306-585-4588, Fax: 306-585-4872, E-mail: dave.broad@uregina.ca. *Information contact:* Ms. Fiona Douglas, Research Coordinator, 306-585-4036, Fax: 306-585-5408, E-mail: fiona.douglas@uregina.ca.

University of Rhode Island, Kingston, RI 02881

Institute for the Study of International Aspects of Competition (ISIAC) Founded in 1980. *Academic areas of research and training:* Industrial organization, international trade. *Degrees offered:* None. *Graduate students served 1997–98:* 8: 2 at the master's level; 4 at the doctoral level; 2 at the postgraduate level. *Faculty:* 3: 1 affiliated solely with the institute. *Faculty affiliations:* Department of Economics. *Annual research budget:* $1,000. *Director:* Dr. John P. Burkett, Executive Director, 401-874-4122, Fax: 401-792-0110, E-mail: burkett@uriacc.uri.edu.

University of Rochester, Rochester, NY 14627-0001

Center for Environmental Health Sciences Founded in 1966. *Academic areas of research and training:* Cellular and molecular toxicology, carcinogenesis, immunotoxicology, neurobehavioral toxicology, pulmonary toxicology, reproductive and developmental toxicology. *Degrees offered:* None. *Faculty:* 38: 30 affiliated solely with the center. *Faculty affiliations:* Departments of Biochemistry and Biophysics, Microbiology and Immunology, Neurobiology and Anatomy, Pathology, Pharmacology and Physiology; Programs in Obstetrics and Gynecology, Pediatrics, Radiation Oncology. *Director:* Thomas Clarkson, 716-274-8820.

Center for Nursing Science and Scholarly Practice Founded in 1994. *Academic areas of research and training:* Health promotion and risk reduction, outcomes management and measurement. *Degrees offered:* None. *Graduate students served 1997–98:* 12 at the doctoral level. *Annual research budget:* $1.3 million. *Director:* Dr. Veronica F. Rempusheski, 716-275-7376, E-mail: vrem@son.rochester.edu.

University of South Alabama, Mobile, AL 36688-0002

Center for Business and Economic Research Founded in 1985. *Academic areas of research and training:* Applied business and economic research. *Degrees offered:* None. *Graduate students served 1997–98:* 1 at the master's level. *Faculty affiliations:* College of Business and Management. *Annual research budget:* $20,000. *Director:* Dr. Semoon Chang, 334-460-6156, Fax: 334-460-6246, E-mail: schang@jaguar1.usouthal.edu.

University of South Carolina, Columbia, SC 29208

Center for Applied Real Estate Education and Research Founded in 1971. *Academic areas of research and training:* Applied real estate research. *Degrees offered:* None. *Graduate students served 1997–98:* 3: 2 at the master's level; 1 at the doctoral level. *Faculty affiliations:* Program in Finance. *Annual research budget:* $50,000. *Director:* Dr. Ronald C. Rogers, 803-777-5960, Fax: 803-777-6876, E-mail: rrogers@darla.badm.sc.edu.

Center for International Business Education and Research (CIBER) Founded in 1989. *Academic areas of research and training:* Promotion of international business; global environment and international marketing; finance; accounting; management science; economics; information management. *Degrees offered:* None. *Graduate students served 1997–98:* 382: 302 at the master's level; 14 at the doctoral level; 66 at the postgraduate level. *Faculty:* 28: 1 affiliated solely with the center. *Faculty affiliations:* Departments of Economics; French and Classics; Germanic, Slavic and Oriental Languages; Government and International Studies; Spanish, Italian, and Portuguese; Programs in Accounting; Chinese; Finance; International Business; Japanese; Management; Management Science; Marketing. *Director:* Dr. William R. Folks Jr., 803-777-3600, Fax: 803-777-3609, E-mail: rfolks@darla.badm.sc.edu.

Center for the Study of Suicide and Life-Threatening Behavior Founded in 1985. *Academic areas of research and training:* Problems of suicide and life-threatening behaviors. *Degrees offered:* MA; PhD. *Graduate students served 1997–98:* 6 at the master's level; 3 at the doctoral level. *Faculty:* 23: 12 affiliated solely with the center. *Faculty affiliations:* College of Nursing, Department of Psychology, Program in Psychiatry, School of Public Health. *Annual research budget:* $50,000. *Director:* Dr. Robert W. Maris, 803-777-6870, Fax: 803-777-1762, E-mail: maris@garnet.cla.sc.edu.

University of Southern California, Los Angeles, CA 90089

Lusk Center for Real Estate Development Founded in 1986. *Academic areas of research and training:* Real estate development, finance, public-private deal structuring, urban research. *Degrees offered:* None. *Graduate students served 1997–98:* 46: 40 at the master's level; 4 at the doctoral level; 2 at the postgraduate level. *Faculty:* 10. *Faculty affiliations:* Graduate School of Business; Leonard Davis School of Gerontology; Schools of Architecture, Urban and Regional Planning. *Annual research budget:* $200,000. *Director:* Dr. Richard Peiser, 213-743-2172, Fax: 213-743-2476, E-mail: peiser@almaak.usc.edu.

University of Southern Maine, Portland, ME 04104-9300

Center for Business and Economic Research (CBER) *Academic areas of research and training:* Technical assistance to economic development agencies and profit/non-profit organizations; business services. *Degrees offered:* None. *Graduate students served 1997–98:* 6: 3 at the master's level. *Faculty:* 6. *Faculty affiliations:* Program in Public Policy and Management, School of Business. *Director:* Dr. Bruce H. Andrews, Co-Director, 207-780-4046, Fax: 207-780-4187, E-mail: usmcber@maine.maine.edu.

University of South Florida, Tampa, FL 33620-9951

Center for Economic Development Research (CEDR) Founded in 1977. *Academic areas of research and training:* Regional economic development. *Degrees offered:* None. *Graduate students served 1997–98:* 4. *Faculty:* 4 affiliated solely with the center. *Annual research budget:* $120,000. *Director:* Kenneth Wieand, 813-974-2377, Fax: 813-974-4978, E-mail: kwieand@coba.usf.edu.

Center for Urban Transportation Research (CUTR) Founded in 1988. *Academic areas of research and training:* Transportation policy and financing. *Degrees offered:* None. *Graduate students served 1997–98:* 25: 17 at the master's level; 2 at the doctoral level; 1 at the postgraduate level. *Faculty:* 60: 40 affiliated solely with the center. *Faculty affiliations:* Colleges of Engineering, Public Health; Department of Economics; Programs in Business Administration, Public Administration. *Annual research budget:* $5 million. *Director:* Mr. Gary L. Brosch, 813-974-3120, Fax: 813-974-5168, E-mail: brosch@cutr.eng.usf.edu.

The University of Tampa, Tampa, FL 33606-1490

Center for Leadership *Academic areas of research and training:* Leadership, organizational behavior, team facilitation. *Degrees offered:* None. *Graduate students served 1997–98:* 240 at the master's level. *Faculty:* 9: 3 affiliated solely with the center. *Faculty affiliations:* Departments of International Business, Management, Marketing, Nursing Administration, Psychology. *Annual research budget:* $20,000. *Director:* Dr. Stephen A. Stumpf, 813-253-6271, E-mail: steve.stumpf@resnet.fmhi.usf.edu. *Information contact:* Dr. Dale Bracken, Associate Director, 813-253-3333 Ext. 3531, Fax: 813-258-7408.

University of Tennessee, Knoxville, Knoxville, TN 37996

Center for Business and Economic Research Founded in 1937. *Academic areas of research and training:* Economic research, economic forecasting. *Degrees offered:* None. *Graduate students served 1997–98:* 4 at the doctoral level. *Faculty:* 3. *Faculty affiliations:* College of Business. *Annual research budget:* $650,000. *Director:* Dr. William Fox, 423-974-1697. *Information contact:* Center Office, 423-974-5441, Fax: 423-974-3100 Ext. 6112, E-mail: billfox@utk.edu.

University of Tennessee, Memphis, Memphis, TN 38163-0002

Boling Center for Developmental Disabilities (BCDD) Founded in 1957. *Academic areas of research and training:* Developmental disabilities, child development, genetics, rehabilitation technology psychiatry. *Degrees offered:* None. *Graduate students served 1997–98:* 228: 31 at the master's level; 169 at the doctoral level; 28 at the postgraduate level. *Faculty:* 25: 9 affiliated solely with the center. *Faculty affiliations:* Programs in Child/Adolescent Psychiatry, Clinical Genetics, Physical and Nutritional Management, Rehabilitation Engineering, Reproductive Genetics. *Director:* Dr. Frederick B. Palmer, 901-448-6511, Fax: 901-448-7097, E-mail: fpalmer@utmem1.utmem.edu.

The University of Texas at Austin, Austin, TX 78712

Bureau of Business Research (BBR) Founded in 1926. *Academic areas of research and training:* Competitiveness of Texas industries, particularly manufacturing; research on the organizational and resource strategies of industries. *Degrees offered:* None. *Graduate students served 1997–98:* 20. *Faculty:* 1. *Faculty affiliations:* Program in Marketing. *Director:* Dr. Raj Srivastava, 512-471-4834. *Information contact:* Dr. Lois Shrout, Associate Director, 512-475-7813, Fax: 512-471-1063, E-mail: shrout@mail.utexas.edu.

Center for Vision and Image Sciences Founded in 1993. *Academic areas of research and training:* Human vision, computer vision, visual neurophysiology, image processing. *Degrees offered:* None. *Graduate students served 1997–98:* 9: 2 at the master's level; 7 at the doctoral level. *Faculty:* 6: 2 affiliated solely with the center. *Faculty affiliations:* Biomedical Research Program; Departments of Electrical and Computer Engineering, Psychology. *Annual research budget:* $800,000. *Director:* Dr. Wilson S. Geisler, E-mail: geisler@psy.utexas.edu. *Information contact:* Ms. Christine Fry, Administrative Assistant, 512-471-5380, Fax: 512-471-7356, E-mail: fry@psy.utexas.edu.

Innovation, Creativity, and Capital Institute (IC&S2 Institute) Founded in 1976. *Academic areas of research and training:* Innovation, creativity, capital, enterprise system, science and technology commercialization, technology transfer, global economic issues, economic wealth creation, regional economic development, experimental learning. *Degrees offered:* MS. *Graduate students served 1997–98:* 98: 80 at the master's level; 15 at the doctoral level; 3 at the postgraduate level. *Faculty:* 28: 3 affiliated solely with the institute. *Faculty affiliations:* Colleges of Business Administration, Communication, Engineering; Lyndon B. Johnson School of Public Affairs. *Annual research budget:* $2.6 million. *Director:* Dr. George Kosmetsky, Interim Director, 512-475-8900, Fax: 512-475-8902, E-mail: georgek@icc.utexas.edu. *Information contact:* Dr. Barbara Fossum, Associate Director for MSSTC, 512-475-8957, Fax: 512-475-8903, E-mail: bfossum@icc.utexas.edu.

J. J. Pickle Research Center Founded in 1963. *Academic areas of research and training:* Engineering science, social sciences. *Degrees offered:* None. *Graduate students served 1997–98:* 550: 200 at the master's level; 300 at the doctoral level; 50 at the postgraduate level. *Faculty:* 200. *Faculty affiliations:* Colleges of Arts and Sciences, Business Administration, Engineering. *Director:* Dr. Marye Anne Fox, Vice President for Research, 512-471-2877, Fax: 512-471-2827, E-mail: vp-research@mail.utexas.edu.

The University of Texas at Dallas, Richardson, TX 75083-0688

Callier Center for Communication Disorders Founded in 1962. *Academic areas of research and training:* Communication disorders, audiology, speech-language pathology. *Degrees offered:* None. *Graduate students served 1997–98:* 145: 125 at the master's level; 20 at the doctoral level. *Faculty:* 34: 17 affiliated solely with the center. *Faculty affiliations:* School of Human

Development. *Annual research budget:* $2.6 million. *Director:* Dr. Ross J. Roeser, 214-883-3000, Fax: 214-883-3022.

Center for Education and Social Policy Founded in 1991. *Academic areas of research and training:* Education policy, reading, literacy. *Degrees offered:* None. *Faculty:* 4. *Faculty affiliations:* School of Social Sciences. *Annual research budget:* $85,000. *Director:* Dr. George Farkas, 972-883-2937, Fax: 972-883-2735, E-mail: farkas@utdallas.edu.

Center for International Accounting Development Founded in 1976. *Academic areas of research and training:* Developing international accounting. *Degrees offered:* None. *Faculty affiliations:* School of Management. *Annual research budget:* $120,000. *Director:* Dr. Adolf Enthoven, 972-883-2320, Fax: 972-883-2192.

Morris Hite Center for Product Development and Marketing Science Founded in 1984. *Academic areas of research and training:* Links between engineering, product design and marketing. *Degrees offered:* None. *Graduate students served 1997–98:* 2 at the doctoral level. *Faculty:* 6. *Faculty affiliations:* School of Management. *Annual research budget:* $75,000. *Director:* Dr. Frank Bass, 972-883-2744, Fax: 972-883-2799, E-mail: mzjb@utdallas.edu.

The University of Texas–Houston Health Science Center, Houston, TX 77225-0036

Houston Biomaterials Research Center Founded in 1994. *Academic areas of research and training:* Oral biomaterials. *Degrees offered:* None. *Graduate students served 1997–98:* 10: 6 at the master's level; 1 at the doctoral level; 3 at the postgraduate level. *Faculty:* 24. *Faculty affiliations:* Dental School, Medical School; Baylor College of Dentistry; Baylor College of Medicine; Rice University Biomedical Engineering; Texas A&M University Biomedical Engineering; University of Munich; University of North Carolina; University of Regensburg; University of Texas Health Science Center at San Antonio. *Annual research budget:* $150,000. *Director:* Dr. John M. Powers, 713-500-4191, Fax: 713-500-4500, E-mail: jpowers@mail.db.uth.tmc.edu.

The University of Texas Medical Branch at Galveston, Galveston, TX 77555

Institute for the Medical Humanities Founded in 1973. *Academic areas of research and training:* Medical humanities, bioethics. *Degrees offered:* MA; PhD; MD/PhD and JD/PhD. *Graduate students served 1997–98:* 25: 2 at the master's level; 23 at the doctoral level. *Faculty:* 12: 10 affiliated solely with the institute. *Faculty affiliations:* Programs in Internal Medicine, Psychiatry. *Director:* Dr. Ronald Carson, 409-772-2376, Fax: 409-772-5640, E-mail: racarson@utmb.edu.

Marine Biomedical Institute Founded in 1969. *Academic areas of research and training:* Neuroscience, pain research, eye movemement control, cephalopod biology, hyperbaric medicine, functional MRI. *Degrees offered:* None. *Graduate students served 1997–98:* 14 at the master's level; 2 at the doctoral level; 20 at the postgraduate level. *Faculty:* 44: 25 affiliated solely with the institute. *Faculty affiliations:* Programs in Anatomy and Neurosciences, Anesthesiology, Biochemistry, Cellular Physiology and Molecular Biophysics, Human Biological Chemistry and Genetics, Internal Medicine, Otolaryngology. *Annual research budget:* $7 million. *Director:* Dr. William D. Willis, 409-772-2103, E-mail: wdwillis@utmb.edu. *Information contact:* Ms. Lori Del Buono, Chief, Administrative Division, 409-772-2101, Fax: 409-772-4687, E-mail: ljdelbuo@utmb.edu.

University of Toledo, Toledo, OH 43606-3398

The Center for Drug Design and Development (CD3) Founded in 1994. *Academic areas of research and training:* Drug discovery and development in all therapeutic areas, oncology, central nervous system, metabolism, diabetes. *Degrees offered:* None. *Graduate students served 1997–98:* 4: 1 at the master's level; 3 at the doctoral level. *Faculty:* 50: 10 affiliated solely with the center. *Faculty affiliations:* Programs in Clinical Pharmacy, Medicinal and Biological Chemistry, Pharmacology, Physical Pharmacy. *Annual research budget:* $100,000. *Director:* Paul W. Erhardt, 419-530-1933, Fax: 419-530-1907, E-mail: perhard@utnet.utoledo.edu.

The International Business Institute (IBI) Founded in 1978. *Academic areas of research and training:* International and global business, competitiveness, international marketing, international management, FDI. *Degrees offered:* None. *Graduate students served 1997–98:* 35 at the master's level. *Faculty:* 25. *Faculty affiliations:* College of Law; Departments of Accounting, Finance, Information Systems and Operation Management, Management; Programs in Marketing, Operations/Production. *Director:* Dr. Don R. Beeman, 419-530-2068, Fax: 419-530-8497, E-mail: dbeeman@pop3.utoledo.edu.

University of Toronto, Toronto, ON M5S 1A1, Canada

Institute for Human Development, Life Course and Aging Founded in 1978. *Academic areas of research and training:* Community health, health administration, nursing, psychology, social work, sociology, rehabilitation science, industrial relations, information studies. *Degrees offered:* None. *Graduate students served 1997–98:* 21: 7 at the master's level; 11 at the doctoral level; 1 at the postgraduate level. *Faculty:* 59: 1 affiliated solely with the institute. *Faculty affiliations:* Departments of Anthropology, Community Health, Economics, Geography, Information Studies, Nursing Science, Nutritional Sciences, Pharmaceutical Sciences, Physiology, Psychology, Social Work, Sociology, Speech Language Pathology; Faculties of Dentistry, Law, Management, Medicine. *Annual research budget:* $.75 million. *Director:* Dr. Victor W. Marshall, 416-978-7910, Fax: 416-978-4771.

Institute for Policy Analysis *Academic areas of research and training:* Contracting theory and economics of restrictive business practices, film organization, impact of federal housing initiatives, insurance law, policy and economic analysis (macroeconomic models). *Degrees offered:* None. *Graduate students served 1997–98:* 10. *Faculty:* 31: 1 affiliated solely with the institute. *Faculty affiliations:* Departments of Community Health, Economics, Political Science, Social Work; Faculty of Law and Management. *Director:* Dr. G. F. Mathewson, 416-978-6127, Fax: 416-978-5519, E-mail: frankm@chass.utoronto.ca.

University of Utah, Salt Lake City, UT 84112-1107

Bureau of Economic and Business Research Founded in 1932. *Academic areas of research and training:* Economic analysis, economic development, research training, economic impact. *Degrees offered:* None. *Graduate students served 1997–98:* 4: 2 at the master's level; 1 at the doctoral level; 1 at the postgraduate level. *Faculty:* 4: 3 affiliated solely with the bureau. *Faculty affiliations:* David Eccles School of Business, Department of Economics. *Annual research budget:* $600,000. *Director:* R. Thayne Robson, 801-581-7274, Fax: 801-581-3354, E-mail: bebrrtr@business.utah.edu.

Matheson Center for Health Care Studies Founded in 1988. *Academic areas of research and training:* Health policy and administration. *Degrees offered:* None. *Graduate students served 1997–98:* 35 at the master's level. *Faculty:* 2. *Faculty affiliations:* Department of Political Science; Program in Public Administration; Schools of Business, Medicine. *Annual research budget:* $100,000. *Director:* Robert P. Huefner, 801-581-6043, E-mail: robert.huefner@geog.utah.edu. *Information contact:* Kim Segal, Program Manager, 801-581-4673, Fax: 801-585-5489, E-mail: kim.segal@cppa.utah.edu.

Social Research Institute (SRI) Founded in 1982. *Academic areas of research and training:* Aging, child welfare, housing, welfare reform, youth corrections. *Degrees offered:* None. *Graduate students served 1997–98:* 25: 20 at the master's level; 5 at the doctoral level. *Faculty:* 25: 3 affiliated solely with the institute. *Faculty affiliations:* Graduate School of Social Work. *Annual research budget:* $1 million. *Director:* Dr. Amanda S. Barusch, 801-581-8842, Fax: 801-585-3219, E-mail: abarusch@socwk.utah.edu.

Western Laboratory for Leisure Research Founded in 1987. *Academic areas of research and training:* Leisure behavior and systems management; consumer services; outdoor education with children and youth, especially "at risk" youth. *Degrees offered:* None. *Graduate students served 1997–98:* 5: 3 at the master's level; 2 at the doctoral level. *Faculty:* 9: 2 affiliated solely with the laboratory. *Faculty affiliations:* Departments of Family and Consumer Studies, Health Education; Gerontology Center. *Annual research budget:* $350,000. *Director:* Dr. David M. Compton, Executive Director, 801-581-8754, Fax: 801-581-8037, E-mail: david.compton@health.utah.edu.

University of Virginia, Charlottesville, VA 22903

Center for Risk Management Founded in 1987. *Degrees offered:* None. *Graduate students served 1997–98:* 5: 3 at the master's level; 2 at the doctoral level. *Faculty:* 3 affiliated solely with the center. *Director:* Yacov Y. Haimes, 804-924-0960, Fax: 804-924-0865.

Center for Transportation Studies Founded in 1975. *Academic areas of research and training:* Civil engineering, planning, systems engineering, intelligent transportation technology, simulation and operations. *Degrees offered:* None. *Graduate students served 1997–98:* 31: 12 at the master's level; 6 at the doctoral level; 13 at the postgraduate level. *Faculty:* 19: 4 affiliated solely with the center. *Faculty affiliations:* Departments of City and Environmental Planning; Electrical Engineering; Environmental Sciences; Mechanical, Aerospace, and Nuclear Engineering; Systems Engineering; Program in Commerce. *Annual research budget:* $1.5 million. *Director:* Dr. Michael J. Demetsky, 804-924-6362, E-mail: mjd@virginia.edu. *Information contact:* Mrs. Cindy Sites, Administrator, 804-924-4775, Fax: 804-982-2951, E-mail: css5b@virginia.edu.

University of Washington, Seattle, WA 98195

Center for Ecogenetics and Environmental Health Founded in 1995. *Academic areas of research and training:* Genetic-environment interactions, toxicology, pharmacology, pathology, environmental health, risk assessment, genetics, epidemiology. *Degrees offered:* None. *Graduate students served 1997–98:* 35: 5 at the master's level; 20 at the doctoral level; 10 at the postgraduate level. *Faculty:* 45. *Faculty affiliations:* Departments of Environmental Health, Epidemiology, Genetics, Pathology, Pharmacology; Programs in Medicinal Chemistry, Pediatrics; School of Medicine. *Annual research budget:* $900,000. *Director:* Dr. David L. Eaton, 206-685-3785, Fax: 206-685-4696, E-mail: deaton@u.washington.edu.

Center for International Trade in Forest Products Founded in 1985. *Academic areas of research and training:* International trade in forest products, marketing, economic research, forest policy, environmental assessments. *Degrees offered:* None. *Graduate students served 1997–98:* 4 at the master's level; 4 at the doctoral level; 1 at the postgraduate level. *Faculty:* 10: 4 affiliated solely with the center. *Faculty affiliations:* College of Forest Resources. *Annual research budget:* $600,000. *Director:* Mr. Bruce R. Lippke, 206-543-8684, Fax: 206-685-0790, E-mail: blippke@u.washington.edu.

Northwest Center for Occupational Health and Safety *Director:* 206-543-1069, E-mail: ce@u.washington.edu.

Social Development Research Group (SDRG) Founded in 1979. *Academic areas of research and training:* Basic research, prevention and treatment of health and behavior problems among young people. *Degrees offered:* None. *Graduate students served 1997–98:* 9 at the doctoral level. *Faculty:* 14: 7 affiliated solely with the group. *Faculty affiliations:* College of Education, Health Services Administration and Planning Group, Program in Biostatistics, School of Social Work. *Annual research budget:* $4.2 million. *Director:* Dr. J. David Hawkins, E-mail: sdrg@u.washington.edu. *Information contact:* Ms. Cynthia Shaw, Public Information Specialist, 206-685-1997, Fax: 206-543-4507, E-mail: cgshaw@u.washington.edu.

University of West Florida, Pensacola, FL 32514-5750

Raymond M. Haas Center for Business Research and Economic Development Founded in 1994. *Academic areas of research and training:* Regional economic development; data collection, analysis, and dissemination; business research. *Degrees offered:* None. *Graduate students served 1997–98:* 12. *Faculty:* 42. *Faculty affiliations:* College of Business. *Annual research budget:* $220,000. *Director:* Dr. Richard K. Harper, Interim Director, 850-474-2657, Fax: 850-474-3174, E-mail: rharper@uwf.edu.

University of Wisconsin–Milwaukee, Milwaukee, WI 53201-0413

University of Wisconsin Institute on Race and Ethnicity Founded in 1987. *Academic areas of research and training:* Research and curricular innovation in racial/ethnic studies. *Degrees offered:* None. *Faculty:* 9. *Faculty affiliations:* Program in Educational Psychology. *Director:* Adrian Chan, 414-229-5053, Fax: 414-229-4581, E-mail: achan@csd.uwm.edu.

University of Wisconsin–Superior, Superior, WI 54880-2873

Center for Economic Development *Degrees offered:* None. *Faculty:* 1 affiliated solely with the center. *Director:* Dr. Don Hinman, 715-394-8208, Fax: 715-394-8277, E-mail: dhinman@staff.uwsuper.edu.

Utah State University, Logan, UT 84322

Center for Persons with Disabilities (CPD) *Academic areas of research and training:* Biological research, instructional development, technology. *Degrees offered:* None. *Graduate students served 1997–98:* 79: 25 at the master's level; 45 at the doctoral level; 1 at the postgraduate level. *Faculty:* 200 affiliated solely with the center. *Faculty affiliations:* Departments of Biology, Communicative Disorders, Computer Science, Family Life, Instructional Technology, Psychology, Special Education and Rehabilitation. *Annual research budget:* $3.47 million. *Director:* Dr. Marvin G. Fifield, 435-797-1982, Fax: 435-797-3944, E-mail: marv@cpd2.usu.edu.

Vanderbilt University, Nashville, TN 37240-1001

The John F. Kennedy Center for Research on Human Development Founded in 1965. *Academic areas of research and training:* Collaborative research, training, and information dissemination on behavioral, intellectual, and brain development; training programs include: research behavioral scientists in mental retardation; developmental psychopathology; vision research; cellular and molecular science, early childhood special education. *Degrees offered:* None. *Graduate students served 1997–98:* 200: 110 at the master's level; 70 at the doctoral level; 20 at the postgraduate level. *Faculty affiliations:* Departments of Cell Biology, Educational Leadership, General Biology, Hearing and Speech Science, Molecular Biology, Molecular Physiology and Biophysics, Pathology, Pediatrics, Pharmacology, Psychiatry, Psychology and Human Development, Radiology, Special Education; Schools of Medicine, Nursing. *Annual research budget:* $11.34 million. *Director:* Dr. Travis I. Thompson. *Information contact:* Dr. Jan Rosemergy, Director of Communications, 615-322-8240, Fax: 615-322-8236, E-mail: jan.rosemergy@vanderbilt.edu.

Virginia Commonwealth University, Richmond, VA 23284-9005

Drug Abuse Training Program Founded in 1988. *Academic areas of research and training:* Drug abuse research, neuroscience, cellular and molecular biology, behavioral studies. *Degrees offered:* None. *Graduate students served 1997–98:* 12: 8 at the doctoral level; 4 at the postgraduate level. *Faculty:* 15. *Faculty affiliations:* Departments of Microbiology and Immunology, Pharmacology and Toxicology; Program in Medicinal Chemistry. *Annual research budget:* $1.14 million. *Director:* Dr. Billy R. Martin, 804-828-8407, Fax: 804-828-2117, E-mail: martinb@hsc.vcu.edu.

Transplant Center Founded in 1962. *Academic areas of research and training:* Solid organ transplantation including Hepatocyte Laboratory, affiliation with Liver Center at Medical Col-

Directory: Research and Training Opportunities

Transplant Center (continued)

lege of Virginia. *Degrees offered:* None. *Graduate students served 1997–98:* 4 at the postgraduate level. *Faculty:* 10: 6 affiliated solely with the center. *Faculty affiliations:* Medical College of Virginia-Professional Programs. *Annual research budget:* $500,000. *Director:* Dr. Marc P. Posner, 804-828-9298, Fax: 804-828-5861, E-mail: mposner@gems.vcu.edu. *Information contact:* Dr. Robert A. Fisher, Associate Professor of Surgery and Pediatrics, 804-828-2461, E-mail: rafisher@gems.vcu.edu.

Wake Forest University, Winston-Salem, NC 27109

Center for Management Communication Founded in 1997. *Academic areas of research and training:* Interpersonal and organizational communication. *Degrees offered:* None. *Graduate students served 1997–98:* 225 at the master's level. *Faculty:* 1 affiliated solely with the center. *Annual research budget:* $1,500. *Director:* Dr. William L. Davis, 336-758-1881, Fax: 336-758-4514, E-mail: bill_davis@mail.mba.wfu.edu. *Information contact:* Ms. Patricia Divine, Assistant Dean, External Relations, 336-758-5421, Fax: 336-758-5830, E-mail: patricia_divine@mail.mba.wfu.edu.

Flow Institute for International Studies Founded in 1988. *Academic areas of research and training:* Other countries' economies, businesses, and cultures. *Degrees offered:* None. *Graduate students served 1997–98:* 90 at the master's level. *Faculty:* 6: 1 affiliated solely with the institute. *Faculty affiliations:* Babcock Graduate School of Management. *Annual research budget:* $40,000. *Director:* Dr. Charles Kennedy, 336-758-5034, Fax: 336-758-4514, E-mail: chuck_kennedy@mail.mba.wfu.edu. *Information contact:* Ms. Patricia Divine, Assistant Dean, External Relations, 336-758-5421, Fax: 336-758-5830, E-mail: patricia_divine@mail.mba.wfu.edu.

Washington University in St. Louis, St. Louis, MO 63130-4899

Center for Optimization and Semantic Control Founded in 1991. *Academic areas of research and training:* Optimization of large scale systems in transportation, health care, and business. *Degrees offered:* None. *Graduate students served 1997–98:* 9 at the doctoral level. *Faculty:* 13: 2 affiliated solely with the center. *Faculty affiliations:* Departments of Computer Science, Physics, Systems Science and Mathematics; John M. Olin School of Business; Program in Health Care. *Annual research budget:* $300,000. *Director:* Dr. Ervin Y. Rodin, 314-935-6007, Fax: 314-935-6121, E-mail: rodin@rodin.wustl.edu.

Center for Social Development (CSD) Founded in 1994. *Academic areas of research and training:* Policy, asset-building strategies, individual development accounts, evaluation. *Degrees offered:* None. *Graduate students served 1997–98:* 35: 20 at the master's level; 15 at the doctoral level. *Faculty:* 9: 1 affiliated solely with the center. *Faculty affiliations:* George Warren Brown School of Social Work, Center for Mental Health Research. *Annual research budget:* $500,000. *Director:* Dr. Michael Sherraden, 314-935-6691, E-mail: sherrad@gwbssw.wustl.edu. *Information contact:* Ms. Karen Edwards, Project Coordinator, 314-935-7433, Fax: 314-935-8661, E-mail: karene@gwbssw.wustl.edu.

Center for the Study of American Business Founded in 1975. *Academic areas of research and training:* Regulation, environmental policy, taxing and spending, global marketplace, issues in management. *Degrees offered:* None. *Graduate students served 1997–98:* 3: 2 at the doctoral level; 1 at the postgraduate level. *Faculty:* 14: 3 affiliated solely with the center. *Faculty affiliations:* Department of Economics. *Director:* Dr. Kenneth W. Chilton, 314-935-5630. *Information contact:* Mr. Robert Batterson, Communications Director, 314-935-5676, Fax: 314-935-5688, E-mail: bat@csab.wustl.edu.

Central Institute for the Deaf (CID) Founded in 1914. *Academic areas of research and training:* Hearing loss, communication sciences, audiology. *Degrees offered:* None. *Graduate students served 1997–98:* 29: 25 at the master's level; 4 at the doctoral level. *Faculty:* 29: 23 affiliated solely with the institute. *Faculty affiliations:* Programs in Anatomy and Physiology, Environmental Health, Speech Pathology. *Director:* Dr. Donald Nielsen, Executive Director, 314-977-0221, Fax: 314-977-0025, E-mail: nielsen@cid.wustl.edu. *Information contact:* Mrs. Cathy Eckenrod, Registrar and Admissions Counselor, 314-977-0240, Fax: 314-977-0027, E-mail: pe@cid.wustl.edu.

Minimally Invasive Surgery Center Founded in 1993. *Academic areas of research and training:* Laparoscopic surgery. *Degrees offered:* None. *Graduate students served 1997–98:* 2 at the postgraduate level. *Faculty affiliations:* School of Medicine. *Annual research budget:* $475,000. *Director:* Dr. Nathaniel Soper, 314-362-8357, Fax: 314-747-0591, E-mail: luttmannd@msnotes.wustl.edu. *Information contact:* Donna Luttman, Research Nurse Coordinator.

Wayne State University, Detroit, MI 48202

Center for Health Research Founded in 1966. *Academic areas of research and training:* Self-care and caregiving, transcultural nursing, adaption to an acute chronic illness, health care systems, urban health. *Degrees offered:* None. *Graduate students served 1997–98:* 45: 25 at the master's level; 18 at the doctoral level; 2 at the postgraduate level. *Faculty:* 38: 3 affiliated solely with the center. *Faculty affiliations:* Department of Adult Health and Administration; Programs in Child Health, Community Health, Gerontology, Nursing Care Administration. *Annual research budget:* $1.5 million. *Director:* Dr. Ada K. Jacox, 313-577-3911, Fax: 313-577-5777.

Center for Legal Studies Founded in 1991. *Academic areas of research and training:* Interdisciplinary legal studies. *Degrees offered:* None. *Faculty:* 12: 2 affiliated solely with the center. *Faculty affiliations:* Law School. *Annual research budget:* $100,000. *Director:* Dr. John Friedl, 313-577-3947, Fax: 313-577-1060, E-mail: jfriedl@novell.law.wayne.edu.

Center for Molecular Medicine and Genetics Founded in 1994. *Academic areas of research and training:* Basic/clinical research in molecular medicine, molecular biology, genetics. *Degrees offered:* MS; PhD. *Graduate students served 1997–98:* 27: 2 at the master's level; 25 at the doctoral level. *Faculty:* 63: 25 affiliated solely with the center. *Faculty affiliations:* College of Science, School of Medicine. *Annual research budget:* $9.2 million. *Director:* Dr. George Grunberger, 313-577-5323, Fax: 313-577-5218, E-mail: geogrun@cmb.biosci.wayne.edu.

Developmental Disabilities Institute (DDI) Founded in 1983. *Academic areas of research and training:* Disabilities, special education, social work, health, employment, occupational therapy. *Degrees offered:* None. *Graduate students served 1997–98:* 25: 17 at the master's level; 5 at the doctoral level; 3 at the postgraduate level. *Faculty affiliations:* Departments of Communication, Occupational Therapy, Physical Therapy, Psychology; Programs in Gerontology, Special Education. *Annual research budget:* $1.6 million. *Director:* Dr. Barbara LeRoy, 313-577-2654, Fax: 313-577-3770, E-mail: b_le_roy@wayne.edu.

Western Michigan University, Kalamazoo, MI 49008

Enabling Technology Center Founded in 1992. *Academic areas of research and training:* Development and use of technologies for persons with disabilities. *Degrees offered:* None. *Faculty:* 30. *Faculty affiliations:* Colleges of Education, Engineering and Applied Sciences, Health and Human Services. *Director:* Dr. Christine M. Bahr, 616-387-5954.

The Evaluation Center Founded in 1973. *Academic areas of research and training:* Program evaluation, personnel evaluation, and research and development in education and human services; evaluation training and capacity building. *Degrees offered:* None. *Graduate students served 1997–98:* 11: 2 at the master's level; 7 at the doctoral level; 2 at the postgraduate level. *Faculty:* 4: 3 affiliated solely with the center. *Faculty affiliations:* Departments of Counselor Education and Counseling Psychology, Educational Leadership. *Annual research budget:* $1 million. *Director:* Dr. Daniel L. Stufflebeam, E-mail: daniel.stufflebeam@wmich.edu. *Information contact:* Mrs. Sally A. Veeder, Assistant Director, 616-387-5895, Fax: 616-387-5923, E-mail: sally.veeder@wmich.edu.

West Virginia University, Morgantown, WV 26506

West Virginia Rehabilitation Research and Training Center (WVRRTC) Founded in 1965. *Academic areas of research and training:* Disability policy, information technology/management, employment of people with disability, assistive technology. *Degrees offered:* None. *Graduate students served 1997–98:* 6: 4 at the master's level; 2 at the doctoral level. *Faculty:* 50: 40 affiliated solely with the center. *Faculty affiliations:* Programs in Counseling Psychology, Educational Psychology, Rehabilitation Counseling, Technology Education. *Annual research budget:* $2 million. *Director:* Dr. Ranjit K. Majumder, 304-776-2680.

Wichita State University, Wichita, KS 67260

Center for Entrepreneurship Founded in 1977. *Academic areas of research and training:* Entrepreneurship and related topics including family business. *Degrees offered:* MS. *Graduate students served 1997–98:* 90 at the master's level. *Faculty:* 9 affiliated solely with the center. *Faculty affiliations:* Program in Marketing and Entrepreneurship. *Director:* Dr. Donald Hackett, E-mail: hackett@twsu.uc.twsu.edu. *Information contact:* Ms. Lara Haywood, Director of Marketing and Public Relations, 316-978-3000, Fax: 316-978-3687, E-mail: haywood@twsuvm.uc.twsu.edu.

Wilkes University, Wilkes-Barre, PA 18766-0002

Allan P. Kirby Center for Free Enterprise and Entrepreneurship Founded in 1994. *Academic areas of research and training:* Entrepreneurship, intrapreneurship, family business, new venture creation, transition management, innovation, financing entrepreneurial ventures. *Degrees offered:* None. *Graduate students served 1997–98:* 10 at the master's level. *Faculty:* 5: 1 affiliated solely with the center. *Faculty affiliations:* Programs in Business Administration. *Annual research budget:* $1,000. *Director:* Dr. Jeffrey R. Alves, 717-408-4590, Fax: 717-408-4591, E-mail: alves@wilkes.edu.

William Paterson University of New Jersey, Wayne, NJ 07470-8420

Center for Research *Academic areas of research and training:* Biology, nursing, communication disorders. *Degrees offered:* None. *Faculty:* 25. *Faculty affiliations:* Departments of Biology, Chemistry, Communication Disorders, Computer Science, Environmental Science, Exercise and Movement Science, Mathematics, Nursing. *Annual research budget:* $91,000. *Director:* Sam Robinson, Co-Director, 973-720-3387, E-mail: robinsons@frontier.wilpaterson.edu.

Yale University, New Haven, CT 06520

Institution for Social and Policy Studies Founded in 1964. *Academic areas of research and training:* Environment, social policy, agrarian studies, health policy, hate crime. *Degrees offered:* None. *Graduate students served 1997–98:* 49: 5 at the master's level; 20 at the doctoral level; 24 at the postgraduate level. *Faculty:* 12. *Faculty affiliations:* Departments of Economics, Epidemiology and Public Health, Political Science, Psychology, Sociology; Law School; Program in Business; Schools of Management, Medicine. *Annual research budget:* $2.65 million. *Director:* Dr. Donald P. Green, 203-432-3237, Fax: 203-432-3296, E-mail: donald.green@yale.edu. *Information contact:* Ms. Carol Pollard, ISPS Coordinator, 203-432-6188, Fax: 203-432-5036, E-mail: carol.pollard@yale.edu.

Appendixes

This section contains two appendixes. The first, Institutional Changes Since the 1998 Edition, lists institutions that have closed, moved, merged, or changed their name or status since the last edition of the guides. The second, Abbreviations Used in the Guides, gives abbreviations of degree names, along with what those abbreviations stand for. These appendixes are identical in all six volumes of the Graduate Guides.

Institutional Changes Since the 1998 Edition

Following is an alphabetical listing of institutions that have recently closed, moved, merged with other institutions, or changed their names or status. In the case of a name change, the former name appears first, followed by the new name.

The American College (Los Angeles, California): name changed to American InterContinental University.
The American College (Atlanta, Georgia): name changed to American InterContinental University.
The American College (London, United Kingdom): name changed to American InterContinental University.
California Baptist College (Riverside, California): name changed to California Baptist University.
College of St. Francis (Joliet, Illinois): name changed to University of St. Francis.
Concordia College (Seward, Nebraska): name changed to Concordia University.
Dakota Wesleyan University (Mitchell, South Dakota): no longer awards graduate degrees.
GMI Engineering & Management Institute (Flint, Michigan): name changed to Kettering University.
Hollins College (Roanoke, Virginia): name changed to Hollins University.
Instituto Tecnológico y de Estudios Superiores de Monterrey, Guaymas Campus (Guaymas, Sonora, Mexico): no longer awards graduate degrees.
Jersey City State College (Jersey City, New Jersey): name changed to New Jersey City University.
Kansas Newman College (Wichita, Kansas): name changed to Newman University.
Keimyung Baylo University (Anaheim, California): name changed to South Baylo University.
Kyung San University (Garden Grove, California): name changed to Kyung San University USA.
Lindenwood College (St. Charles, Missouri): name changed to Lindenwood University.
Mannes College of Music, New School for Social Research (New York, New York): name changed to Mannes College of Music, New School University.
Marylhurst College (Marylhurst, Oregon): name changed to Marylhurst University.
Mount Holyoke College (South Hadley, Massachusetts): no longer accepts graduate students.
New School for Social Research (New York, New York): name changed to New School University.
North Adams State College (North Adams, Massachusetts): name changed to Massachusetts College of Liberal Arts.
Ontario Theological Seminary (Toronto, Ontario, Canada): name changed to Tyndale College & Seminary.
Pennsylvania College of Podiatric Medicine (Philadelphia, Pennsylvania): merged with Temple University (Philadelphia, Pennsylvania).
Pennsylvania State University Great Valley Graduate Center (Malvern, Pennsylvania): name changed to Pennsylvania State University Great Valley School of Graduate Professional Studies.
Philadelphia College of Pharmacy and Science (Philadelphia, Pennsylvania): name changed to University of the Sciences in Philadelphia.
Piedmont Bible College (Winston-Salem, North Carolina): name changed to Piedmont Baptist College.
Point Loma Nazarene College (San Diego, California): name changed to Point Loma Nazarene University.
Saint Francis College (Fort Wayne, Indiana): name changed to University of Saint Francis.
Siena Heights College (Adrian, Michigan): name changed to Siena Heights University.
Simpson College (Redding, California): name changed to Simpson College and Graduate School.
State University of New York College at Plattsburgh (Plattsburgh, New York): name changed to Plattsburgh State University of New York.
Strayer College (Washington, District of Columbia): name changed to Strayer University.
University of Biblical Studies and Seminary (Bethany, Oklahoma): name changed to American Bible College and Seminary.
Western Conservative Baptist Seminary (Portland, Oregon): name changed to Western Seminary.
West Virginia Graduate College (South Charleston, West Virginia): merged with Marshall University (Huntington, West Virginia).

Abbreviations Used in the Guides

The following list includes abbreviations of degree names used in the profiles in the 1999 edition of the guides. Because some degrees (e.g., Doctor of Education) can be abbreviated in more than one way (e.g., D.Ed. or Ed.D.), and because the abbreviations used in the guides reflect the preferences of the individual colleges and universities, the list may include two or more abbreviations for a single degree.

Degrees

AC	Advanced Certificate
AD	Artist's Diploma Doctor of Arts
ADP	Artist's Diploma
Adv C	Advanced Certificate
Adv M	Advanced Master
AE	Aerospace Engineer Agricultural Engineer
AEMBA	Advanced Executive Master of Business Administration
Aerospace E	Aerospace Engineer
AGC	Advanced Graduate Certificate
AGSC	Advanced Graduate Specialist Certificate
ALM	Master of Liberal Arts
AM	Master of Arts
AMPC	Advanced Management Program for Clinician
AMRS	Master of Arts in Religious Studies
A Mus D	Doctor of Musical Arts
APC	Advanced Professional Certificate
App ME	Applied Mechanics
App Sc	Applied Scientist
Au D	Doctor of Audiology
B Th	Bachelor of Theology
CAES	Certificate of Advanced Educational Specialization
CAGS	Certificate of Advanced Graduate Studies
CAL	Certificate of Advanced Librarianship Certificate in Applied Linguistics
CAMS	Certificate of Advanced Management Studies
CAPS	Certificate of Advanced Professional Studies
CAS	Certificate of Advanced Studies
CASPA	Certificate of Advanced Study in Public Administration
CASR	Certificate in Advanced Social Research
CBHS	Certificate in Basic Health Sciences
CCJA	Certificate in Criminal Justice Administration
CE	Civil Engineer
CG	Certificate in Gerontology
CGS	Certificate of Graduate Studies
Ch E	Chemical Engineer
Chem E	Chemical Engineer
CHSS	Counseling and Human Services Specialist
CIF	Certificate in International Finance
CITS	Certificate of Individual Theological Studies
CLIS	Certificate of Library and Information Science
CMH	Certificate in Medical Humanities
CMS	Certificate in Ministerial Studies Certificate in Music Studies
CNM	Certificate in Nonprofit Management
CP	Certificate in Performance
CPC	Certificate in Professional Counseling Certificate in Publications and Communications
CPH	Certificate in Public Health
C Phil	Candidate in Philosophy Certificate in Philosophy
CPI	Certificate in Planning Information
CPM	Certificate in Public Management
CPS	Certificate of Professional Studies
CSD	Certificate in Spiritual Direction
CSE	Computer Systems Engineer
CSS	Certificate of Special Studies
CTS	Certificate of Theological Studies Certified Tax Specialist
CURP	Certificate in Urban and Regional Planning
DA	Doctor of Accounting Doctor of Arts
DA Ed	Doctor of Arts in Education
D Arch	Doctor of Architecture
DAST	Diploma of Advanced Studies in Teaching
DBA	Doctor of Business Administration
DC	Doctor of Chiropractic
DCC	Doctor of Computer Science
D Chem	Doctor of Chemistry
DCL	Doctor of Canon Law Doctor of Civil Law
DCM	Doctor of Church Music
DCS	Doctor of Computer Science
DDN	Diplôme du Droit Notarial
DDS	Doctor of Dental Surgery
DE	Doctor of Engineering
D Ed	Doctor of Education
DEM	Doctor of Educational Ministry
D Eng	Doctor of Engineering
D Env	Doctor of Environment
DEPD	Diplôme Études Spécialisées
DES	Doctor of Engineering Science
DESS	Diplôme Études Supérieures Spécialisées

DF	Doctor of Forestry
DFA	Doctor of Fine Arts
DFES	Doctor of Forestry and Environmental Studies
DGP	Diploma in Graduate and Professional Studies
DHA	Doctor of Health Administration
DHCE	Doctor of Health Care Ethics
DHL	Doctor of Hebrew Letters Doctor of Hebrew Literature
DHS	Doctor of Human Services
DIBA	Doctor of International Business Administration
Dip CS	Diploma in Christian Studies
DIT	Doctor of Industrial Technology
DJ Ed	Doctor of Jewish Education
DJS	Doctor of Jewish Studies
D Jur	Doctor of Jurisprudence
D Law	Doctor of Law
D Litt	Doctor of Letters
DM	Doctor of Management Doctor of Music
DMA	Doctor of Musical Arts
DMD	Doctor of Dental Medicine
DME	Doctor of Music Education
D Med Sc	Doctor of Medical Science
D Min	Doctor of Ministry
D Min PCC	Doctor of Ministry, Pastoral Care, and Counseling
D Miss	Doctor of Missiology
DML	Doctor of Modern Languages
DMM	Doctor of Music Ministry
D Mus	Doctor of Music
D Mus A	Doctor of Musical Arts
D Mus Ed	Doctor of Music Education
DNS	Doctor of Nursing Science
DN Sc	Doctor of Nursing Science
DO	Doctor of Osteopathy
DPA	Diploma in Public Administration Doctor of Public Administration
DPC	Doctor of Pastoral Counseling
DPDS	Doctor of Planning and Development Studies
DPE	Doctor of Physical Education
DPH	Doctor of Public Health
D Phil	Doctor of Philosophy
DPM	Doctor of Podiatric Medicine
DPS	Doctor of Professional Studies
D Ps	Diploma of Psychology Doctor of Psychology
DPT	Doctor of Physical Therapy
Dr DES	Doctor of Design
Dr OT	Doctor of Occupational Therapy
Dr PH	Doctor of Public Health
D Sc	Doctor of Science
D Sc D	Doctor of Science in Dentistry
DSM	Doctor of Sacred Music
DSN	Doctor of Science in Nursing
DS Sc	Doctor of Social Science
DSW	Doctor of Social Work
D Th	Doctor of Theology
DVM	Doctor of Veterinary Medicine
DV Sc	Doctor of Veterinary Science
EAA	Engineer in Aeronautics and Astronautics
EAS	Education Administration Specialist
Ed D	Doctor of Education
Ed DCT	Doctor of Education in College Teaching
EDM	Executive Doctorate in Management
Ed M	Master of Education
Ed S	Specialist in Education
EE	Electrical Engineer
EM	Mining Engineer
EMBA	Executive Master of Business Administration
EMIB	Executive Master of International Business
EMPA	Executive Master of Public Affairs
EMRA	Executive Master of Rehabilitation Administration
EMS	Executive Master of Science
EMSF	Executive Master of Science in Finance
EMSILR	Executive Master of Science in Industrial and Labor Relations
Eng	Engineer
Engr	Engineer
Eng Sc D	Doctor of Engineering Science
Exec Ed D	Executive Doctor of Education
Exec MBA	Executive Master of Business Administration
Exec MGA	Executive Master of General Administration
Exec MIM	Executive Master of International Management
Exec MPA	Executive Master of Public Administration
Exec MPH	Executive Master of Public Health
Exec MS	Executive Master of Science
GDPA	Graduate Diploma in Public Administration
GDRE	Graduate Diploma in Religious Education
Geol E	Geological Engineer
GMBA	Global Master of Business Administration
GPD	Graduate Performance Diploma
GPMBA	Global Professional Master of Business Administration
HSD	Doctor of Health and Safety
HS Dir	Director of Health and Safety
IEMBA	International Executive Master of Business Administration
IMA	Interdisciplinary Master of Arts

IMBA Integrative Master of Business Administration
International Master of Business Administration
IOE Industrial and Operations Engineer
JCD Doctor of Canon Law
JCL Licentiate in Canon Law
JD Juris Doctor
JSD Doctor of Juridical Science
Doctor of Jurisprudence
JSM Master of Science of Law
LL B Bachelor of Laws
LL D Doctor of Laws
LL M Master of Laws
LL M CL Master of Laws in Comparative Law
LL M T Master of Laws in Taxation
L Th Licenciate in Theology
MA Master of Arts
MAA Master of Administrative Arts
Master of Aeronautics and Astronautics
Master of Applied Arts
MAAA Master of Arts in Arts Administration
MAABS Master of Arts in Applied Behavioral Sciences
MAADAM Master of Arts in Alcoholism and Drug Abuse Ministry
MAAE Master of Aeronautical and Astronautical Engineering
Master of Arts in Applied Economics
Master of Arts in Art Education
MAAT Master of Arts in Applied Theology
Master of Arts in Art Therapy
MAB Master of Agribusiness
Master of Arts in Business
MABC Master of Arts in Biblical Counseling
MABM Master of Agribusiness Management
MABS Master of Arts in Behavioral Science
Master of Arts in Biblical Studies
M Ac Master of Accountancy
Master of Accounting
Master of Acupuncture
MAC Master of Arts in Communication
Master of Arts in Counseling
MACAT Master of Arts in Counseling Psychology: Art Therapy
M Acc Master of Accountancy
MACCM Master of Arts in Church and Community Ministry
M Acct Master of Accountancy
Master of Accounting
M Accy Master of Accountancy
MACE Master of Arts in Christian Education
Master of Arts in Computer Education
MACH Master of Arts in Church History
MACL Master of Arts in Classroom Psychology
MACM Master of Arts in Christian Ministries
Master of Arts in Church Music
MACO Master of Arts in Counseling
M Ac OM Master of Acupuncture and Oriental Medicine
MA Comm Master of Arts in Communication
MACP Master of Arts in Community Psychology
Master of Arts in Counseling Psychology
MACT Master of Arts in College Teaching
MACTM Master of Applied Communication Theory and Methodology
M Acy Master of Accountancy
MACY Master of Arts in Accountancy
M Ad Master of Administration
M Ad Ed Master of Adult Education
MADH Master of Applied Development and Health
M Adm Master of Administration
M Admin Master of Administration
M Adm Mgt Master of Administrative Management
MADR Master of Arts in Dispute Resolution
MAE Master of Aerospace Engineering
Master of Agricultural Economics
Master of Agricultural Education
Master of Agricultural Engineering
Master of Art Education
Master of Arts in Education
Master of Arts in English
Master of Automotive Engineering
MA Ed Master of Arts in Education
MA Ed U Master of Arts in Education
M Aero E Master of Aerospace Engineering
MAES Master of Arts in Environmental Sciences
MAF Master of Arts in Finance
MAFIS Master of Accountancy and Financial Information Systems
MAFLL Master of Arts in Foreign Language and Literature
MAFM Master of Accounting and Financial Management
M Ag Master of Agriculture
MAG Master of Applied Geography
M Ag Ed Master of Agricultural Education
MAGP Master of Arts in Gerontological Psychology
M Agr Master of Agriculture
MAGU Master of Urban Analysis and Management
MAH Master of Arts in Humanities
MAHCD Master of Applied Human and Community Development
MAHL Master of Arts in Hebrew Letters
Master of Arts in Hebrew Literature
MAHRM Master of Arts in Human Resources Management
MAIA Master of Arts in Industrial Arts
MAICS Master of Arts in Intercultural Studies
MAIDM Master of Arts in Interior Design and Merchandising
MAIND Master of Arts in Interior Design
MAIR Master of Arts in Industrial Relations

MAIS	Master of Accounting and Information Systems Master of Accounting Information Systems Master of Arts in Interdisciplinary Studies Master of Arts in International Studies
MAJ	Master of Arts in Journalism
MAJC	Master of Arts in Journalism and Communication
MAJCS	Master of Arts in Jewish Communal Service
MAJE	Master of Arts in Jewish Education
MAJ Ed	Master of Arts in Jewish Education
MAJS	Master of Arts in Jewish Studies
MALA	Master of Arts in Liberal Arts Master of Arts in Liturgical Arts
MALAS	Master of Arts in Latin American Studies
MALD	Master of Arts in Law and Diplomacy
MALER	Master of Arts in Labor and Employment Relations
MALIS	Master of Arts in Library and Information Science
MALL	Master of Arts in Liberal Learning
MALS	Master of Arts in Liberal Studies Master of Arts in Library Science
MAM	Master of Agriculture and Management Master of Animal Medicine Master of Applied Mechanics Master of Arts in Management Master of Arts Management Master of Arts in Ministry Master of Association Management Master of Avian Medicine Master of Aviation Management
MAMB	Master of Applied Molecular Biology
MAMC	Master of Arts in Mass Communication
MAME	Master of Arts in Missions/Evangelism
MAMFC	Master of Arts in Marriage and Family Counseling
MAMFCC	Master of Arts in Marriage, Family, and Child Counseling
MAMFT	Master of Arts in Marriage and Family Therapy
MA Min	Master of Arts in Ministry
MAML	Master of Arts in School Media Librarianship
MAMM	Master of Arts in Ministry Management Master of Arts in Music Ministry
MAMS	Master of Applied Mathematical Sciences Master of Associated Medical Sciences
MAM Sc	Master of Applied Mathematical Science
MAMT	Master of Arts in Mathematics Teaching
M Anesth Ed	Master of Anesthesiology Education
MANM	Master of Arts in Nonprofit Management
MANT	Master of Arts in New Testament
MAO	Master of Arts in Organizational Psychology
MAOE	Master of Adult and Occupational Education
MAOM	Master of Arts in Organizational Management
MAOT	Master of Arts in Old Testament
MAP	Master of Applied Psychology Master of Arts in Planning
MAPA	Master of Arts in Public Administration Master of Arts in Public Affairs
MA Past St	Master of Arts in Pastoral Studies
MAPC	Master of Arts in Pastoral Counseling
MAPE	Master of Arts in Physical Education Master of Arts in Political Economy
MAPM	Master of Arts in Pastoral Ministry Master of Arts in Pastoral Music
M Ap Ma	Master of Applied Mathematics
MAP Min	Master of Arts in Pastoral Ministry
MAPP	Master of Arts in Public Policy
M Appl Stat	Master of Applied Statistics
M App St	Master of Applied Statistics
MA Ps	Master of Arts in Psychology
MAPS	Master of Arts in Pastoral Studies
MA Psych	Master of Arts in Psychology
MAPW	Master of Arts in Professional Writing
M Aq	Master of Aquaculture
MAR	Master of Arts in Religion Master of Arts in Research
MA(R)	Master of Arts (Research)
M Arc	Master of Architecture
MARC	Master of Arts in Religious Communication
M Arch	Master of Architecture
M Arch E	Master of Architectural Engineering
M Arch H	Master of Architectural History
M Arch UD	Master of Architecture in Urban Design
MARE	Master of Arts in Religious Education
Mar Eng	Marine Engineer
MARL	Master of Arts in Religious Leadership
MARS	Master of Arts in Religious Studies
MART	Master of Arts in Religion and Theology
MAS	Master of Accounting Science Master of Administrative Science Master of Aeronautical Science Master of American Studies Master of Applied Science Master of Applied Spirituality Master of Applied Statistics Master of Archival Studies
MASA	Master of Advanced Studies in Architecture
MASAC	Master of Arts in Substance Abuse Counseling
MA Sc	Master of Applied Science
MASD	Master of Arts in Spiritual Direction
MASLA	Master of Advanced Studies in Landscape Architecture
MASM	Master of Arts in Specialized Ministries Master of Arts in Special Ministries
MASP	Master of Arts in School Psychology
MASPAA	Master of Arts in Sports and Athletic Administration
MASS	Master of Arts in Social Science Master of Arts in Special Studies

MA(T)	Master of Arts in Teaching
MAT	Master of Arts in Teaching Master of Arts in Theology
MATCM	Master of Acupuncture and Traditional Chinese Medicine
MATE	Master of Arts for the Teaching of English
Mat E	Materials Engineer
MATESL	Master of Arts in Teaching English as a Second Language
MATESOL	Master of Arts in Teaching English to Speakers of Other Languages
MATEX	Master of Arts in Textiles
MATFL	Master of Arts in Teaching Foreign Language
MA Th	Master of Arts in Theology
MATH	Master of Arts in Therapy
MATI	Master of Administration of Information Technology
MATL	Master of Arts in Teaching of Languages
MATM	Master of Arts in Teaching of Mathematics
MATS	Master of Arts in Teaching of Science Master of Arts in Theological Studies Master of Arts in Transforming Spirituality
MAUA	Master of Arts in Urban Affairs
MAUD	Master of Arts in Urban Design
MAURP	Master of Arts in Urban and Regional Planning
MAV Ed	Master of Administration in Vocational Education
MAW	Master of Arts in Worship Master of Arts in Writing
MBA	Master of Business Administration
MBAA	Master of Business Administration in Aviation
MBA Arts	Master of Business Administration in Arts
MBAE	Master of Biological and Agricultural Engineering Master of Biosystems and Agricultural Engineering
MBA-EP	Master of Business Administration–Experienced Professionals
MBAi	Master of Business Administration–International
MBAIB	Master of Business Administration in International Business
MBAPA	Master of Business Administration–Physician Assistant
MBA-PE	Master of Business Administration–Physician's Executive
MBATM	Master of Business in Telecommunication Management
MBC	Master of Building Construction
MBE	Master of Bilingual Education Master of Business Economics Master of Business Education
MBHCM	Master of Behavioral Health Care Management
M Bio E	Master of Bioengineering
M Biomath	Master of Biomathematics
MBMSE	Master of Business Management and Software Engineering
MBOL	Master of Business and Organizational Leadership
MBS	Master of Basic Science Master of Behavioral Science Master of Biblical Studies Master of Biological Science Master of Biomedical Sciences Master of Building Science Master of Business Studies
MBSI	Master of Business Information Science
MBT	Master of Business Taxation
M Bus Ed	Master of Business Education
MC	Master of Communication Master of Counseling
MCA	Master of Commercial Aviation Master of Communication Arts
MCC	Master of Computer Science
MCD	Master of Communications Disorders
MCDCC	Master of Career Development and Community Counseling
MCE	Master of Christian Education Master of Civil Engineering Master of Control Engineering
MC Ed	Master of Continuing Education
MCED	Master of Community Economic Development
MCEM	Master of Construction Engineering Management
MCG	Master of Clinical Gerontology
MCH	Master of Community Health
M Ch E	Master of Chemical Engineering
M Chem E	Master of Chemical Engineering
MCIS	Master of Computer and Information Science Master of Computer Information Systems
M Civil E	Master of Civil Engineering
MCJ	Master of Comparative Jurisprudence Master of Criminal Justice
MCJA	Master of Criminal Justice Administration
MCL	Master of Canon Law Master of Civil Law Master of Comparative Law
M Cl D	Master of Clinical Dentistry
M Cl Sc	Master of Clinical Science
MCM	Master of Christian Ministry Master of Church Management Master of Church Ministry Master of Church Music Master of Clinical Microbiology Master of Construction Management
MCMS	Master of Clinical Medical Science
M Co E	Master of Computer Engineering
M Comp E	Master of Computer Engineering
M Coun	Master of Counseling
MCP	Master of City Planning Master of Community Planning Master of Community Psychology Master of Counseling Psychology

MCPD Master of Community Planning and Development
M Cp E Master of Computer Engineering
MCRP Master of City and Regional Planning
MCS Master of Clinical Science
Master of Communication Studies
Master of Computer Science
MC Sc Master of Computer Science
MCSM Master of Construction Science/Management
MCT Master of Christian Theology
MD Doctor of Medicine
MDA Master of Development Administration
MDE Master of Developmental Economics
Master of Distance Education
M Dec S Master of Decision Sciences
M Dent Sc Master of Dental Sciences
M Des Master of Design
M Des S Master of Design Studies
M Div Master of Divinity
M Div CM Master of Divinity in Church Music
MDR Master of Dispute Resolution
MDS Master of Decision Sciences
Master of Dental Surgery
ME Master of Education
Master of Engineering
MEA Master of Engineering Administration
Master of Engineering Architecture
M Ec Master of Economics
MECE Master of Electrical and Computer Engineering
Mech E Mechanical Engineer
M Econ Master of Economics
MED Master of Education of the Deaf
M Ed Master of Education
MEDS Master of Environmental Design Studies
M Ed T Master of Education in Teaching
MEE Master of Electrical Engineering
Master of Environmental Engineering
ME Ed Master of Agriculture and Extension Education
MEEM Master of Environmental Engineering and Management
MEENE Master of Engineering in Environmental Engineering
MEERM Master of Earth and Environmental Resource Management
MEL Master of Educational Leadership
M Elec E Master of Electrical Engineering
MEM Master of Ecosystem Management
Master of Educational Ministry
Master of Engineering Management
Master of Environmental Management
MEMS Master of Emergency Medical Service
Master of Engineering in Manufacturing Systems
M Eng Master of Engineering
M Eng Mgt Master of Engineering Management
M Engr Master of Engineering
M En S Master of Environmental Sciences
M Env Master of Environment
M Env Des Master of Environmental Design
M Env E Master of Environmental Engineering
MENVEGR Master of Environmental Engineering
M Envir E Master of Environmental Engineering
M Env Sc Master of Environmental Science
MEP Master of Engineering Physics
Master of Environmental Planning
MEPC Master of Environmental Pollution Control
MEPD Master of Education–Professional Development
MEPM Master of Environmental Policy and Management
MER Master of Energy Resources
MES Master of Engineering Science
Master of Environmental Studies
Master of Special Education
ME Sc Master of Engineering Science
MESM Master of Environmental Science and Management
MESS Master of Exercise and Sport Sciences
MET Master of Education in Teaching
Met E Metallurgical Engineer
METM Master of Engineering and Technology Management
MEVE Master of Environmental Engineering
M Ext Ed Master of Extension Education
MF Master of Finance
Master of Forestry
MFA Master of Fine Arts
MFAS Master of Fisheries and Aquatic Science
MFAW Master of Fine Arts in Writing
MFC Master of Forest Conservation
MFCC Marriage and Family Counseling Certificate
Marriage, Family, and Child Counseling
MFCS Master of Family and Consumer Sciences
MFE Master of Financial Economics
Master of Forest Engineering
M Fin Master of Finance
MFR Master of Forest Resources
M Fr Master of French
MFRC Master of Forest Resources and Conservation
MFS Master of Family Studies
Master of Food Science
Master of Forensic Studies
Master of Forest Studies
Master of French Studies
MFT Master of Family Therapy
MGA Master of Government Administration
MGCOD Master of Group Counseling and Organizational Dynamics

MGD	Master of Graphic Design
M Gen E	Master of General Engineering
M Geo E	Master of Geological Engineering
M Geoenv E	Master of Geoenvironmental Engineering
M Geotech E	Master of Geotechnical Engineering
MGIS	Master of Geographic Information Science
MGP	Master of Gestion de Projet
MGPGP	Master of Group Process and Group Psychotherapy
MGS	Master of General Studies Master of Gerontological Studies
MH	Master of Health Master of Humanities
MHA	Master of Health Administration Master of Hospital Administration
MHAMS	Master of Historical Administration and Museum Studies
MHCA	Master of Health Care Administration
MHCI	Master of Human-Computer Interaction
MHD	Master of Human Development
MHE	Master of Health Education Master of Higher Education Master of Home Economics Master of Human Ecology
MHE Ed	Master of Home Economics Education
MHHS	Master of Health and Human Services
MHK	Master of Human Kinetics
MHL	Master of Hebrew Literature
MHM	Master of Hotel Management
MHMS	Master of Health Management Systems
MHP	Master of Health Professions Master of Heritage Preservation Master of Historic Preservation Master of Humanities in Philosophy
MHPE	Master of Health and Physical Education Master of Health Professions Education Master of Health Promotion and Education
MHR	Master of Human Resources
MHRD	Master in Human Resource Development
MHRDOD	Master of Human Resource Development/ Organizational Development
MHRIM	Master of Hotel, Restaurant, and Institutional Management
MHRIR	Master of Human Resources and Industrial Relations
MHRLR	Master of Human Resources and Labor Relations
MHRM	Master of Human Resources Management
MHROD	Master of Human Resources and Organization Development
MHRTA	Master in Hotel, Restaurant, Tourism, and Administration
MHS	Master of Healthcare Systems Master of Health Sciences Master of Hispanic Studies Master of Humane Studies Master of Human Services
MHSA	Master of Health Services Administration Master of Human Services Administration
MH Sc	Master of Health Sciences
MHSE	Master of Health Science Education
M Hum	Master of Humanities
M Hum Svcs	Master of Human Services
MI	Master of Instruction Master of Insurance
MIA	Master of Intercultural Administration Master of Interior Architecture Master of International Administration Master of International Affairs
MI Arch	Master of Interior Architecture
MIB	Master of International Business
MIBA	Master of International Business Administration
MIBS	Master of International Business Studies
MICS	Master of Arts in Intercultural Studies
MID	Master of Industrial Design Master of Interior Design
MIE	Master of Industrial Engineering
MIE Mgmt	Master of Industrial Engineering Management
MIHM	Master of International Health Management
MIIM	Master of International and Intercultural Management
MIJ	Master of International Journalism
MILR	Master of Industrial and Labor Relations
MIM	Master of Industrial Management Master of Information Management Master of International Management
MIMLA	Master of International Management for Latin America
MIMOT	Master of International Management of Technology
MIMS	Master of Information Management and Systems Master of Integrated Manufacturing Systems
M In Ed	Master of Industrial Education
Minl E	Mineral Engineer
MIP	Master of Infrastructure Planning Master of Intellectual Property
MIPP	Master of International Public Policy
MIR	Master of Industrial Relations
MIS	Master of Individualized Studies Master of Industrial Statistics Master of Information Science Master of Information Systems Master of Interdisciplinary Studies Master of International Studies
MISM	Master of Information Systems Management
MI St	Master of Information Studies

MIT	Master in Teaching Master of Information Technology Master of Industrial Technology Master of Initial Teaching
MITA	Master of Information Technology Administration
MITM	Master of International Technology Management
MJ	Master of Journalism Master of Jurisprudence
MJA	Master of Justice Administration
MJ Ed	Master of Jewish Education
MJPM	Master of Justice Policy and Management
MJS	Master of Judaic Studies Master of Juridical Science
M Kin	Master of Kinesiology
MLA	Master of Landscape Architecture Master of Liberal Arts
M Land Arch	Master of Landscape Architecture
ML Arch	Master of Landscape Architecture
MLAS	Master of Laboratory Animal Science
MLAUD	Master of Landscape Architecture in Urban Development
MLD	Master of Leadership Studies
MLE	Master of Applied Linguistics and Exegesis
MLHR	Master of Labor and Human Resources
MLI	Master of Legal Institutions
MLIR	Master of Labor and Industrial Relations
MLIS	Master of Library and Information Science Master of Library and Information Services
M Lit M	Master of Liturgical Music
M Litt	Master of Letters
MLM	Master of Library Media
MLOG	Master of Engineering Logistics
MLRHR	Master of Labor Relations and Human Resources
MLS	Master of Legal Studies Master of Liberal Studies Master of Library Science Master of Library Services Master of Life Sciences Master of Medical Laboratory Sciences
MLSP	Master of Law and Social Policy
MM	Master of Management Master of Ministry Master of Modern Studies Master of Music
MMA	Master of Manpower Administration Master of Marine Affairs Master of Media Arts Master of Musical Arts
MMAE	Master of Mechanical and Aerospace Engineering
MMAS	Master of Military Art and Science
M Math	Master of Mathematics
M Mat SE	Master of Material Science and Engineering
MMC	Master of Managerial Communication Master of Mass Communications
MMCM	Master of Music in Church Music
MME	Master of Manufacturing Engineering Master of Mathematics for Educators Master of Mechanical Engineering Master of Mining Engineering Master of Music Education
M Mech E	Master of Mechanical Engineering
MM Ed	Master of Music Education
M Med Sc	Master of Medical Science
MMF	Master of Mathematical Finance
MMFT	Master of Marriage and Family Therapy
M Mgmt	Master of Management
M Mgt	Master of Management
MMH	Master of Management in Hospitality Master of Medical History Master of Medical Humanities
M Min	Master of Ministries
MMIS	Master of Management Information Systems
M Miss	Master of Missiology
MMM	Master of Management in Manufacturing Master of Manufacturing Management Master of Medical Management Master of Ministry Management
MMME	Master of Metallurgical and Materials Engineering
MMP	Master of Marine Policy Master of Music Performance
MMPA	Master of Management and Professional Accounting
MMR	Master of Marketing Research
MMS	Master of Management Science Master of Management Studies Master of Marine Science Master of Marketing Science Master of Materials Science Master of Medical Science Master of Modern Studies
MM Sc	Master of Medical Science
MMSE	Master of Manufacturing Systems Engineering
MM St	Master of Museum Studies
MMT	Master of Movement Therapy Master of Music Teaching Master of Music Therapy
M Mtl E	Master of Materials Engineering Master of Metal Engineering
M Mu	Master of Music
M Mu Ed	Master of Music Education
M Mus	Master of Music
M Mus Ed	Master of Music Education
MN	Master of Nursing
MNA	Master of Nonprofit Administration Master of Nurse Anesthesia Master of Nursing Administration

MNAS	Master of Natural and Applied Science
M Nat Sci	Master of Natural Science
MNE	Master of Nuclear Engineering
MNM	Master of Nonprofit Management
MNO	Master of Nonprofit Organization
MNPL	Master of Not-for-Profit Leadership
MNR	Master of Natural Resources
MNRM	Master of Natural Resource Management
MNS	Master of Natural Science Master of Nursing Science Master of Nutritional Sciences
MN Sc	Master of Nursing Science
M Nurs	Master of Nursing
MOA	Maître d'Orthophonie et d'Audiologie
MOB	Master of Organizational Behavior
M Oc E	Master of Oceanographic Engineering
MOD	Master of Organizational Development
MOH	Master of Occupational Health
MOL	Master of Organizational Leadership
MOM	Master of Manufacturing
MOR	Master of Operations Research
MOT	Master of Occupational Therapy
MoTM	Master of Technology Management
MP	Master of Planning
MPA	Master of Physician Assistant Master of Professional Accountancy Master of Public Administration Master of Public Affairs
MPA-URP	Master of Public Affairs and Urban and Regional Planning
MP Acc	Master of Professional Accountancy Master of Professional Accounting
MP Acct	Master of Professional Accounting
MP Aff	Master of Public Affairs
MPAS	Master of Physical Activity Studies Master of Physician Assistant Science Master of Physician Assistant Studies Master of Public Art Studies
MPC	Master of Pastoral Counseling Master of Professional Communication Master of Professional Counseling Master of Public Communication
MPDS	Master of Planning and Development Studies
MPE	Master of Physical Education
MPEM	Master of Project Engineering and Management
MPH	Master of Public Health
M Pharm	Master of Pharmacy
MPHE	Master of Public Health Education
M Phil	Master of Philosophy
M Phil F	Master of Philosophical Foundations
MPHTM	Master of Public Health and Tropical Medicine
MPIA	Master of Public and International Affairs
M Pl	Master of Planning
MPM	Master of Personnel Management Master of Pest Management Master of Professional Management Master of Project Management Master of Public Management
M Pol	Master of Political Science
MPP	Master of Public Policy
MPPA	Master of Public Policy Administration
MPPM	Master of Public and Private Management Master of Public Policy and Management
MPPPM	Master of Plant Protection and Pest Management
MPPUP	Master of Public Policy and Urban Planning
M Pr A	Master of Professional Accountancy
M Pr Met	Master of Professional Meteorology
M Prob S	Master of Probability and Statistics
M Prof Past	Master of Professional Pastoral
MPRTM	Master of Parks, Recreation, and Tourism Management
MPS	Master of Pastoral Studies Master of Policy Sciences Master of Political Science Master of Preservation Studies Master of Professional Studies Master of Public Service
M Ps	Master of Psychology
MPSA	Master of Public Service Administration
MPSRE	Master of Professional Studies in Real Estate
M Psych	Master of Psychology
MPT	Master of Pastoral Theology Master of Physical Therapy
MP Th	Master of Pastoral Theology
M Pub	Master of Publishing
MPVM	Master of Preventive Veterinary Medicine
MPW	Master of Public Works
MQM	Master of Quality Management
MQS	Master of Quality Systems
MRC	Master of Rehabilitation Counseling
MRCP	Master of Regional and City Planning Master of Regional and Community Planning
MRE	Master of Religious Education
MRECM	Master of Real Estate and Construction Management
MRED	Master of Real Estate Development
M Rel	Master of Religion
M Rel Ed	Master of Religious Education
MRLS	Master of Resources Law Studies
MRM	Master of Resources Management
MRP	Master of Regional Planning
MRRA	Master of Recreation Resources Administration
MRS	Master of Religious Studies

MRTP Master of Rural and Town Planning

MS Master of Science

MSA Master of School Administration
Master of Science Administration
Master of Science in Accounting
Master of Science in Administration
Master of Science in Anesthesia
Master of Science in Anthropology
Master of Science in Architecture
Master of Science in Aviation
Master of Sports Administration

MSAA Master of Science in Astronautics and Aeronautics

MSAAE Master of Science in Aeronautical and Astronautical Engineering

MSABE Master of Science in Agricultural and Biological Engineering

MSACC Master of Science in Accounting

MS Acct Master of Science in Accounting

MS Accy Master of Science in Accountancy

MS Admin Master of Science in Administration

MSAE Master of Science in Aerospace Engineering
Master of Science in Agricultural Engineering
Master of Science in Architectural Engineering
Master of Science in Art Education

MSAER Master of Science in Aerospace Engineering

MS Ag Master of Science in Agriculture

MSAIS Master of Science in Accounting Information Systems

MSAM Master of Science in Applied Mathematics

MSAP Master of Science in Applied Psychology

MSA Phy Master of Science in Applied Physics

MS Arch Master of Science in Architecture

MS Arch St Master of Science in Architectural Studies

MSAS Master of Science in Architectural Studies

MSAT Master of Science in Advanced Technology

MSB Master of Science in Business

MSBA Master of Science in Business Administration

MSBAE Master of Science in Biological and Agricultural Engineering
Master of Science in Biosystems and Agricultural Engineering

MSBE Master of Science in Biomedical Engineering
Master of Science in Business Education

MSBENG Master of Science in Bioengineering

MS Bio E Master of Science in Bioengineering
Master of Science in Biomedical Engineering

MS Biol Master of Science in Biology

MS Bm E Master of Science in Biomedical Engineering

MSBMS Master of Science in Basic Medical Science

MSBS Master of Science in Biomedical Sciences

MSC Master of Science in Commerce
Master of Science in Communication
Master of Science in Computers
Master of Science in Counseling
Master of Speech and Communication

M Sc Master of Science

M Sc A Master of Science (Applied)

M Sc BMC Master of Science in Biomedical Communications

M Sc CS Master of Science in Computer Science

MSCD Master of Science in Communication Disorders
Master of Science in Community Development

MSCDIS Master of Science in Communication Disorders

MSCE Master of Science in Civil Engineering
Master of Science in Clinical Engineering
Master of Science in Clinical Epidemiology
Master of Science in Computer Engineering
Master of Science in Continuing Education

M Sc E Master of Science in Engineering

MSCEE Master of Science in Civil and Environmental Engineering

M Sc Eng Master of Science in Engineering

M Sc Engr Master of Science in Engineering

M Sc F Master of Science in Forestry

MSCF Master of Science in Computational Finance

M Sc FE Master of Science in Forest Engineering

MS Ch E Master of Science in Chemical Engineering

MS Chem Master of Science in Chemistry

MSCIS Master of Science in Computer and Information Systems
Master of Science in Computer Information Science

MSCJ Master of Science in Criminal Justice

MSCJA Master of Science in Criminal Justice Administration

MSCLS Master of Science in Clinical Laboratory Science
Master of Science in Clinical Laboratory Studies

M Sc N Master of Science in Nursing

MSCNU Master of Science in Clinical Nutrition

MS Coun Master of Science in Counseling

M Sc P Master of Science in Planning

MSCP Master of Science in Clinical Psychology
Master of Science in Counseling Psychology

MS Cp E Master of Science in Computer Engineering

M Sc Pl Master of Science in Planning

M Sc PT Master of Science in Physical Therapy

MSCRP Master of Science in City and Regional Planning
Master of Science in Community and Regional Planning

MSCS Master of Science in Computer Science
Master of Science in Construction Science

MSCSD Master of Science in Communication Sciences and Disorders

MSCSE Master of Science in Computer and Systems Engineering
Master of Science in Computer Science and Engineering

M Sc T Master of Science in Teaching

MSD Master of Science in Dentistry
Master of Science in Design
Master of Science in Dietetics

MSDD Master of Science in Design and Development
Master of Software Design and Development

MSE Master of Science in Education
Master of Science in Engineering
Master of Science Education
Master of Secondary Education
Master of Software Engineering
Master of Special Education

MSEAS Master of Science in Earth and Atmospheric Sciences

MSEC Master of Science in Economic Aspects of Chemistry

MSECE Master of Science in Electrical and Computer Engineering

MS Eco Master of Science in Economics

MS Econ Master of Science in Economics

MS Ed Master of Science in Education

MSED Master of Sustainable Economic Development

MS Ed U Master of Science in Education

MSEE Master of Science in Electrical Engineering
Master of Science in Electronic Engineering
Master of Science in Environmental Engineering

MSEH Master of Science in Environmental Health

MSEL Master of Science in Environmental Law
Master of Studies in Environmental Law

MSEM Master of Science in Engineering and Management
Master of Science in Engineering Management
Master of Science in Engineering Mechanics
Master of Science in Engineering of Mines
Master of Science in Environmental Management

MSE Mgt Master of Science in Engineering Management

MS En E Master of Science in Environmental Engineering

MSENE Master of Science in Environmental Engineering

MS Eng Master of Science in Engineering

MS Engr Master of Science in Engineering

MS Env E Master of Science in Environmental Engineering

MSER Master of Science in Energy Resources

MSES Master of Science in Engineering Science
Master of Science in Environmental Studies

MSESM Master of Science in Engineering Science and Mechanics
Master of Science in Environmental Systems Management

MSESS Master of Science in Exercise and Sport Studies

MSET Master of Science in Engineering Technology

MSETM Master of Science in Environmental Technology Management

MSEV Master of Science in Environmental Engineering

MSF Master of Science in Finance
Master of Science in Forestry

MSFAM Master of Science in Family Studies

MSFM Master of Financial Management

MSFOR Master of Science in Forestry

MSFS Master of Science in Family Studies
Master of Science in Financial Services
Master of Science in Foreign Service
Master of Science in Forensic Science

MSG Master of Science in Gerontology

MSGC Master of Science in Genetic Counseling

MS Geo E Master of Science in Geological Engineering

MSH Master of Science in Hospice

MSHA Master of Science in Health Administration

MSHCI Master of Science in Human Computer Interaction

MSHCPM Master of Science in Health Care Policy and Management

MSHCS Master of Science in Human and Consumer Science

MSH Ed Master of Science in Health Education

MSHES Master of Science in Human Environmental Sciences

MSHP Master of Science in Health Professions

MSHR Master of Science in Human Resources

MSHRM Master of Science in Human Resource Management

MSHROD Master of Science in Human Resources and Organizational Development

MSHS Master of Science in Health and Safety
Master of Science in Health Science
Master of Science in Health Systems

MSHSA Master of Science in Human Service Administration

MSHSE Master of Science in Health Science Education

MSHT Master of Science in History of Technology

MSI Master of Science in Instruction
Master of Science in Insurance

MSIA Master of Science in Industrial Administration
Master of Science in International Administration
Master of Science in International Affairs

MSIB Master of Science in International Business

MSIBK Master of Science in International Banking

MSIDM Master of Science in Interior Design and Merchandising

MSIDT Master of Science in Information Design and Technology

MSIE Master of Science in Industrial Engineering
Master of Science in International Economics

MSIL Master of Science in International Logistics

MSIMC Master of Science in Information Management and Communication
Master of Science in Integrated Marketing Communications

MS Int A Master of Science in International Affairs

MSIO Master of Science in Industrial Optimization

MSIPC Master of Science in Information Processing and Communications

MSIR Master of Science in Industrial Relations

MSIS Master of Science in Information Science
Master of Science in Information Systems
Master of Science in Interdisciplinary Studies

MSIT Master of Science in Industrial Technology
Master of Science in Instructional Technology

MSITM Master of Science in Information Technology Management

MSJ Master of Science in Journalism
Master of Science in Jurisprudence

MSJBS Master of Science in Japanese Business Studies

MSJPS Master of Science in Justice and Public Safety

MSJS Master of Science in Jewish Studies

MSK Master of Science in Kinesiology

MSL Master of School Leadership
Master of Science in Librarianship
Master of Science in Limnology
Master of Studies in Law

MSLA Master of Science in Legal Administration

MSLP Master of Speech-Language Pathology

MSLS Master of Science in Library Science
Master of Science in Logistics Systems

MSM Master of Sacred Ministry
Master of Sacred Music
Master of Science in Management
Master of Service Management

MSMAE Master of Science in Materials Engineering

MS Mat Master of Science in Materials Engineering

MS Mat E Master of Science in Materials Engineering

MS Math Master of Science in Mathematics

MS Mat SE Master of Science in Material Science and Engineering

MSMC Master of Science in Marketing Communications
Master of Science in Mass Communications

MSMCS Master of Science in Management and Computer Science

MSME Master of Science in Mathematics Education
Master of Science in Mechanical Engineering

MS Met E Master of Science in Metallurgical Engineering

MS Metr Master of Science in Meteorology

MSMFE Master of Science in Manufacturing Engineering

MS Mfg E Master of Science in Manufacturing Engineering

MSMfSE Master of Science in Manufacturing Systems Engineering

MSMGEN Master of Science in Management and General Engineering

MS Mgt Master of Science in Management

MSMI Master of Science in Medical Illustration

MS Min Master of Science in Mining

MS Min E Master of Science in Mining Engineering

MSMIS Master of Science in Management Information Systems

MSMM Master of Science in Manufacturing Management

MSMOT Master of Science in Management of Technology

MSMS Master of Science in Management Science
Master of Science in Medical Sciences

MSMSA Master of Science in Management Systems Analysis

MSMSE Master of Science in Manufacturing Systems Engineering
Master of Science in Material Science and Engineering
Master of Science in Material Science Engineering

MSMT Master of Science in Medical Technology

MS Mt E Master of Science in Materials Engineering

MSN Master of Science in Nursing

MSNA Master of Science in Nurse Anesthesia

MSNE Master of Science in Nuclear Engineering

MSN(R) Master of Science in Nursing (Research)

MSNS Master of Science in Natural Science

MS Nsg Master of Science in Nursing

MSOB Master of Science in Organizational Behavior

M Soc Master of Sociology

MSOD Master of Science in Organizational Development

MSOM Master of Science in Organization and Management

MSOR Master of Science in Operations Research

MSOT Master of Science in Occupational Technology
Master of Science in Occupational Therapy

MSP Master of School Psychology
Master of Science in Pharmacy
Master of Science in Planning
Master of Social Psychology
Master of Speech Pathology

MSPA Master of Science in Professional Accountancy
Master of Science in Public Administration
Master of Speech Pathology and Audiology

MSPAS Master of Science in Physician Assistant Studies

MSPC Master of Science in Professional Communications

MSPE Master of Science in Petroleum Engineering
Master of Science in Physical Education

M Sp Ed Master of Special Education

MS Pet E Master of Science in Petroleum Engineering

MSP Ex Master of Science in Exercise Physiology

MSPFP Master of Science in Personal Financial Planning

MSPG Master of Science in Psychology

MSPH Master of Science in Public Health

MS Phr	Master of Science in Pharmacy
MSPHR	Master of Science in Pharmacy
MS Phys	Master of Science in Physics
MS Phys Op	Master of Science in Physiological Optics
MSPNGE	Master of Science in Petroleum and Natural Gas Engineering
MS Poly	Master of Science in Polymers
MSPS	Master of Science in Planning Studies Master of Science in Psychological Services
MS Psy	Master of Science in Psychology
MSPT	Master of Science in Physical Therapy
MS Pub P	Master of Science in Public Policy
MSQSM	Master of Science in Quality Systems Management
MSR	Master of Science in Rehabilitation Sciences
MS(R)	Master of Science (Research)
MSRA	Master of Science in Recreation Administration
MSRC	Master of Science in Resource Conservation
MSRE	Master of Science in Religious Education
MSRMP	Master of Science in Radiological Medical Physics
MS(R)PT	Master of Science (Research) in Physical Therapy
MSRS	Master of Science in Radiological Sciences Master of Science in Recreational Studies
MSRTM	Master of Science in Resort and Tourism Management
MSS	Master of Science in Safety Master of Science in Software Master of Selected Studies Master of Social Science Master of Social Services Master of Special Studies Master of Sports Science
MSSA	Master of Science in Social Administration
MSSE	Master of Science in Software Engineering
MSSI	Master of Science in Strategic Intelligence
MSSL	Master of Science in Speech and Language
MSSM	Master of Science in Science Management Master of Science in Systems Management
MSSPA	Master of Science in Student Personnel Administration
MS Sp Ed	Master of Science in Special Education
MSSS	Master of Science in Systems Science
MS Stat	Master of Science in Statistics
MSSW	Master of Science in Social Work
MST	Master of Science in Taxation Master of Science in Teaching Master of Science in Telecommunications Master of Science in Transportation Master of Science Teaching Master of Science Technology Master of Secondary Teaching Master of Speech Therapy Master of Systems Technology
MSTA	Master of Science in Statistics
M Stat	Master of Statistics
MSTC	Master of Science in Telecommunications
MST Ch	Master of Science in Textile Chemistry
MSTD	Master of Science in Training and Development
MSTE	Master of Science in Technical Education Master of Science in Textile Engineering Master of Science in Transportation Engineering
MS Text	Master of Science in Textiles
MSTM	Master of Science in Teaching Mathematics Master of Science in Technology Management Master of Science in Tropical Medicine
M Struct E	Master of Structural Engineering
MSUD	Master of Science in Urban Design
MSUESM	Master of Science in Urban Environmental Systems Management
MSVE	Master of Science in Vocational Education
MSW	Master of Social Work
M Sw E	Master of Software Engineering
MSWE	Master of Software Engineering
M Sw En	Master of Software Engineering
MSWREE	Master of Science in Water Resources and Environmental Engineering
MT	Master of Taxation Master of Teaching Master of Technology Master of Textiles
MTA	Master of Tax Accounting Master of Teaching Art Master of Theater Arts
M Tax	Master of Taxation
MTC	Master of Technical Communications
MTCM	Master of Traditional Chinese Medicine
MTD	Master of Training and Development
MTE	Master of Teacher Education
M Tech	Master of Technology
MTEL	Master of Telecommunications
MTESL	Master in Teaching English as a Second Language
M Th	Master of Theology
MTHM	Master of Tourism and Hospitality Management
M Th Past	Master of Pastoral Theology
MTI	Master of Information Technology
MTLM	Master of Transportation and Logistics Management
MTM	Master of Telecommunications Management Master of the Teaching of Mathematics Master of Theology and Ministry
MTMH	Master of Tropical Medicine and Hygiene
MTOM	Master of Traditional Oriental Medicine
M Tox	Master of Toxicology
MTP	Master of Transpersonal Psychology
MTPW	Master of Technical and Professional Writing
M Trans E	Master of Transportation Engineering

MTS	Master of Teaching Science Master of Theological Studies
MTSC	Master of Technical and Scientific Communication Master of Theological Studies Counseling
MTX	Master of Taxation
MUA	Master of Urban Affairs Master of Urban Architecture
MUD	Master of Urban Design
MUP	Master of Urban Planning
MUPDD	Master of Urban Planning, Design, and Development
MUPP	Master of Urban Planning and Policy
MURP	Master of Urban and Regional Planning Master of Urban and Rural Planning
MURPL	Master of Urban and Regional Planning
MUS	Master of Urban Studies
Mus AD	Doctor of Musical Arts
Mus Doc	Doctor of Music
Mus M	Master of Music
MVE	Master of Vocational Education
M Vet Sc	Master of Veterinary Science
MVTE	Master of Vocational-Technical Education
MVT Ed	Master of Vocational and Technical Education
MWC	Master of Wildlife Conservation
MWPS	Master of Wood and Paper Science
MWRA	Master of Water Resources Administration
MWS	Master of Women's Studies
MZS	Master of Zoological Science
Naval E	Naval Engineer
Nav Arch	Naval Architecture
ND	Doctor of Naturopathic Medicine Doctor of Nursing
NE	Nuclear Engineer
NPMC	Nonprofit Management Certificate
Nuc E	Nuclear Engineer
Ocean E	Ocean Engineer
OD	Doctor of Optometry
OTD	Doctor of Occupational Therapy
PD	Doctor of Pharmacy Performer Diploma Professional Diploma
PDD	Professional Development Degree
PED	Doctor of Physical Education
PE Dir	Director of Physical Education
PGC	Post-Graduate Certificate
Pharm D	Doctor of Pharmacy
PhD	Doctor of Philosophy
Ph L	Licentiate of Philosophy
PMBA	Professional Master of Business Administration
PMC	Post Master's Certificate
PMSA	Professional Master of Science in Accounting
Psy D	Doctor of Psychology
Psy M	Master of Psychology
Psy S	Specialist in Psychology
Re D	Doctor of Recreation
Re Dir	Director of Recreation
Rh D	Doctor of Rehabilitation
SAS	School Administrator and Supervisor
SCCT	Specialist in Community College Teaching
Sc D	Doctor of Science
Sc M	Master of Science
SD	Doctor of Science Specialist Degree
SJD	Doctor of Juridical Science
SLPD	Doctor of Speech-Language Pathology
SLS	Specialist in Library Science
SM	Master of Science
SM Arch S	Master of Science in Architectural Studies
SMBT	Master of Science in Building Technology
SM Vis S	Master of Science in Visual Studies
SP	Specialist Degree
SPA	Specialist in Public Administration
Sp C	Specialist in Counseling
Sp Ed	Specialist in Education
Sp Ed S	Special Education Specialist
SPS	School Psychology Specialist Special Education Specialist
S Psy S	Specialist in Psychological Services
Spt	Specialist Degree
SSP	Specialist in School Psychology
STB	Bachelor of Sacred Theology
STD	Doctor of Sacred Theology
STL	Licentiate of Sacred Theology
STM	Master of Sacred Theology
Th D	Doctor of Theology
Th M	Master of Theology
TMBA	Transnational Master of Business Administration
V Ed S	Vocational Education Specialist
VMD	Doctor of Veterinary Medicine
WEMBA	Weekend Executive Master of Business Administration
XMA	Executive Master of Arts
XMBA	Executive Master of Business Administration

Indexes

There are three indexes in this section. The first, Index of In-Depth Descriptions and Announcements, gives page references for all programs that have chosen to place in-depth descriptions and announcements in this volume. It is arranged alphabetically by institution; within institutions, the arrangement is alphabetical by subject area. It is not an index to all programs in the book's directories of profiles; readers must refer to the directories themselves for profile information on programs that have not submitted the additional, more individualized statements. The second index, Index of Directories and Subject Areas in Books 2–6, gives book references for the directories in Books 2–6, for example, "Industrial Design—Book 2," and also includes cross-references for subject area names not used in the directory structure, for example, "Computing Technology (*see* Computer Science)." The third index, Index of Directories and Subject Areas in This Book, gives page references for the directories in this volume and cross-references for subject area names not used in this volume's directory structure, for example, "Gas Engineering (*see* Petroleum Engineering)."

Index of In-Depth Descriptions and Announcements

Index of Directories and Subject Areas in Books 2–6

Following is an alphabetical listing of directories and subject areas in Books 2–6. Also listed are cross-references for subject area names not used in the directory structure of the guides, for example, "Arabic (*see* Near and Middle Eastern Languages)."

Index of Directories and Subject Areas in This Book

Notes

Notes

Notes

Notes

FIND A LIFETIME OF LEARNING AT PETERSON'S ON LINE!

Knowledge gives you the power to perform and to succeed—and petersons.com puts the power at your fingertips!

At **petersons.com** you can

- Explore graduate programs
- Discover distance learning programs
- Find out how to finance your education
- Search for career opportunities

Looking for advice on finding the right graduate program?
Look no further than the **Enrollment Message Center at petersons.com!**

- Explore program options by discipline
- E-mail program contacts for more information
- Best of all? **It's FREE**

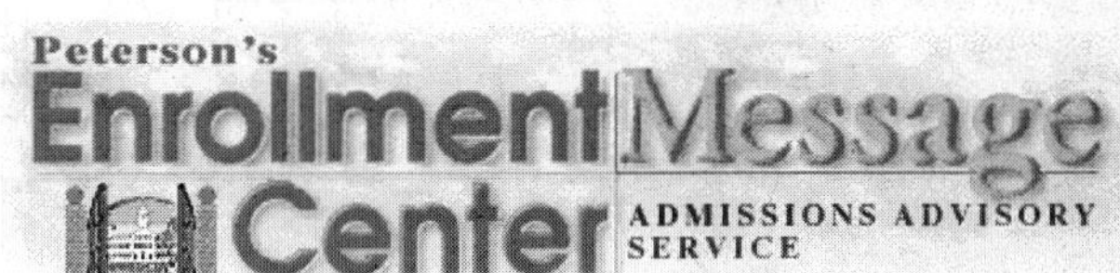

The Enrollment Message Center is an advisory service providing admission news from colleges and graduate schools wanting to contact students like you who are looking for the right institution.

Maybe you are looking to transfer, reassessing your choice of colleges, or just looking to learn more about graduate programs. Whatever your situation, if you're not yet committed to a college or graduate program, use Peterson's Enrollment Message Center, now, to contact institutions that are able to provide you with an enrollment opportunity.

Peterson's gives you everything you need to start a lifetime of learning.

And it's all just a mouse click away!

PETERSON'S
Princeton, New Jersey
www.petersons.com
Keyword on AOL: Petersons

1-800-338-3282

Wait! There's more!→

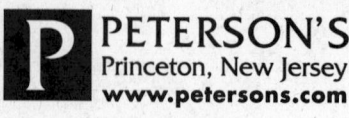

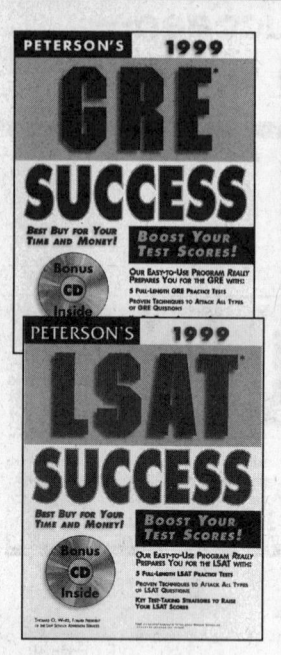